Stanley Gibbons
Stamp Catalogue

Commonwealth and British Empire Stamps 1840 – 1970

111th edition 2009

Stanley Gibbons Ltd
London and Ringwood

By Appointment to Her Majesty The Queen
Stanley Gibbons Ltd, London
Philatelists

Published by Stanley Gibbons Ltd
Editorial, Publications Sales Offices
and Distribution Centre:
Parkside, Christchurch Road, Ringwood,
Hants BH24 3SH

ISBN-13: 978-0-85259-683-8
ISBN: 0-85259-683-9

Item No. 2813-09

Printed and bound in Italy
by Lego SpA

Preface to the 2009 Edition

As catalogue editor, I receive dozens of letters and emails each week, reporting new discoveries for possible catalogue listing, or suggesting how improvements might be made. As editor of *Gibbons Stamp Monthly*, I receive quite a few letters simply thanking us for doing a good job, but before the arrival of the 2008 edition of this catalogue my mailbag was notably lacking in letters of a similar nature addressed to the catalogue editor.

The 2008 edition changed all that, however. Letters, cards and emails came from around the world, welcoming the extension of the period covered by the catalogue to 1970. Naturally, the move did not suit everyone, and one or two were unhappy about its increased size and cost – but they were in a very small minority.

In order to encourage feedback from catalogue users each new edition will now include a small questionnaire. Please use it to let me know what you think of the 2009 edition and how you feel it could be improved for 2010.

Following the success of the 2008 catalogue (we even had to order a reprint), the 2009 edition is very much the same in terms of size, style and content; although, as always, a great deal of the hard work has gone into making improvements.

More early Queen Elizabeth sets are now illustrated in full, and in colour, while thanks largely to our friends at Spink, more of the early issues have now been converted to colour from black and white. Further varieties are now also shown in colour, most notably the re-entries on the 2s.6d. Seahorses of Great Britain.

One change made last year which was approached with a considerable amount of trepidation was the order in which certain countries should be listed. We know this has been the subject of debate in the past and that catalogue users in general do not welcome major changes. However, we felt that it was right to split those countries whose names were changed on independence; so Gold Coast, Ghana, Northern Rhodesia, Zambia, Nyasaland, and Malawi all now appear alphabetically, according to the country name inscribed on the stamp.

Thankfully, these changes also seem to have been welcome – so this year there have been no further changes to the 'running order'.

PRICES

Once again, the past year has seen numerous occasions when significant rarities or stamps in exceptionally fine condition have gone under the auctioneer's hammer and often achieved surprising prices, significantly in excess of those in last year's catalogue. As always, these realisations have been reflected in the price revisions in this edition, although it should be noted that prices are reviewed set at levels which Stanley Gibbons feel are sustainable in the longer term.

However, the market is not defined only by 'blue chip' items which achieve newsworthy prices at auction; it is defined by more 'regularly traded' items at more modest price levels. As demand for such items goes up, so must prices.

In the past year or two, demand has increased in many areas; stocks are running low and 'wants lists' seem to be getting longer. The result has been a widespread marking up of prices with virtually every area and period seeing extensive revision.

The market for **Great Britain** stamps has once again been very strong, with auction prices for the very fine or very rare continuing to rise. This is reflected most obviously in catalogue prices for early issues, high values, and 20th century errors. It has to be noted, however, that serious collectors of Great Britain are increasingly conscious of the condition of their stamps and that anything in less than fine condition will command significantly lower prices that those quoted in this catalogue. The notes on the following pages give helpful guidance on condition and how it affects the price you should have to pay – whether you are buying from a dealer, at auction, or on the internet.

Australia has once again been revised with the help of Simon Dunkerley, and increases are extensive. **New South Wales** sees widespread revision to the letterpress issues from 1862 onwards and contemporary issues of the other states receive similar attention. In **Queensland** the early Chalon heads are marked up mint and **South Australia** and **Western Australia** also see increases to early issues. It is in **Victoria**, however, where the changes are most numerous and significant, with some very substantial increases to the 'Half Lengths', especially mint.

The market in Australia remains as strong as ever with further new records set at auction for anything unusual. Again, this is reflected here with further rises for the scarcer watermark and printing varieties and errors, while there are further increases for more 'basic' stamps, including postage dues and officials, up to about 1940.

Canada is also active, with many price increases in the provinces, including **Newfoundland**, Dominion issues to 1950 and, notably, to the official stamps of King George VI.

In **New Zealand** the Chalon heads have seen extensive revision and, indeed, the whole country has been carefully reviewed throughout, with significant price increases right through to the 1960s. The postal fiscals are nearly all up in price.

South Africa reflects a widespread increase in interest in African stamps generally, with numerous rises to the provinces, especially for unused, with every stamp of **Griqualand West** up, mint and used, and extensive revision to South Africa itself.

Other African countries to have seen significant revision include **Bechuanaland**, where the sale of the Inglefield-Watson collection allowed an accurate assessment of the market for this popular country, while **Gambia, Gold Coast, Kenya, Uganda and Tanganyika, Nigeria, Nyasaland, Rhodesia** and **Zanzibar** have all been extensively reviewed.

The British West Indies have received similar attention, with **Bahamas, Barbados, Bermuda** and **British Guiana** all seeing notable price rises in the period up to 1950, and **Dominica, Jamaica, Leeward Islands, Montserrat, the Saints, Trinidad** and **Turks Island** also worthy of mention.

India sees extensive and significant increases from the earliest issues through to 1950, especially, as increasing demands from collectors in India itself reduces the supply of fine material in the rest of the world. Notably, the 10r. Gandhi stamp (No. 308) has more than doubled in price, mint. Indian Convention States and Indian Feudatory states have again been carefully revised, with thousands of price increases.

If there is a quieter area in this year's catalogue, it has to be the Pacific Islands but, even here, **New Guinea, Papua, Cook Islands, Fiji** and **Tonga** show many increases in the period up to 1950. **Falkland Islands, Mauritius** and **Seychelles**, while, judging from the number of price rises remain as popular as ever.

The 'used abroad' sections have also received considerable attention with Great Britain used in **Ascension, British Levant, Gibraltar, Jamaica, Morocco Agencies** and **Nigeria,** and India used in **Bahrain, Iraq, Straits Settlements** and **Zanzibar** all, or nearly all, being marked up.

Another group notable for almost wholesale price increases are the provisional occupation stamps of World War I, especially those of **New Guinea, Batum, Bushire, Iraq** and **Long Island**.

All in all, therefore, the 2009 edition of this catalogue reflects a continuing healthy market for British and Commonwealth stamps at all levels, based very much on increased collector demand and the spread of the 'global' market, brought about by the increased use of the internet.

REVISIONS TO THIS EDITION

Thanks to the assistance of several collectors and members of the trade, a number of new varieties have been added to this edition of the catalogue, including another 31 newly discovered or reported inverted or reversed watermarks. Other varieties are now illustrated for the first time, notably the 'PALESTINB' flaw on the September 1920 overprints of Palestine.

The 'multipliers' for stamps on cover are also reviewed each year with those for **Australia** now considerably more detailed. For example, on-cover prices for official perfins and overprints have previously been given an across-the-board multiplication factor of '×5'. This year this section has been split into no less than 47 different groups (a few of which are marked as unknown), ranging up to '×200' for an example of No. O128 on cover.

The dates of issue for a number of the early stamps of **Bechuanaland** have been revised following research by Brian Hurst.

In **Hong Kong,** the 'Stop after "CENTS" on the 1941 8c. definitive and the 'Crack in rock' on the 80c. UPU stamp are now listed, thanks to Richard Lockyer and Bill O' Connell, respectively.

India sees the separate listing of the two types of official overprint on the 1926-31 3p., ½a and 1a., more than 70 years after they were first described in *Gibbons Stamp Monthly*.

This edition also sees a major new listing for **Indian stamps used in Iran**, based primarily on the list published by the Iran Philatelic Study Circle, to whom we give our thanks.

In **Kenya, Uganda and Tanganyika**, Ken Lagdon has added a new centre plate to those formerly listed as existing with the retouched value tablet and Peter Brooks has clarified the notes on the King George VI varieties of the **Leeward Islands**.

The vignette re-entry on the 1911 middle-value definitives of **North Borneo**, resulting in extensive doubling of the image, is now listed, adding, with the various subsequent overprints and perforation changes, the addition of no less than 25 new stamps.

Many other additions and amendments have been made throughout the catalogue and we are, as always, grateful to the many study circles, individual collectors and members of the trade who have offered their advice and assistance. I would also like to thank my colleagues, both in Ringwood and London, for their continued help and support in the editing, pricing and production of this catalogue.

Hugh Jefferies,
Catalogue Editor.

Stanley Gibbons Holdings Plc

Stanley Gibbons Limited, Stanley Gibbons Auctions
399 Strand, London WC2R OLX
Telephone 020 7836 8444, Fax 020 7836 7342,
E-mail: *enquiries@stanleygibbons.co.uk*
Internet: *www.stanleygibbons.com*
for all departments,
Auction and Specialist Stamp Departments.
Open Monday–Friday 9.30 a.m. to 5 p.m.
Shop. Open Monday–Friday 9 a.m. to 5.30 p.m. and
Saturday 9.30 a.m. to 5.30 p.m.

Stanley Gibbons Publications
Parkside, Christchurch Road, Ringwood,
Hampshire BH24 3SH.
Telephone 01425 472363 (24 hour answer phone service),
Fax 01425 470247,
E-mail: *info@stanleygibbons.co.uk*
Publications Mail Order. FREEPHONE 0800 611622
Monday–Friday 8.30 a.m. to 5 p.m.

Gibbons Stamp Monthly
Parkside, Christchurch Road, Ringwood,
Hampshire BH24 3SH.
Subscriptions. 01425 481031, Fax 01425 470247
E-mail: *gsm@stanleygibbons.co.uk*

Fraser's
(a division of Stanley Gibbons Ltd)
399 Strand, London WC2R OLX
Autographs, photographs, letters and documents
Telephone 020 7836 8444, Fax 020 7836 7342,
E-mail: *info@frasersautographs.co.uk*
Internet: *www.frasersautographs.com*
Monday–Friday 9 a.m. to 5.30 p.m. and
Saturday 10 a.m. to 4 p.m.

Stanley Gibbons Publications Overseas Representation

Stanley Gibbons Publications are represented overseas by the following sole distributors (*), distributors (**) or licensees (***).

Australia
*Lighthouse Philatelic (Aust.) Pty. Ltd.**
Locked Bag 5900
Botany DC,
New South Wales, 2019.

*Stanley Gibbons (Australia) Pty. Ltd.****
Level 6,
36 Clarence Street, Sydney,
New South Wales 2000,

Belgium and Luxembourg**
Davo c/o Philac, Rue du Midi 48, Bruxelles, 1000.

Canada**
Unitrade,
99 Floral Parkway,
Toronto,
Ontario M6L 264

Denmark**
Samlerforum/Davo,
Ostergade 3,
DK 7470 Karup, Denmark.

Finland**
Davo
c/o Kapylan Merkkiky
Pohjolankatu 00610
Helsinki.

France*
Davo France (Casteilla),
10, Rue Leon Foucault,
78184 St. Quentin Yvelines
Cesex.

Hong Kong**
Po-on Stamp Service,
GPO Box 2498,
Hong Kong.

Italy*
Ernesto Marini Sri,
Via Struppa 300, I-16165,
Genova GE.

Japan**
Japan Philatelic Co. Ltd.,
P.O. Box 2,
Suginami-Minami, Tokyo.

Netherlands*
Davo Publications,
P.O. Box 411,
7400 AK Deventer.

New Zealand***
Mowbray Collectables.
P.O. Box 80, Wellington.

Norway**
Davo Norge A/S,
P.O. Box 738 Sentrum,
N-0105, Oslo.

Saudi Arabia**
Arabian Stamps Centre,
P. O. Box 54645,
Riyadh 11524.

Singapore**
Stamp Inc Collectibles Pte Ltd.,
10 Ubi Cresent, #01-43
Ubi Tech Park, Singapore
408564.

Sweden*
Chr Winther Soerensen AB,
Box 43, S-310 Knaered,
Sweden.

United States**
Filatco Inc,
P. O. Box 520, McLean,
VA 22101-0520.

Stanley Gibbons Stamp Catalogue
Complete list of parts

1 ***Commonwealth & British Empire Stamps 1840–1970*** (formerly Part 1) (Annual)

Foreign Countries

2 ***Austria & Hungary*** (6th edition, 2002)
• Austria • U.N. (Vienna) • Hungary

3 ***Balkans*** (4th edition, 1998) • Albania
• Bosnia & Herzegovina • Bulgaria • Croatia
• Greece & Islands • Macedonia • Romania
• Slovenia • Yugoslavia

4 ***Benelux*** (5th edition 2003)
• Belgium & Colonies • Luxembourg
• Netherlands & Colonies

5 ***Czechoslovakia & Poland*** (6th edition, 2002)
• Czechoslovakia • Czech Republic • Slovakia
• Poland

6 ***France*** (6th edition, 2006)
• France • Colonies • Post Offices •Andorra • Monaco

7 ***Germany*** (8th edition, 2007)
• Germany • States • Colonies • Post Offices

8 ***Italy & Switzerland*** (6th edition, 2003)
• Italy & Colonies • Liechtenstein • San Marino
• Switzerland • U.N. (Geneva) • Vatican City

9 ***Portugal & Spain*** (5th edition, 2004)
• Andorra • Portugal & Colonies • Spain & Colonies

10 ***Russia*** (6th edition, 2008)
• Russia • Armenia • Azerbaijan • Belarus
• Estonia • Georgia • Kazakhstan • Kyrgyzstan
• Latvia • Lithuania • Moldova • Tajikistan
• Turkmenistan • Ukraine • Uzbekistan • Mongolia

11 ***Scandinavia*** (5th edition, 2001)
• Aland Islands • Denmark • Faroe Islands
• Finland • Greenland • Iceland • Norway
• Sweden

12 ***Africa since Independence A-E*** (2nd edition 1983)
• Algeria • Angola • Benin • Burundi • Cameroun
• Cape Verde • Central African Republic • Chad
• Comoro Islands • Congo • Djibouti
• Equatorial Guinea • Ethiopia

13 ***Africa since Independence F-M*** (1st edition, 1981)
• Gabon • Guinea • Guinea-Bissau
• Ivory Coast • Liberia • Libya • Malagasy Republic • Mali
• Mauritania • Morocco • Mozambique

14 ***Africa since Independence N-Z*** (1st edition, 1981)
• Niger Republic • Rwanda • St. Thomas & Prince
• Senegal • Somalia • Sudan • Togo • Tunisia
• Upper Volta • Zaire

15 ***Central America*** (3rd edition, 2007)
• Costa Rica • Cuba • Dominican Republic • El Salvador
• Guatemala • Haiti - Honduras • Mexico • Nicaragua
• Panama

16 ***Central Asia*** (4th edition, 2006)
• Afghanistan • Iran • Turkey

17 ***China*** (7th edition, 2006)
• China • Taiwan • Tibet • Foreign P.O.s • Hong Kong
• Macao

18 ***Japan & Korea*** (5th edition, 2008)
• Japan • Korean Empire • South Korea • North Korea

19 ***Middle East*** (6th edition, 2005)
• Aden • Bahrain • Egypt • Iraq .• Israel • Jordan • Kuwait
• Lebanon • Oman • Qatar • Saudi Arabia • Syria
• U.A.E. • Yemen

20 ***South America*** (3rd edition, 1989)
• Argentina • Bolivia • Brazil • Chile • Colombia • Ecuador
• Paraguay • Peru • Surinam • Uruguay • Venezuela

21 ***South-East Asia*** (4th edition, 2004)
• Bhutan • Cambodia • Indo-China • Indonesia • Laos
• Myanmar • Nepal • Philippines • Thailand • Timor
• Vietnam

22 ***United States*** (6th edition, 2005)
• U.S. & Posessions • Marshall Islands
• Micronesia • Palau • U.N. (New York, Geneva, Vienna)

Great Britain Specialised Catalogues

Volume 1 ***Queen Victoria*** (14th edition, 2006)
Volume 2 ***King Edward VII to King George VI*** (12th edition, 2005)
Volume 3 ***Queen Elizabeth II Pre-decimal Issues*** (11th edition, 2005)
Volume 4 ***Queen Elizabeth II Decimal Definitive Issues – Part 1*** (10th edition, 2008)
Volume 5 ***Queen Elizabeth II Decimal Special Issues*** (3rd edition, 1998 with 1998–99 and 2000/1 Supplements)

Thematic Catalogues
Stanley Gibbons Catalogues for use with ***Stamps of the World.***
Collect Aircraft on Stamps (out of print)
Collect Birds on Stamps (5th edition, 2003)
Collect Chess on Stamps (2nd edition, 1999)
Collect Fish on Stamps (1st edition, 1999)
Collect Fungi on Stamps (2nd edition, 1997)
Collect Motor Vehicles on Stamps (1st edition 2004)
Collect Railways on Stamps (3rd edition, 1999)
Collect Shells on Stamps (Out of Print)
Collect Ships on Stamps (3rd edition, 2001)

Die II

1. There are very few lines of colour in the ball and it appears almost white.
2. A white vertical strand of hair appears in place of the dark shading.
3. The line stops at the eighth line of shading.
4. The white space is oblong, with a line of colour partially dividing it at the left end.

Plates numbered 1 and 2 are both Die I. Plates 3 and 4 are Die II.

GEORGIAN KEY TYPE

Die I

A. The second (thick) line below the name of the country is cut slanting, conforming roughly to the shape of the crown on each side.

B. The labels of solid colour bearing the words "POSTAGE" and "& REVENUE" are square at the inner top corners.

C. There is a projecting "bud" on the outer spiral of the ornament in each of the lower corners.

Die II

A. The second line is cut vertically on each side of the crown.

B. The labels curve inwards at the top.

C. There is no "bud" in this position.

Unless otherwise stated in the lists, all stamps with watermark Multiple Crown CA (w **8**) are Die I while those with watermark Multiple Crown Script CA (w **9**) are Die II. The Georgian Die II was introduced in April 1921 and was used for Plates 10 to 22 and 26 to 28. Plates 23 to 25 were made from Die I by mistake.

2. Paper

All stamps listed are deemed to be on (ordinary) paper of the wove type and white in colour; only departures from this are normally mentioned.

Types. Where classification so requires we distinguish such other types of paper as, for example, vertically and horizontally laid; wove and laid bâtonné; card(board); carton; cartridge; glazed; granite; native; pelure; porous; quadrillé; ribbed; rice; and silk thread.

Wove paper

Laid paper

Granite paper

Quadrillé paper

Burelé band

The various makeshifts for normal paper are listed as appropriate. The varieties of double paper and joined paper are recognised. The security device of a printed burelé band on the back of a stamp, as in early Queensland, qualifies for listing.

Descriptive terms. The fact that a paper is handmade (and thus probably of uneven thickness) is mentioned where necessary. Such descriptive terms as "hard" and "soft"; "smooth" and "rough"; "thick", "medium" and "thin" are applied where there is philatelic merit in classifying papers.

Coloured, very white and toned papers. A coloured paper is one that is coloured right through (front and back of the stamp). In the Catalogue the colour of the paper is given in italics, thus:

black/*rose* = black design on rose paper.

Papers have been made specially white in recent years by, for example, a very heavy coating of chalk. We do not classify shades of whiteness of paper as distinct varieties. There does exist, however, a type of paper from early days called toned. This is off-white, often brownish or buffish, but it cannot be assigned any definite colour. A toning effect brought on by climate, incorrect storage or gum staining is disregarded here, as this was not the state of the paper when issued.

"Ordinary" and "Chalk-surfaced" papers. The availability of many postage stamps for revenue purposes made necessary some safeguard against the illegitimate re-use of stamps with removable cancellations. This was at first secured by using fugitive inks and later by printing on paper surfaced by coatings containing either chalk or china clay, both of which made it difficult to remove any form of obliteration without damaging the stamp design.

This catalogue lists these chalk-surfaced paper varieties from their introduction in 1905. Where no indication is given, the paper is "ordinary".

Our chalk-surfaced paper is specifically one which shows a black mark when touched with a silver wire. The paper used during the Second World War for high values, as in Bermuda, the Leeward Islands, etc., was thinly coated with some kind of surfacing which does not react to silver and is therefore regarded (and listed) as "ordinary". Stamps on chalk-surfaced paper can easily lose this coating through immersion in water.

Another paper introduced during the War as a substitute for chalk-surfaced is rather thick, very white and glossy and shows little or no watermark, nor does it show a black line when touched with silver. In the Bahamas high values this paper might be mistaken for the chalk-surfaced (which is thinner and poorer-looking) but for the silver test.

Some modern coated papers show little or no reaction to the silver test and, therefore, cannot be classed as chalk-surfaced.

Glazed paper. In 1969 the Crown Agents introduced a new general-purpose paper for use in conjunction with all current printing processes. It generally has a marked glossy surface but the degree varies according to the process used, being more marked in recess-printing stamps. As it does not respond to the silver test this presents a further test where previous printings were on chalky paper. A change of paper to the glazed variety merits separate listing.

Green and yellow papers. Issues of the First World War and immediate postwar period occur on green and yellow papers and these are given separate Catalogue listing. The original coloured papers (coloured throughout) gave way to surface-coloured papers, the stamps having "white backs"; other stamps show one colour on the front and a different one at the back. Because of the numerous variations a grouping of colours is adopted as follows:

Yellow papers

(1) The original *yellow* paper (throughout), usually bright in colour. The gum is often sparse, of harsh consistency and dull-looking. Used 1912–1920.
(2) The *white-backs*. Used 1913–1914.
(3) A bright lemon paper. The colour must have a pronounced greenish tinge, different from the "yellow" in (1). As a rule, the gum on stamps using this lemon paper is plentiful, smooth and shiny, and the watermark shows distinctly. Care is needed with stamps printed in green on yellow paper (1) as it may appear that the paper is this lemon. Used 1914–1916.
(4) An experimental *orange-buff* paper. The colour must have a distinct brownish tinge. It is not to be confused with a muddy yellow (1) nor the misleading appearance (on the surface) of stamps printed in red on yellow paper where an engraved plate has been insufficiently wiped. Used 1918–1921.
(5) An experimental *buff* paper. This lacks the brownish tinge of (4) and the brightness of the yellow shades. The gum is shiny when compared with the matt type used on (4). Used 1919–1920.
(6) A *pale yellow* paper that has a creamy tone to the yellow. Used from 1920 onwards.

Green papers

(7) The original "green" paper, varying considerably through shades of blue-green and yellow-green, the front and back sometimes differing. Used 1912–1916.
(8) The *white backs*. Used 1913–1914.
(9) A paper blue-green on the surface with *pale olive* back. The back must be markedly paler than the front and this and the pronounced olive tinge to the back distinguish it from (7). Used 1916–1920.
(10) Paper with a vivid green surface, commonly called *emerald-green*; it has the olive back of (9). Used 1920.
(11) Paper with *emerald-green* both back and front. Used from 1920 onwards.

3. Perforation and Rouletting

Perforation gauge. The gauge of a perforation is the number of holes in a length of 2 cm. For correct classification the size of the holes (large or small) may need to be distinguished; in a few cases the actual number of holes on each edge of the stamp needs to be quoted.

Measurement. The Gibbons *Instanta* gauge is the standard for measuring perforations. The stamp is viewed against a dark background with the transparent gauge put on top of it. Though the gauge measures to decimal accuracy, perforations read from it are generally quoted in the Catalogue to the nearest half. For example:

Just over perf 12¾ to just under 13¼ = perf 13

Perf 13¼ exactly, rounded up = perf 13½
Just over perf 13¼ to just under 13¾ = perf 13½
Perf 13¾ exactly, rounded up = perf 14

However, where classification depends on it, actual quarter-perforations are quoted.

Notation. Where no perforation is quoted for an issue it is imperforate. Perforations are usually abbreviated (and spoken) as follows, though sometimes they may be spelled out for clarity. This notation for rectangular stamps (the majority) applies to diamond shapes if "top" is read as the edge to the top right.

P 14: perforated alike on all sides (read: "perf 14").

P 14×15: the first figure refers to top and bottom, the second to left and right sides (read: "perf 14 by 15"). This is a compound perforation. For an upright triangular stamp the first figure refers to the two sloping sides and second to the base. In inverted triangulars the base is first and the second figure to the sloping sides.

P 14–15: perforation measuring anything between 14 and 15: the holes are irregularly spaced, thus the gauge may vary along a single line or even along a single edge of the stamp (read: "perf 14 to 15").

P 14 *irregular*: perforated 14 from a worn perforator, giving badly aligned holes irregularly spaced (read: "irregular perf 14").

P *comp(ound)* 14×15: two gauges in use but not necessarily on opposite sides of the stamp. It could be one side in one gauge and three in the other; or two adjacent sides with the same gauge. (Read: "perf compound of 14 and 15".) For three gauges or more, abbreviated as "P 12, 14½, 15 *or compound*" for example.

P 14, 14½: perforated approximately 14¼ (read: "perf 14 or 14½"). It does *not* mean two stamps, one perf 14 and the other perf 14½. This obsolescent notation is gradually being replaced in the Catalogue.

Imperf: imperforate (not perforated)

Imperf×P 14: imperforate at top ad bottom and perf 14 at sides.

P 14×*imperf*: perf 14 at top and bottom and imperforate at sides.

Such headings as "P 13×14 (*vert*) and P 14×13 (*horiz*)" indicate which perforations apply to which stamp format—vertical or horizontal.

Some stamps are additionally perforated so that a label or tab is detachable; others have been perforated for use as two halves. Listings are normally for whole stamps, unless stated otherwise.

Imperf×perf

Other terms. Perforation almost always gives circular holes; where other shapes have been used they are specified, e.g. square holes; lozenge perf. Interrupted perfs are brought about by the omission of pins at regular intervals. Perforations merely simulated by being printed as part of the design are of course ignored. With few exceptions, privately applied perforations are not listed.

In the 19th century perforations are often described as clean cut (clean, sharply incised holes), intermediate or rough (rough holes, imperfectly cut, often the result of blunt pins).

Perforation errors and varieties. Authenticated errors, where a stamp normally perforated is accidentally issued imperforate, are listed provided no traces of perforation (blind holes or indentations) remain. They must be provided as pairs, both stamps wholly imperforate, and are only priced in that form.

Stamps imperforate between stamp and sheet margin are not listed in this catalogue, but such errors on Great Britain stamps will be found in the *Great Britain Specialised Catalogue*.

Pairs described as "imperforate between" have the line of perforations between the two stamps omitted.

Imperf between (horiz pair): a horizontal pair of stamps with perfs all around the edges but none between the stamps.

Imperf between (vert pair): a vertical pair of stamps with perfs all around the edges but none between the stamps.

Imperf between (vertical pair)

Imperf horizontally (vertical pair)

Where several of the rows have escaped perforation the resulting varieties are listable. Thus:

Imperf vert (horiz pair): a horizontal pair of stamps perforated top and bottom; all three vertical directions are imperf—the two outer edges and between the stamps.

Imperf horiz (vert pair): a vertical pair perforated at left and right edges; all three horizontal directions are imperf—the top, bottom and between the stamps.

Straight edges. Large sheets cut up before issue to post offices can cause stamps with straight edges, i.e. imperf on one side or on two sides at right angles. They are not usually listable in this condition and are worth less than corresponding stamps properly perforated all round. This does not, however, apply to certain stamps, mainly from coils and booklets, where straight edges on various sides are the manufacturing norm affecting every stamp. The listings and notes make clear which sides are correctly imperf.

Malfunction. Varieties of double, misplaced or partial perforation caused by error or machine malfunction are not listable, neither are freaks, such as perforations placed diagonally from paper folds, nor missing holes caused by broken pins.

Types of perforating. Where necessary for classification, perforation types are distinguished. These include:

Line perforation from one line of pins punching single rows of holes at a time.

Comb perforation from pins disposed across the sheet in comb formation, punching out holes at three sides of the stamp a row at a time.

Harrow perforation applied to a whole pane or sheet at one stroke.

Rotary perforation from toothed wheels operating across a sheet, then crosswise.

Sewing machine perforation. The resultant condition, clean-cut or rough, is distinguished where required.

Pin-perforation is the commonly applied term for pin-roulette in which, instead of being punched out, round holes are pricked by sharp-pointed pins and no paper is removed.

Mixed perforation occurs when stamps with defective perforations are re-perforated in a different gauge.

Punctured stamps. Perforation holes can be punched into the face of the stamp. Patterns of small holes, often in the shape of initial letters, are privately applied devices against pilferage. These (perfins) are outside the scope except for Australia, Canada, Cape of Good Hope, Papua and Sudan where they were used as official stamps by the national administration. Identification devices, when officially inspired, are listed or noted; they can be shapes, or letters or words formed from holes, sometimes converting one class of stamp into another.

Rouletting. In rouletting the paper is cut, for ease of separation, but none is removed. The gauge is measured, when needed, as for perforations. Traditional French terms descriptive of the type of cut are often used and types include:

Arc roulette (percé en arc). Cuts are minute, spaced arcs, each roughly a semicircle.

Cross roulette (percé en croix). Cuts are tiny diagonal crosses.

Line roulette (percé en ligne or *en ligne droite)*. Short straight cuts parallel to the frame of the stamp. The commonest basic roulette. Where not further described, "roulette" means this type.

Rouletted in colour or coloured roulette (percé en lignes colorées or *en lignes de coleur)*. Cuts with coloured edges, arising from notched rule inked simultaneously with the printing plate.

Saw-tooth roulette (percé en scie). Cuts applied zigzag fashion to resemble the teeth of a saw.

Serpentine roulette (percé en serpentin). Cuts as sharply wavy lines.

Zigzag roulette (percé en zigzags). Short straight cuts at angles in alternate directions, producing sharp points on separation. US usage favours "serrate(d) roulette" for this type.

Pin-roulette (originally *percé en points* and now *perforés trous d'epingle*) is commonly called pin-perforation in English.

4. Gum

All stamps listed are assumed to have gum of some kind; if they were issued without gum this is stated. Original gum (o.g.) means that which was present on the stamp as issued to the public. Deleterious climates and the presence of certain chemicals can cause gum to crack and, with early stamps, even make the paper deteriorate. Unscrupulous fakers are adept in removing it and regumming the stamp to meet the unreasoning demand often made for "full o.g." in cases where such a thing is virtually impossible.

The gum normally used on stamps has been gum arabic until the late 1960s when synthetic adhesives were introduced. Harrison and Sons Ltd for instance used *polyvinyl alcohol* known to philatelists as PVA. This is almost invisible except for a slight yellowish tinge which was incorporated to make it possible to see that the stamps had been gummed. It has advantages in hot countries, as stamps do not curl and sheets are less likely to stick together. Gum arabic and PVA are not distinguised in the lists except that where a stamp exists in both forms this is indicated in the footnotes. our more specialised catalogues provide separate listing of gums for Great Britain

5. Watermarks

Stamps are on unwatermarked paper except where the heading to the set says otherwise.

Detection. Watermarks are detected for Catalogue description by one of four methods: (1) holding stamps to the light; (2) laying stamps face down on a dark background; (3) adding a few drops of petroleum ether 40/60 to the stamp laid face down in a watermark tray; (4) by use of the Stanley Gibbons Detectamark, or other equipment, which work by revealing the thinning of the paper at the watermark. (Note that petroleum ether is highly inflammable in use and can damage photogravure stamps.)

Listable types. Stamps occurring on both watermarked and unwatermarked papers are different types and both receive full listing.

Single watermarks (devices occurring once on every stamp) can be modified in size and shape as between different issues; the types are noted but not usually separately listed. Fortuitous absence of watermark from a single stamp or its gross displacement would not be listable.

To overcome registration difficulties the device may be repeated at close intervals *(a multiple watermark)*, single stamps thus showing parts of several devices. Similarly, a *large sheet watermark* (or *all-over watermark*) covering numerous stamps can be used. We give informative notes and illustrations for them. The designs may be such that numbers of stamps in the sheet automatically lack watermark: this is not a listable variety. Multiple and all-over watermarks sometimes undergo modifications, but if the various types are difficult to distinguish from single stamps notes are given but not separate listings.

Papermakers' watermarks are noted where known but not listed separately, since most stamps in the sheet will lack them. Sheet watermarks which are nothing more than officially adopted papermakers' watermarks are, however, given normal listing.

Marginal watermarks, falling outside the pane of stamps, are ignored except where misplacement caused the adjoining row to be affected, in which case they may be footnoted.

Watermark errors and varieties. Watermark errors are recognised as of major importance. They comprise stamps intended to be on unwatermarked paper but issued watermarked by mistake, or stamps printed on paper with the wrong watermark. Varieties showing letters omitted from the watermark are also included, but broken or deformed bits on the dandy roll are not listed unless they represent repairs.

Watermark positions. The diagram shows how watermark position is described in the Catalogue. Paper has a side intended for printing and watermarks are usually impressed so that they read normally when looked through from that printed side. However, since philatelists customarily detect watermarks by looking at the back of the stamp the watermark diagram also makes clear what is actually seen.

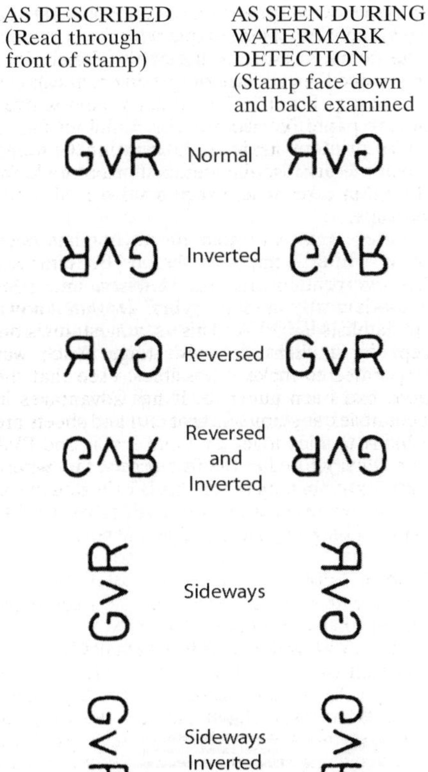

Illustrations in the Catalogue are of watermarks in normal positions (from the front of the stamps) and are actual size where possible.

Differences in watermark position are collectable varieties. This Catalogue now lists inverted, sideways inverted and reversed watermark varieties on Commonwealth stamps from the 1860s onwards except where the watermark position is completely haphazard.

Great Britain inverted and sideways inverted watermarks can be found in the *Great Britain Specialised Catalogue* and the *Great Britain Concise Catalogue.*

Where a watermark comes indiscriminately in various positions our policy is to cover this by a general note: we do not give separate listings because the watermark position in these circumstances has no particular philatelic importance.

There is a general note of this sort in modern Cyprus, for example. Issues printed since 1962 by Aspioti-Elka occur with the vertical stamps having the watermark normal or inverted, while horizontal stamps are likewise found with the watermark reading upwards or downwards.

Standard types of watermark. Some watermarks have been used generally for various British possessions rather than exclusively for a single colony. To avoid repetition the Catalogue classifies 11 general types, as under, with references in the headings throughout the listings being given either in words or in the form ("W w **9**") (meaning "watermark type w **9**"). In those cases where watermark illustrations appear in the listings themselves, the respective reference reads, for example, W **153**, thus indicating that the watermark will be found in the normal sequence of illustrations as (type) **153**.

The general types are as follows, with an example of each quoted.

W	*Description*	*Example*
w **1**	Large Star	St. Helena No. 1
w **2**	Small Star	Turks Is. No. 4
w **3**	Broad (pointed) Star	Grenada No. 24
w **4**	Crown (over) CC, small stamp	Antigua No. 13
w **5**	Crown (over) CC, large stamp	Antigua No. 31
w **6**	Crown (over) CA, small stamp	Antigua No. 21
w **7**	Crown CA (CA over Crown), large stamp	Sierra Leone No. 54
w **8**	Multiple Crown CA	Antigua No. 41
w **9**	Multiple Script CA	Seychelles No. 158
w **9***a*	do. Error	Seychelles No. 158a
w **9***b*	do. Error	Seychelles No. 158b
w **10**	V over Crown	N.S.W. No. 327
w **11**	Crown over A	N.S.W. No. 347

CC in these watermarks is an abbreviation for "Crown Colonies" and CA for "Crown Agents". Watermarks w **1**, w **2** and w **3** are on stamps printed by Perkins, Bacon; w **4** onwards on stamps from De La Rue and other printers.

w **1**
Large Star

w **2**
Small Star

w **3**
Broad-pointed Star

Watermark w **1**, *Large Star*, measures 15 to 16 mm across the star from point to point and about 27 mm from centre to centre vertically between stars in the sheet. It was made for long stamps like Ceylon 1857 and St. Helena 1856.

Watermark w **2**, *Small Star* is of similar design but measures 12 to 13½mm from point to point and 24 mm from centre to centre vertically. It was for use with ordinary-size stamps such as Grenada 1863–71.

When the Large Star watermark was used with the smaller stamps it only occasionally comes in the centre of the paper. It is frequently so misplaced as to show portions of two stars above and below and this eccentricity will very often help in determining the watermark.

Watermark w **3**, *Broad-pointed Star*, resembles w **1** but the points are broader.

w **4**
Crown (over) CC

w **5**
Crown (over) CC

Two *Crown (over) CC* watermarks were used: w **4** was for stamps of ordinary size and w **5** for those of larger size.

w **6**
Crown (over) CA

w **7**
CA over Crown

Two watermarks of *Crown CA* type were used, w **6** being for stamps of ordinary size. The other, w **7**, is properly described as *CA over Crown*. It was specially made for paper on which it was intended to print long fiscal stamps: that some were used postally accounts for the appearance of w **7** in the Catalogue. The watermark occupies twice the space of the ordinary Crown CA watermark, w **6**. Stamps of normal size printed on paper with w **7** watermark show it *sideways*; it takes a horizontal pair of stamps to show the entire watermark.

w **8**
Multiple Crown CA

w **9**
Multiple Script CA

Multiple watermarks began in 1904 with w **8**, *Multiple Crown CA*, changed from 1921 to w **9**, *Multiple Script CA*. On stamps of ordinary size portions of two or three watermarks appear and on the large-sized stamps a greater number can be observed. The change to letters in script character with w **9** was accompanied by a Crown of distinctly different shape.

It seems likely that there were at least two dandy rolls for each Crown Agents watermark in use at any one time with a reserve roll being employed when the normal one was withdrawn for maintenance or repair.

Both the Mult Crown CA and the Mult Script CA types exist with one or other of the letters omitted from individual impressions. It is possible that most of these occur from the reserve rolls as they have only been found on certain issues. The MCA watermark experienced such problems during the early 1920s and the Script over a longer period from the early 1940s until 1951.

During the 1920s damage must also have occurred on one of the Crowns as a substituted Crown has been found on certain issues. This is smaller than the normal and consists of an oval base joined to two upright ovals with a circle positioned between their upper ends. The upper line of the Crown's base is omitted, as are the left and right-hand circles at the top and also the cross over the centre circle.

Substituted Crown

The *Multiple Script CA* watermark, w **9**, is known with two errors, recurring among the 1950–52 printings of several territories. In the first a crown has fallen away from the dandy-roll that impresses the watermark into the paper pulp. It gives w **9a**, *Crown missing*, but this omission has been found in both "Crown only" (*illustrated*) and "Crown CA" rows. The resulting faulty paper was used for Bahamas, Johore, Seychelles and the postage due stamps of nine colonies

w **9a**: Error, Crown missing

w **9b**: Error, St. Edward's Crown

When the omission was noticed a second mishap occurred, which was to insert a wrong crown in the space, giving w 9b, St. Edward's Crown. This produced varieties in Bahamas, Perlis, St. Kitts-Nevis and Singapore and the incorrect crown likewise occurs in (Crown only) and (Crown CA) rows.

w **10**
V over Crown

w **11**
Crown over A

Resuming the general types, two watermarks found in issues of several Australian States are: w **10**, *V over Crown*, and w **11**, *Crown over A*.

w **12**: Multiple
St. Edward's
Crown Block CA

The *Multiple St. Edward's Crown Block CA* watermark, w **12** was introduced in 1957 and besides the change in the Crown (from that used in *Multiple Script CA,* w **9**) the letters reverted to block capitals. The new watermark began to appear sideways in 1966 and these stamps are generally listed as separate sets.

w **13**: Multiple PTM

The watermark w **13**, *Multiple PTM*, was introduced for new Malayan issues in November 1961.

6. Colours

Stamps in two or three colours have these named in order of appearance, from the centre moving outwards. Four colours or more are usually listed as multicoloured.

In compound colour names the second is the predominant one, thus:

orange-red = a red tending towards orange;

red-orange = an orange containing more red than usual.

Standard colours used. The 200 colours most used for stamp identification are given in the Stanley Gibbons Stamp Colour Key. The Catalogue has used the Stamp Colour Key as standard for describing new issues for some years. The names are also introduced as lists are rewritten, though exceptions are made for those early issues where traditional names have become universally established.

Determining colours. When comparing actual stamps with colour samples in the Stamp Colour Key, view in a good north daylight (or its best substitute; fluorescent "colour matching" light). Sunshine is not recommended. Choose a solid portion of the stamp design; if available, marginal markings such as solid bars of colour or colour check dots are helpful. Shading lines in the design can be misleading as they appear lighter than solid colour. Postmarked portions of a stamp appear darker than normal. If more than one colour is present, mask off the extraneous ones as the eye tends to mix them.

Errors of colour. Major colour errors in stamps or overprints which qualify for listing are: wrong colours; one colour inverted in relation to the rest; albinos (colourless impressions), where these have Expert Committee certificates; colours completely omitted, but only on unused stamps (if found on used stamps the information is footnoted) and with good credentials, missing colours being frequently faked.

Colours only partially omitted are not recognised, Colour shifts, however spectacular, are not listed.

Shades. Shades in philately refer to variations in the intensity of a colour or the presence of differing amounts of other colours. They are particularly significant when they can be linked to specific printings. In general, shades need to be quite marked to fall within the scope of this Catalogue; it does not favour nowadays listing the often numerous shades of a stamp, but chooses a single applicable colour name which will indicate particular groups of outstanding shades. Furthermore, the listings refer to colours as issued; they may deteriorate into something different through the passage of time.

Modern colour printing by lithography is prone to marked differences of shade, even within a single run, and variations can occur within the same sheet. Such shades are not listed.

Aniline colours. An aniline colour meant originally one derived from coal-tar; it now refers more widely to colour of a particular brightness suffused on the surface of a stamp and showing through clearly on the back.

Colours of overprints and surcharges. All overprints and surcharges are in black unless stated otherwise in the heading or after the description of the stamp.

7. Specimen Stamps

Originally, stamps overprinted SPECIMEN were circulated to postmasters or kept in official records, but after the establishment of the Universal Postal Union supplies were sent to Berne for distribution to the postal administrations of member countries.

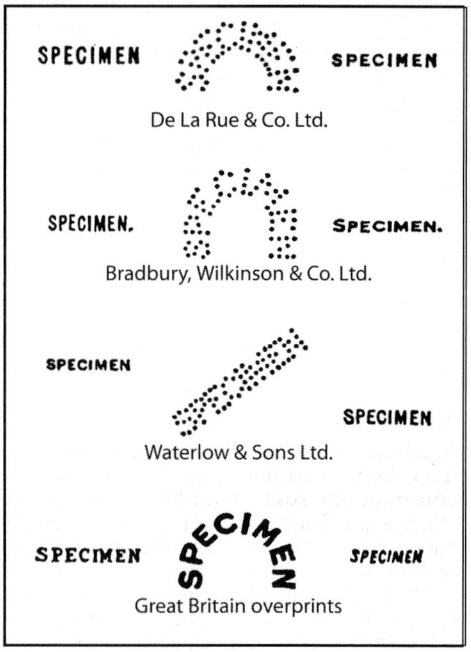

During the period 1884 to 1928 most of the stamps of British Crown Colonies required for this purpose were overprinted SPECIMEN in various shapes and sizes by their printers from typeset formes. Some locally produced provisionals were handstamped locally, as were sets prepared for presentation. From 1928 stamps were punched with holes forming the word SPECIMEN, each firm of printers using a different machine or machines. From 1948 the stamps supplied for UPU distribution were no longer punctured.

Stamps of some other Commonwealth territories were overprinted or handstamped locally, while stamps of Great Britain and those overprinted for use in overseas postal agencies (mostly of the higher denominations) bore SPECIMEN overprints and handstamps applied by the Inland Revenue or the Post Office.

Some of the commoner types of overprints or punctures are illustrated here. Collectors are warned that dangerous forgeries of the punctured type exist.

The *Stanley Gibbons Commonwealth Catalogues* record those Specimen overprints or perforations intended for distribution by the UPU to member countries. In addition the Specimen overprints of Australia and its dependent territories, which were sold to collectors by the Post Office, are also included.

Various Perkins Bacon issues exist obliterated with a "CANCELLED" within an oval of bars handstamp.

Perkins Bacon "CANCELLED" Handstamp

This was applied to six examples of those issues available in 1861 which were then given to members of Sir Rowland Hill's family. 75 different stamps (including four from Chile) are recorded with this handstamp although others may possibly exist. The unauthorised gift of these "CANCELLED" stamps to the Hill family was a major factor in the loss of the Agent General for the Crown Colonies (the forerunner of the

Crown Agents) contracts by Perkins Bacon in the following year. Where examples of these scarce items are known to be in private hands the catalogue provides a price.

For full details of these stamps see *CANCELLED by Perkins Bacon* by Peter Jaffé (published by Spink in 1998).

All other Specimens are outside the scope of this volume.

Specimens are not quoted in Great Britain as they are fully listed in the Stanley Gibbons *Great Britain Specialised Catalogue*.

In specifying type of specimen for individual high-value stamps, "H/S" means handstamped, "Optd" is overprinted and "Perf" is punctured. Some sets occur mixed, e.g. "Optd/Perf". If unspecified, the type is apparent from the date or it is the same as for the lower values quoted as a set.

Prices. Prices for stamps up to £1 are quoted in sets; higher values are priced singly. Where specimens exist in more than one type the price quoted is for the cheapest. Specimen stamps have rarely survived even as pairs; these and strips of three, four or five are worth considerably more than singles.

8. Luminescence

Machines which sort mail electronically have been introduced in recent years. In consequence some countries have issued stamps on flourescent or phosphorescent papers, while others have marked their stamps with phosphor bands.

The various papers can only be distinguished by ultraviolet lamps emitting particular wavelengths. They are separately listed only when the stamps have some other means of distinguishing them, visible without the use of these lamps. Where this is not so, the papers are recorded in footnotes or headings.

For this catalogue we do not consider it appropriate that collectors be compelled to have the use of an ultraviolet lamp before being able to identify stamps by our listings. Some experience will also be found necessary in interpreting the results given by ultraviolet. Collectors using the lamps, nevertheless, should exercise great care in their use as exposure to their light is potentially dangerous to the eyes.

Phosphor bands are listable, since they are visible to the naked eye (by holding stamps at an angle to the light and looking along them, the bands appear dark). Stamps existing with or without phosphor bands or with differing numbers of bands are given separate listings. Varieties such as double bands, bands omitted, misplaced or printed on the back are not listed.

Detailed descriptions appear at appropriate places in the listings in explanation of luminescent papers; see, for example, Australia above No.363, Canada above Nos. 472 and 611, Cook Is. above 249, etc.

For Great Britain, where since 1959 phosphors have played a prominent and intricate part in stamp issues, the main notes above Nos. 599 and 723 should be studied, as well as the footnotes to individual listings where appropriate. In general the classification is as follows.

Stamps with *phosphor bands* are those whre a separate cylinder applies the phosphor after the stamps are printed. Issues with "all-over" phosphor have the "band" covering the entire stamp. Parts of the stamp covered by phosphor bands, or the entire surface for "all-over" phosphor versions, appear matt. Stamps on *phosphorised paper* have the phosphor added to the paper coating before the stamps are printed. Issues on this paper have a completely shiny surface.

Further particularisation of phosphor – their methods of printing and the colours they exhibit under ultraviolet – is outside the scope. The more specialised listings should be consulted for this information.

9. Coil Stamps

Stamps issued only in coil form are given full listing. If stamps are issued in both sheets and coils the coil stamps are listed separately only where there is some feature (e.g. perforation or watermark sideways) by which singles can be distinguished. Coil stamps containing different stamps *se-tenant* are also listed.

Coil join pairs are too random and too easily faked to permit of listing; similarly ignored are coil stamps which have accidentally suffered an extra row of perforations from the claw mechanism in a malfunctioning vending machine.

10. Stamp Booklets

Stamp booklets (with the exception of those from Great Britain for which the current edition of the *Great Britain Concise Catalogue*) are now listed in this catalogue.

Single stamps from booklets are listed if they are distinguishable in some way (such as watermark or perforation) from similar sheet stamps.

Booklet panes are listed where they contain stamps of different denominations *se-tenant*, where stamp-size labels are included, or where such panes are otherwise identifiable. Booklet panes are placed in the listing under the lowest denomination present.

Particular perforations (straight edges) are covered by appropriate notes.

11. Miniature Sheets and Sheetlets

We distinguish between "miniature sheets" and "sheetlets" and this affects the catalogue numbering. An item in sheet form that is postally valid, containing a single stamp, pair, block or set of stamps, with wide, inscribed and/or decorative margins, is a miniature sheet if it is sold at post offices as an indivisable entity. As such the Catalogue allots a single **MS** number and describes what stamps make it up. The sheetlet or small sheet differs in that the individual stamps are intended to be purchased separately for postal purposes. For sheetlets, all the component postage stamps are numbered individually and the composition explained in a footnote. Note that the definitions refer to post office sale—not how items may be subsequently offered by stamp dealers.

12. Forgeries and Fakes

Forgeries. Where space permits, notes are considered if they can give a concise description that will permit unequivocal detection of a forgery. Generalised warnings, lacking detail, are not now-adays inserted, since their value to the collector is problematic.

Forged cancellations have also been applied to genuine stamps. This catalogue includes notes regarding those manufactured by "Madame Joseph", together with the cancellation dates known to exist. It should be remembered that these dates also exist as genuine cancellations.

For full details of these see *Madame Joseph Forged Postmarks* by Derick Worboys (published by the Royal Philatelic Society London and the British Philatelic Trust in 1994) or *Madame Joseph Revisited* by Brian Cartwright (published by the Royal Philatelic Society London in 2005).

Fakes. Unwitting fakes are numerous, particularly "new shades" which are colour changelings brought about by exposure to sunlight, soaking in water contaminated with dyes from adherent paper, contact with oil and dirt from a pocketbook, and so on. Fraudulent operators, in addition, can offer to arrange: removal of hinge marks; repairs of thins on white or coloured papers; replacement of missing margins or perforations; reperforating in true or false gauges; removal of fiscal cancellations; rejoining of severed pairs, strips and blocks; and (a major hazard) regumming. Collectors can only be urged to purchase from reputable sources and to insist upon Expert Committee certification where there is any kind of doubt.

The Catalogue can consider footnotes about fakes where these are specific enough to assist in detection.

Abbreviations

Printers

A.B.N. Co.	American Bank Note Co, New York.
B.A.B.N.	British American Bank Note Co. Ottawa
B.W.	Bradbury Wilkinson & Co, Ltd.
C.B.N.	Canadian Bank Note Co, Ottawa.
Continental B.N. Co.	Continental Bank Note Co.
Courvoisier	Imprimerie Courvoisier S.A., La-Chaux-de-Fonds, Switzerland.
D.L.R.	De La Rue & Co, Ltd, London.
Enschedé	Joh. Enschedé en Zonen, Haarlem, Netherlands.
Harrison	Harrison & Sons, Ltd. London
P.B.	Perkins Bacon Ltd, London.
Waterlow	Waterlow & Sons, Ltd, London.

General Abbreviations

Alph	Alphabet
Anniv	Anniversary
Comp	Compound (perforation)
Des	Designer; designed
Diag	Diagonal; diagonally
Eng	Engraver; engraved
F.C.	Fiscal Cancellation
H/S	Handstamped
Horiz	Horizontal; horizontally
Imp, Imperf	Imperforate
Inscr	Inscribed
L	Left
Litho	Lithographed
mm	Millimetres
MS	Miniature sheet
N.Y.	New York
Opt(d)	Overprint(ed)
P or P-c	Pen-cancelled
P, Pf or Perf	Perforated
Photo	Photogravure
Pl	Plate
Pr	Pair
Ptd	Printed
Ptg	Printing
R	Right
R.	Row
Recess	Recess-printed
Roto	Rotogravure
Roul	Rouletted
S	Specimen (overprint)
Surch	Surcharge(d)
T.C.	Telegraph Cancellation
T	Type
Typo	Typographed
Un	Unused
Us	Used
Vert	Vertical; vertically
W or wmk	Watermark
Wmk s	Watermark sideways

(†) = Does not exist

(–) (or blank price column) = Exists, or may exist, but no market price is known.

/ between colours means "on" and the colour following is that of the paper on which the stamp is printed.

Colours of Stamps

Bl (blue); blk (black); brn (brown); car, carm (carmine); choc (chocolate); clar (claret); emer (emerald); grn (green); ind (indigo); mag (magenta); mar (maroon); mult (multicoloured); mve (mauve); ol (olive); orge (orange); pk (pink); pur (purple); scar (scarlet); sep (sepia); turq (turquoise); ultram (ultramarine); verm (vermilion); vio (violet); yell (yellow).

Colour of Overprints and Surcharges

(B.) = blue, (Blk.) = black, (Br.) = brown, (C.) = carmine, (G.) = green, (Mag.) = magenta, (Mve.) = mauve, (Ol.) = olive, (O.) = orange, (P.) = purple, (Pk.) = pink, (R.) = red, (Sil.) = silver, (V.) = violet, (Vm.) or (Verm.) = vermilion, (W.) = white, (Y.) = yellow.

Arabic Numerals

As in the case of European figures, the details of the Arabic numerals vary in different stamp designs, but they should be readily recognised with the aid of this illustration.

٠	١	٢	٣	٤	٥	٦	٧	٨	٩
0	1	2	3	4	5	6	7	8	9

International Philatelic Glossary

English	*French*	*German*	*Spanish*	*Italian*
Agate	Agate	Achat	Agata	Agata
Air stamp	Timbre de la poste aérienne	Flugpostmarke	Sello de correo aéreo	Francobollo per posta aerea
Apple Green	Vert-pomme	Apfelgrün	Verde manzana	Verde mela
Barred	Annulé par barres	Balkenentwertung	Anulado con barras	Sbarrato
Bisected	Timbre coupé	Halbiert	Partido en dos	Frazionato
Bistre	Bistre	Bister	Bistre	Bistro
Bistre-brown	Brun-bistre	Bisterbraun	Castaño bistre	Bruno-bistro
Black	Noir	Schwarz	Negro	Nero
Blackish Brown	Brun-noir	Schwärzlichbraun	Castaño negruzco	Bruno nerastro
Blackish Green	Vert foncé	Schwärzlichgrün	Verde negruzco	Verde nerastro
Blackish Olive	Olive foncé	Schwärzlicholiv	Oliva negruzco	Oliva nerastro
Block of four	Bloc de quatre	Viererblock	Bloque de cuatro	Bloco di quattro
Blue	Bleu	Blau	Azul	Azzurro
Blue-green	Vert-bleu	Blaugrün	Verde azul	Verde azzuro
Bluish Violet	Violet bleuâtre	Bläulichviolett	Violeta azulado	Violtto azzurrastro
Booklet	Carnet	Heft	Cuadernillo	Libretto
Bright Blue	Bleu vif	Lebhaftblau	Azul vivo	Azzurro vivo
Bright Green	Vert vif	Lebhaftgrün	Verde vivo	Verde vivo
Bright Purple	Mauve vif	Lebhaftpurpur	Púrpura vivo	Porpora vivo
Bronze Green	Vert-bronze	Bronzegrün	Verde bronce	Verde bronzo
Brown	Brun	Braun	Castaño	Bruno
Brown-lake	Carmin-brun	Braunlack	Laca castaño	Lacca bruno
Brown-purple	Pourpre-brun	Braunpurpur	Púrpura castaño	Porpora bruno
Brown-red	Rouge-brun	Braunrot	Rojo castaño	Rosso bruno
Buff	Chamois	Sämisch	Anteado	Camoscio
Cancellation	Oblitération	Entwertung	Cancelación	Annullamento
Cancelled	Annulé	Gestempelt	Cancelado	Annullato
Carmine	Carmin	Karmin	Carmín	Carminio
Carmine-red	Rouge-carmin	Karminrot	Rojo carmín	Rosso carminio
Centred	Centré	Zentriert	Centrado	Centrato
Cerise	Rouge-cerise	Kirschrot	Color de ceresa	Color Ciliegia
Chalk-surfaced paper	Papier couché	Kreidepapier	Papel estucado	Carta gessata
Chalky Blue	Bleu terne	Kreideblau	Azul turbio	Azzurro smorto
Charity stamp	Timbre de bienfaisance	Wohltätigkeitsmarke	Sello de beneficenza	Francobollo di beneficenza
Chestnut	Marron	Kastanienbraun	Castaño rojo	Marrone
Chocolate	Chocolat	Schokolade	Chocolate	Cioccolato
Cinnamon	Cannelle	Zimtbraun	Canela	Cannella
Claret	Grenat	Weinrot	Rojo vinoso	Vinaccia
Cobalt	Cobalt	Kobalt	Cobalto	Cobalto
Colour	Couleur	Farbe	Color	Colore
Comb-perforation	Dentelure en peigne	Kammzähnung, Reihenzähnung	Dentado de peine	Dentellatura e pettine
Commemorative stamp	Timbre commémoratif	Gedenkmarke	Sello conmemorativo	Francobollo commemorativo
Crimson	Cramoisi	Karmesin	Carmesí	Cremisi
Deep Blue	Blue foncé	Dunkelblau	Azul oscuro	Azzurro scuro
Deep bluish Green	Vert-bleu foncé	Dunkelbläulichgrün	Verde azulado oscuro	Verde azzurro scuro
Design	Dessin	Markenbild	Diseño	Disegno
Die	Matrice	Urstempel. Type, Platte	Cuño	Conio, Matrice
Double	Double	Doppelt	Doble	Doppio
Drab	Olive terne	Trüboliv	Oliva turbio	Oliva smorto
Dull Green	Vert terne	Trübgrün	Verde turbio	Verde smorto
Dull purple	Mauve terne	Trübpurpur	Púrpura turbio	Porpora smorto
Embossing	Impression en relief	Prägedruck	Impresión en relieve	Impressione a relievo
Emerald	Vert-eméraude	Smaragdgrün	Esmeralda	Smeraldo
Engraved	Gravé	Graviert	Grabado	Inciso
Error	Erreur	Fehler, Fehldruck	Error	Errore
Essay	Essai	Probedruck	Ensayo	Saggio
Express letter stamp	Timbre pour lettres par exprès	Eilmarke	Sello de urgencia	Francobollo per espresso
Fiscal stamp	Timbre fiscal	Stempelmarke	Sello fiscal	Francobollo fiscale
Flesh	Chair	Fleischfarben	Carne	Carnicino
Forgery	Faux, Falsification	Fälschung	Falsificación	Falso, Falsificazione
Frame	Cadre	Rahmen	Marco	Cornice
Granite paper	Papier avec fragments	Faserpapier	Papel con filamentos	Carto con fili di seta

English	*French*	*German*	*Spanish*	*Italian*
	de fils de soie			
Green	Vert	Grün	Verde	Verde
Greenish Blue	Bleu verdâtre	Grünlichblau	Azul verdoso	Azzurro verdastro
Greenish Yellow	Jaune-vert	Grünlichgelb	Amarillo verdoso	Giallo verdastro
Grey	Gris	Grau	Gris	Grigio
Grey-blue	Bleu-gris	Graublau	Azul gris	Azzurro grigio
Grey-green	Vert gris	Graugrün	Verde gris	Verde grigio
Gum	Gomme	Gummi	Goma	Gomma
Gutter	Interpanneau	Zwischensteg	Espacio blanco entre dos grupos	Ponte
Imperforate	Non-dentelé	Geschnitten	Sin dentar	Non dentellato
Indigo	Indigo	Indigo	Azul indigo	Indaco
Inscription	Inscription	Inschrift	Inscripción	Dicitura
Inverted	Renversé	Kopfstehend	Invertido	Capovolto
Issue	Émission	Ausgabe	Emisión	Emissione
Laid	Vergé	Gestreift	Listado	Vergato
Lake	Lie de vin	Lackfarbe	Laca	Lacca
Lake-brown	Brun-carmin	Lackbraun	Castaño laca	Bruno lacca
Lavender	Bleu-lavande	Lavendel	Color de alhucema	Lavanda
Lemon	Jaune-citron	Zitrongelb	Limón	Limone
Light Blue	Bleu clair	Hellblau	Azul claro	Azzurro chiaro
Lilac	Lilas	Lila	Lila	Lilla
Line perforation	Dentelure en lignes	Linienzähnung	Dentado en linea	Dentellatura lineare
Lithography	Lithographie	Steindruck	Litografía	Litografia
Local	Timbre de poste locale	Lokalpostmarke	Emisión local	Emissione locale
Lozenge roulette	Percé en losanges	Rautenförmiger Durchstich	Picadura en rombos	Perforazione a losanghe
Magenta	Magenta	Magentarot	Magenta	Magenta
Margin	Marge	Rand	Borde	Margine
Maroon	Marron pourpré	Dunkelrotpurpur	Púrpura rojo oscuro	Marrone rossastro
Mauve	Mauve	Malvenfarbe	Malva	Malva
Multicoloured	Polychrome	Mehrfarbig	Multicolores	Policromo
Myrtle Green	Vert myrte	Myrtengrün	Verde mirto	Verde mirto
New Blue	Bleu ciel vif	Neublau	Azul nuevo	Azzurro nuovo
Newspaper stamp	Timbre pour journaux	Zeitungsmarke	Sello para periódicos	Francobollo per giornali
Obliteration	Oblitération	Abstempelung	Matasello	Annullamento
Obsolete	Hors (de) cours	Ausser Kurs	Fuera de curso	Fuori corso
Ochre	Ocre	Ocker	Ocre	Ocra
Official stamp	Timbre de service	Dienstmarke	Sello de servicio	Francobollo di
Olive-brown	Brun-olive	Olivbraun	Castaño oliva	Bruno oliva
Olive-green	Vert-olive	Olivgrün	Verde oliva	Verde oliva
Olive-grey	Gris-olive	Olivgrau	Gris oliva	Grigio oliva
Olive-yellow	Jaune-olive	Olivgelb	Amarillo oliva	Giallo oliva
Orange	Orange	Orange	Naranja	Arancio
Orange-brown	Brun-orange	Orangebraun	Castaño naranja	Bruno arancio
Orange-red	Rouge-orange	Orangerot	Rojo naranja	Rosso arancio
Orange-yellow	Jaune-orange	Orangegelb	Amarillo naranja	Giallo arancio
Overprint	Surcharge	Aufdruck	Sobrecarga	Soprastampa
Pair	Paire	Paar	Pareja	Coppia
Pale	Pâle	Blass	Pálido	Pallido
Pane	Panneau	Gruppe	Grupo	Gruppo
Paper	Papier	Papier	Papel	Carta
Parcel post stamp	Timbre pour colis postaux	Paketmarke	Sello para paquete postal	Francobollo per pacchi
Pen-cancelled	Oblitéré à plume	Federzugentwertung	Cancelado a pluma	Annullato a penna
Percé en arc	Percé en arc	Bogenförmiger Durchstich	Picadura en forma de arco	Perforazione ad arco
Percé en scie	Percé en scie	Bogenförmiger Durchstich	Picado en sierra	Foratura a sega
Perforated	Dentelé	Gezähnt	Dentado	Dentellato
Perforation	Dentelure	Zähnung	Dentar	Dentellatura
Photogravure	Photogravure, Heliogravure	Rastertiefdruck	Fotograbado	Rotocalco
Pin perforation	Percé en points	In Punkten durchstochen	Horadado con alfileres	Perforato a punti
Plate	Planche	Platte	Plancha	Lastra, Tavola
Plum	Prune	Pflaumenfarbe	Color de ciruela	Prugna
Postage Due stamp	Timbre-taxe	Portomarke	Sello de tasa	Segnatasse
Postage stamp	Timbre-poste	Briefmarke, Freimarke, Postmarke	Sello de correos	Francobollo postale
Postal fiscal stamp	Timbre fiscal-postal	Stempelmarke als Postmarke verwendet	Sello fiscal-postal	Fiscale postale
Postmark	Oblitération postale	Poststempel	Matasello	Bollo
Printing	Impression, Tirage	Druck	Impresión	Stampa, Tiratura
Proof	Épreuve	Druckprobe	Prueba de impresión	Prova
Provisionals	Timbres provisoires	Provisorische Marken. Provisorien	Provisionales	Provvisori
Prussian Blue	Bleu de Prusse	Preussischblau	Azul de Prusia	Azzurro di Prussia
Purple	Pourpre	Purpur	Púrpura	Porpora
Purple-brown	Brun-pourpre	Purpurbraun	Castaño púrpura	Bruno porpora

English	*French*	*German*	*Spanish*	*Italian*
Recess-printing	Impression en taille douce	Tiefdruck	Grabado	Incisione
Red	Rouge	Rot	Rojo	Rosso
Red-brown	Brun-rouge	Rotbraun	Castaño rojizo	Bruno rosso
Reddish Lilac	Lilas rougeâtre	Rötlichlila	Lila rojizo	Lilla rossastro
Reddish Purple	Poupre-rouge	Rötlichpurpur	Púrpura rojizo	Porpora rossastro
Reddish Violet	Violet rougeâtre	Rötlichviolett	Violeta rojizo	Violetto rossastro
Red-orange	Orange rougeâtre	Rotorange	Naranja rojizo	Arancio rosso
Registration stamp	Timbre pour lettre chargée (recommandée)	Einschreibemarke	Sello de certificado lettere	Francobollo per
Reprint	Réimpression	Neudruck	Reimpresión	Ristampa
Reversed	Retourné	Umgekehrt	Invertido	Rovesciato
Rose	Rose	Rosa	Rosa	Rosa
Rose-red	Rouge rosé	Rosarot	Rojo rosado	Rosso rosa
Rosine	Rose vif	Lebhaftrosa	Rosa vivo	Rosa vivo
Roulette	Percage	Durchstich	Picadura	Foratura
Rouletted	Percé	Durchstochen	Picado	Forato
Royal Blue	Bleu-roi	Königblau	Azul real	Azzurro reale
Sage green	Vert-sauge	Salbeigrün	Verde salvia	Verde salvia
Salmon	Saumon	Lachs	Salmón	Salmone
Scarlet	Écarlate	Scharlach	Escarlata	Scarlatto
Sepia	Sépia	Sepia	Sepia	Seppia
Serpentine roulette	Percé en serpentin	Schlangenliniger Durchstich	Picado a serpentina	Perforazione a serpentina
Shade	Nuance	Tönung	Tono	Gradazione de colore
Sheet	Feuille	Bogen	Hoja	Foglio
Slate	Ardoise	Schiefer	Pizarra	Ardesia
Slate-blue	Bleu-ardoise	Schieferblau	Azul pizarra	Azzurro ardesia
Slate-green	Vert-ardoise	Schiefergrün	Verde pizarra	Verde ardesia
Slate-lilac	Lilas-gris	Schierferlila	Lila pizarra	Lilla ardesia
Slate-purple	Mauve-gris	Schieferpurpur	Púrpura pizarra	Porpora ardesia
Slate-violet	Violet-gris	Schieferviolett	Violeta pizarra	Violetto ardesia
Special delivery stamp	Timbre pour exprès	Eilmarke	Sello de urgencia	Francobollo per espressi
Specimen	Spécimen	Muster	Muestra	Saggio
Steel Blue	Bleu acier	Stahlblau	Azul acero	Azzurro acciaio
Strip	Bande	Streifen	Tira	Striscia
Surcharge	Surcharge	Aufdruck	Sobrecarga	Soprastampa
Tête-bêche	Tête-bêche	Kehrdruck	Tête-bêche	Tête-bêche
Tinted paper	Papier teinté	Getöntes Papier	Papel coloreado	Carta tinta
Too-late stamp	Timbre pour lettres en retard	Verspätungsmarke	Sello para cartas retardadas	Francobollo per le lettere in ritardo
Turquoise-blue	Bleu-turquoise	Türkisblau	Azul turquesa	Azzurro turchese
Turquoise-green	Vert-turquoise	Türkisgrün	Verde turquesa	Verde turchese
Typography	Typographie	Buchdruck	Tipografia	Tipografia
Ultramarine	Outremer	Ultramarin	Ultramar	Oltremare
Unused	Neuf	Ungebraucht	Nuevo	Nuovo
Used	Oblitéré, Usé	Gebraucht	Usado	Usato
Venetian Red	Rouge-brun terne	Venezianischrot	Rojo veneciano	Rosso veneziano
Vermilion	Vermillon	Zinnober	Cinabrio	Vermiglione
Violet	Violet	Violett	Violeta	Violetto
Violet-blue	Bleu-violet	Violettblau	Azul violeta	Azzurro violetto
Watermark	Filigrane	Wasserzeichen	Filigrana	Filigrana
Watermark sideways	Filigrane couché liegend	Wasserzeichen	Filigrana acostado	Filigrana coricata
Wove paper	Papier ordinaire, Papier uni	Einfaches Papier	Papel avitelado	Carta unita
Yellow	Jaune	Gelb	Amarillo	Giallo
Yellow-brown	Brun-jaune	Gelbbraun	Castaño amarillo	Bruno giallo
Yellow-green	Vert-jaune	Gelbgrün	Verde amarillo	Verde giallo
Yellow-olive	Olive-jaunâtre	Gelboliv	Oliva amarillo	Oliva giallastro
Yellow-orange	Orange jaunâtre	Gelborange	Naranja amarillo	Arancio giallastro
Zig-zag roulette	Percé en zigzag	Sägezahnartiger Durchstich	Picado en zigzag	Perforazione a zigzag

Specialist Philatelic Societies

Requests for inclusion on this page should be sent to the Catalogue Editor.

Great Britain Philatelic Society
Membership Secretary – Mr P. Tanner,
"High Standings" 13 Huberts Close,
Gerards Cross, Bucks SL9 7EN

Great Britain Collectors' Club
Secretary – Mr L Rosenblum
103 East Camino Real PMB, Sunnydale
CA, U.S.A.

Channel Islands Specialists Society
Membership Secretary – Sheila Marshall,
3 La Marette, St. Anne, Alderney
GY9 3UQ

GB Overprints Society
Secretary – Mr A. Stanford,
P. O. Box 2675, Maidenhead, SL6 9ZN.

Aden & Somaliand Study Group
UK Representative – Mr M. Lacey
P.O. Box 9, Winchester, Hampshire
SO22 5RF

Ascension Study Circle
Secretary – Dr. R.C.F. Baker
Greys, Tower Road, Whitstable,
Kent CT5 3ER

Australian States Study Circle
Royal Sydney Philatelic Club
Honorary Secretary – Mr. B. Palmer
G.P.O. Box 1751, Sydney
N.S.W. 1043 Australia

British Society of Australian Philately
Secretary – Mr. A.J. Griffiths
c/o The Royal Philatelic Society
41 Devonshire Place, London W1G 6JY

Society of Australasian Specialists/Oceania
Secretary – Mr. S. Leven
P.O. Box 24764, San Jose, CA 95154-4764
U.S.A.

Bechuanalands and Bostwana Society
Membership Secretary – Mr. N. Midwood
69 Porlock Lane, Furzton,
Milton Keynes MK4 1JY

Bermuda Collectors Society
Secretary – Mr. T.J. McMahon
P.O. Box 1949, Stuart, FL 34995 U.S.A.

British Caribbean Philatelic Study Group
Overseas Director – Mr. D.N. Druett
Pennymead Auctions, 1 Brewerton Street,
Knaresborough, North Yorkshire HG5 8AZ

British West Indies Study Circle
Membership Secretary – Mr. P.G. Boulton
84 Tangier Road, Richmond,
Surrey TW10 5DN

Burma (Myanmar) Philatelic Study Circle
Secretary – Mr. D. Taylor Smith,
30 Seabrook Court,
Norwich NR5 9NQ

Canadian Philatelic Society of Great Britain
Secretary – Mr. J.M. Wright,
12 Milchester House, Staveley Road
Meads, Eastbourne, East Sussex BN20 7JX

Cape and Natal Study Circle
Secretary – Mr. J. Dickson, Lismore House,
Great Lane, Shepton Beauchamp,
Somerset TA19 0LJ

Ceylon Study Circle
Secretary – Mr. R.W.P. Frost
42 Lonsdale Road, Cannington, Bridgewater,
Somerset TA5 2JS

Cyprus Study Circle
Membership Secretary – Mr J. Wigmore
19 Riversmeet, Appledore, Bideford,
North Devon EX39 1RE

East Africa Study Circle
Honorary secretary – Mr. J.P. A. Smalley
1 Lincoln Close, Tewkesbury, Glos
GL20 5TY

Egypt Study Circle
Secretary – Mr M. Murphy,
109 Chadwick Road, Peckham, London SE15
4PY

Falklands Islands Study Group
Membership Secretary – Mr D.W.A. Jeffery,
8 Bridge Court, Bridge Street,
Leatherhead, Surrey KT22 8BW

Gibraltar Study Circle
Membership Secretary – Mr E. D. Holmes,
29 Highgate Road, Woodley, Reading RG5 3ND

Hong Kong Study Circle
Membership Secretary -- Mr. P.V. Ball
37 Hart Court, Newcastle-under-Lyme,
Staffordshire ST5 2AL

Indian Ocean Study Circle
Secretary – Mrs S. Hopson
Field Acre, Hoe Benham, Newbury,
Berkshire RG20 8PD

India Study Circle
Secretary – Mr B. Allcock
9 Golspie Croft, Hodge Lea,
Milton Keynes MK12 6JU

Irish Philatelic Circle
General Secretary – Mr. F. McDonald
63 Rafters Road, Drimnagh, Dublin 12,
Ireland

King George V Silver Jubilee Study Circle
President – Mr. N. Donen
31-4525 Wilkinson Road, Victoria, BC,
V8Z 5C3, Canada

King George VI Collectors Society
Secretary – Mr. J.L. Shaw MBE
17 Balcaskie Road, Eltham
London SE9 1HQ

Kiribati and Tuvalu Philatelic Society
Honorary Secretary – Mr. M.J. Shaw
88 Stoneleigh Avenue, Worcester Park,
Surrey KT4 8XY

Malaya Study Group
Membership Secretary – Mr. D. Morris
1 Howland Place, Woburn,
Bucks MK17 9QR

Malta Study Circle
Honorary Secretary – Mr. D. Crookes
9a Church Street,
Durham DH1 3DG

New Zealand Society of Great Britain
General Secretary – Mr. K.C. Collins
13 Briton Crescent Sanderstead
Surrey CR2 0JN

Orange Free State Study Circle
Secrertary – Mr. J.R. Stroud
28 Oxford Street, Burnham-on-Sea,
Somerset TA8 1LQ

Pacific Islands Study Circle
Honorary Secretary – Mr. J.D. Ray
24 Woodvale Avenue, London SE25 4AE

Papua Philatelic Society
Secretary – Mr. D.C. Ashton
71 Lowerside, Ham, Plymouth
Devon PL2 2HU

Pitcairn Islands Study Group (U.K.)
Honorary Secretary – Mr. D. Sleep
6 Palace Gardens, 100 Court Road, Eltham,
London SE9 5NS

Rhodesian Study Circle
Membership Secretary – Mr. R.G. Barnett
2 Cox Ley, Hatfield Heath,
Bishop's Stortford CM22 7ER

Royal Philatelic Society of New Zealand
Secretary – Mr. W.T.C. Kitching
P.O. Box 1269, Wellington,
New Zealand

St. Helena, Ascension and Tristan da Cunha
Philatelic Society
Secretary – Mr. J. Havill
205 N. Murray Blvd., #221, Colorado Springs,
CO 80916 U.S.A.

Sarawak Specialists Society
(also Brunei, North Borneo and Labuan)
Secretary – Dr. J. Higgins
31 Grimston Road, Kings Lynn,
Norfolk PE30 3HT

South African Collectors' Society
General Secretary – Mr. C. Oliver
Telephone 020 8940 9833

Philatelic Society of Sri Lanka
Secretary – Mr. H. Goonawardena, J.P.
44A Hena Road, Mt. Lavinia 10370,
Sri Lanka

Sudan Study Group
Secretary – Mr B.A. Gardner, Chimneys,
Mapledurwell, Basingstoke, Hants
RG25 2LH

Transvaal Study Circle
Secretary – Mr. J. Woolgar
132 Dale Street, Chatham, Kent
ME4 6QH

West Africa Study Circle
Secretary – Mr. J. Powell
23 Brook Street, Edlesborough, Dunstable,
Bedfordshire LU6 2LG IBAR

Select Bibliography

The literature on British Commonwealth stamps is vast, but works are often difficult to obtain once they are out of print. The selection of books below has been made on the basis of authority together with availability to the general reader, either as new or secondhand. Very specialised studies, and those covering aspects of postal history to which there are no references in the catalogue, have been excluded.

The following abbreviations are used to denote publishers:

- CRL Christie's Robson Lowe;
- HH Harry Hayes;
- PB Proud Bailey Co. Ltd. and Postal History Publications Co.;
- PC Philip Cockrill;
- RPSL Royal Philatelic Society, London;
- SG Stanley Gibbons Ltd.

Where no publisher is quoted, the book is published by its author.

GENERAL

Encylopaedia of British Empire Postage Stamps. Vols 1-6. Edited Robson Lowe. (CRL, 1951–1991)

Specimen Stamps of the Crown Colonies 1857-1948. Marcus Samuel. (RPSL, 1976 and 1984 Supplement)

Cancelled by Perkins Bacon. P. Jaffé. (Spink & Son Ltd., 1998)

U.P.U. Specimen Stamps. J. Bendon. (1988)

King George V Key Plates of the Imperium Postage and Revenue Design. P. Fernbank. (West Africa Study Circle, 1997)

Silver Jubilee of King George V Stamps Handbook. A.J. Ainscough. (Ainweel Developments, 1985)

The Commemorative Stamps of the British Commonwealth. H.D.S. Haverbeck. (Faber, 1955)

The Printings of King George VI Colonial Stamps. W.J.W. Potter & Lt-Col R.C.M. Shelton. (1952 and later facsimile edition)

King George VI Large Key Type Stamps of Bermuda, Leeward Islands, Nyasaland. R.W. Dickgiesser and E.P. Yendall. (Triad Publications, 1985)

Madame Joseph Forged Postmarks. D. Worboys. (RPSL, 1994)

Madame Joseph Revisted. B.M. Cartwright. (RPSL, 2005)

G.B. Used Abroad: Cancellations and Postal Markings. J. Parmenter. (The Postal History Society, 1993)

GREAT BRITAIN

For extensive bibliographies see *G.B. Specialised Catalogues. Vols 1-5.*

Stamps and Postal History of the Channel Islands. W. Newport. (Heineman, 1972)

ADEN

The Postal History of British Aden 1839-1967. Major R.W. Pratt. (PB, 1985)

The Postal History of Aden and Somaliland Protectorate. E. B. Proud. (PB, 2004)

ASCENSION

Ascension. The Stamps and Postal History. J.H. Attwood. (CRL, 1981)

AUSTRALIA

The Postal History of New South Wales 1788-1901. Edited J.S. White. (Philatelic Association of New South Wales, 1988)

South Australia. The Long Stamps 1902-12. J.R.W. Purves. (Royal Philatelic Society of Victoria, 1978)

The Departmental Stamps of South Australia. A.R. Butler. (RPSL, 1978)

A Priced Listing of the Departmental Stamps of South Australia. A.D. Presgrave. (2nd edition, 1999)

Stamps and Postal History of Tasmania. W.E. Tinsley. (RPSL, 1986)

The Pictorial Stamps of Tasmania 1899-1912. K.E. Lancaster. (Royal Philatelic Society of Victoria, 1986)

The Stamps of Victoria. G. Kellow. (B. & K. Philatelic Publishing, 1990)

Western Australia. The Stamps and Postal History. Edited M. Hamilton and B. Pope. (W. Australian Study Group, 1979)

Postage Stamps and Postal History of Western Australia. Vols 1-3. M. Juhl. (1981-83)

The Chapman Collection of Australian Commonwealth Stamps. R. Chapman. (Royal Philatelic Society of Victoria, 1999)

Nauru 1915--1923. K. Buckingham. (The British Philatelic Association Expertising Educational Charity, 2004)

The Postal History of British New Guinea and Papua 1885-1942. R. Lee. (CRL, 1983)

Norfolk Island. A Postal and Philatelic History, 1788-1969. P. Collas & R. Breckon. (B. & K. Philatelic Publishing, 1997)

BAHAMAS

The Postage Stamps and Postal History of the Bahamas. H.G.D. Gisburn, (SG, 1950 and later facsimile edition)

BARBADOS

The Stamps of Barbados. E.A. Bayley. (1989)

Advanced Barbados Philately. H.F. Deakin. (B.W.I. Study Circle, 1997)

BASUTOLAND

The Cancellations and Postal Markings of Basutoland/Lesotho Post Offices. A. H. Scott. (Collectors Mail Auctions (Pty) Ltd., 1980)

BATUM

British Occupation of Batum. P.T. Ashford. (1989)

BECHUANALAND

The Postage Stamps, Postal Stationery and Postmarks of the Bechuanalands. H.R. Holmes. (RPSL, 1971)

BERMUDA

The Postal History and Stamps of Bermuda. M.H. Ludington. (Quarterman Publications Inc., 1978)

The King George V High-value Stamps of Bermuda, 1917-1938. M. Glazer. (Calaby Publishers, 1994)

The Postal History of Bermuda. E.B. Proud. (PB, 2003)

BRITISH GUIANA

The Postage Stamps and Postal History of British Guiana. W.A. Townsend & F.G. Howe. (RPSL, 1970)

BRITISH HONDURAS

The Postal History of British Honduras. E.B. Proud. (PB, 1999)

BRITISH INDIAN OCEAN

THe Postal History of B.I.O.T., Maldive Islands and Seychelles. E. B. Proud (PB, 2006)

BRITISH OCCUPATION OF GERMAN COLONIES

G.R.I. R.M. Gibbs. (CRL, 1989)

BRITISH PACIFIC OCEAN

The Postal History of the British Solomon Islands and Tonga. E.B. Proud (PB, 2006)

The Postal History of the Gilbert and Ellice Islands and new Hebrides. E.B. Proud. (PB, 2006)

BRITISH POSTAL AGENCIES IN EASTERN ARABIA

The Postal Agencies in Eastern Arabia and the Gulf. N. Donaldson. (HH, 1975) and Supplement (Bridger & Kay Guernsey Ltd., 1994)

BRITISH SOLOMON ISLANDS

British Solomon Islands Protectorate. Its Postage Stamps and Postal History. H.G.D. Gisburn. (T. Sanders (Philatelist) Ltd., 1956)

BRITISH WEST AFRICA

The Postal History and Handstamps of British West Africa. C. McCaig. (CRL, 1978)

BRITISH WEST INDIES

The Postal History of the Cayman Islands and Turks & Caicos Islands. E.B. Proud (PB, 2006)

The Postal History of St. Lucia and St. Vincent. E.B. Proud and J. C. Aleong (PB, 2006)

BURMA

Burma Postal History. G. Davis and D Martin. (CRL, 1971 and 1987 Supplement).

The Postal History of Burma. E.B. Proud. (PB, 2002)

CAMEROONS

The Postal Arrangements of the Anglo-French Cameroons Expeditionary Force 1914-1916. R.J. Maddocks. (1996)

CANADA

The Postage Stamps and Postal History of Newfoundland. W.S. Boggs. (Quarterman Publications Inc., 1975)

Stamps of British North America. F. Jarrett. (Quarterman Publications Inc., 1975)

The Postage Stamps and Postal History of Canada. W.S. Boggs. (Quarterman Publications Inc., 1974)

The First Decimal Issue of Canada 1859-68. G. Whitworth. (RPSL, 1966)

The Five Cents Beaver Stamp of Canada. G. Whitworth. (RPSL, 1985)

The Small Queens of Canada. J. Hillson. (CRL, 1989)

Canada Small Queens Re-Appraised. J. Hillson. (Canadian Philatelic Society of Great Britain, 1999)

The Edward VII Issue of Canada, G.C. Marler, (National Postal Museum, Canada, 1975)

The Admiral Issue of Canada. G.C. Marler. (American Philatelic Society, 1982)

CEYLON

The Postal History of Ceylon. E. B. Proud (PB, 2006)

CYPRUS

Cyprus 1353-1986. W. Castle. (CRL 3rd edition, 1987)

DOMINICA

Dominica Postal History, Stamps and Postal Stationery to 1935. E.V. Toeg. (B.W.I. Study Circle, 1994)

EGYPT

Egypt Stamps & Postal History. P.A.S. Smith. (James Bendon, 1999)

The Nile Post. J. H. Chalhoub. (2003)

FALKLAND ISLANDS

The Postage Stamps of the Falkland Islands and Dependencies. B.S.H. Grant. (SG, 1952 and later facsimile edition)

The Falkland Islands Philatelic Digest. Nos. 1 & 2. M. Barton and R Spafford. (HH, 1975 and 1979)

The De La Rue Definitives of the Falkland Islands 1901-1929. J.P. Bunt. (1986 and 1996 Supplement)

The Falkland Islands. The 1891 Provisionals. M. Barton. (BPA Expertising Educational Trust, 2002)

The War Stamp Overprints of the Falkland Islands 1918-1920. J.P. Bunt. (1981)

The Falkland Islands. Printings of the Pictorial Issue of 1938-49. C.E. Glass. (CRL, 1979)

The Postal History of the Falkland Islands and Dependencies. E.B. Proud (PB, 2006)

FIJI

Fiji Philatelics. D.E.F. Alford. (Pacific Islands Study Circle, 1994)

Fiji Queen Victoria One Shilling and Five Shillings Postage Stamps 1881-1902. R.F. Duberal. (Pacific Islands Study Circle, 2003)

The Postal History of Fiji 1911-1952. J.G. Rodger. (Pacific Islands Study Circle, 1991)

GAMBIA

The Stamps and Postal History of the Gambia. Edited J.O. Andrew. (CRL, 1985)

The Postal History of the Gambia. E.B. Proud. (PB, 1994)

GIBRALTAR

Posted in Gibraltar. W. Hine-Haycock. (CRL, 1978 and 1983 Supplement)

Gibraltar. The Postal History and Postage Stamps. Vol 1 to 1885. G. Osborn. (Gibraltar Study Circle, 1995)

The Postal History of Gibraltar. R.J.M. Garcia & E.B. Proud. (PB, 1998)

Gibraltar, Collecting King George VI. E. Chambers. (The Gibraltar Study Circle, 2003)

GOLD COAST

The Postal History of the Gold Coast. E.B. Proud. (PB, 1995)

The Postal Services of the Gold Coast, 1901-1957. Edited M. Ensor. (West Africa Study Circle, 1998)

The Postal Services of the Gold Coast to 1901. Edited J. Sacher. (RPSL, 2003)

HONG KONG

The Philatelic History of Hong Kong. Vol 1. (Hong Kong Study Circle, 1984)

Hong Kong Postage Stamps of the Queen Victoria Period. R.N. Gurevitch. (1993)

Hong Kong. The 1898 10c. on 30c. Provisional Issue. A.M. Chu. (1998)

The Postal History History of Hong Kong. E.B. Proud (PB, 2004)

British Post Offices in the Far East. E.B. Proud. (PB, 1991)

Cancellations of the Treaty Ports of Hong Kong. H. Schoenfield. (1988)

The Crown Colony of Wei Hai Wei. M.Goldsmith and C.W. Goodwyn. (RPSL, 1985)

INDIA

C.E.F. The China Expeditionary force 1900-1923. D.S. Virk, J.C. Hume, G. Sattin. (Philatelic Congress of India, 1992)

India Used Abroad. V.S. Dastur. (Mysore Philatelics, 1982)

The Indian Postal Agencies in the Persian Gulf Area. A. Parsons. (Sahara Publications Ltd., 2001)

A Handbook on Gwalior Postal History and Stamps. V.K. Gupta. (1980)

The Stamps of Jammu & Kashmir. F. Staal. (The Collectors Club, 1983)

Sorath Stamps and Postal History. R.A. Malaviya. (Ravi Prakashan, 1999)

IRAQ

The Postal History of Iraq. P.C. Pearson and E.B. Proud. (PB, 1996)

IRELAND

Irish Stamp Booklets 1931-1991. C.J. Dulin. (1998)

British Stamps Overprinted for use in Ireland during the Transitional Period. Barry Cousins (Irish Philatelic Circle, 2008)

JAMAICA

Encyclopaedia of Jamaican Philately. Vol 1. D.Sutcliffe & S. Jarvis. (1997); *Vol 6.* S. Jarvis. (2001) (B.W.I. Study Circle)

Jamaica, the Definitive and Commemorative Stamps and Postal Stationery of the Reign of King George VI. H.A.H. James. (The King George VI Collectors Society, 1999)

KENYA

British East Africa. The Stamps and Postal Stationery. J. Minns. (RPSL, 1982 and 1990 Supplement) (New edition, revised and updated, George T. Krieger, 2006)

The Postal History of Kenya. E.B. Proud. (PB, 1992)

LEEWARD ISLANDS

The Leeward Islands – Notes for Philatelists. M.N. Oliver. (B.W.I. Study Circle, 2000)

MALAYA

The Postal History of British Malaya. Vols 1-3. E.B. Proud. (PB, 2nd edition, 2000)

The Postage Stamps of Federated Malay States. W.A. Reeves. (Malaya Study Group, 1978)

Kedah and Perlis. D.R.M. Holley. (Malaya Study Group, 1995)

Kelantan. Its Stamps and Postal History. W.A. Reeves and B.E. Dexter. (Malaya Study Group, 1992)

The Postal History of the Occupation of Malaya and British Borneo 1941-1945. E.B. Proud and M.D. Rowell. (PB, 1992)

MALTA

Malta. The Postal History and Postage Stamps. Edited R.E. Martin. (CRL, 1980 and 1985 Supplement)

MAURITIUS

The Postal History and Stamps of Mauritius. P. Ibbotson. (RPSL, 1991); Revisions and additions Supplement (Indian Ocean Study Circle, 1995)

The Postal History of Mauritius. E.B. Proud. (PB, 2001)

MONTSERRAT

Montserrat to 1965. L.E. Britnor. (B.W.I. Study Circle. 2nd edition, 1998)

MOROCCO AGENCIES

British Post Offices and Agencies in Morocco 1857-1907 and Local Posts 1891-1914. R.K. Clough. (Gibraltar Study Circle, 1984)

NEW ZEALAND

The Postage Stamps of New Zealand. Vols I-VII. (Royal Philatelic Society of New Zealand. 1939—98)

The Early Cook Islands Post Office. A.R. Burge (Hawthorn Pres, 1978)

The Postal History and Postage Stamps of the Tokelau/Union Islands. A.H. Burgess. (Pacific Islands Study Circle, 2nd edition, 1998)

A Postal History of the Samoan Islands (Parts I and II). Edited R. Burge. (Royal Philatelic Society of New Zealand, 1987-89)

The Stamps and Postal History of Nineteenth Century Samoa. R.P. Odenweller. (RPSL and The Royal Philatelic Society of New Zealand, 2004)

The 1893 new Zealand Advertisement Stamps. J.A. Robb (Christchurch (N.Z.) Philatelic Society, 2006)

NIGERIA

The Postal Services of the British Nigeria Region. J. Ince and J. Sacher. (RPSL, 1992)

The Postal History of Nigeria. E.B. Proud (PB, 1995)

NORTH BORNEO

A Concise Guide to the Queen Issues of Labuan. R. Price. (Sarawak Specialists Society, 1991)

The Stamps and Postal History of North Borneo. Parts 1-3. L.H. Shipman and P.K. Cassells. (Sarawak Specialists Society, 1976-88)

The Postal History of British Borneo. E.B. Proud. (PB, 2003)

NORTHERN RHODESIA

Northern Rhodesia – The Mkushi Postage Dues and the renamed Old Mkushi Post Office Otto Peetoom (2005)

The King George VI Postage and Revenue Stamps of Northern Rhodesia Alan Drysdall, Ian Lane and Jean Cheston (Rhodesia Study Circle, 2006)

NYASALAND

The Postal History of Nyasaland. E.B. Proud. (PB, 1997)

PALESTINE

The Stamps & Postal Stationery of Palestine Mandate 1918-1948. D. Dorfman. (Edward G. Rosen, 2001)

The Postal History of Palestine and Transjordan. E.B. Proud. (PB, 2006)

PITCAIRN ISLANDS

Pitcairn Islands Philately. D.E. Hume. (3rd edition, 2006)

RHODESIA

Mashonaland. A Postal History 1890—96. Dr. A.R. Drysdall and D. Collis. (CRL, 1990)

Rhodesia. A Postal History. R.C. Smith. (1967 and 1970 Supplement)

The Rhodesia Philatelist. (Ormskirk Stamps)

ST. HELENA

St. Helena, Postal History and Stamps. E. Hibbert. (CRL, 1979)

The Postal History of Ascension, St. Helena & Tristan da Cunha. E.B. Proud. (PB, 2005)

ST. KITTS-NEVIS

A Study of the King George VI Stamps of St. Kitts-Nevis. P.L. Baldwin. (Murray Payne Ltd., 2nd edition, 1997)

The Philately of Nevis. F. Borromeo. (British West Indies Study Circle, 2001)

SARAWAK

The Stamps and Postal History of Sarawak. W.A. Forrester-Wood. (Sarawak Specialists Society, 1959 and 1970 Supplement)

Sarawak: The Issues of 1871 and 1875. W. Batty-Smith and W.E. Watterson. (1990)

SEYCHELLES

Seychelles Postal History and Postage Stamps to 1976. S. Hopson & B.M. McCloy. (Indian Ocean Study Circle, 2002)

The Postal History of B.I.O.T., Maldive Islands and Seychelles. E.B Proud (PB 2006)

SIERRA LEONE

The Postal Service of Sierra Leone. P.O. Beale. (RPSL, 1988)

The Postal History of Sierra Leone. E.B. Proud. (PB, 1994)

Sierra Leone King George VI Definitive Stamps. F. Walton. (West Africa Study Circle, 2001)

SOUTH AFRICA

Postmarks of the Cape of Good Hope. R. Goldblatt. (Reijger Publishers (Pty) Ltd., 1984)

Stamps of the Orange Free State. Parts 1-3. G.D. Buckley & W.B. Marriott. (O.F.S. Study Circle, 1967--80)

Transvaal Philately. Edited I.B. Mathews. (Reijer Publishers (Pty) Ltd., 1986)

Transvaal. The Provisional Issues of the First British Occupation. Dr. A.R. Drysdall. (James Bendon, 1994)

The Wherewithal of Wolmaransstad. H. Birkhead and J. Groenewald. (Philatelic Foundation of Southern Africa, 1999)

SOUTH WEST AFRICA

The Overprinted Stamps of South West Africa to 1930. N. Becker. (Philatelic Holdings (Pty) Ltd., 1990)

SUDAN

Sudan. The Stamps and Postal Stationery of 1867 to 1970. E.C.W. Stagg. (HH, 1977)

The Camel Postman 1898-1998. R. Stock. (Sudan Study Group, 2001)

The Postal History of Sudan. E. B Proud (PB, 2006)

TANGANYIKA

The Postal History of Tanganyika. 1915-1961. E.B. Proud. (PB, 1989)

TOGO

Togo-The Postal History of the Anglo-French Occupation 1914-22. J. Martin and F. Walton. (West Africa S.C., 1995)

Togo Overprints on Stamps of the Gold Coast 1915–1920. P. Duggan. (West Africa S.C. 2005)

TRANSJORDAN

The Stamps of Jordan 1920—1965. A.H. Najjar. (Sahara Publications Ltd., 1998)

TRINIDAD AND TOBAGO

The Postal History of Trinidad and Tobago. J.C. Aleong and E.B. Proud. (PB, 1997)

TRISTAN DA CUNHA

The History and Postal History of Tristan da Cunha. G. Crabb. (1980)

TURKS AND CAICOS ISLANDS

Turks Islands and Caicos Islands to 1950. J.J. Challis. (Roses Caribbean Philatelic Society, 1983)

UGANDA

The Postal History of Uganda and Zanzibar. E.B. Proud. (PB, 1993)

ZANZIBAR

Zanzibar 1895 – 1904. T.W. Hall. (Reprint, East Africa Study Circle, 2002)

Great Britain

STAMPS ON COVER. Prices are quoted, as a third price column, for those Victorian and Edwardian issues usually found used on cover. In general these prices refer to the cheapest version of each basic stamp with other shades, plates or varieties, together with unusual frankings and postmarks, being worth more.

UNITED KINGDOM OF GREAT BRITAIN AND IRELAND

QUEEN VICTORIA
20 June 1837—22 January 1901

MULREADY ENVELOPES AND LETTER SHEETS, so called from the name of the designer, William Mulready, were issued concurrently with the first British adhesive stamps

	1d. black	
Envelopes.	£325 *unused*;	£450 *used*.
Letter Sheets:	£300 *unused*;	£425 *used*.
	2d. blue	
Envelopes.	£400 *unused*;	£1700 *used*.
Letter Sheets:	£375 *unused*;	£1700 *used*.

LINE-ENGRAVED ISSUES

GENERAL NOTES

Brief notes on some aspects of the line-engraved stamps follow, but for further information and a full specialist treatment of these issues collectors are recommended to consult Volume 1 of the Stanley Gibbons *Great Britain Specialised Catalogue*.

Alphabet I

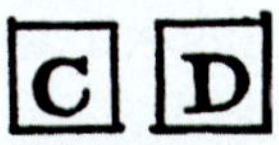

Alphabet II

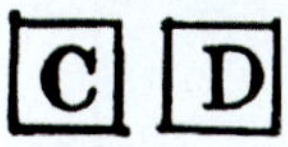

Alphabet III

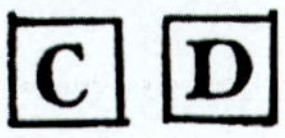

Alphabet IV

Typical Corner Letters of the four Alphabets

Alphabets. Four different styles were used for the corner letters on stamps prior to the issue with letters in all four corners, these being known to collectors as:

Alphabet I. Used for all plates made from 1840 to the end of 1851. Letters small.

Alphabet II. Plates from 1852 to mid-1855. Letters larger, heavier and broader.

Alphabet III. Plates from mid-1855 to end of period. Letters tall and more slender.

Alphabet IV. 1861. 1d. Die II, Plates 50 and 51 only. Letters were hand-engraved instead of being punched on the plate. They are therefore inconsistent in shape and size but generally larger and outstanding.

While the general descriptions and the illustrations of typical letters given above may be of some assistance, only long experience and published aids can enable every stamp to be allocated to its particular Alphabet without hesitation, as certain letters in each are similar to those in one of the others.

Blued Paper. The blueing of the paper of the earlier issues is believed to be due to the presence of prussiate of potash in the printing ink, or in the paper, which, under certain conditions, tended to colour the paper when the sheets were damped for printing. An alternative term is bleuté paper.

Corner Letters. The corner letters on the early British stamps were intended as a safeguard against forgery, each stamp in the sheet having a different combination of letters. Taking the first 1d. stamp, printed in 20 horizontal rows of 12, as an example, the lettering is as follows:

Row 1.	A A,	A B,	A C,	etc. to	A L.
Row 2.	B A,	B B,	B C,	etc. to	B L.
		and so on to			
Row 20.	T A,	T B,	T C,	etc. to	T L.

On the stamps with four corner letters, those in the upper corners are in the reverse positions to those in the lower corners. Thus in a sheet of 240 (12 × 20) the sequence is:

Row 1.	A A	B A	C A		L A
	A A	A B	A C	etc. to	A L
Row 2.	A B	B B	C B		L B
	B A	B B	B C	etc. to	B L
		and so on to			
Row 20.	A T	B T	C T	etc. to	L T
	T A	T B	T C		T L

Placing letters in all four corners was not only an added precaution against forgery but was meant to deter unmarked parts of used stamps being pieced together and passed off as an unused whole.

Dies. The first die of the 1d. was used for making the original die of the 2d., both the No Lines and White Lines issues. In 1855 the 1d. Die I was amended by retouching the head and deepening the lines on a transferred impression of the original. This later version, known to collectors as Die II, was used for making the dies for the 1d. and 2d. with letters in all four corners and also for the 1½d.

The two dies are illustrated above No. 17 in the catalogue.

Double letter

Guide line in corner

Guide line through value

Double Corner Letters. These are due to the workman placing his letter-punch in the wrong position at the first attempt, when lettering the plate, and then correcting the mistake; or to a slight shifting of the punch when struck. If a wrong letter was struck in the first instance, traces of a wrong letter may appear in a corner in addition to the correct one. A typical example is illustrated.

Guide Lines and Dots. When laying down the impressions of the design on the early plates, fine vertical and horizontal guidelines were marked on the plates to assist the operative. These were usually removed from the gutter margins, but could not be removed from the stamp impressions without damage to the plate, so that in such cases they appear on the printed stamps, sometimes in the corners, sometimes through "POSTAGE" or the value. Typical examples are illustrated.

Guide dots or cuts were similarly made to indicate the spacing of the guide lines. These too sometimes appear on the stamps.

Ivory Head

"Ivory Head." The so-called "ivory head" variety is one in which the Queen's Head shows white on the back of the stamp. It arises from the comparative absence of ink in the head portion of the design, with consequent absence of blueing. (*See* "Blued Paper" note above.)

Line-engraving. In this context "line-engraved" is synonymous with recess-printing, in which the engraver cuts recesses in a plate and printing (the coloured areas) is from these recesses. "Line-engraved" is the traditional philatelic description for these stamps; other equivalent terms found are "engraving in *taille-douce*" (French) or in "*intaglio*" (Italian).

Plates. Until the introduction of the stamps with letters in all four corners, the number of the plate was not indicated in the design of the stamp, but was printed on the sheet margin. By long study of identifiable blocks and the minor variations in the design, coupled with the position of the corner letters, philatelists are now able to allot many of these stamps to their respective plates. Specialist collectors often endeavour to obtain examples of a given stamp printed from its different plates and our catalogue accordingly reflects this depth of detail.

Maltese Cross

Type of Town postmark

Type of Penny Post cancellation

Example of 1844 type postmark

Postmarks. The so-called "Maltese Cross" design was the first employed for obliterating British postage stamps and was in use from 1840 to 1844. Being hand-cut, the obliterating stamps varied greatly in detail and some distinctive types can be allotted to particular towns or offices. Local types, such as those used at Manchester, Norwich, Leeds, etc., are keenly sought. A red ink was first employed, but was superseded by black, after some earlier experiments, in February 1841. Maltese Cross obliterations in other colours are rare.

Obliterations of this type, numbered 1 to 12 in the centre, were used at the London Chief Office in 1843 and 1844.

Some straight-line cancellations were in use in 1840 at the Penny Post receiving offices, normally applied on the envelope, the adhesives then being obliterated at the Head Office. They are nevertheless known, with or without Maltese Cross, on the early postage stamps.

In 1842 some offices in S.W. England used dated postmarks in place of the Maltese Cross, usually on the back of the letter since they were not originally intended as obliterators. These town postmarks have likewise been found on adhesives.

In 1844 the Maltese Cross design was superseded by numbered obliterators of varied type, one of which is illustrated. They are naturally comparatively scarce on the first ld. and 2d. stamps. Like the Maltese Cross they are found in various colours, some of which are rare.

Re-entry

"Union Jack" re-entry

Re-entries. Re-entries on the plate show as a doubling of part of the design of the stamp generally at top or bottom. Many re-entries are very slight while others are most marked. A typical one is illustrated.

The "*Union Jack*" *re-entry*, so called owing to the effect of the re-entry on the appearance of the corner stars (*see illustration*) occurs on stamp L K of Plate 75 of the 1d. red, Die I.

T A (T L)

M A (M L)

Varieties of Large Crown Watermark

I

II

Two states of Large Crown Watermark

Watermarks. Two watermark varieties, as illustrated, consisting of crowns of entirely different shape, are found in sheets of the Large Crown paper and fall on stamps lettered M A and T A (or M L and T L when the paper is printed on the wrong side). Both varieties are found on the 1d. rose-red of 1857, while the M A (M L) variety comes also on some plates of the 1d. of 1864 (Nos. 43, 44) up to about Plate 96. On the 2d. the T A (T L) variety is known on plates 8 and 9, and the M A (M L) on later prints of plate 9. These varieties may exist inverted, or inverted reversed, on stamps lettered A A and A L and H A and H L, and some are known.

In 1861 a minor alteration was made in the Large Crown watermark by the removal of the two vertical strokes, representing *fleurs-de-lis*, which projected upwards from the uppermost of the three horizontal curves at the base of the Crown. Hence two states are distinguishable, as illustrated.

CONDITION—IMPERFORATE LINE-ENGRAVED ISSUES

The prices quoted for the 1840 and 1841 imperforate Line-engraved issues are for "fine" examples. As condition is most important in assessing the value of a stamp, the following definitions will assist collectors in the evaluation of individual examples.

Four main factors are relevant when considering quality.

(a) **Impression.** This should be clean and the surface free of any rubbing or unnatural blurring which would detract from the appearance.

(b) **Margins.** This is perhaps the most difficult factor to evaluate. Stamps described as "fine", the standard adopted in this catalogue for pricing purposes, should have margins of the recognised width, defined as approximately one half of the distance between two adjoining unsevered stamps. Stamps described as "very fine" or "superb" should have margins which are proportionately larger than those of a "fine" stamp. Examples with close margins should not, generally, be classified as "fine".

(c) **Cancellation.** On a "fine" stamp this should be reasonably clear and not noticeably smudged. A stamp described as "superb" should have a neat cancellation, preferably centrally placed or to the right.

(d) **Appearance.** Stamps, at the prices quoted, should always be without any tears, creases, bends or thins and should not be toned on either the front or back. Stamps with such defects are worth only a proportion of the catalogue price.

Good

Fine

Very Fine

Superb

The above actual size illustrations of 1840 1d. blacks show the various grades of quality. When comparing these illustrations it should be assumed that they are all from the same plate and that they are free of any hidden defects.

PRINTERS. Nos. 1/53*a* were recess-printed by Perkins, Bacon & Petch, known from 1852 as Perkins, Bacon & Co.

1

1a

2 Small Crown

(Eng Charles and Frederick Heath)

1840 (6 May). *Letters in lower corners.* Wmk Small Crown. W **2**. Imperf.

			Un	*Used*	*Used on cover*
1	**1**	1d. intense black	£15000	£425	
2		1d. black	£8500	£275	£550
3		1d. grey-black (worn plate)	£14000	£400	
4	**1a**	2d. deep full blue	£35000	£900	
5		2d. blue	£27000	£675	£2000
6		2d. pale blue	£35000	£800	

The 1d. stamp in black was printed from Plates 1 to 11. Plate 1 exists in two states (known to collectors as 1a and 1b), the latter being the result of extensive repairs.

Repairs were also made to Plates 2, 5, 6, 8, 9, 10 and 11, and certain impressions exist in two or more states.

The so-called "Royal reprint" of the ld. black was made in 1864, from Plate 66, Die II, on paper with Large Crown watermark, inverted. A printing was also made in carmine, on paper with the same watermark, normal.

For 1d. black with "VR" in upper corners *see* No. Vl under Official Stamps.

The 2d. stamps were printed from Plates 1 and 2.

Plates of 1d. black

Plate	*Un*	*Used*
1a	£10000	£300
1b	£8500	£275
2	£8500	£275
3	£15000	£375
4	£8500	£300
5	£8500	£275
6	£9500	£275
7	£11000	£300
8	£12000	£400
9	£15000	£450
10	£20000	£700
11	£18000	£4000

Varieties of 1d. black.

			Un	*Used*
a.	On *bleuté* paper (Plates 1 to 8)	*from*	60000	£600
b.	Double letter in corner	*from*	£8750	£300
bb.	Re-entry	*from*	£9500	£325
bc.	"PB" re-entry (Plate 5, 3rd state)		—	£6000
c.	Guide line in corner		£8750	£300
cc.	Large letters in each corner (E J, I L, J C and P A) (Plate 1*b*)	*from*	£8750	£425
d.	Guide line through value		£8750	£325
e.	Watermark inverted		£32000	£2000
g.	Obliterated by Maltese Cross			
		In red	—	£300
		In black	—	£275
		In blue	—	£9500
		In magenta	—	£2500
		In yellow	—	—
h.	Obliterated by Maltese Cross with number in centre	*from*		
		No. 1	—	£15000
		No. 2	—	£15000
		No. 3	—	£15000
		No. 4	—	£15000
		No. 5	—	£15000
		No. 6	—	£15000
		No. 7	—	£15000
		No. 8	—	£15000
		No. 9	—	£15000
		No. 10	—	£15000
		No. 11	—	£15000
		No. 12	—	£15000
i.	Obliterated "Penny Post" in black (without Maltese Cross)	*from*	—	£3500
j.	Obliterated by town postmark (without Maltese Cross)			
		In black *from*	—	£12000
		In yellow *from*	—	£40000
		In red *from*	—	£12000
k.	Obliterated by 1844 type postmark in black	*from*	—	£1500

Plates of 2d. blue

Plate		*Un*	*Used*
1	*Shades from*	£27000	£675
2	*Shades from*	£35000	£800

Varieties of 2d. blue.

			Un	*Used*
a.	Double letter in corner		—	£725
aa.	Re-entry		—	£800
b.	Guide line in corner		—	£700
c.	Guide line through value		—	£700
d.	Watermark inverted	*from*	£50000	£4000
e.	Obliterated by Maltese Cross			
		In red	—	£725
		In black	—	£675
		In blue	—	£10000
		In magenta	—	£9000
f.	Obliterated by Maltese Cross with number in centre	*from*		
		No. 1	—	£9500
		No. 2	—	£9500
		No. 3	—	£9500
		No. 4	—	£9500
		No. 5	—	£9500
		No. 6	—	£9500
		No. 7	—	£9500
		No. 8	—	£9500
		No. 9	—	£9500
		No. 10	—	£9500
		No. 11	—	£9500
		No. 12	—	£9500
g.	Obliterated "Penny Post" in black (without Maltese Cross)	*from*	—	£6000
h.	Obliterated by town postmark (without Maltese Cross) in black	*from*	—	£4500
i.	Obliterated by 1844 type postmark			
		In black *from*	—	£1700
		In blue *from*	—	£12000

1841 (10 Feb). *Printed from "black" plates.* Wmk W **2**. Paper more or less blued. Imperf.

			Un	*Used*	*Used on cover*
7	**1**	1d. red-brown (*shades*)	£2500	£110	£225
		a. "PB" re-entry (Plate 5, 3rd state)	—	£2000	

The first printings of the 1d. in red-brown were made from Plates 1b, 2, 5 and 8 to 11 used for the 1d. black.

1d. red-brown from "black" plates.

Plate	*Un*	*Used*
1*b*	£15000	£300
2	£10000	£275
5	£10000	£175
8	£10000	£175
9	£4500	£175
10	£2500	£175
11	£6000	£110

1841 (late Feb). *Plate 12 onwards.* Wmk W **2**. Paper more or less blued. Imperf.

			Un	*Used*	*Used on cover*
8	**1**	1d. red-brown	£500	22·00	30·00
8*a*		1d. red-brown on very blue paper	£600	22·00	
9		1d. pale red-brown (worn plates)	£575	35·00	
10		1d. deep red-brown	£800	40·00	
11		1d. lake-red	£4500	£750	
12		1d. orange-brown	£1800	£225	

Error. No letter "A" *in right lower corner (Stamp* B(A), *Plate 77)*

12*a* **1** 1d. red-brown — £18000

The error "No letter A in right corner" was due to the omission to insert this letter on stamp B A of Plate 77. The error was discovered some months after the plate was registered and was then corrected.

There are innumerable variations in the colour and shade of the 1d. "red" and those given in the above list represent colour groups each covering a wide range.

Varieties of 1d. red-brown, etc.

			Un	*Used*
b.	Major re-entry	*from*	—	80·00
c.	Double letter in corner	*from*	—	30·00
d.	Double Star (Plate 75) "Union Jack" re-entry		£18000	£2700
e.	Guide line in corner		—	22·00
f.	Guide line through value		—	25·00
g.	Thick outer frame to stamp		—	25·00
h.	Ivory head		£525	25·00
i.	Watermark inverted		£3250	£300
j.	Left corner letter "S" inverted (Plates 78, 105, 107)	*from*	—	£150
k.	P converted to R (Plates 30/1,33,83,86)	*from*	—	75·00
l.	Obliterated by Maltese Cross			
		In red	—	£4500
		In black	—	5000
		In blue	—	£500
m.	Obliterated by Maltese Cross with number in centre			
		No. 1	—	£140
		No. 2	—	£140
		No. 3	—	£175
		No. 4	—	£425
		No. 5	—	£140
		No. 6	—	£120
		No. 7	—	£120
		No. 8	—	£120
		No. 9	—	£140
		No. 10	—	£250
		No. 11	—	£250
		No. 12	—	£250
n.	Obliterated "Penny Post" in black (without Maltese Cross)		—	£650
o.	Obliterated by town postmark (without Maltese Cross)			
		In black *from*	—	£650
		In blue *from*	—	£1800
		In green *from*	—	£3200
		In yellow *from*	—	—
		In red *from*	—	£10000
p.	Obliterated by 1844 type postmark			
		In blue *from*	—	£175
		In red *from*	—	£7500
		In green *from*	—	£2500
		In violet *from*	—	£3500
		In black *from*	—	22·00

Stamps with thick outer frame to the design are from plates on which the frame-lines have been strengthened or recut, particularly Plates 76 and 90.

For "Union Jack" re-entry *see* General Notes to Line-engraved Issues.

In "P converted to R" the corner letter "R" is formed from the "P", the distinctive long tail having been hand-cut.

KEY TO LINE-ENGRAVED ISSUES

S.G.No	*Description*	*Date*	*Wmk*	*Perf*	*Die*	*Alphabet*
	THE IMPERFORATE ISSUES					
1/3	1d. black	6.5.40	SC	Imp	I	I
4/6	2d. no lines	8.5.40	SC	Imp	I	I
	PAPER MORE OR LESS BLUED					
7	1d. red-brown	Feb 1841	SC	Imp	I	I
8/12	1d. red-brown	Feb 1841	SC	Imp	I	I
8/12	1d. red-brown	6.2.52	SC	Imp	I	II
13/15	2d. white lines	13.3.41	SC	Imp	I	I
	THE PERFORATED ISSUES					
	ONE PENNY VALUE					
16*a*	1d. red-brown	1848	SC	Roul	I	I
16*b*	1d. red-brown	1850	SC	16	I	I
16*c*	1d. red-brown	1853	SC	16	I	II
17/18	1d. red-brown	Feb 1854	SC	16	I	II
22	1d. red-brown	Jan 1855	SC	14	I	II
24/5	1d. red-brown	28.2.55	SC	14	II	II
21	1d. red-brown	1.3.55	SC	16	II	II
26	1d. red-brown	15.5.55	LC	16	II	II
29/33	1d. red-brown	Aug 1855	LC	14	II	III
	NEW COLOURS ON WHITE PAPER					
37/41	1d. rose-red	Nov 1856	LC	14	II	III
36	1d. rose-red	26.12.57	LC	16	II	III
42	1d. rose-red	1861	LC	14	II	IV
	TWO PENCE VALUE					
19, 20	2d. blue	1.3.54	SC	16	I	I
23	2d. blue	22.2.55	SC	14	I	I
23*a*	2d. blue	5.7.55	SC	14	I	II
20*a*	2d. blue	18.8.55	SC	16	I	II
27	2d. blue	20.7.55	LC	16	I	II
34	2d. blue	20.7.55	LC	14	I	II
35	2d. blue	2.7.57	LC	14	I	III
36*a*	2d. blue	1.2.58	LC	16	I	III
	LETTERS IN ALL FOUR CORNERS					
48/9	½d. rose-red	1.10.70	W **9**	14	—	
43/4	1d. rose-red	1.4.64	LC	14	II	
53*a*	1½d. rosy mauve	1860	LC	14	II	
51/3	1½d. rose-red	1.10.70	LC	14	II	
45	2d. blue	July 1858	LC	14	II	
46/7	2d. thinner lines	7.7.69	LC	14	II	

Watermarks: SC Small Crown, T **2**.
LC Large Crown, T **4**.

Dies: See notes above No. 17 in the catalogue.
Alphabets: See General Notes to this section.

3 White lines added

1841 (13 Mar)–**51**. *White lines added.* Wmk W **2**. Paper more or less blued. Imperf.

			Un	*Used*	*Used on cover*
13	**3**	2d. pale blue	£5000	85·00	
14		2d. blue	£4250	75·00	£250
15		2d. deep full blue	£6000	85·00	
15*aa*		2d. violet-blue (1851)	£20000	£1300	

The 2d. stamp with white lines was printed from Plates 3 and 4.

No. 15*aa* came from Plate 4 and the price quoted is for examples on thicker, lavender tinted paper.

Plates of 2d. blue

Plate		*Un*	*Used*
3	*Shades from*	£4250	85·00
4	*Shades from*	£5000	75·00

Varieties of 2d. blue

		Un	*Used*
a.	Guide line in corner	—	90·00
b.	Guide line through value	£4500	90·00
bb.	Double letter in corner	—	95·00
be.	Re-entry	£6000	£160
c.	Ivory head	£4500	85·00
d.	Watermark inverted	£12500	£600
e.	Obliterated by Maltese Cross		

	In red	—	£20000
	In black	—	£225
	In blue	—	£4000
f.	Obliterated by Maltese Cross with number in centre		
	No. 1	—	£550
	No. 2	—	£550
	No. 3	—	£550
	No. 4	—	£550
	No. 5	—	£650
	No. 6	—	£550
	No. 7	—	£900
	No. 8	—	£700
	No. 9	—	£900
	No. 10	—	£1000
	No. 11	—	£650
	No. 12	—	£375
g.	Obliterated by town postmark (without Maltese Cross)		
	In black *from*	—	£2200
	In blue *from*	—	£3500
h.	Obliterated by 1844 type postmark		
	In black *from*	—	75·00
	In blue *from*	—	£700
	In red *from*	—	£20000
	In green *from*	—	£4000
	In olive-yellow *from*	—	£2000

1841 (Apr). *Trial printing (unissued) on Dickinson silk-thread paper.* No wmk. Imperf.

16	**1**	1d. red-brown (Plate 11)............	£6000

Eight sheets were printed on this paper, six being gummed, two ungummed, but we have only seen examples without gum.

1848. Wmk Small Crown, W **2**. *Rouletted approx 11½ by Henry Archer.*

16a	**1**	1d. red-brown (Plates 70, 71)......	£15000

1850. Wmk Small Crown, W **2**. P 16 by Henry Archer.

			Un	*Used*	*Used on cover*
16*b*	**1**	1d. red-brown (Alph 1) (from Plates 90-101)......... *from*	£2500	£575	£1800

Stamps on cover dated prior to February 1854 are worth a premium of 50% over the price on cover quoted above.

1853. *Government Trial Perforation.* Wmk Small Crown. W **2**.

			Un	*Used*
16*c*	**1**	1d. red-brown (P 16) (Alph II) (*on cover*)................................	†	£17500

SEPARATION TRIALS. Although the various trials of machines for rouletting and perforating were unofficial, Archer had the consent of the authorities in making his experiments, and sheets so experimented upon were afterwards used by the Post Office.

As Archer ended his experiments in 1850 and plates with corner letters Alphabet II did not come into issue until 1852, perforated stamps with corner letters of Alphabet I may safely be assumed to be Archer productions, if genuine.

The Government trial perforation is believed to have been done on Archer's machines after they had been purchased in 1853. As Alphabet II was by that time in use, the trials can only be distinguished from the perforated stamps listed below by being dated prior to 24 February 1854, the date when the perforated stamps were officially issued.

Die I Alphabet I, stamps from plates 74 and 113 perforated 14 have been recorded for many years, but it is now generally recognised that the type of comb machine used, producing one extension hole in the side margins, cannot be contemporary with other trials of this period.

Die I

Die II

Large Crown

Die I: The features of the portrait are lightly shaded and consequently lack emphasis.

Die II (Die I retouched): The lines of the features have been deepened and appear stronger.

The eye is deeply shaded and made more lifelike. The nostril and lips are more clearly defined. the latter appearing much thicker. A strong downward stroke of colour marks the corner of the mouth. There is a deep indentation of colour between lower lip and chin. The band running from the back of the ear to the chignon has a bolder horizontal line below it than in Die I.

The original die (Die I) was used to provide roller dies for the laying down of all the line-engraved stamps from 1840 to 1855. In that year a new master die was laid down (by means of a Die I roller die) and the impression was retouched by hand engraving by William Humphrys. This retouched die, always known to philatelists as Die II, was from that time used for preparing all new roller dies.

One Penny. The numbering of the 1d. plates recommenced at 1 on the introduction of Die II. Plates 1 to 21 were Alphabet II from which a scarce plum shade exists. Corner letters of Alphabet III appear on Plate 22 and onwards.

As an experiment, the corner letters were engraved by hand on Plates 50 and 51 in 1856, instead of being punched (Alphabet IV), but punching was again resorted to from Plate 52 onwards. Plates 50 and 51 were not put into use until 1861.

Two Pence. Unlike the 1d. the old sequence of plate numbers continued. Plates 3 and 4 of the 2d. had corner letters of Alphabet I, Plate 5 Alphabet II and Plate 6 Alphabet III. In Plate 6 the white lines are thinner than before.

1854–57. *Paper more or less blued.*

(a) Wmk Small Crown, W **2**. P 16.

			Un	*Used**	*Used on cover*
17	**1**	1d. red-brown (Die I) (24.2.54)	£275	22·00	45·00
		a. Imperf three sides (horiz pair)..................................	†	—	
18		1d. yellow brown (Die I)	£325	45·00	
19	**3**	2d. deep blue (Plate 4) (12.3.54)	£3500	90·00	£175
		a. Imperf three sides (horiz pair)..................................	†	—	
20		2d. pale blue (Plate 4)...........	£4000	£100	
20*a*		2d. blue (Plate 5) (18.8.55) ...	£6500	£275	£425
21	**1**	1d. red-brown (Die II) (22.2.55)	£400	60·00	£100
		a. Imperf...............................			

(b) Wmk Small Crown, W **2**. P 14.

22	**1**	1d. red-brown (Die I) (1.55)..	£550	70·00	£125
23	**3**	2d. blue (Plate 4) (22.2.55)	£7500	£200	£300
23*a*		2d. blue (Plate 5) (4.7.55).......	£8500	£275	£400
		b. Imperf (Plate 5)................			
24	**1**	1d. red-brown (Die II) (27.2.55)	£500	50·00	90·00
24*a*		1d. deep red-brown (very blue paper) (Die II).........	£600	90·00	
25		1d. orange-brown (Die II).....	£1500	£140	

(c) Wmk Large Crown, W**4**. P 16.

26	**1**	1d. red-brown (Die II) (15.5.55).............................	£900	95·00	£180
		a. Imperf (Plate 7)................			
27	**3**	2d. blue (Plate 5) (20.7.55)	£10000	£350	£450
		a. Imperf...............................	—	£6500	

(d) Wmk Large Crown, W**4**. P 14.

29	**1**	1d. red-brown (Die II) (6.55)	£200	18·00	35·00
		a. Imperf (*shades*) (Plates 22, 24, 25, 32, 43)..............	£3800	£3000	
30		1d. brick-red (Die II)..............	£275	40·00	
31		1d. plum (Die II) (2.56)	£3000	£750	
32		1d. brown-rose (Die II)..........	£275	40·00	
33		1d. orange-brown (Die II) (3.57)	£575	55·00	
34	**3**	2d. blue (Plate 5) (20.7.55).....	£2000	55·00	£140
35		2d. blue (Plate 6) (2.7.57).......	£2400	55·00	£140
		a. Imperf...............................	—	£6500	
		b. Imperf horiz (vert pair)...	†	—	

*17/35a **For well-centred, lightly used +125%**.

1856–58. Wmk Large Crown, W **4**. Paper no longer blued.

(a) P 16.

36	**1**	1d. rose-red (Die II) (26.12.57)	£2000	65·00	£140
36*a*	**3**	2d. blue (Plate 6) (1.2.58).......	£9500	£325	£450

(b) Die II. P 14.

37	**1**	1d. red-brown (11.56)	£950	£250	£600
38		1d. pale red (9.4.57)...............	80·00	18·00	
		a. Imperf...............................	£3500	£2800	
39		1d. pale rose (3.57)	80·00	28·00	
40		1d. rose-red (9.57)..................	45·00	10·00	20·00
		a. Imperf...............................	£3500	£2800	
		b. Imperf vert (horiz pair)...	†	—	
41		1d. deep rose-red (7.57)..........	£140	20·00	

1861. *Letters engraved on plate instead of punched (Alphabet IV).*

42	**1**	1d. rose-red (Die II) (Plates 50 and 51)	£225	35·00	60·00
		a. Imperf...............................	—	£4200	

*36/42a **For well-centred, lightly used +125%**.

In both values, varieties may be found as described in the preceding issues—ivory heads, inverted watermarks, re-entries, and double letters in corners.

The change of perforation from 16 to 14 was decided upon late in 1854 since the closer holes of the former gauge tended to cause the sheets of stamps to break up when handled, but for a time both gauges were in concurrent use. Owing to faulty alignment of the impressions on the plates and to shrinkage of the paper when damped, badly perforated stamps are plentiful in the line-engraved issues.

5

6

Showing position of the plate number on the 1d. and 2d. values. (Plate 170 shown)

1858–79. *Letters in all four corners.* Wmk Large Crown, W **4**. Die II (1d. and 2d.). P 14.

43	**5**	1d. rose-red (1.4.64)	18·00	2·50	6·00
44		1d. lake-red	18·00	2·50	
		a. Imperf from	£6000	£3000	

*43/4a **For well-centred, lightly used +125%**.

Plate	*Un*	*Used*	*Plate*	*Un*	*Used*
71......	40·00	3·50	150......	18·00	2·50
72......	45·00	4·50	151......	65·00	10·00
73......	45·00	3·50	152......	65·00	6·00
74......	45·00	2·50	153......	£110	10·00
76......	40·00	2·50	154......	55·00	2·50
77......	—		155......	55·00	2·75
78......	£100	2·50	156......	50·00	2·50
79......	35·00	2·50	157......	55·00	2·50
80......	50·00	2·50	158......	35·00	2·50
81......	50·00	2·75	159......	35·00	2·50
82......	£100	4·50	160......	35·00	2·50
83......	£125	8·00	161......	65·00	8·00
84......	65·00	2·75	162......	55·00	8·00
85......	45·00	3·75	163......	55·00	3·50
86......	55·00	4·50	164......	55·00	3·50
87......	35·00	2·50	165......	50·00	2·50
88......	£150	8·50	166......	50·00	6·50
89......	45·00	2·50	167......	50·00	2·50
90......	45·00	2·50	168......	55·00	9·00
91......	60·00	6·50	169......	65·00	8·00
92......	40·00	2·50	170......	40·00	2·50
93......	55·00	2·50	171......	18·00	2·50
94......	50·00	5·50	172......	35·00	2·50
95......	45·00	2·50	173......	75·00	10·00
96......	50·00	2·50	174......	35·00	2·50
97......	45·00	4·00	175......	65·00	4·00
98......	55·00	6·50	176......	65·00	2·75
99......	60·00	5·50	177......	45·00	2·50
100......	65·00	2·75	178......	65·00	4·00
101......	65·00	10·00	179......	55·00	2·75
102......	50·00	2·50	180......	65·00	5·50
103......	55·00	4·00	181......	50·00	2·50
104......	80·00	5·50	182......	£100	5·50
105......	£100	8·00	183......	60·00	3·50
106......	60·00	2·50	184......	35·00	2·75
107......	65·00	8·00	185......	55·00	3·50
108......	85·00	2·75	186......	70·00	2·75
109......	90·00	4·00	187......	55·00	2·50
110......	65·00	10·00	188......	75·00	11·00
111......	55·00	2·75	189......	75·00	7·50
112......	75·00	2·75	190......	55·00	6·50
113......	55·00	14·00	191......	35·00	8·00
114......	£280	14·00	192......	55·00	2·50
115......	£100	2·75	193......	35·00	2·50
116......	80·00	10·00	194......	55·00	9·00
117......	50·00	2·50	195......	55·00	9·00
118......	55·00	2·50	196......	55·00	5·50
119......	50·00	2·50	197......	60·00	10·00
120......	18·00	2·50	198......	45·00	6·50
121......	45·00	10·00	199......	60·00	6·50
122......	18·00	2·50	200......	65·00	2·50
123......	45·00	2·50	201......	35·00	5·50
124......	32·00	2·50	202......	65·00	9·00
125......	45·00	2·50	203......	35·00	18·00
127......	60·00	2·75	204......	60·00	2·75
129......	45·00	9·00	205......	60·00	3·00
130......	60·00	2·75	206......	60·00	10·00
131......	70·00	18·00	207......	65·00	10·00
132......	£150	25·00	208......	60·00	18·00
133......	£125	10·00	209......	55·00	10·00
134......	18·00	2·50	210......	70·00	13·00
135......	£100	28·00	211......	75·00	22·00
136......	£100	22·00	212......	65·00	12·00
137......	32·00	2·75	213......	65·00	12·00
138......	22·00	2·50	214......	70·00	20·00
139......	65·00	18·00	215......	70·00	20·00
140......	22·00	2·50	216......	75·00	20·00
141......	£125	10·00	217......	75·00	8·00
142......	75·00	28·00	218......	70·00	9·00
143......	65·00	16·00	219......	£100	75·00
144......	£100	22·00	220......	45·00	8·00
145......	35·00	2·75	221......	75·00	18·00
146......	45·00	6·50	222......	85·00	45·00
147......	55·00	3·50	223......	£100	65·00
148......	45·00	3·50	224......	£125	55·00
149......	45·00	6·50	225......	£2800	£700

The following plate numbers are also known imperf and used (No. 44a); 72, 79, 80, 81, 82, 83, 84, 85, 86, 87, 88, 90, 91, 92, 93, 96, 97, 98, 100, 101, 102, 103, 104, 105, 107, 108, 109, 112, 113, 114, 116, 117, 120, 121, 122, 136, 137, 142, 146, 148, 158, 162, 164, 166, 171, 174, 191 and 202.

The numbering of this series of 1d. red plates follows after that of the previous 1d. stamp, last printed from Plate 68.

Plates 69, 70, 75, 126 and 128 were prepared for this issue but rejected owing to defects, and stamps from these plates do not exist, so that specimens which appear to be from these plates (like many of those which optimistic collectors believe to be from Plate 77) bear other plate numbers. Owing to faulty engraving or printing it is not always easy to identify the plate number. Plate 77 was also rejected but some stamps printed from it were used. One specimen is in the Tapling Collection and six or seven others are known. Plates 226 to 228 were made but not used.

Specimens from most of the plates are known with inverted watermark. The variety of watermark described in the General Notes to this section occurs on stamp M A (or M L) on plates up to about 96 (Prices from £110 used).Re-entries in this issue are few, the best being on stamps M K and T K of Plate 71 and on S L and T L, Plate 83.

			Un	*Used**	*Used on cover*
45	**6**	2d. blue (thick lines) (7.58)	£300	12·00	40·00
		a. Imperf (Plate 9)................		£7000	
		Plate 7................................	£1200	50·00	
		Plate 8................................	£1100	35·00	
		Plate 9................................	£300	12·00	
		Plate 12..............................	£2200	£120	
46		2d. blue (thin lines) (1.7.69) ...	£325	22·00	60·00
47		2d. deep blue (thin lines).......	£325	22·00	
		a. Imperf (Plate 13).............	£8000		
		Plate 13..............................	£325	22·00	
		Plate 14..............................	£425	30·00	
		Plate 15..............................	£400	30·00	

*45/7 **For well-centred, lightly used +125%**.

Plates 10 and 11 of the 2d. were prepared but rejected. Plates 13 to 15 were laid down from a new roller impression on which the white lines were thinner.

There are some marked re-entries and repairs, particularly on Plates 7, 8, 9 and 12.Stamps with inverted watermark may be found

and also the T A (T L) and M A (M L) watermark varieties (see General Notes to this section).

Though the paper is normally white, some printings showed blueing and stamps showing the "ivory head" may therefore be found.

7

Showing the plate number (9)

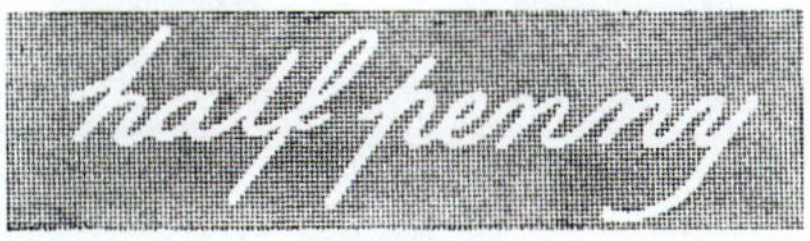

9

1870 (1 Oct). Wmk W **9**, extending over three stamps. P 14.

48	**7**	½d. rose-red	90·00	18·00	60·00
49		½d. rose	90·00	18·00	
		a. Imperf (Plates 1, 4, 5, 6, 8, 14) *from*	£3500	£2500	
		Plate 1	£275	75·00	
		Plate 3	£200	40·00	
		Plate 4	£130	30·00	
		Plate 5	90·00	18·00	
		Plate 6	£100	18·00	
		Plate 8	£500	£200	
		Plate 9	£5500	£700	
		Plate 10	£110	18·00	
		Plate 11	£100	18·00	
		Plate 12	£100	18·00	
		Plate 13	£100	18·00	
		Plate 14	£100	18·00	
		Plate 15	£150	40·00	
		Plate 19	£250	55·00	
		Plate 20	£300	75·00	

*49/9a **For well-centred, lightly used +200%**

The ½d. was printed in sheets of 480 (24 × 20) so that the

check letters run from $\begin{matrix}A A\\A A\end{matrix}$ to $\begin{matrix}X T\\T X\end{matrix}$

Plates 2, 7, 16, 17 and 18 were not completed while Plates 21 and 22, though made, were not used.

Owing to the method of perforating, the outer side of stamps in either the A or X row (ie the left or right side of the sheet) is imperf.

Stamps may be found with watermark inverted or reversed, or without watermark, the latter due to misplacement of the paper when printing.

8

Position of plate Number

1870 (1 Oct). Wmk W **4**. P 14.

51	**8**	1½d. rose-red	£400	50·00	£250
52		1½d. lake-red	£500	50·00	
		a. Imperf (Plates 1 and 3)... *from*	£7500	†	
		Plate (1)	£600	70·00	
		3	£400	50·00	

Error of lettering. OP–PC for CP–PC (Plate 1).

53	**8**	1½d. rose-red	£18000	£1500	£6000

Prepared for use in 1860 but not issued; blued paper.

53*a*	**8**	1½d. rosy mauve (Plate 1)	£7000	
		b. Error of lettering, OP-PC for CP-PC	—	†

*51/3 **For well-centred, lightly used** +125%.

Owing to a proposed change in the postal rates, 1½d. stamps were first printed in 1860, in rosy mauve, No. 53a, but the change was not approved and the greater part of the stock was destroyed, although three or four postally used examples have been recorded.

In 1870 a 1½d. stamp was required and was issued in rose-red.

Plate 1 did not have the plate number in the design of the stamps, but on stamps from Plate 3 the number will be found in the frame as shown above.

Plate 2 was defective and was not used.

The error of lettering OP-PC on Plate 1 was apparently not noticed by the printers, and therefore not corrected.

EMBOSSED ISSUES

Volume 1 of the Stanley Gibbons *Great Britain Specialised Catalogue* gives further detailed information on the embossed issues.

PRICES. The prices quoted are for cut-square stamps with average to fine embossing. Stamps with exceptionally clear embossing are worth more.

10

11

12

13

Position of die number

(Primary die engraved at the Royal Mint by William Wyon. Stamps printed at Somerset House)

1847–54. Imperf. (*For paper and wmk see footnote.*)

			Un	Used	Used on Cover
54	**10**	1s. pale green (11.9.47)	£12000	£750	£1100
55		1s. green	£12000	£800	
56		1s. deep green	£14000	£800	
		Die 1 (1847)	£12000	£750	
		Die 2 (1854)	£14000	£825	
57	**11**	10d. brown (6.11.48)	£8000	£1200	£2200
		Die 1 (1848)	£8500	£1200	
		Die 2 (1850)	£8000	£1200	
		Die 3 1853)	£8000	£1200	
		Die 4 (1854)	£8500	£1200	
		Die 5			
58	**12**	6d. mauve (1.3.54)	£10000	£900	
59		6d. dull lilac	£10000	£900	£1400
60		6d. purple	£10000	£900	
61		6d. violet	£18000	£3500	

The 1s. and 10d. are on "Dickinson" paper with "silk" threads (actually a pale blue twisted cotton yarn). The 6d. is on paper watermarked V R in single-lined letters, W 13, which may be found in four ways—upright, inverted, upright reversed, and inverted reversed, upright reversed being the most common.

The die numbers are indicated on the base of the bust. Only Die 1 (1 WW) of the 6d. was used for the adhesive stamps. The 10d. is from Die 1 (W.W.1 on stamps), and Dies 2 to 5 (2 W.W., 3 W.W., 4 W.W. and 5 W.W.) but the number and letters on stamps from Die 1 are seldom clear and many specimens are known without any trace of them. Because of this the stamp we previously listed as "No die number" has been deleted. That they are from Die I is proved by the existence of blocks showing stamps with and without the die number. The 1s. is from Dies 1 and 2 (W.W.1, W.W.2).

The normal arrangement of the "silk" threads in the paper was in pairs running down each vertical row of the sheet, the space between the threads of each pair being approximately 5 mm and between pairs of threads 20 mm. Varieties due to misplacement of the paper in printing show a single thread on the first stamp from the sheet margin and two threads 20 mm apart on the other stamps of the row. Faulty manufacture is the cause of stamps with a single thread in the middle.

Through bad spacing of the impressions, which were handstruck, all values may be found with two impressions more or less overlapping. Owing to the small margin allowed for variation of spacing, specimens with good margins on all sides are not common. Double impressions are known of all values.

Later printings of the 6d. had the gum tinted green to enable the printer to distinguish the gummed side of the paper.

SURFACE-PRINTED ISSUES

GENERAL NOTES

Volume 1 of the Stanley Gibbons *Great Britain Specialised Catalogue* gives further detailed information on the surface-printed issues.

"Abnormals". The majority of the great rarities in the surface-printed group of issues are the so-called "abnormals", whose existence is due to the practice of printing six sheets from every plate as soon as made, one of which was kept for record purposes at Somerset House, while the others were perforated and usually issued. If such plates were not used for general production or if, before they came into full use, a change of watermark or colour took place, the six sheets originally printed would differ from the main issue in plate, colour or watermark and, if issued, would be extremely rare.

The abnormal stamps of this class listed in this Catalogue and distinguished, where not priced, by an asterisk (*), are:

No.		
78	3d.	Plate 3 (with white dots)
152	4d.	vermilion, Plate 16
153	4d.	sage-green, Plate 17
109	6d.	mauve, Plate 10
124/*a*	6d.	chestnut and 6d. pale chestnut, Plate 12
145	6d.	pale buff, Plate 13
88	9d.	Plate 3 (hair lines) 989d.Plate 5 (*see* footnote to No. 98)
113	10d.	Plate 2 911s.Plate 3 ("Plate 2")
148/50	1s.	green, Plate 14
120	2s.	blue, Plate 3

Those which may have been issued, but of which no specimens are known, are 2½d. wmk Anchor, Plates 4 and 5; 3d. wmk Emblems, Plate 5; 3d. wmk Spray, Plate 21; 6d. grey, wmk Spray, Plate 18; 8d. orange, Plate 2; 1s. wmk Emblems, Plate 5; 5s. wmk Maltese Cross, Plate 4.

The 10d. Plate 1, wmk Emblems (No. 99), is sometimes reckoned among the abnormals, but was an error, due to the use of the wrong paper.

Corner Letters. With the exception of the 4d., 6d. and 1s. of 1855–57, the ½d., 1½d., 2d. and 5d. of 1880, the 1d. lilac of 1881 and the £5 (which had letters in lower corners only, and in the reverse order to the normal), all the surface-printed stamps issued prior to 1887 had letters in all four corners, as in the later line-engraved stamps. The arrangement is the same, the letters running in sequence right across and down the sheets, whether these were divided into panes or not. The corner letters existing naturally depend on the number of stamps in the sheet and their arrangement.

Imprimaturs and Imperforate Stamps. The Post Office retained in their records (now in the National Postal Museum) one imperforate sheet from each plate, known as the Imprimatur (or officially approved) sheet. Some stamps were removed from time to time for presentation purposes and have come on to the market, but these imperforates are not listed as they were not issued. Full details can be found in Volume I of the *Great Britain Specialised Catalogue*.

However, other imperforate stamps are known to have been issued and these are listed where it has been possible to prove that they do not come from the Imprimatur sheets. It is therefore advisable to purchase these only when acccompanied by an Expert Committee certificate of genuineness.

Plate Numbers. All stamps from No. 75 to No. 163 bear in their designs either the plate number or, in one or two earlier instances, some other indication by which one plate can be distinguished from another. With the aid of these and of the corner letters it is thus possible to "reconstruct" a sheet of stamps from any plate of any issue or denomination.

Surface-printing. In this context the traditional designation "surface-printing" is synonymous with typo(graphy)—a philatelic term—or letterpress—the printers' term—as meaning printing from (the surface of) raised type. It is also called relief-printing, as the image is in relief (in French, *en épargne*), unwanted parts of the design having been cut away. Duplicate impressions can be electrotyped or stereotyped from an original die, the resulting *clichés* being locked together to form the printing plate.

Wing Margins. As the vertical gutters (spaces) between the panes, into which sheets of stamps of most values were divided until the introduction of the Imperial Crown watermark, were perforated through the centre with a single row of holes, instead of each vertical row of stamps on the inner side of the panes having its own line of perforation as is now usual, a proportion of the stamps in each sheet have what is called a "wing margin" about 5 mm wide on one or other side.

The stamps with "wing margins" are the watermark Emblems and Spray of Rose series (3d., 6d., 9d., 10d., 1s. and 2s.) with letters D, E, H or I in S.E. corner, and the watermark Garter series (4d. and 8d.) with letters F or G in S.E. corner. Knowledge of this lettering will enable collectors to guard against stamps with wing margin cut down and reperforated, but note that wing margin stamps of Nos. 62 to 73 are also to be found re-perforated.

PRINTERS. The issues of Queen Victoria, Nos. 62/214, were typo by Thomas De La Rue & Co.

PERFORATIONS. All the surface-printed issues of Queen Victoria are Perf 14, with the exception of Nos. 126/9.

KEY TO SURFACE-PRINTED ISSUES 1855–83

S.G. Nos	*Description*	*Watermark*	*Date of Issue*
	NO CORNER LETTERS		
62	4d. carmine	Small Garter	31.7.55
63/5	4d. carmine	Medium Garter	25.2.56
66/*a*	4d. carmine	Large Garter	Jan 1857
69/70	6d. lilac	Emblems	21.10.56
71/3	1s. green	Emblems	1.11.56
	SMALL WHITE CORNER LETTERS		
75/7	3d. carmine	Emblems	1.5.62
78	3d. carmine (dots)	Emblems	Aug 1862
79/82	4d. red	Large Garter	15.1.62
83/5	6d. lilac	Emblems	1.12.62
86/8	9d. bistre	Emblems	15.1.62
89/91	1s. green	Emblems	1.12.62
	LARGE WHITE CORNER LETTERS		
92	3d. rose	Emblems	1.3.65
102/3	3d. rose	Spray	July 1867
93/4	4d. vermilion	Large Garter	4.7.65
96/7	6d. lilac	Emblems	7.3.65
104/7	6d. lilac	Spray	21.6.67
108/9	6d. lilac	Spray	8.3.69
122/4	6d. chestnut	Spray	12.4.72
125	6d.grey	Spray	24.4.73
98	9d.straw	Emblems	30.10.65
110/11	9d. straw	Spray	3.10.67
99	10d. brown	Emblems	11.11.67
112/14	10d. brown	Spray	1.7.67
101	1s. green	Emblems	19.1.65
115/17	1s. green	Spray	13.7.67
118/20*b*	2s. blue	Spray	1.7.67
121	2s. brown	Spray	27.2.80
126/7	5s. rose	Cross	1.7.67
128	10s. grey	Cross	26.9.78
129	£1 brown-lilac	Cross	26.9.78
130, 134	5s. rose	Anchor	25.11.82
131, 135	10s. grey-green	Anchor	Feb 1883
132, 136	£1 brown-lilac	Anchor	Dec 1882
133, 137	£5 orange	Anchor	21.3.82
	LARGE COLOURED CORNER LETTERS		
166	1d. Venetian red	Crown	1.1.80
138/9	2½d. rosy mauve	Anchor	1.7.75
141	2½d. rosy mauve	Orb	1.5.76
142	2½d. blue	Orb	5.2.80
157	2½d. blue	Crown	23.3.81
143/4	3d. rose	Spray	5.7.73
158	3d. rose	Crown	Jan 1881
159	3d. on 3d. lilac	Crown	1.1.83
152	4d. vermilion	Large Garter	1.3.76
153	4d. sage-green	Large Garter	12.3.77
154	4d. brown	Large Garter	15.8.80
160	4d. brown	Crown	9.12.80
145	6d. buff	Spray	15.3.73
146/7	6d. grey	Spray	20.3.74
161	6d. grey	Crown	1.1.81

S.G. Nos	Description	Watermark	Date of Issue
162	6d. on 6d. lilac	Crown	1.1.83
156a	8d. purple-brown	Large Garter	July 1876
156	8d. orange	Large Garter	11.9.76
148/50	1s. green	Spray	1.9.73
151	1s. brown	Spray	14.10.80
163	1s. brown	Crown	24.5.81

	Watermarks:		
		Anchor	W **40**, **47**
		Cross	W **39**
		Crown	W **49**
		Emblems	W **20**
		Large Garter	W **17**
		Medium Garter	W **16**
		Orb	W **48**
		Small Garter	W **15**
		Spray	W **33**

14

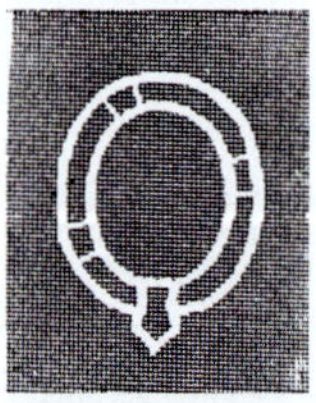
15 Small Garter

16 Medium Garter

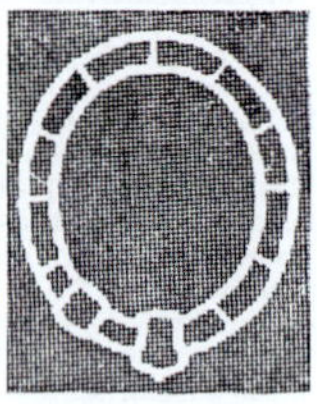
17 Large Garter

1855–57. *No corner letters.*

(a) Wmk Small Garter, W**15**. *Highly glazed, deeply blued paper* (31 July 1855).

			Un	Used*	Used on cover
62	**14**	4d. carmine (*shades*)	£6500	£375	£650
		a. Paper slightly blued	£6750	£375	
		b. White paper	—	£875	

(b) Wmk Medium Garter, W **16**.

(i) *Thick, blued highly glazed paper* (25 February 1856).

63	**14**	4d. carmine (*shades*)	£8000	£450	£650
		a. White paper	£6500		

(ii) *Ordinary thin white paper* (September 1856).

64	**14**	4d. pale carmine	£6500	£350	£550
		a. Stamp printed double	†	—	

(iii) *Ordinary white paper, specially prepared ink* (1 November 1856).

65	**14**	4d. rose or deep rose	£6000	£375	£500

(c) Wmk Large Garter, W**17**. *Ordinary white paper* (January 1857).

66	**14**	4d. rose-carmine	£1700	£100	£175
		a. Rose	£1350	£100	
		b. Thick glazed paper	£4000	£275	

*62/6b **For well-centred, lightly used +125%.**

18

19

20 Emblems wmk (normal)

20a Wmk error, three roses and shamrock

20b Wmk error, three roses and thistle

(d) Wmk Emblems, W**20**.

69	**18**	6d. deep lilac (21.10.56)	£1500	£120	
70		6d. pale lilac	£1100	95·00	£190
		a. Azure paper	£6000	£775	
		b. Thick paper	£3000	£300	
		c. Error. Wmk W **20a**			
71	**19**	1s. deep green (1.11.56)	£3500	£425	
72		1s. green	£1800	£260	£350
73		1s. pale green	£1800	£260	
		a. Azure paper	—	£1800	
		b. Thick paper	—	£300	
		c. Imperf		†	—

*69/73b **For well-centred, lightly used +125%.**

21

22

23

24

25 Plate 2

A. White dots added

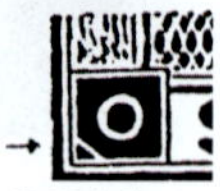
B. Hair lines

1862–64. *A small uncoloured letter in each corner,* the 4d. wmk Large Garter. W**17**, the others Emblems, W**20**.

75	**21**	3d. deep carmine-rose (Plate 2) (1.5.62)	£4000	£425	
76		3d. bright carmine-rose	£2000	£250	£450
		a. Error. Wmk W **20b** (stamp TF)		£7500	
77		3d. pale carmine-rose	£2000	£250	
		b. Thick paper	—	£350	
78		3d. rose (with white dots, Type A, Plate 3) (8.62)	£30000	£11000	
		a. Imperf (Plate 3)	£5500		
79	**22**	4d. bright red (Plate 3) (15.1.62)	£1800	£110	
80		4d. pale red	£1500	90·00	£200
81		4d. bright red (Hair lines, Type B, Plate 4) (16.10.63)	£1900	£120	
82		4d. pale red (Hair lines, Type B, Plate 4)	£1700	90·00	£200
		a. Imperf (Plate 4)	£3500		
83	**23**	6d. deep lilac (Plate 3) (1.12.62)	£2000	£110	
84		6d. lilac	£1700	90·00	£170
		a. Azure paper	—	£1300	
		b. Thick paper	—	£275	
		c. Error. Shamrock missing from wmk (stamp TF)		£7500	
		d. Error. Wmk W **20b** (stamp TF)	—	£7500	
85		6d. lilac (Hair lines, Plate 4) (20.4.64)	£2400	£180	£275
		a. Imperf	£4000		
		c. Thick paper	£3000	£225	
		d. Error. Wmk W **20b** (stamp TF)			
86	**24**	9d. bistre (Plate 2) (15.1.62)	£4500	£450	£750
87		9d. straw	£3250	£350	
		a. On azure paper			
		b. Thick paper	£4750	£425	
		c. Error. Watermark W **20b** (stamp TF)	†	—	
88		9d. bistre (Hair lines, Plate 3) (5.62)	£20000	£10000	
89	**25**	1s. deep green (Plate No. 1 = Plate 2) (1.12.62)	£3500	£350	
90		1s. green (Plate No. 1 = Plate 2)	£2200	£200	£325
		a. "K" in lower left corner in white circle (stamp KD)	£9000	£1300	
		aa. "K" normal (stamp KD)	—	£1600	
		b. On azure paper			
		c. Error. Wmk **20b** (stamp TF)			
		d. Thick paper	—	£275	
		da. Thick paper, "K" in circle as No. 90a	—	£2500	
91		1s. deep green (Plate No. 2 = Plate 3)	£25000		
		a. Imperf	£5000		

*75/91 **For well-centred, lightly used** +**125**%.

The 3d. as Type 21, but with network background in the spandrels which is found overprinted SPECIMEN, was never issued.

The plates of this issue may be distinguished as follows:

3d.	Plate 2.	No white dots.
	Plate 3.	White dots as Illustration A.
4d.	Plate 3.	No hair lines. Roman I next to lower corner letters.
	Plate 4.	Hair lines in corners. (Illustration B.). Roman II.
6d.	Plate 3.	No hair lines.
	Plate 4.	Hair lines in corners.
9d.	Plate 2.	No hair lines.
	Plate 3.	Hair lines in corners. Beware of faked lines.
1s.	Plate 2.	Numbered 1 on stamps.
	Plate 3.	Numbered 2 on stamps and with hair lines.

The 9d. on azure paper (No. 87a) is very rare, only one confirmed example being known.

The variety "K" in circle, No. 90a, is believed to be due to a damaged letter having been cut out and replaced. It is probable that the punch was driven in too deeply, causing the flange to penetrate the surface, producing an indentation showing as an uncoloured circle.

The watermark variety "three roses and a shamrock" illustrated in W **20a** was evidently due to the substitution of an extra rose for the thistle in a faulty watermark bit. It is found on stamp TA of Plate 4 of the 3d., Plates 1 (No. 70c), 3, 5 and 6 of the 6d., Plate 4 of the 9d. and Plate 4 of the 1s.

Similar problems occurred on stamp TF of the 6d. and 9d. Here the shamrock emblem became detached and a used example of the 6d. (No. 84) is known showing it omitted. It was replaced by a third rose (W **20b**) and this variety exists on the 6d. (Nos. 84/5 and 97) and 9d. (Nos. 87 and 98).

26

27

28 (with hyphen)

28a (without hyphen)

29

30

31

1865–67. *Large uncoloured corner letters.* Wmk Large Garter (4d.); others Emblems.

92	**26**	3d. rose (Plate 4) (1.3.65)	£1500	£180	£350
		a. Error. Wmk W **20a**	£3500	£900	
		b. Thick paper	£2500	£200	
93	**27**	4d. dull vermilion (4.7.65)	£525	85·00	
94		4d. vermilion	£450	55·00	£125
		a. Imperf (Plates 11, 12)	£2200		
		Plate			
		7 (1865)	£550	£100	
		8 (1866)	£500	60·00	
		9 (1867)	£500	60·00	
		10 (1868)	£700	£130	
		11 (1869)	£500	60·00	
		12 (1870)	£475	55·00	
		13 (1872)	£550	55·00	
		14 (1873)	£600	85·00	
96	**28**	6d. deep lilac (with hyphen) (7.3.65)	£1500	£150	
97		6d. lilac (with hyphen)	£900	80·00	£150
		a. Thick paper	£1000	£110	
		b. Stamp doubly printed (Pl 6)	—	£12000	
		c. Error. Wmk W **20a** (Pl 5, 6) *from*	—	£900	
		d. Error. Wmk W **20b** (Plate 5)			
		Plate			
		5 (1865)	£800	80·00	
		6 (1867)	£3000	£150	
98	**29**	9d. straw (Plate 4) (30.10.65)	£4000	£500	£1000
		a. Thick paper	£4500	£675	
		b. Error. Wmk W **20a**	—	£1600	
		c. Error. Wmk W **20b** (stamp TF)			
99	**30**	10d. red-brown (Pl 1) (11.11.67)	†	£40000	
101	**31**	1s. green (Plate 4) (19.1.65)	£2000	£200	£350
		a. Error. Wmk W**20a**	—	£1100	
		b. Thick paper	£2500	£275	
		c. Imperf between (vert pair)	—	£12000	

*92/101c **For well-centred, lightly used +100%.**

From mid-1866 to about the end of 1871 4d. stamps of this issue appeared generally with watermark inverted.

Unused examples of No. 98 from Plate 5 exist, but this was never put to press and all evidence points to such stamps originating from a portion of the Imprimatur sheet which was perforated by De La Rue in 1887 for insertion in albums to be presented to members of the Stamp Committee (Price £18000 un).

The 10d. stamps, No. 99, were printed in error on paper watermarked "Emblems" instead of on "Spray of Rose".

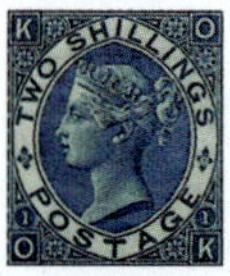

32

33 Spray of Rose

34

1867–80. Wmk Spray of Rose, W **33**.

102	**26**	3d. deep rose (12.7.67)	£800	85·00	
103		3d. rose	£450	55·00	90·00
		a. Imperf (Plates 5, 6, 8) *from*	£3250		
		Plate			
		4 (1867)	£1100	£250	
		5 (1868)	£450	55·00	
		6 (1870)	£475	55·00	
		7 (1871)	£550	60·00	
		8 (1872)	£525	55·00	
		9 (1872)	£525	60·00	
		10 (1873)	£750	£120	
104	**28**	6d. lilac (with hyphen) (Plate 6) (21.6.67)	£1500	80·00	£160
		a. Imperf			
105		6d. deep lilac (with hyphen) (Plate 6)	£1500	80·00	
106		6d. purple (with hyphen) (Pl 6)	£1500	£110	
107		6d. right violet (with hyphen) (Plate 6) (22.7.68)	£1400	90·00	
108		6d. dull violet (without hyphen) (Plate 8) (8.3.69)	£650	80·00	
109		6d. mauve (without hyphen)	£550	80·00	£120

a. Imperf (Plate Nos. 8 and 9) £6000 £4000
Plate
8 (1869, mauve) £550 £120
9 (1870, mauve) £550 80·00
10 (1869, mauve) * £28000
110 **29** 9d. straw (Plate No. 4) (3.10.67) £2000 £275 £425
111 9d. pale straw (Plate No. 4) £1900 £250
a. Imperf (Plate 4) £8000
112 **30** 10d. red-brown (1.7.67) £2800 £300 £700
113 10d. pale red-brown £2800 £325
114 10d. deep red-brown £4000 £525
a. Imperf (Plate 1) £8000
Plate
1 (1867) £2800 £300
2 (1867) £35000 £12000
115 **31** 1s. deep green (13.7.67) £850 40·00
117 1s. green £650 35·00 75·00
a. Imperf between (horiz pair) (Plate 7)
b. Imperf (Plate 4) £6000 £3000
Plate
4 (1867) £1100 60·00
5 (1871) £650 35·00
6 (1871) £1000 35·00
7 (1873) £1200 70·00
118 **32** 2s. dull blue (1.7.67) £2800 £175 £700
119 2s. deep blue £3500 £175
a. Imperf (Plate 1) £11000
120 2s. pale blue £3500 £200
aa. Imperf (Plate 1) £11000
120*a* 2s. cobalt £14000 £2500
120*b* 2s. milky blue £12000 £1700
Plate
1 (1867) £2800 £175
3 (1868) * £11000
121 2s. brown (Plate No. 1) (27.2.80) £20000 £3250
a. Imperf £22000
b. No watermark † –

*102/21 **For well-centred, lightly used +75%.**

Examples of the 1s. from Plates 5 and 6 without watermark are postal forgeries used at the Stock Exchange Post Office in the early 1870's.

1872–73. *Uncoloured letters in corners.* Wmk Spray, W **33**.

122 **34** 6d. deep chestnut (Plate II) (12.4.72) £1100 £110
122*a* 6d. chestnut (Plate II) (22.5.72) £675 50·00 £120
122*b* 6d. pale chestnut (Plate II) (1872) £575 50·00
123 6d. pale buff (19.10.72) £800 £100 £250
Plate
11 (1872, pale buff) £800 £100
12 (1872, pale buff) £2800 £280
124 6d. chestnut (Plate 12) (1872) * £3500
124a 6d. pale chestnut (Plate 12) (1872) * £3200
125 6d. grey (Plate 12) (24.4.73) £1600 £225 £250
a. Imperf £5500

*122/5 **For well-centred, lightly used +50%.**

35
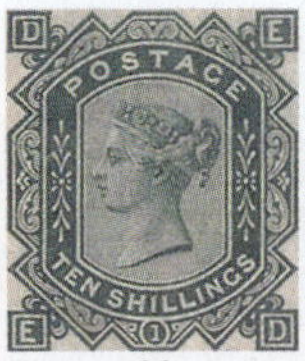
36

37

38
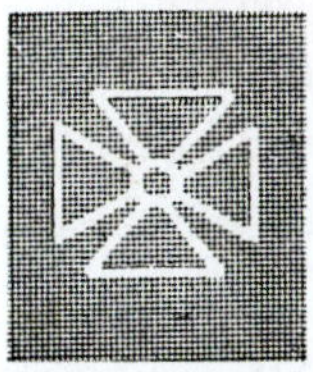
39 Maltese Cross

40 Large Anchor

1867–83. *Uncoloured letters in corners.*

(a) Wmk Maltese Cross, W **39**. P 15½ × 15.

			Un	Used*
126	**35**	5s. rose (1.7.67)	£8250	£600
127		5s. pale rose	£8250	£600
		a. Imperf (Plate 1)	£14000	
		Plate		
		1 (1867)	£8250	£600
		2 (1874)	£12000	£1100
128	**36**	10s. greenish grey (Plate 1) (26.9.78)	£50000	£2800
129	**37**	£1 brown-lilac (Plate 1) (26.9.78)	£80000	£4000

(b) Wmk Anchor, W **40**. P 14.

(i) Blued paper.

130	**35**	5s. rose (Plate 4) (25.11.82)	£28000	£4000
131	**36**	10s. grey-green (Plate 1) (2.83)	£110000	£4800
132	**37**	£1 brown-lilac (Plate 1) (12.82)	£125000	£9000
133	**38**	£5 orange (Plate 1) (21.3.82)	£60000	£13000

(ii) White paper.

134	**35**	5s. rose (Plate 4)	£25000	£3200
135	**36**	10s. greenish grey (Plate 1)	£120000	£4000
136	**37**	£1 brown-lilac (Plate 1)	£150000	£8000
137	**38**	£5 orange (Plate 1)	£12000	£4500

*126/37 **For well-centred, lightly used +75%.**

41

42

43

44

45

46

47 Small Anchor
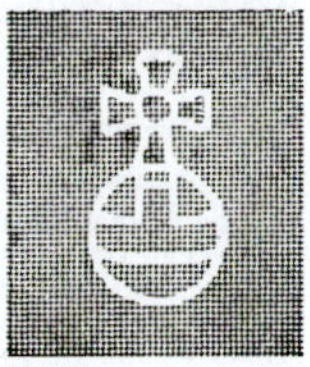
48 Orb

1873–80. *Large coloured letters in the corners.*

(a) Wmk Anchor, W**47**.

			Un	Used*	Used on cover
138	**41**	2½d. rosy mauve (*blued paper*) (1.7.75)	£750	£120	
		a. Imperf			
		Plate			
		1 (*blued paper*) (1875)	£750	£120	
		2 (*blued paper*) (1875)	£7000	£1500	
		3 (*blued paper*) (1875)	–	£5000	
139		2½d. rosy mauve (white paper)	£525	80·00	£140
		Plate			
		1 (*white paper*) (1875)	£525	80·00	
		2 (*white paper*) (1875)	£525	80·00	
		3 (*white paper*) (1875)	£800	£120	

Error of Lettering L H—F L for L H—H L (Plate 2).

140	**41**	2½d. rosy mauve	£18000	£2200	

(b) Wmk Orb, W **48**.

141	**41**	2½d. rosy mauve (1.5.76)	£425	50·00	90·00
		Plate			
		3 (1876)	£1100	£110	
		4 (1876)	£425	50·00	
		5 (1876)	£425	50·00	
		6 (1876)	£425	50·00	
		7 (1877)	£425	50·00	
		8 (1877)	£425	50·00	
		9 (1877)	£425	50·00	
		10 (1878)	£475	65·00	
		11 (1878)	£425	50·00	
		12 (1878)	£425	50·00	
		13 (1878)	£425	50·00	
		14 (1879)	£425	50·00	
		15 (1879)	£425	50·00	
		16 (1879)	£425	50·00	
		17 (1880)	£1400	£275	
142		2½d. blue (5.2.80)	£475	40·00	75·00
		Plate			
		17 (1880)	£475	55·00	
		18 (1880)	£475	40·00	
		19 (1880)	£475	40·00	
		20 (1880)	£475	40·00	

(c) Wmk Spray, W **33**.

143	**42**	3d. rose (5.7.73)	£350	45·00	60·00
144		3d. pale rose	£400	45·00	
		Plate			
		11 (1873)	£350	45·00	
		12 (1873)	£400	45·00	
		14 (1874)	£425	45·00	
		15 (1874)	£350	45·00	
		16 (1875)	£350	45·00	
		17 (1875)	£400	45·00	
		18 (1875)	£400	45·00	
		19 (1876)	£350	45·00	
		20 (1879)	£650	£100	
145	**43**	6d. pale buff (Plate 13) (15.3.73)	*	£20000	
146		6d. deep grey (20.3.74)	£600	90·00	£110
147		6d. grey	£400	60·00	
		Plate			
		13 (1874)	£400	60·00	
		14 (1875)	£400	60·00	
		15 (1876)	£400	60·00	
		16 (1878)	£400	60·00	
		17 (1880)	£750	£140	
148	**44**	1s. deep green (1.9.73)	£900	£140	
150		1s. green	£500	£100	£190
		Plate			
		8 (1873)	£650	£120	
		9 (1874)	£650	£120	
		10 (1874)	£600	£140	
		11 (1875)	£600	£120	
		12 (1875)	£500	£100	
		13 (1876)	£500	£100	
		14 (—)	*	£30000	
151		1s. orange-brown (Plate 13) (14.10.80)	£4000	£600	£1400

(d) Wmk Large Garter, W **17**.

152	**45**	4d. vermilion (1.3.76)	£2400	£425	£850
		Plate			
		15 (1876)	£2400	£425	
		16 (1877)	*	£28000	
153		4d. sage-green (12.3.77)	£1000	£250	£475
		Plate			
		15 (1877)	£1100	£275	
		16 (1877)	£1000	£250	
		17 (1877)	*	£17500	
154		4d. grey-brown (Plate 17) (15.8.80)	£2400	£450	£1300
		a. Imperf	£10000		
156	**46**	8d. orange (Plate 1) (11.9.76)	£1500	£300	£500

*138/56 **For well-centred, lightly used +100%.**

1876 (July). *Prepared for use but not issued.*
156*a* **46** 8d. purple-brown (Plate 1) £8500

49 Imperial Crown

(50)

1880–83. Wmk Imperial Crown. W **49**.

157	**41**	2½d. blue (23.3.81)	£350	28·00	45·00
		Plate			
		21 (1881)	£400	35·00	
		22 (1881)	£350	35·00	
		23 (1881)	£350	28·00	
158	**42**	3d. rose (3.81)	£400	80·00	£140
		Plate			
		20 (1881)	£775	£140	
		21 (1881)	£400	80·00	
159	**50**	3d. on 3d. lilac (C.) (Plate 21) (1.1.83)	£500	£130	£350
160	**45**	4d. grey-brown (8.12.80)	£350	60·00	£140
		Plate			
		17 (1880)	£350	60·00	
		18 (1882)	£350	60·00	
161	**43**	6d. grey (1.1.81)	£350	65·00	£120
		Plate			
		17 (1881)	£400	65·00	
		18 (1882)	£350	65·00	
162	**50**	6d. on 6d. lilac (C.) (Plate 18) (1.1.83)	£550	£130	£350
		a. Slanting dots (various) from	£1200	£350	
		b. Opt double	–	£9000	
163	**44**	1s. orange-brown (24.5.81)	£550	£140	£450
		Plate			
		13 (1881)	£675	£140	
		14 (1881)	£550	£140	

*157/63 **For well-centred, lightly used +75%.**

The 1s. Plate 14 (line perf 14) exists in purple, but was not issued in this shade (*Price* £8000 *unused*). Examples were included in a few of the Souvenir Albums prepared for members of the "Stamp Committee of 1884".

52

53

54

55

56

1880–81. Wmk Imperial Crown, W **49**.

164	**52**	½d. deep green (14.10.80)	45·00	12·00	22·00
		a. Imperf	£2500		
		b. No watermark	£6000		
165		½d. pale green	45·00	18·00	
166	**53**	1d. Venetian red (1.1.80)	22·00	12·00	25·00
		a. Imperf	£2500		
167	**54**	1½d. Venetian red (14.10.80)	£200	45·00	£130
168	**55**	2d. pale rose (8.12.80)	£275	90·00	£225
168a		2d. deep rose	£300	90·00	
169	**56**	5d. indigo (15.3.81)	£675	£110	£225
		a. Imperf	£4250	£3500	

*164/9 **For well-centred, lightly used +75%.**

Two used examples of the 1d. value have been reported on the Orb (fiscal) watermark.

Die I

57

Die II

1881. Wmk Imperial Crown. W **49**.

		(a) 14 dots in each corner, Die I (12 July).			
170	**57**	1d. lilac	£200	30·00	50·00
171		1d. pale lilac	£200	30·00	
		(b) 16 dots in each corner, Die II (13 December).			
172	**57**	1d. lilac	2·50	2·00	3·00
172*a*		1d. bluish lilac	£425	£125	
173		1d. deep purple	2·50	2·00	
		a. Printed both sides	£800	†	
		b. Frame broken at bottom.	£800	£300	
		c. Printed on gummed side.	£800	†	
		d. Imperf three sides (pair)	£6000	†	
		e. Printed both sides but impression on back inverted	£850	†	
		f. No watermark	£5500	†	
		g. Blued paper	£4500		
174		1d. mauve	2·50	1·50	
		a. Imperf (pair)	£4500		

*170/4 **For well-centred, lightly used** +50%.

1d. stamps with the words "PEARS SOAP" printed on the back in orange, blue or mauve price from £525, unused.

The variety "frame broken at bottom" (No. 173b) shows a white space just inside the bottom frame-line from between the "N" and "E" of "ONE" to below the first "N" of "PENNY", breaking the pearls and cutting into the lower part of the oval below "PEN".

KEY TO SURFACE-PRINTED ISSUES 1880–1900

S.G. Nos.	*Description*	*Date of Issue*
164/5	½d. green	14.10.80
187	½d. slate-blue	1.4.84
197/*e*	½d. vermilion	1.1.8
721	3½d. blue-green	17.4.1900
166	1d. Venetian red	1.1.80
170/	11d. lilac, Die 1	12.7.81
172/4	1d. lilac, Die 11	12.12.81
167	1½d. Venetian red	14.10.80
188	1½d. lilac	1.4.84
198	1½d. purple and green	1.1.87
168/*a*	2d. rose	8.12.80
189	2d. lilac	1.4.84
199/200	2d. green and red	1.1.87
190	2½d.lilac	1.4.84
201	2½d purple on blue paper	1.1.87
191	3d. lilac	1.4.84
202/4	3d. purple on yellow paper	1.1.87
192	4d. dull green	1.4.84
205/*a*	4d. green and brown	1.1.87
206	4½d. green and carmine	15.9.92
169	5d. indigo	15.3.81
193	5d. dull green	1.4.84
207	5d. purple and blue, Die I	1.1.87
207*a*	5d. purple and blue, Die II	1888
194	6d. dull green	1.4.84
208/*a*	6d. purple on rose-red paper	1.1.87
195	9d. dull green	1.8.83
209	9d. purple and blue	1.1.87
210/*b*	10d. purple and carmine	24.2.90
196	1s. dull green	1.4.84
211	1s. green	1.1.87
214	1s. green and carmine	11.7.1900
175	2s.6d. lilac on blued paper	2.7.83
178/9	2s.6d. lilac	1884
176	5s. rose on blued paper	1.4.84
180/1	5s. rose	1884
177/*a*	10s. ultramarine on blued paper	1.4.84
182/3*a*	10s. ultramarine	1884
185	£1 brown-lilac, wmk Crowns	1.4.84
186	£1 brown-lilac, wmk Orbs	6.1.88
212	£1 green	28.1.91

Note that the £5 value used with the above series is listed as Nos. 133 and 137.

58

59

60

1883–84. *Coloured letters in the corners.* Wmk Anchor, W **40**.

			Un	*Used*
		(a) Blued paper.		
175	**58**	2s.6d. lilac (2.7.83)	£6000	£1300
176	**59**	5s. rose (1.4.84)	£14000	£3750
177	**60**	10s. ultramarine (1.4.84)	£38000	£8000
177a		10s. cobalt (5.84)	£55000	£13000
		(b) White paper.		
178	**58**	2s.6d. lilac	£500	£140
179		2s.6d. deep lilac	£700	£200
		a. On blued paper	£8000	£3500
180	**59**	5s. rose	£950	£200
181		5s. crimson	£850	£200
182	**60**	10s. cobalt	£32000	£7500
183		10s. ultramarine	£2000	£475
183*a*		10s. pale ultramarine	£2250	£475

*175/83*a* **For well-centred, lightly used** +50%.

For No. 180 perf 12 see second note below No. 196.

61

Broken frames, Plate 2

1884 (1 April). Wmk Three Imperial Crowns, W **49**.

185	**61**	£1 brown-lilac	£28000	£2400
		a. Frame broken	£50000	£4000

1888 (Jan). Wmk Three Orbs, W **48**.

186	**61**	£1 brown-lilac	£60000	£3800
		a. Frame broken	£100000	£6500

*185/6a **For well-centred, lightly used** +50%.

The December 1887 printing of the £1 brown-lilac was produced on paper watermarked Three Orbs in error. The decision was taken to issue date stamps for normal postal use and the earliest recorded postmark is 6 January 1888 at Leadenhall Street, London EC.

The broken-frame varieties, Nos. 185a and 186a, are on Plate 2 stamps JC and TA, as illustrated. See also No. 212a.

62

63

64

65

66

1883 (1 Aug). *(9d.) or* **1884** (1 April) *(others)*. Wmk Imperial Crown, W **49** (sideways on horiz designs).

			Un	*Used**	*Used on cover*
187	**52**	½d. slate-blue	25·00	8·00	15·00
		a. Imperf	£2000		
188	**62**	1½d. lilac	£100	38·00	£100
		a. Imperf	£2500		
189	**63**	2d. lilac	£175	70·00	£125
		a. Imperf	£3000		
190	**64**	2½d. lilac	75·00	15·00	25·00
		a. Imperf	£3000		
191	**65**	3d. lilac	£220	90·00	£150
		a. Imperf	£3000		
192	**66**	4d. dull green	£450	£185	£275
		a. Imperf	£3500		
193	**62**	5d. dull green	£450	£185	£275
		a. Imperf	£4000		
194	**63**	6d. dull green	£475	£200	£300
		a. Imperf	£4000		
195	**64**	9d. dull green (1.8.83)	£950	£400	£2000
196	**65**	1s. dull green	£1100	£250	£475
		a. Imperf	£5500		

*187/96 **For well-centred, lightly used** +100%

The above prices are for stamps in the true dull green colour. Stamps which have been soaked, causing the colour to run, are virtually worthless.

Stamps of the above set and No. 180 are also found perf 12; these are official perforations, but were never issued. A second variety of the 5d. is known with a line instead of a stop under the "d" in the value; this was never issued and is therefore only known unused (Price £28000).

71

72

73

74

75

76

77

78

79

80

81

82

Die I Die II

Die I: Square dots to right of "d". Die II: Thin vertical lines to right of "d".

1887 (1 Jan)–**92**. *"Jubilee" issue. New types. The bicoloured stamps have the value tablets, or the frames including the value tablets, in the second colour.* Wmk Imperial Crown, W **49** (Three Crowns on £1).

197	**71**	½d. vermilion	1·50	1·00	6·00
		a. Printed on gummed side.	£1800		
		b. Printed both sides			
		c. Doubly printed	£15000		
		d. Imperf	£3000		
197*e*		½d. orange-vermilion	1·50	1·00	
198	**72**	1½d. dull purple and pale green	15·00	7·00	22·00
		a. Purple part of design double	—	£6500	
199	**73**	2d. green and scarlet	£350	£225	
200		2d. grey-green and carmine	28·00	12·00	24·00
201	**74**	2½d. purple/*blue*	22·00	3·00	6·00
		a. Printed on gummed side.	£6000		
		b. Imperf three sides	£5000		
		c. Imperf	£7000		
202	**75**	3d. purple/*yellow*	22·00	3.25	30·00
		a. Imperf	£7500		
203		3d. deep purple/*yellow*	22·00	3·25	
204		3d. purple/*orange* (1890)	£600		
205	**76**	4d. green and purple-brown	30·00	13·00	35·00
		aa. Imperf	£7500		
205*a*		4d. green and deep brown	30·00	13·00	
206	**77**	4½d. green and carmine (15.9.92)	10·00	40·00	75·00
206*a*		4½d. green and deep brt carmine	£550	£450	
207	**78**	5d. dull purple and blue (Die I)	£600	£100	£175
207*a*		5d. dull pur and bl (Die II) (1888)	35·00	11·00	40·00
208	**79**	6d. purple/*rose-red*	30·00	10·00	75·00
208*a*		6d. deep purple/*rose-red*	30·00	11·00	
209	**80**	9d. dull purple and blue	60·00	40·00	£200
210	**81**	10d. dull purple and carmine (*shades*) 24.2.90)	45·00	38·00	£225
		aa. Imperf	£12000		
210*a*		10d. dull purple and dp dull carm	£450	£225	
210*b*		10d. dull purple and scarlet	80·00	50·00	
211	**82**	1s. dull green	£200	60·00	£125
212	**61**	£1 green (28.1.91)	£3500	£700	
		a. Frame broken	£7000	£1800	

*197/212a **For well-centred, lightly used +50%**.

The broken-frame varieties, No. 212a, are on Plate 2 stamps JC or TA, as illustrated above No. 185.

½d. stamps with "PEARS SOAP" printed on the back in orange, blue or mauve, price from £525 each.

No used price is quoted for No. 204 as it is not possible to authenticate the paper colour on stamps in used condition.

1900. *Colours changed.* Wmk Imperial Crown, W **49**.

213	**71**	½d. blue-green (17.4)	1·75	2·00	6·00
		a. Printed on gummed side.	—	—	
		b. Imperf	£5500		
214	**82**	1s. green and carmine (11.7)	50·00	£125	£850
197/214 *Set of* 14			£525	£325	

*213/14 **For well-centred, lightly used +50%.**

The ½d., No. 213, in bright blue, is a colour changeling caused by a constituent of the ink used for some months in 1900.

KING EDWARD VII

22 January 1901–6 May 1910

PRINTINGS. Distinguishing De La Rue printings from the provisional printings of the same values made by Harrison & Sons Ltd. or at Somerset House may prove difficult in some cases. For very full guidance Volume 2 of the Stanley Gibbons *Great Britain Specialised Catalogue* should prove helpful.

Note that stamps perforated 15×14 must be Harrison; the 2½d., 3d. and 4d. in this perforation are useful reference material, their shades and appearance in most cases matching the Harrison perf 14 printings.

Except for the 6d. value, all stamps on chalk-surfaced paper were printed by De La Rue.

Of the stamps on ordinary paper, the De La Rue impressions are usually clearer and of a higher finish than those of the other printers. The shades are markedly different except in some printings of the 4d., 6d. and 7d. and in the 5s., 10s. and £1.

Used stamps in good, clean, unrubbed condition and with dated postmarks can form the basis of a useful reference collection, the dates often assisting in the assignment to the printers.

USED STAMPS. For well-centred, lightly used examples of King Edward VII stamps, add the following percentages to the used prices quoted below:

De La Rue printings (Nos. 215/66)—3d. values +35%, 4d. orange + 100%, 6d. +75%, 7d. and 1s. +25%, all other values + 50%.

Harrison printings (Nos. 267/86)—all values and perforations +75%.

Somerset House printings (Nos. 287/320)—1s. values +25%, all other values +50%.

83

84

85

86

87

88

89

90

91

92

93

94

95

96

97

(Des E. Fuchs)

1902 (1 Jan)–**10**. *Printed by De La Rue & Co.* Wmk Imperial Crown (½d. to 1s.); Anchor (2s.6d. to 10s.); Three Crowns (£1). *Ordinary paper*. P 14.

215	**83**	½d. dull blue-green (1.1.02)	2·00	1·50	2·50
216		½d. blue-green	2·00	1·50	
217		½d. pale yellowish green (26.11.04)	2·00	1·50	2·50
218		½d. yellowish green	2·00	1·50	
		a. Booklet pane. Five stamps plus St. Andrew's Cross label (6.06)	£450		
		b. Doubly printed (bottom row on one pane) (Control H9)	£25000		
219		1d. scarlet (1.1.02)	2·00	1·50	2·50
220		1d. bright scarlet	2·00	1·50	
		a. Imperf (pair)	£25000		
221	**84**	1½d. dull purple & green (21.3.02)	40·00	20·00	
222		1½d. slate-purple and green	45·00	20·00	30·00
223		1½d. pale dull pur & green (*chalk-surfaced paper*) (8.05)	40·00	20·00	
224		1½d. slate-purple & bluish green (*chalk-surfaced paper*)	40·00	18·00	
225	**85**	2d. yellowish green & carmine-red (25.3.02)	45·00	20·00	32·00
226		2d. grey-grn & carm-red (1904)	55·00	30·00	
227		2d. pale grey-green & carm-red (*chalk-surfaced paper*) (4.06)	40·00	28·00	
228		2d. pale grey-green & scar (*chalk-surfaced paper*) (1909)	40·00	28·00	
229		2d. dull blue-green & carm (*chalk-surfaced paper*) (1907)	90·00	50·00	
230	**86**	2½d. ultramarine (1.1.02)	20·00	10·00	22·00
231		2½d. pale ultramarine	20·00	10·00	
232	**87**	3d. dull pur/*orge-yell* (20.3.02)	40·00	15·00	30·00
		a. Chalk-surfaced paper (3.06)	£180	75·00	
232*b*		3d. deep purple/*orange-yellow*	40·00	15·00	
232*c*		3d. pale reddish pur/*orge-yell* (*chalk-surfaced paper*) (3.06)	£180	70·00	
233		3d. dull reddish pur/*yell* (*lemon back*) (*chalk-surfaced paper*)	£180	80·00	
233b		3d. pale purple/*lemon* (*chalk-surfaced paper*)	40·00	18·00	
234		3d. pur/*lemon* (*chalk-surfaced paper*)	40·00	18·00	
235	**88**	4d. green & grey-brn (27.3.02)	50·00	30·00	
236		4d. green and chocolate-brown	50·00	30·00	
		a. Chalk-surfaced paper (1.06)	40·00	18·00	40·00
238		4d. dp green & choc-brn (*chalk-surfaced paper*) (1.06)	40·00	18·00	
239		4d. brown-orange (1.11.09)	£180	£140	
240		4d. pale orange (12.09)	20·00	15·00	35·00
241		4d. orange-red (12.09)	20·00	15·00	
242	**89**	5d. dull pur & ultram (14.5.02)	60·00	20·00	50·00
		a. Chalk-surfaced paper (5.06)	50·00	20·00	
244		5d. slate-pur & ultram (*chalk-surfaced paper*) (5.06)	50·00	20·00	
245	**83**	6d. pale dull purple (1.1.02)	40·00	20·00	50·00
		a. Chalk-surfaced paper (1.06)	40·00	20·00	
246		6d. slate-purple	40·00	20·00	
248		6d. dull purple (*chalk-surfaced paper*) (1.06)	40·00	20·00	
249	**90**	7d. grey-black (4.5.10)	12·00	20·00	£195
249*a*		7d. deep grey-black	£110	£100	
250	**91**	9d. dull pur & ultram (7.4.02)	90·00	60·00	£200
		a. Chalk-surfaced paper (6.05)	90·00	60·00	
251		9d. slate-purple & ultramarine	90·00	60·00	
		a. Chalk-surfaced paper (6.05)	90·00	60·00	
254	**92**	10d. dull purple & carm (3.7.02)	90·00	60·00	£225
		a. No cross on crown	£400	£250	
		b. Chalk-surfaced paper (9.06)	90·00	60·00	
255		10d. slate-purple & carm (*chalk-surfaced paper*) (9.06)	90·00	60·00	
		a. No cross on crown	£425	£250	
256		10d. dull purple & scarlet (*chalk-surfaced paper*) (9.10)	95·00	60·00	
		a. No cross on crown	£425	£250	
257	**93**	1s. dull green & carm (24.3.02)	80·00	35·00	£150
		a. Chalk-surfaced paper (9.05)	80·00	35·00	
259		1s. dull green & scarlet (*chalk-surfaced paper*) (9.10)	80·00	50·00	
260	**94**	2s.6d. lilac (5.4.02)	£225	£140	£700
261		2s.6d. pale dull purple (*chalk-surfaced paper*) (7.10.05)	£275	£150	
262		2s.6d. dull pur (*chalk-surfaced paper*)	£250	£150	
263	**95**	5s. bright carmine (5.4.02)	£350	£200	£950
264		5s. deep bright carmine	£350	£200	
265	**96**	10s. ultramarine (5.4.02)	£850	£450	
266	**97**	£1 dull blue-green (16.6.02)	£2000	£750	

97a

1910 (May). *Prepared for use by De La Rue but not issued.* Wmk Imperial Crown, W **49**. P 14.

266*a*	**97**	2d. Tyrian plum	£75000

One example of this stamp is known used, but it was never issued to the public.

1911. *Printed by Harrison & Sons. Ordinary paper.* Wmk Imperial Crown.

(a) P 14

267	**83**	½d. dull yellow-green (3.5.11)	2·75	1·50	4·00
268		½d. dull green	3·00	1·50	
269		½d. deep dull green	11·00	6·00	
270		½d. pale bluish green	40·00	40·00	
		a. Booklet pane. Five stamps plus St. Andrew's Cross label	£700		
		b. Wmk sideways	†	£28000	
		c. Imperf (pair)	£28000	†	
271		½d. brt green (fine impression) (6.11)	£275	£170	
272		1d. rose-red (3.5.11)	8·00	12·00	18·00
		a. No wmk (brick red)	50·00	60·00	
273		1d. deep rose-red	8·00	12·00	
274		1d. rose-carmine	55·00	30·00	
275		1d. aniline pink (5.11)	£600	£350	
275*a*		1d. aniline rose	£180	£140	
276	**86**	2½d. bright blue (10.7.11)	65·00	35·00	50·00
277	**87**	3d. purple/*lemon* (12.9.11)	75·00	£200	£550
277*a*		3d. grey/*lemon*	£3500		
278	**88**	4d. bright orange (12.7.11)	£100	50·00	£175

(b) P 15×14.

279	**83**	½d. dull green (30.10.11)	40·00	45·00	£100
279*a*		½d. deep dull green	40·00	45·00	
280		1d. rose-red (4.10.11)	38·00	25·00	
281		1d. rose-carmine	15·00	15·00	30·00
282		1d. pale rose-carmine	22·00	15·00	
283	**86**	2½d. bright blue (14.10.11)	22·00	15·00	35·00
284		2½d. dull blue	22·00	15·00	
285	**87**	3d. purple/*lemon* (22.9.11)	45·00	15·00	40·00
285*a*		3d. grey/*lemon*	£2250		
286	**88**	4d. bright orange (11.11.11)	30·00	15·00	65·00
279/86 *Set of 5*			£130	90·00	

No. 272a was probably a trial printing.

1911–13. *Printed at Somerset House. Ordinary paper.* Wmk as 1902–1910. P 14.

287	**84**	1½d. reddish purple and bright green (13.7.11)	45·00	35·00	
288		1½d. dull purple and green	30·00	28·00	50·00
289		1½d. slate-purple & grn (9.12)	30·00	28·00	
290	**85**	2d. dp dull green & red (8.8.11)	28·00	20·00	50·00
291		2d. deep dull green & carmine	28·00	20·00	
292		2d. grey-green & bright carmine (carmine shows clearly on back) (11.3.12)	28·00	25·00	
293	**89**	5d. dull reddish purple and bright blue (7.8.11)	30·00	20·00	65·00
294		5d. deep dull reddish purple and bright blue	30·00	20·00	
295	**83**	6d. royal purple (31.10.11)	50·00	85·00	
296		6d. bright magenta (*chalk-surfaced paper*) (31.10.11)	£10000		
297		6d. dull purple	30·00	20·00	85·00
298		6d. reddish purple (11.11)	30·00	25·00	
		a. No cross on crown (*various shades*)	£750		
299		6d. very dp reddish pur (11.11)	40·00	35·00	
300		6d. dark purple (3.12)	30·00	20·00	
301		6d. dull purple ("Dickinson" coated paper) (3.13)	£250	£180	
303		6d. deep plum (7.13)	30·00	70·00	
		a. No cross on crown	£900		
305	**90**	7d. slate-grey (1.8.12)	15·00	22·00	£195
306	**91**	9d. reddish purple and light blue (24.7.11)	80·00	75·00	
306a		9d. deep dull reddish purple & deep bright blue (9.11)	80·00	75·00	
307		9d. dull reddish purple & blue (10.11)	60·00	60·00	£190
307*a*		9d. deep plum and blue (7.13)	60·00	60·00	
308		9d. slate-pur & cobalt-bl (3.12)	£140	£110	
309	**92**	10d. dull purple & scar (9.10.11)	80·00	75·00	
310		10d. dull reddish pur & aniline pink	£275	£225	
311		10d. dull reddish purple & carm (5.12)	80·00	£140	£225
		a. No cross on crown	£1500	60.00	
312	**93**	1s. dark green & scar (13.7.11)	£120	60·00	
313		1s. dp green & scar (9.10.11)	80·00	35·00	
314		1s. green & carmine (15.4.12)	55·00	35·00	£160
315	**94**	2s.6d. dull greyish purple (15.9.11)	£700	£400	
316		2s.6d. dull reddish purple	£275	£180	
317		2s.6d. dark purple	£300	£190	
318	**95**	5s. carmine (29.2.12)	£400	£200	£950
319	**96**	10s. blue (14.1.12)	£900	£600	
320	**97**	£1 deep green (3.9.11)	£2000	£750	

*No. 301 was on an experimental coated paper which does not respond to the silver test.

KING GEORGE V
6 May 1910–20 January 1936

Further detailed information on the issues of King George V will be found in Volume 2 of the Stanley Gibbons *Great Britain Specialised Catalogue*.

PRINTERS. Types **98** to **102** were typographed by Harrison & Sons Ltd, with the exception of certain preliminary printings made at Somerset House and distinguishable by the controls "A.11", "B.11" or "B.12" (the Harrison printings do not have a full stop after the letter). The booklet stamps, Nos. 334/7 and 344/5 were printed by Harrisons only.

WATERMARK VARIETIES. Many British stamps to 1967 exist without watermark owing to misplacement of the paper, and with either inverted, reversed, or inverted and reversed watermarks. A proportion of the low-value stamps issued in booklets have the watermark inverted in the normal course of printing.

Low values with *watermark sideways* are normally from stamp rolls used in machines with sideways delivery or, from June 1940, certain booklets.

STAMPS WITHOUT WATERMARK. Stamps found without watermark, due to misplacement of the sheet in relation to the dandy roll, are not listed here, but will be found in the *Great Britain Specialised Catalogue*.

The 1½d. and 5d. 1912–22, and 2d. and 2½d., 1924–26, listed here, are from *whole* sheets completely without watermark.

98

99

For type differences with T **101/2** *see* notes below the latter.

Die A Die B

Dies of Halfpenny

Die A. The three upper scales on the body of the right hand dolphin form a triangle; the centre jewel of the cross inside the crown is suggested by a comma.

Die B. The three upper scales are incomplete; the centre jewel is suggested by a crescent.

Die A Die B

Dies of One Penny

Die A. The second line of shading on the ribbon to the right of the crown extends right across the wreath; the line nearest to the crown on the right hand ribbon shows as a short line at the bottom of the ribbon.

Die B. The second line of shading is broken in the middle; the first line is little more than a dot.

(Des Bertram Mackennal and G. W. Eve. Head from photograph by W. & D. Downey. Die eng J. A. C. Harrison)

1911–12. Wmk Imperial Crown, W **49**. P 15×14.

No.	Type	Description	*Un*	*Used*
321	**98**	½d. pale green (Die A) (22.6.11) ..	5·00	4·00
322		½d. green (Die A) (22.6.11)	4·00	4·00
		a. Error. Perf 14 (8.11)	£16000	£850
323		½d. bluish green (Die A)	£300	£180
324		½d. yellow-green (Die B)	12·00	1·50
325		½d. bright green (Die B)	8·00	1·50
		a. Wmk sideways	—	£4500
326		½d. bluish green (Die B)	£160	£100
327	**99**	1d. carmine-red (Die A) (22.6.11)	4·50	2·50
		c. Wmk sideways	†	—
328		1d. pale carmine (Die A) (22.6.11)	14·00	3·00
		a. No cross on crown	£575	£350
329		1d. carmine (Die B)	7·00	3·00
330		1d. pale carmine (Die B)	10·00	4·00
		a. No cross on crown	£600	£375
331		1d. rose-pink (Die B)	£125	45·00
332		1d. scarlet (Die B) (6.12)	45·00	18·00
333		1d. aniline scarlet (Die B)	£200	£110

For note on the aniline scarlet No. 333 see below No. 343.

100 Simple Cypher

1912 (Aug). *Booklet stamps.* Wmk Royal Cypher ("Simple"), W **100**. P 15×14.

No.	Type	Description	*Un*	*Used*
334	**98**	½d. pale green (Die B)	40·00	40·00
335		½d. green (Die B)	40·00	40·00
336	**99**	1d. scarlet (Die B)	30·00	30·00
337		1d. bright scarlet (Die B)	30·00	30·00

101

102

103 Multiple Cypher

Type differences

½d. In T **98** the ornament above "P" of "HALFPENNY" has two thin lines of colour and the beard is undefined. In T **101** the ornament has one thick line and the beard is well defined.1d. In T **99** the body of the lion is unshaded and in T **102** it is shaded.

1912 (1 Jan). Wmk Imperial Crown, W **49**. P 15 × 14.

No.	Type	Description	*Un*	*Used*
338	**101**	½d. deep green	15·00	8·00
339		½d. green	8·00	4·00
340		½d. yellow-green	8·00	4·00
		a. No cross on crown	£100	55·00
341	**102**	1d. bright scarlet	5·00	2·00
		a. No cross on crown	80·00	55·00
		b. Printed double, one albino	£180	
342		1d. scarlet	5·00	2·00
343		1d. aniline scarlet*	£175	£100
		a. No cross on crown	£1200	

*Our prices for the aniline scarlet 1d. stamps, Nos. 333 and 343, are for specimens in which the colour is suffused on the surface of the stamp and shows through clearly on the back. Specimens without these characteristics but which show "aniline" reactions under the quartz lamp are relatively common.

1912 (Aug). Wmk Royal Cypher ("Simple"), W **100**. P 15×14.

No.	Type	Description	*Un*	*Used*
344	**101**	½d. green	7·00	3·00
		a. No cross on crown	£100	50·00
345	**102**	1d. scarlet	8·00	4·50
		a. No cross on crown	£100	50·00

1912 (Sept–Oct). Wmk Royal Cypher ("Multiple"), W **103**. P 15×14.

No.	Type	Description	*Un*	*Used*
346	**101**	½d. green (Oct)	12·00	8·00
		a. No cross on crown	£100	60·00
		b. Imperf	£130	
		c. Wmk sideways	†	£3250
		d. Printed on gummed side	—	†
347		½d. yellow-green	15·00	8·00
348		½d. pale green	15·00	8·00
349	**102**	1d. bright scarlet	18·00	10·00
350		1d. scarlet	18·00	10·00
		a. No cross on crown	£120	50·00
		b. Imperf	£130	
		c. Wmk sideways	£130	£150
		d. Wmk sideways. No cross on crown	£750	

104

105

106

No. 357a

No. 357ab

No. 357ac

107

108

Die I

Die II

Dies of 2d.

Die I.— Inner frame-line at top and sides close to solid of background. *Four* complete lines of shading between top of head and oval frame-line. These four lines do *not* extend to the oval itself. White line round "TWOPENCE" thin.

Die II.— Inner frame-line farther from solid of background. *Three* lines between top of head and extending to the oval. White line round "TWOPENCE" thicker.

(Des Bertram Mackennal (heads) and G. W. Eve (frames). Coinage head (½, 1½, 2, 3 and 4d.); large medal head (1d., 2½d.); intermediate medal head (5d. to 1s.); small medal head used for fiscal stamps. Dies eng J. A. C. Harrison)

(Typo by Harrison & Sons Ltd., except the 6d. printed by the Stamping Department of the Board of Inland Revenue, Somerset House. The latter also made printings of the following which can only be distinguished by the controls: ½d. B.13; 1½d. A.12; 2d. C.13; 2½d. A.12; 3d. A.12, B.13, C.13; 4d. B.13; 5d. B.13; 7d. C.13; 8d. C.13; 9d. agate B.13; 10d. C.13; 1s. C.13)

1912–24. Wmk Royal Cypher, W **100**. *Chalk-surfaced paper (6d.).* P 15×14.

No.	Type	Description	*Un*	*Used*
351	**105**	½d. green (16.1.13)	1·00	1·00
		a. Partial double print (half of bottom row from Control G15)	£19000	
		b. Gummed both sides	—	—
352		½d. bright green	1·00	1·00
353		½d. deep green	5·00	2·00
354		½d. yellow-green	6·00	3·00
355		½d. very yellow (Cyprus) green (1914)	£7000	†
356		½d. blue-green	40·00	25·00
357	**104**	1d. bright scarlet (8.10.12)	1·00	1·00
		a. "Q" for "O" (R. 1/4) (Control E14)	£150	£150
		ab. "Q" for "O" (R. 4/11) (Control T22)	£350	£190
		ac. Reversed "Q" for "O" (R. 15/9) (Control T22)	£300	£240
		ad. Inverted "Q" for "O" (R. 20/3)	£375	£240
		b. *Tête-bêche* (pair)	£55000	†
358		1d. vermilion	5·00	2·50
359		1d. pale rose-red	15·00	2·50
360		1d. carmine-red	11·00	5·00
361		1d. scarlet-vermilion	£125	50·00
		a. Printed on back†	£275	†
362	**105**	1½d. red-brown (15.10.12)	4·00	1·50
		a. "PENCF" (R. 15/12)	£200	£150
		b. Booklet pane. Four stamps plus two printed labels (2.24)	£450	
363		1½d. chocolate-brown	11·00	2·00
		a. Without wmk	£180	£125
364		1½d. chestnut	5·00	1·00
		a. "PENCF" (R. 15/12)	£100	80·00
365		1½d. yellow-brown	20·00	16·00
366	**106**	2d. orange-yellow (Die I) (20.8.12)	8·00	3·00
367		2d. reddish orange (Die I) (11.13)	6·00	3·00
368		2d. orange (Die I)	4·00	3·00
369		2d. bright orange (Die I)	5·00	3·00
370		2d. orange (Die II) (9.21)	5·00	3·50
371	**104**	2½d. cobalt-blue (18.10.12)	12·00	4·00
371*a*		2½d. bright blue (1914)	12·00	4·00
372		2½d. blue	12·00	4·00
373		2½d. indigo-blue* (1920)	£2800	£1400
373*a*		2½d. dull Prussian blue* (1921)	£1000	£800
374	**106**	3d. dull reddish violet (9.10.12)	12·00	3·00
375		3d. violet	5·00	3·00
376		3d. bluish violet (11.13)	9·00	3·00
377		3d. pale violet	10·00	3.00
378		4d. deep grey-green (15.1.13)	35·00	10·00
379		4d. grey-green	15·00	2·00
380		4d. pale grey-green	25·00	5·00
381	**107**	5d. brown (30.6.13)	15·00	5·00
382		5d. yellow-brown	15·00	5·00
		a. Without wmk	£900	
383		5d. bistre-brown	£125	65·00
384		6d. dull purple (1.8.13)	25·00	10·00
385		6d. reddish purple (8.13)	15·00	7·00
		a. Perf 14 (9.20)	90·00	£110
386		6d. deep reddish purple	27·00	5·00
387		7d. olive (1.8.13)	20·00	10·00
388		7d. bronze-green (1915)	60·00	25·00
389		7d. sage-green (1917)	70·00	18·00
390		8d. black/*yellow* (1.8.13)	32·00	11·00
391		8d. black/*yellow-buff* (*granite*) (5.17)	40·00	15·00
392	**108**	9d. agate (30.6.13)	15·00	6·00
		a. Printed double, one albino		
393		9d. deep agate	25·00	6·00
393*a*		9d. olive-green (9.22)	£100	30·00
393*b*		9d. pale olive-green	£120	40·00
394		10d. turquoise-blue (1.8.13)	22·00	20·00
394*a*		10d. deep turquoise-blue	90·00	30·00
395		1s. bistre (1.8.13)	20·00	4·00
396		1s. bistre-brown	35·00	12·00
351/95 *Set of* 15			£250	95·00

Imperf stamps of this issue exist but may be war-time colour trials.†

The impression of No. 361a is set sideways and is very pale.

Nos. 362a and 364a occur on Plates 12 and 29 and are known from Controls L18, M18, M19, O19 and Q21. The flaws were corrected by 1921.

*No. 373 comes from Control O20 and also exists on toned paper. No. 373a comes from Control R21 and also exists on toned paper, but both are unlike the rare Prussian blue shade of the 1935 2½d. Jubilee issue.

See also Nos. 418/29.

For the 2d., T 106 bisected, see note under Guernsey, War Occupation Issues.

1913 (1 Aug). Wmk Royal Cypher ("Multiple"). W **103**. P 15×14.

No.	Type	Description	*Un*	*Used*
397	**105**	½d. bright green	£150	£180
		a. Wmk sideways	†	£18000
398	**104**	1d. dull scarlet	£225	£225

Both these stamps were originally issued in rolls only. Subsequently sheets were found, so that horizontal pairs and blocks are known but are of considerable rarity.

109

A

110 Single Cypher

Major Re-entries on 2s.6d.

Nos. 400a and 408a

No. 415b.

(Des Bertram Mackennal. Dies eng J. A. C. Harrison. Recess)

High values, so-called "Sea Horses" design: T **109**. *Background around portrait consists of horizontal lines, Type A.* Wmk Single Cypher, W **110**. P 11×12.

1913 (30 June–Aug). *Printed by Waterlow Bros & Layton.*

399		2s.6d. deep sepia-brown	£280	£180
400		2s.6d. sepia-brown	£225	£140
		a. Re-entry (R. 2/1)	£1500	£700
401		5s. rose-carmine	£500	£300
402		10s. indigo-blue (1 Aug)	£950	£450
403		£1 green (1 Aug)	£2400	£1250
404		£1 dull blue-green (1 Aug)	£2400	£1500

*399/404 **For well-centred, lightly used +35%.**

1915 (Sept–Dec). *Printed by De La Rue & Co.*

405		2s.6d. deep yellow-brown	£300	£225
406		2s.6d. yellow-brown	£250	£200
		a. Re-entry (R. 2/1)	£1400	£750
407		2s.6d. pale brown	£250	£200
		a. Re-entry (R. 2/1)	£1400	£750
408		2s.6d. sepia (seal-brown)	£250	£225
409		5s. bright carmine	£425	£350
410		5s. pale carmine	£500	£325
411		10s. deep blue (Dec)	£2800	£875
412		10s. blue	£2200	£700
413		10s. pale blue	£2500	£700

*405/13 **For well-centred, lightly used + 45%.**

Nos. 406/7 were produced from the original Waterlow plates as were all De La Rue 5s. and 10s. printings. Examples of Nos. 406/7, 410 and 411 occur showing degrees of plate wear.

1918 (Dec)–**19**. *Printed by Bradbury, Wilkinson & Co, Ltd.*

413a		2s.6d.. olive-brown	£100	65·00
414		2s.6d.. chocolate-brown	£125	70·00
415		2s.6d.. reddish brown	£125	70·00
415*a*		2s.6d.. pale brown	£110	65·00
		b. Major re-entry (R. 1/2)	£800	£450
416		5s. rose-red (1.19)	£250	£110
417		10s. dull grey-blue (1.19)	£375	£160
399/417 *Set of* 4			£2500	£1400

*413a/17 **For well-centred, lightly used +35%.**

DISTINGUISHING PRINTINGS. Note that the £1 value was only printed by Waterlow.

Waterlow and De La Rue stamps measure exactly 22 mm vertically. In the De La Rue printings the gum is usually patchy and yellowish, and the colour of the stamp, particularly in the 5s., tends to show through the back. The holes of the perforation are smaller than those of the other two printers, but there is a thick perforation tooth at the top of each vertical side.

In the Bradbury Wilkinson printings the height of the stamp is 22¾ or 23 mm due to the use of curved plates. On most of the 22¾ mm high stamps a minute coloured guide dot appears in the margin just above the middle of the upper frame-line.

For (1934) re-engraved Waterlow printings *see* Nos. 450/2.

UNITED KINGDOM OF GREAT BRITAIN AND NORTHERN IRELAND

111

111a

Block Cypher

The watermark Type **111a**, as compared with Type **111**, differs as follows: Closer spacing of horizontal rows (12½ mm instead of 14½ mm). Letters shorter and rounder. Watermark thicker.

(Typo by Waterlow & Sons, Ltd (all values except 6d.) and later, 1934–35, by Harrison & Sons, Ltd (all values). Until 1934 the 6d. was printed at Somerset House where a printing of the 1½d. was also made in 1926 (identifiable only by control E.26). Printings by Harrisons in 1934–35 can be identified, when in mint condition, by the fact that the gum shows a streaky appearance vertically, the Waterlow gum being uniformly applied, but Harrisons also used up the balance of the Waterlow "smooth gum" paper)

1924 (Feb)–**26**. Wmk Block Cypher, W **111**. P 15×14.

418	**105**	½d. green	1·00	1·00
		a. Wmk sideways (5.24)	9·00	3·25
		b. Doubly printed	£9000	†
419	**104**	1d. scarlet	1·00	1·00
		a. Wmk sideways	20·00	15·00
		b. Experimental paper, W **111a** (10.24)	22·00	
		c. Partial double print, one inverted	£8500	
		d. Inverted "Q" for "O" (R. 20/3)	£400	
420	**105**	1½d. red-brown	1·00	1·00
		a. *Tête-bêche* (pair)	£500	£800
		b. Wmk sideways (8.24)	19·00	3·50
		c. Printed on the gummed side	£550	
		d. Booklet pane. Four stamps plus two printed labels (3.24)	£200	
		e. Ditto. Wmk sideways	£7500	
		f. Experimental paper, W **111a** (10.24)	60·00	70·00
		g. Double impression	£15000	†
421	**106**	2d. orange (Die II) (7.24)	2·50	2·50
		a. No wmk	£850	
		b. Wmk sideways (7.26)	£100	£100
		c. Partial double print	£20000	†
422	**104**	2½d. blue (10.10.24)	5·00	3·00
		a. No wmk	£1600	
		b. Wmk sideways	†	£6500
423	**106**	3d. violet (10.10.24)	10·00	2·50
424		4d. grey-green (23.10.24)	12·00	2·50
		a. Printed on the gummed side	£2800	†
425	**107**	5d. brown (17.10.24)	20·00	3·00
426		6d. reddish purple (*chalk-surfaced paper*) (9.24)	12·00	2·50
426*a*		6d. purple (6.26)	3·00	1·50
427	**108**	9d. olive-green (11.11.24)	12·00	3·50
428		10d. turquoise-blue (28.11.24)	40·00	40·00
429		1s. bistre-brown (10.24)	22·00	3·00
418/29 *Set of* 12			£110	60·00

There are numerous shades in this issue.

The 6d. on both chalk-surfaced and ordinary papers was printed by both Somerset House and Harrisons. The Harrisons printings have streaky gum, differ slightly in shade, and that on chalk-surfaced paper is printed in a highly fugitive ink. The prices quoted are for the commonest (Harrison) printing in each case.

The dandy roll to produce watermark Type **111a** was provided by Somerset House in connection with experiments in paper composition undertaken during 1924–25. These resulted in a change from rag only paper to that made from a mixture including esparto and sulphite.

112

(Des H. Nelson. Eng J. A. C. Harrison, Recess Waterlow)

1924–25. *British Empire Exhibition.* W **111**. P 14.

		(a) Dated "1924" (23.4.24).		
430	**112**	1d. scarlet	10·00	11·00
431		1½d. brown	15·00	15·00
		(b) Dated "1925" (9.5.25).		
432	**112**	1d. scarlet	15·00	30·00
433		1½d. brown	40·00	70·00

113

114

115

116 St. George and the Dragon

117

(Des J. Farleigh (T **113** and **115**), E. Linzell (T **114**) and H. Nelson (T **116**). Eng C. G. Lewis (T **113**), T. E. Storey (T **115**), both at the Royal Mint; J. A. C. Harrison, of Waterlow (T **114** and **116**). Typo by Waterlow from plates made at the Royal Mint, except T **116**, recess by Bradbury, Wilkinson from die and plate of their own manufacture)

1929 (10 May). *Ninth U.P.U. Congress, London.*

		(a) W **111** P 15×14.		
434	**113**	½d. green	2·25	2·25
		a. Wmk sideways	40·00	40·00
435	**114**	1d. scarlet	2·25	2·25
		a. Wmk sideways	75·00	75·00
436		1½d. purple-brown	2·25	1·75
		a. Wmk sideways	40·00	40·00
		b. Booklet pane. Four stamps plus two printed labels	£250	
437	**115**	2½d. blue	10·00	10·00
		(b) W **117**. P 12.		
438	**116**	£1 black	£750	£550
434/7 *Set of* 4 (*to* 2½d.)			15·00	14·50

PRINTERS. All subsequent issues were printed in photogravure by Harrison and Sons Ltd *except where otherwise stated.*

118

119

120

121

122

1934–36. W **111**. P 15×14.

439	**118**	½d. green (17.11.34)	50	50
		a. Wmk sideways	10·00	3·50
		b. Imperf three sides	£2750	
440	**119**	1d. scarlet (24.9.34)	50	50
		a. Imperf (pair)	£2200	
		b. Printed on the gummed side	£600	
		c. Wmk sideways (30.4.35)	20·00	8·00
		d. Double impression	†	£19000
		e. Imperf between (pair)	£3500	
		f. Imperf three sides (pair)	£2400	
441	**118**	1½d. red-brown (20.8.34)	50	50
		a. Imperf (pair)	£700	
		b. Imperf three sides (lower stamp in vert pair)	£1800	
		c. Imperf between (horiz pair)		
		d. Wmk sideways	8·00	4·00
		e. Booklet pane. Four stamps plus two printed labels (1.35).	£110	
442	**120**	2d. orange (19.1.35)	75	75
		a. Imperf (pair)	£4000	
		b. Wmk sideways (30.4.35)	£125	90·00
443	**119**	2½d. ultramarine (18.3.35)	1·50	1·25
444	**120**	3d. violet (18.3.35)	1·50	1·25
445		4d. deep grey-green (2.12.35)	2·00	1·25
446	**121**	5d. yellow-brown (17.2.36)	6·50	2·75
447	**122**	9d. deep olive-green (2.12.35)	12·00	2·25
448		10d. turquoise-blue (24.2.36)	15·00	10·00
449		1s. bistre-brown (24.2.36)	15·00	1·25
		a. Double impression	—	†
439/49 *Set of* 11			50·00	20·00

Owing to the need for wider space for the perforations the size of the designs of the ½d. and 2d. were once, and the 1d. and 1½d. twice, reduced from that of the first printings.

There are also numerous minor variations, due to the photographic element in the process.

The ½d. imperf three sides, No. 439b, is known in a block of four, from a sheet, to which the bottom pair is imperf at top and sides.

For No. 442 bisected, see Guernsey, War Occupation Issues.

B

123

(Eng J. A. C. Harrison. Recess Waterlow)

1934 (16 Oct). *T* **109** *(re-engraved). Background around portrait consists of horizontal and diagonal lines. Type B.* W **110**. P 11×12.

450	**109**	2s.6d. chocolate-brown	80·00	40·00
451		5s. bright rose-red	£175	85·00
452		10s. indigo	£350	80·00
450/2 *Set of* 3			£575	£190

There are numerous other minor differences in the design of this issue.

(Des B. Freedman)

1935 (7 May). *Silver Jubilee.* W **111**. P 15×14.

453	**123**	½d. green	1·00	1·00
454		1d. scarlet	1·50	2·00
455		1½d. red-brown	1·00	1·00
456		2½d. blue	5·00	6·00
456*a*		2½d. Prussian blue	£9500	£9500
453/6 *Set of* 4			8·00	9·25

The 1½d. and 2½d. values differ from T 123 in the emblem in the panel at right.

Four sheets of No. 456a, printed in the wrong shade, were issued in error by the Post Office Stores Department on 25 June 1935. It is known that three of the sheets were sold from the sub-office at 134 Fore Street, Upper Edmonton, London. between that date and 4 July.

Stamps Added

Ascension 55a
Australia
- **Victoria** 162a
- **Western Australia** 94w, 96w, 97w, 100w, 113w
- **Commonwealth of Australia** 393b, 408b, 465ba, O23w, J5d

Bahamas 131ab, 171c
Barbados 252a
British Guiana 202w
Brunei 31x
Canada
- **British Columbia** 22y,
- **Newfoundland** D6ad
- **Dominion of Canada** 359b

Ceylon 173w
Cyprus 7b
Ghana D19c, D20d
Gibraltar 8w
Gold Coast 105w, 133aw
Grenada 159b
Guyana 382w
Hong Kong 144b, 176a, Z596, Z932
India 169a, O38w, O84ab, O109b, O110b, O111b
- **Patiala** O8d
- **Bundi** O40bb, O45a
- **Duttia** 3c, 3d, 21b
- **Faridkot** N5b
- **Hyderabad** O37eb
- **Kishangarh** 22ad
- **Travancore** O66Ab
- **Travancore-Cochin** O6dda, O9b

Iraq Z54, Z197, Z230
Ireland 208a
Jamaica Z161a, 77a, 124a, 124b
Kenya, Uganda and Tanganyika 53aw, 131af
Leeward Islands 79c
Malaya
- **Straits Settlements** 59a, 195w
- **Federated Malay States** 60c
- **Kedah** 22ws
- **Perak** 5w

Malta Z11a, 103g, 111c,
Mauritius 63y, 253b
Nauru 23c, 46a,
New Zealand 274y, 673a, 676a, 679a, 785fa
Niger Coast Protectorate 69x
North Borneo 112asa, 178c, 178e, 179d, 180c, 181a, 201a, 213ab, 229a, 230a, 231b, 232a, 246a, 247a, 248b, 249b, 250a, 255b, 273b, 274b, 274da, 275b, 275cb, 289a, 290a, 291a, 292a
Pakistan O4w
Pitcairn Islands Z14a, 36a
Rhodesia and Nyasaland 32b
St. Helena 97e
St Lucia 43w, DZe
Singapore 72a
Somaliland 18d
South Africa
- **Natal** 73s
- **South Africa** 44c, 44da, 57b, 57c, 114cb, 241a

Swaziland 99w
Transjordan O117b
Trinidad 72w, 74w, 75w
Trinidad and Tobago 187y, 222w, 293w
Uganda 93x, 93y

Catalogue Numbers Altered

The table below is a cross-reference of those catalogue numbers which have been altered in this edition.

	Old	New
Australia	125y	deleted
	O106aw	deleted
India		
Gwalior	16a	deleted
Jaipur	38	deleted
Rajasthan	8	deleted
	9	deleted
	10	deleted
Travancore	O48f	deleted
Travancore-Cochin	O9b	O9c
Jamaica	77a	77b
	77b	77c
	124a	124c
	124ab	124cb
	124b	124d
Kenya Uganda and Tanganyika	53b	deleted
	53a	53aw
	131af	131ag
	131ag	131ah
	131ah	131ai
Malta	45aw	45w
	45ax	45x
	45ay	45y
Mauritius	253b	253c
	253ba	253ca

	Old	New
Nauru	23c	23d
New Zealand	930ba	930a
North Borneo	178c	178d
	274b	274c
	274c	274d
	274ca	274da
	274cb	deleted
	275b	275c
	275ba	275ca
Labuan	96a	96ab
	96b	96a
St. Helena	97cw	97fw
	97e	97g
	97ea	97ga
South Africa		
Natal	73a	deleted
South Africa	44b	44bw
	44cw	44bwa
	57bw	57dw
	57c	57e
	241a	241b
Sudan	A6e	deleted
	A9d	deleted

Contents

General Philatelic Information and Guidelines to the Scope of Stanley Gibbons Commonwealth catalogues

The notes which follow seek to reflect current practice in compiling the Stanley Gibbons Commonwealth Catalogues.

It scarcely needs emphasising that the Stanley Gibbons Stamp Catalogue has a very long history and that the vast quantity of information it contains has been carefully built up by successive generations through the work of countless individuals. Philately is never static and the Catalogue has evolved and developed over the years. These notes relate to the current criteria upon which a stamp may be listed or priced. It should be recognised that these criteria have developed over time and may have differed somewhat in the early years of this catalogue. These notes are not intended to suggest that we plan to make wholesale changes to the listing of classic issues in order to bring them into line with today's listing policy, they are designed to inform catalogue users as to the policies currently in operation.

PRICES

The prices quoted in this Catalogue are the estimated selling prices of Stanley Gibbons Ltd at the time of publication. They are, unless it is specifically stated otherwise, for examples in fine condition for the issue concerned. Superb examples are worth more; those of a lower quality considerably less.

All prices are subject to change without prior notice and Stanley Gibbons Ltd may from time to time offer stamps below catalogue price. Individual low value stamps sold at 399 Strand are liable to an additional handling charge. Purchasers of new issues are asked to note the prices charged for them contain an element for the service rendered and so may exceed the prices shown when the stamps are subsequently catalogued. Postage and handling charges are extra.

No guarantee is given to supply all stamps priced, since it is not possible to keep every catalogued item in stock. Commemorative issues may, at times, only be available in complete sets and not as individual values.

Quotation of prices. The prices in the left-hand column are for unused stamps and those in the right-hand column are for used.

A dagger (†) denotes that the item listed does not exist in that condition and a blank, or dash, that it exists, or may exist, but we are unable to quote a price.

Prices are expressed in pounds and pence sterling. One pound comprises 100 pence (£1 = 100p).

The method of notation is as follows: pence in numerals (e.g. 10 denotes ten pence); pounds and pence, up to £100, in numerals (e.g. 4.25 denotes four pounds and twenty-five pence); prices above £100 are expressed in whole pounds with the '£' sign shown.

Unused stamps. Great Britain and Commonwealth: the prices for unused stamps of Queen Victoria to King George V are for lightly hinged examples. Unused prices for King Edward VIII, King George VI and Queen Elizabeth issues are for unmounted mint.

Some stamps from the King George VI period are often difficult to find in unmounted mint condition. In such instances we would expect that collectors would need to pay a high proportion of the price quoted to obtain mounted mint examples. Generally speaking lightly mounted mint stamps from this reign, issued before 1945, are in considerable demand.

Used stamps. The used prices are normally for stamps postally used but may be for stamps cancelled-to-order where this practice exists.

A pen-cancellation on early issues can sometimes correctly denote postal use. Instances are individually noted in the Catalogue in explanation of the used price given.

Prices quoted for bisects on cover or large piece are for those dated during the period officially authorised.

Stamps not sold unused to the public (e.g. some official stamps) are priced used only.

The use of 'unified' designs, that is stamps inscribed for both postal and fiscal purposes, results in a number of stamps of very high face value. In some instances these may not have been primarily intended for postal purposes, but if they are so inscribed we include them. We only price such items used, however, where there is evidence of normal postal usage.

Cover prices. To assist collectors, cover prices are quoted for issues up to 1945 at the beginning of each country.

The system gives a general guide in the form of a factor by which the corresponding used price of the basic loose stamp should be multiplied when found in fine average condition on cover.

Care is needed in applying the factors and they relate to a cover which bears a single of the denomination listed; if more than one denomination is present the most highly priced attracts the multiplier and the remainder are priced at the simple figure for used singles in arriving at a total.

The cover should be of non-philatelic origin; bearing the correct postal rate for the period and distance involved and cancelled with the markings normal to the offices concerned. Purely philatelic items have a cover value only slightly greater than the catalogue value for the corresponding used stamps. This applies generally to those high-value stamps used philatelically rather than in the normal course of commerce. Low-value stamps, e.g. ¼d. and ½d., are desirable when used as a single rate on cover and merit an increase in 'multiplier' value.

First day covers in the period up to 1945 are not within the scope of the system and the multiplier should not be used. As a special category of philatelic usage, with wide variations in valuation according to scarcity, they require separate treatment.

Oversized covers, difficult to accommodate on an album page, should be reckoned as worth little more than the corresponding value of the used stamps. The condition of a cover also affects its value. Except for 'wreck covers', serious damage or soiling reduce the value where the postal markings and stamps are ordinary ones. Conversely, visual appeal adds to the value and this can include freshness of appearance, important addresses, old-fashioned but legible hand-writing, historic town-names, etc.

The multipliers are a base on which further value would be added to take account of the cover's postal historical importance in demonstrating such things as unusual, scarce or emergency cancels, interesting routes, significant postal markings, combination usage, the development of postal rates, and so on.

Minimum price. The minimum catalogue price quoted is 10p. For individual stamps prices between 10p. and 95p. are provided as a guide for catalogue users. The lowest price charged for individual stamps or sets purchased from Stanley Gibbons Ltd is £1

Set prices. Set prices are generally for one of each value, excluding shades and varieties, but including major colour changes. Where there are alternative shades, etc., the cheapest is usually included. The number of stamps in the set is always stated for clarity. The prices for sets containing *se-tenant* pieces are based on the prices quoted for such combinations, and not on those for the individual stamps.

Varieties. Where plate or cylinder varieties are priced in used condition the price quoted is for a fine used example with the cancellation well clear of the listed flaw.

Specimen stamps. The pricing of these items is explained under that heading.

Stamp booklets. Prices are for complete assembled booklets in fine condition with those issued before 1945 showing normal wear and tear. Incomplete booklets and those which have been 'exploded' will, in general, be worth less than the figure quoted.

Repricing. Collectors will be aware that the market factors of supply and demand directly influence the prices quoted in this Catalogue. Whatever the scarcity of a particular stamp, if there is no one in the market who wishes to buy it cannot be expected to achieve a high price. Conversely, the same item actively sought by numerous potential buyers may cause the price to rise.

All the prices in this Catalogue are examined during the preparation of each new edition by the expert staff of Stanley Gibbons and repriced as necessary. They take many factors into account, including supply and demand, and are in close touch with the international stamp market and the auction world.

Commonwealth cover prices and advice on postal history material originally provided by Edward B Proud.

GUARANTEE

All stamps are guaranteed originals in the following terms:

If not as described, and returned by the purchaser, we undertake to refund the price paid to us in the original transaction. If any stamp is certified as genuine by the Expert Committee of the Royal Philatelic Society, London, or by BPA Expertising Ltd, the purchaser shall not be entitled to make any claim against us for any error, omission or mistake in such certificate.

Consumers' statutory rights are not affected by the above guarantee.

The recognised Expert Committees in this country are those of the Royal Philatelic Society, 41 Devonshire Place, London W1G, 6JY, and BPA Expertising Ltd, PO Box 137, Leatherhead, Surrey KT22 0RG. They do not undertake valuations under any circumstances and fees are payable for their services.

CONDITION GUIDE

To assist collectors in assessing the true value of items they are considering buying or in reviewing stamps already in their collections, we now offer a more detailed guide to the condition of stamps on which this catalogue's prices are based.

For a stamp to be described as 'Fine', it should be sound in all respects, without creases, bends, wrinkles, pin holes, thins or tears. If perforated, all perforation 'teeth' should be intact, it should not suffer from fading, rubbing or toning and it should be of clean, fresh appearance.

Margins on imperforate stamps: These should be even on all sides and should be at least as wide as half the distance between that stamp and the next. To have one or more margins of less than this width, would normally preclude a stamp from being described as 'Fine'. It should be remembered that some early stamps were positioned very close together on the printing plate and in such cases 'Fine' margins would necessarily be narrow. On the other hand, some plates were laid down to give a substantial gap between individual stamps and in such cases margins would be expected to be much wider.

An 'average' four-margin example would have a narrower margin on one or more sides and should be priced accordingly, while a stamp with wider, yet even, margins than 'Fine' would merit the description 'Very Fine' or 'Superb' and, if available, would command a price in excess of that quoted in the catalogue.

Gum: Since the prices for stamps of King Edward VIII, King George VI and Queen Elizabeth are for 'unmounted' or 'never hinged' mint, it should be anticipated that even stamps from these reigns which have been very lightly mounted should be available at a discount from catalogue price, the more obvious the hinge marks, the greater the discount.

Catalogue prices for stamps issued prior to King Edward VIII's reign are for mounted mint, so unmounted examples would be worth a premium. Hinge marks on 20th century stamps should not be too obtrusive, and should be at least in the lightly mounted category. For 19th century stamps more obvious hinging would be acceptable, but stamps should still carry a large part of their original gum—'Large part o.g.'—in order to be described as 'Fine'.

Centring: Ideally, the stamp's image should appear in the exact centre of the perforated area, giving equal margins on all sides. 'Fine' centring would be close to this ideal with any deviation having an effect on the value of the stamp. As in the case of the margins on imperforate stamps, it should be borne in mind that the space between some early stamps was very narrow, so it was very difficult to achieve accurate perforation, especially when the technology was in its infancy. Thus, poor centring would have a less damaging effect on the value of a 19th century stamp than on a 20th century example, but the premium put on a perfectly centred specimen would be greater.

Cancellations: Early cancellation devices were designed to 'obliterate' the stamp in order to prevent it being reused and this is still an important objective for today's postal administrations. Stamp collectors, on the other hand, prefer postmarks to be lightly applied, clear, and to leave as much as possible of the design visible. Dated, circular cancellations have long been 'the postmark of choice', but the definition of a 'Fine' cancellation will depend upon the types of cancellation in use at the time a stamp was current—it is clearly illogical to seek a circular datestamp on a Penny Black.

'Fine', by definition, will be superior to 'Average', so, in terms of cancellation quality, if one begins by identifying what 'Average' looks like, then one will be half way to identifying 'Fine'. The illustrations will give some guidance on mid-19th century and mid-20th century cancellations of Great Britain, but types of cancellation in general use in each country and in each period will determine the appearance of 'Fine'.

As for the factors discussed above, anything less than 'Fine' will result in a downgrading of the stamp concerned, while a very fine or superb cancellation will be worth a premium.

Combining the factors: To merit the description 'Fine', a stamp should be fine in every respect, but a small deficiency in one area might be made up for in another by a factor meriting an 'Extremely Fine' description.

Some early issues are so seldom found in what would normally be considered to be 'Fine' condition, the catalogue prices are for a slightly lower grade, with 'Fine' examples being worth a premium. In such cases a note to this effect is given in the catalogue, while elsewhere premiums are given for well-centred, lightly cancelled examples.

It should be emphasised that stamps graded at less than fine remain collectable and, in the case of more highly priced stamps will continue to hold a value. Nevertheless, buyers should always bear condition in mind.

MARGINS ON IMPERFORATE STAMPS

Superb Very fine Fine Average Poor

GUM

Unmounted Very lightly mounted Lightly mounted Mounted/large part original gum (o.g.). Heavily mounted small part o.g

CENTRING

Superb Very fine Fine Average Poor

CANCELLATIONS

Superb Very fine Fine Average Poor

Superb Very fine

Fine Average Poor

THE CATALOGUE IN GENERAL

Contents. The Catalogue is confined to adhesive postage stamps, including miniature sheets. For particular categories the rules are:
(a) Revenue (fiscal) stamps or telegraph stamps are listed only where they have been expressly authorised for postal duty.
(b) Stamps issued only precancelled are included, but normally issued stamps available additionally with precancel have no separate precancel listing unless the face value is changed.
(c) Stamps prepared for use but not issued, hitherto accorded full listing, are nowadays foot-noted with a price (where possible).
(d) Bisects (trisects, etc.) are only listed where such usage was officially authorised.
(e) Stamps issued only on first day covers or in presentation packs and not available separately are not listed but may be priced in a footnote.
(f) New printings are only included in this Catalogue where they show a major philatelic variety, such as a change in shade, watermark or paper. Stamps which exist with or without imprint dates are listed separately; changes in imprint dates are mentioned in footnotes.
(g) Official and unofficial reprints are dealt with by footnote.
(h) Stamps from imperforate printings of modern issues which occur perforated are covered by footnotes, but are listed where widely available for postal use.

Exclusions. The following are excluded:
(a) non-postal revenue or fiscal stamps;
(b) postage stamps used fiscally;
(c) local carriage labels and private local issues;
(d) bogus or phantom stamps;
(e) railway or airline letter fee stamps, bus or road transport company labels;
(f) cut-outs;
(g) all types of non-postal labels and souvenirs;
(h) documentary labels for the postal service, e.g. registration, recorded delivery, air-mail etiquettes, etc.;
(i) privately applied embellishments to official issues and privately commissioned items generally;
(j) stamps for training postal officers.
(k) Telegraph stamps

Full listing. 'Full listing' confers our recognition and implies allotting a catalogue number and (wherever possible) a price quotation.

In judging status for inclusion in the catalogue broad considerations are applied to stamps. They must be issued by a legitimate postal authority, recognised by the government concerned, and must be adhesives valid for proper postal use in the class of service for which they are inscribed. Stamps, with the exception of such categories as postage dues and officials, must be available to the general public, at face value, in reasonable quantities without any artificial restrictions being imposed on their distribution.

For errors and varieties the criterion is legitimate (albeit inadvertent) sale through a postal administration in the normal course of business. Details of provenance are always important; printers' waste and deliberately manufactured material are excluded.

Certificates. In assessing unlisted items due weight is given to Certificates from recognised Expert Committees and, where appropriate, we will usually ask to see them.

Date of issue. Where local issue dates differ from dates of release by agencies, 'date of issue' is the local date. Fortuitous stray usage before the officially intended date is disregarded in listing.

Catalogue numbers. Stamps of each country are catalogued chronologically by date of issue. Subsidiary classes are placed at the end of the country, as separate lists, with a distinguishing letter prefix to the catalogue number, e.g. D for postage due, O for official and E for express delivery stamps.

The catalogue number appears in the extreme left-column. The boldface Type numbers in the next column are merely cross-references to illustrations.

Once published in the Catalogue, numbers are changed as little as possible; really serious renumbering is reserved for the occasions when a complete country or an entire issue is being rewritten. The edition first affected includes cross-reference tables of old and new numbers.

Our catalogue numbers are universally recognised in specifying stamps and as a hallmark of status.

Illustrations. Stamps are illustrated at three-quarters linear size. Stamps not illustrated are the same size and format as the value shown, unless otherwise indicated. Stamps issued only as miniature sheets have the stamp alone illustrated but sheet size is also quoted. Overprints, surcharges, watermarks and postmarks are normally actual size. Illustrations of varieties are often enlarged to show the detail. Stamp booklet covers are illustrated half-size, unless otherwise indicated.

Designers. Designers' names are quoted where known, though space precludes naming every individual concerned in the production of a set. In particular, photographers supplying material are usually named only where they also make an active contribution in the design stage; posed photographs of reigning monarchs are, however, an exception to this rule.

CONTACTING THE CATALOGUE EDITOR

The editor is always interested in hearing from people who have new information which will improve or correct the Catalogue. As a general rule he must see and examine the actual stamps before they can be considered for listing; photographs or photocopies are insufficient evidence.

Submissions should be made in writing to the Catalogue Editor, Stanley Gibbons Publications at the Ringwood office. The cost of return postage for items submitted is appreciated, and this should include the registration fee if required.

Where information is solicited purely for the benefit of the enquirer, the editor cannot undertake to reply if the answer is already contained in these published notes or if return postage is omitted. Written communications are greatly preferred to enquiries by telephone or e-mail and the editor regrets that he or his staff cannot see personal callers without a prior appointment being made. Correspondence may be subject to delay during the production period of each new edition.

The editor welcomes close contact with study circles and is interested, too, in finding reliable local correspondents who will verify and supplement official information in countries where this is deficient.

We regret we do not give opinions as to the genuineness of stamps, nor do we identify stamps or number them by our Catalogue.

TECHNICAL MATTERS

The meanings of the technical terms used in the catalogue will be found in our *Philatelic Terms Illustrated.*

References below to (more specialised) listings are to be taken to indicate, as appropriate, the Stanley Gibbons *Great Britain Specialised Catalogue* in five volumes or the *Great Britain Concise Catalogue*.

1. Printing

Printing errors. Errors in printing are of major interest to the Catalogue. Authenticated items meriting consideration would include: background, centre or frame inverted or omitted; centre or subject transposed; error of colour; error or omission of value; double prints and impressions; printed both sides; and so on. Designs *tête-bêche*, whether intentionally or by accident, are listable. *Se-tenant* arrangements of stamps are recognised in the listings or footnotes. Gutter pairs (a pair of stamps separated by blank margin) are not included in this volume. Colours only partially omitted are not listed. Stamps with embossing omitted are reserved for our more specialised listings.

Printing varieties. Listing is accorded to major changes in the printing base which lead to completely new types. In recess-printing this could be a design re-engraved; in photogravure or photolithography a screen altered in whole or in part. It can also encompass flat-bed and rotary printing if the results are readily distinguishable.

To be considered at all, varieties must be constant.

Early stamps, produced by primitive methods, were prone to numerous imperfections; the lists reflect this, recognising re-entries, retouches, broken frames, misshapen letters, and so on. Printing technology has, however, radically improved over the years, during which time photogravure and lithography have become predominant. Varieties nowadays are more in the nature of flaws and these, being too specialised for this general catalogue, are almost always outside the scope.

In no catalogue, however, do we list such items as: dry prints, kiss prints, doctor-blade flaws, colour shifts or registration flaws (unless they lead to the complete omission of a colour from an individual stamp), lithographic ring flaws, and so on. Neither do we recognise fortuitous happenings like paper creases or confetti flaws.

Overprints (and surcharges). Overprints of different types qualify for separate listing. These include overprints in different colours; overprints from different printing processes such as litho and typo; overprints in totally different typefaces, etc. Major errors in machine-printed overprints are important and listable. They include: overprint inverted or omitted; overprint double (treble, etc.); overprint diagonal; overprint double, one inverted; pairs with one overprint omitted, e.g. from a radical shift to an adjoining stamp; error of colour; error of type fount; letters inverted or omitted, etc. If the overprint is handstamped, few of these would qualify and a distinction is drawn. We continue, however, to list pairs of stamps where one has a handstamped overprint and the other has not.

Varieties occurring in overprints will often take the form of broken letters, slight differences in spacing, rising spaces, etc. Only the most important would be considered for listing or footnote mention.

Sheet positions. If space permits we quote sheet positions of listed varieties and authenticated data is solicited for this purpose.

De La Rue plates. The Catalogue classifies the general plates used by De La Rue for printing British Colonial stamps as follows:

VICTORIAN KEY TYPE

Die I

1. The ball of decoration on the second point of the crown appears as a dark mass of lines.
2. Dark vertical shading separates the front hair from the bun.
3. The vertical line of colour outlining the front of the throat stops at the sixth line of shading on the neck.
4. The white space in the coil of the hair above the curl is roughly the shape of a pin's head.

KING EDWARD VIII

20 January–10 December 1936

Further detailed information on the stamps of King Edward VIII will be found in Volume 2 of the Stanley Gibbons *Great Britain Specialised Catalogue.*

124

125

(Des H. Brown, adapted Harrison using a photo by Hugh Cecil)

1936. W **125**. P 15×14.

457	**124**	½d. green (1.9.36)	30	30
		a. Double impression		
458		1d. scarlet (14.9.36)	60	50
459		1½d. red-brown (1.9.36)	30	30
		a. Booklet pane. Four stamps plus two printed labels (10.36)	80·00	
		b. Imperf (pair)	£30000	
460		2½d. bright blue (1.9.36)	30	85
457/60 *Set of* 4			1·25	1·75

KING GEORGE VI

11 December 1936–6 February 1952

Further detailed information on the stamps of King George VI will be found in Volume 2 of the Stanley Gibbons *Great Britain Specialised Catalogue.*

126 King George VI and Queen Elizabeth

Colon flaw (Cyl 7 No dot, R 10/1, later corrected

(Des E. Dulac)

1937 (13 May). *Coronation*. W **127**. P 15×14.

461	**126**	1½d. maroon	30	30
		a. Colon flaw	15·00	

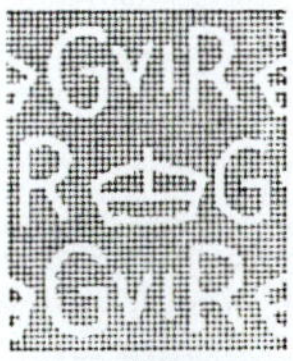

127

128

129

130

King George VI and National Emblems

(Des T **128/9**, E. Dulac (head) and E. Gill (frames). T **130**, E. Dulac (whole stamp))

1937–47. W **127**. P 15×14.

462	**128**	½d. green (10.5.37)	30	25
		a. Wmk sideways (1.38)	50	50
		ab. Booklet pane of 4 (6.40)	50·00	
463		1d. scarlet (10.5.37)	30	25
		a. Wmk sideways (2.38)	20·00	9·00
		ab. Booklet pane of 4 (6.40)	£100	
464		1½d. red-brown (30.7.37)	30	25
		a. Wmk sideways (2.38)	1·00	1·25
		b. Booklet pane. Four stamps plus two printed labels (8.37)	£100	
		c. Imperf three sides (pair)	£3750	
465		2d. orange (31.1.38)	1·20	50
		a. Wmk sideways (2.38)	70·00	38·00
		b. Bisected (on cover)	†	40·00
466		2½d. ultramarine (10.5.37)	40	25
		a. Wmk sideways (6.40)	70·00	32·00
		b. *Tête-bêche* (horiz pair)	£22000	
467		3d. violet (31.1.38)	5·00	1·00
468	**129**	4d. grey-green (21.11.38)	60	75
		a. Imperf (pair)	£5500	
		b. Imperf three sides (horiz pair)	£5500	
469		5d. brown (21.11.38)	3·50	85
		a. Imperf (pair)	£6500	
		b. Imperf three sides (horiz pair)	£5500	
470		6d. purple (30.1.39)	1·50	60
471	**130**	7d. emerald-green (27.2.39)	5·00	60
		a. Imperf three sides (horiz pair)	£5500	
472		8d. bright carmine (27.2.39)	7·50	80
473		9d. deep olive-green (1.5.39)	6·50	80
474		10d. turquoise-blue (1.5.39)	7·00	80
		aa. Imperf (pair)	£6500	
474*a*		11d. plum (29.12.47)	3·00	2·75
475		1s. bistre-brown (1.5.39)	9·00	75
462/75 *Set of* 15			45·00	10·00

For later printings of the lower values in apparently lighter shades and different colours, see Nos. 485/90 and 503/8.

No. 465b was authorised for use in Guernsey. See notes on War Occupation Issues.

Nos. 468b and 469b are perforated at foot only and each occurs in the same sheet as Nos. 468a and 469a.

No. 471a is also perforated at foot only, but occurs on the top row of a sheet.

131 King George VI

132 King George VI

133

(Des E. Dulac (T **131**) and Hon. G. R. Bellew (T **132**). Eng J. A. C. Harrison. Recess Waterlow)

1939–48. W **133**. P 14.

476	**131**	2s.6d. brown (4.9.39)	50·00	6.00
476*a*		2s.6d. yellow-green (9.3.42)	14·00	1·50
477		5s. red (21.8.39)	20·00	2·00
478	**132**	10s. dark blue (30.10.39)	£250	20· 00
478*a*		10s. ultramarine (30.11.42)	35·00	5·00
478*b*		£1 brown (1.10.48)	20·00	26·00
476/8*b* *Set of* 6			£350	55·00

134 Queen Victoria and King George VI.

(Des H. L. Palmer)

1940 (6 May). *Centenary of First Adhesive Postage Stamps*. W **127**. P 14½×14.

479	**134**	½d. green	30	75
480		1d. scarlet	1·00	75
481		1½d. red-brown	50	1·50
482		2d. orange	1·00	75
		a. Bisected (on cover)	†	30·00
483		2½d. ultramarine	2·25	50
484		3d. violet	3·00	3·50
479/84 *Set of* 6			8·75	5·25

No. 482a was authorised for use in Guernsey. See notes on War Occupation Issues.

1941–42. *Head as Nos. 462/7, but with lighter background to provide a more economic use of the printing ink.* W **127**. P 15×14.

485	**128**	½d. pale green (1.9.41)	30	30
		a. *Tête-bêche* (horiz pair)	£16000	
		b. Imperf (pair)	£5500	
486		1d. pale scarlet (11.8.41)	30	30
		a. Wmk sideways (10.42)	5·00	4·50
		b. Imperf (pair)	£6500	
		c. Imperf three sides (horiz pair)	£6500	
487		1½d. pale red-brown (28.9.42)	60	80
488		2d. pale orange (6.10.41)	50	50
		a. Wmk sideways (6.42)	28·00	19·00
		b. *Tête-bêche* (horiz pair)	£16000	
		c. Imperf (pair)	£5500	
		d. Imperf pane*	£16000	
489		2½d. light ultramarine (21.7.41)	30	30
		a. Wmk sideways (8.42)	15·00	12·00
		b. *Tête-bêche* (horiz pair)	£16000	
		c. Imperf (pair)	£4250	
		d. Imperf pane*	£11000	
		e. Imperf three sides (horiz pair)	£6500	
490		3d. pale violet (3.11.41)	2·50	1·00
485/90 *Set of* 6			3·50	2·75

The *tête-bêche* varieties are from defectively made-up stamp booklets.

Nos. 486c and 489e are perforated at foot only and occur in the same sheets as Nos. 486b and 489c.

*BOOKLET ERRORS. Those listed as "imperf panes" show one row of perforations either at the top or at the bottom of the pane of 6.

WATERMARK VARIETIES. Please note that *inverted watermarks* are outside the scope of this listing but are fully listed in the *Great Britain Specialised* and *Great Britain Concise Catalogues*. See also the notes about watermarks at the beginning of the King George V section.

135

136 Symbols of Peace and Reconstruction

Extra porthole aft (Cyl. 11 No dot, R. 16/1)

Extra porthole fore (Cyl. 8 Dot, R. 5/6)

Seven berries (Cyl. 4 No dot, R. 12/5)

(Des H. L. Palmer (T **135**) and R. Stone (T **136**))

1946 (11 June). *Victory*. W **127**. P 15×14.

491	**135**	2½d. ultramarine	20	20
		a. Extra porthole aft	45·00	
		b. Extra porthole fore	65·00	
492	**136**	3d. violet	20	50
		a. Seven berries	22·00	

137

138 King George VI and Queen Elizabeth

(Des G. Knipe and Joan Hassall from photographs by Dorothy Wilding)

1948 (26 Apr). *Royal Silver Wedding*. W **127**. P 15×14 (2½d.) or 14×15 (£1).

493	**137**	2½d. ultramarine	35	20
494	**138**	£1 blue	40·00	40·00

1948 (10 May). Stamps of 1d. and 2½d. showing seaweed-gathering were on sale at eight Head Post Offices in Great Britain, but were primarily for use in the Channel Islands and are listed there (see after Great Britain Postal Fiscals).

139 Globe and Laurel Wreath

140 "Speed"

141 Olympic Symbol

142 Winged Victory

Crown Flaw (Cyl. 1 No dot, R. 20/2, later retouched)

(Des P. Metcalfe (T **139**), A. Games (T **140**), S. D. Scott (T **141**) and E. Dulac (T **142**))

1948 (29 July). *Olympic Games*. W **127**. P 15×14.

495	**139**	2½d. ultramarine	35	10
496	**140**	3d. violet	35	50
		a. Crown flaw	20·00	
497	**141**	6d. bright purple	1·25	40
498	**142**	1s. brown	2·00	1·50
495/8 *Set of* 4			3·50	2·00

143 Two Hemispheres

144 U.P.U. Monument, Berne

145 Goddess Concordia, Globe and Points of Compass

146 Posthorn and Globe

Lake in Asia
(Cyl. 3 Dot, R. 14/1)

Lake in India
(Cyl. 2 No Dot, R. 18/2)

(Des Mary Adshead (T **143**), P. Metcalfe (T **144**), H. Fleury (T **145**) and Hon. G. R. Bellew (T **146**))

1949 (10 Oct). *75th Anniv of Universal Postal Union.* W **127**. P 15×14.

499	**143**	2½d. ultramarine	25	10
		a. Lake in Asia	30·00	
		b. Lake in India	25·00	
500	**144**	3d. violet	25	50
501	**145**	6d. bright purple	50	75
502	**146**	1s. brown	1·00	1·25
499/502 *Set of* 4			1·50	2·50

1950–52. *4d. as Nos. 468 and others as Nos. 485/9, but colours changed.* W **127**. P 15×14.

503	**128**	½d. pale orange (3.5.51)	30	30
		a. Imperf (pair)	£4250	
		b. *Tête-bêche* (horiz pair)	£16000	
		c. Imperf pane	£13000	
504		1d. light ultramarine (3.5.51)	30	30
		a. Wmk sideways (5.51)	1·10	1·25
		b. Imperf (pair)	£4250	
		c. Imperf three sides (horiz pair)	£5500	
		d. Booklet pane. Three stamps plus three printed labels (3.52)	18·00	
		e. Ditto. Partial *tête-bêche* pane .	£6500	
505		1½d. pale green (3.5.51)	65	60
		a. Wmk sideways (9.51)	3·25	5·00
506		2d. pale red-brown (3.5.51)	75	40
		a. Wmk sideways (5.51)	1·75	2·00
		b. *Tête-bêche* (horiz pair)	£16000	
		c. Imperf three sides (horiz pair)	£5500	
507		2½d. pale scarlet (3.5.51)	60	40
		a. Wmk sideways (5.51)	1·75	1·75
		b. *Tête-bêche* (hoiz pair)		
508	**129**	4d. light ultramarine (2.10.50)	2·00	1·75
		a. Double impression	†	£7000
503/8 *Set of* 6			4·00	3·25

No. 504c is perforated at foot only and occurs in the same sheet as No. 504b.No. 506c is also perforated at foot only.

*BOOKLET ERRORS. Those listed as "imperf panes" show one row of perforations either at the top or at the bottom of the pane of 6.

147 H.M.S. *Victory*

148 White Cliffs of Dover

149 St. George and the Dragon

150 Royal Coat of Arms

(Des Mary Adshead (T **147/8**), P. Metcalfe (T **149/50**). Recess Waterlow)

1951 (3 May). W **133**. P 11×12.

509	**147**	2s.6d. yellow-green	7·50	1·00
510	**148**	5s. red	35·00	1·00
511	**149**	10s. ultramarine	15·00	7·50
512	**150**	£1 brown	45·00	18·00
509/12 *Set of* 4			£100	25·00

151 "Commerce and Prosperity"

152 Festival Symbol

(Des E. Dulac (T **151**), A. Games (T **152**))

1951 (3 May). *Festival of Britain.* W **127**. P 15×14.

513	**151**	2½d. scarlet	20	15
514	**152**	4d. ultramarine	30	35

QUEEN ELIZABETH II

6 February 1952

Further detailed information on the stamps of Queen Elizabeth II will be found in volumes 3, 4 and 5 of the Stanley Gibbons *Great Britain Specialised Catalogue.*

USED PRICES. For Nos. 515 onwards the used prices quoted are for examples with circular dated postmarks.

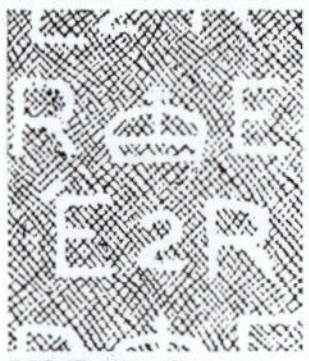

153 Tudor Crown

154

155

156

157

158

159

160

Queen Elizabeth II and National Emblems

I II

Types of 2½d. Type I:—In the frontal cross of the diadem, the top line is only half the width of the cross.

Type II:—The top line extends to the full width of the cross and there are signs of strengthening in other parts of the diadem.

(Des Enid Marx (T **154**), M. Farrar-Bell (T **155/6**), G. Knipe (T **157**), Mary Adshead (T **158**), E. Dulac (T **159/60**). Portrait by Dorothy Wilding)

1952–54. W **153**. P 15×14.

515	**154**	½d. orange-red (31.8.53)	10	15
516		1d. ultramarine (31.8.53)	20	20
		a. Booklet pane. Three stamps plus three printed labels	35·00	
517		1½d. green (5.12.52)	10	20
		a. Wmk sideways (15.10.54)	50	70
		b. Imperf pane*		
518		2d. red-brown (31.8.53)	20	20
		a. Wmk sideways (8.10.54)	1·25	2·00
519	**155**	2½d. carmine-red (Type I) (5.12.52)	15	15
		a. Wmk sideways (15.11.54)	7·00	8·00
		b. Type II (Booklets) (5.53)	1·25	1·25
520		3d. deep lilac (18.1.54)	1·50	90
521	**156**	4d. ultramarine (2.11.53)	3·25	1·25
522	**157**	5d. brown (6.7.53)	75	3·50
523		6d. reddish purple (18.1.54)	4·00	1·00
		a. Imperf three sides (pair)	£1500	
524		7d. bright green (18.1.54)	9·50	5·50
525	**158**	8d. magenta (6.7.53)	75	85
526		9d. bronze-green (8.2.54)	23·00	4·75
527		10d. Prussian blue (8.2.54)	18·00	4·75
528		11d. brown-purple (8.2.54)	35·00	15·00
529	**159**	1s. bistre-brown (6.7.53)	80	50
530	**160**	1s.3d. green (2.11.53)	4·50	3·25
531	**159**	1s.6d. grey-blue (2.11.53)	14·00	3·75
515/31 *Set of* 17			£100	40·00

*BOOKLET ERRORS—This pane of 6 stamps is completely imperf (see No. 540a etc.).

See also Nos. 540/56, 561/6, 570/94 and 599/618*a*.

161

162

163

164

(Des E. Fuller (2½d.), M. Goaman (4d.), E. Dulac (1s.3d.), M. Farrar-Bell (1s.6d.), Portrait (except 1s.3d.) by Dorothy Wilding)

1953 (3 June). *Coronation.* W **153**. P 15×14.

532	**161**	2½d. carmine-red	20	25
533	**162**	4d. ultramarine	1·10	1·90
534	**163**	1s.3d. deep yellow-green	5·00	3·00
535	**164**	1s.6d. deep grey-blue	10·00	4·75
532/5 *Set of* 4			16·00	9·00

165 St. Edward's Crown

166 Carrickfergus Castle

167 Caernarvon Castle

168 Edinburgh Castle

169 Windsor Castle

(Des L. Lamb. Portrait by Dorothy Wilding. Recess Waterlow (until 31.12.57) and De La Rue (subsequently))

1955–58. W **165**. P 11×12.

536	**166**	2s.6d. black-brown (23.9.55)	13·00	2·00
		a. De La Rue printing (17.7.58)	30·00	2·50
537	**167**	5s. rose-carmine (23.9.55)	35·00	4·00
		a. De La Rue printing (30.4.58).	65·00	10·00
538	**168**	10s. ultramarine (1.9.55)	85·00	14·00
		a. De La Rue printing. *Dull ultramarine* (25.4.58)	£225	22·00
539	**169**	£1 black (1.9.55)	£130	35·00
		a. De La Rue printing (28.4.58).	£350	65·00
536/9 *Set of* 4			£225	50·00
536a/9a *Set of* 4			£600	90·00

See also Nos. 595/8a and 759/62.

On 1 January 1958 the contract for printing the high values, T **166** to **169** was transferred to De La Rue & Co, Ltd.

The work of the two printers is very similar, but the following notes will be helpful to those attempting to identify Waterlow and De La Rue stamps of the W **165** issue.

The De La Rue sheets are printed in pairs and have a ⊣ or ⊢ shaped guide-mark at the centre of one side-margin, opposite the middle row of perforations, indicating left- and right-hand sheets respectively.

The Waterlow sheets have a small circle (sometimes crossed) instead of a "⊢" and this is present in both side–margins opposite the 6th row of stamps, though one is sometimes trimmed off. Short dashes are also present in the perforation gutter between the marginal stamps marking the middle of the four sides and a cross is at the centre of the sheet. The four corners of the sheet have two lines forming a right-angle as trimming marks, but some are usually trimmed off. All these gutter marks and sheet-trimming marks are absent in the De La Rue printings.

De La Rue used the Waterlow die and no alterations were made to it, so that no difference exists in the design or its size, but the making of new plates at first resulted in slight but measurable variations in the width of the gutters between stamps, particularly the horizontal, as follows:

	W.	D.L.R.
Horiz gutters, mm	3.8 to 4.0	3.4 to 3.8

Later D.L.R. plates were however less distinguishable in this respect.

For a short time in 1959 the D.L.R. 2s.6d. appeared with one dot in the bottom margin below the first stamp.

It is possible to sort singles with reasonable certainty by general characteristics. The individual lines of the D.L.R. impression are cleaner and devoid of the whiskers of colour of Waterlow's, and the whole impression lighter and softer.

Owing to the closer setting of the horizontal rows the strokes of the perforating comb are closer; this results in the topmost tooth on each side of De La Rue stamps being narrower than the corresponding teeth in Waterlow's which were more than normally broad.

Shades also help. The 2s.6d. D.L.R. is a warmer, more chocolate shade than the blackish brown of W.; the 5s a lighter red with less carmine than W's; the 10s. more blue and less ultramarine; the £1 less intense black.

The paper of D.L.R. printings is uniformly white, identical with that of W. printings from February 1957 onwards, but earlier W. printings are on paper which is creamy by comparison.

In this and later issues of T **166/9** the dates of issue given for changes of watermark or paper are those on which supplies were first sent by the Supplies Department to Postmasters.

1955–58. W **165**. P 15×14.

540	**154**	½d. orange-red (booklets 8.55, sheets 12.12.55)	15	15
		a. Part perf pane*	£4000	
541		1d. ultramarine (19.9.55)	30	15
		a. Booklet pane. Three stamps plus three printed labels	16·00	
		b. *Tête-bêche* (horiz pair)		
542		1½d. green (booklets 8.55, sheets 11.10.55)	25	30
		a. Wmk sideways (7.3.56)	35	70
		b. *Tête-bêche* (horiz pair)	£2500	
543		2d. red-brown (6.9.55)	25	35
		aa. Imperf between (vert pair)	£3500	
		a. Wmk sideways (31.7.56)	55	70
		ab. Imperf between (horiz pair) ..	£3500	
543*b*		2d. light red-brown (17.10.56)	20	20
		ba. *Tête-bêche* (horiz pair)	£1800	
		bb. Imperf pane*	£4500	
		bc. Part perf pane*	£4000	
		d. Wmk sideways (5.3.57)	8·00	7·00

544 **155** 2½d. carmine-red (Type I) (28.9.55) 20 25
a. Wmk sideways (Type I) (23.3.56) 1·50 1·75
b. Type II (booklets 9.55, sheets 1957) 45 45
ba. *Tête-bêche* (horiz pair) £2000
bb. Imperf pane* £3500
bc. Part perf pane* £3250
545 3d. deep lilac (17.7.56) 25 25
aa. *Tête-bêche* (horiz pair) £2000
a. Imperf three sides (pair) £1500
b. Wmk sideways (22.11.57) 18·00 17·00
546 **156** 4d. ultramarine (14.11.55) 1·25 45
547 **157** 5d. brown (21.9.55) 6·00 6·00
548 6d. reddish purple (20.12.55) 4·50 1·25
aa. Imperf three sides (pair) £3000
a. *Deep claret* (8.5.58) 4·50 1·40
ab. Imperf three sides (pair) £3000
549 7d. bright green (23.4.56) 50·00 10·00
550 **158** 8d. magenta (21.12.55) 7·00 1·25
551 9d. bronze-green (15.12.55) 20·00 2·75
552 10d. Prussian blue (22.9.55) 20·00 2·75
553 11d. brown-purple (28.10.55) 50 1·10
554 **159** 1s. bistre-brown (3.11.55) 22·00 65
555 **160** 1s.3d. green (27.3.56) 30·00 1·60
556 **159** 1s.6d. grey-blue (27.3.56) 23·00 1·60
540/56 *Set of* 18 £160 27·00

The dates given for Nos. 540/556 are those on which they were first issued by the Supplies Dept to postmasters.

In December 1956 a completely imperforate sheet of No. 543*b* was noticed by clerks in a Kent post office, one of whom purchased it against P.O. regulations. In view of this irregularity we do not consider it properly issued.

Types of 2½d. In this issue, in 1957, Type II formerly only found in stamps from booklets began to replace Type I on sheet stamps.

*BOOKLET ERRORS. Those listed as "imperf panes" show one row of perforations either at top or bottom of the booklet pane; those as "part perf panes" have one row of 3 stamps imperf on three sides.

170 Scout Badge and "Rolling Hitch"

171 "Scouts coming to Britain"

172 Globe within a Compass

(Des Mary Adshead (2½d.), P. Keely (4d.), W. H. Brown (1s.3d.))

1957 (1 Aug). *World Scout Jubilee Jamboree.* W **165**. P 15×14.
557 **170** 2½d. carmine-red 50 50
558 **171** 4d. ultramarine 75 1·50
559 **172** 1s.3d. green 4·50 4·50
557/9 *Set of* 3 5·00 5·75

173

½d. to 1½d., 2½d 3d. 2d.
Graphite-line arrangements
(Stamps viewed from back)

(Adapted F. Langfield)

1957 (12 Sept). *46th Inter-Parliamentary Union Conference.* W **165**. P 15×14.
560 **173** 4d. ultramarine 1·00 1·00

GRAPHITE-LINED ISSUES. These were used in connection with automatic sorting machinery, first introduced experimentally at Southampton in December 1957.

The graphite lines were printed in black on the back, beneath the gum; two lines per stamp, except for the 2d.

In November 1959 phosphor bands were introduced (see notes after No. 598).

1957 (19 Nov). *Graphite-lined issue. Two graphite lines on the back, except 2d. value, which has one line.* W **165**. P 15×14.
561 **154** ½d. orange-red 25 25
562 1d. ultramarine 40 40
563 1½d. green 1·20 1·40
a. Both lines at left £1200 £450
564 2d. light red-brown 1·60 2·25
a. Line at left £650 £225
565 **155** 2½d. carmine-red (Type II) 8·50 7·00
566 3d. deep lilac 80 50
561/6 *Set of* 6 12·00 10·50

No. 564a results from a misplacement of the line and horizontal pairs exist showing one stamp without line. No. 563a results from a similar misplacement.

See also Nos. 587/94.

176 Welsh Dragon

177 Flag and Games Emblem

178 Welsh Dragon

(Des R. Stone (3d.), W. H. Brown (6d.), P. Keely (1s.3d.))

1958 (18 July). *Sixth British Empire and Commonwealth Games, Cardiff.* W **165**. P 15×14.
567 **176** 3d. deep lilac 20 20
568 **177** 6d. reddish purple 40 45
569 **178** 1s.3d. green 2·25 2·40
567/9 *Set of* 3 2·50 2·75

179 Multiple Crowns

1958–65. W **179**. P 15×14.
570 **154** ½d. orange-red (25.11.58) 10 10
a. Wmk sideways (26.5.61) 30 40
c. Part perf pane* £3000
k. Chalk-surfaced paper (15.7.63) 2·50 2·75
l. Booklet pane. No. 570a×4 7·50
m. Booklet pane. No. 570k×3 *se-tenant* with 574k 9·00
n. Booklet pane. No. 570a×2 *se-tenant* with 574l×2 (1.7.64) 2·25
571 1d. ultramarine (booklets 11.58, sheets 24.3.59) 10 10
aa. Imperf (vert pair from coil)
a. Wmk sideways (26.5.61) 1·50 1·25
b. Part perf pane* £3500
c. Imperf pane £4500
l. Booklet pane. No. 571a×4 10·00
m. Booklet pane. No. 571a×2 *se-tenant* with 575a×2 (1d. values at left) (16.8.65) 10·00
ma. Ditto. 1d. values at right 11·00
572 1½d. green (booklets 12.58, sheets 30.8.60) 10 15
a. Imperf three sides (horiz strip of 3) £5500
b. Wmk sideways (26.5.61) 9·00 5·00
l. Booklet pane. No. 572b×4 35·00
573 2d. light red-brown (4.12.58) 10 10
a. Wmk sideways (3.4.59) 50 1·00
574 **155** 2½d. carmine-red (Type II) (booklets 11.58, sheets 15.9.59) 10 20
a. Imperf strip of 3
b. *Tête-bêche* (horiz pair) £4250
c. Imperf pane £3250
d. Wmk sideways (Type I) (10.11.60) 25 40
da. Imperf strip of 6
e. Type I (wmk upright) (4.10.61) 70 70
k. Chalk-surfaced paper (Type II) (15.7.63) 50 80
l. Wmk sideways (Type II) Ord paper (1.7.64) 70 1·25
575 3d. deep lilac (booklets 11.58, sheets 8.12.58) 10 20
a. Wmk sideways (24.10.58) 25 35
b. Imperf pane* £3250
c. Part perf pane* £3000
d. Phantom "R" (Cyl 41 no dot) £350
e. Phantom "R" (Cyl 37 no dot) 45·00
l. Booklet pane. No. 575a×4 (26.5.61) 3·25
576 **156** 4d. ultramarine (29.10.58) 45 35
a. Deep ultramarine†† (28.4.65) 15 15
ab. Wmk sideways (31.5.65) 70 55
ac. Imperf pane* £4000
ad. Part perf pane* £3000
al. Booklet pane. No. 576ab×4 (16.8.65) 3·25
577 4½d. chestnut (9.2.59) 10 25
578 **157** 5d. brown (10.11.58) 30 40
579 6d. deep claret (23.12.58) 30 25
a. Imperf three sides (pair) £1250
b. Imperf (pair) £1500
580 7d. bright green (26.11.58) 50 45
581 **158** 8d. magenta (24.2.60) 60 40
582 9d. bronze-green (24.3.59) 60 40
583 10d. Prussian blue (18.11.58) 1·00 50
584 **159** 1s. bistre-brown (30.10.58) 45 30
585 **160** 1s.3d. green (17.6.59) 45 30
586 **159** 1s.6d. grey-blue (16.12.58) 4·00 40
570/86 *Set of* 17 8·00 4·25

*BOOKLET ERRORS. See note after No. 556.

††This "shade" was brought about by making more deeply etched cylinders, resulting in apparent depth of colour in parts of the design. There is no difference in the colour of the ink.

Sideways watermark. The 2d., 2½d., 3d. and 4d. come from coils and the ½d., 1d., 1½d., 2½d., 3d. and 4d. come from booklets. In *coil* stamps the sideways watermark shows the top of the watermark to the left *as seen from the front of the stamp*. In the *booklet* stamps it comes equally to the left or right.

Nos. 570k and 574k only come from 2s. "Holiday Resort" Experimental undated booklets issued in 1963, in which one page contained 1×2½d. *se-tenant* with 3×½d. (*See* No. 570l).

No. 574l comes from coils, and the "Holiday Resort" Experimental booklets dated "1964" comprising four panes each containing two of these 2½d. stamps *se-tenant* vertically with two ½d. No. 570a (*See* No. 570m).

2½d. imperf No. 574a comes from a booklet with watermark upright. No. 574da is from a coil with sideways watermark.

No. 574e comes from *sheets* bearing cylinder number 42 and is also known on vertical delivery coils.

Nos. 575d and 615a occurred below the last stamp of the sheet from Cyl 41 (no dot), where an incomplete marginal rule revealed an "R". The cylinder was later twice retouched. The stamps listed show the original, unretouched "R". The rare variety, No. 575d, is best collected in a block of 4 or 6 with full margins in order to be sure that it is not No. 615a with phosphor lines removed.

No. 575e is a similar variety but from Cyl. 37 (no dot). The marginal rule is much narrower and only a very small part of the "R" is revealed. The cylinder was later retouched. The listed variety is for the original, unretouched state.

WHITER PAPER. On 18 May 1962 the Post Office announced that a whiter paper was being used for the current issue (including Nos. 595/8). This is beyond the scope of this catalogue, but the whiter papers are listed in Vol. 3 of the Stanley Gibbons *Great Britain Specialised Catalogue*.

1958 (24 Nov)–**61**. *Graphite-lined issue. Two graphite lines on the back, except 2d. value, which has one line.* W **179**. P 15×14.
587 **154** ½d. orange-red (15.6.59)† 3·25 4·00
588 1d. ultramarine (18.12.58) 2·00 1·50
a. Misplaced graphite lines (7.61)* 80 1·25
589 1½d. green (4.8.59)† 60·00 48·00
590 2d. light red-brown (24.11.58) 9·00 3·50
591 **155** 2½d. carmine-red (Type II) (9.6.59) 10·00 10·00
592 3d. deep lilac (24.11.58) 50 65
a. Misplaced graphite lines (5.61)* £450 £375
593 **156** 4d. ultramarine (29.4.59) 5·50 5·00
a. Misplaced graphite lines (1961)* £1800
594 4½d. chestnut (3.6.59) 6·50 5·00
587/94 *Set of* 8 85·00 70·00

Nos. 587/9 were only issued in booklets or coils (587/8).

*No. 588a (in coils), and Nos. 592a and 593a (both in sheets) result from the use of a residual stock of graphite-lined paper. As the use of graphite lines had ceased, the register of the lines in relation to the stamps was of no importance and numerous misplacements occurred—two lines close together, one line only, etc. No. 588a refers to two lines at left or at right; No. 592a refers to stamps with two lines only at left and both clear of the perforations and No. 593a to stamps with two lines at left (with left line down perforations) and traces of a third line down the opposite perforations.

†The prices quoted are for stamps with the watermark inverted (*Prices for upright watermark ½d. £9 un, £9 us; 1½d. £90 un, £80 us.*)

(Recess D.L.R. (until 31.12.62), then B. W.)

1959–58. W **179**. P 11×12.
595 **166** 2s.6d. black-brown (22.7.59) 10·00 75
a. B.W. printing (1.7.63) 35 40
k. Chalk-surfaced paper (30.5.68) 50 1·50
596 **167** 5s. scarlet-vermilion (15.6.59) 45·00 2·00
a. B. W. ptg. Red (*shades*) (3.9.63) 1·20 50
ab. Printed on the gummed side £1250
597 **168** 10s. blue (21.7.59) 55·00 5·00
a. B.W. ptg. *Bright ultram* (16.10.63) 4·50 4·50
598 **169** £1 black (23.6.59) £120 12·00
a. B. W. printing (14.11.63) 13·00 8·00
595/8 *Set of* 4 £195 17·00
595a/8a *Set of* 4 15·00 11·00

The B.W. printings have a marginal Plate Number. They are generally more deeply engraved than the D.L.R., showing more of the Diadem detail and heavier lines on Her Majesty's face. The vertical perf is 11.9 to 12 as against D.L.R. 11.8.

See also Nos. 759/62.

PHOSPHOR BAND ISSUES. These are printed on the front and are wider than graphite lines. They are not easy to see but show as broad vertical bands at certain angles to the light.

Values representing the rate for printed papers (and when this was abolished in 1968 for second class mail) have one band and others two, three or four bands as stated, according to the size and format.

In the small size stamps the bands are on each side with the single band at left (*except where otherwise stated*). In the large-size commemorative stamps the single band may be at left, centre or right, varying in different designs. The bands are vertical on both horizontal and vertical designs *except where otherwise stated*.

The phosphor was originally applied typographically but later usually by photogravure and sometimes using flexography, a typographical process using rubber cylinders.

Three different types of phosphor have been used, distinguishable by the colour emitted under an ultra-violet lamp, the first being green, then blue and later violet. Different sized bands are also known. All these are fully listed in Vol. 3 of the Stanley Gibbons *Great Britain Specialised Catalogue*.

Varieties. Misplaced and missing phosphor bands are known but such varieties are beyond the scope of this Catalogue.

1959 (18 Nov). *Phosphor-Graphite issue. Two phosphor bands on front and two graphite lines on back, except 2d. value, which has one band on front and one line on back.* P 15×14.

(*a*) W **165**.
599 **154** ½d. orange-red 4·00 3·75
600 1d. ultramarine 11·00 11·00
601 1½d. green 4·00 4·00

(*b*) W **179**.
605 **154** 2d. light red-brown (1 band) 5·00 4·25
a. Error. W **165** £180 £125
606 **155** 2½d. carmine-red (Type II) 22·00 18·00
607 3d. deep lilac 10·00 8·00
608 **156** 4d. ultramarine 20·00 16·00
609 4½d. chestnut 30·00 20·00
599/609 *Set of* 8 85·00 70·00

Examples of the 2½d., No. 606, exist showing watermark W **165** in error. It is believed that phosphor-graphite stamps of this value with this watermark were not used by the public for postal purposes.

1960 (22 June)–**67**. *Phosphor issue. Two phosphor bands on front, except where otherwise stated.* W **179**. P 15×14.

610	**154**	½d. orange-red	10	15
		a. Wmk sideways (14.7.61)	10·00	10·00
		l. Booklet pane. No. 610a×4	40·00	
611		1d. ultramarine	10	10
		a. Wmk sideways (14.7.61)	90	90
		l. Booklet pane. No. 611a×4	9·00	
		m. Booklet pane. No. 611a×2 *se-tenant* with 615d×2 (1d. stamps at left) (16.8.65)	15·00	
		ma. Booklet pane. As. No. 611m, but 1d. stamps at right	15·00	
		n. Booklet pane. No. 611a×2 *se-tenant* with 615b×2†† (11.67)	8·00	
612		1½d. green	15	15
		a. Wmk sideways (14.7.61)	10·00	10·00
		l. Booklet pane. No. 612a×4	42·00	
613		2d. light red-brown (1 band)	16·00	18·00
613*a*	**154**	2d. lt red-brown (two bands) (4.10.61)	10	15
		na. Imperf three sides***		
		ab. Wmk sideways (6.4.67)	30	60
614	**155**	2½d. carmine-red (Type II) (2 bands)*	20	30
614*a*		2½d. carmine-red (Type II) (1 band) (4.10.61)	60	75
614*b*		2½d. carmine-red (Type I) (1 band) (4.10.61)	45·00	40·00
615		3d. deep lilac (2 bands)	60	55
		a. Phantom "R" (Cyl 41 no dot)	40·00	
		b. Wmk sideways (14.7.61)	1·75	1·75
		l. Booklet pane. No. 6156×4	20·00	
615*c*		3d. deep lilac (1 side band) (29.4.65)	60	55
		d. Wmk sideways (16.8.65)	5·50	5·00
		e. One centre band (8.12.66)	40	45
		ea. Wmk sideways (19.6.67)	70	50
616	**156**	4d. ultramarine	3·50	3·50
		a. Deep ultramarine (28.4.65)	25	25
		aa. Part perf pane	£4000	
		ab. Wmk sideways (16.8.65)	35	50
		al. Booklet pane. No. 616ab×4	2·50	
616*b*		4½d. chestnut (13.9.61)	25	30
616*c*	**157**	5d. brown (9.6.67)	25	35
617		6d. deep claret (27.6.60)	30	30
617*a*		7d. bright green (15.2.67)	55	50
617*b*	**158**	8d. magenta (28.6.67)	40	45
617*c*		9d. bronze-green (29.12.66)	60	55
617*d*		10d. Prussian blue (30.12.66)	70	60
617*e*	**159**	1s. bistre-brown (28.6.67)	40	35
618	**160**	1s.3d. green	1·90	2·50
618*a*	**159**	1s.6d. grey-blue (12.12.66)	2·00	2·00
610/18*a* *Set of 17*			7·50	8·00

The automatic facing equipment was brought into use on 6 July 1960 but the phosphor stamps may have been released a few days earlier.

The stamps with watermark sideways are from booklets except Nos. 613ab and 615ea which are from coils. No. 616ab comes from both booklets and coils.

No. 615a. See footnote after No. 586.

*No. 614 with two bands on the creamy paper was originally from cylinder 50 dot and no dot. When the change in postal rates took place in 1965 it was reissued from cylinder 57 dot and no dot on the whiter paper. Some of these latter were also released in error in districts of S. E. London in September 1964. The shade of the reissue is slightly more carmine.

***This comes from the bottom row of a sheet which is imperf at bottom and both sides.

††Booklet pane No. 611n comes from 2s. booklets of January and March 1968. The two bands on the 3d. stamp were intentional because of the technical difficulties in producing one band and two band stamps *se-tenant*.

Unlike previous one-banded phosphor stamps. No. 615*c* has a broad band extending over two stamps so that alternate stamps have the band at left or right (same prices either way).

180 Postboy of 1660

181 Posthorn of 1660

(Des R. Stone (3d.), Faith Jaques (1s.3d.))

1960 (7 July). *Tercentenary of Establishment of General Letter Office.* W **179** (sideways on 1s.3d.). P 15×14 (3d.) or 14×15 (1s.3d.)

619	**180**	3d. deep lilac	50	50
620	**181**	1s.3d. green	3·75	4·25

182 Conference Emblem

(Des R. Stone (emblem, P. Rahikainen))

1960 (19 Sept). *First Anniv of European Postal and Telecommunications Conference. Chalk-surfaced paper.* W **179.** P 15×14.

621	**182**	6d. bronze-green and purple	2·00	50
622		1s.6d. brown and blue	9·50	5·00

183 Thrift Plant

184 "Growth of Savings"

185 Thrift Plant

(Des P. Gauld (2½d.), M. Goaman (others))

1961 (28 Aug). *Centenary of Post Office Saving Bank. Chalk-surfaced paper.* W **179** (sideways on 2½d.). P 14×15 (2½d.) or 15×14 (others).

A. "Timson" Machine

623A	**183**	2½d. black and red	25	25
		a. Black omitted	£22000	
624A	**184**	3d. orange-brown and violet	20	20
		a. Orange-brown omitted	£425	
625A	**185**	1s.6d. red and blue	2·50	2·25
623A/5A *Set of 3*			2·75	2·50

B. "Thrissell" Machine

623B	**183**	2½d. black and red	2·25	2·25
624B	**184**	3d. orange-brown and violet	40	40
		a. Orange-brown omitted	£1500	

2½d. TIMSON. Cyls 1E–1F. Deeply shaded portrait (brownish black).
2½d. THRISSELL. *Cyls* 1D–1B or 1D (dot)–1B (dot). Lighter portrait (grey-black).

3d. TIMSON. Cyls 3D–3E. Clear, well-defined portrait with deep shadows and bright highlights.
3d. THRISSELL. Cyls 3C–3B or 3C (dot)–3B (dot). Dull portrait, lacking in contrast.

Sheet marginal examples without single extension perf hole on the short side of the stamp are always "Timson", as are those with large punch-hole *not* coincident with printed three-sided box guide mark.

The 3d. "Timson" perforated completely through the right-hand side margin comes from a relatively small part of the printing perforated on a sheet-fed machine.

Normally the "Timsons" were perforated in the reel, with three large punch-holes in both long margins and the perforations completely through both short margins. Only one punch-hole coincides with the guide-mark.

The "Thrissells" have one large punch-hole in one long margin, coinciding with guide-mark and one short margin imperf (except sometimes for encroachments).

186 C.E.P.T. Emblem

187 Doves and Emblem

188 Doves and Emblem

(Des M. Goaman (doves T. Kurpershoek))

1961 (18 Sept). *European Postal and Telecommunications (C.E.P.T.) Conference, Torquay. Chalk-surfaced paper.* W **179.** P 15×14.

626	**186**	2d. orange, pink and brown	15	10
		a. Orange omitted	£16000	
627	**187**	4d. buff, mauve and ultramarine	15	15
628	**188**	10d. turquoise, pale green & Prussian bl	15	50
		a. Pale green omitted	£15000	
		b. Turquoise omitted	£4250	
626/8 *Set of 3*			40	60

189 Hammer Beam Roof, Westminster Hall

190 Palace of Westminster

(Des Faith Jaques)

1961 (25 Sept). *Seventh Commonwealth Parliamentary Conference. Chalk-surfaced paper.* W **179** (sideways on 1s.3d.). P 15×14 (6d.) or 14×15 (1s.3d.)

629	**189**	6d. purple and gold	25	25
		a. Gold omitted	£1700	
630	**190**	1s.3d. green and blue	2·50	2·75
		a. Blue (Queen's head) omitted	£20000	

191 "Units of Productivity"

192 "National Productivity"

193 "Unified Productivity"

(Des D. Gentleman)

1962 (14 Nov). *National Productivity Year. Chalk-surfaced paper.* W **179** (inverted on 2½d. and 3d.). P 15×14.

631	**191**	2½d. myrtle-green & carm-red (*shades*)	20	20
		p. One phosphor band	60	50
632	**192**	3d. light blue and violet (*shades*)	50	25
		a. Light blue (Queen's head) omitted	£2750	
		p. Three phosphor bands	1·50	80
633	**193**	1s.3d. carmine, light blue & dp green	1·50	1·75
		a. Light blue (Queen's head) omitted	£12000	
		p. Three phosphor bands	35·00	22·00
631/3 *Set of 3*			2·00	1·90
631p/3p *Set of 3*			30·00	22·00

194 Campaign Emblem and Family

195 Children of Three Races

(Des M. Goaman)

1963 (21 Mar). *Freedom from Hunger. Chalk-surfaced paper.* W **179** (inverted). P 15×14.

634	**194**	2½d. crimson and pink	25	10
		p. One phosphor band	3·00	1·25
635	**195**	1s.3d. bistre-brown and yellow	1·90	1·90
		p. Three phosphor bands	30·00	23·00

196 "Paris Conference"

(Des R. Stone)

1963 (7 May). *Paris Postal Conference Centenary. Chalk-surfaced paper.* W **179** (inverted). P 15×14.

636	**196**	6d. green and mauve	50	50
		a. Green omitted	£4250	
		p. Three phosphor bands	6·00	7·00

197 Posy of Flowers

198 Woodland Life

(Des S. Scott (3d.), M. Goaman (4½d.))

1963 (16 May). *National Nature Week. Chalk-surfaced paper.* W **179.** P 15×14.

637	**197**	3d. yellow, green, brown and black	15	15
		p. Three phosphor bands	60	60
638	**198**	4½d. black, blue, yellow, mag & brn-red	35	35
		p. Three phosphor bands	3·00	3·00

199 Rescue at Sea

200 19th-century Lifeboat

201 Lifeboatmen

(Des D. Gentleman)

1963 (31 May). *Ninth International Lifeboat Conference, Edinburgh. Chalk-surfaced paper.* W **179.** P 15×14.

639	**199**	2½d. blue, black and red	25	25
		p. One phosphor band	50	60
640	**200**	4d. red, yellow, brown, black and blue	50	50
		p. Three phosphor bands	50	60

641 **201** 1s.6d. sepia, yellow and grey-blue .... 3·00 3·25
p. Three phosphor bands .... 48·00 28·00
639/41 *Set of 3* .... 3·25 3·50
639p/41p *Set of 3* .... 48·00 28·00

202 Red Cross

203

204

(Des H. Bartram)

1963 (15 Aug). *Red Cross Centenary Congress. Chalk-surfaced paper.* W **179**. P 15×14.
642 **202** 3d. red and deep lilac 25 25
a. Red omitted £9000
p. Three phosphor bands .... 1·10 1·00
pa. Red omitted £22000
643 **203** 1s.3d. red, blue and grey .... 3·00 3·00
p. Three phosphor bands .... 35·00 27·00
644 **204** 1s.6d. red, blue and bistre .... 3·00 3·00
p. Three phosphor bands .... 35·00 27·00
642/4 *Set of 3* .... 5·00 5·75
642p/4p *Set of 3* .... 65·00 55·00

205 Commonwealth Cable

(Des P. Gauld)

1963 (3 Dec). *Opening of COMPAC (Trans-Pacific Telephone Cable). Chalk-surfaced paper.* W **179**. P 15×14.
645 **205** 1s.6d. blue and black .... 2·75 2·50
a. Black omitted £5500
p. Three phosphor bands .... 16·00 15·50

206 Puck and Bottom (*A Midsummer Night's Dream*)

207 Feste (*Twelfth Night*)

208 Balcony Scene (*Romeo and Juliet*)

209 "Eve of Agincourt" (*Henry V*)

210 Hamlet contemplating Yorick's Skull (*Hamlet*) and Queen Elizabeth II

(Des D. Gentleman. Photo Harrison & Sons (3d., 6d., 1s.3d., 1s.6d.). Des C. and R. Ironside. Recess B.W. (2s.6d.))

1964 (23 April). *Shakespeare Festival. Chalk-surfaced paper.* W **179**. P 11×12 (2s.6d.) or 15×14 (others).
646 **206** 3d. yell-bistre, blk & dp vio-bl (*shades*) 15 15
p. Three phosphor bands 25 30
647 **207** 6d. yellow, orge, blk & yellow-olive (*shades*) 30 30
p. Three phosphor bands .... 75 1·00
648 **208** 1s.3d. cerise, bl-grn, blk & sep (*shades*) .... 75 1·00
p. Three phosphor bands .... 4·00 6·50
649 **209** 1s.6d. violet, turq, blk & blue (*shades*) .... 1·00 85
p. Three phosphor bands .... 8·00 8·00
650 **210** 2s.6d. deep slate-purple (*shades*) ...... 2·75 2·75
646/50 *Set of 5* .... 4·50 4·50
646p/9p *Set of 4* .... 12·00 14·00

211 Flats near Richmond Park ("Urban Development")

212 Shipbuilding Yards, Belfast ("Industrial Activity")

213 Beddgelert Forest Park, Snowdonia ("Forestry")

214 Nuclear Reactor, Dounreay ("Technological Development")

(Des D. Bailey)

1964 (1 July). *20th International Geographical Congress. London. Chalk-surfaced paper.* W **179**. P 15×14.
651 **211** 2½d. black, olive-yell, ol-grey & turq-bl 10 10
p. One phosphor band 40 50
652 **212** 4d. orge-brn, red-brn, rose, blk & vio 30 30
a. Violet (face value) omitted £225
c. Violet and red-brown (dock walls) omitted £450
d. Red-brown (dock walls) omitted
p. Three phosphor bands .... 1·25 1·25
653 **213** 8d. yellow-brown, emerald, grn & blk 75 85
a. Green (lawn) omitted £14000
p. Three phosphor bands .... 2·50 2·75
654 **214** 1s.6d. yellow-brn, pale pk, blk & brn .... 3·50 3·50
p. Three phosphor bands .... 28·00 22·00
651/4 *Set of 4* .... 4·50 4·50
651p/4p *Set of 4* .... 30·00 24·00

A used example of the 4d. is known with the red-brown omitted.

215 Spring Gentian

216 Dog Rose

217 Honeysuckle

218 Fringed Water Lily

(Des M. and Sylvia Goaman)

1964 (5 Aug). *Tenth International Botanical Congress, Edinburgh. Chalk-surfaced paper.* W **179**. P 15×14.
655 **215** 3d. violet, blue and sage-green..... 25 25
a. Blue omitted £12000
b. Sage-green omitted £15000
p. Three phosphor bands 40 40
656 **216** 6d. apple-green, rose, scarlet and green 50 50
p. Three phosphor bands .... 2·50 2·75
657 **217** 9d. lemon, green, lake and rose-red .... 1·75 2·25
a. Green (leaves) omitted £18000
p. Three phosphor bands .... 4·50 4·00
658 **218** 1s.3d. yellow, emerald, reddish violet and grey-green .... 2·50 2·50
a. Yellow (flowers) omitted £40000
p. Three phosphor bands .... 25·00 20·00
655/8 *Set of 4* .... 4·50 4·50
655p/8p *Set of 4* .... 30·00 24·00

219 Forth Road Bridge

220 Forth Road and Railway Bridges

(Des A. Restall)

1964 (4 Sept). *Opening of Forth Road Bridge. Chalk-surfaced paper.* W **179**. P 15×14.
659 **219** 3d. black, blue and reddish violet 10 10
p. Three phosphor bands .... 1·00 1·50
660 **220** 6d. blackish lilac, lt blue & carmine-red 40 40
a. Light blue omitted £4250
p. Three phosphor bands .... 4·50 4·75

221 Sir Winston Churchill

(Des D. Gentleman and Rosalind Dease, from photograph by Karsh)

1965 (8 July). *Churchill Commemoration. Chalk-surfaced paper.* W **179**. P 15×14.

I. "REMBRANDT" Machine.
661 **221** 4d. black and olive-brown............ 10 10
p. Three phosphor bands 25 25

II. "TIMSON" Machine
661*a* **221** 4d. black and olive-brown............ 35 35

III. "L. & M. 4" Machine
662 – 1s.3d. black and grey 30 40
p. Three phosphor bands .... 2·50 3·00

The 1s.3d. shows a closer view of Churchill's head.

4d. REMBRANDT. Cyls 1A–1B dot and no dot. Lack of shading detail on Churchill's portrait. Queen's portrait appears dull and coarse. This is a rotary machine which is sheet-fed.

4d. TIMSON. Cyls 5A–6B no dot. More detail on Churchill's portrait—furrow on forehead, his left eyebrow fully drawn and more shading on cheek. Queen's portrait lighter and sharper. This is a reel-fed, two-colour 12-in, wide rotary machine and the differences in impression are due to the greater pressure applied by this machine.

1s.3d. Cyls 1A–1B no dot. The "Linotype and Machinery No. 4" machine is an ordinary sheet-fed rotary press machine. Besides being used for printing the 1s.3d. stamps it was also employed for overprinting the phosphor bands on both values.

Two examples of the 4d. value exist with the Queen's head omitted, one due to something adhering to the cylinder and the other due to a paper fold. The stamp also exists with Churchill's head omitted, also due to a paper fold.

222 Simon de Montfort's Seal

223 Parliament Buildings (after engraving by Hollar, 1647)

(Des S. Black (6d.), R. Guyatt (2s.6d.))

1965 (19 July). *700th Anniv of Simon de Montfort's Parliament. Chalk-surfaced paper.* W **179**. P 15×14.
663 **222** 6d. olive-green 20 20
p. Three phosphor bands .... 60 1·00
664 **223** 2s.6d. black, grey and pale drab .... 80 1·50

224 Bandsmen and Banner

225 Three Salvationists

(Des M. Farrar-Bell (3d.), G. Trenaman (1s.6d.))

1965 (9 Aug). *Salvation Army Centenary. Chalk-surfaced paper.* W **179**. P 15×14.
665 **224** 3d. indigo, grey-blue, cerise, yell & brn 25 25
p. One phosphor band 25 40
666 **225** 1s.6d. red, blue, yellow and brown ... 1·00 1·50
p. Three phosphor bands .... 2·50 2·75

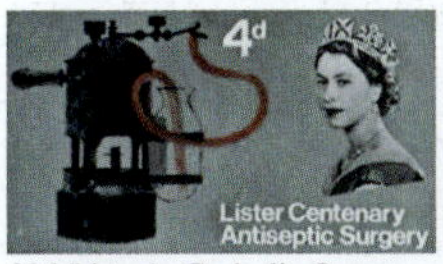

226 Lister's Carbolic Spray

227 Lister and Chemical Symbols

(Des P. Gauld (4d.), F. Ariss (1s.))

1965 (1 Sept). *Centenary of Joseph Lister's Discovery of Antiseptic Surgery. Chalk-surfaced paper.* W **179**. P 15×14.
667 **226** 4d. indigo, brown-red and grey-black 25 15
a. Brown-red (tube) omitted...... £425
b. Indigo omitted.......... £5000
p. Three phosphor bands 25 25
pa. Brown-red (tube) omitted £4500
668 **227** 1s. black, purple and new blue .... 1·00 1·10
p. Three phosphor bands .... 2·00 2·50

228 Trinidad Carnival Dancers

229 Canadian Folk-dancers

(Des D. Gentleman and Rosalind Dease)

1965 (1 Sept). *Commonwealth Arts Festival. Chalk-surfaced paper.* W **179**. P 15×14.
669 **228** 6d. black and orange 20 20
p. Three phosphor bands 30 50
670 **229** 1s.6d. black and light reddish violet. 80 1·10
p. Three phosphor bands .... 2·50 3·50

230 Flight of Supermarine Spitfires

231 Pilot in Hawker Hurricane Mk I

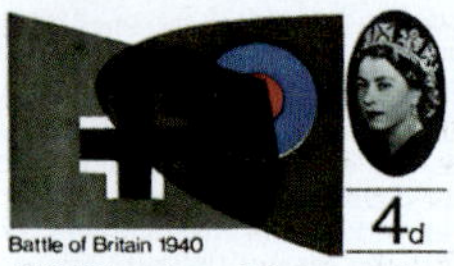

232 Wing-tips of Supermarine Spitfire and Messerschmitt Bf 109

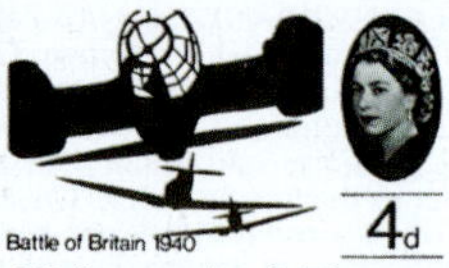

233 Supermarine Spitfires attacking Heinkel HE-111H Bomber

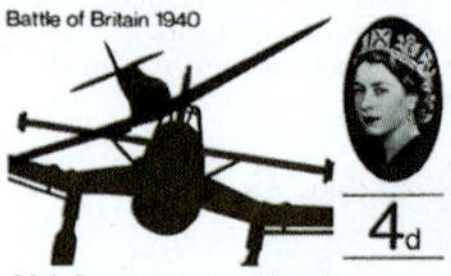

234 Supermarine Spitfire attacking Junkers Ju 87B "Stuka" Dive-bomber

235 Hawker Hurricanes Mk 1 over Wreck of Dornier Do-17Z Bomber

236 Anti-aircraft Artillery in Action

237 Air-battle over St. Paul's Cathedral

(Des D. Gentleman and Rosalind Dease (4d.×6 and 1s.3d.), A. Restall (9d.))

1965 (13 Sept). *25th Anniv of Battle of Britain. Chalk-surfaced paper.* W **179**. P 15×14.

671	**230**	4d. yellow-olive and black	25	25
		a. Block of 6. Nos. 671/6	8·00	8·00
		p. Three phosphor bands	50	50
		pa. Block of 6. Nos. 671p/6p	10·00	12·00
672	**231**	4d. yellow-olive, olive-grey and black	25	25
		p. Three phosphor bands	50	50
673	**232**	4d. red, new blue, yell-ol, ol-grey & blk	25	25
		p. Three phosphor bands	50	50
674	**233**	4d. olive-grey, yellow-olive and black	25	25
		p. Three phosphor bands	50	50
675	**234**	4d. olive-grey, yellow-olive and black	25	25
		p. Three phosphor bands	50	50
676	**235**	4d. olive-grey, yell-olive, new blue & blk	25	25
		a. New blue omitted	†	£5000
		p. Three phosphor bands	50	50
677	**236**	9d. bluish violet, orange and slate-purple	1·75	1·75
		p. Three phosphor bands	1·75	2·50
678	**237**	1s.3d. light grey, deep grey, black, light blue and bright blue	1·75	1·75
		p. Three phosphor bands	1·75	2·50
671/8 *Set of 8*			4·50	4·50
671p/8p *Set of 8*			6·00	7·00

Nos. 671/6 were issued together *se-tenant* in blocks of 6 (3×2) within the sheet.

No. 676a is only known commercially used on cover from Truro.

238 Tower and Georgian Buildings

239 Tower and "Nash" Terrace, Regent's Park

(Des C. Abbott)

1965 (8 Oct). *Opening of Post Office Tower. Chalk-surfaced paper.* W **179** (sideways on 3d.). P 14×14 (1s.3d.).

679	**238**	3d. olive-yell, new blue & bronze-green	10	15
		a. Olive-yellow (Tower) omitted	£4000	£1800
		p. One phosphor band	15	15
680	**239**	1s.3d. bronze-green, yellow-green & bl	30	45
		p. Three phosphor bands	30	50

The one phosphor band on No. 679p was produced by printing broad phosphor bands across alternate vertical perforations. Individual stamps show the band at right or left (same prices either way).

240 U.N. Emblem

241 I.C.Y. Emblem

(Des J. Matthews)

1965 (25 Oct). *20th Anniv of U.N.O. and International Co-operation Year. Chalk-surfaced paper.* W **179**. P 15×14.

681	**240**	3d. black, yellow-orange and light blue	25	20
		p. One phosphor band	25	30
682	**241**	1s.6d. black, bright purple and lt blue	1·00	80
		p. Three phosphor bands	2·75	3·00

242 Telecommunications Network

243 Radio Waves and Switchboard

(Des A. Restall)

1965 (15 Nov). *I.T.U. Centenary. Chalk-surfaced paper.* W **179**. P 15×14.

683	**242**	9d. red, ultram, dp slate vio, blk & pk	50	40
		p. Three phosphor bands	1·00	75
684	**243**	1s.6d. red, greenish bl, ind, blk & lt pk	1·50	1·25
		a. Light pink omitted	£3000	
		p. Three phosphor bands	4·25	5·25

Originally scheduled for issue on 17 May 1965 supplies from the Philatelic Bureau were sent in error to reach a dealer on that date and another dealer received his supply on 27 May.

244 Robert Burns (after Skirving chalk drawing)

245 Robert Burns (after Nasmyth portrait)

(Des G. Huntly)

1966 (25 Jan). *Burns Commemoration. Chalk-surfaced paper.* W **179**. P 15×14.

685	**244**	4d. black, deep violet-blue and new blue	15	15
		p. Three phosphor bands	25	50
686	**245**	1s.3d. black, slate-blue & yellow-orge	40	70
		p. Three phosphor bands	2·25	2·25

246 Westminster Abbey

247 Fan Vaulting, Henry VII Chapel

(Des Sheila Robinson. Photo Harrison (3d.). Des and eng Bradbury, Wilkinson. Recess (2s.6d.))

1966 (28 Feb). *900th Anniv of Westminster Abbey. Chalk-surfaced paper (3d.).* W **179**. P 15×14 (3d.) or 11×12 (2s.6d.).

687	**246**	3d. black, red-brown and new blue	15	20
		p. One phosphor band	20	25
688	**247**	2s.6d. black	55	80

248 View near Hassocks, Sussex

249 Antrim, Northern Ireland

250 Harlech Castle, Wales

251 Cairngorm Mountains, Scotland

(Des L. Rosoman. Queen's portrait, adapted by D. Gentleman from coinage)

1966 (2 May). *Landscapes. Chalk-surfaced paper.* W **179**. P 15×14.

689	**248**	4d. black, yellow-green and new blue	10	15
		p. Three phosphor bands	10	15
690	**249**	6d. black, emerald and new blue	15	20
		p. Three phosphor bands	15	20
691	**250**	1s.3d. blk, greenish yell & greenish bl	25	35
		p. Three phosphor bands	25	35
692	**251**	1s.6d. black, orange and Prussian blue	40	35
		p. Three phosphor bands	40	40
689/92 *Set of 4*			80	95
689p/92p *Set of 4*			80	1·00

A block of four of No. 689 is known with the top right stamp showing the face value and the bottom right the Queen's head and the face value omitted due to a paper fold.

252 Players with Ball

253 Goalmouth Mêlée

254 Goalkeeper saving Goal

(Des D. Gentleman (4d.), W. Kempster (6d.), D. Caplan (1s.3d.). Queen's portrait adapted by D. Gentleman from coinage)

1996 (1 June). *World Cup Football Championship. Chalk-surfaced paper.* W **179** (sideways on 4d.). P 14×15 (4d.) or 15×14 (others).

693	**252**	4d. red, reddish pur, brt bl, flesh & blk	10	25
		p. Two phosphor bands	10	25
694	**253**	6d. black, sepia, red, apple-green & blue	15	25
		a. Black omitted	£150	
		b. Apple-green omitted	£4000	
		c. Red omitted	£7500	
		p. Three phosphor bands	15	25
		pa. Black omitted	£2000	
695	**254**	1s.3d. black, blue, yell, red & lt yell-ol	50	1·00
		a. Blue omitted	£250	
		p. Three phosphor bands	50	1·00
693/5 *Set of 3*			70	1·00
693p/5p *Set of 3*			50	1·00

255 Black-headed Gull

256 Blue Tit

257 European Robin

258 Blackbird

(Des J. Norris Wood)

1966 (8 Aug). *British Birds. Chalk-surfaced paper.* W **179**. P 15×14.

696	**255**	4d. grey, black, red, emerald-green, brt blue, greenish yellow and bistre	20	20
		a. Block of 4. Nos. 696/9	1·00	2·00
		ab. Black (value), etc. omitted* (*block of four*)	£12500	
		ac. Black only omitted*	£12000	
		p. Three phosphor bands	20	20
		pa. Block of 4. Nos. 696p/9p	75	2·00

697 **256** 4d. black, greenish yellow grey, emer-green, bright blue and bistre 20 20
p. Three phosphor bands 20 20
698 **257** 4d. red, greenish yellow, black, grey, bistre, reddish brown & emerald-grn 20 20
a. Black only omitted £12000
p. Three phosphor bands 20 20
699 **258** 4d. black, reddish brown, greenish yellow, grey and bistre** 20 20
p. Three phosphor bands 20 20
696/9 *Set of* 4 .... 1·00 2·00
696p/9p *Set of* 4 .... 75 2·00

Nos. 696/9 were issued together *se-tenant* in blocks of four within the sheet.

*In No. 696ab the blue, bistre and reddish brown are also omitted but in No. 696ac only the black is omitted.

** On No. 699 the black was printed over the bistre.

Other colours omitted, and the stamps affected:
d. Greenish yellow (Nos. 696/9) £900
pd. Greenish yellow (Nos. 696p/9) £1700
e. Red (Nos. 696 and 698) £900
f. Emerald-green (Nos. 696/8) £175
pf. Emerald-green (Nos. 696p/8p) £175
g. Bright blue (Nos. 69617) £550
pg. Bright blue (Nos. 696p/7p) £5000
h. Bistre (Nos. 696/9) £175
ph. Bistre (Nos. 696p/9p) £2500
j. Reddish brown (Nos. 698/9) £100
pj. Reddish brown (Nos. 698p/9p) £140

The prices quoted are for each stamp.

259 Cup Winners

1966 (18 Aug). *England's World Cup Football Victory. Chalk-surfaced paper.* W **179** (sideways). P 14×15.
700 **259** 4d. red, reddish pur, brt bl, flesh & blk 30 30

These stamps were only put on sale at post offices in England, the Channel Islands and the Isle of Man, and at the Philatelic Bureau in London and also, on 22 August, in Edinburgh on the occasion of the opening of the Edinburgh Festival as well as at Army post offices at home and abroad.

260 Jodrell Bank Radio Telescope

261 British Motor-cars

262 "SRN 6" Hovercraft

263 Windscale Reactor

(Des D. and A. Gillespie (4d., 6d.), A. Restall (others))

1966 (19 Sept). *British Technology. Chalk-surfaced paper.* W **179**. P 15×14.
701 **260** 4d. black and lemon 15 10
p. Three phosphor bands 10 10
702 **261** 6d. red, deep blue and orange 25 20
a. Red (Mini-cars) omitted £15000
b. Deep blue (Jaguar and inscr) omitted £12000
p. Three phosphor bands 15 25
703 **262** 1s.3d. black, orange-red, slate and light greenish blue 50 40
p. Three phosphor bands 35 40
704 **263** 1s.6d. black, yellow-green, bronze-green, lilac and deep blue 50 60
p. Three phosphor bands 50 60
701/4 *Set of* 4 .... 1·00 1·10
701p/4p *Set of* 4 .... 1·00 1·10

264

265

266

267

268

269

All the above show battle scenes and they were issued together *se-tenant* in horizontal strips of six within the sheet.

270 Norman Ship

271 Norman Horsemen attacking Harold's Troops

(All the above are scenes from the Bayeux Tapestry)

(Des D. Gentleman. Photo, Queen's head die-stamped (6d., 1s.3d.))

1966 (14 Oct). *900th Anniv of Battle of Hastings. Chalk-surfaced paper.* W **179** (sideways on 1s.3d.). P 15×14.
705 **264** 4d. black, olive-green, bistre, deep blue, orange, mag, grn, blue and grey 10 10
a. Strip of 6. Nos. 705/10 .... 1·90 2·25
p. Three phosphor bands 10 10
pa. Strip of 6. Nos. 705p/10p .... 1·90 2·25
706 **265** 4d. black, olive-green, bistre, deep blue, orange, mag, grn, blue and grey 10 10
p. Three phosphor bands 10 10
707 **266** 4d. black, olive-green, bistre, deep blue, orange, mag, grn, blue and grey 10 10
p. Three phosphor bands 10 10
708 **267** 4d. black, olive-green, bistre, deep blue, magenta, green, blue and grey 10 10
p. Three phosphor bands 10 10
709 **268** 4d. black, olive-green, bistre, deep blue, orange, mag, grn, blue and grey 10 10
p. Three phosphor bands 10 10
710 **269** 4d. black, olive-green, bistre, deep blue, orange, mag, grn, blue and grey 10 10
p. Three phosphor bands 10 25
711 **270** 6d. black, olive-grn, vio, bl, grn & gold 10 10
p. Three phosphor bands 10 10
712 **271** 1s.3d. black, lilac, bronze-green, rosine, bistre-brown and gold 20 75
a. Lilac omitted £2000
p. Four phosphor bands 20 75
pa. Lilac omitted £950
705/12 *Set of* 8 .... 2·00 2·25
705p/12p *Set of* 8 .... 2·00 2·25

Other colours omitted on the 4d. values and the stamps affected:
b. Olive-green (Nos. 705/10) .... 60·00
pb. Olive-green (Nos. 705p/10p) .... 60·00
c. Bistre (Nos. 705/10) .... 60·00
pc. Bistre (Nos. 705p/10) .... 60·00
d. Deep blue (Nos. 705/10) .... 70·00
pd. Deep blue (Nos. 705p/10p) .... 70·00
e. Orange (Nos. 705/7 and 709/10) .... 60·00
pe. Orange (Nos. 705p/7 and 709p/10p) .... 60·00
f. Magenta (Nos. 705/10) .... 60·00
pf. Magenta (Nos. 705 /10p) .... 60·00
g. Green (Nos. 705/10) .... 60·00
pg. Green (Nos. 705/10p) .... 60·00
h. Blue (Nos 705/10) .... 60·00
ph. Blue (Nos. 705/10p) .... 60·00
j. Grey (Nos. 705/10) .... 60·00
pj. Grey (Nos. 705p/10p) .... 60·00
pk. Magenta and green (Nos. 705p/10p) .... 70·00

The prices quoted are for each stamp.

Nos. 705 and 709, with grey and blue omitted, have been seen commercially used, posted from Middleton-inTeesdale.

Three examples of No. 712 in a right-hand top corner block of 10 (2×5) are known with the Queen's head omitted as a result of a double paper fold prior to die-stamping The perforation is normal. Of the other seven stamps, four have the Queen's head misplaced and three are normal.

MISSING GOLD HEADS. The 6d and 1s.3d. were also issued with the die-stamped gold head omitted but as these can also be removed by chemical means we are not prepared to list them unless a way is found of distinguishing the genuine stamps from the fakes which will satisfy the Expert Committees.

The same remarks apply to Nos. 713/14.

272 King of the Orient

273 Snowman

(Des Tasveer Shemza (3d.), J. Berry (1s.6d.) (winners of children's design competition). Photo, Queen's head die-stamped)

1966 (1 Dec). *Christmas. Chalk-surfaced paper.* W **179** (sideways on 3d.). P 14×15.
713 **272** 3d. black, blue, green, yell, red & gold 10 25
a. Queen's head double .... £3750 †
ab. Queen's head double, one albino £650
b. Green omitted ....
p. One phosphor band 10 25
714 **273** 1s.6d. blue, red, pink, black and gold 30 50
a. Pink (hat) omitted £2500
p. Two phosphor bands 30 50

See note below Nos. 679/80 which also applies to No. 713p.

274 Sea Freight

275 Air Freight

(Des C. Abbott)

1967 (20 Feb). *European Free Trade Association (E.F.T.A.). Chalk-surfaced paper.* W **179**. P 15×14.
715 **274** 9d. deep blue, red, lilac, green, brown, new blue, yellow and black 25 20
a. Black (Queen's head, etc.), brown, new blue and yellow omitted £1000
b. Lilac omitted £120
c. Green omitted £120
d. Brown (rail trucks) omitted .... 85·00
e. New blue omitted £120
f. Yellow omitted £120

		p. Three phosphor bands	25	20
		pb. Lilac omitted	£200	
		pc. Green omitted	£120	
		pd. Brown omitted	85·00	
		pe. New blue omitted	£120	
		pf. Yellow omitted	£160	
716	**275**	1s.6d. violet, red, deep blue, brown, green, blue-grey, new bl, yell & blk	50	45
		a. Red omitted		
		b. Deep blue omitted	£475	
		c. Brown omitted	£120	
		d. Blue-grey omitted	£120	
		e. New blue omitted	£120	
		f. Yellow omitted	£120	
		p. Three phosphor bands	25	40
		pa. Red omitted		
		pb. Deep blue omitted	£475	
		pc. Brown omitted	85·00	
		pd. Blue-grey omitted	£120	
		pf. New blue omitted	£120	

276 Hawthorn and Bramble

277 Larger Bindweed and Viper's Bugloss

278 Ox-eye Daisy, Coltsfoot and Buttercup

279 Bluebell, Red Campion and Wood Anemone

The above were issued together *se-tenant* in blocks of four within the sheet.

280 Dog Violet

281 Primroses

(Des Rev. W. Keble Martin (T **276/9**), Mary Grierson (others))

1967 (24 Apr). *British Wild Flowers. Chalk-surfaced paper.* W **179**. P 15×14.

717	**276**	4d. grey, lemon, myrtle-green, red, agate and slate-purple	20	20
		a. Block of 4. Nos. 717/20	80	2·25
		b. Grey double*		
		c. Red omitted	£4000	
		f. Slate-purple omitted	£5500	
		p. Three phosphor bands	10	15
		pa. Block of 4. Nos. 717p/20p	50	2·00
		pd. Agate omitted	£4500	
		pf. Slate-purple omitted	£400	
718	**277**	4d. grey, lemon, myrtle-green, red, agate and violet	20	20
		b. Grey double*		
		p. Three phosphor bands	10	15
		pd. Agate omitted	£4500	
		pe. Violet omitted		
719	**278**	4d. grey, lemon, myrtle-green, red and agate	20	20
		b. Grey double*		
		p. Three phosphor bands	10	15
		pd. Agate omitted	£4500	
720	**279**	4d. grey, lemon, myrtle-green, reddish purple, agate and violet	20	20
		b. Grey double*		
		c. Reddish purple omitted	£1900	
		d. Value omitted†		
		p. Three phosphor bands	10	15
		pd. Agate omitted	£4500	
		pe. Violet omitted		
721	**280**	9d. lavender-grey, green, reddish violet and orange-yellow	20	25
		p. Three phosphor bands	15	25
722	**281**	1s.9d. lavender-grey, green, greenish yellow and orange	25	35
		p. Three phosphor bands	20	30
717/22 *Set of 6*			1·00	2·25
717p/22p *Set of 6*			75	2·00

*The double impression of the grey printing affects the Queen's head, value and inscription.

†No. 720d was caused by something obscuring the face value on R. 14/6 during the printing of one sheet.

PHOSPHOR BANDS. Issues from No. 723 are normally with phosphor bands only, except for the high values. However, most stamps have appeared with the phosphor bands omitted in error, but they are outside the scope of this catalogue. They are listed in Volumes 3, 4 and 5 of the Stanley Gibbons *Great Britain Specialised Catalogue* and in the *Great Britain Concise Catalogue*.

See also further notes after No. X1058.

PHOSPHORISED PAPER. Following the adoption of phosphor bands the Post Office started a series of experiments involving the addition of the phosphor to the paper coating before the stamps were printed. No. 743c was the first of these experiments to be issued for normal postal use. See also notes after No. X1058.

PVA GUM. Polyvinyl alcohol was introduced by Harrisons in place of gum Arabic in 1968. As it is almost invisible a small amount of pale yellowish colouring was introduced to make it possible to check that the stamps had been gummed. Such gum varieties are outside the scope of this catalogue, but they are listed in the *Great Britain Concise Catalogue*. See further notes *re* gum after Nos. 744 and 762.

282

282a

I II

Two types of the 2d.

I. Value spaced away from left side of stamp (cylinders 1 no dot and dot).

II. Value close to left side from new multipositive used for cylinders 5 no dot and dot onwards. The portrait appears in the centre, thus conforming to the other values

(Des after plaster cast by Arnold Machin)

1967 (5 June)–**70**. *Chalk-surfaced paper. Two phosphor hands except where otherwise stated.* No wmk. P 15×14.

723	**282**	½d. orange-brown (5.2.68)	10	20
724		1d. lt olive (*shades*) (2 bands) (5.2.68)	10	10
		a. Imperf (coil strip)	£2000	
		b. Part perf pane*		
		c. Imperf pane*	£4250	
		d. Uncoated paper**	90·00	
		l. Booklet pane. No. 724×2, *se-tenant* with 730×2 (6.3.68)	3·00	
		m. Booklet pane. No. 724×4, *se-tenant* with 734×2 (6.1.69)	3·50	
		n. Booklet pane. No. 724×6, 731×6 and 735×3 *se-tenant* (1.12.69)	8·50	
		na. Uncoated paper**	£900	
725		1d. yellowish olive (1 centre band) (16.9.68)	30	35
		l. Booklet pane. No. 725×d, *se-tenant* with 732×2	4·00	
		m. Coil strip. No. 728×2, *se-tenant* with 729, 725 and 733 (27.8.69)	1·25	
726		2d. lake-brown (Type I) (2 hands) (5.2.68)	10	15
727		2d. lake-brn (Type II) (2 hands) (1969)	15	20
728		2d. lake-brown (Type II) (1 centre band) (27.8.69)	70	90
729		3d. violet (*shades*) (1 centre hand) (8.8.67)	15	10
		a. Imperf (pair)	£700	
730		3d. violet (2 bands) (6.4.68)	30	35
		a. Uncoated paper**	£2000	
731		4d. deep sepia (*shades*) (2 hands)	10	10
		b. Part perf pane*	£2500	
732		4d. dp olive-brown (*shades*) (1 centre band) (16.9.68)	10	10
		a. Part perf pane)	£1750	
		l. Booklet pane. Two stamps plus two printed labels	1·00	
733		4d. brt verm (1 centre band) (6.1.69)	10	10
		a. Tête-bêche (horiz Pair)	£3500	
		b. Uncoated paper**	6·00	
		l. Booklet pane. Two stamps plus two printed labels (3.3.69)	1·00	
734		4d. brt vermilion (1 side band) (6.1.69)	1·50	1·90
		a. Uncoated paper*	£250	
735		5d. royal blue (*shades*) (1.7.68)	10	10
		a. Imperf pane*	£2500	
		b. Part perf pane	£1300	
		c. Imperf (pair)††	£250	
		d. Uncoated paper**	20·00	
736		6d. brt reddish pur (*shades*) (5.2.68)	20	25
737	**282a**	7d. bright emerald (1.7.68)	40	35
738		8d. bright vermilion (1.7.68)	20	45
739		8d. light turquoise-blue (6.1.69)	50	60
740		9d. myrtle-green (8.8.67)	40	25
741	**282**	10d. drab (1.7.68)	50	50
		a. Uncoated paper**	25·00	
742		1s. light bluish violet (*shades*)	45	25
743		1s.6d. greenish blue and deep blue (*shades*) (8.8.67)	50	50
		a. Greenish blue omitted	80·00	
		c. Phosphorised paper. Prussian blue and indigo (10.12.69)	80	80
		ca. Prussian blue omitted	£400	
744		1s.9d. dull orange and black (*shades*)	50	45
723/44 *Set of 16*			4·00	4·00

*BOOKLET ERRORS. See note after No. 556.

**Uncoated paper. This does not respond to the chalky test, and may be further distinguished from the normal chalk-surfaced paper by the fibres which clearly show on the surface, resulting in the printing impression being rougher, and by the screening dots which are not so evident. The 1d., 4d. and 5d. come from the £1 "Stamps for Cooks" Booklet (1970); and the 3d. and 10d. from sheets (1969). The 20p. and 50p. high values (Nos. 830/1) exist with similar errors.

†No. 724a occurs in a vertical strip of four, top stamp perforated on three sides, bottom stamp imperf three sides and the two middle stamps completely imperf.

††No. 735c comes from the original state of cylinder 15 which is identifiable by the screening dots which extend through the gutters of the stamps and into the margins of the sheet. This must not be confused with imperforate stamps from cylinder 10, a large quantity of which was stolen from the printers early in 1970.

The 1d. with centre band (725) only came in the September 1968 booklets (PVA gum) and the coil strip (725m) (gum arabic); the 2d. with centre band (728) was only issued in the coil strip (725m); the 3d. (No. 730) appeared in booklets on 6.4.68 from coils during December 1968 and from sheets in January 1969; and the 4d. with one side band (734) only in 10s. (band at left) and £1 (band at left or right) booklets.

Gum. The 1d. (725), 3d. (729), 4d. (731 and 733), 9d., 1s., 1s.6d. and 1s.9d. exist with gum arabic as well as the PVA gum; the 2d. (728) and coil strip (725m) exist only with gum arabic; and the remainder exist with PVA gum only.

The 4d. (731) in shades of washed-out grey are colour changelings which we understand are caused by the concentrated solvents used in modern dry cleaning methods.

For decimal issue, sec Nos. X841, etc.

283 "Master Lambton" (Sir Thomas Lawrence)

284 "Mares and Foals in a Landscape" (George Stubbs)

285 "Children Coming Out of School" (L. S. Lowry)

(Des S. Rose)

1967 (10 July). *British Paintings. Chalk-surfaced paper. Two phosphor bands.* No wmk. P 14×14 (others).

748	**283**	4d. rose-red, lemon, brown, black, new blue and gold	10	10
		a. Gold (value and Queen's head) omitted	£300	
		b. New blue omitted	£10000	
749	**284**	9d. Venetian red, ochre, grey-black, new blue, greenish yellow and black	15	15
		a. Black (Queen's head and value) omitted	£750	
		ab. Black (Queen's head only) omitted	£1700	
750	**285**	1s.6d. greenish yellow, grey, rose, new blue grey-black and gold	25	35
		a. Gold (Queen's head) omitted	£12000	
		b. New blue omitted	£250	
		c. Grey (clouds and shading) omitted	£125	
748/50 *Set of 3*			30	50

286 *Gypsy Moth IV*

(Des M. and Sylvia Goaman)

1967 (24 July). *Sir Francis Chichester's World Voyage. Chalk-surfaced paper. Three phosphor bands.* No wmk. P 15×14.

751	**286**	1s.9d. black, brown-red, lt emer & blue	20	20

287 Radar Screen

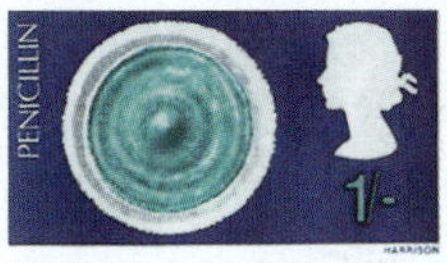

288 *Penicillium notatum*

289 Vickers VC-10 Jet Engines

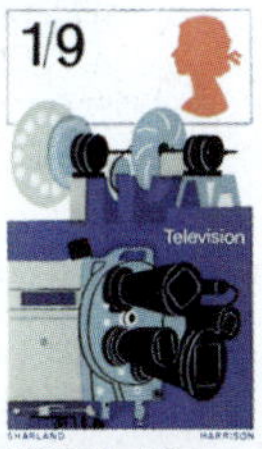

290 Television Equipment

(Des C. Abbott (4d., 1s.), Negus-Sharland team (others))

1967 (19 Sept). *British Discovery and Invention. Chalk-surfaced paper. Three phosphor bands (4d.) or two phosphor bands (others).* W **179** (sideways on 1s.9d.). P 14×15 (1s.9d.) or 15×14 (others).

752	**287**	4d. greenish yellow, black and vermilion	10	10
753	**288**	1s. blue-green, light greenish blue, slate purple and bluish violet	10	20
754	**289**	1s.6d. black, grey, royal blue, ochre and turquoise-blue	20	25
755	**290**	1s.9d. black grey-blue, pale olive-grey, violet and orange	20	30
		a. Grey-blue omitted	£4500	
752/5 *Set of 4*			50	75

WATERMARK. All issues from this date are on unwatermarked paper.

291 "The Adoption of the Sheperds" (School of Seville)

292 "Madonna and Child" (Murillo)

293 "The Adoration of the Shepherds" (Louis le Nain)

(Des S. Rose)

1967. *Christmas. Chalk-surfaced paper. One phosphor band (3d.) or two phosphor bands (others).* P 15×14 (1s.6d.) or 14×15 (others).

756	**291**	3d. ol-yell, rose, bl, blk & gold (27.11)	10	15
		a. Gold (value and Queen's head) omitted	85·00	
		b. Printed on the gummed side	£450	
		c. Rose omitted	£3250	
757	**292**	4d. bright purple, greenish yellow, new blue, grey-black and gold (18.10)	10	15
		a. Gold (value and Queen's head) omitted	75·00	
		b. Gold ("4D" only) omitted	£2750	
		c. Yellow (Child, robe and Madonna's face) omitted	£7500	
		d. Greenish yellow and gold omitted	£15000	
758	**293**	1s.6d. brt purple, bistre, lemon, black, orange-red, ultram & gold (27.11)	15	15
		a. Gold (value and Queen's head) omitted	£7500	
		ab. Gold (Queen's head only) omitted	£2000	
		b. Ultramarine omitted	£500	
		c. Lemon omitted	£18000	
756/8 *Set of 3*			30	30

Distinct shades exist of the 3d. and 4d. values but are not listable as there are intermediate shades. For the 4d. stamps from one machine show a darker background and give the appearance of the yellow colour being omitted, but this is not so and these should not be confused with the true missing yellow No. 757c.

No. 757b comes from stamps in the first vertical row of a sheet.

(Recess Bradbury, Wilkinson)

1967–68. No wmk. *White paper.* P 11×12.

759	**166**	2s.6d. black-brown (1.7.68)	30	45
760	**167**	5s. red (10.4.68)	70	75
761	**168**	10s. bright ultramarine (10.4.68)	7·75	6·25
762	**169**	£1 black (4.12.67)	7·50	6·00
759/62 *Set of 4*			15·00	12·00

PVA GUM. All the following issues from this date have PVA gum *except where footnotes state otherwise.*

294 Tarr Steps, Exmoor

295 Aberfeldy Bridge

296 Menai Bridge

297 M4 Viaduct

(Des A. Restall (9d.), L. Roseman (1s.6d.), J. Matthews (others))

1968 (29 Apr). *British Bridges. Chalk-surfaced paper. Two phosphor bands.* P 15×14.

763	**294**	4d. black, bluish violet, turq-blue & gold	10	10
		a. Printed on gummed side	30·00	
764	**295**	9d. red-brown, myrtle-green, ultramarine, olive-brown, black and gold	10	15
		a. Gold (Queen's head) omitted	£190	
		b. Ultramarine omitted	†	£6000
765	**296**	1s.6d. olive-brown, red-orange, bright green, turquoise-green and gold	15	25
		a. Gold (Queen's head) omitted	£275	
		b. Red-orange (roof tops) omitted	£325	
766	**297**	1s.9d. olive-brown, greenish yellow, dull green, deep ultramarine & gold	20	30
		a. Gold (Queen's head) omitted	£275	
763/6 *Set of 4*			50	70

No. 764b is only known on first day covers posted from Canterbury, Kent. or the Philatelic Bureau, Edinburgh.

298 "T U C" and Trades Unionists

299 Mrs. Emmeline Pankhurst (statue)

300 Sopwith Camel and English Electric Lightning Fighters

301 Captain Cook's *Endeavour* and Signature

(Des D. Gentleman (4d.), C. Abbott (others))

1968 (29 May). *British Anniversaries. Events described on stamps. Chalk-surfaced paper. Two phosphor bands.* P 15×14.

767	**298**	4d. emerald, olive, blue and black	10	10
768	**299**	9d. reddish violet, bluish grey and black	10	15
769	**300**	1s. olive-brown, bl, red, slate-bl & blk	15	15
770	**301**	1s.9d. yellow-ochre and blackish brown	35	35
767/70 *Set of 4*			50	50

302 "Queen Elizabeth I" (unknown artist)

303 "Pinkie" (Lawrence)

304 "Ruins of St. Mary Le Port" (Piper)

305 "The Hay Wain" (Constable)

(Des S. Rose)

1968 (12 Aug). *British Paintings. Queen's head embossed. Chalk-surfaced paper. Two phosphor bands.* P 15×14 (1s.9d.) or 14×15 (others).

771	**302**	4d. blk, verm, greenish yell, grey & gold	10	10
		a. Gold (value and Queen's head) omitted	£250	
		b. Vermilion omitted*	£500	
772	**303**	1s. mauve, new blue, greenish yellow, black, magenta and gold	10	20
		a. Gold (value and Queen's head) omitted	£6000	
773	**304**	1s.6d. slate, orange, black, mauve, greenish yellow, ultramarine & gold	20	25
		a. Gold (value and Queen's head) omitted	£200	
774	**305**	1s.9d. greenish yellow, black, new blue, red and gold	25	40
		a. Gold (value and Queen's head) and embossing omitted	£750	
		b. Red omitted	£12000	
771/4 *Set of 4*			50	85

*The effect of this is to leave the face and hands white and there is more yellow and olive in the costume.

The 4d., 1s. and 1s.9d. are known with the embossing only omitted. No. 774a is only known with the phosphor also omitted. No. 772a exists both with or without embossing or phosphor bands.

306 Boy and Girl with Rocking Horse

307 Girl with Doll's House

308 Boy with Train Set

(Des Rosalind Dease. Head printed in gold and then embossed)

1968 (25 Nov). *Christmas. Chalk-surfaced paper. One centre phosphor band (4d.) or two phosphor bands (others).* P 15×14 (4d.) or 14×15 (others).

775	**306**	4d. black, orange, vermilion, ultramarine, bistre and gold	10	15
		a. Gold omitted	£7000	
		b. Vermilion omitted*	£450	
		c. Ultramarine omitted	£350	
		d. Bistre omitted		
776	**307**	9d. yellow-olive. black, brown, yellow, magenta, orange, turq-green & gold	15	25
		a. Yellow omitted	£110	
		b. Turquoise-green (dress) omitted		
777	**308**	1s.6d. ultramarine. yellow-orange, brt purple. blue-green, black and gold	15	50
775/7 *Set of 3*			30	50

*The effect of the missing vermilion is shown on the rocking horse, saddle and faces which appear orange instead of red.

A single used example of the 4d. exists with the bistre omitted.

No. 775c is only known with the phosphor also omitted. All values exist with the embossing of Queen's head omitted.

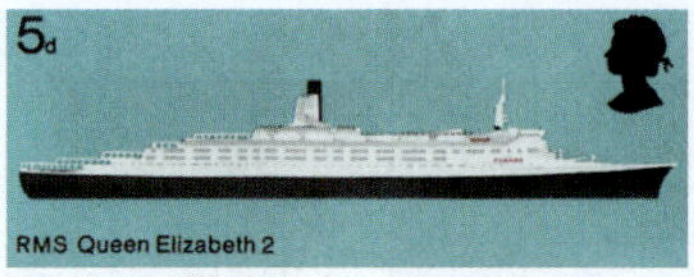

309 *Queen Elizabeth 2*

310 Elizabethan Galleon

311 East Indiaman

312 *Cutty Sark*

313 *Great Britain*

314 *Mauretania I*

(Des D. Gentleman)

1969 (15 Jan). *British Ships. Chalk-surfaced paper. Two vertical phosphor bands at right (1s.), one horizontal phosphor band (5d.) or two phosphor bands (9d.).* P 15×14.

778	**309**	5d. black, grey, red and turquoise	10	15
		a. Black Queen's head, value, (hull and inset) omitted	£1800	
		b. Grey (decks, etc.) omitted	£190	
		c. Red (inscription) omitted	£125	
779	**310**	9d. red, blue, ochre, brown, blk & grey	10	25
		a. Strip of 3. Nos. 779/81	1·25	1·50
		ab. Red and blue omitted	£3000	
		ac. Blue omitted	£3000	
780	**311**	9d. ochre, brown, black and grey	10	25
781	**312**	9d. ochre, brown, black and grey	10	25
782	**313**	1s. brown, blk, grey, grn & greenish yell	40	35
		a. Pair. Nos. 782/3	1·25	1·50
		ab. Greenish yellow omitted	£3250	
783	**314**	1s. red, black, brown, carmine and grey	40	35
		a. Carmine (hull overlay) omitted	£28000	
		b. Red (funnels) omitted	£20000	
		c. Carmine and red omitted	£20000	
778/83 *Set of 6*			2·50	3·00

The 9d. and 1s. values were arranged in horizontal strips of three and pairs respectively throughout the sheet.

No. 779ab is known only with the phosphor also omitted.

315 Concorde in Flight

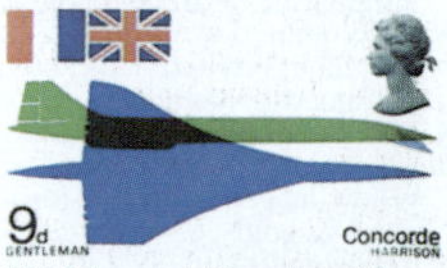

316 Plan and Elevation Views

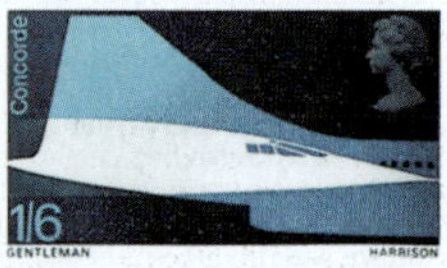

317 Concorde's Nose and Tail

(Des M. and Sylvia Goaman (4d.), D. Gentleman (9d., 1s.6d.))

1969 (3 Mar). *First Flight of Concorde. Chalk-surfaced paper. Two phosphor bands.* P 15×14.

784	**315**	4d. yellow-orange, violet, greenish blue, blue-green and pale green	25	25
		a. Violet (value, etc.) omitted	£500	
		b. Yellow-orange omitted	£500	
785	**316**	9d. ultramarine, emerald, red & grey-bl	55	75
		a. Face value and inscr omitted	£40000	
786	**317**	1s.6d. deep blue, silver-grey & lt blue	75	1·00
		a. Silver-grey omitted	£500	
784/6 *Set of 3*			1·00	1·50

No. 785a is caused by a colour shift of the grey-blue. On the only known example the top of the Queen's head appears across the perforations at foot.

No. 786a affects the Queen's head which appears in the light blue colour.

318 Queen Elizabeth II.
(See also Type **357**)

(Des after plaster cast by Arnold Machin. Recess Bradbury, Wilkinson)

1969 (5 Mar). P 12.

787	**318**	2s.6d. brown	35	30
788		5s. crimson-lake	1·75	60
789		10s. deep ultramarine	6·00	7·00
790		£1 bluish black	3·25	1·50
787/90 *Set of 4*			10·00	8·50

For decimal issue, sec Nos. 829/31b and notes after No. 831*b*.

319 Page from *Daily Mail*, and Vickers FB-27 Vimy Aircraft

320 Europa and CEPT Emblems

321 ILO Emblem

322 Flags of NATO Countries

323 Vickers FB-27 Vimy Aircraft and Globe showing Flight

(Des P. Sharland (5d., 1s., 1s.6d.), M. and Sylvia Goaman (9d., 1s.9d.))

1969 (2 Apr). *Anniversaries. Events described on stamps. Chalk-surfaced paper. Two phosphor bands.* P 15×14.

791	**319**	5d. black, pale sage-green, chestnut and new blue	10	15
792	**320**	9d. pale turq, dp bl, lt emer-grn & blk	15	25
		a. Uncoated paper*	£1800	
793	**321**	1s. bright purple, deep blue and lilac	15	25
794	**322**	1s.6d. red, royal blue, yellow-green, black, lemon and new blue	15	30
		e. Black omitted	£120	
		f. Yellow-green (from flags) omitted	80·00	
		g. Lemon (from flags) omitted	†	£4000
795	**323**	1s.9d. yellow-olive, greenish yellow and pale turquoise-green	20	40
		a. Uncoated paper*	£225	
791/5 *Set of 5*			50	1·00

*Uncoated paper. The second note after No. 744 also applies here.

No. 794g is only known used on first day cover from Liverpool.

324 Durham Cathedral

325 York Minster

326 St. Giles' Cathedral, Edinburgh

327 Canterbury Cathedral

328 St. Paul's Cathedral

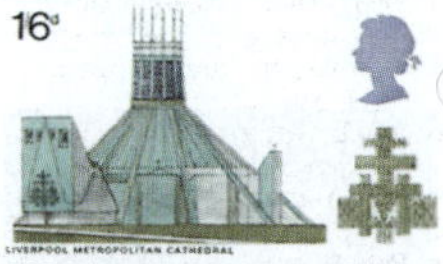

329 Liverpool Metropolitan Cathedral

(Des P. Gauld)

1969 (28 May). *British Architecture. Cathedrals. Chalk-surfaced paper. Two phosphor bands.* P. 15×14.

796	**324**	5d. grey-blk, orge, pale bluish vio & blk	10	10
		a. Block of 4. Nos. 796/9	1·10	1·25
		ab. Block of 4. Uncoated paper**	£1000	
		b. Pale bluish violet omitted	£8000	
797	**325**	5d. grey-black, pale bluish violet, new blue and black	10	10
		b. Pale bluish violet omitted	£7000	
798	**326**	5d. grey-black, purple, green and black	10	10
		c. Green omitted*	80·00	
799	**327**	5d. grey-black, green, new blue & black	10	10
800	**328**	9d. grey-blk,ochre, pale drab, vio & blk	25	30
		a. Black (value) omitted	£150	
801	**329**	1s.6d. grey-black, pale turquoise, pale reddish violet, pale yellow-ol & blk	25	35
		a. Black (value) omitted	£4500	
		b. Black (value) double		
796/801 *Set of 6*			1·10	1·50

The 5d. values were issued together *se-tenant* in blocks of four throughout the sheet.

*The missing green on the roof top is known on R. 2/5, R. 8/5 and R. 10/5, but all from different sheets, and it only occurred in part of the printing, being "probably caused by a batter on the impression cylinder". Examples are also known with the green partly omitted.

**Uncoated paper. The second note after No. 744 also applies here.

330 The King's Gate, Caernarvon Castle

331 The Eagle Tower, Caernarvon Castle

332 Queen Eleanor's Gate, Caernarvon Castle

333 Celtic Cross, Margam Abbey

334 H.R.H. The Prince of Wales (after photo by G. Argent)

(Des D. Gentleman)

1969 (1 July). *Investiture of N.R.H. The Prince of Wales. Chalk-surfaced paper. Two phosphor bands.* P 14×15.

802	**330**	5d. deep olive-grey, light olive-grey, deep grey, light grey, red, pale turquoise-green, black and silver	10	15
		a. Strip of 3. Nos. 802/4	50	1·00
		b. Black (value and inscr) omitted	£350	
		c. Red omitted*	£700	
		d. Deep grey omitted**	£275	
		e. Pale turquoise-green omitted.	£700	
		f. Light grey omitted	£10000	
803	**331**	5d. deep olive-grey, light olive-grey, deep grey, light grey, red, pale turquoise-grccn, black and silver	10	15
		b. Black (value and inscr) omitted	£350	
		c. Red omitted**	£700	
		d. Deep grey omitted**	£275	
		e. Pale turquoise-green omitted.	£700	
		f. Light grey (marks on walls, window frames, etc) omitted..	£10000	£7500
804	**332**	5d. deep olive-grey, light olive-grey, deep grey, light grey, red, pale turquoise-green, black and silver	10	15
		b. Black (value and inscr) omitted	£350	
		c. Red omitted*	£700	
		d. Deep grey omitted**	£275	
		e. Pale turquoise-green omitted.	£700	
		f. Light grey omitted	£10000	
805	**333**	9d. deep grey, light grey, black and gold	15	30
806	**334**	1s. blackish yellow-olive and gold	15	30
802/6 *Set of* 5			60	1·20

The 5d. values were issued together, *se-tenant*, in strips of three throughout the sheet.

*The 5d. value is also known with the red misplaced downwards and where this occurs the red printing does not take very well on the silver background and in some cases is so faint that it could be mistaken for a missing red. However, the red can be seen under a magnifying glass and caution should therefore be exercised when purchasing copies of Nos. 802/4c.

**The deep grey affects the dark portions of the windows and doors.

No. 803f is only known commercially used on cover.

335 Mahatma Gandhi

(Des B. Mullick)

1969 (13 Aug). *Gandhi Centenary Year. Chalk-surfaced paper. Two phosphor bands.* P 15×14.

807	**335**	1s.6d. black, green, red-orange & grey	30	30
		a. Printed on the gummed side..	£750	

336 National Giro "G" Symbol

337 Telecommunications—International Subscriber Dialling

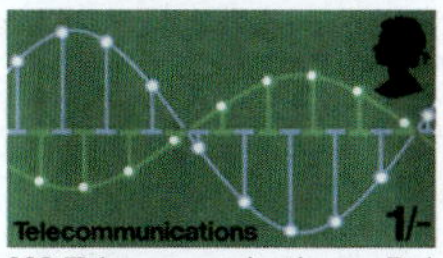

338 Telecommunications—Pulse Code Modulation

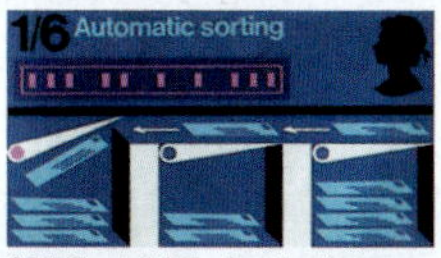

339 Postal Mechanisation—Automatic Sorting

(Des D. Gentleman. Litho De La Rue)

1969 (1 Oct). *Post Office Technology Commemoration. Chalk-surfaced paper. Two phosphor bands.* P 13½×14.

808	**336**	5d. new bl, greenish bl, lavender & blk	10	10
809	**337**	9d. emerald, violet-blue and black	20	25
810	**338**	1s. emerald, lavender and black..	20	25
811	**339**	1s.6d. brt purple, lt blue, grey-bl & blk	25	50
808/11 *Set of* 4			70	1·00

340 Herald Angel

341 The Three Shepherds

342 The Three Kings

(Des F. Wegner. Queen's head (and stars 4d., 5d. and scroll-work 1s.6d.) printed in gold and then embossed)

1969 (26 Nov). *Christmas. Chalk-surfaced paper. Two phosphor bands (5d., 1s.6d.) or one centre band (4d.).* P 15×14.

812	**340**	4d. vermilion, new blue, orange, bright purple, light green, bluish violet, blackish brown and gold	10	10
		a. Gold (Queen's head etc.) omitted	£6500	
813	**341**	5d. magenta, light blue, royal blue, olive-brown, green, greenish yellow, red and gold.	15	15
		a. Light blue (sheep, etc) omitted	90·00	
		b. Red omitted*	£1800	
		c. Gold (Queen's head) omitted	£700	
		d. Green omitted	£350	
		e. Olive-brown, red and gold omitted	£14000	
814	**342**	1s.6d. greenish yell, bright purple, bluish violet, deep slate, orange, green, new blue and gold	20	20
		a. Gold (Queen's head etc.) omitted	£140	
		b. Deep slate (value) omitted	£425	
		c. Greenish yellow omitted	£400	
		e. New blue omitted	£100	
812/14 *Set of* 3			30	30

*The effect of the missing red is shown on the hat, leggings and purse which appear as dull orange.

The 5d. and 1s.6d. values are known with the embossing omitted.

No. 813e was caused by a paper fold and also shows the phosphor omitted.

Used copies of the 5d. have been seen with the olive-brown or greenish yellow (tunic at left) omitted.

343 Fife Harling

344 Cotswold Limestone

345 Welsh Stucco

346 Ulster Thatch

(Des D. Gentleman (5d., 9d.), Sheila Robinson (1s., 1s.6d.))

1970 (11 Feb). *British Rural Architecture. Chalk-surfaced paper. Two phosphor bands.* P 15×14.

815	**343**	5d. grey, grey-blk, blk, lemon, greenish blue, orange-brown, ultram & grn	10	10
		a. Lemon omitted	£110	
		b. Grey (Queen's head and cottage shading) omitted	£9000	
		c. Greenish blue (door) omitted	†	£3500
		d. Grey-black (inscription and face value) omitted	£14000	
		e. Grey-black (face value only) omitted	£14000	
816	**344**	9d. orange-brown, olive-yellow, bright green, black, grey-black and grey	10	25
817	**345**	1s. dp bl, reddish lilac, drab & new bl	15	25
		a. New blue omitted	£110	
818	**346**	1s.6d. greenish yell, blk, turq-bl & lilac	20	40
		a. Turquoise-blue omitted	£13000	
815/18 *Set of* 4			50	75

Used examples of the 5d. exist, one of which is on piece, with the greenish blue colour omitted.

347 Signing the Declaration of Arbroath

348 Florence Nightingale attending Patients

349 Signing of International Co-operative Alliance

350 Pilgrims and *Mayflower*

351 Sir William Herschel, Francis Baily, Sir John Herschel and Telescope

(Des F. Wegner (5d., 9d., and 1s.6d.), Marjorie Saynor (1s., 1s.9d.). Queen's head printed in gold and then embossed)

1970 (1 Apr). *Anniversaries. Events described on stamps. Chalk-surfaced paper. Two phosphor bands.* P 15×14.

819	**347**	5d. blk yell-olive, blue, emer, greenish yellow, rose-red, gold & orange-red	10	10
		a. Gold (Queen's head) omitted	£1800	
		b. Emerald omitted	£400	
820	**348**	9d. ochre, deep blue, carmine, black, blue-green, yellow-olive, gold & blue	15	15
		a. Ochre omitted	£425	

821	**349**	1s. green, greenish yellow, brown, black, cerise, gold and light blue	20	25
		a. Gold (Queen's head) omitted	85·00	
		c. Green omitted	£140	
		d. Brown omitted	£275	
822	**350**	1s.6d. greenish yellow, carmine, deep yellow-olive, emerald, black, blue gold and sage-green	20	30
		a. Gold (Queen's head) omitted	£250	
		b. Emerald omitted	£140	
823	**351**	1s.9d. blk, slate, lemon, gold & brt pur	25	30
		a. Lemon (trousers and document) omitted	£8500	
819/23 *Set of 5*			75	1·00

The 9d., 1s. and 1s.6d. are known with the embossing omitted. No. 821c also exists with embossing omitted.

No. 823a is known mint, or used on first day cover postmarked London WC.

352 "Mr. Pickwick and Sam" (*Pickwick Papers*)

353 "Mr. and Mrs. Micawber" (*David Copperfield*)

354 David Copperfield and Betsy Trotwood" (*David Copperfield*)

355 "Oliver asking for more" (*Oliver Twist*)

356 "Grasmere" (from engraving by J. Farrington, R.A.)

T **352/5** were issued together *se-tenant* in blocks of four throughout the sheet.

(Des Rosalind Dease. Queen's head printed in gold and then embossed)

1970 (3 June). *Literary Anniversaries. Death Centenary of Charles Dickens (novelist) (5d.×4) and Birth Bicentenary of William Wordsworth (poet) (1s.6d.). Chalk-surfaced paper. Two phosphor bands.* P 14×15.

824	**352**	5d. black, orange, silver, gold and mag	10	25
		a. Block of 4. Nos. 824/7	75	1·50
		ab. Imperf (block of four)	£1250	
		ac. Silver (inscr) omitted	£32000	
825	**353**	5d. black, magenta, silver, gold & orge	10	25
826	**354**	5d. black, light greenish blue, silver, gold and yellow-bistre	10	25
		b. Yellow-bistre (value) omitted	£6000	
827	**355**	5d. black, yellow-bistre, silver, gold and light greenish blue	10	25
		b. Yell-bistre (background) omitted	£10000	
		c. Lt greenish blue (value) omitted*	£750	
		d. Light greenish blue and silver (inscr at foot) omitted	£16000	
828	**356**	1s.6d. light yellow-olive, black, silver, gold and bright blue	25	50
		a. Gold (Queen's head) omitted	£4500	
		b. Silver ("Grasmere") omitted	£225	
		c. Bright blue (face value) omitted	£14000	
824/8 *Set of 5*			1·00	1·50

*No 827c (unlike No. 827b) comes from a sheet on which the colour was only partially omitted so that, although No. 827 was completely without the light greenish blue colour, it was still partially present on No. 826.

The 1s.6d. is known with embossing omitted.

Essays exist of Nos. 824/7 showing the Queen's head in silver and with different inscriptions.

357 (Value redrawn)

(Des after plaster cast by Arnold Machin. Recess B.W.)

1970 (17 June)–**72**. *Decimal Currency. Chalk-surfaced paper or phosphorised paper (10p.).* P 12.

829	**357**	10p. cerise	50	75
830		20p. olive-green	60	25
831		50p. deep ultramarine	1·50	40
831*b*		£1 bluish black (6.12.72)	3·50	80
829/316 *Set of 4*			6·00	2·00

The 20p. and 50p. exist on thinner, uncoated paper and are listed in the *Great Britain Concise Catalogue*.

A whiter paper was introduced in 1973. The £1 appeared on 27 Sept. 1973, the 20p. on 30 Nov. 1973 and the 50p. on 20 Feb. 1974.

The 50p. was issued on 1 Feb. 1973 on phosphorised paper. This cannot be distinguished from No. 831 with the naked eye.

The £1, T **318**, was also issued, on 17 June 1970, in sheets of 100 (10×10) instead of panes of 40 (8×5) but it is not easy to distinguish from No. 790 in singles. It can be readily differentiated when in large strips or marginal pieces showing sheet markings or plate numbers.

358 Runners

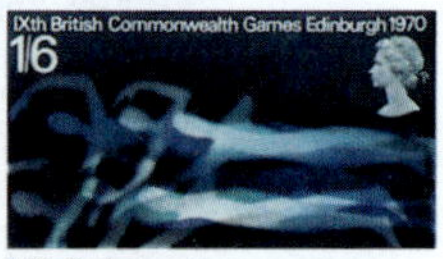

359 Swimmers

360 Cyclists

(Des A. Restall. Litho D.L.R.)

1970 (15 July). *Ninth British Commonwealth Games. Chalk-surfaced paper. Two phosphor bands.* P 13½×14.

832	**358**	5d. pk, emer, greenish yell & dp yell-grn	25	25
		a. Greenish yellow omitted	£18000	
833	**359**	1s.6d. light greenish blue, lilac, bistre brown and Prussian blue	50	50
834	**360**	1s.9d. yellow-orange, lilac, salmon and deep red-brown	50	50
832/4 *Set of 3*			75	75

361 1d. Black (1840)

362 1s. Green (1847)

363 4d. Carmine (1855)

(Des D. Gentleman)

1970 (18 Sept). *"Philympia 70" Stamp Exhibition. Chalk-surfaced paper. Two phosphor bands.* P 14×14½.

835	**361**	5d. grey-black, brownish bistre, black and dull purple	25	10
		a. Grey-black (Queen's head) omitted		
836	**362**	9d. light drab, bluish green, stone, black and dull purple	25	30
837	**363**	1s.6d. carmine, lt drab, blk & dull pur	25	45
835/7 *Set of 3*			50	75

364 Shepherds and Apparition of the Angel

365 Mary, Joseph, and Christ in the Manger

366 The Wise Men bearing gifts

(Des Sally Stiff after De Lisle Psalter. Queen's head printed in gold and then embossed)

1970 (25 Nov). *Christmas. Chalk-surfaced paper. One centre phosphor band (4d.) or two phosphor bands (others).* P 14×15.

838	**364**	4d. brown-red, turquoise-green, pale chestnut, brn, grey-blk, gold & verm	15	10
839	**365**	5d. emerald, gold, blue, brown-red, ochre, grey-black and violet	15	15
		a. Gold (Queen's head) omitted	†	£3500
		b. Emerald omitted	95·00	
		c. Imperf (pair)	£375	
840	**366**	1s.6d. gold, grey-black, pale turq-grn, salmon, ultram, ochre & yellow-grn	25	30
		a. Salmon omitted	£140	
		b. Ochre omitted	95·00	
838/40 *Set of 3*			50	50

The 4d. and 5d. are known with embossing omitted, and the 1s.6d. is known with embossing and phosphor omitted.

REGIONAL ISSUES

For Regional issues of Guernsey and Jersey, *see* after Great Britain Postal Fiscals

Printers (£ s. d. stamps of all regions);—Photo Harrison & Sons. Portrait by Dorothy Wilding Ltd.

DATES OF ISSUE. Conflicting dates of issue have been announced for some of the regional issues, partly explained by the stamps being released on different dates by the Philatelic Bureau in Edinburgh or the Philatelic Counter in London and in the regions. We have adopoted the practice of giving the earliest known dates, since once released the stamps could have been used anywhere in the U.K.

I. ISLE OF MAN

1

2

(Des J. Nicholson. Portrait by Dorothy Wilding Ltd. Photo Harrison)

1958 (18 Aug)–**68**. W **179**. P 15×14.

1	**1**	2½d. carmine-red (8.6.64)	50	1·25
2	**2**	3d. deep lilac	50	20
		a. Chalk-surfaced paper (17.5.63)	12·00	12·00
		p. One centre phosphor band (27.6.68)	20	50
3		4d. ultramarine (7.2.66)	1·50	1·50
		p. Two phosphor bands (5.7.67)	20	30
1/3p *Set of 3*			80	1·60

No. 2a was released in London sometime after 17 May 1963, this being the date of issue in Douglas.

1968–69. *No wmk. Chalk-surfaced paper. PVA gum. One centre phosphor band (Nos. 5/6) or two phosphor bands (others).* P 15×14.

4	**2**	4d. blue (24.6.68)	25	30
5		4d. olive-sepia (4.9.68)	25	30
6		4d. bright vermilion (26.2.69)	45	75
7		5d. royal blue (4.9.68)	45	75
4/7 *Set of 4*			1·25	2·00

II. NORTHERN IRELAND

N 1

N 2

N 3

(Des W. Hollywood (3d., 4d., 5d.), L. Pilton (6d., 9d.), T. Collins (1s.3d., 1s.6d.))

1958–67. W **179**. P 15×14.

NI1	**N 1**	3d. deep lilac (18.8.58)	15	10
		p. One centre phosphor band (9.6.67)	15	15
NI2		4d. ultramarine (7.2.66)	15	15
		p. Two phosphor bands (10.67)	15	15
NI3	**N 2**	6d. deep claret (29.9.58)	30	30
NI4		9d. bronze-green (2 phosphor bands) (1.3.67)	30	70
NI5	**N 3**	1s.3d. green (29.9.58)	30	70
NI6		1s.6d. grey-blue (2 phosphor bands) (1 .3.67)	30	70

1968–69. No wmk. *Chalk-surfaced paper. One centre phosphor band (Nos. NI8/9) or two phosphor bands (others).* P 15×14.

NI7	**N 1**	4d. deep bright blue (27.6.68)	15	15

NI8		4d. olive-sepia (4.9.68)	15	15
NI9		4d. bright vermilion (26.2.69)	20	20
NI10		5d. royal blue (4.9.68)	20	20
NI11	N 3	1s.6d. grey-blue (20.5.69)	2·25	2·50

No. N17 was only issued in Northern Ireland with gum arabic. After it had been withdrawn from Northern Ireland but whilst still on sale at the philatelic counters elsewhere, about fifty sheets with PVA gum were sold over the London Philatelic counter on 23 October 1968, and some were also on sale at the British Philatelic Exhibition Post Office in October, without any prior announcement. The other values exist with PVA gum only.

III. SCOTLAND

S 1

S 2

S 3

(Des G. Huntly (3d., 4d., 5d), J. Fleming (6d., 9d.), A. Imrie (1s.3d., 1s.6d.))

1958–67. W **179**. P 15×14.

S1	S 1	3d. deep lilac (18.8.58)	15	15
		p. Two phosphor bands (29.1.63)	13·00	2·75
		pa. One side phosphor band (30.4.65)	20	25
		pb. One centre phosphor band (9.11.67)	20	25
S2		4d. ultramarine (7.2.66)	15	15
		p. Two phosphor bands	15	15
S3	S 2	6d. deep claret (29.9.58)	20	15
		p. Two phosphor bands (29.1.63)	20	20
S4		9d. bronze-green (2 phosphor bands) (1.3.67)	35	40
S5	S 3	1s.3d. green (29.9.58)	40	40
		p. Two phosphor bands (29.1.63)	40	40
S6		1s.6d. grey-blue (2 phosphor bands) (1.3.67)	45	50

The one phosphor band on No. S1pa was produced by printing broad phosphor bands across alternate vertical perforations. Individual stamps show the band at right or left (same prices either way).

1967–70. No wmk. *Chalk-surfaced paper. One centre phosphor band (S7, S9/10) or two phosphor bands (others).* P 15×14.

S7	S 1	3d. deep lilac (16.5.68)	10	15
S8		4d. deep bright blue (28.11.67)	10	15
S9		4d. olive-sepia (4.9.68)	10	10
S10		4d. bright vermilion (26.2.69)	10	10
S11		5d. royal blue (4.9.68)	20	10
S12	S 2	9d. bronze-green (28.9.70)	6·00	6·00
S13	S 3	1s.6d. grey-blue (12.12.68)	1·75	1·50

Nos. S7/8 exist with both gum arabic and PVA gum; others with PVA gum only.

IV. WALES

From the inception of the Regional stamps, the Welsh versions were tendered to members of the public at all Post Offices within the former County of Monmouthshire but the national alternatives were available on request. By August 1961 the policy of "dual stocking" of definitive stamps was only maintained at Abergavenny, Chepstow, Newport and Pontypool. Offices with a Monmouthshire postal address but situated outside the County, namely Beachley, Brockweir, Redbrook, Sedbury, Tutshill, Welsh Newton and Woodcroft, were not supplied with the Welsh Regional stamps.

W 1

W 2

W 3

(Des R. Stone)

1958–67. W **179**. P 15×14.

W1	W 1	3d. deep lilac (18.8.58)	15	15
		p. One centre phosphor band (16.5.67)	20	15
W2		4d. ultramarine (7.2.66)	20	15
		p. Two phosphor bands (10.67)	20	15
W3	W 2	6d. deep claret (29.9.58)	35	30
W4		9d. bronze-green (2 phosphor bands) (1.3.67)	40	35
W5	W 3	1s.3d. green (29.9.58)	40	40
W6		1s.6d. grey-blue (2 phosphor bands) (1.3.67)	40	40

1967–69. No wmk. *Chalk-surfaced paper. One centre phosphor band (W 7, W 9/10) or two phosphor bands (others).* P 15×14.

W7	W 1	3d. deep lilac (6.12.67)	10	15
W8		4d. ultramarine (21.6.68)	10	15
W9		4d. olive-sepia (4.9.68)	15	15
W10		4d. bright vermilion (26.2.69)	15	15
W11		5d. royal blue (4.9.68)	15	15
W12	W 3	1s.6d. grey-blue (1.8.69)	3·50	3·50

The 3d. exists with gum arabic only; the remainder with PVA gum only.

STAMP BOOKLETS

For a full listing of Great Britain stamp booklets see the *Great Britain Concise Catalogue* published each Spring.

POSTAGE DUE STAMPS

PERFORATIONS. All postage due stamps to No. D39 are perf 14×15.

D1

D2

(Des G. Eve. Typo Somerset House (early trial printings of ½d., 1d., 2d. and 5d.; all printings of 1s.) or Harrison (later printings of all values except 1s.)).

1914 (20 Apr)–**22**. W **100** (Simple Cypher) sideways.

D1	D 1	½d. emerald	50	25
D2		1d. carmine	50	25
		a. Pale carmine	75	50
D3		1½d. chestnut (1922)	48·00	20·00
D4		2d. agate	50	25
D5		3d. violet (1918)	5·00	75
		a. Bluish violet	6·00	2·75
D6		4d. dull grey-green (12.20)	18·00	5·00
D7		5d. brownish cinnamon	7·00	3·50
D8		1s. bright blue (1915)	40·00	5·00
		a. Deep bright blue	40·00	5·00
D1/8 *Set of* 8			£100	32·00

The 1d. is known bisected from various offices between 1914 and 1924, the 2d. bisected for use as a 1d. between 1918 and 1923, the 3d. bisected for use as a 1½d. in 1922 at Warminster and trisected for use as a 1d. in 1921 at Malvern.

(Typo Waterlow)

1924. *As 1914–22, but on thick chalk-surfaced paper.*

D9	D 1	1d. carmine	6·00	6·00

(Typo Waterlow and (from 1934) Harrison)

1924–31. W **111** (Block Cypher) sideways.

D10	D 1	½d. emerald (6.25)	1·25	75
D11		1d. carmine (4.25)	60	25
D12		1½d. chestnut (10.24)	47·00	22·00
D13		2d. agate (7.24)	1·00	25
D14		3d. dull violet (10.24)	1·50	25
		a. Printed on gummed side	£125	†
		b. Experimental paper W **111***a*	55·00	35·00
D15		4d. dull grey-green (10.24)	15·00	4·25
D16		5d. brownish cinnamon (1.31)	65·00	45·00
D17		1s. deep blue (9.24)	8·50	50
D18	D 2	2s.6d. purple/*yellow* (5.24)	85·00	1·75
D10/18 *Set of* 9			£200	60·00

The 1d. is known bisected from various offices between 1925 and 1932 and the 2d. exists bisected to make up the 2½d. rate at Perranwell Station, Cornwall, in 1932.

1936–37. W **125** (E 8 R) sideways.

D19	D 1	½d. emerald (6.37)	12·00	10·50
D20		1d. carmine (5.37)	2·00	1·75
D21		2d. agate (5.37)	12·00	12·00
D22		3d. dull violet (3.37)	2·00	2·00
D23		4d. dull grey-green (12.36)	50·00	34·00
D24		5d. brownish cinnamon (11.36)	75·00	30·00
		a. Yellow-brown (1937)	33·00	28·00
D25		1s. deep blue (12.36)	16·00	8·50
D26	D 2	2s.6d. purple/*yellow* (5.37)	£325	12·00
D19/26 *Set of* 8 (*cheapest*)			£450	90·00

The 1d. is known bisected at Solihull in 1937.

1937–38. W **127** (G VI R) sideways.

D27	D 1	½d. emerald (5.38)	13·00	3·75
D28		1d. carmine (5.38)	3·00	50
D29		2d. agate (5.38)	2·75	30
D30		3d. violet (12.37)	10·50	30
D31		4d. dull grey-green (9.37)	£110	10·00
D32		5d. yellow-brown (11.38)	16·50	75
D33		1s. deep blue (10.37)	78·00	75
D34	D 2	2s.6d. purple/*yellow* (9.38)	85·00	1·25
D27/34 *Set of* 8			£260	18·00

The 2d. is known bisected at various offices between 1951 and 1954.

DATES OF ISSUE. The dates for Nos. D35/9 are those on which stamps were first issued by the Supplies Department to postmasters.

1951–52. *Colours changed and new value (1½d.).* W **127** (G VI R) sideways.

D35	D 1	½d. yellow-orange (18.9.51)	3·50	3·50
		a. Bright orange	25·00	
D36		1d. violet-blue (6.6.51)	1·50	75
D37		1½d. green (11.2.52)	2·00	2·00
D38		4d. blue (14.8.51)	50·00	22·00
D39		1s. ochre (6.12.51)	28·00	5·25
D35/9 *Set of* 5			75·00	28·00

The 1d. is known bisected at Capel, Dorking in 1952 and at Camberley in 1954.

1954–55. *W* **153** *(Mult Tudor Crown and E 2 R) sideways.*

D40	D 1	½d. orange (8.6.55)	7·00	5·25
D41		2d. agate (28.7.55)	26·00	23·00
D42		3d. violet (4.5.55)	75·00	60·00
D43		4d. blue (14.7.55)	26·00	32·00
		a. Imperf (pair)	£250	
D44		5d. yellow-brown (19.5.55)	20·00	20·00
D45	D 2	2s.6d. purple/*yellow* (11.54)	£150	5·75
D40/5 *Set of* 6			£250	£120

1955–57. *W* **165** *(Mult St. Edward's Crown and E 2 R) sideways.*

D46	D 1	½d. orange (16.7.56)	2·75	3·25
D47		1d. violet-blue (7.6.56)	5·00	1·50
D48		1½d. green (13.2.56)	8·50	7·00
D49		2d. agate (22.5.56)	45·00	3·50
D50		3d. violet (5.3.56)	6·00	1·50
D51		4d. blue (24.4.56)	25·00	6·00
D52		5d. brown-ochre (23.3.56)	26·00	20·00
D53		1s. ochre (22.11.55)	65·00	2·25
D54	D 2	2s.6d. purple/*yellow* (28.6.57)	£200	8·25
D55		5s. scarlet/*yellow* (25.1 1.55)	£150	32·00
D46/55 *Set of* 10			£425	65·00

The 1d. is known bisected in September 1956 and June 1957, the 2d. in June and July 1956, the 3d. in May 1957 (London S.E.D.O.) and the 4d. in December 1958 (Poplar).

1959–63. *W* **179** *(Mult St. Edward's Crown) sideways.*

D56	D 1	½d. orange (18.10.61)	15	1·25
D57		1d. violet-blue (9.5.60)	15	50
D58		1½d. green (5.10.60)	2·50	2·50
D59		2d. agate (14.9.59)	1·10	50
D60		3d. violet (24.3.59)	30	30
D61		4d. blue (17.12.59)	30	30
D62		5d. yellow-brown (6.11.61)	45	60
D63		6d. purple (29.3.62)	50	30
D64		1s. ochre (11 .4.60)	90	30
D65	D 2	2s.6d. purple/*yellow* (11.5.61)	3·00	50
D66		5s. scarlet/*yellow* (8.5.61)	8·25	1·00
D67		10s. blue/*yellow* (2.9.63)	11·50	5·75
D68		£1 black/*yellow* (2.9.63)	45·00	8·25
D56/68 *Set of* 13			70·00	20·00

Whiter paper. The note after No. 586 also applies to Postage Due stamps.

The 1d. is known bisected at various offices between November 1961 and July 1964.

1968–69. *Typo.* No wmk. *Chalk-surfaced paper.*

D69	D 1	2d. agate (11.4.68)	75	1·00
D70		3d. violet (9.9.68)	1·00	1·00
D71		4d. blue (6.5.68)	1·00	1·00
D72		5d. orange-brown (3.1.69)	8·00	11·00
D73		6d. purple (9.9.68)	2·25	1·75
D74		1s. ochre (19.11.68)	4·00	2·50
D69/74 *Set of* 6			17·00	20·00

The 2d. and 4d. exist with gum arabic and PVA gum; remainder with PVA gum only.

1968–69. *Photo.* No wmk. *Chalk-surfaced paper. PVA gum.*

D75	D 1	4d. blue (12.6.69)	7·00	6·75
D76		8d. red (3.10.68)	50	1·00

Nos. D75/6 are smaller, 21½×17½ mm.

Both values are known bisected, the 4d. in April 1970 (Northampton) and the 8d. in October 1968 (Kilburn, London NW).

D 3

D 4

(Des J. Matthews. Photo Harrison)

1970 (17 June)–**75**. *Decimal Currency. Chalk-surfaced paper.*

D77	D 3	½p. turquoise-blue (15.2.71)	15	2·50
D78		1p. deep reddish purple (15.2.71)	15	15
D79		2p. myrtle-green (15.2.71)	20	15
D80		3p. ultramarine (15.2.71)	20	15
D81		4p. yellow-brown (15.2.71)	25	15
D82		5p. violet (15.2.71)	25	15
D83		7p. red-brown (21.8.74)	35	1·00
D84	D 4	10p. carmine	30	30
D85		11p. slate-green (18.6.75)	50	1·00
D86		20p. olive-brown	60	25
D87		50p. ultramarine	2·00	1·25
D88		£1 black	4·00	1·00
D89		£5 orange-yellow and black (2.4.73)	36·00	1·50
D77/89 *Set of* 13			40·00	7·75

Later printings were on fluorescent white paper, some with dextrin added to the PVA gum (see notes after X1058 of Great Britain).

The 2p. was bisected at Exeter on 25 October 1977.

OFFICIAL STAMPS

In 1840 the 1d. black (Type **1**), with "V R" in the upper corners, was prepared for official use, but never issued for postal purposes. Obliterated specimens are those which were used for experimental trials of obliterating inks, or those that passed through the post by oversight.

V1

1840. *Prepared for use but not issued; "V" "R" in upper corners. Imperf.*

			Un	Used	Used on cover
V1	V 1	1d. black	£25000	£28000	

The following Official stamps would be more correctly termed Departmental stamps as they were exclusively for the use of certain government departments. Until 1882 official mail used ordinary postage stamps purchased at post offices, the cash being refunded once a quarter. Later the government departments obtained Official stamps by requisition. Official stamps were on sale to the public for a short time at Somerset House but they were not sold from post offices. The system of only supplying the Government departments was open to abuse so that all Official stamps were withdrawn on 13 May 1904.

OVERPRINTS, PERFORATIONS, WATERMARKS. All Official stamps were overprinted by Thomas De La Rue & Co. and are perf 14. They are on Crown watermarked paper unless otherwise stated.

INLAND REVENUE

These stamps were used by revenue officials in the provinces, mail to and from Head Office passing without a stamp. The London Office used these stamps only for foreign mail.

I.R. OFFICIAL (O 1) — I. R. OFFICIAL (O 2)

Optd with Types O **1** (½d. to 1s.) or O **2** (others)

1882–1901. *Stamps of Queen Victoria.*

(a) Issues of 1880–81.

O 1	½d. deep green (1.11.82)	£110	40·00	80·00
O 2	½d. pale green	70·00	28·00	
O 3	1d. lilac (Die II) (1.10.82)	4·50	2·25	22·00
	a. Optd in blue-black	£200	75·00	
	b. "OFFICIAL" omitted	—	£8500	
O 4	6d. grey (Plate 18) (3.11.82)	£450	£110	

No. O3 with the lines of the overprint transposed is an essay.

(b) Issues of 1884–1888.

O 5	½d. slate-blue (8.5.85)	70·00	24·00	£100
O 6	2½d. lilac (12.3.85)	£400	£150	£1000
O 7	1s. dull green (12.3.85)	£5000	£1500	
O 8	5s. rose (*blued paper*) (wmk Anchor) (12.3.85)	£10000	£4250	
O 9	5s. rose (wmk Anchor) (3.90)	£5000	£1600	
	a. Raised stop after "R"	£5500	£2000	
	b. Optd in blue-black	£6500	£2000	
O 9*c*	10s. cobalt (*blued paper*) (wmk Anchor) (12.3.85)	£22000	£7000	
O 9*d*	10s. ultramarine (*blued paper*) (wmk Anchor) (12.3.85)	£17000	£5500	
O10	10s. ultram (wmk Anchor) (3.90)	£7500	£2500	
	a. Raised stop after "R"	£8500	£3250	
	b. Optd in blue-black	£8500	£3250	
O11	£1 brown-lilac (wmk Crowns) (12.3.85)	£55000	£22000	
	a. Frame broken	£60000		
	b. Optd in blue-black	£150000		
O12	£1 brown-lilac (wmk Orbs) (3.90)	£80000	£30000	
	a. Frame broken	£90000		

(c) issues of 1887–92.

O13	½d. vermilion (15.5.88)	9·00	3·25	65·00
	a. Without "I.R."	£4500		
	b. Imperf	£3500		
	c. Opt double (imperf)	£4500		
O14	2½d. purple/*blue* (2.92)	£120	15·00	£325
O15	1s. dull green (9.89)	£750	£250	£2800
O16	£1 green (6.92)	£9000	£2200	
	a. No stop after "R"	—	£3000	
	b. Frame broken	£16000	£4500	

Nos. O3, O13, O15 and O16 may be found showing worn impressions of the overprints with thicker letters.

(d) Issues of 1887 and 1900.

O17	½d. blue-green (4.01)	15·00	10·00	£250
O18	6d. purple/*rose-red* (1.7.01)	£325	90·00	
O19	1s. green and carmine (12.01)	£3500	£1250	

*O1/19 **For well-centred, lightly used +35%.**

1902–04. *Stamps of King Edward VII. Ordinary paper.*

O20	½d. blue-green (4.2.02)	24·00	3·25	£120
O21	1d. scarlet (4.2.02)	17·00	2·25	80·00
O22	2½d. ultramarine (19.2.02)	£900	£250	
O23	6d. pale dull purple (14.3.04)	£250000	£150000	
O24	1s. dull green and carmine (29.4.02)	£3500	£700	
O25	5s. bright carmine (29.4.02)	£14000	£8000	
	a. Raised stop after "R"	£17000	£9000	
O26	10s. ultramarine (29.4.02)	£85000	£35000	
	a. Raised stop after "R"	£95000	£40000	
O27	£1 dull blue-green (29.4.02)	£55000	£22000	

OFFICE OF WORKS

These were issued to Head and Branch (local) offices in London and to Branch (local) offices at Birmingham, Bristol, Edinburgh, Glasgow, Leeds, Liverpool, Manchester and Southampton. The overprints on stamps of value 2d. and upwards were created later in 1902, the 2d. for registration fees and the rest for overseas mail.

O. W. OFFICIAL (O 3)

Optd with Type O **3**

1896 (24 Mar)–**02**. *Stamps of Queen Victoria.*

O31	½d. vermilion	£225	£110	£550
O32	½d. blue-green (2.02)	£325	£160	
O33	1d. lilac (Die II)	£375	£110	£600
O34	5d. dull purple and blue (II) (29.4.02)	£2800	£1000	
O35	10d. dull purple and carmine (28.5.02)	£4800	£1500	

1902 (11 Feb)–**03**. *Stamps of King Edward VII. Ordinary paper.*

O36	½d. blue-green (2.02)	£550	£160	£1600
O37	1d. scarlet	£550	£160	£400
O38	2d. yellowish green and carmine-red (27.4.02)	£1600	£400	£2750
O39	2½d. ultramarine (29.4.02)	£2500	£600	£4000
O40	10d. dull purple & carmine (28.5.03)	£28000	£6000	

*O31/40 **For well-centred, lightly used +25%.**

ARMY

Letters to and from the War Office in London passed without postage. The overprinted stamps were distributed to District and Station Paymasters nationwide, including Cox and Co., the Army Agents, who were paymasters to the Household Division.

ARMY OFFICIAL (O 4) — ARMY OFFICIAL (O 5) — ARMY OFFICIAL (O 6)

1896 (1 Sept)–**01**. *Stamps of Queen Victoria optd with Type* O **4** *(½d., 1d.) or* O**5** *(2½d., 6d.).*

O41	½d. vermilion	5·00	2·50	45·00
	a. "OFFICIAI" (R. 13/7)	£225	£100	
	b. Lines of opt transposed	£3000		
O42	½d. blue-green (6.00)	4·50	7·75	
O43	1d. lilac (Die II)	4·00	2·75	70·00
	a. "OFFICIAI" (R. 13/7)	£180	£110	
O44	2½d. purple/*blue*	32·00	22·00	£500
O45	6d. purple/*rose-red* (20.9.01)	80·00	45·00	£1100

Nos. O41a and O43a occur on sheets overprinted by Forme 1.

1902–03. *Stamps of King Edward VII optd with Type* O **4** *(Nos. O48/50) or Type* O**6** *(No. O52). Ordinary paper.*

O48	½d. blue-green (11.2.02)	5·50	2·25	£100
O49	1d. scarlet (11.2.02)	5·50	2·25	£100
	a. "ARMY" omitted	†	—	
O50	6d. pale dull purple (23.8.02)	£160	75·00	
O52	6d. pale dull purple (12.03)	£2500	£1000	

GOVERNMENT PARCELS

These stamps were issued to all departments, including the Head Office, for use on parcels weighing over 3 lb. Below this weight government parcels were sent by letter post to avoid the 55% of the postage paid from accruing to the railway companies, as laid down by parcel-post regulations. Most government parcels stamps suffered heavy postmarks in use.

GOVT PARCELS (O 7)

Optd as Type O **7**

1883 (1 Aug)–**86**. *Stamps of Queen Victoria.*

		Un	*Used**
O61	1½d. lilac (1.5.86)	£325	65·00
	a. No dot under "T"	£650	£120
	b. Dot to left of "T"	£650	£120
O62	6d. dull green (1.5.86)	£2500	£1000
O63	9d. dull green	£2100	£800
O64	1s. orange-brown (wmk Crown, Pl 13)	£1300	£225
	a. No dot under "T"	£20000	£350
	b. Dot to left of "T"	£2000	£350
O64*c*	1s. orange-brown (Pl 14)	£2750	£400
	ca. No dot under "T"	£3250	£600
	cb. Dot to left of "T"		

1887–90. *Stamps of Queen Victoria.*

O65	1½d. dull purple and pale green (29.10.87)	£110	15·00
	a. No dot under "T"	£175	40·00
	b. Dot to right of "T"	£175	40·00
	c. Dot to left of "T"	£175	40·00
O66	6d. purple/*rose-red* (19.12.87)	£200	50·00
	a. No dot under "T"	£250	75·00
	b. Dot to right of "T"	£300	80·00
	c. Dot to left of "T"	£300	80·00
O67	9d. dull purple and blue (21.8.88)	£300	75·00
O68	1s. dull green (25.3.90)	£550	£225
	a. No dot under "T"	£700	£250
	b. Dot to right of "T"	£700	£350
	c. Dot to left of "T"	£750	£350
	d. Optd in blue-black		

1891–1900. *Stamps of Queen Victoria.*

O69	1d. lilac (Die II) (18.6.97)	75·00	16·00
	a. No dot under "T"	£120	45·00
	b. Dot to left of "T"	£120	45·00
	c. Opt inverted	£5000	£2500
	d. Ditto. Dot to left of "T"	£6000	£3000
O70	2d. grey-green and carmine (24.10.91)	£160	22·00
	a. No dot under "T"	£300	65·00
	b. Dot to left of "T"	£300	65·00
O71	4½d. green and carmine (29.9.92)	£275	£200
	b. Dot to right of "T"		
O72	1s. green and carmine (11.00)	£500	£200
	a. Opt inverted †	†	£13000

*O61/72 **For well-centred, lightly used +100%.**

The "no dot under T" variety occurred on R. 12/3 and 20/2. The "dot to left of T" comes four times in the sheet on R. 2/7, 6/7, 7/9 and 12/9. The best example of the "dot to right of T" is on R. 20/1. All three varieties were corrected around 1897.

1902. *Stamps of King Edward VII. Ordinary paper.*

O74	1d. scarlet (30.10.02)	32·00	13·00
O75	2d. yellowish green & carmine-red (29.4.02)	£150	38·00
O76	6d. pale dull purple (19.2.02)	£250	38·00
O77	9d. dull purple and ultramarine (28.8.02)	£600	£160
O78	1s. dull green and carmine (17.12.02)	£1000	£275

BOARD OF EDUCATION

BOARD OF EDUCATION (O 8)

Optd with Type O **8**

1902 (19 Feb). *Stamps of Queen Victoria.*

		Un	*Used**	*Used on cover*
O81	5d. dull purple and blue (II)	£3000	£850	
O82	1s. green and carmine	£7500	£4500	

1902 (19 Feb)–**04**. *Stamps of King Edward VII. Ordinary paper.*

O83	½d. blue-green	£160	38·00	£375
O84	1d. scarlet	£160	38·00	£400
O85	2½d. ultramarine	£4000	£300	
O86	5d. dull purple & ultram (6.2.04)	£22000	£6000	
O87	1s. dull green & carmine (23.12.02)	£100000		

ROYAL HOUSEHOLD

R.H. OFFICIAL (O 9)

1902. *Stamps of King Edward VII optd with Type* O **9**. *Ordinary paper.*

O91	½d. blue-green (29.4.02)	£375	£200	£1100
O92	1d. scarlet (19.2.02)	£325	£175	£1000

ADMIRALTY

ADMIRALTY OFFICIAL (O 10) — ADMIRALTY OFFICIAL (O 11) (with different "M")

1903 (1 Apr). *Stamps of King Edward VII optd with Type* O **10**. *Ordinary paper.*

O101	½d. blue-green	27·00	13·00	
O102	1d. scarlet	16·00	6·50	£300
O103	1½d. dull purple and green	£300	£140	
O104	2d. yellowish green & carmine-red	£325	£150	
O105	2½d. ultramarine	£450	£140	
O106	3d. purple/*yellow*	£400	£150	

1903–04. *Stamps of King Edward VII optd with Type* O **11**. *Ordinary paper.*

O107	½d. blue-green (9.03)	55·00	22·00	£500
O108	1d. scarlet (12.03)	55·00	22·00	£140
O109	1½d. dull purple and green (2.04)	£900	£600	
O110	2d. yellowish green and carmine red (3.04)	£1500	£650	
O111	2½d. ultramarine (3.04)	£1700	£850	
O112	3d. dull purple/*orange-yell* (12.03)	£1400	£350	

Stamps of various issues perforated with a Crown and initials ("H.M.O.W.", "O.W.", "B.T." or "S.O.") or with initials only ("H.M.S.O." or "D.S.I.R.") have also been used for official purposes, but these are outside the scope of the catalogue.

POSTAL FISCAL STAMPS

PRICES. Prices in the used column are for stamps with genuine postal cancellations dated from the time when they were authorised for use as postage stamps. Beware of stamps with fiscal cancellations removed and fraudulent postmarks applied.

VALIDITY. The 1d. Surface-printed stamps were authorised for postal use from 1 June 1881 and at the same time the 1d. postage issue, No. 166, was declared valid for fiscal purposes. The 3d. and 6d. values, together with the Embossed issues were declared valid for postal purposes by another Act effective from 1 January 1883.

SURFACE-PRINTED ISSUES

(Typo Thomas De La Rue & Co)

F **1** Rectangular Buckle

F **2**

F **3** Octagonal Buckle

F 4

F **5** Double-lined Anchor

F **6** Single-lined Anchor

1853–57. P 15½×15.

(a) Wmk F**5** *(inverted) (1853–55).*

F1	F **1**	1d. light blue (10.10.53).......	40·00	50·00	£190
F2	F **2**	1d. ochre (10.53)...................	£110	£130	£500
		a. *Tête-bêche* (in block of four)................................	£18000		
F3	F **3**	1d. pale turquoise-blue (12.53)	30·00	45·00	£275
F4		1d. light blue/*blue* (12.53) ...	75·00	75·00	£450
F5	F **4**	1d. reddish lilac/*blue glazed paper* (25.3.55)	£110	£120	£375

Only one example is known of No. F2a outside the National Postal Museum and the Royal Collection.

(b) Wmk F**6** *(1856–57).*

F6	F **4**	1d. reddish lilac (*shades*).....	10·00	8·50	£150
F7		1d. reddish lilac/*bluish* (*shades*) (1857)..............	10·00	8·50	£150

(F **7**)

1860 (3 Apr). *No. F7 optd with Type* F**7**, *in red.*

F8	F **4**	1d. dull reddish lilac/*blue*..	£750	£600	£1200

BLUE PAPER. In the following issues we no longer distinguish between bluish and white paper. There is a range of papers from white or greyish to bluish.

F 8

F 9

F **10**

1860–67. *Bluish to white Paper.* P 15½×15.

		(a) Wmk F **6** *(1860).*			
F 9	F **8**	1d. reddish lilac (May)	12·00	12·00	£150
F10	F **9**	3d. reddish lilac (June)........	£375	£250	£450
F11	F **10**	6d. reddish lilac (Oct)..........	£180	£150	£375
		(b) W **40**. (Anchor 16 mm high) *(1864).*			
F12	F **8**	1d. pale reddish lilac (Nov)	10·00	10·00	£150
F13	F **9**	3d. pale reddish lilac...........	£225	£150	£450
F14	F **10**	6d. pale reddish lilac...........	£180	£150	£375

		(c) W **40** (Anchor 18 mm high) *(1867).*			
F15	F **8**	1d. reddish lilac	20·00	20·00	£225
F16	F **9**	3d. reddish lilac	£100	£100	£375
F17	F **10**	6d. reddish lilac	90·00	70·00	£250

For stamps perf 14, see Nos. F24/7.

F 11

F 12

Four Dies of Type F 12

Nos. F19/21 show "O" of "ONE" circular. No. F22 (Die 4) shows a horizontal oval

Die 1. Four lines of shading in left band of ribbon opposite "Y" of "PENNY", small ornaments and heavy shading under chin

Die 2. Two lines of shading in left band of ribbon. Clear line of shading under chin. Small ornaments

Die 3. Ornaments larger and joined; line of shading under chin extended half way down neck

Die 4. Ornaments much larger; straight line of shading continued to bottom of neck

1867–81. *White to bluish paper.* P 14.

		(a) W **47** (Small Anchor).			
F18	F **11**	1d. purple (1.9.67)	18·00	18·00	£120
F19	F **12**	1d. purple (Die 1) (6.68)....	6·00	7·00	£120
F20		1d. purple (Die 2) (6.76)....	22·00	15·00	£250
F21		1d. purple (Die 3) (3.77)....	12·00	12·00	£175
F22		1d. purple (Die 4) (7.78).....	7·00	7·00	£100
		(b) W **48** (Orb).			
F23	F **12**	1d. purple (Die 4) (1.81)................................	7·00	3·50	90·00

1881. *White to bluish paper.* P 14.

		(a) W **40** *(Anchor 18 mm high) (Jan).*			
F24	F **9**	3d. reddish lilac	£700	£375	£800
F25	F **10**	6d. reddish lilac	£325	£150	£375
		(b) **W 40** *(Anchor 20 mm high) (May).*			
F26	F **9**	3d. reddish lilac	£525	£300	£575
F27	F **10**	6d. reddish lilac	£300	£150	£375

ISSUES EMBOSSED IN COLOUR

(Made at Somerset House)

The embossed stamps were struck from dies not appropriated to any special purpose on paper which had the words "INLAND REVENUE" previously printed, and thus became available for payment of any duties for which no special stamps had been provided.

The die letters are included in the embossed designs and holes were drilled for the insertion of plugs showing figures indicating dates of striking.

F **13**

F **14**

(F **15**)

(F **16**)

1860 (3 Apr)–**71**. *Types* F **13/14** *and similar types embossed on bluish paper. Underprint Type* F **15**. No wmk. Imperf.

		Un	*Used*
F28	2d. pink (Die A) (1.1.71)......................	£600	
F29	3d. pink (Die C)......................................	£150	
	a. *Tête-bêche* (vert pair)......................	£1200	
F30	3d. pink (Die D)	£600	
F31	6d. pink (Die T)		
F32	6d. pink (Die U)	£300	
	a. *Tête-bêche* (vert pair)......................		
F33	9d. pink (Die C) (1.1.71)......................	£750	
F34	1s. pink (Die E) (28.6.61)....................	£600	
	a. *Tête-bêche* (vert pair)......................		
F35	1s. pink (Die F) (28.6.61)....................	£225	
	a. *Tête-bêche* (vert pair)......................	£850	
F36	2s. pink (Die K) (6.8.61)	£600	
F37	2s.6d. pink (Die N) (28.6.61)		
F38	2s.6d. pink (Die O) (28.6.61)	£300	

1871 (Aug). *As last but perf 12½.*

F39	2d. pink (Die A)..	£375	
F42	9d. pink (Die C)..	£850	
F43	1s. pink (Die E)..	£600	
F44	1s. pink (Die F)	£525	
F45	2s.6d. pink (Die O)	£300	

1874 (Nov). *Types as before embossed on white paper. Underprint Type* F**16**, *in green.* W **47** (Small Anchor). P 12½.

F46	2d. pink (Die A)..		
F47	9d. pink (Die C)..		
F48	1s. pink (Die F)	£600	
F49	2s.6d. pink (Die O)		

It is possible that the 2d., 9d. and 2s.6d. may not exist with the thin underprint, Type F 16, in this shade

1875 (Nov)–**80**. *As last but colour changed and on white or bluish paper.*

F50	2d. vermilion (Die A) (1880)...............	£450	
F51	9d. vermilion (Die C) (1876)...............	£600	
F52	1s. vermilion (Die E)...........................	£375	
F53	1s. vermilion (Die F)	£850	
F54	2s.6d. vermilion (Die O) (1878)	£375	

1882 (Oct). *As last but* W**48** *(Orbs).*

F55	2d. vermilion (Die A)...........................		
F56	9d. vermilion (Die C)...........................		
F57	1s. vermilion (Die E)...........................		
F58	2s.6d. vermilion (Die O)...........................	£750	£600

Although specimen overprints of Nos. F55/7 are known there is some doubt if these values were issued.

The sale of Inland Revenue stamps up to the 2s. value ceased from 30 December 1882 and stocks were called in and destroyed. The 2s.6d. value remained on sale until 2 July 1883 when it was replaced by the 2s.6d. "Postage & Revenue" stamp. Inland Revenue stamps still in the hands of the public continued to be accepted for revenue and postal purposes.

TELEGRAPH STAMPS. A priced listing of the Post Office telegraph stamps appears in Volume 1 of the Stanley Gibbons *Great Britain Specialised Catalogue*. The last listing for the private telegraph companies in the Part 1 Catalogue was in the 1940 edition and for military telegraphs the 1941 edition.

CHANNEL ISLANDS

GENERAL ISSUE

C**1** Gathering Vraic

C**2** Islanders gathering Vraic

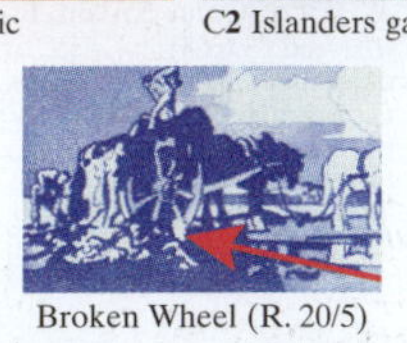
Broken Wheel (R. 20/5)

(Des J. R. R. Stobie (1 d.) or from drawing by E. Blampied (2½d.). Photo Harrison)

1948 (10 May). *Third Anniv of Liberation.* W **127** of Great Britain. P15×14.

C1	C **1**	1d. scarlet	25	30
C2	C **2**	2½d. ultramarine	25	30
		a. Broken Wheel	15·00	

Supplies of these stamps were also available from eight head post offices on the mainland of Great Britain.

GUERNSEY

WAR OCCUPATION ISSUES

Stamps issued under the authority of the Guernsey States during the German Occupation

BISECTS. On 24 December 1940 authority was given, by Post Office notice, that prepayment of penny postage could be effected by using half a British 2d. stamp, diagonally bisected. Such stamps were first used on 27 December 1940.

The 2d. stamps generally available were those of the Postal Centenary issue, 1940 (S.G. 482) and the first colour of the King George VI issue (S.G. 465). These are listed under Nos. 482a and 465b. A number of the 2d. King George V, 1912–22, and of the King George V photogravure stamp (S.G. 442) which were in the hands of philatelists, were also bisected and used.

1

1a Loops (*half actual size*)

(Des E. W. Vaudin. Typo Guernsey Press Co Ltd)

1941–44. *Rouletted.*

(a) White paper. No wmk.

1	1	½d. light green (7.4.41)	6·00	3·50
		a. Emerald-green (6.41)	6·00	2·00
		b. Bluish green (11.41)	32·00	13·00
		c. Bright green (2.42)	22·00	10·00
		d. Dull green (9.42)	4·00	2·00
		e. Olive-green (2.43)	45·00	25·00
		f. Pale yellowish green (7.43 and later) (*shades*)	4·00	3·00
		g. Imperf (pair)	£200	
		h. Imperf between (horiz pair)	£700	
		i. Imperf between (vert pair)	£800	
2		1d. scarlet (18.2.41)	3·25	2·00
		a. Pale vermilion (7.43) (etc.)	5·00	2·00
		b. Carmine (1943)	3·50	2·00
		c. Imperf (pair)	£150	75·00
		d. Imperf between (horiz pair)	£700	
		da. Imperf vert (centre stamp of horiz strip of 3)		
		e. Imperf between (vert pair)	£800	
		f. Printed double (scarlet shade)	£100	
3		2½d. ultramarine (12.4.44)	13·00	12·00
		a. Pale ultramarine (7.44)	10·00	7·00
		b. Imperf (pair)	£500	
		c. Imperf between (horiz pair)	£1000	

(b) Bluish French bank-note paper. W **1a** (sideways).

4	1	½d. bright green (11.3.42)	30·00	22·00
5		1d. scarlet (9.4.42)	16·00	22·00

The dates given for the shades of Nos. 1/3 are the months in which they were printed as indicated on the printer's imprints. Others are issue dates.

REGIONAL ISSUES

DATES OF ISSUE. Conflicting dates of issue have been announced for some of the regional issues, partly explained by the stamps being released on different dates by the Philatelic Bureau in Edinburgh or the Philatelic Counter in London and in the regions. We have adopted the practice of giving the earliest known dates, since once released the stamps could have been used anywhere in the U.K.

2

3

(Des E. A. Piprell. Portrait by Dorothy Wilding Ltd. Photo Harrison & Sons)

1958 (18 Aug)–**67**. W **179** of Great Britain. P 15×14.

6	2	2½d. rose-red (8.6.64)	35	40
7	3	3d. deep lilac	30	30
		p. One centre phosphor band (24.5.67)	15	20
8		4d. ultramarine (7.2.66)	25	30
		p. Two phosphor bands (24.10.67)	15	20
6/8p *Set of* 3			70	80

1968–69. No wmk. *Chalk-surfaced paper. PVA gum*. One centre phosphor band (Nos. 10/11) or two phosphor bands (others).* P 15×14.

9	3	4d. pale ultramarine (16.4.68)	10	20
10		4d. olive-sepia (4.9.68)	10	15
11		4d. bright vermilion (26.2.69)	20	25
12		5d. royal blue (4.9.68)	20	30
9/12 *Set of* 4			50	1·00

No. 9 was not issued in Guernsey until 22 April.

* PVA Gum. See note after No. 722 of Great Britain.

INDEPENDENT POSTAL ADMINISTRATION

4 Castle Cornet and Edward the Confessor

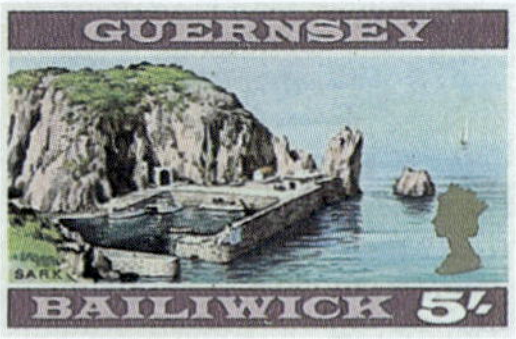

5 View of Sark

Two Types of 1d. and 1s.6d.:

I. Latitude inset "40° 30' N".

II. Corrected to "49° 30' N".

(Des R. Granger Barrett. Photo Harrison (½d. to 2s.6d.); Delrieu (others))

1969 (1 Oct)–**70**. *Designs as T* **4/5**. P 14 (½d. to 2s.6d.) or 12½ (others).

13	½d. deep magenta and black	10	10
14	1d. bright blue and black (I)	10	10
14*b*	1d. bright blue and black (II) (12.12.69)	30	30
	c. Booklet stamp with blank margins	40	40
15	1½d. yellow-brown and black	10	10
16	2d. gold, bright red, deep blue and black	10	10
17	3d. gold, pale greenish yellow, orge-red & blk	15	15
	a. Error. Wmk w **12**	£1200	
18	4d. multicoloured	20	25
	a. Booklet stamp with blank margins (12.12.69)	40	45
	ab. Yellow omitted	£250	
	ac. Emerald (stem) omitted	£110	
19	5d. gold brt vermilion, bluish violet & black	20	20
	a. Booklet stamp with blank margins (12.12.69)	50	50
	b. Gold (inscr etc.) omitted (booklets)	£500	
20	6d. gold, pale greenish yellow, light bronze-green and black	20	30
21	9d. gold, bright red, crimson and black	30	30
22	1s. gold, bright vermilion, bistre and black	30	30
23	1s.6d. turquoise-green and black (I)	25	30
23*b*	1s.6d. turquoise-green and black (II) (4.2.70)	2·00	1·75
24	1s.9d. multicoloured	80	80
	a. Emerald (stem) omitted	£325	
25	2s.6d. bright reddish violet and black	3·25	2·75
26	5s. multicoloured	2·50	2·25
27	10s. multicoloured	16·00	18·00
	a. Perf 13½×13 (4.3.70)	35·00	35·00
28	£1 multicoloured	2·25	2·25
	a. Perf 13½×13 (4.3.70)	2·25	2·25
13/28 *Set of* 16		20·00	26·00

Designs: *Horiz* as T **4**—1d. (*both*), 1s.6d. (*both*), Map and William I; 1½d. Martello Tower and Henry II; 2d. Arms of Sark and King John; 3d. Arms of Alderney and Edward III; 4d. Guernsey Lily and Henry V; 5d. Arms of Guernsey and Elizabeth I; 6d. Arms of Alderney and Charles II; 9d. Arms of Sark and George III; 1s. Arms of Guernsey and Queen Victoria; 1s.9d. Guernsey Lily and Elizabeth I; 2s.6d. Martello Tower and King John. *Horiz* as T **5**—10s. View of Alderney; £1, View of Guernsey.

The booklet panes consist of single perforated stamps with wide margins all round intended to fit automatic machines designed for the Great Britain 2s. booklets. They are therefore found with three margins when detached from booklets or four margins when complete.

There was no postal need for the ½d. and 1½d. values as the ½d. coin had been withdrawn prior to their issue in anticipation of decimalisation. These values were only on sale at the Philatelic Bureau and the Crown Agents as well as in the U.S.A.

Nos. 14*b* and 23*b* are known only on thin paper and Nos. 13, 14, 16, 17, 20, 21, 22, 23, 24 and 25 also exist on thin paper.

19 Isaac Brock as Colonel

23 H.M.S. *L103* (landing craft) entering St. Peter's Harbour

(Litho Format)

1969 (1 Dec). *Birth Bicentenary of Sir Isaac Brock. T* **19** *and similar multicoloured designs.* P 13½×14 (2s.6d.) or 14×13½ (others).

29	4d. Type **19**	20	20
30	5d. Sir Isaac Brock as Major-General	20	20
31	1s.9d. Isaac Brock as Ensign	90	75
32	2s.6d. Arms and flags (*horiz*)	90	75
29/32 *Set of* 4		2·00	1·70

(Des and photo Courvoisier)

1970 (9 May). *25th Anniv of Liberation. T* **23** *and similar designs. Granite paper.* P 11½.

33	4d. blue and pale blue	20	20
34	5d. brown-lake and pale grey	40	20
35	1s.6d. bistre-brown and buff	1·25	90
33/5 *Set of* 3		1·75	1·10

Designs: *Horiz*—5d. H.M.S. *Bulldog* and H.M.S. *Beagle* (destroyers) entering St. Peter's Port. *Vert*—1s.6d. Brigadier Snow reading Proclamation.

26 Guernsey "Toms"

32 St. Peter Church, Sark

(Des and photo Courvoisier)

1970 (12 Aug). *Agriculture and Horticulture. T* **26** *and similar horiz designs. Multicoloured. Granite paper.* P 11½.

36	4d. Type **26**	55	20
37	5d. Guernsey Cow	70	20
38	9d. Guernsey Bull	2·75	1·30
39	1s.6d. Freesias	2·75	2·40
36/9 *Set of* 4		6·00	4·00

(Des and photo Courvoisier)

1970 (11 Nov). *Christmas. Guernsey Churches (1st series). T* **32** *and similar multicoloured designs. Granite paper.* P 11½.

40	4d. St. Anne's Church, Alderney (*horiz*)	20	10
41	5d. St. Peter's Church (*horiz*)	20	10
42	9d. Type **32**	1·25	1·00
43	1s.6d. St. Tugual Chapel, Herm	1·50	1·25
40/3 *Set of* 4		2·50	2·00

STAMP BOOKLETS

For a full listing of Guernsey stamp booklets see *Collect Channel Islands and Isle of Man Stamps* published each February.

POSTAGE DUE STAMPS

D **1** Castle Cornet

(Des R. Granger Barrett. Photo Delrieu)

1969 (1 Oct). *Value in black; background colour given.* No wmk. P 12½×12.

D1	D **1**	1d. plum	2·00	1·25
D2		2d. bright green	2·00	1·25
D3		3d. vermilion	3·00	4·00
D4		4d. ultramarine	4·00	5·00
D5		5d. yellow-ochre	6·00	4·00
D6		6d. turquoise-blue	6·00	4·50
D7		1s. lake-brown	10·00	8·00
D1/7 *Set of* 7			30·00	25·00

JERSEY

WAR OCCUPATION ISSUES

Stamps issued under the authority of the Jersey States during the German Occupation

1

(Des Major N. V. L. Rybot. Typo Jersey Evening Post, St. Helier)

1941–43. *White paper (thin to thick).* No wmk. P 11.

1	1	½d. bright green (29.1.42)	8·00	6·00
		a. Imperf between (vert pair)	£800	
		b. Imperf between (horiz pair)	£700	
		c. Imperf (pair)	£250	
		d. On greyish paper (1.43)	12·00	12·00
2		1d. scarlet (1.4.41)	8·00	5·00
		a. Imperf between (vert pair)	£800	
		b. Imperf between (horiz pair)	£700	
		c. Imperf (pair)	£275	
		d. On chalk-surfaced paper	55·00	48·00
		e. On greyish paper (1.43)	14·00	14·00

2 Old Jersey Farm

3 Portelet Bay

4 Corbière Lighthouse

5 Elizabeth Castle

6 Mont Orgueil Castle

7 Gathering Vraic (seaweed)

(Des E. Blampied. Eng H. Cortot. Typo French Govt Works, Paris)

1943–44. No wmk. P 13½.

3	**2**	½d. green (1 June)	12·00	12·00
		a. Rough, grey paper (6.10.43)	15·00	14·00
4	**3**	1d. scarlet (1 June)	3·00	50
		a. On newsprint (28.2.44)	3·50	75
5	**4**	1½d. brown (8 June)	8·00	5·75
6	**5**	2d. orange-yellow (8 June)	7·50	2·00
7	**6**	2½d. blue (29 June)	3·00	1·00
		a. On newsprint (25.2.44)	1·00	1·75
		ba. Thin paper*	£225	
8	**7**	3d. violet (29 June)	3·00	2·75
3/8 *Set of* 6			30·00	21·00

*On No. 7ba the design shows clearly through the back of the stamp.

REGIONAL ISSUES

DATES OF ISSUE. The note at the beginning of the Guernsey Regional Issues also applies here

INVALIDATION. The regional issues for Jersey were invalidated for use in Jersey and Guernsey on 1 November 1969 but remained valid for use in the rest of the United Kingdom. Nos. 15/41 (except No. 29) and Nos. D1/6 were invalidated on 14 February 1972.

8

9

(Des E. Blampied (T **8**), W Gardner (T **9**) Portrait by Dorothy Wilding Ltd. Photo Harrison & Sons)

1958 (18 Aug)–**67**. W **179** of Great Britain. P 15×14.

9	**8**	2½d. carmine-red (8.6.64)	30	45
		a. Imperf three sides (pair)	£2000	
10	**9**	3d. deep lilac	30	25
		p. One centre phosphor band (9.6.67)	15	15
11		4d. ultramarine (7.2.66)	25	30
		p. Two phosphor bands (5.9.67)	15	25
9/11p *Set of* 3			50	75

1968–69. No wmk. *Chalk-surfaced paper. PVA gum*. One centre phosphor band (4d. values) or two phosphor bands (5d.).* P 15×14.

12	**9**	4d. olive-sepia (4.9.68)	15	25
13		4d. bright vermilion (26.2.69)	15	25
14		5d. royal blue (4.9.68)	15	50
12/14 *Set of* 3			40	1·10

*PVA Gum. See note after No. 722 of Great Britain.

INDEPENDENT POSTAL ADMINISTRATION

10 Elizabeth Castle

11 Queen Elizabeth II (after Cecil Beaton)

13 Queen Elizabeth II (after Cecil Beaton)

12 Jersey Airport

(Des V. Whiteley. Photo Harrison (½d. to 1s.9d.); Courvoisier (others))

1969 (1 Oct). *T* **10/13** *and similar horiz designs as T* **10** *(½d. to 1s.6d.) or T* **12** *(5s., 10s., £1). Multicoloured. Granite paper (2s.6d. to £1).* P 14 (½d. to 1s.9d.) or 12 (others).

15	½d. Type **10**	10	60
16	1d. La Hougue Bie (prehistoric tomb) (*shades*)	10	10
	a. Booklet stamp with blank margins	75	
17	2d. Portelet Bay	10	10
18	3d. La Corbière Lighthouse	10	10
	b. Orange omitted	£120	
19	4d. Mont Orgued Castle by night	10	10
	a. Booklet stamp with blank margins	50	
20	5d. Arms and Royal Mace	10	10
21	6d. Jersey Cow	10	10
22	9d. Chart of English Channel	10	20
23	1s. Mont Orgueil Castle by day	25	25
24	1s.6d. As 9d.	80	75
25	1s.9d. Type **11**	80	75
26	2s.6d. Type **12**	1·25	1·00
27	5s. Legislative Chamber	4·75	3·50
28	10s. The Royal Court	12·00	9·00
	a. Error. Green border*	£4500	
29	£1 Type **13** (*shades*)	1·75	1·50
15/29 *Set of* 15		20·00	16·00

*During the final printing of the 10s. a sheet was printed in the colours of the 50p., No. 56, i.e. green border instead of slate.

The 3d. is known with the orange omitted.

There was no postal need for the ½d. value as the ½d. coin had been withdrawn prior to its issue in anticipation of decimalisation.

Nos. 16a and 19a come from 2s. booklets for the automatic machines formerly used for the Great Britain 2s. booklets (see also note after Guernsey No. 28).

Various papers were used by Harrisons. The ½d. and 1d. exist on much thicker paper from 2s. booklets and the 2d. to 1s.9d. exist on thinner paper having white instead of creamy gum.

24 First Day Cover

25 Lord Coutanche, former Bailiff of Jersey

(Des R. Sellar. Photo Harrison)

1969 (1 Oct). *Inauguration of Post Office.* P 14.

30	**24**	4d. multicoloured	10	15
31		5d. multicoloured	20	10
32		1s.6d. multicoloured	50	75
33		1s.9d. multicoloured	80	1·00
30/3 *Set of* 4			1·40	1·75

(Des Rosalind Dease. Photo Courvoisier)

1970 (9 May). *25th Anniv of Liberation. T* **25** *and similar multicoloured designs. Granite paper.* P 11½.

34	4d. Type **25**	20	20
35	5d. Sir Winston Churchill	20	20
36	1s.6d. "Liberation" (Edmund Blampied) (*horiz*)	90	1·00
37	1s.9d. S.S. *Vega* (*horiz*)	90	1·00
34/7 *Set of* 4		2·00	2·25

29 "A Tribute to Enid Blyton"

(Des Jennifer Toombs. Photo Courvoisier)

1970 (28 July). *"Battle of Flowers" Parade. T* **29** *and similar horiz designs. Multicoloured. Granite paper.* P 11½.

38	4d. Type **29**	20	10
39	5d. "Rags to Riches" (Cinderella and pumpkin)	20	20
40	1s.6d. "Gourmet's Delight" (lobster and cornucopia)	2·75	2·25
41	1s.9d. "We're the Greatest" (ostriches)	2·75	2·25
38/41 *Set of* 4		5·25	4·25

33 Jersey Airport

(Des V. Whiteley. Photo Harrison (½ to 9p.), Courvoisier (others))

1970 (1 Oct)–**74**. *Decimal Currency. Designs as Nos. 15/28, but with values inscr in decimal currency as in T* **33**, *and new horiz design as T* **10** *(6p). Chalk-surfaced paper (4½, 5, 8p.), granite paper (10, 20, 50p.).* P 14 (½p. to 9p.) or 12 (others).

42	½p. Type **10** (15.2.71)	10	10
	a. Booklet stamp with blank margins	20	
43	1p. La Corbière Lighthouse (*shades*) (15.2.71)	10	10
	a. Orange omitted		
44	1½p. Jersey Cow (15.2.71)	10	10
45	2p. Mont Orgueil Castle by night (15.2.71)	10	10
	a. Booklet stamp with blank margins	60	
46	2½p. Arms and Royal Mace (15.2.71)	10	10
	a. Booklet stamp with blank margins	60	
	ab. Gold (Mace) omitted	£375	
	ac. Gold (Mace) printed double	£300	
47	3p. La Hougue Bie (prehistoric tomb) (15.2.71)	10	10
	a. Booklet stamp with blank margins (1.12.72)	60	
48	3½p. Portelet Bay (15.2.71)	10	10
	a. Booklet stamp with blank margins (1.7.74)	25	
49	4p. Chart of English Channel (15.2.71)	10	10
49*a*	4½p. Arms and Royal Mace (1.11.74)	20	20
	ab. Uncoated paper	£400	
50	5p. Mont Orgueil Castle by day (15.2.71)	10	10
50*a*	5½p. Jersey Cow (1.11.74)	40	30
51	6p. Martello Tower, Archirondel (15.2.71)	20	10
52	7½p. Chart of English Channel (15.2.71)	20	15
52*a*	8p. Mont Orgueil Castle by night (1.11.74)	15	15
53	9p. Type **11** (15.2.71)	25	20
54	10p. Type **33**	40	30
55	20p. Legislative Chamber	90	80
56	50p. The Royal Court	1·50	1·25
42/56 *Set of* 18		4·50	3·75

Original printings of the ½p. to 4p.. 5p. and 6p. to 9p. were with PVA gum; printings from 1974 (including original printings of the 4½p. and 5½p.) have dextrin added (see notes after 1971 Great Britain Decimal Machin issue). The 10p. to 50p. have gum arabic.

The border of No. 56 has been changed from turquoise-blue to dull green.

STAMP BOOKLETS

For a full listing of Jersey stamp booklets see Collect Channel Islands and Isle of Man Stamps published each February.

POSTAGE DUE STAMPS

D 1

D 2 Map

(Des F. Gudnier. Litho Bradbury, Wilkinson)

1969 (1 Oct). P 14×13½.

D1	**D 1**	1d. bluish violet	65	1·10
D2		2d. sepia	90	1·10
D3		3d. magenta	1·00	1·10
D4	**D 2**	1s. bright emerald	5·50	5·00
D5		2s.6d. olive-grey	13·00	14·00
D6		5s. vermilion	15·00	16·00
D1/6 *Set of* 6			32·00	35·00

British Post Offices Abroad

The origins of the network of Post Offices, Postal Agencies and Packet Agents can be recognised from the 18th century, but the system did not become established until the expansion of trade, following the end of the Napoleonic Wars in 1815.

Many offices were provided in newly acquired dependent territories, and were then, eventually, transferred from the control of the British Post Office to the evolving local administrations.

Those in foreign countries, nearly always based on existing British Consular appointments, were mostly connected to the network of British Packet lines which had been re-established in 1814. They tended to survive until the country in which they were situated established its own efficient postal service or joined the U.P.U. The term "Post Office Agent" was employed by the British G.P.O. and "Packet Agent" by the shipping lines to describe similar functions.

Listed in this section are the Crowned-circle handstamps and G.B. stamps used in the Post Offices and Agencies situated in foreign countries. Those for the territories within the scope of this catalogue will be found under the following headings:

Prices. Catalogue prices quoted in this section, and throughout the volume, covering Crowned-circle handstamps and stamps of Great Britain used abroad are for used examples with the cancellation or handstamp clearly legible. Poor impressions of the cancellations and handstamps are worth much less than the prices quoted.

They also take into account the fact that many identifiable cancellations of the post offices abroad render the stamps they obliterate in less than 'fine' condition. As a result, some stamps listed in this section are priced at less than the same items used in Great Britain, where the prices are for fine examples. Lightly cancelled stamps used in offices abroad would be worth a premium over the prices quoted.

CROWNED-CIRCLE HANDSTAMPS

Following the introduction, in 1840, of adhesive stamps in Great Britain there was considerable pressure from a number of the dependent territories for the British Post Office to provide something similar for their use.

Such suggestions were resisted, however, because of supposed operational problems, but the decision was taken, in connection with an expansion of the Packet Service, to issue a uniform series of handstamps and date stamps to the offices abroad, both in the dependent territories and in foreign countries.

Under the regulations circulated in december 1841., letters and packets forwarded through these offices to th United Kingdom or any of its territories were to be sent unpaid, the postage being collected delivery. Where this was not possible, for exapmle from a British colony to a foreign colony or between two foreign ports, then a *crowned-circle handstamp* was to be applied with the postage, paid in advance, noted alongside in manuscript.

Examples of these handstamps were supplied over twenty years from 1842, but many continued to fulfil other functions long after the introduction of adhesive stamps in the colony concerned.

Our listings cover the use of these handstamps for their initial purpose and the prices quoted are for examples used on cover during the pre-adhesive period.

In most instances the dates quoted are those on which the handstamp appears in the G.P.O. Record Books, but it seems to have been normal for the handstamps to be sent to the office concerned immediately following this registration. The only known examples of certain hanstamps are those in The Record Books; these include St. Michaels (Azores), Cobija (Bolivia), St Vincent (Cape Verde Islands), Cartagena (CC1) and Chagres (Colombia), Cap Haitien (Haiti), Greytown (Nicaragua), Corunna (Spain), and Charleston, Mobile, New Orleans and Savannah (United States of America).

Many of the handstamps were individually cut by hand, so that each has its own characteristics, but for the purposes of the listing they have been grouped into nine Types as shown in the adjacent column. No attempt has been made to identify them by anything but the most major differences, so that minor differences in size and in the type of the crown have been ignored.

DOUBLE CIRCLE

CC **1**

CC **1a**

Curved "PAID"

CC **1b**

CC **1c**

Curved "PAID"

CC **2**

Straight "PAID"

SINGLE CIRCLE

CC **3**

CC **4**

Straight "PAID"

CC **5**

Curved "PAID"

CC **6** Straight "PAID"

CC **7** Curved "PAID"

GREAT BRITAIN STAMPS USED ABROAD

Prices quoted are for single stamps not on cover unless otherwise stated. Stamps on cover are worth considerably more in most cases.

In many instances obliterators allocated to post offices abroad were, at a later date re-allocated to offices at home. Postmarks on issues later than those included in our lists can therefore safely be regarded as *not* having been "used abroad".

INDEX

TYPES OF OBLITERATOR FOR GREAT BRITAIN STAMPS USED ABROAD

HORIZONTAL OVAL

(1)

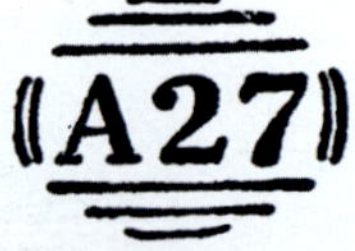

(2)

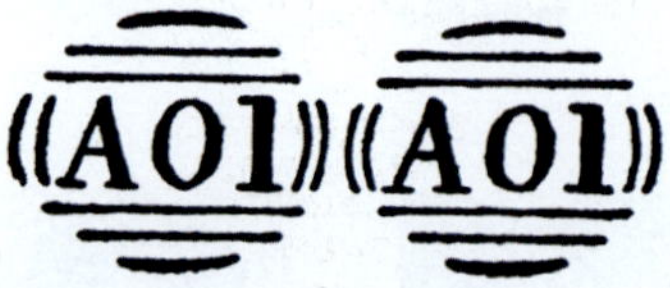

(3)

(4)

(5)

(6)

(7)

VERTICAL OVAL

(8)

(9)

(10)

(11)

(11A)

(12)

(13)

(14)

(14A)

(14B)

(15)

CIRCULAR DATE STAMPS

(16)

(16A)

(17)

(17A)

(17B)

(18)

(19)

(20)

(21)

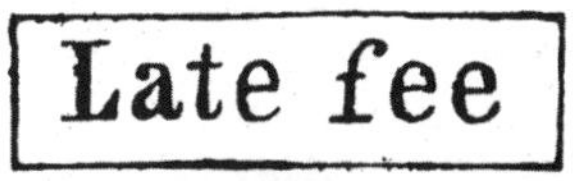

(22)

ARGENTINE REPUBLIC

BUENOS AYRES

The first regular monthly British mail packet service was introduced in 1824, replacing a private arrangement which had previously existed for some years.

Great Britain stamps were used from 1860 until the office closed at the end of June 1873. Until 1878 the British Consul continued to sell stamps which were used in combination with an Argentine value prepaying the internal rate. The British stamps on such covers were cancelled on arrival in England.

CROWNED-CIRCLE HANDSTAMPS

CC1 CC **7** BUENOS AYRES (Black or R.) (5.1.1851) .... *Price on cover* £775

Stamps of GREAT BRITAIN *cancelled* "B 32" *as Types* **2**, **12** *or* **13** *in black or blue.*

1860–73.

Z1	1d. rose-red (1857)		45·00
Z2	1d. rose-red (1864)	*From*	38·00
	Plate Nos. 71, 72, 73, 74, 76, 78, 79, 80, 81, 82, 85, 87, 89, 90, 91, 92, 93, 94, 95, 96, 97, 99, 101, 103, 104, 107, 108, 110, 112, 113, 114, 117, 118, 119, 120, 121, 123, 125, 127, 129, 130, 131, 135, 136, 138, 139, 140, 142, 143, 145, 147, 149, 150, 151, 155, 159, 163, 164, 166, 169, 172.		
Z3	2d. blue (1858–69)	*From*	45·00
	Plate Nos. 8, 9, 12, 13, 14.		
Z4	3d. carmine-rose (1862)		£270
Z5	3d. rose (1865) (Plate No. 4)		£110
Z6	3d. rose (1867–73)	*From*	45·00
	Plate Nos. 4, 5, 6, 7, 8, 9, 10.		
Z7	4d. rose (1857)		£110
Z8	4d. red (1862) (Plate Nos. 3, 4)		£100
Z9	4d. vermilion (1865–73)	*From*	50·00
	Plate Nos. 7, 8, 9, 10, 11, 12, 13.		
Z10	6d. lilac (1856)		£100
Z11	6d. lilac (1862) (Plate Nos. 3, 4)		
Z12	6d. lilac (1865–67) (Plate Nos. 5, 6)	*From*	80·00
Z13	6d. lilac (1867) (Plate No. 6)		90·00
Z14	6d. violet (1867–70) (Plate Nos. 6, 8, 9)	*From*	70·00
Z15	6d. buff (1872) (Plate No. 11)		85·00
Z16	6d. chestnut (1872) (Plate No. 11)		45·00
Z17	9d. bistre (1862)		£325
Z18	9d. straw (1862)		£300
Z19	9d. straw (1865)		£475
Z20	9d. straw (1867)		£300
Z21	10d. red-brown (1867)		£325
Z22	1s. green (1856)		£275
Z23	1s. green (1862)		£170
Z24	1s. green (1865) (Plate No. 4)		£160
Z25	1s. green (1867–73) (Plate Nos. 4, 5, 6, 7)	*From*	45·00
Z26	1s. green (1873–77) (Plate No. 8)		
Z27	2s. blue (1867)		£150
Z28	5s. rose (1867) (Plate No. 1)		£450

A "B 32' obliteration was later used by Mauritius on its own stamps.

AZORES

ST. MICHAELS (SAN MIGUEL)

A British Postal Agency existed at Ponta Delgada, the chief port of the island, to operate with the services of the Royal Mail Steam Packet Company.

CROWNED-CIRCLE HANDSTAMPS

CC1 CC **1b** ST. MICHAELS (27.5.1842) ....

Although recorded in the G.P.O. Proof Books, no example of No. CC1 is known on cover.

BOLIVIA

COBIJA

It is believed that the British Postal Agency opened in 1862. The stamps of Great Britain were used between 1865 and 1878. They can be found used in combination with Bolivia adhesive stamps paying the local postage. The Agency closed in 1881, the town having been occupied by Chile in 1879

CROWNED-CIRCLE HANDSTAMPS

CC1 CC **4** COBIJA (29.3.1862) ....

Although recorded in the G.P.O. Proof Books, no example of No. CC1 is known on cover.

Stamps of GREAT BRITAIN *cancelled* "C 39" *as Types* **4**, **8** or **12**.

1865–78.

Z1	1d. rose-red (Plate Nos. 93, 95)	
Z2	2d. blue (1858–69) (Plate No. 14)	
Z3	3d. rose (1867–73) (Plate No. 6)	
Z4	3d. rose (1873–76) (Plate Nos. 16, 19)	
Z5	4d. sage-green (1877) (Plate No. 15)	£600
Z6	6d. violet (1867–70) (Plate No. 9)	£600

Z7 6d. buff (1872) (Plate No. 11)
Z8 6d. grey (1874–76) (Plate Nos. 13, 14, 15, 16) ... £500
Z9 1s. green (1867–73) (Plate Nos. 4, 5) £500
Z10 1s. green (1873–77) (Plate Nos. 10, 11, 12, 13). £500
Z11 2s. blue (1867) £650
Z12 5s. rose (1867–74) (Plate No. 2) £1200

BRAZIL

The first packets ran to Brazil in 1808 when the Portuguese royal family went into exile at Rio de Janeiro. The Agencies at Bahia and Pernambuco did not open until 1851. All three agencies used the stamps of Great Britain from 1866 and these can be found used in combination with Brazil adhesive stamps paying the local postage. The agencies closed on 30 June 1874

BAHIA

CROWNED-CIRCLE HANDSTAMPS

CC1 CC **7** BAHIA (Black, B. *or* R.) (6.1.1851) *Price on cover* £2750

Stamps of GREAT BRITAIN *cancelled* "C 81" *as Type* **12**.
1866–74.
Z1 1d. rose-red (1864–79) *From* 45·00
Plate Nos. 90, 93, 96, 108, 113, 117, 135, 140, 147, 155.
Z2 1½d. lake-red (1870–74) (Plate No. 3) £110
Z3 2d. blue (1858–59) (Plate Nos. 9, 12, 13, 14) 65·00
Z4 3d. rose (1865) (Plate No. 4)
Z5 3d. rose (1867–73) (Plate Nos. 4, 6, 8, 9, 10) 55·00
Z6 3d. rose (1873–79) (Plate No. 11)
Z7 4d. vermilion (1865–73) *From* 50·00
Plate Nos. 8, 9, 10, 11, 12, 13.
Z8 6d. lilac (1865–67) (Plate No. 5)
Z9 6d. lilac (1867) (Plate No. 6) 90·00
Z10 6d. violet (1867–70) (Plate Nos. 6, 8, 9)... *From* 70·00
Z11 6d. buff (1872–73) (Plate Nos. 11, 12) *From* £100
Z12 6d. chestnut (1872) (Plate No. 11) £100
Z13 6d. grey (1873) (Plate No. 12)
Z14 6d. grey (1874–76) (Plate No. 13)
Z15 9d. straw (1865) £425
Z16 9d. straw (1867) £250
Z17 1s. green (1865) (Plate No. 4) £170
Z18 1s. green (1867–73) (Plate Nos. 4, 5, 6, 7) *From* 50·00
Z19 1s. green (1873–77) (Plate Nos. 8, 9) 85·00
Z20 2s. blue (1867) £275
Z21 5s. rose (1867) (Plate No. 1) £450

PERNAMBUCO

CROWNED-CIRCLE HANDSTAMPS

CC2 CC **7** PERNAMBUCO (Black *or* R.) (6.1.1851) *Price on cover* £2750

Stamps of GREAT BRITAIN *cancelled* "C 82" *as Type* **12** *or with circular date stamp as Type* **16**.
1866–74.
Z22 1d. rose-red (1864–79) *From* 45·00
Plate Nos. 85, 108, 111, 130, 131, 132, 149, 157, 159, 160, 187.
Z23 2d. blue (1858–69) *From* 55·00
Plate Nos. 9, 12, 13, 14.
Z23*a* 3d. rose (1865) (Plate No. 4) £110
Z24 3d. rose (1867–73) (Plate Nos. 4, 5, 6, 7, 10) 55·00
Z25 3d. rose (1873–77) (Plate No. 11)
Z26 4d. vermilion (1865–73) *From* 50·00
Plate Nos. 9, 10, 11, 12, 13, 14.
Z27 6d. lilac (1865–67) (Plate Nos. 5, 6)
Z28 6d. lilac (1867) (Plate No. 6) 80·00
Z29 6d. violet (1867–70) (Plate Nos. 8, 9) *From* 70·00
Z30 6d. buff (1872–73) (Plate Nos. 11, 12) *From* 75·00
Z31 6d. chestnut (1872) (Plate No. 11) 55·00
Z32 6d. grey (1873) (Plate No. 12)
Z33 9d. straw (1865) £425
Z34 9d. straw (1867) £225
Z35 10d. red-brown (1867) £300
Z36 1s. green (1865) (Plate No. 4) £170
Z37 1s. green (1867–73) (Plate Nos. 4, 5, 6, 7) *From* 50·00
Z38 2s. blue (1867) £250
Z39 5s. rose (1867–74) (Plate Nos. 1, 2) *From* £475

RIO DE JANEIRO

CROWNED-CIRCLE HANDSTAMPS

CC3 CC **7** RIO DE JANEIRO (Black, B., G. *or* R.) (6.1.1851) *Price on cover* £500

Stamps of GREAT BRITAIN *cancelled* "C 83" *as Type* **12**.
1866–74.
Z40 1d. rose-red (1857) 45·00
Z41 1d. rose-red (1864–79) *From* 38·00
Plate Nos. 71, 76, 80, 82, 86, 94, 103, 113, 117, 119, 123, 130, 132, 134, 135, 146, 148, 159, 161, 166, 185, 200, 204.
Z42 2d. blue (1858–69) *From* 38·00
Plate Nos. 9, 12, 13, 14.
Z43 3d. rose (1867–73) *From* 45·00
Plate Nos. 4, 5, 6, 7, 8, 9.
Z44 3d. rose (1873–77) (Plate No. 11)
Z45 4d. vermilion (1865–73) *From* 50·00
Plate Nos. 8, 9, 10, 11, 12, 13, 14.
Z46 6d. lilac (1865–67) (Plate No. 5) £100
Z47 6d. lilac (1867) (Plate No. 6) 75·00
Z48 6d. violet (1867–70) (Plate Nos. 6, 8, 9) *From* 70·00
Z49 6d. buff (1872) (Plate No. 11) 75·00
Z50 6d. chestnut (1872) (Plate No. 11) 45·00
Z51 6d. grey (1873) (Plate No. 12)
Z52 9d. straw (1865) £400
Z53 9d. straw (1867) £200
Z54 10d. red-brown (1867) £275
Z55 1s. green (1865) (Plate No. 4) £140
Z56 1s. green (1867–73) (Plate Nos. 4, 5, 6, 7). *From* 45·00
Z57 1s. green (1873–77) (Plate Nos. 8, 9). 70·00
Z58 2s. blue (1867) £130
Z59 5s. rose (1867–74) (Plate Nos. 1, 2) *From* £425

CAPE VERDE ISLANDS

The British Packet Agency at St. Vincent opened in 1851 as part of the revised service to South America. The agency was closed by 1860.

CROWNED-CIRCLE HANDSTAMPS

CC1 CC **6** ST. VINCENT C.DE.V. (6.1.1851)
Although recorded in the G.P.O. Proof Books, no example of No. CC1 is known on cover.

CHILE

The British Postal Agency at Valparaiso opened on 7 May 1846, to be followed by further offices at Caldera (1858) and Coquimbo (1863). The stamps of Great Britain were introduced in 1865 and can be found used in combination with Chile adhesives paying the local postage. All three offices closed on 31 March 1881 when Chile joined the U.P.U.

CALDERA

Stamps of GREAT BRITAIN *cancelled* "C 37" *as in Type* **4** *in black and blue.*
1865–81.
Z1 1d. rose-red (1864–79) *From* 55·00
Plate Nos. 71, 72, 88, 90, 95, 160, 195.
Z2 1½d. lake-red (1870–74) (Plate No. 3)
Z3 2d. blue (1858–69) (Plate No. 9) 60·00
Z4 3d. rose (1865) (Plate No. 4) 90·00
Z5 3d. rose (1867–73) (Plate Nos. 5, 7) 65·00
Z6 3d. rose (1873–76) *From* 55·00
Plate Nos. 11, 12, 16, 17, 18, 19.
Z7 4d. red (1862) (Plate No. 4)
Z8 4d. vermilion (1865–73) *From* 55·00
Plate Nos. 8, 11, 12, 13, 14.
Z9 4d. sage-green (1877) (Plate No. 16)
Z10 6d. lilac (1862) (Plate No. 4) £100
Z11 6d. lilac (1865–67) (Plate Nos. 5, 6) *From* £130
Z12 6d. violet (1867–70) (Plate Nos. 6, 8, 9)... *From* 90·00
Z13 6d. buff (1872) (Plate No. 11)
Z14 6d. chestnut (1872) (Plate No. 11)
Z15 6d. grey (1873) (Plate No. 12)
Z16 6d. grey (1874–80) *From* 55·00
Plate Nos. 13, 14, 15, 16, 17.
Z17 8d. orange (1876) £350
Z18 9d. straw (1867) £250
Z19 10d. red-brown (1867) £275
Z20 1s. green (1865) (Plate No. 4)
Z21 1s. green 1867–73 (Plate Nos. 4, 5, 6) *From* 55·00
Z22 1s. green (1873–77) *From* 85·00
Plate Nos. 8, 10, 11, 12, 13.
Z23 2s. blue (1867) £225
Z23*a* 2s. cobalt (1867)
Z24 2s. brown (1880) £1900
Z25 5s. rose (1867–74) (Plate No. 2) £475

COQUIMBO

Stamps of GREAT BRITAIN *cancelled* "C 40" *as in Type* **4** *or with circular date stamp as Type* **16**.
1865–81.
Z26 ½d. rose-red (1870–79) (Plate No. 14)
Z27 1d. rose-red (1857)
Z28 1d. rose-red (1864–79) (Plate Nos. 85, 204)
Z29 2d. blue (1858–69) (Plate Nos. 9, 14)
Z30 3d. rose (1865)
Z31 3d. rose (1872) (Plate No. 8)
Z32 3d. rose (1873–76) (Plate Nos. 18, 19) *From* 55·00
Z33 4d. red (1863) (Plate No. 4) (*Hair lines*)
Z34 4d. vermilion (1865–73) (Plate Nos. 12, 14) 60·00
Z35 4d. sage-green (1877) (Plate Nos. 15, 16). *From* £200
Z36 6d. lilac (1862) (Plate Nos. 3, 4) *From* 85·00
Z37 6d. lilac (1865–67) (Plate No. 5)
Z38 6d. lilac (1867) (Plate No. 6) 75·00
Z39 6d. violet (1867–70) (Plate Nos. 6, 8, 9)... *From* 70·00
Z40 6d. buff (1872–73) (Plate Nos. 11, 12) *From* 75·00
Z41 6d. chestnut (1872) (Plate No. 11)
Z42 6d. grey (1873) (Plate No. 12) £210
Z43 6d. grey (1874–76) *From* 55·00
Plate Nos. 13, 14, 15, 16.
Z44 8d. orange (1876)
Z45 9d. straw (1862) £300
Z46 9d. straw (1867) £225
Z47 10d. red-brown (1867) £325
Z48 1s. green (1865) (Plate No. 4) £170
Z49 1s. green (1867–73) (Plate Nos. 4, 5, 6) 55·00
Z50 1s. green (1873–77) *From* 80·00
Plate Nos. 8, 10, 11, 12, 13.
Z51 2s. blue (1867) £190
Z51*a* 2s. cobalt (1867)
Z52 2s. brown (1880) £1900
Z53 5s. rose (1867–74) (Plate Nos. 1, 2) *From* £475

VALPARAISO

CROWNED-CIRCLE HANDSTAMPS

CC1 CC **1** VALPARAISO (R.) (*without stop*) (13.1.1846) *Price on cover* £400
CC2 VALPARAISO. (R.) (*with stop*) (16.7.1846) *Price on cover* £450

Stamps of GREAT BRITAIN *cancelled* "C 30", *as in Types* **12**, **14** *and* **14a** (*without* "PAID" *before* 1870) *or with circular date stamp as Type* **16**.
1865–81.
Z54 ½d. rose-red (1870–79) *From* 65·00
Plate Nos. 6,11, 12, 13, 14.
Z55 1d. rose-red (1864–79) *From* 32·00
Plate Nos. 80, 84, 85, 89, 91, 101, 106, 113, 116, 122, 123, 138, 140, 141, 146, 148, 149, 152, 157, 158, 162, 167, 175, 178, 181, 185, 186, 187, 189, 190, 195, 197, 198, 199, 200, 201, 207, 209, 210, 211, 212, 213, 214, 215, 217.
Z56 1½d. lake-red (1870–74) (Plate Nos, 1, 3) *From* 65·00
Z57 2d. blue (1858–69) (Plate Nos. 9, 13, 14, 15) 45·00
Z58 2½d. rosy mauve (1875), white paper £200
Plate No. 2.
Z59 2½d. rosy mauve (1876) (Plate Nos. 4, 8) £165
Z60 3d. carmine-rose (1862)
Z61 3d. rose (1865) (Plate No. 4)
Z62 3d. rose (1867–73) *From* 50·00
Plate Nos. 5, 6, 7, 8, 9, 10.
Z63 3d. rose (1873–76) From 38·00
Plate Nos. 11, 12, 14, 16, 17, 18, 19.
Z63*a* 4d. red (1862) (Plate Nos. 3, 4)
Z64 4d. vermilion (1865–73) *From* 50·00
Plate Nos. 9, 10, 11, 12, 13, 14.
Z65 4d. vermilion (1876) (Plate No. 15) £300
Z66 4d. sage-green (1877) (Plate Nos. 15, 16) *From* £200
Z67 4d. grey-brown (1880) wmk Large Garter
Plate No. 17.
Z68 6d. lilac (1862) (Plate Nos. 3, 4) *From* £100
Z69 6d. lilac (1865) (Plate Nos. 5, 6)
Z70 6d. lilac (1867) (Plate No. 6)
Z71 6d. violet (1867–70) (Plate Nos. 6, 8, 9)... *From* 70·00
Z72 6d. buff (1872–73) (Plate Nos. 11, 12) *From* 80·00
Z73 6d. chestnut (1872) (Plate No. 11) 45·00
Z74 6d. grey (1873) (Plate No. 12) £210
Z75 6d. grey (1874–80) *From* 45·00
Plate Nos. 13, 14, 15, 16, 17.
Z76 6d. grey (1881) (Plate No. 17)
Z77 8d. orange (1876) £300
Z78 9d. straw (1862)
Z79 9d. straw (1865)
Z80 9d. straw (1867) £200
Z81 10d. red-brown (1867) £275
Z82 1s. green (1865) (Plate No. 4)
Z83 1s. green (1867–73) *From* 38·00
Plate Nos. 4, 5, 6, 7.
Z84 1s. green (1873–77) *From* 65·00
Plate Nos. 8, 9, 10, 11, 12, 13.
Z85 1s. orange-brown (1880) (Plate No. 13) £375
Z86 2s. blue (1867) £120
Z86*a* 2s. cobalt (1867) £1500
Z87 2s. brown (1880) £1900
Z88 5s. rose (1867–74) (Plate Nos. 1, 2) *From* £400
Z89 10s. grey-green (1878) (wmk Cross) £2750
Z90 £1 brown-lilac (1878) (wmk Cross) £3750

1880.
Z91 1d. Venetian red 90·00
Z92 1½d. Venetian red £130

COLOMBIA

The system of British Postal Agencies in the area was inaugurated by the opening of the Carthagena office in 1825. In 1842 agencies at Chagres, Panama and Santa Martha were added to the system. A further office opened at Colon in 1852, this port also being known as Aspinwall. During 1872 the system was further enlarged by an office at Savanilla, although this agency was later, 1878, transferred to Barranquilla.

Stamps of Great Britain were supplied to Carthagena, Panama and Santa Martha in 1865, Colon in 1870 and Savanilla in 1872. Combination covers with Colombia stamps paying the local postage are known from Santa Martha and Savanilla as are similar covers from Panama showing Costa Rica and El Salvador stamps.

All offices, except Chagres which had ceased to operate in 1855, closed for public business on 30 June 1881. Colon and Panama continued to exist as transit offices to deal with the mail across the isthmus. Both finally closed on 31 March 1921.

CARTHAGENA

CROWNED-CIRCLE HANDSTAMPS

CC1 CC **1b** CARTHAGENA (R.) (15.1.1841)
CC2 CC **1** CARTHAGENA (1.7.1846) *Price on cover* £1000
Although recorded in the G.P.O. Proof Books, no example of No. CC1 is known on cover.

Stamps of GREAT BRITAIN cancelled "C 56" *as in Type* **4**.
1865–81.
Z1 ½d. rose-red (1870–79) (Plate No. 10)
Z2 1d. rose-red (1864–79) *From* 55·00
Plate Nos. 78, 87, 100, 111, 113, 117, 119, 125, 172, 189, 217.
Z3 2d. blue (1858–69) (Plate Nos. 9, 14) *From* 55·00
Z4 3d. rose (1865) (Plate No. 4)
Z5 3d. rose (1865–68) (Plate Nos. 4, 5)
Z6 3d. rose (1873–79) (Plate Nos. 12, 17, 18) *From* 55·00
Z7 4d. vermilion (1865–73) *From* 55·00
Plate Nos. 7, 8, 9, 10, 11, 12, 13, 14.
Z8 4d. vermilion (1876) (Plate No. 15) £300
Z9 4d. sage-green (1877) (Plate Nos. 15, 16) *From* £200
Z10 6d. lilac (1865–67) (Plate Nos. 5, 6)
Z11 6d. violet (1867–70) (Plate Nos. 6, 8) *From* 75·00
Z12 6d. grey (1873) (Plate No. 12) £210
Z13 6d. grey (1874–76) *From* 55·00
Plate Nos. 13, 14, 15, 16.
Z14 8d. orange (1876) £325
Z15 9d. straw (1865)
Z16 1s. green (1865)
Z17 1s. green (1867–73) (Plate Nos. 4, 5, 7) *From* 60·00
Z18 1s. green (1873–77) *From* 70·00
Plate Nos. 8, 9, 10, 11, 12, 13.
Z19 1s. orange-brown (1880)
Z20 2s. blue (1867) £275
Z21 5s. rose (1867) (Plate No. 1) £500

Cancelled "C 65" (*incorrect handstamp, supplied in error*) *as Type* **12**.

1866–81.
Z22 ½d. rose-red (1870–79) (Plate No. 10)
Z23 1d. rose-red (1864–79) *From* 75·00
Plate Nos. 100, 106, 111, 123.
Z23*a* 1½d. lake-red (1870) (Plate No. 3)
Z24 2d. blue (1858–69) (Plate No. 9) 75·00
Z25 2d. rose (1880)
Z26 2½d. blue (1880) (Plate No. 19)
Z27 3d. rose (1867–73) (Plate No. 9)
Z28 3d. rose (1873–79) (Plate Nos. 14, 17, 19, 20)

(5)

(6)

(7)

VERTICAL OVAL

(8)

(9)

(10)

(11)

(11A)

(12)

(13)

(14)

(14A)

(14B)

(15)

CIRCULAR DATE STAMPS

(16)

(16A)

(17)

(17A)

(17B)

(18)

(19)

(20)

(21)

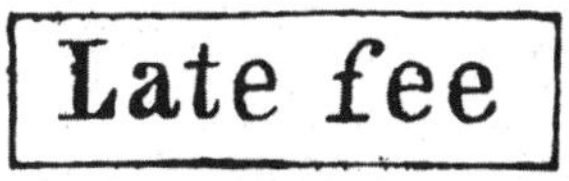

(22)

ARGENTINE REPUBLIC

BUENOS AYRES

The first regular monthly British mail packet service was introduced in 1824, replacing a private arrangement which had previously existed for some years.

Great Britain stamps were used from 1860 until the office closed at the end of June 1873. Until 1878 the British Consul continued to sell stamps which were used in combination with an Argentine value prepaying the internal rate. The British stamps on such covers were cancelled on arrival in England.

CROWNED-CIRCLE HANDSTAMPS

CC1	CC **7** BUENOS AYRES (Black or R.) (5.1.1851) .... *Price on cover*	£775

Stamps of GREAT BRITAIN *cancelled* "B 32" *as Types* **2**, **12** *or* **13** *in black or blue.*

1860–73.

Z1	1d. rose-red (1857)	45·00
Z2	1d. rose-red (1864) .... *From*	38·00
	Plate Nos. 71, 72, 73, 74, 76, 78, 79, 80, 81, 82, 85, 87, 89, 90, 91, 92, 93, 94, 95, 96, 97, 99, 101, 103, 104, 107, 108, 110, 112, 113, 114, 117, 118, 119, 120, 121, 123, 125, 127, 129, 130, 131, 135, 136, 138, 139, 140, 142, 143, 145, 147, 149, 150, 151, 155, 159, 163, 164, 166, 169, 172.	
Z3	2d. blue (1858–69) .... *From*	45·00
	Plate Nos. 8, 9, 12, 13, 14.	
Z4	3d. carmine-rose (1862)	£270
Z5	3d. rose (1865) (Plate No. 4)	£110
Z6	3d. rose (1867–73) .... *From*	45·00
	Plate Nos. 4, 5, 6, 7, 8, 9, 10.	
Z7	4d. rose (1857)	£110
Z8	4d. red (1862) (Plate Nos. 3, 4)	£100
Z9	4d. vermilion (1865–73) .... *From*	50·00
	Plate Nos. 7, 8, 9, 10, 11, 12, 13.	
Z10	6d. lilac (1856)	£100
Z11	6d. lilac (1862) (Plate Nos. 3, 4)	
Z12	6d. lilac (1865–67) (Plate Nos. 5, 6) .... *From*	80·00
Z13	6d. lilac (1867) (Plate No. 6)	90·00
Z14	6d. violet (1867–70) (Plate Nos. 6, 8, 9)... *From*	70·00
Z15	6d. buff (1872) (Plate No. 11)	85·00
Z16	6d. chestnut (1872) (Plate No. 11)	45·00
Z17	9d. bistre (1862)	£325
Z18	9d. straw (1862)	£300
Z19	9d. straw (1865)	£475
Z20	9d. straw (1867)	£300
Z21	10d. red-brown (1867)	£325
Z22	1s. green (1856)	£275
Z23	1s. green (1862)	£170
Z24	1s. green (1865) (Plate No. 4)	£160
Z25	1s. green (1867–73) (Plate Nos. 4, 5, 6, 7) *From*	45·00
Z26	1s. green (1873–77) (Plate No. 8)	
Z27	2s. blue (1867)	£150
Z28	5s. rose (1867) (Plate No. 1)	£450

A "B 32' obliteration was later used by Mauritius on its own stamps.

AZORES

ST. MICHAELS (SAN MIGUEL)

A British Postal Agency existed at Ponta Delgada, the chief port of the island, to operate with the services of the Royal Mail Steam Packet Company.

CROWNED-CIRCLE HANDSTAMPS

CC1	CC **1b** ST. MICHAELS (27.5.1842)	

Although recorded in the G.P.O. Proof Books, no example of No. CC1 is known on cover.

BOLIVIA

COBIJA

It is believed that the British Postal Agency opened in 1862. The stamps of Great Britain were used between 1865 and 1878. They can be found used in combination with Bolivia adhesive stamps paying the local postage. The Agency closed in 1881, the town having been occupied by Chile in 1879

CROWNED-CIRCLE HANDSTAMPS

CC1	CC **4** COBIJA (29.3.1862)	

Although recorded in the G.P.O. Proof Books, no example of No. CC1 is known on cover.

Stamps of GREAT BRITAIN *cancelled* "C 39" *as Types* **4**, **8** *or* **12**.

1865–78.

Z1	1d. rose-red (Plate Nos. 93, 95)	
Z2	2d. blue (1858–69) (Plate No. 14)	
Z3	3d. rose (1867–73) (Plate No. 6)	
Z4	3d. rose (1873–76) (Plate Nos. 16, 19)	
Z5	4d. sage-green (1877) (Plate No. 15)	£600
Z6	6d. violet (1867–70) (Plate No. 9)	£600

Z7	6d. buff (1872) (Plate No. 11)	
Z8	6d. grey (1874–76) (Plate Nos. 13, 14, 15, 16)	£500
Z9	1s. green (1867–73) (Plate Nos. 4, 5)	£500
Z10	1s. green (1873–77) (Plate Nos. 10, 11, 12, 13).	£500
Z11	2s. blue (1867)	£650
Z12	5s. rose (1867–74) (Plate No. 2)	£1200

BRAZIL

The first packets ran to Brazil in 1808 when the Portuguese royal family went into exile at Rio de Janeiro. The Agencies at Bahia and Pernambuco did not open until 1851. All three agencies used the stamps of Great Britain from 1866 and these can be found used in combination with Brazil adhesive stamps paying the local postage. The agencies closed on 30 June 1874

BAHIA

CROWNED-CIRCLE HANDSTAMPS

CC1	CC **7** BAHIA (Black, B. *or* R.) (6.1.1851) *Price on cover*	£2750

Stamps of GREAT BRITAIN *cancelled* "C 81" *as Type* **12**.

1866–74.

Z1	1d. rose-red (1864–79) *From* Plate Nos. 90, 93, 96, 108, 113, 117, 135, 140, 147, 155.	45·00
Z2	1½d. lake-red (1870–74) (Plate No. 3)	£110
Z3	2d. blue (1858–59) (Plate Nos. 9, 12, 13, 14)	65·00
Z4	3d. rose (1865) (Plate No. 4)	
Z5	3d. rose (1867–73) (Plate Nos. 4, 6, 8, 9, 10)	55·00
Z6	3d. rose (1873–79) (Plate No. 11)	
Z7	4d. vermilion (1865–73) *From* Plate Nos. 8, 9, 10, 11, 12, 13.	50·00
Z8	6d. lilac (1865–67) (Plate No. 5)	
Z9	6d. lilac (1867) (Plate No. 6)	90·00
Z10	6d. violet (1867–70) (Plate Nos. 6, 8, 9) *From*	70·00
Z11	6d. buff (1872–73) (Plate Nos. 11, 12) *From*	£100
Z12	6d. chestnut (1872) (Plate No. 11)	£100
Z13	6d. grey (1873) (Plate No. 12)	
Z14	6d. grey (1874–76) (Plate No. 13)	
Z15	9d. straw (1865)	£425
Z16	9d. straw (1867)	£250
Z17	1s. green (1865) (Plate No. 4)	£170
Z18	1s. green (1867–73) (Plate Nos. 4, 5, 6, 7) *From*	50·00
Z19	1s. green (1873–77) (Plate Nos. 8, 9)	85·00
Z20	2s. blue (1867)	£275
Z21	5s. rose (1867) (Plate No. 1)	£450

PERNAMBUCO

CROWNED-CIRCLE HANDSTAMPS

CC2	CC **7** PERNAMBUCO (Black *or* R.) (6.1.1851) *Price on cover*	£2750

Stamps of GREAT BRITAIN *cancelled* "C 82" *as Type* **12** *or with circular date stamp as Type* **16**.

1866–74.

Z22	1d. rose-red (1864–79) *From* Plate Nos. 85, 108, 111, 130, 131, 132, 149, 157, 159, 160, 187.	45·00
Z23	2d. blue (1858–69) *From* Plate Nos. 9, 12, 13, 14.	55·00
Z23a	3d. rose (1865) (Plate No. 4)	£110
Z24	3d. rose (1867–73) (Plate Nos. 4, 5, 6, 7, 10)	55·00
Z25	3d. rose (1873–77) (Plate No. 11)	
Z26	4d. vermilion (1865–73) *From* Plate Nos. 9, 10, 11, 12, 13, 14.	50·00
Z27	6d. lilac (1865–67) (Plate Nos. 5, 6)	
Z28	6d. lilac (1867) (Plate No. 6)	80·00
Z29	6d. violet (1867–70) (Plate Nos. 8, 9) *From*	70·00
Z30	6d. buff (1872–73) (Plate Nos. 11, 12) *From*	75·00
Z31	6d. chestnut (1872) (Plate No. 11)	55·00
Z32	6d. grey (1873) (Plate No. 12)	
Z33	9d. straw (1865)	£425
Z34	9d. straw (1867)	£225
Z35	10d. red-brown (1867)	£300
Z36	1s. green (1865) (Plate No. 4)	£170
Z37	1s. green (1867–73) (Plate Nos. 4, 5, 6, 7) *From*	50·00
Z38	2s. blue (1867)	£250
Z39	5s. rose (1867–74) (Plate Nos. 1, 2) *From*	£475

RIO DE JANEIRO

CROWNED-CIRCLE HANDSTAMPS

CC3	CC **7** RIO DE JANEIRO (Black, B., G. *or* R.) (6.1.1851) *Price on cover*	£500

Stamps of GREAT BRITAIN *cancelled* "C 83" *as Type* **12**.

1866–74.

Z40	1d. rose-red (1857)	45·00
Z41	1d. rose-red (1864–79) *From* Plate Nos. 71, 76, 80, 82, 86, 94, 103, 113, 117, 119, 123, 130, 132, 134, 135, 146, 148, 159, 161, 166, 185, 200, 204.	38·00
Z42	2d. blue (1858–69) *From* Plate Nos. 9, 12, 13, 14.	38·00
Z43	3d. rose (1867–73) *From* Plate Nos. 4, 5, 6, 7, 8, 9.	45·00
Z44	3d. rose (1873–77) (Plate No. 11)	
Z45	4d. vermilion (1865–73) *From* Plate Nos. 8, 9, 10, 11, 12, 13, 14.	50·00
Z46	6d. lilac (1865–67) (Plate No. 5)	£100
Z47	6d. lilac (1867) (Plate No. 6)	75·00
Z48	6d. violet (1867–70) (Plate Nos. 6, 8, 9) *From*	70·00
Z49	6d. buff (1872) (Plate No. 11)	75·00
Z50	6d. chestnut (1872) (Plate No. 11)	45·00
Z51	6d. grey (1873) (Plate No. 12)	
Z52	9d. straw (1865)	£400
Z53	9d. straw (1867)	£200
Z54	10d. red-brown (1867)	£275
Z55	1s. green (1865) (Plate No. 4)	£140
Z56	1s. green (1867–73) (Plate Nos. 4, 5, 6, 7) *From*	45·00
Z57	1s. green (1873–77) (Plate Nos. 8, 9).	70·00
Z58	2s. blue (1867)	£130
Z59	5s. rose (1867–74) (Plate Nos. 1, 2) *From*	£425

CAPE VERDE ISLANDS

The British Packet Agency at St. Vincent opened in 1851 as part of the revised service to South America. The agency was closed by 1860.

CROWNED-CIRCLE HANDSTAMPS

CC1	CC **6** ST. VINCENT C.DE.V. (6.1.1851)	

Although recorded in the G.P.O. Proof Books, no example of No. CC1 is known on cover.

CHILE

The British Postal Agency at Valparaiso opened on 7 May 1846, to be followed by further offices at Caldera (1858) and Coquimbo (1863). The stamps of Great Britain were introduced in 1865 and can be found used in combination with Chile adhesives paying the local postage. All three offices closed on 31 March 1881 when Chile joined the U.P.U.

CALDERA

Stamps of GREAT BRITAIN *cancelled* "C 37" *as in Type* **4** *in black and blue.*

1865–81.

Z1	1d. rose-red (1864–79) *From* Plate Nos. 71, 72, 88, 90, 95, 160, 195.	55·00
Z2	1½d. lake-red (1870–74) (Plate No. 3)	
Z3	2d. blue (1858–69) (Plate No. 9)	60·00
Z4	3d. rose (1865) (Plate No. 4)	90·00
Z5	3d. rose (1867–73) (Plate Nos. 5, 7)	65·00
Z6	3d. rose (1873–76) *From* Plate Nos. 11, 12, 16, 17, 18, 19.	55·00
Z7	4d. red (1862) (Plate No. 4)	
Z8	4d. vermilion (1865–73) *From* Plate Nos. 8, 11, 12, 13, 14.	55·00
Z9	4d. sage-green (1877) (Plate No. 16)	
Z10	6d. lilac (1862) (Plate No. 4)	£100
Z11	6d. lilac (1865–67) (Plate Nos. 5, 6) *From*	£130
Z12	6d. violet (1867–70) (Plate Nos. 6, 8, 9) *From*	90·00
Z13	6d. buff (1872) (Plate No. 11)	
Z14	6d. chestnut (1872) (Plate No. 11)	
Z15	6d. grey (1873) (Plate No. 12)	
Z16	6d. grey (1874–80) *From* Plate Nos. 13, 14, 15, 16, 17.	55·00
Z17	8d. orange (1876)	£350
Z18	9d. straw (1867)	£250
Z19	10d. red-brown (1867)	£275
Z20	1s. green (1865) (Plate No. 4)	
Z21	1s. green 1867–73 (Plate Nos. 4, 5, 6) *From*	55·00
Z22	1s. green (1873–77) *From* Plate Nos. 8, 10, 11, 12, 13.	85·00
Z23	2s. blue (1867)	£225
Z23a	2s. cobalt (1867)	
Z24	2s. brown (1880)	£1900
Z25	5s. rose (1867–74) (Plate No. 2)	£475

COQUIMBO

Stamps of GREAT BRITAIN *cancelled* "C 40" *as in Type* **4** *or with circular date stamp as Type* **16**.

1865–81.

Z26	½d. rose-red (1870–79) (Plate No. 14)	
Z27	1d. rose-red (1857)	
Z28	1d. rose-red (1864–79) (Plate Nos. 85, 204)	
Z29	2d. blue (1858–69) (Plate Nos. 9, 14)	
Z30	3d. rose (1865)	
Z31	3d. rose (1872) (Plate No. 8)	
Z32	3d. rose (1873–76) (Plate Nos. 18, 19) *From*	55·00
Z33	4d. red (1863) (Plate No. 4) (*Hair lines*)	
Z34	4d. vermilion (1865–73) (Plate Nos. 12, 14)	60·00
Z35	4d. sage-green (1877) (Plate Nos. 15, 16). *From*	£200
Z36	6d. lilac (1862) (Plate Nos. 3, 4) *From*	85·00
Z37	6d. lilac (1865–67) (Plate No. 5)	
Z38	6d. lilac (1867) (Plate No. 6)	75·00
Z39	6d. violet (1867–70) (Plate Nos. 6, 8, 9) *From*	70·00
Z40	6d. buff (1872–73) (Plate Nos. 11, 12) *From*	75·00
Z41	6d. chestnut (1872) (Plate No. 11)	
Z42	6d. grey (1873) (Plate No. 12)	£210
Z43	6d. grey (1874–76) *From* Plate Nos. 13, 14, 15, 16.	55·00
Z44	8d. orange (1876)	
Z45	9d. straw (1862)	£300
Z46	9d. straw (1867)	£225
Z47	10d. red-brown (1867)	£325
Z48	1s. green (1865) (Plate No. 4)	£170
Z49	1s. green (1867–73) (Plate Nos. 4, 5, 6)	55·00
Z50	1s. green (1873–77) *From* Plate Nos. 8, 10, 11, 12, 13.	80·00
Z51	2s. blue (1867)	£190
Z51a	2s. cobalt (1867)	
Z52	2s. brown (1880)	£1900
Z53	5s. rose (1867–74) (Plate Nos. 1, 2) *From*	£475

VALPARAISO

CROWNED-CIRCLE HANDSTAMPS

CC1	CC **1** VALPARAISO (R.) (*without stop*) (13.1.1846) *Price on cover*	£400
CC2	VALPARAISO. (R.) (*with stop*) (16.7.1846) *Price on cover*	£450

Stamps of GREAT BRITAIN *cancelled* "C 30", *as in Types* **12**, **14** *and* **14a** (*without* "PAID" *before* 1870) *or with circular date stamp as Type* **16**.

1865–81.

Z54	½d. rose-red (1870–79) *From* Plate Nos. 6, 11, 12, 13, 14.	65·00
Z55	1d. rose-red (1864–79) *From* Plate Nos. 80, 84, 85, 89, 91, 101, 106, 113, 116, 122, 123, 138, 140, 141, 146, 148, 149, 152, 157, 158, 162, 167, 175, 178, 181, 185, 186, 187, 189, 190, 195, 197, 198, 199, 200, 201, 207, 209, 210, 211, 212, 213, 214, 215, 217.	32·00
Z56	1½d. lake-red (1870–74) (Plate Nos, 1, 3) *From*	65·00
Z57	2d. blue (1858–69) (Plate Nos. 9, 13, 14, 15)	45·00
Z58	2½d. rosy mauve (1875), white paper Plate No. 2.	£200
Z59	2½d. rosy mauve (1876) (Plate Nos. 4, 8)	£165
Z60	3d. carmine-rose (1862)	
Z61	3d. rose (1865) (Plate No. 4)	
Z62	3d. rose (1867–73) *From* Plate Nos. 5, 6, 7, 8, 9, 10.	50·00
Z63	3d. rose (1873–76) From Plate Nos. 11, 12, 14, 16, 17, 18, 19.	38·00
Z63a	4d. red (1862) (Plate Nos. 3, 4)	
Z64	4d. vermilion (1865–73) *From* Plate Nos. 9, 10, 11, 12, 13, 14.	50·00
Z65	4d. vermilion (1876) (Plate No. 15)	£300
Z66	4d. sage-green (1877) (Plate Nos. 15, 16). *From*	£200
Z67	4d. grey-brown (1880) wmk Large Garter Plate No. 17.	
Z68	6d. lilac (1862) (Plate Nos. 3, 4) *From*	£100
Z69	6d. lilac (1865) (Plate Nos. 5, 6)	
Z70	6d. lilac (1867) (Plate No. 6)	
Z71	6d. violet (1867–70) (Plate Nos. 6, 8, 9) *From*	70·00
Z72	6d. buff (1872–73) (Plate Nos. 11, 12) *From*	80·00
Z73	6d. chestnut (1872) (Plate No. 11)	45·00
Z74	6d. grey (1873) (Plate No. 12)	£210
Z75	6d. grey (1874–80) *From* Plate Nos. 13, 14, 15, 16, 17.	45·00
Z76	6d. grey (1881) (Plate No. 17)	
Z77	8d. orange (1876)	£300
Z78	9d. straw (1862)	
Z79	9d. straw (1865)	
Z80	9d. straw (1867)	£200
Z81	10d. red-brown (1867)	£275
Z82	1s. green (1865) (Plate No. 4)	
Z83	1s. green (1867–73) *From* Plate Nos. 4, 5, 6, 7.	38·00
Z84	1s. green (1873–77) *From* Plate Nos. 8, 9, 10, 11, 12, 13.	65·00
Z85	1s. orange-brown (1880) (Plate No. 13)	£375
Z86	2s. blue (1867)	£120
Z86a	2s. cobalt (1867)	£1500
Z87	2s. brown (1880)	£1900
Z88	5s. rose (1867–74) (Plate Nos. 1, 2) *From*	£400
Z89	10s. grey-green (1878) (wmk Cross)	£2750
Z90	£1 brown-lilac (1878) (wmk Cross)	£3750

1880.

Z91	1d. Venetian red	90·00
Z92	1½d. Venetian red	£130

COLOMBIA

The system of British Postal Agencies in the area was inaugurated by the opening of the Carthagena office in 1825. In 1842 agencies at Chagres, Panama and Santa Martha were added to the system. A further office opened at Colon in 1852, this port also being known as Aspinwall. During 1872 the system was further enlarged by an office at Savanilla, although this agency was later, 1878, transferred to Barranquilla.

Stamps of Great Britain were supplied to Carthagena, Panama and Santa Martha in 1865, Colon in 1870 and Savanilla in 1872. Combination covers with Colombia stamps paying the local postage are known from Santa Martha and Savanilla as are similar covers from Panama showing Costa Rica and El Salvador stamps.

All offices, except Chagres which had ceased to operate in 1855, closed for public business on 30 June 1881. Colon and Panama continued to exist as transit offices to deal with the mail across the isthmus. Both finally closed on 31 March 1921.

CARTHAGENA

CROWNED-CIRCLE HANDSTAMPS

CC1	CC **1b** CARTHAGENA (R.) (15.1.1841)	
CC2	CC **1** CARTHAGENA (1.7.1846) *Price on cover*	£1000

Although recorded in the G.P.O. Proof Books, no example of No. CC1 is known on cover.

Stamps of GREAT BRITAIN cancelled "C 56" *as in Type* **4**.

1865–81.

Z1	½d. rose-red (1870–79) (Plate No. 10)	
Z2	1d. rose-red (1864–79) *From* Plate Nos. 78, 87, 100, 111, 113, 117, 119, 125, 172, 189, 217.	55·00
Z3	2d. blue (1858–69) (Plate Nos. 9, 14) *From*	55·00
Z4	3d. rose (1865) (Plate No. 4)	
Z5	3d. rose (1865–68) (Plate Nos. 4, 5)	
Z6	3d. rose (1873–79) (Plate Nos. 12, 17, 18). *From*	55·00
Z7	4d. vermilion (1865–73) *From* Plate Nos. 7, 8, 9, 10, 11, 12, 13, 14.	55·00
Z8	4d. vermilion (1876) (Plate No. 15)	£300
Z9	4d. sage-green (1877) (Plate Nos. 15, 16). *From*	£200
Z10	6d. lilac (1865–67) (Plate Nos. 5, 6)	
Z11	6d. violet (1867–70) (Plate Nos. 6, 8) *From*	75·00
Z12	6d. grey (1873) (Plate No. 12)	£210
Z13	6d. grey (1874–76) *From* Plate Nos. 13, 14, 15, 16.	55·00
Z14	8d. orange (1876)	£325
Z15	9d. straw (1865)	
Z16	1s. green (1865)	
Z17	1s. green (1867–73) (Plate Nos. 4, 5, 7) *From*	60·00
Z18	1s. green (1873–77) *From* Plate Nos. 8, 9, 10, 11, 12, 13.	70·00
Z19	1s. orange-brown (1880)	
Z20	2s. blue (1867)	£275
Z21	5s. rose (1867) (Plate No. 1)	£500

Cancelled "C 65" *(incorrect handstamp, supplied in error) as Type* **12**.

1866–81.

Z22	½d. rose-red (1870–79) (Plate No. 10)	
Z23	1d. rose-red (1864–79) *From* Plate Nos. 100, 106, 111, 123.	75·00
Z23a	1½d. lake-red (1870) (Plate No. 3)	
Z24	2d. blue (1858–69) (Plate No. 9)	75·00
Z25	2d. rose (1880)	
Z26	2½d. rose (1880) (Plate No. 19)	
Z27	3d. rose (1867–73) (Plate No. 9)	
Z28	3d. rose (1873–79) (Plate Nos. 14, 17, 19, 20)	

Z29	4d. vermilion (1865–73) *From* Plate Nos. 7, 8, 9, 11, 12, 13 14.	60·00
Z30	4d. vermilion (1876) (Plate No. 15)	£300
Z31	4d. sage-green (1877) (Plate Nos. 15, 16). *From*	£200
Z32	6d. violet (1867–70) (Plate Nos. 6, 8)	90·00
Z33	6d. pale buff (1872) (Plate No. 11)	
Z34	6d. grey (1873) (Plate No. 12)	£210
Z35	6d. grey (1874–80) *From* Plate Nos. 13, 14, 15, 16, 17.	60·00
Z36	8d. orange (1876)	£400
Z37	9d. straw (1865)	£450
Z38	1s. green (1865) (Plate No. 4)	£130
Z39	1s. green (1867) (Plate Nos. 4, 5, 6, 7) *From*	65·00
Z40	1s. green (1873–77) *From* Plate Nos. 8, 11, 12, 13.	75·00
Z41	1s. orange-brown (1880)	
Z42	2s. blue (1867)	£650
Z43	2s. brown (1880)	£2250
Z44	5s. rose (1867) (Plate Nos. 1, 2) *From*	£525

CHAGRES

CROWNED-CIRCLE HANDSTAMPS

CC3 CC **1** CHAGRES (16.9.1846)

Although recorded in the G.P.O. Proof Books, no example of No. CC3 is known on cover.

COLON

CROWNED-CIRCLE HANDSTAMPS

CC4 CC **5** COLON (R.) (21.6.1854) *Price on cover* £4750

Stamps of GREAT BRITAIN *cancelled* "E 88" *as in Type* **12** *or circular date stamp as Type* **16**, **16a** *and* **17a**.

1870–81.

Z45	1d. rose-red (1864–79) *From* Plate Nos. 107, 121, 122, 123, 125, 127, 130, 131, 133, 136, 138, 142, 150, 151, 152, 153, 155, 156, 157, 158, 160, 169, 170, 171, 174, 176, 178, 179, 184, 187, 188, 194, 195, 201, 209, 213, 214, 217.	50·00
Z46	1d. Venetian red (1880)	£110
Z47	1½d. lake-red (1870–74) (Plate No. 3)	£100
Z48	2d. blue (1858–69) (Plate Nos. 14, 15)	50·00
Z49	2d. pale rose (1880)	
Z50	3d. rose (1867–73) (Plate Nos. 6, 9)	
Z51	3d. rose (1873–76) *From* Plate Nos. 11, 12, 16, 18, 19, 20.	55·00
Z52	4d. vermilion (1865–73) *From* Plate Nos. 10, 11, 12, 13 14.	55·00
Z53	4d. vermilion (1876) (Plate No. 15)	
Z54	4d. sage-green (1877) (Plate Nos. 15, 16).. *From*	£200
Z55	4d. grey-brown (1880) wmk Large Garter Plate No. 17.	£325
Z56	4d. grey-brown (1880) wmk Crown Plate No. 17.	75·00
Z57	6d. violet (1867–70) (Plate Nos. 6, 8, 9)	
Z58	6d. buff (1872) (Plate No. 11)	
Z59	6d. chestnut (1872) (Plate No. 11)	65·00
Z60	6d. grey (1873) (Plate No. 12)	
Z61	6d. grey (1874–80) *From* Plate Nos. 13, 14, 15, 16, 17.	55·00
Z62	8d. orange (1876)	
Z63	9d. straw (1867)	£225
Z63*a*	10d. red-brown (1867)	
Z64	1s. green (1867–73) *From* Plate Nos. 4, 5, 6, 7.	50·00
Z65	1s. green (1873–77) *From* Plate Nos. 8, 9, 10, 11, 12, 13.	65·00
Z66	1s. orange-brown (1880) (Plate 13)	£375
Z67	1s. orange-brown (1881) (Plate 13)	£140
Z68	2s. blue (1867)	£150
Z69	2s. brown (1880)	£1900
Z70	5s. rose (1867) (Plate Nos. 1, 2) *From*	£500

PANAMA

CROWNED-CIRCLE HANDSTAMPS

CC5 CC **1** PANAMA (R.) (24.8.1846) *Price on cover* £1900

Stamps of GREAT BRITAIN *cancelled* "C 35" *as in Type* **4**, **11a**, **14b** *or as* **21**.

1865–81.

Z71	½d. rose-red (1870–79) *From* Plate Nos. 10, 11, 12, 13, 14, 15, 19.	50·00
Z72	1d. rose-red (1864–79) *From* Plate Nos. 71, 72, 76, 81, 85, 87, 88, 89, 93, 95, 96, 101, 104, 114, 122, 124, 130, 138, 139, 142, 159, 168, 171, 172, 174, 177, 179, 180, 182, 184, 185, 187, 189, 191, 192, 193, 196, 197, 200, 203, 204, 205, 207, 208, 209, 210, 211, 213, 214, 215, 218, 224.	32·00
Z73	1½d. lake-red (1870–74) (Plate No. 3)	65·00
Z74	2d. blue (1858–69) *From* Plate Nos. 9, 12, 13, 14, 15.	38·00
Z75	2½d. rosy mauve (1875) (Plate No. 1)	£200
Z76	2½d. rosy mauve (1876–80) (Plate Nos. 4, 12,16)	£170
Z77	2½d. blue (1880) (Plate No. 19)	
Z78	2½d. blue (1881) (Plate Nos. 22, 23)	
Z79	3d. carmine-rose (1862)	£250
Z80	3d. rose (1865) (Plate No. 4)	
Z81	3d. rose (1867–73) *From* Plate Nos. 4, 5, 6, 7, 8, 9.	50·00
Z82	3d. rose (1873–76) *From* Plate Nos. 12, 14, 15, 16, 17, 18, 19, 20.	38·00
Z83	3d. rose (1881) (Plate Nos. 20, 21)	
Z84	4d. red (1863) (Plate No. 4) (*Hair lines*)	£110
Z85	4d. vermilion (1865–73) *From* Plate Nos. 7, 8, 9, 10, 11, 12, 13, 14.	50·00
Z86	4d. vermilion (1876) (Plate No. 15)	£300
Z87	4d. sage-green (1877) (Plate Nos. 15, 16). *From*	£200
Z88	4d. grey-brown (1880) *wmk* Crown *From* Plate Nos. 17 18.	55·00
Z89	6d. lilac (1862) (Plate Nos. 3, 4) *From*	95·00
Z90	6d. lilac (1865–67) (Plate Nos. 5, 6) *From*	75·00
Z91	6d. lilac (1867) (Plate No. 6)	
Z92	6d. violet (1867–70) (Plate Nos. 6, 8, 9)	70·00
Z93	6d. buff (1872–73) (Plate Nos. 11, 12) *From*	75·00
Z94	6d. chestnut (Plate No. 11)	50·00
Z95	6d. grey (1873) (Plate No. 12)	£210
Z96	6d. grey (1874–80) *From* Plate Nos. 13, 14, 15, 16, 17.	50·00
Z97	6d. grey (1881) (Plate No. 17)	70·00
Z98	8d. orange (1876)	£300
Z99	9d. straw (1862)	£350
Z100	9d. straw (1867)	£250
Z101	10d. red-brown (1867)	£275
Z102	1s. green (1865) (Plate No. 4)	£140
Z103	1s. green (1867–73) *From* Plate Nos. 4, 5, 6, 7.	45·00
Z104	1s. green (1873–77) *From* Plate Nos. 8, 9, 10, 11, 12, 13.	60·00
Z105	1s. orange-brown (1880) (Plate No. 13)	£400
Z106	1s. orange-brown (1881) (Plate No. 13)	£110
Z107	2s. blue (1867)	£130
Z108	2s. brown (1880)	£1900
Z109	5s. rose (1867–74) (Plate Nos. 1, 2) *From*	£450

1880.

Z110	1d. Venetian red	55·00
Z111	2d. rose	£110
Z112	5d. indigo	£190

Later stamps cancelled "C 35" are believed to originate from sailors' letters or other forms of maritime mail.

SANTA MARTHA

CROWNED-CIRCLE HANDSTAMPS

CC6 CC **1b** SANTA MARTHA (R.) (15.12.1841) *Price on cover* £1900

Stamps of GREAT BRITAIN *cancelled* "C 62" *as in Type* **4**.

1865–81.

Z113	½d. rose-red (1870–79) (Plate No. 6)	90·00
Z114	1d. rose-red (1864–79) (Plate No. 106)	65·00
Z115	2d. blue (1858–69) (Plate Nos. 9, 13)	90·00
Z116	4d. vermilion (1865–73) *From* Plate Nos. 7, 8, 9, 11, 12, 13, 14.	60·00
Z117	4d. sage-green (1877) (Plate No. 15)	£200
Z118	4d. grey-brown (1880) wmk Large Garter Plate No. 17.	£325
Z119	4d. grey-brown (1880) wmk Crown Plate No. 17.	75·00
Z120	6d. lilac (1865–67) (Plate No. 5)	£100
Z121	6d. grey (1873) (Plate No. 12)	
Z122	6d. grey (1874–76) (Plate No. 14)	
Z123	8d. orange (1876)	£350
Z123*a*	9d. bistre (1862)	
Z124	1s. green (1865) (Plate No. 4)	£160
Z125	1s. green (1867–73) (Plate Nos. 5, 7) *From*	75·00
Z126	1s. green (1873–77) (Plate No. 8)	
Z127	2s. blue (1867)	£300
Z128	5s. rose (1867) (Plate No. 2)	£525

SAVANILLA (BARRANQUILLA)

Stamps of GREAT BRITAIN *cancelled* "F 69" *as in Type* **12**.

1872–81.

Z129	½d. rose-red (1870–79) (Plate No. 6)	90·00
Z130	1d. rose-red (1864–79) (Plate Nos. 122, 171)	65·00
Z131	1½d. lake-red (1870–74) Plate No. 3)	£110
Z132	3d. rose (1867–73) (Plate No. 7)	
Z133	3d. rose (1873–76) (Plate No. 20)	£100
Z134	3d. rose (1881) (Plate No. 20)	£100
Z135	4d. verm (1865–73) *From* Plate Nos. 12, 13, 14.	60·00
Z136	4d. vermilion (1876) (Plate No. 15)	£300
Z137	4d. sage-green (1877) (Plate Nos. 15, 16). *From*	£225
Z138	4d. grey-brown (1880) wmk Large Garter Plate No. 17.	£375
Z139	4d. grey-brown (1880) wmk Crown Plate No. 17.	75·00
Z140	6d. buff (1872) (Plate No. 11)	
Z141	6d. grey (1878) (Plate Nos. 16, 17) *From*	80·00
Z142	8d. orange (1876)	£350
Z143	1s. green (1867–73) (Plate Nos. 5,7)	75·00
Z144	1s. green (1873–77) (Plate Nos. 8, 11, 12, 13)	80·00
Z145	1s. orange-brown (1880)	£400
Z146	2s. blue (1867)	£225
Z147	5s. rose (1867–74) (Plate No. 2)	£525

CUBA

The British Postal Agency at Havana opened in 1762, the island then being part of the Spanish Empire. A further office, at St. Jago de Cuba, was added in 1841.

Great Britain stamps were supplied to Havana in 1865 and to St. Jago de Cuba in 1866. They continued in use until the offices closed on 30 May 1877.

HAVANA

CROWNED-CIRCLE HANDSTAMPS

1890.

CC1	CC **1b** HAVANA (13.11.1841) *Price on cover*	£1000
CC2	CC **1c** HAVANA (1848) *Price on cover*	£1000
CC3	CC **2** HAVANA (14.7.1848) *Price on cover*	£825

Stamps of GREAT BRITAIN *cancelled* "C 58" *as in Type* **4**, *or as Type* **14**, **14b**.

1865–77.

Z1	½d. rose-red (1870) (Plate Nos. 6, 12)	75·00
Z2	1d. rose-red (1864–79) Plate Nos. 86, 90, 93, 115, 120, 123, 144, 146, 171, 174, 208.	60·00
Z3	2d. blue (1858–69) (Plate Nos. 9, 14, 15)	75·00
Z4	3d. rose (1867–73) (Plate No. 4)	£140
Z5	3d. rose (1873–76) (Plate Nos. 18, 19)	
Z6	4d. vermilion (1865–73) *From* Plate Nos. 7, 8, 10, 11, 12, 13, 14.	65·00
Z7	4d. vermilion (1876) (Plate No. 15)	£300
Z8	6d. lilac (1865) (with hyphen) (Plate No. 5)	
Z9	6d. grey (1874–76) (Plate No. 15)	
Z10	8d. orange (1876)	
Z11	9d. straw (1867)	£275
Z12	10d. red-brown (1867)	£300
Z13	1s. green (1865) (Plate No. 4)	£160
Z14	1s. green (1867–73) (Plate Nos. 4, 5, 7)... *From*	65·00
Z15	1s. green (1873–77) (Plate Nos. 10, 12, 13) *From*	90·00
Z16	2s. blue (1867)	£225
Z17	5s. rose (1867–74) (Plate Nos. 1, 2) *From*	£475

ST. JAGO DE CUBA

CROWNED-CIRCLE HANDSTAMPS

CC4 CC **1b** ST JAGO-DE-CUBA (R.) (15.12.1841) *Price on cover* £6000

Stamps of GREAT BRITAIN *cancelled* "C 88" *as in Type* **12**.

1866–77.

Z18	½d. rose-red (1870–79) (Plate Nos. 4, 6, 14)	
Z19	1d. rose-red (1864–79) *From* Plate Nos. 100, 105, 106, 109, 111, 120, 123, 138, 144, 146, 147, 148, 171, 208.	£150
Z20	1½d. lake-red (1870–74) (Plate No. 3)	
Z21	2d. blue (1858–69) (Plate Nos. 9, 12, 13, 14)	£200
Z22	3d. rose (1867) (Plate No. 5)	
Z23	4d. vermilion (1865–73) *From* Plate Nos. 9, 10, 11, 12, 13, 14.	£225
Z24	4d. vermilion (1876) (Plate No. 15)	£600
Z25	6d. violet (1867–70) (Plate Nos. 6, 8, 9)... *From*	£450
Z26	6d. buff (Plate No. 11)	
Z27	9d. straw (1865)	
Z27*a*	9d. straw (1867)	
Z28	10d. red-brown (1867)	£600
Z29	1s. green (1867–73) (Plate Nos. 4, 5, 6)... *From*	£450
Z30	1s. green (1873–77) (Plate Nos. 9, 10, 12, 13)...	
Z31	2s. blue (1867)	
Z32	5s. rose (1867) (Plate 1)	

DANISH WEST INDIES

ST. THOMAS

The British Postal Agency at St. Thomas opened in January 1809 and by 1825 was the office around which many of the packet routes were organised.

Great Britain stamps were introduced on 3 July 1865 and can be found used in combination with Danish West Indies adhesives paying the local postage.

Following a hurricane in October 1867 the main British packet office was moved to Colon in Colombia.

The British Post Office at St. Thomas closed to the public on I September 1877, but continued to operate as a transit office for a further two years

CROWNED-CIRCLE HANDSTAMPS

CC1	CC **1** ST. THOMAS (R.) (20.2.49) *Price on cover*	£500
CC2	CC **6** ST. THOMAS (R.) (1.5.1855) *Price on cover*	£1650

Stamps of GREAT BRITAIN *cancelled* "C 51" *as in Types* **4**, **12** *or* **14**.

1865–79.

Z1	½d. rose-red (1870–79) Plate Nos. 5, 6, 8, 10, 11, 12.	38·00
Z2	1d. rose-red (1857)	
Z3	1d. rose-red (1864–79) *From* Plate Nos. 71, 72, 79, 81, 84, 85, 86, 87, 88, 89, 90, 93, 94, 95, 96, 97, 98, 99, 100, 101, 102, 105, 106, 107, 108, 109, 110, 111, 112, 113, 114, 116, 117, 118, 119, 120, 121, 122, 123, 124, 125, 127, 129, 130, 131, 133, 134, 136, 137, 138, 139, 140, 141, 142, 144, 145, 146, 147, 148, 149, 150, 151, 152, 154, 155, 156, 157, 158, 159, 160, 161, 162, 163, 164, 165, 166, 167, 169, 170, 171, 172, 173, 174, 175, 176, 177, 178, 179, 180, 181, 182, 184, 185, 186, 187, 189, 190, 197.	27·00
Z4	1½d. lake-red (1870–74) (Plate Nos. 1, 3)	65·00
Z5	2d. blue (1858–69) *From* Plate Nos. 9, 12, 13, 14, 15.	32·00
Z6	3d. rose (1865) (Plate No. 4)	90·00
Z7	3d. rose (1867–73) *From* Plate Nos. 4, 5, 6, 7, 8, 9, 10.	45·00
Z8	3d. rose (1873–76) *From* Plate Nos. 11, 12, 14, 15, 16, 17, 18, 19.	32·00
Z9	4d. red (1862) (Plate Nos. 3, 4)	75·00
Z10	4d. vermilion (1865–73) *From* Plate Nos. 7, 8, 9, 10, 11, 12, 13, 14.	50·00
Z11	4d. vermilion (1876) (Plate No. 15)	£300
Z12	4d. sage-green (1877) (Plate Nos. 15, 16).. *From*	£200
Z14	6d. lilac (1864) (Plate No. 4)	£150
Z15	6d. lilac (1865–67) (Plate Nos. 5, 6) *From*	75·00
Z16	6d. lilac (1867) (Plate No. 6)	75·00
Z17	6d. violet (1867–70) (Plate Nos. 6, 8, 9)... *From*	70·00
Z18	6d. buff (1872–73) (Plate Nos. 11, 12) *From*	75·00
Z19	6d. chestnut (1872) (Plate No. 11)	45·00
Z20	6d. grey (1873) (Plate No. 12)	£210
Z21	6d. grey (1874–76) *From* Plate Nos. 13, 14, 15, 16.	45·00
Z22	8d. orange (1876)	£275
Z23	9d. straw (1862)	£275
Z24	9d. bistre (1862)	£300
Z25	9d. straw (1865)	£375
Z26	9d. straw (1867)	£200
Z27	10d. red-brown (1867)	£275
Z28	1s. green (1865) (Plate No. 4)	£140
Z29	1s. green (1867–73) (Plate Nos. 4, 5, 6, 7) *From*	32·00
Z30	1s. green (1873–77) *From* Plate Nos, 8, 9, 10, 11, 12, 13.	60·00
Z31	2s. blue (1867)	£130
Z32	5s. rose (1867–74) (Plate Nos. 1, 2) *From*	£450

DOMINICAN REPUBLIC

British Postal Agencies may have existed in the area before 1867, but it is only from that year that details can be found concerning offices at Porto Plata and St. Domingo. Both were closed in 1871, but re-opened in 1876.

Although postmarks were supplied in 1866 it seems likely that Great Britain stamps were not sent until the offices re-opened in 1876.

Covers exist showing Great Britain stamps used in combination with those of Dominican Republic with the latter paying the local postage. Both agencies finally closed in 1881.

PORTO PLATA

Stamps of GREAT BRITAIN *cancelled "C 86" or circular date stamp as in Types* **8** *or* **17**.

1876–81.

Z1	½d. rose-red (1870–79) *From* Plate Nos. 10, 12, 14.	75·00
Z2	1d. rose-red (1864–79) *From* Plate Nos. 123, 130, 136, 146, 151, 178, 199, 200, 205, 217.	60·00
Z3	1½d. lake-red (1870–74) (Plate No. 3)	£110
Z4	2d. blue (1858–69) (Plate Nos. 14, 15)	75·00
Z5	2½d. rosy mauve (1876–79) *From* Plate Nos. 13, 14.	£200
Z6	3d. rose (1873–76) (Plate No. 18)	90·00
Z7	4d. vermilion (1873) (Plate No. 14)	90·00
Z8	4d. vermilion (1876) (Plate No. 15)	£325
Z9	4d. sage-green (1877) (Plate No. 15)	£250
Z10	6d. violet (1867–70) (Plate No. 8)	
Z11	6d. grey (1874–76) (Plate No. 15)	75·00
Z12	8d. orange (1876)	£400
Z13	1s. green (1867–73) (Plate Nos. 4, 7) *From*	65·00
Z14	1s. green (1873–77) *From* Plate Nos. 11, 12, 13.	75·00
Z15	2s. blue (1867)	£275
Z15*a*	5s. rose (1867–83) (Plate No. 2)	

ST. DOMINGO

Stamps of GREAT BRITAIN *cancelled "C 87" or circular date stamp as in Types* **12** *or* **16**.

1876–81.

Z16	½d. rose-red (1870–79) *From* Plate Nos. 5, 6, 8, 10, 11, 13.	90·00
Z17	1d. rose-red (1864–79) *From* Plate Nos. 146, 154, 171, 173, 174, 176, 178, 186, 190, 197, 220.	70·00
Z18	1½d. lake-red (1870–74) (Plate No. 3)	£110
Z19	2d. blue (1858–69) (Plate Nos. 13, 14)	£100
Z20	3d. rose (1873–76) (Plate No. 18)	
Z21	4d. vermilion (1865–73) *From* Plate Nos. 11, 12, 14.	£100
Z22	4d. vermilion (1876) (Plate No. 15)	£450
Z23	4d. sage-green (1877) (Plate No. 15)	£275
Z24	6d. grey (1874–76) (Plate No. 15)	
Z25	9d. straw (1867)	
Z26	1s. green (1867) (Plate No. 4)	
Z27	1s. green (1873–77) *From* Plate Nos. 10, 11, 12, 13.	£100
Z28	2s. blue (1867)	

ECUADOR

GUAYAQUIL

The first British Postal Agent in Guayaquil was appointed in 1848.

Great Britain stamps were supplied in 1865 and continued to be used until the agency closed on 30 June 1880. They can be found used in combination with stamps of Ecuador with the latter paying the local postage.

Stamps of GREAT BRITAIN *cancelled "C 41" as Type* **4**.

1865–80.

Z1	½d. rose-red (1870–79) (Plate Nos. 5, 6)	60·00
Z2	1d. rose-red (1857)	
Z3	1d. rose-red (1864–79) *From* Plate Nos. 74, 78, 85, 92, 94, 105, 110, 115, 133, 140, 145, 166, 174, 180, 216.	45·00
Z4	1½d. lake-red (1870–74) (Plate No. 3)	90·00
Z5	2d. blue (1858–69) (Plate Nos. 9, 13, 14). *From*	45·00
Z6	3d. carmine-rose (1862)	£250
Z7	3d. rose (1865) (Plate No. 4)	£120
Z8	3d. rose (1867–73) (Plate Nos. 6, 7, 9, 10). *From*	50·00
Z9	3d. rose (1873–76) *From* Plate Nos. 11, 12, 15, 16, 17, 18, 19, 20.	50·00
Z10	4d. red (1862) (Plate Nos. 3, 4)	£120
Z11	4d. vermilion (1865–73) *From* Plate Nos. 7, 8, 9, 10, 11, 12, 13, 14.	50·00
Z12	4d. vermilion (1876) (Plate No. 15)	£300
Z13	4d. sage-green (1877) (Plate Nos. 15, 16). *From*	£200
Z14	6d. lilac (1864) (Plate No. 4)	£150
Z15	6d. lilac (1865–67) (Plate Nos. 5, 6) *From*	75·00
Z16	6d. lilac (1867) (Plate No. 6)	
Z17	6d. violet (1867–70) (Plate Nos. 6, 8, 9) *From*	70·00
Z18	6d. buff (1872–73) (Plate Nos. 11, 12) *From*	80·00
Z19	6d. chestnut (1872) (Plate No. 11)	
Z20	6d. grey (1873) (Plate No. 12)	
Z21	6d. grey (1874–76) *From* Plate Nos. 13, 14, 15, 16.	50·00
Z22	8d. orange (1876)	£325
Z23	9d. straw (1862)	£275
Z24	9d. straw (1867)	£200
Z25	10d. red-brown (1867)	£300
Z26	1s. green (1865) (Plate No. 4)	£160
Z27	1s. green (1867–73) (Plate Nos. 4, 5, 6, 7) *From*	45·00
Z28	1s. green (1873–77) *From* Plate Nos. 8, 9, 10, 11, 12, 13.	75·00
Z29	2s. blue (1867)	£150
Z30	2s. brown (1880)	£2250
Z31	5s. rose (1867–74) (Plate Nos. 1, 2) *From*	£450

FERNANDO PO

The British government leased naval facilities on this Spanish island from 1827 until 1834. A British Consul was appointed in 1849 and a postal agency was opened on 1 April 1858.

The use of Great Britain stamps was authorised in 1858, but a cancellation was not supplied until 1874. The office remained open until 1877.

CROWNED-CIRCLE HANDSTAMPS

CC1	CC **4** FERNANDO-PO (R.) (19.2.1859) *Price on cover*	£5500

Stamps of GREAT BRITAIN *cancelled "247" as Type* **9**.

1874–77.

Z1	4d. vermilion (1865–72) (Plate Nos. 13, 14)	
Z2	4d. vermilion (1876) (Plate No. 15)	
Z3	6d. grey (1874–76) (Plate Nos. 13, 14, 15, 16)	

GUADELOUPE

A British Packet Agency was established on Guadeloupe on 1 October 1848 and continued to function until 1874.

No. CC1 is often found used in conjunction with French Colonies (General Issues) adhesive stamps.

A similar packet agency existed on Martinique from 1 October 1848 until 1879, but no crowned-circle handstamp was issued for it.

CROWNED-CIRCLE HANDSTAMPS

CC1	CC **1** GUADALOUPE (R., B. or Black) (9.3.1849) *Price on cover*	£2000

HAITI

The original British Postal Agencies in Haiti date from 1830 when it is known a Packet Agency was established at Jacmel. An office at Port-au-Prince followed in 1842, both these agencies remaining in operation until 30 June 1881.

During this period short-lived agencies also operated in the following Haitian towns: Aux Cayes (1848 to 1863, Cap Haitien (1842 to 1863), Gonaives (1849 to 1857) and St. Marc (1854 to 1861). A further agency may have operated at Le Mole around the year 1841.

Great Britain stamps were supplied to Jacmel in 1865 and to Port-au-Prince in 1869.

CAP HAITIEN

CROWNED-CIRCLE HANDSTAMPS

CC1	CC **1b** CAPE-HAITIEN (R.) (31.12.1841)	

Although recorded in the G.P.O. Proof Books, no example of No. CC1 is known on cover.

JACMEL

CROWNED-CIRCLE HANDSTAMPS

CC2	CC **1b** JACMEL (R.) (29.6.1843) .. *Price on cover*	£900

Stamps of GREAT BRITAIN *cancelled "C 59" as Tvpe* **4** *or with circular date stamp as Type* **16a**.

1865–81.

Z1	½d. rose-red (1870–79) *From* Plate Nos. 4, 5, 6, 10, 11, 12, 14, 15.	60·00
Z2	1d. rose-red (1864–79) *From* Plate Nos. 74, 81, 84, 87, 95, 106, 107, 109, 122, 136, 137, 139, 146, 148, 150, 151, 152, 156, 157, 159, 160, 162, 164, 166, 167, 170, 171, 179, 181, 183, 184, 186, 187, 189, 192, 194, 198, 200, 204, 206, 215, 219.	45·00
Z3	1½d. lake-red (1870–74) (Plate No. 3)	65·00
Z4	2d. blue (1858–69) (Plate Nos. 9, 13, 14, 15)	45·00
Z5	2½d. rosy mauve (1876) (Plate No. 4)	
Z6	3d. rose (1867–73) *From* Plate Nos. 5, 6, 7, 8, 9, 10.	50·00
Z7	3d. rose (1873–76) Plate Nos. 11, 12, 14, 16, 17, 18, 19.	50·00
Z8	4d. red (1863) (Plate No. 4) (*Hair lines*)	£120
Z9	4d. vermilion (1865–73) *From* Plate Nos. 7, 8, 9, 10, 11, 12, 13, 14.	50·00
Z10	4d. vermilion (1876) (Plate No. 15)	£300
Z11	4d. sage-green (1877) (Plate Nos. 15, 16). *From*	£200
Z12	4d. grey-brown (1880) *wmk* Large Garter Plate No. 17.	£325
Z13	4d. grey-brown (1880) *wmk* Crown Plate No. 17.	55·00
Z14	6d. lilac (1867) (Plate Nos. 5, 6)	80·00
Z15	6d. violet (1867–70) (Plate Nos. 8, 9)	75·00
Z16	6d. buff (1872–73) (Plate Nos. 11, 12) *From*	80·00
Z17	6d. chestnut (1872) (Plate No. 11)	
Z18	6d. grey (1873) (Plate No. 12)	
Z19	6d. grey (1874–76) *From* Plate Nos. 13, 14, 15, 16, 17.	55·00
Z20	8d. orange (1876)	£325
Z21	9d. straw (1862)	£275
Z22	9d. straw (1867)	£200
Z23	10d. red-brown (1867)	£300
Z24	1s. green (1865) (Plate No. 4)	£140
Z25	1s. green (1867–73) (Plate Nos. 4, 5, 6, 7) *From*	45·00
Z26	1s. green (1873–77) *From* Plate Nos. 8, 9, 10, 11, 12, 13.	65·00
Z27	1s. orange-brown (1880) (Plate No. 13)	£375
Z28	2s. blue (1867)	£160
Z29	2s. brown (1880)	£2250
Z30	5s. rose (1867–74) (Plate Nos. 1, 2) *From*	£450

1880.

Z31	½d. green (1880)	55·00
Z32	1d. Venetian red	55·00
Z33	1½d. Venetian red	75·00
Z34	2d. rose	£110

PORT-AU-PRINCE

CROWNED-CIRCLE HANDSTAMPS

CC3	CC **1b** PORT-AU-PRINCE (R.) (29.6.1843) *Price on cover*	£2250

Stamps of GREAT BRITAIN *cancelled "E 53" as in Types* **8**, **12** *or* **16**.

1869–81.

Z35	½d. rose-red (1870–79) *From* Plate Nos. 5, 6, 10, 11, 12, 13, 14.	60·00
Z36	1d. rose-red (1864–79) *From* Plate Nos. 87, 134, 154,146, 159, 167, 171, 173, 174, 177, 181, 183, 187, 189, 193, 199, 200, 201, 202, 206, 209, 210, 218, 219.	45·00
Z37	1½d. lake-red (1870–74) (Plate No. 3)	80·00
Z38	2d. blue (1858–69) (Plate Nos. 9, 14, 15)	50·00
Z40	2½d. rosy mauve (1876–79) (Plate Nos. 3, 9) *From*	£150
Z41	3d. rose (1867–73) (Plate Nos. 6, 7)	
Z42	3d. rose (1873–79) (Plate Nos. 17, 18, 20). *From*	50·00
Z43	4d. vermilion (1865–73) *From* Plate Nos. 11, 12, 13, 14.	50·00
Z44	4d. vermilion (1876) (Plate No. 15)	£300
Z45	4d. sage-green (1877) (Plate Nos. 15, 16). *From*	£200
Z46	4d. grey-brown (1880) wmk Large Garter Plate No. 17.	£325
Z47	4d. grey-brown (1880) wmk Crown Plate No. 17.	55·00
Z48	6d. grey (1874–76) (Plate Nos. 15, 16)	
Z49	8d. orange (1876)	£325
Z50	1s. green (1867–73) (Plate Nos. 4, 5, 6, 7) *From*	45·00
Z51	1s. green (1873–77) *From* Plate Nos. 8, 9, 10, 11, 12, 13.	65·00
Z52	1s. orange-brown (1880) (Plate No. 13)	£375
Z53	1s. orange-brown (1880) (Plate No. 13)	£120
Z54	2s. blue (1867)	£160
Z55	2s. brown (1880)	£2250
Z56	5s. rose (1867–74) (Plate Nos. 1, 2) *From*	£450
Z57	10s. greenish grey (1878)	£3250

1880.

Z58	½d. green	55·00
Z59	1d. Venetian red	55·00
Z60	1½d. Venetian red	75·00
Z61	2d. rose	£110

MACAO

A British Consular Post Office opened in 1841. It had been preceded by the Macao Boat Office, possibly a private venture, which operated in the 1830s. The office closed when the consulate closed on 30 September 1845, but was back in operation by 1854.

The Agency continued to function, in conjunction with the Hong Kong Post Office, until 28 February 1884 when Portugal joined the U.P.U.

CROWNED-CIRCLE HANDSTAMPS

Z 2

CC1	– PAID AT MACAO (crowned-oval 20 mm wide) (R.) (1844) *Price on cover*	£32500
CC2	Z **2** Crown and Macao (1881)	

No. CC2 with the Crown removed was used by the Portuguese post office in Macao as a cancellation until 1890.

A locally-cut mark, as Type CC **2**, inscribed "PAGO EM MACAO" is known on covers between 1870 and 1877. It was probably used by the Portuguese postmaster to send letters via the British Post Office (*Price* £10000).

MADEIRA

The British Packet Agency on this Portuguese island was opened in 1767 and was of increased importance from 1808 following the exile of the Portuguese royal family to Brazil. The South American packets ceased to call in 1858. It appears to have closed sometime around 1860.

CROWN-CIRCLE HANDSTAMPS

CC1	CC **1b** MADEIRA (R.) (28.2.1842) *Price on cover*	£17500

MEXICO

The British Postal Agency at Vera Cruz opened in 1825, following the introduction of the Mexican Packet service. No handstamps were supplied, however, until 1842, when a similar agency at Tampico was set up.

Great Britain stamps were used at Tampico from 1867, but, apparently, were never sent to the Vera Cruz office. Combination covers exist showing the local postage paid by Mexican adhesives. The Agency at Vera Cruz closed in 1874 and that at Tampico in 1876.

TAMPICO

CROWNED-CIRCLE HANDSTAMPS

CC1	CC **1b** TAMPICO (R.) (13.11.1841) *Price on cover*	£1750

No. CC1 may be found on cover, used in conjunction with Mexico adhesive stamps.

Stamps of GREAT BRITAIN *cancelled* "C 63" *as Type* **4**.

1867–76.

Z1	1d. rose-red (1864–79) *From* Plate Nos. 81, 89, 103, 117, 139, 147.	£110
Z2	2d. blue (1858–69) (Plate Nos. 9, 14)	£150
Z3	4d. vermilion (1865–73) *From* Plate Nos. 7, 8, 10, 11, 12, 13, 14.	£100
Z4	1s. green (1867–73) (Plate Nos. 4, 5, 7, 8)	£150
Z5	2s. blue (1867)	£500

VERA CRUZ

CROWNED-CIRCLE HANDSTAMPS

CC2	CC **1b** VERA CRUZ (R.) (13.11.1841) *Price on cover*	£1750
CC3	VERA CRUZ (Black) (*circa* 1845) *Price on cover*	£900

NICARAGUA

GREYTOWN

British involvement on the Mosquito Coast of Nicaragua dates from 1655 when contacts were first made with the indigenous Misquito Indians. A formal alliance was signed in 1740 and the area was considered as a British dependency until the Spanish authorities negotiated a withdrawal in 1786.

The Misquitos remained under British protection, however, and, following the revolutionary period in the Spanish dominions, this eventually led to the appropriation, by the Misquitos with British backing, of the town of San Juan del Norte, later renamed Greytown.

The port was included in the Royal West Indian Mail Steam Packet Company's mail network from January 1842, forming part of the Jamaica District. This arrangement only lasted until September of that year, however, although packets were once again calling at Greytown by November 1844. Following the discovery of gold in California the office increased in importance, owing to the overland traffic, although the first distinctive postmark is not recorded in use until February 1856.

A subsidiary agency, without its own postmark, operated at Bluefields from 1857 to 1863.

The British Protectorate over the Misquitos ended in 1860, but the British Post Office at Greytown continued to operate, being supplied with Great Britain stamps in 1865. These are occasionally found used in combination with Nicaragua issues, which had only internal validity.

The British Post Office at Greytown closed on 1 May 1882 when the Republic of Nicaragua joined the U.P.U.

CROWNED-CIRCLE HANDSTAMPS

CC1	C **4** GREYTOWN (R.) (14.4.1859)	

Although recorded in the G.P.O. Proof Books, no example of No. CC1 is known on cover.

Stamps of GREAT BRITAIN *cancelled* "C 57" *as in Types* **4** (*issued* 1865), **14a** (*issued* 1875), *or with circular postmark as Type* **16** (*issued* 1864).

1865–82.

Z1	½d. rose-red (1870–79) (Plate Nos. 5, 10, 11)	80·00
Z2	1d. rose-red (1864–79) Plate Nos. 180, 197, 210.	50·00
Z3	1½d. lake-red (1870) (Plate No. 3)	75·00
Z4	2d. blue (1858–69) (Plate Nos. 9, 14, 15)	
Z5	3d. rose (1873–76) (Plate Nos. 17, 18, 19, 20)	55·00
Z6	3d. rose (1881) (Plate No. 20)	
Z7	4d. vermilion (1865–73) *From* Plate Nos. 8, 10, 11, 12, 13, 14.	55·00
Z8	4d. vermilion (1876) (Plate No. 15)	£300
Z9	4d. sage-green (1877) (Plate Nos. 15, 16) *From*	£200
Z10	4d. grey-brown (1880) wmk Large Garter Plate No. 17.	£325
Z11	4d. grey-brown (1880) wmk Crown Plate No. 17.	90·00
Z12	6d. grey (1874–76) (Plate Nos. 14, 15, 16, 17)	95·00
Z13	8d. orange (1876)	£300
Z14	1s. green (1865) (Plate No. 4)	
Z15	1s. green (1867–73) (Plate Nos. 6, 7)	
Z16	1s. green (1873–77) *From* Plate Nos. 8, 10, 12, 13.	65·00
Z17	1s. orange-brown (1880) (Plate No. 13)	£375
Z18	1s. orange-brown (1881) (Plate No. 13)	£110
Z19	2s. blue (1867)	£160
Z20	2s. brown (1880)	£2250
Z21	5s. rose (1867–74) (Plate Nos. 1, 2) *From*	£450
Z22	5s. rose (1882) (Plate No. 4), *blue paper*	£2250
Z23	10s. greenish grey (1878)	£3250

1880.

Z24	1d. Venetian red	75·00
Z25	1½d. Venetian red	75·00

PERU

British Agencies in Peru date from 1846 when offices were established at Arica and Callao. The network was later expanded to include agencies at Paita (1848), Pisco (1868) and Iquique and Islay (both 1869). This last office was transferred to Mollendo in 1877.

It is believed that a further agency existed at Pisagua, but no details exist.

Great Britain stamps were supplied from 1865 and are often found in combination with Peru adhesives which paid the local postal tax.

The Postal Agency at Pisco closed in 1870 and the remainder in 1879, the towns of Arica, Iquique and Pisagua passing to Chile by treaty in 1883.

ARICA

CROWNED-CIRCLE HANDSTAMPS

CC1	CC **1** ARICA (Black or R.) (5.11.1850) *Price on cover*	£4250

Stamps of Great Britain *cancelled* "C 36" *as Types* **4**, **12**, **14b** *and* **16a** *in black and blue.*

1865–79.

Z1	½d. rose-red (1870–79) *From* Plate Nos. 5, 6, 10, 11, 13.	75·00
Z2	1d. rose-red (1864–79) *From* Plate Nos. 102, 139, 140, 163, 167.	55·00
Z3	1½d. lake-red (1870–74) (Plate No. 3)	
Z4	2d. blue (1858–69) (Plate No. 14)	75·00
Z5	3d. rose (1867–73) (Plate Nos. 5, 9)	
Z6	3d. rose (1873–76) *From* Plate Nos. 11, 12, 17, 18, 19.	55·00
Z7	4d. vermilion (1865–73) *From* Plate Nos. 10, 11, 12, 13, 14.	55·00
Z8	4d. vermilion (1876) (Plate No. 15)	
Z9	4d. sage-green (1877) (Plate Nos. 15, 16)	£225
Z10	6d. lilac (1862) (Plate Nos. 3, 4)	
Z11	6d. lilac (1865–67) (Plate No. 5)	
Z12	6d. violet (1867–70) (Plate Nos. 6, 8, 9) *From*	80·00
Z13	6d. buff (1872) (Plate No. 11)	£100
Z14	6d. chestnut (1872) (Plate No. 11)	£100
Z15	6d. grey (1873) (Plate No. 12)	£210
Z16	6d. grey (1874–76) *From* Plate Nos. 13, 14, 15, 16.	55·00
Z17	8d. orange (1876)	
Z18	9d. straw (1862)	
Z19	9d. straw (1865)	
Z20	9d. straw (1867)	£225
Z21	10d. red-brown (1867)	
Z22	1s. green (1862)	
Z23	1s. green (1865)	
Z24	1s. green (1867–73) (Plate Nos. 4, 5, 6, 7) *From*	55·00
Z25	1s. green (1873–77) *From* Plate Nos. 8, 9, 10, 11, 12, 13.	70·00
Z26	2s. blue (1867)	£175
Z27	5s. rose (1867–74) (Plate Nos. 1, 2) *From*	£450

CALLAO

CROWNED-CIRCLE HANDSTAMPS

CC2	CC **1** CALLAO (R.) (13.1.1846) . *Price on cover*	£650

A second version of No. CC 2, showing "PAID" more curved, was supplied in July 1847.

No. CC2 can be found used on covers from 1865 showing the local postage paid by a Peru adhesive.

Stamps of GREAT BRITAIN *cancelled* "C 38" *as in Types* **4**, **12** *and* **14b**, *with circular date stamp as* **16a** *or with boxed handstamp Type* **22**.

1865–79.

Z28	½d. rose-red (1870–79) *From* Plate Nos. 5, 6, 10, 11, 12, 13, 14.	45·00
Z29	1d. rose-red (1864–79) *From* Plate Nos. 74, 88, 89, 93, 94, 97, 108, 123, 127, 128, 130, 134, 137, 139, 140, 141, 143, 144, 145, 146, 148, 149, 156, 157, 160, 163, 167, 171, 172, 173, 175, 176, 180, 181, 182, 183, 185, 187, 190, 193, 195, 198, 199, 200, 201, 204, 206, 209, 210, 212, 213, 215.	32·00
Z30	1½d. lake-red (1870–74) (Plate No. 3)	
Z31	2d. blue (1858–69) *From* Plate Nos. 9, 12, 13, 14, 15.	32·00
Z32	3d. carmine-rose (1862)	
Z33	3d. rose (1865) (Plate No. 4)	£100
Z34	3d. rose (1867–73) *From* Plate Nos. 5, 6, 7, 8, 9, 10.	45·00
Z35	3d. rose (1873–76) *From* Plate Nos. 11, 12, 14, 15, 16, 17, 18, 19.	45·00
Z36	4d. red (1862) (Plate Nos. 3, 4)	
Z37	4d. vermilion (1865–73) *From* Plate Nos. 8, 10, 11, 12, 13, 14.	38·00
Z38	4d. vermilion (1876) (Plate No. 15)	£300
Z39	4d. sage-green (1877) (Plate Nos. 15, 16)	£200
Z40	6d. lilac (1862) (Plate Nos. 3, 4)	
Z40*a*	6d. lilac (1865) (Plate No. 5)	
Z41	6d. lilac (1867)	
Z42	6d. violet (1867–70) *From* Plate Nos. 6, 8, 9.	70·00
Z43	6d. buff (1872–73) (Plate Nos. 11, 12) *From*	70·00
Z44	6d. chestnut (1872) (Plate No. 11)	50·00
Z45	6d. grey (1873) (Plate No. 12)	£210
Z46	6d. grey (1874–80) *From* Plate Nos. 13, 14, 15, 16.	50·00
Z47	8d. orange (1876)	£275
Z48	9d. straw (1862)	
Z49	9d. straw (1865)	£400
Z50	9d. straw (1867)	£200
Z51	10d. red-brown (1867)	£275
Z52	1s. green (1865)	
Z53	1s. green (1867–73) *From* Plate Nos. 4, 5, 6, 7.	38·00
254	1s. green (1873–77) *From* Plate Nos. 8, 9, 10, 11, 12, 13.	55·00
Z55	2s. blue (1867)	£120
Z56	5s. rose (1867–74) (Plate Nos. 1, 2) *From*	£450

IQUIQUE

Stamps of GREAT BRITAIN *cancelled* "D 87" *as Type* **12**.

1865–79.

Z57	½d. rose-red (1870–79) (Plate Nos. 5, 6, 13, 14)	75·00
Z58	1d. rose-red (1864–79) Plate Nos. 76, 179, 185, 205.	50·00
Z59	2d. blue (1858–69) (Plate Nos. 9, 12, 13, 14)	50·00
Z60	3d. rose (1867–73) (Plate Nos. 5, 6, 7, 8, 9) *From*	60·00
Z61	3d. rose (1873–76) (Plate Nos. 12, 18, 19)	75·00
Z62	4d. vermilion (1865–73) *From* Plate Nos. 12, 13, 14.	65·00
Z63	4d. vermilion (1876) (Plate No. 15)	£300
Z64	4d. sage-green (1877) (Plate Nos. 15, 16) *From*	£200
Z65	6d. mauve (1869) (Plate Nos. 8, 9)	
Z66	6d. buff (1872–73) (Plate Nos. 11, 12) *From*	£110
Z67	6d. chestnut (1872) (Plate No. 11)	
Z68	6d. grey (1873) (Plate No. 12)	£210
Z69	6d. grey (1874–76) (Plate Nos. 13, 14, 15, 16)	80·00
Z70	8d. orange (1876)	£325
Z71	9d. straw (1867)	£200
Z72	10d. red-brown (1867)	
Z73	1s. green (1867–73) (Plate Nos. 4, 6, 7) *From*	60·00
Z74	1s. green (1873–77) *From* Plate Nos. 8, 9, 10, 11, 12, 13.	80·00
Z75	2s. blue (1867)	£225

ISLAY (*later* MOLLENDO)

CROWNED-CIRCLE HANDSTAMPS

CC4	CC **1** ISLAY (Black or R.) (23.10.1850) *Price on cover*	£5000

Stamps of GREAT BRITAIN *cancelled* "C 42" *as Type* **4** *or with circular date stamp as Type* **16**.

1865–79.

Z76	1d. rose-red (1864–79) *From* Plate Nos. 78, 84, 87, 88, 96, 103, 125, 134.	55·00
Z77	1½d. lake-red (1870–74) (Plate No. 3)	
Z78	2d. blue (1858–69) (Plate Nos. 9, 13, 15)	55·00
Z79	3d. carmine-rose (1862)	
Z80	3d. rose (1865)	£110
Z81	3d. rose (1867–73) (Plate Nos. 4, 5, 6, 10) *From*	60·00
Z82	4d. red (1862) (Plate Nos. 3, 4)	£130
Z83	4d. vermilion (1867–73) *From* Plate Nos. 9, 10, 11, 12, 13.	60·00
Z84	4d. vermilion (1876) (Plate No. 15)	
Z85	4d. sage-green (1877) (Plate Nos. 15, 16) *From*	£200
Z86	6d. lilac (1862) (Plate Nos, 3, 4) *From*	90·00
Z87	6d. lilac (1865) (Plate No. 5)	80·00
Z88	6d. violet (1867–70) (Plate Nos. 6, 8, 9) *From*	80·00
Z88*a*	6d. chestnut (1872) (Plate No. 11)	
Z89	6d. buff (1873) (Plate No. 12)	
Z90	6d. grey (1873) (Plate No. 12)	
Z91	6d. grey (1874–76) *From* Plate Nos. 13, 14, 15, 16.	65·00
Z92	9d. straw (1865)	£375
Z93	9d. straw (1867)	£200
Z94	10d. red-brown (1867)	£275
Z95	1s. green (1865) (Plate No. 4)	
Z96	1s. green (1867–73) (Plate Nos. 4, 5, 6, 7) *From*	60·00
Z97	1s. green (1873–77) *From* Plate Nos. 8, 10, 12, 13.	80·00
Z98	2s. blue (1867)	
Z99	5s. rose (1867) (Plate No. 1)	

PAITA

CROWNED-CIRCLE HANDSTAMPS

CC5	CC **1** PAITA (Black or R.) (5.11.1850) *Price on cover*	£6500

Stamps of GREAT BRITAIN *cancelled* "C 43" *as Type* **4** *or with circular date stamp as Type* **16a** *in black or blue.*

1865–79.

Z100	1d. rose-red (1864–79) (Plate Nos. 127, 147)	65·00
Z101	2d. blue (1858–69) (Plate Nos. 9, 14)	65·00
Z102	3d. rose (1867–73) (Plate Nos. 5, 6)	75·00
Z103	3d. rose (1876) (Plate Nos. 17, 18, 19)	75·00
Z104	4d. vermilion (1865–73) *From* Plate Nos. 10, 11, 12, 13, 14, 15.	75·00
Z105	4d. sage-green (1877) (Plate No. 15)	
Z106	6d. lilac (1862) (Plate No. 3)	£110
Z107	6d. lilac (1865–67) (Plate Nos. 5, 6) *From*	£100
Z108	6d. violet (1867–70) (Plate Nos. 6, 8, 9) *From*	90·00
Z109	6d. buff (1872–73) (Plate Nos. 11, 12) *From*	£100
Z110	6d. chestnut (Plate No. 11)	75·00
Z111	6d. grey (1873)	
Z112	6d. grey (1874–76) (Plate Nos. 13, 14, 15)	
Z113	9d. straw (1862)	
Z114	10d. red-brown (1867)	£375
Z115	1s. green (1865) (Plate No. 4)	
Z116	1s. green (1867–73) (Plate No. 4)	75·00
Z117	1s. green (1873–77) (Plate Nos. 8, 9, 10, 13)	90·00
Z118	2s. blue (1867)	£300
Z119	5s. rose (1867) (Plate No. 1)	£650

PISAGUA(?)

Stamps of GREAT BRITAIN *cancelled* "D 65" *as Type* **12**.

Z119*a*	1d. rose-red (1864–79)	
Z119*b*	2d. blue (1858–69)	
Z120	2s. blue (1867)	

There is no record of an office opening at Pisagua. The few known examples of "D 65" in red are on loose stamps. The 2s. blue listing, based on a single cover cancelled "D 65" in black, is without any datestamp confirming its origin.

We continue to list this office pending further research.

PISCO AND CHINCHA ISLANDS

Stamps of GREAT BRITAIN *cancelled* "D 74" *as Type* **12**.

1865–70.

Z121	2d. blue (1858–69) (Plate No. 9)	
Z122	4d. vermilion (1865–73) (Plate Nos. 10, 12)	£800
Z123	6d. violet (1868) (Plate No. 6)	£1500
Z124	1s. green (1867) (Plate No. 4)	
Z125	2s. blue (1867)	£2000

PORTO RICO

A British Postal Agency operated at San Juan from 1844. On 24 October 1872 further offices were opened at Aguadilla, Arroyo, Mayaguez and Ponce, with Naguabo added three years later.

Great Britain stamps were used from 1865 to 1877, but few letters appear to have used the San Juan postal agency between 1866 and 1873 due to various natural disasters and the hostile attitude of the local authorities. All the British Agencies closed on 1 May 1877.

AGUADILLA

Stamps of GREAT BRITAIN *cancelled "F 84" as Type* **8**.

1873–77.

Z1 ½d. rose-red (1870) (Plate No. 6) .... 90·00
Z2 1d. rose-red (1864–79) .... 55·00
Plate Nos. 119, 122, 139, 149, 156, 160.
Z3 2d. blue (1858–69) (Plate No. 14) ....
Z4 3d. rose (1867–73) (Plate Nos. 7, 8, 9) ....
Z5 3d. rose (1873–76) (Plate No. 12) ....
Z6 4d. vermilion (1865–73) .... *From* 65·00
Plate Nos. 12, 13, 14.
Z7 4d. vermilion (1876) (Plate No. 15) £300
Z7*a* 6d. pale buff (1872–73) (Plate No. 11) ....
Z8 6d. grey (1874–76) (Plate Nos. 13, 14) ....
Z9 9d. straw (1867) £350
Z10 10d. red-brown (1867) £350
Z11 1s. green (1867–73) (Plate Nos. 4, 5, 6, 7) *From* 60·00
Z12 1s. green (1873–77) .... *From* 70·00
Plate Nos. 8, 9, 10, 11, 12.
Z13 2s. blue (1867) £275

ARROYO

Stamps of GREAT BRITAIN *cancelled "F 83" as Type* **8** *(black or red) or with circular date stamps as Types* **17** *and* **17b**.

1873–77.

Z14 ½d. rose-red 1870) (Plate No. 5) .... 60·00
Z15 1d. rose-red (1864–79) .... 55·00
Plate Nos. 149, 150, 151, 156, 164, 174, 175..
Z16 1½d. lake-red (1870) (Plate Nos. 1, 3) ....
Z17 2d. blue (1858–69) (Plate No. 14) ....
Z18 3d. rose (1867–73) (Plate Nos. 5, 7, 10).... *From* 60·00
Z19 3d. rose 1873–76 .... *From* 65·00
Plate Nos. 11, 12, 14, 16, 18.
Z20 4d. verm (1865–73) (Plate Nos. 12, 13, 14) *From* 55·00
Z21 4d. vermilion (1876) (Plate No. 15) £300
Z22 6d. chestnut (1872) (Plate No. 11) .... 65·00
Z23 6d. pale buff (1872) (Plate No. 11) .... 80·00
Z23*a* 6d. grey (1873) (Plate No. 12) ....
Z24 6d. grey (1874–76) (Plate Nos. 13, 14, 15) .... 60·00
Z25 9d. straw (1867) £300
Z26 10d. red-brown (1867) £300
Z27 1s. green (1865) (Plate No. 4) ....
Z28 1s. green (1867–73) (Plate Nos. 4, 5, 6, 7) *From* 60·00
Z29 1s. green (1873–77) .... *From* 70·00
Plate Nos. 8, 9, 10, 11, 12, 13.
Z30 2s. blue (1867) £225
Z31 5s. rose (1867–74) (Plate No. 2) ....

MAYAGUEZ

Stamps of GREAT BRITAIN *cancelled "F 85" as Type* **8** *in black or blue.*

1873–77.

Z32 ½d. rose-red (1870) .... *From* 55·00
Plate Nos. 4, 5, 6, 8, 10, 11.
Z33 1d. rose-red (1864–79) .... *From* 38·00
Plate Nos. 76, 120, 121, 122, 124, 134, 137, 140, 146, 149, 150, 151, 154, 155, 156, 157, 160, 167, 170, 171, 174, 175, 176, 178, 180, 182, 185, 186, 189.
Z34 1½d. lake-red (1870–74) (Plate Nos. 1, 3) .... 50·00
Z35 2d. blue (1858–69) (Plate Nos. 13, 14, 15) .... 50·00
Z36 3d. rose (1867–73) (Plate Nos. 7, 8, 9, 10). *From* 55·00
Z37 3d. rose (1873–76) .... *From* 50·00
Plate Nos. 11, 12, 14, 15, 16, 17, 18, 19.
Z38 4d. vermilion (1865–73) .... *From* 50·00
Plate Nos. 11, 12, 13, 14.
Z39 4d. vermilion (1876) (Plate No. 15) £300
Z40 4d. sage-green (1877) (Plate No. 15) ....
Z41 6d. mauve (1870) (Plate No. 9) ....
Z42 6d. buff (1872) (Plate No. 11) .... 80·00
Z43 6d. chestnut (1872) (Plate No. 11) .... 70·00
Z44 6d. grey (1873) (Plate No. 12) £200
Z45 6d. grey (1874–80) .... *From* 50·00
Plate Nos. 13, 14, 15, 16.
Z46 8d. orange (1876) £300
Z47 9d. straw (1867) £225
Z48 10d. red-brown (1867) £300
Z49 1s. green (1867–73) (Plate Nos. 4, 5, 6, 7) *From* 45·00
Z50 1s. green (1873–77) .... *From* 60·00
Plate Nos. 8, 9, 10, 11, 12.
Z51 2s. blue (1867) £180
Z52 5s. rose (1867–74) (Plate Nos. 1, 2) ....

NAGUABO

Stamps of GREAT BRITAIN *cancelled "582" as Type* **9**.

1875–77.

Z53 ½d. rose-red (1870–79) (Plate Nos. 5. 12, 14) ....
Z54 1d. rose-red (1864–79) (Plate Nos. 150, 159, 165) £450
Z55 3d. rose (1873–76) (Plate Nos. 17, 18) £700
Z56 4d. vermilion (1872–73) (Plate Nos. 13, 14) *From* £700
Z57 4d. vermilion (1876) (Plate No. 15) ....
Z58 6d. grey (1874–76) (Plate Nos. 14, 15) ....
Z59 9d. straw (1867) ....
Z60 10d. red-brown (1867) £1100
Z61 1s. green (1873–77) (Plate Nos. 11, 12) ....
Z62 2s. dull blue (1867) (Plate No. 1) £1000

PONCE

Stamps of GREAT BRITAIN *cancelled "F 88" as Type* **8**.

1873–77.

Z63 ½d. rose-red (1870) (Plate Nos. 5, 10, 12) .... 55·00
Z64 1d. rose-red (1864–79) .... *From* 45·00
Plate Nos. 120, 121, 122, 123, 124, 146, 148, 154, 156, 157, 158, 160, 167, 171, 174, 175, 179, 186, 187.
Z65 1½d. lake-red (1870–74) (Plate No. 3) £110
Z66 2d. blue (1858–69) (Plate Nos. 13, 14) .... 55·00
Z67 3d. rose (1867–73) (Plate Nos. 7, 8, 9) ....
Z68 3d. rose (1873–76) .... 50·00
Plate Nos. 12, 16, 17, 18, 19.
Z69 4d. vermilion (1865–73) .... *From* 55·00
Plate Nos. 8, 9, 12, 13, 14.
Z70 4d. vermilion (1876) (Plate No. 15) £300
Z71 4d. sage-green (1877) (Plate Nos. 15, 16). *From* £200
Z72 6d. buff (1872–73) (Plate Nos. 11, 12) ..... *From* 75·00
Z73 6d. chestnut (1872) (Plate No. 11) .... 65·00
Z74 6d. grey (1873) (Plate No. 12) ....
Z75 6d. grey (1874–76) (Plate Nos. 13, 14, 15) *From* 55·00
Z76 9d. straw (1867) £275
Z77 10d. red-brown (1867) £300
Z78 1s. green (1867–73) (Plate Nos. 4, 6, 7) .... 50·00
Z79 1s. green (1873–77) .... *From* 60·00
Plate Nos. 8, 9. 10, 11, 12, 13.
Z80 2s. blue (1867) ....
Z81 5s. rose (1867–74) (Plate Nos. 1, 2) .... *From* £375

SAN JUAN

CROWNED-CIRCLE HANDSTAMPS

CC1 CC **1** SAN JUAN PORTO RICO (R. *or* Black) (25.5.1844) .... *Price on cover* £650

No. CC1 may be found on cover, used in conjunction with Spanish colonial adhesive stamps paying the local postage.

Stamps of GREAT BRITAIN *cancelled "C 61" as in Types* **4**, **8**, **12** *or* **14**a.

1865–77.

Z82 ½d. rose-red (1870) (Plate Nos. 5, 10, 15) *From* 50·00
Z83 1d. rose-red (1857) ....
Z84 1d. rose-red (1864–79) .... *From* 38·00
Plate Nos. 73, 74, 81, 84, 90, 94, 100, 101, 102, 107, 117, 122, 124, 125, 127, 130, 137, 138, 139, 140, 145, 146, 149, 153, 156, 159, 160, 162, 163, 169, 171, 172, 173, 174, 175, 179, 180, 182, 186.
Z85 1½d. lake-red (1870–74) (Plate Nos. 1, 3).. *From* 65·00
Z86 2d. blue (1858–69) (Plate Nos. 9, 13, 14). *From* 38·00
Z87 3d. rose (1865) (Plate No. 4) .... 90·00
Z88 3d. rose (1867–73) .... *From* 50·00
Plate Nos. 5, 6, 7, 8, 9, 10.
Z89 3d. rose (1873–76) .... *From* 45·00
Plate Nos. 11, 12, 14, 15, 16, 17, 18.
Z90 4d. vermilion (1865–73) .... *From* 50·00
Plate Nos. 7, 8, 9, 10, 11, 12, 13, 14.
Z91 4d. vermilion (1876) (Plate No. 15) £300
Z92 6d. lilac (1865–67) (Plate Nos. 5, 6) .... *From* 75·00
Z93 6d. lilac (1867) (Plate No. 6) .... 75·00
Z94 6d. violet (1867–70) (Plate Nos. 6, 8, 9)... *From* 70·00
Z95 6d. buff (1872–73) (Plate Nos. 11, 12) ..... *From* 75·00
Z96 6d. chestnut (1872) (Plate No. 11) .... 50·00
Z97 6d. grey (1873) (Plate No. 12) ....
Z98 6d. grey (1874–76) (Plate Nos. 13, 14, 15) *From* 50·00
Z99 9d. straw (1862) £300
Z100 9d. straw (1865) £375
Z101 9d. straw (1867) £200
Z102 10d. red-brown (1867) £275
Z103 1s. green (1865) (Plate No. 4) £140
Z104 1s. green (1867–73) (Plate Nos. 4, 5, 6, 7) *From* 45·00
Z105 1s. green (1873–77) .... *From* 60·00
Plate Nos. 8, 9, 10, 11, 12, 13.
Z106 2s. blue (1867) £130
Z107 5s. rose (1867) (Plate Nos. 1, 2) .... *From* £450

RUSSIA

ARMY FIELD OFFICES IN THE CRIMEA

1854–57.

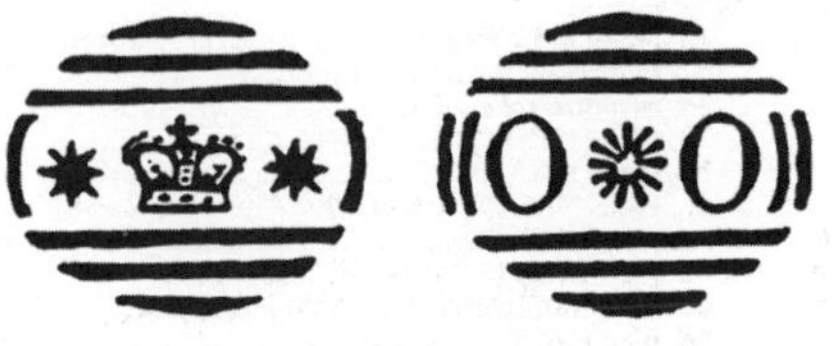

Crown between Stars.

Z1 1d. red-brown (1841), imperf £800
Z2 1d. red-brown (1854), Die I, wmk Small Crown, perf 16 ....
Z3 1d. red-brown (1855), Die II, wmk Small Crown, perf 16 .... £250
Z4 1d. red-brown, Die I, wmk Small Crown, perf 14 ....
Z5 1d. red-brown (1855), Die II, Small Crown, perf 14 ....
Z6 2d. blue (1841) imperf £1500
Z7 2d. blue, Small Crown (1854), perf 16 (Plate No. 4) ....
Z8 1s. green (1847), embossed £2500

Star between Cyphers.

Z9 1d. red-brown (1841), imperf ....
Z10 1d. red-brown (1854), Die I, wmk Small Crown, perf 16 .... 85·00
Z11 1d. red-brown (1855), Die II, wmk Small Crown, perf 16 .... 85·00
Z12 1d. red-brown (1855), Die I, wmk Small Crown, perf 14 .... 85·00
Z13 1d. red-brown (1855), Die II, wmk Small Crown, perf 14 .... 85·00
Z14 1d. red-brown (1855), Die II, wmk Large Crown, perf 16 .... £110
Z15 1d. red-brown (1855), Die II, wmk Large Crown, perf 14 .... 45·00
Z16 2d. blue (1841), imperf £1800
Z17 2d. blue (1854), wmk Small Crown, perf 16 .... *From* £150
Plate Nos. 4, 5.
Z18 2d. blue (1855), wmk Small Crown, perf 14 ...... £225
Plate No. 4.
Z19 2d. blue (1855), wmk Large Crown, perf 16 ..... £250
Plate No. 5.
Z20 2d. blue (1855), wmk Large Crown, perf 14 ..... £150
Plate No. 5.
Z21 4d. rose (1857) £1000
Z22 6d. violet (1854), embossed £1800
Z23 1s. green (1847), embossed £1800

SPAIN

Little is known about the operation of British Packet Agencies in Spain, other than the dates recorded for the various postal markings in the G.P.O. Proof Books. The Agency at Corunna is said to date from the late 17th century when the Spanish packets for South America were based there. No. CC1 was probably issued in connection with the inauguration of the P. & O. service to Spain in 1843. The Spanish port of call was changed to Vigo in 1846 and the office at Corunna was then closed. Teneriffe became a port-of-call for the South American packets in 1817 and this arrangement continued until 1858.

CORUNNA

CROWNED-CIRCLE HANDSTAMPS

CC1 CC **1b** CORUNNA (28.2.1842) ....

Although recorded in the G.P.O. Proof Books no example of No. CC1 on cover is known.

TENERIFFE (CANARY ISLANDS)

CROWNED-CIRCLE HANDSTAMPS

CC2 CC **7** TENERIFFE (6.1.1851)...... *Price on cover* £3750
CC3 CC **4** TENERIFFE (23.10.1857) . *Price on cover* £3750

No. CC2/3 can be found used on covers from Spain to South America with the rate from Spain to Teneriffe paid in Spanish adhesive stamps.

UNITED STATES OF AMERICA

The network of British Packet Agencies, to operate the trans-Atlantic Packet system, was re-established in 1814 after the War of 1812.

The New York Agency opened in that year to be followed by further offices at Boston, Charleston (South Carolina), New Orleans, Savannah (Georgia) (all in 1842), Mobile (Alabama) (1848) and San Francisco (1860). Of these agencies Charleston and Savannah closed the same year (1842) as did New Orleans, although the latter was re-activated from 1848 to 1850. Mobile closed 1850, Boston in 1865, New York in 1882 and San Francisco, for which no postal markings have been recorded, in 1883.

Although recorded in the G.P.O. Proof Books no actual examples of the Crowned-circle handstamps for Charleston, Mobile, New Orleans and Savannah are known on cover.

The G.P.O. Proof Books record, in error, a Crowned-circle handstamp for St. Michaels, Maryland. This handstamp was intended for the agency on San Miguel in the Azores.

CHARLESTON

CROWNED-CIRCLE HANDSTAMPS

CC1 CC **1b** CHARLESTON (15.12.1841) ....

MOBILE

CROWNED-CIRCLE HANDSTAMPS

CC2 CC **1b** MOBILE (15.12.1841) ....

NEW ORLEANS

CROWNED-CIRCLE HANDSTAMPS

CC3 CC **1b** NEW ORLEANS (15.12.1841) ....
CC4 CC **1** NEW ORLEANS (27.4.1848) ....

NEW YORK

CROWNED-CIRCLE HANDSTAMPS

CC5 CC **1b** NEW YORK (R.) (15.12.1841) .... *Price on cover* £27500

SAVANNAH

CROWNED-CIRCLE HANDSTAMPS

CC6 CC **1b** SAVANNAH (15.12.1841) ....

Although recorded in the G.P.O Proof Books, no examples of Nos. CC1/4 or CC6 are known on cover.

URUGUAY

MONTEVIDEO

British packets commenced calling at Montevideo in 1824 on passage to and from Buenos Aires.

Great Britain stamps were in use from 1864. Combination covers exist with the local postage paid by Uruguay adhesive stamps. The agency was closed on 31 July 1873.

CROWNED-CIRCLE HANDSTAMPS

CC1 CC **5** MONTEVIDEO (Black or R.) (6.1.1851) .... *Price on cover* £1000

Stamps of GREAT BRITAIN *cancelled "C 28" as Type* **4**.

1864–73.

Z1 1d. rose-red (1864) .... 55·00
Plate Nos. 73, 92, 93, 94, 119, 148, 154, 157, 171.
Z2 2d. blue (1858–69) (Plate Nos. 9, 13) .... 55·00
Z3 3d. rose (1865) (Plate No. 4) ....
Z4 3d. rose (1867–71) (Plate Nos. 4, 5, 7) ..... *From* 50·00
Z6 4d. rose (1857) ....
Z7 4d. red (1862) (Plate No. 4) ....
Z8 4d. vermilion (1865–70) .... *From* 50·00
Plate Nos. 7, 8, 9, 10, 11, 12.
Z9 6d. lilac (1856) ....
Z10 6d. lilac (1862) (Plate No. 4) £160
Z11 6d. lilac (1865–67) (Plate Nos. 5, 6) .... *From* 90·00
Z12 6d. lilac (1867) (Plate No. 6) ....
Z13 6d. violet (1867–70) (Plate Nos. 8, 9) .... *From* 80·00
Z14 6d. buff (1872) ....
Z15 6d. chestnut (1872) ....
Z16 9d. straw (1862) ....
Z17 9d. straw (1865) ....
Z18 9d. straw (1867) £275

Z19	10d. red-brown (1867)	£325
Z20	1s. green (1862)	£160
Z21	1s. green (1865) (Plate No. 4)	£140
Z22	1s. green (1867–73) (Plate Nos. 4, 5) *From*	60·00
Z23	2s. blue (1867)	£200
Z24	5s. rose (1867) (Plate No. 1)	£450

VENEZUELA

British Postal Agencies were initially opened at La Guayra and Porto Cabello on 1 January 1842. Further offices were added at Maracaibo in 1842 and Ciudad Bolivar during January 1868. Porto Cabello closed in 1858 and Maracaibo was also short-lived. The remaining offices closed at the end of 1879 when Venezuela joined the U.P.U.

Great Britain stamps were used at La Guayra from 1865 and at Ciudad Bolivar from its establishment in 1868. They can be found used in combination with Venezuela adhesives paying the local postage.

CIUDAD BOLIVAR

Stamps of GREAT BRITAIN *cancelled* "D 22" *as Type* **12**, *or circular date stamps as Types* **16** *(black) or* **17** *(red).*

1868–79.

Z1	1d. rose-red (1864–79) (Plate No. 133)	£150
Z2	2d. blue (1858–69) (Plate No. 13)	
Z3	3d. rose (1867–73) (Plate No. 5)	
Z4	3d. rose (1873–79) (Plate No. 11)	£180
Z5	4d. vermilion (1865–73) *From* Plate Nos. 9, 11, 12, 14.	£180
Z6	4d. sage-green (1877) (Plate Nos. 15, 16). *From*	£375
Z7	4d. grey-brown (1880) wmk Crown (Plate No. 17)	£750
Z8	9d. straw (1867)	
Z9	10d. red-brown (1867)	
Z10	1s. green (1867–73) (Plate Nos. 4, 5, 7)... *From*	£250
Z11	1s. green (1873–77) (Plate Nos. 10, 12, 13) *From*	£350
Z12	2s. blue (1867)	£850
Z13	5s. rose (1867–74) (Plate Nos. 1, 2) *From*	£1500

LA GUAYRA

CROWNED-CIRCLE HANDSTAMPS

CC1	CC **1b** LA GUAYRA (R.) (15.12.1841) *Price on cover*	£1300

Stamps of GREAT BRITAIN *cancelled* "C 60" *as Type* **4**, *circular date stamp as Types* **16** *and* **17** *or with No.* CC1.

1865–80.

Z14	½d. rose-red (1870) Plate No. 6)	
Z15	1d. rose-red (1864–79) *From* Plate Nos. 81, 92, 96, 98, 111, 113, 115, 131, 138, 144, 145, 154, 177, 178, 180, 196.	55·00
Z16	1½d. lake-red (1870–74) (Plate No. 3)	
Z17	2d. blue (1858–69) (Plate Nos. 13, 14)	55·00
Z18	3d. rose (1873–76) *From* Plate Nos. 14, 15, 17, 18, 19.	60·00
Z19	4d. vermilion (1865–73) *From* Plate Nos. 7, 9, 11, 12, 13, 14.	55·00
Z20	4d. vermilion (1876) (Plate No. 15)	£300
Z21	4d. sage-green (1877) (Plate Nos. 15, 16). *From*	£225
Z22	6d. lilac (1865) (Plate No. 5)	
Z23	6d. violet (1867–70) (Plate Nos. 6, 8)	
Z24	6d. buff (1872–73) (Plate Nos. 11, 12) *From*	£100
Z25	6d. grey (1873) (Plate No. 12)	£210
Z26	6d. grey (1874–76) (Plate Nos. 13, 14, 15, 16) ...	60·00
Z27	8d. orange (1876)	£300
Z28	9d. straw (1862)	
Z29	9d. straw (1867)	
Z30	10d. red-brown (1867)	
Z31	1s. green (1865) (Plate No. 4)	£160
Z32	1s. green (1867–73) (Plate Nos. 4, 7)	
Z33	1s. green (1873–77) *From* Plate Nos. 8, 9, 10, 11, 12, 13.	55·00
Z34	2s. blue (1867)	£225
Z35	5s. rose (1867–74) (Plate No. 1, 2) *From*	£450

MARACAIBO

CROWNED-CIRCLE HANDSTAMPS

CC2	CC **1b** MARACAIBO (31.12.1841)	

No examples of No. CC2 on cover have been recorded.

PORTO CABELLO

CROWNED-CIRCLE HANDSTAMPS

CC3	CC **1b** PORTO-CABELLO (R.) (15.12.1841) *Price on cover*	£3250

MAIL BOAT OBLITERATIONS

The following cancellations were supplied to G.P.O. sorters operating on ships holding mail contracts from the British Post Office. They were for use on mail posted on board, but most examples occur on letters from soldiers and sailors serving overseas which were forwarded to the mailboats without postmarks.

P. & O. MEDITERRANEAN AND FAR EAST MAILBOATS

The first such cancellation, "A 17" as Type **2**, was issued to the Southampton–Alexandria packet in April 1858, but no examples have been recorded.

The G.P.O. Proof Book also records "B 16", in Type **2**, as being issued for marine sorting in November 1859, but this postmark was subsequently used by the Plymouth and Bristol Sorting Carriage.

Sorting on board P. & O. packets ceased in June 1870 and many of the cancellation numbers were subsequently reallocated using Types **9**, **11** or **12**.

Stamps of GREAT BRITAIN *cancelled* "A 80" *as Type* **2**.

1859 (Mar)–**70**.

Z1	1d. rose-red (1857). Die II, wmk Large Crown, perf 14	40·00
Z2	6d. lilac (1856)	£160

Stamps of GREAT BRITAIN *cancelled* "A 81" *as Type* **2**.

1859 (Mar)–**70**.

Z3	1d. rose-red (1857), Die II, wmk Large Crown, *perf* 14	40·00
Z4	1d. rose-red (1864–79) *From* Plate Nos, 84, 85, 86, 91, 97.	35·00
Z5	2d. blue (1858–69) (Plate No. 9)	50·00
Z6	4d. red (1862) (Plate No. 4)	£120
Z7	4d. vermilion (1865–73) (Plate No. 8)	60·00
Z8	6d. lilac (1856)	£160
Z9	6d. lilac (1862) (Plate No. 3)	£120
Z10	6d. lilac (1865–67) (Plate Nos. 5, 6) *From*	£100
Z11	6d. lilac (1867) (Plate No. 6)	£100
Z12	6d. violet (1867–70) (Plate Nos. 6, 8) *From*	75·00
Z13	10d. red-brown (1867)	£500
Z14	1s. red-brown (1856)	£275

Stamps of GREAT BRITAIN *cancelled* "A 82" *as Type* **2**.

1859 (Mar)–**70**.

Z15	1d. rose-red (1857), Die II, wmk Large Crown, perf 14	50·00
Z16	2d. blue (1858) (Plate No. 7)	55·00
Z17	4d. rose (1856)	£225
Z18	6d. lilac 1856)	£200
Z19	6d. lilac (1865–67) (Plate Nos. 5. 6) *From*	£130
Z20	6d. lilac (1867) (Plate No. 6)	£110

Stamps of GREAT BRITAIN *cancelled* "A 83" *as Type* **2**.

1859 (Apr)–**70**.

Z21	1d. rose-red (1857), Die II, wmk Large Crown, perf 14	40·00
Z22	1d. rose-red (1864–79) *From* Plate Nos. 73, 74, 84, 91, 109.	35·00
Z23	3d. carmine-rose (1862)	£275
Z24	4d. rose (1857)	£200
Z25	4d. red (1862)	£110
Z26	4d. vermilion (1865–73) (Plate Nos. 9, 10) *From*	60·00
Z27	6d. lilac (1856)	£160
Z28	6d. lilac (1862)	£125
Z29	6d. lilac (1865–67) (Plate Nos. 5, 6) *From*	£100
Z30	6d. violet (1867–70) (Plate Nos. 6, 8) *From*	75·00
Z31	10d. red-brown (1867)	£500
Z32	1s. green (1862)	£275

Stamps of GREAT BRITAIN *cancelled* "A 84" *as Type* **2**.

1859 (Apr)–**70**.

Z33	1d. rose-red (1857), Die II, wmk Large Crown, perf 14	£110

Stamps of GREAT BRITAIN *cancelled* "A 85" *as Type* **2**.

1859 (Apr)–**70**.

Z34	1d. rose-red (1857), Die II, wmk Large Crown, perf 14	40·00
Z35	1d. rose-red (1864–79) *From* Plate Nos. 79, 97, 103.	35·00
Z36	3d. carmine-rose (1862)	£275
Z37	4d. red (1862)	£110
Z38	6d. lilac (1856)	£160
Z39	6d. lilac (1862) (Plate Nos. 3, 4) *From*	£120
Z40	6d. lilac (1865–67) (Plate No. 5)	£100
Z41	6d. lilac (1867) (Plate No. 6)	90·00
Z42	1s. green (1862)	£300

Stamps of GREAT BRITAIN *cancelled* "A 86" *as Type* **2**.

1859 (Apr)–**70**.

Z43	1d. rose-red (1857), Die II, wmk Large Crown, perf 14	40·00
Z44	1d. rose-red (1864–79) *From* Plate Nos. 73, 84, 94, 97, 114, 118.	35·00
Z45	3d. rose (1865)	£250
Z46	3d. rose (1867–73) (Plate Nos. 4, 5) *From*	75·00
Z47	4d. rose (1857)	£200
Z48	4d. red (1862) (Plate No. 4)	£110
Z49	4d. vermilion (1865–73) (Plate No. 10)	80·00
Z50	6d. lilac (1856)	£160
Z51	6d. lilac (1862) (Plate Nos. 3, 4) *From*	£120
Z52	6d. lilac (1865–67) (Plate Nos. 5, 6) *From*	£100
Z53	6d. lilac (1867) (Plate Nos. 6, 8) *From*	75·00
Z54	10d. red-brown (1867)	£450
Z55	1s. green (1862)	£275

Stamps of GREAT BRITAIN *cancelled* "A 87" *as Type* **2**.

1859 (Apr)–**70**.

Z56	1d. rose-red (1857), Die II, wmk Large Crown, perf 14	55·00
Z57	4d. rose (1856)	£250
Z58	6d. lilac (1867) (Plate No. 6)	£120

Stamps of GREAT BRITAIN *cancelled* "A 88" *as Type* **2**.

1859 (Apr)–**70**.

Z59	1d. rose-red (1857), Die II, wmk Large Crown, perf 14	40·00
Z60	1d. rose-red (1864–79) *From* Plate Nos. 74, 80, 85.	35·00
Z61	4d. rose (1857)	£225
Z62	4d. red (1862)	£120
Z63	4d. vermilion (1865–73) (Plate No. 8)	60·00
Z64	6d. lilac (1856)	
Z65	6d. lilac (1862) (Plate No. 4)	£160
Z66	6d. lilac (1865–67) (Plate No. 5)	£120
Z67	6d. lilac (1867) (Plate No. 6)	£100
Z68	6d. violet (1867–70) (Plate No. 8)	75·00
Z69	10d. red-brown (1867)	£525
Z70	1s. green (1856)	£300

Stamps of GREAT BRITAIN *cancelled* "A 89" *as Type* **2**.

1859 (Apr)–**70**.

Z71	1d. rose-red (1857), Die II, wmk Large Crown, perf 14	£110
Z72	6d. lilac (1856)	£300

Stamps of GREAT BRITAIN *cancelled* "A 90" *as Type* **2**.

1859 (June)–**70**.

Z73	1d. rose-red (1857), Die II, wmk Large Crown, perf 14	65·00
Z74	4d. rose (1856)	
Z75	6d. lilac (1856)	£250
Z76	6d. lilac (1865–67) (Plate Nos. 5, 6) *From*	£160
Z77	9d. straw (1867)	

Stamps of GREAT BRITAIN *cancelled* "A 99" *as Type* **2**.

1859 (June)–**70**.

Z78	1d. rose-red (1857), Die II, wmk Large Crown, perf 14	40·00
Z79	1d. rose-red (1864–79) *From* Plate Nos. 93, 97, 99, 118.	35·00
Z80	4d. rose (1857)	£200
Z81	4d. red (1862)	£110
Z82	4d. vermilion (1865–73) (Plate No. 11)	60·00
Z83	6d. lilac (1856)	
Z84	6d. lilac (1862)	£160
Z85	6d. lilac (1865–67) (Plate Nos. 5, 6) *From*	£120
Z86	10d. red-brown (1867)	£500

Stamps of GREAT BRITAIN *cancelled* "B 03" *as Type* **2**.

1859 (Aug)–**70**.

Z87	1d. rose-red (1857), Die II, wmk Large Crown, perf 14	55·00
Z88	1d. rose-red (1864–79) (Plate Nos. 109, 116) *From*	40·00
Z89	3d. rose (1865) (Plate No. 4)	£100
Z90	6d. lilac (1856)	£170
Z91	6d. lilac (1867) (Plate No. 6)	£140
Z92	6d. violet (1867–70) (Plate Nos. 6, 8) *From*	£100
Z93	10d. red-brown (1867)	£550

Stamps of GREAT BRITAIN *cancelled* "B 12" *as Type* **2**.

1859 (Oct)–**70**.

Z94	1d. rose-red (1857), Die II, wmk Large Crown, perf 14	55·00
Z95	1d. rose-red (1864–79) (Plate No. 94)	40·00
Z96	3d. rose (1865) (Plate No. 4)	£100
Z97	4d. red (1862)	£120
Z98	4d. vermilion (1865–73) (Plate No. 8)	75·00
Z99	6d. lilac (1856)	
Z100	6d. lilac (1862)	£170
Z101	6d. lilac (1865–67) (Plate Nos. 5, 6) *From*	£140
Z102	6d. violet (1867–70) (Plate No. 8)	95·00

Stamps of GREAT BRITAIN *cancelled* "B 56" *as Type* **2**.

1861 (July)–**70**.

Z103	1d. rose-red (1864–70) (Plate Nos. 84, 97)	40·00
Z104	2d. blue (1858–69) (Plate No. 9)	60·00
Z105	4d. red (1862) (Plate No. 4)	£120
Z106	4d. vermilion (1865–73) (Plate Nos. 7, 8)	65·00
Z107	6d. lilac (1862) (Plate Nos. 3, 4) *From*	£140
Z108	6d. lilac (1865–67) (Plate Nos. 5, 6) *From*	£120
Z109	6d. violet (1867–71) (Plate Nos. 6, 8) *From*	£100

Stamps of GREAT BRITAIN *cancelled* "B 57" *as Type* **2**.

1861 (July)–**70**.

Z110	1d. rose-red (1857), Die II, wmk Large Crown, perf 14	50·00
Z111	1d. rose-red (1864–79) (Plate No. 81)	40·00
Z112	2d. blue (1858–69) (Plate No. 9)	60·00
Z113	4d. red (1862)	£120
Z114	4d. vermilion (1865–73) (Plate Nos. 7, 8)	65·00
Z115	6d. lilac (1865–67) (Plate Nos. 5, 6) *From*	£120

Stamps of GREAT BRITAIN *cancelled* "C 79" *as Type* **12**.

1866 (June)–**70**.

Z116	6d. violet (1867–70) (Plate Nos. 6, 8) *From*	95·00
Z117	10d. red-brown (1867)	£450

CUNARD LINE ATLANTIC MAILBOATS

These were all issued in June 1859. No examples arc known used after August 1868. "B 61" is recorded as being issued in March 1862, but no examples are known. Cancellation numbers were subsequently reallocated to offices in Great Britain or, in the case of "A 91", the British Virgin Islands.

Stamps of GREAT BRITAIN *cancelled* "A 91" *as Type* **2**.

1859 (June)–**68**.

Z130	1d. rose-red (1857), Die II, wmk Large Crown, perf 14	70·00
Z131	1d. rose-red (1864–79) (Plate No. 121)	60·00
Z132	2d. blue (1855), wmk Small Crown, perf 14	
Z133	2d. blue (1858–69) (Plate Nos. 8, 9)	95·00
Z134	4d. rose (1857)	£250
Z135	4d. red (1862)	£130
Z136	6d. lilac (1856)	£175
Z137	6d. lilac (1862)	£150
Z138	6d. lilac (1865–67)	£120
Z139	9d. straw (1862)	
Z140	1s. green (1856)	£325

Stamps of GREAT BRITAIN *cancelled* "A 92" *as Type* **2**.

1859 (June)–**68**.

Z141	1d. rose-red (1857), Die II, wmk Large Crown, perf 14	70·00
Z142	1d. rose-red (1864–79) (Plate Nos. 93, 97) *From*	60·00
Z143	6d. lilac (1856)	£175
Z144	6d. lilac (1862) (Plate No. 3)	£160
Z145	6d. lilac (1865–67) (Plate Nos. 5, 6) *From*	£120

Stamps of GREAT BRITAIN *cancelled* "A 93" *as Type* **2**

1859 (June)–**68**.

Z146	1d. rose-red (1857), Die II, wmk Large Crown, perf 14	70·00
Z147	1d. rose-red (1864–79) (Plate No. 85)	60·00
Z148	6d. lilac (1856)	£175
Z149	6d. lilac (1865–67) (Plate No. 6)	£160
Z150	10d. red-brown (1867)	£525

Stamps of GREAT BRITAIN *cancelled* "A 94" *as Type* **2**

1859 (June)–**68**.

Z151	1d. rose-red (1857), Die II, wmk Large Crown, perf 14	95·00
Z152	1d. rose-red (1864–79) (Plate Nos. 74, 97)	70·00
Z153	4d. vermilion (1865–73) (Plate No. 7)	£100
Z154	6d. lilac (1856)	£200
Z155	6d. lilac (1862)	£160
Z156	6d. lilac (1865–67) (Plate Nos. 5, 6) *From*	£140

Stamps of GREAT BRITAIN *cancelled* "A 95" *as Type* **2**.

1859 (June)–**68**.

Z157	1d. rose-red (1857), Die II, wmk Large Crown, perf 14	65·00
Z158	1d. rose-red (1864–79) *From* Plate Nos. 72, 89, 97.	55·00
Z159	3d. rose (1867–73) (Plate No. 5)	95·00
Z160	4d. red (1862)	£130
Z161	4d. vermilion (1865–73) (Plate No. 8)	70·00
Z162	6d. lilac (1862)	£190
Z163	6d. lilac (1865–67) (Plate No. 5)	£160
Z164	6d. lilac (1867) (Plate No. 6)	£130
Z165	1s. green (1856)	£275

Stamps of GREAT BRITAIN *cancelled* "A 96" *as Type* **2**.

1859 (June)–**68**.

Z166	1d. rose-red (1857), Die II, wmk Large Crown, perf 14	70·00
Z167	4d. vermilion (1865–73) (Plate No. 7)	£100
Z168	6d. lilac (1856)	£180
Z169	1s. green (1856)	£300

Stamps of GREAT BRITAIN *cancelled* "A 97" *as Type* **2**.

1859 (June)–**68**.

Z170	1d. rose-red (1857), Die II, wmk Large Crown, perf 14	70·00
Z171	1d. rose-red (1864–79) (Plate No. 71)	60·00
Z172	4d. Ted (1862) (Plate No. 3)	£140

Stamps of GREAT BRITAIN *cancelled* "A 98" *as Type* **2**.

1859 (June)–**68**.

Z173	1d. rose-red (1857), Die II, wmk Large Crown, perf 14	70·00
Z174	4d. red (1862)	£140
Z175	6d. lilac (1856)	£200
Z176	6d. lilac (1862) (Plate No. 4)	£160
Z177	6d. lilac (1865–67) (Plate Nos. 5, 6) *From*	£120

ALLAN LINE ATLANTIC MAILBOATS

British G.P.O. sorters worked on these Canadian ships between November 1859 and April 1860. Cancellations as Type **2** numbered "B 17", "B 18", "B 27", "B 28", "B 29" and "B 30" were issued to them, but have not been reported used on Great Britain stamps during this period. All were subsequently reallocated to British post offices.

SPANISH WEST INDIES MAILBOATS

"D 26" was supplied for use by British mail clerks employed on ships of the Herrara Line operating between St. Thomas (Danish West Indies), Cuba, Dominican Republic and Porto Rico.

Stamps of GREAT BRITAIN *cancelled* "D 26" *as Type* **12**.

1868–71.

Z190	1d. rose-red (1864–79) (Plate Nos. 98, 125)	
Z191	4d. vermilion (1865–73) (Plate Nos. 9, 10, 11)	£1200
Z192	6d. violet (1867–70) (Plate No. 8)	
Z193	1s. green (1867) (Plate No. 4)	

Abu Dhabi

1964. 100 Naye Paise = 1 Rupee 1966. 1000 Fils = 1 Dinar

Abu Dhabi is the largest of the former Trucial States on the Persian Gulf, which are now combined to form the United Arab Emirates. The others, which all issued stamps, are Ajman (with Manama), Dubai, Fujeira, Ras al Khaima, Sharjah and Umm al Qiwain. They were known as the Trucial States because in May 1853 they all signed the Perpetual Maritime Truce Agreement with the United Kingdom, under which they undertook to give up piracy and the slave trade.

Shaikh Shakhbut bin Sultan

1928–6 August 1966

BRITISH POSTAL ADMINISTRATION

The postal service was established on 30 March 1963 and the stamps of the British Postal Agencies in Eastern Arabia (see *British Postal Agencies in Eastern Arabia* in this catalogue) were used until 29 March 1964.

1 Shaikh Shakhbut bin Sultan

2 Mountain Gazelle

3 Ruler's Palace

4 Oil Rig and Camels

(Des M. C. Farrar-Bell. Photo Harrison (T **1/2**). Des C. T. Kavanagh (T **3**), Miss P. M. Goth (T **4**). Recess Bradbury Wilkinson)

1964 (30 Mar). P 14½ (T **1/2**) or 13×13½ (T **3/4**).

1	**1**	5n.p. green	3·25	3·50
2		15n.p. red-brown	2·75	1·75
3		20n.p. ultramarine	3·25	1·75
		a. Perf 13×13½	£375	
4		30n.p. red-orange	3·50	1·50
5	**2**	40n.p. reddish violet	4·50	1·25
6		50n.p. bistre	6·00	2·75
7		75n.p. black	6·00	4·25
8	**3**	1r. emerald	4·00	2·00
9		2r. black	8·00	3·25
10	**4**	5r. carmine-red	19·00	10·00
11		10r. deep ultramarine	24·00	14·00
1/11 *Set of* 11			75·00	40·00

5

6

7

Saker Falcon on Gloved Hand

(Des V. Whiteley. Photo Harrison)

1965 (30 Mar). *Falconry*. P 14½.

12	**5**	20n.p. light brown and grey-blue	14·00	2·00
13	**6**	40n.p. light brown and blue	17·00	3·00
14	**7**	2r. sepia and turquoise-green	28·00	14·00
12/14 *Set of* 3			55·00	17·00

Shaikh Zaid bin Sultan al Nahayyan

6 August 1966

Fils فلس

(**8**)

(Surch by Arabian Ptg & Publishing House, Bahrain)

1966 (1 Oct). *New Currency. Nos.* 1/11 *surch as T* **8**, *with bars obliterating portrait of deposed shaikh.* P 13×13½ (20f.), others as before.

15	**1**	5f. on 5n.p. green	9·50	5·50
16		15f. on 15n.p. red-brown	12·00	9·50
17		20f. on 20n.p. ultramarine	13·00	8·00
		b. Perf 14½	£160	£170
		ba. Surch inverted	£450	£650
18		30f. on 30n.p. red-orange	12·00	19·00
		a. Arabic "2" for "3" in surch	£5500	
		b. Surch double, one albino	£250	
19	**2**	40f. on 40n.p. reddish violet	14·00	1·00
20		50f. on 50n.p. bistre	35·00	35·00
21		75f. on 75n.p. black	35·00	35·00
		a. Surch double, one albino	£250	
22	**3**	100f. on 1r. emerald	17·00	3·75
23		200f. on 2r. black	18·00	13·00
24	**4**	500f. on 5r. carmine-red	30·00	38·00
25		1d. on 10r. deep ultramarine	48·00	65·00
		a. Short extra bar below portrait (R. 7/3)	£400	
15/25 *Set of* 11			£225	£200

The 40f., 50f. and 75f. are surcharged "Fils" only, as in Type **8**. The remainder have the new value expressed in figures also. On the 1d. the old value is obliterated by bars.

The Abu Dhabi Post Department took over the postal services on 1 January 1967. Later stamp isssues will be found in Part 19 (*Middle East*) of this catalogue.

Aden

The first post office in Aden opened during January 1839, situated in what became known as the Crater district. No stamps were initially available, but, after the office was placed under the Bombay Postal Circle, stocks of the 1854 ½a. and 1a. stamps were placed on sale in Aden from 10 October 1854. Supplies of the 2a. and 4a. values did not arrive until December. Most Indian issues from the 1854 lithographs up to 1935 Silver Jubilee set can be found with Aden postmarks.

During January 1858 a further office, Aden Steamer Point, was opened in the harbour area and much of the business was transferred to it by 1869. The original Aden post office, in Crater, was renamed Aden Cantonment, later to be changed again to Aden Camp.

The first cancellation used with the Indian stamps was a plain diamond of dots. This type was also used elsewhere so that attribution to Aden is only possible when on cover. Aden was assigned "124" in the Indian postal number system, with the sub-office at Aden Steamer Point being "132". After a short period "124" was used at both offices, cancellations being identifiable by the spacing and shape of the numerals. It is possible that "132" was also used at an office in India.

1858 "124" Cancellation

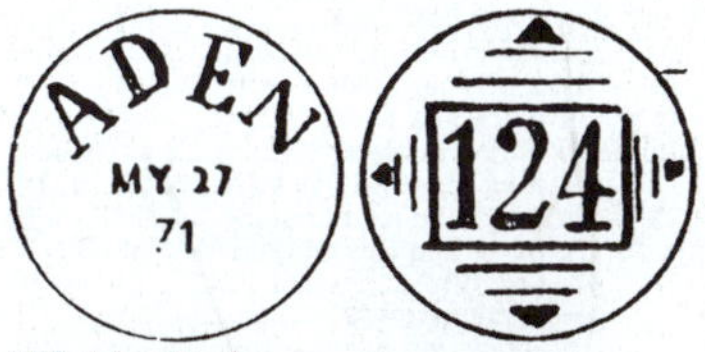

1870 Aden Duplex

1872 Aden Steamer Point Duplex

Both post offices used "124" until 1871 when Aden Cantonment was assigned "125", only to have this swiftly amended to "124A" in the same year.

1871 Aden Cantonment "125" Cancellation

1871 Aden Cantonment "124A" Cancellation

Cancellations inscribed "Aden Steamer Point" disappear after 1874 and this office was then known simply as Aden. Following this change the office was given number "B-22" under the revised Indian P.O. scheme and this number appears as a major part of the cancellations from 1875 to 1886, either on its own or as part of a duplex, Aden Camp, the alternative name for the Cantonment office, became "B-22/1".

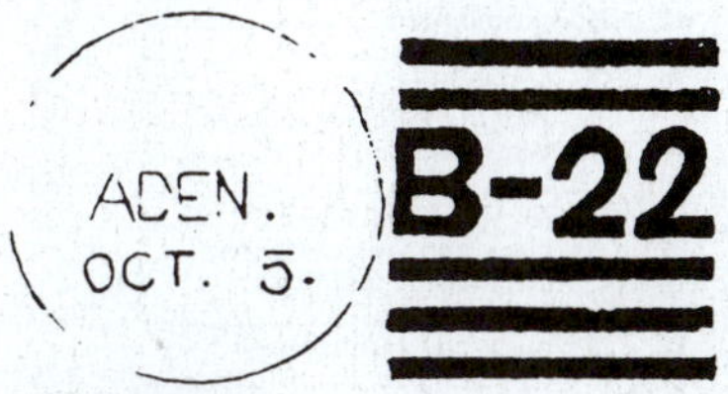

1875 Aden Duplex

Squared-circle types for Aden and Aden Cantonment were introduced in 1884 and 1888 to be in turn replaced by standard Indian double and single circle from 1895 onwards.

A number of other post offices were opened between 1891 and 1937:

- Dthali (*opened* 1903, *initially using* "EXPERIMENTAL P.O. B-84" *postmark*; *closed* 1907)
- Kamaran (*opened c* 1915, *but no civilian postmarks known before* 1925)
- Khormaksar (*opened* 1892; *closed* 1915; *reopened* 1925)
- Maalla (*opened* 1923; *closed* 1931)
- Nobat-Dakim (*opened* 1904, *initially using* "EXPERIMENTAL P.O. B-84" *postmark*; *closed* 1905)
- Perim (*opened* 1915; *closed* 1936)
- Sheikh Othman (*opened* 1891; *closed* 1915; *reopened* 1922; *closed* 1937)

PRICES FOR STAMPS ON COVER TO 1945

Nos. 1/15	*from* × 6
Nos. 16/27	*from* × 3

(Currency. 12 pies = 1 anna; 16 annas = 1 rupee)

1 Dhow

(Recess D.L.R.)

1937 (1 Apr). Wmk Mult Script CA sideways. P 13×12.

1	**1**	½a. yellow-green	3·75	2·75
2		9p. deep green	3·75	3·00
3		1a. sepia	3·75	1·50
4		2a. scarlet	4·00	3·00
5		2½a. bright blue	4·50	2·00
6		3a. carmine	10·00	8·50
7		3½a. grey-blue	7·50	4·50
8		8a. pale purple	24·00	8·00
9		1r. brown	48·00	9·50
10		2r. yellow	80·00	27·00
11		5r. deep purple	£160	95·00
12		10r. olive-green	£425	£425
1/12 *Set of* 12			£700	£550
1s/12s Perf "Specimen" *Set of* 12			£450	

1937 (12 May). *Coronation. As Nos. 95/7 of Antigua, but ptd by D.L.R.* P 14.

13	1a. sepia	65	1·25
14	2½a. light blue	75	1·40
	w. Wmk inverted	£850	
15	3½a. grey-blue	1·00	2·75
13/15 *Set of* 3		2·25	4·75
13s/15s Perf "Specimen" *Set of* 3		£110	

3 Aidrus Mosque, Crater

4 Adenese Camel Corps

5 The Harbour

6 Adenese Dhow

7 Mukalla

8 "Capture of Aden, 1839" (Captain Rundle)

(Recess Waterlow)

1939 (19 Jan)–**48**. Wmk Mult Script CA. P 12½.

16	**3**	½a. yellowish green	1·00	60
		a. Bluish green (13.9.48)	3·25	4·00
17	**4**	¾a. red-brown	2·00	1·25
18	**5**	1a. pale blue	40	40
19	**6**	1½a. scarlet	1·50	60
20	**3**	2a. sepia	40	25
21	**7**	2½a. deep ultramarine	80	30
22	**8**	3a. sepia and carmine	1·00	25
23	**7**	8a. red-orange	1·50	40
23*a*	**8**	14a. sepia and light blue (15.1.45)	2·75	1·00
24	**6**	1r. emerald-green	3·00	2·25
25	**5**	2r. deep blue and magenta	7·00	2·25
26	**4**	5r. red-brown and olive-green	20·00	13·00
27	**8**	10r. sepia and violet	35·00	14·00
16/27 *Set of* 13			65·00	32·00
16s/27s Perf "Specimen" *Set of* 13			£225	

Accent over "D" (R. 7/1, later corrected)

1946 (15 Oct). *Victory. As Nos. 110/11 of Antigua.*

28		1½a. carmine	20	1·60
		a. Accent over "D"	32·00	
29		2½a. blue	30	75
		w. Wmk inverted	£850	
28s/9s Perf "Specimen" *Set of 2*			80·00	

1949 (17 Jan). *Royal Silver Wedding. As Nos. 112/13 of Antigua.*

30		1½a. scarlet (P 14×15)	40	2·00
31		10r. mauve (P 11½×11)	29·00	40·00

1949 (10 Oct). *75th Anniv of U.P.U. As Nos. 114/17 of Antigua, surch with new values by Waterlow.*

32		2½a. on 20c. ultramarine	50	1·50
33		3a. on 30c. carmine-red	2·00	1·50
34		8a. on 50c. orange	1·40	2·00
35		1r. on 1s. blue	1·60	3·25
32/5 *Set of 4*			5·00	7·50

(New Currency. 100 cents = 1 shilling)

5 CENTS
(12)

1951 (1 Oct). *Nos. 18 and 20/7 surch with new values, in cents or shillings, as T* **12**, *or in one line between bars (30c.) by Waterlow.*

36		5c. on 1a. pale blue	25	40
37		10c. on 2a. sepia	15	45
38		15c. on 2½a. deep ultramarine	30	1·25
		a. Surch double	£1100	
39		20c. on 3a. sepia and carmine	30	40
40		30c. on 8a. red-orange (R.)	40	65
41		50c. on 8a. red-orange	70	35
42		70c. on 14a. sepia and light blue	2·25	1·50
43		1s. on 1r. emerald-green	1·00	30
44		2s. on 2r. deep blue and magenta	12·00	3·50
		a. Surch albino	£700	
45		5s. on 5r. red-brown and olive-green	22·00	12·00
46		10s. on 10r. sepia and violet	29·00	13·00
36/46 *Set of 11*			60·00	30·00

1953 (2 June). *Coronation. As No. 120 of Antigua.*

47		15c. black and green	1·00	1·25

14 Minaret

15 Camel transport

16 Crater

17 Mosque

18 Dhow

19 Map

20 Salt works

21 Dhow building

21a Colony's badge

22 Aden Protectorate levy

23 Crater Pass

24 Tribesman

25 "Aden in 1572" (F. Hogenberg)

Crack in wall (R. 1/5)

(Recess Waterlow, D.L.R. from 5 Dec 1961)

1953 (15 June)–**63**. *T* **14** *and similar designs, and T* **25**. *Wmk Mult Script CA. P 13½×13 (No. 72), 12×13½ (Nos. 57, 64, 66, 68) or 12 (others).*

48	**14**	5c. yellowish green	20	10
49		5c. bluish green (1.6.55)	40	3·50
		a. Perf 12×13½ (12.4.56)	10	1·25
50	**15**	10c. orange	40	10
51		10c. vermilion (1.2.55)	10	30
52	**16**	15c. blue-green	1·25	60
53		15c. greenish grey (26.4.59)	5·00	5·50
		a. Deep greenish grey (16.1.62)	18·00	15·00
		b. Greenish slate (13.11.62)	21·00	17·00
54	**17**	25c. carmine-red	85	55
		a. Crack in wall	38·00	27·00
55		25c. deep rose-red (15.3.56)	3·50	1·25
		a. Rose-red (13.3.62)	15·00	6·00
56	**18**	35c. deep ultramarine	2·50	2·00
57		35c. deep blue (15.10.58)	6·00	4·50
		a. Violet-blue (17.2.59)	10·00	3·75
58	**19**	50c. dull blue	20	10
59		50c. deep blue (1.7.55)	75	1·25
		a. Perf 12×13½ (12.4.56)	75	20
		aw. Wmk inverted	†	£600
60	**20**	70c. brown-grey	20	10
61		70c. black (20.9.54)	1·00	35
		a. Perf 12×13½ (12.4.56)	1·00	20
62	**21**	1s. sepia and reddish violet	30	10
63		1s. black and violet (1.7.55)	1·50	10
64	**21a**	1s.25 blue and black (16.7.56)	4·00	60
		a. Dull blue and black (16.1.62)	13·00	70
65	**22**	2s. sepia and rose-carmine	1·25	50
66		2s. black and carmine-red (1.3.56)	9·50	50
		aw. Wmk inverted		
		b. Black and carmine-rose (22.1.63)	30·00	16·00
67	**23**	5s. sepia and dull blue	1·50	1·00
68		5s. black and deep dull blue (11.4.56)	8·00	1·25
		a. Black and blue (11.12.62)	28·00	13·00
69	**24**	10s. sepia and olive	1·75	8·00
70		10s. black and bronze-green (20.9.54)	16·00	1·75
71	**25**	20s. chocolate and reddish lilac	6·50	10·00
72		20s. black and deep lilac (7.1.57)	55·00	14·00
		a. Deep black and deep lilac (14.5.58)	60·00	18·00
48/72 *Set of 25*			£110	45·00

On No. 70 the tribesman's skirt is shaded with cross-hatching instead of with mainly diagonal lines as in No. 69.

1954 (27 Apr). *Royal Visit. As No. 62 but inscr* "ROYAL VISIT 1954" *at top.*

73		1s. sepia and reddish violet	60	60

تعديل
الدستور
١٩٥٩
(26)

REVISED
CONSTITUTION
1959
(27)

1959 (26 Jan). *Revised Constitution. No. 53 optd with T* **26**, *and No. 64 optd with T* **27**, *in red, by Waterlow.*

74		15c. slate-green	30	2·00
75		1s.25 blue and black	1·00	1·00

1963 (4 June). *Freedom from Hunger. As No. 146 of Antigua.*

76		1s.25 bluish green (Protein foods)	1·25	1·75

1964 (5 Feb)–**65**. *As Nos. 48, etc. but wmk w* **12**. *P 12 (10c., 15c., 25c., 1s.) or 12×13½ (others).*

77	**14**	5c. green (16.2.65)	2·50	7·00
78	**15**	10c. bright orange	1·00	1·00
79	**16**	15c. greenish grey	70	3·75
		w. Wmk inverted	£100	
80	**17**	25c. carmine-red	1·25	40
81	**18**	35c. indigo-violet	6·50	3·75
82	**19**	50c. indigo-blue	50	30
		a. Pale indigo-blue (16.2.65)	50	30
		aw. Wmk inverted		
83	**20**	70c. black	60	2·75
		a. Brownish grey (16.2.65)	1·25	3·50
84	**21**	1s. black and violet (10.3.64)	12·00	2·75
85	**21a**	1s.25 ultramarine and black (10.3.64)	17·00	2·25
86	**22**	2s. black and carmine-rose (16.2.65)	3·75	27·00
77/86 *Set of 10*			40·00	45·00

The Stamps of Aden were withdrawn on 31 March 1965 and superseded by those of the South Arabian Federation.

ADEN PROTECTORATE STATES

KATHIRI STATE OF SEIYUN

The stamps of ADEN were used in Kathiri State of Seiyun from 22 May 1937 until 1942. A further office was opened at Tarim on 11 December 1940.

PRICES FOR STAMPS ON COVER TO 1945	
Nos. 1/11	*from* × 10

1 Sultan of Seiyun

2 Seiyun

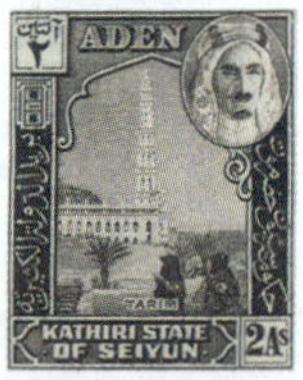
3 Tarim

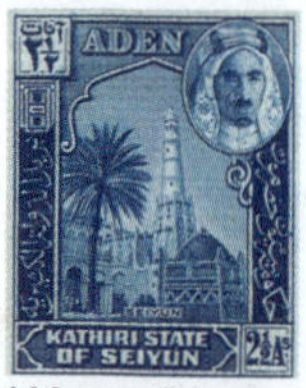
4 Mosque, Seiyun

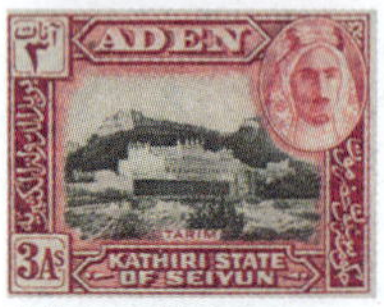
5 Fortress, Tarim

6 Mosque, Seiyun

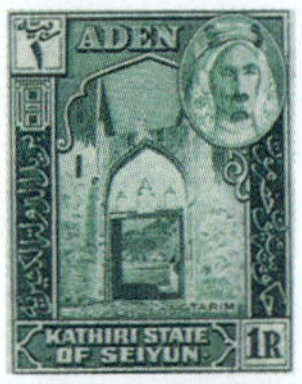
7 South Gate, Tarim

8 Kathiri House

9 Mosque Entrance, Tarim

VICTORY
ISSUE
8TH JUNE 1946
(10)

(Recess D.L.R.)

1942 (July–Oct). Wmk Mult Script CA. *T* **1**, perf 14; others, perf 12×13 (vert) or 13×12 (horiz).

1	**1**	½a. blue-green	20	1·25
2		¾a. brown	40	2·50
3		1a. blue	70	1·25
4	**2**	1½a. carmine	70	2·00
5	**3**	2a. sepia	40	1·75
6	**4**	2½a. blue	1·25	1·75
7	**5**	3a. sepia and carmine	1·75	3·25
8	**6**	8a. red	1·25	70
9	**7**	1r. green	3·75	3·25
10	**8**	2r. blue and purple	9·00	14·00
11	**9**	5r. brown and green	25·00	22·00
1/11 *Set of 11*			40·00	48·00
1s/11s Perf "Specimen" *Set of 11*			£190	

1946 (15 Oct). *Victory. No. 4 optd with T* **10**, *and No. 6 optd similarly but in four lines, by De La Rue.*

12		1½a. carmine	20	65
13		2½a. blue (R.)	20	20
		a. Opt inverted	£700	
		b. Opt double	£1000	
12s/13s Perf "Specimen" *Set of 2*			80·00	

1949 (17 Jan). *Royal Silver Wedding. As Nos. 112/13 of Antigua.*

14		1½a. scarlet	30	3·00
15		5r. green	16·00	9·00

1949 (10 Oct). *75th Anniv of U.P.U. As Nos. 114/17 of Antigua, surch with new values by Waterlow.*

16		2½a. on 20c. ultramarine	15	70
17		3a. on 30c. carmine-red	1·25	1·50
18		8a. on 50c. orange	25	1·60
19		1r. on 1s. blue	30	1·00
16/19 *Set of 4*			1·75	4·25

5 CTS
(11)

50 CENTS
(12)

5/-
(13)

1951 (1 Oct). *Currency changed. Nos. 3 and 5/11 surch as T* **11** (5c.), **12** (10c. ("CTS"), 15c. ("CTS"), 20c. *and* 50c.) *or* **13** (1s. *to* 5s.), *by Waterlow.*

20		5c. on 1a. blue (R.)	15	1·50
21		10c. on 2a. sepia	30	1·00
22		15c. on 2½a. blue	15	1·75
23		20c. on 3a. sepia and carmine	20	2·75
24		50c. on 8a. red	20	1·00
25		1s. on 1r. green	75	3·00
26		2s. on 2r. blue and purple	6·00	32·00
27		5s. on 5r. brown and green	26·00	45·00
20/27 *Set of* 8			30·00	80·00

1953 (2 June). *Coronation. As No. 120 of Antigua.*

28		15c. black and deep green (Queen Elizabeth II)	30	1·75

14 Sultan Hussein

15 Tarim

(Des Freya Stark and H. Ingram. Recess D.L.R.)

1954 (15 Jan). *As Nos. 1/11 (but with portrait of Sultan Hussein as in T* **14/15**). Wmk Mult Script CA. T **14**, perf 12½; others, perf 12×13 (vert) or 13×12 (horiz).

29	**14**	5c. sepia	10	10
30		10c. deep blue	15	10
31	**2**	15c. deep bluish green	15	10
32	**15**	25c. carmine-red	15	10
33	**4**	35c. deep blue	15	10
34	**5**	50c. deep brown and carmine-red	15	10
35	**6**	1s. brown-orange	15	10
36	**7**	2s. deep yellow-green	4·00	2·25
37	**8**	5s. deep blue and violet	8·00	7·00
38	**9**	10s. yellow-brown and violet	8·00	7·00
29/38 *Set of* 10			19·00	15·00

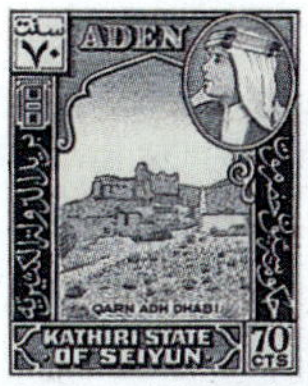
16 Qarn Adh Dhabi

17 Seiyun

18 Gheil Omer

(Recess D.L.R.)

1964 (1 July). *Designs as T* **16/17a**. W w **12**. P 12×13 (70c.) or 13×12 (others).

39	**16**	70c. black	2·50	1·00
40	**17**	1s.25 blue-green	2·50	7·50
41	**18**	1s.50 deep reddish violet	2·50	7·50
39/41 *Set of* 3			6·75	14·50

Stamps after this date can be found listed under South Arabia.

QU'AITI STATE IN HADHRAMAUT

The stamps of ADEN were used in Qu'aiti State in Hadhramaut from 22 April 1937 until 1942. The main post office was at Mukalla. Other offices existed at Du'an (*opened* 1940), Gheil Ba Wazir (*opened* 1942), Haura (*opened* 1940), Shibam (*opened* 1940) and Shihr (*opened* 1939).

PRICES FOR STAMPS ON COVER TO 1945
Nos. 1/11 *from* × 15

I. ISSUES INSCR "SHIHR AND MUKALLA".

1 Sultan of Shihr and Mukalla

2 Mukalla Harbour

3 Gateway of Shihr

4 Shibam

5 Outpost of Mukalla

6 'Einat

7 Du'an

8 Mosque in Hureidha

9 Meshhed

VICTORY
ISSUE
8TH JUNE
1946
(10)

(Recess D.L.R.)

1942 (July)–**46**. *Designs as T* **1** (*½ to 1a.*) *or T* **2** (*others*). Wmk Mult Script CA. P 14 (½ to 1a.), 12×13 (1½, 2, 3a. and 1r.) or 13×12 (others).

1	**1**	½a. blue-green	1·25	50
		a. Olive-green (12.46)	27·00	35·00
2		¾a. brown	2·00	30
3		1a. blue	1·00	1·00
4	**2**	1½a. carmine	1·75	50
5	**3**	2a. sepia	1·75	1·75
6	**4**	2½a. blue	50	30
7	**7**	3a. sepia and carmine	1·00	75
8	**6**	8a. red	70	40
9	**7**	1r. green	5·50	4·00
		a. "A" of "CA" missing from wmk	†	£900
10	**8**	2r. blue and purple	14·00	8·50
11	**9**	5r. brown and green	20·00	12·00
1/11 *Set of* 11			45·00	27·00
1s/11s Perf "Specimen" *Set of* 11			£190	

1946 (15 Oct). *Victory. No. 4 optd. with T* **10** *and No. 6 optd similarly, but to three lines, by De La Rue.*

12		1½a. carmine	15	1·00
13		2½a. blue (R.)	15	15
12s/13s Perf "Specimen" *Set of* 2			80·00	

1949 (17 Jan). *Royal Silver Wedding. As Nos. 112/13 of Antigua.*

14		1½a. scarlet	50	4·50
15		5r. green	17·00	10·00

1949 (10 Oct). *75th Anniv of U.P.U. As Nos. 114/17 of Antigua, surch with new values by Waterlow.*

16		2½a. on 20c. ultramarine	15	20
17		3a. on 30c. carmine-red	1·40	85
18		8a. on 50c. orange	25	85
19		1r. on 1s. blue	30	50
		a. Surch omitted	£2250	
16/19 *Set of* 4			1·90	2·25

1951 (1 Oct). *Currency changed. Surch with new values in cents or shillings as T* **11**(5c.), **12** (10c. ("CTS"), 15c., 20c. *and* 50c.) *or* **13** (1s. *to* 5s.) *of Seiyun, by Waterlow.*

20		5c. on 1a. blue (R.)	15	20
21		10c. on 2a. sepia	15	20
22		15c. on 2½a. blue	15	20
23		20c. on 3a. sepia and carmine	30	75
		a. Surch double, one albino	£325	
24		50c. on 8a. red	50	2·50
25		1s. on 1r. green	2·25	55
26		2s. on 2r. blue and purple	8·50	20·00
27		5s. on 5r. brown and green	16·00	32·00
20/27 *Set of* 8			25·00	50·00

1953 (2 June). *Coronation. As No. 120 of Antigua.*

28		15c. black and deep blue (Queen Elizabeth II)	1·00	55

II. ISSUES INSCR "HADHRAMAUT"

11 Metal Work

22 Metal Work

(Des Mme M. de Sturler Raemaekers. Recess D.L.R.)

1955 (1 Sept)–**63**. *T* **11** *and similar designs.* Wmk Mult Script CA. P 11½×13-13½ (vert) or 14 (horiz).

29		5c. greenish blue	30	10
30		10c. grey-black	1·00	10
31		15c. deep green	50	10
		a. Bronze-green (9.3.63)	40	40
32		25c. carmine-red	40	10
33		35c. blue	70	10
34		50c. orange-red	40	10
		a. Red-orange (9.3.63)	40	30
35		90c. sepia	50	15
36		1s. black and deep lilac	50	10
37		1s.25 black and red-orange	55	55
38		2s. black and indigo	4·00	60
39		5s. black and bluish green	5·00	1·75
40		10s. black and lake	5·50	7·50
29/40 *Set of* 12			17·00	10·00

Designs:*Vert*—10c. Mat-making; 15c. Weaving; 25c. Pottery; 35c. Building; 50c. Date cultivation; 90c. Agriculture. *Horiz*—1s. Fisheries; 1s.25, 10s. Lime-burning; 2s. Dhow building; 5s. Agriculture.

1963 (20 Oct). *As Nos. 29/40 but with inset portrait of Sultan Awadh bin Saleh el-Qu'aiti as in T* **22** *and wmk* w **12**.

41		5c. greenish blue	10	1·75
42		10c. grey-black	10	1·50
43		15c. bronze-green	10	1·75
44		25c. carmine-red	10	75
45		35c. blue	10	2·00
46		50c. red-orange	10	1·00
47		70c. deep brown (as 90c.)	15	75
48		1s. black and deep lilac	20	30
49		1s.25 black and red-orange	45	4·50
50		2s. black and indigo-blue	3·25	1·75
51		5s. black and bluish green	13·00	28·00
52		10s. black and lake	17·00	28·00
41/52 *Set of* 12			32·00	65·00

Stamps after this date can be found listed under South Arabia.

Aitutaki *see* Cook Islands

Anguilla

Following the grant of Associated Statehood to St. Christopher, Nevis and Anguilla, on 27 February 1967 the population of Anguilla agitated for independence and the St. Kitts-Nevis authorities left the island on 30 May 1967. Nos. 1/16 were issued by the Island Council and were accepted for international mail. On 7 July 1969 the Anguilla post office was officially recognised by the Government of St. Christopher, Nevis and Anguilla and normal postal communications via St. Christopher were resumed. By the Anguilla Act of 21 July 1971, Anguilla was restored to direct British control.

A degree of internal self-government with an Executive Council was introduced on 10 February 1976 and the links with St. Kitts-Nevis were officially severed on 18 December 1980.

(Currency. 100 cents = 1 Eastern Carribean dollar)

Independent Anguilla
(1)

2 Mahogany Tree, The Quarter

1967 (4 Sept). *Nos. 129/44 of St. Kitts-Nevis optd as T* **1**, *by Island Press Inc, St. Thomas, U.S. Virgin Islands.*

1		½c. New lighthouse, Sombrero	42·00	26·00
2		1c. Loading sugar cane, St. Kitts	45·00	9·50
3		2c. Pall Mall Square, Basseterre	45·00	2·00
4		3c. Gateway, Brimstone Hill Fort, St. Kitts	45·00	4·50
		w. Wmk inverted	—	42·00
5		4c. Nelson's Spring, Nevis	45·00	5·50
6		5c. Grammar School, St. Kitts	£160	27·00
7		6c. Crater, Mt Misery, St. Kitts	75·00	13·00
8		10c. Hibiscus	45·00	7·50
9		15c. Sea Island cotton, Nevis	85·00	15·00
10		20c. Boat building, Anguilla	£160	17·00
11		25c. White-crowned Pigeon	£130	28·00
		w. Wmk inverted	£170	45·00
12		50c. St. George's Church Tower, Basseterre	£2750	£550
13		60c. Alexander Hamilton	£3500	£1100
14		$1 Map of St. Kitts-Nevis	£2250	£475
15		$2.50 Map of Anguilla	£1900	£350
16		$5 Arms of St. Christopher, Nevis and Anguilla	£2000	£350
1/16 *Set of* 16			£12000	£2750

Owing to the limited stocks available for overprinting, the sale of the above stamps was personally controlled by the Postmaster and no orders from the trade were accepted.

(Des John Lister Ltd. Litho A. & M.)

1967 (27 Nov)–**68**. *T* **2** *and similar horiz designs.* P 12½×13.

17		1c. dull green, bistre-brown and pale orange	10	1·00
18		2c. bluish green and black (21.3.68)	10	2·00
19		3c. black and light emerald (10.2.68)	10	10
20		4c. cobalt-blue and black (10.2.68)	10	10
21		5c. multicoloured	10	10
22		6c. light vermilion and black (21.3.68)	10	10
23		10c. multicoloured	15	10
24		15c. multicoloured (10.2.68)	2·50	20
25		20c. multicoloured	1·25	2·25
26		25c. multicoloured	60	20
27		40c. apple green, light greenish blue and black	1·00	25
28		60c. multicoloured (10.2.68)	4·50	4·50
29		$1 multicoloured (10.2.68)	1·75	3·25
30		$2.50 multicoloured (21.3.68)	2·00	5·50
31		$5 multicoloured (10.2.68)	3·00	4·25
17/31 *Set of* 15			15·00	21·00

Designs:—2c. Sombrero Lighthouse; 3c. St. Mary's Church; 4c. Valley Police Station; 5c. Old Plantation House, Mt Fortune; 6c. Valley Post Office; 10c. Methodist Church, West End; 15c. Wall-Blake Airport; 20c. Beech A90 King Air aircraft over Sandy Ground; 25c. Island Harbour; 40c. Map of Anguilla; 60c. Hermit Crab and Starfish; $1 Hibiscus; $2.50, Local scene; $5, Spiny Lobster.

17 Yachts in Lagoon

18 Purple-throated Carib

(Des John Lister Ltd. Litho A.& M.)

1968 (11 May). *Anguillan Ships. T* **17** *and similar horiz designs. Multicoloured.* P 14.

32	10c. Type **17**	20	10
33	15c. Boat on beach	25	10
34	25c. Warspite (schooner)	35	15
35	40c. Atlantic Star (schooner)	40	20
32/5 *Set of* 4		1·10	50

(Des John Lister Ltd. Litho A. & M.)

1968 (8 July). *Anguillan Birds. T* **18** *and similar multicoloured designs.* P 14.

36	10c. Type **18**	65	15
37	15c. Bananaquit	80	20
38	25c. Black-necked Stilt (horiz)	85	20
39	40c. Royal Tern (horiz)	90	30
36/9 *Set of* 4		3·00	75

19 Guides Badge and Anniversary Years

(Des John Lister Ltd. Litho A. & M.)

1968 (14 Oct). *35th Anniv of Anguillan Girl Guides. T* **19** *and similar multicoloured designs.* P 13×13½ (10, 25c.) *or* 13½×13 *(others).*

40	10c. Type **19**	10	10
41	15c. Badge and silhouettes of Guides (vert)	15	10
42	25c. Guides' badge and Headquarters	20	15
43	40c. Association and Proficiency badges (vert)	25	15
40/3 *Set of* 4		65	45

20 The Three Kings

(Des John Lister Ltd. Litho A. & M.)

1968 (18 Nov). *Christmas. T* **20** *and similar designs.* P 13.

44	1c. black and cerise	10	10
45	10c. black and light greenish blue	10	10
46	15c. black and chestnut	15	10
47	40c. black and blue	15	10
48	50c. black and dull green	20	15
44/8 *Set of* 5		60	50

Designs: *Vert*—10c. The Wise Men; 15c. Holy Family and manger. *Horiz*—40c. The Shepherds; 50c. Holy Family and donkey.

21 Bagging Salt

INDEPENDENCE
JANUARY, 1969
(21a)

(Des John Lister Ltd. Litho A. & M.)

1969 (4 Jan). *Anguillan Salt Industry. T* **21** *and similar horiz designs. Multicoloured.* P 13.

49	10c. Type **21**	25	10
50	15c. Packing salt	30	10
51	40c. Salt pond	35	10
52	50c. Loading salt	35	10
49/52 *Set of* 4		1·10	35

1969 (17 Jan*). *Expiration of Interim Agreement on Status of Anguilla. Nos. 17/24 and 26/7 optd with T* **21a**.

52*a*	1c. dull green, bistre-brown and pale orange	10	40
52*b*	2c. bluish green and black	10	40
52*c*	3c. black and light emerald	10	40
52*d*	4c. cobalt-blue and black	10	40
52*e*	5c. multicoloured	10	20
52*f*	6c. light vermilion and black	10	20
52*g*	10c. multicoloured	10	30
52*h*	15c. multicoloured	90	30
52*i*	25c. multicoloured	80	30
52*j*	40c. apple green, light greenish blue and black	1·00	40
52*a/j Set of* 10		3·00	3·00

*Earliest known postmark date. The remaining values of the 1967–68 series, Nos. 17/31, also come with this overprint. The complete set exists on large first day covers postmarked 9 January 1969. The values listed above have been reported used on commercial mail from Anguilla.

22 "The Crucifixion" (Studio of Massys)

(Des John Lister Ltd. Litho Format)

1969 (31 Mar). *Easter Commemoration. T* **22** *and similar vert design.* P 13½.

53	25c. multicoloured	25	15
54	40c. multicoloured	35	15

Design:—10c. "The Last Supper" (ascribed to Roberti).

23 Amaryllis

(Des John Lister Ltd. Litho Format)

1969 (10 June). *Flowers of the Caribbean. T* **23** *and similar horiz designs. Multicoloured.* P 14.

55	10c. Type **23**	15	20
56	15c. Bougainvillea	20	25
57	40c. Hibiscus	30	50
58	50c. Cattleya orchid	1·25	1·60
55/8 *Set of* 4		1·75	2·25

24 Superb Gaza, Channelled Turban, Chestnut Turban and Carved Star Shell

(Des John Lister Ltd. Litho A. & M.)

1969 (22 Sept). *Sea Shells. T* **24** *and similar horiz designs. Multicoloured.* P 14.

59	10c. Type **24**	20	20
60	15c. American Thorny Oyster	20	20
61	40c. Scotch, Royal and Smooth Scotch Bonnets	30	30
62	50c. Atlantic Trumpet Triton	40	30
59/62 *Set of* 4		1·00	90

(25)

(26)

(27)

(28)

(29)

1969 (1 Oct). *Christmas. Nos. 17, 25/8 optd with T* **25/29**.

63	1c. dull green, bistre-brown & light orange	10	10
64	20c. multicoloured	20	10
65	25c. multicoloured	20	10
66	40c. apple-green, light greenish blue & black	25	15
67	60c. multicoloured	40	20
63/7 *Set of* 5		1·00	55

30 Spotted Goatfish

31 "Morning Glory"

(Des John Lister Ltd. Litho A. & M.)

1969 (1 Dec). *Fishes. T* **30** *and similar horiz designs. Multicoloured.* P 14.

68	10c. Type **30**	30	15
69	15c. Blue-striped Grunt	45	15
70	40c. Nassau Grouper	55	20
71	50c. Banded Butterflyfish	65	20
68/71 *Set of* 4		1·75	65

(Des John Lister Ltd. Litho A. & M.)

1970 (23 Feb). *Flowers. T* **31** *and similar vert designs. Multicoloured.* P 14.

72	10c. Type **31**	25	10
73	15c. Blue Petrea	35	10
74	40c. Hibiscus	50	20
75	50c. "Flame Tree"	60	25
72/5 *Set of* 4		1·50	55

32 "The Crucifixion" (Masaccio)

33 Scout Badge and Map

(Des John Lister Ltd. Litho Format)

1970 (26 Mar). *Easter. T* **32** *and similar multicoloured designs.* P 13½.

76	10c. "The Ascent to Calvary" (Tiepolo) (horiz)	15	10
77	20c. Type **32**	20	10
78	40c. "Deposition" (Rosso Fiorentino)	25	15
79	60c. "The Ascent to Calvary" (Murillo) (horiz)	25	15
76/9 *Set of* 4		75	45

(Des John Lister Ltd. Litho A. & M.)

1970 (10 Aug). *40th Anniv of Scouting in Anguilla. T* **33** *and similar horiz designs. Multicoloured.* P 13.

80	10c. Type **33**	15	15
81	15c. Scout camp and cubs practising first-aid	20	20
82	40c. Monkey Bridge	25	30
83	50c. Scout H.Q. Building and Lord Baden-Powell	35	30
80/3 *Set of* 4		85	85

34 Boatbuilding

(Des John Lister Ltd. Litho Format)

1970 (23 Nov). *Various horiz designs as T* **34**. *Multicoloured.* P 14.

84	1c. Type **34**	30	40
85	2c. Road Construction	30	40
86	3c. Quay, Blowing Point	30	20
87	4c. Broadcaster, Radio Anguilla	30	50
88	5c. Cottage Hospital Extension	40	50
89	6c. Valley Secondary School	30	50
90	10c. Hotel Extension	30	30
91	15c. Sandy Ground	30	30
92	20c. Supermarket and Cinema	70	30
93	25c. Bananas and Mangoes	35	1·00
94	40c. Wall Blake Airport	4·00	3·25
95	60c. Sandy Ground Jetty	65	3·50
96	$1 Administration Buildings	1·25	1·40
97	$2.50 Livestock	1·50	4·00
98	$5 Sandy Hill Bay	3·25	3·75
84/98 *Set of* 15		13·00	18·00

35 "The Adoration of the Shepherds" (Reni)

36 "Ecce Homo" (detail, Correggio)

(Des John Lister Ltd. Litho Questa)

1970 (11 Dec). *Christmas. T* **35** *and similar vert designs. Multicoloured.* P 13½.

99	1c. Type **35**	10	10
100	20c. "The Virgin and Child" (Gozzoli)	30	20
101	25c. "Mystic Nativity" (detail, Botticelli)	30	20
102	40c. "The Santa Margherita Madonna" (detail, Mazzola)	40	25
103	50c. "The Adoration of the Magi" (detail, Tiepolo)	40	25
99/103 *Set of* 5		1·25	90

Antigua

It is believed that the first postmaster for Antigua was appointed under Edward Dummer's scheme in 1706. After the failure of his service, control of the overseas mails passed to the British G.P.O. Mail services before 1850 were somewhat haphazard, until St. John's was made a branch office of the British G.P.O. in 1850. A second office, at English Harbour, opened in 1857.

The stamps of Great Britain were used between May 1858 and the end of April 1860, when the island postal service became the responsibility of the local colonial authorities. In the interim period, between the take-over and the appearance of Antiguan stamps, the crowned-circle handstamps were again utilised and No. CC1 can be found used as late as 1869.

For illustrations of the handstamp and postmark types see BRITISH POST OFFICES ABROAD notes, following GREAT BRITAIN.

ST. JOHN'S

CROWNED-CIRCLE HANDSTAMPS

CC1	CC **1** ANTIGUA (St. John's) (9.3.1850) (R.) *Price on cover*	£650

Stamps of GREAT BRITAIN *cancelled* "A 02" *as Type* **2**.

1858–60.

Z1	1d. rose-red (1857), P 14	£600
Z2	2d. blue (1855), P 14 (Plate No. 6)	£1100
Z3	2d. blue (1858) (Plate Nos. 7, 8, 9)	£750
Z4	4d. rose (1857)	£600
Z5	6d. lilac (1856)	£180
Z6	1s. green (1856)	£2250

ENGLISH HARBOUR

CROWNED-CIRCLE HANDSTAMPS

CC2	CC **3** ENGLISH HARBOUR (10.12.1857) *Price on cover*	£6500

Stamps of GREAT BRITAIN *cancelled* "A 18" *as Type* **2**.

1858–60.

Z6a	1d. rose red (1857)	
Z7	2d. blue (1858) (Plate No. 7)	£6000
Z8	4d. rose (1857)	£6000
Z9	6d. lilac	£2000
Z10	1s. green (1856)	

PRICES FOR STAMPS ON COVER TO 1945

No. 1	*from* × 10
Nos. 2/4	†
Nos. 5/10	*from* × 20
Nos. 13/14	*from* × 30
No. 15	*from* × 60
Nos. 16/18	*from* × 50
Nos. 19/23	*from* × 12
No. 24	*from* × 50
Nos. 25/30	*from* × 10
Nos. 31/51	*from* × 4
Nos. 52/4	*from* × 10
Nos. 55/61	*from* × 4
Nos. 62/80	*from* × 3
Nos. 81/90	*from* × 4
Nos. 91/4	*from* × 5
Nos. 95/7	*from* × 4
Nos. 98/109	*from* × 3

CROWN COLONY

1

3

(Eng C. Jeens after drawing by Edward Corbould. Recess P.B.)

1862 (Aug). No wmk.

(a) Rough perf 14 to 16.

1	**1**	6d. blue-green	£800	£500

(b) P 11 to 12½.

2	**1**	6d. blue-green	£6500	

(c) P 14 to 16×11 to 12½.

3	**1**	6d. blue-green	£3000	

(d) P 14 to 16 compound with 11 to 12½.

4	**1**	6d. blue-green	£3000	

Nos. 2/4 may be trial perforations. They are not known used.

1863 (Jan)–**67**. Wmk Small Star. W w **2** (sideways on 6d.). Rough perf 14 to 16.

5	**1**	1d. rosy mauve	£130	60·00
6		1d. dull rose (1864)	£110	48·00
		a. Imperf between (vert pair)	£24000	
7		1d. vermilion (1867)	£225	27·00
		a. Imperf between (horiz pair)	£24000	
		b. Wmk sideways	£250	42·00
8		6d. green (*shades*)	£600	26·00
		a. Wmk upright	—	£140
9		6d. dark green	£650	26·00
10		6d. yellow-green	£3750	90·00

Caution is needed in buying No. 10 as some of the shades of No. 8 verge on yellow-green.

The 1d. rosy mauve exists showing trial perforations of 11 to 12½ and 14 to 16 (*Price*, £8500 *unused*).

(Recess D.L.R. from P.B. plates)

1872. Wmk Crown CC. P 12½.

13	**1**	1d. lake	£150	15·00
		w. Wmk inverted		
		x. Wmk reversed	£150	15·00
		y. Wmk inverted and reversed		
14		1d. scarlet	£200	21·00
		w. Wmk inverted	£200	60·00
		x. Wmk reversed	—	32·00
15		6d. blue-green	£500	10·00
		w. Wmk inverted	—	80·00
		x. Wmk reversed	£500	13·00
		y. Wmk inverted and reversed	—	90·00

1876. Wmk Crown CC. P 14.

16	**1**	1d. lake	£170	10·00
		a. Bisected (½d.) (1883) (on cover)	†	£5500
		x. Wmk reversed		
17		1d. lake-rose	£170	10·00
		w. Wmk inverted	£250	75·00
		x. Wmk reversed	—	32·00
		y. Wmk inverted and reversed		
18		6d. blue-green	£350	17·00
		w. Wmk inverted	†	£100
		x. Wmk reversed	£350	18·00
		y. Wmk inverted and reversed	£500	70·00

(Recess (T **1**); typo (T **3**) De La Rue & Co).

1879. Wmk Crown CC. P 14.

19	**3**	2½d. red-brown	£600	£170
		a. Large "2" in "2½" with slanting foot	£10000	£2500
20		4d. blue	£250	15·00

Top left triangle detached (Pl 2 R. 3/3 of right panel)

1882. Wmk Crown CA. P 14.

21	**3**	½d. dull green	3·00	16·00
		a. Top left triangle detached	£300	£475
22		2½d. red-brown	£190	55·00
		a. Top left triangle detached		
		b. Large "2" in "2½" with slanting foot	£3250	£1200
23		4d. blue	£275	15·00
		a. Top left triangle detached	—	£650

1884. Wmk Crown CA. P 12.

24	**1**	1d. carmine-red	50·00	15·00
		w. Wmk inverted		
		y. Wmk inverted and reversed		

The 1d. scarlet is a colour changeling.

1884–87. Wmk Crown CA. P 14.

25	**1**	1d. carmine-red	2·25	3·75
		x. Wmk reversed	—	22·00
		y. Wmk inverted and reversed		
26		1d. rose	55·00	12·00
27	**3**	2½d. ultramarine (1887)	7·00	14·00
		a. Large "2" in "2½" with slanting foot	£160	£250
		b. Top left triangle detached	£400	
28		4d. chestnut (1887)	2·25	3·00
		a. Top left triangle detached	£300	£325
29	**1**	6d. deep green	60·00	£120
30	**3**	1s. mauve (1886)	£160	£140
		a. Top left triangle detached	£1600	
25/30 *Set of 5*			£200	£250
27s, 28s, 30s Optd "Specimen" *Set of 3*			£150	

Nos. 25 and 26 postmarked "A 12" in place of "A 02" were used in St. Christopher.

2½ 2½ 2½

A B C

The variety "Large '2' in '2½' with slanting foot" occurs on R. 7/1 of the duty plate on all printings. At this position the "NN" of "PENNY" also sustained damage in about 1882, leaving three vertical strokes shortened. A and B (above) represent two states of the flaw at R. 7/1. Head plate 2, first used for Antigua in 1886, was a double-pane plate of 120, but the same 60-set duty plate remained in use, the variety thus occurring on R. 7/1 of each pane. A very similar flaw (C above) appeared at R. 3/1 of the duty plate (on which the "NN" was undamaged) early in the life of No. 27 and thus occurs on both panes of that stamp.

From 31 October 1890 until July 1903 Leeward Islands general issues were used. Subsequently both general issues and the following separate issues were in concurrent use until July 1956, when the general Leewards Island stamps were withdrawn.

4

5

(Typo D.L.R.)

1903 (July)–**07**. Wmk Crown CC. *Ordinary paper*. P 14.

31	**4**	½d. grey-black and grey-green	3·75	6·50
32		1d. grey-black and rose-red	8·00	1·25
33		2d. dull purple and brown	7·50	24·00
34		2½d. grey-black and blue	9·50	16·00
		a. Chalk-surfaced paper (1907)	30·00	65·00
35		3d. grey-green and orange-brown	11·00	20·00
36		6d. purple and black	32·00	50·00
		w. Wmk inverted	£150	
37		1s. blue and dull purple	45·00	60·00
		a. Chalk-surfaced paper (1907)	55·00	£140
38		2s. grey-green and pale violet	80·00	£100
39		2s.6d. grey-black and purple	23·00	55·00
40	**5**	5s. grey-green and violet	80·00	£120
		a. Chalk-surfaced paper (1907)	£140	£180
31/40 *Set of 10*			£250	£400
31s/40s Optd "Specimen" *Set of 10*			£160	

1908–17. Wmk Mult Crown CA. *Chalk-surfaced paper* (2d., 3d. to 2s.). P 14.

41	**4**	½d. green	3·50	4·50
		w. Wmk inverted		
42		½d. blue-green (1917)	4·50	6·50
43		1d. red (1909)	8·50	2·25
44		1d. scarlet (5.8.15)	7·00	3·25
		w. Wmk inverted		
45		2d. dull purple and brown (1912)	4·75	32·00
46		2½d. ultramarine	17·00	16·00
		a. Blue	23·00	23·00
47		3d. grey-green and orange-brown (1912)	6·50	19·00
48		6d. purple and black (1911)	7·50	40·00
49		1s. blue and dull purple	19·00	70·00
50		2s. grey-green and violet (1912)	95·00	£110
41/50 *Set of 8*			£160	£275
41s, 43s, 46s Optd "Specimen" *Set of 3*			65·00	

1913. *As T* **5**, *but portrait of George V.* Wmk Mult Crown CA. *Chalk-surfaced paper*. P 14.

51		5s. grey-green and violet	80·00	£130
		s. Optd "Specimen"	65·00	

WAR STAMP

(**7**)

8

1916 (Sept)–**17**. *No. 41 optd in London with T* **7**.

52	**4**	½d. green (Bk.)	3·25	2·50
53		½d. green (R.) (1.10.17)	1·50	2·50

1918 (July). *Optd with T* **7**. Wmk Mult Crown CA. P 14.

54	**4**	1½d. orange	1·00	1·25
52s/4s Optd "Specimen" *Set of 3*			80·00	

(Typo D.L.R.)

1921–29. P 14.

(a) Wmk Mult Crown CA. *Chalk-surfaced paper*.

55	**8**	3d. purple/*pale yellow*	4·50	12·00
56		4d. grey-black and red/*pale yellow* (1922)	2·25	5·50
57		1s. black/*emerald*	4·25	9·00
		y. Wmk inverted and reversed	£300	
58		2s. purple and blue/*blue*	13·00	24·00
59		2s.6d. black and red/*blue*	17·00	60·00
60		5s. green and red/*pale yellow* (1922)	8·50	50·00
61		£1 purple and black/*red* (1922)	£225	£325
55/61 *Set of 7*			£250	£425
55s/61s Optd "Specimen" *Set of 7*			£180	

(b) Wmk Mult Script CA. *Chalk-surfaced paper* (3d. to 4s.).

62	**8**	½d. dull green	2·75	50
63		1d. carmine-red	4·00	50
64		1d. bright violet (1923)	5·50	1·50
		a. Mauve	17·00	7·00
65		1d. bright scarlet (1929)	25·00	4·25
67		1½d. dull orange (1922)	5·00	7·00
68		1½d. carmine-red (1926)	8·00	1·75
69		1½d. pale red-brown (1929)	3·00	60
70		2d. grey (1922)	3·75	75
		a. Wmk sideways	†	£2250
71		2½d. bright blue (1922)	6·50	17·00
72		2½d. orange-yellow (1923)	2·50	17·00
73		2½d. ultramarine (1927)	9·00	5·50
74		3d. purple/*pale yellow* (1925)	7·00	8·50
75		6d. dull and bright purple (1922)	5·50	6·50
76		1s. black/*emerald* (1929)	6·00	6·00
77		2s. purple and blue/*blue* (1927)	11·00	60·00
78		2s.6d. black and red/*blue* (1927)	38·00	28·00
79		3s. green and violet (1922)	45·00	95·00
80		4s. grey-black and red (1922)	48·00	70·00
62/80 *Set of 16*			£180	£275
62s/80s Optd or Perf (Nos. 65, 69, 76) "Specimen" *Set of 18*			£375	

9 Old Dockyard, English Harbour

10 Government House, St. John's

11 Nelson's *Victory*

12 Sir Thomas Warner's *Concepcion*

(Des Mrs. J. Goodwin (5s.), Waterlow (others). Recess Waterlow)

1932 (27 Jan). *Tercentenary.* Wmk Mult Script CA. P 12½.

81	**9**	½d. green	3·75	7·50
82		1d. scarlet	4·25	7·50
83		1½d. brown	3·25	4·75
84	**10**	2d. grey	5·50	22·00
85		2½d. deep blue	5·50	8·50
86		3d. orange	5·50	12·00
87	**11**	6d. violet	15·00	12·00
88		1s. olive-green	19·00	28·00
89		2s.6d. claret	50·00	70·00
90	**12**	5s. black and chocolate	£100	£130
81/90 *Set of* 10			£190	£250
81s/90s Perf "Specimen" *Set of* 10			£200	

Examples of all values are known showing a forged St. Johns postmark dated "MY 18 1932".

13 Windsor Castle

(Des H. Fleury. Recess D.L.R.)

1935 (6 May). *Silver Jubilee.* Wmk Mult Script CA. P 13½×14.

91	**13**	1d. deep blue and carmine	2·75	3·50
		f. Diagonal line by turret	85·00	
92		1½d. ultramarine and grey	2·75	65
93		2½d. brown and deep blue	6·50	1·25
		g. Dot to left of chapel	£190	
94		1s. slate and purple	8·50	14·00
		a. Frame printed double, one albino	£1600	
		h. Dot by flagstaff	£300	
91/4 *Set of* 4			18·00	17·00
91s/4s Perf "Specimen" *Set of* 4			95·00	

For illustrations of plate varieties see Omnibus section following Zanzibar.

14 King George VI and Queen Elizabeth

(Des D.L.R. Recess B.W.)

1937 (12 May). *Coronation.* Wmk Mult Script CA. P 11×11½.

95	**14**	1d. carmine	70	2·50
96		1½d. yellow-brown	60	2·50
97		2½d. blue	2·00	2·75
95/7 *Set of* 3			3·00	7·00
95s/7s Perf "Specimen" *Set of* 3			75·00	

15 English Harbour

16 Nelson's Dockyard

16a Fort James

16b St. John's Harbour

(Recess Waterlow)

1938 (15 Nov)–**51**. Wmk Mult Script CA. P 12½.

98	**15**	½d. green	40	1·25
99	**16**	1d. scarlet	3·00	2·50
		a. *Red* (8.42 and 11.47)	4·00	3·00
100		1½d. chocolate-brown	6·50	1·75
		a. *Dull reddish brown* (12.43)	2·75	2·75
		b. *Lake-brown* (7.49)	32·00	13·00
101	**15**	2d. grey	1·00	80
		a. *Slate-grey* (6.51)	8·50	5·00
102	**16**	2½d. deep ultramarine	1·00	80
103	**16a**	3d. orange	1·00	1·00
104	**16b**	6d. violet	3·50	1·25
105		1s. black and brown	6·00	2·00
		a. *Black and red-brown* (7.49)	32·00	11·00
		ab. Frame ptd double, one albino	£5000	
106	**16a**	2s.6d. brown-purple	48·00	16·00
		a. *Maroon* (8.42)	29·00	16·00
107	**16b**	5s. olive-green	14·00	9·00
108	**16a**	10s. magenta (1.4.48)	16·00	28·00
109	–	£1 slate-green (1.4.48)	30·00	45·00
98/109 *Set of* 12			95·00	£100
98s/109s Perf "Specimen" *Set of* 12			£190	

17 Houses of Parliament, London

(Des and recess D.L.R.)

1946 (1 Nov). *Victory.* Wmk Mult Script CA. P 13½×14.

110	**17**	1½d. brown	20	10
111		3d. red-orange	20	50
110s/11s Perf "Specimen" *Set of* 2			70·00	

18 King George VI and Queen Elizabeth

19

(Des and photo Waterlow (T **18**). Design recess; name typo B.W. (T **19**))

1949 (3 Jan). *Royal Silver Wedding.* Wmk Mult Script CA.

112	**18**	2½d. ultramarine (P 14×15)	50	2·75
113	**19**	5s. grey-olive (P 11½×11)	12·00	11·00

20 Hermes, Globe and Forms of Transport

21 Hemispheres, Jet-powered Vickers Viking Airliner and Steamer

22 Hermes and Globe

23 U.P.U. Monument

(Recess Waterlow (T **20**, **23**). Designs recess, name typo B.W. (T **21**/**2**))

1949 (10 Oct). *75th Anniv of Universal Postal Union.* Wmk Mult Script CA.

114	**20**	2½d. ultramarine (P 13½–14)	40	60
115	**21**	3d. orange (P 11×11½)	2·00	2·50
116	**22**	6d. purple (P 11×11½)	45	2·25
117	**23**	1s. red-brown (P 13½–14)	45	1·25
114/17 *Set of* 4			3·00	6·00

(New Currency. 100 cents = 1 West Indian, later Eastern Caribbean, dollar)

24 Arms of University

25 Princess Alice

(Recess Waterlow)

1951 (16 Feb). *Inauguration of B.W.I. University College.* Wmk Mult Script CA. P 14×14½.

118	**24**	3c. black and brown	45	1·50
119	**25**	12c. black and violet	80	1·75

26 Queen Elizabeth II

27 Martello Tower

(Des and eng B.W. Recess D.L.R.)

1953. (2 June). *Coronation.* Wmk Mult Script CA. P 13½×13.

120	**26**	2c. black and deep yellow-green	30	75

(Recess Waterlow until 1961, then D.L.R.)

1953 (2 Nov)–**62**. *Designs previously used for King George VI issue, but with portrait of Queen Elizabeth II as in T* **27**. Wmk Mult Script CA. P 13×13½ (horiz) or 13½×13 (vert).

120*a*	**16a**	½c. brown (3.7.56)	30	30
121	**15**	1c. slate-grey	30	80
		a. *Slate* (7.11.61)	2·00	2·25
122	**16**	2c. green	30	10
123		3c. black and orange-yellow	40	20
		a. *Black and yellow-orange* (5.12.61)	3·00	2·75
124	**15**	4c. scarlet	1·25	10
		a. *Brown-red* (11.12.62)	1·25	50
125	**16**	5c. black and slate-lilac	2·50	40
126	**16a**	6c. yellow-ochre	2·00	10
		a. *Dull yellow-ochre* (5.12.61)	6·50	1·75
127	**27**	8c. deep blue	2·25	10
128	**16b**	12c. violet	2·25	10
129		24c. black and chocolate	2·50	15
130	**27**	48c. purple and deep blue	7·50	2·75
131	**16a**	60c. maroon	7·50	80
132	**16b**	$1.20 olive green	3·00	70
		a. *Yellowish olive* (10.8.55)	3·00	1·00
133	**16**	$2.40 bright reddish purple	11·00	12·00
134	**16a**	$4.80 slate-blue	16·00	24·00
120a/134 *Set of* 15			55·00	38·00

See also Nos. 149/58.

28 Federation Map

COMMEMORATION
ANTIGUA
CONSTITUTION
1960

(29)

(Recess B.W.)

1958 (22 Apr). *Inauguration of British Caribbean Federation.* W w **12**. P 11½×11.

135	**28**	3c. deep green	1·25	30
136		6c. blue	1·40	2·75
137		12c. scarlet	1·60	75
135/7 *Set of* 3			3·75	3·50

MINISTERIAL GOVERNMENT

1960 (1 Jan). *New Constitution. Nos.* 123 *and* 128 *optd with T* **29**.

138		3c. black and orange-yellow (R)	15	15
139		12c. violet	15	15

30 Nelson's Dockyard and Admiral Nelson

31 Stamp of 1862 and R.M.S.P. *Solent I* at English Harbour

(Recess B.W.)

1961 (14 Nov). *Restoration of Nelson's Dockyard.* W w **12**. P 11½×11.

140	**30**	20c. purple and brown	90	1·50
141		30c. green and blue	1·10	1·75

(Des A. W. Money. Recess B.W.)

1962 (1 Aug). *Stamp Centenary.* W w **12**. P 13½.

142	**31**	3c. purple and deep green	85	10
143		10c. blue and deep green	95	10
144		12c. deep sepia and deep green	1·00	10
145		50c. orange-brown and deep green	1·50	2·00
142/5 *Set of* 4			3·75	2·00

32 Protein Foods

33 Red Cross Emblem

(Des M. Goaman. Photo Harrison)

1963 (4 June). *Freedom from Hunger.* W w **12**. P 14×14½.

146	**32**	12c. bluish green	15	15

(Des V. Whiteley. Litho B.W.)

1963 (2 Sept). *Red Cross Centenary.* W w **12**. P 13½.

147	**33**	3c. red and black	30	75
148		12c. red and blue	45	1·25

(Recess D.L.R.)

1963 (16 Sept)–**65**. *As 1953–61 but* wmk w **12**.

149	**16a**	½c. brown (13.4.65)	2·25	75
150	**15**	1c. slate (13.4.65)	1·25	1·00
151	**16**	2c. green	70	30
152		3c. black and yellow-orange	45	20
153	–	4c. brown-red	30	1·25
154	**15**	5c. black and slate-lilac	20	10
		a. *Black and reddish violet* (15.1.65)	20	10
155	**16**	6c. yellow-ochre	60	30
156	**27**	8c. deep blue	30	20
157	**16a**	12c. violet	55	20
158	**16b**	24c. black and deep chocolate	5·00	70
		a. *Black and chocolate-brown* (28.4.65)	6·50	3·25
149/158 *Set of* 10			10·50	4·50

34 Shakespeare and Memorial Theatre, Stratford-upon-Avon

= =

15c.

(35)

(Des R. Granger Barrett. Photo Harrison)

1964 (23 April). *400th Birth Anniv of William Shakespeare.* W w **12**. P 14×14½.

164	**34**	12c. orange-brown	30	10
		w. Wmk inverted	60·00	

1965 (1 April). *No. 157 surch with T* **35**.
165 15c. on 12c. violet 10 10

36 I.T.U. Emblem

(Des M. Goaman. Litho Enschedé)

1965. *I.T.U. Centenary.* W w **12**. P 11×11½.
166 **36** 2c. light blue and light red 25 15
167 50c. orange-yellow and ultramarine 75 95

37 I.C.Y. Emblem

(Des V. Whiteley. Litho Harrison)

1965 (25 Oct). *International Co-operation Year.* W w **12**. P 14½.
168 **37** 4c. reddish purple and turquoise-green 20 10
169 15c. deep bluish green and lavender 30 20

38 Sir Winston Churchill, and St. Paul's Cathedral in Wartime

(Des Jennifer Toombs. Photo Harrison)

1966 (24 Jan). *Churchill Commemoration. Printed in black, cerise and gold and with background in colours stated.* W w **12**. P 14.
170 **38** ½c. new blue .... 10 1·75
a. Value omitted £500
171 4c. deep green 55 10
172 25c. brown .... 1·40 45
173 35c. bluish violet .... 1·40 55
170/3 *Set of* 4 .... 3·00 2·50
No. 170a was caused by misplacement of the gold and also shows "ANTIGUA" moved to the right.

39 Queen Elizabeth II and Duke of Edinburgh

(Des H. Baxter. Litho B.W.)

1966 (4 Feb). *Royal Visit.* W w **12**. P 11×12.
174 **39** 6c. black and ultramarine .... 1·50 1·10
175 15c. black and magenta .... 1·50 1·40

40 Footballer's Legs, Ball and Jules Rimet Cup

(Des V. Whiteley. Litho Harrison)

1966 (1 July). *World Football Cup Championship.* W w **12** (sideways). P 14.
176 **40** 6c. violet, yellow-green, lake and yellow-brown 20 75
177 35c. chocolate, blue-green, lake and yellow-brown 60 25

41 W.H.O. Building

(Des M. Goaman. Litho Harrison)

1966 (20 Sept). *Inauguration of W.H.O. Headquarters, Geneva.* W w **12** (sideways). P 14.
178 **41** 2c. black, yellow-green and light blue 20 25
179 15c. black, light purple and yellow-brown .... 1·10 25

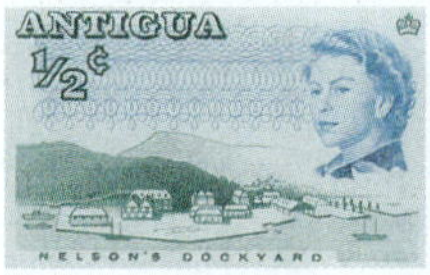

42 Nelson's Dockyard

(Des, eng and recess B.W.)

1966 (1 Nov)–**70**. *Horiz designs as T* **42**. W w **12**. *Ordinary paper.* P 11½×11.
180 ½c. green and turquoise-blue 10 75
a. Perf 13½ (24.6.69) .... 10 2·00
181 1c. purple and cerise 10 30
a. Perf 13½ (24.6.69) .... 10 1·50
ab. Glazed paper (30.9.69) 60 20
182 2c. slate-blue and yellow-orange 10 20
a. Perf 13½ (24.6.69) 10 75
ab. Glazed paper (30.9.69) .... 1·00 10
183 3c. rose-red and black 30 30
a. Perf 13½ (24.6.69) 15 15
184 4c. slate-violet and brown 70 10
a. Perf 13½ (24.6.69) 15 30
ab. Glazed paper (6.4.70) .... 16·00 5·50
185 5c. ultramarine and yellow-olive 10 10
a. Perf 13½ (24.6.69) 15 10
ab. Glazed paper (30.9.69) 40 10
186 6c. salmon and purple .... 1·00 30
a. Perf 13½ (24.6.69) .... 15 1·00
187 10c. emerald and rose-red 15 10
a. Perf 13½ (24.6.69) 15 15
ab. Glazed paper (30.9.69) .... 3·75 10
188 15c. brown and new blue .... 1·75 10
a. Perf 13½ (*glazed paper*) (30.9.69) 55 10
189 25c. slate-blue and sepia 35 20
a. Perf 13½ (*glazed paper*) (30.9.69) 45 10
190 35c. cerise and blackish brown .... 1·50 55
a. Perf 13½ (*glazed paper*) (30.9.69) .... 60 1·00
191 50c. dull green and black .... 2·00 2·50
a. Perf 13½ (*glazed paper*) (30.9.69) .... 70 2·25
192 75c. greenish blue and ultramarine .... 3·00 2·50
193 $1 cerise and yellow-olive .... 8·00 2·50
a. Carmine and yellow-olive (14.5.68) .... 30·00 14·00
b. Perf 13½ (*glazed paper*) (30.9.69) .... 1·25 5·00
194 $2.50 black and cerise .... 5·00 7·50
a. Perf 13½ (*glazed paper*) (30.9.69) .... 1·50 8·00
195 $5 olive-green and slate-violet .... 7·00 6·50
a. Perf 13½ (*glazed paper*) (30.9.69) .... 12·00 24·00
180/195 *Set of* 16 .... 28·00 22·00
180a/195a *Set of* 15 .... 16·00 35·00
Designs:—1c. Old Post Office, St. John's; 2c. Health Centre; 3c. Teachers' Training College; 4c. Martello Tower, Barbuda; 5c. Ruins of Officers' Quarters, Shirley Heights; 6c. Government House, Barbuda; 10c. Princess Margaret School; 15c. Air Terminal building; 25c. General Post Office; 35c. Clarence House; 50c. Government House, St. John's; 75c. Administration Building; $1, Courthouse, St. John's; $2.50, Magistrates' Court; $5, St. John's Cathedral.

54 "Education"

55 "Science"

56 "Culture"

(Des Jennifer Toombs. Litho Harrison)

1966 (1 Dec). *20th Anniv of U.N.E.S.C.O.* W w **12** (sideways). P 14.
196 **54** 4c. slate-violet, red, yellow and orange 15 10
197 **55** 25c. orange-yellow, violet and deep olive 35 10
198 **56** $1 black, bright purple and orange .... 80 2·25
196/8 *Set of* 3 .... 1·10 2·25

ASSOCIATED STATEHOOD

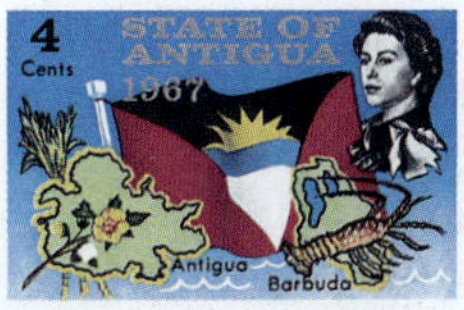

57 State Flag and Maps

(Des W. D. Cribbs. Photo Harrison)

1967 (27 Feb). *Statehood. T* **57** *and similar horiz designs. Multicoloured.* W w **12** (sideways*). P 14.
199 4c. Type **57** 10 10
200 15c. State Flag 10 20
w. Wmk Crown to right of CA .... 1·75
201 25c. Premier's Office and State Flag 10 25
202 35c. As 15c. 15 25
199/202 *Set of* 4 .... 40 70
*The normal sideways watermark shows Crown to left of CA, as seen from the back of the stamp.

60 Gilbert Memorial Church

(Des G. Drummond (from sketches by W. D. Cribbs). Photo Harrison)

1967 (18 May). *Attainment of Autonomy by the Methodist Church. T* **60** *and similar horiz designs.* W w **12**. P 14½×13½.
203 4c. black and orange-red 10 10
204 25c. black and bright green 15 15
205 35c. black and bright blue 15 15
203/5 *Set of* 3 .... 35 35
Designs:—25c. Nathaniel Gilbert's House; 35c. Caribbean and Central American map.

63 Coat of Arms

64 *Susan Constant* (settlers' ship)

(Des V. Whiteley (from sketches by W. D. Cribbs). Photo Harrison)

1967 (21 July). *300th Anniv of Treaty of Breda and Grant of New Arms.* W w **12** (sideways*). P 14½×14.
206 **63** 15c. multicoloured 15 10
w. Wmk Crown to right of CA .... 10·00 10·00
207 35c. multicoloured 15 10
*The normal sideways watermark shows Crown to left of CA, *as seen from the back of the stamp.*

(Des and recess B.W.)

1967 (14 Dec). *300th Anniv of Barbuda Settlement. T* **64** *and similar horiz design.* W w **12**. P 11½×11.
208 **64** 4c. deep ultramarine 40 10
209 – 6c. purple .... 40 1·25
210 **64** 25c. emerald 45 20
211 – 35c. black 45 25
208/11 *Set of* 4 .... 1·50 1·50
Design:—6, 35c. Risen's map of 1665.

66 Tracking Station

70 Limbo-dancing

(Des G. Vasarhelyi. Photo Harrison)

1968 (29 Mar). *N.A.S.A. Apollo Project. Inauguration of Dow Hill Tracking Station. T* **66** *and similar vert designs in deep blue, orange yellow and black.* W w **12** (sideways). P 14½×14.
212 4c. Type **66** 10 10
213 15c. Antenna and spacecraft taking off 20 10
214 25c. Spacecraft approaching Moon 20 10
215 50c. Re-entry of space capsule 30 40
212/15 *Set of* 4 .... 70 60

(Des and photo Harrison)

1968 (1 July). *Tourism. T* **70** *and similar horiz designs. Multicoloured.* W w **12**. P 14½×14.
216 ½c. Type **70** 10 20
217 15c. Water-skiing and bathers 30 10
218 25c. Yachts and beach 30 10
219 35c. Underwater swimming 30 10
220 50c. Type **70** .... 35 1·10
216/20 *Set of* 5 .... 1·25 1·40

74 Old Harbour in 1768

(Des R. Granger Barrett. Recess B.W.)

1968 (31 Oct). *Opening of St. John's Deep Water Harbour. T* **74** *and similar horiz designs.* W w **12**. P 13.

221		2c. light blue and carmine	10	40
222		15c. light yellow-green and sepia	35	10
223		25c. olive-yellow and blue	40	10
224		35c. salmon and emerald	50	10
225		$1 black	90	2·00
221/5 *Set of* 5			2·00	2·25

Designs:—15c. Old Harbour in 1829; 25c. Freighter and chart of New Harbour; 35c. New Harbour, 1968; $1, Type **74**.

78 Parliament Buildings

(Des R. Granger Barrett. Photo Harrison)

1969 (3 Feb). *Tercentenary of Parliament. T* **78** *and similar square designs. Multicoloured.* W w **12** (sideways). P 12½.

226		4c. Type **78**	10	10
227		15c. Antigua Mace and bearer	20	10
228		25c. House of Representatives' Room	20	10
229		50c. Coat of arms and Seal of Antigua	30	1·60
226/9 *Set of* 4			70	1·75

82 Freight Transport

(Des Jennifer Toombs. Litho D.L.R.)

1969 (14 Apr). *1st Anniv of CARIFTA (Caribbean Free Trade Area). T* **82** *and similar design.* W w **12** (sideways on 4c., 15c). P 13.

230		4c. black and reddish purple	10	10
231		15c. black and turquoise-blue	20	30
232		25c. chocolate, black and yellow-ochre	25	30
233		35c. chocolate, black and yellow-brown	25	30
230/3 *Set of* 4			70	90

Designs: *Horiz*—4, 15c. Type **82**. *Vert*—25, 35c. Crate of cargo.

84 Island of Redonda (Chart)

(Des R. Granger Barrett. Photo Enschedé)

1969 (1 Aug). *Centenary of Redonda Phosphate Industry. T* **84** *and similar horiz design.* W w **12** (sideways). P 13×13½.

249		15c. Type **84**	20	10
250		25c. Redonda from the sea	20	10
251		50c. Type **84**	45	75
249/51 *Set of* 3			75	85

86 "The Adoration of the Magi" (Marcillat)

(88)

(Des adapted by V. Whiteley. Litho Enschedé)

1969 (15 Oct). *Christmas. Stained-glass Windows. T* **86** *and similar vert design. Multicoloured.* W w **12** (sideways*). P 13×14.

252		6c. Type **86**	10	10
253		10c. "The Nativity" (unknown German artist, 15th-century)	10	10
254		35c. Type **86**	25	10
255		50c. As 10c.	50	40
		w. Wmk Crown to right of CA	16·00	
252/5 *Set of* 4			85	60

*The normal sideways watermark shows Crown to left of CA, *as seen from the back of the stamp.*

1970 (2 Jan). *No. 189 surch with T* **88**.

256		20c. on 25c. slate-blue and sepia	10	10

89 Coat of Arms

90 Sikorsky S-38 Flying Boat

(Des and photo Harrison)

1970 (30 Jan)–**73**. *Coil Stamps.* W w **12**. P 14½×14.

A. Chalk-surfaced paper. Wmk upright (30.1.70)

257A	**89**	5c. blue	10	25
258A		10c. emerald	10	25
259A		25c. crimson	20	25
257A/9A *Set of* 3			35	65

B. Glazed paper. Wmk sideways (5.3.73)

257B	**89**	5c. blue	1·25	1·75
258B		10c. emerald	1·25	1·75
259B		25c. crimson	1·75	2·00
257B/9B *Set of* 3			3·75	5·00

These stamps were issued on Multiple Crown CA Diagonal paper in 1975.

(Des R. Granger Barrett. Litho J.W.)

1970 (16 Feb). *40th Anniv of Antiguan Air Services. T* **90** *and similar designs. Multicoloured.* W w **12** (sideways). P 14½.

260		5c. Type **90**	50	10
261		20c. Dormer Do-X flying boat	80	10
262		35c. Hawker Siddeley H.S. 748	1·00	10
263		50c. Douglas C-124C Globemaster II	1·00	1·50
264		75c. Vickers Super VC-10	1·25	2·00
260/4 *Set of* 5			4·00	3·50

91 Dickens and Scene from *Nicholas Nickleby*

(Des Jennifer Toombs. Litho Walsall)

1970 (19 May). *Death Centenary of Charles Dickens. T* **91** *and similar horiz designs.* W w **12** (sideways). P 14.

265		5c. bistre, sepia and black	10	10
266		20c. light turquoise-blue, sepia and black	20	10
267		35c. violet-blue, sepia and black	30	10
268		$1 rosine, sepia and black	75	70
265/8 *Set of* 4			1·25	90

Designs:—20c. Dickens and Scene from *Pickwick Papers*; 35c. Dickens and Scene from *Oliver Twist*; $1 Dickens and Scene from *David Copperfield*.

92 Carib Indian and War Canoe

93 "The Small Passion" (detail) (Dürer)

(Des J.W. Litho Questa)

1970 (19 Aug)–**75**. *Horiz designs as T* **92**. *Multicoloured. Toned paper.* W w **12** (sideways*). P 14.

269		½c. Type **92**	10	1·50
270		1c. Columbus and *Nina*	30	1·50
271		2c. Sir Thomas Warner's emblem and *Conception*	40	3·25
		a. Whiter paper (20.10.75)	1·50	3·25
272		3c. Viscount Hood and H.M.S. *Barfleur*	40	1·75
		w. Wmk Crown to right of CA	3·00	3·00
273		4c. Sir George Rodney and H.M.S. *Formidable*	40	3·00
274		5c. Nelson and H.M.S. *Boreas*	50	40
275		6c. William IV and H.M.S. *Pegasus*	1·75	4·00
276		10c. "Blackbeard" and pirate ketch	80	20
277		15c. Captain Collingwood and H.M.S. *Pelican*	7·50	1·00
278		20c. Nelson and H.M.S. *Victory*	1·25	40
279		25c. *Solent I* (paddle-steamer)	1·25	40
280		35c. George V (when Prince George) and H.M.S. *Canada* (screw corvette)	1·75	80
281		50c. H.M.S. *Renown* (battle cruiser)	4·00	6·00
282		75c. *Federal Maple* (freighter)	5·00	6·00
283		$1 *Sol Quest* (yacht) and class emblem	5·00	2·00
284		$2.50 H.M.S. *London* (destroyer)	7·00	7·50
285		$5 *Pathfinder* (tug)	2·50	6·00
269/85 *Set of* 17			35·00	40·00

*The normal sideways watermark shows Crown to left of CA *as seen from the back of the stamp.*

Stamps in these designs were issued with upright watermark between 1972 and 1974 and the $5 value was issued with a change of watermark in 1975.

(Des G. Drummond. Recess and litho D.L.R.)

1970 (28 Oct). *Christmas. T* **93** *and similar vert design.* W w **12**. P 13½×14.

286	**93**	3c. black and turquoise-blue	10	10
287	–	10c. dull purple and pink	10	10
288	**93**	35c. black and rose-red	30	10
289	–	50c. black and lilac	45	50
286/9 *Set of* 4			85	70

Design:—10c., 50c. "Adoration of the Magi" (detail) (Dürer).

94 4th King's Own Regt, 1759

(Des P. W. Kingsland. Litho Questa)

1970 (14 Dec). *Military Uniforms (1st series). T* **94** *and similar vert designs. Multicoloured.* W w **12**. P 14×13½.

290		½c. Type **94**	10	10
291		10c. 4th West India Regiment, 18.04	50	10
292		20c. 60th Regiment, The Royal American, 1809	75	10
293		35c. 93rd Regiment, Sutherland Highlanders, 1826–34	1·00	10
294		75c. 3rd West India Regiment, 1851	1·75	2·00
290/4 *Set of* 5			4·50	2·10
MS295 128×146 mm. Nos. 290/4			5·50	11·00

STAMP BOOKLET

1968 (2 Oct). *Blue cover. Stitched.*

SB1 $1.20 booklet containing 5c., 10c. and 15c. (Nos. 185, 187, 188) in blocks of 4 ... 8·50

BARBUDA

DEPENDENCY OF ANTIGUA

PRICES FOR STAMPS ON COVER TO 1945
Nos. 1/11 *from* × 5

BARBUDA
(1)

1922 (13 July). *Stamps of Leeward Islands optd with T* **1**. *All Die II. Chalk-surfaced paper* (3d. *to* 5s.).

(a) Wmk Mult Script CA.

1	**11**	½d. deep green	1·50	10·00
2		1d. bright scarlet	1·50	10·00
		x. Wmk reversed	£750	£850
3	**10**	2d. slate-grey	1·50	7·00
		x. Wmk reversed	75·00	
4	**11**	2½d. bright blue	1·50	7·50
		w. Wmk inverted	30·00	95·00
5		6d. dull and bright purple	2·00	18·00
6	**10**	2s. purple and blue/*blue*	14·00	48·00
7		3s. bright green and violet	32·00	75·00
8		4s. black and red (R.)	40·00	75·00

(b) Wmk Mult Crown CA.

9	**10**	3d. purple/*pale yellow*	1·75	12·00
10	**12**	1s. black/*emerald* (R.)	1·50	8·00
11		5s. green and red/*pale yellow*	65·00	£130
1/11 *Set of* 11			£140	£350
1s/11s Optd "Specimen" *Set of* 11			£225	

Examples of all values are known showing a forged Barbuda postmark of "JU 1 23".

Stocks of the overprinted stamps were exhausted by October 1925 and issues of Antigua were then used in Barbuda until 1968.

The following issues for Barbuda were also valid for use in Antigua

(New Currency. 100 cents = 1 Eastern Caribbean dollar)

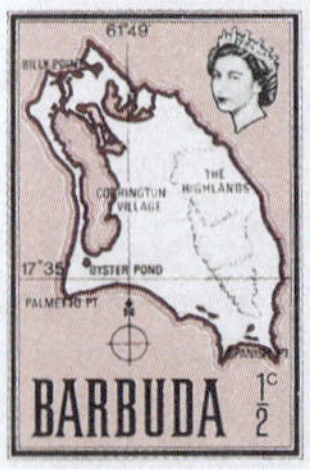

2 Map of Barbuda

3 Greater Amberjack

(Des R. Granger Barrett. Litho Format)

1968 (19 Nov)–**70**. *Designs as T* **2/3**. P 14.

12		½c. brown, black and pink	20	2·25
13		1c. orange, black and flesh	50	25
14		2c. blackish brown, rose-red and rose	1·25	50
15		3c. blackish brown, orange-yellow and lemon	50	25
16		4c. black, bright green and apple-green	1·50	2·25
17		5c. blue-green, black and pale blue-green	1·25	10
18		6c. black, bright purple and pale lilac	75	2·50
19		10c. black, ultramarine and cobalt	60	1·00
20		15c. black, blue-green and turquoise-green	60	2·50
20*a*		20c. multicoloured (22.7.70)	1·50	2·00
21		25c. multicoloured (6.2.69)	60	25
22		35c. multicoloured (5.2.69)	2·00	25

23	50c. multicoloured (5.2.69)	80	70
24	75c. multicoloured (5.2.69)	80	80
25	$1 multicoloured (6.3.69)	50	1·50
26	$2.50 multicoloured (6.3.69)	55	3·00
27	$5 multicoloured (6.3.69)	65	3·50
12/27 *Set of 17*		13·00	21·00

Designs: ½ to 15c. Type **2**. *Horiz as T* **3**—20c. Great Barracuda; 35c. French Angelfish; 50c. Porkfish; 75c. Princess Parrotfish; $1, Long-spined Squirrelfish; $2.50, Bigeye; $5, Blue Chromis.

10 Sprinting and Aztec Sun-stone

14 "The Ascension" (Orcagna)

(Des R. Granger Barrett. Litho Format)

1968 (20 Dec). *Olympic Games, Mexico. T* **10** *and similar horiz designs. Multicoloured.* P 14.

28	25c. Type **10**	45	25
29	35c. High-jumping and Aztec statue	50	25
30	75c. Dinghy-racing and Aztec lion mask	55	45
28/30 *Set of 3*		1·25	85
MS31 85×76 mm. $1 Football and engraved plate		1·75	3·25

(Des R. Granger Barrett. Litho Format)

1969 (24 Mar). *Easter Commemoration.* P 14.

32	**14**	25c. black and light blue	15	45
33		35c. black and deep carmine	15	50
34		75c. black and bluish lilac	15	55
32/4 *Set of 3*			40	1·40

15 Scout Enrolment Ceremony

18 "Sistine Madonna" (Raphael)

(Des R. Granger Barrett. Litho Format)

1969 (7 Aug). *3rd Caribbean Scout Jamboree. T* **15** *and similar horiz designs. Multicoloured.* P 14.

35	25c. Type **15**	35	55
36	35c. Scouts around camp fire	45	65
37	75c. Sea Scouts rowing boat	55	85
35/7 *Set of 3*		1·25	1·90

(Des. R. Granger Barrett. Litho Format)

1969 (20 Oct). *Christmas.* P 14.

38	**18**	½c. multicoloured	10	10
39		25c. multicoloured	10	15
40		35c. multicoloured	10	20
41		75c. multicoloured	20	35
38/41 *Set of 4*			30	60

19 William I (1066–87)

(20)

(Des R. Granger Barrett. Litho Format (Nos. 42/9) or Questa (others))

1970–71. *English Monarchs. T* **19** *and similar vert designs. Multicoloured.* P 14½×14.

42	35c. Type **19** (16.2.70)	30	15
43	35c. William II (2.3.70)	10	15
44	35c. Henry I (16.3.70)	10	15
45	35c. Stephen (1.4.70)	10	15
46	35c. Henry II (15.4.70)	10	15
47	35c. Richard I (1.5.70)	10	15
48	35c. John (15.5.70)	10	15
49	35c. Henry III (1.6.70)	10	15
50	35c. Edward I (15.6.70)	10	15
51	35c. Edward II (1.7.70)	10	15
52	35c. Edward III (15.7.70)	10	15
53	35c. Richard II (1.8.70)	10	15
54	35c. Henry IV (15.8.70)	10	15
55	35c. Henry V (1.9.70)	10	15
56	35c. Henry VI (15.9.70)	10	15
57	36c. Edward IV (1.10.70)	10	15
58	35c. Edward V (15.10.70)	10	15
59	35c. Richard III (2.11.70)	10	15
60	35c. Henry VII (16.11.70)	15	15
61	35c. Henry VIII (1.12.70)	15	15
62	35c. Edward VI (15.12.70)	15	15
63	35c. Lady Jane Grey (2.1.71)	15	15
64	35c. Mary I (15.1.71)	15	15
65	35c. Elizabeth I (1.2.71)	15	15
66	35c. James I (15.2.71)	15	15
67	35c. Charles I (1.3.71)	15	15
68	35c. Charles II (15.3.71)	15	15
69	35c. James II (1.4.71)	15	15
70	35c. William III (15.4.71)	15	15
71	35c. Mary II (1.5.71)	15	15
72	35c. Anne (15.5.71)	15	15
73	35c. George I (1.6.71)	15	15
74	35c. George II (15.6.71)	20	15
75	35c. George III (1.771)	20	15
76	35c. George IV (15.771)	20	15
77	35c. William IV (2.8.71)	20	60
78	35c. Victoria (16.8.71)	20	60
42/75 *Set of 37*		4·25	6·00

See also Nos. 710/15.

1970 (26 Feb). *No.* 12 *surch with T* **20**.

79	**2**	20c. on 1½c. brown, black and pink	10	20
		a. Surch inverted	50·00	
		b. Surch double	50·00	

21 "The Way to Calvary" (Ugolino)

22 Oliver is introduced to Fagin (*Oliver Twist*)

(Des R. Granger Barrett. Litho Questa)

1970 (16 Mar). *Easter Paintings. T* **21** *and similar vert designs. Multicoloured.* P 14.

80	25c. Type **21**	15	30
	a. Horiz strip of 3. Nos. 80/2	40	
81	35c. "The Deposition from the Cross" (Ugolino)	15	30
82	75c. Crucifix (The Master of St. Francis)	15	35
80/2 *Set of 3*		40	85

Nos. 80/2 were printed together, *se-tenant*, in horizontal strips of 3 throughout the sheet.

(Des R. Granger Barrett. Litho Questa)

1970 (10 July). *Death Centenary of Charles Dickens. T* **22** *and similar horiz design. Multicoloured.* P 14.

83	20c. Type **22**	20	25
84	75c. Dickens and Scene from *The Old Curiosity Shop*	45	65

23 "Madonna of the Meadow" (Bellini)

24 Nurse with Patient in Wheelchair

(Des R. Granger Barrett. Litho Questa)

1970 (15 Oct). *Christmas. T* **23** *and similar horiz designs. Multicoloured.* P 14.

85	20c. Type **23**	10	25
86	50c. "Madonna, Child and Angels" (from Wilton diptych)	15	30
87	75c. "The Nativity" (della Francesca)	15	35
85/7 *Set of 3*		30	80

(Des R. Granger Barrett. Litho Questa)

1970 (21 Dec). *Centenary of British Red Cross. T* **24** *and similar multicoloured designs.* P 14.

88	20c. Type **24**	15	30
89	35c. Nurse giving patient magazines (*horiz*)	20	40
90	75c. Nurse and mother weighing baby (*horiz*)	25	70
88/90 *Set of 3*		55	1·25

Ascension

DEPENDENCY OF ST. HELENA

Ascension, first occupied in 1815, was retained as a Royal Navy establishment from 1816 until 20 October 1922 when it became a dependency of St. Helena by Letters Patent.

Under Post Office regulations of 1850 (ratings) and 1854 (officers) mail from men of the Royal Navy serving abroad had the postage repaid in Great Britain stamps, supplies of which were issued to each ship. Great Britain stamps used on Ascension before 1860 may have been provided by the naval officer in charge of the postal service.

The British G.P.O. assumed responsibility for such matters in 1860, but failed to send any stamps to the island until January 1867.

Until about 1880 naval mail, which made up most early correspondence, did not have the stamps cancelled until arrival in England. The prices quoted for Nos. Z1/3 and Z6 are for examples on cover showing the Great Britain stamps cancelled on arrival and an Ascension postmark struck elsewhere on the front of the envelope.

The use of British stamps ceased in December 1922.

The following postmarks were used on Great Britain stamps from Ascension:

Z 1

Z 2

Z 3

Z 4

Z 5

Post-mark Type	*Approx Period of Use*	*Diameter*	*Index Letter*
Z **1**	1862	20 mm	A
Z **2**	1864–1872	20 mm	A
	1872–1878	21½ mm	A
	1879–1889	19½ mm	A
	1891–1894	21½ mm	C
	1894–1902	22 mm	A
	1903–1907	20½ mm	A
	1908–1920	21 mm	A or none
	1909–1920	23 mm	C sideways (1909), none (1910–11), B (1911–20)
Z **3**	1920–1922	24 mm	none
Z **4**	1897–1903 Reg'd	23 mm	none
Z **5**	1900–1902 Reg'd	28 mm	C
	1903–1904 Reg'd	29 mm	A

Postmark Type Z **1** appears in the G.P.O. proof book for 1858, but the first recorded use is 3 November 1862.

Forged postmarks exist. Those found most frequently are genuine postmarks of the post-1922 period with earlier date slugs fraudulently inserted, namely a 20 mm postmark as Type Z **2** (because of the shape of the "O" in "ASCENSION" this is often known as the Square O postmark) and a 24 mm postmark as Type Z **3** but with the index letter A.

Stamps of GREAT BRITAIN cancelled with Types Z 2/5. Prices quoted for Nos. Z 1/6 are for complete covers.

Line-engraved issues.

Z1	1d. red-brown (1855)	£5500
Z2	1d. rose-red (1864–79) From	£2250
	Plate Nos. 71, 74, 76, 78, 83, 85, 96, 100, 102, 103, 104, 122, 134, 138, 154, 155, 157, 160, 168, 178	

Surface-printed issues (1856–1883).

Z2*a*	6d. lilac (1856)	
Z3	6d. lilac (1865) (Plate No. 5)	£5500
Z4	1s. green (1865) (Plate No. 4)	
Z5	1s. green (1867) (Plate No. 7)	
Z6	6d. grey (1874) (Plate Nos. 15, 16)	£4500
Z6*a*	6d. on 6d. lilac (1883)	
Z7	1d. lilac (1881) (16 dots)	60·00

1887–92.

Z8	½d. vermilion	90·00
Z9	1½d. purple and green	£500
Z10	2d. green and carmine	£190
Z11	2½d. purple/*blue*	90·00
Z12	3d. purple/*yellow*	£450
Z13	4d. green and brown	£325
Z14	4½d. green and carmine	£750
Z15	5d. dull purple and blue	£325
Z16	6d. purple/*rose-red*	£250
Z17	9d. purple and blue	£650
Z17*a*	10d. dull purple and carmine	£800
Z18	1s. green	£700

1900.

Z19	½d. blue-green	90·00
Z20	1s. green and carmine	£750

1902–11. *King Edward VII issues.*

Z21	½d. green	65·00
Z22	1d. red	25·00
Z23	1½d. purple and green	£225
Z24	2d. green and carmine	£140
Z25	2½d. blue	£140
Z26	3d. purple/*yellow*	£225
Z27	4d. green and brown	£650
Z28	4d. orange (1909)	£250
Z29	5d. purple and ultramarine	£250
Z30	6d. purple	£225
Z31	7d. grey-black (1910)	£375

Z32	9d. purple and ultramarine (1910)	£400
Z32*a*	10d. dull purple and scarlet	£500
Z33	1s. green and carmine	£140
Z33*a*	2s.6d. dull reddish purple (1911)	£1000
Z34	5s. carmine	£1400
Z35	10s. ultramarine	£2250
Z35*a*	£1 green	£5500

1911–12. *T* **98/9** *of Great Britain.*

Z36	½d. green (Die A)	£150
Z37	½d. yellow-green (Die B)	65·00
Z38	1d. scarlet (Die B)	70·00

1912. *T* **101/2** *of Great Britain.*

Z38*a*	½d. green	70·00
Z38*b*	1d. scarlet	70·00

1912–22.

Z39	½d. green (1913)	55·00
Z40	1d. scarlet	29·00
Z41	1½d. red-brown	80·00
Z42	2d. orange (Die I)	65·00
Z42*a*	2d. orange (Die II) (1921)	£650
Z43	2½d. blue	90·00
Z44	3d. violet	£120
Z45	4d. grey-green (1913)	£160
Z46	5d. brown (1913)	£170
Z47	6d. purple (1913)	£130
Z47*a*	7d. green (1913)	£500
Z47*b*	8d. black/*yellow* (1913)	£550
Z48	9d. agate (1913)	£475
Z49	9d. olive-green (1922)	£1100
Z50	10d. turquoise-blue (1913)	£500
Z51	1s. bistre (1913)	£160
Z52	2s.6d. brown (1918)	£1400
Z53	5s. rose-red (1919)	£2250

Supplies of some values do not appear to have been sent to the island and known examples originate from maritime or, in the case of high values, philatelic mail.

PRICES FOR STAMPS ON COVER	
Nos. 1/34	*from* × 5
Nos. 35/7	*from* × 10
Nos. 38/47	*from* × 6

ASCENSION
(1)

Line through "P" of "POSTAGE" (R. 3/6)

Blot on scroll (R. 3/10)

1922 (2 Nov). *Stamps of St. Helena, showing Government House or the Wharf, optd with T* **1** *by D.L.R.*

(a) Wmk Mult Script CA.

1	½d. black and green	4·75	21·00
	x. Wmk reversed	£850	
2	1d. green	4·75	20·00
3	1½d. rose-scarlet	17·00	48·00
4	2d. black and grey	17·00	13·00
	a. Line through "P" of "POSTAGE"	£325	£325
	b. Blot on scroll	£325	£325
5	3d. bright blue	13·00	21·00
6	8d. black and dull purple	27·00	50·00
7	2s. black and blue/*blue*	95·00	£120
8	3s. black and violet	£140	£160
	(b) Wmk Mult Crown CA.		
9	1s. black/*green* (R.)	28·00	48·00
1/9 *Set of* 9		£300	£450
1s/9s *Set of* 9		£750	

Nos. 1, 4 and 6/8 are on special printings which were not issued without overprint.

Examples of all values are known showing a forged Ascension postmark dated "MY 24 23".

PLATE FLAWS ON THE 1924–33 ISSUE. Many constant plate varieties exist on both the vignette and duty plates of this issue.

The three major varieties are illustrated and listed below.

This issue utilised the same vignette plate as the St. Helena 1922–37 set so that these flaws occur there also.

2 Badge of St. Helena

Broken mainmast. Occurs on R. 2/1 of all values.

Torn flag. Occurs on R. 4/6 of all values except the 5d. Retouched on sheets of ½d., 1d. and 2d. printed after 1927.

Cleft rock. Occurs on R. 5/1 of all values.

Broken scroll. Occurs on R. 1/4 of 1½d. only

(Typo D.L.R.)

1924 (20 Aug)–**33**. Wmk Mult Script CA. *Chalk-surfaced paper.* P 14.

10	**2**	½d. grey-black and black	4·00	16·00
		a. Broken mainmast	85·00	£180
		b. Torn flag	£150	£225
		c. Cleft rock	75·00	£170
11		1d. grey-black and deep blue-green	5·50	11·00
		a. Broken mainmast	£100	£170
		b. Torn flag	£110	£180
		c. Cleft rock	90·00	£160
11*d*		1d. grey-black and bright blue-green (1933)	£110	£500
		da. Broken mainmast	£550	
		dc. Cleft rock	£550	
12		1½d. rose-red	9·00	30·00
		a. Broken mainmast	£110	£225
		b. Torn flag	£110	£225
		c. Cleft rock	£100	£200
		d. Broken scroll	£140	£250
13		2d. grey-black and grey	18·00	10·00
		a. Broken mainmast	£150	£170
		b. Torn flag	£200	£225
		c. Cleft rock	£130	£160
14		3d. blue	8·00	16·00
		a. Broken mainmast	£120	£190
		b. Torn flag	£120	£190
		c. Cleft rock	£100	£170
15		4d. grey-black and black/*yellow*	48·00	80·00
		a. Broken mainmast	£350	£475
		b. Torn flag	£350	£475
		c. Cleft rock	£300	£425
15*d*		5d. purple and olive-green (8.27)	14·00	24·00
		da. Broken mainmast	£190	£300
		dc. Cleft rock	£180	£275
16		6d. grey-black and bright purple	50·00	£100
		a. Broken mainmast	£375	£550
		b. Torn flag	£375	£550
		c. Cleft rock	£350	£500
17		8d. grey-black and bright violet	15·00	45·00
		a. Broken mainmast	£190	£350
		b. Torn flag	£190	£350
		c. Cleft rock	£170	£325
18		1s. grey-black and brown	21·00	55·00
		a. Broken mainmast	£250	£375
		b. Torn flag	£250	£375
		c. Cleft rock	£225	£350
19		2s. grey-black and blue/*blue*	60·00	90·00
		a. Broken mainmast	£400	£550
		b. Torn flag	£400	£550
		c. Cleft rock	£350	£500
20		3s. grey-black and black/*blue*	85·00	90·00
		a. Broken mainmast	£550	£700
		b. Torn flag	£550	£700
		c. Cleft rock	£500	£600
10/20 *Set of* 12			£300	£500
10s/20s Optd "Specimen" *Set of* 12			£700	

3 Georgetown

4 Ascension Island

5 The Pier

6 Long Beach

7 Three Sisters

8 Sooty Tern and Wideawake Fair

9 Green Mountain

"Teardrops" flaw (R. 4/5)

(Des and recess D.L.R.)

1934 (2 July). *T* **3/4** *and similar designs.* Wmk Mult Script CA. P 14.

21	**3**	½d. black and violet	90	80
22	**4**	1d. black and emerald	1·75	1·25
		a. Teardrops flaw	90·00	90·00
23	**5**	1½d. black and scarlet	1·75	2·25
24	**4**	2d. black and orange	1·75	2·50
		a. Teardrops flaw	£130	£150
25	**6**	3d. black and ultramarine	1·75	1·50
26	**7**	5d. black and blue	2·25	3·25
27	**4**	8d. black and sepia	4·25	4·75
		a. Teardrops flaw	£250	£300
28	**8**	1s. black and carmine	18·00	9·00
29	**4**	2s.6d. black and bright purple	45·00	40·00
		a. Teardrops flaw	£750	£800
30	**9**	5s. black and brown	50·00	55·00
21/30 *Set of* 10			£110	£110
21s/30s Perf "Specimen" *Set of* 10			£375	

1935 (6 May). *Silver Jubilee. As Nos. 91/4 of Antigua, but ptd by Waterlow.* P 11×12.

31	1½d. deep blue and scarlet	3·50	9·00
	l. Kite and horizontal log	£275	
32	2d. ultramarine and grey	11·00	25·00
	l. Kite and horizontal log	£425	
33	5d. green and indigo	19·00	28·00
	k. Kite and vertical log	£300	£375
	l. Kite and horizontal log	£475	£550
34	1s. slate and purple	23·00	32·00
	l. Kite and horizontal log	£600	£700
31/4 *Set of* 4		50·00	85·00
31s/4s Perf "Specimen" *Set of* 4		£300	

For illustrations of plate varieties see Omnibus section following Zanzibar.

1937 (19 May). *Coronation. As Nos. 95/7 of Antigua, but printed by D.L.R.* P 14.

35	1d. green	50	1·40
36	2d. orange	1·00	60
37	3d. bright blue	1·00	50
35/7 *Set of* 3		2·25	2·25
35s/7s Perf "Specimen" *Set of* 3		£325	

10 Green Mountain

Long centre bar to "E" in "GEORGETOWN" (R. 2/3)

"Mountaineer" flaw (R. 4/4)

"Davit" flaw (R. 5/1) (all ptgs of 1½d. and 2s.6d.)

"Cut mast and railings" (R. 3/1)

(Recess D.L.R.)

1938 (12 May)–**53**. *Horiz designs as King George V issue, but modified and with portrait of King George VI as in T* **10**. Wmk Mult Script CA. P 13½.

38	**3**	½d. black and violet	4·25	2·00
		a. Long centre bar to E.	£190	£160
		b. Perf 13. *Black and bluish violet* (17.5.44)	1·25	2·50
		ba. Long centre bar to E.	85·00	
39	**10**	1d. black and green	45·00	9·50
39*a*		1d. black and yellow-orange (8.7.40)	14·00	9·00
		b. Perf 13 (5.42)	45	60
		ba. Mountaineer flaw	£120	
		c. Perf 14 (17.2.49)	70	16·00
		ca. Mountaineer flaw	£120	
39*d*	**7**	1d. black and green, P 13 (1.6.49)	60	1·50
40	**5**	1½d. black and vermilion	4·50	1·40
		a. Davit flaw	£325	£170
		b. Perf 13 (17.5.44)	85	80
		ba. Davit flaw	£140	£150
		bb. Cut mast and railings	£140	
		c. Perf 14 (17.2.49)	2·00	13·00
		ca. Davit flaw	£190	
		cb. Cut mast and railings	£190	
40*d*		1½d. black and rose-carmine, P 14 (1.6.49)	70	1·00
		da. Davit flaw	£130	£160
		db. Cut mast and railings	£130	
		e. *Black and carmine*	9·50	5·00
		ea. Davit flaw	£350	£350
		eb. Cut mast and railings	£225	
		f. Perf 13 (25.2.53)	45	6·50
		fa. Davit flaw	£120	
		fb. Cut mast and railings	£120	
41	**10**	2d. black and red-orange	4·25	1·00
		a. Perf 13 (17.5.44)	80	40
		aa. Mountaineer flaw	£190	
		b. Perf 14 (17.2.49)	2·00	35·00
		ba. Mountaineer flaw	£225	
41*c*		2d. black and scarlet, P 14 (1.6.49)	1·00	1·75
		ca. Mountaineer flaw	£170	£225
42	**6**	3d. black and ultramarine	£100	27·00
42*a*		3d. black and grey (8.7.40)	18·00	1·75
		b. Perf 13 (17.5.44)	70	80
42*c*	**10**	4d. black and ultramarine (8.7.40)	16·00	3·25
		d. Perf 13 (17.5.44)	4·50	3·00
		da. Mountaineer flaw	£400	
43	**7**	6d. black and blue	9·00	2·25
		a. Perf 13 (17.5.44)	9·50	6·00
44	**3**	1s. black and sepia	18·00	1·90
		a. Perf 13 (17.5.44)	4·75	2·00
45	**5**	2s.6d. black and deep carmine	42·00	9·50
		a. Frame printed double, one albino	£4250	
		b. Davit flaw	£1200	£475
		c. Perf 13 (17.5.44)	27·00	32·00
		ca. Davit flaw	£950	£1100
		cb. Cut mast and railings	£950	
46	**6**	5s. black and yellow-brown	95·00	9·00
		a. Perf 13 (17.5.44)	38·00	30·00
47	**7**	10s. black and bright purple	£110	42·00
		a. Perf 13 (17.5.44)	45·00	55·00
38b/47a *Set of* 16			£250	£100
38s/47s Perf "Specimen" *Set of* 13			£800	

1946 (21 Oct). *Victory. As Nos. 110/11 of Antigua.*

48	2d. red-orange	40	1·00
49	4d. blue	40	60
48s/9s Perf "Specimen" *Set of* 2		£325	

1948 (20 Oct). *Royal Silver Wedding. As Nos. 112/13 of Antigua.*

50	3d. black	50	30
51	10s. bright purple	50·00	50·00

1949 (10 Oct). *75th Anniv of Universal Postal Union. As Nos. 114/17 of Antigua.*

52	3d. carmine	1·00	2·00
53	4d. deep blue	4·00	1·50
54	6d. olive	2·00	3·50
55	1s. blue-black	2·00	1·50
	a. A of CA missing from Wmk	£1000	
52/5 *Set of* 4		8·00	7·75

1953 (2 June). *Coronation. As No. 120 of Antigua.*

56	3d. black and grey-black	1·00	1·50

15 Water Catchment

16 Map of Ascension

17 View of Georgetown

18 Map showing cable network

19 Mountain road

20 White-tailed Tropic Bird ("Boatswain Bird")

21 Yellow-finned Tuna

22 Rollers on the seashore

23 Young turtles

24 Land Crab

25 Sooty Tern ("Wideawake")

26 Perfect Crater

27 View of Ascension from North-west

(Recess B.W.)

1956 (19 Nov). *T* **19/27**. Wmk Mult Script CA. P 13.

57	**15**	½d. black and brown	10	50
58	**16**	1d. black and magenta	3·00	1·75
59	**17**	1½d. black and orange	1·00	1·00
60	**18**	2d. black and carmine-red	3·50	2·25
61	**19**	2½d. black and orange-brown	1·75	2·50
62	**20**	3d. black and blue	4·00	1·25
63	**21**	4d. black and deep turquoise-green	1·25	2·00
64	**22**	6d. black and indigo	1·25	2·50
65	**23**	7d. black and deep olive	2·25	1·50
66	**24**	1s. black and vermilion	1·00	1·25
67	**25**	2s.6d. black and deep dull purple	27·00	6·50
68	**26**	5s. black and blue-green	35·00	17·00
69	**27**	10s. black and purple	48·00	35·00
57/69 *Set of* 13			£110	65·00

28 Brown Booby

(Des after photos by N. P. Ashmole. Photo Harrison)

1963 (23 May). *T* **28** *and similar horiz designs.* W w **12**. P 14×14½.

70	1d. black, lemon and new blue	1·50	30
71	1½d. black, cobalt and ochre	2·00	1·00
	a. Cobalt omitted	95·00	
72	2d. black, grey and bright blue	1·25	30
73	3d. black, magenta and turquoise-blue	1·75	30
74	4½d. black, bistre-brown and new blue	1·75	30
	w. Wmk inverted	£350	
75	6d. bistre, black and yellow-green	1·25	30
76	7d. black, brown and reddish violet	1·25	30
77	10d. black, greenish yellow and blue-green	1·25	50
78	1s. multicoloured	1·25	30
79	1s.6d. multicoloured	4·50	1·75
80	2s.6d. multicoloured	8·50	11·00
81	5s. multicoloured	9·00	11·00
82	10s. multicoloured	13·00	12·00
83	£1 multicoloured	20·00	13·00
70/83 *Set of* 14		60·00	48·00

Designs:—1½d. White-capped Noddy; 2d. White Tern; 3d. Red billed Tropic Bird; 4½d. Common Noddy; 6d. Sooty Tern; 7d. Ascension Frigate Bird; 10d. Blue-faced Booby; 1s. White-tailed Tropic Bird; 1s.6d. Red-billed Tropic Bird; 2s.6d. Madeiran Storm Petrel; 5s. Red-footed Booby (brown phase); 10s. Ascension Frigate Birds; £1 Red-footed Booby (white phase).

1963 (4 June). *Freedom from Hunger. As Nos. 146 of Antigua.*

84	1s.6d. carmine	75	40

1963 (2 Sept). *Red Cross Centenary. As Nos. 147/8 of Antigua.*

85	3d. red and black	1·75	1·25
86	1s.6d. red and blue	3·25	2·25

1965 (17 May). *I.T.U. Centenary. As Nos. 166/7 of Antigua.*

87	3d. magenta and bluish violet	50	65
88	6d. turquoise-blue and light chestnut	75	65

1965 (25 Oct). *International Co-operation Year. As Nos. 168/9 of Antigua.*

89	1d. reddish purple and turquoise-green	40	60
90	6d. deep bluish green and lavender	60	90

1966 (24 Jan). *Churchill Commemoration. As Nos. 170/3 of Antigua.*

91	1d. new blue	50	75
92	3d. deep green	2·25	1·25
93	6d. brown	2·75	1·50
94	1s.6d. bluish violet	3·50	2·00
91/4 *Set of* 4		8·00	5·00

1966 (1 July). *World Cup Football Championship. As Nos. 176/7 of Antigua.*

95	3d. violet, yellow-green, lake and yell-brn	1·50	60
96	6d. chocolate, blue-green, lake and yellow-brown	1·50	80

1966 (20 Sept). *Inauguration of W.H.O. Headquarters, Geneva. As Nos. 178/9 of Antigua.*

97	3d. black, yellow-green and light blue	1·75	1·00
98	1s.6d. black, light purple and yellow-brown	4·75	2·00

36 Satellite Station

37 B.B.C. Emblem

(Des V. Whiteley. Photo Harrison)

1966 (7 Nov). *Opening of Apollo Communications Satellite Earth Station.* W w **12**. (sideways). P 14×14½.

99	**36**	4d. black and reddish violet	10	10
100		8d. black and deep bluish green	15	15
101		1s.3d. black and olive-brown	15	20
102		2s.6d. black and turquoise-blue	15	20
99/102 *Set of* 4			50	60

(Des B.B.C. staff. Photo, Queen's head and emblem die-stamped, Harrison)

1966 (1 Dec). *Opening of B.B.C. Relay Station.* W w **12**. P 14½.

103	**37**	1d. gold and ultramarine	10	10
104		3d. gold and myrtle-green	15	15
		w. Wmk inverted	50	1·25
105		6d. gold and reddish violet	15	15
106		1s.6d. gold and red	15	15
103/6 *Set of* 4			50	50

1967 (1 Jan). *20th Anniv of U.N.E.S.C.O. As Nos. 196/8 of Antigua.*

107	3d. slate-violet, red, yellow and orange	2·00	1·50
108	6d. orange-yellow, violet and deep olive	2·75	2·00
109	1s.6d. black, bright purple and orange	4·50	2·50
107/9 *Set of* 3		8·50	5·50

44 Human Rights Emblem and Chain Links

(Des and litho Harrison)

1968 (8 July). *Human Rights Year.* W w **12** (sideways*). P 14½×14.

110	**44**	6d. light orange, red and black	15	15
111		1s.6d. light grey-blue, red and black	20	25
112		2s.6d. light green, red and black	20	30
		w. Wmk Crown to right of CA	£400	
110/12 *Set of* 3			50	65

*The normal sideways watermark shows Crown to left of CA, *as seen from the back of the stamp.*

45 Black Durgon ("Ascension Black-Fish")

46 H.M.S. *Rattlesnake*

(Des M. Farrar Bell. Litho D.L.R.)

1968 (23 Oct). *Fishes (1st series). T* **45** *and similar horiz designs.* W w **12** (sideways*). P 13.

113	4d. black, slate and turquoise-blue	30	40
114	8d. multicoloured	35	70
	w. Wmk Crown to right of CA	£325	
115	1s.9d. multicoloured	40	80
116	2s.3d. multicoloured	40	85
113/16 *Set of 4*		1·25	2·50

Designs:—8d. Scribbled Filefish ("Leather-jacket"); 1s.9d. Yellow-finned Tuna; 2s.3d. Short-finned Mako.

*The normal sideways watermark shows Crown to left of CA, *as seen from the back of the stamp.*

See also Nos. 117/20 and 126/9.

(Des M. Farrar Bell. Litho D.L.R.)

1969 (3 Mar). *Fishes (2nd series). Horiz designs as T* **45**. *Multicoloured.* W w **12** (sideways). P 13.

117	4d. Sailfish	75	90
118	6d. White Seabream ("Old Wife")	1·00	1·25
119	1s.6d. Yellowtail	1·25	2·50
120	2s.11d. Rock Hind ("Jack")	1·50	3·00
117/20 *Set of 4*		4·00	7·00

(Des L. Curtis. Photo Harrison)

1969 (1 Oct). *Royal Naval Crests (1st series). T* **46** *and similar vert designs.* W w **12** (sideways*). P 14×14½.

121	4d. multicoloured	60	30
122	9d. multicoloured	75	35
123	1s.9d. deep blue, pale blue and gold	1·10	45
124	2s.3d. multicoloured	1·25	55
121/4 *Set of 4*		3·25	1·50
MS125	165×105 mm. Nos. 121/4. P 14½	6·50	13·00
	w. Wmk Crown to right of CA	£650	

Designs:—9d. H.M.S. *Weston*; 1s.9d. H.M.S. *Undaunted*; 2s.3d. H.M.S. *Eagle*.

*The normal sideways watermark shows Crown to left of CA, *as seen from the back of the stamp.*

See also Nos. 130/4.

(Des M. Farrar Bell. Litho D.L.R.)

1970 (6 Apr). *Fishes (3rd series). Horiz designs as T* **45**. *Multicoloured.* W w **12** (sideways*). P 14.

126	4d. Wahoo	4·50	2·75
	w. Wmk Crown to right of CA	£325	
127	9d. Ascension Jack ("Coalfish")	5·00	2·75
	w. Wmk Crown to right of CA	3·00	1·25
128	1s.9d. Pompano Dolphin	5·50	3·50
129	2s.3d. Squirrelfish ("Soldier")	5·50	3·50
	w. Wmk Crown to right of CA	3·00	1·50
126/9w *Set of 4*		14·00	8·00

*The normal sideways watermark shows Crown to left of CA, *as seen from the back of the stamp.*

(Des L. Curtis. Photo D.L.R.)

1970 (7 Sept). *Royal Naval Crests (2nd series). Designs as T* **46**. *Multicoloured.* W w **12**. P 12½.

130	4d. H.M.S. *Penelope*	1·00	1·00
131	9d. H.M.S. *Carlisle*	1·25	1·50
132	1s.6d. H.M.S. *Amphion*	1·75	2·00
133	2s.6d. H.M.S. *Magpie*	1·75	2·00
130/3 *Set of 4*		5·25	6·00
MS134	153×96 mm. Nos. 130/3	11·00	15·00

STAMP BOOKLET

1963 (23 May). *Buff cover. Stitched.*

SB1	10s.6d. booklet containing 1d., 1½d., 2d., 3d., 6d. and 1s.6d. (Nos. 70/3, 75, 79), each in block of 4	70·00

Australia

The Australian colonies of New South Wales, Queensland, South Australia, Tasmania, Victoria and Western Australia produced their own issues before federation in 1901. Stamps inscribed for the individual states continued in use after federation until the end of December 1912.

INVERTED WATERMARKS. The stamp printers in the various Australian colonies paid little attention to the position of the watermark in the sheets they produced so that some entire printings had the watermark inverted, some 50% upright and 50% inverted while on others the inverted watermarks were restricted to odd sheets. In such circumstances it is impossible to provide adequate prices for such items so only those inverted watermarks occurring on stamps printed in Great Britain are included in the following listings.

NEW SOUTH WALES

PRICES FOR STAMPS ON COVER

Nos. 1/83	*from* × 2
Nos. 84/7	*from* × 3
No. 88	—
Nos. 89/96	*from* × 2
Nos. 97/8	—
Nos. 99/101	*from* × 2
Nos. 102/13	*from* × 3
No. 114	*from* × 10
Nos. 115/17	*from* × 2
Nos. 118/27	*from* × 3
Nos. 131/53	*from* × 2
Nos. 154/70	*from* × 3
Nos. 171/81	—
Nos. 186/202	*from* × 2
Nos. 203/6	*from* × 10
Nos. 207/21	*from* × 5
Nos. 222/37	*from* × 6
Nos. 238/42	—
Nos. 243/4	*from* × 6
Nos. 253/64	*from* × 10
Nos. 265/8	*from* × 15
Nos. 269/70	*from* × 2
Nos. 271/3	*from* × 10
Nos. 280/1	*from* × 2
Nos. 288/97	*from* × 10
Nos. 298/312	*from* × 12
Nos. 313/31	*from* × 10
No. 332	—
Nos. 333/49	*from* × 12
No. 350	—
Nos. 351/63	*from* × 12
No. O1	—
Nos. O2/12	*from* × 4
Nos. O13/18	—
Nos. O19/34	*from* × 20
Nos. O35/8	—
Nos. O39/47	*from* × 40
Nos. O48/53	—
Nos. O54/8	*from* × 20
No. O59	—
Nos. D1/7	*from* × 50
Nos. D8/10	—
Nos. D11/15	*from* × 50

EMBOSSED LETTER SHEETS AND ENVELOPES. From 1 November 1838 the Sydney G.P.O. supplied letter sheets pre-stamped with an albino embossing, as illustrated, at 1½d. each or 1s.3d. per dozen. From January 1841 the price was reduced to 1s. per dozen. The public were also able to present their own stationery for embossing. The circular design measures approximately 29 mm in diameter, and examples are known on laid or wove paper of varying colours. Embossing continued until 1 May 1852 after which the Post Office refused to carry mail which was not franked with postage stamps. The die was used for reprints in 1870 and 1898 before it was destroyed later the same year.

A 1

PRINTERS. The early issues of New South Wales were printed on a press supervised by the Inspector of Stamps. On 1 January 1857 this responsibility passed to the Government printer who produced all subsequent issues, *unless otherwise stated.*

SPECIMEN OVERPRINTS. Those listed are from U.P.U. distributions between 1892 and 1903. Further "Specimen" overprints exist, but these were used for other purposes. From 1891 examples of some of these Specimens, together with cancelled stamps, were sold to collectors by the N.S.W. Post Office.

NEW SOUTH WALES USED IN NEW CALEDONIA. From October 1859 mail for Europe from New Caledonia was routed via Sydney and franked with New South Wales stamps in combination with local issues. Such N.S.W. stamps were cancelled on arrival in Sydney.

1

2

(Eng Robert Clayton, Sydney)

1850 (1 Jan). *T* **1**. *Plate I. No clouds.*

(a) Soft yellowish paper.

1	1d. crimson-lake	£6500	£450
2	1d. carmine	£6000	£400
3	1d. reddish rose	£5500	£375
4	1d. brownish red	£6000	£400

(b) Hard bluish paper.

5	1d. pale red	£5500	£375
6	1d. dull lake	£6000	£400

1850 (Aug). *T* **2**. *Plate I re-engraved by H. C. Jervis, commonly termed Plate II. With clouds.*

(a) Hard toned white to yellowish paper.

7	1d. vermilion	£3750	£300
8	1d. dull carmine	£3750	£300
	a. No trees on hill (R. 2/2)	£6500	£500
	b. Hill unshaded (R. 2/3)	£6500	£500
	c. Without clouds (R. 3/5)	£6500	£500

(b) Hard greyish or bluish paper.

9	1d. crimson-lake	£3750	£300
10	1d. gooseberry-red	£4250	£475
11	1d. dull carmine	£3250	£275
12	1d. brownish red	£3500	£275
	a. No trees on hill (R. 2/2)	£6000	£500
	b. Hill unshaded (R. 2/3)	£6000	£500
	c. Without clouds (R. 3/5)	£6000	£500

(c) Laid paper.

13	1d. carmine	£6000	£475
14	1d. vermilion	£6500	£450
	a. No trees on hill (R. 2/2)	—	£850
	b. Hill unshaded (R. 2/3)	—	£850
	c. Without clouds (R. 3/5)	—	£850

The varieties quoted with the letters "a", "b", "c" of course exist in each shade; the prices quoted are for the commonest shade, and the same applies to the following portions of this list.

Nos. 1/14 were printed in sheets of 25 (5×5).

LAID PAPER. Nos. 13/14, 34/5, 38 and 43*d*/*e* can be found showing parts of the papermaker's watermark (T. H. SAUNDERS 1847 in double-lined capitals and the figure of Britannia seated in an oval beneath a crown).

3

4

A (Pl I)

Illustrations A, B, C and D are sketches of the lower part of the inner circular frame, showing the characteristic variations of each plate.

(Eng John Carmichael)

1850 (1 Jan). *Plate I. Vertical-lined background. T* **3**.

(a) Early impressions, full details of clouds, etc.

15	2d. greyish blue	£7000	£400
16	2d. deep blue	—	£450
	a. Double lines on bale (R. 2/7)	—	£700

(b) Intermediate impressions.

16*b*	2d. greyish blue	£4500	£275
16*c*	2d. deep blue	£4750	£325

(c) Later impressions, clouds, etc., mostly gone, T **4**.

17	2d. greyish blue	£3250	£150
18	2d. dull blue	£2750	£140

(d) Stamps in the lower row partially retouched (end Jan).

19	2d. greyish blue	£4000	£225
20	2d. dull blue	£4250	£275

5

B (Pl II)

C (Pl III)

(Plate entirely re-engraved by H. C. Jervis)

1850 (Apr). *T* **5**. *Plate II. Horizontal-lined background. Bale on left side supporting the seated figure, dated. Dot in centre of the star In each corner.*

(a) Early impressions.

21	2d. indigo	£5000	£275
22	2d. lilac-blue	—	£1200
23	2d. grey-blue	£5000	£225
24	2d. bright blue	£5000	£225
	a. Fan as in Pl III, but with shading outside (R. 1/1)	—	£400
	b. Fan as in Pl III, but without shading, and inner circle intersects the fan (R. 1/2)	—	£400
	c. Fan as B, but inner circle intersects fan (R. 1/3)	—	£400
	d. No whip and inner circle intersects fan (R. 1/4)	—	£400
	e. No whip (R. 1/8, 2/8)	—	£325
	f. Pick and shovel omitted (R. 1/10).	—	£400
	g. "CREVIT" omitted (R. 2/1)	—	£650

(b) Worn impressions.

25	2d. dull blue	£2750	£130
26	2d. Prussian blue	£2750	£170
	a. Fan as in Pl III, but with shading outside (R. 1/1)	—	£325
	b. Fan as in Pl III, but without shading, and inner circle intersects the fan (R. 1/2)	—	£325
	c. Fan as B, but inner circle intersects fan (R. 1/3)	—	£325
	d. No whip and inner circle intersects fan (R. 1/4)	—	£325
	e. No whip (R. 1/8, 2/8)	£4000	£250
	f. Pick and shovel omitted (R. 1/10).	—	£325
	g. "CREVIT" omitted (R. 2/1)	—	£450

(c) Bottom row retouched with dots and dashes in lower spandrels (from July).

27	2d. Prussian blue	£4000	£225
28	2d. dull blue	£3750	£150
	e. No whip (R. 2/8)	—	£275
	g. "CREVIT" omitted (R. 2/1)	—	£400

(Plate re-engraved a second time by H. C. Jervis)

1850 (Sept). *Plate III. Bale not dated and single-lined, except on No. 30c which is doubled-lined. No dots in stars.*

29	2d. ultramarine	£3250	£170
30	2d. deep blue	£3250	£170
	a. No whip (R. 2/3, 2/7)	—	£275
	b. Fan with 6 segments (R. 2/8)	—	£400
	c. Double lines on bale (R. 1/7, 1/10, 1/12)	—	£250

(Plate re-engraved a third time by H. C. Jervis)

1851 (Jan). *Plate IV. Double-lined bale, and circle in centre of each star.*

(a) Hard bluish grey wove paper.

31	2d. ultramarine	£4000	£160
32	2d. Prussian blue	£3250	£130
33	2d. bright blue	£3500	£150
	a. Hill not shaded (R. 1/12)	—	£250
	b. Fan with 6 segments (R. 2/8)	—	£250
	c. No clouds (R. 2/10)	—	£250
	d. Retouch (R. 2/1)	—	£325
	e. No waves (R. 1/9, 2/5)	—	£200

(b) Stout yellowish vertically laid paper.

34	2d. ultramarine	£4500	£170
35	2d. Prussian blue	£4750	£180
	a. Hill not shaded (R. 1/12)	—	£275
	b. Fan with 6 segments (R. 2/8)	—	£275
	c. No clouds (R. 2/10)	—	£275
	d. Retouch (R. 2/1)	—	£350
	e. No waves (R. 1/9, 2/5)	—	£225
	f. "PENOE" (R. 1/10, 2/12)	—	£275

The retouch, Nos. 33d and 35d., occurs outside the left margin line on R. 2/1.

6

D (Pl V)

7

(Plate re-engraved a fourth time by H. C. Jervis)

1851 (Apr). *T* **6**. *Plate V. Pearl in fan.*

(a) Hard greyish wove paper.

36	2d. ultramarine	£3500	£140
37	2d. dull blue	£3500	£140
	a. Pick and shovel omitted (R. 2/5)	—	£275
	b. Fan with 6 segments (R. 2/8)	—	£275

(b) Stout yellowish vertically laid paper.

38	2d. dull ultramarine	£5500	£300
	a. Pick and shovel omitted (R. 2/5)	—	£450
	b. Fan with 6 segments (R. 2/8)	—	£450

Nos. 15/38 were printed in sheets of 24 (12×2), although the existence of an inter-panneau *tête-bêche* pair from Plate II indicates that the printer applied two impressions of the plate to each sheet of paper. The two panes were normally separated before issue. The original plate I was re-cut four times to form Plates II to V. An interesting variety occurs on R. 1/9-11 and 2/7 in all five plates. It consists of ten loops of the engine-turning on each side of the design instead of the normal nine loops.

(Eng H. C. Jervis)

1850. *T* **7**.

(a) Soft yellowish wove paper.

39	3d. yellow-green	£4500	£250
40	3d. myrtle green	£13000	£1000
41	3d. emerald-green	£5000	£275
	a. No whip (R. 4/3–4)	—	£400
	b. "SIGIIIUM" for "SIGILLUM" (R. 5/3)	—	£500

(b) Bluish to grey wove paper.

42	3d. yellow-green	£4000	£225
43	3d. emerald-green	£4750	£225
	b. No whip (R. 4/3–4)	—	£325
	c. "SIGIIIUM" for "SIGILLUM" (R. 5/3)	—	£425

(c) Yellowish to bluish laid paper.

43*d*	3d. bright green	£7500	£500
43*e*	3d. yellowish green	£7000	£450
	f. No whip (R. 4/3–4)	—	£700
	g. "SIGIIIUM " for "SIGILLUM" (R. 5/3)	—	£850

Nos. 39/43*e* were printed in sheets of 25 (5×5).

A used example of No. 42 is known printed double, one albino.

8

9

(Des A. W. Manning from sketch by W. T. Levine; eng on steel by John Carmichael, Sydney)

1851 (18 Dec)–**52**. Imperf.

(a) Thick yellowish paper.

44 **8** 1d. carmine £2000 £225
a. No leaves right of "SOUTH" (R. 1/7, 3/1) – £425
b. Two leaves right of "SOUTH" (R. 2/5) – £600
c. "WALE" (R. 1/9) – £600

(b) Bluish medium wove paper (1852).

45 **8** 1d. carmine £1100 £140
46 1d. scarlet £1100 £140
47 1d. vermilion £1000 £120
48 1d. brick-red £1000 £120
a. No leaves right of "SOUTH" (R. 1/7, 3/1) £2250 £275
b. Two leaves right of "SOUTH" (R. 2/5) – £375
c. "WALE" (R. 1/9) – £375

(c) Thick vertically laid bluish paper (1852?).

49 **8** 1d. orange-brown £3500 £375
50 1d. claret £3500 £400
a. No leaves right of "SOUTH" (R. 1/7, 3/1) – £700
b. Two leaves right of "SOUTH" (R. 2/5) – £900
c. "WALE" (R. 1/9) – £900

Nos. 44/50 were printed in sheets of 50 (10×5).

(Eng John Carmichael (Nos. 51/9), H. C. Jervis (Nos. 60/4))

1851 (24 July)–**55**. Imperf.

(a) Plate I.

(i) Thick yellowish wove paper.

51 **8** 2d. ultramarine £900 85·00

(ii) Fine impressions, blue to greyish medium paper.

52 **8** 2d. ultramarine £800 30·00
53 2d. chalky blue £700 30·00
54 2d. dark blue £700 30·00
55 2d. greyish blue £700 30·00

(iii) Worn plate, blue to greyish medium paper.

56 **8** 2d. ultramarine £475 30·00
57 2d. Prussian blue £475 30·00

(iv) Worn plate, blue wove medium paper.

58 **8** 2d. ultramarine £375 30·00
59 2d. Prussian blue £350 30·00

(b) Plate II. Stars in corners (Oct 1853).

(i) Bluish medium to thick wove paper.

60 **9** 2d. deep ultramarine £1100 £110
61 2d. indigo £1200 90·00
a. "WAEES" (R. 3/3) – £400

(ii) Worn plate, hard blue wove paper.

62 **9** 2d. deep Prussian blue £1100 £100
a. "WAEES" (R. 3/3) – £400

(c) Plate III, being Plate I (T **8***) re-engraved by H. C. Jervis. Background of crossed lines (Sept 1855).*

(i) Medium bluish wove paper.

63 – 2d. Prussian blue £500 60·00
a. "WALES" partly covered with wavy lines (R. 1/3) – £200

(ii) Stout white wove paper.

64 – 2d. Prussian blue £500 60·00
a. "WALES" partly covered with wavy lines (R. 1/3) – £200

Nos. 51/64 were printed in sheets of 50 (10×5).

(Eng John Carmichael)

1852 (3 Dec). Imperf.

(a) Medium greyish blue wove paper.

65 **8** 3d. deep green £2000 £200
66 3d. green £1600 £140
67 3d. dull yellow-green £1500 £100
a. "WAEES" with centre bar of first "E" missing (R. 4/7) – £375

(b) Thick blue wove paper.

69 **8** 3d. emerald-green £1900 £225
71 3d. blue-green £1900 £225
a. "WAEES" with centre bar of first "E" missing (R. 4/7) – £600

Nos. 65/71 were printed in sheets of 50 (10×5).

1852 (Apr)–**53**. Imperf.

(a) Plate I.

(i) Medium white wove paper.

72 **8** 6d. vandyke-brown – £900
a. "WALLS" (R. 2/3) – £1700

(ii) Medium bluish grey wove paper.

73 **8** 6d. vandyke-brown £1900 £250
74 6d. yellow-brown £2000 £275
75 6d. chocolate-brown £1900 £250
76 6d. grey-brown £1800 £250
a. "WALLS" (R. 2/3) – £650

(b) Plate I re-engraved by H. C. Jervis. Coarse background (June 1853).

77 – 6d. brown £2000 £300
78 – 6d. grey-brown £1900 £300

Examples of the 6d. in vandyke-brown on thick yellowish paper are proofs.

Nos. 72/6 and 77/8 were printed in sheets of 25 (5×5).

(Eng H. C. Jervis)

1853 (May). Imperf. *Medium bluish paper.*

79 8d. dull yellow £5000 £600
80 8d. orange-yellow £5000 £600
81 8d. orange £5500 £650
a. No bow at back of head (R. 1/9) – £1600
b. No leaves right of "SOUTH" (R. 3/1) – £1600
c. No lines in spandrel (R. 2/2, 3/2, 4/2) – £900

Nos. 79/81 were issued in sheets of 50 (10×5).

10

NOTE. All watermarked stamps from No. 82 to No. 172 have double-lined figures, as T **10**.

1854 (Jan–Mar). *Yellowish wove paper.* Wmk "**1**", "**2**", or "**3**" as T **10**, to match face value. Imperf.

82 **8** 1d. red-orange (Feb) £225 22·00
83 1d. orange-vermilion £225 22·00
a. No leaves right of "SOUTH" (R. 1/7, 3/1) £475 95·00
b. Two leaves right of "SOUTH" (R. 2/5) £650 £140
c. "WALE" (R. 1/9) £650 £140
84 – 2d. ultramarine (Pl III) (Jan) £150 12·00
85 – 2d. Prussian blue (Pl III) £150 12·00
86 – 2d. chalky blue (Pl III) £150 9·50
a. "WALES" partly covered by wavy lines (R. 1/3) £550 60·00
87 **8** 3d. yellow-green (Mar) £275 32·00
a. "WAEES" with centre bar of first "E" missing (R. 4/7) £950 £140
b. Error. Wmk "**2**" £3500 £1600

Nos. 82/7 were printed in sheets of 50 (10×5).

11

12

13

14

(6d. and 1s. des E. H. Corbould after sketches by T. W. Levinge. Printed by New South Wales Govt Ptg Dept from Perkins Bacon plates)

1854 (1 Feb)–**59**. Wmk "**5**", "**6**", "**8**" or "**12**" to match face value. Imperf.

88 **11** 5d. dull green (1.12.55) £1000 £650
89 **12** 6d. deep slate £750 35·00
a. Wmk sideways † £950
90 6d. greenish grey £600 35·00
91 6d. slate-green £600 35·00
a. Printed both sides
92 6d. bluish grey £650 55·00
93 6d. fawn £700 95·00
a. Wmk "**8**" (15.8.59) £3000 £110
94 6d. grey £650 55·00
95 6d. olive-grey £650 35·00
96 6d. greyish brown £650 35·00
a. Wmk "**8**" (15.8.59) £3000 £110
ab. Wmk sideways – £375
97 **13** 8d. golden yellow (1.12.55) £11000 £1300
98 8d. dull yellow-orange £10000 £1200
99 **14** 1s. rosy vermilion (2.54) £1200 70·00
a. Wmk "**8**" (20.6.57) £3750 £180
100 1s. pale red £1200 70·00
101 1s. brownish red £1300 80·00

Nos. 93a, 96a and 99a come from printings made when supplies of the correct numeral watermarks were unavailable.

Plate proofs of the 6d. in red-brown and of the 1s. in deep blue on unwatermarked paper exist handstamped "CANCELLED" in oval of bars (see note on Perkins Bacon "CANCELLED" in Catalogue introduction) (*Price* £10000 *each*).

For further examples of Types **11/14** on different watermarks see Nos. 141/53, 160/70, 215, 218, 231/3, 236 and 329.

15

16

(Eng John Carmichael)

1856 (1 Jan)–**59**. *For Registered Letters.* No wmk. Imperf.

(a) Soft medium yellowish paper.

102 **15** (6d.) vermilion and Prussian blue £950 £170
a. Frame printed on back £4000 £2250
103 (6d.) salmon and indigo £950 £190
104 (6d.) orange and Prussian blue £950 £225
105 (6d.) orange and indigo £950 £200

(b) Hard medium bluish wove paper, with manufacturer's wmk in sans-serif, double-lined capitals across sheet and only showing portions of letters on a few stamps in a sheet.

106 **15** (6d.) orange and Prussian blue (4.59) £1100 £180

For further examples of Type **15** on different watermarks see Nos. 119/27.

(Printed by New South Wales Govt Ptg Dept from plates engraved by Perkins, Bacon & Co)

1856 (7 Jan)–**60**. Wmk "**1**", "**2**" or "**3**" to match face value. Imperf.

(a) Recess.

107 **16** 1d. orange-vermilion (6.4.56) £170 23·00
a. Error. Wmk "**2**" † £6500
108 1d. carmine-vermilion £170 23·00
109 1d. orange-red £170 23·00
a. Printed on both sides £1800 £1800
110 2d. deep turquoise-blue (Pl I) £160 11·00
111 2d. ultramarine (Pl I) £150 11·00
112 2d. blue (Pl 1) £150 11·00
a. Major retouch (1858) £1800 £450
b. Error. Wmk "**1**" † £6500
c. Wmk "**5**" (3.57) £550 65·00
d. Error. Wmk "**8**" † £6500
113 2d. pale blue (Pl I) £150 11·00
114 2d. blue (Pl II) (1.60) £550 55·00
115 3d. yellow-green (10.10.56) £800 80·00
116 3d. bluish green £850 85·00
117 3d. dull green £850 85·00
a. Error. Wmk "**2**" – £3500

(b) Lithographic transfer of Plate I.

118 **16** 2d. pale blue (3.8.59) – £750
a. Retouched – £2500

For further examples of Type **16** on different watermarks see Nos. 131/40, 154/8, 171/2, 211/12, 226/8 and 327/8.

Two plates were used for the 2d. The 2d. Plate I was retouched, on a total of ten positions, several times as No. 112a. Stamps from Plate II are wider apart and are more regularly spaced. There is also a white patch between "A" of "WALES" and the back of the Queen's head.

On the 3d. the value is in block letters on a white background.

No. 112c comes from a printing made when supplies of the "2" paper were unavailable. Of the errors there are only two known of both Nos. 112b and 112d, all used. One example of each is in the Royal Collection.

The 1d. exists privately rouletted 10, a used pair of which is known postmarked 15 May 1861.

No. 114 was mainly used at post offices in Queensland.

STAMPS WITH STRAIGHT EDGES. Stamps between Nos. 119 and 243 can be found with one or two sides imperforate. These come from the outside rows which were not perforated between the stamps and the sheet margins.

1860 (Feb)–**63**. *For Registered Letters.*

(a) P 12.

(i) Hard medium bluish wove paper with manufacturer's wmk in sans-serif, double-lined capitals across sheet, showing portions of letters on a few stamps.

119 **15** (6d.) orange and Prussian blue £475 60·00
120 (6d.) orange and indigo £450 65·00

(ii) Coarse, yellowish wove paper with manufacturer's wmk in Roman capitals (Feb 1860).

121 **15** (6d.) rose-red and Prussian blue £350 42·00
122 (6d.) rose-red and indigo £425 90·00
123 (6d.) salmon and indigo

(b) P 13. (i) Coarse, yellowish wove paper with manufacturer's wmk in Roman capitals (1862).

124 **15** (6d.) rose-red and Prussian blue £350 60·00

(ii) Yellowish wove paper. Wmk "**6**" (May 1863).

125 **15** (6d.) rose-red and Prussian blue £130 22·00
126 (6d.) rose-red and indigo £190 29·00
127 (6d.) rose-red and pale blue £100 20·00
a. Double impression of frame – £500

1860 (14 Feb)–**72**. Wmk double-lined figure of value.

(a) P 12.

131 **16** 1d. orange-red £200 17·00
a. Imperf between (pair)
b. Double impression
132 1d. scarlet £140 17·00
133 2d. pale blue (Pl I) £550 £140
a. Retouched – £1300
134 2d. greenish blue (Pl II) £130 10·00
136 2d. Prussian blue (Pl II) £130 11·00
a. Error. Wmk "**1**" – £3000
b. Retouched (*shades*) – £400
137 2d. Prussian blue (Pl I) (3.61) £150 12·00
138 2d. dull blue (Pl I) £140 11·00
139 3d. yellow-green (1860) £1200 55·00
140 3d. blue-green £650 42·00
141 **11** 5d. dull green (1863) £250 75·00
142 5d. yellowish green (1863) £250 75·00
143 **12** 6d. grey-brown £400 48·00
144 6d. olive-brown £400 55·00
145 6d. greenish grey £475 45·00
146 6d. fawn £450 65·00
147 6d. mauve £425 35·00
148 6d. violet £400 16·00
a. Imperf between (pair)
149 **13** 8d. lemon-yellow – £1800
150 8d. orange £3750 £1000
151 8d. red-orange £3750 £1000
152 **14** 1s. brownish red £700 48·00
153 1s. rose-carmine £700 48·00
a. Imperf between (pair)

(b) P 13.

154 **16** 1d. scarlet (1862) 90·00 13·00
155 1d. dull red 90·00 13·00
156 3d. blue-green (12.62) 50·00 11·00
157 3d. yellow-green 65·00 8·50
a. Wmk "**6**" (7.72) £120 12·00
158 3d. dull green 65·00 8·00
a. Wmk "**6**" (7.72) £120 15·00
160 **11** 5d. bluish green (12.63) 80·00 20·00
161 5d. bright yellow-green (8.65) £140 50·00
162 5d. sea-green (1866) 80·00 23·00
162*a* 5d. dark bluish green (11.70) 60·00 23·00
163 **12** 6d. reddish purple (Pl I) (7.62) £110 6·00
164 6d. mauve £110 6·00
165 6d. purple (Pl II) (1864) 75·00 4·75
a. Wmk "**5**" (7.66) £600 26·00
ab. Wmk "**5**" sideways † £1000
b. Wmk "**12**" (12.66 and 1868) £500 21·00
166 6d. violet 75·00 6·50
a. Wmk "**5**" (7.66) – 32·00

167		6d. aniline mauve	£1000	£120
167*a*	13	8d. red-orange (1862)	£225	55·00
167*b*		8d. yellow-orange	£250	42·00
167*c*		8d. bright yellow	£225	42·00
168	14	1s. rose-carmine (1862)	£130	7·50
169		1s. carmine	£120	8·00
170		1s. crimson-lake	£110	8·00
		(*c*) Perf compound 12×13.		
171	16	1d. scarlet (1862)	—	£1700
172		2d. dull blue (1.62)	£2250	£180

No. 133 was made by perforating a small remaining stock of No. 113. Nos. 137/8 were printed from the original plate after its return from London, where it had been repaired.

Nos. 157a, 158a and 165a/b come from printings made when supplies of paper with the correct face value were unavailable.

For later printings in these types, with different watermarks and perforations, see Nos. 195, 211/2, 215, 218, 226/8, 231/3, 236, 269/70 and 327/9.

24

25

(Des E. H. Corbould, R.I.)

1861–88. W **25**. Various perfs.

174	24	5s. dull violet, P 12 (1861)	£1400	£325
		a. Perf 13 (1861)	£250	35·00
175		5s. royal purple, P 13 (1872)	£425	60·00
176		5s. deep rose-lilac, P 13 (1875)	£140	35·00
177		5s. deep purple, P 13 (1880)	£225	50·00
		a. Perf 10 (1882)	£225	60·00
178		5s. rose-lilac, P 10 (1883)	£160	50·00
179		5s. purple, P 12 (1885)	—	60·00
		a. Perf 10×12 (1885)	—	£150
180		5s. reddish purple, P 10 (1886)	£160	50·00
		a. Perf 12×10 (1887)	£350	60·00
181		5s. rose-lilac, P 11 (1888)	—	£140

This value was replaced by Nos. 261, etc. in 1888 but reissued in 1897, *see* Nos. 297*c*/*e*.

26

27

28

(Printed by De La Rue & Co, Ltd, London and perf at Somerset House, London)

1862–65. *Surfaced paper*. P 14.

		(*i*) W **27**.		
186	26	1d. dull red (Pl I) (1.4.64)	£130	60·00
		(*ii*) No wmk.		
187	26	1d. dull red (Pl II) (1.65)	£100	48·00
188	28	2d. pale blue (25.3.62)	£100	65·00

(Printed from the De La Rue plates in the Colony)

1862 (12 Apr). Wmk double-lined "**2**" (No. 189) or "**5**" (No. 190). P 13.

189	28	2d. blue	75·00	16·00
		a. Perf 12	£150	35·00
		b. Perf 12×13	£450	£200
190		2d. dull blue (9.62)	80·00	17·00

29

1863–69. W **29**. P 13.

191	26	1d. pale red (3.69)	£130	£220
192	28	2d. pale blue (4.63)	25·00	2·00
		a. Perf 12		
193		2d. cobalt-blue	25·00	2·00
194		2d. Prussian blue	35·00	3·75

1864–65. W **27**. P 13.

195	16	1d. pale red (6.64)	65·00	24·00
196	26	1d. dark red-brown (Pl I)	£180	25·00
197		1d. brownish red (Pl II)	35·00	4·50
		a. Imperf between (horiz pair)	†	£1000
198		1d. brick-red (Pl II)	35·00	4·50
		a. Highly surfaced paper (1865)	£225	
199	28	2d. pale blue	£160	5·00

Plates I and II were made from the same die; they can only be distinguished by the colour or by the marginal inscription.

1865–66. *Thin to very thin wove paper*. No wmk. P 13.

200	26	1d. brick-red	£140	27·00
201		1d. brownish red	£140	27·00
202	28	2d. pale blue (11.65)	85·00	5·00

32

34

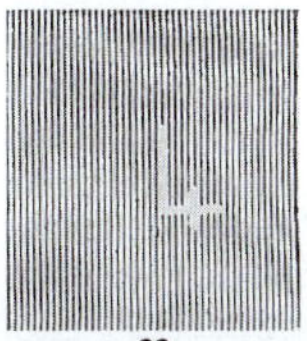
33

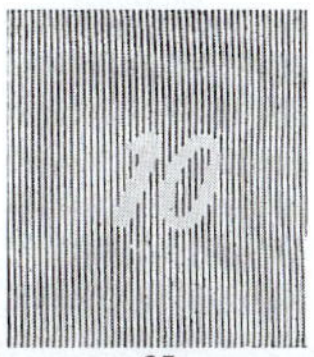
35

1867 (Sept)–**93**. W **33** and **35**.

203	32	4d. red-brown, P 13	70·00	5·00
204		4d. pale red-brown, P 13	70·00	5·00
205	34	10d. lilac, P 13	21·00	6·00
		a. Imperf between (horiz pair)	£1200	
		s. Optd "Specimen"	25·00	
206		10d. lilac, P 11 (1893)	15·00	6·00
		a. Perf 10	16·00	7·50
		b. Perf 10×11 or 11×10	21·00	8·50
		c. Perf 12×11	£110	15·00

36

37

38

NINEPENCE
(39)

From 1871 to 1903 the 9d. is formed from the 10d. by a black surch. (T **39**), 15 mm long on Nos. 219 to 220g, and 13½ mm long on subsequent issues.

1871–1902. W **36**.

207	26	1d. dull red, P 13 (8.71)	15·00	1·75
		a. Imperf vert (horiz pair)	†	£1300
208		1d. salmon, P 13 (1878)	15·00	1·75
		a. Perf 10 (6.80)	£250	32·00
		b. Perf 10×13 (6.80)	50·00	7·00
		ba. Perf 13×10	25·00	1·50
		c. *Scarlet*. Perf 10 (4.82)	—	£180
209	28	2d. Prussian-blue, P 13 (11.71)	20·00	1·50
		a. Perf 11×12, comb (11.84)	£250	40·00
		b. Imperf between (vert pair)	†	—
210		2d. pale blue, P 13 (1876)	20·00	1·50
		a. Perf 10 (6.80)	£250	22·00
		b. Perf 10×13 (6.80)	£100	16·00
		ba. Perf 13×10	20·00	1·25
		c. Surfaced paper. Perf 13		
211	16	3d. yellow-green, P 13 (3.74)	42·00	4·25
		a. Perf 10 (6.80)	75·00	9·00
		b. Perf 11 (1902)	£150	£100
		c. Perf 12 (5.85)	—	£150
		d. Perf 10×12 or 12×10 (5.85)	£150	32·00
		e. Perf 11×12 (1902)	£120	32·00
212		3d. bright green, P 10 (6.80)	£120	15·00
		a. Perf 13×10 (6.80)	£110	19·00
		b. Perf 13		
213	32	4d. pale red-brown, P 13 (8.77)	80·00	12·00
214		4d. red-brown, P 13	80·00	11·00
		a. Perf 10 (6.80)	£190	50·00
		b. Perf 10×13 (6.80)	£120	23·00
		ba. Perf 13×10	90·00	5·50
215	11	5d. bluish green, P 10 (8.84)	24·00	20·00
		a. Perf 12 (5.85)	£250	£100
		b. Perf 10×13 or 13×10		
		c. Perf 10×12 (5.85)	£120	50·00
		ca. Perf 12×10	45·00	21·00
216	37	6d. bright mauve, P 13 (1.1.72)	70·00	2·25
		a. Imperf between (horiz pair)	†	£1200
217		6d. pale lilac, P 13 (1878)	70·00	2·25
		a. Perf 10 (6.80)	£180	12·00
		b. Perf 10×13 (6.80)	90·00	16·00
		ba. Perf 13×10	75·00	2·50
		c. Imperf between (horiz pair). Perf 13×10	†	£1200
218	13	8d. yellow, P 13 (3.77)	£140	17·00
		a. Perf 10 (6.80)	£300	26·00
		b. Perf 13×10 (6.80)	£200	24·00
219	34	9d. on 10d. pale red-brown, P 13 (8.71)	45·00	5·50
220		9d. on 10d. red-brown, P 13 (1878)	45·00	10·00
		a. Perf 10 (6.80)	12·00	9·00
		b. Perf 12 (5.85)	14·00	9·00
		c. Perf 11 (12.85)	45·00	9·00
		ca. Surch in both black and blue (12.85)	£190	
		d. Perf 12×10 (5.85)	£250	£160
		e. Perf 10×11 or 11×10 (12.85)	55·00	15·00
		g. Perf 12×11, comb (1.84)	14·00	6·00
		gs. Optd "Specimen"	25·00	
221	38	1s. black, P 13 (1.4.76)	£100	6·00
		a. Perf 10 (6.80)	£200	16·00
		b. Perf 10×13 (6.80)	£240	28·00
		ba. Perf 13×10	£170	8·50
		c. Perf 11		
		d. Imperf between (vert pair)	†	£1400
		e. Imperf (pair)	†	£1200

Collectors should note that the classification of perforations is that adopted by the Royal Philatelic Society, London. "Perf 12" denotes the perforation formerly called "11½, 12" and "perf 13" that formerly called "12½, 13".

BISECTS. Between 1887 and 1913 various 1d. and 2d. stamps can be found vertically or diagonally bisected. This was unauthorised.

40

1882 (Apr)–**97**. W **40**.

222	26	1d. salmon, P 10	23·00	1·25
		a. Perf 13		
		b. Perf 10×13	†	—
		ba. Perf 13×10	55·00	2·25
223		1d. orange *to* scarlet, P 13	£800	£400
		a. Perf 10	14·00	70
		ab. Imperf between (horiz pair)		
		b. Perf 10×13	£120	8·00
		c. Perf 10×12 or 12×10 (4.85)	£250	65·00
		d. Perf 11×10 (12.85)	£450	£120
		e. Perf 12×11 (12.85)	—	£120
		f. Perf 11×12, comb (1.84)	7·00	60
		h. Perf 11 (12.85)	—	£130
224	28	2d. pale blue, P 13	£450	90·00
		a. Perf 10	29·00	70
		b. Perf 10×13	65·00	3·25
		ba. Perf 13×10		
225		2d. Prussian blue, P 10	38·00	70
		b. Perf 12 (4.85)	—	£225
		c. Perf 11 (12.85)	—	£100
		d. Perf 12×11 (12.85)	£400	£100
		e. Perf 10×12 (4.85)	£225	65·00
		ca. Perf 12×10	£400	£100
		f. Perf 10×11 or 11×10 (12.85)	£450	£150
		g. Perf 11×12, comb (1.84)	13·00	70
		ga. Printed double	†	£650
226	16	3d. yellow-green, P 10 (1886)	14·00	1·75
		a. Double impression	†	£1100
		b. Wmk sideways		
		bs. Optd "Specimen"	25·00	
		c. Perf 10×12	£160	40·00
		ca. Perf 12×10	£120	17·00
		d. Perf 11	7·50	1·00
		da. Imperf vert (horiz pair)	£375	
		e. Perf 11×12 or 12×11	6·00	1·00
		f. Perf 12	11·00	1·75
		g. Imperf (pair)	£275	
227		3d. bluish green, P 10	12·00	1·75
		a. Wmk sideways	55·00	10·00
		b. Perf 11	12·00	2·00
		c. Perf 10×11	24·00	2·75
		ca. Perf 11×10	£100	35·00
		d. Perf 11×12 or 12×11	9·50	2·25
		e. Perf 10×12 or 12×10	35·00	3·75
228		3d. emerald-green, P 10 (1893)	55·00	8·50
		a. Wmk sideways	—	16·00
		b. Perf 10×11	55·00	4·50
		ba. Perf 11×10	£120	38·00
		c. Perf 10×12	50·00	4·50
		ca. Perf 12×10	75·00	7·00
		d. Perf 12×11	—	11·00
229	32	4d. red-brown, P 10	70·00	4·00
		a. Perf 10×12 (4.85)	—	£160
		b. Perf 11×12, comb (1.84)	70·00	2·50
230		4d. dark brown, P 10	70·00	3·50
		a. Perf 12 (4.85)	£300	£180
		b. Perf 10×12 (4.85)	£200	60·00
		ba. Perf 12×10	£300	£150
		c. Perf 11×12, comb (1.84)	48·00	2·25
231	11	5d. dull green, P 10 (1890)	24·00	2·25
		as. Optd. "Specimen"	25·00	
		b. Perf 11×10	50·00	
		c. Perf 12×10 (4.85)	80·00	5·00
232		5d. bright green, P 10	50·00	7·00
		b. Perf 10×11 (12.85)	55·00	6·00
		ba. Perf 11×10	55·00	7·50
		c. Perf 10×12 (4.85)	£150	38·00
		ca. Perf 12×10	£100	70·00
233		5d. blue-green, P 10	17·00	1·75
		a. Perf 12 (4.85)	19·00	1·75
		ab. Wmk sideways	60·00	
		b. Perf 11 (12.85)	10·00	1·25
		c. Perf 10×11 (12.85)	42·00	2·50
		d. Perf 11×12 or 12×11 (12.85)	10·00	1·25
		da. Wmk sideways (P 11×12)	60·00	22·00
		e. Imperf (pair)	£375	
234	37	6d. pale lilac, P 10	65·00	1·25
		a. Perf 10×13 or 13×10	—	£300
		b. Perf 10×12 or 12×10 (4.85)	70·00	1·50
235		6d. mauve, P 10	65·00	1·25
		a. Perf 12 (4.85)	90·00	10·00
		b. Perf 11 (12.85)	90·00	8·00
		c. Perf 10×12 (4.85)	70·00	8·00
		ca. Perf 12×10	65·00	2·25
		cb. Imperf between (horiz pair)	†	£1200
		d. Perf 11×12 (12.85)	90·00	12·00
		da. Perf 12×11	65·00	1·75
		e. Perf 11×10 (12.85)	75·00	2·50
236	13	8d. yellow, P 10 (1883)	£130	18·00
		a. Perf 12 (4.85)	£200	29·00
		b. Perf 11 (12.85)	£130	24·00
		c. Perf 10×12 (4.85)	£160	50·00
		ca. Perf 12×10	£130	42·00
236*d*	34	9d. on 10d. red-brn, P 11×12 (28.2.97)	8·00	11·00
		das. Optd "Specimen"	25·00	
		db. Perf 12	12·00	13·00
		dc. Perf 11	11·00	14·00
		dca. Surch double	£250	£250
236*e*		10d. violet, P 11×12 (1897)	19·00	11·00

		eas. Optd "Specimen"	25·00	
		eb. Perf 12×11½	12·00	11·00
		ec. Perf 12	17·00	12·00
		ed. Perf 11	23·00	13·00
237	38	1s. black, P 10	85·00	4·50
		a. Perf 11 (12.85)	£200	12·00
		b. Perf 10×12	—	£250
		c. Perf 10×13		
		ca. Perf 13×10	£200	23·00
		d. Perf 11×12, comb (1.84)	85·00	4·50

41

42

1885–86. W **41** (sideways).

(i) Optd "POSTAGE", in black.

238	42	5s. lilac and green, P 13 (15.10.85)		
		a. Perf 10		
		b. Perf 12×10	£425	90·00
239		10s. lilac and claret, P 13 (17.5.86)		
		a. Perf 12	£1000	£200
240		£1 lilac and claret, P 13 (17.5.86)	—	£3750
		a. Perf 12	£5000	

(ii) Overprinted in blue.

241	42	10s. mauve and claret, P 10	£750	£200
		as. Optd "Specimen"	60·00	
		b. Perf 12	£225	65·00
		c. Perf 12×11		
242		£1 rose-lilac and claret, P 12×10	£3750	£2250

1886–87. W **41**.

243	26	1d. scarlet, P 10 (12.86)	25·00	7·50
		a. Perf 11×12, comb	8·50	3·75
244	28	2d. deep blue, P 10 (12.87)	65·00	9·50
		a. Perf 11×12, comb	20·00	3·75
		b. Imperf		

45 View of Sydney

46 Emu

47 Captain Cook

48 Queen Victoria and Arms of Colony

49 Superb Lyrebird

50 Eastern Grey Kangaroo

51 Map of Australia

52 Capt. Arthur Phillip, first Governor and Lord Carrington, Governor in 1888

(Des M. Tannenberg (1d., 6d.), Miss Devine (2d., 8d.), H. Barraclough (4d.), Govt Ptg Office (1s.), C. Turner (5s.), Mrs. F. Stoddard (20s.). Eng W. Bell).

1888 (1 May)–**89**. *Centenary of New South Wales.*

(a) W **40**. P 11×12.

253	45	1d. lilac (9.7.88)	7·00	80
		a. Perf 12×11½	18·00	1·00
		b. Perf 12	8·50	30
		c. Imperf (pair)		
		d. Mauve	7·00	30
		da. Imperf between (pair)		
		db. Perf 12×11½	9·50	50
		dc. Perf 12	9·50	50
254	46	2d. Prussian blue (1.9.88)	12·00	30
		a. Imperf (pair)	£190	£300
		b. Imperf between (pair)	£750	
		c. Perf 12×11½	14·00	30
		d. Perf 12	13·00	30
		e. Chalky blue	10·00	30
		ea. Perf 12×11½		
		eb. Perf 12	13·00	50
255	47	4d. purple-brown (8.10.88)	16·00	4·00
		a. Perf 12×11½	38·00	8·00
		b. Perf 12	32·00	4·00
		c. Perf 11	£300	95·00
		d. Red-brown	14·00	4·00
		da. Perf 12×11½	16·00	3·00
		db. Perf 12	16·00	3·00
		e. Orange-brown, P 12×11½	20·00	3·75
		f. Yellow-brown, P 12×11½	18·00	4·00
256	48	6d. carmine (26.11.88)	26·00	3·75
		a. Perf 12×11½	32·00	4·25
		b. Perf 12	26·00	9·00
257	49	8d. lilac-rose (17.1.89)	24·00	4·75
		a. Perf 12×11½	45·00	12·00
		b. Perf 12	24·00	5·50
		c. Magenta	80·00	10·00
		ca. Perf 12×11½	24·00	5·00
		cb. Perf 12	24·00	5·50
258	50	1s. maroon (21.2.89)	38·00	2·25
		a. Perf 12×11½	38·00	2·25
		b. Perf 12	40·00	2·25
		c. Violet-brown	38·00	2·50
		ca. Imperf (pair)	£750	
		cb. Perf 12×11½	55·00	3·00
		cc. Perf 12	55·00	2·50
253s/8s		Optd "Specimen" *Set of* 6	£170	

(b) W **41**. P 11×12.

259	45	1d. lilac (1888)	32·00	
		a. Mauve	24·00	3·00
260	46	2d. Prussian blue (1888)	80·00	4·25

(c) W **25** (sideways on 20s.) P 10.

261	51	5s. deep purple (13.3.89)	£200	48·00
		a. Deep violet	£200	50·00
262	52	20s. cobalt-blue (27.4.88)	£300	£130

Nos. 255c and 261/2 are line perforated, the remainder are comb.

A postal forgery exists of the 2d. on unwatermarked paper and perforated 11.

53

54

1890. W **53** (5s.) or **54** (20s.). P 10.

263	51	5s. lilac	£150	30·00
		a. Perf 11	£200	42·00
		ab. Imperf between (horiz pair)		
		b. Perf 12	£300	48·00
		c. Perf 10×11 or 11×10	£225	30·00
		d. Mauve	£190	30·00
		da. Perf 11	£190	42·00
264	52	20s. cobalt-blue	£325	£140
		a. Perf 11	£275	75·00
		b. Perf 10×11		
		c. Ultramarine, P 11	£225	75·00
		ca. Perf 12	£275	£130
		cb. Perf 11×12 or 12×11	£180	75·00
263s/4s		Optd "Specimen" *Set of* 2	£180	

55 Allegorical figure of Australia

Halfpenny
(56)

SEVEN-PENCE
HALFPENNY
(57)

1890 (22 Dec). W **40**.

265	55	2½d. ultramarine, P 11×12 comb	7·00	50
		as. Optd "Specimen"	25·00	
		b. Perf 12×11½, comb	48·00	48·00
		c. Perf 12, comb	11·00	50

1891 (5 Jan). *Surch as T* **56** *and* **57**. W **40**.

266	26	½d. on 1d. grey, P 11×12 *comb*	3·00	4·00
		a. Surch omitted		
		b. Surch double	£350	
267	37	7½d. on 6d. brown, P 10	5·50	4·50
		a. Perf 11	5·00	3·00
		b. Perf 12	7·00	3·50
		c. Perf 11×12 or 12×11	5·50	3·50
		d. Perf 10×12	6·00	3·50
268	38	12½d. on 1s. red, P 10	12·00	16·00
		a. "HALFPENNY" omitted		
		b. Perf 11	13·00	13·00
		c. Perf 11×12, comb	12·00	11·00
		d. Perf 12×11½, comb	13·00	11·00
		e. Perf 12, comb	16·00	11·00
266/8s		Optd "Specimen" *Set of* 3	70·00	

1891 (1 July). Wmk "10" as W **35**. P 10.

269	16	3d. green	12·00	80·00
270		3d. dark green	5·00	17·00

58

Type I. Narrow "H" in "HALF"

1892 (21 Mar)–**99**. *Type I.* W **40**.

271	58	½d. grey, P 10	40·00	1·50
		a. Perf 11	80·00	6·00
		b. Perf 10×12 or 12×10	75·00	8·50
		c. Perf 11×12	3·00	20
		cs. Optd "Specimen"	20·00	
		d. Perf 12	3·00	30
272		½d. slate, P 11×12 (1897)	2·75	20
		a. Perf 12×11½	3·00	20
		b. Perf 12	3·00	20
		c. Imperf between (horiz pair). Perf 11×12	£700	
273		½d. bluish green, P 11×12 (1.99)	4·75	30
		a. Perf 12×11½	2·00	30
		b. Perf 12	4·25	30

The perforations 11×12, 12×11½, 12, are from comb machines.

The die for Type **58** was constructed from an electro taken from the die of the De La Rue 1d., Type **26**, with "ONE" replaced by "HALF" and two "½" plugs added to the bottom corners. These alterations proved to be less hard-wearing than the remainder of the die and defects were visible by the 1905 plate of No. 333. It seems likely that repairs were undertaken before printing from the next plate in late 1907 which produced stamps as Type II.

59

1894–1904. *Optd* "POSTAGE" *in blue.* W **59** (sideways).

274	42	10s. mauve and claret, P 10	£400	£150
275		10s. violet and claret, P 12	£180	50·00
		a. Perf 11	£325	90·00
		b. Perf 12×11	£200	60·00
276		10s. violet and aniline crimson, P 12×11	£200	55·00
		a. Chalk-surfaced paper (1903)	£225	55·00
		b. Perf 12	£300	85·00
277		10s. violet and rosine (*chalk-surfaced paper*), P 12 (1904)	£225	80·00
		a. Perf 11	£275	85·00
		b. Perf 12×11	£225	50·00
278		10s. violet and claret (*chalk-surfaced paper*), P 12×11 (1904)	£275	90·00
279		£1 violet and claret, P 12×11		

60

61

(Des C. Turner. Litho Govt Printing Office, Sydney)

1897. *Diamond Jubilee and Hospital Charity. T* **60/1**. W **40**. P 12×11 (1d.) or 11 (2½d.).

280	60	1d. (1s.) green and brown (22.6)	40·00	45·00
281	61	2½d. (2s.6d.) gold, carmine & blue (28.6)	£180	£180
280s/1s		Optd "Specimen" *Set of* 2	£200	

These stamps, sold at 1s. and 2s.6d. respectively, paid postage of 1d. and 2½d. only, the difference being given to a Consumptives' Home.

62

63

64

Dies of the 1d.

Die I

Die II

1d. Die I. The first pearl on the crown on the left side is merged into the arch, the shading under the fleur-de-lis is indistinct, the "S" of "WALES" is open.

Die II. The first pearl is circular, the vertical shading under the fleur-de-lis clear, the "S" of "WALES" not so open.

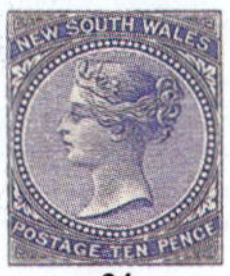

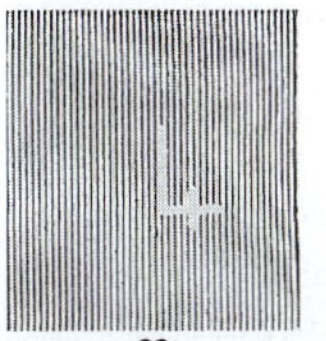

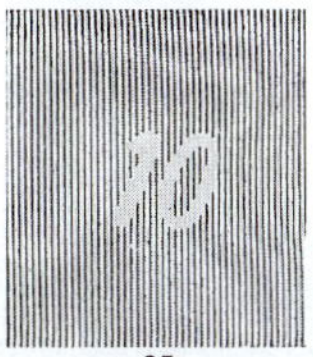

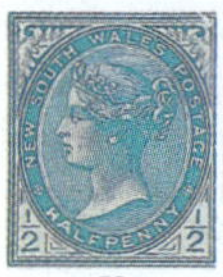

Dies of the 2½d.

Die I

Die II

2½d. Die I. There are 12 radiating lines in the star on the Queen's breast.

Die II. There are 16 radiating lines in the star and the eye is nearly full of colour.

(Des D. Souter (2d., 2½d.). Eng W. Amor)

1897 (22 June)–**99**. W **40** (sideways on 2½d.). P 12×11 (2½d.) or 11×12 (others)

288	**62**	1d. carmine (Die I)	3·00	20
		a. Perf 12×11½	3·00	20
		s. Optd "Specimen"	20·00	
289		1d. scarlet (Die I)	4·25	20
		a. Perf 12×11½	5·50	50
		b. Perf 12	5·50	60
		ba. Imperf horiz (vert pair)	£350	
290		1d. rose-carmine (Die II) (10.97)	3·00	20
		a. Perf 12×11½	2·50	20
		b. Perf 12	3·25	20
		c. Imperf between (pair)	£550	
291		1d. salmon-red (Die II) (P 12×11½)	3·50	20
		a. Perf 12	4·50	40
292	**63**	2d. deep dull blue	5·50	40
		a. Perf 12×11½	5·50	40
		b. Perf 12	7·50	30
		s. Optd "Specimen"	20·00	
293		2d. cobalt-blue	8·00	40
		a. Perf 12×11½	4·50	40
		b. Perf 12	7·00	40
294		2d. ultramarine (1.12.97)	5·50	20
		a. Perf 12×11½	3·00	20
		b. Perf 12	3·00	20
		c. Imperf between (pair)		
		s. Optd "Specimen"	22·00	
295	**64**	2½d. purple (Die I)	15·00	1·75
		a. Perf 11½×12	17·00	1·75
		b. Perf 11	17·00	2·75
		s. Optd "Specimen"	20·00	
296		2½d. deep violet (Die II) (11.97)	15·00	1·25
		a. Perf 11½×12	17·00	1·25
		b. Perf 12	13·00	1·25
297		2½d. Prussian blue (17.1.99)	14·00	2·00
		a. Perf 11½×12	4·75	2·00
		b. Perf 12	4·50	2·00

The perforations 11×12, 12×11½ and 12 are from comb machines, the perforation 11 is from a single-line machine.

1897. *Reissue of T* **24**. W **25**. P 11.

297*c*		5s. reddish purple (*shades*)	48·00	13·00
		ca. Imperf between (horiz pair)	£7000	
		d. Perf 12	65·00	26·00
		e. Perf 11×12 or 12×11	50·00	19·00

1898–99. W **40**. P 11×12.

297*f*	**48**	6d. emerald-green	32·00	15·00
		fa. Perf 12×11½	25·00	10·00
		fb. Perf 12	23·00	10·00
		fs. Optd "Specimen"	22·00	
297*g*		6d. orange-yellow (1899)	19·00	6·50
		ga. Perf 12×11½	15·00	5·50
		gb. Perf 12	26·00	7·00
		gc. Yellow, P 12×11½	17·00	3·75

1899 (Oct). *Chalk-surfaced paper.* W **40** (sideways on 2½d.). P 12×11½ or 11½×12 (2½d.), comb.

298	**58**	½d. blue-green (Type I)	2·00	80
		a. Imperf (pair)	£140	£170
299	**62**	1d. carmine (Die II)	3·50	20
		a. Imperf horiz (vert pair)	£450	
		b. Perf 11		
300		1d. scarlet (Die II)	2·25	20
		a. Perf 11		
301		1d. salmon-red (Die II)	4·75	20
		a. Imperf (pair)	£150	£170
302	**63**	2d. cobalt-blue	3·50	40
		a. Imperf (pair)	£150	
		b. Imperf horiz (vert pair)	£800	
303	**64**	2½d. Prussian blue (Die II)	5·00	70
		a. Imperf (pair)	£190	
303*b*	**47**	4d. red-brown	17·00	7·50
		c. Imperf (pair)	£425	
304		4d. orange-brown	11·00	5·50
305	**48**	6d. deep orange	18·00	3·75
		a. Imperf (pair)	£350	
306		6d. orange-yellow	14·00	3·75
307		6d. emerald-green	75·00	22·00
		a. Imperf (pair)	£425	
308	**49**	8d. magenta	21·00	4·25
309	**34**	9d. on 10d. dull brown	8·00	11·00
		a. Surcharge double	£170	£200
		b. Without surcharge	£180	
310		10d. violet	17·00	11·00
311	**50**	1s. maroon	24·00	3·00
312		1s. purple-brown	24·00	3·50
		a. Imperf (pair)	£375	

65 The spacing between the Crown and "NSW" is 1 mm in T **65** as against 2 mm in T **40**

66 Superb Lyrebird

67

1902–03. *Chalk-surfaced paper.* W **65** (sideways on 2½d.). P 12×11½ or 11½×12 (2½d.), comb

313	**58**	½d. blue-green (Type I)	4·50	40
		a. Perf 12×11	4·50	40
		b. Mixed perfs 12×11½ and 11	£600	
314	**62**	1d. carmine (Die II)	2·50	20
		a. Perf 11	†	£1000
315	**63**	2d. cobalt-blue	3·75	80
		a. Perf 11	—	—
316	**64**	2½d. dark blue (Die II)	8·50	80
317	**47**	4d. orange-brown	42·00	10·00
318	**48**	6d. yellow-orange	18·00	3·50
319		6d. orange	20·00	3·00
320		6d. orange-buff	35·00	3·50
321	**49**	8d. magenta	21·00	4·50
322	**34**	9d. on 10d. brownish orange	9·50	4·00
323		10d. violet	18·00	10·00
324	**50**	1s. maroon	42·00	2·50
325		1s. purple-brown	42·00	2·50
326	**66**	2s.6d. green (1903)	42·00	19·00
		s. Optd "Specimen"	60·00	

1903–08. W **65**.

327	**16**	3d. yellow-green, P 11	9·50	1·50
		b. Perf 12	9·50	1·00
		ba. Imperf between (horiz pair)		
		c. Perf 11×12 or 12×11	9·00	1·00
328		3d. dull green, P 12	30·00	2·75
		a. Perf 11×12 or 12×11	13·00	2·00
		b. Perf 11	13·00	2·00
329	**11**	5d. dark blue-green, P 11×12 or 12×11	9·50	1·25
		a. Wmk sideways	26·00	7·00
		b. Perf 11	22·00	1·25
		ba. Wmk sideways	—	50·00
		c. Perf 12	35·00	4·50
		ca. Wmk sideways	£100	50·00
		d. Imperf (pair)	£200	

Stamps from this series without watermark are from the edge of the sheet.

(Typo Victoria Govt Printer, Melbourne)

1903 (18 July). Wmk double-lined V over Crown. W w **10**.

330	**67**	9d. brown & ultram, P 12¼×12½, *comb*	15·00	3·25
		s. Optd "Specimen"	40·00	
331		9d. brown & dp blue, P 12¼×12½, *comb*	15·00	3·25
332		9d. brown and blue, P 11	£3500	£1500

Type II. Broad "H" in "HALF"

68

1905 (1 Oct)–**10**. W **68** (sideways on 2½d.). Chalk-surfaced paper. P 12×11½ or 11½×12 (2½d.) comb, unless otherwise stated.

333	**58**	½d. blue-green (Type I)	3·00	50
		a. Perf 11½×11	13·00	2·00
		b. Type II (1908)	2·50	50
		ba. Perf 11½×11	3·00	50
334	**62**	1d. rose-carmine (Die II)	2·00	10
		a. Double impression	£375	£425
		b. Perf 11½×11	3·00	20
335	**63**	2d. deep ultramarine	2·00	20
		b. Perf 11½×11	2·50	20
		c. Perf 11		
336		2d. milky blue (1910)	2·75	10
		a. Perf 11	60·00	70·00
		b. Perf 11½×11	2·75	20
337	**64**	2½d. Prussian blue (Die II)	4·00	2·00
338	**47**	4d. orange-brown	10·00	3·50
339		4d. red-brown	12·00	4·00
340	**48**	6d. dull yellow	13·00	2·75
		a. Perf 11½×11	22·00	3·75
341		6d. orange-yellow	16·00	2·25
		a. Perf 11½×11	28·00	4·00
342		6d. deep orange	13·00	2·25
		a. Perf 11	£250	
343		6d. orange-buff	17·00	2·25
		a. Perf 11½×11	27·00	4·00
344	**49**	8d. magenta	23·00	4·75
345		8d. lilac-rose	25·00	6·00
346	**34**	10d. violet	14·00	4·50
		a. Perf 11½×11	13·00	4·00
		b. Perf 11	13·00	4·25
347	**50**	1s. maroon	27·00	1·75
348		1s. purple-brown (1908)	27·00	1·75
349	**66**	2s.6d. blue-green	55·00	27·00
		a. Perf 11½×11	42·00	18·00
		b. Perf 11	35·00	22·00

69

1905 (Dec). W **69**. *Chalk-surfaced paper.* P 11.

350	**52**	20s. cobalt-blue	£190	65·00
		a. Perf 12	£225	75·00
		b. Perf 11×12 or 12×11	£190	60·00

(Typo Victoria Govt Printer, Melbourne)

1905 (Dec). Wmk double-lined "A" and Crown, W w **11**. P 12×12½ comb.

351	**67**	9d. brown and ultramarine	17·00	1·75
		a. Perf 11	85·00	65·00
		b. Mixed perfs 12×12½ and 11	£1300	
352		9d. yellow-brown and ultramarine	14·00	1·75
		a. Perf 11	85·00	65·00

1907 (July). W w **11** (sideways on 2½d.). P 12×11½ or 11½×12 (2½d.), comb, unless otherwise stated

353	**58**	½d. blue-green (Type I)	4·25	2·50
354	**62**	1d. dull rose (Die II)	8·50	1·75
355	**63**	2d. cobalt-blue	7·50	2·00
		a. Wmk sideways	—	£300
356	**64**	2½d. Prussian blue (Die II)	70·00	£120
357	**47**	4d. orange-brown	19·00	17·00
358	**48**	6d. orange-buff	38·00	26·00
359		6d. dull yellow	38·00	26·00
360	**49**	8d. magenta	23·00	26·00
361	**34**	10d. violet, P 11 (12.07)	32·00	48·00
362	**50**	1s. purple-brown	50·00	9·00
		a. Perf 11	†	£1400
363	**66**	2s.6d. blue-green	70·00	70·00

Stamps from this series without watermark are from the edge of the sheet.

STAMP BOOKLETS

There are very few surviving examples of Nos. SB1/4. Listings are provided for those believed to have been issued with prices quoted for those known to still exist.

1904 (May)–**19**. *Black on red cover with map of Australia on front and picture of one of six different State G.P.O's on back. Stapled.*

SB1	£1 booklet containing two hundred and forty 1d. in four blocks of 30 and two blocks of 60	
	a. Red on pink cover (1909)	
	b. Blue on pink cover	

1904 (May). *Black on grey cover as No.* SB1. *Stapled.*

SB2	£1 booklet containing one hundred and twenty 2d. in four blocks of 30	

1910 (May). *Black on cream. cover inscribed* "COMMONWEALTH OF AUSTRALIA/POSTMASTER-GENERAL'S DEPARTMENT". *Stapled.*

SB3	2s. booklet containing eleven ½d. (No. 333), either in block of 6 plus block of 5 or block of 11, and eighteen 1d. (No. 334), either in three blocks of 6 or block of 6 plus block of 12	£4750

Unsold stock of No. SB3 was uprated with one additional ½d. in May 1911.

1911 (Aug). *Red on pink cover as No.* SB3. *Stapled.*

SB4	2s. booklet containing twelve ½d. (No. 333), either in two blocks of 6 or block of 12, and eighteen 1d. (No. 334) either in three blocks of 6 or 1 block of 6 plus block of 12	£4250

OFFICIAL STAMPS

O S (O 1) O S (O 2) O S (O 3)

The space between the letters is normally 7 mm as illustrated, except on the 5d. and 8d. (11–11½ mm), 5s. (12 mm) and 20s. (14 mm). Later printings of the 3d., W **40**, are 5½ mm, and these are listed. Varieties in the settings are known on the 1d. (8 and 8½ mm), 2d. (8½ mm) and 3d. (9 mm).

Varieties of Type O 1 exist with "O" sideways.

Nos. O1/35 overprinted with Type O **1**

1879. Wmk double-lined "**6**". P 13.

O1	**16**	3d. dull green	—	£475

1879 (Oct)–**85**. W **36**. P 13.

O2	**26**	1d. salmon	22·00	2·50
		a. Perf 10 (5.81)	£180	32·00
		b. Perf 13×10 (1881)	40·00	4·00
O3	**28**	2d. blue	24·00	2·25
		a. Perf 10 (7.81)	£225	32·00
		b. Perf 10×13 (1881)	50·00	25·00
		ba. Perf 13×10	40·00	3·25
		d. Perf 11×12 (11.84?)	—	£225
O4	**16**	3d. dull green (R.) (12.79)	£550	£275
O5		3d. dull green (3.80)	£250	55·00
		a. Perf 10 (1881)	£150	50·00
		b. Yellow-green. Perf 10 (10.81)	£150	27·00
		ba. Perf 13×10 (1881)	£150	27·00
		bb. Perf 12 (4.85)	£200	50·00
		be. Perf 10×12 or 12×10 (4.85)	£200	50·00
O6	**32**	4d. red-brown	£180	8·00
		a. Perf 10 (1881)	—	£225
		b. Perf 10×13 (1881)	£225	90·00
		ba. Perf 13×10	£170	12·00
O7	**11**	5d. green, P 10 (8.84)	19·00	20·00
O8	**37**	6d. pale lilac	£250	7·00
		a. Perf 10 (1881)	£375	42·00
		b. Perf 13×10 (1881)	£180	42·00
O9	**13**	8d. yellow (R.) (12.79)	—	£250
O10		8d. yellow (1880)	—	32·00
		a. Perf 10 (1881)	£350	75·00
O11	**34**	9d. on 10d. brown, P 10 (30.5.80)	£500	
		s. Optd "Specimen"	60·00	
O12	**38**	1s. black (R.)	£275	12·00
		a. Perf 10 (1881)	—	23·00
		b. Perf 10×13 (1881)	—	38·00
		ba. Perf 13×10	—	12·00

Other stamps are known with red overprint but their status is in doubt.

1880–88. W **25**.

(a) P 13.

O13 **24** 5s. deep purple (15.2.80) £500 95·00
a. Royal purple — £300
b. Deep rose-lilac £500 95·00

(b) P 10.

O14 **24** 5s. deep purple (9.82) £500 £170
a. Opt double £3000 £1500
b. Rose-lilac (1883) £375 £110

(c) P 10×12.

O15 **24** 5s. purple (10.86)

(d) P 12×10.

O16 **24** 5s. reddish purple (1886) £475 £110

(e) P 12.

O17 **24** 5s. purple † £600

(f) P 11.

O18 **24** 5s. rose-lilac (1888) £225 85·00

1880 (31 May). W **35**. P 13.

O18*a* **34** 10d. lilac £180 £100
ab. Perf 10 and 11, compound £250 £200
ac. Perf 10 £250
aca. Opt double, one albino £350
as. Optd "Specimen" 60·00

1882–85. W **40**. P 10.

O19 **26** 1d. salmon 25·00 3·50
a. Perf 13×10 — £130
O20 1d. orange *to* scarlet 14·00 1·75
a. Perf 10×13 — £130
b. Perf 11×12, comb (1.84) 9·00 1·40
c. Perf 10×12 or 12×10 (4.85) — £110
d. Perf 12×11 (12.85)
O21 **28** 2d. blue 16·00 1·00
a. Perf 10×13 or 13×10 £190 75·00
c. Perf 11×12, comb (1.84) 8·50 1·00
ca. Opt double — £275
e. Perf 12×11 (12.85)
O22 **16** 3d. yellow-green (7 *mm*) 9·50 3·50
a. Wmk sideways
b. Perf 12 (4.85) £120 80·00
c. Perf 12×10 (4.85) — 5·00
ca. Opt double † £500
d. Perf 12×11
O23 3d. bluish green (7 *mm*) 15·00 4·50
a. Perf 12 (4.85) £120 80·00
b. Perf 12×10 (4.85)
c. Perf 10×11 (12.85)
O24 3d. yellow-green (5½ *mm*) 10·00 4·25
a. Wmk sideways 35·00 23·00
as. Optd "Specimen" 35·00
b. Perf 10×12 or 12×10 (4.85) 16·00 4·50
c. Perf 10×11 or 11×10 (12.85) — 5·00
O25 3d. bluish green (5½ *mm*) 7·50 5·50
a. Wmk sideways
b. Perf 10×12 or 12×10 (4.85) 9·50 6·00
c. Perf 10×11 or 11×10 (12.85) 5·00 3·75
O26 **32** 4d. red-brown 38·00 4·00
a. Perf 11×12, comb (1.84) 12·00 3·50
b. Perf 10×12 (4.85) — 70·00
O27 4d. dark brown 18·00 3·50
a. Perf 11×12, comb (1.84) 13·00 3·50
b. Perf 12 (4.85) £200 £150
c. Perf 10×12 (4.85) £200 90·00
O28 **11** 5d. dull green 16·00 16·00
a. Perf 12×10 (4.85)
s. Optd "Specimen" 35·00
O29 5d. blue-green 18·00 21·00
a. Perf 12 (4.85) £100 £100
b. Perf 10×11 14·00 16·00
c. Perf 11 † £150
O30 **37** 6d. pale lilac 20·00 5·50
a. Perf 11 (12.85) 26·00 5·50
O31 6d. mauve 20·00 6·00
a. Perf 12 (4.85) — 45·00
b. Perf 10×12 or 12×10 (4.85) 20·00 5·50
d. Perf 11×10 (12.85) 20·00 6·00
e. Perf 11×12
ea. Perf 12×11 (12.85) 55·00 17·00
O32 **13** 8d. yellow 22·00 11·00
a. Perf 12 (4.85) £130 38·00
b. Perf 10×12 or 12×10 (4.85) 22·00 11·00
ba. Opt double † —
d. Perf 11 (12.85) 22·00 15·00
da. Opt double
db. Opt treble † —
O33 **38** 1s. black (R.) 25·00 9·00
a. Perf 10×13 — 55·00
b. Perf 11×12, comb (1.84) 25·00 8·00
ba. Opt double — £275

1886–87. W **41**. P 10.

O34 **26** 1d. scarlet 60·00 4·50
O35 **28** 2d. deep blue
a. Perf 11×12, comb

1887–90. *Nos. 241/2 optd in black.*

(a) With Type O **1**.

O36 **42** 10s. mauve and claret, P 12 (1890) — £2000

(b) With Type O **2** (30 April 1889).

O37 **42** 10s. mauve and claret P 12 £2750 £1000
as. Optd "Specimen" 80·00
b. Perf 10 £4000 £2000

(c) With Type O **3** (7 Jan 1887).

O38 **42** £1 mauve and claret, P 12×10 £12000 £7000

Only nine examples of No. O38 are recorded, three of which are mint. One of the used stamps, in the Royal Collection, shows overprint Type O **3** double.

1888 (17 July)–**90.** *Optd as Type* O **1**.

(a) W **40**. P 11×12.

O39 **45** 1d. lilac 4·25 75
a. Perf 12 3·00 75
b. Mauve 3·00 75
ba. Perf 12 3·00 75
O40 **46** 2d. Prussian blue (15.10.88) 4·50 40
a. Perf 12 7·00 1·50
O41 **47** 4d. purple-brown (10.10.89) 11·00 3·75
a. Perf 12 17·00 4·75
b. Perf 11
c. Red-brown 12·00 3·75
ca. Opt double † —
cb. Perf 12 15·00 4·50
O42 **48** 6d. carmine (16.1.89) 8·50 6·00
a. Perf 12 13·00 6·00
O43 **49** 8d. lilac-rose (1890) 21·00 12·00
a. Perf 12 35·00 15·00
O44 **50** 1s. maroon (9.1.90) 24·00 4·00
a. Perf 12 24·00 4·00
b. Purple-brown 24·00 4·00
ba. Opt double
bb. Perf 12 24·00 4·00
O39s/44s Optd "Specimen" *Set of* 6 £200

(b) W **41**. P 11×12 (1889).

O45 **45** 1d. mauve
O46 **46** 2d. blue

(c) W **25**. P 10.

O47 **51** 5s. deep purple (R.) (9.1.90) £800 £500
O48 **52** 20s. cobalt-blue (10.3.90) £2250 £800

1890 (15 Feb)–**91.** *Optd as Type* O **1**. W **53** (5s.) or **54** (20s.). P 10.

O49 **51** 5s. lilac £350 £120
a. Mauve £190 70·00
b. Dull lilac, P 12 £500 £130
O50 **52** 20s. cobalt-blue (3.91) £2250 £600
O49s/50s Optd "Specimen" *Set of* 2 £200

1891 (Jan). *Optd as Type* O **1**. W **40**.

(a) On No. 265. P 11×12.

O54 **55** 2½d. ultramarine 11·00 10·00

(b) On Nos. 266/8.

O55 **26** ½d. on 1d. grey, P 11×12 55·00 55·00
a. Opt double — †
O56 **37** 7½d. on 6d. brown, P 10 35·00 48·00
O57 **38** 12½d. on 1s. red, P 11×12 60·00 80·00
O54s/7s Optd "Specimen" *Set of* 4 £140

1892 (May). *No. 271 optd as Type* O **1**. P 10.

O58 **58** ½d. grey 7·50 17·00
a. Perf 11×12 5·00 11·00
as. Optd "Specimen" 30·00
b. Perf 12 6·50 11·00
c. Perf 12×11½ 19·00 13·00

Official stamps were withdrawn from the government departments on 31 December 1894.

POSTAGE DUE STAMPS

D **1**

(Dies eng by A. Collingridge. Typo Govt Printing Office, Sydney)

1891 (1 Jan)–**92.** W **40**. P 10.

D1 **D 1** ½d. green (21.1.92) 6·50 4·50
D2 1d. green 15·00 2·25
a. Imperf vert (horiz pair) † —
b. Perf 11 11·00 2·25
c. Perf 12 24·00 4·00
d. Perf 12×10 30·00 3·25
e. Perf 10×11 16·00 2·75
f. Perf 11×12 or 12×11 11·00 2·25
D3 2d. green 16·00 2·75
a. Perf 11 16·00 2·75
b. Perf 12 — 14·00
c. Perf 12×10 29·00 4·50
d. Perf 10×11 17·00 3·00
e. Perf 11×12 or 12×11 16·00 2·50
f. Wmk sideways 26·00 12·00
D4 3d. green 32·00 6·50
a. Perf 10×11 32·00 6·50
D5 4d. green 24·00 2·75
a. Perf 11 22·00 2·75
b. Perf 10×11 20·00 2·75
D6 6d. green 32·00 8·00
D7 8d. green 90·00 23·00
D8 5s. green £150 50·00
a. Perf 11 £300 90·00
b. Perf 11×12 — £300
D9 10s. green (early 1891) £300 65·00
a. Perf 12×10 £300 £170
D10 20s. green (early 1891) £475 £100
a. Perf 12 £550
b. Perf 12×10 £300 £250
D1s/10s Optd "Specimen" *Set of* 10 £200

Used prices for 10s. and 20s. are for cancelled-to-order stamps. Postally used examples are rare.

1900. *Chalk-surfaced paper.* W **40**. P 11.

D11 **D 1** ½d. emerald-green
D12 1d. emerald-green 14·00 4·25
a. Perf 12 30·00 9·50
b. Perf 11×12 or 12×11 14·00 3·25
D13 2d. emerald-green 16·00 4·75
a. Perf 12 — 40·00
b. Perf 11×12 or 12×11 14·00 4·75
D14 3d. emerald-green, P 11×12 or 12×11 48·00 14·00
D15 4d. emerald-green (7.00) 24·00 6·00

New South Wales became part of the Commonwealth of Australia on 1 January 1901

QUEENSLAND

The area which later became Queensland was previously part of New South Wales known as the Moreton Bay District. The first post office, at Brisbane, was opened in 1834 and the use of New South Wales stamps from the District became compulsory from 1 May 1854.

Queensland was proclaimed a separate colony on 10 December 1859, but continued to use New South Wales issues until 1 November 1860.

Post Offices opened in the Moreton Bay District before 10 December 1859, and using New South Wales stamps, were

Office	*Opened*	*Numeral Cancellation*
Brisbane	1834	95
Burnett's Inn/Goode's Inn/ Nanango	1850	108
Callandoon	1850	74
Condamine	1856	151
Dalby	1854	133
Drayton	1846	85
Gayndah	1850	86
Gladstone	1854	131
Goode's Inn	1858	108
Ipswich	1846	87
Maryborough	1849	96
Rockhampton	1858	201
Surat	1852	110
Taroom	1856	152
Toowoomba	1858	214
Warwick	1848	81

PRICES FOR STAMPS ON COVER

Nos. 1/3	*from* × 2
Nos. 4/56	*from* × 3
Nos. 57/8	—
Nos. 59/73	*from* × 4
Nos. 74/82	*from* × 2
Nos. 83/109	*from* × 3
Nos. 110/13	*from* × 2
Nos. 116/17	*from* × 3
Nos. 118/27	—
Nos. 128/50	*from* × 4
Nos. 151/65	—
Nos. 166/78	*from* × 10
Nos. 179/83	*from* × 4
Nos. 184/206	*from* × 15
No. 207	—
Nos. 208/28	*from* × 15
No. 229	*from* × 100
No. 230	—
Nos. 231/54	*from* × 15
Nos. 256/62c	*from* × 10
Nos. 264a/b	*from* × 2
Nos. 265/6	*from* × 20
Nos. 270/4	—
Nos. 281/5	*from* × 10
Nos. 286/308	*from* × 12
Nos. 309/13	—
Nos. F1/37	—

PERKINS BACON "CANCELLED". For notes on these handstamps, showing "CANCELLED" between horizontal bars forming an oval, see Catalogue Introduction.

1

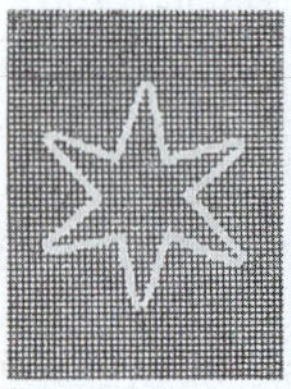

2 Large Star

3 Small Star

(Dies eng W. Humphrys. Recess P.B.)

1860. W **2**.

(a) Imperf.

1 **1** 1d. carmine-rose £3000 £800
2 2d. blue £80 00 £1700
3 6d. green £5500 £800

(b) Clean-cut perf 14–16.

4 **1** 1d. carmine-rose £1800 £300
5 2d. blue £700 £110
a. Imperf between (horiz pair) † —
6 6d. green (15 Nov) £750 70·00

3d. re-entry

3d. retouch (R.2/8)

The 3d. re-entry which occurs on one stamp in the second row, shows doubling of the left-hand arabesque and the retouch has redrawn spandrel dots under "EN" of "PENCE", a single dot in the centre of the circle under "E" and the bottom outer frame line closer to the spandrel's frame line.

1860–61. W **3**.

(a) Clean-cut perf 14–16.

7 **1** 2d. blue £650 £110
a. Imperf between (horiz pair) † £2500

8 | 3d. brown (15.4.61) | £400 | 70·00
a. Re-entry | — | £250
b. Retouch | — | £250
9 | 6d. green | £700 | 75·00
10 | 1s. violet (15.11.60) (H/S "CANCELLED" in oval £9000) | £700 | 95·00
11 | "REGISTERED" (6d.) olive-yellow (1.61) (H/S "CANCELLED" in oval £9000) | £450 | 85·00
a. Imperf between (pair) | £6000

(b) Clean-cut perf 14 at Somerset House (7.61).

12 **1** 1d. carmine-rose (H/S "CANCELLED" in oval £9000) | £160 | 42·00
13 | 2d. blue (H/S "CANCELLED" in oval £9000) | £425 | 55·00

(c) Rough perf 14–16 (9.61).

14 **1** 1d. carmine-rose | 80·00 | 35·00
15 | 2d. blue | £140 | 28·00
a. Imperf between (horiz pair) | £4000
16 | 3d. brown (H/S "CANCELLED" in oval £10000) | 60·00 | 32·00
a. Imperf vert (horiz pair) | £4000
b. Re-entry | £275 | £130
c. Retouch (R. 2/8) | — | £130
17 | 6d. deep green (H/S "CANCELLED" in oval £9000) | £200 | 28·00
18 | 6d. yellow-green | £300 | 28·00
19 | 1s. violet | £475 | 85·00
20 | "REGISTERED" (6d.) orange-yellow | 75·00 | 38·00

The perforation of No. 8 is that known as "intermediate between clean-cut and rough". No. 20 can also be found with a similar perforation.

Line through design

(Printed and perforated by Thomas Ham, Brisbane)

1862–67. *Thick toned paper.* No wmk.

(a) P 13 rough perforations (1862–63).

21 **1** 1d. Indian red (16.12.62) | £325 | 60·00
22 | 1d. orange-vermilion (2.63) | 75·00 | 12·00
a. Imperf (pair) | — | £1200
b. Imperf between (horiz pair) | † | —
23 | 2d. pale blue (16.12.62) | £100 | 27·00
24 | 2d. blue | 50·00 | 9·00
a. Imperf (pair) | — | £1200
b. Imperf between (horiz pair) | † | £2000
c. Imperf between (vert pair) | £3500
25 | 3d. brown | 75·00 | 35·00
a. Re-entry | — | £130
b. Retouch (R. 2/8) | — | £130
26 | 6d. apple green (17.4.63) | £120 | 15·00
a. Line through design at right | — | 85·00
b. Line through design at left | — | 85·00
27 | 6d. yellow-green | £110 | 12·00
a. Imperf between (horiz pair) | † | £1800
b. Line through design at right | — | 75·00
c. Line through design at left | — | 75·00
28 | 6d. pale bluish green | £170 | 30·00
a. Imperf (pair) | — | £1300
b. Line through design at right | — | £130
c. Line through design at left | — | £130
29 | 1s. grey (14.7.63) | £180 | 22·00
a. Imperf between (horiz pair) | † | £2750
b. Imperf between (vert pair) | † | —
s. Handstamped "Specimen" | 40·00

The top or bottom row of perforations was sometimes omitted from the sheet, resulting in stamps perforated on three sides only.

Prior to the plates being printed from in Brisbane, damage occurred to the 6d. plate in the form of a scratch across two adjoining stamps. The position of the pair in the plate is not yet recorded. One joined pair is known.

This flaw was not corrected until around 1869 when, after plate cleaning, only faint traces remain. These are hard to see.

(b) P 12½×13 rough (1863–67).

30 **1** 1d. orange-vermilion | 75·00 | 28·00
31 | 2d. blue | 65·00 | 20·00
32 | 3d. brown | 80·00 | 25·00
a. Re-entry | — | £120
b. Retouch (R. 2/8) | — | £120
33 | 6d. apple green | £120 | 45·00
a. Line through design at right | — | £180
b. Line through design at left | — | £180
34 | 6d. yellow-green | £120 | 45·00
a. Line through design at right | — | £180
b. Line through design at left | — | £180
35 | 6d. pale bluish green
a. Line through design at right
b. Line through design at left
36 | 1s. grey | £250 | 40·00
a. Imperf between (horiz pair)

This paper was used again for a very limited printing in 1867 which can be properly regarded as the First Government Printing. The perforations were now clean-cut. The designs and the background to the head are very well defined, the plates having been cleaned when transferred to the Government Printing Office.

(c) P 13 Clean-cut (1867).

37 | 1d. orange-vermilion | 75·00 | 23·00
38 | 2d. blue | 55·00 | 9·50
40 | 6d. apple green | £130 | 17·00
41 | 6d. yellow-green | £130 | 20·00
42 | 6d. deep green

Previously listed and then removed, the significance of this issue has been reassessed and it is now re-listed under this paper.

Copies of the 3d. and 1s. have been identified with these characteristics but there are no records of them being printed at this time.

1864–65. W **3**.

(a) P 13.

44 **1** 1d. orange-vermilion (1.65) | 70·00 | 30·00
a. Imperf between (horiz pair) | £950
45 | 2d. pale blue (1.65) | 75·00 | 16·00
46 | 2d. deep blue | 75·00 | 16·00
a. Imperf between (vert pair) | £1800
b. Bisected (1d.) (on cover) | † | £3250
47 | 6d. yellow-green (1.65) | £130 | 22·00
a. Line through design at right | — | £110
b. Line through design at left | — | £110
48 | 6d. deep green | £150 | 22·00
a. Line through design at right | — | £110
b. Line through design at left | — | £110
49 | "REGISTERED" (6d.) orge-yell (21.6.64) | 95·00 | 35·00
a. Double printed | £2000 | £2000
b. Imperf

(b) P 12½×13.

50 **1** 1d. orange-vermilion | 95·00 | 55·00
50*a* | 2d. deep blue | £120 | 55·00

The "REGISTERED" stamp was reprinted in 1895. See note below No. 82.

1866 (24 Jan). Wmk "QUEENSLAND/POSTAGE — POSTAGE/STAMPS — STAMPS" in three lines in script capitals with double wavy lines above and below the wmk and single wavy lines with projecting sprays between each line of words. There are ornaments ("fleurons") between "POSTAGE" "POSTAGE" and between "STAMPS" "STAMPS". Single stamps only show a portion of one or two letters of this wmk.

(a) P 13.

51 **1** 1d. orange-vermilion | £140 | 29·00
52 | 2d. blue | 55·00 | 17·00

(b) P 12½×13.

52*a* **1** 1d. orange-vermilion | £170 | 55·00
52*b* | 2d. blue | £170 | 55·00

First transfer

Double transfer

1866. *Lithographed on thick paper. No wmk.* P 13.

(a) First Transfer (Sept 1866) "FOUR" in taller thin letters.

53 | 4d. reddish lilac (*shades*) | £200 | 20·00
a. Re-entry | — | £110
b. Double transfer | — | £150
54 | 4d. grey-lilac (*shades*) | £200 | 20·00
a. Re-entry | — | £110
b. Double transfer | — | £150

Second transfer

(b) Second Transfer (Feb 1867) "FOUR" in shorter letters.

55 | 4d. lilac (*shades*) | £170 | 18·00
a. Retouch (R. 2/8) | — | 95·00
b. "FOUR" missing | — | £300
56 | 4d. grey-lilac (*shades*) | £170 | 18·00
a. Retouch (R. 2/8) | — | 95·00
b. "FOUR" missing | — | £300
s. Handstamped "Specimen" | 45·00
57 | 5s. bright rose | £475 | £130
58 | 5s. pale rose | £400 | 90·00
a. Imperf between (vert pair) | † | £2750
s. Handstamped "Specimen" | 55·00

The 4d. was lithographed from two separate transfers from the 3d. plate and the 5s. was taken from the 1s. plate.

The alterations in values were made by hand on the stones and there are minor varieties in the shape and position of the letters.

4

2d. Pl II. Dot by "U"

2d. Pl II. Dots near arabesque

1868–74. *Wmk small truncated Star,* W **4** *on each stamp, and the word "QUEENSLAND" in single-lined Roman capitals four times in each sheet. A second plate of the 2d. denomination was sent by Perkins, Bacon to the Colony in 1872 and it was first printed from in August of that year. The new plate is helpful in separating many of the 2d. printings up to 1879.* P 13.

59 **1** 1d. orange-vermilion (18.1.71) | 45·00 | 5·00
60 | 2d. pale blue (3.4.68) (Pl I) | 45·00 | 4·75
61 | 2d. blue (18.1.71) (Pl I) | 40·00 | 3·00
62 | 2d. bright blue (Pl I) | 50·00 | 2·75
63 | 2d. greenish blue (Pl I) | 85·00 | 2·75
64 | 2d. dark blue (Pl I) | 45·00 | 2·75
a. Imperf
65 | 3d. olive-green (27.2.71) | 85·00 | 6·00
a. Re-entry | — | 42·00
b. Retouch (R. 2/8) | — | 42·00
66 | 3d. greenish grey | £100 | 5·50
a. Re-entry | — | 40·00
b. Retouch (R. 2/8) | — | 40·00
67 | 3d. brown | 80·00 | 5·50
a. Re-entry | — | 40·00
b. Retouch (R. 2/8) | — | 40·00
68 | 6d. yellow-green (10.11.71) | £140 | 7·00
69 | 6d. green | £130 | 10·00
70 | 6d. deep green | £170 | 17·00
71 | 1s. greenish grey (13.11.72) | £375 | 45·00
72 | 1s. brownish grey | £375 | 45·00
73 | 1s. mauve (19.2.74) | £225 | 22·00
59s/73s H/S "Specimen" *Set of* 5 | £180

(b) P 12 (about Feb 1874).

74 **1** 1d. orange-vermilion | £325 | 25·00
75 | 2d. blue (Pl II) | 75·00 | 55·00
76 | 3d. greenish grey | — | £180
a. Re-entry
b. Retouch (R. 2/8)
77 | 3d. brown | £475 | £180
a. Re-entry
b. Retouch (R. 2/8)
78 | 6d. green | £1200 | 45·00
79 | 1s. mauve | £500 | 48·00

(c) P 13×12.

80 **1** 1d. orange-vermilion | — | £170
81 | 2d. blue (Pl II) | £1200 | 42·00
82 | 3d. greenish grey | — | £275

Plate II of the 2d. may be identified by a smudged dot to the left of "U" in "QUEEN" and tiny dots near the lower curl of the right arabesque.

Reprints were made in 1895 of all five values on Wmk W **4**, and perforated 13; the colours are:—1d. orange and brownish orange, 2d. deep dull blue (Pl II), 3d. brown, 6d green, 1s. red-violet and dull violet. The "Registered" was also reprinted with these on the same paper, but perforated 12. One sheet of the 2d. reprint is known to have had the perforations missing between the fourth and fifth vertical rows.

5

6

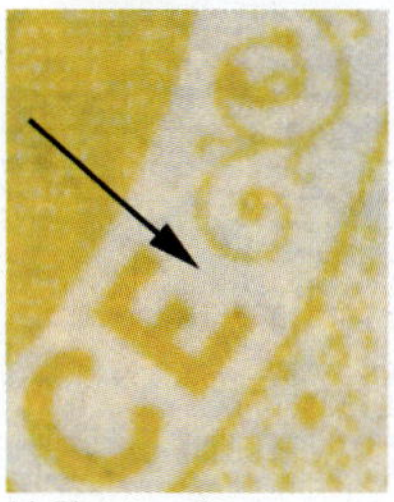
4d. First transfer

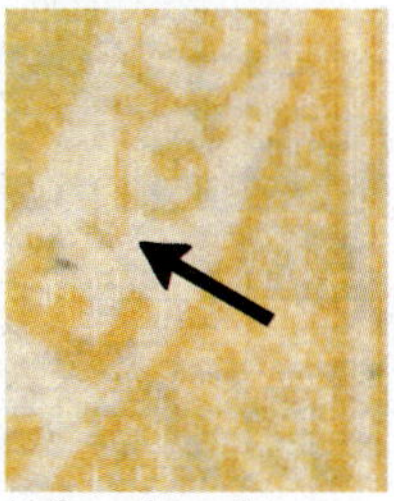
4d. Second transfer

The first transfer of the 4d. was taken from the 3d. plate, identified by the lack of the curl at the foot of the arabesque, the second was from Plate II of the 2d.

(4d., litho. Other values recess)

1868–78. Wmk Crown and Q. W **5**.

(a) P 13 (1868–75).

83 **1** 1d. orange-vermilion (10.11.68) | 60·00 | 4·50
a. Imperf (pair) | £400
84 | 1d. pale rose-red (4.11.74) | 55·00 | 10·00
85 | 1d. deep rose-red | 95·00 | 10·00
86 | 2d. pale blue (20.11.68) (Pl I) | 50·00 | 1·75
87 | 2d. deep blue (4.11.74) (Pl II) | 48·00 | 4·50
a. Imperf (pair) | £500
b. Imperf between (vert pair) | † | —
88 | 3d. brown (11.6.75) | 80·00 | 12·00
a. Re-entry | — | 70·00
b. Retouch (R. 2/8) | — | 70·00
89 | 4d. yellow (*shades*) (1st transfer) (1.1.75) | £850 | 70·00
s. Handstamped "Specimen" | 65·00
90 | 6d. deep green (9.4.69) | £120 | 9·00
91 | 6d. yellow-green | £100 | 6·50
92 | 6d. pale apple-green (1.1.75) | £130 | 9·00
a. Imperf (pair) | £425
93 | 1s. mauve | £200 | 50·00

(b) P 12 (1876–78).

94 **1** 1d. deep orange-vermilion | 38·00 | 5·00
95 | 1d. pale orange-vermilion | 40·00 | 5·00
a. Imperf between (vert pair) | † | —
96 | 1d. rose-red | 48·00 | 10·00
97 | 1d. flesh | 65·00 | 10·00
98 | 2d. pale blue (Pl II) | 85·00 | 15·00
99 | 2d. bright blue (Pl II) | 40·00 | 1·25
100 | 2d. deep blue (Pl II) | 42·00 | 1·50

101		3d. brown	75·00	9·00
		a. Re-entry	—	50·00
		b. Retouch (R. 2/8)	—	50·00
102		4d. yellow (*shades*) (1st transfer).	£700	26·00
103		4d. buff-yellow (*shades*) (2nd transfer)	£700	25·00
104		6d. deep green	£140	8·00
105		6d. green	£130	4·25
106		6d. yellow-green	£140	4·50
107		6d. apple-green	£150	7·00
108		1s. mauve	50·00	9·00
109		1s. purple	£140	5·00
		a. Imperf between (vert pair)	†	—
		(*c*) P 13×12 or 12×13.		
110	1	1d. orange-vermilion	—	£150
110*a*		1d. rose-red	—	£180
111		2d. deep blue (Pl II)	£1100	£250
112		4d. yellow	—	£300
113		6d. deep green	—	£300
		(*d*) P 12½×13 (1868).		
114	1	1d. orange-vermilion	—	£350
115		2d. deep blue (Pl I)	—	£350
115*a*		6d. yellow-green		
		(*e*) P 12½ (1868).		
115*b*	1	2d. deep blue (Pl I)		

Reprints of the above were made in 1895 on thicker paper, Wmk. W **6**, perf 12. The colours are:—1d. vermilion-red, 2d. deep dull blue and pale ultramarine, 3d. brown, 6d. dull yellow-green and 1s. lilac-grey.

1879. No wmk. P 12.

116	1	6d. pale emerald-green	£250	27·00
		a. Imperf between (horiz pair) ..	†	£1600
117		1s. mauve (*fiscal cancel £5*)	£130	75·00

No. 117 has a very indistinct lilac *burelé* band at back.

Nos. 116/17 can be found showing portions of a papermaker's watermark, either T. H. Saunders & Co or A. Pirie & Sons.

1880. *Lithographed from transfers from the 1s. die.* Wmk Crown and Q. W **6**. P 12.

118	1	2s. pale blue	£100	38·00
119		2s. blue (*fiscal cancel £4*)	£100	38·00
		a. Imperf vert (horiz pair)		
120		2s. deep blue (*fiscal cancel £4*)	£120	38·00
121		2s.6d. dull scarlet	£160	60·00
122		2s.6d. bright scarlet (*fiscal cancel £4*)	£190	60·00
123		5s. pale yellow-ochre	£225	95·00
124		5s. yellow-ochre (*fiscal cancel £5*)	£225	95·00
125		10s. reddish brown	£450	£170
		a. Imperf	£500	
126		10s. bistre-brown	£450	£170
127		20s. rose (*fiscal cancel £7*)	£1100	£200

Of the 2s. and 20s. stamps there are five types of each, and of the other values ten types of each.

Beware of fiscally used copies that have been cleaned and provided with forged postmarks.

7

Die I

Die II

Dies I and II often occur in the same sheet.

Die I. The white horizontal inner line of the triangle in the upper right-hand corner merges into the outer white line of the oval above the "L".

Die II. The same line is short and does not touch the inner oval.

1879–80. *Typo.* P 12.

		(*a*) Wmk Crown and Q. W **5**.		
128	7	1d. reddish brown (Die I) (15.5.79)	85·00	26·00
		a. Die II	£130	26·00
		ab. Imperf between (horiz pair) ..		
		ac. "QOEENSLAND"	£1100	£200
129		1d. orange-brown (Die I)	£130	26·00
130		2d. blue (Die I) (10.4.79)	75·00	11·00
		a. "PENGE" (R. 12/6)	£700	£110
		b. "QUEENSbAND" (R. 5/6)	—	£110
		c. "QU" joined	—	£110
131		4d. orange-yellow (6.6.79)	£550	60·00
		(*b*) No wmk, with lilac *burelé* band on back.		
132	7	1d. reddish brown (Die I) (21.10.79)	£400	60·00
		a. Die II	£425	85·00
		ab. "QOEENSLAND"	—	£1500
133		2d. blue (Die I) (21.10.79)	£475	38·00
		a. "PENGE" (R. 12/6)	£3500	£650
		b. "QUEENSbAND" (R. 5/6)		
		(*c*) Wmk Crown and Q. W **6**.		
134	7	1d. reddish brown (Die I) (31.10.79)	50·00	6·50
		a. Imperf between (pair)	†	£750
		b. Die II	65·00	6·50
		ba. "QOEENSLAND"	£275	45·00
		bb. Imperf between (pair)	†	£850
135		1d. dull orange (Die I)	32·00	5·50
		a. Die II	35·00	5·50
		ab. "QOEENSLAND"	90·00	25·00
136		1d. scarlet (Die I) (7.3.81)	27·00	3·25
		a. Die II	29·00	3·75
		ab. "QOEENSLAND"	£120	28·00
137		2d. blue (Die I) (10.4.79)	48·00	2·00
		a. "PENGE"	£160	42·00
		b. "QUEENSbAND"	£160	42·00
		c. Die II	55·00	3·75
138		2d. grey-blue (Die I)	48·00	1·50
		a. "PENGE"	£160	42·00
		b. "QUEENSbAND"	£160	42·00
		c. Die II	55·00	3·50
139		2d. bright blue (Die I)	55·00	1·50
		a. "PENGE"	£170	42·00
		b. "QUEENSbAND"	£170	42·00
		c. Imperf between (pair)	£1100	
		d. Die II	55·00	3·50
140		2d. deep blue (Die I)	55·00	1·50
		a. "PENGE"	£170	42·00
		b. "QUEENSbAND"	£170	42·00
		c. Die II	48·00	5·00
141		4d. orange-yellow	£160	10·00
		a. Imperf between (pair)		
142		6d. deep green	95·00	5·00
143		6d. yellow-green	£100	4·50
		a. Imperf between (pair)		
144		1s. deep violet (3.80)	95·00	5·50
145		1s. pale lilac	85·00	8·50

The variety "QO" is No. 48 in the first arrangement, and No. 44 in a later arrangement on the sheets.

All these values have been seen imperf and unused, but we have no evidence that any of them were used in this condition.

The above were printed in sheets of 120, from plates made up of 30 groups of four electrotypes. There are four different types in each group, and two such groups of four are known of the 1d. and 2d., thus giving eight varieties of these two values. There was some resetting of the first plate of the 1d., and there are several plates of the 2d.; the value in the first plate of the latter value is in thinner letters, and in the last plate three types in each group of four have the "TW" of "TWO" joined, the letters of "PENCE" are larger and therefore much closer together, and in one type the "O" of "TWO" is oval, that letter being circular in the other types.

(8)

9

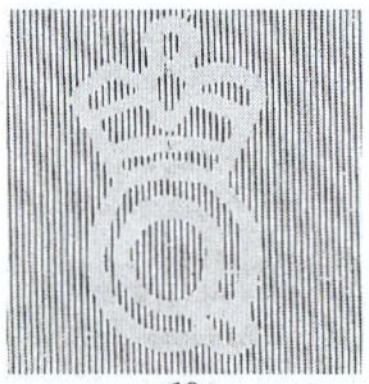

10

1880 (21 Feb). *Surch with T* **8**.

151	7	½d. on 1d. (No. 134) (Die I)	£250	£150
		a. Die II	£600	£425
		ab. "QOEENSLAND"	£1500	£1000

Examples with "Half-penny" reading downwards are forged surcharges.

£1 Re-entry (R. 1/2)

£1 Retouch (R. 6/4)

(Eng H. Bourne. Recess Govt Printing Office, Brisbane, from plates made by B.W.)

1882 (13 Apr)–**95**. P 12.

		(*a*) W **5** (twice sideways). *Thin paper.*		
152	9	2s. bright blue (14.4.82)	£140	38·00
153		2s.6d. vermilion (12.7.82)	90·00	22·00
154		5s. rose	85·00	24·00
155		10s. brown (12.7.82)	£160	42·00
156		£1 deep green (30.5.83)	£400	£140
		a. Re-entry (R. 1/2)	—	£275
		b. Retouch (R. 6/4)	—	£275
152s/6s (*ex* 2s. 6d.) H/S "Specimen" *Set of 4*			£180	
		(*b*) W **10**. *Thick paper* (10.11.86).		
157	9	2s. bright blue	£160	38·00
158		2s.6d. vermilion	45·00	24·00
159		5s. rose	42·00	35·00
160	9	10s. brown	£100	48·00
161		£1 deep green	£250	70·00
		a. Re-entry (R. 1/2)	£700	£150
		b. Retouch (R. 6/4)	£700	£150
		(*c*) W **6** (twice sideways). *Thin paper* (1895).		
162	9	2s.6d. vermilion	60·00	38·00
163		5s. rose	60·00	23·00
164		10s. brown	£375	95·00
165		£1 deep green	£250	90·00
		a. Re-entry (R. 1/2)	£650	£180
		b. Retouch (R. 6/4)	£650	£180

The re-entry on the £1 shows as a double bottom frame line and the retouch occurs alongside the bottom right numeral.

See also Nos. 270/1, 272/4 and 309/12.

11

12

In T **12** the shading lines do not extend entirely across, as in T **11**, thus leaving a white line down the front of the throat and point of the bust.

4d. "PENGE" for "PENCE" (R. 8/1)

4d. "EN" joined in "PENCE" (R. 4/6)

1882 (1 Aug)–**91**. W **6**.

		(*a*) P 12.		
166	11	1d. pale vermilion-red (23.11.82)	5·50	80
		a. Double impression		
167		1d. deep vermilion-red	5·50	80
168		2d. blue	9·00	80
		a. Imperf between (horiz pair) ..		
169		4d. pale yellow (18.4.83)	24·00	2·50
		a. "PENGE" for "PENCE"	£170	48·00
		b. "EN" joined in "PENCE"	£120	32·00
		c. Imperf (11.91)		
170		6d. green (6.11.82)	12·00	1·50
171		1s. violet (6.2.83)	26·00	4·25
172		1s. lilac	13·00	3·75
173		1s. deep mauve	12·00	3·75
174		1s. pale mauve	12·00	3·75
		a. Imperf	†	—
		(*b*) P 9½×12 (1884).		
176	11	1d. pale red	£130	45·00
177		2d. blue	£450	65·00
178		1s. mauve	£225	55·00

The above were printed from plates made up of groups of four electrotypes as previously. In the 1d. the words of value are followed by a full stop. There are four types of the 4d., 6d. and 1s., eight types of the 1d., and twelve types of the 2d.

No. 169c is from a sheet used at Roma post office and comes cancelled with the "46" numeral postmark.

1887 (5 May)–**91**. W **6**.

		(*a*) P 12.		
179	12	1d. vermilion-red	6·00	80
180		2d. blue	7·00	80
		a. Oval white flaw on Queen's head behind diadem (R. 12/5)	28·00	7·50
181		2s. deep brown (12.3.89)	70·00	45·00
182		2s. pale brown	60·00	38·00
		(*b*) P 9½×12.		
183	12	2d. blue	£375	60·00

These are from new plates; four types of each value grouped as before. The 1d. is without stop. In all values No. 2 in each group of four has the "L" and "A" of "QUEENSLAND" joined at the foot, and No. 3 of the 2d. has "P" of word "PENCE" with a long downstroke.

The 2d. is known bisected and used as a 1d. value.

13

14

1890–94. W **6** (sideways on ½d.). P 12½, 13 (comb machine).

184	13	½d. pale green	7·50	1·75
185		½d. deep green	6·50	1·75
186		½d. deep blue-green	5·00	1·75
187	12	1d. vermilion-red	4·00	40
		a. Imperf (pair)	£200	£200
		b. Oval broken by tip of bust (R. 10/3)	30·00	5·00
		c. Double impression	†	£450
188		2d. blue (old plate)	6·50	40
189		2d. pale blue (old plate)	6·50	40
190		2d. pale blue (retouched plate)	7·50	60
		a. "FWO" for "TWO" (R. 8/7)	—	22·00
191	14	2½d. carmine	13·00	2·00
192	12	3d. brown	9·00	3·75
193	11	4d. yellow	13·00	2·50
		a. "PENGE" for "PENCE"	65·00	22·00
		b. "EN" joined in "PENCE"	48·00	16·00
194		4d. orange	19·00	2·75
		a. "PENGE" for "PENCE"	85·00	22·00
		b. "EN" joined in "PENCE"	65·00	16·00
195		4d. lemon	22·00	3·25
		a. "PENGE" for "PENCE"	95·00	28·00
		b. "EN" joined in "PENCE"	75·00	20·00
196		6d. green	11·00	1·50
197	12	2s. red-brown	42·00	26·00
198		2s. pale brown	48·00	28·00

This issue is perforated by a new vertical comb machine, gauging about 12¾×12¾. The 3d. is from a plate similar to those of the last issue, No. 2 in each group of four types having "L" and "A" joined at the foot. The ½d. and 2½d. are likewise in groups of four types, but the differences are very minute. In the retouched plate of the 2d. the letters "L" and "A" no longer touch in No. 2 of each group and the "P" in No. 3 is normal.

1895. *A. Thick paper.* W **10**.

		(*a*) P 12½, 13.		
202	12	1d. vermilion-red (16.1.95)	4·00	50
		a. Oval broken by tip of bust (R. 10/3)	32·00	5·00
203		1d. red-orange	4·00	50
		a. Oval broken by tip of bust (R. 10/3)	32·00	5·00
204		2d. blue (retouched plate) (16.1.95)	4·75	50
		a. "FWO" for "TWO" (R. 8/7)	65·00	22·00
		(*b*) P 12.		
205	11	1s. mauve (8.95)	19·00	7·50
		B. Unwmkd paper; with blue burelé band at back. P 12½, 13.		
206	12	1d. vermilion-red (19.2.95)	2·50	50
		a. Oval broken by tip of bust (R. 10/3)	22·00	5·00
		b. "PE" of "PENNY" omitted (R. 1/2)	£180	£150

206*c*		1d. red-orange	2·50	50

C. Thin paper. Crown and Q faintly impressed. P 12½, 13.

207	**12**	2d. blue (retouched plate) (6.95)	12·00	£150
		a. "FWO" for "TWO" (R. 8/7)	£110	

15

16

17

18

1895–96. *A.* W **6** (sideways on ½d.).

(a) P 12½, 13.

208	**15**	½d. green (11.5.95)	2·25	1·00
		a. Double impression	†	—
209		½d. deep green	2·25	1·00
		a. Printed both sides	£170	
210	**16**	1d. orange-red (28.2.95)	3·50	40
211		1d. pale red	6·50	40
212		2d. blue (19.6.95)	17·00	50
213	**17**	2½d. carmine (8.95)	18·00	4·25
214		2½d. rose	19·00	4·25
215	**18**	5d. purple-brown (10.95)	23·00	4·25

(b) P 12.

217	**16**	1d. red (8.95)	55·00	22·00
218		2d. blue (8.95)	55·00	22·00

B. Thick paper. W **10** (sideways) (part only on each stamp).

(a) P 12½, 13.

219	**15**	½d. green (6.8.95)	2·75	3·25
220		½d. deep green	2·75	3·25

(b) P 12.

221	**15**	½d. green	25·00	
222		½d. deep green	25·00	

C. No wmk*; with blue burelé band at back.*

(a) P 12½, 13.

223	**15**	½d. green (1.8.95)	7·00	3·50
		a. Without *burelé* band	60·00	
224		½d. deep green	7·00	

(b) P 12.

225	**15**	½d. green	21·00	
		a. Without *burelé* band	£110	

Nos. 223a and 225a are from the margins of the sheet.

D. Thin paper, with Crown and Q faintly impressed. P 12½, 13.

227	**15**	½d. green	2·00	3·50
228	**16**	1d. orange-red	3·25	2·00

19

1896–1902. W **6**. P 12½, 13.

229	**19**	1d. vermilion	12·00	60
230		6d. green (1902)	†	£15000

Only used examples of No. 230 are known, mostly with readable postmarks from 1902. It is suggested that electrotypes of this unissued design were inadvertently entered in a plate of No. 249.

20

21

22

23

24

25

"Cracked plate"

Die I

Die II

Two Dies of 4d.:

Die I. Serif of horizontal bar on lower right 4d. is clear of vertical frame line.

Die II. Serif joins vertical frame line.

1897–08. *Figures in all corners.* W **6** (sideways on ½d.). P 12½, 13 (comb).

231	**20**	½d. deep green	3·75	5·50
		a. Perf 12	—	£140
232	**21**	1d. orange-vermilion	2·50	40
233		1d. vermilion	2·50	40
		a. Perf 12 (1899)	8·00	3·25
234		2d. blue	3·50	40
		a. Cracked plate	75·00	25·00
		b. Perf 12 (1905)	£1000	7·00
		ba. Cracked plate		
235		2d. deep blue	3·25	40
		a. Cracked plate	70·00	25·00
236	**22**	2½d. rose (10.98)	17·00	24·00
237		2½d. purple/*blue* (20.1.99)	9·50	2·75
238		2½d. brown-purple/*blue*	9·50	2·75
239		2½d. slate/*blue* (5.08)	12·00	5·50
240	**21**	3d. brown (10.98)	10·00	2·75
241		3d. deep brown	8·00	2·75
242		3d. reddish brown (1906)	9·00	2·75
243		3d. grey-brown (1907)	14·00	2·75
244		4d. yellow (Die I) (10.98)	9·00	2·75
		a. Die II	24·00	6·00
245		4d. yellow-buff (Die I)	9·00	2·75
		a. Die II	22·00	6·00
246	**23**	5d. purple-brown	8·50	2·75
247		5d. dull brown (1906)	9·50	3·75
248		5d. black-brown (1907)	11·00	3·75
249	**21**	6d. green (1.4.98)	8·00	2·75
250		6d. yellow-green	7·00	2·75
251	**24**	1s. pale mauve (1.7.99)	13·00	3·25
252		1s. dull mauve	13·00	3·25
253		1s. bright mauve	15·00	4·25
254	**25**	2s. turquoise-green	30·00	28·00

Stamps of this issue also exist with the irregular line perforation 12½, 13.

The 1d. perf 12×9½ exists used and unused but their status has not yet been established (*price* £110 *unused*).

The cracked plate variety on the 2d. developed during 1901 and shows as a white break on the Queen's head and neck. The electro was later replaced.

1897–98. W **6**

(a) Zigzag roulette in black.
(b) The same but plain.
(c) Roulette *(a)* and also *(b)*.
(d) Roulette *(b)* and perf 12½, 13.
(e) Roulette *(a)* and perf 12½, 13.
(f) Compound of *(a)*, *(b)*, and perf 12½, 13.

256	**21**	1d. vermilion *(a)*	16·00	10·00
257		1d. vermilion *(b)*	9·00	4·50
258		1d. vermilion *(c)*	18·00	19·00
259		1d. vermilion *(d)*	9·00	6·00
260		1d. vermilion *(e)*	65·00	85·00
261		1d. vermilion *(f)*	85·00	90·00

26

27

(Des M. Kellar)

1899 (Sept.)–**1906**. W **6**. P 12½, 13 (comb).

262	**26**	½d. deep green	3·00	2·25
		a. Grey-green	2·50	2·25
		b. Green (P 12) (1905)	£100	50·00
		c. Pale green (1906)	3·50	2·25

Stamps of T **26** without wmk, are proofs.

Stamps of this issue also exist with the irregular line perforation 12½, 12.

(Des F. Elliott)

1900 (19 Jun). *Charity. T* **27** *and horiz design showing Queen Victoria in medallion inscr* "PATRIOTIC FUND 1900". W **6**. P 12.

264*a*		1d. (6d.) claret	£120	£110
264*b*		2d. (1s.) violet	£300	£275

These stamps, sold at 6d. and 1s. respectively, paid postage of 1d. and 2d. only, the difference being contributed to a Patriotic Fund.

28

QUEENSLAND QUEENSLAND
A B

TWO TYPES OF "QUEENSLAND". Three different duty plates, each 120 (12 x 10), were produced for Type **28**. The first contained country inscriptions as Type A and was only used for No. 265. The second duty plate used for Nos. 265/6 and 282/4 contained 117 examples as Type A and 3 as Type B occurring on R. 1/6, R. 2/6 and R. 3/6. The third plate, used for Nos. 266, 283, 284 and 285 had all inscriptions as Type B.

(Typo Victoria Govt Printer, Melbourne)

1903 (4 Jul)–**05**. W w **10**. P 12½.

265	**28**	9d. brown and ultramarine (A)	26·00	4·25
266		9d. brown and ultramarine (B) (1905)	26·00	4·25

1903 (Oct). *As Nos. 162 and 165.* W **6** (twice sideways). P 12½, 13 (irregular line).

270	**9**	2s.6d. vermilion	£120	50·00
271		£1 deep green	£1800	£650
		a. Re-entry (R. 1/2)	£3500	£1200
		b. Retouch (R. 6/4)	£3500	£1200

(Litho Govt Ptg Office, Brisbane, from transfers of the recess plates).

1905 (Nov)–**06**. W **6** (twice sideways).

(a) P 12½, 13 (irregular line).

272	**9**	£1 deep green	£950	£160
		a. Re-entry (R. 1/2)	£1800	£325
		b. Retouch (R. 6/4)	£1800	£325

(b) P 12.

273	**9**	5s. rose (7.06)	95·00	75·00
274		£1 deep green (7.06)	£400	£120
		a. Re-entry (R. 1/2)	£800	£250
		b. Retouch (R. 6/4)	£800	£250

30

32

Redrawn types of T **21**

T **30**. The head is redrawn, the top of the crown is higher and touches the frame, as do also the back of the chignon and the point of the bust. The forehead is filled in with lines of shading, and the figures in the corners appear to have been redrawn also.

T **32**. The forehead is plain (white instead of shaded), and though the top of the crown is made higher, it does not touch the frame; but the point of the bust and the chignon still touch. The figure in the right lower corner does not touch the line below, and has not the battered appearance of that in the first redrawn type. The stamps are very clearly printed, the lines of shading being distinct.

1906 (Sept). W **6**. P 12½, 13 (comb).

281	**30**	2d. dull blue (*shades*)	10·00	4·25

(Typo Victoria Govt Printer, Melbourne)

1906 (Sept)–**10**. Wmk Crown and double-lined A, W w **11**.

(a) P 12×12½.

282	**28**	9d. brown and ultramarine (A)	60·00	6·00
283		9d. brown and ultramarine (B)	16·00	4·50
283*a*		9d. pale brown and blue (A)	55·00	6·00
284		9d. pale brown and blue (B)	13·00	4·50

(b) P 11 (1910).

285	**28**	9d. brown and blue (B)	£4500	£600

(c) Compound perf 12×12½ and 11.

285*a*		9d. brown and ultramarine (B)	†	£1200

33

1907–11. W **33**.

(a) P 12½, 13 (comb).

286	**26**	½d. deep green	1·75	3·25
287		½d. deep blue-green	1·75	3·25
288	**21**	1d. vermilion	3·00	30
		a. Imperf (pair)	£325	
289	**30**	2d. dull blue	13·00	1·75
289*a*		2d. bright blue (3.08)	18·00	8·50
290	**32**	2d. bright blue (4.08)	3·50	30
291	**21**	3d. pale brown (8.08)	15·00	2·75
292		3d. bistre-brown	12·00	3·50
293		4d. yellow (Die I)	11·00	3·25
		a. Die II	38·00	8·00
294		4d. grey-black (Die I) (4.09)	22·00	4·50
		a. Die II	40·00	11·00
295	**23**	5d. dull brown	17·00	8·50
295*a*		5d. sepia (12.09)	17·00	9·50
296	**21**	6d. yellow-green	16·00	4·25
297		6d. bright green	16·00	5·50
298	**24**	1s. violet (1908)	16·00	3·00
299		1s. bright mauve	16·00	3·00
300	**25**	2s. turquoise-green (8.08)	35·00	28·00

Stamps of this issue also exist with the irregular line perforation 12½, 13. This was used when the comb perforation was under repair.

(b) P 13×11 to 12½ (May 1911).

301	**26**	½d. deep green	6·00	8·00
302	**21**	1d. vermilion	7·50	4·25
303	**32**	2d. blue	10·00	8·00
304	**21**	3d. bistre-brown	18·00	15·00
305		4d. grey-black	55·00	60·00
		a. Die II	£120	90·00
306	**23**	5d. dull brown	26·00	42·00
307	**21**	6d. yellow-green	30·00	42·00
308	**23**	1s. violet	50·00	55·00

The perforation *(b)* is from a machine introduced to help cope with the demands caused by the introduction of penny postage. The three rows at top (or bottom) of the sheet show varieties gauging 13×11½, 13×11, and 13×12, respectively, these are obtainable in strips of three showing the three variations.

(Litho Govt Ptg Office, Brisbane)

1907 (Oct)–**11**. W **33** (twice sideways). P 12½, 13 (irregular line).

309	**9**	2s.6d. vermilion	42·00	45·00
		a. Dull orange (1911)	75·00	70·00
		b. Reddish orange (1912)	£170	£200
310		5s. rose (12.07)	65·00	50·00
		a. Deep rose (1910)	75·00	70·00
		b. Carmine-red (1911)	£190	£250
311		10s. blackish brown	£120	65·00
		a. Sepia (1911) (12.07)	£375	£275
312		£1 bluish green	£275	£120
		a. Re-entry (R. 1/2)	£650	£225
		b. Retouch (R. 6/4)	£650	£225
		c. Deep bluish green (1910)	£450	£300
		ca. Re-entry (R. 1/2)	—	£550
		cb. Retouch (R. 6/4)	—	£550
		d. Deep yellowish green (1911)	£1700	£1100
		da. Re-entry (R. 1/2)	£3750	£2000
		db. Retouch (R. 6/4)	£3750	£2000

The 1912 printings are on thinner, whiter paper.

The lithographic stone used for Nos. 272/4 and 309/12 took the full sheet of 30 so the varieties on the £1 recess-printed version also appear on the stamps printed by lithography.

1911. W **33**. Perf irregular compound, 10½ to 12½.

313	**21**	1d. vermilion	£1000	£650

This was from another converted machine, formerly used for perforating Railway stamps. The perforation was very unsatisfactory.

STAMP BOOKLETS

There are very few surviving examples of Nos. SB1/4. Listings are provided for those believed to have been issued with prices quoted for those known to still exist.

1904 (1 Jan)–**09**. *Black on a red cover as No.* SB1 *of New South Wales. Stapled.*

SB1	£1 booklet containing two hundred and forty 1d. in four blocks of 30 and two blocks of 60	
	a. Red on pink cover (1909)	
	b. Blue on pink cover	£15000

1904 (1 Jan). *Black on grey cover as No.* SB1. *Stapled.*

SB2	£1 booklet containing one hundred and twenty 2d. in four blocks of 30	

1910 (May). *Black on cream cover as No.* SB3 *of New South Wales. Stapled.*

SB3	2s. booklet containing eleven ½d. (No. 301), either in block of 6 plus block of 5 or block of 11 and eighteen 1d. (No 302), either in three blocks of 6 or block of 6 plus block of 12	

Unsold stock of No. SB3 was uprated with one additional ½d. in May 1911.

1911 (Aug). *Red on pink cover as No.* SB3. *Stapled.*

SB4	2s. booklet containing twelve ½d. (No. 301), either in two blocks of 6 or block of 12, and eighteen 1d. (No. 302), either in three blocks of 6 or block of 6 plus block of 12	£4250
	a. Red on white	£4250

POSTAL FISCALS

Authorised for use from 1 January 1880 until 1 July 1892

CANCELLATIONS. Beware of stamps which have had pen-cancellations cleaned off and then had faked postmarks applied. Used prices quoted are for postally used examples between the above dates.

F 1

F 2

1866–68.

A. No wmk. P 13.

F1	**F 1**	1d. blue	60·00	15·00
F2		6d. deep violet	70·00	70·00
F3		1s. blue-green	80·00	38·00
F4		2s. brown	£160	£110
F5		2s.6d. dull red	£160	85·00
F6		5s. yellow	£375	£120
F6*a*		6s. light brown	£750	
F7		10s. green	£600	£225
F8		20s. rose	£800	£350

B. Wmk F **2**. P 13.

F9	**F 1**	1d. blue	32·00	35·00
F10		6d. deep violet	70·00	70·00
F11		6d. blue	£150	£110
F12		1s. blue-green	80·00	55·00
F13		2s. brown	£160	80·00
F13*a*		5s. yellow	£375	£130
F14		10s. green	£600	£225
F15		20s. rose	£800	£350

F 3

F 3a

1871–72. P 12 or 13.

A. Wmk Large Crown and Q, Wmk F **3a**.

F16	**F 3**	1d. mauve	26·00	12·00
F17		6d. red-brown	55·00	30·00
F18		1s. green	70·00	30·00
F19		2s. blue	90·00	38·00
F20		2s.6d. brick-red	£140	75·00
F21		5s. orange-brown	£180	85·00
F22		10s. brown	£400	£150
F23		20s. rose	£700	£225

B. No wmk. *Blue burelé band at back.*

F24	**F 3**	1d. mauve	30·00	14·00
F25		6d. red-brown	55·00	30·00
F26		6d. mauve	£130	60·00
F27		1s. green	70·00	30·00
F28		2s. blue	£110	85·00
F29		2s.6d. vermilion	£170	80·00
F30		5s. yellow-brown	£250	90·00
F31		10s. brown	£425	£170
F32		20s. rose	£700	£225

F 4

F 5

1878–79.

A. No wmk. *Lilac burelé band at back.* P 12.

F33	**F 4**	1d. violet	80·00	32·00

B. Wmk Crown and Q, W **5**. P 12.

F34	**F 4**	1d. violet	35·00	24·00

Stamps as Type F **5** may not have been issued until after 1 July 1892 when the proper use of duty stamps for postal service was terminated but there are several examples which appear to have genuinely passed through the post during the 1890's. Unless they are dated during 1892 their postal use was certainly unauthorised although they may have been accepted.

Queensland became part of the Commonwealth of Australia on 1 January 1901.

SOUTH AUSTRALIA

PRICES FOR STAMPS ON COVER

Nos. 1/3	*from* × 3
No. 4	†
Nos. 5/12	*from* × 2
Nos. 13/18	*from* × 3
Nos. 19/43	*from* × 4
Nos. 44/9b	—
Nos. 50/110	*from* × 3
No. 111	—
Nos. 112/34	*from* × 6
Nos. 135/45	*from* × 3
Nos. 146/66	*from* × 5
Nos. 167/70a	*from* × 10
Nos. 171/2a	—
Nos. 173/94a	*from* × 12
Nos. 195/208	—
Nos. 229/31	*from* × 12
No. 232	—
Nos. 233/42	*from* × 12
Nos. 268/75	*from* × 30
Nos. 276/9	—
Nos. 280/8	*from* × 30
Nos. 289/92	—
Nos. 293/304	*from* × 15
No. 305	—
Nos. O1/13	—
Nos. O14/36	*from* × 20
Nos. O37/42	*from* × 5
Nos. O43/4	*from* × 50
Nos. O45/7	—
Nos. O48/52	*from* × 30
No. O53	—
Nos. O54/85	*from* × 50
Nos. O86/7	—

SPECIMEN OVERPRINTS. Those listed are from U.P.U. distributions between 1889 and 1895. Further "Specimen" overprints exist, but these were used for other purposes.

PERKINS BACON "CANCELLED". For notes on these handstamps, showing "CANCELLED" between horizontal bars forming an oval, see Catalogue Introduction.

1

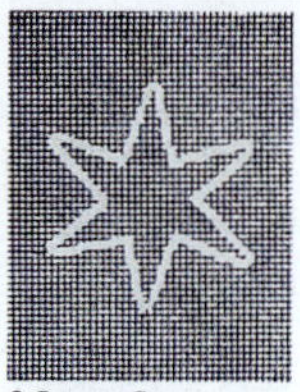
2 Large Star

(Eng Wm Humphrys. Recess P.B.)

1855 (1 Jan–Oct). *Printed in London.* W **2**. Imperf.

1	**1**	1d. dark green (Oct 1855) (H/S "CANCELLED" in oval £10000)	£4750	£475
2		2d. rose-carmine (*shades*) (H/S "CANCELLED" in oval £10000)	£550	80·00
3		6d. deep blue (Oct 1855) (H/S "CANCELLED" in oval £10000)	£2250	£160

Prepared and sent to the Colony, but not issued.

4	**1**	1s. Violet (H/S "CANCELLED" in oval £14000)	£12000	

A printing of 500,000 of these 1s. stamps was delivered, but, as the colour was liable to be confused with that of the 6d. stamp, this stock was destroyed on 5 June 1857. It is believed that surviving examples of No. 4 come from Perkins Bacon remainders which came on to the market in the late 1890s.

Proofs of the 1d. and 6d. without wmk exist, and these are found with forged star watermarks added, and are sometimes offered as originals.

For reprints of the above and later issues, see note after No. 194.

1856–58. *Printed by Printer of Stamps, Adelaide, from Perkins, Bacon plates.* W **2**. Imperf.

5	**1**	1d. deep yellow-green (15.6.58)	£6500	£550
6		1d. yellow-green (11.10.58)	£5500	£650
7		2d. orange-red (23.4.56)	£1500	80·00
8		2d. blood-red (14.11.56)	£1300	60·00
		a. Printed on both sides	†	£950
9		2d. red (shades) (29.10.57)	£650	40·00
		a. Printed on both sides	†	£750
10		6d. slate-blue (7.57)	£2500	£170
11		1s. red-orange (8.7.57)	—	£500
12		1s. orange (11.6.58)	£4500	£400

1858–59. Rouletted. *(This first rouletted issue has the same colours as the local imperf issue).* W **2**.

13	**1**	1d. yellow-green (8.1.59)	£700	60·00
14		1d. light yellow-green (18.3.59)	£700	65·00
		a. Imperf between (pair)		
15		2d. red (17.2.59)	£130	22·00
		a. Printed on both sides	†	£750
17		6d. slate-blue (12.12.58)	£475	42·00
18		1s. orange (18.3.59)	£1000	48·00
		a. Printed on both sides	†	£1400

3

4

(5)

1860–69. Second rouletted issue, *printed (with the exception of No. 24) in colours only found rouletted or perforated. Surch with T* **5** *(Nos. 35/7).* W **2**.

19	**1**	1d. bright yellow-green (22.4.61)	70·00	35·00
20		1d. dull blue-green (17.12.63)	65·00	35·00
21		1d. sage-green	85·00	40·00
22		1d. pale sage-green (27.5.65)	70·00	
23		1d. deep green (1864)	£325	75·00
24		1d. deep yellow-green (1869)	£130	
24*a*		2d. pale red	90·00	4·00
		b. Printed on both sides	†	£425
25		2d. pale vermilion (3.2.63)	75·00	4·00
26		2d. bright vermilion (19.8.64)	70·00	3·50
		a. Imperf between (horiz pair)	£1700	£475
27	**3**	4d. dull violet (24.1.67)	80·00	25·00
28	**1**	6d. violet-blue (19.3.60)	£180	7·00
29		6d. greenish blue (11.2.63)	90·00	4·00
30		6d. dull ultramarine (25.4.64)	85·00	4·00
		a. Imperf between (horiz pair)	†	£475
31		6d. violet-ultramarine (11.4.68)	£170	6·00
32		6d. dull blue (26.8.65)	£130	6·50
		a. Imperf between (pair)	†	£900
33		6d. Prussian blue (7.9.69)	£600	50·00
33*a*		6d. indigo	—	55·00
34	**4**	9d. grey-lilac (24.12.60)	75·00	9·00
		a. Imperf between (horiz pair)	†	£1700
35		10d. on 9d. orange-red (B.) (20.7.66)	£250	38·00
36		10d. on 9d. yellow (B.) (29.7.67)	£400	28·00
37		10d. on 9d. yellow (Blk.) (14.8.69)	£2000	55·00
		a. Surch inverted at the top	†	£4000
		b. Printed on both sides	†	£1000
		c. Roul × perf 10	†	—
38	**1**	1s. yellow (25.10.61)	£500	28·00
		a. Imperf between (vert pair)	†	£1800
39		1s. grey-brown (10.4.63)	£170	21·00
40		1s. dark grey-brown (26.5.63)	£150	21·00
41		1s. chestnut (25.8.63)	£160	11·00
42		1s. lake-brown (27.3.65)	£120	12·00
		a. Imperf between (horiz pair)	†	£650
43	**3**	2s. rose-carmine (24.1.67)	£200	30·00
		a. Imperf between (vert pair)	†	£1200

1868–71. *Remainders of old stock subsequently perforated by the 11½–12½ machine.*

(a) Imperf stamps. P 11½–12½.

44	**1**	2d. pale vermilion (Feb 1868)	—	£900
45		2d. vermilion (18.3.68)	—	£1000

(b) Rouletted stamps. P 11½–12½.

46	**1**	1d. bright green (9.11.69)	—	£550
47		2d. pale vermilion (15.8.68)	£1500	£425

48		6d. Prussian blue (8.11.69)	—	£250
		aa. Horiz pair perf all round, roul between		
48*a*		6d. indigo	—	£325
49	4	9d. grey-lilac (29.3.71)	£1600	£180
		a. Perf × roulette	—	£200
49*b*	1	1s. lake-brown (23.5.70)		

1867–70. W **2**. P 11½–12½ × roulette.

50	1	1d. pale bright green (2.11.67)	£200	24·00
51		1d. bright green (1868)	£180	24·00
52		1d. grey-green (26.1.70)	£200	26·00
		a. Imperf between (horiz pair)		
53		1d. blue-green (29.11.67)	£300	45·00
54	3	4d. dull violet (July 1868)	£1600	£150
55		4d. dull purple (1869)	—	£110
56	1	6d. bright pale blue (29.5.67)	£475	19·00
57		6d. Prussian blue (30.7.67)	£425	19·00
		a. Printed on both sides		
58		6d. indigo (1.8.69)	£550	25·00
59	4	10d. on 9d. yellow (B.) (2.2.69)	£700	35·00
		a. Printed on both sides	—	£800
60	1	1s. chestnut (April 1868)	£275	19·00
61		1s. lake-brown (3.3.69)	£275	19·00

NOTE. The stamps perf 11½, 12½, or compound of the two, are here combined in one list, as both perforations are on the one machine, and all the varieties may be found in each sheet of stamps. This method of classifying the perforations by the machines is by far the most simple and convenient.

(6)

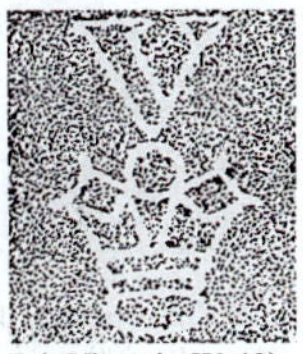
7 (=Victoria W 19)

1868–79. *Surch with T* **6** *(Nos. 66/8)*. W **2**. P 11½–12½.

62	1	1d. pale bright green (8.2.68)	£190	38·00
63		1d. grey-green (18.2.68)	£160	50·00
64		1d. dark green (20.3.68)	90·00	22·00
		a. Printed on both sides	†	£850
65		1d. deep yellow-green (28.6.72)	85·00	22·00
		a. Imperf between (horiz pair)	†	£1800
66	3	3d. on 4d. Prussian blue (Blk.) (7.2.71)	—	£850
67		3d. on 4d. sky-blue (Blk.) (12.8.70)	£300	15·00
		a. Imperf		
		b. Rouletted	—	£800
68		3d. on 4d. deep ultramarine (Blk.) (9.72)	80·00	9·00
		a. Surch double	†	£3500
		b. Additional surch on back	†	£2750
		c. Surch omitted	£22000	£11000
70		4d. dull purple (1.2.68)	70·00	15·00
		a. Imperf between (horiz pair)	†	—
71		4d. dull violet (1868)	65·00	8·00
72	1	6d. bright pale blue (23.2.68)	£350	11·00
73		6d. Prussian blue (29.9.69)	£130	7·00
		a. Perf 11½×imperf (horiz pair)	†	£1300
74		6d. indigo (1869)	£150	17·00
75	4	9d. claret (7.72)	£120	8·00
76		9d. bright mauve (1.11.72)	£120	8·00
		a. Printed on both sides	†	£750
77		9d. red-purple (15.1.74)	70·00	8·00
78		10d. on 9d. yellow (B.) (15.8.68)	£1200	40·00
		a. Wmk Crown and S A (W **10**) (1868)	—	£1100
79		10d. on 9d. yellow (Blk.) (13.9.69)	£250	45·00
80	1	1s. lake-brown (9.68)	£160	12·00
81		1s. chestnut (8.10.72)	£130	17·00
82		1s. dark red-brown	£100	12·00
83		1s. red-brown (6.1.69)	£110	12·00
84	3	2s. pale rose-pink (10.10.69)	£1200	£170
85		2s. deep rose-pink (8.69)	—	£110
86		2s. crimson-carmine (16.10.69)	£100	19·00
87		2s. carmine (1869)	90·00	13·00
		a. Printed on both sides	†	£425

No. 68c comes from two sheets on which, it is believed, some stamps showed the surcharge omitted and others the surcharge double. One of the used examples of No. 68c is known postmarked in 1875 and many of the others in 1879.

No. 78a was a trial printing made to test the perforating machine on the new D.L.R. paper.

1870–71. W **2**. P 10.

88	1	1d. grey-green (6.70)	£160	17·00
89		1d. pale bright green (9.8.70)	£160	17·00
90		1d. bright green (1871)	£140	17·00
91	3	3d. on 4d dull ultramarine (R.) (6.8.70)	£600	85·00
92		3d. on 4d pale ultram (Blk.) (14.2.71)	£350	23·00
93		3d. on 4d ultramarine (Blk.) (14.8.71)	£150	25·00
93*a*		3d. on 4d. Prussian blue (Blk.) (16.12.71)	—	£1000
94		4d. dull lilac (1870)	£120	11·00
95		4d. dull purple (1871)	£110	11·00
96	1	6d. bright blue (19.6.70)	£180	17·00
97		6d. indigo (11.10.71)	£250	16·00
98		1s. chestnut (4.1.71)	£160	29·00

1870–73. W **2**. P 10×11½–12½, 11½–12½×10, or compound.

99	1	1d. pale bright green (11.10.70)	£180	15·00
		a. Printed on both sides		
100		1d. grey-green	£170	16·00
101		1d. deep green (19.6.71)	95·00	11·00
102	3	3d. on 4d. pale ultram (Blk.) (9.11.70)	£300	60·00
103		4d. dull lilac (11.5.72)	—	20·00
104		4d. slate-lilac (5.3.73)	£130	18·00
105	1	6d. Prussian blue (2.3.70)	£150	8·00
106		6d. bright Prussian blue (26.10.70)	£160	10·00
107	4	10d. on 9d. yellow (Blk.) (1.70)	£140	38·00
108	1	1s. chestnut (17.6.71)	£225	60·00
109	3	2s. rose-pink (24.4.71)	—	£190
110		2s. carmine (2.3.72)	£160	42·00

1871 (17 July). W **7**. P 10.

111	3	4d. dull lilac	£2500	£225
		a. Printed on both sides	†	£3500

8 Broad Star

(9)

1876–1900. *Surch with T* **9** *(Nos. 118/21)*. W **8**.

(*a*) P 11½–12½.

112	3	3d. on 4d. ultramarine (1.6.79)	90·00	23·00
		a. Surch double	†	£1600
113		4d. violet-slate (15.3.79)	£110	14·00
114		4d. plum (16.4.80)	60·00	7·00
115		4d. deep mauve (8.6.82)	60·00	5·50
116	1	6d. indigo (2.12.76)	£110	4·75
		a. Imperf between (horiz pair)	†	—
117		6d. Prussian blue (7.78)	80·00	4·25
118	4	8d. on 9d. brown-orange (7.76)	£110	7·00
119		8d. on 9d. burnt umber (1880)	£120	7·00
120		8d. on 9d. brown (9.3.80)	£120	7·00
		a. Imperf between (vert pair)	£900	
121		8d. on 9d. grey-brown (10.5.81)	95·00	7·00
		a. Surch double	—	£1600
122		9d. purple (9.3.80)	60·00	8·50
		a. Printed on both sides	—	£450
123		9d. rose-lilac (21.8.80)	16·00	3·75
124		9d. rose-lilac (large holes) (26.5.00)	10·00	3·50
125	1	1s. red-brown (3.11.77)	50·00	2·75
		a. Imperf between (horiz pair)	†	£550
126		1s. reddish lake-brown (1880)	50·00	3·00
127		1s. lake-brown (9.1.83)	55·00	2·75
		a. Printed double		
128		1s. Vandyke brown (1891)	65·00	8·00
129		1s. dull brown (1891)	48·00	3·00
130		1s. chocolate (large holes) (6.5.97)	25·00	3·00
		a. Imperf vert (horiz pair)	£250	
131		1s. sepia (large holes) (22.5.00)	25·00	3·00
		a. Imperf between (vert pair)	£275	
132	3	2s. carmine (15.2.77)	38·00	5·00
		a. Imperf between (horiz pair)	†	£1500
		b. Imperf (pair)		
133		2s. rose-carmine (1885)	42·00	6·50
134		2s. rose-carmine (*large holes*) (6.12.98)	30·00	6·50

The perforation with larger, clean-cut holes resulted from the fitting of new pins to the machine.

(*b*) P 10.

135	1	6d. Prussian blue (11.11.79)	£110	17·00
136		6d. bright blue (1879)	£130	17·00
136*a*		1s. reddish lake-brown	£300	

(*c*) P 10×11½–12½, 11½–12½×10, or compound.

137	3	4d. violet-slate (21.5.79)	£110	19·00
138		4d. dull purple (4.10.79)	45·00	2·75
139	1	6d. Prussian blue (29.12.77)	70·00	2·50
140		6d. bright blue	90·00	5·50
141		6d. bright ultramarine	60·00	2·50
142		1s. reddish lake-brown (9.2.85)	90·00	10·00
143		1s. dull brown (29.6.86)	£120	12·00
144	3	2s. carmine (27.12.77)	65·00	6·00
145		2s. rose-carmine (1887)	60·00	5·50
		a. Imperf between (horiz pair)	†	£900

10

11

12

1901–02. Wmk Crown SA (wide). W **10**. P 11½–12½ (large holes).

146	4	9d. claret (1.2.02)	18·00	18·00
147	1	1s. dark brown (12.6.01)	22·00	12·00
148		1s. dark reddish brown (1902)	24·00	13·00
		a. Imperf horiz (vert pair)	£1500	£1500
149		1s. red-brown (aniline) (18.7.02)	22·00	16·00
150	3	2s. crimson (29.8.01)	30·00	15·00
151		2s. carmine	25·00	11·00

(Plates and electrotypes by D.L.R. Printed in Adelaide)

1868–76. W **10**.

(*a*) Rouletted.

152	12	2d. deep brick-red (8.68)	85·00	4·50
153		2d. pale orange-red (5.10.68)	80·00	2·75
		a. Printed on both sides	†	£475
		b. Imperf between (horiz pair)	†	£800
		c. Imperf between (vert pair)	†	£1200

(*b*) P 11½–12½.

154	11	1d. blue-green (10.1.75)	95·00	20·00
155	12	2d. pale orange-red (5.5.69)	£950	£200

(*c*) P 11½–12½ × roulette.

156	12	2d. pale orange-red (20.8.69)	—	£150

(*d*) P 10 × roulette.

157	12	2d. pale orange-red (7.5.70)	£325	30·00

(*e*) P 10.

158	11	1d. blue-green (4.75)	55·00	6·00
159	12	2d. brick-red (4.70)	27·00	1·50
160		2d. orange-red (1.7.70)	15·00	1·00
		a. Printed on both sides	†	£375

(*f*) P 10×11½–12½, 11½–12½×10, or compound.

161	11	1d. blue-green (27.8.75)	85·00	23·00
162	12	2d. brick-red (19.1.71)	£450	16·00
163		2d. orange-red (3.2.71)	£120	15·00
		a. Imperf (8.76)	£1000	£1000

1869. Wmk Large Star W **2**.

(*a*) Rouletted.

164	12	2d. orange-red (13.3.69)	90·00	19·00

(*b*) P 11½–12½ × roulette.

165	12	2d. orange-red (1.8.69)	£2000	£100

(*c*) P 11½–12½.

165*a*	12	2d. orange-red (7.69)	—	£1200

1871 (15 July). Wmk V and Crown, W **7**. P 10.

166	12	2d. brick-red	90·00	26·00

13

(14)

1876–1904. Wmk Crown SA (close). W **13**.

(*a*) P 10 (1876–85).

167	11	1d. blue-green (9.2.76)	18·00	60
		a. Yellowish green (11.78)	19·00	40
		b. Deep green (11.79)	17·00	30
		ba. Imperf between (horiz pair)		
		bb. Printed double	†	—
168	12	2d. orange-red (8.76)	20·00	40
		a. Dull brick-red (21.5.77)	21·00	40
		b. Blood-red (31.10.79)	£225	3·50
		c. Pale red (4.85)	12·00	40

(*b*) P 10×11½–12½, 11½–12½×10 or compound (1877–80).

169	11	1d. deep green (11.2.80)	48·00	5·50
		a. Blue-green (2.3.80)	26·00	4·50
170	12	2d. orange-red (4.9.77)	£130	6·00
		a. Dull brick-red (6.80)	£130	6·00

(*c*) P 11½–12½ (1877–84).

171	11	1d. blue-green (2.84)	—	£130
172	12	2d. orange-red (14.9.77)	—	£130
		a. Blood-red (1.4.80)	—	£130

(*d*) P 15 (1893).

173	11	1d. green (8.5.93)	16·00	1·00
174	12	2d. pale orange (9.2.93)	16·00	1·00
		a. Orange-red	16·00	1·00
		b. Imperf between (vert pair)	£500	

(*e*) P 13 (1895–1903).

175	11	1d. pale green (11.1.95)	7·50	20
		a. Green	7·50	20
		b. Imperf between (vert pair)		
176		1d. rosine (8.8.99)	6·00	40
		a. Scarlet (23.12.03)	5·00	50
		b. Deep red	5·00	50
177	12	2d. pale orange (19.1.95)	8·00	10
		a. Orange-red (9.5.95)	11·00	10
178		2d. bright violet (10.10.99)	4·25	10

(*f*) P 12×11½ (comb) (1904).

179	11	1d. rosine (2.2.04)	9·00	80
		a. Scarlet (25.7.04)	7·00	40
180	12	2d. bright violet (11.10.04)	7·50	70

Examples of the 1d. pale green with thicker lettering come from a worn plate.

1882 (1 Jan). *No. 167 surch with T* **14**.

181	11	½d. on 1d. blue-green	13·00	8·00

15

16

17

18

1883–99. W **13** (sideways on ½d.).

(*a*) P 10 (1883–95).

182	15	½d. chocolate (1.3.83)	8·00	1·50
		a. Imperf between (horiz pair)	†	£950
		b. Red-brown (4.4.89)	5·50	1·50
		c. Brown (1895)	4·50	1·50
183	16	3d. sage-green (12.86)	17·00	2·25
		a. Olive-green (6.6.90)	15·00	3·25
		b. Deep green (12.4.93)	11·00	3·25
		s. Optd "Specimen"	30·00	
184	17	4d. pale violet (3.90)	26·00	2·75
		a. Aniline violet (3.1.93)	26·00	3·50
		s. Optd "Specimen"	35·00	
185	18	6d. pale blue (4.87)	24·00	2·25
		a. Blue (5.5.87)	24·00	1·00
		s. Optd "Specimen"	30·00	

(*b*) P 10×11½–12½, 11½–12½×10 or compound (1891).

186	15	½d. red-brown (25.9.91)	16·00	5·50
		a. Imperf between (horiz pair)	£180	

		(c) P 11½–12½ (1890).		
187	15	½d. red-brown (12.10.90)	18·00	2·75
		(d) P 15 (1893–94).		
188	15	½d. pale brown (1.93)	6·50	1·00
		a. Deep brown	6·50	1·00
		b. Imperf between (horiz pair)	£180	
		c. Perf 12½ between (pair)	£190	45·00
189	17	4d. purple (1.1.94)	24·00	3·25
		a. Slate-violet	24·00	3·25
190	18	6d. blue (20.11.93)	42·00	3·50
		(e) P 13 (1895–99).		
191	15	½d. pale brown (9.95)	2·75	30
		a. Deep brown (19.3.97)	4·50	30
192	16	3d. pale olive-green (26.7.97)	9·00	2·25
		a. Deep olive-green (27.11.99)	5·00	2·25
193	17	4d. violet (21.1.96)	6·00	60
194	18	6d. pale blue (3.96)	7·50	1·50
		a. Blue	7·50	1·50

REPRINTS. In 1884, and in later years, reprints on paper wmkd Crown SA, W **10**, were made of Nos. 1, 2, 3, 4, 12, 13, 14, 15, 19, 24, 27, 28, 32, 33, 34, 35, 36, 37, 38, 40, 43, 44, 49a, 53, 65, 67, 67 with surcharge in red, 70, 71, 72, 73, 78, 79, 81, 83, 86, 90, 118, 119, 120, 121, 122, 155, 158, 159, 164, 181, 182. They are overprinted "REPRINT".

In 1889 examples of the reprints for Nos. 1/3, 12, 15, 19, 27, 32/8, 44, 67, 67 surcharged in red, 70/1, 73, 83, 86, 118, 121/2, 158/9, 164 and 181/2, together with No. 141 overprinted "Specimen", were supplied to the U.P.U. for distribution.

19

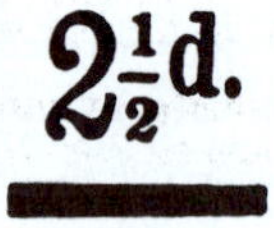

(20)

(21)

(Plates and electrotypes by D.L.R. Printed in Adelaide)

1886 (20 Dec)–**96**. *T* **19** *(inscr* "POSTAGE & REVENUE"*)*. W **13**. Parts of two or more wmks, on each stamp, sometimes sideways. P 10.

195	2s.6d. mauve	60·00	11·00
	a. Perf 11½–12½. *Dull violet*	45·00	8·00
	bb. Bright aniline violet	48·00	9·00
196	5s. rose-pink	80·00	18·00
	a. Perf 11½–12½	60·00	18·00
	ab. Rose-carmine	60·00	20·00
197	10s. green	£170	55·00
	a. Perf 11½–12½	£150	50·00
198	15s. brownish yellow	£425	£275
	a. Perf 11½–12½	£475	£180
199	£1 blue	£375	£140
	a. Perf 11½–12½	£325	£130
200	£2 Venetian red	£1800	£425
	a. Perf 11½–12½	£1600	£375
201	50s. dull pink	£2500	£550
	a. Perf 11½–12½	£2250	£450
202	£3 sage green	£2750	£500
	a. Perf 11½–12½	£2500	£450
203	£4 lemon	£5000	
	a. Perf 11½–12½	£4250	£800
204	£5 grey	£4250	
	a. Perf 11½–12½	£4250	
205	£5 brown (P 11½–12½) (1896)	£2500	£800
206	£10 bronze	£4250	£1000
	a. Perf 11½–12½	£3250	£900
207	£15 silver	£13000	
	a. Perf 11½–12½	£12000	£1500
208	£20 claret	£15000	
	a. Perf 11½–12½	£14000	£1600
195s/208s Optd "Specimen" *Set of* 14		£750	

Variations exist in the length of the words and shape of the letters of the value inscription.

The 2s.6d. dull violet, 5s. rose-pink, 10s., £1 and £5 brown exist perf 11½–12½ with either large or small holes; the 2s.6d. aniline, 5s. rose-carmine, 15s., £2 and 50s. with large holes only and the remainder only with small holes.

Stamps perforated 11½–12½ small holes, are, generally speaking, rather rarer than those with the 1895 (large holes) gauge.

Stamps perf 10 were issued on 20 Dec 1886. Stamps perf 11½–12½ (small holes) are known with earliest dates covering the period from June 1890 to Feb 1896. Earliest dates of stamps with large holes range from July 1896 to May 1902.

1891 (1 Jan)–**93**. *T* **17/18** *surch with T* **20/1**. W **13**.

		(a) P 10.		
229	17	2½d. on 4d. pale green (Br.)	7·50	2·50
		a. Fraction bar omitted	95·00	75·00
		b. Deep green	8·00	1·75
		ba. Fraction bar omitted	95·00	70·00
		bb. "2" and "½" closer together	26·00	18·00
		bc. Imperf between (horiz pair)		
		bd. Imperf between (vert pair)	†	£1400
		s. Optd "Specimen"	30·00	
230	18	5d. on 6d. pale brn (C.)	17·00	5·00
		a. Deep brown	17·00	4·75
		b. No stop after "5D"	£160	
		s. Optd "Specimen"	30·00	
		(b) P 10×11½–12½ or 11½–12½×10.		
231	17	2½d. on 4d. pale green (Br.)	29·00	4·75
		a. Deep green	29·00	4·75
		(c) P 11½–12½.		
232	17	2½d. on 4d. deep green	42·00	55·00
		(d) P 15.		
233	17	2½d. on 4d. green (14.10.93)	29·00	2·75
		a. Fraction bar omitted		
		b. "2" and "½d." closer	70·00	22·00

22 Red Kangaroo

23

24 G.P.O., Adelaide

(Des M. Tannenberg, plates by D.L.R.)

1894 (1 Mar)–**1906**. W **13**.

		(a) P 15.		
234	22	2½d. violet-blue	24·00	3·25
235	23	5d. brown-purple	27·00	3·50
234s/5s Optd "Specimen" *Set of* 2			60·00	
		(b) P 13.		
236	22	2½d. violet-blue (11.2.95)	20·00	70
237		2½d. indigo (25.3.98)	6·00	1·75
238	23	5d. Brown-purple (1.96)	7·00	1·00
		a. Purple	7·00	75
		(c) P 12×11½ (comb).		
239	22	2½d. indigo (4.7.06)	8·50	3·00
240	23	5d. dull purple (1.05)	15·00	2·00

(Typo D.L.R.)

1899 (27 Dec)–**1905**. W **13**.

		(a) P 13.		
241	24	½d. yellow-green	3·00	70
		(b) P 12×11½ (comb).		
242	24	½d. yellow-green (7.05)	4·00	1·50

25

The measurements given indicate the length of the value inscription in the bottom label. The dates are those of the earliest known postmarks.

1902–04. *As T* **19**, *but top tablet as T* **25** *(thin* "POSTAGE"*)*. W **13**.

	(a) P 11½–12½.		
268	3d. olive-green (18½ mm) (1.8.02)	8·50	2·00
	a. Wmk sideways	†	£1600
269	4d. red-orange (17 mm) (29.11.02)	16·00	2·50
270	6d. blue-green (16–16½ mm) (29.11.02)	8·00	2·00
271	8d. ultramarine (19 mm) (25.4.02)	8·50	9·00
272	8d. ultramarine (16½ mm) (22.3.04)	12·00	9·00
	a. "EIGNT" (R.2/9)	£1400	£2500
273	9d. rosy lake (19.9.02)	9·00	5·50
	a. Imperf between (vert pair)	£1100	
	b. Imperf between (horiz pair)		
274	10d. dull yellow (29.11.02)	14·00	10·00
275	1s. brown (18.8.02)	18·00	5·00
	a. Imperf between (horiz pair)		
	b. Imperf between (vert pair)	£1200	
	c. "POSTAGE" and value in red-brown	£900	£900
276	2s.6d. pale violet (19.9.02)	50·00	25·00
	a. Bright violet (2.2.03)	27·00	13·00
277	5s. rose (17.10.02)	80·00	50·00
278	10s. green (1.11.02)	£140	75·00
279	£1 blue (1.11.02)	£350	£190
	(b) P 12.		
280	3d. olive-green (20 mm) (15.4.04)	17·00	2·75
	a. "POSTAGE" omitted; value below "AUSTRALIA"	£1900	
281	4d. orange-red (17½–18 mm) (18.2.03)	15·00	2·25
282	6d. blue-green (15 mm) (14.11.03)	25·00	7·00
283	9d. rosy lake (2.12.03)	75·00	14·00

No. 280a comes from the bottom row of the sheet. Other stamps show the value below "AUSTRALIA" with "POSTAGE" over the bottom frame (*Price* £600, *unused*).

PRINTER. Stamp printing in Adelaide ceased in 1909 when the Printer of Stamps, J. B. Cooke, was appointed head of the Commonwealth Stamp Printing Branch in Melbourne. From 9 March 1909 further printings of current South Australia stamps were made in Melbourne.

26

V

X

In Type X the letters in the bottom line are slightly larger than in Type V, especially the "A", "S" and "P".

Y

Z

In Type Z the letters "S" and "G" are more open than in Type Y.

Nos. 196/a and 277 are similar to Type Y with all letters thick and regular and the last "S" has the top curve rounded instead of being slightly flattened.

1904–11. *As T* **19**, *but top tablet as T* **26** *(thick* "POSTAGE"*)*. W **13**. P 12.

284	6d. blue-green (27.4.04)	19·00	3·00
	a. Imperf between (vert pair)	£3000	
285	8d. bright ultramarine (4.7.05)	10·00	8·00
	a. Value closer (15¼ mm)	35·00	22·00
	b. Dull ultramarine (2.4.08)	21·00	5·00
	ba. Ditto. Value closer (15¼ mm)	65·00	17·00
286	9d. rosy lake (17–17¼ mm) (18.7.04)	15·00	4·75
	a. Value 16½–16¾ mm (2.06)	40·00	6·50
	b. Brown-lake. Perf 12½ small holes (11.3.11)	14·00	16·00
287	10d. dull yellow (8.07)	16·00	15·00
	a. Imperf between (horiz pair)	£1300	£1400
	b. Imperf between (vert pair)	£2500	
288	1s. brown (12.4.04)	23·00	3·25
	a. Imperf between (vert pair)	£1100	
	b. Imperf between (horiz pair)	£1300	
289	2s.6d. bright violet (V.) (14.7.05)	60·00	20·00
	a. Dull violet (X) (8.06)	60·00	20·00
290	5s. rose-scarlet (Y) (8.04)	55·00	35·00
	a. Scarlet (Z) (8.06)	55·00	35·00
	b. Pale rose. Perf 12½ (small holes) (Z) (6.10)	80·00	45·00
291	10s. green (26.8.08)	£140	£140
292	£1 blue (29.12.04)	£250	£140
	a. Perf 12½ (small holes) (6.10)	£150	£130

The "value closer" variety on the 8d. occurs six times in the sheet of 60. The value normally measures 16½ mm but in the variety it is 15¼ mm.

The 9d., 5s. and £1, perf 12½ (small holes), are late printings made in 1910–11 to use up the Crown SA paper.

No. 286*b* has the value as Type C of the 9d. on Crown over A paper.

27

1905–11. W **27**. P 12×11½ (new comb machine).

293	24	½d. pale green (4.07)	6·50	1·25
		a. Yellow-green	6·00	1·25
		b. Thin ready gummed paper (1912)	8·00	3·00
		ba. Mixed perf 12×11½ and 12½	£750	
294	11	1d. rosine (2.12.05)	5·00	20
		a. Scarlet (4.11)	4·00	1·25
295	12	2d. bright violet (2.2.06)	11·00	20
		aa. Imperf three sides (horiz pair)	£1500	
		a. Mauve (4.08)	5·50	20
296	22	2½d. indigo-blue (14.9.10)	9·00	8·50
297	23	5d. brown-purple (11.3.08)	20·00	4·50

No. 295aa is perforated at foot.

Three types of the 9d., perf 12½, distinguishable by the distance between "NINE" and "PENCE".

A. Distance 1¾ mm. B. Distance 2¼ mm. C. Distance 2½ mm.

1906–12. *T* **19** ("POSTAGE" *thick as T* **26**). W **27**. P 12 or 12½ (small holes).

298	3d. sage-green (19 mm) (26.6.06)	9·00	3·75
	a. Imperf between (horiz pair)	†	£4250
	b. Perf 12½. *Sage-green* (17 mm) (9.12.09)	9·00	4·00
	c. Perf 12½. *Deep olive* (20 mm) (7.10)	48·00	11·00
	d. Perf 12½. *Yellow-olive* (19 mm) (16.12.11)	55·00	25·00
	da. Perf 12½. *Bright olive-green* (19–19¾ mm) Thin ready gummed paper (8.9.11)	12·00	16·00
	e. Perf 11 (17 mm) (1910)	£900	£650
299	4d. orange-red (10.9.06)	12·00	2·50
	a. Orange	12·00	2·50
	b. Perf 12½. *Orange*	12·00	4·75
	c. Thin ready gummed paper (19.8.12)	13·00	16·00
300	6d. blue-green (1.9.06)	8·00	2·25
	a. Perf 12½ (21.4.10)	8·00	4·75
	ab. Perf 12½. Imperf between (vert pair)	£1200	£1300
	b. Thin ready gummed paper (3.12)	9·00	11·00
301	8d. bright ultramarine (P 12½) (8.09)	10·00	15·00
	a. Value closer (8.09)	42·00	60·00
302	9d. brown-lake (3.2.06)	13·00	4·25
	a. Imperf between (vert pair)	£950	
	aa. Imperf between (horiz strip of three)	£2750	
	b. Deep lake (9.5.08)	42·00	6·50
	c. Perf 12½. *Lake* (A) (5.9.09)	11·00	5·50
	d. Perf 12½. *Lake* (B) ((7.09)	25·00	6·00
	e. Perf 12½. *Brown-lake*	25·00	6·50
	ea. Perf 12½. *Deep lake*. Thin paper (C)	24·00	6·00
	f. Perf 11 (1909)	†	£1500
303	1s. brown (30.5.06)	12·00	4·75
	a. Imperf between (horiz pair)	£1800	
	aa. Imperf between (vert pair)	£1500	
	b. Perf 12½ (10.3.10)	10·00	5·50
	c. Thin ready gummed paper (4.8.11)	10·00	7·00
304	2s.6d. bright violet (X) (10.6.09)	55·00	16·00
	a. Perf 12½. *Pale violet* (X) (6.10)	55·00	19·00
	ab. Perf 12½. *Deep purple* (X) Thin ready gummed paper (15.11.12)	75·00	50·00
305	5s. bright rose (P 12½) (Z) Thin ready gummed paper (24.4.11)	85·00	80·00

The "value closer" variety of the 8d. occurred 11 times in the sheet of 60 in the later printing only. On No. 301 the value measures 16½ mm while on No. 301a it is 15¼ mm.

The 1s. brown, perf compound of 11½ and 12½, formerly listed is now omitted, as it must have been perforated by the 12 machine, which in places varied from 11½ to 13. The 4d. has also been reported with a similar perforation.

STAMP BOOKLETS

There are very few surviving examples of Nos. SB1/4. Listings are provided for those believed to have been issued with prices quoted for those known still to exist.

1904 (1 Jan)–**09**. *Black on red cover as No.* SB1 *of New South Wales. Stapled.*

SB1 £1 booklet containing two hundred and forty 1d. in four blocks of 30 and two blocks of 60

a. Red on pink cover (1909)

b. Blue on pink cover £15000

1904 (1 Jan). *Black on grey cover as No.* SB1. *Stapled.*

SB2 £1 booklet containing one hundred and twenty 2d. in four blocks of 30

1910 (May). *Black on cream cover as No.* SB3 *of New South Wales. Stapled.*

SB3 2s. booklet containing eleven ½d. (No. 262A), either in block of 6 plus block of 5 or block of 11, and eighteen 1d. (No. 264A), either in three blocks of 6 or block of 6 plus block of 12

Unsold stock of No. SB3 was uprated with one additional ½d. in May 1911.

1911 (Aug). *Red on pink cover as No.* SB3. *Stapled.*

SB4 2s. booklet containing twelve 12d. (No. 262A), either in two blocks of 6 or block of 12 and eighteen 1d. (No. 264A), either in three blocks of 6 or block of 6 plus block of 12.. £6000

OFFICIAL STAMPS

A. Departmentals

Following suspected abuses involving stamps supplied for official use it was decided by the South Australian authorities that such supplies were to be overprinted with a letter, or letters, indicating the department of the administration to which the stamps had been invoiced.

The system was introduced on 1 April 1868 using overprints struck in red. Later in the same year the colour of the overprints was amended blue, and, during the latter months of 1869, to black.

In 1874 the Postmaster-General recommended that this somewhat cumbersome system be replaced by a general series of "O.S." overprints with the result that the separate accounting for the Departmentals ceased on 30 June of that year. Existing stocks continued to be used, however, and it is believed that much of the residue was passed to the Government Printer to pay postage on copies of the *Government Gazette*.

We are now able to provide a check list of these most interesting issues based on the definitive work. *The Departmental Stamps of South Australia* by A. R. Butler, FRPSL, RDP, published by the Royal Philatelic Society, London in 1978.

No attempt has been made to assign the various overprints to the catalogue numbers of the basic stamps, but each is clearly identified by both watermark and perforation. the colours are similar to those of the contemporary postage stamps, but there can be shade variations. Errors of overprint are recorded in footnotes, but not errors occurring on the basic stamps used.

Most departmental overprints are considered to be scarce to rare in used condition, with unused examples, used multiples and covers being regarded as considerable rarities.

Forgeries of a few items do exist, but most can be readily identified by comparison with genuine examples. A number of forged overprints on stamps not used for the genuine issues also occur.

A. (Architect)

Optd in red with stop. W 2. 2d. (Roul), 4d. (P 11½–12½), 6d. (Roul), 1s. (Roul)

Optd in red without stop W 2. Roul. 1d., 2d., 6d., 1s.

Optd in black. (*a*) W 2. 4d. (P 10×11½–12½), 6d. (P 11½–12½), 2s. (Roul)

(*b*) W 10. 2d. D.L.R. (Roul), 2d. D.L.R. (P 10)

A.G. (Attorney-General)

Optd in red. W 2. Roul. 1d., 2d., 6d., 1s.

Optd in blue. (*a*) W 2. Roul. 6d.

(*b*) W 10. Roul. 2d. D.L.R.

Optd in black. (*a*) W 2. 1d (P 11½–12½×Roul), 4d. (P 11½–12½), 4d. (P 10), 6d. (P 11½–12½×Roul), 6d. (P 11½–12½), 1s. (P 11½–12½×Roul), 1s. (P 11½–12½) 1s. (P 10)

(*b*) W 10. 2d. D.L.R. (Roul), 2d. D.L.R. (P 10)

A.O. (Audit Office)

Optd in red. W 2. 2d. (Roul), 4d. (P 11½–12½), 6d. (Roul)

Optd in blue. (*a*) W 2. P 11½–12½. 1d., 6d.

(*b*) W 10. Roul. 2d. D.L.R.

Optd in black. (*a*) W 2. 1d. (P 11½–12½), 1d. (P 10), 2d. D.L.R. (Roul), 4d. (P 11½–12½) 4d. (P 10), 4d. (P 10×11½–12½), 6d. (Roul), 6d. (P 11½–12½), 1s. (P 11½–12½), 1s. (P 11½–12½×Roul)

(*b*) W 7. P 10. 4d.

(*c*) W 10. 2d. D.L.R. (Roul), 2d. D.L.R. (P 10)

B.D. (Barracks Department)

Optd in red. W 2. Roul. 2d., 6d., 1s.

B.G. (Botanic Garden)

Optd in black. (*a*) W 2. 1d. (P 11½–12½×R), 1d. (P 11½–12½), 1d. (P 10×11½–12½), 2d. D.L.R. (Roul), 6d. (Roul), 6d. (P 11½–12½×Roul, 6d. (P 11½–12½), 1s. (P 11½–12½×Roul), 1s. (P 11½–12½), 1s. (P 10), 1s. (P 10×11½–12½)

(*b*) W 7. P 10, 2d. D.L.R.

(*c*) W 10. 2d. D.L.R. (Roul), 2d. D.L.R. (P 10)

The 6d. (W 2. Roul) is known without stamp after "B".

B.M. (Bench of Magistrates)

Optd in red. W 2. Roul. 2d.

Optd in black. W 10. Roul. 2d. D.L.R.

C. (Customs)

Optd in red. W 2. 1d. (Roul), 2d. (Roul), 4d. (P 11½–12½), 6d. (Roul), 1s. (Roul)

Optd in blue (*a*) W 2. Roul. 1d., 4d., 6d., 1s., 2s.

(*b*) W 10. Roul. 2d. D.L.R.

Optd in black. (*a*) W 2. 1d. (Roul), 1d. (P 10), 1d. (P 10×11½–12½), 4d. (P 11½–12½), 4d. (P 10), 4d. (P 10×11½–12½), 6d. (Roul), 6d. (P 11½–12½), 6d. (P 10), 1s. (P 11½–12½×Roul), 1s. (P 11½–12½), 2s. (Roul)

(*b*) W 7. P 10. 2d. D.L.R.

(*c*) W 10. 2d. D.L.R. (Roul), 2d. D.L.R. (P 10×Roul), 2d. D.L.R. (P 10), 2d. D.L.R. (P 10×11½–12½)

The 2d. (W 10. (Roul) with black overprint is known showing the error "G" for "C".

C.D. (Convict Department)

Optd in red. W 2. 2d. (Roul), 4d. (P 11½–12½), 6d. (Roul), 1s. (Roul)

Optd in black. (*a*) W 2. 1d. (P 11½–12½×Roul), 2d. D.L.R. (Roul), 4d. (P 11½–12½), 6d. (Roul), 6d. (P 11½–12½×Roul, 1s. (P 11½–12½×Roul)

(*b*) W 10. 2d. D.L.R. (Roul), 2d. D.L.R. (P 11½–12½), 2d. D.L.R. (P 11½–12½×Roul)

C.L. (Crown Lands)

Optd in red. W 2. 2d. (Roul), 4d. (P 11½–12½), 6d. (Roul), 1s. (Roul)

Optd in blue. (*a*) W 2. Roul. 4d., 6d.

(*b*) W 10. Roul. 2d. D.L.R.

Optd in black. (*a*) W 2. 2d. D.L.R. (Roul), 4d. (P 11½–12½), 4d. (P 10), 4d. (P 10×11½–12½), 6d. (Roul), 6d. (P 11½–12½), 1s. (P 11½–12½×Roul), 2s. (Roul), 2s. (P 11½–12½)

(*b*) W 7. P 10. 2d. D.L.R., 4d.

(*c*) W 10. 2d. D.L.R. (Roul), 2d. D.L.R. (P 10), 2d. D.L.R. (P 10×11½–12½)

The 2s. (W 2. P 11½–12½) with black overprint is known showing the stop omitted after "L".

C.O. (Commissariat Office)

Optd in red. W 2. (Roul), 4d. (P 11½–12½) 6d. (Roul), 1s. (Roul)

Optd in black. (*a*) W 2. 4d. (P 10), 4d. (P 10×11½–12½), 6d. (P 11½–12½), 1s. (P 11½–12½), 2s. (Roul), 2s. (P 11½–12½)

(*b*) W 10. 2d. D.L.R. (Roul), 2d. D.L.R. (P 10)

The 6d. (W 2. Roul) with red overprint is known showing the error "O" for "C", and the 2s. (W 2. P 11½–12½) with black overprint with the stop omitted after "O".

C.P. (Commissioner of Police)

Optd in red. W 2. 2d. (Roul). 4d. (P 11½–12½), 6d. (Roul)

C.S. (Chief Secretary)

Optd in red. W 2. 2d. (Roul), 4d. (P 11½–12½), 6d. (Roul), 1s. (Roul)

Optd in blue. (*a*) W 2. Roul. 4d., 6d.

(*b*) W 10. Roul. 2d. D.L.R.

Optd in black. (*a*) W 2. 2d. D.L.R. (Roul), 4d. (Roul), 4d. (P 11½–12½×Roul), 4d. (P 11½–12½), 4d. (P 10), 4d. (P 10×11½–12½), 6d. (P 11½–12½×Roul), 6d. (P 11½–12½), 6d. (P 10), 6d. (P 10×11½–12½), 1s. (P 11½–12½×Roul), 1s. (P 11½–12½), 1s. (P 10), 1s. (P 10×11½–12½), 2s. (P 10×11½–12½)

(*b*) W 7. P 10. 2d.

(*c*) W 10. 2d. D.L.R. (Roul), 2d. D.L.R. (P 10)

The 6d. and 1s. (W 2. Roul) with red overprint are known showing the error "G" for "C".

C.Sgn. (Colonial Surgeon)

Optd in red. W 2. 2d. (Roul), 4d. (P 11½–12½), 6d. (Roul)

Optd in black. (*a*) W 2. 2d. D.L.R. (Roul), 4d. (P 10), 4d. (P 10×11½–12½), 6d. (Roul), 6d. (P 11½–12½×Roul) 6d. (P 11½–12½)

(*b*) W 10. 2d. D.L.R. (Roul), 2d. D.L.R. (P 11½–12½×Roul), 2d. (P 10×Roul), 2d. D.L.R. (P 10)

Two types of overprint exist on the 2d. D.L.R., the second type having block capitals instead of the serifed type used for the other values.

D.B. (Destitute Board)

Optd in red. W 2. 1d. (Roul), 2d. (Roul), 4d. (P 11½–12½), 6d. (Roul), 1s. (Roul)

Optd in blue. (*a*) W 2. 2d. D.L.R. (Roul), 4d. (P 11½–12½), 6d. (Roul)

(*b*) W 10. Roul. 2d. D.L.R.

Optd in black. (*a*) W 2. 1d. (P 11½–12½), 4d. (P 11½–12½), 4d. (P 10), 6d. (P 10×11½–12½) 1s (P 10)

(*b*) W 10. 2d. D.L.R. (Roul), 2d. D.L.R. (P 11½–12½), 2d. D.L.R. (P 10), 2d. D.L.R. (P 10×11½–12½)

The 2d. D.L.R. (W 10. P 10) with black overprint is known showing the stop omitted after "D".

D.R. (Deeds Registration)

Optd in red. W 2. Roul, 2d., 6d.

E. (Engineer)

Optd in red. W 2. 2d. (Roul), 4d. (P 11½–12½), 6d. (Roul), 1s. (Roul)

Optd in blue. (*a*) W 2. Roul. 1s.

(*b*) W 10. Roul. 2d. D.L.R.

Optd in black. (*a*) W 2. 4d. (P 11½–12½), 4d. (P 10), 4d. (P 10×11½–12½), 6d. (P 11½–12½), 1s. (P 11½–12½×Roul), 1s. (P 11½–12½), 1s. (P 10×11½–12½)

(*b*) W 7. P 10. 4d.

(*c*) W 10. P 10. 2d. D.L.R.

E.B. (Education Board)

Optd in red. W 2. 2d. (Roul), 4d. (P 11½–12½), 6d. (Roul)

Optd in blue. (*a*) W 2. Roul. 4d., 6d.

(*b*) W 10. Roul. 2d. D.L.R.

Optd in black. (*a*) W 2. 2d. D.L.R. (Roul), 4d (Roul), 4d. (P 11½–12½), 4d. (P 10), 6d. (P 11½–12½×Roul), 6d. (P 11½×12½)

(*b*) W 7. P 10. 2d. D.L.R.

(*c*) W 10. 2d. D.L.R. (Roul), 2d. D.L.R. (P 10), 2d. D.L.R. (P 10×11½–12½)

G.F. (Gold Fields)

Optd in black. (*a*) W 2. Roul. 6d.

(*b*) W 10. 2d. D.L.R. (P 10×Roul), 2d. D.L.R. (P 10)

G.P. (Government Printer)

Optd in red. W 2. Roul. 1d., 2d., 6d., 1s.

Optd in blue. (*a*) W 2. Roul. 1d., 6d., 1s., 2s.

(*b*) W 10. Roul. 2d. D.L.R.

Optd in black. (*a*) W 2. 1d. (Roul), 1d. (P 11½–12½×Roul), 1d. (P 11½–12½) 1d. (P 10) 1d. (P 10×11½–12½), 6d. (P 11½–12½×Roul), 1s. (P 10×11½–12½), 2s. (Roul), 2s. (P 11½–12½) 2s. (P 10×11½–12½)

(*b*) W 10. 2d. D.L.R. (Roul), 2d. D.L.R.(P 10)

The 1d. and 1s. (W 2. Roul) with red overprint are known showing "C.P." instead of "G.P.".

G.S. (Government Storekeeper)

Optd in red. W 2. Roul. 2d.

G.T. (Goolwa Tramway)

Optd in red. W 2. 1d. (Roul), 2d. (Roul), 4d. (P 11½–12½), 6d. (Roul), 1s. (Roul)

Optd in black. (*a*) W 2. 2d. D.L.R. (Roul), 4d. (P 11½–12½)

(*b*) W 10. Roul. 2d. D.L.R.

The 2d. and 6d. (both W 2. Roul) with red overprint are known showing the stop omitted after "T". The 6d, and 1s. (W 2. Roul) with red overprint are known showing "C.T.", instead of "G.T.".

H. (Hospitals)

Optd in black. (*a*) W 2. P 10×11½–12½. 4d.

(*b*) W 7. P 10. 2d. D.L.R.

(*c*) W 10. 2d. D.L.R. (P 10), 2d. D.L.R. (P 10×11½–12½)

H.A. (House of Assembly)

Optd in red. W 2. 1d. (Roul), 2d. (Roul), 4d. (P 11½–12½), 6d. (Roul), 1s. (Roul)

Optd in black. (*a*) W 2. 1d. (P 11½–12½), 1d. (P 10) 1d. (P 10×11½–12½), 4d. (P 11½–12½), 4d. (P 10) 6d. (Roul), 6d. (P 11½–12½) 1s. (P 11½–12½×Roul), 1s. (P 11½–12½)

(*b*) W 10. 2d. D.L.R. (Roul), 2d. D.L.R. (P 10)

I.A. (Immigration Agent)

Optd in red. W 2. 1d. (Roul), 2d. (Roul), 4d. (P 11½–12½), 6d. (Roul)

I.E. (Intestate Estates)

Optd in black. W 10. P 10. 2d. D.L.R.

I.S. (Inspector of Sheep)

Optd in red. W 2. Roul. 2d., 6d.

Optd in blue. W 2. P 11½–12½. 6d.

Optd in black. (*a*) W 2. 2d. D.L.R. (Roul), 6d. (P 11½–12½×Roul)

(*b*) W 10. 2d. D.L.R. (Roul). 2d. D.L.R. (P 10)

L.A. (Lunatic Asylum)

Optd in red. W 2. 1d. (Roul), 2d. (Roul), 4d. (P 11½–12½), 6d. (Roul), 1s. (Roul)

Optd in black. (*a*) W 2. 4d. (P 11½–12½), 4d. (P 10), 4d. (P 10×11½–12½), 6d. (P 11½–12½), 1s. (P 11½–12½), 2s. (Roul)

(*b*) W 10. 2d. D.L.R. (Roul), 2d. D.L.R. (P 10)

L.C. (Legislative Council)

Optd in red. W 2. Roul. 2d., 6d.

Optd in black. (*a*) W 2. Roul. 6d.

(*b*) W 10. 2d. D.L.R. (Roul), 2d. D.L.R. (P 10×Roul)

The 2d. and 6d. (both W 2. Roul) with red overprint are known showing the stop omitted after "C".

L.L. (Legislative Librarian)

Optd in red. W 2. 2d. (Roul), 4d. (P 11½–12½), 6d. (Roul)

Optd in black. (*a*) W 2. P 11½–12½. 6d.

(*b*) W 10. P 10. 2d. D.L.R.

The 2d. and 6d. (both W 2. Roul) with red overprint are known showing the stop omitted from between the two letters.

L.T. (Land Titles)

Optd in red. W 2. 2d. (Roul), 4d. (P 11½–12½), 6d. (Roul), 1s. (Roul)

Optd in blue. W 10. Roul. 2d. D.L.R.

Optd in black. (*a*) W 2. 4d. (P 11½–12½), 4d. (P 10), 4d. (P 10×11½–12½), 6d. (P 11½–12½×Roul), 6d. (P 11½–12½), 6d. (P 10), 6d. (P 10×11½–12½)

(*b*) W 7. P 10. 2d. D.L.R.

(*c*) W 10. 2d. D.L.R. (Roul), 2d. D.L.R. (P 10)

The 2d. and 6d. (both W 2. Roul) with red overprint are known showing the stop omitted after "T".

M. (Military)

Optd in red. W 2. Roul. 2d., 6d., 1s.

Optd in black. W 2. 6d. (P 11½–12½×Roul), 1s. (P 11½–12½×Roul), 2s. (Roul)

M.B. (Marine Board)

Optd in red. W 2. 1d. (Roul), 2d. (Roul), 4d. (Roul), 4d. (P 11½–12½), 6d. (Roul), 1s. (Roul)

Optd in black. (*a*) W 2. 1d. (Roul), 1d. (P 11½–12½), 2d. D.L.R. (Roul), 4d. (P 11½–12½×Roul), 4d. (P 11½–12½), 4d. (P 10), 4d. (P 10×11½–12½), 6d. (Roul), 6d. (P 11½–12½), 6d. (P 10), 6d. (P 10×11½–12½), 1s. (P 11½–12½×Roul), 1s. (P 11½–12½) 1s. (P 10), 1s. (P 10×11½–12½)

(*b*) W 7. P 10. 4d.

(*c*) W 10. Roul. 2d. D.L.R.

M.R. (Manager of Railways)

Optd in red. W 2. Roul. 2d., 6d.

Optd in black. (*a*) W 2. 1d. (P 11½–12½), 1d. (P 10), 2d. D.L.R. (Roul), 4d. (Roul), 4d. (P 11½–12½), 6d. (P 11½–12½×Roul), 1s. (P 11½–12½×Roul), 2s. (P 11½–12½ 1, 2s. (P 10×11½–12½)

(*b*) W 10. 2d. D.L.R. (Roul), 2d. D.L.R. (P 10), 2d. D.L.R. (P 10×11½–12½)

M.R.G. (Main Roads Gambierton)

Optd in red without stops. W 2. Roul. 2d., 6d.
Optd in blue without stops. W 10. Roul. 2d. D.L.R.
Optd in black without stops. W 10. 2d. D.L.R. (Roul), 2d. D.L.R. (Roul 10)
Optd in black with stops. W 10. 2d. D.L.R. (Roul), 2d. D.L.R. (Roul 10)

The 2d. D.L.R. (W 10. P 10) with black overprint is known showing the stops omitted after "M" and "R".

N.T. (Northern Territory)

Optd in black (*a*) W 2. P 11½–12½. 1d., 3d. on 4d., 6d., 1s.
(*b*) W 10. 2d. D.L.R. (Roul), 2d. D.L.R. (P 10)

O.A. (Official Assignee)

Optd in red. W 2. 2d. (Roul), 4d. (P 11½–12½)
Optd in blue. W 10. Roul. 2d. D.L.R.
Optd in black. (*a*) W 2. P 10. 4d.
(*b*) W 7. P 10. 2d. D.L.R.
(*c*) W 10. 2d. D.L.R. (Roul), 2d. D.L.R. (P 10×roul), 2d. D.L.R. (P 10)

P. (Police)

Optd in blue. (*a*) W 2. Roul. 6d.
(*b*) W 10. Roul. 2d. D.L.R.
Optd in black. (*a*) W 2. 6d. (P 11½–12½×Roul), 6d. (P 11½–12½), 6d. (P 10)
(*b*) W 7. P 10. 2d. D.L.R.
(*c*) W 10. 2d. D.L.R. (Roul), 2d. D.L.R. (P 11½–12½), 2d. D.L.R. (P 11½–12½×Roul), 2d. D.L.R. (P 10×Roul), 2d. D.L.R. (P 10), 2d. D.L.R. (P 10×11½–12½)

P.A. (Protector of Aborigines)

Optd in red. W 2. Roul. 2d., 6d.
Optd in black. (*a*) W 2. P. 2d. D.L.R., 6d.
(*b*) W 10. 2d. D.L.R. (Roul), 2d. D.L.R. (P 10)

P.O. (Post Office)

Optd in red. W 2. Roul. 1d., 2d., 6d., 1s.
Optd in blue. (*a*) W 2. Roul. 2d.
(*b*) W 10. Roul. 2d. D.L.R.
Optd in black. (*a*) W 2. 1d. (P 10×11½–12½), 2d. D.L.R. (Roul), 2d. D.L.R. (P 11½–12½×Roul), 4d. (P 11½–12½), 6d. (Roul), 6d. (P 11½×12½), 1s. (P 11½–12½×Roul, 1s. (P 11½×12½) 1s. (P 11½–12½), 1s. (P 10) 1s. (P 10×11½–12½)
(*b*) W 10. 2d. D.L.R. (Roul), 2d. (P 11½–12½×Roul), 2d. D.L.R. (P 10×Roul), 2d. D.L.R. (P 10)

The 4d. (W 2. P 11½–12½) with black overprint is known showing the stop omitted after "O".

P.S. (Private Secretary)

Optd in red. W 2. 1d. (Roul), 2d. (Roul), 4d. (P 11½–12½), 6d. (Roul), 1s. (Roul)
Optd in black. (*a*) W 2. 1d. (P 11½–12½×Roul), 1d. (P 11½–12½), 1d. (P 10), 2d. (Roul), 3d. (in black) on 4d. (P 11½–12½), 3d. (in red) on 4d. (P 10), 3d. (in black) on 4d. (P 10), 4d. (P 11½–12½), 4d. (P 10), 4d. (P 10×11½–12½) 6d. (Roul), 6d. (P 11½–12½×Roul), 6d. (P 11½–12½), 6d. (P 10), 9d. (Roul), 9d. (P 11½–12½) 10d. on 9d. (P 10), 10d. on 9d. (P 10×11½–12½), 1s. (P 11½–12½×Roul)
(*b*) W 7. P 10. 2d. D.L.R.
(*c*) W 10. 2d. D.L.R. (Roul), 2d. D.L.R. (P 10)

P.W. (Public Works)

Optd in red without stop after "W". W 2. Roul. 2d., 6d., 1s.
Optd in black. (*a*) W 2. 2d. D.L.R. (Roul), 4d. (P 10), 6d. (Roul), 6d. (P 11½–12½), 1s. (P 11½–12½×Roul)
(*b*) W 10. 2d. D.L.R. (Roul), 2d. D.L.R. (P 10)

R.B. (Road Board)

Optd in red. W 2. 1d. (Roul), 2d. (Roul), 4d. (P 11½–12½), 6d. (Roul), 1s. (Roul)
Optd in blue without stops. W 10. Roul. 2d D.L.R
Optd in black. (*a*) W 2. 1d. (P 11½–12½×Roul), 1d. (P 10), 4d. (Roul), 4d. (P 10), 6d. (P 10), 2s. (Roul)
(*b*) W 7. P 10. 2d. D.L.R.
(*c*) W 10. 2d. D.L.R. (Roul), 2d. (D.L.R.) (P 10×Roul), 2d. D.L.R. (P 10)

The 6d. (W 2. Roul) with red overprint is known showing the stop omitted after "B".

R.G. (Registrar-General)

Optd in red. W 2. Roul. 2d., 6d., 1s.
Optd in blue. (*a*) W 2. P 11½–12½×Roul. 6d.
(*b*) W 10. 2d. D.L.R. (Roul), 2d. D.L.R. (P 11½–12½×Roul)
Optd in black. (*a*) W 2. 2d. D.L.R. (Roul), 6d. (P 10), 6d. (P 10×11½–12½), 1s. (P 11½–12½×Roul), 1s. (P 10)
(*b*) W 7. P 10. 2d. D.L.R.
(*c*) W 10. 2d. D.L.R. (Roul), 2d. D.L.R. (P 10×Roul), 2d. D.L.R. (P 10), 2d. D.L.R. (P 10×11½–12½)

The 2d. (W 2. Roul) with red overprint is known showing "C" for "G".

S. (Sheriff)

Optd in red. W 2. Roul. 2d., 6d.
Optd in blue. W 10. Roul. 2d. D.L.R.
Optd in black. (*a*) W 2. 6d. (Roul), 6d. (P 11½–12½×Roul), 6d. (P 11½–12½), 6d. (P 10)
(*b*) W 10. 2d. D.L.R. (Roul), 2d. D.L.R. (P 10×Roul), 2d. D.L.R. (P 10)

S.C. (Supreme Court)

Optd in red. W 2. Roul. 2d. 6d.
Optd in black. W 10. P 10. 2d. D.L.R.

S.G. (Surveyor-General)

Optd in red. W 2. 2d. (Roul), 4d. (P 11½–12½), 6d. (Roul)
Optd in blue. (*a*) W 2. Roul. 4d.
(*b*) W 10. Roul. 2d. D.L.R.
Optd in black. (*a*) W 2. 2d. D.L.R. (Roul), 4d. (P 11½–12½), 4d. (P 10) 4d. (P 10×11½–12½), 6d. (P 11½–12½×Roul), 6d. (P 11½–12½), 6d. (P 10), 6d. (P 10×11½–12½)
(*b*) W 7. P 10. 2d. D.L.R.
(*c*) W 10. 2d. D.L.R. (Roul), 2d. D.L.R. (P 11½–12½), 2d. D.L.R. (P 10×Roul), 2d. D.L R (P 10)

The 2d. (W 7 and W 10. P 10) with black overprint are known showing "C" for "G".

S.M. (Stipendiary Magistrate)

Optd in red. W 2. Roul. 1d., 2d., 4d., 6d., 1s.
Optd in blue. (*a*) W 2. Roul. 2d., 4d., 6d.
(*b*) W 10. Roul. 2d. D.L.R.
Optd in black. (*a*) W 2. 1d. (P 11½–12½), 1d. (P 10), 2d. D.L.R. (Roul), 4d. (Roul), 4d. (P 11½–12½×Roul), 4d. (P 11½–12½), 4d. (P 10), 4d. (P 10×11½–12½), 6d. (P 11½–12½×Roul), 6d. (P 11½–12½), 6d. (P 10), 6d. (P 10×11½–12½), 1s. (P 11½–12½×Roul)
(*b*) W 7. P 10. 2d. D.L.R.
(*c*) W 10. 2d. D.L.R. (Roul), 2d. D.L.R. (P 11½–12½), 2d. D.L.R. (P 10×Roul) 2d. D.L.R. (P 10), 2d D.L.R. (P 10×11½–12½)

The 2d. and 4d. (both W 2. Roul) with red overprint are known showing the stop omitted after "M".

S.T. (Superintendent of Telegraphs)

Optd in red. W 2. Roul. 2d., 6d.
Optd in blue. W 10. Roul. 2d. D.L.R.
Optd in black. (*a*) W 2. Roul. 2d. D.L.R., 6d.
(*b*) W 7. P 10. 2d. D.L.R.
(*c*) W 10. 2d. D.L.R. (Roul), 2d. D.L.R. (P 10×Roul), 2d. D.L.R. (P 10)

The 2d. and 6d. (both W 2. Roul) with red overprint are known showing the stop omitted after "T".

T. (Treasury)

Optd in red. W 2. 1d. (Roul), 2d. (Roul), 4d. (P 11½–12½×Roul), 6d. (Roul), 1s. (Roul)
Optd in blue. (*a*) W 2. Roul. 1d., 4d., 6d.
(*b*) W 10. Roul. 2d. D.L.R.
Optd in black. (*a*) W 2. 1d. (P 10), 2d. D.L.R. (Roul), 4d. (Roul), 4d. (P 11½–12½), 4d. (P 10), 6d. (Roul), 6d. (P 11½–12½), 1s. (P 11½–12½×Roul), 1s. (P 10×11½–12½), 2s. (Roul), 2s. (P 11½–12½), 2s. (P 10×11½–12½)
(*b*) W 7. P 10. 2d. D.L.R.
(*c*) W 10. 2d. D.L.R. (Roul), 2d. D.L.R. (P 10)

T.R. (Titles Registration)

Optd in black. (*a*) W 2. 4d. (P 11½–12½), 4d. (P 10×11½–12½), 6d. (P 11½–12½), 1s. (P 11½–12½)
(*b*) W 10. P 10. 2d. D.L.R.

V. (Volunteers)

Optd in black. (*a*) W 2. 4d. (P 10×11½–12½), 6d. (P 11½–12½), 1s. (P 11½–12½)
(*b*) W 10. P 10. 2d. D.L.R.
(*c*) W 10. 2d. D.L.R. (Roul), 2d. D.L.R. (P 10×Roul), 2d. D.L.R. (P 10)

The 2d. (W 10. P 10×Roul) overprinted in black is only known showing the stop omitted after "V".

VA. (Valuator of Runs)

Optd in black without stop after "V". (*a*) W 2. Roul. 4d.
(*b*) W 10. P 10. 2d. D.L.R.

VN. (Vaccination)

Optd in black without stop after "V". W 2. 4d. (P 10), 4d. (P 10×11½–12½)

W. (Waterworks)

Optd in red. W 2. Roul. 2d.
Optd in black. W 10. 2d. D.L.R. (Roul), 2d. D.L.R. (P 10)

The 2d. (W 2. Roul) with red overprint is known showing the stop omitted after "W".

B. General

O.S.	**O.S.**
(O **1**)	(O **2**)

1874–77. *Optd with Type* O **1**. W **2**.

(a) P 10.

O1	**3**	4d. dull purple (18.2.74)	£1300	£300

(b) P 11½–12½×10.

O2	**1**	1d. green (2.1.74)	—	£275
O3	**3**	4d. dull violet (12.2.75)	70·00	5·00
O4	**1**	6d. Prussian blue (20.10.75)	90·00	10·00
O4*a*	**3**	2s. rose-pink		
O5		2s. carmine (3.12.76)	—	£120

(c) P 11½–12½.

O6	**1**	1d. deep yellow-green (30.1.74)	£1400	£275
		a. Printed on both sides	—	£900
O7	**3**	3d. on 4d. ultramarine (26.6.77)	£4500	£1400
		a. No stop after "S"	—	£2000
O8		4d. dull violet (13.7.74)	50·00	6·50
		a. No stop after "S"	—	45·00
O9	**1**	6d. bright blue (31.8.75)	£120	15·00
		a. "O.S." double	—	£140
O10		6d. Prussian blue (27.3.74)	£100	8·50
		a. No stop after "S"	—	55·00
O11	**4**	9d. red-purple (22.3.76)	£1800	£800
		a. No stop after "S"	£2500	£1200
O12	**1**	1s. red-brown (5.8.74)	70·00	6·50
		a. "O.S." double	—	£140
		b. No stop after "S"	£200	55·00
O13	**3**	2s. crimson-carmine (13.7.75)	£170	24·00
		a. No stop after "S"	—	85·00
		b. No stops	—	£100
		c. Stops at top of letters		

1876–85. *Optd with Type* O **1**. W **8**.

(a) P 10.

O14	**1**	6d. bright blue (1879)	95·00	14·00

(b) P 10×11½–12½, 11½–12½×10, or compound.

O15	**3**	4d. violet-slate (24.1.78)	70·00	6·50
O16		4d. plum (29.11.81)	42·00	2·75
O17		4d. deep mauve	42·00	2·50
		a. No stop after "S"	£130	35·00
		b. No stop after "O"		
		c. "O.S." double		
		d. "O.S." inverted	—	£170
O18	**1**	6d. bright blue (1877)	85·00	4·75
		a. "O.S." inverted		
		b. No stop after "O"		
O19		6d. bright ultramarine (27.3.85)	80·00	4·50
		a. "O.S." inverted		
		b. "O.S." double		
		c. "O.S." double, one inverted	—	£375
		d. No stop after "S"	—	48·00
		e. No stops after "O" & "S"		
O20		1s. red-brown (27.3.83)	55·00	7·00
		a. "O.S." inverted		
		b. No stop after "O"		
		c. No stop after "S"	—	50·00
O21	**3**	2s. carmine (16.3.81)	£140	8·00
		a. "O.S." inverted	—	£250
		b. No stop after "S"	—	70·00

(c) P 11½–12½.

O22	**3**	3d. on 4d. ultramarine	£4500	
O23		4d. violet-slate (14.3.76)	£140	15·00
O24		4d. deep mauve (19.8.79)	55·00	6·00
		a. "O.S." inverted		
		b. "O.S." double, one inverted		
		c. No stop after "S"	—	42·00
O25	**1**	6d. Prussian blue (6.77)	80·00	7·50
		a. "O.S." double	—	95·00
		b. "O.S." inverted		
O26	**4**	8d. on 9d. brown (9.11.76)	£3000	£950
		a. "O.S." double	£4000	
		b. "O" only	—	£1200
O26*c*		9d. purple	£5000	
O27	**1**	1s. red-brown (12.2.78)	35·00	8·50
		a. "O.S." inverted	£325	£140
		b. No stop after "S"	£200	50·00
O28		1s. lake-brown (8.11.83)	45·00	3·50
O29	**3**	2s. rose-carmine (12.8.85)	£140	8·50
		a. "O.S." double	—	£140
		b. "O.S." inverted	—	£150
		c. No stop after "S"	—	55·00

1891–1903. *Optd with Type* O **2**.

(a) W **8**. P 11½–12½.

O30	**1**	1s. lake-brown (18.4.91)	55·00	10·00
O31		1s. Vandyke brown	65·00	7·00
O32		1s. dull brown (2.7.96)	48·00	5·50
		a. No stop after "S"	—	65·00
O33		1s. sepia (large holes) (4.1.02)	40·00	5·50
		a. "O.S." double	—	£250
		b. No stop after "S"		
O34	**3**	2s. carmine (26.6.00)	90·00	15·00
		a. No stop after "S"		

(b) W **8**. P 10×11½–12½.

O35	**3**	2s. rose-carmine (9.11.95)	80·00	10·00
		a. No stop after "S"	£180	
		b. "O.S." double		

(c) W **10**. P 11½–12½.

O36	**1**	1s. dull brown (1902)	60·00	17·00

1874–76. *Optd with Type* O **1**. W **10**.

(a) P 10.

O37	**11**	1d. blue-green (30.9.75)	£110	25·00
		a. "O.S." inverted		
		b. No stop after "S"		
O38	**12**	2d. orange-red (18.2.74)	27·00	3·50
		a. No stop after "S"	—	32·00
		b. "O.S." double		

(b) P 10×11½–12½, 11½–12½×10, or compound.

O39	**11**	1d. blue-green (16.9.75)		
		a. No stop after "S"		
O40	**12**	2d. orange-red (27.9.76)	—	15·00

(c) P 11½–12½.

O41	**11**	1d. blue-green (13.8.75)	—	35·00
		a. "O.S." inverted		
		b. No stop after "S"		
O42	**12**	2d. orange-red (20.5.74)	—	£100

1876–80. *Optd with Type* O **1**. W **13**.

(a) P 10.

O43	**11**	1d. blue-green (2.10.76)	18·00	1·00
		a. "O.S." inverted	—	60·00
		b. "O.S." double	90·00	50·00
		c. "O.S." double, one inverted		
		d. No stops	—	35·00
		e. No stop after "O"		
		f. No stop after "S"	—	15·00
		g. Deep green	24·00	1·00
		ga. "O.S." double	—	60·00
O44	**12**	2d. orange-red (21.9.77)	9·50	1·00
		a. "O.S." inverted	—	27·00
		b. "O.S." double	95·00	45·00
		c. "O.S." double, one inverted		
		d. "O.S." double, both inverted	—	£150
		e. No stops	—	65·00
		f. No stop after "O"	—	22·00
		g. No stop after "S"		
		h. Dull brick-red	45·00	1·00

(b) P 10×11½–12½, 11½–12½×10 or compound.

O45	**11**	1d. deep green (14.8.80)	—	40·00
		a. "O.S." double		
O46	**12**	2d. orange-red (6.4.78)	65·00	14·00
		a. "O.S." inverted	—	£140
		b. No stop after "S"	—	65·00

(c) P 11½–12½.

O47	**12**	2d. orange-red (15.7.80)	—	70·00

1882 (20 Feb). *No. 181 optd with Type* O **1**.

O48	**11**	½d. on 1d. blue-green	70·00	19·00
		a. "O.S." inverted		

1888 (15 Nov)–**91**. *Nos. 184 and 185a optd with Type* O **1**. P 10.
O49 **17** 4d. pale violet (24.1.91) 75·00 5·00
O50 **18** 6d. blue 28·00 1·25
a. "O.S." double
b. No stop after "S"

1891. *Nos. 229b and 231a/2 optd with Type* O **1**.
(a) P 10.
O51 **17** 2½d. on 4d. deep green (Br.) (1 Aug) 75·00 10·00
a. "2" and "½" closer together — 45·00
b. "O.S." inverted
c. "O.S." double
d. "OS." omitted (in vert pair with normal)
e. No stop after "S"
(b) P 10×11½–12½ or 11½–12½×10.
O52 **17** 2½d. on 4d. deep green (Br.) (1 Oct) 80·00 19·00
(c) P 11½–12½.
O53 **17** 2½d. on 4d. deep green (Br.) (1 June) £150 70·00

1891–96. *Optd with Type* O **2**. W **13**.
(a) P 10.
O54 **11** 1d. deep green (22.4.91) 32·00 2·00
a. "OS." double 85·00 45·00
b. "O.S." double, one inverted
c. No stop after "S" 50·00 12·00
d. Blackish blue opt £200 4·50
O55 **12** 2d. orange-red (22.4.91) 30·00 2·00
a. "O.S." double
b. "O.S." double, both inverted
c. No stop after "S" — 14·00
(b) P 15.
O56 **11** 1d. green (8.9.94) 16·00 1·25
a. "O.S." double
b. No stop after "S"
O57 **12** 2d. orange-red (16.6.94) 16·00 60
a. "O.S." double — 35·00
b. "O.S." inverted — 27·00
(c) P 13.
O58 **11** 1d. green (20.5.95) 25·00 60
a. No stop after "S" 80·00 10·00
O59 **12** 2d. orange-red (11.2.96) 25·00 50
a. "O.S." double £130
b. No stop after "S" 75·00 10·00

1891–99. *Optd with Type* O **2**. W **13** (sideways on ½d.).
(a) P 10.
O60 **15** ½d. brown (2.5.94) 28·00 6·50
a. No stop after "S" 75·00 35·00
O61 **17** 4d. pale violet (13.2.91) 50·00 3·50
a. "O.S." double
b. "S." omitted — 85·00
c. No stop after "S"
d. *Aniline violet* (31.8.93) 50·00 5·50
da. "O.S." double
dc. No stop after "S"
O62 **18** 6d. blue (4.4.93) 25·00 2·50
a. No stop after "S"
b. Blackish blue opt
(b) P 10×11½–12½.
O63 **15** ½d. brown (26.3.95) 25·00 7·50
(c) P 11½–12½.
O64 **15** ½d. red-brown (13.6.91) 50·00 12·00
(d) P 15.
O65 **15** ½d. pale brown (8.6.95) 40·00 12·00
O66 **17** 4d. slate-violet (4.4.95) 65·00 4·50
a. "O.S." double £250 45·00
O67 **18** 6d. blue (20.9.93) 32·00 4·00
(e) P 13.
O68 **15** ½d. deep brown (17.5.98) 27·00 6·00
a. Opt triple, twice sideways £200
O69 **17** 4d. violet (12.96) 75·00 3·00
a. "O.S." double £180 42·00
b. No stop after "S" £180 30·00
O70 **18** 6d. blue (13.9.99) 40·00 2·00
a. No stop after "S" £120 55·00

1891–95. *Nos. 229b, 230a and 231a optd with Type* O **2**.
(a) P 10.
O71 **17** 2½d. on 4d. deep green (Br.) (18.8.94) 42·00 15·00
a. Fraction bar omitted
b. "2" and "½" closer together 95·00 40·00
c. "O.S." inverted £275
d. No stop after "S" — 45·00
O72 **18** 5d. on 6d. deep brown (C.) (2.12.91) 45·00 18·00
a. No stop after "5D" £200
b. No stop after "S" £110 45·00
(b) P 10×11½–12½.
O73 **17** 2½d. on 4d. deep green (Br.) (17.9.95) — 55·00
a. "O.S." double

1897–1901. *Nos. 235/6 and 238a optd with Type* O **2**.
(a) P 15.
O74 **23** 5d. brown-purple (29.3.01) 75·00 12·00
(b) P 13
O75 **22** 2½d. violet-blue (5.7.97) 55·00 7·00
a. No stop after "S" — 40·00
O76 **23** 5d. purple (29.9.01) 75·00 17·00
a. No stop after "S"

O. S.

(O 3)

1899–1901. *Optd with Type* O **3**. W **13**. P 13.
O80 **24** ½d. yellow-green (12.2.00) 16·00 6·00
a. "O.S." inverted 80·00
b. No stop after "S" 48·00
O81 **11** 1d. rosine (22.9.99) 18·00 1·60
a. "O.S." inverted 70·00 45·00
b. "O.S." double † £275
c. No stop after "S" 55·00 16·00
O82 **12** 2d. bright violet (1.6.00) 21·00 80
a. "O.S." inverted 60·00 28·00
b. "O.S." double
c. No stop after "S" 45·00 15·00
O83 **22** 2½d. indigo (2.10.01) 55·00 19·00
a. "O.S." inverted — 90·00
b. No stop after "S" £160
O84 **17** 4d. violet (18.11.00) 50·00 5·50
a. "O.S." inverted £225
b. No stop after "S" £140
O85 **18** 6d. blue (8.10.00) 25·00 5·50
a. No stop after "S" 75·00

1891 (May). *Optd as Type* O **3** *but wider.* W **13**. P 10.
O86 **19** 2s.6d. pale violet £4250 £3750
O87 5s. pale rose £4250 £3750
Only one sheet (60) of each of these stamps was printed.

The use of stamps overprinted "O S" was made invalid by the Posts and Telegraph Act of 1 November 1902.

South Australia became part of the Commonwealth of Australia on 1 January 1901.

TASMANIA

PRICES FOR STAMPS ON COVER	
Nos. 1/4	*from* × 6
Nos. 5/12	*from* × 5
Nos. 14/24	*from* × 3
Nos. 25/56	*from* × 5
Nos. 57/77	*from* × 6
Nos. 78/9	—
Nos. 80/90	*from* × 3
No. 91	—
Nos. 92/109	*from* × 3
No. 110	—
Nos. 111/23	*from* × 3
Nos. 124/6	—
Nos. 127/34	*from* × 5
Nos. 135/55	*from* × 4
Nos. 156/8	*from* × 20
Nos. 159/66	*from* × 10
Nos. 167/9	*from* × 15
Nos. 170/4	*from* × 6
Nos. 216/22	*from* × 15
Nos. 223/5	—
Nos. 226/7	*from* × 15
Nos. 229/36	*from* × 20
Nos. 237/57	*from* × 10
No. 258	—
Nos. 259/62	*from* × 10
Nos. F1/25	—
Nos. F26/9	*from* × 15
Nos. F30/9	—

SPECIMEN OVERPRINTS. Those listed are from U.P.U. distributions between 1892 and 1904. Further "Specimen" overprints exist, but these were used for other purposes.

1 2 3

(Eng C.W. Coard. Recess H. and C. Best at the *Courier* newspaper, Hobart)

1853 (1 Nov). *Twenty-four varieties in four rows of six each.* No wmk. Imperf.
(a) Medium soft yellowish paper with all lines clear and distinct.
1 **1** 1d. pale blue £5500 £1000
2 1d. blue £5500 £1000
(b) Thin hard white paper with lines of the engraving blurred and worn.
3 **1** 1d. pale blue £5000 £900
4 1d. blue £5000 £900

1853 (1 Nov)–**54**. No wmk. Imperf. *In each plate there are twenty-four varieties in four rows of six each.*
(a) Plate I. Finely engraved. All lines in network and background thin, clear, and well defined. (1853).
(i) First state of the plate, brilliant colours.
5 **2** 4d. bright red-orange £4500 £800
a. Double impression
6 4d. bright brownish orange — £950
(ii) Second state of plate, with blurred lines and worn condition of the central background.
7 **2** 4d. red-orange £3000 £450
8 4d. orange £2750 £425
9 4d. pale orange — £425
(b) Plate II. Coarse engraving, lines in network and background thicker and blurred (Dec. 1854).
10 **2** 4d. orange £2750 £400
a. Double print, one albino
11 4d. dull orange £2750 £350
12 4d. yellowish orange £2750 £350

In the 4d. Plate I, the outer frame-line is thin all round. In Plate II it is, by comparison with other parts, thicker in the lower left angle.

The 4d. is known on vertically laid paper from proof sheets. Examples from Plate I have the lines close together and those from Plate II wide apart (Price £6000 *unused*).

In 1879 reprints were made of the 1d. in blue and the 4d., Plate I, in brownish yellow, on thin, tough, white wove paper, and perforated 11½. In 1887, a reprint from the other plate of the 4d. was made in reddish brown and black on thick white paper, imperforate, and in 1889 of the 1d. in blue and in black, and of the 4d. (both plates) in yellow and in black on white card, imperforate. As these three plates were defaced after the stamps had been superseded, all these reprints show two, or three thick strokes across the Queen's head.

All three plates were destroyed in July 1950.

PERKINS BACON "CANCELLED". For notes on these handstamps, showing "CANCELLED" between horizontal bars forming an oval, see Catalogue Introduction.

(Eng W. Humphrys, after water-colour sketch by E. Corbould. Recess P.B.)

1855 (17 Aug–16 Sept). Wmk Large Star. W w **1**. Imperf.
14 **3** 1d. carmine (16.9) (H/S "CANCELLED" in oval £10000) £7500 £800
15 2d. deep green (16.9) £3250 £500
16 2d. green (16.9) (H/S "CANCELLED" in oval £11000) £3250 £450
17 4d. deep blue £2500 £110
18 4d. blue (H/S "CANCELLED" in oval £10000) £2500 £120

Proofs of the 1d. and 4d. on thick paper, *without watermark*, are sometimes offered as the issued stamps. The 6d. dull lilac on this watermark was prepared, but not issued. Examples exist from a creased proof sheet (*Price* £750 *unused*).

(Recess H. and C. Best, Hobart, from P.B. plates)

1856 (Apr)–**57**. No wmk. Imperf.
(a) Thin white paper.
19 **3** 1d. pale brick-red (4.56) £9000 £600
20 2d. dull emerald-green (1.57) £10000 £900
21 4d. deep blue (5.57) £1000 £110
22 4d. blue (5.57) £900 £110
23 4d. pale blue (5.57) — £140
(b) Pelure paper.
24 **3** 1d. deep red-brown (11.56) £6000 £750

4 7 8

(Recess H. Best (August 1857–May 1859), J. Davies (August 1859–March 1862), J. Birchall (March 1863), M. Hood (October 1863–April 1864), Govt Printer (from July 1864), all from P.B. plates)

1857 (Aug)–**69**. Wmk double-lined numerals "1", "2" or "4" as W **4** on appropriate value. Imperf.
25 **3** 1d. deep red-brown £550 40·00
26 1d. pale red-brown £375 29·00
27 1d. brick-red (1863) £180 26·00
28 1d. dull vermilion (1865) £140 26·00
29 1d. carmine (1867) £130 24·00
a. Double print £550 £140
b. Error. Wmkd "2" (1869)
30 2d. dull emerald-green — £120
31 2d. green — 55·00
a. double print — £170
32 2d. yellow-green £450 £100
33 2d. deep green (1858) £400 70·00
34 2d. slate-green (1860) £200 80·00
35 4d. deep blue — 85·00
a. Double print — £170
36 4d. pale blue £170 25·00
37 4d. blue £170 27·00
a. Double print — £170
38 4d. bright blue £170 27·00
a. Printed on both sides † —
b. Double print — £140
39 4d. cobalt-blue — 85·00

Printings before July 1864 were all carried out at the *Courier* printing works which changed hands several times during this period.

CANCELLATIONS. Beware of early Tasmanian stamps with pen-cancellations cleaned off and faked postmarks applied.

(Recess P.B.)

1858. Wmk double-lined numerals "6" or "12" as W **4**. Imperf.
40 **7** 6d. dull lilac (H/S "CANCELLED" in oval £11000) £700 85·00
41 **8** 1s. verm (shades) (H/S "CANCELLED" in oval £10000). £550 75·00

(Recess J. Davies (March 1860), J. Birchall (April 1863), Govt Printer (from February 1865), all from P.B. plates)

1860 (Mar)–**67**. Wmk double-lined "6" as W **4**. Imperf.
44 **7** 6d. dull slate-grey £325 65·00
45 6d. grey — 70·00
46 6d. grey-violet (4.63) £225 65·00
a. Double print — £300
47 6d. dull cobalt (2.65) £475 £100
48 6d. slate-violet (2.65) £350 55·00
49 6d. reddish mauve (4.67) £700 £150

In 1871 reprints were made of the 6d. (in mauve) and the 1s. on white wove paper, and perforated 11½. They are found with or without "REPRINT". In 1889 they were again reprinted on white card, imperforate. These later impressions are also found overprinted "REPRINT" and perforated 11½.

PERFORATED ISSUES. From 1 October 1857 the Tasmania Post Office only supplied purchasers requiring five or more complete sheets of stamps. The public obtained their requirements, at face value, from licensed stamp vendors, who obtained their stocks at a discount from the Post Office.

From 1863 onwards a number of the stamp vendors applied their own roulettes or perforations. The Hobart firm of J. Walch & Sons achieved this so successfully that they were given an official contract in July 1869 to perforate sheets for the Post Office. The Government did not obtain a perforating machine until late in 1871.

1863–71. Double-lined numeral watermarks. Various unofficial roulettes and perforations.

(a) By J. Walch & Sons, Hobart.

(i) Roulette about 8, often imperf × roul (1863–68).

50	3	1d. brick-red	–	£300
51		1d. carmine	£475	£170
52		2d. yellow-green	–	£750
53		2d. slate green		
54		4d. pale blue	–	£275
55	7	6d. dull lilac	–	£325
56	8	1s. vermilion	–	£850

(ii) P 10 (1864–69).

57	3	1d. brick-red	90·00	35·00
58		1d. dull vermilion	90·00	35·00
		a. Double print	†	–
59		1d. carmine	75·00	32·00
60		2d. yellow-green	£450	£130
61		2d. slate-green	£450	£190
62		4d. pale blue	£160	17·00
63		4d. blue	£160	17·00
		a. Double print	–	£130
64	7	6d. grey-violet	£250	24·00
65		6d. dull cobalt	£350	85·00
66		6d. slate-violet	–	32·00
67		6d. reddish mauve	£425	85·00
68	8	1s. vermilion	£200	30·00
		a. Imperf vert (horiz pair)		

(iii) P 12 (1865–71—from July 1869 under contract to the Post Office).

69	3	1d. dull vermilion	85·00	
		a. Double print	†	–
70		1d. carmine	65·00	13·00
		a. Error. Wmkd "2" (*pen cancel* £110)	–	£2000
71		2d. yellow-green	£275	75·00
72		4d. deep blue	£140	21·00
73		4d. blue	£140	23·00
74		4d. cobalt-blue	–	55·00
75	7	6d. slate-violet	£180	29·00
		a. Imperf between (vert pair)		
76		6d. reddish mauve	95·00	42·00
		a. Imperf between (vert or horiz pair) (*pen cancel* £200)		
77	8	1s. vermilion	£180	42·00
		a. Double print	–	£180
		b. Imperf between (horiz pair) (*pen cancel* £200)	–	£1500

(iv) Perf compound 10×12 (1865–69).

78	3	1d. carmine	£1900	
79		4d. blue	–	£1500

(b) P 12½ by R. Harris, Launceston (1864–68).

80	3	1d. brick-red	95·00	40·00
81		1d. dull vermilion	90·00	32·00
82		1d. carmine	55·00	15·00
83		2d. yellow-green	£450	£150
84		2d. slate-green	£375	£170
85		4d. blue	£225	55·00
86		4d. bright blue	£225	55·00
87	7	6d. dull cobalt	£400	£100
88		6d. slate-violet	£300	60·00
89		6d. reddish mauve	£475	£130
90	8	1s. vermilion	£375	£120

(c) Imperf×oblique roulette 11½ at Oatlands (1866).

91	3	4d. blue	–	£650
91*a*	7	6d. dull cobalt	†	–

(d) Oblique roulette 10–10½, possibly at Deloraine (1867).

92	3	1d. brick-red	–	£550
93		1d. carmine	£1500	£450
94		2d. yellow-green	–	£750
95		4d. bright blue	–	£650
96	7	6d. grey-violet	–	£1000

(e) Oblique roulette 14–15, probably at Cleveland (1867–69).

97	3	1d. brick-red	–	£650
98		1d. dull vermilion	–	£650
99		1d. carmine	–	£650
100		2d. yellow-green	–	£800
101		4d. pale blue	–	£600
102	7	6d. grey-violet	–	£1000
103	8	1s. vermilion	–	£1300

(f) Pin-perf 5½ to 9½ at Longford (1867).

104	3	1d. carmine	£600	£160
105		2d. yellow-green		
106		4d. bright blue	–	£325
107	7	6d. grey-violet	–	£300
108		6d. reddish mauve	–	£750
109	8	1s. vermilion		

(g) Pin-perf 12 at Oatlands (1867).

110	3	4d. blue		

(h) Pin-perf 13½ to 14½ (1867).

111	3	1d. brick-red	–	£400
112		1d. dull vermilion	–	£400
113		1d. carmine		
114		2d. yellow-green	–	£600
115		4d. pale blue	–	£350
116	7	6d. grey-violet	–	£700
117	8	1s. vermilion		

(j) Serrated perf 19 at Hobart (1868–69).

118	3	1d. carmine (*pen-cancel* £9)	£425	£160
119		2d. yellow-green	–	£475
120		4d. deep blue	£1000	£160
121		4d. cobalt-blue	–	£160
122	7	6d. slate-violet	–	£700
123	8	1s. vermilion		

(k) Roul 4½, possibly at Macquarie River (1868).

124	3	4d. blue		
125	7	6d. reddish mauve		
126	8	1s. vermilion		

An example of the 1d. carmine is known peforated 10 on three sides and serrated 19 on the fourth.

For stamps perforated 11½ or 12 by the Post Office see Nos. 134a/43.

HAVE YOU READ THE NOTES AT THE BEGINNING OF THIS CATALOGUE?
These often provide answers to the enquiries we receive

11

12

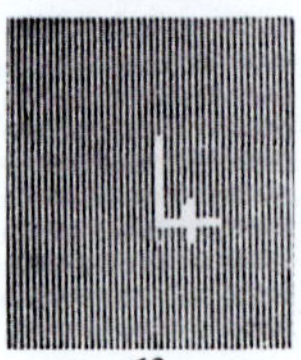
13

14

(Typo Govt Printer, Hobart, from plates made by D.L.R.)

1870 (1 Nov)–**71**. Wmk single-lined numerals W **12** (2d.), **13** (1d., 4d.) or **14** (1d., 10d.).

(a) P 12 by J. Walch & Sons.

127	11	1d. rose-red (wmk "10")	65·00	12·00
		a. Imperf (pair)	£850	£850
		b. Deep rose-red	75·00	9·00
128		1d. rose-red (wmk "4") (3.71)	75·00	25·00
		a. Imperf (pair)	–	£800
129		2d. yellow-green	95·00	8·00
		a. Imperf (pair)		
		b. Blue-green	£100	8·00
130		4d. blue	£750	£425
131		10d. black	24·00	30·00
		a. Imperf (pair)	£400	

(b) P 11½ by the Post Office (1871).

132	11	1d. rose-red (wmk "10")	£1100	
133		2d. yellow-green	£160	8·50
		a. Blue-green	90·00	6·00
		ab. Double print	†	£1200
134		10d. black	30·00	30·00

The above were printed on paper obtained from New South Wales.

See also Nos. 144/55, 156/8, 159/66, 170/4, 226/7, 242 and 255/6.

(Recess P.B.)

1871. Wmk double-lined numeral "**12**". P 11½ by the Post Office.

134*a*	7	1s. vermilion		

(Recess Govt Printer, Hobart)

1871–91. Double-lined numeral watermarks as W **4**. Perforated by the Post Office.

(a) P 11½.

135	7	6d. dull lilac	£130	22·00
136		6d. lilac	£120	22·00
		a. Imperf between (pair)	–	£900
137		6d. deep slate-lilac (3.75)	£120	22·00
		a. Imperf (pair)	–	£650
138		6d. bright violet (5.78)	£120	32·00
		a. Double print	–	£140
		b. Imperf between (horiz pair)	£1500	
139		6d. dull reddish lilac (10.79)	£110	40·00
140	8	1s. brown-red (1.73)	£150	55·00
		a. Imperf between (horiz pair)		
141		1s. orange-red (3.75)	£140	55·00
141*a*		1s. orange (5.78)		

(b) P 12.

142	7	6d. reddish purple (1884)	£100	20·00
		a. Imperf between (horiz pair)	£950	
143		6d. dull claret (7.91)	32·00	13·00

The perforation machine used on Nos. 142/3 was previously owned by J. Walch and Sons and passed to the ownership of the Government in 1884. It may have been used to perforate leftover sheets of previous printings.

15

16

"Wedge" flaw (Right pane R. 10/6)

(Typo Govt Printer, Hobart, from plates made by D.L.R.)

1871 (25 Mar)–**78**. W **15**.

(a) P 11½.

144	11	1d. rose (5.71)	9·00	1·50
		a. Imperf (pair) (*pen cancel* £40)	–	£900
		b. Bright rose	9·00	1·50
		c. Carmine	12·00	1·50
		d. Pink	13·00	2·50
		e. Vermilion (4.75)	£250	75·00
		f. Wedge flaw	£190	35·00
145		2d. deep green (11.72)	45·00	1·50
		a. Blue-green	38·00	1·50
		b. Yellow-green (12.75)	£180	3·25
146		3d. pale red-brown	50·00	4·00
		a. Imperf (pair)	£400	
		b. Imperf horiz (vert pair)	£1700	
		c. Deep red-brown	55·00	4·50
		ca. Purple-brown (1.78)	55·00	4·00
		d. Imperf (pair)	–	£850
		da. Brownish purple	50·00	4·00
147		4d. pale yellow (8.8.76)	80·00	23·00
		a. Ochre (7.78)	75·00	9·00
		b. Buff	65·00	9·50
148		9d. blue (2.10.71)	19·00	7·00
		a. Imperf (pair)	£350	
		b. Double print	†	£2250
149		5s. purple (*pen cancel* £3.75)	£225	65·00
		a. Imperf (pair)		
		b. Mauve	£200	65·00

(b) P 12.

150	11	1d. rose	95·00	13·00
		a. Carmine	£100	15·00
		b. Wedge flaw	–	85·00
151		2d. green	£550	£140
		a. Imperf (pair)	–	£1100
152		3d. red-brown	90·00	18·00
		a. Deep red-brown	90·00	18·00
153		4d. buff	£275	19·00
154		9d. pale blue	32·00	
		a. Imperf between (horiz pair)	£1600	
155		5s. purple	£375	
		a. Mauve	£300	

(Type D.L.R.)

1878 (28 Oct). W **16**. P 14.

156	11	1d. carmine	5·00	75
		a. Rose-carmine	5·00	75
		b. Scarlet	6·50	75
157		2d. pale green	6·50	75
		a. Green	6·50	75
158		8d. dull purple-brown	14·00	6·00

Plate scratch (Left pane R. 10/1)

(Typo Govt Printer, Hobart (some printings of 1d. in 1891 by *Mercury* Press) from plates made by Victoria Govt Printer, Melbourne (½d.) or D.L.R. (others)).

1880 (Apr)–**91**. W **16** (sideways on 1d.).

(a) P 11½.

159	11	½d. orange (8.3.89)	3·00	3·00
		a. Deep orange	3·00	3·00
160		1d. dull red (14.2.89)	9·00	2·75
		a. Vermilion-red	6·50	2·50
		b. Wedge flaw	70·00	25·00
161		3d. red-brown	16·00	4·50
		a. Imperf (pair)	£275	
		b. Plate scratch		
162		4d. deep yellow (1.83)	42·00	16·00
		a. Chrome-yellow	42·00	17·00
		b. Olive-yellow	£120	25·00
		c. Buff	38·00	9·50

(b) P 12.

163	11	½d. orange	2·75	4·25
		a. Deep orange	2·75	4·25
		ab. Wmk sideways		
164		1d. pink (1891)	22·00	6·50
		a. Imperf (pair)	£250	£275
		b. Rosine	20·00	4·50
		c. Dull rosine	20·00	5·50
		ca. Imperf (pair)	£225	
		d. Wedge flaw	£120	35·00
165		3d. red-brown	8·00	5·00
		a. Imperf between (horiz pair)	£1200	
		b. Plate scratch	80·00	45·00
166		4d. deep yellow	85·00	18·00
		a. Chrome-yellow	£100	16·00
		ab. Printed both sides	£850	

SPECIMEN AND PRESENTATION REPRINTS OF TYPE 11. In 1871 the 1d., 2d., 3d., 4d. blue, 9d., 10d. and 5s. were reprinted on soft white wove paper to be followed, in 1879, by the 4d. yellow and 8d. on rough white wove. Both these reprintings were perforated 11½. In 1886 it was decided to overprint remaining stocks with the word "REPRINT".

In 1889 Tasmania commenced sending sample stamps to the U.P.U. in Berne and a further printing of the 4d. blue was made, imperforate, on white card. This, together with the 5s. in mauve on white card, both perforated 11½ and overprinted "REPRINT", were included in presentation sets supplied to members of the states' legislatures in 1901.

Halfpenny	*d.* 2½	*d.* 2½
(17)	(18) (2¼ mm between "d" and "2")	(19) (3½ mm between "d" and "2")

1889 (1 Jan). *No. 156b surch locally with T* **17**.

167	**11**	½d. on 1d. scarlet	9·50	16·00
		a. "al" in "Half" printed sideways (R. 1/2)	£1100	£900

No. 167a occurred in a second printing and was later corrected.

A reprint on white card, perforated 11½ or imperforate, overprinted "REPRINT" was produced in 1901.

1891 (1 Jan–June). *Surch locally.* W **16**.

(a) With T **18**. P 11½.

168	**11**	2½d. on 9d. pale blue	12·00	4·25
		a. Surch double, one inverted	£475	£550
		b. Deep blue (May)	9·00	4·75

(b) With T **19**. P 12.

169	**11**	2½d. on 9d. pale blue (June)	5·00	3·50
		a. Blue surch		

A reprint, using a third setting, perforated 11½ and overprinted "REPRINT" was produced in 1901.

(Typo Govt Printer, Hobart)

1891 (Apr–Aug). W **15**.

(a) P 11½.

170	**11**	½d. orange	42·00	21·00
		a. Brown-orange	27·00	20·00
171		1d. rosine	18·00	8·50
		a. Wedge flaw	£140	55·00

(b) P 12.

172	**11**	½d. orange	32·00	25·00
		a. Imperf (pair)	£170	
173		1d. dull rosine	24·00	23·00
		a. Rosine	35·00	23·00
		b. Wedge flaw	£170	95·00
174		4d. bistre (Aug)	18·00	16·00

20

21

21a

(Typo D.L.R.)

1892 (12 Feb)–**99**. W **16**. P 14.

216	**20**	½d. orange and mauve (11.92)	2·00	1·25
217	**21**	2½d. purple	2·50	1·75
218	**20**	5d. pale blue and brown	7·00	3·00
219		6d. violet and black (11.92)	9·00	3·75
220	**21a**	10d. purple-lake and deep green (30.1.99)	9·00	11·00
221	**20**	1s. rose and green (11.92)	8·50	2·75
222		2s.6d. brown and blue (11.92)	22·00	21·00
223		5s. lilac and red (3.2.97)	60·00	21·00
224		10s. mauve and brown (11.92)	£110	80·00
225		£1 green and yellow (2.97)	£375	£325
216/25 *Set of* 10			£550	£400
216s/25s Optd "Specimen" *Set of* 10			£450	

See also Nos. 243 and 257/8.

(Typo Govt Printer, Hobart)

1896. W **16**. P 12.

226	**11**	4d. pale bistre	12·00	7·00
227		9d. pale blue	8·00	2·75
		a. Blue	8·50	3·25

22 Lake Marion

23 Mount Wellington

24 Hobart

25 Tasman's Arch

26 Spring River, Port Davey

27 Russell Falls

28 Mount Gould, Lake St. Clair

29 Dilston Fall

30

(Eng L. Phillips. Recess D.L.R.)

1899 (Dec)–**1900**. W **30**. P 14.

229	**22**	½d. deep green (31.3.00)	8·50	6·50
230	**23**	1d. bright lake (13.12.99)*	5·50	1·75
231	**24**	2d. deep violet (15.12.99)*	15·00	1·75
232	**25**	2½d. indigo (1900)	22·00	3·75
233	**26**	3d. sepia (1900)	13·00	4·75
234	**27**	4d. deep orange-buff (1900)	18·00	9·00
235	**28**	5d. bright blue (31.3.00)	28·00	11·00
236	**29**	6d. lake (31.3.00)	26·00	24·00
229/36 *Set of* 8			£120	55·00
229s/36s Optd "Specimen" *Set of* 8			£425	

*Earliest known postmark dates.

See also Nos. 237/9, 240/1, 245/8, 249/54, 259 and 261/2.

DIFFERENCES BETWEEN LITHOGRAPHED AND TYPOGRAPHED PRINTINGS OF TYPES 22/9

LITHOGRAPHED	TYPOGRAPHED
General appearance fine.	*Comparatively crude and coarse appearance.*
½d. All "V over Crown" wmk.	All "Crown over A" wmk.
1d. The shading on the path on the right bank of the river consists of very fine dots. In printings from worn stones the dots hardly show.	The shading on the path is coarser, consisting of large dots and small patches of colour.
The shading on the white mountain is fine (or almost absent in many stamps).	The shading on the mountain is coarse, and clearly defined.
2d. Three rows of windows in large building on shore, at extreme left, against inner frame.	Two rows of windows.
3d. Clouds very white.	Clouds dark.
Stars in corner ornaments have long points.	Stars have short points.
Shading of corner ornaments is defined by a coloured outer line.	Shading of ornaments terminates against white background.
4d. Lithographed only.	—
6d. No coloured dots at base of waterfall.	Coloured dots at base of waterfall.
Outer frame of value tablets is formed by outer line of design.	Thick line of colour between value tablets and outer line. Small break in inner frame below second "A" of "TASMANIA".

(Litho, using transfers from D.L.R. plates, Victoria Government Printing Office, Melbourne)

1902 (Jan)–**04**. Wmk V over Crown, W w **10** (sideways on ½d., 2d.). P 12½.

237	**22**	½d. green (2.03)	4·25	1·50
		a. Wmk upright	23·00	23·00
		b. Perf 11 (1904)	5·50	7·50
		c. Perf comp of 12½ and 11	£130	95·00
		d. Perf comp of 12½ and 12	£400	
		s. Optd "Specimen"	90·00	
238	**23**	1d. carmine-red	10·00	1·75
239	**24**	2d. deep reddish violet	9·00	70
		a. Perf 11	9·00	5·00
		b. Perf comp of 12½ and 11	£110	70·00
		c. Wmk upright (2.04)	55·00	12·00
		d. Deep rose-lilac (4.05)	14·00	60
		da. Perf 11	9·00	2·50
		db. Perf comp of 12½ and 11	£150	80·00
		s. Optd "Specimen"	90·00	

As the V and Crown paper was originally prepared for stamps of smaller size, portions of two or more watermarks appear on each stamp.

We only list the main groups of shades in this and the following issues. There are variations of shade in all values, particularly in the 2d. where there is a wide range, also in the 1d. in some issues.

(Typo, using electrotyped plates, Victoria Govt Ptg Office, Melbourne)

1902 (Oct)–**04**. Wmk V over Crown, W w **10**. P 12½.

240	**23**	1d. pale red (wmk sideways)	13·00	2·25
		a. Perf 11	32·00	4·75
		b. Perf comp of 12½ and 11	£300	70·00
		c. Wmk upright (1.03)	27·00	8·00
		ca. Perf 11	42·00	11·00
		d. Rose-red (wmk upright) (4.03)	10·00	2·25
		da. Perf 11	21·00	2·25
		db. Perf comp of 12½ and 11	£300	70·00
		ds. Optd "Specimen"	90·00	
241		1d. scarlet (wmk upright) (9.03)	8·50	1·75
		a. Perf 11	12·00	2·00
		b. Perf comp of 12½ and 11	—	35·00
		c. Rose-scarlet (1904)	8·00	1·75
		ca. Perf 11	7·50	2·00
		cb. Perf comp of 12½ and 11	£100	35·00

The 1d. scarlet of September 1903 was from new electrotyped plates which show less intense shading.

(Typo Victoria Govt Ptg Office, Melbourne)

1903 (Apr–Dec). Wmk V over Crown, W w **10**. P 12½.

242	**11**	9d. blue (Apr)	11·00	3·50
		a. Perf 11	8·00	11·00
		b. Perf comp of 12½ and 11	£750	£750
		c. Wmk sideways	£100	38·00
		d. Pale blue	12·00	8·00
		e. Bright blue	12·00	8·50
		f. Ultramarine	£400	
		g. Indigo	£170	
243	**20**	1s. rose and green (Dec)	24·00	6·00
		a. Perf 11	55·00	50·00
242s/3s Optd "Specimen" *Set of* 2			£180	

1½d.
(31)

ONE PENNY
(32)

1904 (29 Dec). *No. 218 surch with T* **31**.

244	**20**	1½d. on 5d. pale blue and brown	1·50	1·50
		s. Optd "Specimen"	48·00	

Stamps with inverted surcharge or without surcharge *se-tenant* with stamps with normal surcharge were obtained irregularly and were not issued for postal use.

PRINTER. The Victoria Govt Ptg Office became the Commonwealth Stamp Printing Branch in March 1909.

(Litho, using transfers from D.L.R. plates, Victoria Govt Ptg Office, Melbourne)

1905 (Sep)–**12**. Wmk Crown over A, W w **11** (sideways on horiz stamps). P 12½.

245	**24**	2d. deep purple	8·00	65
		a. Perf 11	26·00	1·50
		b. Perf comp of 12½ and 11	24·00	6·00
		c. Perf comp of 12½ and 12	£110	85·00
		d. Perf comp of 11 and 12	£190	£140
		e. Slate-lilac (1906)	9·00	65
		ea. Perf 11	32·00	1·50
		eb. Perf comp of 12½ and 11		
		ed. Perf comp of 11 and 12	£190	£140
		ee. Perf comp of 12½ and 12		
		f. Reddish lilac (1907)	22·00	2·00
		fa. Perf 11	32·00	3·25
		fb. Perf comp of 12½ and 11	95·00	
246	**26**	3d. brown (1906)	8·50	4·50
		a. Perf 11 (9.05)	21·00	19·00
		b. Perf comp of 12½ and 11	£150	£160
247	**27**	4d. pale yellow-brown (3.07)	13·00	4·00
		a. Perf 11	35·00	10·00
		b. Orange-buff (5.09)	27·00	4·25
		ba. Perf 11	35·00	18·00
		bb. Perf comp of 12½ and 11	£300	£350
		c. Brown-ochre (wmk sideways). Perf 11 (6.11)	30·00	38·00
		ca. Perf comp of 12½ and 11	—	£500
		d. Orange-yellow (3.12)	15·00	24·00
		da. Perf 11	40·00	45·00
		db. Perf comp of 12½ and 11	£300	£350
248	**29**	6d. lake (7.08)	50·00	8·00
		a. Perf 11	70·00	8·00
		b. Perf comp of 12½ and 11	£350	£375

Stamps with perf compound of 12½ and 12 or 11 and 12 are found on sheets which were sent from Melbourne incompletely perforated along the outside edge of the pane or sheet. The missing perforations were applied in Hobart using a line machine measuring 12 (11.8 is the exact gauge). This perforation can only occur on one side of a stamp.

(Typo, using electrotyped plates, Victoria Govt Ptg Office, Melbourne).

1905 (Aug)–**11**. Wmk Crown over A, W w **11** (sideways on horiz designs). P 12½.

249	**22**	½d. yellow-green (10.12.08)	1·75	75
		a. Perf 11	1·75	75
		b. Perf comp of 12½ and 11	75·00	23·00
		c. Perf comp of 11 and 12	£170	
		d. Wmk upright (1909)	13·00	5·50
		da. Perf 11	85·00	
250	**23**	1d. rose-red	2·50	30
		a. Perf 11	4·25	30
		b. Perf comp of 12½ and 11	4·50	4·00
		c. Perf comp of 12½ and 12	95·00	38·00
		d. Perf comp of 11 and 12	£120	40·00
		e. Wmk sideways (1907)	13·00	2·25
		ea. Perf 11	14·00	3·25
		eb. Perf comp of 12½ and 11	60·00	21·00
		f. Imperf (pair)	£425	£450
250*g*		1d. carmine-red (3.10)	8·00	2·25
		ga. Perf 11	9·50	2·50
		gb. Perf comp of 12½ and 11	12·00	6·50
		gc. Perf comp of 12½ and 12	95·00	35·00
		gd. Perf comp of 11 and 12	£120	40·00
		ge. Imperf (pair)	£425	
		gf. Wmk sideways	8·50	2·25
		gg. Perf 11	9·50	2·25
		gh. Perf comp of 12½ and 11	12·00	6·50
		h. Carmine-vermilion (1911)	14·00	5·50
		ha. Perf 11	17·00	6·00
		hb. Perf comp of 12½ and 11	40·00	8·50
		hc. Perf comp of 12½ and 12		
		hd. Perf comp of 11 and 12		
251	**24**	2d. plum (8.07)	15·00	70
		a. Wmk upright	22·00	3·75
		b. Perf 11	3·50	30
		ba. Wmk upright (12.07)	19·00	3·25
		c. Perf comp of 12½ and 11	28·00	12·00
		d. Perf comp of 12½ and 12	£275	90·00
		e. Perf comp of 11 and 12	£150	70·00
		f. Bright reddish violet (1910)	7·00	3·00
		fa. Perf 11	7·50	2·00
		fb. Perf comp of 12½ and 11	32·00	18·00
		fc. Perf comp of 12½ and 12	£275	90·00
253	**26**	3d. brown (3.09)	12·00	7·00
		a. Wmk upright		
		b. Perf 11	18·00	8·00
		c. Perf comp of 12½ and 11	£275	£300
254	**29**	6d. carmine-lake (12.10)	20·00	28·00
		a. Perf 11	21·00	40·00
		b. Perf comp of 12½ and 11	£300	
		c. Dull carmine-red (3.11)	23·00	40·00
		ca. Wmk upright	42·00	45·00
		cb. Perf 11	25·00	45·00
		cc. Perf comp of 12½ and 11	£325	£350

The note after No. 248 re perfs compound with perf 12 also applies here.

Nos. 250/f were printed from the same plates as Nos. 241/cb. Nos. 250g/hd are from a further pair of new plates and the images are sharper.

(Typo Victoria Govt Printing Office, Melbourne).

1906–13. Wmk Crown over A, W w **11**. P 12½.

255	**11**	8d. purple-brown (1907)	22·00	11·00
		a. Perf 11	17·00	5·00
256		9d. blue (1907)	7·00	4·75
		a. Perf 11	7·00	5·00
		b. Perf comp of 12½ and 11 (1909)	70·00	
		c. Perf comp of 12½ and 12 (1909)	£250	
		d. Perf comp of 11 and 12	£350	
257	**20**	1s. rose and green (1907)	13·00	5·50
		a. Perf 11 (1907)	27·00	24·00
		b. Perf comp of 12½ and 11	23·00	32·00
		c. Perf comp of 12½ and 12	£150	
258		10s. mauve and brown (1906)	£190	£200
		a. Perf 11	£325	£350
		b. Perf comp of 12½ and 12	£450	

The note after No. 248 re perfs compound with perf 12, also applies here.

(Typo, using stereotyped plates, Commonwealth Stamp Ptg Branch, Melbourne)

1911 (Jan). Wmk Crown over A, W w **11** (sideways). P 12½.

259	**24**	2d. bright violet	11·00	4·50
		a. Wmk upright	28·00	7·00
		b. Perf 11	9·50	4·50
		ba. Wmk upright	28·00	7·00
		c. Perf comp of 12½ and 11	80·00	27·00
		d. Perf comp of 12½ and 12	£325	

Stamps from this stereotyped plate differ from No. 251 in the width of the design (33 to 33¾ mm, against just over 32 mm), in the taller, bolder letters of "TASMANIA", in the slope of the mountain in the left background, which is clearly outlined in white, and in the outer vertical frame-line at left, which appears "wavy". Compare Nos. 260, etc, which are always from this plate.

1912 (Oct). No. 259 *surch with T* **32**. P 12½.

260	**24**	1d. on 2d. bright violet (R.)	1·00	1·00
		a. Perf 11	1·50	2·00
		b. Perf comp of 12½ and 11	£150	£160

(Typo, using electrotyped plates, Commonwealth Stamp Ptg Branch, Melbourne).

1912 (Dec). *Thin ready gummed paper, white gum (as Victoria, 1912).* W w **11** (sideways on 3d.). P 12½.

261	**23**	1d. carmine-vermilion	22·00	14·00
		a. Perf 11	21·00	14·00
		b. Perf comp of 12½ and 11	†	£375
262	**26**	3d. brown	65·00	90·00

STAMP BOOKLETS

There are very few surviving examples of Nos. SB1/4. Listings are provided for those believed to have been issued with prices quoted for those known to still exist.

1904 (1 Jan)–**09**. *Black on red cover as* No. SB1 *of New South Wales. Stapled.*

SB1 £1 booklet containing two hundred and forty 1d. in twelve blocks of 20 (5×4)
a. Red on pink cover (1909)
b. Blue on pink cover

1904 (1 Jan). *Black on grey cover* No. SB1. *Stapled.*

SB2 £1 booklet containing two hundred and twenty 2d. in four blocks of 30

1910 (1 May). *Black on white cover as No.* SB3. *of New South Wales. Stapled.*

SB3 2s. booklet containing eleven ½d. (No. 249), either in block of 6 plus block of 5 or block of 11, and eighteen 1d. (No. 250), either in three blocks of 6 or block of 6 plus block of 12 ... £5500

Unsold stock No. SB3 was uprated with one additional ½d. in May 1911.

1911 (Aug). *Red on pink cover as* No. SB3. *Stapled.*

SB4 2s. booklet containing twelve ½d. (No. 249), either in two blocks of 6 or block of 12, and eighteen 1d. (No. 250), either in three blocks of 6 or block of 6 plus block of 12 ... £4500

POSTAL FISCAL STAMPS

VALIDITY. Nos. F1/29 were authorised for postal purposes on 1 November 1882.

CLEANED STAMPS. Beware of postal fiscal stamps with pen-cancellations removed.

F 1

F 2

F 3

F 4

(Recess Alfred Bock, Hobart)

1863–80. Wmk double-lined "1". W **4**.

(a) Imperf.

F1	F **1**	3d. green (1.65)	£275	£140
F2	F **2**	2s.6d. carmine (11.63)	£275	£140
F3		2s.6d. lake (5.80)		
F4	F **3**	5s. brown (1.64)	£550	£450
F5		5s. sage-green (1880)	£325	£180
F6	F **4**	10s. orange (1.64)	£800	£450
F7		10s. salmon (5.80)	£550	£450

(b) P 10.

F8	F **1**	3d. green	£120	65·00
F9	F **2**	2s.6d. carmine	£140	
F10	F **3**	5s. brown	£225	
F11	F **4**	10s. orange	£160	

(c) P 12.

F12	F **1**	3d. green	£120	85·00
F13	F **2**	2s.6d. carmine	£120	95·00
F14	F **3**	5s. brown	£250	
F15		5s. sage-green	£110	85·00
F16	F **4**	10s. orange	£150	£110
F17		10s. salmon	£110	85·00

(d) P 12½.

F18	F **1**	3d. green	£250	
F19	F **2**	2s.6d. carmine	£225	
F20	F **3**	5s. brown	£350	
F21	F **4**	10s. orange-brown	£225	

(e) P 11½.

F22	F **1**	3d. green	£325	
F23	F **2**	2s.6d. lake	£120	£100
F24	F **3**	5s. sage-green	£110	85·00
F25	F **4**	10s. salmon	£180	£140

See also No. F30.

In 1879, the 3d., 2s.6d., 5s. (brown), and 10s. (orange) were reprinted on thin, tough, white paper, and are found with or without "REPRINT". In 1889 another reprint was made on white card, imperforate and perforated 12. These are also found with or without "REPRINT".

F **5** Duck-billed Platypus

REVENUE (F **6**)

(Typo D.L.R.)

1880 (19 Apr). W **16** (sideways). P 14.

F26	F **5**	1d. slate	25·00	7·00
F27		3d. chestnut	20·00	3·50
F28		6d. mauve	85·00	2·25
F29		1s. rose-pink	£110	17·00
		a. Perf comp of 14 and 11		

All values are known imperf, but not used.

Reprints are known of the 1d. in deep blue and the 6d. in lilac. The former is on yellowish white, the latter on white card. Both values also exist on wove paper, perf 12, with the word "REPRINT".

1888. W **16**. P 12.

F30	F **2**	2s.6d. lake	60·00	45·00
		a. Imperf between (horiz pair)	£900	

1900 (15 Nov). *Optd with Type* F **6**.

(a) On Types F **2** *and* F **4**.

F32	F **2**	2s.6d. lake (No. F30)	£300	
		a. "REVFNUE"	£400	
		b. Opt inverted	£600	
		c. Imperf	£300	
F33	F **4**	10s. salmon (No. F17)	£450	£450
		a. "REVFNUE"		

(b) On Nos. *F27 and F29.*

F34	F **5**	3d. chestnut	27·00	26·00
		a. Double opt, one vertical	90·00	£130
F35		1s. rose-pink		

(c) On stamps as Nos. *F26/9, but typo locally.* W **16**. P 12.

F36	F **5**	1d. blue	20·00	22·00
		a. Imperf between (horiz pair)	£300	
		b. Imperf vert (horiz pair)	£350	
		c. "REVENUE" inverted	£100	
		d. "REVENUE" double	£160	£170
		e. Pale blue	20·00	
F37		6d. mauve	60·00	
		a. Double print	£275	
F38		1s. pink	95·00	£110

(d) On No. 225.

F39	**20**	£1 green and yellow	£140	£130
		a. Opt double, one vertical	£300	£300

It was not intended that stamps overprinted with Type F **6** should be used for postal purposes, but an ambiguity in regulations permitted such usage until all postal fiscal stamps were invalidated for postal purposes on 30 November 1900.

Printings of some of the above with different watermarks, together with a 2d. as Nos. F36/8, did not appear until after the stamps had become invalid for postal purposes.

Tasmania became part of the Commonwealth of Australia on 1 January 1901.

VICTORIA

PRICES FOR STAMPS ON COVER

Nos. 1/17	*from* × 2
Nos. 18/22	*from* × 4
Nos. 23/4	*from* × 2
No. 25	*from* × 3
Nos. 26/32	*from* × 2
No. 33	*from* × 6
No. 34	*from* × 8
Nos. 35/9	*from* × 4
No. 40	*from* × 3
Nos. 41/53	*from* × 2
No. 54	*from* × 3
No. 55	—
No. 56	*from* × 4
Nos. 57/72	*from* × 2
No. 73	*from* × 3
Nos. 74/80	*from* × 2
No. 81	*from* × 3
Nos. 82/7	*from* × 4
Nos. 88/200	*from* × 3
Nos. 201/6	*from* × 5
Nos. 207/8	*from* × 10
Nos. 209/14	*from* × 5
Nos. 215/19	—
Nos. 220/6	*from* × 20
Nos. 227/33	—
Nos. 234/7	*from* × 20
Nos. 238/52	—
Nos. 253/6	*from* × 20
No. 257	*from* × 10
No. 258	*from* × 20
No. 259	*from* × 10
Nos. 260/4	—
Nos. 265/6	*from* × 20
Nos. 267/73	*from* × 10
Nos. 274/91	—
Nos. 292/304	*from* × 10
Nos. 305/9	*from* × 5
Nos. 310/23	*from* × 10
Nos. 324/8	—
No. 329	*from* × 12
Nos. 330/50	*from* × 8
Nos. 351/2	—
Nos. 353/4	*from* × 4
No. 355	*from* × 10
Nos. 356/73	*from* × 15
Nos. 374/5	*from* × 3
Nos. 376/98	*from* × 10
Nos. 399/400	—
Nos. 401/6	*from* × 10
Nos. 407/15	—
Nos. 416/30	*from* × 10
Nos. 431/2	—
Nos. 433/43	*from* × 4
Nos. 444/53	—
Nos. 454/5	*from* × 10
Nos. 456/63	*from* × 6
No. 464	—
Nos. D1/8	*from* × 30
Nos. D9/10	—
Nos. D11/37	*from* × 30

During the expansion of the Australian settlements in the fourth decade of the nineteenth century the growing population of the Port Phillip District in the south of New South Wales led to a movement for its creation as a separate colony. This aspiration received the approval of the British Government in 1849, but the colony of Victoria, as it was to be called, was not to be created until 1 July 1851.

In the meantime the New South Wales Legislative Council voted for the introduction of postal reforms, including the use of postage stamps, from 1 January 1850, and this act was also to apply to the Port Phillip District where stamps inscribed "VICTORIA" would predate the creation of that colony by eighteen months.

Until the end of 1859 the stamps of Victoria, with the exception of Nos. 40 and 73, were produced by local contractors working under the supervision of the colonial administration.

SPECIMEN OVERPRINTS. Those listed are from U.P.U. distributions in 1892 and 1897. Further "Specimen" overprints exist, but these were used for other purposes.

HAM PRINTINGS. The first contractor was Thomas Ham of Melbourne. He was responsible for the initial printings of the "Half-Length" 1d., 2d. and 3d., together with the replacement "Queen on Throne" 2d. The first printings were produced from small sheets of 30 (5×6) laid down directly from the engraved die which showed a single example of each value. Subsequent printings, of which No. 4*a* was the first, were in sheets of 120 (two panes of 60) laid down using intermediate stones of various sizes. Impressions from the first printings were fine and clear, but the quality deteriorated when intermediate stones were used.

1 Queen Victoria ("Half Length")

(Lithographed by Thomas Ham, Melbourne)

1850 (3 Jan)–**53**. Imperf.

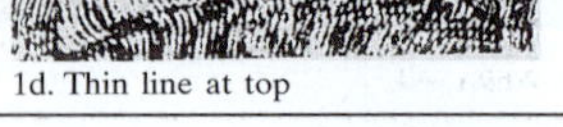
1d. Thin line at top

2d. Fine border and background

3d. White area to left of orb

(a) Original state of dies: 1d. (tops of letters of "VICTORIA" *reach to top of stamp); 2d. (fine border and background); 3d. (thicker white outline around left of orb, central band of orb does not protrude at left). No frame-lines on dies.*

1	1	1d. orange-vermilion	£27000	£5000
		a. Orange-brown	†	£1900
		b. Dull chocolate-brown	£16000	£2250
2		2d. lilac-mauve (*shades*) (Stone A)	£12000	£800
3		2d. brown-lilac (*shades*) (Stone B)	£9000	£450
		a. Grey-lilac	—	£500
4		3d. bright blue (*shades*)	£6000	£550
		a. Blue (*shades*)	£5000	£400
		ab. Retouched (between Queen's head and right border) (No. 11 in transfer group) (8 varieties)	—	£550
		ac. Retouched (under "V") (No. 10 in transfer group)	£12000	£1000

With the exception of No. 4*a* the above were printed from small stones of 30 (5×6) laid down directly from the engraved die which showed a single example of each value. There were two stones of the 2d. and one for each of the other values. No. 4*a* is the second printing of the 3d. for which the sheet size was increased to 120, the printing stone being constructed from an intermediate stone of 15 (5×3).

1d. Thick line at top

2d. Coarse background

3d. White area small and band protruding to left of orb

(b) Second state of dies: 1d. (more colour over top of letters of "VICTORIA"*); 2d. (fine border as (a) but with coarse background); 3d. (thinner white outline around left of orb, central band of orb protrudes at left).*

5	1	1d. red-brown (*shades*) (2.50)	£7500	£425
		a. Pale dull red-brown	£6000	£425
6		2d. grey-lilac (*shades*) (1.50)	£5000	£180
		a. Dull grey	£10000	£200
7		3d. blue (*shades*) (6.51)	£3500	£170
		a. Retouched (22 varieties) *from*	£5000	£350

Printed in sheets of 120 (10×12) with the printing stones constructed from intermediate stones of 30 (5×6) for the 1d. and 2d. or 10 (5×2) for the 3d. It is believed that the use of the smaller intermediate stone for the latter resulted in the many retouches.

Frame-lines added

(c) Third state of dies: As in (b) but with frame-lines added, very close up, on all four sides.

8	1	1d. dull orange-vermilion (11.50).	£4500	£650
		a. Dull red (*shades*)	£3500	£190
9		1d. deep red-brown (5.51)	£10000	£1000
		a. Brownish red (*shades*)	£3000	£170
		b. Dull rose (*shades*)	£3000	£170
10		2d. grey (*shades*) (8.50)	£6000	£190
		a. Olive-grey (*shades*)	£7000	£200
11		3d. blue (*shades*) (12.52)	£1800	80·00
		a. Deep blue (*shades*)	£2250	80·00
		b. Pale greenish blue (*shades*)	£3000	£160

Printed in sheets of 120 (12×10) produced from intermediate stones of 30 (6×5) for No. 8 and 12 (6×2) for the others.

White veil

(d) As (c) but altered to give, for the 1d. and 3d., the so-called "white veils", and for the 2d., the effect of vertical drapes to the veil.

12	1	1d. reddish brown (6.51)	£5000	£160
		a. Bright pinky red (*shades*)	£1500	£160
13		2d. drab (1.51)	£6000	£180
		a. Grey-drab	£6000	£170
		b. Lilac-drab	£6000	£170
		c. Red-lilac	—	£1200
		d. Void lower left corner	†	£20000
14		3d. blue (*shades*) (1.53)	£900	70·00
		a. Deep blue (*shades*)	£950	70·00
		b. Greenish blue (*shades*)	£1200	80·00
		c. Retouched (9 varieties)	£2500	£180

Printed in sheets of 120 (12×10) produced from intermediate stones of 12 (6×2) on which the details of the veil were amended as described above.

The "void corner" error occurred on the printing stone. It is believed that only four examples still exist.

2d. Coarse border and background

(e) Fourth state of 2d. die only: Coarse border and background. Veil details as in original die.

15	1	2d. red-lilac (*shades*) (5.50)	£6000	£300
		a. Lilac	£6000	£325
		b. Grey	£8000	£400
		c. Dull brownish lilac	£6000	£160
		d. Retouched lower label—value omitted *from*	†	£14000
		e. Other retouches (17 varieties) *from*	£9000	£350

Printed in sheets of 120 (12×10) produced from an intermediate stone of 30 (6×5).

(f) 2d. as (e), but with veils altered to give effect of vertical drapes.

16	1	2d. lilac-grey (1.51)	£4250	£160
		a. Deep grey	£4750	£160
		b. Brown-lilac (*shades*)	£3750	£100
17		2d. cinnamon (*shades*) (2.51)	£2500	£160
		a. Drab (*shades*)	£2750	90·00
		b. Pale dull brown (*shades*)	£2500	£110
		c. Greenish grey	£2500	£100
		d. Olive-drab (*shades*)	£2750	£180
		e. Buff	£11000	£225

Printed in sheets of 120 (12×10) produced from two successive intermediate stones of 30 (6×5) on which the details of the veil were amended as described above.

This was the final printing of the 2d. "Half Length" as the die for this value had been damaged. A replacement 2d. design was ordered from Thomas Ham.

For the later printings of the 1d. and 3d. in this design see Nos. 23/4, 26/31, 48/9 and 78/9.

2 Queen on Throne

3

(Recess-printed by Thomas Ham)

1852 (27 Dec). *Imperf.*

18	2	2d. reddish brown	£325	23·00
		a. Chestnut	—	£130
		b. Purple-brown	£400	23·00

Printed in sheets of 50 (10×5) from a hand-engraved plate of the same size. Each stamp in the sheet had individual corner letters made-up of various combinations, none of which contained the letter "J".

Reprints were made in 1891 using the original plate, on paper wmk V over Crown, both imperf and perf 12½.

For later printings of this design see Nos. 19/22 and 36/9.

CAMPBELL & CO PRINTINGS. In May 1853 the Victoria postal authorities placed an order for 1d. and 6d. stamps in the "Queen on Throne" design with Perkins, Bacon in London. These would not arrive for some time, however, and supplies of Ham's printings were rapidly becoming exhausted. Local tenders were, therefore, solicited for further supplies of the 1d. and 3d. "Half Lengths" and the 2d. "Queen on Throne". That received from J. S. Campbell & Co was accepted. The stamps were produced by lithography, using transfers from either the "Half Length" engraved die or the 2d. "Queen on Throne" engraved plate of 50. Stamps from the Campbell & Co printings can be distinguished from later printings in lithography by the good quality paper used.

(Lithographed by J. S. Campbell & Co, Melbourne, using transfers taken from Ham's engraved plate)

1854 (Jan–Jul). *Good quality white or toned paper.* Imperf.

(a) Clear impressions with details around back of throne generally complete.

19	2	2d. brownish purple	£300	30·00
		a. Grey-brown	£400	30·00
		b. Purple-black	—	30·00
		c. Dull lilac-brown (*toned paper only*)	£450	42·00

(b) Poor impressions with details around back of throne not fully defined.

20	2	2d. violet-black (2.54)	£400	30·00
		a. Grey-black	£500	30·00
		b. Grey-lilac	£400	30·00
		c. Dull brown (*on toned*)	£400	30·00
		ca. Substituted transfer (in pair)	—	£2500

(c) Weak impressions with background generally white without details. Toned paper only.

21	2	2d. grey-purple (7.54)	£250	27·00
		a. Purple-black	£250	27·00

(d) Printings using an intermediate stone. Impression flat and blurred. Background details usually complete. Toned paper only.

22	2	2d. grey-drab (*shades*) (5.54)	£375	27·00
		a. Black	—	£130

Nos. 19/21 were produced using transfers taken directly from the original Ham engraved plate. It is believed that the different strengths of the impressions were caused by the amount of pressure exerted when the transfers were taken. The stamps were printed in sheets of 100 (2 panes 10×5). On one stone a block of four at bottom left, lettered "FL GM" over "QV RW", was damaged and the stone was repaired by using a block of four substituted transfers. These were lettered "VZ WA" over "FL GM". No. 20ca covers any one of these substituted transfers in pair with normal. As horizontal pairs these are lettered "WA HN" or "GM SX" and as vertical "VZ" over "VZ" or "WA" over "WA".

For No. 22 an intermediate stone was used to produce a printing stone of 300 (6 panes 10×5). The insertion of a further stage into the process caused the blurred appearance of stamps from this printing. No. 22*a* is believed to come from proof sheets issued to post offices for normal use. Examples are usually cancelled with Barred Oval 108 and Barred Numerals 1 and 2.

(Lithographed by J.S. Campbell & Co, Melbourne)

1854 (Feb–June). *Good quality wove paper.* Imperf.

23	1	1d. orange-red (*shades*)	£2000	£140
		a. Rose	£6000	£750
24		3d. blue (*shades*) (6.54)	£800	48·00
		a. Retouched under "C" of "VICTORIA"	—	£140

The 1d. was produced in sheets of 192 (two panes of 96 (12×8)) and the 3d. in sheets of 320 (two panes of 160 (18×9)). Both printing stones were constructed from transfers taken from intermediate stones of 24 (6×4). The spacing between stamps is far wider than on the Ham printings. The 3d. panes of 160 were constructed using six complete transfers of 24 and three of 6 with the final impression in the bottom two rows removed.

The 1d. Campbell printings have the frame lines almost completely absent due to lack of pressure when taking transfers.

The 3d. retouch, No. 24a, occurs on R. 3/5 of the intermediate stone.

CAMPBELL AND FERGUSSON PRINTINGS. Increased postal rates in early 1854 led to a requirement for a 1s. value and in April a contract for this stamp was awarded to Campbell and Fergusson (the new corporate style of J. S. Campbell & Co). Further contracts to print the 1d. and 3d. "Half Lengths" and the 2d. "Queen on Throne" followed. All were produced by lithography with the two "Half Lengths" using transfers from the original engraved die and the 2d. "Queen on Throne" transfers from Ham's original engraved plate.

All Campbell and Fergusson printings were on paper of a poorer quality than that used for the earlier contract.

(Lithographed by Campbell & Fergusson)

1854 (6 Jul). *Poorer quality paper.* Imperf.

25	3	1s. blue (*shades*)	£700	25·00
		a. Greenish blue	£800	25·00
		b. Indigo-blue	—	£130

No. 25 was produced in sheets of 100 (8×12 with an additional stamp appearing at the end of rows 6 to 9). The printing stones used each contained four such sheets. They were constructed from an intermediate stone of 40 (8×5) taken from a single engraved die. Each pane of 100 showed two complete transfers of 40, one of 20, and one of a vertical strip of 4.

For this stamp rouletted or perforated see Nos. 54 and 81.

(Lithographed by Campbell & Fergusson)

1854 (Jul)–**57**. *Poorer quality paper.* Imperf.

26	1	1d. brown (*shades*)	£2250	£120
		a. Brick-red (*shades*)	£2500	£100
		b. Dull red (*shades*)	£2750	£100
27		1d. *Orange-brown* (*shades*) (8.55)	£2500	£130
		a. Dull rose-red (*shades*)	£2750	75·00
		b. Bright rose-pink	£4000	£140
		c. Retouched (6 varieties)	£5000	£450
28		1d. pink (*shades*) (2.55)	£1000	45·00
		a. Rose (*shades*)	£1000	45·00
		b. Lilac-rose (*shades*)	£1100	45·00
		c. Dull brown-red (*shades*)	£1300	£120
		d. Retouched (8 varieties)	£2000	£325
29		3d. bright blue (*shades*) (7.57)	£1800	65·00
		a. Greenish blue (*shades*)	£1400	50·00
		b. Retouch under "C" of "VICTORIA"	£2500	£130
30		3d. *Prussian blue* (*shades*) (11.56)	£2250	90·00
		a. Milky blue	£3000	£140
		b. Retouch under "C" of "VICTORIA"	—	£275
31		3d. steel-blue (*shades*) (heavier impression) (5.55)	—	60·00
		a. Greenish blue (*shades*)	£1500	45·00
		b. Blue (*shades*)	£1500	45·00
		c. Deep blue (*shades*)	£1100	45·00
		d. Indigo (*shades*)	—	50·00

The 1d. was produced in sheets of 400 (2 panes 20×10) constructed from transfers originating from the J. S. Campbell & Co intermediate stone. Each pane contained six complete transfers of 24, three of 12, two of 8 and one of 4.

The 3d. was produced in sheets of 320 (2 panes of 160) (No. 29), 200 (No. 30) or 400 (2 panes of 200) (No. 31.) The stone for No. 29 was constructed from transfers taken from the J. S. Campbell intermediate stone with the retouch on R. 3/5 still present. The panes of 160 contained six transfers of 24 and three of 6 with the last impression in both rows 8 and 9 removed. Quality of impression is generally poor. The stone for No. 30, once again taken from the Campbell intermediate stone, was laid down in the same combination of transfers as the 1d. value. Impressions from it were, however, so poor that transfers from a new intermediate stone were used for No. 31. Impressions from this stone, on which the panes of 200 were in a similar layout to the 1d. were much further apart than those on the stones used to produce Nos. 29/30.

The Campbell and Fergusson printings of the "Half Lengths" are listed in the order in which they were printed.

CALVERT PRINTINGS. Contracts for the provision of other values required by the postal rate changes in 1853 were placed with Samuel Calvert of Melbourne who used typography as the printing process. Calvert continued to print, and later roulette, stamps for the Victoria Post Office until March 1858 when it was discovered that he had placed some of the stock in pawn.

4 5 6

(Typographed from woodblocks by Samuel Calvert)

1854 (1 Sep)–**55**. Imperf.

32	**4**	6d. reddish brown (13.9.54)	£450	55·00
		a. Dull orange	£200	18·00
		b. Orange-yellow	£200	19·00
33	**5**	6d. ("TOO LATE") lilac and green (1.1.55)	£1400	£200
34	**6**	1s. ("REGISTERED") rose-pink and blue (1.12.54)	£1700	£170
35	**4**	2s. dull bluish green/*pale yellow*	£1800	£180

No. 33 was provided to pay the additional fee on letters posted after the normal closure of the mails. This service was only available in the larger towns; examples are usually postmarked Castlemaine, Geelong or Melbourne. The service was withdrawn on 30 June 1857 and remaining stocks of the "TOO LATE" stamps were used for normal postal purposes.

No. 34 was issued to pay the registration fee and was so used until 5 January 1858 after which remaining stocks were used for normal postage.

These four values were produced from individually-engraved boxwood woodblocks. The 6d. was in sheets of 100 printed by two impressions from two plates of 25. The 2s. was in sheets of 50 from a single plate of 25. The bicoloured "TOO LATE" and "REGISTERED" stamps are unusual in that Calvert used a common woodblock "key" plate of 25 for both values combined with "duty" plates made up from metal stereos. Both values were originally in sheets of 50, but the "REGISTERED" later appeared in sheets of 100 for which a second "key" plate of 25 was utilised.

For these stamps rouletted or perforated see Nos. 53, 55/8, 60/1 and 82.

(Lithographed by Campbell & Fergusson)

1855 (Mar)–**56**. *Poorer quality paper.* Imperf.

(a) Printings from stones which were not over-used; background around top of throne generally full and detail good.

36	**2**	2d. lilac (*shades*) (7.55)	£225	26·00
		a. Purple (shades)	£225	26·00
		b. "TVO" for "TWO"	£8000	£1000

(b) Early printings from stones which were over-used. Similar characteristics to those above, though detail is not quite so full. Distinctive shades.

37	**2**	2d. brown	–	75·00
		a. Brown-purple	£250	24·00
		b. Warm purple	–	24·00
		c. Rose-lilac	–	24·00
		d. Substituted transfer (pair)	–	£700

(c) Later printings from the same stones used for No. 37 *when in a worn condition. Impressions heavy, coarse and overcoloured; details blurred; generally white background around top of throne.*

38	**2**	2d. dull lilac-mauve (1856)	£250	32·00
		a. Dull mauve	£250	32·00
		b. Grey-violet	–	32·00
		c. Red-lilac	–	32·00
		d. Substituted transfer (pair)	–	£700

(d) Printings from a stone giving blotchy and unpleasing results, with poor definition. Mainly shows in extra colour patches found on most stamps.

39	**2**	2d. dull purple (7.55)	–	55·00
		a. Dull grey-lilac	£275	55·00
		b. On thick card paper	–	£600

The Campbell and Fergusson 2d. "Queen on Throne" printings were in sheets of 200 (4 panes 10×5) constructed from transfers taken from the original Ham engraved plate.

Four separate stones were used. On Stone A a creased transfer running through R. 4/8, 4/9 and 5/8 caused the "TVO" variety on the stamp from the bottom row of one pane. On Stone C the impression in the first vertical row of one pane were found to be so faulty that they were replaced by substituted transfers taken from elsewhere on the sheet causing abnormal horizontal pairs lettered "UY BF", "TX MQ", "DI WA", "SW GM" and "CH RW". The vertical pairs from the substituted transfers are lettered "UY" over "TX" and "DI" over "SW".

PERKINS BACON "CANCELLED". For notes on these handstamps, showing "CANCELLED" between horizontal bars forming an oval, see Catalogue Introduction.

7 Queen on Throne

8 "Emblems"

(Recess Perkins, Bacon & Co, London)

1856 (23 Oct). Wmk Large Star. Imperf.

40	**7**	1d. yellow-green (H/S "CANCELLED" in oval £10000)	£180	27·00

Supplies of this stamp, and the accompanying 6d. which was only issued rouletted (see No. 73), arrived in the colony at the end of 1854, but the 1d. was not placed on sale until almost two years later.

No. 40 was reprinted from the original plate in 1891. Examples, in either dull yellow-green or bright blue-green, are imperforate and on V over Crown watermarked paper.

(Typographed from electrotypes by Calvert)

1857 (26 Jan–6 Sept). Imperf.

(a) Wmk Large Star, W w **1**.

41	**8**	1d. yellow-green (18 Feb)	£130	18·00
		a. Deep green	£150	30·00
		b. Printed on both sides	†	£1600
42		4d. vermilion	£325	10·00
		a. Brown-vermilion	£300	9·00
		b. Printed on both sides	†	£1600
43		4d. dull red (20 July)	£200	7·50
44		4d. dull rose (6 Sept)	£300	7·50

(b) No wmk. Good quality medium wove paper.

45	**8**	2d. pale lilac (25 May)	£300	11·00
		a. Grey-lilac	£300	11·00

Nos. 41/5 were produced in sheets of 120, arranged as four panes of 30 (6×5) (1d. and 4d.) or twelve panes of 10 (2×5) (2d.), using electrotypes taken from a single engraved die of each value.

The setting of the 4d. was rearranged before the printing of Nos. 43/4.

Only two examples of No. 41b and No. 42b have been recorded.

For this printing rouletted or perforated see Nos. 46/7, 50/2, 59, 74 and 77.

ROULETTES AND PERFORATIONS. In August 1857 a rouletting machine was provided at the G.P.O., Melbourne, to enable the counter clerks to separate stamp stocks before sale to the public. This machine produced roulettes of 7½–9 in one direction across six rows at a time. There was also a single wheel device which gauged 7–7½. Both were in use between the earliest known date of 12 August and the end of 1857.

Calvert was granted a separate contract in October 1857 to roulette the stamps he printed, but only Nos. 57/61 had been produced when it was found, in April 1858, that he had pawned a quantity of the sheets. His contracts were terminated and his successor, F. W. Robinson, used a roulette machine of a different gauge before switching to a gauge 12 perforating machine in January 1859.

1857 (12 Aug–Sept). Rouletted 7–9 by counter clerks at G.P.O., Melbourne.

46	**8**	1d. yellow-green (No. 41)	£450	90·00
47		2d. pale lilac (No. 45)	–	38·00
		a. Grey-lilac	–	38·00
48	**1**	3d. blue (*shades*) (No. 24)	£2000	£225
		a. Retouch under "C" of "VICTORIA"	†	£450
49		3d. bright blue (*shades*) (No. 29)	–	£250
		a. Greenish blue (shades)	£2000	£225
		b. Retouch under "C" of "VICTORIA"	†	£600
50	**8**	4d. vermilion (No. 42)	–	£100
51		4d. dull red (No. 43)	–	40·00
52		4d. dull rose (No. 44) (Sept)	–	27·00
53	**4**	6d. reddish brown (No. 32)	–	75·00
		a. Dull orange	–	50·00
		b. Orange-yellow	–	60·00
54	**3**	1s. blue (*shades*) (No. 25)	–	95·00
		a. Greenish blue	–	95·00
55	**6**	1s. ("REGISTERED") rose-pink and blue (No. 34)	£6500	£325
56	**4**	2s. dull bluish green/*pale yellow* (No. 35)	£5500	£475

With the exception of the 1s., Nos. 54/a, these stamps are normally found rouletted on one or two sides only.

1857 (Oct). Rouletted by Calvert.

(a) Rouletted 7–9 on all four sides and with finer points than No. 53*b.*

57	**4**	6d. orange-yellow (No. 32*b*)	–	70·00

(b) Serpentine roulette 10–10½.

58	**4**	6d. orange-yellow (No. 32*b*)	–	90·00

(c) Serrated 18–19.

59	**8**	2d. grey-lilac (No. 45*a*)	£800	£475
60	**4**	6d. orange-yellow (No. 32*b*)	–	95·00

(d) Compound of serrated 18–19 and serpentine 10–10½.

61	**4**	6d. orange-yellow (No. 32*b*)	–	£150

No. 59 was not covered by the contract given to Calvert, but it is believed to be a test run for the rouletting machine. No. 61 always shows serrated 18–19 on three sides and the serpentine roulette at the top or bottom of the stamp.

(Typo from electrotypes by Calvert)

1858 (14 Jan–Apr). *Good quality white wove paper.* No wmk.

(a) Rouletted 7–9 on all four sides.

62	**8**	1d. pale emerald	£375	23·00
		a. Emerald-green	£375	23·00
63		4d. rose-pink (18 Jan)	£275	6·00
		a. Bright rose	£275	6·00
		b. Reddish pink	–	11·00
		c. Imperf horiz (vert pair)	†	£600

(b) Imperf (Apr).

64	**8**	1d. pale emerald	£250	13·00
		a. Emerald-green	–	16·00
65		4d. rose-pink	£325	23·00
		a. Bright rose	–	23·00
		b. Reddish pink	–	30·00

Nos. 62/5 were produced in sheets of 120, arranged as four panes of 30 (6×5).

The Royal Collection contains a used horizontal pair of the 4d. showing the vertical roulettes omitted.

The majority of Nos. 64/5 were issued in April after Calvert's contracts had been terminated, although there is some evidence that imperforate sheets of the 4d., at least, were issued earlier.

For the 1d. of this issue perforated see No. 75.

ROBINSON PRINTINGS. Calvert's contracts were cancelled in April 1858 and the work was then placed with F. W. Robinson, who had unsuccessfully tendered in 1856. The same electrotypes were used, but a perforating machine was introduced from January 1859. Robinson continued to print and perforate stamps under contract until the end of 1859 when the Victoria Post Office purchased his equipment to set up a Stamp Printing Branch and appointed him Printer of Postage Stamps.

(Typo from electrotypes by Robinson)

1858 (May–Dec).

(a) Imperf.

(i) Coarse quality wove paper.

66	**8**	4d. dull rose (*oily ink*)	–	70·00

(ii) Smooth vertically-laid paper.

67	**8**	4d. dull rose (*oily ink*)	–	42·00
		a. Dull rose-red	–	42·00
68		4d. dull rose-red (*normal ink*) (20 May)	£475	22·00

(b) Rouletted 5½–6½.

(i) Smooth-laid paper.

69	**8**	2d. brown-lilac (*shades*) (*horiz laid*) (June)	£150	8·50
		a. Vert laid paper (21 Sept)	£250	10·00
70		2d. violet (*horiz laid*) (27 Nov)	£180	6·00
		a. Dull violet	£225	18·00
71		4d. pale dull rose (*vert laid*) (1 June)	£180	3·75
		a. Horiz laid paper	†	£900
		b. Dull rose-red	£150	3·75
		c. Rose-red	£150	3·50
		ca. Serrated 19	†	£500

(ii) Good quality wove paper.

72	**8**	1d. yellow-green (24 Dec)	£350	27·00

Nos. 66/72 were produced in sheets of 120, arranged as four panes of 30 (6×5).

For stamps of this issue perforated see Nos. 76 and 80.

(Recess Perkins, Bacon & Co, London)

1858 (1 Nov). Wmk Large Star, W w **1**. Rouletted 5½–6½.

73	**7**	6d. bright blue	£250	14·00
		a. Light blue	£300	25·00

No. 73 was received from London at the same time as the 1d., No. 40, but was kept in store until November 1858 when the stock was rouletted by Robinson. When issued the gum was in a poor state.

Imperforate examples exist from Perkins Bacon remainders. Examples are known handstamped "CANCELLED" in oval of bars. *Price* £10000.

Imperforate reprints, in shades of indigo, were made from the original plate in 1891 on V over Crown watermarked paper.

1859 (Jan–May). P 12 by Robinson.

74	**8**	1d. yellow-green (No. 41)	–	£300
75		1d. emerald-green (No. 64*a*)	–	£300
		a. Imperf between (horiz pair)		
76		1d. yellow-green (as No. 72) (11 Jan)	£225	14·00
		a. Imperf horiz (vert pair)	–	£425
		b. Thin, glazed ("Bordeaux") paper	†	£160
77		2d. pale lilac (No. 45)	–	£275
		a. Grey-lilac	–	£275
78	**1**	3d. blue (shades) (No. 24) (2 Feb)	£1500	£130
		a. Retouch under "C" of "VICTORIA"	–	£400
79		3d. greenish blue (*shades*) (No. 29*a*)	†	£425
		a. Retouch under "C" of "VICTORIA"	†	£1200
80	**8**	4d. dull rose-red (No. 68)	–	£325
81	**3**	1s. blue (*shades*) (No. 25) (4 Feb)	£170	15·00
		a. Greenish blue	£190	12·00
		b. Indigo-blue	–	32·00
82	**4**	2s. dull bluish green/*pale yellow* (No. 35) (May)	£350	42·00

The 1s. was reprinted in 1891 using transfers taken from the original die. These reprints were on V over Crown watermarked paper and perforated 12½.

For perforated 6d. black and 2s. blue both as Type **4** see Nos. 102 and 129/30.

(Typo from electrotypes by Robinson)

1859 (17 May–23 Dec). P 12.

(a) Good quality wove paper.

83	**8**	4d. dull rose	£180	4·50
		a. Roul 5½–6½	†	£850

(b) Poorer quality wove paper.

84	**8**	1d. dull green (July)	£150	15·00
		a. Green (11 Nov)	£150	15·00
85		4d. rose-carmine (16 July)	£180	5·00
		a. Rose-pink (thick paper) (30 Nov)	–	11·00

(c) Horizontally laid paper with the lines wide apart.

86	**8**	1d. dull green (18 July)		
		a. Laid lines close together	–	28·00
		b. Green (shades) (Oct)	£160	16·00
87		4d. rose-pink (*shades*) (23 Dec)	£150	7·50
		a. Laid lines close together	–	10·00

STAMP PRINTING BRANCH. On 1 January 1860 F. W. Robinson was appointed Printer of Postage Stamps and his equipment purchased by the Post Office to establish the Stamp Printing Branch. All later Victoria issues were printed by the Branch which became part of the Victoria Government Printing Office in December 1885. In 1909 the Commonwealth Stamp Printing Office under J. B. Cooke was established in Melbourne and produced stamps for both the states and Commonwealth until 1918.

9

10

11

(Des and eng F. Grosse. Typo from electrotypes)

1860 (31 Jan)–**66**. P 12.

(a) No wmk.

88	**9**	3d. deep blue (*horiz laid paper*) ..	£400	45·00
		a. Light blue		
89		4d. rose-pink (*thin glazed Bordeaux paper*) (21.4.60)	—	16·00
		a. Rose	£375	19·00
		ab. Thicker coarser paper (7.60)	£375	16·00

(b) On paper made by T. H. Saunders of London wmkd with the appropriate value in words as W **10**.

90	**9**	3d. pale blue (1.61)	£160	7·00
		a. Bright blue (10.61)	£160	8·50
		b. Blue (4.63)	£170	6·00
		c. Deep blue (4.64)	£170	6·00
		d. "TRREE" for "THREE" in wmk	—	£500
91		3d. maroon (13.2.66)	£150	27·00
		a. Perf 13	£150	29·00
92		4d. rose-pink (1.8.60)	—	9·00
		a. Rose-red	£100	4·75
		b. Rose-carmine	—	9·50
		c. Dull rose	£100	4·75
		d. Printed on "FIVE SHILLINGS" diagonal wmk paper (11.9.62)	£2000	20·00
93		6d. orange (25.10.60)	£4500	£300
94		6d. black (20.8.61)	£150	5·50
		a. Grey-black	£150	5·50

(c) On paper made by De La Rue wmkd with the appropriate value as a single-lined numeral as W **11**.

95	**9**	4d. dull rose-pink (9.10.62)	£120	5·50
		a. Dull rose	£130	6·00
		b. Rose-red	—	5·50
		c. Roul 8 (28.7.63)	—	£250
		d. Imperf (31.7.63)	—	75·00
		e. Perf 13×12		

All three values were produced in sheets of 120, initially as four panes of 30 (6×5). Printings of the 3d. from 1864 were in a changed format of six panes of 20 (4×5).

The "TRREE" watermark error comes from early printings of No. 90 on R. 10/7.

Two examples of the 4d. on Saunders paper are known bisected in 1863, but such use was unauthorised.

Nos. 95c/e were issued during July and August 1863 when the normal perforating machine had broken down.

Reprints, from new plates, were made of the 3d. and 4d. in 1891 on "V over Crown" paper and perforated 12½.

1860 (Apr)–**63**. P 12.

(a) No wmk.

96	**8**	1d. bright green (*horiz laid paper*)		
97		1d. bright green (*thin, glazed Bordeaux paper*) (25.5.60)	—	42·00

(b) On paper made by T. H. Saunders of London wmkd with the appropriate value in words as W **10**.

98	**8**	1d. pale yellowish green (8.7.60) ..	85·00	4·50
		a. Yellow-green	95·00	4·75
		b. Error. Wmkd "FOUR PENCE"	†	£7500
99		2d. brown-lilac (7.7.61)	—	35·00
100		2d. bluish slate (8.61)	£140	6·00
		a. Greyish lilac (9.61)	£150	6·00
		b. Slate-grey (1.62)	—	6·00
		c. Printed on "THREE PENCE" wmkd paper. *Pale slate* (27.12.62)	£150	16·00
		ca. Bluish grey (2.63)	£160	18·00

*(c) On paper made by De La Rue wmkd single-lined "***2***",* W **11**.

101	**8**	2d. dull reddish lilac (24.4.63)	£200	11·00
		a. Grey-lilac (10.63)	£190	17·00
		ab. Error. Wmkd "6"	†	£6000
		b. Grey-violet (11.63)	£140	14·00
		c. Slate (12.63)	£190	23·00

Only two examples of No. 98b have been recorded, one of which is in the Royal Collection.

1861 (22 Jun). *On paper made by T. H. Saunders of London wmkd "SIX PENCE" as* W **10**. P 12.

102	**4**	6d. black	£200	48·00

No. 102 was produced as an emergency measure after the decision had been taken to change the colour of the current 6d. from orange (No. 93) to black (No. 94). During the changeover the old Calvert "woodblock" plates were pressed into service to provide two months' supply.

12

13

(Des, eng and electrotyped De Gruchy & Leigh, Melbourne. Typo)

1861 (1 Oct)–**64**. P 12.

(a) On paper made by T. H. Saunders of London. Wmk "ONE PENNY" as W **10**.

103	**12**	1d. pale green	95·00	11·00
		a. Olive-green	—	12·00

(b) On paper made by De La Rue. Wmk single-lined "1" as W **11**.

104	**12**	1d. olive-green (1.2.63)	75·00	14·00
		a. Pale green (9.63)	75·00	8·50
		b. Apple-green (4.64)	75·00	8·00

(c) On paper supplied to Tasmania by Perkins, Bacon. Wmk double-lined "1", W **4** *of Tasmania.*

105	**12**	1d. yellow-green (10.12.63)	£140	12·00
		a. Dull green	—	12·00
		b. Imperf between (pair)	†	—

All printings were in sheets of 120 containing four panes of 30 (6×5).

Reprints from new plates were made in 1891 on paper watermarked "V over Crown" and perforated 12½.

(Frame die eng F. Grosse. Typo from electrotypes)

1862 (26 Apr)–**64**. *Centre vignette cut from* T **9** *with a new frame as* T **13**.

(a) On paper made by T. H. Saunders of London. Wmk "SIX PENCE" as W **10**. P 12.

106	**13**	6d. grey	£100	9·50
		a. Grey-black	£100	11·00
		b. Jet-black	£110	13·00

(b) On paper made by De La Rue. Wmk single-lined "6" as W **11**.

107	**13**	6d. grey (p 12) (18.6.63)	90·00	6·50
		a. Jet-black	—	8·50
		b. Grey-black	90·00	7·00
		c. Perf 13. *Jet-black*	£100	8·50
		ca. Grey-black	£100	8·50

Printings before August 1863 were in sheets of 120 containing four panes of 30 (6×5). For subsequent printings of No. 107 the format was changed to six panes of 20 (4×5).

Reprints from new plates were made in 1891 on paper watermarked "V over Crown" and perforated 12½.

SINGLE-LINED NUMERAL WATERMARK PAPERS. The first consignment of this paper, showing watermarks as W **11**, arrived in Victoria during October 1862. Five further consignments followed, all but the last supplied by De La Rue.

The complexity of the scheme for different watermarks for each value, together with the time required to obtain further supplies from Great Britain, resulted in the emergency use of paper obtained from Tasmania and of the wrong numeral watermark on certain printings.

The final order for this paper was placed, in error with the firm of T. H. Saunders of London. Although the actual watermarks are the same (the dandy rolls were the property of the Victoria Government and supplied to each firm in turn) there are considerable differences between the two types of paper. That manufactured by Saunders is of a more even quality and is smoother, thicker, less brittle and less white than the De La Rue type.

De La Rue supplied white paper watermarked "1", "2", "4", "6" and "8", blue paper watermarked "1" and green paper watermarked "2". The Saunders consignment of October 1865 contained white paper watermarked "1", "4" and "6", blue paper watermarked "1", green paper watermarked "2" and pink paper watermarked "10".

It is helpful for comparison purposes to note that all white paper watermarked "2" or "8" can only be De La Rue and all pink paper watermarked "10" can only be Saunders.

14

15

16

17

18

(Des and eng F. Grosse. Typo from electrotypes)

1863–74. *"Laureated" series.*

(a) On paper made by De La Rue wmkd with the appropriate value in single-lined numerals as W **11**.

108	**14**	1d. pale green (P 12) (9.9.64)	80·00	9·00
		a. Perf 12½×12 (9.64)		
		b. Perf 13 (10.10.64)	75·00	5·50
		c. Bluish green (P 13)	70·00	4·50
		ca. Printed double	†	£1000
		d. Green (P 12) (7.65)	75·00	4·50
		da. Perf 13	70·00	4·75
		e. Deep green (P 12) (12.65)	90·00	4·75
		ea. Perf 13	—	4·75
		eb. Perf 12×13	—	9·50
		f. Bright yellow-green (P 13)	—	19·00
109		2d. violet (P 12) (1.4.64)	80·00	8·50
		a. Dull violet (P 12) (10.64)	85·00	8·50
		ab. Perf 12½×12		
		ac. Perf 12½		
		ad. Perf 13	85·00	7·00
		b. Dull lilac (P 13) (4.65)	70·00	7·00
		ba. Perf 12 (7.66)	—	12·00
		bb. Perf 12×13 (7.66)	—	13·00
		c. Reddish mauve (P 13) (11.65)	75·00	9·50
		d. Rose-lilac (P 13) (1.66)	70·00	8·50
		da. Perf 12×13 or 13×12	70·00	8·50
		e. Grey (P 12) (7.66)	£110	11·00
		ea. Perf 13	70·00	4·75
110		4d. deep rose (P 12) (11.9.63)	£140	4·50
		a. Printed double	†	£1100
		b. Rose-pink (P 12) (9.63)	£110	2·50
		c. Pink (P 12) (7.5.64)	£110	2·50
		ca. Error. Wmkd single-lined "8"	†	£7500
		cb. Perf 12½×12 (9.64)		
		d. Dull rose (P 13) (10.64)	95·00	2·50
		e. Dull rose-red (P 13)	95·00	2·50
		ea. Perf 12 (8.65)	£150	75·00
111	**16**	6d. blue (P 12) (13.2.66)	65·00	7·00
		a. Perf 13	65·00	3·75
		b. Perf 12×13	60·00	4·50
112	**14**	8d. orange (P 13) (22.2.65)	£400	60·00
113	**17**	1s. blue/*blue* (P 13) (10.4.65)	£140	4·50
		a. Perf 12×13 (4.66)	£140	4·50
		ab. Imperf between (vert pair)	†	£3750
		b. Bright blue/blue (P 13) (6.67)	£110	4·00
		c. Indigo-blue/blue (P 13) (3.68)	—	4·00
		d. Dull blue/blue (P 12) (6.74)	—	3·75

(b) Emergency printings on Perkins, Bacon paper borrowed from Tasmania. Wmk double-lined "4" as W **4** of Tasmania.

114	**14**	4d. deep rose (P 12) (7.1.64)	£150	6·00
		a. Pale rose (P 12)	—	5·50
		b. Dull reddish rose (P 13) (11.8.65)	£150	6·00
		ba. Perf 12	—	6·00
		bb. Perf 12×13	—	15·00
		bc. Perf 12½, 12 and 13 compound		
		c. Red (P 13) (4.12.65)	£160	6·00

(c) Emergency printings on De La Rue paper as W **11**, *but showing incorrect single-lined numeral.* P 13.

115	**14**	1d. bright yellow-green (wmkd "8") (27.12.66)	£160	16·00
116		1d. bright yellow-green (wmkd "6") (6.67)	—	30·00
117		2d. grey (wmkd "8") (18.1.67)	£150	5·00
118	**15**	3d. lilac (wmkd "8") (29.9.66)	£150	32·00
119	**16**	10d. grey (wmkd "8") (21.10.65)	£600	£120
		a. Grey-black	£600	£130

(d) On paper made by T. H. Saunders wmkd with the appropriate value in single-lined numerals as W **11**.

120	**14**	1d. deep yellow-green (P 12×13) (1.66)	£130	14·00
		a. Perf 13 (3.66)	70·00	7·00
		b. Perf 12 (7.66)	—	15·00
121		4d. rose-red (P 13) (12.12.65)	90·00	3·25
		a. Perf 12×13 or 13×12 (2.66)	£140	7·00
		b. Perf 12 (4.66)	—	7·00
122	**16**	6d. blue (P 13) (28.5.66)	60·00	1·75
		a. Perf 12	65·00	4·25
		b. Perf 12×13	60·00	2·75
		ba. Imperf between (horiz pair) ..	†	£2000
123		10d. dull purple/*pink* (P 13) (22.3.66)	£110	5·00
		a. Perf 12×13	£150	6·50
		b. Blackish brown/pink (P 13) (12.69)	£120	5·50
		c. Purple-brown/pink (P 13) (11.70)		
124	**17**	1s. bright blue/*blue* (P 13) (5.12.70)	75·00	3·50
		a. Pale dull blue/blue (P 12) (1.73)	£150	4·50
		ab. Perf 13	—	11·00
		b. Indigo-blue/blue (P 12) (9.73)	—	7·50
		ba. Perf 13	75·00	4·75

(e) Emergency printings on Saunders paper as W **11**, *but showing incorrect single-lined numeral.* P 13.

125	**14**	1d. bright yellow-green (wmkd "4") (6.3.67)	£120	20·00
126		1d. bright yellow-green (wmkd "6") (6.67)	£170	27·00
127		2d. grey (wmkd "4") (21.2.67)	£120	6·50
128		2d. grey (wmkd "6") (13.5.67)	£190	7·00

The 1d., 2d., 4d. and 8d. were originally produced in sheets of 120 containing eight panes of 15 (3×5). The 3d. and 6d. were in sheets of 120 (12×10) and the 1d. (from February 1866), 2d. (from July 1866) and 4d. (from April 1866) subsequently changed to this format. The 10d. was in sheets of 120 containing twenty panes of 6 (2×3). The 1s. was originally in sheets of 60 containing three panes of 20 (4×5), but this changed to 120 (12×10) in April 1866.

Only single examples are thought to exist of Nos. 110a, 110ca, 113ab, and 122ba and two of No. 108ca.

For later emergency printings on these papers see Nos. 153/66.

(Typo from composite woodblock and electrotype plate)

(a) On De La Rue paper. Wmk single-lined "2" as W **11**.

129	**4**	2s. light blue/*green* (P 13) (22.11.64)	£180	7·00
		a. Dark blue/green (P 12) (9.65)	£200	14·00
		ab. Perf 13 (6.66)	£180	8·00
		b. Blue/green (P 13) (6.68)	£170	6·00
		c. Greenish blue/green (P 13) (7.73)	£170	7·50
		ca. Perf 12	£190	8·50
		d. Deep greenish blue/green (P 12½)	£170	6·50

(b) On Saunders paper. Wmk single-lined "2" as W **11**.

130	**4**	2s. dark blue/*green* (P 13) (23.11.67)	£190	7·00
		a. Blue/green (P 13) (10.71)	£190	7·00
		ab. Perf 12 (8.74)	£225	8·00
		c. Deep greenish blue/green (P 12½) (7.80)	£170	5·50

Nos. 129/30 were produced in sheets of 30 containing two panes of 15 (3×5). The plate contained eighteen of the original woodblock impressions and twelve electrotypes taken from them.

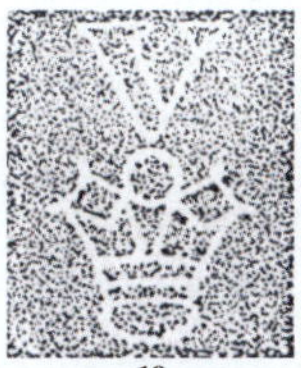

19

20

V OVER CROWN WATERMARKS. The changeover from the numeral watermarks to a general type to be used for all values was first suggested at the end of 1865, but the first supplies did not reach Melbourne until April 1867. Five different versions were used before the V over Crown watermark was superseded by the Commonwealth type in 1905. The five versions are listed as follows:

Type **19** De La Rue paper supplied 1867 to 1882. Shows four points at the top of the crown with the left and right ornaments diamond-shaped

Type **33** De La Rue paper supplied 1882 to 1895. No points at the top of the crown with the left and right ornaments oval-shaped

Type **82** Waterlow paper supplied 1896 to 1899. Wide base to crown

Type **85** Waterlow paper used for postal issues 1899 to 1905. Wide top to crown

Type **104** James Spicer and Sons paper used for postal issues August and September 1912. Narrow crown

The 1d. scarlet of September 1903 was from new electrotyped plates which show less intense shading.

(Type from electrotypes)

1867–81. Wmk. V over Crown. W **19**.

(a) P 13.

131 **14** 1d. bright yellow-green (10.8.67) . 70·00 3·50
a. Bright olive-green (1.69) £100 20·00
b. Yellow-green (4.69) 70·00 3·25
c. Dull green (3.70) 70·00 3·25
d. Pale green (10.70) 65·00 3·25
e. Grass-green (1871) 65·00 3·50
f. Bluish green (shades) (7.72) 65·00 3·50
g. Green (shades) (9.72) 65·00 3·25
132 2d. slate-grey *(shades)* (26.8.67) 75·00 3·50
a. Grey-lilac (29.1.68) 75·00 5·00
b. Lilac (26.8.68) 55·00 3·25
c. Dull mauve (shades) (10.68) 55·00 3·25
d. Lilac-grey (1.69) – 3·50
e. Lilac-rose (2.69) 60·00 3·00
f. Mauve (4.69) 75·00 3·25
g. Red-lilac (5.69) 60·00 3·00
h. Dull lilac (6.69) 60·00 2·50
i. Silver-grey (9.69) £120 7·50
133 **15** 3d. lilac (28.8.67) £225 38·00
a. Grey-lilac (6.68) £250 40·00
134 3d. yellow-orange (12.6.69) 32·00 5·50
a. Dull orange (6.70) 30·00 4·75
b. Orange (3.73) – 4·75
c. Bright orange (3.73) 35·00 4·75
d. Orange-brown (glazed paper) (10.78) 30·00 11·00
135 **14** 4d. dull rose (28.11.67) 80·00 6·50
a. Wmk sideways † 65·00
b. Aniline red (shades) (21.4.69) – 8·50
c. Rose-pink (11.69) – 5·00
d. Rose (shades) (8.71) 75·00 3·25
e. Dull rose (glazed paper) (5.3.79) 75·00 3·75
f. Dull rose-red (glazed paper) (11.79) – 5·50
g. Bright lilac-rose (aniline) (glazed paper) (2.80) 85·00 4·00
h. Rosine (aniline) (glazed paper) (9.80) £225 6·00
136 **16** 6d. deep blue (15.1.68) – 4·25
a. Blue (21.12.68) 42·00 3·00
b. Indigo-blue (10.69) 42·00 3·00
c. Prussian blue (9.72) 38·00 3·00
d. Indigo (4.73) 42·00 3·50
e. Dull blue (worn plate) (3.74) – 3·00
f. Dull ultramarine (2.12.75) 55·00 3·00
g. Light Prussian blue (12.75) 75·00 3·00
h. Dull violet-blue (7.77) – 10·00
i. Blue (glazed paper) (6.78) 55·00 3·00
j. Dull milky-blue (glazed paper) (9.79) 55·00 3·00
k. Prussian blue (glazed paper) (4.80) – 3·00
l. Light blue (glazed paper) (4.81) 55·00 3·00
m. Deep blue (glazed paper) (10.81) 55·00 3·00
137 **14** 8d. lilac-brown/*pink* (24.1.77) 90·00 5·50
a. Purple-brown/pink (2.78) 90·00 5·50
b. Chocolate/pink (8.78) 95·00 7·00
ba. Compound perf 13×12 † £325
c. Red-brown/pink (12.78) 90·00 5·00
d. Wmk sideways † £400
138 **17** 1s. light blue/*blue* (11.5.75) £130 12·00
139 **18** 5s. blue/*yellow* (26.12.67) £2250 £325
a. Wmk reversed – £500
140 5s. indigo-blue and carmine (I) (8.10.68) £325 32·00
a. Blue and carmine (4.69) £275 22·00
b. Pale bright blue and carmine (glazed paper) (24.7.77) – 28·00
c. Grey-blue and carmine (glazed paper) (4.78) £275 24·00
d. Wmk sideways. *Deep lavender-blue and carmine* (4.6.80) £275 28·00
141 5s. bright blue and red (II) *(glazed paper)* (12.5.81) £250 23·00
a. Indigo-blue and red (glazed paper) – 29·00

(b) P 12.

142 **14** 1d. pale green (10.71) 75·00 5·50
a. Grass-green (1871) 65·00 5·50
b. Bluish green (shades) (7.72) – 5·50
c. Green (shades) (9.72) 65·00 5·00
143 **15** 3d. dull orange (5.72) 35·00 3·00
a. Orange (3.73) – 2·10
b. Bright orange (3.73) – 2·50
c. Dull orange-yellow (glazed paper) (12.80)
144 **14** 4d. rose *(shades)* (8.71) 75·00 3·00
a. Compound perf 12×13 – £400
b. Dull rose (glazed paper) (3.79) – 3·25
c. Dull rose-red (glazed paper) (11.79) – 4·25
d. Bright lilac-rose (aniline) (glazed paper) (2.80) – 11·00
e. Rosine (aniline) (glazed paper) (9.80) 85·00 7·50
145 **16** 6d. deep blue (2.2.72)
a. Prussian blue (9.72) 42·00 4·00
b. Indigo (4.73) 55·00 4·25
c. Dull blue (worn plate)
d. Blue (glazed paper) (6.78) – 4·00
e. Dull milky-blue (glazed paper) – 4·00
f. Light blue (glazed paper) (4.81) – 5·00
146 **14** 8d. red-brown/*pink (glazed paper)* (11.80) 90·00 11·00
147 **17** 1s. light blue/*blue* (5.75) – 10·00
148 **18** 5s. bright blue and red (II) *(glazed paper)* (5.81) £250 15·00
a. Indigo-blue and red £350 19·00

(c) P 12½.

149 **15** 3d. dull orange-yellow *(glazed paper)* (12.80) 55·00 6·00
150 **14** 4d. rosine *(aniline) (glazed paper)* (9.80)
151 **16** 6d. Prussian blue *(glazed paper)* (4.80)
a. Light blue (glazed paper) (4.81)
b. Deep blue (glazed paper) (10.81) 55·00 4·50
152 **14** 8d. lilac-brown/*pink* (8.77) 90·00 12·00
a. *Red-brown/pink (glazed paper)* (11.80) † £500

The same electrotypes as the previous issues were used for this series with the exception of the 5s. which was a new value. The 1d., 2d., 3d., 4d., 6d. and 1s. plates were arranged to print sheets of 120 (12×10) and the 8d. conformed to this when reintroduced in 1877. New plates for the 1d. (1868), 2d. (1869) and 6d. (1875) were constructed by Robinson's successor, J. P. Atkinson, using the improved facilities then available.

Atkinson was also responsible for the printing of the 5s. value. The original printings in blue on yellow paper were produced in sheets of 25, or possibly 50, using a vertical strip of five electrotypes. Due to its size the 5s. did not exactly fit the watermarked paper and, to avoid a preprinted sheet number, a proportion of the printing was made on the back of the paper creating the reversed watermark variety, No. 139a. These varieties occur in the first printing only as Atkinson created a plate of 25 for the second printing in March 1868. Printings of the 5s. bicoloured to April 1880 were made from electrotypes taken from the monocoloured plate. These showed a blue line beneath the crown (Type I). In early 1881 this plate was found to be too worn for further use and a new die was made from which a plate of 100 was constructed. Stamps from this plate are without the blue line beneath the crown (Type II).

PERFORATIONS. Various perforating machines were in use during this period. The use of line machines gauging 12 ceased around 1883. Of the line machines gauging 13 two were converted to comb types in 1873 and were eventually replaced by the 12½ gauge line and comb machines first used in 1876.

(Typo from electrotypes)

1867–70. *Emergency printings on various papers due to shortages of V over Crown paper.* P 13.

(a) Perkins, Bacon paper borrowed from Tasmania. Wmkd double-lined numerals as W **4** of Tasmania.

153 **14** 1d. pale yellowish green (wmkd "1") (24.9.67) 75·00 5·00
a. Deep yellow-green (10.67) 75·00 5·00
154 1d. pale yellow-green (wmkd "4") (27.5.68) £1700 £100
155 2d. grey-lilac (wmkd "4") (3.2.68) £140 4·25
a. Slate (4.68) £140 3·50
b. Mauve (7.68) – 4·50
c. Imperf (pair) † £4250
156 2d. mauve (wmkd "1") (30.6.68) £140 5·50
157 **15** 3d. grey-lilac (wmkd "1") (8.68) £180 60·00
158 **14** 4d. dull rose-red (wmkd "4") (5.68) £140 5·00
159 **16** 6d. blue (wmkd "4") (20.6.68) £180 22·00
a. Indigo-blue – 24·00
160 6d. blue (wmkd "1") (28.7.68) 70·00 5·50
161 6d. dull blue (wmkd "2") (1870) † £3500

(b) Saunders paper. Wmkd in words as W **10**.

162 **14** 1d. pale yellow-green (wmkd "SIX PENCE") (23.3.68) £650 40·00
a. Wmk sideways † –
163 2d. slate-grey (wmkd "SIX PENCE") (6.68) † £8000
164 **16** 6d. blue (wmkd "SIX PENCE") (20.5.68) £450 28·00
a. Indigo-blue – 30·00
165 6d. dull blue (wmkd "THREE PENCE") (6.12.69) £275 13·00
a. Deep blue – 14·00
166 6d. dull blue (wmkd "FOUR PENCE") (21.5.70) £450 35·00
a. Deep blue – 38·00

(c) V over Crown, W **19**, *coloured paper.*

167 **14** 2d. mauve/*lilac* (7.68) 75·00 6·50
a. *Lilac/lilac* 75·00 6·50

(d) Saunders single-lined numeral "4" as W **11**.

168 **16** 6d. dull blue (21.5.70) † £1250

The supply of paper was so short during 1868 that many odds and ends were utilised. Nos. 161 (five known), 163 (one known) and 168 (ten known) are the rarest of these emergency printings.

(Printed in Melbourne from a double electrotyped plate of 240 supplied by D.L.R.)

1870 (28 Jan)–**73**. Wmk V over Crown. W **19**.

169 **20** 2d. brown-lilac (P 13) 75·00 1·75
a. Dull lilac-mauve (9.70) 65·00 1·00
b. Mauve (worn plate) (3.73) 65·00 1·25
170 2d. dull lilac-mauve (P 12) (28.7.71) 70·00 2·50
a. Mauve (worn plate) (3.73) 70·00 2·25

9 9

NINEPENCE

(21)

1871 (22 Apr). No. 123c *surch with T* **21** *in blue.*

171 **16** 9d. on 10d. purple-brown/*pink* £375 10·00
a. Blackish brown/pink £450 12·00
b. Surch double † £1500

22 23 24

25 26 27

(Des and eng W. Bell. Typo from electrotyped plates)

1873 (25 Mar)–**74**. *Saunders paper.* Wmk single-lined "10" as W **11**.

172 **25** 9d. pale brown/*pink* (P 13) 90·00 21·00
a. Red-brown/pink (7.74) 85·00 20·00
173 9d. pale brown/*pink* (P 12) 95·00 21·00

½ ½

HALF

(28)

1873 (25 Jun). No. 131g *surch with T* **28** *in red.*

174 **14** ½d. on 1d. green (P 13) 50·00 14·00
a. Grass-green 55·00 14·00
b. Short "1" at right (R. 1/3) – 70·00
175 ½d. on 1d. green (P 12) 70·00 14·00
a. Grass-green 70·00 14·00
b. Short "1" at right (R. 1/3) – 75·00

Die I

Die II

Two Dies of 2d.:

Die I. Single-lined outer oval

Die II. Double-lined outer oval

(Des and eng W. Bell. Typo from electrotyped plates)

1873–87. Wmk V over Crown, W **19** (sideways on ½d.).

(a) P 13.

176 **22** ½d. rose-red (10.2.74) 17·00 1·25
a. Lilac-rose (1874) 18·00 1·75
b. Rosine (shades) (glazed paper) 16·00 1·25
c. Pale red (glazed paper) (1882) 17·00 1·25
d. Mixed perf 13 and 12 † £400
177 **23** 1d. *dull bluish green* (14.12.75) 35·00 2·00
a. Green (shades) (1877) 35·00 2·00
b. Yellow-green (glazed paper) 35·00 1·75
c. Mixed perf 13 and 12
178 **24** 2d. deep lilac-mauve (I) (1.10.73) 48·00 1·00
a. Dull violet-mauve 48·00 1·00
b. Dull mauve 48·00 1·00
c. Pale mauve (worn plate) (glazed paper) (1.79) 48·00 1·25
d. Mixed perf 13 and 12 £375 £275
179 2d. lilac-mauve (II) *(glazed paper)* (17.12.78) 48·00 1·00
a. Grey-mauve (1.80) – 1·25
b. Pale mauve (6.80) 60·00 1·25
c. Vert pair, lower stamp imperf horiz † £2000
180 **26** 1s. indigo-blue/*blue* (16.8.76) 80·00 3·75
a. Wmk sideways † £750
b. Deep blue/blue (7.77) 85·00 3·75
c. Pale blue/blue (3.80) 90·00 3·75
d. Bright blue/blue (9.80) 95·00 7·50
e. Bright blue/blue (glazed paper) (21.11.83) 95·00 5·00
f. Pale blue/blue (glazed paper).
g. Mixed perf 13 and 12 † –

(b) P 12.

181 **22** ½d. rose-red (1874) 17·00 3·25
a. Lilac-rose (1874) 17·00 3·25
b. Rosine (shades) (glazed paper) 17·00 3·00
c. Pale red (glazed paper) (1882) 17·00 3·25
182 **23** 1d. dull bluish green (1875) 42·00 3·75
a. Green (shades) (1877) 38·00 7·00
b. Yellow-green (glazed paper) – 4·75
183 **24** 2d. deep lilac-mauve (I) (1873) – 7·00
a. Dull violet-mauve – 7·00
b. Dull mauve 65·00 3·25
c. Pale mauve (worn plate) (glazed paper) (1879) 75·00 3·50
184 2d. lilac-mauve (II) *(glazed paper)* (1878) 70·00 3·25
a. Grey-mauve (glazed paper) (1880) – 3·25
b. Pale mauve (glazed paper) (1880) – 4·25
185 **25** 9d. lilac-brown/*pink* (1.12.75) £130 16·00
186 **26** 1s. deep blue/*blue* (1880) – 7·50
a. Bright blue/blue (1880) – 7·50

(c) P 12½.

187 **22** ½d. rosine *(shades) (glazed paper)* (1880)
a. Pale red (glazed paper) (1882)

188	23	1d. yellow-green (*glazed paper*) (1880)		
189	24	2d. grey-mauve (II) (*glazed paper*) (1880)		
		a. Pale mauve (1880)		
190	27	2s. deep blue/*green* (*glazed paper*) (8.7.81)	£140	20·00
		a. Light blue/green (glazed paper) (4.83)		
		ab. Wmk sideways	£150	22·00
		b. Ultramarine/green (glazed paper) (6.84)	—	28·00
		ba. Wmk sideways	—	50·00

8d 8d

EIGHTPENCE

(29)

1876 (1 Jul). No. 185 *surch with T* **29** *in blue.*

191	25	8d. on 9d. lilac-brown/*pink*	£250	19·00
		a. "F.IGHTPENCE"	—	£300

No. 191a was caused by a broken "E" and it occurred once in each sheet of 120.

1877. *Saunders paper.* Wmk "10" as W **11**.

192	14	8d. lilac-brown/*pink* (P 13)	—	£500
		a. Purple-brown/pink (2.78)	£120	12·00
		b. Chocolate/pink (8.78)	†	£600
		c. Red-brown/pink (8.79)	95·00	6·50
193		8d. red-brown/*pink* (P 12) (8.79)	£200	18·00
194		8d. red-brown/*pink* (P 12½) (8.79)	—	50·00

Nos. 192/4 occur amongst the V over Crown printings, the two types of pink paper having become mixed.

1878. *Emergency printings on coloured papers.* Wmk V over Crown, W **19** (sideways on ½d.). P 13.

195	22	½d. rose-red/*pink* (1.3.78)	45·00	26·00
196	23	1d. yellow-green/*yellow* (5.3.78)	95·00	18·00
197		1d. yellow-green/*drab* (5.4.78)	£150	60·00
198	24	2d. dull violet-mauve/*lilac* (21.2.78)	—	£800
199		2d. dull violet-mauve/*green* (23.2.78)	£190	25·00
200		2d. dull violet-mauve/*brown* (21.3.78)	£180	25·00

There was a shortage of white V over Crown, W **19**, watermarked paper in the early months of 1878 and various coloured papers were used for printings of the ½d., 1d. and 2d. values until fresh stocks of white paper were received.

No. 198 is often misidentified. It can be confused with discoloured examples of Nos. 178/b, and has often been faked.

30

31

32

(Des and eng C. Naish. Typo from electrotyped plates)

1880 (3 Nov)–**84**. Wmk V over Crown. W **19**.

201	30	1d. green (P 12½) (2.84)	£120	16·00
202	31	2d. sepia (P 12½)	35·00	1·00
		a. Sepia-brown (2.81)	32·00	1·00
		b. Brown (aniline) (5.81)	35·00	1·00
		c. Dull black-brown (10.81)	—	1·00
		d. Dull grey-brown (3.82)	30·00	1·00
203		2d. sepia (P 13)		
		a. Mixed perf 13 and 12	†	£650
204		2d. sepia (P 12)	—	£120
		a. Sepia-brown (2.81)	—	£120
		b. Brown (aniline) (5.81)	—	£120
205		2d. mauve (*worn plate*) (P 12½) (2.84)	£275	9·00
206	32	4d. rose-carmine (P 12½) (10.81)	75·00	6·50
		a. Rosine (7.82)	75·00	6·00

Nos. 201 and 205 are subsequent printings of stamps first produced on watermark W **33**.

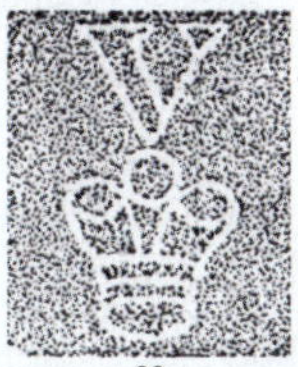
33

1882–84. Wmk V over Crown W **33** (sideways on ½d.). P 12½.

207	22	½d. rosine (3.83)	25·00	8·00
		a. Perf 12	—	24·00
208	23	1d. yellow-green (9.82)	40·00	3·25
		a. Perf 12		
209	30	1d. yellow-green (29.10.83)	35·00	2·00
		a. Green (1.84)	32·00	2·00
		b. Pale green (5.84)	32·00	1·75
210	31	2d. dull grey-brown (15.8.82)	30·00	1·50
		a. Chocolate (3.83)	30·00	1·50
		ab. Perf 12	†	£375
211		2d. mauve (20.12.83)	29·00	1·75
		a. Worn plate (2.84)	29·00	1·75
		b. Perf 12	†	£750
		c. Mixed perf 12 and 12½	†	£750
212	15	3d. yellow-orange (13.4.83)	60·00	14·00
		a. Dull brownish orange	60·00	17·00
213	32	4d. rose-red (3.83)	70·00	10·00
214	16	6d. dull violet-blue (10.11.82)	35·00	2·25
		a. Indigo-blue (11.83)	35·00	2·25
		b. Light ultramarine (8.84)	35·00	2·25

Reprints were made in 1891 of the "Laureated" 1d., 2d., 3d. (in yellow), 4d., 6d., 8d. (in orange-yellow), 10d. (in greenish slate) and 5s. (in blue and red), of the Bell ½d., 1d., 2d. (Die II), 9d. and 1s. and of the Naish 2d. (in brown), 4d. (in pale red) and 2s. With the exception of the Bell 9d., which was watermarked W **19**, all were watermarked W **33** and perforated 12½. Some were from new plates.

THE POST OFFICE ACT OF 1883. Following official concern as to the number of different series of adhesive stamps, both fiscal and postal, used in Victoria it was decided that the system should be unified to the extent that the postage stamps, Stamp Statute fiscals and Stamp Duty fiscals should be replaced by a single series valid for all three purposes. As the Stamp Duty series contained the largest number of values it was adopted as the basis of the new range.

The regulations for the changeover were detailed in the Post Office Act of 1883 which came into force on 1 January 1884. From that date all existing Stamp Statute (first produced in 1871) and Stamp Duty (first produced in 1879) issues became valid for postal purposes, and the previous postage stamps could be used for fiscal fees.

Until matters could be organised printings of some of the existing postage values continued and these will be found included in the listings above.

Printing of the Stamp Statute series was discontinued in early 1884.

The existing Stamp Duty range was initially supplemented by postage stamps overprinted "STAMP DUTY" for those values where the available fiscal design was considered to be too large to be easily used on mail. These overprints were replaced by smaller designs inscribed "STAMP DUTY".

Stamp Statute and Stamp Duty values which became valid for postal purposes on 1 January 1884 have previously been listed in this catalogue as Postal Fiscals. Under the circumstances this distinction appears somewhat arbitrary and all such stamps are now shown in the main listing. Used prices quoted are for examples with postal cancellations. In some instances prices are also provided for fiscally used and these are marked "F.C.".

Nos 215/92 were extensively used for fiscal purposes. Collectors are warned against the many examples of these stamps which have been cleaned and provided with fake gum or forged cancels.

34

35

36

37

(Des and dies eng J. Turner (3d., 2s.6d.), W. Bell (others). Typo from electrotypes)

1884 (1 Jan*). *Stamp Statute series. Vert designs as T* **34/6**, *and others showing Queen Victoria, and T* **37**. P 13.

(*a*) Wmk single-lined numerals according to face value, as W **11**, (sideways). *Paper manufactured by T. H. Saunders unless otherwise stated.*

215	1s. blue/*blue*	90·00	28·00
	a. Perf 12	£110	35·00
216	2s. blue/*green* (*D.L.R. paper*)	£150	90·00
	a. Perf 12	£150	90·00
217	2s. deep blue/*green*	£150	
	a. Perf 12	—	90·00
	b. Wmk upright		
218	10s. brown-olive/*pink*		
219	10s. red-brown/*pink*	£1100	£300
	a. Wmk upright Perf 12		

(*b*) Wmk V over Crown W **19** (sideways). P 13.

220	1d. pale green	60·00	42·00
	a. Green (wmk upright) (P 12½)	95·00	75·00
221	3d. mauve	£750	£400
222	4d. rose	£650	£325
	a. Wmk upright	£750	
223	6d. blue	85·00	28·00
	a. Ultramarine	75·00	24·00
	ab. Perf 12	85·00	25·00
224	1s. blue/*blue*	85·00	28·00
	a. Perf 12	90·00	32·00
	b. Ultramarine/blue (P 12½)	—	55·00
	ba. Perf 12	—	40·00
	c. Deep blue/blue (P 12½)	85·00	28·00
	ca. Perf 12	90·00	28·00
225	2s. blue/*green*	£140	85·00
	a. Perf 12	£140	
	b. Deep blue/blue-green (glazed paper)	£140	90·00
	ba. Perf 12	£140	95·00
226	2s.6d. orange	—	£160
	a. Perf 12		
	b. Yellow (glazed paper)	£400	
	ba. Perf 12	£400	£160
	c. Orange-yellow (glazed paper) (P 12½)	—	£170
	ca. Perf 12		
227	5s. blue/*yellow*	£375	90·00
	a. Perf 12	£375	
	b. Wmk upright		
	ba. Perf 12		
	c. Ultramarine/lemon (glazed paper) (P 12½)	£375	90·00
	ca. Wmk upright		
228	10s. brown/*pink*	£1100	£300
	a. Purple-brown/pink	£1100	£300
	ab. Perf 12		
229	£1 slate-violet/*yellow*	£800	£225
	a. Wmk upright		
	b. Mauve/yellow		
	ba. Perf 12	£800	£225
	bb. Perf 12½	£800	£225
230	£5 black and yellow-green	£5500	£1200
	a. Perf 12		
	b. Wmk upright. Perf 12½	£5500	£1200

(*c*) Wmk V over Crown (sideways) W **33**.

231	1d. yellowish green (P 12½)	75·00	75·00
232	2s.6d. pale orange-yellow (P 12)	£375	£160
233	£5 black and yellow-green (wmk upright) (P 12)	—	£1100

½d

HALF

(38)

1884 (1 Jan*). *No.* 220 *surch with T* **38** *in red.*

234	½d. on 1d. pale green	75·00	75·00

*The dates quoted are those on which the stamps became valid for postal purposes. The ½d., 1d., 4d., 6d., 1s., 5s. and £1 were issued for fiscal purposes on 26 April 1871. The 10s. was added to the series in June 1871, the £5 in September 1871, the 2s.6d. in July 1876 and the 3d. in October 1879.

All values of the Stamp Statute series were reprinted in 1891 on paper watermarked W **19** (5s., 10s., £1) or W **33** (others). The £5 was pulled from the original plate, but the others were produced from new electrotypes taken from the original dies.

39

40

41

42

43

44

45

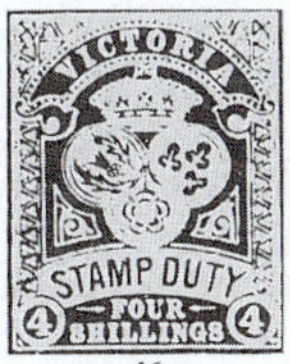
46

47

48

49

50

51

52

53

54

55

56

57

58

59

60

61

(Des H. Samson and F. Oxenbould (T **39**), C. Jackson and L. Lang (all others except T **40**). Dies eng C. Jackson, J. Turner, J. Whipple, A. Williams and other employees of Sands & MacDougall. T **40** die eng C. Naish)

1884 (1 Jan*)–**96**. *Existing Stamp Duty series.*

(*a*) *Litho.* Wmk V over Crown. W **19** (sideways). P 13.

235	**39**	1d. blue-green	85·00	29·00
		a. Perf 12	85·00	29·00
		b. Perf 12½		
236	**43**	1s.6d. rosine	£200	32·00
		a. Perf 12	–	42·00
		b. Perf 12½		
237	**45**	3s. purple/*blue*	£550	55·00
		a. Perf 12	£600	60·00
		b. Perf 12½		
238	**46**	4s. orange-red	£110	21·00
		a. Perf 12	£110	21·00
		b. Perf 12½		
239	**48**	6s. apple-green	£350	42·00
		a. Perf 12½		
240	**49**	10s. brown/*rose (glazed paper)*	£550	95·00
		a. Perf 12		
		b. Perf 12½		
		c. Wmk upright		
		cb. Perf 12½		
241	**50**	15s. mauve	£1600	£275
242	**51**	£1 red-orange	£550	90·00
		a. Perf 12½	£550	90·00
243	**52**	£1.5s. dull rose (wmk upright)	£1600	£300
244	**53**	£1.10s. deep grey-olive	£1600	£170
		a. Wmk upright	–	£200
245	–	35s. grey-violet (wmk upright) (F.C. £250)	£7500	
246	**54**	£2 blue	–	£150
247	**55**	45s. dull brown-lilac	£3500	£300
248	**56**	£5 rose-red (wmk upright) (F.C. £70)	£4500	£700
249	**57**	£6 blue/*pink* (wmk upright) (*glazed paper*) (F.C. £130)	–	£1000
250	**58**	£7 violet/*blue* (wmk upright) (F.C. £130)	–	£1000
251	**59**	£8 brownish red/*yellow* (wmk upright) (*glazed paper*) (F.C. £130)	–	£1200
252	**60**	£9 yellow-green/*green* (wmk upright) (*glazed paper*) (F.C. £130)	–	£1200

(*b*) *Typo from electrotypes.*

(*i*) Wmk V over Crown. W **19** (sideways). P 13.

253	**39**	1d. yellowish green	70·00	29·00
		a. Perf 12	70·00	29·00
		b. Perf 12½		
254	**40**	1d. pale bistre	28·00	4·50
		a. Perf 12	28·00	5·50
		b. Perf 12½		
255	**41**	6d. dull blue	85·00	14·00
		a. Perf 12	90·00	24·00
		b. Perf 12½		
256	**42**	1s. deep blue/*blue*	95·00	6·50
		a. Perf 12	95·00	8·00
		b. Perf 12½		
		c. *Bright blue/blue* (*glazed paper*) (P 12½)	95·00	7·50
		ca. Perf 12	–	8·00
		d. *Ultramarine/blue* (*glazed paper*) (P 12½) (11.84)	£150	8·00
257		1s. chalky blue/*lemon* (*glazed paper*) (P 12½) (3.3.85)	£120	27·00
258	**44**	2s. deep blue/*green* (*glazed paper*)	£180	27·00
		a. Perf 12	–	29·00
		b. Perf 12½	£180	32·00
		c. *Indigo/green*	£160	32·00
		ca. Perf 12	£200	35·00
		cb. Perf 12½		
259	**45**	3s. maroon/*blue* (*glazed paper*) (P 12½) (8.8.84)	£425	42·00
260	**47**	5s. claret/*yellow* (*glazed paper*)	65·00	7·00
		a. Perf 12	80·00	14·00
		b. Perf 12½		
		c. *Pale claret/yellow* (P 12½)	65·00	15·00
		ca. Perf 12	85·00	15·00
		d. *Reddish purple/lemon* (P 12½) (6.87)	60·00	14·00
		e. *Brown-red/yellow* (P 12½) (5.93)	90·00	38·00
261	**49**	10s. *chocolate/rose* (*glazed paper*)	–	90·00
		a. Perf 12		
		b. Perf 12½		
		c. Wmk upright		
262	**51**	£1 yellow-orange/*yellow* (P 12)	£700	80·00
		a. *Orange/yellow* (P 12½) (8.84)	£650	55·00
		b. *Reddish orange/yellow* (P 12½) (9.88)	£400	55·00
263	**54**	£2 deep blue (P 12)	–	£140
264	**61**	£10 dull mauve (P 12)		
		a. *Deep red-lilac* (P 12)	£3750	£200

(*ii*) Wmk V over Crown W **33** (sideways). P 12½.

265	**40**	1d. ochre	42·00	7·00
		a. Perf 12	42·00	7·00
266	**41**	6d. ultramarine	90·00	13·00
		a. Perf 12	90·00	13·00
267	**43**	1s.6d. pink (1.85)	£160	28·00
		a. *Bright rose-carmine* (4.86)	£180	24·00
268	**45**	3s. drab (20.10.85)	85·00	16·00
		a. *Olive-drab* (1.93)	80·00	16·00
269	**46**	4s. red-orange (5.86)	90·00	16·00
		a. *Yellow-orange* (12.94)		
		ab. Wmk upright	£120	14·00
270	**47**	5s. rosine (8.5.96)	85·00	20·00
271	**48**	6s. pea-green (12.11.91)	£130	45·00
		a. *Apple-green* (wmk upright)	£200	42·00
272	**49**	10s. dull bluish green (10.85)	£225	45·00
		a. *Grey-green* (5.86)	£170	35·00
273	**50**	15s. purple-brown (12.85)	£800	90·00
		a. *Brown* (wmk upright) (5.95)	£800	95·00
274	**52**	£1.5s. pink (wmk upright) (6.8.90)	£1600	£110
275	**53**	£1.10s. pale olive (6.88)	£1100	95·00
276	**54**	£2 bright blue	–	90·00
		a. *Blue* (7.88)	£900	90·00
277	**55**	45s. lilac (15.8.90)	£3500	£130
278	**56**	£5 rose-pink (P 12)	–	£600
		a. *Pink* (P 12½)	–	£750
279	**61**	£10 mauve (3.84)	£3750	£140
		a. *Lilac* (6.85)	–	£150

*This is the date on which the stamps became valid for postal use. The 1d., 6d., 1s., 1s.6d., 2s., 3s., 4s., 5s., 10s., 15s., £1, £1.10s., £2, £5 and £10 were issued for fiscal purposes on 18 December 1879 with the £1.5s., 35s., 45s., £6 and £9 added to the range later the same month and the 6s., £7 and £8 in January 1880.

Used prices for the £1.5s., £1.10s., £2 (No. 276a), 45s. and £10 watermarked W **33** are for examples from the cancelled-to-order sets sold to collectors by the Victoria postal authorities between September 1900 and 30 June 1902.

Similar Stamp Duty designs were prepared for 7s., 8s., 9s., 11s., 12s., 13s., 14s., 16s., 17s., 18s., and 19s., but were never issued.

The two different 1d. designs were reprinted in 1891 on W **33** paper.

For these designs with later watermarks see Nos. 345/50 and 369/71.

62

(Des C. Jackson and L. Lang. Dies eng C. Jackson)

1884 (1 Jan*)–**00**. *High value Stamp Duty series.*

(*a*) *Recess-printed direct from the die.*

(*i*) Wmk V over Crown W **19** (sideways). P 12½.

280	**62**	£25 yellow-green (F.C. £85)		
		a. Wmk upright		
		b. Perf 13		
		c. *Deep green* (F.C. £85)		
		ca. Wmk upright		
281		£50 bright mauve (F.C. £120)		
		a. Wmk upright		
		b. Perf 13		
282		£100 crimson-lake (F.C. £170)		
		a. Wmk upright		
		b. Perf 13		

(*ii*) Wmk V over Crown W **33** (sideways). P 12½.

283	**62**	£25 yellow-green		
		a. Perf 12		
		b. *Deep green* (1.85) (F.C. £85)	–	£700
		c. *Bright blue-green* (10.90) (F.C £85)		
		ca. Wmk upright		
284		£50 dull lilac-mauve (wmk upright) (F.C. £120)		
		a. *Black-violet* (10.90) (F.C £95)	–	£700
		ab. Wmk upright		
285		£100 crimson (F.C. £170)		
		a. Wmk upright		
		b. Perf 12 (F.C. £170)		
		c. *Aniline crimson* (wmk upright) (2.85) (F.C. £170)	–	£850
		d. *Scarlet-red* (5.95)	–	£850
		da. Wmk upright	–	£700

(*b*) *Litho.* Wmk V over Crown W **33** (sideways). P 12½.

286	**62**	£25 dull yellowish green (1.86) (F.C. £60)		
		a. Wmk upright (11.87)		
		b. *Dull blue-green* (9.88) (F.C £60)		
		ba. Wmk upright		
287		£50 dull purple (1.86) (F.C. £80)		
		a. Wmk upright		
		b. *Bright violet* (11.89) (F.C. £80)		
		ba. Wmk upright		
288		£100 rosine (1.86) (F.C. £130)		
		a. Wmk upright		

(*c*) *Typo from electrotyped plates.* Wmk V over Crown. W **33**. P 12½.

289	**62**	£25 dull blue-green (12.97)	–	£225
290		£50 bright mauve (10.97)	–	£325
291		£100 pink-red (10.19.00)	–	£400

*This is the date on which the stamps became valid for postal use. All three values were issued for fiscal purposes on 18 December 1879.

Used prices for Nos. 283*b*, 284*a*, 285*c/d* and 289/91 are for examples from the cancelled-to-order sets described beneath No. 279*a*. "F.C." indicates that the price quoted is for a stamp with a fiscal cancellation.

For the £25 and £50 with watermark W **82** see Nos. 351/2.

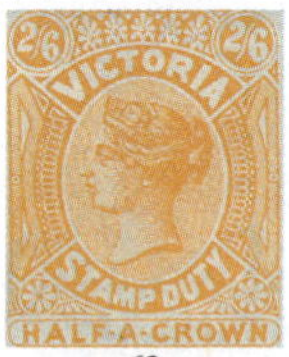
63

(Des and die eng C. Naish. Typo from electrotyped plates)

1884 (23 Apr)–**92**. *New design inscr* "STAMP DUTY". Wmk V over Crown, W **33** (sideways). P 12½.

292	**63**	2s.6d. brown-orange	90·00	16·00
		a. *Yellow* (8.85)	85·00	13·00
		b. *Lemon-yellow* (2.92)	85·00	14·00

For this design on later watermarks see Nos. 344 and 370.

64

65

66

67

68

(Des and dies eng C. Naish. Typo from electrotyped plates)

1885 (1 Jan)–**95**. *New designs inscr* "STAMP DUTY". P 12½.

(*a*) W **19**.

293	**68**	8d. rose/*pink*	32·00	8·00
		a. *Rose-red/pink* (2.88)	35·00	8·00
294	**66**	1s. deep dull blue/*lemon* (11.85)	95·00	10·00
		a. *Dull blue/yellow* (6.86)	95·00	11·00
295	**68**	2s. olive/*bluish green* (12.85)	85·00	3·75

(*b*) W **33**.

296	**64**	½d. pale rosine	16·00	1·25
		a. *Deep rosine* (7.85)	18·00	1·50
		b. *Salmon* (9.85)	18·00	1·50
297	**65**	1d. yellowish green (1.85)	20·00	1·25
		a. *Dull pea-green* (2.85)	21·00	1·75
298	**66**	2d. lilac	22·00	60
		a. *Mauve* (1886)	22·00	60
		b. *Rosy-mauve* (1886)	24·00	80

299	65	3d. yellowish brown	24·00	1·50
		a. Pale ochre (9.86)	11·00	1·50
		b. Bistre-yellow (9.92)	11·00	1·50
300	67	4d. magenta	70·00	3·75
		a. Bright mauve-rose (12.86)	70·00	4·25
		b. Error. *Lilac* (12.86)	£4250	£850
301	65	6d. chalky blue (1.85)	90·00	3·50
		a. Bright blue (3.85)	60·00	3·00
		b. Cobalt (7.85)	60·00	3·00
302	68	8d. bright scarlet/*pink* (3.95)	30·00	11·00
303		2s. olive-green/*pale green* (1.90)	38·00	6·00
304		2s. apple-green (12.8.95)	25·00	60·00
		a. Blue-green (29.10.95)	19·00	16·00

The plates for the 1d., 6d., 1s. and 2s. were derived from the dies of the 2d. (1s.), 3d. (1d. and 6d.) and 8d. (2s.). In each instance lead moulds of six impressions were taken from the original die and the face values altered by hand creating six slightly different versions.

Two states of the 2d. die exist with the second showing a break in the top frame line near the right-hand corner. This damaged die was used for seven impressions on Plate 1 and all 120 on Plate 2.

No. 300b occurred during the December 1886 printing of the 4d. when about fifty sheets were printed in the colour of the 2d. by mistake. The sheets were issued to Melbourne post offices and used examples are known postmarked between 21 December 1886 and 4 March 1887. Nine unused are also believed to exist.

Reprints of the ½d., 1d., 2d., 4d., 6d. and 1s. values were made in 1891 from the existing plates. The 1s. was watermarked W **19** and the remainder W **33**.

For some of these values used with later watermarks see Nos. 336, 343, 361 and 369.

STAMP DUTY

(69)

1885 (Feb–Nov). *Optd with T* **69**. P 12½.

(a) W **19**.

305	15	3d. dull orange-yell (*glazed paper*) (B.) (Nov)	—	£140
306	26	1s. pale blue/*blue* (*glazed paper*) (P 13)	95·00	23·00
		a. Deep blue/*blue*	—	25·00
		b. Blue opt (F.C. £14)	£1700	£900
307	27	2s. ultramarine/*green* (*glazed paper*) (Mar)	£100	18·00
		a. Wmk sideways	£120	25·00

(b) W **33**.

308	15	3d. yellow-orange (B.) (Nov)	60·00	28·00
		a. Dull brownish orange (B.)	65·00	29·00
309	32	4d. rose-red (B.) (Nov)	55·00	45·00

Unauthorised reprints of the 4d. and 1s., both with blue overprints and watermarked W **33**, were made during 1895–96. The 4d. reprint, which is in pale red, also exists without the overprint.

70

71

72

73

74

75

76

77

78

79

80

(Des S. Reading (1d.) (No. 313), M. Tannenberg (2½d., 5d.), C. Naish (1s.6d.), P. Astley (others). Dies eng C. Naish (2d., 4d. (both existing dies with lines added behind Queen's head) and 1s.6d.), S. Reading (originally as an employee of Fergusson & Mitchell) (others). Typo from electrotyped plates)

1886 (26 Jul)–**96**. W **33** (sideways on ½d., 1s., £5, £7 to £9). P 12½.

310	70	½d. lilac-grey (28.8.86)	24·00	6·50
		a. Grey-black	—	35·00
311		½d. pink (15.2.87)	17·00	70
		a. Rosine (aniline) (1889)	9·00	40
		b. Rose-red (1891)	9·00	40
		c. Vermilion (1896)	9·50	45
312	71	1d. green	12·00	1·50
		a. Yellow-green (1887)	12·00	1·50
313	72	1d. dull chestnut (1.1.90)	13·00	50
		a. Deep red-brown (1890)	13·00	50
		b. Orange-brown (1890)	13·00	30
		c. Brown-red (1890)	13·00	30
		d. Yellow-brown (1891)	13·00	30
		e. Bright yellow-orange	50·00	12·00
		f. Brownish orange (1894)	7·50	30
314	73	2d. pale lilac (17.12.86)	17·00	20
		a. Pale mauve (1887)	18·00	20
		b. Deep lilac (1888, 1892)	9·50	20
		c. Purple (1894)	7·50	25
		d. Violet (1895)	7·50	20
		e. Imperf	—	£900
315	74	2½d. red-brown/*lemon* (1.1.91)	27·00	3·25
		a. Brown-red/yellow (1892)	20·00	80
		b. Red/yellow (1893)	17·00	70
316	75	4d. rose-red (1.4.87)	27·00	1·00
		a. Red (1893)	16·00	1·00
317	76	5d. purple-brown (1.1.91)	14·00	2·75
		a. Pale reddish brown (1893)	9·00	2·75
318	77	6d. bright ultramarine (27.8.86)	28·00	2·25
		a. Pale ultramarine (1887)	24·00	50
		b. Dull blue (1891)	23·00	60
319	25	9d. apple-green (18.10.92)	27·00	11·00
320		9d. carmine-rose (15.10.95)	40·00	11·00
		a. Rosine (aniline) (1896)	42·00	10·00
321	78	1s. dull purple-brown (14.3.87)	70·00	2·75
		a. Lake (1890)	55·00	3·50
		b. Carmine-lake (1892)	28·00	1·50
		c. Brownish red (1896)	28·00	2·00
322	79	1s.6d. pale blue (9.88)	£140	70·00
323		1s.6d. orange (19.9.89)	22·00	11·00
		a. Red-orange (1893)	22·00	8·50
324	80	£5 pale blue and maroon (7.2.88)†	£2500	£110
325		£6 yellow and pale blue (1.10.87)†	£3000	£150
326		£7 rosine and black (17.10.89)†	£3250	£160
327		£8 mauve and brown-orange (2.8.90)†	£3500	£190
328		£9 apple-green and rosine (21.8.88)†	£3750	£200

†The used prices provided for these stamps are for cancelled-to-order examples.

Unauthorised reprints of the ½d. lilac-grey and 1s.6d. pale blue were made in 1894–95 on W **33** paper and perforated 12½. These differ in shade from the originals and have rougher perforations. It should be noted that the original printing of No. 322 does not occur with inverted watermark, but the reprint does.

A single example of No. 314e is known postmarked "737" (Foster). A second, postmarked "249" (Mortlake), was reported in 1892. It is known that an imperforate sheet was sold at Mortlake P.O. in 1890. Other examples are believed to be clandestine.

Later printings of the £5 to £9 values, as No. 324/8 but on W **85** paper perforated 12½ or 11, were not valid for postal use (*Unused prices, £275 for £5 value, from £375 for £6 to £9 values*).

A £10 value as Type **80** was prepared, but not issued.

1891 (17 Jun). W **19**. P 12½.

329	72	1d. orange-brown/*pink*	8·00	3·00

No. 329 was an emergency printing during a shortage of white W **33** paper.

81

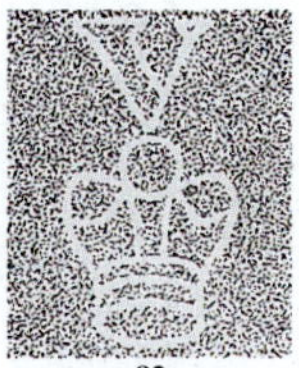

82

(Die eng A. Williams (1½d.). Typo from electrotyped plates).

1896 (11 Jun)–**99**. W **82** (sideways on ½d., 1½d., 1s., 2s.6d. to 15s.). P 12½.

330	70	½d. light scarlet (1.7.96)	5·50	1·25
		a. Carmine-rose (1897)	5·50	1·25
		b. Deep carmine-red (coarse impression) (1899)	—	2·75
		c. Wmk upright	£100	65·00
331		½d. emerald (1.8.99)	18·00	3·75
		a. Wmk upright		
332	72	1d. brown-red (13.6.96)	7·50	20
		a. Brownish orange (1897)	7·50	10
		b. Wmk sideways		
333	81	1½d. apple-green (7.10.97)	3·00	4·75
334	73	2d. violet	14·00	10
		a. Wmk sideways	†	85·00
335	74	2½d. blue (1.8.99)	11·00	10·00
336	65	3d. ochre (11.96)	11·00	1·50
		a. Buff (1898)	9·00	1·50
		b. Wmk sideways		
337	75	4d. red (6.97)	23·00	4·00
338	76	5d. red-brown (7.97)	22·00	1·75
339	77	6d. dull blue (9.96)	20·00	1·25
340	25	9d. rosine (8.96)	35·00	4·00
		a. Rose-carmine (1898)	—	4·00
		b. Dull rose (1898)	28·00	4·00
		c. Wmk sideways		
341	78	1s. brownish red (3.97)	18·00	2·75
		a. Wmk upright		
342	79	1s.6d. brown-orange (8.98)	48·00	28·00
343	68	2s. blue-green (4.97)	45·00	8·50
344	63	2s.6d. yellow (9.96)	95·00	16·00
		a. Wmk upright (1898)	£110	16·00
345	45	3s. olive-drab (12.96)	65·00	22·00
		a. Wmk upright (1898)	65·00	22·00
346	46	4s. orange (9.97)	95·00	19·00
347	47	5s. rosine (2.97)	95·00	16·00
		a. Rose-carmine (1897)	95·00	16·00
		b. Wmk upright. *Rosine* (1899)	95·00	17·00
348	48	6s. pale yellow-green (4.99)†	95·00	26·00
349	49	10s. grey-green (4.97)	£180	22·00
		a. Blue-green (1898)	£180	20·00
350	50	15s. brown (4.97)†	£500	70·00
351	62	£25 dull bluish green (1897)†	—	£190
352		£50 dull purple (1897)†	—	£275

†The used prices provided for these stamps are for cancelled-to-order examples.

83

84

(Des M. Tannenberg. Dies eng A. Mitchelhill. Typo from electrotyped plates)

1897 (22 Oct). *Hospital Charity Fund*. W **82** (sideways). P 12½.

353	83	1d. (1s.) blue	18·00	21·00
354	84	2½d. (2s.6d) red-brown	95·00	80·00
353s/4s		Optd "Specimen" *Set of 2*	£160	

These stamps were sold at 1s. and 2s.6d., but only had postal validity for 1d. and 2½d. with the difference going to the Fund.

1899 (1 Aug). W **33** (sideways). P 12½.

355	81	1½d. brown-red/*yellow*	3·00	2·25

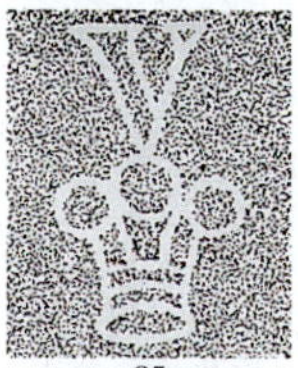

85

1899 (1 Aug)–**1901**. W **85** (sideways on ½d., 1s. and 2s.6d. to 10s.). P 12½.

356	70	½d. emerald (12.99)	4·75	50
		a. Deep blue-green	5·00	50
		b. Wmk upright	—	10·00
357	72	1d. rose-red	7·50	25
		a. Rosine (1900)	4·50	10
		b. Wmk sideways		
358		1d. olive (6.6.01)	7·50	4·00
359	73	2d. violet	18·00	20
		a. Wmk sideways	†	—
360	74	2½d. blue (10.99)	21·00	1·75
361	65	3d. bistre-yellow (9.99)	7·00	3·00
		a. Wmk sideways		
362		3d. slate-green (20.6.01)	25·00	13·00
363	75	4d. rose-red (12.99)	12·00	3·00
364	76	5d. red-brown (10.99)	22·00	3·00
365	77	6d. dull ultramarine (1.00)	13·00	2·75
366	25	9d. rose-red (9.99)	18·00	2·25
		a. Wmk sideways		
367	78	1s. brown-red (5.00)	24·00	3·50
368	79	1s.6d. orange (2.00)	24·00	22·00
369	68	2s. blue-green (6.00)	24·00	12·00
370	63	2s.6d. yellow (1.00)	£350	23·00
371	45	3s. pale olive (4.00)†	£150	27·00
372	47	5s. rose-red (4.00)	£120	27·00
373	49	10s. green (3.00)†	£190	27·00

†The used prices provided for these stamps are for cancelled-to-order examples.

From 1 July 1901 stamps inscribed "STAMP DUTY" could only be used for fiscal purposes.

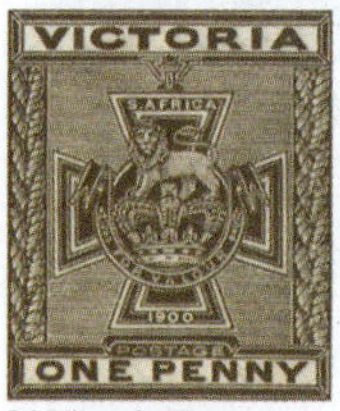

86 Victoria Cross

87 Australian Troops in South Africa

(Des Sands and MacDougall (1d.), J. Sutherland (2d.). Dies eng S. Reading. Typo from electrotyped plates).

1900 (22 May). *Empire Patriotic Fund*. W **85** (sideways). P 12½.

374	86	1d. (1s.) olive-brown	90·00	55·00
375	87	2d. (2s.) emerald-green	£170	£180

These stamps were sold at 1s. and 2s., but only had postal validity for 1d. and 2d. with the difference going to the Fund.

FEDERATION. The six Australian colonies were federated as the Commonwealth of Australia on 1 January 1901. Under the terms of the Post and Telegraph Act their postal services were amalgamated on 1 March 1901, but other clauses to safeguard the financial position of the individual States provided them with a large degree of independence until 13 October 1910 when issues of each state could be used throughout Australia. Postage stamps for the Commonwealth of Australia did not appear until January 1913.

It was agreed in 1901 that stamp printing should be centralised at Melbourne under J. B. Cooke of South Australia who was appointed Commonwealth Stamp Printer. By 1909 the Commonwealth Stamp Printing Branch in Melbourne was producing stamps for Papua, South Australia, Tasmania and Western Australia in addition to those of Victoria.

On federation it was decided to separate postal and fiscal stamp issues so Victoria needed urgent replacements for the current Stamp Duty series which reverted to fiscal use only on 30 June 1901.

1901 (29 Jan). *Re-use of previous designs without* "POSTAGE" *inscr.* W **82** (2s.) or W **85** (others) (sideways on ½d.). P 12×12½.

376	**22**	½d. bluish green	2·00	2·25
		a. "VICTCRIA" (R. 7/19)	40·00	45·00
377	**31**	2d. reddish violet	8·00	2·25
378	**15**	3d. dull orange	15·00	3·50
379	**32**	4d. bistre-yellow	25·00	17·00
380	**16**	6d. emerald	9·00	8·50
381	**26**	1s. yellow	60·00	42·00
382	**27**	2s. blue/*pink*	42·00	38·00
383	**18**	5s. pale red and deep blue	50·00	48·00

88

89

90

91

92

93

94

95

96

97

98

99

100

101

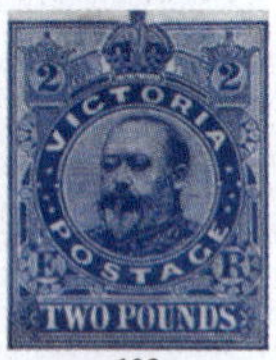

102

I II III

Three die states of ½d.:

I. Outer vertical line of colour to left of "V" continuous except for a break opposite the top of "V". Triangles either end of "VICTORIA" are more or less solid colour.

II. Die re-engraved. Three breaks in outer line of colour left of "V". White lines added to left triangle.

III. Die re-engraved. As II, but equivalent triangle at right also contains white lines.

I

II

III

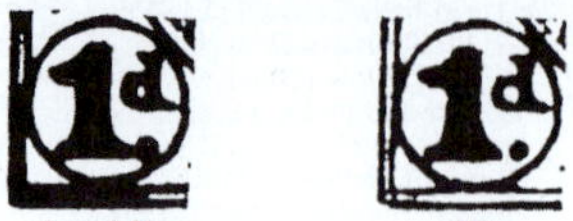
I and II III

Three die states of 1d.:

I. Thick lines fill top of oval above Queen's head.

II. Die re-engraved. Lines thinner, showing white space between.

III. Die re-engraved. As II, but with bottom left value tablet recut to show full point separated from both "1" and the circular frame.

Two die states of 2d.:

I. Frame line complete at top right corner. Bottom right corner comes to a point.

II. Break in right frame line just below the top corner. Bottom right corner is blunted.

Two types of 1s.:

A. "POSTAGE" 6 mm long (produced by a hand punch applied twice to each impression on the previous 1s. electrotyped plate. Slight variations in position occur).

B. "POSTAGE" 7 mm long (produced from new electrotyped plates incorporating the "POSTAGE" inscriptions).

(Eng S. Reading after photo by W. Stuart (£1, £2))

1901 (29 Jan)–**10**. *Previous issues with* "POSTAGE" *added and new designs (£1, £2).* W **85** (sideways on ½d., 1½d., £1, £2).

(*a*) P 12×12½ (½d. to 2s.) or 12½ (½d., 5s. to £2).

384	**88**	½d. blue-green (I) (26.6.01)	3·75	70
		a. Wmk upright (1903)	3·25	70
		b. Die state II (6.04)	6·50	70
		ba. Wmk upright	6·50	40
		c. Die state III (6.05)	12·00	1·25
385	**89**	1d. rose (I)	10·00	50
		a. Dull red (12.02)	9·00	50
		ab. Wmk sideways	£200	75·00
		b. Die state II (4.01)	3·25	15
		ba. Dull red (12.02)	3·00	15
		bb. Wmk sideways	£200	75·00
		c. Die state III. *Pale rose-red*	5·50	2·00
		ca. Wmk sideways	60·00	60·00
386	**90**	1½d. maroon/*yellow* (9.7.01)	10·00	7·00
		a. Wmk upright. *Brown-red/yellow* (9.01)	3·25	55
		b. Dull red-brown/yellow (1906)	2·10	55
		ba. *On yellow-buff back* (1908)	3·75	1·25
387	**91**	2d. lilac (I) (26.6.01)	16·00	70
		a. Die state II	32·00	2·00
		b. Reddish violet (1902)	14·00	70
		ba. Die state II	32·00	2·00
		c. Bright purple (II) (1905)	7·00	40
		d. Rosy mauve (II) (1905)		
		e. Wmk sideways	30·00	
388	**92**	2½d. dull blue	12·00	35
		a. Deep blue (1902)	12·00	35
		b. Wmk sideways	†	£950
389	**93**	3d. dull orange-brown (5.7.01)	11·00	1·75
		a. Chestnut (1901)	12·00	80
		b. Yellowish brown (1903)	12·00	80
		ba. Wmk sideways	14·00	22·00
390	**94**	4d. bistre-yellow (26.6.01)	8·00	65
		a. Brownish bistre (1905)	11·00	1·25
391	**95**	5d. reddish brown	13·00	40
		a. Purple-brown (1903)	10·00	60
392	**96**	6d. emerald (5.7.01)	12·00	1·00
		a. Dull green (1904)	14·00	1·00
393	**97**	9d. dull rose-red (5.7.01)	18·00	3·00
		a. Wmk sideways (1901)	30·00	13·00
		b. Pale red (1901)	16·00	1·25
		c. Dull brownish red (1905)	22·00	3·25
394	**98**	1s. yellow-orange (A) (5.7.01)	22·00	2·00
		a. Yellow (1902)	19·00	2·00
		b. Type B (4.03)	19·00	3·00
		ba. Orange (1904)	18·00	2·50
		bb. Wmk sideways (1905)	42·00	16·00
395	**99**	2s. blue/*rose* (5.7.01)	23·00	2·00
		a. Wmk sideways	†	£900
398	**100**	5s. rose-red and pale blue (5.7.01)	60·00	16·00
		a. Scarlet and deep blue	70·00	16·00
		b. Rosine and blue (12.04)	70·00	16·00
399	**101**	£1 carmine-rose (18.11.01)	£250	£120
400	**102**	£2 deep blue (2.6.02)	£500	£300
		(*b*) P 11.		
401	**88**	½d. blue-green (I) (9.02)	10·00	4·00
		a. Wmk upright (1903)	3·25	2·25
		b. Die state II (6.04)	9·00	2·25
		ba. Wmk upright	11·00	3·00
		c. Die state III (6.05)	10·00	2·50
402	**89**	1d. dull red (I) (12.02)	85·00	45·00
		a. Die state II	25·00	8·00
		ab. Pale red (aniline) (3.03)	13·00	2·75
		ac. Pale rose (aniline) (1904)	28·00	6·00
		b. Die state III. *Pale rose-red* (7.05)	85·00	45·00
403	**90**	1½d. dull red-brown/*yellow* (1910)	£100	80·00
404	**91**	2d. bright purple (II) (1905)	£750	£300
		a. Rosy mauve (II) (1905)	†	£250
405	**93**	3d. yellowish brown (1903)	5·50	8·50
		a. Wmk sideways	18·00	35·00
406	**96**	6d. emerald (2.03)	12·00	21·00
		a. Dull green (1905)	£1000	£550
407	**101**	£1 rose (5.05)	£375	£150
408	**102**	£2 deep blue (1905)	£1500	£1100
		(*c*) Compound or mixed perfs of 12×12½ or 12½ and 11.		
409	**88**	½d. blue-green (I) (1901)	40·00	15·00
		a. Wmk upright (1903)	40·00	15·00
		b. Die state II (1904)	38·00	28·00
		ba. Wmk upright	48·00	38·00
410	**89**	1d. dull red (I) (1902)	—	£450
		a. Die state II	£900	£225
411	**90**	1½d. maroon/*yellow* (1903)	£1000	£600
412	**91**	2d. reddish violet (I) (1903)	†	£850
413	**93**	3d. dull orange-brown (1902)	—	£1000
414	**96**	6d. emerald (1903)	†	£1000
415	**100**	5s. rosine and blue (12.04)	£2000	

Examples of the 1d. Die state II perforated 12×12½ exist with two black lines printed across the face of the stamp. These were prepared in connection with stamp-vending machine trials.

1905–13. Wmk Crown over A, W w **11** (sideways on ½d., £1, £2).

(*a*) P 12×12½ (½d. to 1s.) or 12½ (½d., 1d., 2½d., 6d., 5s. to £2)

416	**88**	½d. blue-green (shades) (III) (21.10.05)	2·50	50
		a. Wmk upright	15·00	4·50
		b. Thin, ready gummed paper (6.12)	5·00	6·00
		ba. Wmk upright	4·50	7·00
417	**89**	1d. rose-red (III) (16.7.05)	2·50	20
		a. Pale rose (1907)	1·25	10
		b. Rose-carmine (1911)	10·00	2·75
		c. Wmk sideways	14·00	7·50
		d. Thin, ready gummed paper (10.12)	4·50	2·50
418	**91**	2d. dull mauve (II) (13.9.05)	6·00	30
		a. Lilac (1906)	6·00	25
		b. Reddish violet (1907)	6·00	25
		c. Bright mauve (1910)	5·50	1·00
		ca. Thin, ready gummed paper (8.12)	32·00	7·00
419	**92**	2½d. deep dull blue (10.08)	5·00	1·25
		a. Dull blue (11.09)	3·00	40
		b. Indigo (7.09)	17·00	2·75
420	**93**	3d. orange-brown (11.11.05)	11·00	1·25
		a. Yellow-orange (1908)	10·00	1·25
		b. Dull orange-buff (1909)	8·00	1·25
		c. Ochre (1912)	8·00	6·00
421	**94**	4d. yellow-bistre (15.1.06)	8·50	65
		a. Olive-bistre (1908)	7·00	65
		b. Yellow-olive (1912)	7·00	3·25
422	**95**	5d. chocolate (14.8.06)	7·00	3·25
		a. Dull reddish brown (1908)	7·00	3·25
		b. Wmk sideways	†	£750
		c. Thin, ready gummed paper (19.10.12)	13·00	16·00
423	**96**	6d. dull green (25.10.05)	15·00	80
		a. Dull yellow-green (1907)	13·00	80
		b. Emerald (1909)	13·00	1·10
		c. Yellowish green (1911)	13·00	3·25
		d. Emerald. Thin, ready gummed paper (11.12)	24·00	24·00
424	**97**	9d. brown-red (11.12.05)	18·00	3·25
		a. Orange-brown (1906)	17·00	3·00
		b. Red-brown (1908)	20·00	3·00
		c. Pale dull rose (1909)	16·00	4·25
		d. Rose-carmine (1910)	9·50	1·25
		e. Wmk sideways	£200	75·00
425	**98**	1s. orange (B) (13.2.06)	8·00	2·00
		a. Yellow-orange (1906)	11·00	2·00
		b. Yellow (1908)	13·00	2·00
		ba. Thin, ready gummed paper (11.12)	30·00	25·00
		c. Pale orange. Thin, ready gummed paper (1913)	30·00	32·00
430	**100**	5s. rose-red and ultramarine (12.07)	70·00	19·00
		a. Rose-red and blue (1911)	80·00	24·00
		ab. Wmk sideways	90·00	27·00
431	**101**	£1 salmon (12.2.07)	£250	£130
		a. Dull rose (1910)	£250	£130
		ab. Wmk upright (1911)	£300	£150
432	**102**	£2 dull blue (18.7.06)	£550	£375
		(*b*) P 11.		
433	**88**	½d. blue-green (shades) (III) (1905)	1·60	30
		a. Wmk upright. Thin, ready gummed paper (1912)	18·00	22·00
434	**89**	1d. rose-red (III) (1905)	4·50	1·75
		a. Pale rose (1907)	4·00	1·75
		b. Rose-carmine (1911)	7·00	4·25
		ba. Wmk sideways	22·00	15·00
		c. Thin, ready gummed paper (10.12)	11·00	5·00
435	**91**	2d. lilac (II) (1906)	†	£375
		a. Reddish violet (1907)	75·00	21·00
		b. Bright mauve (1910)	29·00	17·00
436	**92**	2½d. blue (1908)	60·00	17·00
		a. Indigo (1909)	17·00	11·00
437	**93**	3d. orange-brown (1905)	10·00	14·00
		a. Yellow-orange (1908)	†	£200
		b. Dull orange-buff (1909)	15·00	22·00
		c. Ochre (1912)	9·00	10·00
		d. Wmk sideways	†	£200
438	**94**	4d. yellow-bistre (1906)	11·00	19·00
		a. Olive-bistre (1909)		
		b. Yellow-olive (1912)	8·50	19·00
439	**95**	5d. chocolate (1906)	†	£1000
		a. Dull reddish brown (1908)	†	£1000
440	**96**	6d. emerald (1909)	10·00	21·00
		a. Yellowish green (1911)	16·00	25·00
441	**97**	9d. rose-carmine (1910)	†	£850
442	**98**	1s. yellow-orange (B) (1906)	†	£300
		a. Orange (1910)	£1000	
443	**100**	5s. rose-red and ultramarine (12.07)	75·00	9·50
444	**101**	£1 salmon (12.2.07)	£400	£140
445	**102**	£2 dull blue (1.07)	£850	£450
		(*c*) Compound or mixed perfs of 12×12½ or 12½ and 11.		
446	**88**	½d. blue-green (*shades*) (III) (1905)	23·00	16·00
		a. Wmk upright. Thin, ready gummed paper (1912)	£200	£160
447	**89**	1d. rose-red (III) (1905)	75·00	75·00
		a. Pale rose (1907)	—	75·00
		b. Rose-carmine (1911)	—	75·00

448 **91** 2d. reddish violet (II) (1907) £600 £375
449 **93** 3d. orange-brown (1905) .... † £850
a. Ochre (1912) £450
450 **94** 4d. bistre (1908) .... † £1000
451 **96** 6d. emerald (1909) .... — £1000
a. Yellowish green (1911) .... † £600
452 **97** 9d. orange-brown (1906) .... † £1100
a. Red-brown (1908) .... † £1100
453 **98** 1s. yellow-orange (1906) £1200
453*a* £1 dull rose .... † £10000

(*d*) Rotary comb perf 11½×12¼.

454 1d. scarlet-red .... 4·00 1·25
a. Thin, ready gummed paper (Rose-carmine) .... 2·75 3·25
ab. Rose-red.................................... 2·75 3·25
ac. Wmk sideways.......................... 35·00 25·00
455 **91** 2d. lilac (II) (1910)........................ 20·00 1·75

The original Crown over A watermark paper used by Victoria was of medium thickness and had toned gum applied after printing. Stocks of this paper lasted until 1912 when further supplies were ordered from a new papermakers, Cowan and Sons. This paper was much thinner and was supplied with white gum already applied. The first delivery arrived in June 1912 and a second in September of the same year.

The rotary comb perforating machine gauging 11½×12¼ was transferred from South Australia in 1909 when J. B. Cooke moved to Melbourne.

Examples of the 1d. perforated 12½ or 11 exist with two black lines across the face of the stamp. These were prepared in connection with stamp-vending machine trials.

ONE PENNY

(**103**)

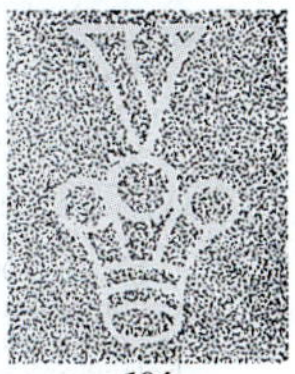

104

1912 (29 Jun). No. 455 *surch with T* **103** *in red.*

456 **91** 1d. on 2d. lilac (II) .... 1·00 60

1912 (1 Aug). W **104**.

(*a*) P 12½ (½d.) or 12×12½.

457 **88** ½d. bluish green (III) .... 3·00 5·50
458 **89** 1d. rose-carmine (III).................... 5·00 4·25
a. Wmk sideways.......................... 50·00 50·00
459 **91** 2d. reddish violet (II) (Sept) .... 3·00 4·75
a. Lilac.. 5·50 7·00
460 **97** 9d. rose-carmine............................ 22·00 23·00

(*b*) P 11.

461 **88** ½d. bluish green (III) .... 20·00 30·00
462 **89** 1d. rose-carmine (III).................... 45·00 25·00
a. Wmk sideways.......................... £110 £110
463 **97** 9d. rose-carmine............................ 38·00 45·00

(*c*) Compound perfs of 12×12½ or 12½ and 11.

464 **97** 9d. rose-carmine............................ † £1100

Nos. 457/64 were emergency printings caused by the non-arrival of stocks of the Cowan thin, ready gummed Crown over A watermarked paper. Paper watermarked W **104** had been introduced in 1911 and was normally used for Victoria fiscal stamps. This watermark can be easily distinguished from the previous W **85** by its narrow crown.

STAMP BOOKLETS

There are very few surviving examples of Nos. SB1/4. Listings are provided for those believed to have been issued with prices quoted for those known to still exist.

1904 (Mar)–**09**. *Black on red cover as* No. SB1 *of New South Wales. Stapled.*

SB1 £1 booklet containing two hundred and forty 1d. in four blocks of 30 and two blocks of 60 ....
a. Red on pink cover (1909)............................ £22000
b. Blue on pink cover....................................... £20000

1904 (Mar). *Black on grey cover as* No. SB1. *Stapled.*

SB2 £1 booklet containing one hundred and twenty 2d. in four blocks of 30 ....

1910 (May). *Black on white cover as* No. SB3 *of New South Wales. Stapled.*

SB3 2s. booklet containing eleven ½d. (No. 426), either in block of 6 plus block of 5 or block of 11, and eighteen 1d. (No. 427), either in three blocks of 6 or block of 6 plus block of 12.. £4250
a. Black on pale green cover........................... £4500

Unsold stock of No. SB3 was uprated with one additional ½d. in May 1911.

1911 (1 Aug). *Red on pink cover as* No. SB3. *Stapled.*

SB4 2s. Booklet containing twelve ½d. (No. 426), either in two blocks of 6 or block of 12, and eighteen 1d. (No. 427), either in three blocks of 6 or block of 6 plus block of 12.. £4750

POSTAGE DUE STAMPS

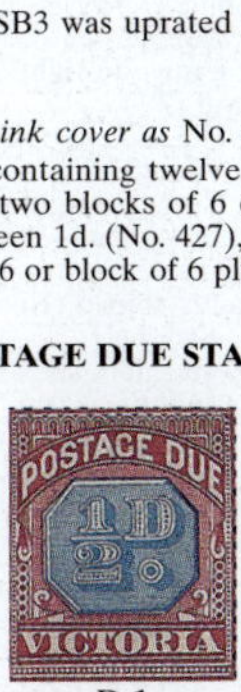

D 1

(Dies eng A. Williams (values) and J. McWilliams (frame). Typo)

1890 (12 Oct)–**94**. Wmk V over Crown, W **33**. P 12×12½.

D1 **D 1** ½d. dull blue and brown-lake (24.12.90) .... 5·00 4·25
a. Dull blue and deep claret........ 3·50 4·50
D2 1d. dull blue and brown-lake........ 6·50 1·60
a. Dull blue and brownish red (1.93)... 8·50 1·75
D3 2d. dull blue and brown-lake........ 11·00 1·75
a. Dull blue and brownish red (3.93) .... 17·00 1·00
D4 4d. dull blue and brown-lake........ 17·00 3·00
a. Dull blue and pale claret (5.94) .... 18·00 6·00
D5 5d. dull blue and brown-lake........ 16·00 2·00
D6 6d. dull blue and brown-lake........ 15·00 4·00
D7 10d. dull blue and brown-lake........ 75·00 50·00
D8 1s. dull blue and brown-lake........ 48·00 8·50
D9 2s. dull blue and brown-lake........ £110 50·00
D10 5s. dull blue and brown-lake........ £160 90·00
D1/10 *Set of* 10.. £400 £170
D1as/10s Optd "Specimen" *Set of* 10................... £300

A used example of the 6d. showing compound perforation of 12×12½ and 11 exists in the Royal Collection.

1895 (17 Jan)–**96**. *Colours changed.* Wmk V over Crown. W **33**. P 12×12½.

D11 **D 1** ½d. rosine and bluish green........... 6·00 1·60
a. Pale scarlet and yellow-green (3.96) .... 3·75 2·25
D12 1d. rosine and bluish green........... 6·00 1·75
a. Pale scarlet and yellow-green (3.96) .... 5·50 1·75
D13 2d. rosine and bluish green........... 14·00 2·25
a. Pale scarlet and yellow-green (3.96) .... 13·00 1·50
D14 4d. rosine and bluish green........... 12·00 1·50
a. Pale scarlet and yellow-green (3.96) .... 9·50 2·25
D15 5d. rosine and bluish green........... 16·00 16·00
a. Pale scarlet and yellow-green (3.96) .... 12·00 9·50
D16 6d. rosine and bluish green........... 13·00 9·50
D17 10d. rosine and bluish green........... 26·00 10·00
D18 1s. rosine and bluish green........... 18·00 3·25
D19 2s. pale red and yellowish green (28.3.95) .... 65·00 20·00
D20 5s. pale red and yellowish green (28.3.95) .... £110 40·00
D11/20 *Set of* 10.. £250 90·00

1897 (1 July)–**99**. Wmk V over Crown. W **82**. P 12×12½.

D21 **D 1** 1d. pale scarlet and yellow-green 9·00 1·25
a. Dull red and bluish green (8.99) .... 9·50 1·25
D22 2d. pale scarlet and yellow-green 13·00 1·25
a. Dull red and bluish green (6.99) .... 14·00 1·00
D23 4d. pale scarlet and yellow-green 27·00 2·25
a. Dull red and bluish green (8.99) .... 27·00 2·00
D24 5d. pale scarlet and yellow-green 27·00 4·25
D25 6d. pale scarlet and yellow-green 10·00 4·50
D21/5 *Set of* 5.. 75·00 11·50

1900 (1 Jun)–**04**. Wmk V over Crown. W **85**. P 12×12½.

D26 **D 1** ½d. rose-red and pale green .... 13·00 5·50
a. Pale red and deep green (8.01) .... 6·00 5·00
b. Scarlet and deep green (1.03).. — 27·00
c. Aniline rosine and green (6.04) .... 10·00 9·00
D27 1d. rose-red and pale green .... 13·00 1·25
a. Pale red and deep green (9.01) .... 12·00 55
b. Scarlet and deep green (2.02). 13·00 70
c. Aniline rosine and green (9.03) .... 13·00 1·25
D28 2d. rose-red and pale green (7.00) 13·00 1·75
a. Pale red and deep green (9.01) .... 15·00 1·75
b. Scarlet and deep green (2.02). 15·00 1·00
c. Aniline rosine and green (9.03) .... 15·00 1·75
D29 4d. rose-red and pale green (5.01) .... 27·00 7·50
a. Pale red and deep green (9.01) .... 26·00 2·75
b. Scarlet and deep green (6.03). 26·00 4·00
c. Aniline rosine and green (6.04) .... 26·00 4·25
D30 5d. scarlet and deep green (1.03). 21·00 9·00
D31 1s. scarlet and deep green (3.02). 23·00 8·50
D32 2s. scarlet and deep green (1.03). £140 80·00
D33 5s. scarlet and deep green (1.03). £160 80·00
D26/33 *Set of* 8.. £350 £170

1905 (Dec)–**09**. Wmk Crown over A, W w **11**. P 12×12½.

D34 **D 1** ½d. aniline rosine and pale green (1.06)... 16·00 14·00
a. Scarlet and pale yellow-green (7.07) .... 5·50 7·50
b. Dull scarlet and pea-green (3.09) .... 6·50 8·50
ba. Compound perf 12×12½ and 11... £425 £300
D35 1d. aniline rosine and pale green. 50·00 7·00
a. Scarlet and pale yellow-green (5.06) .... 6·50 2·50
b. Dull scarlet and pea-green (1.07)... 10·00 2·50
D36 2d. aniline scarlet and deep yellow-green (5.06)............... 22·00 3·25
a. Dull scarlet and pea-green (11.07)... 12·00 2·50
D37 4d. dull scarlet and pea-green (1908)... 22·00 13·00
D34/7 *Set of* 4.. 35·00 23·00

A printing of the 5d. in dull scarlet and pea-green on this paper was prepared in 1907–08, but not put into use. A few examples have survived, either mint or cancelled-to-order from presentation sets (*Price £1800 mint, £1200 cancelled-to-order*).

WESTERN AUSTRALIA

PRICES FOR STAMPS ON COVER

Nos. 1/6	*from* × 6
Nos. 15/32	*from* × 4
Nos. 33/46	*from* × 5
Nos. 49/51	*from* × 6
Nos. 52/62	*from* × 10
Nos. 63/*a*	*from* × 8
No. 67	—
Nos. 68/92*a*	*from* × 10
Nos. 94/102	*from* × 40
Nos. 103/5	*from* × 8
Nos. 107/10*a*	*from* × 12
Nos. 111*a*/*b*	—
Nos. 112/16	*from* × 25
Nos. 117/25	*from* × 10
Nos. 126/8	—
Nos. 129/34	*from* × 8
Nos. 135/6	—
Nos. 138/48	*from* × 12
Nos. 151/63	*from* × 5
Nos. 168/9	*from* × 20
Nos. 170/1	*from* × 4
Nos. 172/3	*from* × 40
Nos. F11/22	*from* × 10
Nos. T1/2	—

SPECIMEN OVERPRINTS. Those listed are from U.P.U. distributions between 1889 and 1892. Further "Specimen" overprints exist, but those were used for other purposes.

1

2

3

4

GUM. The 1854 and 1857–59 issues are hardly ever seen with gum, so the unused prices quoted are for examples without gum.

(Eng W. Humphrys. Recess P.B.)

1854 (1 Aug). W **4** (sideways).

(*a*) Imperf.

1 **1** 1d. black £900 £225

(*b*) Rouletted 7½ to 14 and compound.

2 **1** 1d. black £2500 £550

In addition to the supplies received from London a further printing, using the original plate and watermarked paper from Perkins, Bacon, was made in the colony before the date of issue.

The 1d. is also known pin-perforated.

(Litho H. Samson (later A. Hillman), Government Lithographer)

1854 (1 Aug)–**55**. W **4** (sideways).

(*a*) Imperf.

3 **2** 4d. pale blue £325 £190
a. Blue.. £375 £225
b. Deep dull blue............................. £2250 £850
c. Slate-blue (1855) £2500 £1000
d. "T" of "POSTAGE" shaved off to a point at foot (R. 7/5, 7/10, 7/15, 7/20)..................... £1400 £900
e. Top of letters of "AUSTRALIA" cut off so that they are barely 1 mm high.. † £15000
f. "PEICE" instead of "PENCE".. † £15000
g. "CE" of "Pence" close together.. † £18000
h. Frame inverted (R. 8/1, 8/6, 8/11, 8/16)...................................... † £75000
i. Tilted border (R. 7/4, 7/9, 7/14, 7/19)...................................... £1600 £1100
j. "WEST" in squeezed-down letters and "F" of "FOUR" with pointed foot (R. 2/17)..... £1700 £1200
k. "ESTERN" in squeezed-down letters and "U" of "FOUR" squeezed up (R. 3/17) £3250 £1900
l. Small "S" in "POSTAGE" (R. 4/17) £1700 £1200
m. "EN" of "PENCE" shorter (R. 6/4).. £1500 £1000
n. "N" of "PENCE" tilted to right with thin first downstroke (R. 6/16)............... £1500 £1000
o. Swan and water above "ENCE" damaged (R. 6/20)... £1500 £1000
p. "F" of "FOUR" slanting to left (R. 7/17) £1500 £1000
q. "WESTERN" in squeezed-down letters only 1½ mm high (R. 8/17)........................... £1800 £1300
r. "P" of "PENCE" with small head (R. 9/15)........................... £1500 £1000
s. "RALIA" in squeezed-down letters only 1½ mm high (R. 9/16) £1700 £1100

t. "PE" of "PENCE" close together (R. 10/15) £1500 £1000
u. "N" of "PENCE" narrow (R. 10/16) £1500 £1000
v. Part of right cross-stroke and downstroke of "T" of "POSTAGE" cut off (R. 11/15) £1500 £1000
w. "A" in "POSTAGE" with thin right limb (R. 11/16) £1500 £1000
x. Coloured line above "AGE" of "POSTAGE" (R. 8/6) £1600 £1100
y. No outer line above "GE" of "POSTAGE" and coloured line under "FOU" of "FOUR" (R. 8/11) £1600 £1200

4 3 1s. salmon £17000 £3250
a. Deep red-brown £1600 £800
b. Grey-brown (1.55) £550 £375
c. Pale brown (10.55) £400 £325

(*b*) Rouletted 7½ to 14 and compound.

5 2 4d. pale blue £1900 £550
a. Blue — £550
b. Slate-blue (1855) — £1900
6 3 1s. grey-brown (1.55) £4000 £1000
a. Pale brown (10.55) £3750 £850

Both values are also known pin-perforated.

The 4d. value was prepared by Horace Samson from the Perkins, Bacon 1d. plate. A block of 60 (5×12, cols 16-20) was taken as a "plate to stone" transfer and each frame was then erased. A new lithographic frame, drawn on stone, was transferred 60 times to make up the intermediate stone.

There were a number of transfer varieties, one of the most prominent being the "T" of "POSTAGE" shaved at foot (No. 3d).

Four transfers were taken from the intermediate stone to make printing stone No. l with 240 impressions. Samson printed the initial supply of 100 sheets in deep dull blue (No. 3b) in July 1854.

Printing stone No. 1 had three scarce creased transfers whose positions in the sheet have yet to be established (Nos. 3e/g).

Further supplies were printed in January 1855 by Alfred Hillman, Samson's successor. A severe interruption to printing, almost certainly a broken stone, occurred when the fourth sheet was being pulled. On examining the intermediate stone preparatory to making a new printing stone it was found that the frame of R. 8/1 had been damaged and needed replacing.

This was done, but in so doing, Hillman accidentally produced the transfer error "Inverted Frame" (No. 3h). Printing Stone No. 2 was made as before and bore a range of transfer varieties (Nos. 3j/w) along with four "Inverted Frames". This printing was in blue (No. 3a). Some time after completion of the required 97 sheets, the "Inverted Frame" was corrected on each of the four positions to make printing stone No. 2A. All four corrections are identifiable and on two of them, traces of the inverted frame remain visible (Nos. 3x/y).

Printing stone No. 2A was used for the third printing undertaken in October 1855, producing 175 sheets of slate-blue (No. 3c.) stamps and for the fourth and final printing, totalling 1500 sheets in pale blue (No. 3), undertaken in December 1855.

The 1s. value was produced in much the same way, based on a transfer of cols. 10-14 from the Perkins, Bacon 1d. plate.

5

(Litho A. Hillman, Government Lithographer)

1857 (7 Aug)–**59**. W **4** (sideways).

(*a*) Imperf.

15 5 2d. brown-black/*red* (26.2.58) £2750 £550
a. Printed both sides £3500 £800
16 2d. brown-black/*Indian red* (26.2.58) £3250 £800
a. Printed both sides £3750 £850
17 6d. golden bronze £12000 £1800
18 6d. black-bronze £4500 £650
19 6d. grey-black (1859) £4500 £550

(*b*) Rouletted 7½ to 14 and compound.

20 5 2d. brown-black/*red* £8000 £1700
a. Printed both sides — £2000
21 2d. brown-black/*Indian red* — £1800
22 6d. black-bronze £8000 £950
23 6d. grey-black — £1000

The 2d. and 6d. are known pin-perforated.

Prices quoted for Nos. 15/23 are for "cut-square" examples. Collectors are warned against "cut-round" copies with corners added.

(Recess in the colony from P.B. plates)

1860 (11 Aug)–**64**. W **4** (sideways on 2d. and 6d.).

(*a*) Imperf.

24 1 2d. pale orange 85·00 75·00
25 2d. orange-vermilion 85·00 75·00
a. Wmk upright
25*b* 2d. deep vermilion £1600 £800
26 4d. blue (Wmk upright) (21.6.64) £250 £1800
a. Wmk sideways £425
27 4d. deep blue (Wmk upright) £250 £1700
28 6d. sage-green (27.7.61) £1800 £400
28*a* 6d. deep sage-green — £550

(*b*) Rouletted 7½ to 14.

29 1 2d. pale orange £500 £200
30 2d. orange-vermilion £550 £200
31 4d. deep blue (Wmk upright) £4250
32 6d. sage-green £3500 £600

PERKINS BACON "CANCELLED". For notes on these handstamps, showing "CANCELLED" between horizontal bars forming an oval, see Catalogue Introduction.

(Recess P.B.)

1861. W **4** (sideways).

(*a*) Intermediate perf 14–16.

33 1 1d. rose £475 £140
34 2d. blue £160 40·00
35 4d. vermilion £950 £1800
36 6d. purple-brown £650 £100
37 1s. yellow-green £750 £200

(*b*) P 14 at Somerset House.

38 1 1d. rose £275 65·00
39 2d. blue £100 40·00
40 4d. vermilion £300 £180

(*c*) Perf clean-cut 14–16.

41 1 2d. blue 80·00 24·00
a. Imperf between (pair)
42 6d. purple-brown £375 50·00
43 1s. yellow-green £500 80·00
a. Wmk upright — 90·00

(*d*) P 14–16 very rough (July).

44 1 1d. rose-carmine (H/S "CANCELLED" in oval £17000) £250 50·00
45 6d. purple/*blued* (H/S "CANCELLED" in oval £11000) £2750 £475
46 1s. deep green (H/S "CANCELLED" in oval £10000) £1600 £350

Perkins, Bacon experienced considerable problems with their perforating machine during the production of these stamps.

The initial printing showed intermediate perforation 14–16. Further supplies were then sent, in late December 1860, to Somerset House to be perforated on their comb 14 machine. The Inland Revenue Board were only able to process the three lower values, although the 6d. purple-brown and 1s. yellow-green are known from this perforation overprinted "SPECIMEN".

The Perkins, Bacon machine was repaired the following month and the 6d., 1s. and a further supply of the 2d. were perforated on it to give a clean-cut 14-16 gauge.

A final printing was produced in July 1861, but by this time the machine had deteriorated so that it produced a very rough 14–16.

(Recess D.L.R. from P.B. plates)

1863 (16 Dec)–**64**. No wmk. P 13.

49 1 1d. carmine-rose 65·00 3·50
50 1d. lake 65·00 3·50
51 6d. deep lilac (15.4.64) £160 42·00
51*a* 6d. dull violet (15.4.64) £225 48·00

Both values exist on thin and on thick papers, the former being the scarcer.

Both grades of paper show a marginal sheet watermark, "T H SAUNDERS 1860" in double-lined large and small capitals, but parts of this watermark rarely occur on the stamps.

(Recess D.L.R. from P.B. plates)

1864 (27 Dec)–**79**. Wmk Crown CC (sideways* on 1d.). P 12½.

52 1 1d. bistre 60·00 6·50
w. Wmk Crown to right of CC 60·00 6·50
x. Wmk sideways reversed 60·00 7·00
53 1d. yellow-ochre (16.10.74) 75·00 9·00
w. Wmk Crown to right of CC 75·00 9·00
54 2d. chrome-yellow (18.1.65) 70·00 3·50
55 2d. yellow 70·00 3·50
a. Wmk sideways (5.79) — 21·00
aw. Wmk Crown to right of CC — 21·00
b. Error. Mauve (1879) £12000 £11000
x. Wmk reversed 70·00 3·50
56 4d. carmine (18.1.65) 85·00 6·00
a. Doubly printed £25000
w. Wmk inverted — 30·00
x. Wmk reversed — 7·50
57 6d. violet (18.1.65) £100 6·00
a. Doubly printed † £20000
b. Wmk sideways — £275
x. Wmk reversed — 6·00
58 6d. indigo-violet £350 32·00
x. Wmk reversed — 32·00
59 6d. lilac (1872) £180 6·00
60 6d. mauve (12.5.75) £170 6·00
x. Wmk reversed — 6·00
61 1s. bright green (18.1.65) £140 15·00
s. Handstamped "Specimen" £160
62 1s. sage-green (10.68) £325 28·00

*The normal sideways watermark shows Crown to left of CC, *as seen from the back of the stamp.*

Beware of fakes of No. 55b made by altering the value tablet of No. 60.

7

ONE PENNY
(8)

(Typo D.L.R)

1871 (29 Oct)–**73**. Wmk Crown CC (sideways). P 14.

63 7 3d. pale brown 45·00 4·75
a. Cinnamon (1873) 45·00 4·00
s. Handstamped "Specimen" £130

1874 (10 Dec). No. 55 *surch with T* **8** *by Govt Printer.*

67 1 1d. on 2d. yellow (G.) £475 55·00
a. Pair, one without surch
b. Surch triple † £4500
c. "O" of "ONE" omitted

Forged surcharges of T **8** are known on stamps wmk Crown CC perf 14, and on Crown CA, perf 12 and 14.

(Recess D.L.R. from P.B. plates)

1876–81. Wmk Crown CC (sideways*). P 14.

68 1 1d. ochre 60·00 3·25
w. Wmk Crown to right of CC 60·00 3·25
69 1d. bistre (1878) £100 4·25
w. Wmk Crown to right of CC — 4·75
70 1d. yellow-ochre (1879) 70·00 2·00
71 2d. chrome-yellow 75·00 1·50
a. Wmk upright (1877) 90·00 2·75
bw. Wmk Crown to right of CC — 1·75
by. Wmk Crown to right of CC and reversed — 20·00
74 4d. carmine (1881) £425 £100
75 6d. lilac (1877) £140 4·00
a. Wmk upright (1879) £550 15·00
bw. Wmk Crown to right of CC — 4·00
75*c* 6d. reddish lilac (1879) £130 6·00

*The normal sideways watermark shows Crown to left of CC, *as seen from the back of the stamp.*

(Recess D.L.R. from P.B. plates)

1882 (Mar)–**85**. Wmk Crown CA (sideways*).

(*a*) P 14.

76 1 1d. yellow-ochre 26·00 2·00
w. Wmk Crown to right of CA 26·00 2·00
x. Wmk sideways reversed
77 2d. chrome-yellow 30·00 2·00
a. Wmk upright † —
w. Wmk Crown to right of CA — 2·50
78 4d. carmine (8.82) £120 8·50
a. Wmk upright (1885) — 85·00
w. Wmk Crown to right of CA £120 8·50
79 6d. reddish lilac (1882) 95·00 3·00
80 6d. lilac (1884) 95·00 4·00
s. Handstamped "Specimen" £130
w. Wmk Crown to right of CA — 5·00
y. Wmk sideways inverted and reversed — 30·00

(*b*) P 12×14.

81 1 1d. yellow-ochre (2.83) £1800 £150

(*c*) P 12.

82 1 1d. yellow-ochre (2.83) 70·00 5·00
83 2d. chrome-yellow (6.83) £100 5·00
a. Imperf between (pair)
w. Wmk Crown to right of CA — 5·50
84 4d. carmine (5.83) £180 38·00
w. Wmk Crown to right of CA — 38·00
85 6d. lilac (6.83) £350 38·00
w. Wmk Crown to right of CA — 38·00

*The normal sideways watermark shows Crown to left of CA, *as seen from the back of the stamp.*

(Typo D.L.R.)

1882 (July)–**95**. Wmk Crown CA (sideways). P 14.

86 7 3d. pale brown 16·00 3·00
87 3d. red-brown (12.95) 8·50 3·00

The 3d. stamps in other colours, watermark Crown CA and perforated 12, are colour trials dating from 1883.

½ (9) 1d. (10) 1d. (11)

1884 (19 Feb). *Surch with T* **9**, *in red, by Govt Printer.*

89 1 ½d. on 1d. yellow-ochre (No. 76) 18·00 26·00
a. Thin bar 80·00 £100
90 ½d. on 1d. yellow-ochre (No. 82) 13·00 21·00

Inverted or double surcharges are forgeries made in London about 1886.

The "Thin bar" varieties occur on R. 12/3, R. 12/8, R. 12/13 and R. 12/18, and show the bar only 0.2 mm thick.

1885 (May). Nos. 63/*a surch, in green, by Govt Printer.*

(*a*) *Thick "1" with slanting top, T* **10** *(Horizontal Rows 1/5).*

91 1d. on 3d. pale brown 70·00 18·00
a. Cinnamon 60·00 17·00
b. Vert pair. Nos. 91/2 £250

(*b*) *Thin "1" with straight top, T* **11** *(Horizontal Row 6).*

92 1d. on 3d. pale brown £170 50·00
a. Cinnamon £140 50·00

12

13

14

15

(Typo D.L.R.)

1885 (May)–**93**. Wmk Crown CA (sideways). P 14.

94 12 ½d. yellow-green 4·75 70
a. Green 4·00 70
w. Wmk Crown to right of CA — 50·00
95 13 1d. carmine (2.90) 25·00 60
w. Wmk Crown to right of CA — 30·00
96 14 2d. bluish grey (6.90) 29·00 2·00
a. Grey 26·00 2·00
w. Wmk Crown to right of CA — 50·00
97 15 2½d. deep blue (1.5.92) 17·00 2·25
a. Blue 15·00 2·25
w. Wmk Crown to right of CA — 50·00
98 4d. chestnut (7.90) 10·00 2·00
99 5d. bistre (1.5.92) 11·00 3·75
100 6d. bright violet (1.93) 16·00 1·75
w. Wmk Crown to right of CA — 70·00
101 1s. pale olive-green (4.90) 28·00 5·00
102 1s. olive-green 20·00 4·75
94s/101s (ex 1d., 6d.) Handstamped (Nos. 96, 98, 101) or optd "Specimen" *Set of* 6 £425

The normal sideways watermark shows Crown to left of CA, *as seen from the back of the stamp.*

(Recess D.L.R. from P.B. plates)

1888 (Mar–Apr). Wmk Crown CA (sideways). P 14.

103 1 1d. carmine-pink 23·00 3·50
104 2d. grey 55·00 1·25
105 4d. red-brown (April) 75·00 22·00
103s/5s H/S "Specimen" *Set of* 3 £225

The watermark shows Crown to right of CA on No. 103 and to the left of CA on 104/5, *as seen from the back of the stamp.*

ONE PENNY (16) **Half-penny** (17)

1893 (Feb). *Surch with T* **16**, *in green, by Govt Printer.*

107	**7**	1d. on 3d. pale brown (No. 63)	13·00	5·00
108		1d. on 3d. cinnamon (No. 63*a*)	13·00	5·00
		a. Double surcharge	£1300	
109		1d. on 3d. pale brown (No. 86)	55·00	6·50

1895 (21 Nov). *Surch with T* **17** *by Govt Printer.*

		(a) In green.		
110	**7**	½d. on 3d. pale brown (No. 63)	9·00	27·00
110*a*		½d. on 3d. cinnamon (No. 63*a*)	7·50	27·00
		b. Surcharge double	£900	
		(b) In red and in green.		
111*a*	**7**	½d. on 3d. cinnamon (No. 63*a*)	85·00	£275
111*b*		½d. on 3d. red-brown (No. 87)	65·00	£180

Green was the adopted surcharge colour but a trial had earlier been made in red on stamps watermarked Crown CC. As they proved unsatisfactory they were given another surcharge in green. The trial stamps were inadvertently issued and, to prevent speculation, a further printing of the duplicated surcharge was made, but on both papers, Crown CC (No. 111*a*) and Crown CA (No. 111*b*).

18

19

20

21

(Typo D.L.R.)

1898 (Dec)–**1907**. Wmk W Crown A, W **18**. P 14.

112	**13**	1d. carmine	5·50	20
113	**14**	2d. bright yellow (1.99)	20·00	2·50
		w. Wmk inverted	—	75·00
114	**19**	2½d. blue (1.01)	11·00	1·25
115	**20**	6d. bright violet (10.06)	25·00	2·25
		w. Wmk inverted	—	£130
116	**21**	1s. olive-green (4.07)	28·00	3·75
		w. Wmk inverted	—	75·00

22

23

24

25

26

27

28

29

30

31

32

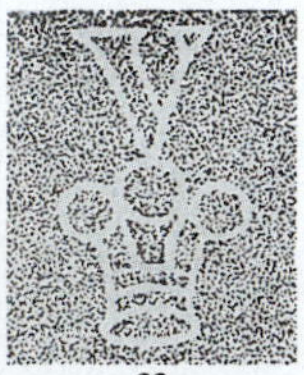
33

(Typo Victoria Govt Printer, Melbourne, Commonwealth Stamp Ptg Branch from March 1909)

1902 (Oct)–**12**. Wmk V and Crown, W **33** (sideways on horiz designs).

		(a) P 12½ or 12½×12 (horiz), 12×12½ (vert).		
117	**22**	1d. carmine-rose (1.03)	15·00	60
		a. Wmk upright (10.02)	19·00	70
118	**23**	2d. yellow (4.1.03)	16·00	3·25
		a. Wmk upright (1903)	32·00	4·50
119	**24**	4d. chestnut (4.03)	20·00	2·75
		a. Wmk upright	£375	
120	**15**	5d. bistre (4.9.05)	£110	75·00
121	**25**	8d. apple-green (3.03)	19·00	3·00
122	**26**	9d. yellow-orange (5.03)	27·00	12·00
		a. Wmk upright (11.03)	75·00	28·00
123	**27**	10d. red (3.03)	32·00	8·00
124	**28**	2s. bright red/*yellow*	85·00	25·00
		a. Wmk sideways	£200	20·00
		b. Orange/yellow (7.06)	45·00	12·00
		c. Brown-red/yellow (5.11)	45·00	13·00
125	**29**	2s.6d. deep blue/*rose*	45·00	9·00
126	**30**	5s. emerald-green	70·00	29·00
127	**31**	10s. deep mauve	£160	80·00
		a. Bright purple (1910)	£550	£325
128	**32**	£1 orange-brown (1.11.02)	£350	£170
		a. Orange (10.7.09)	£600	£325
		(b) P 11.		
129	**22**	1d. carmine-rose	£275	24·00
		a. Wmk upright	†	£375
130	**23**	2d. yellow	£300	40·00
		a. Wmk upright	†	£375
131	**24**	4d. chestnut	£900	£375
132	**15**	5d. bistre	48·00	65·00
133	**26**	9d. yellow-orange	£110	£130
134	**28**	2s. bright red/*yellow*	£180	£120
		a. Orange/yellow	£300	£150
		(c) Perf compound of 12½ or 12½×12 and 11.		
135	**22**	1d. carmine-rose	£850	£450
136	**23**	2d. yellow	£1200	£750
137	**24**	4d. chestnut		

Type **22** is similar to Type **13** but larger.

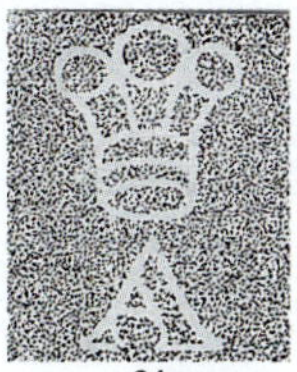
34

35

1905–12. Wmk Crown and A, W **34** (sideways).

		(a) P 12½ or 12½×12 (horiz), 12×12½ (vert).		
138	**12**	½d. green (6.10)	4·25	6·00
139	**22**	1d. rose-pink (10.05)	13·00	1·00
		a. Wmk upright (1.06)	9·00	1·00
		b. Carmine (1909)	12·00	1·00
		c. Carmine-red (1912)	13·00	8·00
140	**23**	2d. yellow (15.11.05)	7·00	2·00
		a. Wmk upright (4.10)	†	£250
141	**7**	3d. brown (2.06)	26·00	3·00
142	**24**	4d. bistre-brown (12.06)	27·00	9·50
		a. Pale chestnut (1908)	25·00	9·00
		b. Bright brown-red (14.10.10)	13·00	3·25
143	**15**	5d. pale olive-bistre (8.05)	19·00	11·00
		a. Olive-green (1.09)	19·00	11·00
		b. Pale greenish yellow (5.12)	55·00	85·00
144	**25**	8d. apple-green (22.4.12)	18·00	60·00
145	**26**	9d. orange (11.5.06)	27·00	6·00
		a. Red-orange (6.10)	45·00	5·50
		b. Wmk upright (7.12)	60·00	28·00
146	**27**	10d. rose-orange (16.2.10)	23·00	21·00
148	**30**	5s. emerald-green (wmk upright) (9.07)	£140	£100
		(b) P 11.		
150	**12**	½d. green	£1700	
151	**22**	1d. rose-pink	38·00	16·00
		a. Carmine-red	48·00	15·00
		b. Wmk upright	70·00	19·00
152	**23**	2d. yellow	35·00	23·00
153	**7**	3d. brown	19·00	7·00
154	**24**	4d. yellow-brown	£750	£250
		a. Pale chestnut	—	£375
155	**15**	5d. pale olive-bistre	38·00	10·00
		a. Olive-green	19·00	15·00
157	**26**	9d. orange	£130	£160
		a. Red-orange	—	£170
		b. Wmk upright (1912)	†	£700
		(c) Perf compound of 12½ or 12½×12 and 11.		
161	**22**	1d. rose-pink (wmk upright)	£700	£350
		a. Wmk sideways	—	£600
162	**23**	2d. yellow	£650	£375
163	**7**	3d. brown	—	£850
164	**26**	9d. red-orange		

The prices provided for Nos. 154/a are for examples perforated "OS".

1912 (Mar). Wmk Crown and A W **35** (sideways). P 11½×12.

168	**20**	6d. bright violet	12·00	13·00
169	**21**	1s. sage-green	27·00	20·00
		a. Perf 12½ (single line)	—	£1600

1912 (7 Aug). *Thin, ready gummed paper with white gum (as Victoria).* W **34** (sideways).

170	**7**	3d. brown (P 12½)	60·00	65·00
		a. Wmk upright	£130	£130
171		3d. brown (P 11)		
		a. Wmk upright		

ONE PENNY
(36)

1912 (6 Nov). Nos. 140 *and* 162 *surch with T* **36** *in Melbourne.*

		(a) P 12½ ×12.		
172	**23**	1d. on 2d. yellow	1·50	1·75
		a. Wmk upright	4·50	8·00
		(b) Perf compound of 12½×12 and 11.		
173	**23**	1d. on 2d. yellow	£475	£325

STAMP BOOKLETS

There are very few surviving examples of Nos. SB1/4. Listings are provided for those believed to have been issued with prices quoted for those known to still exist.

1904 (1 Jan)–**09**. *Black on red cover as* No. SB1 *of New South Wales. Stapled.*

SB1	£1 booklet containing two hundred and forty 1d. in four blocks of 30 and two blocks of 60	
	a. Red on pink cover (1909)	£20000
	b. blue on pink cover	

1904 (1 Jan). *Black on grey cover as* No. SB1. *Stapled.*

SB2	£1 Booklet containing one hundred and twenty 2d. in four blocks of 30	

1910 (May). *Black on cream cover as* No. SB3 *of New South Wales. Stapled.*

SB3	2s. booklet containing eleven ½d. (No. 138), either in block of 6 plus block of 5 or block of 11, and eighteen 1d. (No. 139) either in three blocks of 6 or block of 6 plus block of 12	£5500

Unsold stock of No. SB3 was uprated with one additional ½d. in May 1911.

1911 (1 Aug). *Red on pink cover as* No. SB3. *Stapled.*

SB4	2s. Booklet containing twelve ½d. (No. 138), either in two blocks of 6 or block of 12, and eighteen 1d. (No. 139), either in three blocks of 6 or block of 6 plus block of 12	£4750

POSTAL FISCAL STAMPS

By the Post and Telegraph Act of 5 September 1893 the current issue of fiscal stamps up to and including the 1s. value, Nos. F11/15, was authorised for postal use.

These stamps had been initially supplied, for fiscal purposes, in February 1882 and had been preceded by a series of "I R" surcharges and overprints on postage stamps which were in use for a period of about six months. Examples of these 1881–82 provisionals can be found postally used under the terms of the 1893 Act but, as they had not been current for fiscal purposes for over eleven years, we no longer list them.

F 3

(Typo D.L.R.)

1893 (5 Sep). *Definitive fiscal stamps of Feb 1882.* Wmk CA over Crown. P 14.

F11	**F 3**	1d. dull purple	20·00	3·25
F12		2d. dull purple	£190	60·00
F13		3d. dull purple	65·00	4·25
F14		6d. dull purple	80·00	6·00
F15		1s. dull purple	£140	12·00

The 1s. value is as Type **F 3** but with rectangular outer frame and circular frame surrounding swan.

Higher values in this series were not validated by the Act for postal use.

Two varieties of watermark exist on these stamps. Initial supplies showed an indistinct watermark with the base of the "A" 4 mm wide. From 1896 the paper used showed a clearer watermark on which the base of the "A" was 5 mm wide.

1897. Wmk W Crown A, W **18**. P 14.

F19	**F 3**	1d. dull purple	15·00	3·25
F20		3d. dull purple	60·00	4·25
F21		6d. dull purple	60·00	4·50
F22		1s. dull purple	£140	16·00

The above were invalidated for postal purposes from 1 January 1901.

TELEGRAPH STAMPS USED FOR POSTAGE

The 1d. Telegraph stamps were authorised for postal purposes from 25 October 1886.

T 1

1886 (25 Oct). Wmk Crown CC.

T1	**T 1**	1d. bistre (P 12½)	50·00	6·00
T2		1d. bistre (P 14)	50·00	6·00

Copies of a similar 6d. value are known postally used, but such use was unauthorised.

OFFICIAL STAMPS

From 1 August 1862 stamps of various issues were punched with a circular hole, the earlier size being about 3 mm. in diameter and the latter 4 mm. These were used on official correspondence by the Commissariat and Convict Department, branches of the Imperial administration separate from the colonial government. This system of punching ceased in March 1886. Subsequently many stamps between Nos. 94 and 148 may be found punctured, "PWD", "WA" or "OS".

Western Australia became part of the Commonwealth of Australia on 1 January 1901.

COMMONWEALTH OF AUSTRALIA

On 1 March 1901 control of the postal service passed to the federal administration although it was not until 13 October 1910 that the issues of the various states became valid for use throughout Australia. Postal rates were standardised on 1 May 1911.

The first national postage due stamps appeared in July 1902, but it was not until January 1913 that postage stamps inscribed "AUSTRALIA" were issued.

PRICES FOR STAMPS ON COVER TO 1945

Nos. 1/3	*from* × 10
No. 4	*from* × 4
Nos. 5/12	*from* × 10
Nos. 13/16	—
Nos. 17/19	*from* × 10
Nos. 20/3	*from* × 10
No. 24	*from* × 8
No. 25	*from* × 2
Nos. 26/7	*from* × 8
Nos. 28/30	—
Nos. 35/7	*from* × 5
Nos. 38/9	*from* × 8
Nos. 40/1	*from* × 20
Nos. 42/5	—
No. 47	*from* × 5
Nos. 48/51	*from* × 8
Nos. 52/3	*from* × 5
Nos. 56/7	*from* × 10
Nos. 58/61	*from* × 8
No. 62	*from* × 5
No. 63	*from* × 2
No. 64	*from* × 15
No. 65	*from* × 5
No. 66	—
No. 73	*from* × 20
Nos. 74/5	*from* × 5
Nos. 76/7	*from* × 4
Nos. 78/81	*from* × 8
Nos. 82/4	*from* × 6
Nos. 85/104	*from* × 4
No. 105	*from* × 15
Nos. 106/10	*from* × 6
Nos. 111/14	—
No. 115	*from* × 3
Nos. 116/18	*from* × 5
Nos. 119/20	*from* × 8
Nos. 121/9	*from* × 5
Nos. 130/1	*from* × 25
No. 132	*from* × 3
Nos. 133/5	*from* × 10
Nos. 136/8	*from* × 4
Nos. 139/*a*	*from* × 3
No. 140	*from* × 8
Nos. 141/2	*from* × 4
No. 143	*from* × 6
No. 146	*from* × 20
Nos. 147/8	*from* × 3
No. 149	*from* × 6
Nos. 150/2	*from* × 3
Nos. 153/*a*	*from* × 12
No. 154	*from* × 15
No. 155	*from* × 4
No. 156	*from* × 15
Nos. 157/8	*from* × 3
Nos. 159/60	*from* × 6
No. 161	*from* × 10
Nos. 162/3	*from* × 4
Nos. 164/211	*from* × 2
Nos. D1/118	*from* × 8
Nos. O1/3	*from* × 10
Nos. O4/6	*from* × 4
Nos. O7/8	*from* × 10
Nos. O9/15	—
Nos. O16/18	*from* × 10
No. O19	*from* × 3
No. O20	*from* × 15
No. O21	*from* × 3
Nos. O22/3	*from* × 10
No. O24/30	—
Nos. O31/4	*from* × 10
Nos. O35/7	—
Nos. O38/42	*from* × 15
Nos. O43/7	*from* × 10
No. O48	*from* × 30
Nos. O49/53	—
No. O54	*from* × 6
No. O60	*from* × 4
No. O61	*from* × 30
No. O62	—
No. O63	*from* × 5
Nos. O64/5	*from* × 15
Nos. O66/7	*from* × 8
No. O68	*from* × 20
No. O69	*from* × 10
Nos. O70/4	*from* × 15
No. O75	—
Nos. O76/7	*from* × 15
No. O78	—
Nos. O79/84	*from* × 8
No. O85	*from* × 6
Nos. O86/7	*from* × 3
No. O88	—
No. O89	*from* × 15
Nos. O90/6	*from* × 6
No. O97	*from* × 20
Nos. O98/110	*from* × 6
Nos. O111	*from* × 10
Nos. O112/17	*from* × 20
Nos. O118/*b*	—
Nos. O119/2	*from* × 20
Nos. O126	*from* × 100
Nos. O127	*from* × 5
Nos. O128	*from* × 200
Nos. O129/31	*from* × 50
Nos. O132/3	*from* × 10
Nos. O134/6	*from* × 40

PRINTERS. Except where otherwise stated, all Commonwealth stamps to No. 581 were printed under Government authority at Melbourne. Until 1918 there were two establishments (both of the Treasury Dept)—the Note Printing Branch and the Stamp Printing Branch. The former printed T **3** and **4**.

In 1918 the Stamp Printing Branch was closed and all stamps were printed by the Note Printing Branch. In 1926 control was transferred from the Treasury to the Commonwealth Bank of Australia, and on 14 January 1960 the branch was attached to the newly established Reserve Bank of Australia.

Until 1942 stamps bore in the sheet margin the initials or names of successive managers and from 1942 to March 1952 the imprint "Printed by the Authority of the Government of the Commonwealth of Australia". After November 1952 (or Nos. D129/31 for Postage Dues) imprints were discontinued.

SPECIMEN OVERPRINTS. These come from Specimen sets, first made available to the public on 15 December 1913. In these sets the lower values were cancelled-to-order, but stamps with a face value of 7s.6d. or 75c. were overprinted "Specimen" in different types. These overprints are listed as they could be purchased from the Australian Post Office.

It is, however, believed that examples of No. 112 overprinted "Specimen" were distributed by the U.P.U. in 1929. Supplies of the 1902 and 1902–04 postage due stamps overprinted "Specimen" were supplied to the U.P.U. by some of the states.

1

2

Die I

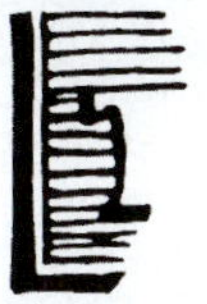
Die II

Dies of Type 1 (mono-coloured values only):—

Die I. Break in inner frame line at lower left level with top of words of value.

Die II. Die repaired showing no break.

Die I was only used for the ½d., 1d., 2d. and 3d. Several plates were produced for each except the 3d. When the second plate of the 3d. was being prepared the damage became aggravated after making 105 out of the 120 units when the die was returned for repair. This gave rise to the *se-tenant* pairs showing the two states of the die.

Die II was used until 1945 and deteriorated progressively with damage to the frame lines and rounding of the corners.

Specialists recognise seven states of this die, but we only list the two most major of the later versions.

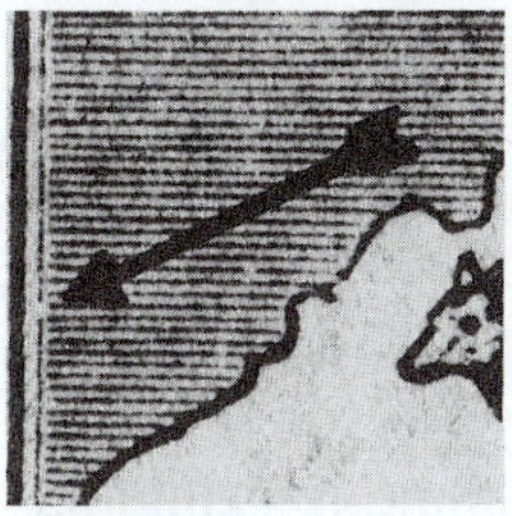

Die IIA. This state is as Die II, but, in addition, shows a break in the inner left-hand frame line, 9 mm from the top of the design (occurs on 1d., 2d. and 6d.).

Die IIB. As Die IIA, but now also showing break in outer frame line above "ST", and (not illustrated) an incomplete corner to the inner frame line at top right (occurs on 3d., 6d., 9d., Is. and £1 (No. 75)).

(Des B. Young. Eng S. Reading. Typo J. B. Cooke)

1913 (2 Jan)–**14**. W **2**. P 12.

1	**1**	½d. green (Die I) (14.1.13)	6·50	3·75
		bw. Wmk inverted	48·00	17·00
		c. Wmk sideways	†	£25000
		cw. Wmk sideways inverted	†	£15000
2		1d. red (Die I)	10·00	1·00
		a. Wmk sideways	£1100	£250
		aw. Wmk sideways inverted	£1200	£275
		b. Carmine	10·00	1·00
		cw. Wmk inverted	40·00	8·50
		d. Die II Red (16.1.13)	10·00	1·00
		da. Wmk sideways	£1200	£275
		daw. Wmk sideways inverted	£1300	£300
		db. Carmine	9·50	1·25
		dw. Wmk inverted	40·00	13·00
		e. Die IIA. *Red* (4.14)	16·00	1·25
		eb. Carmine	16·00	1·25
		ew. Wmk inverted	55·00	9·50
3		2d. grey (Die I) (15.1.13)	40·00	5·50
		w. Wmk inverted	85·00	24·00
4		2½d. indigo (Die II) (27.1.13)	35·00	14·00
5		3d. olive (Die I) (28.1.13)	55·00	9·00
		a. Imperf three sides (horiz pair)	£42000	
		aa. Imperf three sides (lower stamp of vert pair)	£21000	
		b. in pair with Die II	£600	£300
		c. Yellow-olive	55·00	9·50
		ca. In pair with Die II	£600	£300
		dw. Wmk inverted	£150	60·00
		e. Die II *Olive*	£200	65·00
		ea. Yellow-olive	£200	65·00
		ew. Wmk inverted	£500	£200
6		4d. orange (Die II) (19.2.13)	60·00	22·00
		a. Orange-yellow	£300	70·00
8		5d. chestnut (Die II) (18.1.13)	55·00	32·00
9		6d. ultramarine (Die II) (18.1.13)	55·00	20·00
		a. Retouched "E"	£2000	£750
		b. Die IIA (substituted cliché) (11.13)	£3000	£900
		w. Wmk inverted	£650	£325
10		9d. violet (Die II) (1.2.13)	60·00	24·00
11		1s. emerald (Die II) (25.1.13)	70·00	19·00
		a. Blue-green	80·00	19·00
		w. Wmk inverted	£1000	70·00
12		2s. brown (Die II) (28.1.13)	£190	80·00
13		5s. grey and yellow (Die II) (20.3.13)	£325	£170
14		10s. grey and pink (Die II) (20.3.13)	£650	£500
15		£1 brown and ultram (Die II) (20.3.13)	£1800	£1900
16		£2 black and rose (Die II) (8.4.13)	£4000	£2500
1/16 *Set of* 15			£6750	£4750
14s/16s Optd "Specimen" *Set of* 3			£800	

The watermark on Nos. 1c, 2a and 2da shows the Crown pointing to the left and on Nos. 1cw, 2aw and 2daw pointing to the right, *as seen from the back of the stamp.* One example of 1c and two examples of 1cw are known, all used.

The 3d. was printed from two plates, one of which contained 105 stamps as Die I and 15 as Die II. The other plate contained Die I stamps only.

No. 5a. is from the top row of a sheet, with perforations at foot only. No. 5aa is from the bottom two rows of a different sheet.

No. 9a shows a badly distorted second "E" in "PENCE", which is unmistakable. It occurs on the upper plate right pane R. 10/6 and was replaced by a substitute cliché in Die IIA (No. 9b) in the November 1913 printing.

See also Nos. 24/30 (W **5**), 35/45*b* (W **6**), 73/5 (W **6**, new colours), 107/14 (W **7**), 132/8 (W **15**), 212 (2s. re-engraved).

3

4 Laughing Kookaburra

(Des R. A. Harrison. Eng and recess T. S. Harrison)

1913 (9 Dec)–**14**. No wmk. P 11.

17	**3**	1d. red	2·50	4·50
		a. Imperf between (horiz pair)	£3750	
		b. Imperf horiz (vert pair)	£1800	
		c. Pale rose-red	7·50	13·00
		ca. Imperf between (vert pair)	£2250	
		cb. Imperf between (horiz pair)	£3750	
19	**4**	6d. claret (26.8.14)	75·00	50·00

All printings from Plate 1 of the 1d. were in the shade of No. 17*c*. This plate shows many retouches.

5

5a

1d. Die II

Thin "1" in fraction at right (Plate 5 right pane R. 8/1)

Dot before "1"
(Plate 3 right pane R. 4/3)

"Secret mark"
(Plate 4 left pane R. 1/1)

Flaw under neck
(Plate 4 left pane R. 7/1)

"RA" joined
(Plate 4 left pane R. 10/6)

1d. Die II. The flaw distinguishing the so-called Die II, a white upward spur to the right of the base of the "1" in the left value tablet, is now known to be due to a defective roller-die. It occurred on all stamps in the second and third vertical rows of upper left plate, right pane. Each of the twenty defective impressions differs slightly; a typical example is illustrated above.

(Dies eng P.B. Typo J. B. Cooke until May 1918, then T. S. Harrison)

1914 (17 Jul)–**20**. W **5**. P 14¼×14 (comb).

20	**5a**	½d. bright green (22.2.15)	3·75	1·00
		a. Perf 14¼ (line) (12.15)	£5500	£450
		b. Green (1916)	3·75	1·00
		c. Yellow-green (1916)	24·00	10·00
		d. Thin "1" in fraction at right	£12000	£4250
		w. Wmk inverted	16·00	9·00
21		1d. carmine-red (*shades*) (Die I) (P 14¼ (line))	26·00	5·00
		a. Die II	£8500	£1600
		bw. Wmk inverted	†	£10000
		c. Perf 14¼×14 (comb)	7·50	60
		ca. Rusted cliché (Pl 2 rt pane R. 6/4 and 5) (9.16)	£10000	£375
		cb. Substituted cliché (Pl 2 rt pane R. 6/5) (2.18)	£1100	60·00
		cc. Pale carmine (*shades*) (1917)	10·00	60
		cd. Rose-red (1917)	11·00	2·50
		ce. Carmine-pink (1918)	£120	11·00
		cf. Carmine (*aniline*) (1920)	16·00	3·25
		cg. Dot before "1"	55·00	8·50
		ch. "Secret mark"	55·00	8·50
		ci. Flaw under neck	55·00	8·50
		cj. "RA" joined	55·00	8·50
		cw. Wmk inverted	15·00	2·50
		d. Die II *Carmine-red* (*shades*)	£325	6·00
		db. Substituted cliché (Pl 2 right pane R. 6/4) (2.18)	£1100	60·00
		dc. Pale carmine (*shades*)	£375	7·00
		dw. Wmk inverted	£650	45·00
22		4d. orange (6.1.15)	27·00	2·50
		a. Yellow-orange (1915)	27·00	3·25
		b. Lemon-yellow (3.16)	75·00	14·00
		c. Pale orange-yellow (1.17)	90·00	12·00
		d. Dull orange (1920)	45·00	3·25
		e. Line through "FOUR PENCE" (Pl 2 right pane R. 2/6) (*all shades*) *From*	£300	£100
		w. Wmk inverted	40·00	12·00
23		5d. brown (*p* 14¼ (line)) (22.2.15)	27·00	4·00
		aw. Wmk inverted	£500	£350
		b. Perf 14¼×14 (comb)	20·00	2·00
		ba. Yellow-brown (1920)	25·00	2·75
		bw. Wmk inverted	£325	£150

The variety No. 20d was caused by the engraving of a new fraction in a defective electro in 1918.

No. 21ca was caused by rusting on two positions of the steel plate 2 and shows as white patches on the back of the King's neck and on, and beside, the top of the right frame (right pane R. 6/4) and on the left frame, wattles, head and ears of kangaroo (right pane R. 6/5). These were noticed in December 1916 when the damaged impressions were removed and replaced by a pair of copper electros (Die II for R. 6/4 and Die I for R. 6/5), showing rounded corners and some frame damage, the former also showing a white spot under tail of emu. In time the tops of the crown quickly wore away.

Most of Nos. 20/3 were perforated 14 by a comb machine (exact gauge 14.25×14), but printings of the ½d. in December 1915, of the 1d. in July and August 1914 and of the 5d. until June 1917 were perforated by a line machine measuring 14.2.

See also Nos. 47/fa (W **5**, rough paper), 48/52 (W **6a**), 53/*ba* (1d. Die III), 56/66*b* and 76/81 (W **5**, new colours), 82 (W **6a**), 83/4 (no wmk), 85/104 (W **7**), 124/31 (W **15**).

(Typo J. B. Cooke)

1915 (15 Jan–Aug). W **5**. P 12.

24	**1**	2d. grey (Die I)	70·00	12·00
		w. Wmk inverted	†	£8000
25		2½d. indigo (Die II) (July)	60·00	30·00
26		6d. ultramarine (Die II) (April)	£170	22·00
		a. Bright blue	£275	65·00
		b. Die IIA. *Ultramarine* (substituted cliché) (Upper plate rt pane R. 10/6)	£3250	£1000
		ba. Bright blue	£4000	£1400
		w. Wmk inverted	†	£11000
27		9d. violet (Die II) (9 July)	£180	40·00
		w. Wmk inverted	£3000	£1600
28		1s. blue-green (Die II) (Apr)	£160	26·00
29		2s. brown (Die II) (March)	£475	90·00
30		5s. grey and yellow (Die II) (12 Feb)	£750	£325
		a. Yellow portion doubly printed	£13000	£3500
		w. Wmk inverted	£850	£375
24/30 *Set of* 7			£1700	£500

6

6a

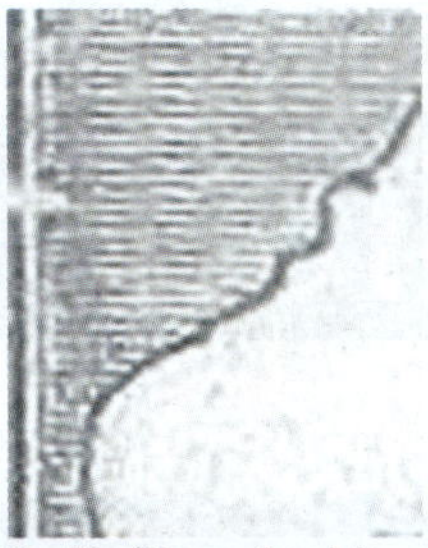

No. 35a (Upper plate left pane R. 10/1)

Nos. 38da and 73a (Upper plate left pane R. 1/6)

(Typo J. B. Cooke (to May 1918), T. S. Harrison to February 1926), A. J. Mullett (to June 1927) and thereafter J. Ash).

1915 (8 Oct)–**28**. W **6** (narrow Crown). P 12.

35	**1**	2d. grey (Die I) (11.15)	35·00	6·50
		a. Die IIA subsituted cliché (upper plate left pane R. 10/1)*	£4000	£1100
		bw. Wmk inverted	48·00	18·00
		c. Silver-grey (*shiny paper*)	38·00	14·00
		d. Die IIA. *Silver-grey* (*shiny paper*) (3.18)	55·00	15·00
		daw. Wmk inverted	†	£8000
		dba. Grey (1920)	60·00	15·00
36		2½d. deep blue (Die II) (9.17)	23·00	10·00
		aw. Wmk inverted	85·00	40·00
		b. Deep indigo (1919)	38·00	8·50
		ba. "1" of fraction omitted (Lower plate left pane R. 6/3)	£30000	£10000
37		3d. yellow-olive (Die I)	28·00	4·75
		a. In pair with Die II	£250	£150
		b. Olive-green (1917)	30·00	4·50
		ba. In pair with Die II	£250	£140
		cw. Wmk inverted	65·00	35·00
		d. Die II *Yellow-olive*	80·00	27·00
		da. Olive-green	85·00	27·00
		dw. Wmk inverted	£275	£160
		e. Die IIB. *Light olive* (12.22)	45·00	12·00
38		6d. ultramarine (Die II) (15.12.15)	55·00	7·50
		a. Die IIA (substituted cliché) (Upper plate rt pane R. 10/6)	£3000	£850
		b. Dull blue (6.18)	70·00	11·00
		ba. Die IIA (substituted cliché)	£3000	£900
		cw. Wmk inverted	£325	80·00
		d. Die IIB. *Bright ultramarine* (23.7.21)	60·00	12·00
		da. Leg of kangaroo broken	£2250	£550
		dw. Wmk inverted	—	£170
39		9d. violet (Die II) (29.7.16)	38·00	11·00
		aw. Wmk inverted	£225	65·00
		b. Die IIB. *Violet* (16.4.19)	50·00	9·50
		bw. Wmk inverted	£140	45·00
		c. Die II (substituted cliché) in pair with Die IIB	£350	£200
40		1s. blue-green (Die II) (6.16)	38·00	4·25
		aw. Wmk inverted	£140	50·00
		b. Die IIB (9.12.20)	55·00	4·25
		ba. Wmk sideways (13.12.27)	60·00	£400
		bw. Wmk inverted	£150	50·00
41		2s. brown (Die II) (6.16)	£190	13·00
		a. Imperf three sides (horiz pair)	£55000	
		b. Red-brown (*aniline*)	£1600	£225
		w. Wmk inverted	£2250	£275
42		5s. grey and yellow (Die II) (4.18)	£190	75·00
		a. Grey and orange (1920)	£250	95·00
		b. Grey and deep yellow	£200	90·00
		ba. Wmk sideways	†	£50000
		c. Grey and pale yellow	£190	75·00
		w. Wmk inverted	£750	£450
43		10s. grey and pink (Die II) (5.2.17)	£450	£275
		a. Grey and bright aniline pink (10.18)	£400	£250
		ab. Wmk sideways	£20000	£10000
		aw. Wmk inverted	£1600	£1000
		b. Grey and pale aniline pink (1922)	£500	£275
44		£1 chocolate & dull blue (Die II) (7.16)	£2250	£1300
		a. Chestnut and bright blue (6.17)	£2500	£1300
		ab. Wmk sideways	†	£25000
		aw. Wmk inverted	£3250	£1900
		b. Bistre-brown and bright blue (7.19)	£2250	£1500
		ba. Frame printed double, one albino	£5000	
45		£2 black and rose (Die II) (12.19)	£3500	£2250
		a. Grey and crimson (1921)	£3000	£2000
		b. Purple-black and pale rose (6.24)	£2750	£1600
35/45*b* *Set of* 11			£5500	£3000
43s/5s Optd "Specimen" *Set of* 3			£550	

*The Die IIA of No. 35a is a substituted cliché introduced to repair a crack which occurred on R. 10/1 of the upper plate left pane. Its Die IIA characteristics are more pronounced than on the sheet stamps from this die, with the break at left with the extending to the outer, in addition to the inner, frame line.

One plate of the 3d. contained mixed Die I and Die II stamps as described.

No. 39c comes from six substituted clichés taken from plate 2 (Die II) and inserted in plate 4 (Die IIB) at positions left pane R. 1/3-4, 2/3-4 and 8/6 and right pane R. 2/1 This substitution tok place towards the end of the printings on W **6**. The variety can also be found on stamps with W **7** and W **15**, see Nos. 108a and 133a.

All values were printed by both Cooke and Harrison, and the 9d., 1s. and 5s. were also printed by Mullett and Ash.

The watermark on No. 40ba shows the Crown printing to the right, that on Nos. 42ba and 43ab shows the Crown pointing to the left *as seen from the back of the stamp*.

1916 (Nov)–**18**. *Rough, unsurfaced paper, locally gummed*. W **5**. P 14.

47	**5a**	1d. scarlet (Die I)	19·00	2·50
		a. Deep red (1917)	19·00	2·50
		b. Rose-red (1918)	28·00	2·75
		ba. Substituted cliché (Pl 2 rt pane R. 6/5)	£1100	65·00
		c. Rosine (1918)	£200	20·00
		ca. Substituted cliché (Pl 2 rt pane R. 6/5)	£2000	£300
		d. Dot before "1"	70·00	14·00
		e. Secret mark	70·00	14·00
		f. Flaw under neck	70·00	14·00
		g. "RA" joined	70·00	14·00
		hw. Wmk inverted	45·00	11·00
		i. Die II *Rose-red* (1918)	£350	23·00
		ia. Substituted cliché (Pl 2 rt pane R. 6/4)	£1100	65·00
		iw. Wmk inverted	£600	70·00
		j. Die II *Rosine* (1918)	£600	90·00
		ja. Substituted cliché (Pl 2 rt pane R. 6/4)	£2000	£300
		k. No wmk	£1500	£1500

All examples of the 5d. on this paper were perforated "OS" and will be found listed as No. O60.

No. 47k is the result of misplacement of the sheet during printing. To qualify, there should be no trace of the Crown over A or a line watermark.

(Typo J. B. Cooke to May 1918 thereafter T. S. Harrison)

1918 (4 Jan)–**20**. W **6a** (Mult). P 14.

48	**5a**	½d. green (*shades*)	5·00	2·50
		a. Thin 1 in fraction at right	£100	£130
		b. Wmk sideways	†	£15000
		bw. Wmk sideways inverted	†	£15000
		w. Wmk inverted	20·00	13·00
49		1d. carmine-pink (Die I) (23.1.18)	£180	£130
		aw. Wmk inverted	†	£10000
		b. Deep red (1918)	£3750	£2250
		bw. Wmk inverted	†	£15000
		c. Dot before "1"	£700	£375
		d. Secret mark	£700	£375
		e. Flaw under neck	£700	£375
		f. "RA" joined	£700	£375
50		1d. carmine (10.12.19)	25·00	10·00
		aw. Wmk inverted	£900	£2500
		b. Deep red (*aniline*) (1920)	£550	£200
		c. Dot before "1"	£140	65·00
		d. Secret mark	£140	65·00
		e. Flaw under neck	£140	65·00
		f. "RA" joined	£140	65·00
51		1½d. black-brown (30.1.19)	4·00	3·50
		a. Very thin paper (2.19)	20·00	13·00
		w. Wmk inverted	20·00	15·00
52		1½d. red-brown (4.19)	10·00	2·25
		a. Chocolate (1920)	10·00	2·25
		w. Wmk inverted	55·00	20·00

No. 48 was printed by Cooke and Harrison, Nos. 49/*b* by Cooke only and Nos. 50/2*a* by Harrison only. Nos. 49/*b* have rather yellowish gum, that of No. 50 being pure white.

The watermark on No. 48b shows the Crown pointing to the left and on No. 48bw pointing to the right, *as seen from the back of the stamp*. One example of each is known.

1d. Die III

1d. Die III. In 1917 a printing (in sheets of 120) was made on paper originally prepared for printing War Savings Stamps, with watermark T **5**. A special plate was made for this printing, differing in detail from those previously used. The shading round the head is even; the solid background of the words "ONE PENNY" is bounded at each end by a white vertical line; and there is a horizontal white line cutting the vertical shading lines at left on the King's neck.

(Typo J. B. Cooke)

1918 (15 Jul). *Printed from a new Die III plate on white unsurfaced paper, locally gummed.* W **5**. P 14.

53 **5a** 1d. rose-red .... 60·00 30·00
a. *Rose-carmine* .... 60·00 30·00
w. Wmk inverted .... £120 75·00

(Typo T. S. Harrison or A. J. Mullett (1s.4d. from March 1926))

1918 (9 Nov)–**23**. W **5**. P 14.

56 **5a** ½d. orange (8.11.23) .... 2·50 2·75
w. Wmk inverted .... 6·00 7·50
57 1d. violet (shades) (12.2.22) .... 5·00 1·50
a. Imperf three sides (horiz pair) £40000
b. *Red-violet* .... 6·50 2·25
c. Dot before "1" .... 38·00 14·00
d. Secret mark .... 38·00 14·00
e. Flaw under neck .... 38·00 14·00
f. "RA" joined .... 38·00 14·00
58 1½d. black-brown .... 8·50 1·50
w. Wmk inverted .... 21·00 7·00
59 1½d. deep red-brown (4.19) .... 6·50 70
a. *Chocolate* (1920) .... 6·50 60
w. Wmk inverted .... 26·00 10·00
60 1½d. bright red-brown (20.1.22) .... 20·00 3·75
61 1½d. green (7.3.23) .... 4·00 80
a. Coarse unsurfaced paper (1923) £200 £100
w. Wmk inverted .... † £9000
62 2d. brown-orange (9.20) .... 12·00 1·00
a. *Dull orange* (1921) .... 14·00 1·00
w. Wmk inverted .... † £5000
63 2d. bright rose-scarlet (19.1.22) .... 9·50 1·50
a. *Dull rose-scarlet* .... 9·50 1·50
w. Wmk inverted £12000
64 4d. violet (21.6.21) .... 13·00 15·00
a. Line through "FOUR PENCE" (Pl 2 rt pane R. 2/6) £14000 £3750
b. "FOUR PENCE" in thinner letters (Pl 2 rt pane R. 2/6) £425 £275
65 4d. ultramarine (*shades*) (23.3.22) .... 48·00 8·50
a. "FOUR PENCE" in thinner letters (Pl 2 rt pane R. 2/6) £400 £150
b. *Pale milky blue* .... 80·00 13·00
w. Wmk inverted .... 75·00 £225
66 1s.4d. pale blue (2.12.20) .... 55·00 27·00
a. *Dull greenish blue* .... 65·00 25·00
b. *Deep turquoise* (1922) £2250 £1900
56/66 *Set of* 11 .... £160 55·00

In addition to a number of mint pairs from two sheets purchased at Gumeracha, South Australia, with the bottom row imperforate on three sides, a single used example of No. 57 imperforate on three sides is known.

No. 61a was printed on a batch of coarse unsurfaced paper during 1923. Examples may be indentified by a clear vertical mesh in the paper, with mint stamps having a yellowish gum.

The 4d. ultramarine was originally printed from the Cooke plates but the plates were worn in mid-1923 and Harrison prepared a new pair of plates. Stamps from these plates can only be distinguished by the minor flaws which are peculiar to them.

The variety of Nos. 64 and 65 with "FOUR PENCE" thinner, was caused by the correction of the line through "FOUR PENCE" flaw early in the printing of No. 64.

(Typo T. S. Harrison (to February 1926), A. J. Mullett (to June 1927), thereafter J. Ash)

1923 (6 Dec)–**24**. W **6**. P 12.

73 **1** 6d. chestnut (Die IIB) .... 24·00 1·75
a. Leg of kangaroo broken (Upper plate lt pane R. 1/6) .... 75·00 £110
w. Wmk inverted .... † £15000
74 2s. maroon (Die II) (1.5.24) .... 55·00 30·00
w. Wmk inverted £950 £400
75 £1 grey (Die IIB) (1.5.24) £550 £275
s. Optd "Specimen" .... 75·00

The 6d. and 2s. were printed by all three printers, but the £1 only by Harrison.

No. 73a was corrected during the Ash printing.

(Typo T. S. Harrison (to February 1926), thereafter A. J. Mullett)

1924 (1 May–18 Aug). P 14.

(*a*) W **5**.

76 **5a** 1d. sage-green .... 3·00 1·50
a. Dot before "1" .... 30·00 11·00
b. Secret mark .... 30·00 11·00
c. Flaw under neck .... 30·00 11·00
d. "RA" joined .... 30·00 11·00
w. Wmk inverted .... 13·00 7·00
77 1½d. scarlet (*shades*) .... 2·25 40
a. Very thin paper .... 75·00 35·00
b. "HALEPENCE" (Pl 22 left pane R. 4/4) .... 30·00 28·00
c. "RAL" of AUSTRALIA" thin (Pl 22 Left pane R. 5/4) .. 32·00 28·00
d. Curved "1" and thin fraction at left (Pl 24 rt pane R. 7/5) ... 32·00 28·00
w. Wmk inverted .... 40·00 15·00
78 2d. red-brown .... 17·00 7·00
a. *Bright red-brown* .... 22·00 8·00
w. Wmk inverted .... † £13000
79 3d. dull ultramarine .... 26·00 2·00
a. Imperf three sides (horiz pair) £7000
80 4d. olive-yellow .... 29·00 5·50
a. *Olive-green* .... 29·00 6·00
w. Wmk inverted .... † £9000
81 4½d. violet .... 23·00 3·50

(*b*) W **6a**.

82 **5a** 1d. sage-green (20 May) .... 9·00 8·50
a. Dot before "1" .... 50·00 60·00
b. Secret mark .... 50·00 60·00
c. Flaw under neck .... 50·00 60·00
d. "RA" joined .... 50·00 60·00
w. Wmk inverted .... † £10000

(*c*) No wmk.

83 **5a** 1d. sage-green (18 August) .... 5·50 9·50
a. Dot before "1" .... 35·00 60·00
b. Secret mark .... 35·00 60·00
c. Flaw under neck .... 35·00 60·00
d. "RA" joined .... 35·00 60·00
84 1½d. scarlet (14 August) .... 15·00 9·50
76/84 *Set of* 9 .... £120 42·00

Nos. 78/*a* and 82/4 were printed by Harrison only but the remainder were printed by both Harrison and Mullett.

In the semi-transparent paper of Nos. 51a and 77a the watermark is almost indistinguishable.

Nos. 77b, 77c and 77d are typical examples of retouching of which there are many others in these issues. In No. 77c the letters "RAL" differ markedly from the normal. There is a white stroke cutting the oval frame-line above the "L", and the right-hand outer line of the Crown does not cut the white frame-line above the "A".

It is believed that No. 79a occurs on the bottom row of at least four sheets purchased from post offices in Victoria during 1926.

7

I

II

New Dies

1d. For differences see note above No. 20.

1½d. From new steel plates made from a new die. Nos. 87*a* and 96*a* are the Ash printings, the ink of which is shiny.

2d. Die I. Height of frame 25.6 mm. Left-hand frame-line thick and uneven behind Kangaroo. Pearls in Crown vary in size.
Die II. Height of frame 25.6 mm. Left-hand frame-line thin and even. Pearls in Crown are all the same size.
Die III. Height 25.1 mm; lettering and figures of value bolder than Die I.

3d. Die II has bolder letters and figures than Die I, as illustrated above.

5d. Die II has a bolder figure "5" with flat top compared with Die I of the earlier issues.

(Typo A. J. Mullett or J. Ash (from June 1927))

1926–30. W **7**.

(*a*) P 14.

85 **5a** ½d. orange (10.3.27) .... 6·00 7·50
w. Wmk inverted .... 90·00 75·00
86 1d. sage-green (23.10.26) .... 3·25 1·00
a. Dot before "1" .... 50·00 17·00
b. Secret mark .... 50·00 17·00
c. Flaw under neck .... 75·00 29·00
d. "RA" joined .... 75·00 29·00
w. Wmk inverted .... 17·00 7·00
87 1½d. scarlet (5.11.26) .... 7·50 2·00
a. *Golden scarlet* (1927) .... 13·00 2·50
w. Wmk inverted .... 18·00 4·50
89 2d. red-brown (Die I) (17.8.27) .... 30·00 40·00
90 3d. dull ultramarine (12.26) .... 24·00 5·00
w. Wmk inverted .... † £10000
91 4d. yellow-olive (17.1.28) .... 48·00 40·00
92 4½d. violet (26.10.27) .... 18·00 3·75
93 1s.4d. pale greenish blue (6.9.27) .... 90·00 80·00
w. Wmk inverted .... † £10000
85/93 *Set of* 8 .... £200 £160

(*b*) P 13½×12½.

94 **5a** ½d. orange (21.11.28) .... 2·25 1·40
95 1d. sage-green (Die I) (23.12.26) .... 2·75 70
aa. Dot before "1" .... 85·00 40·00
ab. Secret mark .... £110 65·00
ac. Flaw under neck .... £110 55·00
ad. "RA" joined .... £110 55·00
aw. Wmk inverted .... 18·00 18·00
b. Die II (6.28) .... 50·00 80·00
bw. Wmk inverted £1100 £1100
96 1½d. scarlet (14.1.27) .... 2·25 1·00
a. *Golden scarlet* (1927) .... 2·50 1·00
w. Wmk inverted .... 13·00 2·50
97 1½d. red-brown (16.9.30) .... 5·50 5·50
98 2d. red-brown (Die II) (28.4.28) .. 9·00 9·50
99 2d. golden scarlet (Die II) (2.8.30) .... 13·00 2·25
a. Die III (9.9.30) .... 7·50 85
ab. No wmk £1100 £2500
ac. Tête-bêche (pair) £120000
aw. Wmk inverted (*from booklets*) .... 9·00 1·40
100 3d. dull ultramarine (Die I) (28.2.28) .... 38·00 6·50
aw. Wmk inverted £150 £3000
b. Die II *Deep ultramarine* (28.9.29) .... 20·00 1·40
bw. Wmk inverted .... † £8500
102 4d. yellow-olive (19.4.29) .... 23·00 3·25
w. Wmk inverted .... † £7500
103 4½d. violet (11.28) .... 48·00 24·00
103*a* 5d. orange-brown Die II (27.8.30) 26·00 7·00
104 1s.4d. turquoise (30.9.28) .... 80·00 26·00
w. Wmk inverted .... † £14000
94/104 *Set of* 11 .... £200 70·00

Owing to defective manufacture, part of the sheet of the 2d. (Die III), discovered in July 1931, escaped unwatermarked; while the watermark in other parts of the same sheet was faint or normal.

Only one example of No. 99ac is known.

8 Parliament House, Canberra

9 "DH66" Biplane and Pastoral Scene

(Des R. A. Harrison. Die eng J. A. C. Harrison (Waterlow, London). Plates and printing by A. J. Mullett)

1927 (9 May). *Opening of Parliament House, Canberra.* No wmk. P 11.

105 **8** 1½d. brownish lake 50 50
a. Imperf between (vert pair) £2750
b. Imperf between (horiz pair) .. £5500 £5500

(Eng H. W. Bell. Recess J. Ash)

1928 (29 Oct–2 Nov). *4th National Stamp Exhibition, Melbourne. As T* **4**. No wmk. P 11.

106 3d. blue (2 Nov) .... 4·25 6·50
MS106*a* 65×70 mm. No. 106×4 .... £110 £200
ab. Imperf (pane of four) £75000

No. **MS**106*a* comes from special sheets of 60 stamps divided into 15 blocks of 4 (5×3) and separated by wide gutters perforated down the middle, printed and sold at the Exhibition.

(Typo J. Ash)

1929 (Feb)–**30**. W **7**. P 12.

107 **1** 6d. chestnut (Die IIB) (25.9.29) .... 23·00 4·50
108 9d. violet (Die IIB) .... 30·00 21·00
a. Die II (substituted cliché) in pair with Die IIB £275 £200
109 1s. blue-green (Die IIB) (12.6.29) .... 45·00 6·50
w. Wmk inverted .... † £15000
110 2s. maroon (Die II) (3.29) .... 50·00 15·00
111 5s. grey and yellow (Die II) (30.11.29) .... £200 85·00
112 10s. grey and pink (Die II) £400 £450
114 £2 black and rose (Die II) (11.30) £3250 £650
107/14 *Set of* 7 .... £3750 £1100
112s/14s Optd "Specimen" *Set of* 2 .... £325

(Des R. A. Harrison and H. Herbert. Eng A. Taylor. Recess J. Ash)

1929 (20 May). *Air.* No wmk. P 11.

115 **9** 3d. green (*shades*) .... 8·00 4·00

Variations of up to ¾ mm in the design size of No. 115 are due to paper shrinkage on the printings produced by the "wet" process. The last printing, in 1935, was printed by the "dry" method.

10 Black Swan

11 "Capt. Charles Sturt" (J. H. Crossland)

Re-entry ("T" of "AUSTRALIA" clearly double) (Pl 2 R. 7/4)

(Des G. Pitt Morrison. Eng F. D. Manley. Recess J. Ash)

1929 (28 Sep). *Centenary of Western Australia.* No wmk. P 11.

116	**10**	1½d. dull scarlet	1·25	1·60
		a. Re-entry	55·00	65·00

(Des R. A. Harrison. Eng F. D. Manley. Recess J. Ash)

1930 (2 Jun). *Centenary of Exploration of River Murray by Capt. Sturt.* No wmk. P 11.

117	**11**	1½d. scarlet	1·00	1·00
118		3d. blue	4·25	7·50

No. 117 with manuscript surcharge of "2d. paid P M L H I" was issued by the Postmaster of Lord Howe Island during a shortage of 2d. stamps between 23 August and 17 October 1930 (*Price £700 un. or used*). A few copies of the 1½d. value No. 96*a* were also endorsed (*Price £1500 un. or used*). These provisionals are not recognized by the Australian postal authorities.

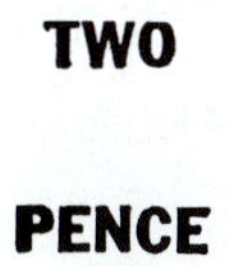

(12)

13 Fokker F. VIIa/3m *Southern Cross* above Hemispheres

1930 (28 Jul–2 Aug). *T* **5a** *surch as T* **12**. W **7**. P 13½×12½.

119	2d. on 1½d. golden scarlet	1·50	1·00
120	5d. on 4½d. violet (2 Aug)	7·00	11·00

No. 120 is from a redrawn die in which the words "FOURPENCE HALFPENNY" are noticeably thicker than in the original die and the figure "4" has square instead of tapering serifs. The redrawn die also shows thin white lines to the left and right of the tablet carrying "FOURPENCE HALFPENNY".

Stamps from the redrawn die without the surcharge were printed, but not issued thus. Some stamps, *cancelled to order*, were included in sets supplied by the post office. A few mint copies, which escaped the cancellation were found and some may have been used postally (*Price £2500 unused, £35 used c.t.o.*).

Re-entry ("FO" and "LD" double) (Pl 1 R. 5/5)

(Des and eng F. D. Manley. Recess John Ash)

1931 (19 Mar). *Kingsford Smith's Flights.* No wmk. P 11.

(a) Postage.

121	**13**	2d. rose-red	1·00	1·00
122		3d. blue	4·75	5·00

(b) Air. Inscr "AIR MAIL SERVICE" *at sides.*

123	**13**	6d. violet	5·50	15·00
		a. Re-entry	50·00	90·00
121/3 *Set of* 3			10·00	19·00

15

17 Superb Lyrebird

(Typo John Ash).

1931–36. W **15**.

(a) P 13½×12½.

124	**5a**	½d. orange (2.33)	5·00	6·00
125		1d. green (Die I) (10.31)	1·75	20
		w. Wmk inverted	24·00	3·75
		x. Wmk reversed	£1800	£1200
126		1½d. red-brown (10.36)	6·00	12·00
127		2d. golden scarlet (Die III) (18.12.31)	1·75	10
		w. Wmk inverted (from booklets)	2·25	50
128		3d. ultramarine (Die II) (30.9.32)	18·00	1·25
		w. Wmk inverted	£11000	£11000
129		4d. yellow-olive (2.33)	18·00	1·25
		w. Wmk inverted	†	£6500
130		5d. orange-brown (Die II) (25.2.32)	15·00	20
		w. Wmk inverted	†	£5000
131		1s.4d. turquoise (18.8.32)	50·00	3·50
		w. Wmk inverted	†	£6000
124/31 *Set of* 8			£100	22·00

(b) P 12.

132	**1**	6d. chestnut (Die IIB) (20.4.32)	23·00	29·00
133		9d. violet (Die IIB) (20.4.32)	29·00	1·50
		a. Die II (substituted cliché) in pair with Die IIB	£250	£130
134		2s. maroon (Die II) (6.8.35)	5·50	60
135		5s. grey and yellow (Die II) (12.32)	£130	14·00
136		10s. grey and pink (Die II) (31.7.32)	£325	£130
137		£1 grey (Die IIB) (11.35)	£550	£225
138		£2 black and rose (Die II) (6.34)	£2750	£450
132/8 *Set of* 7			£3500	£750
136s/8s Optd "Specimen" *Set of* 3			75·00	

Stamps as No. 127, but without watermark and perforated 11, are forgeries made in 1932 to defraud the P.O. (*Price £300, unused*).

For re-engraved type of No. 134, see No. 212.

For 133a/ab see note below No 114.

(Des and eng F. D. Manley. Recess John Ash)

1931 (4 Nov). *Air Stamp. As T* **13** *but inscr* "AIR MAIL SERVICE" *in bottom tablet.* No wmk. P 11.

139	6d. sepia	14·00	14·00

1931 (17 Nov). *Air.* No. 139 *optd with Type* O **4**.

139*a*	6d. sepia	25·00	48·00

This stamp was not restricted to official use but was on general sale to the public.

(Des and eng F. D. Manley. Recess John Ash)

1932 (15 Feb). No wmk. P 11.

140	**17**	1s. green	35·00	2·50
		a. Yellow-green	48·00	3·25

18 Sydney Harbour Bridge

19 Laughing Kookaburra

(Des R. A. Harrison. Eng F. D. Manley. Printed John Ash)

1932 (14 Mar). *Opening of Sydney Harbour Bridge.*

(a) Recess. No wmk. P 11.

141	**18**	2d. scarlet	3·50	3·75
142		3d. blue	5·50	7·50
143		5s. blue-green	£400	£190

(b) Typo. W **15**. P 10½.

144	**18**	2d. scarlet	3·00	1·40
141/4 *Set of* 4			£400	£190

Stamps as No. 144 without wmk and perf 11 are forgeries made in 1932 to defraud the P.O. (*Price £650, unused*).

(Des and eng F. D. Manley. Recess John Ash)

1932 (1 June). W **15**. P 13½×12½.

146	**19**	6d. red-brown	16·00	55
		w. Wmk inverted	†	£4250

20 Melbourne and R. Yarra

21 Merino Ram

(Des and eng F. D. Manley. Recess John Ash)

1934 (2 Jul–Aug). *Centenary of Victoria.* W **15**. P 10½.

147	**20**	2d. orange-vermilion	2·50	1·75
		a. Perf 11½ (Aug)	8·00	1·75
148		3d. blue	4·00	5·50
		a. Perf 11½ (Aug)	4·00	8·00
149		1s. black	45·00	20·00
		a. Perf 11½ (Aug)	48·00	22·00
147/9 *Set of* 3			48·00	25·00
147a/9a *Set of* 3			55·00	28·00

Stamps were originally issued perforated 10½, but the gauge was subsequently changed to 11½ in August 1934 due to difficulties in separating stamps in the first perforation.

(Des and eng F. D. Manley. Recess John Ash)

1934 (1–26 Nov). *Death Centenary of Capt. John Macarthur (founder of Australian sheep farming).* W **15**. P 11½.

150	**21**	2d. carmine-red (A)	6·50	1·50
150*a*		2d. carmine-red (B) (26 Nov)	20·00	3·25
151		3d. blue	10·00	14·00
152		9d. bright purple	27·00	45·00
150/2 *Set of* 3			40·00	55·00

Type A of the 2d. shows shading on the hill in the background varying from light to dark (as illustrated). Type B has the shading almost uniformly dark.

22 Hermes

23 Cenotaph, Whitehall

(Des F. D. Manley. Eng E. Broad and F. D. Manley. Recess John Ash until April 1940; W. C. G. McCracken thereafter)

1934 (1 Dec)–**48**.

(a) No wmk. P 11.

153	**22**	1s.6d. dull purple	42·00	1·00

(b) W **15**. *Chalk-surfaced paper.* P 13½×14.

153*a*	**22**	1s.6d. dull purple (22.10.37)	9·00	45
		b. Thin rough ordinary paper (12.2.48)	2·00	1·40

(Des B Cottier; adapted and eng F. D. Manley. Recess John Ash)

1935 (18 Mar). *20th Anniv of Gallipoli Landing.* W **15**. P 13½×12½ or 11 (1s.).

154	**23**	2d. scarlet	1·75	30
155		1s. black (chalk-surfaced)	48·00	42·00

The 1s. perforated 13½×12½ is a plate proof (*Price £1500, unused*).

24 King George V on "Anzac"

25 Amphitrite and Telephone Cable

(Des and eng F. D. Manley. Recess John Ash)

1935 (2 May). *Silver Jubilee. Chalk-surfaced paper.* W **15** (sideways). P 11½.

156	**24**	2d. scarlet	2·00	30
		a. Printed double, one albino	£200	30·00
157		3d. blue	6·00	9·00
158		2s. bright violet	30·00	45·00
156/8 *Set of* 3			35·00	50·00

(Des and eng F. D. Manley. Recess John Ash)

1936 (1 Apr). *Opening of Submarine Telephone Link to Tasmania.* W **15**. P 11½.

159	**25**	2d. scarlet	1·25	50
160		3d. blue	3·25	2·75

26 Site of Adelaide, 1836; Old Gum Tree, Glenelg; King William St, Adelaide

(Des and eng F. D. Manley. Recess John Ash)

1936 (3 Aug). *Centenary of South Australia.* W **15**. P 11½.

161	**26**	2d. carmine	2·00	40
162		3d. blue	6·00	3·50
163		1s. green	12·00	8·50
161/3 *Set of* 3			18·00	11·00

27 Wallaroo

28 Queen Elizabeth

28a Queen Elizabeth

29

30 King George VI

30a

31 King George VI

32 Koala

33 Merino Ram

34 Laughing Kookaburra

35 Platypus

36 Superb Lyrebird

38 Queen Elizabeth

39 King George VI

40 King George VI and Queen Elizabeth

Dies of 3d.:

Die I Die Ia Die II

Die I. The letters "TA" of "POSTAGE" at right are joined by a white flaw; the outline of the chin consists of separate strokes.

No. 168a is a preliminary printing made with unsuitable ink and may be detected by the absence of finer details; the King's face appears whitish and the wattles are blank. The greater part of this printing was distributed to the Press with advance notices of the issue.

Die Ia. As Die I, but "T" and "A" have been clearly separated by individual retouches made on the plates.

Die II A completely new die. "T" and "A" are separate and a continuous line has been added to the chin. The outline of the cheek extends to about 1 mm above the lobe of the King's right ear.

Die III. Differs from Dies I and II in the King's left eyebrow which is shaded downwards from left to right instead of from right to left.

Line to Kangaroo's ear (Right pane R. 6/8)

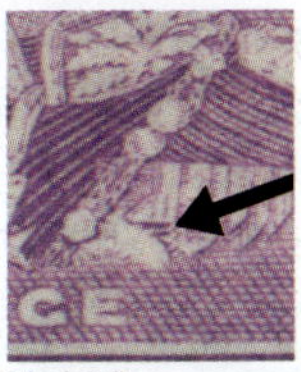

Medal flaw (Right pane R. 2/5)

Top hat flaw (Lower plate, right pane R. 3/3)

Roller flaw over "o" of "one" (upper plate, right pane R. 1-6/6)

(Des R. A. Harrison (T **28/30**), F. D. Manley (T **27**, **31/6**), H. Barr (T **38/9**), H. Barr and F. D. Manley (T **40**). Eng F. D. Manley and T. C. Duffell (T **34**), T. C. Duffell (revised lettering for T **28a**, **30a**), F. D. Manley (others). All recess with John Ash, W. C. G. McCracken or "By Authority ..." imprints)

1937–49. *Chalk-surfaced paper (3d.* (No. 168), *5s., 10s., £1).* W **15** (sideways on 5d., 9d., 5s. and 10s.).

(a) P 13½×14 (vert designs) or 14×13½ (horiz).

164	**27**	½d. orange (3.10.38)	2·50	50
165	**28**	1d. emerald-green (10.5.37)	80	50
166	**29**	1½d. maroon (20.4.38)	9·00	4·50
167	**30**	2d. scarlet (10.5.37)	80	50
168	**31**	3d. blue (Die I) (2.8.37)	60·00	18·00
		a. "White wattles" (from 1st ptg)	£120	80·00
		b. Die Ia	£140	7·50
		c. Die II (3.38)	60·00	5·50
		ca. Bright blue (ordinary thin paper) (20.12.38)	60·00	3·75
170	**32**	4d. green (1.2.38)	7·00	2·25
171	**33**	5d. purple (1.12.38)	1·50	60
172	**34**	6d. purple-brown (2.8.37)	20·00	1·50
173	**35**	9d. chocolate (1.9.38)	4·50	1·50
174	**36**	1s. grey-green (2.8.37)	48·00	2·50
175	**31**	1s. 4d. pale magenta (3.10.38)	2·00	2·50
		a. Deep magenta (1943)	3·25	2·50

(b) P 13½.

176	**38**	5s. claret (1.4.38)	20·00	2·00
		a. Thin rough ordinary paper (4.2.48)	3·75	2·50
177	**39**	10s. dull purple (1.4.38)	42·00	16·00
		a. Thin rough ordinary paper (11.48)	45·00	32·00
		s. Optd "Specimen"	30·00	
178	**40**	£1 bluish slate (1.11.38)	60·00	35·00
		a. Thin rough ordinary paper (4.4.49)	60·00	65·00
		s. Optd "Specimen"	£425	
164/78 *Set of* 14			£225	65·00

(c) P 15×14 (vert designs) or 14×15 (horiz) (1d. and 2d. redrawn with background evenly shaded and lettering strengthened).

179	**27**	½d. orange (28.1.42)	55	20
		a. Line to kangaroo's ear	18·00	
		b. Coil pair (1942)	17·00	26·00
		ba. Coil block of four (1943)	£600	
180	**28a**	1d. emerald-green (1.8.38)	4·75	60
181		1d. maroon (10.12.41)	1·50	50
		a. Coil pair (1942)	14·00	26·00
182	**29**	1½d. maroon (21.11.41)	4·75	10·00
183		1½d. emerald-green (10.12.41)	1·00	1·75
184	**30a**	2d. scarlet (11.7.38)	3·75	20
		a. Coil pair (10.41)	£350	£425
		b. Medal flaw	£180	60·00
		w. Wmk inverted (*from booklets*)	8·00	75
185		2d. bright purple (10.12.41)	50	1·75
		a. Coil pair (1942)	45·00	65·00
		b. Medal flaw	60·00	65·00
		w. Wmk inverted (*from coils*)	£130	65·00
186	**31**	3d. bright blue (Die III) (11.40)	45·00	3·75
187		3d. purple-brown (Die III) (10.12.41)	40	10
188	**32**	4d. green (10.42)	1·00	10
		w. Wmk inverted	£2250	£1600
189	**33**	5d. purple (17.12.45)	50	2·00
190	**34**	6d. red-brown (6.42)	2·25	10
		a. Purple-brown (1944)	1·75	10
		b. "top hat" flaw	£325	£200
191	**35**	9d. chocolate (12.9.43)	1·00	30
192	**36**	1s. grey-green (29.3.41)	1·25	10
		a. Roller flaw	21·00	11·00
		w. Wmk inverted	£2250	£1600
179/92 *Set of* 14			60·00	19·00

The watermark on No. 191 shows Crown to the left of C of A, on Nos. 171, 173 and 189 it is to the right, *as seen from the back of the stamp.*

For unwmkd issue, see Nos. 228/30*d*.

Thin paper. Nos. 176a, 177a, 178a. In these varieties the watermark is more clearly visible on the back and the design is much less sharp. On early printings of No. 176a the paper appears tinted.

SPECIAL COIL PERFORATION. This special perforation of large and small holes on the narrow sides of the stamps was introduced after 1939 for stamps issued in coils and was intended to facilitate separation. Where they exist they are listed as "Coil pairs".

The following with "special coil" perforation were placed on sale in *sheets*: Nos. 179, 205, 222a (1952), 228, 230, 237, 262 (1953), 309, 311, and 314. These are listed as "Coil blocks of four".

Coils with "normal" perforations also exist for Nos. 180 and 184.

41 "Governor Phillip at Sydney Cove" (J. Alcott)

"Tail" flaw (Left pane R. 7/1. Later retouched)

(Des and eng E. Broad and F. D. Manley. Recess J. Ash)

1937 (1 Oct). *150th Anniv of Foundation of New South Wales.* W **15**. P 13½×14.

193	**41**	2d. scarlet	2·25	30
		a. "Tail" flaw	£425	£100
194		3d. bright blue	6·00	2·25
195		9d. purple	18·00	10·00
193/5 *Set of* 3			24·00	11·00

42 A.I.F. and Nurse

(Des and eng F. D. Manley from drawing by Virgil Reilly. Recess W. C. G. McCracken)

1940 (15 Jul). *Australian Imperial Forces.* W **15** (sideways). P 14×13½.

196	**42**	1d. green	1·75	2·50
197		2d. scarlet	1·75	1·50
198		3d. blue	12·00	10·00
199		6d. brown-purple	23·00	20·00
196/9 *Set of* 4			35·00	30·00

(43) (44) (45)

(Opts designed by F. D. Manley)

1941 (10 Dec). Nos. 184, 186 and 171 *surch with T* **43/5**.

200	**30a**	2½d. on 2d. scarlet (V.)	75	70
		a. Pair, one without surcharge	£8000	
		b. Medal flaw	£250	£150
201	**31**	3½d. on 3d. bright blue (Y. on Black)	1·00	2·25
202	**33**	5½d. on 5d. purple (V.)	4·00	5·50
200/2 *Set of* 3			5·25	7·50

Nos. 200/2 were prepared in connection with the imposition of a ½d. "war tax" increase on most postage rates.

One sheet of the 2½d. on 2d. was discovered showing the surcharge omitted on R. 1/4 and R. 1/5.

46 Queen Elizabeth

46a Queen Elizabeth

47 King George VI

48 King George VI

49 King George VI

50 Emu

(Des F. D. Manley. Eng F. D. Manley and T. C. Duffell (T **46/a**) or F. D. Manley (others))

1942–50. *Recess.* W **15**. P 15×14.

203	**46**	1d. brown-purple (2.1.43)	1·25	10
		a. Coil pair (1944)	22·00	35·00
204	**46a**	1½d. green (1.12.42)	1·50	10
205	**47**	2d. bright purple (4.12.44)	1·00	1·75
		b. Coil pair (1.49)	90·00	£120
		ba. Coil block of four (5.50)	£1600	
206	**48**	2½d. scarlet (7.1.42)	40	10
		a. Imperf (pair)*	£4500	
		w. Wmk inverted (*from booklets*)	4·75	1·25
207	**49**	3½d. bright blue (3.42)	1·00	60
		a. Deep blue	1·25	60
208	**50**	5½d. slate-blue (12.2.42)	1·00	20
203/8 *Set of* 6			5·50	2·50

*No. 206a comes in horizontal pair with the right-hand stamp completely imperforate and the left-hand stamp imperforate at right only.

Coils with normal perforations exist for 1d.

For stamps as Nos. 204/5 but without watermark see Nos. 229/30.

The following items are understood to have been the subject of unauthorised leakages from the Commonwealth Note and Stamp Printing Branch and are therefore not listed by us.

It is certain that none of this material was distributed to post offices for issue to the public.

Imperforate all round. 1d. Princess Elizabeth; 1½d. Queen; 2½d. King; 4d. Koala; 6d. Kookaburra; 9d. Platypus; 1s. Lyrebird (small) (also imperf three sides); 1s.6d. Air Mail (Type **22**); 2½d. Mitchell; 2½d. Newcastle (also imperf three sides or imperf vertically).

Also 2½d. Peace, unwatermarked; 2½d. King, *tête-bêche*; 3½d. Newcastle, in dull ultramarine; 2½d. King on "toned" paper.

52 Duke and Duchess of Gloucester

(Des F. D. Manley. Eng F. D. Manley and T. C. Duffell. Recess)

1945 (19 Feb). *Arrival of Duke and Duchess of Gloucester in Australia.* W **15**. P 14½.

209	**52**	2½d. lake	15	10
210		3½d. ultramarine	20	1·10
211		5½d. indigo	25	1·10
209/11 *Set of* 3			55	2·00

A

B

1945 (24 Dec). *Kangaroo type, as* No. 134, *but re-engraved as* B. W **15**. P 12.

212	**1**	2s. maroon	2·50	5·00
		w. Wmk inverted	†	£15000

No. 134 has two background lines between the value circle and "TWO SHILLINGS"; No. 212 has only one line in this position. There are also differences in the shape of the letters.

53 Star and Wreath

56 Sir Thomas Mitchell and Queensland

54 Flag and dove

55 Angel

(Des F. D. Manley (2½d.), F. D. Manley and G. Lissenden (3½d.), G. Lissenden (5½d.). Eng F. D. Manley. Recess)

1946 (18 Feb). *Victory Commemoration.* W **15** (sideways on 5½d.). P 14½.

213	**53**	2½d. scarlet	15	10
214	**54**	3½d. blue	45	1·50
215	**55**	5½d. green	50	90
213/15 *Set of 3*			1·00	2·25

These designs were re-issued in 1995 with face values in decimal currency.

(Des F. D. Manley. Eng F. D. Manley and T. C. Duffell. Recess)

1946 (14 Oct). *Centenary of Mitchell's Exploration of Central Queensland.* W **15**. P 14½.

216	**56**	2½d. scarlet	15	10
217		3½d. blue	50	1·25
218		1s. grey-olive	50	50
216/18 *Set of 3*			1·00	1·60

57 Lt. John Shortland R.N.

58 Steel Foundry

59 Coal Carrier/Cranes

(Des and eng G. Lissenden (5½d.), F. D. Manley (others). Recess)

1947 (8 Sep). *150th Anniv of City of Newcastle, New South Wales.* W **15** (sideways on 3½d.). P 14½ or 15×14 (2½d.).

219	**57**	2½d. lake	15	10
220	**58**	3½d. blue	50	1·25
221	**59**	5½d. green	50	65
219/21 *Set of 3*			1·00	1·75

60 Queen Elizabeth II when Princess

(Des R. A. Harrison. Eng. F. D. Manley. Recess)

1947 (20 Nov)–**52**. *Marriage of Princess Elizabeth.* P 14×15.

		(a) W **15** (sideways).		
222	**60**	1d. purple	15	30
		(b) No wmk.		
222*a*	**60**	1d. purple (8.48)	10	10
		b. Coil pair (1.50)	2·25	5·00
		c. Coil block of four (9.52)	5·00	

61 Hereford Bull

61a Hermes and Globe

62 Aboriginal Art

62a Commonwealth Coat of Arms

Roller flaw below "E" of "POSTAGE" (R. 4/1 and 5/1). Later retouched.

(Des G. Sellheim (T **62**), F.D. Manley (others). Eng G. Lissenden (T **62**), F. D. Manley (1s.3d., 1s.6d., 5s.), F. D. Manley and R. J. Becker (10s., £1, £2). Recess)

1948 (16 Feb)–**56**. W **15** (sideways).

		(a) P 14½.		
223	**61**	1s.3d. brown-purple	1·75	1·10
223*a*	**61a**	1s.6d. blackish brown (1.9.49)	70	10
224	**62**	2s. chocolate	1·50	10
		(b) P 14½×13½.		
224*a*	**62a**	5s. claret (11.4.49)	3·00	20
		ab. Thin paper (1951)	60·00	45·00
224*b*		10s. purple (3.10.49)	15·00	85
224*c*		£1 blue (28.11.49)	32·00	3·75
224*d*		£2 green (16.1.50)	80·00	14·00
		da. Roller flaw	£120	75·00
223/24*d* *Set of 7*			£120	18·00
224bs/ds Optd "Specimen" *Set of 3*			£140	
		(c) No wmk. P 14½.		
224*e*	**61a**	1s.6d. blackish brown (2.12.56)	7·00	1·50
224*f*	**62**	2s. chocolate (27.6.56)	7·00	70

No. 224ab is an emergency printing on white Harrison paper instead of the toned paper used for No. 224a.

No. 224b exists with watermark inverted and overprinted "SPECIMEN".

63 William J. Farrer

64 F. von Mueller

65 Boy Scout

(Des and eng F. D. Manley. Recess)

1948 (12 Jul). *William J. Farrer (wheat research) Commemoration.* W **15**. P 15×14.

225	**63**	2½d. scarlet	30	10

(Des and eng F. D. Manley. Recess)

1948 (13 Sep). *Sir Ferdinand von Mueller (botanist) Commemoration.* W **15**. P 15×14.

226	**64**	2½d. lake	20	10

(Des and eng F. D. Manley. Recess)

1948 (15 Nov). *Pan-Pacific Scout Jamboree, Wonga Park.* W **15** (sideways). P 14×15.

227	**65**	2½d. lake	20	10

See also No. 254.

Sky retouch (normally unshaded near hill) (Rt pane R. 6/8) (No. 228a retouched in 1951)

"Green mist" retouch. A large area to the left of the bird's feathers is recut (upper plate left pane R. 9/3)

1948–56. No wmk. P 15×14 or 14×15 (9d.).

228	**27**	½d. orange (15.9.49)	20	10
		a. Line to kangaroo's ear	25·00	
		b. Sky retouch	38·00	
		c. Coil pair (1950)	75	2·75
		ca. Line to kangaroo's ear	65·00	
		cb. Sky retouch (in pair)	£190	
		d. Coil block of four (1953)	2·75	
229	**46a**	1½d. green (17.8.49)	1·00	1·75
230	**47**	2d. bright purple (20.12.48)	80	1·75
		aa. Coil pair	3·00	10·00
230*a*	**32**	4d. green (18.8.56)	2·00	2·25
230*b*	**34**	6d. purple-brown (18.8.56)	5·50	1·00
230*c*	**35**	9d. chocolate (13.12.56)	22·00	3·75
230*d*	**36**	1s. grey-green (13.12.56)	4·00	1·25
		da. "Green mist" retouch	£2000	£1200
		db. Roller flaw	32·00	18·00
228/30*d* *Set of 7*			32·00	10·00

66 "Henry Lawson" (Sir Lionel Lindsay)

67 Mounted Postman and Convair CV 240 Aircraft

(Des F. D. Manley. Eng. E. R. M. Jones. Recess)

1949 (17 Jun). *Henry Lawson (poet) Commemoration.* P 15×14.

231	**66**	2½d. maroon	30	10

(Des Sir Daryl Lindsay and F. D. Manley. Eng F. D. Manley. Recess)

1949 (10 Oct). *75th Anniv of Founding of U.P.U.* P 15×14.

232	**67**	3½d. ultramarine	40	60

68 John, Lord Forrest of Bunbury

69 Queen Elizabeth

70 King George VI

(Des and eng F. D. Manley. Recess)

1949 (28 Nov). *John, Lord Forrest of Bunbury (explorer and politician) Commemoration.* W **15**. P 15×14.

233	**68**	2½d. lake	30	10

(Des and eng F. D. Manley. Recess)

1950 (12 Apr)–**52**.

		(a) W **15**. P 15×14.		
234	**70**	2½d. scarlet (12.4.50)	10	10
235		3d. scarlet (28.2.51)	15	25
		aa. Coil pair (4.51)	17·00	38·00
		(b) No wmk.		
236	**69**	1½d. green (19.6.50)	40	40
237		2d. yellow-green (28.3.51)	15	10
		a. Coil pair	6·00	9·50
		b. Coil block of four (11.52)	12·00	
237*c*	**70**	2½d. purple-brown (23.5.51)	15	35
237*d*		3d. grey-green (14.11.51)	15	10
		da. Coil pair (12.51)	24·00	38·00
234/7*d* *Set of 6*			1·00	1·10

On 14 October 1951 No. 235 was placed on sale in sheets of 144 originally intended for use in stamp booklets. These sheets contain 3 panes of 48 (16×3) with horizontal gutter margin between.

71 Aborigine

72 Reproduction of First Stamps of New South Wales

73 Reproduction of First Stamps of Victoria

(Des and eng F. D. Manley. Recess)

1950 (14 Aug). W **15**. P 15×14.

238	**71**	8½d. brown	20	1·00

For T **71** in a larger size, see Nos. 253/*b*.

(Des and eng G. Lissenden (T **72**), E. R. M. Jones (T **73**). Recess)

1950 (27 Sep). *Centenary of First Adhesive Postage Stamps in Australia.* P 15×14.

239	**72**	2½d. maroon	25	10
		a. Horiz pair. Nos. 239/40	50	70
240	**73**	2½d. maroon	25	10

Nos. 239/40 were printed alternately in vertical columns throughout the sheet.

74 Sir Edmund Barton

75 Sir Henry Parkes

76 "Opening First Federal Parliament" (T. Roberts)

77 Federal Parliament House, Canberra

(Des and eng F. D. Manley. Recess)

1951 (1 May). *50th Anniv of Commonwealth of Australia.* P 15×14.

241	**74**	3d. lake	60	10
		a. Horiz pair. Nos. 241/2	2·25	2·50
242	**75**	3d. lake	60	10
243	**76**	5½d. blue	30	2·25
244	**77**	1s.6d. purple-brown	50	50
241/4 *Set of 4*			2·75	2·75

Nos. 241/2 were printed alternately in vertical columns throughout the sheet.

78 E. H. Hargraves

79 C. J. Latrobe

(Des and eng F. D. Manley. Recess)

1951 (2 Jul). *Centenaries of Discovery of Gold in Australia and of Responsible Government in Victoria.* P 15×14.

245	**78**	3d. maroon	50	10
		a. Horiz pair. Nos. 245/6	1·50	2·75
246	**79**	3d. maroon	50	10

Nos. 245/6 were printed alternately in vertical columns throughout the sheet.

80

81 King George VI

82

(Des E. R. M. Jones (7½d.), F. D. Manley (others) Eng. F. D. Manley. Recess)

1951–52. W **15** (sideways on 1s.0½d.). P 14½ (1s.0½d.) or 15×14 (others).

247 **80** 3½d. brown-purple (28.11.51) 10 10
a. Imperf between (horiz pair) .. £10000
248 4½d. scarlet (20.2.52) .... 15 1·25
249 6½d. brown (20.2.52) .... 15 1·00
250 6½d. emerald-green (9.4.52) 10 35
251 **81** 7½d. blue (31.10.51) 15 80
a. Imperf three sides (vert pair) £13000
252 **82** 1s.0½d. indigo (19.3.52) 60 60
247/52 *Set of* 6 .... 1·10 3·50

No. 251a occurs on the left-hand vertical row of one sheet.

(Des F. D. Manley. Eng E. R. M. Jones. Recess)

1952 (19 Mar)–**65**. P 14½.

(*a*) W **15** (sideways*).

253 2s.6d. deep brown .... 1·50 70
aw. Wmk Crown to left of C of A .... † £2500

(*b*) No wmk.

253*b* 2s.6d. deep brown (30.1.57) .... 4·50 75
ba. Sepia (10.65) .... 13·00 13·00

Design:—2s.6d. As T **71** but larger (21×25½ mm).

*The normal sideways watermark on No. 253 shows Crown to right of C of A, *as seen from the back of the stamp*.

No. 253*ba* was an emergency printing and can easily be distinguished from No. 253*b* as it is on white Harrison paper, No. 253*b* being on toned paper.

(Des and eng F. D. Manley. Recess)

1952 (19 Nov). *Pan-Pacific Scout Jamboree, Greystanes. As T* **65**, *but inscr* "1952–53". W **15** (sideways). P 14×15.

254 3½d. brown-lake 20 10

83 Butter

84 Wheat

85 Beef

(Des P.O. artists; adapted G. Lissenden. Typo)

1953 (11 Feb). *Food Production*. P 14½.

255 **83** 3d. emerald 30 10
a. Strip of 3. Nos. 255/7 .... 1·40 2·50
256 **84** 3d. emerald 30 10
257 **85** 3d. emerald 30 10
258 **83** 3½d. scarlet 30 10
a. Strip of 3. Nos. 258/60 .... 1·40 2·50
259 **84** 3½d. scarlet 30 10
260 **85** 3½d. scarlet 30 10
255/60 *Set of* 6 .... 2·75 55

The three designs in each denomination appear in rotation, both horizontally and vertically, throughout the sheet.

86 Queen Elizabeth II

87 Queen Elizabeth II

(Des F. D. Manley from photograph by Dorothy Wilding Ltd. Eng D. Cameron. Recess)

1953–56. P 15×14.

(*a*) No wmk.

261 **86** 1d. purple (19.8.53) 15 15
261*a* 2½d. blue (23.6.54) 20 15
262 3d. deep green (17.6.53) 20 10
aa. Coil pair .... 5·00 7·50
ab. Coil block of four (9.53) .... 13·00
262*a* 3½d. brown-red (2.7.56) .... 1·25 30
262*b* 6½d. orange (9.56) .... 1·75 2·00

(*b*) W **15**.

263 **86** 3½d. brown-red (21.4.53) 20 10
263*a* 6½d. orange (23.6.54) .... 2·50 50
261/3*a* *Set of* 7 .... 5·50 3·00

(Des and eng F. D. Manley. Recess)

1953 (25 May). *Coronation*. P 15×14.

264 **87** 3½d. scarlet 40 10
265 7½d. violet .... 75 1·40
266 2s. dull bluish green .... 2·50 1·40
264/6 *Set of* 3 .... 3·25 2·50

88 Young Farmers and Calf

(Des P.O. artist; adapted P. E. Morriss. Eng E. R. M. Jones. Recess)

1953 (3 Sept). *25th Anniv of Australian Young Farmers' Clubs*. P 14½.

267 **88** 3½d. red-brown and deep green 10 10

89 Lt.-Gov. D. Collins

90 Lt.-Gov. W. Paterson

91 Sullivan Cove, Hobart, 1804

(Des E. R. M. Jones, eng D. Cameron (T **89/90**); des and eng G. Lissenden (T **91**). Recess)

1953 (23 Sept). *150th Anniv of Settlement in Tasmania*. P 15×14.

268 **89** 3½d. brown-purple 30 10
a. Horiz pair. Nos. 268/9 .... 70 1·50
269 **90** 3½d. brown-purple 30 10
270 **91** 2s. green .... 1·25 2·75
268/70 *Set of* 3 .... 1·75 2·75

Nos. 268/9 were printed alternately in vertical columns throughout the sheet.

92 Stamp of 1853

(Des R. L. Beck; eng G. Lissenden. Recess)

1953 (11 Nov). *Tasmanian Postage Stamp Centenary*. P 14½.

271 **92** 3d. rose-red 10 40

93 Queen Elizabeth II and Duke of Edinburgh

94 Queen Elizabeth II

Re-entry (lower plate left pane R. 8/2)

(Des and eng F. D. Manley; border and lettering on 7½d. des by R. M. Warner. Recess)

1954 (2 Feb). *Royal Visit*. P 14.

272 **93** 3½d. scarlet 20 10
a. Re-entry .... 40·00 14·00
273 **94** 7½d. purple .... 30 1·25
274 **93** 2s. dull bluish green 60 65
272/4 *Set of* 3 .... 1·00 1·75

95 "Telegraphic Communications"

96 Red Cross and Globe

(Des R. M. Warner. Eng P. E. Morriss. Recess)

1954 (7 Apr). *Australian Telegraph System Centenary*. P 14.

275 **95** 3½d. brown-red 10 10

(Des B. Stewart. Eng P. E. Morriss. Design recess: cross typo)

1954 (9 June). *40th Anniv of Australian Red Cross Society*. P 14½.

276 **96** 3½d. ultramarine and scarlet 10 10

97 Mute Swan

98 Locomotives of 1854 and 1954

(Des R. L. Beck. Eng G. Lissenden. Recess)

1954 (2 Aug). *Western Australian Postage Stamp Centenary*. P 14½.

277 **97** 3½d. black 20 10

(Des R. M. Warner. Eng G. Lissenden. Recess)

1954 (13 Sept). *Australian Railways Centenary*. P 14.

278 **98** 3½d. purple-brown 30 10

99 Territory Badge

100 Olympic Games Symbol

101 Rotary Symbol, Globe and Flags

(Des F. D. Manley. Eng G. Lissenden. Recess)

1954 (17 Nov). *Australian Antarctic Research*. P 14½×13½.

279 **99** 3½d. grey-black 15 10

(Des R. L. Beck. Eng P. E. Morriss. Recess)

1954 (1 Dec)–**55**. *Olympic Games Propaganda*. P 14.

280 **100** 2s. deep bright blue .... 1·00 1·00
280*a* 2s. deep bluish green (30.11.55) .... 1·75 2·25

(Des and eng D. Cameron. Recess)

1955 (23 Feb). *50th Anniv of Rotary International*. P 14×14½.

281 **101** 3½d. carmine 10 10

101a Queen Elizabeth II

101b Queen Elizabeth II

102 Queen Elizabeth II

(Des F. D. Manley from bas-relief by W. L. Bowles. Eng D. Cameron (7½d.), G. Lissenden (others). Recess)

1955 (9 Mar)–**57**. P 15×14 (T **101a/b**) or 14½ (T **102**).

(*a*) W **15** (sideways).

282 **102** 1s.0½d. deep blue .... 1·25 1·25

(*b*) No wmk.

282*a* **101a** 4d. lake (13.3.57) 20 10
ab. Booklet pane of 6 .... 7·50
282*b* **101b** 7½d. violet (13.11.57) .... 60 1·50
ba. Double print £4000
282*c* **101a** 10d. deep grey-blue (6.3.57) .... 60 1·25
282*d* **102** 1s.7d. red-brown (13.3.57) .... 1·25 45
282/*d* *Set of* 5 .... 3·50 4·00

No. 282ab from booklet SB33 has the outer edges of the pane imperforate, producing single stamps with one or two adjacent sides imperforate.

103 American Memorial, Canberra

104 Cobb & Co. Coach (from etching by Sir Lionel Lindsay)

(Des R. L. Beck (head by F. D. Manley). Eng F. D. Manley. Recess)

1955 (4 May). *Australian–American Friendship*. P 14×14½.

283 **103** 3½d. violet-blue 10 10

(Design adapted and eng by F. D. Manley. Recess)

1955 (6 July). *Mail-coach Pioneers Commemoration*. P 14½×14.

284 **104** 3½d. blackish brown 25 10
285 2s. reddish brown .... 50 1·40

105 Y.M.C.A. Emblem and Map of the World

106 Florence Nightingale and Young Nurse

(Des E. Thake. Eng P. E. Morriss. Design recess; emblem typo)

1955 (10 Aug). *World Centenary of Y.M.C.A.* P 14½×14.

286 **105** 3½d. deep bluish green and red 10 10
a. Red (emblem) omitted £13000

(Des and eng F. D. Manley. Recess)

1955 (21 Sept). *Nursing Profession Commemoration*. P 14×14½.

287 **106** 3½d. reddish violet 10 10

107 Queen Victoria

108 Badges of New South Wales, Victoria and Tasmania

(Des and eng D. Cameron. Recess)

1955 (17 Oct). *Centenary of First South Australian Postage Stamps.* P 14½.

288	**107**	3½d. green	10	10

(Des and eng F. D. Manley. Recess)

1956 (26 Sept). *Centenary of Responsible Government in New South Wales, Victoria and Tasmania.* P 14½×14.

289	**108**	3½d. brown-lake	10	10

109 Arms of Melbourne

110 Olympic Torch and Symbol

111 Collins Street, Melbourne

112 Melbourne across R. Yarra

(Des P. E. Morriss; eng F. D. Manley (4d.). Des and eng F. D. Manley (7½d.) Recess. Des and photo Harrison from photographs by M. Murphy and sketches by L. Coles (1s.). Des and photo Courvoisier from photographs by M. Murphy (2s.))

1956 (31 Oct). *Olympic Games, Melbourne.* P 14½ (4d.), 14×14½ (7½d., 1s.) or 11½ (2s.).

290	**109**	4d. carmine-red	25	10
291	**110**	7½d. deep bright blue	50	1·40
292	**111**	1s. multicoloured	60	30
293	**112**	2s. multicoloured	85	1·40
290/3 *Set of* 4			2·00	2·75

115 South Australia Coat of Arms

116 Map of Australia and Caduceus

(Des and eng P. E. Morriss. Recess)

1957 (17 Apr). *Centenary of Responsible Government in South Australia.* P 14½.

296	**115**	4d. red-brown	10	10

(Des J. E. Lyle; adapted B. Stewart. Eng D. Cameron. Recess)

1957 (21 Aug). *Flying Doctor Service.* P 14½×14.

297	**116**	7d. ultramarine	15	10

117 "The Spirit of Christmas"

Re-entry (upper plate left pane R. 10/1)

(Des and eng D. Cameron from a painting by Sir Joshua Reynolds. Recess)

1957 (6 Nov). *Christmas.* P 14½×14.

298	**117**	3½d. scarlet	10	20
		a. Re-entry	9·00	13·00
299		4d. purple	10	10

118 Lockheed L.1049 Super Constellation Airliner

Re-entry on final "A" of "AUSTRALIA" (R. 7/6)

(Des and eng P. E. Morriss. Recess)

1958 (6 Jan). *Inauguration of Australian "Round the World" Air Service.* P 14½×14.

301	**118**	2s. deep blue	75	1·00
		a. Re-entry	28·00	32·00

119 Hall of Memory, Sailor and Airman

120 Sir Charles Kingsford Smith and Fokker F.VIIa/3m *Southern Cross*

(Des and eng G. Lissenden. Recess)

1958 (10 Feb). *T* **119** *and similar horiz design.* P 14½×14.

302		5½d. brown-red	40	30
		a. Horiz pair. Nos. 302/380	1·25	5·50
303		5½d. brown-red	40	30

No. 303 shows a soldier and service-woman respectively in place of the sailor and airman. Nos. 302/3 are printed alternately in vertical columns throughout the sheet.

(Des J. E. Lyle. Eng F. D. Manley. Recess)

1958 (27 Aug). *30th Anniv of First Air Crossing of the Tasman Sea.* P 14×14½.

304	**120**	8d. deep ultramarine	60	1·00

121 Silver Mine, Broken Hill

122 The Nativity

(Des R. H. Evans; adapted and eng F. D. Manley. Recess)

1958 (10 Sept). *75th Anniv of Founding of Broken Hill.* P 14½×14.

305	**121**	4d. chocolate	30	10

(Des D. Cameron. Eng P. E. Morriss. Recess)

1958 (5 Nov). *Christmas.* P 14½×15.

306	**122**	3½d. deep scarlet	20	30
307		4d. deep violet	20	10

123

124

126

127

128 Queen Elizabeth II

129

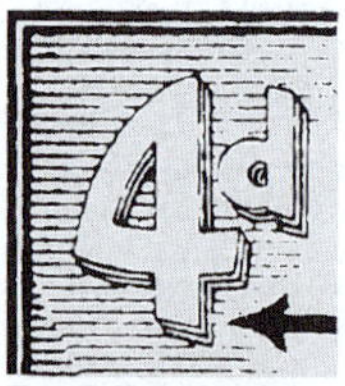

Type I Short break in outer line to bottom right of "4"

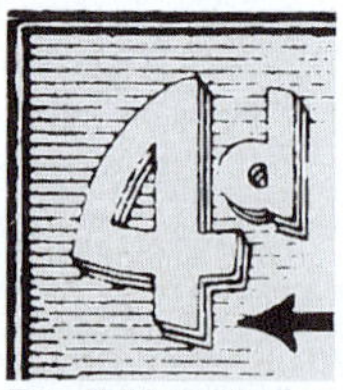

Type II Line unbroken

Type A Four short lines inside "5"

Type B Five short lines inside "5"

1d. Re-entry. Line running through base of "RALIA" (Lower right plate, right pane R. 1/8).

3½d. Re-entry to "E" and left frame (R. 1/10)

(Des G. Lissenden from photographs by Baron Studios. Eng F. D. Manley (2d.), D. Cameron (3d.). P. E. Morriss (others). Recess)

1959–63. P 14×15 (horiz) or 15×14 (vert).

308	**123**	1d. deep slate-purple (2.2.59)	10	10
		a. Deep slate-lilac (1961)	1·25	30
		b. Re-entry	8·50	
309	**124**	2d. brown (21.3.62)	50	20
		a. Coil pair (1962)	4·00	4·75
		b. Coil block of four (1963)	8·00	
311	**126**	3d. blue-green (20.5.59)	15	10
		a. Coil pair (8.59)	4·00	5·50
		b. Coil block of four	10·00	
312	**127**	3½d. deep green (18.3.59)	15	15
		a. Re-entry	9·50	
313	**128**	4d. carmine-lake (Type I) (2.2.59)	1·75	10
		a. Carmine-red	1·75	10
		ab. Booklet pane of 6 (18.3.59)	19·00	
		b. Type II	1·75	10
		ba. Carmine-red	1·75	10
314	**129**	5d. deep blue (Type A or B) (1.10.59)	1·00	10
		a. Vert *se-tenant* pair (A and B)	2·25	2·75
		b. Coil pair (18.7.60)	9·50	13·00
		c. Coil block of four (7.61)	40·00	
		d. Booklet pane of 6 (23.3.60)	10·00	
308/14 *Set of* 6			3·25	65

No. 313. Produced in printer's sheets, of 640 split into sheets of 160 for issue. Type I occurs on the two upper sheets from the printers' sheet and on ten positions from the left pane of the lower right sheet. Type II occurs on all stamps from the lower sheets except for ten positions from the left pane of lower right sheet.

No. 314. Both types occur in alternate horizontal rows in the sheet (Type A in Row 1, Type B in Row 2, and so on), and their value is identical. Booklet pane No. 314d from SB35/6a contains two Type A and four Type B.

Nos. 309a/b, 311a/b and 314b/c have horizontal coil perforations as described after No. 191.

Nos. 313ab from booklets SB34/a and 314d from booklets SB35/6a have the outer edges of the panes imperforate, producing stamps with one or two adjacent sides imperforate.

Printings of the 2d. (from March 1965) and of the 3d. (from April 1965), both including coils, were on Helecon paper.

131 Numbat

132 Tiger Cat

133 Eastern Grey Kangaroos

134 Common Rabbit-Bandicoot

135 Platypus

136 Thylacine

137 Christmas Bells

138 Flannel Flower

139 Wattle

140 Banksia

141 Waratah

142 Aboriginal Stockman

"T" retouch (Right plate R. 6/8)

(Des Eileen Mayo (6d., 8d., 9d., 11d., 1s., 1s.2d.), B. Stewart (5s.), Margaret Stones (others). Eng P. Morriss (11d.) F. D. Manley (1s.), B. Stewart (others). Recess)

1959–64. *T* **131/42**. W **15** (5s.), no wmk (others). P 14×15 (1s.2d.), 15×14 (6d. to 1s.), 14½×14 (5s.) or 14½ (others).

316 **131** 6d. brown (30.9.60) ... 1·50 10
317 **132** 8d. red-brown (11.5.60) ... 75 10
a. Pale red-brown (9.61) ... 75 10
318 **133** 9d. deep sepia (21.10.59) ... 1·50 55
319 **134** 11d. deep blue (3.5.61) ... 1·00 15
320 **135** 1s. deep green (9.9.59) ... 1·75 40
321 **136** 1s.2d. deep purple (21.3.62) ... 1·00 15
322 **137** 1s.6d. crimson/*yellow* (3.2.60) ... 1·50 1·00
323 **138** 2s. grey-blue (8.4.59) ... 70 10
a. "T" retouch ... 20·00
324 **139** 2s.3d. green/*maize* (9.9.59) ... 1·00 10
324*a* 2s.3d. yellow-green (28.10.64) ... 2·50 75
325 **140** 2s.5d. brown/*yellow* (16.3.60) ... 3·50 75
326 **141** 3s. scarlet (15.7.59) ... 1·00 20
327 **142** 5s. red-brown (26.7.61) ... 11·00 2·25
a. White paper. *Brown-red* (17.6.64) ... 85·00 7·50
316/327 *Set of* 13 ... 25·00 5·75

No. 327 is on toned paper. No. 327a was a late printing on the white paper referred to in the note below No. 360.

An experimental printing of the 11d. was made on Helecon paper in December 1963. See note below No. 362.

All printings of the 8d., 11d., 1s.2d. and 2s.3d. (No. 324a) were on Helecon paper from April 1965.

143 Postmaster Isaac Nichols boarding the brig *Experiment*

144 Parliament House, Brisbane, and Arms of Queensland

(Des R. Shackel; adapted and eng F. D. Manley. Recess)

1959 (22 Apr). *150th Anniv of the Australian Post Office.* P 14½×14.
331 **143** 4d. slate ... 15 10

(Des and eng G. Lissenden. Recess and typo)

1959 (5 June). *Centenary of Self-Government in Queensland.* P 14×14½.
332 **144** 4d. lilac and green ... 10 10

145 "The Approach of the Magi"

146 Girl Guide and Lord Baden-Powell

(Des and eng F. D. Manley. Recess)

1959 (4 Nov). *Christmas.* P 15×14.
333 **145** 5d. deep reddish violet ... 10 10

(Des and eng B. Stewart. Recess)

1960 (18 Aug). *50th Anniv of Girl Guide Movement.* P 14½×14.
334 **146** 5d. deep ultramarine ... 30 15

147 "The Overlanders" (Sir Daryl Lindsay)

148 "Archer" and Melbourne Cup

Two types:

I Mane rough

II Mane smooth

Major re-entry below rider's right arm (Lower left plate R. 4/4). This occurs only on Type I.

Type II occurs on Pane A, Row 2 Nos. 8 and 9, Row 4 Nos. 1 to 12, Row 5 Nos. 10 to 12, and on Pane C, Row 4 Nos. 5 to 12, Row 5 Nos. 1 to 9, and Rows 6 to 10 inclusive; the stamps in Row 4 Nos. 5 to 12 and Row 5 Nos. 1 to 9 are considered to be of an intermediate type with the mane as in Type II but the ear and rein being as in Type I. All the rest are Type I.

(Adapted and eng P. E. Morriss. Recess)

1960 (21 Sept). *Centenary of Northern Territory Exploration.* P 15×14½.
335 **147** 5d. magenta (I) ... 40 15
a. Major re-entry ... 25·00
b. Type II ... 2·00 1·00

(Des F. D. Manley. Eng G. Lissenden. Recess)

1960 (12 Oct). *100th Melbourne Cup Race Commemoration.* P 14½.
336 **148** 5d. sepia ... 20 10

149 Queen Victoria

150 Open Bible and Candle

(Des F. D. Manley. Eng B. Stewart. Recess)

1960 (2 Nov). *Centenary of First Queensland Postage Stamp.* P 14½×15.
337 **149** 5d. deep myrtle-green ... 25 10

Re-entry. "19" of "1960" partially double (Lower left plate R. 5/2). On upper left plate R. 10/10 there is a similar partial doubling of "19" but to right of "1" and inside "9". Same price for either variety.

(Des K. McKay. Adapted and eng B. Stewart. Recess)

1960 (9 Nov). *Christmas.* P 15×14½.
338 **150** 5d. carmine-red ... 10 10
a. Re-entry ... 8·00

151 Colombo Plan Bureau Emblem

152 Melba (after bust by Sir Bertram Mackennal)

(Des and eng G. Lissenden. Recess)

1961 (30 June). *Colombo Plan.* P 14×14½.
339 **151** 1s. red-brown ... 10 10

No. 339 was issued on Helecon paper in April 1965. See note after No. 362.

(Des and eng B. Stewart. Recess)

1961 (20 Sept). *Birth Centenary of Dame Nellie Melba (singer).* P 14½×15.
340 **152** 5d. blue ... 30 15

153 Open Prayer Book and Text

(Des G. Lissenden. Eng P. E. Morriss. Recess)

1961 (8 Nov). *Christmas.* P 14½×14.
341 **153** 5d. brown ... 10 10

154 J. M. Stuart

155 Flynn's Grave and Nursing Sister

(Des W. Jardine. Eng P. E. Morriss. Recess)

1962 (25 July). *Centenary of Stuart's Crossing of Australia from South to North.* P 14½×15.
342 **154** 5d. brown-red ... 15 10

(Des F. D. Manley. Photo)

1962 (5 Sept). *50th Anniv of Australian Inland Mission.* P 13½.
343 **155** 5d. multicoloured ... 30 15
a. Red omitted ... † £1000

The note below No. 372b also applies to No. 343a.

156 "Woman"

157 "Madonna and Child"

(Des D. Dundas. Eng G. Lissenden. Recess)

1962 (26 Sept). *"Associated Country Women of the World" Conference, Melbourne.* P 14×14½.
344 **156** 5d. deep green ... 10 10

(Des and eng G. Lissenden. Recess)

1962 (17 Oct). *Christmas.* P 14½.
345 **157** 5d. violet ... 15 10

158 Perth and Kangaroo Paw (plant)

159 Arms of Perth and Running Track

(Des R. M. Warner (5d.), G. Hamori (2s.3d.) Photo Harrison)

1962 (1 Nov). *Seventh British Empire and Commonwealth Games, Perth.* P 14 (5d.) or 14½×14 (2s.3d.).
346 **158** 5d. multicoloured ... 40 10
a. Red omitted ... £3000
347 **159** 2s.3d. black, red, blue and green ... 1·50 2·75

160 Queen Elizabeth II

161 Queen Elizabeth II and Duke of Edinburgh

(Des and eng after portraits by Anthony Buckley, P. E. Morriss (5d.), B. Stewart (2s.3d.). Recess)

1963 (18 Feb). *Royal Visit.* P 14½.
348 **160** 5d. deep green ... 35 10
349 **161** 2s.3d. brown-lake ... 1·50 3·00

162 Arms of Canberra and W. B. Griffin (architect)

163 Centenary Emblem

(Des and eng B. Stewart. Recess)

1963 (8 Mar). *50th Anniv of Canberra.* P 14½×14.
350 **162** 5d. deep green ... 15 10

(Des G. Hamori. Photo)

1963 (8 May). *Red Cross Centenary.* P 13½×13.
351 **163** 5d. red, grey-brown and blue ... 40 10

164 Blaxland, Lawson and Wentworth on Mt. York

(Des T. Alban. Eng P. E. Morriss. Recess)

1963 (28 May). *150th Anniv of First Crossing of Blue Mountains.* P 14½×14.

352	**164**	5d. ultramarine	15	10

165 "Export"

166 Queen Elizabeth II

(Des and eng B. Stewart. Recess)

1963 (28 Aug). *Export Campaign.* P 14½×14.

353	**165**	5d. red	10	10

(Des and eng P. E. Morriss from photograph by Anthony Buckley. Recess)

1963 (9 Oct)–**65**. P 15×14.

354	**166**	5d. deep green	75	10
		a. Booklet pane of 6	21·00	
		b. Imperf between (horiz pair) (31.7.64)	1·25	2·50
354*c*		5d. red (30.6.65)	55	10
		ca. Coil pair	18·00	27·00
		cb. Booklet pane of 6	21·00	

The 5d. deep green exists from both sheets and booklets on Helecon paper produced in error.

The 5d. red was issued with or without Helecon added to the ink. All coil and booklet printings included Helecon in the ink, except for a small printing produced in error. Examples of the sheet and booklet printings with Helecon ink have been found on Helecon *paper*.

Nos. 354a and 354cb have the outer edges of the panes imperforate producing single stamps with one or two adjacent sides imperforate. They come from booklets SB37/8a.

No. 354b comes from sheets of uncut booklet panes containing 288 stamps (16×18) with wide margins intersecting the sheet horizontally below each third row, alternate rows of stamps imperforate between vertically and the outer left, right and bottom margins imperforate. This means that in each sheet there are 126 pairs of stamps imperf between vertically, plus a number with wide imperforate margins attached, as shown in the illustration.

A 5d. in a similar design, printed in blue and brown with vertical edges imperforate, was prepared, but not issued.

167 Tasman and *Heemskerk*

168 Dampier and *Roebuck*

169 Captain Cook (after painting by Nathaniel Dance)

170 Flinders and *Investigator*

171 Bass and *Tom Thumb* (whaleboat)

172 Admiral King and *Mermaid* (survey cutter)

£2 Roller flaw, right-hand frame line at top (R. 1/3).

(Des W. Jardine. Eng B. Stewart (4s.), P. E. Morriss (5s., 7s., 6d., £1), M. Jones (10s). Recess)

1963–65. *T* **167/72**. No wmk (4s.) or W **15** (others), (sideways on 5s., £1). P 14 or 14½ (5s., £1, £2).

355	**167**	4s. ultramarine (9.10.63)	3·00	55
356	**168**	5s. red-brown (25.11.64)	3·25	1·75
357	**169**	7s.6d. olive (26.8.64)	19·00	16·00
358	**170**	10s. brown-purple (26.2.64)	25·00	5·00
		a. White paper. *Deep brown-purple* (14.1.65)	25·00	7·50
359	**171**	£1 deep reddish violet (26.2.64)	32·00	16·00
		a. White paper. *Deep bluish violet* (16.11.64)	42·00	29·00
360	**172**	£2 sepia (26.8.64)	55·00	75·00
		a. Roller flaw	£130	
355/60 *Set of 6*			£120	£100
357s/60s Optd "Specimen" *Set of 4*			£450	

Nos. 358 and 359 were printed on a toned paper but all the other values are on white paper, the 4s. being on rather thicker paper.

173 "Peace on Earth ..."

174 "Commonwealth Cable"

(Des R. M. Warner. Eng B. Stewart. Recess)

1963 (25 Oct). *Christmas.* P 14½.

361	**173**	5d. greenish blue	10	10

(Des P. E. Morriss. Photo)

1963 (3 Dec). *Opening of COMPAC (Trans-Pacific Telephone Cable). Chalk-surfaced paper.* P 13½.

362	**174**	2s.3d. red, blue, black and pale blue	1·00	2·75

HELECON (PHOSPHOR) STAMPS. "Helecon", a chemical substance of the zinc sulphide group, has been incorporated in stamps in two different ways, either in the ink with which the stamps are printed, or included in the surface coating of the stamp paper.

Owing to the difficulty of identification without the use of a U.V. lamp we do not list the Helecon stamps separately but when in stock can supply them after testing under the lamp.

The first stamp to be issued on helecon was the 11d. Bandicoot (No. 319) from an experimental printing of four million released to the public in December 1963. The next printing, on ordinary paper, was released in September 1964. The experimental printing was coarse, showing a lot of white dots and the colour is slate-blue, differing from both the ordinary and the later Helecon paper.

Further Helecon printings followed from March 1965. Almost all issues from No. 378 onwards were on Helecon paper or paper coated with Derby Luminescence.

175 Yellow-tailed Thornbill

176 Black-backed Magpie

(Des Betty Temple-Watts. Photo)

1964 (11 Mar)–**65**. *Birds. T* **175/6** *and similar designs. Chalk-surfaced paper.* P 13½.

363		6d. brown, yellow, black and bluish green (19.8.64)	1·00	25
		a. Brown, yellow, black & emer-grn	2·75	2·00
364		9d. black, grey and pale green	1·00	2·75
365		1s.6d. pink, grey, dull purple and black	75	1·40
366		2s. yellow, black and pink (21.4.65)	1·40	50
367		2s.5d. deep royal blue, light violet-blue, yellow-orange, grey and black	1·75	3·50
		a. Ordinary paper. *Deep blue, light blue, orange-brown, blue-grey and black* (7.65)	11·00	11·00
368		2s.6d. black, red, grey and green (21.4.65)	2·50	3·75
		a. Red omitted (white breast)	£5500	
369		3s. black, red, buff and yellow-green (21.4.65)	2·50	1·75
363/9 *Set of 7*			9·75	12·50

Designs: *Vert*—1s.6d. Galah; 2s. Golden Whistler; 2s.5d. Blue Wren; 3s. Straw-necked Ibis. *Horiz*—2s.6d. Scarlet Robin.

No. 367a was from a printing, made in 1962, on unsurfaced Wiggins Teape paper, the rest of the set being on chalk-surfaced Harrison paper. Apart from the differences in shade, the inscriptions, particularly "BLUE WREN", stand out very much more clearly on No. 367a. Although two colours are apparent in both stamps, the grey and black were printed from one cylinder.

The 6d. (No. 363) and 2s.5d. were only issued on ordinary paper. The 9d. and 1s.6d. exist on ordinary or Helecon paper. The 6d. (No. 363a), 1s., 2s.6d. and 3s. were issued on Helecon paper only.

182 Bleriot XI Aircraft (type flown by M. Guillaux, 1914)

Re-entry (upper right plate, R. 4/4)

(Des K. McKay. Adapted and eng P. E. Morriss. Recess)

1964 (1 July). *50th Anniv of First Australian Airmail Flight.* P 14½×14.

370	**182**	5d. olive-green	30	10
		a. Re-entry	£225	£130
371		2s.3d. scarlet	1·50	2·75

183 Child looking at Nativity Scene

184 "Simpson and his Donkey"

(Des P. E. Morriss and J. Mason. Photo)

1964 (21 Oct). *Christmas. Chalk-surfaced paper.* P 13½.

372	**183**	5d. red, blue, buff and black	10	10
		a. Red omitted	£2500	£1400
		b. Black omitted	£1500	

The red ink is soluble and can be removed by bleaching and it is therefore advisable to obtain a certificate from a recognised expert committee before purchasing No. 372a. The used price quoted is for an example on cover.

(Des C. Andrew (after statue, Shrine of Remembrance, Melbourne). Eng E. R. M. Jones. Recess)

1965 (14 Apr). *50th Anniv of Gallipoli Landing.* P 14×14½.

373	**184**	5d. drab	50	10
374		8d. blue	75	2·50
375		2s.3d. reddish purple	1·50	2·50
373/5 *Set of 3*			2·50	4·50

185 "Telecommunications"

186 Sir Winston Churchill

(Des J. McMahon and G. Hamori. Photo)

1965 (10 May). *I.T.U. Centenary. Chalk-surfaced paper.* P 13½.

376	**185**	5d. black, brown, orange-brown and blue	40	10
		a. Black (value and pylon) omitted	£3000	

(Des P. E. Morriss from photo by Karsh. Photo)

1965 (24 May). *Churchill Commemoration. Chalk-surfaced paper.* P 13½.

377	**186**	5d. black, pale grey, grey and light blue	15	10
		a. Pale grey (facial shading) omitted	£4000	
		b. Grey ("AUSTRALIA") omitted	†	£3500

No. 377a occurred on stamps from the bottom row of one sheet.

No. 377 exists on ordinary or Helecon paper in approximately equal quantities.

HELECON PAPER. All stamps from No. 378 were on Helecon paper, *unless otherwise stated.*

187 General Monash

188 Hargrave and "Multiplane" Seaplane (1902)

(Des O. Foulkes and W. Walters. Photo)

1965 (23 June). *Birth Centenary of General Sir John Monash (engineer and soldier).* P 13½.

378	**187**	5d. multicoloured	15	10

(Des G. Hamori. Photo)

1965 (4 Aug). *50th Death Anniv of Lawrence Hargrave (aviation pioneer).* P 13½.

379	**188**	5d. purple-brown, blk, yell-ochre and purple	15	10
		a. Purple (value) omitted	£350	

189 I.C.Y. Emblem

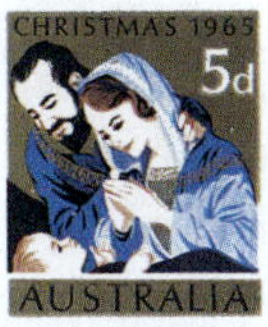

190 "Nativity Scene"

(Des H. Fallu from U.N. theme. Photo)

1965 (1 Sept). *International Co-operation Year.* P 13½.

380	**189**	2s.3d. emerald and light blue	65	1·50

(Des J. Mason. Photo)

1965 (20 Oct). *Christmas.* P 13½.

381	**190**	5d. multicoloured	15	10
		a. Gold omitted	£3000	
		b. Blue omitted	£600	

No. 381a comes from the bottom row of a sheet in which the gold is completely omitted, the background appearing as black with "CHRISTMAS 1965" and "AUSTRALIA" omitted. The row above had the gold missing from the lower two-fifths of the stamp.

(New Currency. 100 cents = 1 dollar)

191 Queen Elizabeth II

192 Blue-faced Honeyeater

193 White-tailed Dascyllus ("Humbug Fish")

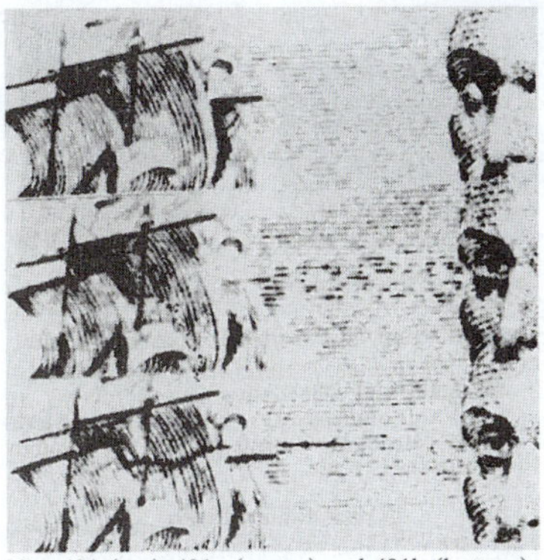

Nos. 401 (top), 401a (centre) and 401b (bottom). No. 401b shows the final form of the variety with a plate crack visible in sky and across sail (Lower sheet left pane. R. 10/1)

(Des Betty Temple-Watts (6c. (No. 387), 13c., 24c.), Eileen Mayo (7c. (No. 388) to 10c.). Recess (T **191**, 40c. to $4). Photo (others))

1966 (14 Feb)–**73**. *Decimal currency. T* **191/3** *and similar designs, some reused from previous issues.* P 15×14 (T **191**), 14 (40c., 75c., $1), 14½ (50c., $2, $4) or 13½ (others).

382	**191**	1c. deep red-brown	25	10
383		2c. olive-green	70	10
384		3c. slate-green	70	10
385		4c. red	20	10
		a. Booklet pane. Five stamps plus one printed label	16·00	
386	**175**	5c. brown, yellow, black and emerald-green	25	10
		a. Brown (plumage) omitted	£2250	
		b. Brown, yellow, black and blue-green (1.67)	25	20
386c	**191**	5c. deep blue (29.9.67)	70	10
		ca. Booklet pane. Five stamps plus one printed label	8·00	
		cb. Imperf in horiz strip of 3*	£2250	
387	**192**	6c. olive-yellow, black, blue and pale grey	1·25	1·00
		aa. Blue (eye markings) omitted	£1400	
387*a*	**191**	6c. orange (28.9.70)	1·00	10
388	**193**	7c. black, grey, salmon and brown	60	10
388*a*	**191**	7c. purple (1.10.71)	1·50	10
389	–	8c. red, yellow, blue-green and blackish green	60	1·00
390	–	9c. brown-red, purple-brown, black and light yellow-olive	60	20
391	–	10c. orange, blackish brown, pale turquoise blue and olive-brown	60	10
392	–	13c. red black, grey and light turq-green	1·50	25
		a. Red omitted	£2000	
		b. Grey (plumage and legs) omitted	£1800	
393	–	15c. rose-carmine, black, grey and light bluish green	1·25	1·50
		a. Rose-carmine omitted	£4000	
		b. Grey omitted	£1800	
394	–	20c. yellow, black and pink	2·00	15
		a. Yellow (plumage) omitted	£2500	
395	–	24c. ultramarine, yellow, black and light brown	65	1·25
396	–	25c. black, red, grey and green	2·00	30
		a. Red omitted	£5000	
397	–	30c. black, red, buff and light yellow-green	4·50	1·25
		a. Red omitted	£2000	
398	**167**	40c. ultramarine	3·00	10
399	**168**	50c. red-brown	3·00	10
400	**169**	75c. olive	1·00	1·00
401	**170**	$1 brown-purple (*shades*)	1·50	20
		a. Recut lines in sky	75·00	
		b. Recut lines and plate crack	£100	
		c. Perf 15×14† (9.73)	85·00	22·00
402	**171**	$2 deep reddish violet	6·00	1·00
403	**172**	$4 sepia	5·50	6·50
382/403 *Set of 25*			35·00	14·00
400/3 Optd "Specimen" *Set of 4*			75·00	

Designs: *Vert (as T* **193**)—8c. Copper-banded Butterflyfish ("Coral Fish"); 9c. Hermit Crab; 10c. Orange Clownfish ("Anemone Fish"). (*As T* **192**)—13c. Red-necked Avocet; 15c. Galah; 20c. Golden Whistler; 30c. Straw-necked Ibis. *Horiz* (*as T* **192**)—24c. Azure Kingfisher; 25c. Scarlet Robin. *As T* **167**—75c. Captain Cook; $1 Flinders and *Investigator*. *As T* **168**—$2 Bass and whaleboat; $4 Admiral King and *Mermaid* (survey cutter).

*This shows two stamps imperforate all round and one imperforate at left only.

†The note below No. 553 also applies to No. 401c, its exact gauge being 14.8×14.1. No. 401 is 14.25×13.95.

Nos. 385a (from booklets SB39/a) and 386ca (from booklets SB42/3a) have the outer edges of the pane imperforate producing single stamps with one or two adjacent sides imperforate.

No. 385 was normally printed in Helecon ink. Early in 1967 experimental printings on different kinds of paper coated with Helecon or Derby Luminescents phosphor were put on sale. These cannot be distinguished by the naked eye.

199 Queen Elizabeth II

200 "Saving Life"

1966 (14 Feb)–**67**. *Coil stamps. Photo.* P 15×imperf.

404	**199**	3c. black, light brown and green	45	1·25
405		4c. black, light brown and light vermilion	35	60
405*a*		5c. black, light brown and new blue (1.10.67)	40	10
404/5a *Set of 3*			1·10	1·75

(Des L. Mason. Photo)

1966 (6 July). *75th Anniv of Royal Life Saving Society.* P 13½.

406	**200**	4c. black, bright blue and blue	15	10

201 "Adoration of the Shepherds"

202 *Eendracht*

(Des L. Stirling, after medieval engraving. Photo)

1966 (19 Oct). *Christmas.* P 13½.

407	**201**	4c. black and yellow-olive	10	10
		a. Value omitted	£3000	

No. 407a was caused by a partial omission of the yellow-olive so that there was no colour surrounding the white face value.

(Des F. Eidlitz. Photo)

1966 (24 Oct). *350th Anniv of Dirk Hartog's Landing in Australia.* P 13½.

408	**202**	4c. multicoloured	10	10
		a. Red (sphere) omitted	£3000	
		b. Gold omitted	£1200	

203 Open Bible

204 Ancient Keys and Modern Lock

(Des L. Stirling. Photo)

1967 (7 Mar). *150th Anniv of British and Foreign Bible Society in Australia.* P 13½.

409	**203**	4c. multicoloured	10	10

Broken frame between "R" and "S" of "YEARS" (Left-hand pane, R. 8/1)

(Des G. Andrews. Photo)

1967 (5 Apr). *150th Anniv of Australian Banking.* P 13½.

410	**204**	4c. black, light blue and emerald	10	10
		a. Broken frame	3·00	

205 Lions Badge and 50 Stars

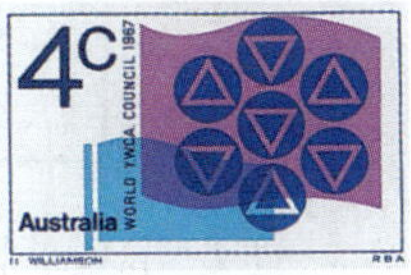

206 Y.W.C.A. Emblem

(Des M. Ripper. Photo)

1967 (7 June). *50th Anniv of Lions International.* P 13½.

411	**205**	4c. black, gold and blue	10	10

(Des H. Williamson. Photo)

1967 (21 Aug). *World Y.M.C.A. Council Meeting, Monash University, Melbourne.* P 13½.

412	**206**	4c. deep blue, ultramarine, light purple and light blue	10	10

207 Anatomical Figures

5c
(208)

(Des R. Ingpen. Photo)

1967 (20 Sept). *Fifth World Gynaecology and Obstetrics Congress, Sydney.* P 13½.

413	**207**	4c. black, blue and light reddish violet	10	10

1967 (29 Sept). *No. 385 surch with T* **208**.

414	**191**	5c. on 4c. red	35	10
		a. Booklet pane. Five stamps plus one printed label	1·25	

No. 414 was only issued in 50c. or $1 booklets, Nos. SB40/1ab, with the outer edges of the pane imperforate so all stamps have one or two adjacent sides imperforate. It only exists printed in Helecon ink.

209 Christmas Bells and Gothic Arches

210 Religious Symbols

(Des M. Ripper (5c.), Erica McGilchrist (25c.). Photo)

1967. *Christmas.* P 13½.

415	**209**	5c. multicoloured (18.10.67)	20	10
		a. Imperf three sides (vert pair)	£9000	
416	**210**	25c. multicoloured (27.11.67)	1·00	1·90

No. 415a show the stamps perforated at left only.

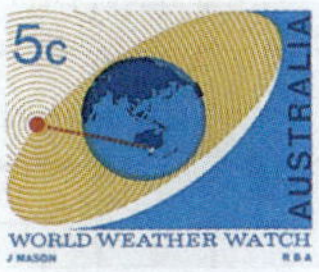

211 Satellite in Orbit

212 World Weather Map

(Des J. Mason. Photo)

1968 (20 Mar). *World Weather Watch.* P 13½.

417	**211**	5c. orange-brown, pale blue, black and ochre	30	10
418	**212**	20c. orange-brown, blue and black	1·10	2·75
		a. White (radio waves) omitted	£1000	
		b. Orange-brown (triangle) omitted	£2750	

213 Radar Antenna

214 Kangaroo Paw (Western Australia)

(Des R. Ingpen. Photo)

1968 (20 Mar). *World Telecommunications via Intelsat II.* P 13½.
419 **213** 25c. greenish blue, black and light blue-green ... 1·25 2·50

Type I

Type II

The 30c. was reprinted in 1971 from new cylinders so that Type II shows greater areas of white in the pink tones of the petals.

(Des Nell Wilson (6c., 30c.); R. and P. Warner (13c., 25c.); Dorothy Thornhill (15c., 20c.). Photo)

1968 (10 July)–**71**. *State Floral Emblems. T* **214** *and similar vert designs. Multicoloured.* P 13½.
420 6c. Type **214** ... 45 1·25
421 13c. Pink Heath (Victoria) ... 50 70
422 15c. Tasmanian Blue Gum (Tasmania) ... 70 40
423 20c. Sturt's Desert Pea (South Australia) ... 1·50 75
424 25c. Cooktown Orchid (Queensland) ... 1·10 75
425 30c. Waratah (New South Wales) (Type I) ... 50 10
a. Green (leaves) omitted ... £2000
b. Type II (29.6.71) ... 4·75 2·00
420/5 *Set of* 6 ... 4·25 3·50

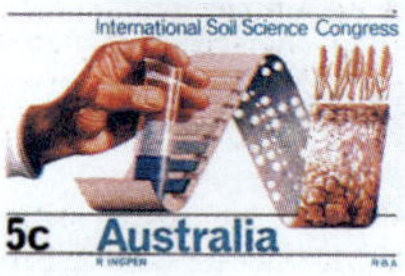

220 Soil Sample Analysis

(Des R. Ingpen. Photo)

1968 (6 Aug). *International Soil Science Congress and World Medical Association Assembly. T* **220** *and similar horiz design.* P 13½.
426 **220** 5c. orange-brown, stone, greenish blue and black ... 10 10
a. Nos. 426/7 *se-tenant* with gutter margin between ... 8·00 15·00
427 – 5c. greenish blue, dull ol-yell, rose and black ... 10 10

Design:—No. 427, Rubber-gloved hands, syringe and head of Hippocrates.

The above were printed in sheets of 100 containing a pane of 50 of each design.

The major shades formerly listed have been deleted as there is a range of intermediate shades.

222 Athlete carrying Torch, and Sunstone Symbol

223 Sunstone Symbol and Mexican Flag

(Des H. Williamson. Photo)

1968 (2 Oct). *Olympic Games, Mexico City.* P 13½.
428 **222** 5c. multicoloured ... 30 10
429 **223** 25c. multicoloured ... 40 1·50
a. Green (left-hand panel) omitted ... £1500

224 Houses and Dollar Signs

225 Church Window and View of Bethlehem

(Des Erica McGilchrist. Photo)

1968 (16 Oct). *Building and Savings Societies Congress.* P 13½.
430 **224** 5c. multicoloured ... 10 40

(Des G. Hamori. Photo)

1968 (23 Oct). *Christmas.* P 13½.
431 **225** 5c. multicoloured ... 10 10
a. Green window (gold omitted) ... £600
b. Red (inscr) omitted ... £1500

226 Edgeworth David (geologist)

(Des Note Ptg Branch (Nos. 432, 434) A. Cook (others). Recess, background litho)

1968 (6 Nov). *Famous Australians (1st series). T* **226** *and similar vert portraits.* P 15×14.
432 5c. myrtle-green/*pale green* ... 25 20
a. Booklet pane. Five stamps plus one printed label ... 1·40
433 5c. black/*pale blue* ... 25 20
a. Booklet pane. Five stamps plus one printed label ... 1·40
434 5c. blackish brown/*pale buff* ... 25 20
a. Booklet pane. Five stamps plus one printed label ... 1·40
435 5c. deep violet/*pale lilac* ... 25 20
a. Booklet pane. Five stamps plus one printed label ... 1·40
432/5 *Set of* 4 ... 90 70

Designs:—No. 432, Type **226**; No. 433, A. B. Paterson (poet); No. 434, Albert Namatjira (artist); No. 435, Caroline Chisholm (social worker).

Nos. 432/5 were only issued in $1 booklets, Nos. SB44/a, with the outer edges of the pane imperforate so all stamps have one or two adjacent sides imperforate.

See also Nos. 446/9, 479/82, 505/8, 537/40, 590/5, 602/7 and 637/40.

230 Macquarie Lighthouse

231 Pioneers and Modern Building, Darwin

(Des and eng Note Ptg Branch. Recess; background litho)

1968 (27 Nov). *150th Anniv of Macquarie Lighthouse.* P 14½×13½.
436 **230** 5c. black and pale yellow ... 30 70

Used examples are known with the pale yellow background colour omitted.

(Des Marietta Lyon. Photo)

1969 (5 Feb). *Centenary of Northern Territory Settlement.* P 13½.
437 **231** 5c. blackish brown, yellow-olive and yellow-ochre ... 10 10

232 Melbourne Harbour

233 Concentric Circles (symbolising Management, Labour and Government)

(Des J. Mason. Photo)

1969 (26 Feb). *Sixth Biennial Conference of International Association of Ports and Harbours, Melbourne.* P 13½.
438 **232** 5c. multicoloured ... 20 10

(Des G. Hamori. Photo)

1969 (4 June). *50th Anniv of International Labour Organisation.* P 13½.
439 **233** 5c. multicoloured ... 15 10
a. Gold (middle circle) omitted ... £2250

234 Sugar Cane

238 "The Nativity" (stained-glass window)

240 Edmund Barton

(Des R. Ingpen. Photo)

1969 (17 Sept). *Primary Industries. T* **234** *and similar vert designs. Multicoloured.* P 13½.
440 7c. Type **234** ... 50 1·50
441 15c. Timber ... 75 2·50
a. Black ("Australia" and value) omitted ... £1400
442 20c. Wheat ... 30 60
443 25c. Wool ... 50 1·50
440/3 *Set of* 4 ... 1·90 5·50

(Des G. Hamori (5c.), J. Coburn (25c.). Photo)

1969 (15 Oct). *Christmas. T* **238** *and similar multicoloured designs.* P 13½.
444 5c. Type **238** ... 20 10
a. Magenta (robe) omitted ... £800
b. Yellow omitted ... £850
445 25c. "Tree of Life", Christ in Crib and Christmas Star (abstract) ... 1·00 2·00

(Des from drawings by J. Santry. Recess, background litho)

1969 (22 Oct). *Famous Australians (2nd series). Prime Ministers. T* **240** *and similar vert designs each black on pale green.* P 15×14.
446 5c. Type **240** ... 40 20
a. Booklet pane. Five stamps plus one printed label ... 1·75
447 5c. Alfred Deakin ... 40 20
a. Booklet pane. Five stamps plus one printed label ... 1·75
448 5c. J. C. Watson ... 40 20
a. Booklet pane. Five stamps plus one printed label ... 1·75
449 5c. G. H. Reid ... 40 20
a. Booklet pane. Five stamps plus one printed label ... 1·75
446/9 *Set of* 4 ... 1·40 70

Nos. 446/9 were only issued in $1 booklets, Nos. SB45/a, with the outer edges of the pane imperforate so all stamps have one or two adjacent sides imperforate.

244 Capt. Ross Smith's Vickers Vimy, 1919

247 Symbolic Track and Diesel Locomotive

(Des E. Thake. Photo)

1969 (12 Nov). *50th Anniv of First England–Australia Flight. T* **244** *and similar horiz designs.* P 13½.
450 5c. olive-green, pale blue, black and red ... 15 10
a. Strip of 3. Nos. 450/2 ... 1·50 1·75
451 5c. black, red and olive-green ... 15 10
452 5c. olive-green, black, pale blue and red ... 15 10
450/2 *Set of* 3 ... 1·50 25

Designs:—No. 450, Type **244**; No. 451, Lt. H. Fysh and Lt. P. McGinness on 1919 survey with Ford Model T runabout; No. 452, Capt. Wrigley and Sgt. Murphy in Royal Aircraft Factory B.E.2E taking off to meet the Smiths.

The three designs appear *se-tenant*, both horizontally and vertically, throughout the sheet.

(Des B. Sadgrove. Photo)

1970 (11 Feb). *Sydney–Perth Standard Gauge Railway Link.* P 13½.
453 **247** 5c. multicoloured ... 15 10

248 Australian Pavilion, Osaka

251 Australian Flag

(Des J. Copeland (5c.), A. Leydin (20c.). Photo)

1970 (16 Mar). *World Fair, Osaka. T* **248** *and similar horiz design.* P 13½.
454 5c. multicoloured ... 15 10
455 20c. orange-red and black ... 35 65

Design:—20c. "Southern Cross" and "from the Country of the South with warm feelings" (message).

(Des P.O. Artists (5c.), J. Mason (30c.). Photo)

1970 (31 Mar). *Royal Visit. T* **251** *and similar horiz design.* P 13½.
456 5c. black and deep ochre ... 35 15
457 30c. multicoloured ... 1·10 2·50

Design:—5c. Queen Elizabeth II and Prince Philip.

252 Lucerne Plant, Bull and Sun

253 Captain Cook and H.M.S. *Endeavour*

5c. (No. 459). Red mark on sail at left (Top pane, R. 5/1)

(Des R. Ingpen. Photo)

1970 (13 Apr). *Eleventh International Grasslands Congress, Queensland.* P 13½.
458 **252** 5c. multicoloured 10 80

(Des R. Ingpen and "Team" (T. Keneally, A. Leydin, J. R. Smith). Photo)

1970 (20 Apr). *Bicentenary of Captain Cook's Discovery of Australia's East Coast. T* **253** *and similar multicoloured designs.* P 13½.
459 5c. Type **253** 35 10
a. Strip of 5. Nos. 459/63 .... 1·60 1·50
aa. Black omitted £12000
b. Red mark on sail .... 2·00
460 5c. Sextant and H.M.S. *Endeavour* 35 10
461 5c. Landing at Botany Bay 35 10
462 5c. Charting and exploring 35 10
463 5c. Claiming possession 35 10
464 30c. Captain Cook, H.M.S. *Endeavour*, sextant, aborigines and kangaroo (63 × 30 mm) .... 1·25 2·50
459/64 *Set of* 6 .... 2·75 2·75
MS465 157×129 mm. Nos. 459/64. Imperf .... 7·50 9·00

The 5c. stamps were issued horizontally *se-tenant* within the sheet, to form a composite design in the order listed.

Three used single 5c. stamps are also known with the black omitted.

50,000 miniature sheets were made available by the Post Office to the organisers of the Australian National Philatelic Exhibition which overprinted them in the white margin at each side of the 30c. stamp with "Souvenir Sheet AUSTRALIAN NATIONAL PHILATELIC EXHIBITION" at left and "ANPEX 1970 SYDNEY 27 APRIL–1 MAY" at right in light red-brown and they were also serially numbered. These were put on sale at the exhibition on the basis of one sheet to each visitor paying 30c. for admission. Although still valid for postage, since the stamps themselves had not been defaced, these sheets were not sold at post offices.

Subsequently further supplies were purchased and similarly overprinted and numbered by a private firm without the authority of the Post Office and ANPEX took successful legal action to stop their further sale to the public. This firm also had the unoverprinted sheets rouletted in colour between the stamps whilst further supplies of the normal sheets were overprinted with reproductions of old coins and others with an inscription commemorating the opening of Melbourne Airport on 1st July 1970, but all these are private productions. Further private productions have been reported.

259 Sturt's Desert Rose

AUSTRALIA **AUSTRALIA**
I. II.

Two types of 2c.

I. "AUSTRALIA" thin: "2c" thin; flower name lightly printed.
II. Redrawn. "AUSTRALIA" thicker; "2c" much more heavily printed; flower name thicker and bolder.

(Des Note Ptg Branch. Photo)

1970–75. *Coil Stamps. Vert designs as T* **259**. *Multicoloured. White fluorescent paper (10c.).* Perf 15×imperf.
465*a* 2c. Type **259** (I) (1.10.71) 40 20
ab. White fluorescent paper 40
b. Type II (white fluorescent paper) .... 1·00 45
ba. Yellow omitted £1500
466 4c. Type **259** (27.4.70) .... 85 1·75
467 5c. Golden Wattle (27.4.70) 20 10
a. White fluorescent paper 20
468 6c. Type **259** (28.9.70) .... 1·25 1·00
a. Green (leaves) omitted £2000
468*b* 7c. Sturt's Desert Pea (1.10.71) 40 70
ba. Black (berries, "7c." and inscr) omitted £1700
bb. Buff (shadows on flowers) omitted £225
bc. Buff and green (leaves) omitted .... 75·00
bd. White fluorescent paper (10.73) 40
468*d* 10c. As 7c. (15.1.75) .... 60 1·25
465a/8d *Set of* 6 .... 3·25 4·50

Nos. 465*a*/8*d* have horizontal coil perforations described after No. 191.

One used example of No. 468 is known with the magenta omitted.

Examples of No. 468bb also show the green colour displaced downwards.

For notes on white fluorescent paper see after No. 504.

264 Snowy Mountains Scheme

265 Rising Flames

7c. Broken pylon leg (Left pane, R. 7/4).

(Des L. Mason (7c.), R. Ingpen (8c., 9c.), B. Sadgrove (10c.). Photo)

1970 (31 Aug). *National Development (1st series). T* **264** *and similar horiz designs. Multicoloured.* P 13½.
469 7c. Type **264** 20 80
a. Broken pylon leg .... 6·00
470 8c. Ord River Scheme 10 15
471 9c. Bauxite to aluminium 15 15
472 10c. Oil and Natural Gas 30 10
469/72 *Set of* 4 .... 65 1·10

See also Nos. 541/4.

(Des G. Hamori, Photo)

1970 (2 Oct). *16th Commonwealth Parliamentary Association Conference, Canberra.* P 13½.
473 **265** 6c. multicoloured 10 10

266 Milk Analysis and Dairy Herd

267 "The Nativity"

(Des R. Honisett. Photo)

1970 (7 Oct). *18th International Dairy Congress, Sydney.* P 13½.
474 **266** 6c. multicoloured 10 10

(Des W. Beasley. Photo)

1970 (14 Oct). *Christmas.* P 13½.
475 **267** 6c. multicoloured 10 10

268 U.N. "Plant" and Dove of Peace

269 Boeing 707 and Avro 504

(Des Monad Design and Visual Graphics. Photo)

1970 (19 Oct). *25th Anniv of United Nations.* P 13½.
476 **268** 6c. multicoloured 15 10

(Des G. Hamori. Photo)

1970 (2 Nov). *50th Anniv of QANTAS Airline. T* **269** *and similar horiz design. Multicoloured.* P 13½.
477 6c. Type **269** 30 10
478 30c. Avro 504 and Boeing 707 .... 70 1·50

270 The Duigan Brothers (Pioneer Aviators)

(Des A. Cook (No. 480), T. Adams (No. 482), Note Ptg Branch (others). Recess (background litho))

1970 (16 Nov). *Famous Australians (3rd series). T* **270** *and similar vert designs.* P 15×14.
479 6c. blue 50 20
a. Booklet pane. Five stamps plus one printed label .... 2·50
480 6c. black/*cinnamon* 50 20
a. Booklet pane. Five stamps plus one printed label .... 2·50
481 6c. purple/*pale pink* 50 20
a. Booklet pane. Five stamps plus one printed label .... 2·50
482 6c. brown-lake/*flesh* 50 20
a. Booklet pane. Five stamps plus one printed label .... 2·50
479/82 *Set of* 4 .... 1·75 75

Designs:—No. 479 Type **270**; No. 480 Lachlan Macquarie (Governor of N.S.W.); No. 481 Adam Lindsay Gordon (poet); No. 482 E.J. Eyre (explorer).

Nos. 479/82 were only issued in 60c. or $1.20 booklets, Nos. SB46/8a, with the outer edges of the pane imperforate so all stamps have one or two adjacent sides imperforate.

STAMP BOOKLETS

Illustrations of booklet covers are reduced to ½ size, *unless otherwise stated.*

All booklets from 1913 to 1949 were stapled.

1913 (17 Jan). *Red on pink cover* (SB1) *or blue on pink cover with map of Australia on front and picture of State G.P.O. on back* (SB2).
SB1 2s. booklet containing twelve ½d. and eighteen 1d. (Nos. 1/2) in blocks of 6 .... £1700
SB2 £1 booklet containing two hundred and forty 1d. (No. 2) in blocks of 30 .... £17000

1914 (6 Oct)–**18**. *Red on pink cover* (Nos. SB2*a*/3), *black on red cover* (No. SB4) *or blue on pink cover with map of Australia on front and picture of State G.P.O. on back* (No. SB5).
SB2*a* 2s. booklet containing twelve ½d. and eighteen 1d. (Nos. 1, 21c) in blocks of 6 .... £3750
SB3 2s. booklet containing twelve ½d. and eighteen 1d. (Nos. 20, 21c) in blocks of 6 (1915) £3250
SB4 2s. booklet containing twenty-four 1d. (No. 21c) in blocks of 6 (10.5.17) £3250
a. Black on green cover £3750
b. Red on green cover £3500
SB5 £1 booklet containing two hundred and forty 1d. (No. 21c) in blocks of 30 .... £17000
a. Back cover without G.P.O. picture (1918) .. £19000

Records show that a £1 booklet containing one hundred and twenty 2d. stamps was issued in very limited quantities during 1914. No examples are known to have survived.

1919 (Jan–Apr). *Black on pink* (Nos. SB6/7) *or black on green* (*Nos.* SB8/9c) *covers.*
SB6 2s.3d. booklet containing eighteen 1½d. (No. 58) in blocks of 6 .... £2750
a. Black on green cover £2750
SB7 2s.3d. booklet containing eighteen 1½d. (No. 51) in blocks of 6 .... £2750
a. Black on green cover £2750
SB8 2s.3d. booklet containing eighteen 1½d. (No. 59) in blocks of 6 (Apr) £2750
a. Black on pink cover £2750
SB9 2s.3d. booklet containing eighteen 1½d. (No. 52) in blocks of 6 (Apr) £2750
a. Black on pink cover ....
b. Black on blue cover £2750
SB9*c* £1 booklet containing one hundred and sixty 1½d. (No. 51) in blocks of 20 .... £19000
SB9*d* £1 booklet containing one hundred and sixty 1½d. (No. 52) in blocks of 20 (Apr) £17000

1920 (Dec)–**22**. *Black on blue* (Nos. SB10, SB12), *black on white* (No. SB11) *or black on brown* (No. SB14) *covers.*
SB10 2s. booklet containing twelve 2d. (No. 62) in blocks of 6 .... £3250
a. Black on pink cover £3250
b. Black on orange cover (3.22) £3750
SB11 2s. booklet containing twelve 2d. (No. 63) in blocks of 6 (3.22) £4000
a. Black on orange cover (7.22) £3500
b. Black on pink cover £3250
c. Brown on buff cover £3500
d. Brown on pink cover £3500
SB12 £1 booklet containing one hundred and twenty 2d. (No. 62) in blocks of 15 (1.21) £18000
a. Black on pink cover ....
SB13 £1 booklet containing ninety 2d. and fifteen 4d. (Nos. 63, 65) in blocks of 15 (3.22) ....
SB14 £1 booklet containing one hundred and twenty 2d. (No. 63) in blocks of 15 (8.22) £17000

1923 (Oct)–**24**. *Black on rose* (No. SB15), *or green on pale green* (Nos. SB16/18) *covers.*
SB15 2s.3d. booklet containing eighteen 1½d. (No. 61) in blocks of 6 .... £2750
a. Black on pale green cover £2750
b. Green on pale green cover £2250
SB16 2s.3d. booklet containing eighteen 1½d. (No. 77) in blocks of 6 (5.24) £2000
SB17 £1 booklet containing one hundred and sixty 1½d. (No. 61) in blocks of 20 (3.24) £15000
SB18 £1 booklet containing one hundred and sixty 1½d. (No. 77) in blocks of 20 (5.24) £15000

1927 (Jan–June). *Green on pale green covers.*
SB19 2s.3d. booklet containing eighteen 1½d. (No. 87) in blocks of 6 .... £1400
SB20 2s.3d. booklet containing eighteen 1½d. (No. 96) in blocks of 6 .... £1400
SB21 £1 booklet containing one hundred and sixty 1½d.(No. 96) in blocks of 20 (June) £12000

1927 (9 May). *Opening of Parliament House, Canberra. Green on pale green cover with picture of H.M.S.* Renown *on back (2s.).*
SB22 2s. booklet containing sixteen 1½d. (No. 105) in blocks of 8 .... 85·00

Examples of a 10s. booklet containing eighty 1½d. (No. 105) are known without a front cover and with the back cover blank. There is no record that this was an official issue.

1928 (Nov). *Green on pale green cover.*
SB23 2s.3d. booklet containing eighteen 1½d. (No. 96a or 96w) in blocks of 6 .... £400

1930 (July)–**35**. *Air. Black on blue cover inscr "*AIR MAIL. SAVES TIME*" and biplane.*
SB24 3s. booklet containing twelve 3d. (No. 115) in blocks of 4 plus two panes of air mail labels £750
a. Black on pale green cover inscr "USE THE AIR MAIL" and monoplane (5.35) £1400

1930 (9 Sep)–**33**. *Green on pale green covers inscr* "USE THE AIR MAIL" *on the back (2s).*

SB25 2s. booklet containing twelve 2d. (No. 99a or 99aw) in blocks of 6 .... £350
SB25*a* 2s. booklet containing twelve 2d. (No. 127 or 127w) in blocks of 6 (1.32) £350
ab. Cover with parcel rates on back (1933) £475
SB26 £1 booklet containing one hundred and twenty 2d. (No. 99) in blocks of 20 .... £9500
SB26*a* £1 booklet containing one hundred and twenty 2d. (No. 99a) in blocks of 20 .... £9500

1934 (June). *Black on cream cover inscr* "Address your mail fully..." *on front.*

SB26*b* 2s. booklet containing twelve 2d. (No. 127 or 127w) in blocks of 6 .... £600

1935–38. *Black on green cover with Commonwealth Savings Bank advertisement on front inscr* "WHEREVER THERE IS A MONEY ORDER POST OFFICE".

SB26*c* 2s. booklet containing twelve 2d. (No. 127 or 127w) in blocks of 6 .... £425
ca. Front cover inscr "IN MOST MONEY ORDER OFFICES" (1936) £400
cb. Ditto with waxed interleaves (1938) £475

1938 (Dec). *Black on green cover as No.* SB26*c*. *Postal rates on interleaves.*

SB27 2s. booklet containing twelve 2d. (No. 184 or 184w) in blocks of 6 .... £450
a. With waxed interleaves. Postal rates on back cover £600
b. Black on buff cover £600

1942 (Aug). *Black on buff cover, size 73×47½ mm. Postal rates on interleaves.*

SB28 2s.6d. booklet containing twelve 2½d. (No. 206 or 206w) in blocks of 6, upright within the booklet £110
a. With waxed interleaves. Postal rates on back cover £225

1949 (Sept). *Black on buff cover, size 79½×42½ mm including figure of Hermes.*

SB29 2s.6d. booklet containing twelve 2½d. (No. 206) in blocks of 6, sideways within the booklet .... 80·00

B 1

1952 (24 June). *Vermilion and deep blue on green cover as Type* B **1**.

SB30 3s.6d. booklet containing twelve 3½d. (No. 247) in blocks of 6 .... 17·00
a. With waxed interleaves .... 90·00

B **1a**

1953 (8 July)–**56**. *Vermilion and deep blue on green cover as Type* B **1a**.

SB31 3s. on 6d. booklet containing twelve 3½d. (No. 263) in blocks of 6 .... 11·00
a. With waxed interleaves .... 23·00
SB32 3s. on 6d. booklet containing twelve 3½d. (No. 262a) in blocks of 6 (7.56) .... 23·00
a. With waxed interleaves .... 80·00

B 2

1957 (13 Mar)–**59**. *Vermilion and deep blue on green cover as Type* B **2**.

SB33 4s. booklet containing two panes of 6 4d. (No. 282ab) .... 15·00
a. With waxed interleaves .... 45·00
SB34 4s. booklet containing two panes of 6 4d. (No. 313ab) (18.3.59) .... 38·00
a. With waxed interleaves .... 80·00

B 3

1960 (23 Mar). *Vermilion and deep blue on green cover as Type* B **3**.

SB35 5s. booklet containing two panes of 6 5d. (No. 314d) .... 20·00
a. With waxed interleaves .... 45·00

B 4

1962 (1 July)–**65**. *Rose and emerald on green cover as Type* B **4**.

SB36 5s. booklet containing two panes of 6 5d. (No. 314d) .... 45·00
a. With waxed interleaves (1963) £100
SB37 5s. booklet containing two panes of 6 5d. (No. 354a) (17.6.64) .... 40·00
a. With waxed interleaves £100
SB38 5s. booklet containing two panes of 6 5d. (No. 354cb) (13.7.65) .... 50·00
a. With waxed interleaves £120

B 5

1966 (14 Feb). *Greenish blue and black on yellow-olive cover as Type* B **5**.

SB39 60c. booklet containing three panes of 5 4c. and 1 label (No. 385a) .... 45·00
a. With waxed interleaves £130

1967 (29 Sept). *Greenish blue and black on yellow-olive covers as Type* B **5**.

(a) Surcharged covers.

SB40 50c. booklet containing two panes of 5 5c. on 4c. and 1 label (No. 414a) .... 12·00
SB41 $1 booklet containing four panes of 5 5c. on 4c. and 1 label (No. 414a) .... 5·50
a. Normal cover as Type B **5** .... 6·00
ab. With waxed interleaves .... 55·00

(b) Normal covers.

SB42 50c. booklet containing two panes of 5 5c. and 1 label (No. 386ca) .... 15·00
SB43 $1 booklet containing four panes of 5 5c. and 1 label (No. 386ca) .... 23·00
a. With waxed interleaves .... 65·00

Booklets SB40/1ab were intended as provisional issues until supplies of the new 5c. became available in booklet form, but in the event these were put on sale on the same date.

B 6

1968 (6 Nov). *Famous Australians (1st series). Black, red, white and blue cover as Type* B **6**.

SB44 $1 booklet containing four panes of 5 5c. and 1 label (Nos. 432a, 433a, 434a, 435a) .... 5·00
a. With waxed interleaves .... 50·00

B 7

1969 (22 Oct). *Famous Australians (2nd series). Olive-green, gold and black cover as Type* B **7**.

SB45 $1 booklet containing four panes of 5 5c. and 1 label (Nos. 446a, 447a, 448a, 449a) .... 6·00
a. With waxed interleaves .... 60·00

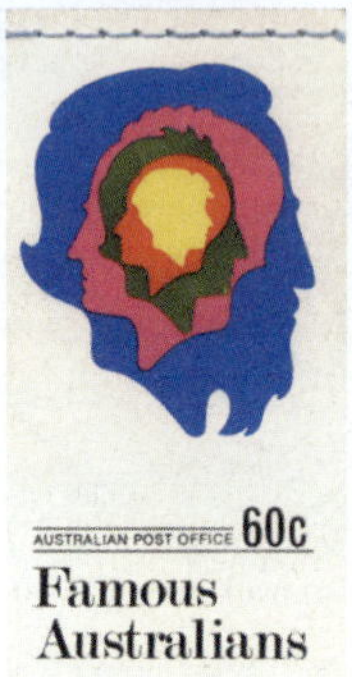

B **8**

(Des B. Young. Eng S. Reading. Typo J. B. Cooke)

1970 (16 Nov). *Famous Australians (3rd series). Multicoloured on white covers as Type* B **8**.

SB46 60c. booklet containing two panes of 5 6c. and 1 label (Nos. 479a, 480a) .... 11·00
SB47 60c. booklet containing two panes of 5 6c. and 1 label (Nos. 481a, 482a) .... 11·00
SB48 $1.20 booklet containing four panes of 5 6c. and 1 label (Nos. 479a, 480a, 481a, 482a) .... 9·00
a. With waxed interleaves .... 60·00

Military Post Booklets

Issued for the use of Australian Forces in Vietnam

MB 1

1967 (30 May–Sept). *Yellow-green and black on white cover as Type* MB **1**. *Pane attached by selvedge.*

MB1 50c. booklet containing 5c. (No. 386) in block of 10 .... 80·00
a. Containing No. 386b (Sept) .... 80·00

1968 (1 Mar). *Yellow-green and black on white cover as Type* MB **1**. *Pane attached by selvedge.*

MB2 50c. booklet containing 5c. (No. 386c) in block of 10 .... 50·00

POSTAGE DUE STAMPS

POSTAGE DUE PRINTERS. Nos. D1/62 were typographed at the New South Wales Government Printing Office, Sydney. They were not used in Victoria.

D 1

D 2

D 3

Type D **1** adapted from plates of New South Wales Type D **1**. No letters at foot.

1902 (1 Jul). *Chalk-surfaced paper.* Wmk Type D **2** (inverted on 1d., 3d. and 4d.).

(a) P 11½, 12.

D1	D **1**	½d. emerald-green *or* dull green	3·25	4·50
D2		1d. emerald-green	13·00	8·00
		w. Wmk upright	32·00	21·00
D3		2d. emerald-green	45·00	9·00
		w. Wmk inverted	£110	
D4		3d. emerald-green	35·00	23·00
		w. Wmk upright	38·00	27·00
D5		4d. emerald-green	42·00	12·00
		w. Wmk upright	50·00	22·00
D6		6d. emerald-green	55·00	9·50
		w. Wmk inverted	55·00	9·50
D7		8d. emerald-green *or* dull green	95·00	75·00
D8		5s. emerald-green *or* dull green	£180	70·00
D1/8 *Set of* 8			£400	£180
D1s/7s Opt "Specimen" *Set of* 7			£275	
		(b) P 11½, 12, compound with 11.		
D9	D **1**	1d. emerald-green	£275	£150
		w. Wmk upright	£300	£140
D10		2d. emerald-green	£400	£150
		w. Wmk inverted	£450	£170
		(c) P 11.		
D12	D **1**	1d. emerald-green (*wmk upright*)	£1300	£550

Stamps may be found showing portions of the marginal watermark "NEW SOUTH WALES POSTAGE".

1902 (July)–**04**. *Type* D **3** *(with space at foot filled in). Chalk-surfaced paper.* Wmk Type D **2** (inverted on 3d., 4d., 6d., 8d. and 5s.).

(a) P 11½, 12.

D13	D **3**	1d. emerald-green (10.02)	£200	95·00
D14		2d. emerald-green (3.03)	–	£120
D15		3d. emerald-green (3.03)	£250	80·00

No.	Type	Description	Unused	Used
D17		5d. emerald-green	50·00	10·00
D18		10d. emerald-green *or* dull green	75·00	17·00
D19		1s. emerald-green	55·00	14·00
D20		2s. emerald-green	£100	18·00
		(b) P 11½, 12, compound with 11.		
D22	D 3	½d. emerald-green *or* dull green (3.04)	10·00	8·00
		w. Wmk inverted	12·00	8·00
D23		1d. emerald-green *or* dull green (10.02)	10·00	3·00
		w. Wmk inverted	10·00	3·00
D24		2d. emerald-green *or* dull green (3.03)	27·00	3·00
		w. Wmk inverted	27·00	3·00
D25		3d. emerald-green *or* dull green (3.03)	65·00	16·00
		w. Wmk upright	85·00	27·00
D26		4d. emerald-green *or* dull green (5.03)	55·00	13·00
		w. Wmk upright	55·00	14·00
D27		5d. emerald-green	55·00	23·00
D28		6d. emerald-green (3.04)	55·00	10·00
D29		8d. emerald-green (3.04)	£120	50·00
D30		10d. emerald-green *or* dull green	£100	18·00
D31		1s. emerald-green	90·00	20·00
D32		2s. emerald-green	£130	27·00
D33		5s. emerald-green *or* dull green (5.03)	£250	22·00
		(c) P 11.		
D34	D 3	½d. emerald-green *or* dull green (wmk inverted) (3.04)	£350	£200
D35		1d. emerald-green *or* dull green (10.02)	£100	27·00
		w. Wmk inverted	£140	40·00
D36		2d. emerald-green (3.03)	£150	29·00
		w. Wmk inverted	£150	29·00
D37		3d. emerald-green *or* dull green (3.03)	80·00	42·00
		w. Wmk upright	80·00	42·00
D38		4d. emerald-green *or* dull green (5.03)	£170	60·00
		w. Wmk upright	£170	60·00
D39		5d. emerald-green	£275	48·00
D40		6d. emerald-green (3.04)	95·00	16·00
D41		1s. emerald-green	£325	38·00
D42		5s. emerald-green (5.03)	£800	£140
D43		10s. dull green (10.03)	£1800	£1800
D44		20s. dull green (10.03)	£4000	£2250
D13/44 *Set of* 14			£6000	£3750
D13s/44s Opt "Specimen" *Set of* 14			£850	

The 10s. and 20s. values were only issued in New South Wales.

The used prices quoted for Nos. D43/4 are for cancelled to order.

D 4

D 6

1906 (Jan)–**08**. *Chalk-surfaced paper.* Wmk Type D **4**.

No.	Type	Description	Unused	Used
		(a) P 11½, 12, compound with 11.		
D45	D 3	½d. green (1.07)	9·50	11·00
		w. Wmk inverted	9·50	11·00
D46		1d. green	18·00	3·75
		w. Wmk inverted	18·00	3·75
D47		2d. green	45·00	5·50
		w. Wmk inverted	45·00	5·50
D48		3d. green (7.08)	£600	£300
D49		4d. green (4.07)	60·00	23·00
		w. Wmk inverted	60·00	23·00
D50		6d. green (3.08)	£180	25·00
		w. Wmk inverted	£180	25·00
D45/50 *Set of* 6			£750	£300
		(b) P 11.		
D51	D 3	1d. dull green	£1800	£800
		aw. Wmk inverted	—	£800
D51*b*		2d. green	†	£1900
D52		4d. dull green (4.07)	£3500	£1800

No. D51*b* is only known pen-cancelled.

Shades exist.

1907 (July–Sept). *Chalk-surfaced paper.* Wmk Type **w 11** (Crown over double lined A) (inverted on ½d.). P 11½×11.

No.	Type	Description	Unused	Used
D53	D 3	½d. dull green	27·00	65·00
		w. Wmk upright	48·00	95·00
D54		1d. dull green (August)	75·00	45·00
		w. Wmk inverted	75·00	45·00
D55		2d. dull green (Sept)	£140	£110
		w. Wmk inverted	£160	£110
D56		4d. dull green (Sept)	£200	£100
		w. Wmk inverted	£200	£100
		y. Wmk inverted and reversed	£450	
D57		6d. dull green (Sept)	£225	£140
		w. Wmk inverted	—	£275
D53/7 *Set of* 5			£600	£400

1908 (Sept)–**09**. *Stroke after figure of value. Chalk-surfaced paper.* Wmk Type D **4** (inverted on 10s.).

No.	Type	Description	Unused	Used
		(a) P 11½×11.		
D58	D 6	1s. dull green (1909)	75·00	9·00
D59		5s. dull green	£225	48·00
		(b) P 11.		
D60	D 6	2s. dull green (1909)	£1000	£6000
D61		10s. dull green (1909)	£2500	£15000
D62		20s. dull green (1909)	£6500	£30000
D58/62 *Set of* 5			£9000	£48000

Nos. D61/2 were only issued in New South Wales. The used prices quoted for Nos. D60/2 are for examples with verified postal cancellations from the period of issue.

D 7

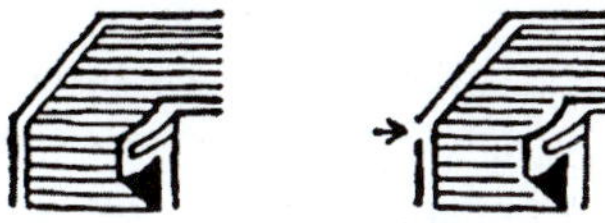
Die I Die II

1d.

Die I Die II

2d.

(Typo J. B. Cooke, Melbourne)

1909 (1 Jul)–**10**. Wmk Crown over A, Type **w 11**.

No.	Type	Description	Unused	Used
		(a) P 12×12½ (comb).		
D63	D 7	½d. rosine and yellow-green (8.09)	14·00	27·00
D64		1d. rosine and yellow-green (I)	14·00	4·00
		b. Die II (7.10)	22·00	1·75
D65		2d. rosine and yellow-green (I)	28·00	3·75
		a. Die II (8.10)	32·00	1·75
		aw. Wmk inverted		
D66		3d. rosine and yellow-green (9.09)	29·00	14·00
D67		4d. rosine and yellow-green (8.09)	30·00	5·00
D68		6d. rosine and yellow-green (8.09)	27·00	3·25
D69		1s. rosine and yellow-green (8.09)	30·00	2·75
D70		2s. rosine and yellow-green (8.09)	70·00	9·50
D71		5s. rosine and yellow-green (10.09)	90·00	13·00
D72		10s. rosine and yellow-green (11.09)	£250	£150
D73		£1 rosine and yellow-green (11.09)	£475	£275
D63/73 *Set of* 11			£900	£450
		(b) P 11.		
D74	D 7	1d. rose and yellow-green (II)	£2250	£1000
D74*a*		2d. rose and yellow-green (II)	£12000	£4500
D75		6d. rose and yellow-green	£16000	£13000

Only one unused example, without gum, and another pen-cancelled are known of No. D74*a*.

The 1d. of this printing is distinguishable from No. D78 by the colours, the green being very yellow and the rose having less of a carmine tone. The paper is thicker and slightly toned, that of No D78 being pure white; the gum is thick and yellowish, No. D78 having thin white gum.

All later issues of the 1d. and 2d. are Die II.

(Typo J.B. Cooke (later ptgs by T.S. Harrison))

1912 (Dec)–**23**. *Thin paper. White gum.* W **w 11**.

No.	Type	Description	Unused	Used
		(a) P 12½ (line).		
D76	D 7	½d. scarlet and pale yellow-green (7.13)	25·00	26·00
		w. Wmk inverted	42·00	35·00
		(b) P 11.		
D77	D 7	½d. rosine & bright apple-green (10.14)	11·00	17·00
		a. Wmk sideways	6·50	8·50
D78		1d. rosine & bright apple-green (8.14)	12·00	2·25
		a. Wmk sideways	16·00	2·25
		w. Wmk inverted	48·00	17·00
		(c) P 14.		
D79	D 7	½d. rosine and bright apple-green (11.14)	£130	£170
		a. Carmine and apple-green (Harrison) (1919)	9·00	16·00
D80		1d. rosine and bright apple-green (9.14)	60·00	14·00
		a. Scarlet and pale yellow-green (2.18)	20·00	7·00
		aw. Wmk inverted	†	£450
		b. Carmine and apple-green (Harrison) (1919)	13·00	3·75
D81		2d. scarlet and pale yellow-green (1.18)	17·00	9·00
		a. Carmine and apple-green (Harrison) (10.18)	20·00	4·25
D82		3d. rosine and apple-green (5.16)	75·00	32·00
		a. Wmk sideways	£5000	£3000
D83		4d. carmine and apple-green (Harrison) (5.21)	90·00	55·00
		b. Carmine and pale yellow-green	65·00	50·00
		ba. Wmk sideways	£800	£400
D85		1s. scarlet and pale yellow-green (6.23)	25·00	13·00
D86		10s. scarlet and pale yellow-green (5.21)	£1000	
D87		£1 scarlet and pale yellow-green (5.21)	£800	£1400
		(d) Perf 14 compound with 11.		
D88	D 7	1d. carmine and apple-green	£4000	
D76/88 *Set of* 8			£1800	

(Typo T. S. Harrison (to Feb 1926), A. J. Mullett (to June 1927) and J. Ash (thereafter))

1922 (1 May)–**30**. W **6**.

No.	Type	Description	Unused	Used
		(a) P 14.		
D91	D 7	½d. carmine and yellow-green (17.5.23)	2·50	6·50
D92		1d. carmine and yellow-green	4·00	1·00
D93		1½d. carmine and yellow-green (3.25)	1·50	9·00
D94		2d. carmine and yellow-green (3.3.22)	3·50	2·25
D95		3d. carmine and yellow-green	9·50	3·50
D96		4d. carmine and yellow-green (7.2.22)	35·00	15·00
D97		6d. carmine and yellow-green (8.22)	26·00	13·00
		(b) P 11.		
D98	D 7	4d. carmine and yellow-green (22.9.30)	7·00	4·50
D91/8 *Set of* 8			80·00	50·00

All values perforated 14 were printed by Harrison and all but the 1d. by Mullett and Ash. The 4d. perforated 11 was produced by J. Ash. There is a wide variation of shades in this issue.

(Typo J. Ash)

1931 (Oct)–**36**. W **15**.

No.	Type	Description	Unused	Used
		(a) P 14.		
D100	D 7	1d. carmine and yellow-green (10.31)	7·00	11·00
		a. Imperf between (horiz pair)	†	£13000
D102		2d. carmine and yellow-green (19.10.31)	7·00	11·00
		(b) P 11.		
D105	D 7	½d. carmine and yellow-green (4.34)	12·00	14·00
D106		1d. carmine and yellow-green (21.11.32)	7·50	2·25
D107		2d. carmine and yellow-green (1933)	10·00	75
D108		3d. carmine and yellow-green (5.36)	70·00	70·00
D109		4d. carmine and yellow-green (23.5.34)	6·50	3·25
D110		6d. carmine and yellow-green (4.36)	£375	£325
D111		1s. carmine and yellow-green (8.34)	50·00	35·00
D105/11 *Set of* 7			£475	£400

D 8

D 9

A B C

Type A. Solid rectangle inside "D" (ptgs of ½d., 1d., 2d., 4d. and 6d. from 1909 to 1945)

Type B. Shaded area inside "D" (ptgs of 3d. from 1909 to 1945)

Type C. Solid segment of circle inside "D" (ptgs of all values below 1s. from 1946)

D E

Type D. Six lines of shading above numeral and four below (ptgs of 1s. from 1909 to 1945)

Type E. Larger "1" with only three background lines above; hyphen more upright (ptgs of 1s. from 1946 to 1953)

(Frame recess. Value typo J. Ash (to 1940, then W. C. G. McCracken)).

1938 (1 Jul). W **15**. P 14½×14.

No.	Type	Description	Unused	Used
D112	D 8	½d. carmine and green (A) (Sept)	3·00	2·75
D113		1d. carmine and green (A)	10·00	60
D114		2d. carmine and green (A)	15·00	2·25
D115		3d. carmine and green (B) (Aug)	35·00	18·00
D116		4d. carmine and green (A) (Aug)	13·00	60
D117		6d. carmine and green (A) (Aug)	70·00	45·00
D118		1s. carmine and green (D) (Aug)	50·00	12·00
D112/18 *Set of* 7			£170	70·00

Shades exist.

1946–57. *Redrawn as Type C and E (1s).* W **15**. P 14½×14.

No.	Type	Description	Unused	Used
D119	D 9	½d. carmine and green (9.56)	1·25	3·25
D120		1d. carmine and green (17.6.46)	1·25	80
		w. Wmk inverted		
D121		2d. carmine and green (9.46)	5·50	1·25

D122		3d. carmine and green (6.8.46)	4·50	1·25
D123		4d. carmine and green (30.7.52)	8·00	2·50
D124		5d. carmine and green (16.12.48).	12·00	4·00
D125		6d. carmine and green (9.47)	11·00	2·00
D126		7d. carmine and green (26.8.53)	2·25	3·00
D127		8d. carmine and green (24.4.57)	4·00	16·00
D128		1s. carmine and green (9.47)	17·00	1·75
D119/28 *Set of* 10			60·00	32·00

There are many shades in this issue.

D 10

1953 (26 Aug)–**59**. W **15**. P 14½×14.

D129		1s. carmine & yellow-green (17.2.54)	7·50	2·00
		a. *Carmine and deep green*	12·00	5·50
D130		2s. carmine and yellow-green	14·00	8·00
		a. *Carmine and deep green*	£225	£100
D131		5s. carmine and green	14·00	4·00
		a. *Carmine and deep green* (6.59)	12·00	70
D129/31 *Set of* 3			32·00	12·50
D129a/31a *Set of* 3			£225	95·00

A new die was introduced for No. D131a. This differs from the original in having a distinct gap between the two arms of the "5". On No. D131 these two features are joined.

Two Dies of ½d.:
Die I. Six dots in base of "2"
Die II. Seven dots in base of "2"

I II

Two Dies of 1d. to 10d.:
Die I. Numeral, "D" and stop, generally unoutlined.
Die II. Clear white line separates numeral, etc. from background.

1958–60. No wmk. P 14½×14.

D132		½d. carmine & dp grn (I) (27.2.58)	3·00	2·50
		a. Die II (6.59)	2·50	1·25
D133		1d. carmine & dp green (I) (25.2.58)	2·50	3·00
D133*a*		Die II (6.59)	2·25	75
D134		3d. carmine & dp grn (II) (25.5.60)	1·75	3·00
D135		4d. carmine & dp green (I) (27.2.58)	4·75	7·00
		a. Die II (6.59)	2·50	5·00
D136		5d. carmine & dp green (I) (27.2.58)	11·00	15·00
		a. Die II (6.59)	60·00	60·00
D137		6d. carmine & dp grn (II) (25.5.60)	2·50	2·00
D138		8d. carmine & dp grn (II) (25.2.58)	6·00	28·00
D139		10d. carmine & dp grn (II) (9.12.59)	3·25	1·75
D140		1s. carmine and deep green (6.5.58)	5·50	2·25
		a. *Deep carmine & dp green* (6.59)	6·50	1·50
D141		2s. dp carmine & dp green (8.3.60)	12·00	10·00
D132/41 *Set of* 10			45·00	60·00

Nos. D140a and D141. Value tablets are re-engraved and have thicker and sharper printed lines than before.

The use of Postage Due stamps ceased on 13 January 1963.

OFFICIAL STAMPS

From 1902 the departments of the Commonwealth government were issued with stamps of the various Australian States perforated "OS" to denote official use. These were replaced in 1913 by Commonwealth of Australia issues with similar perforated initials as listed below.

During the same period the administrations of the Australian States used their own stamps and those of the Commonwealth perforated with other initials for the same purpose. These States issues are outside the scope of this catalogue.

Most shades listed under the postage issues also exist perforated "OS". Only those which are worth more than the basic colours are included below.

(O 1) (O 2) (11 holes in "S". Examples with 12 holes in "S" are N.S.W. state issues) (O 3)

1913 (Jan–Apr). *Nos. 1/16 punctured as Type* O **1**. W **2**. P 12.

O1	1	½d. green (Die I)	18·00	11·00
		w. Wmk inverted	†	90·00
O2		1d. red (Die I)	15·00	3·50
		cw. Wmk inverted	90·00	12·00
		d. Die II	22·00	7·00
		da. Wmk sideways	†	£600
		dw. Wmk inverted	90·00	17·00
O3		2d. grey (Die I)	32·00	14·00
O4		2½d. indigo (Die II)	£325	£140
O5		3d. olive (Die I)	£120	48·00
		ca. In pair with Die II	£800	
		dw. Wmk inverted	£170	65·00
		e. Die II	£350	£120
		ew. Wmk inverted	£600	£170
O6		4d. orange (Die II)	£180	21·00
		a. Orange-yellow	£300	90·00
O7		5d. chestnut (Die II)	£160	38·00
O8		6d. ultramarine (Die II)	£130	19·00
		w. Wmk inverted	£700	£275
O9		9d. violet (Die II)	£140	50·00
		w. Wmk inverted	†	£6000
O10		1s. emerald (Die II)	£180	25·00
		w. Wmk inverted	£1000	£400
O11		2s. brown (Die II)	£325	£140
		a. Double print	†	£3000
O12		5s. grey and yellow	£800	£425
O13		10s. grey and pink	£2500	£1300
O14		£1 brown and ultramarine	£3750	£2750
O15		£2 black and rose	£12000	£8000
O1/15 *Set of* 15			£18000	£11000

1914. *Nos. 1/16 punctured as Type* O **2**. W **2**. P 12.

O16	1	½d. green (Die I)	17·00	10·00
		w. Wmk inverted	†	55·00
O17		1d. red (Die I)	18·00	7·00
		d. Die II	25·00	3·75
		e. Die IIA	20·00	2·25
O18		2d. grey (Die I)	70·00	4·50
		w. Wmk inverted	£120	19·00
O19		2½d. indigo (Die II)	£300	£120
O20		3d. olive (Die I)	£100	15·00
		dw. Wmk inverted	£170	38·00
		e. Die II	£275	£110
		ew. Wmk inverted	£425	£160
O21		4d. orange (Die II)	£200	80·00
		a. Orange-yellow	£300	£110
O22		5d. chestnut (Die II)	£180	50·00
O23		6d. ultramarine (Die II)	£120	13·00
		w. Wmk inverted	†	£500
O24		9d. violet (Die II)	£130	30·00
O25		1s. emerald (Die II)	£130	22·00
O26		2s. brown (Die II)	£400	£100
O27		5s. grey and yellow		
O28		10s. grey and pink	£4000	
O29		£1 brown and ultramarine	£5000	£3000
O30		£2 black and rose	£14000	

1915. *Nos. 24 and 26/30 punctured as Type* O **2**. W **5**. P 12.

O31	1	2d. grey (Die I)	£120	11·00
O33		6d. ultramarine (Die II)	£200	15·00
		b. Die IIA	£3000	£850
O34		9d. violet (Die II)	£550	85·00
O35		1s. blue-green (Die II)	£550	75·00
O36		2s. brown (Die II)	£900	£130
O37		5s. grey and yellow	£1000	£150
		a. Yellow portion doubly printed	†	£3750
		w. Wmk inverted	£1100	£200

1914–21. *Nos. 20/3 punctured as Type* O **2**. W **5**. P 14¼×14 (comb).

O38	5a	½d. bright green	12·00	2·75
		a. Perf 14¼ (line)	†	£1700
		w. Wmk inverted	20·00	9·00
O39		1d. carmine-red (I) (No. 21c)	12·00	1·00
		gw. Wmk inverted	20·00	3·50
		h. Die II	£375	35·00
O41		4d. orange	50·00	3·50
		a. Yellow-orange	65·00	7·50
		b. Pale orange-yellow	£150	18·00
		c. Lemon-yellow	£375	60·00
		w. Wmk inverted	£100	25·00
O42		5d. brown (P 14¼ (line))	60·00	3·75
		aw. Wmk inverted	£400	£275
		b. Printed on the gummed side (wmk inverted)	£2500	
		c. Perf 14¼×14 (comb)	60·00	3·25
		cw. Wmk inverted	£325	£140

1915–28. *Nos. 35/45 punctured as Type* O **2**. W **6**. P 12.

O43	1	2d. grey (Die I)	27·00	7·00
		bw. Wmk inverted	48·00	38·00
		d. Die IIA	42·00	18·00
		da. Printed double	†	£2000
O44		2½d. deep blue (Die II)	65·00	16·00
		w. Wmk inverted	†	45·00
O45		3d. yellow-olive (Die I)	38·00	5·50
		cw. Wmk inverted	60·00	35·00
		d. Die II	£130	65·00
		dw. Wmk inverted	£225	£130
		e. Die IIB	32·00	20·00
		ew. Wmk inverted	70·00	45·00
O46		6d. ultramarine (Die II)	45·00	6·50
		a. Die IIA	£2250	£700
		d. Die IIB	75·00	25·00
		dw. Wmk inverted	£450	£180
O47		9d. violet (Die II)	40·00	18·00
		b. Die IIB	55·00	19·00
		bw. Wmk inverted	†	45·00
O48		1s. blue-green (Die II)	26·00	3·00
		aw. Wmk inverted	£750	£500
		b. Die IIB	26·00	3·50
O49		2s. brown (Die II)	£250	17·00
		b. Red-brown (aniline)	£650	£170
		w. Wmk inverted	£1400	£300
O50		5s. grey and yellow	£325	48·00
		w. Wmk inverted	£700	£425
O51		10s. grey and pink	£550	65·00
O52		£1 chocolate and dull blue	£3250	£1800
		ab. Wmk sideways. *Chestnut and bright blue*	£30000	
		aw. Wmk inverted	£3750	£2750
O53		£2 black and rose	£2500	£1200
O43/53 *Set of* 11			£6500	£3000

1916–20. *Nos. 47/f and 5d. as No. 23 punctured as Type* O **2**. *Rough paper*. W **5**. P 14.

O54	5a	1d. scarlet (Die I)	23·00	7·00
		a. Deep red	23·00	7·00
		b. Rose-red	23·00	7·00
		c. Rosine	65·00	14·00
		dw. Wmk inverted	30·00	11·00
		e. Die II. *Rose-red*	£250	18·00
		f. Die II. *Rosine*	£450	48·00
		fw. Wmk inverted		
O60		5d. bright chestnut (P 14¼ (line) (9.20)	£2250	£160

All examples of the 5d. on this paper were perforated "OS".

1918–20. *Nos. 48/52 punctured as Type* O **2**. W **6a**. P 14.

O61	5a	½d. green	18·00	2·00
		w. Wmk inverted	25·00	11·00
O62		1d. carmine-pink (I)	†	£1100
O63		1d. carmine (I)	£180	75·00
O64		1½d. black-brown	18·00	4·00
		a. Very thin paper	60·00	30·00
		w. Wmk inverted	65·00	35·00
O65		1½d. red-brown	24·00	2·50
		w. Wmk inverted	55·00	30·00
O61/5 *Set of* 4			£200	75·00

1918–23. *Nos. 56/9 and 61/6 punctured as Type* O **2**. W **5**. P 14.

O66	5a	½d. orange	17·00	10·00
O67		1d. violet	26·00	14·00
		w. Wmk inverted	†	£13000
O68		1½d. black-brown	29·00	2·75
		w. Wmk inverted	48·00	18·00
O69		1½d. deep red-brown	25·00	2·50
		aw. Wmk inverted	55·00	30·00
O69*b*		1½d. bright red-brown	—	65·00
O70		1½d. green	16·00	3·00
O71		2d. brown-orange	13·00	1·25
		w. Wmk inverted	£250	75·00
O72		2d. bright rose-scarlet	20·00	4·00
		w. Wmk inverted	£750	£130
O73		4d. violet	55·00	13·00
O74		4d. ultramarine	65·00	11·00
O75		1s.4d. pale blue	60·00	17·00
		b. Deep turquoise	£2000	£1700
O66/75 *Set of* 10			£300	65·00

1923–24. *Nos. 73/5 punctured as Type* O **2**. W **6**. P 12.

O76	1	6d. chestnut (Die IIB)	25·00	2·50
O77		2s. maroon (Die II)	90·00	12·00
O78		£1 grey (Die IIB)	£900	£475
O76/8 *Set of* 3			£950	£475

1924. *Nos. 76/84 punctured as Type* O **2**. P 14.

(*a*) W **5**.

O79	5a	1d. sage-green	11·00	2·50
O80		1½d. scarlet	7·50	70
		w. Wmk inverted	65·00	18·00
		wa. Printed on the gummed side	£300	
O81		2d. red-brown	20·00	17·00
		a. Bright red-brown	42·00	25·00
O82		3d. dull ultramarine	35·00	6·00
O83		4d. olive-yellow	48·00	6·00
O84		4½d. violet	£130	16·00
		w. Wmk inverted	†	£6500

(*b*) W **6a**.

O85	5a	1d. sage-green	19·00	17·00

(*c*) No wmk.

O86		1d. sage-green	75·00	70·00
O87		1½d. scarlet	80·00	70·00
O79/87 *Set of* 9			£375	£180

1926–30. *Nos. 85/104 punctured as Type* O **2**. W **7**.

(*a*) P 14.

O88	5a	½d. orange	£225	£100
O89		1d. sage-green	11·00	1·50
O90		1½d. scarlet	24·00	2·50
		a. Golden scarlet	27·00	4·75
		w. Wmk inverted	27·00	5·50
O92		2d. red-brown (Die I)	£180	45·00
O93		3d. dull ultramarine	80·00	13·00
		w. Wmk inverted	80·00	60·00
O94		4d. yellow-olive	£180	40·00
O95		4½d. violet	£170	35·00
O96		1s.4d. pale greenish blue	£375	£160
O88/96 *Set of* 8			£1100	£350

(*b*) P 13½×12½.

O97	5a	½d. orange	5·50	1·25
O98		1d. sage-green (Die I)	5·50	1·50
		b. Die II	£110	£130
O100		1½d. scarlet	9·50	2·50
		a. Golden scarlet	6·00	3·00
		w. Wmk inverted	12·00	4·00
O102		1½d. red-brown	20·00	5·00
O103		2d. red-brown (Die II)	32·00	16·00
O104		2d. golden scarlet (Die II)	16·00	4·00
		a. Die III	14·00	4·00
		aw. Wmk inverted	23·00	8·00
O106		3d. dull ultramarine (Die I)	32·00	5·00
		b. Die II. *Deep ultramarine*	15·00	1·50
		bw. Wmk inverted	£11000	£8500
O108		4d. yellow-olive	23·00	3·75
O109		4½d. violet	£190	£160
O110		5d. orange-brown (Die II)	60·00	7·00
O111		1s.4d. turquoise	£300	27·00
O97/111 *Set of* 11			£600	£200

1927 (9 May). *Opening of Parliament House, Canberra. No. 105 punctured as Type* O **3**.

O112	8	1½d. brownish lake	18·00	7·50

1928 (29 Oct). *National Stamp Exhibition, Melbourne. No. 106 punctured as Type* O **2**.

O113		3d. blue	13·00	9·00

1929–30. *Nos. 107/14 punctured as Type* O **2**. W **7**. P 12.

O114	1	6d. chestnut (Die IIB)	26·00	4·25
O115		9d. violet (Die IIB)	55·00	5·50
O116		1s. blue-green (Die IIB)	23·00	5·00
O117		2s. maroon (Die II)	£110	8·00
O118		5s. grey and yellow	£325	40·00
O118*a*		10s. grey and pink	£5000	£6000
O118*b*		£2 black and rose	£10000	£10000

1929 (20 May). *Air. No. 115 punctured as Type* O **3**.

O119	9	3d. green	25·00	12·00

1929 (28 Sep). *Centenary of Western Australia. No. 116 punctured as Type* O **3**.

O120	10	1½d. dull scarlet	19·00	14·00

1930 (2 Jun). *Centenary of Exploration of River Murray by Capt. Sturt. Nos. 117/18 punctured as Type* O **2**.

O121	11	1½d. scarlet	14·00	7·50
O122		3d. blue	17·00	8·00

(O 4)

1931 (4 May). *Nos. 121/2 optd with Type* O **4**.

O123	**13**	2d. rose-red	55·00	19·00
O124		3d. blue	£200	27·00

For No. 139 overprinted with Type O **4**, see No. 139*a*.

1932 (Feb)–**33**. *Optd as Type* O **4**.

(a) W **7**.

(i) P 13½×12½.

O125	**5a**	2d. golden scarlet (Die III)	14·00	1·50
		a. Opt inverted	†	£30000
		w. Wmk inverted	£4000	£3000
O126		4d. yellow-olive (3.32)	16·00	3·00
		(ii) P 12.		
O127	**1**	6d. chestnut (3.32)	50·00	50·00
		(b) W **15**.		
		(i) P 13½×12½.		
O128	**5a**	½d. orange (11.7.32)	4·75	1·50
		a. Opt inverted	£14000	£7000
O129		1d. green (3.32)	3·25	45
		w. Wmk inverted	£1100	£800
		x. Wmk reversed	£2000	£900
O130		2d. golden scarlet (Die III)	12·00	55
		a. Opt inverted	†	£24000
O131		3d. ultramarine (Die II) (2.33)	7·50	4·00
O132		5d. orange-brown (7.32)	35·00	27·00
		(ii) P 12.		
O133	**1**	6d. chestnut (9.32)	24·00	20·00
		a. Opt inverted	†	£32000
		(c) Recess. No wmk. P 11.		
O134	**18**	2d. scarlet (3.32)	5·00	2·00
O135		3d. blue (3.32)	14·00	5·00
O136	**17**	1s. green (4.32)	42·00	27·00

No. O128a and probably the other inverted overprints were caused by the insertion of a stamp upside down into sheets repaired before surcharging.

Issue of overprinted official stamps ceased in February 1933 and remaining supplies were withdrawn from sale on 1 October 1935, thereafter mail from the federal administration was carried free.

BRITISH COMMONWEALTH OCCUPATION FORCE (JAPAN)

Nos. J1/7 were used by the Australian forces occupying Japan after the Second World War. Initially their military post offices supplied unoverprinted Australian stamps, but it was decided to introduce the overprinted issue to prevent currency speculation.

(1)

(2)

Wrong fount "6" (left pane R. 9/4) Normal Narrow "N" (right pane R. 1/8)

1946 (11 Oct)–**48**. *Stamps of Australia optd as T* **1** *(1d., 3d.,) or T* **2** *(others) at Hiroshima Printing Co, Japan.*

J1	**27**	½d. orange (No. 179)	4·50	8·00
		a. Wrong fount "6"	£120	£140
		b. Narrow "N"	£130	£150
		c. Stop after "JAPAN" (right pane R.5/5)	£130	£150
J2	**46**	1d. brown-purple (No. 203)	3·75	4·50
		a. Blue-black overprint	55·00	95·00
J3	**31**	3d. purple-brown (No. 187)	2·75	3·50
		a. Opt double	£850	
J4	**34**	6d. purple-brown (No. 189*a*) (8.5.47)	19·00	15·00
		a. Wrong fount "6"	£200	£200
		b. Stop after "JAPAN" (right pane R. 5/5)	£250	£225
		c. Narrow "N"	£225	£200
J5	**36**	1s. grey-green (No. 192) (8.5.47)	17·00	17·00
		a. Wrong fount "6"	£250	£250
		b. Stop after "JAPAN" (right pane R. 5/5)	£300	£300
		c. Narrow "N"	£250	£250
		d. Roller flaw	£110	
J6	**1**	2s. maroon (No. 212) (8.5.47)	42·00	50·00
J7	**38**	5s. claret (No. 176) (8.5.47)	£100	£130
		a. Thin rough paper (No. 176a)	80·00	£130
J1/7a *Set of* 7			£150	£200

The ½d., 1d. and 3d. values were first issued on 11 October 1946, and withdrawn two days later, but were re-issued together with the other values on 8 May 1947.

The following values with T **2** in the colours given were from proof sheets which, however, were used for postage: ½d. (red) 1d. (red or black) and 3d. (gold, red or black). (*Prices for black opts* £100, *each, and for red or gold from* £300 each, *all un*).

The use of B.C.O.F. stamps ceased on 12 February 1949.

AUSTRALIAN ANTARCTIC TERRITORY

For use at the Antarctic bases of Casey (opened early 1969: used Wilkes postmark until early 1970), Davis (closed from 1965 until early 1969), Heard Island (seasonal occupation only), Macquarie Island, Mawson and Wilkes (closed January 1969). Stamps of Australia were used from the bases before 27 March 1957 and remained valid for use there after the introduction of Australian Antarctic Territory issues.

The following are also valid for use in Australia, where they are put on sale for a limited period when first issued.

DATES OF ISSUE. The dates given refer to release dates in Australia. Local release dates are usually later and where known they are given in footnotes.

1 1954 Expedition at Vestfold Hills and Map

(Des. T. Lawrence: adapted by artist of the Printing Branch. Recess)

1957 (27 Mar). P 14½.

1	**1**	2s. ultramarine	80	50

Issued Macquarie Island 11.12.57, Davis 6.2.58, Mawson 18.2.58, Wilkes 1.2.59.

2 Members of Shackleton Expedition at South Magnetic Pole, 1909

3 Weazel and Team

4 Dog team and iceberg

5 Map of Antarctica and Emperor Penguins

1959 (16 Dec). *T* **2/4**. *T* **3**. *Recess; new values surch typo (5d., 8d.).* P 14½ (5d.), 14½×14 (8d.) or 14×14½ (others).

2	**2**	5d. on 4d. black and sepia	60	15
3	**3**	8d. on 7d. black and indigo	1·75	2·25
4	**4**	1s. deep green	2·25	2·00
5	**5**	2s.3d. green	7·00	4·00
2/5 *Set of* 4			10·50	7·50

Issued Macquarie Island 26.12.59, Davis 30.1.60, Mawson 10.2.60, Wilkes 13.2.60.

6

7 Sir Douglas Mawson (Expedition leader)

1961 (5 July). *Recess.* P 14½.

6	**6**	5d. deep blue	1·00	20

Issued Macquarie Island 6.12.61, Wilkes 10.1.62, Davis 20.1.62, Mawson 30.1.62.

1961 (18 Oct). *50th Anniv of 1911–14 Australasian Antarctic Expedition. Recess.* P 14½.

7	**7**	5d. myrtle-green	35	20

Issued Macquarie Island 6.12.61, Wilkes 10.1.62, Davis 20.1.62, Mawson 30.1.62.

(New Currency. 100 cents = 1 Australian dollar)

8 Aurora and Camera Dome

9 Bell 47G Trooper Helicopter

(Des J. Mason. Photo)

1966 (28 Sept)–**68**. *Vert designs as T* **8** *(1c. to 15c.) or horiz as T* **9** *(20c. to $1). Multicoloured. Helecon paper (5c.).* P 13½.

8	1c. Type **8** (*shades*)	70	30
9	2c. Emperor Penguins (*shades*)	3·00	80
10	4c. Ship and iceberg	1·00	90
11	5c. Banding Elephant-seals (25.9.68)	2·25	1·75
12	7c. Measuring snow strata	80	80
13	10c. Wind gauges	1·00	1·10
14	15c. Weather balloon	5·00	2·00
15	20c. Type **9**	7·50	2·50
16	25c. Radio operator	1·75	2·25
17	50c. Ice compression tests	2·50	4·00
18	$1 Parahelion ("mock sun")	19·00	12·00
8/18 *Set of* 11		38·00	25·00

Nos. 13/15 and 17 have parts of the designs printed in bright orange fluorescent ink.

Nos. 8/10 and 12/18 placed on sale locally at Macquarie Island on 11.12.66, Wilkes 9.2.67 and Mawson 16.2.67.

No. 11 issued Macquarie Island 4.12.68, Mawson 13.1.69, Wilkes/Casey 9.2.69 and Davis 20.2.69.

CHRISTMAS ISLAND

Formerly a part of the Straits Settlements and then of the Colony of Singapore, Christmas Island was occupied by the Japanese from 31 March, 1942, until September, 1945. It reverted to Singapore after liberation, but subsequently became an Australian territory on 15 October 1958.

Stamps of the STRAITS SETTLEMENTS were used on Christmas Island from 1901 until 1942. Following liberation issues of MALAYA (BRITISH MILITARY ADMINISTRATION) and then SINGAPORE were used from 1946 to 1958.

(Currency. 100 cents = 1 Malayan dollar)

1 Queen Elizabeth II

(Des G. Lissenden. Recess with name and value typo in black. Note Printing Branch, Commonwealth Bank, Melbourne)

1958 (15 Oct). No wmk. P 14½.

1	**1**	2c. yellow-orange	55	80
2		4c. brown	60	30
3		5c. deep mauve	60	50
4		6c. grey-blue	1·00	30
5		8c. black-brown	1·75	50
6		10c. violet	1·00	30
7		12c. carmine	1·75	1·75
8		20c. blue	1·00	1·75
9		50c. yellow-green	1·75	1·75
10		$1 deep bluish green	1·75	1·75
1/10 *Set of* 10			10·50	8·75

PRINTERS. Nos. 11/32 were printed by the Note Printing Branch, Reserve Bank of Australia, Melbourne. Nos. 33/82 were printed in photogravure by Harrison and Sons, Ltd, London.

2 Map

3 Moonflower

4 Robber crab

5 Island scene

6 Phosphate train

7 Raising phosphate

8 Flying Fish Cove

9 Loading cantilever

10 Christmas Island Frigate Bird

11 White-tailed Tropic Bird

(Des G. Lissenden (2, 8c.), P. Morriss (4, 5, 10, 20c.), B. Stewart (others). Recess)

1963 (28 Aug). *T* **2/11**. P 14½ × 14 ($1) or 14½ (others).

11	**2**	2c. orange	1·25	35
12	**3**	4c. red-brown	50	15
13	**4**	5c. purple	50	20
14	**5**	6c. indigo	30	35
15	**6**	8c. black	2·50	35

16	7	10c. violet	40	15
17	8	12c. brown-red	40	25
18	9	20c. blue	1·00	20
19	10	50c. green	1·00	20
20	11	$1 yellow	1·75	35
11/20		*Set of* 10	8·50	2·25

I Thick lettering

II Thinner lettering

1965. *50th Anniversary of Gallipoli Landing. As T* **184** *of Australia but slightly larger (22×34½ mm) and colour changed. Photo.* P 13½.

21		10c. sepia, black and emerald (I) (14.4)	30	1·25
		a. *Black-brown, black and light emerald* (II) (24.4)	2·25	2·00

(New Currency. 100 cents = 1 Australian dollar)

12 Golden-striped Grouper 13 "Angel" (mosaic)

(Des G. Hamori. Photo)

1968 (6 May)–**70**. *Fishes. T* **12** *and similar horiz designs. Multicoloured.* P 13½.

22		1c. Type **12**	45	45
23		2c. Moorish Idol	60	20
24		3c. Long-nosed Butterflyfish	60	30
25		4c. Pink-tailed Triggerfish	60	20
		a. Deep blue (face value) omitted	£1200	
26		5c. Regal Angelfish	60	20
27		9c. White-cheeked Surgeonfish	60	40
28		10c. Lionfish	60	20
28*a*		15c. Saddle Butterflyfish (14.12.70)	5·50	2·50
29		20c. Ornate Butterflyfish	1·50	55
29*a*		30c. Giant Ghost Pipefish (14.12.70)	5·50	2·50
30		50c. Clown Surgeonfish	1·75	1·50
31		$1 Meyer's Butterflyfish	1·75	2·00
22/31		*Set of* 12	18·00	10·00

(Des G. Hamori. Photo)

1969 (10 Nov). *Christmas.* P 13½.

32	13	5c. red, deep blue and gold	20	30

14 "The Ansidei Madonna" (Raphael)

(Des Harrison)

1970 (26 Oct). *Christmas. Paintings. T* **14** *and similar vert design. Multicoloured.* P 14×14½.

33		3c. Type **14**	20	15
34		5c. "The Virgin and Child, St. John the Baptist and an Angel" (Morando)	20	15

COCOS (KEELING) ISLANDS

The Cocos (Keeling) Islands, which had been settled by the Clunies Ross family in the 1820s, were annexed by Great Britain in 1857. In 1878 the group was attached to Ceylon, but was transferred to the Straits Settlements on 7 February 1886. During the Second World War the islands were under British military control exercised from Ceylon. At the end of hostilities administration from Singapore was continued until the islands were transferred to Australia on 23 November 1955.

The stamps of the STRAITS SETTLEMENTS were used by a postal agency operating on Cocos (Keeling) Islands from 1 April 1933 until 1 March 1937. The postal agency reopened on 2 September 1952 and used the stamps of SINGAPORE until the islands were transferred to Australia in 1955. From 1955 until 1963 stamps of AUSTRALIA were in use.

Nos. 1/31 were also valid for use in Australia.

PRINTERS. All the following stamps to No. 31 were printed by the Note Printing Branch, Reserve Bank of Australia, Melbourne.

1 Copra Industry 2 "Super Constellation"

(Des K. McKay and E. Jones (5d.), E. Jones (others). Eng E. Jones. Recess)

1963 (11 June). *T* **1/2** *and similar designs.* P 14½×14 (5d., 2s.3d.) or 14½ (others).

1		3d. chocolate	1·00	1·50
2		5d. ultramarine	1·50	80
3		8d. scarlet	1·00	1·75
4		1s. green	1·00	75
5		2s. deep purple	9·00	2·75
6		2s.3d. deep green	12·00	2·75
1/6		*Set of* 6	23·00	9·25

Designs: *Vert (as T* **1**)—8d. Map of islands; 2s. Jukong (sailboat). *Horiz (as T* **1**)—1s. Palms. (*as T* **2**)—2s.3d. White Tern.

I Thick lettering

II Thinner lettering

1965 (14 Apr). *50th Anniv of Gallipoli Landing. As T* **184** *of Australia, but slightly larger (22×34½ mm) and colour changed. Photo.* P 13½.

7		5d. sepia, black and emerald (I)	60	45
		a. *Black-brown, black and light emerald* (II)	2·75	1·75

No. 7a comes from a second printing, using a new black cylinder, which was available from the end of April.

With the introduction of decimal currency on 14 February 1966, Australian stamps were used in Cocos Islands, until the appearance of the new definitives on 9 July 1969.

(New Currency. 100 cents = 1 Australian dollar)

7 Reef Clam (*Tridacna derasa*) 8 Great Frigate Bird

(Des L. Annois (1c. to 6c.), P. Jones (10c. to $1). Photo)

1969 (9 July). *Decimal Currency. T* **8** *or designs as T* **7**. *Multicoloured.* P 13½.

8		1c. Lajonkaines Turbo shell (*Turbo lajonkairii*) (*vert*)	30	60
9		2c. Elongate or Small Giant Clam (*Tridacna maxima*) (*vert*)	75	80
10		3c. Type **7**	40	20
11		4c. Floral Blenny (fish)	30	50
		a. Salmon-pink omitted	£1200	
12		5c. *Porites cocosensis* (coral)	35	30
13		6c. Atrisignis Flyingfish	75	75
14		10c. Buff-banded Rail	75	70
15		15c. Java Sparrow	75	30
16		20c. Red-tailed Tropic Bird	75	30
17		30c. Sooty Tern	75	30
18		50c. Eastern Reef Heron (*vert*)	75	30
19		$1 Type **8**	1·50	75
8/19		*Set of* 12	7·25	5·25

NEW GUINEA

Stamps of Germany and later of GERMAN NEW GUINEA were used in New Guinea from 1888 until 1914.

During the interim period between the "G.R.I." surcharges and the "N.W. PACIFIC ISLANDS" overprints, stamps of AUSTRALIA perforated "OS" were utilised.

PRICES FOR STAMPS ON COVER

Nos. 1/30	*from* × 3
Nos. 31/2	—
Nos. 33/49	*from* × 3
Nos. 50/9	*from* × 2
Nos. 60/2	—
Nos. 63/4	*from* × 2
Nos. 64*c*/*q*	—
Nos. 65/81	*from* × 5
Nos. 83/5	—
Nos. 86/97	*from* × 5

PRICES FOR STAMPS ON COVER

No. 99	—
Nos. 100/16	*from* × 4
Nos. 117/18	—
Nos. 119/24	*from* × 4
Nos. 125/203	*from* × 2
Nos. 204/5	—
Nos. 206/11	*from* × 8
Nos. 212/25	*from* × 2
Nos. O1/33	*from* × 8

AUSTRALIAN OCCUPATION

Stamps of German New Guinea surcharged

G.R.I. **G.R.I.**

2d. (1) **1s.** (2) **1** (3)

SETTINGS. The "G.R.I" issues of New Guinea were surcharged on a small hand press which could only accommodate one horizontal row of stamps at a time. In addition to complete sheets the surcharges were also applied to multiples and individual stamps which were first lightly affixed to plain paper backing sheets. Such backing sheets could contain a mixture of denominations, some of which required different surcharges.

Specialists recognise twelve settings of the low value surcharges (1d. to 8d.):

Setting 1 (Nos. 1/4 7/11) shows the bottom of the "R" 6 mm from the top of the "d"
Setting 2 (Nos. 16/19, 22/6) shows the bottom of the "R" 5 mm from the top of the "d"
Setting 3 was used for the Official stamps (Nos. O1/2)
Setting 4, which included the 2½d. value for the first time, and Setting 5 showed individual stamps with either 6 mm or 5 mm spacing.

These five settings were for rows of ten stamps, but the remaining seven, used on odd stamps handed in for surcharging, were applied as strips of five only. One has, so far, not been reconstructed, but of the remainder three show the 6 mm spacing, two the 5 mm and one both.

On the shilling values the surcharges were applied as horizontal rows of four and the various settings divide into two groups, one with 3½ to 4½ mm between the bottom of the "R" and the top of numeral, and the second with 5½ mm between the "R" and numeral. The first group includes the very rare initial setting on which the space is 4 to 4½ mm.

G.R.I. **G.R.I.** **G.R.I.**

2d. "1" for "I" (Setting 1) **1d.** Short "1" (Setting 1) **1s.** Large "S" (Setting 1)

1914 (17 Oct)–**15**. *Stamps of 1901 surch.*

(a) As T **1**. *"G.R.I." and value 6 mm apart.*

1		1d. on 3pf. brown	£475	£550
		a. "1" for "I"	£1300	
		b. Short "1"	£1300	
		c. "1" with straight top serif (Setting 6)	£1300	
		d. "I" for "1" (Setting 12)	£1700	
2		1d. on 5pf. green	60·00	75·00
		a. "1" for "I"	£250	£325
		b. Short "1"	£250	£325
		c. "1" with straight top serif (Settings 6 and 9)	£375	£425
3		2d. on 10pf. carmine	65·00	90·00
		a. "1" for "I"	£300	£375
4		2d. on 20pf. ultramarine	65·00	75·00
		a. "1" for "I"	£275	£325
		e. Surch double, one "G.R.I." albino	£4000	
		f. Surch inverted	£10000	
5		2½d. on 10pf. carmine (27.2.15)	75·00	£160
		a. Fraction bar omitted (Setting 9)	£1700	£1800
6		2½d. on 20pf. ultramarine (27.2.15)	85·00	£170
		a. Fraction bar omitted (Setting 9)		
7		3d. on 25pf. black and red/*yellow*	£225	£325
		a. "1" for "I"	£850	£950
8		3d. on 30pf. black and orange/*buff*	£300	£350
		a. "1" for "I"	£900	£1000
		e. Surch double	£9000	£9000
9		4d. on 40pf. black and carmine	£300	£375
		a. "1" for "I"	£1000	
		e. Surch double	£2500	£3250
		f. Surch inverted	£10000	
10		5d. on 50pf. black and purple/*buff*	£500	£800
		a. "1" for "I"	£1600	£2000
		e. Surch double	£10000	
		f. Surch inverted		
11		8d. on 80pf. black and carmine/*rose*	£750	£1100
		a. "1" for "I"	£2250	£3000
		d. No stop after "d"	£3500	
		e. Error. Surch "G.R.I. 4d."	£9000	

(b) As T **2**. *"G.R.I." and value 3½ to 4 mm apart.*

12		1s. on 1m. carmine	£2000	£3000
		a. Large "s"	£8000	£8000
13		2s. on 2m. blue	£2000	£3000
		a. Large "s"	£8000	£10000
		c. Error. Surch "G.R.I. 5s."	£30000	
		d. Error. Surch "G.R.I. 2d." corrected by handstamped "S"	£35000	
14		3s. on 3m. violet-black	£3750	£4750
		a. Large "s"	£10000	
		b. No stop after "I" (Setting 3)	£10000	£10000
15		5s. on 5m. carmine and black	£9000	£11000
		a. Large "s"	£20000	
		b. No stop after "I" (Setting 3)	£12000	£14000
		c. Error. Surch "G.R.I. 1s."	£55000	

G.R.I. 3d. — Thick "3" (Setting 2)

G.R.I. 5d. — Thin "5" (Setting 2)

1914 (16 Dec)–**15**. *Stamps of 1901 surch.*

(a) As T **1**. *"G.R.I." and value 5 mm apart.*

16 1d. on 3pf. brown 48·00 60·00
a. "I" for "1" (Setting 11) £500
b. Short "1" (Setting 2) £250
c. "1" with straight top serif (Settings 2 and 6) 85·00 £100
e. Surch double £900 £1200
f. Surch double, one inverted £4750
g. Surch inverted £3500
h. Error. Surch "G.R.I. 4d." £11000
17 1d. on 5pf. green 21·00 38·00
b. Short "1" (Setting 2) £120 £170
c. "1" with straight top serif (Setting 2) 38·00 65·00
e. "d" inverted † £2000
f. "1d" inverted † £7500
g. "G.R.I." without stops or spaces £7500
ga. "G.R.I." without stops, but with normal spaces — £7500
h. "G.I.R." instead of "G.R.I." £8000 £9000
i. Surch double £3500
18 2d. on 10pf. carmine 28·00 45·00
e. No stop after "d" (Setting 2) £140 £190
f. Stop before, instead of after, "G" (Settings 4 and 5) £7500
g. Surch double £11000 £11000
h. Surch double, one inverted — £9000
i. In vert pair with No. 20 £17000
j. In horiz pair with No. 20 £24000
k. Error. Surch "G.R.I. 1d." £8000 £7000
l. Error. Surch "G.I.R. 3d." £9000
19 2d. on 20pf. ultramarine 32·00 50·00
e. No stop after "d" (Setting 2) £100 £140
f. No stop after "I" (Setting 11) £1000
g. "R" inverted (Settings 4 and 5) — £6000
h. Surch double £2000 £3000
i. Surch double, one inverted £3250 £4000
j. Surch inverted £7000
k. Albino surch (in horiz pair with normal) £20000
l. In vert pair with No. 21 £15000 £18000
m. Error. Surch "G.R.I. 1d." £8000 £9000
20 2½d. on 10pf. carmine (27.2.15) £180 £300
21 2½d. on 20pf. ultramarine (27.2.15) £1700 £2000
a. Error. Surch "G.R.I. 3d." (in vert pair with normal) £32000
22 3d. on 25pf. black and red/*yellow* £130 £180
e. Thick "3" £550 £700
f. Surch double £7500 £9000
g. Surch inverted £7500 £9000
h. Surch omitted (in horiz pair with normal) £12000
i. Error. Surch "G.R.I. 1d." £16000
23 3d. on 30pf. black and orange/*buff* £110 £160
e. No stop after "d" (Setting 2) £600
f. Thick "3" £500
g. Surch double £2500 £3000
h. Surch double, one inverted £2750 £3250
i. Surch double, both inverted £8000 £9000
j. Surch inverted £6500
k. Albino surch £11000
l. Surch omitted (in vert pair with normal) £10000
m. Error. Surch "G.R.I. 1d." £8000 £9000
24 4d. on 40pf. black and carmine £120 £190
e. Surch double £2000
f. Surch double, one inverted £3500
g. Surch double, both inverted £9000
h. Surch inverted £6000
i. Error. Surch "G.R.I. 1d." £5500
ia. Surch "G.R.I. 1d." inverted £12000
j. Error. Surch "G.R.I. 3d." double £20000
k. No stop after "I" (Setting 11) £2750
25 5d. on 50pf. black and purple/*buff* £190 £250
e. Thin "5" £1000 £2500
f. Surch double £2750
g. Surch double, one inverted £7500 £7000
h. Surch double, both inverted £8000 £9000
i. Surch inverted £6500
j. Error. Surch "G.I.R. 3d." £16000
26 8d. on 80pf. black and carmine/*rose* £350 £450
e. Surch double £4500 £5000
f. Surch double, one inverted £4500 £5000
g. Surch triple £5500 £6000
h. Surch inverted £9000
i. Error. Surch "G.R.I. 3d." £13000

(b) As T **2**. *"G.R.I." and value 5½ mm apart.*

27 1s. on 1m. carmine £3500 £4750
a. No stop after "I" (Setting 7) £8000
28 2s. on 2m. blue £3750 £5500
a. No stop after "I" (Setting 7) £8500
29 3s. on 3m. violet-black £6500 £10000
a. "G.R.I." double £30000
30 5s. on 5m. carmine and black £25000 £30000

1915 (1 Jan). *Nos. 18 and 19 further surch with T* **3**.

31 1d. on 2d. on 10pf. £22000 £22000
32 1d. on 2d. on 20pf. £22000 £14000

German New Guinea Registration Labels surcharged

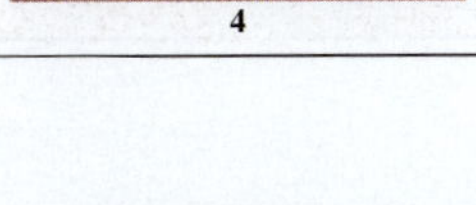

4

4a

G.R.I. 3d. — Sans serif "G" and different "3"

1915 (Jan). *Registration Labels surch "G.R.I. 3d." in settings of five or ten and used for postage. Each black and red on buff. Inscr "(Deutsch Neuguinea)" spelt in various ways as indicated. P 14 (No. 43) or 11½ (others).*

I. With name of town in sans-serif letters as T **4**.

33 **Rabaul** "(Deutsch Neuguinea)" £200 £250
a. "G.R.I. 3d." double £3750 £4750
b. No bracket before "Deutsch" £750 £1000
ba. No bracket and surch double £10000
d. "(Deutsch-Neuguinea)" £300 £425
da. "G.R.I. 3d." double £10000 £10000
db. No stop after "I" £750
dc. "G.R.I. 3d" inverted £10000
dd. No bracket before "Deutsch" £1100 £1500
de. No bracket after "Neuguinea" £1100 £1500
34 **Deulon** "(Deutsch Neuguinea)" £20000 £22000
35 **Friedrich-Wilhelmshafen** "(Deutsch Neuguinea)" £180 £600
a. No stop after "d" £350
b. "G" omitted £6000
c. Sans-serif "G" £11000
d. Sans-serif "G" and different "3" £95000
e. Surch inverted † £10000
f. "(Deutsch-Neuguinea)" £190 £600
fa. No stop after "d" £400
36 **Herbertshohe** "(Deutsch Neuguinea)" £200 £550
a. No stop after "d" £400
b. No stop after "I" £750
c. "G" omitted £6500
d. Surch omitted (in horiz pair with normal) £12000
e. "(Deutsch Neu-Guinea)" £375 £750
37 **Kawieng** "(Deutsch-Neuguinea)" £750
a. No bracket after "Neuguinea" £3000
b. "Deutsch Neu-Guinea" £250 £500
ba. No stop after "d" £450
bb. "G.R.I." double £5500
bc. "3d." double £5500
bd. "G" omitted £6500
38 **Kieta** "(Deutsch-Neuguinea)" £375 £650
a. No bracket before "Deutsch" £1300 £2000
b. No stop after "d" £700
c. Surch omitted (right hand stamp of horiz pair) £11000
e. No stop after "I" £1000
f. "G" omitted £6000
39 **Manus** "(Deutsch Neuguinea)" £225 £700
a. "G.R.I. 3d." double £6000
b. No bracket before "Deutsch" £950 £1700
40 **Stephansort** "(Deutsch Neu-Guinea)" † £2250
a. No stop after "d" † £5000

II. With name of town in letters with serifs as T **4a**.

41 **Friedrich Wilhelmshafen** "(Deutsch-Neuguinea)" £180 £550
b. No stop after "d" £350 £800
c. No stop after "I" £700 £1200
d. No bracket before "Deutsch" £1100 £1700
e. No bracket after "Neuguinea" £1100 £1700
42 **Kawieng** "(Deutsch Neuguinea)" £170 £475
a. No stop after "d" £375
b. No stop after "I"
43 **Manus** "(Deutsch-Neuguinea)" £2500 £3500
a. No stop after "I" £5000 £4500

Examples of Nos. 33db, 36b, 38e, 41c and 43a also show the stop after "R" either very faint or missing completely.

Stamps of Marshall Islands surcharged

SETTINGS. The initial supply of Marshall Islands stamps, obtained from Nauru, was surcharged with Setting 2 (5 mm between "R" and "d") on the penny values and with the 3½ to 4 setting on the shilling stamps.

Small quantities subsequently handed in were surcharged, often on the same backing sheet as German New Guinea values, with Settings 6, 7 or 12 (all 6 mm between "R" and "d") for the penny values and with a 5½ mm setting for the shilling stamps.

1914 (16 Dec). *Stamps of 1901 surch.*

(a) As T **1**. *"G.R.I." and value 5 mm apart.*

50 1d. on 3pf. brown 60·00 95·00
c. "1" with straight top serif (Setting 2) £130 £200
d. "G.R.I." and "1" with straight top serif (Settings 4 and 5) † £9000
e. Surch inverted £6000
51 1d. on 5pf. green 60·00 65·00
c. "1" with straight top serif (Settings 2 and 11) £120 £140
d. "I" for "1" (Setting 11) £850
e. "1" and "d" spaced £275 £300
f. Surch double £2250 £3000
g. Surch inverted £3500
52 2d. on 10pf. carmine 20·00 29·00
e. No stop after "G" (Setting 2) £750
f. Surch double £2250
g. Surch double, one inverted £3250
h. Surch inverted £4500
i. Surch sideways £7000
53 2d. on 20pf. ultramarine 21·00 32·00
e. No stop after "d" (Setting 2) 50·00 85·00
g. Surch double £2500 £3500
h. Surch double, one inverted £6500 £7000
i. Surch inverted £7000 £7000
54 3d. on 25pf. black and red/*yellow* £325 £425
e. No stop after "d" (Settings 2 and 11) £650 £850
f. Thick "3" £900 £1200
g. Surch double £2500 £3250
h. Surch double, one inverted £2500
i. Surch inverted £8000
55 3d. on 30pf. black and orange/*buff* £350 £450
e. No stop after "d" (Setting 2) £700 £900
f. Thick "3" £950
g. Surch inverted £5500 £6000
h. Surch double £4500
56 4d. on 40pf. black and carmine £120 £160
e. No stop after "d" (Setting 2) £325 £475
f. "d" omitted (Setting 2) † £6000
g. Surch double £4500 £5000
h. Surch triple £9000
i. Surch inverted £6500
j. Error. Surch "G.R.I. 1d." £12000
k. Error. Surch "G.R.I. 3d." £12000
57 5d. on 50pf. black and purple/*buff* £160 £225
e. Thin "5" £3500
f. "d" omitted (Setting 2) £1700
g. Surch double £7000
h. Surch inverted £1000
58 8d. on 80pf. black and carmine/*rose* £400 £550
e. Surch double £6500
f. Surch double, both inverted £8000 £9000
g. Surch triple £10000
h. Surch inverted £7000

(b) As T **2**. *"G.R.I." and value 3½–4 mm apart.*

59 1s. on 1m. carmine £2500 £3750
b. No stop after "I" £4250 £6000
e. Surch double £30000
f. Error. Additional surch "1d." £32000
60 2s. on 2m. blue £1300 £3000
b. No stop after "I" £2750 £4500
e. Surch double £30000
f. Surch double, one inverted £30000 £30000
61 3s. on 3m. violet-black £4250 £6500
b. No stop after "I" £6000
e. Surch double £25000 £30000
62 5s. on 5m. carmine and black £8500 £10000
e. Surch double, one inverted † £45000

1915 (Jan). *Nos. 52 and 53 further surch with T* **3**.

63 1d. on 2d. on 10pf. carmine £160 £190
a. "1" double £11000
b. "1" inverted £14000 £14000
c. Small "1" £400
64 1d. on 2d. on 20pf. ultramarine £3250 £2250
a. On No. 53e £7500 £3500
b. "1" inverted £14000 £14000

The surcharged "1" on No. 63c is just over 4 mm tall. Type **3** is 6 mm tall.

1915. *Stamps of 1901 surch.*

(a) As T **1**. *"G.R.I." and value 6 mm apart.*

64*c* 1d. on 3pf. brown £2000
cc. "1" with straight top serif (Setting 6)
cd. "I" for "1" (Setting 12) £2750
ce. Surch inverted £10000
64*d* 1d. on 5pf. green £2000
dc. "1" with straight top serif (Setting 6) £2750
dd. "I" for "1" (Setting 12) £2750
de. Surch inverted £10000
df. Surch double £10000
64*e* 2d. on 10pf carmine £3000
ea. Surch sideways £11000
64*f* 2d. on 20pf. ultramarine £2500
fe. Surch inverted £10000
64*g* 2½d. on 10pf. carmine £18000
64*h* 2½d. on 20pf. ultramarine £27000
64*i* 3d. on 25pf. black and red/*yellow* £3500
64*j* 3d. on 30pf. black and orange/*buff* £3750
je. Error. Surch "G.R.I. 1d." £12000
64*k* 4d. on 40pf. black and carmine £3750
ke. Surch double £11000
kf. Surch inverted £11000
64*l* 5d. on 50pf. black and purple/*buff* £3500
le. Surch double £11000
64*m* 8d. on 80pf. black and carmine/*rose* £4250
me. Surch inverted £12000

(b) As T **2**. *"G.R.I." and value 5½ mm apart.*

64*n* 1s. on 1m. carmine £11000
na. Large "s" (Setting 5) £15000
nb. No stop after "I" (Setting 7) £15000
64*o* 2s. on 2m. blue £9000
a. Large "s" (Setting 5) £13000
b. Surch double, one inverted £38000
64*p* 3s. on 3m. violet-black £18000
pa. Large "s" (Setting 5) £24000
pb. No stop after "I" (Setting 7) £24000
pe. Surch inverted £42000
64*q* 5s. on 5m. carmine and black £25000
qa. Large "s" (Setting 5) £32000

Stamps of Australia overprinted

N. W. PACIFIC ISLANDS. (a) — N. W. PACIFIC ISLANDS. (b) — N. W. PACIFIC ISLANDS. (c)

(6)

1915–16. *Stamps of Australia optd in black as T* **6** *(a), (b) or (c).*

(i) T **5a**. *W* **5** *of Australia. P 14¼×14 (4 Jan–15 Mar 1915).*

65 ½d. green 2·75 8·50
a. Bright green 3·00 9·50
aw. Wmk inverted £140
67 1d. pale rose (Die I) (4.1) 7·00 6·50
a. Dull red 7·00 6·50
b. Carmine-red 7·00 6·50
ba. Substituted cliché (Pl 2 rt pane R. 6/5) £1200 £1000
bb. Dot before "1" 70·00 80·00

bc. "Secret mark" 70·00 80·00
bd. Flaw under neck 70·00 80·00
be. "RA" joined 70·00 80·00
c. Die II. *Carmine-red* £100 £140
ca. Substituted cliché (Pl 2 rt pane R. 6/4) £1200 £1000
70 4d. yellow-orange 4·00 15·00
a. Pale orange-yellow 18·00 35·00
b. Chrome-yellow £250 £275
c. Line through "FOUR PENCE" (PL 2 rt pane R. 2/6) (*all shades*) *from* £375 £600
72 5d. brown (P 14¼ (line)) 2·25 16·00

(ii) T **1**. W **2** of Australia. P 12 (4 Jan 1915–March 1916).

73 2d. grey (Die I) 19·00 50·00
74 2½d. indigo (Die II) (4.1.15) 2·75 16·00
76 3d. yellow-olive (Die I) 21·00 50·00
a. Die II £300 £450
ab. In pair with Die I £600 £900
c. Greenish olive £190 £275
ca. Die II £1300
cb. In pair with Die I £2250
78 6d. ultramarine (Die II) 90·00 95·00
a. Retouched "E" £6000 £7000
w. Wmk inverted £150 £225
79 9d. violet (Die II) 48·00 55·00
81 1s. green (Die II) 50·00 55·00
83 5s. grey and yellow (Die II) (3.16) £1600 £2250
84 10s. grey and pink (Die II) (12.15) £110 £160
85 £1 brown and ultramarine (Die II) (12.15) £425 £600

(iii) T **1**. W **5** of Australia. P 12 (Oct 1915–July 1916).

86 2d. grey (Die I) 18·00 26·00
87 2½d. indigo (Die II) (7.16) £15000 £15000
88 6d. ultramarine (Die II) 10·00 12·00
89 9d. violet (Die II) (12.15) 16·00 21·00
90 1s. emerald (Die II) (12.15) 11·00 24·00
91 2s. brown (Die II) (12.15) 95·00 £110
92 5s. grey and yellow (Die II) (12.15) 70·00 £100

(iv) T **1**. W **6** of Australia. P 12 (Dec 1915–1916).

94 2d. grey (Die I) 6·00 19·00
a. Die IIA (substituted cliché) £600
96 3d. yellow-olive (Die I) 5·50 11·00
a. Die II 85·00 £130
ab. In pair with Die I £180
97 2s. brown (Die II) (8.16) 35·00 50·00
w. Wmk inverted 30·00 75·00
99 £1 chocolate and dull blue (Die II) (8.16) £250 £400

Dates for Nos. 67 and 74 are issue dates at Rabaul. The stamps were in use from 2 January 1915 on Nauru. All other dates are those of despatch. Nos. 65/6, 68/73, 76/81 were despatched on 15 March 1915.

For Die IIA of 2d. see note below Australia No. 45.

SETTINGS. Type **6** exists in three slightly different versions, illustrated above as (*a*), (*b*), and (*c*). These differ in the letters "S" of "ISLANDS" as follows:

(*a*) Both "SS" normal.

(*b*) First "S" with small head and large tail and second "S" normal.

(*c*) Both "SS" with small head and large tail.

Type **11**, which also shows the examples of "S" as the normal version, can be identified from Type **6** (*a*) by the relative position of the second and third lines of the overprint. On Type **6** (*a*) the "P" of "PACIFIC" is exactly over the first "S" of "ISLANDS". On Type **11** the "F" appears over the space between "I" and "S".

It has been established, by the study of minor variations, that there are actually six settings of the "N.W. PACIFIC ISLANDS" overprint, including that represented by T **11**, but the following are the different arrangements of Type **6** (*a*), (*b*), and (*c*) which occur.

A. Horizontal rows 1 and 2 all Type (*a*). Row 3 all Type (*b*). Rows 4 and 5 all Type (*c*).

B. (½d. green only). As A, except that the types in the bottom row run (*c*) (*c*) (*c*) (*c*) (*b*) (*c*).

C. As A, but bottom row now shows types (*a*) (*c*) (*c*) (*c*) (*b*) (*c*).

Horizontal strips and pairs showing varieties (*a*) and (*c*), or (*b*) and (*c*) *se-tenant* are scarce.

The earliest printing of the 1d. and 2½d. values was made on sheets with margin attached on two sides, the later printings being on sheets from which the margins had been removed. In this printing the vertical distances between the overprints are less than in later printings, so that in the lower horizontal rows of the sheet the overprint is near the top of the stamp.

The settings used on King George stamps and on the Kangaroo type are similar, but the latter stamps being smaller the overprints are closer together in the vertical rows.

PURPLE OVERPRINTS. We no longer differentiate between purple and black overprints in the above series. In our opinion the two colours are nowadays insufficiently distinct to warrant separation.

PRICES. The prices quoted for Nos. 65 to 101 apply to stamps with opts Types **6** (*a*) or **6** (*c*). Stamps with opt Type **6** (*b*) are worth a 25 per cent premium. Vertical strips of three, showing (*a*), (*b*) and (*c*), are worth from four times the prices quoted for singles as Types **6** (*a*) or **6** (*c*).

One Penny
(**10**)

N. W.
PACIFIC
ISLANDS.
(**11**)

1918 (23 May). *Nos. 72 and 81 surch locally with T* **10**.

100 1d. on 5d. brown 90·00 80·00
101 1d. on 1s. green 90·00 75·00

Types **6** (*a*), (*b*), (*c*) occur on these stamps also.

1918–23. *Stamps of Australia optd with T* **11** *("P" of "PACIFIC" over space between "I" and "S" of "ISLANDS").*

(i) T **5a**. W **5** of Australia. P 14¼×14.

102 ½d. green 1·50 3·50
103 1d. carmine-red (Die I) 3·75 1·60
a. Substituted cliché (Pl 2 rt pane R. 6/5) £750 £450
ab. Dot before "1" 50·00 40·00
ac. "Secret mark" 50·00 40·00
ad. Flaw under neck 50·00 40·00
ae. "RA" joined 50·00 40·00
b. Die II £110 75·00
ba. Substituted cliché (Pl 2 rt pane R. 6/4) £750 £450
104 4d. yellow-orange (1919) 3·25 16·00
a. Line through "FOUR PENCE" (Pl 2 rt pane R. 2/6) £800 £1200
105 5d. brown (1919) 3·50 12·00

(ii) T **1**. W **6** of Australia. P 12.

106 2d. grey (Die I) (1919) 7·00 22·00
a. Die II 11·00 42·00
107 2½d. indigo (Die II) (1919) 4·50 16·00
a. "1" of "½" omitted £7500 £10000
b. Blue (1920) 8·00 32·00
109 3d. greenish olive (Die I) (1919) 23·00 26·00
a. Die II 60·00 70·00
ab. In pair with Die I £375 £475
110 6d. ultramarine (Die II) (1919) 4·50 14·00
a. Greyish ultramarine (1922) 42·00 65·00
112 9d. violet (Die IIB) (1919) 9·00 45·00
113 1s. emerald (Die II) 6·50 30·00
a. Pale blue-green 14·00 30·00
115 2s. brown (Die II) (1919) 21·00 38·00
116 5s. grey and yellow (Die II) (1919) 60·00 65·00
117 10s. grey and bright pink (Die II) (1919) £150 £200
118 £1 bistre-brown and grey-blue (Die II) (1922) £2750 £4000

(iii) T **5a**. W **6a**. of Australia (Mult Crown A). P 14.

119 ½d. green (1919) 2·25 4·00
w. Wmk inverted 65·00

(iv) T **5a**. W **5** of Australia. *Colour changes and new value.*

120 1d. violet (*shades*) (1922) 2·00 6·50
a. Dot before "1" 32·00 75·00
b. "Secret mark" 32·00 75·00
c. Flaw under neck 32·00 75·00
d. "RA" joined 32·00 75·00
121 2d. orange (1921) 8·00 2·75
122 2d. rose-scarlet (1922) 9·50 3·75
123 4d. violet (1922) 20·00 40·00
a. "FOUR PENCE" in thinner letters (Pl 2 rt pane R. 2/6) £750 £1200
124 4d. ultramarine (1922) 11·00 60·00
a. "FOUR PENCE" in thinner letters (Pl 2 rt pane R. 2/6) £850 £1400
120/4 *Set of* 5 45·00 £100

Type **11** differs from Type **6** (*a*) in the position of the "P" of "PACIFIC", which is further to the left in Type **11**.

For 1d. rosine Dies I and II on rough unsurfaced paper see Nos. O16/b.

MANDATED TERRITORY OF NEW GUINEA

A civil administration for the Mandated Territory of New Guinea was established on 9 May 1921.

PRINTERS. See note at the beginning of Australia.

12 Native Village

(**13**)

(Des R. Harrison. Eng T. Harrison. Recess Note Printing Branch, Treasury, Melbourne, from 1926 Note Ptg Branch, Commonwealth Bank of Australia, Melbourne)

1925 (23 Jan)–**28**. P 11.

125 **12** ½d. orange 2·50 7·00
126 1d. green 2·50 5·50
126*a* 1½d. orange-vermilion (1926) 3·25 2·75
127 2d. claret 2·75 4·50
128 3d. blue 4·50 4·00
129 4d. olive-green 13·00 21·00
130 6d. dull yellow-brown 20·00 48·00
a. Olive-bistre (1927) 6·00 50·00
b. Pale yellow-bistre (1928) 6·00 48·00
131 9d. dull purple (*to* violet) 13·00 45·00
132 1s. dull blue-green (6.4.25) 15·00 27·00
133 2s. brown-lake (6.4.25) 30·00 48·00
134 5s. olive-bistre (6.4.25) 48·00 65·00
135 10s. dull rose (6.4.25) £110 £180
136 £1 dull olive-green (6.4.25) £190 £300
125/36 *Set of* 13 £400 £650

1931 (8 June). *Air. Optd with T* **13**. P 11.

137 **12** ½d. orange 1·50 7·50
138 1d. green 1·60 5·00
139 1½d. orange-vermilion 1·25 5·00
140 2d. claret 1·25 7·00
141 3d. blue 1·75 13·00
142 4d. olive-green 1·25 9·00
143 6d. pale yellow-bistre 1·75 14·00
144 9d. violet 3·00 17·00
145 1s. dull blue-green 3·00 17·00
146 2s. brown-lake 7·00 42·00
147 5s. olive-bistre 20·00 65·00
148 10s. bright pink 80·00 £110
149 £1 olive-grey £140 £250
137/49 *Set of* 13 £225 £500

14 Raggiana Bird of Paradise (Dates either side of value)

(**15**)

(Recess John Ash, Melbourne)

1931 (2 Aug). *Tenth Anniv of Australian Administration. T* **14** *(with dates).* P 11.

150 **14** 1d. green 4·00 2·50
151 1½d. vermilion 5·00 10·00
152 2d. claret 5·00 2·25
153 3d. blue 5·00 4·75
154 4d. olive-green 6·50 23·00
155 5d. deep blue-green 5·00 21·00
156 6d. bistre-brown 5·00 19·00
157 9d. violet 8·50 19·00
158 1s. pale blue-green 6·00 15·00
159 2s. brown-lake 10·00 38·00
160 5s. olive-brown 42·00 55·00
161 10s. bright pink 95·00 £130
162 £1 olive-grey £200 £250
150/62 *Set of* 13 £350 £500

1931 (2 Aug). *Air. Optd with T* **15**.

163 **14** ½d. orange 3·25 3·25
164 1d. green 4·00 4·75
165 1½d. vermilion 3·75 10·00
166 2d. claret 3·75 3·00
167 3d. blue 6·00 6·50
168 4d. olive-green 6·00 6·00
169 5d. deep blue-green 6·00 11·00
170 6d. bistre-brown 7·00 26·00
171 9d. violet 8·00 15·00
172 1s. pale blue-green 7·50 15·00
173 2s. dull lake 16·00 48·00
174 5s. olive-brown 42·00 70·00
175 10s. bright pink 70·00 £120
176 £1 olive-grey £120 £250
163/76 *Set of* 14 £275 £500

1932 (30 June)–**34**. *T* **14** *(redrawn without dates).* P 11.

177 1d. green 3·00 20
178 1½d. claret 3·00 12·00
179 2d. vermilion 3·00 20
179*a* 2½d. green (14.9.34) 6·50 21·00
180 3d. blue 3·75 1·00
180*a* 3½d. aniline carmine (14.9.34) 13·00 12·00
181 4d. olive-green 3·50 6·00
182 5d. deep blue-green 4·25 70
183 6d. bistre-brown 5·00 3·25
184 9d. violet 9·50 22·00
185 1s. blue-green 4·50 10·00
186 2s. dull lake 4·00 17·00
187 5s. olive 27·00 45·00
188 10s. pink 55·00 70·00
189 £1 olive-grey £110 £100
177/89 *Set of* 15 £225 £275

1932 (30 June)–**34**. *Air. T* **14** *(redrawn without dates), optd with T* **15**. P 11.

190 ½d. orange 60 1·50
191 1d. green 1·25 1·50
192 1½d. claret 1·75 7·50
193 2d. vermilion 1·75 30
193*a* 2½d. green (14.9.34) 6·50 2·50
194 3d. blue 3·25 3·00
194*a* 3½d. aniline carmine (14.9.34) 4·50 3·25
195 4d. olive-green 4·50 10·00
196 5d. deep blue-green 7·00 7·50
197 6d. bistre-brown 4·50 15·00
198 9d. violet 6·00 9·00
199 1s. pale blue-green 6·00 9·00
200 2s. dull lake 10·00 48·00
201 5s. olive-brown 48·00 60·00
202 10s. pink 90·00 85·00
203 £1 olive-grey 80·00 55·00
190/203 *Set of* 16 £250 £275

The ½d. orange redrawn without dates exists without overprint, but it is believed that this was not issued (*Price* £100 *un*).

16 Bulolo Goldfields

(Recess John Ash, Melbourne)

1935 (1 May). *Air.* P 11.

204 **16** £2 bright violet £275 £140
205 £5 emerald-green £600 £400

HIS MAJESTY'S
JUBILEE.
1910 — 1935
(**17**)

18

1935 (27 June). *Silver Jubilee. As Nos. 177 and 179, but shiny paper. Optd with T* **17**.

206 1d. green 1·00 65
207 2d. vermilion 2·25 65

Re-entry (design completely duplicated) (Pl 2a R. 5/2)

(Recess John Ash, Melbourne)

1937 (18 May). *Coronation.* P 11.

208 **18** 2d. scarlet 50 1·50
209 3d. blue 50 1·75

210		5d. green	50	1·75
		a. Re-entry	60·00	90·00
211		1s. purple	50	2·00
208/11 *Set of 4*			1·75	6·25

(Recess John Ash, Melbourne)

1939 (1 Mar). *Air. Inscr* "AIRMAIL POSTAGE" *at foot.* P 11.

212	**16**	½d. orange	3·75	7·00
213		1d. green	3·25	4·50
214		1½d. claret	4·00	11·00
215		2d. vermilion	8·00	3·50
216		3d. blue	14·00	18·00
217		4d. yellow-olive	14·00	8·50
218		5d. deep green	13·00	4·00
219		6d. bistre-brown	28·00	22·00
220		9d. violet	28·00	28·00
221		1s. pale blue-green	29·00	23·00
222		2s. dull lake	65·00	50·00
223		5s. olive-brown	£140	£110
224		10s. pink	£425	£275
225		£1 olive-green	£100	£110
212/25 *Set of 14*			£800	£600

OFFICIAL STAMPS

O. S.

G.R.I.

1d. (O 1) **O S** (O 2) **O S** (O 3)

1915 (27 Feb). *Stamps of 1901 surch as Type* O **1**. "G.R.I." *and value 3½ mm apart.*

O1		1d. on 3pf. brown	26·00	75·00
		a. "1" and "d" spaced	75·00	£170
		b. Surch double	£3750	
O2		1d. on 5pf. green	80·00	£140
		a. "1" and "d" spaced	£160	£300

1919–23. *Stamps of Australia optd with T* **11** *and punctured* "O S" *(8×15½ mm with eleven holes in the perforated* "S"*).*

		(i) T **5a** *of Australia.* W **5**. P 14¼×14.		
O3		1d. carmine-red (Die I)	£150	38·00
		ab. Dot before "1"		
		ac. "Secret mark"		
		ad. Flaw under neck	£550	
		b. Die II	—	£300
O4		4d. yellow-orange	£160	65·00
		a. Line through "FOUR PENCE" (Pl 2 rt pane R. 2/6)	—	£3250
O5		5d. brown (1921)	£250	65·00
		(ii) T **1** *of Australia.* W **6**. P 12.		
O6		2d. grey (Die I)	£250	55·00
O7		2½d. indigo (Die II)	£400	£250
O8		3d. greenish olive (Die I) (1921)	£450	£100
O9		6d. ultramarine (Die II) (1921)	£450	£160
		a. Greyish ultramarine	£400	£170
O10		9d. violet (Die IIB) (1921)	£140	£100
O11		1s. emerald (Die II) (1921)	£250	£110
		a. Pale blue-green	£300	£120
O12		2s. brown (Die II) (1922)	£325	£200
O13		5s. grey and yellow (Die II) (1922)	—	£600
O14		10s. grey and bright pink (Die II) (1921)		
		(iii) T **5a** *of Australia.* W **5**. *Rough unsurfaced paper, locally gummed.* P 14.		
O16		1d. rosine (Die I) (1920)	£600	£170
		b. Die II	£2500	£600
		(iv) T **5a** *of Australia.* W **5**. *Colour changes and new value.* P 14.		
O17		1d. violet (*shades*) (1923)	£250	38·00
O18		2d. orange (1921)	£100	38·00
O19		2d. rose-scarlet (1923)	£250	27·00
O20		4d. violet (1921)	£160	85·00
		a. "FOUR PENCE" in thinner letters (Pl 2 rt pane R. 2/6)		
O21		4d. ultramarine (1922)	£225	£100

Dates quoted for Nos. O3/21 are those of despatch from Australia. The earliest postmark date recorded is 2 April 1919 on No. O3. Their continued use on mail from government departments after the establishment of the civil administration is confirmed by a notice in the official *New Guinea Gazette* of 1 August 1921.

Australian postal archives indicate that nine sheets of the £1 Type **1** perforated "O S" were sent to New Guinea in September 1921. There is a pane of 30 of this stamp in the Royal Collection, but as no other examples are known it may not have been issued for postal purposes.

1925 (6 Apr)–**31**. *Optd with Type* O **2**. P 11.

O22	**12**	1d. green	1·00	4·50
O23		1½d. orange-vermilion (1931)	5·50	17·00
O24		2d. claret	1·75	3·75
O25		3d. blue	3·50	9·00
O26		4d. olive-green	4·50	8·50
O27		6d. olive-bistre	20·00	35·00
		a. Pale yellow-bistre (1931)	7·00	35·00
O28		9d. violet	4·00	35·00
O29		1s. dull blue-green	5·50	35·00
O30		2s. brown-lake	28·00	60·00
O22/30 *Set of 9*			65·00	£180

1931 (2 Aug). *Optd with Type* O **3**. P 11.

O31	**14**	1d. green	8·00	13·00
O32		1½d. vermilion	9·00	12·00
O33		2d. claret	10·00	7·00
O34		3d. blue	6·50	6·00
O35		4d. olive-green	6·50	8·50
O36		5d. deep blue-green	10·00	12·00
O37		6d. bistre-brown	14·00	17·00
O38		9d. violet	16·00	28·00
O39		1s. pale blue-green	16·00	28·00
O40		2s. brown-lake	40·00	70·00
O41		5s. olive-brown	£100	£170
O31/41 *Set of 11*			£200	£325

1932 (30 June)–**34**. *T* **14** *(redrawn without dates), optd with Type* O **3**. P 11.

O42		1d. green	11·00	12·00
O43		1½d. claret	12·00	13·00
O44		2d. vermilion	12·00	3·25
O45		2½d. green (14.9.34)	4·25	6·50
O46		3d. blue	9·50	30·00
		a. Double opt, one albino	£1000	
O47		3½d. aniline carmine (14.9.34)	4·25	9·00
O48		4d. olive-green	12·00	23·00
O49		5d. deep blue-green	9·00	23·00
O50		6d. bistre-brown	17·00	42·00
O51		9d. violet	15·00	42·00
O52		1s. pale blue-green	15·00	29·00
O53		2s. dull lake	30·00	75·00
O54		5s. olive-brown	£110	£170
O42/54 *Set of 13*			£225	£400

Civil Administration in New Guinea was suspended in 1942, following the Japanese invasion.

Various New Guinea stamps exist overprinted with an anchor and three Japanese characters in a style similar to the Japanese Naval Control Area overprints found on the stamps of Netherlands Indies. These overprints on New Guinea are bogus. Two different versions are known, one produced in Japan during 1947 and the other in Australia during the late 1980s.

On resumption, after the Japanese defeat in 1945, Australian stamps were used until the appearance of the issue for the combined territories of Papua & New Guinea.

NORFOLK ISLAND

Norfolk Island, first settled in 1788 from New South Wales, was transferred to Tasmania on 29 September 1844. It became a separate settlement on 1 November 1856 under the control of the Governor of New South Wales. The island was declared an Australian Territory on 1 July 1914. Unlike the other External Territories it retains an independent postal administration.

A Post Office was opened on Norfolk Island in 1832. The stamps of TASMANIA were used on Norfolk Island from July 1854 until May 1855, such use being identified by the "72" numeral cancellation. Stamps of NEW SOUTH WALES were first used on the island in 1877, but were not regularly available until 1898. The first "NORFOLK ISLAND" cancellation was supplied in 1892, but not used until 1898. Stamps of AUSTRALIA were in use from 1913 to 1947.

1 Ball Bay

(Des and eng F. Manley. Recess Note Printing Branch, Reserve Bank of Australia)

1947 (10 June)–**59**. *Toned paper.* P 14.

1	**1**	½d. orange	85	60
		a. White paper (11.56)	1·60	7·00
2		1d. bright violet	50	60
		a. White paper (8.57)	5·00	18·00
3		1½d. emerald-green	50	70
		a. White paper (11.56)	7·50	21·00
4		2d. reddish violet	55	40
		a. White paper (11.56)	90·00	£130
5		2½d. scarlet	80	30
6		3d. chestnut	70	70
6*a*		3d. emerald-green (*white paper*) (6.7.59)	11·00	7·50
7		4d. claret	1·75	40
8		5½d. indigo	70	30
9		6d. purple-brown	70	30
10		9d. magenta	1·25	40
11		1s. grey-green	70	40
12		2s. yellow-bistre	1·00	1·00
12*a*		2s. deep blue (*white paper*) (6.7.59)	14·00	8·00
1/12*a* *Set of 14*			30·00	19·00

Stamps as Type **1**, some in different colours, perforated 11 were prepared in 1940 but never issued. Examples exist from sheets stolen prior to the destruction of these stocks.

2 Warder's Tower

3 Airfield

4 Old Stores (Crankmill)

5 Barracks entrance

6 Salt House

7 Bloody Bridge

(Des B. Stewart, eng. G. Lissenden (3½d.), D. Cameron (7½d.). Des and eng D. Cameron (6½d.), P. Morriss (8½d., 10d.) or G. Lissenden (5s.))

1953 (10 June). *T* **2/7**. P 14½×15 (vert) or 15×14½ (horiz).

13	**2**	3½d. brown-lake	1·00	90
14	**3**	6½d. deep green	2·25	3·25
15	**4**	7½d. deep blue	1·50	3·00
16	**5**	8½d. chocolate	1·75	4·75
17	**6**	10d. reddish violet	1·00	75
18	**7**	5s. sepia	32·00	8·00
13/18 *Set of 6*			35·00	18·00

8 Norfolk Island Seal and Pitcairners Landing

Two types of 2s.:

Type I

Type II

Alternate stamps on each horizontal row are with or without a dot in bottom right corner.

(Des and eng F. Manley)

1956 (8 June). *Centenary of Landing of Pitcairn Islanders on Norfolk Island.* P 15×14½.

19	**8**	3d. deep bluish green	75	40
20		2s. violet (I)	1·00	1·00
		a. Type II	1·00	75
		b. Deep violet (I)	2·50	1·75
		ba. Type II	2·50	1·75

7d (9) **8d** (10) **NORFOLK ISLAND 5D** (11)

1958 (1 July). *Nos. 15/16 surch with T* **9/10**.

21		7d. on 7½d. deep blue	1·00	1·00
22		8d. on 8½d. chocolate	1·00	1·00

1959 (7 Dec). *150th Anniv of Australian Post Office. No. 331 of Australia surch with T* **11**.

23		5d. on 4d. slate (R.)	35	30

12 *Hibiscus insularis*

13 *Lagunaria patersonii*

14 White Tern

15 Lantana

16 Red Hibiscus

17 Queen Elizabeth II and Cereus

18 Fringed Hibiscus

19 Solander's Petrel

20 Passion Flower

21 Rose Apple

22 Red-tailed Tropic Bird

(Des G. Lissenden, eng P. Morriss (5s.). Des and eng G. Lissenden (10s.), P. Morriss (others). Recess and typo (2s.8d.), recess (others))

1960–62. *T* **6/7** and **12/22**. P 14½ or 14½×14 (10s.).

24	**12**	1d. bluish green (23.5.60)	15	10
25	**13**	2d. rose and myrtle-green (23.5.60)	20	10
26	**14**	3d. green (1.5.61)	70	15
27	**15**	5d. bright purple (20.6.60)	55	20
28	**16**	8d. red (20.6.60)	80	50
29	**17**	9d. ultramarine (23.5.60)	80	45
30	**6**	10d. brown and reddish violet (as No. 17) (27.2.61)	1·25	1·00
31	**18**	1s.1d. carmine-red (16.10.61)	80	35
32	**19**	2s. sepia (1.5.61)	4·00	1·00
33	**20**	2s.5d. deep violet (5.2.62)	1·00	40
34	**21**	2s.8d. cinnamon and deep green (9.4.62)	2·25	55
35	**7**	5s. sepia and deep green (as No. 18) (27.2.61)	2·75	75
36	**22**	10s. emerald-green (14.8.61)	26·00	32·00
		s. Optd "Specimen"	42·00	
24/36 *Set of* 13			38·00	32·00

Nos. 30 and 35 are redrawn.

The Specimen overprint on No. 36 is from sets sold by the Australian Post Office.

For Nos. 25 and 28 with face values in decimal currency see Nos. 600/1.

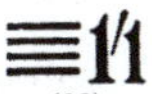

(23) **(24)** **(25)**

1960. *As Nos. 13/15 but colours changed, surch with T* **23/5**.

37		1s.1d. on 3½d. deep ultramarine (26.9.60)	2·00	1·00
38		2s.5d. on 6½d. bluish green (26.9.60)	3·00	1·00
39		2s.8d. on 7½d. sepia (29.8.60)	6·00	5·50
37/9 *Set of* 3			10·00	6·75

26 Queen Elizabeth II and Map

27 Open Bible and Candle

(Des and eng P. Morriss)

1960 (24 Oct). *Introduction of Local Government.* P 14.

40	**26**	2s. 8d. reddish purple	4·50	6·50

(Des K. McKay. Adapted and eng B. Stewart. Recess)

1960 (21 Nov). *Christmas.* P 15×14½.

41	**27**	5d. bright purple	60	50

28 Open Prayer Book and Text

29 Stripey (*Atypichthys latus*)

(Des G. Lissenden. Eng P. Morriss. Recess)

1961 (20 Nov). *Christmas.* P 14½×14.

42	**28**	5d. slate-blue	30	70

PRINTERS. All the following issues to No. 233 were printed in photogravure by Harrison and Sons, Ltd, London, *except where otherwise stated.*

1962–63. *Fishes. Horiz designs as T* **29**. P 14½×14.

43		6d. sepia, yellow and deep bluish green (16.7.62)	60	25
44		11d. red-orange, brown and blue (25.2.63)	1·00	80
45		1s. blue, pink and yellow-olive (17.9.62)	60	25
46		1s.3d. blue, red-brown and green (15.7.63)	1·00	1·75
47		1s.6d. sepia, violet and light blue	1·25	80
48		2s.3d. deep blue, red and greenish yellow (23.9.63)	2·50	80
43/8 *Set of* 6			6·25	4·25

Designs:—11d. Gold-mouthed Emperor (*Lethrinus chrysostomus*); 1s. Surge Wrasse ("Po'ov"); 1s.3d. Seachub ("Dreamfish"); 1s.6d. Giant Grouper (*Promicrops lanceolatus*); 2s.3d. White Trevally (*Carangidae*).

30 "Madonna and Child"

31 "Peace on Earth..."

(Des and eng G. Lissenden. Recess Note Ptg Branch, Reserve Bank of Australia)

1962 (19 Nov). *Christmas.* P 14½.

49	**30**	5d. ultramarine	45	80

(Des R. Warner. Eng B. Stewart. Recess Note Ptg Branch, Reserve Bank of Australia)

1963 (11 Nov). *Christmas.* P 14½.

50	**31**	5d. red	40	70

32 Overlooking Kingston

33 Norfolk Pine

1964 (24 Feb). *Views. Horiz designs as T* **32**. *Multicoloured.* P 14½×14.

51		5d. Type **32**	60	60
52		8d. Kingston	1·00	1·50
53		9d. The Arches (Bumboras) (11.5)	1·00	30
54		10d. Slaughter Bay (28.9)	1·00	30
51/4 *Set of* 4			3·25	2·50

(Photo Note Ptg Branch, Reserve Bank of Australia, Melbourne)

1964 (1 July). *50th Anniv of Norfolk Island as Australian Territory.* P 13½.

55	**33**	5d. black, red and orange	40	15
56		8d. black, red and grey-green	40	1·10

34 Child looking at Nativity Scene

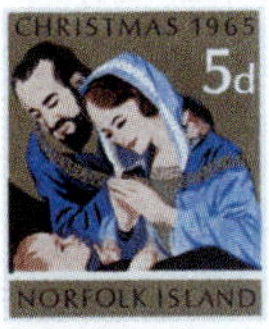

35 Nativity Scene

(Des P. Morriss and J. Mason. Photo Note Ptg Branch, Reserve Bank of Australia)

1964 (9 Nov). *Christmas.* P 13½.

57	**34**	5d. green, blue, buff and violet	30	40

1965 (14 Apr). *50th Anniv of Gallipoli Landing. As T* **22** *of Nauru.* P 13½.

58		5d. sepia, black and emerald	15	10

(Des J. Mason. Photo Note Ptg Branch, Reserve Bank of Australia)

1965 (25 Oct). *Christmas. Helecon paper.* P 13½.

59	**35**	5d. multicoloured	15	10

(New Currency. 100 cents = 1 Australian dollar)

38 *Hibiscus insularis*

39 Headstone Bridge

1966 (14 Feb). *Decimal currency. Various stamps surch in black on silver tablets, which vary slightly in size, obliterating old value as in T* **38**. *Surch typo.*

60	**38**	1c. on 1d. bluish green (*value tablet* 4×5 mm)	20	10
		a. Value tablet larger, 5½×5½ mm	40	30
61	–	2c. on 2d. rose and myrtle-green (No. 25)	20	10
62	**14**	3c. on 3d. green	75	90
		a. Silver tablet omitted	£450	
63	–	4c. on 5d. bright purple (No. 27)	25	10
64	**16**	5c . on 8d.red	30	10
65	–	10c. on 10d. brown and reddish violet (No. 30)	1·00	15
66	–	15c. on 1s.1d. carmine-red (No. 31)	50	70
67	–	20c. on 2s. sepia (No. 32)	2·75	2·75
68	–	25c. on 2s.5d. deep violet (No. 33)	1·00	40
69	**21**	30c. on 2s.8d. cinnamon and deep green	1·00	50
70	–	50c. on 5s. sepia and deep green (No. 35)	2·50	75
71	**22**	$1 on 10s. emerald-green (*value tablet* 7×6½ mm)	3·00	2·50
		a. Value tablet smaller, 6½×4 mm	2·25	3·00
60/71a *Set of* 12			11·50	8·00

1966 (27 June). *Horiz designs as T* **39**. *Multicoloured.* P 14½×14.

72		7c. Type **39**	40	15
73		9c. Cemetery Road	40	15

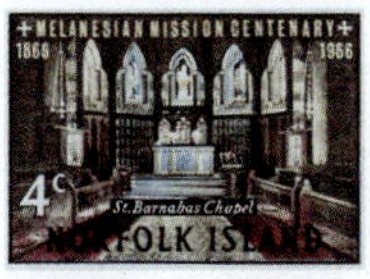

41 St. Barnabas' Chapel (interior)

42 St. Barnabas' Chapel (exterior)

1966 (23 Aug). *Centenary of Melanesian Mission.* P 14×14½.

74	**41**	4c. multicoloured	10	10
75	**42**	25c. multicoloured	20	20

43 Star over Philip Island

44 H.M.S. *Resolution*, 1774

(Des B. G. W. McCoy)

1966 (24 Oct). *Christmas.* P 14½.

76	**43**	4c. multicoloured	10	10

(Des V. Whiteley)

1967 (17 Apr)–**68**. *T* **44** *and similar horiz designs showing ships. Multicoloured.* P 14×14½.

77		1c. Type **44**	10	10
78		2c. *La Boussole and L'Astrolabe*, 1788	15	10
79		3c. H.M.S. *Supply*, 1788	15	10
80		4c. H.M.S. *Sirius*, 1790	75	10
81		5c. *Norfolk* (sloop), 1798 (14.8.67)	20	10
82		7c. H.M.S. *Mermaid* (survey cutter), 1825 (14.8.67)	20	10
83		9c. *Lady Franklin*, 1853 (14.8.67)	20	10
84		10c. *Morayshire*, 1856 (14.8.67)	20	50
85		15c. *Southern Cross*, 1866 (18.3.68)	50	30
86		20c. *Pitcairn*, 1891 (18.3.68)	60	40
87		25c. *Black Billy* (Norfolk Island whaleboat), 1895 (18.3.68)	1·50	75
88		30c. *Iris* (cable ship), 1907 (18.6.68)	1·50	2·00
89		50c. *Resolution*, 1926 (18.6.68)	2·50	2·75
90		$1 *Morinda*, 1931 (18.6.68)	3·00	2·75
77/90 *Set of* 14			10·50	9·00

45 Lions Badge and 50 Stars

46 Prayer of John Adams and Candle

(Des M. Ripper. Photo Note Ptg Branch, Reserve Bank of Australia)

1967 (7 June). *50th Anniv of Lions International.* P 13½.

91	**45**	4c. black, bluish green and olive-yellow	10	10

(Des B. G. W. McCoy)

1967 (16 Oct). *Christmas.* P 14.

92	**46**	5c. black, light yellow-olive and red	10	10

47 Queen Elizabeth II

(Photo Note Ptg Branch, Reserve Bank of Australia)

1968 (5 Aug)–**71**. *Coil stamps.* P 15×imperf.

93	**47**	3c. black, light brown and vermilion	10	10
94		4c. black, light brown and blue-green	10	10
95		5c. black, light brown and deep violet	10	10
95*a*		6c. black, light brown and lake-brown (25.8.71)	30	60
93/5a *Set of* 4			55	80

59 Avro Type 691 Lancastrian and Douglas DC-4 Aircraft

60 Bethlehem Star and Flowers

(Des Harrison)

1968 (25 Sept). *21st Anniv of QANTAS Air Service, Sydney-Norfolk Island.* P 14.

96	**59**	5c. bluish black, carmine-red and light blue	15	10
97		7c. blackish brown, carmine-red ad turquoise	15	10

(Des Betty Laing)

1968 (24 Oct). *Christmas.* P 14×14½.

98	**60**	5c. multicoloured	10	10

61 Captain Cook, Quadrant and Chart of Pacific Ocean Island

62 Van Diemen's Land, Norfolk and Sailing Cutter

(Des V. Whiteley from sketch by J. Cowap)

1969 (3 June). *Captain Cook Bicentenary (1st issue). Observation of the transit of Venus across the Sun, from Tahiti.* P 14.

99	**61**	10c. multicoloured	10	10

See also Nos. 118/19, 129, 152/5, 200/2 and 213/14.

(Des Mrs. A. Bathie and Mrs. M. J. McCoy)

1969 (29 Sept). *125th Anniv of the Annexation of Norfolk Island to Van Diemen's Land.* P 14×14½.

100	**62**	5c. multicoloured	10	10
101		30c. multicoloured	50	1·00
		a. Inscr "VAN DIFMEN'S LAND" (R. 8/5)	11·00	

63 "The Nativity" (carved mother-of-pearl plaque)

64 New Zealand Grey Flyeater

(Des J. Cowap)

1969 (27 Oct). *Christmas.* P 14½×14.

102	**63**	5c. multicoloured	10	10

(Des G. Mathews)

1970–71. *Birds. T* **64** *and similar multicoloured designs. Chalk-surfaced paper.* P 14.

103	1c. Scarlet Robins (22.7.70)	30	10
104	2c. Golden Whistler (24.2.71)	30	20
105	3c. Type **64** (25.2.70)	30	10
106	4c. Long-tailed Koels (25.2.70)	60	10
107	5c. Red-fronted Parakeet (24.2.71)	1·50	60
108	7c. Long-tailed Triller (22.7.70)	45	10
109	9c. Island Thrush (25.2.70)	70	10
110	10c. Boobook Owl (22.7.70)	1·75	3·00
111	15c. Norfolk Island Pigeon (24.2.71)	1·25	65
112	20c. White-chested White Eye	7·00	3·50
113	25c. Norfolk Island Parrots (22.7.70)	1·75	40
	a. Error. Glazed, ordinary paper	£400	
114	30c. Collared Grey Fantail (16.6.71)	7·00	2·00
115	45c. Norfolk Island Starlings (25.2.70)	1·25	80
116	50c. Crimson Rosella (24.2.71)	1·50	2·00
117	$1 Sacred Kingfisher (16.6.71)	8·00	10·00
103/17 *Set of* 15		30·00	21·00

Nos. 105, 106, 109, 112, 114, 115 and 117 are horizontal, and the remainder vertical designs.

It is believed that only one sheet of No. 113a was issued.

65 Capt. Cook and Map of Australia

66 First Christmas Service, 1788

(Des R. Bates)

1970 (29 Apr). *Captain Cook Bicentenary (2nd issue). Discovery of Australia's East Coast. T* **65** *and similar horiz design. Multicoloured.* P 14.

118		5c. Type **65**	15	10
119		10c. H.M.S. *Endeavour* and aborigine	40	10

(Des R. Bates)

1970 (15 Oct). *Christmas.* P 14.

120	**66**	5c. multicoloured	10	10

PAPUA (BRITISH NEW GUINEA)

Stamps of QUEENSLAND were used in British New Guinea (Papua) from at least 1885 onwards. Post Offices were opened at Daru (1894), Kulumadau (Woodlarks) (1899), Nivani (1899), Port Moresby (1885), Samarai (1888), Sudest (1899) and Tamata (1899). Stamps were usually cancelled "N.G." (at Port Moresby from 1885) or "BNG" (without stops at Samarai or with stops at the other offices) from 1888. Queensland stamps were replaced in Papua by the issue of 1901.

PRICES FOR STAMPS ON COVER

Nos. 1/7	*from* × 15
No. 8	—
Nos. 9/15	*from* × 20
No. 16	—
Nos. 17/27	*from* × 6
No. 28	—
Nos. 39/45*a*	*from* × 5
Nos. 47/71	*from* × 8
Nos. 72/4	—
Nos. 75/92*a*	*from* × 8
Nos. 93/103	*from* × 6
Nos. 104/5	—
Nos. 106/11	*from* × 10
Nos. 112/14	*from* × 6
No. 115	—
Nos. 116/28	*from* × 5
Nos. 130/53	*from* × 4
Nos. 154/7	*from* × 12
Nos. 158/67	*from* × 4
No. 168	*from* × 3
Nos. O1/54	*from* × 10
Nos. O55/66*a*	*from* × 7

1 Lakatoi (trading canoe) with Hanuabada Village in Background

2 (Horizontal)

Deformed "d" at left (R. 4/3)

(Recess D.L.R.)

1901 (1 July)–**05**. Wmk Mult Rosettes, W **2**. P 14.

A. Wmk horizontal. Thick paper. Line perf.

1	**1**	½d. black and yellow-green	15·00	21·00
		a. Thin paper	£180	£140
2		1d. black and carmine	12·00	13·00
3		2d. black and violet	15·00	7·00
4		2½d. black and ultramarine	22·00	10·00
		a. Thin paper	£250	£160
		ab. Black and dull blue	£600	£400
5		4d. black and sepia	48·00	35·00
		a. Deformed "d" at left	£300	£250
6		6d. black and myrtle-green	48·00	35·00
7		1s. black and orange	60·00	65·00
8		2s.6d. black and brown (1.1.05)	£550	£500
1/8 *Set of* 8			£700	£600

B. Wmk vertical. Medium to thick paper. Line or comb perf.

9	**1**	½d. black and yellow-green	12·00	3·75
		a. Thin paper (*comb perf*) (1905)	18·00	25·00
10		1d. black and carmine	4·75	2·00
11		2d. black and violet	10·00	4·00
		a. Thin paper (*comb perf*) (1905)	55·00	16·00
12		2½d. black and ultramarine (*shades*)	17·00	12·00
13		4d. black and sepia	35·00	50·00
		a. Deformed "d" at left	£250	£325
		b. Thin paper (*comb perf*) (1905)	£225	
		ba. Deformed "d" at left	£1100	
14		6d. black and myrtle-green	48·00	75·00
		a. Thin paper (*comb perf*) (1905)	£700	
15		1s. black and orange	55·00	85·00
		a. Thin paper (*comb perf*) (1905)	£650	
16		2s.6d. black and brown (1905)	£3500	£2500
		a. Thin paper (*comb perf*)	£500	£1000
9/16a *Set of* 8			£600	£1100

The paper used for Nos. 1/8 is white, of consistent thickness and rather opaque. The thin paper used for the horizontal watermark printings is of variable thickness, readily distinguishable from the thick paper by its greater transparency and by the gum which is thin and smooth.

Nos. 9/16 were initially printed on the same thick paper as the stamps with horizontal watermark and were line perforated. Values from ½d. to 2½d. were subsequently printed on medium paper on which the watermark was more visible. These were comb perforated. The thin paper with vertical watermark, produced in 1905, is much more transparent and has smooth gum. Printings were made on this paper for all values except the 2½d., but only the ½d. and 2d. were issued in Papua although used examples of the 2s.6d. are also known. The entire printing of the 1d. on thin paper with vertical watermark was used for subsequent overprints.

The sheets of the ½d., 2d. and 2½d. show a variety known as "white leaves" on R. 4/5, while the 2d. and 2½d. (both R. 6/2) and the ½d. and 1s. (both R. 6/3) show what is known as the "unshaded leaves" variety.

Papua. (3) **Papua.** (4)

1906–07. *I. Optd with T* **3** *(large opt), at Port Moresby (8 Nov 1906).*

A. Wmk horizontal. Thick paper. Line perf.

17	**1**	4d. black and sepia	£190	£150
		a. Deformed "d" at left	£600	£500
18		6d. black and myrtle-green	50·00	48·00
19		1s. black and orange	20·00	38·00
20		2s.6d. black and brown	£140	£150

B. Wmk vertical. Thin paper (½d., 1d., 2d.) or medium to thick paper (others). Comb perf (½d. to 2½d.) or line perf (others).

21	**1**	½d. black and yellow-green	5·50	20·00
22		1d. black and carmine	16·00	18·00
23		2d. black and violet	7·00	3·00
24		2½d. black and ultramarine	3·75	15·00
25		4d. black and sepia	£170	£130
		a. Deformed "d" at left	£550	
26		6d. black and myrtle-green	28·00	60·00
27		1s. black and orange	£1200	£900
28		2s.6d. black and brown	£9500	£8500
19/26 *Set of* 8			£350	£375

II. Optd with T **4** *(small opt), at Brisbane (May-June 1907).*

A. Wmk horizontal. Thick paper. Line perf.

34	**1**	½d. black and yellow-green		
		a. Thin paper	60·00	80·00
35		2½d. black and ultramarine		
		a. Thin paper	48·00	60·00
		ac. Black and dull blue	£160	£170
36		1s. black and orange	£180	£275
37		2s.6d. black and brown	38·00	60·00
		a. Opt reading downwards	£4750	
		c. Opt double (horiz)	†	£3750
		d. Opt triple (horiz)	†	£3000

B. Wmk vertical. Thin paper (½d., 1d., 2d., 4d., 6d.) or medium to thick paper (2½d., 1s., 2s.6d.). Line or comb perf (2½d.), line perf (1s., 2s.6d.) or comb perf (others).

38	**1**	½d. black and yellow-green	13·00	14·00
		a. Opt double	£2750	
39		1d. black and carmine	5·50	5·00
		a. Opt reading upwards	£4000	£2250
40		2d. black and violet	4·50	2·25
		a. Opt double	£2750	
41		2½d. black and ultramarine	11·00	18·00
42		4d. black and sepia	35·00	55·00
		a. Deformed "d" at left	£190	£325
43		6d. black and myrtle-green	35·00	42·00
		a. Opt double	£4000	£7000
44		1s. black and orange	65·00	80·00
		b. Thin paper (*comb perf*)	28·00	40·00
		ba. Opt double, one diagonal	£13000	£7500
45		2s.6d. black and brown	£10000	£6000
		a. Thin paper (*comb perf*)	38·00	50·00
38/45a *Set of* 8			£150	£200

In the setting of this overprint Nos. 10,16, and 21 have the "p" of "Papua" with a defective foot or inverted "d" for "p", and in No. 17 the "pua" of "Papua" is a shade lower than the first "a".

No. 37a comes from a single sheet on which the overprints were sideways. Examples exist showing one, two or four complete or partial overprints.

PRINTERS. All the following issues were printed at Melbourne by the Stamp Ptg Branch (to 1928) or Note Ptg Branch.

WATERMARK VARIETIES. When printing the lithographed issues, Nos. 47/83, little attention was paid to the position of the watermark. Nos. 47, 49/58 and 75/83 all come either upright or inverted while Nos. 48 and 59/71 all occur with watermark sideways to left or right. Nos. 51/2 are known with watermark reversed and others may well exist.

5 Large "PAPUA"

B

C

Three types of the 2s.6d.:—

A. Thin top to "2" and small ball. Thin "6" and small ball. Thick uneven stroke.

B. Thin top to 2" and large, well shaped ball. Thin "6" and large ball. Very thick uneven stroke.

C. Thick top to "2" and large, badly shaped ball. Thick "6" and uneven ball. Thin even line.

Type A is not illustrated as the stamp is distinguishable by perf and watermark.

The litho stones were prepared from the engraved plates of the 1901 issue, value for value except the 2s.6d. for which the original plate was mislaid. No. 48 containing Type A was prepared from the original ½d. plate with the value inserted on the stone and later a fresh stone was prepared from the 1d. plate and this contained Type B. Finally, the original plate of the 2s.6d. was found and a third stone was prepared from this, and issued in 1911. These stamps show Type C.

6 Small "PAPUA"

(Litho Stamp Ptg Branch, Melbourne, from transfers taken from original engraved plates)

1907–10. *A. Large "PAPUA". Wmk Crown over A, W w* **11**.

(a) Wmk upright. P 11.

47 5 ½d. black and yellow-green (11.07) 2·00 3·50

(b) Wmk sideways. P 11.

48 5 2s.6d. black and chocolate (A) (12.09) 48·00 60·00
a. "POSTAGIE" at left (R.1/5) £550 £650

B. Small "PAPUA" I. Wmk upright.

(a) P 11 (1907–8).

49 6 1d. black and rose (6.08) 4·75 5·00
50 2d. black and purple (10.08) 14·00 4·50
51 2½d. black and bright ultramarine (7.08) 21·00 28·00
a. Black and pale ultramarine 8·00 6·50
52 4d. black and sepia (20.11.07) 4·25 11·00
a. Deformed "d" at left 32·00 55·00
53 6d. black and myrtle-green (4.08) 11·00 16·00
54 1s. black and orange (10.08) 28·00 20·00

(b) P 12½ (1907–9).

55 6 2d. black and purple (10.08) 27·00 6·50
56 2½d. black and bright ultramarine (7.08) £130 £140
a. Black and pale ultramarine 60·00 80·00
57 4d. black and sepia (20.11.07) 8·00 8·00
a. Deformed "d" at left 55·00 55·00
58 1s. black and orange (1.09) 65·00 85·00

II. Wmk sideways.

(a) P 11 (1909–10).

59 6 ½d. black and yellow-green (12.09) 2·25 2·75
a. Black and deep green (1910) 28·00 42·00
60 1d. black and carmine (1.10) 9·00 8·00
61 2d. black and purple (1.10) 15·00 8·00
62 2½d. black and dull blue (1.10) 4·25 23·00
63 4d. black and sepia (1.10) 4·75 9·00
a. Deformed "d" at left 32·00 50·00
64 6d. black and myrtle-green (11.09) 10·00 21·00
65 1s. black and orange (3.10) 48·00 60·00

(b) P 12½ (1909–10).

66 6 ½d. black and yellow-green (12.09) 1·75 3·75
a. Black and deep green (1910) 30·00 38·00
67 1d. black and carmine (12.09) 7·50 12·00
68 2d. black and purple (1.10) 4·25 6·50
69 2½d. black and dull blue (1.10) 9·00 40·00
70 6d. black and myrtle-green (11.09) £3250 £5000
71 1s. black and orange (3.10) 16·00 42·00

(c) Perf compound of 11 and 12½.

72 6 ½d. black and yellow-green £2500 £2500
73 2d. black and purple £1000

(d) Mixed perfs 11 and 12½.

74 6 4d. black and sepia £11000

Compound perforations on the 4d. are fakes.

The only known examples of No. 74 come from the top row of a sheet perforated 11 and with an additional line perf 12½ in the top margin.

(Litho Stamp Ptg Branch, Melbourne, by J. B. Cooke, from new stones made by fresh transfers)

1910 (Sept)–**11**. *Large "PAPUA".* W w **11** (upright). P 12½.

75 5 ½d. black and green (12.10) 3·50 11·00
76 1d. black and carmine 10·00 8·50
77 2d. black and dull purple (*shades*) (12.10) 6·00 5·00
a. "C" for "O" in "POSTAGE" (R. 4/3) 65·00 65·00
78 2½d. black and blue-violet (10.10) 7·00 17·00
79 4d. black and sepia (10.10) 7·00 10·00
a. Deformed "d" at left 38·00 55·00
80 6d. black and myrtle-green 8·50 7·50
81 1s. black and deep orange (12.10) 8·00 19·00
82 2s.6d. black and brown (B) 38·00 48·00
83 2s.6d. black and brown (C) (1911) 45·00 55·00
75/82 *Set of* 8 80·00 £110

A variety showing a white line or "rift" in clouds occurs on R. 5/3 in Nos. 49/74 and the "white leaves" variety mentioned below No. 16 occurs on the 2d. and 2½d. values in both issues. They are worth about three times the normal price.

8

ONE PENNY
(9)

(Eng S. Reading. Typo J. B. Cooke)

1911–15. *Printed in one colour.* W **8** (sideways*).

(a) P 12½ (1911–12).

84 6 ½d. yellow-green 1·50 3·75
a. Green 50 2·25
w. Wmk Crown to right of A 10·00
85 1d. rose-pink 70 75
w. Wmk Crown to right of A 20·00 20·00
86 2d. bright mauve 1·00 75
w. Wmk Crown to right of A 60·00 40·00
87 2½d. bright ultramarine 4·75 8·50
a. Dull ultramarine 5·50 8·50
aw. Wmk Crown to right of A 50·00
88 4d. pale olive-green 2·25 11·00
w. Wmk Crown to right of A 60·00 40·00
89 6d. orange-brown 3·75 5·00
w. Wmk Crown to right of A 75·00
90 1s. yellow 9·00 15·00
w. Wmk Crown to right of A 75·00
91 2s.6d. rose-carmine 32·00 38·00
w. Wmk Crown to right of A £170
84/91 *Set of* 8 48·00 70·00

(b) P 14.

92 6 1d. rose-pink (6.15) 23·00 6·00
a. Pale scarlet 6·50 2·00
w. Wmk Crown to right of A — 40·00

*The normal sideways watermark shows Crown to left of A, *as seen from the back of the stamp.*

(Typo J. B. Cooke (1916–18), T. S. Harrison (1918–26), A. J. Mullett (No. 95*b* only) (1926–27), or John Ash (1927–31))

1916 (Aug)–**31**. *Printed in two colours.* W **8** (sideways*). P 14.

93 6 ½d. myrtle and apple green (Harrison and Ash) (1919) 80 1·00
a. Myrtle and pale olive-green (1927) 1·75 2·25
w. Wmk Crown to right of A 5·50 8·00
94 1d. black and carmine-red 1·40 1·25
a. Grey-black and red (1918) 1·60 1·25
aw. Wmk Crown to right of A 3·25 50
b. Intense black and red (Harrison) (*wmk Crown to right of A*) (1926) 2·50 2·50
95 1½d. pale grey-blue (*shades*) and brown (1925) 1·50 80
aw. Wmk Crown to right of A 15·00 5·00
b. Cobalt and light brown (Mullett) (*wmk Crown to right of A*) (1927) 6·00 3·25
c. Bright blue and bright brown (1929) 2·75 2·00
d. "POSTACE" at right (R.1/1) (all printings) *From* 32·00 32·00
96 2d. brown-purple and brown-lake (1919) 1·75 75
a. Deep brown-purple and lake (1931) 25·00 1·75
aw. Wmk Crown to right of A 30·00 2·50
b. Brown-purple and claret (1931) 2·00 75
97 2½d. myrtle and ultramarine (1919) 4·75 12·00
98 3d. black and bright blue-green (12.16) 2·50 1·75
a. Error. Black and deep greenish Prussian blue† £500 £500
b. Sepia-black and bright blue-green (Harrison) 22·00 19·00
c. Black and blue-green (1927) 4·50 8·00
99 4d. brown and orange (1919) 2·50 5·00
a. Light brown and orange (1927) 9·50 17·00
aw. Wmk Crown to right of A 8·50 17·00
100 5d. bluish slate and pale brown (1931) 4·25 16·00
101 6d. dull and pale purple (*wmk Crown to right of A*) (1919) 3·25 9·50
aw. Wmk Crown to left of A 13·00
b. Dull purple and red-purple (*wmk Crown to left of A*) (1927) 15·00 16·00
c. "POSTACE" at left (R. 6/2) (all printings) *From* 75·00 £110
102 1s. sepia and olive (1919) 3·50 7·00
a. Brown and yellow-olive (1927) 7·00 14·00
103 2s.6d. maroon and pale pink (1919) 22·00 40·00
a. Maroon and bright pink (*shades*) (1927) 19·00 50·00
104 5s. black and deep green (12.16) 48·00 48·00
105 10s. green and pale ultramarine (1925) £140 £160
93/105 *Set of* 13 £200 £275

*The normal sideways watermark shows Crown to left of A, *as seen from the back of the stamp.*

†Beware of similar shades produced by removal of yellow pigment. No 98a is a colour trial, prepared by Cooke, of which, it is believed, five sheets were sold in error.

The printers of various shades can be determined by their dates of issue. The Ash printings are on whiter paper.

For 9d. and 1s.3d. values, see Nos. 127/8.

1917 (Oct). *Nos. 84, 86/9 and 91 surch with T* **9** *by Govt Ptg Office, Melbourne.*

106 6 1d. on ½d. yellow-green 1·50 1·60
a. Green 1·00 1·25
w. Wmk Crown to right of A 4·25 5·50
107 1d. on 2d. bright mauve 12·00 15·00
108 1d. on 2½d. ultramarine 1·25 3·75
109 1d. on 4d. pale olive-green 1·75 4·50
w. Wmk Crown to right of A — 40·00
110 1d. on 6d. orange-brown 8·50 17·00
111 1d. on 2s.6d. rose-carmine 1·50 6·00
106/11 *Set of* 6 23·00 42·00

AIR MAIL
(10)

(11)

1929 (Oct)–**30**. *Air. Optd with T* **10** *by Govt Printer, Port Moresby.*

(a) Cooke printing. Yellowish paper.

112 6 3d. black and bright blue-green 1·25 13·00
a. Opt omitted in vert pair with normal £5000

(b) Harrison printing. Yellowish paper.

113 6 3d. sepia-black and bright blue-green 50·00 65·00

(c) Ash printing. White paper.

114 6 3d. black and blue-green 1·00 7·00
a. Opt omitted (in horiz pair with normal) £5500
b. Ditto, but vert pair £5000
c. Opt vertical, on back £4500
d. Opts *tête-bêche* (vert pair) £7000

1930 (15 Sept). *Air. Optd with T* **11**, *in carmine by Govt Printer, Port Moresby.*

(a) Harrison printings. Yellowish paper.

115 6 3d. sepia-black and bright blue-green £2000 £3250
116 6d. dull and pale purple 3·00 16·00
a. "POSTACE" at left (R. 6/2) 65·00 £110
117 1s. sepia and olive 7·00 20·00
a. Opt inverted £8500

(b) Ash printings. White paper.

118 6 3d. black and blue-green 1·00 6·00
119 6d. dull purple and red-purple 5·50 8·00
a. "POSTACE" at left (R. 6/2) 70·00 £100
120 1s. brown and yellow-olive 4·25 13·00
118/20 *Set of* 3 11·00 24·00

The rare Harrison printing with this overprint, No. 115, should not be confused with examples of the Ash printing, No. 118, which have been climatically toned.

5d.

TWO PENCE
(12)

FIVE PENCE
(13)

1931 (1 Jan). *Surch with T* **12** *by Govt Printer, Port Moresby.*

(a) Mullett printing.

121 6 2d. on 1½d. cobalt and light brown 12·00 24·00
a. "POSTACE" at right (R. 1/1) £140 £225

(b) Ash printing.

122 6 2d. on 1½d. bright blue and bright brown 1·00 2·00
a. "POSTACE" at right (R. 1/1) 25·00 42·00

1931. *Surch as T* **13** *by Govt Printer, Port Moresby.*

(a) Cooke printing.

123 6 1s.3d. on 5s. black and deep green 4·25 9·00

(b) Harrison printing. Yellowish paper.

124 6 9d. on 2s.6d. maroon and pale pink (Dec) 6·00 24·00

(c) Ash printings. White paper.

125 6 5d. on 1s. brown and yellow-olive (26.7) 1·00 1·75
126 9d. on 2s.6d. maroon and bright pink 5·50 8·50

(Typo J. Ash)

1932. W **15** of Australia (Mult "C of A"). P 11.

127 5 9d. lilac and violet 4·50 32·00
128 1s.3d. lilac and pale greenish blue 7·50 32·00
127s/8s Optd "Specimen" *Set of* 2 £500

15 Motuan girl

16 A Chieftain's son

17 Tree houses

18 Raggiana Bird of Paradise

19 Papuan dandy

20 Native mother and child

21 Masked dancer

22 Papuan motherhood

23 Papuan shooting fish

24 *Dubu—or ceremonial platform*

25 "Lakatoi"

26 Papuan art

27 Pottery making

28 Native policeman

29 Lighting a fire

30 Delta house

(Des F. E. Williams (2s., £1 and frames of other values), E. Whitehouse (2d., 4d., 6d., 1s., and 10s.); remaining centres from photos by Messrs F. E. Williams and Gibson. Recess J. Ash (all values) and W. C. G. McCracken (½d., 1d., 2d., 4d.))

1932 (14 Nov)–**40**. *T* **15/30**. No wmk. P 11.

130	**15**	½d. black and orange	1·75	3·25
		a. Black and buff (McCracken) (1940)	13·00	24·00
131	**16**	1d. black and green	1·75	60
132	**17**	1½d. black and lake	1·75	8·00
133	**18**	2d. red	11·00	30
134	**19**	3d. black and blue	3·25	6·50
135	**20**	4d. olive-green	8·00	9·50
136	**21**	5d. black and slate-green	3·25	3·00
137	**22**	6d. bistre-brown	7·50	5·50
138	**23**	9d. black and violet	10·00	21·00
139	**24**	1s. dull blue-green	4·75	8·50
140	**25**	1s.3d. black and dull purple	15·00	27·00
141	**26**	2s. black and slate-green	15·00	24·00
142	**27**	2s.6d. black and rose-mauve	25·00	38·00
143	**28**	5s. black and olive-brown	55·00	55·00
144	**29**	10s. violet	95·00	95·00
145	**30**	£1 black and olive-grey	£225	£170
130/145 *Set of* 16			£425	£425

31 Hoisting the Union Jack

32 Scene on H.M.S. *Nelson*

(Recess J. Ash)

1934 (6 Nov). *50th Anniv of Declaration of British Protectorate.* P 11.

146	**31**	1d. green	1·00	3·50
147	**32**	2d. scarlet	1·75	3·00
148	**31**	3d. blue	1·75	3·00
149	**32**	5d. purple	11·00	16·00
146/9 *Set of* 4			14·00	23·00

HIS MAJESTY'S JUBILEE.

1910 1935

(33)

HIS MAJESTY'S JUBILEE. 1910 — 1935

(34)

MAJESTY'S Normal

MAJESTY'S "Accent" flaw (R.5/4)

1935 (9 July). *Silver Jubilee. Nos.* 131, 133/4 *and* 136 *optd with T* **33** *or* **34** *(2d.).*

150	1d. black and green	1·00	3·00
	a. "Accent" flaw	32·00	55·00
151	2d. scarlet	3·50	3·50
152	3d. black and blue	2·50	3·00
	a. "Accent" flaw	55·00	70·00
153	5d. black and slate-green	2·50	3·00
	a. "Accent" flaw	60·00	80·00
150/3 *Set of* 4		8·50	11·00

35

36 Port Moresby

(Recess J. Ash)

1937 (14 May). *Coronation.* P 11.

154	**35**	1d. green	45	20
155		2d. scarlet	45	1·25
156		3d. blue	45	1·25
157		5d. purple	45	1·75
154/7 *Set of* 4			1·60	4·00

Some covers franked with these stamps and posted on 2 June 1937 were postmarked 2 April 1937 in error.

(Recess J. Ash)

1938 (6 Sept). *Air. 50th Anniv of Declaration of British Possession.* P 11.

158	**36**	2d. rose-red	3·00	3·00
159		3d. bright blue	3·00	2·25
160		5d. green	3·00	3·50
161		8d. brown-lake	6·00	16·00
162		1s. mauve	19·00	17·00
158/62 *Set of* 5			30·00	38·00

37 Natives poling Rafts

(Recess J. Ash)

1939 (6 Sept). *Air.* P 11.

163	**37**	2d. rose-red	3·00	5·00
164		3d. bright blue	3·00	10·00
165		5d. green	3·00	2·50
166		8d. brown-lake	8·00	3·50
167		1s. mauve	10·00	9·00

(Recess W. C. G. McCracken)

1941 (2 Jan). *Air.* P 11½.

168	**37**	1s.6d. olive-green	30·00	35·00
163/168 *Set of* 6			50·00	60·00

OFFICIAL STAMPS

1908 (Oct). *Punctured "OS".*

O1	**1**	2s.6d. black and brown (No. 37)	£700	35·00
O2		2s.6d. black and brown (No. 45)	£3000	£2500
		a. Thin paper (No. 45a)	£800	£650

1908 (Dec)–**10**. *Nos.* 49/71 *punctured "OS".*

I. Wmk upright.

(a) P 11.

O4	**6**	1d. black and rose	19·00	6·00
O5		2d. black and purple	28·00	4·50
O6		2½d. black and bright ultramarine	45·00	35·00
		a. Black and pale ultramarine	21·00	4·25
O7		4d. black and sepia	21·00	4·50
		a. Deformed "d" at left	£100	32·00
O8		6d. black and myrtle-green	55·00	28·00
O9		1s. black and orange	55·00	18·00
O4/9 *Set of* 6			£180	60·00

(b) P 12½.

O10	**6**	2d. black and purple	50·00	13·00
O11		2½d. black and bright ultramarine	£150	90·00
		a. Black and pale ultramarine	85·00	60·00
O12		4d. black and sepia	50·00	9·00
		a. Deformed "d" at left	£170	65·00
O13		1s. black and orange	£140	55·00
O10/13 *Set of* 4			£300	£120

II. Wmk sideways.

(a) P 11.

O14	**6**	½d. black and yellow-green	23·00	4·50
		a. Black and deep green	55·00	30·00
O15		1d. black and carmine	50·00	15·00
O16		2d. black and purple	17·00	2·00
O17		2½d. black and dull blue	30·00	5·00
O18		4d. black and sepia	25·00	10·00
		a. Deformed "d" at left	£110	60·00
O19		6d. black and myrtle-green	45·00	5·00
O20		1s. black and orange	£140	50·00
O14/20 *Set of* 7			£300	80·00

(b) P 12½.

O21	**6**	½d. black and yellow-green	18·00	1·50
		a. Black and deep green	50·00	30·00
O22		1d. black and carmine	45·00	4·00
O23		2d. black and purple	26·00	3·00
O24		2½d. black and dull blue	50·00	14·00
O25		6d. black and myrtle-green	—	£1100
O26		1s. black and orange	55·00	16·00

1910. *Nos.* 47/8 *punctured "OS".*

O27	**5**	½d. black and yellow-green (wmk upright)	20·00	13·00
O28		2s.6d. black and chocolate (wmk sideways)	£120	85·00

1910–11. *Nos.* 75/83 *punctured "OS".*

O29	**5**	½d. black and green	23·00	12·00
O30		1d. black and carmine	50·00	9·00
O31		2d. black and dull purple	19·00	12·00
		a. "C" for "O" in "POSTAGE"	£160	80·00
O32		2½d. black and blue-violet	27·00	6·50
O33		4d. black and sepia	32·00	6·00
		a. Deformed "d" at left	£150	42·00
O34		6d. black and myrtle-green	35·00	6·00
O35		1s. black and deep orange	50·00	9·00
O36		2s.6d. black and brown (B)	85·00	30·00
O37		2s.6d. black and brown (C)	£100	65·00
O29/36 *Set of* 8			£275	75·00

1911–12. *Nos.* 84/91 *punctured "OS".*

O38	**6**	½d. yellow-green	12·00	2·00
O39		1d. rose-pink	17·00	1·25
O40		2d. bright mauve	17·00	1·25
		w. Wmk Crown to right of A	—	26·00
O41		2½d. bright ultramarine	21·00	8·50
O42		4d. pale olive-green	27·00	16·00
O43		6d. orange-brown	26·00	6·00
O44		1s. yellow	42·00	11·00
O45		2s.6d. rose-carmine	75·00	80·00
O38/45 *Set of* 8			£225	£110

1930. *Nos.* 93/6a *and* 98c/103 *punctured "OS".*

O46	**6**	½d. myrtle and apple green	11·00	16·00
O47		1d. intense black and red	18·00	3·50
O48		1½d. bright blue and bright brown	13·00	18·00
		a. "POSTACE" at right	£100	£140
O49		2d. deep brown-purple and lake	24·00	38·00
O50		3d. black and blue-green	65·00	80·00
O51		4d. light brown and orange	38·00	42·00
O52		6d. dull purple and pale purple	19·00	38·00
		a. "POSTACE" at left	£180	£275
O53		1s. brown and yellow-olive	40·00	60·00
O54		2s.6d. maroon and pale pink	£100	£130
O46/54 *Set of* 9			£300	£375

O S

(O 1)

(Typo T. S. Harrison (1d. and 2s.6d.) and J. Ash)

1931 (29 July)–**32**. *Optd with Type* O **1**. W **7** or W **15** of Australia (9d., 1s.3d.). P 14 or 11 (9d., 1s.3d.).

O55	**6**	½d. myrtle and apple-green	2·25	4·75
O56		1d. grey black and red		
		a. Intense black and red	4·00	11·00
O57		1½d. bright blue and bright brown	1·60	12·00
		a. "POSTACE" at right	48·00	£140
O58		2d. brown-purple and claret	3·75	13·00
O59		3d. black and blue-green	2·50	22·00
O60		4d. light brown and orange (No. 99aw)	2·50	18·00
O61		5d. bluish slate and pale brown	6·00	38·00
O62		6d. dull purple and red-purple	4·00	8·50
		a. "POSTACE" at left	£100	£190
O63		9d. lilac and violet (1932)	30·00	48·00
O64		1s. brown and yellow-olive	9·00	30·00
O65		1s.3d. lilac & pale greenish blue (1932)	30·00	48·00
O66		2s.6d. maroon and pale pink (Harrison)	42·00	85·00
		a. Maroon and bright pink (Ash)	45·00	85·00
O55/66 *Set of* 12			£120	£300

Civil Administration in Papua was suspended in 1942. On resumption, after the Japanese defeat in 1945, Australian stamps were used until the appearance of the issue of the combined territories of Papua & New Guinea.

PAPUA NEW GUINEA

AUSTRALIAN TRUST TERRITORY

Stamps of Australia were used in the combined territory following the defeat of the Japanese in 1945. They remained valid for postal purposes from Papua and New Guinea until 1 March 1953.

The name of the combined territory was changed from "Papua and New Guinea" to "Papua New Guinea" at the beginning of 1972.

SPECIMEN OVERPRINTS. These come from specimen sets in which the lower values were cancelled-to-order, but stamps above the value of 10s. were overprinted "Specimen". These overprints are listed as they could be purchased from the Post Office.

1 Matschie's Tree Kangaroo

2 Buka Head-dresses

3 Native Youth

4 Greater Bird of Paradise

5 Native policeman

6 Papuan Head-dress

7 Kiriwana Chief house

8 Kiriwana Yam house

9 Copra making

10 Lakatoi

11 Rubber tapping

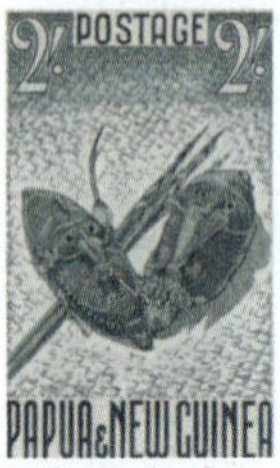

12 Sepik dancing masks

13 Native shepherd and flock

14 Map of Papua and New Guinea

15 Papuan shooting Fish

(Recess Note Printing Branch, Commonwealth Bank, Melbourne)

1952 (30 Oct)–**58**. *T* **1/15**. P 14.

1	**1**	½d. emerald	30	10
2	**2**	1d. deep brown	20	10
3	**3**	2d. blue	35	10
4	**4**	2½d. orange	3·75	50
5	**5**	3d. deep green	50	10
6	**6**	3½d. carmine-red	50	10
6*a*		3½d. black (2.6.58)	6·00	90
7	**7**	6½d. dull purple	1·25	10
		a. Maroon (1956)	6·50	25
8	**8**	7½d. blue	2·50	1·00
9	**9**	9d. brown	2·75	40
10	**10**	1s. yellow-green	1·75	10
11	**11**	1s.6d. deep green	4·00	60
12	**12**	2s. indigo	3·00	10
13	**13**	2s.6d. brown-purple	3·00	40
14	**14**	10s. blue-black	32·00	13·00
15	**15**	£1 deep brown	35·00	13·00
1/15 *Set of* 16			85·00	27·00
14a/15s Optd "Specimen" *Set of* 2			£120	

(**16**)

(**17**)

1957 (29 Jan). *Nos. 4 and 10 surch with T* **16** *or T* **17**.

16	4d. on 2½d. orange	1·50	10
17	7d. on 1s. yellow-green	40	10

18 Cacao Plant

19 Klinki Plymill

20 Cattle

21 Coffee Beans

(Recess Note Ptg Branch, Commonwealth Bank, Melbourne)

1958 (2 June)–**60**. *New values.* P 14.

18	**18**	4d. vermilion	75	10
19		5d. green (10.11.60)	75	10
20	**19**	7d. bronze-green	3·25	10
21		8d. deep ultramarine (10.11.60)	75	1·50
22	**20**	1s.7d. red-brown	7·50	3·75
23		2s.5d. vermilion (10.11.60)	1·75	1·25
24	**21**	5s. crimson and olive-green	5·50	1·00
18/24 *Set of* 7			19·00	7·00

(**22**)

23 Council Chamber, Port Moresby

1959 (1 Dec). *No. 1 surch with T* **22**.

25	**1**	5d. on ½d. emerald	75	10

(Photo Harrison)

1961 (10 Apr). *Reconstitution of Legislative Council.* P 15×14.

26	**23**	5d. deep green and yellow	75	25
27		2s.3d. deep green and light salmon	2·00	1·50

24 Female, Goroka, New Guinea

25 Tribal elder, Tari, Papua

26 Female Dancer

27 Male Dancer

28 Traffic Policeman

(Des Pamela M. Prescott, Recess Note Ptg Branch, Reserve Bank of Australia, Melbourne)

1961 (26 July)–**62**. *T* **24/8**. P 14½×14 (1d., 3d., 3s.) or 14×14½ (others).

28	1d. lake	70	10
29	3d. indigo	30	10
30	1s. bronze-green	1·00	15
31	2s. maroon	45	15
32	3s. deep bluish green (5.9.62)	1·00	2·00
28/32 *Set of* 5		3·00	2·25

29 Campaign Emblem

30 Map of South Pacific

(Recess Note Ptg Branch, Reserve Bank of Australia, Melbourne)

1962 (7 Apr). *Malaria Eradication.* P 14.

33	**29**	5d. carmine-red and light blue	30	15
34		1s. red and sepia	50	25
35		2s. black and yellow-green	60	70
33/5 *Set of* 3			1·25	1·00

(Des Pamela M. Prescott. Recess Note Ptg Branch, Reserve Bank of Australia, Melbourne)

1962 (9 July). *Fifth South Pacific Conference, Pago Pago.* P 14½×14.

36	**30**	5d. scarlet and light green	50	15
37		1s.6d. deep violet and light yellow	75	70
38		2s.6d. deep green and light blue	75	1·40
36/8 *Set of* 3			1·75	2·00

31 Throwing the Javelin

33 Runners

(Des G. Hamori. Photo Courvoisier)

1962 (24 Oct). *Seventh British Empire and Commonwealth Games, Perth. T* **31**, **33** *and similar design.* P 11½.

39	5d. brown and light blue	20	10
	a. Pair. Nos. 39/40	40	50
40	5d. brown and orange	20	10
41	2s.3d. brown and light green	70	75
39/41 *Set of* 3		1·00	85

Design: (*As T* **31**)—5d. High jump.

Nos. 39/40 are arranged together *se-tenant* in sheets of 100.

34 Raggiana Bird of Paradise

35 Common Phalanger

36 Rabaul

37 Queen Elizabeth II

(Des S. T. Cham (10s.), A. Buckley (photo) (£1). Photo Harrison (£1), Courvoisier (others))

1963. P 14½ (£1) or 11½ (others).

42	**34**	5d. yellow, chestnut and sepia (27 Mar)	70	10
43	**35**	6d. red, yellow-brown and grey (27 Mar)	50	1·25
44	**36**	10s. multicoloured (13 Feb)	12·00	6·00
45	**37**	£1 sepia, gold and blue-green (3 July)	1·50	1·75
		a. Gold ptd double		
42/5 *Set of* 4			13·00	8·00
44a/5s Optd "Specimen" *Set of* 2			90·00	

38 Centenary Emblem

39 Waterfront, Port Moresby

(Des G. Hamori. Photo Note Ptg Branch, Reserve Bank of Australia, Melbourne)

1963 (1 May). *Red Cross Centenary.* P 13½×13.

46	**38**	5d. red, grey-brown and bluish green	60	10

(Des J. McMahon (8d.), Pamela M. Prescott (2s.3d.). Recess Note Ptg Branch, Reserve Bank of Australia, Melbourne)

1963 (8 May). *T* **39** *and similar horiz design.* P 14×13½.

47	**39**	8d. green	30	15
48	–	2s.3d. ultramarine	30	30

Design:—2s.3d. Piaggio P-166B Portofino aircraft landing at Tapini.

40 Games Emblem

41 Watarn Head

(Des Pamela M. Prescott. Recess Note Ptg Branch, Reserve Bank of Australia, Melbourne)

1963 (14 Aug). *First South Pacific Games, Suva.* P 13½×14½.

49	**40**	5d. bistre	10	10
50		1s. deep green	30	60

(Des Pamela M. Prescott. Photo Courvoisier)

1964 (5 Feb). *Native Artefacts. T* **41** *and similar vert designs. Multicoloured.* P 11½.

51	11d. Type **41**	25	10
52	2s.5d. Watam Head (*different*)	30	1·75
53	2s.6d. Bosmun Head	30	10
54	5s. Medina Head	35	20
51/4 *Set of 4*		1·10	1·75

45 Casting Vote

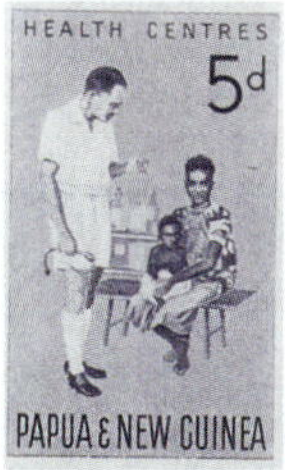

46 "Health Centres"

(Photo Courvoisier)

1964 (4 Mar). *Common Roll Elections.* P 11½.

55	**45**	5d. brown and drab	10	10
56		2s.3d. brown and pale blue	20	25

(Recess Note Ptg Branch, Reserve Bank of Australia, Melbourne)

1964 (5 Aug). *Health Services. T* **46** *and similar vert designs.* P 14.

57	5d. violet	10	10
58	8d. bronze-green	10	10
59	1s. blue	15	10
60	1s.2d. brown-red	20	35
57/60 *Set of 4*		50	60

Designs:—8d. "School health"; 1s. "Infant, child and maternal health"; 1s.2d. "Medical training".

50 Striped Gardener Bowerbird

51 Emperor of Germany Bird of Paradise

(Photo Courvoisier)

1964 (28 Oct)–**65**. *Vert designs as T* **50** *(1d. to 8d.) or* **51** *(others). Multicoloured; background colours given.* P 11½ (1d. to 8d.) or 12×11½ (1s. to 10s.).

61	1d. pale olive-yellow (20.1.65)	40	10
62	3d. light grey (20.1.65)	50	10
63	5d. pale red (20.1.65)	55	10
64	6d. pale green	75	10
65	8d. lilac	1·00	20
66	1s. salmon	1·00	10
67	2s. light blue (20.1.65)	75	30
68	2s.3d. light green (20.1.65)	75	85
69	3s. pale yellow (20.1.65)	75	1·25
70	5s. cobalt (20.1.65)	7·00	1·50
71	10s. pale drab	2·75	9·00
	s. Optd "Specimen"	£120	
61/71 *Set of 11*		14·00	12·00

Designs:—3d. Adelbert Bowerbird; 5d. Blue Bird of Paradise; 6d. Lawes's Parotia; 8d. Black-billed Sicklebill; 2s. Brown Sicklebill; 2s.3d. Lesser Bird of Paradise; 3s. Magnificent Bird of Paradise; 5s. Twelve-wired Bird of Paradise; 10s. Magnificent Riflebird.

61 Canoe Prow

(Des Pamela M. Prescott. Photo Courvoisier)

1965 (24 Mar). *Sepik Canoe Prows in Port Moresby Museum. T* **61** *and similar horiz designs showing carved prows.* P 11½.

72	4d. multicoloured	50	10
73	1s.2d. multicoloured	1·00	1·75
74	1s.6d. multicoloured	50	10
75	4s. multicoloured	50	50
72/5 *Set of 4*		2·25	2·25

1965 (14 Apr). *50th Anniv of Gallipoli Landing. As T* **22** *of Nauru.* P 13½.

76	2s.3d. sepia, black and emerald	20	10

65 Urban Plan and Native House

(Des G. Hamori. Photo Courvoisier)

1965 (7 July). *Sixth South Pacific Conference, Lae. T* **65** *and similar horiz design.* P 11½.

77	6d. multicoloured	10	10
78	1s. multicoloured	10	10

No. 78 is similar to T **65** but with the plan on the right and the house on the left. Also "URBANISATION" reads downwards.

66 Mother and Child

67 Globe and U.N. Emblem

(Photo Courvoisier)

1965 (13 Oct). *20th Anniv of U.N.O. T* **66/7** *and similar vert design.* P 11½.

79	6d. sepia, blue and pale turquoise-blue	10	10
80	1s. orange-brown, blue and reddish violet	10	10
81	2s. blue, blue-green and light yellow-olive	10	10
79/81 *Set of 3*		25	25

Design:—2s. U.N. Emblem and globes.

(New Currency. 100 cents = 1 Australian dollar)

69 *Papilio ulysses*

71 *Ornithoptera priamus*

(Photo Courvoisier)

1966 (14 Feb). *Decimal Currency. Butterflies. Vert designs as T* **69** *(1 to 5c.), or horiz as T* **71** *(others). Multicoloured.* P 11½.

82	1c. Type **69**	40	1·00
83	3c. *Cyrestis acilia*	40	1·00
84	4c. *Graphium weiskei*	40	1·00
85	5c. *Terinos alurgis*	40	10
86	10c. Type **71**	50	30
86*a*	12c. *Euploea callithoe* (12.10)	2·50	2·25
87	15c. *Papilio euchenor*	1·00	80
88	20c. *Parthenos sylvia*	50	25
89	25c. *Delias aruna*	70	1·25
90	50c. *Apaturina erminea*	10·00	1·25
91	$1 *Doleschallia dascylus*	3·00	1·75
92	$2 *Ornithoptera paradises*	6·00	8·50
82/92 *Set of 12*		23·00	17·50

80 "Molala Harai"

84 Throwing the Discus

(Des Rev. H. A. Brown. Photo Courvoisier)

1966 (8 June). *Folklore. Elema Art (1st series). T* **80** *and similar vert designs.* P 11½.

93	2c. black and carmine	10	10
94	7c. black, light yellow and light blue	10	65
95	30c. black, carmine and apple-green	15	15
96	60c. black, carmine and yellow	40	65
93/6 *Set of 4*		65	1·40

Designs:—7c. "Marai"; 30c. "Meavea Kivovia"; 60c. "Toivita Tapaivita".

Nos. 93/6 were supplementary values to the decimal currency definitive issue.

See also Nos. 152/5 and 342/5.

(Photo Courvoisier)

1966 (31 Aug). *South Pacific Games, Noumea. T* **84** *and similar vert designs. Multicoloured.* P 11½.

97	5c. Type **84**	10	10
98	10c. Football	15	10
99	20c. Tennis	20	40
97/9 *Set of 3*		40	55

87 *Mucuna novoguineensis*

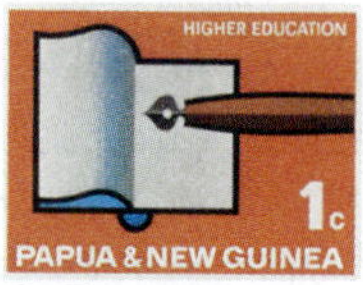

91 "Fine Arts"

(Des Mrs. D. Pearce. Photo Courvoisier)

1966 (7 Dec). *Flowers. T* **87** *and similar vert designs. Multicoloured.* P 11½.

100	5c. Type **87**	15	10
101	10c. *Tecomanthe dendrophila*	15	10
102	20c. *Rhododendron macgregoriae*	20	10
103	60c. *Rhododendron konori*	50	1·40
100/3 *Set of 4*		90	1·50

(Des G. Hamori. Photo Courvoisier)

1967 (8 Feb). *Higher Education. T* **91** *and similar horiz designs. Multicoloured.* P 12½×12.

104	1c. Type **91**	10	10
105	3c. "Surveying"	10	10
106	4c. "Civil Engineering"	10	10
107	5c. "Science"	10	10
108	20c. "Law"	10	10
104/8 *Set of 5*		45	45

96 *Sagra speciosa*

100 Laloki River

(Des Pamela M. Prescott. Photo Courvoisier)

1967 (12 Apr). *Fauna Conservation (Beetles). T* **96** *and similar vert designs. Multicoloured.* P 11½.

109	5c. Type **96**	15	10
110	10c. *Eupholus schoenherri*	15	10
111	20c. *Sphingnotus albertisi*	25	10
112	25c. *Cyphogastra albertisi*	25	10
109/12 *Set of 4*		70	35

(Des G. Wade. Photo Courvoisier)

1967 (28 June). *Laloki River Hydro-Electric Scheme, and "New Industries". T* **100** *and similar vert designs. Multicoloured.* P 12½.

113	5c. Type **100**	10	10
114	10c. Pyrethrum	10	10
115	20c. Tea Plant	15	10
116	25c. Type **100**	15	10
113/16 *Set of 4*		45	35

103 Air Attack at Milne Bay

107 Papuan Lory

(Des R. Hodgkinson (2c.), F. Hodgkinson (5c.), G. Wade (20c., 50c.). Photo Courvoisier)

1967 (30 Aug). *25th Anniv of the Pacific War. T* **103** *and similar multicoloured designs.* P 11½.

117	2c. Type **103**	10	50
118	5c. Kokoda Trail (*vert*)	10	10
119	20c. The Coast Watchers	25	10
120	50c. Battle of the Coral Sea	80	70
117/20 *Set of 4*		1·10	1·25

(Des T. Walcot. Photo Courvoisier)

1967 (29 Nov). *Christmas. Territory Parrots. T* **107** *and similar vert designs. Multicoloured.* P 12½.

121	5c. Type **107**	20	10
122	7c. Pesquet's Parrot	25	90
123	20c. Dusky Lory	30	10
124	25c. Edward's Fig Parrot	35	10
121/4 *Set of 4*		1·00	1·10

111 Chimbu Head-dresses

112

(Des P. Jones. Photo Courvoisier)

1968 (21 Feb). *"National Heritage". T* **111/12** *and similar multicoloured designs.* P 12×12½ (5, 60c.) or 12½×12 (10, 20c.).

125	5c. Type **111**	10	10
126	10c. Southern Highlands Head-dress (*horiz*)	15	10
127	20c. Western Highlands Head-dress (*horiz*)	15	10
128	60c. Type **112**	40	45
125/8 *Set of* 4		70	65

115 *Hyla thesaurensis*

119 Human Rights Emblem and Papuan Head-dress (abstract)

(Des and photo Courvoisier)

1968 (24 Apr). *Fauna Conservation (Frogs). T* **115** *and similar horiz designs. Multicoloured.* P 11½.

129	5c. Type **115**	15	50
130	10c. *Hyla iris*	15	10
131	15c. *Ceratobatrachus guentheri*	15	10
132	20c. *Nyctimystes narinosa*	20	50
129/32 *Set of* 4		60	1·10

(Des G. Hamori. Litho Enschedé)

1968 (26 June). *Human Rights Year. T* **119** *and similar horiz design. Multicoloured.* P 13½×12½.

133	5c. Type **119**	10	20
134	10c. Human Rights in the World (abstract)	10	10

121 Leadership (abstract)

123 Common Egg Cowrie (*Ovula ovum*)

(Des G. Hamori. Litho Enschedé)

1968 (26 June). *Universal Suffrage. T* **121** *and similar horiz design. Multicoloured.* P 13½×12½.

135	20c. Type **121**	15	20
136	25c. Leadership of the community (abstract)	15	30

(Des P. Jones. Photo Courvoisier)

1968–69. *Sea Shells. Multicoloured designs as T* **123**. P 12×12½ ($2), 12½×12 (1c. to 20c.) or 11½ (others).

137	1c. Type **123** (29.1.69)	10	10
138	3c. Laciniate Conch (*Strombus sinuatus*) (30.10.68)	30	1·25
139	4c. Lithograph Cone (*Conus litoglyphus*) (29.1.69)	20	1·25
140	5c. Marbled Cone (*Cones marmoreus marmoreus*) (28.8.68)	25	10
141	7c. Episcopal Mitre (*Mitra mitra*) (29.1.69)	35	10
142	10c. *Cymbiola rutila ruckeri* (30.10.68)	45	10
143	12c. Checkerboard Bonnet (*Phalium areola*) (29.1.69)	1·25	2·00
144	15c. Scorpion Conch (*Lambis scorpius*) (30.10.68)	60	1·00
145	20c. Fluted Giant Clam or Scale Tridacna (*Tridacna sqamosa*) (28.8.68)	70	10
146	25c. Camp Pitar Venus (*Lioconcha castrensis*) (28.8.68)	70	1·75
147	30c. Ramose Murex (*Murex ramosus*) (28.8.68)	70	1·00
148	40c. Chambered or Pearly Nautilus (*Nautilus pompilius*) (30.10.68)	75	1·25
149	60c. Trumpet Triton (*Charonia tritonis*) (28.8.68)	70	60
150	$1 Manus Green Papuina (*Papuina pulcherrima*) (30.10.68)	1·00	75
151	$2 Glory of the Sea Cone (*Cones gloriamaris*) (*vert*) (29.1.69)	10·00	2·00
137/51 *Set of* 15		16·00	12·00

The 1, 5, 7, 15, 40, 60c. and $1 exist with PVA gum as well as gum arabic.

138 Tito Myth

139 Iko Myth

140 Luvuapo Myth

141 Miro Myth

(Des from native motifs by Revd. H. A. Brown. Litho Enschedé)

1969 (9 Apr). *Folklore. Elema Art (2nd series).* P 12½×13½×Roul 9 between *se-tenant* pairs.

152	**138**	5c. black, yellow and red	10	60
		a. Pair. Nos. 152/3	20	1·10
153	**139**	5c. black, yellow and red	10	60
154	**140**	10c. black, grey and red	15	60
		a. Pair. Nos. 154/5	30	1·10
155	**141**	10c. black, grey and red	15	60
152/5 *Set of* 4			45	2·00

Nos. 152/3 and 154/5 were issued in vertical *se-tenant* pairs, separated by a line of roulette.

142 "Fireball" class Dinghy

145 *Dendrobium ostrinoglossum*

(Des J. Fallas. Recess Note Ptg Branch, Reserve Bank of Australia)

1969 (25 June). *Third South Pacific Games, Port Moresby. T* **142** *and similar designs.* P 14×14½ (5c.) or 14½×14 (others).

156	5c. black	10	25
157	10c. deep bluish violet	10	10
158	20c. myrtle-green	15	20
156/8 *Set of* 3		30	50

Designs: *Horiz*—10c. Swimming pool, Boroko; 20c. Games arena, Konedobu.

(Des P. Jones. Photo Courvoisier)

1969 (27 Aug). *Flora conservation (Orchids). T* **145** *and similar vert designs. Multicoloured. P 11½.*

159	5c. Type **145**	25	10
160	10c. *Dendrobium lawesii*	25	70
161	20c. *Dendrobium pseudofrigidum*	30	90
162	30c. *Dendrobium conanthum*	30	70
159/62 *Set of* 4		1·00	2·25

149 Bird of Paradise

150 Native Potter

(Des G. Hamori. Photo Note Ptg Branch, Reserve Bank of Australia)

1969 (24 Sept)–**71**. *Coil stamps.* P 15×imperf.

162*a*	**149**	2c. blue, black and red (1.4.71)	10	65
163		5c. bright green, brown and red-orange	10	10

(Des G. Hamori. Photo Courvoisier)

1969 (24 Sept). *50th Anniv of International Labour Organization.* P 11½.

164	**150**	5c. multicoloured	10	10

151 Tareko

155 Prehistoric Ambun Stone

(Des G. Hamori. Photo Courvoisier)

1969 (29 Oct). *Musical Instruments. T* **151** *and similar horiz designs.* P 12½×12.

165	5c. multicoloured	10	10
166	10c. black, olive-green and pale yellow	10	10
167	25c. black, yellow and brown	15	15
168	30c. multicoloured	25	15
165/8 *Set of* 4		55	45

Designs:—10c. Garamut; 25c. Iviliko; 30c. Kundu.

(Des R. Bates. Photo Courvoisier)

1970 (11 Feb). *"National Heritage". T* **155** *and similar horiz designs. Multicoloured.* P 12½×12.

169	5c. Type **155**	10	10
170	10c. Masawa canoe of Kula circuit	10	10
171	25c. Torres' Map, 1606	40	15
172	30c. H.M.S. *Basilisk* (paddle-sloop), 1873	65	25
169/72 *Set of* 4		1·10	55

159 King of Saxony Bird Paradise

(Des T. Walcot. Photo Courvoisier)

1970 (13 May). *Fauna Conservation (Birds of Paradise). T* **159** *and similar vert designs. Multicoloured.* P 12.

173	5c. Type **159**	60	15
174	10c. King Bird of Paradise	60	60
175	15c. Raggiana Bird of Paradise	80	1·00
176	25c. Sickle-crested Bird of Paradise	1·00	70
173/6 *Set of* 4		2·75	2·25

163 Douglas Dc-6B and Mt Wilhelm

164 Lockheed L.188 Electra and Mt Yule

165 Boeing 727-100 and Mt Giluwe

166 Fokker F.27 Friendship and Manam Island

(Des D. Gentleman. Photo Harrison)

1970 (8 July). *Australian and New Guinea Air Services. T* **163/6** *and similar horiz designs. Multicoloured.* P 14½×14.

177	5c. Type **163**	25	30
	a. Block of 4. Nos. 177/80	1·00	2·00
178	5c. Type **164**	25	30
179	5c. Type **165**	25	30
180	5c. Type **166**	25	30
181	25c. Douglas DC-3 and Matupi Volcano	35	40
182	30c. Boeing 707 and Hombrom's Bluff	35	60
177/82 *Set of* 6		1·50	2·50

Nos. 177/80 were issued together, *se-tenant*, in blocks of 4 throughout the sheet.

169 N. Miklouho-Maclay (scientist) and Effigy

170 Wogeo Island Food Bowl

(Des D. Gentleman. Photo Courvoisier)

1970 (19 Aug). *42nd ANZAAS (Australian—New Zealand Association for the Advancement of Science) congress, Port Moresby. T* **169** *and similar horiz designs.* P 11½.

183	5c. multicoloured	10	10
184	10c. multicoloured	20	10
185	15c. multicoloured	90	25
186	20c. multicoloured	60	25
183/6 *Set of* 4		1·60	60

Designs:—10c. B. Malinowski (anthropologist) and native hut; 15c. T. Salvadori (ornithologist) and Double-wattled Cassowary; 20c. F.R.R. Schlechter (botanist) and flower.

(Des P. Jones. Photo Courvoisier)

1970 (28 Oct). *Native Artefacts. T* **170** *and similar multicoloured designs.* P 12½×12 (30c.) or 12×12½ (others).

187	5c. Type **170**	10	10
188	10c. Lime Pot	20	10
189	15c. Aibom Sago Storage Pot	20	10
190	30c. Manus Island Bowl (*horiz*)	25	30
187/90 *Set of* 4		65	55

STAMP BOOKLETS

B 1

1970 (28 Jan). *Green on olive-yellow cover as Type* B **1**, *but* "POSTAGE STAMP" *in seriffed type. Stamps attached by selvedge.*

SB1	50c. booklet containing 5c. (No. 140) in block of 10	£375

1970 (25 May). *Green on cream cover as Type* B **1** *with* "POSTAGE STAMP" *without serifs. Stamps attached by selvedge.*

SB2	50c. booklet containing 5c. (No. 140) in block of 10	16·00

No. SB2 shows "GP-P&NG/B112" imprint on reverse.

An example of No. SB2 has been reported containing No. 187 in block of 10.

POSTAGE DUE STAMPS

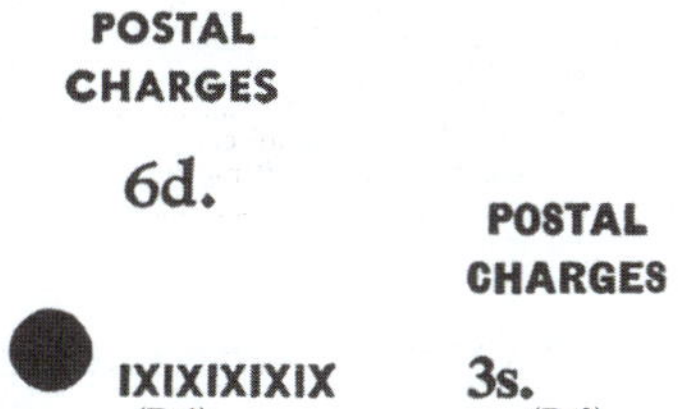

(D 1) (D 2)

1960 (1 Mar). *Postage stamps surcharged.*

(a) No. 8 with Type D **1**.

D1	6d. on 7½d. blue (R.)	£800	£425
	a. Surch double	£3750	£2000

(b) Nos. 1, 4, 6a, 7/8 as Type D **2**.

D2	1d. on 6½d. maroon	3·00	4·00
D3	3d. on ½d. emerald (B.)	3·00	1·50
	a. Surch double	£850	
D4	6d. on 7½d. blue (R.)	28·00	6·00
	a. Surch double	£900	
D5	1s. 3d. on 3½d. black (O.)	3·25	1·50
D6	3s. on 2½d. orange	14·00	3·00
D2/6 *Set of 5*		45·00	14·50

Genuine used examples of No. D1a should be postmarked at Goroko or Kawieng.

Examples of Nos. D1, D1a, D3a and D4a should only be purchased if accompanied by an expert committee's certificate.

D 3

(Typo Note Ptg Branch, Reserve Bank of Australia, Melbourne)

1960 (2 June). W **15** of Australia. P 14.

D7	D **3**	1d. orange	65	75
D8		3d. yellow-brown	70	75
D9		6d. blue	75	40
D10		9d. deep red	75	1·75
D11		1s. light emerald	75	50
D12		1s.3d. violet	1·00	2·00
D13		1s.6d. pale blue	4·00	6·00
D14		3s. yellow	2·50	75
D7/14 *Set of 8*			10·00	11·50

The use of Postal Charge stamps was discontinued on 12 February 1966, but they remained on sale at the Philatelic Bureau until 31 August 1966.

Bahamas

The British Post Office at Nassau was established during the early days of the West Indies packet system, and was certainly operating by 1733. The first known local postmark dates from 1802.

The crowned-circle handstamp No. CC1 was issued in 1846 and was generally replaced, for the public mails, by various stamps of Great Britain in 1858.

Local mail deliveries were rudimentary until 1859 when Nos. 1/2 were issued by the colonial authorities for interisland mails. Examples used for this purpose are usually cancelled in manuscript or with a "27" postmark. The "local" 1d. stamp became valid for overseas mails in May, 1860, when the colonial authorities took over this service from the British G.P.O.

For illustrations of the handstamp and postmark types see BRITISH POST OFFICES ABROAD notes, following GREAT BRITAIN.

NASSAU

CROWNED-CIRCLE HANDSTAMPS

CC1 CC **2** BAHAMAS (Nassau) (18.5.1846) (R.) *Price on cover* £2250

No. CC1 was later struck in black and used as an Official Paid mark between July 1899 and September 1935. Handstamps as Types CC **1** and CC **3** (only three known) struck in black were used for the same purpose from 1933 until 1953; but it is believed that these were never employed during the pre-stamp period. *Price on cover from* £50.

Stamps of GREAT BRITAIN *cancelled* "A 05" *as Type* **2**.

1858–60.

Z1	1d. rose-red (1857), perf 14	£2250
Z2	2d. blue (1858) (Plate Nos. 7, 8)	£1300
Z3	4d. rose (1857)	£450
Z3*a*	6d. purple (1854), embossed	£4250
Z4	6d. lilac (1856)	£350
Z5	1s. green (1856)	£2250

PRICES FOR STAMPS ON COVER TO 1945

No. 1	*from* × 8
No. 2	—
Nos. 3/6	*from* × 8
No. 7	—
Nos. 8/11	*from* × 10
Nos. 12/15	*from* × 4
Nos. 16/19*a*	*from* × 6
Nos. 20/5	*from* × 15
Nos. 26/8	*from* × 4
No. 29	—
Nos. 30/2	*from* × 15
No. 33	*from* × 30
Nos. 35/7	*from* × 6
Nos. 38/9	*from* × 10
No. 39b	*from* × 30
No. 40	*from* × 50
No. 41	*from* × 6
No. 42	*from* × 15
No. 43	*from* × 5
Nos. 44/*a*	*from* × 10
No. 45	*from* × 40
Nos. 47/57	*from* × 4
Nos. 58/89	*from* × 2
Nos. 90/130	*from* × 3
Nos. 131/2	*from* × 10
Nos. 141/5	*from* × 4
Nos. 146/8	*from* × 6
Nos. 149/57	*from* × 3
Nos. 158/60	*from* × 4
No. 161	*from* × 8
Nos. 162/75	*from* × 5
Nos. S1/3	*from* × 20

CROWN COLONY

1

2

3

(Eng and recess P.B.)

1869 (10 June)–**60**. No wmk. Imperf.

(a) Thick, opaque paper.

1	**1**	1d. reddish lake (*shades*)	£5000	£2250

(b) Thin paper.

2	**1**	1d. dull lake (4.60)	60·00	£1500

No. 1, the printing on thick opaque paper, is very rare in unused condition. Unused remainders, on medium to thick, but slightly transparent, paper are worth about £250.

Collectors are warned against false postmarks upon the remainder stamps of 1d., imperf, on thin paper.

1860 (Oct). No wmk. Clean-cut perf 14 to 16.

3	**1**	1d. lake (H/S "CANCELLED" in oval £8000)	£5500	£750

For notes on "CANCELLED" examples see Catalogue Introduction. Examples with this handstamp on No. 3 are imperforate horizontally.

1861 (June)–**62**. No wmk.

(a) Rough perf 14 to 16.

4	**1**	1d. lake	£650	£325
5	**2**	4d. dull rose (Dec, 1861)	£1400	£400
		a. Imperf between (pair)	£30000	
6		6d. grey-lilac (Dec, 1861)	£4250	£600
		a. Pale dull lilac	£3250	£500

(b) P 11 to 12½ (1862).

7	**1**	1d. lake	£2250	

No. 7 was a perforation trial on a new machine at Perkins, Bacon. It was not sent out to the Colony and is also known part perforated.

(Recess D.L.R.)

1862. No wmk.*

(a) P 11½, 12.

8	**1**	1d. carmine-lake	£1000	£180
9		1d. lake	£1500	£250
10	**2**	4d. dull rose	£3500	£400
11		6d. lavender-grey	£11000	£500

(b) P 11½, 12, compound with 11.

12	**1**	1d. carmine-lake	£2000	£850
13		1d. lake	£2250	£950
14	**2**	4d. dull rose	£20000	£1900
15		6d. lavender-grey	£20000	£1800

(c) P 13.

16	**1**	1d. lake	£900	£160
17		1d. brown-lake	£750	£130
18	**2**	4d. dull rose	£2750	£375
19		6d. lavender-grey	£3250	£475
		a. Lilac	£2750	£450

*Stamps exist with part of papermaker's sheet wmk ("T. H. SAUNDERS" and date).

1863–77. Wmk Crown CC.

(a) P 12½.

20	**1**	1d. brown-lake	95·00	65·00
		w. Wmk inverted	£150	£100
		x. Wmk reversed		
		y. Wmk inverted and reversed	—	£160
21		1d. carmine-lake	£110	70·00
		w. Wmk inverted	£150	90·00
		x. Wmk reversed	£120	70·00
22		1d. carmine-lake (aniline)	£130	75·00
		w. Wmk inverted	£180	
		x. Wmk reversed		
23		1d. rose-red	65·00	45·00
		w. Wmk inverted	£110	
		x. Wmk reversed	65·00	45·00
24		1d. red	65·00	45·00
		w. Wmk inverted		
		x. Wmk reversed	—	45·00
25		1d. vermilion	70·00	45·00
		w. Wmk inverted	£110	80·00
		x. Wmk reversed	70·00	45·00
		y. Wmk inverted and reversed	£160	95·00
26	**2**	4d. bright rose	£300	60·00
		w. Wmk inverted	—	£200
		x. Wmk reversed		
27		4d. dull rose	£400	60·00
		w. Wmk inverted	—	£200
		x. Wmk reversed	£375	60·00
		y. Wmk inverted and reversed	£900	£200
28		4d. brownish rose (*wmk reversed*)	£450	80·00
		w. Wmk inverted	—	£200
29		6d. rose-lilac	—	£2250
		w. Wmk inverted	£6500	
30		6d. lilac (*shades*)	£375	70·00
		w. Wmk inverted	—	£200
		x. Wmk reversed		
31		6d. deep violet	£160	60·00
		w. Wmk inverted	£550	£200
		x. Wmk reversed	£180	65·00
		y. Wmk inverted and reversed		
32		6d. violet (aniline)	£250	90·00
		x. Wmk reversed	£250	95·00

(b) P 14.

33	**1**	1d. scarlet-vermilion (1877)	55·00	15·00
		x. Wmk reversed	65·00	23·00
34		1d. scarlet (or scarlet-vermilion) (aniline)	£1000	
		x. Wmk reversed		
35	**2**	4d. bright rose (1876)	£375	40·00
		w. Wmk inverted	£800	£200
36		4d. dull rose	£1500	40·00
		w. Wmk inverted		
37		4d. rose-lake	£425	40·00

No. 29 is believed to be the first printing only and should not be confused with other lilac shades of the 6d.

No. 34 is not known postally used, although manuscript fiscal cancellations on this shade do exist.

(Typo D.L.R.)

1863–80. Wmk Crown CC.

(a) P 12½.

38	**3**	1s. green (1865)	£2500	£300

(b) P 14.

39	**3**	1s. deep green	£300	40·00
		aw. Wmk inverted		
		b. Green	£120	26·00
		ba. Thick paper (1880)	8·00	8·00
		bw. Wmk inverted (thick paper)	—	£150

1882 (Mar). Wmk Crown CA.

(a) P 12.

40	**1**	1d. scarlet-vermilion	48·00	12·00
		x. Wmk reversed	—	60·00
41	**2**	4d. rose	£550	45·00

(b) P 14.

42	**1**	1d. scarlet-vermilion	£450	60·00
		x. Wmk reversed	£550	
43	**2**	4d. rose	£800	60·00
		x. Wmk reversed	£900	70·00

1882 (Mar)–**98**. Wmk Crown CA. P 14.

44	**3**	1s. green	42·00	14·00
44*a*		1s. blue-green (1898)	35·00	28·00

FOURPENCE

(**4**)

5

1883. *No. 31 surch with T* **4**.

45	**2**	4d. on 6d. deep violet	£550	£400
		a. Surch inverted	£17000	£10000
		x. Wmk reversed	£600	£450

Type **4** was applied by handstamp and occurs in various positions.

Caution is needed in buying Nos. 45/x.

Sloping "2" (R. 10/6)

Malformed "E"

(Typo D.L.R.)

1884–90. Wmk Crown CA. P 14.

47	**5**	1d. pale rose	75·00	13·00
48		1d. carmine-rose	7·00	2·50
49		1d. bright carmine (aniline)	2·75	6·50
50		2½d. dull blue (1888)	75·00	18·00
51		2½d. blue	42·00	7·50
		a. Sloping "2"	£450	£120
52		2½d. ultramarine	9·50	2·25
		a. Sloping "2"	£160	70·00
		s. Optd "Specimen"	65·00	
		w. Wmk inverted	£170	85·00
53		4d. deep yellow	9·50	4·00
54		6d. mauve (1890)	6·00	30·00
		a. Malformed "E" (R. 6/6)	£180	£350
		s. Optd "Specimen"	65·00	
56		5s. sage-green	65·00	75·00
57		£1 Venetian red	£275	£225
47/57 *Set of* 6			£325	£300

Examples of Nos. 54/7 are known showing a forged Bahamas postmark dated "AU 29 94".

6 Queen's Staircase, Nassau

7

8

(Recess D.L.R.)

1901 (23 Sept)–**03**. Wmk Crown CC. P 14.

58	**6**	1d. black and red	12·00	2·00
		w. Wmk inverted	£120	£120
59		5d. black and orange (1.03)	8·50	48·00
		y. Wmk inverted and reversed	£150	£200
60		2s. black and blue (1.03)	27·00	50·00
		x. Wmk reversed	£300	
61		3s. black and green (1.03)	38·00	60·00
		w. Wmk inverted		
		y. Wmk inverted and reversed	£110	£120
58/61 *Set of* 4			75·00	£140
58s/61s Optd "Specimen" *Set of* 4			£130	

For stamps in this design, but with Mult Crown CA or Mult Script CA watermarks see Nos. 75/80 and 111/14.

(Typo D.L.R.)

1902 (18 Dec)–**10**. Wmk Crown CA. P 14.

62	**7**	1d. carmine	1·50	2·00
63		2½d. ultramarine	6·50	1·25
		a. Sloping "2"	£250	£120
64		4d. orange	15·00	60·00
65		4d. deep yellow (3.10)	23·00	70·00
66		6d. brown	3·50	24·00
		a. Malformed "E" (R. 6/6)	£150	£225
67		1s. grey-black and carmine	20·00	50·00
68		1s. brownish grey and carmine (6.07)	22·00	50·00
69		5s. dull purple and blue	65·00	85·00
70		£1 green and black	£250	£325
62/70 *Set of* 7			£325	£500
62s/70s Optd "Specimen" *Set of* 7			£275	

Examples of most values are known showing a forged Nassau postmark dated "2 MAR 10".

1906 (Apr)–**11**. Wmk Mult Crown CA. P 14.

71	**7**	½d. pale green (5.06)	5·00	3·00
		s. Optd "Specimen"	55·00	
72		1d. carmine-rose	25·00	1·25
73		2½d. ultramarine (4.07)	25·00	26·00
		a. Sloping "2"	£350	£400
		w. Wmk inverted	£150	£150
74		6d. bistre-brown (8.11)	17·00	48·00
		a. Malformed "E" (R. 6/6)	£275	£475
71/4 *Set of* 4			65·00	70·00

1911 (Feb)–**19**. Wmk Mult Crown CA. P 14.

75	**6**	1d. black and red	18·00	2·75
		a. Grey-black and scarlet (1916)	4·75	2·50
		b. Grey-black & deep carmine-red (1919)	8·50	6·00
76		3d. purple/*yellow* (*thin paper*) (18.5.17)	4·75	30·00
		a. Reddish pur/buff (thick paper) (1.19)	5·50	5·50
		s. Optd "Specimen"	40·00	
		x. Wmk reversed	†	£375

77 3d. black and brown (23.3.19) 2·00 2·25
s. Optd "Specimen" 40·00
w. Wmk inverted
x. Wmk reversed † £375
78 5d. black and mauve (18.5.17) 2·75 5·50
s. Optd "Specimen" 40·00
79 2s. black and blue (11.16) 29·00 55·00
w. Wmk inverted £350
80 3s. black and green (8.17) 65·00 55·00
w. Wmk inverted £200 £200
y. Wmk inverted and reversed £140 £140
75/80 *Set of* 6 95·00 £110

(Typo D.L.R.)

1912–19. Wmk Mult Crown CA. *Chalk-surfaced paper (1s. to £1)*. P 14.
81 **8** ½d. green 80 10·00
a. Yellow-green 2·50 15·00
82 1d. carmine (aniline) 3·50 30
a. Deep rose 8·00 2·25
b. Rose 11·00 3·00
w. Wmk inverted £225 95·00
83 2d. grey (1919) 2·25 3·00
84 2½d. ultramarine 4·75 28·00
a. Deep dull blue 17·00 38·00
b. Sloping "2" £275 £400
85 4d. orange-yellow 5·50 20·00
a. Yellow 2·50 15·00
86 6d. bistre-brown 1·75 4·75
a. Malformed "E" (R. 6/6) £120 £170
87 1s. grey-black and carmine 1·75 9·00
a. Jet-black and carmine 14·00 22·00
88 5s. dull purple and blue 40·00 70·00
a. Pale dull purple and deep blue 50·00 75·00
89 £1 dull green and black £170 £300
a. Green and black £225 £325
81/9 *Set of* 9 £200 £400
81s/9s Optd "Specimen" *Set of* 9 £300

1.1.17. (9) WAR TAX (10)

1917 (18 May). *No. 75b optd with T* **9** *in red by D.L.R.*
90 **6** 1d. grey-black and deep carmine-red 40 2·00
a. Long stroke to "7" (R. 4/6) 40·00 75·00
s. Optd "Specimen" 65·00

It was originally intended to issue No. 90 on 1 January 1917, but the stamps were not received in the Bahamas until May. Half the proceeds from their sale were donated to the British Red Cross Society.

1918 (21 Feb–10 July). *Nos. 75/6, 81/2 and 87 optd at Nassau with T* **10**.
91 **8** ½d. green 9·00 42·00
92 1d. carmine (aniline) 1·00 50
w. Wmk inverted £250
x. Wmk reversed £300
93 **6** 1d. black and red (10 July) 3·50 5·50
a. Opt double, one inverted £850
b. Opt double £1700 £1800
c. Opt inverted £1500 £1600
x. Wmk reversed £275
94 3d. purple/*yellow* (*thin paper*) 2·25 2·25
a. Opt double £1600 £1700
b. Opt inverted £1100 £1200
c. "W" of "WAR" inserted by hand £3250
95 **8** 1s. grey-black and carmine £100 £140
91/5 *Set of* 5 £110 £170

No. 93 was only on sale for ten days.
No. 94c occured on R. 1/1 of one sheet, the original "W" having been omitted as a result of a paper fold.
Examples of Nos. 91/2 with overprint inverted, and of Nos. 91/2 and 95 with overprint double, are now considered to be forgeries.

WAR TAX (11) WAR TAX (12) WAR CHARITY 3.6.18. (13)

1918 (1 June–20 July). *Optd by D.L.R. in London with T* **11** *or* **12** *(3d)*.
96 **8** ½d. green 1·75 1·75
w. Wmk inverted
x. Wmk reversed
97 1d. carmine 2·00 35
a. Wmk sideways £300
w. Wmk inverted
y. Wmk inverted and reversed £300
98 **6** 3d. purple/*yellow* (20 July) 1·00 1·50
w. Wmk inverted £110
x. Wmk reversed
99 **8** 1s. grey-black and carmine (R.) 9·00 2·75
96/9 *Set of* 4 12·00 5·75
96s/9s Optd "Specimen" *Set of* 4 £140

1919 (21 Mar). *No. 77 optd with T* **12** *by D.L.R.*
100 **6** 3d. black and brown 60 4·00
a. "C" and "A" missing from wmk £1700
s. Optd "Specimen" 50·00
w. Wmk inverted 60·00

No. 100a shows the "C" omitted from one impression and the "A" missing from the next one to the right (as seen from the front of the stamp). The "C" is badly distorted in the second watermark.

1919 (1 Jan). *No. 75b optd with T* **13** *by D.L.R.*
101 **6** 1d. grey-black and deep carmine-red (R.) 30 2·50
a. Opt double £1800
s. Optd "Specimen" 55·00
w. Wmk inverted 60·00
x. Wmk reversed 60·00
y. Wmk inverted and reversed £110

The date is that originally fixed for the issue of the stamp. The year 1918 was also the bicentenary of the appointment of the first Royal governor.

WAR TAX (14) WAR TAX (15)

1919 (14 July).

(a) Optd with T **14** *by D.L.R.*
102 **8** ½d. green (R.) 30 1·25
103 1d. carmine 1·50 1·50
104 – 1s. grey-black and carmine (R.) 22·00 42·00

(b) No. 77 optd with T **15**.
105 **6** 3d. black and brown 75 8·00
w. Wmk inverted 60·00
ws. Ditto. Optd "Specimen" 60·00
x. Wmk reversed 65·00
y. Wmk inverted and reversed 85·00
102/5 *Set of* 4 22·00 48·00
102s/5s Optd "Specimen" *Set of* 4 £140

16

17 Great Seal of the Bahamas.

(Recess D.L.R.)

1920 (1 Mar). *Peace Celebration*. Wmk Mult Crown CA (sideways*). P 14.
106 **16** ½d. green 1·00 5·50
a. "A" of "CA" missing from wmk £800
x. Wmk sideways reversed £325 £325
107 1d. carmine 2·75 1·00
a. "A" of "CA" missing from wmk † £600
x. Wmk sideways reversed £375
y. Wmk Crown to right of CA and reversed £375
108 2d. slate-grey 2·75 7·50
a. "C" of "CA" missing from Wmk £850
109 3d. deep brown 2·75 9·00
a. "C" of "CA" missing from wmk £900
w. Wmk Crown to right of CA £250
110 1s. deep myrtle-green 12·00 35·00
a. Substituted crown in wmk £1400
b. "C" of "CA" missing from wmk £1400
x. Wmk sideways reversed £500
106/10 *Set of* 5 19·00 50·00
106s/10s Optd "Specimen" *Set of* 5 £160

*The normal sideways watermark shows Crown to left of CA, *as seen from the back of the stamp*.
For illustration of the substituted watermark crown see Catalogue Introduction.

1921 (29 Mar)–**29**. Wmk Script CA. P 14.
111 **6** 1d. grey and rose-red 1·75 2·00
112 5d. black and purple (8.29) 3·75 45·00
113 2s. black and blue (11.22) 19·00 22·00
114 3s. black and green (9.24) 48·00 65·00
111/14 *Set of* 4 65·00 £120
111s/14s Optd or Perf (5d.) "Specimen" *Set of* 4. £170

Examples of all values are known showing a forged Nassau postmark dated "2 MAR 10".

Elongated "E" (left pane R. 9/6)

1921 (8 Sept)–**37**. Wmk Mult Script CA. *Chalk-surfaced paper (3d., 1s., 5s., £1)*. P 14.
115 **8** ½d. green (1924) 50 40
a. Elongated "E" 55·00 60·00
116 1d. carmine 1·00 15
117 1½d. brown-red (1934) 9·00 1·00
118 2d. grey (1927) 1·50 2·25
119 2½d. ultramarine (1922) 1·00 2·25
y. Wmk inverted and reversed † £600
120 3d. purple/*pale yellow* (1931) 6·50 16·00
a. Purple/orange-yellow (1937) 7·50 17·00
121 4d. orange-yellow (1924) 1·50 4·00
122 6d. bistre-brown (1922) 70 1·25
a. Malformed "E" (R.6/6) 90·00 £130
123 1s. black and carmine (1926) 2·75 5·50
124 5s. dull purple and blue (1924) 35·00 65·00
125 £1 green and black (1926) £170 £325
115/25 *Set of* 11 £200 £375
115s/25s Optd or Perf (1½d., 3d.) "Specimen" *Set of* 11 £400

(Recess B.W.)

1930 (2 Jan). *Tercentenary of Colony*. Wmk Mult Script CA. P 12.
126 **17** 1d. black and scarlet 2·25 2·75
127 3d. black and deep brown 4·25 15·00
128 5d. black and deep purple 4·25 15·00
129 2s. black and deep blue 18·00 50·00
130 3s. black and green 45·00 85·00
126/30 *Set of* 5 65·00 £150
126s/30s Perf "Specimen" *Set of* 5 £150

18

(Recess B.W.)

1931 (14 July)–**46**. Wmk Mult Script CA. P 12.
131 **18** 2s. slate-purple and deep ultramarine 24·00 29·00
a. Slate-purple and indigo (9.42) 90·00 40·00
ab. "A" of "CA" missing from wmk £1500
b. Brownish black and indigo (13.4.43) 11·00 5·00
c. Brownish black and steel-blue (6.44) 14·00 3·00
132 3s. slate-purple and myrtle-green 29·00 27·00
a. Brownish black and green (13.4.43) 9·00 3·50
b. Brownish black and myrtle-green (1.10.46) 8·00 5·00
131s/2s Perf "Specimen" *Set of* 2 80·00

Most of the stamps from the September 1942 printing (No. 131*a* and further stocks of the 3s. similar to No. 132) were used for the 1942 "LANDFALL" overprints.

1935 (6 May). *Silver Jubilee. As Nos. 91/4 of Antigua.*
141 1½d. deep blue and carmine 1·00 3·50
h. Dot by flagstaff 95·00 £160
i. Dash by turret £190
142 2½d. brown and deep blue 5·00 9·50
f. Diagonal line by turret £140 £190
g. Dot to left of chapel £275
143 6d. light blue and olive-green 7·00 14·00
g. Dot to left of chapel £200 £275
h. Dot by flagstaff £300
144 1s. slate and purple 7·00 13·00
h. Dot by flagstaff £250 £350
i. Dash by turret £325
141/4 *Set of* 4 18·00 35·00
141s/4s Perf "Specimen" *Set of* 4 £120

For illustrations of plate varieties see Omnibus section following Zanzibar.

19 Greater Flamingos in flight

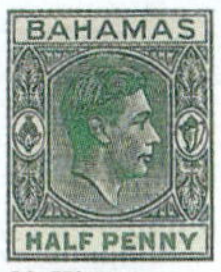

20 King George VI

(Recess Waterlow)

1935 (22 May). Wmk Mult Script CA. P 12½.
145 **19** 8d. ultramarine and scarlet 6·00 3·25
s. Perf "Specimen" 50·00

1937 (12 May). *Coronation. As Nos. 95/7 of Antigua.* P 14.
146 ½d. green 15 15
147 1½d. yellow-brown 30 1·10
148 2½d. bright blue 50 1·10
146/8 *Set of* 3 85 2·10
146s/8s Perf "Specimen" *Set of* 3 90·00

Accent flaw (right pane R. 1/5) (1938 ptg only)

Short "T" in "TWO" (right pane R. 3/6) (Retouched on No. 152*c*, although bottom of letter is still pointed)

"RENCE" flaw (Right pane R. 9/3. Later corrected.

(Typo D.L.R.)

1938 (11 Mar)–**52**. Wmk Mult Script CA. *Chalk-surfaced paper (1s. to £1)*. P 14.
149 **20** ½d. green 1·50 1·25
a. Elongated "E" £130
b. Accent flaw £400
c. Bluish green (11.9.42) 2·00 2·25
ca. Elongated "E" £160
d. Myrtle-green (11.12.46) 7·00 7·00
da. Elongated "E" £275
149*e* ½d. brown-purple (18.2.52) 1·00 2·50
ea. Error. Crown missing £9500
eb. Error. St Edward's Crown £3750
ec. Elongated "E" £150
150 1d. carmine 8·50 2·50

150*a*		1d. olive-grey (17.9.41)	3·25	3·25
		ab. Pale slate (11.9.42)	60	70
151		1½d. red-brown (19.4.38)	1·50	1·25
		a. Pale red-brown (19.4.48)	6·50	2·50
152		2d. pale slate (19.4.38)	18·00	4·00
		a. Short "T"	£750	
152*b*		2d. scarlet (17.9.41)	1·00	65
		ba. Short "T"	£120	
		bb. "TWO PENCE" printed double	†	£9000
		bc. Dull rose-red (19.4.48)	3·25	3·25
152*c*		2d. green (1.5.51)	1·75	80
153		2½d. ultramarine	3·25	1·50
153*a*		2½d. violet (1.7.43)	1·25	1·25
		ab. "2½ PENNY" printed double	£4000	
154		3d. violet (19.4.38)	16·00	3·00
154*a*		3d. blue (4.43)	70	1·25
		aa. "RENCE" flaw		
		ab. Bright ultramarine (19.4.48)	4·25	4·75
154*b*		3d. scarlet (1.2.52)	70	3·25
154*c*		10d. yellow-orange (18.11.46)	2·50	20
155		1s. grey-black and carmine (*thick paper*) (15.9.38)	24·00	6·00
		a. Brownish grey and scarlet (4.42)	£475	80·00
		b. Ordinary paper. *Black and carmine* (9.42)	22·00	7·00
		c. Ordinary paper. *Grey-black and bright crimson* (6.3.44)	15·00	75
		d. Pale brownish grey and crimson (19.4.48)	14·00	1·50
156		5s. lilac & blue (*thick paper*) (19.4.38)	£170	£100
		a. Reddish lilac and blue (4.42)	£2500	£650
		b. Ordinary paper. *Purple and blue* (9.42)	28·00	22·00
		c. Ordinary paper. *Dull mauve and deep blue* (11.46)	£100	60·00
		d. Brown-purple and deep bright blue (19.4.48)	35·00	13·00
		e. Red-purple and deep bright blue (8.51)	24·00	17·00
157		£1 deep grey-green and black (*thick paper*) (15.9.38)	£250	£140
		a. Ordinary paper. *Blue-green and black* (13.4.43)	60·00	55·00
		b. Ordinary paper. *Grey-green and black* (3.44)	£170	£100
149/57a *Set of* 17			£140	80·00
149s/57s Perf "Specimen" *Set of* 14			£500	

Nos. 149/50*a* exist in coils, constructed from normal sheets.

No. 149eb occurs on a row in the watermark in which the crowns and letters "CA" alternate.

The thick chalk-surfaced paper, used for the initial printing of the 1s., 5s. and £1, was usually toned and had streaky gum. The April 1942 printing for the 1s. and 5s., which was mostly used for the "LANDFALL" overprints, was on thin, white chalk-surfaced paper with clear gum. Printings of the three values between September 1942 and November 1946 were on a thick, smooth, opaque ordinary paper.

21 Sea Garden, Nassau

22 Fort Charlotte

23 Greater Flamingos in flight

3d.
(24)

(Recess Waterlow)

1938 (1 July). Wmk Mult Script CA. P 12½.

158	**21**	4d. light blue and red-orange	1·00	1·00
159	**22**	6d. olive-green and light blue	75	1·00
160	**23**	8d. ultramarine and scarlet	9·50	2·50
158/60 *Set of* 3			10·00	4·00
158s/60s Perf "Specimen" *Set of* 3			£120	

1940 (28 Nov). *No.* 153 *surcharged with T* **24** *by The Nassau Guardian.*

161	**20**	3d. on 2½d. blue	1·50	1·75

1492
LANDFALL
OF
COLUMBUS
1942
(25)

Broken "OF" and "US" (R.2/5, late printing)

1942 (12 Oct). *450th Anniv of Landing of Columbus in New World. Optd as T* **25** *by The Nassau Guardian.*

162	**20**	½d. bluish green	30	60
		a. Elongated "E"	60·00	
		b. Opt double	£1700	
163		1d. pale slate	30	60
164		1½d. red-brown	40	60
165		2d. scarlet	50	65
		a. Short "T"	£100	
166		2½d. ultramarine	50	65
167		3d. ultramarine	30	65
		a. "RENCE" flaw	£350	
168	**21**	4d. light blue and red-orange	40	90
		a. "COIUMBUS" (R. 5/2)	£850	£950
169	**22**	6d. olive-green and light blue	40	1·75
		a. "COIUMBUS" (R. 5/2)	£850	£1000
170	**23**	8d. ultramarine and scarlet	1·50	70
		a. "COIUMBUS" (R. 5/2)	£8500	£3000
171	**20**	1s. brownish grey and scarlet	8·50	4·25
		a. Ordinary paper. *Black and carmine*	8·50	9·00
		b. Ordinary paper. *Grey-black and bright crimson*	17·00	9·00
		c. Broken "OF" and "US"	£180	
172	**18**	2s. slate-purple and indigo	16·00	21·00
		a. Brownish black and indigo	8·00	10·00
		b. Brownish black and steel-blue	30·00	26·00
		c. Stop after "COLUMBUS" (R. 2/12)	£4250	
173		3s. slate-purple and myrtle-green	8·00	6·50
		a. Brownish black and green	42·00	35·00
		b. Stop after "COLUMBUS" (R. 2/12)	£2250	
174	**20**	5s. reddish lilac and blue	48·00	17·00
		a. Ordinary paper. *Purple and blue*	23·00	14·00
175		£1 deep grey-green & blk (*thick paper*)	80·00	90·00
		a. Ordinary paper. *Grey-green & black*	30·00	25·00
162/75a *Set of* 14			70·00	60·00
162s/75s Perf "Specimen" *Set of* 14			£475	

These stamps replaced the definitive series for a period of six months. Initially stocks of existing printings were used, but when further supplies were required for overprinting a number of new printings were produced, some of which, including the new colour of the 3d., did not appear without overprint until much later.

1946 (11 Nov). *Victory. As Nos.* 110/11 *of Antigua.*

176		1½d. brown	10	60
177		3d. blue	10	60
176s/7s Perf "Specimen" *Set of* 2			80·00	

26 Infant Welfare Clinic

27 Agriculture (combine harvester)

28 Sisal

29 Straw work

30 Dairy farm

31 Fishing fleet

32 Hatchet Bay, Eleuthera

33 Tuna fishing

34 Paradise Beach

35 Modern hotels

36 Yacht racing

37 Watersports—skiing

38 Shipbuilding

39 Transportation

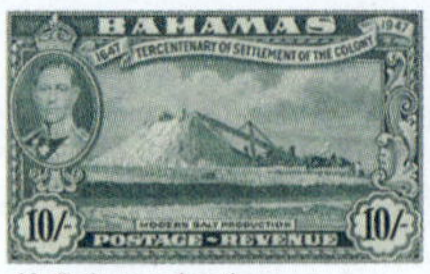
40 Salt production

41 Parliament buildings

(Recess C.B.N.)

1948 (11 Oct). *Tercentenary of Settlement of Island of Eleuthera. T* **26/41**. P 12.

178	**26**	½d. orange	40	1·50
179	**27**	1d. sage-green	40	35
180	**28**	1½d. yellow	40	80
181	**29**	2d. scarlet	40	40
182	**30**	2½d. brown-lake	70	75
183	**31**	3d. ultramarine	2·50	85
184	**32**	4d. black	60	70
185	**33**	6d. emerald-green	2·50	80
186	**34**	8d. violet	1·25	70
187	**35**	10d. carmine	1·25	35
188	**36**	1s. sepia	2·75	50
189	**37**	2s. magenta	4·25	8·50
190	**38**	3s. blue	11·00	8·50
191	**39**	5s. mauve	18·00	4·50
192	**40**	10s. grey	15·00	11·00
193	**41**	£1 vermilion	15·00	16·00
178/93 *Set of* 16			65·00	50·00

1948 (1 Dec). *Royal Silver Wedding. As Nos.* 112/13 *of Antigua.*

194		1½d. red-brown	20	25
195		£1 slate-green	38·00	32·00

1949 (10 Oct). *75th Anniv of Universal Postal Union. As Nos.* 114/17 *of Antigua.*

196		2½d. violet	35	75
197		3d. deep blue	2·25	3·25
198		6d. greenish blue	55	3·00
199		1s. carmine	55	75
196/9 *Set of* 4			3·25	7·00

Des and eng B.W. Recess D.L.R.)

1953 (3 June). *Coronation. As No.* 120 *of Antigua.*

200		6d. black and pale blue	1·50	60

42 Infant Welfare Clinic

43 Queen Elizabeth II

(Recess B.W.)

1954 (1 Jan)–**63**. *Designs previously used for King George VI issue, but bicoloured with portrait of Queen Elizabeth II as in T* **42**, *and commemorative inscr omitted.* Wmk Mult Script CA. P 11×11½.

201	**42**	½d. black and red-orange	10	1·50
202	**27**	1d. olive-green and brown	10	30
203	**28**	1½d. blue and black	15	80
204	**29**	2d. yellow-brown and myrtle-green	15	30
		a. Yellow-brn & dp myrtle-grn (23.1.62)	7·50	9·50
205	**30**	3d. black and carmine-red	65	1·25
206	**31**	4d. turquoise-green and deep reddish purple	30	30
		a. Turq-blue and dp reddish pur (23.1.62)	18·00	19·00
207	**32**	5d. red-brown and deep bright blue	1·40	2·25
208	**33**	6d. light blue and black	2·25	20
		w. Wmk inverted	—	£650
209	**34**	8d. black and reddish lilac	70	40
		a. Black and deep reddish lilac (21.11.56)	3·50	2·75
210	**35**	10d. black and ultramarine	30	10
		a. Black and deep ultramarine (8.1.63)	7·00	2·75
211	**36**	1s. ultramarine and olive-brown	1·50	10
		a. Ultramarine and dp ol-sepia (19.2.58)	4·25	70
212	**37**	2s. orange-brown and black	2·00	70
		a. Chestnut and black (19.2.58)	12·00	2·00
213	**38**	2s.6d. black and deep blue	3·50	2·00
214	**39**	5s. bright emerald and orange	19·00	75
		a. Brt emerald & reddish orange (14.1.59)	60·00	6·50
215	**40**	10s. black and slate-black	26·00	2·50
216	**41**	£1 slate-black and violet	24·00	6·50
201/16 *Set of* 16			70·00	18·00

Nos. 201/2, 205, 208 and 211 exist in coils, constructed from normal sheets.

See also No. 246.

(Recess Waterlow)

1959 (10 June). *Centenary of First Bahamas Postage Stamp.* W w **12**. P 13½.

217	**43**	1d. black and scarlet	45	20
218		2d. black and blue-green	45	1·00
219		6d. black and blue	55	40
220		10d. black and chocolate	55	1·00
217/20 *Set of* 4			1·80	2·40

44 Christ Church Cathedral

(Photo Enschedé)

1962 (30 Jan). *Nassau Centenary. T* **44** *and similar horiz design.* P 14×13.

221	8d. green	50	55
222	10d. bluish violet	50	25

Design:—10d. Nassau Public Library.

1963 (4 June). *Freedom from Hunger. As No. 146 of Antigua.*

223	8d. sepia	40	40
	a. Name and value omitted	£900	£1700

BAHAMAS TALKS 1962 (46) **NEW CONSTITUTION 1964** (47)

1963 (15 July). *Bahamas Talks, 1962. Nos. 209/10 optd with T* **46**.

224	8d. black and reddish lilac	50	75
225	10d. black and deep ultramarine	50	75

1963 (2 Sept). *Red Cross Centenary. As Nos. 147/8 of Antigua.*

226	1d. red and black	50	50
227	10d. red and blue	1·75	2·50

SELF GOVERNMENT

1964 (7 Jan). *New Constitution. As Nos. 201/16 but* W w **12**, optd with *T* **47**, by B.W.

228	½d. black and red-orange	15	1·50
229	1d. olive-green and brown	15	15
230	1½d. blue and black	70	1·50
231	2d. yellow-brown and deep myrtle-green	15	20
232	3d. black and carmine-red	2·00	1·75
233	4d. turquoise-blue and deep reddish purple	70	55
234	5d. red-brown and deep bright blue	70	1·50
235	6d. light blue and black	3·25	30
236	8d. black and reddish lilac	70	30
237	10d. black and deep ultramarine	30	15
238	1s. ultramarine and olive-brown	1·50	15
239	2s. chestnut and black	2·00	1·75
240	2s.6d. black and deep blue	3·00	2·75
241	5s. bright emerald and orange	7·00	3·25
242	10s. black and slate black	7·00	5·50
243	£1 slate-black and violet	7·50	19·00
228/243 *Set of* 16		32·00	35·00

1964 (23 April). *400th Birth Anniv of William Shakespeare. As No. 244 of Antigua.*

244	6d. turquoise	30	10
	w. Wmk inverted	55·00	

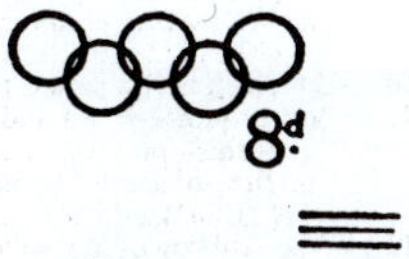

(48)

1964 (1 Oct). *Olympic Games, Tokyo. As No. 211 but* W w **12**, surch with *T* **48**.

245	8d. on 1s. ultramarine and olive-brown	45	15

1964 (6 Oct). *As No. 204a, but wmk w* **12**.

246	2d. yellow-brown and deep myrtle-green	45	30

49 Colony's Badge

50 Out Island regatta

51 Hospital

52 High School

53 Greater Flamingo

54 RMS *Queen Elizabeth*

55 "Development"

56 Yachting

57 Public square

58 Sea Gardens

59 Old cannons at Fort Charlotte

60 Sikorsky S-38 flying boat, 1929 and Boeing 707 airliner

61 Williamson Film Project, 1914 and Undersea Post Office, 1939

62 Queen or Pink Conch

63 Columbus's flagship

(Queen's portrait by Anthony Buckley. Litho and recess (portrait and "BAHAMAS") B.W.)

1965 (7 Jan–14 Sept). *Horiz designs as* T **49/63**. W w **12**. P 13½.

247	**49**	½d. multicoloured	15	2·25
248	**50**	1d. slate, light blue and orange	30	1·00
249	**51**	1½d. rose-red, green and brown	15	2·75
250	**52**	2d. slate, green and turquoise-blue	15	10
251	**53**	3d. red, light blue and purple	4·00	20
252	**54**	4d. green, blue and orange-brown	4·75	3·00
253	**55**	6d. dull green, light blue and rose	1·25	10
254	**56**	8d. reddish purple, light blue and bronze green	50	30
255	**57**	10d. orange-brown, green and violet	25	10
256	**58**	1s. red, yellow, torquoise-blue and deep emer	50	20
		a. Red, yellow, dull blue & emer (14.9.65)	40	10
257	**59**	2s. brown, light blue and emerald	1·00	1·25
258	**60**	2s.6d. yellow-olive, blue and carmine	2·50	3·00
259	**61**	5s. orange-brown, ultramarine and green	2·75	1·00
260	**62**	10s. rose, blue and chocolate	16·00	3·50
261	**63**	£1 chestnut, blue and rose-red	19·00	9·00
247/261 *Set of* 15			48·00	24·00

Nos. 247/8, 251, 253 and 256 exist in coils, constructed from normal sheets.

1965 (17 May). *I.T.U Centenary. As Nos. 262/3 of Antigua.*

262	1d. light emerald and orange	15	10
	w. Wmk inverted	80·00	
263	2s. purple and yellow-olive	65	45
	w. Wmk inverted	16·00	

9d. (64)

1965 (12 July). *No. 254 surch with T* **64**.

264	9d. on 8d. reddish purple, light blue and bronze-green	30	15

1965 (25 Oct). *International Co-operation Year. As Nos. 168/9 of Antigua.*

265	½d. reddish purple and turquoise-green	10	1·10
266	1s. deep bluish green and lavender	30	40

1966 (24 Jan). *Churchill Commemoration. As Nos. 267/70 of Antigua.*

267	½d. new blue	10	75
	w. Wmk inverted	42·00	
268	2d. deep green	50	30
269	10d. brown	85	85
270	1s. bluish violet	85	1·40
267/70 *Set of* 4		2·00	3·00

1966 (4 Feb). *Royal Visit. As Nos. 174/5 of Antigua, but inscr "to the Caribbean" omitted.*

271	6d. black and ultramarine	1·00	50
272	1s. black and magenta	1·25	1·25

(New Currency. 100 cents = 1 Bahamas dollar)

1c (65) 3c (66)

1966 (25 May). *Decimal Currency. Nos. 247/61 variously surch as T* **55/6**, *by B.W.*

273	1c. on ½d. multicoloured	10	30
274	2c. on 1d. slate, light blue and orange	75	30
275	3c. on 2d. slate, green and turquoise-blue	10	10
276	4c. on 3d. red, light blue and purple	2·00	20
277	5c. on 4d. green, blue and orange-brown	2·00	3·00
	a. Surch omitted (vert strip of 10)	£3250	
278	8c. on 6d. dull green, light blue and rose	20	20
279	10c. on 8d. reddish purple, light blue and bronze-green	30	75
280	11c. on 1½d. rose-red, green and brown	15	30
281	12c. on 10d. orange-brown, green and violet	15	10
282	15c. on 1s. multicoloured	25	10
283	22c. on 2s. brown, light blue and emerald	60	1·25
284	50c. on 2s.6d. yellow-olive, blue and carmine	1·00	1·40
285	$1 on 5s. orange-brown, ultram and green	1·75	1·50
286	$2 on 10s. rose, blue and chocolate	7·50	4·50
287	$3 on £1 chestnut, blue and rose-red	7·50	4·50
273/287 *Set of* 15		22·00	16·00

The above were made on new printings, some of which vary slightly in shade, and in No. 273 the shield appears as vermilion and green instead of carmine and blue-green due to a different combination of the printing colours.

No. 277a. One sheet exists and the stamp can be distinguished from No. 252 when in a vertical strip of ten as these were printed in sheets of 100 whereas No. 252 was printed in sheets of 60 (six rows often across).

1966 (1 July). *World Cup Football Championship. As Nos. 176/7 of Antigua.*

288	8c. violet, yellow-green, lake and yellow-brown	35	15
289	15c. chocolate, blue-green, lake and yellow-brown	40	25

1966 (20 Sept). *Inauguration of W.H.O. Headquarters, Geneva. As Nos. 178/9 of Antigua.*

290	11c. black, yellow-green and light blue	50	90
291	15c. black, light purple and yellow-brown	50	50

1966 (1 Dec). *20th Anniv of U.N.E.S.C.O. As Nos. 196/8 of Antigua.*

292	3c. slate-violet, red, yellow and orange	10	10
293	15c. orange-yellow, violet and deep olive	35	20
294	$1 black, bright purple and orange	1·10	2·00
292/4 *Set of* 3		1·40	2·00

67 *Oceanic*

68 Conch Shell

(Portrait by Anthony Buckley. Litho and recess (portrait, "BAHAMAS" and value), B.W.)

1967 (25 May)–**71**. *As T* **49/63** *and additional design (T* **67**) *but values in decimal currency, as T* **68** *and colours changed. Toned paper.* W w **12**. P 13½.

295	**49**	1c. multicoloured (as ½d.)	10	3·25
		a. Whiter paper (1970)	45	3·25
296	**50**	2c. slate, light blue & deep emerald (as 1d.)	50	60
		a. Whiter paper (1970)	1·40	6·50
297	**52**	3c. slate, green and violet (as 2d.)	10	10
		a. Whiter paper (1970)	48·00	5·00
298	**53**	4c. red, light blue and ultramarine (as 3d.)	4·75	50
		a. Whiter paper (9.70*)	12·00	18·00
299	**67**	5c. black, greenish blue and purple	1·00	3·50
		a. Whiter paper (1970)	1·50	6·50
300	**55**	8c. dull green, light blue and sepia (as 6d.)	25	10
		a. Whiter paper (1970)	£180	18·00
301	**56**	10c. reddish purple, greenish blue & carmine (as 8d.)	30	70
		a. Whiter paper (1970)	1·00	4·00
302	**51**	11c. rose-red, green and blue (as 1½d.)	25	80
		a. Whiter paper (1970)	80	2·50
303	**57**	12c. orange-brown green and olive (as 10d.)	25	10
		a. Whiter paper (4.71)	12·00	27·00
304	**58**	15c. red, yellow, turquoise-blue and carmine (as 1s.)	55	10
		a. Whiter paper (1970)	£225	23·00

305 **59** 22c. brown, new blue and rose-red (as 2s.) 70 65
a. Whiter paper (1970) .... 1·50 7·00
306 **60** 50c. yellow-olive, new blue and emerald (as 2s.6d.) .... 2·25 1·00
a. Whiter paper (1970) .... 2·25 4·00
307 **61** $1 orange-brown ultramarine and slate-purple (as 5s.) .... 2·00 60
a. Whiter paper (4.71) .... 19·00 65·00
308 **68** $2 multicoloured .... 13·00 3·00
a. Whiter paper (4.71) .... 30·00 75·00
309 **63** $3 chestnut, new blue and purple (as £1) .... 3·75 2·00
a. Whiter paper (4.71) .... 30·00 75·00
295/309 *Set of* 15 .... 26·00 15·00
295a/309a *Set of* 15 (whiter paper) £500 £300

*This is the earliest known date recorded in the Bahamas.

The 3c. has the value at right instead of at left as on No. 250.

The 1970–71 printings on whiter paper were released as needed, the 12c., $1, $2 and $3 only a week or two before the issue was withdrawn. Due to the marked difference in paper and the use of some new plates there are marked differences in shade in nearly all values.

69 Bahamas Crest

(Des R. Granger Barrett. Photo Enschedé)

1967 (1 Sept). *Diamond Jubilee of World Scouting. T* **69** *and similar horiz design. Multicoloured.* W w **12** (sideways*). P 14×13.

310 3c. Type **69** 35 15
w. Wmk Crown to left of CA .... 35·00
311 15c. Scout badge 40 15

*The normal sideways watermark shows Crown to right of CA, *as seen from the back of the stamp.*

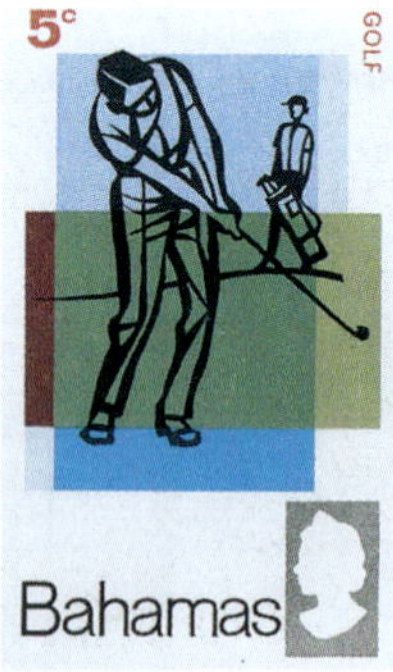

71 Globe and Emblem **74** Golf

(Des R. Granger Barrett, Litho D.L.R)

1968 (13 May). *Human Rights Year. T* **71** *and similar horiz designs. Multicoloured.* W w **12** (sideways*). P 14×13½.

312 3c. Type **71** 10 10
313 12c. Scales of Justice and emblem 20 10
314 $1 Bahamas Crest and emblem 70 80
312/14 *Set of* 3 .... 90 85

*The normal sideways watermark shows Crown to right of CA on the 12c. and Crown to left of CA on the others, *each when seen from the back of the stamp.*

(Litho B.W.)

1968 (20 Aug). *Tourism. T* **74** *and similar vert designs. Multicoloured.* P 13.

315 5c. Type **74** .... 1·75 1·75
316 11c. Yachting .... 1·25 40
317 15c. Horse-racing .... 1·75 45
318 50c. Water-skiing .... 2·50 6·50
315/18 *Set of* 4 .... 6·50 8·00

78 Racing Yacht and Olympic Monument

(Photo Harrison)

1968 (29 Sept). *Olympic Games, Mexico City. T* **78** *and similar horiz designs.* No wmk. P 14½×13½.

319 5c. red-brown, orange-yellow and blue-green 40 75
320 11c. multicoloured 40 25
321 50c. multicoloured .... 60 1·75
322 $1 olive-grey, greenish blue and violet .... 2·00 3·75
319/22 *Set of* 4 .... 3·00 6·00

Designs:—11c. Long-jumping and Olympic Monument; 50c. Running and Olympic Monument; $1 Type **78**.

It is understood that the above were released by the Philatelic Agency in the U.S.A. on 1st September.

81 Legislative Building

(Des J. Cooter, Litho Format)

1968 (1 Nov). *14th Commonwealth Parliamentary Conference. T* **81** *and similar multicoloured designs.* P 14.

323 3c. Type **81** 10 30
324 10c. Bahamas Mace and Westminster Clock Tower (*vert*) 15 30
325 12c. Local straw market (*vert*) 15 25
326 15c. Horse-drawn Surrey 20 35
323/6 *Set of* 4 .... 55 1·10

85 Obverse and reverse of $100 Gold Coin

(Recess D.L.R.)

1968 (2 Dec). *Gold Coins commemorating the first General Election under the New Constitution. T* **85** *and similar "boomerang" shaped designs.* P 13½.

327 3c. red/*gold* 40 40
328 12c. blue-green/*gold* 45 50
329 15c. dull purple/*gold* 50 60
330 $1 black/*gold* .... 1·25 3·25
327/30 *Set of* 4 .... 2·40 4·00

Designs:—12c. Obverse and reverse of $50 gold coin; 15c. Obverse and reverse of $20 gold coin; $1 Obverse and reverse of $10 gold coin.

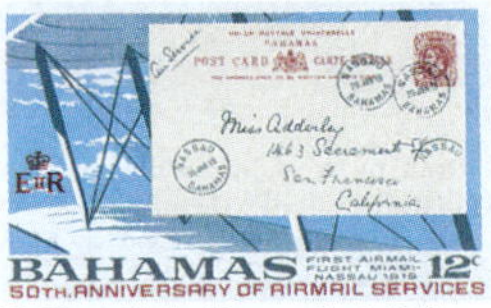

89 First Flight Postcard of 1919

90 Sikorsky S-38 Flying Boat of 1929

(Des V. Whiteley. Litho Format)

1969 (30 Jan). *50th Anniv of Bahamas Airmail Service.* P 14.

331 **89** 12c. multicoloured 50 50
332 **90** 15c. multicoloured .... 60 1·75

91 Game-fishing Boats **92** "The Adoration of the Shepherds" (Louis le Nain)

(Des J. Cooter. Litho Format)

1969 (26 Aug). *Tourism. One Millionth Visitor to Bahamas. T* **91** *and similar horiz designs. Multicoloured.* W w **12** (sideways). P 14½.

333 3c. Type **91** 25 10
334 11c. Paradise Beach 35 15
335 12c. "Sunfish" sailing boats 35 15
336 15c. Rawson Square and Parade 45 25
333/6 *Set of* 4 .... 1·25 60
MS337 130×96 mm. Nos. 333/6 .... 2·75 3·50

(Des G. Drummond. Litho D.L.R.)

1969 (15 Oct). *Christmas. T* **92** *and similar vert designs.* W w **12**. P 12.

338 3c. Type **92** 10 20
339 11c. "The Adoration of the Shepherds" (Poussin) 15 30
340 12c. "The Adoration of the Kings" (Gerard David) 15 20
341 15c. "The Adoration of the Kings" (Vincenzo Foppa) 20 65
338/41 *Set of* 4 .... 55 1·25

93 Badge of Girl Guides

(Des Mrs. R. Sands. Litho Harrison)

1970 (23 Feb). *Girl Guides Diamond Jubilee. T* **93** *and similar designs. Multicoloured.* W w **12**. P 14½.

342 3c. Type **93** 30 10
w. Wmk inverted ....
343 12c. Badge of Brownies 45 20
344 15c. Badge of Rangers 50 35
w. Wmk inverted .... 14·00
342/4 *Set of* 3 .... 1·10 55

94 U.P.U. Headquarters and Emblem

(Des L. Curtis, Litho J.W.)

1970 (20 May). *New U.P.U. Headquarters Building.* W w **12** (sideways). P 14.

345 **94** 3c. multicoloured 10 40
346 15c. multicoloured 20 60

95 Coach and Globe

(Des G. Drummond. Litho B.W.)

1970 (14 July). *"Goodwill Caravan". T* **95** *and similar horiz designs. Multicoloured.* W w **12** (sideways*). P 13½×13.

347 3c. Type **95** 75 20
w. Wmk Crown to right of CA ....
348 11c. Diesel train and globe .... 1·50 60
349 12c. *Canberra* (liner), yacht and globe .... 1·50 60
w. Wmk Crown to right of CA .... 3·50
350 15c. B.A.C. One Eleven airliner and globe .... 1·50 1·75
347/50 *Set of* 4 .... 4·75 2·75
MS351 165×125 mm. Nos. 347/50 .... 9·50 17·00

*The normal sideways watermark shows Crown to left of CA, *as seen from the back of the stamp.*

96 Nurse, Patients and Greater Flamingo **97** "The Nativity" (detail, Pittoni)

(Photo Harrison)

1970 (1 Sept). *Centenary of British Red Cross. T* **96** *and similar horiz design. Multicoloured.* W w **12** (sideways*). P 14½.

352 3c. Type **96** 75 50
a. Gold ("EIIR", etc) omitted £400
w. Wmk Crown to right of CA .... 38·00
353 15c. Hospital and Blue Marlin .... 75 1·75

*The normal sideways watermark shows Crown to left of CA, *as seen from the back of the stamp.*

(Des G. Drummond. Litho D.L.R.)

1970 (3 Nov). *Christmas. T* **97** *and similar vert designs. Multicoloured.* W w **12**. P 13.

354 3c. Type **97** 15 15
355 11c. "The Holy Family" (detail, Anton Raphael Mengs) 20 25
356 12c. "The Adoration of the Shepherds" (detail, Giorgione) 20 20
357 15c. "The Adoration of the Shepherds" (detail, School of Seville) 30 75
354/7 *Set of* 4 .... 75 1·25
MS358 114×140 mm. Nos. 354/7 plus two labels .... 1·40 4·25

STAMP BOOKLETS

1938. *Black on pink cover with map and* "BAHAMAS ISLES OF JUNE" *on reverse. Stapled.*

SB1 2s. booklet containing twelve 1d. (No. 150) in blocks of 6 and eight 1½d. (No. 151) in folded block of 8 .... £10000

1961. (15 Aug). *Brown-purple cover (3s.) or green cover (6s.) Stitched.*

SB2 3s. booklet containing eight each of 1d., 1½d. and 2d. (Nos. 202/4) in blocks of 4 .... 28·00
SB3 6s. booklet containing four of each of 4d., 6d. and 8d. (Nos. 206, 208/9) in blocks of 4 .... 35·00

1965. (23 Mar). *Pink cover (3s.) or green cover (6s.).*

SB4	3s. booklet containing eight each of 1d., 1½d. and 2d. (Nos. 248/50) in blocks of 4	19·00
SB5	6s. booklet containing four each of 4d., 6d. and 8d. (Nos. 252/4) in blocks of 4	19·00

SPECIAL DELIVERY STAMPS

SPECIAL DELIVERY

(S **1**)

1916 (1 May). *No. 59 optd with Type* S **1** *by The Nassau Guardian.*

S1	**6**	5d. black and orange	6·00	38·00
		a. Opt double	£800	£1200
		b. Opt double, one inverted	£950	£1300
		c. Opt inverted	£1300	£1400
		d. Pair, one without opt	£26000	£35000
		x. Wmk reversed	£650	

There were three printings from similar settings of 30, and each sheet had to pass through the press twice. The first printing of 600 was on sale from 1 May 1916 in Canada at Ottawa, Toronto, Westmount (Montreal) and Winnipeg; and under an agreement with the Canadian P.O. were used in combination with Canadian stamps and were cancelled in Canada. The second printing (number unknown) was made about the beginning of December 1916, and the third of 6000, issued probably on 1 March 1917, were on sale only in the Bahamas. These printings caused the revocation, in mid-December 1916, of the agreement by Canada, which no longer accepted the stamps as payment of the special delivery fee and left them to be cancelled in the Bahamas.

It is not possible to identify the printings of the normal stamps without plating both the basic stamp and the overprint, though, in general, the word "SPECIAL" is further to the right in relation to "DELIVERY" in the third printing than in the first or second. Our prices for No. S1 are for the third printing and any stamps which can be positively identified as being from the first or second printings would be worth about eight times as much unused, and any on cover are very rare. All the errors appear to be from the third printing.

SPECIAL DELIVERY (S **2**)

SPECIAL DELIVERY (S **3**)

1917 (2 July). *As No. 59, but Wmk Mult Crown CA. Optd with Type* S **2** *by D.L.R.*

S2	**6**	5d. black and orange	50	9·00
		s. Optd "Specimen"	65·00	

1918. *No. 78 optd with Type* S **3** *by D.L.R.*

S3	**6**	5d. black and mauve (R.)	30	3·25
		s. Optd "Specimen"	65·00	

Nos. S2/3 were only on sale in the Bahamas.

Bahrain

An independent shaikhdom, with an Indian postal administration from 1884. A British postal administration operated from 1 April 1948 to 31 December 1965.

The first, and for 62 years the only, post office in Bahrain opened at the capital, Manama, on 1 August 1884 as a sub-office of the Indian Post Office at Bushire (Iran), both being part of the Bombay Postal Circle.

Unoverprinted postage stamps of India were supplied to the new office, continuing on sale there until 1933.

Z 1

Z 2

Stamps of INDIA *cancelled with Type* Z **1** (*this was normally struck elsewhere on the envelope with the stamps obliterated with "B" enclosed in a circular background of horizontal bars*) (1884–86)

1882–90. *Queen Victoria* (Nos. 84/101).

Z1	½a. deep blue-green	£325
Z2	2a. pale blue	£325

Stamps of INDIA *cancelled with Type* Z **2** (*squared-circle*) (1886–1909)

1882–90. *Queen Victoria* (Nos. 84/101).

Z5	½a. deep blue-green	9·00
Z5a	½a. blue-green	10·00
Z6	1a. brown-purple	11·00
Z6a	1a. plum	11·00
Z7	1a.6p. sepia	35·00
Z8	2a. pale blue	17·00
Z8a	2a. blue	18·00
Z9	3a. orange	35·00
Z9a	3a. brown-orange	16·00
Z10	4a. olive-green	30·00
Z11	8a. dull mauve	40·00

1891. *Surch on Queen Victoria* (No. 102).

Z12	2½a. on 4a.6p. yellow-green	30·00

1892–97. *Queen Victoria* (Nos. 103/6).

Z13	2a.6p. yellow-green	11·00
Z14	1r. green and aniline carmine	55·00

1900–02. *Queen Victoria* (Nos. 112/18).

Z15	½a. pale yellow-green	15·00
Z15a	½a. yellow-green	17·00
Z16	1a. carmine	16·00
Z17	2½a. ultramarine	28·00

OFFICIAL STAMPS

1883–99. *Queen Victoria* (Nos. O37*a*/48).

Z18	½a. blue-green	50·00
Z19	1a. brown-purple	55·00

Z 3

Z 4

Stamps of INDIA *cancelled with Type* Z **3** (*single circle, principally intended for use as a backstamp*) (1897–1920)

1882–90. *Queen Victoria* (Nos. 84/101).

Z21	½a. blue-green	25·00
Z22	3a. brown-orange	30·00

1892–97. *Queen Victoria* (Nos. 103/6).

Z23	1r. green and aniline carmine	65·00

1899. *Queen Victoria* (No. 111).

Z24	3p. aniline carmine	25·00

1900–02. *Queen Victoria* (Nos. 112/18).

Z25	½a. pale yellow-green	22·00
Z25*a*	½a. yellow-green	24·00
Z26	1a. carmine	23·00
Z26*a*	2a. pale violet	50·00
Z27	2a.6p. ultramarine	35·00

1902–11. *King Edward VII* (Nos. 119/47).

Z28	½a. green	22·00
Z29	2a. mauve	23·00
Z30	2a.6p. ultramarine	18·00

1906–07. *King Edward VII* (Nos. 149/50).

Z31	½a. green	12·00
Z32	1a. carmine	14·00

1911–22. *King George V*. Wmk Star (Nos. 151/91).

Z33	3p. grey	17·00
Z34	½a. light green	14·00
Z35	2a. purple	27·00
Z36	2a.6p. ultramarine (No. 171)	27·00

OFFICIAL STAMPS

1902–09. *King Edward VII* (Nos. O54/65).

Z37	2a. mauve	60·00

1906–07. *King Edward VII* (Nos. O66/7).

Z38	1a. carmine	60·00

Stamps of INDIA *cancelled with Type* Z **4** (*double circle with date band and black lines in centre*) (1902–24)

1876. *Queen Victoria* (Nos. 80/2).

Z40	6a. pale brown	55·00

1882–90. *Queen Victoria* (Nos. 84/101).

Z40*a*	½a. blue-green	18·00
Z41	3a. brown-orange	27·00
Z42	4a. slate-green	32·00
Z43	8a. dull mauve	40·00
Z44	12a. purple/red	70·00

1895. *Queen Victoria* (Nos. 107/9).

Z45	2r. carmine and yellow-brown	£225
Z46	5r. ultramarine and violet	£250

1899. *Queen Victoria* (No. 111).

Z47	3p. aniline carmine	13·00

1900–02. *Queen Victoria* (Nos. 112/18).

Z48	½a. pale yellow-green	12·00
Z48*a*	½a. yellow-green	14·00
Z49	1a. carmine	15·00
Z50	2a. pale violet	38·00
Z51	2a.6p. ultramarine	30·00

1902–11. *King Edward VII* (Nos. 119/47).

Z52	3p. grey	9·00
Z52*a*	3p. slate-grey	10·00
Z53	½a. yellow-green	6·50
Z53*a*	½a. green	6·50
Z54	1a. carmine	8·00
Z55	2a. violet	16·00
Z55*a*	2a. mauve	16·00
Z56	2a.6p. ultramarine	9·50
Z57	3a. orange-brown	25·00
Z58	4a. olive	26·00
Z59	6a. olive-bistre	40·00
Z60	8a. purple	50·00
Z60*a*	1r. green and carmine	75·00
Z61	2r. rose-red and yellow-brown	£150

1905. *Surcharged on King Edward VII* (No. 148).

Z62	¼a. on ½a. green	22·00

1906–07. *King Edward VII* (Nos. 149/50).

Z63	½a. green	8·00
Z64	1a. carmine	11·00

1911–22. *King George V*. Wmk Star (Nos. 151/91).

Z65	3p. grey	14·00
Z66	½a. light green	7·50
Z67	1a. carmine	9·00
Z67*a*	1a. rose-carmine	9·00
Z68	1½a. chocolate (Type A)	30·00
Z69	2a. purple	18·00
Z70	2a.6p. ultramarine (No. 171)	13·00
Z71	3a. orange	23·00
Z72	6a. yellow-bistre	35·00

1922–26. *King George V*. Wmk Star (Nos. 197/200).

Z73	1a. chocolate	16·00

OFFICIAL STAMPS

1902–09. *King Edward VII* (Nos. O54/65).

Z74	2a. mauve	42·00
Z74*a*	4a. olive	80·00

1906. *King Edward VII* (Nos. O66/7).

Z75	1a. carmine	38·00

1912–13. *King George V* (No. O85).

Z77	1a. carmine	32·00

1921. *King George V* (No. O97).

Z78	9p. on 1a. rose-carmine	45·00

Z 5

Stamps of INDIA *cancelled with type* Z **5** (*double circle without arc*) (*previously intended for use as a backstamp*) (1915–33)

1911–22. *King George V*. Wmk Star (Nos. 151/91).

Z79	3p. grey	18·00
Z80	½a. light green	12·00
Z80*a*	½a. emerald	13·00
Z81	1a. aniline carmine	15·00
Z81*a*	1a. pale rose-carmine	16·00
Z82	1½a. chocolate (Type A)	38·00
Z83	2a. purple	22·00
Z83*a*	2a. reddish purple	21·00
Z83*b*	2a. bright reddish violet	22·00
Z84	2a.6p. ultramarine (No. 171)	17·00
Z85	3a. orange	29·00
Z86	6a. yellow-bistre	42·00
Z87	1r. brown and green (*shades*)	55·00

1922–26. *King George V*. Wmk Star (Nos. 197/200).

Z88	1a. chocolate	20·00
Z89	3a. ultramarine	35·00

1926–33. *King George V*. Wmk Multiple Star (Nos. 201/19).

Z90	3p. slate	9·00
Z91	½a. green	9·00
Z92	1a. chocolate	8·00
Z93	2a. bright purple (No. 205)	45·00
Z94	2a. purple (No. 206)	17·00
Z95	3a. ultramarine	27·00
Z95*a*	3a. blue	25·00
Z96	4a. sage-green (No. 211)	21·00
Z97	8a. reddish purple	29·00
Z98	1r. chocolate and green	35·00
Z99	2r. carmine and orange	60·00
Z100	5r. ultramarine and purple	£100

The 1a. is known with inverted watermark.

1929. *Air* (Nos. 220/5).

Z101	2a. deep blue-green	24·00
Z102	3a. blue	23·00
Z103	4a. olive-green	26·00
Z104	6a. bistre	35·00

1931. *Inauguration of New Delhi* (Nos. 226/31).

Z105	¼a. olive-green and orange-brown	35·00
Z106	1a. mauve and chocolate	21·00

Nos. Z101/6 come with watermark sideways to left or right.

OFFICIAL STAMPS

1902–09. *King Edward VII* (Nos. O54/65).

Z107	2a. mauve	42·00

1912–13. *King George V*. Wmk Star (Nos. O73/96).

Z108	½a. light green	27·00
Z109	1a. rose-carmine	27·00
Z110	2a. reddish purple	35·00

Z 6

Stamps of INDIA *cancelled with Type* Z **6** (*double circle with black arc in lower segment*) (1924–33)

1911–22. *King George V*. Wmk Star (Nos. 151/91).

Z115	3p. grey	16·00
Z116	½a. light green	10·00
Z117	1a. aniline carmine	12·00
Z118	2a. purple	18·00
Z119	6a. yellow-bistre	27·00

1921. *King George V*. (No. 192).

Z119*a*	9p. on 1a. rose-carmine	35·00

1922–26. *King George V*. Wmk Star (Nos. 197/200).

Z120	1a. chocolate	11·00
Z121	3a. ultramarine	22·00

1926–33. *King George V*. Wmk Multiple Star (Nos. 201/19).

Z122	3p. slate	6·00
Z123	½a. green	7·00
Z124	1a. chocolate	6·00
Z124*a*	*Tête-Bêche* (pair)	
Z125	1½a. rose-carmine	30·00
Z126	2a. bright purple (No. 205)	30·00
Z127	2a. purple (No. 206)	10·00
Z128	3a. blue	12·00
Z130	4a. sage-green (No. 211)	15·00
Z131	8a. reddish purple	22·00

The ½a. and 1a. are known with watermark inverted.

1929. *Air* (Nos. 220/5).

Z132	2a. deep blue-green	13·00
Z133	3a. blue	14·00
Z134	4a. olive-green	17·00
Z135	6a. bistre	21·00

1931. *Inauguration of New Delhi* (Nos. 226/31).

Z136	½a. violet and green	22·00
Z137	2a. green and blue	26·00
Z137*a*	3a. chocolate and carmine	40·00

Nos. Z132/5 and Z136/7*a* exist with watermark showing stars pointing left or right.

1932–36. *King George V*. Wmk Multiple Star (Nos. 232/9).

Z138	1a. chocolate	13·00
Z139	1a.3p. mauve	12·00
Z140	2a. vermilion	20·00
Z141	3a. carmine	23·00

PRICES FOR STAMPS ON COVER TO 1945

Nos. 1/14	*from* × 5
Nos. 15/19	*from* × 6
Nos. 20/37	*from* × 2
Nos. 38/50	*from* × 6

(Currency. 12 pies = 1 anna; 16 annas = 1 rupee)

BAHRAIN (1) BAHRAIN (2)

Stamps of India overprinted with T 1 or T 2 (rupee values).

1933 (10 Aug)–**37**. *King George V.* Wmk Mult Star, T **69**.

1	**55**	3p. slate (11.33)	3·50	45
2	**56**	½a. green	7·50	3·25
		w. Wmk inverted	50·00	26·00
3	**80**	9p. deep green (*litho*)	3·75	3·50
		a. Typo ptg (1937)	14·00	14·00
4	**57**	1a. chocolate	7·00	2·50
		w. Wmk inverted	29·00	10·00
5	**82**	1a.3p. mauve	10·00	2·75
		w. Wmk inverted	10·00	2·75
6	**70**	2a. vermilion	10·00	19·00
		w. Wmk inverted	17·00	19·00
7	**62**	3a. blue	19·00	55·00
8	**83**	3a.6p. ultramarine	3·75	30
		w. Wmk inverted	14·00	60
9	**71**	4a. sage-green	18·00	55·00
10	**65**	8a. reddish purple	6·00	30
		w. Wmk inverted	†	80·00
11	**66**	12a. claret	7·50	1·25
		w. Wmk inverted	†	75·00
12	**67**	1r. chocolate and green	16·00	10·00
13		2r. carmine and orange	28·00	35·00
14		5r. ultramarine and purple	£160	£160
		w. Wmk inverted	£120	£140
1/14w *Set of* 14			£225	£275

1934–37. *King George V.* Wmk Mult Star. T **69**.

15	**79**	½a. green (1935)	4·50	1·75
		w. Wmk inverted	9·00	1·00
16	**81**	1a. chocolate	10·00	40
		w. Wmk inverted (from booklets)	26·00	38·00
17	**59**	2a. vermilion (1935)	45·00	7·50
17*a*		2a. vermilion (*small die*) (1937)	90·00	25
18	**62**	3a. carmine	4·75	60
19	**63**	4a. sage-green (1935)	5·00	40
15/19 *Set of* 6			£150	9·00

1938–41. *King George VI.*

20	**91**	3p. slate (5.38)	16·00	4·50
21		½a. red-brown (5.38)	7·00	20
22		9p. green (5.38)	11·00	9·00
23		1a. carmine (5.38)	10·00	20
24	**92**	2a. vermilion (1939)	5·00	3·50
26	**94**	3a. yellow-green (1941)	12·00	8·00
27	**95**	3a.6p. bright blue (7.38)	6·00	5·00
28	**96**	4a. brown (1941)	£150	70·00
30	**98**	8a. slate-violet (1940)	£200	35·00
31	**99**	12a. lake (1940)	£130	45·00
32	**100**	1r. grey and red-brown (1940)	5·50	1·75
33		2r. purple and brown (1940)	15·00	8·00
34		5r. green and blue (1940)	15·00	13·00
35		10r. purple and claret (1941)	75·00	42·00
36		15r. brown and green (1941)	£190	£200
		w. Wmk inverted	70·00	75·00
37		25r. slate-violet and purple (1941)	£120	90·00
20/37 *Set of* 16			£750	£375

1942–45. *King George VI on white background.*

38	**100a**	3p. slate	3·00	2·50
39		½a. purple	4·25	3·00
40		9p. green	15·00	19·00
41		1a. carmine	6·50	1·00
42	**101**	1a.3p. bistre	8·50	21·00
43		1½a. dull violet	6·00	8·00
44		2a. vermilion	6·00	1·50
45		3a. bright violet	18·00	7·50
46		3½a. bright blue	4·75	21·00
47	**102**	4a. brown	4·00	2·00
48		6a. turquoise-green	17·00	12·00
49		8a. slate-violet	7·00	4·00
50		12a. lake	9·50	6·00
38/50 *Set of* 13			£100	95·00

Unoverprinted India Victory stamps, Nos. 278/81, were placed on sale in Bahrain during January 1946.

Although the stamps of Pakistan were never placed on sale in Bahrain examples of the 1947 "PAKISTAN" overprints on India can be found cancelled in Bahrain from air mail originating at Dubai or Sharjah.

Stamps of Great Britain surcharged

For similar surcharges without the name of the country, see BRITISH POSTAL AGENCIES IN EASTERN ARABIA.

BAHRAIN 1 ANNA (3)

BAHRAIN 5 RUPEES (4)

1948 (1 Apr)–**49**. *Surch as T* **3**, **4** *(2r. and 5r.) or similar surch with bars at foot (10r.).*

51	**128**	½a. on ½d. pale green	50	1·25
52		1a. on 1d. pale scarlet	50	2·75
53		1½a. on 1½d. pale red-brown	50	3·75
54		2a. on 2d. pale orange	50	20
55		2½a. on 2½d. light ultramarine	50	4·50
56		3a. on 3d. pale violet	50	10
57	**129**	6a. on 6d. purple	50	10
58	**130**	1r. on 1s. bistre-brown	1·25	10
59	**131**	2r. on 2s.6d. yellow-green	5·50	4·75
60		5r. on 5s. red	5·50	4·75
60*a*	**132**	10r. on 10s. ultramarine (4.7.49)	80·00	60·00
51/60a *Set of* 11			85·00	75·00

BAHRAIN 2½ ANNAS (5)

BAHRAIN 15 RUPEES (6)

1948 (26 Apr). *Silver Wedding, surch as T* **5** *or* **6**.

61	**137**	2½a. on 2½d. ultramarine	1·00	2·50
62	**138**	15r. on £1 blue	30·00	48·00

1948 (29 July). *Olympic Games, surch as T* **5**, *but in one line (6a.) or two lines (others); the 1r. also has a square of dots as T* **7**.

63	**139**	2½a. on 2½d. ultramarine	1·00	4·00
		a. Surch double	£1900	£2750
64	**140**	3a. on 3d. violet	1·00	3·75
65	**141**	6a. on 6d. bright purple	1·50	3·75
66	**142**	1r. on 1s. brown	2·50	4·00
63/6 *Set of* 4			5·50	14·00

Fifteen used examples of No. 63a are known, of which thirteen, including a block of 4, were postmarked at Experimental P.O. K-121 (Muharraq), one on cover from F.P.O. 756 (Shaibah) on 25 October 1948 and one apparently cancelled-to-order at Bahrain on 10 October 1949.

BAHRAIN 3 ANNAS (7)

1949 (10 Oct). *75th Anniv of U.P.U., surch as T* **7**, *in one line (2½a.) or in two lines (others).*

67	**143**	2½a. on 2½d. ultramarine	60	2·25
		a. Lake in India	90·00	
68	**144**	3a. on 3d. violet	70	4·00
69	**145**	6a. on 6d. bright purple	60	3·00
70	**146**	1r. on 1s. brown	1·25	2·75
67/70 *Set of* 4			2·75	11·00

BAHRAIN 2 RUPEES (7a)

BAHRAIN 2 RUPEES Type II

BAHRAIN Extra bar (R. 6/1)

Three Types of 2r.:

Type I. As Type **7a** showing "2" level with "RUPEES" and "BAHRAIN" sharp.

Type II. "2" raised. "BAHRAIN" worn. 15 mm between "BAHRAIN" and "2 RUPEES".

Type III. As Type II, but 16 mm between "BAHRAIN" and "2 RUPEES". Value is set more to the left of "BAHRAIN".

1950 (2 Oct)–**55**. *Surch as T* **3** *or* **7a** *(rupee values).*

71	**128**	½a. on ½d. pale orange (3.5.51)	2·50	3·00
72		1a. on 1d. light ultramarine (3.5.51)	3·00	20
73		1½a. on 1½d. pale green (3.5.51)	3·00	13·00
74		2a. on 2d. pale red-brown (3.5.51)	1·50	30
75		2½a. on 2½d. pale scarlet (3.5.51)	3·00	14·00
76	**129**	4a. on 4d. light ultramarine	4·00	1·50
77	**147**	2r. on 2s.6d. yellow-green (3.5.51)	26·00	12·00
		a. Surch Type II (1953)	£110	42·00
		b. Surch Type III (1955)	£900	£100
		ba. "I" inverted and raised (R. 2/1)	£6500	£800
78	**148**	5r. on 5s. red (3.5.51)	14·00	4·25
		a. Extra bar	£475	
79	**149**	10r. on 10s. ultramarine (3.5.51)	30·00	8·50
71/79 *Set of* 9			80·00	50·00

1952 (5 Dec)–**54**. *Q.E. II* (**W153**), *surch as T* **3** *(in two lines on 2½ and 6a.).*

80	½a. on ½d. orange-red (31.8.53)	10	1·00
	a. Fraction "½" omitted	£140	£250
81	1a. on 1d. ultramarine (31.8.53)	10	10
82	1½a. on 1½d. green	10	30
83	2a. on 2d. red-brown (31.8.53)	30	10
84	2½a. on 2½d. carmine-red	20	1·75
85	3a. on 3d. deep lilac (B.) (18.1.54)	3·00	10
86	4a. on 4d. ultramarine (2.11.53)	13·00	30
87	6a. on 6d. reddish purple (18.1.54)	3·25	10
88	12a. on 1s.3d. green (2.11.53)	3·25	20
89	1r. on 1s.6d. grey-blue (2.11.53)	3·25	10
80/89 *Set of* 10		24·00	3·25

Designs:—Nos. 80/89, Queen Elizabeth II.

The word BAHRAIN is in taller letters on the 1½a., 2½a., 3a. and 6a.

2½ BAHRAIN ANNAS (8)

1953 (3 June). *Coronation. Surch as T* **8**, *or similarly.*

90	2½a. on 2½d. carmine-red	1·25	75
91	4a. on 4d. ultramarine	2·25	6·50
92	12a. on 1s.3d. deep yellow-green	3·25	4·50
93	1r. on 1s.6d. deep grey-blue	7·50	50
90/3 *Set of* 4		13·00	11·00

Designs:—Nos. 90/93, Queen Elizabeth II.

BAHRAIN 2 RUPEES I

BAHRAIN 2 RUPEES II

BAHRAIN 2 RUPEES (9) III

BAHRAIN 5 RUPEES I

BAHRAIN 5 RUPEES (10) II

BAHRAIN 10 RUPEES I

BAHRAIN 10 RUPEES (11) II

TYPE I (T **9/11**). Type-set surch by Waterlow. Bold thick letters with sharp corners and straight edges.

TYPE II (T **9/11**). Plate-printed surch by Harrison. Thinner letters, rounded corners and rough edges. Bars wider apart.

TYPE III (T **9**). Plate-printed surch by Harrison. Similar to Type II as regards the position of the bars on all 40 stamps of the sheet, but the letters are thinner and with more rounded corners than in II, while the ink of the surcharge is less black.

The general characteristics of Type II of the 2r. are less pronounced than in the other values, but a distinguishing test is in the relative position of the bars and the "U" of "RUPEES". In Type B (except for the 1st stamp, 5th row) the bars start immediately beneath the left-hand edge of the "U". In Type I they start more to the right.

In the 10r. the "1" and the "0" are spaced 0.9 mm in Type I and only 0.6 mm in Type II.

1955 (23 Sept)–**60**. *T* **166/8** *(Waterlow ptgs) surch as T* **9/11**.

94	2r. on 2s.6d. black-brown (Type I)	5·50	2·00
	a. Type II (13.5.58)	12·00	12·00
	b. Type III (No. 536a, D.L.R.) (29.1.60)	25·00	48·00
95	5r. on 5s. rose-red (Type I)	13·00	2·75
	a. Type II (19.8.57)	11·00	8·00
96	10r. on 10s. ultramarine (Type I)	20·00	2·75
	a. Type II (13.5.58)	50·00	£100
	ab. Type II. Surch on No. 538a (D.L.R. ptg) (1960)	£130	
94/6 *Set of* 3		32·00	6·25
94a/6a *Set of* 3		65·00	£110

Designs:—No. 94, Carrickfergus Castle; No. 95, Caernarvon Castle; No. 96, Edinburgh Castle.

1956–57. *Q.E. II* (**W165**), *surch as T* **3** *(in two lines on 6a.).*

97	½ a. on ½d. orange-red (1.57)	10	15
98	4a. on 4d. ultramarine (8.6.56)	5·50	21·00
99	6a. on 6d. reddish purple (5.12.56)	50	75
100	12a. on 1s.3d. green (2.8.56)	7·50	11·00
101	1r. on 1s.6d. grey-blue (4.3.57)	10·00	10
	a. Surch double	†	£3250
97/101 *Set of* 5		21·00	30·00

Designs:—Nos. 97/101, Queen Elizabeth II.

New Currency. 100 naye paise = 1 rupee.

BAHRAIN NP 1 NP (12)

BAHRAIN NP 3 NP (13)

BAHRAIN 75 NP (14)

1957 (1 Apr)–**59**. *Q.E. II* (**W165**), *surch as T* **12** *(1n.p., 15n.p., 25n.p., 40n.p., and 50n.p.), T* **14** *(75n.p.) or T* **13** *(others).*

102	1n.p. on 5d. brown	10	10
103	3n.p. on 1½d. orange-red	50	3·00
104	6n.p. on 1d. ultramarine	50	3·00
105	9n.p. on 1½d. green	50	3·25
106	12n.p. on 2d. light red-brown	30	70
107	15n.p. on 2½d. carmine-red (Type I)	30	15
	a. Type II (1959)	1·00	3·25
108	20n.p. on 3d. deep lilac (B.)	30	10
109	25n.p. on 4d. ultramarine	1·25	2·50
110	40n.p. on 6d. reddish purple	40	10
	a. *Deep claret* (1959)	65	10
111	50n.p. on 9d. bronze-green	3·75	4·50
112	75n.p. on 1s.3d. green	2·50	50
102/112 *Set of* 11		9·25	16·00

Designs:—Nos. 102/112, Queen Elizabeth II.

(15)

1957 (1 Aug). *World Scout Jubilee Jamboree. Surch in two lines as T* **15** *(15n.p.), or in three lines (others).*

113	15n.p. on 2½d. carmine-red	25	35
114	25n.p. on 4d. ultramarine	30	35
115	75n.p. on 1s.3d. green	40	45
113/15 *Set of* 3		85	1·00

Designs:—No. 113, Scout badge and "Rolling Hitch"; No. 114, "Scouts coming to Britain"; No. 115, Globe within a Compass.

1960 (24 May). *QE. II* (W**179**), *surch as T* **12**.

116	15n.p. on 2½d. carmine-red (Type II) .	2·25	8·00

Design:—No. 116, Queen Elizabeth II.

16 Shaikh Sulman bin Hamed al-Khalifa

17

(Des M. Farrar Bell. Photo Harrison (T **16**). Des O. C. Meronti. Recess D.L.R. (T **17**))

1960 (1 July). P 15×14 (T **16**) or 13½×13 (T **17**).

117	**16**	5n.p. bright blue	20	10
118		15n.p. red-orange	20	10
119		20n.p. reddish violet	20	10
120		30n.p. bistre-brown	20	10
121		40n.p. grey	20	10
122		50n.p. emerald-green	20	10
123		75n.p. chocolate	30	15
124	**17**	1r. black	3·00	30
125		2r. rose-red	3·00	2·25
126		5r. deep blue	5·00	3·00
127		10r. bronze-green	12·00	5·50
117/127 *Set of* 11			22·00	10·00

Shaikh Isa bin Sulman al-Khalifa

2 November 1961–6 March 1999

18 Shaikh Isa bin Sulman al-Khalifa

19 Air Terminal, Muharraq

20 Deep Water Harbour

(Des M. Farrar Bell. Photo Harrison (5 to 75n.p.). Des D. C. Rivett. Recess B.W. (others))

1964 (22 Feb). P 15×14 (T **18**) or 13½×13 (T **19/20**).

128	**18**	5n.p. bright blue	10	10
129		15n.p. orange red	10	70
130		20n.p. reddish violet	10	10
131		30n.p. olive-brown	10	10
132		40n.p. slate	15	10
133		50n.p. emerald-green	15	1·50
134		75n.p. brown	25	10
135	**19**	1r. black	11·00	2·25
136		2r. carmine-red	11·00	2·75
137	**20**	5r. ultramarine	14·00	15·00
138		10r. myrtle-green	14·00	15·00
128/138 *Set of* 11			45·00	32·00

LOCAL STAMPS

The following stamps were issued primarily for postage within Bahrain, but apparently also had franking value when used on external mail.

L **1** Shaikh Sulmanbin Hamed al-Khalifa

L **2** Shaikh Sulmanbin Hamed al-Khalifa

(Types L **1/2**. Rccess De La Rue)

1953–56. P 12×12½.

L1	L **1**	½a. deep green (1.10.56)	3·75	75
L2		1a. deep blue (1.10.56)	3·75	60
L3		1½a. carmine (15.2.53)	50	4·25
L1/3 *Set of* 3			7·25	5·00

1957 (16 Oct). *As Nos.* L1/3 *but values in new currency.*

L4	3p. deep green	4·25	1·25
L5	6p. carmine	4·25	1·25
L6	9p. deep blue	4·25	1·25
L4/6 *Set of* 3		11·50	3·25

1961 (20 Mar). P 12×12½.

L7	L **2**	5p. green	1·25	30
L8		10p. carmine-red	2·25	30
L9		15p. grey	1·50	25
L10		20p. blue	1·75	25
L11		30p. sepia	1·50	25
L12		40p. ultramarine	3·50	30
L7/12 *Set of* 6			10·50	1·50

STAMP BOOKLET

1934. *Red and black on tan cover. Mysore Sandal Soap advertisement on front.*

SB1	16a. booklet containing sixteen 1a. (Nos. 16 and/or 16w) in blocks of 4	£1500

The Bahrain Post Department took over the postal services on 1 January 1966. Later stamp issues wil be found in Part 19 (*Middle East*) of the Stanley Gibbons catalogue.

Barbados

Regular mails between Barbados and Great Britain were established at an early date in the island's development and it is believed that the British Mail Packet Agency at Bridgetown was opened in 1688 as part of the considerable expansion of the Packet Service in that year.

From 1 August 1851 the colonial authorities were responsible for the internal post system, but the British G.P.O. did not relinquish control of the overseas post until 1858.

For illustrations of the handstamp types see BRITISH POST OFFICES ABROAD notes, following GREAT BRITAIN.

CROWNED-CIRCLE HANDSTAMPS

CC1 CC **1** BARBADOES (3.10.1849) (R.)
Price on cover £450

Combination covers exist with the local postage paid by a Barbados 1d. stamp and the overseas fee by an example of No. CC1.

During shortages of ½d. stamps in 1893 (17 February to 15 March) and of the ¼d. in 1896 (23 January to 4 May) No. CC1 was utilised, struck in black, on local mail. *Price on cover from* £90.

PRICES FOR STAMPS ON COVER TO 1945

Nos. 1/35	*from* × 5
Nos. 43/63	*from* × 4
Nos. 64/6	*from* × 10
Nos. 67/83	*from* × 5
Nos. 86/8	*from* × 3
Nos. 89/103	*from* × 4
No. 104	*from* × 20
Nos. 105/15	*from* × 4
Nos. 116/24	*from* × 8
Nos. 125/33	*from* × 5
Nos. 135/44	*from* × 4
Nos. 145/52	*from* × 6
No. 153	*from* × 8
Nos. 158/62	*from* × 5
Nos. 163/9	*from* × 3
Nos. 170/96	*from* × 4
Nos. 197/8	*from* × 10
Nos. 199/212	*from* × 6
Nos. 213/39	*from* × 3
No. 240	*from* × 10
Nos. 241/4	*from* × 5
Nos. 245/7	*from* × 6
Nos. 248/56a	*from* × 4
Nos. 257/61	*from* × 5
Nos. D1/3	*from* × 25

PERKINS BACON "CANCELLED". For notes on these handstamps, showing "CANCELLED" between horizontal bars forming an oval, see Catalogue Introduction.

CROWN COLONY

1 Britannia

2 Britannia

(Recess Perkins, Bacon & Co)

1852 (15 April)–**55**. *Paper blued.* No wmk. Imperf.

1	**1**	(½d.) yellow-green (1855)	–	£700
2		(½d.) deep green	£120	£325
3		(1d.) blue	50·00	£190
4		(1d.) deep blue	32·00	70·00
4*a*		(2d.) greyish slate	£250	£1200
		b. Bisected (1d.) (on cover) (1854)	†	£7500
5		(4d.) brownish red (1855)	£100	£275

The bisect, No. 4b was authorised for use between 4 August and 21 September 1854 during a shortage of 1d. stamps.

Prepared for use but not issued.

5a	**1**	(No value), slate-blue (*shades*)	26·00
5b		(No value), deep slate	£225

Nos. 5*a*/*b* were never sent to Barbados and come from the Perkins Bacon remainders sold in the 1880's.

Apart from the shade, which is distinctly paler, No. 4*a* can be distinguished from No. 5*b* by the smooth even gum, the gum of No. 5*b* being yellow and patchy, giving a mottled appearance to the back of the stamp. No. 5*a* also has the latter gum.

1855–58. *White paper.* No wmk. Imperf.

7	**1**	(½d.) yellow-green (1857)	£550	£110
8		(½d.) green (shades) (1858)	£170	£200
9		(1d.) pale blue	£120	70·00
10		(1d.) deep blue (H/S "CANCELLED" in oval £12000)	50·00	60·00

No. 8 exists in a yellowish green shade which should not be confused with No. 7.

1858 (10 Nov). No wmk. Imperf.

11	**2**	6d. pale rose-red	£750	£120
11*a*		6d. deep rose-red	£750	£180
12		1s. brown-black	£250	£110
12*a*		1s. black	£225	75·00

BISECTS. The various 1d. bisects recorded between Nos. 14a and 73a were principally used for the ½d. inland rate, covering newspapers from 1854 onwards.Prices for Nos. 24a, 52a, 66a and 73a are for examples on dated piece, undated pieces being worth considerably less. Nos. 14a, 15a and 19a are only known on undated piece and the prices for these bisects are for items in this condition.

1860. No wmk.

(a) Pin-perf 14.

13	**1**	(½d.) yellow-green	£2500	£425
14		(1d.) pale blue	£2000	£150
		a. Bisected (½d.) (on piece)	†	£750
15		(1d.) deep blue	£2250	£180
		a. Bisected (½d.) (on piece)	†	£750

(b) Pin-perf 12½.

16	**1**	(½d.) yellow-green	£8500	£650
16*a*		(1d.) blue	–	£1500

(c) Pin-perf 14×12½.

16*b*	**1**	(½d.) yellow-green	–	£7500

1861. No wmk. Clean-cut perf 14 to 16.

17	**1**	(½d.) deep green (H/S "CANCELLED" in oval £12000)	£140	14·00
18		(1d.) pale blue	£750	65·00
19		(1d.) blue	£850	70·00
		a. Bisected (½d.) (on piece)	†	£550

1861–70. No wmk.

(a) Rough perf 14 to 16.

20	**1**	(½d.) deep green	25·00	30·00
21		(½d.) green	20·00	21·00
21*a*		(½d.) blue-green	55·00	75·00
		b. Imperf (pair)	£650	
22		(½d.) grass-green	32·00	32·00
		a. Imperf (pair)	£750	
23		(1d.) blue (1861)	55·00	2·25
		a. Imperf (pair) (pale blue, worn plate)	£750	
24		(1d.) deep blue	45·00	3·75
		a. Bisected diag (½d.) (on piece) (1863)	†	£500
25		(4d.) dull rose-red (1861)	£110	50·00
		a. Imperf (pair)	£900	
26		(4d.) dull brown-red (1865)	£140	55·00
		a. Imperf (pair)	£1400	
27		(4d.) lake-rose (1868)	£150	80·00
		a. Imperf (pair)	£1400	
28		(4d.) dull vermilion (1869)	£275	90·00
		a. Imperf (pair)	£1300	
29	**2**	6d. rose-red (1861) (Handstamped "CANCELLED" in oval £12000)	£350	17·00
30		6d. orange-red (1864)	£120	24·00
31		6d. bright orange-vermilion (1868)	£100	25·00
32		6d. dull orange-vermilion (1870)	£120	22·00
		a. Imperf (pair)	£650	
33		6d. orange (1870)	£140	40·00
34		1s. brown-black (1863)	75·00	7·50
		a. Error. Blue	£17000	
35		1s. black (1866)	60·00	7·50
		a. Imperf between (horiz pair)	£7500	

(b) Prepared for use, but not issued. P 11 to 12.

36	**1**	(½d.) grass-green	£12000
37		(1d.) blue	£2000

The (1d.) deep blue No. 24, also exists imperforate, from a new plate, but examples cannot readily be distinguished from No. 10.

The bisect, No. 24a, was first authorised for use in April 1863 and further examples have been reported up to January 1869 during shortages of ½d. stamps.

No. 34a was an error on the part of the printer who supplied the first requisition of the 1s. value in the colour of the 1d. The 1s. blue stamps were never placed on sale, but the Barbados Colonial Secretary circulated some samples which were defaced by a manuscript corner-to-corner cross. A number of these samples subsequently had the cross removed.

Nos. 36/7 were never sent to Barbados and come from the

Perkins Bacon remainders. It is believed that the imperforate pairs came from the same source.

1870. Wmk Large Star, Type w **1**. Rough perf 14 to 16.

43 **1** (½d.) green £140 7·50
43*b* (½d.) yellow-green £180 45·00
44 (1d.) blue £2000 55·00
a. Blue paper £3250 £110
45 (4d.) dull vermilion £1200 £120
46 **2** 6d. orange-vermilion £900 75·00
47 1s. black £450 18·00

No. 43 exists imperforate (*Price* £1200, unused pair).

1871. Wmk Small Star, Type w **2**. Rough perf 14 to 16.

48 **1** (1d.) blue £160 2·75
49 (4d.) dull rose-red £1000 45·00
50 **2** 6d. orange-vermilion £650 18·00
51 1s. black £190 11·00

1872. Wmk Small Star, Type w **2**.

(*a*) Clean-cut perf 14½ to 15½.

52 **1** (1d.) blue £300 2·00
a. Bisected diag (½d.) (on piece) † £750
53 **2** 6d. orange-vermilion £900 70·00
54 1s. black £170 11·00

(*b*) P 11 to 13×14½ to 15½.

56 **1** (½d.) green £325 50·00
57 (4d.) dull vermilion £750 £110

1873. Wmk Large Star, Type w **1**.

(*a*) Clean-cut perf 14½ to 15½.

58 **1** (½d.) green £375 19·00
59 (4d.) dull rose-red £1200 £190
60 **2** 6d. orange-vermilion £750 75·00
a. Imperf between (horiz pair) £8000
b. Imperf (pair) 95·00
61 1s. black £150 16·00
a. Imperf between (horiz pair) £7500

(*b*) *Prepared for use, but not issued*. P 11 to 12.

62 **2** 6d. orange-vermilion £8000

Only eight mint examples, in two strips of four, are known of No. 62.

Two used singles of No. 60b have been seen.

1873 (June). Wmk Small Star, Type w **2** (sideways = two points upwards). P 14.

63 **2** 3d. brown-purple £325 £110

3

1873 (June). Wmk Small Star, Type w **2** (sideways). P 15½×15.

64 **3** 5s. dull rose £950 £300
s. Handstamped "Specimen" £300

1874 (May)–**75**. Wmk Large Star, Type w **1**.

(*a*) Perf 14.

65 **2** ½d. deep green 40·00 9·00
66 1d. deep blue £100 3·25
a. Bisected (½d.) (on piece) (5.75) † £600

(*b*) Clean-cut perf 14½ to 15½.

66*b* **2** 1d. deep blue † £18000
c. Imperf (pair)

(Recess D.L.R)

1875–80. Wmk Crown CC (sideways* on 6d., 1s.).

(*a*) P 12½.

67 **2** ½d. bright green 65·00 6·00
x. Wmk reversed 80·00 13·00
68 4d. deep red £275 18·00
w. Wmk inverted £375 40·00
x. Wmk reversed £275 20·00
69 6d. bright yellow (aniline) £950 90·00
70 6d. chrome-yellow £650 70·00
a. Wmk upright † £2500
w. Wmk Crown to right of CC — 75·00
x. Wmk sideways reversed
71 1s. violet (aniline) £500 3·50
x. Wmk sideways reversed £500 3·00
y. Wmk sideways inverted and reversed — 10·00

(*b*) P 14.

72 **2** ½d. bright green (1876) 15·00 50
s. Handstamped "Specimen" in red £100
sa. Handstamped "Specimen" in black £130
w. Wmk inverted — 17·00
x. Wmk reversed 15·00 75
73 1d. dull blue 80·00 1·75
a. Bisected (½d.) (on piece) (3.77) † £300
s. Handstamped "Specimen" in red £100
sa. Handstamped "Specimen" in black £130
w. Wmk inverted
x. Wmk reversed 95·00 2·25
74 1d. grey-blue 80·00 1·25
a. Wmk sideways † £850
w. Wmk inverted £140 23·00
x. Wmk reversed 95·00 1·50
y. Wmk inverted and reversed — 40·00
75 3d. mauve-lilac (1878) £130 9·00
s. Handstamped "Specimen" in black £140
w. Wmk inverted † 95·00
76 4d. red (1878) £140 11·00
s. Handstamped "Specimen" in black £150
x. Wmk reversed — 15·00
77 4d. carmine £200 3·00
w. Wmk inverted † 70·00
x. Wmk reversed £200 6·00
78 4d. crimson-lake £500 3·25
79 6d. chrome-yellow (1876) £140 2·25
s. Handstamped "Specimen" in black £150
w. Wmk Crown to right of CC £140 3·00
x. Wmk sideways reversed — 3·00
80 6d. yellow £325 7·50
w. Wmk Crown to right of CC — 11·00
81 1s. purple (4.78) £150 5·00
s. Handstamped "Specimen" in red £150
w. Wmk Crown to right of CC £140 5·00
x. Wmk sideways reversed — 7·50
82 1s. violet (aniline) (6.77) £3750 40·00
w. Wmk Crown to right of CC — 40·00
x. Wmk sideways reversed — 45·00
83 1s. dull mauve (1879) £500 4·25
a. Bisected (6d.) (on piece) (1.80) † —
x. Wmk sideways reversed — 12·00

(*c*) P 14×12½.

84 **2** 4d. red £6000

*The normal sideways watermark shows Crown to left of CC, *as seen from the back of the stamp*.

Only two examples, both used, of No. 70a have been reported.

Nos. 72sa/3sa were from postal stationery and are without gum.

Very few examples of No. 84 have been found unused and only one used specimen is known.

1D. (3a) 1D. (3b) 1D. (3c)

1878 (28 Mar). *No. 64 surch by West Indian Press with T* **3a/c** *sideways twice on each stamp and then divided vertically by 11½ to 13 perforations. The lower label, showing the original face value, was removed before use.*

(*a*) *With T* **3a.** *Large numeral "1", 7 mm high with curved serif, and large letter "D", 2¾ mm high.*

86 **3** 1d. on half 5s. dull rose £4750 £650
a. No stop after "D" £14000 £1800
b. Unsevered pair (both No. 86) £22000 £2250
c. Ditto, Nos. 86 and 87 — £4500
ca. Pair without dividing perf † £32000
d. Ditto, Nos. 86 and 88 £32000 £7500

(*b*) *With T* **3b.** *As last, but numeral with straight serif.*

87 **3** 1d. on half 5s. dull rose £6000 £850
a. Unsevered pair † £3500

(*c*) *With T* **3c.** *Smaller numeral "1", 6 mm high and smaller "D", 2½ mm high.*

88 **3** 1d. on half 5s. dull rose £7500 £950
a. Unsevered pair £26000 £4500

All types of the surcharge are found reading upwards as well as downwards, and there are minor varieties of the type.

4

HALF-PENNY
(5)

(Typo D.L.R)

1882 (28 Aug)–**86**. Wmk Crown CA. P 14.

89 **4** ½d. dull green (1882) 20·00 1·50
w. Wmk inverted
90 ½d. green 20·00 1·50
91 1d. rose (1882) 65·00 2·25
a. Bisected (½d.) (on cover) † £1500
w. Wmk inverted
92 1d. carmine 26·00 1·00
93 2½d. ultramarine (1882) 90·00 1·50
w. Wmk inverted — £110
94 2½d. deep blue £110 1·50
95 3d. deep purple (1885) £110 35·00
96 3d. reddish purple 4·50 22·00
97 4d. grey (1882) £350 4·25
98 4d. pale brown (1885) 17·00 4·00
w. Wmk inverted — 90·00
x. Wmk reversed † £150
y. Wmk inverted and reversed † £300
99 4d. deep brown 8·00 1·50
100 6d. olive-black (1886) 75·00 45·00
102 1s. chestnut (1886) 29·00 21·00
103 5s. bistre (1886) £160 £200
89/103 *Set of* 9 £700 £275
95s/103s (ex 4d. grey) Optd "Specimen" *Set of* 5 £400

1892 (July). *No. 99 surch with T* **5** *by West Indian Press.*

104 **4** ½d. on 4d. deep brown 2·25 6·00
a. No hyphen 15·00 26·00
b. Surch double (R.+Bk.) £850 £1000
ba. Surch double (R.+Bk.) both without hyphen £2500 £3000
c. Surch double, one albino
d. Surch "PENNY HALF" £375 £225

Nos. 104b/ba come from a sheet with a trial surcharge in red which was subsequently surcharged again in black and put back into stock.

No. 104c is known in a horizontal pair (*Price*, £2500, *unused*) with the left hand stamp showing the first two letters of the second impression inked. The right hand stamp shows a complete albino surcharge.

6 Seal of Colony

7

(Typo D.L.R.)

1892 (July)–**1903**. Wmk Crown CA. P 14.

105 **6** ¼d. slate-grey and carmine (5.5.96) 2·50 10
w. Wmk inverted
106 ½d. dull green 2·50 10
w. Wmk inverted — 95·00
107 1d. carmine 4·75 10
108 2d. slate-black and orange (5.99) 8·00 75
109 2½d. ultramarine 17·00 20
110 5d. grey-olive 7·00 4·50
111 6d. mauve and carmine 16·00 2·00
112 8d. orange and ultramarine 4·00 25·00
113 10d. dull blue-green and carmine 8·00 7·00
114 2s.6d. blue-black and orange 48·00 55·00
w. Wmk inverted £150 £160
115 2s.6d. violet and green (29.5.03) £120 £200
105/15 *Set of* 11 £200 £275
105s/15s Optd "Specimen" *Set of* 11 £225

See also Nos. 135/44 and 163/9.

(Typo D.L.R.)

1897 (16 Nov)–**98**. *Diamond Jubilee. T* **7**. Wmk Crown CC. P 14.

(*a*) *White paper.*

116 ¼d. grey and carmine 6·00 60
117 ½d. dull green 6·00 60
118 1d. rose 6·00 60
119 2½d. ultramarine 8·50 85
w. Wmk inverted — £120
120 5d. olive-brown 23·00 20·00
121 6d. mauve and carmine 30·00 25·00
122 8d. orange and ultramarine 15·00 27·00
123 10d. blue-green and carmine 48·00 55·00
124 2s.6d. blue-black and orange 85·00 60·00
w. Wmk inverted
116/24 *Set of* 9 £200 £170
116s/24s Optd "Specimen" *Set of* 9 £180

(*b*) *Paper blued.*

125 ¼d. grey and carmine 30·00 30·00
126 ½d. dull green 30·00 30·00
127 1d. carmine 40·00 40·00
128 2½d. ultramarine 42·00 45·00
129 5d. olive-brown £225 £250
130 6d. mauve and carmine £130 £140
131 8d. orange and ultramarine £140 £150
132 10d. dull green and carmine £190 £225
133 2s.6d. blue-black and orange £130 £140

1905. Wmk Mult Crown CA. P 14.

135 **6** ¼d. slate-grey and carmine 11·00 2·75
136 ½d. dull green 21·00 10
137 1d. carmine 21·00 10
139 2½d. blue 24·00 15
141 6d. mauve and carmine 23·00 22·00
142 8d. orange and ultramarine 60·00 £120
144 2s.6d. violet and green 65·00 £140
135/144 *Set of* 7 £200 £250

See also Nos. 163/9.

8 Nelson Monument

(Des Mrs. G. Goodman. Recess D.L.R.)

1906 (1 Mar). *Nelson Centenary*. Wmk Crown CC. P 14.

145 **8** ¼d. black and grey 12·00 1·75
w. Wmk inverted 45·00 48·00
146 ½d. black and pale green 11·00 15
w. Wmk inverted
x. Wmk reversed £160 80·00
147 1d. black and red 12·00 15
w. Wmk inverted 65·00
x. Wmk reversed † 80·00
148 2d. black and yellow 1·75 4·50
149 2½d. black and bright blue 3·75 1·25
w. Wmk inverted
150 6d. black and mauve 18·00 26·00
151 1s. black and rose 21·00 50·00
145/51 *Set of* 7 70·00 75·00
145s/51s Optd "Specimen" *Set of* 7 £160

Two sets may be made of the above: one on thick, opaque,

creamy white paper; the other on thin, rather transparent, bluish white paper.
See also Nos. 158/62*a*.

9 *Olive Blossom*, 1605

Kingston Relief Fund. 1d.
(10)

(Des Lady Carter. Recess D.L.R.)

1906 (15 Aug). *Tercentenary of Annexation.* Wmk Multiple Crown CA (sideways). P 14.
152 **9** 1d. black, blue and green .... 12·00 25
s. Optd "Specimen" .... 65·00

1907 (25 Jan–25 Feb). *Kingston Relief Fund. No. 108 surch with T* **10** *by T. E. King & Co., Barbados.*
153 **6** 1d. on 2d. slate-black and orange (R.) .... 3·75 9·50
a. Surch inverted (25.2.07) 1·75 6·50
b. Surch double £850 £950
c. Surch double, both inverted £850
d. Surch *tête-bêche* (vert pair) £1400
e. No stop after "1d." .... 55·00 90·00
ea. Do., surch inverted (25.2.07) .... 40·00 95·00
eb. Do., surch double.......... — £1800
f. Vert pair, one normal, one surch double .... — £1200

The above stamp was sold for 2d. of which 1d. was retained for the postal revenue, and the other 1d. given to a fund for the relief of the sufferers by the earthquake in Jamaica.
An entire printing as No. 153a was created after a sheet of inverted surcharges was found in the initial supply.

1907 (6 July). *Nelson Centenary.* Wmk Mult Crown CA. P 14.
158 **8** ¼d. black and grey........................... 5·00 7·50
161 2d. black and yellow .... 30·00 35·00
162 2½d. black and bright blue .... 8·00 35·00
a. Black and indigo...................... £700 £800
158/62 *Set of* 3 .... 38·00 70·00

1909 (July)–**10**. Wmk Mult Crown CA. P 14.
163 **6** ¼d. brown... 9·50 30
164 ½d. blue-green.................................. 25·00 1·50
165 1d. red... 24·00 10
166 2d. greyish slate (8.10).................. 7·50 15·00
167 2½d. bright blue (1910) .... 50·00 10·00
168 6d. dull and bright purple (1910). 17·00 22·00
169 1s. black/*green* (8.10) .... 13·00 14·00
163/9 *Set of* 7 .... £130 55·00
163s/9s (ex ½d., 2½d.) Optd "Specimen" *Set of* 5... £140

11

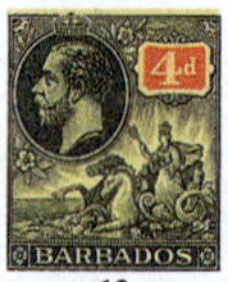
12

13

(Typo D.L.R.)

1912 (23 July)–**16**. Wmk Mult Crown CA. P 14.
170 **11** ¼d. brown... 1·50 1·50
a. Pale brown (1916).................... 1·50 2·50
aw. Wmk inverted ....
171 ½d. green... 3·75 10
a. Wmk sideways........................... † —
172 1d. red (13.8.12).............................. 11·00 10
a. Scarlet (1915)........................... 30·00 3·75
173 2d. greyish slate (13.8.12)............ 4·50 15·00
174 2½d. bright blue (13.8.12)................ 1·50 50
175 **12** 3d. purple/*yellow* (13.8.12)............ 1·50 14·00
176 4d. black and red/*yellow* (13.8.12) .... 3·00 20·00
177 6d. dull purple and purple (13.8.12) .... 12·00 12·00
178 **13** 1s. black/*green* (13.8.12) .... 9·00 18·00
179 2s. purple and blue/*blue* (13.8.12) .... 55·00 60·00
180 3s. green and violet (13.8.12)....... £110 £120
170/80 *Set of* 11 .... £190 £225
170s/80s Optd "Specimen" *Set of* 11...................... £160

14

WAR TAX
(15)

(Recess D.L.R.)

1916 (16 June)–**19**. Wmk Mult Crown CA. P 14.
181 **14** ¼d. deep brown.................................. 75 40
a. Chestnut-brown (9.17) .... 1·50 35
b. Sepia-brown (4.18)................... 4·00 2·75
w. Wmk inverted .... 17·00 18·00
y. Wmk inverted and reversed....... 42·00 48·00
182 ½d. green... 2·00 15
a. Deep green (9.17)..................... 1·60 15
b. Pale green (4.18)...................... 2·25 80
w. Wmk inverted .... 35·00
x. Wmk reversed .... 80·00
y. Wmk inverted and reversed... 60·00 60·00
183 1d. deep red .... 17·00 6·00
a. Bright carmine-red (4.17)......... 2·50 15
b. Pale carmine-red (9.17) .... 6·00 65
w. Wmk inverted .... 38·00
x. Wmk reversed............................
y. Wmk inverted and reversed... 38·00
184 2d. grey.. 8·50 26·00
a. Grey-black (9.19) .... 45·00 70·00
y. Wmk inverted and reversed...
185 2½d. deep ultramarine....................... 4·75 3·25
a. Royal blue (11.17) .... 5·50 3·50
w. Wmk inverted ....
y. Wmk inverted and reversed... 40·00 40·00
186 3d. purple/*yellow* (thin paper)...... 5·00 9·50
a. Dp purple/yell (thick paper) (9.19).. 30·00 45·00
187 4d. red/*yellow*................................. 1·00 14·00
188 6d. purple .... 6·50 5·00
189 1s. black/*green*............................... 7·00 12·00
190 2s. purple/*blue*............................... 16·00 7·50
y. Wmk inverted and reversed... 90·00
191 3s. deep violet.................................. 65·00 £160
w. Wmk inverted ....
y. Wmk inverted and reversed... £1200
181/91 *Set of* 11 .... £110 £200
181s/91s "Specimen" *Set of* 11.............................. £225

Dates quoted for shades are those of despatch from Great Britain.
Examples of the ½d. and 1d. values can be found perforated either by line or by comb machines.
No. 191y is gummed on the printed side.
See also Nos. 199/200*a*.

1917 (10 Oct)–**18**. *War Tax. Optd in London with T* **15**.
197 **11** 1d. bright red 50 15
s. Optd "Specimen"..................... 55·00
w. Wmk inverted .... — £140
198 1d. pale red (*thicker bluish paper*) (4.18)....................................... 4·75 60

1918 (18 Feb)–**20**. *Colours changed.* Wmk Mult Crown CA. P 14.
199 **14** 4d. black and red............................ 1·00 3·75
x. Wmk reversed £180
y. Wmk inverted and reversed.. † £325
200 3s. green and deep violet............. 22·00 90·00
a. Green and bright violet (1920).. £250 £375
199s/200s Optd "Specimen" *Set of* 2 .... £130

The centres of these are from a new die having no circular border line.

16 Winged Victory from the Louvre

17 Victory from Victoria Memorial, London

(Recess D.L.R.)

1920 (9 Sept)–**21**. *Victory.* P 14.

(*a*) Wmk Mult Crown CA (sideways* on T **17**).
201 **16** ¼d. black and bistre-brown 30 70
a. "C" of "CA" missing from wmk £325
c. Substituted crown in wmk...... £375
w. Wmk inverted £100
x. Wmk reversed........................... 45·00
y. Wmk inverted and reversed... 50·00
202 ½d. black and bright yellow-green .... 1·00 15
a. "C" of "CA" missing from wmk £350 £300
b. "A" of "CA" missing from wmk £350
c. Substituted crown in wmk...... £475
w. Wmk inverted .... — £110
x. Wmk reversed........................... £100
y. Wmk inverted and reversed... £100 £100
203 1d. black and vermilion................. 4·00 10
a. "A" of "CA" missing from wmk .... † £425
c. Substituted crown in wmk...... † £425
w. Wmk inverted .... 40·00 42·00
y. Wmk inverted and reversed... £100
204 2d. black and grey.......................... 2·25 10·00
a. "C" of "CA" missing from wmk £400
205 2½d. indigo and ultramarine .... 2·75 22·00
a. "C" of "CA" missing from wmk £425
w. Wmk inverted .... — £110
y. Wmk inverted and reversed... £100 £120
206 3d. black and purple....................... 3·00 6·50
w. Wmk inverted .... 30·00 45·00
207 4d. black and blue-green.............. 3·25 7·00
208 6d. black and brown-orange .... 3·75 18·00
w. Wmk inverted .... 65·00 £110
wa. "C" of "CA" missing from wmk £1300
wb. Substituted crown in wmk...... £1300
209 **17** 1s. black and bright green .... 12·00 38·00
a. "C" of "CA" missing from wmk £1000
w. Wmk Crown to left of CA .....
x. Wmk sideways reversed £150
y. Wmk sideways inverted and reversed.................................... £160
210 2s. black and brown........................ 38·00 50·00
w. Wmk Crown to left of CA ..... 75·00 £110
x. Wmk sideways reversed £150
y. Wmk sideways inverted and reversed.................................... £150
211 3s. black and dull orange.............. 40·00 70·00
a. "C" of "CA" missing from wmk £950
w. Wmk Crown to left of CA £100
x. Wmk sideways reversed .... — £170
y. Wmk sideways inverted and reversed....................................

(*b*) Wmk Mult Script CA.
212 **16** 1d. black and vermilion (22.8.21) 17·00 30
201/12 *Set of* 12.. £110 £200
201s/12s Optd "Specimen" *Set of* 12 .... £225

*The normal sideways watermark on Nos. 209/11 shows Crown to right of CA, *as seen from the back of the stamp*.
For illustration of the substituted watermark crown see Catalogue Introduction.

18

19

(Recess D.L.R.)

1921 (14 Nov)–**24**. P 14.

(*a*) Wmk Mult Crown CA.
213 **18** 3d. purple/*pale yellow*................... 2·00 7·00
a. "A" of "CA" missing from wmk ....
x. Wmk reversed........................... † £180
214 4d. red/*pale yellow* .... 1·75 18·00
215 1s. black/*emerald* .... 5·50 18·00
w. Wmk inverted .... † £300
x. Wmk reversed........................... £325 £275

(*b*) Wmk Mult Script CA.
217 **18** ¼d. brown... 25 10
x. Wmk reversed........................... 30·00
y. Wmk inverted and reversed... 48·00
219 ½d. green.. 1·50 10
220 1d. red... 80 10
aw. Wmk inverted .... 25·00 32·00
ax. Wmk reversed........................... — £120
ay. Wmk inverted and reversed... — £120
b. Bright rose-carmine .... 7·50 1·00
bw. Wmk inverted .... 25·00
221 2d. grey... 1·75 20
y. Wmk inverted and reversed...
222 2½d. ultramarine .... 1·50 9·00
225 6d. reddish purple .... 3·50 5·50
226 1s. black/*emerald* (18.9.24) .... 50·00 £140
227 2s. purple/*blue*............................... 10·00 19·00
228 3s. deep violet .... 16·00 75·00
y. Wmk inverted and reversed...
213/28 *Set of* 12 .... 85·00 £275
213s/28s Optd "Specimen" *Set of* 12 .... £180

1925 (1 Apr)–**35**. Wmk Mult Script CA. P 14.
229 **19** ¼d. brown... 25 10
230 ½d. green.. 50 10
a. Perf 13½×12½ (2.32)............... 8·50 10
231 1d. scarlet 50 10
ax. Wmk reversed........................... † £300
b. Perf 13½×12½ (2.32)............... 8·50 50
231*c* 1½d. orange (1933) .... 14·00 3·25
ca. Perf 13½×12½ (15.8.32).......... 2·50 1·00
232 2d. grey... 50 3·25
233 2½d. blue 50 80
a. Bright ultramarine (1933) .... 16·00 2·25
ab. Perf 13½×12½ (2.32)............... 10·00 5·50
234 3d. purple/*pale yellow*................... 1·00 45
a. Reddish purple/yellow (1935). 6·00 6·50
235 4d. red/*pale yellow* .... 75 1·00
236 6d. purple .... 1·00 90
237 1s. black/*emerald* .... 2·00 7·50
a. Perf 13½×12½ (8.32)............... 65·00 40·00
b. Brownish black/bright yellow-green (1934)............................ 4·50 10·00
238 2s. purple/*blue*.............................. 7·00 7·00
238*a* 2s.6d. carmine/*blue* (1.9.32) .... 24·00 30·00
239 3s. deep violet .... 11·00 15·00
229/39 *Set of* 13 .... 45·00 60·00
229s/39s Optd or Perf (1½d., 2s.6d.) "Specimen" *Set of* 13 .... £200

Nos. 230/1 exist in coils constructed from normal sheets.

20 King Charles I and King George V

21 Badge of the Colony

(Recess B.W.)

1927 (17 Feb). *Tercentenary of Settlement of Barbados.* Wmk Mult Script CA. P 12½.
240 **20** 1d. carmine....................................... 1·00 75
s. Optd "Specimen"...................... 50·00

1935 (6 May). *Silver Jubilee. As Nos. 91/4 of Antigua, but ptd by Waterlow.* P 11×12.
241 1d. deep blue and scarlet 75 20
j. Damaged turret............................. £325
242 1½d. ultramarine and grey..................... 4·00 7·00
j. Damaged turret............................. £400
243 2½d. brown and deep blue .... 2·50 5·00
m. "Bird" by turret............................ £250 £300
244 1s. slate and purple .... 20·00 24·00
l. Kite and horizontal log.................. £475 £500
241/4 *Set of* 4 .... 24·00 32·00
241s/4s Perf "Specimen" *Set of* 4 .... £110

For illustrations of plate varieties see Omnibus section following Zanzibar.

1937 (14 May). *Coronation. As Nos. 95/7 of Antigua, but printed by D.L.R.* P 14.

245	1d. scarlet	30	15
246	1½d. yellow-brown	55	65
247	2½d. bright blue	1·25	75
245/7 *Set of* 3		1·90	1·40
245s/7s Perf "Specimen" *Set of* 3		80·00	

Recut line (R. 10/6)

Extra frame line (R. 11/9)

Mark on central ornament (R. 1/3, 2/3, 3/3)

Vertical line over horse's head (R. 4/10) (corrected on Dec 1947 ptg)

"Flying mane" (R. 4/1) (corrected on Dec 1947 ptg)

Curved line at top right (R. 7/8) (corrected on Dec 1947 ptg)

Cracked plate (extends to top right ornament) (R. 6/10))

(Recess D.L.R.)

1938 (3 Jan)–**47**. Wmk Mult Script CA. P 13½×13.

248	**21**	½d. green	6·00	15
		a. Recut line	£130	40·00
		b. Perf 14 (8.42)	70·00	1·25
		ba. Recut line	£400	75·00
248*c*		½d. yellow-bistre (16.10.42)	15	30
		ca. "A" of "CA" missing from wmk	£1100	
		cb. Recut line	22·00	26·00
249		1d. scarlet (12.40)	£275	4·00
		a. Perf 14 (3.1.38)	16·00	10
249*b*		1d. blue-green (1943)	5·00	1·25
		c. Perf 14 (16.10.42)	15	10
		ca. "A" of "CA" missing from wmk	£1100	
250		1½d. orange	15	40
		a. "A" of "CA" missing from wmk	£1100	
		b. Perf 14 (11.41)	4·75	75
250*c*		2d. claret (3.6.41)	50	2·50
		ca. Extra frame line	45·00	75·00
250*d*		2d. carmine (20.9.43)	20	70
		da. Extra frame line	30·00	42·00
		db. "A" of "CA" missing from wmk	†	—
		e. Perf 14 (11.9.44)	60	1·75
		ea. Extra frame line	40·00	70·00
251		2½d. ultramarine	50	60
		a. Mark on central ornament	45·00	45·00
		b. Blue (17.2.44)	1·75	5·00
		ba. "A" of "CA" missing from wmk	£1000	
		bb. Mark on central ornament	65·00	85·00
252		3d. brown	20	2·50
		a. Vertical line over horse's head	90·00	£140
		ab. "A" of "CA" missing from wmk		
		b. Perf 14 (4.41)	20	60
		ba. Vertical line over horse's head	90·00	£110
252*c*		3d. blue (1.4.47)	20	1·75
		ca. Vertical line over horse's head	90·00	£120
253		4d. black	20	10
		a. Flying mane	£120	60·00
		b. Curved line at top right	£100	50·00
		c. Cracked plate	£100	50·00
		d. Perf 14 (11.9.44)	20	6·00
		da. Flying mane	£120	£170
		db. Curved line at top right	£100	£150
		dc. Cracked plate	£100	£150
254		6d. violet	80	40
254*a*		8d. magenta (9.12.46)	55	2·00
255		1s. olive-green	16·00	2·50
		a. Deep brown-olive (19.11.45)	1·00	10
256		2s.6d. purple	7·00	1·50
256*a*		5s. indigo (3.6.41)	4·50	9·00
		ab. "A" of "CA" missing from wmk	£2000	
248/56*a Set of* 16			32·00	18·00
248s/56as Perf "Specimen" *Set of* 16			£325	

No. 249a was perforated by two machines, one gauging 13.8×14.1 line (1938), the other 14.1 comb (October 1940).

Nos. 248/*c* and 249/*c* exist in coils constructed from normal sheets.

22 Kings Charles I, George VI, Assembly Chamber and Mace

(Recess D.L.R.)

1939 (27 June). *Tercentenary of General Assembly.* Wmk Mult Script CA. P 13½×14.

257	**22**	½d. green	2·75	1·00
258		1d. scarlet	2·75	1·25
259		1½d. orange	2·75	60
260		2½d. bright ultramarine	3·25	7·00
261		3d. brown	3·50	5·50
257/61 *Set of* 5			13·50	14·00
257s/61s Perf "Specimen" *Set of* 5			£170*	

Two flags on tug (R. 5/2)

1946 (18 Sept). *Victory. As Nos. 110/11 of Antigua.*

262	1½d. red-orange	15	40
	a. Two flags on tug	25·00	
263	3d. brown	15	40
262s/3s Perf "Specimen" *Set of* 2		70·00	

ONE
PENNY
(**23**)

Short "Y" (R. 6/2)

Broken "E" (R. 7/4 and 11/4)

Broken "N"s (R. 2/8, later sheets only)

(Surch by Barbados Advocate Co.)

1947 (21 Apr). *Surch with T* **23**.

(*a*) P 14.

264	**21**	1d. on 2d. carmine (No. 250*e*)	2·00	3·00
		a. Extra frame line	90·00	£100
		b. Broken "N"s	£110	
		c. Short "Y"	90·00	£100
		d. Broken "E"	48·00	55·00

(*b*) P 13½×13.

264*e*	**21**	1d. on 2d. carmine (No. 250*d*)	3·00	5·00
		ea. Extra frame line	£180	£225
		eb. Broken "N"s	£200	
		ec. Short "Y"	£180	£225
		ed. Broken "E"	£110	£140
		f. Surch double	£2500	

The relationship of the two words in the surcharge differs on each position of the sheet.

1948 (24 Nov). *Royal Silver Wedding. As Nos. 112/13 of Antigua.*

265	1½d. orange	30	50
266	5s. indigo	14·00	10·00

1949 (10 Oct). *75th Anniv of Universal Postal Union. As Nos. 114/17 of Antigua.*

267	1½d. red-orange	50	2·00
268	3d. deep blue	2·50	4·00
269	4d. grey	50	3·25
270	1s. olive	50	60
267/70 *Set of* 4		3·50	9·00

(New Currency. 100 cents = 1 West Indian, later Barbados, dollar)

24 Dover Fort

25 Sugar cane breeding

26 Public buildings

27 Statue of Nelson

28 Casting net

29 *Frances W. Smith* (schooner)

30 Four-winged Flying Fish

31 Old Main Guard Garrison

32 St. Michael's Cathedral

33 Careenage

34 Map of Barbados and wireless mast

35 Seal of Barbados

(Recess B.W.)

1950 (1 May). *T* **24/35**. Wmk Mult Script CA. P 11×11½ (*horiz*), 13½ (*vert*).

271	**24**	1c. indigo	35	3·75
272	**25**	2c. emerald-green	15	2·50
273	**26**	3c. reddish brown and blue-green	1·25	3·50
274	**27**	4c. carmine	15	40
275	**28**	6c. light blue	15	2·25
276	**29**	8c. bright blue and purple-brown	1·50	3·00
277	**30**	12c. greenish blue and brown-olive	1·00	1·25
278	**31**	24c. scarlet and black	1·00	50
279	**32**	48c. violet	9·00	6·50
280	**33**	60c. green and claret	10·00	11·00
281	**34**	$1.20 carmine and olive-green	10·00	4·25
282	**35**	$2.40 black	23·00	29·00
271/282 *Set of* 12			50·00	60·00

1951 (16 Feb). *Inauguration of B.W.I. University College. As Nos. 118/19 of Antigua.*

283	3c. brown and blue-green	30	40
284	12c. blue-green and brown-olive	70	2·25

36 King George VI and Stamp of 1852

(Recess Waterlow)

1952 (15 Apr). *Barbados Stamp Centenary.* Wmk Mult Script CA. P 13½.

285	**36**	3c. green and slate-green	35	40
286		4c. blue and carmine	35	1·00
287		12c. slate-green and bright green	35	1·00
288		24c. red-brown and brownish black	35	55
285/8 *Set of* 4			1·25	2·75

37 Harbour Police

(Recess B.W.)

1953 (13 Apr)–**61**. *Designs previously used for King George VI issue, but with portrait or cypher ($2.40) of Queen Elizabeth II, as in T* **37**. Wmk Mult Script CA. P 11×11½ (*horiz*) or 13½ (*vert*).

289	**24**	1c. indigo	10	80
290	**25**	2c. orange and deep turquoise (15.4.54)	15	1·00
291	**26**	3c. black and emerald (15.4.54)	1·00	90
292	**27**	4c. black and orange (15.4.54)	20	20
		a. Black and reddish orange (18.3.59)	2·75	1·50
293	**37**	5c. blue and deep carmine-red (4.1.54)	1·00	60
294	**28**	6c. red-brown (15.4.54)	1·25	60
		w. Wmk inverted		
295	**29**	8c. black and blue (15.4.54)	2·00	40
296	**30**	12c. turquoise-blue & brown-olive (15.4.54)	1·00	10
		a. Turquoise-grn & brown-olive (18.3.59)	14·00	3·00
		b. Turquoise-blue & bronze-grn (13.6.61)	16·00	2·00
297	**31**	24c. rose-red and black (2.3.56)	60	10
298	**32**	48c. deep violet (2.3.56)	7·00	1·00
299	**33**	60c. blue-green and brown-purple (3.4.56)	25·00	5·50
		a. Blue-green and pale maroon (17.5.60)	40·00	9·00
300	**34**	$1.20 carmine and bronze-green (3.4.56)	19·00	4·50
301	**35**	$2.40 black (1.2.57)	7·50	1·75
289/301 *Set of* 13			55·00	15·00

See also Nos. 312/19.

1953 (4 June). *Coronation. As No. 120 of Antigua.*

302	4c. black and red-orange	75	10

1958 (23 Apr). *Inauguration of British Caribbean Federation. As Nos. 135/7 of Antigua.*

303	3c. deep green	35	20
304	6c. blue	50	2·25
305	12c. scarlet	50	30
303/5 *Set of* 3		1·25	2·50

38 Deep Water Harbour, Bridgetown

(Recess B.W.)

1961 (6 May). *Opening of Deep Water Harbour, Bridgetown.* W w **12**. P 11×12.

306	**38**	4c. black and red-orange	25	50
307		8c. black and blue	25	60
308		24c. carmine-red and black	25	60
306/8 *Set of* 3			65	1·50

SELF-GOVERNMENT

39 Scout Badge and Map of Barbados

40 Deep Sea Coral

(Recess B.W)

1962 (9 Mar). *Golden Jubilee of Barbados Boy Scout Association.* W w **12**. P 11½×11.

309	**39**	4c. black and orange	70	10
310		12c. blue and olive-brown	1·00	15
311		$1.20 carmine and olive-green	1·60	3·75
309/11 *Set of* 3			3·00	3·75

1964 (14 Jan)–**65**. *As Nos. 289, etc., but wmk w* **12**.

312	**24**	1c. indigo (6.10.64)	50	3·00
313	**27**	4c. black and orange	30	50
314	**29**	8c. black and blue (29.6.65)	60	35
315	**30**	12c. turquoise-blue and brown-olive (29.6.65)	50	50
316	**31**	24c. rose-red and black (6.10.64)	65	70
317	**32**	48c. deep violet	5·00	1·50
318	**33**	60c. blue-green and brown-purple (6.10.64)	10·00	4·00
319	**35**	$2.40 black (29.6.65)	1·25	1·75
312/19 *Set of* 8			17·00	11·00

The above dates are for Crown Agents releases. The 14.1.64 printings were not released in Barbados until April 1964 the 6.10.64 printings until December 1964 and of the stamps released in London on 29 June 1965 the 8c. and $2.40 were released from about 15 June 1965, but the 12c. value was never put on sale in Barbados.

1965 (17 May). *I.T.U. Centenary. As Nos. 166/7 of Antigua.*

320	2c. lilac and red	20	40
321	48c. yellow and grey-brown	45	1·00

HAVE YOU READ THE NOTES AT THE BEGINNING OF THIS CATALOGUE?
These often provide answers to the enquiries we receive

(Des V. Whiteley, from drawings by Mrs. J. Walker. Photo Harrison)

1965 (15 July). *Marine Life. Horiz designs as T* **40**. W w **12** (upright). P 14×13½.

322	1c. black, pink and blue	20	30
323	2c. olive-brown, yellow and magenta	20	15
324	3c. olive-brown and orange	45	60
325	4c. deep blue and olive-green	15	10
	a. Imperf (pair)	£275	£170
	w. Wmk inverted	—	16·00
326	5c. sepia, rose and lilac	30	20
327	6c. multicoloured	45	20
	w. Wmk inverted	1·25	1·00
328	8c. multicoloured	25	10
	w. Wmk inverted	3·50	
329	12c. multicoloured	35	10
	a. Grey printing double	50·00	
	w. Wmk inverted		
330	15c. black, greenish yellow and red	2·75	30
331	25c. ultramarine and yellow-ochre	1·00	30
332	35c. brown-red and deep green	1·50	15
	w. Wmk inverted		
333	50c. bright blue and apple-green	2·00	40
334	$1 multicoloured	3·25	2·00
335	$2.50 multicoloured	2·75	4·25
322/35 *Set of* 14		14·00	8·00

Designs:—2c. Lobster; 3c. Lined Seahorse; 4c. Sea Urchin; 5c. Staghorn Coral; 6c. Spot-finned Butterflyfish; 8c. Rough File shell; 12c. Porcupinefish ("Balloon Fish"); 15c. Grey Angelfish; 25c. Brain Coral; 35c. Brittle Star; 50c. Four-winged Flyingfish; $1 Queen or Pink Conch shell; $2.50 Fiddler Crab.

The 3c. value is wrongly inscribed "Hippocanpus", the correct spelling "Hippocampus" was used for subsequent printings, see No. 344.

See also Nos. 342, etc.

1966 (24 Jan). *Churchill Commemoration. As Nos. 170/3 of Antigua.*

336	1c. new blue	10	2·75
	w. Wmk inverted	22·00	
337	4c. deep green	30	10
338	25c. brown	70	50
339	35c. bluish violet	80	60
336/9 *Set of* 4		1·75	3·50

1966 (4 Feb). *Royal Visit. As Nos. 174/5 of Antigua.*

340	3c. black and ultramarine	35	1·00
341	35c. black and magenta	1·40	1·00

41 Dolphin

54 Arms of Barbados

1966 (15 Mar)–**69**. *As Nos. 322/35 but wmk w* **12** *(sideways*). New value and design (as T* **41**).

342	1c. black, pink and blue	10	20
	w. Wmk Crown to right of CA		
343	2c. olive-brn, yellow & magenta (16.5.67)	30	80
344	3c. olive-brown and orange (4.12.67)	30	2·75
345	4c. deep blue and olive-green	50	10
	w. Wmk Crown to right of CA	55·00	
346	5c. sepia, rose and lilac (23.8.66)	45	10
347	6c. multicoloured (31.1.67)	70	10
348	8c. multicoloured (19.9.67)	75	10
349	12c. multicoloured (31.1.67)	45	10
350	15c. black, greenish yellow and red	2·25	10
351	25c. ultramarine and yellow-ochre	2·25	40
	aw. Wmk Crown to right of CA	8·50	
	b. Deep ultram and yellow-ochre (26.9.66)	9·00	2·25
352	35c. brown-red and deep green (23.8.66)	2·50	65
	a. Chestnut and deep green (26.11.68)	7·00	3·25
353	50c. bright blue and apple-green	1·75	3·50
	w. Wmk Crown to right of CA	65·00	
354	$1 multicoloured (23.8.66)	6·00	1·00
355	$2.50 multicoloured (23.8.66)	7·00	3·00
355*a*	$5 multicoloured (9.1.69)	16·00	9·00
342/55a *Set of* 15		35·00	19·00

*The normal sideways watermark shows Crown to left of CA, *as seen from the back of the stamp.*

The 3c. value is correctly inscribed "Hippocampus".

All values except the 50c. exist with PVA gum as well as gum arabic but the $5 exists with PVA gum only.

The $5 was released by the Crown Agents on 6 January but was not put on sale locally until 9 January.

INDEPENDENT

(Des. V. Whiteley. Photo Harrison)

1966 (2 Dec). *Independence. T* **54** *and similar multicoloured designs.* P 14.

356	4c. Type **54**	10	10
357	25c. Hilton Hotel (*horiz*)	15	10
358	35c. G. Sobers (Test cricketer)	1·50	65
359	50c. Pine Hill Dairy (*horiz*)	70	1·10
356/9 *Set of* 4		2·25	1·75

1967 (6 Jan). *20th Anniv of U.N.E.S.CO. As Nos. 196/8 of Antigua.*

360	4c. slate-violet, red, yellow and orange	20	10
361	12c. orange-yellow, violet and deep olive	45	50
362	25c. black, bright purple and orange	75	1·25
360/2 *Set of* 3		1·25	1·60

58 Policeman and Anchor

62 Governor-General Sir Winston Scott, G.C.M.G.

(Des V. Whiteley. Litho D.L.R.)

1967 (16 Oct). *Centenary of Harbour Police. T* **58** *and similar multicoloured designs.* P 14.

363	4c. Type **58**	25	10
364	25c. Policeman with telescope	40	15
365	35c. *BP1* (police launch) (*horiz*)	45	15
366	50c. Policeman outside H.Q.	60	1·60
363/6 *Set of* 4		1·50	1·75

(Des V. Whiteley. Photo Harrison)

1967 (4 Dec). *First Anniv of Independence. T* **62** *and similar multicoloured designs.* P 14½×14 (4c.) or 14×14½ (others).

367	4c. Type **62**	15	10
368	25c. Independence Arch (*horiz*)	25	10
369	35c. Treasury Building (*horiz*)	30	10
370	50c. Parliament Building (*horiz*)	40	90
367/70 *Set of* 4		1·00	1·00

66 U.N. Building, Santiago, Chile

67 Radar Antenna

(Des G. Vasarhelyi. Photo Harrison)

1968 (27 Feb). *20th Anniv of the Economic Commission for Latin America.* P 14½.

371	**66**	15c. multicoloured	10	10

(Des G. Vasarhelyi. Photo Harrison)

1968 (4 June). *World Meteorological Day. T* **67** *and similar multicoloured designs.* P 14×14½ (25c.) or 14½×14 (others).

372	3c. Type **67**	10	10
373	25c. Meteorological Institute (*horiz*)	25	10
374	50c. Harp Gun and coat of arms	30	90
372/4 *Set of* 3		55	1·00

70 Lady Baden-Powell, and Guide at Camp Fire

(Des. V. Whiteley (from local designs). Photo Harrison)

1968 (29 Aug). *50th Anniv of Girl Guiding in Barbados. T* **70** *and similar horiz designs.* P 14.

375	3c. ultramarine, black and gold	20	60
376	25c. turquoise-blue, black and gold	30	60
377	35c. orange-yellow, black and gold	35	60
375/7 *Set of* 3		75	1·60

Designs:—25c. Lady Baden-Powell and Pax Hill; 35c. Lady Baden-Powell and Guide Badge.

73 Hands breaking Chain, and Human Rights Emblem

(Des V. Whiteley. Litho B.W.)

1968 (10 Dec*). *Human Rights Year. T* **73** *and similar horiz designs.* P 11×12.

378	4c. violet, brown and light green	10	20
379	25c. black, blue and orange-yellow	10	25
380	35c. multicoloured	15	25
378/80 *Set of* 3		30	60

Designs:—25c. Human Rights emblem and family enchained; 35c. Shadows of refugees beyond opening fence.

*This was the local release date but the Crown Agents issued the stamps on 29 October.

76 Racehorses in the Paddock

(Des J. Cooter. Litho Format)

1969 (20 Mar*). *Horse-Racing. T* **76** *and similar horiz designs. Multicoloured.* P 14.

381	4c. Type **76**	25	15
382	25c. Starting-gate	25	15
383	35c. On the flat	30	15
384	50c. Winning post	35	2·00
381/4 *Set of* 4		1·00	2·25
MS385 117×85 mm. Nos. 381/4		2·00	2·75

*This was the local release date but the Crown Agents issued the stamps on 15 March.

80 Map showing "CARIFTA" Countries

81 "Strength in Unity"

(Des J. Cooter. Photo Harrison)

1969 (6 May). *First Anniv of CARIFTA (Caribbean Free Trade Area).* W w **12** (sideways on T **80**). P 14.

386	**80**	5c. multicoloured	10	10
387	**81**	12c. multicoloured	10	10
388	**80**	25c. multicoloured	10	10
389	**81**	50c. multicoloured	15	20
386/9 *Set of* 4			30	30

82 I.L.O. Emblem and "1919–1969".

ONE
CENT
(83)

(Des Sylvia Goaman. Litho Enschedé)

1969 (12 Aug). *50th Anniv of International Labour Organisation.* P 14×13.

390	**82**	4c. black, emerald and turquoise-blue	10	10
391		25c. black, cerise and brown-red	20	10

Although released by the Crown Agents on 5 August, the above were not put on sale in Barbados until 12 August.

1969 (30 Aug). *No. 363 surch with T* **83**.

392	1c. on 4c. Type **58**	10	10
	a. Surch double	75·00	

84 National Scout Badge

(Des J. Cooter. Litho Enschedé)

1969 (16 Dec). *Independence of Barbados Boy Scouts Association and 50th Anniv of Barbados Sea Scouts. T* **84** *and similar horiz designs. Multicoloured.* P 13×13½.

393	5c. Type **84**	15	10
394	25c. Sea Scouts rowing	45	10
395	35c. Scouts around camp fire	55	10
396	50c. Scouts and National Scout Headquarters	80	1·25
393/6 *Set of* 4		1·75	1·40
MS397 155×115 mm. Nos. 393/6		14·00	13·00

4 x
(88)

89 Lion at Gun Hill

1970 (11 Mar). *No. 346 surch locally with T* **88**.

398	4c. on 5c. sepia, rose and lilac	10	10
	a. Vert pair, one without surch	38·00	
	b. Surch double	27·00	
	c. Vert pair, one normal, one surch double	70·00	
	d. Surch triple	£225	£110
	e. Surch normal on front, inverted on back	14·00	
	f. Surch omitted on front, inverted on back	18·00	

(Des J.W. Photo D.L.R.)

1970 (4 May)–**71**. *Multicoloured designs as T* **89**. W w **12** (sideways on 12c. to $5). *Chalk-surfaced paper.* P 12½.

399	1c. Type **89**	10	1·50
	a. Glazed, ordinary paper (15.3.71)	10	1·50
400	2c. Trafalgar Fountain	30	1·25
	a. Glazed, ordinary paper (15.3.71)	10	1·75
401	3c. Montefiore Drinking Fountain	10	1·00
	a. Glazed, ordinary paper (15.3.71)	10	1·75
	aw. Wmk inverted	7·50	
402	4c. St. James' Monument	1·00	15
	a. Glazed, ordinary paper (15.3.71)	30	10
403	5c. St. Anne's Fort	10	10
	a. Glazed, ordinary paper (15.3.71)	10	10
404	6c. Old Sugar Mill, Morgan Lewis	35	3·00
405	8c. Cenotaph	10	10
	a. Glazed, ordinary paper (15.3.71)	10	10
406	10c. South Point Lighthouse	3·00	50
	a. Glazed, ordinary paper (15.3.71)	1·25	15
407	12c. Barbados Museum (*horiz*)	1·50	10
	a. Glazed, ordinary paper (13.12.71)	3·00	30
408	15c. Sharon Moravian Church (*horiz*)	30	15
	a. Glazed, ordinary paper (13.12.71)	60	30
409	25c. George Washington House (*horiz*)	25	15
	a. Glazed, ordinary paper (15.3.71)	50	35
410	35c. Nicholas Abbey (*horiz*)	30	85
	a. Glazed, ordinary paper (15.3.71)	45	70
411	50c. Bowmanston Pumping Station (*horiz*)	40	1·00
	a. Glazed, ordinary paper (15.3.71)	70	4·00
412	$1 Queen Elizabeth Hospital (*horiz*)	70	2·50
	a. Glazed, ordinary paper (15.3.71)	4·00	9·00
413	$2.50 Modern sugar factory (*horiz*)	1·50	4·00
	a. Glazed, ordinary paper (13.12.71)	27·00	16·00
414	$5 Seawell International Airport (*horiz*)	6·00	11·00
	a. Glazed, ordinary paper (15.3.71)	13·00	15·00
399/414 *Set of* 16		14·00	24·00
399a/414a *Set of* 15		45·00	45·00

Stamps in this set were re-issued between 1972 and 1974 with watermark *w* **12** sideways on 4c. to 10c.; upright on 12c. to $5.

105 Primary Schoolgirl

(Des V. Whiteley. Litho J.W.)

1970 (26 June). *25th Anniv of United Nations. T* **105** *and similar horiz designs. Multicoloured.* W w **12**. P 14.

415	4c. Type **108**	10	10
416	5c. Secondary Schoolboy	10	10
417	25c. Technical Student	35	10
418	50c. University Buildings	55	1·50
415/18 *Set of* 4		90	1·60

106 Minnie Root

(Des and litho JW.)

1970 (24 Aug). *Flowers of Barbados. T* **106** *and similar designs. Multicoloured.* W w **12** (sideways on horiz designs). P 14½.

419	1c. Barbados Easter Lily (*vert*)	10	2·00
420	5c. Type **106**	40	10
421	10c. Eyelash Orchid	1·75	30
422	25c. Pride of Barbados (*vert*)	1·25	75
423	35c. Christmas Hope	1·25	85
419/23 *Set of* 5		4·25	3·50
MS424 162×101 mm. Nos. 419/23. Imperf		2·00	6·00

STAMP BOOKLETS

1906 (Feb).

SB1	2s.½d. booklet containing twenty-four 1d. (No. 137) in blocks of 6	

1909. *Black on red cover. Stapled.*

SB1*a*	1s.6d. booklet containing eighteen 1d. (No. 165) in blocks of 6	

1913 (June). *Black on red cover. Stapled.*

SB2	2s. booklet containing twelve ½d. and eighteen 1d. (Nos. 171/2) in blocks of 6	£3000

1916 (16 June). *Black on red cover. Stapled.*

SB3	2s. booklet containing twelve ½d. and eighteen 1d. (Nos. 182/3) in pairs	£1000

1920 (Sept). *Black on red cover. Stapled.*

SB4	2s. booklet containing twelve ½d. and eighteen 1d. (Nos. 202/3) in pairs	£2500

1932 (12 Nov). *Black on pale green cover. Austin Cars and Post Office Guide advertisements on front. Stapled.*

SB5	2s. booklet containing ½d. and 1d. (Nos. 230a, 231a) each in block of 10 and 1½d. (No. 231ba) in block of 6	£2250

1933 (4 Dec). *Black on pale green cover. Advocate Co. Ltd. advertisement on front. Stapled.*

SB6	2s. booklet containing ½d. and 1d. (Nos. 230/1) each in block of 10 and 1½d. (No. 231*b*) in block of 6	£2500

1938 (3 Jan). *Black on light blue cover. Advocate Co. Ltd. advertisement on front. Stapled.*

SB7	2s. booklet containing ½d. and 1d. (Nos. 248, 249a) each in block of 10 and 1½d. (No. 250) in block of 6	£2750

POSTAGE DUE STAMPS

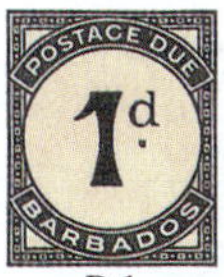

D 1

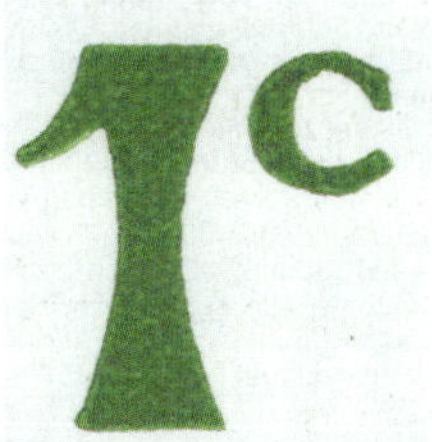

Missing top serif on "c" (R. 2/4)

(Typo D.L.R.)

1934 (2 Jan)–**47**. Wmk Mult Script CA. P 14.

D1	D **1**	½d. green (10.2.35)	1·25	8·50
D2		1d. black	1·25	1·25
		a. Bisected (½d.) (on cover)	†	£1700
D3		3d. carmine (11.3.47)	20·00	21·00
D1/3 *Set of* 3			20·00	28·00
D1s/3s Perf "Specimen" *Set of* 3			90·00	

The bisected 1d. was officially authorised for use between March 1934 and February 1935. Some specimens had the value "½d." written across the half stamp in red or black ink (*Price on cover* £2250).

(Typo D.L.R.)

1950 (8 Dec)–**53**. *Values in cents.* Wmk Mult Script CA. *Ordinary paper.* P 14.

D4	D **1**	1c. green	3·75	30·00
		a. Chalk-surfaced paper. *Deep green* (29.11.51)	30	3·00
		ab. Error. Crown missing, W **9a**	£650	
		ac. Error. St. Edward's Crown, W **9b**	£325	
D5		2c. black	7·00	16·00
		a. Chalk-surfaced paper (20.1.53)	1·00	6·50
		ac. Error. St. Edward's Crown, W **9b**	£600	
D6		6c. carmine	16·00	17·00
		a. Chalk-surfaced paper (20.1.53)	1·00	8·50
		ab. Error. Crown missing, W **9a**	£300	
		ac. Error. St. Edward's Crown, W **9b**	£180	
D4/6 *Set of* 3			24·00	55·00
D4a/6a *Set of* 3			2·10	16·00

The 1c. has no dot below "c".

1965 (3 Aug)–**68**. *As Nos.* D4/6 *but wmk* w **12** *(upright). Chalk-surfaced paper.*

D7	D **1**	1c. deep green	30	4·00
		a. Missing top serif on "C" (R. 2/4)	6·50	
		b. Green	2·00	6·50
		c. Centre inverted	£16000	
D8		2c. black	30	5·00
D9		6c. carmine	50	7·00
		a. Carmine-red (14.5.68)	1·40	12·00
D7/9 *Set of* 3			1·00	13·50

Barbuda (*see after* Antigua)

Basutoland

Stamps of CAPE OF GOOD HOPE were used in Basutoland from about 1876, initially cancelled by upright oval with framed number type postmarks of that colony. Cancellation numbers known to have been used in Basutoland are 133 (Quthing), 156 (Mafeteng), 210 (Mohaleshoek), 277 (Morija), 281 (Maseru), 317 (Thlotse Heights) and 688 (Teyateyaneng).

From 1910 until 1933 the stamps of SOUTH AFRICA were in use. Stamps of the Union provinces are also known used in Basutoland during the early years of this period and can also be found cancelled-to-order during 1932–33.

The following post offices and postal agencies existed in Basutoland before December 1933. Stamps of Cape of Good Hope or South Africa with recognisable postmarks from them are worth a premium. For a few of the smaller offices or agencies there are, as yet, no actual examples recorded. Dates given are those generally accepted as the year in which the office was first opened.

Bokong (1931)	Motsekuoa (1915)
Butha Buthe (1907)	Mount Morosi (1918)
Jonathan's (1927)	Mphotos (1914)
Khabos (1927)	Peka (1908)
Khetisas (1930)	Phamong (1932)
Khukhune (1933)	Pitseng (1921)
Kolonyama (1914)	Qachasnek (1895)
Kueneng (1914)	Qalo (1923?)
Leribe (1890)	Quthing (1882)
Mafeteng (1874)	Rankakalas (1933)
Majara (1912)	Roma Mission (1913)
Makhoa (1932)	Sebapala (1930)
Makoalis (1927)	Seforong (1924)
Mamathes (1919)	Sehlabathebe (1921)
Mapoteng (1925)	Sekake (1931)
Marakabeis (1932)	Teyateyaneng (1886)
Maseru (1872)	Thaba Bosigo (1913)
Maseru Rail (1915?)	Thabana Morena (1922)
Mashai (1929)	Thabaneng (1914)
Matsaile (1930)	Thaba Tseka (1929)
Mekading (1914)	Thlotse Heights (1872)
Mofokas (1915)	Tsepo (1923)
Mohaleshoek (1873)	Tsoelike (1927)
Mokhotlong (1921)	Tsoloane (1918)
Morija (1884)	

For further details of the postal history of Basutoland see *The Cancellations and Postal Markings of Basutoland/Lesotho* by A. H. Scott, published by Collectors Mail Auctions (Pty) Ltd, Cape Town, from which the above has been, with permission, extracted.

PRICES FOR STAMPS ON COVER TO 1945

Nos. 1/19	*from* × 5
Nos. 11/14	*from* × 6
Nos. 15/17	*from* × 10
Nos. 18/28	*from* × 6
Nos. 29/31	*from* × 10
Nos. O1/4	*from* × 4
Nos. D1/2	*from* × 25

CROWN COLONY

1 King George V, Nile Crocodile and Mountains

(Recess Waterlow)

1933 (1 Dec). Wmk Mult Script CA. P 12½.

1	1	½d. emerald	1·00	1·75
2		1d. scarlet	75	1·25
3		2d. bright purple	1·00	80
4		3d. bright blue	75	1·25
5		4d. grey	2·00	7·00
6		6d. orange-yellow	2·25	1·75
7		1s. red-orange	2·25	4·50
8		2s.6d. sepia	25·00	48·00
9		5s. violet	50·00	75·00
10		10s. olive-green	£150	£160
1/10 *Set of* 10			£200	£275
1s/10s Perf "Specimen" *Set of* 10			£300	

1935 (4 May). *Silver Jubilee. As Nos. 91/4 of Antigua.* P 13½×14.

11	1d. deep blue and carmine	55	2·25
	f. Diagonal line by turret	£110	£160
12	2d. ultramarine and grey	65	2·25
	f. Diagonal line by turret	£110	£170
	g. Dot to left of chapel	£190	£250
13	3d. brown and deep blue	3·75	5·50
	g. Dot to left of chapel	£200	
	h. Dot by flagstaff	£250	
	i. Dash by turret	£275	
14	6d. slate and purple	3·75	5·50
	g. Dot to left of chapel	£300	
	h. Dot by flagstaff	£275	£325
	i. Dash by turret	£300	
11/14 *Set of* 4		8·00	14·00
11s/14s Perf "Specimen" *Set of* 4		£120	

For illustrations of plate varieties see Omnibus section following Zanzibar.

1937 (12 May). *Coronation. As Nos. 95/7 of Antigua, but printed by D.L.R.* P 14.

15	1d. scarlet	35	1·25
16	2d. bright purple	50	1·25
17	3d. bright blue	60	1·25
15/17 *Set of* 3		1·25	3·25
15s/17s Perf "Specimen" *Set of* 3		85·00	

2 King George VI, Nile Crocodile and Mountains

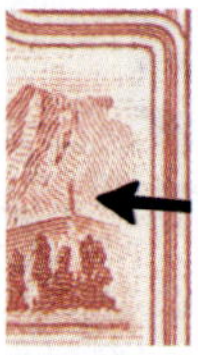

Tower flaw (R. 2/4)

(Recess Waterlow)

1938 (1 Apr). Wmk Mult Script CA. P 12½.

18	2	½d. green	30	1·25
19		1d. scarlet	50	70
		a. Tower flaw	£150	£170
20		1½d. light blue	40	50
21		2d. bright purple	30	60
22		3d. bright blue	30	1·25
23		4d. grey	1·50	3·50
24		6d. orange-yellow	1·50	1·50
25		1s. red-orange	1·50	1·00
26		2s.6d. sepia	13·00	8·50
27		5s. violet	32·00	9·50
28		10s. olive-green	32·00	17·00
18/28 *Set of* 11			75·00	40·00
18s/28s Perf "Specimen" *Set of* 11			£275	

Basutoland
(3)

1945 (3 Dec). *Victory. Stamps of South Africa, optd with T* **3**, *inscr alternately in English and Afrikaans.*

			Un pair	*Used pair*	*Used single*
29	**55**	1d. brown and carmine	50	80	10
30	**56**	2d. slate-blue and violet	50	60	10
31	**57**	3d. deep blue and blue	50	85	15
29/31 *Set of* 3			1·40	2·00	30

4 King George VI

5 King George VI and Queen Elizabeth

6 Queen Elizabeth II as Princess, and Princess Margaret

7 The Royal Family

(Recess Waterlow)

1947 (17 Feb). *Royal Visit.* Wmk Mult Script CA. P 12½.

32	4	1d. scarlet	10	10
33	5	2d. green	10	10
34	6	3d. ultramarine	10	10
35	7	1s. mauve	15	10
32/5 *Set of* 4			40	30
32s/5s Perf "Specimen" *Set of* 4			95·00	

1948 (1 Dec). *Royal Silver Wedding. As Nos. 112/13 of Antigua.*

36	1½d. ultramarine	20	10
37	10s. grey-olive	38·00	38·00

1949 (10 Oct). *75th Anniv of Universal Postal Union. As Nos. 114/17 of Antigua.*

38	1½d. blue	20	1·50
39	3d. deep blue	2·00	2·00
40	6d. orange	1·00	4·00
41	1s. red-brown	50	1·25
38/41 *Set of* 4		3·25	8·00

1953 (3 June). *Coronation. As No. 153 of Jamaica.*

42	2d. black and reddish purple	40	40

8 Qiloane

9 Orange River

10 Mosuto horseman

11 Basuto household

12 Maletsunyane Falls

13 Herd-boy playing lesiba

14 Pastoral scene

15 Aeroplane over Lancers Gap

16 Old Fort, Leribe

17 Mission Cave House

18 Mohair (Shearing Angora Goats)

(Recess D.L.R.)

1954 (18 Oct)–**58**. T **8/18** Wmk Mult Script CA. P 11½ (10s.) or 13½ (others).

43	**8**	½d. grey-black and sepia	20	10
44	**9**	1d. grey-black and bluish green	20	10
45	**10**	2d. deep bright blue and orange	60	10
46	**11**	3d. yellow-green and deep rose-red	80	30
		a. Yellow-green and rose (27.11.58)	9·00	1·75
47	**12**	4½d. indigo and deep ultramarine	70	15
48	**13**	6d. chestnut and deep grey-green	1·25	15
49	**14**	1s. bronze-green and purple	1·25	30
50	**15**	1s.3d. brown and turquoise-green	22·00	6·50
51	**16**	2s.6d. deep ultramarine and crimson	22·00	8·50
		a. Brt ultram & crimson-lake (27.11.58)	65·00	19·00
52	**17**	5s. black and carmine-red	6·00	8·50
53	**18**	10s. black and maroon	27·00	23·00
43/53 *Set of* 11			75·00	42·00

½d. ▬
(19)

20 "Chief Moshoeshoe I" (engraving by Delangle)

1959 (1 Aug). *No. 45 surch with T* **19**, *by South African Govt Ptr, Pretoria.*

54	½d. on 2d. deep bright blue and orange	10	15

(Des from drawings by James Walton. Recess Waterlow)

1959 (15 Dec). *Basutoland National Council. T* **20** *and similar vert designs.* W w **12**. P 13×13½.

55	3d. black and yellow-olive	40	10
56	1s. carmine and yellow-green	40	20
57	1s.3d. ultramarine and red-orange	60	45
55/7 *Set of* 3		1·25	65

Designs:—1s. Council house; 1s.3d. Mosuto horseman.

(New Currency. 100 cents = 1 rand)

½c. (23) 1c. (24) 2c (25)

2½c (I) 2½c (II) 3½c (I) 3½c (II)

5c (I) 5c (II) 10c (I) 10c (II)

12½c (I) 12½c (II) 50c (I) 50c (II)

25c (I) 25c (II) 25c (III)

R1 (I) R1 (II) R1 (III)

1961 (14 Feb). *Nos. 43/53 surch with T* **23** *(½c.),* **24** *(1c.) or as T* **25** *(others) by South African Govt Printer, Pretoria.*

58		½c. on ½d. grey-black and sepia	10	10
		a. Surch double	£475	
59		1c. on 1d. grey-black and bluish green	10	10
60		2c. on 2d. deep bright blue and orange	10	10
		a. Surch inverted	£140	
61		2½c. on 3d. yellow-green and rose (Type I)	10	10
		a. Type II	10	10
		b. Type II inverted	†	£1600
62		3½c. on 4½d. indigo & deep ultram (Type I)	10	10
		a. Type II	1·50	5·00
63		5c. on 6d. chestnut & dp grey-green (Type I)	10	10
		a. Type II	15	10
64		10c. on 1s. bronze-green and purple (Type I)	10	10
		a. Type II	£100	£120
65		12½c. on 1s.3d. brown & turq-green (Type I)	4·50	1·25
		a. Type II	3·75	1·25
66		25c. on 2s.6d. bright ultramarine and crimson-lake (Type I)	30	60
		a. Type II	32·00	9·50
		b. Type III	30	75
67		50c. on 5s. black and carmine-red (Type I)	1·75	1·40
		a. Type II	1·75	2·50
68		1r. on 10s. black and maroon (Type I)	32·00	18·00
		a. Type II	17·00	40·00
		b. Type III	17·00	18·00
58/68b *Set of 11*			21·00	19·00

There were two printings of the 2½c. Type II, differing in the position of the surcharge on the stamps.

Examples of the 2c. surcharge are known in a fount similar to Type **24** (*Price* £160 *unused*).

26 Basuto Household

(Recess D.L.R.)

1961–63. *As Nos. 43/53 but values in cents as in T* **26**. Wmk Mult Script CA. P 13½ or 11½ (1r.).

69		½c. grey-black and sepia (as ½d.) (25.9.62)	20	20
		a. Imperf (pair)	£300	
70		1c. grey-blk & bluish grn (as 1d.) (25.9.62)	20	40
71		2c. dp but blue & orange (as 2d.) (25.9.62)	1·25	1·40
72		2½c. yellow-green & deep rose-red (14.2.61)	1·00	30
		a. Pale yellow-green & rose-red (22.5.62)	13·00	1·50
73		3½c. indigo & dp ultram (as 4½d.) (25.9.62)	30	1·50
74		5c. chestnut and deep grey-green (as 6d.) (10.8.62)	60	75
75		10c. bronze-green & pur (as 1s.) (22.10.62)	30	40
76		12½c. brown and turquoise-green (as 1s.3d.) (17.12.62)	17·00	8·00
77		25c. deep ultramarine and crimson (as 2s.6d.) (25.9.62)	6·50	6·50
78		50c. black & carmine-red (as 5s.) (22.10.62)	18·00	16·00
79		1r. black and maroon (as 10s.) (4.2.63)	45·00	17·00
		a. Black and light maroon (16.12.63)	65·00	25·00
69/79 *Set of 11*			80·00	48·00

1963 (4 June). *Freedom from Hunger. As No. 146 of Antigua.*

80		12½c. reddish violet	40	15

1963 (2 Sept). *Red Cross Centenary. As Nos. 147/8 of Antigua.*

81		2½c. red and black	20	10
82		12½c. red and blue	80	60

1964. *As Nos. 70, 72, 74, 76 and 78, but* W w **12**.

84		1c. grey-black and bluish green (11.8.64)	10	20
86		2½c. pale yellow-green and rose-red (10.3.64)	15	25
88		5c. chestnut and deep grey-green (10.11.64)	30	50
90		12½c. brown and turquoise-green (10.11.64)	5·00	1·50
92		50c. black and carmine-red (29.9.64)	7·25	11·00
84/92 *Set of 5*			11·50	12·00

SELF-GOVERNMENT

28 Mosotho Woman and Child

29 Maseru Border Post

1965 (10 May). *New Constitution. T* **28/9** *and similar horiz designs. Multicoloured.* W w **12**. P 14×13½.

94		2½c. Type **28**	20	10
		w. Wmk inverted	26·00	15·00
95*a*		3½c. Type **29**	25	20
96		5c. Mountain scene	25	20
		w. Wmk inverted	26·00	15·00
97		12½c. Legislative Buildings	45	70
94/7 *Set of 4*			1·10	1·10

1965 (17 May). *I.T.U. Centenary. As Nos. 166/7 of Antigua.*

98		1c. orange-red and bright purple	15	10
99		20c. light blue and orange-brown	50	30

1965 (25 Oct). *International Co-operation Year. As Nos. 168/9 of Antigua.*

100		½c. reddish purple & turquoise-green	10	10
101		12½c. deep bluish green and lavender	45	35

1966 (24 Jan). *Churchill Commemoration. Printed in black, cerise, gold and background in colours stated. As Nos. 170/3 of Antigua.*

102		1c. new blue	15	70
103		2½c. deep green	50	10
104		10c. brown	75	30
105		22½c. bluish violet	1·25	90
102/5 *Set of 4*			2·40	1·75

OFFICIAL STAMPS

OFFICIAL
(O 1)

1934 (Feb). *Nos. 1/3 and 6 optd with Type* O **1**, *by Govt printer, Pretoria.*

O1	**1**	½d. emerald	£11000	£7000
O2		1d. scarlet	£2750	£2500
O3		2d. bright purple	£3000	£850
O4		6d. orange-yellow	£11000	£4750
O1/4 *Set of 4*			£25000	£13500

Collectors are advised to buy these stamps only from reliable sources. They were not sold to the public.

300 of each value were supplied in January 1934 for use by the Secretariat in Maseru. Limited usage is recorded between 28 Feb 1934 and 8 June 1934. The issue was then withdrawn and the remainders destroyed. Only the following numbers appear to have been issued: ½d. 24, 1d. 34, 2d. 54, 6d. 27, from which a maximum of ten mint sets exist.

POSTAGE DUE STAMPS

D 1

2d Normal

2d Large "d." (R. 9/6, 10/6)

(Typo D.L.R.)

1933 (1 Dec)–**52**. *Ordinary paper.* Wmk Mult Script CA. P 14.

D1	D **1**	1d. carmine	1·75	10·00
		a. Scarlet (1938)	42·00	50·00
		b. Chalk-surfaced paper. *Deep carmine* (24.10.51)	1·50	4·00
		ba. Error. Crown missing, W **9a**	£225	
		bb. Error. St. Edward's Crown, W **9b**	£100	
D2		2d. violet	7·50	19·00
		a. Chalk-surfaced paper (6.11.52)	30	17·00
		ab. Error. Crown missing, W **9a**	£250	
		ac. Error. St. Edward's Crown, W **9b**	£110	
		ad. Large "d"	6·50	
D1s/2s Perf "Specimen" *Set of 2*			50·00	

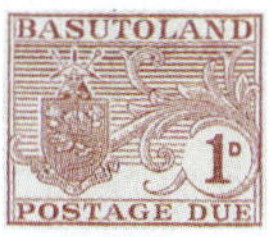

D 2

(Typo D.L.R.)

1956 (1 Dec). Wmk Mult Script CA. P 14.

D3	D **2**	1d. carmine	30	3·00
D4		2d. deep reddish violet	30	6·00

5c (I) 5c (II)

1961 (14 Feb). *Surch as T* **24**, *but without stop.*

D5	D **2**	1c. on 1d. carmine	10	35
D6		1c. on 2d. deep reddish violet	10	1·25
D7		5c. on 2d. deep reddish violet (Type I)	15	45
		a. Type II	12·00	45·00
D5/7 *Set of 3*			30	1·90

1961 (1 June). *No. D2a surch as T* **24** *(without stop).*

D8	D **1**	5c. on 2d. violet	1·00	6·50
		a. Error. Missing Crown, W9a	£1400	
		b. Error. St. Edward's Crown, W9b	£275	
		c. Large "d"	16·00	

1964. *As No. D3/4 but values in cents and* W w **12** *(sideways on 1c.).*

D9	D **2**	1c. carmine	3·00	19·00
D10		5c. deep reddish violet	3·00	19·00

POSTAL FISCAL

In July 1961 the 10s. stamp, T **9**, surcharged "R1 Revenue", was used for postage at one post office at least, but such usage was officially unauthorised.

Basutoland attained independence on 4 October 1966 as the Kingdom of Lesotho.

Batum

Batum, the outlet port on the Black Sea for the Russian Transcaucasian oilfields, was occupied by the Turks on 15 April 1918.

Under the terms of the armistice signed at Mudros on 30 October 1918 the Turks were to withdraw and be replaced by an Allied occupation of Batum, the Baku oilfields and the connecting Transcaucasia Railway. British forces arrived off Batum in early December and the oblast, or district, was declared a British military governorship on 25 December 1918. The Turkish withdrawal was complete five days later.

The provision of a civilian postal service was initially the responsibility of the Batum Town Council. Some form of mail service was in operation by February 1919 with the postage prepaid in cash. Letters are known showing a framed oblong handstamp, in Russian, to this effect. The Town Council was responsible for the production of the first issue, Nos. 1/6, but shortly after these stamps were placed on sale a strike by Council employees against the British military governor led to the postal service being placed under British Army control.

SURCHARGES. Types **2** and **4/8** were all applied by handstamp. Most values from No. 19 to 40 are known showing the surcharge inverted, surcharge double or in pairs with surcharge *tête-bêche*. Inverted surcharges are worth from 2×normal, *tête-bêche* pairs from four times the price of a single stamp.

FORGERIES. Collectors are warned that all the stamps, overprints and surcharges of Batum have been extensively forged. Even the Type 1 stamps should be purchased with caution, and rarities should not be acquired without a reliable guarantee.

BRITISH OCCUPATION

(Currency. 100 kopeks = 1 rouble)

PRICES FOR STAMPS ON COVER

Nos. 1/6	*from* × 50
Nos. 7/10	*from* × 15
Nos. 11/28	*from* × 50
Nos. 19/20	*from* × 15
Nos. 21/44	—
Nos. 45/53	*from* × 100

1 Aloe Tree

БАТУМ. ОБ.

Руб 10 Руб
(**2**)

1919 (4 Apr). *Litho.* Imperf.

1	**1**	5k. green	6·50	15·00
2		10k. ultramarine	6·50	15·00
3		50k. yellow	3·75	6·00
4		1r. chocolate	5·50	6·00
5		3r. violet	9·50	16·00
6		5r. brown	10·00	28·00
1/6 *Set of 6*			38·00	80·00

Nos. 1/6 were printed in sheets of 198 (18×11).

1919 (13 Apr). *Russian stamps (Arms types) handstamped with T* **2**.

7		10r. on 1k. orange (imperf)	60·00	70·00
8		10r. on 3k. carmine-red (imperf)	24·00	29·00
9		10r. on 5k. brown-lilac (perf)	£375	£400
10		10r. on 10 on 7k. deep blue (perf)	£425	£450

A similar handstamped surcharge, showing the capital letters without serifs, is bogus.

BRITISH OCCUPATION
(**3**)

1919 (10 Nov). *Colours changed and new values. Optd with T* **3**.

11	**1**	5k. yellow-green	22·00	17·00
12		10k. bright blue	15·00	17·00
13		25k. orange-yellow	22·00	17·00
14		1r. pale blue	5·50	17·00
15		2r. pink	1·00	6·00
16		3r. bright violet	1·00	6·00
17		5r. brown	1·25	6·00
		a. "CCUPATION" (R. 5/1)	£400	
18		7r. brownish red	4·50	9·00

11/18	*Set of* 8	65·00	85·00

Nos. 11/18 were printed in sheets of 432 (18×24).

(4)

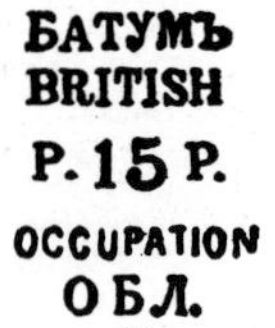

(5)

1919 (27 Nov)–**20**. *Russian stamps (Arms types) handstamped with T* **4** *or* **5**. Imperf.

19	10r. on 3k. carmine-red	20·00	24·00
20	15r. on 1k. orange	70·00	75·00
	a. Red surch	55·00	60·00
	b. Violet surch (10.3.20)	70·00	85·00

Nos. 20a/b have the handstamp in soluble ink.

1920 (12 Jan). *Russian stamps (Arms types) handstamped as T* **4**.

(a) Imperf.

21	50r. on 1k. orange	£475	£550
22	50r. on 2k. yellow-green (R.)	£650	£800

(b) Perf.

23	50r. on 2k. yellow-green	£650	£700
24	50r. on 3k. carmine-red	£1200	£1300
25	50r. on 4k. red	£800	£850
26	50r. on 5k. brown-lilac	£425	£500
27	50r. on 10k. deep blue (R.)	£1800	£1900
28	50r. on 15k. blue and red-brown	£650	£750

(6)

1920 (30 Jan–21 Feb). *Russian stamps (Arms types) handstamped as T* **6**.

(a) Perf.

29	25r. on 5k. brown-lilac (21 Feb)	42·00	55·00
	a. Blue surch	42·00	55·00
30	25r. on 10 on 7k. blue (21 Feb)	£120	£140
	a. Blue surch	70·00	80·00
31	25r. on 20 on 14k. dp carmine & bl (21 Feb)	75·00	90·00
	a. Blue surch	85·00	£100
32	25r. on 25k. deep violet & lt green (21 Feb)	£150	£160
	a. Blue surch	95·00	£120
33	25r. on 50k. green and copper-red (21 Feb)	90·00	£100
	a. Blue surch	75·00	90·00
34	50r. on 2k. yellow-green	£110	£140
35	50r. on 3k. carmine-red	£110	£140
36	50r. on 4k. red	£100	£120
37	50r. on 5k. brown-lilac	80·00	95·00

(b) Imperf.

38	50r. on 2k. yellow-green	£375	£475
39	50r. on 3k. carmine-red	£475	£600
40	50r. on 5k. brown-lilac	£1400	£1500

1920 (10 Mar). *Romanov issue, as T* **25** *of Russia, handstamped with T* **6**.

41	50r. on 4k. rose-carmine (B.)	70·00	90·00

(7)

(8)

1920 (1 Apr). *Nos. 3, 11 and 13 handstamped with T* **7** *(Nos. 42/3) or* **8** *(No. 44).*

42	25r. on 5k. yellow-green	38·00	40·00
	a. Blue surch	55·00	60·00
43	25r. on 25k. orange-yellow	28·00	30·00
	a. Blue surch	£130	£140
44	50r. on 50k. yellow	22·00	26·00
	a. "50" cut	17·00	18·00
	b. Blue surch	£110	£110
	ba. "50"cut	£200	£200

Nos. 44a and 44ba show the figures broken by intentional file cuts applied as a protection against forgery. The "5" is cut at the base and on the right side of the loop. The "0" is chipped at top and foot, and has both vertical lines severed.

1920 (19 June). *Colours changed and new values. Optd with T* **3**. Imperf.

45	**1**	1r. chestnut	2·00	11·00
		a. "BPITISH"	75·00	
46		2r. pale blue	2·00	11·00
		a. "BPITISH"	85·00	
47		3r. pink	2·00	11·00
		a. "BPITISH"	85·00	
48		5r. black-brown	2·00	11·00
		a. "BPITISH"	85·00	
49		7r. yellow	2·00	11·00
		a. "BPITISH"	85·00	
50		10r. myrtle-green	2·00	11·00
		a. "BPITISH"	85·00	
51		15r. violet	2·50	15·00
		a. "BPITISH"	£180	
52		25r. scarlet	2·25	14·00
		a. "BPITISH"	£160	
53		50r. deep blue	2·50	17·00
		a. "BPITISH"	£300	
45/53		*Set of* 9	17·00	£100

Nos. 45/53 were printed in sheets of 308 (22×14). The "BPITISH" error occurs on R. 1/19 of the overprint.

POSTCARD STAMPS

When Nos. 7/10 were issued on 13 April 1919 a similar 35k. surcharge was applied to stocks of various Russian postcards held by the post office. The majority of these had stamp impressions printed directly on to the card, but there were also a few cards, originally intended for overseas mail, on which Russia 4k. stamps had been affixed.

PRICES. Those in the left-hand column are for unused examples on complete postcard; those on the right for used examples off card. Examples used on postcard are worth more.

1919 (13 Apr). *Russian stamps handstamped as T* **2**.

P1	35k. on 4k. red (Arms type)	£4750	£5500
P2	35k. on 4k. carmine-red (Romanov issue)	£11000	£11000

Batum was handed over to the National Republic of Georgia on 7 July 1920.

Bechuanaland

Before the 1880s the only Europeans in the area which became Bechuanaland were scattered hunters and traders, together with the missionaries who were established at Kuruman as early as 1816.

Tribal conflicts in the early years of the decade led to the intervention of Boers from the Transvaal who established the independent republics of Goshen and Stellaland.

STELLALAND

The Boer republic of Stellaland was proclaimed towards the end of 1882. A postal service was organised from the capital, Vryburg, and stamps were ordered from a firm in Cape Town. These were only valid within the republic. Until June 1885 mail to other parts of South Africa was sent through Christiana, in the Transvaal, and was franked with both Stellaland and Transvaal stamps.

No date stamps or obliterators were used by the Stellaland Post Office. Stamps were pen-cancelled with the initials of a postal official and the date.

PRICES FOR STAMPS ON COVER

The issues of Stellaland are very rare on cover.

1 Arms of the Republic

(Litho by Van der Sandt, de Villiers & Co., Cape Town)

1884 (29 Feb). P 12.

1	**1**	1d. red	£180	£325
		a. Imperf between (horiz pair)	£3750	
		b. Imperf between (vert pair)	£4000	
2		3d. orange	23·00	£325
		a. Imperf between (horiz pair)	£750	
		b. Imperf between (vert pair)	£1700	
		c. Imperf vert (horiz pair)	£1100	
3		4d. olive-grey	21·00	£350
		a. Imperf between (horiz pair)	£650	
		b. Imperf between (vert pair)	£1800	
4		6d. lilac-mauve	23·00	£350
		a. Imperf between (horiz pair)	£1300	
		b. Imperf between (vert pair)	£1500	
5		1s. green	60·00	£650

In 1884 the British Government, following appeals from local chiefs for protection, decided to annex both Goshen and Stellaland. A force under Sir Charles Warren from the Cape reached Vryburg on 7 February 1885 and continued to Mafeking, the principal town of Goshen.

On 30 September 1885 Stellaland and other territory to the south of the Molopo River was constituted the Crown Colony of British Bechuanaland. A protectorate was also proclaimed over a vast tract of land to the north of the Molopo.

Stellaland stamps continued to be used until 2 December 1885 with external mail, franked with Stellaland and Cape of Good Hope stamps, postmarked at Barkly West and Kimberley in Griqualand West.

1885 (Oct). *Handstamped "Twee" sideways in violet-lake.*

6	**1**	2d. on 4d. olive-grey	£3500	

On 2 December 1885 Cape of Good Hope stamps overprinted "British Bechuanaland" were placed on sale at the Vryburg post office.

BRITISH BECHUANALAND

CROWN COLONY

PRICES FOR STAMPS ON COVER

Nos. 1/8	*from* × 12
No. 9	*from* × 80
Nos. 10/21	*from* × 8
Nos. 22/8	*from* × 10
No. 29	*from* × 10
No. 30	*from* × 10
Nos. 31/2	*from* × 12
Nos. 33/7	*from* × 20
Nos. 38/9	*from* × 25

British
Bechuanaland
(1)

BRITISH
BECHUANALAND
(2)

1885 (3 Dec)–**87**. *Stamps of Cape of Good Hope ("Hope" seated) optd with T* **1**, *by W. A. Richards & Sons, Cape Town.*

(*a*) Wmk Crown CC (No. 3) or Crown CA (others).

1		½d. grey-black (No. 40a) (R.)	19·00	26·00
		a. Opt in lake	£3750	£4500
		b. Opt double (Lake+Black)	£750	
2		3d. pale claret (No. 43)	35·00	50·00
		a. No dot to 1st "i" of "British"	£550	
3		4d. dull blue (No. 30) (2.6.87)	65·00	75·00

(*b*) Wmk Anchor (Cape of Good Hope. Type **13**).

4		½d. grey-black (No. 48*a*) (24.12.86)	8·50	16·00
		a. Error. "ritish"	£2250	
		b. Opt double	£3250	
5		1d. rose-red (No. 49)	16·00	9·00
		a. Error. "ritish"	£3750	£2250
		b. No dot to 1st "i" of "British"	£250	£225
		c. Opt double	†	£2000
6		2d. pale bistre (No. 50)	35·00	8·00
		a. Error. "ritish"	£6500	£3750
		b. No dot to 1st "i" of "British"	£550	£225
		c. Opt double	†	£1800
7		6d. reddish purple (No. 52)	£120	38·00
		a. No dot to 1st "i" of "British"	£1500	£650
8		1s. green (No. 53) (26.11.86)	£300	£170
		a. Error. "ritish"	£20000	£13000

Nos. 1/8 were overprinted from settings of 120. The missing "B" errors are believed to have occurred on one position for one of these settings only. The 'No dot to 1st "i"' variety occurs on R. 10/3 of the left pane.

Overprints with stop after "Bechuanaland" are forged.

1888 (19 Jan). *No. 197 of Great Britain optd with T* **2**, *by D.L.R.*

9		½d. vermilion	1·25	1·25
		a. Opt double	£2250	
		s. Handstamped "Specimen"	85·00	

3

4

5

(Typo D.L.R.)

1888 (19 Jan).

(*a*) Wmk Orb (Great Britain Type **48**). P 14.

10	**3**	1d. lilac and black	15·00	2·00
11		2d. lilac and black	75·00	1·75
		a. Pale dull lilac and black	60·00	23·00
12		3d. lilac and black	4·00	5·50
		a. Pale reddish lilac and black	65·00	22·00
13		4d. lilac and black	50·00	2·25
14		6d. lilac and black	60·00	2·50

(*b*) Wmk Script "V R" (sideways, reading up). P 13½.

15	**4**	1s. green and black	29·00	7·00
16		2s. green and black	50·00	42·00
17		2s.6d. green and black	65·00	65·00
18		5s. green and black	90·00	£150
19		10s. green and black	£180	£350

(*c*) Two Orbs (sideways). P 14×13½.

20	**5**	£1 lilac and black	£800	£750
21		£5 lilac and black	£3250	£1500
10s/21s H/S "Specimen" *Set of* 12			£900	

Nos. 10/21 were produced by overprinting a series of "Unappropriated Die" designs originally produced by the Board of Inland Revenue for use as Great Britain fiscal stamps.

Several values are known on blued paper. No. 11*a* is the first printing of the 2d. (on safety paper?) and has a faded appearance.

When purchasing Nos. 20/21 in used condition beware of copies with fiscal cancellations cleaned off and bearing forged postmarks.

For No. 15 surcharged "£5" see No. F2.

1d.
(6)

1s.
(7)

Curved foot to "2"

1888 (7 Aug). *Nos. 10/11 and 13/15 surch as T* **6** *or* **7**, *by P. Townshend & Co., Vryburg.*

22	**3**	1d. on 1d. lilac and black	7·50	6·50
23		2d. on 2d. lilac and black (R.)	29·00	3·00
		a. Pale dull lilac and black (No. 11a)	90·00	48·00
		b. Curved foot to "2"	£300	£150
		c. Surch in green	†	£4000
25		4d. on 4d. lilac and black (R.)	£350	£450
26		6d. on 6d. lilac and black	£130	12·00
		a. Surch in blue	†	£13000
28	**4**	1s. on 1s. green and black	£180	85·00

Nos. 23c and 26a are from two sheets of surcharge trials subsequently put into stock and used at Vryburg (2d.) or Mafeking (6d.) during 1888–89.

It should be noted that, in addition to its curved foot, the "2" on No. 23b is distinctly shorter than the "d".

One
Half-
Penny
(8)

1888 (7 Dec). *No. 12a surch with T* **8**, *by P. Townshend & Co, Vryburg.*

29	**3**	½d. on 3d. pale reddish lilac and black	£180	£200
		a. Broken "f" in "Half"	£12000	

No. 29 was produced from a setting of 60 (12×5).

No. 29a shows the letter "f" almost completely missing and occurs on R. 5/11 of the setting. Five examples are known, one being in the Royal Collection.

Errors of spelling on this surcharge are bogus.

British
Bechuanaland.
(9)

British
Bechuanaland.
(10)

BRITISH
BECHUANALAND
(11)

1889 (Jan). *No. 48a of Cape of Good Hope* (wmk Anchor) *optd with T* **9**, *by P. Townshend & Co, Vryburg.*

30		½d. grey-black (G.)	3·25	27·00
		a. Opt "Bechuanaland British"	£2500	
		ab. "British" omitted	£5500	
		b. Opt double, one inverted, inverted opt "Bechuanaland British"	£2500	
		ba. Opt double, one inverted, inverted "British" omitted	£5500	
		c. Opt double, one vertical	£850	
		ca. *Se-tenant* with stamp without opt.	£7000	

No. 30 was produced using a setting of 30 (6×5).

The overprint was misplaced upwards on at least one pane, giving the overprint "Bechuanaland British" (No. 30a) on rows 1 to 4 and "British" omitted on row 5 (No. 30ab). "British" was also omitted on R. 5/1 of the setting on some sheets only.

On one pane on which the overprint was applied double, one inverted, the inverted overprint was misplaced downwards, giving No. 30ba on rows 7 to 10 and "British" omitted (No. 30bb) on row 6.

n
Normal "n"

u
Inverted "u"

1891 (Nov). *Nos. 49/50 of Cape of Good Hope* (wmk Anchor), *optd with T* **10**, *reading upwards.*

31		1d. rose-red	10·00	10·00
		a. Horiz pair, one without opt		
		b. "British" omitted	–	£2500
		c. "Bechuanaland" omitted	£2500	
		d. Inverted "u" for 2nd "n"	£170	£170
32		2d. pale bistre	3·25	2·25
		a. No stop after "Bechuanaland"	£275	£325
		b. Inverted "u" for 2nd "n"	£250	£250
31s/2s H/S "Specimen" *Set of* 2			£130	

The overprint on Nos. 31 and 32 was of 120 impressions in two panes of 60 (6×10). That on No. 32 was applied both by a stereo plate and by a forme made up from loose type. No. 31 was overprinted only with the latter. No. 32a is from the stereo overprinting (left pane, R. 3/3), 31d and 32b are from the typeset overprinting (left pane, R. 10/4).

See also Nos. 38 and 39.

1891 (1 Dec)–**1904**. *Nos. 172, 200, 205, 208 and 211 of Great Britain optd with T* **11**, *by D.L.R.*

33		1d. lilac	6·00	1·50
34		2d. grey-green and carmine	14·00	4·00
35		4d. green and purple-brown	2·50	60
		a. Bisected (2d.) (on cover) (11.99)	†	£2500
36		6d. purple/*rose-red*	3·75	2·00
37		1s. dull green (7.94)	13·00	16·00
		a. Bisected (6d.) (on cover) (12.04)	†	–
33/7 *Set of* 5			35·00	22·00
33s/6s H/S "Specimen" *Set of* 4			£170	

No. 35a was used at Palapye Station and No. 37a at Kanye, both in the Protectorate.

1893 (Dec)–**95**. *As Nos. 31/2, but T* **10** *reads downwards.*

38		1d. rose-red	2·25	2·25
		a. Pair, one without opt		
		b. "British" omitted	£3500	£3500
		c. Optd "Bechuanaland. British"	£1400	£1500
		d. Inverted "u" for 2nd "n"	£130	£140
		e. No dots to "i" of "British"	£130	£140
		f. "s" omitted	£325	£325
		g. Opt reading up, no dots to "i" of "British"	£3250	
39		2d. pale bistre (12.3.95)	5·00	2·25
		a. Opt double	£1400	£700
		b. "British" omitted	£750	£500
		c. "Bechuanaland" omitted	–	£500
		d. Optd "Bechuanaland. British"	£425	£225
		e. Inverted "u" for 2nd "n"	£190	£140
		f. No dots to "i" of "British"	£190	£140
		g. Opt reading up, no dots to "i" of "British"	£3500	

The same typeset overprint was used for Nos. 38 and 39 as had been employed for Nos. 31 and 32 but applied the other way up; the inverted "u" thus falling on the right pane, R. 1/3. The no dots to "i" variety only occurs on this printing (right pane, R. 1/4). Some sheets of both values were overprinted the wrong way up, resulting in Nos. 38g. and 39g.

No. 38g. developed gradually on right pane R. 10/8. The variety is not known on Nos. 31, 32 or 39.

On 16 November 1895 British Bechuanaland was annexed to the Cape of Good Hope and ceased to have its own stamps, but they remained in use in the Protectorate until superseded in 1897. The Postmaster-General of Cape Colony had assumed control of the Bechuanaland postal service on 1 April 1893 and the Cape, and subsequently the South African, postal authorities continued to be responsible for the postal affairs of the Bechuanaland Protectorate until 1963.

BECHUANALAND PROTECTORATE

PRICES FOR STAMPS ON COVER TO 1945

Nos. 40/51	*from* × 10
Nos. 52/71	*from* × 6
Nos. 72/82	*from* × 5
Nos. 83/98	*from* × 4
Nos. 99/110	*from* × 6
Nos. 111/17	*from* × 10
Nos. 118/28	*from* × 4
Nos. 129/31	*from* × 10
Nos. D1/3	*from* × 50
Nos. D4/6	*from* × 60
No. F1	*from* × 5
No. F2	—
No. F3	*from* × 5

This large area north of the Molopo River was proclaimed a British Protectorate on 30 September 1885 at the request of the native chiefs.

A postal service using runners was inaugurated on 9 August 1888 and Nos. 40 to 55 were issued as a temporary measure with the object of assessing the cost of this service

Protectorate
(12) 15½ mm

(13)

13a Small figure "1" (R. 7/2)

13b Small figure "1" (R. 10/2)

1888 (7 Aug). *No. 9 optd with T* **12** *and Nos. 10/19 surch or optd only as T* **13** *by P. Townshend & Co. Vryburg.*

40 – ½d. vermilion 6·00 38·00
a. "Protectorate" double £350
s. Handstamped "Specimen" 85·00
41 3 1d. on 1d. lilac and black 9·00 15·00
a. Small figure "1" (R. 7/2, 10/2) £425 £500
b. Space between "1" and "d" (R. 10/9) £600
42 2d. on 2d. lilac and black 30·00 17·00
b. Curved foot to "2" £800 £550
43 3d. on 3d. pale reddish lilac and black £140 £190
44 4d. on 4d. lilac and black £400 £425
a. Small figure "4" £4500 £4500
45 6d. on 6d. lilac and black 75·00 48·00
46 4 1s. green and black 95·00 55·00
a. First "o" omitted £6500 £3750
s. Handstamped "Specimen" £110
47 2s. green and black £600 £950
a. First "o" omitted £18000
48 2s.6d. green and black £550 £850
a. First "o" omitted £15000
49 5s. green and black £1200 £2000
a. First "o" omitted £22000
50 10s. green and black £4000 £6000
a. First "o" omitted £30000

Nos. 40/5 were produced from a basic setting of 120 (12×10) on which a faulty first "o" in "Protectorate" occurred on R. 5/12. For Nos. 46/50 the setting was reduced to 84 (12×7) and on many sheets the first "o" on R. 5/12 failed to print.

There are a number of smaller than normal "1"s in the setting, usually identifiable by the upper serif of the "1" which is pointed and slopes sharply downwards at the left. R. 7/2 and 10/2 are quite distinct and are as shown.

The normal space between "1" and "d" measures 1 mm. On No. 41b it is 1.7 mm.

It should be noted that, like No. 23b, the "2" on No. 42b is distinctly shorter than the "d".

See also Nos. 54/5.

1888 (Dec). *No. 25 optd with T* **12** *by P. Townshend & Co., Vryburg.*

51 3 4d. on 4d. lilac and black 85·00 45·00

Bechuanaland

Protectorate

Protectorate.
(14)

Fourpence
(15)

1889 (Jan). *No. 48a of Cape of Good Hope* (wmk Anchor), *optd with T* **14** *by P. Townshend & Co., Vryburg.*

52 ½d. grey-black (G.) 3·50 48·00
a. Opt double £475 £750
ab. Ditto, one reading "Protectorate Bechuanaland" £1100
ac. Ditto, one reading "Bechuanaland" only £2500
b. "Bechuanaland" omitted £1700
c. Optd "Protectorate Bechuanaland" £800 £900

1889 (Mar). *No. 9 surch with T* **15** *by P. Townshend & Co., Vryburg.*

53 4d. on ½d. vermilion 29·00 4·25
a. "rpence" omitted (R. 9/2) † £6000
b. "ourpence" omitted (R. 9/2) £10000
c. Surch (T **15**) inverted † £4000
cb. Ditto. "ourpence" omitted † £16000
s. Handstamped "Specimen" £130

The lines of the surcharge are normally 6 mm apart, but 5 mm and 4.5 mm spacings are known.

Examples of No. 53c are postmarked "679" (Tati).

The surcharge is known printed in green, due to faulty cleaning of the inking roller. All examples known were cancelled at Shoshong. (*Price £1500 used*)

Protectorate
(16) 15 mm

Protectorate
(17)

1890. *No. 9 optd.*

54 16 ½d. vermilion £160 £180
a. Type **16** inverted 75·00 £100
b. Type **16** double £110 £170
c. Type **16** double and inverted £600 £750
d. Optd "Portectorate" inverted £18000
w. Wmk inverted
55 17 ½d. vermilion £200 £400
a. Type **17** double £1500 £1600
b. Optd "Protectorrte"
c. Optd "Protectorrte" double £18000

These were trial printings made in 1888 which were subsequently issued.

In June 1890 the Bechuanaland Protectorate and the Colony of British Bechuanaland came under one postal administration and the stamps of British Bechuanaland were used in the Protectorate until 1897.

BRITISH

BECHUANALAND
(18)

BECHUANALAND PROTECTORATE
(19)

1897. *No. 61 of Cape of Good Hope* (wmk Anchor), *optd as T* **18**.

(a) Lines 13 mm apart, bottom line 16 mm long, by Taylor & Marshall, Cape Town.

56 ½d. yellow-green (July?) 2·50 14·00

(b) Lines 13½ mm apart bottom line 15 mm long, by P. Townshend & Co, Vryburg.

57 ½d. yellow-green (April) 25·00 85·00
a. Opt double, one albino inverted £225

(c) Lines 10½ mm apart, bottom line 15 mm long, by W. A. Richards & Sons, Cape Govt Printers.

58 ½d. yellow-green (July?) 11·00 55·00

Although issued only in the Protectorate, the above were presumably overprinted "BRITISH BECHUANALAND" because stamps bearing this inscription were in use there at the time.

1897 (Oct)–**1902**. *Nos. 172, 197, 200, 202, 205 and 208 of Great Britain (Queen Victoria) optd with T* **19** *by D.L.R.*

59 ½d. vermilion 1·25 2·25
60 ½d. blue-green (25.2.02) 1·40 3·50
61 1d. lilac 4·00 75
62 2d. grey-green and carmine 5·00 3·50
63 3d. purple/*yellow* (12.97) 5·50 8·50
64 4d. green and purple-brown 17·00 16·00
65 6d. purple/*rose-red* 23·00 11·00
59/65 *Set of 7* 50·00 40·00
59s/65s Optd or H/S (No. 60s) "Specimen" *Set of 7* £225

BECHUANALAND PROTECTORATE
(20)

BECHUANALAND PROTECTORATE
(21)

1904 (29 Nov)–**13**. *Nos. 216, 218/19, 230 and 313/14 (Somerset House ptgs) of Great Britain (King Edward VII) optd with T* **20**, *by D.L.R.*

66 ½d. blue-green (3.06) 2·00 2·00
67 ½d. yellowish green (11.08) 3·75 3·50
68 1d. scarlet (4.05) 8·00 30
s. Optd "Specimen" 60·00
69 2½d. ultramarine 8·00 5·50
a. Stop after "P" in "PROTECTORATE" £1000 £1300
70 1s. deep green and scarlet (10.12) 45·00 £140
a. Opt double, one albino £200
71 1s. green and carmine (1913) 48·00 £120
s. Optd "Specimen" £100

No. 69a occurs on R. 5/9 of the lower pane.

1912 (Sept)–**14**. *No. 342 of Great Britain (King George V, wmk Crown) optd with T* **20**.

72 1d. scarlet 2·00 60
a. No cross on crown £150 75·00
b. Aniline scarlet (No. 343) (1914) £180 90·00

1913 (1 July)–**24**. *Stamps of Great Britain (King George V) optd.*

(a) Nos. 351, 357, 362, 367, 370/1, 376, 379, 385 and 395 (wmk Simple Cypher, T **100**) *optd with T* **20**.

73 ½d. green (*shades*) 1·25 1·50
74 1d. scarlet (*shades*) (4.15) 2·75 75
a. Carmine-red (1922) 28·00 2·50
75 1½d. red-brown (12.20) 5·00 3·00
76 2d. reddish orange (Die I) 7·00 3·25
a. Orange (Die I) (1921) 17·00 3·00
aw. Wmk inverted
77 2d. orange (Die II) (1924) 38·00 2·75
78 2½d. cobalt-blue 3·50 23·00
a. Blue (1915) 14·00 23·00
79 3d. bluish violet 6·00 12·00
80 4d. grey-green 6·50 24·00
81 6d. reddish purple (*shades*) 8·00 19·00
a. Opt double, one albino £250
82 1s. bistre 13·00 26·00
a. Bistre-brown (1923) 28·00 32·00
s. Optd "Specimen" 75·00
73/82 *Set of 9* 48·00 £100

(b) With T **21**.

(i) Waterlow printings (Nos. 399 and 401) (1914–15).

83 2s.6d. deep sepia-brown (1.15) £130 £250
a. Re-entry (R. 2/1) £1200 £1800
b. Opt double, one albino £300
84 5s. rose-carmine (1914) £160 £375
a. Opt double, one albino £375
83s/4s Optd "Specimen" *Set of 2* £275

(ii) *D.L.R. printings (Nos. 407/8 and 409)* (1916–19).

85 2s.6d. pale brown (7.16) £120 £250
a. Re-entry (R. 2/1) £1200 £1700
86 2s.6d. sepia (1917) £130 £225
a. Opt treble, two albino
b. Re-entry (R. 2/1) £1400 £1700
87 5s. bright carmine (8.19) £300 £425
a. Opt double, one albino £450

(iii) *B.W. printings (Nos. 414 and 416)* (1920–23).

88 2s.6d. chocolate-brown (7.23) 85·00 £160
a. Major re-entry (R. 1/2) £2250
b. Opt double, one albino £550
c. Opt treble, two albino £550
89 5s. rose-red (7.20) £110 £275
a. Opt treble, two albino £375
b. Opt double, one albino

Examples of Nos. 83/9 are known showing a forged Lobatsi postmark dated "6 MAY 35" or "6 MAY 39".

1925 (July)–**27**. *Nos. 418/19, 421, 423/4, 426/a and 429 of Great Britain* (wmk Block Cypher, *T* **111**) *optd with T* **20**.

91 ½d. green (1927) 1·50 1·75
92 1d. scarlet (8.25) 2·00 70
w. Wmk inverted
93 2d. orange (Die II) 1·75 1·00
94 3d. violet (10.26) 4·75 22·00
a. Opt double, one albino £200
w. Wmk inverted £200
95 4d. grey-green (10.26) 4·75 45·00
a. Printed on the gummed side
96 6d. reddish purple (*chalk-surfaced paper*) (12.25) 48·00 75·00
97 6d. purple (*ordinary paper*) (1926) 48·00 50·00
98 1s. bistre-brown (10.26) 9·00 24·00
w. Wmk inverted £325 £300
91/8 *Set of 8* £100 £190

No. 94w. also usually shows the variety, opt double, one albino.

22 King George V, Baobab Tree and Cattle drinking

23 King George VI, Baobab Tree and Cattle drinking

(Des from photo by Resident Commissioner, Ngamiland, Recess Waterlow)

1932 (12 Dec). Wmk Mult Script CA. P 12½.

99 22 ½d. green 1·75 30
a. Imperf between (horiz pair) £21000
100 1d. scarlet 1·00 25
101 2d. brown 1·00 30
102 3d. ultramarine 2·00 3·25
103 4d. orange 2·00 7·50
104 6d. purple 3·00 5·50
105 1s. black and olive-green 3·00 7·00
106 2s. black and orange 24·00 48·00
107 2s.6d. black and scarlet 19·00 35·00
108 3s. black and purple 35·00 48·00
109 5s. black and ultramarine 80·00 85·00
110 10s. black and brown £150 £160
99/110 *Set of 12* £275 £350
99s/110s Perf "Specimen" *Set of 12* £300

Examples of most values are known showing a forged Lobatsi postmark dated "6 MAY 35" or "6 MAY 39".

1935 (4 May). *Silver Jubilee. As Nos. 91/4 of Antigua but ptd by B.W.* P 11×12.

111 1d. deep blue and scarlet 75 4·50
a. Extra flagstaff £250 £350
b. Short extra flagstaff £425
c. Lightning conductor £375
d. Flagstaff on right-hand turret £400
e. Double flagstaff £400
112 2d. ultramarine and grey-black 1·25 4·50
a. Extra flagstaff £100 £160
b. Short extra flagstaff £160 £190
c. Lightning conductor £130 £180
113 3d. brown and deep blue 2·75 5·00
a. Extra flagstaff £140 £200
b. Short extra flagstaff £190
c. Lightning conductor £160 £200
114 6d. slate and purple 6·00 5·00
a. Extra flagstaff £150 £180
b. Short extra flagstaff £170
c. Lightning conductor £170 £180
111/14 *Set of 4* 9·75 17·00
111s/14s Perf "Specimen" *Set of 4* £100

For illustrations of plate varieties see Omnibus section following Zanzibar.

1937 (12 May). *Coronation. As Nos. 95/7 of Antigua, but printed by D.L.R.* P 14.

115 1d. scarlet 45 40
116 2d. yellow-brown 60 1·00
117 3d. bright blue 60 1·25
115/17 *Set of 3* 1·50 2·40
115s/17s Perf "Specimen" *Set of 3* 90·00

(Recess Waterlow)

1938 (1 Apr)–**52**. Wmk Mult Script CA. P 12½.

118 23 ½d. green 2·25 3·25
a. Light yellowish green (1941) 8·50 7·50
b. Yellowish green (4.43) 8·50 4·25

c. Deep green (4.49) ... 3·75 9·50
119 1d. scarlet ... 75 50
120 1½d. dull blue ... 10·00 2·00
a. Light blue (4.43) ... 1·00 1·00
121 2d. chocolate-brown ... 75 50
122 3d. deep ultramarine ... 1·00 2·50
123 4d. orange ... 2·00 3·50
124 6d. reddish purple ... 5·00 3·00
a. Purple (1944) ... 4·00 2·50
ab. "A" of "CA" missing from wmk ... † —
125 1s. black and brown-olive ... 4·00 7·00
a. Grey-black & olive-green (21.5.52) ... 18·00 27·00
126 2s.6d. black and scarlet ... 14·00 15·00
127 5s. black and deep ultramarine ... 30·00 22·00
a. Grey-black & dp ultram (10.46) ... 75·00 50·00
128 10s. black and red-brown ... 19·00 25·00
118/28 *Set of* 11 ... 70·00 75·00
118s/28s Perf "Specimen" *Set of* 11 ... £250

Bechuanaland

(24)

1945 (3 Dec). *Victory. Stamps of South Africa optd with T* **24**. *Inscr alternately in English and Afrikaans.*

			Un pair	*Used pair*	*Used single*
129	**55**	1d. brown and carmine	75	1.25	10
130	**56**	2d. slate-blue and violet	50	1.25	10
131	**57**	3d. deep blue and blue	50	1.50	10
		a. Opt omitted (in vert pair with normal)	£11000		
129/31 *Set of* 3			1·60	3.50	25

No. 131a comes from a sheet on which the overprint was displaced downwards so that it is omitted from stamps in the top row and shown on the sheet margin at foot.

(Recess Waterlow)

1947 (17 Feb). *Royal Visit. As Nos. 32/5 of Basutoland.* Wmk Mult Script CA. P 12½.
132 1d. scarlet ... 10 10
133 2d. green ... 10 10
134 3d. ultramarine ... 10 10
135 1s. mauve ... 10 10
132/5 *Set of* 4 ... 35 30
132s/5s Perf "Specimen" *Set of* 4 ... 95·00

1948 (1 Dec). *Royal Silver Wedding. As Nos. 112/13 of Antigua.*
136 1½d. ultramarine ... 30 10
137 10s. black ... 35·00 40·00

1949 (10 Oct). *75th Anniv of Universal Postal Union. As Nos. 114/17 of Antigua.*
138 1½d. blue ... 30 1·25
139 3d. deep blue ... 1·50 2·50
140 6d. magenta ... 60 3·00
141 1s. olive ... 60 1·50
138/41 *Set of* 4 ... 2·75 7·50

1953 (3 June). *Coronation. As No. 120 of Antigua.*
142 2d. black and brown ... 1·00 30

25 Queen Elizabeth II, Baobab Tree and Cattle drinking

26 Queen Victoria, Queen Elizabeth II and Landscape

(Des from photo by Resident Commissioner, Ngamiland. Recess Waterlow)

1955 (3 Jan)–**58**. Wmk Mult Script CA. P 13½×14.
143 **25** ½d. green ... 50 30
144 1d. rose-red ... 80 10
145 2d. red-brown ... 1·25 30
146 3d. ultramarine ... 3·00 2·00
a. Bright ultramarine (16.1.57) ... 9·00 3·25
146*b* 4d. red-orange 11.12.58) ... 6·50 9·00
147 4½d. blackish blue ... 1·50 35
148 6d. purple ... 1·25 60
149 1s. black and brown-olive ... 1·25 80
150 1s.3d. black and lilac ... 14·00 9·50
151 2s.6d. black and rose-red ... 12·00 9·50
152 5s. black and violet-blue ... 15·00 9·50
153 10s. black and red-brown ... 32·00 15·00
143/53 *Set of* 12 ... 80·00 50·00

(Photo Harrison)

1960 (21 Jan). *75th Anniv of Bechuanaland Protectorate.* W w **12**. P 14½×14.
154 **26** 1d. sepia and black ... 40 50
155 3d. magenta and black ... 40 30
156 6d. bright blue and black ... 40 50
154/6 *Set of* 3 ... 1·10 1·10

(New Currency. 100 cents = 1 rand)

1c (27) | 1c (I) | 1c (II) | 2½c (I) | 2½c (II)

3 (I) | 3 (II) | 3 (III) | 5c (I) | 5c (II) | R1 (I) | R1 (II)

2½c

Spaced "c" (R. 10/3)

1961. *Nos. 144/6a and 148/53 surch as T* **27** *by South African Govt Printer, Pretoria.*
157 **25** 1c. on 1d. rose-red (Type I) ... 30 10
a. Type II (6 June) ... 40 10
158 2c. on 2d. red-brown ... 20 10
159 2½c. on 2d. red-brown (Type I) ... 30 10
a. Type II (26 July) ... 85 1·25
b. Vert pair, one without surch ... £8500
160 2½c. on 3d. bright ultramarine ... 2·00 5·50
a. Spaced "c" (R. 10/3) ... 55·00
161 3½c. on 4d. red-orange (Type I) ... 50 2·00
a. Type II ... 2·00 7·00
b. Wide surch (I) ... 17·00 26·00
c. Wide surch (II) ... 60·00 80·00
d. Type III (6 June) ... 20 60
162 5c. on 6d. purple (Type I) ... 65 60
a. Type II (12 May) ... 20 10
163 10c. on 1s. black and brown-olive ... 20 10
a. Horiz pair, righthand stamp without surch ... £6000
164 12½c. on 1s.3d. black and lilac ... 65 20
165 25c. on 2s.6d. black and rose-red ... 1·50 50
166 50c. on 5s. black and violet-blue ... 2·00 2·00
167 1r. on 10s. black & red-brown (Type I) ... £375 £110
a. Type II (surch at bottom left) (17 Mar) ... 11·00 12·00
b. Type II (surch at foot, either to right or central) (Apr) ... 11·00 6·50
157/67b *Set of* 11 ... 17·00 14·00

Nos. 161/c occur from the same printing each sheet containing thirty-three examples of Type I, five of Type I with wide spacing, nineteen of Type II and three of Type II with wide spacing. The wide surcharge measures 9½ mm overall (with "C' paced 1½ mm from "½") and comes on 8 of the 10 stamps in the last vertical row. The surcharge on the remainder of the sheet varies between 8½ and 9½ mm.

No. 163a was caused by a shift of the surcharge so that the last vertical row on the sheet is without "10 c".

A later printing of the 12½ c. on 1s.3d. was from a fresh setting of type, but is insufficiently different for separate listing. Later printings of the 10c. and 25c. were identical with the originals.

28 African Golden Oriole

29 Hoopoe

30 Scarlet-chested Sunbird

31 Yellow-rumped Bishop

32 Swallow-tailed Bee Eater

33 African Grey Hornbill

34 Red-headed Weaver

35 Brown-hooded Kingfisher

36 Woman Musician

37 Baobab Tree

38 Woman grinding maize

39 Bechuana Ox

40 Lion

41 Police Camel Patrol

(Des P. Jones (1c. to 12½c.). Photo Harrison)

1961 (2 Oct). *T* **28/41**. W w **12**. P 14½×14 (25, 50c.) or 14×14½ (others).
168 **28** 1c. yellow, red, black and lilac ... 1·50 40
169 **29** 2c. orange, black and yellow-olive ... 2·00 3·75
170 **30** 2½c. carmine, green, black and bistre ... 1·75 10
171 **31** 3½c. yellow, black, sepia and pink ... 2·50 3·75
172 **32** 5c. yellow, blue, black and buff ... 3·25 1·00
173 **33** 7½c. brown, red, black and apple-green ... 2·25 2·25
174 **34** 10c. red, yellow, sepia & turquoise-green ... 2·25 60
175 **35** 12½c. buff, blue, red and grey-black ... 18·00 5·50
176 **36** 20c. yellow-brown and drab ... 3·00 2·75
177 **37** 25c. deep brown and lemon ... 3·50 1·50
178 **38** 35c. deep blue and orange ... 3·00 3·00
179 **39** 50c. sepia and olive ... 1·75 2·25
180 **40** 1r. black and cinnamon ... 6·50 2·50
181 **41** 2r. brown and turquoise-blue ... 18·00 9·00
168/81 *Set of* 14 ... 60·00 35·00

1963 (4 June). *Freedom from Hunger. As No. 146 of Antigua.*
182 12½c. bluish green ... 30 15

1963 (2 Sept). *Red Cross Centenary. As Nos. 147/8 of Antigua.*
183 2½c. red and black ... 20 10
184 12½c. red and blue ... 40 50

1964 (23 April). *400th Birth Anniv of William Shakespeare. As No. 164 of Antigua.*
185 12½c. light brown ... 15 15

INTERNAL SELF–GOVERNMENT

42 Map and Gaberones Dam

(Des Mrs. M. Townsend, adapted V. Whiteley. Photo Harrison)

1965 (1 Mar). *New Constitution.* W w **12**. P 14½×14.
186 **42** 2½c. red and gold ... 20 10
w. Wmk inverted ... 16·00 3·75
187 5c. ultramarine and gold ... 20 40
188 12½c. brown and gold ... 30 40
189 25c. green and gold ... 40 55
186/9 *Set of* 4 ... 1·00 1·25

1965 (17 May). *I.T.U. Centenary. As Nos. 166/7 of Antigua.*
190 2½c. red and bistre-yellow ... 20 10
191 12½c. mauve and brown ... 45 30

1965 (25 Oct). *International Co-operation Year. As Nos. 168/9 of Antigua.*
192 1c. reddish purple and turquoise-green ... 10 20
193 12½c. deep bluish green and lavender ... 60 55

1966 (24 Jan). *Churchill Commemoration. As Nos. 170/3 of Antigua.*
194 1c. new blue ... 15 1·25
195 2½c. deep green ... 35 10
196 12½c. brown ... 70 30
197 20c. bluish violet ... 75 50
194/7 *Set of* 4 ... 1·75 1·90

43 Haslar Smoke Generator

(Des V. Whiteley. Photo Harrison)

1966 (1 June). *Bechuanaland Royal Pioneer Corps. T* **43** *and similar horiz designs.* W w **12**. P 14½.
198 2½c. Prussian blue, red and light emerald ... 25 10
199 5c. brown and light blue ... 25 20
200 15c. Prussian blue, rosine and emerald ... 30 25
201 35c. buff, blackish brown, red and green ... 30 1·00
198/201 *Set of* 4 ... 1·00 1·25
Designs:—5c. Bugler; 15c. Gun-site; 35c. Regimental cap badge.

POSTAGE DUE STAMPS

BECHUANALAND (D 1) PROTECTORATE

BECHUANALAND PROTECTORATE (D 2)

1926 (1 Jan). *Nos. D9/10 and D13 of Great Britain, optd with Types* D **1** *or* D **2** *(2d.).*

D1		½d. emerald (wmk sideways - inverted)	7·50	£100
D2		1d. carmine	7·50	60·00
D3		2d. agate	7·50	85·00
D1/3 *Set of 3*			20·00	£225

The watermark shows Crown to the left of GvR on D1 and to the right og GvR of D2/3, *as seen from the back of the stamp.*

D 3

2d Normal — 2d Large "d." (R. 9/6, 10/6)

Serif on "d" (R. 1/6)

(Typo D.L.R.)

1932 (12 Dec)–**58**. *Ordinary paper.* Wmk Mult Script CA. P 14.

D4	D 3	½d. sage-green	6·00	55·00
D5		1d. carmine	7·00	9·00
		a. Chalk-surfaced paper (27.11.58)	1·50	24·00
D6		2d. violet	9·00	55·00
		a. Large "d"	£130	
		b. Serif on "d"	£180	
		c. Chalk-surfaced paper (27.11.58)	1·75	20·00
		ca. Large "d"	38·00	
		cb. Serif on "d"	50·00	
D4/6b *Set of 3*			8·50	70·00
D4s/6s Perf "Specimen" *Set of 3*			75·00	

No. D6a first occurred on the 1947 printing.

1c 1c
I (Small) II (Large)

1961 (14 Feb). *Surch as T* **27**. *Chalk-surfaced paper (Nos. D7/8).*

D7	D 3	1c. on 1d. (Type I)	25	50
		a. Type II (Apr)	15	1·75
		ab. Double surch	£200	
		ac. Ordinary paper	16·00	50·00
D8		2c. on 2d. (Type I)	25	1·50
		a. Large "d"	8·00	
		b. Serif on "d"	12·00	
		c. Type II	15	2·00
		ca. Large "d"	5.00	
		cb. Serif on "d"	8·50	
		d. Ordinary paper. Type II	£110	£120
		da. Large "d"	£450	
D9		5c. on ½d.	20	60
D7/9 *Set of 3*			45	2·40

1961 (15 Nov). *As Type* D **3** *but values in cents. Chalk-surfaced paper.* Wmk Mult Script CA. P 14.

D10		1c. carmine	20	2·00
D11		2c. violet	20	2·00
D12		5c. green	40	2·00
D10/12 *Set of 3*			70	5·50

POSTAL FISCAL STAMPS

The following stamps issued for fiscal purposes were each allowed to be used for postal purposes for a short time. No. F2 was used by the public because the word "POSTAGE" had not been obliterated and No. F3 because the overprint did not include the words "Revenue only" as did the contemporary fiscal overprints for Basutoland and Swaziland.

Bechuanaland Protectorate (F 1)

£5 (F 2)

Bechuanaland Protectorate. (F 3)

1910 (July). *No. 266a of Transvaal optd with Type* F **1** *by Transvaal Govt Ptg Wks, Pretoria.*

F1		6d. black and brown-orange (Bl-Blk)	£160	£325

No. F1 was supplied to Assistant Commissioners in January 1907 for revenue purposes. The "POSTAGE" inscription was not oobliterated, however, and the stamp is known postally used for a period of a year from July 1910.

1918. *No. 15 surch with Type* F **2** *at top.*

F2	4	£5 on 1s. green and black (F.C. £700)		

1921. *No. 4b of South Africa optd with Type* F **3**, *in varying positions.*

F3		1d. scarlet	42·00	£130
		a. Opt double, one albino	£160	

Bechuanaland became the independent republic of Botswana, within the Commonwealth, on 30 September 1966.

Bermuda

The first internal postal system for Bermuda was organised by Joseph Stockdale, the proprietor of the *Bermuda Gazette*, in January 1784. This service competed with that of the colonial post office, set up in May 1812, until 1818.

Control of the overseas postal services passed to the British G.P.O. in 1818. The internal delivery system was discontinued between 1821 and 1830. The overseas posts became a colonial responsibility in September 1859.

For illustrations of the handstamp types see BRITISH POST OFFICES ABROAD notes, following GREAT BRITAIN.

CROWNED-CIRCLE HANDSTAMPS

CC1	CC **1** ST. GEORGES BERMUDA (R.) (1.8.1845)	*Price on cover*	£7500
CC2	IRELAND ISLE BERMUDA (R.) (1.8.1845)	*Price on cover*	£7000
CC3	HAMILTON BERMUDA (R.) (13.11.1846)	*Price on cover*	£3750

For Nos. CC1 and CC3 used as adhesive Postmasters' Stamps see Nos. O7 and O6.

PRICES FOR STAMPS ON COVER TO 1845	
Nos. 1/11	*from* × 5
Nos. 12/17	*from* × 10
Nos. 19/29*a*	*from* × 8
Nos. 30/a	*from* × 10
Nos. 31/4	*from* × 4
Nos. 34*a*/55	*from* × 3
Nos. 56/8	*from* × 10
Nos. 59/76	*from* × 4
Nos. 76*a*/93	*from* × 3
Nos. 94/7	*from* × 4
Nos. 98/106	*from* × 3
Nos. 107/15	*from* × 4
Nos. 116/21	*from* × 5
No. 122	*from* × 20

COLONY

O 1

O 2

1848–61. *Postmasters' Stamps. Adhesives prepared and issued by the postmasters at Hamilton and St. Georges. Dated as given in brackets.*

(a) By W. B. Perot at Hamilton.

O1	O 1	1d. black/*bluish grey* (1848)	–	£130000
O2		1d. black/*bluish grey* (1849)	–	£150000
O3		1d. red/*thick white* (1853)	–	£110000
O4		1d. red/*bluish wove* (1854)	–	£275000
O5		1d. red/*bluish wove* (1856)	–	£170000
O6	O 2	(1d.) carmine-red/*bluish laid* (1861)	£100000	£80000

(b) By J. H. Thies at St. Georges. As Type O **2** *but inscr* "ST. GEORGES".

O7	–	(1d.) carmine-red/*buff* (1860)	†	£75000

Stamps of Type O **1** bear manuscript value and signature, the dates being those shown on the eleven known examples. The stamps are distributed between the dates as follows: 1848 three examples, 1849 two examples, 1853 three examples, 1854 two examples, 1856 one example.

It is believed that the franking value of Nos. O6/7 was 1d., although this is not shown on the actual stamps. Four examples are known of this type used from Hamilton, from March 1861 (and one unused), and five used from St. Georges between July 1860 and January 1863, both issues being cancelled by pen.

Prices shown reflect our estimation of value based on known copies. For instance of the two copies known of No. O4, one is in the Royal collection and the other is on entire.

It is possible that a fourth postmaster's provisional was used by Robert Ward at Hamilton in late 1862 when two examples of Type O **2** on laid paper are known cancelled by blue crayon.

1

2

3

4

5

(Typo D.L.R.)

1865–1903. Wmk Crown CC.

(a) P 14.

1	1	1d. rose-red (25.9.65)	90·00	1·25
		a. Imperf	£30000	£15000
		w. Wmk inverted	£400	£150
2		1d. pale rose	£130	7·50
		w. Wmk inverted	£425	£170
3	2	2d. dull blue (14.3.66)	£450	28·00
		w. Wmk inverted	–	£450
4		2d. bright blue (1877)	£475	21·00
		w. Wmk inverted	–	£450
5	3	3d. yellow-buff (10.3.73)	£475	65·00
		aw. Wmk inverted	£1300	£250
		ax. Wmk reversed		
5*b*		3d. orange (1875)	£2000	£160
6	4	6d. dull purple (25.9.65)	£1000	75·00
		w. Wmk inverted	–	£950
7		6d. dull mauve (2.7.74)	23·00	12·00
		w. Wmk inverted	£130	£160
8	5	1s. green (25.9.65)	£325	55·00
		w. Wmk inverted	£700	£300
		(b) P 14×12½.		
10	3	3d. yellow-buff (12.81)	£180	60·00
10*a*	4	6d. bright mauve (1903)	13·00	22·00
		aw. Wmk inverted	£850	
11	5	1s. green (11.93)	12·00	£120
		a. Imperf between (vert strip of 3)	£12000	
		w. Wmk inverted		

No. 11a occurs from Rows 8, 9, and 10 of four panes, possibly from a single sheet. Some of the stamps have become partially separated. One *used* vertical pair is known (*Price* £12000).

Although they arrived in Bermuda in March 1880, stamps perforated 14×12½ were not issued until the dates given above.

THREE PENCE (6) THREE PENCE (6a)

THREE PENCE (7) One Penny. (8)

1874 (12 Mar–19 May). *Nos. 1 and 8 surch diagonally.*

		(a) With T **6** *("P" and "R" different type).*		
12	1	3d. on 1d. rose-red	£18000	
13	5	3d. on 1s. green	£2500	£850
		(b) With T **6a** *("P" same type as "R").*		
13*b*	5	3d. on 1s. green	£2000	£800
		(c) With T **7** *(19 May).*		
14	5	3d. on 1s. green	£1500	£650

The 3d. on 1d. was a trial surcharge which was not regularly issued, though a few specimens were postally used before 1879. Nos. 13, 13*b* and 14, being handstamped, are found with double or partial double surcharges.

(Surch by Queens Printer, Donald McPhee Lee)

1875 (March–May). *Surch with T* **8**.

15	2	1d. on 2d. (No. 3) (23 Apr)	£700	£375
		a. No stop after "Penny"	£25000	£13000
16	3	1d. on 3d. (No. 5) (8 May)	£450	£350
17	5	1d. on 1s. (No. 8) (11 Mar)	£500	£250
		a. Surch inverted	†	£42000
		b. No stop after "Penny"	£30000	£17000

It is emphasised that the prices quoted for Nos. 12/17 are for fine examples. The many stamps from these provisional issues which are in inferior condition are worth much less.

9

10

11

(Typo D.L.R.)

1880 (25 Mar). Wmk Crown CC. P 14.

19	9	½d. stone	4·75	4·75
		w. Wmk inverted	85·00	£160
		y. Wmk inverted and reversed		
20	10	4d. orange-red	17·00	1·75
		w. Wmk inverted		
		x. Wmk reversed		

(Typo D.L.R.)

1883–1904. Wmk Crown CA. P 14.

21	9	½d. dull green (10.92)	4·75	3·50
21*a*		½d. deep grey-green (1893)	3·50	80
22	1	1d. dull rose (12.83)	£160	4·25
		w. Wmk inverted	–	£275
23		1d. rose-red	80·00	3·25
		w. Wmk inverted	–	£275
24		1d. carmine-rose (3.86)	50·00	1·00
24*a*		1d. aniline carmine (1889)	11·00	20
		aw. Wmk inverted	£300	£150
25	2	2d. blue (12.86)	60·00	4·75
		x. Wmk reversed	†	£800
26		2d. aniline purple (7.93)	14·00	4·00
26*a*		2d. brown purple (1898)	3·50	1·50
27	11	2½d. deep ultramarine (10.11.84)	16·00	2·75
		aw. Wmk inverted	£450	£180
27*b*		2½d. pale ultramarine	9·00	40
		bw. Wmk inverted	–	£160

28	3	3d. grey (20.1.86)	22·00	7·00
28*a*	10	4d. orange-brown (18.1.04)	35·00	60·00
		ax. Wmk reversed	£450	
29	5	1s. yellow-brown (1893)	19·00	17·00
		ax. Wmk reversed	£1100	£750
29*b*		1s. olive-brown	13·00	16·00
		bx. Wmk reversed		
21/9b *Set of* 8			£140	80·00
21s, 26s & 29s Optd "Specimen" *Set of* 3			£375	

1893 PROVISIONAL POSTCARD. Following the reduction of the overseas postcard rate to 1d. in 1893 existing stocks of postal stationery postcards, including some from the September 1880 issue franked with Nos. 19 and 22, were surcharged "One Penny". This surcharge was applied by the *Royal Gazette* press. It is generally believed that an individual in the Post Office acquired all the examples showing Nos. 19 and 22, but provisional postcards are known used to Europe or locally. *Price from* £550 *unused*, £1400 *used*.

(12)

13 Dry Dock

14

1901. *As Nos. 29/a but colour changed, surch with T* **12** *by D.L.R.*

30	5	¼d. on 1s. dull grey (11.1.01)	3·25	50
		as. Optd "Specimen"	80·00	
30*b*		¼d. on 1s. bluish grey (18.3.01)	3·75	1·00
		ba. "F" in "FARTHING" inserted by handstamp	£7000	£8000

Eight examples of No. 30ba are known, six unused (one being in the Royal Collection) and two used (one on postcard). It would appear that the "F" in position one of an unspecified horizontal row was damaged and an additional impression of the letter was then inserted by a separate handstamp.

(Typo D.L.R.)

1902 (Nov)–**03**. Wmk Crown CA. P 14.

31	13	½d. black and green (12.03)	12·00	2·75
32		1d. brown and carmine	8·00	10
33		3d. magenta and sage-green (9.03)	3·75	2·00
31/3 *Set of* 3			21·00	4·25
31s/3s Optd "Specimen" *Set of* 3			£140	

1906–10. Wmk Mult Crown CA. P 14.

34	13	¼d. brown and violet (9.08)	1·75	1·50
35		½d. black and green (12.06)	19·00	65
36		½d. green (3.09)	16·00	3·00
37		1d. brown and carmine (4.06)	29·00	20
		w. Wmk inverted	£475	£325
38		1d. red (5.08)	19·00	10
39		2d. grey and orange (10.07)	7·50	10·00
40		2½d. brown and ultramarine (12.06)	22·00	7·00
41		2½d. blue (14.2.10)	14·00	7·00
42		4d. blue and chocolate (11.09)	3·00	16·00
34/42 *Set of* 9			£120	40·00
34s, 36s, 38s/42s Optd "Specimen" *Set of* 7			£375	

(Recess D.L.R.)

1910–25. Wmk Mult Crown CA. P 14.

44	14	¼d. brown (26.3.12)	1·75	2·50
		a. Pale brown	60	1·50
45		½d. green (4.6.10)	1·50	25
		a. Deep green (1918)	10·00	1·25
		w. Wmk inverted		
		x. Wmk reversed	£475	£375
		y. Wmk inverted and reversed		
46		1d. red (I) (15.10.10)	15·00	30
		a. Rose-red (1916)	24·00	30
		b. Carmine (12.19)	55·00	8·00
		w. Wmk inverted	£550	£450
		x. Wmk reversed		
		y. Wmk inverted and reversed	£500	
47		2d. grey (1.13)	3·00	14·00
		x. Wmk reversed		
48		2½d. blue (273.12)	3·50	60
		w. Wmk inverted		
		x. Wmk reversed	—	£400
		y. Wmk inverted and reversed	£300	£200
49		3d. purple/*yellow* (1.13)	2·00	6·00
49*a*		4d. red/*yellow* (1.9.19)	7·00	13·00
50		6d. purple (26.3.12)	16·00	20·00
		a. Pale claret (2.6.24)	11·00	8·00
51		1s. black/*green* (26.3.12)	4·25	4·25
		a. Jet black/olive (1925)	4·75	17·00
44/51 *Set of* 9			42·00	42·00
44s/51s Optd "Specimen" *Set of* 9			£425	

Nos. 44 to 51a are comb-perforated 13.8×14 or 14. No. 45 exists also line-perforated 14 probably from the printing dispatched to Bermuda on 13 March 1911.

See also Nos. 76b/87a.

15

HIGH VALUE KEY TYPES. The reign of King Edward VII saw the appearance of the first in a new series of "key type" designs, initially for Nyasaland, to be used for high value denominations where a smaller design was felt to be inappropriate. The system was extended during the reign of King George V, using the portrait as Bermuda Type **15**, to cover Bermuda, Ceylon, Leeward Islands, Malaya — Straits Settlements, Malta and Nyasaland. A number of these territories continued to use the key type concept for high value King George VI stamps and one, Leeward Islands, for stamps of Queen Elizabeth II.

In each instance the King George V issues were printed in sheets of 60 (12×5) on various coloured papers. The system utilised a common "head" plate used with individual "duty" plates which printed the territory name and face value.

Many of the major plate flaws on the King George V head plate occur in different states, having been repaired and then damaged once again, perhaps on several occasions. Later printings of R. 1/12 show additional damage to the crown and upper scrolls. The prices quoted in the listings are for examples approximately as illustrated.

Break in scroll (R. 1/12)

Broken crown and scroll (R. 2/12)

Nick in top right scroll (R. 3/12) (Some printings from 1920 onwards show attempts at repair)

Break through scroll (R. 1/9. Ptgs from June 1929. Some show attempts at repair)

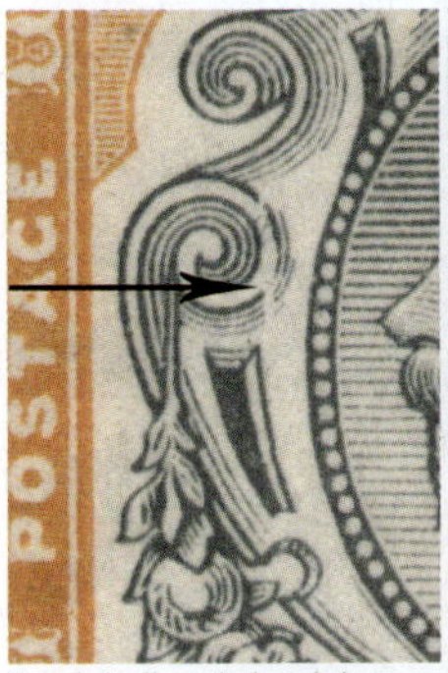
Break in lines below left scroll (R. 4/9. Ptgs from May 1920)

Damaged leaf at bottom right (R. 5/6. Ptgs from April 1918)

Gash in fruit and leaf (R. 5/12. Ptgs from November 1928)

(Typo D.L.R)

1918 (1 Apr)–**22**. Wmk Mult Crown CA. *Chalk-surfaced paper.* P 14.

51*b*	15	2s. purple and blue/*blue* (19.6.20)	20·00	50·00
		ba. Break in scroll	£275	
		bb. Broken crown and scroll	£225	
		bc. Nick in top right scroll	£275	
		be. Break in lines below left scroll	£275	£375
		bf. Damaged leaf at bottom right	£275	
		bx. Wmk reversed	£1900	£2500
52		2s.6d. black and red/*blue*	30·00	80·00
		a. Break in scroll	£325	
52*b*		4s. black and carmine (19.6.20)	60·00	£160
		ba. Break in scroll	£300	
		bb. Broken crown and scroll	£300	£600
		bc. Nick in top right scroll	£325	£600
		be. Break in lines below left scroll	£350	
		bf. Damaged leaf at bottom right	£350	
53		5s. deep green and deep red/*yellow*	70·00	£140
		a. Break in scroll	£425	
		c. Nick in top right scroll	£425	
		d. Green and carmine-red/pale yellow (1920)	50·00	£120
		da. Break in scroll	£375	£550
		db. Broken crown and scroll	£375	£550
		de. Break in lines below left scroll	£400	
		df. Damaged leaf at bottom right	£400	
		dw. Wmk inverted	£425	
		dx. Wmk reversed	£3750	
		dy. Wmk inverted and reversed	£3750	
54		10s. green and carmine/*pale bluish green*	£180	£350
		a. Break in scroll	£750	
		c. Green and red/pale bluish green (10.22)	£275	£425
		ca. Break in scroll	£950	
		cb. Broken crown and scroll	£950	
		ce. Break in lines below left scroll	£1000	
		cf. Damaged leaf at bottom right	£1000	
		cw. Wmk inverted		
55		£1 purple and black/*red*	£325	£550
		a. Break in scroll	£850	
		b. Broken crown and scroll	£1000	
		c. Nick in top right scroll	£1000	
		d. Break through scroll	£2000	
		e. Break in lines below left scroll	£1500	
		f. Damaged leaf at bottom right	£1200	
		g. Gash in fruit and leaf	£2000	
		w. Wmk inverted	£1800	
51*b*/5 *Set of* 6			£600	£1100
51*bs*/5s Optd "Specimen" *Set of* 6			£800	

Beware of cleaned copies of the 10s. with faked postmarks.

Examples of Nos. 51*b*/5 are known showing a forged Hamilton double ring postmark dated "22 JAN 13".

See also Nos. 88/93.

WAR TAX (16)

WAR TAX (17)

1918 (4 May). *Nos. 46 and 46a optd with T* **16** *by the Bermuda Press.*

56	14	1d. red	50	1·00
		a. Rose-red	50	1·25
		ay. Wmk inverted and reversed		

1920 (5 Feb). *No. 46b optd with T* **17** *by the Bermuda Press.*

58	14	1d. carmine	1·50	2·25

The War Tax stamps represented a compulsory levy on letters to Great Britain and often Empire Countries in addition to normal postal fees until 31 Dec 1920. Subsequently they were valid for ordinary postage.

18

19

(Des by the Governor (Gen. Sir James Willcocks). Typo D.L.R.)

1920 (11 Nov)–**21**. *Tercentenary of Representative Institutions (1st issue). Chalk-surfaced paper (3d. to 1s.).* P 14.

(*a*) Wmk Mult Crown CA (sideways*) (19.1.21).

59	18	¼d. brown	3·25	23·00
		a. "C" of "CA" missing from wmk	£650	
		b. "A" of "CA" missing from wmk	£650	
		w. Wmk Crown to right of CA	£225	
		x. Wmk sideways reversed	£225	
		y. Wmk sideways inverted and reversed	£275	
60		½d. green	6·00	14·00
		a. "C" of "CA" missing from wmk	£900	
		b. "A" of "CA" missing from wmk		
		w. Wmk Crown to right of CA	£350	
		x. Wmk sideways reversed	£300	
		y. Wmk sideways inverted and reversed		
61		2d. grey	14·00	48·00
		a. "C" of "CA" missing from wmk	£900	
		w. Wmk Crown to right of CA	£450	
		y. Wmk sideways inverted and reversed	£500	
62		3d. dull and deep purple/*pale yellow*	12·00	45·00
		w. Wmk Crown to right of CA		
		x. Wmk sideways reversed		
63		4d. black and red/*pale yellow*	12·00	35·00
		a. "C" of "CA" missing from wmk	£1400	
		x. Wmk reversed		
64		1s. black/*blue-green*	16·00	48·00

(*b*) Wmk Mult Script CA (sideways).

65	18	1d. carmine	4·00	30
		w. Wmk inverted	†	£550

		y. Wmk inverted and reversed...	†	£550
66		2½d. bright blue	16·00	17·00
67		6d. dull and bright purple (19.1.21)	28·00	85·00
59/67 Set of 9			£100	£275
59s/67s Optd "Specimen" *Set of 9*			£375	

*The normal sideways watermark shows Crown to left of CA, *as seen from the back of the stamp.*

(Des H. J. Dale. Recess D.L.R.)

1921 (12 May). *Tercentenary of Representative Institutions (2nd issue).* P 14.

(*a*) Wmk Mult Crown CA (sideways*).

68	19	2d. slate-grey	9·00	38·00
		a. "C" of "CA" missing from wmk	—	£800
		w. Wmk Crown to left of CA	£550	
69		2½d. bright ultramarine	11·00	3·50
		a. "C" of "CA" missing from wmk	£950	
		b. "A" of "CA" missing from wmk	£950	
		x. Wmk sideways reversed	—	£500
70		3d. purple/*pale yellow*	5·50	16·00
		w. Wmk Crown to left of CA		
71		4d. red/*pale yellow*	19·00	25·00
		x. Wmk sideways reversed	£250	
72		6d. purple	16·00	50·00
		a. "C" of "CA" missing from wmk	£1200	
		b. "A" of "CA" missing from wmk	£1300	
		c. Substituted crown in wmk	†	£1900
73		1s. black/*green*	24·00	50·00

(*b*) Wmk Mult Script CA (sideways*).

74	19	¼d. brown	3·00	3·75
		w. Wmk Crown to left of CA		
		x. Wmk sideways reversed		
75		½d. green	3·00	7·50
		w. Wmk Crown to left of CA	£200	£225
		y. Wmk sideways inverted and reversed	£375	
		ys. Optd "Specimen"	£110	
76		1d. deep carmine	4·25	35
		a. "C" of "CA" missing from wmk		
		w. Wmk Crown to left of CA	—	£475
		x. Wmk sideways reversed		
		y. Wmk sideways inverted and reversed	£900	£500
68/76 Set of 9			85·00	£170
68s/76s Optd "Specimen" *Set of 9*			£325	

*The normal sideways watermark shows Crown to right of CA, *as seen from the back of the stamp.*

For illustration of the substituted watermark crown see Catalogue Introduction.

Examples of most values of Nos. 59/76 are known showing part strikes of the forged Hamilton postmark mentioned below Nos. 51*b*/5.

I II III

Three Types of the 1d.

I. Scroll at top left very weak and figure "1" has pointed serifs.

II. Scroll weak. "1" has square serifs and "1d" is heavy.

III. Redrawn. Scroll is completed by a strong line and "1" is thinner with long square serifs.

I II

Two Types of the 2½d.

I. Short, thick figures, especially of the "1", small "d".

II. Figures taller and thinner, "d" larger.

1922–34. Wmk Mult Script CA. P 14.

76*b*	14	¼d. brown (7.28)	1·50	3·00
77		½d. green (11.22)	1·50	15
		w. Wmk inverted		
		x. Wmk reversed		
78		1d. scarlet (I) (11.22)	17·00	60
		a. Carmine (7.24)	18·00	60
		bx. Wmk reversed		
78*c*		1d. carmine (II) (12.25)	45·00	6·50
		cx. Wmk reversed		
		d. Scarlet (8.27)	15·00	80
79		1d. scarlet (III) (10.28)	12·00	30
		a. Carmine-lake (1934)	25·00	2·25
79*b*		1½d. red-brown (27.3.34)	9·00	35
80		2d. grey (12.23)	1·50	1·50
		x. Wmk reversed	70·00	
81		2½d. pale sage-green (12.22)	2·25	1·50
		a. Deep sage-green (1924)	1·75	1·50
		aw. Wmk inverted		
		ax. Wmk reversed		
		ay. Wmk inverted and reversed		
82		2½d. ultramarine (I) (1.12.26)	2·75	50
		aw. Wmk inverted	£190	
82*b*		2½d. ultramarine (II) (3.32)	1·75	70
83		3d. ultramarine (12.24)	16·00	26·00
		w. Wmk inverted	£130	
84		3d. purple/*yellow* (10.26)	4·00	1·00
85		4d. red/*yellow* (8.24)	2·00	1·00
		x. Wmk reversed		
86		6d. purple (8.24)	1·00	80
87		1s. black/*emerald* (10.27)	5·00	9·00
		a. Brownish black/yellow-green (1934)	35·00	50·00
76b/87 Set of 12			50·00	40·00
76*b*s/87s Optd or Perf (1½d.) "Specimen" *Set of 12*			£500	

Both comb and line perforations occur on Nos. 76*b*/87*a*.

Detailed gauges are as follows:

13.7×13.9 comb	—	Nos. 77, 78/*a*, 80, 81/*a*, 83, 84, 85, 86, 87
13.75 line	—	Nos. 76*b*, 77, 78*c*/*d*, 79/*a*, 79*b*, 80, 82, 82*b*, 84, 85, 86, 87/*a*
13.75×14 line	—	Nos. 77, 78*c*/*d*, 79*b*, 80, 82*b*, 86, 87*a*
14×13.75 line	—	Nos. 79/*a*
14 line	—	Nos. 81/*a*

Breaks in scrolls at right (R. 1/3. Ptgs of 12s.6d. from July 1932)

1924–32. Wmk Mult Script CA. *Chalk-surfaced paper.* P 14.

88	15	2s. purple and bright blue/*pale blue* (1.9.27)	45·00	75·00
		a. Break in scroll	£250	
		b. Broken crown and scroll	£250	
		c. Nick in top right scroll	£275	
		e. Break in lines below left scroll	£275	
		f. Damaged leaf at bottom right	£275	
		g. Purple and blue/grey-blue (1931)	55·00	85·00
		ga. Break in scroll	£300	
		gb. Broken crown and scroll	£300	
		gd. Break through scroll	£350	
		ge. Break in lines below left scroll	£350	
		gf. Damaged leaf at bottom right	£350	
		gg. Gash in fruit and leaf	£350	
89		2s.6d. black and carmine/*pale blue* (4.27)	60·00	£100
		a. Break in scroll	£300	
		b. Broken crown and scroll	£300	
		e. Break in lines below left scroll	£350	
		f. Damaged leaf at bottom right	£350	
		g. Black and red/blue to deep blue (6.29)	75·00	£110
		ga. Break in scroll	£350	
		gb. Broken crown and scroll	£350	
		gd. Break through scroll	£400	
		ge. Break in lines below left scroll	£400	
		gf. Damaged leaf at bottom right	£400	
		gg. Gash in fruit and leaf	£400	
		h. Grey-black and pale orange-vermilion/grey-blue (3.30)	£2750	£2750
		ha. Break in scroll	£5500	
		hb. Broken crown and scroll	£5500	
		hd. Break through scroll	£5500	
		he. Break in lines below left scroll	£5500	
		hf. Damaged leaf at bottom right	£5500	
		hg. Gash in fruit and leaf	£5500	
		i. Black and carmine-red/deep grey-blue (8.30)	£100	£140
		ia. Break in scroll	£500	
		ib. Broken crown and scroll	£500	
		id. Break through scroll	£600	
		ie. Break in lines below left scroll	£600	
		if. Damaged leaf at bottom right	£600	
		ig. Gash in fruit and leaf	£600	
		j. Black and scarlet-vermilion/dp bl (9.31)	90·00	£130
		ja. Break in scroll	£450	
		jb. Broken crown and scroll	£450	
		jc. Nick in top right scroll	£500	£600
		jd. Break through scroll	£550	
		je. Break in lines below left scroll	£550	
		jf. Damaged leaf at bottom right	£550	
		jg. Gash in fruit and leaf	£550	
		k. Black & brt orange-vermilion/deep blue (8.32)	£3250	£3000
		kb. Broken crown and scroll	£6000	
		kc. Nick in top right scroll	£6000	
		kd. Break through scroll	£6000	
		ke. Break in lines below left scroll	£6000	
		kf. Damaged leaf at bottom right	£6000	
		kg. Gash in fruit and leaf	£6000	
92		10s. green and red/*pale emerald* (12.24)	£130	£250
		a. Break in scroll	£650	
		b. Broken crown and scroll	£550	
		e. Break in lines below left scroll	£650	
		f. Damaged leaf at bottom right	£600	
		g. Green and red/deep emerald (1930)	£140	£275
		ga. Break in scroll	£650	
		gb. Broken crown and scroll	£600	
		gc. Nick in top right scroll	£650	
		gd. Break through scroll	£750	
		ge. Break in lines below left scroll	£750	
		gf. Damaged leaf at bottom right	£700	
		gg. Gash in fruit and leaf	£700	
93		12s.6d. grey and orange (8.32)	£250	£375
		a. Break in scroll	£700	£900
		b. Broken crown and scroll	£750	£950
		c. Nick in top right scroll	£800	
		d. Break through scroll	£900	
		e. Break in lines below left scroll	£900	
		f. Damaged leaf at bottom right	£800	
		g. Gash in fruit and leaf	£800	
		h. Break in scrolls at right	£900	
		i. Error. Ordinary paper		
88/93 Set of 4			£425	£700
88s/93s Optd or Perf (12s.6d) "Specimen" *Set of 4*			£500	

The true No. 89*h* is the only stamp on grey-blue paper, other deeper orange-vermilion shades exist on different papers. No. 89k was despatched to Bermuda in July/August 1932, but is not known used before 1937.

Beware of fiscally used 2s.6d. 10s. and 12s.6d. stamps cleaned and bearing faked postmarks. Large quantities were used for a "head tax" levied on travellers leaving the country.

For 12s.6d. design inscribed "Revenue" at both sides see No. F1 under POSTAL FISCAL.

1935 (6 May). *Silver Jubilee. As Nos. 91/4 of Antigua, but ptd by Waterlow.* P 11×12.

94		1d. deep blue and scarlet	55	1·75
		j. Damaged turret	£350	
		m. "Bird" by turret	£150	£180
95		1½d. ultramarine and grey	80	3·25
		m. "Bird" by turret	£160	
96		2½d. brown and deep blue	1·40	2·25
		m. "Bird" by turret	£250	£275
97		1s. slate and purple	17·00	35·00
		k. Kite and vertical log	£200	£300
		l. Kite and horizontal log	£450	
94/7 Set of 4			18·00	38·00
94s/7s Perf "Specimen" *Set of 4*			£200	

For illustrations of plate varieties see Omnibus section following Zanzibar.

20 Red Hole, Paget

21 South Shore

22 *Lucie* (yacht)

23 Grape Bay, Paget Parish

24 Point House, Warwick Parish

25 Gardener's Cottage, Par-la-Ville, Hamilton

(Recess B.W.)

1936 (14 Apr)–**47.** *T* 12. Wmk Mult Script CA (sideways on horiz designs).

98	20	½d. bright green	10	10
99	21	1d. black and scarlet	50	30
100		1½d. black and chocolate	1·00	50
101	22	2d. black and pale blue	5·00	1·50
102	23	2½d. light and deep blue	1·00	25
103	24	3d. black and scarlet	3·00	2·25
104	25	6d. carmine-lake and violet	80	10
		a. Claret and dull violet (6.47)	4·25	2·50
105	23	1s. green	8·00	14·00
106	20	1s.6d. brown	50	10
98/106 Set of 9			18·00	17·00
98s/106s Perf "Specimen" *Set of 9*			£275	

All are line-perf 11.9, except printings of the 6d. from July 1951 onwards, which are comb-perf 11.9×11.75.

1937 (14 May). *Coronation. As Nos. 95/7 of Antigua, but printed by D.L.R.* P 14.

107 1d. scarlet 70 1·25
108 1½d. yellow-brown 60 1·75
109 2½d. bright blue 70 1·75
107/9 *Set of 3* 1·75 4·25
107s/9s Perf "Specimen" *Set of 3* £180

26 Ships in Hamilton Harbour

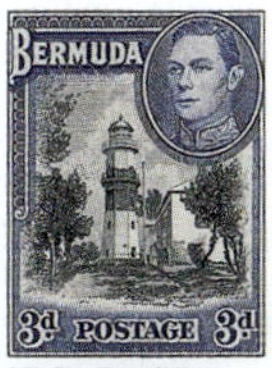

27 St. David's Lighthouse

28 White-tailed Tropic Bird, Arms of Bermuda and Native Flower

29 King George VI

(Des Miss Higginbotham (T **28**). Recess B.W.)

1938 (20 Jan)–**52**. *T* **22**, *T* **23** *(but with portrait of King George VI) and T* **26** *to* **28**. Wmk Mult Script CA. P 12.

110 **26** 1d. black and red (*a*) (*b*) 1·00 20
111 1½d. deep blue and purple-brown (*a*) (*b*) 7·00 1·50
a. Blue and brown (*a*) (3.43) 8·50 3·50
b. lt blue & purple-brn (*a*) (*b*) (9.45) 2·25 1·50
ba. "A" of "CA" missing from wmk £1600
112 **22** 2d. light blue and sepia (*a*) 50·00 9·00
112*a* 2d. ultramarine and scarlet (*a*) (*b*) (8.11.40) 1·50 1·00
113 **23** 2½d. light and deep blue (*a*) 11·00 1·25
113*a* 2½d. lt blue & sepia-black (*a*) (18.12.41) 3·00 2·75
b. Pale blue & sepia-black (*a*) (3.43) 2·75 2·75
c. Bright blue and deep sepia-black (*b*) (23.9.52) 5·50 6·50
114 **27** 3d. black and rose-red (*a*) 27·00 4·00
114*a* 3d. black & deep blue (*a*) (*b*) (16.7.41) 1·75 40
114*b* **28** 7½d. black, blue & brt grn (*a*) (18.12.41) 7·50 2·75
c. Black, blue & yellow-grn (*a*) (3.43) 6·00 2·75
115 **23** 1s. green (*a*) (*b*) 2·00 50
a. Bluish green (*b*) (20.6.52) 7·00 6·50

Perforations. Two different perforating machines were used on the various printings of these stamps: (*a*) the original 11.9 line perforation; (*b*) 11.9×11.75 comb perforation, introduced in July 1950. These perforations occur as indicated above.

Shading omitted from top right scroll (R. 1/1. March 1943 ptgs of 2s. and £1)

Lower right scroll with broken tail (R. 2/10. Line perforated printings only)

Broken top right scroll (R. 5/11. Line perforated ptgs only. A retouched state of the flaw is visible in later ptgs up to March 1943)

Broken lower right scroll (R. 5/12. Occurs on printings made between May 1941 and March 1943)

Gash in chin (R. 2/5. Ptgs between May 1941 and March 1943)

Missing pearl (R. 5/1, Nov 1945 ptg of 5s. only)

"ER" joined (R. 1/2. Occurs in its complete state on 1938 ptg only. Subsequent ptgs show it incomplete)

Damaged left value tablet (R. 1/11. Part of 1951 ptg only)

(Typo D.L.R.)

1938 (20 Jan)–**53**. *T* **29**. Wmk Mult Crown CA (£1) or Mult Script CA (others). *Chalk-surfaced paper.* P 14 (comb).

116 2s. deep purple and ultramarine/*grey-blue* £110 14·00
a. Deep reddish purple and ultram/grey-blue (21.11.40)* £350 29·00
b. Perf 14¼ line. *Deep purple and ultram/grey-blue* (14.11.41)* £300 85·00
bc. Lower right scroll with broken tail £3000 £1100
bd. Broken top right scroll £1700 £700
be. Broken lower right scroll £1700 £700
bf. Gash in chin £2000 £850
c. Ordinary paper. *Pur & bl/dp bl* (7.6.42) 8·00 1·50
ce. Broken lower right scroll £225 £110
cf. Gash in chin £275 £130
d. Ordinary paper. *Purple and deep blue/pale blue* (5.3.43) 12·00 1·50
db. Shading omitted from top right scroll £1700 £900
de. Broken lower right scroll £700 £425
df. Gash in chin £750 £450
e. Perf 13. Ordinary paper. *Dull purple and blue/pale blue* (15.2.50) 14·00 15·00
f. Perf 13. Ordinary paper. *Reddish purple and blue/pale blue* (10.10.50) 9·00 23·00
117 2s.6d. black and red/*grey-blue* 70·00 12·00
a. Perf 14¼ line. *Black and red/grey-blue* (21.2.42)* £550 £110
ac. Lower right scroll with broken tail £3250 £1200
ad. Broken top right scroll £2000 £850
ae. Broken lower right scroll £2000 £850
af. Gash in chin £2250 £950
b. Ordinary paper. *Black and red/pale blue* (5.3.43) 19·00 7·00
be. Broken lower right scroll £650 £375
bf. Gash in chin £750 £400
c. Perf 13. Ordinary paper. *Black and orange-red/pale blue* (10.10.50) 17·00 11·00
d. Perf 13. Ordinary paper. *Black and red/ pale blue* (18.6.52) 16·00 15·00
118 5s. green and red/*yellow* £140 32·00
a. Pale green & red/yellow (14.3.39)* £350 85·00
b. Perf 14¼ line. *Dull yellow-green and red/yellow* (5.1.43)* £275 40·00
bc. Lower right scroll with broken tail £2500 £800
bd. Broken top right scroll £1000 £400
be. Broken lower right scroll £1000 £400
bf. Gash in chin £1300 £475
c. Ordinary paper. *Dull yellow-green & carmine-red/pale yellow* (5.42)* £950 £140
ce. Broken lower right scroll £6000 £1600
cf. Gash in chin £6000 £1600
d. Ordinary paper. *Pale bluish green and carmine-red/pale yellow* (5.3.43) £100 50·00
de. Broken lower right scroll £1000 £550
df. Gash in chin £1000 £550
e. Ordinary paper. *Green and red/pale yellow* (11.45)* 50·00 22·00
ea. Missing pearl £850
f. Perf 13. Ordinary paper. *Yellow-green and red/pale yellow* (15.2.50) 28·00 24·00
g. Perf 13. *Green and scarlet/yellow (chalk-surfaced)* (10.10.50) 48·00 65·00
119 10s. green and deep lake/*pale emerald* £450 £325
a. Bluish green & deep red/green (8.39)* £225 £130
b. Perf 14¼ line. Ordinary paper. *Yellow green and carmine/green* (1942)* £500 £120
bc. Lower right scroll with broken tail £3500 £1400
bd. Broken top right scroll £1900 £900
be. Broken lower right scroll £1900 £900
bf. Gash in chin £2250 £950
c. Ordinary paper. *Yellowish green and deep carmine-red/green* (5.3.43) 70·00 65·00
ce. Broken lower right scroll £2750
cf. Gash in chin £2750
d. Ordinary paper. *Deep green and dull red/green (emerald back)* (11.12.46) 80·00 65·00
e. Perf 13. Ordinary paper. *Green and vermilion/green* (19.9.51) 42·00 45·00
f. Perf 13. Ordinary paper. *Green and dull red/green* (16.4.53) 42·00 50·00
120 12s.6d. deep grey and brownish orange £550 £425
a. Grey and brownish orange (shades) £200 75·00
b. Grey and pale orange (9.11.40)* £100 55·00
c. Ordinary paper (2.3.44)* £110 65·00
ce. Broken lower right scroll £2250 £2500
cf. Gash in chin £2500
d. Ordinary paper. *Grey and yell*† (17.9.47)* £700 £500
e. Perf 13. *Grey and pale orange (chalk surfaced)* (10.10.50) 95·00 75·00
121 £1 purple and black/*red* £275 £100
a. "ER" joined £900 £550
b. Pale purple & black/pale red (13.5.43)* 85·00 70·00
ba. "ER" joined £600 £475
bb. Shading omitted from top right scroll £3250
be. Broken lower right scroll £1900 £1400
bf. Gash in chin £1900 £1400
c. Dp reddish pur and blk/pale red (5.3.43)* 60·00 70·00
ca. "ER" joined £600 £600
ce. Broken lower right scroll £1800
cf. Gash in chin £1800
d. Perf 13. *Violet & black/scarlet* (7.12.51) 50·00 75·00
da. Damaged left value tablet £3250
e. Perf 13. *Brt violet & blk/scar* (10.12.52) £160 £170
110/21d *Set of 16* £300 £200
110s/21s Perf "Specimen" *Set of 16* £1800

Following extensive damage to their printing works on 29 December 1940 much of De La Rue's work was transferred to other firms operating under their supervision. It is understood that Williams Lea & Co produced those new printings ordered for the Bermuda high value stamps during 1941. The first batch of these printings showed the emergency use, by Williams Lea, of a 14¼ line perforating machine (exact gauge 14.15) instead of the comb perforation (exact gauge 13.9×13.8).

Dates marked * are those of earliest known use.

In No. 116c the coloured surfacing of the paper is mottled with white specks sometimes accompanied by very close horizontal lines. In Nos. 116d, 117b and 118c/d the surfacing is the same colour as the back, sometimes applied in widely spaced horizontal lines giving the appearance of laid paper.

†No. 120d is the so-called "lemon" shade.

HALF
PENNY

X X

30

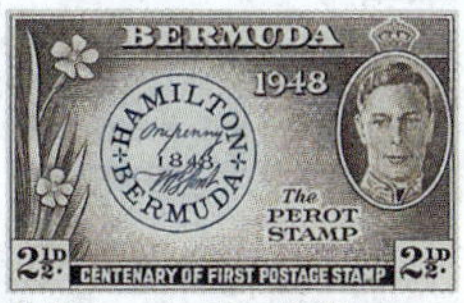

31 Postmaster Perot's Stamp

1940 (20 Dec). *No. 110 surch with T* **30** *by Royal Gazette, Hamilton.*

122 **26** ½d. on 1d. black and red (*shades*) 40 2·00

The spacing between "PENNY" and "X" varies from 12½ mm to 14 mm.

1946 (6 Nov). *Victory. As Nos. 110/11 of Antigua.*

123 1½d. brown 15 15
124 3d. blue 15 30
123s/4s Perf "Specimen" *Set of 2* £120

1948 (1 Dec). *Royal Silver Wedding. As Nos. 112/13 of Antigua.*

125 1½d. red-brown 30 50
126 £1 carmine 42·00 50·00

(Recess B.W.)

1949 (11 Apr). *Centenary of Postmaster Perot's Stamp.* Wmk Mult Script CA. P 13½.

127 **31** 2½d. blue and brown 35 35
128 3d. black and blue 35 15
129 6d. violet and green 40 15
127/9 *Set of 3* 1·00 60

1949 (10 Oct). *75th Anniv of Universal Postal Union. As Nos. 114/17 of Antigua.*

130 2½d. blue-black 30 2·00
131 3d. deep blue 1·75 1·25
132 6d. purple 40 75
133 1s. blue-green 40 1·50
130/3 *Set of 4* 2·50 5·00

1953 (4 June). *Coronation. As No. 200 of Bahamas, but ptd by B. W.*

134 1½d. black and blue 60 30

32 Easter Lilies

33 Postmaster Perot's stamp

34 Easter Lily

35 *Victory II* (racing dinghy)

36 Sir George Somers and *Sea Venture*

37 Map of Bermuda

38 *Sea Venture* (galleon), coin and Perot stamp

39 White-tailed Tropic Bird

40 Early Bermudan coinage

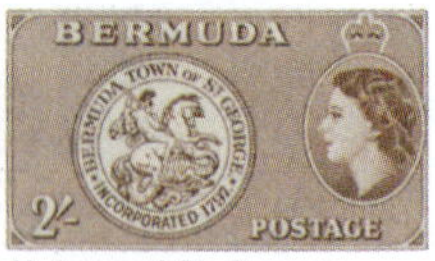

41 Arms of St. Georges

42 Warwick Fort

43 1 tog coin

44 Obverse and reverse of 1 tog coin

45 Arms of Bermuda

Die I "Sandy's"

Die II "Sandys"

(Des C. Deakins (½d., 3d., 1s.3d., 5s.), J. Berry (1d., 1½d., 2½d., 4d., 1s.). B. Brown (2d., 6d., 8d.), D. Haig (4½d., 9d.), Pamela Braley-Smith (2s.6d.) and E. C. Leslie (10s.) Recess (except £1, centre typo), B.W.)

1953 (9 Nov)–**62**. *T* **32**,/**45**. Wmk Mult Script CA. P 13½.

135	**32**	½d. olive-green	60	3·00
		a. Yellow-olive (19.5.54)	40	1·25
136	**33**	1d. black and red	2·00	50
		a. Black and deep red (19.5.54)..	3·75	1·00
137	**34**	1½d. green	30	10
138	**35**	2d. ultramarine and brown-red	50	40
139	**36**	2½d. rose-red	2·00	50
140	**37**	3d. deep purple (I)	30	10
140*a*		3d. deep purple (II) (2.1.57)	1·00	20
141	**33**	4d. black and bright blue	55	1·25
142	**38**	4½d. emerald	1·50	1·00
143	**39**	6d. black and deep turquoise	6·00	60
143*a*		8d. black and red (16.5.55)	3·25	30
143*b*	**38**	9d. violet (6.1.58)	9·00	2·50
144	**40**	1s. orange	50	15
145	**37**	1s.3d. blue (I)	3·75	30
		a. Greenish blue (21.9.54)	10·00	1·50
145*b*		1s.3d. blue (II) (2.1.57)	7·00	50
		bc. Bright blue (14.8.62)	15·00	4·50
146	**41**	2s. brown	4·00	85
147	**42**	2s.6d. scarlet	7·00	45
148	**43**	5s. carmine	19·00	85
149	**44**	10s. deep ultramarine	16·00	6·00
		a. Ultramarine (13.2.57)	65·00	15·00
150	**45**	£1 brown, blue, red, grn and bronze-grn	30·00	21·00
135/150 *Set of* 18			95·00	32·00

Nos. 136, 138 and 143 exist in coils, constructed from normal sheets.

1953 (26 Nov). *Royal Visit. As No. 143 but inscr* "ROYAL VISIT 1953" *in top left corner.*

151		6d. black and deep turquoise	60	20

Three Power Talks December, 1953. (46)

Three Power Talks December, 1953. (46a)

First setting (Type **46**). First line 24½ mm long.
Second setting (Type **46***a*). First line 25¼ mm long.

1953 (8 Dec). *Three Power Talks. Nos. 140 and 145 optd with T* **46** *by Royal Gazette, Hamilton.*

152	**37**	3d. deep purple (Type **46**) (B.)	10	10
		a. Optd with Type **46a**	1·00	15
153		1s.3d. blue (Type **46**) (R.)	10	10
		a. Optd with Type **46a**	3·00	3·00

50TH ANNIVERSARY U S – BERMUDA OCEAN RACE 1956 (47)

48 Perot's Post Office

1956 (22 June). *50th Anniv of United States–Bermuda Yacht Race. Nos. 143a and 145a optd with T* **47** *by the Bermuda Press.*

154		8d. black and red (Bk.)	20	45
155		1s.3d. greenish blue (R.)	20	55

(Des W. Harrington. Recess B.W.)

1959 (1 Jan). Wmk Mult Script CA. P 13½.

156	**48**	6d. black and deep mauve	1·25	15

49 Arms of King James I and Queen Elizabeth II

(Des W. Harrington. Recess; arms litho D.L.R.)

1959 (29 July). *350th Anniv of First Settlement. Arms, red, yellow and blue; frame colours below.* W w **12**. P 13.

157	**49**	1½d. grey-blue	25	10
158		3d. drab-grey	30	50
159		4d. reddish purple	35	55
160		8d. slate-violet	35	15
161		9d. olive-green	35	1·25
162		1s.3d. brown	35	30
157/162 *Set of* 6			1·75	2·50

50 The Old Rectory, St. George's, *circa* 1730

51 Church of St. Peter, St. George's

52 Government House, 1892

53 The Cathedral, Hamilton, 1894

54 H.M. Dockyard, 1811

55 Perot's Post Office, 1848

56 G.P.O Hamilton, 1869

57 Library, Par-la-Ville

58 Bermuda cottage, *circa* 1705

59 Christchurch, Warwick, 1719

60 City Hall Hamilton, 1960

61 Town of St. George

62 Bermuda house, *circa* 1710

63 Bermuda house, early 18th century

64 Colonial Secretariat, 1833

65 Old Post Office, Somerset, 1890

66 The House of Assembly, 1815

(Des W. Harrington. Photo Harrison)

1962 (26 Oct)–**68**. T **50/66**. W w **12** (upright). P 12½.

163	**50**	1d. reddish purple, black and orange	10	75
		w. Wmk inverted	†	—
164	**51**	2d. lilac, indigo, yellow and green	1·00	35
		a. Lilac omitted	£1000	£850
		b. Green omitted	†	£6000
		c. Imperf (pair)	£1800	
		d. *Pale lilac, indigo, yell and grn* (22.10.68)	2·50	1·00
		w. Wmk inverted	—	£200
165	**52**	3d. yellow-brown and light blue	10	10
166	**53**	4d. red-brown and magenta	20	40
167	**54**	5d. grey-blue and rose	75	2·50
168	**55**	6d. grey-blue, emerald and light blue	30	30
		w. Wmk inverted	£120	
169	**56**	8d. bright blue, bright green and orange	30	35
170	**57**	9d. light blue and brown	30	60
170*a*	**58**	10d. violet and ochre (8.2.65)	10·00	1·50
		aw. Wmk inverted		
171	**59**	1s. black, emerald, bright blue and orange	30	10
172	**60**	1s.3d. lake, grey and bistre	75	15
173	**58**	1s.6d. violet and ochre	75	1·00
174	**61**	2s. red-brown and orange	3·00	1·25
175	**62**	2s.3d. bistre-brown and yellow-green	1·00	6·50
176	**63**	2s.6d. bistre-brn, bluish grn & olive-yell	55	50
177	**64**	5s. brown-purple and blue-green	1·25	1·50
		w. Wmk inverted	£110	
178	**65**	10s. magenta, deep bluish green and buff	4·50	7·00
		w. Wmk inverted	£425	£475
179	**66**	£1 black, yellow-olive and yellow-orange	14·00	14·00
163/79 *Set of* 18			35·00	32·00

Three examples of No. 164b are known, all used on piece. The 3d. value with the yellow-brown omitted, previously No. 165a, is no longer listed as this is believed to be a dry print. All reported examples show traces of the yellow-brown.

See also Nos. 195/200 and 246a.

1963 (4 June). *Freedom from Hunger. As No. 146 of Antigua.*

180		1s.3d. sepia	60	40

1963 (2 Sept). *Red Cross Centenary. As Nos. 147/8 of Antigua.*

181		3d. red and black	50	25
182		1s.3d. red and blue	1·00	2·50

(Des V. Whiteley. Photo D.L.R.)

1964 (28 Sept). *Olympic Games, Tokyo.* W w **12**. P 14×13½.

183	**67**	3d. red, violet and blue	10	10

1965 (17 May). *I.T.U. Centenary. As Nos. 166/7 of Antigua.*

184		3d. light blue and emerald	35	25
185		2s. yellow and ultramarine	65	1·25

68 Scout Badge and St. Edward's Crown

(Des W. Harrington. Photo Harrison)

1965 (24 July). *50th Anniv of Bermuda Boy Scouts Association.* W w **12**. P 12½.
186 **68** 2s. multicoloured 50 50
w. Wmk inverted .... 50·00

1965 (25 Oct). *International Co-operation Year. As Nos. 168/9 of Antigua.*
187 4d. reddish purple and turquoise-green 40 20
188 2s.6d. deep bluish green and lavender 60 80

1966 (24 Jan). *Churchill Commemoration. As Nos. 170/3 of Antigua.*
189 3d. new blue 30 20
190 6d. deep green .... 70 1·00
191 10d. brown .... 1·00 75
192 1s.3d. bluish violet .... 1·25 2·50
189/92 *Set of* 4 .... 3·00 4·00

1966 (1 July). *World Cup Football Championship. As Nos. 176/7 of Antigua.*
193 10d. violet, yellow-green, lake and yellow-brn .... 1·00 15
194 2s.6d. chocolate, blue-grn, lake & yell-brn .... 1·25 1·25

1966 (25 Oct)–**69**. *Designs as Nos. 164, 167 (1s.6d.), 169, 170a/1 and 174 but* W w **12** *(sideways*).*
195 **51** 2d. lilac, indigo, yellow and green (20.5.69) .... 5·00 6·00
196 **56** 8d. brt blue, brt green and orange (14.2.67) .... 50 1·50
197 **58** 10d. violet and ochre (1.11.66) 75 60
w. Wmk Crown to right of CA £950 £950
198 **59** 1s. black, emerald, brt bl and orge (14.2.67) .... 70 1·40
199 **54** 1s.6d. grey-blue and rose (1.11.66) .... 1·50 50
w. Wmk Crown to right of CA .... 75·00
200 **61** 2s. red-brown and orange .... 1·50 75
195/200 *Set of* 6 .... 9·00 9·75

*The normal sideways watermark shows Crown to left of CA, *as seen from the back of the stamp.*

The 2d. value exists with PVA gum only, and the 8d. exists with PVA gum as well as gum arabic.

1966 (1 Dec). *20th Anniv of U.N.E.S.C.O. As Nos. 196/8 of Antigua.*
201 4d. slate-violet, red, yellow and orange 45 15
202 1s.3d. orange-yellow, violet and deep olive 75 50
203 2s. black, bright purple and orange .... 1·00 1·10
201/3 *Set of* 3 .... 2·00 1·60

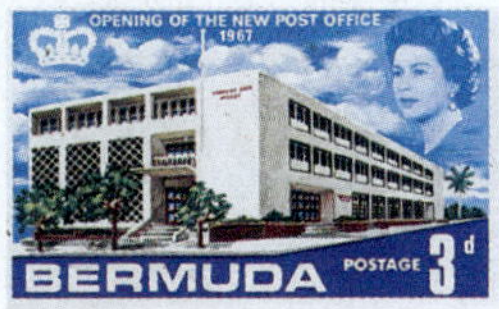

69 G.P.O. Building

(Des G. Vasarhelyi. Photo Harrison)

1967 (23 June). *Opening of New General Post Office, Hamilton.* W w **12**. P 14½.
204 **69** 3d. multicoloured 10 10
205 1s. multicoloured 10 10
206 1s.6d. multicoloured 20 25
207 2s.6d. multicoloured 20 70
204/7 *Set of* 4 .... 50 1·00

70 *Mercury* (cable ship) and Chain Links

(Des V. Whiteley. Photo Harrison)

1967 (14 Sept). *Inauguration of Bermuda–Tortola Telephone Service. T* **70** *and similar horiz designs. Multicoloured.* W w **12**. P 14½×14.
208 3d. Type **70** 15 10
209 1s. Map, telephone and microphone 25 10
210 1s.6d. Telecommunications media 25 25
211 2s.6d. *Mercury* (cable ship) and marine fauna 40 70
208/11 *Set of* 4 .... 1·00 1·00

74 Human Rights Emblem and Doves

(Des M. Farrar Bell. Litho Harrison)

1968 (1 Feb). *Human Rights Year.* W w **12**. P 14×14½.
212 **74** 3d. indigo, blue and dull green 10 10
213 1s. yellow-brown, blue and light blue 10 10
214 1s.6d. black, blue and rose 10 15
215 2s.6d. grey-green, blue and yellow 15 25
212/15 *Set of* 4 .... 30 55

REPRESENTATIVE GOVERNMENT

75 Mace and Queen's Profile

(Des R. Granger Barrett. Photo Harrison)

1968 (1 July). *New Constitution. T* **75** *and similar horiz design.* W w **12**. P 14.
216 **75** 3d. multicoloured 10 10
217 1s. multicoloured 10 10
218 – 1s.6d. greenish yellow, black and turq-bl 10 20
219 – 2s. 6d. lilac, black and orange-yellow 15 75
216/19 *Set of* 4 .... 30 1·00
Design:—1s.6d., 2s.6d. Houses of Parliament and House of Assembly, Bermuda.

77 Football, Athletics and Yachting

(Des V. Whiteley. Photo Harrison)

1968 (24 Sept). *Olympic Games, Mexico.* W w **12**. P 12½.
220 **77** 3d. multicoloured 15 10
a. Red-brown ("BERMUDA" and value) omitted £4500
221 1s. multicoloured 25 10
222 1s.6d. multicoloured 50 30
223 2s.6d. multicoloured .... 50 1·40
220/3 *Set of* 4 .... 1·25 1·75

78 Brownie and Guide

80 Emerald-studded Gold Cross and Seaweed

(Des Harrison. Litho Format)

1969 (17 Feb). *50th Anniv of Bermuda Girl Guides.* P 14.
224 **78** 3d. multicoloured 10 10
225 1s. multicoloured 20 10
226 – 1s.6d. multicoloured 25 40
227 – 2s.6d. multicoloured .... 35 1·40
224/7 *Set of* 4 .... 80 1·75
Design:—1s.6d., 2s.6d. Guides and badge.

(Des K. Giles adapted by V. Whiteley. Photo Harrison)

1969 (29 Sept). *Underwater Treasure. T* **80** *and similar vert design. Multicoloured.* W w **12** (sideways). P 14½×14.
228 4d. Type **80** 20 10
229 1s.3d. Emerald-studded gold cross and seabed 35 15
230 2s. Type **80** 45 90
231 2s.6d. As 1s.3d. .... 45 1·75
228/31 *Set of* 4 .... 1·25 2·50

(New Currency. 100 cents = 1 Bermuda dollar)

1c

(82)

2c
Tall "2" (Pl 1A. R. 2/2)

1970 (6 Feb). *Decimal Currency. As Nos. 163, 165/6, 168, 170, 172, 175/9 and 195/200 surch as T* **82**. W w **12** (sideways* on 2, 5, 10, 12, 15, 18, 24, 30, 60c., $1.20 and $2.40).
232 1c. on 1d. reddish purple, black and orange .... 10 1·75
w. Wmk inverted .... 50·00 27·00
233 2c. on 2d. lilac, indigo, yellow and green 10 10
a. Lilac omitted £900
b. Vert pair, one without surch £5500
c. Tall "2" .... 7·50
dw. Wmk Crown to right of CA .... 85·00
e. Wmk upright (No. 164) .... 1·75 3·50
ea. Tall "2" .... 24·00
f. Wmk upright (No. 164d) .... 2·50 3·75
fa. Tall "2" .... 27·00
234 3c. on 3d. yellow-brown and light blue 10 30
235 4c. on 4d. red-brown and magenta (Br.) 10 10
236 5c. on 8d. bright blue, brt green and orange .... 15 2·25
237 6c. on 6d. grey-blue, emerald & light blue .... 15 1·75
a. Horiz pair, one with albino surch, the other with albino bar ....
w. Wmk inverted .... † £170
238 9c. on 9d. light blue and brown (Br.) .... 30 2·75
239 10c. on 10d. violet and ochre 30 25
240 12c. on 1s. black, emerald, brt blue and orge .... 30 1·25
241 15c. on 1s.3d. lake, grey and bistre .... 1·50 1·50
242 18c. on 1s.6d. grey-blue and rose 80 65
243 24c. on 2s. red-brown and orange .... 85 2·75
w. Wmk Crown to right of CA .... 95·00
244 30c. on 2s.6d. bistre-brown, bluish green and olive-yellow .... 1·00 3·00
245 36c. on 2s.3d. bistre-brown & yellow-green .... 1·75 8·00
246 60c. on 5s. brown-purple and blue-green .... 2·25 4·50
a. Surch omitted £1000
247 $1.20 on 10s. mag, dp bluish green and buff .... 4·00 15·00
248 $2.40 on £1 black, yellow-olive and yellow-orange .... 5·50 19·00
232/48 *Set of* 17 .... 17·00 55·00

*The normal sideways watermark shows Crown to left of CA, *as seen from the back of the stamp.*

†No. 246a differs from the normal No. 177 by its watermark, which is sideways, and its gum, which is PVA.

83 Spathiphyllum

(Des W. Harrington. Photo D.L.R.)

1970 (6 July)–**75**. *Flowers. Multicoloured designs as T* **83**. W w **12** (sideways on horiz designs). P 14.
249 1c. Type **83** 10 20
250 2c. Bottlebrush 20 25
251 3c. Oleander (*vert*) 15 10
252 4c. Bermudiana 15 10
253 5c. Poinsettia 30 20
254 6c. Hibiscus 30 30
255 9c. Cereus 20 45
256 10c. Bougainvillea (*vert*) 20 15
257 12c. Jacaranda 60 60
258 15c. Passion-Flower .... 90 1·40
258*a* 17c. As 15c. (2.6.75) .... 2·75 4·00
259 18c. Coralita .... 2·25 1·50
259*a* 20c. As 18c. (2.6.75) .... 2·75 4·00
260 24c. Morning Glory .... 1·50 4·75
260*a* 25c. As 24c. (2.6.75) .... 2·75 4·50
261 30c. Tecoma .... 1·00 1·25
262 36c. Angel's Trumpet .... 1·25 1·75
262*a* 40c. As 36c. (2.6.75) .... 2·75 5·50
263 60c. Plumbago .... 1·75 1·50
263*a* $1 As 60c. (2.6.75) .... 3·25 6·50
264 $1.20 Bird of Paradise flower .... 2·25 1·75
264*a* $2 As $1.20 (2.6.75) .... 7·50 8·50
265 $2.40 Chalice Cup .... 6·00 4·00
265*a* $3 As $2.40 (2.6.75) .... 11·00 11·00
249/65*a* *Set of* 24 .... 45·00 55·00
See also Nos. 303/6 and 340/1.

84 The State House, St. George's

(Des G. Drummond. Litho Questa)

1970 (12 Oct). *350th Anniv of Bermuda Parliament. T* **84** *and similar horiz designs. Multicoloured.* W w **12** (sideways). P 14.
266 4c. Type **84** 10 10
267 15c. The Sessions House, Hamilton 25 20
268 18c. St. Peter's Church, St. George's 25 25
269 24c. Town Hall, Hamilton 35 75
266/9 *Set of* 4 .... 85 1·00
MS270 131×95 mm. Nos. 266/9 .... 1·10 1·50

STAMP BOOKLETS

1948 (5 Apr–10 May). *Pink (No. SB1), or light blue (No. SB2) covers. Stapled.*

SB1	5s. booklet containing six 1d., 1½d., 2d., 2½d. and 3d. (Nos. 110, 111*b*, 112*a*, 113*b*, 114*a*) in blocks of 6 (10 May)	£140	
SB2	10s.6d. booklet containing six 3d. and eighteen 6d. (Nos. 114*a*, 104) in blocks of 6 with twelve air mail labels	£150	

POSTAL FISCAL

1937 (1 Feb). *As T* **15**, *but inscr* "REVENUE" *at each side.* Wmk Mult Script CA. *Chalk-surfaced paper.* P 14

F1	12s.6d. grey and orange	£1100	£1400
	a. Break in scroll (R. 1/12)	£4000	£6000
	b. Broken crown and scroll (R. 2/12)	£4000	
	d. Break through scroll (R. 1/9)	£4000	
	e. Break in lines below left scroll	£4000	
	f. Damaged leaf at bottom right	£4000	
	g. Gash in fruit and leaf	£4000	
	h. Breaks in scrolls at right (R. 1/3)	£4000	

No. F1 was issued for fiscal purposes towards the end of 1936. Its use as a postage stamp was authorised from 1 February to April 1937. The used price quoted above is for examples postmarked during this period. Later in the same year postmarks with other dates were obtained by favour.

For illustration of No. F1a/h see above Nos. 51*b* and 88.

Botswana

INDEPENDENCE

47 National Assembly Building

(Des R. Granger Barrett. Photo Harrison)

1966 (30 Sept). *Independence. T* **47** *and similar horiz designs. Multicoloured.* P 14½.

202	2½c. Type **47**	15	10
	a. Imperf (pair)	£375	
203	5c. Abattoir Lobatsi	20	10
204	15c. National Airways Douglas DC-3	65	20
205	35c. State House, Gaberones	40	30
202/5 *Set of 4*		1·25	55

REPUBLIC OF BOTSWANA

(**51**)

52 Golden Oriole

1966 (30 Sept). *Nos. 168/81 optd as T* **51**.

206	1c. yellow, red, black and lilac	25	10
207	2c. orange, black and yellow-olive	30	1·75
208	2½c. carmine, green, black and bistre	30	10
209	3½c. yellow, black, sepia and pink	1·25	20
	a. Yellow, black, sepia and flesh	2·00	1·25
210	5c. yellow, blue, black and buff	1·50	1·50
211	7½c. brown, red, black and apple-green	50	1·75
	a. Blue-green omitted		
212	10c. red, yellow, sepia & turquoise-green	1·00	20
213	12½c. buff, blue, red and grey-black	2·00	2·75
214	20c. yellow-brown and drab	20	1·00
215	25c. deep brown and lemon	20	2·00
216	35c. deep blue and orange	30	2·25
217	50c. sepia and olive	20	70
218	1r. black and cinnamon	40	1·25
219	2r. brown and turquoise-blue	60	2·50
206/19 *Set of 14*		8·00	16·00

No. 209*a* was a special printing produced to make up quantities. It does not exist without the overprint.

No. 211a shows the background in yellow instead of apple-green, the blue-green overlay being omitted.

(Des D. M. Reid-Henry. Photo Harrison)

1967 (3 Jan). *Birds. Vert designs as T* **52**. *Multicoloured.* P 14×14.

220	1c. Type **52**	30	15
	a. Error. Wmk **105** of Malta	†	£750
221	2c. Hoopoe	60	70
222	3c. Groundscraper Thrush	55	10
223	4c. Cordon-bleu ("Blue Waxbill")	55	10
224	5c. Secretary Bird	55	10
225	7c. Yellow-billed Hornbill	60	1·00
226	10c. Burchell's Gonolek ("Crimson-breasted Shrike")	60	15
227	15c. Malachite Kingfisher	7·50	3·00
228	20c. African Fish Eagle	7·50	2·00
229	25c. Go-away Bird ("Grey Loerie")	4·00	1·50
230	35c. Scimitar-bill	6·00	2·25
231	50c. Comb Duck	2·75	2·75
232	1r. Levaillant's Barbet	5·00	3·50
233	2r. Didric Cuckoo	7·00	16·00
220/33 *Set of 14*		38·00	30·00

A used copy of the 20c. has been seen with the pale brown colour missing, resulting in the value (normally shown in white) being omitted.

The 1, 2, 4, 7 and 10c. values exist with PVA gum as well as gum arabic.

66 Students and University

(Des V. Whiteley. Photo Harrison)

1967 (7 Apr). *First Conferment of University Degrees.* P 14×14½.

234	**66** 3c. sepia, ultramarine and light orange-yell	10	10
235	7c. sepia, ultram & lt greenish bl.	10	10
236	15c. sepia, ultramarine and rose	10	10
237	35c. sepia, ultramarine and light violet	20	20
234/7 *Set of 4*		30	30

67 Bushbuck

(Des G. Vasarhelyi. Photo Harrison)

1967 (2 Oct). *Chobe Game Reserve. T* **67** *and similar horiz designs. Multicoloured.* P 14.

238	3c. Type **67**	10	20
239	7c. Sale Antelope	15	30
240	35c. Fishing on Chobe River	80	1·10
238/40 *Set of 3*		90	1·40

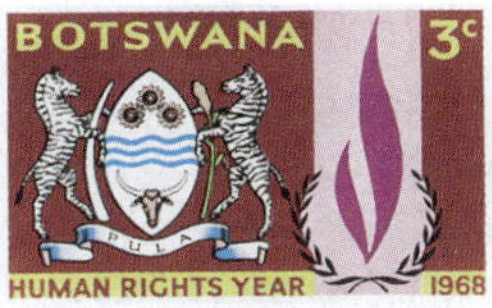

70 Arms of Botswana and Human Rights Emblem

(Litho D.L.R.)

1968 (8 Apr). *Human Rights Year. T* **70** *and similar horiz designs showing Anniv of Botswana and Human Rights emblem arranged differently.* P 13½×13.

241	3c. multicoloured	10	10
242	15c. multicoloured	25	45
243	25c. multicoloured	25	60
241/3 *Set of 3*		50	1·00

73 Eland and Giraffe Rock

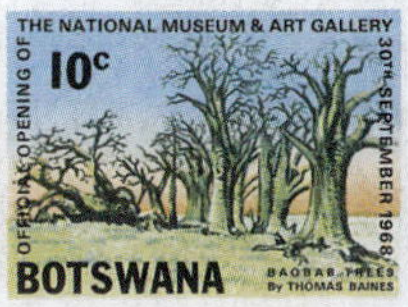

75 "Baobab Trees" (Thomas Paintings, Tsodilo Hills Baines)

76 National Museum and Art Gallery

(Litho D.L.R.)

1968 (30 Sept). *Opening of National Museum and Art Gallery. T* **73/6** *and similar multicoloured design.* P 12½ (7c.), 12½×13½ (15c.), or 13×13½ (others).

244	3c. Type **73**	20	20
245	7c. Girl wearing ceremonial beads (30×48 *mm*)	25	40
246	10c. Type **75**	25	30
247	15c. Type **76**	40	1·50
244/7 *Set of 4*		1·00	2·25
MS248 132×82 mm. Nos. 244/7. P 13		1·00	2·25

77 African Family, and Star over Village

(Des Mrs M. E. Townsend, adapted J. Cooter. Litho Enschedé)

1968 (11 Nov). *Christmas.* P 13×14.

249	**77** 1c. multicoloured	10	10
250	2c. multicoloured	10	10
251	5c. multicoloured	10	10
252	25c. multicoloured	15	50
249/52 *Set of 4*		30	70

78 Scout, Lion and Badge in Frame

(Des D.L.R. Litho Format)

1969 (21 Aug). *22nd World Scout Conference, Helsinki. T* **78** *and similar multicoloured designs.* P 13½.

253	3c. Type **78**	30	30
254	15c. Scouts cooking over open fire (*vert*)	35	1·00
255	25c. Scouts around camp fire	35	1·00
253/5 *Set of 3*		90	2·00

81 Woman, Child and Christmas Star

82 Diamond Treatment Plant, Orapa

(Des A. Vale, adapted V. Whiteley. Litho Harrison)

1969 (6 Nov). *Christmas.* P 14½×14.

256	**81** 1c. pale blue and chocolate	10	10
257	2c. pale yellow-olive and chocolate	10	10
258	4c. yellow and chocolate	10	10
259	35c. chocolate and bluish violet	20	20
256/9 *Set of 4*		30	30
MS260 86×128 mm. Nos. 256/9. P 14½ (*shades*)		70	1·10

(Des J.W. Litho Harrison)

1970 (23 Mar). *Developing Botswana. T* **82** *and similar designs. Multicoloured.* P 14½×14 (3c., 7c.) or 14×14½ (others).

261	3c. Type **82**	70	20
262	7c. Copper-nickel mining	95	20
263	10c. Copper-nickel mine, Selebi–Pikwe (*horiz*)	1·25	15
264	35c. Orapa diamond mine, and diamonds (*horiz*)	2·75	1·25
261/4 *Set of 4*		5·00	1·60

83 Mr. Micawber (*David Copperfield*)

(Des V. Whiteley. Litho Walsall)

1970 (6 July). *Death Centenary of Charles Dickens. T* **83** *and similar horiz designs. Multicoloured.* P 11.

265	3c. Type **83**	25	10
266	7c. Scrooge (*A Christmas Carol*)	25	10
267	15c. Fagin (*Oliver Twist*)	45	40
268	25c. Bill Sykes (*Oliver Twist*)	70	60
265/8 *Set of 4*		1·50	1·00
MS269 114×81 mm. Nos. 265/8		2·75	4·00

84 U.N. Building and Emblem

(Des J. Cooter. Litho Walsall)

1970 (24 Oct). *25th Anniv of United Nations.* P 11.

270	**84** 15c. bright blue, chestnut and silver	70	30

85 Crocodile

(Des A. Vale. Litho Questa)

1970 (3 Nov). *Christmas. T* **85** *and similar horiz designs. Multicoloured.* P 14.

271	1c. Type **85**	10	10
272	2c. Giraffe	10	10
273	7c. Elephant	15	15

274	25c. Rhinoceros	60	80
271/4	*Set of 4*	80	1·00
MS275	128×90 mm. Nos. 271/4	1·00	3·00

POSTAGE DUE STAMPS

REPUBLIC OF

BOTSWANA

(D **4**)

1967 (1 Mar). *Nos. D10/12 optd with Type* D **4**.

D13	1c. carmine	15	1·75
D14	2c. violet	15	1·75
D15	5c. green	20	1·75
D13/15	*Set of 3*	45	4·75

British Antarctic Territory

1963. 12 pence (d.) = 1 shilling;
20 shillings = £11971. 100 pence (p.) = £1

For use at the following bases:

Adelaide Island (Graham Land) (*closed* 1977)
Argentine Islands ("Faraday" *from* 1981), (Graham Land) (*closed* 8 February 1996 *and transferred to Ukraine*)
Brabant Island (Graham Land) (*opened* 1984, *closed* 1985)
Deception Island (South Shetlands) (*closed* December 1967, *opened* 4 December 1968, *closed* 23 February 1969)

Halley Bay (Coats Land)
Hope Bay (Graham Land) (*closed* 12 February 1964)
Port Lockroy (Graham Land) (*opened* 25 November 1996)
Rothera Point (Graham Land) (*opened* 1977)
Signy Island (South Orkneys)
Stonington Island (Graham Land) (*closed* February 1975)

1 M.V. *Kista Dan*

2 Manhauling

3 Muskeg (tractor)

4 Skiing

5 De Havilland D.H.C.2 Beaver

6 R.R.S. *John Biscoe II*

7 Camp scene

8 H.M.S. *Protector*

9 Sledging

10 De Havilland D.H.C.3 Otter

11 Huskies

12 Westland Whirlwind

13 Snocat

14 R.R.S. *Shackleton*

15 Antarctic map

16 H.M.S. *Endurance*

(Des B.W. (No. 15*a*), M. Goaman (others). Recess B.W.)

1963 (1 Feb)–**69**. *Horiz designs as T* **1**. W w **12**. P 11×11½.

1	**1**	½d. deep blue	1·25	1·75
2	**2**	1d. brown	1·25	80
3	**3**	1½d. orange-red and brown-purple	1·25	1·50
4	**4**	2d. purple	1·50	80
5	**5**	2½d. myrtle-green	3·25	1·25
6	**6**	3d. deep blue	3·75	1·50
7	**7**	4d. sepia	2·75	1·50
8	**8**	6d. olive and deep ultramarine	4·75	2·50
9	**9**	9d. olive-green	3·50	2·00
10	**10**	1s. deep turquoise-blue	4·25	1·50
11	**11**	2s. deep violet and orange-sepia	20·00	10·00
12	**12**	2s.6d. blue	22·00	13·00
13	**13**	5s. red-orange and rose-red	22·00	17·00
14	**14**	10s. deep ultramarine and emerald	45·00	26·00
15	**15**	£1 black and light blue	48·00	48·00
15*a*	**16**	£1 red and brownish black (1.12.69)	£130	£120
1/15*a* *Set of* 16			£275	£225

1966 (24 Jan). *Churchill Commemoration. As Nos. 223/6 of Falkland Islands.*

16	½d. new blue	80	3·25
17	1d. deep green	3·00	3·25
18	1s. brown	21·00	6·50
19	2s. bluish violet	24·00	7·00
16/19 *Set of* 4		45·00	18·00

17 Lemaire Channel and Icebergs

(Des R. Granger Barrett. Litho Format)

1969 (6 Feb). *25th Anniv of Continuous Scientific Work. T* **17** *and similar horiz designs.* W w **12** (sideways). P 14.

20	3½d. black, pale blue and ultramarine	2·50	3·00
21	6d. multicoloured	1·00	2·50
22	1s. black, pale blue and vermilion	1·00	2·00
23	2s. black, orange and turquoise-blue	1·00	3·00
20/3 *Set of* 4		5·00	9·50

Designs:—6d. Radio Sonde balloon; 1s. Muskeg pulling tent equipment; 2s. Surveyors with theodolite.

British Guiana

The postal service from what was to become British Guiana dates from 1796, being placed on a more regular basis after the final British occupation.

An inland postal system was organised in 1850, using the adhesive stamps of British Guiana, but, until 1 May 1860, overseas mails continued to be the province of the British G.P.O. The stamps of Great Britain were supplied for use on such letters from 11 May 1858 and examples of their use in combination with British Guiana issues have been recorded.

For illustration of the handstamp and postmark type see BRITISH POST OFFICES ABROAD notes, following GREAT BRITAIN.

CROWNED-CIRCLED HANDSTAMPS

The provision of a handstamp, probably as Type CC **1**, inscribed "DEMERARA", is recorded in the G.P.O. proof book under 1 March 1856. No examples have been reported. A further handstamp, as Type CC **6**, recorded in the proof book on 17 February 1866, is known used as a cancellation in at least two instances, *circa* 1868.

GEORGETOWN (DEMERARA)

Stamps of GREAT BRITAIN *cancelled* "A 03" *as Type* **2**.

1858–60.

Z1	1d. rose-red (1857), *perf* 14	£350
Z2	4d. rose (1857)	£180
Z3	6d. lilac (1856)	£120
	a. Azure paper	
Z4	1s. green (1856)	£1500

NEW AMSTERDAM (BERBICE)

Stamps of GREAT BRITAIN *cancelled* "A 04" *as Type* **2**.

1858–60.

Z5	1d. rose-red (1857), *perf* 14	£850
Z6	2d. blue (1858) (Plate Nos. 7, 8)	£1000
Z7	4d. rose (1857)	£375
Z8	6d. lilac (1856)	£250
Z9	1s. green (1856)	£1900

PRICES FOR STAMPS ON COVER TO 1945

No. 1	*from* × 1
Nos. 2/8	*from* × 4
Nos. 9/21	*from* × 3
No. 23	†
Nos. 24/7	*from* × 3
Nos. 29/115	*from* × 5
Nos. 116/24	*from* × 8
Nos. 126/36	*from* × 7
Nos. 137/59	*from* × 8
Nos. 162/5	*from* × 10
Nos. 170/4	*from* × 8
Nos. 175/89	*from* × 10
No. 192	*from* × 30
Nos. 193/210	*from* × 5
Nos. 213/15	*from* × 8
Nos. 216/21	*from* × 5
Nos. 222/4	*from* × 10
Nos. 233/50	*from* × 4
No. 251	—
Nos. 252/7	*from* × 4
Nos. 259/82	*from* × 5
Nos. 283/7	*from* × 8
Nos. 288/300	*from* × 5
Nos. 301/4	*from* × 6
Nos. 305/7	*from* × 8
Nos. 308/19	*from* × 5
Nos. D1/4	*from* × 15
Nos. O1/12	*from* × 15

CROWN COLONY

(Currency. 100 cents = 1 dollar)

1

2

(Set up and printed at the office of the *Royal Gazette*, Georgetown, British Guiana)

1850 (1 July)–**51**. *Type-set. Black impression.*

(a) Medium wove paper. Prices are for—I. *Cut square.* II. *Cut round.*

			I *Used*	II *Used*
1	**1**	2c. *rose* (1.3.51)	—	£170000
2		4c. *orange*	£48000	£8000
3		4c. *lemon-yellow* (1851)	£75000	£12000
4		8c. *green*	£32000	£7000
5		12c. *blue*	£13000	£4750
6		12c. *indigo*	£18000	£5500
7		12c. *pale blue* (1851)	£18000	£6000
		a. "2" of "12" with straight foot	£50000	£13000
		b. "1" of "12" omitted	†	£85000
		(b) Pelure paper (1851).		
8	**1**	4c. *pale yellow*	£85000	£12000

These stamps were usually initialled by the postmaster, or the Post Office clerks, before they were issued. The initials are—E. T. E. D(alton), E. D. W(ight), J. B. S(mith), H. A. K(illikelley), and W. H. L(ortimer). There are several types of each value and it has been suggested that the setting contained one horizontal row of four slightly different impressions.

Ten examples of No. 1 have been recorded, including three pairs on separate covers.

(Litho Waterlow)

1852 (1 Jan). *Surface-coloured paper.* Imperf.

9	**2**	1c. black/*magenta*	£8500	£4250
10		4c. black/*deep blue*	£14000	£9000

There are two types of each value.

Reprints on thicker paper, and perf 12½, were made in 1865 (*Price £18 either value*).

Such reprints with the perforations removed are sometimes offered as genuine originals.

CONDITION. Prices for Nos. 9 to 21 are for fine copies. Poor to medium specimens can be supplied when in stock at much lower rates.

3

4

5

(Dies eng and stamps litho Waterlow)

1853–59. Imperf.

(a) Original printing.

11	**3**	1c. vermilion	£3750	£1100

This 1c. in *reddish brown* is probably a proof (*Price* £750).

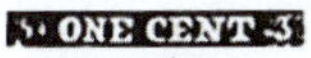
A

B

C

D

A. "O" large and 1 mm from left corner.
B. "O" small and ¾ mm from left corner.
C. "O" small and ¾ mm from left corner. "NT" widely spaced.
D. "ONE" close together, "O" 1¼ mm from left corner.

(b) Fresh lithographic transfers from the 4c. with varying labels of value. White line above value (1857–59).

12	**3**	1c. dull red (A)	£3500	£1300
13		1c. brownish red (A)	£7500	£1700
14		1c. dull red (B)	£4000	£1400
15		1c. brownish red (B)	£8000	£1800
16		1c. dull red (C)	£5000	£1700
16*a*		1c. brownish red (C)	—	£2250
17		1c. dull red (D)	£19000	£8000

1853–55. Imperf.

18	**4**	4c. deep blue	£2750	£750
		a. Retouched	£3750	£1000
19		4c. blue (1854)	£1500	£500
		a. Retouched	£2250	£700
20		4c. pale blue (1855)	£1100	£425
		a. Retouched	£1600	£600

The 4c. value was produced from transfers from the original 1c., with the bottom inscription removed, teamed with a new face value. The join often shows as a white line or traces of it above the label of value and lower corner figures. In some stamps on the sheet this line is missing, owing to having been retouched, and in these cases a line of colour usually appears in its place.

The 1c. and 4c. stamps were printed in 1865 from fresh transfers of five varieties. These are on thin paper and perf 12½ (*Price £16 each unused*).

1860 (May). *Figures in corners framed.* Imperf

21	**5**	4c. blue	£4000	£550

6

(Type-set and printed at the *Official Gazette* by Baum and Dallas, Georgetown).

1856.

		(a) Surface-coloured paper.		
23	6	1c. black/*magenta*	†	–
24		4c. black/*magenta* (Jan)	–	£8500
25		4c. black/*rose-carmine* (Aug)	£28000	£12000
26		4c. black/*blue* (Sept)	†	£65000
		(b) Paper coloured through.		
27	6	4c. black/*deep blue* (Aug)	†	£90000

Since only one example of No. 23 is known, no market price can be given. This celebrated stamp frequently termed "the world's rarest", was last on the market in 1980. It is initialled by E. D. Wight and postmarked at Demerara on 4 April 1856.

These stamps, like those of the first issue, were initialled before being issued; the initials are—E.T.E.D (alton), E.D.W. (ight), C.A.W (atson), and W.H.L (ortimer). C.A.W. only appears on stamps postmarked between 14 March and 4 April and also 16–20 May. E.T.E.D. is only known on stamps between 1–5 July and on 1 August. All examples on the rose-carmine or blue papers show E.D.W.

Stamps as Type **6** were printed in sheets of 4 (2×2) each stamp differing slightly in the position of the inscriptions. There is evidence that the setting was re-arranged at some point before August, *possibly* to accommodate the production of the 1c.

PAPERMAKERS' WATERMARKS. Seven different papermakers' watermarks were used in the period 1860 to 1875 and stamps bearing portions of these are worth a premium.

7

A

B

C

D

E

F

(Dies eng and litho Waterlow)

1860 (July)–**63**. *Tablets of value as illustrated. Thick paper.* P 12.

29	7	1c. pale rose	£2000	£225
30		2c. deep orange (8.60)	£225	48·00
31		2c. pale orange	£250	50·00
32		4c. deep blue (8.60)	£550	85·00
33		4c. blue	£325	55·00
34		8c. brownish rose	£700	£110
35		8c. pink	£550	75·00
36		12c. lilac	£650	45·00
37		12c. grey-lilac	£550	42·00
38		24c. deep green (6.63)	£1700	£110
39		24c. green	£1300	65·00

The 1c. was reprinted in 1865 on *thin* paper, P 12½–13, and in a different shade. *Price* £17.

The 12c. in both shades is frequently found surcharged with a large "5d" in *red*; this is to denote the proportion of postage repayable by the colony to Great Britain for overseas letters.

1861 (3 Aug*). *Colour changed. Thick paper.* P 12.

40	7	1c. reddish brown	£350	95·00

*Earliest known postmark date.

1862–65.

		(a) Thin paper. P 12.		
41	7	1c. brown	£600	£190
42		1c. black (1863)	£100	50·00
43		2c. orange	90·00	50·00
44		4c. blue	£110	45·00
45		4c. pale blue	95·00	32·00
46		8c. pink (1863)	£170	60·00
47		12c. dull purple (1863)	£225	28·00
48		12c. purple	£250	32·00
49		12c. lilac	£275	42·00
50		24c. green	£1100	90·00
		(b) Thin paper. P 12½–13 (1863).		
51	7	1c. black	60·00	20·00
52		2c. orange	75·00	22·00
53		4c. blue	75·00	17·00
54		8c. pink	£250	80·00
55		12c. brownish lilac	£750	£110
56		24c. green	£700	65·00

Copies are found on *pelure* paper.

		(c) Medium paper. P 12½–13.		
57	7	1c. black (1864)	50·00	45·00
58		2c. deep orange (1864)	65·00	27·00
59		2c. orange	70·00	25·00
60		4c. greyish blue (1864)	80·00	21·00
61		4c. blue	95·00	27·00
62		8c. pink (1864)	£180	60·00
63		12c. brownish lilac (1865)	£700	£100
64		24c. green (1864)	£250	50·00
65		24c. deep green	£300	75·00
		(d) Medium paper. P 10 (No. 1865).		
65*a*	7	12c. grey-lilac	£600	80·00

8

9

G

H

I

K

New transfers for the 1c., 2c., 8c., and 12c. with the spaces between values and the word "CENTS" about 1 mm.

1863–76. *Medium paper.*

		(a) P 12½–13 (1863–68).		
66	8	1c. black (1866)	50·00	30·00
67		2c. orange-red (1865)	55·00	8·00
68		2c. orange	55·00	8·00
69	9	6c. blue (1865)	£140	60·00
70		6c. greenish blue	£150	65·00
71		6c. deep blue	£225	75·00
72		6c. milky blue	£140	60·00
73	8	8c. pink (1868)	£250	22·00
74		8c. carmine	£325	24·00
75		12c. grey-lilac (1867)	£475	35·00
76		12c. brownish purple	£600	45·00
77	9	24c. green (*perf* 12)	£275	21·00
78		24c. yellow-green (*perf* 12)	£180	13·00
79		24c. yellow-green (*perf* 12½–13)	£180	13·00
80		24c. green (*perf* 12½–13) (1864)	£180	13·00
81		24c. blue-green (*perf* 12½–13)	£225	21·00
82		48c. pale red	£275	60·00
83		48c. deep red	£300	60·00
84		48c. carmine-rose	£325	60·00

The 4c. corresponding to this issue can only be distinguished from that of the previous issue by minor plating flaws.

There is a variety of the 6c. with stop before "VICISSIM".

Varieties of most of the values of issues of 1863–64 and 1866 are to be found on both very thin and thick papers.

		(b) P 10 (1866–71).		
85	8	1c. black (1869)	15·00	6·50
86		1c. grey-black	17·00	14·00
87		2c. orange (1868)	35·00	4·25
88		2c. reddish orange	48·00	6·00
89		4c. slate-blue	£100	13·00
90		4c. blue	90·00	9·00
		a. Bisected (on cover)	†	£6000
		b. Ditto. Imperf (on cover)	†	–
91		4c. pale blue	85·00	9·50
92	9	6c. milky blue (1867)	£150	32·00
93		6c. ultramarine	£160	55·00
94		6c. dull blue	£150	35·00
95	8	8c. pink (5.71)	£170	29·00
96		8c. brownish pink	£200	32·00
96*a*		8c. carmine	£275	45·00
97		12c. pale lilac (1867)	£250	20·00
98		12c. grey-lilac	£200	19·00
99		12c. brownish grey	£200	21·00
100		12c. lilac	£200	21·00
101	9	24c. deep green	£275	9·50
102		24c. bluish green	£250	8·00
103		24c. yellow-green	£200	7·50
104		48c. crimson (1867)	£325	32·00
		s. Handstamped "Specimen"	£225	
		as. Perf "Specimen"	£180	
105		48c. red	£300	27·00
		(c) P 15 (1875–76).		
106	8	1c. black	50·00	7·50
107		2c. orange-red	£130	11·00
108		2c. orange	£130	11·00
109		4c. bright blue	£225	95·00
111	9	6c. ultramarine	£750	£100
112	8	8c. deep rose (1876)	£250	85·00
113		12c. lilac	£650	75·00
114	9	24c. yellow-green	£650	35·00
115		24c. deep green	£1100	80·00

There is a variety of the 48c. with stop after "P" in "PETIMUSQUE".

Imperforate stamps of this and of the previous issue are considered to be proofs, although examples of the 24c. imperforate from the 1869–73 period are known commercially used.

PRICES for stamps of the 1862 issue are for good average copies. Copies with roulettes on all sides very seldom occur and do not exist in marginal positions.

10

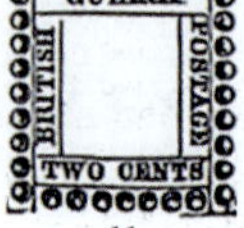

11

12

13

14

15

(Type-set and printed at the Office of the *Royal Gazette*, Georgetown)

1862 (Sept). *Black on coloured paper. Roul* 6.

116	10	1c. *rose*	£3750	£650
		a. Unsigned	£450	
		b. Wrong ornament (as T **13**) at left (R. 1/1)	–	£950
		c. "1" for "I" in "BRITISH" (R. 1/5)	–	£950
117	11	1c. *rose*	£4500	£800
		a. Unsigned	£500	
		b. Narrow "T" in "CENTS" (R. 3/1)	–	£950
		c. Wrong ornament (as T **15**) at top (R. 3/3)	–	£950
		d. "1" for "I" in "BRITISH" and italic "S" in "POSTAGE" (R. 3/5)	–	£950
118	12	1c. *rose*	£7000	£1000
		a. Unsigned	£850	
		b. "1" for "I" in "GUIANA" (R. 4/4)	–	£1000
		c. Wrong ornament (as T **15**) at left (R. 4/5)	–	£1000
		d. "C" for "O" in "POSTAGE" (R. 4/6)	–	£1000
119	10	2c. *yellow*	£3750	£375
		a. Unsigned	£1600	
		b. Wrong ornament (as T **13**) at left (R. 1/1)	–	£650
		c. "1" for "I" in "BRITISH" (R. 1/5)	–	£650
120	11	2c. *yellow*	£4500	£450
		a. Unsigned	£1700	
		b. "C" for "O" in "TWO" and narrow "T" in "CENTS" (R. 3/1)	–	£650
		c. Wrong ornament (as T **15**) at top (R. 3/3)	–	£650
		d. Italic "S" in "CENTS" (R. 3/4)	£6000	£650
		e. "1" for "I" in "BRITISH" and italic "S" in "POSTAGE" (R. 3/5)	–	£650
		f. Italic "T" in "TWO" (R. 3/6)	–	£650
121	12	2c. *yellow*	£7000	£750
		a. Unsigned	£2250	
		b. "1" for "I" in "GUIANA" (R. 4/4)	–	£750
		c. Wrong ornament (as T **15**) at left (R. 4/5)	–	£750
		d. "C" for "O" in "POSTAGE" (R. 4/6)	–	£750
122	13	4c. *blue*	£4000	£750
		a. Unsigned	£850	
		b. Wrong ornament (as T **15**) at left (R. 1/6)	£5500	£1300
		c. Wrong ornament (as T **15**) at top and italic "S" in "CENTS" (R. 2/2)	–	£1300
		d. Ornament omitted at right (R. 2/4)	–	£1300
123	14	4c. *blue*	£5000	£1000
		a. Unsigned	£900	
		b. With inner frame lines (as in T **10/13**) (R. 2/5–6)	£8000	£1700
		ba. "1" for "I" in "BRITISH" (R. 2/5)	£8000	£1700
		c. "1" for "I" in "BRITISH" and "GUIANA" (R. 4/1)	–	£1300
124	15	4c. *blue*	£5000	£1000
		a. Unsigned	£950	
		b. Wrong ornament (as T **12**) at foot (R. 3/1)	–	£1300
		c. Italic "S" in "CENTS" (R. 3/2)	–	£1300
		d. Italic "S" in "BRITISH" (R. 3/3)	–	£1300

Stamps were initialled across the centre before use by the Acting Receiver-General, Robert Mather. Black was used on the 1c., red for the 2c. and an ink which appears white for the 4c.

The three values of this provisional were each printed in sheets of 24 (6×4). The 1c. and 2c. were produced from the same setting of the border ornaments which contained 12 examples as Type **10** (Rows 1 and 2), 8 as Type **11** (R. 3/1 to R. 4/2) and 4 as Type **12** (R. 4/3-6).

The setting of the 4c. contained 10 examples as Type **13** (R. 1/1 to R. 2/4), 8 as Type **14** (R. 2/5–6 and Row 4) and 6 as Type **15** (Row 3).

16

(17)

(Typo D.L.R.)

1876 (1 July)–**79**. Wmk Crown CC.

		(a) P 14.		
126	16	1c. slate	2·75	1·40
		w. Wmk inverted	£180	£180
127		2c. orange	70·00	2·75
		w. Wmk inverted		
128		4c. blue	£120	9·00
129		6c. brown	75·00	8·50
130		8c. rose	£120	75
		w. Wmk inverted		
131		12c. pale violet	50·00	1·25
		w. Wmk inverted		
132		24c. emerald-green	60·00	3·00
		w. Wmk inverted		
133		48c. red-brown	£130	35·00
134		96c. olive-bistre	£475	£250
126/34 *Set of* 9			£950	£250

126s/32s, 134s Handstamped "Specimen" *Set of 8* £750
131sa/2sa Perf "Specimen" *Set of 2* £200

(b) P 12½ (1877).

135 **16** 4c. blue £1200 £200

(c) Perf compound of 14×12½ (1879).

136 **16** 1c. slate .... — £200

1878. *Provisionals. Various stamps with old values ruled through with thick bars, in black ink, the bars varying in depth of colour.*

(a) With two horiz bars (17 Apr).

137 **16** (1c.) on 6c. brown .... 38·00 £110

(b) Official stamps with horiz bars across "OFFICIAL" *(end Aug).*

138 **8** 1c. black .... £250 75·00
139 **16** 1c. slate .... £180 65·00
140 2c. orange .... £350 65·00

(c) With horiz and vert bars as T **17** *(6 Nov).*

141 **9** (1c.) on 6c. ultramarine (93) .... £190 75·00
142 **16** (1c.) on 6c. brown £325 £110
a. Optd with vert bar only .... † £6000

(d) Official stamps with bars across "OFFICIAL" *(23 Nov).*

(i) With two horiz bars and one vert.

144 **16** (1c.) on 4c. blue £325 £100
145 (1c.) on 6c. brown £475 £110
146 **8** (2c.) on 8c. rose £3000 £325

(ii) With one horiz bar and one vert.

147 **16** (1c.) on 4c. blue .... † £4000
148 (2c.) on 8c. rose £450 £120

1 2 2
(18) **(19)** **(20)**

1881 (21 Dec). *No. 134 with old value ruled through with bar in black ink and surch.*

149 **18** 1c. on 96c. olive-bistre .... 3·50 6·50
a. Bar in red ....
b. Bar omitted ....
150 **19** 2c. on 96c. olive-bistre .... 7·00 12·00
a. Bar in red ....
b. Bar omitted ....
151 **20** 2c. on 96c. olive-bistre .... 50·00 £100
a. Bar in red ....

In the setting of 60 Type **19** occurs on the first five vertical rows and Type **20** on the sixth.

1 2 2
(21) **(23)** **(24)**

1881 (28 Dec). *Various stamps with old value ruled with bar and surch.*

(a) On No. 105.

152 **21** 1c. on 48c. red .... 45·00 5·00
a. Bar omitted .... — £600

(b) On Official stamps (including unissued 48c. optd with Type O **2**).

153 **21** 1 on 12c. brownish purple (O4) .... £130 70·00
154 1 on 48c. red-brown £170 £100
155 **23** 2 on 12c. pale violet (O11) .... 75·00 38·00
a. Pair. Nos. 155/6 .... £1200 £1400
b. Surch double £800 £450
c. Surch double (T **23** + **24**) £4250
d. Extra bar through "OFFICIAL" ....
156 **24** 2 on 12c. pale violet (O11) £550 £350
157 **23** 2 on 24c. emerald-green (O12) .... 85·00 48·00
a. Pair. Nos. 157/8 .... £1500 £1600
b. Surch double £1100
158 **24** 2 on 24c. emerald-green (O12) £700 £750
159 **19** 2 on 24c. green (O5) £300 £150

On Nos. 149/59 the bar is found in various thicknesses ranging from 1 to 4 mm.

It is believed that the same composite surcharge setting of 60 (6×10) was used for Nos. 155/6 and 157/8. Type **24** occurs on R. 7/2, 4-6 and R. 8/1.

26

27

(Type-set, Baldwin & Co. Georgetown)

1882 (9 Jan). *Black impression.* P 12. *Perforated with the word* "SPECIMEN" *diagonally.*

162 **26** 1c. *magenta* .... 48·00 28·00
a. Imperf between (horiz pair) .... † —
b. Without "SPECIMEN" £800 £450
c. "1" with foot .... £110 70·00
163 2c. *yellow* .... 85·00 50·00
a. Without "SPECIMEN" £700 £550
b. Small "2" .... 85·00 50·00
164 **27** 1c. *magenta* .... 48·00 28·00
a. Without "SPECIMEN" £800 £450
b. "1" with foot .... £110 70·00
c. Imperf between (horiz pair) .... † £6500
165 2c. *yellow* .... 80·00 50·00
a. Bisected diagonally (1c.) (on cover) .... † —
b. Without "SPECIMEN" £700 £550
c. Small "2" .... £140 95·00

These stamps were perforated "SPECIMEN" as a precaution against fraud. Stamps are known with "SPECIMEN" double.

The 1c. and 2c. stamps were printed in separate sheets; but utilising the same clichés, these being altered according to the face value required. Two settings were used, common to both values:—

1st setting. Four rows of three, T **26** being Nos. 5, 6, 7, 8, 11 and 12, and T **27** the remainder.

From this setting there were two printings of the 2c., but only one of the 1c.

2nd setting. Six rows of two, T **26** being Nos. 3, 7, 8, 9, 11 and 12, and T **27** the remainder.

There were two printings of each value from this setting.

Se-tenant pairs are worth about 20% more.

The "1" with foot occurs on T **27** on No. 9 in the first setting and on T **26** on No. 7 in the first printing only of the second setting.

The small "2" appears on T **26** in the first setting on Nos. 6, 7 8 and 12 in the first printing and on Nos. 7, 8 and 12 only in the second printing: in the second setting it comes on Nos. 3, 9 and 12 in the first printing and on Nos. 9, 11 and 12 in the second printing. On T **27** the variety occurs in the first setting on No. 9 of the second printing only and in the second setting on No. 10 in both printings.

(Typo D.L.R.)

1882. Wmk Crown C.A. P 14.

170 **16** 1c. slate (27 Jan) .... 9·00 30
x. Wmk reversed .... — £170
171 2c. orange (27 Jan) .... 27·00 15
a. Value doubly printed .... † £7000
x. Wmk reversed .... — £180
172 4c. blue .... 90·00 5·00
173 6c. brown .... 5·00 6·50
w. Wmk inverted ....
174 8c. rose .... 90·00 40
x. Wmk reversed .... — £170
170/4 *Set of 5* .... £200 11·00
170s/4s Perf "Specimen" *Set of 5* £300

INLAND

2 CENTS
REVENUE
(28)

4 CENTS *(a)* 4 CENTS *(b)*

Two types of "4"

6 *(c)* 6 *(d)*

Two types of "6"

1888–89. *T* **16** *(without value in lower label) optd* "INLAND REVENUE", *and surch with value as T* **28**, *by* D.L.R. Wmk Crown CA. P 14.

175 1c. dull purple (8.89) .... 1·50 20
176 2c. dull purple (25.5.89) .... 1·50 85
177 3c. dull purple .... 1·00 20
178 4c. dull purple *(a)* .... 10·00 30
a. Larger figure "4" *(b)* .... 20·00 6·00
179 6c. dull purple *(c)* .... 9·00 3·75
a. Figure 6 with straight top *(d)* .... 19·00 5·00
180 8c. dull purple (8.89) .... 1·50 30
181 10c. dull purple .... 6·00 2·50
182 20c. dull purple .... 20·00 16·00
183 40c. dull purple .... 22·00 25·00
184 72c. dull purple (1.10.88) .... 50·00 60·00
185 $1 green (1.10.88) £425 £550
186 $2 green (1.10.88) £200 £250
187 $3 green (1.10.88) £180 £200
188 $4 green *(a)* (1.10.88) £475 £650
a. Larger figure "4" *(b)* £1600 £2000
189 $5 green (1.10.88) £300 £325
175/89 *Set of 15* £1500 £1800

Nos. 175/89 were surcharged in settings of 60 (6×10). No. 178a occurs on all stamps in the third vertical row, No. 179a in the fourth and sixth vertical rows and No. 188a in the second vertical row.

2
(29)

30

INLAND
One
Cent
~~1 DOLLAR~~
REVENUE
(31)

1889 (6 June). *No. 176 surch with T* **29** *in red by* Official *Gazette.*

192 "2" on 2c. dull purple .... 3·00 15

The varieties with figure "2" *inverted* or *double* were made privately by a postal employee in Demerara.

1889 (Sept). Wmk Crown CA. P 14.

193 **30** 1c. dull purple and slate-grey .... 4·75 2·00
194 2c. dull purple and orange .... 3·00 10
w. Wmk inverted ....
195 4c. dull purple and ultramarine .... 4·50 2·75
196 4c. dull purple and cobalt .... 21·00 2·75
197 6c. dull purple and brown .... 35·00 20·00
198 6c. dull purple and maroon .... 7·00 16·00
199 8c. dull purple and rose .... 12·00 2·50
w. Wmk inverted .... — 90·00
200 12c. dull purple and bright purple .... 18·00 3·00
200*a* 12c. dull purple and mauve .... 8·50 2·75
201 24c. dull purple and green .... 6·00 2·75
202 48c. dull purple and orange-red .... 20·00 9·50
w. Wmk inverted ....
x. Wmk reversed ....
203 72c. dull purple and red-brown .... 28·00 40·00
204 72c. dull purple and yellow-brown .... 65·00 75·00
205 96c. dull purple and carmine .... 65·00 70·00
x. Wmk reversed ....
206 96c. dull purple and rosine .... 75·00 80·00
193/205 *Set of 10* £140 £120
193s/205s Optd "Specimen" *Set of 10* £140

1890 (15 July). *Stamps of 1888-89 surch locally "One Cent", in red, as in T* **31**.

207 1c. on $1 (No. 185) .... 1·50 35
a. Surch double £250 £150
208 1c. on $2 (No. 186) .... 2·00 60
a. Surch double £100
209 1c. on $3 (No. 187) .... 2·00 1·25
a. Surch double £140
210 1c. on $4 (No. 188) .... 2·50 7·50
a. Surch double £120
b. Larger figure "4" *(b)* .... 12·00 35·00
207/10 *Set of 4* .... 7·25 9·00

1890–91. *Colours changed.* Wmk Crown CA. P 14

213 **30** 1c. sea-green (12.90) 75 10
214 5c. ultramarine (1.91) .... 2·75 10
215 8c. dull purple and greenish black (10.90) .... 3·00 1·10
213/15 *Set of 3* .... 6·00 1·10
213s/15s Optd "Specimen" *Set of 3* .... 60·00

32 Mount Roraima

33 Kaieteur Falls

(Recess D.L.R.)

1898 (18 July). *Queen Victoria's Jubilee.* Wmk Crown CC (sideways* on T **32**). P 14.

216 **32** 1c. blue-black and carmine-red .... 5·50 1·75
w. Wmk Crown to left of CC .... 6·50 1·90
x. Wmk sideways reversed ....
y. Wmk sideways inverted and reversed ....
217 **33** 2c. brown and indigo .... 25·00 3·50
a. Imperf between (horiz pair) £10000
x. Wmk reversed .... — £140
218 2c. brown and blue .... 28·00 3·50
219 **32** 5c. deep green and sepia .... 48·00 4·50
a. Imperf between (horiz pair) ....
w. Wmk Crown to left of CC .... 45·00 4·25
220 **33** 10c. blue-black and brown-red .... 25·00 22·00
221 **32** 15c. red-brown and blue .... 30·00 19·00
216/21 *Set of 5* .... £120 45·00
216s/21s Optd "Specimen" *Set of 5* £120

*The normal sideways watermark on Type **32** shows Crown to right of CC, *as seen from the back of the stamp.*

A second plate was later used for the 1c. on which the lines of shading on the mountains in the background are strengthened, and those along the ridge show distinct from each other, whereas, in the original, they are more or less blurred. In the second plate the shading of the sky is less pronounced.

TWO CENTS.
(34)

CE
Shaved "E"

35

(Surch at Printing Office of the *Daily Chronicle*, Georgetown)

1899 (24 Feb–15 June). *Surch with T* **34**.

222 **32** 2c. on 5c. (No. 219) (15 June) .... 3·25 2·00
a. No stop after "CENTS" .... £140 95·00
b. Comma after "CENTS" (R. 7/2) .... 70·00
c. "CINTS" (R. 4/1) £140
d. Shaved "E" (R. 6/2) .... 45·00
w. Wmk Crown to left of CC .... 3·75 2·25
223 **33** 2c. on 10c. (No. 220) .... 2·50 2·25
a. No stop after "CENTS" (R. 5/5 or 2/9) .... 20·00 50·00
b. "GENTS" for "CENTS" (R. 5/7) .... 50·00 70·00
c. Surch inverted £550 £650
ca. Surch inverted and stop omitted £4500
d. Shaved "E" (R. 4/2 or 3/8) .... 28·00
x. Wmk reversed £110
224 **32** 2c. on 15c. (No. 221) .... 2·25 1·25
a. No stop after "CENTS" (R. 9/2) .... 65·00 65·00
b. Surch double £850 £1100
ba. Surch double, one without stop £8500
d. Surch inverted £650 £850
da. Surch inverted and stop omitted ....
f. Shaved "E" (R. 6/2) .... 40·00
222/4 *Set of 3* .... 7·25 5·00

No. 222c was caused by damage to the first "E" of "CENTS" which developed during surcharging. The listing is for an example with only the upright stroke of the letter visible.

There were two settings of No. 223 with the no stop and shaved "E" varieties occurring on R. 5/5 and R. 4/2 of the first and on R. 2/9 and R. 3/8 of the second.

No. 224b occurred on the first five vertical columns of one sheet, the surcharges on the right hand vertical column being normal.

Only two examples of No. 224ba are known.

There is only one known example of No. 224da.

1900–03. Wmk Crown CA. P 14.

233 **30** 1c. grey-green (1902) .... 1·75 4·00
234 2c. dull purple and carmine .... 3·25 30

235 2c. dull purple and black/*red* (1901) 1·25 10
w. Wmk inverted — 85·00
236 6c. grey-black and ultramarine (1902) 6·50 11·00
237 48c. grey and purple-brown (1901) 50·00 35·00
a. Brownish grey and brown 29·00 28·00
238 60c. green and rosine (1903) 60·00 £180
233/8 *Set of* 6 90·00 £200
233s/8s Optd "Specimen" *Set of* 6 95·00

No. 233 is a reissue of No. 213 in non-fugitive ink.

1905–07. Wmk Multiple Crown CA. *Ordinary paper (1c. to 60c.) or chalk-surfaced paper (72, 96c.).*

240 **30** 1c. grey-green 4·25 30
aw. Wmk inverted
b. Chalk-surfaced paper 7·00 30
241 2c. purple and black/*red* 10·00 10
a. Chalk-surfaced paper 3·50 10
242 4c. dull purple and ultramarine 8·50 15·00
a. Chalk-surfaced paper 6·00 12·00
243 5c. dull purple and blue/*blue* (1.5.05) 11·00 15·00
a. Chalk-surfaced paper 3·50 6·50
s. Optd "Specimen" 21·00
244 6c. grey-black and ultramarine 16·00 45·00
aw. Wmk inverted — £225
b. Chalk-surfaced paper 15·00 42·00
bw. Wmk inverted
245 12c. dull and bright purple 22·00 32·00
a. Chalk-surfaced paper 22·00 42·00
246 24c. dull purple and green (1906) 11·00 14·00
a. Chalk-surfaced paper 3·75 4·50
247 48c. grey and purple-brown 25·00 35·00
a. Chalk-surfaced paper 14·00 20·00
248 60c. green and rosine 25·00 90·00
a. Chalk-surfaced paper 14·00 90·00
249 72c. purple and orange-brown (1907) 32·00 70·00
250 96c. black and vermilion/*yellow* (20.11.05) 35·00 45·00
s. Optd "Specimen" 32·00
240/50 *Set of* 11 £140 £300

1905. *Optd* "POSTAGE AND REVENUE". Wmk Multiple Crown CA. *Chalk-surfaced paper*. P 14.

251 **35** $2.40, green and violet £160 £325
s. Optd "Specimen" 75·00

1907–10. *Colours changed*. Wmk Mult Crown CA. P 14

252 **30** 1c. blue-green 15·00 2·75
253 2c. rose-red 16·00 30
a. Redrawn (1910) 8·50 10
254 4c. brown and purple 2·25 60
255 5c. ultramarine 14·00 3·50
256 6c. grey and black 13·00 7·00
257 12c. orange and mauve 4·00 4·50
252/7 *Set of* 6 50·00 16·00
253s/7s Optd "Specimen" *Set of* 5 75·00

In No. 253a the flag at the main truck is close to the mast, whereas in the original type it appears to be flying loose from halyards. There are two background lines above the value "2 CENTS" instead of three and the "S" is further away from the end of the tablet.

37

War
Tax
(38)

(Typo D.L.R.)

1913–21. Wmk Mult Crown CA. *Chalk-surfaced paper (4c. and 48c. to 96c.)*. P 14.

259 **37** 1c. yellow-green 2·50 80
a. Blue-green (1917) 1·50 25
ay. Wmk inverted and reversed † £325
260 2c. carmine 1·25 10
a. Scarlet (1916) 3·00 10
b. Wmk sideways † £2500
261 4c. brown and bright purple (1914) 5·50 25
aw. Wmk inverted
b. Deep brown and purple 3·75 25
262 5c. bright blue 1·75 1·00
263 6c. grey and black 2·75 1·50
264 12c. orange and violet 1·25 1·00
265 24c. dull purple and green (1915) 3·25 4·25
266 48c. grey and purple-brown (1914) 22·00 17·00
267 60c. green and rosine (1915) 15·00 50·00
268 72c. purple and orange-brown (1915) 42·00 80·00
269 96c. black and vermilion/*yellow* (1915) 30·00 60·00
a. White back (1913) 22·00 48·00
b. On lemon (1916) 19·00 48·00
bs. Optd "Specimen" 32·00
c. On pale yellow (1921) 20·00 60·00
cs. Optd "Specimen" 32·00
259/69a *Set of* 11 £110 £180
259s/69as Optd "Specimen" *Set of* 11 £140

Examples of Nos. 267/9c are known with part strikes of forged postmarks of Grove dated "29 OCT 1909" and of Georgetown dated "30 OCT 1909".

1918 (4 Jan). *No. 260a optd with T* **38**, *by D.L.R.*

271 **37** 2c. scarlet 1·50 15

The relative position of the words "WAR" and "TAX" vary considerably in the sheet.

1921–27. Wmk Mult Script CA. *Chalk-surfaced paper (24c. to 96c.)*. P 14.

272 **37** 1c. green (1922) 4·75 30
273 2c. rose-carmine 4·25 20
w. Wmk inverted † £180
274 2c. bright violet (1923) 2·50 10
275 4c. brown and bright purple (1922) 4·75 10
276 6c. bright blue (1922) 3·00 30
277 12c. orange and violet (1922) 2·75 1·50
278 24c. dull purple and green 2·00 4·50
279 48c. black and purple (1926) 9·50 3·50
280 60c. green and rosine (1926) 10·00 48·00
281 72c. dull purple & orange-brown (1923) 26·00 65·00
282 96c. black and red/*yellow* (1927) 21·00 45·00
272/82 *Set of* 11 80·00 £150
272s/82s Optd "Specimen" *Set of* 11 £160

39 Ploughing a Rice Field

40 Indian shooting Fish

41 Kaieteur Falls

42 Public buildings, Georgetown

(Recess Waterlow)

1931 (21 July). *Centenary of County Union*. *T* **39/42**. Wmk Mult Script CA. P 12½.

283 **39** 1c. emerald-green 2·50 1·25
284 **40** 2c. brown 2·00 10
285 **41** 4c. carmine 1·75 45
286 **42** 6c. blue 2·25 2·75
287 **41** $1 violet 32·00 48·00
283/7 *Set of* 5 35·00 48·00
283s/7s Perf "Specimen" *Set of* 5 85·00

43 Ploughing a Rice Field

44 Gold Mining

45 Shooting logs over falls

46 Stabrock Market

47 Sugar canes in punts

48 Forest road

49 Victoria Regis Lilies

50 Mount Roraima

51 Sir Walter Raleigh and his son

52 Botanical Gardens

(Recess Waterlow)

1934 (1 Oct)–**51**. *T* **40** *(without dates at top of frame) and* **43/52**. Wmk Mult Script CA (sideways on horiz designs). P 12½.

288 **43** 1c. green 60 1·50
289 **40** 2c. red-brown 1·50 1·00
290 **44** 3c. scarlet 30 10
aa. Wmk error. Crown missing £3250 £2250
a. Perf 12½×13½ (30.12.43) 60 80
b. Perf 13×14 (28.4.49) 60 10
291 **41** 4c. slate-violet 2·00 3·00
a. Imperf between (vert pair) † £25000
b. Imperf horiz (vert pair) £11000 £12000
292 **45** 6c. deep ultramarine 3·25 6·00
293 **46** 12c. red-orange 20 20
a. Perf 14×13 (16.4.51) 50 1·00
294 **47** 24c. purple 3·50 9·00
295 **48** 48c. black 7·00 8·50
296 **41** 50c. green 10·00 17·00
297 **49** 60c. red-brown 26·00 27·00
298 **50** 72c. purple 1·25 2·25
299 **51** 96c. black 21·00 30·00
300 **52** $1 bright violet 32·00 32·00
288/300 *Set of* 13 95·00 £120
288s/300s Perf "Specimen" *Set of* 13 £180

Examples of Nos. 295/300 are known with forged Georgetown postmarks dated "24 JY 31" or "6 MY 35".

1935 (6 May). *Silver Jubilee. As Nos. 91/4 of Antigua.*

301 2c. ultramarine and grey 20 20
f. Diagonal line by turret 38·00
h. Dot by flagstaff 90·00 90·00
302 6c. brown and deep blue 1·75 3·75
f. Diagonal line by turret £100
g. Dot to left of chapel £120 £160
h. Dot by flagstaff £140
303 12c. green and indigo 5·00 8·00
f. Diagonal line by turret £120 £160
h. Dot by flagstaff £190 £225
i. Dash by turret £225
304 24c. slate and purple 9·00 11·00
h. Dot by flagstaff £250
i. Dash by turret £300
301/4 *Set of* 4 14·50 21·00
301s/4s Perf "Specimen" *Set of* 4 £110

For illustrations of plate varieties see Omnibus section following Zanzibar.

1937 (12 May). *Coronation. As Nos. 95/7 of Antigua, but ptd by D.L.R.* P 14.

305 2c. yellow-brown 15 10
306 4c. grey-black 50 40
307 6c. bright blue 60 1·75
305/7 *Set of* 3 1·10 2·00
305s/7s Perf "Specimen" *Set of* 3 85·00

53 South America

54 *Victoria Regia*, water-lilies

(Recess Waterlow)

1938 (1 Feb)–**52**. *As earlier types but with portrait of King George VI as in T* **53/4**. Wmk Mult Script CA. P 12½

308 **43** 1c. yellow-green 18·00 55
a. Green (1940) 30 10
ab. Perf 14×13 (1949) 30 80
309 **41** 2c. slate-violet 60 10
a. Perf 13×14 (28.4.49) 30 10
310 **53** 4c. scarlet and black 70 30
a. Imperf horiz (vert pair) £27000 £21000
b. Perf 13×14 (1952) 50 15
311 **40** 6c. deep ultramarine 40 10
a. Perf 13×14 (24.10.49) 50 30
312 **47** 24c. blue-green 26·00 10·00
a. Wmk sideways 1·50 10
313 **41** 36c. bright violet (7.3.38) 2·00 20
a. Perf 13×14 (13.12.51) 3·00 30
314 **48** 48c. orange 60 50
a. Perf 14×13 (8.5.51*) 1·50 1·25
315 **49** 60c. red-brown 16·00 8·50
316 **51** 96c. purple 5·00 2·75
a. Perf 12½×13½ (1944) 6·00 8·50
b. Perf 13×14 (8.2.51) 2·75 6·50
317 **52** $1 bright violet 18·00 35
a. Perf 14×13 (1951) £400 £550
318 **50** $2 purple (11.6.45) 7·50 22·00
a. Perf 14×13 (9.8.50) 14·00 22·00
319 **54** $3 red-brown (2.7.45) 29·00 29·00
a. Bright red-brown (12.46) 35·00 28·00
b. Perf 14×13. *Red-brown* (29.10.52) 30·00 45·00
308a/19 *Set of* 12 70·00 55·00
308s/19s Perf "Specimen" *Set of* 12 £275

*Earliest known postmark date.

1946 (21 Oct). *Victory. As Nos. 110/11 of Antigua.*

320 3c. carmine 10 40
321 6c. blue 50 85
320s/1s Perf "Specimen" *Set of* 2 75·00

1948 (20 Dec). *Royal Silver Wedding. As Nos. 112/13 of Antigua, but $3 in recess.*

322 3c. scarlet 10 40
323 $3 red-brown 17·00 23·00

1949 (10 Oct). *75th Anniv of Universal Postal Union. As Nos. 114/17 of Antigua.*

324 4c. carmine 10 50
325 6c. deep blue 1·75 1·75
326 12c. orange 15 50
327 24c. blue-green 15 70
324/7 *Set of* 4 1·90 3·00

1951 (16 Feb). *University College of B.W.I. As Nos. 118/19 of Antigua.*

328 3c. black and carmine 30 50
329 6c. black and blue 30 65

1953 (2 June). *Coronation. As No. 120 of Antigua.*

330 4c. black and scarlet 30 10

55 G.P.O., Georgetown

56 Botanical Gardens

57 *Victoria Regia* water-lilies

58 Amerindian shooting fish

59 Map of Caribbean

60 Rice combine harvester

61 Sugar cane entering factory

62 Felling Greenheart

63 Mining for bauxite

64 Mount Roraima

65 Kaieteur Falls

66 Arapaima

67 Channel-billed Toucan

68 Dredging gold

69 Arms of British Guiana

(Centre litho, frame recess ($1); recess (others). Waterlow (until 1961), then D.L.R.)

1954 (1 Dec)–**63**. *T* **55/69** *and similar designs.* Wmk Mult Script CA. P 12½×13* (horiz) or 13 (vert).

331	**55**	1c. black	10	10
332	**56**	2c. myrtle-green	10	10
333	**57**	3c. brown-olive and red-brown	3·50	20
		w. Wmk inverted		
334	**58**	4c. violet	75	10
		a. D.L.R. ptg (5.12.61)	10·00	3·00
		ab. Deep violet (3.1.63)	13·00	2·50
335	**59**	5c. scarlet and black	1·00	10
		w. Wmk inverted		
336	**60**	6c. yellow-green	50	10
		a. D.L.R. ptg. *Green* (22.5.62)	1·50	2·50
337	**61**	8c. ultramarine	30	20
		a. D.L.R. ptg. *Blue* (19.9.61)	11·00	1·50
338	**62**	12c. black and reddish brown	60	40
		a. Black and light brown (13.6.56)	20	10
		b. D.L.R. ptg. *Black and brown* (11.7.61)	24·00	3·75
339	**63**	24c. black and brownish orange	4·50	10
		a. Black and orange (13.6.56)	7·00	10
340	**64**	36c. rose-carmine and black	6·00	1·25
		w. Wmk inverted		
341	**65**	48c. ultramarine and brown-lake	1·00	1·00
		a. Brt ultram & pale brown-lake (13.6.56)	1·00	1·00
		ab. D.L.R. ptg (19.9.61)	29·00	23·00
342	**66**	72c. carmine and emerald	12·00	2·75
		a. D.L.R. ptg (17.7.62)	12·00	20·00
343	**67**	$1 pink. yellow. green and black	20·00	3·75
344	**68**	$2 deep mauve	20·00	7·50
		a. D.L.R. ptg. *Reddish mauve* (11.7.61)	48·00	8·50
345	**69**	$5 ultramarine and black	18·00	28·00
		a. D.L.R. ptg (19.9.61)	48·00	35·00
331/45 *Set of* 15			75·00	35·00

On the Waterlow printings there is *always* a single wide-tooth perforation on each side at the top of the stamps. For the De La Rue stamps these teeth can occur *either* at the top or the bottom. Those listed De La Rue printings, which do not differ in shade, are for examples with the wide-tooth perforation at the bottom.

*All the Waterlow printing and early De La Rue printings of the horizontal designs measure 12.3×12.8, but De La Rue printings from 22 May 1962 (including those on the Block CA watermark) measure 12.3×12.6.

The 1c. and 2c., printed by Waterlow, exist in coils constructed from normal sheets.

See also Nos. 354/65.

SELF-GOVERNMENT

70

71 Weightlifting

(Photo Harrison)

1961 (23 Oct). *History and Culture Week.* W w **12**. P 14½×14.

346	**70**	5c. sepia and orange-red	20	10
347		6c. sepia and blue-green	20	15
348		30c. sepia and yellow-orange	45	45
346/8 *Set of* 3			75	60

1963 (14 July). *Freedom from Hunger. As No. 146 of Antigua.*

349	20c. reddish violet	30	10

1963 (2 Sept). *Red Cross Centenary. As Nos. 147/8 of Antigua.*

350	5c. red and black	20	20
351	20c. red and blue	55	35

1963–65. *As Nos. 333/44, but wmk* w **12**.

354	**57**	3c. brown-olive and red-brown (12.65)	3·50	4·00
356	**59**	5c. scarlet and black (28.5.64)	30	10
		w. Wmk inverted		
359	**62**	12c. black and yellowish brown (6.10.64)	20	10
360	**63**	24c. black and bright orange (10.12.63)	4·00	10
361	**64**	36c. rose-carmine and black (10.12.63)	60	60
362	**65**	48c. brt ultram & Venetian red (25.11.63)	1·25	2·25
		w. Wmk inverted		
363	**66**	72c. carmine and emerald (25.11.63)	4·25	20·00
364	**67**	$1 pink, yellow, green & black (10.12.63)	7·00	90
365	**68**	$2 reddish mauve (10.12.63)	11·00	14·00
354/65 *Set of* 9			29·00	38·00

There was no London release of No. 354.

The 5c. exists in coils constructed from normal sheets.

For 1c. value, see No. 429a.

(Photo D.L.R.)

1964 (1 Oct). *Olympic Games, Tokyo.* W w **12**. P 13×13½.

367	**71**	5c. orange	10	10
368		8c. blue	15	35
369		25c. magenta	25	40
367/9 *Set of* 3			45	75

1965 (17 May). *I.T.U. Centenary. As Nos. 166/7 of Antigua.*

370	5c. emerald and yellow-olive	10	15
371	25c. light blue and magenta	20	15

1965 (25 Oct). *International Co-operation Year. As Nos. 168/9 of Antigua.*

372	5c. reddish purple and turquoise-green	15	10
373	25c. deep bluish green and lavender	30	20

72 St. George's Cathedral, Georgetown

(Des Jennifer Toombs, Photo Harrison)

1966 (24 Jan). *Churchill Commemoration.* W w **12**. P 14×14½.

374	**72**	5c. black, crimson and gold	50	10
375		25c. black, blue and gold	2·00	50

1966 (3 Feb). *Royal Visit. As Nos. 174/5 of Antigua.*

376	3c. black and ultramarine	75	15
377	25c. black and magenta	1·50	60

STAMP BOOKLETS

1909 (14 June). *Black on pink cover without face value. Stapled.*

SB1 49c. booklet containing twelve 1c. and eighteen 2c. (Nos. 252/3) in blocks of 6 ...... £2250

1923. *Black on pink cover without face value. Stapled.*

SB2 30c. booklet containing six 1c. and twelve 2c. (Nos. 272, 274) in blocks of 6

1923. *Black on pink without face value. Stapled.*

SB3 48c. booklet containing twelve 1c. and eighteen 2c. (Nos. 272, 274) in blocks of 6 . £1700
a. With face value on front cover

1923. *Black on red cover without face value. Stapled.*

SB4 72c. booklet containing twelve 1c., six 2c. and twelve 4c. (Nos. 272, 274/5) in blocks of 6.. £2750

1934. *Black on orange cover. Stitched.*

SB5 24c. booklet containing eight 1c. and eight 2c. (Nos. 288/9) in blocks of 4

1934. *Black on orange cover. Stitched.*

SB6 36c. booklet containing four 1c., eight 2c. and four 4c. (Nos. 288/9, 291) in blocks of 4

1938. *Black on orange cover. Stitched.*

SB7 36c. booklet containing four 1c., eight 2c. and four 4c. (Nos. 308/10) in blocks of 4 ...... £500

1944. *Black on orange cover. Stitched.*

SB8 24c. booklet containing eight 1c. and eight 2c. (Nos. 308/9) in blocks of 4 ...... £450

1945–49. *Black on red cover. Stitched.*

SB9 24c. booklet containing 1c., 2c. and 3c. (Nos. 290, 308, 309), each in block of 4
- a. Containing Nos. 290, 308*a*, 309 ...... 65·00
- b. Containing Nos. 290, 308*a*, 309a ...... 65·00
- c. Containing Nos. 290a, 308*a*, 309 ...... 65·00
- d. Containing Nos. 290b, 308*a*, 309 ...... 85·00
- e. Containing Nos. 290b, 308*a*, 309a ...... 80·00
- f. Containing Nos. 290b, 308*ab*, 309a ...... 85·00

POSTAGE DUE STAMPS

D 1

(Typo D.L.R.)

1940 (Mar)–**55**. Wmk Mult Script CA. *Chalk-surfaced paper (4c.)*. P 14.

D1	D **1**	1c. green	6·00	7·50
		a. Chalk-surfaced paper. *Deep green*, (30.4.52)	1·50	16·00
		ab. W **9a** (Crown missing)	£375	
		ac. W **9b** (St. Edward's Crown)	£120	
D2		2c. black	24·00	2·00
		a. Chalk-surfaced paper (30.4.52)	2·75	5·00
		ab. W **9a** (Crown missing)	£300	
		ac. W **9b** (St. Edward's Crown)	£120	
D3		4c. bright blue (1.5.52)	30	12·00
		a. W **9a** (Crown missing)	£250	
		b. W **9b** (St. Edward's Crown)	£100	
D4		12c. scarlet	30·00	4·50
		a. Chalk-surfaced paper (19.7.55)	17·00	30·00
D1, D2, D4 *Set of 3*			55·00	12·50
D1a/4a *Set of* 4			19·00	55·00
D1s, D2s and D4s Perf "Specimen" *Set of 3*			70·00	

OFFICIAL STAMPS

OFFICIAL (O **1**) OFFICIAL (O **1a**) OFFICIAL (O **2**)

1875. *Optd with Type* O **1** *(1c.) or* O **1a** *(others) by litho.* P 10.

O1	**8**	1c. black (R.)	55·00	19·00
		a. Imperf between (horiz pair)	†	£14000
O2		2c. orange	£180	14·00
O3		8c. rose	£325	£120
O4	**7**	12c. brownish purple	£2500	£500
O5	**9**	24c. green	£1800	£225

Two types of the word "OFFICIAL" are found on each value. On the 1c. the word is either 16 or 17 mm long. On the other values the chief difference is in the shape and position of the letter "o" in "OFFICIAL". In one case the "o" is upright, in the other it slants to the left.

1877. *Optd with Type* O **2** *by typo.* Wmk Crown CC. P 14.

O6	**16**	1c. slate	£250	65·00
		a. Imperf between (vert pair)	†	£19000
O7		2c. orange	£120	15·00
O8		4c. blue	85·00	20·00
O9		6c. brown	£5500	£600
O10		8c. rose	£2000	£450

Prepared for use, but not issued.

O11	**16**	12c. pale violet	£1500
O12		24c. green	£1800

The "OFFICIAL" overprints have been extensively forged.

The use of Official stamps was discontinued in June 1878.

British Guiana became independent as Guyana on 25 May 1966.

British Honduras

It is recorded that the first local post office was established by the inhabitants in 1809, but Belize did not become a regular packet port of call until December 1829. The post office came under the control of the British G.P.O. in April 1844 and the stamps of Great Britain were supplied for use on overseas mail from May 1858.

The colonial authorities took over the postal service on 1 April 1860, the Great Britain stamps being withdrawn at the end of the month. There was no inland postal service until 1862.

For illustrations of the handstamp and postmark types see BRITISH POST OFFICES ABROAD notes, following GREAT BRITAIN.

BELIZE

CROWNED-CIRCLE HANDSTAMPS

CC1 CC **1** BELIZE (R.) (13.11.1841). *Price on cover* £4000

Stamps of GREAT BRITAIN *cancelled* "A 06" *as Type* **2**.

1858–60.

Z1	1d. rose-red (1857), *perf* 14	£950
Z2	4d. rose (1857)	£400
Z3	6d. lilac (1856)	£375
Z4	1s. green (1856)	£1800

PRICES FOR STAMPS ON COVER TO 1945

Nos. 1/4	*from* × 20
Nos. 5/16	*from* × 25
Nos. 17/22	*from* × 20
Nos. 23/6	*from* × 10
Nos. 27/30	*from* × 15
Nos. 35/42	*from* × 20
Nos. 43/4	*from* × 30
Nos. 49/50	*from* × 25
Nos. 51/69	*from* × 15
Nos. 80/100	*from* × 6
Nos. 101/10	*from* × 5
Nos. 111/20	*from* × 15
Nos. 121/2	*from* × 8
No. 123	*from* × 10
Nos. 124/37	*from* × 6
Nos. 138/42	*from* × 10
Nos. 143/9	*from* × 8
Nos. 150/61	*from* × 5
Nos. D1/3	*from* × 30

CROWN COLONY

1

(Typo D.L.R.)

1865 (1 Dec). No wmk. P 14.

1	**1**	1d. pale blue	60·00	60·00
		a. Imperf between (pair)		
2		1d. blue	90·00	70·00
3		6d. rose	£375	£160
4		1s. green	£350	£120
		a. In horiz pair with 6d.	£48000	
		b. In vert pair with 1d.	£60000	

In the first printing all three values were printed in the same sheet separated by horizontal and vertical gutter margins. The sheet comprised two panes of 60 of the 1d. at the top with a pane of 60 of the 1s. at bottom left and another of 6d. at bottom right. Copies of 1d. *se-tenant* with the 6d. are not known. There were two later printings of the 1d. but they were in sheets without the 6d. and 1s.

1872–79. Wmk Crown CC.

(a) P 12½.

5	**1**	1d. pale blue	85·00	21·00
		w. Wmk inverted	£300	
		y. Wmk inverted and reversed		
6		1d. deep blue (1874)	95·00	21·00
7		3d. red-brown	£150	75·00
8		3d. chocolate (1874)	£170	95·00
9		6d. rose	£350	45·00
9*a*		6d. bright rose-carmine (1874)	£500	60·00
10		1s. green	£500	30·00
10*a*		1s. deep green (1874)	£425	24·00
		b. Imperf between (horiz pair)	†	£24000
		w. Wmk inverted		

(b) P 14 (1877–79).

11	**1**	1d. pale blue (1878)	80·00	19·00
12		1d. blue	75·00	14·00
		a. Imperf between (horiz strip of 3)	£24000	
13		3d. chestnut	£140	21·00
14		4d. mauve (1879)	£225	8·50
		x. Wmk reversed		
15		6d. rose (1878)	£425	£190
		w. Wmk inverted	—	£425
16		1s. green	£275	11·00
		a. Imperf between (pair)		

1882–87. Wmk Crown CA. P 14.

17	**1**	1d. blue (4.84)	55·00	15·00
18		1d. rose (1884)	23·00	13·00
		a. Bisected (½d.) (on cover)	†	—
		s. Optd "Specimen"	£200	
19		1d. carmine (1887)	55·00	20·00
20		4d. mauve (7.82)	85·00	4·75
		w. Wmk inverted	—	£140
21		6d. yellow (1885)	£275	£200
22		1s. grey (1.87)	£250	£160
		s. Optd "Specimen"	75·00	

(New Currency. 100 cents = 1 British Honduras dollar)

2 CENTS (2) **TWO** (3) **2 CENTS** (4)

1888 (1 Jan). *Stamps of 1872–79* (wmk Crown CC), *surch locally as T* **2**.

(a) P 12½.

23	**1**	2c. on 6d. rose	£300	£200
24		3c. on 3d. chocolate	£17000	£5500

(b) P 14.

25	**1**	2c. on 6d. rose	£160	£150
		a. Surch double	£2250	
		b. Bisected (1c.) (on cover)	†	£250
		c. Slanting "2" with curved foot	£3000	
		w. Wmk inverted	—	£450
26		3c. on 3d. chestnut	95·00	£100

There are very dangerous forgeries of these surcharges.

No. 25c may be a trial.

1888. *Stamps of 1882–87* (wmk Crown CA), *surch locally as T* **2**, P 14.

27	**1**	2c. on 1d. rose	8·50	26·00
		a. Surch inverted	£3500	£3250
		b. Surch double	£900	£900
		c. Bisected (1c.) (on cover)	†	£180
28		10c. on 4d. mauve	50·00	16·00
29		20c. on 6d. yellow	27·00	35·00
30		50c. on 1s. grey	£400	£600
		a. Error. "5" for "50"	£15000	

Various settings were used for the surcharges on Nos. 23/30, the most common of which was of 36 (6×6) impressions. For No. 29 this setting was so applied that an albino surcharge occurs in the margin above each stamp in the first horizontal row.

The same setting was subsequently amended, by altering the "2" to "1", to surcharge the 4d. value. As this was in sheets of 30 it was only necessary to alter the values on the bottom five rows of the setting. Albino surcharges once again occur in the top margin of the sheet, but, as the type in the first horizontal row remained unaltered, these read "20 CENTS" rather than the "10 CENTS" on the actual stamps.

1888 (Mar). *No. 30 further surch locally with T* **3**.

35	**1**	"TWO" on 50c. on 1s. grey (R.)	50·00	95·00
		a. Bisected (1c.) (on cover)	†	£275
		b. Surch in black	£15000	£13000
		c. Surch double (R.+Blk.)	£15000	£13000

1888 (July)–**91**. *Surch in London as T* **4**. Wmk Crown CA. P 14.

36	**1**	1c. on 1d. dull green (?12.91)	80	1·50
37		2c. on 1d. carmine	60	2·25
		a. Bisected (1c.) (on cover)	†	90·00
		w. Wmk inverted		
38		3c. on 3d. red-brown	3·25	1·40
39		6c. on 3d. ultramarine (?4.91)	3·00	19·00
40		10c. on 4d. mauve	15·00	50
		a. Surch double	£3250	
41		20c. on 6d. yellow (2.89)	14·00	14·00
42		50c. on 1s. grey (11.88)	29·00	85·00
36/42 *Set of* 7			60·00	£110
36s/42s Optd "Specimen" *Set of* 7			£350	

6
~~10~~
CENTS
(5)

FIVE (6) **15** (7)

1891. *Stamps of 1888–9 surch locally.*

(a) With T **5** *(May).*

43	**1**	6c. on 10c. on 4d. mauve (R.)	1·50	2·00
		a. "6" and bar inverted	£600	£600
		b. "6" only inverted	†	£6000
44		6c. on 10c. on 4d. mauve (Blk.)	1·25	1·50
		a. "6" and bar inverted	£4500	£1000
		b. "6" only inverted	†	£6000

Of variety (b) only six copies of each can exist, as one of each of these errors came in the first six sheets, and the mistake was then corrected. Of variety (a) more copies exist.

Essays are known with "SIX" in place of "6" both with and without bars (*price* £120 *and* £500 *respectively*). Although not issued we mention them, as three contemporary covers franked with them are known.

(b) With T **6/7** *(23 Oct).*

49	**1**	5c. on 3c. on 3d. red-brown	1·25	1·40
		a. Wide space between "I" and "V"	60·00	75·00
		b. "FIVE" and bar double	£375	£425
50		15c. on 6c. on 3d. ultramarine (R.)	13·00	28·00
		a. Surch double		

8

9

10

11

(Typo D.L.R.)

1891 (July)–**1901**. Wmk Crown CA. P 14.

51	**8**	1c. dull green (4.95)	2·50	1·25
		a. Malformed "S"	£300	£160
		w. Wmk inverted		
52		2c. carmine-rose	3·00	20
		a. Malformed "S"	£300	£110
		b. Repaired "S"	£275	£110
53		3c. brown	7·00	4·00
		w. Wmk inverted	£190	
54		5c. ultramarine (4.95)	12·00	75
		a. Malformed "S"	£500	£190
55	**11**	5c. grey-black & ultram/*blue* (10.00)	17·00	2·50
56	**8**	6c. ultramarine	9·00	2·00
57	**9**	10c. mauve and green (4.95)	10·00	11·00
58	**10**	10c. dull purple and green (1901)	11·00	7·50
59	**9**	12c. reddish lilac and green	2·50	2·25
60		24c. yellow and blue	5·50	17·00
		a. Orange and blue	30·00	55·00
61		25c. red-brown and green (4.95)	80·00	£130
62	**10**	50c. green and carmine (3.98)	25·00	60·00
63	**11**	$1 green and carmine (12.99)	80·00	£130
64		$2 green and ultramarine (12.99)	£120	£170
65		$5 green and black (12.99)	£300	£400
51/65 *Set of* 15			£600	£850
51s/65s Optd "Specimen" *Set of* 15			£350	

For illustrations of Nos. 51a, 52a/b and 54a see above Gambia No. 37.

Most values are known with a forged Belize postmark dated "OC 23 09".

1899 (1 July). *Optd* "REVENUE" *12 mm long.*

66	**8**	5c. ultramarine	17·00	2·50
		a. "BEVENUE"	£130	£140
		b. Malformed "S" at right	£500	£350
		c. Repaired "S" at right	£500	
		d. Opt 11 mm long	23·00	8·50
67	**9**	10c. mauve and green	8·00	16·00
		a. "BEVENUE"	£250	£350
		b. "REVENU"	£650	
		c. Opt 11 mm long	19·00	45·00
		cb. "REVENU"	£750	£850
68		25c. red-brown and green	2·75	35·00
		a. "BEVENUE"	£150	£375
		b. "REVE UE"	£2500	
		c. Repaired "S" at right	£700	
		d. Opt 11 mm long	4·00	55·00
69	**1**	50c. on 1s. grey	£180	£350
		a. "BEVENUE"	£4750	
		c. Opt 11 mm long	£300	£450

Two minor varieties, a small "U" and a tall, narrow "U" are found in the word "REVENUE".

The overprint setting of 60 (6×10) contained 43 examples of the 12 mm size and 17 of the 11 mm. The smaller size overprints occur on R. 8/1, R. 8/3 to 6 and on all positions in Rows 9 and 10.

The "BEVENUE" error appears on R. 6/4 and, it is believed, "REVE UE" comes from R. 6/6. Both occur on parts of the printing only. The missing "E" developed during the overprinting and damage to this letter can be observed on at least eight positions in the setting.

14

15

(Typo D.L.R.)

1902 (10 Oct)–**04**. Wmk Crown CA. P 14.

80	**14**	1c. grey-green and green (28.4.04)	1·25	23·00
81		2c. purple and black/*red* (18.3.03)	75	25
		w. Wmk inverted	£140	85·00
82		5c. grey-black and blue/*blue*	9·50	30
		w. Wmk inverted		
83	**15**	20c. dull and bright purple (28.4.04)	7·50	17·00
80/3 *Set of* 4			17·00	35·00
80s/3s Optd "Specimen" *Set of* 4			60·00	

1904 (Dec)–**07**. Wmk Mult Crown CA. *Ordinary paper (1, 2c.) or chalk-surfaced paper (others).* P 14.

84	**14**	1c. grey-green and green (8.05)	11·00	15·00
		a. Chalk-surfaced paper (1906)	1·50	2·25
85		2c. purple and black/*red*	2·75	30
		a. Chalk-surfaced paper (1906)	1·00	20
86		5c. grey-black and blue/*blue* (5.2.06)	1·75	20
87	**15**	10c. dull purple & emerald-green (20.9.07)	4·00	12·00
89		25c. dull purple and orange (20.9.07)	7·00	48·00
90		50c. grey-green and carmine (20.9.07)	15·00	75·00

91	**14**	$1 grey-green and carmine (20.9.07)	55·00	85·00
92		$2 grey-green and blue (20 9 07)	£110	£170
93		$5 grey-green and black (20.9.07)	£300	£350
84/93 *Set of* 9			£450	£650
87s/93s Optd "Specimen" *Set of* 6			£225	

Examples of most values are known showing a forged Belize postmark dated "OC 23 09".

1908 (7 Dec)–**11**. *Colours changed.* Wmk Mult Crown CA. *Chalk-surfaced paper (25c.).* P 14.

95	**14**	1c. blue-green (1.7.10)	14·00	50
96		2c. carmine	12·00	10
		w. Wmk inverted		
97		5c. ultramarine (1.6.09)	1·75	10
100	**15**	25c. black/*green* (14.10.11)	3·25	45·00
95/100 *Set of* 4			28·00	45·00
96s/100s Optd "Specimen" *Set of* 3			70·00	

16

17

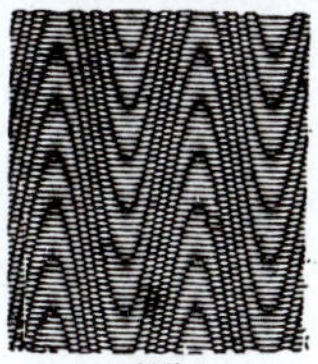
(18)

1913–21. Wmk Mult Crown CA. *Chalk-surfaced paper (10c. to $5).* P 14.

101	**16**	1c. blue-green	3·75	1·50
		a. Yellow-green (13.3.17)	8·00	2·75
		w. Wmk inverted		
102		2c. red	3·50	1·00
		a. Bright scarlet (1915)	6·00	1·00
		b. Dull scarlet (8.17)	3·00	1·50
		c. Red/bluish	13·00	8·00
		w. Wmk inverted		
103		3c. orange (16.4.17)	1·00	20
104		5c. bright blue	2·00	85
105	**17**	10c. dull purple and yellow-green	3·25	6·50
		a. Dull purple and bright green (1917)	18·00	25·00
106		25c. black/*green*	1·25	12·00
		a. On blue-green, olive back (8.17)	5·00	11·00
		b. On emerald back (1921)	1·75	28·00
107		50c. purple and blue/*blue*	17·00	15·00
108	**16**	$1 black and carmine	19·00	55·00
109		$2 purple and green	65·00	80·00
110		$5 purple and black/*red*	£250	£275
101/10 *Set of* 10			£325	£400
101s/10s Optd "Specimen" *Set of* 10			£225	

1915–16. *Optd with T* **18**, *in violet.*

111	**16**	1c. green (30.12.15)	3·75	18·00
		a. Yellow-green (6.6.16)	50	15·00
112		2c. scarlet (3.11.15)	3·50	50
113		5c. bright blue (29.7.15)	30	6·00
111s/13s Optd "Specimen" *Set of* 3			£100	

These stamps were shipped early in the 1914–18 war, and were thus overprinted, so that if seized by the enemy, they could be distinguished and rendered invalid.

WAR
(19)

WAR
(20)

21

1916 (23 Aug). *No. 111 optd locally with T* **19**.

114	**16**	1c. green	10	2·00
		a. Opt inverted	£275	£325

1917–18. *Nos. 101 and 103 optd with T* **19**.

116	**16**	1c. blue-green (6.17)	1·50	4·50
		aw. Wmk inverted	£200	
		ax. Wmk reversed	£200	
		b. Yellow-green (3.3.17)	20	2·75
118		3c. orange (12.3.18)	4·75	8·00
		a. Opt double	£375	

1918. *Nos. 101 and 103 optd with T* **20**.

119	**16**	1c. blue-green (25.4.18)	20	30
		a. Yellow-green	3·50	4·50
120		3c. orange (9.18)	80	2·50
		y. Wmk inverted and reversed	£200	
119s/20s Optd "Specimen" *Set of* 2			£100	

(Recess D.L.R.)

1921 (28 Apr). *Peace Commemoration.* Wmk Mult Crown CA (sideways). P 14.

121	**21**	2c. rose-red	4·25	50
		a. "C" of "CA" missing from wmk	£325	
		s. Optd "Specimen"	48·00	

1921 (26 Nov). Wmk Mult Script CA. P 14.

122	**16**	1c. green	4·75	12·00
		s. Optd "Specimen"	45·00	

1922 (4 Jan). *As T* **21** *but with words* "PEACE" *omitted.* Wmk Mult Script CA (sideways). P 14.

123		4c. slate	10·00	50
		s. Optd "Specimen"	48·00	

22

BELIZE
RELIEF FUND
PLUS
3 CENTS
(23)

(Typo D.L.R.)

1922 (1 Aug)–**33**. *Ordinary paper (1c. to 5c.) or chalk-surfaced paper (others).* P 14.

(*a*) Wmk Mult Crown CA.

124	**22**	25c. black/*emerald*	6·50	45·00
125		$5 purple and black/*red* (1.10.24)	£200	£250

(*b*) Wmk Mult Script CA.

126	**22**	1c. green (2.1.29)	10·00	6·50
127		2c. brown (1.3.23)	1·50	1·50
128		2c. rose-carmine (10.12.26)	4·50	1·50
129		3c. orange (1933)	23·00	4·00
130		4c. grey (1.10.29)	12·00	85
131		5c. ultramarine	1·50	55
		a. Milky blue (1923)	4·75	3·75
132		10c. dull purple and sage-green (1.12.22)	2·50	30
133		25c. black/*emerald* (1.10.24)	1·75	8·50
134		50c. purple and blue/*blue* (1.11.23)	4·75	16·00
136		$1 black and scarlet (2.1.25)	9·00	26·00
137		$2 yellow-green and bright purple	35·00	95·00
124/37 *Set of* 13			£275	£400
124s/37s Optd or Perf (1c., 3c., 4c.) "Specimen" *Set of* 13			£275	

1932 (2 May). *Belize Relief Fund. Surch as T* **23**. Wmk Mult Script CA. P 14.

138	**22**	1c.+1c. green	1·00	10·00
139		2c.+2c. rose-carmine	1·00	10·00
140		3c.+3c. orange	1·00	23·00
141		4c.+4c. grey (R.)	11·00	25·00
142		5c.+5c. ultramarine	6·50	14·00
138/42 *Set of* 5			18·00	75·00
138s/42s Perf "Specimen" *Set of* 5			£110	

1935 (6 May). *Silver Jubilee. As Nos. 91/4 of Antigua, but ptd by B.W. & Co.* P 11×12.

143	3c. ultramarine and grey-black	2·00	50
	a. Extra flagstaff	55·00	75·00
	b. Short extra flagstaff	95·00	£110
	c. Lightning conductor	65·00	85·00
	d. Flagstaff on right-hand turret	£170	
144	4c. green and indigo	3·25	4·00
	a. Extra flagstaff	£180	£225
	c. Lightning conductor	£200	£225
	d. Flagstaff on right-hand turret	£275	
	e. Double flagstaff	£300	£325
145	5c. brown and deep blue	2·00	2·25
146	25c. slate and purple	5·00	5·50
	a. Extra flagstaff	£250	£300
	b. Short extra flagstaff	£400	
	c. Lightning conductor	£275	
	d. Flagstaff on right-hand turret	£375	
	e. Double flagstaff	£400	
143/6 *Set of* 4		11·00	11·00
143s/6s Perf "Specimen" *Set of* 4		£100	

For illustrations of plate varieties see Omnibus section following Zanzibar.

1937 (12 May). *Coronation. As Nos. 95/7 of Antigua, but printed by D.L.R.* P 14.

147	3c. orange	30	30
148	4c. grey-black	70	30
149	5c. bright blue	80	1·90
147/9 *Set of* 3		1·60	2·25
147s/9s Perf "Specimen" *Set of* 3		80·00	

24 Maya Figures

25 Chicle Tapping

26 Cohune palm

27 Local products

28 Grapefruit

29 Mahogany logs in river

30 Sergeant's Cay

31 Dorey

32 Chicle industry

33 Court House Belize

34 Mahogany felling

35 Arms of Colony

(Recess B.W.)

1938 (10 Jan)–**47**. *T* **24/35**. Wmk Mult Script CA (sideways on horizontal stamps). P 11½×11 (horiz designs) or 11×11½ (vert designs).

150	**24**	1c. bright magenta and green (14.2.38)	30	1·50
151	**25**	2c. black and scarlet (14.2.38)	30	1·00
		a. Perf 12 (1947)	2·75	1·00
152	**26**	3c. purple and brown	1·00	80
153	**27**	4c. black and green	1·00	70
154	**28**	5c. mauve and dull blue	2·25	1·00
155	**29**	10c. green and reddish brown (14.2.38)	2·50	60
156	**30**	15c. brown and light blue (14.2.38)	4·50	70
157	**31**	25c. blue and green (14.2.38)	3·25	1·25
158	**32**	50c. black and purple (14.2.38)	15·00	3·50
159	**33**	$1 scarlet and olive (28.2.38)	28·00	10·00
160	**34**	$2 deep blue and maroon (28.2.38)	45·00	20·00
161	**35**	$5 scarlet and brown (28.2.38)	42·00	32·00
150/61 *Set of* 12			£130	65·00
150s/61s Perf "Specimen" *Set of* 12			£225	

1946 (9 Sept). *Victory. As Nos. 110/11 of Antigua.*

162	3c. brown	10	20
163	5c. blue	10	20
162s/3s Perf "Specimen" *Set of* 2		75·00	

1948 (1 Oct). *Royal Silver Wedding. As Nos. 112/13 of Antigua.*

164	4c. green	15	60
165	$5 brown	19·00	48·00

36 Island of St. George's Cay

37 H.M.S. *Merlin*

(Recess Waterlow)

1949 (10 Jan). *150th Anniv of Battle of St. George's Cay.* Wmk Mult Script CA. P 12½.

166	**36**	1c. ultramarine and green	10	1·25
167		3c. blue and yellow-brown	10	1·50
168		4c. olive and violet	10	1·50
169	**37**	5c. brown and deep blue	1·50	75
170		10c. green and red-brown	1·50	30
171		15c. emerald and ultramarine	1·50	30
166/71 *Set of* 6			4·00	5·00

1949 (10 Oct). *75th Anniv of U.P.U. As Nos. 114/17 of Antigua.*

172	4c. blue-green	30	30
173	5c. deep blue	1·50	50
174	10c. red-brown	40	3·00
175	25c. blue	35	50
172/5 *Set of* 4		2·25	3·75

1951 (16 Feb). *Inauguration of B.W.I. University College. As Nos. 118/19 of Antigua.*

176	3c. reddish violet and brown	45	1·50
177	10c. green and brown	45	30

1953 (2 June). *Coronation. As No. 120 of Antigua.*

178	4c. black and green	40	30

38 Arms of British Honduras

39 Baird's Tapir ("Mountain Cow")

40 Mace and Legislative Council Chamber

41 Pine industry

42 Spiny Lobster

43 Stanley Field Airport

44 Maya frieze, Xunantunich

45 *Morpho peleides*

46 Maya Indian

47 Nine-banded Armadillo

48 Hawkesworth Bridge

49 Mountain Orchid

(Recess Waterlow (until 20.6.1961), then D.L.R.)

1953 (2 Sept)–**62**. *T* **38/39**. Wmk Mult Script CA. P 13½.

179	**38**	1c. green and black	10	40
		a. Perf 13½×13 (3.10.61)	1·00	1·25
180	**39**	2c. yellow-brown and black	30	2·00
		a. Perf 14 (18.9.57)	85	30
		b. Perf 13½×13 (20.6.61)	10	50
181	**40**	3c. reddish violet and bright purple	30	20
		a. Perf 14 (18.9.57)	10	10
		b. Perf 13½×13 (20.6.61)	5·00	12·00
		ba. Reddish lilac and pale magenta (19.1.62)	60	1·00
182	**41**	4c. brown and green	1·00	30
183	**42**	5c. deep olive-green and scarlet	10	10
		a. Perf 14 (15.5.57)	30	10
		ab. D.L.R. ptg (3.10.61)	5·00	12·00
184	**43**	10c. slate and bright blue	10	10
		a. Perf 13½×13 (19.1.62)	10	10
185	**44**	15c. green and violet	15	10
186	**45**	25c. bright blue and yellow-brown	6·00	3·00
187	**46**	50c. yellow-brown and reddish purple	14·00	3·00
		a. Pale yellow-brown and pale purple (22.3.60)	26·00	9·00
188	**47**	$1 slate-blue and red-brown	6·00	5·00
189	**48**	$2 scarlet and grey	6·50	4·50
190	**49**	$5 purple and slate	48·00	17·00
179/90 *Set of* 12			75·00	30·00

Nos. 179/90 were released a day earlier by the Crown Agents in London.

Stamps from the Waterlow printings perforated 13½×13 or 14 have a very fine perforation tooth at the *top* of each vertical side. On the De La Rue printings this tooth is at the *bottom*.

50 "Belize from Fort George, 1842" (C. J. Hullmandel)

51 Public Seals, 1860 and 1960.

52 Tamarind Tree, Newtown Barracks.

(Recess B.W.)

1960 (1 July). *Post Office Centenary.* W w **12**. P 11½×11.

191	**50**	2c. green	45	1·25
192	**51**	10c. deep carmine	45	10
193	**52**	15c. blue	45	35
191/3 *Set of* 3			1·25	1·50

NEW CONSTITUTION
1960
(53)

HURRICANE
HATTIE
(54)

1961 (1 Mar). *New Constitution. Nos. 180a, 181a and 184/5 optd with T* **53** *by Waterlow.*

194	2c. yellow-brown and black	25	20
195	3c. reddish violet and bright purple	30	20
196	10c. slate and bright blue	30	10
197	15c. green and violet	30	20
194/7 *Set of* 4		1·00	60

1962 (15 Jan). *Hurricane Hattie Relief Fund. Nos. 179a, 184a, 186 and 187 optd with T* **54** *by D.L.R.*

198	1c. green and black	10	65
199	10c. slate and bright blue	30	10
200	25c. bright blue and yellow-brown	1·75	80
201	50c. yellow-brown and reddish purple	75	1·00
198/201 *Set of* 4		2·50	2·25

55 Great Curassow

(Des D. R. Eckelberry. Photo Harrison)

1962 (2 Apr). *Horiz designs on T* **55**. *Multicoloured.* W w **12** (upright). P 14×14½.

202		1c. Type **55**	1·50	75
		a. Orange-yellow (knob) omitted	£400	
		w. Wmk inverted		
203		2c. Red-legged Honey-creeper	2·00	10
		a. Turquoise-blue (bird's head) omitted	£425	
204		3c. Northern Jacana	3·50	3·00
		a. Blue-green (legs) omitted	£450	
205		4c. Great Kiskadee	3·75	3·75
206		5c. Scarlet-rumped Tanager	2·75	10
		w. Wmk inverted		
207		10c. Scarlet Macaw	4·50	10
		a. Blue omitted	£550	
		w. Wmk inverted	†	—
208		15c. Slaty-tailed Trogon	1·50	10
		w. Wmk inverted	25·00	15·00
209		25c. Red-footed Booby	4·50	30
		w. Wmk inverted		
210		50c. Keel-billed Toucan	6·00	35
		a. Pale blue (claw and beak) omitted	£600	
211		$1 Magnificent Frigate Bird	9·00	1·00
212		$2 Rufous-tailed Jacamar	17·00	3·25
		*a. Shade**	55·00	16·00
		w. Wmk inverted	80·00	
213		$5 Montezuma Oropendola	26·00	16·00
202/13 *Set of* 12			75·00	26·00

*On No. 212a, the bird is myrtle-green and red-brown instead of yellow-green and orange-brown.

See also Nos. 239/45.

1963 (4 June). *Freedom from Hunger. As No. 146 of Antigua.*

214	22c. bluish green	30	15

1963 (2 Sept). *Red Cross Centenary. As Nos. 147/8 of Antigua.*

215	4c. red and black	20	75
216	22c. red and blue	40	1·25

SELF-GOVERNMENT

SELF GOVERNMENT
1964
(56)

DEDICATION OF SITE
NEW CAPITAL
9th OCTOBER 1965
(57)

1964. *New Constitution. Nos. 202, 204/5, 207 and 209 optd with T* **56**.

217	1c. Type **55** (20.4)	10	30
	a. Opt inverted	£350	
	b. Orange-yellow (knob) omitted	£120	
218	3c. Northern Jacana (20.4)	45	30
219	4c. Great Kiskadee (3.2)	45	30
220	10c. Scarlet Macaw (20.4)	45	10
221	25c. Red-footed Booby (3.2)	55	30
217/21 *Set of* 5		1·75	1·10

1965 (17 May). *I.T.U Centenary. As Nos. 166/7 of Antigua.*

222	2c. orange-red and light green	10	10
223	50c. yellow and light purple	35	25

1965 (25 Oct). *International Co-operation Year. As Nos. 168/9 of Antigua.*

224	1c. reddish purple and turquoise-green	10	15
225	22c. deep bluish green and lavender	20	15

1966 (24 Jan). *Churchill Commemoration. As Nos. 170/3 of Antigua.*

226	1c. new blue	10	75
227	4c. deep green	50	10
228	22c. brown	75	10
229	25c. bluish violet	95	45
226/9 *Set of* 4		2·00	1·10

1966 (1 July). *Dedication of New Capital Site. As Nos. 202, 204/5, 207 and 209, but wmk sideways, optd with T* **57** *by Harrison.*

230	1c. Type **55**	10	40
	a. Orange-yellow (knob) omitted	£180	
	w. Wmk Crown to right of CA	70	
231	3c. Northern Jacana	45	40
232	4c. Great Kiskadee	45	40
233	10c. Scarlet Macaw	45	10
234	25c. Red-footed Booby	55	35
230/4 *Set of* 5		1·75	1·50

*The normal sideways watermark shows Crown to left of CA, *as seen from the back of the stamp.*

58 Citrus Grove

(Des V. Whiteley. Photo Harrison)

1966 (1 Oct). *Stamp Centenary. T* **58** *and similar horiz designs. Multicoloured.* W w **12**. P 14×14½.

235	5c. Type **58**	10	10
236	10c. Half Moon Cay	10	10
237	22c. Hidden Valley Falls	10	10
238	25c. Maya Ruins, Xunantunich	15	45
235/8 *Set of* 4		30	65

1967. *As Nos. 202, etc, but* W w **12** (sideways).

239	1c. Type **55** (16.2)	10	50
240	2c. Red-legged Honey-creeper (28.11)	30	1·00
241	4c. Great Kiskadee (16.2)	1·75	2·00
242	5c. Scarlet-rumped Tanager (16.2)	40	10
243	10c. Scarlet Macaw (28.11)	40	10
244	15c. Slaty-tailed Trogon (28.11)	40	10
245	50c. Keel-billed Toucan (16.2)	2·00	3·50
239/45 *Set of* 7		4·75	4·75

The 15c. value exists with PVA gum as well as gum arabic.

59 Sailfish

60 *Schomburgkia tibicinis*

(Des R. Granger Barrett. Photo Harrison)

1967 (1 Dec). *International Tourist Year. T* **59** *and similar horiz designs.* W w **12**. P 12½.

246	5c. deep violet-blue black and light yellow	15	30
247	10c. brown, black and orange-red	15	10
248	22c. yellow-orange, black and bright green	30	10
249	25c. lt greenish blue, black & greenish yell	30	60
246/9 *Set of* 4		80	1·00

Designs:—10c. Red Brocket; 22c. Jaguar; 25c. Atlantic Tarpon.

(Des Sylvia Goaman. Photo Harrison)

1968 (16 Apr). *20th Anniv of Economic Commission for Latin America. T* **60** *and similar vert designs showing orchids. Multicoloured.* W w **12** (sideways). P 14½×14.

250	5c. Type **60**	20	15
251	10c. *Muxillaria tenuifolia*	25	10
252	22c. *Bletia purpurea*	30	10
253	25c. *Sobralia macrantha*	40	20
250/3 *Set of* 4		1·10	40

61 Monument to Belizean Patriots

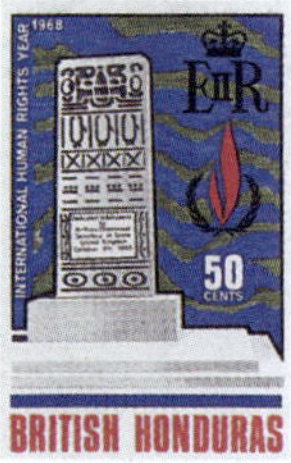

62 Monument at Site of New Capital

(Des G. Vasarhelyi. Litho B.W.)

1968 (15 July). *Human Rights Year.* W w **12**. P 13½.

254	**61**	22c. multicoloured	15	10
255	**62**	50c. multicoloured	15	20

63 Spotted Jewfish

(Des J. W. Litho D.L.R.)

1968 (15 Oct). *Wildlife. Horiz designs as T* **63**. *Multicoloured.* No wmk. P 13×12½.

256	1c. Type **63**	30	10
257	2c. White-Tipped Peccary ("Warree")	10	10
258	3c. Misty Grouper	20	10
259	4c. Collared Anteater	15	1·25
260	5c. Bonefish	15	1·25
261	10c. Para ("Gibnut")	15	10

262	15c. Dolphin	2·00	20
263	25c. Kinkajou ("Night Walker")	30	20
264	50c. Mutton Snapper	70	1·25
265	$1 Tayra ("Bush Dog")	2·50	1·25
266	$2 Great Barracuda	2·50	2·00
267	$5 Puma	13·00	6·50
256/67	*Set of* 12	20·00	12·00

See also Nos. 276/8.

The 3c., 5c. and 10c. were re-issued in 1972 with watermark W **12** upright.

64 *Rhyncholaelia digbyana*

65 Ziricote Tree

(Des Sylvia Goaman. Photo Harrison)

1969 (9 Apr). *Orchids of Belize (1st series). T* **64** *and similar vert designs. Multicoloured.* W w **12** (sideways). P 14½×14.

268	5c. Type **64**	60	20
269	10c. *Cattleya bowringiana*	65	15
270	22c. *Lycaste cochleatum*	95	15
271	25c. *Coryanthes speciosum*	1·10	1·10
268/71	*Set of* 4	3·00	1·40

See also Nos. 287/90.

(Des V. Whiteley. Litho D.L.R.)

1969 (1 Sept). *Indigenous Hardwoods (1st series). T* **65** *and similar vert designs. Multicoloured.* W w **12**. P 14.

272	5c. Type **65**	10	20
273	10c. Rosewood	10	10
274	22c. Mayflower	20	10
275	25c. Mahogany	20	45
272/5	*Set of* 4	45	70

See also Nos. 291/4, 315/18 and 333/7.

1969–72. *As Nos. 257/8, 261, 267 and new value and design (½ c.), but* W w **12** (sideways*).

276	½c. Mozambique Mouthbrooder ("Crana") (ultramarine background) (1.9.69)	10	10
277	½c. Mozambique Mouthbrooder ("Crana") (yellow-olive background) (1.2.71)	2·50	1·00
	a. Black (inscr and value) omitted	£325	
	bw. Wmk Crown to right of CA	3·00	
277*c*	2c. White-tipped Peccary (5.5.72)	3·75	3·75
277*d*	3c. Misty Grouper (6.5.72)	3·75	3·75
277*e*	10c. Paca (5.5.72)	3·75	3·75
278	$5 Puma (12.5.70)	2·50	10·00
276/8	*Set of* 6	17·00	22·00

*The normal sideways watermark shows Crown to left of CA, *as seen from the back of the stamp.*

66 "The Virgin and Child" (Bellini

POPULATION CENSUS 1970

(68)

(Des adapted by G. Drummond. Litho Format)

1969 (1 Nov). *Christmas. Paintings. T* **66** *and similar vert design. Multicoloured.* W w **12**. P 14×14½.

279	5c. Type **66**	10	10
280	15c. Type **66**	10	10
281	22c. "The Adoration of the Kings" (Veronese)	10	10
282	25c. As 22c.	10	20
279/82	*Set of* 4	30	30

Although released by the Crown Agents on 1 October this issue was not put on sale locally until 1 November.

1970 (2 Feb). *Population Census. As Nos. 260 and 262/3 but* W w **12** (sideways) *and No. 277e optd with T* **68**.

283	5c. Bonefish	10	10
284	10c. Paca	15	10
285	15c. Dolphin	20	10
286	25c. Kinkajou	20	15
283/6	*Set of* 4	55	30

(Des G. Drummond. Litho Format)

1970 (2 Apr). *Orchids of Belize (2nd series). As T* **64**. *Multicoloured.* W w **12**. P 14.

287	5c. Black Orchid	35	15
288	15c. White Butterfly Orchid	50	10
289	22c. Swan Orchid	70	10
290	25c. Butterfly Orchid	70	40
287/90	*Set of* 4	2·00	60

69 Santa Maria

70 "The Nativity" (A. Hughes).

(Des Jennifer Toombs, Litho Questa)

1970 (7 Sept). *Indigenous Hardwoods (2nd series). T* **69** *and similar vert designs. Multicoloured.* W w **12** (sideways). P 14×14½.

291	5c. Type **69**	25	10
292	15c. Nargusta	40	10
293	22c. Cedar	45	10
294	25c. Sapodilla	45	35
291/4	*Set of* 4	1·40	55

(Des J. Cooter Litho J.W.)

1970 (7 Nov*). *Christmas. T* **70** *and similar vert design. Multicoloured.* W w **12**. P 14.

295	½c. Type **70**	10	10
296	5c. "The Mystic Nativity" (Botticelli).	10	10
297	10c. Type **70**	10	10
298	15c. As 5c.	20	10
299	22c. Type **70**	25	10
300	50c. As 5c.	40	85
295/300	*Set of* 6	85	1·10

*These stamps were released by the Crown Agents in London on 2 November.

STAMP BOOKLETS

1920. *Black on pink cover inscr* "British Honduras–100–Two Cent Stamps". *Stapled.*

SB1 $2 booklet containing one hundred 2c. (No. 102*b*) in blocks of 10 (5×2) £4000

1920. *Grey-blue cover inscr* "British Honduras–100–Three Cent Stamps". *Stapled.*

SB2 $3 booklet containing one hundred 3c. (No. 103) in blocks of 10 (5×2)

1923. *Black on pink cover inscr* "British Honduras–100–Two Cent Stamps". *Stapled.*

SB3 $2 booklet containing one hundred 2c. brown (No. 127) in blocks of 10 (5×2)

1927. *Black on pink cover inscr* "British Honduras–100–Two Cent Stamps". *Stapled.*

SB4 $2 booklet containing one hundred 2c. rose-carmine (No. 128) in blocks of 10 (5×2)

POSTAGE DUE STAMPS

D **1**

(Typo D.L.R.)

1923–64. Wmk Mult Script CA. *Ordinary paper.* P 14.

D1	D **1**	1c. black	2·25	13·00
		a. Chalk-surfaced paper (25.9.56)	50	24·00
		b. White uncoated paper (9.4.64)	14·00	29·00
D2		2c. black	2·25	7·50
		a. Chalk-surfaced paper (25.9.56)	50	19·00
D3		4c. black	1·25	6·00
		a. Missing top serif on "C" (R. 6/6)	30·00	
		bw. Wmk inverted	£250	
		c. Chalk-surfaced paper (25.9.56)	90	18·00
		ca. Missing top serif on "C" (R. 6/6)	29·00	
D1/3		*Set of* 3	5·25	24·00
D1a/3c		*Set of* 3	1·75	55·00
D1s/3s		Optd "Specimen" *Set of* 3	60·00	

The early ordinary paper printings were yellowish and quite distinct from No. D1*b*.

1965 (3 Aug)–**72**. *As Nos. D2a and D3c, but* Wmk w **12** (sideways on 2c.). P 13½×13 (2c.) or 13½×14 (4c.).

D4	D **1**	2c. black (10.1.72)	2·75	5·50
D5		4c. black	1·25	6·00

The missing top serif on "C" variety of R. 6/6 was corrected before No. D5 was printed.

British Indian Ocean Territory

This Crown Colony was created on 8 November 1965 when it comprised the Chagos Archipelago, previously administered by Mauritius, together with the islands of Aldabra, Farquhar and Desroches, previously administered by Seychelles.

(Currency. 100 cents=1 rupee).

B.I.O.T.

(**1**)

1968 (17 Jan). *As Nos. 196/200, 202/4 and 206/12 of Seychelles, optd with T* **1**. W w **12** (sideways* on 5, 10, 15, 20, 25, 50, 75c. and 10r.).

1	5c. multicoloured	1·00	1·50
	a. No stop after "I"	11·00	14·00
	b. No stop after "O"	6·50	8·50
	w. Wmk Crown to right of CA	45·00	
2	10c. multicoloured	10	15
	a. No stop after "I"	14·00	16·00
	b. No stop after "O"	5·50	8·50
3	15c. multicoloured	10	15
	a. No stop after "I"	10·00	13·00
	b. No stop after "O"	5·50	8·50
4	20c. multicoloured	15	15
	a. No stop after "I"	12·00	13·00
	b. No stop after "O"	6·00	8·50
5	25c. multicoloured	15	15
	a. No stop after "I"	11·00	14·00
	b. No stop after "O"	5·50	9·00
6	40c. multicoloured	20	20
	a. No stop after "I"	16·00	18·00
	b. No stop after "O"	7·50	10·00
7	45c. multicoloured	20	30
	a. No stop after "I"	16·00	18·00
	b. No stop after "B"	22·00	22·00
	c. No stop after "O"	25·00	25·00
8	50c. multicoloured	20	30
	a. No stop after "I"	14·00	17·00
	b. No stop after "O"	7·00	9·50
9	75c. multicoloured	60	35
10	1r. multicoloured	70	35
	a. No stop after "I"	15·00	17·00
	b. No stop after "O"	7·50	10·00
11	1r.50 multicoloured	1·75	1·50
	a. No stop after "I"	32·00	32·00
	b. No stop after "O"	17·00	17·00
12	2r.25 multicoloured	3·00	3·75
	a. No stop after "I"	80·00	85·00
	b. No stop after "O"	38·00	38·00
13	3r.50 multicoloured	3·00	4·50
	a. No stop after "I"	80·00	85·00
	b. No stop after "O"	30·00	35·00
14	5r. multicoloured	10·00	7·50
	a. No stop after "I"	£120	£120
	b. No stop after "O"	45·00	48·00
15	10r. multicoloured	20·00	20·00
	a. No stop after "B"	£150	£150
	b. No stop after "I"	£150	£150
	c. No stop after "O"	80·00	85·00
1/15	*Set of* 15	38·00	35·00

*The normal sideways watermark shows Crown to left of CA, *as seen from the back of the stamp.*

These were issued by the Crown Agents on 15 January but owing to shipping delays they were not put on sale locally until 17 January.

The positions of the "no stop" varieties are as follows:

After "I": R. 2/4 on horiz stamps except 45c. where it occurs on R. 3/3, and R. 8/5 on vert stamps except 10r. where it occurs on R. 4/3.

After "O": R. 3/2 and 5/1 on vert stamps, R. 2/1 and 4/4 on horiz stamps (only occurs on R. 2/1 for 45c.), and R. 2/7 and 5/9 on 10r. value.

After "B": R. 10/4 (45c.) or R. 1/8 (10r.).

As sheets of all values from 5c. to 50c. are known with all stops in place the no stop varieties either developed during printing or their omission was discovered and replacements inserted.

2 Lascar

(Des G. Drummond, based on drawings by Mrs. W. Veevers-Carter. Litho D.L.R.)

1968 (23 Oct)–**70**. *Marine Life. Multicoloured designs as T* **2**. *White paper (Nos. 20a, 23a, 24a) or cream paper (others).* W w **12** (sideways on horiz, inverted on vert designs). P 14.

16	5c. Type **2**	1·00	2·00
17	10c. Smooth Hammerhead (*vert*)	30	1·25
18	15c. Tiger Shark	30	1·50
19	20c. Spotted Eagle Ray ("Bat Ray")	30	1·00
20	25c. Yellow-finned Butterflyfish and Earspotted Angelfish (*vert*)	80	1·00
20*a*	30c. Robber Crab (7.12.70)	3·50	2·75
21	40c. Blue-finned Trevally ("Caranx")	2·00	40
22	45c. Crocodile Needlefish ("Garfish") (*vert*)	2·25	2·50
23	50c. Pickhandle Barracuda	2·00	30
23*a*	60c. Spotted Pebble Crab (7.12.70)	3·50	3·25
24	75c. Indian Ocean Steep-headed Parrotfish	2·50	2·75
24*a*	85c. Rainbow Runner ("Dorado") (7.12.70)	4·50	3·50
25	1r. Giant Hermit Crab	1·75	35
26	1r.50 Parrotfish ("Humphead")	2·50	3·00
27	2r.25 Yellow-edged Lyretail and Areolate Grouper ("Rock Cod")	12·00	10·00

28 3r.50 Black Marlin .... 4·00 3·75
29 5r. black, blue-green and greenish blue (Whale Shark) (*vert*) .... 15·00 11·00
30 10r. Lionfish .... 6·00 8·00
a. Imperf (pair) £800
16/30 *Set of* 18 .... 55·00 50·00

The 5c. was re-issued in 1973 on white paper with watermark w **12** upright.

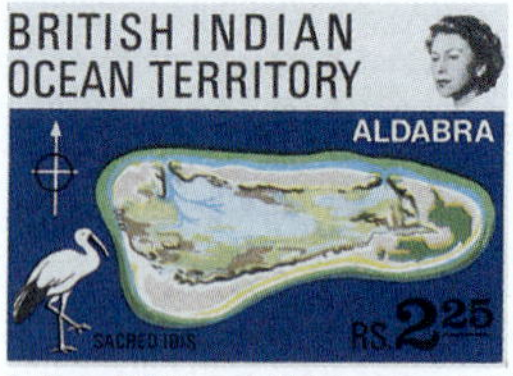

3 Sacred Ibis and Aldabra Coral Atoll

(Des and litho D.L.R.)

1969 (10 July). *Coral Atolls.* W w **12** (sideways). P 13½×13.
31 **3** 2r.25 multicoloured .... 1·75 1·00

4 Outrigger Canoe

(Des Mrs. M. Hayward adapted by V. Whiteley. Litho D.L.R.)

1969 (15 Dec). *Ships of the Islands. T* **4** *and similar horiz designs. Multicoloured.* W w **12** (sideways). P 13½×14.
32 45c. Type **4** 55 75
33 75c. Pirogue 55 80
34 1r. M. V. *Nordvaer* 60 90
35 1r.50 *Isle of Farquhar* .... 65 1·00
32/5 *Set of* 4 .... 2·10 3·00

British Levant

The term "British Levant" is used by stamp collectors to describe the issues made by various British Post Offices within the former Turkish Empire.

Arrangements for the first such service were included amongst the terms of a commercial treaty between the two countries in 1832, but the system did not start operations until September 1857 when a post office for civilian use was opened in Constantinople, replacing the Army Post Office which had existed there since June 1854.

Eventually the number of British Post Offices grew to five:

Beyrout (Beirut, Lebanon). Opened 1873, closed 30 September 1914.

Constantinople (Istanbul). Opened 1 September 1857, closed 30 September 1914, re-opened 4 February 1919, finally closed 27 September 1923.

Salonica (Thessalonika, Greece). Opened 1 May 1900, closed October 1914. The city was captured by Greek troops on 7 November 1912 and incorporated into Greece by the Treaty of London (July 1913).

Smyrna (Izmir). Opened 1872, closed 30 September 1914, re-opened 1 March 1919, finally closed September 1922. Between 15 May 1919 and 8 September 1922 the city was under Greek occupation.

Stamboul (a sub-office of Constantinople). Opened 1 April 1884, closed 25 August 1896, re-opened 10 February 1908, finally closed 30 September 1914.

Stamps from the two British Post Offices in Egypt still technically part of the Turkish Empire, are listed under EGYPT.

A. BRITISH POST OFFICES IN TURKISH EMPIRE, 1857–1914

For illustrations of the postmark types see BRITISH POST OFFICES ABROAD notes, following GREAT BRITAIN.

From 1 August 1885 letter and registered charges were prepaid with surcharged stamps (No. 1 onwards). Until 14 August 1905 postcards and parcels continued to be franked with unoverprinted Great Britain stamps. Only a limited range of values were stocked for this purpose and these are listed. Other values exist with Levant postmarks, but these stamps did not originate from the local post offices.

After 15 August 1905 the post offices were supplied with Great Britain stamps overprinted "LEVANT". Subsequent examples of unoverprinted stamps with Levant postmarks are omitted from the listing. The use of such stamps during 1919–22 at Constantinople and Smyrna is, however, covered by a later note.

BEYROUT (BEIRUT)

Between 1873 and 1876 much of the mail from the British Post Office in Beyrout sent to European addresses was forwarded through the French or Italian Post Offices at Alexandria. Such covers show Great Britain stamps used in combination with those of French or Italian P.O's in the Turkish Empire.

Stamps of GREAT BRITAIN *cancelled* "G 06" *or circular postmark as in Types* **8**, **18** or **20**.

1873–81.
Z1 ½d. rose-red (1870–79) .... *From* 45·00
Plate Nos. 12, 13, 14, 19, 20.
Z2 1d. rose-red (1864–79) .... *From* 18·00
Plate Nos. 107, 118, 130, 140, 145, 148, 155, 157, 162, 167, 177, 179, 180, 184, 185, 186, 187, 195, 198, 200, 203, 204, 211, 213, 215, 218, 220, 222.
Z3 1½d. lake-red (1870–74) (Plate 3) £300
Z4 2d. blue (1858–69) .... *From* 26·00
Plate Nos. 13, 14, 15.
Z5 2½d. rosy mauve (1875) (*blued paper*) .... 75·00
Plate No. 1.
Z6 2½d. rosy mauve (1875–76) .... *From* 32·00
Plate Nos. 1, 2, 3.
Z7 2½d. rosy mauve (1876–79) .... *From* 25·00
Plate Nos. 3, 4, 5, 6, 7, 8, 9, 10, 11, 12, 13, 14, 15, 16, 17.
Z8 2½d. blue (1880) .... *From* 15·00
Plate Nos. 17, 18, 19, 20.
Z9 2½d. blue (1881) .... *From* 11·00
Plate Nos. 21, 22, 23.
Z10 3d. rose (1867–73) (Plate No. 10) ....
Z11 3d. rose (1873–76) .... 45·00
Plate Nos. 12, 15, 16, 18, 19, 20.
Z12 3d. rose (1881) (Plate Nos. 20, 21)
Z13 4d. vermilion (1865–73) .... *From* 40·00
Plate Nos. 11, 12, 13, 14.
Z14 4d. vermilion (1876) (Plate No. 15) £180
Z15 4d. sage-green (1877) £120
Plate Nos. 15, 16.
Z16 4d. grey-brown (1880) wmk Large Garter (Plate No. 17)
Z17 4d. grey-brown (1880) wmk Crown .... 55·00
Plate Nos. 17, 18.
Z18 6d. mauve (1870) (Plate Nos. 8, 9) ....
Z19 6d. buff (1872–73) .... *From* 85·00
Plate Nos. 11, 12.
Z20 6d. chestnut (1872) (Plate No. 11) .... 45·00
Z21 6d. grey (1873) (Plate No. 12) £150
Z22 6d. grey (1874–80) .... *From* 32·00
Plate Nos. 13, 14, 15, 16, 17.
Z23 8d. orange (1876) £425
Z24 10d. red-brown (1867) £160
Z25 1s. green (1867–73) .... 32·00
Plate Nos. 6, 7.
Z26 1s. green (1873–77) .... *From* 45·00
Plate Nos. 8, 9, 10, 12, 13.
Z27 1s. orange-brown (1880) (Plate No. 13) ....
Z28 1s. orange-brown (1881) .... 65·00
Plate Nos. 13, 14.
Z29 2s. blue (1867) £150
Z30 5s. rose (1867) (Plate Nos. 1, 2) .... *From* £700

1880.
Z31 ½d. deep green .... 11·00
Z32 ½d. pale green .... 12·00
Z33 1d. Venetian red .... 15·00
Z34 1½d. Venetian red £180
Z35 2d. pale rose .... 60·00
Z36 2d. deep rose .... 60·00
Z37 5d. indigo .... 95·00

1881.
Z38 1d. lilac (14 dots) ....
Z39 1d. lilac (16 dots) .... 6·00

1884.
Z40 ½d. slate-blue .... 18·00
Z41 1½d. lilac .... 90·00
Z42 2d. lilac .... 75·00
Z43 2½d. lilac .... 11·00
Z44 4d. dull green £190
Z45 5d. dull green £110
Z46 1s. dull green £325

1887–92.
Z47 ½d. vermilion .... 9·00
Z54 6d. purple/*rose-red* .... 25·00
Z55 1s. dull green £150

1900.
Z56 ½d. blue-green .... 12·00
Z57 1s. green and carmine £180

1902–04. *De La Rue ptgs.*
Z58 ½d. blue-green .... 4·75
Z59 ½d. yellowish green .... 5·00
Z60 1d. scarlet .... 4·25
Z64 1s. dull green and carmine .... 32·00

CONSTANTINOPLE

Stamps of GREAT BRITAIN *cancelled* "C" *or circular postmark as in Types* **1**, **10**, **18** or **19**.

1857–83.
Z68 ½d. rose-red (1870–79) .... *From* 25·00
Plate Nos. 5, 6, 10, 11, 12, 13, 14, 15, 20.
Z69 1d. red-brown (1854), Die I, wmk Small Crown, perf 16 ....
Z70 1d. red-brown (1855), Die II, wmk Small Crown, perf 14 ....
Z71 1d. red-brown, (1855), Die II, wmk Large Crown, perf 14 .... 20·00
Z72 1d. rose-red (1857) .... 7·00
Z73 1d. rose-red (1861) Alphabet IV ....
Z74 1d. rose-red (1864–79) .... *From* 8·50
Plate Nos. 71, 72, 73, 74, 76, 78, 79, 80, 81, 83, 85, 87, 89, 90, 92, 93, 94, 95, 96, 97, 99, 101, 102, 105, 106, 108, 109, 110, 113, 116, 118, 119, 120, 121, 122, 123, 124, 125, 127, 129, 130, 131, 134, 135, 136, 137, 138, 140, 141, 143, 144, 145, 146, 147, 148, 149, 150, 151, 152, 155, 156, 157, 158, 159, 160, 161, 162, 163, 164, 165, 166, 167, 170, 171, 172, 173, 174, 175, 176, 177, 178, 179, 180, 181, 183, 184, 186, 187, 188, 189, 190, 191, 192, 193, 194, 195, 196, 197, 198, 200, 201, 203, 204, 205, 206, 207, 208, 210, 212, 214, 215, 216, 220, 222, 224.
Z75 1½d. rose-red (1870) (Plate 1) £225
Z76 2d. blue (1855), wmk Large Crown, perf 14. (Plate Nos. 5, 6) ....
Z77 2d. blue (1858–69) .... *From* 12·00
Plate Nos. 7, 8, 9, 12, 13, 14, 15.
Z78 2½d. rosy mauve (1875–76) (*blued paper*) (Plate Nos. 1, 2) .... *From* 55·00
Z79 2½d. rosy mauve (1875–76) .... *From* 30·00
Plate Nos. 1, 2, 3.
Z80 2½d. rosy mauve (*Error of Lettering*) ....
Z81 2½d. rosy mauve (1876–79) .... *From* 23·00
Plate Nos. 3 to 17.
Z82 2½d. blue (1880–81) .... *From* 11·00
Plate Nos. 17, 18, 19, 20.
Z83 2½d. blue (1881) (Plate Nos. 21, 22, 23) .... 7·50
Z84 3d. carmine-rose (1862) (Plate No. 2) £140
Z85 3d. rose (1865) (Plate No. 4) .... 80·00
Z86 3d. rose (1867–73) (Plate Nos. 4 to 10) .... 75·00
Z87 3d. rose (1873–76) .... 24·00
Plate Nos. 11, 12, 15, 16, 17, 18, 19.
Z88 3d. rose (1881) (Plate No. 21) ....
Z89 3d. on 3d. lilac (1883) (Plate No. 21) ....
Z90 4d. rose (1857) .... 45·00
a. Rose-carmine ....
Z91 4d. red (1862) (Plate Nos. 3, 4) .... *From* 38·00
Z92 4d. vermilion (1865–73) .... *From* 26·00
Plate Nos. 7 to 14.
Z93 4d. vermilion (1876) (Plate No. 15) £150
Z94 4d. sage-green (1877) £100
Plate Nos. 15, 16. ....
Z95 4d. grey-brown (1880) wmk Large Garter (Plate No. 17) ....
Z96 4d. grey-brown (1880) wmk Crown (Plate Nos. 17, 18) .... *From* 42·00
Z97 6d. lilac (1856) .... 60·00
Z98 6d. lilac (1862) (Plate Nos. 3, 4) .... *From* 38·00
Z99 6d. lilac (1865–67) .... 35·00
Plate Nos. 5, 6.
Z100 6d. lilac (1867) (Plate No. 6) .... 40·00
Z101 6d. violet (1867–70) .... *From* 32·00
Plate Nos. 6, 8, 9.
Z102 6d. buff (1872–73) .... 55·00
Plate Nos. 11, 12.
Z103 6d. chestnut (1872) (Plate No. 11) .... 30·00
Z104 6d. grey (1873) (Plate No. 12) .... 75·00
Z105 6d. grey (1874–76) .... *From* 26·00
Plate Nos. 13, 14, 15, 16.
Z106 6d. grey (1881–82) (Plate Nos. 17, 18) .... 28·00
Z107 6d. on 6d. lilac (1883) .... 80·00
a. Dots slanting (Letters MI or SJ) £150
Z108 8d. orange (1876) £400
Z109 10d. red-brown (1867), wmk Emblems £25000
Z110 10d. red-brown (1867) £160
Z111 1s. green (1856) £110
Z112 1s. green (1862) .... 60·00
Z113 1s. green (1862) ("K" variety) ....
Z114 1s. green (1862) (*thick paper*) ....
Z115 1s. green (1865) (Plate No. 4) .... 65·00
Z116 1s. green (1867–73) .... *From* 16·00
Plate Nos. 4, 5, 6, 7.
Z117 1s. green (1873–77) .... *From* 27·00
Plate Nos. 8, 9, 10, 11, 12, 13.
Z118 1s. orange-brown (1880) (Plate No. 13) £180
Z119 1s. orange-brown (1881) .... *From* 48·00
Plate Nos. 13, 14.
Z120 2s. blue (1867) .... 95·00
Z121 5s. rose (1867–74) .... *From* £250
Plate Nos. 1, 2.
Z122 5s. rose (1882) (*white paper*) £850
Z123 5s. rose (1882) (*blued paper*) £1200

1880.
Z124 ½d. deep green .... 7·50
Z125 ½d. pale green .... 10·00
Z126 1d. Venetian red .... 10·00
Z127 2d. pale rose .... 45·00
Z128 2d. deep rose .... 45·00
Z129 5d. indigo ....

1881.
Z130 1d. lilac (14 *dots*) ....
Z131 1d. lilac (16 *dots*) .... 2·50

1883–84.
Z132 ½d. slate-blue .... 8·00
Z133 1½d. lilac ....
Z134 2d. lilac .... 60·00
Z135 2½d. lilac .... 7·00
Z136 3d. lilac ....
Z137 4d. dull green ....
Z138 5d. dull green .... 90·00
Z139 6d. dull green ....
Z140 9d. dull green ....
Z141 1s. dull green £250
Z142 2s.6d. lilac (*blued paper*) £600
Z143 2s.6d. lilac (*white paper*) .... 85·00
Z144 5s. rose (*blued paper*) ....
Z145 5s. rose (*white paper*) ....

1887–92.
Z146 ½d. vermilion .... 3·25
Z154 6d. purple/rose-red .... 12·00
Z157 1s. dull green .... 85·00

1900.
Z158 ½d. blue-green .... 6·00
Z159 1s. green and carmine £140

1902–04. *De La Rue ptgs.*
Z160 ½d. blue-green .... 3·00
Z161 ½d. yellowish green .... 3·50
Z162 1d. scarlet .... 2·50
Z169 6d. purple .... 12·00
Z172 1s. green and carmine .... 19·00
Z173 2s.6d. lilac ....
Z174 5s. carmine ....

POSTAL FISCALS

Z175 1d. purple (wmk Anchor) (1868)
Z176 1d. purple (wmk Orb) (1881) £600

SALONICA

Stamps of GREAT BRITAIN *cancelled with circular postmark as in Type* **18** *or double-circle datestamp.*

1900.
Z202 ½d. vermilion (1887) 20·00
Z203 ½d. blue-green (1900) 22·00
Z204 1d. lilac (1881) 22·00
Z205 6d. purple/red (1887) 30·00
Z206 1s. green and carmine (1900) £190
Z207 5s. rose (white paper) (1883) £900

1902.
Z208 ½d. blue-green 25·00
Z209 ½d. yellow-green 19·00
Z209a 1d. scarlet 19·00
Z209c 1s. green and carmine 50·00

SMYRNA (IZMIR)

Stamps of GREAT BRITAIN *cancelled* "F 87" *or circular postmark as in Type* **8**, **16** *or* **18**.

1872–83.
Z210 ½d. rose-red (1870–79) *From* 30·00
Plates 11, 12, 13, 14, 15.
Z211 1d. rose-red (1864–79) *From* 14·00
Plate Nos. 120, 124, 134, 137, 138, 139, 140, 142, 143, 145, 146, 148, 149, 150, 151, 152, 153, 155, 156, 157, 158, 159, 160, 161, 162, 163, 164, 166, 167, 168, 169, 170, 171, 172, 173, 174, 175, 176, 177, 178, 183, 184, 185, 186, 187, 188, 191, 193, 195, 196, 198, 200, 201, 204, 210, 212, 215, 217, 218.
Z212 1½d. lake-red (1870–74) (Plate Nos. 1, 3).. *From* £250
Z213 2d. blue (1858) wmk Large Crown, perf 16
Z214 2d. blue (1858–69) *From* 16·00
Plate Nos. 13, 14, 15.
Z215 2½d. rosy mauve (1875) (*blued paper*) 60·00
Plate No. 1.
Z216 2½d. rosy mauve (1875–76) *From* 27·00
Plate Nos. 1, 2, 3.
Z217 2½d. rosy mauve (*Error of lettering*)
Z218 2½d. rosy mauve (1876–79) *From* 22·00
Plate Nos. 3, 4, 5, 6, 7, 8, 9, 10, 11, 12, 13, 14, 15, 16, 17.
Z219 2½d. blue (1880) *From* 11·00
Plate Nos. 17, 18,19, 20.
Z220 2½d. blue (1881) 9·00
Plate Nos. 21, 22, 23.
Z221 3d. rose (1867–73) 40·00
Plate Nos. 5, 7, 9, 10.
Z222 3d. rose (1873–76) (Plate No. 14)
Z223 4d. vermilion (1865–73) 26·00
Plate Nos. 12, 13, 14.
Z224 4d. vermilion (1876) (Plate No. 15) £150
Z225 4d. sage-green (1877) 95·00
Plate Nos. 15, 16.
Z226 4d. grey-brown (1880) wmk Large Garter (Plate No. 17)
Z227 4d. grey-brown (1880) wmk Crown (Plate Nos. 17, 18) *From* 38·00
Z228 6d. buff (1872–73) *From* 70·00
Plate Nos. 11, 12.
Z229 6d. chestnut (1872) (Plate No. 11)
Z230 6d. grey (1873) (Plate No. 12) 75·00
Z231 6d. grey (1874–80) *From* 27·00
Plate Nos. 13, 14, 15, 16, 17.
Z232 6d. grey (1881–82) (Plate Nos. 17, 18) 50·00
Z233 6d. on 6d. lilac (1883) £100
Z234 8d. orange (1876)
Z235 9d. straw (1867) £300
Z236 10d. red-brown (1867) £140
Z237 1s. green (1867–73) (Plate Nos. 6, 7)
Z238 1s. green (1873–77) *From* 32·00
Plate Nos. 8, 9, 10, 11, 12, 13.
Z239 1s. orange-brown (1880) (Plate No. 13) £160
Z240 1s. orange-brown (1881) (Plate Nos. 13, 14) 50·00
Z241 5s. rose (1867–74) (Plate No. 2)

1880.
Z242 ½d. deep green 9·00
Z243 ½d. pale green 9·00
Z244 1d. Venetian red 13·00
Z245 1½d. Venetian red £120
Z246 2d. pale rose 45·00
Z247 2d. deep rose 45·00
Z248 5d. indigo 70·00

1881.
Z249 1d. lilac (16 dots) 4·50

1884.
Z250 ½d. slate-blue 15·00
Z251 2d. lilac 70·00
Z252 2½d. lilac 10·00
Z253 4d. dull green
Z254 5d. dull green £100
Z255 1s. dull green £300

1887.
Z256 ½d. vermilion 5·50
Z263 6d. purple/*rose-red* 20·00
Z264 1s. dull green £110

1900.
Z265 ½d. blue-green 8·00
Z266 1s. green and carmine

1902–04. *De La Rue ptgs.*
Z267 ½d. blue-green 4·50
Z268 ½d. yellowish green 5·00
Z269 1d. scarlet 4·00
Z276 6d. purple 15·00
Z279 1s. green and carmine 26·00
Z280 2s.6d. purple
Z281 5s. carmine

STAMBOUL (CONSTANTINOPLE)

Stamps of GREAT BRITAIN *cancelled* "S" *as Type* **10**, *or circular postmarks inscribed either* "BRITISH POST OFFICE CONSTANTINOPLE S" *or* "BRITISH POST OFFICE STAMBOUL" *as Type* **18**.

1884.
Z296 ½d. slate-blue 25·00
Z297 1d. lilac 12·00
Z298 2d. lilac
Z299 2½d. lilac 15·00
Z300 5d. dull green £150

1887–92.
Z306 ½d. vermilion 15·00
Z314 6d. purple/*rose-red* 35·00
Z317 1s. dull green

The "S" cancellation was in use from 1885 to 1891 and the "Stamboul" mark from 1892 to 1896, when the office was closed, and from its reopening in 1908 to 1914. The "CONSTANTINOPLE S" handstamp was normally used as a back stamp, but can be found cancelling stamps in the period 1885 to 1892.

PRICES FOR STAMPS ON COVER	
Nos. 1/3a	*from* × 8
Nos. 4/6*a*	*from* × 5
Nos. 7/40	*from* × 3
Nos. L1/10	*from* × 6
Nos. L11/17	*from* × 3

I. TURKISH CURRENCY

(40 paras = 1 piastre)

Following the depreciation of the Turkish piastre against sterling in 1884 it was decided to issue stamps surcharged in Turkish currency to avoid speculation. During the early period unsurcharged stamps of Great Britain remained on sale from the British Post Offices at the current rate of exchange until replaced by "LEVANT" overprints.

80 PARAS (1) **4 PIASTRES** (2) **12 PIASTRES** (3)

PRINTERS. Nos. 1/24 were surcharged or overprinted by De La Rue, *unless otherwise stated.*

Stamps of Great Britain (Queen Victoria) surch as T 1 to 3

1885 (1 Aug)–**88.**
1 **64** 40pa. on 2½d. lilac £110 1·25
2 **62** 80pa. on 5d. green £200 9·50
3 **58** 12pi. on 2s.6d. lilac/*bluish* £400 £250
a. On white paper (4.88) 48·00 24·00

Nos. 3, 11 and 33 were surcharged from a horizontal setting of eight clichés of which three showed a small final 'S'.

1887 (June)–**96.**
4 **74** 40pa. on 2½d. purple/*blue* 6·50 10
a. Surch double £1900 £2500
5 **78** 80pa. on 5d. purple and blue (7.90) 15·00 30
a. Small "0" in "80" £275 85·00
w. Wmk inverted † £550
6 **81** 4pi. on 10d. dull purple & carm (10.10.96) 42·00 8·00
a. Dull purple and deep bright carmine 42·00 11·00
b. Large, wide "4" (R. 1/2, 1/4) £190 65·00

No. 5a first appeared on the June 1895 printing when the size of the surcharge plate was increased from 60 to 120. On the Victorian stamp the variety comes on R. 4/1 and 4/7. The same setting was used for the first printing of the Edward VII surcharge, but here the sheet size was further increased to 240 so that No. 9a occurs on R. 4/1, 4/7, 14/1 and 14/7.

1893 (25 Feb). *Roughly handstamped at Constantinople, as T* **1**.
7 **71** 40pa. on ½d. vermilion £425 £100

This provisional was in use for five days only at the Constantinople and Stamboul offices. As fraudulent copies were made with the original handstamp, and can be found "used" on piece cancelled by fraudulent use of the usual canceller, this stamp should only be purchased from undoubted sources.

The handstamp became damaged during use so that by 1 March the top of the "S" was broken. Used examples dated 25 or 26 February showing the broken "S" *must* be fraudulent. It is also known with genuine handstamp inverted (*Price* £850 *unused*, £325 *used*).

1902–05. *Stamps of King Edward VII surch as T* **1** *to* **3**.
8 **86** 40pa. on 2½d. ultramarine (3.02) 17·00 10
a. Pale ultramarine 19·00 10
ab. Surch double † £2250
9 **89** 80pa. on 5d. dull purple and ultram (5.6.02) 11·00 2·50
a. Small "0" in "80" £275 £190
10 **92** 4pi. on 10d. dull purple and carmine (6.9.02) 15·00 4·00
a. No cross on crown £140 90·00
b. Chalk-surfaced paper 6·00 10·00
ba. Chalk-surfaced paper. No cross on crown 90·00 £110
11 **94** 12pi. on 2s.6d. lilac (29.8.03) 35·00 35·00
a. Chalk-surfaced paper. *Pale dull purple* 70·00 75·00
b. Chalk-surfaced paper. *Dull purple* 38·00 35·00
12 **95** 24pi. on 5s. bright carmine (15.8.05) 32·00 40·00
8/12 *Set of* 5 90·00 70·00
9s/11s Optd "Specimen" *Set of* 3 £150

No. 9a only occurs on the first printing of 80pa. on 5d.

1 PIASTRE
(4)

1905–08. *Surch in* "PIASTRES" *instead of* "PARAS" *as T* **4** *and* **2**.
13 **86** 1pi. on 2½d. ultramarine (17.4.06) 18·00 10
a. Surch double † £1600
w. Wmk inverted £750 £750
14 **89** 2pi. on 5d. dull purple & ultram (11.11.05) 35·00 2·50
a. Chalk-surfaced paper (1.08) 27·00 3·50
ab. Slate-purple and ultramarine 35·00 7·00

1 Piastre (5) **1 PIASTRE 10 PARAS** (6)

1906 (2 July). *Issued at Beyrout. No. L4 surch with T* **5** *by American Press, Beyrout.*
15 **85** 1pi. on 2d. grey-green and carmine £1300 £600

1909 (16 Nov–Dec). *Stamps of King Edward VII surch as T* **1** *(30pa.)* **6**, *and* **2** *(5 pi). Ordinary paper (No. 19) or chalk-surfaced paper (others).*
16 **84** 30pa. on 1½d. pale dull purple and green 14·00 1·25
a. Surch double, one albino
17 **87** 1pi.10pa. on 3d. dull purple/*orange-yellow* 12·00 40·00
18 **88** 1pi.30pa. on 4d. green and chocolate-brown 5·00 17·00
19 1pi.30pa. on 4d. brown-orange (16.12.09) 17·00 65·00
20 **83** 2pi.20pa. on 6d. dull purple 23·00 65·00
21 **93** 5pi. on 1s. dull green and carmine 4·25 12·00
s. Optd "Specimen" 60·00
16/21 *Set of* 6 65·00 £180

1¾ PIASTRE (7) **4** Normal "4" **4** Pointed "4"

1910 (24 Jan). *Stamps of King Edward VII surch as T* **7**. *Chalk-surfaced paper (Nos. 22 and 24).*
22 **87** 1¼pi. on 3d. dull purple/*orange-yellow* 50 1·00
23 **88** 1¾pi. on 4d. pale orange 50 60
a. Orange-red 5·50 6·00
b. Thin, pointed "4" in fraction 5·50 26·00
24 **83** 2½pi. on 6d. dull purple 1·40 65
22/4 *Set of* 3 2·25 2·00

No. 23b occurs in the first and seventh vertical rows of the sheet. The variety also occurs on No. 38, but not on No. 38b.

1 PIASTRE (8) **1 PIASTRE** (9)

TYPE DIFFERENCES. In T **4** the letters are tall and narrow and the space enclosed by the upper part of the "A" is small.

In T **8** the opening of the "A" is similar but the letters are shorter and broader, the "P" and the "E" being particularly noticeable.

In T **9** the letters are short and broad, but the "A" is thin and open.

1911–13. *Stamps of King Edward VII, Harrison or Somerset House ptgs, surch at Somerset House.*

(a) Surch with T **4** *(20 July).*
25 **86** 1pi. on 2½d. bright blue (perf 14) 16·00 9·00
a. Surch double, one albino £225
26 1pi. on 2½d. bright blue (perf 15×14) (14.10.11) 22·00 2·75
a. Dull blue 22·00 2·25

(b) Surch with T **8**.
27 **86** 1pi. on 2½d. bright blue (perf 15×14) (3.12) 16·00 3·50
a. Dull blue 24·00 4·00

(c) Surch with T **9** *(7.12).*
28 **86** 1pi. on 2½d. bright blue (perf 15×14) 70·00 75
a. Dull blue 70·00 75

(d) Surch with T **1** *to* **3** *(1911–13).*
29 **84** 30pa. on 1½d. reddish purple and bright green (22.8.11) 6·50 55
a. Slate-purple and green 12·00 2·25
b. Surch double, one albino 55·00
30 **89** 2pi. on 5d. dull reddish purple and bright blue (13.5.12) 16·00 2·25
a. Deep dull reddish purple and bright blue 19·00 2·25

31	92	4pi. on 10d. dull purple & scarlet (26.6.12)	40·00	17·00
		a. Dull reddish purple & aniline pink	£275	£100
		b. Dull reddish purple and carmine	14·00	11·00
		c. No cross on crown		
32	93	5pi. on 1s. green and carmine (1913)	23·00	5·50
		a. Surch double, one albino	£250	
33	94	12pi. on 2s.6d. dull reddish purple (3.2.12)	55·00	38·00
		a. Dull greyish purple	55·00	38·00
34	95	24pi. on 5s. carmine (1913)	60·00	80·00
		a. Surch double, one albino	£300	
29/34 *Set of 6*			£160	£120

1913 (Apr)–**14**. *Stamps of King George V, wmk Royal Cypher, surch as T* **1** *(30pa.),* **9** *(1pi.)* **7** *or* **2** *(4 and 5pi.).*

35	105	30pa. on 1½d. red-brown (4.13)	3·50	14·00
		a. Surch double, one albino	£110	
36	104	1pi. on 2½d. cobalt-blue (6.13)	11·00	10
		a. Bright blue	9·00	15
37	106	1¼pi. on 3d. dull reddish violet (9.13)	5·00	4·25
		a. Violet	7·50	6·00
		b. Surch double, one albino	£300	
38		1¾pi. on 4d. deep grey-green (7.13)	3·00	7·50
		a. Thin, pointed "4" in fraction	45·00	85·00
		b. Grey-green	7·00	5·50
39	108	4pi. on 10d. turquoise-blue (12.13)	8·00	23·00
40		5pi. on 1s. bistre-brown (1.14)	40·00	60·00
35/40 *Set of 6*			65·00	95·00

II. BRITISH CURRENCY

Stamps overprinted "LEVANT" were for use on parcels, with the ½d. and 1d. principally used for printed paper and post cards. They replaced unoverprinted Great Britain stamps, Nos. Z58/64, Z160/74, Z208/9c and Z267/81, which had previously been used for these purposes.

From October 1907 the three lowest values were also used for certain other amended postal rates until Nos. 16/21 were introduced.

LEVANT

(L **1**)

1905 (15 Aug)–**12**. *Stamps of King Edward VII optd with Type* L **1**.

(a) De La Rue ptgs.

L1	83	½d. pale yellowish green	8·50	15
		a. Yellowish green	8·50	15
L2		1d. scarlet	11·00	15
		a. Bright scarlet	11·00	90
L3	84	1½d. dull purple and green	6·00	2·00
		a. Chalk-surfaced paper. *Pale dull purple and green*	16·00	3·00
L4	85	2d. grey-green and carmine-red	9·50	32·00
		a. Chalk-surfaced paper. *Pale grey-green and carmine-red*	3·50	7·50
		ab. Dull blue-green and carmine	3·50	8·00
L5	86	2½d. ultramarine	8·50	20·00
L6	87	3d. dull purple/*orange-yellow*	6·00	12·00
L7	88	4d. green and grey-brown	9·50	50·00
		a. Green and chocolate-brown	20·00	55·00
L8	89	5d. dull purple and ultramarine	16·00	32·00
L9	83	6d. slate-purple	12·00	25·00
L10	93	1s. dull green and carmine	40·00	50·00
		a. Chalk-surfaced paper	40·00	50·00
L1/10 *Set of* 10			£110	£180

(b) Harrison ptgs optd at Somerset House.

L11	83	½d. dull yellow-green (*p.* 14) (2.12)	30·00	29·00
		a. Dull green	30·00	29·00
		b. Deep dull green	45·00	35·00

On 28 December 1909 all values, except for the ½d. and 1d. were withdrawn from sale. A further consignment of the 2d, No. L4*ab*, probably ordered in error was however, received, and, as there was no requirement for this value, sold mainly to collectors. Subsequently dated cancellations on the withdrawn values are philatelic, being worth much less than the used prices quoted.

ANT

Distorted "N" (R. 2/10, 12/10)

1911–13. *Stamps of King George V optd with Type* L **1** *at Somerset House.*

(a) Die A. Wmk Crown.

L12	98	½d. green (No. 322) (12.9.11)	2·25	2·00
		a. Distorted "N"	35·00	
L13	99	1d. carmine-red (No. 327) (1.1.12)	50	7·00
		a. No cross on crown	£150	
		b. Opt double, one albino	£100	
		c. Distorted "N"	18·00	

(b) Redrawn types. Wmk Crown.

L14	101	½d. green (No. 339) (19.3.12)	1·00	20
		a. Yellow-green	2·25	75
		b. Distorted "N"	20·00	
L15	102	1d. bright scarlet (No. 341) (24.2.12)	1·50	1·60
		a. Scarlet (No. 342)	2·50	1·60
		b. Opt triple, two albino	42·00	
		c. Distorted "N"	25·00	

(c) New types. Wmk Royal Cypher (7.13).

L16	105	½d. green (No. 351)	1·00	2·00
		a. Yellow-green	2·50	2·75
		b. Distorted "N"	21·00	
L17	104	1d. scarlet (No. 357)	30	6·00
		a. Vermilion	12·00	12·00
		b. Distorted "N"	15·00	

Similar overprints were issued when the British Post Offices reopened in 1919, and are listed below.

B. BRITISH POST OFFICES IN CONSTANTINOPLE AND SMYRNA, 1919–1923

CONSTANTINOPLE

Following the occupation of Constantinople by Allied forces a British Military Post Office was opened for civilian use on 4 February 1919. During the period of its existence stamps of Great Britain with face values to 10s. were available and such use can be identified by the following cancellations:

"FIELD POST OFFICE H12" (4 February 1919 to 18 March 1919)

"ARMY POST OFFICE Y" (20 March 1919 to June 1920)

"ARMY POST OFFICE S.X.3" (March 1919 to April 1920)

"British A.P.O. CONSTANTINOPLE" (July 1919 to July 1920).

Of these four marks the first two types were also used for military mail.

The office reverted to civilian control on 29 July 1920, Nos. 41/50 and L18/24 being intended for its use.

Z 1

Z 2

Z 3

Z 4

1919–20. *Used at the Army Post Office. Stamps of* GREAT BRITAIN *cancelled with Types* Z **1**, Z **2**, Z **3**, Z **4**.

Z176	½d. green	2.00
Z177	1d. scarlet	2·00
Z178	1½d. brown	3·25
Z179	2d. orange (Die I)	2·50
Z180	2½d. blue	4·00
Z181	4d. grey-green	8·50
Z182	6d. purple	4·50
Z183	9d. agate	22·00
Z184	1s. bistre	5·50
Z185	2s.6d. brown	42·00
Z186	5s. rose-red	70·00
Z187	10s. dull grey-blue	£120

1920–21. *Used at the Civilian Post Office. Stamps of* GREAT BRITAIN *cancelled with Type* **18** *or double-circle datestamp.*

Z188	½d. green	2·00
Z189	1d. scarlet	2·00
Z190	1½d. brown	3·25
Z191	2d. orange (Die I)	2·50
Z192	2½d. blue	4·00
Z193	3d. violet	6·50
Z194	4d. grey-green	8·50
Z195	5d. brown	13·00
Z196	6d. purple	4·50
Z197	10d. turquoise-blue	22·00
Z198	1s. bistre	5·50
Z199	2s.6d. brown	42·00
Z200	5s. rose-red	70·00
Z201	10s. dull grey-blue	£120

PRICES FOR STAMPS ON COVER	
Nos. 41/50	*from* × 2
Nos. L18/24	*from* × 5

Stamps of Great Britain surch at Somerset House

I. TURKISH CURRENCY

1½ PIASTRES

(**10**)

15 PIASTRES

(**11**)

18¾

Short fraction bar (R. 4/12, 14/12)

1921 (Aug). *Stamps of King George V, wmk Royal Cypher, surch as T* **1** *(30pa.),* **10** *and* **11** *(15 and 18¾pi.).*

41	105	30pa. on ½d. green	75	13·00
		a. Yellow-green	3·50	15·00
42	104	1½pi. on 1d. bright scarlet	1·50	1·25
		a. Vermilion	12·00	4·25
		b. Scarlet-vermilion	10·00	4·75
43		3¾pi. on 2½d. blue	1·25	25
		a. Dull Prussian blue	38·00	2·75
44	106	4½pi. on 3d. violet	2·00	3·75
		a. Bluish violet	4·00	3·00
45	107	7½pi. on 5d. brown	50	10
		a. Yellow-brown	3·00	40
46	108	15pi. on 10d. turquoise-blue	70	15
47		18¾pi. on 1s. bistre-brown	4·25	4·25
		a. Short fraction bar	55·00	
		b. Olive-bistre	7·00	4·75
		ba. Short fraction bar	75·00	

45 PIASTRES

(**12**)

45

Joined figures (second stamp in each horiz row)

1921. *Stamps of King George V (Bradbury, Wilkinson printing) surch as T* **12**.

48	109	45pi. on 2s.6d. chocolate-brown	20·00	45·00
		a. Joined figures	35·00	65·00
		b. Olive-brown	55·00	65·00
		ba. Joined figures	75·00	90·00
49		90pi. on 5s. rose-red	25·00	30·00
		a. Surch double, one albino	£250	
50		180pi. on 10s. dull grey-blue	45·00	40·00
		a. Surch double, one albino	£250	
41/50 *Set of* 10			90·00	£120
47s/50s Optd "Specimen" *Set of* 4			£275	

II. BRITISH CURRENCY

1921. *Stamps of King George V optd as Type* L **1**.

L18	106	2d. reddish orange (Die I)	2·30	32·00
		a. Bright orange	2·25	32·00
L19		3d. bluish violet	7·50	10·00
L20		4d. grey-green	5·00	15·00
L21	107	5d. yellow-brown	12·00	28·00
L22		6d. dull purple (*chalk-surfaced paper*)	24·00	42·00
		a. Reddish purple	26·00	8·50
L23	108	1s. bistre-brown	14·00	8·50
		a. Olive-bistre	14·00	8·50
		s. Optd "Specimen"	65·00	
L24	109	2s.6d. chocolate-brown	38·00	90·00
		a. Olive-brown	65·00	£120
		s. Optd "Specimen"	£140	
L18/24 *Set of* 7			85·00	£170

On No. L24 the letters of the overprint are shorter, being only 3 mm high.

Nos. 41/50 and L18/24 were used at the Constantinople office only.

SMYRNA

When the office re-opened on 1 March 1919 existing stocks of surcharged or overprinted issues were utilised until they were exhausted in mid-1920. During this period examples of Nos. 24, 29*a*, 30*a*, 33*b*/7, 39/40, L4*b*, L14/17 are known with commercial postmarks. These stamps were supplemented and finally replaced in mid-1920 by ordinary stamps of Great Britain.

1919–22. *Stamps of* GREAT BRITAIN *cancelled with circular postmark as Type* **18** *or with* "REGISTERED" *oval.*

Z282	½d. green	2·50
Z283	1d. scarlet	2·50
Z284	1½d. brown	3·50
Z285	2d. orange (Die I)	3·00
Z286	2d. orange (Die II)	26·00
Z287	2½d. blue (shades)	5·00
Z288	2½d. dull Prussian blue	£500
Z289	4d. grey-green	11·00
Z290	6d. purple	8·00
Z291	10d. turquoise-blue	30·00
Z292	1s. bistre	8·50
Z293	2s.6d. brown	75·00
Z294	5s. rose-red	£110
Z295	10s. dull grey-blue	£180

C. BRITISH FIELD OFFICE IN SALONICA

These overprints were originally prepared for use by a civilian post office to be set up on Mt. Athos, Northern Greece. When the project was abandoned they were placed on sale at the Army Field Office in Salonica.

PRICES FOR STAMPS ON COVER	
Nos. S1/8	*from* × 6

Levant

(S **1**)

1916 (end Feb–9 Mar). *Stamps of Gt. Britain, optd with Type* S **1** *by Army Printing Office, Salonica.*

S1	105	½d. green	55·00	£250
		a. Opt double	£3500	£4250
		b. Vert pair, one without opt	£1800	£2250
S2	104	1d. scarlet	55·00	£250
		a. Opt double	£2250	£2750
S3	106	2d. reddish orange (Die I)	£160	£375
S4		3d. bluish violet	£130	£375
S5		4d. grey-green	£160	£375

S6	**107**	6d. reddish pur (*chalk-surfaced paper*)	90·00	£325
		a. Vert pair, one without opt	£2000	£2750
S7	**108**	9d. agate	£325	£600
		a. Opt double	£12000	£9000
S8		1s. bistre-brown	£275	£500
S1/8 *Set of* 8			£1100	£2750

There are numerous forgeries of this overprint.

All values can be found with an additional albino overprint, inverted on the gummed side. These are worth a 25% premium.

British New Guinea
see **Papua** *after* **Australia**

British Occupation of Iraq *see* Iraq

British Occupation of Italian Colonies

PRICES FOR STAMPS ON COVER TO 1945	
Nos. M1/21	*from* × 4
Nos. MD1/5	*from* × 10
Nos. S1/9	*from* × 4

The above prices refer to covers from the territories concerned, not examples used in Great Britain.

MIDDLE EAST FORCES

For use in territory occupied by British Forces in Eritrea (1942), Italian Somaliland (from 13 April 1942), Cyrenaica (1943), Tripolitania (1943), and some of the Dodecanese Islands (1945).

PRICES. Our prices for used stamps with "M.E.F." overprints are for specimens with identifiable postmarks of the territories concerned. These stamps were also used in the United Kingdom with official sanction, from the summer of 1950 onwards, and with U.K. postmarks are worth considerably less.

PRINTERS. Considerable research has been undertaken to discover the origins of Nos. M1/10. It is now suggested that Nos. M1/5, previously assigned to Harrison and Sons, were produced by the Army Printing Services, Cairo, and that the smaller printing, Nos. M6/10, previously identified as the work of the Army Printing Services, Cairo, was from an unidentified printer within the Middle East Forces area.

M.E.F. **M.E.F.**

(M **1**) Opt. 14 mm long. Regular lettering and upright oblong stops.

(M **2**) Opt. 13½ mm long. Regular lettering and square stops.

M.E.F.

(M **2a**) Opt. 13½ mm long. Rough lettering and round stops.

M.E.F.

Sliced "M" (R. 6/10)

(Illustrations twice actual size)

1942 (2 Mar). *Stamps of Great Britain optd.* W **127**. P 15×14.

(a) With Type M **1**.

M1	**128**	1d. scarlet (No. 463)	1·75	2·75
		a. Sliced "M"	90·00	£110
M2		2d. orange (No. 465)	1·25	4·00
		a. Sliced "M"	65·00	
M3		2½d. ultramarine (No. 466)	1·00	1·25
		a. Sliced "M"	70·00	
M4		3d. violet (No. 467)	80	30
M5	**129**	5d. brown	80	30
		a. Sliced "M"	65·00	70·00

(b) With Type M **2**.

M6	**128**	1d. scarlet (No. 463)	55·00	17·00
		a. Optd with Type M **2a**	45·00	12·00
		b. Nos. M6/a *se-tenant* vert	£200	95·00
M7		2d. orange (No. 465)	80·00	£110
		a. Optd with Type M **2a**	70·00	95·00
		b. Nos. M7/a *se-tenant* vert	£350	£425
M8		2½d. ultramarine (No. 466)	60·00	7·50
		a. Optd with Type M **2a**	55·00	5·50
		b. Nos. M8/a *se-tenant* vert	£225	60·00
M9		3d. violet (No. 467)	£130	45·00
		a. Optd with Type M **2a**	£120	42·00
		ab. Opt double	†	£4500
		b. Nos. M9/a *se-tenant* vert	£475	£200
M10	**129**	5d. brown	£425	95·00
		a. Optd with Type M **2a**	£400	85·00
		b. Nos. M10/a *se-tenant* vert	£1300	£700

See note after No. M21.

Nos. M6/10 were issued in panes of 60 (6×10), rows 2, 3, and 7 being overprinted with Type M **2** and the other seven rows with Type M **2a**.

M.E.F.

(M **3**) Optd 13½ mm long. Regular lettering and upright oblong stops.

(Illustration twice actual size)

1943 (1 Jan)–**47**. *Stamps of Great Britain optd with Type* M **3** *by Harrison & Sons.* W **127**, P 15×14 (1d. to 1s.); W **133**, P 14 (others).

M11	**128**	1d. pale scarlet (No. 486)	1·50	10
M12		2d. pale orange (No. 488)	1·50	1·25
M13		2½d. light ultramarine (No. 489)	50	10
M14		3d. pale violet (No. 490)	1·50	10
M15	**129**	5d. brown	4·00	10
M16		6d. purple	40	10
M17	**130**	9d. deep olive-green	85	10
M18		1s. bistre-brown	50	10
M19	**131**	2s.6d. yellow-green	7·00	1·00
M20		5s. red (1947)	18·00	17·00
M21	**132**	10s. ultramarine (1947)	29·00	10·00
M11/21 *Set of* 11			55·00	27·00
M18s/21s Optd "Specimen" *Set of* 4			£550	

The overprint on No. M15 should not be confused with the other overprints on the 5d. value. It can be distinguished from No. M5 by the ½ mm difference in length; and from No. M10 by the more intense colour, thicker lettering and larger stops.

POSTAGE DUE STAMPS

M.E.F.

(MD **1**)

1942. *Postage Due stamps of Great Britain Nos. D27/30 and D33 optd with Type* MD **1**, *in blue-black.*

MD1	D **1**	½d. emerald	30	13·00
MD2		1d. carmine	30	1·75
		w. Wmk sideways inverted*	–	60·00
MD3		2d. agate	1·25	1·25
MD4		3d. violet	50	4·25
MD5		1s. deep blue	3·75	13·00
		s. Optd "Specimen"	£160	
MD1/5 *Set of* 5			5·50	30·00

*No. MD2w shows the Crown pointing to the left, *as seen from the back of the stamp.*

CYRENAICA

In June 1949 the British authorities recognised the leader of the Senussi, Amir Mohammed Idris Al-Senussi, as Amir of Cyrenaica with autonomy in internal affairs.

(Currency. 10 millièmes = 1 piastre, 100 piastres = 1 Egyptian pound)

24 Mounted Warrior

25 Mounted Warrior

(Recess Waterlow)

1950 (16 Jan). P 12½.

136	**24**	1m. brown	3·00	5·50
137		2m. carmine	3·00	5·50
138		3m. orange-yellow	3·00	5·50
139		4m. blue-green	3·00	5·50
140		5m. grey-black	3·00	3·75
141		8m. orange	3·00	2·75
142		10m. violet	3·00	2·25
143		12m. scarlet	3·00	2·25
144		20m. blue	3·00	2·25
145	**25**	50m. ultramarine and purple-brown	7·00	6·50
146		100m. carmine and black	14·00	9·00
147		200m. violet and deep blue	18·00	25·00
148		500m. orange-yellow and green	48·00	65·00
136/148 *Set of* 13			£100	£130

POSTAGE DUE STAMPS

D **26**

(Recess Waterlow)

1950 (16 Jan). P 12½.

D149	D **26**	2m. brown	48·00	£100
D150		4m. blue-green	48·00	£100
D151		8m. scarlet	48·00	£110
D152		10m. orange	48·00	£110
D153		20m. orange-yellow	48·00	£120
D154		40m. blue	48·00	£160
D155		100m. grey-brown	48·00	£170
D149/155 *Set of* 7			£300	£750

On 24 December 1951 Cyrenaica united with Tripolitania, Fezzan and Ghadames to form the independent Kingdom of Libya, whose issues are listed in our Part 13 (*Africa since Independence F—M*) catalogue.

ERITREA

From early 1950 examples of Nos. E1/32 exist precancelled in manuscript by a black or blue horizontal line for use by British troops on concession rate mail.

BRITISH MILITARY ADMINISTRATION

(Currency. 100 cents = 1 shilling)

B. M. A.
ERITREA
10
CENTS
(E **1**)

B. M. A.
ERITREA
5 SHILLINGS
(E **2**)

SH. 50 Normal

SH .50 Misplaced Stop

1948–49. *Stamps of Great Britain surch as Types* E **1** *or* E **2**.

E1	**128**	5c. on ½d. pale green	1·75	65
E2		10c. on 1d. pale scarlet	1·50	2·50
E3		20c. on 2d. pale orange	1·50	2·25
E4		25c. on 2½d. light ultramarine	1·25	60
E5		30c. on 3d. pale violet	1·50	4·50
E6	**129**	40c. on 5d. brown	1·50	4·25
E7		50c. on 6d. purple	65	1·00
E7*a*	**130**	65c. on 8d. bright carmine (1.2.49)	7·00	2·00
E8		75c. on 9d. deep olive-green	1·75	75
E9		1s. on 1s. bistre-brown	1·50	50
E10	**131**	2s.50c. on 2s.6d. yellow-green	8·50	10·00
		a. Misplaced stop (R. 4/7)	£140	£160
E11		5s. on 5s. red	8·50	17·00
E12	**132**	10s. on 10s. ultramarine	22·00	22·00
E1/12 *Set of* 13			55·00	60·00

BRITISH ADMINISTRATION

1950 (6 Feb). *As Nos. E1/12, but surch* "B.A. ERITREA" *and new values instead of* "B.M.A." *etc.*

E13	**128**	5c. on ½d. pale green	1·50	8·00
E14		10c. on 1d. pale scarlet	40	3·00
E15		20c. on 2d. pale orange	50	80
E16		25c. on 2½d. light ultramarine	50	60
E17		30c. on 3d. pale violet	40	2·25
E18	**129**	40c. on 5d. brown	1·00	1·75
E19		50c. on 6d. purple	40	20
E20	**130**	65c. on 8d. bright carmine	3·25	1·50
E21		75c. on 9d. deep olive-green	60	25
E22		1s. on 1s. bistre-brown	40	15
E23	**131**	2s.50c. on 2s.6d. yellow-green	7·00	4·75
E24		5s. on 5s. red	7·00	12·00
E25	**132**	10s. on 10s. ultramarine	60·00	55·00
E13/25 *Set of* 13			75·00	80·00

1951 (28 May*). *Nos. 503/4, 506/7 and 509/11 of Great Britain surch* "B.A. ERITREA" *and new values.*

E26	**128**	5c. on ½d. pale orange	75	75
E27		10c. on 1d. light ultramarine	75	75
E28		20c. on 2d. pale red-brown	75	30
E29		25c. on 2½d. pale scarlet	75	30
E30	**147**	2s.50c. on 2s.6d. yellow-green	12·00	24·00
E31	**148**	5s. on 5s. red	21·00	24·00
E32		10s. on 10s. ultramarine	22·00	24·00
E26/32 *Set of* 7			55·00	65·00

*This is the local release date. The stamps were placed on sale in London on 3 May.

POSTAGE DUE STAMPS

B. M. A.
ERITREA
10 CENTS
(ED **1**)

1948. *Postage Due stamps of Great Britain Nos. D27/30 and D33 surch as Type* ED **1**.

ED1	D **1**	5c. on ½d. emerald	9·50	22·00
		a. No stop after "A"	–	£325
ED2		10c. on 1d. carmine	9·50	24·00
		a. No stop after "B"	£160	
ED3		20c. on 2d. agate	13·00	16·00
		a. No stop after "A"	65·00	
		b. No stop after "B" (R. 1/9)	£170	
ED4		30c. on 3d. violet	10·00	17·00
ED5		1s. on 1s. deep blue	18·00	32·00
ED1/5 *Set of* 5			55·00	£100

1950 (6 Feb). *As Nos. ED1/5, but surch* "B.A. ERITREA" *and new values instead of* "B.M.A." *etc.*

ED6	D **1**	5c. on ½d. emerald	13·00	48·00
ED7		10c. on 1d. carmine	13·00	18·00
		a. "C" of "CENTS" omitted	£2750	
		ab. "C" omitted and vertical oblong for "E" of "CENTS"	£4500	
ED8		20c. on 2d. agate	13·00	20·00
ED9		30c. on 3d. violet	17·00	28·00
		w. Wmk sideways-inverted*	–	55·00
ED10		1s. on 1s. deep blue	17·00	28·00
		a. Stop after "A" omitted (R. 2/13)	£425	
ED6/10 *Set of* 5			65·00	£130

No. ED7a, and probably No. ED7ab, occurred on R. 7/17, but the error was quickly corrected.

*No. ED9w shows the Crowns pointing to the left, *as seen from the back of the stamp.*

Stamps of Ethiopia were used in Eritrea after 15 September 1952 following federation with Ethiopia.

SOMALIA

BRITISH OCCUPATION

E.A.F.

(S 1 "East Africa Forces")

1943 (15 Jan)–**46**. *Stamps of Great Britain optd with Type* S **1**, *in blue.*

S1	**128**	1d. pale scarlet	1·00	60
S2		2d. pale orange	1·50	1·50
S3		2½d. light ultramarine	1·25	3·50
S4		3d. pale violet	1·25	15
S5	**129**	5d. brown	2·00	40
S6		6d. purple	1·50	1·25
S7	**130**	9d. deep olive-green	2·00	2·25
S8		1s. bistre-brown	3·00	15
S9	**131**	2s.6d. yellow-green (1946)	17·00	8·50
S1/9 *Set of* 9			27·00	16·00
S8s/9s Optd "Specimen" *Set of* 2			£275	

The note *re* used prices above Type M **1** of Middle East Forces also applies to the above issue.

BRITISH MILITARY ADMINISTRATION

(Currency. 100 cents = 1 shilling)

1948 (27 May). *Stamps of Great Britain surch* "B.M.A./ SOMALIA" *and new values, as Types* E **1** *and* E **2** *of Eritrea.*

S10	**128**	5c. on ½d. pale green	1·25	2·00
S11		15c. on 1½d. pale red-brown	1·75	15·00
S12		20c. on 2d. pale orange	3·00	4·50
S13		25c. on 2½d. light ultramarine	2·25	4·50
S14		30c. on 3d. pale violet	2·25	9·00
S15	**129**	40c. on 5d. brown	1·25	20
S16		50c. on 6d. purple	50	2·00
S17	**130**	75c. on 9d. deep olive-green	2·00	19·00
S18		1s. on 1s. bistre-brown	1·25	20
S19	**131**	2s.50c. on 2s.6d. yellow-green	4·25	25·00
		a. Misplaced stop (R. 4/7)	£100	£250
S20		5s. on 5s. red	11·00	42·00
S10/20 *Set of* 11			26·00	£110

For illustration of No. S19a, see previous column above No. E1 of Eritrea.

BRITISH ADMINISTRATION

1950 (2 Jan). *As Nos. S10/20, but surch* "BA./SOMALIA" *and new values, instead of* "B.M.A." *etc.*

S21	**128**	5c. on ½d. pale green	20	3·00
S22		15c. on 1½d. pale red-brown	75	17·00
S23		20c. on 2d. pale orange	75	7·50
S24		25c. on 2½d. light ultramarine	50	8·50
S25		30c. on 3d. pale violet	1·25	5·00
S26	**129**	40c. on 5d. brown	55	1·00
S27		50c. on 6d. purple	50	1·00
S28	**130**	75c. on 9d. deep olive-green	2·00	7·50
S29		1s. on 1s. bistre-brown	60	1·50
S30	**131**	2s.50c. on 2s.6d. yellow-green	4·00	25·00
S31		5s. on 5s. red	11·00	38·00
S21/31 *Set of* 11			20·00	£100

Somalia reverted to Italian Administration on 1 April 1950 later becoming independent. Later issues will be found listed in our Part 8 (*Italy and Switzerland*) catalogue.

TRIPOLITANIA

BRITISH MILITARY ADMINISTRATION

(Currency. 100 centesimi = 1 Military Administration lira)

4 M.A.L. — Normal

4 M.A.L. — Misaligned surcharge (R. 8/8, 18/8)

1948 (1 July). *Stamps of Great Britain surch* "B.M.A./ TRIPOLITANIA" *and new values, as Types* E **1** *and* E **2** *of Eritrea, but expressed in M(ilitary) A(dministration) L(ire).*

T1	**128**	1l. on ½d. pale green	1·00	1·75
T2		2l. on 1d. pale scarlet	50	15
T3		3l. on 1½d. pale red-brown	50	50
		a. Misaligned surch	35·00	45·00
T4		4l. on 2d. pale orange	50	70
		a. Misaligned surch	35·00	55·00
T5		5l. on 2½d. light ultramarine	50	20
T6		6l. on 3d. pale violet	50	40
T7	**129**	10l. on 5d. brown	50	15
T8		12l. on 6d. purple	50	20
T9	**130**	18l. on 9d. deep olive-green	1·00	65
T10		24l. on 1s. bistre-brown	1·00	1·50
T11	**131**	60l. on 2s.6d. yellow-green	4·00	12·00
T12		120l. on 5s. red	16·00	24·00
T13	**132**	240l. on 10s. ultramarine	24·00	£100
T1/13 *Set of* 13			45·00	£130

BRITISH ADMINISTRATION

1950 (6 Feb). *As Nos. T1/13, but surch* "B.A. TRIPOLITANIA" *and new values, instead of* "B.M.A." *etc.*

T14	**128**	1l. on ½d. pale green	3·50	13·00
T15		2l. on 1d. pale scarlet	3·00	40
T16		3l. on 1½d. pale red-brown	1·75	13·00
		a. Misaligned surch	70·00	£170
T17		4l. on 2d. pale orange	2·25	4·50
		a. Misaligned surch	80·00	£120
T18		5l. on 2½d. light ultramarine	1·00	70
T19		6l. on 3d. pale violet	1·75	3·25
T20	**129**	10l. on 5d. brown	1·25	4·00
T21		12l. on 6d. purple	2·75	50
T22	**130**	18l. on 9d. deep olive-green	3·25	2·75
T23		24l. on 1s. bistre-brown	3·25	3·75
T24	**131**	60l. on 2s.6d. yellow-green	10·00	12·00
T25		120l. on 5s. red	22·00	23·00
T26	**132**	240l. on 10s. ultramarine	38·00	70·00
T14/26 *Set of* 13			85·00	£140

1951 (3 May). *Nos. 503/7 and 509/11 of Great Britain surch* "B.A. TRIPOLITANIA" *and new values.*

T27	**128**	1l. on ½d. pale orange	20	6·50
T28		2l. on 1d. light ultramarine	20	1·00
T29		3l. on 1½d. pale green	30	8·00
T30		4l. on 2d. pale red-brown	20	1·25
T31		5l. on 2½d. pale scarlet	30	7·50
T32	**147**	60l. on 2s.6d. yellow-green	8·00	23·00
T33	**148**	120l. on 5s. red	9·50	27·00
T34	**149**	240l. on 10s. ultramarine	40·00	60·00
T27/34 *Set of* 8			55·00	£120

POSTAGE DUE STAMPS

1948. *Postage Due stamps of Great Britain Nos. D27/30 and D33 surch* "B.M.A./TRIPOLITANIA" *and new values, as Type* ED **1** *of Eritrea, but expressed in M(ilitary) A(dministration) L(ire).*

TD1	D **1**	1l. on ½d. emerald	5·50	55·00
		a. No stop after "A"	70·00	
TD2		2l. on 1d. carmine	2·50	42·00
		a. No stop after "A"	48·00	
		b. No stop after "M" (R. 1/17)	£130	
TD3		4l. on 2d. agate	11·00	42·00
		a. No stop after "A"	£150	
		b. No stop after "M"	£200	
TD4		6l. on 3d. violet	7·50	23·00
TD5		24l. on 1s. deep blue	29·00	£100
TD1/5 *Set of* 5			50·00	£225

1950 (6 Feb). *As Nos. TD1/5, but surch* "B.A. TRIPOLITANIA" *and new values, instead of* "B.M.A." *etc.*

TD6	D **1**	1l. on ½d. emerald	13·00	85·00
		a. No stop after "B"	£160	
TD7		2l. on 1d. carmine	5·50	27·00
		a. No stop after "B"	90·00	
TD8		4l. on 2d. agate	6·50	38·00
		a. No stop after "B"	95·00	
TD9		6l. on 3d. violet	18·00	65·00
		a. No stop after "B"	£225	
		w. Wmk sideways-inverted*	35·00	
TD10		24l. on 1s. deep blue	48·00	£140
		a. No stop after "A"	£500	
		b. No stop after "B"	£500	
TD6/10 *Set of* 5			80·00	£325

*No. TD9w shows the Crowns pointing to the left, *as seen from the back of the stamp*.

Tripolitania became part of the independent kingdom of Libya on 24 December 1951.

British P.Os in Crete

BRITISH ADMINISTRATION OF CANDIA PROVINCE (HERAKLEION)

Crete, formerly part of the Turkish Empire, was made autonomous, under Turkish suzerainty, in November 1898 with British, French, Italian and Russian troops stationed in separate zones to keep the peace.

Overseas mail franked with Nos. B1/5 was forwarded through the Austrian post office at Canea, being additionally franked with stamps of the Austro-Hungarian Post Offices in the Turkish Empire.

(Currency. 40 pares = 1 piastre)

PRICES FOR STAMPS ON COVER

No. B1	*from* × 8
Nos. B2/5	—

B 1

B 2

1898 (25 Nov). *Handstruck locally.* Imperf.

B1	B **1**	20pa. bright violet	£425	£225

1898 (3 Dec). *Litho by M. Grundmann, Athens.* P 11½.

B2	B **2**	10pa. blue	8·00	19·00
		a. Imperf (pair)	£250	
B3		20pa. green	14·00	17·00
		a. Imperf (pair)	£250	

1899. P 11½.

B4	B **2**	10pa. brown	8·50	26·00
		a. Imperf (pair)	£250	
B5		20pa. rose	19·00	15·00
		a. Imperf (pair)	£250	

The British postal service closed at the end of 1899.

British P.O. in Siam

(Bangkok)

An overseas postal service for foreign residents was operated by the British Consulate at Bangkok from 1858. Mail was despatched by steamer to Singapore and from 1876 onwards was increasingly franked with Straits Settlements stamps. These were initially cancelled on arrival at Singapore, but later an oval postmark inscribed "BRITISH CONSULATE BANGKOK" was used. In 1883 a circular "BANGKOK" datestamp was introduced for use with Nos. 1/23. Both cancellations can also be found used on Hong Kong stamps between 1881 and 1885.

(Currency. 100 cents = 1 Straits dollar)

Stamps of Straits Settlements (see Malaysia) cancelled with oval postmark inscribed "BRITISH CONSULATE BANGKOK" *around Royal Arms.*

1882. Wmk Crown CC (Nos. 11/15, 33, 35).

Z1	2c. brown	£400
Z2	4c. rose	£400
Z3	6c. dull lilac	£450
Z4	8c. orange-yellow	£400
Z5	10c. on 30c. claret (thin "0") (No. 33)	£1000
Z6	10c. on 30c. claret (thick "10") (No. 34)	£1000
Z7	10c. on 30c. claret (thin "1", thick "0") (No. 35)	£1200
Z8	12c. blue	£600

Subsequent Straits Settlements values to 8c. watermarked Crown CA are known used at Bangkok in 1883 and 1884. During this period the stamps overprinted "B" were on sale at the British Post Office.

PRICES FOR STAMPS ON COVER

The issues of the British Post Offices in Siam are worth from × 100 the prices quoted for used stamps when on cover.

B

(1)

1882 (May)–**85**. *Stamps of Straits Settlements optd with T* **1**.

(a) On No. 9 of 1867.

1	32c. on 2a. yellow (1885)	£35000	

(b) On Nos. 11/13, 14a, 15/17 and 19 of 1867–72 and Nos. 48/9 of 1882. Wmk Crown CC.

2	2c. brown	£3500	£1500
3	4c. rose	£3250	£1300
	a. Opt double	—	£7500
4	5c. purple-brown	£375	£400
5	6c. lilac	£250	£120
6	8c. orange	£2500	£225
7	10c. slate	£425	£150
8	12c. blue	£950	£475
9	24c. green	£700	£150
10	30c. claret	£45000	£30000
11	96c. grey	£7500	£3000

(c) On Nos. 59/60 of April 1883.

12	2c. on 32c. pale red (*Wide "S"*)	£2750	£2750
13	2c. on 32c. pale red (*Wide "E"*)	£3500	£3500

(d) On Nos. 50/3 of 1882 and Nos. 63/7 of 1883–84. Wmk Crown CA.

14	2c. brown	£475	£350
15	2c. pale rose (1883)	55·00	45·00
	a. Opt inverted	—	£12000
	b. Opt double	£2750	£2750
	c. Opt treble	£10000	
16	4c. rose (1883)	£600	£325
17	4c. pale brown (1883)	80·00	70·00
	a. Opt double	£3500	
	b. Broken oval	£1100	£1100
18	5c. blue (1884)	£250	£170
19	6c. lilac (1884)	£180	£110
20	8c. orange (1883)	£160	65·00
	a. Opt inverted	£22000	£12000
21	10c. slate (1883)	£160	85·00
22	12c. brown-purple (1883)	£300	£150
23	24c. yellow-green (1884?)	£6000	£3000

The prices quoted for the overprint double errors, Nos. 3a, 15b and 17a, are for stamps showing two clear impressions of the overprint. Examples showing partial doubling, on these and other values, are worth a small premium over the price quoted for normal stamps.

No. 17b shows the edge of the central oval broken above the "O" of "POSTAGE". It occurs on R. 10/5 of the lower right pane.

The use of these stamps ceased on 30 June 1885. Siam joined the Universal Postal Union on 1 July 1885.

British Postal Agencies in Eastern Arabia

Certain Arab States in Eastern Arabia, whilst remaining independent, had British postal administrations replacing Bahrain, and subsequently Indian, post offices at Dubai and Muscat.

Bahrain and Kuwait (from 1948) and Qatar (from 1957) used British stamps overprinted and surcharged in local currency. Abu Dhabi (from 1964) and Trucial States (from 1961 and used only in Dubai) had definitive issues made under the auspices of the British Agencies.

In addition, British stamps were surcharged with value only for use in Muscat and certain other states. They were formerly listed under Muscat as they were first put on sale there, but in view of their more extended use, the list has been transferred here, retaining the same numbering.

The stamps were used in Muscat from 1 April 1948 to 29 April 1966; in Dubai from 1 April 1948 to 6 January 1961; in Qatar: Doha from August 1950, Umm Said from February 1956, to 31 March 1957; and in Abu Dhabi from 30 March 1963 (Das Island from December 1960) to 29 March 1964.

Nos. 21/2 were placed on sale in Kuwait Post Offices in April and May 1951 and from February to November 1953 due to shortages of stamps with "KUWAIT" overprint. Isolated examples of other values can be found commercially used from Bahrain or Kuwait.

(Currency. 12 pies = 1 anna; 16 annas = 1 rupee)

Stamps of Great Britain surcharged

1 ANNA (3) 2 RUPEES (4)

1½ I 1½ II

Two types of 1½a. surcharge:

I. "1" 3¼ mm high and aligns with top of "2" in "½" (Rows 1 to 10).

II. "1" 3½ mm high with foot of figure below top of "2" (Rows 11 to 20).

1948 (1 Apr). *Surch with T* **3** *(½a. to 1r.) or* **4** *(2r.).*

16	**128**	½a. on ½d. pale green	2·75	7·50
17		1a. on 1d. pale scarlet	3·00	30
18		1½a. on 1½d. pale red-brown (I)	11·00	3·75
		a. Type II	11·00	3·75
		b. Vert pair. Nos. 18/a	75·00	
19		2a. on 2d. pale orange	2·00	3·25
20		2½a. on 2½d. light ultramarine	3·50	8·00
21		3a. on 3d. pale violet	3·50	10
22	**129**	6a. on 6d. purple	4·00	10
23	**130**	1r. on 1s. bistre-brown	4·50	60
24	**131**	2r. on 2s.6d. yellow-green	10·00	42·00
16/24 *Set of 9*			40·00	60·00

One example of No. 22 is known with the surcharge almost completely omitted from position R. 20/2 in the sheet.

2½ ANNAS (5) 15 RUPEES (6)

1948 (26 Apr). *Royal Silver Wedding. Nos. 493/4 surch with T* **5** *or* **6**.

25	**137**	2½a. on 2½d. ultramarine	2·75	3·75
26	**138**	15r. on £1 blue	25·00	35·00

1948 (29 July). *Olympic Games. Nos. 495/8 surch with new values in* "ANNAS" *or* "1 RUPEE", *as T* **5/6**, *but in one line on 2½a. (vert) or 6a. and 1r. (horiz) and grills obliterating former values of all except 2½a.*

27	**139**	2½a. on 2½d. ultramarine	35	2·50
28	**140**	3a. on 3d. violet	45	2·50
		a. Crown flaw	65·00	
29	**141**	6a. on 6d. bright purple	45	2·75
30	**142**	1r. on 1s. brown	1·25	3·50
		a. Surch double	£1200	
27/30 *Set of 4*			2·25	10·00

1949 (10 Oct). *75th Anniv of Universal Postal Union. Nos. 499/502 surch with new values in* "ANNAS" *or* "1 RUPEE" *as T* **3/4**, *but all in one line, with grills obliterating former values.*

31	**143**	2½a. on 2½d. ultramarine	50	3·00
		a. Lake in India	75·00	
32	**144**	3a. on 3d. violet	60	3·75
33	**145**	6a. on 6d. bright purple	60	2·75
34	**146**	1r. on 1s. brown	2·00	6·00
31/4 *Set of 4*			3·25	14·00

2 RUPEES (6a) 2 RUPEES (6b)

Type **6a**. "2" and "RUPEES" level and in line with lower of the two bars.

Type **6b**. "2" raised in relation to "RUPEES" and whole surcharge below the lower bar.

1950 (2 Oct)–**55**. *Nos. 503/8 surch as T* **3** *and No. 509 with T* **6a**.

35	**128**	½a. on ½d. pale orange (3.5.51)	70	9·00
36		1a. on 1d. light ultramarine (3.5.51)	30	7·50
37		1½a. on 1½d. pale green (I) (3.5.51)	11·00	26·00
		a. Type II	11·00	26·00
		b. Vert pair. Nos. 37/a	75·00	
38		2a. on 2d. pale red-brown (3.5.51)	30	8·50
39		2½a. on 2½d. pale scarlet (3.5.51)	30	16·00
40	**129**	4a. on 4d. light ultramarine	45	3·50
41	**147**	2r. on 2s.6d. yellow-green (3.5.51)	30·00	7·00
		a. Surch with Type *6b* (1955)	£250	65·00
35/41 *Set of 7*			38·00	70·00

1952. *Queen Elizabeth.*

42	½a. on ½d. orange	10	2·25
43	1a. on 1d. blue	10	2·25
44	1½a. on 1½d. green	10	2·25
45	2a. on 2d. brown	20	10
46	2½a. on 2½d. red	10	10
47	3a. on 3d. lilac	20	1·25
48	4a. on 4d. blue	1·50	4·00
49	6a. on 6d. purple	35	10
50	12a. on 1s.3d. green	4·75	30
51	1r. on 1s.6d. blue	2·25	10
42/51 *Set of 10*		8·50	11·50

Designs:—Nos. 42/51, Queen Elizabeth II.

1953 (10 June). *Coronation. Nos. 532/5 surch with new values.*

52	2½a. on 2½d. carmine-red	1·75	2·50
53	4a. on 4d. ultramarine	1·75	1·00
54	12a. on 1s.3d. deep yellow-green	2·25	1·00
55	1r. on 1s.6d. deep grey-blue	2·50	50
52/5 *Set of 4*		7·50	4·50

Designs:—Nos. 52/55, Queen Elizabeth II.

2 RUPEES 2 RUPEES 2 RUPEES (7)

5 RUPEES 5 RUPEES (8)

Types of surcharges

2 rupees.

Type I. On *Waterlow ptg*. Top of "R" level with top of "2" and other letters of "RUPEES". Bars 7 mm long.

Type II. On *Waterlow ptg* by Harrison: "R" dropped out of alignment with 2" and other letters of RUPEES". Bars 6½ mm long.

Type III. On *De La Rue ptg* by Harrison. Top of "R" below level of top of "2". Bars 7–7¼ mm long and with left sides aligned with "S".

5 rupees.

Type I. On *Waterlow ptg* by Harrison. Ends of letters square and sharp. There were two printings made in March and May 1957.

Type II. On *De La Rue ptg* by Harrison. Type is thicker and ends of letters are relatively rounded.

For differences between Waterlow and De La Rue printings of the basic stamps see notes in Great Britain after No. 539.

1955–60. *T* **166/7** *(Waterlow ptgs) (W* **165**, St. Edward's Crown*) surch with T* **7/8**.

56	2r. on 2s.6d. black-brown (Type I) (23.9.55)	6·50	70
	a. Type II (2.57)	7·00	4·00
	b. Type III (No. 536a D.L.R.) (6.60)	25·00	60·00
57	5r. on 5s. rose-red (Type I) (1.3.57)	10·00	2·25
	a. Wide surcharge	£325	£225
	b. Type II (No. 537a D.L.R.) (27.1.60)	20·00	55·00

Designs:—No. 56, Carrickfergus Castle; No. 57, Caernarvon Castle.

No. 57a ("5" and "R" spaced 2¼ mm instead of 1¼ mm) occurred on R. 8/4 of the first surcharging of No. 57 only.

1956–57. *Stamps of Queen Elizabeth II, W* **165**, St. Edward's Crown, *surch as T* **3** *(in one line on 2½a and 6a.).*

58	1a. on 1d. ultramarine (4.3.57)	35	50
58*a*	1½a. on 1½d. green (1956)	£5500	£800
59	2a. on 2d. red-brown (8.6.56)	70	2·50
60	2½a. on 2½d. carmine-red (8.6.56)	80	4·00
61	3a. on 3d. deep lilac (B.) (3.2.57)	1·00	8·50
62	4a. on 4d. ultramarine (9.12.56)	5·00	20·00
63	6a. on 6d. red-purple (10.2.57)	1·10	7·00
64	1r. on 1s.6d. grey-blue (2.8.56)	5·50	15
58/64 *(ex 58a) Set of 7*		13·00	38·00

Designs:—Nos. 58/64, Queen Elizabeth II.

No. 58a came from a few sheets of the St. Edward's Crown watermark included, in error, with a printing of No. 44. Most examples were used in Dubai, but two are known from Muscat, a pair and a single on separate covers from Bahrain and a single postmarked F.P.O. 936 (Sharjah). A single mint example also exists.

NP 1 NP (9) 3 NP NP (10) 75 NP (11)

1957 (1 Apr)–**59**. *Value in naye paise. Stamps of Queen Elizabeth II, W* **165**, St. Edward's Crown, *surch as T* **9** *(1, 15, 25, 40, 50n.p.),* **11** *(75n.p.) or* **10** *(others).*

65	1n.p. on 5d. brown	10	1·00
66	3n.p. on ½d. orange-red	20	2·50
67	6n.p. on 1d. ultramarine	20	2·75
68	9n.p. on 1½d. green	20	2·50
69	12n.p. on 2d. light red-brown	30	2·75
70	15n.p. on 2½d. carmine-red (Type I)	30	10
	a. Type II (4.59)	30	3·75
71	20n.p. on 3d. deep lilac (B.)	20	10
72	25n.p. on 4d. ultramarine	70	6·00
73	40n.p. on 6d. reddish purple	30	10
	a. Deep claret (3.59)	35	10
74	50n.p. on 9d. bronze-green	1·25	2·75
75	75n.p. on 1s.3d. green	2·00	40
65/75 *Set of 11*		5·00	19·00

Designs:—Nos. 65/75, Queen Elizabeth II.

15 NP

(12)

1957 (1 Aug). *World Scout Jubilee Jamboree. Nos. 557/9 surch in one line as T* **12** *(15np.) or in two lines (others).*

76	15n.p. on 2½d. carmine-red	25	85
77	25n.p. on 4d. ultramarine	30	85
78	75n.p. on 1s.3d. green	35	85
76/8 *Set of 3*		80	2·25

Designs:—No. 76, Scout badge and "Rolling Hitch"; No. 77, "Scouts coming to Britain"; No. 78, Globe within a compass.

1960 (26 Apr)–**61**. *Stamps of Queen Elizabeth II. W* **179**, Mult Crown, *surch as T* **9** *(1, 15, 30, 40, 50n.p.),* **11** *(75n.p.),* **3** *(1r.),* **7** *(2r., 5r.) or* **10** *(others).*

79	1n.p. on 5d. brown (30.8.60)	10	20
80	3n.p. on ½d. orange-red (21.6.60)	55	80
81	5n.p. on 1d. ultramarine (8.4.61)	1·75	2·75
82	6n.p. on 1d. ultramarine (21.6.60)	1·25	90
83	10n.p. on 1½d. green (8.4.61)	1·00	2·75
84	12n.p. on 2d. light red-brown (21.6.60)	2·00	2·50
85	15n.p. on 2½d. carmine-red (Type II)	25	10
86	20n.p. on 3d. deep lilac (B.) (28.9.60)	25	10
87	30n.p. on 4½d. chestnut (8.4.61)	40	50
88	40n.p. on 6d. deep claret (28.9.60)	45	10
89	50n.p. on 9d. bronze-green (8.4.61)	1·00	2·50
90	75n.p. on 1s.3d. green (8.4.61)	3·50	1·75
91	1r. on 1s.6d. grey-blue (8.4.61)	22·00	5·00
92	2r. on 2s.6d. black-brown (No. 595) (8.4.61)	12·00	40·00
93	5r. on 5s. rose-red (No. 596) (8.4.61)	24·00	55·00
79/93 *Set of 15*		65·00	£100

Designs:—Nos. 79/91, Queen Elizabeth II; No. 92, Carrickfergus Castle; No. 93, Caernarvon Castle.

The "5" on No. 93 differs from that on Nos. 57/b, being the same height as "RUPEES".

British Solomon Islands

The first British Resident Commissioner, Charles Woodford, was appointed in 1896 and an administrative centre established at Tulagi.

Mail was initially sent unstamped by sealed bag to Sydney where New South Wales stamps were applied and cancelled. Later the Resident Commissioner kept a stock of New South Wales stamps which were still not cancelled until arrival at Sydney. From April 1906 Mr. Woodford used a vertical oblong "BRITISH SOLOMON ISLANDS PAID" handstamp in place of New South Wales stamps which were then added to many of the covers by the postal authorities in Sydney.

PRICES FOR STAMPS ON COVER TO 1945

Nos. 1/7	*from* × 12
Nos. 8/17	*from* × 25
Nos. 18/36	*from* × 6
Nos. 37/8	—
Nos. 39/51	*from* × 6
No. 52	—
Nos. 53/6	*from* × 2
Nos. 57/9	*from* × 6
Nos. 60/72	*from* × 2
Nos. D1/8	*from* × 5

BRITISH PROTECTORATE

1

2

(Des C. M. Woodford. Litho W. E. Smith & Co. Sydney)

1907 (14 Feb). No wmk. P 11.

1	**1**	½d. ultramarine	9·00	14·00
2		1d. rose-carmine	23·00	25·00
3		2d. indigo	30·00	30·00
		a. Imperf between (horiz pair)	£14000	
4		2½d. orange-yellow	32·00	42·00
		a. Imperf between (vert pair)	£6500	
		b. Imperf between (horiz pair)	£9000	£6500
5		5d. emerald-green	55·00	65·00
6		6d. chocolate	50·00	60·00
		a. Imperf between (vert pair)	£6000	
7		1s. bright purple	70·00	75·00
1/7 *Set of 7*			£250	£275

Nos. 1/7 did not become valid for international postage until early September 1907. Overseas covers before that date show additional New South Wales values.

Three types exist of the ½d. and 2½d., and six each of the other values, differing in minor details.

Forgeries of Nos. 1/7 show different perforations and have the boat paddle touching the shore. Genuine stamps show a gap between the paddle and the shore.

(Recess D.L.R.)

1908 (1 Nov)–**11**. Wmk Mult Crown CA (sideways). P 14.

8	**2**	½d. green	1·50	1·00
9		1d. red	1·25	1·00
10		2d. greyish slate	1·25	1·00
11		2½d. ultramarine	3·75	2·00
11*a*		4d. red/*yellow* (6.3.11)	3·25	9·00
12		5d. olive	10·00	5·00
13		6d. claret	10·00	5·50
14		1s. black/*green*	8·50	5·00
15		2s. purple/*blue* (7.3.10)	40·00	55·00
16		2s.6d. red/*blue* (7.3.10)	50·00	70·00
17		5s. green/*yellow* (7.3.10)	80·00	£110
8/17 *Set of* 11			£190	£225
8s/17s Optd "Specimen" *Set of* 11			£275	

The ½d. and 1d. were issued in 1913 on rather thinner paper and with brownish gum.

3

4

(T **3** and **4**. Typo D.L.R.)

1913. *Inscribed* "POSTAGE POSTAGE". Wmk Mult Crown CA. P 14.

18	**3**	½d. green (1.4)	80	3·50
19		1d. red (1.4)	1·50	14·00
20		3d. purple/*yellow* (27.2)	80	4·00
		a. On orange-buff	8·00	24·00
21		11d. dull purple and scarlet (27.2)	3·00	12·00
18/21 *Set of* 4			5·50	30·00
18s/21s Optd "Specimen" *Set of* 4			70·00	

1914 (Mar)–**23**. *Inscribed* "POSTAGE REVENUE". *Chalk-surfaced paper (3d. to £1).* Wmk Mult Crown CA. P 14.

22	**4**	½d. green	1·00	12·00
23		½d. yellow-green (1917)	4·50	18·00
24		1d. carmine-red	1·50	1·25
25		1d. scarlet (1917)	4·75	6·50
26		2d. grey (7.14)	3·00	9·00
27		2½d. ultramarine (7.14)	2·25	5·00
28		3d. purple/*pale yellow* (3.23)	20·00	90·00
29		4d. black and red/*yellow* (7.14)	2·00	2·50
30		5d. dull purple and olive-green (7.14)	20·00	30·00
31		5d. brown-purple and olive-green (7.14)	20·00	30·00
32		6d. dull and bright purple (7.14)	6·00	14·00
33		1s. black/*green* (7.14)	4·75	7·00
		a. On blue-green, olive back (1923)	7·50	24·00
34		2s. purple and blue/*blue* (7.14)	7·00	10·00
35		2s.6d. black and red/*blue* (7.14)	9·50	20·00
36		5s. green and red/*yellow* (7.14)	35·00	48·00
		a. On orange-buff (1920)	50·00	70·00
37		10s. green and red/*green* (7.14)	85·00	65·00
38		£1 purple and black/*red* (7.14)	£250	£120
22/38 *Set of* 14			£400	£375
22s/38s Optd "Specimen" *Set of* 14			£400	

Variations in the coloured papers are mostly due to climate and do not indicate separate printings.

1922–31. *Chalk-surfaced paper (4d. and 5d. to 10s).* Wmk Mult Script CA. P 14.

39	**4**	½d. green (10.22)	30	3·50
40		1d. scarlet (4.23)	9·00	11·00
41		1d. dull violet (2.27)	1·00	7·50
42	**3**	1½d. bright scarlet (7.24)	2·25	60
43	**4**	2d. slate-grey (4.23)	4·50	15·00
44		3d. pale ultramarine (11.23)	70	4·50
45		4d. black and red/*yellow* (7.27)	3·50	23·00
45*a*		4½d. red-brown (1931)	3·00	20·00
46		5d. dull purple and olive-green (12.27)	3·00	27·00
47		6d. dull and bright purple (12.27)	3·75	27·00
48		1s. black/*emerald* (12.27)	2·75	12·00
49		2s. purple and blue/*blue* (2.27)	11·00	38·00
50		2s.6d. black and red/*blue* (12.27)	7·50	45·00
51		5s. green and red/*pale yellow* (12.27)	26·00	55·00
52		10s. green and red/*emerald* (1.25)	£110	95·00
39/52 *Set of* 15			£170	£325
39s/52s Optd or Perf (4½d.) "Specimen" *Set of* 16			£350	

1935 (6 May). *Silver Jubilee. As Nos. 91/4 of Antigua.* P 13½×14.

53	1½d. deep blue and carmine	1·00	1·00
	a. Frame printed double, one albino		
	f. Diagonal line by turret	70·00	80·00
	h. Dot by flagstaff	£130	
54	3d. brown and deep blue	3·50	7·00
	f. Diagonal line by turret	£110	£160
	h. Dot by flagstaff	£225	£275
55	6d. light blue and olive-green	11·00	12·00
	a. Frame printed double, one albino		
	b. Frame printed triple, two albino	£1300	
	h. Dot by flagstaff	£325	£325
	i. Dash by turret	£375	
56	1s. slate and purple	7·50	13·00
	a. Frame printed double, one albino	£1800	
	f. Diagonal line by turret	£250	
	h. Dot by flagstaff	£325	£375
	i. Dash by turret	£350	
53/6 *Set of* 4		21·00	30·00
53s/6s Perf "Specimen" *Set of* 4		£120	

The second albino impression on No. 55b is sometimes almost co-incidental with the inked impression of the frame.

For illustrations of plate varieties see Omnibus section following Zanzibar.

1937 (13 May). *Coronation. As Nos. 95/7 of Antigua.* P 11×11½.

57	1d. violet	30	1·25
58	1½d. carmine	30	60
59	3d. blue	50	50
57/9 *Set of* 3		1·00	2·10
57s/9s Perf "Specimen" *Set of* 3		90·00	

5 Spears and Shield

6 Native Constable and Chief

7 Artificial Island, Malaita

8 Canoe House

9 Roviana Canoe

10 Roviana Canoes

11 Native House, Reef Islands

12 Coconut Plantation

13 Breadfruit

14 Tinakula Volcano

15 Bismarck Scrub Fowl

16 Malaita Canoe

(Recess D.L.R. (2d., 3d., 2s. and 2s.6d.), Waterlow (others))

1939 (1 Feb)–**51**. *T* **5/16**. Wmk Mult Script CA. P 13½ (2d., 3d., 2s. and 2s.6d.) or 12½ (others).

60	**5**	½d. blue and blue-green	15	1·00
61	**6**	1d. brown and deep violet	30	1·50
62	**7**	1½d. blue-green and carmine	70	1·75
63	**8**	2d. orange-brown and black	1·00	1·75
		a. Perf 12 (7.11.51)	30	1·50
64	**9**	2½d. magenta and sage-green	2·75	2·25
		a. Imperf horiz (vert pair)	£19000	
65	**10**	3d. black and ultramarine	1·25	1·75
		a. Perf 12 (29.11.51)	1·50	2·50
66	**11**	4½d. green and chocolate	4·00	13·00
67	**12**	6d. deep violet and reddish purple	1·00	1·00
68	**13**	1s. green and black	1·25	1·00
69	**14**	2s. black and orange	11·00	5·50
70	**15**	2s.6d. black and violet	28·00	4·50
71	**16**	5s. emerald-green and scarlet	32·00	11·00
72	**11**	10s. sage-green and magenta (27.4.42)	4·00	8·50
60/72 *Set of* 13			75·00	48·00
60s/72s Perf "Specimen" *Set of* 13			£375	

Examples of No. 64a from the first two rows of the only known sheet are perforated between stamp and top margin.

1946 (15 Oct). *Victory. As Nos. 110/1 of Antigua.*

73	1½d. carmine	15	1·25
74	3d. blue	15	20
73s/4s Perf "Specimen" *Set of* 2		80·00	

Pocket handkerchief flaw (R. 1/6)

1949 (14 Mar). *Royal Silver Wedding. As Nos. 112/3 of Antigua.*

75	2d. black	50	50
	a. Pocket handkerchief flaw	38·00	38·00
76	10s. magenta	10·00	8·50

1949 (10 Oct). *75th Anniv of U.P.U. As Nos. 114/7 of Antigua.*

77	2d. red-brown	50	1·00
78	3d. deep blue	2·25	1·50
79	5d. deep blue-green	50	1·75
80	1s. blue-black	50	1·75
77/80 *Set of* 4		3·25	5·50

1953 (2 June). *Coronation. As No. 120 of Antigua.*

81	2d. black and grey-black	50	1·25

17 Ysabel Canoe

18 Roviana Canoe

19 Map

20 *Miena* (schooner)

21 Henderson Airfield

22 Voyage of H.M.S. *Swallow*

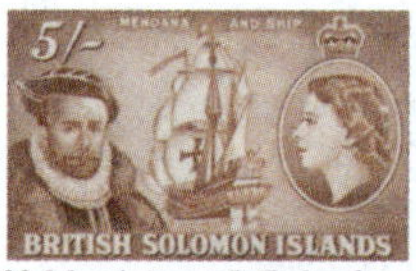
23 Mendaña and *Todos los Santos*

24 Native Constable and Malaita Chief

25 Arms of the Protectorate

(Des Miss I. R. Stinson (½d.), R. Bailey (2½d.), R. A. Sweet (5d., 1s., 1s.3d.), Capt. J. Brett Hilder (6d., 8d., 9d., 5s.). Recess B.W. (½d., 2½d., 5d., 6d., 8d., 9d., 1s., 1s.3d., 5s.), D.L.R. (1d., 2d., 2s.), Waterlow (1½d., 3d., 2s.6d., 10s., £1), until 1962, then D.L.R.)

1956 (1 Mar)–**63**. *T* **17/25** *and similar horiz designs.* Wmk Mult Script CA. P 12 (1d., 2d., 2s.), 13 (1½d., 3d., 2s.6d., 10s., £1) or 11½ (others).

82	**17**	½d. orange and purple	15	50
83	**10**	1d. yellow-green and red-brown	15	15
84	**7**	1½d. slate-green and carmine-red	15	1·00
		a. Slate-green and brown-red (31.7.63)	2·00	40
85	**8**	2d. deep brown and dull green	30	30
86	**18**	2½d. black and blue	1·00	60
87	**16**	3d. blue-green and red	85	15
88	**19**	5d. black and blue	30	55
89	**20**	6d. black and turquoise-green	50	25
90	**21**	8d. bright blue and black	25	15
90*a*		9d. emerald and black (28.1.60)	3·25	80

91 **22** 1s. slate and yellow-brown .... 2·25 50
a. Slate and orange-brown (13.6.61) .... 5·00 3·25
91*b* **19** 1s.3d. black and blue (28.1.60) .... 6·00 1·75
ba. Black and pale ultramarine (11.12.62) .... 12·00 3·50
92 **14** 2s. black and carmine .... 13·00 3·25
93 **11** 2s.6d. emerald and bright purple .... 7·50 45
a. Emerald and reddish purple (19.2.63) .... 17·00 2·25
94 **23** 5s. red-brown .... 15·00 5·50
95 **24** 10s. sepia .... 20·00 6·50
96 **25** £1 black and blue (5.11.58) .... 30·00 35·00
82/96 *Set of* 17 .... 90·00 50·00

See also Nos. 103/11.

LEGISLATIVE COUNCIL

32 Great Frigate Bird

(Litho Enschedé)

1961 (19 Jan). *New Constitution, 1960.* W w **12** (sideways*). P 13×12½.

97 **32** 2d. black and turquoise-green 10 30
w. Wmk Crown to right of CA 10 30
98 3d. black and rose-carmine 10 10
w. Wmk Crown to right of CA 10 10
99 9d. black and reddish purple 15 30
w. Wmk Crown to right of CA 15 30
97/9 *Set of* 3 .... 30 60

*This issue with watermark sideways exists in almost equal quantities with the watermark showing Crown to left or right of CA.

1963 (4 June). *Freedom from Hunger. As No. 146 of Antigua.*

100 1s.3d. ultramarine 75 35

1963 (2 Sept). *Red Cross Centenary. As Nos. 147/8 of Antigua.*

101 2d. red and black 25 20
102 9d. red and blue 50 90

1963–64. *As Nos. 83/5, 87, 89, 90a and 91a/3, but wmk* w **12**.

103 **10** 1d. yellow-green and red-brown (9.7.64) 25 30
104 **7** 1½d. slate-green and red (9.7.64) .... 1·00 50
105 **8** 2d. deep brown and dull green (9.7.64) 20 20
106 **16** 3d. light blue-green and scarlet (16.11.63) 55 15
a. Yellowish green and red (9.7.64) .... 2·25 2·50
107 **20** 6d. black and turquoise (7.7.64) 60 40
108 **21** 9d. emerald and black (7.7.64) 40 35
109 **19** 1s.3d. black and blue (7.7.64) 60 70
110 **14** 2s. black and carmine (9.7.64) .... 1·00 5·50
111 **11** 2s.6d. emerald and reddish purple (9.7.64) .... 15·00 14·00
103/11 *Set of* 9 .... 18·00 20·00

33 Makira Food Bowl

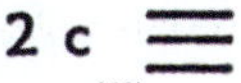
(**48**)

(Des M. Farrar-Bell. Litho D.L.R.)

1965 (24 May). *Horiz designs as T* **33**. W w **12**. P 13×12½.

112 ½d. black, deep slate-blue and light blue .... 10 1·40
113 1d. black, orange and yellow 70 60
114 1½d. black, blue and yellow-green 35 65
115 2d. black, ultramarine and light blue .... 60 1·75
116 2½d. black, light brown & pale yellow-brown .... 10 1·25
117 3d. black, green and light green 10 10
118 6d. black, magenta and yellow-orange 35 80
119 9d. brownish blk, dp bluish grn & pale yell 40 15
120 1s. black, chocolate and magenta .... 1·00 15
121 1s.3d. black and rose-red .... 4·00 2·25
122 2s. black, bright purple and lilac .... 8·50 2·75
123 2s.6d. black, olive-brown and light brown .... 1·00 70
124 5s. black, ultramarine and violet .... 14·00 4·25
125 10s. black, olive-green and yellow .... 17·00 3·00
126 £1 black, deep reddish violet and pink .... 10·00 4·00
112/126 *Set of* 15 .... 50·00 21·00

Designs:—1d. *Dendrobium veratrifolium* (orchid); 1½d. Chiragra Spider Conch; 2d. Blyth's Hornbill; 2½d. Ysabel shield; 3d. Rennellese club; 6d. Moorish Idol; 9d. Lesser Frigate Bird; 1s. *Dendrobium macrophyllum* (orchid); 1s.3d. *Dendrobium spectabilis* (orchid); 2s. Sanford's Sea Eagle; 2s.6d. Malaita belt; 5s. *Ornithoptera victoreae* (butterfly); 10s. Ducorp's Cockatoo; £1, Western canoe figurehead.

1965 (28 June). *I.T.U. Centenary. As Nos. 166/7 of Antigua.*

127 2d. orange-red and turquoise-blue 20 15
128 3d. turquoise-blue and olive-brown 20 15

1965 (25 Oct). *International Co-operation Year. As Nos. 168/9 of Antigua.*

129 1d. reddish purple and turquoise-green 10 10
130 2s.6d. deep bluish green and lavender 45 20

1966 (24 Jan). *Churchill Commemoration. As Nos. 170/3 of Antigua.*

131 2d. new blue 15 10
132 9d. deep green 25 10
133 1s.3d. brown 35 10
134 2s.6d. bluish violet 40 25
131/4 *Set of* 4 .... 1·00 50

(New Currency. 100 cents = 1 Australian, later Solomon Islands dollar)

8 c. Normal "8"

8 c. Inverted "8" (No. 142a) (R. 9/2. Later corrected)

1966 (14 Feb)–**67**. *Decimal Currency. Nos. 112/26 variously surch as T* **48** *by De La Rue.*

A. Wmk upright.

135A 1c. on ½d. black, dp slate-blue and light blue 10 10
136A 2c. on 1d. black, orange and yellow 10 10
137A 3c. on 1½d. black, blue and yellow-green 10 10
138A 4c. on 2d. black, ultramarine and light blue 15 10
139A 5c. on 6d. black, magenta and yellow-orge 15 10
140A 6c. on 2½d. black, lt brn & pale yell-brn 15 10
141A 7c. on 3d. black, green and light green 15 10
142A 8c. on 9d. brownish black, deep bluish green and pale yellow 25 10
a. Inverted "8" .... 35·00 18·00
b. Surch omitted (vert pair with normal) £3500
143A 10c. on 1s. black, chocolate and magenta 30 10
145A 13c. on 1s.3d. black and rose-red .... 2·50 15
147A 20c. on 2s. black, bright purple and lilac .... 2·50 25
148A 25c. on 2s.6d. black, olive-brown and light brown 60 40
150A 50c. on 5s. black, ultramarine and violet (R.) .... 4·50 1·50
151A $1 on 10s. black, olive-green and yellow .... 2·50 1·50
152A $2 on £1 black, dp reddish violet and pink .... 2·25 3·00
135A/52A *Set of* 15 .... 14·00 7·00

B. Wmk sideways

135B 1c. on ½d. black, dp slate-bl & lt bl (6.66) 10 10
136B 2c. on 1d. black, orange and yellow (6.66) 10 10
137B 3c. on 1½d. black, bl & yellow-grn (6.66) 15 10
138B 4c. on 2d. black, ultram & lt blue (6.66) 15 10
139B 5c. on 6d. black, mag & yell-orge (6.66) 15 10
140B 6c. on 2½d. black, light brown and pale yellow-brown (6.66) 10 10
141B 7c. on 3d. black, green & lt green (6.66) 10 10
142B 8c. on 9d. brownish black, deep bluish green and pale yellow (6.66) 15 10
143B 10c. on 1s. black, chocolate & mag (6.66) 40 10
144B 12c. on 1s.3d. black and rose-red (1.3.67) 65 10
145B 13c. on 1s.3d. black and rose-red (6.66) .... 4·50 1·75
146B 14c. on 3d. black, green & lt green (1.3.67) 40 10
147B 20c. on 2s. black, brt purple & lilac (6.66) .... 3·25 30
148B 25c. on 2s.6d. blk, olive-brn & lt brn (6.66) .... 2·50 35
149B 35c. on 2d. black, ultram & lt blue (1.3.67) .... 2·00 25
a. Surch omitted (horiz pair with normal) £3000
b. Surch value only omitted ....
150B 50c. on 5s. black, ultram & vio (R.) (6.66) .... 10·00 4·00
151B $1 on 10s. black, olive-green & yell (6.66) .... 7·00 1·25
152B $2 on £1 black, dp reddish vio and pink (6.66) .... 5·00 2·00
135B/52B *Set of* 18 .... 30·00 9·00

The positions of the bars in the surcharge vary considerably from stamp to stamp within the sheets.

The stamps with sideways watermark are all from new printings and in some instances there are marked shade variations from Nos. 112/26 which were used for making Nos. 135A/152A.

No. 142Ab comes from the bottom left-hand corner of the sheet and was covered by a paper fold. The bottom stamp in the pair is completely without surcharge and the upper has the surcharge value and one bar missing.

1966 (1 July). *World Cup Football Championship. As Nos. 176/7 of Antigua.*

153 8c. violet, yellow-green, lake and yellow-brn 15 15
154 35c. chocolate, blue-green, lake and yellow-brn 30 15

1966 (20 Sept). *Inauguration of W.H.O. Headquarters, Geneva. As Nos. 178/9 of Antigua.*

155 3c. black, yellow-green and light blue 20 10
156 50c. black, light purple and yellow-brown 60 20

1966 (1 Dec). *20th Anniv of U.N.E.S.C.O. As Nos. 196/8 of Antigua.*

157 3c. slate-violet, red, yellow and orange 15 10
158 25c. orange-yellow, violet and deep olive 30 15
159 $1 black, bright purple and orange 75 70
157/9 *Set of* 3 .... 1·10 85

49 Henderson Field

(Des V. Whiteley. Photo Harrison)

1967 (28 Aug). *25th Anniv of Guadalcanal Campaign (Pacific War). T* **49** *and similar horiz design. Multicoloured.* W w **12**. P 14×14½.

160 8c. Type **49** 15 15
161 35c. Red Beach landings 15 15

51 Mendaña's *Todos los Santos* off Point Cruz

(Des V. Whiteley. Photo Harrison)

1968 (7 Feb). *Quatercentenary of the Discovery of Solomon Is. T* **51** *and similar horiz designs. Multicoloured.* W w **12**. P 14.

162 3c. Type **51** 20 10
163 8c. Arrival of missionaries 20 10
164 35c. Pacific Campaign, World War II 40 10
165 $1 Proclamation of the Protectorate .... 60 1·00
162/5 *Set of* 4 .... 1·25 1·10

55 Vine Fishing

(Des R. Granger Barrett. Photo Harrison)

1968 (20 May)–**71**. *Horiz designs as T* **55**. *Chalk-surfaced paper.* W w **12**. P 14½.

166 1c. turquoise-blue, black and brown 10 10
a. Glazed, ordinary paper (9.8.71) .... 1·00 1·00
aw. Wmk inverted .... 1·50
167 2c. apple-green, black and brown 10 10
aw. Wmk inverted. Glazed, ordinary paper (9.8.71) .... 1·50 1·00
168 3c. green, myrtle-green and black 10 10
a. Glazed, ordinary paper (9.8.71) .... 1·00 1·00
169 4c. bright purple, black and brown 15 10
a. Glazed, ordinary paper (9.8.71) .... 1·00 1·00
170 6c. multicoloured 30 10
171 8c. multicoloured 25 10
a. Glazed, ordinary paper (9.8.71) .... 1·50 1·60
172 12c. yellow-ochre, brown-red and black 65 50
a. Glazed, ordinary paper (9.8.71) .... 2·25 2·50
aw. Wmk inverted .... 4·50
173 14c. orange-red, chocolate and black .... 2·50 3·50
174 15c. multicoloured 80 80
a. Glazed, ordinary paper (9.8.71) .... 2·50 3·75
175 20c. bright blue, red and black .... 4·50 3·00
a. Glazed, ordinary paper (9.8.71) .... 4·25 7·00
176 24c. rose-red, black and yellow .... 2·00 3·25
177 35c. multicoloured .... 2·00 30
178 45c. multicoloured .... 1·50 30
179 $1 violet-blue light green and black .... 2·50 1·50
180 $2 multicoloured .... 6·50 3·50
w. Wmk inverted £100
166/80 *Set of* 15 .... 21·00 15·00
166a/75a *Set of* 8 .... 13·50 17·00

Designs:—2c. Kite fishing; 3c. Platform fishing; 4c. Net fishing; 6c. Gold Lip shell diving; 8c. Night fishing; 12c. Boat building; 14c. Cocoa; 15c. Road building; 20c. Geological survey; 24c. Hauling timber; 35c. Copra; 45c. Harvesting rice; $1, Honiara Port; $2, Internal air service.

The stamps on glazed, ordinary paper exist with PVA gum only. The 1c. to 12c. and 20c. on chalk-surfaced paper exist with PVA gum as well as gum arabic, but the others exist with gum arabic only.

70 Map of Australasia and Diagram

71 Basketball Player

(Des R. Gates. Litho Enschedé)

1969 (10 Feb). *Inaugural Year of the South Pacific University.* P 12½×12.

181 **70** 3c. multicoloured 10 10
182 12c. multicoloured 10 10
183 35c. multicoloured 15 10
181/3 *Set of* 3 .... 30 25

(Des J. Cooter. Photo Harrison)

1969 (13 Aug). *Third South Pacific Games, Port Moresby. T* **71** *and similar vert designs. Multicoloured.* W w **12** (sideways*). P 14½×14.

184	3c. Type **71**	10	10
	w. Wmk Crown to right of CA	65	80
185	8c. Footballer	10	10
186	14c. Sprinter	10	10
187	45c. Rugby player	20	15
184/7	*Set of* 4	45	40
MS188	126×120 mm. Nos. 184/7	2·75	8·00

*The normal sideways watermark shows Crown to left of CA, *as seen from the back of the stamp.*

Stamps from the miniature sheets differ slightly from those in the ordinary sheets, particularly the 14c. value, which has a shadow below the feet on the runner. The footballer and rugby player on the 8c. and 45c. values also have shadows below their feet, but these are more pronounced than on the stamps from the ordinary sheets.

75 South Sea Island with Star of Bethlehem

76 Southern Cross, "PAX" and Frigatebird (stained glass window)

(Des L. Curtis. Photo Harrison)

1969 (21 Nov). *Christmas.* W w **12** (sideways). P 14½×14.

189	**75**	8c. black, violet and turquoise-green	10	10
190	**76**	35c. multicoloured	20	20

77 "Paid" Stamp, New South Wales 1896–1906 2d. Stamp and 1906–07 Tulagi Postmark

(Des G. Drummond. Litho B.W.)

1970 (15 Apr). *Inauguration of New G.P.O. Honiara. T* **77** *and similar horiz designs.* W w **12** (sideways). P 13.

191	7c. light magenta, deep blue and black	15	15
192	14c. sage-green, deep blue and black	20	15
193	18c. multicoloured	20	15
194	23c. multicoloured	20	20
191/4	*Set of* 4	65	60

Designs:—14c. 1906–07 2d. stamp and C. M. Woodford; 18c. 1910–14 5s. stamp and Tulagi postmark, 1913; 23c. New G.P.O., Honiara.

81 Coat of Arms

83 British Red Cross H.Q., Honiara

(Des V. Whiteley. Photo Harrison)

1970 (15 June). *New Constitution. T* **81** *and similar design.* W w **12** (sideways on 18c.). P 14½×14 (18c.) or 14×14½ (35c.).

195	18c. multicoloured	15	10
196	35c. pale apple-green, deep blue and ochre	35	20

Design: *Horiz*—35c. Map.

(Des L. Curtis. Litho Questa)

1970 (17 Aug). *Centenary of British Red Cross. T* **83** *and similar horiz design.* W w **12** (sideways). P 14×14½.

197	3c. multicoloured	10	10
198	35c. blue, vermilion and black	25	20

Design:—35c. Wheelchair and map.

86 Reredos (Altar Screen)

(Des L. Curtis. Litho J.W.)

1970 (19 Oct). *Christmas. T* **86** *and similar design.* W w **12** (sideways on 45c.). P 14×13½ (8c.) or 13½×14 (45c.).

199	8c. ochre and bluish violet	10	10
200	45c. chestnut, yellow-orange & blackish brn	25	20

Design: *Vert*—8c. Carved angel.

STAMP BOOKLETS

1959 (1 Apr). *Black on buff (No. SB1) or grey (No. SB2) covers. Stapled.*

SB1	4s. booklet containing eight 1d., 2d. and 3d. (Nos. 83, 85, 87) in blocks of 4	30·00
SB2	11s. booklet containing eight 1d. and 8d., and four 3d. and 1s. (Nos. 83, 87, 90/1) in blocks of 4	40·00

1960 (1 May)–**64**. *Black on green (No. SB3) or orange (No. SB4) covers. Stapled.*

SB3	5s. booklet containing eight 1d., 1½d., 2d. and 3d. (Nos. 83/5, 87) in blocks of 4	45·00
SB4	£1 booklet containing eight 1d., 2d., 3d., 9d. and 1s.3d. (Nos. 83, 85, 87, 90*a*, 91*a*) in blocks of 4	75·00
	a. Contents as No. SB4, but Nos. 103, 85, 106a, 108/9 (1964)	

POSTAGE DUE STAMPS

D 1

(Typo B.W.)

1940 (1 Sept). Wmk Mult Script CA. P 12.

D1	D **1**	1d. emerald-green	6·50	7·00
D2		2d. scarlet	7·00	7·00
D3		3d. brown	7·00	11·00
D4		4d. blue	11·00	11·00
D5		5d. grey-green	12·00	21·00
D6		6d. purple	12·00	15·00
D7		1s. violet	14·00	26·00
D8		1s.6d. turquoise-green	29·00	48·00
D1/8		*Set of* 8	85·00	£130
D1s/8s		Perf "Specimen" *Set of* 8	£180	

British Virgin Islands

CROWN COLONY

Apart from the 1951 Legislative Council issue, the word "BRITISH" did not appear regularly on the stamps until 1968 when it was introduced to avoid confusion with the nearby Virgin Islands of the United States (the former Danish West Indies).

Most mail from the early years of the islands' history was sent via the Danish island of St. Thomas.

It is not known exactly when the first post office, or agency, was established on Tortola, but an entry in a G.P.O. account book suggest that it was operating by 1787 and the earliest letter postmarked "TORTOLA" dates from June of that year. The stamps of Great Britain were used from 1858 to May 1860, when the colonial authorities assumed responsibility for the overseas mails from the British G.P.O.

For illustrations of the handstamp and postmark types see BRITISH POST OFFICES ABROAD notes, following GREAT BRITAIN.

TORTOLA

CROWNED-CIRCLE HANDSTAMPS

CC1 CC **1** TORTOLA (R.) (15.12.1842)
Price on cover £5500

CC2 CC **5** TORTOLA (R.) (21.6.1854)
Price on cover £10000

No. CC2 is known used as an Official Paid mark during the years 1900 to 1918. *Price on cover* £950.

Stamps of GREAT BRITAIN *cancelled* "A 13" *as Type* **2**.

1858–60.

Z1	1d. rose-red (1857), perf 14	£3750
Z2	4d. rose (1857)	£4000
Z3	6d. lilac (1856)	£1400
Z4	1s. green (1856)	

PRICES FOR STAMPS ON COVER TO 1945

Nos. 1/7	*from* × 30
Nos. 8/9	*from* × 40
No. 10	—
No. 11	*from* × 10
No. 12	*from* × 30
No. 13	—
Nos. 14/b	*from* × 10
Nos. 15/17	*from* × 30
Nos. 18/19	*from* × 40
No. 20	—
Nos. 21/b	*from* × 20
Nos. 22/b	*from* × 30
Nos. 24/31	*from* × 25
Nos. 32/4	*from* × 50
Nos. 35/7	*from* × 30
Nos. 38/41	*from* × 15
No. 42	*from* × 20
Nos. 43/50	*from* × 8
Nos. 54/77	*from* × 6
Nos. 78/81	*from* × 6
Nos. 82/101	*from* × 3
Nos. 103/6	*from* × 4
Nos. 107/9	*from* × 6
Nos. 110/21	*from* × 2

1 St. Ursula

2 St. Ursula

(Litho Nissen & Parker from original dies by Waterlow)

1866 (Dec). No wmk. P 12.

		(a) White wove paper.		
1	**1**	1d. green	45·00	60·00
2		1d. deep green	55·00	65·00
3	**2**	6d. rose	90·00	£110
		a. Large "V" in "VIRGIN" (R. 2/1)	£375	£475
4		6d. deep rose	£130	£140
		a. Large "V" in "VIRGIN" (R. 2/1)	£425	£500
		(b) Toned paper.		
5	**1**	1d. green	48·00	60·00
		a. Perf 15×12	£5500	£7000
6		1d. deep green	£100	£120
7	**2**	6d. rose-red	60·00	90·00
		a. Large "V" in "VIRGIN" (R. 2/1)	£275	£375

The above were printed in sheets of 25.

6d. stamps showing part of the papermaker's watermark ("A. Cowan & Sons Extra Superfine A. C. & S.") are worth 50% more.

Beware of fakes of No. 5a made from perf 12 stamps.

3

4

Normal

Variety

1s. Long-tailed "S" in "ISLANDS" (R. 3/1)

(Litho and typo (figure of the Virgin) (1s.) or litho (others) Nissen and Parker from original dies by Waterlow)

1867–70. No wmk. P 15. *1s. with double-lined frame.*

		(a) White wove paper.		
8	**1**	1d. yellow-green (1868)	80·00	80·00
9		1d. blue-green (1870)	65·00	70·00
10	**2**	6d. pale rose	£600	£600
11	**4**	1s. black and rose-carmine	£275	£375
		a. Long-tailed "S"	£900	£1100
		(b) Greyish (No. 14) or toned paper (others).		
12	**1**	1d. yellow-green (1868)	85·00	80·00
13	**2**	6d. dull rose (1868)	£300	£350
14	**4**	1s. black & rose-carmine (*greyish paper*)	£275	£375
		a. Long-tailed "S"	£900	£1100
14*b*		1s. black and rose-carmine (*toned paper*)	£325	£375
		ba. Long-tailed "S"	£900	£1100
		(c) Pale rose paper.		
15	**3**	4d. lake-red	50·00	70·00
		(d) Buff paper.		
16	**3**	4d. lake-red	40·00	60·00
17		4d. lake-brown	40·00	60·00

The thin lines of the frame on the 1s. are close together and sometimes merge into one.

The 1d. from the 1868 printing was in sheets of 20 (5×4) with narrow margins between the stamps. Later printings were in sheets of 12 (3×4) with wider margins. The 4d. was in sheets of 25; and the remaining two values in sheets of 20 (5×4).

The greyish paper used for Nos. 14 and 20 often shows traces of blue.

1867. *Nos. 11 and 14/b with crimson frames superimposed extending into margins.* P 15.

18	**4**	1s. black and rose-carmine (*white paper*)	75·00	85·00
		a. Long-tailed "S"	£250	£300
		b. Figure of Virgin omitted	£85000	
19		1s. black and rose-carmine (*toned paper*)	65·00	75·00
		a. Long-tailed "S"	£200	£250
20		1s. black and rose-carmine (*greyish paper*)	£750	£900
		a. Long-tailed "S"	£2000	£2250

1868. *Nos. 11 and 14b with frame lines retouched so as to make them single lines. Margins remain white.* P 15.

21	**4**	1s. black and rose-carmine (*white paper*)	£140	£170
		a. Long-tailed "S"	£450	£550
21*b*		1s. black and rose-carmine (*toned paper*)	£140	£170
		ba. Long-tailed "S"	£450	£550

(Litho D.L.R.)

1878. Wmk Crown CC (sideways). P 14.

22	**1**	1d. green	80·00	£100
		a. Yellow-green	£170	£130
		b. Wmk upright	90·00	£120

6 (Die I)

4D
(7)

(Typo D.L.R.)

1879–80. Wmk Crown CC. P 14.
24 6 1d. emerald-green (1880) .... 75·00 90·00
25 2½d. red-brown £100 £130

1883 (June)–**84**. Wmk Crown CA. P 14.
26 6 ½d. yellow-buff .... 85·00 85·00
27 ½d. dull green (*shades*) (11.83) ..... 6·50 11·00
b. Top left triangle detached £275 £350
29 1d. pale rose (15.9.83) .... 26·00 30·00
a. Deep rose (1884) .... 55·00 60·00
31 2½d. ultramarine (9.84) .... 2·75 16·00
b. Top left triangle detached £275
w. Wmk inverted £170

For illustration of "top left triangle detached" variety see above No. 21 of Antigua.

(Litho D.L.R.)

1887–89. Wmk Crown CA. P 14.
32 1 1d. red (5.89) .... 3·75 9·00
x. Wmk reversed £150
33 1d. rose-red .... 3·25 8·50
34 1d. rose .... 5·50 14·00
35 3 4d. chestnut .... 35·00 65·00
x. Wmk reversed £180
36 4d. pale chestnut .... 35·00 65·00
37 4d. brown-red .... 45·00 70·00
38 2 6d. dull violet .... 19·00 50·00
39 6d. deep violet .... 18·00 50·00
40 4 1s. sepia (2.89) .... 80·00 £100
41 1s. brown *to* deep brown .... 45·00 70·00
34s/40s Optd "Specimen" *Set of 4* £300

The De La Rue transfers of T **1** to **4** are new transfers and differ from those of Messrs. Nissen and Parker, particularly T **4**.

1888 (July). *Nos. 18/19. Surch with T* **7**, *in violet, in Antigua.*
42 4 4d. on 1s. black and rose-car (*toned paper*) £130 £160
a. Surch double £6500
b. Surch inverted (in pair with normal) £48000
c. Long-tailed "S" £450 £550
42*d* 4d. on 1s. black and rose-car (*white paper*) £180 £225
dc. Long-tailed "S" £550 £700

The special issues for Virgin Islands were superseded on 31 October 1890, by the general issue for Leeward Islands. In 1899, however, a new special issue, Nos. 43/50, appeared; it did not supersede the general issue for Leeward Islands, but was used concurrently, as were all subsequent issues, until 1 July 1956 when the general Leeward Islands stamps were withdrawn.

8

9

10

(Recess D.L.R.)

1899 (Jan). Wmk Crown CA. P 14.
43 8 ½d. yellow-green .... 3·25 55
a. Error. "HALFPFNNY" (R. 10/1) .... 85·00 £120
b. Error. "HALΓPENNY" (R. 8/2) .... 85·00 £120
c. Imperf between (horiz pair) .. £12000
44 1d. brick-red .... 3·75 2·50
45 2½d. ultramarine .... 12·00 2·75
46 4d. brown .... 4·00 18·00
a. Error "FOURPENCF" (R.10/3) £750 £1100
47 6d. dull violet .... 4·50 3·00
48 7d. deep green .... 10·00 6·00
49 1s. brown-yellow .... 22·00 35·00
50 5s. indigo .... 70·00 85·00
43/50 *Set of 8* £110 £140
43s/50s Optd "Specimen" *Set of 8* £160

Nos. 43a/b and 46a were corrected after the first printing.

(Typo D.L.R.)

1904 (1 June). Wmk Mult Crown CA. P 14.
54 9 ½d. dull purple and green .... 1·00 40
55 1d. dull purple and scarlet .... 2·50 35
56 10 2d. dull purple and ochre .... 6·50 3·50
57 9 2½d. dull purple and ultramarine ... 2·25 2·00
58 10 3d. dull purple and black .... 3·50 2·50
59 9 6d. dull purple and brown .... 2·75 2·50
60 10 1s. green and scarlet .... 4·25 5·00
61 2s.6d. green and black .... 28·00 55·00
62 9 5s. green and blue .... 48·00 65·00
54/62 *Set of 9* .... 90·00 £120
54s/62s Optd "Specimen" *Set of 9* £140

11

12

(Typo D.L.R.)

1913 (Feb)–**19**. *Die I. Chalk-surfaced paper (3d. to 5s.).* Wmk Mult Crown CA. P 14.
69 11 ½d. green .... 2·00 4·00
a. Yellow-green (8.16) .... 3·00 12·00
b. Blue-green and deep green (3.19) .... 1·25 6·00
70 1d. deep red .... 8·50 11·00
a. Deep red and carmine (10.17) 2·25 14·00
b. Scarlet (10.17) .... 2·25 14·00
c. Carmine-red (3.19) .... 48·00 27·00
71 12 2d. grey .... 4·00 26·00
a. Slate-grey (1919) .... 4·25 30·00
72 11 2½d. bright blue .... 5·50 9·00
73 12 3d. purple/*yellow* .... 2·75 6·50
74 11 6d. dull and bright purple .... 5·50 13·00
75 12 1s. black/*blue-green* .... 3·25 9·00
76 2s.6d. black and red/*blue* .... 48·00 50·00
77 11 5s. green and red/*yellow* .... 35·00 £110
69/77 *Set of 9* .... 95·00 £200
69s/77s Optd "Specimen" *Set of 9* £180

Stock of the original printing of the ½d., No. 69 was exhausted by January 1916 and Leeward Islands ½d. stamps were used until the yellow-green printing, No. 69*a*, arrived in August 1916.

WAR STAMP
(13)

14

1916 (20 Oct)–**19**. *Optd with T* **13**.
78 11 1d. carmine .... 1·75 19·00
a. Watermark sideways £1100
b. Pale red/bluish .... 50 7·00
bw. Wmk inverted .... 55·00
by. Wmk inverted and reversed ...
c. Scarlet (11.3.19) .... 30 3·75
d. Short opt (right pane R.10/1) 21·00
79 12 3d. purple/*yellow* .... 3·50 19·00
a. Purple/lemon (12.3.17) .... 3·50 15·00
b. Purple/buff-yellow (11.3.19) .... 4·00 20·00
bw. Wmk inverted .... 10·00 45·00
by. Wmk inverted and reversed ...
c. Short opt (right pane R. 10/1) 45·00
78s/9s Optd "Specimen" *Set of 2* .... 70·00

Nos. 78d and 79c show the overprint 2 mm high instead of 2½ mm.

No. 78c is known with the "A" of the "CA" watermark sideways.

1921 (18 Nov). *As 1913–19, but Die II and* wmk Mult Script CA.
80 11 ½d. green .... 6·00 35·00
w. Wmk inverted ....
81 1d. scarlet and deep carmine .... 4·25 27·00
80s/1s Optd "Specimen" *Set of 2* .... 70·00

(Typo D.L.R.)

1922 (Mar)–**28**. P 14.
(*a*) Wmk Mult Crown CA. *Chalk surfaced paper.*
82 14 3d. purple/*pale yellow* (15.6.22) .... 65 17·00
83 1s. black/*emerald* (15.6.22) .... 75 14·00
84 2s.6d. black and red/*blue* (15.6.22) ... 5·50 11·00
85 5s. green and red/*pale yellow* (15.6.22) .... 30·00 £100
82/5 *Set of 4* .... 32·00 £130
82s/5s Optd "Specimen" *Set of 4* .... 90·00
(*b*) Wmk Mult Script CA. *Chalk-surfaced paper (5d. to 5s.).*
86 14 ½d. dull green .... 85 2·75
87 1d. rose-carmine 60 60
88 1d. bright violet (1.27) .... 1·25 3·50
89 1d. scarlet (12.28) .... 17·00 14·00
90 1½d. carmine-red (1.27) .... 1·75 2·50
91 1½d. Venetian red (11.28) .... 2·00 1·50
92 2d. grey .... 1·25 6·00
93 2½d. pale bright blue .... 2·25 19·00
94 2½d. dull orange (1.9.23) .... 1·25 1·75
95 2½d. bright blue (1.27) .... 6·50 3·50
96 3d. purple/*pale yellow* (2.28) .... 2·25 11·00
97 5d. dull purple and olive (6.22) .... 5·50 45·00
98 6d. dull and bright purple (6.22) .. 1·75 6·50
99 1s. black/*emerald* (2.28) .... 2·50 14·00
100 2s.6d. black and red/*blue* (2.28) .... 19·00 48·00
101 5s. green and red/*yellow* (1.9.23) . 19·00 70·00
86/101 *Set of 16* .... 75·00 £225
86s/101s Optd or Perf (Nos. 89, 91) "Specimen" *Set of 16* £275

In the 1½d. stamps the value is in colour on a white ground.

1935 (6 May). *Silver Jubilee. As Nos. 91/4 of Antigua but printed by Waterlow.* P 11×12.
103 1d. deep blue and scarlet .... 1·25 5·00
k. Kite and vertical log .... 95·00
l. Kite and horizontal log £100 £170
104 1½d. ultramarine and grey .... 1·25 4·50
k. Kite and vertical log £110
l. Kite and horizontal log £110 £180
m. "Bird" by turret £150 £170
105 2½d. brown and deep blue .... 2·25 4·50
k. Kite and vertical log £130
l. Kite and horizontal log £140 £190
106 1s. slate and purple .... 14·00 23·00
k. Kite and vertical log £275
l. Kite and horizontal log £250 £350
103/6 *Set of 4* .... 17·00 32·00
103s/6s Perf "Specimen" *Set of 4* £130

For illustrations of plate varieties see Omnibus section following Zanzibar.

1937 (12 May). *Coronation. As Nos. 95/7 of Antigua.* P 11×11½.
107 1d. carmine .... 40 3·25
108 1½d. yellow-brown .... 60 3·00
109 2½d. blue .... 50 1·50
107/9 *Set of 3* .... 1·40 7·00
107s/9s Perf "Specimen" *Set of 3* .... 85·00

15 King George VI and Badge of Colony

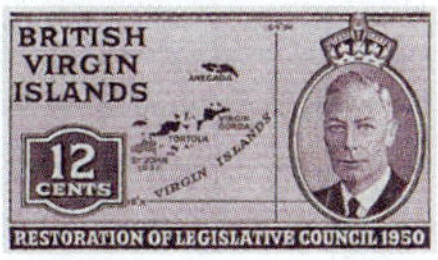

16 Map

(Photo Harrison)

1938 (1 Aug)–**47**. *Chalk-surfaced paper.* Wmk Mult Script CA. P 14.
110 15 ½d. green .... 2·50 3·00
a. Ordinary paper (10.43) .... 75 1·00
111 1d. scarlet .... 3·50 1·25
a. Ordinary paper (10.43) .... 1·50 60
112 1½d. red-brown .... 5·50 6·00
a. Ordinary paper (10.43) .... 1·50 1·00
w. Wmk inverted .... † £1300
113 2d. grey .... 4·75 2·25
a. Ordinary paper (10.43) .... 1·75 90
114 2½d. ultramarine .... 4·00 1·25
a. Ordinary paper (10.43) .... 2·00 2·50
115 3d. orange .... 5·50 70
a. Ordinary paper (10.43) .... 1·00 80
116 6d. mauve .... 6·50 1·00
a. Ordinary paper (10.43) .... 4·00 80
117 1s. olive-brown .... 16·00 3·25
a. Ordinary paper (8.42) .... 1·80 70
118 2s.6d. sepia .... 50·00 8·00
a. Ordinary paper (8.42) .... 17·00 3·00
119 5s. carmine .... 50·00 9·00
a. Ordinary paper (8.42) .... 14·00 4·00
120 10s. blue (1.12.47) .... 6·00 8·00
121 £1 black (1.12.47) .... 8·00 20·00
110a/21 *Set of 12* .... 55·00 38·00
110s/21s Perf "Specimen" *Set of 12* £275

The ordinary paper, used as a substitute for the chalk-surfaced for printings between 1942 and 1945, is thick, smooth and opaque.

1946 (1 Nov). *Victory. As Nos. 110/11 of Antigua.*
122 ½d. lake-brown 10 10
123 3d. orange 10 30
122s/3s Perf "Specimen" *Set of 2* .... 75·00

1949 (3 Jan). *Royal Silver Wedding. As Nos. 112/13 of Antigua.*
124 2½d. ultramarine 10 10
125 £1 black .... 13·00 16·00

1949 (10 Oct). *75th Anniv of U.P.U. As Nos. 114/17 of Antigua.*
126 2½d. ultramarine .... 30 1·00
127 3d. orange .... 1·50 2·50
128 6d. magenta 45 40
129 1s. olive 35 50
126/9 *Set of 4* .... 2·40 4·00

(New Currency. 100 cents = 1 B.W.I. dollar)

1951 (16 Feb–10 Apr). *Inauguration of B.W.I. University College. As Nos. 118/19 of Antigua.*
130 3c. black and brown-red (10 Apr) .... 40 2·25
131 12c. black and reddish violet .... 60 1·75

Issue of the 3c. value was delayed when the supplies were sent to Puerto Rico by mistake.

(Recess Waterlow)

1951 (2 Apr). *Restoration of Legislative Council.* Wmk Mult Script CA. P 14½×14.
132 16 6c. orange .... 50 1·50
133 12c. purple 50 50
134 24c. olive 50 50
135 $1.20 carmine .... 1·25 1·00
132/5 *Set of 4* .... 2·50 3·25

17 Sombrero Lighthouse

18 Map of Jost Van Dyke

19 Sheep industry

20 Map of Anegada

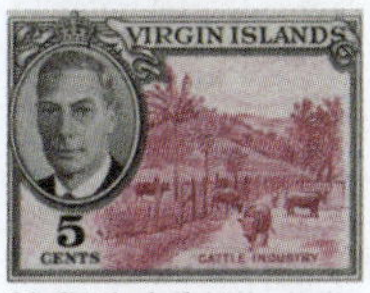

21 Cattle industry

22 Map of Virgin Gorda

23 Map of Tortola

24 Badge of the Presidency

25 Dead Man's Chest

26 Sir Francis Drake Channel

27 Road Town

28 Map of Virgin Islands

(Recess D.L.R.)

1952 (15 Apr). *T* **17/28**. Wmk Mult Script CA. P 12½×13 (vert) or 13×12½ (horiz).

136	**17**	1c. black	80	2·25
137	**18**	2c. deep green	70	30
138	**19**	3c. black and brown	80	2·00
139	**20**	4c. carmine-red	70	2·00
140	**21**	5c. claret and black	1·50	50
141	**22**	8c. bright blue	70	1·25
142	**23**	12c. dull violet	80	1·60
143	**24**	24c. deep brown	70	50
144	**25**	60c. yellow-green and blue	4·50	11·00
145	**26**	$1.20 black and bright blue	5·00	12·00
146	**27**	$2.40 yellowish green and red-brown	11·00	16·00
147	**28**	$4.80 bright blue and carmine	12·00	17·00
136/47 *Set of* 12			35·00	60·00

1953 (2 June). *Coronation. As No.* 120 *of Antigua.*

148	2c. black and green	30	1·25

29 Map of Tortola

30 Virgin Islands sloop

31 Nelthrop Red Poll bull

32 Road Harbour

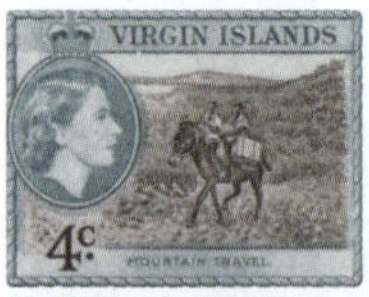

33 Mountain travel

34 Badge of the Presidency

35 Beach scene

36 *New Idea* (sloop) under construction

37 White Cedar tree

38 Skipjack Tuna ("Bonito")

39 Coronation celebrations, Treasury Square

40 Brown Pelican

41 Magnficent Frigate Bird

(Recess D.L.R.)

1956 (1 Nov)–**62**. *T* **29/41**. Wmk Mult Script CA. P 13×12½ (½c. to $1.20) or 12×11½ ($2.40 and $4.80).

149	**29**	½c. black and reddish purple	1·00	20
		a. Black and deep reddish purple (19.4.60)	2·00	3·00
150	**30**	1c. turquoise-blue and slate	1·50	75
		a. Turquoise and slate-violet (26.11.62)	17·00	11·00
151	**31**	2c. vermilion and black	30	10
152	**32**	3c. blue and deep olive	30	30
153	**33**	4c. deep brown and turquoise-green	70	30
154	**34**	5c. grey-black	50	10
155	**35**	8c. yellow-orange and deep blue	2·00	40
156	**36**	12c. ultramarine and rose-red	4·00	75
157	**37**	24c. myrtle-green and brown-orange	1·00	65
158	**38**	60c. indigo and yellow-orange	8·50	8·00
159	**39**	$1.20 deep yellow-green and carmine-red	2·00	8·00
160	**40**	$2.40 lemon and deep dull purple	40·00	13·00
161	**41**	$4.80 blackish brown and turquoise-blue	40·00	13·00
149/61 *Set of* 13			90·00	40·00

(New Currency. 100 cents = 1 U.S. dollar)

≡ 1¢

(42)

1962 (10 Dec). *As Nos.* 149/53 *and* 155/61, *but* W w **12**, *surch in U.S. currency as T* **42** *by D.L.R.*

162	1c. on ½c. black and deep reddish purple	30	10
163	2c. on 1c. turquoise and slate-violet	1·75	10
164	3c. on 2c. vermilion and black	70	10
165	4c. on 3c. black and deep olive	30	10
166	5c. on 4c. deep brown and turquoise-green	30	10
167	8c. on 8c. yellow-orange and deep blue	30	10
168	10c. on 12c. ultramarine and rose-red	2·00	10
169	12c. on 24c. myrtle-green and brown-orange	30	10
170	25c. on 60c. indigo and yellow-orange	2·75	45
171	70c. on $1.20 deep yellow-green and carmine-red	35	45
	a. Stop to right of C in surcharge instead of beneath it (in pair with normal)	9·50	5·50
172	$1.40 on $2.40 lemon and deep dull purple	9·50	4·00
173	$2.80 on $4.80 blackish brown and turquoise-blue	9·50	4·00
162/73 *Set of* 12		25·00	8·00

No. 171a occurs on the first stamp on Rows 1 to 10.

1963 (4 June). *Freedom from Hunger. As No.* 146 *of Antigua.*

174	25c. reddish violet	20	10

1963 (2 Sept). *Red Cross Centenary. As Nos.* 147/8 *of Antigua.*

175	2c. red and black	15	20
176	25c. red and blue	50	20

1964 (23 Apr). *400th Birth Anniv of William Shakespeare. As No.* 164 *of Antigua.*

177	10c. bright blue	20	10

43 Skipjack Tuna

44 Soper's Hole

45 Brown Pelican

46 Dead Man's Chest

47 Road Harbour

48 Fallen Jerusalem

49 The Baths, Virgin Gorda

50 Map of Virgin Islands

51 *Youth of Tortola*, Tortola-St. Thomas ferry

52 The Towers, Tortola

53 Beef Island Airfield

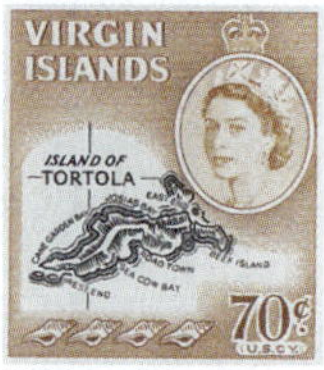

54 Map of Tortola

55 Virgin Gorda

56 Yachts at anchor

57 Badge of the Colony

(Des and recess D.L.R.)

1964 (2 Nov)–**68**. *T* **43/57**. W w **12**. P 11½×12 ($2.80), 13×13½ (70c., $1, $1.40), or 13×12½ (others).

178	**43**	1c. blue and olive-green	30	1·75
179	**44**	2c. yellow-olive and rose-red	15	30
180	**45**	3c. sepia and turquoise-blue	4·75	1·25
181	**46**	4c. black and carmine-red	80	2·25
182	**47**	5c. black and deep bluish green	1·25	2·25
183	**48**	6c. black and brown-orange	30	85
184	**49**	8c. black and magenta	30	50
185	**50**	10c. lake and deep lilac	3·75	30
		a. Bright lake and reddish lilac (26.11.68)	13·00	2·50
186	**51**	12c. deep bluish green and deep violet-blue	2·00	2·75
187	**52**	15c. yellow-green and grey-black	35	2·75
188	**53**	25c. green and purple	11·00	1·75
189	**54**	70c. black and yellow-brown	4·25	8·00
190	**55**	$1 yellow-green and chestnut	3·00	2·00
191	**56**	$1.40 light blue and rose	24·00	9·00
192	**57**	$2.80 black and bright purple	25·00	9·00
178/92 *Set of* 15			70·00	40·00

1965 (17 May). *I.T.U. Centenary. As Nos.* 166/7 *of Antigua.*

193	4c. yellow and turquoise	20	10
194	25c. light blue and orange-buff	45	20

1965 (25 Oct). *International Cooperation Year. As Nos.* 168/9 *of Antigua.*

195	1c. reddish purple and turquoise-green	10	15
196	25c. deep bluish green and lavender	30	15

1966 (24 Jan). *Churchill Commemoration. As Nos.* 170/3 *of Antigua.*

197	1c. new blue	10	30
198	2c. deep green	15	30
199	10c. brown	30	10
200	25c. bluish violet	60	25
197/200 *Set of* 4		1·00	75

1966 (22 Feb). *Royal Visit. As Nos.* 174/5 *of Antigua.*

201	4c. black and ultramarine	40	10
202	70c. black and magenta	1·40	45

58 *Atrato I* (paddle-steamer), 1866

(Des R. Granger Barrett. Litho B.W.)

1966 (25 Apr). *Stamp Centenary. T* **58** *and similar horiz designs.* W w **12** (sideways). P 13.

203	5c. black, red, yellow and emerald	35	10
204	10c. black, green and rose-red/*cream*	35	10
205	25c. black, rose-red and blue/*pale green*	55	10
206	60c. black, red and green/*pale blue*	1·00	2·50
203/6 *Set of* 4		2·00	2·50

Design:—10c. 1d. and 6d. stamps of 1866; 25c. Air mail transport, Beef Island, and 6d. stamp of 1866; 60c. Landing mail at Roadtown, 1866 and 1d. stamp of 1866.

50c.

(**62**)

1966 (15 Sept). *As Nos.* 189 *and* 191/2 *but wmk sideways, surch as T* **62**.

207	50c. on 70c. black and yellow-brown	1·25	90
208	$1.50 on $1.40 light blue and rose	2·25	2·00
209	$3 on $2.80 black and bright purple	2·25	2·75
207/9 *Set of* 3		5·00	5·00

1966 (1 Dec). *20th Anniv of U.N.E.S.C.O. As Nos.* 196/8 *of Antigua.*

210	2c. slate-violet, red, yellow and orange	10	10
211	12c. orange-yellow, violet and deep olive	25	10
212	60c. black, bright purple and orange	75	45
210/12 *Set of* 3		1·00	60

63 Map of Virgin Islands

(Des G. Vasarhelyi. Photo Harrison)

1967 (18 Apr). *New Constitution.* W w **12**. P 14½.

213	**63**	2c. multicoloured	10	10
214		10c. multicoloured	15	10
		w. Wmk inverted	15·00	
215		25c. multicoloured	15	10
		w. Wmk inverted	9·00	
216		$1 multicoloured	55	40
213/16 *Set of* 4			75	55

64 *Mercury* (cable ship) and Bermuda-Tortola Link

(Des G. Drummond, Photo Harrison)

1967 (14 Sept). *Inauguration of Bermuda-Tortola Telephone Service. T* **64** *and similar horiz designs. Multicoloured.* W w **12**. P 14½.

217	4c. Type **64**	30	10
218	10c. Chalwell Telecommunications Station	20	10
219	50c. *Mercury* (cable ship)	60	30
217/19 *Set of* 3		1·00	40

67 Blue Marlin

(Des V. Whiteley. Photo Enschedé)

1968 (2 Jan). *Game Fishing. T* **67** *and similar horiz designs.* W w **12** (sideways). P 12½×12.

220	2c. multicoloured	10	65
221	10c. multicoloured	25	10
222	25c. black, blue and bright violet	55	10
223	40c. multicoloured	85	75
220/3 *Set of* 4		1·60	1·40

Designs—10c. Cobia; 25c. Wahoo; 40c. Fishing launch and map.

1968
INTERNATIONAL
YEAR FOR
HUMAN RIGHTS

(**71**)

72 Dr. Martin Luther King, Bible, Sword and Armour Gauntlet

1968 (29 July). *Human Rights Year. Nos.* 185 *and* 188 *optd with T* **71**.

224	10c. lake and deep lilac	20	10
225	25c. green and purple	30	40

29 July was the date of issue in the islands. The Crown Agents supplies went on sale in London on 1 July, the local consignment being delayed in transit.

(Des V. Whiteley. Litho Format)

1968 (15 Oct). *Martin Luther King Commemoration.* W w **12** (sideways). P 14.

226	**72**	4c. multicoloured	25	20
227		25c. multicoloured	40	40

73 De Havilland D.H.C.6 Twin Otter 100

(Des R. Granger Barrett. Litho Format)

1968 (16 Dec). *Opening of Beef Island Airport Extension. T* **73** *and similar horiz designs. Multicoloured.* P 14.

228	2c. Type **73**	15	1·25
229	10c. Hawker Siddeley H.S.748 airliner	20	10
230	25c. De Havilland D.H.114 Heron 2	40	10
231	$1 Royal Engineers cap badge	50	2·00
228/31 *Set of* 4		1·10	3·00

77 Long John Silver and Jim Hawkins

78 Jim Hawkins escaping from the Pirates

(Des Jennifer Toombs. Photo Enschedé)

1969 (18 Mar). *75th Death Anniv of Robert Louis Stevenson. Scenes from Treasure Island. T* **77/8** *and similar designs.* W w **12** (sideways on 10c., $1). P 13½×13 (4c., 40c.) or 13×13½ (others).

232	4c. indigo, pale yellow and carmine-red	20	15
233	10c. multicoloured	20	10
234	40c. brown, black and blue	25	30
235	$1 multicoloured	45	1·00
232/5 *Set of* 4		1·00	1·40

Designs: *Vert*—40c. The fight with Israel Hands. *Horiz*—$1 Treasure trove.

82 Yachts in Road Harbour, Tortola

(Des J. Cooter, Litho P.B.)

1969 (20 Oct). *Tourism. T* **82** *and similar multicoloured designs.* W w **12** (sideways on 2c., $1). P 12½.

236	2c. Tourist and Yellow-finned Grouper (fish) (*vert*)	15	50
237	10c. Type **82**	30	10
238	20c. Sun-bathing at Virgin Gorda National Park	40	20
239	$1 Tourist and Pipe Organ Cactus at Virgin Gorda (*vert*)	90	1·50
236/9 *Set of* 4		1·60	2·00

85 Carib Canoe

(Des and litho J.W.)

1970 (16 Feb)–**74**. *Horiz designs as T* **85**. W w **12** (sideways*). P 14.

240	½c. buff, red-brown and sepia	10	1·50
241	1c. new blue, apple-green and chalky blue	15	30
	a. Perf 13½ (12.11.74)	1·25	2·00
242	2c. yellow-orange, red-brown and slate	40	1·00
243	3c. orange-red, cobalt and sepia	30	1·25
244	4c. greenish blue, chalky blue and bistre-brown	30	50
	w. Wmk Crown to right of CA		
245	5c. emerald, pink and black	30	10
246	6c. reddish violet mauve and myrtle-green	40	2·00
247	8c. apple-green, greenish yellow and sepia	50	4·25
248	10c. greenish blue, yellow-brown and red-brown	50	15
	a. Perf 13½ (12.11.74)	2·50	2·25
249	12c. yellow, crimson and brown	65	1·50
	a. Perf 13½ (12.11.74)	2·50	3·25
250	15c. turquoise-green, orange and bistre-brownn	6·00	85
	a. Perf 13½ (12.11.74)	3·50	3·25
251	25c. grey-green, steel-blue and plum	4·00	1·75
252	50c. magenta, dull green and purple-brown	3·25	1·50
253	$1 salmon, olive-green and red-brown	4·00	3·75
254	$2 buff, slate and grey	7·50	7·00
255	$3 ochre, deep blue and sepia	2·75	4·50
256	$5 violet and grey	2·75	5·00
240/56 *Set of* 17		30·00	32·00

Designs:—1c. *Santa Maria*. (Columbus' flagship); 2c. *Elizabeth Bonaventure* (Drake's flagship); 3c. Dutch Buccaneer, *circa* 1660; 4c. *Thetis*, 1827 (after etching by E. W. Cooke); 5c. Henry Morgan's ship (17th century); 6c. H.M.S. *Boreas* (Captain Nelson, 1784); 8c. H.M.S. *Eclair*, 1804; 10c. H.M.S. *Formidable*, 1782; 12c. H.M.S. *Nymph*, 1778; 15c. *Windsor Castle* (sailing packet) engaging *Jeune Richard* (French brig), 1807; 25c. H.M.S. *Astrea*, 1808; 50c. Wreck of R.M.S. *Rhone*, 1867; $1 Tortola sloop; $2 H.M.S. *Frobisher*; $3 *Booker Viking* (cargo liner), 1967; $5 Hydrofoil *Sun Arrow*.

*The normal sideways watermark shows Crown to left of CA, *as seen from the back of the stamp*.

The ½c., 3c., 4c., 5c., 10c., and 12c. were reissued in 1973 with W w **12** upright.

102 *A Tale of Two Cities*

(Des W. G. Brown. Litho D.L.R.)

1970 (4 May). *Death Centenary of Charles Dickens. T* **102** *and similar horiz designs showing original book illustrations.* W w **12** (sideways). P 14.

257	5c. black, light rose and grey	10	1·00
258	10c. black, light blue and pale green	20	10
259	25c. black, light green and pale yellow	30	25
257/9 *Set of* 3		55	1·00

Designs:—10c. *Oliver Twist*; 25c. *Great Expectations*.

103 Hospital Visit

(Des R. Granger Barrett. Litho Questa)

1970 (10 Aug). *Centenary of British Red Cross. T* **103** *and similar horiz designs. Multicoloured.* W w **12** (sideways*). P 14.

260	4c. Type **103**	20	45
261	10c. First Aid Class	20	10
262	25c. Red Cross and Coat of Arms	50	55
	w. Wmk Crown to right of CA	50·00	
260/2 *Set of* 3		1·00	1·00

*The normal sideways watermark shows Crown to left of CA, *as seen from the back of the stamp*.

104 Mary Read

105 Children and "UNICEF"

(Des and litho J. W.)

1970 (16 Nov). *Pirates. T* **104** *and similar vert designs. Multicoloured.* W w **12**. P 14×14½.

263	½c. Type **104**	10	15
264	10c. George Lowther	30	10
265	30c. Edward Teach (Blackbeard)	60	25
266	60c. Henry Morgan	80	1·00
263/6 *Set of* 4		1·50	1·40

Brunei

Sultan Hashim Jalil-ul-alam Akamudin, 1885–1906

(Currency. 100 cents = 1 Straits, later Malayan and Brunei, dollar)

For many years the status of the 1895 issue remained uncertain to such an extent that the 1906 provisionals on Labuan were taken to be the first issue of Brunei.

The 1895 "Star and Crescent" design stamps were, from their first appearance, considered bogus or, at best, as an issue made purely for philatelic purposes. Research into the background of the events surrounding the set led to the publication, in 1933, of the original agreement between Sultan Hashim and J. C. Robertson, dated 20 August 1894, which made clear that the stamps fulfilled a genuine postal purpose. Although Robertson and his partners intended to exploit the philatelic sales for their own benefit, the agreement testifies, as does other evidence, to the use of the stamps by the Sultan for his postal service. As Brunei did not, at that time, belong to any local or international postal union, the stamps were only valid within the state or on mail to Labuan or Sarawak. Items for further afield required franking with Labuan stamps in addition. Although most covers surviving are addressed to Robertson's associates, enough commercial covers and cards exist to show that there was, indeed, a postal service.

PRICES FOR STAMPS ON COVER TO 1945

Nos. 1/10 are rare used on cover.

Nos. 11/22	*from* × 30
Nos. 23/33	*from* × 25
Nos. 34/50	*from* × 10
Nos. 51/9	*from* × 12
Nos. 60/78	*from* × 8

The Sarawak Government maintained a post office at the coal mining centre of Brooketon, and the stamps of SARAWAK were used there from 1893 until the office was handed over to Brunei in February 1907.

1 Star and Local Scene

(Litho in Glasgow)

1895 (22 July). P 13–13½.

1	1	½c. brown	4·25	20·00
2		1c. brown-lake	3·25	15·00
3		2c. black	4·00	16·00
4		3c. deep blue	3·75	14·00
5		5c. deep blue-green	6·50	17·00
6		8c. plum	6·50	35·00
7		10c. orange-red	8·00	32·00
		a. Imperf (pair)	£1900	
8		25c. turquoise-green	75·00	90·00
9		50c. yellow-green	20·00	£100
10		$1 yellow-olive	22·00	£110
1/10 *Set of* 10			£140	£400

BRUNEI. BRUNEI.

BRUNEI. (2) TWO CENTS. (3) 25 CENTS. (4)

Line through "B" (R. 5/10)

(Optd by Govt Printer, Singapore)

1906 (1 Oct). *Nos. 117/26 of Labuan (see North Borneo), optd with T* **2**, *or surch as T* **3** *or* **4** *(25c.), in red.* P 13½ or 14 (1c.).

11		1c. black and purple	35·00	55·00
		a. Error. Opt in black	£2250	£2750
		b. Line through "B"	£500	
		c. Perf 13½–14, comp 12–13	£160	
12		2c. on 3c. black and sepia	3·50	13·00
		a. "BRUNEI" double	£3750	£2500
		b. "TWO CENTS" double	£5000	
		c. Line through "B"	£170	
13		2c. on 8c. black and vermilion	27·00	80·00
		a. "TWO CENTS" double	£12000	
		b. "TWO CENTS" omitted (in vert pair with normal)	£13000	
		c. Line through "B"	£475	
14		3c. black and sepia	35·00	85·00
		a. Line through "B"	£475	
15		4c. on 12c. black and yellow	5·00	5·00
		a. Line through "B"	£180	
16		5c. on 16c. green and brown	45·00	75·00
		a. Line through "B"	£550	
17		8c. black and vermilion	10·00	32·00
		a. Line through "B"	£325	
18		10c. on 16c. green and brown	6·50	22·00
		a. Line through "B"	£275	
19		25c. on 16c. green and brown	£100	£120
		a. Line through "B"	£1000	
20		30c. on 16c. green and brown	£100	£120
		a. Line through "B"	£1000	
21		50c. on 16c. green and brown	£100	£120
		a. Line through "B"	£1000	
22		$1 on 8c. black and vermilion	£100	£120
		a. Line through "B"	£1000	
11/22 *Set of* 12			£500	£750

Only one sheet of the 1c. received the black overprint.

The surcharges were applied in settings of 50. Nos. 13a/b occur from one sheet on which the surcharge from the second impression of the setting was misplaced to give two surcharges on row five and none on row ten.

Examples of all values are known showing a forged Brunei postmark dated "13 JUL".

Sultan Mohamed Jemal-ul-Alam, 1906–1924

PRINTERS. All Brunei stamps from Nos. 23 to 113 were recess-printed by De La Rue.

5 View on Brunei River

1907 (26 Feb)–**10**. Wmk Mult Crown CA. P 14.

23	5	1c. grey-black and pale green	2·25	11·00
		x. Wmk reversed	15·00	
		xs. Ditto, optd "Specimen"	40·00	
24		2c. grey-black and scarlet	2·50	3·75
		x. Wmk reversed	32·00	
25		3c. grey-black and chocolate	10·00	22·00
		x. Wmk reversed	40·00	
26		4c. grey-black and mauve	7·50	10·00
		a. Grey-black and reddish purple (1910)	60·00	45·00
		w. Wmk inverted	£190	
		x. Wmk reversed	70·00	
27		5c. grey-black and blue	50·00	90·00
		x. Wmk reversed	95·00	£150
		y. Wmk inverted and reversed	£250	
28		8c. grey-black and orange	7·50	23·00
29		10c. grey-black and deep green	4·50	5·00
30		25c. pale blue and ochre-brown	32·00	48·00
31		30c. violet and black	25·00	22·00
		x. Wmk reversed		
32		50c. green and deep brown	15·00	22·00
33		$1 red and grey	60·00	90·00
23/33 *Set of* 11			£190	£300
23s/33s Optd "Specimen" *Set of* 11			£275	

I

II

I Double plate. Lowest line of shading on water is dotted.

II Single plate. Dotted line of shading removed.

Stamps printed in two colours are as I.

1908 (12 June)–**22**. *Colours changed. Double or single plates.* Wmk Mult Crown CA. P 14.

34	5	1c. green (I)	80	2·25
35		1c. green (II) (1911)	60	2·00
		a. "A" missing from wmk	£225	
		b. "C" missing from wmk	£225	
36		2c. black and brown (5.4.11)	4·00	1·25
		w. Wmk inverted	85·00	
37		3c. scarlet (I)	5·50	1·25
		a. Substituted crown in wmk	£700	
38		3c. scarlet (II) (1916)	£110	38·00
39		4c. claret (II) (17.4.12)	4·75	75
40		5c. black and orange (1916)	7·00	7·00
41		8c. blue and indigo-blue (10.08)	7·00	11·00
42		10c. purple/*yellow* (II) (11.12)	3·00	1·75
		a. On pale yellow (1922)	2·50	4·00
		as. Optd "Specimen"	50·00	
		w. Wmk inverted	£150	
		x. Wmk reversed	£120	
		y. Wmk inverted and reversed	£300	£300
43		25c. deep lilac (II) (30.5.12)	5·00	18·00
		a. Deep dull purple (1920)	13·00	18·00
44		30c. purple and orange-yellow (18.3.12)	9·00	12·00
45		50c. black/*green* (II) (1912)	27·00	65·00
		a. On blue-green (1920)	8·50	35·00
46		$1 black and red/*blue* (18.3.12)	21·00	48·00
47		$5 carmine/*green* (I) (1910)	£160	£250
48		$25 black/*red* (I) (1910)	£550	£1000
34/47 *Set of* 12			£200	£350
34s/48s Optd "Specimen" *Set of* 13			£550	

The used price for No. 48 is for a cancelled-by-favour example, dated before December 1941; there being no actual postal rate for which this value could be used. Examples dated after 1945 are worth much less.

For illustration of the substituted watermark crown see Catalogue Introduction.

Retouch Normal

MALAYA-BORNEO EXHIBITION, 1922.

(6)

RETOUCHES. We list the very distinctive 5c. Retouch (top left value tablet, R. 1/8), but there are others of interest, notably in the clouds.

1916. *Colours changed. Single plates.* Wmk Mult Crown CA. P 14.

49	5	5c. orange	16·00	22·00
		a. "5c." retouch	£475	£550
50		8c. ultramarine	6·00	29·00
49s/50s Optd "Specimen" *Set of* 2			£110	

MALAYA-BORNEO EXHIBITION OVERPRINTS. These were produced from a setting of 30 examples, applied twice to overprint the complete sheet of 60 stamps. Three prominent overprint flaws exist, each occurring on all the stamps in two vertical rows of the sheet.

HI	EX	NE
Short "I" (all stamps in 2nd and 8th vertical rows)	Broken "E" (all stamps in 4th and 10th vertical rows)	Broken "N" (all stamps in 6th and 12th vertical rows)

(Optd by Govt Printer, Singapore)

1922 (31 Mar). *Optd with T* **6**, *in black.*

51	5	1c. green (II)	6·00	35·00
		a. Short "I"	8·00	48·00
		b. Broken "E"	8·00	48·00
		c. Broken "N"	8·00	48·00
52		2c. black and brown	6·00	42·00
		a. Short "I"	10·00	55·00
		b. Broken "E"	10·00	55·00
		c. Broken "N"	10·00	55·00
53		3c. scarlet (II)	7·00	48·00
		a. Short "I"	12·00	70·00
		b. Broken "E"	12·00	70·00
		c. Broken "N"	12·00	70·00
54		4c. claret (II)	13·00	50·00
		a. Short "I"	17·00	75·00
		b. Broken "E"	17·00	75·00
		c. Broken "N"	17·00	75·00
55		5c. orange (II)	18·00	55·00
		a. "5c." retouch (and short "I")	£475	£900
		b. Short "I"	23·00	85·00
		c. Broken "E"	23·00	85·00
		d. Broken "N"	23·00	85·00
56		10c. purple/*yellow* (II)	6·50	55·00
		a. Short "I"	14·00	85·00
		b. Broken "E"	14·00	85·00
		c. Broken "N"	14·00	85·00
57		25c. deep dull purple (II)	14·00	80·00
		a. Short "I"	30·00	£130
		b. Broken "E"	30·00	£130
		c. Broken "N"	30·00	£130
		d. "C" missing from wmk	£1100	
		x. Wmk reversed	£300	
58		50c. black/*blue-green* (II)	45·00	£150
		a. Short "I"	80·00	£225
		b. Broken "E"	80·00	£225
		c. Broken "N"	80·00	£225
59		$1 black and red/*blue*	70·00	£190
		a. Short "I"	£120	£275
		b. Broken "E"	£120	£275
		c. Broken "N"	£120	£275
51/9 *Set of* 9			£160	£600

Examples of all values are known showing a forged Brunei postmark dated "13 JUL".

Sultan Ahmed Tajudin Akhazul Khairi Wadin, 1924–1950

7 Native houses, Water Village

1924 (Feb)–**37**. *Printed from single plates as Type* **II**, *except* 30c. *and* $1 *as Type* **I**. Wmk Mult Script CA. P 14.

60	5	1c. black (9.26)	1·00	75
		a. "A" of "CA" missing from wmk	£750	
61		2c. brown (3.24)	1·00	8·00
62		2c. green (3.33)	2·00	1·00
63		3c. green (3.24)	1·00	6·50
64		4c. maroon (3.24)	1·50	1·25
65		4c. orange (1929)	2·00	1·00
66		5c. orange-yellow* (3.24)	7·00	1·50
		a. "5c." retouch	£250	£130
67		5c. grey (1931)	19·00	12·00
		a. "5c." retouch	£500	£425
68		5c. chocolate (1933)	19·00	1·00
		a. "5c." retouch	£275	65·00
69	7	6c. intense black** (3.24)	14·00	10·00
		x. Wmk reversed		
70		6c. scarlet (1931)	6·00	11·00
71	5	8c. ultramarine (9.27)	6·00	5·00
72		8c. grey-black (1933)	16·00	75
73		10c. purple/*yellow* (3.37)	17·00	27·00
74	7	12c. blue	4·50	9·00
		a. Pale greenish blue (1927)	£130	£200
75	5	25c. slate-purple (1931)	11·00	13·00
76		30c. purple and orange-yellow (1931)	20·00	16·00
77		50c. black/*emerald* (1931)	11·00	15·00
78		$1 black and red/*blue* (1931)	24·00	75·00

60/78 *Set of* 19			£170	£190
60s/78s (*ex* 10c.) Optd (Nos. 60/1, 63/4, 66, 69, 71, 74) or Perf "Specimen" *Set of* 18			£400	

*For 5 c, orange, see No. 82. No. 66 is a "Wet" printing and No. 82 a "Dry".

**For 6c. black, see No. 83. Apart from the difference in shade there is a variation in size, No. 69 being 37¾ mm long and No. 83 39 mm.

The 2c. orange and 3c. blue-green in Type **5**, and the 6c. greenish grey, 8c. red and 15c. ultramarine in Type **7** were not issued without the Japanese Occupation overprint, although unoverprinted examples exist. It is believed that these 1941 printings were produced and possibly perforated, by other firms in Great Britain following bomb damage to the De La Rue works at the end of 1940 (*Price for set of* 5, £475 *un*).

During the life of this issue De La Rue changed the method of production from a "Wet" to a "Dry" process. Initially the stamps were printed on ungummed paper which was dampened before being put on the press. Once the paper had dried, and contracted in the process, the gum was then applied. "Dry" printings, introduced around 1934, were on pre-gummed paper. The contraction of the "Wet" printings was considerable and usually involves a difference of between 0.5 mm and 1 mm when compared with the larger "Dry" printings. The following stamps occur from both "Wet" and "Dry" versions: 1c., 2c. green, 4c. orange, 5c. chocolate, 6c. scarlet, 8c. grey-black, 10c. and 25c.

Stamps of this issue can be found either line or comb perforated.

Brunei was occupied by the Japanese Army in January 1942 and remained under Japanese administration until liberated by the 9th Australian Division in June 1945.

After the cessation of hostilities with the Japanese postal services were re-introduced by the British Military Administration. Post offices under B.M.A. control were opened at Brunei Town and Kuala Belait on 17 December 1945 where B.M.A. overprints on the stamps of NORTH BORNEO and SARAWAK were used until the reappearance of Brunei issues on 2 January 1947.

Redrawn clouds (R. 1/1 of No. 80*ab* only)

1947 (2 Jan)–**51**. *Colours changed and new values.* Wmk Mult Script CA. P 14.

79	5	1c. chocolate	50	2·00
		a. "A" of "CA" missing from wmk	£1100	
80		2c. grey	60	5·00
		a. Perf 14½×13½ (25.9.50)	2·00	4·50
		ab. Black (27.6.51)	2·00	6·50
		ac. Redrawn clouds	75·00	
81	7	3c. green	1·00	5·50
82	5	5c. orange*	80	1·25
		a. "5c." retouch	65·00	85·00
		b. Perf 14½×13½ (25.9.50)	4·00	15·00
		c. Ditto "5c." retouch	£130	£225
83	7	6c. black*	1·00	4·25
84	5	8c. scarlet	50	1·00
		a. Perf 13 (25.1.51)	55	9·00
85		10c. violet	2·00	30
		a. Perf 14½×13½ (25.9.50)	2·00	5·50
86		15c. ultramarine	1·75	70
87		25c. deep claret	2·75	1·00
		a. Perf 14½×13½ (25.1.51)	2·75	9·00
88		30c. black and orange	2·50	1·00
		a. Perf 14½×13½ (25.1.51)	2·00	13·00
89		50c. black	4·00	80
		a. Perf 13 (25.9.50)	1·75	17·00
90		$1 black and scarlet	10·00	75
91		$5 green and red-orange (2.2.48)	18·00	19·00
92		$10 black and purple (2.2.48)	75·00	30·00
79/92 *Set of* 14			£110	65·00
79s/92s Perf "Specimen" *Set of* 14			£275	

*See also Nos. 66 and 69.

The 1, 2, 3, 5, 6, 10 and 25c. values utilised the plates of the pre-war issue and were line perforated until the introduction of the 14½×13½ comb machine for some values in 1950–51. The 8, 15, 50c., $1, $5 and $10 were from new plates with the sheets comb perforated. The 30c. was initially a pre-war plate, but it is believed that a new plate was introduced in 1951.

8 Sultan Ahmed Tajudin and Water Village

1949 (22 Sept). *Sultan's Silver Jubilee.* Wmk Mult Script CA. P 13.

93	8	8c. black and carmine	1·00	1·25
94		25c. urple and red-orange	1·00	1·60
95		50c. black and blue	1·00	1·60
93/5 *Set of* 3			2·75	4·00

1949 (10 Oct). *75th Anniv of Universal Postal Union. As Nos. 114/17 of Antigua.*

96		8c. carmine	1·00	1·50
97		15c. deep blue	3·50	1·50
98		25c. magenta	1·00	1·50
99		50c. blue-black	1·00	1·25
96/9 *Set of* 4			6·00	5·25

Sultan Sir Omar Ali Saifuddin-Wasa'adul Khairi Wadin, 1950-1967

9 Sultan Omar Ali Saifuddin **10** Native houses, Water Village

1952 (1 Mar)–**58**. Wmk Mult Script CA. P 13.

100	9	1c. black	10	50
101		2c. black and orange	10	50
102		3c. black and lake-brown	10	30
103		4c. black and green	10	20
104		6c. black and grey	50	10
105		8c. black and crimson	50	60
		a. *Black and crimson-lake* (15.2.56)	9·50	20
106		10c. black and sepia	15	10
107		12c. black and violet	5·50	10
108		15c. black and pale blue	3·25	10
109		25c. black and purple	2·50	10
		a. *Black and reddish purple* (8.10.53)	4·50	90
110		50c. black and ultramarine	2·25	10
		a. *Black and blue* (22.6.55)	7·00	10
111	10	$1 black and green	1·50	1·40
		a. *Black and bronze-green* (23.7.58)	6·00	3·00
112		$2 black and scarlet	4·50	2·50
113		$5 black and maroon	18·00	8·50
		a. *Black and brown-purple* (15.2.56)	24·00	8·50
100/13 *Set of* 14			35·00	13·00

No. 106 exists in coils constructed from normal sheets.

See also Nos. 118/31.

11 Brunei Mosque and Sultan Omar

(Recess B.W.)

1958 (24 Sept). *Opening of Brunei Mosque.* W w **12**. P 13½.

114	11	8c. black and myrtle-green	20	65
115		15c. black and carmine	25	15
116		35c. black and deep lilac	30	90
114/16 *Set of* 3			65	1·50

12 "Protein Foods"

(Des M. Goaman. Photo Harrison)

1963 (4 June). *Freedom from Hunger.* W w **12**. P 14×14½.

117	12	12c. sepia	2·75	1·00

1964–72. *As Nos. 100/13, but* W w **12**. *Glazed paper ($2, 5) or ordinary paper (others).*

118	9	1c. black (17.3.64)	50	70
		a. Glazed paper. Grey (28.11.69)	2·00	2·75
		ab. *Slate grey* (30.6.72)	15	2·25
119		2c. black and orange (17.3.64)	1·50	20
		a. Glazed paper (27.5.70)	2·50	10
120		3c. black and lake-brown (10.11.64)	1·50	60
		a. Glazed paper (27.5.70)	2·50	10
121		4c. black and green (12.5.64)	30	10
		a. Glazed paper (6.3.70)	50	10
		ab. *Black and emerald* (19.11.71)	1·50	4·00
122		6c. black and grey (12.5.64)	3·00	10
		a. *Black* (28.11.69)	8·00	8·50
		b. Glazed paper (28.11.69)	35	30
		ba. *Light grey* (19.11.71)	2·00	3·75
123		8c. black and crimson-lake (12.5.64)	1·00	10
		a. Glazed paper (27.5.70)	1·00	15
		ab. *Black and brown-red* (19.11.71)	3·50	4·50
124		10c. black and sepia (12.5.64)	65	10
		a. Glazed paper (31.3.70)	2·75	10
		ab. *Grey and pale brown* (coil) (11.10.71)	3·50	4·50
125		12c. black and violet (12.5.64)	1·50	10
		a. Glazed paper (5.11.70)	14·00	1·00
126		15c. black and pale blue (12.5.64)	55	10
		a. Glazed paper (28.11.69)	65	20
127		25c. black and purple (12.5.64)	7·50	10
		a. Glazed paper (18.5.70)	14·00	7·00
		ab. Glazed paper. *Black and reddish violet* (30.4.71)	15·00	1·25
128		50c. black and ultramarine (10.11.64)	2·50	10
		a. *Black & brt ultramarine* (17.3.69)	7·00	1·50
		b. Glazed paper (5.11.70)	15·00	4·00
		ba. *Grey and indigo* (21.12.71)	12·00	4·00
129	10	$1 black and bronze-green (14.5.68)	3·00	6·00
		a. Glazed paper (5.11.70)	8·50	7·00
130		$2 black and scarlet (5.11.70)	38·00	20·00
131		$5 black and maroon (5.11.70)	45·00	35·00
118/29 *Set of* 12			20·00	7·00
118ab/29a, 130/1 *Set of* 14			£120	65·00

Printings of the 6 and 15c. issued on 28 November 1969 were on both ordinary and glazed paper, the 6c. on ordinary producing a distinct shade.

No. 124a exists in coils constructed from normal sheets.

The 2c., 3c.,4c.,6c.,8c.,10c.,12c. and 15c. were reissued between 1972 and 1974 with Ww**12** sideways.

13 I.T.U. Emblem

(Des M. Goaman. Litho Enschedé)

1965 (17 May). *I.T.U. Centenary.* W w **12**. P 11×11½.

132	13	4c. mauve and orange-brown	35	10
133		75c. orange-yellow and light emerald	1·00	75

14 I.C.Y. Emblem

(Des V. Whiteley. Litho Harrison)

1965 (25 Oct). *International Co-operation Year.* W w **12**. P 14.

134	14	4c. reddish purple and turquoise-green	20	10
135		15c. deep bluish green and lavender	55	35

15 Sir Winston Churchill and St. Paul's Cathedral in Wartime

(Des Jennifer Toombs. Photo Harrison)

1966 (24 Jan). *Churchill Commemoration.* W w **12**. P 14.

136	15	3c. black, cerise, gold and new blue	30	50
137		10c. black, cerise, gold and deep green	1·50	20
138		15c. black, cerise, gold and brown	1·75	35
139		75c. black, cerise, gold and bluish violet	4·25	3·00
136/9 *Set of* 4			7·00	3·50

16 Footballer's Legs, Ball and Jules Rimet Cup

(Des V. Whiteley. Litho Harrison)

1966 (4 July). *World Cup Football Championships.* W w **12** (side ways). P 14.

140	16	4c. violet, yellow-green, lake & yell-brn	20	15
141		75c. chocolate, blue-grn, lake & yell-brn	80	60

17 W.H.O. Building

(Des M. Goaman. Litho Harrison)

1966 (20 Sept). *Inauguration of W.H.O. Headquarters, Geneva.* W w **12** (sideways). P 14.

142	17	12c. black, yellow-green and light blue	40	65
143		25c. black, light purple and yellow-brown	60	1·25

18 "Education"

19 "Science"

20 "Culture"

(Des Jennifer Toombs. Litho Harrison)

1966 (1 Dec). *20th Anniv of U.N.E.S.C.O.* W w **12** (sideways). P 14.

144	**18**	4c. slate-violet, red, yellow and orange	35	10
145	**19**	15c. orange-yellow, violet and deep olive	75	50
146	**20**	75c. black, bright purple and orange	2·50	6·00
144/6 *Set of 3*			3·25	6·00

Sultan Sir Hassanal Bolkiah Mu'izzadin Waddaulah, 1967

21 Religious Headquarters Building

(Des and photo Harrison)

1967 (19 Dec). *1400th Anniv of Revelation of the Koran.* W w **12** (sideways). P 12½.

147	**21**	4c. multicoloured	10	10
148		10c. multicoloured	15	10
149	–	25c. multicoloured	20	30
150	–	50c. multicoloured	35	1·50
147/50 *Set of 4*			70	1·75

Nos. 149/50 are as T **21** but have sprigs of laurel flanking the main design (which has a smaller circle) in place of flagpoles.

22 Sultan of Brunei, Mosque and Flags

(Des V. Whiteley. Photo Enschedé)

1968 (9 July). *Installation of Y.T.M. Seri Paduka Duli Pengiran Temenggong. T* **22** *and similar multicoloured design.* P 14×13 (12c.) or 13×14 (others).

151	4c. Type **22**	15	60
152	12c. Sultan of Brunei, Mosque and Flags (*horiz*)	40	1·50
153	25c. Type **22**	55	2·00
151/3 *Set of 3*		1·00	3·75

23 Sultan of Brunei

24 Sultan of Brunei

(Des V. Whiteley. Litho D.L.R.)

1968 (15 July). *Sultan's Birthday.* W w **12** (sideways). P 12.

154	**23**	4c. multicoloured	10	35
155		12c. multicoloured	20	75
156		25c. multicoloured	30	1·40
154/6 *Set of 3*			55	2·25

(Des V. Whiteley. Photo Harrison)

1968 (1 Aug). *Coronation of the Sultan of Brunei.* W w **12** (sideways). P 14½×14.

157	**24**	4c. multicoloured	15	25
158		12c. multicoloured	25	50
159		25c. multicoloured	40	75
157/9 *Set of 3*			70	1·40

25 New Building and Sultan's Portrait

26 New Building and Sultan's Portrait

(Photo Enschedé)

1968 (29 Sept). *Opening of Language and Literature Bureau.* W w **12** (sideways). P 13½ (10c.) or 12½×13½ (others).

160	**25**	10c. multicoloured	20	1·75
		a. *Tête-bêche* (pair)	40	3·50
161	**26**	15c. multicoloured	20	35
162		30c. multicoloured	45	90
160/2 *Set of 3*			75	2·75

The above were scheduled for release in 1967, and when finally issued had the year altered by overprinting.

27 Human Rights Emblem and struggling Man

28 Sultan of Brunei and W.H.O. Emblem

(Des V. Whiteley. Litho Harrison)

1968 (16 Dec). *Human Rights Year.* W w **12**. P 14.

163	**27**	12c. black, yellow and green	10	20
164		25c. black, yellow and blue	15	25
165		75c. black, yellow and dull purple	45	1·75
163/5 *Set of 3*			65	2·00

(Des V. Whiteley. Litho Format)

1968 (19 Dec). *20th Anniv of World Health Organization.* P 14.

166	**28**	4c. yellow, black and cobalt	30	30
167		15c. yellow, black and deep bluish violet	55	65
168		25c. yellow, black and pale yellow-olive	65	1·25
166/8 *Set of 3*			1·40	2·00

29 Deep Sea Oil-Rig, Sultan of Brunei and inset portrait of Pengiran Di-Gadong

(Des adapted by V. Whiteley. Photo Enschedé)

1969 (10 July). *Installation (9th May, 1968) of Pengiran Shahbandar as Y.T.M. Seri Paduka Duli Pengiran Di-Gadong Sahibol Mal.* W w **12**. P 14×13.

169	**29**	12c. multicoloured	85	50
170		40c. multicoloured	1·25	2·00
171		50c. multicoloured	1·25	2·00
169/71 *Set of 3*			3·00	4·00

30 Aerial View of Parliament Buildings

(Des Harrison. Litho D.L.R.)

1969 (23 Sept). *Opening of Royal Audience Hall and Legislative Council Chamber.* P 15.

172	**30**	12c. multicoloured	20	25
173		25c. multicoloured	30	45
174	–	50c. rose-red and bluish violet	60	3·25
172/4 *Set of 3*			1·00	3·50

Design:—50c. Elevation of new buildings.

32 Youth Centre and Sultan's Portrait

(Des V. Whiteley. Litho D.L.R.)

1969 (20 Dec). *Opening of the New Youth Centre.* W w **12**. P 15×14½.

175	**32**	6c. flesh, slate-lilac and black	20	1·00
176		10c. olive-yellow, grey-green and blackish brown	25	10
177		30c. yellow-olive, yellow-brown & black	70	1·00
175/7 *Set of 3*			1·00	1·90

JAPANESE OCCUPATION OF BRUNEI

Japanese forces landed in Northern Borneo on 15 December 1941 and the whole of Brunei had been occupied by 6 January 1942.

Brunei, North Borneo, Sarawak and, after a short period, Labuan, were administered as a single territory by the Japanese. Until September-October 1942, previous stamp issues, without overprint, continued to be used in conjunction with existing postmarks. From the Autumn of 1942 onwards unoverprinted stamps of Japan were made available and examples can be found used from the area for much of the remainder of the War. Japanese Occupation issues for Brunei, North Borneo and Sarawak were equally valid throughout the combined territory but not, in practice, equally available.

PRICES FOR STAMPS ON COVER

Nos. J1/16	*from* × 8
Nos. J17/20	—

(1) ("Imperial Japanese Government")

(2) ("Imperial Japanese Postal Service $3")

1942 (Oct)–**44**. *Stamps of Brunei handstamped with T* **1** *in violet to blue.* Wmk Mult Script CA (except Nos. J18/19, Mult Crown CA). P 14.

J1	**5**	1c. black	8·00	23·00
		a. Red opt	£100	£120
J2		2c. green	50·00	£110
J3		2c. orange (1943)	4·50	9·00
J4		3c. blue-green	28·00	75·00
		a. Opt omitted (in pair with normal)	£2750	
J5		4c. orange	3·25	13·00
J6		5c. chocolate	3·25	13·00
		a. "5c." retouch	£150	£375
J7	**7**	6c. greenish grey (P 14×11½) (1944)	40·00	£225
J8		6c. scarlet	£550	£550
J9	**5**	8c. grey-black	£700	£850
J10	**7**	8c. red	6·00	12·00
		a. Opt omitted (in pair with normal)	£2000	
J11	**5**	10c. purple/*yellow*	9·00	26·00
J12	**7**	12c. blue	26·00	26·00
		a. Red opt	£300	£400
J13		15c. ultramarine (1944)	19·00	26·00
J14	**5**	25c. slate-purple	25·00	50·00
		a. Red opt	£425	£500
J15		30c. purple and orange-yellow	95·00	£180
J16		50c. black/*emerald*	38·00	60·00
		a. Red opt	£450	
J17		$1 black and red/*blue* (1944)	55·00	70·00
		a. Red opt	–	£950
J18		$5 carmine/*green* (1944)	£900	£2250
J19		$25 black/*red* (1944)	£900	£2250

The overprint varies in shade from violet to blue, and being handstamped, exists inverted, double, double one inverted and treble.

Nos. J3, J4, J7, J10 and J13 were not issued without the overprint (See footnote below Brunei No. 78).

1944 (11 May). *No.* J1 *surch with T* **2** *in orange-red.*

J20	**5**	$3 on 1c. black	£7000	£7000
		a. Surch on No. 60 of Brunei	£8500	

Three separate handstamps were used to apply Type **2**, one for the top line, one for the bottom and the third for the two central characters.

Burma

(Currency. 12 pies = 1 anna; 16 annas = 1 rupee)

Stamps of India were used in Burma from 1854 and, after 1856, individual examples can be identified by the use of the concentric octagonal postmarks of the Bengal Postal Circle of which the following were supplied to Burmese post offices:

Type A No. B156 (Rangoon)

Type B No. B5 (Akyab)

B5	Akyab	B146	Pegu
B12*	Bassein	B150	Prome
B22	Nga Thine Khyoung	B156*	Rangoon
B56	Amherst	B159	Sandoway
B108	Kyouk Phyoo	B165	Sarawah (*to* 1860)
B111	Meeaday	B165	Henzada (*from* 1861)
B112	Mengyee	B171	Shoay Gyeen
B127	Moulmein	B173	Sittang
B128	Mergui	B179	Thayetmyo
B129	Tavoy	B181	Toungoo
B133	Myanoung	B227	Port Blair
B136	Namayan		

*Exists in black or blue. Remainder in black only.

Akyab, Moulmein and Rangoon used postmarks as both Type A and Type B, Port Blair as Type B only and the remainder as Type A only.

From 1860 various types of duplex cancellations were introduced and Burmese examples can be identified when sufficient of the left-hand portion is visible on the stamp. Such marks were issued for the following offices:

Akyab	Rangoon
Bassein	Rangoon C.R.H. (Cantonment Receiving House)
Mandalay	Thayetmyo
Moulmein	Toungoo
Port Blair	
Prome	

1862 Duplex from Toungoo

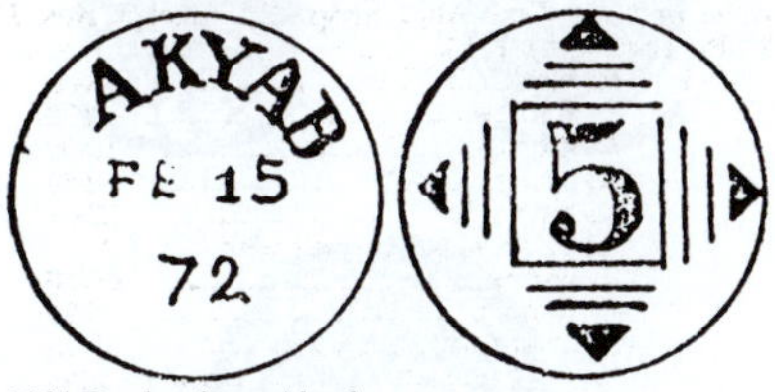

1865 Duplex from Akyab

During 1875, a further series of duplex marks was introduced in which the right-hand portion of the cancellation included the office code number, prefixed by the letter "R" for Rangoon:

R-1	Rangoon	R-9	Myanoung
R-1/1	Rangoon Cantonment	R-10	Port Blair
R-2	Akyab	1/R-10	Nancowry
R-3	Bassein	R-11	Prome
R-4	Henzada	R-12	Sandoway
R-5	Kyouk Phyoo	R-13	Shwegyeen
R-6	Mandalay	R-14	Tavoy
R-7	Mergui	R-15	Thayetmyo
R-8	Moulmein	R-16	Tounghoo
1/R-8	Amherst		

1875 type from Rangoon

1875 type from Rangoon Cantonment Receiving House

From 1886 the whole of Burma was united under the Crown and the post offices were supplied with circular date stamps giving the name of the town.

Most Indian stamps, both postage and official, issued during the period were supplied to post offices in Burma. None of the imperforates printed by De La Rue have been seen however, and from the later issues the following have not been recorded with Burma postmarks:

Nos. 39a, 66a, 68, 85a, 92a, 110a/b, 148a, 155a, 165, 192a/c, 195a/b, O15, O38, O40b, O50a/b, O76a, O101a, O102, O103/a, O104/5 and O142.

The value of most India stamps used in Burma coincides proportionately with the used prices quoted for India, but some, especially the provisional surcharges, are extremely rare with Burmese postmarks. Stamps of the face value of 2 r. and above from the reigns of Victoria and Edward VII are more common with telegraph cancellations than with those of the postal service.

PRICES FOR STAMPS ON COVER TO 1945	
Nos. 1/18	*from* × 6
Nos. 18*a*/33	*from* × 4
No. 34	*from* × 5
Nos. 35/50	*from* × 8
Nos. O1/27	*from* × 15

BRITISH ADMINISTRATION

From 1 January 1886 Burma was a province of the Indian Empire but was separated from India and came under direct British administration on 1 April 1937.

BURMA (1) **BURMA** (1a)

1937 (1 Apr). *Stamps of India. (King George V inscr* "INDIA POSTAGE"*) optd with T* **1** *or* **1a** *(rupee values).* W **69**. P 14.

1	3p. slate	1·00	10
	w. Wmk inverted	4·50	1·25
2	½a. green	1·00	10
	w. Wmk inverted	4·75	1·25
3	9p. deep green (*typo*)	1·00	10
	w. Wmk inverted	4·50	1·25
4	1a. chocolate	2·50	10
	w. Wmk inverted	4·50	1·25
5	2a. vermilion (*small die*)	75	10
6	2½a. orange	60	10
	w. Wmk inverted	4·50	1·25
7	3a. carmine	2·25	30
	w. Wmk inverted	7·50	2·25
8	3½a. deep blue	3·50	10
	aw. Wmk inverted	4·25	30
	b. Dull blue	12·00	8·00
	bw. Wmk inverted	10·00	4·00
9	4a. sage-green	1·00	10
	w. Wmk inverted	—	65·00
10	6a. bistre	1·00	35
	w. Wmk inverted	—	65·00
11	8a. reddish purple	2·00	10
12	12a. claret	7·50	1·75
	w. Wmk inverted	20·00	3·25
13	1r. chocolate and green	32·00	3·75
14	2r. carmine and orange	32·00	18·00
	w. Wmk inverted	45·00	18·00
15	5r. ultramarine and purple	38·00	23·00
	w. Wmk inverted	—	£170
16	10r. green and scarlet	£120	70·00
	w. Wmk inverted	†	—
17	15r. blue and olive (wmk inverted)	£450	£130
18	25r. orange and blue	£850	£325
	w. Wmk inverted	£850	£325
1/18 *Set of* 18		£1400	£500

The opt is at top on all values except the 3a.

The 1a. has been seen used from Yenangyaung on 22 Mar 1937.

2 King George VI and "Chinthes"

3 King George VI and "Nagas"

4 *Karaweik* (royal barge)

5 Burma teak

6 Burma rice

7 River Irrawaddy

8 King George VI and Peacock

9 King George VI and "Nats"

10 Elephants' Heads

Extra trees flaw (R. 11/8)

(Des Maung Kyi (2a.6p.), Maung Hline (3a.), Maung Ohn Pe (3a.6p.) and N. K. D. Naigamwalla (8a.). Litho Security Ptg Press, Nasik)

1938 (15 Nov)–**40**. *T* **2/9**. W **10**. P 14 (vert) or 13½ × 13 (horiz).

18*a*	**2**	1p. red-orange (1.8.40)	3·00	1·00
19		3p. bright violet	20	2·00
20		6p. bright blue	20	10
21		9p. yellow-green	1·00	1·50
22	**3**	1a. purple-brown	20	10
23		1½a. turquoise-green	20	2·50
24		2a. carmine	1·00	50
25	**4**	2a.6p. claret	14·00	2·50
26	**5**	3a. dull violet	14·00	3·00
27	**6**	3a.6p. light blue and blue	2·50	6·50
		a. Extra trees flaw	85·00	
28	**3**	4a. greenish blue	1·75	10
29	**7**	8a. myrtle-green	4·00	55
30	**8**	1r. purple and blue	4·00	55
31		2r. brown and purple	16·00	3·50
32	**9**	5r. violet and scarlet	55·00	35·00
33		10r. brown and myrtle	60·00	65·00
18*a*/33 *Set of* 16			£160	£110

The 1a. exists lithographed or typographed, the latter having a "Jubilee" line in the sheet margin.

COMMEMORATION POSTAGE STAMP 6th MAY 1840

3 ONE ANNA 1A

(11)

1940 (6 May). *Centenary of First Adhesive Postage Stamps. No. 25 surch with T* **11**.

34	**4**	1a. on 2a.6p. claret	4·00	2·00

For stamps issued in 1942–45 see under Japanese Occupation.

CHIN HILLS DISTRICT. This area, in the far north-west of the country, remained in British hands when the Japanese overran Burma in May 1942.

During the period July to December 1942 the local officials were authorised to produce provisional stamps and the letters "OHMS" are known overprinted by typewriter on Nos. 3, 20, 22/4, 28/9 and 31 of Burma or handstamped, in violet, on Nos. 25, 27 and 29. The two types can also occur together or in combination with a handstamped "SERVICE".

From early in 1943 ordinary postage stamps of India were used from the Chin Hills post offices of Falam, Haka, Fort White and Tiddim, this expedient continuing until the fall of Falam to the Japanese on 7 November 1943.

The provisional stamps should only be collected on Official cover (*Price*, from £2000) where dates and the sender's handwriting can be authenticated.

BRITISH MILITARY ADMINISTRATION

Preparations for the liberation of Burma commenced in February 1943 when the Civil Affairs Service (Burma) (CAS(B)) was set up at Delhi as part of the proposed military administration structure. One of the specific tasks assigned to CAS(B) was the operation of a postal service for the civilian population.

Operations against the Japanese intensified during the second half of 1944. The port of Akyab in the Arakan was reoccupied in January 1945. The 14th Army took Mandalay on 29 March and Rangoon was liberated from the sea on 3 May.

Postal services for the civilian population started in Akyab on 13 April 1945, while post offices in the Magwe Division around Meiktila were operating from 4 March. Mandalay post offices opened on 8 June and those in Rangoon on 16 June, but the full network was only completed in December 1945, just before the military administration was wound up.

MILY ADMN (12) MILY ADMN (13)

1945 (from 11 Apr). *Nos. 18a to 33 optd with T* **12** *(small stamps) or* **13** *(others) by Security Printing Press, Nasik.*

35	2	1p. red-orange	10	10
		a. Opt omitted (in pair with normal)	£1600	
36		3p. bright violet	10	1·25
37		6p. bright blue	10	30
38		9p. yellow-green	30	1·25
39	3	1a. purple-brown (16.6)	10	10
40		1½a. turquoise-green (16.6)	10	15
41		2a. carmine	10	15
42	4	2a.6p. claret	2·00	2·25
43	5	3a. dull violet	1·50	20
44	6	3a.6p. light blue and blue	10	70
		a. Extra trees flaw	32·00	
45	3	4a. greenish blue	10	70
46	7	8a. myrtle-green	10	1·25
47	8	1r. purple and blue	40	50
48		2r. brown and purple	40	1·25
49	9	5r. violet and scarlet	40	1·25
50		10r. brown and myrtle	40	1·25
35/50 *Set of* 16			4·75	11·00

Only the typographed version of the 1a., No. 22, received this overprint.

The missing overprints on the 1p. occur on the stamps from the bottom row of one sheet. A further block with two examples of the variety caused by a paper fold also exists.

The exact dates of issue for Nos. 35/50 are difficult to establish.

The initial stock of overprints is known to have reached CAS(B) headquarters, Imphal, at the beginning of April 1945. Postal directives issued on 11 April refer to the use of the overprints in Akyab and in the Magwe Division where surcharged pre-war postal stationery envelopes had previously been in use. The 6p., 1a., 1½a. and 2a.values were placed on sale at Mandalay on 8 June and the 1a. and 2a. at Rangoon on 16 June. It has been suggested that only a limited service was initially available in Rangoon. All values were on sale by 9 August 1945.

BRITISH CIVIL ADMINISTRATION

1946 (1 Jan). *As Nos. 19/33, but colours changed.*

51	2	3p. brown	10	3·00
52		6p. deep violet	10	30
53		9p. green	15	4·50
54	3	1a. blue	15	20
55		1½a. orange	15	10
56		2a. claret	15	50
57	4	2a.6p. greenish blue	2·75	5·50
57*a*	5	3a. blue-violet	6·50	7·00
57*b*	6	3a.6p. black and ultramarine	1·50	3·25
		ba. Extra trees flaw	75·00	
58	3	4a. purple	50	60
59	7	8a. maroon	1·75	4·75
60	8	1r. violet and maroon	1·25	2·00
61		2r. brown and orange	6·50	5·00
62	9	5r. green and brown	7·00	22·00
63		10r. claret and violet	16·00	30·00
51/63 *Set of* 15			40·00	80·00

No. 54 was printed in typography only.

14 Burman

(Des A. G. I. McGeogh. Litho Nasik)

1946 (2 May). *Victory. T* **14** *and similar vert designs.* W **10** (sideways). P 13.

64	9p. turquoise-green	20	20
65	1½a. violet	20	10
66	2a. carmine	20	10
67	3a.6p. ultramarine	50	20
64/7 *Set of* 4		1·00	50

Designs:—1½a. Burmese woman; 2a. Chinthe; 3a.6p. Elephant.

INTERIM BURMESE GOVERNMENT

(**18** *Trans.* "Interim Government") **18a** **18b**

Type **18a** shows the first character transposed to the end of the top line (R. 6/15).

Type **18b** shows the last two characters transposed to the front of the top line (R. 14/14).

Some sheets of the 3p. show both errors corrected by a handstamp as Type **18**.

1947 (1 Oct). *Stamps of 1946 optd with T* **18** *(small stamps) or larger opt (others).*

68	2	3p. brown	1·25	70
		a. Opt Type **18a**	60·00	
		ab. Corrected by handstamp as Type **18**	£160	
		b. Opt Type **18b**	60·00	
		ba. Corrected by handstamp as Type **18**	£160	
69		6p. deep violet	10	30
		a. Opt Type **18a**	38·00	
70		9p. green	10	30
		a. Opt inverted	22·00	28·00
71	3	1a. blue	10	30
		a. Vert pair, one with opt omitted	£1000	
72		1½a. orange	1·75	10
73		2a. claret	30	15
		a. Horiz pair, one with opt omitted	£1000	
		b. Opt Type **18a**	55·00	
74	4	2a.6p. greenish blue	1·75	1·00
75	5	3a. blue-violet	2·50	1·75
76	6	3a.6p. black and ultramarine	1·25	2·25
		a. Extra trees flaw	70·00	
77	3	4a. purple	1·75	30
78	7	8a. maroon	1·75	2·75
79	8	1r. violet and maroon	5·50	2·25
80		2r. brown and orange	5·50	6·00
81	9	5r. green and brown	5·50	5·50
82		10r. claret and violet	3·75	5·50
68/82 *Set of* 15			29·00	26·00

The 3p., 6p., 2a., 2a.6p., 3a.6p. and 1r. are also known with overprint inverted.

OFFICIAL STAMPS

BURMA BURMA

SERVICE (O **1**) SERVICE (O **1a**)

1937 (Apr–June). *Stamps of India. (King George V inscr "INDIA POSTAGE") optd with Type* O **1** *or* O **1a** *(rupee values).* W **69**. P 14.

O1	3p. slate	3·50	10
	w. Wmk inverted	—	30·00
O2	½a. green	14·00	10
	w. Wmk inverted	†	—
O3	9p. deep green	5·00	1·00
O4	1a. chocolate	7·00	10
O5	2a. vermilion (*small die*)	15·00	45
	w. Wmk inverted	—	30·00
O6	2½a. orange	7·00	2·50
O7	4a. sage-green	7·00	10
O8	6a. bistre	7·00	12·00
O9	8a. reddish purple (1.4.37)	7·00	2·50
O10	12a. claret (1.4.37)	7·00	10·00
O11	1r. chocolate and green (1.4.37)	20·00	7·00
O12	2r. carmine and orange	40·00	55·00
	w. Wmk inverted	40·00	60·00
O13	5r. ultramarine and purple	£130	55·00
O14	10r. green and scarlet	£375	£180
O1/14 *Set of* 14		£600	£275

For the above issue the stamps were either overprinted "BURMA" and "SERVICE" at one operation or had the two words applied separately. Research has yet to establish if all values exist with both forms of overprinting.

SERVICE (O **2**) SERVICE (O **3**)

1939. *Nos. 19/24 and 28 optd with Type* O **2** *(typo) and Nos. 25 and 29/33 optd with Type* O **3** *(litho).*

O15	2	3p. bright violet	15	20
O16		6p. bright blue	15	20
O17		9p. yellow-green	4·00	5·00
O18	3	1a. purple-brown	15	15
O19		1½a. turquoise-green	3·50	2·25
O20		2a. carmine	1·25	20
O21	4	2a.6p. claret	21·00	18·00
O22	3	4a. greenish blue	4·50	1·25
O23	7	8a. myrtle-green	15·00	4·00
O24	8	1r. purple and blue	16·00	5·50
O25		2r. brown and purple	30·00	16·00
O26	9	5r. violet and scarlet	25·00	32·00
O27		10r. brown and myrtle	£130	38·00
O15/27 *Set of* 13			£225	£110

Both versions of the 1a. value exist with this overprint.

1946. *British Civil Administration. Nos. 51/6 and 58 optd with Type* O **2** *(typo) and Nos. 57 and 59/63 optd with Type* O **3** *(litho).*

O28	2	3p. brown	3·00	4·50
O29		6p. deep violet	2·25	2·25
O30		9p. green	65	4·50
O31	3	1a. blue	20	2·00
O32		1½a. orange	20	20
O33		2a. claret	20	2·00
O34	4	2a.6p. greenish blue	2·00	9·00
O35	3	4a. purple	20	70
O36	7	8a. maroon	3·75	5·00
O37	8	1r. violet and maroon	80	7·50
O38		2r. brown and orange	8·00	45·00
O39	9	5r. green and brown	15·00	55·00
O40		10r. claret and violet	17·00	65·00
O28/40 *Set of* 13			48·00	£180

1947. *Interim Burmese Government. Nos. O28/40 optd with T* **18** *(small stamps) or larger opt (others).*

O41	2	3p. brown	1·00	40
O42		6p. deep violet	3·75	10
O43		9p. green	5·00	90
O44	3	1a. blue	5·00	80
O45		1½a. orange	8·50	30
O46		2a. claret	5·00	15
O47	4	2a.6p. greenish blue	29·00	13·00
O48	3	4a. purple	18·00	40
O49	7	8a. maroon	18·00	4·00
O50	8	1r. violet and maroon	15·00	2·25
O51		2r. brown and orange	15·00	20·00
O52	9	5r. green and brown	15·00	20·00
O53		10r. claret and violet	15·00	30·00
O41/53 *Set of* 13			£140	80·00

Later stamp issues will be found listed in Part 21 (*South-East Asia*) of this catalogue.

JAPANESE OCCUPATION OF BURMA

PRICES FOR STAMPS ON COVER

Nos. J1/44	—
Nos. J45/6	*from* × 6
Nos. J47/56	*from* × 8
No. J56g	—
Nos. J57/72	*from* × 6
Nos. J73/5	*from* × 25
No. J76	*from* × 8
No. J77	*from* × 20
Nos. J78/81	*from* × 25
Nos. J82/4	*from* × 10
Nos. J85/7	*from* × 40
No. J88	*from* × 12
Nos. J89/97	*from* × 30
Nos. J98/104	*from* × 50
Nos. J105/111	*from* × 30

BURMA INDEPENDENCE ARMY ADMINISTRATION

The Burma Independence Army, formed by Aung San in 1941, took control of the Delta area of the Irrawaddy in May 1942. They reopened a postal service in the area and were authorised by the Japanese to overprint local stocks of stamps with the Burmese emblem of a peacock.

Postage and Official stamps with the peacock overprints or handstamps were used for ordinary postal purposes with the probable exception of No. J44.

DISTINGUISHING FEATURES. Type **1**. Body and head of Peacock always clearly outlined by broad uncoloured band. There are four slightly different sub-types of overprint Type **1**.

Type **2**. Peacock with slender neck and more delicately detailed tail. Clear spur on leg at right. Heavy fist-shaped blob of ink below and parallel to beak and neck.

Type **4**. No basic curve. Each feather separately outlined. Straight, short legs.

Type **5**. Much fine detail in wings and tail in clearly printed overprints. Thin, long legs ending in claws which, with the basic arc, enclose clear white spaces in well printed copies. Blob of colour below beak shows shaded detail and never has the heavy fist-like appearance of this portion in Type **2**.

Two sub-types may be distinguished in Type **5**, the basic arc of one having a chord of 14–15 mm and the other 12½–13 mm.

Type **6**. Similar to Type **5**, but with arc deeply curved and reaching nearly to the top of the wings. Single diagonal line parallel to neck below beak.

Collectors are warned against forgeries of these overprints, often in the wrong colours or on the wrong values.

(**1**)

(**2**)

(**3**)

1942 (May). *Stamps of Burma overprinted with the national device of a Peacock.*

I. Overprinted at Myaungmya.

A. With Type **1** *in black.*

		On Postage Stamps of King George V.		
J1		9p. deep green (No. 3)	£110	
J2		3½a. deep blue (No. 8)	70·00	
		On Official Stamp of King George V.		
J3		6a. bistre (No. O8)	80·00	
		On Postage Stamps of King George VI.		
J4	2	9p. yellow-green	£150	
J5	3	1a. purple-brown	£550	
J6		4a. greenish blue (opt black on red)	£160	
		a. Triple opt, black on double red	£450	
		On Official Stamps of King George VI.		
J7	2	3p. bright violet	30·00	90·00
J8		6p. bright blue	21·00	65·00
J9	3	1a. purple-brown	22·00	55·00
J9*a*		1½a. turquoise-green	£700	£1000
J10		2a. carmine	28·00	£100
J11		4a. greenish blue	28·00	80·00

The overprint on No. J6 was apparently first done in red in error, and then corrected in black. Some stamps have the black overprint so accurately superimposed that the red hardly shows. These are rare.

Nos. J5 and J9 exist with the Peacock overprint on both the typographed and the litho printings of the original stamps.

*B. With Types **2** or **3** (rupee values), in black.*

On Postage Stamps of King George VI.

J12 2 3p. bright violet ... 18·00 75·00
J13 6p. bright blue ... 50·00 £110
J14 9p. yellow-green ... 22·00 70·00
J15 3 1a. purple-brown ... 14·00 65·00
J16 2a. carmine ... 25·00 85·00
J17 4a. greenish blue ... 50·00 £110
a. Opt double ...
b. Opt inverted ... £750
c. Opt double, one inverted ... £450
d. Opt double, both inverted ... £700
J18 1r. purple and blue ... £325 £500
J19 8 2r. brown and purple ... £180 £375

The Myaungmya overprints (including No. J44) are usually clearly printed.

(4)

(5)

(6)

Type **5** generally shows the details of the peacock much less clearly and, due to heavy inking, or careless impression, sometimes appears as almost solid colour.

Type **6** was officially applied only to postal stationery. However, the handstamp remained in the possession of a postal official who used it on postage stamps after the war. These stamps are no longer listed.

*II. Handstamped (at Pyapon?) with T **4**, in black (so-called experimental type).*

On Postage Stamps of King George VI.

J19*a* 2 6p. bright blue ... 85·00
J19*b* 3 1a. purple-brown ... £100 £250
J20 2a. carmine ... £130 £300
J21 4a. greenish blue ... £700 £700

Unused specimens of Nos. J20/1 are usually in poor condition.

*III. Overprinted at Henzada with T **5** in blue, or blue-black.*

On Postage Stamps of King George V.

J22 3p. slate (No. 1) ... 3·75 22·00
a. Opt double ... 10·00 50·00
J23 9p. deep green (No. 3) ... 26·00 65·00
a. Opt double ... 80·00
J24 2a. vermilion (No. 5) ... £110 £190

On Postage Stamps of King George VI.

J25 2 1p. red-orange ... £225 £325
J26 3p. bright violet ... 40·00 80·00
J27 6p. bright blue ... 25·00 55·00
a. Opt double ... £100 £150
b. Clear opt, on back and front ... £325
J28 9p. yellow-green ... £900
J29 3 1a. purple-brown ... 9·00 42·00
a. Opt inverted ... £1700 £900
J30 1½a. turquoise-green ... 22·00 70·00
a. Opt omitted (in pair with normal) ... £3250
J31 2a. carmine ... 22·00 70·00
a. Opt double ... £1800
J32 4a. greenish blue ... 42·00 £100
a. Opt double ... £250
b. Opt inverted ... £2750

On Official Stamps of King George VI.

J33 2 3p. bright violet ... £140 £275
J34 6p. bright blue ... £150 £275
J35 3 1½a. turquoise-green ... £180 £325
J35*a* 2a. carmine ... £350 £450
J36 4a. greenish blue ... £1000

(6a) ("Yon Thon" = "Office use")

*V. Official Stamp of King George VI optd at Myaungmya with Type **6a** in black.*

J44 7 8a. myrtle-green ... 95·00

No. J44 was probably for official use.

There are two types of T **6a**, one with base of peacock 8 mm long and the other with base about 5 mm long. The neck and other details also vary. The two types are found *se-tenant* in the sheet. Stocks of the peacock types were withdrawn when the Japanese Directorate-General took control of the postal services in the Delta in August 1942.

JAPANESE ARMY ADMINISTRATION

7

8 Farmer

1942 (1 June). *Impressed by hand. Thick yellowish paper. No gum.* P 12×11.

J45 **7** (1a.) red ... 42·00 70·00

This device was the personal seal of Yano Sitza, the Japanese official in charge of the Posts and Telegraphs department of the Japanese Army Administration. It was impressed on paper already perforated by a line machine. Some stamps show part of the papermaker's watermark, either "ABSORBO DUPLICATOR" or "ELEPHANT BRAND", each with an elephant.

Other impressions of this seal on different papers, and showing signs of wear, were not valid for postal purposes.

(Des T. Kato. Typo *Rangoon Gazette* Press)

1942 (15 June). *Value in annas.* P 11 or 11×11½. *Laid bâtonné paper. No gum.*

J46 **8** 1a. scarlet ... 20·00 20·00

Some stamps show part of the papermaker's watermark, either "ELEPHANT BRAND" or "TITAGHUR SUPERFINE", each with an elephant.

(9)

(10)

1942 (22 Sept). *(a) Nos. 314/17, 320/2, 325, 327 and 396 of Japan surch as T* **9/10**.

J47 **9** ¼a. on 1s. chestnut (Rice harvesting) ... 38·00 45·00
a. Surch inverted ... £120 £120
b. Surch double, one inverted ... £170
J48 ½a. on 2s. bright scarlet (General Nogi) ... 45·00 48·00
a. Surch inverted ... £110 £120
b. Surch double, one inverted ... £170
J49 ¾a. on 3s. green (Power station) ... 70·00 75·00
a. Surch inverted ... £140 £140
b. Surch double, one inverted ... – £180
J50 1a. on 5s. claret (Admiral Togo) ... 70·00 60·00
a. Surch inverted ... £190 £190
b. Surch double, one inverted ... £225 £200
c. Surch omitted (in pair with normal) ... £375 £325
J51 3a. on 7s. green (Diamond Mts) ... £110 £130
a. Surch inverted ... £225
J52 4a. on 4s. emerald (Togo) ... 55·00 60·00
a. Surch inverted ... £190
J53 8a. on 8s. violet (Meiji Shrine) ... £150 £150
a. Surch inverted ... £250 £250
b. Surch double, one inverted ... £375
c. Surch in red ... £250 £275
d. Red surch inverted ... £375
e. Surch double (black and red) ... £900
J54 **10** 1r. on 10s. deep carmine (Yomei Gate) ... 23·00 26·00
a. Surch inverted ... 85·00 95·00
b. Surch double ... 80·00 £100
c. Surch double (black and red) ... £475 £475
d. Surch omitted (in pair with normal) ... £325 £325
e. Surch omitted (in pair with inverted surch) ... £450
J55 2r. on 20s. ultramarine (Mt Fuji) ... 50·00 50·00
a. Surch inverted ... £120 £120
b. Surch double, one inverted ... £150
c. Surch omitted (in pair with normal black surch) ... £200 £200
d. Surch in red ... 50·00 50·00
e. Red surch inverted ... £120 £120
f. Red surch double ... £120 £120
g. Surch omitted (in pair with normal red surch) ... £275 £275
ga. Surch omitted (in pair with double red surch) ..
h. Surch double (black and red) ... £425
J56 **9** 5r. on 30s. turquoise (Torii Shrine) ... 13·00 27·00
a. Surch inverted ... 85·00
b. Surch double ... £110
c. Surch double, one inverted ... £150
d. Surch omitted (in pair with normal surch) ... £250 £250
e. Surch omitted (in pair with inverted black surch) ... £350
f. Surch in red ... 26·00 32·00
fa. Red surch inverted ... 90·00 90·00
fb. J56a and J56fa *se-tenant* ... £500 £500
fc. Surch omitted (in pair with normal red surch) ... £250 £250

(b) No. 386 of Japan commemorating the fall of Singapore similarly surch.

J56*g* **9** 4a. on 4+2s. green and red ... £160 £170
h. Surch omitted (in pair with normal) ... £600
ha. Surch omitted (in pair with inverted surch) ... £650
i. Surch inverted ... £375

(New Currency. 100 cents = 1 rupee)

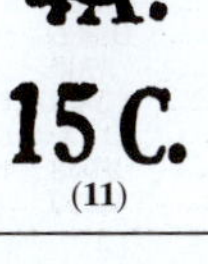
(11)

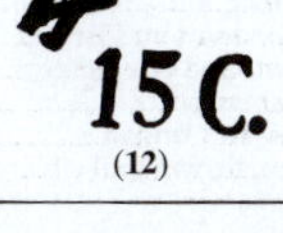
(12)

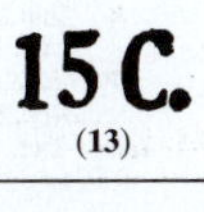
(13)

1942 (15 Oct). *Previous issues, with "anna" surcharges obliterated, handstamped with new value in cents, as T* **11** *and* **12** *(No. J57 handstamped with new value only).*

(a) On No. J46.

J57 5c. on 1a. scarlet ... 18·00 22·00
a. Surch omitted (in pair with normal) ... £1600

(b) On Nos. J47/53.

J58 1c. on ¼a. on 1s. chestnut ... 50·00 50·00
a. "1 c." omitted (in pair with normal) ... £850
b. "¼ a." inverted ... £275
J59 2c. on ½a. on 2s. bright scarlet ... 50·00 50·00
J60 3c. on ¾a. on 3s. green ... 55·00 55·00
a. Surch in blue ... £190
J61 5c. on 1a. on 5s. claret ... 75·00 65·00
J62 10c. on 3a. on 7s. green ... £140 £130
J63 15c. on 4a. on 4s. emerald ... 48·00 50·00
J64 20c. on 8a. on 8s. violet ... £700 £600
a. Surch on No. J53c (surch in red) ... £325 £160

The "anna" surcharges were obliterated by any means available, in some cases by a bar or bars, and in others by the butt of a pencil dipped in ink. In the case of the fractional surcharges, the letter "A" and one figure of the fraction, were sometimes barred out, leaving the remainder of the fraction to represent the new value, e.g. the "1" of "½" deleted to create the 2c. surcharge or the "4" of "¾" to create the 3c. surcharge.

1942. *Nos. 314/17, 320/1 and 396 of Japan surcharged in cents only as T* **13**.

J65 1c. on 1s. chestnut (Rice harvesting) .. 28·00 20·00
a. Surch inverted ... £120 £120
J66 2c. on 2s. brt scarlet (General Nogi) ... 55·00 35·00
J67 3c. on 3s. green (Power station) ... 80·00 55·00
a. Pair, with and without surch ... – £300
b. Surch inverted ... £150
c. Surch in blue ... 95·00 £100
d. Surch in blue inverted ... £250 £275
J68 5c. on 5s. claret (Admiral Togo) ... 85·00 50·00
a. Pair, with and without surch ... £375
b. Surch in violet ... £150 £170
ba. Surch inverted ... – £275
J69 10c. on 7s. green (Diamond Mts) ... £100 70·00
J70 15c. on 4s. emerald (Togo) ... 22·00 23·00
a. Surch inverted ... £140 £150
b. Pair, with and without surch ... – £275
J71 20c. on 8s. violet (Meiji Shrine) ... £180 85·00
a. Surch double ... £375

Nos. J67c and J68b were issued for use in the Shan States.

BURMESE GOVERNMENT

On 1 November 1942 the Japanese Army Administration handed over the control of the postal department to the Burmese Government. On 1 August 1943 Burma was declared by the Japanese to be independent.

14 Burma State Crest

15 Farmer

(Des U Tun Tin and Maung Tin from drawing by U Ba Than. Typo Rangoon)

1943 (15 Feb). *No gum.* P 11.

J72 **14** 5c. scarlet ... 22·00 26·00
a. Imperf ... 23·00 26·00
ab. Printed on both sides ... 90·00

No. J72 was usually sold affixed to envelopes, particularly those with the embossed 1a. King George VI stamp, which it covered. Unused specimens off cover are not often seen and blocks are scarce.

1943. *Typo. No gum.* P 11½.

J73 **15** 1c. orange (22 March) ... 3·75 6·00
a. Brown-orange ... 3·00 6·50
J74 2c. yellow-green (24 March) ... 60 1·00
a. "3" for "2" in face value (R. 2/10) ... £325
b. Blue-green ... 12·00
J75 3c. light blue (25 March) ... 3·25 1·00
a. On laid paper ... 20·00 29·00
b. Imperf between (horiz pair) .. – £300
J76 5c. carmine (small "c") (17 March) ... 23·00 15·00
J77 5c. carmine (large "C") ... 3·25 5·00
a. Imperf (pair) ... £110
b. "G" for "C" (R. 2/6) ... £180
J78 10c. grey-brown (25 March) ... 6·50 6·00
a. Imperf (pair) ... £110
b. Imperf between (horiz pair) .. – £300
J79 15c. magenta (26 March) ... 30 3·00
b. On laid paper ... 6·00 20·00
ba. Inverted "C" in value (R. 2/3) ... £180
J80 20c. grey-lilac (29 March) ... 30 1·00
J81 30c. deep blue-green (29 March) ... 30 1·50

The 1c., 2c. and 3c. have large "C" in value as illustrated. The 10c. and higher values have small "c". Nos. J73/81 had the face values inserted individually into the plate used for No. J46 with the original face value removed. There were a number of printings for each value, often showing differences such as missing stops, various founts of figures or "c", etc., in the value tablets.

The face value error, No. J74a, was later corrected.

Some sheets of No. J75a show a sheet watermark of Britannia seated within a crowned oval spread across fifteen stamps in each sheet. This paper was manufactured by T. Edmonds and the other half of the sheet carried the watermark inscription "FOOLSCAP LEDGER". No stamps have been reported showing letters from this inscription, but a block of 25 is known on laid paper showing a different sheet watermark "HERTFORDSHIRE LEDGER MADE IN ENGLAND". Examples showing parts of these sheet watermarks are rare.

There are marked varieties of shade in this issue.

16 Soldier carving word "Independence"

17 Rejoicing Peasant

18 Boy with National Flag

Normal

Skyline flaw (R. 5/6)

(Des Maung Ba Thit (**16**), Naung Ohn Maung (**17**), and Maung Soi Yi (**18**). Typo State Press, Rangoon)

1943 (1 Aug). *Independence Day.*

(a) P 11.

J82	**16**	1c. orange	9·50	16·00
J83	**17**	3c. light blue	10·00	17·00
J84	**18**	5c. carmine	18·00	8·50
		a. Skyline flaw	£100	
J82/4 *Set of 3*			35·00	38·00

(b) Rouletted.

J85	**16**	1c. orange	1·25	1·75
		b. Perf × roul	£110	£110
		c. Imperf (pair)	45·00	55·00
J86	**17**	3c. light blue	2·50	2·75
		b. Perf × roul	90·00	90·00
		c. Imperf (pair)	45·00	55·00
J87	**18**	5c. carmine	2·50	3·00
		b. Perf × roul	60·00	60·00
		c. Imperf (pair)	45·00	55·00
		d. Skyline flaw	24·00	26·00
J85/7 *Set of 3*			5·50	6·50

The stamps perf × rouletted may have one, two or three sides perforated.

The rouletted stamps often appear to be roughly perforated owing to failure to make clean cuts. These apparent perforations are very small and quite unlike the large, clean holes of the stamps perforated 11.

A few imperforate sets, mounted on a special card folder and cancelled with the commemorative postmark were presented to officials. These are rare.

19 Burmese Woman

20 Elephant carrying Log

21 Watch Tower, Mandalay

(Litho G. Kolff & Co, Batavia)

1943 (1 Oct). P 12½.

J88	**19**	1c. red-orange	20·00	15·00
J89		2c. yellow-green	50	2·00
J90		3c. deep violet	50	2·25
		a. Bright violet	1·75	4·00
J91	**20**	5c. carmine	65	60
J92		10c. blue	1·75	1·10
J93		15c. red-orange	1·00	3·00
J94		20c. yellow-green	1·00	1·75
J95		30c. olive-brown	1·00	2·00
J96	**21**	1r. red-orange	30	2·00
J97		2r. bright violet	30	2·25
J88/97 *Set of 10*			25·00	29·00

22 Bullock Cart

23 Shan Woman

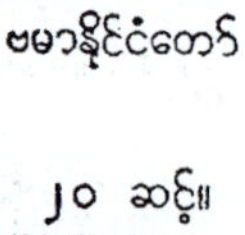
(**24** "Burma State" and value)

(Litho G. Kolff & Co, Batavia)

1943 (1 Oct). *Issue for Shan States.* P 12½.

J98	**22**	1c. olive-brown	30·00	38·00
J99		2c. yellow-green	35·00	38·00
J100		3c. bright violet	4·75	10·00
J101		5c. ultramarine	2·25	6·50
J102	**23**	10c. blue	14·00	18·00
J103		20c. carmine	32·00	18·00
J104		30c. olive-brown	21·00	50·00
J98/104 *Set of 7*			£120	£160

The Shan States, except for the frontier area around Keng Tung which was ceded to Thailand on 20 August 1943, were placed under the administration of the Burmese Government on 24 December 1943, and these stamps were later overprinted as T **24** for use throughout Burma.

1944 (1 Nov). *Optd as T* **24** *(the lower characters differ for each value).*

J105	**22**	1c. olive-brown	3·50	6·00
J106		2c. yellow-green	50	3·25
		a. Opt inverted	£425	£700
J107		3c. bright violet	2·25	7·00
J108		5c. ultramarine	1·25	2·25
J109	**23**	10c. blue	3·25	2·00
J110		20c. carmine	50	1·50
J111		30c. olive-brown	50	1·75
J105/11 *Set of 7*			10·50	21·00

Bushire

BRITISH OCCUPATION

(Currency. 20 chahis = 1 kran; 10 kran = 1 toman)

Bushire, a seaport town of Persia, was occupied by the British on 8 August 1915. The Persian postal authorities resumed control on 18 October 1915. British forces returned to Bushire during 1916, but mail from this period was carried by Indian Army F.P.O. No. 319.

PRICES FOR STAMPS ON COVER	
Nos. 1/29	*from* × 5

Types of Iran (Persia) overprinted

57

66

67

68

BUSHIRE
Under British
Occupation.

(1)

1915 (15 Aug). *Nos. 361/3, 365, 367/70, 372, 374/6 and 378/9 of Iran optd with T* **1** *at the British Residency.*

1	**57**	1ch. orange and green	55·00	60·00
		a. No stop	£160	£170
2		2ch. sepia and carmine	55·00	50·00
		a. No stop	£160	£160
3		3ch. green and grey	70·00	70·00
		a. No stop	£200	£225
4		5ch. carmine and brown	£375	£350
5		6ch. brown-lake and green	50·00	38·00
		a. No stop	£160	£140
6		9ch. indigo-lilac and brown	50·00	65·00
		a. No stop	£170	£190
		b. Opt double		
7		10ch. brown and carmine	50·00	60·00
		a. No stop	£170	£180
8		12ch. blue and green	70·00	70·00
		a. No stop	£200	£225
9		24ch. green and purple	£120	75·00
		a. No stop	£350	£225
10		1kr. carmine and blue	£110	42·00
		a. Double overprint	£8000	
		b. No stop	£325	£140
11		2kr. claret and green	£325	£200
		a. No stop	£950	£600
12		3kr. black and lilac	£250	£250
		a. No stop	£750	£750
13		5kr. blue and red	£170	£150
		a. No stop	£600	£500
14		10kr. rose and bistre-brown	£150	£130
		a. No stop	£550	£475

Nos. 1/3 and 5/14 were overprinted in horizontal strips of 10 and No. 4 in horizontal strips of 5. Eight different settings are recognized with the "No stop" variety occurring on stamp 9 from four settings with 3 mm between "Under" and "British" and on stamp 10 from one setting where the gap is 2 mm.

1915 (Sept). *Nos. 426/40 and 441 of Iran optd with T* **1**.

15	**66**	1ch. deep blue and carmine	£475	£425
16		2ch. carmine and deep blue	£8500	£9000
17		3ch. deep green	£650	£600
18		5ch. vermilion	£7500	£7500
19		6ch. carmine and green	£6500	£6500
20		9ch. deep violet and brown	£900	£850
21		10ch. brown and deep green	£1400	£1400
22		12ch. ultramarine	£1700	£1700
23		24ch. sepia and brown	£650	£500
24	**67**	1kr. black, brown and silver	£650	£650
25		2kr. carmine, slate and silver	£650	£650
26		3kr. sepia, dull lilac and silver	£750	£750
27		5kr. slate, sepia and silver	£700	£750
		a. Opt inverted	–	£18000
28	**68**	1t. black, violet and gold	£650	£650
29		3t. red, crimson and gold	£4750	£4750

Nos. 15/29 were overprinted in strips of 5.

Examples of overprint Type **1** on Iran No. 414, 1ch. on 5ch. (previously No. 30), are now believed to be forged.

Cameroon

Allied operations against the German protectorate of Kamerun commenced in September 1914 and were completed in 18 February 1916. The territory was divided, under an Anglo-French agreement, on 31 March 1916, with the British administering the area in the west along the Nigerian border. League of Nations mandates were issued for the two sections of Cameroon, which were converted into United Nations trusteeships in 1946.

Supplies of Kamerun stamps were found on the German steamer *Professor Woermann*, captured at Freetown, and these were surcharged, probably in Sierra Leone, and issued by the Cameroons Expeditionary Force at Duala in July 1915.

A French post office opened in Duala on 10 November 1915 using stamps of Gabon overprinted "Corps Expeditionnaire Franco Anglais Cameroun". Although under the overall control of the British combined force commander, this office remained part of the French postal system.

PRICES FOR STAMPS ON COVER

The stamps of British Occupation of Cameroons are rare used on cover.

CAMEROONS EXPEDITIONARY FORCE

A

B

C.E.F.

1d.

(1)

C.E.F.

1s.

(2)

SETTINGS. Nos. B1/3 were surcharged from a setting of 100 (10×10) with the face value changed for the 1d.

Nos. B4 and B6/9 were surcharged from a common setting of 50 (5×10) with the face value amended.

No. B5 was surcharged from a setting of 10 in a vertical strip repeated across the sheet. The figures of the surcharge on this are in a different style from the remainder of the pence stamps.

Nos. B10/13 were surcharged from a common setting of 20 (4×5) with the face value amended.

Different font "d" (R. 1/10, 6/9, 10/10)

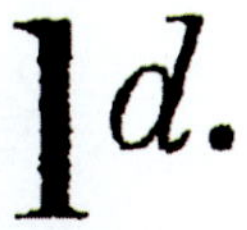

"1" with thin serifs (R. 5/1)

Short "4" (R. 10/2, 10/7)

"s" broken at top (R. 3/1)

"s" inverted (R. 3/4)

1915 (12 July). *Stamps of German Kamerun. Types* A *and* B, *surch as T* **1** *(Nos. B1/9) or* **2** *(Nos. B10/13) in black or blue.*

B1	A	½d. on 3pf. brown (No. K7) (B.)	13·00	42·00
		a. Different fount "d"	£150	£350
B2		½d. on 5pf. green (No. K21 wmk lozenges) (B.)	3·25	9·50
		a. Different fount "d"	45·00	£110
		b. Surch double	†	£900
		ba. Surch double, one albino	£275	
B3		1d. on 10pf. carmine (No. K22 wmk lozenges) (B.)	1·25	9·50
		a. "1" with thin serifs	13·00	65·00
		b. Surch double	£325	
		ba. Surch double, one albino	£120	
		c. "1d." only double	£1900	
		d. Surch triple, two albino	£275	
		e. Surch in black	14·00	55·00
		ea. "1" with thin serifs	£225	
B4		2d. on 20pf. ultramarine (No. K23 wmk lozenges)	3·50	22·00
		a. Surch double, one albino	£275	
B5		2½d. on 25pf. black and red/*yellow* (No. K11)	12·00	50·00
		a. Surch double	£9000	
		ab. Surch double, one albino		
B6		3d. on 30pf. black and orange/*buff* (No. K12)	12·00	55·00
		a. Large "3" (R. 3/5, 3/10)	£950	
		b. Surch triple, two albino	£325	
B7		4d. on 40pf. black and carmine (No. K13)	12·00	55·00
		a. Short "4"	£800	£1200
		b. Surch triple, two albino	£300	
		c. Surch quadruple, three albino	£2000	
B8		6d. on 50pf. black and purple/*buff* (No. K14)	12·00	55·00
		a. Surch double, one albino	£225	
B9		8d. on 80pf. black and carmine/*rose* (No. K15)	12·00	55·00
		a. Surch triple, two albino	£1400	
B10	B	1s. on 1m. carmine (No. K16)	£180	£750
		a. "s" inverted	£900	£3000
B11		2s. on 2m. blue (No. K17)	£180	£750
		a. "s" inverted	£900	£3000
		b. Surch double, one albino	£1800	
B12		3s. on 3m. violet-black(No. K18)	£180	£750
		a. "s" inverted	£900	£3000
		b. "s" broken at top	£700	
		c. Surch double	£11000	
		ca. Surch triple, two albino	£1800	
B13		5s. on 5m. carmine and black (No. K25a wmk lozenges)	£250	£800
		a. "s" inverted	£1100	£3250
		b. "s" broken at top	£800	
B1/13 *Set of 13*			£800	£3000

The 1d. on 10pf. was previously listed with "C.E.F." omitted. This was due to misplacement, so that all stamps (except for a pair in the Royal Collection) from the bottom row show traces of the overprint on the top perforations.

Examples of all values exist showing a forged Duala, Kamerun postmark dated "11 10 15". Another forged cancel dated "16 11 15" is also known. This can be identified by the lack of a serif on the index letter "b".

The stamps of Nigeria were subsequently used in British Cameroons and the area was administered as part of Nigeria from February 1924.

For issues of Cameroon under French administration see *Part 6 (France)*.

II. CAMEROONS TRUST TERRITORY

Following the independence of the French Trust Territory of Cameroun on 1 January 1960 the United Nations directed that a plebiscite should be held in the British Trust Territory whose postal service continued, for the time being, to run by Nigeria. The northern area voted to join Nigeria, but the southern part of the territory decided to join the Cameroun Republic.

The following issue, although ordered by the Southern Cameroons authorities, was also on sale in Northern Cameroons, until the latter joined Nigeria on 1 June 1961. The stamps therefore can be found with Nigerian postmarks.

CAMEROONS
U.K.T.T.

(1)

1960 (1 Oct)–**61**. *Nos. 69/71, 72ca/cc and 73/80 of Nigeria optd with T* **1**, *in red.*

T1	**18**	½d. black and orange	10	1·50
T2	–	1d. black and bronze-green	10	70
		a. Grey-black and dull bronze-green (19.9.61)	60	2·00
T3	–	1½d. blue-green	10	20
T4	**21**	2d. grey (Type B)	10	1·50
		a. Slate-blue (Type A)	£800	£250
		b. Bluish grey (Type B)	65·00	17·00
		c. Pale grey (Type B) (19.9.61)	70	1·25
T5	–	3d. black and deep lilac	15	10
T6	–	4d. black and blue	10	1·75
T7	**24**	6d. orange-brown and black (p 14)	30	20
		a. Perf 13×13½ (19.9.61)	20	2·25
T8	–	1s. black and maroon	15	10
T9	**26**	2s.6d. black and green	1·50	1·00
T10	–	5s. black and red-orange	2·00	3·50
T11	–	10s. black and red-brown	2·75	6·50
T12	**29**	£1 black and violet	9·50	23·00
T1/12 *Set of 12*			15·00	35·00

Nos. T2 and T4/*b* were overprinted on stamps printed by Waterlows' subsidiary, Imprimerie Belge de Securité.

Nos. T2*a*, T4*c* and T7a were from new printings produced by De La Rue instead of Waterlow.

The above stamps were withdrawn on 30 September 1961, when Southern Cameroons became part of the Cameroun Republic, although some post offices had been using unoverprinted Nigerian stamps for some months previously.

Canada

Separate stamp issues appeared for British Columbia and Vancouver Island, Canada, New Brunswick, Newfoundland, Nova Scotia and Prince Edward Island before these colonies joined the Dominion of Canada.

BRITISH COLUMBIA & VANCOUVER ISLAND

Vancouver Island was organised as a Crown Colony in 1849 and the mainland territory was proclaimed a separate colony as British Columbia in 1858. The two colonies combined, as British Columbia, on 19 November 1866.

PRICES FOR STAMPS ON COVER

Nos. 2/3	*from* × 6
Nos. 11/12	*from* × 2
Nos. 13/14	*from* × 6
Nos. 21/2	*from* × 10
Nos. 23/7	*from* × 6
Nos. 28/9	*from* × 10
No. 30	—
No. 31	*from* × 10
Nos. 32/3	—

1

(Typo D.L.R.)

1860. No wmk. P 14.

2	**1**	2½d. deep reddish rose	£375	£180
3		2½d. pale reddish rose	£375	£180

When Vancouver Island adopted the dollar currency in 1862 the 2½d. was sold at 5c. From 18 May until 1 November 1865 examples of Nos. 2/3 were used to prepay mail from Vancouver Island to British Columbia at the price of 15 cents a pair.

From 20 June 1864 to 1 November 1865, the 2½d. was sold in British Columbia for 3d. and was subsequently used for the same purpose during a shortage of 3d. stamps in 1867.

Imperforate plate proofs exist in pale dull red (*Price* £4000 *un*).

VANCOUVER ISLAND

(New Currency. 100 cents = 1 dollar)

2

3

(Typo D.L.R.)

1865 (19 Sept). Wmk Crown CC.

		(a) Imperf (1866).		
11	**2**	5c. rose	£30000	£9000
12	**3**	10c. blue	£1800	£850
		(b) P 14.		
13	**2**	5c. rose	£275	£160
		w. Wmk inverted	£1400	£750
		x. Wmk reversed	†	£750
14	**3**	10c. blue	£225	£140
		w. Wmk inverted	£800	£600

Medium or poor copies of Nos. 11 and 12 can be supplied at much lower prices, when in stock.

After the two colonies combined Nos. 13/14 were also used in British Columbia.

BRITISH COLUMBIA

4

(Typo D.L.R.)

1865 (1 Nov)–**67**. Wmk Crown CC. P 14.

21	**4**	3d. deep blue	95·00	65·00
22		3d. pale blue (19.7.67)	90·00	65·00
		w. Wmk inverted	£350	£225
		y. Wmk inverted and reversed	†	£375

British Columbia changed to the dollar currency on 1 January 1866. Remaining stocks of No. 21 and the supply of No. 22, when it finally arrived, were sold at 12½c. a pair.

(New Currency. 100 cents = 1 dollar)

TWO CENTS

(5)

5.CENTS.5

(6)

1868–71. *T* **4** *in various colours. Surch as T* **5** *or* **6**. Wmk Crown CC.

	(a) P 12½ (3.69).		
23	5c. red (Bk.)	£1300	£1000
24	10c. lake (B.)	£900	£700
25	25c. yellow (V.)	£600	£600
26	50c. mauve (R.)	£750	£650
27	$1 green (G.)	£1200	£1300
	(b) P 14.		
28	2c. brown (Bk.) (1.68)	£160	£140
29	5c. pale red (Bk.) (5.69)	£200	£150
30	10c. lake (B.)	£1200	
31	25c. yellow (V.) (21.7.69)	£200	£150
32	50c. mauve (R.) (23.2.71)	£600	£1100
	w. Wmk inverted	£1000	
33	$1 green (G.)	£1000	

Nos. 30 and 33 were not issued.

British Columbia joined the Dominion of Canada on 20 July 1871.

COLONY OF CANADA

The first British post offices in what was to become the colony of Canada were opened at Quebec, Montreal and Trois Rivières during, 1763. These, and subsequent, offices remained part of the British G.P.O. system until 6 April 1851.

The two provinces of Upper Canada (Ontario) and Lower Canada (Quebec) were united in 1840.

For illustration of the handstamp types see BRITISH POST OFFICES ABROAD notes, following GREAT BRITAIN.

NEW CARLISLE, GASPÉ

POSTMASTER'S PROVISIONAL ENVELOPE

1

1851 (7 April).

1	1	3d. black		

Only one example is known, addressed to Toronto, with the impression cancelled by the signature of the postmaster, R. W. Kelly.

QUEBEC

CROWNED-CIRCLE HANDSTAMPS

CC1	CC 1	QUEBEC L.C. (R.) (13.1.1842)	
		Price on cover	£150

PRICES FOR STAMPS ON COVER	
Nos. 1/23	*from* × 2
Nos. 25/8	*from* × 3
Nos. 29/43*a*	*from* × 3
Nos. 44/5	*from* × 8

1 American Beaver (Designed by Sir Sandford Fleming)

2 Prince Albert

3

Major re-entry: Line through "EE PEN" (Upper pane R. 5/7)

(T **1/6**. Eng and recess Rawdon, Wright, Hatch and Edson, New York)

1851. *Laid paper.* Imperf.

1	1	3d. red (23 April)	£18000	£800
1*a*		3d. orange-vermilion	£18000	£800
		b. Major re-entry	—	£2000
2	2	6d. slate-violet (15 May)	£24000	£1000
3		6d. brown-purple	£26000	£1200
		a. Bisected (3d.) on cover	†	£26000
4	3	12d. black (14 June)	£130000	£60000

There are several re-entries on the plate of the 3d. in addition to the major re-entry listed. All re-entries occur in this stamp on all papers.

Forgeries of the 3d. are known without the full stop after "PENCE". They also omit the foliage in the corners, as do similar forgeries of the 6d.

4

5

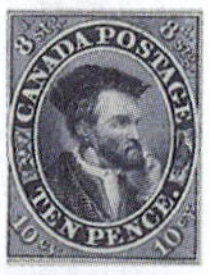

6 Jacques Cartier

Re-entry (R. 10/12)

1852–57. Imperf.

		A. Handmade wove paper, varying in thickness (1852–56).		
5	1	3d. red	£1600	£170
		a. Bisected (1½d.) on cover (1856)	†	£26000
6		3d. deep red	£1800	£190
7		3d. scarlet-vermilion	£2250	£190
8		3d. brown-red	£1700	£190
		a. Bisected (1½d.) on cover (1856)	†	£26000
		b. Major re-entry (*all shades*) *from*	£3750	£650
9	2	6d. slate-violet	£21000	£950
		a. Bisected (3d.) on cover	†	£14000
10		6d. greenish grey	£21000	£1000
11		6d. brownish grey	£22000	£1200
12	5	7½d. yellow-green (*shades*) (2.6.57)	£9000	£1700
13	6	10d. bright blue (1.55)	£9000	£1300
14		10d. dull blue	£8500	£1200
15		10d. blue *to* deep blue	£9000	£1300
		a. Major re-entry (*all shades*) *from*	—	£2250
16	3	12d. black	—	£85000
		B. Machine-made medium to thick wove paper of a more even hard texture with more visible mesh. Clearer impressions (1857).		
17	4	½d. deep rose (1.8.57)	£800	£500
		a. Re-entry	£2000	£1000
18	1	3d. red	£2250	£450
		a. Bisected (1½d.) on cover	†	£26000
		b. Major re-entry	—	£1300
19	2	6d. grey-lilac	£27000	£2000
20	6	10d. blue *to* deep blue	£10000	£2000
		a. Major re-entry	£16000	£2500
		C. Thin soft horizontally ribbed paper (1857).		
21	4	½d. deep rose	£7000	£1700
		a. Vertically ribbed paper	£7500	£2500
22	1	3d. red	£3500	£400
		a. Major re-entry	—	£1200
		D. Very thick soft wove paper (1857).		
23	2	6d. reddish purple	£30000	£3000
		a. Bisected (3d.) on cover	†	£21000

Bisected examples of the 3d. value were used to make up the 7½d. Canadian Packet rate to England from May 1856 until the introduction of the 7½d. value on 2 June 1857.

The 7½d. and 10d. values can be found in wide and narrow versions. These differences are due to shrinkage of the paper, which was wetted before printing and then contracted unevenly during drying. The width of these stamps varies between 17 and 18 mm.

The listed major re-entry on the 10d. occurs on R. 3/5 and shows strong doubling of the top frame line and the left-hand "8d. stg." with a line through the lower parts of "ANAD" and "ENCE". Smaller re-entries occur on all values.

Examples of the 12d. on wove paper come from a proof sheet used for postal purposes by the postal authorities.

The 3d. is known perforated 14 and also *percé en scie* 13. Both are contemporary, but were unofficial.

1858–59. P 11¾.

		A. Machine-made medium to thick wove paper with a more even hard texture.		
25	4	½d. deep rose (12.58)	£3000	£700
		a. Lilac-rose	£3000	£750
		b. Re-entry (R. 10/10)	£5500	£1500
26	1	3d. red (1.59)	£3750	£300
		a. Major re-entry	—	£1100
27	2	6d. brownish grey (1.59)	£11000	£3000
		a. Slate-violet	£11000	£2750
		B. Thin soft horizontally ribbed paper.		
27*b*	4	½d. deep rose-red	—	£3750
28	1	3d. red	—	£1400
		a. Major re-entry		

The re-entry on the imperforate and perforated sheets was the same, but occurred on R. 10/10 of the perforated sheets because the two left-hand vertical rows were removed prior to perforation.

(New Currency. 100 cents = 1 dollar)

7

8 American Beaver

9 Prince Albert

10

11 Jacques Cartier

(On 1 May 1858, Messrs. Rawdon, Wright, Hatch and Edson joined with eight other firms to form "The American Bank Note Co" and the "imprint" on sheets of the following stamps has the new title of the firm with "New York" added.)

(Recess A.B.N. Co)

1859 (1 July). P 12.

29	7	1c. pale rose (to rose-red)	£325	38·00
30		1c. deep rose (to carmine-rose)	£400	50·00
		a. Imperf (pair)	£3250	
		b. Imperf×perf		
31	8	5c. pale red	£350	16·00
32		5c. deep red	£350	16·00
		a. Re-entry* (R.3/8)	£3000	£450
		b. Imperf (pair)	£11000	
		c. Bisected (2½c.) with 10c. on cover	†	£4750
33	9	10c. black-brown	£9500	£1600
		a. Bisected (5c.), on cover	†	£7000
33*b*		10c. deep red-purple	£3500	£550
		ba. Bisected (5c.), on cover	†	£4500
34		10c. purple (*shades*)	£1000	60·00
		a. Bisected (5c.), on cover	†	£4500
35		10c. brownish purple	£950	60·00
36		10c. brown (to pale)	£950	60·00
		a. Bisected (5c.), on cover	†	£5500
37		10c. dull violet	£1000	65·00
38		10c. bright red-purple	£1000	60·00
		a. Imperf (pair)	£10000	
39	10	12½c. deep yellow-green	£900	55·00
40		12½c. pale yellow-green	£850	55·00
41		12½c. blue-green	£1000	70·00
		a. Imperf (pair)	£4000	
		b. Imperf between (vert pair)		
42	11	17c. deep blue	£1100	75·00
		a. Imperf (pair)	£4250	
43		17c. slate-blue	£1400	£100
43*a*	4	17c. indigo	£1300	80·00

*The price of No. 32a is for the very marked re-entry showing oval frame line doubled above "CANADA". Slighter re-entries are worth from £30 upwards in used condition.

As there were numerous P.O. Dept. orders for the 10c., 12½c. and 17c. and some of these were executed by more than one separate printing, with no special care to ensure uniformity of colour, there is a wide range of shade, especially in the 10c., and some shades recur at intervals after periods during which other shades predominated. The colour-names given in the above list therefore represent groups only.

It has been proved by leading Canadian specialists that the perforations may be an aid to the approximate dating of a particular stamp, the gauge used measuring 11¾×11¾ from mid-July 1859 to mid-1863, 12×11¾ from March 1863 to mid-1865 and 12×12 from April 1865 to 1868. Exceptionally, in the 5c. value many sheets were perforated 12×12 between May and October, 1862, whilst the last printings of the 12½c. and 17c. perf 11¾×11¾ were in July 1863, the perf 12×11¾ starting towards the end of 1863.

12

(Recess A.B.N. Co)

1864 (1 Aug). P 12.

44	12	2c. rose-red	£500	£160
45		2c. bright rose	£500	£160
		a. Imperf (pair)	£2000	

The Colony of Canada became part of the Dominion of Canada on 1 July 1867.

NEW BRUNSWICK

New Brunswick, previously part of Nova Scotia, became a separate colony in June 1784. The colony became responsible for its postal service on 6 July 1851.

PRICES FOR STAMPS ON COVER	
Nos. 1/4	*from* × 2
Nos. 5/6	*from* × 3
Nos. 7/9	*from* × 10
Nos. 10/12	*from* × 30
No. 13	—
Nos. 14/17	*from* × 2
No. 18	*from* × 5
No. 19	*from* × 100

1 Royal Crown and Heraldic Flowers of the United Kingdom

(Recess P.B.)

1851 (5 Sept). *Blue paper.* Imperf.

1	1	3d. bright red	£2500	£350
2		3d. dull red	£2250	£325
		a. Bisected (1½d.) (on cover)	†	£2750
2*b*		6d. mustard-yellow	£7000	£1500
3		6d. yellow	£4500	£800
4		6d. olive-yellow	£4500	£700
		a. Bisected (3d.) (on cover)	†	£3000
		b. Quartered (1½d.) (on cover)	†	£42000
5		1s. reddish mauve	£15000	£4000
6		1s. dull mauve	£16000	£4500
		a. Bisected (6d.) (on cover)	†	£24000
		b. Quartered (3d.) (on cover)	†	£35000

Reprints of all three values were made in 1890 on thin, hard, white paper. The 3d. is bright orange, the 6d. and 1s. violet-black.

Nos. 2a and 4b were to make up the 7½d. rate to Great Britain, introduced on 1 August 1854.

(New Currency. 100 cents = 1 dollar)

2 Locomotive

3

3a Charles Connell

4

5

6 Paddle-steamer *Washington*

7 King Edward VII when Prince of Wales

(Recess A.B.N. Co)

1860 (15 May)–**63**. No wmk. P 12.

7	**2**	1c. brown-purple	60·00	45·00
8		1c. purple	50·00	42·00
9		1c. dull claret	50·00	42·00
		a. Imperf vert (horiz pair)	£550	
10	**3**	2c. orange (1863)	25·00	23·00
11		2c. orange-yellow	29·00	23·00
12		2c. deep orange	30·00	23·00
		a. Imperf horiz (vert pair)	£450	
13	**3a**	5c. brown	£6000	
14	**4**	5c. yellow-green	23·00	15·00
15		5c. deep green	23·00	15·00
16		5c. sap-green (deep yellowish green)	£300	40·00
17	**5**	10c. red	48·00	50·00
		a. Bisected (5c.) (on cover) (1860)	†	£600
18	**6**	12½c. indigo	65·00	40·00
19	**7**	17c. black	38·00	55·00

Beware of forged cancellations.

No. 13 was not issued due to objections to the design showing Charles Connell, the Postmaster-General. Most of the printing was destroyed.

New Brunswick joined the Dominion of Canada on 1 July 1867 and its stamps were withdrawn in March of the following year.

NEWFOUNDLAND

Newfoundland became a self-governing colony in 1855 and a Dominion in 1917. In 1934 the adverse financial situation led to the suspension of the constitution.

The first local postmaster, at St. John's, was appointed in 1805, the overseas mails being routed via Halifax, Nova Scotia. A regular packet service was established between these two ports in 1840, the British G.P.O. assuming control of the overseas mails at the same time.

The responsibility for the overseas postal service reverted to the colonial administration on 1 July 1851.

For illustrations of the handstamp types see BRITISH POST OFFICES ABROAD notes, following GREAT BRITAIN.

ST. JOHN'S

CROWNED-CIRCLE HANDSTAMPS

CC1	CC **1**	ST. JOHN'S NEWFOUNDLAND (R.) (27.6.1846) ... *Price on cover*	£950

PRICES FOR STAMPS ON COVER TO 1945

No. 1	*from* × 30
Nos. 2/4	*from* × 3
No. 5	*from* × 20
No. 6	*from* × 10
No. 7	*from* × 3
No. 8	*from* × 30
No. 9	*from* × 8
No. 10	—
No. 11	*from* × 8
No. 12	*from* × 3
Nos. 13/14	*from* × 20
Nos. 15/17	—
Nos. 18/20	*from* × 20
No. 21	*from* × 15
Nos. 22/3	—
No. 25	*from* × 30
No. 26	*from* × 5
No. 27	*from* × 8
No. 28	*from* × 3
Nos. 29/30	*from* × 10
No. 31	*from* × 30
No. 32	*from* × 8
No. 33	*from* × 5
No. 33*a*	—
Nos. 34/9	*from* × 8
Nos. 40/1	*from* × 5
Nos. 42/3	*from* × 30
Nos. 44/8	*from* × 8
No. 49	*from* × 50
Nos. 50/3	*from* × 10
No. 54	*from* × 4
Nos. 55/8*b*	*from* × 10
No. 59	*from* × 100
No. 59*a*	*from* × 10
Nos. 60/1	*from* × 4
Nos. 62/5	*from* × 8
Nos. 65*a*/79	*from* × 3
Nos. 83/90	*from* × 10
Nos. 91/3	*from* × 2
No. 94	*from* × 50
Nos. 95/141	*from* × 3
Nos. 142/*a*	*from* × 1½
No. 143	*from* × 8
Nos. 144/8*f*	*from* × 2
Nos. 149/62	*from* × 3
No. 163	—
Nos. 164/78	*from* × 2
Nos. 179/90	*from* × 3
No. 191	—
Nos. 192/220	*from* × 2
No. 221	—
Nos. 222/9	*from* × 3
Nos. 230/4	*from* × 2
No. 235	—
Nos. 236/91	*from* × 2
Nos. D1/6	*from* × 10

1

2

3

4

5

Royal Crown and Heraldic flowers of the United Kingdom

(Recess P.B.)

1857 (1 Jan)–**64**. *Thick, machine-made paper with a distinct mesh.* No wmk. Imperf.

1	**1**	1d. brown-purple	£130	£200
		a. Bisected (½d.) (1864) (on cover)	†	£35000
2	**2**	2d. scarlet-vermilion (15 Feb)	£16000	£5500
3	**3**	3d. yellowish green (H/S "CANCELLED" in oval £12000)	£1200	£425
4	**4**	4d. scarlet-vermilion	£9500	£2500
5	**1**	5d. brown-purple	£250	£425
6	**4**	6d. scarlet-vermilion	£18000	£3500
7	**5**	6½d. scarlet-vermilion	£3000	£3250
8	**4**	8d. scarlet-vermilion	£300	£550
		a. Bisected (4d.) (1859) (on cover)	†	£4250
9	**2**	1s. scarlet-vermilion	£18000	£6000
		a. Bisected (6d.) (1860) (on cover)	†	£15000

The 6d. and 8d. differ from the 4d. in many details, as does also the 1s. from the 2d.

PERKINS BACON "CANCELLED". For notes on these handstamps, showing "CANCELLED" between horizontal bars forming an oval, see Catalogue Introduction.

1860 (15 Aug–Dec). *Medium, hand-made paper without mesh.* Imperf.

10	**2**	2d. orange-vermilion	£425	£550
11	**3**	3d. grn *to* dp grn* (H/S "CANCELLED" in oval £11000)	85·00	£170
12	**4**	4d. orange-verm (H/S "CANCELLED" in oval £14000)	£2750	£900
		a. Bisected (2d.) (12.60) (on cover)	†	£20000
13	**1**	5d. Venetian red (H/S "CANCELLED" in oval £13000)	£110	£375
14	**4**	6d. orange-vermilion	£3500	£600
15	**2**	1s. orange-verm (H/S "CANCELLED" in oval £17000)	£28000	£9000
		a. Bisected (6d.) (12.60) (on cover)	†	£42000

*No. 11 includes stamps from the July and November 1861 printings which are very difficult to distinguish.

The 1s. on horizontally or vertically *laid* paper is now considered to be a proof (*Price* £17000).

Stamps of this and the following issue may be found with part of the paper-maker's watermark "STACEY WISE 1858".

BISECTS. Collectors are warned against buying bisected stamps of these issues without a reliable guarantee.

1862–64. *New colours. Hand-made paper without mesh.* Imperf.

16	**1**	1d. chocolate-brown	£250	£400
		a. Red-brown	£6000	
17	**2**	2d. rose-lake	£250	£500
18	**4**	4d. rose-lake (H/S "CANCELLED" in oval £13000)	42·00	£110
		a. Bisected (2d.) (1864) (on cover)	†	£35000
19	**1**	5d. chocolate-brown (*shades*)	85·00	£325
		a. Red-brown (shades)	70·00	£200
20	**4**	6d. rose-lake (H/S "CANCELLED" in oval £11000)	27·00	£100
		a. Bisected (3d.) (1863) (on cover)	†	£9000
21	**5**	6½d. rose-lake (H/S "CANCELLED" in oval £11000)	85·00	£450
22	**4**	8d. rose-lake	£100	£650
23	**2**	1s. rose-lake (H/S "CANCELLED" in oval £12000)	45·00	£300
		a. Bisected (6d.) (1863) (on cover)	†	£22000

Nos. 16/23 come from printings made in July (2d., 4d., 6d., 6½d., and 1s. only) or November 1861 (all values). The paper used was from the same manufacturer as that for Nos. 11/15, but was of more variable thickness and texture, ranging from a relatively soft medium paper, which can be quite opaque, to a thin hard transparent paper. The rose-lake stamps also show a considerable variation in shade ranging from pale to deep. The extensive remainders of this issue were predominantly in pale shades on thin hard paper, but it is not possible to distinguish between stamps from the two printings with any certainty. Deep shades of the 2d., 4d., 6d., 6½d. and 1s. on soft opaque paper do, however, command a considerable premium.

Beware of buying used specimens of the stamps which are worth much less in unused condition, as many unused stamps have been provided with faked postmarks. A guarantee should be obtained.

(New Currency. 100 cents = 1 dollar)

6 Atlantic Cod

7 Common Seal on Ice-floe

8 Prince Consort

9 Queen Victoria

10 Schooner

11 Queen Victoria

(Recess A.B.N. Co, New York)

1865 (15 Nov)–**71**. P 12.

		(a) Thin yellowish paper.		
25	**6**	2c. yellowish green	£130	70·00
		a. Bisected (1c.) (on cover) (1870)	†	£7500
26	**7**	5c. brown	£550	£170
		a. Bisected (2½c.) (on cover)	†	£9000
27	**8**	10c. black	£325	95·00
		a. Bisected (5c.) (on cover) (1869)	†	£6000
28	**9**	12c. red-brown	£475	£150
		a. Bisected (6c.) (on cover)	†	£4000
29	**10**	13c. orange-yellow	£110	95·00
30	**11**	24c. blue	38·00	38·00
		(b) Medium white paper.		
31	**6**	2c. bluish green (*to* deep) (1870)	90·00	45·00
32	**8**	10c. black (1871)	£250	48·00
33	**9**	12c. chestnut (1870)	50·00	48·00

The inland postage rate was reduced to 3c. on 8 May, 1870. Until the 3c. value became available examples of No. 25 were bisected to provide 1c. stamps.

12 King Edward VII when Prince of Wales

14 Queen Victoria

I

II

In Type II the white oval frame line is unbroken by the scroll containing the words "ONE CENT", the letters "N.F." are smaller and closer to the scroll, and there are other minor differences.

(Recess National Bank Note Co, New York)

1868 (Nov). P 12.

34	**12**	1c. dull purple (I)	70·00	55·00

(Recess A.B.N. Co)

1868 (Nov)–**73**. P 12.

35	**12**	1c. brown-purple (II) (5.71)	£120	65·00
36	**14**	3c. vermilion (7.70)	£300	£100
37		3c. blue (1.4.73)	£275	24·00
38	**7**	5c. black	£250	£110
39	**14**	6c. rose (7.70)	10·00	23·00

1876–79. Rouletted.

40	**12**	1c. lake-purple (II) (1877)	£100	55·00
41	**6**	2c. bluish green (1879)	£140	48·00

42	**14**	3c. blue (1877)	£300	5·00
43	**7**	5c. blue	£180	3·50
		a. Imperf (pair)		

15 King Edward VII when Prince of Wales

16 Atlantic Cod

17

18 Common Seal on Ice-floe

(Recess British American Bank Note Co, Montreal)

1880–82. P 12.

44	**15**	1c. dull grey-brown	32·00	12·00
		a. Dull brown	32·00	12·00
		b. Red-brown	35·00	17·00
46	**16**	2c. yellow-green (1882)	50·00	27·00
47	**17**	3c. pale dull blue	95·00	8·50
		a. Bright blue	80·00	5·50
48	**18**	5c. pale dull blue	£300	10·00

19 Newfoundland Dog

20 Atlantic Brigantine

21 Queen Victoria

(Recess British American Bank Note Co, Montreal)

1887 (15 Feb)–**88**. *New colours and values.* P 12.

49	**19**	½c. rose-red	15·00	8·00
50	**15**	1c. blue-green (1.88)	12·00	8·00
		a. Green	6·00	3·50
		b. Yellow-green	11·00	9·50
51	**16**	2c. orange-vermilion (1.88)	22·00	6·50
		a. Imperf (pair)	£300	
52	**17**	3c. deep brown (1.88)	65·00	2·25
53	**18**	5c. deep blue (1.88)	£110	5·50
54	**20**	10c. black (1.88)	60·00	55·00
49/54 *Set of* 6			£250	70·00

For reissues of 1880/8 stamps in similar colours, see Nos. 62/5*a*.

(Recess B.A.B.N.)

1890 (Nov). P 12.

55	**21**	3c. deep slate	40·00	2·50
		a. Imperf (pair)		
56		3c. slate-grey (*to* grey)	40·00	2·50
		a. Imperf horiz (vert pair)	£475	
57		3c. slate-violet	50·00	5·00
58		3c. grey-lilac	48·00	2·50
58*a*		3c. brown-grey	50·00	6·00
58*b*		3c. purple-grey	50·00	6·00

There is a very wide range of shades in this stamp, and those given only cover the main groups.

Stamps on pink paper are from a consignment recovered from the sea and which were affected by the salt water.

(Recess British American Bank Note Co, Montreal)

1894 (Aug–Dec). *Changes of colour.* P 12.

59	**19**	½c. black (11.94)	9·50	6·00
59*a*	**18**	5c. bright blue (12.94)	70·00	4·75
60	**14**	6c. crimson-lake (12.94)	21·00	19·00
61	**9**	12c. deep brown	65·00	65·00

The 6c. is printed from the old American Bank Note Company's plates.

1896 (Jan)–**98**. *Reissues.* P 12.

62	**19**	½c. orange-vermilion	55·00	55·00
63	**15**	1c. deep brown	75·00	55·00
63*a*		1c. deep green (1898)	22·00	13·00
64	**16**	2c. green	£100	60·00
65	**17**	3c. deep blue	80·00	24·00
65*a*		3c. chocolate-brown	95·00	85·00
62/5*a* *Set of* 6			£400	£250

The above were *reissued* for postal purposes. The colours were generally brighter than those of the original stamps.

22 Queen Victoria

23 John Cabot

24 Cape Bonavista

25 Caribou hunting

26 Mining

27 Logging

28 Fishing

29 *Matthew* (Cabot)

30 Willow Grouse

31 Group of Grey Seals

32 Salmon-fishing

33 Seal of the Colony

34 Iceberg off St. John's

35 Henry VII

(Des R. O. Smith. Recess A.B.N. Co)

1897 (24 June). *400th Anniv of Discovery of Newfoundland and 60th year of Queen Victoria's reign.* P 12.

66	**22**	1c. green	3·75	8·50
67	**23**	2c. bright rose	2·25	2·75
		a. Bisected (1c.) on cover	†	£300
68	**24**	3c. bright blue	3·50	1·00
		a. Bisected (1½c.) on cover	†	£300
69	**25**	4c. olive-green	9·50	6·00
70	**26**	5c. violet	14·00	3·00
71	**27**	6c. red-brown	9·50	3·25
		a. Bisected (3c.) on cover	†	£325
72	**28**	8c. orange	21·00	9·00
73	**29**	10c. sepia	42·00	9·00
74	**30**	12c. deep blue	35·00	8·00
75	**31**	15c. bright scarlet	20·00	18·00
76	**32**	24c. dull violet-blue	25·00	25·00
77	**33**	30c. slate-blue	50·00	80·00
78	**34**	35c. red	60·00	70·00
79	**35**	60c. black	21·00	15·00
66/79 *Set of* 14			£275	£225

The 60c. surcharged "TWO—2—CENTS" in three lines is an essay made in December 1918 (*Price* £375).

ONE CENT

(36)

ONE CENT

(37)

ONE CENT

(38)

1897 (19 Oct). *T* **21** *surch with T* **36/8** *by* Royal Gazette, *St. Johns, on stamps of various shades.*

80	**36**	1c. on 3c. grey-purple	60·00	26·00
		a. Surch double, one diagonal	£1300	
		d. Vert pair, one without lower bar and "ONE CENT"	£4000	
81	**37**	1c. on 3c. grey-purple	£130	95·00
82	**38**	1c. on 3c. grey-purple	£550	£475

Nos. 80/2 occur in the same setting of 50 (10×5) applied twice to each sheet. Type **36** appeared in the first four horizontal rows, Type **37** on R. 5/1–8 and Type **38** on R. 5/9 and 10.

Trial surcharges in red or red and black were not issued. (*Price*: Type **36** *in red* £900, *in red and black* £900: Type **37** *in red* £3000, *in red and black* £30000: Type **38** *in red* £7500, *in red and black* £8000).

These surcharges exist on stamps of various shades, but those on brown-grey are clandestine forgeries, having been produced by one of the printers at the *Royal Gazette*.

39 Prince Edward later Duke of Windsor

40 Queen Victoria

41 King Edward VII when Prince of Wales

42 Queen Alexandra when Princess of Wales

43 Queen Mary when Duchess of York

44 King George V when Duke of York

(Recess A.B.N. Co)

1897 (4 Dec)–**1918**. P 12.

83	**39**	½c. olive (8.98)	2·25	1·50
		a. Imperf (pair)	£475	
84	**40**	1c. carmine	3·75	4·00
85		1c. blue-green (6.98)	16·00	20
		a. Yellow-green	13·00	20
		b. Imperf horiz (vert pair)	£250	
86	**41**	2c. orange	6·00	6·50
		a. Imperf (pair)	–	£425
87		2c. scarlet (6.98)	18·00	40
		a. Imperf (pair)	£325	£325
		b. Imperf between (pair)	£450	
88	**42**	3c. orange (6.98)	24·00	30
		a. Imperf horiz (vert pair)	£400	
		b. Imperf (pair)	£325	£325
		c. Red-orange/bluish (6.18)	38·00	2·75
89	**43**	4c. violet (21.10.01)	28·00	5·50
		a. Imperf (pair)	£550	
90	**44**	5c. blue (6.99)	45·00	3·00
83/90 *Set of* 8			£130	19·00

No. 88*c* was an emergency war-time printing made by the American Bank Note Co from the old plate, pending receipt of the then current 3c. from England.

The imperforate errors of this issue are found used, but only as philatelic "by favour" items. It is possible that No. 86a only exists in this condition.

45 Map of Newfoundland

(Recess A.B.N. Co)

1908 (31 Aug). P 12.

94	**45**	2c. lake	27·00	1·00

46 King James I

47 Arms of Colonisation Co

48 John Guy

49 *Endeavour* (immigrant ship), 1610

50 Cupids

51 Sir Francis Bacon

52 View of Mosquito

53 Logging Camp, Red Indian Lake

54 Paper Mills, Grand Falls

55 King Edward VII

56 King George V

6c. (A) "Z" in "COLONIZATION" reversed. (B) "Z" correct.

(Litho Whitehead, Morris & Co Ltd)

1910 (15 Aug).

(a) P 12.

95	**46**	1c. green	13·00	2·50
		a. "NFWFOUNDLAND" (Right pane R. 5/1)	75·00	£100
		b. "JAMRS" (Right pane R. 5/2)	75·00	£100
		c. Imperf between (horiz pair)	£325	£350
96	**47**	2c. rose-carmine	19·00	2·00
97	**48**	3c. olive	7·00	19·00
98	**49**	4c. violet	18·00	18·00
99	**50**	5c. bright blue	35·00	11·00
100	**51**	6c. claret (A)	45·00	£160
100*a*		6c. claret (B)	26·00	95·00
101	**52**	8c. bistre-brown	50·00	£110
102	**53**	9c. olive-green	50·00	90·00
103	**54**	10c. purple-slate	55·00	£120
104	**55**	12c. pale red-brown	55·00	90·00
		a. Imperf (pair)	£325	
105	**56**	15c. black	65·00	£120
95/105 *Set of* 11			£350	£600

(b) P 12×14.

106	**46**	1c. green	5·00	10·00
		a. "NFWFOUNDLAND"	55·00	£150
		b. "JAMRS"	55·00	£150
		c. Imperf between (horiz pair)	£550	£600
107	**47**	2c. rose-carmine	5·50	40
		a. Imperf between (horiz pair)	£600	
108	**50**	5c. bright blue (P 14×12)	8·00	2·75

(c) P 12×11.

109	**46**	1c. green	2·50	30
		a. Imperf between (horiz pair)	£300	
		b. Imperf between (vert pair)	£350	
		c. "NFWFOUNDLAND"	32·00	55·00
		e. "JAMRS"	32·00	55·00

(d) P 12×11½.

110	**47**	2c. rose-carmine	£325	£200

(Dies eng Macdonald & Sons. Recess A. Alexander & Sons, Ltd)

1911 (7 Feb). *As T* **51** *to* **56**, *but recess printed.* P 14.

111		6c. claret (B)	18·00	50·00
112		8c. yellow-brown	50·00	75·00
		a. Imperf between (horiz pair)	£900	
		b. Imperf (pair)	£300	
113		9c. sage-green	50·00	£130
		a. Imperf between (horiz pair)	£900	
114		10c. purple-black	90·00	£140
		a. Imperf between (horiz pair)	£900	
		b. Imperf (pair)	£250	
115		12c. red-brown	65·00	70·00
116		15c. slate-green	65·00	£130
111/16 *Set of* 6			£300	£550

The 9c. and 15c. exist with papermaker's watermark "E. TOWGOOD FINE".

57 Queen Mary

58 King George V

59 Duke of Windsor when Prince of Wales

60 King George VI when Prince Albert

61 Princess Mary, the Princess Royal

62 Prince Henry, Duke of Gloucester

63 Prince George, Duke of Kent

64 Prince John

65 Queen Alexandra

66 Duke of Connaught

67 Seal of Newfoundland

(1c. to 5c., 10c. eng and recess D.L.R.; others eng Macdonald & Co, recess A. Alexander & Sons)

1911 (19 June)–**16**. *Coronation.* P 13½×14 (comb) (1c. to 5c., 10c.) or 14 (line) (others).

117	**57**	1c. yellow-green	10·00	30
		a. Blue-green (1915)	17·00	30
118	**58**	2c. carmine	7·50	20
		a. Rose-red (blurred impression). Perf 14 (1916)	14·00	65
119	**59**	3c. red-brown	21·00	40·00
120	**60**	4c. purple	19·00	29·00
121	**61**	5c. ultramarine	7·00	1·50
122	**62**	6c. slate-grey	13·00	25·00
123	**63**	8c. aniline blue	60·00	80·00
		a. Greenish blue	80·00	£100
124	**64**	9c. violet-blue	23·00	48·00
125	**65**	10c. deep green	35·00	42·00
126	**66**	12c. plum	26·00	48·00
127	**67**	15c. lake	24·00	48·00
117/27 *Set of* 11			£225	£325

The 2c. rose-red, No. 118*a* is a poor war-time printing by Alexander & Sons.

Although No. 123 has a typical aniline appearance it is believed that the shade results from the thinning of non-aniline ink.

68 Caribou

FIRST TRANS-ATLANTIC AIR POST April, 1919.

(69)

(Des J. H. Noonan. Recess D.L.R.)

1919 (2 Jan). *Newfoundland Contingent, 1914–1918.* P 14.

130	**68**	1c. green *(a) (b)*	3·75	20
131		2c. scarlet *(a) (b)*	3·75	85
		a. Carmine-red (b)	17·00	45
132		3c. brown *(a) (b)*	8·00	20
		a. Red-brown (b)	12·00	50
133		4c. mauve *(a)*	10·00	80
		a. Purple (b)	17·00	30
134		5c. ultramarine *(a) (b)*	11·00	1·25
135		6c. slate-grey *(a)*	12·00	50·00
136		8c. bright magenta *(a)*	12·00	55·00
137		10c. deep grey-green *(a)*	7·00	6·00
138		12c. orange *(a)*	19·00	75·00
139		15c. indigo *(a)*	16·00	75·00
		a. Prussian blue (a)	90·00	£150
140		24c. bistre-brown *(a)*	24·00	32·00
141		36c. sage-green *(a)*	16·00	38·00
130/41 *Set of* 12			£130	£300

Each value bears with "Trail of the Caribou" the name of a different action: 1c. Suvla Bay; 3c. Gueudecourt; 4c. Beaumont Hamel; 6c. Monchy; 10c. Steenbeck; 15c. Langemarck; 24c. Cambrai; 36c. Combles; 2c., 5c., 8c., and 12c. inscribed "Royal Naval Reserve-Ubique".

Perforations. Two perforating heads were used: *(a)* comb 14×13.9; *(b)* line 14.1×14.1.

1919 (12 Apr). *Air. No. 132 optd with T* **69**, *by Robinson & Co Ltd, at the offices of the "Daily News".*

142	**68**	3c. brown	£17000	£8500

These stamps franked correspondence carried by Lieut. H. Hawker on his Atlantic flight. 18 were damaged and destroyed, 95 used on letters, 11 given as presentation copies, and the remaining 76 were sold in aid of the Marine Disasters Fund.

1919 (19 April). *Nos. 132 optd in MS.* "Aerial Atlantic Mail. J.A.R.".

142*a*	**68**	3c. brown	£65000	£20000

This provisional was made by W. C. Campbell, the Secretary of the Postal Department, and the initials are those of the Postmaster, J. A. Robinson, for use on correspondence intended to be carried on the abortive Morgan-Raynham Trans-Atlantic flight. The mail was eventually delivered by sea.

In addition to the 25 to 30 used examples, one unused, no gum, copy of No. 142*a* is known.

Single examples of a similar overprint on the 2c., (No. 131) and 5c. (No. 134) are known used on cover, the former with an unoverprinted example of the same value.

Trans-Atlantic AIR POST, 1919. ONE DOLLAR.

(70)

THREE CENTS

(71)

1919 (9 June). *Air. No. 75 surch with T* **70** *by* Royal Gazette, *St. John's.*

143	**31**	$1 on 15c. bright scarlet	£120	£120
		a. No comma after "AIR POST"	£150	£160
		b. As var a and no stop after "1919"	£350	£400
		c. As var a and "A" of "AIR" under "a" of "Trans"	£350	£400

These stamps were issued for use on the mail carried on the first successful flight across the Atlantic by Capt. J. Alcock and Lieut. A. Brown, and on other projected Trans-Atlantic flights (Alcock flown cover, *Price* £3000).

The surcharge was applied in a setting of which 16 were normal, 7 as No. 143a, 1 as No. 143b and 1 as No. 143c.

1920 (Sept). *Nos. 75 and 77/8 surch as T* **71**, *by* Royal Gazette *(2c. with only one bar, at top of stamp).*

A. *Bars of surch 10½ mm apart.* B. *Bars 13½ mm apart.*

144	**33**	2c. on 30c. slate-blue (24 Sept)	4·75	23·00
		a. Surch inverted	£950	£1100
145	**31**	3c. on 15c. bright scarlet (A) (13 Sept)	£250	£250
		a. Surch inverted	£2500	
146		3c. on 15c. bright scarlet (B) (13 Sept)	26·00	24·00
147	**34**	3c. on 35c. red (15 Sept)	12·00	20·00
		a. Surch inverted	£1900	
		b. Lower bar omitted	£170	£225
		c. "THREE" omitted	£1200	

Our prices for Nos. 147b and 147c are for stamps with lower bar or "THREE" entirely missing. The bar may be found in all stages of incompleteness and stamps showing broken bar are not of much value.

On the other hand, stamps showing either only the top or bottom of the letters "THREE" are scarce, though not as rare as No. 147c.

The 6c. T **27** surcharged "THREE CENTS", in red or black, is an essay (*Price* £650). The 2c. on 30c. with red surcharge is a colour trial (*Price* £850).

AIR MAIL to Halifax, N.S. 1921.

(72)

1921 (16 Nov). *Air. No. 78 optd with T* **72** *by* Royal Gazette.

I. *2¾ mm between "AIR" and "MAIL".*

148	**34**	35c. red	£130	90·00
		a. No stop after "1921"	£110	80·00
		b. No stop and first "1" of "1921" below "f" of "Halifax"	£300	£200
		c. As No. 148, inverted	£5500	
		d. As No. 148a, inverted	£4500	
		e. As No. 148b, inverted	£17000	

II. *1½ mm between "AIR" and "MAIL".*

148*f*	**34**	35c. red	£150	£100
		g. No stop after "1921"	£180	£130
		h. No stop and first "1" of "1921" below "f" of "Halifax"	£300	£200
		i. As No. 148f, inverted	£6500	
		k. As No. 148g, inverted	£10000	
		l. As No. 148h, inverted	£17000	

Type **72** was applied as a setting of 25 which contained ten stamps as No. 148a, seven as No. 148, four as No. 148*f*, two as No. 148g, one as No. 148b and one as No. 148h.

73 Twin Hills, Tor's Cove

74 South-West Arm, Trinity

75 Statue of the Fighting Newfoundlander St. John's

76 Humber River

77 Coast at Trinity

78 Upper Steadies, Humber River

79 Quidi Vidi, near St. John's

80 Caribou crossing lake

81 Humber River Cañon

82 Shell Bird Island

83 Mount Moriah, Bay of Islands

84 Humber River nr. Little Rapids

85 Placentia

86 Topsail Falls

(Recess D.L.R.)

1923 (9 July)–**24**. *T* **73/86**. P 14 (comb or line).

149	**73**	1c. green	2·00	20
150	**74**	2c. carmine	1·00	10
		a. Imperf (pair)	£170	
151	**75**	3c. brown	1·50	10
152	**76**	4c. deep purple	1·00	30
153	**77**	5c. ultramarine	2·75	1·75
154	**78**	6c. slate	7·50	11·00
155	**79**	8c. purple	9·00	3·50
156	**80**	9c. slate-green	18·00	29·00
157	**81**	10c. violet	9·50	4·50
		a. Purple	12·00	2·75
158	**82**	11c. sage-green	3·75	22·00
159	**83**	12c. lake	4·00	13·00
160	**84**	15c. Prussian blue	4·00	26·00
161	**85**	20c. chestnut (28.4.24)	15·00	15·00
162	**86**	24c. sepia (22.4.24)	48·00	75·00
149/62 *Set of* 14			£110	£180

Perforations. Three perforating heads were used: comb 13.8×14 (all values); line 13.7 and 14, and combinations of these two (for all except 6, 8, 9 and 11c.).

Air Mail
DE PINEDO
1927
(**87**)

1927 (18 May). *Air. No. 79 optd with T* **87**, *by Robinson & Co, Ltd.*

163	**35**	60c. black (R.)	£32000	£9000

For the mail carried by De Pinedo to Europe 300 stamps were overprinted, 230 used on correspondence, 66 presented to De Pinedo, Government Officials, etc., and 4 damaged and destroyed. Stamps without overprint were also used.

88 Newfoundland and Labrador

89 S.S. *Caribou*

90 King George V and Queen Mary

91 Duke of Windsor when Prince of Wales

92 Express Train

93 Newfoundland Hotel, St. John's

94 Heart's Content

95 Cabot Tower, St. John's

96 War Memorial, St. John's

97 G.P.O., St. John's

98 Vickers "Vimy" Aircraft

99 Parliament House, St. John's

100 Grand Falls, Labrador

(Recess D.L.R.)

1928 (3 Jan)–**29**. *Publicity issue.* P 14 (1c.) 13½×13 (2, 3, 5, 6, 10, 14, 20c.), 13×13½ (4c.) (all comb), or 14–13½* (line) (others).

164	**88**	1c. deep green	2·75	1·25
165	**89**	2c. carmine	3·50	50
166	**90**	3c. brown	8·00	1·25
		a. Perf 14–13½ (line)	2·25	1·25
167	**91**	4c. mauve	7·50	3·25
		a. Rose-purple (1929)	9·50	8·50
168	**92**	5c. slate-grey	13·00	7·50
		a. Perf 14–13½ (line)	30·00	9·00
169	**93**	6c. ultramarine	8·00	35·00
		a. Perf 14–13½ (line)	18·00	30·00
170	**94**	8c. red-brown	4·00	38·00
171	**95**	9c. deep green	2·00	20·00
172	**96**	10c. deep violet	18·00	21·00
		a. Perf 14–13½ (line)	6·00	23·00
173	**97**	12c. carmine-lake	2·00	23·00
174	**95**	14c. brown-purple (8.28)	19·00	12·00
		a. Perf 14–13½ (line)	10·00	8·50
175	**98**	15c. deep blue	6·00	35·00
176	**99**	20c. grey-black	20·00	18·00
		a. Perf 14–13½ (line)	4·00	7·50
177	**97**	28c. deep green (12.28)	28·00	60·00
178	**100**	30c. sepia	6·00	17·00
164/78 (*cheapest*) *Set of* 15			95·00	£250

*Exact gauges for the various perforations are: 14 comb = 14×13.9; 13½×13 comb = 13.5×12.75; 14–13½ line = 14–13.75.

See also Nos. 179/87 and 198/208.

D 1c. P

D 2c. P

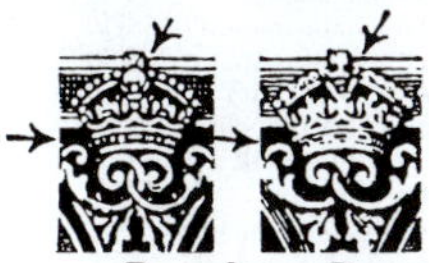

D 3c. P

D 4c. P

D 5c. P

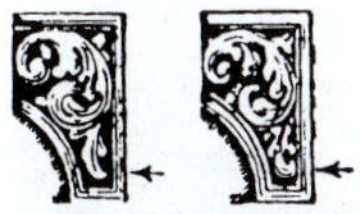

D 6c. P

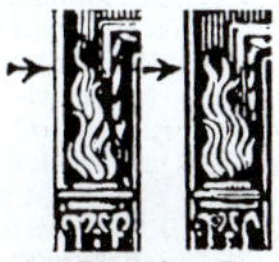

D 10c. P

D 15c. P

D 20c. P

D. De La Rue printing

P. Perkins, Bacon printing

1929 (10 Aug)–**31**. *Perkins, Bacon printing. Former types re-engraved.* No wmk. P 14 (comb) (1c.), 13½ (comb) (2, 6c.), 14–13½ (line) (20c.) or 13½×14 (comb) (others)*.

179	**88**	1c. green (26.9.29)	3·75	75
		a. Perf 14–13½ (line)	3·50	30
		b. Imperf between (vert pair)	£180	
		c. Imperf (pair)	£150	
180	**89**	2c. scarlet	1·75	40
		a. Imperf (pair)	£160	
		b. Perf 14–13½ (line)	3·75	1·00
181	**90**	3c. red-brown	1·00	20
		a. Imperf (pair)	£140	
182	**91**	4c. reddish purple (26.8.29)	2·75	80
		a. Imperf (pair)	£160	
183	**92**	5c. deep grey-green (14.9.29)	7·00	4·25
184	**93**	6c. ultramarine (8.11.29)	9·00	18·00
		a. Perf 14–13½ (line)	2·25	21·00
185	**96**	10c. violet (5.10.29)	4·50	4·00
186	**98**	15c. blue (1.30)	17·00	85·00
187	**99**	20c. black (1.1.31)	55·00	60·00
179/87 *Set of* 9			85·00	£150

*Exact gauges for the various perforations are: 14 comb = 14×13.9; 13½ comb = 13.6×13.5; 14–13½ line = 14–13.75; 13½ ×14 comb = 13.6×13.8.

THREE
CENTS
(**101**)

Trans-Atlantic
AIR MAIL
By B. M.
"Columbia"
September
1930
Fifty Cents
(**102**)

(Surch by Messrs D. R. Thistle, St. John's)

1929 (23 Aug). *No. 154 surch with T* **101**.

188		3c. on 6c. slate (R.)	1·25	7·00
		a. Surch inverted	£800	£1200
		b. Surch in black	£900	

The issued surcharge shows 3 mm. space between "CENTS" and the bar. The black surcharge also exists with 5 mm. space, from a trial setting (*Price*, £800).

1930 (25 Sept). *Air. No.* 141 *surch with T* **102** *by Messrs D. R. Thistle.*

191	**68**	50c. on 36c. sage-green	£5500	£4750

103 Aeroplane and Dog-team

104 Vickers-Vimy Biplane and early Sailing Packet

105 Routes of historic Transatlantic Flights

106

(Des A. B. Perlin. Recess P.B.)

1931. *Air.* P 14.

(*a*) Without wmk (2.1.31).

192	**103**	15c. chocolate	9·00	17·00
		a. Imperf between (horiz pair)	£900	
		b. Imperf between (vert pair)	£900	
		c. Imperf (pair)	£550	
193	**104**	50c. green	32·00	55·00
		a. Imperf between (horiz pair)	£950	£1000
		b. Imperf between (vert pair)	£1300	
		c. Imperf (pair)	£750	
194	**105**	$1 deep blue	50·00	95·00
		a. Imperf between (horiz pair)	£1000	
		b. Imperf between (vert pair)	£1000	
		c. Imperf (pair)	£750	
192/4 *Set of* 3			80·00	£150

(*b*) Wmk W **106**, (sideways*) (13.3.31).

195	**103**	15c. chocolate	9·00	24·00
		a. Pair, with and without wmk	35·00	
		b. Imperf between (horiz pair)	£850	
		c. Imperf between (vert pair)	£900	
		ca. Ditto, one without wmk (vert pair)	£1400	
		d. Imperf (pair)	£550	
		e. Wmk Cross (pair)	£140	
196	**104**	50c. green	32·00	65·00
		a. Imperf between (horiz pair)	£950	
		b. Imperf between (vert pair)	£1200	
		c. Imperf (pair)		
		d. Pair, with and without wmk	£400	
		w. Wmk top of shield to right	75·00	
197	**105**	$1 deep blue	80·00	£140
		a. Imperf between (horiz pair)	£1000	
		b. Imperf between (vert pair)	£950	
		c. Imperf horiz (vert pair)	£800	
		d. Pair, with and without wmk	£650	
		e. Imperf (pair)	£700	
195/7 *Set of* 3			£110	£200

The normal sideways wmk on this issue shows the top of the shield to right on the 15c., but top of the shield to left on the 50c. and $1.

"WITH AND WITHOUT WMK" PAIRS listed in the issues from No. 195a onwards must have one stamp *completely* without any trace of watermark.

1931 (25 March–July). *Perkins, Bacon printing (re-engraved types).* W **106** (sideways on 1c., 4c., 30c.). P 13½ (1c.) or 13½×14 (others), both comb*.

198	**88**	1c. green (7.31)	9·50	3·00
		a. Imperf between (horiz pair)	£600	
199	**89**	2c. scarlet (7.31)	6·00	5·50
		w. Wmk inverted	50·00	
200	**90**	3c. red-brown (7.31)	2·50	3·50
		w. Wmk inverted	50·00	
201	**91**	4c. reddish purple (7.31)	2·00	1·25
202	**92**	5c. deep grey-green (7.31)	7·00	17·00
203	**93**	6c. ultramarine	7·00	29·00
		w. Wmk inverted	60·00	
204	**94**	8c. chestnut (1.4.31)	32·00	42·00
		w. Wmk inverted	65·00	
205	**96**	10c. violet (1.4.31)	18·00	19·00
206	**98**	15c. blue (1.7.31)	21·00	70·00
207	**99**	20c. black (1.7.31)	60·00	26·00
208	**100**	30c. sepia (1.7.31)	28·00	50·00
198/208 *Set of* 11			£170	£250

*Exact gauges for the two perforations are: 13½ = 13.6×13.5; 13½×14 = 13.6×13.8.

107 Atlantic Cod

108 King George V

109 Queen Mary

110 Duke of Windsor when Prince of Wales

111 Caribou

112 Queen Elizabeth II when Princess

113 Atlantic Salmon

114 Newfoundland Dog

115 Harp Seal

116 Cape Race

117 Sealing Fleet

118 Fishing Fleet

(Recess P.B.)

1932 (2 Jan). W **106** (sideways* on vert designs). P 13½ (comb).

209	**107**	1c. green	3·25	30
		a. Imperf (pair)	£150	
		b. Perf 13 (line)	21·00	35·00
		ba. Imperf between (vert pair)	£130	
		w. Wmk top of shield to right	50·00	
210	**108**	2c. carmine	1·50	20
		a. Imperf (pair)	£170	
		c. Perf 13 (line)	15·00	25·00
		w. Wmk top of shield to right	50·00	
211	**109**	3c. orange-brown	1·50	20
		a. Imperf (pair)	95·00	
		c. Perf 13 (line)	23·00	35·00
		ca. Imperf between (vert pair)	£250	
		d. Perf 14 (line). Small holes	25·00	29·00
		w. Wmk top of shield to right	50·00	
212	**110**	4c. bright violet	8·50	2·25
		w. Wmk top of shield to right		
213	**111**	5c. maroon	7·50	3·25
		a. Imperf (pair)	£160	
		w. Wmk top of shield to right		
214	**112**	6c. light blue	4·00	14·00
215	**113**	10c. black-brown	70	65
		a. Imperf (pair)	70·00	
		w. Wmk inverted	10·00	
216	**114**	14c. black	4·25	5·50
		a. Imperf (pair)	£160	
217	**115**	15c. claret	1·25	2·00
		a. Imperf (pair)	£180	
		b. Perf 14 (line)	8·00	10·00
218	**116**	20c. green	1·00	1·00
		a. Imperf (pair)	£150	
		b. Perf 14 (line)	£110	£110
		w. Wmk inverted	27·00	
219	**117**	25c. slate	2·00	2·25
		a. Imperf (pair)	£170	
		b. Perf 14 (line)	50·00	70·00
		ba. Imperf between (vert pair)	£425	
220	**118**	30c. ultramarine	40·00	35·00
		a. Imperf (pair)	£450	
		b. Imperf between (vert pair)	£1100	
		c. Perf 14 (line)	£375	
209/20 *Set of* 12			65·00	60·00

*The normal sideways watermark shows the top of the shield to left, *as seen from the back of the stamp*.

Nos. 209b, 210c and 211c were only issued in stamp booklets.

For similar stamps in different perforations see Nos. 222/8*c* and 276/89.

TRANS-ATLANTIC
WEST TO EAST
Per Dornier DO-X
May, 1932.
One Dollar and Fifty Cents

(**119**)

1932 (19 May). *Air. No. 197 surch as T* **119**, *by Messrs. D. R. Thistle.* P 14.

221	**105**	$1.50 on $1 deep blue (R.)	£225	£225
		a. Surch inverted	£16000	

120 Queen Mother, when Duchess of York

121 Corner Brook Paper Mills

122 Loading Iron Ore, Bell Island

(Recess P.B.)

1932 (15 Aug)–**38**. W **106** (sideways* on vert designs). P 13½ (comb).

222	**107**	1c. grey	3·25	10
		a. Imperf (pair)	45·00	
		c. Perf 14 (line)	7·00	15·00
		d. Perf 14 (line). Small holes	15·00	32·00
		e. Pair, with and without wmk	65·00	
		w. Wmk top of shield to right	55·00	
223	**108**	2c. green	2·50	10
		a. Imperf (pair)	35·00	
		c. Perf 14 (line)	8·00	15·00
		ca. Imperf between (horiz pair)	£275	
		d. Perf 14 (line). Small holes	19·00	35·00
		e. Pair, with and without wmk	65·00	
		w. Wmk top of shield to right	42·00	
224	**110**	4c. carmine (21.7.34)	5·50	40
		a. Imperf (pair)	55·00	
		b. Perf 14 (line)	6·50	8·00
		ba. Imperf between (horiz pair)	£180	
		bb. Imperf between (vert pair)	£130	
		c. Pair, with and without wmk	70·00	
		w. Wmk top of shield to right	60·00	
225	**111**	5c. violet (Die I)	3·50	1·75
		a. Imperf (pair)	65·00	
		b. Perf 14 (line). Small holes	25·00	32·00
		c. Die II	1·00	30
		ca. Imperf (pair)	65·00	
		cb. Perf 14 (line)	22·00	28·00
		cbw. Wmk top of shield to right	55·00	
		cc. Imperf between (horiz pair)	£250	
		cd. Pair, with and without wmk	£150	
226	**120**	7c. red-brown	3·00	3·75
		b. Perf 14 (line)	£170	
		ba. Imperf between (horiz pair)	£550	
		c. Imperf (pair)	£180	
		w. Wmk top of shield to right		
227	**121**	8c. brownish red	3·75	2·00
		a. Imperf (pair)	£100	
		w. Wmk inverted		
228	**122**	24c. bright blue	1·00	3·25
		a. Imperf (pair)	£325	
		b. Doubly printed	£1200	
		w. Wmk inverted	38·00	
228*c*	**118**	48c. red-brown (1.1.38)	11·00	10·00
		ca. Imperf (pair)	£110	
222/8*c* *Set of* 8			27·00	18·00

*The normal sideways watermark shows the top of the shield to left, *as seen from the back of the stamp*.

No. 223. Two dies exist of the 2c. Die I was used for No. 210 and both dies for No. 223. The differences, though numerous, are very slight.

No. 225. There are also two dies of the 5c., Die I only being used for No. 213 and both dies for the violet stamp. In Die II the antler pointing to the "T" of "POSTAGE" is taller than the one pointing to the "S" and the individual hairs on the underside of the caribou's tail are distinct.

For similar stamps in a slightly larger size and perforated 12½ or 13½ (5c.) see Nos. 276/89.

L. & S. Post.

(**123**) "L.&S."—Land and Sea

1933 (9 Feb). *No. 195 optd with T* **123** *for ordinary postal use, by Messrs D. R. Thistle.* W **106** (sideways top of shield to right from back). P 14.

229	**103**	15c. chocolate	4·25	15·00
		a. Pair, one without wmk	25·00	
		b. Opt reading up	£3500	
		c. Vertical pair, one without opt	£6000	

124 Put to Flight

125 Land of Heart's Delight

126 Spotting the Herd

127 News from Home

128 Labrador

(Des J. Scott. Recess P.B.)

1933 (9 June). *Air. T* **124/8** *and similar horiz designs.* W **106** (sideways*). P 14 (5c., 30c., 75c.) or 11½ (10c., 60c.).

230	5c. red-brown	20·00	22·00
	a. Imperf (pair)	£170	
	b. Imperf between (horiz pair)	£1000	
	c. Imperf between (vert pair)	£1000	
231	10c. orange-yellow	16·00	35·00
	a. Imperf (pair)	£140	
232	30c. light blue	32·00	48·00
	a. Imperf (pair)	£450	
233	60c. green	50·00	£110
	a. Imperf (pair)	£500	
234	75c. yellow-brown	50·00	£110
	a. Imperf (pair)	£450	
	b. Imperf between (horiz or vert pair)	£4000	
230/4 *Set of* 5		£150	£300

*The normal sideways watermark shows the top of the shield to right, *as seen from the back of the stamp*.

1933
GEN. BALBO
FLIGHT.
$4.50

(**129**)

(Surch by Robinson & Co, St. John's)

1933 (24 July). *Air. Balbo Transatlantic Mass Formation Flight. No. 234 surch with T* **129**. W **106**. P 14.

235	$4.50 on 75c. yellow-brown	£275	£325
	a. Surch inverted	£70000	
	b. Surch on 10c. (No. 231)	£70000	
	w. Wmk top of shield to left		

No. 235a. When this error was discovered the stamps were ordered to be officially destroyed but four copies which had been torn were recovered and skilfully repaired. In addition, four undamaged examples exist and the price quoted is for one of these (*Price for repaired example*, £20000, *unused*).

130 Sir Humphrey Gilbert

131 Compton Castle, Devon

132 Gilbert Coat of Arms

133 Eton College

134 Anchor token

135 Gilbert commissioned by Elizabeth I

136 Fleet leaving Plymouth, 1583

137 Arrival at St. John's

138 Annexation, 5th August, 1583

139 Royal Arms

140 Gilbert in the *Squirrel*

141 Map of Newfoundland, 1626

142 Queen Elizabeth

143 Gilbert's statue at Truro

(Recess P.B.)

1933 (3 Aug). *350th Anniv of the Annexation by Sir Humphrey Gilbert. T* **130/43**. W **106** (sideways* on vert designs). P 13½ (comb†).

236	**130**	1c. slate	1·00	1·50
		a. Imperf (pair)	50·00	
237	**131**	2c. green	2·00	70
		a. Imperf (pair)	50·00	
		b. Doubly printed	£400	
238	**132**	3c. chestnut	2·50	1·25
239	**133**	4c. carmine	1·00	50
		a. Imperf (pair)	50·00	
240	**134**	5c. violet	2·00	80
241	**135**	7c. greenish blue	15·00	17·00
		a. Perf 14 (line)	15·00	48·00
242	**136**	8c. vermilion	8·00	17·00
		a. Brownish red	£400	
		b. Bisected (4c.) (on cover)	†	£425
243	**137**	9c. ultramarine	7·00	18·00
		a. Imperf (pair)	£250	
		b. Perf 14 (line)	75·00	90·00
244	**138**	10c. brown-lake	4·00	12·00
		a. Imperf (pair)	£275	
		b. Perf 14 (line)	90·00	£100
245	**139**	14c. grey-black	19·00	30·00
		a. Perf 14 (line)	24·00	55·00
246	**140**	15c. claret	17·00	32·00
		w. Wmk top of shield to right	7·50	26·00
247	**141**	20c. grey-green	15·00	19·00
		a. Perf 14 (line)	25·00	45·00
		w. Wmk inverted	60·00	
248	**142**	24c. maroon	19·00	25·00
		a. Imperf (pair)	£110	
		b. Perf 14 (line)	32·00	48·00
		w. Wmk top of shield to right	40·00	
249	**143**	32c. olive-black	8·50	50·00
		a. Perf 14 (line)	22·00	75·00
		w. Wmk top of shield to right	20·00	60·00
236/49 *Set of* 14			£100	£200

*The normal sideways watermark shows the top of the shield to left, *as seen from the back of the stamp*.

†Exact gauges for the two perforations are: 13½ comb = 13.4; 14 line = 13.8.

1935 (6 May). *Silver Jubilee. As Nos. 91/4 of Antigua, but ptd by B.W.* P 11×12.

250	**133**	4c. rosine	1·00	1·75
251		5c. bright violet	1·25	3·50
252		7c. blue	3·25	7·00
253		24c. olive-green	5·00	16·00
250/3 *Set of* 4			9·50	25·00
250s/3s Perf "Specimen" *Set of* 4			£170	

1937 (12 May). *Coronation Issue. As Nos. 95/7 of Antigua, but name and value uncoloured on coloured background.* P 11×11½.

254	**134**	2c. green	1·00	3·00
255		4c. carmine	1·60	4·00
256		5c. purple	3·00	4·00
254/6 *Set of* 3			5·00	10·00
254s/6s Perf "Specimen" *Set of* 3			£110	

144 Atlantic Cod

145 Map of Newfoundland

146 Caribou

147 Corner Brook Paper Mills

148 Atlantic Salmon

149 Newfoundland Dog

150 Harp Seal

151 Cape Race

152 Bell Island

153 Sealing Fleet

154 The Banks Fishing Fleet

Die I

Die II

No. 258. In Die II the shading of the King's face is heavier and dots have been added down the ridge of the nose. The top frame line is thicker and more uniform.

Fish-hook flaw (R. 1/7 or 3/3)

Re-entry to right of design (inscr oval, tree and value) (R. 4/8)

Extra chimney (R. 6/5)

(Recess P.B.)

1937 (12 May). *Additional Coronation Issue. T* **144/54**. W **106**. P 14 (line)*.

257	**144**	1c. grey	3·00	30
		a. Pair, with and without wmk	25·00	
		b. Fish-hook flaw	27·00	
		cw. Wmk inverted	50·00	
		d. Perf 13½ (line)	4·00	75
		da. Pair, with and without wmk	32·00	
		db. Fish-hook flaw	38·00	
		e. Perf 13 (comb)	29·00	55·00
		ea. Pair, with and without wmk		
		eb. Fish-hook flaw	£170	
258	**145**	3c. orange-brown (I)	19·00	4·75
		a. Pair, with and without wmk	90·00	
		b. Imperf between (horiz pair)		
		c. Perf 13½ (line)	17·00	6·50
		ca. Pair, with and without wmk		
		cb. Imperf between (vert pair)	£450	
		d. Perf 13 (comb)	8·50	4·00
		e. Die II (P 14, *line*)	9·00	5·50
		ea. Pair, with and without wmk	£140	
		ec. Perf 13½ (line)	9·00	5·50
		eca. Pair, with and without wmk	£160	
		ecb. Imperf between (vert pair)	£550	
		ed. Perf 13 (comb)	9·00	4·00
		eda. Pair, with and without wmk	£140	
259	**146**	7c. bright ultramarine	2·75	1·25
		a. Pair, with and without wmk		
		b. Re-entry at right	75·00	75·00
		c. Perf 13½ (line)	3·00	1·75
		ca. Pair, with and without wmk		
		cb. Re-entry at right	80·00	
		d. Perf 13 (comb)	£450	£550
		db. Re-entry at right	£1900	
260	**147**	8c. scarlet	3·00	4·00
		a. Pair, with and without wmk	80·00	
		b. Imperf between (horiz pair)	£900	
		c. Imperf between (vert pair)	£900	
		d. Imperf (pair)	£425	
		e. Perf 13½ (line)	3·75	5·50
		ea. Pair, with and without wmk	90·00	
		eb. Imperf between (vert pair)		
		f. Perf 13 (comb)	9·00	16·00
261	**148**	10c. blackish brown	6·00	9·00
		a. Pair, with and without wmk	£110	
		b. Perf 13½ (line)	6·00	11·00
		ba. Pair, with and without wmk	£100	
		c. Perf 13 (comb)	3·25	15·00
		cw. Wmk inverted	75·00	
262	**149**	14c. black	1·60	3·50
		a. Pair, with and without wmk	90·00	
		b. Perf 13½ (line)	1·75	4·50
		ba. Pair, with and without wmk	90·00	
		c. Perf 13 (comb)	£17000	£10000
263	**150**	15c. claret	16·00	7·00
		a. Pair, with and without wmk	£100	
		bw. Wmk inverted	95·00	
		c. Perf 13½ (line)	17·00	7·50
		ca. Pair, with and without wmk	£100	
		cb. Imperf between (vert pair)	£850	
		d. Perf 13 (comb)	26·00	35·00
		da. Pair, with and without wmk	£170	
264	**151**	20c. green	5·00	13·00
		a. Pair, with and without wmk		
		c. Extra chimney	85·00	
		dw. Wmk inverted	£110	
		e. Perf 13½ (line)	4·00	15·00
		ea. Pair, with and without wmk	£170	
		eb. Imperf between (vert pair)	£1200	
		ec. Extra chimney	75·00	£100
		f. Perf 13 (comb)	3·25	9·50
		fc. Extra chimney	70·00	
265	**152**	24c. light blue	2·50	3·00
		a. Pair, with and without wmk	£190	
		c. Perf 13½ (line)	2·50	3·00
		ca. Pair, with and without wmk	£190	
		cb. Imperf between (vert pair)	£1700	
		d. Perf 13 (comb)	32·00	35·00
266	**153**	25c. slate	3·25	3·25
		a. Pair, with and without wmk	£170	
		b. Perf 13½ (line)	4·00	3·75
		ba. Pair, with and without wmk	£170	
		c. Perf 13 (comb)	35·00	80·00
267	**154**	48c. slate-purple	10·00	6·50
		a. Pair, with and without wmk	£250	
		c. Perf 13½ (line)	10·00	9·00
		ca. Pair, with and without wmk	£250	
		cb. Imperf between (vert pair)	£1800	
		d. Perf 13 (comb)	45·00	95·00
257/67 *Set of* 11			50·00	48·00

The line perforations measure 14.1 (14) or 13.7 (13½). The comb perforation measures 13.3×13.2. One example of the 7c. has been reported perforated 13½×14.

The paper used had the watermarks spaced for smaller format stamps. In consequence, the individual watermarks are out of alignment so that stamps from the second vertical row were sometimes without watermark.

155 King George VI

156 Queen Mother

157 Queen Elizabeth II as princess

158 Queen Mary

(Recess P.B.)

1938 (12 May). *T* **155/8**. W **106** (sideways*). P 13½ (comb).

268	**155**	2c. green	3·25	1·25
		a. Pair, with and without wmk	£180	
		b. Imperf (pair)	£130	
		w. Wmk top of shield to right	85·00	
269	**156**	3c. carmine	1·00	1·00
		a. Perf 14 (line)	£550	£350
		b. Pair, with and without wmk	£275	
		c. Imperf (pair)	£130	
270	**157**	4c. light blue	2·50	60
		a. Pair, with and without wmk	£120	
		b. Imperf (pair)	£100	
		w. Wmk top of shield to right	80·00	
271	**158**	7c. deep ultramarine	1·00	8·00
		a. Pair, with and without wmk	£180	
		b. Imperf (pair)	£170	
268/71 *Set of 4*			7·00	9·75

* The normal sideways watermark shows the top of the shield to left, *as seen from the back of the stamp*.

For similar designs, perf 12½, see Nos. 277/81.

159 King George VI and Queen Elizabeth

(Recess B.W.)

1939 (17 June). *Royal Visit*. No wmk. P 13½.

272	**159**	5c. deep ultramarine	3·25	1·00

2

CENTS

(160)

1939 (20 Nov). *No. 272 surch as T* **160**, *at St. John's*.

273	**159**	2c. on 5c. deep ultramarine (Br.)	2·50	50
274		4c. on 5c. deep ultramarine (C.)	2·00	1·00

161 Grenfell on the *Strathcona* (after painting by Gribble)

162 Memorial University College

(Recess C.B.N.)

1941 (1 Dec). *50th Anniv of Sir Wilfred Grenfell's Labrador Mission*. P 12.

275	**161**	5c. blue	30	1·00

Damaged "A" (R. 5/9)

(Recess Waterlow)

1941–44. W **106** (sideways* on vert designs). P 12½ (line).

276	**107**	1c. grey	20	2·25
277	**155**	2c. green	30	75
		w. Wmk top of shield to right	40·00	
278	**156**	3c. carmine	30	30
		a. Pair, with and without wmk	£100	
		b. Damaged "A"	65·00	35·00
		w. Wmk top of shield to right	40·00	
279	**157**	4c. blue (As No. 270)	2·50	40
		a. Pair, with and without wmk	£190	
		w. Wmk top of shield to right	45·00	
280	**111**	5c. violet (Die I) (P 13½ *comb*)	£150	
		a. Perf 12½ (line) (6.42)	2·75	85
		ab. Pair, with and without wmk	£170	
		ac. Printed double	£550	
		ad. Imperf vert (horiz pair)	£500	
		b. Imperf (pair)	£180	
281	**158**	7c. deep ultramarine (As No. 271)	6·00	20·00
		a. Pair, with and without wmk	£200	
282	**121**	8c. rose-red	2·25	4·00
		a. Pair, with and without wmk	£190	
283	**113**	10c. black-brown	1·75	2·25
284	**114**	14c. black	6·50	8·50
285	**115**	15c. claret	6·00	8·50
286	**116**	20c. green	6·00	8·00
287	**122**	24c. blue	3·25	22·00
		w. Wmk inverted	70·00	
288	**117**	25c. slate	8·50	16·00
289	**118**	48c. red-brown (1944)	4·00	8·00
276/89 *Set of 14*			45·00	90·00

*The normal sideways watermark shows the top of the shield to left, *as seen from the back of the stamp*.

Nos. 276/89 are redrawn versions of previous designs with slightly larger dimensions; the 5c. for example, measures 21 mm in width as opposed to the 20.4 mm of the Perkins Bacon printings.

No. 280. For Die I see note relating to No. 225.

(Recess C.B.N.)

1943 (1 Jan). P 12.

290	**162**	30c. carmine	1·50	3·75

163 St. John's

TWO

CENTS

(164)

(Recess C.B.N.)

1943 (1 June). *Air*. P 12.

291	**163**	7c. ultramarine	50	1·00

1946 (21 Mar). *No. 290 surch locally with T* **164**.

292	**162**	2c. on 30c. carmine	30	1·25

165 Queen Elizabeth II when Princess

166 Cabot off Cape Bonavista

(Recess Waterlow)

1947 (21 Apr). *Princess Elizabeth's 21st Birthday*. W **106** (sideways). P 12½.

293	**165**	4c. light blue	40	1·00
		a. Imperf vert (horiz pair)	£425	

(Recess Waterlow)

1947 (24 June). *450th Anniv of Cabot's Discovery of Newfoundland*. W **106** (sideways). P 12½.

294	**166**	5c. mauve	50	1·00

STAMP BOOKLETS

1926. *Black on pink cover with Ayre and Sons advertisement on front. Stapled.*

SB1	40c. booklet containing eight 1c. and sixteen 2c. (Nos. 149/50) in blocks of 8	£1600

B 1

1932 (2 Jan). *Black on buff cover as Type* B **1**. *Stapled.*

SB2	40c. booklet containing four 1c., twelve 2c. and four 3c. (Nos. 209b, 210c, 211c) in blocks of 4	£450
	a. Contents as No. SB2, but containing Nos. 209b, 210 and 211c	£550
	b. Contents as No. SB2, but containing Nos. 222d, 223d and 211d	£500

B 2

1932. *Black on cream cover as Type* B **2**. *Stapled.*

SB3	40c. booklet containing four 1c., twelve 2c. and four 3c. (Nos. 222, 223, 211) in blocks of 4	£450

POSTAGE DUE STAMPS

D 1

"POSTAGE LUE" (R.3/3 and 3/8)

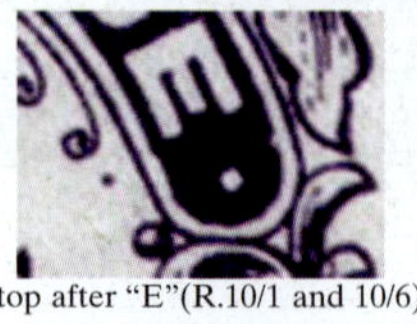

Stop after "E"(R.10/1 and 10/6)

(Litho John Dickinson & Co, Ltd)

1939 (1 May)–**49**. P 10.

D1	D **1**	1c. green	2·25	14·00
		a. Perf 11 (1949)	3·25	16·00
D2		2c. vermilion	13·00	7·50
		a. Perf 11×9 (1946)	14·00	22·00
D3		3c. ultramarine	5·00	27·00
		a. Perf 11×9 (1949)	13·00	48·00
		b. Perf 9	£850	
D4		4c. orange	9·00	24·00
		a. Perf 11×9 (May 1948)	12·00	60·00
D5		5c. brown	5·50	30·00
D6		10c. violet	8·00	23·00
		a. Perf 11 (W **106**) (1949)	18·00	85·00
		ab. Ditto. Imperf between (vert pair)	£1000	
		ac. "POSTAGE LUE"	£140	£375
		ad. Stop after "E"	£100	£250
D1/6 *Set of 6*			38·00	£110

Newfoundland joined the Dominion of Canada on 31 March 1949.

NOVA SCOTIA

Organised postal services in Nova Scotia date from April 1754 when the first of a series of Deputy Postmasters was appointed, under the authority of the British G.P.O. This arrangement continued until 6 July 1851 when the colony assumed responsibility for its postal affairs.

For illustrations of the handstamp types see BRITISH POST OFFICES ABROAD notes, following GREAT BRITAIN.

AMHERST

CROWNED-CIRCLE HANDSTAMPS

CC1 CC **1** AMHERST. N.S.(R) (25.2.1845) *Price on cover* £1000

ST. MARGARETS BAY

CROWNED-CIRCLE HANDSTAMPS

CC2 CC **1** ST. MARGARETS BAY. N.S.(R) (30.6.1845) *Price on cover* £9500

Nos. CC1/2 were later used during temporary shortages of stamps, struck in red or black.

PRICES FOR STAMPS ON COVER

No. 1	*from* × 5
Nos. 2/4	*from* × 2
Nos. 5/8	*from* × 4
Nos. 9/10	*from* × 10
Nos. 11/13	*from* × 2
Nos. 14/15	—
No. 16	*from* × 4
Nos. 17/19	*from* × 10
Nos. 20/5	*from* × 2
No. 26	*from* × 50
Nos. 27/8	*from* × 4
No. 29	*from* × 10

1

2

Crown and Heraldic Flowers of United Kingdom and Mayflower of Nova Scotia.

(Recess P.B.)

1851 (1 Sept)–**60**. *Bluish paper*. Imperf.

1	**1**	1d. red-brown (12.5.53)	£2250	£400
		a. Bisected (½d.) (on cover) (1857)	†	£50000
2	**2**	3d. deep blue	£1200	£160
		a. Bisected (1½d.) (on cover)	†	£2500
3		3d. bright blue	£1000	£120
		a. Bisected (1½d.) (on cover)	†	£2500
4		3d. pale blue (1857)	£850	£140
		a. Bisected (1½d.) (on cover)	†	£2500
5		6d. yellow-green	£4750	£475
		a. Bisected (3d.) (on cover)	†	£3250
		b. Quartered (1½d.) (on cover) (1860)	†	£60000
6		6d. deep green (1857)	£10000	£750
		a. Bisected (3d.) (on cover)	†	£5000
7		1s. cold violet	£25000	£5000
7*c*		1s. deep purple (1851)	£17000	£3750
		d. Watermarked	£22000	£5000
8		1s. purple (1857)	£16000	£2750
		a. Bisected (6d.) (on cover) (1860)	†	£38000
		b. Quartered (3d.) (on cover) (1858)	†	£80000

The watermark on No. 7d consists of the whole or part of a letter from the name "T. H. SAUNDERS" (the papermakers).

The stamps formerly catalogued on almost white paper are probably some from which the bluish paper has been discharged.

Reprints of all four values were made in 1890 on thin, hard, white paper. The 1d. is brown, the 3d. blue, the 6d. deep green, and the 1s. violet-black.

The 3d. bisects, which were authorised on 19 October 1854, are usually found used to make up the 7½d. rate.

(New Currency. 100 cents = 1 dollar)

3

4

5

(Recess American Bank Note Co, New York)

1863. P 12.

(a) Yellowish paper.

9	3	1c. jet black	4·00	16·00
		a. Bisected (½c.) (on cover)	†	£8000
10		1c. grey-black	4·00	16·00
11		2c. grey-purple	11·00	16·00
11*a*		2c. purple	17·00	15·00
12		5c. blue	£450	21·00
13		5c. deep blue	£450	21·00
14	4	8½c. deep green	3·75	45·00
15		8½c. yellow-green	3·50	45·00
16		10c. scarlet	21·00	29·00
17	5	12½c. black	30·00	28·00
17*a*		12½c. greyish black	—	28·00

(b) White paper.

18	3	1c. black	4·00	18·00
		a. Imperf vert (horiz pair)	£160	
19		1c. grey	4·00	18·00
20		2c. dull purple	4·50	14·00
21		2c. purple	4·50	14·00
22		2c. grey-purple	4·50	14·00
		a. Bisected (1c.) (on cover)	†	£3500
23		2c. slate-purple	4·50	12·00
24		5c. blue	£475	25·00
25		5c. deep blue	£475	25·00
26	4	8½c. deep green	20·00	45·00
27		10c. scarlet	8·00	30·00
28		10c. vermilion	4·75	30·00
		a. Bisected (5c.) (on cover)	†	£750
29	5	12½c. black	55·00	32·00

Nova Scotia joined the Dominion of Canada on 1 July 1867.

PRINCE EDWARD ISLAND

Prince Edward Island, previously administered as part of Nova Scotia, became a separate colony in 1769.

PRICES FOR STAMPS ON COVER

Nos. 1/4	*from* × 4
No. 5	—
No. 6	*from* × 5
Nos. 7/8	*from* × 10
Nos. 9/11	*from* × 8
Nos. 12/18	*from* × 6
Nos. 19/20	*from* × 10
Nos. 21/6	*from* × 4
Nos. 27/31	*from* × 8
Nos. 32/3	*from* × 40
Nos. 34/7	*from* × 8
No. 38	*from* × 30
Nos. 39/41	*from* × 20
No. 42	*from* × 50
Nos. 43/7	*from* × 8

1

2

3

4

5

6

Two Dies of 2d.:
Die I. Left-hand frame and circle merge at centre left (all stamps in the sheet of 60 (10×6) except R. 2/5)
Die II. Left-hand frame and circle separate at centre left (R. 2/5). There is also a break in the top frame line.

(Typo Charles Whiting, London)

1861 (1 Jan). *Yellowish toned paper.*

(a) P 9.

1	1	2d. rose (I)	£400	£170
		a. Imperf between (horiz pair)	£7500	
		b. Imperf horiz (vert pair)		
		c. Bisected (1d.) (on cover)	†	£4500
		d. Die II		
2		2d. rose-carmine (I)	£425	£180
		a. Die II		
3	2	3d. blue	£850	£350
		a. Bisected (1½d.) (on cover)	†	£4000
		b. Double print	£2500	
4	3	6d. yellow-green	£1400	£550

(b) Rouletted.

5	1	2d. rose (I)	†	£8500

The 2d. and 3d., perf 9, were authorised to be bisected and used for half their normal value.

1862–69. *Yellowish toned paper.*

(a) P 11 (1862) or 11¼ (1869).

6	4	1d. brown-orange	55·00	85·00
6*a*		2d. rose (I) (1869)	†	£500
7	6	9d. bluish lilac (29.3.62)	£100	80·00
8		9d. dull mauve	£100	80·00

(b) P 11½–12 (1863-69).

9	4	1d. yellow-orange (1863)	40·00	50·00
		a. Bisected (½d.) (on cover)	†	£2750
		b. Imperf between (horiz pair)	£500	
10		1d. orange-buff	42·00	50·00
11		1d. yellow	48·00	50·00
12	1	2d. rose (I) (1863)	17·00	14·00
		a. Imperf vert (horiz pair)		
		b. Bisected (1d.) (on cover)	†	£2250
		c. Die II	95·00	95·00
13		2d. deep rose (I)	18·00	17·00
		a. Die II	£100	£100
14	2	3d. blue (1863)	25·00	25·00
		a. Imperf horiz (vert pair)		
		b. Bisected (1½d.) (on cover)		
15		3d. deep blue	25·00	25·00
16	5	4d. black (1869)	25·00	32·00
		a. Imperf vert (horiz pair)	£350	
		b. Bisected (2d.) (on cover)	†	£2000
		c. Imperf between (horiz strip of 3)	£450	
17	3	6d. yellow-green (15.12.66)	£130	£110
		a. Bisected (3d.) (on cover)	†	£4000
18		6d. blue-green (1868)	£110	£110
19	6	9d. lilac (1863)	90·00	90·00
20		9d. reddish mauve (1863)	90·00	90·00
		a. Imperf vert (horiz pair)	£750	
		b. Bisected (4½d.) (on cover)	†	£3500

A new perforator, gauging exactly 11¼, was introduced in 1869. Apart from No. 6a, it was used in compound with the perf 11½–12 machine.

(c) Perf compound of 11 or 11¼ (1869) and 11½–12.

21	4	1d. yellow-orange	£200	85·00
22	1	2d. rose (I)	£180	70·00
		a. Die II		
23	2	3d. blue	£225	70·00
24	5	4d. black	£325	£250
25	3	6d. yellow-green	£300	£300
26	6	9d. reddish mauve	£350	£300

1870. *Coarse, wove bluish white paper.* P 11½–12.

27	1	2d. rose (I)	14·00	15·00
		a. Die II	90·00	£100
28		2d. rose-pink (I)	8·50	12·00
		a. Die II	70·00	80·00
		b. "TWC" (R. 6/4)	75·00	85·00
		c. Imperf between (horiz pair)	£250	
		d. Imperf horiz (vert pair)	£250	
29	2	3d. pale blue	11·00	16·00
30		3d. blue	11·00	16·00
		a. Imperf between (horiz pair)	£375	
31	5	4d. black	5·50	30·00
		a. Imperf between (horiz pair)	£225	
		b. Bisected (2d.) (on cover)	†	£2000

(New Currency. 100 cents = 1 dollar)

7

(Recess British-American Bank Note Co., Montreal and Ottawa)

1870 (1 June). P 12.

32	7	4½d. (3d. stg), yellow-brown	50·00	60·00
33		4½d. (3d. stg), deep brown	50·00	65·00

8

9

10

11

12

13

(Typo Charles Whiting, London)

1872 (1 Jan).

(a) P 11½–12.

34	8	1c. orange	7·00	23·00
35		1c. yellow-orange	7·00	20·00
36		1c. brown-orange	7·00	23·00
37	10	3c. rose	22·00	30·00
		a. Stop between "PRINCE. EDWARD"	65·00	85·00
		b. Bisected (1½c.) (on cover)		
		c. Imperf horiz (vert pair)	£550	

(b) Perf 12 to 12¼ large holes.

38	9	2c. blue	23·00	45·00
		a. Bisected (1c.) (on cover)	†	£3500
39	11	4c. yellow-green	7·50	25·00
40		4c. deep green	8·00	22·00
		a. Bisected (2c.) (on cover)	†	£3250
41	12	6c. black	5·50	23·00
		a. Bisected (3c.) (on cover)	†	£1800
		b. Imperf between (horiz pair)	£300	
		c. Imperf vert (horiz pair)		
42	13	12c. reddish mauve	6·00	42·00

(c) P 12½–13, smaller holes.

43	8	1c. orange	17·00	
44		1c. brown-orange	7·50	24·00
45	10	3c. rose	21·00	38·00
		a. Stop between "PRINCE. EDWARD"	75·00	£100
45*b*	12	6c. black	—	£250

(d) Perf compound of (a) and (c) 11½–12×12½–13.

46	8	1c. orange	45·00	50·00
47	10	3c. rose	50·00	55·00
		a. Stop between "PRINCE. EDWARD"	£200	£225

Prince Edward Island joined the Dominion of Canada on 1 July 1873.

DOMINION OF CANADA

On 1 July 1867, Canada, Nova Scotia and New Brunswick were united to form the Dominion of Canada.

The provinces of Manitoba (1870), British Columbia (1871), Prince Edward Island (1873), Alberta (1905), Saskatchewan (1905), and Newfoundland (1949) were subsequently added, as were the Northwest Territories (1870) and Yukon Territory (1898).

PRICES FOR STAMPS ON COVER TO 1945

Nos. 46/67	*from* × 2
Nos. 68/71	*from* × 10
Nos. 72/89	*from* × 3
Nos. 90/100	*from* × 2
Nos. 101/2	*from* × 5
Nos. 103/11	*from* × 3
Nos. 115/20	*from* × 6
Nos. 121/49	*from* × 3
Nos. 150/65	*from* × 2
Nos. 166/72	*from* × 3
Nos. 173/87	*from* × 5
Nos. 188/95	*from* × 2
Nos. 196/215	*from* × 3
Nos. 219/224*b*	*from* × 4
Nos. 225/45	*from* × 2
Nos. 246/55	*from* × 8
Nos. 256/310	*from* × 2
No. 312	*from* × 20
No. 313	*from* × 10
Nos. 315/18	*from* × 2
Nos. 319/28	*from* × 3
Nos. 329/40	*from* × 2
Nos. 341/400	*from* × 1
Nos. R1/7*a*	*from* × 5
Nos. R8/9	*from* × 50
Nos. R10/11	*from* × 20
Nos. S1/3	*from* × 8
No. S4	*from* × 6
No. S5	*from* × 5
Nos. S6/11	*from* × 3
Nos. S12/14	*from* × 5
Nos. D1/8	*from* × 4
Nos. D9/13	*from* × 5
Nos. D14/24	*from* × 4

13

14

15

Large types

PRINTERS. Nos. 46/120 were recess-printed by the British American Bank Note Co at Ottawa or Montreal.

1868 (1 Apr)–**90**. *As T* **13/15** *(various frames).*

I. *Ottawa printings.* P 12.

(a) Thin rather transparent crisp paper.

46	13	½c. black (1.4.68)	80·00	75·00
47	14	1c. red-brown (1.4.68)	£450	60·00
48		2c. grass-green (1.4.68)	£500	50·00
49		3c. red-brown (1.4.68)	£950	28·00
50		6c. blackish brown (1.4.68)	£1400	£170
51		12½c. bright blue (1.4.68)	£950	£130
52		15c. deep reddish purple	£1200	£180

In these first printings the impression is generally blurred and the lines of the background are less clearly defined than in later printings.

(b) Medium to stout wove paper (1868–71).

53	13	½c. black	60·00	60·00
54		½c. grey-black	60·00	60·00
		a. Imperf between (pair)		
		b. Watermarked	£15000	£7500
55	14	1c. red-brown	£350	45·00
		a. Laid paper	£13000	£3000
		b. Watermarked (1868)	£2750	£275
56		1c. deep orange (Jan, 1869)	£1000	95·00
56*a*		1c. orange-yellow (May (?), 1869)	£850	80·00
56*b*		1c. pale orange-yellow	£900	90·00
		ba. Imperf		
57		2c. deep green	£450	38·00
57*a*		2c. pale emerald-green (1871)	£550	55·00
		ab. Bisected (1c. with 2c. to make 3c. rate) on cover	†	£4750
		ac. Laid paper	†	£85000

57*d*		2c. bluish green	£475	38·00
		da. Watermarked (1868)	£2500	£250
58		3c. brown-red	£850	18·00
		a. Laid paper	£9500	£475
		b. Watermarked (1868)	£3000	£225
59		6c. blackish brown (*to* chocolate)	£950	50·00
		a. Watermarked (1868)	£5000	£900
59*b*		6c. yellow-brown (1870)	£950	45·00
		ba. Bisected (3c.), on cover	†	£3000
60		12½c. bright blue	£700	48·00
		a. Imperf horiz (vert pair)	†	£15000
		b. Watermarked (1868)	£3000	£275
60*c*		12½c. pale dull blue (milky)	£750	60·00
61		15c. deep reddish purple	£700	60·00
61*a*		15c. pale reddish purple	£600	60·00
		ab. Watermarked (1868)	—	£1400
61*b*		15c. dull violet-grey	£250	30·00
		ba. Watermarked (1868)	£4000	£800
61*c*		15c. dull grey-purple	£325	30·00

The official date of issue was 1 April 1868. Scattered examples of most values can be found used in the second half of March.

The watermark on the stout paper stamps consists of the words "E & G BOTHWELL CLUTHA MILLS," in large double-lined capitals which can be found upright, inverted or reversed. Portions of one or two letters only may be found on these stamps, which occur in the early printings of 1868.

The paper may, in most cases, be easily divided if the stamps are laid face downwards and carefully compared. The thin hard paper is more or less transparent and shows the design through the stamp; the thicker paper is softer to the feel and more opaque.

Of the 2c. laid paper No. 57ac two examples only are known.

II. *Montreal printings. Medium to stout wove paper.*

(*a*) P 11½×12 or 11¾×12.

62	**13**	½c. black (1873)	75·00	75·00
63	**15**	5c. olive-green (28.9.75)	£750	75·00
		a. Perf 12	£3500	£800
64	**14**	15c. dull grey-purple (1874)	£900	£170
65		15c. lilac-grey (3.77)	£1000	£160
		a. Script watermark	£23000	£2250
		b. "BOTHWELL" watermark	†	£750
66		15c. slate	£1000	£300

(*b*) P 12.

67	**14**	15c. clear deep violet (1879)	£3250	£600
68		15c. deep slate (1881)	£160	32·00
69		15c. slaty blue (1887)	£160	32·00
70		15c. slate-purple (*shades*) (7.88–92)	65·00	19·00

No. 63a gauges 12 or above on all four sides.

The watermark on No. 65a is part of "Alex.Pirie & Sons" which appeared as script letters once per sheet in a small batch of the paper used for the 1877 printing. For a description of the sheet watermark on No. 65b, see note after No. 61*c*.

Several used examples of the 12½c. have been reported perforated 11½×12 or 11¾×12.

The last printing of the 15c. slate-purple, No. 70, took place at Ottawa.

III. *Ottawa printings. Thinnish paper of poor quality, often toned grey or yellowish.* P 12.

71	**14**	15c. slate-violet (*shades*) (5.90)	65·00	21·00
		a. Imperf (pair). *Brown-purple*	£1400	

Examples of No. 71 are generally found with yellowish streaky gum.

21 *Small type*

Strand of hair

Straw in hair

1870–88. *As T* **21** *(various frames). Ottawa (1870–73) and Montreal printings.* P 12 (or slightly under).

Papers (*a*) 1870–80. *Medium to stout wove.*
(*b*) 1870–72. *Thin, soft, very white.*
(*c*) 1878–97. *Thinner and poorer quality.*

72	**21**	1c. bright orange (*a, b*) (2.1870–73)	£170	29·00
		a. Thick soft paper (1871)	£475	£130
73		1c. orange-yellow (*a*) (1876–79)	65·00	3·50
74		1c. pale dull yellow (*a*) (1877–79)	45·00	2·75
75		1c. bright yellow (*a, c*) (1878–97)	30·00	1·25
		a. Imperf (pair) (*c*)	£475	
		b. Bisected (½c.) (on *Railway News*)	†	£4250
		c. Printed both sides	£1800	
		d. Strand of hair	£750	£250
76		1c. lemon-yellow (*c*) (1880)	£100	16·00
77		2c. dp green (*a, b*) (1872–73 and 1876–78)	85·00	3·25
78		2c. grass-green (*c*) (1878–88)	50·00	1·50
		a. Imperf (pair)	£500	
		b. Bisected on cover	†	£2500
		c. Stamp doubly printed	†	£5000
79		3c. Indian red (*a*) (1.70)	£950	50·00
		a. Perf 12½ (2.70)	£6500	£600
80		3c. pale rose-red (*a*) (9.70)	£325	10·00
81		3c. deep rose-red (*a, b*) (1870–73)	£350	10·00
		a. Thick soft paper (1.71)	—	£150
82		3c. dull red (*a, c*) (1876–88)	75·00	2·75
83		3c. orange-red (*shades*) (*a, c*) (1876–88)	50·00	2·25
84		3c. rose-carm (*c*) (10.88.–4.89)	£375	12·00
85		5c. olive-green (*a, c*) (2.76–88)	£275	11·00
		a. Straw in hair	£1500	£475
86		6c. yellowish brown (*a, b, c*) (1872–73 and 1876–90)	£225	15·00
		a. Bisected (3c.) on cover	†	£1200
		b. Perf 12×11½ (1873)	†	—
		c. Perf 12×12½	†	£2500
87		10c. pale lilac-magenta (*a*) (1876–?)	£550	50·00
88		10c. deep lilac-magenta (*a, c*) (3.76–88)	£650	60·00
89		10c. lilac-pink (3.88)	£300	38·00

Nos. 75 and 78 were printed in the same shades during the second Ottawa period. Nos. 75a and 78a date from *circa* 1894–95.

There are four variants of the Strand of Hair, with the strand in the same position but varying in length. R. 2/13 and R. 3/16 have been identified. The illustration shows the "Long Strand".

Examples of paper (*a*) can often be found showing traces of ribbing, especially on the 2c. value.

No. 79a was issued in New Brunswick and Nova Scotia.

One used copy of the 10c. perf 12½ has been reported.

1873–79. *Montreal printings. Medium to stout wove paper.* P 11½×12 or 11¾×12.

90	**21**	1c. bright orange	£200	45·00
91		1c. orange-yellow (1873–79)	£170	16·00
92		1c. pale dull yellow (1877–79)	£160	20·00
93		1c. lemon-yellow (1879)	£200	20·00
94		2c. deep green (1873–78)	£250	21·00
95		3c. dull red (1875–79)	£250	21·00
96		3c. orange-red (1873–79)	£250	21·00
97		5c. olive-green (1.2.76–79)	£450	29·00
98		6c. yellowish brown (1873–79)	£450	42·00
99		10c. very pale lilac magenta (1874)	£1200	£250
100		10c. deep lilac-magenta (1876–79)	£900	£200

27

5c. on 6c. re-entry (R. 3/5)

1882–97. *Montreal (to March 1889) and Ottawa printings. Thinnish paper of poor quality.* P 12.

101	**27**	½c. black (7.82–97)	15·00	9·00
102		½c. grey-black	15·00	9·00
		ab. Imperf (pair) (1891–93?)	£600	
		ac. Imperf between (horiz pair)	£900	

1889–97. *Ottawa printings. Thinnish paper of poor quality, often toned grey or yellowish.* P 12.

103	**21**	2c. dull sea-green	50·00	1·50
104		2c. blue-green (7.89–91)	40·00	2·50
105		3c. bright vermilion (4.89–97)	38·00	80
		a. Imperf (pair) (1891–93?)	£450	
106		5c. brownish grey (5.89)	70·00	1·75
		a. Imperf (pair) (1891–93)	£550	
107		6c. deep chestnut (10.90)	38·00	11·00
		a. "5c." re-entry*	£3000	£1400
		b. Imperf (pair) (1891–93?)	£600	
108		6c. pale chestnut	45·00	11·00
109		10c. salmon-pink	£275	£110
110		10c. carmine-pink (4.90)	£225	29·00
		a. Imperf (pair) (1891–93?)	£700	
111		10c. brownish red (1894?)	£225	28·00
		a. Imperf (pair)	£600	

On No. 107a the top portion of the 5c. design cuts across "CANADA POSTAGE", the white circle surrounding the head, and can be seen on the top of the head itself. Lesser re-entries are visible on R. 2/10 and R. 3/1 from another plate.

The 1c. showed no change in the Ottawa printings, so is not included. The 2c. reverted to its previous grass-green shade in 1891.

28

29

(Recess B.A.B.N.)

1893 (17 Feb). P 12.

115	**28**	20c. vermilion	£225	48·00
		a. Imperf (pair)	£1400	
116		50c. blue	£250	35·00
		a. Imperf (*Prussian blue*) (pair).	£1500	

1893 (1 Aug). P 12.

117	**29**	8c. pale bluish grey	£120	6·50
		a. Imperf (pair)	£750	
118		8c. bluish slate	£120	6·50
119		8c. slate-purple	£100	6·50
120		8c. blackish purple	85·00	6·50
		a. Imperf (pair)	£750	

PRINTERS. The following stamps to No. 287 were recess-printed by the American Bank Note Co, Ottawa, which in 1923 became the Canadian Bank Note Co.

30

(Des L. Pereira and F. Brownell)

1897 (19 June). *Jubilee issue.* P 12.

121	**30**	½c. black	50·00	50·00
122		1c. orange	10·00	4·50
123		1c. orange-yellow	10·00	4·50
		a. Bisected (½c.) (on *Railway News*)	†	£4500
124		2c. green	20·00	9·00
125		2c. deep green	20·00	9·00
126		3c. carmine	12·00	2·25
127		5c. slate-blue	40·00	14·00
128		5c. deep blue	40·00	14·00
129		6c. brown	90·00	90·00
130		8c. slate-violet	32·00	30·00
131		10c. purple	55·00	48·00
132		15c. slate	90·00	90·00
133		20c. vermilion	90·00	90·00
134		50c. pale ultramarine	£130	95·00
135		50c. bright ultramarine	£130	£100
136		$1 lake	£450	£450
137		$2 deep violet	£750	£350
138		$3 bistre	£950	£700
139		$4 violet	£900	£600
140		$5 olive-green	£900	£600
121/40 *Set of* 16			£4000	£2750
133s/40s Handstamped "Specimen" *Set of* 7			£1900	

No. 123a was used on issues of the *Railway News* of 5, 6 and 8 November 1897 and must be on a large part of the original newspaper with New Glasgow postmark.

31

32

(From photograph by W. & D. Downey, London)

1897–98. P 12.

141	**31**	½c. grey-black (9.11.97)	7·50	5·00
142		½c. black	8·00	5·00
		a. Imperf (pair)	£400	
143		1c. blue-green (12.97)	19·00	90
		a. Imperf (pair)	£400	
144		2c. violet (12.97)	18·00	1·50
		a. Imperf (pair)	£400	
145		3c. carmine (1.98)	30·00	1·50
		a. Imperf (pair)	£750	
146		5c. deep blue/*bluish* (12.97)	65·00	2·75
		a. Imperf (pair)	£400	
147		6c. brown (12.97)	60·00	26·00
		a. Imperf (pair)	£750	
148		8c. orange (12.97)	80·00	7·00
		a. Imperf (pair)	£450	
149		10c. brownish purple (1.98)	£130	55·00
		a. Imperf (pair)	£475	
141/9 *Set of* 8			£350	90·00

BOOKLET PANES. Most definitive booklets issued from 1900 onwards had either the two horizontal sides or all three outer edges imperforate. Stamps from the panes show one side or two adjacent sides imperforate.

Two types of the 2c.

Die Ia. Frame consists of four fine lines.

Die Ib. Frame has one thick line between two fine lines.

The die was retouched in 1900 for Plates 11 and 12, producing weak vertical frame lines and then retouched again in 1902 for Plates 15 to 20 resulting in much thicker frame lines. No. 155*b* covers both states of the retouching.

1898–1902. P 12.

150	**32**	½c. black (9.98)	5·00	1·10
		a. Imperf (pair)	£425	
151		1c. blue-green (6.98)	26·00	50
152		1c. deep green/*toned paper*	28·00	1·75
		a. Imperf (pair)	£900	
153		2c. dull purple (Die Ia) (9.98)	28·00	30
		a. Thick paper (6.99)	90·00	10·00
154		2c. violet (Die Ia)	24·00	30
154*a*		2c. reddish purple (Die Ia)	45·00	1·25
155		2c. rose-carmine (Die Ia) (20.8.99)	38·00	30
		a. Imperf (pair)	£375	
155*b*		2c. rose-carmine (Die Ib) (1900).	55·00	75
		ba. Booklet pane of 6 (11.6.00)	£750	
156		3c. rose-carmine (6.98)	60·00	1·00

157		5c. slate-blue/*bluish*	£110	3·00
		a. Imperf (pair)	£950	
158		5c. Prussian blue/*bluish*	£120	3·00
159		6c. brown (9.98)	95·00	55·00
		a. Imperf (pair)	£850	
160		7c. greenish yellow (23.12.02)	65·00	18·00
161		8c. orange-yellow (10.98)	£120	32·00
162		8c. brownish orange	£110	32·00
		a. Imperf (pair)	£850	
163		10c. pale brownish purple (11.98)	£170	14·00
164		10c. deep brownish purple	£170	14·00
		a. Imperf (pair)	£900	
165		20c. olive-green (29.12.00)	£300	50·00
150/65 *Set of* 11			£900	£160

The 7c. and 20c. also exist imperforate, but unlike the values listed in this condition, they have no gum. (*Price*, 7c. £425, 20c. £2000 *pair*, *un*).

33

(Des R. Weir Crouch, G. Hahn, A. H. Howard and R. Holmes. Eng C. Skinner. Design recess, colours added by typo)

1898 (7 Dec). *Imperial Penny Postage. Design in black. British possessions in red. Oceans in colours given.* P 12.

166	**33**	2c. lavender	29·00	5·50
		a. Imperf (pair)	£375	
167		2c. greenish blue	27·00	5·50
		a. Imperf (pair)	£425	
168		2c. blue	27·00	5·50
		a. Imperf (pair)	£425	

Forgeries of Type **33** are without horizontal lines across the continents and have a forged Montreal postmark of 24.12.98.

1899 (4 Jan). *Provisionals used at Port Hood, Nova Scotia. No. 156 divided vertically and handstamped.*

169	**32**	"1" in blue, on 13 of 3c.	–	£3500
170		"2" in violet, on 23 of 3c.	–	£3000

Nos. 169/70 were prepared by the local postmaster during a shortage of 2c. stamps caused by the change in postage rates.

2 CENTS
(**34**)

35 King Edward VII

1899. *Surch with T* **34**, *by Public Printing Office.*

171	**31**	2c. on 3c. carmine (8 Aug)	17·00	8·00
		a. Surch inverted	£350	
172	**32**	2c. on 3c. rose-carmine (28 July)	17·00	4·25
		a. Surch inverted	£350	

(Des King George V when Prince of Wales and J. A. Tilleard)

1903 (1 July)–**12**. P 12.

173	**35**	1c. pale green	27·00	50
174		1c. deep green	25·00	50
175		1c. green	25·00	50
176		2c. rose-carmine	20·00	50
		a. Booklet pane of 6	£750	£950
177		2c. pale rose-carmine	20·00	50
		a. Imperf (pair) (18.7.09)	28·00	35·00
178		5c. blue/*bluish*	80·00	2·50
179		5c. indigo/*bluish*	80·00	2·75
180		7c. yellow-olive	65·00	2·75
181		7c. greenish bistre	75·00	2·75
181*a*		7c. straw (1.12)	£120	42·00
182		10c. brown-lilac	£130	16·00
183		10c. pale dull purple	£130	16·00
184		10c. dull purple	£130	16·00
185		20c. pale olive-green (27.9.04)	£225	25·00
186		20c. deep olive-green	£250	25·00
		s. Handstamped "Specimen"	80·00	
187		50c. deep violet (19.11.08)	£350	85·00
173/87 *Set of* 7			£800	£110

The 1c., 5c., 7c. and 10c. exist imperforate but are believed to be proofs. (*Prices per pair*, 1c. £475, 5c. £800. 7c. £550, 10c. £800).

IMPERFORATE AND PART-PERFORATED SHEETS. Prior to 1946 many Canadian issues exist imperforate, or with other perforation varieties, in the colours of the issued stamps and, usually, with gum. In the years before 1927 such examples are believed to come from imprimatur sheets, removed from the Canadian Post Office archives. From 1927 until 1946 it is known that the printers involved in the production of the various issues submitted several imperforate plate proof sheets of each stamp to the Post Office authorities for approval. Some of these sheets or part sheets were retained for record purposes, but the remainder found their way on to the philatelic market.

Part-perforated sheets also occur from 1927–29 issues.

From 1908 until 1946 we now only list and price such varieties of this type which are known to be genuine errors, sold from post offices. Where other imperforate or similar varieties are known they are recorded in footnotes.

It is possible, and in some cases probable, that some imperforate varieties listed before 1908 may have also been removed from the archives as mentioned above, but it is far harder to be explicit over the status of this earlier material.

36 King George V and Queen Mary when Prince and Princess of Wales

37 Jacques Cartier and Samuel Champlain

Re-entry (R. 5/4)

38 King Edward VII and Queen Alexandra

39 Champlain's house in Quebec

40 Generals Montcalm and Wolfe

41 Quebec in 1700

42 Champlain's departure for the West

43 Cartier's arrival before Quebec

(Des Machado)

1908 (16 July). *Quebec Tercentenary. T* **36/43**. P 12.

188	**36**	½c. sepia	3·75	3·50
		a. Re-entry	45·00	45·00
189	**37**	1c. blue-green	16·00	2·75
190	**38**	2c. carmine	19·00	1·00
191	**39**	5c. indigo	48·00	26·00
192	**40**	7c. olive-green	65·00	48·00
193	**41**	10c. violet	70·00	55·00
194	**42**	15c. brown-orange	85·00	70·00
195	**43**	20c. dull brown	£120	£100
188/95 *Set of* 8			£375	£275

Some values exist on both toned and white papers.

Nos. 188/95 exist imperforate. (*Price £475*, *un*, *for each pair*).

WET AND DRY PRINTINGS. Until the end of December 1922 all Canadian stamps were produced by the "wet" method of recess-printing in which the paper was dampened before printing, dried and then gummed.

In late December 1922 the Canadian Bank Note Co. began to use the "dry" process in which the paper was gummed before printing. Late printings of the 3c. brown were the first stamps to be produced by this method, but the changeover was not completed until January 1926.

"Dry" printings have a sharper appearance and can often be found with a degree of embossing showing on the reverse. Stamps from "wet" printings shrink during drying and are narrower than "dry" examples. In many cases the difference can be as great as 0.5 mm. On some early booklet panes the difference is in the vertical, rather than the horizontal, measurement.

On Nos. 196/215 all values only exist from "wet" printings, except the 3c., 20c. and 50c. which come from both types of printing.

44

1911–22. P 12.

196	**44**	1c. yellow-green (22.12.11)	6·00	50
		a. With fine horiz lines across stamp	40·00	8·50
197		1c. bluish green	5·50	50
		a. Booklet pane of 6 (1.5.13)	50·00	
198		1c. deep bluish green	6·00	50
199		1c. deep yellow-green	6·00	65
		a. Booklet pane of 6	18·00	
200		2c. rose-red (15.12.11)	5·50	50
201		2c. deep rose-red	5·50	50
		a. Booklet pane of 6 (1.12)	32·00	
202		2c. pale rose-red	5·50	50
		a. With fine horiz lines across stamp	25·00	14·00
203		2c. carmine	6·50	50
204		3c. brown (6.8.18)	6·00	50
205		3c. deep brown	5·50	50
		a. Booklet pane of 4+2 labels (2.22)	50·00	
205*b*		5c. deep blue (17.1.12)	60·00	75
206		5c. indigo	90·00	5·00
206*a*		5c. grey-blue	85·00	3·25
206*b*		7c. straw (12.1.12)	75·00	15·00
207		7c. pale sage-green (1914)	£200	38·00
208		7c. olive-yellow (1915)	20·00	3·00
209		7c. yellow-ochre (1916)	20·00	3·00
210		10c. brownish purple (12.1.12)	90·00	2·75
211		10c. reddish purple	£100	5·00
212		20c. olive-green (23.1.12)	32·00	1·50
213		20c. olive	32·00	1·75
214		50c. grey-black (26.1.12)	£100	8·00
215		50c. sepia	50·00	3·75
196/215 *Set of* 8			£225	11·00

The 20c. and 50c. values exist imperforate (*Price* £2250 *un*, *for each pair*).

1912 (1 Nov)–**21**. *For use in coil-machines.*

(*a*) P 12×imperf.

216	**44**	1c. yellow-green (1914)	3·50	11·00
217		1c. blue-green	17·00	24·00
		a. Two large holes at top and bottom (vert pair) (7.18)	75·00	90·00
218		2c. deep rose-red (1914)	27·00	21·00
218*a*		3c. brown (1921)	3·50	6·50

No. 217a has two large holes about 3½ mm in diameter in the top and bottom margins. They were for experimental use in a vending machine at Toronto in July 1918 and were only in use for two days.

The 1c. and 2c. also exist with two small "V" shaped holes about 9.5 mm apart at top which are gripper marks due to modifications made in vending machines in 1917.

(*b*) Imperf×perf 8.

219	**44**	1c. yellow-green (9.12)	15·00	5·00
220		1c. blue-green	19·00	5·00
		a. With fine horiz lines across stamp	60·00	
221		2c. carmine (9.12)	12·00	1·50
222		2c. rose-red	13·00	2·25
223		2c. scarlet	32·00	5·00
224		3c. brown (8.18)	5·00	2·00

(*c*) P 8×imperf.

224a	**44**	1c. blue-green (15.2.13)	60·00	48·00
224b		2c. carmine (15.2.13)	60·00	48·00

The stamps imperf×perf 8 were sold in coils over the counter; those perf 8×imperf were on sale in automatic machines. Varieties showing perf 12 on 2 or 3 adjacent sides and 1 or 2 sides imperf are from booklets, or the margins of sheets.

(**45**)

46

47

1915 (12 Feb). *Optd with T* **45**.

225	**44**	5c. blue	£110	£200
226		20c. olive-green	55·00	£100
227		50c. sepia (R.)	£110	£160
225/7 *Set of* 3			£250	£425

These stamps were intended for tax purposes, but owing to ambiguity in an official circular dated 16 April 1915, it was for a time believed that their use for postal purposes was authorised. The position was clarified by a further circular on 20 May 1916 which made clear that Nos. 225/7 were for fiscal use only.

1915. P 12.

228	**46**	1c. green (15.4.15)	8·00	50
229		2c. carmine-red (16.4.15)	17·00	1·50
230		2c. rose-carmine	19·00	3·50

Die I

Die II

In Die I there is a long horizontal coloured line under the foot of the "T", and a solid bar of colour runs upwards from the "1" to the "T".

In Die II this solid bar of colour is absent, and there is a short horizontal line under the left side of the "T", with two short vertical dashes and a number of dots under the right-hand side.

1916 (1 Jan). P 12.

231	**47**	2c. +1c. rose-red (Die I)	35·00	1·25
232		2c. +1c. bright carmine (Die I)	32·00	1·25
233		2c. +1c. scarlet (Die I)	30·00	1·25

1916 (Feb). Imperf×perf 8 (coils).

234	**47**	2c. +1c. rose-red (Die I)	55·00	12·00

1916 (July). P 12×8.

235	**47**	2c. +1c. carmine-red (Die I)	24·00	50·00
236		2c. +1c. bright rose-red (Die I)	24·00	50·00

1916 (Aug). P 12.

237	**47**	2c. +1c. carmine-red (Die II)	£110	22·00

1916 (Aug). *Colour changed.*

(*a*) P 12.

238	**47**	2c. + 1c. brown (Die I)	£200	20·00
239		2c. + 1c. yellow-brown (Die II)	4·25	50
		a. Imperf (pair)	£1000	
240		2c. + 1c. deep brown (Die II)	12·00	50

(*b*) Imperf×perf 8.

241	**47**	2c. + 1c. brown (Die I)	£100	8·00
		a. Pair, 241 and 243	£350	
243		2c. + 1c. deep brown (Die II)	48·00	3·50

No. 239a, which is a genuine error, should not be confused with ungummed proofs of the Die I stamp, No. 238 (*Price per pair*, £140).

This value also exists p 12×imperf or imperf×p 12, but was not issued with these perforations (*Price*, *in either instance*, £325, *un*, *per pair*).

48 Quebec Conference, 1864, from painting "The Fathers of Confederation", by Robert Harris

The Philalux 3

The only detector with built in short wave and long wave UV lights allowing you to see every phosphor from around the world

This Multifunction Detector has a built in short-wave UV light tube with a filter for Great Britain “all over” phosphor and phosphor band detection. It also has a long-wave tube for identifying fluorescent paper (tagging) on stamps from Germany, France, Canada, China and Mexico as well as enabling you to detect repairs, forgeries and ink variations. The magnetic sensor can be used to detect magnetism on counterfeit bank notes.

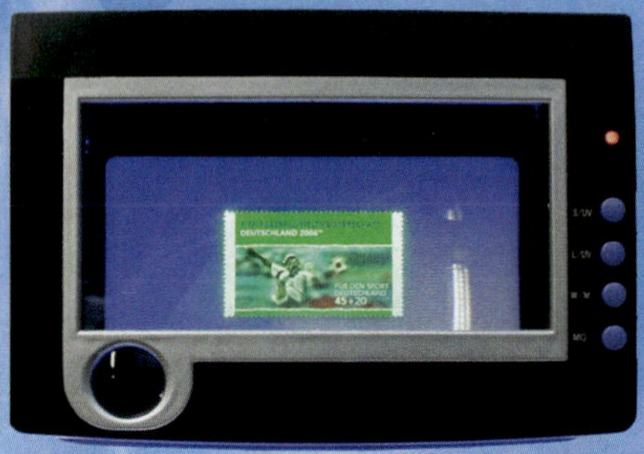

View from above

S9865 The Philalux 3 **£125**

Stanley Gibbons Publications
7 Parkside, Christchurch Road, Ringwood, Hampshire, BH24 3SH
Tel: +44 (0)1425 472 363 Email: info@stanleygibbons.co.uk
www.stanleygibbons.com

1917 (15 Sept). *50th Anniv of Confederation.* P 12.

244	**48**	3c. bistre-brown	18·00	2·50
245		3c. deep brown	20·00	2·75

No. 244 exists imperforate, without gum (*Price per pair, £350 un*).

Die I (top). Space between top of "N" and oval frame line and space between "CENT" and lower frame line.

Die II (bottom). "ONE CENT" appears larger so that "N" touches oval and "CENT" almost touches frame line. There are other differences but this is the most obvious one.

Die I (top). The lowest of the three horizontal lines of shading below the medals does not touch the three heavy diagonal lines; three complete white spaces over both "E's" of "THREE"; long centre bar to figures "3". Vertical spandrel lines fine.

Die II (bottom). The lowest horizontal line of shading touches the first of the three diagonal lines; two and a half spaces over first "E" and spaces over second "E" partly filled by stem of maple leaf; short centre bar to figures "3". Vertical spandrel lines thick. There are numerous other minor differences.

WET AND DRY PRINTINGS. See notes above No. 196.

On Nos. 246/63 all listed items occur from both "wet" and "dry" printings except Nos. 246aa/ab, 248aa, 256, 259, 260 and 262 which come "wet" only, and Nos. 246a, 248/a, 252/4*a*, 256b and 263 which are "dry" only.

1922–31. *As T* **44**.

(a) P 12.

246	**44**	1c. chrome-yellow (Die I) (7.6.22)	2·50	60
		aa. Booklet pane of 4+2 labels (7.22)	60·00	
		ab. Booklet pane of 6 (12.22)	30·00	
		a. Die II (1925)	5·50	30
247		2c. deep green (6.6.22)	2·25	10
		aa. Booklet pane of 4+2 labels (7.22)	45·00	
		ab. Booklet pane of 6 (12.22)	£300	
		b. Thin paper (9.24)	3·00	4·50
248		3c. carmine (Die I) (18.12.23)	3·75	10
		aa. Booklet pane of 4+2 labels (12.23)	38·00	
		a. Die II (11.24)	24·00	80
249		4c. olive-yellow (7.7.22)	8·00	3·50
		a. Yellow-ochre	8·00	3·50
250		5c. violet (2.2.22)	5·00	1·75
		a. Thin paper (9.24)	5·00	8·00
		b. Reddish violet (1925)	7·00	2·00
251		7c. red-brown (12.12.24)	12·00	7·50
		a. Thin paper	£140	35·00
252		8c. blue (1.9.25)	19·00	11·00
253		10c. blue (20.2.22)	17·00	3·25
254		10c. bistre-brown (1.8.25)	19·00	3·25
		a. Yellow-brown	18·00	3·25
255		$1 brown-orange (22.7.23)	55·00	8·00
246/55 *Set of* 10			£130	32·00

The $1 differs from T **44** in that the value tablets are oval.

Nos. 249/52 and 254/5 exist imperforate (*Prices per un pair* 4c. *to* 8c. *£1600 each*, 10c. *£1700*, $1 *£1900*).

(b) Imperf×perf 8.

256	**44**	1c. chrome-yellow (Die I) (1922)	4·00	6·00
		a. Imperf horiz (vert pair) (1924)	£160	
		b. Die II (1925)	4·50	7·00
		c. Do. Imperf horiz (vert pair) (1927)	8·00	27·00
257		2c. deep green (26.7.22)	7·00	2·25
		b. Imperf horiz (vert pair) (1927)	9·00	27·00
258		3c. carmine (Die I) (9.4.24)	70·00	11·00
		a. Imperf horiz (vert pair) (1924)	£250	
		b. Die II (1925)	90·00	27·00
256/8 *Set of* 3			75·00	17·00

Nos. 256a, 256c, 257b and 258a come from coil printings sold in sheet form. Those issued in 1924 were from "wet" printings and those in 1927 from "dry". A "wet" printing of No. 257b, issued in 1924, also exists (*Price £160 mint*), but cannot be identified from that issued in 1927 except by the differences between "wet" and "dry" stamps.

(c) Imperf (pairs).

259	**44**	1c. chrome-yellow (Die I) (6.10.24)	50·00	70·00
260		2c. deep green (6.10.24)	50·00	70·00
261		3c. carmine (Die I) (31.12.23)†	29·00	45·00

(d) P 12×imperf.

262	**44**	2c. deep green (9.24)	65·00	65·00

(e) P 12×8.

263	**44**	3c. carmine (Die II) (24.6.31)	2·75	3·25

†Earliest known postmark.

Nos. 259 to 261 were on sale only at the Philatelic Branch, P.O. Dept, Ottawa.

No. 263 was produced by adding horizontal perforations to unused sheet stock of No. 258b. The stamps were then issued in 1931 pending the delivery of No. 293.

2 CENTS (49) **2 CENTS** (50)

1926. *No. 248 surch.*

(a) With T **49**, *by the Govt Printing Bureau.*

264	**44**	2c. on 3c. carmine (12.10.26)	50·00	60·00
		a. Pair, one without surch	£450	
		b. On Die II	£375	

(b) With T **50**, *by the Canadian Bank Note Co.*

265	**44**	2c. on 3c. carmine (4.11.26)	16·00	25·00
		a. Surch double (partly treble)	£200	

51 Sir J. A. Macdonald

52 "The Fathers of Confederation"

53 Parliament Buildings, Ottawa

54 Sir W. Laurier

55 Canada, Map 1867–1927

1927 (29 June). *60th Anniv of Confederation.* P 12.

I. *Commemorative Issue. Inscr* "1867–1927 CANADA CONFEDERATION".

266	**51**	1c. orange	2·50	1·50
267	**52**	2c. green	2·25	30
268	**53**	3c. carmine	7·50	5·00
269	**54**	5c. violet	4·00	3·50
270	**55**	12c. blue	24·00	5·00
266/70 *Set of* 5			35·00	14·00

Nos. 266/70 exist imperforate, imperf×perf or perf×imperf (*Prices from £85, un, per pair*).

56 Darcy McGee

57 Sir W. Laurier and Sir J. A. Macdonald

58 R. Baldwin and L. H. Lafontaine

II. *Historical Issue.*

271	**56**	5c. violet	3·00	2·50
272	**57**	12c. green	17·00	4·50
273	**58**	20c. carmine	17·00	12·00
271/3 *Set of* 3			32·00	17·00

Nos. 271/3 exist imperforate, imperf×perf or perf×imperf (*Prices from £85, un, per pair*).

59

(Des H. Schwartz)

1928 (21 Sept). *Air.* P 12.

274	**59**	5c. olive-brown	6·50	4·25

No. 274 exists imperforate, imperf×perf or perf×imperf (*Price per pair, £170, un*).

60 King George V

61 Mt Hurd and Indian Totem Poles

62 Quebec Bridge

63 Harvesting with Horses

64 *Bluenose* (fishing schooner)

65 Parliament Buildings, Ottawa

1928–29.

(a) P 12.

275	**60**	1c. orange (25.10.28)	2·75	1·50
		a. Booklet pane of 6	18·00	
276		2c. green (16.10.28)	1·25	20
		a. Booklet pane of 6	18·00	
277		3c. lake (12.12.28)	17·00	18·00
278		4c. olive-bistre (16.8.29)	13·00	8·00
279		5c. violet (12.12.28)	6·50	4·25
		a. Booklet pane of 6 (6.1.29)	£100	
280		8c. blue (21.12.28)	7·50	6·00
281	**61**	10c. green (5.12.28)	8·50	1·50
282	**62**	12c. grey-black (8.1.29)	23·00	13·00
283	**63**	20c. lake (8.1.29)	28·00	14·00
284	**64**	50c. blue (8.1.29)	£130	42·00
285	**65**	$1 olive-green (8.1.29)	£120	70·00
		a. Brown-olive	£225	£100
275/85 *Set of* 11			£325	£160

(b) Imperf×perf 8 (5.11.28).

286	**60**	1c. orange	13·00	22·00
287		2c. green	14·00	6·50

Slight differences in the size of many Canadian stamps, due to paper shrinkage, are to be found.

Nos. 275/85 exist imperforate, imperf×perf or perf×imperf (*Prices per unused pair*, 1c. to 8c., *from £90*, 10c. to 20c., *from £150*, 50c. and $1, *from £450*). *Tête-bêche* horizontal pairs of the 1c., 2c. and 5c. are also known from uncut booklet sheets (*Prices per pair, £300, un*).

PRINTERS. The following stamps to No. 334 were recess-printed by the British American Bank Note Co, Ottawa.

66

67 Parliamentary Library, Ottawa

68 The Old Citadel, Quebec

69 Harvesting with Tractor

70 Acadian Memorial Church and Statue of "Evangeline", Grand Pre, Nova Scotia

71 Mt Edith Cavell, Canadian Rockies

Die I 1c. Die II Die I 2c. Die II

1c. Die I. Three thick coloured lines and one thin between "P" and ornament, at right. Curved line in ball-ornament short.

Die II. Four thick lines. Curved line longer.

2c. Die I. Three thick coloured lines between "P" and ornament, at left. Short line in ball.

Die II. Four thick lines. Curved line longer.

1930–31.

(a) P 11.

288	**66**	1c. orange (I) (17.7.30)	1·75	1·00
289		1c. green (I) (6.12.30)	1·50	10
		b. Booklet pane of 6 (21.7.31)	27·00	
		d. Die II (8.31)	1·75	10
		da. Imperf (pair)	£1800	
		db. Booklet pane of 4+2 labels (13.11.31)	85·00	
290		2c. green (I) (6.6.30)	1·75	10
		a. Booklet pane of 6 (17.6.30)	38·00	
291		2c. scarlet (I) (17.11.30)	1·50	2·25
		a. Booklet pane of 6 (17.11.30)	24·00	
		b. Die II	1·00	10
292		2c. deep brown (I) (4.7.31)	1·50	3·75
		a. Booklet pane of 6 (23.7.31)	40·00	
		b. Die II (4.7.31)	1·25	10

		ba. Booklet pane of 4+2 labels (13.11.31)	£130	
293		3c. scarlet (13.7.31)	1·00	10
		a. Booklet pane of 4+2 labels	40·00	
294		4c. yellow-bistre (5.11.30)	7·00	4·50
295		5c. violet (18.6.30)	2·75	5·00
296		5c. deep slate-blue (13.11.30)	5·50	20
		a. Dull blue	19·00	75
297		8c. blue (13.8.30)	11·00	16·00
298		8c. red-orange (5.11.30)	7·50	5·50
299	**67**	10c. olive-green (15.9.30)	17·00	1·00
		a. Imperf (pair)	£1500	
300	**68**	12c. grey-black (4.12.30)	14·00	5·50
301	**69**	20c. red (4.12.30)	22·00	1·25
302	**70**	50c. blue (4.12.30)	80·00	17·00
303	**71**	$1 olive-green (4.12.30)	£100	27·00
288/303 *Set of* 16			£250	75·00
		(b) Imperf×perf 8½.		
304	**66**	1c. orange (I) (14.7.30)	11·00	16·00
305		1c. green (I) (4.2.31)	6·00	7·00
306		2c. green (I) (27.6.30)	4·00	6·00
307		2c. scarlet (I) (19.11.30)	4·50	7·50
308		2c. deep brown (I) (4.7.31)	9·00	1·50
309		3c. scarlet (13.7.31)	14·00	1·50
304/9 *Set of* 6			42·00	35·00

Nos. 300/3 exist imperforate (*Prices per unused pair*, 12c. £650, 20c. £650, 50c. £750, $1 £950).

Some low values in the above and subsequent issues have been printed by both Rotary and "Flat plate" processes. The former can be distinguished by the gum, which has a striped appearance.

For 13c. bright violet, T **68**, see No. 325.

72 Mercury and Western Hemisphere

73 Sir Georges Etienne Cartier

(Des H. Schwartz)

1930 (4 Dec). *Air.* P 11.

310	**72**	5c. deep brown	19·00	18·00

1931 (30 Sept). P 11.

312	**73**	10c. olive-green	10·00	20

No. 312 exists imperforate (*Price per pair*, £450, *un*).

6 (74)

3 (75)

1932 (22 Feb). *Air. No. 274 surch with T* **74**.

313	**59**	6c. on 5c. olive-brown	3·00	2·50

Examples of this stamp with surcharge inverted, surcharge double, surcharge triple or surcharge omitted in pair with normal are not now believed to have been regularly issued. Such "errors" have also been forged and collectors are warned against forged examples, some of which bear unauthorized markings which purport to be the guarantee of Stanley Gibbons Ltd.

1932 (21 June). *Nos. 291/b surch with T* **75**.

314	**66**	3c. on 2c. scarlet (I)	3·50	3·00
		a. Die II	1·00	60

76 King George V

77 Duke of Windsor when Prince of Wales

78 Allegory of British Empire

6 OTTAWA CONFERENCE 1932 6

(79)

1932 (12 July). *Ottawa Conference.* P 11.

		(a) Postage stamps.		
315	**76**	3c. scarlet	70	80
316	**77**	5c. blue	9·50	5·00
317	**78**	13c. green	9·50	6·00
		(b) Air. No. 310 surch with T **79**.		
318	**72**	6c. on 5c. deep brown (B.)	10·00	15·00
315/18 *Set of* 4			27·00	24·00

80 King George V

"3" level Die I

"3" raised Die II

1932 (1 Dec)–**33**.

		(a) P 11.		
319	**80**	1c. green	60	10
		a. Booklet pane of 6 (28.12.33)	15·00	
		b. Booklet pane of 4+2 labels (19.9.33)	85·00	
320		2c. sepia	70	10
		a. Booklet pane of 6 (7.9.33)	16·00	
		b. Booklet pane of 4+2 labels (19.9.33)	85·00	
321		3c. scarlet (Die I)	1·25	10
		a. Booklet pane of 4+2 labels (22.8.33)	60·00	
		b. Die II (29.11.32)	85	10
		ba. Booklet pane of 4+2 labels (19.9.33)	38·00	
322		4c. yellow-brown	35·00	9·00
323		5c. blue	10·00	10
		a. Imperf vert (horiz pair)	£1400	
324		8c. red-orange	26·00	4·25
325	**68**	13c. bright violet	50·00	2·25
319/25 *Set of* 7			£110	14·00

Nos. 319/25 exist imperforate (*Prices per unused pair*, 1c. to 8c. £225, 13c. £650).

		(b) Imperf×perf 8½ (1933).		
326	**80**	1c. green (3.11.33)	16·00	4·00
327		2c. sepia (15.8.33)	20·00	4·00
328		3c. scarlet (Die II) (16.8.33)	12·00	1·75
326/8 *Set of* 3			42·00	8·75

81 Parliament Buildings, Ottawa

1933 (18 May). *U.P.U. Congress Preliminary Meeting.* P 11.

329	**81**	5c. blue	7·50	3·00

No. 329 exists imperforate (*Price per pair £650, un*).

WORLD'S GRAIN EXHIBITION & CONFERENCE

REGINA 1933

(82)

1933 (24 July). *World's Grain Exhibition and Conference, Regina. No. 301 optd with T* **82** *in blue.*

330	**69**	20c. red	16·00	7·00

No. 330 exists imperforate (*Price per pair £650, un*).

83 S.S. *Royal William* (after S. Skillett)

84 Jacques Cartier approaching Land

1933 (17 Aug). *Centenary of First Trans-Atlantic Steamboat Crossing.* P 11.

331	**83**	5c. blue	15·00	3·25

No. 331 exists imperforate (*Price per pair £650, un*).

1934 (1 July). *Fourth Centenary of Discovery of Canada.* P 11.

332	**84**	3c. blue	4·00	1·50

No. 332 exists imperforate (*Price per pair £650, un*).

85 U.E.L. Statue, Hamilton

86 Seal of New Brunswick

1934 (1 July). *150th Anniv of Arrival of United Empire Loyalists.* P 11.

333	**85**	10c. olive-green	8·50	6·00

No. 333 exists imperforate (*Price per pair £1200, un*).

1934 (16 Aug). *150th Anniv of Province of New Brunswick.* P 11.

334	**86**	2c. red-brown	1·50	2·50

No. 334 exists imperforate (*Price per pair £650, un*).

PRINTERS. The following stamps were recess-printed (except where otherwise stated) by the Canadian Bank Note Co, Ottawa, until No. 616.

87 Queen Elizabeth II when Princess

88 King George VI when Duke of York

89 King George V and Queen Mary

90 King Edward VIII when Prince of Wales

91 Windsor Castle

92 Royal Yacht *Britannia*

1935 (4 May). *Silver Jubilee. T* **87/92**. P 12.

335	**87**	1c. green	60	80
336	**88**	2c. brown	60	80
337	**89**	3c. carmine-red	2·00	80
338	**90**	5c. blue	5·50	7·00
339	**91**	10c. green	6·00	7·00
340	**92**	13c. blue	6·50	7·00
335/40 *Set of* 6			19·00	21·00

Nos. 335/40 exist imperforate (*Price £250, un, for each pair*).

93 King George V

94 Royal Canadian Mounted Policeman

95 Confederation Conference, Charlottetown, 1864

96 Niagara Falls

97 Parliament Buildings, Victoria, British Columbia

98 Champlain Monument, Quebec

99 Daedalus

1935 (1 June–5 Nov). *T* **93/99**.

		(a) Postage. (i) P 12.		
341	**93**	1c. green	1·75	10
		a. Booklet pane of 6 (19.8.35)	26·00	
		b. Booklet pane of 4+2 labels (22.7.35)	60·00	
342		2c. brown	1·75	10
		a. Booklet pane of 6 (16.11.35)	26·00	
		b. Booklet pane of 4+2 labels (22.7.35)	60·00	
343		3c. scarlet	1·75	10
		a. Booklet pane of 4+2 labels	35·00	
		b. Printed on the gummed side	£250	
344		4c. yellow	3·50	2·00
345		5c. blue	3·50	10
		a. Imperf vert (horiz pair)	£200	
346		8c. orange	4·25	4·25
347	**94**	10c. carmine	6·50	50
348	**95**	13c. purple	7·50	65
349	**96**	20c. olive-green	21·00	70
350	**97**	50c. deep violet	25·00	5·50
351	**98**	$1 bright blue	40·00	11·00
341/51 *Set of* 11			£100	22·00
		(ii) *Coil stamps.* Imperf×perf 8.		
352	**93**	1c. green (5.11.35)	14·00	8·50
353		2c. brown (14.10.35)	9·50	4·50
354		3c. scarlet (20.7.35)	9·00	1·75
352/4 *Set of* 3			29·00	13·00
		(b) Air. P 12.		
355	**99**	6c. red-brown	3·00	1·00
		a. Imperf vert (horiz pair)	£7000	

Nos. 341/51 (*Prices per pair*, 1c. *to* 8c. *each* £150, 10c. *to* 50c. *each* £275, $1 £325, *un*) and 355 (*Price per pair* £500, *un*) exist imperforate.

100 King George VI and Queen Elizabeth

1937 (10 May). *Coronation.* P 12.

356	**100**	3c. carmine	1·75	1·50

No. 356 exists imperforate (*Price per pair £650, un*).

101 King George VI

102 Memorial Chamber, Parliament Buildings, Ottawa

103 Entrance to Halifax Harbour

104 Fort Garry Gate, Winnipeg

105 Entrance, Vancouver Harbour

106 Chateau de Ramezay, Montreal

107 Fairchild 45-80 Sekani Seaplane over *Distributor* on River Mackenzie

Crease on collar (Pl upper right pane R.9/5)

(T **101**. Photograph by Bertram Park)

1937–38. *T* **101/107**.

(a) Postage. (i) P 12.

357	**101**	1c. green (1.4.37)	1·50	10
		a. Booklet pane of 4+2 labels (14.4.37)	28·00	
		b. Booklet pane of 6 (18.5.37)	5·00	
358		2c. brown (1.4.37)	1·75	10
		a. Booklet pane of 4+2 labels (14.4.37)	60·00	
		b. Booklet pane of 6 (3.5.38)	11·00	
359		3c. scarlet (1.4.37)	1·75	10
		a. Booklet pane of 4+2 labels (14.4.37)	4·25	
		b. Crease on collar	55·00	30·00
360		4c. yellow (10.5.37)	5·50	1·75
361		5c. blue (10.5.37)	5·50	10
362		8c. orange (10.5.37)	5·50	3·00
363	**102**	10c. rose-carmine (15.6.38)	5·00	30
		a. Red	5·00	10
364	**103**	13c. blue (15.11.38)	22·00	2·00
365	**104**	20c. red-brown (15.6.38)	22·00	2·00
366	**105**	50c. green (15.6.38)	48·00	13·00
367	**106**	$1 violet (15.6.38)	60·00	13·00
		a. Imperf horiz (vert pair)	£3500	
357/67 *Set of* 11			£160	32·00

Nos. 357/67 exist imperforate (*Prices per pair* 1c. to 8c. *each* £275, 10c. to 50c. *each* £400, $1 £500 *un*).

(ii) *Coil stamps.* Imperf×perf 8.

368	**101**	1c. green (15.6.37)	3·75	3·75
369		2c. brown (18.6.37)	3·75	4·50
370		3c. scarlet (15.4.37)	23·00	1·25
368/70 *Set of* 3			27·00	8·50

(b) Air. P 12.

371	**107**	6c. blue (15.6.38)	13·00	1·50

No. 371 exists imperforate (*Price per pair £600, un*).

108 Queen Elizabeth II when Princess and Princess Margaret

109 National War Memorial

110 King George VI and Queen Elizabeth

1939 (15 May). *Royal Visit.* P 12.

372	**108**	1c. black and green	2·00	20
373	**109**	2c. black and brown	2·00	1·25
374	**110**	3c. black and carmine	1·50	20
372/4 *Set of* 3			5·00	1·50

Nos. 372/4 exist imperforate (*Price £475, un, for each pair*).

111 King George VI in Naval uniform

112 King George VI in Military uniform

113 King George VI in Air Force uniform

114 Grain Elevator

115 Farm Scene

116 Parliament Buildings

117 Ram Tank

118 Launching of Corvette H.M.C.S. *La Malbaie*, Sorel

119 Munitions Factory

120 H.M.S. *Cossack* (destroyer)

121 Air Training Camp

1942 (1 July)–**48**. *War Effort. T* **111/121** *and similar designs.*

(a) Postage. (i) P 12.

375	**111**	1c. green	1·50	10
		a. Booklet pane of 4+2 labels (12.9.42)	28·00	
		b. Booklet pane of 6 (24.11.42)	2·50	
376	**112**	2c. brown	1·75	10
		a. Booklet pane of 4+2 labels (12.9.42)	32·00	
		b. Booklet pane of 6 (6.10.42)	21·00	
377	**113**	3c. carmine-lake	1·25	60
		a. Booklet pane of 4+2 labels (20.8.42)	4·25	
378		3c. purple (30.6.43)	90	10
		a. Booklet pane of 4+2 labels (28.8.43)	6·00	
		b. Booklet pane of 6 (24.11.47)	14·00	
379	**114**	4c. slate	5·50	1·50
380	**112**	4c. carmine-lake (9.4.43)	70	10
		a. Booklet pane of 6 (3.5.43)	3·50	
381	**111**	5c. blue	3·00	10
382	**115**	8c. red-brown	5·50	75
383	**116**	10c. brown	9·50	10
384	**117**	13c. dull green	7·50	8·50
385		14c. dull green (16.4.43)	22·00	1·00
386	**118**	20c. chocolate	18·00	45
387	**119**	50c. violet	26·00	5·50
388	**120**	$1 blue	42·00	8·00
375/88 *Set of* 14			£130	23·00

Nos. 375/88 exist imperforate (*Prices per pair* 1c. to 8c. *each* £275, 10c. to 20c. *each* £400, 50c. and $1 *each* £475, *un*).

(ii) *Coil stamps.* Imperf×perf 8.

389	**111**	1c. green (9.2.43)	1·00	1·50
390	**112**	2c. brown (24.11.42)	2·25	2·00
391	**113**	3c. carmine-lake (23.9.42)	2·00	7·00
392		3c. purple (19.8.43)	10·00	6·00
393	**112**	4c. carmine-lake (13.5.43)	7·00	1·50
389/93 *Set of* 5			21·00	16·00

(iii) *Booklet stamps.* Imperf×perf 12 (1.9.43).

394	**111**	1c. green	3·25	1·25
		a. Booklet pane of 3	9·00	
395	**113**	3c. purple	3·25	1·50
		a. Booklet pane of 3	9·00	
396	**112**	4c. carmine-lake	3·25	1·75
		a. Booklet pane of 3	9·00	
394/6 *Set of* 3			9·00	4·00

Nos. 394/6 are from booklets in which the stamps are in strips of three, imperforate at top and bottom and right-hand end.

(iv) *Coil stamps.* Imperf×perf 9½.

397	**111**	1c. green (13.7.48)	3·00	4·00
397*a*	**112**	2c. brown (1.10.48)	7·50	19·00
398	**113**	3c. purple (2.7.48)	4·75	6·00
398*a*	**112**	4c. carmine-lake (22.7.48)	7·00	3·75
397/8*a Set of* 4			20·00	29·00

(b) Air. P 12.

399	**121**	6c. blue (1.7.42)	26·00	9·50
400		7c. blue (16.4.43)	4·00	20

Nos. 399/400 exist imperforate (*Price £650, un, for each pair*).

122 Ontario Farm Scene

123 Great Bear Lake

124 St. Maurice River Power Station

125 Combine Harvester

126 Lumbering in British Columbia

127 *Abegweit* (train ferry), Prince Edward Is.

128 Canada Geese in Flight

129 Alexander Graham Bell and "Fame"

1946 (16 Sept)–**47**. *Peace Re-conversion. T* **122/128**. P 12.

(a) Postage.

401	**122**	8c. brown	1·25	2·50
402	**123**	10c. olive-green	2·00	10
403	**124**	14c. sepia	4·25	2·25
404	**125**	20c. slate	3·00	10
405	**126**	50c. green	16·00	4·25
406	**127**	$1 purple	25·00	4·25

(b) Air.

407	**128**	7c. blue	5·00	20
		a. Booklet pane of 4 (24.11.47)	9·00	
401/7 *Set of* 7			50·00	12·00

1947 (3 Mar). *Birth Centenary of Bell (inventor of telephone).* P 12.

408	**129**	4c. blue	15	30

130 "Canadian Citizenship"

131 Queen Elizabeth II when Princess

1947 (1 July). *Advent of Canadian Citizenship and Eightieth Anniv of Confederation.* P 12.

409	**130**	4c. blue	10	25

(From photograph by Dorothy Wilding)

1948 (16 Feb). *Princess Elizabeth's Marriage.* P 12.

410	**131**	4c. blue	10	15

132 Queen Victoria, Parliament Building, Ottawa, and King George VI

133 Cabot's Ship *Matthew*

1948 (1 Oct). *One Hundred Years of Responsible Government.* P 12.

411	**132**	4c. grey	10	10

1949 (1 Apr). *Entry of Newfoundland into Canadian Confederation.* P 12.

412	**133**	4c. green	30	10

134 "Founding of Halifax, 1749" (C. W. Jefferys)

1949 (21 June). *Bicentenary of Halifax, Nova Scotia.* P 12.

413	**134**	4c. violet	30	10

135

136

137

138 King George VI

139 King George VI

(From photographs by Dorothy Wilding)

1949 (15 Nov)–**51**.

(i) P 12.

414	**135**	1c. green	25	10
415	**136**	2c. sepia	1·75	45
415*a*		2c. olive-green (25.7.51)	1·50	10
416	**137**	3c. purple	30	10
		a. Booklet pane of 4+2 labels (12.4.50)	2·25	
417	**138**	4c. carmine-lake	20	10
		a. Booklet pane of 6 (5.5.50)	27·00	
417*b*		4c. vermilion (2.6.51)	50	10
		ba. Booklet pane of 6	6·00	
418	**139**	5c. blue	2·00	40
414/18 *Set of* 7			6·00	80

(ii) Imperf×perf 9½ (coil stamps).

419	**135**	1c. green (18.5.50)	2·75	1·50
420	**136**	2c. sepia (18.5.50)	8·00	6·00
420*a*		2c. olive-green (9.10.51)	1·75	3·75
421	**137**	3c. purple (18.5.50)	2·25	3·00
422	**138**	4c. carmine-lake (20.4.50)	14·00	9·00
422*a*		4c. vermilion (27.11.51)	3·00	2·75
419/22*a Set of* 6			28·00	23·00

(iii) Imperf×perf 12 (booklets).

422*b*	**135**	1c. green (18.5.50)	50	1·75
		ba. Booklet pane of 3	1·50	
423	**137**	3c. purple (18.5.50)	1·25	1·00
		a. Booklet pane of 3	3·75	
423*b*	**138**	4c. carmine-lake (18.5.50)	15·00	9·00
		ba. Booklet pane of 3	45·00	
423*c*		4c. vermilion (25.10.51)	8·00	7·50
		ca. Booklet pane of 3	24·00	
422*b*/3*c Set of* 4			22·00	17·00

These booklet panes are imperforate at top, bottom and right-hand end.

140 King George VI

141 Oil Wells in Alberta

(From photograph by Dorothy Wilding)

1950 (19 Jan). *As T* **135/9** *but without* "POSTES POSTAGE", *as T* **140**.

(i) P 12.

424		1c. green	50	65
425		2c. sepia	50	3·50
426		3c. purple	50	65
427		4c. carmine-lake	50	20
428		5c. blue	50	1·50
424/8 *Set of* 5			2·25	6·00

(ii) Imperf×perf 9½ (coil stamps).

429		1c. green	30	1·00
430		3c. purple	80	1·50

1950 (1 Mar). P 12.

431	**141**	50c. green	6·00	1·00

142 Drying Furs

143 Fisherman

1950 (2 Oct). P 12.

432	**142**	10c. brown-purple	3·75	10

1951 (1 Feb). P 12.

433	**143**	$1 ultramarine	38·00	5·00

144 Sir R. L. Borden

145 W. L. Mackenzie King

1951 (25 June). *Prime Ministers (1st issue).* P 12.

434	**144**	3c. blue-green	10	75
435	**145**	4c. rose-carmine	10	10

See also Nos. 444/5, 475/6 and 483/4.

146 Mail Trains, 1851 and 1951

147 SS. *City of Toronto* and SS. *Prince George*

148 Mail Coach and DC-4M North Star

149 Reproduction of 3d., 1851

1951 (24 Sept). *Canadian Stamp Centenary.* P 12.

436	**146**	4c. black	50	10
437	**147**	5c. violet	1·00	2·00
438	**148**	7c. blue	50	1·25
439	**149**	15c. scarlet	1·60	10
436/9 *Set of* 4			3·25	3·00

150 Queen Elizabeth II when Princess and Duke of Edinburgh

151 Forestery Products

1951 (26 Oct). *Royal Visit.* P 12.

440	**150**	4c. violet	20	15

(Des A. L. Pollock)

1952 (1 Apr). P 12.

441	**151**	20c. grey	2·00	10

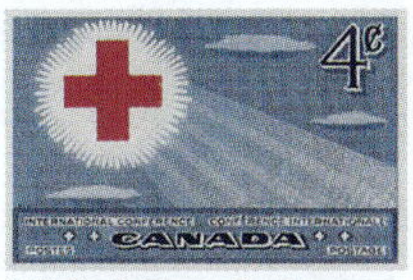
152 Red Cross Emblem

1952 (26 July). *18th International Red Cross Conference, Toronto. Design recess; cross litho.* P 12.

442	**152**	4c. scarlet and blue	15	10

153 Canada Goose

154 Pacific Coast Indian House and Totem Pole

(Des E. Hahn)

1952 (3 Nov). P 12.

443	**153**	7c. blue	1·25	10

1952 (3 Nov). *Prime Ministers (2nd issue). Various portraits as T* **144**. P 12.

444		3c. reddish purple	25	65
445		4c. orange-red	25	25

Portraits:—3c. Sir John J. C. Abbott; 4c. A. Mackenzie.

(Des E. Hahn)

1953 (2 Feb). P 12.

446	**154**	$1 black	3·25	20

155 Polar Bear

156 Elk

157 American Bighorn

(Des J. Crosby (2c.), E. Hahn (others))

1953 (1 Apr). *National Wild Life Week.* P 12.

447	**155**	2c. blue	10	10
448	**156**	3c. sepia	10	60
449	**157**	4c. slate	15	10
447/9 *Set of* 3			30	60

158 Queen Elizabeth II

159 Queen Elizabeth II

(From photograph by Karsh, Ottawa)

1953 (1 May–3 Sept).

(*a*) *Sheet stamps.* P 12.

450	**158**	1c. purple-brown	10	10
451		2c. green	15	10
452		3c. carmine	15	15
		a. Booklet pane of 4+2 labels (17.7)	1·90	
453		4c. violet	20	10
		a. Booklet pane of 6 (6.7)	3·75	
454		5c. ultramarine	20	10
450/4 *Set of* 5			70	30

(*b*) *Coil stamps.* Imperf×perf 9½

455	**158**	2c. green (30.7)	2·00	1·25
456		3c. carmine (27.7)	2·00	1·00
457		4c. violet (3.9)	1·50	1·25
455/7 *Set of* 3			5·00	3·25

(*c*) *Booklet stamps.* Imperf×perf 12

458	**158**	1c. purple-brown (12.8)	2·00	1·50
		a. Booklet pane of 3	5·50	
459		3c. carmine (17.7)	2·00	1·50
		a. Booklet pane of 3	5·50	
460		4c. violet (6.7)	2·00	1·50
		a. Booklet pane of 3	5·50	
458/60 *Set of* 3			5·50	4·00

These booklet stamps have top and bottom or top, bottom and right-hand sides imperforate.

(Des E. Hahn)

1953 (1 June). *Coronation.* P 12.

461	**159**	4c. violet	10	10

160 Textile Industry

161 Queen Elizabeth II

(Des A. L. Pollock)

1953 (2 Nov). P 12.

462	**160**	50c. deep bluish green	1·50	10

(From photograph by Dorothy Wilding)

1954–62.

(i) P 12.

463	**161**	1c. purple-brown (10.6.54)	10	10
		a. Booklet pane. Five stamps plus printed label (1.6.56)	1·50	
		p. Two phosphor bands (13.1.62)	80	3·00
464		2c. green (10.6.54)	20	10
		a. Pack. Two blocks of 25 (12.61)	6·00	
		p. Two phosphor bands (13.1.62)	80	3·25
465		3c. carmine (10.6.54)	70	10
		a. Imperf vert (horiz pair)	£1700	
		p. Two phosphor bands (13.1.62)	1·50	3·50
466		4c. violet (10.6.54)	30	10
		a. Booklet pane of 6 (7.7.55)	4·75	
		b. Booklet pane. Five stamps plus printed label (1.6.56)	1·50	
		p. One phosphor band (13.1.62)	2·00	9·00
467		5c. bright blue (1.4.54)	30	10
		a. Booklet pane. Five stamps plus printed label (14.7.54)	2·75	
		b. Pack. One block of 20 (12.61)	5·00	
		c. Imperf vert (horiz pair)	£4000	
		p. Two phosphor bands (13.1.62)	2·75	8·00
468		6c. red-orange (10.6.54)	1·50	55
463/8 *Set of* 6			2·75	70
463p/7p *Set of* 5			7·00	24·00

(ii) Imperf×perf 9½ (coil stamps)

469	**161**	2c. green (9.9.54)	70	75
470		4c. violet (23.8.54)	55	1·60
471		5c. bright blue (6.7.54)	1·75	45
469/71 *Set of* 3			2·75	2·50

No. 467c is from the left side of a sheet and shows perforations between the stamps and the sheet margin.

Nos. 464a and 467b are blocks with the outer edges imperf. These come from "One Dollar Plastic Packages" sold at post offices.

WINNIPEG PHOSPHOR BANDS. In 1962 facer-cancelling machines were introduced in Winnipeg which were activated by phosphor bands on the stamps. Under long or short wave ultra-violet light the phosphor glows and there is also a short after-glow when the lamp is turned off. This should not be confused with the fluorescent bands introduced in Ottawa in 1971.

162 Walrus

163 American Beaver

164 Northern Gannet

(Des E. Hahn)

1954 (1 Apr). *National Wild Life Week.* P 12.

472	**162**	4c. slate-black	35	20
473	**163**	5c. ultramarine	35	10
		a. Booklet pane. Five stamps plus one printed label	2·00	

(Des L. Hyde)

1954 (1 Apr). P 12.

474	**164**	15c. black	1·00	10

1954 (1 Nov). *Prime Ministers (3rd issue). Various portraits as T* **144**. P 12.

475		4c. violet	15	35
476		5c. bright blue	15	20

Portraits:—4c. Sir John Thompson; 5c. Sir Mackenzie Bowell.

165 Eskimo Hunter

(Des H. Beament)

1955 (21 Feb). P 12.

477	**165**	10c. purple-brown	50	10

166 Musk Ox

167 Whooping Cranes

(Des E. Hahn (4c.), Dr. W. Rowan (5c.))

1955 (4 Apr). *National Wild Life Week.* P 12.

478	**166**	4c. violet	30	10
479	**167**	5c. ultramarine	1·00	20

168 Dove and Torch

169 Pioneer Settlers

(Des W. Lohse)

1955 (1 June). *Tenth Anniv of International Civil Aviation Organisation.* P 12.

480	**168**	5c. ultramarine	20	20

(Des L. Hyde)

1955 (30 June). *50th Anniv of Alberta and Saskatchewan Provinces.* P 12.

481	**169**	5c. ultramarine	15	20

170 Scout Badge and Globe

173 Ice-hockey Players

(Des L. Hyde)

1955 (20 Aug). *Eighth World Scout Jamboree, Niagara-on-the-Lake.* P 12.

482	**170**	5c. orange-brown and green	25	10

1955 (8 Nov). *Prime Ministers (4th issue). Various portraits as T* **144**. P 12.

483		4c. violet	10	40
484		5c. bright blue	10	10

Portraits:—4c. R. B. Bennett; 5c. Sir Charles Tupper.

(Des J. Simpkins)

1956 (23 Jan). *Ice-hockey Commemoration.* P 12.

485	**173**	5c. ultramarine	20	20

174 Reindeer

175 Mountain Goat

(Des E. Hahn)

1956 (12 Apr). *National Wild Life Week.* P 12.

486	**174**	4c. violet	20	15
487	**175**	5c. bright blue	20	10

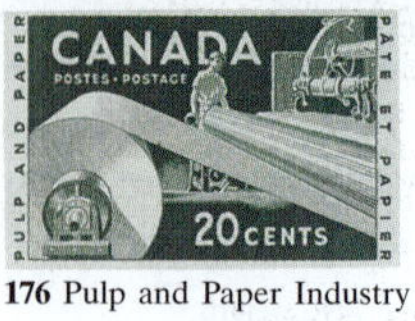

176 Pulp and Paper Industry

177 Chemical Industry

(Des A. J. Casson (20c.), A. L. Pollock (25c.))

1956 (7 June). P 12.

488	**176**	20c. green	60	10
489	**177**	25c. red	70	10

178

(Des A. Price)

1956 (9 Oct). *Fire Prevention Week.* P 12.

490	**178**	5c. red and black	30	10

179 Fishing

180 Swimming

(Des L. Hyde)

1957 (7 Mar). *Outdoor Recreation. T* **179/180** *and similar horiz designs.* P 12.

491	**179**	5c. ultramarine	25	10
		a. Block of 4. Nos. 491/4	1·25	1·50
492	**180**	5c. ultramarine	25	10
493	–	5c. ultramarine	25	10
494	–	5c. ultramarine	25	10
491/4 *Set of 4*			1·25	35

Designs:—No. 493, Hunting. No. 494, Skiing.

Nos. 491/4 are printed together in sheets of 50 (5×10). In the first, second, fourth and fifth vertical rows the four different designs are arranged in *se-tenant* blocks, whilst the central row is made up as follows (reading downwards):—Nos. 491/4, 491/2 (or 493/4), 491/4.

183 White-billed Diver

184 Thompson with Sextant, and North American Map

(Des L. Hyde)

1957 (10 Apr). *National Wild Life Week.* P 12.

495	**183**	5c. black	50	20

(Des G. A. Gundersen)

1957 (5 June). *Death Centenary of David Thompson (explorer).* P 12.

496	**184**	5c. ultramarine	25	30

185 Parliament Buildings, Ottawa

186 Globe within Posthorn

(Des Carl Mangold)

1957 (14 Aug). *14th U.P.U. Congress, Ottawa.* P 12.

497	**185**	5c. grey-blue	15	10
498	**186**	15c. blackish blue	55	1·75

187 Miner

188 Queen Elizabeth II and Duke of Edinburgh

(Des A. J. Casson)

1957 (5 Sept). *Mining Industry.* P 12.

499	**187**	5c. black	35	20

(From photographs by Karsh, Ottawa)

1957 (10 Oct). *Royal Visit.* P 12.

500	**188**	5c. black	30	10

189 "A Free Press"

190 Microscope

(Des A. L. Pollock)

1958 (22 Jan). *The Canadian Press.* P 12.

501	**189**	5c. black	15	70

(Des A. L. Pollock)

1958 (5 Mar). *International Geophysical Year.* P 12.

502	**190**	5c. blue	20	10

191 Miner panning for Gold

192 La Verendrye (statue)

(Des J. Harman)

1958 (8 May). *Centenary of British Columbia.* P 12.

503	**191**	5c. deep turquoise-green	20	10

(Des G. Trottier)

1958 (4 June). *La Verendrye (explorer) Commemoration.* P 12.

504	**192**	5c. ultramarine	15	10

193 Samuel de Champlain and the Heights of Quebec

194 Nurse

(Des G. Trottier)

1958 (26 June). *350th Anniv of Founding of Quebec.* P 12.

505	**193**	5c. brown-ochre and deep green	30	10

(Des G. Trottier)

1958 (30 July). *National Health.* P 12.

506	**194**	5c. reddish purple	30	10

195 "Petroleum 1858–1958"

196 Speaker's Chair and Mace

(Des A. L. Pollock)

1958 (10 Sept). *Centenary of Canadian Oil Industry.* P 12.

507	**195**	5c. scarlet and olive	30	10

(Des G. Trottier and C. Dair)

1958 (2 Oct). *Bicentenary of First Elected Assembly.* P 12.

508	**196**	5c. deep slate	30	10

197 John McCurdy's *Silver Dart* Biplane

198 Globe showing N.A.T.O. Countries

1959 (23 Feb). *50th Anniv of First Flight of the Silver Dart in Canada.* P 12.

509	**197**	5c. black and ultramarine	30	10

(Des P. Weiss)

1959 (2 Apr). *Tenth Anniv of North Atlantic Treaty Organisation.* P 12.

510	**198**	5c. ultramarine	40	10

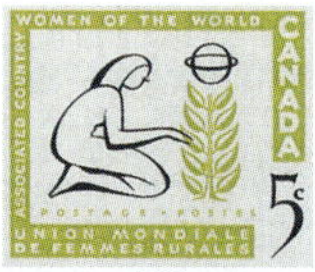

199

200 Queen Elizabeth II

(Des Helen Fitzgerald)

1959 (13 May). *"Associated Country Women of the World" Commemoration.* P 12.

511	**199**	5c. black and yellow-olive	15	10

(Des after painting by Annigoni)

1959 (18 June). *Royal Visit.* P 12.

512	**200**	5c. lake-red	30	10

201 Maple Leaf linked with American Eagle

202 Maple Leaves

(Des A. L. Pollock, G. Trottier (of Canada); W. H. Buckley, A. J. Copeland, E. Metzl (of the United States))

1959 (26 June). *Opening of St. Lawrence Seaway.* P 12.

513	**201**	5c. ultramarine and red	20	10
		a. Centre inverted	£9000	£5000

It is believed that No. 513a occurred on two printer's sheets, each of 200 stamps. About 230 examples have been discovered.

(Des P. Weiss)

1959 (10 Sept). *Bicentenary of Battle of Plains of Abraham (Quebec).* P 12.

514 **202** 5c. deep green and red................. 30 10

203

204 Dollard des Ormeaux

(Des Helen Fitzgerald)

1960 (20 Apr). *Golden Jubilee of Canadian Girl Guides Movement.* P 12.

515 **203** 5c. ultramarine and orange-brown.. 20 10

(Des P. Weiss)

1960 (19 May). *Tercentenary of Battle of the Long Sault.* P 12.

516 **204** 5c. ultramarine and light brown .. 20 10

205 Surveyor, Bulldozer and Compass Rose

206 E. Pauline Johnson

(Des B. J. Reddie)

1961 (8 Feb). *Northern Development.* P 12.

517 **205** 5c. emerald and red...................... 15 10

(Des B. J. Reddie)

1961 (10 Mar). *Birth Centenary of E. Pauline Johnson (Mohawk poetess).* P 12.

518 **206** 5c. green and red 15 10

207 Arthur Meighen (statesman)

208 Engineers and Dam

1961 (19 Apr). *Arthur Meighen Commemoration.* P 12.

519 **207** 5c. ultramarine 15 10

(Des B. J. Reddie)

1961 (28 June). *Tenth Anniv of Colombo Plan.* P 12.

520 **208** 5c. blue and brown 30 10

209 "Resources for Tomorrow"

210 "Education"

(Des A. L. Pollock)

1961 (12 Oct). *Natural Resources.* P 12.

521 **209** 5c. blue-green and brown 15 10

(Des Helen Fitzgerald)

1962 (28 Feb). *Education Year.* P 12.

522 **210** 5c. black and orange-brown......... 15 10

211 Lord Selkirk and Farmer

212 Talon bestowing Gifts on Married Couple

(Des Phillips-Gutkin Ltd)

1962 (3 May). *150th Anniv of Red River Settlement.* P 12.

523 **211** 5c. chocolate and green 20 10

(Des P. Weiss)

1962 (13 June). *Jean Talon Commemoration.* P 12.

524 **212** 5c. blue 20 10

213 Br Columbia & Vancouver Is 2½d. stamp of 1860, and Parliament Buildings, B.C.

214 Highway (map version) and Provincial Arms

(Des Helen Bacon)

1962 (22 Aug). *Centenary of Victoria, B.C.* P 12.

525 **213** 5c. red and black........................... 30 10

(Des A. L. Pollock)

1962 (31 Aug). *Opening of Trans-Canada Highway.* P 12.

526 **214** 5c. black and orange-brown......... 15 10

215 Queen Elizabeth II and Wheat (agriculture) Symbol

216 Sir Casimir Gzowski

(From drawing by Ernst Roch)

1962–64. *Horiz designs as T* **215** *showing Queen Elizabeth II and industry symbols.*

(i) P 12

527	1c. chocolate (4.2.63)............................	10	10
	a. Booklet pane. Five stamps plus one printed label (15.5.63)	3·50	
	p. Two phosphor bands (15.5.63).......	15	45
528	2c. green (2.5.63)..................................	15	10
	a. Pack. Two blocks of 25..................	9·00	
	p. Two phosphor bands (15.5.63).......	30	60
529	3c. reddish violet† (2.5.63)	15	10
	p. Two phosphor bands (15.5.63).......	30	1·00
530	4c. carmine-red (4.2.63)	15	10
	a. Booklet pane. Five stamps plus one printed label (15.5.63)	3·50	
	b. Pack. One block of 25.....................	6·00	
	p. One centre phosphor band (*narrow*)* (2.63)................................	50	3·00
	pa. One centre phosphor band (*wide*) (8.64)	4·25	6·50
	pb. One side phosphor band (12.64)...	50	2·75
531	5c. ultramarine (3.10.62)......................	15	10
	a. Booklet pane. Five stamps plus one printed label (5.63)	3·75	
	b. Pack. One block of 20.....................	7·00	
	c. Imperf horiz (vert pair)	£2500	£700
	p. Two phosphor bands (31.1.63?)	35	75
	pa. Pack. One block of 20....................	15·00	
	pb. Imperf (pair)	£2250	
527/31 *Set of* 5	....	65	15
527p/31p *Set of* 5	....	1·25	5·00

(ii) P 9½×imperf (coil stamps)

532	2c. green (1963)......................................	6·50	8·50
532*a*	3c. reddish violet (1964)......................	4·75	3·50
533	4c. carmine-red (15.5.63)	2·50	3·50
	a. Imperf (pair)	£2500	
534	5c. ultramarine (15.5.63)......................	4·50	1·50
532/4 *Set of* 4	....	16·00	15·00

Symbols:—1c. Crystals (Mining); 2c. Tree (Forestry); 3c. Fish (Fisheries); 4c. Electricity pylon (Industrial power).

Nos. 528a, 530b, 531b and 531pa are blocks with the outer edges imperf. These come from "One Dollar Plastic Packages" sold at post offices.

†This is a fugitive colour which tends to become reddish on drying. In successive printings the violet colour became more and more reddish as the printer tried to match the shade of each previous printing instead of referring back to the original shade. A deep reddish violet is also known from Plate 3. As there is such a range of shades it is not practical to list them.

*On No. 530p the band is 4 mm wide as against 8 mm on No. 530pa. No. 530pb exists with the band at either left or right side of the stamp, the bands being applied across alternate vertical perforations.

Postal forgeries are known of the 4c. showing a coarser background and lack of shading on the Queen's face.

(Des P. Weiss)

1963 (5 Mar). *150th Birth Anniv of Sir Casimir Gzowski (engineer).* P 12.

535 **216** 5c. reddish purple 10 10

217 "Export Trade"

218 Frobisher and barque *Gabriel*

(Des A. L. Pollock)

1963 (14 June). P 12.

536 **217** $1 carmine.................................... 4·75 2·00

(Des P. Weiss)

1963 (21 Aug). *Sir Martin Frobisher Commemoration.* P 12.

537 **218** 5c. ultramarine 20 10

219 Horseman and Map

220 Canada Geese

(Des B. J. Reddie)

1963 (25 Sept). *Bicentenary of Quebec–Trois-Rivieres–Montreal Postal Service.* P 12.

538 **219** 5c. red-brown and deep green 15 10

(Des A. Short and P. Arthur)

1963 (30 Oct). P 12.

539 **220** 15c. blue .... 1·00 10

221 Douglas DC-9 Airliner and Uplands Airport, Ottawa

222 "Peace on Earth"

1964. P 12.

540 **221** 7c. blue (11 Mar) 35 70

540*a* 8c. blue (18 Nov) 50 50

1964 (8 Apr). *"Peace". Litho and recess.* P 12.

541 **222** 5c. ochre, blue and turquoise-blue 15 10

223 Maple Leaves

1964 (14 May). *"Canadian Unity".* P 12.

542 **223** 5c. lake-red and light blue........... 10 10

224 White Trillium and Arms of Ontario

236 Maple Leaf and Arms of Canada

1964–66. *Provincial Emblems. T* **224**, **236** *and similar horiz designs. Recess (No. 555) or litho and recess (others).* P 12.

543	5c. green, brown and orange (30.6.64)	40	20
544	5c. green, orange-brown and yellow (30.6.64)	40	20
545	5c. carmine-red, green and bluish violet (3.2.65)	30	20
546	5c. blue, red and green (3.2.65)...........	30	20
547	5c. purple, green and yellow-brown (28.4.65)	30	20
548	5c. red-brown, deep bluish green and mauve (28.4.65)..............................	30	20
549	5c. slate-lilac, green and light reddish purple (21.7.65)	50	20
550	5c. green, yellow and rose-red (19.1.66)...	30	20
551	5c. sepia, orange and green (19.1.66) ..	30	20
552	5c. black, green and red (23.2.66).........	30	20
553	5c. drab, green and yellow (23.3.66)....	30	20
554	5c. blue, green and rose-red (23.3.66).	30	20
555	5c. red and blue (30.6.66)	30	20
543/55 *Set of* 13	....	4·00	2·40

Designs:—No. 543, Type **224**; No. 544, Madonna Lily and Arms of Quebec; No. 545, Purple Violet and Arms of New Brunswick; No. 546, Mayflower and Arms of Nova Scotia; No. 547, Dogwood and Arms of British Columbia; No. 548, Prairie Crocus and Arms of Manitoba; No. 549, Lady's Slipper and Arms of Prince Edward Island; No. 550, Wild Rose and Arms of Alberta; No. 551, Prairie Lily and Arms of Saskatchewan; No. 552, Pitcher Plant and Arms of Newfoundland; No. 553, Mountain Avens and Arms of Northwest Territories; No. 554, Fireweed and Arms of Yukon Territory; No. 555, Type **236**.

8
═

(237)

238 Fathers of the Confederation Memorial, Charlottetown

1964 (15 July). *No. 540 surch with T* **237**.

556 **221** 8c. on 7c. blue............................... 15 15

a. Surch omitted (left-hand stamp of horiz pair)................ £7000

(Des P. Weiss)

1964 (29 July). *Centenary of Charlottetown Conference.* P 12.

557 **238** 5c. black 10 10

239 Maple Leaf and Hand with Quill Pen

240 Queen Elizabeth II

(Des P. Weiss)

1964 (9 Sept). *Centenary of Quebec Conference.* P 12.
558 **239** 5c. light red and chocolate 15 10

(Portrait by Anthony Buckley)

1964 (5 Oct). *Royal Visit.* P 12.
559 **240** 5c. reddish purple 15 10

241 "Canadian Family"

242 "Co-operation"

1964 (14 Oct). *Christmas.* P 12.
560 **241** 3c. scarlet 10 10
a. Pack. Two blocks of 25 .... 7·00
p. Two phosphor bands .... 60 2·50
pa. Pack. Two blocks of 25 .... 13·00
561 5c. ultramarine 10 10
p. Two phosphor bands .... 90 3·25
Nos. 560a and 560pa are blocks with the outer edges imperf. These come from "$1.50 Plastic Packages" sold at post offices.

1965 (3 Mar). *International Co-operation Year.* P 12.
562 **242** 5c. grey-green 35 10

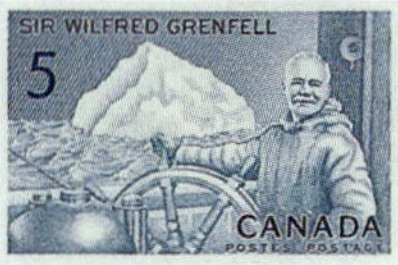

243 Sir W. Grenfell

244 National Flag

1965 (9 June). *Birth Centenary of Sir Wilfred Grenfell (missionary).* P 12.
563 **243** 5c. deep bluish green..................... 20 10

1965 (30 June). *Inauguration of National Flag.* P 12.
564 **244** 5c. red and blue 15 10

245 Sir Winston Churchill

246 Peace Tower, Parliament Buildings, Ottawa

(Des P. Weiss from photo by Karsh. Litho)

1965 (12 Aug). *Churchill Commemoration.* P 12.
565 **245** 5c. purple-brown........................... 15 10

(Des Philips-Gutkin)

1965 (8 Sept). *Inter-Parliamentary Union Conference, Ottawa.* P 12.
566 **246** 5c. deep green 10 10

247 Parliament Buildings, Ottawa, 1865

248 "Gold, Frankincense and Myrrh"

(Des G. Trottier)

1965 (8 Sept). *Centenary of Proclamation of Ottawa as Capital.* P 12.
567 **247** 5c. brown... 10 10

(Des Helen Fitzgerald)

1965 (13 Oct). *Christmas.* P 12.
568 **248** 3c. olive-green 10 10
a. Pack. Two blocks of 25 .... 5·00
p. Two phosphor bands .... 10 1·30
pa. Pack. Two blocks of 25 .... 5·50
569 5c. ultramarine 10 10
p. Two phosphor bands 25 35
Nos. 568a and 568pa are blocks with the outer edges imperf. These come from "$1.50 Plastic Packages" sold at post offices.

249 "Alouette 2" over Canada

250 La Salle

1966 (5 Jan). *Launching of Canadian Satellite, "Alouette 2".* P 12.
570 **249** 5c. ultramarine 15 10

(Des Brigdens Ltd., Toronto)

1966 (13 Apr). *300th Anniv of La Salle's Arrival in Canada.* P 12.
571 **250** 5c. deep bluish green.................... 15 10

251 Road Signs

252 Canadian Delegation and Houses of Parliament

(Des Helen Fitzgerald)

1966 (2 May). *Highway Safety. Invisible gum.* P 12.
572 **251** 5c. yellow, blue and black............ 15 10

(Des P. Pederson (Brigdens Ltd.))

1966 (26 May). *London Conference Centenary.* P 12.
573 **252** 5c. red-brown 10 10

253 Douglas Point Nuclear Power Station

254 Parliamentary Library, Ottawa

(Des A. L. Pollock)

1966 (27 July). *Peaceful Uses of Atomic Energy.* P 12.
574 **253** 5c. ultramarine 10 10

(Des Brigdens Ltd.)

1966 (8 Sept). *Commonwealth Parliamentary Association Conference, Ottawa.* P 12.
575 **254** 5c. purple 10 10

255 "Praying Hands", after Dürer

256 Flag and Canada on Globe

(Des G. Holloway)

1966 (12 Oct). *Christmas.* P 12.
576 **255** 3c. carmine...................................... 10 10
a. Pack. Two blocks of 25 .... 4·50
p. Two phosphor bands 70 65
pa. Pack. Two blocks of 25 .... 6·50
577 5c. orange.. 10 10
p. Two phosphor bands .... 70 1·00
Nos. 576a and 576pa are blocks with the outer edges imperf. These come from "$1.50 Plastic Packages" sold at post offices.

(Des Brigdens Ltd.)

1967 (11 Jan). *Canadian Centennial. Invisible gum.* P 12.
578 **256** 5c. scarlet and blue........................ 10 10
p. Two phosphor bands .... 30 1·25

257 Northern Lights and Dog-team

258 Totem pole

259 Combine-harvester and oil derrick

260 Ship in lock

261 Harbour scene

261a "Transport"

262 "Alaska Highway" (A.Y. Jackson)

263 The Jack Pine (T. Thomson)

264 "Bylot Island" (L. Harris)

265 "Quebec Ferry" (J. W. Morrice)

266 "The Solemn Land (J. E. H MacDonald)

267 "Summer's Stores" (grain elevators) (J. Ensor)

268 "Oilfield" (near Edmonton) (H. G. Glyde)

268a Library of Parliament

1967 (8 Feb)–**73**. *T* **257/68a**.

A. *Recess C.B.N.*

(i) P 12.

579 1c. brown.. 10 10
a. Booklet pane. Five stamps plus one printed label (2.67) 75
b. Printed on the gummed side......... £600
p. Two phosphor bands .... 30 1·00
pa. Centre phosphor band (12.68)....... 30 1·50
q. Two fluorescent bands (11.71)........ 30 10
580 2c. green 10 10
a. Booklet pane. No. 580×4 *se-tenant* with No. 581×4 with gutter margin between (26.10.70)......................... 1·75
p. Two phosphor bands .... 30 1·00
pa. Centre phosphor band (12.68)....... 30 70
q. Two fluorescent bands (12.72) 40 10
581 3c. slate-purple.. 30 20
p. Two phosphor bands .... 30 1·75
q. Two fluorescent bands (1972?) ...... 1·50 1·00
582 4c. red.. 20 10
a. Booklet pane. Five stamps plus one printed label (2.67) .... 1·75
b. Pack. One block of 25 (8.2.67)....... 10·00
p. One side phosphor band .... 1·25 2·75
pa. Centre phosphor band (3.69).......... 30 1·00
q. Two fluorescent bands (4.73) 40 10
583 5c. blue 20 10
a. Booklet pane. Five stamps plus one printed label (3.67) .... 5·50
b. Pack. One block of 20 (2.67).......... 17·00
p. Two phosphor bands .... 50 1·50
pa. Pack. One block of 20 (8.2.67)....... 35·00
pb. Centre phosphor band (12.68)....... 30 1·50
583*c* 6c. black (2.72)....................................... 70 30
ca. Printed on the gummed side.......... 9·50
cp. Centre phosphor band .... 3.00 3·25
cq. Two fluorescent bands.................... 40 40
584 8c. purple-brown....................................... 25 80
585 10c. olive-green 25 10
p. Two phosphor bands (9.12.69)....... 1·50 2·50
q. Two fluorescent bands (1.72).......... 75 50
586 15c. dull purple 30 10
p. Two phosphor bands (9.12.69)....... 1·50 2·75
q. Two fluorescent bands (2.72) .... 80 1·25
587 20c. deep blue .... 1·40 10
p. Two phosphor bands (9.12.69)....... 2·50 3·50
588 25c. myrtle-green... 75 10
p. Two phosphor bands (9.12.69)....... 4·25 6·50
589 50c. cinnamon .... 1·50 10
590 $1 scarlet .... 1·50 65
579/90 *Set of* 13 .... 6·50 2·00
579pa/588p *Set of* 10.. 13·00 22·00

(ii) Perf 9½×imperf (coil stamps)

591 3c. slate-purple (3.67).............................. 2·00 3·50
592 4c. red (3.67)... 2·00 2·50
593 5c. blue (2.67)... 2·00 2·50

(iii) Perf 10×imperf (coil stamps)

594 6c. orange-red (1.69).................................. 90 35
a. Imperf (vert pair) £190
595 6c. black (8.70)... 35 1·50
a. Imperf (vert pair) £1500
596 7c. green (30.6.71)...................................... 40 1·75
a. Imperf (vert pair) £650
597 8c. black (30.12.71).................................... 1·00 1·25
a. Imperf (vert pair) £325
q. Two fluorescent bands.................... 30 30
qa. Imperf (vert pair) £600

B. *Recess B.A.B.N.*

(i) P 10 (sheets (601/p) or booklets)

598 1c. brown (9.68) .... 30 2·50
a. Booklet pane. No. 598×5 *se-tenant* with No. 599×5 (9.68)...................... 1·75
b. Booklet pane. No. 601×4 *se-tenant* with No. 598 plus one printed label (10.68)....................................... 2·00

599 4c. red (9.68) ... 20 2·00
a. Booklet pane. 25 stamps plus two printed labels ... 6·50
600 5c. blue (9.68) ... 30 2·00
a. Booklet pane of 20 ... 4·50
601 6c. orange-red (10.68) ... 45 10
a. Booklet pane. 25 stamps plus two printed labels (1.69) ... 9·00
p. Two phosphor bands (1.11.68) ... 75 85
602 6c. black (1.70) ... 75 1·40
a. Booklet pane. 25 stamps plus two printed labels ... 14·00
603 6c. black (*re-engraved die*) (8.70) ... 2·50 3·50
a. Booklet pane of 4 ... 10·00

(ii) P 12½×12 (sheets (606/10) or booklets)

604 1c. brown (30.6.71) ... 50 2·50
a. Booklet pane. Nos. 604×4, 605×4 and 609×12 *se-tenant* ... 13·00
b. Booklet pane. Nos. 604/5 and 609×3 *se-tenant* plus one printed label ... 4·00
c. Booklet pane. Nos. 604×3, 608 and 610×2 *se-tenant* (30.12.71) ... 1·50
d. Booklet pane. Nos. 604×6, 608 and 610×11 *se-tenant* (30.12.71) ... 6·50
e. Booklet pane. Nos. 604×4, 608 and 610×5 *se-tenant* (8.72) ... 4·50
q. Two fluorescent bands (30.12.71) ... 40 10
qc. Booklet pane. Nos. 604q×3, 608q and 610q×2 *se-tenant* ... 2·00
qd. Booklet pane. Nos. 604q×6, 608q and 610q×11 *se-tenant* ... 5·00
qe. Booklet pane. Nos. 604q×4, 608q and 610q×5 *se-tenant* (8.72) ... 4·50
605 3c. slate-purple (30.6.71) ... 3·50 5·00
606 6c. orange-red (3.69) ... 60 10
p. Two phosphor bands ... 1·00 1·25
607 6c. black (7.1.70) ... 30 10
a. Booklet pane. 25 stamps plus two printed labels (8.70) ... 15·00
p. Two phosphor bands ... 1·00 2·00
608 6c. black (*re-engraved die*) (9.70) ... 1·00 10
a. Booklet pane of 4 (11.70) ... 4·00
p. One centre phosphor band (9.71) ... 1·75 3·00
q. Two fluorescent bands (30.12.71) ... 1·00 20
609 7c. myrtle-green (30.6.71) ... 30 20
p. Two phosphor bands ... 60 2·50
610 8c. slate-black (30.12.71) ... 30 10
p. Two phosphor bands ... 60 1·00
q. Two fluorescent bands (30.12.71) ... 45 15

No. 581q only exists as a pre-cancel.

Nos. 582b, 583b, 583pa are blocks with the outer edges imperf. These come from "One Dollar Plastic Packages" sold at post offices.

No. 582p comes with the band to the left or right of the stamp, the phosphor having been applied across alternate vertical perforations.

Postal forgeries exist of the 6c. orange printed in lithography and perforated 12½.

Normal

Re-engraved

When the basic postal rate was changed to 6c. the C.B.N. lent their die to B.A.B.N. who made a duplicate die from it by transfer. Parts of this proved to be weak, but it was used for Nos. 601/2 and 606/7. B.A.B.N. later re-engraved their die to make fresh plates which were used for Nos. 603 and 608. No. 608 first appeared on sheets from Plate 4.

There are no records of dates of issue of the booklets, packs and coils, but supplies of these were distributed to depots in the months indicated.

IMPERF BETWEEN PAIRS FROM COIL STAMPS. Nos. 594/7 are known in blocks or horizontal pairs imperf between vertically. Coils are supplied to post offices in batches of ten coils held together by roulettes between every fourth stamp so that they can easily be split apart. If two or more unsplit coils are purchased it is possible to obtain blocks or pairs imperf between vertically.

Vertical coil stamps are also known imperf between horizontally or with some stamps apparently completely imperf. These can result from blind perforations identifiable by slight indentations.

WHITE FLUORESCENT PAPER. Different papers with varying degrees of whiteness have been used for Canadian stamps, but during 1968–70 a distinctive very white and highly fluorescent paper was used known as "hybrite"; this fluoresces on the back and front. This paper has also been employed for commemorative issues, some of which exist on more than one type of paper.

FLUORESCENT BANDS. During the second half of 1971 new sorting machines were installed in the Ottawa area which were activated by stamps bearing fluorescent bands. These differ from the Winnipeg phosphor bands in that they react green and have no after-glow. To the naked eye the fluorescent bands appear shiny when compared with the remainder of the stamp when looking along its surface. Winnipeg phosphor bands appear matt.

The experiments were successful and what was at first called "Ottawa tagging" has since come into more general use and the Winnipeg phosphor was phased out. However, the substance at first used (known as OP-4) was found to migrate to envelopes, documents, album pages, etc. as well as to adjoining stamps. Late in 1972 this fault was cured by using another substance (called OP-2). The migrating bands were used on early printings of Nos. 604q, 608q and 610q as well as certain stamps referred to in a footnote after No. 692. It is most advisable to use plastic mounts for housing stamps with migrating bands or else clear acetate should be affixed to the album leaves.

269 Canadian Pavilion

270 Allegory of "Womanhood" on Ballot-box

(Des C.B.N.)

1967 (28 Apr). *World Fair, Montreal.* P 12.
611 **269** 5c. blue and red ... 10 10

(Des Helen Fitzgerald. Litho)

1967 (24 May). *50th Anniv of Women's Franchise.* P 12.
612 **270** 5c. reddish purple and black ... 10 10

271 Queen Elizabeth II and Centennial Emblem

272 Athlete

(Portrait from photo by Anthony Buckley)

1967 (30 June). *Royal Visit.* P 12.
613 **271** 5c. plum and orange-brown ... 15 10

(Des Brigdens Ltd.)

1967 (19 July). *Fifth Pan-American Games, Winnipeg.* P 12.
614 **272** 5c. rose-red ... 10 10

273 "World News"

274 Governor-General Vanier

(Des W. McLauchlan)

1967 (31 Aug). *50th Anniv of the Canadian Press.* P 12.
615 **273** 5c. blue ... 10 10

(Des from photo by Karsh)

1967 (15 Sept). *Vanier Commemoration.* P 12.
616 **274** 5c. black ... 10 10

PRINTERS. The following were printed either by the Canadian Bank Note Co, Ottawa (C.B.N.) or the British American Bank Note Co, Ottawa (B.A.B.N.), *except where otherwise stated.*

275 People of 1867 and Toronto, 1967

276 Carol Singers

(Des and recess C.B.N.)

1967 (28 Sept). *Centenary of Toronto as Capital City of Ontario.* P 12.
617 **275** 5c. myrtle-green and vermilion ... 10 10

(Des and recess B.A.B.N.)

1967 (11 Oct). *Christmas.* P 12.
618 **276** 3c. scarlet ... 10 10
a. Pack. Two blocks of 25 ... 3·25
p. Two phosphor bands ... 20 60
pa. Pack. Two blocks of 25 ... 3·25
619 5c. emerald-green ... 10 10
p. Two phosphor bands ... 70 60

Nos. 618a and 618pa are blocks with the outer edges imperf. These come from "$1.50 Plastic Packs" sold at post offices.

277 Grey Jays

278 Weather Map and Instruments

(Des M. G. Loates. Litho C.B.N.)

1968 (15 Feb). *Wild Life.* P 12.
620 **277** 5c. multicoloured ... 30 10
See also Nos. 638/40.

(Des and litho B.A.B.N.)

1968 (13 Mar). *Bicentenary of First Meteorological Readings.* P 11.
621 **278** 5c. multicoloured ... 15 10

279 Narwhal

280 Globe, Maple Leaf and Rain Gauge

(Des J. A. Crosby. Litho B.A.B.N.)

1968 (10 Apr). *Wildlife.* P 11.
622 **279** 5c. multicoloured ... 15 10

No. 622 has a background of yellow-green and pale blue but copies are known with the yellow-green apparently missing. This "yellow-green" is produced by an overlay of yellow on the blue but we have not come across any copies where the yellow is completely missing and the wide range of colour variation is due to technical difficulties in maintaining an exact blend of the two colours.

(Des I. von Mosdossy. Litho B.A.B.N.)

1968 (8 May). *International Hydrological Decade.* P 11.
623 **280** 5c. multicoloured ... 15 10

IMPERF EDGES. On Nos. 624/54, 657 and 659 (stamps printed by the B.A.B.N. Co.) the outer edges of the sheets were guillotined to remove the imprints for P.O. stock so that single stamps may, therefore, be found with either one, or two adjacent sides imperforate.

281 *Nonsuch*

282 Lacrosse Players

(Recess and photo B.A.B.N.)

1968 (5 June). *300th Anniv of Voyage of the "*Nonsuch*".* P 10.
624 **281** 5c. multicoloured ... 20 10

(Des J. E. Aldridge. Recess and photo B.A.B.N.)

1968 (3 July). *Lacrosse.* P 10.
625 **282** 5c. black, red and lemon ... 15 10

283 Front Page of *The Globe*, George Brown and Legislative Building

284 H. Bourassa

(Des N. Sabolotny. Recess and photo B.A.B.N.)

1968 (21 Aug). *150th Birth Anniv of George Brown (politician and journalist).* P 10.
626 **283** 5c. multicoloured ... 10 10

(Des, recess and litho C.B.N.)

1968 (4 Sept). *Birth Centenary of Henri Bourassa (journalist and politician).* P 12.
627 **284** 5c. black, red and pale cream ... 10 10

285 John McCrae, Battlefield and First Lines of "In Flanders Fields"

286 Armistice Monument, Vimy

(Des I. von Mosdossy. Litho C.B.N.)

1968 (15 Oct). *50th Death Anniv of John McCrae (soldier and poet).* P 12.
628 **285** 5c. multicoloured ... 10 10

(Des and recess C.B.N.)

1968 (15 Oct). *50th Anniversary of 1918 Armistice.* P 12.
629 **286** 15c. slate-black ... 30 40

287 Eskimo Family (carving)

288 "Mother and Child" (carving)

(Designs from Eskimo carvings by Munamee (6c.) and unknown carver (5c.). Photo C.B.N.)

1968. *Christmas.* P 12.

630	**287**	5c. black and new blue (1.11.68)..	10	10
		a. Booklet pane of 10 (15.11.68)	2·25	
		p. One centre phosphor band	10	1·00
		pa. Booklet pane of 10 (15.11.68)	3·00	
631	**288**	6c. black and ochre (15.11.68)......	10	10
		p. Two phosphor bands	20	1·00

289 Curling

290 Vincent Massey

(Des D. Eales. Recess and photo B.A.B.N.)

1969 (15 Jan). *Curling.* P 10.

632	**289**	6c. black, new blue and scarlet	15	10

(Des I. von Mosdossy. Recess and litho C.B.N.)

1969 (20 Feb). *Vincent Massey, First Canadian-born Governor-General.* P 12.

633	**290**	6c. sepia and yellow-ochre...........	10	10

291 "Return from the Harvest Field" (Suzor-Côté)

292 Globe and Tools

(Photo C.B.N.)

1969 (14 Mar). *Birth Centenary of Marc Aurèle de Foy Suzor-Côté (painter).* P 12.

634	**291**	50c. multicoloured	70	2·00

(Des J. Hébert. Recess B.A.B.N.)

1969 (21 May). *50th Anniv of International Labour Organisation.* P 12½×12.

635	**292**	6c. bronze-green...........................	10	10

293 Vickers FB-27 Vimy Aircraft over Atlantic Ocean

294 "Sir William Osler" (J. S. Sargent)

(Des R. W. Bradford. Recess and photo B.A.B.N.)

1969 (13 June). *50th Anniv of First Non-stop Transatlantic Flight.* P 12×12½.

636	**293**	15c. chocolate, bright green and pale blue	40	55

(Des, recess and photo B.A.B.N.)

1969 (23 June). *50th Death Anniv of Sir William Osler (physician).* P 12½×12.

637	**294**	6c. deep blue, light blue and chestnut	20	10

295 White-throated Sparrows

298 Flags of Winter and Summer Games

(Des M. G. Loates. Litho C.B.N.)

1969 (23 July). *Birds. T* **295** *and similar multicoloured designs.* P 12.

638		6c. Type **295**..	25	10
639		10c. Savannah Sparrow ("Ipswich Sparrow") (*horiz*)............................	35	1·10
640		25c. Hermit Thrush (*horiz*)	1·10	3·50
638/40 *Set of 3*		....	1·50	4·25

(Des C. McDiarmid. Recess and litho C.B.N.)

1969 (15 Aug). *Canadian Games.* P 12.

641	**298**	6c. emerald, scarlet and blue........	10	10

299 Outline of Prince Edward Island showing Charlottetown

300 Sir Isaac Brock and Memorial Column

(Des L. Fitzgerald. Recess and photo B.A.B.N.)

1969 (15 Aug). *Bicentenary of Charlottetown as Capital of Prince Edward Island.* P 12×12½.

642	**299**	6c. yellow-brown, black and blue	20	20

(Des I. von Mosdossy. Recess and litho C.B.N.)

1969 (12 Sept). *Birth Bicentenary of Sir Isaac Brock.* P 12.

643	**300**	6c. orange, bistre and bistre-brown.......................................	10	10

301 Children of the World in Prayer

302 Stephen Butler Leacock, Mask and "Mariposa"

(Des Rapid Grip and Batten Ltd. Litho C.B.N.)

1969 (8 Oct). *Christmas.* P 12.

644	**301**	5c. multicoloured	10	10
		a. Booklet pane of 10..................	1·50	
		p. One centre phosphor band	10	1·25
		pa. Booklet pane of 10.................	2·50	
645		6c. multicoloured	10	10
		a. Black (inscr, value and frame omitted).................................	£1400	£850
		p. Two phosphor bands	20	1·25

(Des, recess and photo B.A.B.N.)

1969 (12 Nov). *Birth Centenary of Stephen Butler Leacock (humorist).* P 12×12½.

646	**302**	6c. multicoloured	10	10

303 Symbolic Cross-roads

304 "Enchanted Owl" (Kenojuak)

(Des K. C. Lochhead. Litho C.B.N.)

1970 (27 Jan). *Centenary of Manitoba.* P 12.

647	**303**	6c. ultramarine, lemon and vermilion................................	15	10
		p. Two phosphor bands	15	80

(Des N. E. Hallendy and Miss S. Van Raalte. Recess C.B.N.)

1970 (27 Jan). *Centenary of Northwest Territories.* P 12.

648	**304**	6c. carmine, red and black	10	10

305 Microscopic View of Inside of Leaf

306 Expo 67 Emblem and Stylized Cherry Blossom

(Des I. Charney. Recess and photo B.A.B.N.)

1970 (18 Feb). *International Biological Programme.* P 12×12½.

649	**305**	6c. emerald, orange-yellow and ultramarine................................	15	10

(Des E. R. C. Bethune. Litho C.B.N.)

1970 (18 Mar). *World Fair, Osaka. T* **306** *and similar horiz designs. Multicoloured; colour of Cherry Blossom given.* P 12.

650		25c. red..	1·50	2·25
		a. Block of 4. Nos. 650/3............	5·50	8·00
		p. Two phosphor bands	1·50	2·50
		pa. Block of 4. Nos. 650p/3p	5·50	9·00
651		25c. violet..	1·50	2·25
		p. Two phosphor bands	1·50	2·50
652		25c. green...	1·50	2·25
		p. Two phosphor bands	1·50	2·50
653		25c. blue...	1·50	2·25
		p. Two phosphor bands	1·50	2·50
650/3 *Set of 4*		....	5·50	8·00
650p/3p *Set of 4*		....	5·50	9·00

Designs:—No. 650, Type **306**; No. 651, Dogwood and stylized cherry blossom; No. 652, White Trillium and stylized cherry blossom; No. 653, White Garden Lily and stylized cherry blossom.

Nos. 650/3 and 650p/3p are printed together in sheets of 50 (5×10). In the first, second, fourth and fifth vertical rows the four different designs are arranged in *se-tenant* blocks, whilst the centre row is composed as follows (reading downwards:—650(p)/3(p), 650(p) ×2, 653(p), 651(p), 652(p) and 650(p).

310 Henry Kelsey

311 "Towards Unification"

(Des D. Burton. Recess and photo B.A.B.N.)

1970 (15 Apr). *300th Birth Anniv of Henry Kelsey (explorer).* P 12×12½.

654	**310**	6c. multicoloured	10	10

(Des B. Fisher. Litho B.A.B.N.)

1970 (13 May). *25th Anniv of United Nations.* P 11.

655	**311**	10c. blue..	75	75
		p. Two phosphor bands	80	2·00
656		15c. magenta and bluish lilac	75	50
		p. Two phosphor bands	80	2·00

312 Louis Riel (Métis leader)

313 Mackenzie's Inscription, Dean Channel

(Des R. Derreth. Photo B.A.B.N.)

1970 (19 June). *Louis Riel Commemoration.* P 12½×12.

657	**312**	6c. greenish blue and vermilion...	10	10

(Design from Government Archives photo. Recess C.B.N.)

1970 (25 June). *Sir Alexander Mackenzie (explorer).* P 12×11½.

658	**313**	6c. bistre-brown	15	10

314 Sir Oliver Mowat (statesman)

315 "Isles of Spruce"(A. Lismer)

(Des E. Roch. Recess and photo B.A.B.N.)

1970 (12 Aug). *Sir Oliver Mowat Commemoration.* P 12×12½.

659	**314**	6c. vermilion and black................	10	10

(Litho Ashton-Potter)

1970 (18 Sept). *50th Anniv of "Group of Seven" (artists).* P 11.

660	**315**	6c. multicoloured	10	10

316 "Horse-drawn Sleigh" (D. Niskala)

317 "Christ in Manger"(C. Fortier)

(Des from children's drawings. Litho C.B.N.)

1970 (7 Oct). *Christmas. Horiz designs as T* **316/17**, *showing children's drawings. Multicoloured.* P 12.

661		5c. Type **316**......................................	50	20
		a. Strip of 5. Nos. 661/5	2·25	2·50
		p. One centre phosphor band	90	1·25
		pa. Strip of 5. Nos. 661p/5p............	4·00	5·00
662		5c. "Stable and Star of Bethlehem"(L. Wilson) (26×21 *mm*)...	50	20
		p. One centre phosphor band	90	1·25
663		5c. "Snowmen" (M. Lecompte) (26×21 *mm*)......................................	50	20
		p. One centre phosphor band	90	1·25
664		5c. "Skiing" (D. Durham) (26×21 *mm*)	50	20
		p. One centre phosphor band	90	1·25
665		5c. "Santa Claus" (A. Martin) (26×21 *mm*)...	50	20
		p. One centre phosphor band	90	1·25
666		6c. "Santa Claus" (E. Bhattacharya) (26×21 *mm*)..................................	50	20
		a. Strip of 5. Nos. 666/70	2·25	2·50
		p. Two phosphor bands	90	1·25
		pa. Strip of 5. Nos. 666p/70p............	4·00	5·00
667		6c. "Christ in Manger" (J. McKinney) (26×21 *mm*)..................................	50	20
		p. Two phosphor bands	90	1·25

668 6c. "Toy Shop" (N. Whateley) (26×21 *mm*) ... 50 20
p. Two phosphor bands ... 90 1·25
669 6c. "Christmas Tree" (J. Pomperleau) (26×21 *mm*) ... 50 20
p. Two phosphor bands ... 90 1·25
670 6c. "Church" (J. McMillan) (26×21 *mm*) ... 50 20
p. Two phosphor bands ... 90 1·25
671 10c. Type **317** ... 30 30
p. Two phosphor bands ... 55 1·25
672 15c. "Trees and Sledge" (J. Dojcak) (35×21 *mm*) ... 45 60
p. Two phosphor bands ... 70 1·75
661/72 *Set of* 12 ... 4·75 2·50
661p/672p *Set of* 12 ... 8·50 12·50

The designs of the 5c. and 6c. were each issued with the various designs *se-tenant* in a diamond shaped arrangement within the sheet. This generally results in *se-tenant* pairs both vert and horiz, but due to the sheet arrangement vert and horiz pairs of the same design exist from the two centre vert and horiz rows.

328 Sir Donald A. Smith

329 "Big Raven" (E. Carr)

(Des Dora de Pédery-Hunt. Litho C.B.N.)

1970 (4 Nov). *150th Birth Anniv of Sir Donald Alexander Smith. P* 12.
673 **328** 6c. yellow, brown and bronze-green ... 15 10

STAMP BOOKLETS

Booklet Nos. SB1/48 are stapled.

All booklets up to and including No. SB41 contain panes consisting of two rows of three (3×2).

B **1**

1900 (11 June). *Red on pink cover. Two panes of six 2c. (No. 155ba).*
SB1 25c. booklet. Cover as Type B **1** with English text ... £1800

1903 (1 July). *Red on pink cover. Two panes of six 2c. (No. 176a).*
SB2 25c. booklet. Cover as Type B **1** with English text ... £1900

1912 (Jan)–**16**. *Red on pink cover. Two panes of six 2c. (No. 201a).*
SB3 25c. booklet. Cover as Type B **1** with English text ... 60·00
a. Cover handstamped "NOTICE Change in Postal Rates For New Rates See Postmaster" ... 60·00
b. French text (4.16) ... £130
ba. Cover handstamped "AVIS Changement des tarifs Postaux Pour les nouveaux tarifs consulter le maitre de poste" ... £100

1913 (1 May)–**16**. *Green on pale green cover. Four panes of six 1c. (No. 197a).*
SB4 25c. booklet. Cover as Type B **1** with English text ... £375
a. Containing pane No. 199a ... 75·00
ab. Cover handstamped "NOTICE Change in Postal Rates For New Rates See Postmaster" ... 75·00
b. French text (28.4.16) ... £600
ba. Containing pane No. 199a ... £180
bb. Cover handstamped "AVIS Changement des tarifs Postaux Pour les nouveaux tarifs consulter le maitre de poste" ... £550

1922 (Mar). *Black on brown cover. Two panes of four 3c. and 2 labels (No. 205a).*
SB5 25c. booklet. Cover as Type B **1** with English text ... £300
a. French text ... £600

1922 (July–Dec). *Black on blue cover. Panes of four 1c., 2c. and 3c. (Nos. 246aa, 247aa, 205a) and 2 labels.*
SB6 25c. booklet. Cover as Type B **1** with English text ... £300
a. French text (Dec) ... £500

1922 (Dec). *Black on orange cover. Four panes of six 1c. (No. 246ab).*
SB7 25c. booklet. Cover as Type B **1** with English text ... £100
a. French text ... £130

1922 (Dec). *Black on green cover. Two panes of six 2c. (No. 247ab).*
SB8 25c. booklet. Cover as Type B **1** with English text ... £600
a. French text ... £700

1923 (Dec). *Black on blue cover. Panes of four 1c., 2c. and 3c. (Nos. 246aa, 247aa, 248aa) and 2 labels.*
SB9 25c. booklet. Cover as Type B **1** with English text ... £200
a. French text ... £475

1923 (Dec)–**24**. *Black on brown cover. Two panes of four 3c. (No. 248aa) and 2 labels.*
SB10 25c. booklet. Cover as Type B **1** with English text ... £180
a. French text (5.24) ... £275

B **2**

1928 (16 Oct). *Black on green cover. Two panes of six 2c. (No. 276a).*
SB11 25c. booklet. Cover as Type B **2** with English text ... 55·00
a. French text ... 85·00

1928 (25 Oct). *Black on orange cover. Four panes of six 1c. (No. 275a).*
SB12 25c. booklet. Cover as Type B **2** with English text ... £100
a. French text ... £190

1929 (6 Jan). *Plain manilla cover. Three panes of six 1c., two panes of six 2c. and one pane of six 5c. (Nos. 275a, 276a, 279a).*
SB13 72c. booklet. Plain cover ... £325
a. With "Philatelic Div., Fin. Br. P.O. Dept., Ottawa" circular cachet on front cover ... £850
b. With "1928" in the centre of the circular cachet ... £1300

1930 (17 June). *Black on green cover. Two panes of six 2c. (No. 290a).*
SB14 25c. booklet. Cover as Type B **2** with English text ... 90·00
a. French text ... £160

1930 (17 Nov). *Black on red cover. Two panes of six 2c. (No. 291a).*
SB15 25c. booklet. Cover as Type B **2** with English text ... 55·00
a. French text ... £130

1931 (13 July). *Black on red cover. Two panes of four 3c. (No. 293a) and 2 labels.*
SB16 25c. booklet. Cover as Type B **2** with English text ... 80·00
a. French text ... £110

1931 (21 July). *Black on green cover. Four panes of six 1c. (No. 289b).*
SB17 25c. booklet. Cover as Type B **2** with English text ... £120
a. French text ... £170

1931 (23 July). *Black on brown cover. Two panes of six 2c. (No. 292a).*
SB18 25c. booklet. Cover as Type B **2** with English text ... £110
a. French text ... £350

1931 (13 Nov). *Black on blue cover. Panes of four 1c., 2c. and 3c. (Nos. 289db, 292ba, 293a) and 2 labels.*
SB19 25c. booklet. Cover as Type B **2** with English text ... £250
a. French text ... £350

1933 (22 Aug–13 Nov). *Black on red cover. Two panes of four 3c. (No. 321a) and 2 labels.*
SB20 25c. booklet. Cover as Type B **2** with English text (13 Nov) ... 85·00
a. French text (22 Aug) ... £160

1933 (7 Sept). *Black on brown cover. Two panes of six 2c. (No. 320a).*
SB21 25c. booklet. Cover as Type B **2** with English text ... £180
a. French text ... £375

1933 (19 Sept–5 Dec). *Black on blue cover. Panes of four 1c., 2c. and 3c. (Nos. 319b, 320b, 321ba) and 2 labels.*
SB22 25c. booklet. Cover as Type B **2** with English text ... £200
a. French text (5 Dec) ... £300

1933 (28 Dec)–**34**. *Black on green cover. Four panes of six 1c. (No. 319a).*
SB23 25c. booklet. Cover as Type B **2** with English text ... £120
a. French text (26.3.34) ... £170

B **3**

1935 (1 June–8 Aug). *Red on white cover. Two panes of four 3c. (No. 343a) and 2 labels.*
SB24 25c. booklet. Cover as Type B **3** with English text (8 Aug) ... 60·00
a. French text (1 June) ... £100

1935 (22 July–1 Sept). *Blue on white cover. Panes of four 1c., 2c. and 3c. (Nos. 341b, 342b, 343a) and 2 labels.*
SB25 25c. booklet. Cover as Type B **3** with English text ... £140
a. French text (1 Sept) ... £180

1935 (19 Aug–18 Oct). *Green on white cover. Four panes of six 1c. (No. 341a).*
SB26 25c. booklet. Cover as Type B **3** with English text ... 90·00
a. French text (18 Oct) ... £130

1935 (16–18 Mar). *Brown on white cover. Two panes of six 2c. (No. 342a).*
SB27 25c. booklet. Cover as Type B **3** with English text ... 70·00
a. French text (18 Mar) ... £120

B **4**

1937 (14 Apr)–**38**. *Blue and white cover. Panes of four 1c., 2c. and 3c. (Nos. 357a, 358a, 359a) and 2 labels.*
SB28 25c. booklet. Cover as Type B **3** with English text ... 85·00
a. French text (4.1.38) ... £130
SB29 25c. booklet. Cover as Type B **4** with English text 57 mm wide ... 70·00
a. English text 63 mm wide ... £110
b. French text 57 mm wide (4.1.38) ... 90·00
ba. French text 63 mm wide ... £170

1937 (23–27 Apr). *Red and white cover. Two panes of four 3c. (No. 359a) and 2 labels.*
SB30 25c. booklet. Cover as Type B **3** with English text (27 Apr) ... 27·00
a. French text (23 Apr) ... 55·00
SB31 25c. booklet. Cover as Type B **4** with English text 57 mm wide (27 Apr) ... 10·00
a. English text 63 mm wide ... 50·00
b. French text 57 mm wide (23 Apr) ... 13·00
ba. French text 63 mm wide ... £170

1937 (18 May)–**38**. *Green and white cover. Four panes of six 1c. (No. 357b).*
SB32 25c. booklet. Cover as Type B **3** with English text ... 45·00
a. French text (14.10.38) ... 60·00
SB33 25c. booklet. Cover as Type B **4** with English text 57 mm wide ... 24·00
a. English text 63 mm wide ... 60·00
b. French text 57 mm wide (14.10.38) ... 18·00
ba. French text 63 mm wide ... £150

1938 (3 May)–**39**. *Brown and white cover. Two panes of six 2c. (No. 358b).*
SB34 25c. booklet. Cover as Type B **3** with English text ... 55·00
a. French text (3.3.39) ... 75·00
SB35 25c. booklet. Cover as Type B **4** with English text 57 mm wide ... 23·00
a. English text 63 mm wide ... 70·00
b. French text 57 mm wide ... 42·00
ba. French text 63 mm wide ... £100

1942 (20–29 Aug). *Red and white cover. Two panes of four 3c. (No. 377a) and 2 labels.*
SB36 25c. booklet. Cover as Type B **4** with English text ... 8·50
a. French text (29 Aug) ... 12·00

1942 (12–14 Sept). *Violet and white cover. Panes of four 1c., 2c. and 3c. (Nos. 375a, 376a, 377a), each with 2 labels.*
SB37 25c. booklet. Cover as Type B **4** with English text (14 Sept) ... 48·00
a. French text (12 Sept) ... 90·00

1942 (6 Oct)–**43**. *Brown and white cover. Two panes of six 2c. (No. 376b).*
SB38 25c. booklet. Cover as Type B **4** with English text ... 48·00
a. French text (6.4.43) ... 70·00

1942 (24 Nov)–**46**. *Green and white cover. Four panes of six 1c. (No. 375b).*
SB39 25c. booklet. Cover as Type B **4** with English text ... 11·00
a. French text (16.2.43) ... 17·00
b. Bilingual text (8.1.46) ... 25·00

1943 (3 May)–**46**. *Orange and white cover. One pane of six 4c. (No. 380a).*
SB40 25c. booklet. Cover as Type B **4** with English text ... 4·00
a. French text (12.5.43) ... 15·00
b. Bilingual text (8.1.46) ... 18·00

1943 (28 Aug)–**46**. *Purple and white cover. Two panes of four 3c. (No. 378a) and 2 labels.*
SB41 25c. booklet. Cover as Type B **4** with English text ... 10·00
a. French text (7.9.43) ... 28·00
b. Bilingual text (8.1.46) ... 22·00

B **5**

1943 (1 Sept)–**46**. *Black and white cover. Panes of three 1c., 3c. and 4c. (Nos. 394a, 395a, 396a) (3×1).*

SB42	25c. booklet. Cover as Type B **5** with English text	30·00
	a. French text (18.9.43)	42·00
	c. Bilingual text (23.1.46)	40·00

B **6**

1947 (24 Nov). *Brown on orange cover. Panes of six 3c. and 4c. (3×2) and two panes of four 7c. (2×2) (Nos. 378b, 380a, 407a).*

SB43	$1 booklet. Cover as Type B **6** with English text	25·00
	a. French text	40·00

1950 (12 Apr–18 May). *Purple and white cover. Two panes of four 3c. (No. 416a) and 2 labels (3×2).*

SB44	25c. booklet. Cover as Type B **4** with English text	5·00
	a. Bilingual text (18 May)	5·00

1950 (5–10 May). *Orange and white cover. One pane of six 4c. (No. 417a) (3×2).*

SB45	25c. booklet, Cover as Type B **4** with English text	38·00
	a. Stitched	60·00
	b. Bilingual text (10 May)	40·00

1950 (18 May). *Black and white cover. Panes of three 1c., 3c. and 4c. (Nos. 422ba, 423a, 423ba) (3×1).*

SB46	25c. booklet. Cover as Type B **5** with English text	50·00
	a. Bilingual text	55·00

1951 (2 June). *Orange and white cover. One pane of six 4c. (No. 417ba) (3×2).*

SB47	25c. booklet. Cover as Type B **4** with English text	6·00
	a. Stitched	12·00
	b. Bilingual text	12·00

1951 (25 Oct)–**52**. *Black and white cover. Panes of three 1c., 3c. and 4c. (Nos. 422ba, 423a, 423ca) (3×1).*

SB48	25c. booklet. Cover as Type B **5** with English text	38·00
	a. Bilingual text (9.7.52)	42·00

1953 (6 July–19 Aug). *Orange cover. One pane of six 4c. (No. 453a) (3×2).*

SB49	25c. booklet. Cover as Type B **4** with English text	4·00
	a. Bilingual text (19 Aug)	6·50

1953 (17 July–20 Oct). *Purple cover. Two panes of four 3c. (No. 452a) and 2 labels (3×2).*

SB50	25c. booklet. Cover as Type B **4** with English text	3·75
	a. Bilingual text (20 Oct)	11·00

1953 (12 Aug). *Grey cover. Panes of three 1c., 3c. and 4c. (Nos. 458a, 459a, 460a) (3×1).*

SB51	25c. booklet. Cover as Type B **5** with English text	16·00
	a. Bilingual text	26·00

All the following booklets are bilingual

1954 (1 Apr–Nov). *Blue cover as Type* B **4**.

SB52	25c. booklet containing pane of five 5c. and 1 label (No. 473a) (3×2)	2·00
	a. Stitched (Nov)	3·25

1954 (14 July–Nov). *Blue cover as Type* B **4**.

SB53	25c. booklet containing pane of five 5c. and 1 label (No. 467a) (3×2)	2·00
	a. Stitched (Nov)	3·50

1955 (7 July). *Violet cover as Type* B **4**.

SB54	25c. booklet containing pane of six 4c. (No. 466a) (3×2)	4·75

B **7**

1956 (1 June). *Red and white cover as Type* B **7**.

SB55	25c. booklet containing two panes of five 1c. and five 4c., each with 1 label (Nos. 463a, 466b) (3×2)	3·00

1956 (July). *Blue and white cover as Type* B **7**.

SB56	25c. booklet containing pane of five 5c. and 1 label (No. 467a) (3×2)	2·75

B **8**

1963 (May)–**67**. *Blue and white cover as Type* B **7**.

SB57	25c. booklet containing pane of five 5c. and 1 label (No. 531a) (2×3)	3·75
	a. Cover Type B 8 (1.67)	32·00

1963 (15 May). *Red and white cover as Type* B **7**.

SB58	25c. booklet containing two panes of five 1c. and five 4c., each with 1 label (Nos. 527a, 530a) (2×3)	7·00

1967 (Feb). *Red cover as Type* B **8**.

SB59	25c. booklet containing two panes of five 1c. and five 4c., each with 1 label (Nos. 579a, 582a) (2×3)	2·50

1967 (Mar). *Blue cover as Type* B **8**.

SB60	25c. booklet containing pane of five 5c. and 1 label (No. 583a) (2×3)	5·50

B **9**

1968 (Sept). *Brown and cream cover, 70×48 mm, as Type* B **9**.

SB61	25c. booklet containing se-tenant pane of five 1c. and five 4c. (No. 598a) (2×5)	1·75

1968 (Sept). *Red and cream cover as Type* B **9**.

SB62	$1 booklet containing pane of twenty-five 4c. and 2 labels (No. 599a) (3×9)	6·50

1968 (Sept). *Blue and cream cover, 82×48 mm, as Type* B **9**.

SB63	$1 booklet containing pane of twenty 5c. (No. 600a) (2×10)	4·50

1968 (Oct). *Orange and cream cover, 70×48 mm, as Type* B **9**, *but without border.*

SB64	25c. booklet containing se-tenant pane of one 1c., four 6c. and 1 label (No. 598b) (2×3)	2·00

B **10** (*Illustration reduced. Actual size 128×60 mm*)

1968 (15 Nov). *Christmas. Red and green cover as Type* B **10**.

SB65	$1 booklet containing two panes of ten 5c. (No. 630a) (5×2)	4·50
	p. Phosphor (No. 630pa)	6·00

Nos. SB65/p exist with left or right opening (i.e. with selvedge at left or right of pane).

1969 (Jan). *Orange-red on cream cover as Type* B **9**, *but without border.*

SB66	$1.50, booklet containing pane of twenty-five 6c. and 2 labels (No. 601a) (3×9)	9·00

1969 (8 Oct). *Christmas. Red cover size as Type* B **10**.

SB67	$1 booklet containing two panes of ten 5c. (No. 644a) (5×2)	3·00
	p. Phosphor (No. 644pa)	5·00

1970 (Jan). *Black on cream cover as Type* B **9**, *but without border.*

SB68	$1.50 booklet containing pane of twenty-five 6c. and 2 labels (No. 602a) (3×9)	14·00

1970 (Aug). *Black on cream cover, 70×48 mm, as Type* B **9**, *but without border.*

SB69	25c. booklet containing pane of four 6c. (No. 603a) (2×2)	10·00

1970 (Aug). *Black on cream cover as Type* B **9**, *but without border.*

SB70	$1.50 booklet containing pane of twenty-five 6c. and 2 labels (No. 607a) (3×9)	15·00

1970 (26 Oct). *Indigo on cream cover, 70×50mm. Inscr* "CANADIAN POSTAGE STAMPS ... MADE EXPRESSLY FOR OPAL MANUFACTURING CO. LIMITED".

SB71	25c. booklet containing four 2c. and four 3c. (No. 580a) (2×2) with gutter margin between	1·75

No. SB71 was produced by the Canadian Bank Note Co for use in the private stamp-vending machines owned by the Opal Manufacturing Co Ltd, Toronto. To cover the cost of manufacture and installation these booklets were sold at 25c. each. They were not available from the Canadian Post Office.

1970 (Nov). *Black on cream cover, 70×48 mm, as Type* B **9**, *but without border.*

SB72	25c. booklet containing pane of four 6c. (No. 608a) (2×2)	4·00

REGISTRATION STAMPS

R **1**

(Eng and recess-printed British-American Bank Note Co, Montreal and Ottawa)

1875 (15 Nov)–**92**. *White wove paper.*

		(a) P 12 (or slightly under).		
R1	R **1**	2c. orange	60·00	1·00
R2		2c. orange-red (1889)	70·00	6·00
R3		2c. vermilion	75·00	7·50
		a. Imperf (pair)	†	£3750
R4		2c. rose-carmine (1888)	£150	55·00
R5		5c. yellow-green (1878)	£110	1·50
R6		5c. deep green	85·00	1·25
		a. Imperf (pair)	£750	
R7		5c. blue-green (1888)	90·00	1·50
R7*a*		5c. dull sea-green (1892)	£140	3·25
R8		8c. bright blue	£375	£275
R9		8c. dull blue	£350	£250
		(b) P 12×11½ or 12×11¾.		
R10	R **1**	2c. orange	£325	60·00
R11		5c. green (*shades*)	£900	£150

SPECIAL DELIVERY STAMPS

PRINTERS. The following Special Delivery and Postage Due Stamps were recess-printed by the American Bank Note Co (to 1928), the British American Bank Note Co (to 1934), and the Canadian Bank Note Co (1935 onwards).

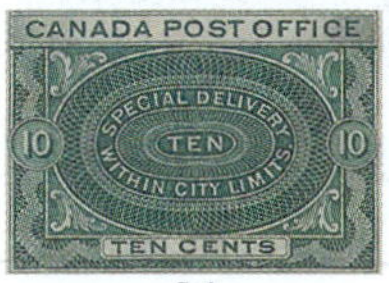

S **1**

1898–1920. P 12.

S1	S **1**	10c. blue-green (28.6.98)	80·00	10·00
S2		10c. deep green (12.13)	50·00	9·00
S3		10c. yellowish green (8.20)	60·00	9·00

The differences between Types I and II (figures "10" with and without shading) formerly illustrated were due to wear of the plate. There was only one die.

S **2**

S **3** Mail-carrying, 1867 and 1927

1922 (21 Aug). P 12.

S4	S **2**	20c. carmine-red	35·00	6·50

No. S4 exists in two slightly different sizes due to the use of "wet" or "dry" printing processes. See note below No. 195.

1927 (29 June). *60th Anniversary of Confederation.* P 12.

S5	S **3**	20c. orange	11·00	10·00

No. S5 exists imperforate, imperf×perf or perf×imperf (*Price, in each instance,* £150 *per pair, un*).

S **4**

1930 (2 Sept). P 11.

S6	S **4**	20c. brown-red	42·00	7·00

1932 (24 Dec). *Type as* S **4**, *but inscr* "CENTS" *in place of* "TWENTY CENTS". P 11.

S7	20c. brown-red	45·00	17·00

No. S7 exists imperforate (*Price per pair* £500, *un*).

S 5 Allegory of Progress

(Des A. Foringer)

1935 (1 June). P 12.

S8	S 5	20c. scarlet	3·75	3·50

No. S8 exists imperforate (*Price per pair £600, un*).

S 6 Canadian Coat of Arms

1938–39. P 12.

S9	S 6	10c. green (1.4.39)	21·00	4·00
S10		20c. scarlet (15.6.38)	40·00	28·00

Nos. S9/10 exist imperforate (*Price £600, un, for each pair*).

≡10 10≡

(S 7)

1939 (1 Mar). *Surch with Type* S **7**.

S11	S 6	10c. on 20c. scarlet	10·00	14·00

S 8 Coat of Arms and Flags

S 9 Lockheed L.18 Lodestar

1942 (1 July)–**43**. *War Effort*. P 12.

		(a) Postage.		
S12	S 8	10c. green	8·00	30
		(b) Air.		
S13	S 9	16c. ultramarine	6·00	45
S14		17c. ultramarine (1.4.43)	4·50	55

Nos. S12/14 exist imperforate (*Prices per un pair* 10c. £600, 16c. £650, 17c. £650).

S 10 Arms of Canada and Peace Symbols

S 11 Canadair DC-4M North Star

1946 (16 Sept–5 Dec). P 12.

		(a) Postage.		
S15	S 10	10c. green	5·00	30
		(b) Air. (i) Circumflex accent in "EXPRÊS".		
S16	S 11	17c. ultramarine	4·50	6·50
		(ii) Grave accent in "EXPRÈS".		
S17	S 11	17c. ultramarine (5.12.46)	7·00	5·50

POSTAGE DUE STAMPS

PRINTERS. See note under "Special Delivery Stamps".

D 1

D 2

1906 (1 July)–**28**. P 12.

D1	D 1	1c. dull violet	10·00	2·75
D2		1c. red-violet (1916)	12·00	3·75
		a. Thin paper (10.24)	15·00	20·00
D3		2c. dull violet	25·00	1·00
D4		2c. red-violet (1917)	26·00	1·50
		a. Thin paper (10.24)	32·00	20·00
D5		4c. violet (3.7.28)	45·00	50·00
D6		5c. dull violet	30·00	4·00
D7		5c. red-violet (1917)	32·00	4·00
		a. Thin paper (10.24)	20·00	32·00
D8		10c. violet (3.7.28)	32·00	20·00
D1/8 *Set of* 5			£120	70·00

The 1c., 2c. and 5c. values exist imperforate, without gum (*Price £325 for each un pair*).

Printings up to October 1924 used the "wet" method, those from mid 1925 onwards the "dry". For details of the differences between these two methods, see above No. 196.

1930–32. P 11.

D9	D 2	1c. bright violet (14.7.30)	8·50	11·00
D10		2c. bright violet (21.8.30)	7·50	1·90
D11		4c. bright violet (14.10.30)	15·00	6·50
D12		5c. bright violet (12.12.31)	16·00	32·00
D13		10c. bright violet (24.8.32)	65·00	32·00
D9/13 *Set of* 5			£100	75·00

Nos. D9/11 and D13 exist imperforate, No. D13 also exists imperf×perf (*Price for vertical pair £700, un*).

D 3

D 4

1933–34. P 11.

D14	D 3	1c. violet (5.5.34)	9·50	16·00
D15		2c. violet (20.12.33)	7·50	4·75
D16		4c. violet (12.12.33)	12·00	15·00
D17		10c. violet (20.12.33)	24·00	40·00
D14/17 *Set of* 4			48·00	65·00

No. D14 exists imperforate (*Price per pair £350, un*).

1935–65. P 12.

D18	D 4	1c. violet (14.10.35)	80	10
D19		2c. violet (9.9.35)	3·50	10
D20		3c. violet (4.65)	6·00	5·00
D21		4c. violet (2.7.35)	1·50	10
D22		5c. violet (12.48)	6·00	3·75
D23		6c. violet (1957)	2·00	3·00
D24		10c. violet (16.9.35)	70	10
D18/24 *Set of* 7			18·00	11·00

The 1c., 2c., 4c. and 10c. exist imperforate (*Price £190 for each un pair*).

D 5

1967–78. *Litho*. P 12½×12 (20c., 24c., 50c.) or 12 (others).

		(a) Size 20×17½ mm.		
D25	D 5	1c. scarlet (3.67)	1·75	4·00
D26		2c. scarlet (3.67)	1·00	1·00
D27		3c. scarlet (3.67)	1·00	4·25
D28		4c. scarlet (2.67)	2·75	1·25
D29		5c. scarlet (3.67)	4·25	4·75
D30		6c. scarlet (2.67)	1·60	3·75
D31		10c. scarlet (1.67)	2·00	2·50
D25/31 *Set of* 7			13·00	19·00
		(b) Size 19½×16 mm.		
D32	D 5	1c. scarlet (12.70)	30	30
		a. Perf 12½×12 (11.77)	15	1·25
D33		2c. scarlet (1972)	1·00	3·00
D34		3c. scarlet (1.74)	2·50	3·50
D35		4c. scarlet (4.69)	30	60
		a. Printed on the gummed side	£550	
		b. Perf 12½×12 (11.77)	30	1·00
D36		5c. scarlet (2.69)	22·00	35·00
		a. Perf 12½×12 (11.77)	30	2·00
D37		6c. scarlet (1972)	2·75	3·75
D38		8c. scarlet (1.69)	30	45
		a. Perf 12½×12 (28.6.78)	75	1·40
D39		10c. scarlet (4.69)	40	45
		a. Perf 12½×12 (9.77)	40	60
D40		12c. scarlet (1.69)	30	50
		a. Perf 12½×12 (9.77)	80	1·50
D41		16c. scarlet (1.74)	3·00	4·00
D42		20c. scarlet (10.77)	30	1·25
D43		24c. scarlet (10.77)	30	1·75
D44		50c. scarlet (10.77)	40	2·25
D32/44 *Set of* 13			10·00	21·00

There are no records of dates of issue of the above but supplies were distributed to depots in the months indicated.

Both white and ordinary papers have been used for Nos. D32/41.

OFFICIAL STAMPS

Stamps perforated "O H M S" were introduced in May 1923 for use by the Receiver General's department in Ottawa and by the Assistant Receiver Generals' offices in provincial cities. From 1 July 1939 this use was extended to all departments of the federal government and such stamps continued to be produced until replaced by the "O.H.M.S." overprinted issue of 1949.

The perforated initials can appear either upright, inverted or sideways on individual stamps. The prices quoted are for the cheapest version. Stamps perforated with Type O **1** are only priced used. Only isolated examples are known mint and these are very rare.

A number of forged examples of the perforated "O.H.M.S." are known, in particular of Type O **1**. Many of these forged perforated initials were applied to stamps which had already been used and this can aid their detection. Genuine examples, postmarked after the perforated initials were applied, often show the cancellation ink bleeding into the holes.

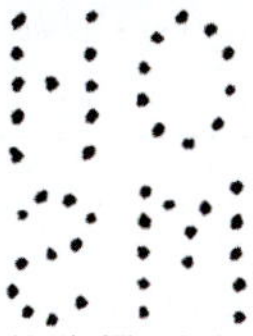

(O **1**) (Five holes in vertical bars of "H")

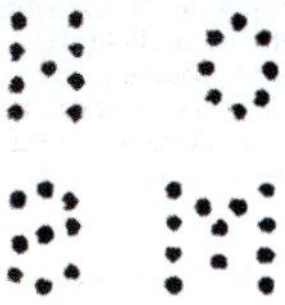

(O **2**) (Four holes in vertical bars of "H")

1923 (May). *Nos. 196/215 punctured as Type* O **1**.

O1	44	1c. yellow-green	–	22·00
O2		2c. carmine	–	20·00
O3		3c. deep brown	–	18·00
O4		5c. deep blue	–	22·00
O5		7c. yellow-ochre	–	35·00
O6		10c. reddish purple	–	35·00
O7		20c. olive	–	22·00
O8		50c. sepia	–	38·00
O1/8 *Set of* 8			–	£190

1923 (May). *50th Anniv of Confederation. No. 244 punctured as Type* O **1**.

O9	48	3c. bistre-brown	–	£120

1923 (May)–**31**. *Nos. 246/55 and 263 punctured as Type* O **1**.

		(a) P 12.		
O10	44	1c. chrome-yellow (Die I)	–	20·00
		a. Die II (1925)	–	20·00
O11		2c. deep green	–	15·00
O12		3c. carmine (Die I) (12.23)	–	15·00
		a. Die II (1924)	–	18·00
O13		4c. olive-yellow	–	20·00
O14		5c. violet	–	20·00
		a. Thin paper (1924)	–	22·00
O15		7c. red-brown (1924)	–	27·00
O16		8c. blue (1925)	–	32·00
O17		10c. blue	–	22·00
O18		10c. bistre-brown (1925)	–	15·00
O19		$1 brown-orange (7.23)	–	55·00
O10/19 *Set of* 10			–	£200
		(b) P 12×8.		
O20	44	3c. carmine (Die II) (1931)	–	45·00

1927 (29 June). *60th Anniv of Confederation. Nos. 266/73 punctured as Type* O **1**.

		(a) Commemorative issue.		
O21	51	1c. orange	–	20·00
O22	52	2c. green	–	27·00
O23	53	3c. carmine	–	35·00
O24	54	5c. violet	–	24·00
O25	55	12c. blue	–	£150
O21/5 *Set of* 5			–	£225
		(b) Historical issue.		
O26	56	5c. violet	–	20·00
O27	57	12c. green	–	£120
O28	58	20c. carmine	–	70·00
O26/8 *Set of* 3			–	£190

1928 (21 Sept). *Air. No. 274 punctured as Type* O **1**.

O29	59	5c. olive-brown	–	95·00

1928–29. *Nos. 275/85 punctured as Type* O **1**.

O30	60	1c. orange	–	25·00
O31		2c. green	–	17·00
O32		3c. lake	–	40·00
O33		4c. olive-bistre	–	50·00
O34		5c. violet	–	18·00
O35		8c. blue	–	48·00
O36	61	10c. green	–	15·00
O37	62	12c. grey-black	–	£150
O38	63	20c. lake	–	42·00
O39	64	50c. blue	–	£200
O40	65	$1 olive-green	–	£150
O30/40 *Set of* 11			–	£650

1930–31. *Nos. 288/97 and 300/5 punctured as Type* O **1**.

O41	66	1c. orange (Die I)	–	25·00
O42		1c. green (Die I)	–	15·00
		a. Die II	–	13·00
O43		2c. green (Die I)	–	42·00
O44		2c. scarlet (Die I)	–	20·00
		a. Die II	–	18·00
O45		2c. deep brown (Die I)	–	22·00
		a. Die II	–	20·00
O46		3c. scarlet	–	15·00
O47		4c. yellow-bistre	–	45·00
O48		5c. violet	–	30·00
O49		5c. deep slate-blue	–	25·00
O50		8c. blue	–	55·00
O51		8c. red-orange	–	40·00
O52	67	10c. olive-green	–	20·00
O53	68	12c. grey-black	–	85·00
O54	69	20c. red	–	42·00
O55	70	50c. blue	–	60·00
O56	71	$1 olive-green	–	£140
O41/56 *Set of* 15			–	£600

1930 (4 Dec). *Air. No. 310 punctured as Type* O **1**.

O57	72	5c. deep brown	–	£150

1931 (30 Sept). *No. 312 punctured as Type* O **1**.

O58	73	10c. olive-green	–	20·00

1932 (22 Feb). *Air. No. 313 punctured as Type* O **1**.

O59	59	6c. on 5c. olive-brown	–	£100

1932 (21 June). *Nos. 314/a punctured as Type* O **1**.

O60	66	3c. on 2c. scarlet (Die I)	–	30·00
		a. Die II	–	25·00

1932 (12 July). *Ottawa Conference. Nos. 315/18 punctured as Type* O **1**.

(a) Postage.

O61	**76**	3c. scarlet	–	17·00
O62	**77**	5c. blue	–	27·00
O63	**78**	13c. green	–	£170
		(b) Air.		
O64	**72**	6c. on 5c. deep brown	–	£130
O61/4 *Set of* 4			–	£300

1932–33. *Nos. 319/25 punctured as Type* O **1**.

O65	**80**	1c. green	–	15·00
O66		2c. sepia	–	15·00
O67		3c. scarlet	–	15·00
O68		4c. yellow-brown	–	45·00
O69		5c. blue	–	22·00
O70		8c. red-orange	–	45·00
O71	**68**	13c. bright violet	–	45·00
O65/71 *Set of* 7			–	£180

1933 (18 May). *U.P.U. Congress Preliminary Meeting. No. 329 punctured as Type* O **1**.

O72	**81**	5c. blue	–	42·00

1933 (24 July). *World's Grain Exhibition and Conference, Regina. No. 330 punctured as Type* O **1**.

O73	**69**	20c. red	–	48·00

1933 (17 Aug). *Centenary of First Trans-Atlantic Steamboat Crossing. No. 331 punctured as Type* O **1**.

O74	**83**	5c. blue	–	42·00

1934 (1 July). *Fourth Centenary of Discovery of Canada. No. 332 punctured as Type* O **1**.

O75	**84**	3c. blue	–	48·00

1934 (1 July). *150th Anniv of Arrival of United Empire Loyalists. No. 333 punctured as Type* O **1**.

O76	**85**	10c. olive-green	–	50·00

1934 (16 Aug). *150th Anniv of Province of New Brunswick. No. 334 punctured as Type* O **1**.

O77	**86**	2c. red-brown	–	60·00

1935 (4 May). *Silver Jubilee. Nos. 335/40 punctured as Type* O **1**.

O78	**87**	1c. green	–	27·00
O79	**88**	2c. brown	–	35·00
O80	**89**	3c. carmine-red	–	45·00
O81	**90**	5c. blue	–	42·00
O82	**91**	10c. green	–	£110
O83	**92**	13c. blue	–	£110
O78/83 *Set of* 6			–	£325

1935. *Nos. 341/51 and 355 punctured as Type* O **1**.

		(a) Postage.		
O84	**93**	1c. green	–	17·00
O85		2c. brown	–	30·00
O86		3c. scarlet	–	27·00
O87		4c. yellow	–	48·00
O88		5c. blue	–	27·00
O89		8c. orange	–	48·00
O90	**94**	10c. carmine	–	38·00
O91	**95**	13c. purple	–	48·00
O92	**96**	20c. olive-green	–	50·00
O93	**97**	50c. deep violet	–	35·00
O94	**98**	$1 bright blue	–	£100
		(b) Air.		
O95	**99**	6c. red-brown	–	80·00
O84/95 *Set of* 12			–	£500

1937 (10 May). *Coronation. No. 356 punctured as Type* O **1**.

O96	**100**	3c. carmine	–	45·00

1937–38. *Nos. 357/67, 370 and 371 punctured as Type* O **1**.

		(a) Postage.		
O97	**101**	1c. green	–	2·75
O98		2c. brown	–	3·00
O99		3c. scarlet	–	2·75
O100		4c. yellow	–	9·50
O101		5c. blue	–	7·00
O102		8c. orange	–	16·00
O103	**102**	10c. rose-carmine	–	22·00
		a. Red	–	25·00
O104	**103**	13c. blue	–	30·00
O105	**104**	20c. red-brown	–	30·00
O106	**105**	50c. green	–	70·00
O107	**106**	$1 violet	–	£100
O97/107 *Set of* 11			–	£275
		(b) Coil stamp.		
O108	**101**	3c. scarlet	–	65·00
		(c) Air.		
O109	**107**	6c. blue	–	32·00

1939 (15 May). *Royal Visit. Nos. 372/4 punctured as Type* O **1**.

O110	**108**	1c. black and green	–	42·00
O111	**109**	2c. black and brown	–	50·00
O112	**110**	3c. black and carmine	–	42·00
O110/12 *Set of* 3			–	£120

1939 (1 July). *Air. No. 274 punctured as Type* O **2**.

O113	**59**	5c. olive-brown	24·00	16·00

1939 (1 July). *Nos. 347/50 and 355 punctured as Type* O **2**.

		(a) Postage.		
O114	**94**	10c. carmine	60·00	40·00
O115	**95**	13c. purple	70·00	40·00
O116	**96**	20c. olive-green	90·00	50·00
O117	**97**	50c. deep violet	70·00	40·00
		(b) Air.		
O118	**99**	6c. red-brown	55·00	45·00
O114/18 *Set of* 5			£300	£190

1939 (1 July). *Coronation. No. 356 punctured as Type* O **2**.

O119	**100**	3c. carmine	80·00	48·00

1939 (1 July). *Nos. 357/67, 369/70 and 371 punctured as Type* O **2**.

		(a) Postage.		
O120	**101**	1c. green	1·75	30
O121		2c. brown	2·50	30
O122		3c. scarlet	2·75	30
O123		4c. yellow	5·50	2·50
O124		5c. blue	3·75	45
O125		8c. orange	14·00	4·50
O126	**102**	10c. rose-carmine	60·00	3·25
		a. Red	12·00	40
O127	**103**	13c. blue	19·00	1·75
O128	**104**	20c. red-brown	38·00	2·50
O129	**105**	50c. green	55·00	8·50
O130	**106**	$1 violet	£120	32·00
O120/30 *Set of* 11			£250	48·00
		(b) Coil stamps.		
O131	**101**	2c. brown	75·00	50·00
O132		3c. scarlet	75·00	50·00
		(c) Air.		
O133	**107**	6c. blue	3·50	1·00

1939 (1 July). *Royal Visit. Nos. 372/4 punctured as Type* O **2**.

O134	**108**	1c. black and green	90·00	38·00
O135	**109**	2c. black and brown	90·00	38·00
O136	**110**	3c. black and carmine	90·00	38·00
O134/6 *Set of* 3			£250	£100

1942–43. *War Effort. Nos. 375/88 and 399/400 punctured as Type* O **2**.

		(a) Postage.		
O137	**111**	1c. green	70	20
O138	**112**	2c. brown	70	10
O139	**113**	3c. carmine-lake	2·30	75
O140		3c. purple	1·50	10
O141	**114**	4c. slate	6·00	1·50
O142	**112**	4c. carmine-lake	70	10
O143	**111**	5c. blue	1·50	30
O144	–	8c. red-brown	8·50	2·30
O145	**116**	10c. brown	5·00	20
O146	**117**	13c. dull green	9·50	8·00
O147		14c. dull green	10·00	1·30
O148	**118**	20c. chocolate	17·00	1·00
O149	**119**	50c. violet	40·00	6·00
O150	**120**	$1 blue	90·00	26·00
		(b) Air.		
O151	**121**	6c. blue	4·25	3·50
O152		7c. blue	4·00	35
O137/52 *Set of* 16			£180	45·00

1946. *Peace Re-conversion. Nos. 401/7 punctured as Type* O **2**.

		(a) Postage.		
O153	**122**	8c. brown	24·00	4·25
O154	**123**	10c. olive-green	3·25	15
O155	**124**	14c. sepia	7·50	1·50
O156	**125**	20c. slate	8·50	50
O157	**126**	50c. green	32·00	8·50
O158	**127**	$1 purple	65·00	16·00
		(b) Air.		
O159	**128**	7c. blue	3·50	1·50
O153/9 *Set of* 7			£130	29·00

1949. *Nos. 415 and 416 punctured as Type* O **2**.

O160	**136**	2c. sepia	2·00	2·50
O161	**137**	3c. purple	2·00	2·50

O.H.M.S.
(O **3**)

1949. *Nos. 375/6, 378, 380 and 402/7 optd as Type* O **3** *by typography.*

		(a) Postage.		
O162	**111**	1c. green	3·75	3·50
		a. Missing stop after "S"	£190	70·00
O163	**112**	2c. brown	12·00	12·00
		a. Missing stop after "S"	£170	95·00
O164	**113**	3c. purple	2·00	2·50
O165	**112**	4c. carmine-lake	3·00	2·50
O166	**123**	10c. olive-green	4·50	15
		a. Missing stop after "S"	£120	45·00
O167	**124**	14c. sepia	6·50	3·75
		a. Missing stop after "S"	£140	65·00
O168	**125**	20c. slate	12·00	60
		a. Missing stop after "S"	£190	60·00
O169	**126**	50c. green	£160	£120
		a. Missing stop after "S"	£1300	£750
O170	**127**	$1 purple	45·00	48·00
		a. Missing stop after "S"	£4250	
		(b) Air.		
O171	**128**	7c. blue	24·00	7·00
		a. Missing stop after "S"	£150	70·00
O162/71 *Set of* 10			£225	£140

Forgeries exist of this overprint. Genuine examples are 2.3×15 mm and show the tops of all letters aligned, as are the stops.

Only a few sheets of the $1 showed the variety, No. O170a.

MISSING STOP VARIETIES. These occur on R. 6/2 of the lower left pane (Nos. O162a, O163a and O176a) or R. 10/2 of the lower left pane (O166a, O167a, O168a, O169a, O170a and O171a). No. O176a also occurs on R. 8/8 of the upper left pane in addition to R. 6/2 of the lower left pane.

1949–50. *Nos. 414/15, 416/17, 418 and 431 optd as Type* O **3** *by typography.*

O172	**135**	1c. green	3·25	1·50
O173	**136**	2c. sepia	3·50	1·50
O174	**137**	3c. purple	2·75	1·50
O175	**138**	4c. carmine-lake	2·75	15
O176	**139**	5c. blue (1949)	6·00	2·00
		a. Missing stop after "S"	90·00	42·00
O177	**141**	50c. green (1950)	32·00	28·00
O172/7 *Set of* 6			45·00	32·00

G (O **4**) **G** (O **5**)

Variations in thickness are known in Type O **4** these are due to wear and subsequent cleaning of the plate. All are produced by typography. Examples showing the "G" applied by lithography are forgeries.

1950 (2 Oct)–**52.** *Nos. 402/4, 406/7, 414/18 and 431 optd with Type* O **4** *(1 to 5c.) or* O **5** *(7c. to $1).*

		(a) Postage.		
O178	**135**	1c. green	1·50	10
O179	**136**	2c. sepia	3·00	3·75
O180		2c. olive-green (11.51)	1·75	10
O181	**137**	3c. purple	2·25	10
O182	**138**	4c. carmine-lake	3·00	1·00
O183		4c. vermilion (1.5.52)	3·00	60
O184	**139**	5c. blue	3·50	1·75
O185	**123**	10c. olive-green	3·00	10
O186	**124**	14c. sepia	19·00	8·00
O187	**125**	20c. slate	35·00	30
O188	**141**	50c. green	15·00	16·00
O189	**127**	$1 purple	75·00	75·00
		(b) Air.		
O190	–	7c. blue	24·00	15·00
O178/90 *Set of* 13			£160	£110

1950–51. *Nos. 432/3 optd with Type* O **5**.

O191	**142**	10c. brown-purple	4·00	30
		a. Opt omitted in pair with normal	£700	£450
O192	**143**	$1 ultramarine (1.2.51)	65·00	75·00

On a small number of sheets of 10c. the opt was omitted from R7/1.

1952–53. *Nos. 441, 443 and 446 optd with Type* O **5**.

O193	**153**	7c. blue (3.11.52)	2·00	2·75
O194	**151**	20c. grey (1.4.52)	2·00	10
O195	**154**	$1 black (2.2.53)	10·00	13·00
O193/5 *Set of* 3			12·50	14·00

1953 (1 Sept)–**61.** *Nos. 450/4 and 462 optd with Type* O **4** *(1 to 5c.) or* O **5** *(50c.).*

O196	**158**	1c. purple-brown	15	10
O197		2c. green	20	10
O198		3c. carmine	20	10
O199		4c. violet	30	10
O200		5c. ultramarine	30	10
O201	**160**	50c. deep bluish green (2.11.53)	3·00	3·00
		a. Opt Type O **6** (24.4.61*)	2·25	3·50
O196/201 *Set of* 6			3·00	3·00

*Earliest recorded date.

1955–56. *Nos. 463/4 and 466/7 optd with Type* O **4**.

O202	**161**	1c. purple-brown (12.11.56)	65	20
O203		2c. green (19.1.56)	15	10
O204		4c. violet (23.7.56)	40	10
O205		5c. bright blue (11.1.55)	15	10
O202/5 *Set of* 4			1·25	30

1955–62. *Nos. 477 and 488 optd with Type* O **5**.

O206	**165**	10c. purple-brown (21.2.55)	70	20
		a. Opt Type O **6** (28.3.62*)	40	1·50
O207	**176**	20c. green (4.12.56)	2·50	20
		a. Opt Type O **6** (10.4.62*)	5·50	1·00

*Earliest recorded date.

1963 (15 May). *Nos. 527/8 and 530/1 optd as Type* O **4**.

O208		1c. chocolate	40	4·25
O209		2c. green	40	4·00
		a. Type O **4** omitted (vert pair with normal)	£750	
O210		4c. carmine-red	40	2·25
O211		5c. ultramarine	40	1·75
O208/11 *Set of* 4			1·40	11·00

No. O209a comes from the top row of an upper pane on which the overprint was misplaced downwards by one row. Owing to the margin between the panes the top row of the bottom pane had the overprint at the top of the stamp.

OFFICIAL SPECIAL DELIVERY STAMPS

1923 (May). *Nos. S3/4 punctured as Type* O **1**.

OS1	**S 1**	10c. yellowish green	–	£110
OS2	**S 2**	20c. carmine-red	–	85·00

1927 (29 June). *60th Anniv of Confederation. No. S5 punctured as Type* O **1**.

OS3	**S 3**	20c. orange	–	85·00

1930 (2 Sept). *Inscr* "TWENTY CENTS" *at foot. No. S6 punctured as Type* O **1**.

OS4	**S 4**	20c. brown-red	–	70·00

1932 (24 Dec). *Inscr* "CENTS" *at foot. No. S7 punctured as Type* O **1**.

OS5	**S 4**	20c. brown-red	–	70·00

1935 (1 June). *No. S8 punctured as Type* O **1**.

OS6	**S 5**	20c. scarlet	–	70·00

1938–39. *Nos. S9/10 punctured as Type* O **1**.

OS7	**S 6**	10c. green	–	45·00
OS8		20c. scarlet	–	70·00

1939 (1 Mar). *No. S11 punctured as Type* O **1**.

OS9	**S 6**	10c. on 20c. scarlet	–	70·00

1939 (1 July). *Inscr* "CENTS" *at foot. No. S7 punctured as Type* O **2**.

OS10	**S 4**	20c. brown-red	£180	90·00

1939 (1 July). *No. S8 punctured as Type* O **2**.

OS11	**S 5**	20c. scarlet	95·00	45·00

1939 (1 July). *No. S9 punctured as Type* O **2**.

OS12	**S 6**	10c. green	7·50	6·50

1939 (1 July). *No. S11 punctured as Type* O **2**.

OS13	**S 6**	10c. on 20c. scarlet	£120	60·00

1942–43. *Nos. S12/14 punctured as Type* O **2**.

		(a) Postage.		
OS14	**S 8**	10c. green	9·50	8·00
		(b) Air.		
OS15	**S 9**	16c. ultramarine	18·00	16·00
OS16		17c. ultramarine	12·00	9·00

1946–47. *Nos. S15/17 punctured as Type* O **2**.

(a) Postage.

OS17	S **10**	10c. green	8·50	5·00

(b) Air.

OS18	S **11**	17c. ultramarine (circumflex accent)	42·00	25·00
OS19		17c. ultramarine (grave accent)	70·00	70·00

1950. *No. S15 optd as Type* O **3**, *but larger.*

OS20	S **10**	10c. green	17·00	26·00

1950 (2 Oct). *No. S15 optd as Type* O **4**, *but larger.*

OS21	S **10**	10c. green	26·00	30·00

The use of official stamps was discontinued on 31 December 1963.

Cape of Good Hope *see* **South Africa**

Cayman Islands

The first post office was opened at Georgetown in April 1889. The stamps of Jamaica with the following cancellations were used until 19 February 1901. At some stage, probably around 1891, a supply of the Jamaica 1889 1d., No. 27, was overprinted "CAYMAN ISLANDS", but these stamps were never issued. Two surviving examples are known, one unused and the other cancelled at Richmond in Jamaica.

Types of Jamaica

2

3

4

8

11

13

PRICES OF NOS. Z1/27. These are for a single stamp showing a clear impression of the postmark. Nos. Z1, 2, 6/8, 11/13, 18, 22, Z25 and Z26 are known used on cover and these are worth considerably more.

GEORGETOWN, GRAND CAYMAN

Z 1

Z 2

Z 3

Stamps of JAMAICA *cancelled with Type* Z **1** *in purple.*

1889–94.

Z1	**8**	½d. yellow-green (No. 16)	£550
Z2	**11**	1d. purple and mauve (No. 27)	£550
Z2*a*	**2**	2d. slate (No. 20*a*)	£6000
Z3	**11**	2d. green (No. 28)	£950
Z4		2½d. dull purple and blue (No. 29)	£1200
Z5	**4**	4d. red-orange (No. 22)	£3500

Stamps of JAMAICA *cancelled with Type* Z **2** *in purple or black.*

1895–98.

Z6	**8**	½d. yellow-green (No. 16)	£650
Z7	**11**	1d. purple and mauve (No. 27)	£500
Z8		2½d. dull purple and blue (No. 29)	£850
Z9	**3**	3d. sage-green (No 21)	£4500

Stamps of JAMAICA *cancelled with Type* Z **3**

1898–1901.

Z10	**8**	½d. yellow-green (No. 16)	£500
		a. Green (No. 16*a*)	£500
Z11	**11**	1d. purple and mauve (No. 27)	£500
Z12	**13**	1d. red (No. 31) (1900)	£550
Z13	**11**	2½d. dull purple and blue (No. 29)	£750

OFFICIAL STAMPS

Stamps of JAMAICA *cancelled with Type* Z **1** *in purple.*

1890–94.

Z14	**8**	½d. green (No. O1) (*opt 17–17½ mm long*)	£1300
Z15		½d. green (No. O3) (*opt 16 mm long*) (1893)	£3250
Z16	**11**	1d. rose (No. O4)	£1300
Z17		2d. grey (No. O5)	£4250

Stamps of JAMAICA *cancelled with Type* Z **2** *in purple or black.*

1895–98.

Z18	**8**	½d. green (No. O3)	£3000
Z19	**11**	1d. rose (No. O4)	£4500
Z20		2d. grey (No. O5)	£4750

STAKE BAY, CAYMAN BRAC

Z 4

Z 5

Stamps of JAMAICA *cancelled with Type* Z **4**.

1898–1900.

Z21	**8**	½d. yellow-green (No. 16)	£3750
Z22	**11**	1d. purple and mauve (No. 27)	£3750
Z23		2d. green (No. 28)	£5000
Z24		2½d. dull purple and blue (No. 29)	£3750

Stamps of JAMAICA *cancelled with Type* Z **5**.

1900–01.

Z25	**8**	½d. yellow-green (No. 16)	£3750
Z26	**11**	1d. purple and mauve (No. 27)	£4000
Z27	**13**	1d. red (No. 31)	£4000
Z28	**11**	2½d. dull purple and blue (No. 29)	£3500

PRICES FOR STAMPS ON COVER TO 1945	
Nos. 1/2	*from* × 25
Nos. 3/12	*from* × 5
Nos. 13/16	*from* × 4
Nos. 17/19	*from* × 12
Nos. 25/34	*from* × 5
Nos. 35/52*b*	*from* × 4
Nos. 53/67	*from* × 5
Nos. 69/83	*from* × 4
Nos. 84/95	*from* × 6
Nos. 96/9	*from* × 5
Nos. 100/11	*from* × 4
Nos. 112/14	*from* × 6
Nos. 115/26	*from* × 2

DEPENDENCY OF JAMAICA

1

2

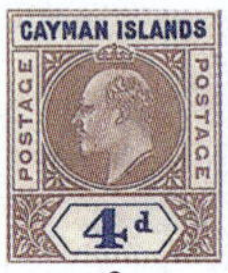

3

(T **1/3**, **8/9** and **12/13** typo D.L.R.)

1900 (1 Nov). Wmk Crown CA. P 14.

1	**1**	½d. deep green	14·00	20·00
		a. Pale green	8·00	16·00
2		1d. rose-carmine	8·00	2·25
		a. Pale carmine	14·00	13·00
1s/2s Optd "Specimen" *Set of* 2			£140	

(Dented frame under "A" (R. 1/6 of left pane). (The variety is believed to have occurred at some point between 9 January and 9 April 1902 and is then present on all subsequent printings of the "POSTAGE POSTAGE" design)

1902 (1 Jan)–**03**. Wmk Crown CA. P 14.

3	**2**	½d. green (15.9.02)	4·50	25·00
		a. Dented frame	£190	
4		1d. carmine (6.3.03)	10·00	9·00
		a. Dented frame	£275	£275
5		2½d. bright blue	10·00	13·00
		a. Dented frame	£275	
6		6d. brown	29·00	60·00
		a. Dented frame	£500	£750
7	**3**	1s. orange	60·00	£110
		a. Dented frame	£700	£1000
3/7 *Set of* 5			£100	£190
3s/7s Optd "Specimen" *Set of* 5			£200	

1905 (Feb–Oct). Wmk Mult Crown CA. P 14.

8	**2**	½d. green	7·00	9·50
		a. Dented frame	£250	£275
9		1d. carmine (18 Oct)	14·00	17·00
		a. Dented frame	£375	£425
10		2½d. bright blue	7·00	3·25
		a. Dented frame	£275	£250
11		6d. brown	16·00	38·00
		a. Dented frame	£375	£550
12	**3**	1s. orange	32·00	48·00
		a. Dented frame	£550	
8/12 *Set of* 5			70·00	£100

1907 (13 Mar). Wmk Mult Crown CA. P 14.

13	**3**	4d. brown and blue	32·00	60·00
		a. Dented frame	£700	£850
14	**2**	6d. olive and rose	32·00	70·00
		a. Dented frame	£650	£850
15	**3**	1s. violet and green	55·00	80·00
		a. Dented frame	£800	
16		5s. salmon and green	£190	£300
		a. Dented frame	£4250	£4750
13/16 *Set of* 4			£275	£450
13s/16s Optd "Specimen" *Set of* 4			£200	

(4)

(5)

(6)

1907 (30 Aug). *No.* 9 *surch at Govt Printing Office, Kingston, with T* **4**.

17	**2**	½d. on 1d. carmine	50·00	80·00
		a. Dented frame	£800	£1100

1907 (Nov). *No.* 16 *handstamped at Georgetown P.O. with T* **5** *or* **6**.

18	**3**	½d. on 5s. salmon and green (25 Nov)	£275	£425
		a. Surch inverted	£55000	
		b. Surch double	£12000	£11000
		c. Surch double, one inverted		
		d. Surch omitted (in pair with normal)	£70000	
		e. Dented frame	£4250	
19		1d. on 5s. salmon and green (23 Nov)	£250	£375
		a. Surch double	£22000	
		b. Surch inverted	£90000	
		c. Dented frame	£3750	£4250

The ½d. on 5s. may be found with the figures "1" or "2" omitted, owing to defective handstamping.

8

9

(10)

1907 (27 Dec)–**09**. *Chalk-surfaced paper (3d. to 10s.).* P 14.

(*a*) Wmk Mult Crown CA.

25	**8**	½d. green	2·50	4·00
26		1d. carmine	1·50	75
27		2½d. ultramarine (30.3.08)	3·50	3·50
28	**9**	3d. purple/*yellow* (30.3.08)	3·25	5·50
29		4d. black and red/*yellow* (30.3.08)	55·00	70·00
30	**8**	6d. dull purple and violet purple (2.10.08)	12·00	35·00
		a. Dull and bright purple	32·00	55·00
31	**9**	1s. black/*green* (5.4.09)	8·50	22·00
32		5s. green and red/*yellow* (30.3.08)	38·00	65·00

(*b*) Wmk Crown CA (30.3.08).

33	**9**	1s. black/*green*	65·00	85·00
34	**8**	10s. green and red/*green*	£170	£225
25/34 *Set of* 10			£325	£450
25s/30s, 32s/4s Optd "Specimen" *Set of* 9			£325	

1908 (12 Feb). *No.* 13 *handstamped locally with T* **10**.

35	**3**	2½d. on 4d. brown and blue	£1700	£3000
		a. Surch double	£35000	£20000
		b. Dented frame	£16000	

No. 35 should only be purchased when accompanied by an expert committee's certificate or similar form of guarantee.

MANUSCRIPT PROVISIONALS. During May and June 1908 supplies of ½d. and 1d. stamps became exhausted, and the payment of postage was indicated by the postmistress, Miss Gwendolyn Parsons, using a manuscript endorsement. Such endorsements were in use from 12 May to 1 June.

MP1	"(Postage Paid G.A.P.)" (12 May to 1 June)	£5000
MP1*a*	"(Postage Paid G.A.P.)½" (23 May to 1 June)	£7500
MP1*b*	"(Postage Paid G.A.P.)1" (23 May to 1 June)	£6500

In October of the same year there was a further shortage of ¼d. stamps and the manuscript endorsements were again applied by either the new Postmaster, William Graham McCausland or by Miss Parsons who remained as his assistant.

MP2	"Pd ¼d.W.G. McC" (4 to 27 October)	£250
MP2*a*	"¼d. Pd. W.G. McC" (14 October)	£1500
MP2*b*	"Pd ¼d.W.G. McC" (6 October)	£2000
MP3	"Paid" (7 October)	£9000
MP4	"Pd ¼d." (8 October)	£7500
MP5	"Paid ¼d/ GAP. asst." (15 October)	£8500

No. MP2 exists in different inks and formats. Nos. MP2 and MP2*a* show the endorsement in two lines, whereas it is in one line on No. MP2*b*.

Manuscript endorsement for the 2½d. rate is also known, but this is thought to have been done by oversight.

A 1d. surcharge on 4d. (No. 29), issued in mid-May, was intended as a revenue stamp and was never authorised for postal use (*price* £225 *un.*). Used examples were either cancelled by favour or passed through the post in error. Exists with surcharge inverted (*price* £1800 *un.*), surcharge double (*price* £2750 *un.*) or surcharge double, both inverted (*price* £2750 *un.*).

11

12

13

1908 (30 June)–**09**. Wmk Mult Crown CA. *Litho*. P 14.
38 **11** ¼d. brown .... 3·00 50
a. Grey-brown (2.09) .... 3·75 1·00
s. Optd "Specimen" .... 85·00

1912 (24 Apr)–**20**. *Die I*. Wmk Mult Crown CA. *Chalk-surfaced paper* (*3d. to 10s.*). P 14.
40 **13** ¼d. brown (10.2.13) .... 1·00 40
41 **12** ½d. green .... 2·75 5·00
w. Wmk inverted .... † £475
42 1d. red (25.2.13) .... 3·25 2·50
43 **13** 2d. pale grey .... 1·00 10·00
44 **12** 2½d. bright blue (26.8.14) .... 7·00 11·00
a. Deep bright blue (9.11.17) .... 18·00 25·00
45 **13** 3d. purple/*yellow* (26.11.14) .... 15·00 40·00
a. White back (19.11.13) .... 3·50 8·00
b. On lemon (12.3.18) .... 2·50 18·00
bs. Optd "Specimen" .... 65·00
c. On orange-buff (1920) .... 10·00 30·00
d. On buff (1920) ....
e. On pale yellow (1920) .... 3·50 30·00
46 4d. black and red/*yellow* (25.2.13) .... 1·00 10·00
47 **12** 6d. dull and bright purple (25.2.13) .... 3·75 7·50
48 **13** 1s. black/*green* (15.5.16) .... 3·50 26·00
as. Optd "Specimen" .... 65·00
b. White back (19.11.13) .... 3·50 3·50
49 2s. purple and bright blue/*blue* .... 12·00 50·00
50 3s. green and violet .... 19·00 65·00
51 5s. green and red/*yellow* (26.8.14) .... 75·00 £170
52 **12** 10s. deep green and red/*green* (26.11.14) £120 £225
as. Optd "Specimen" £100
b. White back (19.11.13) .... 95·00 £160
c. On blue-green, olive back (5.10.18) £100 £200
40/52*b* *Set of* 13 .... £200 £450
40s/4s, 45as, 46s/7s, 48bs, 49s/51s, 52bs Optd "Specimen" *Set of* 13 .... £375

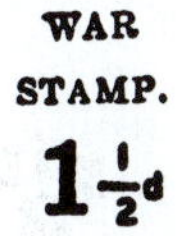
(14)

(15)

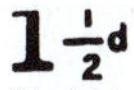
Straight serif (Left-hand pane R. 10/2)

1917 (26 Feb). *T* **12** *surch with T* **14** *or* **15** *at Kingston, Jamaica.*
53 **14** 1½d. on 2½d. deep blue .... 13·00 13·00
a. No fraction bar £170 £190
b. Missing stop after "STAMP" (R. 1/4) £700
54 **15** 1½d. on 2½d. deep blue .... 1·75 6·00
a. No fraction bar .... 70·00 £130
b. Straight serif .... 85·00 £160

On No. 53 "WAR STAMP" and "1½d." were applied separately.

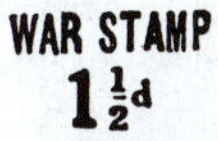
(16)

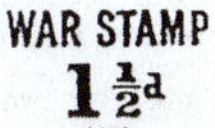
(17)

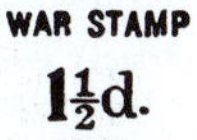
(18)

1917 (4 Sept). *T* **12** *surch with T* **16** *or* **17** *by D.L.R.*
55 **16** 1½d. on 2½d. deep blue £750 £2000
56 **17** 1½d. on 2½d. deep blue 30 60
s. Optd "Specimen" £120
x. Wmk reversed £110

De La Rue replaced surcharge Type **16** by Type **17** after only a few sheets as it did not adequately obliterate the original face value. A small quantity, said to be 3½ sheets, of Type **16** was included in the consignment in error.

1919–20. *T* **12** *and* **13** *(2½d. special printing), optd only, or surch in addition at Kingston (No. 58) or by D.L.R. (others).*
57 – ½d. green (4.2.19) .... 60 2·50
a. Short opt (right pane R. 10/1) .... 24·00
58 **18** 1½d. on 2d. grey (10.3.20) .... 2·50 7·00
59 **17** 1½d. on 2½d. orange (4.2.19) .... 80 1·25
57s, 59s Optd "Specimen" *Set of* 2 .... £110

No. 57 was overprinted with T **13** of British Virgin Islands.

The ½d. stamps on *buff* paper, and later consignments of the 2d. T **13** on *pinkish*, derived their colour from the paper in which they were packed for despatch from England.

No. 57a shows the overprint 2 mm high instead of 2½ mm.

A further surcharge as No. 58, but in red, was prepared in Jamaica during April 1920, but these were not issued.

19

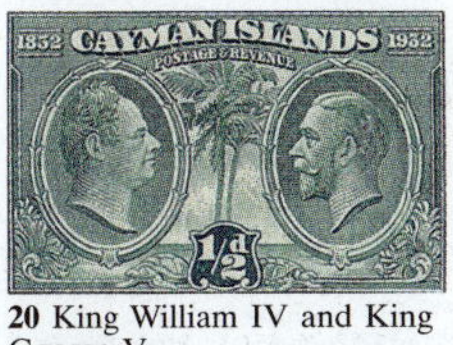
20 King William IV and King George V

1921 (4 Apr)–**26**. P 14.

(*a*) Wmk Mult Crown CA.
60 **19** 3d. purple/*orange-buff* .... 1·50 8·00
aw. Wmk inverted £190 £250
ay. Wmk inverted and reversed £110 £160
b. Purple/pale yellow .... 45·00 60·00
bw. Wmk inverted ....
62 4d. red/*yellow* (1.4.22) .... 1·00 4·00
63 1s. black/*green* .... 1·25 9·50
x. Wmk reversed £375
64 5s. yellow-green/*pale yellow* .... 16·00 70·00
a. Deep green/pale yellow .... 95·00 £150
b. Blue-green/pale yellow £100 £170
c. Deep green/orange-buff (19.11.21) £150 £225
67 10s. carmine/*green* (19.11.21) .... 60·00 £110
60/7 *Set of* 5 .... 75·00 £180
60s/7s Optd "Specimen" *Set of* 5 .... £200

(*b*) Wmk Mult Script CA.
69 **19** ¼d. yellow-brown (1.4.22) .... 50 1·50
y. Wmk inverted and reversed £275
70 ½d. pale grey-green (1.4.22) 50 30
w. Wmk inverted ....
y. Wmk inverted and reversed ....
71 1d. deep carmine-red (1.4.22) .... 1·40 85
72 1½d. orange-brown .... 1·75 30
73 2d. slate-grey (1.4.22) .... 1·75 4·00
74 2½d. bright blue (1.4.22) 50 50
x. Wmk reversed £375
75 3d. purple/*yellow* (29.6.23) .... 1·25 4·00
y. Wmk inverted and reversed £400
76 4½d. sage-green (29.6.23) .... 2·75 3·00
77 6d. claret (1.4.22) .... 5·50 32·00
a. Deep claret .... 19·00 40·00
79 1s. black/*green* (15.5.25) .... 9·50 32·00
80 2s. violet/*blue* (1.4.22) .... 14·00 24·00
81 3s. violet (1.4.22) .... 23·00 16·00
82 5s. green/*yellow* (15.2.25) .... 24·00 45·00
83 10s. carmine/*green* (5.9.26) .... 60·00 85·00
69/83 *Set of* 14 .... £130 £225
69s/83s Optd "Specimen" *Set of* 14 .... £350

An example of the 4d, No. 62, is known with the 'C' missing from the watermark in the top sheet margin.

"A.S.R." PROVISIONAL. On the night of 9/10 November 1932 the Cayman Brac Post Office at Stake Bay, and its contents, was destroyed by a hurricane. Pending the arrival of replacement stamp stocks and cancellation the Postmaster, Mr A. S. Rutty, initialled covers to indicate that postage had been paid. Those destined for overseas addresses additionally received a "Postage Paid" machine postmark in red when they passed through Kingston, Jamaica.

MP6 Endorsed "A.S.R." in manuscript £7500
MP7 Endorsed "A.S.R." in manuscript and "Postage Paid" machine postmark in red £10000

These emergency arrangements lasted until 19 December.

(Recess Waterlow)

1932 (5 Dec). *Centenary of the "Assembly of Justices and Vestry"*. Wmk Mult Script CA. P 12½.
84 **20** ¼d. brown .... 1·50 1·00
a. "A" of "CA" missing from wmk. £1200 £1200
85 ½d. green .... 2·75 8·00
a. "A" of "CA" reversed in wmk £1500
86 1d. scarlet .... 2·75 11·00
87 1½d. red-orange .... 2·75 2·75
a. "A" of "CA" missing from wmk.
88 2d. grey .... 2·75 3·50
89 2½d. ultramarine .... 2·75 1·50
90 3d. olive-green .... 4·00 5·00
91 6d. purple .... 9·50 23·00
92 1s. black and brown .... 17·00 32·00
93 2s. black and ultramarine .... 45·00 75·00
94 5s. black and green .... 85·00 £120
95 10s. black and scarlet £275 £350
84/95 *Set of* 12 .... £400 £550
84s/95s Perf "Specimen" *Set of* 12 .... £550

The design of Nos. 92/5 differs slightly from Type **20**.

No. 85a shows one "A" of the watermark reversed so that its head points to right when seen from the back. It is believed that this stamp may also exist with "A" missing.

Examples of all values are known showing a forged George Town postmark dated "DE 31 1932".

21 Cayman Islands

22 Cat Boat

23 Red-footed Booby

24 Queen or Pink Conch Shells

25 Hawksbill Turtles

(Recess Waterlow)

1935 (1 May). *T* **21**, **24** *and similar designs.* Wmk Mult Script CA. P 12½.
96 **21** ¼d. black and brown .... 50 1·00
97 **22** ½d. ultramarine and yellow-green .... 1·00 1·00
98 **23** 1d. ultramarine and scarlet .... 4·00 2·25
99 **24** 1½d. black and orange .... 1·50 1·75
100 **22** 2d. ultramarine and purple .... 3·75 1·10
101 **25** 2½d. blue and black .... 3·25 1·25
102 **21** 3d. black and olive-green .... 2·50 3·00
103 **25** 6d. bright purple and black .... 8·50 4·00
104 **22** 1s. ultramarine and orange .... 6·00 6·50
105 **23** 2s. ultramarine and black .... 45·00 35·00
106 **25** 5s. green and black .... 50·00 50·00
107 **24** 10s. black and scarlet .... 85·00 95·00
96/107 *Set of* 12 .... £190 £180
96s/107s Perf "Specimen" *Set of* 12 .... £300

Examples of all values are known showing a forged George Town postmark dated "AU 23 1936".

1935 (6 May). *Silver Jubilee. As Nos. 91/4 of Antigua.*
108 ½d. black and green .... 15 1·00
f. Diagonal line by turret .... 45·00 65·00
h. Dot by flagstaff .... 80·00
i. Dash by turret .... 95·00
109 2½d. brown and deep blue .... 2·50 1·00
110 6d. light blue and olive-green .... 1·50 5·50
h. Dot by flagstaff £225
i. Dash by turret £250
111 1s. slate and purple .... 8·00 8·00
h. Dot by flagstaff £375
i. Dash by turret £425
108/11 *Set of* 4 .... 11·00 14·00
108s/11s Perf "Specimen" *Set of* 4 .... £140

For illustrations of plate varieties see Omnibus section following Zanzibar.

1937 (13 May). *Coronation Issue. As Nos. 95/7 of Antigua.*
112 ½d. green .... 30 1·90
113 1d. carmine 50 20
114 2½d. blue 95 40
112/14 *Set of* 3 .... 1·60 2·25
112s/14s Perf "Specimen" *Set of* 3 .... £130

26 Beach View

27 Dolphin (fish) (*Coryphaena hippurus*)

28 Cayman Islands map

29 Hawksbill Turtles

30 *Rembro* (schooner)

(Recess D.L.R. (½d., 2d., 6d., 1s., 10s.), Waterlow (others))

1938 (5 May)–**48**. *T* **26/7** *and similar designs.* Wmk Mult Script CA (sideways on ¼d., 1d., 1½d., 2½d., 3d., 2s., 5s.). Various perfs.
115 **26** ¼d. red-orange (P 12½) 70 55
a. Perf 13½×12½ (16.7.43) 10 65
116 **27** ½d. green (P 13×11½) .... 1·00 55
a. Perf 14 (16.7.43) .... 1·50 1·40
ab. "A" of "CA" missing from wmk £1200
117 **28** 1d. scarlet (P 12½) 30 75
118 **26** 1½d. black (P 12½) 30 10
119 **29** 2d. violet (P 11½×13) .... 3·00 40
a. Perf 14 (16.7.43) 60 30
120 **30** 2½d. bright blue (P 12½) 40 20
120*a* 2½d. orange (P 12½) (25.8.47) .... 3·00 50
121 **28** 3d. orange (P 12½) 40 15
121*a* 3d. bright blue (P 12½) (25.8.47) .... 3·00 30
122 **29** 6d. olive-green (P 11½×13) .... 11·00 4·00
a. Perf 14 (16.7.43) .... 3·25 1·25
b. Brownish olive (P 11½× 13) (8.7.47) .... 3·00 1·50
123 **27** 1s. red-brown (P 13×11½) .... 6·50 1·50
a. Perf 14 (16.7.43) .... 5·00 2·00
ab. "A" of "CA" missing from wmk £1500
124 **26** 2s. yellow-green (*shades*) (P 12½) .... 50·00 14·00
a. Deep green (16.7.43) .... 25·00 9·00
125 **30** 5s. carmine-lake (P 12½) .... 32·00 15·00
a. Crimson (1948) .... 70·00 22·00
126 **29** 10s. chocolate (P 11½×13) .... 25·00 9·00
a. Perf 14 (16.7.43) .... 26·00 9·00
aw. Wmk inverted ....
115/26a *Set of* 14 .... 90·00 35·00
115s/26s Perf "Specimen" *Set of* 14 .... £425

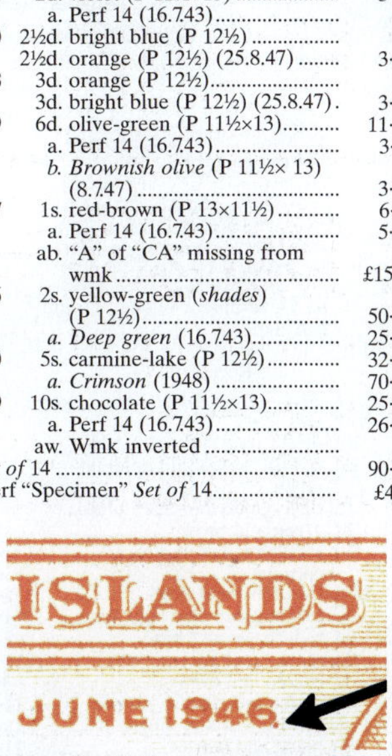

Stop after "1946" (Plate B1 R. 2/1)

1946 (26 Aug). *Victory. As Nos. 110/11 of Antigua.*

127	1½d. black	30	20
128	3d. orange-yellow	30	20
	a. Stop after "1946"	24·00	
127s/8s	Perf "Specimen" *Set of* 2	£100	

1948 (29 Nov). *Royal Silver Wedding. As Nos. 112/13 of Antigua.*

129	½d. green	10	1·00
130	10s. violet-blue	18·00	23·00

1949 (10 Oct). *75th Anniv of Universal Postal Union. As Nos. 114/17 of Antigua.*

131	2½d. orange	30	1·00
132	3d. deep blue	1·50	2·25
133	6d. olive	60	2·25
134	1s. red-brown	60	50
131/4	*Set of* 4	2·75	5·50

31 Cat Boat

32 Coconut Grove, Cayman Brac

33 Green Turtle

34 Thatch Rope Industry

35 Cayman Seamen

36 Map of Cayman Islands

37 Parrotfish

38 Bluff, Cayman Brac

39 Georgetown Harbour

40 Turtle in "crawl"

41 *Ziroma* (schooner)

42 Boat-building

43 Government Offices, Grand Cayman

(Recess B.W.)

1950 (2 Oct). *T* **31/2** *and similar horiz designs.* Wmk Mult Script CA. P 11½ × 11.

135	**31**	¼d. bright blue and pale scarlet	15	60
136	**32**	½d. reddish violet and emerald-green	15	1·25
137	**33**	1d. olive-green and deep blue	60	75
138	**34**	1½d. green and brown	40	75
139	**35**	2d. reddish violet and rose-carmine	1·25	1·50
140	**36**	2½d. turquoise and black	1·25	60
141	**37**	3d. bright green and light blue	1·40	1·50
142	**38**	6d. red-brown and blue	2·00	1·25
143	**39**	9d. scarlet and grey-green	11·00	2·00
144	**40**	1s. brown and orange	3·25	2·75
145	**41**	2s. violet and reddish purple	11·00	11·00
146	**42**	5s. olive-green and violet	18·00	7·00
147	**43**	10s. black and scarlet	21·00	16·00
135/47		*Set of* 13	65·00	42·00

44 South Sound Lighthouse, Grand Cayman

45 Queen Elizabeth II

1953 (2 Mar)–**62**. *Designs previously used for King George VI issue but with portrait of Queen Elizabeth II as in T* **44/5**. Wmk Mult Script CA. P 11½×11 or 11×11½ (4d., £1).

148	**31**	¼d. deep bright blue & rose-red (21.2.55)	1·00	50
		a. Bright blue and bright rose-red (5.12.56)	3·00	1·75
149	**32**	½d. purple and bluish green (7.7.54)	75	50
150	**33**	1d. brown-olive and indigo (7.7.54)	70	40
151	**34**	1½d. deep green and red-brown (7.7.54)	60	20
152	**35**	2d. reddish violet and cerise (2.6.54)	3·00	85
153	**36**	2½d. turquoise-blue and black (2.6.54)	3·50	80
154	**37**	3d. bright green and blue (21.2.55)	4·00	60
155	**44**	4d. black and deep blue	2·00	40
		a. Black and greenish blue (13.10.54)	20·00	20·00
		b. Black and deep bright blue (10.7.62)	15·00	15·00
156	**38**	6d. lake-brown and deep blue (7.7.54)	1·75	30
157	**39**	9d. scarlet and bluish green (2.6.54)	7·50	30
158	**40**	1s. brown and red-orange (21.2.55)	3·75	20
159	**41**	2s. slate-violet and reddish purple (21.2.55)	13·00	8·00
160	**42**	5s. olive-green and slate-violet (21.2.55)	15·00	7·00
161	**43**	10s. black and rose-red (21.2.55)	18·00	7·50
161*a*	**45**	£1 blue (6.1.59)	32·00	10·00
148/61*a*		*Set of* 15	95·00	32·00

1953 (2 June). *Coronation. As No. 120 of Antigua, but printed by B.W.*

162	1d. black and emerald	30	2·00

46 Arms of the Cayman Islands

(Photo D.L.R.)

1959 (4 July). *New Constitution.* Wmk Mult Script CA. P 12.

163	**46**	2½d. black and light blue	45	2·50
164		1s. black and orange	55	50

CROWN COLONY

47 Cuban Amazon

48 Cat Boat

49 *Schomburgkia thomsoniana* (orchid)

50 Map of Cayman Islands

51 Fisherman casting net

52 West Bay Beach

53 Green Turtle

54 *Kirk B* (schooner)

55 Angler with King Mackerel

56 Iguana

57 Swimming pool, Cayman Brac

58 Water sports

59 Fort George

60 Coat of Arms

61 Queen Elizabeth II

(Recess B.W.)

1962 (28 Nov)–**64**. *T* **47/61**. W w **12**. P 11×11½ (vert) or 11½×11 (horiz).

165	**47**	¼d. emerald and red	55	1·00
		a. Emerald and rose (18.2.64)	2·75	3·50
166	**48**	1d. black and yellow-olive	80	20
167	**49**	1½d. yellow and purple	2·75	80
168	**50**	2d. blue and deep brown	1·00	30
169	**51**	2½d. violet and bluish green	85	1·00
170	**52**	3d. bright blue and carmine	30	10
171	**53**	4d. deep green and purple	2·25	60
172	**54**	6d. bluish green and sepia	3·25	30
173	**55**	9d. ultramarine and purple	3·50	40
174	**56**	1s. sepia and rose-red	1·25	10
175	**57**	1s.3d. bluish green and orange-brown	4·50	2·25
176	**58**	1s.9d. deep turquoise and violet	18·00	1·25
177	**59**	5s. plum and deep green	11·00	11·00
178	**60**	10s. olive and blue	20·00	9·50
179	**61**	£1 carmine and black	20·00	21·00
165/79		*Set of* 15	80·00	45·00

1963 (4 June). *Freedom from Hunger. As No. 146 of Antigua.*

180	1s.9d. carmine	30	15

1963 (2 Sept). *Red Cross Centenary. As Nos. 147/8 of Antigua.*

181	1d. red and black	30	75
182	1s.9d. red and blue	70	1·75

1964 (23 April). *400th Birth Anniv of William Shakespeare. As No. 164 of Antigua.*

183	6d. magenta	20	10

1965 (17 May). *I.T.U. Centenary. As Nos. 166/7 of Antigua.*

184	1d. blue and light purple	15	10
185	1s.3d. bright purple and green	55	45

1965 (25 Oct). *International Co-operation Year. As Nos. 168/9 of Antigua.*

186	1d. reddish purple and turquoise-green	15	10
187	1s. deep bluish green and lavender	50	25

1966 (24 Jan). *Churchill Commemoration. As Nos. 170/3 of Antigua.*

188	¼d. new blue	10	1·75
	w. Wmk inverted	35·00	
189	1d. deep green	60	15
190	1s. brown	1·50	15
	w. Wmk inverted	3·00	4·25
191	1s.9d. bluish violet	1·60	75
188/91	*Set of* 4	3·25	2·50

1966 (4 Feb). *Royal Visit. As Nos. 174/5 of Antigua.*

192	1d. black and ultramarine	75	35
193	1s.9d. black and magenta	2·50	1·25

1966 (1 July). *World Cup Football Championships. As Nos. 176/7 of Antigua.*

194	1½d. violet, yellow-green, lake and yellow-brown	15	10
195	1s.9d. chocolate, blue-green, lake and yellow-brown	50	25

1966 (20 Sept). *Inauguration of W.H.O. Headquarters, Geneva. As Nos. 178/9 of Antigua.*

196	2d. black, yellow-green and light blue	60	15
197	1s.3d. black, light purple and yellow-brown	1·40	60

62 Telephone and Map

(Des V. Whiteley. Litho Harrison)

1966 (5 Dec). *International Telephone Links.* W w **12**. P 14½×14.

198 **62** 4d. red, black, greenish blue and olive-green ... 20 20
199 9d. violet-blue, black, brown-red and light green ... 20 30

1966 (12 Dec*). *20th Anniv of U.N.E.S.C.O. As Nos. 196/8 of Antigua.*

200 1d. slate-violet, red, yellow and orange ... 15 10
201 1s.9d. orange-yellow, violet and deep olive ... 60 10
202 5s. black, bright purple and orange ... 1·50 70
200/2 *Set of* 3 ... 2·00 80

*This is the local date of issue; the Crown Agents released the stamps on 1 December.

63 B.A.C. One Eleven 200/400 Airliner over *Ziroma* (Cayman schooner)

(Des V. Whiteley. Photo Harrison)

1966 (17 Dec). *Opening of Cayman Jet Service.* W w **12**. P 14½.

203 **63** 1s. black, new blue and olive-green ... 35 30
204 1s.9d. deep purple-brown, ultramarine and emerald ... 40 35

64 Water-skiing

(Des G. Vasarhelyi. Photo Harrison)

1967 (1 Dec). *International Tourist Year. T* **64** *and similar horiz designs. Multicoloured.* W w **12**. P 14½×14.

205 4d. Type **64** ... 35 10
a. Gold omitted ... £275 £275
206 6d. Skin diving ... 35 30
207 1s. Sport fishing ... 35 30
208 1s.9d. Sailing ... 40 75
205/8 *Set of* 4 ... 1·25 1·25

A used copy of No. 207 is known with yellow omitted.

68 Former Slaves and Emblem

(Des and photo Harrison)

1968 (3 June). *Human Rights Year.* W w **12**. P 14½×14.

209 **68** 3d. deep bluish green, black and gold ... 10 10
w. Wmk inverted ... 60 80
210 9d. brown, gold and myrtle-green ... 10 10
211 5s. ultramarine, gold and myrtle-green ... 30 90
209/11 *Set of* 3 ... 40 1·00

69 Long jumping

(Des R. Granger Barrett. Litho P.B.)

1968 (1 Oct). *Olympic Games, Mexico. T* **69** *and similar multicoloured designs.* W w **12**. P 13½.

212 1s. Type **69** ... 15 10
213 1s.3d. High jumping ... 20 25
214 2s. Pole vaulting (*vert*) ... 20 75
212/14 *Set of* 3 ... 50 1·00

72 "The Adoration of the Shepherds" (Fabritius)

(Des and photo Harrison)

1968–69. *Christmas. T* **72** *and similar horiz design. Centres multicoloured; country name and frames in gold; value and background in colours given.* P 14×14½.

(*a*) W w **12**. (18.11.68)

215 **72** ¼d. brown ... 10 20
a. Gold omitted ... £225
216 – 1d. bluish violet ... 10 10
217 **72** 6d. bright blue ... 15 10
218 – 8d. cerise ... 15 15
219 **72** 1s.3d. bright green ... 20 25
220 – 2s. grey ... 25 35

(*b*) No wmk (8.1.69)

221 **72** ¼d. bright purple ... 10 20
215/21 *Set of* 7 ... 80 1·10

Design:—1d., 8d., 2s. "The Adoration of the Shepherds" (Rembrandt).

74 Grand Cayman Thrush

76 Arms of the Cayman Islands

(Des G. Vasarhelyi. Litho Format)

1969 (5 June). *Designs as T* **74** *and T* **76** *in black, ochre and red (£1) or multicoloured (others).* No wmk. P 14.

222 ¼d. Type **74** ... 10 75
223 1d. Brahmin Cattle (*horiz*) ... 10 10
224 2d. Blowholes on the coast (*horiz*) ... 10 10
225 2½d. Map of Grand Cayman (*horiz*) ... 15 10
226 3d. Georgetown scene (*horiz*) ... 10 10
227 4d. Royal Poinciana (*horiz*) ... 15 10
228 6d. Cayman Brac and Little Cayman on Chart (*horiz*) ... 20 10
229 8d. Motor vessels at berth (*horiz*) ... 25 10
230 1s. Basket-making (*horiz*) ... 15 10
231 1s.3d. Beach scene (*horiz*) ... 35 1·00
232 1s.6d. Straw-rope making (*horiz*) ... 35 1·00
233 2s. Great Barracuda (*horiz*) ... 1·25 80
234 4s. Government House (*horiz*) ... 35 80
235 10s. Type **76** ... 1·00 1·50
236 £1 Queen Elizabeth II (*vert*) ... 1·25 2·00
222/36 *Set of* 15 ... 5·00 7·00

1969 (11 Aug). *As No. 222, but wmk* w **12** (sideways).

237 **74** ¼d. multicoloured ... 30 65

(New Currency. 100 cents = 1 dollar.)

C-DAY
8th September 1969

¼c

(89)

1969 (8 Sept). *Decimal Currency. No. 237, and as Nos. 223/36, but* wmk w **12** (sideways on horiz designs), *surch as T* **89**.

238 ¼c. on ¼d. Type **74** ... 10 75
239 1c. on 1d. Brahmin Cattle ... 10 10
240 2c. on 2d. Blowholes on the coast ... 10 10
241 3c. on 4d. Royal Poinciana ... 10 10
242 4c. on 2½d. Map of Grand Cayman ... 10 10
243 5c. on 6d. Cayman Brac and Little Cayman on Chart ... 10 10
244 7c. on 8d. Motor vessels at berth ... 10 10
245 8c. on 3d. Georgetown scene ... 15 10
246 10c. on 1s. Basket-making ... 25 10
247 12c. on 1s.3d. Beach scene ... 35 1·75
248 15c. on 1s.6d. Straw-rope making ... 45 1·50
249 20c. on 2s. Great Barracuda ... 1·25 1·75
250 40c. on 4s. Government House ... 45 85
251 $1 on 10s. Type **76** ... 1·00 2·50
w. Wmk inverted ...
252 $2 on £1 Queen Elizabeth II ... 1·50 3·25
238/52 *Set of* 15 ... 5·00 11·00

90 "Virgin and Child" (Vivarini)

92 "Noli me tangere" (Titian)

(Des adapted by G. Drummond. Photo Harrison)

1969 (14 Nov*). *Christmas. Multicoloured; background colours given.* W w **12** (sideways on 1, 7 and 20c.). P 14½.

253 **90** ¼c. orange-red ... 10 10
w. Wmk inverted ... 2·75 5·00
254 ¼c. magenta ... 10 10
w. Wmk inverted ... 2·75 5·00
255 ¼c. emerald ... 10 10
a. Gold frame omitted ... £200
w. Wmk inverted ... 1·00 1·75
256 ¼c. new blue ... 10 10
w. Wmk inverted ... 2·75 5·00
257 – 1c. ultramarine ... 10 10
258 **90** 5c. orange-red ... 10 10
259 – 7c. myrtle-green ... 10 10
260 **90** 12c. emerald ... 15 15
261 – 20c. brown-purple ... 20 25
253/61 *Set of* 9 ... 45 45

Design:—1, 7, 20c. "The Adoration of the Kings" (Gossaert).

*This is the local release date. The Crown Agents released the stamps on 4 November.

(Des L. Curtis. Litho D.L.R.)

1970 (23 Mar). *Easter. Paintings multicoloured; frame colours given.* P 14.

262 **92** ¼c. carmine-red ... 10 10
263 ¼c. deep green ... 10 10
264 ¼c. yellow-brown ... 10 10
265 ¼c. pale violet ... 10 10
266 10c. chalky blue ... 35 10
267 12c. chestnut ... 40 10
268 40c. plum ... 55 60
262/8 *Set of* 7 ... 1·25 75

93 Barnaby (*Barnaby Rudge*)

97 Grand Cayman Thrush

(Des Jennifer Toombs. Photo Harrison)

1970 (17 June). *Death Centenary of Charles Dickens. T* **93** *and similar vert designs.* W w **12** (sideways*). P 14½×14.

269 1c. black, olive-green and greenish yellow ... 10 10
w. Wmk Crown to right of CA ... – 2·25
270 12c. black, lake-brown and red ... 35 10
271 20c. black, ochre-brown and gold ... 40 10
272 40c. black, bright ultramarine and new blue ... 45 25
269/72 *Set of* 4 ... 1·00 50

Designs:—12c. Sairey Gamp (*Martin Chuzzlewit*); 20c. Mr. Micawber and David (*David Copperfield*); 40c. The "Marchioness" (*The Old Curiosity Shop*).

*The normal sideways watermark shows Crown to left of CA, *as seen from the back of the stamp.*

1970 (8 Sept). *Decimal Currency. Designs as Nos. 223/37, but with values inscr in decimal currency as T* **97**. W w **12** (sideways* on cent values).

273 ¼c. Type **97** ... 65 30
274 1c. Brahmin Cattle ... 10 10
275 2c. Blowholes on the coast ... 10 10
276 3c. Royal Poinciana ... 20 10
277 4c. Map of Grand Cayman ... 20 10
278 5c. Cayman Brac and Little Cayman on Chart ... 35 10
w. Wmk Crown to right of CA ... 15·00
279 7c. Motor vessels at berth ... 30 10
280 8c. Georgetown scene ... 30 10
281 10c. Basket-making ... 30 10
282 12c. Beach scene ... 90 1·00
283 15c. Straw-rope making ... 1·25 4·00
284 20c. Great Barracuda ... 3·25 1·25
285 40c. Government House ... 85 75
286 $1 Type **76** ... 1·25 4·75
w. Wmk inverted ... 9·50 6·50
287 $2 Queen Elizabeth II ... 2·00 4·75
273/87 *Set of* 15 ... 10·50 15·00

*The normal sideways watermark shows Crown to left of CA, *as seen from the back of the stamp.*

98 The Three Wise Men

(Des G. Drummond. Litho Format)

1970 (8 Oct). *Christmas. T* **98** *and similar horiz design.* W w **12** (sideways*). P 14.

288 **98** ¼c. apple-green, grey and emerald ... 10 10
w. Wmk Crown to right of CA ... 5·00 5·00
289 – 1c. black, lemon and turquoise-green ... 10 10
290 **98** 5c. grey, red-orange and crimson ... 10 10
291 – 10c. black, lemon and orange-red ... 10 10
292 **98** 12c. grey, pale turquoise and ultramarine ... 15 10
293 – 20c. black, lemon and green ... 20 15
288/93 *Set of* 6 ... 55 30

Design:—1, 10, 20c. Nativity scene and Globe.

*The normal sideways watermark shows Crown to left of CA, *as seen from the back of the stamp.*

Ceylon

PRICES FOR STAMPS ON COVER TO 1945

No. 1	*from* × 5
Nos. 2/12	*from* × 4
Nos. 16/17	*from* × 5
Nos. 18/59	*from* × 8
Nos. 60/2	*from* × 15
Nos. 63/72	*from* × 8
Nos. 121/38	*from* × 6
Nos. 139/41	†
Nos. 142/3	*from* × 10
Nos. 146/51	*from* × 6
Nos. 151a/2	†
Nos. 153/93	*from* × 8
Nos. 195/201	*from* × 12
Nos. 202/43	*from* × 6
Nos. 245/9	*from* × 4
Nos. 250/5	*from* × 5
Nos. 256/64	*from* × 4
Nos. 265/76	*from* × 3
Nos. 277/88	*from* × 4
Nos. 289/300	*from* × 8
Nos. 301/18	*from* × 2
Nos. 319/23	—
Nos. 330/7b	*from* × 4
Nos. 338/56	*from* × 2
Nos. 357/60	—
Nos. 361/2	*from* × 5
Nos. 363/7	*from* × 3
Nos. 368/78	*from* × 2
Nos. 379/82	*from* × 4
Nos. 383/5	*from* × 3
Nos. 386/97	*from* × 2
Nos. 398/9	*from* × 8
Nos. O1/7	†
Nos. O11/27	*from* × 30

CROWN COLONY

PRICES. The prices of the imperf stamps of Ceylon vary greatly according to condition. The following prices are for fine copies with four margins.

Poor to medium specimens can be supplied at much lower prices.

1

2

3

NOTE. Beware of stamps of Type **2** which are often offered with corners added.

(Recess P.B.)

1857 (1 Apr). *Blued paper.* Wmk Star W w **1**. Imperf.

1	1	6d. purple-brown	£8000	£450

Collectors should beware of proofs with faked watermark, often offered as originals.

PERKINS BACON "CANCELLED". For notes on these handstamps, showing "CANCELLED" between horizontal bars forming an oval, see Catalogue Introduction.

1857 (2 July)–**59**. Wmk Star, W w **1**. *White paper.*

		(a) Imperf.		
2	1	1d. deep turquoise-blue (24.8.57)	£750	38·00
		a. Blue	£850	60·00
		b. Blued paper	—	£225
3		2d. green (*shades*) (24.8.57)	£170	60·00
		a. Yellowish green	£500	90·00
4	2	4d. dull rose (23.4.59)	£65000	£4500
5	1	5d. chestnut	£1500	£150
6		6d. purple-brown (1859)	£2000	£140
		a. Brown	£7000	£475
		b. Deep brown	£9000	£1000
		c. Light brown	—	£1100
7	2	8d. brown (23.4.59)	£28000	£1500
8		9d. purple-brown (23.4.59)	£45000	£900
9	3	10d. dull vermilion	£800	£300
10		1s. slate-violet	£4750	£200
11	2	1s.9d. green (H/S "CANCELLED" in oval £9000)	£800	£800
		a. Yellow-green	£4500	£3000
12		2s. dull blue (23.4.59)	£6000	£1200
		(b) Unofficial perf 7½ (1s.9d.) or roul (others).		
13	1	1d. blue	£6500	
14		2d. green	£3000	£1400
15	2	1s.9d. green	£8500	

Nos. 13/15 were privately produced, probably by commercial firms for their own convenience.

The 10d. also exists with "CANCELLED" in oval, but no examples are believed to be in private hands.

4

(Typo D.L.R.)

1857 (Oct)–**64**. No wmk. *Glazed paper.*

		(a) Imperf.		
16	4	½d. reddish lilac (*blued paper*)	£3750	£550
17		½d. dull mauve (1858)	£180	£225
		a. Private roul	£6000	
		(b) P 12½.		
18	4	½d. dull mauve (1864)	£225	£180

(Recess P.B.)

1861–64. Wmk Star, W w **1**.

		(a) Clean-cut and intermediate perf 14 to 15½.		
19	1	1d. light blue	£1300	£250
		a. Dull blue (H/S "CANCELLED" in oval £10000)	£160	12·00
20		2d. green (*shades*)	£200	28·00
		a. Imperf between (vert pair)	†	—
		b. Yellowish green (H/S "CANCELLED" in oval £11000)	£225	24·00
21	2	4d. dull rose (H/S "CANCELLED" in oval £11000)	£2000	£300
22	1	5d. chestnut (H/S "CANCELLED" in oval £8000)	90·00	8·00
23		6d. brown (H/S "CANCELLED" in oval £9000)	£2500	£130
		a. Bistre-brown	—	£180
24	2	8d. brown (H/S "CANCELLED" in oval £10000)	£2000	£500
25		9d. purple-brown	£7500	£225
26	3	1s. slate-violet (H/S "CANCELLED" in oval £10000)	£110	13·00
27	2	2s. dull blue	£3250	£650
		(b) Rough perf 14 to 15½.		
28	1	1d. dull blue	£130	9·50
		a. Blued paper	£600	22·00
29		2d. green	£400	80·00
30	2	4d. rose-red	£475	£100
		a. Deep rose-red	£500	£120
31	1	6d. deep brown	£900	£100
		a. Light brown	£1600	£150
		b. Olive-sepia	£800	90·00
32	2	8d. brown	£1500	£550
		a. Yellow-brown	£1500	£350
33		9d. deep brown (H/S "CANCELLED" in oval £9000)	95·00	80·00
		a. Light brown	£850	£100
		b. Olive-sepia	£600	70·00
34	3	10d. dull vermilion	£250	24·00
		a. Imperf vert (horiz pair)	†	—
35		1s. slate-violet	£225	15·00
36	2	1s.9d. light green (*prepared for use, but not issued*)	£700	
37		2s. dull blue (H/S "CANCELLED" in oval £10000)	£600	£140
		a. Deep dull blue	£850	£170
		(c) P 12½ by D.L.R.		
38	3	10d. dull vermilion (9.64)	£250	18·00

The line machine used for Nos. 19/37 produced perforations of variable quality due to wear, poor cleaning and faulty servicing, but it is generally accepted that the clean-cut and intermediate versions occurred on stamps perforated up to March 1861 and the rough variety when the machine was used after that date.

(Recess D.L.R.)

1862. No wmk. *Smooth paper.*

		(a) P 13.		
39	1	1d. dull blue	£150	6·00
40		5d. lake-brown	£1700	£150
41		6d. brown	£190	27·00
		a. Deep brown	£170	27·00
42	2	9d. brown	£1200	£100
43	3	1s. slate-purple	£1800	80·00
		(b) P 11½, 12.		
44	1	1d. dull blue	£1500	£130
		a. Imperf between (horiz pair)	†	£14000

Nos. 39/44 were printed on paper showing a papermaker's watermark of "T H SAUNDERS 1862", parts of which can be found on individual stamps. Examples are rare and command a premium.

The 1s. is known imperforate, but was not issued in this condition.

5 (23 mm high. "CC" oval)

6 (21½ mm high. "CC" round and smaller)

(Typo (½d.) or recess (others) D.L.R.)

1863–65. W **5**. *Paper medium thin and slightly soft.*

		(a) P 11½, 12.		
45	1	1d. deep blue	£2500	£325
		x. Wmk reversed	£3250	£450
		(b) P 13.		
46	1	6d. sepia	£1700	£200
		x. Wmk reversed	—	£180
		y. Wmk inverted and reversed	£2500	£450
47	2	9d. sepia	£4500	£800
		(c) P 12½.		
48	4	½d. dull mauve (1864)	55·00	40·00
		aw. Wmk inverted	£250	80·00
		b. Reddish lilac	65·00	48·00
		c. Mauve	40·00	40·00
49	1	1d. deep blue	£140	7·00
		a. Imperf		
		w. Wmk inverted	†	40·00
		x. Wmk reversed	£160	7·00
		y. Wmk inverted and reversed	†	60·00
50		2d. grey-green (1864)	80·00	13·00
		a. Imperf		
		bw. Wmk inverted	£275	65·00
		by. Wmk inverted and reversed	†	£130
		c. Bottle-green	†	£3500
		d. Yellowish green	£8500	£400
		dx. Wmk reversed	†	£850
		e. Emerald (wmk reversed)	£160	£100
		ew. Wmk inverted	£550	£325
51		2d. ochre (*wmk reversed*) (1866)	£275	£250
		w. Wmk inverted	£650	£650
		y. Wmk inverted and reversed	£500	£475
52	2	4d. rose-carmine (1865)	£750	£180
		ax. Wmk reversed	£900	
		b. Rose	£475	95·00
		bx. Wmk reversed	£550	£130
53	1	5d. red-brown (*shades*) (1865)	£225	80·00
		w. Wmk inverted	†	£200
		x. Wmk reversed	£300	65·00
54		5d. grey-olive (1866)	£1800	£375
		ax. Wmk reversed	£1500	£325
		b. Yellow-olive	£750	£250
		bx. Wmk reversed	£750	£250
55		6d. sepia	£170	4·00
		aw. Wmk inverted	†	80·00
		ax. Wmk reversed		
		b. Reddish brown	£225	12·00
		c. Blackish brown	£180	10·00
		ca. Double print	†	£3500
		cw. Wmk inverted	†	65·00
		cx. Wmk reversed	£250	48·00
		cy. Wmk inverted and reversed	†	£140
56	2	8d. reddish brown (*shades*) (1864)	£120	55·00
		x. Wmk reversed	£160	85·00
		y. Wmk inverted and reversed	£350	£110
57		9d. sepia	£300	48·00
		x. Wmk reversed	£500	90·00
58	3	10d. vermilion (1866)	£2250	65·00
		ax. Wmk reversed	†	£160
		b. Orange-red	£4500	£425
		bx. Wmk reversed	†	£600
59	2	2s. steel-blue (*shades*) (1864)	£275	40·00
		x. Wmk reversed	†	£100
		y. Wmk inverted and reversed	£650	£200

Watermarks as Type **5** were arranged in four panes, each of 60, with the words "CROWN COLONIES" between the panes. Parts of this marginal watermark often appear on the stamps.

De La Rue had considerable difficulty matching the standard Crown CC watermark to the plates received from Perkins Bacon with the result that the watermark W **5** is frequently found misplaced.

A further aid to identifying the two watermarks is the distance between the top of the cross and the foot of "CC", which measures 2 mm on W **5** and 6.5 mm on W **6**.

The ½d. dull mauve, 2d. ochre and 5d. grey-olive with this watermark also exist imperforate, but are not known used. The 6d. sepia and 2s. steel-blue also exist imperforate on wove paper without watermark.

One used example of the 2d. grey-green is known showing private roulettes added to an imperforate stamp (*Price* £3250).

7

8

(Typo D.L.R.)

1866–68. Wmk Crown CC.

		(a) P 12½.		
60	7	3d. rose	£225	90·00
		(b) P 14.		
61	8	1d. blue (*shades*) (1868)	23·00	10·00
		w. Wmk inverted	†	£140
62	7	3d. carmine-rose (1867)	85·00	45·00
		a. Bright rose	90·00	50·00

Nos. 60/1 exist imperforate.

(Recess D.L.R.)

1867–70. W **6**. *Specially produced hand-made paper.* P 12½.

63	1	1d. dull blue	£190	14·00
		aw. Wmk inverted	£450	£100
		ax. Wmk reversed	£190	14·00
		ay. Wmk inverted and reversed	†	£170
		b. Deep blue	£180	11·00
		bw. Wmk inverted	—	£110
		bx. Wmk reversed	£300	35·00
64		2d. ochre	£150	13·00
		aw. Wmk inverted		
		ax. Wmk reversed	—	40·00
		b. Bistre	70·00	8·00
		bw. Wmk inverted	£120	
		c. Olive-bistre	£150	20·00
		cw. Wmk inverted	£150	
		d. Yellow	£100	6·50
		dx. Wmk reversed	65·00	20·00
65	2	4d. rose	£250	55·00
		ax. Wmk reversed	£225	45·00
		b. Rose-carmine	65·00	19·00
		bw. Wmk inverted	†	95·00
		bx. Wmk reversed	75·00	19·00
		by. Wmk inverted and reversed	£450	£140
66	1	5d. yellow-olive	£110	17·00
		ax. Wmk reversed	£100	21·00
		ay. Wmk inverted and reversed		
		b. Olive-green	£110	17·00
		bx. Wmk reversed		
		c. Bronze-green	42·00	50·00
67		6d. deep brown (1869)	95·00	10·00
		a. Blackish brown	£130	8·50

		aw. Wmk inverted	†	£110
		ax. Wmk reversed	£150	17·00
		b. Red-brown	42·00	35·00
68	2	8d. chocolate	85·00	65·00
		ax. Wmk reversed	—	£100
		b. Lake-brown	£130	75·00
		bx. Wmk reversed	£250	£100
69		9d. bistre-brown (12.68)	£500	35·00
		ax. Wmk reversed	£400	25·00
		b. Blackish brown	55·00	6·00
70	3	10d. dull vermilion (*wmk reversed*)	£3500	£140
		ay. Wmk inverted and reversed	†	£250
		b. Red-orange	60·00	16·00
		bx. Wmk reversed	—	13·00
		by. Wmk inverted and reversed	£600	
		c. Orange	£100	13·00
71		1s. reddish lilac (1870)	£275	28·00
		ax. Wmk reversed	£425	60·00
		b. Reddish violet	£100	9·50
		bw. Wmk inverted	†	£150
		bx. Wmk reversed	£300	55·00
72	2	2s. steel-blue	£250	20·00
		ax. Wmk reversed	†	50·00
		b. Deep blue	£140	14·00
		bx. Wmk reversed	£180	20·00

Watermarks as Type **6** were arranged in one pane of 240 (12×20) with the words "CROWN COLONIES" twice in each side margin.

Unused examples of the 1d. dull blue, 1d. deep blue, 5d. yellow-olive, 6d. deep brown, 9d. blackish brown and 10d. red orange with this watermark exist imperforate.

PRINTERS. All stamps from No. 121 to 367 were typographed by De La Rue & Co. Ltd, London.

A wide variety of shades may be found on stamps of this period. We only list the most significant.

(New Currency. 100 cents = 1 rupee)

9

10

11

12

13

14

15

16

17

18

19

1872–80. Wmk Crown CC.

(a) P 14.

121	9	2c. pale brown (*shades*)	24·00	3·50
		w. Wmk inverted	£120	60·00
122	10	4c. grey	40·00	1·50
		w. Wmk inverted	—	65·00
123		4c. rosy-mauve (1880)	65·00	1·50
		w. Wmk inverted	£250	£130
124	11	8c. orange-yellow	42·00	5·50
		a. Yellow	32·00	6·00
		w. Wmk inverted	†	£150
126	12	16c. pale violet	95·00	2·75
		w. Wmk inverted	†	£150
127	13	24c. green	60·00	2·00
		w. Wmk inverted	†	£150
128	14	32c. slate (1877)	£150	15·00
		w. Wmk inverted	£425	£150
129	15	36c. blue	£160	24·00
		x. Wmk reversed	£375	£100
130	16	48c. rose	80·00	7·50
		w. Wmk inverted	—	55·00
131	17	64c. red-brown (1877)	£300	70·00
132	18	96c. drab	£225	26·00
		w. Wmk inverted	—	£180
121/32 *Set of* 11			£1100	£140

(b) P 14×12½.

133	9	2c. brown	£350	65·00
134	10	4c. grey	£1600	30·00
135	11	8c. orange-yellow	£400	48·00
		w. Wmk inverted	†	£250

(c) P 12½.

136	9	2c. brown	£3000	£190
		w. Wmk inverted	†	£400
137	10	4c. grey	£1800	£275

(d) P 12½×14.

138	19	2r.50 dull-rose (1879)	£550	£300

(e) Prepared for use and sent out to Ceylon, but not issued unsurcharged.

139	14	32c. slate (P 14×12½)	£1300	
140	17	64c. red-brown (P 14×12½)	£1500	
141	19	2r.50 dull rose (P 12½)	£2000	

FORGERIES—Beware of forged overprint and surcharge varieties on Victorian issues.

SIXTEEN

16

CENTS
(20)

1882 (Oct). *Nos. 127 and 131 surch as T* **20** *by Govt Printer.*

142	13	16c. on 24c. green	27·00	7·00
		a. Surch inverted		
143	17	20c. on 64c. red-brown	11·00	7·00
		a. Surch double	†	£1300

1883–98. Wmk Crown CA.

(a) P 14.

146	9	2c. pale brown	60·00	2·50
147		2c. dull green (1884)	2·50	15
		s. Optd "Specimen"	£375	
		w. Wmk inverted	£170	70·00
148	10	4c. rosy mauve	4·00	30
		w. Wmk inverted	†	£170
149		4c. rose (1884)	4·75	12·00
		s. Optd "Specimen"	£375	
150	11	8c. orange-yellow	5·00	10·00
		a. Yellow (1898)	4·00	8·50
151	12	16c. pale violet	£1700	£160

(b) Trial perforation. P 12.

151*a*	9	2c. dull green	£4750	
151*b*	10	4c. rose	£4750	
151*c*	13	24c. brown-purple	£5000	

(c) Prepared for use and sent out to Ceylon, but not issued unsurcharged. P 14.

152	13	24c. brown-purple	£1400	
		s. Optd "Specimen"	£600	

Although delivered in 1884 it is believed that the 4c. rose, No. 149, was not used until the early 1890s.

See also Nos. 246, 256 and 258 for the 2c. and 4c. in different colours.

Postage &

FIVE
CENTS

Revenue
(21)

TEN
CENTS
(22)

Twenty
Cents
(23)

One Rupee
Twelve
Cents
(24)

1885 (1 Jan–Mar). *T* **10/19** *surch locally as T* **21/24**.

I.Wmk Crown CC.

(a) P 14.

153	21	5c. on 16c. pale violet	†	£3000
154		5c. on 24c. green	£3250	£110
155		5c. on 32c. slate	65·00	15·00
		a. Surch inverted	†	£2000
		b. Dark grey	£180	45·00
156		5c. on 36c. blue	£300	13·00
		a. Surch inverted	†	£2500
		x. Wmk reversed	†	£120
157		5c. on 48c. rose	£1600	60·00
158		5c. on 64c. red-brown	£120	9·00
		a. Surch double	†	£1700
159		5c. on 96c. drab	£500	70·00
161	22	10c. on 16c. pale violet	£7000	£2500
162		10c. on 24c. green	£450	£120
163		10c. on 36c. blue	£375	£200
164		10c. on 64c. red-brown	£425	£190
165		20c. on 24c. green	60·00	19·00
166	23	20c. on 32c. slate	75·00	60·00
		a. Dark grey	85·00	50·00
		aw. Wmk inverted	£250	
167		25c. on 32c. slate	20·00	5·00
		a. Dark grey	28·00	8·50
168		28c. on 48c. rose	40·00	8·00
		a. Surch double	†	£2000
		w. Wmk inverted	†	£275
169	22	30c. on 36c. blue	17·00	12·00
		x. Wmk reversed	12·00	9·00
		xa. Surch inverted	£250	£110
170		56c. on 96c. drab	26·00	22·00

(b) P 14×12½.

172	21	5c. on 32c. slate	£750	50·00
173		5c. on 64c. red-brown	£800	48·00
		w. Wmk inverted		
174	22	10c. on 64c. red-brown	70·00	£130
		a. Imperf between (vert pair)	£3750	
175	24	1r.12 on 2r.50 dull rose (P 12½)	£550	£100
176		1r.12 on 2r.50 dull rose (P 12½×14)	£110	45·00

II. Wmk Crown CA. P 14.

178	21	5c. on 4c. rose (3.85)	24·00	4·50
		a. Surch inverted	†	£300
179		5c. on 8c. orange-yellow	80·00	9·00
		a. Surch double	†	£2250
		b. Surch inverted	†	£2750
180		5c. on 16c. pale violet	£130	14·00
		a. Surch inverted	†	£225
182		5c. on 24c. brown-purple	—	£500
184	22	10c. on 16c. pale violet	£7000	£1500
185		10c. on 24c. brown-purple	15·00	8·00
186		15c. on 16c. pale violet	12·00	9·00

The 5c. on 4c. rosy mauve and 5c. on 24c. green, both watermarked Crown CA, previously catalogued are now known to be forgeries.

REVENUE AND POSTAGE

5 CENTS (25) 10 CENTS (26) 1 R. 12 C. (27)

1885. *T* **11/15**, **18** *and* **19** *surch with T* **25/7** *by D.L.R.* P 14.

(a) Wmk Crown CA.

187	25	5c. on 8c. lilac	21·00	1·50
		w. Wmk inverted	†	90·00
		x. Wmk reversed	†	£200
188	26	10c. on 24c. brown-purple	11·00	8·50
189		15c. on 16c. orange-yellow	60·00	13·00
190		28c. on 32c. slate	26·00	2·50
191		30c. on 36c. olive-green	28·00	15·00
192		56c. on 96c. drab	50·00	16·00

(b) Wmk Crown CC (sideways).

193	27	1r.12 on 2r.50 dull rose	50·00	£110
187/93 *Set of* 7			£225	£150
187s/93s Optd "Specimen" *Set of* 7			£900	

28

29

1886. Wmk Crown CA. P 14.

195	28	5c. dull purple	2·75	10
		w. Wmk inverted	£160	£100
196	29	15c. sage-green	7·00	1·80
		w. Wmk inverted	†	£170
197		15c. olive-green	7·50	1·60
198		25c. yellow-brown	4·50	1·10
		a. Value in yellow	£120	75·00
199		28c. slate	22·00	1·40
195s, 197s/9s Optd "Specimen" *Set of* 4			£250	

Six plates were used for the 5c., No. 195, between 1885 and 1901, each being replaced by its successor as it became worn. Examples from the worn plates show thicker lines in the background and masses of solid colour under the chin, in front of the throat, at the back of the neck and at the base.

30

1887. Wmk Crown CC (sideways). *White or blued paper.* P 14.

201	30	1r.12 dull rose	28·00	25·00
		aw. Wmk Crown to left of CA	55·00	55·00
		b. Wmk upright	50·00	60·00
		bw. Wmk inverted	†	£225
		s. Optd "Specimen"	£140	

The normal sideways watermark shows Crown to right of CC, *as seen from the back of the stamp.*

TWO CENTS (31) TWO (32) 2 Cents (33)

Two Cents (34) 2 Cents (35)

1888–90. *Nos. 148/9 surch with T* **31/5**.

202	31	2c. on 4c. rosy mauve	1·40	80
		a. Surch inverted	21·00	20·00
		b. Surch double, one inverted	—	£300
203		2c. on 4c. rose	2·25	30
		a. Surch inverted	17·00	18·00
		b. Surch double	—	£325
204	32	2(c). on 4c. rosy mauve	75	30
		a. Surch inverted	35·00	35·00
		b. Surch double	85·00	90·00
		c. Surch double, one inverted	70·00	70·00
205		2(c). on 4c. rose	7·00	20
		a. Surch inverted	£325	
		b. Surch double	90·00	£100
		c. Surch double, one inverted	90·00	£100
206	33	2c. on 4c. rosy mauve	70·00	32·00
		a. Surch inverted	£140	42·00
		b. Surch double, one inverted	£170	
207		2c. on 4c. rose	2·75	75
		a. Surch inverted	16·00	8·50
		b. Surch double	£170	£140
		c. Surch double, one inverted	8·00	12·00
		w. Wmk inverted	£140	
208	34	2c. on 4c. rosy mauve	55·00	25·00
		a. Surch inverted	£170	30·00
209		2c. on 4c. rose	2·50	1·10
		a. Surch inverted	16·00	6·50
		b. Surch double	£120	£110
		c. Surch double, one inverted	16·00	8·00
210	35	2c. on 4c. rosy mauve	60·00	32·00
		a. Surch inverted	85·00	42·00

b. Surch double, one inverted £100 £100
c. Surch double — £325
d. "s" of "Cents" inverted (R. 3/5) — £500
e. As d. Whole surch inverted
211 2c. on 4c. rose 11·00 1·00
a. Surch inverted 21·00 5·50
b. Surch double £110 £110
c. Surch double, one inverted 23·00 11·00
d. "s" of "Cents" inverted (R. 3/5) £375 £225
x. Wmk reversed † £180
209s, 211s Optd "Specimen" *Set of 2* 65·00

The 4c. rose and the 4c. rosy mauve are found surcharged "Postal Commission 3 (or "Three") Cents". They denote the extra commission charged by the Post Office on postal orders which had not been cashed within three months of the date of issue. For a short time the Post Office did not object to the use of these stamps on letters.

POSTAGE

Five Cents

REVENUE
(36)

FIFTEEN
CENTS
(37)

1890. *No. 197 surch with T* **36**.
233 5c. on 15c. olive-green 3·25 2·00
a. Surch inverted 50·00 55·00
b. Surch double £100 £120
c. "Flve" for "Five" (R. 1/1) £120 85·00
d. Variety as c, inverted — £1500
e. "REVENUE" omitted £170 £160
f. Inverted "s" in "Cents" (R. 10/2) 90·00 90·00
g. Variety as f, and whole surch inverted £1800
h. "REVENUE" omitted and inverted "s" in "Cents" £1300
i. "POSTAGE" spaced between "T" and "A" (R. 1/5) 75·00 80·00
j. Variety as i, and whole surch inverted — £1400
s. Optd "Specimen" 30·00

1891. *Nos. 198/9 surch with T* **37**.
239 **29** 15c. on 25c. yellow-brown 15·00 14·00
240 15c. on 28c. slate 17·00 8·50

3 Cents
(38)

39

1892. *Nos. 148/9 and 199 surch with T* **38**.
241 **10** 3c. on 4c. rosy mauve 1·00 3·25
242 3c. on 4c. rose 5·50 8·50
s. Optd "Specimen" 38·00
w. Wmk inverted £140
ws. Optd "Specimen" 95·00
243 **29** 3c. on 28c. slate 4·75 4·50
a. Surch double £160
241/3 *Set of 3* 10·00 14·50

1893–99. Wmk Crown CA. P 14.
245 **39** 3c. terracotta and blue-green 4·00 45
246 **10** 4c. carmine-rose (1898) 9·00 9·00
247 **29** 30c. bright mauve and chestnut 4·25 2·50
a. Bright violet and chestnut 5·00 2·75
249 **19** 2r.50 purple/red (1899) 32·00 50·00
245/9 *Set of 4* 45·00 55·00
245s, 247s/9s Optd "Specimen" *Set of 3* 60·00

Six Cents
(40)

2 R. 25 C.
(41)

1898 (Dec)–**99**.

(a) No. 196 surch with T **40**.
250 **29** 6c. on 15c. sage-green 1·00 75

(b) As No. 138, but colour changed and perf 14, surch as T **41** *(1899)*.
254 **19** 1r.50 on 2r.50 slate 20·00 48·00
w. Wmk inverted £160 £225
255 2r.25 on 2r.50 yellow 38·00 80·00
250s/5s Optd "Specimen" *Set of 3* 70·00

43

1899–1900. Wmk Crown CA (1r.50, 2r.25 wmk Crown CC). P 14.
256 **9** 2c. pale orange-brown 3·50 30
257 **39** 3c. deep green 3·50 55
258 **10** 4c. yellow 3·00 2·75
259 **29** 6c. rose and black 1·75 45
260 **39** 12c. sage-green and rose (1900) 4·00 7·50
261 **29** 15c. blue 6·00 1·25
262 **39** 75c. black and red-brown 6·50 7·50
263 **43** 1r.50 rose 26·00 42·00
264 2r.25 dull blue 35·00 42·00
256/64 *Set of 9* 80·00 95·00
256s/64s Optd "Specimen" *Set of 9* £180

44

45

46

47

48

1903 (29 May)–**05**. Wmk Crown CA. P 14.
265 **44** 2c. red-brown (21.7.03) 2·00 20
266 **45** 3c. green (11.6.03) 2·00 1·00
267 4c. orange-yellow and blue 2·00 4·00
268 **46** 5c. dull purple (2.7.03) 1·50 60
269 **47** 6c. carmine (5.11.03) 9·50 1·50
w. Wmk inverted 85·00
270 **45** 12c. sage-green and rosine (13.8.03) 5·00 11·00
271 **48** 15c. blue (2.7.03) 6·50 3·00
272 25c. bistre (11.8.03) 4·00 8·00
273 30c. dull violet and green 3·25 4·00
274 **45** 75c. dull blue and orange (31.3.05) 3·00 21·00
275 **48** 1r.50 greyish slate (7.4.04) 65·00 55·00
276 2r.25 brown and green (12.4.04) 75·00 50·00
265/76 *Set of 12* £160 £140
265s/76s Optd "Specimen" *Set of 12* £150

1904 (13 Sept)–**05**. Wmk Mult Crown CA. *Ordinary paper*. P 14.
277 **44** 2c. red-brown (17.11.04) 1·50 10
278 **45** 3c. green (17.11.04) 1·50 15
279 4c. orange and ultramarine 2·50 1·50
w. Wmk inverted — £160
280 **46** 5c. dull purple (29.11.04) 2·50 1·25
a. Chalk-surfaced paper (5.10.05) 5·00 70
281 **47** 6c. carmine (11.10.04) 3·00 15
282 **45** 12c. sage-green and rosine (29.9.04) 1·50 1·75
283 **48** 15c. blue (1.12.04) 2·75 60
284 25c. bistre (5.1.05) 6·00 3·75
285 30c. violet and green (7.9.05) 2·50 3·00
286 **45** 75c. dull blue and orange (25.5.05) 5·25 8·00
287 **48** 1r.50 grey (5.1.05) 28·00 10·00
288 2r.25 brown and green (22.12.04) 22·00 30·00
277/88 *Set of 12* 70·00 55·00

50

51

1908. Wmk Mult Crown CA. P 14.
289 **50** 5c. deep purple (26 May) 3·75 10
290 5c. dull purple 4·75 30
291 **51** 6c. carmine (6 June) 1·50 10
289s, 291s Optd "Specimen" *Set of 2* 65·00

1910 (1 Aug)–**11**. Wmk Mult Crown CA. P 14.
292 **44** 2c. brown-orange (20.5.11) 1·50 50
293 **48** 3c. green (5.7.11) 1·00 75
294 10c. sage-green and maroon 2·50 2·50
295 25c. grey 2·50 2·00
296 50c. chocolate 4·00 7·50
297 1r. purple/*yellow* 7·50 10·00
298 2r. red/*yellow* 15·00 28·00
299 5r. black/*green* 38·00 75·00
300 10r. black/*red* 90·00 £190
292/300 *Set of 9* £150 £275
292s/300s Optd "Specimen" *Set of 9* £190

Examples of Nos. 298/300 are known showing a forged Colombo registered postmark dated '27.1.10'.

52

53

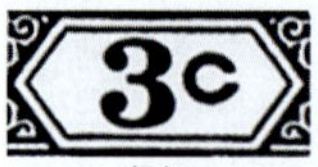

(A)

(B)

Most values in Type **52** were produced by two printing operations, using "Key" and "Duty" plates. Differences in the two Dies of the Key plate are described in the introduction to this catalogue.

In the Ceylon series, however, the 1c. and 5c. values, together with later printings of the 3c. and 6c., were printed from special plates at one operation. These plates can be identified by the large "C" in the value tablet (see illustration A). Examples of these values from Key and Duty plates printing have value tablet as illustration B. The 3c. and 5c. stamps from the single plates *resemble* Die I, and the 1c. and 6c. Die II, although in the latter case the inner top corners of the side panels are square and not curved.

1912–25. Wmk Mult Crown CA. *Chalk-surfaced paper (30c. to 100r.)*. P 14.

(a) Printed from single plates. Value tablet as A.
301 **52** 1c. brown (1919) 1·00 10
w. Wmk inverted 22·00
302 3c. blue-green (1919) 4·00 45
w. Wmk inverted 20·00 32·00
y. Wmk inverted and reversed 28·00 48·00
303 5c. purple 9·00 2·75
a. Wmk sideways (Crown to right of CA) £500
x. Wmk reversed † £160
y. Wmk inverted and reversed £100
304 5c. bright magenta 1·00 60
w. Wmk inverted £120 £100
305 6c. pale scarlet (1919) 12·00 85
a. Wmk sideways (Crown to left of CA) 45·00 90·00
w. Wmk inverted 30·00 48·00
306 6c. carmine 18·00 1·25
a. Wmk sideways (Crown to right of CA) 55·00
aw. Wmk sideways (Crown to left of CA) 90·00
y. Wmk inverted and reversed 42·00

(b) Printed from Key and Duty plates. Die I. 3c. and 6c. have value tablet as B.
307 **52** 2c. brown-orange 40 30
a. Deep orange-brown 30 20
308 3c. yellow-green 6·50 2·25
a. Deep green (1917) 4·50 1·10
309 6c. scarlet (*shades*) 1·10 50
a. Wmk sideways † —
310 10c. sage-green 3·00 1·75
a. Deep sage-green (1917) 5·50 2·50
w. Wmk inverted £140
311 15c. deep bright blue 2·75 1·25
a. Ultramarine (1918) 1·75 1·25
aw. Wmk inverted 24·00
312 25c. orange and blue 6·50 4·50
a. Yellow and blue (1917) 1·75 1·75
aw. Wmk inverted £140 £140
313 30c. blue-green and violet 4·00 3·25
a. Yellow-green and violet (1915) 7·00 4·00
ab. Wmk sideways (Crown to right of CA) 32·00
abw. Wmk Crown to left of CA 35·00
aw. Wmk inverted 48·00
314 50c. black and scarlet 1·50 1·75
w. Wmk inverted 19·00 38·00
315 1r. purple/*yellow* 4·50 3·50
a. White back (1913) 4·50 4·75
as. Optd "Specimen" 50·00
b. On lemon (1915) 4·25 8·00
bs. Optd "Specimen" 45·00
c. On orange-buff (1918) 26·00 35·00
cw. Wmk inverted 75·00
d. On pale yellow (1922) 4·50 10·00
ds. Optd "Specimen" 42·00
316 2r. black and red/*yellow* 3·25 14·00
a. White back (1913) 2·75 14·00
as. Optd "Specimen" 50·00
b. On lemon (1915) 25·00 27·00
bs. Optd "Specimen" 40·00
c. On orange-buff (1919) 40·00 42·00
cw. Wmk inverted 65·00
d. On pale yellow (1921) 40·00 40·00
317 5r. black/*green* 18·00 32·00
a. White back (1914) 23·00 35·00
as. Optd "Specimen" 48·00
b. On blue-grn (olive back) (1917) 20·00 40·00
bs. Optd "Specimen" 60·00
bw. Wmk inverted 80·00 95·00
c. Die II. *On emerald back* (1923) 45·00 £100
cs. Optd "Specimen" 60·00
318 10r. purple and black/*red* 70·00 90·00
aw. Wmk inverted £180
b. Die II (1923) 85·00 £150
bw. Wmk inverted £400
319 20r. black and red/*blue* £150 £160
320 **53** 50r. dull purple £450
a. Break in scroll £1100
b. Broken crown and scroll £1100
f. Damaged leaf at bottom right £1100
s. Optd "Specimen" £180
321 100r. grey-black £1800
a. Break in scroll £3500
b. Broken crown and scroll £3500
f. Damaged leaf at bottom right £3500
s. Optd "Specimen" £325
w. Wmk inverted £4250
322 500r. dull green £6000
a. Break in scroll £11000
b. Broken crown and scroll £11000
f. Damaged leaf at bottom right
s. Optd "Specimen" £500
323 1000r. purple/*red* (1925) £23000
b. Broken crown and scroll £30000
e. Break in lines below left scroll
f. Damaged leaf at bottom right
s. Optd "Specimen" £950
301/18 *Set of 14* £100 £130
301s/19s Optd "Specimen" *Set of 15* £400

For illustrations of the varieties on Nos. 320/3 see above No. 51*b* of Bermuda.

The 2c. and 5c. exist in coils, constructed from normal sheets, used in stamp-affixing machines introduced in 1915.

Sideways watermark varieties are described *as seen from the back of the stamp*.

The "substituted crown" watermark variety is known on the sheet margin of the 1c., No. 301.

WAR STAMP
(54)

WAR STAMP ONE CENT
(55)

1918 (18 Nov)–**19**.

(a) Optd with T **54** *by Govt Printer, Colombo.*

330	**52**	2c. brown-orange	20	40
		a. Opt inverted	55·00	65·00
		b. Opt double	30·00	40·00
		c. Opt omitted in pair with opt inverted	£950	
331		3c. blue-green (No. 302) (1919)	2·50	40
		a. Opt double	£110	
332		3c. deep green (No. 308*a*)	20	50
		a. Opt double	85·00	95·00
333		5c. purple	50	30
		a. Opt double	50·00	60·00
		w. Wmk inverted	£100	
334		5c. bright magenta	3·25	2·75
		a. Opt inverted	55·00	65·00
		b. Opt double	38·00	48·00
		(b) Surch with T **55**.		
335	**52**	1c. on 5c. purple	50	40
		w. Wmk inverted	£140	
		by. Wmk inverted and reversed	£110	
336		1c. on 5c. bright magenta	2·00	20
330s, 332s/3s, 335s Optd "Specimen" *Set of 4*			£120	

Collectors are warned against forgeries of the errors in the "WAR STAMP" overprints.

1918. *Surch as T* **55**, *but without* "WAR STAMP".

337	**52**	1c. on 5c. purple	15	25
		a. Surch double	£190	
		bs. Optd "Specimen"	40·00	
		by. Wmk inverted and reversed	£140	
337*c*		1c. on 5c. bright magenta	2·75	3·25

1921–32. Wmk Mult Script CA. *Chalk-surfaced paper (30c. to 100r.).* P 14.

		(a) Printed from single plates. Value tablet as A.		
338	**52**	1c. brown (1927)	1·00	35
339		3c. green (5.5.22)	3·50	75
		w. Wmk inverted	19·00	35·00
340		3c. slate-grey (1923)	75	20
		a. Wmk sideways	£1500	
		w. Wmk inverted	30·00	
341		5c. purple (1927)	60	15
342		6c. carmine-red (3.8.21)	2·25	75
		w. Wmk inverted	20·00	35·00
		y. Wmk inverted and reversed	45·00	
343		6c. bright violet (1922)	1·75	15
		w. Wmk inverted	30·00	
		y. Wmk inverted and reversed	45·00	
		(b) Printed from Key and Duty plates.		
344	**52**	2c. brown-orange (Die II) (1927)	70	25
345		9c. red/*pale yellow* (Die II) (1926)	1·25	30
346		10c. sage-green (Die I) (16.9.21)	1·40	40
		aw. Wmk inverted	32·00	
		ay. Wmk inverted and reversed	28·00	45·00
		b. Die II (1924)	1·75	60
		c. Vert gutter pair. Die I and Die II. Nos. 346 and 346b	£350	
347		12c. rose-scarlet (Die I) (1925)	5·50	5·50
		a. Die II	1·00	2·25
		as. Optd "Specimen"	95·00	
		b. Vert gutter pair. Die I and Die II. Nos. 347/a	£150	
348		15c. ultramarine (Die I) (30.5.22)	3·25	13·00
349		15c. green/*pale yellow* (Die I) (1923)	3·00	1·25
		a. Die II (1924)	3·00	1·00
		aw. Wmk inverted	30·00	
		b. Vert gutter pair. Die I and Die II. Nos. 349/a	£300	
350		20c. bright blue (Die I) (1922)	4·00	6·00
		aw. Wmk inverted	55·00	
		b. Die II (1924)	3·50	45
		c. Vert gutter pair. Die I and Die II. Nos. 350 and 350b	£350	
351		25c. orange-yellow and blue (Die I) (17.10.21)	2·00	1·90
		aw. Wmk inverted	75·00	
		b. Die II (1924)	3·75	1·25
		c. Vert gutter pair. Die I and Die II. Nos. 351/b	£170	
352		30c. yellow-green & vio (Die I) (15.3.22)	1·60	3·75
		a. Die II (1924)	4·50	1·25
		b. Vert gutter pair. Die I and Die II. Nos. 352/a	£550	
353		50c. black and scarlet (Die II) (1922)	1·75	80
		a. Die I (1932)	60·00	80·00
354		1r. purple/*pale yellow* (Die I) (1923)	15·00	30·00
		a. Die II (1925)	20·00	26·00
		b. Vert gutter pair. Die I and Die II. Nos. 354/a	£375	
355		2r. black & red/*pale yell* (Die II) (1923)	7·00	9·00
356		5r. black/*emerald* (Die II) (1924)	38·00	65·00
357		20r. black and red/*blue* (Die II) (1924)	£190	£250
358	**53**	50r. dull purple (1924)	£550	£950
		a. Break in scroll	£1100	
		b. Broken crown and scroll	£1100	
		e. Break in lines below left scroll	£1100	
		f. Damaged leaf at bottom right	£1100	
		g. Gash in fruit and leaf	£1100	
		s. Optd "Specimen"	£180	
359		100r. brownish grey (1924)	£1900	
		a. Break in scroll	£3500	
		b. Broken crown and scroll	£3500	
		e. Break in lines below left scroll	£3500	
		f. Damaged leaf at bottom right	£3500	
		h. Grey-black	£1900	
		ha. break in scroll	£3500	
		hb. broken crown and scroll	£3500	
		he. break in lines below left scroll	£3500	
		hf. Damaged leaf at bottom right	£3500	
		s. Optd "Specimen"	£375	
360		100r. dull purple and blue (24.10.27)	£1400	
		a. Break in scroll	£3000	
		b. Broken crown and scroll	£3000	
		e. Break in lines below left scroll	£3000	
		f. Damaged leaf at bottom right	£3000	
		g. Gash in fruit and leaf	£3000	
		s. Optd "Specimen"	£375	
338/56 *Set of 19*			80·00	£110
338s/57s Optd "Specimen" *Set of 20*			£500	

The 2c. to 30c. and 1r. values produced from Key and Duty plates were printed in sheets of 240 using two plates one above the other. Nos. 346c, 347b, 349b, 350c, 351b, 353b and 354b come from printings in 1924 and 1925 which combined Key Plate 7 (Die I) with Key Plate 12 (Die II).

No. 353a, from Key Plate 23, was a mistake; the "retired" Die I being issued in error when it became necessary to replace Key Plate 21.

For illustrations of the varieties on Nos. 358/60 see above No. 51*b* of Bermuda.

2 Cents.
(56)

57

(Surch at Ceylon Govt Printing Works)

1926 (27 Nov). *Surch as T* **56**.

361	**52**	2c. on 3c. slate-grey	1·00	1·00
		a. Surch double	70·00	
		b. Bar omitted	80·00	90·00
362		5c. on 6c. bright violet	50	40
361s/2s Optd "Specimen" *Set of 2*			60·00	

No. 361b comes from the bottom horizontal row of the sheet which was often partially obscured by the selvedge during surcharging.

1927 (27 Nov)–**29**. Wmk Mult Script CA. *Chalk-surfaced paper.* P 14.

363	**57**	1r. dull and bright purple (1928)	2·50	1·25
364		2r. green and carmine (1929)	3·75	2·75
365		5r. green and dull purple (1928)	14·00	21·00
366		10r. green and brown-orange	42·00	90·00
367		20r. dull purple and blue	£140	£250
363/7 *Set of 5*			£180	£325
363s/7s Optd "Specimen" *Set of 5*			£160	

No. 364. Collectors are warned against faked 2r. stamps, showing what purports to be a double centre.

58 Tapping Rubber

59 Adam's Peak

60 Colombo Harbour

61 Plucking tea

62 Hill paddy (rice)

63 River scene

64 Coconut Palms

65 Temple of the Tooth, Kandy

66 Ancient irrigation tank

67 Wild elephants

68 Trincomalee

(Recess D.L.R. (2, 3, 20, 50c.), B.W. (others))

1935 (1 May)–**36**. *T* **58/68**. Wmk Mult Script CA (sideways on 10, 15, 25, 30c. and 1r.). Various perfs.

368	**58**	2c. black and carmine (P 12×13)	30	40
		a. Perf 14	9·00	40
369	**59**	3c. blk & ol-green (P 13×12) (1.10.35)	35	40
		a. Perf 14	28·00	35
370	**60**	6c. black & blue (P 11×11½) (1.1.36)	30	30
371	**61**	9c. green & orange (P 11×11½) (1.1.36)	1·00	65
372	**62**	10c. black & purple (P 11½×11) (1.6.35)	1·25	2·75
373	**63**	15c. red-brown and green (P 11½×11)	1·00	50
374	**64**	20c. black & grey-blue (P 12×13) (1.1.36)	1·75	3·00
375	**65**	25c. deep blue & chocolate (P 11½×11)	1·40	1·25
376	**66**	30c. carm & green (P 11½×11) (1.8.35)	2·25	3·25
377	**67**	50c. black and mauve (P 14) (1.1.36)	13·00	1·75
378	**68**	1r. vio-bl & chocolate (P 11½×11) (1.7.35)	24·00	18·00
368/78 *Set of 11*			42·00	29·00
368s/78s Perf "Specimen" *Set of 11*			£225	

1935 (6 May). *Silver Jubilee. As Nos. 91/4 of Antigua.* P 13½×14.

379	6c. ultramarine and grey	75	30
	f. Diagonal line by turret	70·00	32·00
	g. Dot to left of chapel	£100	50·00
	h. Dot by flagstaff	£100	50·00
	i. Dash by turret	£120	70·00
380	9c. green and indigo	75	2·25
	f. Diagonal line by turret	90·00	£130
	g. Dot to left of chapel	£160	£200
	h. Dot by flagstaff	£160	£200
381	20c. brown and deep blue	4·25	2·75
	f. Diagonal line by turret	£190	£130
	g. Dot to left of chapel	£350	£200
382	50c. slate and purple	5·25	12·00
	f. Diagonal line by turret	£350	£425
	h. Dot by flagstaff	£400	£450
379/82 *Set of 4*		10·00	15·00
379s/82s Perf "Specimen" *Set of 4*		£130	

For illustrations of plate varieties, see Omnibus section following Zanzibar.

1937 (12 May). *Coronation. As Nos. 95/7 of Antigua.* P 11×11½.

383	6c. carmine	65	1·00
384	9c. green	2·50	4·50
385	20c. blue	3·50	4·00
383/5 *Set of 3*		6·00	8·50
383s/5s Perf "Specimen" *Set of 3*		£100	

69 Tapping Rubber

70 Sigiriya (Lion Rock)

71 Ancient Guard-stone, Anuradhapura

72 King George VI

HAVE YOU READ THE NOTES AT THE BEGINNING OF THIS CATALOGUE?
These often provide answers to the enquiries we receive

Comma flaw (Pl 2A R. 5/6)

Apostrophe flaw (Frame Pl 1A R. 6/6) (ptg of 1 Jan 1943 only)

(Recess B.W. (6, 10, 15, 20, 25, 30c., 1r., 2r. (both)), D.L.R (others) T **72** typo D.L.R.)

1938–49. *T* **69/72** *and designs as 1935–36, but with portrait of King George VI instead of King George V,* "POSTAGE & REVENUE" *omitted and some redrawn.* Wmk Mult Script CA (sideways on 10, 15, 25, 30c. and 1r.). *Chalk-surfaced paper (5r.).* P 11×11½ (6, 20c., 2r. (both)), 11½×11 (10, 15, 25, 30c., 1r.), 11½×13 (2c.), 13×11½ (3, 50c.), 13½ (5c.) or 14 (5r.).

386	**69**	2c. black and carmine (25.4.38)	17·00	1·75
		aa. Comma flaw		
		a. Perf 13½×13 (1938)	£120	1·75
		ab. Comma flaw		
		b. Perf 13½ (25.4.38)	2·00	10
		c. Perf 11×11½ (17.2.44)	80	85
		cw. Wmk inverted	—	£850
		d. Perf 12 (22.4.49)	2·25	3·50
387	**60**	3c. black and deep blue-green (21.3.38)	11·00	1·50
		a. Perf 13×13½ (1938)	£250	12·00
		b. Perf 13½ (21.3.38)	4·25	10
		c. Perf 14 (line) (7.41)	£120	1·00
		d. Perf 11½×11 (14.5.42)	80	10
		da. "A" of "CA" missing from wmk	£950	£950
		dw. Wmk inverted	†	—
		e. Perf 12 (14.1.46)	80	85
387*f*	**64**	5c. sage-green & orange (1.1.43)	30	10
		fa. Apostrophe flaw	75·00	38·00
		g. Perf 12 (1947)	1·75	30
388	**60**	6c. black and blue (1.1.38)	30	10
389	**70**	10c. black and light blue (1.2.38)	3·25	10
		a. Wmk upright (1.6.44)	2·50	50
390	**63**	15c. green and red-brown (1.1.38)	2·00	10
		a. Wmk upright (23.7.45)	2·75	60
391	**61**	20c. black and grey-blue (15.1.38)	3·25	10
392	**65**	25c. deep blue and chocolate (15.1.38)	5·00	30
		a. Wmk upright (1944)	4·25	10
393	**66**	30c. carmine and green (1.2.38)	12·00	3·00
		a. Wmk upright (16.4.45)	13·00	4·50
394	**67**	50c. black and mauve (25.4.38)	£160	45·00
		a. Perf 13×13½ (25.4.38)	£375	2·75
		b. Perf 13½ (25.4.38)	20·00	30
		c. Perf 14 (line) (4.42)	£100	27·00
		d. Perf 11½×11 (14.5.42)	5·00	3·75
		da. "A" of "CA" missing from wmk	£1100	
		e. Perf 12 (14.1.46)	5·00	20
395	**68**	1r. blue-violet and chocolate (1.2.38)	17·00	1·25
		a. Wmk upright (1944)	18·00	2·25
396	**71**	2r. black and carmine (1.2.38)	13·00	3·00
		a. "A" of "CA" missing from wmk		
396*b*		2r. black and violet (15.3.47)	2·25	2·25
397	**72**	5r. green and purple (1.7.38)	42·00	8·50
		a. Ordinary paper. *Green and pale purple* (19.2.43)	18·00	5·50
386/97a (*cheapest*) *Set of* 14			70·00	13·50
386s/97s Perf "Specimen" *Set of* 14			£400	

Printings of the 2c., 3c. and 50c. perforated 11×11½ or 11½×11 were produced by Bradbury, Wilkinson after the De La Rue works had been bombed in December 1940.

(73)

(74)

1940–41. *Nos. 388 and 391 surch by Govt Ptg Office, Colombo.*

398	**73**	3c. on 6c. black and blue (10.5.41)	65	10
399	**74**	3c. on 20c. black and grey-blue (5.11.40)	4·00	2·00

1946 (10 Dec). *Victory. As Nos. 110/11 of Antigua.*

400	6c. blue	30	35
401	15c. brown	30	1·75
400s/1s Perf "Specimen" *Set of* 2		80·00	

75 Parliament Building

76 Adam's Peak

77 Temple of the Tooth

78 Anuradhapura

(Des R. Tenison and M. S. V. Rodrigo. Recess B.W.)

1947 (25 Nov). *Inauguration of New Constitution. T* **75/8**. Wmk Mult Script CA. P 11×12 (horiz) or 12×11 (vert).

402	**75**	6c. black and blue	20	15
403	**76**	10c. black, orange and carmine	25	40
404	**77**	15c. green and purple	25	80
405	**78**	25c. ochre and emerald-green	25	1·75
402/5 *Set of* 4			85	2·75
402s/5s Perf "Specimen" *Set of* 4			90·00	

DOMINION

79 Lion Flag of Dominion

80 D. S. Senanayake

81 Lotus Flowers and Sinhalese Letters "Sri"

(Recess (flag typo) B.W.)

1949 (4 Feb–5 Apr). *First Anniv of Independence.*

(*a*) Wmk Mult Script CA (sideways on 4c.). P 12½×12 (4c.) or 12×12½ (5c.).

406	**79**	4c. yellow, carmine and brown	20	20
407	**80**	5c. brown and green	10	10

(*b*) W **81** (sideways on 15c.). P 13×12½ (15c.) or 12×12½ (25c.) (5 April).

408	**79**	15c. yellow, carmine and vermilion	1·00	40
409	**80**	25c. brown and blue	15	1·00
406/9 *Set of* 4			1·25	1·50

The 15c. is larger, measuring 28×12 mm.

82 Globe and Forms of Transport

83

84

(Recess U.L.R.)

1949 (10 Oct). *75th Anniv of Universal Postal Union.* W **81**. P 13 (25c.) or 12 (others).

410	**82**	5c. brown and bluish green	75	10
411	**83**	15c. black and carmine	1·10	2·75
412	**84**	25c. black and ultramarine	1·10	1·10
410/12 *Set of* 3			2·75	3·50

85 Kandyan Dancer

86 Kiri Vehera Polonnaruwa

87 Vesak Orchid

88 Sigiriya (Lion Rock)

89 Octagon Library, Temple of the Tooth

90 Ruins at Madirigiriya

(Recess B.W.)

1950 (4 Feb). *T* **85/90**. W **81**. P 11×11½ (75c.), 11½×11 (1r.), 12×12½ (others).

413	**85**	4c. purple and scarlet	10	10
414	**86**	5c. green	10	10
415	**87**	15c. blue-green and violet	2·50	50
416	**88**	30c. carmine and yellow	30	70
417	**89**	75c. ultramarine and orange	7·50	20
418	**90**	1r. deep blue and brown	1·75	30
413/18 *Set of* 6			11·00	1·50

These stamps were issued with redrawn inscriptions in 1958/9. See Nos. 448/65.

91 Sambars, Ruhuna National Park

92 Ancient Guard-stone, Anuradhapura

93 Harvesting rice

94 Coconut trees

95 Sigiriya fresco

96 Star Orchid

97 Rubber Plantation

98 Outrigger canoe

99 Tea Plantation

100 River Gal Dam

101 Bas-relief, Anuradhapura

102 Harvesting rice

I. No. 424

II. No. 424a (Dot added)

(Photo Courvoisier)

1951 (1 Aug)–**54**. *T* **91/102**. No wmk. P 11½.

419	**91**	2c. brown and blue-green (15.5.54)	10	1·25
420	**92**	3c. black and slate-violet (15.5.54)	10	1·00
421	**93**	6c. brown-black & yellow-green (15.5.54)	10	30
422	**94**	10c. green and blue-grey	1·00	65
423	**95**	25c. orange-brown & bright blue (15.3.54)	10	20
424	**96**	35c. red and deep green (I) (1.2.52)	1·50	1·50
		a. Type II (1954)	6·00	60
425	**97**	40c. deep brown (15.5.54)	5·00	1·00
426	**98**	50c. indigo and slate-grey (15.3.54)	30	10
427	**99**	85c. black and deep blue-green (15.5.54)	75	30
428	**100**	2r. blue and deep brown (15.5.54)	7·50	1·25
429	**101**	5r. brown and orange (15.3.54)	5·00	1·40
430	**102**	10r. red-brown and buff (15.3.54)	50·00	16·00
419/30 *Set of* 12			65·00	21·00

Nos. 413/30 (except 422) were reissued in 1958–62, redrawn with ‘CEYLON’ much smaller and other inscriptions in Sinhalese. See Nos. 448/65.

103 Ceylon Mace and symbols of Progress

(Photo Harrison)

1952 (23 Feb). *Colombo Plan Exhibition. Chalk-surfaced paper.* W **81** (sideways). P 14½×14.

431	**103**	5c. green	10	30
432		15c. ultramarine	10	60

104 Queen Elizabeth II

105 Ceremonial Procession

(Recess B.W.)

1953 (2 June). *Coronation.* W **81**. P 12×13.

433	**104**	5c. green	1·25	10

(Recess D.L.R.)

1954 (10 Apr). *Royal Visit.* W **81** (sideways). P 13×12½.

434	**105**	10c. deep blue	1·00	10

106 King Coconuts

107 Farm Produce

(Photo Courvoisier)

1954 (1 Dec). No wmk. P 11½.

435	**106**	10c. orange, bistre-brown and buff	10	10

For this design with redrawn inscription see No. 453.

(Photo Harrison)

1955 (10 Dec). *Royal Agricultural and Food Exhibition.* W **81** (sideways). P 14×14½.

436	**107**	10c. brown and orange	10	10

108 Sir John Kotelawala and House of Representatives

(Photo Courvoisier)

1956 (26 Mar). *Prime Minister's 25 Years of Public Service.* P 11½.

437	**108**	10c. deep bluish green	10	10

109 Arrival of Vijaya in Ceylon

110 Lampstand and Dharmachakra

111 Hand of Peace and Dharmachakra

112 Dharmachakra encircling the Globe

(Photo Courvoisier)

1956. *Buddha Jayanti.* P 11½.

438	**109**	3c. blue and brownish grey (23 May)	15	15
439	**110**	4c.+2c. grnish yell & dp bl (10 May)	20	75
440	**111**	10c.+5c. carm, yellow & grey (10 May)	20	1·00
441	**112**	15c. bright blue (23 May)	25	10
438/41 *Set of* 4			70	1·75

113 Mail Transport

114 Stamp of 1857

(Photo Enschedé (4c., 10c.), Courvoisier (others))

1957 (1 Apr). *Centenary of First Ceylon Postage Stamp.* P 12½×13 (4 c., 10 c.) or 11½ (others).

442	**113**	4c. orange-red and deep bluish green	75	50
443		10c. vermilion and blue	75	10
444	**114**	35c. brown, yellow and blue	30	50
445		85c. brown, yellow and grey-green	80	1·60
442/5 *Set of* 4			2·40	2·40

(115)

(116)

117 Kandyan Dancer

1958 (15 Jan). *Nos. 439/40 with premium obliterated as T* **115** *(4c.) or T* **116** *(10c.).*

446	**110**	4c. greenish yellow and deep blue	10	10
		a. Opt inverted	15·00	20·00
		b. Opt double	20·00	26·00
447	**111**	10c. carmine, yellow and grey	10	10
		a. Opt inverted	13·00	16·00
		b. Narrower square (R. 2/3 and R. 10/1)	1·25	

The 4c. exists with opt misplaced to right so that some stamps show the vertical bar on the left (*Price* £19 *un.*).

On No. 447b the obliterating square is 3 mm. wide instead of 4 mm.

(Recess B.W. (4c., 5c., 15c., 30c., 75c., 1r.). Photo Courvoisier (others))

1958 (14 May)–**62**. *As earlier types, but inscriptions redrawn as in T* **117**. W **81** (4, 5, 15, 30, 75c., 1r.) or no wmk (others). P 11×11½ (75c.), 11½×11 (1r.), 12×12½ (4, 5, 15, 30c.), or 11½ (others).

448	**91**	2c. brown and blue-green	10	50
449	**92**	3c. black and slate-violet	10	70
450	**117**	4c. purple and scarlet	10	10
451	–	5c. green (1.10.58)	10	1·60
		a. Yellow-green (13.6.61)	40	2·00
		b. Deep green (19.6.62)	3·75	3·00
452	–	6c. brown-black and yellow-green	10	65
453	**106**	10c. orge, bistre-brown & buff (1.10.58)	10	10
454	–	15c. blue-green and violet (1.10.58)	3·50	80
455	–	25c. orange-brown and bright blue	15	10
456	**88**	30c. carmine and yellow (1.5.59)	20	1·40
457	**96**	35c. red and deep green (II) (15.7.58)	6·50	30
459	**89**	50c. indigo and slate-grey (15.7.58)	30	10
460	**89**	75c. ultramarine and orange (1.5.59)	9·00	2·75
		a. Ultramarine & brown-orge (3.4.62)	9·00	2·25
461	**99**	85c. black and deep blue-green (1.5.59)	3·75	7·00
462	**90**	1r. deep blue and brown (1.10.58)	60	10
463	–	2r. blue and deep brown	1·75	30
464	–	5r. brown and orange	7·50	30
465	–	10r. red-brown and buff	10·00	1·00
448/65 *Set of* 17			40·00	15·00

Designs: *Vert* (*as T* **117**)—5c. Kiri Vehera Polonnaruwa; 6c. Harvesting rice; 15c. Vesak Orchid; 25c. Sigiriya fresco. (*as T* **99**)—5r. Bas-relief, Anuradhapura; 10r. Harvesting rice. Horiz (*as T* **97**)—50c. Outrigger canoe. (*as T* **99**)—2r. River Gal Dam.

118 “Human Rights”

119 Portraits of Founders and University Buildings

(Photo Enschedé)

1958 (10 Dec). *Tenth Anniv of Declaration of Human Rights.* P 13×12½.

466	**118**	10c. vermilion and dull purple	10	10
467		85c. vermilion and deep blue-green	30	55

(Photo Enschedé)

1959 (31 Dec). *Institution of Pirivena Universities.* P 13×12½.

468	**119**	10c. red-orange and ultramarine	10	10

120 Uprooted Tree

121 S. W. R. D. Bandaranaike

(Des W. A. Ariyasena. Photo Courvoisier)

1960 (7 Apr). *World Refugee Year.* P 11½.

469	**120**	4c. red-brown and gold	10	85
470		25c. blackish violet and gold	10	15

(Photo Courvoisier)

1961 (8 Jan). *Prime Minister Bandaranaike Commemoration.* P 11½.

471	**121**	10c. deep blue and greenish blue	10	10
		a. Portrait redrawn (15.6.61)*	10	10

*Earliest known postmark date.

No. 471a can be identified by Mr. Bandaranaike's dark hair at temples.

122 Ceylon Scout Badge

123 Campaign Emblem

(Des W. A. Ariyasena. Photo Courvoisier)

1962 (26 Feb). *Golden Jubilee of Ceylon Boy Scouts Association.* P 11½.

472	**122**	35c. buff and blue	15	10

(Photo Harrison)

1962 (7 Apr). *Malaria Eradication.* W **81**. P 14½×14.

473	**123**	25c. red-orange and sepia	10	10

124 De Havilland D.H.85 Leopard Moth and Hawker Siddeley Comet 4

125 “Produce” and Campaign Emblem

(Photo Courvoisier)

1963 (28 Feb). *25th Anniv of Airmail.* P 11½.

474	**124**	50c. black and light blue	50	50

(Photo Courvoisier)

1963 (21 Mar). *Freedom from Hunger.* P 11½.

475	**125**	5c. vermilion and blue	75	2·00
476		25c. brown and yellow-olive	3·00	30

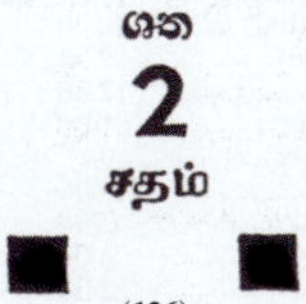

(126)

127 “Rural Life”

1963 (1 June). *No. 450 surch with T* **126**.

477	**117**	2c. on 4c. purple and scarlet	10	10
		a. Surch inverted	16·00	
		b. Surch double	32·00	

(Photo Harrison)

1963 (5 July). *Golden Jubilee of Ceylon Co-operative Movement (1962).* W **81**. P 14×14½.

478	**127**	60c. rose-red and black	2·00	50

128 S. W. R. D. Bandaranaike

129 Terrain, Elephant and Tree

(Recess Courvoisier)

1963 (26 Sept). P 11½.

479	**128**	10c. light blue	10	10

(Photo Harrison)

1963 (9 Dec). *National Conservation Week.* W **81** (sideways). P 14×14½.

480	**129**	5c. sepia and blue	60	40

130 S. W. R. D. Bandaranaike

131 Anagarika Dharmapala (Buddhist missionary)

(T **130/1**. Photo Courvoisier)

1964 (1 July). P 11½

481	**130**	10c. deep violet-blue and greenish grey	10	10

1964 (16 Sept). *Birth Centenary of Anagarika Dharmapala (founder of Maha Bodhi Society).* P 11½.

482	**131**	25c. sepia and olive-yellow	10	10

134 Southern Grackle

135 D. S. Senanayake

136

138 Ruins at Madirigiriya

146 Tea Plantation

149 Map of Ceylon

(Des A. Dharmasiri (5r.); P. A. Miththapala (10r.). Photo Courvoisier (10c. (486), 20c.), Harrison (10c. (487), 60c., 1r., 5r., 10r.), D.L.R. (others incl sheet))

1964 (1 Oct)–**72**. *T* **134/6**, **138**, **146**, **149** *and similar designs.* No wmk (Nos. 486, 489). W **81** (others; sideways on Nos. 487, 494 499). P 11½ (Nos. 486, 489), 14½×14 (No. 494) or 14 (others).

485	**134**	5c. multicoloured (5.2.66)	2·00	1·00
486	**135**	10c. myrtle-green (22.3.66)	80	10
487	**136**	10c. myrtle-green (23.9.68)	10	10
		a. Imperf (pair)	48·00	
		b. Horiz pair, one stamp imperf 3 sides	£120	
488	–	15c. multicoloured (5.2.66)	3·00	30
489	**138**	20c. brown-purple and buff	20	25
494	–	60c. multicoloured (5.2.66)	4·00	1·25
		a. Red omitted	40·00	
		b. Blue and green omitted*	40·00	
495	–	75c. multicoloured (5.2.66)	2·75	70
		a. No wmk (8.6.72)	12·00	13·00
497	**146**	1r. brown and bluish green	1·00	30
		a. Brown (tea picker, etc) omitted	£600	
		b. Bluish green omitted	£700	
499	–	5r. multicoloured (15.8.69)	6·00	6·50
500	**149**	10r. multicoloured (1.10.69)	22·00	3·50
485/500 *Set of* 10			38·00	12·50

MS500*a* 148×174 mm. As Nos. 485, 488, 494 and 495. Imperf	7·00	14·00

Designs: *Horiz* (*as T* **134**)—15c. Common Peafowl; 60c. Ceylon Junglefowl; 75c. Asian Black-headed Oriole. (*As T* **138**)—5r. Girls transplanting rice.

*Actually only the blue printing is omitted on this sheet, but where this was printed over the yellow to form the leaves it appeared as green.

The 5c., 75c. and 1r. exist with PVA gum as well as gum arabic.

No. 487b comes from a sheet which showed stamps in the third vertical row imperforate at top, bottom and at right.

In the miniature sheet the inscriptions on the 60c. have been rearranged to conform with the style of the other values.

150 Exhibition Buildings and Cogwheels

151 Trains of 1864 and 1964

(Photo State Printing Works, Budapest)

1964 (1 Dec). *Industrial Exhibition. T* **150** *and similar horiz design.* No wmk. P 11.

501	–	5c. multicoloured	10	75
		a. Pair. Nos. 501/2	35	2·50
502	**150**	5c. multicoloured	10	75

No. 501 is inscribed "INDUSTRIAL EXHIBITION" in Sinhala and Tamil, No. 502 in Sinhala and English. The stamps were issued together *se-tenant* in alternate vertical rows, producing horizontal pairs.

(Photo Harrison)

1964 (21 Dec). *Centenary of Ceylon Railways. T* **151** *and similar horiz design.* W **81** (sideways). P 14×14½.

503	–	60c. blue, reddish purple and yellow-green	2·75	40
		a. Pair. Nos. 503/4	5·50	5·50
504	**151**	60c. blue, reddish purple and yellow-green	2·75	40

No. 503 is inscribed "RAILWAY CENTENARY" in Sinhala and Tamil, No. 504 in Sinhala and English. The stamps were issued together *se-tenant* in alternate horizontal rows, producing vertical pairs.

152 ITU Emblem and Symbols

153 ICY Emblem

(Photo Harrison)

1965 (17 May). *ITU Centenary.* W **81** (sideways). P 14½.

505	**152**	2c. bright blue and red	1·00	1·10
506		30c. brown and red	3·00	45
		a. Value omitted	£160	

No. 506a was caused by the misplacement of the red.

(Photo Courvoisier)

1965 (26 June). *International Co-operation Year. T* **153** *and similar horiz design.* P 11½.

507		3c. deep blue and rose-carmine	1·25	1·00
508		50c. black, rose-carmine and gold	3·25	50

No. 508 is similar to T **153** but has the multilingual inscription "CEYLON" rearranged.

154 Town Hall, Colombo

5 ■

(**155**)

(Photo Courvoisier)

1965 (29 Oct). *Centenary of Colombo Municipal Council.* P 11×11½.

509	**154**	25c. myrtle-green and sepia	20	20

1965 (18 Dec). *No. 481 surch with T* **155**.

510	**130**	5c. on 10c. deep violet-blue and greenish grey	10	1·00

157 Kandy and Council Crest

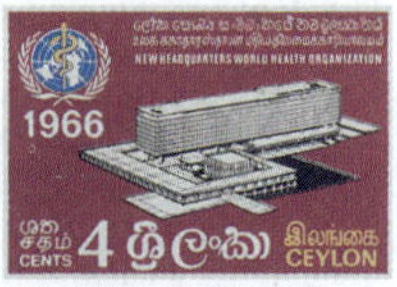

158 WHO Building

(Photo Harrison)

1966 (15 June). *Kandy Municipal Council Centenary.* W **81**. P 14×13½.

512	**157**	25c. multicoloured	20	20

(Litho D.L.R.)

1966 (8 Oct). *Inauguration of WHO Headquarters. Geneva.* P 14.

513	**158**	4c. multicoloured	1·75	3·00
514		1r. multicoloured	6·75	1·50

159 Rice Paddy and Map of Ceylon

160 Rice Paddy and Globe

(Photo Courvoisier)

1966 (25 Oct). *International Rice Year.* P 11½.

515	**159**	6c. multicoloured	20	75
516	**160**	30c. multicoloured	30	15

161 UNESCO Emblem

162 Water-resources Map

(Litho State Ptg Wks, Vienna)

1966 (3 Nov). *20th Anniv of UNESCO.* P 12.

517	**161**	3c. multicoloured	2·75	3·75
518		50c. multicoloured	8·00	50

(Litho D.L.R.)

1966 (1 Dec). *International Hydrological Decade.* P 14.

519	**162**	2c. orange-brown, greenish yellow and blue	30	85
520		2r. orange-brown, greenish yellow, blue and yellow-green	1·50	2·25

163 Devotees at Buddhist Temple

167 Galls Fort and Clock Tower

(Photo State Ptg Wks, Vienna)

1967 (2 Jan). *Poya Holiday System. T* **163** *and similar horiz designs. Multicoloured.* P 12.

521	5c. Type **163**	15	60
522	20c. Mihintale	15	10
523	35c. Sacred Bo-tree, Anuradhapura	15	15
524	60c. Adam's Peak	15	10
521/4 *Set of* 4		55	85

(Litho Rosenbaum Brothers, Vienna)

1967 (5 Jan). *Centenary of Galle Municipal Council.* P 13½.

525	**167**	25c. multicoloured	70	20

168 Field Research

(Litho Rosenbaum Bros, Vienna)

1967 (1 Aug). *Centenary of Ceylon Tea Industry. T* **168** *and similar horiz designs. Multicoloured.* P 13½.

526	4c. Type **168**	60	80
527	40c. Tea-tasting equipment	1·75	1·50
528	50c. Leaves and bud	1·75	20
529	1r. Shipping tea	1·75	10
526/9 *Set of* 4		5·25	2·25

169 Elephant Ride

170 Ranger, Jubilee Emblem and Flag

(Litho Rosenbaum Bros, Vienna)

1967 (15 Aug). *International Tourist Year.* P 13½.

530	**169**	45c. multicoloured	2·25	80

1967 (16 Sept). *1st National Stamp Exhibition. No.* **MS**500*a optd "FIRST NATIONAL STAMP EXHIBITION 1967".*

MS531 148×174 mm. Nos. 485, 488, 494/5. Imperf	8·50	9·00

(Litho D.L.R.)

1967 (19 Sept). *Golden Jubilee of Ceylon Girl Guides Association*. P 12½×13.

532	**170**	3c. multicoloured	50	20
533		25c. multicoloured	75	10

171 Col. Olcott and Buddhist Flag

(Litho Rosenbaum Bros, Vienna)

1967 (8 Dec). *60th Death Anniv of Colonel H. S. Olcott (theosophist)*. P 13½.

534	**171**	15c. multicoloured	30	20

172 Independence Hall

173 Lion Flag and Sceptre

(Photo Harrison)

1968 (2 Feb). *20th Anniv of Independence*. W **81** (sideways). P 14.

535	**172**	5c. multicoloured	10	55
536	**173**	1r. multicoloured	50	10

174 Sir D. B. Jayatilleke

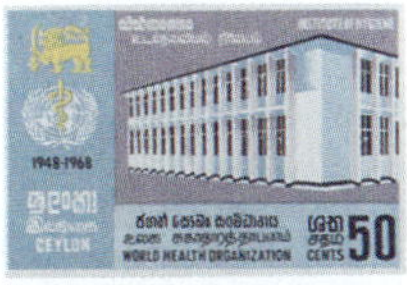

175 Institute of Hygiene

(Litho D.L.R.)

1968 (14 Feb). *Birth Centenary of Sir Baron Jayatilleke (scholar and statesman)*. P 14.

537	**174**	25c. yellow-brown and sepia	10	10

(Litho B.W.)

1968 (7 Apr). *20th Anniv of World Health Organization*. W **81**. P 12.

538	**175**	50c. multicoloured	10	10

176 Vickers Super VC-10 Aircraft over Terminal Building

177 Open Koran and "1400"

(Des and litho B.W.)

1968 (5 Aug). *Opening of Colombo Airport*. W **81**. P 13½.

539	**176**	60c. grey-blue, chestnut, red and yellow	1·00	10

(Des M. I. M. Mohideen. Photo Harrison)

1968 (14 Oct). *1400th Anniv of the Holy Koran*. W **81**. P 14.

541	**177**	25c. multicoloured	10	10

178 Human Rights Emblem

179 All Ceylon Buddhist Congress Headquarters

(Photo Pakistan Security Printing Corp)

1968 (10 Dec). *Human Rights Year*. P 12½×13½.

542	**178**	2c. multicoloured	10	15
543		20c. multicoloured	10	10
544		40c. multicoloured	10	10
545		2r. multicoloured	70	4·00
542/5 *Set of 4*			90	4·00

(Des A. Dharmasiri. Litho Rosenbaum Bros, Vienna)

1968 (19 Dec). *Golden Jubilee of All Ceylon Buddhist Congress*. P 13½.

546	**179**	5c. multicoloured	10	50

A 50c. value showing a footprint was prepared but its release was stopped the day before it was due for issue. However, some are known to have been released in error at rural offices (*Price £30 mint*).

180 E. W. Perera (patriot)

181 Symbols of Strength in Savings

(Photo Harrison)

1969 (17 Feb). *E. W. Perera Commemoration*. W **81**. P 14×13½.

547	**180**	60c. brown	10	30

(Des A. Dharmasiri. Photo Harrison)

1969 (20 Mar). *Silver Jubilee of National Savings Movement*. W **81**. P 14.

548	**181**	3c. multicoloured	10	30

182 Seat of Enlightenment under Sacred Bodhi Tree

183 Buduresmala (Six fold Buddha-Rays)

(Des L. T. P. Manjusree. Litho D.L.R.)

1969 (10 Apr). *Vesak Day (inscr "Wesak")*. W **81** (sideways). P 15.

549	**182**	4c. multicoloured	10	50
550	**183**	6c. multicoloured	10	50
551	**182**	35c. multicoloured	10	10
549/51 *Set of 3*			25	1·00

No. 549 exists with the gold apparently omitted. Normally the gold appears (without a seperate plate number) over an underlay of olive-green on carmine. In one sheet we have seen, the gold only shows as tiny specks under a strong magnifying glass and as there may be intermediate stages of faint printing we do not list this.

184 A. E. Goonesinghe

185 ILO Emblem

(Des and photo Harrison)

1969 (29 Apr). *Commemoration of Goonesinghe (founder of Labour Movement in Ceylon)*. W **81**. P 14.

552	**184**	15c. multicoloured	10	10

(Photo Harrison)

1969 (4 May). *50th Anniv of International Labour Organisation*. W **81** (sideways). P 14.

553	**185**	5c. black and turquoise-blue	10	10
554		25c. black and carmine-red	10	10

186 Convocation Hall, University of Ceylon

187 Uranium Atom

(Des Ahangama Edward (35c.); L. D. P. Jayawardena (50 c.); A. Dharmasiri (60c.); 4c. from photograph. Litho Rosenbaum Bros, Vienna)

1969 (1 Aug). *Educational Centenary*. *T* **190**, **192** *and similar multicoloured designs*. P 13½.

555		4c. Type **186**	10	80
556		35c. Lamp of Learning, Globe and flags (*horiz*)	20	10
557		50c. Type **187**	20	10
558		60c. Symbols of Scientific education	30	10
555/8 *Set of 4*			70	1·00

188 Ath Pana (Elephant Lamp)

189 Rock Fortress of Sigiriya

(Des from photographs. Litho Rosenbaum Bros, Vienna)

1969 (1 Aug). *Archaeological Centenary*. P 13½.

559	**188**	6c. multicoloured	25	1·50
560	**189**	1r. multicoloured	25	10

190 Leopard

191 Emblem and Symbols

(Litho Rosenbaum Bros, Vienna)

1970 (11 May). *Wildlife Conservation*. *T* **196** *and similar horiz designs. Multicoloured*. P 13½.

561		5c. Water Buffalo	1·25	1·25
562		15c. Slender Loris	2·00	75
		a. Brown-black and orange-brown colours omitted	£150	
563		50c. Spotted Deer	1·40	1·25
		a. Imperf (in vert pair with stamp perf 3 sides)	£425	
564		1r. Type **190**	1·40	1·75
561/4 *Set of 4*			5·50	4·50

In No. 562a the sky is blue instead of violet and the animal is in green and yellow only.

(Des A. Dharmasiri. Litho Rosenbaum Bros, Vienna)

1970 (17 June). *Asian Productivity Year*. P 13½.

565	**191**	60c. multicoloured	10	10

192 New UPU HQ Building

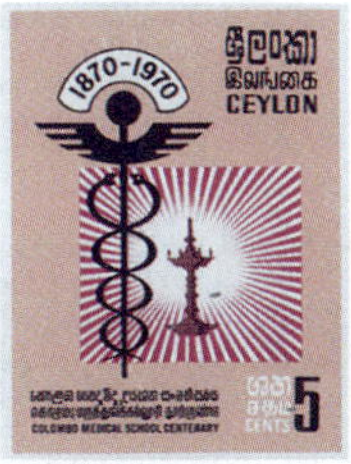

193 Oil Lamp and Caduceus

(Litho Rosenbaum Bros, Vienna)

1970 (14 Aug). *New UPU Headquarters Building*. P 13½.

566	**192**	50c. yellow-orange, black and new blue	50	10
		a. New blue (Building) omitted	£150	
567		1r.10 vermilion, black and new blue	4·50	40

(Des A. Dharmasiri. Litho Rosenbaum Bros, Vienna)

1970 (1 Sept). *Centenary of Colombo Medical School*. P 13½.

568	**193**	5c. multicoloured	1·25	80
		a. Vert pair, bottom stamp imperf	£350	
569		45c. multicoloured	1·50	60

194 Victory March and S. W. R. D. Bandaranaike

195 UN Emblem and Dove of Peace

(Des A. Dharmasiri. Litho D.L.R.)

1970 (25 Sept). *Definitive issue marking establishment of United Front Government*. P 13½.

570	**194**	10c. multicoloured	10	10

(Des A. Dharmasiri. Photo Pakistan Security Printing Corp)

1970 (24 Oct). *25th Anniv of United Nations*. P 12½×13½.

571	**195**	2r. multicoloured	2·00	3·50

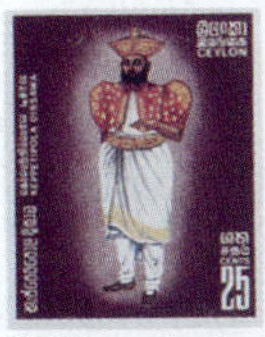

196 Keppetipola Dissawa

197 Ola Leaf Manuscript

(Des A. Dharmasiri. Litho Harrison)

1970 (26 Nov). *152nd Death Anniv of Keppetipola Dissawa (Kandyan patriot)*. P 14×14½.

572	**196**	25c. multicoloured	10	10

(Des A. Dharmasiri. Photo Pakistan Security Printing Corp)

1970 (21 Dec). *International Education Year*. P 13.

573	**197**	15c. multicoloured	2·75	1·25

STAMP BOOKLETS

1905 (Oct). *Black on grey (No. SB1) or black on buff (No. SB1a) covers. Stapled.*

SB1	1r.21, booklet containing twenty-four 5c. (No. 280) in blocks of 12	
SB1*a*	1r.45, booklet containing twenty-four 6c. (No. 281) in blocks of 6	£4500

1908. *Black on grey cover. Advertisement on back cover. Stapled.*

SB2	1r.20, booklet containing twenty-four 5c. (No. 289) in blocks of 12	

1912. *Black on grey cover. Advertisement on back cover, Stapled.*

SB2*a*	1r.20, booklet containing twenty-four 5c. (No. 304) in blocks of 12	

1919. *Black on orange covers. Telegraph details on back cover. Stapled.*

SB3	1r.44, booklet containing twenty-four 6c. (No. 311) in blocks of 6	
	a. Black on grey cover. Advertisement on back cover	
SB4	1r.44, booklet containing twenty-four 3c. and twelve 6c. (Nos. 310/11) in blocks of 6	
	a. Advertisement on back cover	

1922. *Black on green covers. "Fiat" advertisement on back cover. Stapled.*

SB5	1r.44, booklet containing twenty-four 6c. (No. 343) in blocks of 6	
SB6	1r.46, booklet containing twenty-four 6c. (No. 343) in blocks of 6	£3500
SB6*a*	1r.46, booklet containing twenty-four 3c. and twelve 6c. (Nos. 340/3) in blocks of 6	£3750
	b. Black on orange cover. "Colombo Jewelry Store" advertisement on back cover	

1926. *Black on green covers. Kennedy & Co. (No. SB7) or Fiat (No. SB8) advertisements on back cover. Stapled.*

SB7	2r.06, booklet containing twelve 3c., 5c. on 6c. and 9c. (Nos. 340, 362 and 345) in blocks of 6	£3250
SB8	2r.16, booklet containing twenty-four 9c. (No. 345) in blocks of 6	

1932. *Black on green covers. Stapled.*

SB9	1r.80, booklet containing thirty 6c. (No. 343) in blocks of 6 and pane of three airmail labels	£1400
SB10	2r.70, booklet containing thirty 9c. (No. 345) in blocks of 6 and pane of three airmail labels	£1800

1935 (May). *Silver Jubilee of King George V. Black on light blue (No. SB11) or light green (No. SB12) covers. Stapled.*

SB11	1r.80, booklet containing thirty 6c. (No. 379) in blocks of 6	£1400
SB12	2r.70, booklet containing thirty 9c. (No. 380) in blocks of 6	£1700

1935 (Dec)–**36**. *Black on blue (No. SB13) or green (No. SB14) covers. Stapled.*

SB13	1r.80, booklet containing thirty 6c. (No. 370) in blocks of 6 and pane of four airmail labels	£850
	a. Stamps in blocks of 10	£850
SB14	2r.70, booklet containing thirty 9c. (No. 371) in blocks of 6 and pane of four airmail labels	£1000
	a. Stamps in blocks of 10 (1936)	£1000

1937 (Apr–June). *Coronation of King George VI. Black on blue (No. SB15) or olive-green (No. SB16) covers. Stapled.*

SB15	1r.80, booklet containing thirty 6c. (No. 383) in blocks of 10 and pane of four airmail labels (June)	£1100
SB16	2r.70, booklet containing thirty 9c. (No. 384) in blocks of 10 and pane of four airmail labels	£1200

1938. *Black on blue (No. SB17) or grey (No. SB18) covers. Stapled.*

SB17	1r.80, booklet containing thirty 6c. (No. 388) in blocks of 10 and pane of four airmail labels	£1300
SB18	3r. booklet containing fifteen 20c. (No. 391) in blocks of 5 or 10 and pane of four airmail labels	£1400

1941. *Black on pink cover, with contents amended in manuscript. Stapled.*

SB19	1r.80, booklet containing sixty 3c. on 6c. (No. 398) in blocks of 10	
	a. Black on blue cover	

1951 (5 Dec). *Black on buff cover. Stitched.*

SB20	1r. booklet containing twenty 5c. (No. 414) in blocks of four and pane of airmail labels	12·00
	a. Containing two blocks of ten 5c. stamps and no airmail labels	45·00

1952 (21 Jan). *Black on green cover. Stitched.*

SB21	6r. booklet containing eight 75c. (No. 417) in blocks of 4 and two panes of four airmail labels	18·00

OFFICIAL STAMPS

1869. Issues of 1867–68 overprinted "SERVICE" in block letters. Although these stamps were prepared for use and sent out to the colony, they were never issued.

SERVICE

Type O **1**

Narrow "SERVICE". Wmk **6**. P 12½.

O1	**1**	2d. yellow	75·00	
		x. Wmk reversed	£200	
O2		6d. deep brown (R.)	75·00	
O3	**2**	8d. chocolate	75·00	
O4	**1**	1s. pale lilac	£160	
O5	**2**	2s. deep blue (R.)	£120	
		a. Imperf	£950	

SERVICE

Type O **2**

Wide "SERVICE". Wmk Crown CC. P 14.

O6	**8**	1d. blue	75·00	
O7	**7**	3d. carmine-rose	£140	

Until 1 October 1895 all Official mail was carried free. After that date postage was paid on Official letters to the general public, on certain interdepartmental mail and on all packets over 1lb in weight. Nos. O11/27 were provided for this purpose.

On

Service

(O **3**)

1895. *Optd with Type* O **3** *by the Govt Printer, Colombo.*

Type O1

Narrow "SERVICE". Wmk **6**. *P12½.*

O11	**9**	2c. green (No. 147)	12·00	60
		w. Wmk inverted	†	—
O12	**39**	3c. terracotta and blue-green (No. 245)	10·00	1·50
O13	**28**	5c. dull purple (No. 195)	4·00	30
O14	**29**	15c. sage-green (No. 196)	16·00	50
O15		25c. yellow-brown (No. 198)	11·00	2·00
O16		30c. bright mauve and chestnut (No. 247)	13·00	60
O17	**30**	1r.12 dull rose (*wmk sideways*) (No. 201)	90·00	60·00
		a. Opt double, one albino	£300	
		b. Wmk upright	£100	80·00
O11/17 *Set of 7*			£140	60·00

1899 (June)–**1900**. *Nos. 256/7 and 261/2 optd with Type* O **3**.

O18	**9**	2c. pale orange-brown (3.00)	9·00	60
O19	**39**	3c. deep green (9.00)	10·00	3·50
O20	**29**	15c. blue (9.00)	21·00	60
O21	**39**	75c. black and red-brown (R.)	6·00	7·00
O18/21 *Set of 4*			42·00	10·50

1903 (26 Nov)–**04**. *Nos. 265/6, 268 and 271/3 optd with Type* O **3**.

O22	**44**	2c. red-brown (4.1.04)	16·00	1·00
O23	**45**	3c. green	10·00	2·00
O24	**46**	5c. dull purple	23·00	1·50
O25	**48**	15c. blue	32·00	2·50
O26		25c. bistre (15.7.04)	26·00	18·00
O27		30c. dull violet and green (14.3.04)	15·00	1·50
O22/27 *Set of 6*			£110	25·00

Stamps overprinted "On Service" were withdrawn on 1 October 1904.

POSTAL FISCAL

1952 (1 Dec). *As T* **72** *but inscr* "REVENUE" *at sides. Chalk-surfaced paper.*

F1	10r. dull green and yellow-orange	85·00	40·00

This revenue stamp was on sale for postal use from 1 December 1952 until 14 March 1954.

Used price for stamp with identifiable postal cancellation.

Cook Islands

COOK ISLANDS

A British Protectorate was declared over this group of fifteen islands by the local Vice-Consul on 20 September 1888.

Before the introduction of the Cook Islands Post Office, mail was forwarded via Auckland, New Zealand.

PRICES FOR STAMPS ON COVER TO 1945	
Nos. 1/4	*from* × 5
Nos. 5/74	*from* × 4
Nos. 75/145	*from* × 3

BRITISH PROTECTORATE

1

2 Queen Makea Takau

3 White Tern or Torea

(Des F. Moss. Typo Govt Printing Office, Wellington)

1892 (19 Apr). No wmk. *Toned or white paper.* P 12½.

1	**1**	1d. black	27·00	26·00
		a. Imperf between (vert pair)	£9500	
2		1½d. mauve	40·00	38·00
		a. Imperf (pair)	£16000	
3		2½d. blue	40·00	38·00
4		10d. carmine	£140	£130
1/4 *Set of* 4			£225	£200

Nos. 1/4 were printed in sheets of 60 (6×10) from plates constructed from a matrix of 6 slightly different types.

(Eng A. E. Cousins. Typo Govt Printing Office, Wellington)

1893 (28 July)–**1900**. W **12**b of New Zealand (N Z and Star wide apart) (sideways on *T* **3**).

(a) P 12×11½.

5	**2**	1d. brown	42·00	45·00
6		1d. blue (3.4.94)	12·00	2·00
		a. Perf 12×11½ and 12½ mixed	†	£1700
7		1½d. mauve	10·00	7·00
8		2½d. rose	40·00	23·00
		a. Rose-carmine	60·00	48·00
		ab. Perf 12×11½ and 12½ mixed	£2500	
9		5d. olive-black	20·00	15·00
10		10d. green	70·00	48·00
5/10 *Set of* 6			£170	£120

(b) P 11 (July 1896–1900).

11	**3**	½d. steel blue (1st setting) (11.99)	32·00	45·00
		a. Upper right "d" omitted	£1500	
		b. Second setting	21·00	22·00
		ba. Deep blue (1900)	5·50	8·00
12	**2**	1d. blue	5·00	5·00
13		1d. deep brown/*cream* (4.99)	19·00	19·00
		a. Wmk sideways		
		b. Bistre-brown (1900)	22·00	23·00
14		1½d. deep lilac	9·50	6·50
		a. Deep mauve (1900)	9·50	6·50
15	**3**	2d. brown/*thin toned* (7.98)	11·00	6·50
		a. Deep brown (1900)	9·50	8·00
16	**2**	2½d. pale rose	48·00	38·00
		a. Deep rose (1900)	20·00	9·00
17		5d. olive-black	24·00	18·00
18	**3**	6d. purple/*thin toned* (7.98)	26·00	29·00
		a. Bright purple (1900)	19·00	25·00
19	**2**	10d. green	18·00	48·00
20	**3**	1s. red/*thin toned* (7.98)	60·00	70·00
		a. Deep carmine (1900)	48·00	48·00
11/20*a* *Set of* 10			£160	£170

Examples of the 1d., 1½d., 2½d. and 5d. perforated 11 and on laid paper are perforation trials. On the 1st setting of the ½d. the face values are misplaced in each corner. As corrected in the second setting the face values are correctly positioned in each corner.

ONE
HALF
PENNY
(4)

(5)

1899 (24 Apr). *No.* 12 *surch with T* **4** *by Govt Printer, Rarotonga.*

21	**2**	½d. on 1d. blue	32·00	42·00
		a. Surch inverted	£850	£900
		b. Surch double	£1000	£850

NEW ZEALAND TERRITORY

On 8 and 9 October 1900 the chiefs of all the main islands, except Aitutaki, ceded their territory to the British Crown. On 11 June 1901 all the islands, including Aitutaki, were transferred by Great Britain to New Zealand control.

1901 (8 Oct). *No.* 13 *optd with T* **5** *by Govt Printer, Rarotonga.*

22	**2**	1d. brown	£180	£140
		a. Crown inverted	£2000	£1600
		c. Optd with crown twice	£1600	£1600

1902. No wmk. P 11.

(a) Medium white Cowan paper (Feb).

23	**3**	½d. blue-green	6·50	7·00
		a. Imperf horiz (vert pair)	£1300	
24	**2**	1d. dull rose	9·00	15·00

(b) Thick white Pirie paper (May).

25	**3**	½d. yellow-green	5·00	4·25
26	**2**	1d. rose-red	12·00	11·00
		a. Rose-lake	11·00	6·50
27		2½d. dull blue	13·00	21·00

NEW ZEALAND WATERMARKS. In W **43** the wmk units are in vertical columns widely spaced and the sheet margins are unwatermarked or wmkd "NEW ZEALAND POSTAGE" in large letters.

In W **98** the wmk units are arranged alternately in horizontal rows closely spaced and are continued into the sheet margins. Stamps with W **98** sideways show the star to the left of NZ, *as seen from the back.* Sideways inverted varieties have the star to the right, *as seen from the back.*

1902 (Sept). W **43** of New Zealand (single-lined NZ and Star, close together; sideways on *T* **2**). P 11.

28	**3**	½d. yellow-green	2·75	3·25
		a. Grey-green	23·00	48·00
29	**2**	1d. rose-pink	4·00	3·00
30		1½d. deep mauve	4·00	8·50
31	**3**	2d. deep brown	6·00	10·00
		a. No figures of value	£2250	£3000
		b. Perf 11×14	£2000	
32	**2**	2½d. deep blue	3·75	7·00
33		5d. olive-black	35·00	48·00
34	**3**	6d. purple	32·00	28·00
35	**2**	10d. green	48·00	£100
36	**3**	1s. carmine	48·00	75·00
		a. Perf 11×14	£2500	
28/36 *Set of* 9			£160	£250

Stamps in Type **3** were printed from a master plate with the value added by a series of separate duty plates. One sheet of the 2d. missed this second pass through the press and was issued without value.

For Nos. 28/36 Type **2** exists with the watermark in equal quantities either upright or inverted and for Type **3**, on which the watermark is sideways, in equal quantities with the star to the right or left of NZ.

1909–11. W **43** of New Zealand.

37	**3**	½d. green (P 14½×14) (1911)	6·50	8·00
38	**2**	1d. deep red (P 14)	35·00	30·00
		a. Wmk sideways (24.12.09)	14·00	6·00

For Nos. 37/8 the watermark is either upright or inverted. For No. 38a it is sideways, either with star to right or left of NZ.

1913–19. W **43** of New Zealand (sideways on *T* **3**). *Chalk-surfaced paper.*

39	**3**	½d. deep green (P 14) (1915)	6·50	15·00
		a. Wmk upright	8·00	15·00
40	**2**	1d. red (P 14) (7.13)	6·50	4·25
41		1d. red (P 14×14½) (1914)	6·00	6·00
42		1½d. deep mauve (P 14) (1915)	75·00	28·00
43		1½d. deep mauve (P 14×15) (1916)	12·00	4·00
44	**3**	2d. deep brown (P 15×14) (1919).	5·00	48·00
45	**2**	10d. green (P 14×15) (1918)	21·00	95·00
46	**3**	1s. carmine (P 15×14) (1919)	27·00	95·00
39/46 *Set of* 6			70·00	£225

RAROTONGA

APA PENE
(8)

1919 (Apr–July). *Stamps of New Zealand surch as T* **8**.

(a) T **53**. W **43**. *De La Rue chalk-surfaced paper.* P 14×15.

47	1d. carmine (No. 405) (B.) (June)	1·00	3·00

(b) T **60** *(recess).* W **43**. *Cowan unsurfaced paper.* P 14×13½.

48	2½d. blue (No. 419) (R.) (June)	2·25	6·50
	a. Perf 14×14½	2·00	2·25
	b. Vert pair. Nos. 48/a	20·00	50·00
49	3d. chocolate (No. 420) (B.)	2·00	8·00
	a. Perf 14×14½	2·50	2·00
	b. Vert pair. Nos. 49/a	22·00	60·00
50	4d. bright violet (No. 422) (B.)	2·00	5·50
	a. Re-entry (Pl 20 R. 1/6)	60·00	
	b. Re-entry (Pl 20 R. 4/10)	60·00	
	c. Perf 14×14½	1·75	4·25
	d. Vert (pair Nos. 50 and 50c)	20·00	65·00
51	4½d. deep green (No. 423) (B.)	2·00	7·00
	a. Perf 14×14½	1·75	8·00
	b. Vert pair. Nos. 51/a	20·00	75·00
52	6d. carmine (No. 425) (B.) (June)	3·00	8·50
	a. Perf 14×14½	1·75	5·50
	b. Vert pair. Nos. 52/a	38·00	90·00
53	7½d. red-brown (No. 426a) (B.)	1·50	5·50
54	9d. sage-green (No. 429) (R.)	3·25	15·00
	a. Perf 14×14½	2·00	15·00
	b. Vert pair. Nos. 54/a	38·00	£120
55	1s. vermilion (No. 430) (B.) (June)	11·00	30·00
	a. Perf 14×14½	2·75	18·00
	b. Vert pair. Nos. 55/a	48·00	£130

(c) T **61** *(typo).* W **43**. *De La Rue chalk-surfaced paper.* P 14×15.

56	½d. green (No. 435) (R.) (June)	40	1·00
57	1½d. orange-brown (No. 438) (R.) (June)	50	75
58	2d. yellow (No. 439) (R.)	1·50	1·75
59	3d. chocolate (No. 440) (B.) (July)	2·75	13·00
47/59 *Set of* 13		20·00	70·00

9 Capt. Cook landing

10 Wharf at Avarua

11 "Capt. Cook" (Dance)

12 Palm Tree

13 Huts at Arorangi

14 Avarua Harbour

R. 2/8

R. 3/6 Double derrick flaws

R. 5/2

(Des, eng and recess Perkins, Bacon & Co)

1920 (23 Aug). No wmk. P 14.

70	**9**	½d. black and green	4·00	22·00
71	**10**	1d. black and carmine-red	4·75	22·00
		a. Double derrick flaw (R. 2/8, 3/6 or 5/2)	13·00	
72	**11**	1½d. black and dull blue	8·50	8·50
73	**12**	3d. black and chocolate	2·25	5·50
74	**13**	6d. brown and yellow-orange	3·00	8·50
75	**14**	1s. black and violet	5·00	17·00
70/5 *Set of* 6			24·00	75·00

Examples of the 1d. and 1s. with centre inverted were not supplied to the Post Office (*Price £500 each, unused).*

RAROTONGA
(15)

RAROTONGA

Trimmed overprint (R. 1/6 and R. 3/7)

1921 (Oct)–**23**. *Postal Fiscal stamps as Type* F **4** *of New Zealand optd with T* **15**. W **43** (sideways). *Chalk-surfaced "De La Rue" paper.* P 14½×14.

76	2s. deep blue (No. F111) (R.)	27·00	55·00
	a. Trimmed opt	£110	
	b. Carmine opt (1923)	£160	£180
	ba. Trimmed opt	£450	£500
77	2s.6d. grey-brown (No. F112) (B.)	19·00	50·00
	a. Trimmed opt	85·00	
78	5s. yellow-green (No. F115) (R.)	27·00	65·00
	a. Trimmed opt	£110	
79	10s. maroon (No. F120) (B.)	75·00	£120
	a. Trimmed opt	£200	
80	£1 rose-carmine (No. F123) (B.)	£120	£200
	a. Trimmed opt	£325	
76/80 *Set of* 5		£250	£450

See also Nos. 85/9.

16 Te Po, Rarotongan Chief

17 Harbour, Rarotonga and Mt. Ikurangi

(2½d. from a print; 4d. des A. H. Messenger. Plates by P.B. Recess Govt Ptg Office, Wellington)

1924–27. W **43** of New Zealand (sideways on 4d.). P 14.

81	**9**	½d. black and green (13.5.26)	4·50	8·50
82	**10**	1d. black and deep carmine (10.11.24)	6·00	2·25
		a. Double derrick flaw (R. 2/8, 3/6 or 5/2)	16·00	
		x. Wmk reversed	£180	
83	**16**	2½d. red-brown and steel blue (15.10.27)	6·00	24·00
84	**17**	4d. green and violet (15.10.27)	10·00	16·00
81/4 *Set of* 4			24·00	45·00

1926 (Feb–May). *As Nos.* 76/80, *but on thick, opaque white chalk-surfaced "Cowan" paper.*

85	2s. blue (No. F131) (C.)	£150	£225
	a. Trimmed opt	£425	
86	2s.6d. deep grey-brown (No. F132) (B.)	80·00	£140
87	5s. yellow-green (No. F135) (R.) (May)	90·00	£140
	a. Trimmed opt	£250	
88	10s. brown-red (No. F139) (B.) (May)	£100	£160
89	£1 rose-pink (No. F142) (B.) (May)	£140	£225
	a. Trimmed opt	£425	
85/9 *Set of* 5		£500	£800

1926 (Oct)–**28**. *T* **72** *of New Zealand, overprinted with T* **15**.

(a) Jones chalk-surfaced paper.

90	2s. deep blue (No. 466) (R.)	10·00	40·00
	w. Wmk inverted		

(b) Cowan thick, opaque chalk-surfaced paper.

91		2s. light blue (No. 469) (R.) (18.6.27)	15·00	40·00
92		3s. pale mauve (No. 470) (R.) (30.1.28)	16·00	42·00
90/2 *Set of 3*			38·00	£110

TWO PENCE (18)   **COOK ISLANDS.** (19)

1931 (1 Mar). *Surch with T* **18**. P 14.

(a) No wmk.

93	**11**	2d. on 1½d. black and blue (R.)	9·50	2·75

(b) W **43** of New Zealand.

94	**11**	2d. on 1½d. black and blue (R.)	4·75	11·00

1931 (12 Nov)–**32**. *Postal Fiscal stamps as Type* F **6** *of New Zealand.* W **43**. *Thick, opaque, white chalk-surfaced "Cowan" paper.* P 14.

(a) Optd with T **15**.

95		2s.6d. deep brown (No. F147) (B.)	10·00	22·00
96		5s. green (No. F149) (R.)	19·00	55·00
97		10s. carmine-lake (No. F155) (B.)	38·00	95·00
98		£1 pink (No. F158) (B.)	95·00	£160

(b) Optd with T **19** *(3.32).*

98*a*		£3 green (No. F164) (R.)	£400	£600
98*b*		£5 indigo-blue (No. F168) (R.)	£200	£325

The £3 and £5 values were mainly used for fiscal purposes.

20 Capt. Cook landing

21 Capt. Cook

22 Double Maori Canoe

23 Natives working Cargo

24 Port of Avarua

25 R.M.S. *Monowai*

26 King George V

(Des L. C. Mitchell. Recess P.B.)

1932 (15 Mar–2 May). No wmk. P 13.

99	**20**	½d. black and deep green	3·50	16·00
		a. Perf 14	28·00	90·00
100	**21**	1d. black and lake	6·50	4·50
		a. Centre inverted	£6000	£6000
		b. Perf compound of 13 and 14	£190	£225
		c. Perf 14	15·00	25·00
101	**22**	2d. black and brown	3·00	5·50
		a. Perf 14	9·00	20·00
102	**23**	2½d. black and deep blue	15·00	55·00
		a. Perf 14	15·00	55·00
103	**24**	4d. black and bright blue	22·00	65·00
		a. Perf 14	10·00	55·00
		b. Perf 14×13	30·00	£110
		c. Perf compound of 14 and 13	50·00	£120
104	**25**	6d. black and orange	26·00	48·00
		a. Perf 14	4·25	15·00
105	**26**	1s. black and violet (P 14) (2 May)	13·00	22·00
99/105 *Set of 7*			50·00	£150

Nos. 100b and 103c come from sheets reperforated 14 on arrival at Wellington. No. 100b comes from the first vertical column of a sheet and has 14 at left and No. 103c from the third or fourth vertical column with 13 at left or right.

Other major errors exist on this issue, but these are not listed as they originated from printer's waste which appeared on the market in 1935. They include the ½d. in vertical pair, imperforate horizontally (*price £350, unused*), and the ½d. 2d. and 2½d. with centre inverted (*prices from £250 each, unused*).

(Recess from P.B. plates at Govt Printing Office, Wellington)

1933–36. W **43** of New Zealand (Single N Z and Star). P 14.

106	**20**	½d. black and deep green	1·00	4·50
		w. Wmk inverted	—	75·00
107	**21**	1d. black and scarlet (1935)	1·25	2·00
		w. Wmk inverted and reversed		
108	**22**	2d. black and brown (1936)	1·50	50
		w. Wmk inverted		
109	**23**	2½d. black and deep blue	1·50	2·25
110	**24**	4d. black and bright blue	1·50	50
111	**25**	6d. black and orange-yellow (1936)	1·75	2·25
112	**26**	1s. black and violet (1936)	22·00	38·00
106/12 *Set of 7*			28·00	45·00

SILVER JUBILEE OF KING GEORGE V. 1910-1935.
(27)

Normal Letters
B K E N
B K E N
Narrow Letters

1935 (7 May). *Silver Jubilee. Optd with T* **27** *(wider vertical spacing on 6d.). Colours changed.* W **43** of New Zealand. P 14.

113	**21**	1d. red-brown and lake	60	1·40
		a. Narrow "K" in "KING"	2·75	5·50
		b. Narrow "B" in "JUBILEE"	10·00	12·00
114	**23**	2½d. dull and deep blue (R.)	1·50	2·50
		a. Narrow first "E" in "GEORGE"	3·50	6·00
115	**25**	6d. green and orange	3·75	6·00
		a. Narrow "N" in KING"	13·00	20·00
113/15 *Set of 3*			5·25	9·00

1936 (15 July)–**44**. *Stamps of New Zealand optd with T* **19**. W **43.** P 14.

(a) T **72**. *Cowan thick, opaque chalk-surfaced paper.*

116		2s. light blue (No. 469)	13·00	45·00
117		3s. pale mauve (No. 470)	13·00	70·00

(b) Type F **6**. *Cowan thick, opaque chalk-surfaced paper.*

118		2s.6d. deep brown (No. F147)	25·00	80·00
119		5s. green (No. F149) (R.)	29·00	£100
120		10s. carmine-lake (No. F155)	65·00	£190
121		£1 pink (No. F158)	95·00	£225
118/21 *Set of 4*			£190	£550

(c) Type F **6**. *Thin, hard, chalk-surfaced Wiggins Teape paper.*

122		2s.6d. dull brown (No. F170) (12.40)	£130	£120
123		5s. green (No. F172) (R.) (10.40)	£450	£375
123*a*		10s. pale carmine-lake (No. F177) (11.44)	£140	£190
123*b*		£3 green (No. F183) (R.) (date?)	£375	£600
122/3*b* *Set of 4*			£1000	£1200

COOK IS'DS.
(28)

IS'DS.
Small second "S" (R. 1/2)

1937 (1 June). *Coronation. Nos. 599/601 of New Zealand (inscr "12th MAY 1937") optd with T* **28**.

124		1d. carmine	40	80
		a. Small second "S"	14·00	
125		2½d. Prussian blue	80	1·40
		a. Small second "S"	24·00	
126		6d. red-orange	80	60
		a. Small second "S"	24·00	
124/6 *Set of 3*			1·75	2·50

29 King George VI

30 Native Village

31 Native Canoe

32 Tropical Landscape

(Des J. Berry (2s., 3s., and frame of 1s.). Eng B.W. Recess Govt Ptg. Office, Wellington)

1938 (2 May). W **43** of New Zealand. P 14.

127	**29**	1s. black and violet	8·50	12·00
128	**30**	2s. black and red-brown	18·00	13·00
		w. Wmk inverted		
129	**31**	3s. greenish blue and green	48·00	38·00
127/9 *Set of 3*			65·00	55·00

(Recess B.W.)

1940 (2 Sept). *Surch as in T* **32**. W **98** of New Zealand. P 13½×14.

130	**32**	3d.on 1½d. black and purple	75	60

Type **32** was not issued without surcharge.

1943–54. *Postal Fiscal stamps as Type* F **6** *of New Zealand optd with T* **19**. W **98**. *Wiggins Teape chalk-surfaced paper.* P 14.

131		2s.6d. dull brown (No. F193) (3.46)	80·00	85·00
		w. Wmk inverted (2.4.51)	24·00	24·00
132		5s. green (No. F195) (R.) (11.43)	11·00	24·00
		w. Wmk inverted (5.54)	27·00	30·00
133		10s. pale carmine-lake (No. F201) (10.48)	90·00	£120
		w. Wmk inverted (10.51)	65·00	90·00
134		£1 pink (No. F203) (11.47)	65·00	£100
		w. Wmk inverted (19.5.54)	£100	£110
135		£3 green (No. F208) (R.) (1946?)	£800	£950
		w. Wmk inverted (28.5.53)	60·00	£160
136		£5 indigo-blue (No. F211) (R.) (25.10.50)	£325	£425
		w. Wmk inverted (19.5.54)	£250	£375
131w/6w *Set of 6*			£425	£700

The £3 and £5 were mainly used for fiscal purposes.

(Recess Govt Ptg Office, Wellington)

1944–46. W **98** of New Zealand (sideways on ½d. 1d., 1s., and 2s.). P 14.

137	**20**	½d. black and deep green (11.44)	1·75	4·00
		w. Wmk sideways inverted	5·00	9·00
138	**21**	1d. black and scarlet (3.45)	2·00	1·00
		w. Wmk sideways inverted	7·00	2·50
		x. Wmk sideways reversed		
139	**22**	2d. black and brown (2.46)	2·25	10·00
140	**23**	2½d. black and deep blue (5.45)	1·00	2·00
141	**24**	4d. black and blue (4.44)	5·50	18·00
		y. Wmk inverted and reversed	40·00	42·00
142	**25**	6d. black and orange (6.44)	3·50	2·00
143	**29**	1s. black and violet (9.44)	3·00	2·50
144	**30**	2s. black and red-brown (8.45)	35·00	48·00
145	**31**	3s. greenish blue and green (6.45)	38·00	32·00
		w. Wmk inverted	£100	
137/45 *Set of 9*			80·00	£110

The normal sideways watermark shows the star to the left of NZ *as seen from the back of the stamp.*

COOK ISLANDS
(33)

1946 (4 June). *Peace. Nos. 668, 670, 674/5 of New Zealand optd with T* **33** *(reading up and down at sides on 2d.).*

146		1d. green (Parliament House)	30	10
147		2d. purple (Royal family) (B.)	30	50
148		6d. chocolate and vermilion (Coat of arms, foundry and farm)	1·00	1·25
149		8d. black and carmine ("St. George") (B.)	60	1·25
146/9 *Set of 4*			2·00	2·75

34 Ngatangiia Channel, Rarotonga

35 Capt. Cook and map of Hervey Islands

36 Raratonga and Revd. John Williams

37 Aitutaki and palm trees

38 Rarotonga Airfield

39 Penrhyn village

40 Native hut

41 Map and Statue of Capt. Cook

42 Native hut and palms

43 *Matua* (inter-island freighter)

(Des J. Berry. Recess Waterlow)

1949 (1 Aug)–**61**. *T* **34/43**. W **98** of New Zealand (sideways on shilling values). P 13½×13 (horiz) or 13×13½ (vert).

150	**34**	½d. violet and brown	10	1·25
151	**35**	1d. chestnut and green	3·50	2·25
152	**36**	2d. reddish brown and scarlet	2·00	2·25
153	**37**	3d. green and ultramarine	2·75	2·00
		aw. Wmk inverted	£100	
		b. Wmk sideways (white opaque paper) (22.5.61)	4·25	2·50
154	**38**	5d. emerald-green and violet	6·00	1·50
155	**39**	6d. black and carmine	5·50	2·75
156	**40**	8d. olive-green and orange	55	3·75
		w. Wmk inverted	£120	60·00
157	**41**	1s. light blue and chocolate	4·25	3·75
158	**42**	2s. yellow-brown and carmine	3·00	13·00
		w. Wmk sideways inverted		
159	**43**	3s. light blue and bluish green	14·00	24·00
150/9 *Set of 10*			38·00	50·00

43a Queen Elizabeth II

(Des J. Berry. Photo Harrison)

1953 (25 May). *Coronation. T* **43a** *and similar vert design.* W **98**. P 14×14½.

160 3d. brown 1·00 85
161 6d. slate-grey 1·25 1·50

Design:—6d. Westminster Abbey.

1/6

(**44**)

1960 (1 Apr). *No. 154 surch with T* **44**.

162 1s.6d. on 5d. emerald-green and violet 75 40

45 Tiare Maori

48 White Tern

52 Queen Elizabeth II

53 Island Scene

(Des J. Berry. Recess (1s.6d.), litho (others) B.W.)

1963 (4 June). *T* **45**, **48**, **52/3** *and similar designs.* W **98** of New Zealand (sideways). P 13½×13 (1d., 2d., 8d.), 13×13½ (3d., 5d., 6d., 1s.) or 13½ (others).

163 1d. emerald-green and yellow 45 65
164 2d. brown-red and yellow 20 50
165 3d. yellow, yellow-green & reddish violet 70 65
166 5d. blue and black 8·00 2·25
167 6d. red, yellow and green 1·00 60
168 8d. black and blue 4·25 1·50
169 1s. orange-yellow and yellow-green 1·00 60
170 1s.6d. bluish violet 2·75 2·00
171 2s. bistre-brown and grey-blue 1·75 1·00
172 3s. black and yellow-green 1·75 1·75
173 5s. bistre-brown and blue 13·00 4·00
163/73 *Set of* 11 32·00 14·00

Designs: *Vert* (*as T* **45**)—2d. Fishing god; 8d. Long-tailed Tuna. *Horiz* (*as T* **48**)—3d. Frangipani; 6d. Hibiscus; 1s. Oranges. (*As T* **53**)—3s. Administration Centre, Mangaia; 5s. Rarotonga.

56 Eclipse and Palm

57 N.Z. Ensign and Map

(Des L. C. Mitchell. Litho B.W.)

1965 (31 May). *Solar Eclipse Observation, Manuae Island.* W **98** of New Zealand. P 13½.

174 **56** 6d. black, yellow and light blue 20 10

The Cook Islands became a self-governing territory in "free association" with New Zealand on 16 September 1965.

SELF-GOVERNMENT

(Des R. M. Conly (4d.), L. C. Mitchell (10d., 1s.), J. Berry (1s.9d.). Litho B.W.)

1965 (16 Sept). *Internal Self-Government. T* **57** *and similar horiz designs.* W **98** of New Zealand (sideways). P 13½.

175 4d. red and blue 20 10
176 10d. multicoloured 20 15
177 1s. multicoloured 20 15
178 1s.9d. multicoloured 50 1·25
175/8 *Set of* 4 1·00 1·50

Designs:—10d. London Missionary Society Church; 1s. Proclamation of Cession, 1900; 1s.9d. Nikao School.

In Memoriam
SIR WINSTON CHURCHILL
1874 - 1965
(**61**)

Airmail
(**62**)

1966 (24 Jan). *Churchill Commemoration. Nos. 171/3 and 175/7 optd with T* **61**, *in red.*

179 4d. red and blue 1·00 30
a. "l" for "1" in "1874" 3·50
180 10d. multicoloured 2·00 45
a. Opt inverted £160
b. "l" for "1" in "1874" 6·00
181 1s. multicoloured 2·00 65
a. Opt inverted £100
b. "l" for "1" in "1874" 6·00
182 2s. bistre-brown and grey-blue 2·00 1·50
a. "l" for "1" in "1874" 6·00
183 3s. black and yellow-green 2·00 1·50
a. "l" for "1" in "1874" 6·00
184 5s. bistre-brown and blue 2·25 2·00
a. "l" for "1" in "1874" 11·00
179/84 *Set of* 6 10·00 5·75

The lower case "l" for "1" in "1874" occurred on R. 6/5 for all values and additionally on R. 12/5 for the 2s., 3s. and 5s.

1966 (22 Apr). *Air. Various stamps optd with T* **62** *or surch also.*

185 6d. red, yellow and green (No. 167) 1·25 20
186 7d. on 8d. black and blue (No. 168) 2·00 25
187 10d. on 3d. yellow, yellow-green and reddish violet (No. 165) 1·00 15
188 1s. orange-yellow & yellow-green (No. 169) 1·00 15
189 1s.6d. bluish violet (No. 170) 1·50 1·25
190 2s.3d. on 3s. black & yellow-grn (No. 172) 1·00 65
191 5s. bistre-brown and blue (No. 173) 1·75 1·50
192 10s. on 2s. bistre-brown & grey-bl (No. 171) 1·75 14·00
193 £1 pink (No. 134) 13·00 17·00
a. Aeroplane omitted 35·00 48·00
w. Wmk inverted 13·00 17·00
wa. Aeroplane omitted 35·00 48·00
185/93 *Set of* 9 22·00 32·00

No. 193a occurred in all stamps of the last vertical row as insufficient aeroplane symbols were available. There are also numerous other varieties on all values, notably aeroplanes of different sizes and broken first 'i' with dot missing owing to damaged type.

PRINTERS. The following stamps were printed by Heracho Fournier, Spain except *where otherwise stated*. The process used was photogravure until No. **MS**1247 and lithography thereafter.

63 "Adoration of the Magi" (Fra Angelico)

1966 (28 Nov). *Christmas. T* **63** *and similar multicoloured designs.* P 13×12 (horiz) or 12×13 (vert).

194 1d. Type **63** 50 60
a. Perf 13×14½ 10 10
195 2d. "The Nativity" (Memling) (*vert*) 12·00 12·00
a. Perf 14½×13 20 10
196 4d. "Adoration of the Magi" (Velazquez) 1·00 1·00
a. Perf 13×14½ 30 15
197 10d. "Adoration of the Magi" (Bosch) 2·00 4·75
a. Perf 13×14½ 30 20
198 1s.6d. "Adoration of the Shepherds" (J. de Ribera) (*vert*) 27·00 7·00
a. Perf 14½×13 40 35
194/8 *Set of* 5 38·00 23·00
194a/8a *Set of* 5 1·10 80

68 Tennis, and Queen Elizabeth II

(Des V. Whiteley)

1967 (12 Jan). *2nd South Pacific Games, Nouméa. T* **68** *and similar horiz designs in orange-brown, black and new blue (1d.) or multicoloured (others).* P 13½.

(a) Postage.

199 ½d. Type **68** 10 10
200 1d. Netball and Games emblem 10 10
201 4d. Boxing and Cook Islands' team badge 10 10
202 7d. Football and Queen Elizabeth II 20 15

(b) Air.

203 10d. Running and Games emblem 20 15
204 2s.3d. Running and Cook Islands' team badge 25 65
199/204 *Set of* 6 70 1·00

(New Currency, 100 cents = 1 dollar)

1c (**74**) 2½c (I) 2½c (II)

1967 (3 Apr). *Decimal Currency. Nos. 134, 135w, 136, 163/70 and 172/5 surch as T* **74** *by the Government Printer. Sterling values unobliterated except No. 218.*

205 1c. on 1d. emerald-green and yellow (4.5) 45 1·50
206 2c. on 2d. brown-red and yellow 10 10
207 2½c. on 3d. yell, yellow-grn & reddish vio (I) 20 10
a. Horiz pair. Nos. 207/8 40 20
208 2½c. on 3d. yellow, yellow-green & reddish violet (II) 20 10
209 3c. on 4d. red and blue 15 10
210 4c. on 5d. blue and black (4.5) 10·00 30
211 5c. on 6d. red, yellow and green 15 10
212 5c. on 6d. black, yellow and light blue 5·00 1·25
213 7c. on 8d. black and blue 30 10
214 10c. on 1s. orange-yellow and yellow-green 15 10
215 15c. on 1s.6d. bluish violet (R.) (4.5.67) 2·00 1·00
216 30c. on 3s. black & yellow-green (R.) (4.5.67) 24·00 4·50
217 50c. on 5s. bistre-brown & blue (R.) (4.5.67) 4·00 1·25
218 $1 and 10s. on 10d. mult (R.) (4.5.67) 17·00 5·50
219 $2 on £1 pink (R.) (6.6.67) 55·00 75·00
220 $6 on £3 green (R.) (6.6.67) £100 £140
221 $10 on £5 blue (R.) (6.6.67) £150 £170
w. Wmk inverted £150 £190
205/18 *Set of* 14 55·00 14·00

The two types of the 2½c. occur on alternate vertical rows within the sheet.

The surcharge on No. 218 is $1 and its equivalent of 10s. in the old currency. The "10d." is obliterated by three bars.

A large number of minor varieties exist in these surcharges, such as wrong fount letter "C" and figures.

75 Village Scene. Cook Islands 1d. Stamp of 1892 and Queen Victoria (from "Penny Black")

(Des V. Whiteley)

1967 (3 July). *75th Anniv of First Cook Islands Stamps. T* **75** *and similar horiz designs. Multicoloured.* P 13½.

222 1c. (1d.) Type **75** 10 10
223 3c. (4d.) Post Office, Avarua, Rarotonga and Queen Elizabeth II 15 10
224 8c. (10d.) Avarua, Rarotonga and Cook Islands 10d. stamp of 1892 30 15
225 18c. (1s.9d.) *Moana Roo* (inter-island ship), Douglas DC-3 aircraft, map and Captain Cook 1·40 30
222/5 *Set of* 4 1·75 60
MS226 134×109 mm. Nos. 222/5 1·75 2·75

The face values are expressed in decimal currency and in the sterling equivalent.

Each value was issued in sheets of 8 stamps and 1 label.

79 Hibiscus

80 Queen Elizabeth II

81 Queen Elizabeth and Flowers

Two types of $4

I. Value 32½ mm long. Coarse screen.
II. Value 33½ mm long. Finer screen.

(Floral designs from paintings by Kay Billings)

1967 (31 July)–**71**. *Multicoloured designs as T* **79/81**. P 14×13½.

A. Without fluorescent security markings.

227A ½c. Typa **79** 10 10
228A 1c. *Hibiscus syriacus* (*27×37 mm*) 10 10
229A 2c. Frangipani (*27×37 mm*) 10 10
230A 2½c. *Clitoria ternatea* (*27×37 mm*) 20 10
231A 3c. "Suva Queen" (*27×37 mm*) 55 10
232A 4c. Water Lily ("WALTER LILY") (*27×37 mm*) 70 1·00
233A 4c. Water Lily (*27×37 mm*) 2·00 2·00
234A 5c. *Bauhinia bipianata rosea* (*27×37 mm*) 35 10
235A 6c. Hibiscus (*27×37 mm*) 40 10
236A 8c. *Allamanda cathartica* (*27×37 mm*) 40 10
237A 9c. Stephanotis (*27×37 mm*) 40 10
238A 10c. *Poinciana regia flamboyant* (*27×37 mm*) 40 10
239A 16c. Frangipani (*27×37 mm*) (11.8.67) 40 10
240A 20c. Thunbergia (*27×37 mm*) (11.8.67) 4·50 1·50
241A 26c. Canna Lily (*27×37 mm*) (11.8.67) 80 30
242A 30c. *Euphorbia pulcherrima poinsettia* (*27×37 mm*) (11.8.67) 65 50
243A 50c. *Gardinia taitensis* (*27×37 mm*) (11.8.67) 1·00 55
244A $1 Type **80** (31.8.67) 2·25 80

245A	$2 Type **80** (31.8.67)	4·75	1·50
246A	$4 Type **81** (I) (30.4.68)	1·50	4·25
247A	$6 Type **81** (30.4.68)	1·75	5·50
247cA	$8 Type **81** (21.4.69)	5·00	16·00
248A	$10 Type **81** (12.7.65)	3·25	12·00
227A/48A	*Set of* 22	26·00	40·00
	B. With fluorescent security markings.		
227B	½c. Type **78** (9.2.70)	20	10
228B	1c. *Hibiscus syriacus* (27×37 *mm*) (9.2.70)	20	10
229B	2c. Frangipani (27×37 *mm*) (9.2.70)	20	10
230B	2½c. *Clitoria ternatea* (27×37 *mm*) (9.2.70)	20	10
231B	3c. "Suva Queen" (27×37 *mm*) (9.2.70)	40	10
233B	4c. Water Lily (27×37 *mm*) (9.2.70)	2·50	10
234B	5c. *Bauhinia bipirsnata roses* (27×37 *mm*) (9.2.70)	30	10
235B	6c. Hibiscus (27×37 *mm*) (9.2.70)	30	10
236B	8c. *Allemanda cathartica* (27×37 *mm*) (9.2.70)	30	10
237B	9c. Stephanotis (27×37 *mm*) (9.2.70)	30	10
238B	10c. *Poinciana regia flamboyant* (27×37 *mm*) (9.2.70)	30	10
239B	15c. Frangipani (27×37 *mm*) (9.2.70)	40	10
240B	20c. Thunbergia (27×37 *mm*) (9.2.70)	3·50	1·50
241B	25c. Canna Lily (27×37 *mm*) (9.2.70)	1·00	15
242B	30c. *Euphorbia pulcherrima poinsettia* (27×37 *mm*) (9.2.70)	1·25	40
243B	50c. *Gardinia taitensis* (27×37 *mm*) (9.2.70)	1·25	40
244B	$1 Type **80** (12.10.70)	1·25	80
245B	$2 Type **80** (12.10.70)	2·25	1·50
246B	$4 Type **81** (I) (11.11.70)	35·00	48·00
	a. Type II (14.7.71)	5·50	8·50
247B	$6 Type **81** (12.2.71)	11·00	6·00
247cB	$8 Type **81** (3.5.71)	12·00	10·00
248B	$10 Type **81**(14.6.71)	16·00	12·00
227B/48B	*Set of* 22	55·00	38·00

The "WALTER" spelling error occurred on all stamps in one of the four post office sheets which went to make up the printing sheet and this was corrected in later supplies.

FLUORESCENT PAPER. This is on paper treated with fluorescent security markings, in the form of faint multiple coats of arms. Stamps exist with these markings inverted. In addition an invisible synthetic gum has been used which prevents curling and is suitable for use in the tropics without interleaving the sheets.

Some of the above are known with these markings omitted and can be distinguished when in unused condition from the original printings without markings by their synthetic invisible gum.

97 "Ia Oraria Maria"

1967 (24 Oct). *Gauguin's Polynesian Paintings. T* **97** *and similar designs. Multicoloured.* P 13.

249	1c. Type **97**	10	10
250	3c. "Riders on the Beach"	15	10
251	5c. "Still Life with Flowers"	20	10
252	8c. "Whispered Words"	25	10
253	15c. "Maternity"	50	15
254	22c. "Why are you angry?"	65	20
249/54	*Set of* 6	1·60	65
MS255	156×132 mm. Nos. 249/54	1·75	1·50

The 5c. includes an inset portrait of Queen Elizabeth.

98 "The Holy Family" (Rubens)

HURRICANE
RELIEF
PLUS 5c

(**99**)

1967 (4 Dec). *Christmas. Renaissance Paintings. T* **98** *and similar designs. Multicoloured.* P 12×13.

256	1c. Type **98**	10	10
257	3c. "Adoration of the Magi" (Dürer)	10	10
258	4c. "The Lucca Madonna" (J. van Eyck)	10	10
259	8c. "The Adoration of the Shepherds" (J. da Bassano)	20	15
260	15c. "Adoration of the Shepherds" (El Greco)	35	15
261	25c. "Madonna and Child" (Correggio)	40	15
256/61	*Set of* 6	1·10	65

1968 (12 Feb). *Hurricane Relief. Nos. 231A, 233A, 251, 238A, 241A and 243/4A suroh as T* **99** *by Govt Printer, Rarotonga.*

262	3c.+1c. "Suva Queen"	15	15
263	4c.+1c. Water Lily	15	15
264	5c.+2c. "Still Life with Flowers"	15	15
	a. Black surch albino		
265	10c.+2c. *Poinciana regia flamboyant*	15	15
266	25c.+5c. Canna Lily	20	20
267	50c.+10c. *Gardinia taitensis*	25	30
268	$1+10c. Type **80**	35	50
262/8	*Set of* 7	1·25	1·40

The surcharge on No. 268 is as T **99**, but with seriffed letters. On No. 264 silver blocking obliterates the design area around the lettering.

100 "Matavai Bay, Tahiti" (J. Barralet)

101 "*Resolution and Discovery*" (J. Webber)

(Des J. Berry)

1968 (12 Sept). *Bicentenary of Captain Cook's First Voyage of Discovery. Multicoloured. Invisible gum.* P 13.

	(a) Postage. Vert designs as T **100**.		
269	½c. Type **100**	10	10
270	1c. "Island of Huaheine" (John Cleveley)	15	10
271	2c. "Town of St. Peter and St. Paul, Kamchatka" (J. Webber)	30	20
272	4c. "The Ice Islands" (Antarctica: W. Hodges)	40	20
	(b) Air. Horiz designs as T **101**.		
273	6c. Type **101**	45	25
274	10c. "The Island of Tahiti" (W. Hodges)	45	25
275	15c. "Karakakooa, Hawaii" (J. Webber)	50	35
276	25c. "The Landing at Middleburg" (J. Shemin)	60	55
269/76	*Set of* 8	2·50	1·75

Each value was issued in sheets of 10 stamps and 2 labels.

FLUORESCENT PAPER. From No. 277, *unless otherwise stated*, all issues are printed on paper treated with fluorescent security markings with invisible synthetic gum. These markings may be inverted or omitted in error.

102 Dinghy-sailing

103 "Madonna and Child" (Titian)

1968 (21 Oct). *Olympic Games, Mexico. T* **102** *and similar horiz designs. Multicoloured.* P 13.

277	1c. Type **102**	10	10
278	5c. Gymnastics	10	10
279	15c. High jumping	25	10
280	20c. High-diving	25	10
281	30c. Cycling	60	20
282	50c. Hurdling	50	25
277/82	*Set of* 6	1·50	75

Each value was issued in sheets of 10 stamps and 2 labels.

1968 (2 Dec). *Christmas. Paintings. T* **103** *and similar vert designs. Multicoloured.* P 13½.

283	1c. Type **103**	10	10
284	4c. "The Holy Family with Lamb" (Raphael)	15	10
285	10c. "The Virgin of the Rosary" (Murillo)	25	10
286	20c. "Adoration of the Kings" (Memling)	40	10
287	30c. "Adoration of the Magi" (Ghirlandaio)	45	10
283/7	*Set of* 5	1·25	45
MS288	114×177 mm. Nos. 283/7 plus label	1·25	1·60

104 Camp-fire Cooking

1969 (6 Feb). *Diamond Jubilee of New Zealand Scout Movement and Fifth National (New Zealand) Jamboree. T* **104** *and similar square designs. Multicoloured.* P 13½.

289	½c. Type **104**	10	10
290	1c. Descent by rope	10	10
291	5c. Semaphore	15	10
292	10c. Tree-planting	20	10
293	20c. Constructing a shelter	25	15
294	30c. Lord Baden-Powell and island scene	45	25
289/94	*Set of* 6	1·00	50

Each value was issued in sheets of 10 stamps and 2 labels.

105 High Jumping

1969 (7 July). *Third South Pacific Games, Port Moresby. T* **105** *and similar triangular designs. Multicoloured. Without fluorescent security markings.* P 13×13½.

295	½c. Type **105**	10	40
296	½c. Footballer	10	40
297	1c. Basketball	50	40
298	1c. Weightlifter	50	40
299	4c. Tennis-player	50	50
300	4c. Hurdler	50	50
301	10c. Javelin-thrower	55	50
302	10c. Runner	55	50
303	15c. Golfer	1·75	1·50
304	15c. Boxer	1·75	1·50
295/304	*Set of* 10	6·00	5·75
MS305	174×129 mm. Nos. 295/304 plus two labels	7·50	6·00

Each value was issued in sheets containing 5 *se-tenant* pairs of both designs and 2 labels.

106 Flowers, Map and Captain Cook

1969 (8 Oct). *South Pacific Conference, Nouméa. T* **106** *and similar horiz designs. Multicoloured. Without fluorescent security markings.* P 13.

306	5c. Flowers, map and Premier Albert Henry	20	20
307	10c. Type **106**	80	40
308	25c. Flowers, map and N.Z. arms	30	40
309	30c. Queen Elizabeth II, map and flowers	30	40
306/9	*Set of* 4	1·40	1·25

107 "Virgin and Child with Saints Jerome and Dominic" (Lippi)

108 "The Resurrection of Christ" (Raphael)

1969 (21 Nov). *Christmas. Paintings. T* **107** *and similar designs. Multicoloured. Without fluorescent security markings.* P 13.

310	1c. Type **107**	10	10
311	4c. "The Holy Family" (Fra Bartolomeo)	10	10
312	10c. "The Adoration of the Shepherds" (A. Mengs)	15	10
313	20c. Madonna and Child with Saints" (R. Campin)	25	20
314	30c. "The Madonna of the Basket" (Correggio)	25	30
310/14	*Set of* 5	75	70
MS315	132×97 mm. Nos. 310/14	1·00	1·50

Each value was issued in sheets of 9 stamps and 1 label.

1970 (12 Mar). *Easter. Paintings. T* **108** *and similar perf designs showing "The Resurrection of christ" by the artists named. Multicoloured.* P 13.

316	4c. Type **108**	10	10
317	8c. Dirk Bouts	10	10
318	20c. Altdorfer	15	10
319	25c. Murillo	20	10
316/19	*Set of* 4	50	35
MS320	132×162 mm. Nos. 316/19	1·25	1·25

Each value was issued in sheets of 8 stamps and 1 label.

KIA ORANA
APOLLO 13
ASTRONAUTS
Te Atua to
Tatou Irinakianga
(109)

1970 (17–30 Apr). *Apollo 13. Nos.* 233, 236, 239/40, 242 *and* 245/6 *optd with T* **109** *(4c. to $2) or with first three lines only in larger type ($4), by Govt Printer. Without fluorescent security markings.*

321 4c. Water Lily ... 10 10
a. Opt albino ... 26·00
322 8c. *Allamanda cathartics* ... 10 10
323 15c. Frangipani ... 10 10
324 20c. Thunbergia ... 40 15
325 30c. *Euphorbia pulcherrima poinsettia* . 20 20
326 $2 Type **80** ... 50 90
327 $4 Type **81** (30.4) ... 29·00 45·00
a. With fluorescent security markings ... 1·00 2·75
ab. Opt double, one albino ... † —
321/7a *Set of* 7 ... 2·00 3·75

110 The Royal Family

(Des V. Whiteley (5c.), J. Berry ($1))

1970 (12 June). *Royal Visit to New Zealand. T* **110** *and similar horiz designs. Multicoloured.* P 13.

328 5c. Type **110** ... 50 30
329 30c. Captain Cook and H.M.S. *Endeavour* ... 2·00 1·75
330 $1 Royal Visit commemorative coin .. 3·00 3·00
328/30 *Set of* 3 ... 5·00 4·50
MS331 145×97 mm. Nos. 328/30 ... 9·50 10·00

Each value was issued in sheets of 8 stamps and 1 label.

FOUR
DOLLARS

FIFTH ANNIVERSARY
SELF-GOVERNMENT
AUGUST 1970
(113)

$4.00
(114)

1970 (27 Aug). *5th Anniv of Self-Government. Nos. 328/30 optd with T* **113** *(30c. and $1), or in single line in silver around frame of stamp (5c.).*

332 5c. Type **110** ... 40 15
333 30c. Captain Cook and H.M.S. *Endeavour* ... 80 35
334 $1 Royal Visit commemorative coin .. 1·00 90
332/4 *Set of* 3 ... 2·00 1·25

1970 (11 Nov). *Nos. 247c and 248 surch with T* **114** *by Govt Printer, Rarotonga. Without fluorescent security markings.*

335 **81** $4 on $8 multicoloured ... 35·00 28·00
a. With fluorescent security markings ... 1·25 1·75
336 $4 on $10 multicoloured ... 35·00 48·00
a. With fluorescent security markings ... 1·25 1·50

There are variations in the setting of this surcharge and also in the rule.

115 Mary, Joseph and Christ in Manger

(Des from De Lisle Psalter)

1970 (30 Nov). *Christmas. T* **115** *and similar square designs. Multicoloured.* P 13.

337 1c. Type **115** ... 10 10
338 4c. Shepherds and Apparition of the Angel ... 10 10
339 10c. Mary showing Chid to Joseph ... 15 10
340 20c. The Wise Men bearinG Gifts ... 20 20
341 30c. Parents wrapping Child in swaddling clothes ... 25 35
337/41 *Set of* 5 ... 70 75
MS342 100×139 mm. Nos. 337/41 plus label ... 1·00 1·50

Each value was issued in sheets of 5 stamps and 1 label. Stamps from the miniature sheet are smaller, since they do not have the buff parchment border as on the stamps from the sheets.

AITUTAKI

The island of Aitutaki, under British protection from 1888, was annexed by New Zealand on 11 June 1901.

NEW ZEALAND DEPENDENCY

Stamps of COOK ISLANDS were used in Aitutaki from 1892 until 1903.

PRICES FOR STAMPS ON COVER TO 1945

Nos. 1/7	*from* × 4
Nos. 9/14	*from* × 3
Nos. 15/29	*from* × 4
Nos. 30/2	*from* × 6

Stamps of New Zealand overprinted or surcharged. For illustrations of watermarks and definitive types see New Zealand.

AITUTAKI. (1)
Ava Pene. (2) ½d.
Tai Pene. (3) 1d.
Rua Pene Ma Te Ava. (4) 2½d.
Toru Pene. (5) 3d.
Ono Pene. (6) 6d.
Tai Tiringi. (7) 1s.

1903 (29 June)–**11**. *T* **23**, **27/8**, **31**, **34** *and* **42** *surch with T* **1** *at top and T* **2** *to* **7** *at foot. Thin, hard Cowan paper.* W **43**.

(a) P 14.

1 ½d. green (No. 302) (R.) ... 4·50 6·50
2 1d. carmine (No. 303) (B.) ... 4·75 5·50
3 2½d. deep blue (No. 320*a*) (R.) (9.11) ... 8·00 18·00
a. "Ava" without stop ... £150 £250
1/3 *Set of* 3 ... 15·50 27·00

(b) P 11.

4 2½d. blue (No. 308) (R.) ... 12·00 12·00
5 3d. yellow-brown (No. 309) (B.) ... 18·00 15·00
6 6d. rose-red (No. 312*a*) (B.) ... 30·00 25·00
7 1s. bright red (No. 315*a*) (B.) ... 50·00 85·00
a. "Tiringi" without stop (R. 7/12) ... £600 £800
b. Orange-red ... 65·00 95·00
ba. "Tiringi" without stop (R. 7/12) ... £750 £900
4/7 *Set of* 4 ... £100 £120

Nos. 1/2 and 4/7 were placed on sale in Auckland on 12 June 1903. There were four states of the overprint used for No. 3. On the first the "no stop" variety (No. 3a) occurs on R. 6/8, on the second it appears on R. 1/4, 2/4 and 6/8, on the third on R. 5/8 and 6/8, and on the fourth all stops are present.

AITUTAKI.

Ono Pene.
(8)

1911–16. *T* **51** *and* **53** *surch with T* **1** *at top and T* **2** *or* **3** *at foot and T* **52** *surch as T* **8**. P 14×15 (½d., 1d.) or 14×14½ (others).

9 ½d. green (No. 387) (R.) (9.11) ... 1·00 5·50
10 1d. carmine (No. 405) (B.) (2.13) ... 3·00 13·00
11 6d. carmine (No. 392) (B.) (23.5.16) ... 45·00 £130
12 1s. vermilion (No. 394) (B.) (9.14) ... 50·00 £150
9/12 *Set of* 4 ... 90·00 £275

1916–17. *T* **60** *(recess) surch as T* **8**. W **43**. P 14×13½.

13 6d. carmine (No. 425) (B.) (6.6.16) ... 10·00 50·00
a. Perf 14×14½ ... 7·50 27·00
b. Vert pair. Nos. 13/13a ... 50·00 £170
14 1s. vermilion (No. 430) (B.) (3.17) ... 12·00 90·00
a. Perf 14×14½ ... 14·00 90·00
ab. "Tai" without dot (R. 8/9, 9/12, 10/12) ... £225 £600
ac. "Tiringi" without dot on second "i" (R. 8/12, 10/7) ... £300 £700
ad. "Tiringi" without dot on third "i" (R. 8/11) ... £425 £900
b. Vert pair. Nos. 14/14a ... £120 £400

1917–18. *T* **60** *(recess) optd "AITUTAKI" only, as in T* **8**. W **43**. P 14×13½.

15 2½d. blue (No. 419) (R.) (12.18) ... 2·00 20·00
a. Perf 14×14½ ... 1·75 15·00
b. Vert pair. Nos. 15/15a ... 30·00 £140
16 3d. chocolate (No. 420) (B.) (1.18) ... 1·75 28·00
a. Perf 14×14½ ... 1·50 26·00
b. Vert pair. Nos. 16/16a ... 30·00 £150
17 6d. carmine (No. 425) (B.) (11.17) ... 6·00 21·00
a. Perf 14×14½ ... 4·75 21·00
b. Vert pair. Nos. 17/17a ... 40·00 £140
18 1s. vermilion (No. 430) (B.) (11.17) ... 14·00 45·00
a. Perf 14×14½ ... 12·00 32·00
b. Vert pair. Nos. 18/18a ... 65·00 £200
15/18 *Set of* 4 ... 21·00 £100
15a/18a *Set of* 4 ... 18·00 85·00

1917–20. *T* **53** *and* **61** *(typo) optd "AITUTAKI" only, as in T* **8**. W **43**. P 14×15.

19 ½d. green (No. 435) (R.) (2.20) ... 1·00 6·00
20 1d. carmine (No. 405) (B.) (5.20) ... 4·25 30·00
21 1½d. slate (No. 437) (R.) (11.17) ... 3·75 30·00
22 1½d. orange-brown (No. 438) (R.) (2.19) ... 80 7·00
23 3d. chocolate (No. 440) (B.) (6.19) ... 3·50 17·00
19/23 *Set of* 5 ... 12·00 80·00

(Des and recess Perkins, Bacon & Co)

1920 (23 Aug). *T* **9/14** *of Cook Islands, but inscr "AITUTAKI".* No wmk. P 14.

24 ½d. black and green ... 3·50 25·00
25 1d. black and dull carmine ... 3·50 17·00
a. Double derrick flaw (R. 2/8, 3/6 or 5/2) ... 11·00
26 1½d. black and sepia ... 6·00 12·00
27 3d. black and deep blue ... 2·50 14·00
28 6d. red-brown and slate ... 5·50 14·00
29 1s. black and purple ... 9·50 16·00
24/9 *Set of* 6 ... 27·00 90·00

Examples of the 6d. with centre inverted (*price* £550, *unused*) and the 1s. with frame printed double (*price* £200, *unused*) come from printer's waste and were not issued.

(Recess Govt Printing Office, Wellington)

1924–27. *T* **9/10** *and* **16** *of Cook Islands, but inscr "AITUTAKI".* W **43** of New Zealand. P 14.

30 ½d. black and green (5.27) ... 2·00 17·00
31 1d. black and deep carmine (10.24) ... 6·00 7·50
a. Double derrick flaw (R. 2/8, 3/6 or 5/2) ... 16·00
32 2½d. black and dull blue (10.27) ... 7·50 70·00
30/2 *Set of* 3 ... 14·00 85·00

Cook Islands stamps superseded those of Aitutaki on 15 March 1932.

PENRHYN ISLAND

Stamps of COOK ISLANDS were used on Penrhyn Island from late 1901 until the issue of the surcharged stamps in May 1902.

PRICES FOR STAMPS ON COVER TO 1945

No. 1	*from* × 25
No. 3	—
Nos. 4/5	*from* × 25
Nos. 6/8	—
Nos. 9/10	*from* × 50
Nos. 11/13	—
Nos. 14/18	*from* × 3
Nos. 19/23	*from* × 2
Nos. 24/37	*from* × 3
Nos. 38/40	*from* × 5

NEW ZEALAND DEPENDENCY The island of Penrhyn, under British protection from 20 September 1888, was annexed by New Zealand on 11 June 1901.

Stamps of New Zealand overprinted or surcharged. For illustrations of New Zealand watermarks and definitive types see New Zealand.

PENRHYN ISLAND. ½ PENI. (1)
PENRHYN ISLAND. TAI PENI. (2) 1d.
PENRHYN ISLAND. 2½ PENI. (3)

1902 (5 May). *T* **23**, **27** *and* **42** *surch with T* **1**, **2** *and* **3**.

(a) Thick, soft Pirie paper. No wmk. P 11.

1 2½d. blue (No. 260) (R.) ... 5·00 8·00
a. "½" and "P" spaced (all stamps in 8th vert row) ... 18·00 32·00

(b) Thin, hard Basted Mills paper. W **38** of New Zealand.

(i) P 11.

3 1d. carmine (No. 286) (Br.) ... £850 £1200

(ii) P 14.

4 ½d. green (No. 287) (R.) ... 80 8·50
a. No stop after "ISLAND" ... £150 £250
5 1d. carmine (No. 288) (Br.) ... 3·25 19·00

(iii) Perf compound of 11 and 14.

6 1d. carmine (No. 290) (Br.) ... £1100 £1300

(iv) Mixed perfs.

7 ½d. green (No. 291) (R.) ... £2250
8 1d. carmine (No. 292) (Br.) ... £2500

(c) Thin, hard Cowan paper. W **43** of New Zealand.

(i) P 14.

9 ½d. green (No. 302) (R.) ... 2·25 8·00
a. No stop after "ISLAND" (R. 10/6) ... £140 £275
10 1d. carmine (No. 303) (B.) ... 1·25 5·50
a. No stop after "ISLAND" (R. 10/6) ... 48·00 £110

(ii) Perf compound of 11 and 14.

11 1d. carmine (No. 305) (B.) ... £15000

(iii) Mixed perfs.

12 ½d. green (No. 306) (R.) ... £2250 £2500
13 1d. carmine (No. 307) (B.) ... £800 £950

PENRHYN ISLAND. (4)
Toru Pene. (5) 3d.
Ono Pene. (6) 6d.
Tahi Silingi. (7) 1s.

1903 (28 Feb). *T* **28**, **31** *and* **34** *surch with name at top, T* **4**, *and values at foot, T* **5/7**. *Thin, hard Cowan paper.* W **43** (sideways) of New Zealand. P 11.

14 3d. yellow-brown (No. 309) (B.) ... 10·00 26·00
15 6d. rose-red (No. 312*a*) (B.) ... 15·00 40·00
16 1s. brown-red (No. 315) (B.) ... 55·00 55·00
a. Bright red ... 42·00 42·00
b. Orange-red ... 55·00 55·00
14/16a *Set of* 3 ... 60·00 95·00

1914 (May)–**15**. *T* **51/2** *surch with T* **1** *(½d.) or optd with T* **4** *at top and surch with T* **6/7** *at foot.*

19 ½d. yellow-green (No. 387) (C.) (5.14) ... 80 8·00
a. No stop after "ISLAND" ... 25·00 80·00
b. No stop after "PENI" (R. 3/17) ... £100 £200
c. Vermilion opt (1.15) ... 80 8·00
ca. No stop after "ISLAND" ... 10·00 50·00
cb. No stop after "PENI" (R. 3/5, 3/17) ... 48·00 £150
22 6d. carmine (No. 393) (B.) (8.14) ... 23·00 75·00
23 1s. vermilion (No. 394) (B.) (8.14) ... 42·00 £100
19/23 *Set of* 3 ... 60·00 £160

The "no stop after ISLAND" variety occurs on R. 1/4, 1/10, 1/16, 1/22, 6/4, 6/10, 6/16 and 6/22 of the carmine surcharge, No. 19, and on these positions plus R. 1/12, 1/24, 6/12 and 6/24 for the vermilion, No. 19c.

1917 (Nov)–**20**. *Optd as T* **4**.

(a) T **60** *(recess).* W **43** of New Zealand. P 14×13½.

24 2½d. blue (No. 419) (R.) (10.20) ... 3·00 13·00
a. Perf 14×14½ ... 2·00 7·00
ab. No stop after "ISLAND" (R. 10/8) ... £190 £425
b. Vert pair. Nos. 24/4a ... 45·00 95·00
25 3d. chocolate (No. 420) (B.) (6.18) ... 12·00 70·00
a. Perf 14×14½ ... 9·50 70·00
b. Vert pair. Nos. 25/5a ... 70·00 £250
26 6d. carmine (No. 425) (B.) (1.18) ... 8·00 25·00
a. Perf 14×14½ ... 5·00 20·00
ab. No stop after "ISLAND" (R. 10/8) ... £450 £800
b. Vert pair. Nos. 26/6a ... 55·00 £150
27 1s. vermilion (No. 430) (B.) (12.17) ... 15·00 42·00
a. Perf 14×14½ ... 12·00 32·00
ab. No stop after "ISLAND" (R. 10/8) ... £550 £900
b. Vert pair. Nos. 27/7a ... £100 £250
24/7 *Set of* 4 ... 35·00 £130
24a/7a *Set of* 4 ... 26·00 £110

(b) T **61** *(typo).* W **43** of New Zealand. P 14×15.

28 ½d. green (No. 435) (R.) (2.20) ... 1·00 2·00
a. No stop after "ISLAND" (R. 2/24) ... £140 £190
b. Narrow spacing ... 7·00 12·00
29 1½d. slate (No. 437) (R.) ... 6·50 22·00
a. Narrow spacing ... 18·00 48·00
30 1½d. orange-brown (No. 438) (R.) (2.19) ... 60 22·00
a. Narrow spacing ... 5·00 48·00
31 3d. chocolate (No. 440) (B.) (6.19) ... 3·50 28·00
a. Narrow spacing ... 16·00 65·00
28/31 *Set of* 4 ... 10·50 65·00

The narrow spacing variety occurs on R. 1/5–8, 4/21–4, 7/5–8 and 9/21–4.

(Recess P.B.)

1920 (23 Aug). *As T* **9/14** *of Cook Islands, but inscr* "PENRHYN". No wmk. P 14.

32 ½d. black and emerald ... 1·00 18·00
a. Part imperf block of 4 ... £1500
33 1d. black and deep red ... 1·50 15·00
a. Double derrick flaw (R. 2/8, 3/6 or 5/2) ... 5·50 45·00
34 1½d. black and deep violet ... 6·50 19·00
35 3d. black and red ... 2·50 9·00
36 6d. red-brown and sepia ... 3·25 20·00
37 1s. black and slate-blue ... 10·00 26·00
32/7 *Set of* 6 ... 22·00 95·00

No. 32a comes from sheets on which two rows were imperforate between horizontally and the second row additionally imperforate vertically.

Examples of the ½d. and 1d. with centre inverted were not supplied to the Post Office (*Price £550 each, unused*).

(Recess Govt Printing Office, Wellington)

1927–29. *As T* **9/10** *and* **16** *of Cook Islands, but inscr* "PENRHYN". W **43**. P 14.

38 ½d. black and green (5.29) ... 5·50 21·00
39 1d. black and deep carmine (14.3.28) ... 5·50 18·00
a. Double derrick flaw (R. 2/8, 3/6 or 5/2) ... 16·00
40 2½d. red-brown and dull blue (10.27) ... 7·00 29·00
38/40 *Set of* 3 ... 16·00 60·00

Cook Islands stamps superseded those of Penrhyn Island on 15 March 1932.

Cyprus

Cyprus was part of the Turkish Ottoman Empire from 1571.

The first records of an organised postal service date from 1871 when a post office was opened at Nicosia (Lefkosa) under the jurisdiction of the Damascus Head Post Office. Various stamps of Turkey from the 1868 issue onwards are known used from this office, cancelled "KIBRIS", in Arabic, within a double-lined oblong. Manuscript cancellations have also been reported. The records report the opening of a further office at Larnaca (Tuzla) in 1873, but no cancellation for this office has been identified.

To provide an overseas postal service the Austrian Empire opened a post office in Larnaca during 1845. Stamps of the Austrian Post Offices in the Turkish Empire were placed on sale there from 1 June 1864 and were cancelled with an unframed straight-line mark or circular date stamp. This Austrian post office closed on 6 August 1878.

BRITISH ADMINISTRATION

Following the convention with Turkey, Great Britain assumed the administration of Cyprus on 11 July 1878 and the first post office, as part of the British G.P.O. system, was opened at Larnaca on 27 July 1878. Further offices at Famagusta, Kyrenia, Limassol, Nicosia and Paphos followed in September 1878.

The stamps of Great Britain were supplied to the various offices as they opened and continued to be used until the Cyprus Administration assumed responsibility for the postal service on 1 April 1880. With the exception of "969" (Nicosia) similar numeral cancellations had previously been used at offices in Great Britain.

Numeral postmarks for Headquarters Camp, Nicosia ("D48") and Polymedia (Polemidhia) Camp, Limassol ("D47") were supplied by the G.P.O. in London during January 1881. These cancellations had three bars above and three bars below the numeral. Similar marks, but with four bars above and below, had previously been used in London on newspapers and bulk mail.

Although both three bar cancellations subsequently occur on Cyprus issues only, isolated examples have been found on loose Great Britain stamps and there are no known covers or pieces which confirm such usage in Cyprus.

For illustrations of the postmark types see BRITISH POST OFFICES ABROAD notes, following GREAT BRITAIN.

FAMAGUSTA

Stamps of GREAT BRITAIN *cancelled* "982" *as Type* **9**.

1878–80.

Z1 ½d. rose-red (1870–79) (Plate Nos. 11, 13) ... £700
Z2 1d. rose-red (1864–79) ... £500
Plate Nos. 145, 174, 181, 193, 202, 204, 206, 215, 217.
Z3 2d. blue (1858–69) (Plate Nos. 13, 14, 15) ... £1000
Z4 2½d. rosy mauve (1876) (Plate Nos. 13, 16) ... £1100
Z5 6d. grey (1874–80) (Plate No. 15)
Z6 1s. green (1873–77) (Plate No. 12) ... £2250

KYRENIA

Stamps of GREAT BRITAIN *cancelled* "974" *as Type* **9**.

1878–80.

Z8 ½d. rose-red (1870–79) (Plate No. 13) ... £900
Z9 1d. rose-red (1864–79) ... *From* £600
Plate Nos. 168, 171, 193, 196, 206, 207, 209, 220.
Z10 2d. blue (1858–69) (Plate Nos. 13, 15) ... *From* £900
Z11 2½d. rosy mauve (1876–79) (Plate Nos. 12, 13, 14, 15) ... *From* £1000
Z12 4d. sage-green (1877) (Plate No. 16)
Z13 6d. grey (1874–80) (Plate No. 16)

LARNACA

Stamps of GREAT BRITAIN *cancelled* "942" *as Type* **9**.

1878–80.

Z14 ½d. rose-red (1870–79) ... *From* £250
Plate Nos. 11, 12, 13, 14, 15, 19, 20.
Z15 1d. rose-red (1864–79) ... *From* £170
Plate Nos. 129, 131, 146, 154, 170, 171, 174, 175, 176, 177, 178, 179, 181, 182, 183, 184, 187, 188, 190, 191, 192, 193, 194, 195, 196, 197, 198, 199, 200, 201, 202, 203, 204, 205, 206, 207, 208, 209, 210, 212, 213, 214, 215, 216, 217, 218, 220, 221, 222, 225.
Z16 1½d. lake-red (1870) (Plate No. 3) ... £1900
Z17 2d. blue (1858–69) (Plate Nos. 9, 13, 14, 15) ... £250
Z18 2½d. rosy mauve (1876–79) ... *From* 75·00
Plate Nos. 4, 5, 6, 8, 9, 10, 11, 12, 13, 14, 15, 16, 17.
Z19 2½d. blue (1880) (Plate Nos. 17, 18) ... £500
Z21 4d. sage-green (1877) (Plate Nos. 15, 16) ... £550
Z22 6d. grey (1874–76) (Plate Nos. 15, 16, 17) ... £500
Z23 6d. pale buff (1872–73) (Plate No. 11) ... £2250
Z24 8d. orange (1876) ... £5000
Z25 1s. green (1873–77) (Plate Nos. 12, 13) ... £950
Z27 5s. rose (1874) (Plate No. 2) ... £5000

LIMASSOL

Stamps of GREAT BRITAIN *cancelled* "975" *as Type* **9**.

1878–80.

Z28 ½d. rose-red (1870–79) (Plate Nos. 11, 13, 15, 19) ... £450
Z29 1d. rose-red (1864–79) ... *From* £275
Plate Nos. 159, 160, 171, 173, 174, 177, 179, 184, 187, 190, 193, 195, 196, 197, 198, 200, 202, 206, 207, 208, 209, 210, 213, 215, 216, 218, 220, 221, 222, 225.
Z30 1½d. lake-red (1870–74) (Plate No. 3) ... £2000
Z31 2d. blue (1858–69) (Plate Nos. 14, 15) ... *From* £450
Z32 2½d. rosy-mauve (1876–80) ... *From* £225
Plate Nos. 11, 12, 13, 14, 15, 16.
Z33 2½d. blue (1880) (Plate No. 17) ... £1200
Z34 4d. sage-green (Plate No. 16) ... £800

NICOSIA

Stamps of GREAT BRITAIN *cancelled* "969" *as Type* **9**.

1878–80.

Z35 ½d. rose-red (1870–79) ... £450
Plate Nos. 12, 13, 14, 15, 20.
Z36 1d. rose-red (1864–79) ... *From* £275
Plate Nos. 170, 171, 174, 189, 190, 192, 193, 195, 196, 198, 200, 202, 203, 205, 206, 207, 210, 212, 214, 215, 218, 221, 222, 225.
Z36*a* 1½d. lake red (1870) (Plate No. 3) ... £2750
Z37 2d. blue (1858–69) (Plate Nos. 14, 15) ... £475
Z38 2½d. rosy mauve (1876–79) ... *From* £200
Plate Nos. 10, 11, 12, 13, 14, 15, 16.
Z39 2½d. blue (1880) (Plate No. 17) ... £750
Z42 4d. sage-green (1877) (Plate No. 16) ... £850
Z43 6d. grey (1873) (Plate No. 16) ... £900

PAPHOS

Stamps of GREAT BRITAIN *cancelled* "981" *as Type* **9**.

1878–80.

Z44 ½d. rose-red (1870–79) (Plate Nos. 13, 15)
Z45 1d. rose-red (1864–79) ... *From* £600
Plate Nos. 196, 201, 202, 204, 206, 213, 217.
Z46 2d. blue (1858–69) (Plate No. 15) ... £950
Z47 2½d. rosy mauve (1876–79) ... *From* £600
Plate Nos. 13, 14, 15, 16.

PRICES FOR STAMPS ON COVER TO 1945	
Nos. 1/4	*from* × 50
Nos. 5/6	—
Nos. 7/10	*from* × 25
Nos. 11/15	*from* × 8
No. 16	—
Nos. 16*a*/24	*from* × 12
No. 25	*from* × 100
No. 26	—
No. 27	*from* × 15
No. 28	—
No. 29	*from* × 60
Nos. 31/5*a*	*from* × 10
Nos. 36/7	—
Nos. 40/9	*from* × 8
Nos. 50/71	*from* × 5
Nos. 74/99	*from* × 4
Nos. 100/2	—
Nos. 103/17	*from* × 4
No. 117*a*	—
Nos. 118/31	*from* × 5
No. 132	—
Nos. 133/43	*from* × 5
Nos. 144/7	*from* × 6
Nos. 148/63	*from* × 5

PERFORATION. Nos. 1/122 are perf 14.

Stamps of Great Britain overprinted

CYPRUS (1) CYPRUS (2)

(Optd by D.L.R.)

1880 (1 April).

1 **1** ½d. rose ... £110 £100
a. Opt double (Plate 15) ... † £22000

Plate No.	*Un.*	*Used.*	*Plate No.*	*Un.*	*Used*
12.	£200	£250	19.	£5000	£700
15.	£110	£100			

2 **2** 1d. red ... 14·00 38·00
a. Opt double (Plate 208) ... £19000
aa. Opt double (Plate 218) ... £4250
b. Vert pair, top stamp without opt (Plate 208) ... £21000

Plate No.	*Un.*	*Used.*	*Plate No.*	*Un.*	*Used*
174.	£1400	£1400	208.	£110	55·00
181.	£475	£190	215.	14·00	55·00
184.	£15000	£2500	216.	16·00	38·00
193.	£750	†	217.	15·00	50·00
196.	£650	†	218.	22·00	55·00
201.	17·00	55·00	220.	£350	£375
205.	70·00	50·00			

3 **2** 2½d. rosy mauve ... 3·00 10·00
a. Large thin "C" (Plate 14) (BK, JK) ... 65·00 £250
b. Large thin "C" (Plate 15) (BK, JK) ... £110 £600
w. Wmk inverted (Plate 15) ... £425

Plate No.	*Un.*	*Used.*	*Plate No.*	*Un.*	*Used*
14.	3·00	10·00	15.	4·25	29·00

4 **2** 4d. sage-green (Plate 16) ... £130 £225
5 6d. grey (Plate 16) ... £500 £650
6 1s. green (Plate 13) ... £700 £450

HALF-PENNY (3) 18 mm HALF-PENNY (4) 16 or 16½ mm

HALF-PENNY (5) 13 mm 30 PARAS (6)

(Optd by Govt Ptg Office, Nicosia)

1881 (Feb–June). *No. 2 surch.*

7 **3** ½d. on 1d. red (Feb) ... 75·00 85·00
a. "HALFPENN" (BG, LG) (*all plates*) ... *From* £2750 £2750
b. Surch double (Plate 220) ... £1600

Plate No.	*Un.*	*Used.*	*Plate No.*	*Un.*	*Used*
174.	£200	£375	215.	£750	£850
181.	£170	£200	216.	75·00	85·00
201.	£100	£130	217.	£900	£800
205.	75·00	85·00	218.	£500	£600
208.	£200	£325	220.	£300	£375

8 **4** ½d. on 1d. red (Apr) ... £120 £160
a. Surch double (Plates 201 and 216) ... £3250 £2500

Plate No.	*Un.*	*Used.*	*Plate No.*	*Un.*	*Used*
201.	£120	£160	218.	—	£10000
216.	£350	£425			

9 **5** ½d. on 1d. red (1 June) ... 45·00 65·00
aa. Surch double (Plate 205) ... £800
ab. Surch double (Plate 215) ... £450 £650
b. Surch treble (Plate 205) ... £4250
ba. Surch treble (Plate 215) ... £800
bc. Surch treble (Plate 218) ... £4250
c. Surch quadruple (Plate 205) ... £5500
ca. Surch quadruple (Plate 215) ... £5500

Plate No.	*Un.*	*Used.*	*Plate No.*	*Un.*	*Used*
205.	£350	—	217.	£160	90·00
215.	45·00	65·00	218.	80·00	£110

The surcharge on No. 8 was handstamped; the others were applied by lithography.

(New Currency: 40 paras = 1 piastre, 180 piastres = £1)

1881 (June). *No. 2 surch with T* **6** *by lithography.*

			Un.	Used
10	6	30 paras on 1d. red	£120	85·00
		a. Surch double, one invtd (Plate 216)	£5000	
		aa. Surch double, one invtd (Plate 220)	£1600	£1300

Plate No.	*Un.*	*Used.*	*Plate No.*	*Un.*	*Used*
201.	£140	£100	217.	£190	£190
216.	£120	85·00	220.	£160	£170

7

"US" damaged at foot (R. 5/5 of both panes)

(Typo D.L.R)

1881 (1 July). *Die I.* Wmk Crown CC.

			Un.	Used
11	7	½pi. emerald-green	£180	45·00
		w. Wmk inverted	£750	£425
12		1pi. rose	£375	32·00
13		2pi. blue	£450	35·00
		w. Wmk inverted	—	£850
14		4pi. pale olive-green	£900	£275
15		6pi. olive-grey	£1700	£475

Stamps of Queen Victoria initialled "J.A.B." or overprinted "POSTAL SURCHARGE" with or without the same initials were employed for accounting purposes between the Chief Post Office and sub-offices, the initials are those of the then Postmaster, Mr. J. A. Bulmer.

1882 (May)–**86**. *Die I*.* Wmk Crown CA.

			Un.	Used
16	7	½pi. emerald-green (5.82)	£5000	£500
		a. Dull green (4.83)	20·00	2·25
		ab. Top left triangle detached	—	£275
17		30pa. pale mauve (7.6.82)	70·00	23·00
		a. Top left triangle detached	£1400	£750
		b. Damaged "US"	£900	£450
18		1pi. rose (3.83)	£100	3·00
		a. Top left triangle detached	—	£325
19		2pi. blue (4.83)	£140	3·00
		a. Top left triangle detached	—	£325
20		4pi. deep olive-green (10.83)	£550	40·00
		a. Pale olive-green	£350	29·00
		ab. Top left triangle detached	£3750	£800
21		6pi. olive-grey (7.82)	60·00	17·00
		a. Top left triangle detached	—	£650
22		12pi. orange-brown (1886)	£180	40·00
		s. Optd "Specimen"	£950	
16a/22 *Set of 7*			£800	£110

*For description and illustrations of Dies I and II see Introduction.

For illustration of "top left triangle detached" variety see above No. 21 of Antigua.

No. 21 with manuscript "Specimen" endorsement is known with "CYPRUS" and value double.

See also Nos. 31/7.

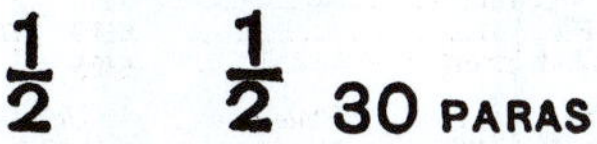

(8) (9)

Spur on "1" (position 3 in setting)

(Surch litho by Govt Ptg Office, Nicosia)

1882. *Surch with T* **8/9**.

(a) Wmk crown CC.

			Un.	Used
23		½ on ½pi. emerald-green (6.82)	£650	75·00
		c. Spur on "1"	£950	£130
		w. Wmk inverted		
24		30pa. on 1pi. rose (22.5.82)	£1500	£110

(b) Wmk Crown CA.

			Un.	Used
25	7	½ on ½pi. emerald-green (27.5.82)	£150	6·50
		a. Surch double	†	£2750
		b. "½" inserted by hand	†	£5000
		c. Spur on "1"	£250	12·00

Nos. 23 and 25 were surcharged by a setting of 6 arranged as a horizontal row.

No. 25b shows an additional handstamped "½" applied to examples on which the surcharge was so misplaced as to almost omit one of the original "½"s.

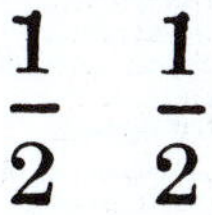

(10)

11

Varieties of numerals:

Normal Large Small

Normal Large

1886 (Apr). *Surch with T* **10** *(fractions approx 6 mm apart) in typography.*

(a) Wmk Crown CC.

			Un.	Used
26	7	½ on ½pi. emerald-green	£21000	

(b) Wmk Crown CA.

			Un.	Used
27	7	½ on ½pi. emerald-green	£250	70·00
		a. Large "2" at right (R. 10/1)	£2500	£750

1886 (May–June). *Surch with T* **10** *(fractions approx 8 mm apart) in typography.*

(a) Wmk Crown CC.

			Un.	Used
28	7	½ on ½pi. emerald-green	£8000	£425
		a. Large "1" at left	—	£1900
		b. Small "1" at right	£15000	£2250
		c. Large "2" at left	—	£2250
		d. Large "2" at right	†	£2250

(b) Wmk Crown CA.

			Un.	Used
29	7	½ on ½pi. emerald-green (June)	£425	12·00
		a. Large "1" at left	£3500	£250
		b. Small "1" at right	£3250	£275
		c. Large "2" at left	£3500	£325
		d. Large "2" at right	£3500	£325

Nos. 28/9 were surcharged in a setting of 60. The large "1" at left and large "2" at right both occur in the fourth vertical row, the large "2" at left in the fifth vertical row and the small "1" at right in the top horizontal row.

A third type of this surcharge is known with the fractions spaced approximately 10 mm apart on CA paper with postmarks from August 1886. This may be due to the shifting of type.

1892–94. *Die II.* Wmk Crown CA.

			Un.	Used
31	7	½pi. dull green	7·00	1·25
32		30pa. mauve	6·50	9·00
		a. Damaged "US"	£225	£250
33		1pi. carmine	14·00	4·00
34		2pi. ultramarine	14·00	1·75
35		4pi. olive-green	50·00	32·00
		a. Pale olive-green	18·00	28·00
36		6pi. olive-grey (1894)	£200	£650
37		12pi. orange brown (1893)	£160	£375
31/7 *Set of 7*			£375	£950

1894 (14 Aug)–**96**. *Colours changed and new values. Die II.* Wmk Crown CA.

			Un.	Used
40	7	½pi. green and carmine (1896)	4·00	1·25
		w. Wmk inverted	†	£1800
41		30pa. bright mauve and green (1896)	2·00	2·00
		a. Damaged "US"	£150	£140
42		1pi. carmine and blue (1896)	6·50	1·25
43		2pi. blue and purple (1896)	9·00	1·25
44		4pi. sage-green and purple (1896)	17·00	8·00
45		6pi. sepia and green (1896)	16·00	25·00
46		9pi. brown and carmine	19·00	23·00
47		12pi. orange-brown and black (1896)	19·00	60·00
48		18pi. greyish slate and brown	50·00	55·00
49		45pi. grey-purple and blue	95·00	£150
40/9 *Set of 10*			£200	£300
40s/9s Optd "Specimen" *Set of 10*			£325	

LIMASSOL FLOOD HANDSTAMP. Following a flood on 14 November 1894, which destroyed the local stamp stocks, the postmaster of Limassol produced a temporary handstamp showing "½C.P." which was applied to local letters with the usual c.d.s.

(Typo D.L.R.)

1902–04. Wmk Crown CA.

			Un.	Used
50	11	½pi. green and carmine (12.02)	6·50	1·25
		w. Wmk inverted	95·00	65·00
51		30pa. violet and green (2.03)	13·00	3·50
		a. Mauve and green	20·00	8·00
		b. Damaged "US"	£300	£140
52		1pi. carmine and blue (9.03)	24·00	3·50
53		2pi. blue and purple (2.03)	75·00	14·00
54		4pi. olive-green and purple (9.03)	35·00	19·00
55		6pi. sepia and green (9.03)	42·00	£130
56		9pi. brown and carmine (5.04)	£100	£200
57		12pi. chestnut and black (4.03)	17·00	65·00
58		18pi. black and brown (5.04)	85·00	£160
59		45pi. dull purple and ultramarine (10.03)	£200	£500
50/9 *Set of 10*			£550	£1000
50sw/9s Optd "Specimen" *Set of 10*			£450	

The ½pi "SPECIMEN" is only known with watermark inverted.

Broken top left triangle (Left pane R. 7/5)

1904–10. Wmk Mult Crown CA.

			Un.	Used
60	11	5pa. bistre and black (14.1.08)	1·00	1·25
		a. Broken top left triangle	70·00	80·00
		w. Wmk inverted	£1500	
61		10pa. orange and green (12.06)	4·25	1·00
		aw. Wmk inverted	—	£100
		b. Orange-yellow and green	38·00	5·50
		bw. Wmk inverted	—	£120
		c. Broken top left triangle	£100	55·00
62		½pi. green and carmine (1.7.04)	7·00	60
		a. Broken top left triangle	£130	40·00
		w. Wmk inverted	£130	90·00
		y. Wmk inverted and reversed	†	£750
63		30pa. purple and green (1.7.04)	18·00	2·00
		a. Violet and green (1910)	20·00	2·50
		b. Broken top left triangle	£275	85·00
		c. Damaged "US"	£225	70·00
		w. Wmk inverted	†	£1300
64		1pi. carmine and blue (11.04)	9·00	1·00
		a. Broken top left triangle	£140	65·00
65		2pi. blue and purple (11.04)	10·00	1·75
		a. Broken top left triangle	£180	85·00
66		4pi. olive-green and purple (2.05)	18·00	9·50
		a. Broken top left triangle	£275	£200
67		6pi. sepia and green (17.7.04)	22·00	15·00
		a. Broken top left triangle	£300	£300
68		9pi. brown and carmine (30.5.04)	45·00	8·50
		a. Yellow-brown and carmine	42·00	22·00
		aw. Wmk inverted	£180	95·00
		b. Broken top left triangle	£450	£250
69		12pi. chestnut and black (4.06)	29·00	45·00
		a. Broken top left triangle	£425	
70		18pi. black and brown (16.6.04)	40·00	12·00
		a. Broken top left triangle	£500	£300
71		45pi. dull purple & ultram (15.6.04)	95·00	£140
		a. Broken top left triangle.	£950	
60/71 *Set of 12*			£250	£200
60s/1s Optd "Specimen" *Set of 2*			£130	

12

13

Broken bottom left triangle (Right pane R. 10/6)

(Typo D.L.R.)

1912 (July)–**15**. Wmk Mult Crown CA.

			Un.	Used
74	12	10pa. orange and green (11.12)	4·00	2·50
		a. Wmk sideways	†	£3000
		b. Orange-yellow & brt green (8.15)	2·25	1·25
		ba. Broken bottom left triangle	90·00	55·00
75		½pi. green and carmine	2·00	30
		a. Yellow-green and carmine	7·50	1·90
		ab. Broken bottom left triangle	£110	60·00
		w. Wmk inverted	†	£1400
76		30pa. violet and green (3.13)	3·00	1·50
		a. Broken bottom left triangle	95·00	55·00
		w. Wmk inverted		
77		1pi. rose-red and blue (9.12)	4·75	1·75
		a. Broken bottom left triangle	£130	60·00
		b. Carmine and blue (1.15?)	13·00	4·25
		ba. Broken bottom left triangle	£200	85·00
78		2pi. blue and purple (7.13)	6·50	2·00
		a. Broken bottom left triangle	£150	65·00
79		4pi. olive-green and purple	4·25	4·75
		a. Broken bottom left triangle	£120	£130
80		6pi. sepia and green	4·00	9·00
		a. Broken bottom left triangle	£120	
81		9pi. brown and carmine (3.15)	30·00	26·00
		a. Yellow-brown and carmine	35·00	29·00
		b. Broken bottom left triangle	£400	
82		12pi. chestnut and black (7.13)	21·00	48·00
		a. Broken bottom left triangle	£275	£425
83		18pi. black and brown (3.15)	32·00	40·00
		a. Broken bottom left triangle	£375	
84		45pi. dull purple and ultramarine (3.15)	95·00	£140
		a. Broken bottom left triangle	£800	
74/84 *Set of 11*			£180	£250
74s/84s Optd "Specimen" *Set of 11*			£500	

1921–23.

(a) Wmk Mult Script CA.

			Un.	Used
85	12	10pa. orange and green	11·00	10·00
		a. Broken bottom left triangle	£150	£150
		w. Wmk inverted	£2750	
86		10pa. grey and yellow (1923)	13·00	8·00
		a. Broken bottom left triangle	£180	£140
87		30pa. violet and green	2·50	1·25
		a. Broken bottom left triangle	95·00	50·00
		w. Wmk inverted	£2250	£2250
		y. Wmk inverted and reversed	†	£1700
88		30pa. green (1923)	7·00	1·25
		a. Broken bottom left triangle	£160	50·00
89		1pi. carmine and blue	23·00	35·00
		a. Broken bottom left triangle	£250	
90		1pi. violet and red (1922)	3·50	4·00
		a. Broken bottom left triangle	£110	£120
91		1½pi. yellow and black (1922)	9·00	5·50
		a. Broken bottom left triangle	£160	£130
92		2pi. blue and purple	27·00	19·00
		a. Broken bottom left triangle	£325	£225
93		2pi. carmine and blue (1922)	13·00	23·00
		a. Broken bottom left triangle	£225	
94		2¾pi. blue and purple (1922)	8·00	9·00
		a. Broken bottom left triangle	£180	£200
95		4pi. olive-green and purple	16·00	21·00
		a. Broken bottom left triangle	£225	
		w. Wmk inverted	†	£1700
96		6pi. sepia and green (1923)	24·00	80·00
		a. Broken bottom left triangle	£275	
97		9pi. brown and carmine (1922)	35·00	85·00
		a. Yellow-brown and carmine	£100	£150
		b. Broken bottom left triangle	£425	
98		18pi. black and brown (1923)	70·00	£150
		a. Broken bottom left triangle	£600	
99		45pi. dull purple & ultramarine (1923)	£225	£275
		a. Broken bottom left triangle	£1200	£1500

85/99 *Set of* 15			£425	£650
85s/99s Optd "Specimen" *Set of* 15			£650	

(*b*) Wmk Mult Crown CA (1923).

100	12	10s. green and red/*pale yellow*	£375	£750
		a. Broken bottom left triangle ...	£2500	
101		£1 purple and black/*red*	£1200	£2250
		a. Broken bottom left triangle ...	£4750	£7500
100s/1s Optd "Specimen" *Set of* 2			£550	

Examples of Nos. 96/101 are known showing a forged Limassol postmark dated "14 MR 25".

1924–28. *Chalk-surfaced paper.*

(*a*) Wmk Mult Crown CA.

102	13	£1 purple and black/*red*	£300	£750

(*b*) Wmk Mult Script CA.

103	13	¼pi. grey and chestnut	1·25	50
		w. Wmk inverted	†	£1100
104		½pi. black	4·00	12·00
105		¾pi. green	2·50	1·00
106		1pi. purple and chestnut	2·00	1·25
107		1½pi. orange and black	2·25	11·00
108		2pi. carmine and green	2·75	17·00
109		2¾pi. bright blue and purple	3·25	4·00
110		4pi. sage-green and purple	3·75	4·00
111		4½pi. black and orange/*emerald*	3·50	4·25
112		6pi. olive-brown and green	3·75	7·00
113		9pi. brown and purple	6·50	4·50
114		12pi. chestnut and black	10·00	60·00
115		18pi. black and orange	20·00	5·00
116		45pi. purple and blue	48·00	38·00
117		90pi. green and red/*yellow*	£100	£200
117*a*		£5 black/*yellow* (1928) (F.C. £250)	£3000	£7000
		as. Optd "Specimen"	£1000	

Examples of No. 102 are known showing a forged Limassol postmark dated "14 MR 25" and of No. 117*a* showing a forged Registered Nicosia postmark dated "6 MAY 35".

CROWN COLONY

1925. Wmk Mult Script CA. *Chalk-surfaced paper (½, ¾ and 2pi.).*

118	13	½pi. green	2·25	1·00
119		¾pi. brownish black	3·00	50
120		1½pi. scarlet	4·00	1·00
121		2pi. yellow and black	11·00	3·25
122		2½pi. bright blue	3·75	1·00
102/22 (*ex* £5) *Set of* 21			£475	£1000
102s/22s (*ex* £5) Optd "Specimen" *Set of* 21			£850	

In the above set the fraction bar in the value is horizontal. In Nos. 91, 94, 107 and 109 it is diagonal.

14 Silver Coin of Amathus, 6th-cent B.C.

15 Zeno (philosopher)

16 Map of Cyprus

17 Discovery of body of St. Barnabas

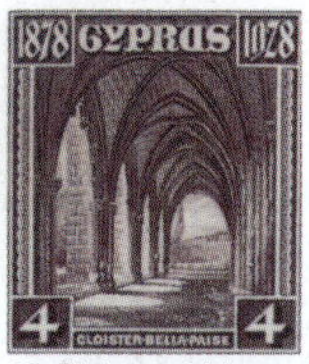
18 Cloister, Abbey of Bella Paise

19 Badge of Cyprus

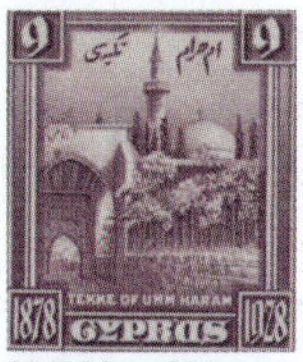
20 Tekke of Umm Haram

21 Statue of Richard I, Westminster

22 St. Nicholas Cathedral (now Lala Mustafa Pasha Mosque), Famagusta

23 King George V

(Recess B.W.)

1928 (1 Feb). *50th Anniv of British Rule. T* **14/23**. Wmk Mult Script CA. P 12.

123	14	¾pi. deep dull purple	2·75	1·50
124	15	1pi. black and greenish blue	3·00	1·50
125	16	1½pi. scarlet	4·50	2·00
126	17	2½pi. light blue	3·50	2·25
127	18	4pi. deep brown	7·00	8·00
128	19	6pi. blue	10·00	25·00
129	20	9pi. maroon	8·00	12·00
130	21	18pi. black and brown	23·00	26·00
131	22	45pi. violet and blue	40·00	48·00
132	23	£1 blue and bistre-brown	£225	£300
123/32 *Set of* 10			£300	£375
123s/32s Optd "Specimen" *Set of* 10			£650	

24 Ruins of Vouni Palace

25 Small Marble Forum, Salamis

26 Church of St. Barnabas and St. Hilarion, Peristerona

27 Roman theatre, Soli

28 Kyrenia Harbour

29 Kolossi Castle

30 St. Sophia Cathedral, Nicosia (now Selimiye Mosque)

31 Bayraktar Mosque, Nicosia

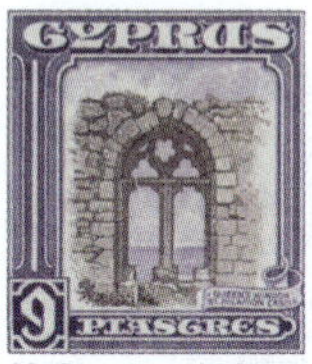
32 Queen's window, St. Hilarion Castle

33 Buyuk Khan, Nicosia

34 Forest scene, Troodos

(Recess Waterlow)

1934 (1 Dec). *T* **24/34**. Wmk Mult Script CA (sideways on ½pi., 1½pi., 2½pi., 4½pi., 6pi., 9pi. and 18pi.). P 12½.

133	24	¼pi. ultramarine and orange-brown	1·25	1·00
		a. Imperf between (vert pair)	£35000	£21000
134	25	½pi. green	1·50	1·00
		a. Imperf between (vert pair)	£16000	£17000
135	26	¾pi. black and violet	2·50	40
		a. Imperf between (vert pair)	£38000	
136	27	1pi. black and red-brown	2·25	1·50
		a. Imperf between (vert pair)	£19000	£19000
		b. Imperf between (horiz pair)	£16000	
137	28	1½pi. carmine	3·25	1·25
138	29	2½pi. ultramarine	4·00	1·75
139	30	4½pi. black and crimson	4·00	4·25
140	31	6pi. black and blue	10·00	16·00
141	32	9pi. sepia and violet	10·00	6·50
142	33	18pi. black and olive-green	45·00	38·00
143	34	45pi. green and black	85·00	70·00
133/43 *Set of* 11			£150	£130
133s/43s Perf "Specimen" *Set of* 11			£450	

1935 (6 May). *Silver Jubilee. As Nos. 91/4 of Antigua, but ptd by Waterlow & Sons.* P 11×12.

144		¾pi. ultramarine and grey	3·00	1·50
145		1½pi. deep blue and scarlet	4·75	2·50
		l. Kite and horizontal log	£325	£275
146		2½pi. brown and deep blue	4·25	1·50
147		9pi. slate and purple	18·00	22·00
144/7 *Set of* 4			27·00	25·00
144s/7s Perf "Specimen" *Set of* 4			£180	

For illustration of plate variety see Omnibus section following Zanzibar.

1937 (12 May). *Coronation. As Nos. 95/7 of Antigua.* P 11×11½.

148		¾pi. grey	1·50	75
149		1½pi. carmine	2·00	1·50
150		2½pi. blue	2·75	2·50
148/50 *Set of* 3			5·50	4·25
148s/50s Perf "Specimen" *Set of* 3			£160	

35 Vouni Palace

36 Map of Cyprus

37 Othello's Tower, Famagusta

38 King George VI

(Recess Waterlow)

1938 (12 May)–**51**. *T* **35** *to* **38** *and other designs as 1934, but with portrait of King George VI.* Wmk Mult Script CA. P 12½.

151	35	¼pi. ultramarine and orange-brown	1·00	40
152	25	½pi. green	1·50	30
152*a*		½pi. violet (2.7.51)	2·25	40
153	26	¾pi. black and violet	17·00	1·00
154	27	1pi. orange	1·75	25
		a. Perf 13½×12½ (4.44)	£550	27·00
155	28	1½pi. carmine	5·50	1·50
155*a*		1½pi. violet (15.3.43)	1·75	55
155*ab*		1½pi. green (2.7.51)	3·50	80
155*b*	26	2pi. black and carmine (2.2.42)	2·00	25
		c. Perf 12½×13½ (10.44)	2·75	9·50
156	29	2½pi. ultramarine	35·00	2·50
156*a*		3pi. ultramarine (2.2.42)	2·75	40
156*b*		4pi. ultramarine (2.7.51)	3·00	60
157	36	4½pi. grey	1·75	25
158	31	6pi. black and blue	2·50	1·00
159	37	9pi. black and purple	2·75	40
160	33	18pi. black and olive-green	11·00	1·00
		a. Black and sage-green (19.8.47)	14·00	1·50
161	34	45pi. green and black	32·00	3·75
162	38	90pi. mauve and black	29·00	6·50
163		£1 scarlet and indigo	60·00	25·00
151/63 *Set of* 19			£190	42·00
151s/63s Perf "Specimen" *Set of* 16			£550	

Dot between "1" and "½" in right-hand value tablet (Pl B1 R. 7/1)

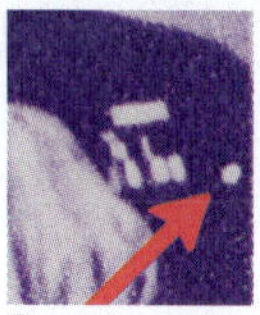
Extra decoration (R. 3/5)

1946 (21 Oct). *Victory. As Nos. 110/11 of Antigua.*

164		1½pi. deep violet	30	10
		a. Dot between "1" and "½"	35·00	
165		3pi. blue	30	30
164s/5s Perf "Specimen" *Set of* 2			£140	

1948 (20 Dec). *Royal Silver Wedding. As Nos. 112/13 of Antigua.*

166		1½pi. violet	75	40
		a. Extra decoration	45·00	48·00
167		£1 indigo	50·00	70·00

1949 (10 Oct). *75th Anniv of Universal Postal Union. As Nos. 114/17 of Antigua but inscr "CYPRUS" (recess).*

168		1½pi. violet	60	1·25
169		2pi. carmine-red	1·50	1·50
170		3pi. deep blue	1·00	1·00
171		9pi. purple	1·00	2·75
168/71 *Set of* 4			3·50	6·00

1953 (2 June). *Coronation. As No. 120 of Antigua.*

172		1½pi. black and emerald	1·50	10

(New Currency = 1000 mils = £1)

39 Carobs

40 Grapes

41 Oranges

42 Mavrovouni Copper Pyrites Mine

43 Troodos Forest

44 Beach of Aphrodite

45 5th-century B.C. coin of Paphos

46 Kyrenia

47 Harvest in Mesaoria

48 Famagusta Harbour

49 St. Hilarion Castle

50 Hala Sultan Tekke

51 Kanakaria Church

52 Coins of Salamis, Paphos, Citium and Idalium

53 Arms of Byzantium, Lusignan, Ottoman Empire and Venice

1955 (1 Aug)–**60**. *T* **39/53**. Wmk Mult Script CA. P 13½ (Nos. 183/5) or 11½ (others).

173	**39**	2m. blackish brown	30	40
174	**40**	3m. blue-violet	30	15
175	**41**	5m. brown-orange	1·75	10
		a. Orange-brown (17.9.58)	6·00	40
176	**42**	10m. deep brown and deep green	2·00	10
177	**43**	15m. olive-green and indigo	3·75	45
		aa. Yellow-olive and indigo (17.9.58)	23·00	4·00
		a. Bistre and indigo (14.6.60)	26·00	8·50
178	**44**	20m. brown and deep bright blue	1·50	15
179	**45**	25m. deep turquoise-blue	3·50	60
		a. Greenish blue (17.9.58)	19·00	4·75
180	**46**	30m. black and carmine-lake	3·00	10
181	**47**	35m. orange-brown and deep turquoise-blue	2·00	40
182	**48**	40m. deep green and sepia	2·00	60
183	**49**	50m. turquoise-blue and reddish brown	2·00	30
184	**50**	100m. mauve and bluish green	13·00	60
185	**51**	250m. deep grey-blue and brown	13·00	10·00
186	**52**	500m. slate and purple	32·00	12·00
187	**53**	£1 brown-lake and slate	26·00	45·00
173/87		*Set of* 15	95·00	65·00

ΚΥΠΡΙΑΚΗ
ΔΗΜΟΚΡΑΤΙΑ
KIBRIS
CUMHURIYETI

(**54** "Cyprus Republic")

55 Map of Cyprus

(Recess B.W.)

1960 (16 Aug)–**61**. *Nos. 173/87 optd as T* **54** *in blue by B.W. Opt larger on Nos. 191/7 and in two lines on Nos 198/202.*

188	2m. blackish brown	20	75
189	3m. blue-violet	20	15
190	5m. brown-orange	1·00	10
	a. Orange-brown (15.8.61)	5·50	70
191	10m. deep brown and deep green	1·00	10
192	15m. yellow-bistre and indigo	2·00	10
	a. Olive-green and indigo	£120	60·00
	b. Brownish bistre and deep indigo (10.10.61)	7·00	3·25
193	20m. brown and deep bright blue	1·75	1·50
	a. Opt double	†	£10000
194	25m. deep turquoise-blue	1·75	1·75
	a. Greenish blue (7.2.61)	27·00	10·00
195	30m. black and carmine-lake	1·75	10
	a. Opt double	†	£18000
196	35m. orange-brown and deep turquoise-blue	1·75	70
197	40m. deep green and sepia	2·00	2·50
198	50m. turquoise-blue and reddish brown	2·00	60
199	100m. mauve and bluish green	9·00	1·00
200	250m. deep grey-blue and brown	28·00	4·25
201	500m. slate and purple	40·00	22·00
202	£1 brown-lake and slate	48·00	50·00
188/202	*Set of* 15	£120	75·00

Only two used examples of No. 195a are known.

(Recess B.W.)

1960 (16 Aug). *Constitution of Republic.* W w **12**. P 11½.

203	**55**	10m. sepia and deep green	30	10
204		30m. ultramarine and deep brown	65	10
205		100m. purple and deep slate	2·00	2·00
203/5		*Set of* 3	2·75	2·00

PRINTERS. All the following stamps to No. 715 were designed by A. Tassos and lithographed by Aspioti-Elka, Athens, unless otherwise stated.

56 Doves

(Des T. Kurpershoek)

1962 (19 Mar). *Europa.* P 14×13.

206	**56**	10m. purple and mauve	10	10
207		40m. ultramarine and cobalt	20	15
208		100m. emerald and pale green	20	20
206/8		*Set of* 3	45	40

57 Campaign Emblem

1962 (14 May). *Malaria. Eradication.* P 14×13½.

209	**57**	10m. black and olive-green	15	15
210		30m. black and brown	30	15

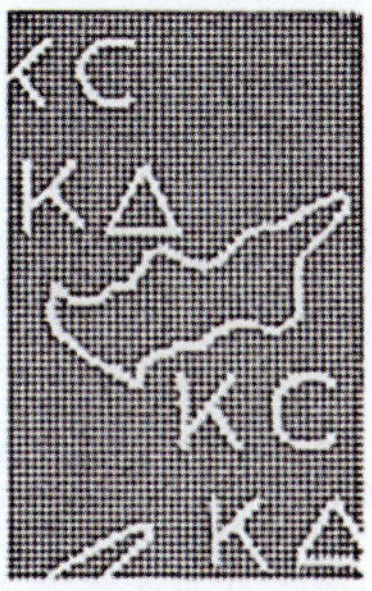

58 Mult K C K Δ and Map

WATERMARK VARIETIES. The issues printed by Aspioti-Elka with W **58** are known with the vertical stamps having the watermark normal or inverted and the horizontal stamps with the watermark reading upwards or downwards. Such varieties are not given separate listing.

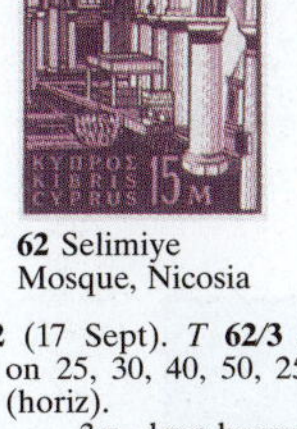

62 Selimiye Mosque, Nicosia

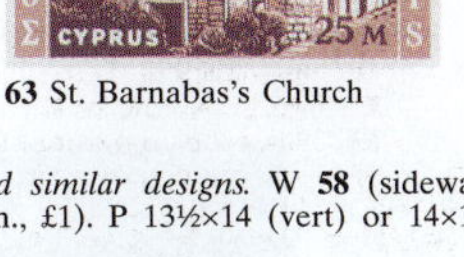

63 St. Barnabas's Church

1962 (17 Sept). *T* **62/3** *and similar designs.* W **58** (sideways) on 25, 30, 40, 50, 250m., £1). P 13½×14 (vert) or 14×13½ (horiz).

211	3m. deep brown and orange-brown	10	30
212	5m. purple and grey-green	10	10
213	10m. black and yellow-green	15	10
214	15m. black and reddish purple	50	15
215	25m. deep brown and chestnut	60	20
216	30m. deep blue and light blue	20	10
217	35m. light green and blue	35	10
218	40m. black and violet-blue	1·25	1·75
219	50m. bronze-green and bistre	50	10
220	100m. deep brown and yellow-brown	3·50	30
221	250m. black and cinnamon	13·00	2·25
222	500m. deep brown and light green	19·00	9·00
223	£1 bronze-green and grey	17·00	30·00
211/23	*Set of* 13	50·00	40·00

Designs: *Vert*—3m. Iron Age jug; 5m. Grapes; 10m. Bronze head of Apollo; 35m. Head of Aphrodite; 100m. Hala Sultan Tekke; 500m. Mouflon. *Horiz*—30m. Temple of Apollo Hylates; 40m. Skiing, Troodos; 50m. Salamis Gymnasium; 250m. Bella Paise Abbey; £1 St. Hilarion Castle.

72 Europa "Tree"

(Des L. Weyer)

1963 (28 Jan). *Europa.* W **58** (sideways). P 14×13½.

224	**72**	10m. bright blue and black	1·75	20
225		40m. carmine-red and black	9·00	2·00
226		150m. emerald-green and black	27·00	6·00
224/6		*Set of* 3	35·00	7·25

73 Harvester

75 Wolf Cub in Camp

1963 (21 Mar). *Freedom from Hunger. T* **73** *and similar vert design.* W **58**. P 13½×14.

227	25m. ochre, sepia and bright blue	30	25
228	75m. grey, black and lake	1·75	1·00

Design:—75m. Demeter, Goddess of Corn.

1963 (21 Aug). *50th Anniv of Cyprus Scout Movement and Third Commonwealth Scout Conference, Platres. T* **75** *and similar vert designs. Multicoloured.* W **58**. P 13½×14.

229	3m. Type **75**	10	20
230	20m. Sea Scout	35	10
231	150m. Scout with Mouflon	1·00	2·50
229/31	*Set of* 3	1·25	2·50
MS231*a*	110×90 mm. Nos. 229/31 (*sold at 250m.*). Imperf	£100	£180

78 Nurse tending Child

79 Children's Centre, Kyrenia

1963 (9 Sept). *Centenary of Red Cross.* W **58** (sideways on 100m.). P 13½×14 (10m.) or 14×13½ (100m.).

232	**78**	10m. red, blue, grey-blue, chestnut and black	50	15
233	**79**	100m. red, green, black and blue	2·00	3·50

80 "Co-operation" (emblem)

(**81**)

(Des A. Holm)

1963 (4 Nov). *Europa.* W **58** (sideways). P 14×13½.

234	**80**	20m. buff, blue and violet	2·50	40
235		30m. grey, yellow and blue	2·50	40
236		150m. buff, blue and orange-brown	26·00	9·00
234/6		*Set of* 3	28·00	9·00

1964 (5 May). *U.N. Security Council's Cyprus Resolutions, March, 1964. Nos. 213, 216, 218/20 optd with T* **81** *in blue by Govt Printing Office, Nicosia.*

237	10m. black and yellow-green	15	10
238	30m. deep blue and light blue	20	10
239	40m. black and violet-blue	25	30
240	50m. bronze-green and bistre	25	10
241	100m. deep brown and yellow-brown	25	50
237/41	*Set of* 5	1·00	1·00

82 Soli Theatre

1964 (15 June). *400th Birth Anniv of Shakespeare. T* **82** *and similar horiz designs. Multicoloured.* W **58**. P 13½×13.

242	15m. Type **82**	70	15
243	35m. Curium Theatre	70	15
244	50m. Salamis Theatre	70	15
245	100m. Othello Tower and scene from *Othello*	1·10	2·25
242/5	*Set of* 4	2·75	2·50

86 Running

89 Europa "Flower"

10m. Brown flaw covering face of right-hand runner gives the appearance of a mask (R. 9/2).

As these stamps were printed in sheets of 400, divided into four post office sheets of 100, the variety was only constant on one sheet in four. Moreover, it was quickly discovered and many were removed from the sheets by post office clerks.

1964 (6 July). *Olympic Games, Tokyo. T* **86** *and similar designs.* W **58** (sideways, 25m., 75m.). P 13½×14 (10m.) or 14×13½ (others).

246	10m. brown, black and yellow	10	10
	a. Blind runner	£375	
247	25m. brown, blue and blue-grey	20	10
248	75m. brown, black and orange-red	35	65
246/8	*Set of* 3	60	75
MS248*a*	110×90 mm. Nos. 246/8 (*sold at 250m.*). Imperf.	6·00	15·00

Designs: *Horiz*—25m. Boxing; 75m. Charioteers.

(Des G. Bétemps)

1964 (14 Sept). *Europa.* W **58**. P 13½×14.

249	**89**	20m. chestnut and light ochre	1·50	10
250		30m. ultramarine and light blue	1·50	10
251		150m. olive and light blue-green	18·00	5·50
249/51		*Set of* 3	19·00	5·50

90 Dionysus and Acme

91 Silenus (satyr)

1964 (26 Oct). *Cyprus Wines. T* **90/1** *and similar multicoloured designs.* W **58** (sideways, 10m. or 100m.). P 14×13½ (horiz) or 13½×14 (vert).

252	10m. Type **90**	30	10
253	40m. Type **91**	65	1·25
254	50m. Commandaria Wine (*vert*)	65	10
255	100m. Wine factory (*horiz*)	1·50	2·00
252/5	*Set of* 4	2·75	3·00

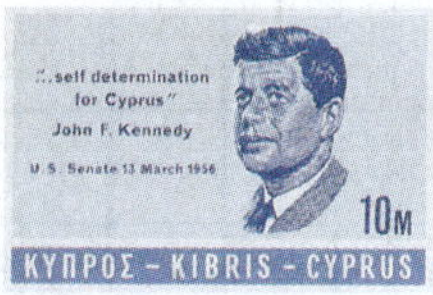

94 President Kennedy

1965 (16 Feb). *President Kennedy Commemoration.* W **58** (sideways). P 14×13½.

256	**94**	10m. ultramarine	10	10
257		40m. green	25	35
258		100m. carmine-lake	30	35
256/8		*Set of* 3	60	70
MS258*a*		110×90 mm. Nos. 256/8 (*sold at 250m.*). Imperf.	3·25	8·00

95 "Old Age"

96 "Maternity"

1965 (12 Apr). *Introduction of Social Insurance Law. T* **95/6** *and similar design.* W **58**. P 13½×12 (75m.) or 13½×14 (others).

259	30m. drab and dull green	15	10
260	45m. light grey-green, blue and deep ultramarine	20	10
261	75m. red-brown and flesh	1·25	2·50
259/61	*Set of* 3	1·40	2·50

Design: *Vert as T* **95**—45m. "Accident".

98 I.T.U. Emblem and Symbols

1965 (17 May). *I.T.U. Centenary.* W **58** (sideways). P 14×13½.

262	**98**	15m. black, brown and yellow	75	20
263		60m. black, green and light green	7·50	3·25
264		75m. black, indigo and light blue	8·50	4·75
262/4		*Set of* 3	15·00	7·25

99 I.C.Y. Emblem

1965 (17 May). *International Co-operation Year.* W **58** (sideways). P 14×13½.

265	**99**	50m. brown, deep green and light yellow-brown	75	10
266		100m. purple, deep green and light purple	1·25	50

100 Europa "Sprig"

U. N.
Resolution
on Cyprus
18 Dec. 1965

(101)

(Des H. Karlsson)

1965 (27 Sept). *Europa.* W **58** (sideways). P 14×13½.

267	**100**	5m. black, orange-brown and orange	50	10
268		45m. black, orange-brown and light emerald	7·00	1·50
269		150m. black, orange-brown and light grey	13·00	3·75
267/9		*Set of* 3	18·00	4·75

1966 (31 Jan). *U.N. General Assembly's Cyprus Resolution, 18 December 1965. Nos. 211, 213, 216 and 221 optd with T* **101** *in blue by Govt Printing Office, Nicosia.*

270	3m. deep brown and orange-brown	10	50
271	10m. black and yellow-green	10	10
272	30m. deep blue and light blue	15	15
273	250m. black and cinnamon	80	2·25
270/3	*Set of* 4	1·00	2·75

102 Discovery of St. Barnabas's Body

104 St. Barnabas (icon)

103 St. Barnabas's Chapel

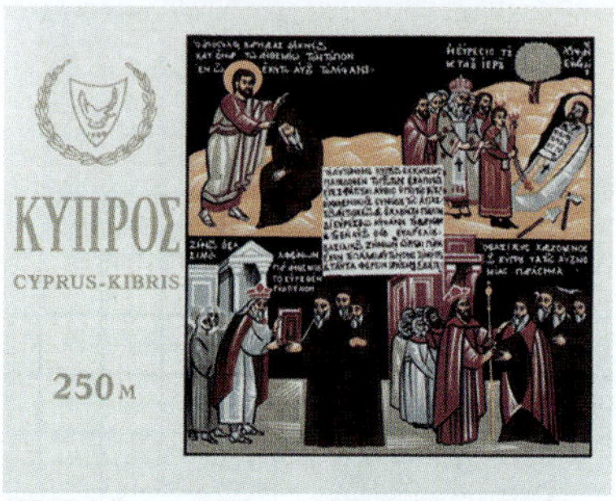

105 "Privileges of Cyprus Church" (*Actual size* 102×82 *mm*)

1966 (25 Apr). *1900th Death Anniv of St. Barnabas.* W **58** (sideways on 15m., 100m., 250m). P 14×13 (25m) or 13×14 (others).

274	**102**	15m. multicoloured	10	10
275	**103**	25m. drab, black and blue	15	10
276	**104**	100m. multicoloured	45	2·00
274/6		*Set of* 3	60	2·00
MS277		110×91 mm. **105** 250m. mult. Imperf.	3·50	13·00

5 M

Ξ

(106)

107 General K. S. Thimayya and U.N. Emblem

1966 (30 May). *No. 211 surch with T* **106** *by Govt Printing Office, Nicosia.*

278	5m. on 3m. deep brown and orange-brown	10	10

1966 (6 June). *General Thimayya Commemoration.* W **58** (sideways). P 14×13.

279	**107**	50m. black and light orange-brown	30	10

108 Europa "Ship"

(Des G. and J. Bender)

1966 (26 Sept). *Europa.* W **58**. P 13½×14.

280	**108**	20m. green and blue	40	10
281		30m. bright purple and blue	40	10
282		150m. bistre and blue	3·25	3·00
280/2		*Set of* 3	3·50	3·00

110 Church of St. James, Trikomo

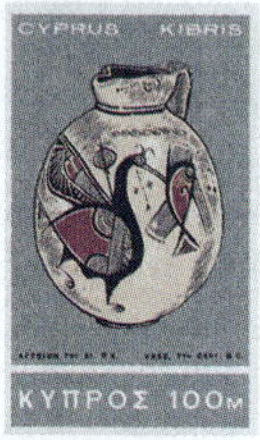

119 Vase of 7th Century B.C.

120 Bronze Ingot-stand

1966 (21 Nov)–**69**. *T* **110**, **119/20** *and similar designs.* W **58** (sideways on 3, 15, 25, 50, 250, 500m., £1. P 12×13 (3m.), 13×12 (5, 10m.), 14×13½ (15, 25, 50m.), 13½×14 (20, 30, 35, 40, 100m.) or 13×14 (others).

283	3m. grey-green, buff, black and light blue	40	10
284	5m. bistre, black and steel-blue	10	10
	a. Brownish bistre, black and steel-blue (18.4.69)	75	20
285	10m. black and bistre	15	10
286	15m. black, chestnut and light orange-brown	15	10
287	20m. black, slate and brown	1·25	1·00
288	25m. black, drab and lake-brown	30	10
289	30m. black, yellow-ochre and turquoise	50	20
290	35m. yellow, black and carmine-red	50	30
291	40m. black, grey and new blue	70	30
	a. Grey (background) omitted		

292	50m. black, slate and brown	90	10
293	100m. black, red, pale buff and grey	4·00	15
294	250m. olive-green, black and light yellow-ochre	1·00	40
295	500m. multicoloured	2·75	70
296	£1 black, drab and slate	2·25	6·50
283/96	*Set of* 14	13·00	8·50

Designs: *Horiz* (*as T* **110**)—3m. Stavrovouni Monastery. (*As T* **119**)—15m. Minoan wine ship of 700 B.C. (painting); 25m. Sleeping Eros (marble statue); 50m. Silver coin of Alexander the Great. *Vert* (*as T* **110**)—10m. Zeno of Cibium (marble bust). (*As T* **119**)—20m. Silver coin of Evagoras I; 30m. St. Nicholas Cathedral, Famagusta; 35m. Gold sceptre from Curium; 40m. Silver dish from 7th century. (*As T* **120**)—500m. "The Rape of Ganymede" (mosaic); £1 Aphrodite (marble statue).

123 Power Station, Limassol

124 Cogwheels

1967 (10 Apr). *First Development Programme. T* **123** *and similar designs but horiz. Multicoloured.* W **58** (sideways on 15 to 100m.). P 13½×14 (10m.) or 14×13½ (others).

297	10m. Type **123**	10	10
298	15m. Arghaka-Maghounda Dam	15	10
299	35m. Troodos Highway	20	10
300	50m. Hilton Hotel, Nicosia	20	10
301	100m. Famagusta Harbour	20	1·10
297/301	*Set of* 5	75	1·25

(Des O. Bonnevalle)

1967 (2 May). *Europa.* W **58**. P 13½×14.

302	**124**	20m. olive-green, green and pale yellow-green	30	10
303		30m. reddish violet, lilac and pale lilac	30	10
304		150m. brown, light reddish brown and pale yellow-brown	2·25	2·25
302/4		*Set of* 3	2·50	2·25

125 Throwing the Javelin

126 Running (amphora) and Map of Eastern Mediterranean (*Actual size* 97×77 *mm*)

1967 (4 Sept). *Athletic Games, Nicosia. T* **125** *and similar designs and T* **126**. *Multicoloured.* W **58**. P 13½×13.

305	15m. Type **125**	20	10
306	35m. Running	20	35
307	100m. High jumping	30	1·00
305/7	*Set of* 3	60	1·25
MS308	110×90 mm. 250m. Type **126** (wmk sideways). Imperf	1·25	6·50

127 Ancient Monuments

128 St. Andrew Mosaic

1967 (16 Oct). *International Tourist Year. T* **127** *and similar horiz designs. Multicoloured.* W **58**. P 13×13½.

309	10m. Type **127**	10	10
310	40m. Famagusta Beach	15	90
311	50m. Hawker Siddeley Comet 4 at Nicosia Airport	15	10
312	100m. Skier and youth hostel	20	95
309/12	*Set of* 4	55	1·75

1967 (8 Nov). *Centenary of St. Andrew's Monastery.* W **58** (sideways). P 13×13½.

313	**128**	25m. multicoloured	10	10

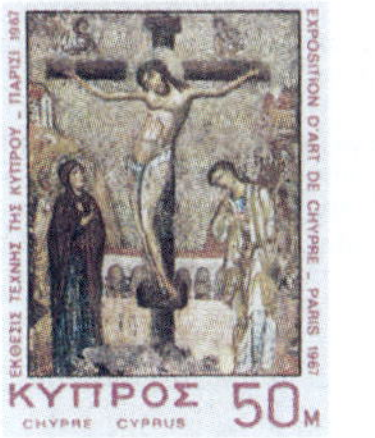

129 "The Crucifixion" (icon)

130 The Three Magi

(Photo French Govt Ptg Wks, Paris)

1967 (8 Nov). *Cyprus Art Exhibition, Paris.* P 12½×13½.

314	**129**	50m. multicoloured	10	10

1967 (8 Nov). *20th Anniv of U.N.E.S.C.O.* W **58** (sideways). P 13×13½.

315	**130**	75m. multicoloured	20	20

131 Human Rights Emblem over Stars

132 Human Rights and U.N. Emblems

133 Scroll of Declaration (*Actual size* 95×75½ *mm*)

1968 (18 Mar). *Human Rights Year.* W **58**. P 13×14.

316	**131**	50m. multicoloured	10	10
317	**132**	90m. multicoloured	30	70
MS318		95×75½ mm. **133** 250m. multicoloured. W **58** (sideways). Imperf	60	4·75

134 Europa "Key"

(Des H. Schwarzenbach)

1968 (29 Apr). *Europa.* W **58** (sideways). P 14×13.

319	**134**	20m. multicoloured	25	10
320		30m. multicoloured	25	10
321		150m. multicoloured	1·00	2·25
319/21		*Set of* 3	1·40	2·25

135 U.N. Children's Fund Symbol and Boy drinking Milk

136 Aesculapius

1968 (2 Sept). *21st Anniv of U.N.I.C.E.F.* W **58** (sideways). P 14×13.

322	**135**	35m. yellow-brown, carmine-red and black	10	10

1968 (2 Sept). *20th Anniv of W.H.O.* W **58**. P 13×14.

323	**136**	50m. black, green and light olive	10	10

137 Throwing the Discus

138 I.L.O. Emblem

1968 (24 Oct). *Olympic Games, Mexico. T* **137** *and similar designs. Multicoloured.* W **58** (sideways on 100m.). P 14×13 (100m.) or 13×14 (others).

324	10m. Type **137**	10	10
325	25m. Sprint finish	10	10
326	100m. Olympic Stadium (*horiz*)	20	1·25
324/6	*Set of* 3	35	1·25

1969 (3 Mar). *50th Anniv of International Labour Organization.* W **58**. P 12×13½.

327	**138**	50m. yellow-brown, blue and light blue	15	10
328		90m. yellow-brown, black and pale grey	15	55

139 Mercator's Map of Cyprus, 1554

140 Blaeu's Map of Cyprus, 1635

1969 (7 Apr). *First International Congress of Cypriot Studies.* W **58** (sideways). P 14×14½.

329	**139**	35m. multicoloured	20	30
330	**140**	50m. multicoloured	20	10
		a. Wmk upright	—	2·75
		ab. Grey (shading on boats and cartouche) omitted	£275	

141 Europa Emblem

142 European Roller

(Des L. Gasbarra and G. Belli)

1969 (28 Apr). *Europa.* W **58** (sideways). P 14×13½.

331	**141**	20m. multicoloured	30	10
332		30m. multicoloured	30	10
333		150m. multicoloured	1·00	2·00
331/3		*Set of* 3	1·40	2·00

1969 (7 July). *Birds of Cyprus. T* **142** *and similar designs. Multicoloured.* W **58** (sideways on horiz designs). P 13½×12 (horiz designs) or 12×13½ (vert designs).

334	5m. Type **142**	40	15
335	15m. Audouin's Gull	60	15
336	20m. Cyprus Warbler	60	15
337	30m. Jay (*vert*)	60	15
338	40m. Hoopoe (*vert*)	65	30
339	90m. Eleanora's Falcon (*vert*)	1·50	5·00
334/9	*Set of* 6	4·00	5·50

The above were printed on glazed Samuel Jones paper with very faint watermark.

143 "The Nativity" (12th-century Wall Painting)

145 "Virgin and Child between Archangels Michael and Gabriel" (6th–7th-century Mosaic) (*Actual size* 102×81 *mm*)

1969 (24 Nov). *Christmas. T* **143** *and similar horiz design, and T* **145**. *Multicoloured.* W **58** (sideways). P 13½×13.

340	20m. Type **143**	15	10
341	45m. "The Nativity" (14th-century wall painting)	15	20
MS342	110×90 mm. 250m. Type **145**. Imperf	3·00	12·00
	a. Grey and light brown omitted	£2250	

146 Mahatma Gandhi

1970 (26 Jan). *Birth Centenary of Mahatma Gandhi.* W **58** (sideways). P 14×13½.

343	**146**	25m. ultramarine, drab and black ...	50	10
344		75m. yellow-brown, drab and black	75	65

147 "Flaming Sun"

148 Gladioli

(Des L. le Brocquy)

1970 (4 May). *Europa.* W **58** (sideways). P 14×13.

345	**147**	20m. brown, greenish yellow and orange	30	10
346		30m. new blue, greenish yellow and orange	30	10
347		150m. bright purple, greenish yellow and orange	1·00	2·50
345/7 *Set of 3*			1·40	2·50

1970 (3 Aug). *European Conservation Year. T* **148** *and similar vert designs. Multicoloured.* W **58**. P 13×13½.

348	10m. Type **148**	10	10
349	50m. Poppies	15	10
350	90m. Giant fennel	50	1·40
348/50 *Set of 3*		65	1·40

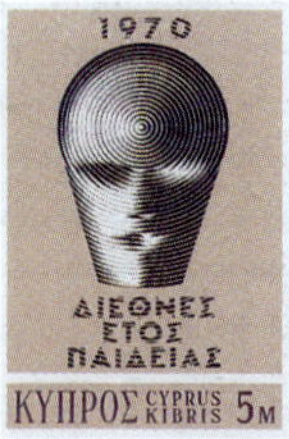

149 I.E.Y. Emblem

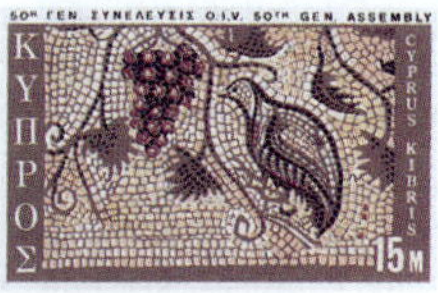

150 Mosaic

151 Globe, Dove and U.N. Emblem

(Des G. Simonis (75m.))

1970 (7 Sept). *Anniversaries and Events.* W **58** (sideways on horiz designs). P 13×14 (5m.) or 14×13 (others).

351	**149**	5m. black, red-brown and light yellow-brown	10	10
352	**150**	15m. multicoloured	10	10
353	**151**	75m. multicoloured	15	75
351/3 *Set of 3*			30	85

Events:—5m. International Education Year; 15m. 50th General Assembly of International Vine and Wine Office; 75m. 25th anniv of United Nations.

152 Virgin and Child

(Photo Harrison)

1970 (23 Nov). *Christmas. Wall-painting from Church of Panayia Podhythou, Galata. T* **152** *and similar multicoloured designs.* P 14×14½.

354	25m. Archangel (facing right)	15	20
	a. Horiz strip of 3. Nos. 354/6	40	55
355	25m. Type **152**	15	20
356	25m. Archangel (facing left)	15	20
357	75m. Virgin and Child between Archangels	15	30
354/7 *Set of 4*		55	80

The 75m. is horiz, size 42×30 mm, and the 25m. values are vert, size as T **152**.

Nos. 354/6 were issued in *se-tenant* strips of three, throughout the sheet. The triptych thus formed is depicted in its entirety on the 75m. value.

STAMP BOOKLETS

Booklet vending machines, originally fitted to provide stamps to the value of 50m., were introduced by the Cyprus Post Office in 1962.

The stamps contained in these booklets were a haphazard selection of low values to the required amount, attached by their sheet margins to the cardboard covers. From 1968 these covers carried commercial advertising and details of postage rates.

Dominica

CROWN COLONY

A British packet agency was operating on Dominica from about 1778, the date of the earliest known use of a postal marking. This was replaced by a branch office of the British G.P.O. which opened at Roseau on 8 May 1858. The stamps of Great Britain were used from that date until 1 May 1860, after which the colonial authorities assumed responsibility for the postal service. Until the introduction of Nos. 1/3 in 1874 No. CC1 and later handstamps were utilised.

For illustrations of handstamp and postmark types see BRITISH POST OFFICES ABROAD notes, following GREAT BRITAIN.

ROSEAU

CROWNED/CIRCLE HANDSTAMPS

CC1 CC **1** DOMINICA (Black or R.) (17.5.1845)
Price on cover £550

No. CC1 is also known struck in black on various adhesive stamps as late as 1883.

Stamps of GREAT BRITAIN *cancelled* "A 07" *as Type* **2**.

1858–60.

Z1	1d. rose-red (1857), *perf* 14	£300
Z2	2d. blue (1858) (Plate No. 7)	£800
Z3	4d. rose (1857)	£325
Z4	6d. lilac (1856)	£300
Z5	1s. green	£1600

PRICES FOR STAMPS ON COVER TO 1945

Nos. 1/3	*from* × 25
No. 4	*from* × 40
No. 5	*from* × 100
No. 6	*from* × 40
Nos. 7/8	*from* × 100
No. 9	*from* × 40
Nos. 10/12	*from* × 15
Nos. 13/15	*from* × 100
No. 17	*from* × 50
Nos. 18/a	—
No. 19	*from* × 40
Nos. 20/5	*from* × 30
No. 26	—
Nos. 27/90	*from* × 5
No. 91	—
Nos. 92/8	*from* × 10
Nos. 99/109	*from* × 3
Nos. R1/3	*from* × 15
No. R4	*from* × 50
No. R6	*from* × 3

1

½ (2) 1/2 (3) HALF PENNY (4)

(Typo D.L.R.)

1874 (4 May). Wmk Crown CC. P 12½.

1	1	1d. lilac	£150	50·00
		a. Bisected vert (½d.) (on cover)	†	£8000
2		6d. green	£550	£100
3		1s. dull magenta	£325	70·00

NCE Normal NCE Malformed "CE" (R. 10/6)

1877–79. Wmk Crown CC. P 14.

4	1	½d. olive-yellow (1879)	15·00	55·00
5		1d. lilac	8·00	2·25
		a. Bisected vert or diag (½d.) (on cover or card)	†	£2500
		w. Wmk inverted	90·00	
6		2½d. red-brown (1879)	£225	29·00
		w. Wmk inverted	†	£150
7		4d. blue (1879)	£110	3·00
		a. Malformed "CE" in "PENCE"	£1500	£130
8		6d. green	£150	20·00
9		1s. magenta	£120	50·00

1882 (25 Nov)–**83**. *No. 5 bisected vertically and surch.*

10	2	½(d.), in *black*, on half 1d.	£200	48·00
		a. Surch inverted	£1100	£800
		b. Surcharges *tête-bêche* (pair)	£2250	
11	3	½(d.), in *red*, on half 1d. (12.82)	30·00	19·00
		a. Surch inverted	£1100	£475
		c. Surch double	£1600	£650
12	4	½d. in *black*, on half 1d. (3.83)	65·00	26·00
		b. Surch double	£800	

Type **4** is found reading up or down.

1883–86. Wmk Crown CA. P 14.

13	1	½d. olive-yellow	4·25	10·00
14		1d. lilac (1886)	38·00	14·00
		a. Bisected (½d.) (on cover)	†	£2250
15		2½d. red-brown (1884)	£140	2·25
		w. Wmk inverted	£425	

Half Penny (5) One Penny (6)

1886 (1 Mar). *Nos. 8 and 9 surch locally.*

17	5	½d. on 6d. green	6·00	5·00
18	6	1d. on 6d. green	£24000	£10000
		a. Thick bar (approx 1 mm)	†	£18000
19		1d. on 1s. magenta	16·00	19·00
		a. Surch double	£10000	£4000

It is believed that only two sheets of the 1d. on 6d. were surcharged. On one of these sheets the six stamps in the top row showed the thick bar variety, No. 18a.

1886–90. Wmk Crown CA. P 14.

20	1	½d. dull green	2·25	5·50
22		1d. rose (1887)	17·00	19·00
		a. Deep carmine (1889)	3·25	8·00
		b. Bisected (½d.) (on cover)	†	£1900
		w. Wmk inverted	£160	
23		2½d. ultramarine (1888)	3·75	5·50
24		4d. grey	4·50	7·00
		a. Malformed "CE" in "PENCE"	£160	£250
25		6d. orange (1888)	13·00	60·00
26		1s. dull magenta (1890)	£160	£325
20/6 *Set of* 6			£170	£375
20s/5s Optd "Specimen" *Set of* 5			£225	

The stamps of Dominica were superseded by the general issue for Leeward Islands on 31 October 1890, but the sets following were in concurrent use with the stamps inscribed "LEEWARD ISLANDS" until 31 December 1939, when the island came under the administration of the Windward Islands.

9 "Roseau from the Sea" (Lt. Caddy)

10

(T **9** to **11** typo D.L.R.)

1903 (1 Sept)–**07**. Wmk Crown CC (sideways* on T **9**). *Ordinary paper.* P 14.

27	9	½d. green and grey-green	4·00	2·50
		a. Chalk-surfaced paper (1906)	15·00	18·00
28		1d. grey and red	8·00	75
		a. Chalk-surfaced paper (1906)	30·00	6·00
29		2d. green and brown	2·50	4·50
		a. Chalk-surfaced paper (1906)	28·00	38·00
30		2½d. grey and bright blue	5·50	4·00
		a. Chalk-surfaced paper (3.9.07)	23·00	50·00
31		3d. dull purple and grey-black	8·00	3·25
		a. Chalk-surfaced paper (1906)	40·00	30·00
32		6d. grey and chestnut	7·00	18·00
33		1s. magenta and grey-green	27·00	42·00
		a. Chalk-surfaced paper (1906)	75·00	£150
34		2s. grey-black and purple	26·00	29·00
35		2s.6d. grey-green and maize	18·00	75·00
36	10	5s. black and brown	95·00	£150
27/36 *Set of* 10			£180	£275
27s/36s Optd "Specimen" *Set of* 10			£150	

*The normal sideways watermark shows Crown to right of CC, *as seen from the back of the stamp.* No. 34 exists overprinted "SPECIMEN" with watermark showing Crown to left of CC (*Price*, £100).

1907–08. Wmk Mult Crown CA (sideways* on T **9**). *Chalk-surfaced paper.* P 14.

37	9	½d. green	5·00	3·25
38		1d. grey and red	2·00	40
39		2d. green and brown	6·50	16·00
40		2½d. grey and bright blue	4·50	21·00
41		3d. dull purple and grey-black	4·00	14·00
42		6d. black and chestnut	50·00	85·00
43		1s. magenta and grey-green (1908)	3·75	55·00
44		2s. grey-black and purple (1908)	22·00	32·00
45		2s.6d. grey-green and maize (1908)	22·00	65·00
46	10	5s. black and brown (1908)	60·00	60·00
37/46 *Set of* 10			£160	£300

*The normal sideways watermark shows Crown to right of CA, *as seen from the back of the stamp.*

Examples of Nos. 27/36 and 37/46 are known showing a forged Gen. Post Office Dominica postmark dated "JU 1 11".

11

WAR TAX ONE HALFPENNY (12)

1908–21. Wmk Mult Crown CA (sideways* on T **9**). *Chalk-surfaced paper (3d., 6d., 1s.).* P 14.

47	9	½d. blue-green	5·00	4·50
		aw. Wmk Crown to left of CA	2·50	3·25
		ay. Wmk sideways inverted and reversed		
		b. Dp green (wmk Crown to left of CA)	3·50	2·25
48		1d. carmine-red	3·00	30
		aw. Wmk Crown to left of CA	3·75	40
		b. Scarlet (1916)	1·50	40
		bw. Wmk Crown to left of CA	1·25	50
49		2d. grey (1909)	4·00	12·00
		aw. Wmk Crown to left of CA	4·00	16·00
		b. Slate (wmk Crown to left of CA) (1918)	3·50	12·00
50		2½d. blue	8·50	6·00
		aw. Wmk Crown to left of CA	—	9·00
		b. Bright blue (1918)	5·00	9·00
		bw. Wmk Crown to left of CA	6·00	13·00
51		3d. purple/*yellow* (1909)	3·00	4·25
		a. Ordinary paper (wmk Crown to left of CA) (1912)	3·00	4·50
		ab. *On pale yellow* (1920)	8·50	17·00
52		6d. dull and bright purple (1909)	10·00	13·00
		a. Ordinary paper. *Dull purple* (wmk Crown to left of CA) (1915)	3·50	18·00
53		1s. black/*green* (1910)	3·00	2·75
		a. Ordinary paper (wmk Crown to left of CA) (1912)	3·00	4·00
		as. Optd "Specimen" in red	65·00	
53*b*		2s. purple and deep blue/*blue* (wmk Crown to left of CA) (1919)	25·00	85·00
53*c*		2s.6d. black and red/*blue* (wmk Crown to left of CA) (1921)	25·00	90·00
54	11	5s. red and green/*yellow* (1914)	55·00	85·00
47/54 *Set of* 10			£110	£275
48s/54s Optd "Specimen" (1s. optd in blk)*Set of* 9			£180	

The watermark orientation differs according to the printings. Unless otherwise stated the watermark shows the Crown to right of CA *as seen from the back of the stamp.*

1916 (Sept). *No. 47b surch with T* **12** *by De La Rue.*

55	9	½d. on ½d. deep green (R.)	2·00	75
		a. Small "O" in "ONE"	6·50	7·50

No. 55a occurs on ten stamps within each sheet of 60.

1918 (18 Mar). *No. 47b optd with T* **12** *locally, from D.L.R. plate, but with* "ONE HALF-PENNY" *blanked out.*

56	9	½d. deep green (Blk.)	4·00	6·00
		w. Wmk Crown to right of CA		

The blanking out of the surcharge was not completely successful so that it almost always appears as an albino to a greater or lesser extent.

WAR TAX (14)

1918 (1 June)–**19**. *Nos. 47b and 51a optd with T* **14** *by De La Rue.*

57	9	½d. deep green	15	50
		w. Wmk Crown to right of CA	50·00	
		x. Wmk reversed		
58		3d. purple/*yellow* (R.) (1919)	3·00	4·00

WAR TAX =1½D.= (15) 1½D. Short Fraction Bar (R. 6/4)

1919. *As No. 50aw, but colour changed, surch with T* **15** *by De La Rue.*

59	9	1½d. on 2½d. orange (R.)	15	55
		a. Short fraction bar	8·00	35·00
		b. "C" and "A" missing from wmk	£500	

No. 59b shows the "C" omitted from one impression with the "A" missing from the next one to the left (as seen from the back of the stamp). The "C" is badly distorted in the second watermark.

1920 (1 June). *As No. 59, but without* "WAR TAX".

60	9	1½d. on 2½d. orange (Blk.)	4·50	4·50
		a. Short fraction bar	55·00	70·00
		b. "A" of "CA" missing from wmk		
55s/60s Optd "Specimen" *Set of* 6			£170	

1921–22. Wmk Mult Script CA (sideways*). *Chalk-surfaced paper (6d.).* P 14.

62	9	½d. blue-green	2·50	16·00
63		1d. carmine-red	2·00	3·75
		w. Wmk Crown to right of CA	—	16·00
64		1½d. orange	3·00	12·00
65		2d. grey	2·75	3·25
66		2½d. bright blue	2·00	9·00
67		6d. purple	2·50	38·00
69		2s. purple and blue/*blue* (1922)	35·00	90·00
70		2s.6d. black and red/*blue*	32·00	£100
62/70 *Set of* 8			70·00	£225
62s/70s Optd "Specimen" *Set of* 8			£140	

*The normal sideways watermark shows Crown to left of CA, *as seen from the back of the stamp.*

The 1½d. has figures of value in the lower corner and no ornamentation below words of value.

Examples of some values are known showing a forged G.P.O. Dominica postmark dated "MY 19 27".

16

(Typo D.L.R.)

1923 (1 Mar)–**33**. *Chalk-surfaced paper.* P 14.

(*a*) Wmk Mult Script CA (sideways*).

71	16	½d. black and green	1·75	60
72		1d. black and bright violet	3·75	1·75
73		1d. black and scarlet (1933)	13·00	1·00
74		1½d. black and scarlet	4·75	65
75		1½d. black and red-brown (1933)	13·00	70
76		2d. black and grey	2·75	50
77		2½d. black and orange-yellow	2·75	9·00

78 2½d. black and ultramarine (1927). 7·00 2·00
79 3d. black and ultramarine 2·75 12·00
80 3d. black and red/*yellow* (1927) 3·00 1·00
81 4d. black and brown 3·50 5·50
82 6d. black and bright magenta 3·50 7·00
83 1s. black/*emerald* 2·50 2·75
84 2s. black and blue/*blue* 10·00 23·00
85 2s.6d. black and red/*blue* 18·00 23·00
86 3s. black and purple/*yellow* (1927) 3·25 12·00
87 4s. black and red/*emerald* 15·00 26·00
88 5s. black and green/*yellow* (1927) 22·00 48·00
(b) Wmk Mult Crown CA (sideways*).
89 **16** 3s. black and purple/*yellow* 4·00 65·00
90 5s. black and green/*yellow* 9·00 50·00
91 £1 black and purple/*red* £225 £350
71/91 *Set of* 21 £325 £550
71s/91s Optd or Perf (Nos. 73s, 75s) "Specimen" *Set of* 21 £375

*The normal sideways watermark shows Crown to left of CA, *as seen from the back of the stamp.*

Examples of most values are known showing a forged G.P.O. Dominica postmark dated "MY 19 27".

1935 (6 May). *Silver Jubilee. As Nos. 91/4 of Antigua.*
92 1d. deep blue and carmine 1·00 30
f. Diagonal line by turret 50·00
h. Dot by flagstaff 80·00 60·00
93 1½d. ultramarine and grey 3·50 2·25
f. Diagonal line by turret 75·00
h. Dot by flagstaff 95·00
94 2½d. brown and deep blue 3·50 3·50
95 1s. slate and purple 3·50 7·00
h. Dot by flagstaff £160 £250
i. Dash by turret £180
92/5 *Set of* 4 10·50 11·50
92s/5s Perf "Specimen" *Set of* 4 £110

For illustrations of plate varieties see Omnibus section following Zanzibar.

1937 (12 May). *Coronation. As Nos. 95/7 of Antigua.* P 11×11½.
96 1d. carmine 40 10
97 1½d. yellow-brown 40 10
98 2½d. blue 60 1·75
96/8 *Set of* 3 1·25 1·75
96s/8s Perf "Specimen" *Set of* 3 85·00

17 Fresh Water Lake

18 Layou River

19 Picking limes

20 Boiling Lake

(Recess Waterlow)

1938 (15 Aug)–**47**. *T* **17/20**. Wmk Mult Script CA. P 12½.
99 **17** ½d. brown and green 10 15
100 **18** 1d. grey and scarlet 25 25
101 **19** 1½d. green and purple 45 70
102 **20** 2d. carmine and grey-black 50 2·00
103 **19** 2½d. purple and bright blue 4·00 1·75
a. purple & bright ultramarine (8.42) 20 1·75
104 **18** 3d. olive-green and brown 30 50
104*a* **19** 3½d. ultramarine and purple (15.10.47) 2·25 2·00
105 **17** 6d. emerald-green and violet 1·75 1·50
105*a* 7d. green and yellow-brown (15.10.47) 2·25 1·50
106 **20** 1s. violet and olive-green 4·25 1·50
106*a* **18** 2s. slate and purple (15.10.47) 8·00 9·00
107 **17** 2s.6d. black and vermilion 14·00 5·00
108 **18** 5s. light blue and sepia 9·50 8·50
108*a* **20** 10s. black and brown-orange (15.10.47) 16·00 17·00
99/108*a Set of* 14 55·00 45·00

21 King George VI

(Photo Harrison)

1940 (15 Apr)–**42**. Wmk Mult Script CA. *Chalk-surfaced paper.* P 15×14.
109 **21** ¼d. chocolate 1·00 20
a. Ordinary paper (1942) 10 35
99s/109s Perf "Specimen" *Set of* 15 £250

1946 (14 Oct). *Victory. As Nos. 110/11 of Antigua.*
110 1d. carmine 20 10
111 3½d. blue 20 10
110s/11s Perf "Specimen" *Set of* 2 75·00

1948 (1 Dec). *Royal Silver Wedding. As Nos. 112/13 of Antigua.*
112 1d. scarlet 15 10
113 10s. red-brown 18·00 24·00

(New Currency. 100 cents = 1 B.W.I., later East Caribbean dollar)

1949 (10 Oct). *75th Anniv of Universal Postal Union. As Nos. 114/17 of Antigua.*
114 5c. blue 20 15
115 6c. brown 1·25 2·75
116 12c. purple 45 1·75
a. "A" of "CA" missing from wmk — £550
117 24c. olive 30 30
114/17 *Set of* 4 2·00 4·50

1951 (16 Feb). *Inauguration of B.W.I. University College. As Nos. 118/19 of Antigua.*
118 3c. yellow-green and reddish violet 50 1·25
119 12c. deep green and carmine 75 40

22 King George VI

23 Drying Cocoa

24 Making Carib baskets

25 Lime plantation

26 Picking oranges

27 Bananas

28 Botanical Gardens

29 Drying vanilla beans

30 Fresh Water Lake

31 Layou River

32 Boiling Lake

33 Picking oranges

(Photo Harrison (½c.). Recess B.W. (others))

1951 (1 July). *T* **22/33**. Wmk Mult Script CA. *Chalk-surfaced paper (½c.).* P 15×14 (½c.), 13½×13 ($2.40), 13×13½ (others).
120 **22** ½c. chocolate 10 30
121 **23** 1c. black and vermilion 10 30
b. "A" of "CA" missing from wmk £500
c. "JA" for "CA" in wmk £500
122 **24** 2c. red-brown and deep green 10 40
a. "C" of "CA" missing from wmk £600
b. "A" of "CA" missing from wmk £600
c. "JA" for "CA" in wmk — £600
123 **25** 3c. green and reddish violet 25 2·75
a. "C" of "CA" missing from wmk £500
c. "JA" for "CA" in wmk £500
124 **26** 4c. brown-orange and sepia 70 3·00
a. "C" of "CA" missing from wmk £600
b. "A" of "CA" missing from wmk £600
125 **27** 5c. black and carmine 85 30
a. "C" of "CA" missing from wmk £800
b. "A" of "CA" missing from wmk £800
c. "JA" for "CA" in wmk
126 **28** 6c. olive and chestnut 1·00 30
a. "C" of "CA" missing from wmk £600
b. "A" of "CA" missing from wmk £1000
127 **29** 8c. blue-green and blue 2·00 85
b. "A" of "CA" missing from wmk
128 **30** 12c. black and bright green 70 1·25
a. "C" of "CA" missing from wmk £1200
129 **31** 14c. blue and violet 1·25 2·75
a. "C" of "CA" missing from wmk £1200
b. "A" of "CA" missing from wmk † £750
c. "JA" for "CA" in wmk £1000
130 **32** 24c. reddish violet and rose-carmine 75 30
a. "C" of "CA" missing from wmk £1200 £1000
131 **25** 48c. bright green and red-orange 3·75 10·00
a. "C" of "CA" missing from wmk £1200
b. "A" of "CA" missing from wmk £1200
c. "JA" for "CA" in wmk
132 **24** 60c. carmine and black 3·75 7·50
c. "JA" for "CA" in wmk £800
133 **30** $1.20 emerald and black 5·00 6·50
a. "C" of "CA" missing from wmk £1400
b. "A" of "CA" missing from wmk £1400
134 **33** $2.40 orange and black 24·00 45·00
120/34 *Set of* 15 38·00 70·00

Examples of Nos. 121, 122, 124, 125, 126, 129, 131 and 133 show traces of the *left leg* of the "A", *the listed variety shows no trace of the letter.*

Nos. 121c, 122c, 123c, 125c, 129c, 131c and 132c may represent an attempt to repair the missing "C" variety.

NEW CONSTITUTION 1951

(34)

1951 (15 Oct). *New Constitution. Nos. 123, 125, 127 and 129 optd with T* **34** *by B.W.*
135 3c. green and reddish violet 15 70
a. "C" of "CA" missing from wmk £600 £650
136 5c. black and carmine 15 1·25
a. "JA" for "CA" in wmk £700
137 8c. blue-green and blue (R.) 15 15
a. "JA" for "CA" in wmk
138 14c. blue and violet (R.) 1·00 20
b. "A" of "CA" missing from wmk £900
135/8 *Set of* 4 1·25 2·10

1953 (2 June). *Coronation. As No. 120 of Antigua.*
139 2c. black and deep green 20 10

35 Queen Elizabeth II

36 Mat Making

37 Canoe Making

38 Cutting bananas

(Photo Harrison (½c.). Recess B.W. (others))

1954 (1 Oct)–**62**. *Designs previously used for King George VI issue, but with portrait of Queen Elizabeth II as in T* **35/8**. Wmk Mult Script CA. P 15×14 (½c.), 13½×13 ($2.40), 13×13½ (others).
140 **35** ½c. brown 10 50
141 **23** 1c. black and vermilion 30 20
142 **24** 2c. chocolate and myrtle-green 75 2·50
a. Chocolate and grey-green (13.3.62) 8·50 8·50
143 **25** 3c. green and purple 1·50 40
144 **36** 3c. black and carmine (15.10.57) 3·25 2·25
145 **37** 4c. brown-orange and sepia 30 10
146 **27** 5c. black and carmine-red 3·00 60
147 **37** 5c. light blue & sepia-brown (15.10.57) 10·00 1·00
a. Blue and sepia (13.3.62) 23·00 8·00
148 **28** 6c. bronze-green and red-brown 40 10
149 **29** 8c. deep green and deep blue 1·00 10
150 **38** 10c. green and brown (15.10.57) 5·00 3·25
a. Green and deep brown (17.7.62) 10·00 3·75
151 **30** 12c. black and emerald 50 10
152 **31** 14c. blue and purple 50 10
153 **32** 24c. purple and carmine 50 10
154 **35** 48c. green and red-orange 2·25 11·00
155 **36** 48c. deep brown and violet (15.10.57) 1·25 1·50
156 **24** 60c. rose-red and black 1·50 1·00
157 **30** $1.20 emerald and black 17·00 7·00
158 **33** $2.40 yellow-orange and black 17·00 14·00
140/58 *Set of* 19 60·00 40·00

1958 (22 Apr). *Inauguration of British Caribbean Federation. As Nos. 135/7 of Antigua.*
159 3c. deep green 45 10
160 6c. blue 60 1·25
161 12c. scarlet 70 15
159/61 *Set of* 3 1·60 1·40

40 Seashore at Rosalie

48 Traditional Costume

Two types of 14c.

I. Eyes of model looking straight ahead.

II. Eyes looking to her right.

(Des S. Scott. Photo Harrison)

1963 (16 May)–**65**. *T* **40**, **48** *and similar designs.* W w **12** (upright). P 14×14½ (vert) or 14½×14 (horiz).

162	1c. green, blue and sepia	10	85
163	2c. bright blue	30	10
	w. Wmk inverted	—	11·00
164	3c. blackish brown and blue	1·75	1·25
165	4c. green, sepia and slate-violet	10	10
166	5c. magenta	30	10
167	6c. green, bistre and violet	10	80
168	8c. green, sepia and black	30	20
169	10c. sepia and pink	10	20
170	12c. green, blue and blackish brown	1·00	10
171	14c. multicoloured (I)	70	10
171*a*	14c. multicoloured (II) (1.4.65)	2·50	2·25
172	15c. yellow, green and brown	1·50	10
	w. Wmk inverted	—	20·00
173	24c. multicoloured	9·00	20
174	48c. green, blue and black	75	1·00
175	60c. orange, green and black	1·00	70
176	$1.20 multicoloured	6·50	1·00
177	$2.40 blue, turquoise and brown	3·50	2·75
178	$4.80 green, blue and brown	12·00	22·00
162/78 *Set of* 17		35·00	27·00

Designs: *Vert*—2c., 5c. Queen Elizabeth II; 24c. Imperial Amazon; $2.40, Trafalgar Falls; $4.80, Coconut Palm. *Horiz*—3c. Sailing canoe; 4c. Sulphur springs; 6c. Road making; 8c. Dug-out canoe; 10c. Crapaud (toad); 12c. Scott's Head; 15c. Bananas; 48c. Goodwill; 60c. Cocoa tree; $1.20, Coat of Arms.

See also Nos. 200/4.

1963 (4 June). *Freedom from Hunger. As No. 146 of Antigua.*

179	15c. reddish violet	15	10

1963 (2 Sept). *Red Cross Centenary. As Nos. 147/8 of Antigua.*

180	5c. red and black	20	40
181	15c. red and blue	40	60

1964 (23 April). *400th Birth Anniv of William Shakespeare. As No. 164 of Antigua.*

182	15c. bright purple	10	10
	w. Wmk inverted	1·50	

1965 (17 May). *I.T.U. Centenary. As Nos. 166/7 of Antigua.*

183	2c. light emerald and blue	10	10
184	48c. turquoise-blue and grey	45	20

1965 (25 Oct). *International Co-operation Year. As Nos. 168/9 of Antigua.*

185	1c. reddish purple and turquoise-green	10	20
186	15c. deep bluish green and lavender	35	10

1966 (24 Jan). *Churchill Commemoration. As Nos. 170/3 of Antigua.*

187	1c. new blue	10	1·25
	a. Gold omitted	£700	
188	5c. deep green	30	10
189	15c. brown	60	10
190	24c. bluish violet	75	20
	w. Wmk inverted	£150	
187/90 *Set of* 4		1·50	1·50

No. 187a occured on the bottom row of a sheet.

An example of the 1c. is known showing the gold face value printed double.

1966 (4 Feb). *Royal Visit. As Nos. 174/5 of Antigua.*

191	5c. black and ultramarine	75	30
192	15c. black and magenta	1·00	30

1966 (1 July). *World Cup Football Championships. As Nos. 176/7 of Antigua.*

193	5c. violet, yellow-green, lake & yellow-brown	25	15
194	24c. chocolate, blue-green, lake & yell-brown	85	15

1966 (20 Sept). *Inauguration of W.H.O. Headquarters, Geneva. As Nos. 178/9 of Antigua.*

195	5c. black, yellow-green and light blue	15	15
196	24c. black, light purple and yellow-brown	30	15

1966 (1 Dec). *20th Anniv of U.N.E.S.C.O. As Nos. 196/8 of Antigua.*

197	5c. slate-violet, red, yellow and orange	20	15
198	15c. orange-yellow, violet and deep olive	50	10
199	24c. black, bright purple and orange	60	15
197/9 *Set of* 3		1·10	30

1966 (30 Dec)–**67**. *As Nos. 165, 167/9 and 172 but* wmk w **12** sideways.

200	4c. green, sepia and slate-violet (16.5.67)	1·25	90
201	6c. green, bistre and violet	20	15
202	8c. green, sepia and black	40	10
203	10c. sepia and pink (16.5.67)	70	10
204	15c. yellow, green and brown (16.5.67)	70	10
200/4 *Set of* 5		3·00	1·25

ASSOCIATED STATEHOOD

56 Children of Three Races

(Des and photo Harrison)

1967 (2 Nov). *National Day. T* **56** *and similar horiz designs. Multicoloured.* W w **12**. P 14½.

205	5c. Type **56**	10	10
206	10c. The *Santa Maria* and motto	40	15
207	15c. Hands holding motto ribbon	15	15
208	24c. Belaire dancing	15	20
205/8 *Set of* 4		70	45

57 John F. Kennedy

(Des G. Vasarhelyi. Litho D.L.R.)

1968 (20 Apr). *Human Rights Year. T* **57** *and similar horiz designs. Multicoloured.* W w **12** (sideways). P 14×13½.

209	1c. Type **57**	10	10
210	10c. Cecil A. E. Rawle	10	10
	a. Imperf (pair)	90·00	
211	12c. Pope John XXIII	50	15
212	48c. Florence Nightingale	35	25
213	60c. Albert Schweitzer	35	25
209/13 *Set of* 5		1·25	75

ASSOCIATED STATEHOOD (**58**)

NATIONAL DAY 3 NOVEMBER 1968 (**59**)

1968 (8 July). *Associated Statehood. As Nos. 162, 170 and 174, but wmk sideways, or Nos. 163/4, 166, 170, 171a, 173, 175/8 and 200/4 optd with T* **58**.

214	1c. green, blue and sepia (Sil.)	10	10
215	2c. right blue (Sil.)	10	10
216	3c. blackish brown and blue (Sil.)	10	10
217	4c. green, sepia and slate-violet (Sil.)	10	10
218	5c. magenta (Sil.)	10	10
219	6c. green, bistre and violet	10	10
220	8c. green, sepia and black	10	10
221	10c. sepia and pink (Sil.)	55	10
222	12c. green, blue and blackish brown (Sil.) (wmk sideways)	10	10
	a. Wmk upright	10	10
224	14c. multicoloured (II) (Sil.)	10	10
225	15c. yellow, green and brown (Sil.)	10	10
226	24c. multicoloured (Sil.)	4·25	10
227	48c. green, bl & blk (Sil.) (wmk sideways)	55	1·75
	a. Wmk upright	90	1·00
228	60c. orange, green and black	90	70
229	$1.20 multicoloured	1·00	3·25
230	$2.40 blue, turquoise and brown (Sil.)	1·00	2·50
231	$4.80 green, blue and brown (Sil.)	1·25	8·50
214/31 *Set of* 17		9·00	15·00

The 2, 5, 6, 8 and 10c. values exist with PVA gum as well as gum arabic.

1968 (3 Nov). *National Day. Nos. 162/4, 171 and 176 optd with T* **59**.

232	1c. green, blue and sepia	10	10
	a. Opt inverted	45·00	
	b. Opt double		
233	2c. bright blue	10	10
	a. Opt double	30·00	
234	3c. blackish brown and blue	10	10
	a. Opt inverted	30·00	
235	14c. multicoloured (I)	10	10
	a. Opt double	70·00	
236	$1.20 multicoloured	55	40
	a. Opt double	30·00	
	b. Vert pair, one opt omitted, other opt double	£150	
232/6 *Set of* 5		60	40

The above set was put on sale by the New York Agency on 1 November but not sold locally until the 3 November.

60 Forward shooting at Goal

(Des M. Shamir (1c., 60c.), K. Plowitz (5c., 48c.). Litho B.W.)

1968 (25 Nov). *Olympic Games, Mexico. T* **60** *and similar horiz designs. Multicoloured.* P 11½×11.

237	1c. Type **60**	10	10
	a. Horiz pair. Nos. 237/8	10	10
238	1c. Goalkeeper trying to save goal	10	10
239	5c. Swimmers about to dive	10	10
	a. Horiz pair. Nos. 239/40	10	10
240	5c. Swimmers diving	10	10
241	48c. Javelin-throwing	15	15
	a. Horiz pair. Nos. 241/2	30	30
242	48c. Hurdling	15	15
243	60c. Basketball	90	25
	a. Horiz pair. Nos. 243/4	1·75	50
244	60c. Basketball players	90	25
237/44 *Set of* 8		2·00	85

Nos. 237/44 were issued in sheets of 40 containing two panes of *se-tenant* pairs.

61 "The Small Cowper Madonna" (Raphael)

62 "Venus and Adonis" (Rubens)

(Photo Delrieu, Paris)

1968 (23 Dec). *Christmas.* P 12½×12.

245	**61** 5c. multicoloured	10	10

Three other values were issued: 12c. "Madonna of the Chair" (Raphael); 24c. "Madonna and Child" (Italo-Byzantine, XVI century); $1.20 "Madonna and Child" (Byzantine, XIII century). Sizes as T **61**.

These only come from miniature sheets, containing two *se-tenant* strips of each value.

(Litho D.L.R.)

1969 (30 Jan). *20th Anniv of World Health Organisation. Paintings. T* **62** *and similar vert designs. Multicoloured.* W w **12**. P 15.

246	5c. Type **62**	20	10
247	15c. "The Death of Socrates" (J.-L. David)	30	10
248	24c. "Christ and the Pilgrims of Emmaus" (Velasquez)	30	10
249	50c. "Pilate washing his Hands" (Rembrandt)	50	40
246/9 *Set of* 4		1·10	50

66 Picking Oranges

67 "Strength in Unity" Emblem and Fruit Trees

(Des K. Plowitz. Litho Harrison)

1969 (10 Mar). *Tourism. T* **66** *and similar horiz designs. Multicoloured.* W w **12**. P 14½.

250	10c. Type **66**	15	10
	a. Horiz pair. Nos. 250/1	30	15
251	10c. Woman, child and ocean scene	15	10
252	12c. Fort Yeoung Hotel	50	10
	a. Horiz pair. Nos. 252/3	1·00	20
253	12c. Red-necked Amazons	50	10
254	24c. Calypso band	30	15
	a. Horiz pair. Nos. 254/5	60	30
	w. Wmk inverted	35·00	
255	24c. Women dancing	30	15
	w. Wmk inverted	35·00	
256	48c. Underwater life	30	25
	a. Horiz pair. Nos. 256/7	60	50
257	48c. Skin-diver and turtle	30	25
250/7 *Set of* 8		2·25	1·00

Each denomination was printed *se-tenant* throughout the sheet. The 12c. values are on cream coloured paper.

(Litho B.W.)

1969 (July). *First Anniv of CARIFTA (Caribbean Free Trade Area). T* **67** *and similar horiz designs. Multicoloured.* P 13½×13.

258	5c. Type **67**	10	10
259	8c. Hawker Siddeley H.S.748 aircraft, emblem and island	30	20
260	12c. Chart of Caribbean Sea and emblem	30	25
261	24c. Steamship unloading, tug and emblem	40	25
258/61 *Set of* 4		1·00	70

71 "Spinning"

72 Mahatma Gandhi Weaving and Clock Tower, Westminster

(Litho B.W.)

1969 (10 July). *50th Anniv of International Labour Organisation. T* **71** *and similar vert designs showing paintings of people at work by J. Millet, bordered by flags of member-nations of the I.L.O. Multicoloured.* No wmk. P 13×13½.

262	15c. Type **71**	10	10
263	30c. "Threshing"	15	15
264	38c. "Flax-pulling"	15	15
262/4 *Set of* 3		30	30

(Des G. Vasarhelyi. Litho Format)

1969 (20 Oct). *Birth Centenary of Mahatma Gandhi. T* **72** *and similar horiz designs. Multicoloured.* P 14½.

265	6c. Type **72**	45	10
266	38c. Gandhi, Nehru and Mausoleum	65	15

267	$1.20 Gandhi and Taj Mahal	1·00	1·00
265/7 *Set of 3*		1·90	1·00

Nos. 265/7 are incorrectly inscribed "Ghandi".

75 "Saint Joseph"

(Des G. Vasarhelyi. Litho Govt Printer, Jerusalem)

1969 (3 Nov). *National Day. Stained Glass Windows. T* **75** *and similar vert designs. Multicoloured.* P 14.

268	6c. Type **75**	10	10
269	8c. "Saint John"	10	10
270	12c. "Saint Peter"	10	10
271	60c. "Saint Paul"	30	50
268/71 *Set of 4*		40	60

Nos. 268/71 were printed in sheets of 16 (4×4) containing 12 stamps and four printed labels in the top row. The labels each contain two lines of a patriotic poem by W. O. M. Pond, the first letter from each line spelling "DOMINICA".

79 Queen Elizabeth II

80 Purple-throated Carib and Flower

81 Government Headquarters

82 Coat of Arms

(Photo D.L.R.)

1969 (26 Nov)–**72**. *T* **79/82** *and similar horiz designs. Multicoloured.* W **41** of Singapore (Half-check Pattern) (60c. to $4.80) or no wmk (others). *Chalk-surfaced paper.* P 13½×14 (½c.), 14×13½ (1 to 50c.) or 14 (60c. to $4.80).

272	½c. Type **79**	10	2·25
	a. Glazed paper (1972)	30	1·75
273	1c. Type **80**	1·00	2·50
	a. Glazed paper (1972)	1·50	1·50
274	2c. Poinsettia	15	10
	a. Glazed paper (1972)	50	40
275	3c. Red-necked Pigeon	2·75	2·75
	a. Glazed paper (1972)	3·00	1·50
276	4c. Imperial Amazon	2·75	2·75
	a. Glazed paper (1972)	3·00	1·50
277	5c. *Battus polydamas* (butterfly)	2·75	2·00
	a. Glazed paper (1972)	2·75	1·75
278	6c. *Dryas julia* (butterfly)	2·75	3·25
	a. Glazed paper (1972)	2·75	2·75
279	8c. Shipping Bananas	20	10
	a. Glazed paper (1972)	40	50
280	10c. Portsmouth Harbour	20	10
	a. Glazed paper (1972)	35	20
281	12c. Copra processing plant	20	10
	a. Glazed paper (1972)	35	20
282	15c. Straw workers	20	10
	a. Glazed paper (1972)	35	25
283	25c. Timber plant	30	10
	a. Glazed paper (1972)	40	25
284	30c. Pumice mine	1·50	90
	a. Glazed paper (1972)	1·50	70
285	38c. Grammar school and playing field	9·50	1·75
	a. Glazed paper (1972)	8·50	15·00
286	50c. Roseau Cathedral	50	45
	a. Glazed paper (1972)	80	1·00
287	60c. Type **81**	55	1·50
288	$1.20 Melville Hall Airport (40×27 *mm*)	1·25	1·75
289	$2.40 Type **82**	1·00	4·00
290	$4.80 Type **79** (26×39 *mm*)	1·25	7·00
272/90 *Set of 19*		25·00	30·00
272a/86a *Set of 15*		22·00	26·00

99 "Virgin and Child with St. John" (Perugino)

101 Astronaut's First Step onto the Moon

(Des G. Vasarhelyi. Litho B.W.)

1969 (19 Dec). *Christmas. Paintings. T* **99** *and similar perf designs. Multicoloured.* P 14×14½.

291	6c. "Virgin and Child with St. John" (Lippi)	10	10
292	10c. "Holy Family with the Lamb" (Raphael)	10	10
293	15c. Type **99**	10	10
294	$1.20 "Madonna of the Rose Hedge" (Botticelli)	35	40
291/4 *Set of 4*		35	40
MS295 89×76 mm. Nos. 293/4. Imperf		75	1·00

(Des G. Vasarhelyi. Photo Banknote Printing Office, Helsinki)

1970 (6 Feb*). *Moon Landing. T* **101** *and similar horiz designs. Multicoloured.* P 12½.

296	½c. Type **101**	10	10
297	5c. Scientific Experiment on the Moon, and Flag	15	10
298	8c. Astronauts collecting Rocks	15	10
299	30c. Module over the Moon	30	15
300	50c. Moon Plaque	40	25
301	60c. Astronauts	40	30
296/301 *Set of 6*		1·25	80
MS302 116×112 mm. Nos. 298/301. Imperf		2·00	2·00

*This is the date of release in Dominica, but the above were released by the Philatelic Agency in the U.S.A. on 2 February.

107 Giant Green Turtle

(Des G. Drummond. Litho Kyodo Printing Co, Tokyo)

1970 (7 Sept). *Flora and Fauna. T* **107** *and similar horiz designs. Multicoloured.* P 13.

303	6c. Type **107**	30	20
304	24c. Atlantic Flyingfish	40	45
305	38c. Anthurium lily	50	65
306	60c. Imperial and Red-necked Amazons	2·75	5·50
303/6 *Set of 4*		4·50	6·00
MS307 160×111 mm. Nos. 303/6		5·50	6·50

108 18th-Century National Costume

109 Scrooge and Marley's Ghost

(Des G. Drummond from local designs. Litho Questa)

1970 (30 Oct). *National Day. T* **108** *and similar horiz designs. Multicoloured.* P 14.

308	5c. Type **108**	10	10
309	8c. Carib Basketry	10	10
310	$1 Flag and Chart of Dominica	30	40
308/10 *Set of 3*		30	40
MS311 150×85 mm. Nos. 308/10 plus three labels		50	1·75

(Des R. Granger Barrett. Litho Questa)

1970 (23 Nov). *Christmas and Charles Dickens' Death Centenary. T* **109** *and similar vert designs showing scenes from "A Christmas Carol". Multicoloured.* P 14×14½.

312	2c. Type **109**	10	10
313	15c. Fezziwig's Ball	20	10
314	24c. Scrooge and his Nephew's Party	20	10
315	$1.20 Scrooge and the Ghost of Christmas Present	65	90
312/15 *Set of 4*		1·00	1·00
MS316 142×87 mm. Nos. 312/15		1·00	3·75

110 "The Doctor" (Sir Luke Fildes)

(Des G. Vasarhelyi. Litho Questa)

1970 (28 Dec). *Centenary of British Red Cross. T* **110** *and similar horiz designs. Multicoloured.* P 14½×14.

317	8c. Type **110**	10	10
318	10c. Hands and Red Cross	10	10
319	15c. Flag of Dominica and Red Cross Emblem	15	10
320	50c. "The Sick Child" (E. Munch)	50	45
317/20 *Set of 4*		75	50
MS321 108×76 mm. Nos. 317/20		1·00	3·00

POSTAL FISCALS

REVENUE (R **1**) **Revenue** (R **2**)

1879–88. *Optd with Type* R **1** *by De La Rue.* P 14.

(a) Wmk Crown CC.

R1	1	1d. lilac	80·00	8·00
		a. Bisected vert (½d.) on cover..	†	£2750
R2		6d. green	3·00	24·00
		w. Wmk inverted	£130	
R3		1s. magenta	9·00	16·00
R1/3 *Set of 3*			85·00	42·00

(b) Wmk Crown CA.

R4	1	1d. lilac (1888)	6·00	5·50

1888. *Optd with Type* R **2** *locally.* Wmk Crown CA.

R6	1	1d. rose	£250	70·00

East Africa (G.E.A.) *see* **Tanganyika**

East Africa and Uganda Protectorates *see* **Kenya, Uganda and Tanganyika**

Egypt

TURKISH SUZERAINTY

In 1517 Sultan Selim I added Egypt to the Ottoman Empire, and it stayed more or less under Turkish rule until 1805, when Mohammed Ali became governor. He established a dynasty of governors owing nominal allegiance to the Sultan of Turkey until 1914.

Khedive Ismail

18 January 1863–26 June 1879

He obtained the honorific title of Khedive (viceroy) from the Sultan in 1867.

The operations of British Consular Post Offices in Egypt date from August 1839 when the first packet agency, at Alexandria, was opened. Further agencies at Suez (1 January 1847) and Cairo (1856) followed. Alexandria became a post office on 17 March 1858 with Cairo following on 23 February 1859 and Suez on 1 January 1861.

Great Britain stamps were issued to Alexandria in March 1858 and to the other two offices in August/September 1859. "B O1" cancellations as Type **2** were issued to both Alexandria and Cairo. Cancellations with this number as Types **8**, **12** and **15** were only used at Alexandria.

Before 1 July 1873 combination covers showing Great Britain stamps and the first issue of Egypt exist with the latter paying the internal postage to the British Post Office at Alexandria.

The Cairo office closed on 30 June 1873 and the other two on 30 March 1878. Suez continued to function as a transit office for a number of years.

Stamps issued after 1877 can be found with the Egyptian cancellation "Port Said", but these are on letters posted from British ships.

For cancellations used during the 1882 and 1885 campaigns, see BRITISH FORCES IN EGYPT at the end of the listing.

For illustrations of the handstamp and postmark types see BRITISH POST OFFICES ABROAD notes following GREAT BRITAIN.

ALEXANDRIA

CROWNED-CIRCLE HANDSTAMPS

CC1	CC **1b**	ALEXANDRIA (R.) (13.5.1843) *Price on cover*	£2750

Stamps of GREAT BRITAIN *cancelled* "B 01" *as in Types* **2** *(also used at Cairo),* **8**, **12** *or* **15**.

1858 (Mar)–**78**.

Z1	½d. rose-red (1870–79) *From* Plate Nos. 5, 6, 8, 10, 13, 14, 15, 19, 20.	20·00
Z2	1d. rose-red (1857)	7·00
Z3	1d. rose-red (1861) (Alph IV)	
Z4	1d. rose-red (1864–79) *From* Plate Nos. 71, 72, 73, 74, 76, 78, 79, 80, 81, 82, 83, 84, 85, 86, 87, 88, 89, 90, 91, 92, 93, 94, 95, 96, 97, 98, 99, 101, 102, 103, 104, 106, 107, 108, 109, 110, 111, 112, 113, 114, 115, 117, 118, 119, 120, 121, 122, 123, 124, 125, 127, 129, 130, 131, 133, 134, 136, 137, 138, 139, 140, 142, 143, 144, 145, 146, 147, 148, 149, 150, 152, 154, 156, 157, 158, 159, 160, 162, 163, 165, 168, 169, 170, 171, 172, 174, 175, 177, 179, 180, 181, 182, 183, 185, 188, 190, 198, 200, 203, 206, 210, 220.	9·50
Z5	2d. blue (1858–69) *From* Plate Nos. 7, 8. 9, 13, 14, 15.	9·50

Z6	2½d. rosy mauve (1875) (blued *paper*)..... *From* Plate Nos. 1, 2.	60·00
Z7	2½d. rosy mauve (1875–6) (Plate Nos. 1, 2, 3)	35·00
Z8	2½d. rosy mauve (*Error of Lettering*)..................	£1500
Z9	2½d. rosy mauve (1876–79) .... *From* Plate Nos. 3, 4, 5, 6, 7, 8, 9.	25·00
Z10	3d. carmine-rose (1862).......................................	£120
Z11	3d. rose (1865) (Plate No. 4)..............................	60·00
Z12	3d. rose (1867–73) .... Plate Nos. 4, 5, 6, 7, 8, 9.	24·00
Z13	3d. rose (1873–76)..................................... *From* Plate Nos. 11, 12, 14, 15, 16, 18, 19.	26·00
Z15	4d. rose (1857)..	42·00
Z16	4d. red (1862) (Plate Nos. 3, 4)................ *From*	42·00
Z17	4d. vermilion (1865–73)............................ *From* Plate Nos. 7, 8, 9, 10, 11, 12, 13, 14.	29·00
Z18	4d. vermilion (1876) (Plate No. 15)	£160
Z19	4d. sage-green (1877) (Plate No. 15)	£110
Z20	6d. lilac (1856)..	48·00
Z21	6d. lilac (1862) (Plate Nos. 3, 4) .... *From*	42·00
Z22	6d. lilac (1865–67) (Plate Nos. 5, 6) .... *From*	32·00
Z23	6d. lilac (1867) (Plate No. 6).............................	42·00
Z24	6d. violet (1867–70) (Plate Nos. 6, 8, 9).. *From*	38·00
	a. Imperf (Plate No. 8).....................................	£3500
Z25	6d. buff (1872–73) (Plate Nos. 11, 12) .... *From*	55·00
Z26	6d. chestnut (1872) (Plate No. 11)	27·00
Z27	6d. grey (1873) (Plate No. 12)	80·00
Z28	6d. grey (1874–76) Plate Nos. 13, 14, 15 . *From*	23·00
Z29	9d. straw (1862)...	£150
Z30	9d. bistre (1862)..	
Z31	9d. straw (1865)...	
Z32	9d. straw (1867)...	
Z33	10d. red-brown (1867)	£140
Z34	1s. green (1856)..	£130
Z35	1s. green (1862)..	75·00
Z36	1s. green (1862) ("K" *variety*)............................	
Z37	1s. green (1865) (Plate No. 4)	35·00
Z38	1s. green (1867–73) Plate Nos. 4, 5, 6, 7. *From*	15·00
Z39	1s. green (1873–77).................................. *From* Plate Nos. 8, 9, 10, 11, 12, 13.	27·00
Z40	2s. blue (1867)..	£110
Z41	5s. rose (1867–74) (Plate Nos. 1, 2) .... *From*	£250

CAIRO

CROWNED-CIRCLE HANDSTAMPS

CC2 CC **6** CAIRO (R. or Blk.) (23.3.1859)
Price on cover £4000

Cancellation "B 01" as Type **2** (also issued at Alexandria) was used to cancel mail franked with Great Britain stamps between April 1859 and June 1873.

SUEZ

CROWNED-CIRCLE HANDSTAMPS

CC3 CC **1** SUEZ (B. or Black) (16.7.1847)
Price on cover £4500

Stamps of GREAT BRTAIN *cancelled* "B 02" *as in Types* **2** *and* **8**, *or with circular date stamp as Type* **5**.

1859 (Aug)–**78**.

Z42	½d. rose-red (1870–79)...................................... Plate Nos. 6, 10, 11, 12, 13, 14.	30·00
Z43	1d. rose-red (1857)	10·00
Z44	1d. rose-red (1864–79) .... *From* Plate Nos. 73, 74, 78, 79, 80, 81, 83, 84, 86, 87, 90, 91, 93, 94, 96, 97, 100, 101, 106, 107, 108, 110, 113, 118, 119, 120, 121, 122, 123, 124, 125, 129, 130, 131, 134, 136, 137, 138, 140, 142, 143, 144, 145, 147, 148, 149, 150, 151, 152, 153, 154, 156, 158, 159, 160, 161, 162, 163, 164, 165, 166, 167, 168, 170, 174, 176, 177, 178, 179, 180, 181, 182, 184, 185, 186, 187, 189, 190, 205.	12·00
Z45	2d. blue (1858–69)...................................... *From* Plate Nos. 8, 9, 13, 14, 15.	15·00
Z46	2½d. rosy mauve (1875) (blued *paper*) ..... *From* Plate Nos. 1, 2, 3.	65·00
Z47	2½d. rosy mauve (1875–76) .... *From* Plate Nos. 1, 2, 3.	35·00
Z48	2½d. rosy mauve (*Error of Lettering*)..................	£1700
Z49	2½d. rosy mauve (1876–79) .... *From* Plate Nos. 3, 4, 5, 6, 7, 8, 9, 10.	27·00
Z50	3d. carmine-rose (1862).......................................	£140
Z51	3d. rose (1865) (Plate No. 4)..............................	75·00
Z52	3d. rose (1867–73) (Plate Nos. 5, 6, 7, 8, 10)......	
Z53	3d. rose (1873–76) (Plate Nos. 12, 16) .... *From*	26·00
Z54	4d. rose (1857)..	55·00
Z55	4d. red (1862) (Plate Nos. 3, 4)................ *From*	48·00
Z56	4d. vermilion (1865–73)............................ *From* Plate Nos. 7, 8, 9, 10, 11, 12, 13, 14.	29·00
Z57	4d. vermilion (1876) (Plate No. 15)	
Z58	4d. sage-green (1877) (Plate No. 15)	£130
Z59	6d. lilac (1856)..	55·00
Z60	6d. lilac (1862) (Plate Nos. 3, 4) .... *From*	45·00
Z61	6d. lilac (1865–67) (Plate Nos. 5, 6) .... *From*	38·00
Z62	6d. lilac (1867) (Plate No. 6).............................	48·00
Z63	6d. violet (1867–70) (Plate Nos. 6, 8, 9).. *From*	38·00
Z64	6d. buff (1872–73) (Plate Nos. 11, 12) .... *From*	65·00
Z65	6d. pale chestnut (Plate No. 12) (1872)..............	£2750
Z66	6d. chestnut (1872) (Plate No. 11)	32·00
Z67	6d. grey (1873) (Plate No. 12)	95·00
Z68	6d. grey (1874–76) .... *From* Plate Nos, 13, 14, 15, 16.	28·00
Z69	8d. orange (1876)	
Z70	9d. straw (1862)...	£180
	a. Thick paper..	
Z71	9d. bistre (1862)..	
Z72	9d. straw (1867)...	
Z73	10d. red-brown (1867)	£200
Z74	1s. green (1856)..	£150
Z75	1s. green (1862)..	85·00
Z76	1s. green (1862) ("K" *variety*)............................	
Z77	1s. green (1865) (Plate No. 4)	48·00
Z78	1s. green (1867–73) Plate Nos. 4, 5, 6, 7. *From*	20·00
Z79	1s. green (1873–77).................................. *From* Plate Nos. 8, 9, 10, 11, 12.	30·00
Z80	2s. blue (1867)..	£160
Z81	5s. rose (1867–74) (Plate Nos. 1, 2) .... *From*	£350

PRICES FOR STAMPS ON COVER	
Nos. 1/41	*from* × 8
Nos. 42/3	*from* × 30
Nos. 44/83	*from* × 5
Nos. 84/97	*from* × 2
Nos. D57/70	*from* × 12
Nos. D71/86	*from* × 5
Nos. D84/103	*from* × 2
Nos. O64/87	*from* × 5
Nos. O88/101	*from* × 2

(Currency: 40 paras = 1 piastre)

1

2

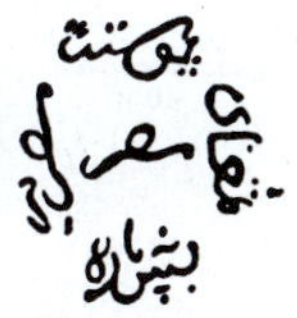
(3)

(Typo (1pi) or litho (others) Pellas Brothers, Genoa. Inscr (T **3**) applied typo (1, 2pi.) or litho (others))

1866 (1 Jan). *Various designs as T* **1** *with black inscriptions as T* **3**. *The lowest group of characters indicates the value. 1pi.* no wmk, others W **2** (inverted). P 12½.

1		5pa. grey.....................................	45·00	28·00
		a. Greenish grey	45·00	28·00
		b. Imperf (pair)	£180	
		c. Imperf between (pair)	£300	
		d. Perf 12½×13 and compound...........	55·00	48·00
		e. Perf 13	£250	£300
		w. Wmk upright	£275	£200
2		10pa. brown..................................	55·00	30·00
		a. Imperf (pair)	£160	
		b. Imperf between (pair)	£350	
		c. Perf 12½×13 and compound...........	80·00	48·00
		d. Perf 12½×15	£250	£275
		e. Perf 13	£170	£190
		w. Wmk upright	65·00	30·00
3		20pa. pale blue	70·00	32·00
		a. Greenish blue	70·00	32·00
		b. Imperf (pair)	£240	
		c. Imperf between (pair)	£400	
		d. Perf 12½×13 and compound...........	£100	80·00
		e. Perf 13	£425	£250
		w. Wmk upright	70·00	32·00
4		1pi. claret.....................................	60·00	5·00
		a. Imperf (pair)	£100	
		b. Imperf between (pair)	£400	
		c. Perf 12½×13 and compound...........	90·00	20·00
		d. Perf 13	£300	£190
		e. Perf 12½×15..............................	£300	
5		2pi. yellow....................................	90·00	45·00
		a. Orange-yellow	90·00	45·00
		b. Imperf (pair)		
		c. Imperf between (pair)	£350	£350
		d. Bisected diag (1pi.) (on cover)......	†	£2250
		e. Perf 12½×13 and compound...........	£120	48·00
		f. Perf 12½×15..............................	£130	
		w. Wmk upright	90·00	45·00
6		5pi. rose	£250	£170
		a. Imperf (pair)		
		b. Imperf between (pair)	£1000	
		c. Perf 12½×13 and compound...........	£275	
		d. Error. Inscr 10pi., perf 12½×15......	£900	£750
		da. Imperf....................................	£500	
		e. Perf 13	£450	
		w. Wmk upright	£250	£170
7		10pi. slate....................................	£275	£250
		a. Imperf (pair)	£600	
		b. Imperf between (pair)	£2000	
		c. Perf 12½×13 and compound...........	£425	£425
		d. Perf 13	£1600	
		w. Wmk upright	£275	£250

The 2pi. bisected was authorised for use between 16 and 31 July 1867 at Alexandria or Cairo.

Stamps perforated 12½, 12½×13 and compound, and 13 occur in the same sheets with the 13 gauge usually used on the top, left-hand, right-hand or bottom rows. Each sheet of 200 contained one stamp perforated 13 all round, two 13 on three sides, one 13 on two adjacent sides, eighteen 13×12½, eight 12½×13, eight 13 on one side and eighteen 13 at top or bottom. So many sheets were received imperforate or part-perforated that some stock was passed to V. Penasson of Alexandria who applied the 12½×15 gauge.

The two halves of each background differ in minor details of the ornamentation. All values can be found with either half at the top.

Proofs of all values exist on smooth paper, without watermark. Beware of forgeries.

All values also exist with the watermark reversed (*same price as upright*) or inverted and reversed (*same price as inverted*).

4

5

6

(Des F. Hoff. Litho V. Penasson, Alexandria)

1867 (1 Aug)–**71**. W **6** (*impressed on reverse*). P 15×12½.

11	**4**	5pa. orange-yellow........................	32·00	8·00
		a. Imperf (pair)		
		b. Imperf between (horiz pair) ..	£170	
		x. Wmk impressed on face		
12		10pa. dull lilac..............................	75·00	9·50
		b. Bright mauve (7.69)................	55·00	9·00
		ba. Bisected diag (5pa.) (on piece) (17.11.71)............................	†	£750
		w. Wmk inverted	£300	£200
		x. Wmk impressed on face		
13		20pa. deep blue-green	£100	13·00
		a. Pale blue-green	£100	13·00
		b. Yellowish green (7.69).............	£110	12·00
		x. Wmk impressed on face		
14	**5**	1pi. dull rose-red *to* rose	19·00	1·00
		a. Lake...	£150	32·00
		b. Imperf (pair)	£100	
		c. Imperf between (horiz pair) ..	£170	
		d. Bisected diag (20pa.) (on piece)......................................	†	£750
		e. Rouletted	55·00	
		w. Wmk inverted	50·00	30·00
		x. Wmk impressed on face		
15		2pi. bright blue	£110	17·00
		a. Pale blue..................................	£110	17·00
		b. Imperf (pair)		
		c. Imperf between (pair)	£425	
		d. Bisected diag (1pi.) (on cover)..	†	—
		e. Perf 12½	£225	
16		5pi. brown....................................	£300	£180
		x. Wmk impressed on face		

Each value was engraved four times, the resulting blocks being used to form sheets of 200. There are therefore four types showing minor variations for each value.

No. 12ba was used on newspapers from Alexandria between 17 November 1871 and 20 January 1872.

Stamps printed both sides, both imperf and perf, come from printer's waste. The 1pi. rose without watermark is a proof.

7

8 (Side panels transposed and inverted)

8*a* (I)

8*a* (II)

WATERMARK 8*a*. There are two types of this watermark which, as they are not always easy to distinguish, we do not list separately. Type II is slightly wider and less deep and the crescent is flatter than in Type I. The width measurement for Type I is generally about 14 mm and for Type II about 15 mm, but there is some variation within the sheets for both types.

Nos. 26/43, 45/7*a*, 49/*a*, 50/1 and 57 come with Type I only. Nos. 44*a*, 48/*a*, 52, 54*b*, 73/7 and 78 exist with both types of watermark (but No. 83 and official overprints on these stamps still require research); our prices are generally for Type II. Other watermarked issues between 1888 and 1907 have Type II watermarks only.

1872 (1 Jan)–**75**. *T* **7** (*the so-called "Penasson" printing**). *Thick opaque paper.* W **8***a*. P 12½×13½.

A. LITHOGRAPHED.

26	**7**	20pa. blue (*shades*)	£120	55·00
		a. Imperf (pair)		
		b. Imperf between (pair)	—	£2000
		c. Perf 13½..................................	£200	60·00
		w. Wmk inverted	£200	80·00
27		1pi. red (*shades*)	£225	11·00
		a. Perf 13½..................................	£500	24·00
		w. Wmk inverted	£600	32·00

B. TYPOGRAPHED.

28	**7**	5pa. brown (*shades*)......................	7·00	4·50
		a. Perf 13½..................................	24·00	9·50
		w. Wmk inverted	£100	60·00
29		10pa. mauve..................................	6·00	3·00
		a. Perf 13½..................................	6·00	3·25
		w. Wmk inverted	40·00	25·00
30		20pa. blue (*shades*)	60·00	4·50
		a. Perf 13½..................................	85·00	20·00
		w. Wmk inverted	55·00	30·00
31		1pi. rose-red	60·00	1·00
		a. Bisected (20pa.) (on piece with No. 31) (7.75)	†	£600
		b. Perf 13½..................................	85·00	3·50
		w. Wmk inverted	45·00	25·00
32		2pi. chrome-yellow.......................	90·00	4·00
		a. Bisected (1pi.) (on piece) (7.74)......................................	†	£650
		b. Perf 13½..................................	18·00	4·00
		w. Wmk inverted		
33		2½pi. violet...................................	85·00	20·00
		a. Perf 13½..................................	£700	£190
		w. Wmk inverted	95·00	32·00
34		5pi. yellow-green	£180	35·00
		a. Tête-bêche (pair)......................	£8000	
		b. Perf 13½..................................	£300	55·00
		w. Wmk inverted	£200	90·00

*It is now accepted that stamps in both processes were printed by the Goverment Printing Works at Bûlâq, Cairo, although Penasson may have been involved in the production of the dies.

The lithographed and typographed stamps show the characteristic differences between these two processes:—

The typographed stamps show the coloured lines of the design impressed into the paper and an accumulation of ink along the margins of the lines.

The lithographed stamps are essentially flat in appearance, without the heaping of the ink. Many of the 20pa. show evidence of retouching, particularly of the outer frame lines.

The 1p. bisected was used at Gedda, on 5 July 1875, or Scio, and the 2pi. vertically bisected at Gallipolli or Scio.

See also footnote below No. 41

1874 (Nov)–**75**. *Typo from new stereos at Bûlâq, on thinner paper.* W **8***a*. P 12½.

35	**8**	5pa. brown (3.75)	13·00	3·75
		a. *Tête-bêche* (vert pair)	35·00	35·00
		b. *Tête-bêche* (horiz pair)	£275	£300
		c. Imperf (pair)		
		d. Imperf between (pair)	£100	£120
		ew. Wmk inverted	13·00	3·75
		f. Perf 13½×12½	18·00	3·75
		fa. *Tête-bêche* (vert pair)	60·00	60·00
		fb. *Tête-bêche* (horiz pair)	£325	£350
		fw. Wmk inverted	18·00	3·75
36	**7**	10pa. grey-lilac (*shades*) (8.75)	13·00	3·25
		a. *Tête-bêche* (vert pair)	£140	£160
		b. *Tête-bêche* (horiz pair)		
		c. Imperf (pair)		
		dw. Wmk inverted	13·00	3·25
		e. Perf 13½×12½	27·00	3·25
		ea. *Tête-bêche* (vert pair)	£140	£160
		eb. *Tête-bêche* (horiz pair)		
		ew. Wmk inverted	27·00	3·50
37		20pa. grey-blue (*shades*) (2.75)	95·00	3·00
		b. Bisected diag (10pa.) (on cover)	†	—
		cw. Wmk inverted	95·00	3·00
		d. Perf 13½×12½	10·00	2·50
		da. Imperf between (pair)	£300	
38		1pi. red (*shades*) (4.75)	11·00	65
		a. *Tête-bêche* (vert pair)	90·00	90·00
		b. *Tête-bêche* (horiz pair)	£300	£300
		c. Imperf (pair)		
		d. Imperf between (pair)	£400	£400
		ew. Wmk inverted	13·00	1·50
		f. Perf 13½×12½	75·00	1·25
		fa. *Tête-bêche* (vert pair)	£350	£350
		fb. *Tête-bêche* (horiz pair)		
		fw. Wmk inverted	85·00	7·50
39		2pi. yellow (12.74)	75·00	3·25
		a. *Tête-bêche* (pair)	£400	£400
		bw. Wmk inverted	95·00	7·50
		c. Perf 13½×12½	5·50	6·00
		ca. *Tête-bêche* (pair)	£425	£400
		cb. Bisected diag (1pi.) (on cover) (4.75)	†	£2500
		cw. Wmk inverted	7·50	6·50
		d. Perf 12½×13½	70·00	15·00
		da. *Tête-bêche* (pair)	£950	
		dw. Wmk inverted	85·00	18·00
40		2½pi. violet	8·50	5·00
		a. *Tête-bêche* (pair)	£350	
		bw. Wmk inverted	12·00	7·50
		c. perf 12½×13½	65·00	19·00
		ca. *Tête-bêche* (pair)	£1000	90·00
		cw. Wmk inverted	55·00	25·00
41		5pi. green	55·00	19·00
		a. Imperf (pair)	†	—
		bw. Wmk inverted	£100	50·00
		c. Perf 12½×13½	£325	£275

The 2pi. bisected was used at Gedda and are all postmarked 13 April.

The 1872 printings have a thick line of colour in the top margin of the sheet and the other margins are all plain, an exception being the 5pa., which on the majority of the sheets has the line at the right-hand side of the sheet. The 1874–75 printings have a wide fancy border all round every sheet.

The 1872 printings are on thick opaque paper, with the impressions sharp and clear. The 1874–75 printings are on thinner paper, often semi-transparent and oily in appearance, and having the impressions very blurred and badly printed. These are only general distinctions and there are a number of exceptions.

The majority of the 1874–75 stamps have blind or defective perforations, while the 1872 stamps have clean-cut perfs.

The two printings of the 5pa. to 1pi. values can be identified by their perforation gauges, which are always different; the 5pa. also differs in the side panels (Types **7** and **8**). Only the perf 12½×13½ varieties of the three higher values may need to be distinguished. As well as the general points noted above the following features are also helpful:

2pi. In the 1872 issue the left-hand Arabic character in the top inscription is one complete shape, resembling an inverted "V" with a horizontal line on top. In the 1874 issue the character has three separate components, a line with two dots below.

2½ pi. There is a distinct thinning of the frame line in the top right-hand corner of the 1872 issue. This sometimes takes the form of a short white line within the frame.

5pi. In the 1872 issue the top frame line is split for its entire length; in the 1874 issue the line is solid for all or most of its length. The 1872 printing always has a white dot above the "P" of "PIASTRE"; this dot appears on only a few positions of the 1874 printing.

There seem to be many different compositions of the sheets containing the *tête-bêche* varieties, settings being known with 1, 3, 9 and 10 inverted stamps in various sheets. Sheets of the 5pa. are known with 9 of the 20 horizontal rows inverted, giving vertical *tête-bêche* pairs; four stamps were inverted within their row giving four horizontal *tête-bêche* pairs.

Examples of some values exist without watermark due to the paper being misplaced on the press.

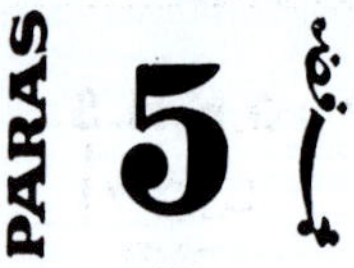

(9)

1878 (Dec). *No. 40 surch as T* **9** *at Bûlâq.* P 12½.

42	**7**	5pa. on 2½pi. violet	6·00	6·00
		a. Surch inverted	70·00	70·00
		b. *Tête-bêche* (pair)	£3500	
		c. Imperf (pair)	£900	
		dw. Wmk inverted	7·50	7·50
		e. Perf 12½×13½	6·50	8·00
		ea. Surch inverted	£140	£140
		eb. *Tête-bêche* (pair)		
		ew. Wmk inverted	8·00	10·00
43		10pa. on 2½ pi. violet	11·00	10·00
		a. Surch inverted	75·00	75·00
		b. *Tête-bêche* (pair)	£1500	
		dw. Wmk inverted	15·00	15·00
		e. Perf 12½×13½	15·00	15·00
		ea. Surch inverted	£110	£110
		eb. *Tête-bêche* (pair)	£1500	
		ew. Wmk inverted	25·00	25·00

10

11

12

13

14

15

(Typo De La Rue)

1879 (1 Apr). *Ordinary paper.* W **8***a* (*inverted on* 10*pa.*). P 14.

44	**10**	5pa. deep brown	3·25	60
		a. *Pale brown*	3·25	60
		w. Wmk inverted	£120	£100
45	**11**	10pa. reddish lilac	50·00	3·00
		w. Wmk upright	†	£100
46	**12**	20pa. pale blue	60·00	1·75
		w. Wmk inverted	90·00	15·00
47	**13**	1pi. rose	29·00	20
		a. *Pale rose*	29·00	20
		w. Wmk inverted	60·00	10·00
48	**14**	2pi. orange	32·00	50
		a. *Orange-yellow*	30·00	80
		w. Wmk inverted	35·00	2·00
49	**15**	5pi. green	55·00	11·00
		a. *Blue-green*	55·00	10·00
		w. Wmk inverted	50·00	11·00

See also Nos. 50/6.

Khedive Tewfik

26 June 1879–7 January 1892

British troops were landed in Egypt in 1882 to secure the Suez Canal against a nationalist movement led by Arab Pasha. Arabi was defeated at Tel-el-Kebir and British troops remained in Egypt until 1954. A British resident and consul-general advised the Khedive. Holders of this post were Sir Evelyn Baring (Lord Cromer), 1883–1907; Sir Eldon Gorst, 1907–11; and Lord Kitchener, 1911–14.

1881–1902. *Colours changed. Ordinary paper.* W **8***a* (*inverted on* No. 50). P 14.

50	**11**	10pa. claret (1.81)	50·00	8·00
51		10pa. bluish grey (25.1.82)	13·00	1·75
		w. Wmk inverted	40·00	3·00
52		10pa. green (15.12.84)	2·00	1·25
		w. Wmk inverted	30·00	10·00
53	**12**	20pa. rose-carmine (15.12.84)	18·00	55
		a. *Bright rose*	18·00	50
		w. Wmk inverted	35·00	7·00
54	**13**	1pi. blue (15.12.84)	6·50	20
		a. *Deep ultramarine*	7·00	20
		b. *Pale ultramarine*	5·50	20
		cw. Wmk inverted	26·00	10·00
		d. Chalk-surfaced paper. *Ultramarine* (1902)	3·00	10
		da. *Blue*	3·00	10
		dw. Wmk inverted	75·00	40·00
55	**14**	2pi. orange-brown (1.8.93)	12·00	30
		aw. Wmk inverted	80·00	40·00
		b. Chalk-surfaced paper (1902)	12·00	10
		ba. *Orange*	23·00	1·00
		bw. Wmk inverted	—	30·00
56	**15**	5pi. pale grey (15.12.84)	13·00	50
		a. *Slate*	11·00	50
		bw. Wmk inverted		
		c. Chalk-surfaced paper. *Slate-grey* (1902)	16·00	15
		cw. Wmk inverted	—	£100

(17)

1884 (1 Feb). *Surch with T* **17** *at Bûlâq.*

57	**15**	20pa. on 5pi. green	7·00	1·25
		a. Surch inverted	65·00	60·00
		w. Wmk inverted	50·00	30·00

(New Currency: 1000 milliemes = 100 piastres = £1 Egyptian)

18

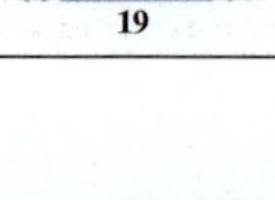
19

20

21

22

1888 (1 Jan)–**1909**. *Ordinary paper.* W **8***a*. P 14.

58	**18**	1m. pale brown	3·00	10
		a. *Deep brown*	3·25	10
		bw. Wmk inverted	25·00	4·00
		c. Chalk-surfaced paper. *Pale brown* (1902)	3·25	10
		ca. *Deep brown*	3·25	10
		cw. Wmk inverted	40·00	5·00
59	**19**	2m. blue-green	2·25	10
		a. *Green*	1·25	10
		bw. Wmk inverted	40·00	5·00
		c. Chalk-surfaced paper. *Green* (1902)	1·00	10
		cw. Wmk inverted	40·00	5·00
60	**20**	3m. maroon (1.1.92)	4·25	1·00
61		3m. yellow (1.8.93)	5·00	50
		a. *Orange-yellow*	4·75	15
		bw. Wmk inverted	45·00	15·00
		c. Chalk-surfaced paper. *Orange-yellow* (1902)	2·75	10
		cw. Wmk inverted	75·00	30·00
62	**21**	4m. verm (*chalk-surfaced paper*) (1906)	3·75	10
		a. Bisected (2m.) (on cover) (11.09)	†	—
		w. Wmk inverted	—	60·00
63		5m. rose-carmine	3·75	10
		a. *Bright rose*	3·75	10
		b. *Aniline rose*	4·75	10
		cw. Wmk inverted	—	75·00
		d. Chalk-surfaced paper. *Rose* (1902)	2·75	10
		da. *Deep aniline rose*	4·50	20
64	**22**	10p. mauve (1.1.89)	15·00	80
		a. *Aniline mauve*	18·00	80
		bw. Wmk inverted	—	50·00
		c. Chalk-surfaced paper. *Mauve* (1902)	22·00	50

No. 62a was used at Gizira in conjunction with the 1m. value and the Official, No. O64.

No. 63d exists in coils constructed from normal sheets.

Kedive Abbas Hilmi

7 January 1892–19 December 1914

A set of three values, in a common design showing Cleopatra and a Nile boat, was prepared in 1895 for the Nile Winter Fête, but not issued. Examples survive from the De La Rue archives.

29 Nile Feluccas

30 Cleopatra from Temple of Dendera

31 Ras-el-Tin Palace, Alexandria

32 Pyramids of Giza

33 Sphinx

34 Colossi of Amenophis III at Thebes

35 Archway of Ptolemy III, Karnak

36 Citadel, Cairo

37 Rock Temple of Abu Simbel

38 Aswân Dam

(Typo D.L.R.)

1914 (8 Jan). W **8***a*. P 13½×14 (1m. to 10m.) or 14 (20m. to 200m.).

73	**29**	1m. sepia	1·25	40
		w. Wmk inverted	—	75·00
74	**30**	2m. green	3·25	20
		w. Wmk inverted	—	40·00
75	**31**	3m. yellow-orange	2·75	35
		a. Double impression		
		w. Wmk inverted	—	40·00
76	**32**	4m. vermilion	3·25	65
		w. Wmk inverted	—	40·00

77 **33** 5m. lake ... 3·50 10
a. Wmk sideways star to right* (booklets) ... 10·00 22·00
aw. Wmk sideways star to left ... 10·00 22·00
w. Wmk inverted ... 15·00 10·00
78 **34** 10m. dull blue ... 5·50 10
w. Wmk inverted ... 25·00 25·00
79 **35** 20m. olive ... 6·50 30
w. Wmk inverted ... 60·00 40·00
80 **36** 50m. purple ... 17·00 55
w. Wmk inverted ... — 50·00
81 **37** 100m. slate ... 17·00 75
82 **38** 200m. maroon ... 26·00 3·50
73/82 *Set of* 10 ... 75·00 6·00

*The normal sideways watermark shows the star to the right of the crescent, *as seen from the back of the stamp*.

All the above exist imperforate, but imperforate stamps without watermark are proofs.

See also Nos. 84/95.

BRITISH PROTECTORATE

On 18 December 1914, after war with Turkey had begun, Egypt was declared to be a British protectorate. Abbas Hilmi was deposed, and his uncle, Hussein Kamil, was proclaimed Sultan of Egypt.

Sultan Hussain Kamil
19 December 1914–9 October 1917

(39)

1915 (15 Oct). *No. 75 surch with T* **39**, *at Bûlâq*.
83 **31** 2m. on 3m. yellow-orange ... 55 2·25
a. Surch inverted ... £200 £200
b. Surch double, one albino ... £120
w. Wmk inverted ... 4·00

Sultan Ahmed Fuad
9 October 1917–15 March 1922

40

(A)

(B)

41 Statue of Rameses II, Luxor

42

(Typo Harrison)

1921–22. *As Nos. 73/82 and new designs (15m.)*. W **40**. P 14 (20, 50, 100m.) or 13½×14 (others).
84 **29** 1m. sepia (A) ... 1·50 2·75
a. Two dots omitted (B) (R. 10/10) ... 35·00 45·00
w. Wmk inverted ... 10·00 7·50
85 **30** 2m. green ... 5·50 3·75
a. Imperf between (pair) ...
w. Wmk inverted ... 15·00 10·00
86 2m. vermilion (1922) ... 4·25 1·25
w. Wmk inverted ... 15·00 10·00
87 **31** 3m. yellow-orange ... 6·00 3·00
w. Wmk inverted ... 16·00 10·00
88 **32** 4m. green (1922) ... 5·50 6·50
w. Wmk inverted ... — 10·00
89 **33** 5m. lake (1.21) ... 4·75 45
a. Imperf between (pair) ...
w. Wmk inverted ... 15·00 10·00
90 5m. pink (11.21) ... 7·00 20
w. Wmk inverted ... 15·00 10·00
91 **34** 10m. dull blue ... 7·00 20
w. Wmk inverted ... — 10·00
92 10m. lake (9.22) ... 1·75 30
w. Wmk inverted ... — 10·00
93 **41** 15m. indigo (3.22) ... 6·50 15
w. Wmk inverted ... — 8·00
94 **42** 15m. indigo ... 27·00 3·50
w. Wmk inverted ... 28·00 10·00
95 **35** 20m. olive ... 9·50 30
w. Wmk inverted ... 20·00 10·00
96 **36** 50m. purple ... 10·00 1·25
w. Wink inverted ... 18·00 12·00
97 **37** 100m. slate (1922) ... 85·00 7·50
84/97 *Set of* 14 ... £160 28·00

Type **42** was printed first; but because the Arabic inscription at right was felt to be unsuitable the stamps were withheld and the corrected Type **41** printed and issued. Type **42** was released later.

STAMP BOOKLETS

1903 (1 Jan). *Black on pink cover inscr* "Egyptian Post Office" *in English and French. Stapled.*
SB1 121m. booklet containing twenty-four 5m. (No. 63c) in blocks of 6 ... £4000

1903 (1 July). *Black on blue cover inscr* "Egyptian Post Office" *in English and French. Stapled.*
SB2 73m. booklet containing twenty-four 3m. (No. 61ab) in blocks of 6 ...

1911 (1 July). *Black on pink cover inscr* "Egyptian Post Office" *in English and Arabic. Stapled.*
SB3 120m. Contents as No. SB1 ... £3000

1914 (8 Jan). *Black on pink cover inscr* "Egyptian Post Office" *in English and Arabic. Stapled.*
SB4 125m. booklet containing twenty-four 5m. (No. 77a) in blocks of 6 ...

1919 (1 Jan). *Black on pink cover inscr* "Egyptian Post Office" *in English and Arabic. Stapled.*
SB5 120m. Contents as No. SB4 ... £2000

1921 (12 June). *Deep blue on pink cover inscr* "POST OFFICE" *in English and Arabic. Stapled.*
SB6 120m. booklet containing twenty-four 5m. (No. 89) in blocks of 6 ...
a. Stitched ... £1600

1921 (Nov). *Deep blue or pink cover inscr* "POST OFFICE" *in English and Arabic. Stapled.*
SB7 120m. booklet containing twenty-four 5m. (No. 90) in blocks of 6 ... £1200

POSTAGE DUE STAMPS

D 16

D 23

D 24

(Des L. Barkhausen. Litho V. Penasson, Alexandria)

1884 (1 Jan). W **6** (*impressed on reverse*). P 10½.
D57 **D 16** 10pa. red ... 45·00 9·00
a. Imperf (Pair) ... £110
b. Imperf between (pair) ... £110
x. Wmk impressed on face ...
D58 20pa. red ... £110 29·00
x. Wmk impressed on face ...
D59 1pi. red ... £130 48·00
x. Wmk impressed on face ...
D60 2pi. red ... £225 10·00
w. Wmk inverted ... £325 20·00
x. Wmk impressed on face ...
D61 5pi. red ... 14·00 42·00
x. Wmk impressed on face ...

1886 (1 Aug)–**87**. No wmk. P 10½.
D62 **D 16** 10pa. rose-red (1887) ... 70·00 14·00
a. Imperf between (pair) ... 90·00
D63 20pa. rose-red ... £250 42·00
a. Imperf between (pair) ...
D64 1pi. rose-red ... 30·00 8·00
a. Imperf between (pair) ... £120 £120
D65 2pi. rose-red ... 30·00 3·75
a. Imperf between (pair) ... £120

Specialists distinguish four types of each value in both these issues.

(Litho V. Penasson, Alexandria)

1888 (1 Jan). No wmk. P 11½.
D66 **D 23** 2m. green ... 17·00 23·00
a. Imperf between (pair) ... £170 £170
b. Imperf (pair) ...
D67 5m. rose-carmine ... 35·00 23·00
a. Imperf (pair) ...
D68 1p. blue ... £130 35·00
a. Imperf between (pair) ... £170
D69 2p. orange ... £150 13·00
D70 5p. grey ... £200 £180
a. With stop after left-hand "PIASTRES" ... £275 £225

Specialists distinguish four types of each value. No. D70a occurs on all examples of one of these types in the sheet except that on R. 2/1.

Beware of forgeries of the 5p.

(Typo De La Rue)

1889 (Apr)–**1907**. *Ordinary paper.* W **8***a*. P 14.
D71 **D 24** 2m. green ... 7·00 50
a. Bisected (1m.) (on cover with unbisected 2m.) (2.98). † £250
bw. Wmk inverted ... 8·00 3·00
c. Chalk-surfaced paper (1906) 15·00 50
D72 4m. maroon ... 2·25 50
aw. Wmk inverted ... 4·00 1·00
b. Chalk-surfaced paper (1906) 2·75 50
D73 1p. ultramarine ... 5·50 50
aw. Wmk inverted ... 8·50 3·00
b. Chalk-surfaced paper (1906) 6·50 50
D74 2p. orange ... 5·50 70
bw. Wmk inverted ... 5·00 70
c. Chalk-surfaced paper (1907) 5·00 70

No. D71a was authorised for use on Egyptian Army letters from the Sudan campaign which were only charged 3m. postage due.

See also Nos. 84/6 for stamps with watermark sideways.

(D 26)

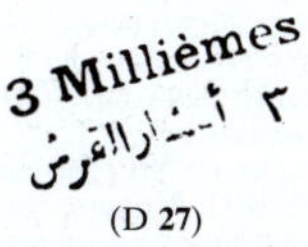

(D 27)

Type D 26

The Arabic figure at right is less than 2 mm from the next character, which consists of a straight stroke only.

Type D 27

The distance is 3 mm and the straight character has a comma-like character above it. There are other minor differences.

1898 (7 May)–**1907**. *No.* D74 *surch at Bûlâq. Ordinary paper.*

(*a*) *With Type* D **26**.
D75 **D 24** 3m. on 2p. orange ... 1·25 4·50
a. Surch inverted ... 60·00 75·00
b. Pair, one without surch ...
c. Arabic "2" for "3" ...
d. Arabic "3" over "2" ... £100

No. D75c occurred in the first printing on positions 10, 20, 30, 40, 50 and 60 of the pane of 60 (the Arabic figure is the right-hand character of the second line—see illustration on page xvii). In the second printing the correct figure was printed on top to form No. D75d The error was corrected in subsequent printings.

(*b*) *With Type* D **27** (*11.04*).
D76 **D 24** 3m. on 2p. orange ... 4·75 17·00
a. Surch inverted ... 50·00 60·00
b. Chalk-surfaced paper (1907)
ba. Surch inverted ...
bb. Surch double ...

1914–15. *As Nos. D71/3 but wmk sideways**.
D84 **D 24** 2m. bright green (1915) ... 16·00 4·25
w. Wmk star to left of crescent 22·00 14·00
D85 4m. maroon ... 16·00 17·00
w. Wmk star to left of crescent 26·00
D86 1p. dull ultramarine ... 25·00 11·00
w. Wmk star to left of crescent 20·00 12·00

*The normal sideways watermark shows star to right of crescent, *as seen from the back of the stamp*.

D 43

D 44

(Typo Harrison)

1921 (Apr)–**22**. *Chalk-surfaced paper.* W **40** (sideways*). P 14×13½.
D98 **D 43** 2m. green ... 2·75 4·75
w. Wmk stars below crescents 9·00 4·75
D99 2m. scarlet (1922) ... 1·00 2·00
w. Wmk stars below crescents 7·50 4·25
D100 4m. scarlet ... 5·50 16·00
D101 4m. green (1922) ... 6·00 1·75
w. Wmk stars below crescents 12·00 5·50
D102 **D 44** 10m. deep slate-blue (11.21) ... 9·00 21·00
D103 10m. lake (1922) ... 5·50 1·25
w. Wmk stars below crescents 10·00 4·00
D98/103 *Set of* 6 ... 27·00 42·00

*The normal sideways watermark shows the stars above the crescents.

OFFICIAL STAMPS

O 25

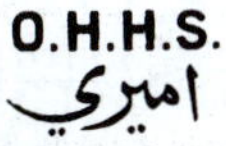

(O 28)

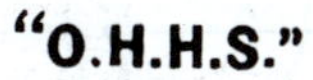

(O 29)

(Typo De La Rue)

1893 (1 Jan)–**1914**. *Ordinary paper.* W **8***a*. P 14.
O64 **O 25** (–) chestnut ... 2·75 10
a. Chalk-surfaced paper (1903) ... 4·00 50
bw. Wmk inverted ... 9·00
c. Wmk sideways star to right. Chalk-surfaced paper (1914) ... 10·00 9·00
cw. Wmk sideways star to left ..

From January 1907 No. O64 was used on most official mail to addresses within Egypt. In 1907 it was replaced by Nos. O73/8, but the use of No. O64 for unregistered official mail to Egyptian addresses was resumed on 1 January 1909.

After No. O64c was withdrawn in 1915 the remaining stock was surcharged 1p., 2p., 3p. or 5p. for fiscal use.

1907 (1 Feb–Aug). *Nos. 54da, 56c, 58c, 59c, 61c and 63d optd with Type* O **28** *by De La Rue.*
O73 **18** 1m. pale brown ... 1·75 30
O74 **19** 2m. green ... 4·00 10
a. Opt double ...
O75 **20** 3m. orange-yellow ... 2·75 1·25
O76 **21** 5m. rose ... 5·00 10
O77 **13** 1p. blue ... 2·00 20
O78 **15** 5p. slate-grey (Aug) ... 16·00 4·50
O73/8 *Set of* 6 ... 28·00 5·75

Nos. O73/8 were used on all official mail from February 1907 until 1 January 1909 after which their use was restricted to registered items and those sent to addresses overseas.

1913 (Nov). *No. 63d optd at Bûlâq.*

(*a*) *With Type* O **29**.
O79 **21** 5m. rose ... — £325
a. Opt inverted ... — £6000

(*b*) *As Type* O **29** *but without inverted commas.*
O80 **21** 5m. rose ... 8·50 60
a. No stop after "S" (R. 11/10) ... 55·00 16·00
b. Opt inverted ... — 75·00

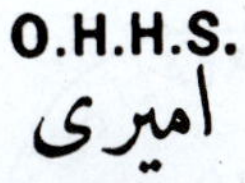

(O 38)

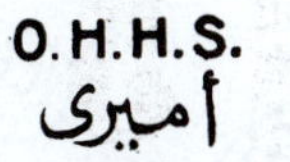

(O 39)

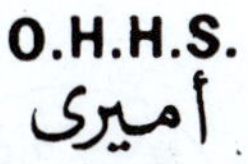

(O 43)

1914 (Dec)–**15**. *Stamps of 1902–6 and 1914 optd with Type* O **38** *at Bûlâq.*
O83 **29** 1m. sepia (1.15) ... 1·50 4·25
a. No stop after "S" (R. 10/10) ... 12·00 25·00
w. Wmk inverted ... † —
O84 **19** 2m. green (3.15) ... 4·25 8·00
a. No stop after "S" ... 14·00 23·00

		b. Opt inverted	35·00	35·00
		c. Opt double	£325	
O85	**31**	3m. yellow-orange (3.15)	2·50	4·50
		a. No stop after "S" (R. 10/10)	14·00	25·00
O86	**21**	4m. vermilion (12.14)	5·00	3·00
		a. Opt inverted	£190	£140
		b. Pair, one without opt		
O87	**33**	5m. lake (1.15)	4·00	1·50
		a. No stop after "S" (R. 10/10)	15·00	22·00
O83/7 *Set of* 5			15·00	19·00

No. O84a occurs on three positions from the first printing and on two different positions from the second. Nos. O83a, O85a and O87a usually show a faint trace of the stop.

1915 (Oct). *Nos. 59ab, 62 and 77 optd lithographically with Type* O **39** *at Bûlâq.*

O88	**19**	2m. green	2·75	4·25
		a. Opt inverted	20·00	20·00
		b. Opt double	25·00	
O89	**21**	4m. vermilion	7·00	8·00
O90	**33**	5m. lake	9·50	1·25
		a. Pair, one without opt	£275	

1922. *Nos. 84, etc optd lithographically with Type* O **43** *at Bûlâq.*

O98	**29**	1m. sepia (A) (28.6)	3·50	12·00
		a. Two dots omitted (B)	£200	
		w. Wmk inverted		
O99	**30**	2m. vermilion (16.6)	8·00	18·00
O100	**31**	3m. yellow-orange (28.6)	65·00	£130
O101	**33**	5m. pink (13.3)	17·00	4·50

Egypt was declared to be an independent kingdom on 15 March 1922, and Sultan Ahmed Fuad became king.

Later stamp issues will be found listed in Part 19 (*Middle East*) of this catalogue.

EGYPTIAN POST OFFICES ABROAD

From 1865 Egypt operated various post offices in foreign countries. No special stamps were issued for these offices and use in them of unoverprinted Egyptian stamps can only be identified by the cancellation. Stamps with such cancellations are worth more than the used prices quoted in the Egypt listings.

Such offices operated in the following countries. An * indicates that details will be found under that heading elsewhere in the catalogue.

ETHIOPIA

A

B

C

D

MASSAWA. *Open Nov* 1867 *to* 5 Dec 1885. *Postmark types* A (*also without* REGIE), B, C, D. *An Arabic seal type is also known on stampless covers.*

SENHIT (near Keren). *Open* 1878 *to* April 1885. *Only one cover, cancelled* "Mouderie Senhit" *in* 1879, *is known, together with one showing possible hand-drawn cancellation.*

A post office is also recorded at Harar in 1878, but no postal marking has so far been reported

SOMALILAND*

Unoverprinted stamps of Egypt used from 1876 until 1884.

SUDAN*

Unoverprinted stamps of Egypt used from 1867 until 1897.

TURKISH EMPIRE

E

F

G

H

I

J

K

L

M

N

O

The offices are listed according to the spelling on the cancellation. The present-day name (if different) and country are given in brackets.

ALESSANDRETTA (Iskenderun, Turkey). *Open* 14 July 1870 *to* Feb 1872. *Postmark types* E, I.

BAIROUT (Beirut, Lebanon). *Open* 14 July 1870 *to* Feb 1872. *Postmark types* E, J.

CAVALA (Kavala, Greece). *Open* 14 July 1870 *to* Feb 1872. *Postmark type* E.

COSTANTINOPOLI (Istanbul, Turkey). *Open* 13 June 1865 *to* 30 June 1881. *Postmark types* E, F, O.

DARDANELLI (Canakkle, Turkey). *Open* 10 June 1868 *to* 30 June 1881. *Postmark types* H, K.

DJEDDAH, *see* GEDDA.

GALIPOLI (Gelibolu, Turkey). *Open* 10 June 1868 *to* 30 June 1881. *Postmark types* E, L.

GEDDA, DJEDDAH (Jeddah, Saudi Arabia). *Open* 8 June 1865 *to* 30 June 1881. *Postmark types* F, G (*also with year replacing solid half-circle*), O (*all spelt* GEDDA), D (*spelt* DJEDDAH).

JAFFA (Jaffa, Israel). *Open* 14 July 1870 *to* Feb 1872. *Postmark type* E.

LAGOS (Port Logo, Greece). *Open* 14 July 1870 *to* Feb 1872. *Postmark type* E.

LATAKIA (Syria). *Open* 14 July 1870 *to* Feb 1872. *Postmark type* E.

LEROS (Aegean Is). *Open* July 1873 *to* January 1874 *and* May *to* October 1874. *Postmark type* E.

MERSINA (Mersin, Turkey). *Open* 14 July 1870 *to* Feb 1872. *Postmark type* E.

METELINO (Lesbos, Greece). *Open* 14 July 1870 *to* 30 June 1881. *Postmark types* E, M.

RODI (Rhodes, Greece). *Open* 13 Aug 1872 *to* 30 June 1881. *Postmark type* E.

SALONNICCHI (Thessaloniki, Greece). *Open* 14 July 1870 *to* Feb 1872. *Postmark type* E.

SCIO (Chios, Aegean Is.). *Open* 14 July 1870 *to* 30 June 1881. *Postmark types* E, N.

SMIRNE (Izmir, Turkey). *Open* 14 Nov 1865 *to* 30 June 1881. *Postmark types* E (*also without* "V. R."), F.

TENEDOS (Bozcaada, Turkey). *Open* 14 July 1870 *to* March 1871. *Postmark type* E.

TRIPOLI (Lebanon). *Open* 14 July 1870 *to* Feb 1872. *Postmark type* E.

VOLO (Volos, Greece). *Open* 14 July 1870 *to* Feb 1872. *Postmark type* E.

BRITISH FORCES IN EGYPT

Following the rise of a nationalist movment led by Arabi Pasha, and serious disturbances in Alexandria, British troops landed at Ismalia in August 1882 and defeated the nationalists at Tel-el-Kebir on 13 September. A British Army Post Office detachment landed at Alexandria on 21 August and provided a postal service for the troops, using Great Britain stamps, from various locations until it was withdrawn on 7 October

During the Gordon Relief Expedition of 1884–85 a postal detachment was sent to Suakin on the Red Sea. This operated between 25 March and 30 May 1885 using Great Britain stamps.

ZA 1

Stamps of GREAT BRITAIN *cancelled with Type* ZA **1**.

1882 (Aug–Oct).

ZA1	½d. rose-red (Plate No. 20)	
ZA2	½d. green (1880)	£300
ZA3	1d. Venetian red (1880)	
ZA4	1d. lilac (1881)	£175
ZA5	2½d. blue (1881) (Plate Nos. 21, 22, 23)	£100

1885. *Used at Suakin.*

ZA6	½d. slate-blue (1884)	
ZA7	1d. lilac (1881)	£300
ZA8	2½d. lilac (1884)	£225
ZA9	5d. dull green (1884)	£500

From 1 November 1932 to 29 February 1936 members of the British Forces in Egypt and their families were allowed to send letters to the British Isles at reduced rates. Special seals, which were on sale in booklets at N.A.A.F.I. Institutes and Canteens, were used instead of Egyptian stamps. These seals were stuck on the back of the envelopes, letters bearing the seals being franked on the front with a hand-stamp inscribed "EGYPT POSTAGE PREPAID" in a double circle surmounted by a crown.

PRICES FOR STAMPS ON COVER

Nos. A1/9	*from* × 5
No. A10	*from* × 1·5
No. A11	*from* × 5
No. A12	*from* × 75
No. A13	*from* × 20
No. A14	*from* × 100
No. A15	*from* × 20

A 1

A 2

(Des Lt-Col. C. Fraser. Typo Hanbury, Tomsett & Co. Ltd, London)

1932 (1 Nov)–**33**. P 11.

		(a) Inscr "POSTAL SEAL"		
A1	A **1**	1p. deep blue and red	95·00	3·50
		(b) Inscr "LETTER SEAL"		
A2	A **1**	1p. deep blue and red (8.33)	38·00	85

(Des Sgt. W. F. Lait. Litho Walker & Co, Amalgamated Press, Cairo)

1932 (26 Nov)–**35**. *Christmas Seals.* P 11½.

A3	A **2**	3m. black/*azure*	50·00	70·00
A4		3m. brown-lake (13.11.33)	7·50	50·00
A5		3m. deep blue (17.11.34)	7·00	28·00
A6		3m. vermilion (23.11.35)	1·25	42·00
		a. Pale vermilion (19.12.35)	9·50	25·00

A 3

(Des Miss Waugh. Photo Harrison)

1934 (1 June)–**35**.

		(a) P 14½ x 14.		
A7	A **3**	1p. carmine	48·00	85
A8		1p. green (5.12.34)	4·00	4·00
		(b) P 13½×14.		
A9	A **3**	1p. carmine (24.4.35)	2·75	3·25

(A **4**)

1935 (6 May). *Silver Jubilee. As No. A9, but colour changed and optd with Type* A **4**, *in red.*

A10	A **3**	1p. ultramarine	£250	£180

Xmas 1935
3 Milliemes
(A 5)

1935 (16 Dec). *Provisional Christmas Seal. No. A9 surch with Type* A **5**.

A11	A **3**	3m. on 1p. carmine	16·00	70·00

The seals and letter stamps were replaced by the following Army Post stamps issued by the Egyptian Postal Administration. No. A9 was accepted for postage until 15 March 1936.

A **6** King Fuad I

A **7** King Farouk

W **48** of Egypt

(Types A **6**/A **7**. Photo Survey Dept, Cairo)

1936. W **48** of Egypt. P 13½ × 14.

A12	A **6**	3m. green (1.12.36)	1·00	1·50
A13		10m. carmine (1.3.36)	5·50	10
		w. Wmk inverted		

1939 (16 Dec). W **48** of Egypt. P 13×13½.

A14	A **7**	3m. green	4·50	7·00
A15		10m. carmine	6·50	10
		w. Wmk inverted		

These stamps were withdrawn in April 1941 but the concession, without the use of special stamps, continued until October 1951 when the postal agreement was abrogated.

SUEZ CANAL COMPANY

PRICES FOR STAMPS ON COVER	
Nos. 1/4	*from* × 20

100 Centimes = 1 Franc

On 30 November 1855 a concession to construct the Suez Canal was granted to Ferdinand de Lesseps and the Compagnie Universelle du Canal Maritime de Suez was formed. Work began in April 1859 and the canal was opened on 17 November 1869. In November 1875 the Khedive sold his shares in the company to the British Government, which then became the largest shareholder.

The company transported mail free of charge between Port Said and Suez from 1859 to 1867, when it was decided that payment should be made for the service and postage stamps were introduced in July 1868. Letters for destinations beyond Port Said or Suez required additional franking with Egyptian or French stamps.

The imposition of charges for the service was not welcomed by the public and in August the Egyptian Government agreed to take it over.

1

(Litho Chezaud, Aine & Tavernier, Paris)

1868 (8 July). Imperf.

1	**1**	1c. black	£250	£1000
2		5c. green	85·00	£500
3		20c. blue	75·00	£500
4		40c. pink	£130	£750

Shades of all values exist.

Stamps can be found showing parts of the papermaker's watermark "LA+-F" (La Croix Frères).

These stamps were withdrawn from sale on 16 August 1868 and demonetised on 31 August.

Many forgeries exist, unused and cancelled. The vast majority of these forgeries show vertical lines, instead of cross-hatching, between "POSTES" and the central oval. It is believed that other forgeries, which do show cross-hatching, originate from the plate of the 40c. value which is missing from the company's archives. These are, however, on thin, brittle paper with smooth shiny gum.

Falkland Islands

PRICES FOR STAMPS ON COVER TO 1945	
No. 1	*from* × 100
No. 2	*from* × 50
Nos. 3/4	*from* × 10
No. 5	—
Nos. 6/10	*from* × 30
Nos. 11/12	*from* × 15
Nos. 13/14	*from* × 15
Nos. 15/17	*from* × 20
Nos. 17*b*/*c*	*from* × 100
Nos. 18/21	*from* × 10
Nos. 22/*b*	*from* × 30
Nos. 23/4	*from* × 100
Nos. 25/6	*from* × 30
No. 27	*from* × 20
No. 28	*from* × 40
No. 29	*from* × 5
Nos. 30/*b*	*from* × 50
No. 30*c*	*from* × 15
No. 31	*from* × 5
Nos. 32/8	*from* × 15
Nos. 41/2	—
Nos. 43/8	*from* × 12
Nos. 49/50	—
Nos. 60/5	*from* × 10
Nos. 66/9	—
Nos. 70/1	*from* × 10
Nos. 72/*b*	—
Nos. 73/9	*from* × 4
No. 80	—
No. 115	*from* × 2
Nos. 116/19	*from* × 20
Nos. 120/2	*from* × 6
Nos. 123/6	—
Nos. 127/34	*from* × 5
Nos. 135/8	—
Nos. 139/45	*from* × 50
Nos. 146/63	*from* × 5

CROWN COLONY

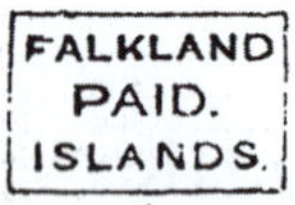

1

2

1869–76. *The Franks.*

FR1	1	In black, *on cover*	£11000
FR2	2	In red, *on cover* (1876)	£18000

On *piece*, No. FR1 on white or coloured paper £110; No. FR2 on white £180.

The first recorded use of No. FR1 is on a cover to London datestamped 4 January 1869. The use of these franks ceased when the first stamps were issued.

3

½d.
(4)

In the ½d., 2d., 2½d. and 9d. the figures of value in the lower corners are replaced by small rosettes and the words of value are in colour.

NOTE. Nos. 1, 2, 3, 4, 8, 10, 11 and 12 exist with one or two sides imperf from the margin of the sheets.

(Recess B.W.)

1878–79. No wmk. P 14, 14½.

1	3	1d. claret (19.6.78)	£750	£425
2		4d. grey-black (Sept 1879)	£1200	£150
		a. On wmkd paper	£2750	£500
3		6d. blue-green (19.6.78)	95·00	75·00
4		1s. bistre-brown (1878)	75·00	65·00

No. 2a shows portions of the papermaker's watermark—"R. TURNER, CHAFFORD MILLS"—in ornate double-lined capitals.

NOTES. The dates shown for Nos. 5/12 and 15/38 are those on which the printer delivered the various printings to the Crown Agents. Several months could elapse before the stamps went on sale in the Colony, depending on the availability of shipping.

The plates used for these stamps did not fit the paper so that the watermark appears in all sorts of positions on the stamp. Well centred examples are scarce. Examples can also be found showing parts of the marginal watermarks, either CROWN AGENTS horizontally in letters 12 mm high or "CROWN AGENTS FOR THE COLONIES" vertically in 7 mm letters. Both are in double-lined capitals.

1882 (22 Nov). Wmk Crown CA (upright). P 14, 14½.

5	3	1d. dull claret	£325	£170
		a. Imperf vert (horiz pair)	£65000	
		x. Wmk reversed	£950	
		y. Wmk inverted and reversed	£550	£350
6		4d. grey-black	£475	90·00
		w. Wmk inverted	£750	£275

1885 (23 Mar)–**91**. Wmk Crown CA (sideways*). P 14, 14½.

7	3	1d. pale claret	90·00	60·00
		w. Wmk Crown to right of CA	90·00	70·00
		x. Wmk sideways reversed	£250	£120
		y. Wmk Crown to right of CA and reversed	£190	£130
8		1d. brownish claret (3.10.87)	£110	50·00
		a. Bisected (on cover) (1.1891)	†	£3250
		w. Wmk Crown to right of CA	£130	50·00
		x. Wmk sideways reversed	£250	£100
		y. Wmk Crown to right of CA and reversed	£250	£150
9		4d. pale grey-black	£700	80·00
		w. Wmk Crown to right of CA	£700	90·00
		x. Wmk sideways reversed	£750	£190
		y. Wmk Crown to right of CA and reversed	£650	£140
10		4d. grey-black (3.10.87)	£400	50·00
		w. Wmk Crown to right of CA	£450	50·00
		x. Wmk sideways reversed	£850	£120
		y. Wmk Crown to right of CA and reversed	£750	90·00

*The normal sideways watermark shows Crown to left of CA, *as seen from the back of the stamp*.

For No. 8a see note below No. 14.

1889 (26 Sept)–**91**. Wmk Crown CA (upright). P 14, 14½.

11	3	1d. red-brown (21.5.91)	£200	85·00
		a. Bisected (on cover) (7.91)	†	£3500
		x. Wmk reversed	£500	£200
12		4d. olive grey-black	£160	60·00
		w. Wmk inverted	£750	£375
		x. Wmk reversed	£450	£180

For No. 11a see note below No. 14.

1891 (Jan–11 July). *Nos. 8 and 11 bisected diagonally and each half handstamped with T* **4**.

13	3	½d. on half of 1d. brownish claret (No. 8)	£600	£300
		a. Unsevered pair	£3250	£1000
		b. Unsevered pair *se-tenant* with unsurcharged whole stamp	£27000	
		c. Bisect *se-tenant* with unsurcharged whole stamp	†	£1700
14		½d. on half of 1d. red-brown (No. 11) (11 July)	£700	£275
		a. Unsevered pair	£3750	£1500
		b. Bisect *se-tenant* with unsurcharged whole stamp	†	£1600

1891 PROVISIONALS. In 1891 the postage to the United Kingdom and Colonies was reduced from 4d. to 2½d. per half ounce. As no ½d. or 2½d. stamps were available the bisection of the 1d. was authorised from 1 January 1891. This authorisation was withdrawn on 11 January 1892, although bisects were accepted for postage until July of that year. The ½d. and 2½d. stamps were placed on sale from 10 September 1891.

Cork Cancel used in 1891

The Type **4** surcharge was not used regularly; unsurcharged bisects being employed far more frequently. Genuine bisects should be cancelled with the cork cancel illustrated above. The use of any other postmark, including a different cork cancel or an "F.I." obliterator, requires date evidence linked to known mail ship sailings to prove authenticity.

After 10 September 1891 the post office supplied "posthumous" examples of the surcharged bisects to collectors. These were without postal validity and differ from Type **4** by showing a large full stop, long fraction bar or curly tail to "2". Some of the posthumous surcharges were applied to No. 18 which was not used for the original bisects. Examples are also known showing the surcharge double, inverted or sideways.

1891 (10 Sept)–**1902**. Wmk Crown CA (upright). P 14, 14½.

15	3	½d. blue-green (10 Sept–Nov 1891)	25·00	27·00
		x. Wmk reversed	£400	£375
		y. Wmk inverted and reversed	£425	£425
16		½d. green (20.5.92)	16·00	15·00
		ax. Wmk reversed	£180	£180
		ay. Wmk inverted and reversed	£375	£375
		b. Deep dull green (15.4.96)	40·00	30·00
17		½d. deep yellow-green (1894–95)	17·00	21·00
		ay. Wmk inverted and reversed	£180	£180
		b. Yellow-green (19.6.99)	2·00	3·25
		c. Dull yellowish green (13.1.1902)	6·00	4·75
		cx. Wmk reversed	£400	£400
18		1d. orange red-brown (14.10.91)	95·00	75·00
		a. Brown	£140	75·00
		w. Wmk inverted	£950	£425
		x. Wmk reversed	£250	£250
19		1d. reddish chestnut (20.4.92)	45·00	42·00
20		1d. orange-brn (wmk reversed) (18.1.94)	55·00	50·00
21		1d. claret (23.7.94)	£110	80·00
		x. Wmk reversed	80·00	50·00
22		1d. Venetian red (pale to deep) (1895–96)	22·00	17·00
		ax. Wmk reversed	10·00	12·00
		b. Venetian claret (1898?)	32·00	15·00
23		1d. pale red (19.6.99)	8·50	2·75
		x. Wmk reversed	£325	£325
24		1d. orange-red (13.1.1902)	15·00	4·25
25		2d. purple (pale to deep) (1895–98)	6·50	12·00
		x. Wmk reversed	£475	£500
26		2d. reddish purple (15.4.96)	5·00	11·00
27		2½d. pale chalky ultramarine (10.9.91)	£180	50·00
28		2½d. dull blue (19.11.91)	£180	27·00
		x. Wmk reversed	£375	£275
29		2½d. Prussian blue (18.1.94)	£225	£130
30		2½d. ultramarine (1894–96)	38·00	13·00
		ax. Wmk reversed	70·00	16·00
		ay. Wmk inverted and reversed	£800	
		b. Pale ultramarine (10.6.98)	40·00	17·00
		bx. Wmk reversed	£120	75·00
		c. Deep ultramarine (18.9.1901)	42·00	35·00
		cx. Wmk reversed	£350	£350
31		4d. brownish black (wmk reversed) (18.1.94)	£750	£350
32		4d. olive-black (11.5.95)	13·00	21·00
33		6d. orange-yellow (19.11.91)	£200	£160
		x. Wmk reversed	75·00	50·00
34		6d. yellow (15.4.96)	48·00	48·00
35		9d. pale reddish orange (15.11.95)	48·00	55·00
		x. Wmk reversed	£375	£425
		y. Wmk inverted and reversed	£550	£550
36		9d. salmon (15.4.96)	50·00	55·00
		x. Wmk reversed	£375	£425
37		1s. grey-brown (15.11.95)	60·00	55·00
		x. Wmk reversed	£180	£180
38		1s. yellow-brown (15.4.96)	60·00	48·00
		x. Wmk reversed	£160	£180
17b/38 *Set of* 8			£200	£180
15s, 26s, 28s, 33s, 35s Optd "Specimen" *Set of* 5			£600	

The ½d. and 2½d. were first placed on sale in the Falkland Islands on 10 September 1891. Such stamps came from the August 1891 printing. The stock of the May printings sent to the Falkland Islands was lost at sea.

The 2½d. ultramarine printing can sometimes be found in a violet shade, but the reason for this is unknown.

5

6

(Recess B.W.)

1898 (5 Oct). Wmk Crown CC. P 14, 14½.

41	5	2s.6d. deep blue	£250	£250
42	6	5s. red	£225	£225
41s/2s Optd "Specimen" *Set of* 2			£475	

7

8

(Recess D.L.R.)

1904 (16 July)–**12**. Wmk Mult Crown CA. P 14.

43	7	½d. yellow-green	4·50	1·50
		aw. Wmk inverted	£375	£225
		ax. Wmk reversed	£900	
		b. Pale yellow-green (on thick paper) (6.08)	16·00	7·50
		bw. Wmk inverted		
		c. Deep yellow-green (7.11)	11·00	3·00
44		1d. vermilion	13·00	1·50
		aw. Wmk inverted	£325	£200
		ax. Wmk reversed	£475	£375
		b. Wmk sideways (7.06)	1·00	3·00
		c. Thick paper (1908)	20·00	1·75
		cw. Wmk inverted	£475	£375
		cx. Wmk reversed	£550	£400
		d. Dull coppery red (on thick paper) (3.08)	£200	35·00
		dx. Wmk reversed	£850	£450
		e. Orange-vermilion (7.11)	22·00	2·75
		ex. Wmk reversed	£475	£450
45		2d. purple (27.12.04)	19·00	23·00
		ax. Wmk reversed	£160	£160
		b. Reddish purple (13.1.12)	£225	£275
46		2½d. ultramarine (*shades*)	29·00	7·50
		aw. Wmk inverted	£375	£225
		ay. Wmk inverted and reversed	—	£800
		b. Deep blue (13.1.12)	£275	£150
47		6d. orange (27.12.04)	42·00	48·00
48		1s. brown (27.12.04)	42·00	32·00
49	8	3s. green	£160	£150
		aw. Wmk inverted	£1900	£1500
		b. Deep green (4.07)	£140	£120
		bx. Wmk reversed	£1900	£1400
50		5s. red (27.12.04)	£200	£150
43/50 *Set of* 8			£425	£350
43s/50s Optd "Specimen" *Set of* 8			£600	

Examples of Nos. 41/50 and earlier issues are known with a forged Falkland Islands postmark dated "OCT 15 10".

For details of South Georgia underprint, South Georgia provisional handstamps and Port Foster handstamp see under FALKLAND ISLANDS DEPENDENCIES.

9

10

(Des B. MacKennal. Eng J. A. C. Harrison. Recess D.L.R.)

1912 (3 July)–**20**. Wmk Mult Crown CA. P 13¾×14 (comb) (½d. to 1s.) or 14 (line) (3s. to £1).

60	**9**	½d. yellow-green	2·75	3·50
		a. Perf 14 (line). *Dp yell-green* (1914)	18·00	35·00
		b. Perf 14 (line). *Deep olive* (1918)	24·00	£130
		c. Deep olive (4.19)	3·50	38·00
		ca. Printed both sides	†	£6500
		d. Dull yellowish green (on thick greyish paper) (1920)	4·50	35·00
61		1d. orange-red	5·00	2·50
		a. Perf 14 (line). *Orange-vermilion* (1914, 1916)	32·00	2·50
		b. Perf 14 (line). *Vermilion* (1918)	†	£900
		c. Orange-vermilion (4.19)	4·25	3·00
		d. Orange-vermilion (on thick greyish paper) (1920)	7·00	2·00
		dx. Wmk reversed	£225	
62		2d. maroon	26·00	23·00
		a. Perf 14 (line). *Deep reddish purple* (1914)	£190	£110
		b. Perf 14 (line). *Maroon* (4.18)	£200	£120
		c. Deep reddish purple (4.19)	8·00	16·00
63		2½d. deep bright blue	21·00	24·00
		a. Perf 14 (line). *Deep bright blue* (1914)	30·00	35·00
		b. Perf 14 (line). *Deep blue* (1916, 4.18)	35·00	48·00
		c. Deep blue (4.19)	7·00	17·00
64		6d. yellow-orange (6.7.12)	15·00	20·00
		aw. Wmk inverted	£550	£450
		b. Brown-orange (4.19)	15·00	42·00
65		1s. light bistre-brown (6.7.12)	32·00	30·00
		a. Pale bistre-brown (4.19)	70·00	£120
		b. Brown (on thick greyish paper) (1920)	32·00	£140
66	**10**	3s. slate-green	85·00	85·00
67		5s. deep rose-red	£100	£100
		a. Reddish maroon (1914)	£225	£225
		b. Maroon (1916)	£100	£110
		bx. Wmk reversed	£3750	£2250
68		10s. red/*green* (11.2.14)	£160	£250
69		£1 black/*red* (11.2.14)	£450	£550
60/9 (*inc 67b*) *Set of* 11			£850	£1000
60s/9s (*inc both 67s and 67as*) Optd "Specimen" *Set of* 11			£1500	

The exact measurement of the comb perforation used for Type **9** is 13.7×13.9. The line perforation, used for the 1914, 1916 and 1918 printings and for all the high values in Type **10**, measured 14.1×14.1.

It was previously believed that all examples of the 1d. in vermilion with the line perforation were overprinted to form No. 71, but it has now been established that some unoverprinted sheets of No. 61b were used during 1919.

Many of the sheets showed stamps from the left-hand side in a lighter shade than those from the right. It is believed that this was due to the weight of the impression. Such differences are particularly noticeable on the 2½d. 1916 and 1918 printings where the lighter shades, approaching milky blue in appearance, are scarce.

All 1919 printings show weak impressions of the background either side of the head caused by the poor paper quality.

Examples of all values are known with forged postmarks, including one of Falkland Islands dated "5 SP 19" and another of South Shetlands dated "20 MR 27".

WAR STAMP
(**11**)

2½D
(**12**)

1918 (22 Oct*)–**20**. *Optd by Govt Printing Press, Stanley, with T* **11**.

70	**9**	½d. deep olive (line perf) (No. 60b)	1·00	11·00
		a. Yellow-green (No. 60) (4.19)	21·00	£600
		ab. Albino opt	£1900	
		b. Deep olive (comb perf) (No. 60c) (4.19)	50	6·50
		c. *Dull yellowish green* (on thick greyish paper) (No. 60*d*) (5.20)	8·00	55·00
		cx. Wmk reversed	£325	
71		1d. vermilion (line perf) (No. 61b)	2·00	18·00
		a. Opt double, one albino	£400	
		b. Orange-verm (line perf) (No. 61a) (4.19)	24·00	†
		c. Orange-verm (comb perf) (No. 61*c*) (4.19)	50	3·75
		ca. Opt double	£2750	
		cx. Wmk reversed	£550	
		d. Orange-vermilion (on thick greyish paper) (No. 61*d*) (5.20)	£110	£200
72		1s. light bistre-brown (No. 65)	35·00	80·00
		a. Pale bistre-brown (No. 65*a*) (4.19)	4·00	50·00
		ab. Opt double, one albino	£1800	
		ac. Opt omitted (in pair with normal)	£11000	
		b. Brown (on thick greyish paper) (No. 65*b*) (5.20)	5·50	45·00
		ba. Opt double, one albino	£1900	
		bw. Wmk inverted	£275	£375
		bx. Wmk reversed	£1500	

*Earliest known postal use. Cancellations dated 8 October were applied much later.

There were five printings of the "WAR STAMP" overprint, but all, except that in May 1920, used the same setting. Composition of the five printings was as follows:

October 1918. Nos. 70, 71 and 72.
January 1919. Nos. 70, 71 and 72.
April 1919. Nos. 70/*b*, 71*b*/*c* and 72*a*.
October 1919. Nos. 70*b*, 71c and 72*a*.
May 1920. Nos. 70*c*, 71*d* and 72*b*.

It is believed that the entire stock of No. 70*a* was sold to stamp dealers. Only a handful of used examples are known which may have subsequently been returned to the colony for cancellation.

No. 71ca exists in a block of 12 (6×2) from the bottom of a sheet on which the first stamp in the bottom row shows a single overprint, but the remainder have overprint double.

Examples of Nos. 70/2 are known with a forged Falkland Islands postmark dated "5 SP 19".

1921–28. Wmk Mult Script CA. P 14.

73	**9**	½d. yellowish green	3·00	4·00
		a. Green (1925)	3·00	4·00
74		1d. dull vermilion (1924)	5·00	1·75
		aw. Wmk inverted	†	£2250
		ay. Wmk inverted and reversed	£450	
		b. Orange-vermilion (shades) (1925)	5·50	1·25
75		2d. deep brown-purple (8.23)	18·00	8·00
		aw. Wmk inverted	–	£2250
		ax. Wmk reversed	£2250	
		b. Purple-brown (1927)	28·00	26·00
		c. Reddish maroon (1.28)	8·50	24·00
		cy. Wmk inverted and reversed		
76		2½d. deep blue	22·00	16·00
		a. Indigo (28.4.27)	17·00	21·00
		b. Deep steel-blue (1.28)	10·00	16·00
77		2½d. deep purple/*pale yellow* (8.23)	4·50	38·00
		a. Pale purple/pale yellow (1925)	4·50	38·00
		ay. Wmk inverted and reversed	£500	
78		6d. yellow-orange (1925)	8·50	38·00
		w. Wmk inverted	£350	
		x. Wmk reversed	£1800	
79		1s. deep ochre	20·00	48·00
80	**10**	3s. slate-green (8.23)	90·00	£160
73/80 *Set of* 8			£140	£275
73s/80s (*inc both 76s and 76as*) Optd "Specimen" *Set of* 9			£750	

Dates quoted above are those of despatch from Great Britain.

No. 76*b* includes the so-called "Prussian blue" shades (formerly listed as No. 76*c*) which formed part of a second printing in Oct 1928.

1928 (7 Feb). *No. 75b surch with T* **12**.

115	**9**	2½d. on 2d. purple-brown	£1000	£1100
		a. Surch double	£40000	

No. 115 was produced on South Georgia during a shortage of 2½d. stamps. The provisional was withdrawn on 22 February 1928.

13 Fin Whale and Gentoo Penguins

14

(Recess P.B.)

1929 (2 Sept)–**36**. P 14 (comb).

(*a*) Wmk Mult Script CA.

116	**13**	½d. green	1·25	3·00
		a. Line perf (1936)	4·00	8·00
117		1d. scarlet	3·75	80
		a. Line perf. *Deep red* (1936)	7·00	14·00
118		2d. grey	3·00	2·75
119		2½d. blue	3·00	2·25
120	**14**	4d. orange (*line perf*) (18.2.32)	18·00	13·00
		a. Deep orange (1936)	42·00	48·00
121	**13**	6d. purple	17·00	13·00
		a. Line perf. *Reddish purple* (1936)	48·00	25·00
122		1s. black/*emerald*	23·00	35·00
		a. Line perf. *On bright emerald* (1936)	23·00	27·00
123		2s.6d. carmine/*blue*	55·00	55·00
124		5s. green/*yellow*	85·00	£100
125		10s. carmine/*emerald*	£180	£225
		(*b*) Wmk Mult Crown CA.		
126	**13**	£1 black/*red*	£300	£375
116/26 *Set of* 11			£600	£700
116s/26s Perf "Specimen" *Set of* 11			£1000	

Two kinds of perforation exist:

A. Comb perf 13.9:—original values of 1929.

B. Line perf 13.9, 14.2 or compound (small holes)—4d. and 1936 printings of ½d., 1d., 6d. and 1s. On some sheets the last vertical row of perforations shows larger holes.

Examples of most values are known with forged postmarks, including one of Port Stanley dated "14 JY 31" and another of South Georgia dated "AU 30 31".

15 Romney Marsh Ram

16 Iceberg

17 Whale-catcher *Bransfield*

18 Port Louis

19 Map of Falkland Islands

20 South Georgia

21 Fin Whale

22 Government House, Stanley

23 Battle Memorial

24 King Penguin

25 Coat of Arms

26 King George V

Thick serif to "1" at left (R. 1/3, first printing only)

(Des (except 6d.) by G. Roberts. Eng and recess B.W.)

1933 (2 Jan–Apr). *Centenary of British Administration. T* **15/26**. Wmk Mult Script CA. P 12.

127	**15**	½d. black and green	2·75	7·00
128	**16**	1d. black and scarlet	3·50	2·25
		a. Thick serif to 1 at left	£190	£130
129	**17**	1½d. black and blue	17·00	18·00
130	**18**	2d. black and brown	11·00	23·00
131	**19**	3d. black and violet	19·00	24·00
132	**20**	4d. black and orange	19·00	19·00
133	**21**	6d. black and slate	50·00	70·00
134	**22**	1s. black and olive-green	50·00	80·00
135	**23**	2s.6d. black and violet	£170	£250
136	**24**	5s. black and yellow	£650	£950
		a. Black and yellow-orange (Apr)	£1900	£2250
137	**25**	10s. black and chestnut	£600	£1000
138	**26**	£1 black and carmine	£1800	£2500
127/38 *Set of* 12			£3000	£4500
127s/38s Perf "Specimen" *Set of* 12			£2750	

Examples of all values are known with forged Port Stanley postmarks dated "6 JA 33". Some values have also been seen with part strikes of the forged Falkland Islands postmark mentioned below Nos. 60/9 and 70/2.

(Des H. Fleury. Recess B.W.)

1935 (7 May). *Silver Jubilee. As Nos. 91/4 of Antigua, but printed by B.W.* P 11×12.

139	1d. deep blue and scarlet	3·25	40
	b. Short extra flagstaff	£700	£500
	d. Flagstaff on right-hand turret	£350	£275
	e. Double flagstaff	£375	£300
140	2½d. brown and deep blue	12·00	1·75
	b. Short extra flagstaff	£2000	£1600
	d. Flagstaff on right-hand turret	£400	£300
	e. Double flagstaff	£650	£400
	l. Re-entry on value tablet (R. 8/1)	£200	£110
141	4d. green and indigo	14·00	5·50
	b. Short extra flagstaff	£900	£600
	d. Flagstaff on right-hand turret	£650	£400
	e. Double flagstaff	£700	£450
142	1s. slate and purple	11·00	3·50
	a. Extra flagstaff	£3500	£2500
	b. Short extra flagstaff	£800	£450
	c. Lightning conductor	£2750	£1300
	d. Flagstaff on right-hand turret	£950	£550
	e. Double flagstaff	£1000	£600
139/42 *Set of* 4		35·00	10·00
139s/42s Perf "Specimen" *Set of* 4		£400	

For illustrations of plate varieties see Omnibus section following Zanzibar.

1937 (12 May). *Coronation. As Nos. 95/7 of Antigua.* P 11×11½.

143	½d. green	30	10
144	1d. carmine	1·00	50
145	2½d. blue	1·50	1·40
143/5 *Set of* 3		2·50	1·75
143s/5s Perf "Specimen" *Set of* 3		£350	

27 Whale's Jawbones

28 Black-necked Swan

29 Battle Memorial

30 Flock of sheep

31 Magellan Goose

32 *Discovery II* (polar supply vessel)

33 *William Scoresby* (supply ship)

34 Mount Sugar Top

34a Turkey Vultures

35 Gentoo Penguins

36 Southern Sealion

37 Deception Island

38 Arms of the Falkland Islands

(Des G. Roberts (Nos. 146, 148/9, 158 and 160/3), K. Lellman (No. 159). Recess B.W.)

1938 (3 Jan)–**50**. *T* **27/38**. Wmk Mult Script CA. P 12.

146	**27**	½d. black and green (*shades*)	30	75
147	**28**	1d. black and carmine	35·00	80
		a. Black and vermilion	3·75	85
148	**29**	1d. black and violet (14.7.41)	2·50	1·75
		a. Black and purple-violet	8·50	2·00
149		2d. black and deep violet	1·25	50
150	**28**	2d. black and carmine-red (14.7.41)	1·50	2·75
		a. Black and red	3·25	1·50
151	**30**	2½d. black and bright blue	1·25	30
152	**31**	2½d. black and blue (15.6.49)	6·50	7·50
153	**30**	3d. black and blue (14.7.41)	6·50	3·50
		a. Black and deep blue	12·00	3·00
154	**31**	4d. black and purple	3·25	1·25
155	**32**	6d. slate-black and deep brown	10·00	2·50
		a. Black and sepia (shades)	2·50	1·50
156		6d. black (15.6.49)	6·50	4·25
157	**33**	9d. black and grey-blue	24·00	3·25
158	**34**	1s. light dull blue	75·00	19·00
		a. Dull greenish blue	45·00	3·75
		b. Dull blue (greyish paper)	26·00	£110
		c. Deep dull blue (thin paper) (1948)	75·00	£100
159	**34a**	1s.3d. black and carmine-red (11.12.46)	2·50	1·40
160	**35**	2s.6d. slate	55·00	16·00
161	**36**	5s. blue and chestnut	£140	70·00
		b. Indigo and pale yellow-brown	£900	90·00
		c. Dull blue and yellow brown (greyish paper) (1949)	£120	£350
		d. Steel blue and buff-brown (thin paper) (9.50)	£200	£325
162	**37**	10s. Black and orange-brown	£140	48·00
		a. Black and orange (1942?)	£300	42·00
		b. Black and red-orange (greyish paper) (1949)	85·00	£325
		c. Black and deep reddish orange (thin paper) (1950)	£425	£350
163	**38**	£1 Black and violet	£130	55·00
146/63 *Set of* 18			£425	£190
146s/51s, 153s/5s, 157s/63s Perf "Specimen" *Set of* 16			£1600	

The 'thin paper' referred to will aid identification of Nos. 158c, 161d and 162c. It is more transparent than previous papers and has white gum.

Examples of values issued before 1946 are known with forged Port Stanley postmarks dated "14 JY 41" and "28 JY 43".

Crown flaw and re-entry (Pl 1, R. 8/5)

1946 (7 Oct). *Victory. As Nos. 110/11 of Antigua.* P 13½–14.

164	1d. dull violet	30	65
165	3d. blue	45	50
	a. Crown flaw and re-entry	55·00	55·00
164s/5s Perf "Specimen" *Set of* 2		£325	

1948 (1 Nov). *Royal Silver Wedding. As Nos. 112/13 of Antigua.*

166	2½d. ultramarine	2·00	1·00
167	£1 mauve	90·00	60·00

1949 (10 Oct). *75th Anniv of Universal Postal Union. As Nos. 114/17 of Antigua.*

168	1d. violet	1·75	1·00
169	3d. deep blue	5·00	2·75
170	1s.3d. deep blue-green	3·25	2·25
171	2s. blue	3·00	8·00
168/71 *Set of* 4		11·50	12·50

39 Sheep

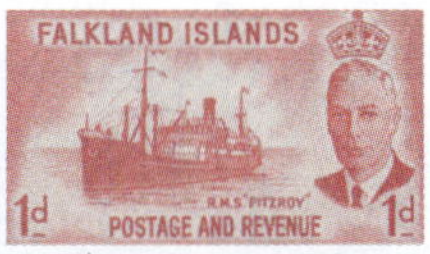

40 *Fitzroy* (supply ship)

41 Magellan Goose

42 Map of Falkland Islands

43 Arms of the Colony

44 Auster Autocrat Aircraft

45 *John Biscoe* (research ship)

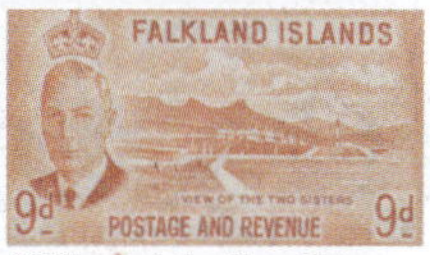

46 View of the Two Sisters

47 Gentoo Penguins

48 Kelp Goose and Gander

49 Sheep shearing

50 Battle Memorial

51 Southern Sealion and South American Fur Seal

52 Hulk of *Great Britain*

(Des from sketches by V. Spencer. Recess Waterlow)

1952 (2 Jan). *T* **39/52**. Wmk Mult Script CA. P 13×13½ (vert) or 13½×13 (horiz).

172	**39**	½d. green	1·25	70
173	**40**	1d. scarlet	2·50	40
174	**41**	2d. violet	4·50	2·50
175	**42**	2½d. black and light ultramarine	1·75	50
176	**43**	3d. deep ultramarine	2·25	1·00
177	**44**	4d. reddish purple	11·00	1·50
178	**45**	6d. bistre-brown	12·00	1·00
179	**46**	9d. orange-yellow	9·00	2·00
180	**47**	1s. black	24·00	80
181	**48**	1s.3d. orange	16·00	5·00
182	**49**	2s.6d. olive-green	20·00	11·00
183	**50**	5s. purple	17·00	9·00
184	**51**	10s. grey	28·00	12·00
185	**52**	£1 black	32·00	19·00
172/185 *Set of* 14			£160	60·00

1953 (4 June). *Coronation. As No. 120 of Antigua.*

186	1d. black and scarlet	80	1·50

53 *John Biscoe I* (research ship)

(Recess Waterlow)

1955–57. *Designs previously used for King George VI issue but with portrait of Queen Elizabeth II as in T* **53**. Wmk Mult Script CA. P 13×13½ (vert) or 13½×13 (horiz).

187	**53**	½d. green (2.9.57)	70	1·25
188	**40**	1d. scarlet (2.9.57)	1·25	1·25
189	**41**	2d. violet (3.9.56)	3·25	4·50
190	**45**	6d. deep yellow-brown (1.6.55)	7·00	60
191	**46**	9d. orange-yellow (2.9.57)	10·00	17·00
192	**47**	1s. black (15.7.55)	7·50	1·25
187/92 *Set of* 6			27·00	23·00

54 Austral Thrush

55 Southern Black-backed Gull

56 Gentoo Penguins

57 Long-tailed Meadowlark

58 Magellan Geese

59 Falkland Islands Flightless Steamer Ducks

60 Rockhopper Penguin

61 Black-browed Albatross

62 Silvery Grebe

63 Magellanic Oystercatchers

64 Chilean Teal

65 Kelp Geese

66 King Cormorants

67 Common Caracara

68 Black-necked Swan

variety normal

½d., 1d., 2d., 2s. Weak entry under "FA" of "FALKLAND" (D.L.R. Pl. 2, R. 12/5).

(Des from sketches by S. Scott. Recess Waterlow, then D.L.R. (from 9.1.62 onwards))

1960 (10 Feb)–**66**. *T* **54/68**. W w **12** (upright). P 13½.

193	**54**	½d. black and myrtle-green	5·00	1·00
		a. Black and green (DLR) (9.1.62)	15·00	6·00
		ab. Weak entry	42·00	16·00
		aw. Wmk inverted	£4000	£2000
194	**55**	1d. black and scarlet	3·00	1·25
		a. Black and carmine-red (DLR) (15.7.63)	10·00	4·50
		ab. Weak entry	42·00	15·00
195	**56**	2d. black and blue	4·50	1·25
		a. Black and deep blue (DLR) (25.10.66)	19·00	17·00
		ab. Weak entry	75·00	55·00
196	**57**	2½d. black and yellow-brown	2·50	75
197	**58**	3d. black and olive	1·25	50
198	**59**	4d. black and carmine	1·50	1·25
199	**60**	5½d. black and violet	3·25	2·50
200	**61**	6d. black and sepia	3·50	30
201	**62**	9d. black and orange-red	2·50	1·25
202	**63**	1s. black and maroon	1·25	40
203	**64**	1s.3d. black and ultramarine	11·00	13·00
204	**65**	2s. black and brown-red	32·00	2·50
		a. Black and lake-brown (DLR) (25.10.66)	£160	48·00
		ab. Weak entry	£350	£130
205	**66**	5s. black and turquoise	28·00	11·00
206	**67**	10s. black and purple	48·00	17·00
207	**68**	£1 black and orange-yellow	48·00	27·00
193/207 *Set of* 15			£170	70·00

Waterlow

De La Rue

Waterlow printings were from Frame Plates 1 or 2. The De La Rue printings of the ½d., 1d., 2d. and 2s. are all from Frame Plate 2 and can be distinguished by the finer lines of shading on the Queen's face, neck and shoulders (appearing as a white face) and also the very faint cross hatching left of the face. Apart from this the shades differ in varying degrees. Frame Plate 1 was used by De La Rue to print initial supplies of the 6d. and these stamps have little to distinguish them from the original printing. Frame Plate 2 was subsequently used for this value which, although it shows the usual plate characteristics, does not differ in shade from the Waterlow printing.

For the ½d. with watermark sideways see No. 227.

69 Morse Key

70 One-valve Receiver

(Des M. Goaman. Photo Enschedé)

1962 (5 Oct). *50th Anniv of Establishment of Radio Communications. T* **69/70** *and similar vert design.* W w **12**. P 11½×11.

208	**69**	6d. carmine-lake and orange	75	40
209	**70**	1s. deep bluish green and yellow-olive	80	40
210	–	2s. deep violet and ultramarine	90	1·75
		w. Wmk inverted	£100	£250
208/10 *Set of* 3			2·25	2·25

Design:—2s. Rotary Spark Transmitter.

1963 (4 June). *Freedom from Hunger. As No. 146 of Antigua.*

211	1s. ultramarine	10·00	1·50

1963 (2 Sept). *Red Cross Centenary. As Nos. 147/8 of Antigua.*

212	1d. red and black	3·00	75
213	1s. red and blue	13·00	4·75

1964 (23 Apr). *400th Birth Anniv of William Shakespeare. As No. 164 of Antigua.*

214	6d. black	1·50	50

72 H.M.S. *Glasgow*

(Recess D.L.R.)

1964 (8 Dec). *50th Anniv of the Battle of the Falkland Islands. T* **72** *and similar designs.* W w **12**. P 13×14 (2s.) or 13 (others).

215	2½d. black and red	11·00	3·75
216	6d. black and light blue	50	25
	a. Centre Type **72**	£40000	
217	1s. black and carmine-red	50	1·00
	w. Wmk inverted	£2000	
218	2s. black and blue	35	75
215/18 *Set of* 4		11·00	5·25

Designs: Horiz—6d. H.M.S. *Kent*; 1s. H.M.S. *Invincible*. *Vert*—2s. Battle Memorial.

It is believed that No. 216a came from a sheet which was first printed with the centre of the 2½d. and then accidentally included among the supply of the 6d. value and thus received the wrong frame. There have been seventeen reports of stamps showing the error, although it is believed that some of these may refer to the same example.

1965 (26 May). *I.T.U. Centenary. As Nos. 166/7 of Antigua.*

219	1d. light blue and deep blue	50	30
	w. Wmk inverted	£1000	
220	2s. lilac and bistre-yellow	4·50	1·75

1965 (25 Oct). *International Co-operation Year. As Nos. 168/9 of Antigua.*

221	1d. reddish purple and turquoise-green	1·50	40
222	1s. deep bluish green and lavender	4·00	1·10

1966 (24 Jan). *Churchill Commemoration. As Nos. 170/3 of Antigua. Printed in black, cerise and gold with background in colours stated.* W w **12**. P 14.

223	½d. new blue	65	2·25
224	1d. deep green	1·75	20
	w. Wmk inverted	8·50	4·50
225	1s. brown	6·00	3·00
	w. Wmk inverted	85·00	85·00
226	2s. bluish violet	4·00	3·50
223/6 *Set of* 4		11·00	8·00

1966 (25 Oct). *As No. 193a, but wmk w* **12** *sideways.*

227	**54**	½d. black and green	30	40
		a. Weak entry	22·00	17·00

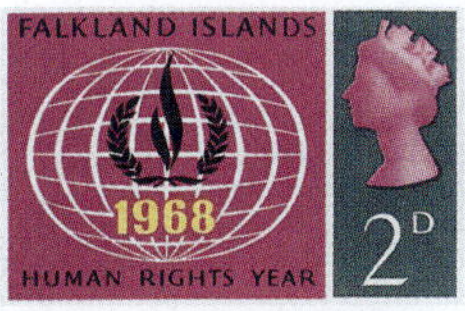

76 Globe and Human Rights Emblem

77 Dusty Miller

(Des M. Farrar Bell. Photo Harrison)

1968 (4 July). *Human Rights Year.* W w **12**. P 14×14½.

228	**76**	2d. multicoloured	40	20
		a. Yellow omitted ("1968" white)	£1500	
229		6d. muticoloured	40	20
230		1s. multicoloured	50	20
231		2s. multicoloured	65	30
228/31 *Set of* 4			1·75	80

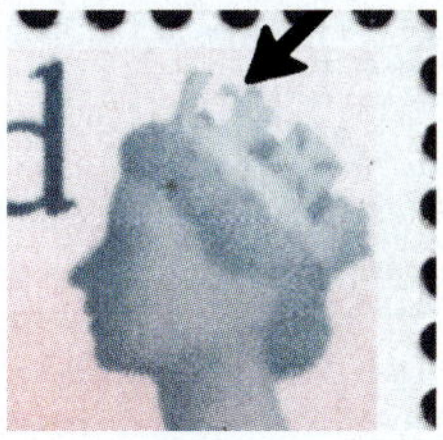

½d. Missing grey colour in diadem appears as a damaged crown (Pl. 1A, R. 2/2).

(Des Sylvia Goaman)

1968 (9 Oct). *Flowers. Designs as T* **77**. *Chalk-surfaced paper.* W w **12** (sideways on vert designs). P 14.

232	½d. multicoloured	15	1·75
	a. Crown damaged	7·00	
233	1½d. multicoloured	40	15
234	2d. multicoloured	50	15
235	3d. multicoloured	6·00	1·00
236	3½d. multicoloured	30	75
237	4½d. multicoloured	1·50	2·00
238	5½d. olive-green, brown and yellow-green	1·50	2·00
239	6d. carmine, black and yellow-green	75	20
240	1s. multicoloured	75	1·50
	w. Wmk inverted	£160	
241	1s.6d. multicoloured	4·50	13·00
242	2s. multicoloured	5·50	6·50
243	3s. multicoloured	8·00	8·00
244	5s. multicoloured	30·00	13·00
245	£1 multicoloured	13·00	2·50
232/45 *Set of* 14		65·00	45·00

Designs: *Horiz*—1½d. Pig Vine; 3½d. Sea Cabbage; 5½d. Arrowleaf Marigold; 6d. Diddle Dee; 1s. Scurvy Grass; 5s. Felton's Flower. *Vert*—2d. Pale Maiden; 3d. Dog Orchid; 4½d. Vanilla Daisy; 1s.6d. Prickly Burr; 2s. Fachine; 3s. Lavender; £1 Yellow Orchid.

A further printing of the £1 took place with the decimal surcharges issued 15 February 1971. It was for some time believed that stamps from this printing could be identified by the brown shading which extended to the foot of the design, instead of stopping short as on the original printing, but this test has now been shown to be inconsistent.

For stamps inscribed in decimal currency see Nos. 276/88, 293/5 and 315.

91 De Havilland D.H.C.2 Beaver Seaplane

(Des V. Whiteley. Litho Format)

1969 (8 Apr). *21st Anniv of Government Air Services. T* **91** *and similar horiz designs. Multicoloured.* W w **12** (sideways). P 14.

246	2d. Type **91**	50	30
247	6d. Noorduyn Norseman V	50	35
248	1s. Auster Autocrat	50	35
249	2s. Falkland Islands Arms	1·50	2·00
246/9 *Set of* 4		2·75	2·75

92 Holy Trinity Church, 1869

(Des G. Drummond. Litho Format)

1969 (30 Oct). *Centenary of Bishop Stirling's Consecration. T* **92** *and similar horiz designs.* W w **12** (sideways). P 14.

250	2d. black, grey and apple-green	40	60
251	6d. black, grey and orange-red	40	60
252	1s. black, grey and lilac	40	60
253	2s. multicoloured	50	75
250/3 *Set of* 4		1·50	2·25

Designs:—6d. Christ Church Cathedral, 1969; 1s. Bishop Stirling; 2s. Bishop's Mitre.

96 Mounted Volunteer

97 S.S. *Great Britain* (1843)

(Des R. Granger Barrett. Litho B.W.)

1970 (30 Apr). *Golden Jubilee of Defence Force. T* **96** *and similar designs. Multicoloured.* W w **12** (sideways on 2d. and 1s.). P 13.

254	2d. Type **96**	1·50	70
255	6d. Defence Post (*horiz*)	1·50	70
256	1s. Corporal in Number One Dress Uniform	1·50	70
257	2s. Defence Force Badge (*horiz*)	1·50	75
254/7 *Set of* 4		5·50	2·50

(Des V. Whiteley. Litho J.W.)

1970 (30 Oct). *Restoration of S.S. "Great Britain". T* **97** *and views of the ship at different dates. Multicoloured.* W w **12** (sideways*). P 14½×14.

258	2d. Type **97**	80	40
259	4d. In 1845	80	75
	w. Wmk Crown to right of CA	17·00	2·75
260	9d. In 1876	80	75
261	1s. In 1886	80	75
	w. Wmk Crown to right of CA	£1000	
262	2s. In 1970	1·10	75
258/62 *Set of* 5		3·75	3·00

*The normal sideways watermark shows Crown to left of CA, *as seen from the back of the stamp.*

FALKLAND ISLANDS DEPENDENCIES

PRICES FOR STAMPS ON COVER TO 1945
Nos. A1/D8 *from* × 20

A. GRAHAM LAND

For use at Port Lockroy (established 1 February 1944) and Hope Bay (established 12 February 1945) bases.

Falkland Islands definitive stamps with face values of 1s.3d. and above were valid for use from Graham Land in conjunction with Nos. A1/8 and subsequently Nos. G1/16.

Stamps of FALKLAND ISLANDS *cancelled at Port Lockroy or Hope Bay with Graham Land circular datestamps between* 12 February 1944 *and* 31 January 1954.

1938–50. *King George VI (Nos. 159/63).*

Z1	1s.3d. black and carmine-red	£140
Z2	2s.6d. slate	60·00
Z3	5s. indigo and yellow-brown	£160
Z4	10s. black and orange	75·00
Z5	£1 black and violet	95·00

1952. *King George VI (Nos. 181/5).*

Z6	1s.3d. orange	£120
Z7	2s.6d. olive-green	£130
Z8	5s. purple	£150
Z9	10s. grey	£160
Z10	£1 black	£170

GRAHAM LAND

DEPENDENCY OF

(A 1)

1944 (12 Feb)**–45.** *Falkland Islands Nos. 146, 148, 150, 153/5, 157 and 158a optd with Type A* **1**, *in red, by B.W.*

A1	½d. black and green	30	1·75
	a. Blue-black and green	£1100	£600
A2	1d. black and violet	30	1·00
A3	2d. black and carmine-red	50	1·00
A4	3d. black and blue	50	1·00
A5	4d. black and purple	2·00	1·75
A6	6d. black and brown	18·00	2·25
	a. Blue-black and brown (24.9.45)	18·00	
A7	9d. black and grey-blue	1·25	1·25
A8	1s. deep blue	1·25	1·25
A1/8 *Set of* 8		22·00	10·00
A1s/8s Perf "Specimen" *Set of* 8		£500	

B. SOUTH GEORGIA

The stamps of Falkland Islands were used at the Grytviken whaling station on South Georgia from 3 December 1909.

Mr. J. Innes Wilson, the Stipendary Magistrate whose duties included those of postmaster, was issued with a stock of stamps, values ½d. to 5s., together with an example of the current "FALKLAND ISLANDS" circular datestamp. This was used to cancel the stamps, but, as it gave no indication that mail had originated at South Georgia, a straight-line handstamp inscribed "SOUTH GEORGIA", or subsequently "South Georgia", was also supplied. It was intended that this should be struck directly on to each letter or card below the stamp, but it can sometimes be found struck across the stamp instead.

The use of the "South Georgia" handstamp continued after the introduction of the "SOUTH GEORGIA" circular datestamp in June 1910 apparently for philatelic purposes, but no example has been reported used after June 1912.

SOUTH GEORGIA.

Z 1

South Georgia.

Z 2

		On piece	On cover/ card
ZU1	Example of Type Z **1** used in conjunction with "FALKLAND ISLANDS" postmark (22 Dec 1909 to 30 March 1910) *Price from*	£1500	£7000
ZU2	Example of Type Z **2** used in conjunction with "FALKLAND ISLANDS" postmark (May 1910) *Price from*	£1000	£4250
ZU3	Example of Type Z **2** used in conjunction with "SOUTH GEORGIA" postmark (June 1910 to June 1912) *Price from*	£275	£900

Stamps of FALKLAND ISLANDS *cancelled at Grytviken with South Georgia circular datestamps between* June 1910 *and* 31 January 1954.

1891–1902. *Queen Victoria (Nos. 17/38).*

Z11	½d. yellow-green	£160
Z11*a*	1d. pale red	£160
Z11*b*	2d. purple	£200
Z11*c*	2½d. deep ultramarine	£225
Z12	4d. olive-black	£300
Z12*a*	6d. yellow	£300
Z12*b*	9d. salmon	£300
Z12*d*	1s. yellow-brown	£300

1898. *Queen Victoria (No. 42).*

Z13	5s. red	£600

1904–12. *King Edward VII (Nos. 43/50).*

Z14	½d. green	21·00
Z15	1d. vermilion	21·00
	d. Dull coppery red (on thick paper)	55·00
Z16	2d. purple	80·00
	b. Reddish purple	£325
Z17	2½d. ultramarine	30·00
	b. Deep blue	£200
Z18	6d. orange	£170
Z19	1s. brown	£170
Z20	3s. green	£375
Z21	5s. red	£425

SOUTH GEORGIA PROVISIONAL HANDSTAMPS

During October 1911 the arrival of the German South Polar Expedition at Grytviken, South Georgia, resulted in the local supply of stamps becoming exhausted. The Acting Magistrate, Mr. E. B. Binnie, who was also responsible for the postal facilities, produced a handstamp reading "Paid at (or At) SOUTH GEORGIA" which, together with a manuscript indication of the postage paid and his signature, was used on mail from 18 October 1911 to January 1912. Further examples, signed by John Innes Wilson, are known from February 1912.

PH1	"Paid 1 at SOUTH GEORGIA EBB" *Price on cover*	£4750
PH1*a*	"Paid 1 At SOUTH GEORGIA EBB" (16 Dec) *Price on cover*	£5000
PH2	"Paid 2½ at SOUTH GEORGIA EBB" *Price on cover*	£5500
PH2*a*	"Paid 2½ At SOUTH GEORGIA EBB" (16 Dec) *Price on cover*	£6000
PH3	"Paid 1 At SOUTH GEORGIA JIW" *Price on cover*	£7500
PH4	"Paid 2½ At SOUTH GEORGIA JIW" *Price on cover*	£7500

1912–23. *King George V.* Wmk Mult Crown CA (Nos. 60/9).

Z22	½d. green	20·00
	a. Perf 14 (line). *Deep yellow-green*	38·00
	d. Dull yellowish green (on thick greyish paper)	48·00
Z23	1d. orange-red	13·00
	a. Perf 14 (line). *Orange-vermilion*	13·00
	d. Orange-vermilion	13·00
Z24	2d. maroon	55·00
Z25	2½d. deep bright blue	38·00
	c. Deep blue	35·00
Z26	6d. yellow-orange	70·00
	b. Brown-orange	80·00
	ba. Bisected (diag) (3d.) (on cover) (3.23)	£16000
Z27	1s. light bistre-brown	£130
	a. Pale bistre-brown	£160
	b. Brown (on thick greyish paper)	£180
Z28	3s. slate-green	£225
Z29	5s. deep rose-red	£275
	a. Reddish maroon	£375
	b. Maroon	£350
Z30	10s. red/*green*	£475
Z31	£1 black/*red*	£750

1918–20. "WAR STAMP" *ovpts (Nos. 70/2).*

Z32	½d. deep olive	24·00
Z33	1d. vermilion	24·00
Z34	1s. light bistre-brown	£120

1921–28. *King George V.* Wmk Mult Script CA (Nos. 73/80).

Z35	½d. yellowish green	7·50
Z36	1d. dull vermilion	6·00
Z37	2d. deep brown-purple	32·00
Z38	2½d. deep blue	28·00
	a. Bisected (diag) (1d.) (on cover) (3.23)	£13000
Z39	2½d. deep purple/*pale yellow*	55·00
Z40	6d. yellow-orange	60·00
Z41	1s. deep ochre	70·00
Z42	3s. slate-green	£275

1928 PROVISIONAL. For listing of the 2½d. on 2d. surcharge issued at Grytviken on 7 February 1928 see No. 115 of Falkland Islands.

1929–36. *King George V. Whale and Penguins design (Nos. 116/26).*

Z43	½d. green	8·00
Z44	1d. scarlet	6·50
Z45	2d. grey	16·00
Z46	2½d. blue	8·00
Z47	4d. orange	30·00
Z48	6d. purple	42·00
Z49	1s. black/*emerald*	55·00
Z50	2s.6d. carmine/*blue*	£120
Z51	5s. green/*yellow*	£180
Z52	10s. carmine/*emerald*	£375
Z53	£1 black/*red*	£700

Examples of most values are known with forged postmarks dated "Au 30" in 1928, 1930 and 1931.

1933. *Centenary of British Administration (Nos. 127/38).*

Z54	½d. black and green	11·00
Z55	1d. black and scarlet	6·00
Z56	1½d. black and blue	28·00
Z57	2d. black and brown	32·00
Z58	3d. black and violet	32·00
Z59	4d. black and orange	27·00
Z60	6d. black and slate	95·00
Z61	1s. black and olive-green	£110
Z62	2s.6d. black and violet	£350
Z63	5s. black and yellow	£1200
	a. Black and yellow-orange	£2750
Z64	10s. black and chestnut	£1400
Z65	£1 black and carmine	£3250

1935. *Silver Jubilee (Nos. 139/42).*

Z66	1d. deep blue and scarlet	6·00
Z67	2½d. brown and deep blue	7·00
Z68	4d. green and indigo	8·50
Z69	1s. slate and purple	8·00

1937. *Coronation (Nos. 143/5).*

Z70	½d. green	3·50
Z71	1d. carmine	3·50
Z72	2½d. blue	3·50

1938–50. *King George VI (Nos. 146/63).*

Z73	½d. black and green	6·00
Z74	1d. black and carmine	9·00
	a. Black and scarlet	5·00
Z75	1d. black and violet	10·00
Z76	2d. black and deep violet	10·00
Z77	2d. black and carmine-red	13·00
Z78	2½d. black and bright blue (No. 151)	5·00
Z79	3d. black and blue	15·00
Z80	4d. black and purple	11·00
Z81	6d. black and brown	13·00
Z82	9d. black and grey-blue	18·00
Z83	1s. light dull blue	45·00
	a. Dull greenish blue	45·00
Z84	1s.3d. black and carmine-red	60·00
Z85	2s.6d. slate	42·00
Z86	5s. blue and chestnut	£170
	a. Indigo and yellow-brown	£140
	b. Steel blue and buff-brown	£400
Z87	10s. black and orange-brown	95·00
	a. Black and orange	70·00
Z88	£1 black and violet	90·00

Falkland Islands definitive stamps with values of 1s.3d. and above continued to be valid from South Georgia after the introduction of Nos. B1/8 and subsequently Nos. G1/16. Forged South Georgia postmarks exist dated "30 MR 49".

1952. *King George VI (Nos. 181/5).*

Z89	1s.3d. orange	65·00
Z90	2s.6d. olive-green	£120
Z91	5s. purple	£130
Z92	10s. grey	£150
Z93	£1 black	£160

1944 (24 Feb)**–45.** *Falkland Islands Nos. 146, 148, 150, 153/5, 157 and 158a optd* "SOUTH GEORGIA/DEPENDENCY OF", *in red, as Type A* **1** *of Graham Land.*

B1	½d. black and green	30	1·75
	a. Wmk sideways	£3750	
B2	1d. black and violet	30	1·00
B3	2d. black and carmine-red	50	1·00
B4	3d. black and blue	50	1·00
B5	4d. black and purple	2·00	1·75
B6	6d. black and brown	18·00	2·25
	a. Blue-black and brown (24.9.45)	18·00	
B7	9d. black and grey-blue	1·25	1·25
B8	1s. deep blue	1·25	1·25
B1/8 *Set of* 8		22·00	10·00
B1s/8s Perf "Specimen" *Set of* 8		£500	

C. SOUTH ORKNEYS

Used from the *Fitzroy* in February 1944 and at Laurie Island (established January 1946).

Falkland Islands definitive stamps with face values of 1s.3d. and above were valid for use from the South Orkneys in conjunction with Nos. C1/8 and subsequently Nos. G1/16.

Stamps of FALKLAND ISLANDS *cancelled on the Fitzroy, at Laurie Island or at Signy Island with South Orkneys circular datestamps between* 21 February 1944 *and* 31 January 1954.

1938–50. *King George VI (Nos. 160/3).*

Z94	1s.3d. black and carmine-red	£180
Z95	2s.6d. slate	60·00
Z96	5s. indigo and yellow-brown	£160
Z97	10s. black and orange	75·00
Z98	£1 black and violet	95·00

1952. *King George VI (Nos. 181/5).*

Z99	1s.3d. orange	£120
Z100	2s.6d. olive-green	£130
Z101	5s. purple	£150
Z102	10s. grey	£160
Z103	£1 black	£170

1944 (21 Feb)**–45.** *Falkland Islands Nos. 146, 148, 150, 153/5, 157 and 158a optd* "SOUTH ORKNEYS/DEPENDENCY OF", *in red, as Type A* **1** *of Graham Land.*

C1	½d. black and green	30	1·75
C2	1d. black and violet	30	1·00
	w. Wmk inverted	£5000	
C3	2d. black and carmine-red	50	1·00
C4	3d. black and blue	50	1·00
C5	4d. black and purple	2·00	1·75
C6	6d. black and brown	18·00	2·25
	a. Blue-black and brown (24.9.45)	18·00	
C7	9d. black and grey-blue	1·25	1·25
C8	1s. deep blue	1·25	1·25
C1/8 *Set of* 8		22·00	10·00
C1s/8s Perf "Specimen" *Set of* 8		£500	

D. SOUTH SHETLANDS

Postal facilities were first provided at the Port Foster whaling station on Deception Island for the 1912–13 whaling season and were available each year between November and the following April until March 1931.

No postmark was provided for the 1912–13 season and the local postmaster was instructed to cancel stamps on cover with a straight-line "PORT FOSTER" handstamp. Most letters so cancelled subsequently received a "FALKLAND ISLANDS" circular postmark dated between 19 and 28 March 1913. It is known that only low value stamps were available at Port Foster. Higher values, often with other "FALKLAND ISLANDS" postmark dates, were, it is believed, subsequently "made to order".

Stamps of FALKLAND ISLANDS *cancelled at Port Foster, Deception Island with part of* "PORT FOSTER" *straightline handstamp.*

1904–12. *King Edward VII (Nos. 43c, 44e).*

Z104	½d. deep yellow-green	£1500
Z105	1d. orange-vermilion	£1500

1912. *King George V.* Wmk Mult Crown CA (Nos. 60/1).

Z106	½d. yellow-green	£1500
Z107	1d. orange-red	£1500

Stamps of FALKLAND ISLANDS *cancelled at Port Foster with part of oval* "DECEPTION ISLAND SOUTH SHETLANDS" *postmark in black or violet between 1914 and 1927.*

1904–12. *King Edward VII (No. 43c).*

Z108	½d. deep yellow-green	£400

1912–20. *King George V.* Wmk Mult Crown CA (Nos. 60/9).

Z110	½d. yellow-green	£130
Z111	1d. orange-red	£130
Z112	2d. maroon	£160
Z113	2½d. deep bright blue	£160
Z114	6d. yellow-orange	£200
Z115	1s. light bistre-brown	£250
Z116	3s. slate-green	£500
Z117	5s. deep rose-red	£600
Z118	10s. red/*green*	£800
Z119	£1 black/*red*	£1000

1918–20. "WAR STAMP" *ovpts (Nos. 70/2).*

Z120	½d. deep olive	£160
Z121	1d. vermilion	£160
Z122	1s. light bistre-brown	£375

1921–28. *King George V.* Wmk Mult Script CA (Nos. 73/80).

Z123	½d. yellowish green	£160
Z126	2½d. deep blue	£190
Z129	1s. deep ochre	£250

Stamps of FALKLAND ISLANDS *cancelled at Port Foster with* "SOUTH SHETLANDS" *circular datestamp between* 1923 *and* March 1931.

1912–20. *King George V.* Wmk Mult Crown CA (Nos. 60/9).

Z129*a*	½d. dull yellowish green (on thick greyish paper)	£100
Z130	1d. orange-vermilion	85·00
Z131	2d. deep reddish purple	95·00
Z132	2½d. deep bright blue	£130
	c. Deep blue	£130
Z133	6d. brown-orange	£140
Z134	1s. bistre-brown	
Z135	3s. slate-green	£325
Z136	5s. maroon	£375
Z137	10s. red/*green*	£550
Z138	£1 black/*red*	£950

Examples of all values are known with forged postmarks dated "20 MR 27".

1918–20. "WAR STAMP" *ovpts (Nos. 70/2).*

Z138*a*	½d. deep olive	£140
Z139	1d. vermilion	£130
Z140	1s. light bistre-brown	£300

1921–28. *King George V.* Wmk Mult Script CA (Nos. 73/80).

Z141	½d. yellowish green	48·00
Z142	1d. dull vermilion	48·00
Z143	2d. deep brown-purple	75·00
Z144	2½d. deep blue	65·00
Z145	2½d. deep purple/*pale yellow*	85·00
Z146	6d. yellow-orange	£100
Z147	1s. deep ochre	£100
Z148	3s. slate-green	£350

1929. *King George V. Whale and Penguins design (Nos. 116/26).*

Z149	½d. green	80·00
Z150	1d. scarlet	80·00
Z151	2d. grey	£100
Z152	2½d. blue	90·00
Z153	6d. purple	£120
Z154	1s. black/*emerald*	£130
Z155	2s.6d. carmine/*blue*	£200
Z156	5s. green/*yellow*	£250
Z157	10s. carmine/*emerald*	£475
Z158	£1 black/*red*	£850

The whaling station at Port Foster was abandoned at the end of the 1930–31 season.

It was reoccupied as a Falkland Islands Dependencies Survey base on 3 February 1944.

Falkland Islands definitive stamps with face values of 1s.3d. and above were valid for use from the South Shetlands in conjunction with Nos. D1/8 and subsequently Nos. G1/16.

Stamps of FALKLAND ISLANDS *cancelled at Port Foster or Admiralty Bay with South Shetlands circular datestamps between* 5 February 1944 *and* 31 January 1954.

1938–50. *King George VI (Nos. 160/3).*

Z159	2s.6d. slate	60·00
Z160	5s. indigo and yellow-brown	£160
Z161	10s. black and orange	75·00
Z162	£1 black and violet	95·00

1952. *King George VI (Nos. 181/5).*

Z163	1s.3d. orange	£110
Z164	2s.6d. olive-green	£120
Z165	5s. purple	£140
Z166	10s. grey	£150
Z167	£1 black	£160

1944 (5 Feb)–**45.** *Falkland Islands Nos.* 146, 148, 150, 153/5, 157 *and* 158*a optd* "SOUTH SHETLANDS/DEPENDENCY OF", *in red, as Type A* **1** *of Graham Land.*

D1	½d. black and green	30	1·75
D2	1d. black and violet	30	1·00
D3	2d. black and carmine-red	50	1·00
D4	3d. black and blue	50	1·00
D5	4d. black and purple	2·00	1·75
D6	6d. black and brown	18·00	2·25
	a. Blue-black and brown (24.9.45)	18·00	
D7	9d. black and grey-blue	1·25	1·25
D8	1s. deep blue	1·25	1·25
D1/8 *Set of* 8		22·00	10·00
D1s/8s Perf "Specimen" *Set of* 8		£500	

From 12 July 1946 to 16 July 1963, Graham Land, South Georgia, South Orkneys and South Shetlands used FALKLAND ISLANDS DEPENDENCIES stamps.

E. FALKLAND ISLANDS DEPENDENCIES

For use at the following bases:

Admiralty Bay (South Shetlands) (*opened* January 1948, *closed* January 1961)
Argentine Islands (Graham Land) (*opened* 1947)
Deception Island (South Shetlands)
Grytviken (South Georgia)
Hope Bay (Graham Land) (*closed* 4 February 1949, *opened* February 1952)
Laurie Island (South Orkneys) (*closed* 1947)
Port Lockroy (Graham Land) (*closed* 16 January 1962)
Signy Island (South Orkneys) (*opened* 1946)
Stonington Island (Graham Land) (*opened* 1946, *closed* 1950, *opened* 1958, *closed* 1959, *opened* 1960)

G **1**

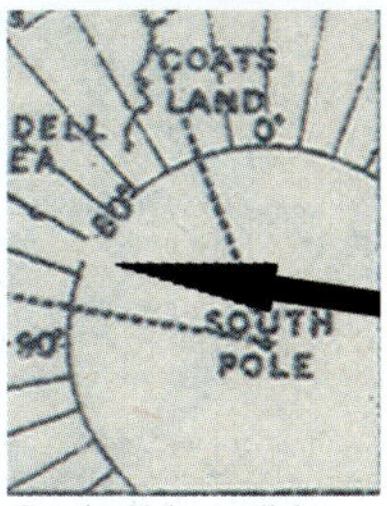

Gap in 80th parallel (R. 1/4, 1/9, 3/4, 3/9, 5/4 and 5/9)

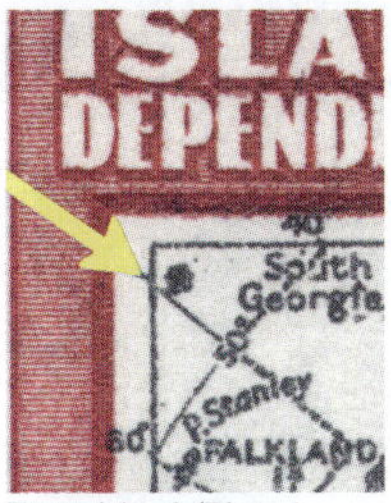

Extra island (Plate 1 R. 3/9)

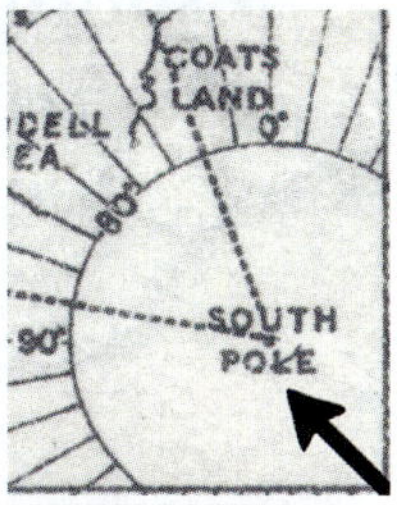

"SOUTH POKE" flaw (Plate 2 R. 6/8)

Missing "I" in "S. Shetland Is." (Plate 1 R. 1/2)

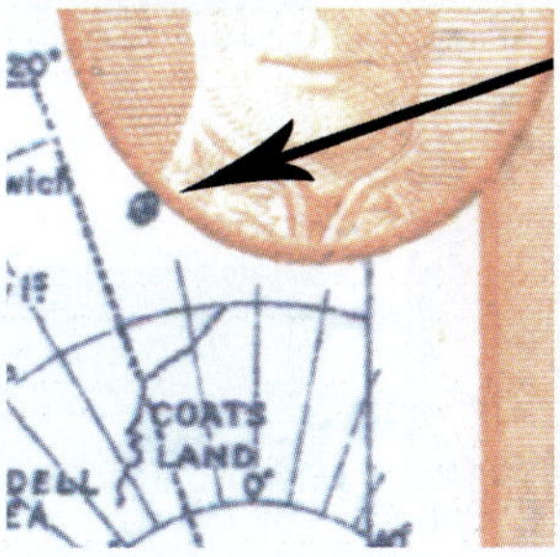

Extra dot by oval (Plate 1 R. 4/6)

(Map litho, frame recess D.L.R.)

1946 (12 July*)–**49.** Wmk Mult Script CA (sideways). P 12.

(a) Map thick and coarse.

G1	G **1**	½d. black and green	1·00	3·50
		a. Gap in 80th parallel	3·00	6·50
		aa. Extra island	£170	£190
		b. Missing "I"	£160	£180
		c. "SOUTH POKE"	£140	£190
		d. Extra dot by oval	£170	£190
G2		1d. black and violet	1·25	1·75
		a. Gap in 80th parallel	3·50	4·50
		aa. Extra island	£110	£130
		b. Missing "I"	£100	£120
		d. Extra dot by oval	£110	£130
G3		2d. black and carmine	1·25	2·50
		a. Gap in 80th parallel	3·50	5·50
		aa. Extra island	£180	£200
		b. Missing "I"	£170	£190
		d. Extra dot by oval	£180	£200
G4		3d. black and blue	1·25	5·00
		a. Gap in 80th parallel	3·50	8·50
		aa. Extra island	£150	£190
		b. Missing "I"	£140	£180
		d. Extra dot by oval	£150	£190
G5		4d. black and claret	2·25	4·75
		a. Gap in 80th parallel	6·00	9·50
		c. "SOUTH POKE"	£170	£190
G6		6d. black and orange	3·50	4·75
		a. Gap in 80th parallel	7·50	9·50
		aa. Extra island	£180	£190
		b. Missing "I"	£170	£190
		c. "SOUTH POKE"	£160	£200
		d. Extra dot by oval	£180	£190
		e. Black and ochre	50·00	95·00
		ea. Gap in 80th parallel	85·00	£150
		eaa. Extra island	£425	
		eb. Missing "I"	£425	
		ec. "SOUTH POKE"	£425	
		ed. Extra dot by oval	£425	
G7		9d. black and brown	2·00	3·75
		a. Gap in 80th parallel	5·50	8·50
		c. "SOUTH POKE"	£160	£200
G8		1s. black and purple	2·00	4·25
		a. Gap in 80th parallel	5·50	9·00
		c. "SOUTH POKE"	£140	£200
G1/8 *Set of* 8			13·00	27·00
G1s/8s Perf "Specimen" *Set of* 8			£850	

*This is the date of issue for South Georgia. Nos. G1/8 were released in London on 11 February.

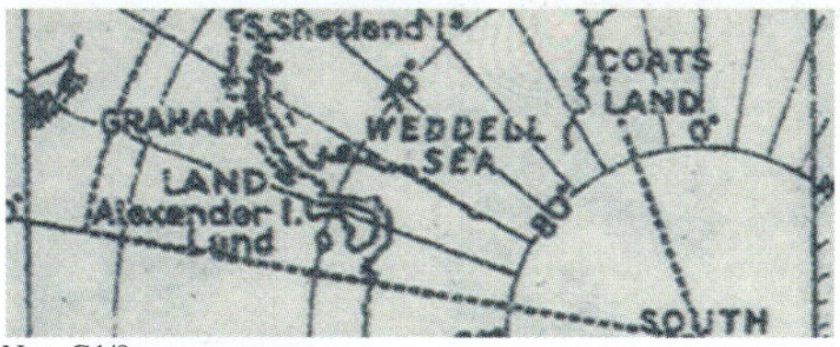

Nos. G1/8

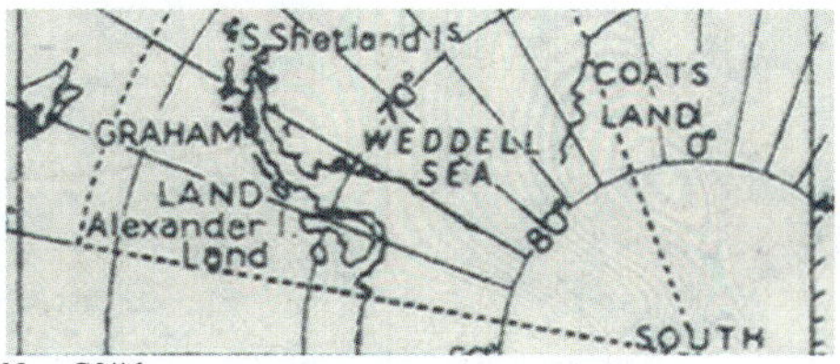

Nos. G9/16

On Nos. G9 to G16 the map is redrawn; the "0°" meridian does not pass through the "S" of "COATS", the "n" of "Alexander" is not joined to the "L" of "Land" below, and the loops of letters "s" and "t" are generally more open.

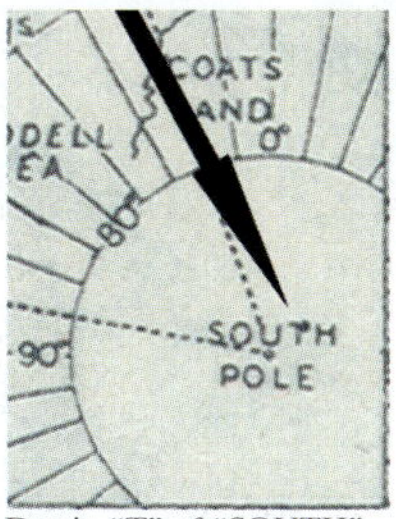

Dot in "T" of "SOUTH" (R. 5/2, 5/4, 5/6, 5/8 and 5/10)

(b) Map thin and clear (16.2.48).

G9	G **1**	½d. black and green	2·25	14·00
		a. Recess frame printed double, one albino and inverted	£1700	
		b. Dot in "T"	5·50	35·00
G10		1d. black and violet	1·50	17·00
		a. Dot in "T"	3·75	40·00
G11		2d. black and carmine	2·75	24·00
		a. Dot in "T"	6·50	55·00
G11*b*		2½d. black and deep blue (6.3.49)	6·50	4·00
G12		3d. black and blue	2·75	4·00
		a. Dot in "T"	6·50	11·00
G13		4d. black and claret	17·00	27·00
		a. Dot in "T"	35·00	60·00
G14		6d. black and orange	24·00	7·00
		a. Dot in "T"	50·00	19·00
G15		9d. black and brown	24·00	7·00
		a. Dot in "T"	50·00	19·00
G16		1s. black and purple	24·00	7·00
		a. Dot in "T"	50·00	19·00
G9/16 *Set of* 9			95·00	£100

1946 (4 Oct*). *Victory. As Nos. 110/11 of Antigua.*

G17	1d. deep violet	50	50
G18	3d. blue	75	50
G17s/18s Perf "Specimen" *Set of* 2		£250	

*This is the date of issue for South Georgia. The stamps were placed on sale from the South Orkneys on 17 January 1947, from the South Shetlands on 30 January 1947 and from Graham Land on 10 February 1947.

1948 (6 Dec). *Royal Silver Wedding. As Nos. 112/13 of Antigua, but 1s. in recess.*

G19	2½d. ultramarine	1·75	2·50
G20	1s. violet-blue	1·75	2·50

1949 (10 Oct). *75th Anniv of U.P.U. As Nos. 114/17 of Antigua.*

G21	1d. violet	1·00	2·50
G22	2d. carmine-red	5·00	3·75
G23	3d. deep blue	3·50	1·25
G24	6d. red-orange	4·00	3·00
G21/4 *Set of* 4		12·00	9·50

1953 (4 June). *Coronation. As No. 120 of Antigua.*

G25	1d. black and violet	1·10	1·25

G **2** *John Biscoe I*, 1947–52

G **3** *Trepassey*, 1945–47

G **4** *Wyatt Earp*, 1934–36

G **5** *Eagle*, 1944–45

G **6** *Penola*, 1934–37

G **7** *Discovery II*, 1929–37

G **8** *William Scoresby*, 1926–46

G **9** *Discovery*, 1925–27

G **10** *Endurance*, 1914–16

G **11** *Deutschland*, 1910–12

G **12** *Pourquoi-pas?*, 1908–10

G **13** *Francais*, 1903–05

G **14** *Scotia*, 1902–04

G **15** *Antarctic*, 1901–03

G **16** *Belgica* 1897–99

1d. There are a number of retouches of the cross-hatching in the clouds where lines have been deepened. The one illustrated is on R. 12/1 and other prominent retouches occur on R. 8/1 and R. 10/1 but there are other less marked ones. These were corrected in the D.L.R. printing.

(Recess Waterlow, then D.L.R. (from 27.3.62))

1954 (1 Feb)–**62**. *Types* G **2/16**. Wmk Mult Script CA. P 12½.

G26	G **2**	½d. black and bluish green	30	3·25
		a. Black and deep green (DLR) (17.4.62)	6·50	16·00
G27	G **3**	1d. black and sepia-brown	1·75	2·25
		aa. Retouches to cross-hatching *from*	10·00	
		a. Black and sepia (DLR) (27.3.62)	16·00	24·00
G28	G **4**	1½d. black and olive	2·50	3·25
		a. Black and yellow-olive (DLR) (21.9.62)	8·50	3·00
G29	G **5**	2d. black and rose-red	2·75	2·50
G30	G **6**	2½d. black and yellow-ochre	1·25	35
G31	G **7**	3d. black and deep bright blue	1·75	35
G32	G **8**	4d. black and bright reddish purple	6·00	2·50
G33	G **9**	6d. black and deep lilac	6·00	2·50
G34	G **10**	9d. black	6·00	3·25
G35	G **11**	1s. black and brown	4·75	2·50
G36	G **12**	2s. black and carmine	19·00	12·00
G37	G **13**	2s.6d. black and pale turquoise	21·00	10·00
G38	G **14**	5s. black and violet	42·00	12·00
G39	G **15**	10s. black and blue	60·00	24·00
G40	G **16**	£1 black	85·00	48·00
G26/40 *Set of* 15			£225	£110

TRANS-ANTARCTIC EXPEDITION 1955-1958

(G **17**)

1956 (30 Jan). *Trans-Antarctic Expedition. Nos. G27, G30/1 and G33 optd with Type* G **17**.

G41	1d. black and sepia-brown	10	35
G42	2½d. black and yellow-ochre	50	60
G43	3d. black and deep bright blue	50	30
G44	6d. black and deep lilac	50	30
G41/4 *Set of* 4		1·40	1·25

The stamps of Falkland Islands Dependencies were withdrawn on 16 July 1963 after Coats Land, Graham Land, South Orkneys and South Shetlands had become a separate colony, known as British Antarctic Territory.

F. SOUTH GEORGIA

From 17 July 1963 South Georgia and South Sandwich Islands used stamps inscribed "South Georgia".

1 Reindeer

2 South Sandwich Islands

3 Sperm Whale

4 Chinstrap and King Penguins

5 South American Fur Seal

6 Fin Whale

7 Southern Elephant-seal

8 Light-mantled Sooty Albatross

9 *R2* (Whale catcher)

10 Leopard Seal

11 Shackleton's Cross

12 Wandering Albatross

13 Southern Elephant-seal and South American Fur Seal

14 Plankton and Krill

15 Blue Whale

16 King Penguins

(Des D.L.R. (No. 16), M. Goaman (others). Recess D.L.R.)

1963 (17 July)–**69**. *T* **1/16**. *Ordinary or glazed paper (No. 16).* W w **12**. P 15.

1	**1**	½d. brown-red	50	1·25
		a. Perf 14×15 (13.2.67)	70	1·50
2	**2**	1d. violet-blue	2·50	1·25
3	**3**	2d. turquoise-blue	1·25	1·25
4	**4**	2½d. black	5·50	2·50
5	**5**	3d. bistre	2·75	30
6	**6**	4d. bronze-green	5·00	1·50
7	**7**	5½d. deep violet	2·50	30
8	**8**	6d. orange	75	50
9	**9**	9d. blue	6·50	2·00
10	**10**	1s. purple	75	30
11	**11**	2s. yellow-olive and light blue	26·00	6·50
12	**12**	2s.6d. blue	25·00	4·00
13	**13**	5s. orange-brown	22·00	4·00
14	**14**	10s. magenta	45·00	11·00
15	**15**	£1 ultramarine	90·00	48·00
16	**16**	£1 grey-black (1.12.69)	10·00	16·00
1/16 *Set of* 16			£200	90·00

1970 (22 Jan). *As No. 1, but wmk w* **12** *sideways and on glazed paper.*

17	½d. brown-red	1·50	2·00

Fiji

PRICES FOR STAMPS ON COVER TO 1945

Nos. 1/9	*from* × 6
Nos. 10/34	*from* × 5
Nos. 35/59	*from* × 8
Nos. 60/3	—
Nos. 64/9	*from* × 20
Nos. 70/5	*from* × 5
Nos. 76/103	*from* × 8
Nos. 104/14	*from* × 5
Nos. 115/24	*from* × 4
Nos. 125/37	*from* × 3
Nos. 138/241	*from* × 4
Nos. 242/5	*from* × 3
Nos. 246/8	*from* × 8
Nos. 249/66*b*	*from* × 2
No. 267	*from* × 8
Nos. D1/5*c*	*from* × 5
Nos. D6/10	*from* × 20
Nos. D11/18	*from* × 15

King Cakobau 1852–Oct 1874

Christian missionaries reached Fiji in 1835 and early letters are known to and from their mission stations, sent via Sydney, Hobart or Auckland.

In 1852 Cakobau, the chief of the island of Bau, declared himself King of Fiji and converted to Christianity two years later. Internal problems and difficulties with the American government led the king to offer to cede Fiji to Great Britain. The offer was refused, but resulted in the appointment of a British Consul in 1858. A Consular Post Office operated from September 1858 until 1872 and franked mail with New South Wales stamps from 1863.

The destruction of plantations in the Confederacy during the American Civil War led to an increased demand for Fijian cotton and this upsurge in commercial activity encouraged *The Fiji Times* newspaper on Levuka to establish a postal service on 1 November 1870.

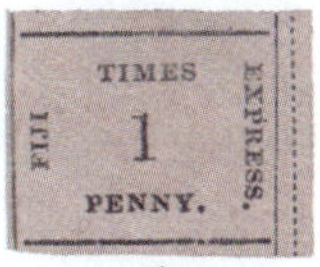

1

(Type-set and printed at the office of *The Fiji Times*, Levuka, Ovalau, Fiji)

1870 (1 Nov)–**71**. *Rouletted in the printing.*

(a) Quadrillé paper.

1	1	1d. black/*rose*	£3250	£3500
2		3d. black/*rose*	£3500	£3500
		a. Comma after "EXPRESS" (R. 4/4)	£4500	£4500
3		6d. black/*rose*	£2000	£2000
4		1s. black/*rose*	£1500	£1800
		(b) Laid bâtonné paper (1871).		
5	1	1d. black/*rose*	£900	£1800
		a. Vert strip of 4. Nos. 5, 7/9	£35000	
6		3d. black/*rose*	£1500	£2750
7		6d. black/*rose*	£1200	£1800
8		9d. black/*rose*	£2500	£3000
		a. Comma after "EXPRESS" (R. 4/4)	£3250	
9		1s. black/*rose*	£1300	£1400

Nos. 1/4 were printed *se-tenant* as a sheet of 24 (6×4) with the 6d. stamps in the first horizontal row, the 1s. in the second, the 1d. in the third and the 3d. in the fourth. Nos. 5/9 were produced from the same plate on which three of the 3d. impressions had been replaced with three 9d. values.

The issued stamps showed the vertical frame lines continuous from top to bottom of the sheet with the horizontal rules broken and not touching the verticals. Used examples are cancelled in manuscript, by an Australian arrival mark or by the star cancellation used at Bua.

There are no reprints of these stamps, but the 1d., 3d., 6d. and 1s. are known in the correct type on *yellow wove* paper and are believed to be proofs.

There are also three different sets of imitations made by the proprietors of *The Fiji Times* to meet the demands of collectors:—

The first was produced in 1876 on *white wove* paper, surfaced to simulate the appearance of vertically ribbed when viewed with light reflecting off its surface. Rouletted on dotted lines and arranged in sheets of 40 (5 rows of 8) comprising 1d., 3d., 6d., 9d. and 1s.; the horizontal frame lines are continuous and the vertical ones broken.

The second was produced before 1888 on *thick rosy mauve wove* paper, rouletted on dotted lines and arranged in sheets of 30 (5 rows of 6) comprising 1s., 9d., 6d., 3d. and 1d.; the vertical frame lines are continuous and the horizontal ones broken.

The third only came to light in the 1960s and is rare, only one complete sheet being recorded, which has since been destroyed. The sheet arrangement is the same as Nos. 1/4, which suggests that this was the first imitation to be produced. It is on *off-white wove* paper, rouletted on closely dotted or solid lines, with vertical frame lines continuous and the horizontal ones broken, as in the originals. These differ from the proofs mentioned above in that the lettering is slightly larger and the figures also differ.

King Cakobau established a formal government in June 1871 and stamps for the royal post office were ordered from Sydney. These arrived in October 1871 and the postal service was placed on a firm basis by the First Postal Act in December of that year. Under its terms *The Fiji Times* service closed on 17 January 1872 and the British Consular Post Office followed six months later.

2

3

Two

Cents

(4)

(Eng and electrotyped by A. L. Jackson. Typo Govt Printing Office, Sydney)

1871 (Oct). *Wove paper.* Wmk impressed "FIJI POSTAGE" in small sans serif capitals across the middle row of stamps in the sheet. P 12½.

10	2	1d. blue	50·00	£120
11		3d. pale yellow-green	£110	£350
12	3	6d. rose	£140	£300

The 3d. differs from T **2** in having a white circle containing square dots surrounding the centre.

All three values are known *imperf*, but were not issued in that condition.

See notes after No. 33b.

1872 (13 Jan). *Surch as T* **4**, *in local currency, by Govt Ptg Office, Sydney.*

13	2	2c. on 1d. pale blue	50·00	65·00
		a. Deep blue	42·00	50·00
14		6c. on 3d. yellow-green	70·00	70·00
15	3	12c. on 6d. carmine-rose	£100	80·00

CROWN COLONY

King Cakobau renewed his offer to cede Fiji to Great Britain and this took place on 12 October 1874.

V.R. (5) V.R. (6) 2d. (7)

V.R. (Enlarged) Cross pattée stop — V.R. Inverted "A"

Cross pattée stop after "R" (R. 3/6).
Round raised stop after "V" (R. 3/8)
Round raised stops after "V" and "R" (R. 3/9).
Inverted "A" for "V" (R. 3/10).
No stop after "R" (R. 2/3 on T **5**, R. 5/3 on T **6**).
Large stop after "R" (R. 5/10).

(Optd at *Polynesian Gazette* Office, Levuka)

1874 (21 Oct). *Nos. 13/15 optd.*

		(a) With T **5**.		
16	2	2c. on 1d. blue	£950	£250
		a. No stop after "R"	£2250	£1000
		b. Cross pattée stop after "R"	£2250	£1000
		c. Round raised stop after "V"	£2250	£1000
		d. Round raised stops after "V" and "R"	£2250	£1000
		e. Inverted "A" for "V"	£2250	£1000
		f. Vert pair. Nos. 16 and 19	£7000	
17		6c. on 3d. green	£1600	£650
		a. No stop after "R"	£4000	£1600
		b. Cross pattée stop after "R"	£4000	£1600
		c. Round raised stop after "V"	£4000	£1600
		d. Round raised stops after "V" and "R"	£4000	£1600
		e. Inverted "A" for "V"	£4000	£1600
		f. Vert pair. Nos. 17 and 20	£9000	
18	3	12c. on 6d. rose	£700	£200
		a. No stop after "R"	£2000	£1000
		b. Cross pattée stop after "R"	£2000	£1000
		c. Round raised stop after "V"	£2000	£1000
		d. Round raised stops after "V" and "R"	£2000	£1000
		e. Inverted "A" for "V"	£2000	£1000
		f. Opt inverted	—	£4500
		g. Vert pair. Nos. 18 and 21	£5000	
		(b) With T **6**.		
19	2	2c. on 1d. blue	£1100	£275
		a. No stop after "R"	£2250	£1000
		f. Large stop after "R"	—	£1000
20		6c. on 3d. green	£2000	£900
		a. No stop after "R"	£4000	£1600
21	3	12c. on 6d. rose	£850	£225
		a. No stop after "R"	£2000	£1000
		b. Opt inverted	£5500	

Nos. 16/21 were produced in sheets of 50 (10×5) of which the top three rows were overprinted with Type **5** and the lower two with Type **6**.

1875. *Stamps of 1874 surch at Polynesian Gazette Office, Levuka, with T* **7**.

		(a) In red (April).		
22	2	2d. on 6c. on 3d. green (No. 17)	£600	£190
		a. No stop after "R"	£1600	£650
		b. Cross pattée stop after "R"	£1600	£650
		c. Round raised stop after "V"	£1600	£650
		d. Round raised stops after "V" and "R"	£1600	£650
		e. Inverted "A" for "V"	£1600	£650
		f. No stop after "2d" (R. 1/2)	£1600	£650
		g. Vert pair. Nos. 22/3	£4000	
23		2d. on 6c. on 3d. green (No. 20)	£750	£275
		a. No stop after "R"	£1600	£650
		b. Stop between "2" and "d" (R. 5/7)	£1600	£650
		(b) In black (30 Sept).		
24	2	2d. on 6c. on 3d. green (No. 17)	£1600	£550
		a. No stop after "R"	£3250	£1300
		b. Cross pattée stop after "R"	£3250	£1300
		c. Round raised stop after "V"	£3250	£1300
		d. Round raised stops after "V" and "R"	£3250	£1300
		e. Inverted "A" for "V"	£3250	£1300
		f. No stop after "2d" (R. 1/2)	£3250	£1300
		g. "V.R." double		
		h. Vert pair. Nos. 24/5	£8500	
25		2d. on 6c. on 3d. green (No. 20)	£2000	£750
		a. No stop after "R"	£3250	£1300
		b. Stop between "2" and "d" (R. 5/7)	£3250	£1300
		c. "V.R." double	£4000	£3500

1875 (20 Nov). *No. 15 surch at Polynesian Gazette Office, Levuka, with T* **7** *and "V.R." at one operation.*

		(a) "V.R." T **5**.		
26	3	2d. on 12c. on 6d. rose	£2000	£850
		a. No stop after "R"	—	£2250
		b. Round raised stop after "R"	—	£1400
		c. Inverted "A" for "V" (R. 1/3, 2/8, 4/4)	£2750	£1200
		d. Do. and round raised stop after "V" (R. 3/3, 3/6, 3/8, 3/10)	£2500	£1000
		e. As "c" and round raised stops after "R" and "V" (R. 3/2, 3/9)	£3000	£1300
		f. Surch double	—	£4000
		g. Vert pair. Nos. 26/7	£9000	
		(b) "V.R." T **6**.		
27	3	2d. on 12c. on 6d. rose	£2250	£900
		a. Surch double	—	£4250

The setting used for Nos. 26/7 was similar to that of Nos. 16/21, but the fourth stamp in the fourth row had a Type **5** "V.R." instead of a Type **6**.

The position of No. 26b is not known.

(8)

Two Pence

(9)

Void corner (R. 2/1)

(Typo Govt Printing Office, Sydney, from plates of 1871)

1876–77. *On paper previously lithographed "VR" as T* **8**, *the 3d. surch with T* **9**. P 12½.

		(a) Wove paper (31.1.76).		
28	2	1d. grey-blue	50·00	50·00
		a. Dull blue	50·00	50·00
		b. Doubly printed	£550	
		c. Void corner	£650	£375
		d. Imperf vert (horiz pair)	£850	
29		2d. on 3d. pale green	55·00	55·00
		a. Deep green	50·00	55·00
30	3	6d. pale rose	65·00	65·00
		a. Dull rose	50·00	55·00
		b. Carmine-rose	55·00	55·00
		c. Doubly printed	£2500	
		(b) Laid paper (5.1.77).		
31	2	1d. blue	22·00	35·00
		a. Deep blue	23·00	35·00
		b. Void corner (R. 2/1)	£400	£300
		c. Imperf vert (horiz pair)	£700	
32		2d. on 3d. yellow-green	60·00	70·00
		a. Deep yellow-green	60·00	70·00
		b. Imperf between (pair)	£850	
		c. Perf 10	£375	
		ca. Imperf vert (horiz pair)	£950	
		d. Perf 11	£350	
33	3	6d. rose	50·00	30·00
		a. Carmine-rose	50·00	35·00
		b. Imperf vert (horiz pair)	£700	

The extent of the void area on Nos. 28c and 31b varies.

The 3d. *green* is known without the surcharge T **9** on wove paper and also without the surcharge and the monogram. In this latter condition it can only be distinguished from No. 11 by its colour, which is a fuller, deeper yellow-green.

Stamps on both wove and laid paper *imperf* are from printer's trial or waste sheets and were not issued.

All values are known on laid paper without the monogram "VR" and the 3d. stamp also without the surcharge but these are also believed to be from printer's trial sheets which were never issued for postal purposes. Being on laid paper they are easily distinguishable from Nos. 10/12.

1877 (12 Oct). *Optd with T* **8** *and surch as T* **9**. *Laid paper.* P 12½.

34	2	4d. on 3d. mauve	85·00	25·00
		a. Imperf vert (horiz pair)	£850	

10

11

A Four Pence

B Four Pence

Type A: Length 12½ mm
Type B: Length 14 mm

Note also the different shape of the two "e"s.

(Typo from new plates made from original dies of 1871 with "CR" altered to "VR" at Govt Printing Office, Sydney. 2d. and 4d. made from old 3d. die.)

1878–99. *Surcharges as T* **9** *or as Types A or B for 4d. value. Wove paper with paper-maker's name "T. H. SAUNDERS" or "SANDERSON" in double-lined capitals extending over seven stamps in each full sheet.*

(a) P 12½ (1878–80).

35	10	1d. pale ultramarine (19.2.79)	11·00	11·00
		a. Ultramarine	14·00	11·00
36		2d. on 3d. green (17.10.78)	8·00	25·00
37		2d. yellow-green (1.9.79)	22·00	12·00
		a. Blue-green	38·00	17·00
		b. Error. Ultramarine	£25000	
38	11	6d. rose (30.7.80)	£100	24·00
		(b) P 10 (1881–90).		
39	10	1d. dull blue (11.5.82)	55·00	3·00
		a. Ultramarine	20·00	3·00
		b. Cambridge blue (12.7.83)	50·00	4·25
40		2d. yellow-green (20.10.81)	20·00	1·00
		a. Blue-green	29·00	5·50
41		4d. on 1d. mauve (29.1.90)	50·00	40·00
42		4d. on 2d. pale mauve (A) (23.5.83)	75·00	12·00
		a. Dull purple	75·00	12·00
43		4d. on 2d. dull purple (B) (7.11.88)	—	£140
44		4d. mauve (13.9.90)	65·00	
		a. Deep purple	65·00	65·00
45	11	6d. pale rose (11.3.85)	70·00	22·00
		a. Bright rose	21·00	21·00
		(c) P 10×12½ (1881–82).		
46	10	1d. ultramarine (11.5.82)	£100	38·00
47		2d. green (20.10.81)	£160	60·00
48	11	6d. rose (20.10.81)	£350	55·00
		a. Pale rose	£350	55·00
		(d) P 12½×10 (1888–90).		
49	10	1d. ultramarine (1890)	—	£300
49*a*		2d. green (1888)		
49*b*		4d. on 2d. dull purple (A)	†	—
		(e) P 10×11¾ (3.9.86).		
50	10	1d. dull blue	70·00	16·00
		a. Ultramarine		
51		2d. yellow-green	65·00	9·00
		(f) P 11¾×10 (1886–88).		
51*a*	10	1d. dull blue (7.11.88)	£225	48·00
		ab. Ultramarine		
51*b*		2d. yellow-green (3.9.86)	—	£500
52	11	6d. rose (1887)	†	£750
		(g) P 11×10 (1892–93).		
53	10	1d. ultramarine (18.8.92)	18·00	14·00
54		4d. pale mauve (18.8.92)	15·00	16·00
55	11	6d. pale rose (14.2.93)	11·00	22·00
		a. Rose	16·00	24·00
		(h) P 11 (1897–99).		
56	10	4d. mauve (14.7.96)	17·00	11·00
57	11	6d. dull rose (14.7.96)	32·00	50·00
		a. Printed both sides (12.99)	£2000	£1500
		b. Bright rose	48·00	55·00
		(i) P 11×11¾ (1896).*		
58	10	4d. deep purple (14.7.96)	40·00	
		a. Bright purple	12·00	7·00
59	11	6d. rose (23.7.96)	35·00	
		a. Bright rose	11·00	3·75
		(j) Imperf (pairs) (1882–90).		
60	10	1d. ultramarine		
61		2d. yellow-green		
62		4d. on 2d. pale mauve		
63	11	6d. rose	—	£1400

*Under this heading are included stamps from several perforating machines with a gauge varying between 11.6 and 12.

No. 37b was printed in the colour of the 1d. in error. Only four examples have been reported, one of which was subsequently destroyed.

In the absence of detailed information on dates of issue printing dates are quoted for Nos. 35/63 and 76/103.

12

13

(Eng A. L. Jackson. Typo Govt Printing Office, Sydney)

1881–99. Paper-maker's name wmkd as previous issue.

(a) P 10 (19.10.81).

64	12	1s. pale brown	90·00	22·00
		a. Deep brown	90·00	25·00
		(b) P 11×10 (1894).		
65	12	1s. pale brown	50·00	50·00
		(c) P 11 (1897).		
66	12	1s. pale brown	50·00	15·00
		(d) P 11×11¾ (5.99).		
67	12	1s. pale brown	45·00	12·00
		a. Brown	45·00	12·00
		b. Deep brown	48·00	48·00
		(e) P 11¾×11 (3.97).		
68	12	1s. brown	60·00	50·00

Dates given of earliest known use.
Forgeries exist.

(Centre typo, frame litho Govt Printing Office, Sydney)

1882 (23 May). Toned paper wmkd with paper-maker's name "Cowan" in old English outline type once in each sheet. P 10.

69	13	5s. dull red and black	55·00	29·00

An unknown quantity of the 1s. and 264 sheets (13,200 stamps) of the 5s., both perf 10 and imperf, were cancelled by the Fiji Post Office and sold as remainders. A number of different "SUVA" remainder cancellations have been recorded between "15 DEC 00" and "21 DE 1902".

An electrotyped plate was also produced for the frame of the 5s. This printing was not used for postal purposes but examples were included among the remainders, all cancelled "15 DEC 00". The electrotyped printing, in dull orange and black, is on paper watermarked "NEW SOUTH WALES GOVERNMENT" in double-line capitals and, apart from the colour of the medallion, differs in a number of respects from the original, most notably in the circular frame surrounding the Queen's head, which is notably thicker than the litho printing. Examples are rare.

2½d. (14) **2½d.** (15)

Types **14** (fraction bar 1 mm from "2") and **15** (fraction bar 2 mm from "2") are from the same setting of 50 (10×5) with Type **15** occurring on R. 1/2, 2/2, 3/2 and 4/2.

(Stamps typo in Sydney and surch at Govt Printing Office, Suva)

1891 (1 Jan). *T* **10** *surch.* P 10.

70	14	2½d. on 2d. green	50·00	50·00
71	15	2½d. on 2d. green	£130	£140

½d. (16) **5d** (17)

FIVE PENCE (18) 2 mm spacing **FIVE PENCE** (19) 3 mm spacing

1892 (1 Mar)–**93**. P 10.

(a) Surch on T **10**.

72	16	½d. on 1d. dull blue	50·00	75·00
		a. Ultramarine	50·00	70·00
73	17	5d. on 4d. deep purple (25.7.92)	50·00	70·00
		a. Dull purple	50·00	70·00
		(b) Surch on T **11**.		
74	18	5d. on 6d. brownish rose (30.11.92)	55·00	65·00
		a. Bright rose	55·00	60·00
		b. Perf 10×12½		
75	19	5d. on 6d. rose (4.1.93)	70·00	80·00
		a. Deep rose	60·00	70·00
		b. Brownish rose	60·00	

20

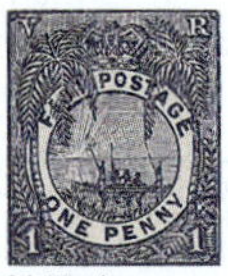

21 Native Canoe

22

(Typo in Sydney)

1891–1902. Wmk in sheet, either "SANDERSON" or "NEW SOUTH WALES GOVERNMENT" in outline capitals.

(a) P 10 (1891–94).

76	20	½d. slate-grey (26.4.92)	4·50	5·50
77	21	1d. black (19.9.94)	15·00	4·50
78		2d. pale green (19.9.94)	£100	15·00
79	22	2½d. chocolate (8.6.91)	45·00	20·00
80	21	5d. ultramarine (14.2.93)	80·00	55·00
		(b) P 11×10 (1892–93).		
81	20	½d. slate-grey (20.10.93)	8·50	20·00
82	21	1d. black (14.2.93)	9·00	4·75
83		2d. green (14.2.93)	17·00	7·00
84	22	2½d. chocolate (17.8.92)	20·00	28·00
		a. Brown	12·00	12·00
		b. Yellowish brown		
85	21	5d. ultramarine (14.2.93)	15·00	7·50
		(c) P 11 (1893–96).		
86	20	½d. slate-grey (2.6.96)	3·00	6·50
		a. Greenish slate	2·50	6·50
87	21	1d. black (31.10.95)	8·00	7·00
88		1d. pale mauve (2.6.96)	8·50	1·00
		a. Rosy mauve	9·50	1·00
89		2d. dull green (17.3.94)	8·50	80
		a. Emerald-green	8·50	2·00
90	22	2½d. brown (31.10.95)	29·00	12·00
		a. Yellowish brown	19·00	22·00
91	21	5d. ultramarine (14.2.93)	£150	
		(d) P 10×11¾ (1893–94).		
92	20	½d. greenish slate	£1000	
93	21	1d. black (20.7.93)	22·00	6·00
94		2d. dull green (19.9.94)	£650	£375
		(e) P 11¾×10 (19.9.94).		
94*a*	20	½d. greenish slate	—	£1000
		(f) P 11¾ (1894–98).		
95	20	½d. greenish slate (19.9.94)	2·75	11·00
		a. Grey	40·00	
96	21	1d. black (19.9.94)	£225	42·00
97		1d. rosy mauve (4.5.98)	7·00	8·00
98		2d. dull green (19.9.94)	95·00	48·00
		(g) P 11×11¾ (1895–97).		
99	20	½d. greenish slate (8.10.97)	1·00	4·25
100	21	1d. black (31.10.95)	£3000	£1500
101		1d. rosy mauve (14.7.96)	7·50	1·00
		a. Pale rosy mauve	4·50	2·00
102		2d. dull green (26.7.97)	40·00	4·00
103	22	2½d. brown (26.7.97)	11·00	18·00
		a. Yellow-brown	5·00	5·00
		(h) P 11¾×11 (1897–98).		
103*b*	20	½d. greenish slate (8.10.97)	5·00	10·00
103*c*	21	1d. rosy mauve (10.2.97)	15·00	5·00
103*d*		2d. dull green (4.5.98) (*shades*)	£225	£100

The 2½d. brown is known doubly printed, but only occurs in the remainders and with the special obliteration (*Price £130 cancelled-to-order*). It was never used for postal use.

23

24

(Typo D.L.R.)

1903 (1 Feb). Wmk Crown CA. P 14.

104	23	½d. green and pale green	2·25	2·00
105		1d. dull purple and black/*red*	13·00	55
106	24	2d. dull purple and orange	3·75	1·25
107	23	2½d. dull purple and blue/*blue*	14·00	1·75
108		3d. dull purple and purple	1·50	3·25
109	24	4d. dull purple and black	1·50	2·50
110	23	5d. dull purple and green	1·50	2·50
111	24	6d. dull purple and carmine	1·50	1·75
112	23	1s. green and carmine	11·00	70·00
113	24	5s. green and black	70·00	£160
114	23	£1 grey-black and ultramarine	£325	£400
104/14 *Set of* 11			£400	£550
104s/14s Optd "Specimen" *Set of* 11			£300	

1904–09. Wmk Mult Crown CA. *Chalk-surfaced paper (1s.).* P 14.

115	23	½d. green and pale green	15·00	3·00
116		1d. purple and black/*red*	27·00	10
117		1s. green and carmine (1909)	28·00	40·00
115/17 *Set of* 3			60·00	40·00

1906–12. *Colours changed.* Wmk Mult Crown CA. *Chalk surfaced paper (6d. to £1).* P 14.

118	23	½d. green (1908)	11·00	3·25
119		1d. red (1906)	12·00	10
		w. Wmk inverted	†	—
120		2½d. bright blue (1910)	6·50	7·50
121	24	6d. dull purple (1910)	17·00	32·00
122	23	1s. black/*green* (1911)	6·00	10·00
123	24	5s. green and red/*yellow* (1911)	60·00	80·00
124	23	£1 purple and black/*red* (1912)	£300	£275
118/24 *Set of* 7			£350	£350
119s/24s Optd "Specimen" *Set of* 6			£325	

Nos. 112/14, 117 and 120/4 are known with a forged registered postmark of Suva dated "10 DEC 1909".

25

26

WAR STAMP (27)

(Typo D.L.R.)

1912 (Oct)–**23**. *Die I.* Wmk Mult Crown CA. *Chalk-surfaced paper (5d. to £1).* P 14.

125	26	¼d. brown (1.4.16)	2·50	30
		a. Deep brown (1917)	1·50	40
		y. Wmk inverted and reversed		
126	25	½d. green	1·50	1·00
		a. Yellow-green (1916)	8·50	8·50
		b. Blue-green (1917)	1·25	50
		w. Wmk inverted	£130	
		y. Wmk inverted and reversed	£130	
127		1d. carmine	2·00	10
		a. Bright scarlet (1916)	2·00	75
		ax. Wmk reversed	†	—
		b. Deep rose (1916)	9·50	2·00
		bw. Wmk inverted	†	—
128	26	2d. greyish slate (5.14)	1·75	10
		a. Wmk sideways		
		b. "C" of "CA" missing from wmk	†	—
		w. Wmk inverted	—	£275
129	25	2½d. bright blue (5.14)	3·00	3·50
130		3d. purple/*yellow* (5.14)	4·25	6·00
		a. Wmk sideways	£350	£475
		b. On lemon (1915)	2·00	8·50
		c. On pale yellow (1921)	1·75	14·00
		ca. "A" of "CA" missing from wmk		
		cw. Wmk inverted		
		d. Die II. *On pale yellow* (1922)	2·50	24·00
131	26	4d. black and red/*yellow* (5.14)	23·00	20·00
		a. On lemon	3·00	16·00
		b. On orange-buff (1920)	50·00	65·00
		c. On pale yellow (1921)	6·50	14·00
		cw. Wmk inverted	£400	
		d. Die II. *On pale yellow* (1922)	3·00	27·00
		ds. Optd "Specimen"	40·00	
132	25	5d. dull purple and olive-green (5.14)	4·75	11·00
133	26	6d. dull and bright purple (5.14)	2·00	5·50
134	25	1s. black/*green* (10.13)	1·25	14·00
		a. White back (4.14)	1·00	11·00
		b. On blue-green, olive back (1916)	3·00	10·00
		c. On emerald back (1921)	4·50	48·00
		cs. Optd Specimen"	45·00	
		d. Die II. *On emerald back* (1922)	2·25	27·00
135	26	2s.6d. black and red/*blue* (19.1.16)	32·00	30·00
136		5s. green and red/*yellow*	32·00	40·00
137	25	£1 purple and black/*red* (5.14)	£275	£275
		a. Die II (1923)	£250	£275
125/37 *Set of* 13			£300	£350
125s/37s Optd "Specimen" *Set of* 13			£425	

Bold "TA" (left pane, R. 5/4)

1915 (1 Dec)–**19**. *Optd with T* **27** *by Govt Printer, Suva.*

138	**25**	½d. green		
		a. Yellow-green (1916)	1·50	6·00
		b. Blue-green (1917)	75	3·00
		c. Opt inverted	£600	
		d. Opt double		
		e. Bold "TA"		
139		1d. carmine	28·00	23·00
		a. Bright scarlet	2·00	75
		ab. Horiz pair, one without opt	£6000	
		c. Opt inverted	£700	
		d. Deep rose (1919)	4·25	2·25
		e. Bold "TA"		
138s/9s H/S "Specimen" *Set of* 2			£120	

No. 139ab occurred on one pane of 120 only, the overprint being so misplaced that all the stamps of the last vertical row escaped it entirely.

The bold "TA" variety only occurs on later printings of Nos. 138/9.

Nos. 140/227 are no longer used.

1922–29. *Die II.* Wmk Mult Script CA. *Chalk-surfaced paper (1s. to 5s.).* P 14.

228	**26**	¼d. deep brown (1923)	2·50	24·00
229	**25**	½d. green (1923)	75	1·00
		w. Wmk inverted		
230		1d. carmine-red	2·75	50
231		1d. violet (6.1.27)	1·25	10
232	**26**	1½d. scarlet (6.1.27)	4·00	1·00
233		2d. grey	1·25	10
		a. Face value omitted	£22000	
234	**25**	3d. bright blue (1924)	2·75	1·00
235	**26**	4d. black and red/*lemon* (1924)	7·00	7·00
		a. On pale yellow (1929)	50·00	24·00
236	**25**	5d. dull purple and sage-green (1927)	1·50	1·50
237	**26**	6d. dull and bright purple	2·00	1·25
238	**25**	1s. black/*emerald* (1924)	6·50	5·00
		w. Wmk inverted		
239	**26**	2s. purple and blue/*blue* (6.1.27)	25·00	65·00
240		2s.6d. black and red/*blue* (1925)	11·00	32·00
241		5s. green and red/*pale yellow* (1926)	32·00	70·00
228/41 *Set of* 14			90·00	£190
228s/41s Optd "Specimen" *Set of* 14			£300	

The 2d. imperforate with watermark Type **10** of Ireland came from a trial printing and was not issued.

Only one example of No. 233a is known. It was caused by an obstruction during the printing of the duty plate.

1935 (6 May). *Silver Jubilee. As Nos. 91/4 of Antigua.* P 13½×14.

242	1½d. deep blue and carmine	1·00	8·50
	a. Deep blue and aniline red	9·00	24·00
	b. Frame printed double, one albino	£1000	
	f. Diagonal line by turret	75·00	
	h. Dot by flagstaff	£150	
	i. Dash by turret	£150	
243	2d. ultramarine and grey	1·50	35
	f. Diagonal line by turret	85·00	60·00
	g. Dot to left of chapel	£190	
244	3d. brown and deep blue	2·50	3·50
	f. Diagonal line by turret	£140	
	h. Dot by flagstaff	£275	£325
	i. Dash by turret	£275	
245	1s. slate and purple	7·50	10·00
	a. Frame printed double, one albino	£1600	
	f. Diagonal line by turret	£225	
	h. Dot by flagstaff	£350	
	i. Dash by turret	£400	
242/5 *Set of* 4		11·50	20·00
242s/5s Perf "Specimen" *Set of* 4		£120	

For illustrations of plate varieties see Omnibus section following Zanzibar.

1937 (12 May). *Coronation. As Nos. 95/7 of Antigua.*

246	1d. purple	60	1·25
247	2d. grey-black	60	2·25
248	3d. Prussian blue	60	2·25
246/8 *Set of* 3		1·60	5·25
246s/8s Perf "Specimen" *Set of* 3		90·00	

28 Native sailing Canoe

29 Native Village

30 Camakua (canoe)

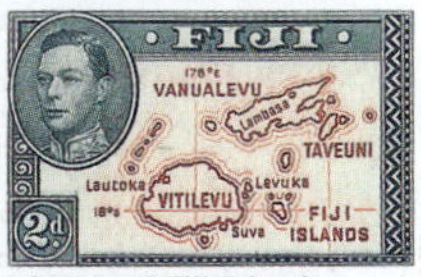

31 Map of Fiji Islands

Two Dies of Type **30**:

Die I Empty Canoe   Die II Native in Canoe

Two Dies of Type **31**:

Die I Without "180°" Die II With "180°"

32 Government Offices

33 Canoe and arms of Fiji

34 Sugar cane

35 Arms of Fiji

36 Spearing fish by torchlight

37 Suva Harbour

38 River scene

39 Chief's hut

40 Paw-paw tree

41 Police bugler

Extra palm frond (R. 5/8)

Extra line (R. 10/2)

Scratch through value (R. 5/1)

Extra island (R. 10/5)

Spur on arms medallion (Pl 2 R. 4/2) (ptg of 26 Nov 1945)

(Des V. E. Ousey (½d., 1s., 2s.6d.), Miss C. D. Lovejoy (1d., 1½d., 5d.), Miss I. Stinson (3d., 5s.) and A. V. Guy (2d. (Nos. 253/4), 2½d., 6d., 2s.). Recess De La Rue (½d., 1½d., 2d., (Nos. 253/5a), 2½d., 6d., 8d., 1s.5d., 1s.6d.), Waterlow (others))

1938 (5 Apr)–**55**. *T* **28/41**. Wmk Mult Script CA. Various perfs.

249	**28**	½d. green (P 13½)	20	75
		a. Perf 14 (5.41)	20·00	3·50
		b. Perf 12 (8.48)	1·00	3·00
		ba. Extra palm frond	80·00	
250	**29**	1d. brown and blue (P 12½)	50	20
251	**30**	1½d. carmine (Die I) (P 13½)	15·00	35
252		1½d. carmine (Die II) (P 13½) (1.10.40)	1·40	3·00
		a. Deep carmine (10.42)	4·00	1·25
		b. Perf 14 (6.42)	22·00	19·00
		c. Perf 12 (21.7.49)	1·50	1·25
253	**31**	2d. brown and green (Die I) (P 13½)	40·00	40
		a. Extra line	£600	75·00
		b. Scratch through value	£600	75·00
254		2d. brown and green (Die II) (P 13½) (1.10.40)	16·00	16·00
255	**32**	2d. green & mag (P 13½) (19.5.42)	40	60
		a. Perf 12 (27.5.46)	1·00	70
256	**31**	2½d. brown & grn (Die II) (P 14) (6.1.42)	1·50	1·00
		a. Extra island	55·00	48·00
		b. Perf 13½ (6.1.42)	1·00	80
		ba. Extra island	48·00	45·00
		c. Perf 12 (19.1.48)	1·00	50
		ca. Extra island	48·00	28·00
257	**33**	3d. blue (P 12½)	1·00	30
		a. Spur on arms medallion	£350	£160
258	**34**	5d. blue and scarlet (P 12½)	42·00	11·00
259		5d. yell-green & scar (P 12½) (1.10.40)	20	30
260	**31**	6d. black (Die I) (P 13×12)	60·00	12·00
261		6d. black (Die II) (P 13½) (1.10.40)	4·00	2·25
		a. Violet-black (1.44)	25·00	28·00
		b. Perf 12. *Black* (5.6.47)	1·50	1·50
261*c*	**35**	8d. carmine (P 14) (15.11.48)	1·00	2·50
		d. Perf 13 (7.6.50)	70	2·75
262	**36**	1s. black and yellow (P 12½)	1·00	70
263	**35**	1s.5d. black & carm (P 14) (13.6.40)	20	10
263*a*		1s.6d. ultramarine (P 14) (1.8.50)	3·50	2·75
		b. Perf 13 (16.2.55)	1·25	15·00
264	**37**	2s. violet and orange (P 12½)	2·50	40
265	**38**	2s.6d. green and brown (P 12½)	3·25	1·50
266	**39**	5s. green and purple (P 12½)	3·00	1·75
266*a*	**40**	10s. orange & emer (P 12½) (13.3.50)	35·00	40·00
266*b*	**41**	£1 ultram & carm (P 12½) (13.3.50)	48·00	50·00
249/66*b* *Set of* 22			£250	£120
249s/66s (*excl* 8d. *and* 1s.6d.) Perf "Specimen" *Set of* 18			£550	

2½d.

(**42**)

1941 (10 Feb). *No. 254 surch with T* **42** *by Govt Printer, Suva.*

267	**31**	2½d. on 2d. brown and green	2·25	65

1946 (17 Aug). *Victory. As Nos. 110/11 of Antigua.*

268	2½d. green	10	1·50
	a. Printed double, one albino	£425	
269	3d. blue	10	10
268s/9s Perf "Specimen" *Set of* 2		90·00	

1948 (17 Dec). *Royal Silver Wedding. As Nos. 112/13 of Antigua.*

270	2½d. green	40	1·75
271	5s. violet-blue	14·00	8·00

1949 (10 Oct). *75th Anniv of Universal Postal Union. As Nos. 114/17 of Antigua.*

272	2d. bright reddish purple	30	75
273	3d. deep blue	2·00	3·75
274	8d. carmine-red	30	4·00
275	1s.6d. blue	35	1·75
272/5 *Set of* 4		2·75	9·25

43 Children Bathing

44 Rugby Football

(Recess B.W.)

1951 (17 Sept). *Health Stamps.* Wmk Mult Script CA. P 13½.

276	**43**	1d.+1d. brown	10	1·00
277	**44**	2d.+1d. green	40	1·00

45 Arms of Fiji

(Des and eng B.W. Recess D.L.R.)

1953 (2 June). *Coronation. As No. 120 of Antigua.*

278		2½d. black and green	1·75	50

(Recess D.L.R.)

1953 (16 Dec). *Royal Visit.* Wmk Mult Script CA. P 13.

279	**45**	8d. deep carmine-red	30	15

46 Queen Elizabeth II (after Annigoni)

47 Government Offices

48 Loading Copra

49 Sugar Cane Train

50 Preparing Bananas for Export

51 Gold Industry

(Des V. E. Ousey (½d., 1s., 2s.6d.), A. V. Guy (6d.). Recess D.L.R. (½d., 2d., 6d., 8d.), Waterlow (1s., 2s.6d., 10s., £1) B.W. (others))

1954 (1 Feb)–**59**. *T* **46/51** *and similar designs previously used for King George VI issue (but with portrait of Queen Elizabeth II as in T* **47**). Wmk Mult Script CA. P 12 (2d.),13 (8d.), 12½ (1s., 2s.6d., 10s., £1), 11½×11 (3d., 1s.6d., 2s., 5s.) or 11½ (½d. 1d., 1½d., 2½d, 6d.).

280	**28**	½d. myrtle-green (1.7.54)	75	1·50
281	**46**	1d. turquoise-blue (1.6.56)	1·75	10
282		1½d. sepia (1.10.56)	1·75	65
283	**47**	2d. green and magenta	1·25	40
284	**46**	2½d. blue-violet (1.10.56)	3·00	10
285	**48**	3d. brown and reddish violet (1.10.56)	4·25	20
		a. *Brown & dp reddish vio* (10.11.59)	13·00	80
287	**31**	6d. black (1.7.54)	2·50	85
288	**35**	8d. deep carmine-red (1.7.54)	6·50	1·25
		a. *Carmine-lake* (6.3.58)	9·00	2·00
289	**36**	1s. black and yellow	2·50	10
290	**49**	1s.6d. blue and myrtle-green (1.10.56)	19·00	1·00
291	**50**	2s. black and carmine (1.10.56)	5·50	60
292	**38**	2s.6d. bluish green and brown	1·25	50
		a. *Bluish green & red-brown* (14.9.54)	1·25	10
293	**51**	5s. ochre and blue (1.10.56)	13·00	1·25
294	**40**	10s. orange and emerald (1.7.54)	7·00	20·00
295	**41**	£1 ultramarine and carmine (1.7.54)	38·00	19·00
280/95 *Set of* 15			95·00	42·00

Designs: *Vert* (22½×36 *mm*)—½d. Fijians sailing canoe. (25×31 *mm*)—1s. Spearing fish by torchlight; 10s. Paw-paw tree; £1 Police bugler. *Horiz* (36×22½ *mm*)—6d. Map of Fiji. (31×25 *mm*)—8d. Arms of Fiji; 2s.6d. River scene.

52 River Scene

53 Cross of Lorraine

(Recess B.W.)

1954 (1 Apr). *Health Stamps.* Wmk Mult Script CA. P 11×11½.

296	**52**	1½d.+½d. bistre-brown and green	10	1·00
297	**53**	2½d.+½d. orange and black	10	20

54 Queen Elizabeth II (after Annigoni)

55 Fijian beating Lali

56 Hibiscus

57 Yagona ceremony

58 Location Map

59 Nadi Airport

60 Red Shining Parrot

61 Cutting Sugar-cane

62 Arms of Fiji

(Des M. Goaman: Photo Harrison (8d., 4s.). Recess. B.W. (others))

1959–63. *T* **54/6**, **60** *and similar designs.* Wmk Mult Script CA. P 11½ (T **46** and **54**), 11½×11 (6d., 10d., 1s., 2s.6d., 10s. £1), 14½×14 (8d.) or 14×14½ (4s).

298	**46**	½d. emerald-green (14.11.61)	15	2·50
299	**54**	1d. deep ultramarine (3.12.62)	3·50	2·50
300		1½d. sepia (3.12.62)	3·50	2·50
301	**46**	2d. rose-red (14.11.61)	50	10
302		2½d. orange-brown (3.12.62)	1·50	3·50
303	**55**	6d. carmine and black (14.11.61)	1·50	10
304	**56**	8d. scarlet, yellow, green & blk (1.8.61)	50	25
305	**57**	10d. brown and carmine (1.4.63)	1·75	60
306	**58**	1s. light blue and blue (14.11.61)	1·50	10
307	**59**	2s.6d. black and purple (14.11.61)	12·00	10
308	**60**	4s. red, green, blue & slate-grn (13.7.59)	1·75	1·50
309	**61**	10s. emerald and deep sepia (14.11.61)	3·50	1·25
310	**62**	£1 black and orange (14.11.61)	9·00	3·50
298/310 *Set of* 13			35·00	16·00

Nos. 299 and 311 have turtles either side of "Fiji" instead of shells.

63 Queen Elizabeth II

64 International Dateline

65 White Orchid

66 Orange Dove

(Des M. Goaman. Photo Harrison (3d., 9d., 1s.6d., 2s., 4s., 5s.). Recess B.W. (others))

1962 (3 Dec)–**67**. W w **12** (upright). P 11½ (1d., 2d.), 12½ (3d.), 11½×11 (6d., 10d., 1s., 2s.6d., 10s., £1), 14½×14 (9d., 2s.) or 14×14½ (1s.6d., 4s., 5s.).

311	**54**	1d. deep ultramarine (14.1.64)	70	3·25
312	**46**	2d. rose-red (3.8.65)	50	10
313	**63**	3d. multicoloured	25	10
		w. Wmk inverted		
314	**55**	6d. carmine and black (9.6.64)	1·50	10
315	**56**	9d. scarlet, yellow, grn & ultram (1.4.63)	90	65
316	–	10d. brown and carmine (14.1.64)	60	50
317	–	1s. light blue and blue (24.1.66*)	1·25	45
318	**64**	1s.6d. red, yellow, gold, black & blue	1·50	90
		a. Error. Wmk sideways	£750	
319	**65**	2s. yellow-green, green and copper	10·00	3·50
		a. *Apple-green, grn & copper* (16.5.67)	23·00	4·25
320	–	2s.6d. black and purple (3.8.65)	2·75	1·00
		a. *Black and deep purple* (8.67)	4·50	2·00
321	**60**	4s. red, yellow-green, blue & grn (1.4.64)	7·00	2·00
322		4s. red, green, blue & slate-grn (1.3.66)	4·50	2·75
323	**66**	5s. red, yellow and grey	10·00	35
		w. Wmk inverted	£140	£110
324	–	10s. emerald and deep sepia (14.1.64)	5·50	3·00
325	–	£1 black and orange (9.6.64)	14·00	9·00
311/25 *Set of* 15			55·00	25·00

Designs: *Horiz* (*as T* **55**)—10d. Yaqona Ceremony; 1s. Location map; 2s.6d. Nadi Airport; 10s. Cutting sugar-cane; £1 Arms of Fiji.

*This is the earliest known used date in Fiji and it was not released by the Crown Agents until 1 November.

The 3d. value exists with PVA gum as well as gum arabic.

For 4s. with watermark sideways see No. 359.

ROYAL VISIT
1963

(67)

ROYAL VISIT 1963

(68)

1963 (1 Feb). *Royal Visit. Nos. 313 and 306 optd with T* **67/8**.

326	**67**	3d. multicoloured	40	20
327	**68**	1s. light blue and blue	60	20

1963 (4 June). *Freedom from Hunger. As No. 146 of Antigua.*

328		2s. ultramarine	1·00	1·50

69 Running

(73 C.S. *Retriever*.)

(Des M. Goaman. Photo Harrison)

1963 (6 Aug). *First South Pacific Games, Suva. T* **69** *and similar designs.* W w **12**. P 14½.

329		3d. red-brown, yellow and black	25	10
330		9d. red-brown, violet and black	25	1·50
331		1s. red-brown, green and black	25	10
332		2s.6d. red-brown, light blue and black	60	60
329/32 *Set of* 4			1·25	2·00

Designs: *Vert*—9d. Throwing the discus; 1s. Hockey. *Horiz*—2s.6d. High-jumping.

1963 (2 Sept). *Red Cross Centenary. As Nos. 147/8 of Antigua.*

333		2d. red and black	35	10
334		2s. red and blue	75	2·50

1963 (3 Dec). *Opening of COMPAC (Trans-Pacific Telephone Cable). No. 317 optd with T* **73** *by B.W.*

335		1s. light blue and blue	55	10

74 Jamborette Emblem

75 Scouts of Three Races

(Des V. Whiteley assisted by Norman L. Joe Asst. D.C., Fiji Scouts for Jamboree emblem. Photo Harrison)

1964 (4 Aug). *50th Anniv of Fijian Scout Movement.* W w **12**. P 12½.

336	**74**	3d. multicoloured	15	25
337	**75**	1s. violet and yellow-brown	15	30

76 Flying-boat *Aotearoa*

78 *Aotearoa* and Map

(Des V. Whiteley. Photo Harrison)

1964 (24 Oct). *25th Anniv of First Fiji-Tonga Airmail Service. T* **76**, **78** *and similar design.* W w **12**. P 14½×14 (1s.) or 12½ (others).

338		3d. black and vermilion	40	10
339		6d. vermilion and bright blue	70	1·00
340		1s. black and turquoise-blue	70	1·00
338/40 *Set of* 3			1·60	1·75

Design: *Vert* (*as T* **76**)—6d. De Havilland D.H.114 Heron 2.

1965 (17 May). *I.T.U. Centenary. As Nos. 166/7 of Antigua.*

341		3d. blue and rose-carmine	20	10
342		2s. orange-yellow and bistre	50	25

1965 (25 Oct). *International Co-operation Year. As Nos. 168/9 of Antigua.*

343		2d. reddish purple and turquoise-green	20	10
344		2s.6d. deep bluish green and lavender	80	25

AFFIX
STAMP
HERE

Stanley Gibbons (Guernsey) Limited
18 Le Bordage
St Peter Port
Guernsey
Channel Islands
United Kingdom
GY1 1DE

AFFIX
STAMP
HERE

Stanley Gibbons Mail Order
399 Strand
London
England
WC2R 0LX

AFFIX
STAMP
HERE

Stanley Gibbons A & A Department
399 Strand
London
England
WC2R 0LX

1966 (24 Jan). *Churchill Commemoration. As Nos. 170/3 of Antigua.*
345 3d. new blue 70 10
346 9d. deep green 90 85
347 1s. brown 90 10
348 2s.6d. bluish violet .... 1·00 85
345/8 *Set of* 4 .... 3·25 1·60

1966 (1 July). *World Cup Football Championship. As Nos. 176/7 of Antigua.*
349 2d. violet, yellow-green, lake & yellow-brn 25 10
350 2s. chocolate, blue-green, lake & yellow-brn 75 20

79 H.M.S. *Pandora* approaching Split Island, Rotuma

(Des V. Whiteley. Photo Enschedé)

1966 (29 Aug). *175th Anniv of Discovery of Rotuma. T* **79** *and similar horiz designs. Multicoloured.* W w **12** (sideways). P 14×13.
351 3d. Type **79** 30 10
352 10d. Rotuma Chiefs 30 10
353 1s.6d. Rotumans welcoming H.M.S. *Pandora* 50 30
351/3 *Set of* 3 .... 1·00 40

1966 (20 Sept). *Inauguration of W.H.O. Headquarters, Geneva. As Nos. 178/9 of Antigua.*
354 6d. black, yellow-green and light blue .... 1·25 25
355 2s.6d. black, light purple and yellow-brown .... 2·75 2·50

LEGISLATIVE ASSEMBLY

82 Running

(Des V. Whiteley. Photo Harrison)

1966 (5 Dec*). *2nd South Pacific Games, Nouméa. T* **82** *and similar designs.* W w **12** (sideways on 9d.). P 14½×14 (9d.) or 14×14½ (others).
356 3d. black, chestnut and yellow-olive 10 10
357 9d. black, chestnut and greenish blue 15 15
358 1s. multicoloured 15 15
356/8 *Set of* 3 .... 30 30
Designs: *Vert*—9d. Putting the shot. *Horiz*—1s. Diving.
*These were not released in London until 8.12.66.

1967 (16 Feb). *As No. 321 but* wmk w **12** sideways.
359 **60** 4s. red, yellow-green, blue and green .... 2·75 1·00

85 Military Forces Band

(Des G. Vasarhelyi. Photo Enschedé)

1967 (20 Oct). *International Tourist Year. T* **85** *and similar horiz designs. Multicoloured.* W w **12** (sideways). P 14×13.
360 3d. Type **85** 40 10
361 9d. Reef diving 15 10
362 1s. Beqa fire walkers 15 10
363 2s. *Oriana* (cruise liner) at Suva 40 15
360/3 *Set of* 4 .... 1·00 30

89 Bligh (bust), H.M.S. *Providence* and Chart

91 Bligh's Tomb

90 "*Bounty's* longboat being chased in Fiji waters"

(Des V. Whiteley. Photo Harrison)

1967 (11 Dec). *150th Death Anniv of Admiral Bligh.* W w **12** (sideways on 1s.). P 12½×13 (1s.) or 15×14 (others).
364 **89** 4d. multicoloured 10 10
365 **90** 1s. multicoloured 10 10
366 **91** 2s.6d. multicoloured 15 15
364/6 *Set of* 3 .... 30 30

92 Simmonds Spartan Seaplane

(Des V. Whiteley. Photo Harrison)

1968 (5 June). *40th Anniv of Kingsford Smith's Pacific Flight via Fiji. T* **92** *and similar horiz designs.* W w **12**. P 14×14½.
367 2d. black and green 15 10
368 6d. greenish blue, black and lake 15 10
369 1s. deep violet and turquoise-green 20 10
370 2s. orange-brown and blue 30 15
367/70 *Set of* 4 .... 70 30
Designs:—6d. Hawker Siddeley H.S.748 and airline insignias; 1s. Fokker F.VIIa/3M *Southern Cross* and crew; 2s. Lockheed 8D Altair *Lady Southern Cross* monoplane.

96 Bure Huts

97 Eastern Reef Heron (after Belcher)

98 Sea Snake

99 Queen Elizabeth and Arms of Fiji

(Des G. Hamori (½d., 1d., 9d.), W. O. Cernohorsky (2d., 4s.) H. S. Robinson (4d., 10d.), D. W. Blair (6d., 5s.), P. D. Clarke (1s.), G. Vasarhelyi (2s.6d.), W. O. Cernohorsky and E. Jones (3s.), E. Jones and G. Hamori (10s.), E. Jones (£1) Adapted V. Whiteley. Photo D.L.R.)

1968 (15 July). *T* **96/9** *and similar designs.* W w **12** (sideways on all vert designs). P 14×13½ (2s., 2s.6d., 5s., £1), 13½×14 (3d., 1s., 1s.6d., 4s., 10s.) or 13½×13 (others).
371 ½d. multicoloured 10 10
372 1d. deep greenish blue, red and yellow 10 10
373 2d. new blue, brown and ochre 10 10
374 3d. blackish green, blue and ochre 35 10
375 4d. multicoloured .... 80 2·00
376 6d. multicoloured 25 10
377 9d. multicoloured .... 15 2·00
378 10d. royal blue, orange and blackish brown .... 1·25 20
379 1s. Prussian blue and brown-red 20 10
380 1s.6d. multicoloured .... 4·00 4·50
381 2s. turquoise, black and rosine .... 75 2·00
382 2s.6d. multicoloured 75 30
383 3s. multicoloured .... 2·00 6·00
384 4s. yellow-ochre, black and olive .... 5·00 2·75
385 5s. multicoloured .... 2·50 1·50
386 10s. lake-brown, black and ochre .... 1·00 2·50
387 £1 multicoloured .... 1·25 3·00
371/87 *Set of* 17 .... 18·00 24·00
Designs: *Horiz (as T* **96**)—1d. Passion Flowers; 2d. Chambered or Pearly Nautilus; 4d. *Psilogramma jordana* (moth); 6d. Pennant Coralfish; 9d. Bamboo raft; 10d. *Asota woodfordi* (moth); 3s. Golden Cowrie shell. *Vert (as T* **97**)—1s. Black Marlin; 1s.6d. Orange-breasted Honeyeaters (after Belcher); 4s. Mining industry; 10s. Ceremonial whale's tooth. *Horiz (as T* **98**)—2s.6d. Outrigger canoes; 5s. Bamboo Orchids.

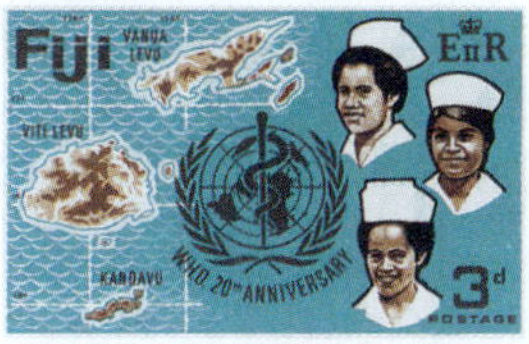

113 Map of Fiji, W.H.O. Emblem and Nurses

(Des V. Whiteley. Litho D.L.R.)

1968 (9 Dec). *20th Anniv of World Health Organization. T* **113** *and similar horiz designs. Multicoloured.* W w **12** (sideways). P 14.
388 3d. Type **113** 15 10
389 9d. Transferring patient to Medical Ship *Vuniwai* 20 15
390 3s. Recreation 25 30
388/90 *Set of* 3 .... 55 40

(New Currency. 100 cents = 1 dollar.)

116 Passion Flowers

117 Fijian Soldiers overlooking the Solomon Islands

1969 (13 Jan)–**70**. *Decimal Currency. Designs as Nos. 371/87, but with values inscr in decimal currency as T* **116**. W w **12** (sideways on vert designs). *Chalk-surfaced paper.* P 14×13½ (20, 25, 50c. $2) 13½×14 (3, 10, 15, 40c., $1) or 13½×13 (others).
391 **116** 1c. deep greenish blue, red and yellow 10 10
392 – 2c. new blue, brown and ochre (as 2d.) 10 10
393 **97** 3c. blackish green, blue and ochre .... 1·25 1·50
394 – 4c. multicoloured (as 4d.) .... 1·50 1·50
395 – 5c. multicoloured (as 6d.) 20 10
396 **96** 6c. multicoloured 10 10
397 – 8c. multicoloured (as 9d.) 10 10
398 – 9c. royal blue, orange and blackish brown (as 10d.) .... 1·50 2·75
399 – 10c. Prussian blue and brown-red (as 1s.) 20 10
400 – 15c. multicoloured (as 1s.6d.) .... 9·00 4·75
401 **98** 20c. turquoise, black and rosine .... 1·25 80
402 – 25c. multicoloured (as 2s.6d.) .... 1·00 20
403 – 30c. multicoloured (as 3s.) .... 6·50 1·50
404 – 40c. yellow-ochre, black and olive (as 4s.) .... 7·50 4·00
405 – 50c. multicoloured (as 5s.) .... 4·50 20
a. Glazed, ordinary paper (3.9.70) .... 10·00 1·50
406 – $1 lake-brown, black and ochre (as 10s.) .... 1·50 40
a. Glazed, ordinary paper (3.9.70) .... 2·00 2·75
407 **99** $2 multicoloured .... 1·50 1·50
391/407 *Set of* 17 .... 32·00 17·00

(Des G. Drummond. Photo Harrison)

1969 (23 June). *25th Anniv of Fijian Military Forces' Solomons Campaign. T* **117** *and similar horiz designs.* W w **12**. P 14.
408 3c. yellow-brown, black and bright emerald 20 10
409 10c. multicoloured 25 10
410 25c. multicoloured 35 20
408/10 *Set of* 3 .... 70 30
Designs:—10c. Regimental Flags and Soldiers in full dress and battledress; 25c. Cpl. Sefanaia Sukanaivalu and Victoria Cross.

120 Javelin Thrower

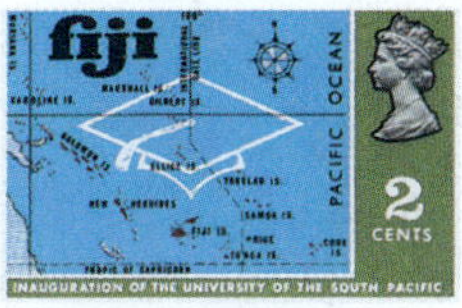

123 Map of South Pacific and "Mortar-board"

(Des L. Curtis. Photo Harrison)

1969 (18 Aug). *3rd South Pacific Games. Port Moresby. T* **120** *and similar vert designs.* W w **12** (sideways*). P 14½×14.
411 4c. black, brown and vermilion 10 10
w. Wmk Crown to right of CA .... 3·00
412 8c. black, grey and new blue 10 10
413 20c. multicoloured 20 20
411/13 *Set of* 3 .... 30 30
Designs:—8c. Sailing dinghy; 20c. Games medal and winners' rostrum.
*The normal sideways watermark shows Crown to left of CA, *as seen from the back of the stamp.*

(Des G. Drummond. Photo Harrison)

1969 (10 Nov). *Inauguration of University of the South Pacific. T* **123** *and similar horiz designs. Multicoloured.* W w **12**. P 14×15.
414 2c. Type **123** 10 15
415 8c. R.N.Z.A.F badge and Short S.25 Sunderland flying boat over Laucala Bay (site of University) 15 10
416 25c. Science students at work 25 15
w. Wmk inverted .... 2·00 1·50
414/16 *Set of* 3 .... 45 30

ROYAL VISIT 1970

(**126**)

127 Chaulmugra Tree, Makogai

1970 (4 Mar). *Royal Visit. Nos. 392, 399 and 402 optd with T* **126**.
417 2c. new blue, brown and ochre 10 20
418 10c. Prussian blue and brown-red 10 10
419 25c. multicoloured 20 10
417/19 *Set of* 3 .... 35 30

(Des G. Drummond. Photo Harrison)

1970 (25 May). *Closing of Leprosy Hospital Makogai. T* **127** *and similar designs.* W w **12** (sideways* on 10c.). P 14×14½.
420 2c. multicoloured 10 50
421 10c. pale turquoise-green and black 40 65
a. Pair. Nos. 421/2 .... 80 1·25
w. Wmk Crown to right of CA .... 5·50 5·50
422 10c. turquoise-blue, black and magenta 40 65
w. Wmk Crown to right of CA .... 5·50 5·50
423 30c. multicoloured 70 50
420/3 *Set of* 4 .... 1·40 2·10
Designs: *Vert*—No. 421, "Cascade" (Semisi Maya); No. 422, "Sea Urchins" (Semisi Maya). *Horiz*—No. 423, Makogai Hospital.
*The normal sideways watermark shows Crown to left of CA, *as seen from the back of the stamp.*
Nos. 421/2 were printed together, *se-tenant*, throughout the sheet.

131 Abel Tasman and Log, 1643

(Des V. Whiteley. Litho D.L.R.)

1970 (18 Aug). *Explorers and Discoverers. T* **131** *and similar horiz designs.* W w **12** (sideways*). P 13×12½.

424	2c. black, brown and turquoise	30	25
	w. Wmk Crown to right of CA	70·00	
425	3c. multicoloured	60	25
426	8c. multicoloured	60	15
427	25c. multicoloured	30	15
424/7	*Set of* 4	1·60	70

Designs:—3c. Captain Cook and H.M.S. *Endeavour*, 1774; 8c. Captain Bligh and longboat, 1789; 25c. Fijian and ocean-going canoe.

*The normal sideways watermark shows Crown to left of CA, *as seen from the back of the stamp*.

INDEPENDENT

135 King Cakobau and Cession Stone

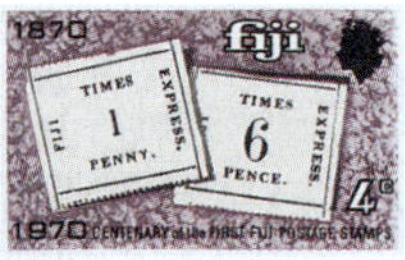

139 1d. and 6d. Stamps of 1870

(Des J. W. Litho Format)

1970 (10 Oct). *Independence. T* **135** *and similar horiz designs. Multicoloured.* W w **12** (sideways). P 14.

428	2c. Type **135**	10	10
429	3c. Children of the World	10	10
430	10c. Prime Minister and Fijian flag	10	10
431	25c. Dancers in costume	20	20
428/31	*Set of* 4	30	30

The design for the 10c. value does not incorporate the Queen's head profile.

(Des V. Whiteley. Photo Harrison)

1970 (2 Nov). *Stamp Centenary. T* **139** *and similar horiz designs. Multicoloured.* W w **12** (sideways on 15c.). P 14½×14.

432	4c. Type **139**	15	10
433	15c. Fijian stamps of all reigns (61×21 *mm*)	40	15
434	20c. *Fiji Times* office and modern GPO	40	15
	w. Wmk inverted	65·00	
432/4	*Set of* 3	85	35

STAMP BOOKLETS

1909. *Black and red cover. Stapled.*

SB1 2s. booklet containing eleven ½d. (No. 118) in blocks of 5 and 6, and eighteen 1d. (No. 119) in blocks of 6 .... £3000

1914. *Black on red cover. Stapled.*

SB2 2s. booklet containing eleven ½d. (No. 126) in blocks of 5 and 6, and eighteen 1d. (No. 127) in blocks of 6 .... £2750

1939 (10 Mar)–**40**. *Black on deep green covers. No advertising pages. Stapled.*

SB3 3s. booklet containing eight ½d. and eight 1d. (Nos. 249/50) in blocks of 8 and twelve 2d. (No. 253) in blocks of 6 .... £1100
a. Including four advertising pages (black on pale greenish buff cover) (1940) £900

SB4 5s.9d. booklet containing ten ½d. and ten 1d. (Nos. 249/50) in blocks of 10 and twenty-seven 2d. (No. 253) in blocks of 9 .... £3750
a. Including four advertising pages (black on pink cover) (1940) £3250

Nos. SB3/4 were produced locally and Nos. SB3a/4a by De La Rue.

1967 (23 Jan). *Black on salmon cover. Stitched.*

SB5 2s. booklet containing eight 3d. (No. 313) in blocks of four .... 9·00

The first printing was not released by the Crown Agents, but a second printing was released in London on 30.6.67. The first printing had 4d. as the surface-rate for letters to the British Commonwealth on the inside back cover (*Price* £12); in the second printing this was corrected to 3d.

1969 (27 Feb). *Black on salmon cover. Stitched.*

SB6 20c. booklet containing ten 2c. (No. 392) in two blocks of 4 and a vert pair .... 4·50

1970 (27 Oct). *Black on salmon cover. Stitched.*

SB7 20c. booklet containing four 1c. and eight 2c. (Nos. 391/2) in blocks of 4 .... 5·50

POSTAGE DUE STAMPS

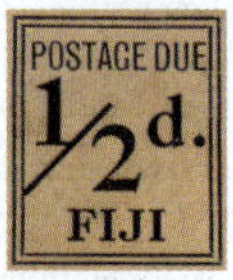

D 1

D 2

(Typo Govt Printer, Suva)

1917 (1 Jan). *Thick yellowish white laid paper. No gum.* P 11.

D1	D **1**	½d. black	£900	£475
		a. *Se-tenant* strip of 8: 1d.(×3)+½d.+4d.+3d.(×3)	£13000	
D2		1d. black	£400	£130
D3		2d. black	£300	80·00
D4		3d. black	£400	£110
D5		4d. black	£950	£550

Nos. D1/2 and D4/5 were printed, *se-tenant*, in sheets of 96 (8×12) with each horizontal row containing three 1d., one ½d., one 4d. and three 3d. in that order. Only thirty-one such sheets were issued. The 2d. was printed separately in sheets of 84 (7×12). On all these sheets marginal copies were imperforate on the outer edge.

1917 (21 April)–**18**. *As Nos. D1/3 but narrower setting, value in ½d. as Type* D **2**.

D5*a*	½d. black	£475	£300
D5*b*	1d. black	£300	£140
D5*c*	2d. black (5.4.18)	£1000	£650

1d. and 2d. stamps must have wide margins (3½ to 4 mm) on the vertical sides to be Nos. D2 or D3. Stamps with narrow margins of approximately the same width on all four sides are Nos. D5*b* or D5*c*.

Nos. D5*a*/*c* were printed in separate sheets of 84 (7×12). The marginal copies are perforated on all sides.

D 3

D 4

(Typo D.L.R.)

1918 (1 June). Wmk Mult Crown CA. P 14.

D6	D **3**	½d. black	3·00	24·00
D7		1d. black	3·50	5·00
D8		2d. black	3·25	7·50
D9		3d. black	3·25	48·00
D10		4d. black	6·00	27·00
D6/10		*Set of* 5	17·00	£100
D6s/10s		Optd "Specimen" *Set of* 5	£150	

D9 exists with watermark sideways (Crown to right of CA *as seen from the back of the stamp*) and overprinted "SPECIMEN". (*Price*, £550).

No postage due stamps were in use between 31 August 1931 and 3 July 1940.

(Typo Waterlow)

1940 (3 July). Wmk Mult Script CA. P 12½.

D11	D **4**	1d. emerald-green	8·00	70·00
D12		2d. emerald-green	12·00	70·00
D13		3d. emerald-green	15·00	75·00
D14		4d. emerald-green	16·00	80·00
D15		5d. emerald-green	18·00	85·00
D16		6d. emerald-green	20·00	85·00
D17		1s. carmine-lake	23·00	£110
D18		1s.6d. carmine-lake	23·00	£160
D11/18		*Set of* 8	£120	£650
D11s/18s		Perf "Specimen" *Set of* 8	£190	

All values are known with forged postmarks, including one of Levuka dated "8 APR 41" and others of Suva dated "12 AUG 42", "14 AU 42" or "20 MR 45".

The use of postage due stamps was discontinued on 30 April 1946.

Gambia

PRICES FOR STAMPS ON COVER TO 1945

Nos. 1/4	*from* × 25
Nos. 5/8	*from* × 20
Nos. 10/20	*from* × 25
Nos. 21/31	*from* × 50
Nos. 32/6	*from* × 20
Nos. 37/44	*from* × 10
Nos. 45/68	*from* × 8
Nos. 69/70	*from* × 25
Nos. 72/85	*from* × 8
Nos. 86/142	*from* × 5
Nos. 143/6	*from* × 6
Nos. 147/9	*from* × 8
Nos. 150/61	*from* × 3

WEST AFRICAN SETTLEMENT

British traders were active in the River Gambia area from the beginning of the 17th century, but it was not until 1808 that it was officially recognised as a Settlement. Administration passed from the merchants to the Governor of Freetown (Sierra Leone) in 1821 and in 1843 Gambia became a separate colony with a Protectorate declared over the banks of the river for 300 miles inland in 1857. A period of colonial retrenchment in 1865 saw a return to Settlement status under Sierra Leone, but Gambia once again became a Crown Colony in 1888.

There was no government postal service before 1858.

PRICES. The prices of Nos. 1 to 8 are for fine copies, with good margins and embossing. Brilliant or poor copies can be supplied at prices consistent with their condition.

DOUBLE EMBOSSING. The majority of the stamps of T **1** with so-called "double embossing" are merely specimens in which the printing and embossing do not register accurately and have no special value. We no longer list "twice embossed" or "twice embossed, once inverted" varieties as they are considered to be outside the scope of this catalogue.

1

(Typo and embossed by D.L.R.)

1869 (18 Mar)–**72**. No wmk. Imperf.

1	**1**	4d. brown	£500	£190
2		4d. pale brown (1871)	£450	£200
3		6d. deep blue	£475	£200
3*a*		6d. blue	£550	£170
4		6d. pale blue (17.2.72)	£2750	£1000

Our prices for the 6d. pale blue, No. 4, are for stamps which are pale by comparison with specimens of the "deep blue" and "blue" colour groups listed under Nos. 3 and 3*a*. The date given is the earliest known postmark. An exceptionally pale shade is recognized by specialists and this is rare.

1874 (Aug). Wmk Crown CC. Imperf.

5	**1**	4d. brown	£375	£190
		w. Wmk inverted	£600	£325
		x. Wmk reversed	£600	£325
		y. Wmk inverted and reversed	£700	£375
6		4d. pale brown	£400	£200
7		6d. deep blue	£325	£200
		w. Wmk inverted	£475	£325
		x. Wmk reversed	£550	£350
		y. Wmk inverted and reversed	£500	£325
8		6d. blue	£325	£190
		a. Sloping label	£700	£400
		b. Wmk sideways	†	—
		w. Wmk inverted	£475	£325

SLOPING LABEL VARIETY. Traces of this flaw first occur in the 6d. imperforate on R. 1/1 and R. 1/5. In the perforated printings the variety on R. 1/5 is much more pronounced and appears as illustrated above. Our listings are these examples from R.1/5, less noticeable varieties of this type from R. 1/1, which slope from right to left, being worth less. These varieties continued to appear until the introduction of a new 6d. plate in 1893, used for No. 34.

1880–81. Wmk Crown CC. P 14*.

A. Wmk sideways†.

10A	**1**	½d. orange	£350	£300
		w. Wmk Crown to left of CC		
12A		1d. maroon	£600	£500
		w. Wmk Crown to left of CC		
		y. Wmk sideways inverted and reversed		
13A		2d. rose	£160	80·00
		w. Wmk Crown to left of CC		
14A		3d. bright ultramarine	£450	£450
		w. Wmk Crown to left of CC		
15A		4d. brown	£500	65·00
		w. Wmk Crown to left of CC	£475	60·00
16A		4d. pale brown	£475	60·00
		w. Wmk Crown to left of CC	£450	55·00
17A		6d. deep blue	£200	90·00
		c. Sloping label	£550	£275
18A		6d. blue	£180	90·00
		c. Sloping label	£550	£275
		w. Wmk Crown to left of CC		
19A		1s. green	£425	£300
20A		1s. deep green	£450	£300
		w. Wmk Crown to left of CC	£600	
10A/20A *Set of* 7			£2250	£1600

B. Wmk upright.

10B	**1**	½d. orange	11·00	18·00
11B		½d. dull orange	11·00	18·00
		w. Wmk inverted	80·00	
		x. Wmk reversed	70·00	
12B		1d. maroon	5·50	6·00
		w. Wmk inverted	£130	£130
13B		2d. rose	30·00	11·00
		w. Wmk inverted	†	£325
14B		3d. bright ultramarine	80·00	40·00
14cB		3d. pale dull ultramarine	65·00	30·00
		w. Wmk inverted	80·00	55·00
15B		4d. brown	£250	17·00
		w. Wmk inverted	†	£200
16B		4d. pale brown	£250	18·00
17B		6d. deep blue	£100	45·00
		c. Sloping label	£275	£150
18B		6d. blue	£100	45·00
		c. Sloping label	£275	£150
19B		1s. green	£275	£150
		w. Wmk inverted	†	£450
20B		1s. deep green	£275	£150
10B/20B *Set of* 7			£650	£250

*There were three different printings of these stamps. The original supply, sent in June 1880 and covering all seven values, had watermark sideways and was perforated by a line machine. In October of the same year a further printing of the lowest five values had the watermark changed to upright, but was still with line perforation. The final printing, sent May 1881 and containing all values, also had watermark upright, but was perforated on a comb machine.

†The normal sideways watermark shows Crown to right of CC, *as seen from the back of the stamp*.

1886–93. Wmk Crown CA (sideways*). P 14.

21	**1**	½d. myrtle-green (1887)	4·25	2·25
		w. Wmk Crown to right of CA	55·00	
		x. Wmk sideways reversed	75·00	
22		½d. grey-green	4·25	3·25
22*b*		1d. maroon	†	£15000
23		1d. crimson (1887)	8·00	9·50
23*a*		1d. aniline crimson	7·00	11·00
23*b*		1d. pale carmine	6·00	11·00
24		2d. orange (1887)	11·00	5·00
25		2d. deep orange	2·25	8·50
26		2½d. ultramarine (1887)	6·50	2·00
27		2½d. deep bright blue	6·00	1·25
		w. Wmk Crown to right of CA	£140	
28		3d. slate-grey (1886)	9·00	14·00
29		3d. grey	7·50	15·00
30		4d. brown (1887)	10·00	2·00
31		4d. deep brown	10·00	2·00
		a. Wmk upright	†	£2000
		w. Wmk Crown to right of CA	£110	£110
32		6d. yellowish olive-green (1886)	85·00	35·00
		a. Sloping label	£225	90·00
		bw. Wmk Crown to right of CA	£225	
32*d*		6d. olive-green (1887)	70·00	60·00
		da. Sloping label	£190	£150
33		6d. bronze-green (1889)	32·00	60·00
		a. Sloping label	75·00	£120
		bw. Wmk Crown to right of CA	£225	
33*c*		6d. deep bronze-green (1889)	35·00	60·00
		ca. Sloping label	75·00	£120
34		6d. slate-green (1893)	15·00	55·00
35		1s. violet (1887)	3·25	18·00
36		1s. deep violet	7·00	22·00
36*b*		1s. aniline violet	£1100	
21/36 *Set of* 8			48·00	80·00
21s/4s, 32cs Optd "Specimen" *Set of* 4			£400	

*The normal sideways watermark shows Crown to left of CA, *as seen from the back of the stamp*.

The above were printed in panes of 15 on paper intended for larger panes. Hence the watermark is sometimes misplaced or omitted and letters from "CROWN AGENTS FOR THE COLONIES" from the margin may appear on the stamps.

The ½d., 2d., 3d., 4d., 6d. (No. 32) and 1s. with watermark Crown CA are known imperforate (*price from* £1100, *unused*).

Only three examples, all used, are recorded of the 1d. maroon, No. 22*b*.

The previously listed 3d. "pearl-grey" shade has been deleted as it is impossible to distinguish from other 3d. shades when it occurs on a single stamp. Sheets from this late printing can be identified by three coloured dots in the left sheet margin and one in the right, this being the reverse of the normal arrangement.

Only three used examples are known of the 4d. with upright watermark, No. 31a.

CROWN COLONY

2

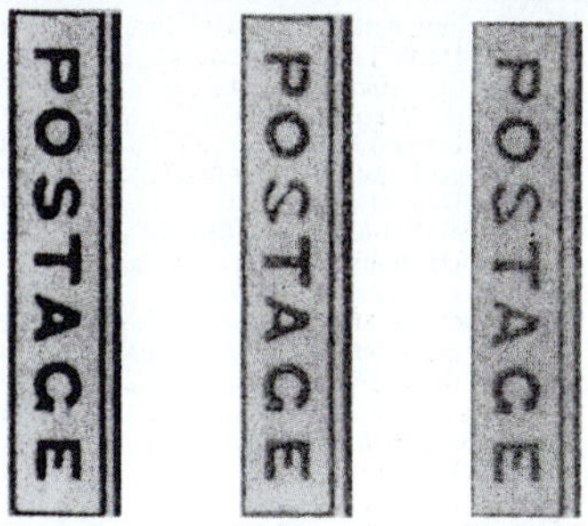

Normal — Malformed "S" — Repaired "S"

The Malformed "S" occurs on R. 7/3 of the left pane from Key Plate 2. This was used to print the initial supply of all values. Printings of the ½d., 1d. and 2½d. despatched on 24 September 1898 had the "S" repaired as shown above. Subsequent printings of the ½d., 1d. and 3d. were from Key Plate 3.

(Typo D.L.R.)

1898 (2 May)–**1902**. Wmk Crown CA. P 14.

37	**2**	½d. dull green (*shades*)	2·75	1·75
		a. Malformed "S"	£350	
		b. Repaired "S"	£375	£325
38		1d. carmine (*shades*)	2·50	75
		a. Malformed "S"	£350	
		b. Repaired "S"	£375	£375
39		2d. orange and mauve	6·00	3·50
		a. Malformed "S"	£400	£400
40		2½d. ultramarine	2·00	2·50
		a. Malformed "S"	£350	
		b. Repaired "S"	£400	
41		3d. reddish purple and blue	32·00	12·00
		a. Malformed "S"	£500	
		b. Deep purple and ultramarine (1902)	90·00	£100
42		4d. brown and blue	12·00	35·00
		a. Malformed "S"	£475	
43		6d. olive-green and carmine	12·00	32·00
		a. Malformed "S"	£475	
44		1s. violet and green	32·00	70·00
		a. Malformed "S"	£650	
37/44 *Set of* 8			90·00	£140
37s/44s Optd "Specimen" *Set of* 8			£160	

3

4

Dented frame (R. 1/6 of left pane)

1902 (13 Mar)–**05**. Wmk Crown CA. P 14.

45	**3**	½d. green (19.4.02)	3·75	2·50
		a. Dented frame	£110	£110
46		1d. carmine	7·00	1·00
		a. Dented frame	£150	90·00
47		2d. orange and mauve (14.6.02)	3·25	2·00
		a. Dented frame	£160	£150
48		2½d. ultramarine (14.6.02)	32·00	18·00
		a. Dented frame	£400	£275
49		3d. purple and ultramarine (19.4.02)	13·00	3·50
		a. Dented frame	£300	£180
50		4d. brown and ultramarine (14.6.02)	3·75	27·00
		a. Dented frame	£200	
51		6d. pale sage-green & carmine (14.6.02)	8·00	12·00
		a. Dented frame	£250	
52		1s. violet and green (14.6.02)	42·00	80·00
		a. Dented frame	£475	
53	**4**	1s.6d. green and carmine/*yellow* (6.4.05)	7·50	19·00
		a. Dented frame	£300	
54		2s. deep slate and orange (14.6.02)	48·00	65·00
		a. Dented frame	£500	
55		2s.6d. purple and brown/*yellow* (6.4.05)	15·00	65·00
		a. Dented frame	£375	
56		3s. carmine and green/*yellow* (6.4.05)	20·00	65·00
		a. Dented frame	£400	
45/56 *Set of* 12			£180	£325
45s/56s Optd "Specimen" *Set of* 12			£190	

1904 (Aug)–**06**. Wmk Mult Crown CA. P 14.

57	**3**	½d. green (9.05)	4·50	30
		a. Dented frame	£140	85·00
58		1d. carmine	4·50	15
		a. Dented frame	£150	70·00
59		2d. orange and mauve (23.2.06)	12·00	2·25
		a. Dented frame	£300	£150
60		2½d. bright blue (8.05)	8·00	4·75
		a. Bright blue and ultramarine	18·00	25·00
		b. Dented frame	£190	£170
61		3d. purple and ultramarine (9.05)	9·50	2·00
		a. Dented frame	£200	£150
62		4d. brown and ultramarine (23.2.06)	18·00	42·00
		a. Dented frame	£350	

63	4	5d. grey and black (6.4.05)	14·00	24·00
		a. Dented frame	£325	
64	3	6d. olive-green and carmine (23.2.06)	18·00	60·00
		a. Dented frame	£350	
65	4	7½d. green and carmine (6.4.05)	13·00	48·00
		a. Dented frame	£250	
66		10d. olive and carmine (6.4.05)	21·00	40·00
		a. Dented frame	£375	
67	3	1s. violet and green (9.05)	27·00	55·00
		a. Dented frame	£375	
68	4	2s. deep slate and orange (7.05)	80·00	£100
		a. Dented frame	£600	
57/68 *Set of* 12			£200	£350
63s, 65s/6s Optd "Specimen" *Set of* 3			70·00	

See also Nos. 72/85.

(5)

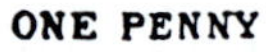

(6)

1906 (10 Apr). *Nos. 55 and 56 surch with T* **5** *or* **6** *by Govt Printer.*

69		½d. on 2s.6d. purple and brown/*yellow*	50·00	60·00
		a. Dented frame	£600	
70		1d. on 3s. carmine and green/*yellow*	55·00	30·00
		a. Surch double	£1800	£5000
		b. Dented frame	£700	

No. 69 was surcharged in a setting of 30 (6×5), the spacing between the words and the bars being 5 mm on rows 1, 2 and 5; and 4 mm on rows 3 and 4. Constant varieties occur on R. 2/1 (broken "E") and R. 5/1 (dropped "Y") of the setting.

No. 70 was surcharged in a setting of 60 (6×10) and a similar dropped "Y" variety occurs on R. 6/3 and R. 8/4, the latter in conjunction with a dropped "E".

Both values were withdrawn on 24 April when fresh supplies of ½d. and 1d. definitives were received from London.

1909 (1 Oct). *Colours changed.* Wmk Mult Crown CA. P 14.

72	3	½d. blue-green	8·00	4·00
		a. Dented frame	£150	£130
73		1d. red	11·00	15
		a. Dented frame	£190	85·00
74		2d. greyish slate	2·00	11·00
		a. Dented frame	£160	
75		3d. purple/yellow	4·50	1·00
		a. Purple/lemon-yellow	5·50	1·75
		b. Dented frame	£170	£130
76		4d. black and red/*yellow*	1·75	65
		a. Dented frame	£170	£130
77	4	5d. orange and purple	1·50	1·25
		a. Dented frame	£180	£180
78	3	6d. dull and bright purple	2·25	2·25
		a. Dented frame	£190	£200
79	4	7½d. brown and blue	2·75	2·50
		a. Dented frame	£190	£200
80		10d. pale sage-green and carmine	3·25	7·00
		a. Dented frame	£200	
81	3	1s. black/*green*	3·25	17·00
		a. Dented frame	£200	
82	4	1s.6d. violet and green	21·00	65·00
		a. Dented frame	£350	
83		2s. purple and bright blue/*blue*	14·00	20·00
		a. Dented frame	£325	
84		2s.6d. black and red/*blue*	21·00	20·00
		a. Dented frame	£400	
85		3s. yellow and green	30·00	48·00
		a. Dented frame	£425	
72/85 *Set of* 14			£110	£180
73s/85s Optd "Specimen" *Set of* 13			£250	

Most values between Nos. 45 and 85 are known with forged postmarks. These include circular types of Bathurst, dated "JA 2 97", and Macarthy Island, dated "FE 17 10", and an oval registered Gambia postmark dated "22 JU 10".

7

8

Split "A" (R. 8/3 of left pane) (ptgs to 1918)

(Type D.L.R)

1912 (1 Sept)–**22**. Wmk Mult Crown CA. *Chalk-surfaced paper* (5s.) P 14.

86	7	½d. deep green	2·25	1·50
		a. Green	3·00	1·50
		b. Pale green (1916)	4·00	3·25
		c. Split "A"	£100	
87		1d. red	2·50	80
		a. Rose-red	3·50	30
		b. Scarlet (1916)	5·50	90
		c. Split "A"	£120	
88	8	1½d. olive-green and blue-green	50	30
		a. Split "A"	£120	
89	7	2d. greyish slate	50	2·75
		a. Split "A"	£120	
90		2½d. deep bright blue	4·00	3·00
		a. Bright blue	4·50	2·50
		b. Split "A"	£180	
91		3d. purple/*yellow*	50	30
		a. On lemon (1917)	14·00	18·00
		b. On orange-buff (1920)	10·00	8·50
		c. On pale yellow	1·25	1·00
		d. Split "A"	£150	
92		4d. black and red/*yellow*	1·00	10·00
		a. On lemon (1917)	2·75	7·50
		b. On orange-buff (1920)	8·00	11·00
		c. On pale yellow	1·50	9·50
		d. Split "A"	£160	
		w. Wmk inverted	£150	
93	8	5d. orange and purple	1·00	2·00
		a. Split "A"	£170	
94	7	6d. dull and bright purple	1·00	2·50
		a. Split "A"	£170	
95	8	7½d. brown and blue	2·00	7·00
		a. Split "A"	£250	
96		10d. pale sage-green and carmine	3·00	17·00
		a. Deep sage-green and carmine	3·00	15·00
		b. Split "A	£300	
97	7	1s. black/*green*	2·00	1·00
		a. On emerald back (1921)	1·00	20·00
		b. Split "A"	£200	
98	8	1s.6d. violet and green	12·00	10·00
		a. Split "A"	£475	
99		2s. purple and blue/*blue*	3·75	6·00
		a. Split "A"	£450	
100		2s.6d. black and red/*blue*	4·00	14·00
		a. Split "A"	£450	
101		3s. yellow and green	9·50	32·00
		a. Split "A"	£650	
102		5s. green and red/*pale yellow* (1922)	95·00	£170
86/102 *Set of* 17			£130	£250
86s/102s Optd "Specimen" *Set of* 17			£350	

1921–22. Wmk Mult Script CA. *Chalk-surfaced paper (4s.).* P 14.

108	7	½d. dull green	30	20·00
		x. Wmk reversed	£130	
109		1d. carmine-red	1·00	7·50
		x. Wmk reversed	£120	£120
110	8	1½d. olive-green and blue-green	1·25	14·00
111	7	2d. grey	1·00	2·50
		x. Wmk reversed	£110	
112		2½d. bright blue	50	8·00
113	8	5d. orange and purple	1·75	18·00
		x. Wmk reversed	50·00	
114	7	6d. dull and bright purple	1·75	18·00
		x. Wmk reversed	25·00	
115	8	7½d. brown and blue	2·00	38·00
		x. Wmk reversed	26·00	
116		10d. pale sage-green and carmine	7·00	21·00
		x. Wmk reversed	£100	
117		4s. black and red (1922)	90·00	£170
		w. Wmk inverted	85·00	£190
108/17 *Set of* 10			90·00	£275
108s/17s Optd "Specimen" *Set of* 10			£200	

Forged postmarks of the types mentioned below No. 85 have also been seen on various values between No. 86 and 117. Collectors should beware of partial strikes which do not show the year date.

9

10

(Recess D.L.R.)

1922 (1 Sept)–**29**. *Portrait and shield in black.* P 14*.

(a) Wmk Mult Crown CA.

118	9	4d. red/*yellow* (*a*)	3·00	4·25
119		7½d. purple/*yellow* (*a*)	5·00	7·00
120	10	1s. purple/*yellow* (*a*)	17·00	30·00
		w. Wmk inverted	£120	£160
121		5s. green/*yellow* (*c*)	48·00	£150
		w. Wmk inverted		
118/21 *Set of* 4			65·00	£170
118s/21s Optd or H/S (5s.) "Specimen" *Set of* 4			£140	

(b) Wmk Mult Script CA.

122	9	½d. green (*abd*)	55	55
123		½d. deep green (*bd*) (1925)	6·00	1·50
124		1d. brown (*abd*)	1·00	30
125		1½d. bright rose-scarlet (*abd*)	1·00	30
		w. Wmk inverted	†	£400
126		2d. grey (*ab*)	1·00	3·75
127		2½d. orange-yellow (*b*)	1·25	11·00
		w. Wmk inverted	£120	
128		3d. bright blue (*abd*)	1·00	20
129		4d. red/*yellow* (*bd*) (1.3.27)	10·00	20·00
130		5d. sage-green (*a*)	2·50	11·00
131		6d. claret (*ad*)	1·25	30
132		7½d. purple/*yellow* (*ab*) (1927)	12·00	75·00
133		10d. blue (*a*)	4·50	18·00
134	10	1s. purple/*yellow* (*aef*) (9.24)	2·50	1·75
		a. Blackish purple/yell-buff (*c*) (1929)	45·00	45·00
135		1s.6d. blue (*af*)	14·00	14·00
136		2s. purple/*blue* (*ac*)	7·00	5·50
137		2s.6d. deep green (*a*)	8·00	9·50
138		3s. bright aniline violet (*a*)	18·00	65·00
139		3s. slate-purple (*c*) (1928)	£200	£400
140		4s. brown (*ace*)	9·50	18·00
141		5s. green/*yellow* (*acf*) (9.26)	18·00	48·00
142		10s. sage-green (*ce*)	75·00	£110
122/42 *Set of* 19			£170	£375
122s/42s Optd "Specimen" *Set of* 19			£400	

Perforations. A number of different perforating machines were used for the various printings of these stamps and the following varieties are known: (*a*) the original 14 line perforation; (*b*) 14×13.8 comb perforation used for Type **9**; (*c*) 13.8×13.7 comb perforation used for Type **10**; (*d*) 13.7 line perforation used for Type **9**; (*e*) 14×13.8 compound line perforation used for Type **10**; (*f*) 13.8×14 compound line perforation used for Type **10**. The occurrence of these perforations on the individual values is indicated by the letters shown after the colour descriptions above.

No. 139 has been faked, but note that this stamp is comb perf 13.8×13.7 whereas No. 138 is line perf 14 exactly. There are also shades of the slate-purple.

Most values of the above issue are known with a forged oval registered Gambia postmark dated "22 JU 10", often with the year date not shown. Collectors should exercise particular caution in buying used examples of No. 139.

1935 (6 May). *Silver Jubilee. As Nos. 91/4 of Antigua, but printed by B.W.* P 11×12.

143		1½d. deep blue and scarlet	70	1·25
		a. Extra flagstaff	£275	£350
		b. Short extra flagstaff	£250	£300
		c. Lightning conductor	£400	
		d. Flagstaff on right-hand turret	£325	
		e. Double flagstaff	£325	
144		3d. brown and deep blue	1·25	1·25
		a. Extra flagstaff	£180	£200
		b. Short extra flagstaff	£200	£225
		c. Lightning conductor	£200	
145		6d. light blue and olive-green	1·50	5·00
		a. Extra flagstaff	£170	£250
		b. Short extra flagstaff	£275	£325
		c. Lightning conductor	£225	£275
		d. Flagstaff on right-hand turret	£475	
146		1s. slate and purple	8·50	10·00
		a. Extra flagstaff	£225	£275
		b. Short extra flagstaff	£325	£375
		c. Lightning conductor	£300	£350
		d. Flagstaff on right-hand turret	£600	
143/6 *Set of* 4			10·50	16·00
143s/6s Perf "Specimen" *Set of* 4			£110	

For illustrations of plate varieties see Omnibus section following Zanzibar.

Sheets from the second printing of the 6d. and 1s. in November 1935 had the extra flagstaff partially erased with a sharp point.

1937 (12 May). *Coronation. As Nos. 95/7 of Antigua.* P 11×11½

147		1d. yellow-brown	30	1·25
148		1½d. carmine	30	1·25
149		3d. blue	55	2·00
147/9 *Set of* 3			1·00	4·00
147s/9s Perf "Specimen" *Set of* 3			90·00	

11 Elephant (from Colony Badge)

(Recess B.W.)

1938 (1 Apr)–**46**. Wmk Mult Script CA. P 12.

150	11	½d. black and emerald-green	15	70
151		1d. purple and brown	30	50
152		1½d. brown-lake and bright carmine	£180	12·00
		a. Brown-lake and scarlet	3·75	3·00
		b. Brown-lake and vermilion	30	2·00
152*c*		1½d. blue and black (2.1.45)	30	1·50
153		2d. blue and black	10·00	3·25
153*a*		2d. lake and scarlet (1.10.43)	60	2·25
154		3d. light blue and grey-blue	30	10
154*a*		5d. sage-green & purple-brn (13.3.41)	50	50
155		6d. olive-green and claret	1·50	35
156		1s. slate-blue and violet	3·50	20
156*a*		1s.3d. chocolate & lt blue (28.11.46)	3·25	2·50
157		2s. carmine and blue	6·00	3·25
158		2s.6d. sepia and dull green	12·00	2·50
159		4s. vermilion and purple	25·00	2·50
160		5s. blue and vermilion	26·00	4·00
161		10s. orange and black	25·00	7·00
150/61 *Set of* 16			£100	28·00
150s/61s Perf "Specimen" *Set of* 16			£375	

1946 (6 Aug). *Victory. As Nos. 110/11 of Antigua.*

162		1½d. black	10	25
163		3d. blue	10	40
162s/3s Perf "Specimen" *Set of* 2			80·00	

1948 (24 Dec). *Royal Silver Wedding. As Nos. 112/13 of Antigua.*

164		1½d. black	25	10
165		£1 mauve	18·00	16·00

1949 (10 Oct). *75th Anniv of Universal Postal Union. As Nos. 114/17 of Antigua.*

166		1½d. blue-black	30	1·50
167		3d. deep blue	1·25	2·00
168		6d. magenta	75	2·75
169		1s. violet	45	60
166/9 *Set of* 4			2·50	6·25

1953 (2 June). *Coronation. As No. 120 of Antigua, but ptd by B. W.*

170		1½d. black and deep bright blue	65	1·25

12 Tapping for Palm Wine

13 Cutter

14 Wollof woman

15 Barra canoe

16 S.S. *Lady Wright*

17 James Island

18 Woman hoeing

19 Elephant and Palm (from colony badge)

(Des Mrs O. W. Meronti. Recess D.L.R.)

1953 (2 Nov)–**59**. *T* **12/13** *and similar horiz designs.* Wmk Mult Script CA. P 13½.

171	**12**	½d. carmine-red and bluish green	30	20
		a. Carmine and bluish green (7.1.59)	2·25	3·00
172	**13**	1d. deep ultramarine and deep brown	40	40
		a. Deep ultramarine & choc (22.8.56)	3·00	2·25
173	**14**	1½d. deep brown and grey-black	20	1·00
174	**15**	2½d. black and carmine-red	45	70
175	**16**	3d. deep blue and slate-lilac	35	10
176	**17**	4d. black and deep blue	60	3·00
177	**12**	6d. brown and reddish purple	35	15
178	**18**	1s. yellow-brown and yellow-green	60	60
179	**13**	1s.3d. ultramarine and pale blue	10·00	60
		a. Ultramarine and light blue (22.2.56)	15·00	55
180	**15**	2s. indigo and carmine	7·00	3·50
181	**13**	2s.6d. deep bluish green and sepia	4·00	1·50
182	**17**	4s. grey-blue and Indian red	11·00	3·25
183	**14**	5s. chocolate and bright blue	2·50	1·75
184	**16**	10s. deep blue and myrtle-green	22·00	10·00
185	**19**	£1 green and black	22·00	10·00
171/85 *Set of* 15			75·00	32·00

20 Queen Elizabeth II and Palm

21 Queen Elizabeth II and West African Map

(Des J. R. F. Ithier (T **20**), A. W. Morley (T **21**). Recess B.W.)

1961 (2 Dec). *Royal Visit.* W w **12**. P 11½.

186	**20**	2d. green and purple	30	40
187	**21**	3d. turquoise-blue and sepia	75	15
188		6d. blue and cerise	75	70
189	**20**	1s.3d. violet and myrtle-green	75	2·25
186/9 *Set of* 4			2·25	3·25

1963 (4 June). *Freedom from Hunger. As No. 146 of Antigua.*

190	1s.3d. carmine	55	15

1963 (2 Sept). *Red Cross Centenary. As Nos. 147/8 of Antigua.*

191	2d. red and black	20	10
192	1s.3d. red and blue	40	55

SELF-GOVERNMENT

22 Beautiful Sunbird

SELF GOVERNMENT
1963

(**35**)

(Des V. Whiteley. Photo Harrison)

1963 (4 Nov). *Birds. Horiz designs as T* **22**. *Multicoloured.* W w **12**. P 12½×13.

193	½d. Type **22**	75	1·00
194	1d. Yellow-mantled Whydah	75	30
195	1½d. Cattle Egret	2·50	70
196	2d. Senegal Parrot	2·50	70
197	3d. Rose-ringed Parakeet	2·50	1·00
198	4d. Violet Starling	2·50	80
199	6d. Village Weaver	2·50	10
200	1s. Rufous-crowned Roller	2·50	10
201	1s.3d. Red-eyed Dove	14·00	2·00
202	2s.6d. Double-spurred Francolin	9·00	2·50
203	5s. Palm-nut Vulture	9·00	3·50
204	10s. Orange-cheeked Waxbill	14·00	8·00
205	£1 African Emerald Cuckoo	29·00	14·00
193/205 *Set of* 13		80·00	30·00

1963 (7 Nov). *New Constitution. Nos. 194, 197, 200/1 optd with T* **35**.

206	1d. Yellow-mantled Whydah	15	50
207	3d. Rose-ringed Parakeet	35	35
208	1s. Rufous-crowned Roller	35	10
	a. Opt double	†	£4500
209	1s.3d. Red-eyed Dove	35	45
206/9 *Set of* 4		1·10	1·00

1964 (23 Apr). *400th Birth Anniv of William Shakespeare. As No. 164 of Antigua.*

210	6d. bright blue	20	10
	w. Wmk inverted	35·00	35·00

INDEPENDENT

36 Gambia Flag and River

37 Arms

(Des V. Whiteley. Photo Harrison)

1965 (18 Feb). *Independence.* P 14½.

211	**36**	½d. multicoloured	10	40
212	**37**	2d. multicoloured	15	10
213	**36**	7½d. multicoloured	40	35
214	**37**	1s.6d. multicoloured	50	30
211/14 *Set of* 4			1·00	1·00

INDEPENDENCE
1965

(**38**)

39 I.T.U Emblem and Symbols

1965 (18 Feb). *Nos. 193/205 optd with T* **38** *or with date centred (1d., 2d., 3d., 4d., 1s., 5s.).*

215	½d. Type **22**	30	1·00
216	1d. Yellow-mantled Whydah	30	20
217	1½d. Cattle Egret	60	1·00
218	2d. Senegal Parrot	70	30
219	3d. Rose-ringed Parakeet	70	15
220	4d. Violet Starling	70	1·75
221	6d. Village Weaver	70	10
222	1s. Rufous-crowned Roller	70	10
223	1s.3d. Red-eyed Dove	70	10
224	2s.6d. Double-spurred Francolin	70	60
225	5s. Palm-nut Vulture	70	75
226	10s. Orange-cheeked Waxbill	1·75	3·25
227	£1 African Emerald Cuckoo	7·50	8·50
215/27 *Set of* 13		14·50	16·00

(Des V. Whiteley. Photo Harrison)

1965 (17 May). *I.T.U. Centenary.* P 14½.

228	**39**	1d. silver and Prussian blue	25	10
229		1s.6d. gold and bluish violet	1·00	40

THE GAMBIA. From this point onwards stamps are inscribed "The Gambia".

40 Sir Winston Churchill and Houses of Parliament

(Des Jennifer Toombs. Photo Harrison)

1966 (24 Jan). *Churchill Commemoration.* P 14×14½.

230	**40**	1d. multicoloured	15	10
231		6d. multicoloured	35	15
232		1s.6d. multicoloured	60	75
230/2 *Set of* 3			1·00	85

41 Red-cheeked Cordon Bleu

42 Pin-tailed Whydah

(Des V. Whiteley. Photo Harrison)

1966 (18 Feb). *Birds. Horiz designs as T* **41**, *and T* **42**. *Multicoloured.* P 14×14½ (£1) or 12×13 (others).

233	½d. Type **41**	90	40
234	1d. White-faced Whistling Duck	30	50
235	1½d. Red-throated Bee Eater	30	40
236	2d. Lesser Pied Kingfisher	4·25	75
237	3d. Golden Bishop	30	10
238	4d. African Fish Eagle	50	30
239	6d. Yellow-bellied Green Pigeon	40	10
240	1s. Blue-bellied Roller	40	10
241	1s.6d. African Pygmy Kingfisher	50	30
242	2s.6d. Spur-winged Goose	50	70
243	5s. Cardinal Woodpecker	50	75
244	10s. Violet Turaco	50	2·75
245	£1 Type **42**	75	6·50
233/45 *Set of* 13		9·00	12·00

The ½d., 1d. and 2d. to 1s. values exist with PVA gum as well as gum arabic.

54 Arms, Early Settlement and Modern Buildings

(Photo, arms die-stamped Harrison)

1966 (24 June). *150th Anniv of Bathurst.* P 14½×14.

246	**54**	1d. silver, brown and yellow-orange	10	10
247		2d. silver, brown and light blue	10	10
248		6d. silver, brown and light emerald	10	10
249		1s.6d. silver, brown and light magenta	15	15
246/9 *Set of* 4			30	30

55 I.T.Y. Emblem and Hotels

(Des and photo (emblem die-stamped) Harrison)

1967 (20 Dec). *International Tourist Year.* P 14½×14.

250	**55**	2d. silver, brown and apple-green	10	10
251		1s. silver, brown and orange	10	10
252		1s.6d. silver, brown and magenta	15	35
250/2 *Set of* 3			30	40

56 Handcuffs

(Des V. Whiteley. Photo Enschede)

1968 (15 July). *Human Rights Year. T* **56** *and similar horiz designs. Multicoloured.* P 14×13.

253	1d. Type **56**	10	10
254	1s. Fort Bullen	10	10
255	5s. Methodist Church	30	1·00
253/5 *Set of* 3		35	1·00

59 Queen Victoria, Queen Elizabeth II and 4d. Stamp of 1869

(Des G. Drummond. Photo and embossing (cameo head) Harrison)

1969 (20 Jan). *Gambia. Stamp Centenary.* P 14½×13½.

256	**59**	4d. sepia and yellow-ochre	20	10
257		6d. Prussian blue and deep yellow-green	20	10
258	–	2s.6d. multicoloured	70	1·60
256/8 *Set of* 3			1·00	1·60

Design:—2s.6d. Queen Elizabeth II with 4d. and 6d. stamps of 1869.

In the 6d. value the stamp illustrated is the 6d. of 1869.

61 Catapult-Ship *Westfalen* launching Dornier DO-J II 10-t Wal

(Des L. Curtis. Litho Format)

1969 (15 Dec). *35th Annie of Pioneer Air Services. T* **61** *and similar horiz designs showing various forms of transport, map of South Atlantic and Lufthansa emblem. Multicoloured.* P 13½×14.

259	2d. Type **61**	50	20
260	1s. Dornier Do-J II 10-t Wal *Boreas* flying boat	50	20
261	1s.6d. Airship LZ-127 *Graf Zeppelin*	60	1·60
259/61 *Set of* 3		1·40	1·75

REPUBLIC

63 Athlete and Gambian Flag

(Des Jennifer Toombs. Litho Format)

1970 (16 July). *Ninth British Commonwealth Games, Edinburgh.* P 14.

262	**63**	1d. multicoloured	10	10
263		1s. multicoloured	10	10
264		5s. multicoloured	30	1·25
262/4 *Set of 3*			35	1·25

64 President Sir Dawda Kairaba Jawara and State House

(Des G. Vasarhelyi. Litho Questa)

1970 (2 Nov). *Republic Day. T* **64** *and similar multicoloured designs.* P 14.

265	2d. Type **64**	10	10
266	1s. President Sir Dawda Jawara	15	10
267	1s.6d. President and flag of Gambia	50	60
265/7 *Set of 3*		65	65

The 1s. and 1s.6d. are both vertical designs.

Ghana

DOMINION

***CANCELLED REMAINDERS.** In 1961 remainders of some issues of 1957 to 1960 were put on the market cancelled-to-order in such a way as to be indistinguishable from genuine postally used copies for all practical purposes. Our used quotations which are indicated by an asterisk are the same for cancelled-to-order or postally used copies.

29 Dr. Kwame Nkrumah, Palmnut Vulture and Map of Africa

GHANA
INDEPENDENCE
6TH MARCH,
1957.

(30)

(Photo Harrison)

1957 (6 Mar). *Independence.* Wmk Mult Script CA. P 14×14½.

166	**29**	2d. scarlet	10	10*
167		2½d. green	10	15*
168		4d. brown	10	15*
169		1s.3d. deep blue	15	15*
166/9 *Set of* 4			40	45*

1957 (6 Mar)–**58.** *Nos.* 153a/64 *of Gold Coast optd as T* **30**.

170	½d. bistre-brown and scarlet	10	10*
	a. Olive-brown and scarlet	10	10*
171	1d. deep blue (R.)	10	10*
172	1½d. emerald-green	10	10*
173	2d. chocolate (26.5.58)	30	30
174	2½d. scarlet (26.5.58)	1·00	1·25
175	3d. magenta	30	10*
176	4d. blue (26.5.58)	6·00	7·50*
177	6d. black and orange (R.)	10	10*
	a. Opt double	†	£375*
178	1s. black and orange-red	10	10*
179	2s. brown-olive and carmine	60	10*
180	5s. purple and black	1·00	10*
181	10s. black and olive-green	1·50	70*
170/81 *Set of* 12		9·50	8·75*

Nos. 173/4 and 176 were officially issued on 26 May 1958 although, in error, small quantities were sold at certain post offices when the rest of the set appeared.

Nos. 170 and 171 exist in coils constructed from normal sheets.

31 Viking Ship

(Des W. Wind. Recess E. A. Wright Bank Note Co., Philadelphia)

1957 (27 Dec). *Inauguration of Black Star Shipping Line. T* **31** *and similar horiz designs.* No wmk. P 12.

182		2½d. emerald-green	30	20
		a. Imperf between (vert pair)	£400	
		b. Imperf between (horiz pair)	£400	
183		1s.3d. deep blue	35	1·25
		a. Imperf horiz (vert pair)	£450	
184		5s. bright purple	45	3·00
		a. Imperf vert (horiz pair)	£550	
182/4 *Set of* 3			1·00	4·00

Designs:—1s.3d. Galleon; 5s. M.V.*Volta River.*

PRINTERS. Nos. 185/**MS**568 were printed in photogravure by Harrison & Sons *except where otherwise stated.*

34 Ambassador Hotel, Accra

35 Ghana Coat of Arms

1958 (6 Mar). *First Anniv of Independence. T* **34/5** *and similar designs.* Wmk Mult Script CA. P 14½×14 (2s.) or 14×14½ (others).

185	½d. black, red, yellow, green and carmine	10	10
186	2½d. black, red, green and yellow	10	10
187	1s.3d. black, red, yellow, green and blue	30	10
188	2s. red, yellow, blue, green, brown and black	45	35
185/8 *Set of* 4		75	70

Designs: *Horiz as T***34**—2½d. State Opening of Parliament; 1s.3d. National Monument.

38 Map showing the Independent African States

39 Map of Africa and Flaming Torch

(Des R. Milton)

1958 (15 Apr). *First Conference of Independent African States, Accra.* Wmk Mult Script CA. P 13½×14½ (2½d., 3d) or 14½×13½ (others).

189	**38**	2½d. black, bistre and bright carmine-red	10	10
190		3d. black, bistre, brown and bright green	10	10
191	**39**	1s. black, yellow, red and dull blue	20	10
192		2s.6d. black, yelow, red and dull violet	40	65
189/92 *Set of* 4			60	75

40 Palm-nut Vulture over Globe

41 Bristol 175 Britannia 309 Airliner

(Des M. Goaman (2½d., 2s.6d.), R. Milton (1s.3d.), W. Wind (2s.))

1958 (15 July). *Inauguration of Ghana Airways. T* **40/1** *and similar designs.* Wmk Mult Script CA. P 15×14 (2s.6d.) or 14×15 (others).

193	2½d. black, yellow-bistre & rose-carmine	45	10
194	1s.3d. multicoloured	75	20
195	2s. multicoloured	80	55
196	2s.6d. black and bistre	80	95
193/6 *Set of* 4		2·50	1·60

Designs: *Horiz* (*as T* **41**)—2s. Boeing 377 Stratocruiser and Yellow-nosed Albatross. (*As T* **40**)—2s.6d. Palm-nut Vulture and Vickers VC-10 aircraft.

PRIME
MINISTER'S
VISIT,
U.S.A. AND
CANADA

(44)

45

1958 (18 July). *Prime Minister's Visit to the United States and Canada. Nos.* 166/9 *optd with T* **44**.

197	**29**	2d. scarlet	10	40
198		2½d. green	10	30
199		4d. brown	10	50
200		1s.3d. deep blue	15	25
197/200 *Set of* 4			30	1·25

(Des W. Wind)

1958 (24 Oct). *United Nations Day.* Wmk Mult Script CA. P 14×14½.

201	**45**	2½d. purple-brown, green and black	10	10
202		1s.3d. purple-brown, blue and black	15	10
203		2s.6d. purple-brown, violet and black	15	35
201/3 *Set of* 3			30	40

46 Dr. Nkrumah and Lincoln Statue, Washington

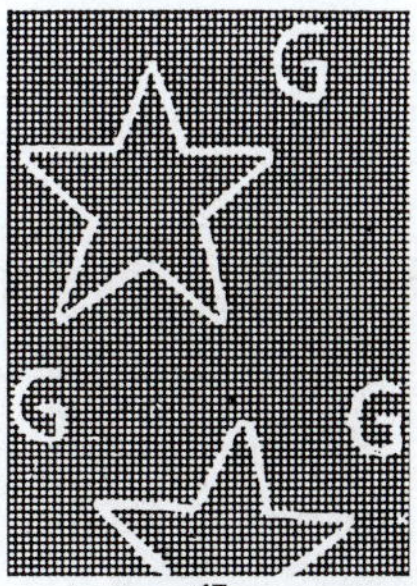

47

(Des M. Goaman)

1959 (12 Feb). *150th Birth Anniv of Abraham Lincoln.* W **47**. P 14×14½.

204	**46**	2½d. pink and deep purple	10	10
205		1s.3d. light blue and blue	10	10
206		2s.6d. orange-yellow & dp olive-green	15	35
204/6 *Set of* 3			30	45
MS206a		102×77 mm. Nos. 204/6. Imperf	55	2·25

48 Kente Cloth and Traditional Symbols

(Des Mrs. T. Sutherland (½d.), M. Karoly (2½d.), K. Antubam (1s.3d.), A. M. Medina (2s.))

1959 (6 Mar). *Second Anniv of Independenee. T* **48** *and similar multicoloured designs.* W **47**. P 14½×14 (2s.) or 14×14½ (others)

207	1½d. Type **48**	10	10
208	2½d. Talking drums and elephant-horn blower	10	10
209	1s.3d. "Symbol of Greeting" (*vert*)	15	10
210	2s. Map of Africa, Ghana flag and palms	30	1·25
207/10 *Set of* 4		50	1·40

52 Globe and Flags

(Des Mrs. H. Potter)

1959 (15 Apr). *Africa Freedom Day.* W **47** (sideways). P 14½×14.

211	**52**	2½d. multicoloured	15	10
212		8½d. multicoloured	15	20

53 "God's Omnipotence"

54 Nkrumah Statue, Accra

55 Ghana Timber

56 Volta River

65a Red-fronted Gazelle

Two Types of ½d. and 3d:

I. Inscr "GOD'S OMNIPOTENCE"

II. Inscr "GYE NYAME"

(Des Mrs. T. Sutherland (½d., 3d.), Ghana Information Bureau (source of 1d. and 2d.), O. Haulkland (1½d.), A. Medina (2½d., 4d.), M. Goaman (6d., 1s.3d., 2s.6d.), W. Wind (11d., 1s., 2s., 5s.), W. H. Brown (10s), M. Shamir (£1)).

1959 (5 Oct)–**61.** *T* **53/6**, **65a**, *and similar multicoloured designs.* W **47** (sideways on horiz designs). P 11½×12 (½d.), 12×11½ (1d.), 14×14½ (½d., 11d., 1s., 2s. and 5s.), 14×15 (10s.) or 14½×14 (others). *(a) Postage.*

213	½d. Type **53** (I)	10	10
	a. Type II (29.4.61)	30	10
214	1d. Type **54**	10	10
215	1½d. Type **55**	10	10
216	2d. Type **56**	10	10
217	2½d. Cocoa bean	10	10
218	3d. "God's Omnipotence" (I)	10	10
	a. Type 11(29.4.61)	30	10
219	4d. Diamond and Mine	4·50	65
220	6d. Red-crowned Bishop	50	10
	a. Green (flag) omitted	£100	
221	11d. Golden Spider Lily	25	10
222	1s. Shell Ginger	25	10
223	2s.6d. Great Blue Turaco	2·00	15
224	5s. Tiger Orchid	2·25	65
225	10s. Jewel Cichlid	75	70
225*a*	£1 Type **65a** (29.4.61)	2·25	4·75
	(b) Air		
226	1s.3d. Pennant-winged Nightjar	2·00	10
227	2s. Crowned Cranes	1·75	10
213/27 *Set of* 16		15·00	6·00

Nos. 217/224 and 226/7 are as Types **55/6**, the 11d., 1s., 5s. and 2s. (air) being vertical and the remainder horizontal. No. 225 is as Type **65a**.

68 Gold Cup and West African Map

(Des K. Lehmann (½d., 3d.), M. & G. Shamir (1d.), W. Wind (8d.), and K. Antubam (2s.6d.))

1959 (15 Oct). *West African Football Competition, T* **68** *and similar multicoloured designs.* W **47** (sideways on horiz designs). P 14×14½ (1d., 2s. 6d) or 14½×14 (others).

228	½d. Type **68**	10	10*
229	1d. Footballers (*vert*)	10	10*
230	3d. Goalkeeper saving ball	10	10*
231	8d. Forward attacking goal	40	15*
232	2s.6d. "Kwame Nkrumah" Gold Cup (*vert*)	50	15*
228/32	*Set of* 5	1·00	40*

73 The Duke of Edinburgh and Arms of Ghana

(Des A. S. B. New)

1959 (24 Nov). *Visit of the Duke of Edinburgh to Ghana.* W **47** (sideways). P 15×14.

233	**73**	3d. black and magenta	30	10*

74 Ghana Flag and Talking Drums

75 Ghana Flag and U.N. Emblem

(Des K. Antubam (2e.6d.), A. Medina (others))

1959 (10 Dec). *United Nations Trusteeship Council. T* **74/5** *and similar multicoloured designs.* W **47** (sideways on 3d). P 14½×14 (3d) or 14×14½) (others).

234	3d. Type **74**	10	10*
235	6d. Type **75**	10	10*
236	1s.3d. Ghana flag and U.N. emblem (*vert*)	20	15*
237	2s.6d. "Totem Pole" (*vert*)	25	15*
234/7	*Set of* 4	55	45*

78 Eagles in Flight

79 Fireworks

(Des A. Medina (½d), M. Goaman (3d), W. Wind (1s.3d., 2s.))

1960 (6 Mar). *Third Anniv of Independence. T* **78/9** *and similar vert designs. Multicoloured.* W **47**. P 14×14½.

238	½d. Type **78**	10	10*
239	3d. Type **79**	10	10*
240	1s.3d. "Third Anniversary"	30	10*
241	2s. "Ship of State"	30	15*
238/41	*Set of* 4	70	30*

82 "A" of National Flags

85 President Nkrumah

(Des W. Wind)

1960 (15 Apr). *Africa Freedom Day. T* **82** *and similar horiz designs. Multicoloured.* W **47** (sideways). P 14½×14.

242	3d. Type **82**	10	10*
243	6d. Letter "f"	20	10*
244	1s. Letter "d"	20	10*
242/4	*Set of* 3	40	20*

REPUBLIC

(Des A. Medina (3d., 10s.), W. Wind (1s.3d., 2s))

1960 (1 July). *Republic Day. T* **85** *and similar multicoloured designs.* W **47**. P 14½×14 (10s) or 14×14½ (others).

245	3d. Type **85**	10	10
246	1s.3d. Ghana flag	30	10
247	2s. Torch of Freedom	20	20
248	10s. Arms of Ghana (*horiz*)	50	80
245/8	*Set of* 4	1·00	1·00
MS248*a*	102×77 mm. Nos. 245/8. Imperf	40	1·50

89 Olympic Torch

90 Athlete

(Des A. Medina (T **89**), W. Wind (T **90**))

1960 (15 Aug). *Olympic Games.* W **47** *(sideways on T* **90**). *P 14×14½ (T* **89**) *or 14½×14 (T* **90**).

249	**89**	3d. multicoloured	10	10
250		6d. multicoloured	15	10
251	**90**	1s.3d. multicoloured	25	10
252		2s.6d. multicoloured	35	60
249/52		*Set of* 4	70	70

91 President Nkrumah

94 U.N. Emblem and Ghana Flag

(Des M. Goaman (3d., 6d.), W. Wind (1s.3d.))

1960 (21 Sept). *Founder's Day. T* **91** *and similar multicoloured designs.* W **47** (sideways on 3d.). P 14½×14 (3d.) or 14×14½ (others).

253	3d. Type **91**	10	10
254	6d. President Nkrumah (*vert*)	10	15
255	1s.3d. Flag-draped column over map of African (*vert*)	20	30
253/5	*Set of* 3	30	45

(Des M. Goaman (3d., 1s.3d.), W. Wind (6d.))

1960 (10 Dec). *Human Rights Day. T* **94** *and similar vert designs.* W **47**. P 14×14½.

256	3d. multicoloured	10	10
257	6d. yellow, black and blue	15	15
258	1s.3d. multicoloured	25	55
256/8	*Set of* 3	40	65

Designs:—6d. U.N. emblem and Torch; 1s.3d. U.N. emblem.

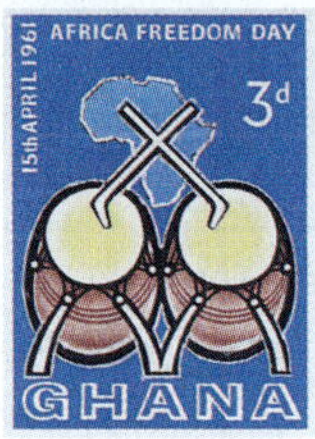

97 Talking Drums

100 Eagle on Column

(Des M. Goaman (3d.), A. S. B. New (6d.), W. Wind (2s.))

1961 (15 Apr). *Africa Freedom Day. T* **97** *and similar designs.* W **47** (sideways on 2s.). P 14½×14 (2s.) or 14×14½ (others).

259	3d. multicoloured	10	10
260	6d. red, black and green	20	10
261	2s. multicoloured	50	45
259/61	*Set of* 3	70	50

Designs: *Vert.*—6d. Map of Africa. *Horiz*—2s. Flags and map.

(Des A. S. B. New (3d.), M. Shamir (Is. 3d.), W. Wind (2s.))

1961 (1 July). *First Anniv of Republic. T* **100** *and similar vert designs. Multicoloured.* W **47**. P 14×14½.

262	3d. Type **100**	10	10
263	1s.3d. "Flower"	10	10
264	2s. Ghana flags	20	1·25
262/4	*Set of* 3	30	1·25

103 Dove with Olive Branch

106 Pres. Nkrumah and Globe

(Des V. Whiteley)

1961 (1 Sept). *Belgrade Conference. T* **103** *and similar designs.* W **47** (sideways on 1s.3d., 5s.). P 14×14½ (3d.) or 14½×14 (others).

265	3d. yellow-green	10	10
266	1s.3d. deep blue	15	10
267	5s. bright reddish purple	40	1·00
265/7	*Set of* 3	50	1·00

Designs: *Horiz.*—1s.3d. World map, chain and olive branch; 5s. Rostrum, conference room.

(Des A. Medina (3d.), M. Goaman (1s.3d.), Miriam Karoly (5s.))

1961 (21 Sept). *Founder's Day. T* **106** *and similar multicoloured designs.* W **47** (sideways on 3d.). P 14½×14 (3d.) or 14×14½ (others).

268	3d. Type **106**	10	10
269	1s.3d. President and Kente Cloth (*vert*)	20	10
270	5s. President in national costume (*vert*)	65	2·50
268/70	*Set of* 3	75	2·50
MS270*a*	Three sheets 106×86 mm (3d.) or 86×106 mm (others) each with Nos. 268/70 in block of four. Imperf. *Three sheets*	3·25	14·00

The 1s.3d. Miniature Sheet is known with the brown colour omitted. (*Price,* £2000, *unused*)

109 Queen Elizabeth II and African Map

(Des M. Goaman)

1961 (9 Nov). *Royal Visit.* W **47**. P 14½×14.

271	**109**	3d. multicoloured	15	10
272		1s.3d. multicoloured	30	20
273		5s. multicoloured	65	3·75
271/3		*Set of* 3	1·00	3·75
MS273*a*		106×84 mm. No. 273 in block of four. Imperf	2·25	7·50

110 Ships in Tema Harbour

(Des C. Bottiau. Litho Enschedé & Sons)

1962 (10 Feb). *Opening of Tema Harbour. T* **110** *and similar horiz designs. Multicoloured.* No wmk. P 14×13.

(a) Postage.

274	3d. Type **110**	15	10

(b) Air

275	1s.3d. Douglas DC-8 aircraft and ships at Tema	65	15
276	2s.6d. As 1s.3d.	80	2·50
274/6	*Set of* 3	1·40	2·50

112 Africa and Peace Dove

113 Compass over Africa

(Des R. Hegeman. Litho Enschedé)

1962 (6 Mar). *First Anniv of Casablanca Conference.* No wmk. P 13×14. *(a) Postage.*

277	**112**	3d. multicoloured	10	10

(b) Air

278	**112**	1s.3d. multicoloured	20	15
279		2s.6d. multicoloured	30	2·00
277/9		*Set of* 3	55	2·00

(Des R. Hegeman)

1962 (24 Apr). *Africa Freedom Day.* W **47**. P 14×14½.

280	**113**	3d. sepia, blue-green and reddish purple	10	10
281		6d. sepia, blue-green and orange-brown	10	15
282		1s.3d. sepia, blue-green and red	15	15
280/2		*Set of* 3	30	30

114 Ghana Star and "Five Continents"

115 Atomic Bomb-burst "Skull"

(Des M. Goaman (3d.), M. Shamir (6d.), W. Wind (1s. 3d))

1962 (21 June). *Accra Assembly, T* **114/15** *and similar vert design.* W **47**. P 14×14½.

283		3d. black and lake-red	10	10
284		6d. black and scarlet	25	35
285		1s.3d. turquoise	30	50
283/5 *Set of* 3			55	80

Design:—1s.3d. Dove of Peace.

117 Patrice Lumumba

118 Star over Two Columns

(Des A. S. B. New)

1962 (30 June). *1st Death Anniv of Lumumba.* W **47**. P 14½×14.

286	**117**	3d. black and orange-yellow	10	10
287		6d. black, green and lake	10	30
288		1s.3d. black, pink and black-green	15	35
286/8 *Set of* 3			30	60

(Des A. S. B. New (3d.), A. Medina (6d), M. Goaman (1s.3d) Litho Enschede)

1962 (1 July). *2nd Anniv of Republic. T* **118** *and similar multicoloured designs.* P 14×13½ (1s.3d) or 13½×14 (others).

289		3d. Type **118**	10	10
290		6d. Flaming torch	20	20
291		1s.3d. Eagle trailing flag (*horiz*)	40	40
289/91 *Set of* 3			60	60

121 President Nkrumah

125 Campaign Emblem

(Litho Enschedé)

1962 (21 Sept). *Founder's Day. T* **121** *and similar vert designs.* P 13×14½.

292		1d. multicoloured	10	10
293		3d. multicoloured	10	10
294		1s.3d. black and bright blue	30	15
295		2s. multicoloured	30	1·25
292/5 *Set of* 4			70	1·25

Designs:—3d. Nkrumah medallion; 1s.3d. President Nkrumah and Ghana Star; 2s. Laying "Ghana" Brick.

1962 (3 Dec). *Malaria Eradication.* W **47**. P 14×14½.

296	**125**	1d. cerise	10	10
297		4d. yellow-green	20	1·25
298		6d. bistre	20	30
299		1s.3d. bluish violet	25	90
296/9 *Set of* 4			65	2·25
MS299*a* 90×115 mm. Nos. 296/9. Imperf			75	1·50

126 Campaign Emblem

129 Map of Africa

1963 (21 Mar). *Freedom from Hunger. T* **126** *and similar designs.* W **47** (sideways on 4d., 1s.3d.). P 14×14½ (1d.) or 14½×14(others).

300		1d. multicoloured	15	25
301		4d. sepia, yellow and orange	75	1·25
302		1s.3d. ochre, black and green	1·60	1·25
300/2 *Set of* 3			2·25	2·50

Designs: *Horiz*—4d. Emblem in hands; 1s.3d. World map and emblem.

1963 (15 Apr). *Africa Freedom Day. T* **129** *and similar designs.* W **47** (sideways on 4d.). P 14½×14 (4d.) or 14×14½ (others).

303		1d. gold and red	10	10
304		4d. red, black and yellow	10	10
305		1s.3d. multicoloured	20	10
306		2s.6d. multicoloured	35	1·25
303/6 *Set of* 4			65	1·40

Designs: *Horiz*—4d. Carved stool. *Vert*—1s.3d. Map and bowl of fire; 2s.6d. Topi (antelope) and flag.

133 Red Cross

137 "3rd Anniversary"

(Des R. Hegeman (4d.), M. Shamir (others))

1963 (28 May). *Red Cross Centenary. T* **133** *and similar multicoloured designs.* W **47** (sideways on 1½d., 4d.). P 14½×14 (1d., 1s.3d.) or 14×14½ (others).

307		1d. Type **133**	40	15
308		1½d. Centenary emblem (*horiz*)	55	2·25
309		4d. Nurses and child (*horiz*)	75	20
310		1s.3d. Emblem, globe and laurel	1·75	2·00
307/10 *Set of* 4			3·00	4·25
MS310*a* 102×127 mm. Nos. 307/10. Imperf			2·75	12·00

(Des M. Goaman (1d., 4d.), R. Hegeman (others))

1963 (1 July). *3rd Anniv of Republic. T* **137** *and similar multicoloured designs.* W **47** (*sideways on 1d., 4d.*). P 14½×14 (horiz) or 14×14½ (vert).

311		1d. Type **137**	10	10
312		4d. Three Ghanaian flags	10	10
		a. Black (stars on flag) omitted	†	£350
313		1s.3d. Map, flag and star (*vert*)	20	15
314		2s.6d. Flag and torch (*vert*)	35	2·25
311/14 *Set of* 4			60	2·25

141 President Nkrumah and Ghana Flag

145 Rameses II, Abu Simbel

(Des R. Hegeman (1d., 4d.), M. Shamir (1s.3d.), G. Rose (5s.))

1963 (21 Sept). *Founder's Day. T* **141** *and similar designs.* W **47** (sideways on 1s.3d., 5s.). P 14×14½ (vert) or 14½×14 (horiz).

315		1d. multicoloured	10	10
316		4d. multicoloured	15	10
317		1s.3d. multicoloured	30	10
		a. Green omitted	£150	
318		5s. yellow and bright reddish purple	65	75
315/18 *Set of* 4			1·00	80

Designs: *Vert*—4d. Nkrumah and flag. *Horiz*—1s.3d. Nkrumah and fireworks; 5s. Symbol of Wisdom.

(Des M. Farrar Bell and R. Hegeman. Litho (1½d., 2d.) or photo (others) Enschedé)

1963 (1 Nov). *Nubian Monuments Preservation. T* **145** *and similar multicoloured designs.* No wmk. P 11½×11 (vert) or 11×11½ (horiz).

319		1d. Type **145**	15	10
320		1½d. Rock paintings (*horiz*)	20	65
321		2d. Queen Nefertari (*horiz*)	20	10
322		4d. Sphinx, Selina	35	15
323		1s.3d. Rock Temple, Abu Simbel (*horiz*)	80	90
319/23 *Set of* 5			1·50	1·75

150 Class 248 Steam Locomotive and Diesel–electric Locomotive No. 1401

151 Eleanor Roosevelt and "Flame of Freedom"

(Des H. L. W. Stevens)

1963 (1 Dec). *60th Anniv of Ghana Railway.* W **47** (sideways). P 14½×14.

324	**150**	1d. multicoloured	10	10
325		6d. multicoloured	40	10
326		1s.3d. multicoloured	45	40
327		2s.6d. multicoloured	75	1·90
324/7 *Set of* 4			1·50	2·25

(Des R. Hegeman and F. H. Savage. Photo Enschedé)

1963 (10 Dec). *15th Anniv of Declaration of Human Rights. T* **151** *and similar multicoloured designs.* No wmk. P 11×11½ (1s.3d.) or 11½×11 (others).

328		1d. Type **151**	10	10
329		4d. Type **151**	10	30
330		6d. Eleanor Roosevelt	10	10
331		1s.3d. Eleanor Roosevelt and emblems (*horiz*)	15	15
328/31 *Set of* 4			30	50

No. 329 differs from No. 328 in the arrangement of the trailing "flame" and of the background within the circular emblem.

154 Sun and Globe Emblem

155 Harvesting Corn on State Farm

1964 (15 June). *International Quiet Sun Years.* W **47** *(sideways). Each blue, yellow, red and green; background colours given.* P 14½.

332	**154**	3d. pale brown	15	10
333		6d. pale grey	25	10
334		1s.3d. mauve	25	15
332/4 *Set of* 3			60	30
MS334*a* 90×90 mm. No. 334 in block of four. Imperf			75	2·50

Nos. 332/4 each exist in a miniature sheet of 12 in different colours (i.e. 3d. in colours of 6d.; 6d. in colours of 1s.3d.; 1s.3d. in colours of 3d.) but these were not generally available to the public.

(Des M. Shamir. Photo Govt Printer, Israel)

1964 (1 July). *4th Anniv of Republic. T* **155** *and similar horiz designs.* P 13×14.

335		3d. olive brown and yellow-olive	10	10
336		6d. bluish green, brown and turquoise-green	10	10
337		1s.3d. brown-red, brown and salmon-red	10	10
338		5s. multicoloured	40	1·25
335/8 *Set of* 4			55	1·40
MS338*a* 126×100 mm. Nos. 335/8. Imperf			85	2·00
		ab. Olive (central design and face value of 3d.) omitted	£550	
		ac. Green (face value of 5s.) omitted	£650	

Designs:—6d. Oil refinery, Tema; 1s.3d. "Communal Labour"; 5s. Procession headed by flag.

159 Globe and Dove

163 Pres. Nkrumah and Hibiscus Flowers

(Des M. Shamir. Litho Lewin-Epstein Ltd, Bat Yam, Israel)

1964 (15 July). *1st Anniv of African Unity Charter. T* **159** *and similar designs.* P 14.

339		3d. multicoloured	10	10
340		6d. deep bronze-green and red	10	10
341		1s.3d. multicoloured	15	10
342		5s. multicoloured	45	70
339/42 *Set of* 4			65	75

Designs: *Vert*—6d. Map of Africa and quill pen; 5s. Planting flower. *Horiz*—1s.3d. Hitched rope on map of Africa.

1964 (21 Sept). *Founder's Day.* W **47** (sideways). P 14×14½.

343	**163**	3d. sepia, red, deep green and light blue	10	10
344		6d. sepia, red, deep green and yellow	15	10
345		1s.3d. sepia, red, deep green and grey	25	10
346		2s.6d. sepia, red, dp grn & light emerald	40	1·00
343/6 *Set of* 4			75	1·10
MS346*a* 90×122 mm. No. 346 in block of four. Imperf			70	2·50

IMPERFORATE STAMPS. Many issues, including miniature sheets, from here onwards exist imperforate, but these were not sold at post offices.

164 Hurdling

(Des A. S. B. New (No. 352))

1964 (25 Oct). *Olympic Games, Tokyo. T* **164** *and similar multicoloured designs.* W **47** (sideways on 1d., 2½d., 6d., 5s.). P 14½×14 (horiz) or 14×14½ (vert).

347		1d. Type **164**	10	10
348		2½d. Running	10	1·50
349		3d. Boxing (*vert*)	10	10
350		4d. Long-jumping (*vert*)	10	10
351		6d. Football (*vert*)	15	10
352		1s.3d. Athlete holding Olympic Torch (*vert*)	20	10
353		5s. Olympic Rings and flags	55	3·25
347/53 *Set of* 7			1·00	4·50
MS353*a* 128×102 mm. Nos. 351/3. Imperf			75	2·50
		ab. Brown omitted	£650	

171 G. Washington Carver (botanist) and Plant

173 African Elephant

(Des M. Shamir)

1964 (7 Dec). *U.N.E.S.C.O. Week.* W **47**. P 14½.

354 **171** 6d. deep blue and green ... 15 10
355 – 1s.3d. reddish purple & greenish blue ... 30 10
w. Wmk inverted ... 11·00
356 **171** 5s. sepia and orange-red ... 50 4·25
354/6 *Set of 3* ... 85 4·25
MS356*a* 127×77 mm. Nos. 354/6. Imperf ... 75 2·00

Design:—1s.3d. Albert Einstein (scientist) and atomic symbol.

(Des A. S. B. New (No. 360). Photo Enschedé))

1964 (14 Dec). *Multicoloured designs as T* **173**. P 11½×11 (vert) or 11×11½ (horiz).

357 1d. Type **173** ... 50 50
358 1½d. Secretary Bird (*horiz*) ... 75 2·50
359 2½d. Purple Wreath (flower) ... 30 2·50
360 3d. Grey Parrot ... 75 50
361 4d. Blue-naped Mousebird (*horiz*) ... 75 70
362 6d. African Tulip Tree (*horiz*) ... 30 30
363 1s.3d. Violet Starling (*horiz*) ... 1·00 1·25
364 2s.6d. Hippopotamus (*horiz*) ... 1·00 5·50
357/64 *Set of 8* ... 4·75 12·00
MS364*a* (a) 150×86 mm. Nos. 357/9. (b) 150×110 mm. Nos. 360/4. Imperf *Set of 2 sheets* ... 4·75 14·00

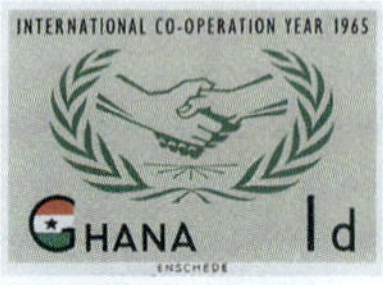

181 I.C.Y. Emblem

182 I.T.U. Emblem and Symbols

(Litho Enschedé)

1965 (22 Feb). *International Co-operation Year.* P 14×12½.

365 **181** 1d. multicoloured ... 35 70
366 4d. multicoloured ... 1·00 1·60
367 6d. multicoloured ... 1·00 70
368 1s.3d. multicoloured ... 1·25 2·75
365/8 *Set of 4* ... 3·25 5·25
MS368*a* 100×100 mm. No. 368 in block of four. Imperf ... 2·75 5·00

(Litho Enschedé)

1965 (12 Apr). *I.T.U. Centenary.* P 13½.

369 **182** 1d. multicoloured ... 15 15
370 6d. multicoloured ... 30 15
371 1s.3d. multicoloured ... 55 25
372 5s. multicoloured ... 1·25 3·25
369/72 *Set of 4* ... 2·00 3·50
MS372*a* 132×115 mm. Nos. 369/72. Imperf ... 7·50 10·00

183 Lincoln's Home.

(Des M. Farrar Bell (6d.), A. S. B. New (1s.3d., 5s.), R. Hegeman (2s.))

1965 (17 May). *Death Centenary of Abraham Lincoln. T* **183** *and similar square-shaped designs.* W **47** (sideways). P 12½.

373 6d. multicoloured ... 10 10
374 1s.3d. black, red and blue ... 15 15
375 2s. black, orange-brown and greenish yellow ... 15 35
376 5s. black and red ... 30 1·75
373/6 *Set of 4* ... 60 2·00
MS376*a* 115×115 mm. Nos. 373/6. Imperf ... 75 3·50
ab. Green (part of flag on 6d.) omitted ... £550

Designs:—1s.3d. Lincolns Inaugural Address; 2s. Abraham Lincoln: 5s. Adaptation of U.S. 90c Lincoln Stamp of 1899.

(New Currency. 100 pesewas = 1 cedi)

187 Obverse (Pres. Nkrumah) and Reverse of 5p. Coin

(Photo Enschedé)

1965 (19 July). *Introduction of Decimal Currency. T* **187** *and similar horiz designs. Multicoloured.* P 11×13 (5p., 10p.), 13×12½ (25p.) or 13½×14 (50p.)

377 5p. Type **187** ... 20 10
378 10p. As Type **187** ... 25 10
379 25p. Size 63×39 mm ... 55 1·00
380 50p. Size 71×43½ mm ... 1·00 2·50
377/80 *Set of 4* ... 1·75 3·25

The coins in Nos. 378/80 are all circular and express the same denominations as on the stamps.

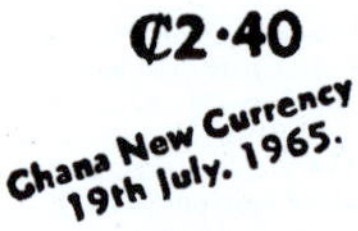

(188)

1965 (19 July). *Nos. 214, 216 and 218a/27 surch as T* **188** *diagonally upwards, (D) or horizontally, (H), by Govt Printer, Accra.*

(a) Postage

381 1p. on 1d. multicoloured (R.) (D) ... 10 10
a. Surch inverted ... 15·00
b. Surch double ... 60·00
382 2p. on 2d. multicoloured (Ultram.) (H) ... 10 10
a. Surch inverted ... 20·00
b. Surch double ... 11·00
c. Surch on back only ... £200
d. Surch on front and back ... £200
e. Red surch ... 28·00
f. Orange surch ... 28·00
g. Indigo surch ...
ga. Surch sideways ...
383 3p. on 3d. multicoloured (II) (Br.) (H) ... 1·00 5·50
a. Surch inverted ... 20·00
b. Indigo surch ...
384 4p. on 4d. multicoloured (B.) (H) ... 5·00 45
a. Surch inverted ... 65·00 65·00
b. Surch double ... 50·00
c. Red surch ...
385 6p. on 6d. multicoloured (Blk.) (H) ... 50 10
a. Surch inverted ... 8·50 10·00
b. Surch double ... 15·00
c. Horiz pair, one without surch ... 80·00
d. Green (flag) omitted ... £110
386 11p. on 11d. multicoloured (W.) (D) ... 25 10
a. Surch inverted ... 13·00 9·00
387 12p. on 1s. multicoloured (B.) (D) ... 25 10
a. Surch double ... 55·00
b. Surch double, one albino inverted
c. Black surch ... 10·00
ca. Surch inverted ... 10·00 10·00
388 30p. on 2s.6d. multicoloured (B.) (H) ... 4·75 9·00
389 60p. on 5s. multicoloured (B.) (D) ... 4·50 70
a. Surch double (G.+B.) ... 35·00
390 1c.20 on 10s. multicoloured (B.) (D) ... 75 2·25
a. Surch double (G.+B.) ... £120
391 2c.40 on £1 multicoloured (B.) (D) ... 1·00 6·50

(b) Air

392 15p. on 1s.3d. multicoloured (W.) (H) ... 2·50 70
a. Surch inverted
393 24p. on 2s. multicoloured (G.) (D) ... 2·50 30
a. Surch on front and back ... 35·00
381/93 *Set of 13* ... 20·00 22·00

On the diagonal surcharges the values are horizontal.

The 30p. was not released in Ghana until 30 July and the 3p. sometime later.

Numerous minor varieties exist.

189 "OAU" and Flag

190 "OAU", Heads and Flag

191 "OAU" Emblem and Flag

192 African Map and Flag

1965 (21 Oct). *O.A.U. Summit Conference, Accra. T* **189/92** *and similar horiz designs. Multicoloured.* W **47** (sideways* except on 6p.). P 14 (T **189/91**) or 14½×14 (others).

394 1p. Type **189** ... 10 10
a. Red (part of flag) omitted ... £110
395 2p. Type **190** ... 10 10
396 5p. Type **191** ... 10 10
397 6p. Type **192** ... 10 10
398 15p. "Sunburst", map and flag ... 20 30
399 24p. "O.A.U." on map, and flag ... 35 60
w. Wmk top of G to left ...
394/9 *Set of 6* ... 75 1·10

*The 1p. also exists with the watermark facing left or right, but positional blocks are required to show the two types. The normal sideways watermark has top of G to right, *as seen from the back of the stamp*.

195 Goalkeeper saving Ball

198 Pres. Kennedy and Grave Memorial

(Photo Enschedé)

1965 (15 Nov). *African Soccer Cup Competition. T* **195** *and similar multicoloured designs.* P 13×14 (15p.) or 14×13 (others).

400 6p. Type **195** ... 25 10
401 15p. Player with ball (*vert*) ... 40 30
402 24p. Players, ball and soccer cup ... 45 70
400/2 *Set of 3* ... 1·00 1·00

(Des A. S. B. New (No. 405))

1965 (15 Dec)–**68**. *2nd Anniv of President Kennedy's Death. T* **198** *and similar square-shaped designs.* W **47** (sideways). P 12½.

403 6p. multicoloured ... 15 10
404 15p. violet, red and green ... 20 35
405 24p. black and reddish violet ... 20 60
406 30p. dull purple and black ... 25 1·25
403/6 *Set of 4* ... 70 2·00
MS407 114½×114 mm. Nos. 40316. Imperf (21.3.66) ... 3·00 6·50

Designs:—15p. Pres. Kennedy and Eternal Flame; 24p. Pres. Kennedy and memorial inscription; 30p. President Kennedy.

202 Section of Dam and Generators

(206)

(Des A. S. B. New (No. 411). Photo Enschedé))

1966 (22 Jan). *Volta River Project. T* **202** *and similar horiz designs.* P 11×11½.

408 6p. multicoloured ... 15 10
409 15p. multicoloured ... 20 15
410 24p. multicoloured ... 25 20
411 30p. black and new blue ... 35 50
408/11 *Set of 4* ... 85 85

Designs:—15p. Dam and Lake Volta; 24p. Word "GHANA" as dam; 30p. "Fertility".

1966 (7 Feb). *"Black Stars" Victory in African Soccer Cup Competition. Nos. 400/2 aptd with T* **206**, *in black.*

412 6p. Type **195** ... 40 15
a. Green opt ... 22·00
b. Green opt double, one inverted ... 55·00
c. Stop after "Nov" omitted (R. 5/1) ... 11·00
413 15p. Player with ball ... 60 30
414 24p. Players, ball and cup ... 65 70
a. Opt inverted* ... 30·00
ab. Vert pair, one without opt, the other with opt inverted ... £150
b. Error. Opt for 15p. on 24p. inverted* ... 30·00
c. Stop after "Nov" omitted (R. 5/1) ... 15·00
412/14 *Set of 3* ... 1·50 1·00

*In No. 414a the overprint reads downwards (top right to bottom left), but in No. 414b it reads upwards (bottom right to top left).

DATES OF ISSUE of miniature sheets are approximate as they are generally released some time after the related ordinary stamps, but it is known that the G.P.O. sometimes applied first-day cancellations months after the dates shown on the cancellations.

207 W.H.O. Building and Ghana Flag

1966 (1 July). *Inauguration of W.H.O. Headquarters, Geneva. T* **207** *and similar horiz design. Multicoloured.* W **47**. P 14½×14.

415	6p. Type **207**	50	10
416	15p. Type **207**	1·25	65
417	24p. W.H.O. Building and emblem	1·40	1·60
418	30p. As 24p.	1·60	3·75
415/18 *Set of 4*		4·25	5·50
MS419	120×101 mm. Nos. 415/18. Imperf (11.66)	20·00	21·00

209 Atlantic Herring

214 African "Links" and Ghana Flag

(Des O. Hamann. Photo Enschedé)

1966 (10 Aug). *Freedom from Hunger. T* **209** *and similar horiz designs. Multicoloured.* P 14×13.

420	6p. Type **209**	25	10
421	15p. Turbot	45	15
422	24p. Spadefish	45	35
423	30p. Red Snapper	50	1·25
424	60p. Blue-finned Tuna	70	4·75
420/4 *Set of 5*		2·10	6·00
MS425	126×109 mm. No. 423 in block of four. Imperf (Nov)	10·00	13·00

(Photo Enschedé)

1966 (11 Oct). *Third Anniv of African Charter. T* **214** *and similar multicoloured designs.* P 13½.

426	6p. Type **214**	15	10
427	15p. Flags as "Quill", and diamond (*horiz*)	35	55
428	24p. Ship's wheel, map and cocoa bean (*horiz*)	40	70
426/8 *Set of 3*		80	1·25

217 Player heading Ball, and Jules Rimet Cup

1966 (14 Nov). *World Cup Football Championships, England. T* **217** *and similar horiz designs. Multicoloured.* W **47**. P 14½×14.

429	5p. Type **217**	40	10
430	15p. Goalkeeper clearing ball	80	20
	w. Wmk inverted	1·60	1·60
431	24p. Player and Jules Rimet Cup (replica)	1·00	35
432	30p. Players and Jules Rimet Cup (replica)	1·40	1·25
433	60p. Players with ball	2·00	7·50
	w. Wmk inverted	10·00	
429/33 *Set of 5*		5·00	8·50
MS434	120×102 mm. 60p. (block of four). Imperf	24·00	26·00

222 U.N.E.S.C.O. Emblem

1966 (23 Dec). *20th Anniv of U.N.E.S.C.O.* W **47** (sideways). P 14½.

435	**222**	5p. multicoloured	70	15
436		15p. multicoloured	1·50	50
437		24p. multicoloured	2·00	1·00
438		30p. multicoloured	2·25	2·75
439		60p. multicoloured	3·00	9·00
435/9 *Set of 5*			8·50	12·00
MS440		140×115 mm. Nos. 435/9. Imperf	25·00	26·00

223 Fair Emblem and Crates

1967 (1 Feb). *Ghana Trade Fair, Accra. T* **223** *and similar multicoloured designs.* W **47** (sideways on 24p.). P 14×14½ (24p.) or 14½×14 (others).

441	5p. Type **223**	10	10
442	15p. Fair emblem and world map	15	20
443	24p. Shipping and flags (*vert*)	25	30
444	36p. Fair emblem and hand-held hoist	40	2·50
441/4 *Set of 4*		70	2·75

(New Currency. 100 new pesewae = 1 new cedi (1.2 old cedi))

1½Np (227) N₵2.00 (228)

229 Ghana Eagle and Flag

1967 (23 Feb). *Nos. 216, 219/23, 225/6 and 393 surch as T* **227/8**.

(a) Postage

445	1½n.p. on 2d. multicoloured (Blk.)	2·00	7·00
446	3½n.p. on 4d. multicoloured (R)	7·00	4·00
	a. Surch double, one sideways		
	b. Surch double	—	65·00
447	5n.p. on 6d. multicoloured (R.)	2·75	2·25
448	9n.p. on 11d. multicoloured (W)	30	50
449	10n.p. on 1s. multicoloured (W)	30	1·25
450	25n.p. on 2s.6d. multicoloured (R.)	3·50	6·50
451	1n.c. on 10s. multicoloured (R.)	3·00	15·00
452	2n.c. on £1 on 10s. multicoloured (R.)	6·00	24·00

(b) Air

453	12½n.p. on 1s.3d. multicoloured (W.)	4·00	4·25
454	20n.p. on 24p. on 2s. multicoloured (R.1)	6·50	7·50
445/54 *Set of 10*		30·00	65·00

Inverted surcharges in a different type face on the 3½, 5 and 25n.p. are fakes.

(Des M. Shamir)

1967 (24 Feb). *First Anniv of February 24 Revolution.* W **47** (sideways). P 14×14½.

455	**229**	1n.p. multicoloured	10	90
456		4n.p. multicoloured	10	10
457		12½n.p. multicoloured	35	60
458		25n.p. multicoloured	65	3·50
455/8 *Set of 4*			1·00	4·50
MS459		89×108 mm. Nos. 455/8. Perf or imperf	5·00	12·00

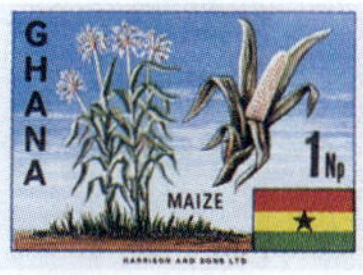

230 Maize

231 Forest Kingfisher

235 Rufous-crowned Roller

236 Akasombo Dam

1967 (1 June). *T* **230/1**, **235/6** *and similar designs.* W **47** (1½, 2, 4, 50n.p. and 1n.c.) or sideways (others). P 11½×12 (1, 8n.p), 12×11½ (4n.p), 14×14½ (1½ 2, 2½, 20n.p., 2n.c. 50) or 14½×14 (others).

460	1n.p. multicoloured	10	10
	a. Salmon omitted**	£400	
461	1½n.p. multicoloured	1·00	2·75
	a. Blue omitted*	£250	
	b. Green printed double, once inverted	—	£225
	c. Green omitted	—	£110
462	2n.p. multicoloured (4.9)	10	10
	a. Green (part of flag) omitted	£170	
	b. Gold (frame) omitted	£140	
	w. Wmk inverted	10·00	
463	2½n.p. multicoloured (4.9)	35	10
	a. Wmk upright	10·00	
	ab. Face value omitted	£275	
464	3n.p. multicoloured	20	40
	a. Green (part of flag) omitted	—	£375
465	4n.p. multicoloured	1·50	10
	a. Green (part of flag) omitted	70·00	
	b. Red (part of flag) omitted	£325	
	c. Black (star, bird markings and shadow) omitted	£110	
466	6n.p. multicoloured	15	2·25
467	8n.p. multicoloured	15	75
468	9n.p. multicoloured (4.9)	75	10
469	10n.p. multicoloured	15	10
470	20n.p. deep blue and new blue (4.9)	20	10
471	50n.p. multicoloured	8·50	2·50
472	1n.c. multicoloured (4.9.)	2·00	1·00
473	2n.c. multicoloured (4.9.)	2·00	3·50
474	2n.c. 50 multicoloured	1·75	9·00
460/74 *Set of 15*		16·00	20·00

Designs:—Vert (*as T* **231**)—2n.p. The Ghana Mace; 2½ n.p Commelina; 20n.p. Bush Hare; 2n.c. Frangipani; 2n.c. 50, Seat of State. Horiz (*as T* **236**) 3n.p. West African Lungfish; 9n.p. Chameleon; 10n.p Tema Harbour; 50n.p. Black-winged Stilt; 1n.c. Wooden Stool. (*As T* **230**)—8n.p. Adomi Bridge.

*In this stamp the blue not only affects the bird but is printed over the yellow background to give the value in green, so that its omission results in the value also being omitted.

**This affects the maize flowers, corn and foreground.

†This affects the feather-tips and the flag.

The 2n.p. and 20n.p. were officially issued on 4 September but small quantities of both were released in error on 1 June. The 2½ n.p. is also known to have been released in error in June.

245 Kumasi Fort

249 "Luna 10"

(Des O. Hamann)

1967 (1 July). *Castles and Forts. T* **245** *and similar designs. Multicoloured.* W **47** (diagonal). P 14½.

475	4n.p. Type **245**	25	10
476	12½n.p. Cristiansborg Castle and British galleon	60	1·00
477	20n.p. Elmina Castle and Portuguese galleon	75	2·75
478	25n.p. Cape Coast Castle and Spanish galleon	75	3·50
475/8 *Set of 4*		2·10	6·50

(Des M. Shamir. Photo Enschedé)

1967 (16 Aug). *"Peaceful Use of Outer Space". T* **249** *and similar square designs. Multicoloured.* P 13½×14.

479	4n.p. Type **249**	10	10
480	10n.p. "Orbiter 1"	10	45
481	12½n.p. Man in Space	20	80
479/81 *Set of 3*		35	1·25
MS482	140×90 mm. Nos. 479/81. Imperf	1·75	4·00

252 Scouts and Camp-fire

(Photo Enschedé)

1967 (18 Sept). *50th Anniv of Ghanaian Scout Movement. T* **252** *and similar horiz designs. multicoloured.* P 14½×13.

483	4n.p. Type **252**	20	10
484	10n.p. Scout on march	40	50
485	12½n.p. Lard Baden-Powell	50	1·75
483/5 *Set of 3*		1·00	2·00
MS486	167×95 mm. Nos. 453/5. Imperf	6·00	10·00

255 U.N. Headquarters Building

256 General View of U.N. H.Q., Manhattan

(Litho D.L.R.)

1967 (20 Nov). *United Nations Day (24 October).* P 13½.

487	**255**	4n.p. multicoloured	10	10
488		10n.p. multicoloured	10	15
489	**256**	50n.p. multicoloured	20	70
490		2n.c.50 multicoloured	55	4·00
487/90 *Set of 4*			75	4·50
MS491		76×75 mm. No. 490. Imperf (4.12.67)	2·25	9·50

257 Leopard

1967 (28 Dec). *International Tourist Year. T* **257** *and similar diamond-shaped designs. Multicoloured.* W **47** (diagonal). P 12½.

492	4n.p. Type **257**	1·00	20
493	12½n.p. *Papilio demodocus* (butterfly)	2·25	1·50
494	20n.p. Carmine Bee Eater	2·50	3·75
495	50n.p. Waterbuck	2·50	9·00
492/5 *Set of 4*		7·50	13·00
MS496	126×126 mm. Nos. 493/S. Imperf	18·00	21·00

261 Revolutionaries entering Accra

(Litho D.L.R.)

1968 (24 Feb). *2nd Anniv of February Revolution. T* **261** *and similar horiz designs. Multicoloured.* P 14.

497		4n.p. Type **261**	10	10
498	**12**	½n.p. Marching troops	20	20
499		20n.p. Cheering people	30	40
500		40n.p. Victory celebrations	50	2·25
497/500 *Set of* 4			1·00	2·50

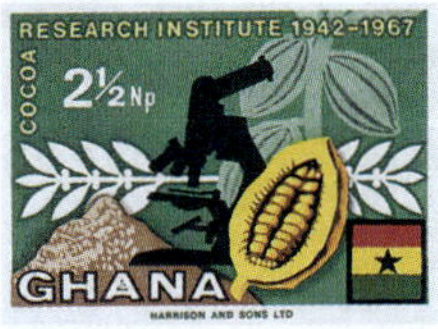

265 Microscope and Cocoa Beans

1968 (18 Mar). *Cocoa Reseach. T* **265** *and similar horiz design. Multicoloured.* W **47** (sideways). P 14½×14.

501	2½n.p. Type **265**	10	1·00
502	4n.p. Microscope and cocoa tree, beans and pods	10	10
503	10n.p. Type **265**	15	20
504	25n.p. As 4n.p.	60	1·50
501/4 *Set of* 4		80	2·50
MS505 102×102 mm. Nos. 501/4. Imperf		2·25	5·00

267 Kotoka and Flowers

271 Tobacco

(Des A. S. B. New (No. 508) and F. Mate (others) Litho D.L.R.))

1968 (17 Apr). *1st Death Anniv of Lt.–Gen. E. K. Kotoka. T* **267** *and similar multicoloured designs.* P 14.

506	4n.p. Type **267**	10	10
507	12½n.p. Kotoka and wreath	20	30
508	20n.p. Kotoka in civilian clothes	35	75
509	40n.p. Lt.-Gen. Kotoka (*vert*)	50	2·25
506/9 *Set of* 4		1·00	3·00

(Des A. S. B. New (5n.p.))

1968 (19 Aug). *Flora and Fauna. T* **271** *and similar vert designs. Multicoloured.* W **47** (sideways). P 14×14½.

510	4n.p. Type **271**	15	10
511	5n.p. North African Crested Porcupine	15	1·25
512	12½n.p. Rubber	30	75
513	20n.p. *Cymothoe sangaris* (butterfly)	1·25	2·75
514	40n.p. *Charaxes ameliae* (butterfly)	1·50	5·00
510/14 *Set of* 5		3·00	8·50
MS515 88×114 mm. Nos. 510, 512/14. Imperf		3·75	9·00

276 Surgeons, Flag and W.H.O. Emblem

277 Hurdling

(Photo Enschedé)

1968 (11 Nov). *20th Anniv of World Health Organization.* P 14×13.

516	**276**	4n.p. multicoloured	20	10
517		12½n.p. multicoloured	40	40
518		20n.p. multicoloured	60	1·25
519		40n.p. multicoloured	1·00	3·75
516/19 *Set of* 4			2·00	5·00
MS520 132×110 mm. Nos. 516/19. Imperf			2·75	7·00

1969 (10 Jan). *Olympic Games, Mexico (1968). T* **277** *and similar vert designs. Multicoloured.* W **47** (sideways). P 14×14½.

521	4n.p. Type **277**	10	10
522	12½n.p. Boxing	20	30
523	20n.p. Torch, Olympic Rings and flags	40	75
524	40n.p. Football	70	3·25
521/4 *Set of* 4		1·25	4·00
MS525 89×114 mm. Nos. 521/4 Imperf (17.1.69)		3·50	8·00

281 U.N. Building

285 Dr. J. B. Danquah

(Litho D.L.R.)

1969 (1 Feb). *United Nations Day (1968). T* **281** *and similar square-shaped designs. Multicoloured.* P 13½.

526	4n.p. Type **281**	10	10
527	12½n.p. Native stool, staff and U.N. emblem	15	25
528	20n.p. U.N. building and emblem over Ghanaian flag	20	45
529	40n.p. U.N. emblem encircled by flags	40	2·50
526/9 *Set of* 4		75	3·00
MS530 127×117 mm. No. 526/9. Imperf		75	3·50

1969 (7 Mar). *Human Rights Year. T* **285** *and similar horiz design. Multicoloured.* W **47** (sideways on **MS**535). P 14½×14.

531	4n.p. Type **285**	10	10
532	12½n.p. Dr. Martin Luther king	20	35
533	20n.p. As 12½n.p.	35	75
534	40n.p. Type **285**	50	2·75
531/4 *Set of* 4		1·00	3·50
MS535 116×50 mm. Nos. 531/4. Imperf (17.4.69)		80	3·75

287 Constituent Assembly Building

1969 (10 Sept). *Third Anniv of the Resolution. T* **287** *and srmilar horiz design.* W **47** (sideways on **MS**540). P 14½×14.

536	4n.p. Type **287**	10	10
537	12½n.p. Arms of Ghana	10	15
538	20n.p. Type **287**	15	20
539	40n.p. As 12½n.p.	20	75
536/9 *Set of* 4		40	80
MS540 114×89 mm. Nos. 536/9. Imperf		70	2·75

NEW CONSTITUTION
1969
(289)

290 Map of Africa and Flags

1969 (1 Oct). *New Constitution. Nos. 460/74 optd with T* **289** *in various positions by Government Press, Accra.*

541	1n.p. multicoloured (Horiz)	10	2·00
542	1½n.p. multicoloured (Vert down)	2·00	4·50
	a. Opt Vert up	4·50	
	b. Horiz opt	25·00	
	ba. Opt omitted (in Vert pair with normal)	£250	
543	2n.p. multicoloured (Vert up)	10	4·00
	a. Opt Vert down	5·00	
	b. Opt double	12·00	
544	2½n.p. multicoloured (Vert up)	10	2·25
	a. Opt Vert down	22·00	
545	3n.p. multicoloured (Horiz)	1·00	2·25
	a. Opt inverted	17·00	
546	4n.p. multicoloured (Y.) (Vert down)	3·00	60
	a. Black opt (Vert down)	7·00	1·25
	b. Black opt (Vert up)	13·00	
	c. Red opt (Vert down)	20·00	
	d. Opt double (White Vert down+yellow Vert up)	30·00	
547	6n.p. multicoloured (Horiz)	15	3·00
548	8n.p. multicoloured (Horiz)	15	3·50
549	9n.p. multicoloured (Horiz)	15	3·75
550	10n.p. multicoloured (Horiz)	20	3·50
551	20n.p. deep blue and new blue (Vert up)	35	2·25
	a. Opt Vert down	24·00	
552	50n.p. multicoloured (Horiz)	7·00	6·50
	a. Opt double	28·00	
553	1n.c. multicoloured (Horiz)	1·50	7·50
554	2n.c. multicoloured (R.) (Vert up)	1·50	9·00
	a. Opt double (Vert up and down)	42·00	
	b. Opt triple (Red Vert up and down+yellow Vert up)	55·00	
555	2n.c. 50 multicoloured (Vert down)	1·50	9·50
541/55 *Set of* 15		17·00	55·00

The 1n.p is known with the overprint inverted, "NEW CONSTITUTION" appearing between the stamps across the perforations.

(Litho D.L.R.)

1969 (4 Dec). *Inauguration of Second Republic. T* **290** *and similar vert designs. Multicoloured.* P 14.

556	4n.p. Type **290**	10	10
557	12½n.p. Figure "2", branch and Ghanaian colours	20	10
558	20n.p. Hands receiving egg	35	35
559	40n.p. Type **290**	60	1·50
556/9 *Set of* 4		1·10	1·75

293 I.L.O. Emblem and Cog-wheels

1970 (5 Jan). *50th Anniv of International Labour Organisation.* W **47** (sideways). P 14½×14.

560	**293**	4n.p. multicoloured	10	10
561		12½n.p. multicoloured	20	55
562		20n.p. multicoloured	30	1·25
560/2 *Set of* 3			55	1·60
MS563 117×89 mm. Nos. 560/2. Imperf			70	3·00

294 Red Cross and Globe

298 General Kotoka, Vickers VC-10 and Airport

1970 (2 Feb). *50th Anniv of League of Red Cross Societies. T* **294** *and similar multicoloured designs.* W **47** (sideways on 4n.p.). P 14×14½ (4n.p) or 14½×14 (others).

564	4n.p. Type **294**	20	10
565	12½n.p. Henri Dunant and Red Cross emblem (*horiz*)	25	25
	w. Wmk inverted		
566	20n.p. Patient receiving medicine (*horiz*)	30	75
567	40n.p. Patient having arm bandaged (*horiz*)	35	2·50
564/7 *Set of* 4		1·00	3·25
MS568 114×89 mm. Nos. 564/7. Imperf		1·50	6·00

(Des G. Vasarhelyi. Litho D.L.R.)

1970 (17 Apr). *Inauguration of Koto Airport. T* **298** *and similar horiz designs. Multicoloured.* P 13×13½.

569	4n.p. Type **298**	15	10
570	12½n.p. Control tower and tail of Vickers VC-10	25	15
571	20n.p. Aerial view of airport	40	30
572	40n.p. Airport and flags	75	80
569/72 *Set of* 4		1·40	1·25

302 Lunar Module landing on Moon

306 Adult Education

(Des A. Medina (4n.p., 12½ n.p), G. Vasarhelyi (others). Litho D.L.R)

1970 (15 June). *Moon Landing. T* **302** *and similar multicoloured designs.* P 12½.

573	4n.p. Type **302**	30	10
574	12½n.p. Astronaut's first step onto the Moon	50	60
575	20n.p. Astronaut with equipment on Moon (*horiz*)	60	1·40
576	40n.p. Astronauts (*horiz*)	70	3·25
573/6 *Set of* 4		1·90	4·75
MS577 142×142 mm. Nos. 573/6. Imperf (with or without simulated perfs)		2·25	12·00

On 18 September 1970 Nos. 573/6 were issued overprinted "PHILYMPIA LONDON 1970" but it is understood that only 900 sets were made available for sale in Ghana and we do not consider that this is sufficient to constitute normal postal use. The miniature sheet was also overprinted but not issued in Ghana.

(Litho D.L.R)

1970 (10 Aug). *International Education Year. T* **306** *and similar horiz designs. Multicoloured.* P 13.

578	4n.p. Type **306**	10	10
579	12½n.p. International education	20	20
580	20n.p. "Ntesie" and I.E.Y. symbols	35	30
581	40n.p. Nursery schools	60	1·00
578/81 *Set of* 4		1·10	1·40

310 Saluting March-Past

314 *Crinum ornatum*

(Litho D.L.R)

1970 (1 Oct). *First Anniv of the Second Republic. T* **310** *and similar horiz designs. Multicoloured.* P 13×13½.

582	4n.p. Type **310**	20	10
583	12½n.p. Busia declaration	15	15

584 20n.p. Doves symbol 25 30
585 40n.p. Opening of Parliament .... 50 1·00
582/5 *Set of 4* .... 1·00 1·40

(Des G. Vasarhelyi. Photo Harrison)

1970 (2 Nov). *Flora and Fauna. T* **314** *and similar horiz designs. Multicoloured.* W **47** (sideways). P 14½×14.

586 4n.p. Type **314** .... 1·75 25
w. Wmk inverted .... 9·00
587 12½n.p. Lioness .... 1·25 85
588 20n.p. *Aaselia africana* (flower) .... 1·25 1·50
589 40n.p. African Elephant .... 2·00 6·00
586/9 *Set of 4* .... 5·50 7·75

315 Kuduo Brass Casket

(Des G. Vasarhelyi. Photo Harrison)

1970 (7 Dec). *Monuments and Archaeological Sites in Ghana. T* **315** *and similar horiz designs. Multicoloured.* W **47**. P 14½×14.

590 4n.p. Type **315** 15 10
w. Wmk inverted .... 20·00
591 12½n.p. Akan traditional house 30 20
592 20n.p. Larabanga Mosque 35 50
593 40n.p. Funerary clay head .... 50 1·40
590/3 *Set of 4* .... 1·10 2·00
MS594 89×71 mm. Nos. 590, 592 and 12½n.p. Basilica of Pompeii, 40n.p. Pistrinum of Pompeii (wmk sideways). Imperf (2.71) .... 6·50 9·50

STAMP BOOKLETS

1961. *Red (No.* SB2*), yellow (No.* SB3*) or green (No.* SB4*) covers. Stitched.*

SB2 3s. booklet containing twelve 3d. (No. 218a) in blocks of 4 .... 6·00
SB3 6s. booklet containing eight 3d. and eight 1d. (Nos. 218a, 220) in blocks of 4 .... 7·50
SB4 10s. booklet containing four 3d., eight 6d. and four 1s.3d. (Nos. 218a, 220, 226) in blocks of 4 .... 9·50

POSTAGE DUE STAMPS

GHANA
(D 2)

D 3

1958 (25 June). *Nos.* D5/8 *of Gold Coast and similar 1d. value optd with Type* D **2** *in red.*

D9 D **1** 1d. black 10 30
D10 2d. black 10 30
c. Large "d" .... 2·25
D11 3d. black 10 30
a. Missing serif .... 4·50
D12 6d. black 15 65
D13 1s. black .... 20 1·50
c. Upright stroke .... 1·50
D9/13 *Set of 5* .... 50 2·75

(Typo De La Rue)

1958 (1 Dec). *Chalk-surfaced paper.* Wmk Mult Script CA. P 14.

D14 D **3** 1d. carmine 10 30
D15 2d. green 10 30
c. Large "d" .... 2·25
D16 3d. orange 10 30
a. Missing serif .... 4·25
D17 6d. bright ultramarine 10 50
D18 1s. reddish violet .... 15 2·00
c. Upright stroke .... 1·50
D14/18 *Set of 5* .... 45 3·00

3p.
Ghana New Currency
19th July. 1965.
(D 4)

1½Np
(D 5)

1965 (19 July). *Nos.* D14/18 *surch as Type* D **4** *diagonally upwards (D) or horiz (H), by Govt Printer, Accra.*

D19 D **3** 1p. On 1d. (D) 10 75
a. Surch inverted .... 10·00
b. Surch double ....
c. Surch omitted (in horiz pair with normal) £100
D20 2p. on 2d. (B.) (H) .... 10 1·10
a. Surch inverted .... 8·00
c. Large "d" .... 2·25
d. Surch omitted (in horiz pair with normal) .... 75·00
D21 3p. on 3d. (indigo) (H) .... 10 1·10
a. Surch inverted .... 12·00
b. Surch omitted (in horiz pair with normal) ....
c. Ultramarine surch ....
ca. Surch inverted .... 9·00
cb. Surch on front and back .... 15·00
d. Black surch ....
e. Missing serif .... 3·00
D22 6p. on 6d. (R) (H) .... 10 2·25
a. Surch inverted .... 14·00
b. Purple-brown surch .... 11·00
ba. Surch double .... 22·00
c. Green surch .... 13·00
D23 12p. on 1s. (B) (D) .... 15 2·50
c. Upright stroke .... 1·50
D19/23 *Set of 5* .... 45 7·00

On the diagonal surcharges the figures of value are horizontal.

No. D21b occurs in the first or second vertical row of one sheet which shows the surcharges shifted progressively to the right.

1968 (1 Feb)–**70**. *Nos.* D20/2 *additionally surch as Type* D **5**, *in red (1½ n.p., 5n.p.), or black (2½ n.p.).*

D24 D **3** 1½n.p. on 2p. on 2d. .... 5·50 4·25
a. Type D **5** double, one albino.
b. Albino surch (Type D **4**) ....
c. Large "d" .... 20·00
D25 2½n.p. on 3p. on 3d. (4.70?) .... 1·00 5·00
a. Type D **5** double, one albino. 5·50
b. Missing serif .... 5·00
D26 5n.p. on 6p. on 6d. (1970) .... 1·25
D24/6 *Set of 3* .... 7·00

The above were three in a series of surcharges, the others being 1n.p on 1p. and 10n.p. on 12 p, which were prepared, but owing to confusion due to the two surcharges in similar currency it was decided by the authorities not to issue the stamps, however, Nos. D24/6 were issued in error.

(Litho D.L.R)

1970. *Inscr in new currency.* P 14½×14.

D27 D **3** 1n.p. carmine-red .... 1·25 4·50
D28 1½n.p. green .... 1·50 5·00
D29 2½n.p. yellow-orange .... 1·75 6·50
D30 5n.p. ultramarine .... 2·50 6·50
D31 10n.p. reddish violet .... 3·25 8·00
D27/31 *Set of 5* .... 9·00 27·00

Gibraltar

CROWN COLONY

Early details of postal arrangements in Gibraltar are hard to establish, although it is known that postal facilities were provided by the Civil Secretary's Office from 1749. Gibraltar became a packet port in July 1806, although the Civil Secretary's office continued to be responsible for other mail. The two services were amalgamated on 1 January 1857 as a Branch Office of the British G.P.O., the control of the postal services not reverting to Gibraltar until 1 January 1886.

Spanish stamps could be used at Gibraltar from their introduction in 1850 and, indeed, such franking was required on letters weighing over ½ oz. sent to Spain after 1 July 1854. From 1 July 1856 until 1 January 1876 all mail to Spain required postage to be prepaid by Spanish stamps and these issues were supplied by the Gibraltar postal authorities, acting as a Spanish Postal Agent. The mail forwarded under this system was cancelled at San Roque with a horizontal barred oval, later replaced by a cartwheel type mark showing numeral 63. From 1857 combination covers showing the 2d. ship mail fee paid in British stamps and the inland postage by Spanish issues exist.

Stamps of Great Britain were issued for use in Gibraltar from 3 September 1857 (earliest recorded cover is dated 7 September 1857) to the end of 1885.

The initial supply contained 1d., 4d. and 6d. values. No supplies of the 2d. or 1s. were sent until the consignment of October 1857. No other values were supplied until early 1862.

For illustrations of the postmark types see BRITISH POST OFFICES ABROAD notes following GREAT BRITAIN.

Stamps of GREAT BRITAIN cancelled "G" as Type **1** *(3 Sept 1857 to 19 Feb 1859).*

Z1	1d. red-brown (1854) Die I, *wmk* Small Crown, *perf* 16	£400
Z2	1d. red-brown (1855), Die II, *wmk* Small Crown, *perf* 16	£700
Z3	1d. red-brown (1855), Die II, *wmk* Small Crown *perf* 14	£350
Z4	1d. red-brown (1855), Die II, *wmk* Large Crown, *perf* 14	90·00
Z5	1d. rose-red (1857), Die II, *wmk* Large Crown, *perf* 14	24·00
Z6	2d. blue (1855), *wmk* Small Crown, *perf* 14	£450
Z7	2d. blue (1855–58), *wmk* Large Crown, *perf* 16	£375
Z8	2d. blue (1855), *wmk* Large Crown, *perf* 14 ... *From* Plate Nos. 5, 6.	75·00
Z9	2d. blue (1858) (Plate No. 7)	£325
Z10	4d. rose (1857)	60·00
	a. Thick glazed paper	
Z11	6d. lilac (1856)	42·00
Z12	6d. lilac (1856) (blued *paper*)	£850
Z13	1s. green (1856)	£120
	a. Thick paper	
Z14	1s. green (1856) (blued *paper*)	£1500

Stamps of GREAT BRITAIN cancelled "A 26" as in Types **2**, **5**, **11** *or* **14** *(20 Feb 1859 to 31 Dec 1885).*

Z15	½d. rose-red (1870–79) ... *From* Plate Nos. 4, 5, 6, 8, 10, 11, 12, 13, 14, 15, 19, 20.	32·00
Z16	1d. red-brown (1841), *imperf*	£1800
Z17	1d. red-brown (1855), *wmk* Large Crown, *perf* 14	£200
Z18	1d. rose-red (1857), *wmk* Large Crown, *perf* 14	13·00
Z19	1d. rose-red (1864–79) ... *From* Plate Nos. 71, 72, 73, 74 ,76, 78, 79, 80, 81, 82, 83, 84, 85, 86, 87, 88, 89, 90, 91, 92, 93, 94, 95, 96, 97, 98, 99, 100, 101, 102, 103, 104, 105, 106, 107, 108, 109, 110, 111, 112, 113, 114, 115, 116, 117, 118, 119, 120, 121, 122, 123, 124, 125, 127, 129, 130, 131, 132, 133, 134, 135, 136, 137, 138, 139, 140, 141, 142, 143, 144, 145, 146, 147, 148, 149, 150, 151, 152, 153, 154, 155, 156, 157, 158, 159, 160, 161, 162, 163, 164, 165, 166, 167, 168, 169, 170, 171, 172, 173, 174, 175, 176, 177, 178, 179, 180, 181, 182, 183, 184, 185, 186, 187, 188, 189, 190, 191, 192, 193, 194, 195, 196, 197, 198, 199, 200, 201, 202, 203, 204, 205, 206, 207, 208, 209, 210, 211, 212, 213, 214, 215, 216, 217, 218, 219, 220, 221, 222, 223, 224, 225.	22·00
Z20	1½d. lake-red (1870) (Plate No. 3)	£600
Z21	2d. blue (1855), *wmk* Large Crown, *perf* 14. Plate No. 6.	£150
Z22	2d. blue (1858–69) ... *From* Plate Nos. 7, 8, 9, 12, 13, 14, 15.	22·00
Z23	2½d. rosy mauve (1875) (blued *paper*) ... *From* Plate Nos. 1, 2, 3.	£100
Z24	2½d. rosy mauve (1875–76) ... *From* Plate Nos. 1, 2, 3.	28·00
Z25	2½d. rosy mauve (*Error of Lettering*)	£2250
Z26	2½d. rosy mauve (1876–79) ... *From* Plate Nos. 3, 4, 5, 6, 7, 8, 9, 10, 11, 12, 13, 14, 15, 16, 17.	21·00
Z27	2½d. blue (1880–81) ... *From* Plate Nos. 17, 18, 19, 20.	13·00
Z28	2½d. blue (1881) (Plate Nos. 21, 22, 23) ... *From*	10·00
Z29	3d. carmine-rose (1862)	£250
Z30	3d. rose (1865) (Plate No. 4)	70·00
Z31	3d. rose (1867–73) ... *From* Plate Nos. 4, 5, 6, 7, 8, 9, 10.	48·00
Z32	3d. rose (1873–76) ... *From* Plate Nos. 11, 12, 14, 15, 16, 17, 18, 19, 20.	60·00
Z33	3d. rose (1881) (Plate Nos. 20, 21)	
Z34	3d. lilac (1883) (3d. *on* 3d.)	£160
Z35	4d. rose (1857)	80·00
Z36	4d. red (1862) (Plate Nos. 3, 4) ... *From*	48·00
Z37	4d. vermilion (1865–73) ... *From* Plate Nos. 7, 8, 9, 10, 11, 12, 13, 14.	30·00
Z38	4d. vermilion (1876) (Plate No. 15)	£300
Z39	4d. sage-green (1877) (Plate Nos. 15, 16)	£130
Z40	4d. grey-brown (1880) *wmk* Large Garter. Plate No. 17.	£300
Z41	4d. grey-brown (1880) *wmk* Crown ... *From* Plate Nos. 17, 18.	65·00
Z42	6d. lilac (1856)	42·00
Z43	6d. lilac (1862) (Plate Nos. 3, 4) ... *From*	38·00
Z44	6d. lilac (1865–67) (Plate Nos. 5, 6) ... *From*	32·00
Z45	6d. lilac (1867) (Plate No. 6)	45·00
Z46	6d. violet (1867–70) (Plate Nos. 6, 8, 9).. *From*	32·00
Z47	6d. buff (1872–73) (Plate Nos. 11, 12) .... *From*	£150
Z48	6d. chestnut (1872) (Plate No. 11)	35·00
Z49	6d. grey (1873) (Plate No. 12)	95·00
Z50	6d. grey (1874–80) ... *From* Plate Nos. 13, 14, 15, 16, 17.	32·00
Z51	6d. grey (1881) (Plate Nos. 17, 18)	£275
Z52	6d. lilac (1883) (6d. *on* 6d.)	£110
Z53	8d. orange (1876)	£550
Z54	9d. bistre (1862)	£325
Z55	9d. straw (1862)	£700
Z56	9d. straw (1865)	£650
Z57	9d. straw (1867)	£200
Z58	10d. red-brown (1867)	£150
Z59	1s. green (1856)	£110
Z60	1s. green (1862)	70·00
Z61	1s. green (1862) ("K" *variety*)	£2250
Z62	1s. green (1865) (Plate No. 4)	60·00
Z63	1s. green (1867–73) (Plate Nos. 4, 5, 6, 7) ... *From*	28·00
Z64	1s. green (1873–77) ... *From* Plate Nos. 8, 9, 10, 11, 12, 13.	70·00
Z65	1s. orange-brown (1880) (Plate No. 13)	£400
Z66	1s. orange-brown (1881) ... *From* Plate Nos. 13, 14.	£110
Z67	2s. blue (1867)	£275
Z68	5s. rose (1867) (Plate No. 1)	£900

1880.

Z69	½d. deep green	27·00
Z70	½d. pale green	27·00
Z71	1d. Venetian red	26·00
Z72	1½d. Venetian red	£300
Z73	2d. pale rose	70·00
Z74	2d. deep rose	70·00
Z75	5d. indigo	£140

1881.

Z76	1d. lilac (14 *dots*)	32·00
Z77	1d. lilac (16 *dots*)	10·00

1884.

Z78	½d. slate-blue	25·00
Z79	2d. lilac	£100
Z80	2½d. lilac	18·00
Z81	3d. lilac	
Z82	4d. dull green	£180
Z83	6d. dull green	

POSTAL FISCAL

Z83*a*	1d. purple (Die 4) (1878) *wmk* Small Anchor.	£700
Z84	1d. purple (1881), *wmk* Orb	£1100

PRICES FOR STAMPS ON COVER TO 1945

Nos. 1/2	*from* × 25
No. 3	*from* × 10
No. 4	*from* × 25
Nos. 5/6	*from* × 8
Nos. 7/33	*from* × 6
Nos. 39/45	*from* × 5
Nos. 46/109	*from* × 3
Nos. 110/13	*from* × 4
Nos. 114/17	*from* × 3
Nos. 118/20	*from* × 5
Nos. 121/31	*from* × 3

(1)

1886 (1 Jan). *Contemporary types of Bermuda optd with T* **1** *by D.L.R.* Wmk Crown CA. P 14.

1	**9**	½d. dull green	16·00	8·00
2	**1**	1d. rose-red	70·00	4·25
3	**2**	2d. purple-brown	£130	80·00
		w. Wmk inverted		
4	**11**	2½d. ultramarine	£160	3·25
		a. Optd in blue-black	£500	£150
		w. Wmk inverted	—	£450
5	**10**	4d. orange-brown	£170	95·00
6	**4**	6d. deep lilac	£275	£200
7	**5**	1s. yellow-brown	£450	£375
1/7 *Set of 7*			£1100	£700
1s/3s, 4as/7s Optd "Specimen" *Set of 7*			£3500	

PRINTER. All Gibraltar stamps to No. 109 were typographed by De La Rue & Co, Ltd.

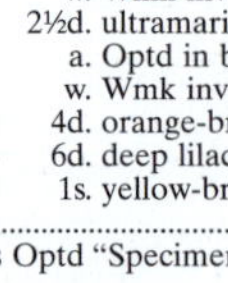

2

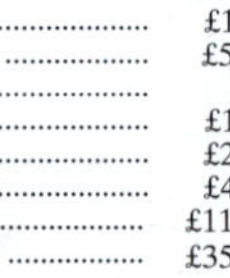

3

4

5

1886 (Nov)–**87**. Wmk Crown CA. P 14.

8	**2**	½d. dull green (1.87)	11·00	4·00
		w. Wmk inverted	†	£750
9	**3**	1d. rose (2.87)	45·00	4·50
10	**4**	2d. brown-purple (12.86)	30·00	24·00
		w. Wmk inverted	£550	
11	**5**	2½d. blue	80·00	2·75
		w. Wmk inverted	£275	75·00
12	**4**	4d. orange-brown (16.4.87)	80·00	75·00
13		6d. lilac (16.4.87)	£130	£130
14		1s. bistre (2.87)	£250	£200
		w. Wmk inverted		
8/14 *Set of 7*			£550	£400
8s/14s Optd "Specimen" *Set of 7*			£500	

Examples of Nos. 3, 6/7 and 14 are known showing a forged Gibraltar postmark dated "JU-13 87".

See also Nos. 39/45.

(6)

"5" with short foot (all stamps in 1st, 5th and 6th vertical columns (5c. on ½d.) or all stamps in 2nd vertical column (25c. on 2d., 25c. on 2½d., 50c. on 6d. and 75c. on 1s.)

1889 (1 Aug). *Surch as T* **6**.

15	**2**	5c. on ½d. green	7·00	25·00
		a. "5" with short foot	7·00	25·00
16	**3**	10c. on 1d. rose	12·00	13·00
17	**4**	25c. on 2d. brown-purple	4·75	9·00
		a. "5" with short foot	10·00	17·00
		ab. Small "I" (R. 6/2)	£100	£160
		b. Broken "N" (R. 10/5)	£100	£160
18	**5**	25c. on 2½d. bright blue	22·00	2·25
		a. "5" with short foot	38·00	5·00
		ab. Small "I" (R. 6/2)	£325	£100
		b. Broken "N" (R. 10/5)	£325	£100
19	**4**	40c. on 4d. orange-brown	50·00	70·00
20		50c. on 6d. bright lilac	55·00	75·00
		a. "5" with short foot	£110	£140
21		75c. on 1s. bistre	55·00	65·00
		a. "5" with short foot	£110	£130
15/21 *Set of 7*			£180	£225
15s/21s Optd "Specimen" *Set of 7*			£350	

10c., 40c. and 50c. values from this issue and that of 1889–96 are known bisected and used for half their value from various post offices in Morocco (*price on cover from* £500). These bisects were never authorised by the Gibraltar Post Office.

Broken "M" (Pls 1 & 2 R. 4/5)

7

Flat top to "C" (Pl 2 R. 4/4)

1889 (8 Oct*)–**96**. *Issue in Spanish currency.* Wmk Crown CA. P 14.

22	**7**	5c. green	4·50	80
		a. Broken "M"	£150	75·00
		w. Wmk inverted	£250	£200
23		10c. carmine	4·50	50
		b. Value omitted	£5500	
24		20c. olive-green and brown (2.1.96)	45·00	20·00
		w. Wmk inverted	—	£450
25		20c. olive-green (8.7.96)	13·00	75·00
		a. Flat top to "C"	£250	
26		25c. ultramarine	21·00	70
		a. Deep ultramarine	32·00	80
27		40c. orange-brown	3·75	3·25
28		50c. bright lilac (1890)	3·25	2·00
29		75c. olive-green (1890)	32·00	32·00
30		1p. bistre (11.89)	75·00	20·00
31		1p. bistre and ultramarine (6.95)	4·75	6·50
32		2p. black and carmine (2.1.96)	11·00	30·00
33		5p. slate-grey (12.89)	42·00	£100
22/33 *Set of 12*			£225	£250
22s/4s, 26s/33s Optd "Specimen" *Set of 11*			£400	

*Earliest recorded postmark date.

1898 (1 Oct). *Reissue in Sterling currency.* Wmk Crown CA. P 14.

39	**2**	½d. grey-green	9·00	1·75
		w. Wmk inverted		
40	**3**	1d. carmine	9·00	50
		w. Wmk inverted	†	£1400
41	**4**	2d. brown-purple and ultramarine	22·00	1·75
42	**5**	2½d. bright ultramarine	32·00	50
		w. Wmk inverted	£250	80·00
43	**4**	4d. orange-brown and green	18·00	5·50
		a. "FOUR PENCE" trimmed at top (Pl 2 R. 8/4)	£475	
44		6d. violet and red	42·00	22·00
45		1s. bistre and carmine	38·00	16·00
		w. Wmk inverted		
39/45 *Set of 7*			£150	42·00
39s/45s Optd "Specimen" *Set of 7*			£275	

No. 39 is greyer than No. 8, No. 40 brighter and deeper than No. 9 and No. 42 much brighter than No. 11.

8

9

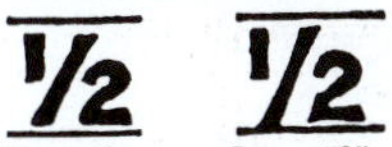

Normal Large "2"
2½d.

This occurs on R. 10/1 in each pane of 60. The diagonal stroke is also longer.

1903 (1 May). Wmk Crown CA. P 14.

46	**8**	½d. grey-green and green	10·00	9·50
47		1d. dull purple/*red*	30·00	60
48		2d. grey-green and carmine	22·00	28·00
49		2½d. dull purple and black/*blue*	7·50	60
		a. Large "2" in "½"	£325	£130
50		6d. dull purple and violet	24·00	21·00
51		1s. black and carmine	28·00	35·00
52	**9**	2s. green and blue	£150	£225
53		4s. dull purple and green	£100	£180
54		8s. dull purple and black/*blue*	£140	£160
55		£1 dull purple and black/*red*	£550	£650
46/55 *Set of* 10			£950	£1200
46s/55s Optd "Specimen" *Set of* 10			£500	

1904–08. Wmk Mult Crown CA. *Ordinary paper (½d. to 2d. and 6d. to 2s.) or chalk-surfaced paper (others)*. P 14.

56	**8**	½d. dull and bright green (4.4.04*)	15·00	2·50
		a. Chalk-surfaced paper (10.05)	13·00	7·00
57		1d. dull purple/*red* (6.9.04*)	17·00	50
		a. Bisected (½d.) (on card)	†	£1500
		bw. Wmk inverted	†	£750
		c. Chalk-surfaced paper (16.9.05)	6·50	85
58		2d. grey-green and carmine (9.1.05)	19·00	8·00
		a. Chalk-surfaced paper (2.07)	10·00	8·50
59		2½d. purple and black/*blue* (4.5.07)	35·00	90·00
		a. Large "2" in "½"	£600	£950
60		6d. dull purple and violet (19.4.06)	45·00	26·00
		a. Chalk-surfaced paper (4.08)	32·00	15·00
61		1s. black and carmine (13.10.05)	60·00	17·00
		a. Chalk-surfaced paper (4.06)	55·00	17·00
62	**9**	2s. green and blue (2.2.05)	90·00	£120
		a. Chalk-surfaced paper (10.07)	85·00	£100
63		4s. deep purple and green (6.08)	£300	£375
64		£1 deep purple and black/*red* (15.3.08)	£550	£650
56/64 *Set of* 9			£950	£1100

*Earliest known date of use.

1906 (Oct)–**12**. *Colours changed.* Wmk Mult Crown CA. *Chalk-surfaced paper (6d. to 8s.)*. P 14.

66	**8**	½d. blue-green (1907)	7·00	1·75
		x. Wmk reversed	†	£1400
67		1d. carmine	5·50	60
		a. Wmk sideways	£3750	£3500
		w. Wmk inverted	†	£550
68		2d. greyish slate (5.10)	8·50	11·00
69		2½d. ultramarine (6.07)	5·50	1·60
		a. Large "2" in "½"	£250	£120
70		6d. dull and bright purple (18.3.12)	£140	£375
71		1s. black/*green* (1910)	23·00	21·00
72	**9**	2s. purple and bright blue/*blue* (4.10)	50·00	48·00
73		4s. black and carmine (4.10)	£130	£160
		x. Wmk reversed	£1700	£1800
74		8s. purple and green (1911)	£200	£225
66/74 *Set of* 9			£500	£750
67s/74s Optd "Specimen" *Set of* 8			£600	

Examples of Nos. 54, 55, 64 and 73/4 are known showing a forged oval registered postmark dated "6 OC 10".

10

11

1912 (17 July)–**24**. Wmk Mult Crown CA. *Ordinary paper (½d. to 2½d) or chalk-surfaced paper (others)*. P 14.

76	**10**	½d. blue-green	3·25	70
		a. Yellow-green (4.17)	5·50	1·75
		w. Wmk inverted	†	£1100
		x. Wmk reversed	†	£1500
77		1d. carmine-red	3·50	75
		a. Scarlet (6.16)	4·00	1·25
		ay. Wmk inverted and reversed		
78		2d. greyish slate	9·50	1·50
79		2½d. deep bright blue	9·00	2·00
		a. Large "2" in "½"	£250	£140
		b. Pale ultramarine (1917)	7·00	2·00
		ba. Large "2" in "½"	£275	£140
80		6d. dull purple and mauve	9·00	17·00
81		1s. black/*green*	10·00	3·25
		a. Ordinary paper (8.18)	£600	
		b. On blue-green, olive back (1919)	18·00	26·00
		c. On emerald surface (12.23)	27·00	65·00
		d. On emerald back (3.24)	20·00	95·00
		ds. Optd "Specimen"	75·00	
82	**11**	2s. dull purple and blue/*blue*	26·00	3·50
83		4s. black and carmine	32·00	55·00
84		8s. dull purple and green	80·00	£100
85		£1 dull purple and black/*red*	£140	£225
76/85 *Set of* 10			£275	£375
76s/85s Optd "Specimen" *Set of* 10			£500	

WAR TAX
(12)

1918 (15 Apr). *Optd with T* **12** *by Beanland, Malin & Co, Gibraltar.*

86	**10**	½d. green	1·00	1·75
		a. Opt double	£850	
		w. Wmk inverted	£550	
		y. Wmk inverted and reversed	£475	

Two printings of this overprint exist, the second being in slightly heavier type on a deeper shade of green.

3 PENCE **THREE PENCE**
(I) (II)

1921–27. Wmk Mult Script CA. *Chalk-surfaced paper (6d. to 8s.)*. P 14.

89	**10**	½d. green (25.4.27)	1·50	1·50
90		1d. carmine-red (2.21)	1·75	1·00
91		1½d. chestnut (1.12.22)	2·00	55
		a. Pale chestnut (7.24)	1·75	30
		w. Wmk inverted	†	£900
93		2d. grey (17.2.21)	1·25	1·25
94		2½d. bright blue (2.21)	20·00	45·00
		a. Large "2" in "½"	£500	£700
95		3d. bright blue (I) (1.1.22)	3·00	4·25
		a. Ultramarine	2·50	1·50
97		6d. dull purple and mauve (1.23)	6·00	4·25
		a. Bright purple & magenta (22.7.26)	1·60	3·50
98		1s. black/*emerald* (20.6.24)	10·00	21·00
99	**11**	2s. grey-purple and blue/*blue* (20.6.24)	19·00	70·00
		a. Reddish purple and blue/blue (1925)	7·00	42·00
100		4s. black and carmine (20.6.24)	65·00	£110
101		8s. dull purple and green (20.6.24)	£250	£425
89/101 *Set of* 11			£325	£600
89s/101s Optd "Specimen" *Set of* 11			£600	

The ½d. exists in coils, constructed from normal sheets, first issued in 1937.

1925 (15 Oct)–**32**. *New values and colours changed.* Wmk Mult Script CA. *Chalk-surfaced paper*. P 14.

102	**10**	1s. sage-green and black (8.1.29)	14·00	26·00
		a. Olive and black (1932)	14·00	15·00
103	**11**	2s. red-brown and black (8.1.29)	10·00	32·00
104		2s.6d. green and black	10·00	21·00
105		5s. carmine and black	16·00	60·00
106		10s. deep ultramarine and black	32·00	70·00
107		£1 red-orange and black (16.11.27)	£160	£250
108		£5 violet and black	£1400	£5000
		s. Optd "Specimen"	£700	
102/7 *Set of* 6			£200	£400
102s/7s Optd or Perf (1s., 2s.) "Specimen" *Set of* 6			£425	

Examples of Nos. 83/5, 99/101 and 102/8 are known showing forged oval registered postmarks dated "24 JA 25" or "6 MY 35".

1930 (11 Apr). *T* **10** *inscribed "THREE PENCE".* Wmk Mult Script CA. P 14.

109		3d. ultramarine (II)	7·50	2·00
		s. Perf "Specimen"	75·00	

13 The Rock of Gibraltar

(Des Capt. H. St. C. Garrood. Recess D.L.R.)

1931–33. Wmk Mult Script CA. P 14.

110	**13**	1d. scarlet (1.7.31)	2·50	2·50
		a. Perf 13½×14	16·00	6·50
111		1½d. red-brown (1.7.31)	1·75	2·25
		a. Perf 13½×14	13·00	4·00
112		2d. pale grey (1.11.32)	6·50	1·75
		a. Perf 13½×14	17·00	3·25
113		3d. blue (1.6.33)	5·50	3·00
		a. Perf 13½×14	26·00	40·00
110/13 *Set of* 4			15·00	8·50
110a/13a *Set of* 4			65·00	48·00
110s/13s Perf "Specimen" *Set of* 4			£170	

Figures of value take the place of both corner ornaments at the base of the 2d. and 3d.

1935 (6 May). *Silver Jubilee. As Nos. 91/4 of Antigua but ptd by B.W.* P 11×12.

114		2d. ultramarine and grey-black	1·60	2·50
		a. Extra flagstaff	65·00	90·00
		b. Short extra flagstaff	£140	£160
		c. Lightning conductor	85·00	£110
		d. Flagstaff on right-hand turret	£250	£275
		e. Double flagstaff	£250	£275
115		3d. brown and deep blue	3·25	3·75
		a. Extra flagstaff	£325	£375
		b. Short extra flagstaff	£300	£350
		c. Lightning conductor	£350	£400
116		6d. green and indigo	10·00	14·00
		a. Extra flagstaff	£250	£300
		b. Short extra flagstaff	£450	£450
		c. Lightning conductor	£250	£300
117		1s. slate and purple	12·00	15·00
		a. Extra flagstaff	£225	£250
		b. Short extra flagstaff	£450	£450
		c. Lightning conductor	£250	£275
114/17 *Set of* 4			24·00	32·00
114s/17s Perf "Specimen" *Set of* 4			£200	

For illustrations of plate varieties see Omnibus section following Zanzibar.

1937 (12 May). *Coronation. As Nos. 95/7 of Antigua.* P 11×11½.

118		½d. green	25	50
119		2d. grey-black	1·50	3·25
120		3d. blue	2·75	3·25
118/20 *Set of* 3			4·00	6·25
118s/20s Perf "Specimen" *Set of* 3			£150	

14 King George VI

15 Rock of Gibraltar

16 The Rock (North Side)

17 Europa Point

18 Moorish Castle

19 Southport Gate

20 Eliott Memorial

21 Government House

22 Catalan Bay

Ape on rock (R. 1/5)

Bird on memorial (R. 9/3)

Broken second "R" in "GIBRALTAR" (Frame Pl 2 R. 9/4)

(Des Captain H. St. C. Garrood. Recess D.L.R.)

1938 (25 Feb)–**51**. *T* **14/22**. *Mult Script CA.*

121	**14**	½d. deep green (P 13½×14)	10	40
122	**15**	1d. yellow-brown (P 14)	26·00	2·25
		a. Perf 13½ (1940)	27·00	2·25
		ab. Perf 13½. Wmk sideways (1940)	6·50	7·00
		b. Perf 13. Wmk sideways. *Red-brown* (1942)	50	60
		c. Perf 13. Wmk sideways. *Deep brown* (1944)	2·00	3·50
		d. Perf 13. *Red-brown* (1949)	3·50	1·50
123		1½d. carmine (P 14)	35·00	75
		a. Perf 13½	£250	30·00
123*b*		1½d. slate-violet (P 13) (1.1.43)	50	1·50
124	**16**	2d. grey (P 14)	29·00	40
		aa. Ape on rock	£350	55·00
		a. Perf 13½ (1940)	3·50	35
		ab. Perf 13½. Wmk sideways (1940)	£700	42·00
		b. Perf 13. Wmk sideways (1943)	1·00	1·50
		ba. "A" of "CA" missing from wmk	£1200	
124*c*		2d. carm (P 13) (*wmk sideways*) (15.7.44)	50	60
125	**17**	3d. light blue (P 13½)	27·00	1·00
		a. Perf 14	£130	5·00
		b. Perf 13 (1942)	50	30
		ba. Greenish blue (2.51)	4·00	1·50
125*c*		5d. red-orange (P 13) (1.10.47)	1·25	1·25
126	**18**	6d. carm & grey-violet (P 13½) (16.3.38)	48·00	3·00
		a. Perf 14	£120	1·25
		b. Perf 13 (1942)	5·50	1·75
		c. Perf 13. *Scarlet and grey-violet* (1945)	6·00	3·75
127	**19**	1s. black and green (P 14) (16.3.38)	42·00	24·00
		a. Perf 13½	70·00	6·00
		b. Perf 13 (1942)	3·25	4·25

		ba. Broken "R"	£375	
128	20	2s. black and brown (P 14) (16.3.38)	65·00	22·00
		a. Perf 13½	£130	35·00
		b. Perf 13 (1942)	5·00	6·50
		ba. Broken "R"	£400	
		bb. Bird on memorial	£300	
129	21	5s. black and carmine (P 14) (16.3.38)	95·00	£160
		a. Perf 13½	42·00	14·00
		b. Perf 13 (1944)	23·00	17·00
		ba. Broken "R"	£600	
130	22	10s. black and blue (P 14) (16.3.38)	65·00	£120
		a. Perf 13 (1943)	38·00	25·00
		ab. Broken "R"	£850	
131	14	£1 orange (P 13½×14) (16.3.38)	38·00	48·00
121/31 Set of 14			£130	90·00
121s/31s Perf "Specimen" *Set of* 14			£750	

The ½d., 1d. and both colours of the 2d. exist in coils constructed from normal sheets. These were originally joined vertically, but, because of technical problems, the 1d. and 2d. grey were subsequently issued in horizontal coils. The 2d. carmine only exists in the horizontal version.

Examples of Nos. 129/31 are known showing forged oval registered postmarks dated "6 OC 43", "18 OC 43", "3 MR 44" and "4 AU 44".

1946 (12 Oct). *Victory. As Nos. 110/11 of Antigua.*

132	½d. green	10	1·25
133	3d. ultramarine	50	1·25
132s/3s Perf "Specimen" *Set of* 2		£110	

1948 (1 Dec). *Royal Silver Wedding. As Nos. 112/13 of Antigua.*

134	½d. green	1·25	2·50
135	£1 brown-orange	55·00	75·00

1949 (10 Oct). *75th Anniv of Universal Postal Union. As Nos. 114/17 of Antigua.*

136	2d. carmine	1·00	1·25
137	3d. deep blue	2·00	1·50
138	6d. purple	1·25	2·00
139	1s. blue-green	1·00	3·25
136/9 *Set of* 4		4·75	7·25

NEW CONSTITUTION 1950

(23)

1950 (1 Aug). *Inauguration of Legislative Council. Nos. 124c, 125ba, 126b and 127b optd as T* **23**.

140	16	2d. carmine	30	1·50
141	–	3d. greenish blue	65	1·00
142	–	6d. carmine and grey-violet	75	2·00
		a. Opt double	£950	£1100
143	–	1s. black and green (R.)	75	2·00
		a. Broken "R"	£100	
140/3 *Set of* 4			2·25	6·00

On some examples of No. 142a the two impressions are almost coincident.

Stop before "2" in "½" in right-hand value tablet (Pl. 1A–5A, R. 4/4)

1953 (2 June). *Coronation. As No. 120 of Antigua.*

144	½d. black and bronze-green	50	1·50
	a. Stop before "2" in "½"	6·00	

24 Cargo and Passenger Wharves

25 South View from Straits

26 Gibraltar Fish Canneries

27 Southport Gate

28 Sailing in the Bay

29 *Saturnia* (liner)

30 Coaling wharf

31 Airport

32 Europa Point

33 Straits from Buena Vista

34 Rosia Bay and Straits

35 Main Entrance, Government House

36 Tower of Homage, Moorish Castle

37 Arms of Gibraltar

Major re-entry causing doubling of "ALTA" in "GIBRALTAR" (R. 4/6)

(Des N. Cummings. Recess (except £1, centre litho) De La Rue)

1953 (19 Oct)–**59**. *T* **24/37**. Wmk Mult Script CA. P 13.

145	24	½d. indigo and grey-green	15	30
146	25	1d. bluish green	1·50	40
		a. Deep bluish green (31.12.57)	3·00	1·00
147	26	1½d. black	1·00	1·50
148	27	2d. deep olive-brown	1·75	1·00
		a. Sepia (18.6.58)	2·75	1·25
149	28	2½d. carmine	4·25	1·25
		a. Deep carmine (11.9.56)	5·00	1·25
		aw. Wmk inverted	£400	
150	29	3d. light blue	4·00	10
		a. Deep greenish blue (8.6.55)	7·50	25
		b. Greenish blue (18.6.58)	15·00	1·40
151	30	4d. ultramarine	5·50	3·50
		a. Blue (17.6.59)	18·00	8·00
152	31	5d. maroon	1·25	1·00
		a. Major re-entry	35·00	
		b. Deep maroon (31.12.57)	2·50	2·25
		ba. Major re-entry	50·00	
153	32	6d. black and pale blue	2·50	1·25
		a. Black and blue (24.4.57)	5·00	1·75
		b. Black and grey-blue (17.6.59)	8·00	4·50
154	33	1s. pale blue and red-brown	50	80
		a. Pale blue and deep red-brown (27.3.56)	50	1·00
155	34	2s. orange and reddish violet	32·00	8·50
		a. Orange and violet (17.6.59)	24·00	5·50
156	35	5s. deep brown	35·00	13·00
157	36	10s. reddish brown and ultramarine	45·00	38·00
158	37	£1 scarlet and orange-yellow	45·00	45·00
145/58 *Set of* 14			£150	£100

Nos. 145/6, 148 and 150 exist in coils, constructed from normal sheets.

1954 (10 May). *Royal Visit. As No. 150 but inscr "ROYAL VISIT 1954" at top.*

159	3d. greenish blue	20	20

38 Gibraltar Candytuft

39 Moorish Castle

40 Rock and Badge of Gibraltar Regiment

1d. Retouch right of flag appears as an extra flag (Pl. 1B, R. 5/5)

1d. Jagged brown flaw in wall to right of gate appears as a crack (Pl. 1B, R. 2/5)

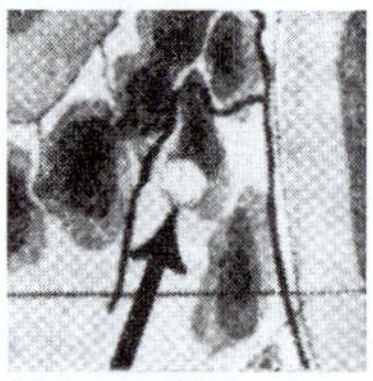

6d. Large white spot on map S.W. of "CEUTA" (Pl. 1B, R. 4/5)

(Des J. Celecia (½d. 2d., 2½d., 2s., 10s.), N. A. Langdon 1d. 3d., 6d. 7d. 9d., 1s.), M. Bonilla (4d.), L. V. Gomez (5s.), Sgt. T. A. Griffths (£1). Recess (£1) or photo (others) D.L.R.)

1960 (29 Oct)–**62**. *Designs as T* **38/9**, *and T* **40**. W w **12** (upright). P 14 (£1) or 13 (others).

160	½d. bright purple and emerald-green	15	50
161	1d. black and yellow-green	20	10
	a. Crack in wall	5·00	
	b. "Phantom flag"	5·00	
162	2d. indigo and orange-brown	70	20
163	2½d. black and blue	75	80
	a. Black and grey-blue (16.10.62)	65	30
164	3d. deep blue and red-orange	30	10
165	4d. deep red-brown and turquoise	2·75	70
166	6d. sepia and emerald	70	70
	a. White spot on map	14·00	
167	7d. indigo and carmine-red	2·00	1·75
168	9d. grey-blue and greenish blue	1·00	1·00
169	1s. sepia and bluish green	1·50	70
170	2s. chocolate and ultramarine	16·00	2·75
171	5s. turquoise-blue and olive-brown	8·00	6·00
172	10s. yellow and blue	21·00	15·00
173	£1 black and brown-orange	15·00	14·00
160/73 *Set of* 14		60·00	40·00

Designs: *Horiz*—2d. St. George's Hall; 3d. The Rock by moonlight; 4d. Catalan Bay; 1s. Barbary Ape; 2s. Barbary Partridge; 5s. Blue Rock Thrush. *Vert*—2½d. The Keys; 6d. Map of Gibraltar; 7d. Air terminal; 9d. American War Memorial; 10s. Rock Lily (*Narcissus niveus*).

The 1d. imperforate comes from stolen printer's waste.

Vignette cylinders 2A and 2B, used for printings of the 9d. from 13 March 1962 onwards, had a finer screen (250 dots per inch instead of the 200 of the original printing) (*Price* £1.50 *un* or *us*).

Nos. 160/2, 164 and 166 exist in coils, constructed from normal sheets.

See also No. 199.

1963 (4 June). *Freedom from Hunger. As No. 146 of Antigua.*

174	9d. sepia	3·00	1·50

1963 (2 Sept). *Red Cross Centenary. As Nos. 147/8 of Antigua.*

175	1d. red and black	1·00	1·75
176	9d. red and blue	3·00	3·75

1964 (23 Apr). *400th Birth Anniv of William Shakespeare. As No. 164 of Antigua.*

177	7d. bistre-brown	50	20

NEW CONSTITUTION 1964.

(44)

1964 (16 Oct). *New Constitution. Nos. 164 and 166 optd with T* **44**.

178	3d. deep blue and red-orange	20	10
179	6d. sepia and emerald	20	60
	a. No stop after "1964" (R.2/5)	16·00	28·00
	b. White spot on map	12·00	

1965 (17 May). *I.T.U. Centenary. As Nos. 166/7 of Antigua.*

180	4d. light emerald and yellow	2·00	50
	w. Wmk inverted	28·00	
181	2s. apple-green and deep blue	5·50	3·25

1965 (25 Oct). *International Co-operation Year. As Nos. 168/9 of Antigua.*

182	½d. deep bluish green and lavender	20	2·25
183	4d. reddish purple and turquoise-green	70	50

The value of the ½d. stamp is shown as "1/2".

1966 (24 Jan). *Churchill Commemoration. As Nos. 170/3 of Antigua. Printed in black, cerise and gold and with background in colours stated.*

184	½d. new blue	20	2·25
	w. Wmk inverted	45·00	
185	1d. deep green	30	10
186	4d. brown	1·25	10
187	9d. bluish violet	1·25	2·50
184/7 *Set of* 4		2·75	4·50

1966 (1 July). *World Cup Football Championship. As Nos. 176/7 of Antigua.*

188	2½d. violet, yellow-green, lake and yellow and brown	75	1·00
189	6d. chocolate, blue-green, lake and yellow and brown	1·00	50

PRINTERS. All stamps from here to No. 239 were printed in photogravure by Harrison and Sons Ltd, London.

53 Red Seabream

4d. Break at top right corner of "d" of value (R. 9/3).

(Des A. Ryman)

1966 (27 Aug). *European Sea Angling Championships, Gibraltar. T* **53** *and similar designs.* W w **12** (sideways on 1s.). P 13½×14(1s.) or 14×13½ (others)

190	4d. rosine, bright blue and black	30	10
	a. Broken "d"	4·00	
191	7d. rosins, deep olive-green and black	30	70
	a. Black (value and inscr) omitted	£1300	
	w. Wmk inverted	3·00	
192	1s. lake-brown, emerald and black	50	30
190/2	*Set of* 3	1·00	1·00

Designs: *Horiz*—7d. Red Scorpionfish. *Vert*—1s. Stone Bass.

1966 (20 Sept). *Inauguration of W.H.O. Headquarters, Geneva. As Nos. 178/9 of Antigua.*

193	6d. black, yellow-green and light blue	2·75	1·75
194	9d. black, light purple and yellow-brown	3·25	2·25

56 "Our Lady of Europa"

(Des A. Ryman)

1966 (15 Nov). *Centenary of Re-enthronement of "Our Lady of Europa".* W w **12**. P 14×14½.

195	**56**	2s. bright blue and black	30	80

1966 (1 Dec). *20th Anniv of U.N.E.S.C.O. As Nos. 196/8 of Antigua.*

196	2d. slate-violet, red, yellow and orange	35	10
197	7d. orange-yellow, violet and deep olive	1·75	10
198	5s. black, bright purple and orange	3·75	3·00
196/8	*Set of* 3	5·25	3·00

1966 (23 Dec). *As No. 165 but* wmk w **12** sideways.

199	4d. deep red-brown and turquoise	30	1·75

57 H.M.S. *Victory*

½d. Gash in shape of boomerang in topsail (Pl. 1A, R. 8/4).

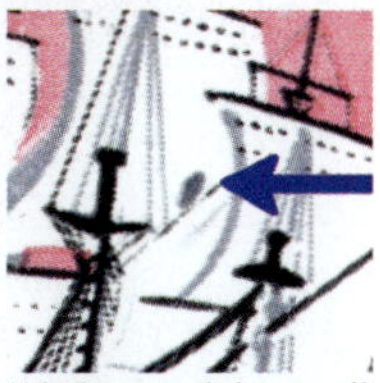

½d. Grey mark in topsail resembling a stain (Pl. 1A, R. 8/6).

7d. Bold shading on sail appearing as patch (Pl. 1A, R. 10/5).

(Des A. Ryman)

1967 (3 Apr)–**69**. *Horiz designs as T* **57**. *Multicoloured.* W w **12**. P 14×14½.

200	½d. Type **57**	10	20
	a. Grey (sails, etc) omitted	£500	
	b. Gash in sail	1·50	
	c. Stained sail	1·50	
201	1d. *Arab* (early steamer)	10	10
	w. Wmk inverted	3·25	2·75
202	2d. H.M.S. *Carmania* (merchant cruiser)	15	10
	a. Grey-blue (hull) omitted	£3750	
203	2½d. *Mons Calpe* (ferry)	40	30
204	3d. *Canberra* (liner)	20	10
	w. Wmk inverted	27·00	7·00
205	4d. H.M.S. *Hood* (battle cruiser)	30	10
	w. Wmk inverted		
205*a*	5d. *Mirror* (cable ship) (7.7.69)	2·00	55
	aw. Wmk inverted		
206	6d. *Xebec* (sailing vessel)	30	50
207	7d. *Amerigo Vespucci* (Italian cadet ship)	30	70
	a. Patched sail	10·00	
	w. Wmk inverted	17·00	
208	9d. *Raffaello* (liner)	30	1·25
209	1s. *Royal Katherine* (galleon)	30	35
210	2s. H.M.S. *Ark Royal* (aircraft carrier), 1937	3·50	2·50
211	5s. H.M.S. *Dreadnought* (nuclear submarine)	3·50	7·00
212	10s. *Neuralia* (liner)	14·00	23·00
213	£1 *Mary Celeste* (sailing vessel)	14·00	23·00
200/13	*Set of* 15	35·00	55·00

No. 202a results from the misaligning of the grey-blue cylinder. The bottom horizontal row of the sheet involved has this colour completely omitted except for the example above the cylinder numbers which shows the grey-blue "1A" towards the top of the stamp.

The ½d., 1d., 2d. 3d. 6d. 2s. 5s. and £1 exist with PVA gum as well as gum arabic, but the 5d. exists with PVA gum only.

Nos. 201/2, 204/5 and 206 exist in coils constructed from normal sheets.

58 Aerial Ropeway

(Des A. Ryman)

1967 (15 June). *International Tourist Year. T* **58** *and similar designs but horiz. Multicoloured.* W w **12** (sideways on 7d.). P 14½×14 (7d.) or 14×14½ (others).

214	7d. Type **58**	15	10
215	9d. Shark fishing	15	10
216	1s. Skin-diving	20	15
214/16	*Set of* 3	45	30

59 Mary, Joseph and Child Jesus

60 Church Window

1967 (1 Nov). *Christmas.* W w **12** (sideways* on 6d.). P 14.

217	**59**	2d. multicoloured	15	10
		w. Wmk inverted	1·25	
218	**60**	6d. multicoloured	15	10
		w. Wmk Crown to right of CA	£250	

*The normal sideways watermark shows Crown to left of CA, *as seen from the back of the stamp.*

61 Gen. Elliott and Route Map

62 Eliott directing Rescue Operations

(Des A. Ryman)

1967 (11 Dec). *250th Birth Anniv of General Eliott. Multicoloured designs as T* **61** *(4d. to 1s.) or T* **62**. W w **12** (sideways on horiz designs). P 14×15 (1s.) or 15×14 (others).

219	4d. Type **61**	15	10
220	9d. Heathfield Tower and Monument, Sussex (38×22 mm)	15	10
221	1s. General Eliott (22×38 mm)	15	10
222	2s. Type **62**	25	50
219/22	*Set of* 4	65	70

65 Lord Baden-Powell

(Des A. Ryman)

1968 (27 Mar). *60th Anniv of Gibraltar Scout Association. T* **65** *and similar horiz designs.* W w **12**. P 14×14½.

223	4d. buff and bluish violet	15	10
224	7d. ochre and blue-green	15	20
225	9d. bright blue, yellow-orange and black	15	30
226	1s. greenish yellow and emerald	15	30
223/6	*Set of* 4	55	75

Designs:—7d. Scout Flag over the Rock; 9d. Tent, scouts and salute; 1s. Scout badges.

66 Nurse and W.H.O. Emblem

68 King John signing Magna Carta

(Des A. Ryman)

1968 (1 July). *20th Anniv of World Health Organization. T* **66** *and similar horiz design.* W w **12**. P 14×14½.

227	2d. ultramarine, black and yellow	10	15
228	4d. slate, black and pink	10	10

Design:—4d. Doctor and W.H.O. emblem.

(Des A. Ryman)

1968 (26 Aug). *Human Rights Year. T* **68** *and similar vert design.* W w **12** (sideways). P 13½×14.

229	1s. yellow-orange, brown and gold	15	10
230	2s. myrtle and gold	15	20

Design:—2s. "Freedom" and Rock of Gibraltar.

70 Shepherd, Lamb and Star

72 Parliament Houses

(Des A. Ryman)

1968 (1 Nov). *Christmas. T* **70** *and similar vert design. Multicoloured.* W w **12**. P 14½×13½.

231	4d. Type **70**	10	10
	a. Gold (star) omitted	£475	
232	9d. Mary holding Holy Child	15	20

(Des A. Ryman)

1969 (26 May). *Commonwealth Parliamentary Association Conference. T* **72** *and similar designs.* W w **12** (sideways on 2s.). P 14×14½ (2s.) or 14½×14 (others).

233	4d. green and gold	10	10
234	9d. bluish violet and gold	10	10
235	2s. multicoloured	15	20
233/5	*Set of* 3	30	30

Designs: *Horiz*—9d. Parliamentary emblem and outline of "The Rock". *Vert*—2s. Clock Tower, Westminster (Big Ben) and arms of Gibraltar.

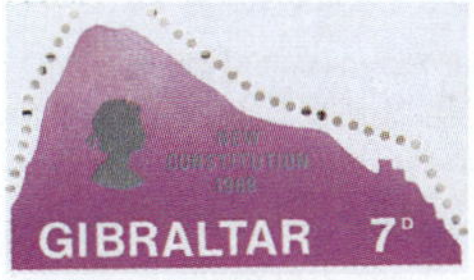

75 Silhouette of Rock, and Queen Elizabeth II

77 Soldier and Cap Badge, Royal Anglian Regiment, 1969

(Des A. Ryman)

1969 (30 July). *New Constitution.* W w **12**. P 14×13½ (in addition, the outline of the Rock is perforated).

236	**75**	½d. gold and orange	10	10
237		5d. silver and bright green	20	10
		a. Portrait and inscr in gold and silver*		
238		7d. silver and bright purple	20	10
239		5s. gold and ultramarine	65	1·10
236/9		*Set of* 4	1·00	1·25

*No. 237a was first printed with the head and inscription in gold and then in silver but displaced slightly to lower left.

(Des A. Ryman. Photo D.L.R.)

1969 (6 Nov). *Military Uniforms (1st series). T* **77** *and similar vert designs. Multicoloured.* W w **12**. P 14.

240	1d. Royal Artillery officer, 1758 and modern cap badge	15	10
241	6d. Type **77**	20	15

242 9d. Royal Engineers' Artificer, 1786 and modern cap badge 30 15
243 2s. Private, Fox's Marines, 1704 and modern Royal Marines cap badge 75 70
240/3 *Set of* 4 .... 1·25 1·00

Nos. 240/3 have a short history of the Regiment printed on the reverse side over the gum, therefore, once the gum is moistened the history disappears.

See also Nos. 248/51, 290/3, 300/3, 313/16, 331/4, 340/3 and 363/6.

80 "Madonna of the Chair" (detail, Raphael)

83 Europa Point

(Des A. Ryman. Photo Enschedé)

1969 (1 Dec). *Christmas. T* **80** *and similar vert designs. Multicoloured.* W w **12** (sideways). P 14 × Roulette 9.

244 5d. Type **80** 10 35
a. Strip of 3. Nos. 244/6 .... 45 1·00
245 7d. "Virgin and Child" (detail, Morales) 20 35
246 1s. "The Virgin of the Rocks" (detail, Leonardo da Vinci) 20 40
244/6 *Set of* 3 .... 45 1·00

Nos. 244/6 were issued together in *se-tenant* strips of three throughout the sheet.

(Des A. Ryman. Photo Enschedé)

1970 (8 June). *Europa Point.* W w **12**. P 13½.

247 **83** 2s. multicoloured 45 30
w. Wmk inverted .... 2·00 1·90

(Des A. Ryman. Photo D.L.R.)

1970 (28 Aug). *Military Uniforms (2nd series). Vert designs as T* **77**. *Multicoloured.* W w **12**. P 14.

248 2d. Royal Scots officer, 1839 and cap badge 25 10
249 5d. South Wales Borderers private, 1763 and cap badge 35 10
250 7d. Queens Royal Regiment private, 1742 and cap badge 35 10
251 2s. Royal Irish Rangers piper, 1969 and cap badge .... 1·00 90
248/51 Set of 4 .... 1·75 1·00

Nos. 248/51 have a short history of the Regiment printed on the reverse side under the gum.

88 No. 191a and Rock of Gibraltar

(Des A. Ryman. Litho D.L.R.)

1970 (18 Sept). *"Philympia 1970" Stamp Exhibition, London. T* **88** *and similar horiz design.* W w **12** (sideways). P 13.

252 1s. vermilion and bronze-green 15 10
253 2s. bright blue and magenta 25 65

Design:—2s. Victorian stamp (No. 23b) and Moorish Castle.

The stamps shown in the designs are well-known varieties with values omitted.

90 "The Virgin Mary" (stained-glass window by Gabriel Loire)

(Photo Enschedé)

1970 (1 Dec). *Christmas.* W w **12**. P 13×14.

254 **90** 2s. multicoloured 30 40

STAMP BOOKLETS

1906 (Oct). *Black on red cover. Stapled.*

SB1 2s.½d. booklet containing twenty-four ½d. and twelve 1d. (Nos. 56a, 67) in blocks of 6 ......

1912 (17 July). *Black on red cover with Edwardian cypher. Stapled.*

SB2 2s.½d. booklet containing twenty-four ½d. and twelve 1d. (Nos. 76/7) in blocks of 6 ....

POSTAGE DUE STAMPS

D 1

Normal

Large "d." (R. 9/6, 10/6)

4d. Ball of "d" broken and serif at top damaged (R. 9/5). Other stamps in 9th vertical row show slight breaks to ball of "d".

(Typo D.L.R.)

1956 (1 Dec). *Chalk-surfaced paper.* Wmk Mult Script CA. P 14.

D1 **D 1** 1d. green .... 1·50 4·25
D2 2d. sepia .... 1·50 2·75
a. Large "d" (R. 9/6, 10/6) .... 25·00
D3 4d. blue .... 1·75 5·00
a. Broken "d" .... 35·00
D1/3 *Set of* 3 .... 4·25 11·00

Gilbert and Ellice Islands

No organised postal service existed in the Gilbert and Ellice Islands before the introduction of stamp issues in January 1911. A New Zealand Postal Agency was, however, provided on Fanning Island, one of the Line Islands, primarily for the use of the staff of the Pacific Cable Board cable station which was established in 1902. The agency opened on 29 November 1902 and continued to operate until replaced by a Protectorate post office on 14 February 1939. The cable station closed on 16 January 1964. Fanning Island is now known as Tabuaeran.

Z 1

The following NEW ZEALAND *stamps are known postmarked on Fanning Island with Type* Z **1** (*in use from November 1902 until November 1936. The earliest known cover is postmarked 20 December 1902.*

1882–1900 Q.V. (P 11) ½d., 1d., 2d. (*Nos.* 236/8)
1898 Pictorials (*no wmk*) 1d., 2d. (*Nos.* 247/8)
1900 Pictorials (*W* **38**) ½d. 1½d., 2d. (*Nos.* 273, 275b, 276)
1901 1d. "Universal" (*W* **38**) (*No.* 278)
1902 1d. "Universal" (*no wmk*) (*No.* 295)
1902 ½d. Pictorial (*W* **43**) (*No.* 302b)
1902–09 Pictorials (*W* **43**) 2d., 2½d., 3d., 6d., 8d., 9d., 1s., 2s., 5s. (*Nos.* 309, 312/13, 315, 319/20, 326, 328/9)
1907–08 Pictorials (*W* **43**) 4d. (*No.* 379)
1908 1d. "Universal" (*De La Rue paper*) 1d. (*No.* 386)
1909–12 King Edward VII (*typo*) ½d. (*No.* 387)
1909–16 King Edward VII (*recess*) 2d., 3d., 4d., 5d., 6d., 8d., 1s. (*Nos.* 388/91, 393/6, 398)
1909–26 1d. "Universal" (*W* **43**) 1d. (*Nos.* 405, 410)
1915–30 King George V (*recess*) 1½d., 2d. bright violet, 2½d., 3d., 4d. bright violet, 4½d., 6d., 7½d., 9d., 1s. (*Nos.* 416/17, 419/20, 422/3, 425/6, 429/30)
1915–34 King George V (*typo*) ½d., 1½d. (all 3), 2d., 3d. (*Nos.* 435/40, 446, 448, 449)
1915 "WAR STAMP" opt ½d. (*No.* 452)
1920 Victory 1d., 1½d. (*Nos.* 454/5)
1922 2d. on ½d. (*No.* 459)
1923–25 Penny Postage 1d. (*No.* 460)
1926–34 Admiral design 1d. (*No.* 468)
1935–36 Pictorials ½d., 2d., 4d., 8d., 1s. (*Nos.* 556, 559, 562, 565, 567)
1935 Silver Jubilee ½d., 1d., 6d. (*Nos.* 573/5)
1936 Anzac 1d. + 1d. (*No.* 592)

Z 2

The following NEW ZEALAND *stamps are known postmarked on Fanning Island with Type* Z **2** (*in use from 7 December 1936 to 13 February 1939*):

1935–36 Pictorials (*W* **43**) 1d (*No.* 557)
1936–39 Pictorials (*W* **98**) ½d., 1d., 1½d. (*Nos.* 577/9)
1936 Chambers of Commerce Congress ½d. (*No.* 593)
1936 Health 1d.+1d. (*No.* 598)
1937 Coronation 1d., 2½d., 6d. (*Nos.* 599/601)
1938–39 King George VI ½d., 1d., 1½d. (*Nos.* 603, 605, 607)

The schooner which carried the mail from Fanning Island also called at Washington Island, another of the Line group. Problems arose, however, as the authorities insisted that mail from Washington must first pass through the Fanning Island Postal Agency before being forwarded which resulted in considerable delays. Matters were resolved by the opening of a New Zealand Postal Agency on Washington Island which operated from 1 February 1921 until the copra plantations were closed in early 1923. The postal agency was re-established on 15 May 1924, but finally closed on 30 March 1934. Covers from this second period occur with incorrectly dated postmarks. Manuscript markings on New Zealand Nos. 578, 599/600 and 692 are unofficial and were applied during the resettlement of the island between 1937 and 1948. Washington Island is now known as Teraina.

Z 3

The following NEW ZEALAND stamps are known postmarked on Washington Island with Type Z **3**:

1909–16 King Edward VII 5d., 8d. (*Nos.* 402, 404*b*)
1915–30 King George V (*recess*) 6d., 7½d., 8d., 9d., 1s. (*Nos.* 425/7, 429/30)
1915–34 King George V (*typo*) ½d., 1½d., 2d., 3d. (*Nos.* 435, 438/9, 449)
1915 "WAR STAMP" opt ½d (*No.* 452)
1920 Victory 1d., 1½d., 6d. (*Nos.* 454/5, 457)
1922 2d. on ½d. (*No.* 459)
1926–34 Admiral design 1d. (*No.* 468/*a*)

The above information is based on a special survey undertaken by members of the Kiribati & Tuvalu Philatelic Society and the Pacific Islands Study Circle, co-ordinated by Mr. Michael Shaw.

PRICES FOR STAMPS ON COVER TO 1945

Nos. 1/7	*from* × 5
Nos. 8/11	*from* × 10
Nos. 12/23	*from* × 6
No. 24	—
No. 26	*from* × 15
Nos. 27/30	*from* × 6
No. 35	—
Nos. 36/9	*from* × 4
Nos. 40/2	*from* × 12
Nos. 43/54	*from* × 4
Nos. D1/8	*from* × 5

BRITISH PROTECTORATE

GILBERT&ELLICE

PROTECTORATE

(1)

2 Pandanus Pine

1911 (1 Jan). *Stamps of Fiji optd with T* **1**. Wmk Mult Crown CA. *Chalk-surfaced paper (5d. to 1s.).*

1	**23**	½d. green	4·75	45·00
2		1d. red	48·00	28·00
3	**24**	2d. grey	12·00	15·00
4	**23**	2½d. ultramarine	13·00	38·00
5		5d. purple and olive-green	50·00	80·00
6	**24**	6d. dull and bright purple	22·00	45·00
7	**23**	1s. black/*green* (R.)	22·00	60·00
1/7 *Set of* 7			£150	£275
1s/7s Optd "Specimen" *Set of* 7			£300	

The 2d. to 6d. are on special printings which were not issued without overprint.

Examples of Nos. 1/7 are known showing a forged Ocean Island postmark dated "JY 15 11".

(Recess D.L.R.)

1911 (Mar). Wmk Mult Crown CA. P 14.

8	**2**	½d. green	4·75	17·00
9		1d. carmine	2·00	7·00
		w. Wmk inverted	£425	
10		2d. grey	1·50	7·00
11		2½d. blue	5·00	11·00
8/11 *Set of* 4			11·50	38·00
8s/11s Optd "Specimen" *Set of* 4			£140	

3

WAR TAX

(5)

(Typo D.L.R.)

1912 (May)–**24**. *Die I (½d. to 5s.) or Die II (£1).* Wmk Mult Crown CA. *Chalk-surfaced paper (3d. to £1).* P 14.

12	**3**	½d. green (7.12)	50	4·50
		a. Yellow-green (1914)	4·50	11·00
13		1d. carmine (12.12)	2·25	7·00
		a. Scarlet (1915)	3·75	11·00
14		2d. greyish slate (1.16)	15·00	26·00
15		2½d. bright blue (1.16)	1·75	11·00
16		3d. purple/*yellow* (1918)	2·50	8·50
17		4d. black and red/*yellow* (10.12)	75	7·00
18		5d. dull purple and sage-green	1·75	6·00
19		6d. dull and bright purple	1·25	6·50
20		1s. black/*green*	1·25	5·50
21		2s. purple and blue/*blue* (10.12)	14·00	30·00
22		2s.6d. black and red/*blue* (10.12)	17·00	25·00
23		5s. green and red/*yellow* (10.12)	32·00	65·00
24		£1 purple and black/*red* (Die II) (3.24)	£550	£1400
12/24 Set of 13			£600	£1400
12s/24s Optd "Specimen" Set of 13			£600	

CROWN COLONY

1918 (June). *Optd with T* **5**.

26	**3**	1d. red	50	6·50
		s. Optd "Specimen"	65·00	

1922–27. *Die II.* Wmk Mult Script CA. *Chalk-surfaced paper (10s.).* P 14.

27	**3**	½d. green (1923)	3·25	3·25
28		1d. violet (1927)	4·50	5·50
29		1½d. scarlet (1924)	4·50	2·25
30		2d. slate-grey	7·00	30·00
35		10s. green and red/*emerald* (3.24)	£150	£350
27s/35s Optd "Specimen" *Set of* 5			£275	

Examples of most values between Nos. 12 and 35 are known showing part strikes of the forged postmark mentioned below Nos. 1/7. Collectors should exercise particular caution when buying used examples of Nos. 24 and 35.

1935 (6 May). *Silver Jubilee. As Nos. 91/4 of Antigua, but ptd by B.W.* P 11×12.

36	1d. ultramarine and grey-black	2·25	9·50
	d. Flagstaff on right-hand turret	£225	£325
	e. Double flagstaff	£350	
37	1½d. deep blue and scarlet	1·75	3·75
	d. Flagstaff on right-hand turret	£225	
	e. Double flagstaff	£350	
38	3d. brown and deep blue	5·50	16·00
	d. Flagstaff on right-hand turret	£350	
	e. Double flagstaff	£400	£500
39	1s. slate and purple	20·00	20·00
	d. Flagstaff on right-hand turret	£475	£500
	e. Double flagstaff	£550	£600
36/9 *Set of* 4		26·00	45·00
36s/9s Perf "Specimen" *Set of* 4		£150	

For illustrations of plate varieties see Omnibus section following Zanzibar.

1937 (12 May). *Coronation. As Nos. 95/7 of Antigua, but ptd by D.L.R.* P 14.

40	1d. violet	35	65
41	1½d. scarlet	35	65
42	3d. bright blue	40	70
40/2 *Set of* 3		1·00	1·75
40s/2s Perf "Specimen" *Set of* 3		£120	

6 Great Frigate Bird

7 Pandanus Pine

8 Canoe crossing Reef

9 Canoe and boat-house

10 Native house

11 Seascape

12 Ellice Islands canoe

13 Coconut palms

14 Cantilever jetty, Ocean Island

15 H.M.C.S. *Nimanoa*

16 Gilbert Islands canoe

17 Coat of arms

(Recess B.W. (½d., 2d., 2s.6d.), Waterlow (1d., 5d., 6d., 2s., 5s.), D.L.R. (1½d., 2½d., 3d., 1s.))

1939 (14 Jan)–**55**. *T* **6/17**. Wmk Mult Script CA (sideways on ½d., 2d. and 2s.6d.). P 11½×11 (½d., 2d., 2s.6d.), 12½ (1d., 5d., 6d., 2s., 5s.) or 13½ (1½d., 2½d., 3d., 1s.).

43	**6**	½d. indigo and deep bluish green.	60	1·00
		a. "A" of "CA" missing from wmk		
44	**7**	1d. emerald and plum	30	1·50
45	**8**	1½d. brownish black and bright carmine	30	1·25
46	**9**	2d. red-brown and grey-black	75	1·00
47	**10**	2½d. brownish black and deep olive	50	70
		a. Brownish black & olive-green (12.5.43)	4·75	5·00
48	**11**	3d. brownish black and ultramarine	50	1·00
		a. Perf 12. *Black and bright blue* (24.8.55)	60	2·25
49	**12**	5d. deep ultramarine and sepia	4·75	1·50
		a. Ultramarine and sepia (12.5.43)	5·50	8·00
		b. Ultramarine & blackish brn (20.10.44)	4·75	5·50
50	**13**	6d. olive-green and deep violet	60	60
51	**14**	1s. brownish black and turquoise-green	18·00	2·25
		a. Brownish black & turquoise-bl (12.5.43)	9·00	3·25
		ab. Perf 12 (8.5.51)	2·75	16·00
52	**15**	2s. deep ultramarine and orange-red	10·00	10·00

53	16	2s.6d. deep blue and emerald	10·00	11·00
54	17	5s. deep rose-red and royal blue	13·00	14·00
43/54 *Set of* 12			40·00	40·00
43s/54s Perf "Specimen" *Set of* 12			£375	

1946 (16 Dec). *Victory. As Nos. 110/11 of Antigua.*

55	1d. purple	15	50
56	3d. blue	15	50
55s/6s Perf "Specimen" *Set of* 2		90·00	

1949 (29 Aug). *Royal Silver Wedding. As Nos. 112/13 of Antigua.*

57	1d. violet	50	75
58	£1 scarlet	14·00	23·00

1949 (10 Oct). *75th Anniv of U.P.U. As Nos. 114/17 of Antigua.*

59	1d. purple	40	1·25
60	2d. grey-black	2·00	3·00
61	3d. deep blue	50	3·00
62	1s. blue	50	2·00
59/62 *Set of* 4		3·00	8·25

1953 (2 June). *Coronation. As No. 120 of Antigua.*

63	2d. black and grey-black	55	2·25

18 Great Frigate Bird

19 Loading Phosphate from Cantilever

(Recess B.W. (½d., 2d., 2s.6d.), Waterlow (1d., 5d., 6d., 2s., 5s.), D.L.R. (2½d., 3d., 1s., 10s. and after 1962, 1d., 5d.))

1956 (1 Aug)–**62**. *Designs previously used for King George VI issue; but with portrait of Queen Elizabeth II as in T* **18**. Wmk Mult Script CA. P 11½×11 (½d., 2d., 2s.6d.), 12½ (1d., 5d., 6d., 2s., 5s.) or 12 (2½d., 3d., 1s., 10s.).

64	18	½d. black and deep bright blue	65	1·25
65	7	1d. brown-olive and deep violet	60	1·25
66	9	2d. bluish green and deep purple	90	2·50
		a. Bluish green and purple (30.7.62)	27·00	27·00
67	10	2½d. black and myrtle-green	50	60
68	11	3d. black and carmine-red	50	60
69	12	5d. ultramarine and red-orange	8·50	2·00
		a. Ultramarine & brown-orange (DLR) (30.7.62)	18·00	25·00
70	13	6d. chestnut and black-brown	55	2·75
71	14	1s. black and bronze-green	2·50	60
72	15	2s. deep bright blue and sepia	6·00	4·00
73	16	2s.6d. scarlet and deep blue	7·00	4·00
74	17	5s. greenish blue and bluish green	7·00	5·00
75	8	10s. black and turquoise	28·00	8·50
64/75 *Set of* 12			55·00	29·00

See also Nos. 85/6.

(Des R. Turrell (2d.), M. Thoma (2½d), M. A. W. Hook and A. Larkins (1s.). Photo D.L.R.)

1960 (1 May). *Diamond Jubilee of Phosphate Discovery at Ocean Island. T* **19** *and similar horiz designs.* W w **12**. P 12.

76	2d. green and carmine-rose	70	85
77	2½d. black and olive-green	70	85
78	1s. black and deep turquoise	70	85
76/8 *Set of* 3		1·90	2·40

Designs:—2½d. Phosphate rock; 1s. Phosphate mining.

1963 (1 Aug). *Freedom from Hunger. As No. 146 of Antigua.*

79	10d. ultramarine	75	30

1963 (5 Oct). *Red Cross Centenary. As Nos. 147/8 of Antigua.*

80	2d. red and black	50	75
81	10d. red and blue	75	2·50

22 De Havilland D.H.114 Heron 2 and Route Map

24 De Havilland D.H.114 Heron 2 over Tarawa Lagoon

23 Eastern Reef Heron in Flight

(Des Margaret Barwick. Litho Enschedé)

1964 (20 July). *First Air Service.* W w **12** (sideways* on 3d., 3s.7d.). P 11×11½ (1s.) or 11½×11 (others).

82	22	3d. blue, black and light blue	70	30
		w. Wmk Crown to right of CA	70	30
83	23	1s. light blue, black and deep blue	90	30
84	24	3s.7d. deep green, black and light emerald	1·40	1·50
82/4 *Set of* 3			2·75	1·90

*The normal sideways watermark shows Crown to left of CA, *as seen from the back of the stamp.*

(Recess B.W. (2d.), D.L.R. (6d.))

1964 (30 Oct)–**65**. *As Nos. 66a and 70 but wmk* w **12**.

85	9	2d. bluish green and purple	1·00	2·00
86	13	6d. chestnut and black-brown (26.4.65)*	1·25	2·25

*Earliest known postmark date.

1965 (4 June). *I.T.U. Centenary. As Nos. 166/7 of Antigua.*

87	3d. red-orange and deep bluish green	15	10
88	2s.6d. turquoise-blue and light purple	45	20

25 Maneaba and Gilbertese Man blowing Bu Shell

26 Gilbertese Women's Dance

(Des V. Whiteley from drawings by Margaret Barwick. Litho B.W.)

1965 (16 Aug). *Vert designs as T* **25** *(½d. to 2s.) or horiz designs as T* **26** *(3s.7d. to £1). Centres multicoloured.* W w **12**. P 12×11 (½d. to 2s.) or 11×12 (3s.7d. to £1).

89	½d. turquoise-green	10	10
90	1d. deep violet-blue	10	10
91	2d. bistre	10	10
92	3d. rose-red	10	10
93	4d. purple	15	10
94	5d. cerise	20	10
95	6d. turquoise-blue	20	10
96	7d. bistre-brown	25	10
97	1s. bluish violet	50	10
98	1s.6d. lemon	1·00	1·00
99	2s. yellow-olive	1·00	1·40
100	3s.7d. new blue	1·75	65
101	5s. light yellow-olive	1·75	80
102	10s. dull green	2·50	1·00
103	£1 light turquoise-blue	3·00	1·75
89/103 *Set of* 15		11·00	6·00

Designs:—1d. Ellice Islanders reef fishing by flare; 2d. Gilbertese girl weaving head garland; 3d. Gilbertese woman performing Ruoia; 4d. Gilbertese man performing Kamei; 5d. Gilbertese girl drawing water; 6d. Ellice islander performing a Fatele; 7d. Ellice youths performing spear dance; 1s. Gilbertese girl tending Ikaroa Babai plant; 1s.6d. Ellice islanders dancing a Fatele; 2s. Ellice islanders pounding Pulaka; 5s. Gilbertese boys playing stick game; 10s. Ellice youths beating the box for the Fatele; £1 Coat of arms.

1965 (25 Oct). *International Co-operation Year. As Nos. 168/9 of Antigua.*

104	½d. reddish purple and turquoise-green	10	10
105	3s.7d. deep bluish green and lavender	50	20

1966 (24 Jan). *Churchill Commemoration. As Nos. 170/3 of Antigua.*

106	½d. new blue	10	10
107	3d. deep green	20	10
108	3s. brown	40	35
109	3s.7d. bluish violet	45	35
106/9 *Set of* 4		1·00	75

(New Currency, 100 cents = 1 Australian dollar)

≡2c

(40)

1966 (14 Feb). *Decimal currency. Nos. 89/103 surch as T* **40**.

110	1c. on 1d. deep violet-blue	10	10
111	2c. on 2d. bistre	10	10
112	3c. on 3d. rose-red	10	10
113	4c. on ½d. turquoise-green	10	10
114	5c. on 6d. turquoise-blue	15	10
115	6c. on 4d. purple	15	10
116	8c. on 5d. cerise	15	10
117	10c. on 1s. bluish violet	15	10
118	15c. on 7d. bistre-brown	60	40
119	20c. on 1s.6d. lemon	30	25
120	25c. on 2s. yellow-olive	30	20
121	35c. on 3s.7d. new blue	1·00	20
122	50c. on 5s. light yellow-olive	55	35
123	$1 on 10s. dull green	55	40
124	$2 on £1 light turquoise-blue	1·25	2·50
110/24 *Set of* 15		4·75	4·25

1966 (1 July). *World Cup Football Championship. As Nos. 176/7 of Antigua.*

125	3c. violet, yellow-green, lake and yellow-brown	20	10
126	35c. chocolate, blue-green, lake and yellow-brown	55	20

1966 (20 Sept). *Inauguration of W.H.O. Headquarters, Geneva. As Nos. 178/9 of Antigua.*

127	3c. black, yellow-green and light blue	20	10
128	12c. black, light purple and yellow-brown	45	40

1966 (1 Dec). *20th Anniv of UNESCO. As Nos. 196/8 of Antigua.*

129	5c. slate-violet, red, yellow and orange	25	35
130	10c. orange-yellow, violet and deep olive	35	10
131	20c. black, bright purple and orange	60	45
129/31 *Set of* 3		1·10	80

41 H.M.S. *Royalist*

(Des V. Whiteley. Photo Harrison)

1967 (1 Sept). *75th Anniv of the Protectorate. T* **41** *and similar horiz designs.* W w **12**. P 14½.

132	3c. red, blue and myrtle-green	30	50
133	10c. multicoloured	15	15
134	35c. sepia, orange-yellow and deep bluish green	30	50
132/4 *Set of* 3		65	1·00

Designs:—10c. Trading Post; 35c. Island family.

44 Gilbertese Women's Dance

1968 (1 Jan). *Decimal Currency. Designs as Nos. 89/103 but with values inscr in decimal currency as T* **44**. W w **12** (sideways on horiz designs). P 12×11 (vert) or 11×12 (horiz).

135	1c. deep violet-blue (as 1d.)	10	15
136	2c. bistre (as 2d.)	15	10
137	3c. rose-red (as 3d.)	15	10
138	4c. turquoise-green (as ½d.)	15	10
139	5c. turquoise-blue (as 6d.)	15	10
140	6c. purple (as 4d.)	20	10
141	8c. cerise (as 5d.)	20	10
142	10c. bluish violet (as 1s.)	20	10
143	15c. bistre-brown (as 7d.)	50	20
144	20c. lemon (as 1s.6d.)	65	15
	w. Wmk inverted	14·00	14·00
145	25c. yellow-olive (as 2s.)	1·25	20
146	35c. new blue	1·50	20
147	50c. light yellow-olive (as 5s.)	1·50	2·50
148	$1 dull green (as 10s.)	1·50	3·75
149	$2 light turquoise-blue (as £1)	4·00	3·75
135/49 *Set of* 15		11·00	10·00

45 Map of Tarawa Atoll

(Des V. Whiteley. Photo D.L.R.)

1968 (21 Nov). *25th Anniv of the Battle of Tarawa. T* **45** *and similar designs. Multicoloured.* W w **12** (sideways). P 14.

150	3c. Type **45**	20	30
151	10c. Marines landing	20	20
152	15c. Beach-head assault	20	35
153	35c. Raising U.S. and British flags	25	50
150/3 *Set of* 4		75	1·25

46 Young Pupil against outline of Abemama Island

47 "Virgin and Child" in Pacific Setting

(Des J.W. (from original designs by Mrs V. J. Anderson and Miss A. Loveridge) Litho D.L.R.)

1969 (2 June). *End of Inaugural Year of South Pacific University. T* **46** *and similar horiz designs.* W w **12** (sideways). P 12½.

154	3c. multicoloured	10	25
155	10c. multicoloured	10	10
156	35c. black, brown and grey-green	15	30
154/6 *Set of* 3		30	55

Designs:—10c. Boy and girl students and Tarawa atoll; 35c. University graduate and South Pacific islands.

(Des Jennifer Toombs. Litho B.W.)

1969 (20 Oct). *Christmas.* W w **12** (sideways). P 11½.

157	–	2c. olive-grn and multicoloured (shades)	15	20
158	47	10c. olive-grn and multicoloured (shades)	15	10

Design:—2c. As T **47** but foreground has grass instead of sand.

48 "The Kiss of Life"

(Des Manate Tenang Manate. Litho J.W.)

1970 (9 Mar*). *Centenary of British Red Cross.* W w **12** (sideways). P 14.

159	**48**	10c. multicoloured	20	10
160	–	15c. multicoloured	30	45
161	–	35c. multicoloured	60	90
159/61 *Set of* 3			1·00	1·25

Nos. 160/1 are as T **48**, but arranged differently.

*The above were released by the Crown Agents on 2 March, but not sold locally until the 9 March.

49 Foetus and Patients

(Des Jennifer Toombs. Litho Enschedé)

1970 (26 June). *25th Anniv of United Nations. T* **49** *and similar horiz designs.* W w **12** (sideways). P 12½×13.

162		5c. multicoloured	15	30
163		10c. black, grey and red	15	15
164		15c. multicoloured	20	30
165		35c. new blue, black and turquoise-green	30	45
162/5 *Set of* 4			70	1·10

Designs:—10c. Nurse and surgical instruments; 15c. X-ray plate and technician; 35c. U.N. emblem and map.

53 Map of Gilbert Islands

57 "Child with Halo" (T. Collis)

(Des G. Vasarhelyi. Litho Harrison)

1970 (1 Sept). *Centenary of Landing in Gilbert Islands by London Missionary Society. T* **53** *and similar designs.* W w **12** (sideways on vert designs). P 14½×14 (2c., 35c.) or 14×14½ (others).

166		2c. multicoloured	15	90
		w. Wmk inverted		
167		10c. black and pale green	25	15
168		25c. chestnut and cobalt	20	20
169		35c. turquoise-blue, black and red	50	70
166/9 *Set of* 4			1·00	1·75

Designs: *Vert*—10c. Sailing-ship *John Williams III*; 25c. Rev. S. J. Whitmee. *Horiz*—35c. M. V. *John Williams VII.*

(Des L. Curtis. Litho Format)

1970 (3 Oct). *Christmas. Sketches. T* **57** *and similar vert designs. Multicoloured.* W w **12**. P 14½.

170		2c. Type **57**	10	60
171		10c. "Sanctuary, Tarawa Cathedral" (Mrs. A. Burroughs)	10	10
172		35c. "Three ships inside star" (Mrs. C. Barnett)	20	20
170/2 *Set of* 3			35	80

POSTAGE DUE STAMPS

D 1

(Typo B.W.)

1940 (Aug). Wmk Mult Script CA. P 12.

D1	D **1**	1d. emerald-green	10·00	25·00
D2		2d. scarlet	11·00	25·00
D3		3d. brown	15·00	26·00
D4		4d. blue	17·00	35·00
D5		5d. grey-green	22·00	35·00
D6		6d. purple	22·00	35·00
D7		1s. violet	24·00	48·00
D8		1s.6d. turquoise-green	48·00	90·00
D1/8 *Set of* 8			£150	£275
D1s/8s Perf "Specimen" *Set of* 8			£190	

Examples of all values are known showing a forged Post Office Ocean Island postmark dated "16 DE 46".

Stamps for the Gilbert and Ellice Islands were withdrawn on 31 December 1975 when the separate colonies of KIRIBATI (GILBERT ISLANDS) and TUVALU were created.

Gold Coast

Gold Coast originally consisted of coastal forts, owned by the Royal African Company, trading with the interior. In 1821, due to raids by the Ashanti king, the British Government took over the forts, together with some of the hinterland, and the Gold Coast was placed under the Governor of Sierra Leone.

The administration was handed back to a merchantile company in 1828, but the forts returned to British Government rule in 1843. The colony was reconstituted by Royal Charter on 24 July 1874, and at that time also included the settlement at Lagos which became a separate colony in January 1886.

Following the end of the final Ashanti War the whole of the territory was annexed in September 1901.

A postal service was established at Cape Coast Castle in 1853. There is no record of British stamps being officially issued in the Colony before 1875, apart from those used on board the ships of the West African Squadron, but examples do, however, exist cancelled by Gold Coast postmarks.

CROWN COLONY

PRICES FOR STAMPS ON COVER TO 1945

Nos. 1/3	*from* × 125
Nos. 4/8	*from* × 40
Nos. 9/10	*from* × 15
Nos. 11/20	*from* × 30
Nos. 22/5	—
Nos. 26/34	*from* × 10
Nos. 35/6	*from* × 20
Nos. 38/69	*from* × 6
Nos. 70/98	*from* × 3
Nos. 100/2	—
Nos. 103/12	*from* × 5
Nos. 113/16	*from* × 3
Nos. 117/19	*from* × 4
Nos. 120/32	*from* × 3
No. D1	*from* × 6
No. D2	*from* × 20
Nos. D3/4	*from* × 12

1

(2)

(Typo D.L.R.)

1875 (1 July). Wmk Crown CC. P 12½.

1	**1**	1d. blue	£475	80·00
2		4d. magenta	£450	£120
3		6d. orange	£700	65·00

1876–84. Wmk Crown CC. P 14.

4	**1**	½d. olive-yellow (1879)	80·00	28·00
		w. Wmk inverted	£300	
5		1d. blue	27·00	6·50
		a. Bisected (½d.) (on cover) (1884)	†	£3750
		w. Wmk inverted	£450	£180
6		2d. green (1879)	£100	9·00
		a. Bisected (1d.) (on cover) (1884)	†	£3250
		b. Quartered (½d.) (on cover) (1884)	†	£6000
7		4d. magenta	£250	6·00
		a. Bisected (2d.) (on cover) (1884)	†	£7000
		b. Quartered (1d.) (on cover) (1884)	†	£9000
		c. Tri-quadrisected (3d.) (on cover) (1884)	†	—
		w. Wmk inverted	£950	£300
8		6d. orange	£190	19·00
		a. Bisected (3d.) (on cover) (1884)	†	£8500
		b. Sixth (1d.) (on cover) (1884)	†	£10000

During 1884 some values were in short supply and the use of bisects and other divided stamps is known as follows:

No. 5a.	Used as part of 2½d. rate from Accra and Quittah
No. 6a.	Used as 1d. rate from Addah, Cape Coast Castle, Quittah, Salt Pond, Secondee and Winnebah
No. 6b.	Used as part of 2½d. rate from Cape Coast Castle
No. 7a.	Used as 2d. or as part of 2½d. rate from Quittah
No. 7b.	Used as 1d. rate from Appam, Axim, Cape Coast Castle, Elmina and Winnebah
No. 7c.	Used as 3d. rate from Winnebah
No. 8a.	Used as 3d. rate from Secondee
No. 8b.	Used as 1d. rate from Cape Coast Castle and Winnebah.

Examples of bisects used on piece are worth about 15% of the price quoted for those on cover.

The 4d., No. 7, is known surcharged "1 d". This was previously listed as No. 8c, but there are now serious doubts as to its authenticity. The three examples reported of this stamp all show *different* surcharges!

1883. Wmk Crown CA. P 14.

9	**1**	½d. olive-yellow (January)	£180	65·00
10		1d. blue (May)	£850	70·00

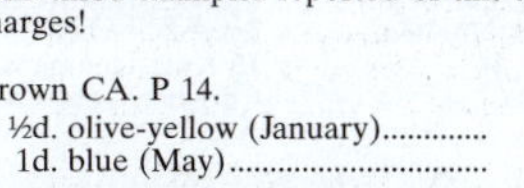

Short "P" and distorted "E" (Pl 1 R. 5/6) ("P" repaired for Pl 2)

1884 (Aug)–**91**. Wmk Crown CA. P 14.

11	**1**	½d. green	3·50	1·25
		a. Dull green	3·50	1·00
		w. Wmk inverted	£180	£180
		x. Wmk reversed		
12		1d. rose-carmine	4·00	50
		a. Carmine	4·00	50
		b. Bisected (½d.) (on cover)	†	£4250
		c. Short "P" and distorted "E"	£160	55·00
13		2d. grey	18·00	4·50
		aw. Wmk inverted	£250	£250
		b. Slate	7·00	50
		c. Bisected (1d.) (on cover)	†	£4750
		d. Quartered (½d.) (on cover)	†	—
14		2½d. ultramarine and orange (13.3.91)	7·00	70
		w. Wmk inverted	†	£225
15		3d. olive-yellow (9.89)	15·00	6·50
		a. Olive	15·00	6·00
16		4d. deep mauve (3.85)	15·00	2·50
		a. Rosy mauve	18·00	4·00
17		6d. orange (1.89)	15·00	5·00
		a. Orange-brown	15·00	5·00
		b. Bisected (3d.) (on cover)	†	£9000
18		1s. violet (1888)	32·00	12·00
		a. Bright mauve	8·00	1·25
19		2s. yellow-brown (1888)	85·00	35·00
		a. Deep brown	50·00	15·00
11/19*a Set of* 9			£110	29·00
14s/15s, 18s/19s Optd "Specimen" *Set of* 4			£150	

During 1884 to 1886 and in 1889 some values were in short supply and the use of bisects and other divided stamps is known as follows:

No. 12b.	Used as part of 2½d. rate from Cape Coast Castle
No. 13c.	Used as 1d. or as part of 2d. rate from Cape Coast Castle, Chamah, Dixcove and Elmina
No. 13d.	Used as part of 2½d. rate from Cape Coast Castle
No. 17b.	Used as 3d. from Appam

1889 (Mar). *No. 17 surch with T* **2**.

20	**1**	1d. on 6d. orange	£120	50·00
		a. Surch double	†	£4000

In some sheets examples may be found with the bar and "PENNY" spaced 8 mm, the normal spacing being 7 mm.

USED HIGH VALUES. Until the introduction of airmail in 1929 there was no postal use for values over 10s. Post Offices did, however, apply postal cancellations to high value stamps required for telegram fees.

3 **4**

1889 (Sept)–**94**. Wmk Crown CA. P 14.

22	**3**	5s. dull mauve and blue	65·00	18·00
23		10s. dull mauve and red	80·00	15·00
		a. Dull mauve and carmine	£700	£250
24		20s. green and red	£3250	
25		20s. dull mauve and black/*red* (4.94)	£160	35·00
		w. Wmk inverted	£475	£100
22a/5s Optd "Specimen" *Set of* 4			£400	

No. 24 was withdrawn from sale in April 1893 when a large part of the stock was stolen. No 20s. stamps were available until the arrival of the replacement printing a year later.

1898 (May)–**1902**. Wmk Crown CA. P 14.

26	**3**	½d. dull mauve and green	3·50	1·00
27		1d. dull mauve and rose	4·00	50
		aw. Wmk inverted	–	£150
27*b*	**4**	2d. dull mauve and orange-red (1902)	50·00	£150
28	**3**	2½d. dull mauve and ultramarine	6·50	6·50
29	**4**	3d. dull mauve and orange	7·00	2·25
30		6d. dull mauve and violet	7·50	2·25
31	**3**	1s. green and black (1899)	11·00	22·00
32		2s. green and carmine	18·00	23·00
33		5s. green and mauve (1900)	60·00	38·00
34		10s. green and brown (1900)	£160	60·00
26/34 *Set of* 10			£300	£275
26s/34s Optd "Specimen" *Set of* 10			£180	

1901 (6 Oct). *Nos. 28 and 30 surch with T* **2**.

35		1d. on 2½d. dull mauve and ultramarine	4·50	4·25
		a. "ONE" omitted	£1000	
36		1d. on 6d. dull mauve and violet	4·50	3·50
		a. "ONE" omitted	£275	£550

6 **7** **8**

1902. Wmk Crown CA. P 14.

38	**6**	½d. dull purple and green (Aug)	1·50	40
39		1d. dull purple and carmine (May)	1·50	15
		w. Wmk inverted	£150	£100
40	**7**	2d. dull purple and orange-red (Apr)	23·00	7·00
		w. Wmk inverted		
41	**6**	2½d. dull purple and ultramarine (Aug)	4·50	9·00
42	**7**	3d. dull purple and orange (Aug)	3·25	1·50
43		6d. dull purple and violet (Aug)	4·00	1·50
		w. Wmk inverted	–	£140
44	**6**	1s. green and black (Aug)	14·00	3·25

45		2s. green and carmine (Aug)	16·00	22·00
46		5s. green and mauve (Aug)	50·00	95·00
47		10s. green and brown (Aug)	60·00	£130
48		20s. purple and black/*red* (Aug)	£140	£180
38/48 *Set of* 11			£275	£400
38s/48s Optd "Specimen" *Set of* 11			£200	

Examples of Nos. 45/8 are known showing a forged Accra postmark dated "25 MAR 1902".

1904–06. Wmk Mult Crown CA. *Ordinary paper (½d. to 6d.) or chalk-surfaced paper (2s.6d.).*

49	6	½d. dull purple and green (3.06)	2·50	7·00
50		1d. dull purple and carmine (10.04)	11·00	30
		a. Chalk-surfaced paper (5.06)	10·00	2·00
		w. Wmk inverted		
51	7	2d. dull purple and orange-red (11.04)	6·50	60
		a. Chalk-surfaced paper (8.06)	28·00	2·50
52	6	2½d. dull purple and ultramarine (6.06)	50·00	50·00
53	7	3d. dull purple and orange (8.05)	65·00	6·00
		a. Chalk-surfaced paper (4.06)	18·00	60
54		6d. dull purple and violet (3.06)	75·00	3·50
		a. Chalk-surfaced paper (9.06)	40·00	2·00
57		2s.6d. green and yellow (3.06)	28·00	£110
		s. Optd Specimen"	45·00	
49/57 *Set of* 7			£140	£150

1907–13. Wmk Mult Crown CA. *Ordinary paper (½d. to 2½d. and 2s.) or chalk-surfaced paper (3d. to 1s., 2s.6d., 5s.).* P 14.

59	6	½d. dull green (5.07)	7·00	30
		a. Blue-green (1909)	12·00	2·00
60		1d. red (2.07)	11·00	40
61	7	2d. greyish slate (4.09)	2·25	40
62	6	2½d. blue (4.07)	12·00	3·00
		w. Wmk inverted	†	£325
63	7	3d. purple/*yellow* (16.4.09)	8·50	55
64		6d. dull and deep purple (12.08)	20·00	55
		a. Dull and bright purple (1911)	4·00	3·75
65	6	1s. black/*green* (10.09)	16·00	50
66		2s. purple and blue/*blue* (1910)	8·50	16·00
		a. Chalk-surfaced paper (1912)	18·00	16·00
67	7	2s.6d. black and red/*blue* (1911)	32·00	90·00
68	6	5s. green and red/*yellow* (1913)	55·00	£200
59/68 *Set of* 10			£140	£275
59s/68s Optd "Specimen" *Set of* 10			£275	

A 10s. green and red on green, and a 20s. purple and black on red, both Type **6**, were prepared for use but not issued. Both exist overprinted "SPECIMEN" (*Price for* 10s. *in this condition*, £275). An example of the 10s. exists without "SPECIMEN" overprint.

(Typo D.L.R.)

1908 (Nov). Wmk Mult Crown CA. P 14.

69	8	1d. red	5·00	10
		a. Wmk sideways	†	£2000
		s. Optd "Specimen"	45·00	

9

10

11

(Typo D.L.R.)

1913–21. *Die I.* Wmk Mult Crown CA. *Chalk-surfaced paper (3d. to 20s.).* P 14.

70	9	½d. green	2·50	1·00
		a. Yellow-green (1916)	3·00	1·25
72	10	1d. red	1·25	10
		a. Scarlet (1917)	1·75	50
74	11	2d. grey	5·00	2·50
		a. Slate-grey (1920)	11·00	11·00
		w. Wmk inverted	†	£250
76	9	2½d. bright blue	8·00	1·00
		a. "A" of "CA" missing from wmk	£550	
		x. Wmk reversed	†	£250
77	11	3d. purple/*yellow* (8.15)	2·50	80
		as. Optd "Specimen"	35·00	
		aw. Wmk inverted	—	£140
		b. White back (9.13)	1·75	40
		c. On orange-buff (1919)	8·50	7·50
		cw. Wmk inverted		
		d. On buff (1920)		
		e. Die II. *On pale yellow* (1921)	50·00	5·00
		ew. Wmk inverted	†	£325
78		6d. dull and bright purple	4·75	2·25
79	9	1s. black/*green*	4·00	1·25
		a. Wmk sideways	†	£1300
		bw. Wmk inverted		
		c. On blue-green, olive back (1916)	9·00	75
		cs. Optd "Specimen"	48·00	
		cw. Wmk inverted	—	£190
		d. On emerald back (1920)	2·00	2·00
		ds. Optd "Specimen"	42·00	
		e. Die II. *On emerald back* (1921)	1·50	50
		es. Optd "Specimen"	48·00	
		ew. Wmk inverted		
80		2s. purple and blue/*blue*	9·00	3·25
		aw. Wmk inverted	—	£300
		b. Die II (1921)	£160	65·00
81	11	2s.6d. black and red/*blue*	8·00	13·00
		a. Die II (1921)	24·00	42·00
82	9	5s. green and red/*yellow* (1916)	18·00	60·00
		as. Optd "Specimen"	50·00	
		b. White back (10.13)	16·00	60·00
		c. On orange-buff (1919)	75·00	85·00
		d. On buff (1920)		
		e. On pale yellow (1921)	£100	£150
		f. Die II. *On pale yellow* (1921)	30·00	£150
		fw. Wmk inverted	£300	
83		10s. green and red/*green*	50·00	90·00
		a. On blue-green, olive back (1916)	22·00	75·00
		aw. Wmk inverted	£800	
		b. On emerald back (1921)	32·00	£160
84		20s. purple and black/*red*	£150	95·00
70/84 *Set of* 12			£200	£225
70s/6s, 77bs, 78s/81s, 82bs/4s Optd "Specimen" *Set of* 12			£275	

The 10s. and 20s. were withdrawn locally from September 1920 and, in common with other Gold Coast stamps, were not available to stamp dealers from the Crown Agents in London.

WAR TAX

ONE PENNY

(**12**)

13 King George V and Christiansborg Castle

1918 (17 June). *Surch with T* **12**.

85	10	1d. on 1d. red	2·75	75
		s. Optd "Specimen"	50·00	

1921–24. *Die I (15s., £2) or Die II (others).* Wmk Mult Script CA. *Chalk-surfaced paper (6d. to £2).* P 14.

86	9	½d. green	80	50
87	10	1d. chocolate-brown (1922)	70	10
88	11	1½d. red (1922)	1·75	10
89		2d. grey	1·75	30
90	9	2½d. yellow-orange (1922)	1·25	9·50
91	11	3d. bright blue (1922)	1·75	60
94		6d. dull and bright purple	2·50	3·00
95	9	1s. black/*emerald* (1924)	3·75	3·25
96		2s. purple and blue/*blue* (1923)	3·25	3·25
97	11	2s.6d. black and red/*blue* (1924)	7·00	29·00
98	9	5s. green and red/*pale yellow* (1924)	16·00	70·00
100	11	15s. dull purple and green (Die I)	£160	£425
		a. Die II (1924)	£130	£425
		as. Optd "Specimen"	£100	
102		£2 green and orange (Die I)	£450	£1200
86/100a *Set of* 12			£150	£500
86s/102s Optd "Specimen" *Set of* 13			£450	

The Duty plate for the 1½d., 15s. and £2 has the words "GOLD COAST" in distinctly larger letters.

Examples of Nos. 100/a and 102 are known showing parts of forged Accra postmarks. These are dated "3 MAY 44" and "8 MAY 44", but are invariably positioned so that the year date is not shown.

(Des W. Palmer. Photo Harrison)

1928 (1 Aug). Wmk Mult Script CA. P 13½×14½.

103	13	½d. blue-green	1·00	40
104		1d. red-brown	85	10
105		1½d. scarlet	2·00	1·50
		w. Wmk inverted	†	£300
106		2d. slate	2·00	20
107		2½d. orange-yellow	2·25	3·50
108		3d. bright blue	2·00	40
109		6d. black and purple	2·00	40
110		1s. black and red-orange	3·50	75
111		2s. black and bright violet	26·00	4·75
112		5s. carmine and sage-green	60·00	45·00
103/12 *Set of* 10			90·00	50·00
103s/12s Optd "Specimen" *Set of* 10			£200	

1935 (6 May). *Silver Jubilee. As Nos. 91/4 of Antigua, but printed by B.W.* P 11×12.

113		1d. ultramarine and grey-black	60	50
		a. Extra flagstaff	£130	£100
		b. Short extra flagstaff	£190	
		c. Lightning conductor	£140	
		d. Flagstaff on right-hand turret	£300	
114		3d. brown and deep blue	3·00	6·00
		a. Extra flagstaff	£140	£170
		c. Lightning conductor	£190	
115		6d. green and indigo	12·00	18·00
		a. Extra flagstaff	£170	£225
		b. Short extra flagstaff	£375	
		c. Lightning conductor	£250	£300
		d. Flagstaff on right-hand turret	£500	
116		1s. slate and purple	5·00	27·00
		a. Extra flagstaff	£180	£325
		b. Short extra flagstaff	£275	
		c. Lightning conductor	£275	£375
113/16 *Set of* 4			19·00	45·00
113s/16s Perf "Specimen" *Set of* 4			£120	

For illustrations of plate varieties see Omnibus section following Zanzibar.

1937 (12 May). *Coronation. As Nos. 95/7 of Antigua.* P 11×11½.

117		1d. buff	1·75	2·50
118		2d. slate	1·75	4·50
119		3d. blue	2·00	2·75
117/19 *Set of* 3			5·00	8·75
117s/19s Perf "Specimen" *Set of* 3			85·00	

14

15 King George VI and Christiansborg Castle, Accra

(Recess B.W.)

1938 (1 Apr)–**44**. Wmk Mult Script CA. P 11½×12 (comb) (1s.3d., 10s.) or 12 (line) (others).

120	14	½d. green	6·00	2·25
		a. Perf 12×11½ (1940)	40	50
121		1d. red-brown	8·50	30
		a. Perf 12×11½ (1939)	40	10
122		1½d. scarlet	9·00	3·75
		a. Perf 12×11½ (1940)	40	50
123		2d. slate	9·00	1·50
		a. Perf 12×11½ (1940)	40	10
124		3d. blue	6·50	1·00
		a. Perf 12×11½ (1940)	40	35
125		4d. magenta	7·50	3·00
		a. Perf 12×11½ (1942)	80	1·25
126		6d. purple	13·00	50
		a. Perf 12×11½ (1939)	80	20
127		9d. orange	7·00	1·75
		a. Perf 12×11½ (1944)	1·25	55
128	15	1s. black and olive-green	16·00	2·25
		a. Perf 11½×12 (1940)	1·50	65
129		1s.3d. brown & turquoise-bl (12.4.41)	2·00	50
130		2s. blue and violet	38·00	21·00
		a. Perf 11½×12 (1940)	5·00	17·00
131		5s. olive-green & carmine	70·00	25·00
		a. Perf 11½×12 (1940)	10·00	19·00
132		10s. black and violet (7.40)	7·00	27·00
120a/32 *Set of* 13			27·00	60·00
120s/32s Perf "Specimen" *Set of* 13			£250	

The exact measurement of the comb perforated stamps is 12×11.8 (vertical designs) or 11.8×12 (horizontal designs).

The ½d. and 1d. values exist in coils constructed from normal sheets.

1946 (14 Oct). *Victory. As Nos. 110/11 of Antigua.* P 13½×14.

133		2d. slate-violet	17·00	2·75
		a. Perf 13½	10	10
		aw. Wmk inverted	£500	
134		4d. claret	2·50	3·75
		a. Perf 13½	1·50	3·25
133s/4as Perf "Specimen" *Set of* 2			85·00	

16 Northern Territories Mounted Constabulary

17 Christiansborg Castle

18 Emblem of Joint Provincial Council

19 Talking drums

20 Map showing position of Gold Coast

21 Nsuta manganese mine

22 Lake Bosumtwi

23 Cocoa farmer

24 Breaking cocoa pods

25 Gold Coast Regt Trooping the Colour

26 Surfboats

27 Forest

(Des B. A. Johnston (1½d.), M. Ziorkley and B. A. Abban (2d.), P.O. draughtsman (2½d.), C. Gomez (1s.), M. Ziorkley (10s.); others from photographs. Recess B.W.)

1948 (1 July). *T* **16/27**. Wmk Mult Script CA. P 12×11½ (vert) or 11½×12 (horiz).

135	16	½d. emerald-green	20	30
136	17	1d. blue	15	15
137	18	1½d. scarlet	1·25	80
138	19	2d. purple-brown	55	10
139	20	2½d. yellow-brown and scarlet	2·00	4·25

140	**21**	3d. light blue	4·00	50
141	**22**	4d. magenta	3·50	3·25
142	**23**	6d. black and orange	40	30
143	**24**	1s. black and vermilion	1·50	30
144	**25**	2s. sage-green and magenta	3·50	3·00
145	**26**	5s. purple and black	28·00	8·50
146	**27**	10s. black and sage-green	11·00	8·50
135/46 *Set of* 12			50·00	26·00
135s/46s Perf "Specimen" *Set of* 12			£300	

Nos. 135/6 exist in coils constructed from normal sheets.

1948 (20 Dec). *Royal Silver Wedding. As Nos. 112/13 of Antigua.*

147	1½d. scarlet	30	70
148	10s. grey-olive	23·00	30·00

1949 (10 Oct). *75th Anniv of U.P.U. As Nos. 114/17 of Antigua.*

149	2d. red-brown	25	20
	a. "A" of "CA" missing from wmk		
150	2½d. orange	1·50	4·25
151	3d. deep blue	35	1·75
152	1s. blue-green	35	30
149/52 *Set of* 4		2·25	6·00

As on other examples of this variety No. 149a shows traces of the left leg of the "A".

28 Northern Territories Mounted Constabulary

(Recess B.W.)

1952 (19 Dec)–**54**. *Designs previously used for King George VI issue, but with portrait of Queen Elizabeth II, as in T* **28**. *Portrait faces left on ½d., 4d., 6d., 1s. and 5s.* Wmk Mult Script CA. P 12×11½ (vert) or 11½×12 (horiz).

153	**20**	½d. yellow-brown and scarlet (1.4.53)	10	20
		a. Bistre-brown and scarlet (7.4.54)	40	20
154	**17**	1d. deep blue (1.3.54)	30	10
155	**18**	1½d. emerald-green (1.4.53)	30	1·50
156	**19**	2d. chocolate (1.3.54)	30	10
157	**28**	2½d. scarlet	35	1·50
158	**21**	3d. magenta (1.4.53)	75	10
159	**22**	4d. blue (1.4.53)	35	30
160	**23**	6d. black and orange (1.3.54)	40	15
161	**24**	1s. black and orange-red (1.3.54)	75	15
162	**25**	2s. brown-olive and carmine (1.3.54)	12·00	85
163	**26**	5s. purple and black (1.3.54)	19·00	7·00
164	**27**	10s. black and olive-green (1.3.54)	17·00	12·00
153/64 *Set of* 12			45·00	21·00

Nos. 153*a*/4 exist in coils constructed from normal sheets.

1953 (2 June). *Coronation. As No. 120 of Antigua, but ptd by B. W.*

165	2d. black and sepia	1·00	10

STAMP BOOKLETS

1916 (Dec).

SB1 2s. booklet containing twelve ½d. and eighteen 1d. (Nos. 70*a*, 72) in blocks of 6...

POSTAGE DUE STAMPS

D 1

(Typo D.L.R.)

1923 (6 Mar). *Yellowish toned paper.* Wmk Mult Script CA. P 14.

D1	**D 1**	½d. black	15·00	£120
D2		1d. black	75	1·25
D3		2d. black	13·00	3·75
D4		3d. black	22·00	2·25
D1/4 *Set of* 4			45·00	£120
D1s/4s Optd "Specimen" *Set of* 4			75·00	

A bottom marginal strip of six of No. D2 is known showing the "A" of "CA" omitted from the watermark in the margin below the third vertical column.

Normal

Lower serif at left of "3" missing (R. 9/1)

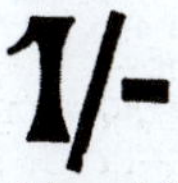

Column 4 (No. D8)

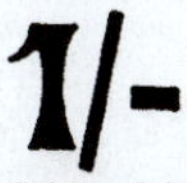

Column 5 (No. D8c)

The degree of inclination of the stroke on the 1s. value varies for each column of the sheet: Column 1, 2 and 6 104°, Column 3 108°, Column 4 107° and Column 5 (No. D8c) 100°.

1951–52. Wmk Mult Script CA. *Chalk-surfaced paper.* P 14.

D5	**D 1**	2d. black (13.12.51)	3·75	25·00
		a. Error. Crown missing, W **9***a*	£950	
		b. Error. St. Edward's Crown, W **9***b*	£475	
		c. Large "d" (R. 9/6, 10/6)	28·00	
		d. Serif on "d" (R. 1/6)	50·00	
D6		3d. black (13.12.51)	3·00	23·00
		a. Error. Crown missing, W **9***a*	£900	
		b. Error. St. Edward's Crown, W **9***b*	£450	
		c. Missing serif	42·00	
D7		6d. black (1.10.52)	1·75	9·00
		a. Error. Crown missing, W **9***a*	£1300	
		b. Error. St. Edward's Crown, W **9***b*	£850	
D8		1s. black (1.10.52)	1·75	65·00
		b. Error. St. Edward's Crown, W **9***b*	£1000	
		c. Upright stroke	12·00	
D5/8 *Set of* 4			9·25	£110

For illustration of Nos. D5c/d see Nos. D4/6 of Bechuanaland.

Gold Coast became the Dominion of Ghana on 6 March 1957.

Grenada

The earliest recorded postmark of the British administration of Grenada dates from 1784, and, although details of the early period are somewhat sparse, it would appear that the island's postal service was operated at a branch of the British G.P.O. In addition to a Packet Agency at St. George's, the capital, there was a further agency at Carriacou, in the Grenadines, which operated for a few years from 15 September 1847.

Stamps of Great Britain were supplied to the St. George's office from April 1858 until the colony assumed responsibility for the postal service on 1 May 1860. Following the take-over the crowned-circle handstamp, No. CC2, was again used until the Grenada adhesives were issued in 1861.

There was no internal postal service before 1861.

For illustrations of the handstamp and postmark types see BRITISH POST OFFICES ABROAD notes, following GREAT BRITAIN.

CARRIACOU

CROWNED-CIRCLE HANDSTAMPS

A crowned-circle handstamp for Carriacou is recorded in the G.P.O. proof book but no example has been reported used from Grenada.

ST. GEORGE'S

CROWNED-CIRCLE HANDSTAMPS

CC2 CC **1** GRENADA (R.) (24.10.1850)
Price on cover £2000

Stamps of GREAT BRITAIN *cancelled* "A 15" *as Type* **2**.

1858–60.

Z1	1d. rose-red (1857), perf 14	£425
Z2	2d. blue (1858) (Plate No. 7)	£1100
Z3	4d. rose (1857)	£275
Z4	6d. lilac (1856)	£120
Z5	1s. green (1856)	£1300

PRICES FOR STAMPS ON COVER TO 1945

Nos. 1/19	*from* × 15
Nos. 20/3	*from* × 20
Nos. 24/6	*from* × 10
No. 27	*from* × 15
No. 28	—
No. 29	*from* × 10
Nos. 30/6	*from* × 20
Nos. 37/9	*from* × 10
No. 40	*from* × 30
Nos. 41/7	*from* × 10
Nos. 48/101	*from* × 4
Nos. 109/11	*from* × 8
Nos. 112/48	*from* × 4
Nos. 149/51	*from* × 10
No. 152/63	*from* × 4
Nos. D1/3	*from* × 25
Nos. D4/7	*from* × 12
Nos. D8/14	*from* × 20

CROWN COLONY

PRINTERS. Types **1** and **5** recess-printed by Perkins, Bacon and Co.

PERKINS BACON "CANCELLED". For notes on these handstamps, showing "CANCELLED" between horizontal bars forming an oval, see Catalogue Introduction.

1

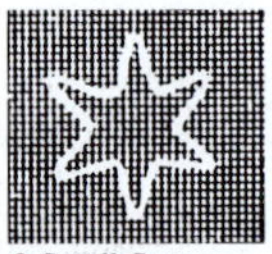

2 Small Star

(Eng C. Jeens)

1861 (3 June)–**62**. No wmk. *Wove paper.*

(a) Rough perf 14 to 16.

1	**1**	1d. bluish green	£4500	£300
2		1d. green (5.62)	50·00	45·00
		a. Imperf between (horiz pair) ..		
3		6d. rose (*shades*) (H/S "CANCELLED" in oval £10000)	£900	90·00

(b) Perf 11 to 12½.

3*a*	**1**	6d. lake-red (6.62)	£750	

The 1d. bluish green also exists handstamped "CANCELLED" in oval, but the only known example is in the Royal Collection.

No. 3*a* is only known unused, and may be the result of perforating machine trials undertaken by Perkins, Bacon. It has also been seen on horizontally laid paper (*Price* £1200).

SIDEWAYS WATERMARK. W **2/3** when sideways show two points of star downwards.

1863–71. W **2** (Small Star). Rough perf 14 to 16.

4	**1**	1d. green (3.64)	90·00	13·00
		a. Wmk sideways	—	26·00
5		1d. yellowish green	£110	26·00
6		6d. rose (*shades*) (5.63)	£600	13·00
		a. Wmk sideways	—	65·00
7		6d. orange-red (*shades*) (5.66)	£650	12·00
8		6d. dull rose-red (*wmk sideways*)	£3500	£225
9		6d. vermilion (5.71)	£750	12·00
		a. Double impression	—	£2000

1873 (Jan). W **2** (Small Star, sideways). Clean-cut perf 15.

10	**1**	1d. deep green	£110	42·00
		a. Bisected diag (on cover)	†	£9000
		b. Imperf between (pair)	—	£9000

No. 10a, and later bisected 1d. values, were authorised until 1881 to pay the island newspaper rate (½d.) or the newspaper rate to Great Britain (1½d.). Examples also exist on covers to France.

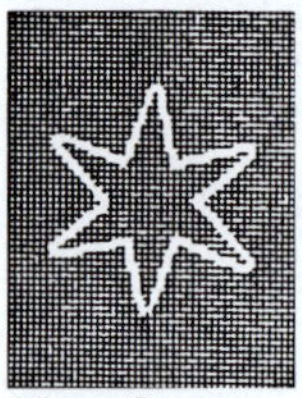

3 Large Star

4 Broad-pointed Star

1873 (Sept)–**74**. W **3** (Large Star). Intermediate perf 15.

11	**1**	1d. blue-green (*wmk sideways*) (2.74)	95·00	19·00
		a. Double impression		
		b. Bisected diag (on cover)	†	£9000
12		6d. orange-vermilion	£700	26·00

5

POSTAGE

ONE SHILLING

(6)

NOTE. The early ½d., 2½d., 4d. and 1s. postage stamps were made by surcharging the undenominated Type **5** design.

The surcharges were from two founts of type—one about 1½ mm high, the other 2 mm high—so there are short and tall letters on the same stamp; also the spacing varies considerably, so that the length of the words varies.

Examples of Type **5** with surcharges, but without the "POSTAGE" inscription, are revenue stamps.

1875 (July). *Surch with T* **6**. W **3**. P 14.

13	**5**	1s. deep mauve (B.)	£700	12·00
		a. "SHLLIING"	£6000	£700
		b. "NE SHILLING"	†	£3000
		c. Inverted "S" in "POSTAGE"	£4000	£500
		d. "OSTAGE"	£6500	£2750

1875 (Dec). W **3** (Large Star, upright).

14	**1**	1d. green to yellow-green (P 14)	80·00	8·00
		a. Bisected diag (on cover)	†	£9000
15		1d. green (P 15)	£9000	£2250

No. 14 was perforated at Somerset House. 40 sheets of No. 15 were perforated by Perkins, Bacon to replace spoilages and to complete the order.

1878 (Aug). W **2** (Small Star, sideways). Intermediate perf 15.

16	**1**	1d. green	£250	42·00
		b. Bisected diag (on cover)	†	£9000
17		6d. deep vermilion	£850	38·00
		a. Double impression	—	£2000

1879 (Dec). W **2** (Small Star, upright). Rough perf 15.

18	**1**	1d. pale green (*thin paper*)	£300	27·00
		a. Double impression		
		b. Bisected diag (on cover)	†	—

1881 (Apr). W **2** (Small Star, sideways). Rough perf 14½.

19	**1**	1d. green	£160	9·00
		a. Bisected diag (on cover)	†	£9000

POSTAGE HALF-PENNY **(7)**

POSTAGE TWO PENCE HALF-PENNY. **(8)**

POSTAGE FOUR PENCE **(9)**

1881 (Apr). *Surch with T* **7/9**. P 14½.

(a) W **3** (Large Star, sideways on ½d.)

20	**5**	½d. pale mauve	32·00	10·00
21		½d. deep mauve	14·00	5·50
		a. Imperf (pair)	£300	
		ab. Ditto. "OSTAGE" (R. 9/4)	£5000	
		b. Surch double	£300	
		c. "OSTAGE" (R. 9/4)	£190	£130
		d. No hyphen	£190	£130
		e. "ALF-PENNY"	£3500	
		f. Wmk upright	£300	£140
		g. Ditto. "OSTAGE" (R. 9/4)	£1800	£800
22		2½d. rose-lake	60·00	7·50
		a. Imperf (pair)	£600	
		b. Imperf between (horiz pair) ..	£4500	
		c. No stop	£250	75·00
		d. "PENCF" (R. 8/12)	£450	£180
23		4d. blue	£110	8·00
		a. Wmk sideways	†	£500
		b. Inverted "S" in "POSTAGE".		

(b) W **4** (Broad-pointed Star).

24	**5**	2½d. rose-lake	£160	50·00
		a. No stop	£550	£200
		b. "PENCF" (R. 8/12)	£750	£275
25		2½d. claret	£425	£120
		a. No stop	£1100	£500
		b. "PENCF" (R. 8/12)	£1600	£700
25*c*		2½d. deep claret	£650	£225
		d. No stop	£2250	£900
		e. "PENCF" (R. 8/12)	£2750	£1100
26		4d. blue	£275	£180

Examples of the "F" for "E" error on the 2½d. value should not be confused with a somewhat similar broken "E" variety. The latter is always without the stop and shows other damage to the "E". The authentic error always occurs with the full stop shown.

The "no stop" variety occurs on R. 3/4, R. 6/2, R. 8/3 and R. 9/7.

ONE PENNY **(10)**

POSTAGE. **(11)**

POSTAGE POSTAGE **(12)**

1883 (Jan). *Revenue stamps* (*T* **5** *with green surcharge as in T* **10**) *optd for postage*. W **2** (Small Star). P 14½.

(a) Optd horizontally with T **11**.

27	**5**	1d. orange	£375	60·00
		a. "POSTAGE" inverted	£3250	£2250
		b. "POSTAGE" double	£1400	£1100
		c. Inverted "S" in "POSTAGE".	£1000	£600
		d. Bisected diag (on cover)	†	£3000

(b) Optd diagonally with T **11** *twice on each stamp, the stamp being cut and each half used as ½d.*

28	**5**	Half of 1d. orange	£650	£225
		a. Unsevered pair	£4250	£1200
		b. "POSTAGE" inverted	—	£1200

(c) Optd with T **12**, *the stamps divided diagonally and each half used as ½d.*

29	**5**	Half of 1d. orange	£275	£110
		a. Unsevered pair	£1500	£450

Nos. 27/9 exist with wmk either upright or sideways.

1d. Revenue stamps with "POSTAGE" added in black manuscript were used at Gouyave during February and March 1883 (*Price* £54000, *used*). Similar manuscript overprints, in red were also used at Grenville in June 1883 and in black or red at Sauteurs in September 1886 (*Price from* £7500, *used*).

13

d. 1 POSTAGE. **(14)**

15

(Typo D.L.R.)

1883. Wmk Crown CA. P 14.

30	**13**	½d. dull green (February)	1·50	1·00
		a. *Tête-bêche* (vert pair)	4·50	16·00
31		1d. carmine (February)	75·00	3·25
		a. *Tête-bêche* (vert pair)	£225	£250
32		2½d. ultramarine (May)	7·00	1·00
		a. *Tête-bêche* (vert pair)	26·00	50·00
33		4d. greyish slate (May)	7·00	2·00
		a. *Tête-bêche* (vert pair)	20·00	55·00
34		6d. mauve (May)	3·25	4·25
		a. *Tête-bêche* (vert pair)	18·00	55·00
35		8d. grey-brown (February)	10·00	13·00
		a. *Tête-bêche* (vert pair)	38·00	80·00
36		1s. pale violet (April)	£130	55·00
		a. *Tête-bêche* (vert pair)	£1700	£2000
30/36 *Set of* 7			£200	70·00

Types **13** and **15** were printed in rows *tête-bêche* in the sheets, so that 50% of the stamps have inverted watermarks.

1886 (1 Oct–Dec). *Revenue stamps* (*T* **5** *with green surch as T* **10**), *surch with T* **14**. P 14.

(a) Wmk Large Star, T **3**.

37	**5**	1d. on 1½d. orange	48·00	35·00
		a. Surch inverted	£300	£300
		b. Surch double	£550	£300
		c. "THRFE"	£275	£225
		d. "PFNCE"	£275	£225
		e. "HALH"	£275	£225
		f. Bisected diag (on cover)	†	£2250
38		1d. on 1s. orange (December)	42·00	32·00
		a. "POSTAGE" (no stop)	£450	
		b. "SHILLNG"	£450	£375
		c. Wide space (3½ mm) between "ONE" and "SHILLING"	£325	£250
		d. Bisected diag (on cover)	†	£2250

(b) Wmk Small Star, T **2**.

39	**5**	1d. on 4d. orange (November)	£160	90·00

1887 (Jan). Wmk Crown CA. P 14.

40	**15**	1d. carmine	2·50	1·75
		a. *Tête-bêche* (vert pair)	9·50	22·00
		s. Optd "Specimen"	50·00	

Due to the sheet formation 50% of the stamps have inverted watermarks.

4d. POSTAGE **(16)**

HALF PENNY POSTAGE **(17)**

1888 (31 Mar)–**91**. *Revenue stamps* (*T* **5** *with green surch as T* **10**) *further surcharged*. W **2**. P 14½, and No. 35.

I. *Surch with T* **16**.

(a) 4 mm between value and "POSTAGE".

41	**5**	4d. on 2s. orange	40·00	19·00
		a. Upright "d" (R. 5/6)	£750	£450
		b. Wide space (2¼ mm) between "TWO" and "SHILLINGS"	£275	£150
		c. First "S" in "SHILLINGS" inverted	£475	£325
		d. Imperf between (horiz pair) ..	£7500	

(b) 5 mm between value and "POSTAGE".

42	5	4d. on 2s. orange	70·00	32·00
		a. Wide space	£350	£225
		b. "S" inverted	£700	£550

II. *Surch as T* **17** *(December 1889).*

43	5	½d. on 2s. orange	14·00	23·00
		a. Surch double	£300	£325
		b. Wide space	£110	£130
		c. "S" inverted	£275	£300

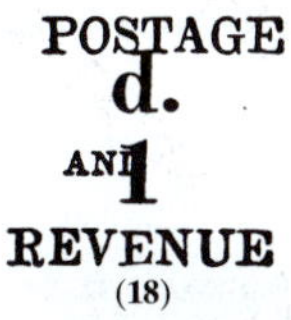

(18)

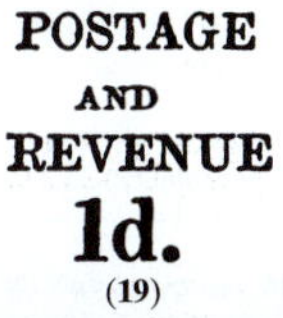

(19)

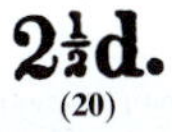

(20)

III. *Surch with T* **18** *(December 1890).*

44	5	1d. on 2s. orange	80·00	80·00
		a. Surch inverted	£750	
		b. Wide space	£325	£325
		c. "S" inverted	£700	£650

IV. *Surch with T* **19** *(January 1891).*

45	5	1d. on 2s. orange	60·00	60·00
		a. No stop after "1d" (R. 3/8)	£375	
		b. Wide space	£250	£250
		c. "S" inverted	£500	£500
46	13	1d. on 8d. grey-brown	11·00	15·00
		a. *Tête-bêche* (vert pair)	40·00	60·00
		b. Surch inverted	£325	£275
		c. No stop after "1d" (R. 6/5)	£250	£250

V. *Surch with T* **20** *(December 1891).*

47	13	2½d. on 8d. grey-brown	10·00	11·00
		a. *Tête-bêche* (vert pair)	40·00	60·00
		b. Surch inverted		
		c. Surch double	£850	£800
		d. Surch double, one inverted	£550	£500
		e. Surch treble	—	£900
		f. Surch treble, two inverted	—	£1000
		s. Optd "Specimen"	65·00	

The surcharges, Types **16/19**, were applied to half sheets as a setting of 60 (12×5).

The wide space between "TWO" and "SHILLINGS" occurs on R. 1/4 and 10/3 of the original 2s. Revenue stamp which was printed in sheets of 120 (12×10).

Type **18** was a two-step surcharge comprising "1d./Revenue", followed by "POSTAGE/AND". An example of No. 44 is known with the "POSTAGE" omitted due to faulty registration and the word applied by hand in a slightly different type style.

There are two varieties of fraction in Type **20**, which each occur 30 times in the setting; in one the "1" has horizontal serif and the "2" commences in a ball; in the other the "1" has sloping serif and the "2" is without ball.

See also D4/7.

21

22

23 Flagship of Columbus. (Columbus named Grenada "La Concepcion")

(Typo D.L.R.)

1895 (6 Sept)–**99**. Wmk Crown CA. P 14.

48	22	½d. mauve and green (9.99)	2·75	1·75
49	21	1d. mauve and carmine (5.96)	4·50	75
50		2d. mauve and brown (9.99)	40·00	32·00
		x. Wmk reversed	£350	£250
51		2½d. mauve and ultramarine	7·50	1·50
52	22	3d. mauve and orange	6·50	16·00
53	21	6d. mauve and green	15·00	45·00
54	22	8d. mauve and black	12·00	45·00
55		1s. green and orange	21·00	50·00
48/55 *Set of* 8			£100	£170
48s/55s Optd "Specimen" *Set of* 8			£150	

(Recess D.L.R.)

1898 (15 Aug). *400th Anniv of Discovery of Grenada by Columbus.* Wmk Crown CC. P 14

56	23	2½d. ultramarine	16·00	6·00
		a. Bluish paper	32·00	40·00
		s. Optd "Specimen"	85·00	

24

25

(Typo D.L.R.)

1902. Wmk Crown CA. P 14.

57	24	½d. dull purple and green	3·25	1·25
58	25	1d. dull purple and carmine	4·50	30
59		2d. dull purple and brown	3·00	10·00
60		2½d. dull purple and ultramarine	3·50	2·75
61	24	3d. dull purple and orange	3·75	9·00
62	25	6d. dull purple and green	2·50	17·00
63	24	1s. green and orange	6·00	28·00
64		2s. green and ultramarine	25·00	55·00
65	25	5s. green and carmine	42·00	70·00
66	24	10s. green and purple	£130	£250
57/66 *Set of* 10			£200	£400
57s/66s Optd "Specimen" *Set of* 10			£190	

1904–06. Wmk Mult Crown CA. *Ordinary paper.* P 14.

67	24	½d. purple and green (1905)	17·00	30·00
68	25	1d. purple and carmine	13·00	2·50
69		2d. purple and brown (1905)	55·00	£120
70		2½d. purple and ultramarine (1905)	55·00	65·00
71	24	3d. purple and orange (1905)	2·75	7·50
		a. Chalk-surfaced paper	3·00	8·50
72	25	6d. purple and green (1906)	7·00	19·00
		a. Chalk-surfaced paper	8·50	26·00
73	24	1s. green and orange (1905)	6·00	30·00
74		2s. green and ultramarine (1906)	50·00	80·00
		a. Chalk-surfaced paper	35·00	75·00
75	25	5s. green and carmine (1906)	65·00	£100
76	24	10s. green and purple (1906)	£160	£250
67/76 *Set of* 10			£375	£600

Examples of most values between Nos. 57 and 76 are known showing a forged G.P.O. Grenada B.W.I. postmark dated "OC 6 09".

26 Badge of the Colony

27 Badge of the Colony

(Recess D.L.R.)

1906. Wmk Mult Crown CA. P 14.

77	26	½d. green	4·50	30
78		1d. carmine	6·50	10
		y. Wmk inverted and reversed		
79		2d. orange	3·00	3·00
80		2½d. blue	6·00	1·75
		a. Ultramarine	9·00	3·50

(Typo D.L.R.)

1908. Wmk Crown CA. *Chalk-surfaced paper.* P 14.

82	27	1s. black/*green*	32·00	60·00
83		10s. green and red/*green*	£110	£225

1908–11. Wmk Mult Crown CA. *Chalk-surfaced paper.* P 14.

84	27	3d. dull purple/*yellow*	4·75	1·75
85		6d. dull purple and purple	20·00	16·00
86		1s. black/*green* (1911)	7·00	4·50
87		2s. blue and purple/*blue*	23·00	12·00
88		5s. green and red/*yellow*	60·00	75·00
77/88 *Set of* 11			£250	£350
77s/80s, 82s/5s, 87s/8s Optd "Specimen" *Set of* 10			£200	

Examples of Nos. 82/8 are known showing a forged G.P.O. Grenada B.W.I. postmark dated "OC 6 09".

28

WAR TAX
(29)

WAR TAX
(30)

(Typo D.L.R.)

1913 (3 Jan)–**22**. Wmk Mult Crown CA. *Chalk-surfaced paper (3d. to 10s.).* P 14.

89	28	½d. yellow-green	1·00	1·60
90		½d. green	1·00	1·00
91		1d. red	2·25	30
92		1d. scarlet (1916)	7·00	1·50
		w. Wmk inverted		
93		2d. orange	1·75	30
94		2½d. bright blue	1·75	2·25
95		2½d. dull blue (1920)	4·75	5·50
96		3d. purple/*yellow*	65	85
		a. White back (3.14)	65	1·50
		as. Optd "Specimen"	32·00	
		b. On lemon (1917)	4·00	9·00
		c. On pale yellow (1921)	6·00	28·00
97		6d. dull and bright purple	1·50	9·00
98		1s. black/*green*	1·00	10·00
		a. White back (3.14)	1·25	7·50
		as. Optd "Specimen"	35·00	
		b. On blue-green, olive back (1917)	35·00	80·00
		c. On emerald surface	1·50	17·00
		d. On emerald back (6.22)	1·00	15·00
		ds. Optd "Specimen"	35·00	
		dw. Wmk inverted	90·00	
99		2s. purple and blue/*blue*	6·50	12·00
100		5s. green and red/*yellow*	17·00	60·00
		a. On pale yellow (1921)	25·00	75·00
		as. Optd "Specimen"	48·00	
101		10s. green and red/*green*	55·00	95·00
		a. On emerald back (6.22)	55·00	£160
		as. Optd "Specimen"	60·00	
89/101 *Set of* 10			80·00	£170
89s/101s Optd "Specimen" (1s. optd in red) *Set of* 10			£180	
98sa 1s. optd in black			35·00	

1916 (1 June). *Optd with T* **29** *by Govt Press, St. George's.*

109	28	1d. red (*shades*)	2·25	1·75
		a. Opt inverted	£275	
		b. Triangle for "A" in "TAX"	55·00	70·00
		s. Handstamped "Specimen"	50·00	

A small "A" in "WAR", 2 mm high is found on Nos. 29, 38 and 48 of the setting of 60 and a very small "A" in "TAX", 1½ mm high, on No. 11. Value about twice normal. The normal "A" is 2¼ mm high.

No. 109b is on No. 56 of the setting.

1916 (1 Sept)–**18**. *Optd with T* **30** *in London.*

111	28	1d. scarlet	30	20
		a. Carmine-red/bluish (5.18)	4·00	1·50
		s. Optd "Specimen"	40·00	
		w. Wmk inverted	£130	

1921–32. Wmk Mult Script CA. *Chalk-surfaced paper (3d. (No. 122) to 10s.)* P 14.

112	28	½d. green	1·25	30
113		1d. carmine-red	80	75
114		1d. brown (1923)	1·50	30
115		1½d. rose-red (6.22)	1·50	1·50
116		2d. orange	1·25	30
117		2d. grey (1926)	2·50	2·75
117*a*		2½d. dull blue	4·50	3·50
118		2½d. grey (6.22)	1·00	9·00
119		2½d. bright blue (1926)	4·50	3·75
120		2½d. ultramarine (1931)	4·50	8·50
120*a*		2½d. chalky blue and blue (1932)	50·00	50·00
121		3d. bright blue (6.22)	1·25	11·00
122		3d. purple/*yellow* (1926)	3·00	5·00
123		4d. black and red/*yellow* (1926)	1·00	3·75
124		5d. dull purple & sage-green (27.12.22)	1·50	4·25
125		6d. dull and bright purple	1·25	23·00
126		6d. black and carmine (1926)	2·25	2·50
127		9d. dull purple and black (27.12.22)	2·25	9·50
128		1s. black/*emerald* (1923)	2·50	50·00
		y. Wmk inverted and reversed	£160	
129		1s. chestnut (1926)	3·00	10·00
130		2s. purple and blue/*black* (1922)	6·00	17·00
131		2s.6d. black and carmine/*blue* (1929)	7·00	23·00
132		3s. green and violet (27.12.22)	8·00	27·00
133		5s. green and red/*pale yellow* (1923)	12·00	35·00
134		10s. green and red/*emerald* (1923)	50·00	£130
112/19, 121/34 *Set of* 22			£110	£325
112s/34s Optd or Perf (2s.6d.) "Specimen" *Set of* 23			£375	

Some values of Nos. 89/101 and 112/34 have been seen with part strikes of the forged postmark mentioned after Nos. 67/76 and 77/88.

31 Grand Anse Beach

32 Badge of the Colony

33 Grand Etang

34 St. George's

(Recess Waterlow)

1934 (23 Oct)–**36**. Wmk Mult Script CA (sideways on T **32**). P 12½.

135	31	½d. green	15	1·25
		a. Perf 12½×13½ (1936)	5·00	50·00
136	32	1d. black and sepia	1·50	3·25
		a. Perf 13½×12½ (1936)	60	35
137	33	1½d. black and scarlet	4·75	3·50
		a. Perf 12½×13½ (1936)	1·25	40
138	32	2d. black and orange	1·00	75
139	34	2½d. blue	50	50
140	32	3d. black and olive-green	1·00	2·75
141		6d. black and purple	2·00	1·75
142		1s. black and brown	2·00	4·00
143		2s.6d. black and ultramarine	8·00	28·00
144		5s. black and violet	42·00	50·00
135/44 *Set of* 10			55·00	80·00
135s/44s Perf "Specimen" *Set of* 10			£160	

1935 (6 May). *Silver Jubilee. As Nos. 91/4 of Antigua but ptd by Waterlow.* P 11×12.

145		½d. black and green	80	1·25
		k. Kite and vertical log	55·00	75·00
		l. Kite and horizontal log	75·00	£110
146		1d. ultramarine and grey	1·25	1·75
		l. Kite and horizontal log	£100	£120
147		1½d. deep blue and scarlet	1·25	3·50
		l. Kite and horizontal log	£110	£180
148		1s. slate and purple	9·00	26·00
		l. Kite and horizontal log	£225	£325
145/8 *Set of* 4			11·00	29·00
145s/8s Perf "Specimen" *Set of* 4			95·00	

For illustrations of plate varieties see Omnibus section following Zanzibar.

1937 (12 May). *Coronation. As Nos. 95/7 of Antigua.* P 11×11½.

149		1d. violet	40	1·75
150		1½d. carmine	40	50
151		2½d. blue	80	1·25
149/51 *Set of* 3			1·40	3·25
149s/51s Perf "Specimen" *Set of* 3			85·00	

35 King George VI

(Photo Harrison)

1937 (12 July)–**50**. Wmk Mult Script CA. *Chalk-surfaced paper.* P 15×14.

152	35	¼d. brown	1·75	20
		a. Ordinary paper (11.42)	30	1·50

		b. Ordinary paper. *Chocolate* (1.45)	20	1·50
		c. Chalk-surfaced paper. *Chocolate* (8.50)	70	3·75

The ordinary paper is thick, smooth and opaque.

36 Grand Anse Beach

40 Badge of the Colony

Line on sail (Centre Pl 3 R. 1/1. Later partially retouched)

Colon flaw (R. 5/6. Corrected on ptg of Nov 1950)

(Recess D.L.R. (10s.), Waterlow (others))

1938 (16 Mar)–**50**. *As T* **31/4** *(but portrait of King George VI as in T* **36***) and T* **40**. Wmk Mult Script CA (sideways on T **32**). P 12½ or 12×13 (10s.).

153	**36**	½d. yellow-green	8·00	1·50
		a. Blue-green (10.9.43)	60	1·25
		b. Perf 12½×13½ (1938)	6·00	80
		ba. Blue-green	6·50	5·00
154	**32**	1d. black and sepia	1·00	20
		a. Perf 13½×12½ (1938)	50	50
		ab. Line on sail	90·00	
155	**33**	1½d. black and scarlet	50	1·00
		a. Perf 12½×13½ (1938)	2·25	30
156	**32**	2d. black and orange	30	50
		a. Perf 13½×12½ (1938)	2·50	85
		ab. Line on sail	£110	
157	**34**	2½d. bright blue	30	30
		a. Perf 12½×13½ (?March 1950)	£6500	£180
158	**32**	3d. black and olive-green	14·00	1·40
		a. Perf 13½×12½ (16.3.38)	6·00	1·00
		ab. Black and brown-olive (1942)	30	80
		ac. Line on sail	85·00	
		b. Perf 12½. *Black & brn-ol* (16.8.50)	30	1·90
		ba. Colon flaw	85·00	
159		6d. black and purple	2·00	40
		a. Perf 13½×12½ (1942)	2·25	50
		b. Line on sail	£200	
160		1s. black and brown	3·00	40
		a. Perf 13½×12½ (1941)	4·00	1·75
161		2s. black and ultramarine	27·00	1·75
		a. Perf 13½×12½ (1941)	29·00	1·50
162		5s. black and violet	3·75	3·25
		a. Perf 13½×12½ (1947)	3·00	5·50
163	**40**	10s. steel blue and carmine (*narrow*) (P 12×13)	55·00	9·00
		a. Perf 14. *Steel blue and bright carmine (narrow)*	£180	45·00
		b. Perf 14. *Slate-blue and bright carmine (narrow)* (1943)	£200	£120
		c. Perf 12. *Slate-blue and bright carmine (narrow)* (1943)	£650	£1600
		d. Perf 14. *Slate-blue and carmine lake (wide)* (1944)	£110	9·00
		e. Perf 14. *Blue-black and carmine (narrow)* (1943)	32·00	9·00
		ea. Frame printed double, one albino	£3750	
		f. Perf 14. *Blue-black and bright carmine (wide)* (1947)	25·00	25·00
152/63e *Set of* 12			55·00	16·00
152s/63s Perf "Specimen" *Set of* 12			£250	

In the earlier printings of the 10s. the paper was dampened before printing and the subsequent shrinkage produced narrow frames 23½ to 23¾ mm wide. Later printings were made on dry paper producing wide frames 24¼ mm wide.

No. 163a is one of the earlier printings, line perf 13.8×14.1. Later printings of the 10s. are line perf 14.1.

Nos. 163b/c show a blurred centre caused by the use of a worn plate.

Nos. 163a and 163b may be found with gum more or less yellow due to local climatic conditions.

Examples of No. 163c are known showing forged St. George's postmarks dated "21 AU 42", "21 AU 43" or "2 OC 43".

1946 (25 Sept). *Victory. As Nos. 110/11 of Antigua.*

164	1½d. carmine	10	50
165	3½d. blue	10	1·00
164s/5s Perf "Specimen" *Set of* 2		75·00	

1948 (27 Oct). *Royal Silver Wedding. As Nos. 112/13 of Antigua.*

166	1½d. scarlet	15	10
167	10s. slate-green	16·00	17·00

(New Currency. 100 cents = 1 West Indian, later Eastern Caribbean, dollar)

1949 (10 Oct). *75th Anniv of Universal Postal Union. As Nos. 114/17 of Antigua.*

168	5c. ultramarine	15	10
169	6c. olive	1·50	2·50
170	12c. magenta	15	30
171	24c. red-brown	15	40
168/71 *Set of* 4		1·75	3·00

41 King George VI

42 Badge of the Colony

43 Badge of the Colony

(Recess B.W. (T **41**), D.L.R. (others))

1951 (8 Jan). Wmk Mult Script CA. P 11½ (T **41**), 11½×12½ (T **42**), and 11½×13 (T **43**).

172	**41**	½c. black and red-brown	15	1·60
173		1c. black and emerald-green	15	25
174		2c. black and brown	15	50
175		3c. black and rose-carmine	15	10
176		4c. black and orange	35	40
177		5c. black and violet	20	10
178		6c. black and olive	30	60
179		7c. black and light blue	1·75	10
180		12c. black and purple	2·25	30
181	**42**	25c. black and sepia	2·25	80
182		50c. black and blue	6·50	40
183		$1.50 black and yellow-orange	7·50	7·00
184	**43**	$2.50 slate-blue and carmine	6·50	5·50
172/184 *Set of* 13			25·00	15·00

1951 (16 Feb). *Inauguration of B.W.I. University College. As Nos. 118/19 of Antigua.*

185	3c. black and carmine	45	1·25
186	6c. black and olive	45	50

NEW CONSTITUTION

1951

(44)

1951 (21 Sept). *New Constitution. Nos. 175/7 and 180 optd with T* **44** *by B.W.*

187	**41**	3c. black and rose-carmine	20	60
188		4c. black and orange	20	60
189		5c. black and violet (R.)	20	80
190		12c. black and purple	20	1·00
187/90 *Set of* 4			70	2·75

1953 (3 June). *Coronation. As No. 120 of Antigua.*

191	3c. black and carmine-red	20	10

45 Queen Elizabeth II

46 Badge of the Colony

47 Badge of the Colony

(Recess B.W. (T **45**), D.L.R. (T **46/7**))

1953 (15 June)–**59**. Wmk Mult Script CA. P 11½ (T **45**), 11½×12½ (T **46**), or 11½×13 (T **47**).

192	**45**	½c. black and brown (28.12.53)	10	10
193		1c. black and deep emerald	10	10
194		2c. black and sepia (15.9.53)	30	10
195		3c. black and carmine-red (22.2.54)	10	10
196		4c. black and brown-orange (22.2.54)	10	10
197		5c. black and deep violet (22.2.54)	10	10
198		6c. black and olive-green (28.12.53)	1·00	1·25
199		7c. black and blue (6.6.55)	1·50	10
200		12c. black and reddish purple	30	10
201	**46**	25c. black and sepia (10.1.55)	1·25	20
202		50c. black and deep blue (2.12.55)	5·50	40
203		$1.50 black & brown-orange (2.12.55)	11·00	14·00
204	**47**	$2.50 slate-blue & carmine (16.11.59)	21·00	10·00
192/204 *Set of* 13			38·00	24·00

On 23 December 1965, No. 203 was issued surcharged "2" but this was intended for fiscal and revenue purposes and it was not authorised to be used postally, although some are known to have passed through the mail.

For stamps in Types **45/6** watermarked w **12** see Nos. 214/20.

1958 (22 Apr). *Inauguration of British Caribbean Federation. As Nos. 135/7 of Antigua.*

205	3c. deep green	35	10
206	6c. blue	45	60
207	12c. scarlet	55	10
205/7 *Set of* 3		1·25	70

48 Queen Victoria, Queen Elizabeth II, Mail Van and Post Office, St George's

(Photo Harrison)

1961 (1 June). *Grenada Stamp Centenary. T* **48** *and similar horiz designs.* W w 12. P 14½×14.

208	3c. crimson and black	25	10
209	8c. bright blue and orange	55	25
210	25c. lake and blue	55	25
208/10 *Set of* 3		1·25	55

Designs:—8c. Queen Victoria, Queen Elizabeth II and flagship of Columbus; 25c. Queen Victoria, Queen Elizabeth II, *Solent I* (paddle-steamer) and Douglas DC-3 aircraft.

1963 (4 June). *Freedom from Hunger. As No. 146 of Antigua.*

211	8c. bluish green	30	15

1963 (2 Sept). *Red Cross Centenary. As Nos. 147/8 of Antigua.*

212	3c. red and black	20	15
213	25c. red and blue	40	15

1964 (12 May)–**66**. *As Nos. 194/8, 201/1, but wmk w* **12**.

214	**45**	2c. black and sepia	25	10
215		3c. black and carmine-red	25	10
216		4c. black and brown-orange	25	1·25
217		5c. black and deep violet	25	10
218		6c. black and olive-green (4.1.66)	£190	65·00
219		12c. black and reddish purple	35	30
220	**46**	25c. black and sepia	3·25	1·25
214/20 *Set of* 7			£190	65·00

1965 (17 May). *I.T.U. Centenary. As Nos. 166/7 of Antigua.*

221	2c. red-orange and yellow-olive	10	10
222	50c. lemon and light red	25	20

1965 (25 Oct). *International Co-operation Year. As Nos. 168/9 of Antigua.*

223	1c. reddish purple and turquoise-green	10	15
224	25c. deep bluish green and lavender	20	15

1966 (24 Jan). *Churchill Commemoration. As Nos. 170/3 of Antigua.*

225	1c. new blue	10	15
226	3c. deep green	10	15
227	25c. brown	15	10
228	35c. bluish violet	25	15
225/8 *Set of* 4		45	40

1966 (4 Feb). *Royal Visit. As Nos. 174/5 of Antigua.*

229	3c. black and ultramarine	25	15
230	35c. black and magenta	65	15

52 Hillsborough, Carriacou

53 Badge of the Colony

54 Queen Elizabeth II

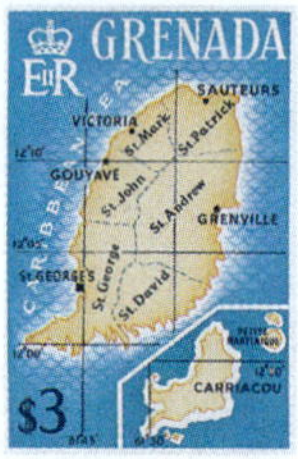

55 Map of Grenada

(Des V. Whiteley. Photo Harrison)

1966 (1 Apr). *Horiz designs as T* **52**, *and T* **53/5**. *Multicoloured.* W w **12**. P 14½ ($1, $2, $3) or 14½×13½ (others).

231	1c. Type **52**	20	1·25
232	2c. Bougainvillea	20	10
233	3c. Flamboyant plant	1·00	1·00
234	5c. Levera beach	1·25	10
235	6c. Carenage, St George's	1·00	10
236	8c. Annandale Falls	1·00	10
	w. Wmk inverted		
237	10c. Cocoa pods	50	10
	w. Wmk inverted		
238	12c. Inner Harbour	30	1·25
239	15c. Nutmeg	30	1·25
240	25c. St George's	30	10
241	35c. Grand Anse beach	30	10
242	50c. Bananas	1·25	2·00
243	$1 Type **53**	7·00	3·75
244	$2 Type **54**	5·00	8·50
245	$3 Type **55**	4·50	15·00
231/45 *Set of* 15		21·00	30·00

1966 (1 July). *World Cup Football Championship. As Nos. 176/7 of Antigua.*

246	5c. violet, yellow-green, lake and yellow-brown	10	10
247	50c. chocolate, blue-green, lake and yellow-brown	40	90

1966 (20 Sept). *Inauguration of W.H.O. Headquarters, Geneva. As Nos. 178/9 of Antigua.*

248	8c. black, yellow-green and light blue	20	10
249	25c. black, light purple and yellow-brown	45	20

1966 (1 Dec). *20th Anniv of U.N.E.S.C.O. As Nos. 196/8 of Antigua.*

250	2c. slate-violet, red, yellow and orange	10	10
251	15c. orange-yellow, violet and deep olive	15	10
257	50c. black, bright purple and orange	30	90
250/2	*Set of 3*	45	1·00

ASSOCIATED STATEHOOD

ASSOCIATED STATEHOOD 1967
(67)

(68)

1967 (3 Mar). *Statehood. Nos. 232/3, 236 and 240 optd with T* **67**, *in silver.*

253	2c. Bougainvillea	10	15
254	3c. Flamboyant plant	10	10
255	8c. Annandale Falls	15	10
256	25c. St George's	15	15
253/6	*Set of 4*	30	30

1967 (1 June). *World Fair, Montreal. Nos. 232, 237, 239 and 243/4 surch as T* **68** *or optd with "Expo" emblem only.*

257	1c. on 15c. Nutmeg	10	20
	a. Surch and opt albino	14·00	
258	2c. Bougainvillea	10	20
259	3c. on 10c. Cocoa pods	10	20
	w. Wmk inverted	8·00	
260	$1 Type **53**	30	25
261	$2 Type **54**	45	30
257/61	*Set of 5*	70	1·00

ASSOCIATED STATEHOOD
(69)

70 Kennedy and Local Flower

1967 (1 Oct). *Statehood. Nos. 231/45 optd with T* **69**.

262	1c. Type **52**	10	10
263	2c. Bougainvillea	10	10
264	3c. Flamboyant plant	10	10
265	5c. Levers each	10	10
266	6c. Carenaga St George's	10	10
267	8c. Annandale Falls	10	10
268	10c. Cocoa pods	10	10
269	12c. Inner harbour	10	10
270	15c. Nutmeg	15	10
271	25c. St George's	20	10
272	35c. Grand Anse beach	55	10
273	50c. Bananas	1·00	20
274	$1 Type **53**	1·50	60
275	$2 Type **54**	1·25	3·75
276	$3 Type **55**	2·25	5·50
262/76	*Set of 15*	6·50	10·00

See also No. 295.

(Des M. Shamir. Photo Harrison)

1968 (13 Jan). *50th Birth Anniv of President Kennedy. T* **70** *and similar horiz designs. Multicoloured.* P 14½×14.

277	1c. Type **70**	10	25
278	15c. Type **70**	10	10
279	25c. Kennedy and strelitzia	10	10
280	35c. Kennedy and roses	10	10
281	50c. As 25c.	15	20
282	$1 As 35c.	25	60
277/82	*Set of 6*	55	1·00

73 Scout Bugler

76 "Near Antibes"

(Des K. Plowitz. Photo Govt Printer, Israel)

1968 (17 Feb). *World Scout Jamboree, Idaho. T* **73** *and similar vert designs. Multicoloured.* P 13×13½.

283	1c. Type **73**	10	10
284	2c. Scouts camping	10	10
285	3c. Lord Baden-Powell	10	10
286	35c. Type **73**	25	10
287	50c. As 2c.	35	20
288	$1 As 3c.	50	55
283/8	*Set of 6*	1·10	80

(Des G. Vasarhelyi. Photo Harrison)

1968 (23 Mar). *Paintings by Sir Winston Churchill. T* **76** *and similar horiz designs. Multicoloured.* P 14×14½.

289	10c. Type **76**	10	10
290	12c. "The Mediterranea"	15	10
291	15c. "St Jean Cap Ferratt"	15	10
292	25c. Type **76**	20	10
293	35c. As 15c.	25	10
294	50c. Sir Winston painting	35	25
289/94	*Set of 6*	1·10	45

$5
(80)

CHILDREN NEED MILK
2cts. + 3cts.
(81)

CHILDREN NEED MILK
1c. + 3cts.
(82)

1968 (18 May). *No. 275 surch with T* **80**.

295	**54**	$5 on $2 multicoloured	1·25	2·25

1968 (22 July–19 Aug). *"Children Need Milk".*

(a) Nos. 244/5 surch locally as T **81** *(22 July).*

296	**54**	2c.+3c. on $2 multicoloured	10	10
297	**55**	3c.+3c. on $3 multicoloured	10	10
		a. Surch inverted	50·00	15·00
		b. Surch double	22·00	
		c. Surch double, one albino		

(b) Nos. 243/4 surch locally as T **82** *(19 Aug).*

298	**53**	1c.+3c. on $1 multicoloured	10	40
		a. Surch on No. 274	75·00	75·00
		b. Surch double	35·00	
299	**54**	2c.+3c. on $2 multicoloured	16·00	55·00
		a. Surch on No. 275	80·00	
296/9		*Set of 4*	16·00	55·00

83 Edith McGuire (U.S.A.)

86 Hibiscus

(Des M. Shamir. Photo Harrison)

1968 (24 Sept). *Olympic Games, Mexico. T* **83** *and similar square designs.* P 12½.

300	1c. brown, black and blue	10	50
301	2c. orange, brown, blue and lilac	10	50
	a. Orange (badge, etc.) omitted		
302	3c. scarlet, brown and dull green	10	50
	a. Scarlet (rings, "MEXICO" etc.) omitted	£750	
303	10c. brown, black, blue and vermilion	15	50
304	50c. orange, brown, blue and turquoise	55	75
305	60c. scarlet, brown and red-orange	60	80
300/5	*Set of 6*	1·25	3·25

Designs:—2, 50c. Arthur Wint (Jamaica); 3, 60c. Ferreira da Silva (Brazil); 10c. Type **83**.

Nos. 300/2 and 303/5 were issued in separate composite sheets containing three strips of three with three *se-tenant* labels showing Greek athlete (Nos. 300/2) or Discobolos (Nos. 303/5). (*Price for two sheets £6 mint, £8 used*).

(Des G. Vasarhelyi (No. 314a), V. Whiteley (75c.), M. Shamir (others). Litho Format (Nos. 314a and 317a). Photo Harrison (others))

1968 (1 Oct)–**71**. *Multicoloured designs as T* **86**. P 13½ (Nos. 314a. and 317a), 13½×14½ (vert except No. 314a) or 14½×13½ (horiz except No. 317a).

306	1c. Type **86**	10	10
307	2c. Strelitzia	10	10
308	3c. Bougainvillea (1.7.69)	10	10
309	5c. Rock Hind (*horiz*) (4.2.69)	10	10
310	6c. Sailfish	10	10
311	8c. Red Snapper (*horiz*) (1.7.69)	10	60
312	10c. Marine Toad (*horiz*) (4.2.69)	10	10
313	12c. Turtle	15	10
314	15c. Tree Boa (*horiz*)	1·00	60
314*a*	15c. Thunbergia (1970)	2·75	2·50
315	25c. Greater Trinidadian Murine Opossum (4.2.69)	30	10
316	35c. Nine-banded Armadillo (*horiz*) (1.7.69)	35	10
317	50c. Mona Monkey	45	25
317*a*	75c. Yacht in St. George's Harbour (*horiz*) (9.10.71)	14·00	8·50
318	$1 Bananaquit	3·00	1·50
319	$2 Brown Pelican (4.2.69)	8·00	12·00
320	$3 Magnificent Frigate Bird	4·50	6·00
321	$5 Bare-eyed Thrush (1.7.69)	10·00	24·00
306/21	*Set of 18*	40·00	50·00

Nos. 314*a*, 317*a* and the dollar values are larger—29×45½, 44×28½ and 25½×48 mm respectively.

No. 317*a* exists imperforate from stock dispersed by the liquidator of Format International Security Printers Ltd.

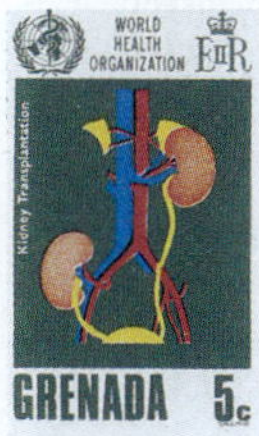

102 Kidney Transplant

106 "The Adoration of the Kings" (Veronese)

(Des M. Shamir. Litho B.W.)

1968 (25 Nov). *20th Anniv of World Health Organization. T* **102** *and similar vert designs. Multicoloured.* P 13×13½.

322	5c. Type **102**	20	10
323	25c. Heart transplant	30	10
324	35c. Lung transplant	30	10
325	50c. Eye transplant	35	50
322/5	*Set of 4*	1·10	60

(Photo Harrison)

1968 (3 Dec). *Christmas. T* **106** *and similar square designs.* P 12½.

326	5c. multicoloured	10	10
327	15c. multicoloured	10	10
328	35c. multicoloured	10	10
329	$1 multicoloured	30	40
326/9	*Set of 4*	40	45

Designs:—15c. "Madonna and Child with Sts John and Catherine" (Titian); 35c. "Adoration of the Kings" (Botticelli); $1 "A Warrior Adoring" (Catena).

VISIT CARIFTA EXPO '69
April 5-30
5c
(110)

1969 (1 Feb). *Caribbean Free Trade Area Exhibition. Nos. 300/5 surch in red as T* **110**.

330	5c. on 1c. brown, black and blue	10	10
	a. Surch double		
331	8c. on 2c. orange, brown, blue and lilac	10	10
	a. Surch double		
332	25c. on 3c. scarlet, brown and dull green	10	10
	a. Surch double		
333	35c. on 10c. brown, black, blue and vermilion	10	10
334	$1 on 50c. orange, brown, blue and turquoise	20	30
335	$2 on 60c. scarlet, brown and red-orange	35	60
	a. Scarlet (rings, "MEXICO" etc) omitted	†	—
330/5	*Set of 6*	65	1·00

The centre of the composite sheets is also overprinted with a commemorative inscription publicising CARIFTA EXPO 1969 (*Price for two sheets £11 mint or used*).

111 Dame Hylda Bynoe (Governor) and Island Scene

(Des and litho D.L.R.)

1969 (1 May). *Carifta Expo 1969. T* **111** *and similar horiz designs. Multicoloured.* P 13×13½.

336	5c. Type **111**	10	10
337	15c. Premier E. M. Gairy and Island scene	10	10
338	50c. Type **111**	10	30
339	60c. Emblems of 1958 and 1967 World's Fairs	10	65
336/9	*Set of 4*	30	70

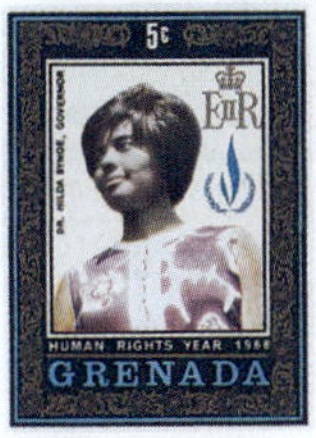

114 Dame Hylda Bynoe

115 "Balshazzar's Feast" (Rembrandt)

(Photo Enschedé)

1969 (8 June). *Human Rights Year. T* **114/15** *and similar multicoloured design.* P 12½×13 ($1) or 13×12½ (others).

340	5c. Type **114**	10	10
341	25c. Dr Martin Luther King (*vert*)	15	10
342	35c. Type **114**	15	10
343	$1 Type **115**	30	45
340/3	*Set of 4*	55	55

117 Batsman and Wicket-keeper

(Des M. Shamir and L. W. Denyer. Photo Harrison)

1969 (1 Aug). *Cricket. T* **117** *and similar horiz designs.* P 14×14½.

344	3c. yellow, brown and ultramarine	25	1·00
	a. Yellow (caps and wicket) omitted	£475	
345	10c. multicoloured	25	40
346	25c. brown, ochre and myrtle-green	45	85
347	35c. multicoloured	65	90
344/7	*Set of 4*	1·75	2·75

Designs:—10c. Batsman playing defensive stroke; 25c. Batsman sweeping ball; 35c. Batsman playing on-drive.
Nos. 344/7 were each issued in small sheets of 9 (3×3) with decorative borders.

129 Astronaut handling Moon Rock

(Des G. Vasarhelyi. Photo)

1969 (24 Sept). *First Man on the Moon. T* **129** *and similar multicoloured designs.* P 13½ (½c.) or 12½ (others).

348	½c. As Type **129** but larger (56×35 mm.)	10	10
349	1c. Moon rocket and moon	10	10
350	2c. Module landing	10	10
351	3c. Declaration left on moon	10	10
352	8c. Module leaving rocket	10	10
353	25c. Rocket lifting-off (*vert*)	25	10
354	35c. Spacecraft in orbit (*vert*)	25	10
355	50c. Capsule with parachutes (*vert*)	35	30
356	$1 Type **129**	50	1·25
348/56 *Set of 9*		1·40	1·60
MS357 115×90 mm. Nos. 351 and 356. Imperf.		1·00	2·75

130 Gandhi

(Des A. Robledo. Litho B.W.)

1969 (8 Oct). *Birth Centenary of Mahatma Gandhi. T* **130** *and similar designs.* P 11½.

358	**130** 6c. multicoloured	35	20
359	– 15c. multicoloured	45	10
360	– 25c. multicoloured	50	10
361	– $1 multicoloured	80	60
358/61 *Set of 4*		1·90	75
MS362 155×122 mm. Nos. 358/61. Imperf.		2·25	3·50

Designs: *Vert*—15c. Gandhi standing; 25c. Gandhi waking. *Horiz*—$1 Head of Gandhi.

(**134**)

135 "Blackbeard" (Edward Teach)

1969 (23 Dec). *Christmas. Nos. 326/9 surch with T* **134** *in black (2c.) or optd with new date only in silver (others).*

363	2c. on 15c. multicoloured	10	1·40
	a. Surch inverted	40·00	
364	5c. multicoloured	10	10
	a. Opt double	40·00	
365	35c. multicoloured	20	10
	a. Opt inverted	40·00	
	b. Horiz pair, one with opt omitted	£200	
	c. Opt double, one vertical	45·00	
366	$1 multicoloured	80	1·90
	a. Opt inverted	40·00	
363/6 *Set of 4*		1·00	3·00

(Des K. Plowitz. Recess B.W.)

1970 (2 Feb). *Pirates. T* **135** *and similar vert designs.* P 13½.

367	15c. black	35	10
368	25c. dull green	50	10
369	50c. lilac	90	20
370	$1 carmine	1·50	75
367/70 *Set of 4*		3·00	1·00

Designs:—25c. Anne Bonney; 50c. Jean Lafitte; $1 Mary Read.

(**139**)

(**140**)

1970 (18 Mar). *No. 348 surch with T* **139**.

371	5c. on ½c. multicoloured	10	10
	a. Surch double	25·00	
	b. Surch with T **140**	70	70
	ba. Surch double, one inverted	40·00	

141/2 "The Last Supper" (detail, Del Sarto)

(Des and litho B.W.)

1970 (13 Apr). *Easter. Paintings. T* **141/2** *and similar vert design. Mulicoloured.* P 11½.

372	5c. Type **141/2**	10	40
373	5c. Type **142**	10	40
374	15c. "Christ crowned with Thorns" (detail, Van Dyck)	15	40
375	15c. As No. 374	15	40
376	25c. "The Passion of Christ" (detail, Memling)	15	40
377	25c. As No. 376	15	40
378	60c. "Christ in the Tomb" (detail, Rubens)	20	60
379	60c. As No. 378	20	60
372/9 *Set of 8*		1·00	3·25
MS380 120×140 mm. Nos. 376/9		75	1·75

Nos. 372/9 were issued with each design spread over two *se-tenant* stamps of the same denomination.

149 Girl with Kittens in Pram

(Des A. Robledo. Litho Questa)

1970 (27 May). *Birth Bicentenary of William Wordsworth (poet). "Children and Pets". T* **149** *and similar horiz designs. Multicoloured.* P 11.

381	5c. Type **149**	15	15
382	15c. Girl with puppy and kitten	25	15
383	30c. Boy with fishing rod and cat	30	30
384	60c. Boys and girls with cats and dogs	40	1·75
381/4 *Set of 4*		1·00	2·10
MS385 Two sheets each 114×126 mm. Nos. 381, 383 and Nos. 382, 384. Imperf		1·00	2·00

153 Parliament of India

(Des G. Vasarhelyi. Litho Questa)

1970 (15 June). *Seventh Regional Conference of Commonwealth Parliamentary Association. T* **153** *and similar horiz designs. Multicoloured.* P 14.

386	5c. Type **153**	10	10
387	25c. Parliament of Great Britain, Westminster	10	10
388	50c. Parliament of Canada	20	15
389	60c. Parliament of Grenada	20	15
386/9 *Set of 4*		50	35
MS390 126×90 mm. Nos. 386/9		50	90

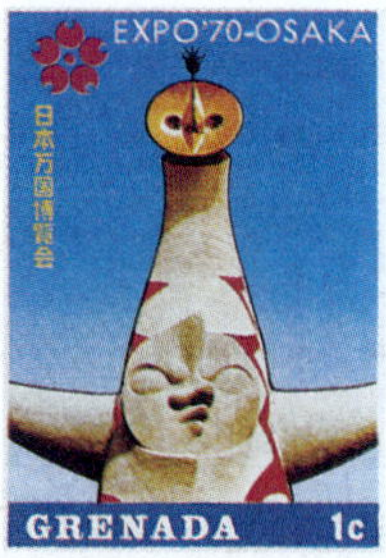
157 Tower of the Sun

(Litho Kyodo Printing Co, Tokyo)

1970 (8 Aug). *World Fair, Osaka. T* **157** *and similar multicoloured designs.* P 13.

391	1c. Type **157**	10	55
392	2c. Livelihood and Industry Pavilion (*horiz*)	10	55
393	3c. Flower painting, 1634	10	55
394	10c. "Adam and Eve" (Tintoretto) (*horiz*)	10	10
395	25c. OECD (Organisation for Economic Co-operation and Development) Pavilion (*horiz*)	15	10
396	50c. San Francisco Pavilion	30	1·60
391/6 *Set of 6*		65	3·00
MS397 121×91 mm. $1 Japanese Pavilion (56×34 mm)		55	1·50

164 Roosevelt and "Raising U.S. Flag on Iwo Jima"

(Litho Questa)

1970 (3 Sept). *25th Anniv of Ending of World War II. T* **164** *and similar horiz designs. Multicoloured.* P 11.

398	½c. Type **164**	10	1·25
399	5c. Zhukov and "Fall of Berlin"	70	65
400	15c. Churchill and "Evacuation at Dunkirk"	1·50	60
401	25c. De Gaulle and "Liberation of Paris"	1·25	60
402	50c. Eisenhower and "D-Day Landing"	1·50	1·50
403	60c. Montgomery and "Battle of Alamein"	1·50	3·25
398/403 *Set of 6*		7·00	7·00
MS404 163×113 mm. Nos. 398, 400, 402/3		2·75	7·00
	a. Brown (panel) on 60c. value omitted	£700	

PHILYMPIA
LONDON 1970
(**169**)

170 U.P.U. Emblem, Building and Transport

1970 (18 Sept). *"Philympia 1970" Stamp Exhibition, London. Nos. 353/6 optd with T* **169**.

405	25c. Rocket lifting-off	10	10
	a. Albino opt	4·75	
	b. Opt inverted	17·00	
406	35c. Spacecraft in orbit	10	10
	a. Opt inverted	45·00	
	b. Opt double, one albino, one inverted		
407	50c. Capsule with parachutes	15	15
	a. Albino opt	3·50	
408	$1 Type **129** (Sil.) (optd vert upwards)	20	30
	a. Albino opt	6·50	
405/8 *Set of 4*		40	50

The miniature sheet was also overprinted but we understand that only 300 of these were put on sale in Grenada.

(Litho Questa)

1970 (17 Oct). *New U.P.U. Headquarters Building. T* **170** *and similar multicoloured designs.* P 14.

409	15c. Type **170**	1·00	30
410	25c. As Type **170**, but modern transport	1·00	30
411	50c. Sir Rowland Hill and U.P.U. Building	35	45
412	$1 Abraham Lincoln and U.P.U. Building	45	2·50
409/12 *Set of 4*		2·50	3·25
MS413 79×85 mm. Nos. 411/12		1·00	3·50

The 50c. and $1 are both vertical designs.

171 "The Madonna of the Goldfinch" (Tiepolo)

172 19th-Century Nursing

(Des G. Vasarhelyi. Litho Questa)

1970 (5 Dec). *Christmas. T* **171** *and similar vert designs. Multicoloured.* P 13½.

414	½c. Type **171**	10	35
415	½c. "The Virgin and Child with St Peter and St. Paul" (Bouts)	10	35
416	½c. "The Virgin and Child" (Bellini)	10	35
417	2c. "The Madonna of the Basket" (Correggio)	10	35
418	3c. Type **171**	10	35
419	35c. As No. 415	20	10
420	50c. As 2c.	30	40
421	$1 As No. 416	50	1·60
414/21 *Set of 8*		1·10	3·50
MS422 102×87 mm. Nos. 420/1		1·00	3·00

(Des G. Vasarhelyi. Litho Questa)

1970 (12 Dec). *Centenary of British Red Cross. T* **172** *and similar horiz designs. Multicoloured.* P 14½×14.

423	5c. Type **172**	20	10
424	15c. Military Ambulance, 1918	25	10
425	25c. First-Aid Post, 1941	35	10
426	60c. Red Cross Transport, 1970	90	1·50

423/6 *Set of* 4 ... 1·50 1·60
MS427 113×82 mm. Nos. 423/6 ... 2·00 1·60
a. Error. Imperf ... 25·00

POSTAGE DUE STAMPS

D 1

1d.
SURCHARGE
POSTAGE
(D 2)

(Typo D.L.R.)

1892 (18 Apr–Oct).

(a) Type D **1**. Wmk Crown CA. P 14.

D1	D **1**	1d. blue-black	27·00	1·50
D2		2d. blue-black	£190	1·50
D3		3d. blue-black	£200	2·50
D1/3 *Set of* 3			£375	5·00

(b) Nos. 34 and 35 surch locally as Type D **2**.

D4	**13**	1d. on 6d. mauve (10.92)	90·00	1·25
		a. *Tête-bêche* (vert pair)	£1700	£1100
		b. Surch double	—	£160
D5		1d. on 8d. grey-brown (8.92)	£1000	3·25
		a. *Tête-bêche* (vert pair)	£5000	£1800
D6		2d. on 6d. mauve (10.92)	£170	2·50
		a. *Tête-bêche* (vert pair)	£2500	£1400
D7		2d. on 8d. grey-brown (8.92)	£2000	10·00
		a. *Tête-bêche* (vert pair)	£7500	£3500

Nos. D4/7 were in use from August to November 1892. As supplies of Nos. D1/3 were available from April or May of that year it would not appear that they were intended for postage due purposes. There was a shortage of 1d. postage stamps in July and August, but this was alleviated by Nos. 44/5 which were still available. The provisionals may have been intended for postal purposes, but the vast majority appear to have been used philatelically.

1906 (1 July)–**11**. Wmk Mult Crown CA. P 14.

D8	D **1**	1d. blue-black (1911)	3·50	7·50
D9		2d. blue-black	11·00	1·75
D10		3d. blue-black (9.06)	13·00	6·00
D8/10 *Set of* 3			25·00	13·50

1921 (1 Dec)–**22**. *As Type* D **1**, *but inscr* "POSTAGE DUE". Wmk Mult Script CA. P 14.

D11	1d. black	1·50	1·00
D12	1½d. black (15.12.22)	8·50	23·00
D13	2d. black	2·00	1·75
D14	3d. black	2·00	4·50
D11/14 *Set of* 4		12·50	27·00
D11s/14s Optd "Specimen" *Set of* 4		80·00	

1952 (1 Mar). *As Type* D **1**, *but inscr* "POSTAGE DUE". *Value in cents. Chalk-surfaced paper.* Wmk Mult Script CA. P 14.

D15	2c. black	30	8·00
	a. Error. Crown missing. W **9a**	£150	
	b. Error. St. Edward Crown. W **9b**	55·00	
D16	4c. black	30	15·00
	a. Error. Crown missing. W **9a**	£140	
	b. Error. St Edward Crown. W **9b**	55·00	
D17	6c. black	45	12·00
	a. Error. Crown missing. W **9a**	£225	
	b. Error. St. Edward Crown. W **9b**	£100	
D18	8c. black	75	12·00
	a. Error. Crown missing. W **9a**	£400	
	b. Error. St. Edward Crown. W **9b**	£190	
D15/18 *Set of* 4		1·60	42·00

Griqualand West *see* **South Africa**

Guyana

GUYANA
INDEPENDENCE
1966
(73)

1966 (26 May)–**67**. *Various stamps of British Guiana as Nos. 331/45 optd with T* **73** *by De La Rue. (a)* Wmk Mult Script CA.

378		2c. myrtle-green	30	40
379		3c. brown-olive and red-brown	2·50	6·00
380		4c. violet	1·50	75
381		6c. yellow-green	40	10
382		8c. ultramarine	1·50	1·50
		w. Wmk inverted	†	£275
383		12c. black and reddish brown	1·50	1·25
384		$5 ultramarine and black	24·00	48·00
378/84 *Set of* 7			28·00	50·00

(b) Wmk w **12** (upright)

385		1c. black (28.2.67)	10	30
386		3c. brown-olive and red-brown	1·25	10
387		4c. violet (28.2.67)	20	1·25
388		5c. scarlet and black	40	10
389		6c. green (28.2.67)	10	20
390		8c. ultramarine (14.3.67)	1·00	1·75
391		12c. black and yellowish brown	10	10
392		24c. black and bright orange	4·50	20
393		36c. rose-carmine and black	30	30
394		48c. bright ultramarine and Venetian red	3·50	8·50
395		72c. carmine and emerald	50	65
396		$1 pink, yellow, green and black	4·00	35
397		$2 reddish mauve	1·50	1·00
398		$5 ultramarine and black	1·00	2·50
385/98 *Set of* 14			16·00	15·00

(c) Wmk w **12** (sideways)

399		1c. black	10	10
400		4c. violet	10	10
401		8c. ultramarine	10	10
402		12c. black and yellowish brown (28.2.67)	10	10
403		24c. black and bright orange	2·00	60
404		36c. rose-carmine and black (28.2.67)	30	1·50
405		48c. bright ultramarine and Venetian red	30	30
406		72c. carmine and emerald (28.2.67)	1·75	4·00
407		$1 pink, yellow, green and black (14.3.67)	3·00	4·25
407*a*		$2 reddish mauve (28.2.67)	3·00	3·75
407*b*		$5 ultramarine and black (28.2.67)	1·50	3·25
399/407b *Set of* 11			11·00	16·00

See also Nos. 420/40.

74 Flag and Map

75 Arms of Guyana

(Des V. Whiteley. Photo Harrison)

1966 (26 May). *Independence.* P 14½.

408	**74**	5c. multicoloured	20	10
409		15c. multicoloured	25	10
410	**75**	25c. multicoloured	25	10
411		$1 multicoloured	85	1·25
408/11 *Set of* 4			1·40	1·25

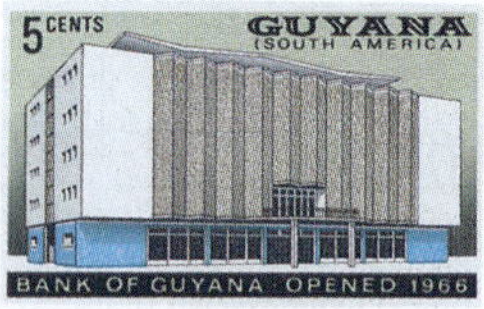

76 Bank Building

(Des B. Granger Barrett. Photo Enschedé)

1966 (11 Oct). *Opening of Bank of Guyana.* P 13½×14.

412	**76**	5c. multicoloured	10	10
413		25c. multicoloured	10	10

CANCELLED REMAINDERS.* In 1969 remainders of some issues were put on the market cancelled-to-order in such a way as to be indistinguishable from genuine postally used copies for all practical purposes. Our used quotations which are indicated by an asterisk are the same for cancelled-to-order or postally used copies.

77 British Guiana One Cent Stamp of 1856

(Des V. Whiteley. Litho D.L.R.)

1967 (23 Feb). *World's Rarest Stamp Commemoration.* P 12½.

414	**77**	5c. black, magenta, silver & light ochre	10	10*
415		25c. black, magenta, gold and light green	10	10*

78 Chateau Margot

GUYANA
INDEPENDENCE
1966
(82)

(Des R. Granger Barrett. Photo Harrison)

1967 (26 May). *First Anniv of Independence. T* **78** *and similar multicoloured designs.* P 14 (6c.), 14½×14 (15c.) or 14×14½ (others).

416		6c. Type **78**	10	10*
417		15c. Independence Arch	10	10*
418		25c. Fort Island (*horiz*)	10	10*
419		$1 National Assembly (*horiz*)	20	15
416/19 *Set of* 4			30	15

1967–68. *Stamps as Nos. 331/45 optd with T* **82** *locally.*

(i) Wmk Mult Script CA

420		1c. black (3.10.67)	10	10
		a. Opt inverted	45·00	
		b. Date misplaced 5 mm	12·00	
		c. Date misplaced 2 mm	12·00	
421		2c. myrtle-green (3.10.67)	10	10
		a. "1966" for "GUYANA"	18·00	
		b. Date misplaced 5 mm	10·00	
		c. Date misplaced 2 mm	10·00	
422		3c. brown-olive and red-brown (3.10.67)	30	10
		a. "1966" for "GUYANA"	15·00	15·00
		b. Vert pair, one without opt	£450	
		c. Date misplaced 2 mm	9·50	
423		4c. violet (10.67)	10	10
		a. Deep violet	65	65
		b. Opt inverted	60·00	65·00
424		6c. yellow-green (11.67)	10	10
		a. "1966" for "GUYANA"	25·00	25·00
		b. Opt inverted	50·00	55·00
		c. Opt double	65·00	70·00
425		8c. ultramarine (12.67)	10	10
426		12c. black and brown (12.67)	10	10
426*a*		24c. black and orange (date?)	£375	£100
427		$2 reddish mauve (12.67)	1·25	1·75
428		$5 ultramarine and black (12.67)	1·50	2·25

(ii) Wmk w **12** (upright)

429		1c. black (2.68)	10	1·00
		a. Opt omitted	£200	
430		2c. myrtle-green (2.68)	40	2·50
431		3c. brown-olive and red-brown (3.10.67)	30	10
		a. "1966" for "GUYANA"	80·00	
		b. Opt inverted	30·00	
432		4c. violet (2.68)	10	2·50
433		5c. scarlet and black (3.10.67)	2·00	2·25
		a. Deep scarlet and black	1·00	2·25
		aw. Wmk inverted	55·00	
		c. Date misplaced 2 mm	10·00	
434		6c. yellow-green (2.68)	30	1·25
		a. Opt double, one diagonal	85·00	
435		24c. black and bright orange (11.12.67)	5·00	10
		a. Opt double, one diagonal (horiz pair)	£180	
436		36c. rose-carmine and black (12.67)	2·00	10
437		48c. bright ultram & Venetian red (12.67)	2·25	50
		a. Opt inverted	80·00	
438		72c. carmine and emerald (12.67)	2·25	50
439		$1 pink, yellow, green and black (12.67)	3·00	50
440		$2 reddish mauve (12.67)	3·00	4·00
420/40 (*excl.* 426a) *Set of* 21			20·00	18·00

The "1966" errors occurred on R. 7/10 and were later corrected. Nos. 425/8 and 436/40 were issued in mid-December, but some were cancelled-to-order with a November date in error.

On Nos. 420b and 421b the "1" of "1966" is below the second "D" of "INDEPENDENCE" (R. 6/3). On Nos. 420c, 421c, 422c and 433c it is below the second "E" (R. 6/1). Lesser misplacements exist in other positions.

No. 433*a* is from a printing made specially for this overprint.

83 "Millie " (Blue and Yellow Macaw)

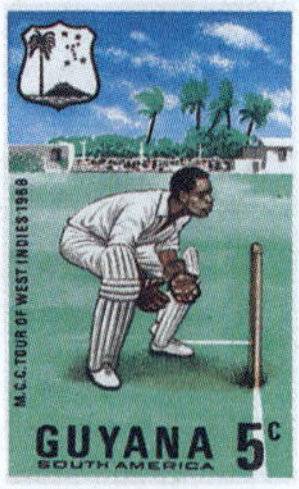

84 Wicket-keeping

(Des V. Whiteley. Photo Harrison)

1967–68. *Christmas.* P 14½×14. *(a) First issue (6 Nov 1967).*

441	**83**	5c. yellow, new blue, black and bronze-green	10	10
442		25c. yellow, new blue, black and violet	15	10

(b) Second issue. Colours changed (22 Jan 1968)

443	**83**	5c. yellow, new blue, black and red	10	10*
444		25c. yellow, new blue, black and apple-green	15	10*

(Des V. Whiteley. Photo Harrison)

1968 (8 Jan). *M.C.C.'s West Indies Tour. T* **84** *and similar vert designs.* P 14.

445		5c. Type **84**	10	10*
		a. Strip of 3. Nos. 445/7	45	
446		6c. Batting	10	10*
447		25c. Bowling	30	10*
445/7 *Set of* 3			45	15*

Nos. 445/7 were issued in small sheets of 9 containing three *se-tenant* strips.

87 Pike Cichlid

102 "Christ of St John of the Cross" (Salvador Dali)

(Des R. Granger Barrett. Photo Harrison)

1968 (4 Mar). *Multicoloured designs as T* **87**, *showing fish (1 to 6c.), birds (10 to 40c.) or animals (others).* No wmk. P 14×14½.

448		1c. Type **87**	10	10
449		2c. Red Piranha ("Pirai")	10	10
450		3c. Peacock Cichlid ("Lukunani ")	10	10
451		5c. Armoured Catfish ("Hassar")	10	10
452		6c. Black Acara ("Patna")	55	10
453		10c. Spix's Guan (*vert*)	55	10
454		15c. Harpy Eagle (*vert*)	1·60	10
455		20c. Hoatzin (*vert*)	60	10
456		25c. Guianan Cock of the Rock (*vert*)	60	10
457		40c. Great Kiskadee (*vert*)	1·50	75
458		50c. Brazilian Agouti ("Accouri")	80	50
459		60c. White-lipped Peccary	80	10
460		$1 Paca ("Labba")	80	10
461		$2 Nine-banded Armadillo	1·00	2·00
462		$5 Ocelot	1·00	3·00
448/62 *Set of* 15			9·00	6·00

For Nos. 448/62 with W **106** see Nos. 485/99.

(Des and photo Harrison)

1968 (25 Mar). *Easter.* P 14.

463	**102**	5c. multicoloured	10	10*
464		25c. multicoloured	20	10*

103 "Efficiency Year"

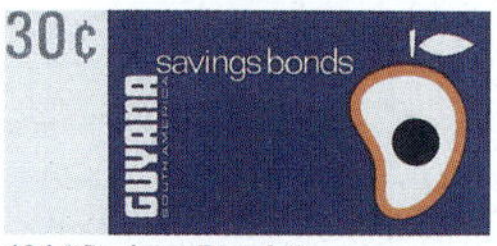

104 "Savings Bonds"

(Des W. Starzmann. Litho B.W.)

1968 (22 July). *"Savings Bonds and Efficiency".* P 14.

465	**103**	6c. multicoloured	10	10*
466		25c. multicoloured	10	10*
467	**104**	30c. multicoloured	10	10*
468		40c. multicoloured	10	10*
465/8 *Set of* 4			30	15*

105 Open Book, Star and Crescent

(Des R. Gates. Photo D.L.R.)

1968 (9 Oct). *1400th Anniv of the Holy Quran.* P 14.

469	**105**	6c. black, gold and flesh	10	10*
470		25c. black, gold and lilac	10	10*
471		30c. black, gold and light apple-green	10	10*
472		40c. black, gold and cobalt	10	10*
469/72 *Set of* 4			30	15*

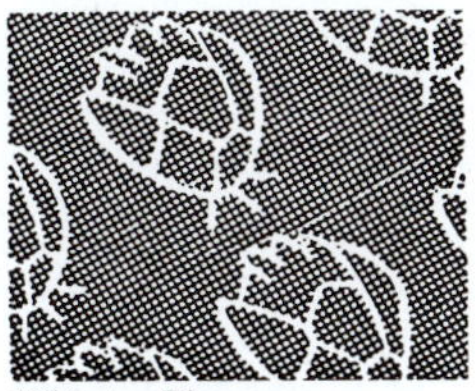

106 Lotus Blossoms

107 Broadcasting Greetings

(Des L. Pritchard; adapted G. Vasarhelyi. Litho D.L.R.)

1968 (11 Nov). *Christmas. T* **107** *and similar vert design.* W **106**. P 14.

473	6c. brown, blue and green	10	10*
474	25c. brown, reddish violet and green	10	10*
475	30c. blue-green and turquoise-green	10	10*
476	40c. red and turquoise-green	10	10*
473/6 *Set of* 4		30	15*

Designs:—25c. Type **107**; 30, 40c. Map showing radio link, Guyana-Trinidad.

109 Festival Ceremony

(Des J. Cooter. Litho P.B.)

1969 (26 Feb). *Hindu Festival of Phagwah. T* **109** *and similar horiz design. Multicoloured.* W **106** (sideways). P 13½.

477	6c. Type **109**	10	10
478	25c. Ladies spraying scent	10	10
479	30c. Type **109**	10	10
480	40c. As 25c.	10	10
477/80 *Set of* 4		30	20

111 "Sacrament of the Last Supper" (Dali)

112 Map showing "CARIFTA" Countries

(Photo D.L.R.)

1969 (10 Mar). *Easter.* W **106** (sideways). P 13½×13.

481	**111**	6c. multicoloured	10	10
482		25c. multicoloured	10	10
483		30c. multicoloured	10	10
484		40c. multicoloured	10	10
481/4 *Set of* 4			30	15

1969–71. *As Nos. 448/62, but Wmk* **106** *(sideways* on 1 to 6c. and 50c. to $5). Chalk-surfaced paper.*

485	1c. Type **87**	10	10
486	2c. Red Piranha ("Pirai")	10	30
487	3c. Peacock Cichlid ("Lukunani")	10	75
488	5c. Armoured Catfish ("Hassar")	10	10
489	6c. Black Acara ("Patna")	10	1·00
490	10c. Spix's Guan	30	60
	a. Glazed paper (*wmk inverted*) (21.12.71)	1·00	3·75
491	15c. Harpy Eagle	30	10
	aw. Wmk inverted		
	b. Glazed paper (*wmk inverted*) (21.12.71)	1·25	3·75
492	20c. Hoatzin	30	80
493	25c. Guianan Cock of the Rock	30	10
	a. Glazed paper (*wmk inverted*) (21.12.71)	1·50	4·50
494	40c. Great Kiskadee	60	1·00
495	50c. Brazilian Agouti ("Accouri")	35	15
496	60c. White-lipped Peccary	35	1·00
497	$1 Paca ("Labba")	70	1·25
	a. Glazed paper (*wmk top of blossom to right*) (21.12.71)	1·75	11·00
498	$2 Nine-banded Armadillo	1·00	3·25
499	$5 Ocelot	1·00	5·00
485/99 *Set of* 15		4·50	13·00

*The normal sideways watermark shows the top of the blossom to the left, *as seen from the back of the stamp*.

These were put on sale by the Crown Agents on 25 March 1969 but although supplies were sent to Guyana in time they were not released there until needed as ample supplies remained of the stamps without watermark. It is understood that the 3c. and 5c. were put on sale in early May 1969 followed by the 25c. but there are no records of when the remainder were released.

(Des J. Cooter. Litho P.B.)

1969 (30 Apr). *First Anniv of CARIFTA (Caribbean Free Trade Area). T* **112** *and similar design.* W **106** (sideways on 25c.). P 13½.

500	6c. rose-red, ultramarine and turquoise-blue	15	15
501	25c. lemon, brown and rose-red	15	15

Design: *Horiz*—25c. "Strength in Unity".

114 Building *Independence* (first aluminium ship)

116 Scouts raising Flag

(Des R. Gates. Litho B.W.)

1969 (30 Apr). *50th Anniv of International Labour Organization. T* **114** *and similar design.* W **106** (sideways on 40c.). P 12×11 (30c.) or 11×12 (40c.).

502	30c. turquoise-blue, black and silver	40	25
503	40c. multicoloured	50	25

Design: *Horiz*—40c. Bauxite processing plant.

(Des Jennifer Toombs. Litho B.W.)

1969 (13 Aug). *Third Caribbean Scout Jamboree and Diamond Jubilee of Scouting in Guyana. T* **116** *and similar horiz design. Multicoloured.* W **106** (sideways). P 13.

504	6c. Type **116**	10	10
505	8c. Camp-fire cooking	10	10
506	25c. Type **116**	10	10
507	30c. As 8c.	10	10
508	50c. Type **116**	15	15
504/8 *Set of* 5		30	30

118 Gandhi and Spinning-wheel

119 "Mother Sally Dance Troupe"

(Des G. Drummond. Litho Format)

1969 (1 Oct). *Birth Centenary of Mahatma Gandhi.* W **106** (sideways). P 14½.

509	**118**	6c. black, brown and yellowish olive	65	65
510		15c. black, brown and lilac	65	65

(Des V. Whiteley (5, 25c.), J.W. (others). Litho B.W. (5, 25c.), D.L.R. (others))

1969 (17 Nov). *Christmas. T* **119** *and similar vert designs. Multicoloured.* No wmk (5, 25c.) or W **106** (others). P 13½ (5, 25c.) or 13×13½ (others).

511	5c. Type **119**	10	10
	a. Opt omitted	28·00	
	b. Opt double	25·00	
512	6c. City Hall, Georgetown	10	10
	a. Opt omitted	28·00	
	b. Opt inverted	30·00	
513	25c. Type **119**	10	10
	a. Opt omitted	28·00	
514	60c. As 6c.	20	25
511/14 *Set of* 4		30	30

Nos. 511/14 are previously unissued stamps optd as in T **119** by Guyana Lithographic Co, Ltd.

REPUBLIC

121 Forbes Burnham and Map

125 "The Descent from the Cross"

(Des L. Curtis. Litho D.L.R.)

1970 (23 Feb). *Republic Day. T* **121** *and similar designs.* W **106** (sideways on 15 and 25c.). P 14.

515	5c. sepia, ochre and pale blue	10	10
516	6c. multicoloured	10	10
517	15c. multicoloured	15	10
518	25c. multicoloured	20	15
515/18 *Set of* 4		40	30

Designs: *Vert*—6c. "Rural Self-help". *Horiz*—15c. University of Guyana; 25c. Guyana House.

(Des J. Cooter. Litho Questa)

1970 (24 Mar). *Easter. Paintings by Rubens. T* **125** *and similar vert design. Multicoloured.* W **106** (inverted). P 14×14½.

519	5c. Type **125**	10	10
520	6c. "Christ on the Cross"	10	10
521	15c. Type **125**	20	15
522	25c. As 6c.	20	15
519/22 *Set of* 4		45	40

127 "Peace" and U.N. Emblem

128 "Mother and Child" (Philip Moore)

(Des and litho Harrison)

1970 (26 Oct). *25th Anniv of United Nations. T* **127** *and similar horiz design. Multicoloured.* W **106** (inverted). P 14.

523	5c. Type **127**	10	10
524	6c. U.N. Emblem, Gold-panning and Drilling	10	10
525	15c. Type **127**	10	10
526	25c. As 6c.	15	15
523/6 *Set of* 4		30	30

(Des Harrison. Litho J.W.)

1970 (8 Dec). *Christmas.* W **106**. P 13½.

527	**128**	5c. multicoloured	10	10
528		6c. multicoloured	10	10
529		15c. multicoloured	15	15
530		25c. multicoloured	15	15
527/30 *Set of* 4			30	30

POSTAGE DUE STAMPS

D2

(Typo D.L.R.)

1967–68. *Chalk-surfaced paper.* W w **12**. P 14.

D5	D **2**	2c. black (11.12.68)	1·50	17·00
D6		4c. deep ultramarine	30	5·50
D7		12c. reddish scarlet	30	5·50
D5/7 *Set of* 3			1·90	25·00

Heligoland

Stamps of HAMBURG (see Part 7 (Germany) of this catalogue) were used in Heligoland until 16 April 1867. The Free City of Hamburg ran the Heligoland postal service between 1796 and 1 June 1866. Its stamps continued in use on the island until replaced by Heligoland issues.

PRICES FOR STAMPS ON COVER

Nos. 1/19	*from* × 3

PRINTERS. All the stamps of Heligoland were typographed at the Imperial Printing Works, Berlin.

REPRINTS. Many of the stamps of Heligoland were subsequently reprinted at Berlin (between 1875 and 1885), Leipzig (1888) and Hamburg (1892 and 1895). Of these only the Berlin productions are difficult to distinguish from the originals so separate notes are provided for the individual values. Leipzig reprints can be identified by their highly surfaced paper and those from Hamburg by their 14 perforation. All of these reprints are worth much less than the original stamps priced below.

There was, in addition, a small reprinting of Nos. 13/19, made by the German government in 1890 for exchange purposes, but examples of this printing are far scarcer than the original stamps.

Forgeries, printed by lithography instead of typography, also exist for Nos. 1/4, 6 and 8 perforated 12½ or 13. Forged cancellations can also be found on originals and, on occasion, genuine postmarks on reprints.

1

(Currency. 16 schillings = 1 mark)

Three Dies of Embossed Head for Types **1** and **2**:

Die I Die II

Die III

Die I. Blob instead of curl beneath the chignon. Outline of two jewels at top of diadem.
Die II. Curl under chignon. One jewel at top of diadem.
Die III. Shorter curl under chignon. Two jewels at top of diadem.

(Des Wedding. Die eng E. Schilling)

1867 (Mar)–**68**. *Head Die I embossed in colourless relief. Roul.*

1	**1**	½sch. blue-green and rose	£300	£800
		a. Head Die II (7.68)	£700	£1100
2		1sch. rose and blue-green (21.3.67)	£160	£180
3		2sch. rose and grass-green (21.3.67)	13·00	55·00
4		6sch. green and rose	15·00	£250

For Nos. 1/4 the second colour given is that of the spandrels on the ½ and 1sch., and of the spandrels and central background for the 2 and 6sch.

All four values exist from the Berlin, Leipzig and Hamburg reprintings. The following points are helpful in identifying originals from Berlin reprints; for Leipzig and Hamburg reprints see general note above:

½sch. – Reprints are all in yellowish green and show Head Die II
1sch. – All reprints are Head Die III
2sch. – Berlin reprints are in dull rose with a deeper blue-green
6sch. – Originals show white specks in green. Berlin reprints have a more solid bluish green

1869 (Apr)–**73**. *Head embossed in colourless relief.* P 13½×14½.

5	**1**	¼sch. rose and green (background) (I) (*quadrillé paper*) (8.73)	28·00	£1500
		a. Error. Green and rose (background) (9.73)	£120	£3000
		b. Deep rose and pale green (background) (11.73)	85·00	£1500
6		½sch. blue-green and rose (II)	£190	£200
		a. Yellow green and rose (7.71)	£140	£190
		b. Quadrille paper (6.73)	95·00	£150
7		¾sch. green and rose (I) (*quadrillé paper*) (12.73)	32·00	£1100
8		1sch. rose and yellow-green (III) (7.71)	£140	£180
		a. Quadrillé paper. *Rose and pale blue-green* (6.73)	£120	£180
9		1½sch. grn & rose (I) (*quadrillé paper*) (9.73)	65·00	£250

For Nos. 5/9 the second colour given is that of the spandrels on the ½ and 1sch., of the central background on the ¼ and 1½sch., and of the central background, side labels and side marginal lines of the ¾sch.

No. 5a was a printing of the ¼sch. made in the colour combination of the 1½sch. by mistake.

A further printing of the ½sch. (head die I) in deep rose-red and yellowish green (background), on non-*quadrillé* paper, was made in December 1874, but not issued (*Price* £15, *unused*).

All five values exist from the Berlin, Leipzig and Hamburg reprintings. The following points are helpful in identifying originals from Berlin reprints; for Leipzig and Hamburg reprints see general note above:

¼sch. – All Berlin and some Hamburg reprints are Head Die II
½sch. – Berlin reprints on thinner paper with solid colour in the spandrels
¾sch. – Berlin reprints on thinner, non-quadrille paper
1sch. – Berlin reprints are on thinner paper or show many breaks in the rose line beneath "SCHILLING" at the top of the design or in the line above it at the foot
1½sch. – All Berlin and some Hamburg reprints are Head Die II

Berlin, Leipzig and Hamburg reprints also exist of the 2 and 6sch., but these values do not come as perforated originals.

(New Currency. 100 pfennig = 1 mark)

2

3

4

5

(Des H. Gätke. Die eng E. Schilling (T **2**), A. Schiffner (others))

1875 (Feb)–**90**. *Head Die II on T* **2** *embossed in colourless relief.* P 13½×14½.

10	**2**	1pf. (¼d.) deep green and rose	13·00	£500
11		2pf. (½d.) deep rose and deep green	13·00	£600
12	**3**	3pf. (⅝d.) pale green, red and yellow (6.76)	£225	£1100
		a. Green, red and orange (6.77)	£160	£850
13	**2**	5pf. (¾d.) deep yellow-green and rose	13·00	19·00
		a. Deep green and rose (6.90)	17·00	42·00
14		10pf. (1½d.) deep rose and deep green	32·00	22·00
		a. Scarlet and pale blue-green (5.87)	12·00	22·00
15	**3**	20pf. (2½d.) rose, green and yellow (6.76)	£200	£120
		a. Rose-carmine, deep green and orange (4.80)	£150	50·00
		b. Dull red, pale green and lemon (7.88)	15·00	29·00
		c. Aniline verm, brt grn and lemon (6.90)	13·00	50·00
16	**2**	25pf. (3d.) deep green and rose	15·00	28·00
17		50pf. (6d.) rose and green	20·00	35·00
18	**4**	1m. (1s.) deep green, scarlet and black (8.79)	£140	£200
		a. Perf 11½	£1100	
		b. Deep green, aniline rose and black (5.89)	£140	£200
19	**5**	5m. (5s.) deep green, aniline rose, black and yellow (8.79)	£170	£950
		a. Perf 11½	£1100	
		ab. Imperf between (horiz pair)	£4500	

For stamps as Type **2** the first colour is that of the central background and the second that of the frame. On the 3pf. the first colour is of the frame and the top band of the shield, the second is the centre band and the third the shield border. The 20pf. is similar, but has the centre band in the same colour as the frame and the upper band on the shield in the second colour.

The 1, 2 and 3pf. exist from the Berlin, Leipzig and Hamburg reprintings. There were no such reprints for the other values. The following points are helpful in identifying originals from Berlin reprints; for Leipzig and Hamburg reprints see general note above:

1pf. – Berlin printings show a peculiar shade of pink
2pf. – All reprints are much lighter in shade than the deep rose and deep green of the originals
3pf. – Berlin reprints either show the band around the shield in brownish orange, or have this feature in deep yellow with the other two colours lighter

Heligoland was ceded to Germany on 9 August 1890.

Hong Kong

CROWN COLONY

Hong Kong island was formally ceded to Great Britain on 26 January 1841. The Hong Kong Post Office was established in October 1841, when much of the business previously transacted through the Macao postal agency was transferred to the island. The first cancellation is known from April 1842, but local control of the posts was short-lived as the Hong Kong Office became a branch of the British G.P.O. on 15 April 1843.

The colonial authorities resumed control of the postal service on 1 May 1860 although the previously established postal agencies in the Chinese Treaty Ports remained part of the British G.P.O. system until 1 May 1868.

For illustrations of the handstamp types see BRITISH POST OFFICES ABROAD notes following GREAT BRITAIN.

CROWNED-CIRCLE HANDSTAMPS

CC1	CC **1b**	HONG KONG (R.) (17.10.1843)	
		Price on cover	£800
CC2	CC **1**	HONG KONG (R.) (21.8.1844)	
		Price on cover	£1000
CC3	CC **3**	HONG KONG (R.) (16.6.1852)	
		Price on cover	£475

We no longer list the Great Britain stamps with obliteration "B 62" within oval. The Government notification dated 29 November 1862 stated that only the Hong Kong stamps to be issued on 8 December would be available for postage and the stamps formerly listed were all issued in Great Britain later than the date of the notice.

(Currency. 100 cents = 1 Hong Kong dollar)

PRICES FOR STAMPS ON COVER TO 1945

Nos. 1/7	*from* × 6
Nos. 8/12	*from* × 15
No. 13	*from* × 6
Nos. 14/17	*from* × 15
No. 18	*from* × 50
No. 19	*from* × 15
Nos. 20/27	*from* × 10
Nos. 28/36	*from* × 8
Nos. 37/9	*from* × 10
Nos. 40/4	*from* × 8
Nos. 45/50	*from* × 10
No. 51	*from* × 20
No. 52	*from* × 10
Nos. 53/4	—
No. 55	*from* × 10
Nos. 56/61	*from* × 10
Nos. 62/99	*from* × 4
Nos. 100/32	*from* × 3
Nos. 133/6	*from* × 2
Nos. 137/9	*from* × 4
Nos. 140/68	*from* × 2
Nos. D1/12	*from* × 10
Nos. F1/11	*from* × 20
No. F12	*from* × 4
Nos. P1/3	*from* × 2

PRINTERS. All definitive issues up to 1962 were typographed by De La Rue and Co., *except for some printings between 1941 and 1945.*

1

2

3

1862 (8 Dec)–**63**. No wmk. P 14.

1	**1**	2c. brown	£450	£100
		a. Deep brown (1863)	£600	£130
2		8c. yellow-buff	£700	75·00
3		12c. pale greenish blue	£600	60·00
4	**3**	18c. lilac	£600	55·00
5		24c. green	£1000	£100
6		48c. rose	£2750	£350
7		96c. brownish grey	£3750	£450

"GKON" of "HONGKONG" damaged at foot (Pl 1 lower right pane R. 9/5)

1863 (Aug)–**71**. Wmk Crown CC. P 14.

8	**1**	2c. deep brown (11.64)	£325	30·00
		a. Brown	£130	7·00
		b. Pale yellowish brown	£160	12·00
		w. Wmk inverted	£650	90·00
		y. Wmk inverted and reversed	†	£800
		x. Wmk reversed	—	£160
9	**2**	4c. grey	£150	16·00
		ay. Wmk inverted and reversed	†	£800
		b. Slate	£120	8·00
		bw. Wmk inverted	£475	90·00
		c. Deep slate	£160	14·00
		d. Greenish grey	£325	50·00
		dw. Wmk inverted	†	£400
		e. Bluish slate	£475	23·00
		ew. Wmk inverted	£1200	£160
		f. Perf 12½. *Slate* (8.70)	£12000	£275
		fw. Wmk inverted	—	£750
10		6c. lilac	£425	16·00
		a. Mauve	£600	17·00
		w. Wmk inverted	£1300	90·00
		x. Wmk reversed	£1600	£120
11	**1**	8c. pale dull orange (10.64)	£550	9·50
		a. Brownish orange	£500	11·00
		b. Bright orange	£450	11·00
		w. Wmk inverted	£1300	£110
		x. Wmk reversed	£1400	£160
12		12c. pale greenish blue (4.65)	£1000	32·00
		a. Pale blue	32·00	5·50
		b. Deep blue	£275	12·00
		w. Wmk inverted	—	95·00
		x. Wmk reversed	—	£110
13	**3**	18c. lilac (1866)	£7000	£300
		w. Wmk inverted	£10000	£1000
		x. Wmk reversed	£18000	£1500
		y. Wmk inverted and reversed	†	£2500
14		24c. green (10.64)	£500	9·50
		a. Pale green	£650	16·00
		b. Deep green	£1000	30·00
		w. Wmk inverted	£2500	£110
		x. Wmk reversed	£2250	£150
15	**2**	30c. vermilion	£900	14·00
		a. Orange-vermilion	£800	15·00
		b. "GKON" of "HONGKONG" damaged at foot	—	£1300
		w. Wmk inverted	£2500	£130
		x. Wmk reversed	—	£160
16		30c. mauve (14.8.71)	£250	5·50
		a. "GKON" of "HONGKONG" damaged at foot	—	£500
		w. Wmk inverted	£1200	£100
		x. Wmk reversed	—	£160
17		48c. pale rose (1.65)	£1200	55·00
		a. Rose-carmine	£900	28·00
		w. Wmk inverted	£2250	£150
		x. Wmk reversed	—	£200
18		96c. olive-bistre (1.65)	£55000	£700
		w. Wmk inverted	†	£2750
19		96c. brownish grey (1865)	£1400	60·00
		a. Brownish black	£1700	50·00
		w. Wmk inverted	£2000	£180
		y. Wmk inverted and reversed	†	£1800

There is a wide range of shades in this issue, of which we can only indicate the main groups.

No. 12 is the same shade as No. 3 without wmk, the impression having a waxy appearance.

A single used example of the 48c. in a bright claret shade is known. No other stamps in this shade, either mint or used, have been discovered.

See also Nos. 22 and 28/31.

16 cents. (4) | 28 cents. (5) | 5 cents. (6) | 10 cents. (7)

ts. No. 20b

1876 (Aug)–**77**. *Nos.* 13 *and* 16 *surch with T* **4** *or* **5** *by Noronha and Sons, Hong Kong.*

20	**3**	16c. on 18c. lilac (1.4.77)	£2250	£150
		a. Space between "n" and "t"	£8000	£900
		b. Space between "s" and stop	£8000	£900
		w. Wmk inverted	£5500	£900
21	**2**	28c. on 30c. mauve	£1500	50·00
		a. "GKON" of "HONGKONG" damaged at foot	—	£850

1877 (Aug). *New value.* Wmk Crown CC. P 14.

22	**3**	16c. yellow	£1900	65·00
		w. Wmk inverted	£3750	£400

1880 (1 Mar–Sept). *Surch with T* **6** *or* **7** *by Noronha and Sons.*

23	**1**	5c. on 8c. brt orange (No. 11*b*) (Sept)	£1000	£100
		a. Surch inverted	†	£17000
		b. Surch double	†	£18000
24	**3**	5c. on 18c. lilac (No. 13)	£950	60·00
		x. Wmk reversed	£2250	£1000
		y. Wmk inverted and reversed	†	£3000
25	**1**	10c. on 12c. pale blue (No. 12*a*)	£1000	55·00
		a. Blue	£1600	£100
26	**3**	10c. on 16c. yellow (No. 22) (May)	£4250	£150
		a. Surch inverted	†	£80000
		b. Surch double	†	£75000
		w. Wmk inverted	†	£1700
27		10c. on 24c. green (No. 14) (June)	£1400	85·00
		w. Wmk inverted	†	£500

Two examples of No. 26b are known, both used in Shanghai.

1880 (Mar–Dec). *Colours changed and new values.* Wmk Crown CC. P 14.

28	**1**	2c. dull rose	£170	27·00
		a. Rose	£180	28·00
		w. Wmk inverted	†	£350
29	**2**	5c. blue (Dec)	£550	55·00
		w. Wmk inverted	—	£250
30		10c. mauve (Nov)	£650	15·00
		w. Wmk inverted	—	£225
31	**3**	48c. brown	£1400	£100

1882 (May)–**96**. Wmk Crown CA. P 14.

32	**1**	2c. rose-lake (7.82)	£190	30·00
		a. Rose-pink	£200	32·00
		ab. Perf 12	£75000	£70000
		w. Wmk inverted	—	£150
		x. Wmk reversed	†	£450
33		2c. carmine (1884)	45·00	2·00
		a. Aniline carmine	48·00	2·00
		w. Wmk inverted	—	£120
34	**2**	4c. slate-grey (1.4.96)	17·00	2·00
		w. Wmk inverted	—	£130
35		5c. pale blue	30·00	85
		a. Blue	32·00	85
		aw. Wmk inverted	£375	80·00
		x. Wmk reversed	—	£250
36		10c. dull mauve (8.82)	£800	17·00
		w. Wmk inverted	—	£225
37		10c. deep blue-green (1884)	£1800	38·00
		a. Green (2.84)	£140	1·25
		aw. Wmk inverted	†	£550
38		10c. purple/*red* (1.1.91)	30·00	1·25
		w. Wmk inverted	£475	80·00
		x. Wmk reversed	£850	£130
		y. Wmk inverted and reversed		
39		30c. yellowish green (1.1.91)	£130	38·00
		a. Grey-green	85·00	25·00
38s, 39as Optd "Specimen" *Set of* 2			£400	

Examples of No. 39 should not be confused with washed or faded stamps from the grey-green shade which tend to turn to a very yellow-green when dampened.

For other stamps with this watermark, but in colours changed to the U.P.U. scheme see Nos. 56/61.

20 CENTS (8) | 50 CENTS (9) | 1 DOLLAR (10)

1885 (Sept). *As Nos.* 15, 19 *and* 31, *but wmk Crown CA, surch with T* **8** *to* **10** *by De La Rue.*

40	**2**	20c. on 30c. orange-red	£150	5·50
		a. Surch double		
		w. Wmk inverted	£1000	£350
41	**3**	50c. on 48c. yellowish brown	£400	40·00
		w. Wmk inverted	—	£300
42		$1 on 96c. grey-olive	£750	85·00
40s/2s Optd "Specimen" *Set of* 3			£1300	

7 cents. (11) | 14 cents. (12)

弍 (13) (20c.) | 五十 (14) (50c.) | 壹員 (15) ($1)

1891 (1 Jan–Mar).

(a) Nos. 16 and 37 surch with T **11** *or* **12** *by Noronha and Sons, Hong Kong.*

43	**2**	7c. on 10c. green	75·00	8·00
		a. Antique "t" in "cents" (R. 1/1)	£600	£150
		b. Surch double	£6500	£1300
44		14c. on 30c. mauve (Feb)	£180	70·00
		a. Antique "t" in "cents" (R. 1/1)	£2750	£900
		b. "GKON" of "HONGKONG" damaged at foot	£4750	£1600

(b) As Nos. 40/2 (surch with T **8** *to* **10** *by De La Rue), but colours changed.*

45	**2**	20c. on 30c. yellowish green (No. 39)	£170	£160
		a. Grey-green (No. 39*a*)	£110	£150
46	**3**	50c. on 48c. dull purple	£275	£300
47		$1 on 96c. purple/*red*	£800	£350
45as/7s Optd "Specimen" *Set of* 3			£850	

(c) Nos. 45/7 with further surch, T **13/15**, *in Chinese characters, handstamped locally (Mar).*

48	**2**	20c. on 30c. yellowish green	55·00	9·50
		a. Grey-green	42·00	8·00
		b. Surch double	£25000	
49	**3**	50c. on 48c. dull purple	80·00	5·50
50		$1 on 96c. purple/*red*	£450	22·00
		w. Wmk inverted		

The true antique "t" variety (Nos. 43a and 44a) should not be confused with a small "t" showing a short foot. In the antique "t" the crossbar is accurately bisected by the vertical stroke, which is thicker at the top. The lower curve bends towards the right and does not turn upwards to the same extent as on the normal.

The handstamped surcharges on Nos. 48/50 were applied over the original Chinese face values. The single character for "2" was intended to convert "30c." to "20c." There were six slightly different versions of the "2" handstamp and three for the "50c."

The errors of the Chinese surcharges previously listed on the above issue and also on Nos. 52 and 55 are now omitted as being outside the scope of the catalogue. While some without doubt possess philatelic merit, it is impossible to distinguish between the genuine errors and the clandestine copies made to order with the original chops. No. 55c is retained as this represents a distinctly different chop which was used for the last part of the printing.

1841 Hong Kong JUBILEE 1891 (16) | 10 CENTS (17) | 拾 (18) | 拾 (19)

1891 (22 Jan). *50th Anniversary of Colony. Optd with T* **16** *by Noronha and Sons, Hong Kong.*

51	**1**	2c. carmine (No. 33)	£450	£120
		a. Short "J" in "JUBILEE" (R. 1/6)	£700	£180
		b. Short "U" in "JUBILEE" (R. 1/1)	£700	£180
		c. Broken "1" in "1891" (R. 2/1)	£850	£275
		d. Tall narrow "K" in "Kong" (R. 1/3)	£1200	£450
		e. Opt double	£16000	£12000
		f. Space between "O" and "N" of "Hong" (R. 1/5)	£1600	£700

Most of the supply of No. 51, which was only on sale for three days, was overprinted from a setting of 12 (6×2) applied five times to complete each sheet. There were six printings from this setting, but a second setting, possibly of 30 or 60, was used for the seventh. Positions quoted are from the setting of twelve. Most varieties only occur in some printings and many less marked overprint flaws also exist.

The prices quoted for No. 51e are for examples on which the two impressions are distinctly separated. Examples on which the two impressions are almost coincidental are worth considerably less.

1898 (1 Apr). Wmk Crown CA. P 14.

(a) Surch with T **10** *by D.L.R. and handstamped Chinese characters as T* **15**.

52	3	$1 on 96c. black	£180	27·00
		a. Grey-black	£170	27·00

(b) Surch with T **10** *only.*

53	3	$1 on 96c. black	£3250	£4000
		a. Grey-black	£2750	£3750
		as. Optd "Specimen"	£600	

1898 (1 Apr).

(a) Surch with T **17** *by Noronha and Sons, Hong Kong.*

54	2	10c. on 30c. grey-green (No. 39*a*)	£550	£1100
		a. Figures "10" widely spaced (1½ mm)	£7500	
		b. Surch double		

(b) As No. 54, but with handstamped Chinese characters, T **18**, *in addition.*

55	2	10c. on 30c. grey-green (No. 39*a*)	55·00	80·00
		a. Yellowish green	80·00	£110
		b. Figures "10" widely spaced (1½ mm)	£700	£900
		c. Chinese character large (Type **19**)	£900	£1000
		d. Surch Type **17** double	£11000	
		s. Handstamped "Specimen"	£140	

Type **17** was applied in a horizontal setting of 12, Nos. 54a and 55b appearing on position 12 for the early printings only. The true 1½ mm wide spacing is not known on No. 55c. Examples showing spacing of 1.2-1.3 mm are worth a premium over the normal prices.

1900 (Aug)–**01**. Wmk Crown CA. P 14.

56	1	2c. dull green	27·00	85
		w. Wmk inverted	£190	90·00
57	2	4c. carmine (1901)	19·00	85
		w. Wmk inverted	†	—
58		5c. yellow	22·00	6·50
		w. Wmk inverted	—	£425
59		10c. ultramarine	50·00	1·75
		w. Wmk inverted	—	£100
60	1	12c. blue (1901)	48·00	60·00
61	2	30c. brown (1901)	50·00	22·00
56/61 *Set of 6*			£200	85·00
56s/9s, 61s Optd "Specimen" *Set of 5*			£550	

20

21

22

23

1903 (Jan–July). Wmk Crown CA. P 14.

62	20	1c. dull purple and brown	2·00	50
63		2c. dull green (July)	14·00	1·50
		w. Wmk inverted	†	£1000
64	21	4c. purple/*red* (July)	17·00	40
65		5c. dull green and brown-orange (July)	15·00	9·00
66		8c. slate and violet (12 Feb)	11·00	1·25
67	20	10c. purple and blue/*blue* (July)	48·00	1·50
68	23	12c. green and purple/*yellow* (12 Feb)	9·00	4·25
69		20c. slate and chestnut (June)	50·00	3·25
70	22	30c. dull green and black (21 May)	50·00	20·00
71	23	50c. dull green and magenta (June)	48·00	48·00
72	20	$1 purple and sage-green (June)	90·00	22·00
73	23	$2 slate and scarlet (July)	£300	£275
74	22	$3 slate and dull blue (July)	£375	£375
75	23	$5 purple and blue-green (June)	£500	£500
76	22	$10 slate and orange/*blue* (July)	£1200	£425
		w. Wmk inverted	†	—
62/76 *Set of 15*			£2500	£1500
62s/76s Optd "Specimen" *Set of 15*			£1800	

No. 63w is known used at Shanghai.

1904 (4 Oct)–**06**. Wmk Mult Crown CA. *Chalk-surfaced paper (8, 12c., $3, $5) or ordinary paper (others).* P 14.

77	20	2c. dull green	14·00	1·75
		a. Chalk-surfaced paper (1906)	15·00	4·25
		aw. Wmk inverted	†	£950
78	21	4c. purple/*red*	26·00	40
		a. Chalk-surfaced paper (1906)	13·00	75
79		5c. dull green and brown-orange	40·00	11·00
		a. Chalk-surfaced paper (1906)	18·00	5·00
		aw. Wmk inverted		
80		8c. slate and violet (1906)	15·00	2·00
81	20	10c. purple and blue/*blue* (3.05)	24·00	1·25
82	23	12c. green and purple/*yellow* (1906)	16·00	5·50
83		20c. slate and chestnut	48·00	2·75
		a. Chalk-surfaced paper (1906)	40·00	2·25
		aw. Wmk inverted	†	£650
84	22	30c. dull green and black	48·00	25·00
		a. Chalk-surfaced paper (1906)	50·00	18·00
85	23	50c. green and magenta	85·00	10·00
		a. Chalk-surfaced paper (1906)	80·00	13·00
86	20	$1 purple and sage-green	£140	29·00
		a. Chalk-surfaced paper (1906)	£150	29·00
87	23	$2 slate and scarlet	£325	£130
		a. Chalk-surfaced paper (1905)	£250	£110
88	22	$3 slate and dull blue (1905)	£275	£225
89	23	$5 purple and blue-green (1905)	£450	£400
90	22	$10 slate and orange/*blue* (5.05)	£1800	£1300
		aw. Wmk inverted	†	—
		b. Chalk-surfaced paper (1906)	£2000	£1100
77/90 *Set of 14*			£2750	£1700

No. 77aw is known used at Shanghai in October 1908 and 83aw at Hoihow in March 1908.

1907–11. *Colours changed and new value.* Wmk Mult Crown CA. *Chalk-surfaced paper (6c. and 20c. to $2).* P 14.

91	20	1c. brown (9.10)	5·50	1·00
		x. Wmk reversed	†	£1400
92		2c. deep green	28·00	1·75
		a. Green	28·00	1·50
		w. Wmk inverted	£1400	£850
93	21	4c. carmine-red	12·00	40
94	22	6c. orange-vermilion and purple (10.07)	26·00	6·00
95	20	10c. bright ultramarine	35·00	40
96	23	20c. purple and sage-green (3.11)	45·00	42·00
97	22	30c. purple and orange-yellow (3.11)	55·00	29·00
98	23	50c. black/*green* (3.11)	42·00	15·00
99		$2 carmine-red and black (1910)	£325	£325
91/9 *Set of 9*			£500	£375
91s, 93s/9s Optd "Specimen" *Set of 8*			£950	

No. 91x is known used at Canton in December 1912 and January 1913 and No. 92w at Shanghai in 1908.

24

25

26

27

28

(A)

(B)

In Type A of the 25c. the upper Chinese character in the left-hand label has a short vertical stroke crossing it at the foot. In Type B this stroke is absent.

Crown broken at right (R. 9/2)

Broken flower at top right (Upper left pane R. 1/3)

1912 (9 Nov)–**21**. Wmk Mult Crown CA. *Chalk-surfaced paper (12c. to $10).* P 14.

100	24	1c. brown	3·25	55
		a. Black-brown	4·50	2·50
		b. Crown broken at right (R. 9/2)	£250	£170
101		2c. deep green	10·00	30
		a. Green	10·00	30
		w. Wmk inverted	†	—
		y. Wmk inverted and reversed	†	—
102	25	4c. carmine-red	5·00	30
		a. Scarlet (1914)	24·00	2·00
103	26	6c. yellow-orange	4·75	1·75
		a. Brown-orange	6·50	2·50
		w. Wmk inverted	£850	£850
104	25	8c. grey	25·00	6·50
		a. Slate (1914)	40·00	5·50
105	24	10c. ultramarine	38·00	30
		a. Deep bright ultramarine	24·00	30
106	27	12c. purple/*yellow*	7·00	9·00
		a. White back (1914)	8·00	16·00
		as. Optd "Specimen"	£120	
107		20c. purple and sage-green	9·00	1·00
108	28	25c. purple & magenta (Type A) (1.14)	26·00	27·00
109		25c. purple & magenta (Type B) (8.19)	£190	75·00
		a. Broken flower	£3250	
110	26	30c. purple and orange yellow	40·00	9·50
		a. Purple and orange	26·00	7·50
		w. Wmk inverted		
111	27	50c. black/*blue-green*	23·00	1·75
		a. White back (5.14)	19·00	4·25
		as. Optd "Specimen"	£160	
		b. On blue-green, olive back (1917)	£1300	30·00
		c. On emerald surface (9.19)	28·00	8·00
		d. On emerald back (7.12.21)	25·00	7·00
		ds. Optd "Specimen"	£170	
		w. Wmk inverted	£3000	
		y. Wmk inverted and reversed		
112	24	$1 purple and blue/*blue*	50·00	4·50
		w. Wmk inverted	£180	£130
113	27	$2 carmine-red and grey-black	£170	65·00
114	26	$3 green and purple	£275	95·00
115	27	$5 green and red/*green*	£650	£400
		a. White back (5.14)	£600	£325
		as. Optd "Specimen"	£375	
		b. On blue-green, olive back (1917)	£1100	£350
		bs. Optd "Specimen"	£425	
		bw. Wmk inverted	£4000	
116	26	$10 purple and black/*red*	£600	85·00
100/16 *Set of 17*			£1800	£650
100s/16s Optd "Specimen" *Set of 17*			£1900	

No. 100b occurred in 1916 on R. 9/2 of the lower right pane before being retouched.

1921 (Jan)–**37**. Wmk Mult Script CA. *Chalk-surfaced paper (12c. to $5).* P 14.

117	24	1c. brown	1·00	40
118		2c. blue-green	3·00	60
		a. Yellow-green (1932)	13·00	1·75
		bw. Wmk inverted	85·00	
118*c*		2c. grey (14.4.37)	20·00	8·00
119	25	3c. grey (8.10.31)	9·00	1·00
120		4c. carmine-rose	4·50	70
		a. Carmine-red (1932)	5·00	30
		b. Top of lower Chinese characters at right broken off (R. 9/4)	£100	80·00
121		5c. violet (16.10.31)	15·00	30
122		8c. grey	18·00	38·00
123		8c. orange (7.12.21)	4·50	1·50
		w. Wmk inverted	£1000	
124	24	10c. bright ultramarine	6·00	30
		aw. Wmk inverted	£250	
124*b*	27	12c. purple/*yellow* (3.4.33)	17·00	3·00
125		20c. purple and sage-green (7.12.21)	7·50	30
126	28	25c. purple and magenta (B) (7.12.21)	6·50	70
		a. Broken flower	42·00	55·00
		w. Wmk inverted	†	£450
127	26	30c. purple and chrome-yellow (7.12.21)	11·00	1·50
		a. Purple and orange-yellow	29·00	7·50
		w. Wmk inverted	£250	
128	27	50c. black/*emerald* (1924)	19·00	30
129	24	$1 purple and blue/*blue* (7.12.21)	40·00	50
130	27	$2 carmine-red and grey-black (7.12.21)	£130	6·50
131	26	$3 green and dull purple (1926)	£170	60·00
132	27	$5 green and red/*emerald* (1925)	£475	75·00
117/32 *Set of 18*			£800	£170
117s/32s Optd or Perf (2c. grey, 3c., 5c., 12c.) "Specimen" *Set of 18*			£1900	

No. 120b occurs on R. 9/4 of the lower left pane.

1935 (6 May). *Silver Jubilee. As Nos. 91/4 of Antigua, but ptd by B.W.* P 11×12.

133	3c. ultramarine and grey-black	4·00	3·50
	c. Lightning conductor	£375	£225
134	5c. green and indigo	8·50	3·50
	a. Extra flagstaff	£325	£275
	b. Short extra flagstaff	£400	
	c. Lightning conductor	£350	£275
	d. Flagstaff on right-hand turret	£450	£300
	e. Double flagstaff	£550	
135	10c. brown and deep blue	20·00	1·75
136	20c. slate and purple	38·00	8·00
	b. Short extra flagstaff	£800	£350
	d. Flagstaff on right-hand turret	£850	£375
	e. Double flagstaff	£950	£425
133/6 *Set of 4*		60·00	15·00
133s/6s Perf "Specimen" *Set of 4*		£450	

For illustrations of plate varieties see Omnibus section following Zanzibar.

1937 (12 May). *Coronation. As Nos. 95/7 of Antigua.* P 11×11½.

137	4c. green	4·50	5·50
138	15c. carmine	10·00	3·25
139	25c. blue	13·00	4·00
137/9 *Set of 3*		25·00	11·50
137s/9s Perf "Specimen" *Set of 3*		£275	

29 King George VI

Short right leg to "R" (Right pane R. 7/3, left pane R. 3/1)

Normal

Broken character (left pane R. 6/6, later repaired)

Stop after "CENTS" (Left pane R. 4/2)

1938–52. Wmk Mult Script CA. *Chalk-surfaced paper (80c., $1 (No. 155), $2 (No. 157), $5 (No. 159), $10 (No. 161)).* P 14.

140	29	1c. brown (24.5.38)	1·75	3·50
		a. Pale brown (4.2.52)	2·50	7·00
141		2c. grey (5.4.38)	2·00	30
		a. Perf 14½×14 (28.9.45)	1·75	5·00
142		4c. orange (5.4.38)	4·50	3·00
		a. Perf 14½×14 (28.9.45)	4·50	3·25
143		5c. green (24.5.38)	1·25	20
		a. Perf 14½×14 (28.9.45)	2·50	5·00
144		8c. red-brown (1.11.41)	1·75	2·50
		a. Imperf (pair)	£28000	
		b. Stop after "CENTS"	£180	£120

145		10c. bright violet (13.4.38)	50·00	75
		a. Perf 14½×14. *Dull violet* (28.9.45)	9·50	20
		b. Dull reddish violet (8.4.46)	7·00	1·00
		c. Reddish lilac (9.4.47)	16·00	20
146		15c. scarlet (13.4.38)	2·00	30
		a. Broken character	75·00	28·00
147		20c. black (1.2.46)	1·25	30
148		20c. scarlet-vermilion (1.4.48)	7·00	40
		a. Rose-red (25.4.51)	20·00	5·50
149		25c. bright blue (5.4.38)	29·00	2·75
150		25c. pale yellow-olive (24.9.46)	4·75	2·25
151		30c. yellow-olive (13.4.38)	£150	3·50
		a. Perf 14½×14. *Yellowish olive* (28.9.45)	24·00	8·50
152		30c. blue (27.12.46)	7·00	20
153		50c. purple (13.4.38)	55·00	70
		a. Perf 14½×14. *Deep magenta* (28.9.45)	30·00	1·10
		ab. Printed both sides, inverted on reverse	£1200	
		b. Reddish purple (9.4.46)	17·00	2·00
		c. Chalk-surfaced paper. *Brt purple* (9.4.47)	9·00	20
154		80c. carmine (2.2.48)	5·00	1·00
155		$1 dull lilac and blue (*chalk-surfaced paper*) (27.4.38)	8·00	3·25
		a. Short right leg to "R"	£140	£110
		b. Ordinary paper. *Pale reddish lilac and blue* (28.9.45)	13·00	13·00
		ba. Short right leg to "R"	£180	£190
156		$1 red-orange and green (8.4.46)	18·00	30
		a. Short right leg to "R"	£190	50·00
		b. Chalk-surfaced paper (21.6.48)	48·00	1·75
		ba. Short right leg to "R"	£350	75·00
		c. Chalk-surfaced paper. *Yellow orange and green* (6.11.52)	80·00	15·00
		ca. Short right leg to "R"	£550	£200
157		$2 red-orange and green (24.5.38)	75·00	22·00
158		$2 reddish violet and scarlet (8.4.46)	38·00	5·50
		a. Chalk-surfaced paper (9.4.47)	38·00	1·00
159		$5 dull lilac and scarlet (2.6.38)	60·00	50·00
160		$5 green and violet (8.4.46)	80·00	12·00
		a. Yellowish green and violet (8.4.46)	£250	24·00
		ab. Chalk-surfaced paper (9.4.47)	£110	4·00
161		$10 green and violet (2.6.38)	£500	£120
162		$10 bright lilac and blue (8.4.46)	£140	38·00
		a. Chalk-surfaced paper. *Reddish violet and blue* (9.4.47)	£180	18·00
140/62 *Set of* 23			£900	£200
140s/62s Perf "Specimen" *Set of* 23			£2250	

Following bomb damage to the De La Rue works on the night of 29 December 1940 various emergency arrangements were made to complete current requisitions for Hong Kong stamps:

Nos. 141a, 143a, 145a, 151a and 153a (all printings perforated 14½×14 except the 4c.) were printed and perforated by Bradbury, Wilkinson & Co. Ltd. using De La Rue plates. These stamps are on rough-surfaced paper.

Nos. 142a and 144 were printed by Harrison & Sons in undivided sheets of 120 (12×10) instead of the normal two panes of 60 (6×10).

Printings of the $1 and $2 values were made by Williams, Lea & Co. using De La Rue plates.

With the exception of the 8c. it is believed that none of these printings were issued in Hong Kong before its occupation by the Japanese on 25 December 1941, although examples could be obtained in London from late 1941. The issue dates quoted are those on which the stamps were eventually released in Hong Kong following liberation in 1945.

Nos. 160/*a* were separate printings released in Hong Kong on the same day.

No. 144a. One imperforate sheet was found and most of the stamps were sold singly to the public at a branch P.O. and used for postage.

30 Street Scene

31 *Empress of Japan* (liner) and Junk

32 The University

33 The Harbour

34 The Hong Kong Bank

35 *Falcon* (clipper) and Short S.23 Empire "C" class flying boat

(Des W. E. Jones. Recess B.W.)

1941 (26 Feb). *Centenary of British Occupation. T* **30/35**. Wmk Mult Script CA (sideways on horiz designs). P 13½×13 (2c. and 25c.) or 13×13½ (others).

163		2c. orange and chocolate	6·00	2·00
164		4c. bright purple and carmine	7·00	4·00
165		5c. black and green	3·00	50
166		15c. black and scarlet	6·50	2·00
167		25c. chocolate and blue	15·00	7·00
168		$1 blue and orange	48·00	9·50
163/8 *Set of* 6			75·00	22·00
163s/8s Perf "Specimen" *Set of* 6			£450	

Hong Kong was under Japanese occupation from 25 December 1941 until 30 August 1945. The Japanese post offices in the colony were closed from 31 August and mail was carried free, marked with cachets reading "HONG KONG/1945/POSTAGE PAID". Military administration lasted until 1 May 1946. Hong Kong stamps were re-introduced on 28 September 1945.

36 King George VI and Phoenix

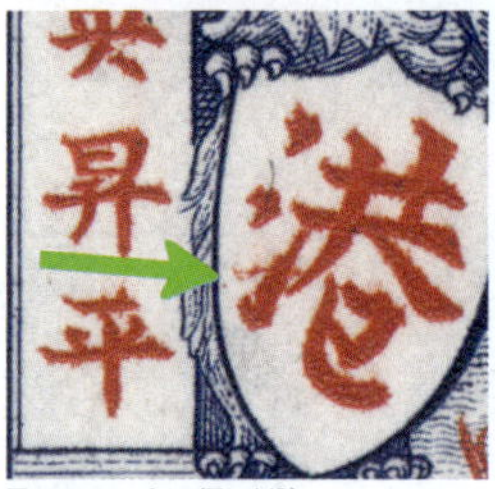

Extra stroke (R. 1/2)

(Des W. E. Jones. Recess D.L.R.)

1946 (29 Aug). *Victory*. Wmk Mult Script CA. P 13.

169	**36**	30c. blue and red (*shades*)	2·75	1·75
		a. Extra stroke	75·00	60·00
170		$1 brown and red	3·75	75
		a. Extra stroke	£100	50·00
169s/70s Perf "Specimen" *Set of* 2			£200	

Spur on "N" of "KONG" (R. 2/9)

1948 (22 Dec). *Royal Silver Wedding. As Nos. 112/13 of Antigua.*

171		10c. violet	3·00	1·00
		a. Spur on "N"	70·00	55·00
172		$10 carmine	£300	£100

Crack in rock (R. 12/5)

1949 (10 Oct). *75th Anniv of Universal Postal Union. As Nos. 114/17 of Antigua.*

173		10c. violet	4·50	1·00
174		20c. carmine-red	17·00	4·50
175		30c. deep blue	15·00	4·50
176		80c. bright reddish purple	35·00	8·00
		a. Crack in rock	£180	£110
173/6 *Set of* 4			65·00	16·00

1953 (2 June). *Coronation. As No. 120 of Antigua.*

177		10c. black and slate-lilac	4·50	30

37a Queen Elizabeth II

$2 The top stroke in the right-hand upper character is shortened (Pl. 1-1, R. 6/4)

1954 (5 Jan)–**62**. *Chalk-surfaced paper (20c. to $10)*. Wmk Mult Script CA. P 14.

178	**37a**	5c. orange	1·75	20
		a. Imperf (pair)	£1500	
179		10c. lilac	2·50	10
		aw. Wmk inverted	£180	
		b. Reddish violet (18.7.61)	8·00	10
180		15c. green	4·50	65
		a. Pale green (6.12.55)	4·50	65
181		20c. brown	6·00	30
182		25c. scarlet	4·25	2·50
		a. Rose-red (26.6.58)	4·00	2·50
183		30c. grey	5·00	20
		a. Pale grey (26.2.58)	8·00	60
184		40c. bright blue	6·00	40
		a. Dull blue (10.1.61)	11·00	1·75
185		50c. reddish purple	6·50	20
186		65c. grey (20.6.60)	19·00	11·00
187		$1 orange and green	7·50	20
		a. Short right leg to "R"	£110	20·00
188		$1.30 blue and red (20.6.60)	23·00	2·00
		a. Bright blue and red (23.1.62)	45·00	4·00
189		$2 reddish violet and scarlet	12·00	60
		a. Short character	£130	40·00
		b. Lt reddish violet & scarlet (26.2.65)	13·00	60
		ba. Short character	£130	40·00
190		$5 green and purple	75·00	2·75
		a. Yellowish green and purple (7.3.61)	£100	4·00
191		$10 reddish violet and bright blue	60·00	9·00
		a. Lt reddish violet & brt blue (26.2.58)	70·00	10·00
178/91 *Set of* 14			£200	26·00

No. 178a exists from two sheets, each of which had 90 stamps imperforate and 10 perforated on three sides only.

The 10c. exists in coils constructed from normal sheets.

The duty plates for the King George VI issue were reformatted to reduce the sheet size from 120 (two panes of 60) to 100. In doing so, one of the 'short "R"' clichés was discarded. The other occurs on R. 10/9 of No. 187.

38 University Arms

39 Statue of Queen Victoria

(Des and photo Harrison)

1961 (11 Sept). *Golden Jubilee of Hong Kong University.* W w **12**. P 11½×12.

192	**38**	$1 multicoloured	5·00	2·00
		a. Gold ptg omitted	£1800	

Normal Spot on character 10c. White spot over character in lower right corner (Pl. 1A-1A, R. 1/3)

(Des Cheung Yat-man. Photo Harrison)

1962 (4 May). *Stamp Centenary.* W w **12**. P 14½.

193	**39**	10c. black and magenta	45	10
		a. Spot on character	8·00	
194		20c. black and light blue	1·50	2·00
195		50c. black and bistre	2·75	40
193/5 *Set of* 3			4·25	2·25

40 Queen Elizabeth II (after Annigoni)

41 Queen Elizabeth II (after Annigoni)

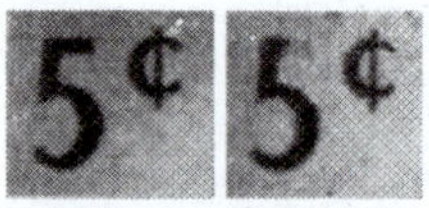

Normal Broken "5" 5c.
The horizontal bar of the "5" is missing (Pl. 1A, R. 3/1 and Pl. 1B, R. 2/2)

(Photo Harrison)

1962 (4 Oct)–**73**. *Chalk-surfaced paper.* W w **12** (upright). P 15×14 (5c. to $1) or 14×14½ (others).

196	**40**	5c. red-orange	75	60
		a. Broken "5"	20·00	
197		10c. bright reddish violet	1·50	10
		a. Reddish violet (19.11.71)	4·50	30
		ab. Glazed paper (14.4.72)	8·50	2·00
198		15c. emerald	3·25	2·25
199		20c. red-brown	2·50	1·25
		a. Brown (13.12.71)	7·00	2·75
		ab. Glazed paper (27.9.72)	13·00	9·00
200		25c. cerise	3·00	3·50
201		30c. deep grey-blue	2·50	10
		a. Chalky blue (19.11.71)	6·60	3·00
		ab. Glazed paper (27.9.72)	14·00	5·50
202		40c. deep bluish green	3·25	70
203		50c. scarlet	1·75	30
		a. Vermilion (13.12.71)	17·00	2·75
		ab. Glazed paper (27.9.72)	10·00	3·00
204		65c. ultramarine	18·00	2·00
205		$1 sepia	18·00	40
206	**41**	$1.30 multicoloured	4·00	20
		a. Pale yellow omitted	42·00	

b. Pale yellow inverted (horiz pair) £4000
c. Ochre (sash) omitted .... 30·00
d. Glazed paper (3.2.71) .... 16·00 2·50
da. Ochre (sash) omitted .... 40·00
dw. Wmk inverted .... 22·00
207 $2 multicoloured .... 6·00 65
a. Pale yellow omitted† .... 42·00
b. Ochre (sash) omitted .... 40·00
c. Pale yellow† and ochre (sash) omitted £180
dw. Wmk inverted .... 11·00
e. Glazed paper (1973)* .... £190 8·00
208 $5 multicoloured .... 17·00 1·25
a. Ochre (sash) omitted .... 40·00
bw. Wmk inverted .... 30·00
c. Glazed paper (3.2.71) .... 29·00 10·00
cw. Wmk inverted .... 50·00
209 $10 multicoloured .... 32·00 2·50
a. Ochre (sash) omitted £150
b. Pale yellow† and ochre (sash) omitted £200
cw. Wmk inverted .... 95·00
d. Glazed paper (1973)* £2250 £140
210 $20 multicoloured .... £140 24·00
w. Wmk inverted £700
196/210 *Set of* 15 .... £225 35·00

*These are from printings which were sent to Hong Kong in March 1973 but not released in London.

†This results in the Queen's face appearing pinkish.

It is believed that No. 206b comes from the last two vertical rows of a sheet, the remainder of which had the pale yellow omitted.

The $1.30 to $20 exist with PVA gum as well as gum arabic. The glazed paper printings are with PVA gum only.

See also Nos. 222, etc.

1963 (4 June). *Freedom from Hunger. As No. 14b of Antigua, but additionally inscr in Chinese characters.*
211 **42** $1.30 bluish green .... 30·00 8·00

1963 (2 Sept). *Red Cross Centenary. As Nos. 147/8 of Antigua, but additionally inscr in Chinese characters at right.*
212 10c. red and black .... 2·00 30
213 $1.30 red and blue .... 12·00 8·00

1965 (17 May). *I.T.U. Centenary. As Nos. 166/7 of Antigua.*
214 **44** 10c. light purple and orange-yellow .... 2·00 25
w. Wmk inverted .... 45·00
215 $1.30 olive-yellow and deep bluish green .... 11·00 5·50

1965 (25 Oct). *International Co-operation Year. As Nos. 168/9 of Antigua.*
216 **45** 10c. reddish purple and turquoise-green .... 1·50 25
w. Wmk inverted .... 3·25
217 $1.30 dp bluish green & lavender (shades) .... 10·00 5·50

1966 (24 Jan). *Churchill Commemoration. As Nos. 170/3 of Antigua, but additionally inscr in Chinese characters.*
218 10c. new blue .... 2·50 15
w. Wmk inverted .... 20·00
219 50c. deep green .... 2·75 30
w. Wmk inverted .... 2·75 4·50
220 $1.30 brown .... 10·00 3·00
221 $2 bluish violet .... 20·00 10·00
w. Wmk inverted £180
218/21 *Set of* 4 .... 32·00 12·00

10c. Large white dot to right of upper white Chinese character (Pl. 2B, R. 3/4).

1966 (1 Aug)–**72**. *As Nos. 196/208 and 210 but wmk* W w **12** (sideways*). *Chalk-surfaced paper (5c. to $1) or glazed, ordinary paper ($1.30 to $20).*
222 **40** 5c. red-orange (6.12.66) .... 65 1·25
223 10c. reddish violet (31.3.67)† 70 60
a. Imperf (horiz pair) £900
b. dot beside character .... 10·00
w. Wmk Crown to right of CA £180
224 15c. emerald (31.3.67)† .... 2·00 2·75
225 20c. red-brown .... 1·75 2·50
a. Glazed, ordinary paper (14.4.72) .... 8·50 11·00
226 25c. cerise (31.3.67)† .... 3·00 4·00
aw. Wmk Crown to right of CA .... 16·00
b. Glazed, ordinary paper (14.4.72) .... 15·00 16·00
227 30c. deep grey-blue (31.3.70) .... 10·00 3·00
a. Glazed, ordinary paper (14.4.72) .... 14·00 10·00
228 40c. deep bluish green (1967) .... 3·75 2·50
a. Glazed, ordinary paper (14.4.72) .... 14·00 15·00
229 50c. scarlet (31.3.67)† .... 2·75 1·00
w. Wmk Crown to right of CA (13.5.69) .... 4·00 1·75
230 65c. ultramarine (29.3.67) .... 6·50 8·00
a. Bright blue (16.7.68) .... 8·00 9·00
231 $1 sepia (29.3.67)† .... 18·00 1·75
w. Wmk Crown to right of CA .... 60·00
232 **41** $1.30 multicoloured (14.4.72) .... 10·00 2·75
w. Wmk Crown to right of CA (17.11.72) .... 12·00 2·75
233 $2 multicoloured (13.12.71) .... 14·00 3·00
a. Ochre (sash) omitted .... 55·00
w. Wmk Crown to right of CA (17.11.72) .... 12·00 4·25
234 $5 multicoloured (13.12.71) .... 70·00 16·00
236 $20 multicoloured (14.4.72) .... £150 65·00
222/36 *Set of* 14 .... £250 £100

*The normal sideways watermark shows Crown to left of CA, *as seen from the back of the stamp.*

†Earliest known postmark dates.

The 5c. to 25c., 40c. and 50c. exist with PVA gum as well as gum arabic, but the 30c., and all stamps on glazed paper exist with PVA gum only.

1966 (20 Sept). *Inauguration of W.H.O. Headquarters, Geneva. As Nos. 178/9 of Antigua.*
237 10c. black, yellow-green and light blue .... 1·50 30
238 50c. black, light purple and yellow-brown .... 4·50 1·75

1966 (1 Dec). *20th Anniv of U.N.E.S.C.O. As Nos. 196/8 of Antigua.*
239 10c. slate-violet, red, yellow and orange .... 2·50 20
240 50c. orange-yellow, violet and deep olive .... 5·50 90
241 $2 black, light purple and orange .... 32·00 20·00
239/41 *Set of* 3 .... 35·00 20·00

49 Rams' Heads on Chinese Lanterns

10c. White dot after "1967" (R. 2/2)

(Des V. Whiteley. Photo Harrison)

1967 (17 Jan). *Chinese New Year ("Year of the Ram"). T* **49** *and similar horiz design.* W w **12** (sideways). P 14½.
242 10c. rosine, olive-green and light yellow-olive .... 2·00 50
a. Dot after "1967" .... 12·00
243 $1.30 emerald, rosine and light yellow-olive .... 13·00 9·00
Design:—$1.30, Three rams.

50 Cable Route Map

(Des V. Whiteley. Photo Harrison)

1967 (30 Mar). *Completion of Malaysia–Hong Kong Link of SEACOM Telephone Cable.* W w **12**. P 12½.
244 **50** $1.30 new blue and red .... 7·50 3·50

51 Rhesus Macaques in Tree ("Year of the Monkey")

(Des R. Granger Barrett. Photo Harrison)

1968 (23 Jan). *Chinese New Year ("Year of the Monkey"). T* **51** *and similar horiz design.* W w **12** (sideways). P 14½.
245 10c. gold, black and scarlet .... 2·50 50
246 $1.30 gold, black and scarlet .... 15·00 10·00
Design:—$1.30, Family of Rhesus Macaques.

52 *Iberia* (liner) at Ocean Terminal

(Des and litho D.L.R.)

1968 (24 Apr). *Sea Craft. T* **52** *and similar horiz design.* P 13.
247 10c. multicoloured .... 1·75 15
a. Dull orange and new blue omitted £1300
248 20c. cobalt-blue, black and brown .... 2·50 1·00
249 40c. orange, black and mauve .... 8·00 10·00
250 50c. orange-red, black and green .... 5·00 75
a. Green omitted £1000
251 $1 greenish yellow, black and red .... 9·00 5·50
252 $1.30 Prussian blue, black and pink .... 27·00 4·25
247/52 *Set of* 6 .... 45·00 19·00
Designs:—20c. Pleasure launch; 40c. Car ferry, 50c. Passenger ferry; $1, Sampan; $1.30, Junk.

53 *Bauhinia blakeana*

54 Arms of Hong Kong

(Des V. Whiteley. Photo Harrison)

1968 (25 Sept)–**73**. W w **12**. P 14×14½.
(a) *Upright wmk. Chalk-surfaced paper.*
253 **53** 65c. multicoloured .... 8·00 50
aw. Wmk inverted .... 24·00
b. Glazed, ordinary paper (3.73) .... 60·00 19·00
254 **54** $1 multicoloured .... 8·00 40
(b) *Sideways wmk. Glazed, ordinary paper.*
254*a* **53** 65c. multicoloured (27.9.72) .... 45·00 23·00
254*b* **54** $1 multicoloured (13.12.71) .... 8·00 2·50

Nos. 253/4 exist with PVA gum as well as gum arabic; Nos. 254*a/b* with PVA gum only.

55 "Aladdin's Lamp" and Human Rights Emblem

(Des R. Granger Barrett. Litho B.W.)

1968 (20 Nov). *Human Rights Year.* W w **12** (sideways). P 13½.
255 **55** 10c. orange, black and myrtle-green 75 75
256 50c. yellow, black and deep reddish purple .... 1·75 2·25

56 Cockerel

(Des R. Granger Barrett. Photo Enschedé)

1969 (11 Feb). *Chinese New Year ("Year of the Cock"). T* **56** *and similar multicoloured design.* P 13½.
257 10c. Type **56** .... 2·00 1·00
a. Red omitted £250
258 $1.30 Cockerel (*vert*) .... 26·00 9·00

58 Arms of Chinese University

59 Earth Station and Satellite

(Des V. Whiteley. Photo Govt Ptg Bureau, Tokyo)

1969 (26 Aug). *Establishment of Chinese University of Hong Kong.* P 13½.
259 **58** 40c. violet, gold and pale turquoise-blue .... 3·50 3·00

(Des V. Whiteley. Photo Harrison)

1969 (24 Sept). *Opening of Communications Satellite Tracking Station.* W w **12**. P 14½.
260 **59** $1 multicoloured .... 10·00 4·50

60 Chow's Head

62 "Expo 70" Emblem

(Des R. Granger Barrett. Photo D.L.R.)

1970 (28 Jan). *Chinese New Year ("Year of the Dog"). T* **60** *and similar design.* W w **12** (sideways on $1.30). P 14½×14 (10c.) or 14×14½ ($1.30).
261 10c. lemon-yellow, orange-brown and black .... 2·50 1·00
262 $1.30 multicoloured .... 30·00 10·00
Design: *Horiz*—$1.30, Chow standing.

(Des and litho B.W.)

1970 (14 Mar). *World Fair Osaka. T* **62** *and similar multicoloured design.* W w **12** (sideways on 25c.). P 13½×13 (15c.) or 13×13½ (26c.).
263 15c. Type **62** 65 85
264 25c. "Expo '70" emblem and junks (*horiz*) .... 1·40 1·50

64 Plaque in Tung Wah Hospital

65 Symbol

(Des M. F. Griffith. Photo Harrison)

1970 (9 Apr). *Centenary of Tung Wah Hospital.* W w **12** (*sideways**). P 14½.
265 **64** 10c. multicoloured ... 50 25
266 50c. multicoloured ... 1·00 1·50
w. Wmk Crown to right of CA... 8·50

*The normal sideways watermark shows Crown to left of CA, *as seen from the back of the stamp.*

(Des J. Cooter. Litho B.W.)

1970 (5 Aug). *Asian Productivity Year.* W w **12**. P 14×13½.
267 **65** 10c. multicoloured ... 1·00 60

STAMP BOOKLETS

BOOKLET CONTENTS. In Nos. SB1/4 and SB6/7 the 1c. and 2c. were normally each in blocks of 12 or two blocks of 6 and the 4c. in blocks of 12 and 4 or two blocks of 8, all having been taken from normal sheets. No. SB5 had both the 2c. and 4c. in blocks of 12 and 4 or as two blocks of 8. Other content formats exist.

1904 (1 Jan). *Black on white cover showing contents and postage rates with "K & W LD" imprint on front. Stapled.*
SB1 $1 booklet containing twelve 1c. (No. 62), twelve 2c. (No. 56) and sixteen 4c. (No. 57)
a. 4c. No. 64 (King Edward VII) instead of No. 57 (Q.V.) ... £7000

1905–06. *Black on white cover showing contents and postage rates with "Hongkong Printing Press" imprint on front. Metal fastener.*
SB2 $1 booklet containing twelve 1c., twelve 2c. and sixteen 4c. (Nos. 62/4) ... £6000
a. 2c. and 4c. (Nos. 77/8) (MCA ordinary paper) instead of Nos. 63/4 (CA) (1906) ... £8000
b. 2c. and 4c. (Nos. 77a/8a) (MCA chalk-surfaced paper) instead of Nos. 77/8 (MCA ordinary paper) (1906) ...

Some examples of No. SB2 show the reference to Australia on the front cover deleted in manuscript. No. SB2a has the rate information reset to omit "EXCEPT AUSTRALIA".

1907 (Dec). *Black on white cover showing contents and postage rates for both Hong Kong and Agencies in China with "Hongkong Printing Press" imprint. Metal fastener.*
SB3 $1 booklet containing twelve 1c. (No. 62), twelve 2c. (No. 92) and sixteen 4c. (No. 93) ...
a. Stapled ... £4000

1910 (May)–**11**. *Black on white cover showing contents, but no postage rates, with "Hongkong Printing Press" imprint on front. Stapled.*
SB4 $1 booklet containing twelve 1c. (No. 62), twelve 2c. (No. 92) and sixteen 4c. (No. 93)
a. 1c. No. 91 (MCA) instead of No. 62 (CA) (9.11) ... £4000

1912 (Apr). *Black on cream cover showing contents, but no postage rates, with "Hongkong Printing Press" imprint on front. Stapled.*
SB5 $1 booklet containing four 1c., sixteen 2c. and sixteen 4c. (Nos. 91/3) ... £4750

1913 (Feb). *Black on cream cover showing contents, but no postage rates, with "Hongkong Printing Press" imprint on front. Stapled.*
SB6 $1 booklet containing twelve 1c., twelve 2c. and sixteen 4c. (Nos. 100/2) (MCA wmk) .. £3750

1922–24. *Black on cream cover showing contents, but no postage rates, with "Hongkong Printing Press" imprint on front. Stapled.*
SB7 $1 booklet containing twelve 1c., twelve 2c. and sixteen 4c. (Nos. 117/18, 120) (Script wmk) ... £4000
a. With Ye Olde Printers Ltd imprint (1924).

1965 (10 May). *Orange-brown (No. SB8) or yellow-green (No. SB9) covers. Stitched.*
SB8 $2 booklet containing eight 5c. and sixteen 10c. (Nos. 196/7) in blocks of 4 ... 35·00
SB9 $5 booklet containing twelve 5c., eight 10c., eight 20c. and four 50c. (Nos. 196/7, 199, 203) in blocks of 4 ... £120

POSTAGE DUE STAMPS

PRINTERS. Nos. D1/12 were typographed by De La Rue & Co.

D **1** Post-office Scales

1923 (Dec)–**56**. Wmk Mult Script CA. Ordinary paper. P 14.
D1 D **1** 1c. brown ... 2·50 65
a. Wmk sideways (1931) ... 1·50 3·25
ab. Chalk-surfaced paper (21.3.56) ... 30 1·00
D2 2c. green ... 28·00 7·50
a. Wmk sideways (1928) ... 11·00 5·00
D3 4c. scarlet ... 42·00 7·00
a. Wmk sideways (1928) ... 28·00 6·00
D4 6c. yellow ... 28·00 13·00
a. Wmk sideways (1931) ... 75·00 35·00
D5 10c. bright ultramarine ... 25·00 8·50
a. Wmk sideways (1934) ... £100 16·00
D1/5 *Set of* 5 ... £110 32·00
D1a/5a *Set of* 5 ... £190 55·00
D1s/5s Optd "Specimen" *Set of* 5 ... £350

1938 (Feb)–**63**. Wmk Mult Script CA (sideways). Ordinary paper. P 14.
D6 D **1** 2c. grey ... 14·00 9·00
a. Chalk-surfaced paper (21.3.56) ... 1·10 10·00
D7 4c. orange ... 19·00 6·50
a. Chalk-surfaced paper. *Orange-yellow* (23.5.61) ... 2·50 10·00
D8 6c. scarlet ... 8·50 5·50
D9 8c. chestnut (26.2.46) ... 5·50 32·00
D10 10c. violet ... 35·00 50
a. Chalk-surfaced paper (17.9.63) ... 16·00 16·00
D11 20c. black (26.2.46) ... 13·00 3·00
D12 50c. blue (7.47) ... 55·00 15·00
D6a/12 *Set of* 7 ... 90·00 65·00
D6s/12s Perf "Specimen" *Set of* 7 ... £400

1965 (15 Apr)–**72**. *Chalk-surfaced paper.* P 14.
(*a*) Wmk w **12** (sideways).
D13 4c. yellow-orange ... 8·00 29·00
D14 5c. red (13.5.69) ... 3·25 5·00
a. Glazed paper (17.11.72) ... 12·00 40·00
D15 10c. violet (27.6.67) ... 3·50 4·75
D16 20c. black (1965) ... 6·00 4·25
D17 50c. deep blue (1965) ... 27·00 8·00
a. Blue (13.5.69) ... 20·00 8·00
D13/17a *Set of* 5 ... 35·00 45·00
(*b*) Wmk w **12** (upright).
D18 D **1** 5c. red (20.7.67) ... 2·50 5·50
D19 50c. deep blue (26.8.70) ... 38·00 10·00

The 5c. is smaller, 21×18 mm.

POSTCARD STAMPS

Stamps specially surcharged for use on Postcards.

PRICES. Those in the left-hand column are for unused examples on complete postcards; those on the right for used examples off card. Examples used on postcards are worth much more.

3 CENTS
(P **1**)

THREE
(P **2**)

1879 (1 Apr). *Nos. 22 and 13 surch as Type* P **1** *by Noronha & Sons.*
P1 **3** 3c. on 16c. yellow (No. 22) ... £350 £425
P2 5c. on 18c. lilac (No. 13) ... £350 £450

1879 (Nov). *No. P2 handstamped with Type* P **2**.
P3 **3** 3c. on 5c. on 18c. lilac ... £7500 £8000

POSTAL FISCAL STAMPS

I. Stamps inscribed "STAMP DUTY"

NOTE. The dated circular "HONG KONG" cancellation with "PAID ALL" in lower segment was used for fiscal purposes, in black, from 1877. Previously it appears in red on mail to the U.S.A., but is usually not used as a cancellation.

F **1**

F **2**

F **3**

1874–1902. Wmk Crown CC.
(*a*) P 15½×15.
F1 F **1** $2 olive-green ... £375 65·00
F2 F **2** $3 dull violet ... £350 48·00
b. Bluish paper ...
F3 F **3** $10 rose-carmine ... £8000 £700
(*b*) P 14.
F4 F **1** $2 dull bluish green (10.97) ... £425 £250
F5 F **2** $3 dull mauve (3.02) ... £600 £500
a. Bluish paper ... £2000
F6 F **3** $10 grey-green ... £12000 £11000
F4s/5s Optd "Specimen" *Set of* 2 ... £450

Nos. F1/3 and F7 exist on various papers, ranging from thin to thick.

All three of the values perforated 15½×15 were authorised for postal use in 1874. The $10 rose-carmine was withdrawn from such use in 1880, the $2 in September 1897 and the $3 in 1902.

The $2 and $3 perforated 14 were available for postal purposes until July 1903. The $10 in grey-green was issued for fiscal purposes in 1884 and is known with postal cancellations.

12 CENTS.
(F **4**)

(F **5**)

1880. *No. F3 surch with type* F **4** *by Noronha and Sons, Hong Kong.*
F7 F **3** 12c. on $10 rose-carmine ... £900 £300

1890 (24 Dec). Wmk Crown CA. P 14.
F8 F **5** 2c. dull purple ... £130 28·00
w. Wmk inverted ...

No. F8 was authorised for postal use between 24 and 31 December 1890.

5 DOLLARS
(F **6**)

ONE DOLLAR
(F **7**)

(F **8**)

1891 (1 Jan). *Surch with Type* F **6** *by D.L.R.* Wmk Crown CA. P 14.
F9 F **3** $5 on $10 purple/*red* ... £325 £100
s. Optd "Specimen" ... £200

No. F9 was in use for postal purposes until June 1903.

1897 (Sept). *Surch with Type* F **7** *by Noronha and Sons, Hong Kong, and with the value in Chinese characters subsequently applied twice by handstamp as T* **15**.
F10 F **1** $1 on $2 olive-green (No. F1) £225 £120
a. Both Chinese handstamps omitted ... £4000 £2750
F11 $1 on $2 dull bluish green (No. F4) ... £250 £140
a. Both Chinese handstamps omitted ... £1900 £1600
b. Diagonal Chinese handstamp omitted ... £15000
c. Vertical Chinese handstamp omitted ...
s. Handstamped "Specimen" ... £140

1938 (11 Jan). Wmk Mult script CA. P 14.
F12 F **8** 5c. green ... 75·00 13·00

No. F12 was authorised for postal use between 11 and 20 January 1938 due to a shortage of 5c., No 121.

Forged cancellations are known on this stamp inscribed "VICTORIA 9.AM 11 JA 38 HONG KONG" without side bars between the rings.

II. Stamps overprinted "S.O." (Stamp Office) or "S.D." (Stamp Duty)

S. O.   S. D.

(S **1**)   (S **2**)

1891 (1 Jan). *Optd with Types* S **1** *or* S **2**.
S1 S **1** 2c. carmine (No. 33) ... £900 £375
S2 S **2** 2c. carmine (No. 33) ... £400 £200
a. Opt inverted ... † £6500
S3 S **3** 10c. purple/*red* (No. 38) ... £1600 £450

Examples of No. S1 exist the "O" amended to "D" in manuscript.

Other fiscal stamps are found apparently postally used, but there is no evidence that this use was authorised.

JAPANESE OCCUPATION OF HONG KONG

Hong Kong surrendered to the Japanese on 25 December 1941. The postal service was not resumed until 22 January 1942 when the G.P.O. and Kowloon Central Office re-opened.

Japanese postmarks used in Hong Kong can be identified by the unique combination of horizontal lines in the central circle and three stars in the lower segment of the outer circle. Dates shown on such postmarks are in the sequence Year/Month/Day with the first shown as a Japanese regnal year number so that Showa 17 = 1942 and so on.

Initially six current Japanese definitives, 1, 2, 3, 4, 10 and 30s. (Nos. 297, 315/17, 322 and 327) were on sale, but the range gradually expanded to cover all values between ½s. and 10y. with Nos. 313/14, 318, 325, 328/31, 391, 395/6, 398/9 and 405 of Japan also available from Hong Kong post offices during the occupation. Philatelic covers exist showing other Japanese stamps, but these were not available from the local post offices. Supply of these Japanese stamps was often interrupted and, during the period between 28 July 1942 and 21 April 1943, circular "Postage Paid" handstamps were sometimes used. A substantial increase in postage rates on 16 April 1945 led to the issue of the local surcharges, Nos. J1/3.

PRICES FOR STAMPS ON COVER	
Nos. J1/3	*from* × 7

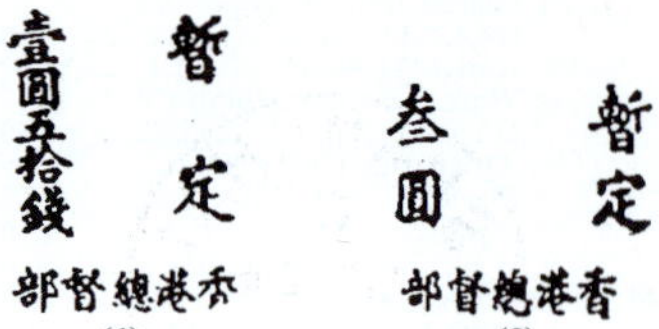

(**1**)   (**2**)

1945 (16 Apr). *Stamps of Japan surch with T* **1** *(No. J1) or as T* **2**.
J1 1.50 yen on 1s. brown ... 35·00 29·00
J2 3 yen on 2s. scarlet ... 12·00 23·00
J3 5 yen on 5s. claret ... £900 £150

Designs (18½×22 mm):—1s. Girl Worker; 2s. Gen. Nogi; 5s. Admiral Togo.

No. J3 has four characters of value similarly arranged but differing from T **2**.

BRITISH POST OFFICES IN CHINA

Under the terms of the 1842 Treaty of Nanking China granted Great Britain and its citizens commercial privileges in five Treaty Ports, Amoy, Canton, Foochow, Ningpo and Shanghai. British Consuls were appointed to each Port and their offices, as was usual during this period, collected and distributed mail for the British community. This system was formally recognised by a Hong Kong Government notice published on 16 April 1844. Mail from the consular offices was postmarked when it passed through Hong Kong.

The number of Chinese Treaty Ports was increased to sixteen by the ratification of the Treaty of Peking in 1860 with British postal facilities being eventually extended to the Ports of Chefoo, Hankow, Kiungchow (Hoihow), Swatow, Tainan (Anping) and Tientsin.

As postal business expanded the consular agencies were converted into packet agencies or post offices which passed under the direct control of the Hong Kong postal authorities on 1 May 1868.

In May 1898 the British Government leased the territory of Wei Hai Wei from China for use as a naval station to counter the Russian presence at Port Arthur.

The opening of the Trans-Siberia Railway and the extension of Imperial Penny Postage to the Treaty Port agencies resulted in them becoming a financial burden on the colonial post office. Control of the agencies reverted to the G.P.O., London, on 1 January 1911.

The pre-adhesive postal markings of the various agencies are a fascinating, but complex, subject. Full details can be found in *Hong Kong & the Treaty Ports of China & Japan* by F. W. Webb (reprinted edition J. Bendon, Limassol, 1992) and in various publications of the Hong Kong Study Circle.

From 15 October 1864 the use of Hong Kong stamps on mail from the Treaty Ports became compulsory, although such stamps were, initially, not cancelled (with the exception of Amoy) until they reached Hong Kong where the "B62" killer was applied. Cancellation of mail at the actual Ports commenced during 1866 at Shanghai and Ningpo, spreading to all the agencies during the next ten years. Shanghai had previously used a c.d.s. on adhesives during 1863 and again in 1865–66.

The main types of cancellation used between 1866 and 1930 are illustrated below. The illustrations show the style of each postmark and no attempt has been made to cover differences in type letters or figures, arrangement, diameter or colour.

Until 1885 the vertical and horizontal killers were used to obliterate the actual stamps with an impression of one of the circular date stamps shown elsewhere on the cover. Many of the early postmarks were also used as backstamps or transit marks and, in the notes which follow, references to use are for the first appearance of the mark, not necessarily its first use as an obliterator.

Illustrations in this section are taken from *Hong Kong & the Treaty Ports of China & Japan* by F. W. Webb and are reproduced with the permission of the Royal Philatelic Society, London.

Details of the stamps known used from each post office are taken, with permission, from *British Post Offices in the Far East* by Edward B. Proud, published by Proud-Bailey Co. Ltd.

Postmark Types

Type **A** Vertical killer

Type **B** Horizontal killer

Type **C** Name horizontal

Type **D** Name curved

Type **E** Double circle Name at top

Type **F** Double circle Name at foot

Type **G** Single circle Name at top

PRICES. The prices quoted in this section are for fine used stamps which show a clear impression of a substantial part of the cancellation.

AMOY

One of the five original Treaty Ports, opened to British trade by the Treaty of Nanking in 1842. A consular postal agency was established in 1844 which expanded in 1876 into two separate offices, one on the off-shore island of Ku Lang Seu and the other in Amoy itself.

Amoy "PAID" (*supplied* 1858) *used* 1859–67
Type **A** ("A1") (*supplied* 1866) *used at Ku Lang Seu* 1869–82
Type **D** (*supplied* 1866) *used* 1867–1922
Type **B** ("D27") (*supplied* 1876) *used at Amoy* 1876–84
Type **C** *used* 1876–94
Type **F** (*supplied* 1913) *used* 1916–22

Stamps of HONG KONG *cancelled at Amoy between* 1864 *and* 1916 *with postmarks detailed above.*

1862. No wmk (Nos. 1/7).

Z1	2c. brown	£225
Z2	8c. yellow-buff	£200
Z3	12c. pale greenish blue	£180
Z4	18c. lilac	£140
Z5	24c. green	£225
Z6	48c. rose	£1200
Z7	96c. brownish grey	£950

1863–71. Wmk Crown CC (Nos. 8/19).

Z8	2c. brown	35·00
Z9	4c. grey	40·00
	a. Perf 12½	
Z10	6c. lilac	65·00
Z11	8c. orange	45·00
Z12	12c. blue	20·00
Z13	18c. lilac	£900
Z14	24c. green	55·00
Z15	30c. vermilion	£110
Z16	30c. mauve	16·00
Z17	48c. rose	65·00
Z18	96c. olive-bistre	£3000
Z19	96c. brownish grey	£300

1876–77. (Nos. 20/1).

Z20	16c. on 18c. lilac	£350
Z21	28c. on 30c. mauve	£150

1877. Wmk Crown CC (No. 22).

Z22	16c. yellow	£130

1880. (Nos. 23/7).

Z23	5c. on 8c. orange	£140
Z24	5c. on 18c. lilac	£100
Z25	10c. on 12c. blue	£100
Z26	10c. on 16c. yellow	£225
Z27	10c. on 24c. green	£130

1880. Wmk Crown CC (Nos. 28/31).

Z28	2c. rose	50·00
Z29	5c. blue	80·00
Z30	10c. mauve	70·00
Z31	48c. brown	£200

1882–96. Wmk Crown CA (Nos. 32/9).

Z31a	2c. rose-lake	60·00
Z32	2c. carmine	4·25
Z33	4c. slate-grey	11·00
Z34	5c. blue	4·25
Z35	10c. dull mauve	38·00
Z36	10c. green	4·75
Z37	10c. purple/red	4·75
Z38	30c. green	35·00

1885. (Nos. 40/2).

Z39	20c. on 30c. orange-red	14·00
Z40	50c. on 48c. yellowish brown	70·00
Z41	$1 on 96c. grey-olive	£110

1891. (Nos. 43/50).

Z42	7c. on 10c. green	22·00
Z43	14c. on 30c. mauve	£100
Z44	20c. on 30c. green (No. 48)	15·00
Z45	50c. on 48c. dull purple (No. 49)	16·00
Z46	$1 on 96c. purple/*red* (No. 50)	45·00

1891. *50th Anniv of Colony* (No. 51).

Z47	2c. carmine	£950

1898. (No. 52).

Z48	$1 on 96c. black	60·00

1898. (No. 55).

Z49	10c. on 30c. green	£225

1900–01. Wmk Crown CA (Nos. 56/61).

Z50	2c. dull green	4·25
Z51	4c. carmine	3·00
Z52	5c. yellow	17·00
Z53	10c. ultramarine	4·75
Z54	12c. blue	£150
Z55	30c. brown	65·00

1903. Wmk Crown CA (Nos. 62/76).

Z56	1c. dull purple and brown	4·50
Z57	2c. dull green	4·25
Z58	4c. purple/red	2·75
Z59	5c. dull green and brown-orange	19·00
Z60	8c. slate and violet	7·00
Z61	10c. purple and blue/blue	4·00
Z62	12c. green and purple/yellow	13·00
Z63	20c. slate and chestnut	9·50
Z64	30c. dull green and black	48·00
Z65	50c. dull green and magenta	80·00
Z67	$2 slate and scarlet	£425
Z68	$3 slate and dull blue	£650

1904–06. Wmk Mult Crown CA (Nos. 77/90).

Z71	2c. dull green	4·00
Z72	4c. purple/red	2·75
Z73	5c. dull green and brown-orange	15·00
Z74	8c. slate and violet	9·50
Z75	10c. purple and blue/blue	4·00
Z76	12c. green and purple/yellow	17·00
Z77	20c. slate and chestnut	9·00
Z78	30c. dull green and black	32·00
Z79	50c. green and magenta	29·00
Z80	$1 purple and sage-green	80·00
Z81	$2 slate and scarlet	£325
Z83	$5 purple and blue-green	£550

1907–11. Wmk Mult Crown CA (Nos. 91/9).

Z85	1c. brown	4·50
Z86	2c. green	4·00
Z87	4c. carmine-red	2·75
Z88	6c. orange-vermilion and purple	15·00
Z89	10c. bright ultramarine	3·75
Z90	20c. purple and sage-green	65·00
Z91	30c. purple and orange-yellow	60·00
Z92	50c. black/green	

1912–15. Wmk Crown CA (Nos. 100/16).

Z93	1c. brown	5·50
Z94	2c. green	5·00
Z95	4c. red	2·75
Z96	6c. orange	5·00
Z97	8c. grey	20·00
Z98	10c. ultramarine	4·00
Z99	12c. purple/yellow	24·00
Z100	20c. purple and sage-green	7·00
Z102	30c. purple and orange-yellow	20·00
Z103	50c. black/green	12·00
Z104	$1 purple and blue/blue	25·00
Z105	$3 green and purple	£160

POSTCARD STAMPS

1879. (Nos. P1/2).

ZP106	3c. on 16c. yellow	£650
ZP107	5c. on 18c. lilac	£750

POSTAL FISCAL STAMPS

1874–1902. Wmk Crown CC. P 15½×15 (Nos. F1/3)

ZF109	$2 olive-green	£170
ZF110	$3 dull violet	£170

1891. (No. F9).

ZF116	$5 on $10 purple/red	£300

1897. (Nos. F10/11).

ZF118	$1 on $2 olive-green	
ZF119	$1 on $2 dull bluish green	

ANPING

Anping is the port for Tainan, on the island of Formosa, opened to British trade in 1860. A British Vice-consulate operated in the port and mail is known postmarked there between 1889 and 1895. Formosa passed under Japanese control in 1895 and British Treaty Port rights then lapsed.

Type **D** *used* 1889–95

Stamps of HONG KONG *cancelled at Anping between* 1889 *and* 1895 *with postmark detailed above.*

1882–91. Wmk Crown CA (Nos. 32/9).

Z120	2c. carmine	£900
Z121	5c. blue	£750
Z123	10c. green	£850
Z124	10c. purple/*red*	£1000

1885. (Nos. 40/2).

Z126	20c. on 30c. orange-red	£950
Z127	50c. on 48c. yellowish brown	£1500

CANTON

A British postal service was organised in Canton from 1834, but was closed when the foreign communities were evacuated in August 1839. The city was one of the original Treaty Ports and a consular agency was opened there in 1844. The consulate closed during the riots of December 1856, being replaced by a temporary postal agency at Whampoa, further down the river. When British forces reached Canton a further temporary agency was set up on 23 March 1859, but both closed in July 1863 when the consulate was re-established.

Type **A** ("C1") (*supplied* 1866) *used* 1875–84
Type **C** (*supplied* 1866) *used* 1870–1901
Type **D** *used* 1890–1922

Stamps of HONG KONG *cancelled at Canton between* 1870 *and* 1916 *with postmarks detailed above.*

1862. No wmk (Nos. 1/7).

Z135	18c. lilac	£140

1863–71. Wmk Crown CC (Nos. 8/19).

Z136	2c. brown	40·00
Z137	4c. grey	42·00
Z138	6c. lilac	55·00
Z139	8c. orange	45·00
Z140	12c. blue	21·00
Z142	24c. green	65·00
Z143	30c. vermilion	
Z144	30c. mauve	20·00
Z145	48c. rose	95·00
Z147	96c. brownish grey	£250

1876–77. (Nos. 20/1).

Z148	16c. on 18c. lilac	£300
Z149	28c. on 30c. mauve	£120

1877. Wmk Crown CC (No. 22).

Z150	16c. yellow	£160

1880. (Nos. 23/7).

Z151	5c. on 8c. orange	£170
Z152	5c. on 18c. lilac	£130
Z153	10c. on 12c. blue	£120
Z154	10c. on 16c. yellow	£275
Z155	10c. on 24c. green	£160

1880. Wmk Crown CC (Nos. 28/31).

Z156	2c. rose	42·00
Z157	5c. blue	65·00
Z158	10c. mauve	50·00

1882–96. Wmk Crown CA (Nos. 32/9).

Z159	2c. rose-lake	38·00
Z160	2c. carmine	3·00
Z161	4c. slate-grey	12·00
Z162	5c. blue	4·75
Z163	10c. dull mauve	28·00
Z164	10c. green	9·00
Z165	10c. purple/red	4·50
Z166	30c. green	38·00

1886. (Nos. 40/2).

Z167	20c. on 30c. orange-red	13·00
Z168	50c. on 48c. yellowish brown	70·00
Z169	$1 on 96c. grey-olive	£120

1891. (Nos. 43/50).

Z170	7c. on 10c. green	22·00
Z171	14c. on 30c. mauve	£110
Z171*a*	20c. on 30c. green (No. 45)	£275
Z172	20c. on 30c. green (No. 48)	18·00
Z173	50c. on 48c. dull purple (No. 49)	20·00
Z174	$1 on 96c. purple/*red* (No. 50)	60·00

1891. *50th Anniv of Colony* (No. 51).

Z175	2c. carmine	£900

1898. (No. 52).

Z176	$1 on 96c. black	£130

1898. (No. 55).

Z177	10c. on 30c. grey-green	£170

1900–01. Wmk Crown CA (Nos. 56/61)

Z178	2c. dull green	4·00
Z179	4c. carmine	3·75
Z180	5c. yellow	27·00
Z181	10c. ultramarine	3·75
Z182	12c. blue	£100
Z183	30c. brown	60·00

1903. Wmk Crown CA (Nos. 62/76).

Z184	1c. dull purple and brown	4·25
Z185	2c. dull green	4·25
Z186	4c. purple/*red*	3·00
Z187	5c. dull green and brown-orange	19·00
Z188	8c. slate and violet	8·50
Z189	10c. purple and blue/*blue*	4·25
Z190	12c. green and purple/*yellow*	14·00
Z191	20c. slate and chestnut	8·00
Z192	30c. dull green and black	45·00

1904–06. Wmk Mult Crown CA (Nos. 77/90).

Z199	2c. dull green	4·00
Z200	4c. purple/*red*	3·00
Z201	5c. dull green and brown-orange	18·00
Z202	8c. slate and violet	13·00
Z203	10c. purple and blue/blue	4·00
Z204	12c. green and purple/*yellow*	21·00
Z205	20c. slate and chestnut	11·00
Z206	30c. dull green and black	32·00
Z207	50c. green and magenta	35·00
Z208	$1 purple and sage-green	65·00
Z209	$2 slate and scarlet	£450
Z210	$3 slate and dull blue	£550
Z212	$10 slate and orange/blue	£1600

1907–11. Wmk Mult Crown CA (Nos. 91/9).

Z213	1c. brown	4·25
Z214	2c. green	4·25
Z215	4c. carmine-red	3·00
Z216	6c. orange-vermilion and purple	17·00
Z217	10c. bright ultramarine	3·75
Z218	20c. purple and sage-green	70·00
Z219	30c. purple and orange-yellow	50·00
Z220	50c. black/*green*	42·00
Z221	$2 carmine-red and black	£425

1912–15. Wmk Mult Crown CA (Nos. 100/16).

Z222	1c. brown	4·25
Z223	2c. green	3·50
Z224	4c. red	2·50
Z225	6c. orange	4·50
Z226	8c. grey	18·00
Z227	10c. ultramarine	4·00
Z228	12c. purple/yellow	18·00
Z229	20c. purple and sage-green	6·00
Z230	25c. purple and magenta (type A)	70·00
Z231	30c. purple and orange-yellow	19·00
Z232	50c. black/*green*	6·50
Z233	$1 purple and blue/*blue*	35·00
Z234	$2 carmine red and grey-black	95·00
Z235	$3 green and purple	£170

POSTCARD STAMPS

1879. (Nos. P1/2).

ZP236	3c. on 16c. yellow	£600
ZP237	5c. on 18c. lilac	£750

POSTAL FISCAL STAMPS

1874–1902. Wmk Crown CC. P 15½×15 (Nos. F1/3)

ZF238	$2 olive-green	£180

1891. (No. F9).

ZF246	$5 on $10 purple/*red*	£375

1897. (No. F10).

ZF247	$1 on $2 olive-green	

CHEFOO

Chefoo was opened to British trade in 1860. Although a consulate was established in 1863 no organised postal agency was provided until 1 January 1903 when one was opened at the premises of Curtis Brothers, a commercial firm.

Type **E** (*supplied* 1902) *used* 1903–20
Type **D** (*supplied* 1907) *used* 1907–13
Type **F** *used* 1916–22

Stamps of HONG KONG *cancelled at Chefoo between* 1903 *and* 1916 *with postmarks detailed above.*

1882–96. Wmk Crown CA (Nos. 32/9).

Z249	5c. blue	35·00

1891. (Nos. 43/50).

Z250	20c. on 30c. grey-green (No. 48*a*)	50·00

1898. (No. 52).

Z251	$1 on 96c. black	£100

1900–01. Wmk Crown CA (Nos. 56/61).

Z252	2c. dull green	27·00
Z253	4c. carmine	26·00
Z254	5c. yellow	60·00
Z255	10c. ultramarine	27·00
Z257	30c. brown	£130

1903. Wmk Crown CA (Nos. 62/76).

Z258	1c. dull purple and brown	10·00
Z259	2c. dull green	9·00
Z260	4c. purple/*red*	8·50
Z261	5c. dull green and brown-orange	22·00
Z262	8c. slate and violet	18·00
Z263	10c. purple and blue/*blue*	10·00
Z264	12c. green and purple/*yellow*	28·00
Z268	$1 purple and sage-green	

1904–06. Wmk Mult Crown CA (Nos. 77/90).

Z273	2c. dull green	9·00
Z274	4c. purple/*red*	7·50
Z275	5c. dull green and brown-orange	16·00
Z276	8c. slate and violet	17·00
Z277	10c. purple and blue/*blue*	9·00
Z278	12c. green and purple/*yellow*	25·00
Z279	20c. slate and chestnut	20·00
Z280	30c. dull green and black	50·00
Z281	50c. green and magenta	50·00
Z282	$1 purple and sage-green	90·00
Z283	$2 slate and scarlet	£225
Z284	$3 slate and dull blue	£450
Z285	$5 purple and blue-green	

1907–11. Wmk Mult Crown CA (Nos. 91/9).

Z287	1c. brown	10·00
Z288	2c. green	9·50
Z289	4c. carmine-red	8·50
Z290	6c. orange-vermilion and purple	27·00
Z291	10c. bright ultramarine	9·00
Z292	20c. purple and sage-green	80·00
Z293	30c. purple and orange-yellow	60·00
Z295	$2 carmine-red and black	

1912–15. Wmk Mult Crown CA (Nos. 100/16).

Z296	1c. brown	8·00
Z297	2c. green	7·50
Z298	4c. red	6·00
Z299	6c. orange	14·00
Z300	8c. grey	28·00
Z301	10c. ultramarine	7·50
Z302	12c. purple/*yellow*	30·00
Z303	20c. purple and sage-green	11·00
Z305	30c. purple and orange-yellow	17·00
Z306	50c. black/*green*	10·00
Z307	$1 purple and blue/*blue*	15·00
Z308	$2 carmine-red and grey-black	90·00
Z309	$3 green and purple	£140
Z310	$5 green and red/*green*	£500
Z311	$10 purple and black/*red*	£325

FOOCHOW

Foochow, originally known as Foochowfoo, was one of the original Treaty Ports opened to British trade in 1842. A British consulate and postal agency was established in June 1844.

Type **A** ("F1") (*supplied* 1866) *used* 1873–84
Type **D** (inscr "FOOCHOWFOO") (*supplied* 1866) *used* 1867–1905
Type **D** (inscr "FOOCHOW") (*supplied* 1894) *used* 1894–1917
Type **E** (inscr "B.P.O.") *used* 1906–10
Type **F** *used* 1915–22

Stamps of HONG KONG *cancelled at Foochow between* 1867 *and* 1916 *with postmarks detailed above.*

1882. No wmk (Nos. 1/7).

Z312	18c. lilac	£170

1863–71. Wmk Crown CC (Nos. 8/19).

Z313	2c. brown	35·00
Z314	4c. grey	35·00
Z315	6c. lilac	45·00
Z316	8c. orange	50·00
Z317	12c. blue	18·00
Z318	18c. lilac	£850
Z319	24c. green	75·00
Z320	30c. vermilion	£170
Z321	30c. mauve	15·00
Z322	48c. rose	£100
Z324	96c. brownish grey	£375

1876–77. (Nos. 20/1).

Z325	16c. on 18c. lilac	£325
Z326	28c. on 30c. mauve	£150

1877. Wmk Crown CC (No. 22).

Z327	16c. yellow	£140

1880. (Nos. 23/7).

Z328	5c. on 8c. orange	£350
Z329	5c. on 18c. lilac	£130
Z330	10c. on 12c. blue	£130
Z331	10c. on 16c. yellow	
Z332	10c. on 24c. green	£170

1880. Wmk Crown CC (Nos. 28/31).

Z333	2c. rose	38·00
Z334	5c. blue	75·00
Z335	10c. mauve	45·00
Z336	48c. brown	£200

1882–96. Wmk Crown CA (Nos. 32/9).

Z336a	2c. rose-lake	35·00
Z337	2c. carmine	2·50
Z338	4c. slate-grey	7·50
Z339	5c. blue	3·25
Z340	10c. dull mauve	32·00
Z341	10c. green	11·00
Z342	10c. purple/*red*	4·00
Z343	30c. green	40·00

1885. (Nos. 40/2).

Z344	20c. on 30c. orange-red	15·00
Z345	50c. on 48c. yellowish brown	60·00
Z346	$1 on 96c. grey-olive	£100

1891. (Nos. 43/50).

Z347	7c. on 10c. green	
Z348	14c. on 30c. mauve	95·00
Z348*a*	20c. on 30c. green (No. 45)	£250
Z349	20c. on 30c. green (No. 48)	21·00
Z350	50c. on 48c. dull purple	25·00
Z351	$1 on 96c. purple/*red*	60·00

1898. (No. 52).

Z353	$1 on 96c. black	80·00

1898. (No. 55).

Z354	10c. on 30c. green	£225

1900–01. Wmk Crown CA (Nos. 56/61).

Z355	2c. dull green	3·75
Z356	4c. carmine	4·25
Z357	5c. yellow	19·00
Z358	10c. ultramarine	3·75
Z360	30c. brown	75·00

1903. Wmk Crown CA (Nos. 62/76).

Z361	1c. dull purple and brown	4·50
Z362	2c. dull green	4·00
Z363	4c. purple/*red*	2·75
Z364	5c. dull green and brown-orange	19·00
Z365	8c. slate and violet	10·00
Z366	10c. purple and blue/*blue*	4·25
Z367	12c. green and purple/*yellow*	16·00
Z368	20c. slate and chestnut	10·00
Z369	30c. dull green and black	40·00
Z370	50c. dull green and magenta	65·00

1904–06. Wmk Mult Crown CA (Nos. 77/90).

Z376	2c. dull green	4·00
Z377	4c. purple/red	2·75
Z378	5c. dull green and brown-orange	13·00
Z379	8c. slate and violet	9·00
Z380	10c. purple and blue/blue	4·25
Z381	12c. green and purple/yellow	19·00
Z382	20c. slate and chestnut	9·00
Z383	30c. dull green and black	38·00
Z384	50c. green and magenta	32·00
Z385	$1 purple and sage-green	60·00

1907–11. Wmk Mult Crown CA (Nos. 91/9).

Z390	1c. brown	3·75
Z391	2c. green	3·75
Z392	4c. carmine-red	2·75
Z393	6c. orange-vermilion and purple	16·00
Z394	10c. bright ultramarine	3·50
Z395	20c. purple and sage-green	70·00
Z396	30c. purple and orange-yellow	50·00
Z397	50c. black/*green*	40·00

1912–15. Wmk Mult Crown CA (Nos. 100/16).

Z399	1c. brown	4·50
Z400	2c. green	4·00
Z401	4c. red	2·75
Z402	6c. orange	9·50
Z403	8c. grey	21·00
Z404	10c. ultramarine	4·00
Z406	20c. purple and sage-green	6·00
Z407	25c. purple and magenta (Type A)	
Z408	30c. purple and orange-yellow	15·00

POSTCARD STAMPS

1874–1902. (Nos. P1/2).

ZP413	3c. on 16c. yellow	£700

POSTAL FISCAL STAMPS

1874–1902. Wmk Crown CC. P 15½×15 (Nos. F1/3)

ZF415	$2 olive-green	£160
ZF416	$3 dull violet	£140

HANKOW

Hankow, on the Yangtse River 600 miles from the sea, became a Treaty Port in 1860. A British consulate opened the following year, but no organised British postal agency was established until 1872.

Type **D** (*supplied* 1874) *used* 1874–1916
Type **B** ("D29") (*supplied* 1876) *used* 1878–83
Type **F** *used* 1916–22

Stamps of HONG KONG *cancelled at Hankow between* 1874 *and* 1916 *with postmarks detailed above.*

1862. No wmk (Nos. 1/7).

Z426	18c. lilac	£250

1863–71. Wmk Crown CC (Nos. 8/19).

Z427	2c. brown	90·00
Z428	4c. grey	90·00
Z429	6c. lilac	£120
Z430	8c. orange	£110
Z431	12c. blue	38·00
Z432	18c. lilac	£900
Z433	24c. green	£160
Z435	30c. mauve	£100
Z436	48c. rose	£225
Z438	96c. brownish grey	

1876–77. (Nos. 20/1).

Z439	16c. on 18c. lilac	£400
Z440	28c. on 30c. mauve	£225

1877. Wmk Crown CC (No. 22).

Z441	16c. yellow	£500

1880. (Nos. 23/7).

Z442	5c. on 8c. orange	£225
Z443	5c. on 18c. lilac	£170
Z444	10c. on 12c. blue	£180
Z445	10c. on 16c. yellow	£375
Z446	10c. on 24c. green	£200

1880. Wmk Crown CC (Nos. 28/31).

Z447	2c. rose	75·00
Z448	5c. blue	85·00
Z449	10c. mauve	90·00
Z450	48c. brown	£325

1882–96. Wmk Crown CA (Nos. 32/9).

Z451	2c. carmine	7·50
Z452	4c. slate-grey	16·00
Z453	5c. blue	8·00
Z454	10c. dull mauve	75·00
Z455	10c. green	9·50
Z456	10c. purple/*red*	8·50
Z457	30c. green	50·00

1885. (Nos. 40/2).

Z458	20c. on 30c. orange-red	29·00
Z459	50c. on 48c. yellowish brown	75·00
Z460	$1 on 96c. grey-olive	£140

1891. (Nos. 43/50).

Z461	7c. on 10c. green	28·00
Z462	14c. on 30c. mauve	£120
Z463	20c. on 30c. green	21·00
Z464	50c. on 48c. dull purple	21·00
Z465	$1 on 96c. purple/*red*	60·00

1898. (No. 52).

Z467	$1 on 96c. black	80·00

1898. (No. 55).

Z468	10c. on 30c. green	£225

1900–01. Wmk Crown CA (Nos. 56/61).

Z469	2c. dull green	4·75
Z470	4c. carmine	5·00
Z471	5c. yellow	25·00
Z472	10c. ultramarine	6·50
Z473	12c. blue	£130
Z474	30c. brown	75·00

1903. Wmk Crown CA (Nos. 62/76).

Z475	1c. dull purple and brown	5·00
Z476	2c. dull green	4·75
Z477	4c. purple/*red*	4·00
Z478	5c. dull green and brown-orange	19·00
Z479	8c. slate and violet	15·00
Z480	10c. purple and blue/*blue*	4·50
Z481	12c. green and purple/*yellow*	18·00
Z482	20c. slate and chestnut	13·00
Z483	30c. dull green and black	42·00
Z484	50c. dull green and magenta	75·00
Z485	$1 purple and sage-green	60·00

1904–06. Wmk Mult Crown CA (Nos. 77/90).

Z490	2c. dull green	4·50
Z491	4c. purple/red	4·00
Z492	5c. dull green and brown-orange	18·00
Z493	8c. slate and violet	9·00
Z494	10c. purple and blue/blue	4·50
Z495	12c. green and purple/yellow	20·00
Z496	20c. slate and chestnut	15·00
Z497	30c. dull green and black	38·00
Z498	50c. green and magenta	28·00
Z499	$1 purple and sage-green	60·00
Z500	$2 slate and scarlet	£375
Z502	$5 purple and blue-green	£700
Z503	$10 slate and orange/blue	£1800

1907–11. Wmk Mult Crown CA (Nos. 91/9).

Z504	1c. brown	4·75
Z505	2c. green	4·25
Z506	4c. carmine-red	3·00
Z507	6c. orange-vermilion and purple	20·00
Z508	10c. bright ultramarine	4·50
Z509	20c. purple and sage-green	80·00
Z510	30c. purple and orange-yellow	65·00

1912–15. Wmk Mult Crown CA (Nos. 100/16).

Z513	1c. brown	5·50
Z514	2c. green	4·75
Z515	4c. red	3·75
Z516	6c. orange	10·00
Z518	10c. ultramarine	4·25
Z520	20c. purple and sage-green	11·00
Z522	30c. purple and orange-yellow	22·00
Z523	50c. black/*green*	13·00
Z524	$1 purple and blue/*blue*	50·00
Z527	$5 green and red/*green*	£550

POSTCARD STAMPS

1879. (Nos. P1/2).

ZP528	3c. on 16c. yellow	£950

POSTAL FISCAL STAMPS

1874–1902. Wmk Crown CC.

(*a*) P 15½×15 (Nos. F1/3).

ZF529	$2 olive-green	£200

(*b*) P 14 (Nos. F4/6).

ZF532	$2 dull bluish green	£425

1897. (No. F11).

ZF533	$1 on $2 dull bluish green	£550

KIUNGCHOW (HOIHOW)

Kiungchow, a city on the island of Hainan, and its port of Hoihow was added to the Treaty Port system in 1860. A consular postal agency was opened at Kiungchow in 1876, being transferred to Hoihow in 1878. A second agency was opened at Kiungchow in 1879.

Type **B** ("D28") (*supplied* 1876) *used* 1879–83
Type **D** (inscr "KIUNG-CHOW") (*supplied* 1878) *used* 1879–81

"REGISTERED KIUNG-CHOW" with "REGISTERED" removed (*originally supplied* 1876) *used* 1883–85
Type **D** (inscr "HOIHOW") *used* 1885–1922

Stamps of HONG KONG *cancelled at Kiungchow (Hoihow) between* 1879 *and* 1916 *with postmarks detailed above.*

1863–71. Wmk Crown CC (Nos. 8/19).

Z540	2c. brown	£750
Z541	4c. grey	£550
Z542	6c. lilac	£1200
Z543	8c. orange	£1200
Z544	12c. blue	£550
Z546	24c. green	£1200
Z547	30c. vermilion	
Z548	30c. mauve	£300
Z549	48c. rose	£1600
Z551	96c. brownish grey	£1800

1876–77. (Nos. 20/1).

Z552	16c. on 18c. lilac	£1300
Z553	28c. on 30c. mauve	£1100

1877. (No. 22).

Z554	16c. yellow	£2250

1880. (Nos. 23/7).

Z555	5c. on 8c. orange	£800
Z556	5c. on 18c. lilac	£700
Z557	10c. on 12c. blue	£700
Z558	10c. on 16c. yellow	£1400
Z559	10c. on 24c. green	

1880. Wmk Crown CC (Nos. 28/31).

Z561	5c. blue	£600
Z562	10c. mauve	£750

1882–96. Wmk Crown CA (Nos. 32/9).

Z564	2c. carmine	48·00
Z565	4c. slate-grey	65·00
Z566	5c. blue	48·00
Z567	10c. dull mauve	£550
Z568	10c. green	60·00
Z569	10c. purple/*red*	48·00
Z570	30c. green	£100

1886. (Nos. 40/2).

Z571	20c. on 30c. orange-red	£100
Z572	50c. on 48c. yellowish brown	£120
Z573	$1 on 96c. grey-olive	£200

1891. (Nos. 43/50).

Z574	7c. on 10c. green	£150
Z576	20c. on 30c. green	48·00
Z577	50c. on 48c. dull purple	65·00
Z578	$1 on 96c. purple/*red*	£130

1891. *50th Anniv of Colony* (No. 51).

Z579	2c. carmine	£2750

1898. (No. 52).

Z580	$1 on 96c. black	£250

1898. (No. 55).

Z581	10c. on 30c. green	£450

1900–01. Wmk Crown CA (Nos. 56/61).

Z582	2c. dull green	70·00
Z583	4c. carmine	32·00
Z584	5c. yellow	75·00
Z585	10c. ultramarine	38·00
Z587	30c. brown	£160

1903. Wmk Crown CA (Nos. 62/76).

Z588	1c. dull purple and brown	23·00
Z589	2c. dull green	23·00
Z590	4c. purple/*red*	18·00
Z591	5c. dull green and brown-orange	42·00
Z592	8c. slate and violet	40·00
Z593	10c. purple and blue/*blue*	21·00
Z594	12c. green and purple/*yellow*	48·00
Z596	30c. dull green and black	£100
Z597	50c. dull green & magenta	£160
Z598	$1 purple and sage-green	£225
Z599	$2 slate and scarlet	£750

1904. Wmk Mult Crown CA (Nos. 77/90).

Z603	2c. dull green	22·00
Z604	4c. purple/*red*	18·00
Z605	5c. dull green and brown-orange	42·00
Z606	8c. slate and violet	27·00
Z607	10c. purple and blue/*blue*	20·00
Z608	12c. green and purple/*yellow*	45·00
Z609	20c. slate and chestnut	55·00
Z610	30c. dull green and black	75·00
Z612	$1 purple and sage-green	£375

1907–11. Wmk Mult Crown CA (Nos. 91/9).

Z617	1c. brown	22·00
Z618	2c. green	21·00
Z619	4c. carmine-red	18·00
Z620	6c. orange-vermilion and purple	45·00
Z621	10c. bright ultramarine	20·00
Z622	20c. purple and sage-green	85·00

1912–15. Wmk Mult Crown CA (Nos. 100/16).

Z625	1c. brown	20·00
Z626	2c. green	19·00
Z627	4c. red	18·00
Z628	6c. orange	27·00
Z629	8c. grey	
Z630	10c. ultramarine	18·00
Z631	12c. purple/*yellow*	48·00
Z632	20c. purple and sage-green	38·00
Z633	25c. purple and magenta (Type A)	85·00
Z634	30c. purple and orange-yellow	
Z635	50c. black/*green*	55·00
Z636	$1 purple and blue/blue	60·00

POSTAL FISCAL STAMPS

1874–1902. Wmk Crown CC.

(*a*) P 15½×15 (Nos. F1/3).

ZF641	$2 olive-green	£350

(*b*) P 14 (Nos. F4/6).

ZF644	$2 dull bluish green	£475

1897. (Nos. F10/11).

ZF650	$1 on $2 olive-green	£425

NINGPO

Ningpo was one of the 1842 Treaty Ports and a consular postal agency was established there in 1844.

Type **A** ("N1") (*supplied* 1866) *used* 1870–82
Type **C** (*supplied* 1866) *used* 1870–99
Type **D** *used* 1899–1922

Stamps of HONG KONG *cancelled at Ningpo between* 1866 *and* 1916 *with postmarks detailed above.*

1862. No wmk (Nos. 1/7).

Z652	18c. lilac	£800

1863–71. Wmk Crown CC (Nos. 8/19).

Z653	2c. brown	£300
Z654	4c. grey	£300
	a. Perf 12½	
Z655	6c. lilac	£350
Z656	8c. orange	£300
Z657	12c. blue	£140
Z658	18c. lilac	
Z659	24c. green	£325
Z660	30c. vermilion	£400
Z661	30c. mauve	£120
Z662	48c. rose	£550
Z663.	96c. olive-bistre	
Z664	96c. brownish grey	£700

1876–77. (Nos. 20/1).

Z665	16c.. on 18c lilac	£550
Z666	28c.. on 30c mauve	£325

1877. Wmk Crown CC (No. 22).

Z667	16c. yellow	£400

1880. (Nos. 23/7).

Z668	5c. on 8c. orange	£375
Z669	5c. on 18c. lilac	£300
Z670	10c. on 12c. blue	£325
Z672	10c. on 24c. green	£375

1880. Wmk Crown CC (Nos. 28/31).

Z674	5c. blue	£160
Z675	10c. mauve	£160
Z676	48c. brown	£700

1882–96. Wmk Crown CA (Nos. 32/9).

Z677	2c. carmine	45·00
Z678	4c. slate-grey	70·00
Z679	5c. blue	45·00
Z680	10c. dull mauve	£170
Z681	10c. green	50·00
Z682	10c. purple/red	50·00
Z683	30c. green	£100

1885. (Nos. 40/2).
Z685 50c. on 48c. yellowish brown £130

1891. (Nos. 43/50).
Z686 7c. on 10c. green .... 55·00
Z687 14c. on 30c. mauve ....
Z688 20c. on 30c. green .... 40·00
Z689 50c. on 48c. dull purple .... 65·00
Z690 $1 on 96c. purple/*red* £120

1898. (No. 52).
Z692 $1 on 96c. black £140

1898. (No. 55).
Z693 10c. on 30c. green £300

1900–01. Wmk Crown CA (Nos. 56/61).
Z694 2c. dull green .... 25·00
Z695 4c. carmine .... 22·00
Z697 10c. ultramarine .... 25·00

1903. Wmk Crown CA (Nos. 62/76).
Z700 1c. dull purple and brown .... 23·00
Z701 2c. dull green .... 23·00
Z702 4c. purple/*red* .... 17·00
Z703 5c. dull green and brown-orange .... 45·00
Z704 8c. slate and violet .... 26·00
Z705 10c. purple and blue/*blue* .... 19·00
Z706 12c. green and purple/*yellow* .... 55·00
Z709 50c. dull green and magenta .... 95·00

1904–06. Wmk Mult Crown CA (Nos. 77/90).
Z715 2c. dull green .... 21·00
Z716 4c. purple/*red* .... 19·00
Z718 8c. slate and violet .... 40·00
Z720 12c. green and purple/*yellow* .... 50·00
Z721 20c. slate and chestnut .... 50·00
Z722 30c. dull green and black .... 75·00
Z723 50c. green and magenta .... 65·00
Z724 $1 purple and sage-green .... 95·00

1907–11. Wmk Mult Crown CA (Nos. 91/9).
Z729 1c. brown .... 18·00
Z730 2c. green .... 18·00
Z731 4c. carmine-red .... 16·00
Z733 10c. bright ultramarine .... 18·00
Z734 20c. purple and sage-green .... 95·00
Z735 30c. purple and orange-yellow .... 80·00

1912–15. Wmk Mult Crown CA (Nos. 100/16).
Z738 1c. brown .... 19·00
Z739 2c. green .... 18·00
Z740 4c. red .... 17·00
Z742 8c. grey .... 55·00
Z743 10c. ultramarine .... 18·00
Z745 20c. purple and sage-green ....
Z747 30c. purple and orange-yellow ....
Z749 $1 purple and blue/*blue* .... 60·00

POSTCARD STAMPS

1879. (Nos. P1/2).
ZP751 3c. on 16c. yellow £1200

POSTAL FISCAL STAMPS

1874–1902. Wmk Crown CC. P 15½×15 (Nos. F1/3).
ZF754 $2 olive-green £325

1881. (No. F7).
ZF760 12c. on $10 rose-carmine ....

1897. (No. F10).
ZF763 $1 on $2 olive-green ....

SHANGHAI

Shanghai was one of the original Treaty Ports of 1842 and a packet agency was opened at the British consulate in April 1844. It moved to a separate premises in 1861 and was upgraded to a Post Office in September 1867.

British military post offices operated in Shanghai from 1927 until 1940.

Type **D** (inscr "SHANGHAE" (*supplied* 1861) *used* 1861–99

Sunburst *used* 1864–65
Type **A** ("S1") (*supplied* 1866) *used* 1866–85
Type **D** (inscr "SHANGHAI) (*supplied* 1885) *used* 1886-1906
Type **G** (inscr "B.R.O." at foot) (*supplied* 1904) *used* 1904–21
Type **G** (inscr "Br.P.O." at foot) (*supplied* 1907) *used* 1907–22
Type **E** (figures "I" to "VIII" at foot) *used* 1912–22

Stamps of HONG KONG *cancelled at Shanghai between* 1863 *and* 1916 *with postmarks detailed above.*

1862. No wmk (Nos. 1/7).
Z765 2c. brown £100
Z766 8c. yellow-buff £120
Z767 12c. pale greenish blue .... 90·00
Z768 18c. lilac .... 80·00
Z769 24c. green £150
Z770 48c. rose £450
Z771 96c. brownish grey £550

1863–71. Wmk Crown CC (Nos. 8/19).
Z772 2c. brown .... 9·00
Z773 4c. grey .... 8·50
a. Perf 12½ £275
Z774 6c. lilac .... 18·00
Z775 8c. orange .... 14·00
Z776 12c. blue .... 7·50
Z777 18c. lilac £350
Z778 24c. green .... 13·00
Z779 30c. vermilion .... 20·00
Z780 30c. mauve .... 6·50
Z781 48c. rose .... 35·00
Z782 96c. olive-bistre £950
Z783 96c. brownish grey .... 50·00

1876–77. (Nos. 20/1).
Z784 16c. on 18c. lilac £170
Z785 28c. on 30c. mauve .... 55·00

1877. Wmk Crown CC (No. 22).
Z786 16c. yellow .... 70·00

1880. (Nos. 23/7).
Z787 5c. on 8c. orange £100
Z788 5c. on 18c. lilac .... 60·00
Z789 10c. on 12c. blue .... 55·00
Z790 10c. on 16c. yellow £170
Z791 10c. on 24c. green .... 85·00

1880. Wmk Crown CC (Nos. 28/31).
Z792 2c. rose .... 28·00
Z793 5c. blue .... 55·00
Z794 10c. mauve .... 18·00
Z795 48c. brown £120

1882–96. Wmk Crown CA (Nos. 32/9).
Z795a 2c. rose-lake .... 32·00
Z796 2c. carmine .... 2·25
Z797 4c. slate-grey .... 2·75
Z798 5c. blue .... 1·10
Z799 10c. dull mauve .... 18·00
Z800 10c. green .... 1·50
Z801 10c. purple/red .... 1·40
Z802 30c. green .... 27·00

1885. (Nos. 40/2).
Z803 20c. on 30c. orange-red .... 7·00
Z804 50c. on 48c. yellowish brown .... 45·00
Z805 $1 on 96c. grey-olive .... 90·00

1891. (Nos. 43/50).
Z806 7c. on 10c. green .... 12·00
Z807 14c. on 30c. mauve .... 75·00
Z807a 20c. on 30c. green (No. 45) ....
Z807b 50c. on 48c. dull purple (No. 46) £325
Z807c $1 on 96c. purple/*red* (No. 47) £400
Z808 20c. on 30c. green .... 8·00
Z809 50c. on 48c. dull purple (No. 49) .... 7·00
Z810 $1 on 96c. purple/*red* (No. 50) .... 26·00

1898. (No. 52).
Z812 $1 on 96c. black .... 35·00

1898. (No. 55).
Z813 10c. on 30c. green .... 90·00

1900–01. Wmk Crown CA (Nos. 56/61).
Z814 2c. dull green .... 1·10
Z815 4c. carmine .... 1·10
Z816 5c. yellow .... 7·50
Z817 10c. ultramarine .... 2·25
Z818 12c. blue .... 75·00
Z819 30c. brown .... 29·00

1903. Wmk Crown CA (Nos. 62/76).
Z820 1c. dull purple and brown 75
Z821 2c. dull green .... 1·75
Z822 4c. purple/*red* 60
Z823 5c. dull green and brown-orange .... 11·00
Z824 8c. slate and violet .... 2·25
Z825 10c. purple and blue/*blue* .... 1·75
Z826 12c. green and purple/*yellow* .... 6·00
Z827 20c. slate and chestnut .... 4·25
Z828 30c. dull green and black .... 28·00
Z829 50c. dull green and magenta .... 50·00
Z830 $1 purple and sage-green .... 30·00
Z831 $2 slate and scarlet £350
Z832 $3 slate and dull blue £475
Z833 $5 purple and blue-green £600
Z834 $10 slate and orange/*blue* £650

1904–06. Wmk Mult Crown CA (Nos. 77/90).
Z835 2c. dull green .... 1·75
Z836 4c. purple/*red* 60
Z837 5c. dull green and brown-orange .... 7·50
Z838 8c. slate and violet .... 2·75
Z839 10c. purple and blue/*blue* .... 1·75
Z840 12c. green and purple/*yellow* .... 8·00
Z841 20c. slate and chestnut .... 2·75
Z842 30c. dull green and black .... 25·00
Z843 50c. green and magenta .... 13·00
Z844 $1 purple and sage-green .... 32·00
Z845 $2 slate and scarlet £140
Z846 $3 slate and dull blue £325
Z847 $5 purple and blue-green £475
Z848 $10 slate and orange/*blue* £1300

1907–11. Wmk Mult Crown CA (Nos. 91/9).
Z849 1c. brown .... 1·50
Z850 2c. green .... 1·90
Z851 4c. carmine-red 60
Z852 6c. orange-vermilion and purple .... 6·50
Z853 10c. bright ultramarine 60
Z854 20c. purple and sage-green .... 50·00
Z855 30c. purple and orange-yellow .... 32·00
Z856 50c. black/*green* .... 21·00
Z857 $2 carmine-red and black £400

1912–15. Wmk Mult Crown CA (Nos. 100/16).
Z858 1c. brown .... 1·00
Z859 2c. green 60
Z860 4c. red 45
Z861 6c. orange .... 2·00
Z862 8c. grey .... 9·00
Z863 10c. ultramarine 50
Z864 12c. purple/*yellow* .... 10·00
Z865 20c. purple and sage-green .... 1·40
Z867 30c. purple and orange-yellow .... 10·00
Z868 50c. black/*green* .... 3·75
Z869 $1 purple and blue/*blue* .... 5·50

POSTCARD STAMPS

1879. (Nos. P1/2).
ZP871 3c. on 16c. yellow £450
ZP872 5c. on 18c. lilac £500

POSTAL FISCAL STAMPS

1874–1902. Wmk Crown CC.

(a) P 15½×15 (Nos. F1/5).
ZF874 $2 olive-green .... 70·00
ZF875 $3 dull violet .... 48·00
ZF876 $10 rose-carmine £700

(b) P 14.
ZF877 $2 dull bluish green £275
ZF878 $3 dull mauve £500

1881. (No. F7).
ZF880 12c. on $10 rose-carmine £300

1891. (No. F9).
ZF882 $5 on $10 purple/red £140

1897. (No. F10/11).
ZF883 $1 on $2 olive-green £180
ZF884 $1 on $2 dull bluish green £275

SWATOW

Swatow became a Treaty Port in 1860 and a consular packet agency was opened in the area made available for foreign firms during the following year. In 1867 the original agency was transferred to the Chinese city on the other side of the Han river, but a second agency was subsequently opened in the foreign concession during 1883.

Type **A** ("S2") (*supplied* 1866) *used* 1875–85
Type **C** (*supplied* 1866) *used* 1866–90
Type **D** (*supplied* 1883) *used* 1884–1922
Type **F** *used* 1916–22

Stamps of HONG KONG *cancelled at Swatow between* 1866 *and* 1916 *with postmarks detailed above.*

1862. No wmk (Nos. 1/7).
Z885 18c. lilac £300

1863–71. Wmk Crown CC (Nos. 8/19).
Z886 2c. brown £120
Z887 4c. grey £120
a. Perf 12½ ....
Z888 6c. lilac £450
Z889 8c. orange £120
Z890 12c. blue .... 45·00
Z891 18c. lilac £900
Z892 24c. green £150
Z893 30c. vermilion ....
Z894 30c. mauve .... 45·00
Z895 48c. rose £180
Z897 96c. brownish grey £750

1876–77. (Nos. 20/1).
Z898 16c. on 18c. lilac £475
Z899 28c. on 30c. mauve £250

1877. Wmk Crown CC (No. 22).
Z900 16c. yellow £500

1880. (Nos. 23/7).
Z901 5c. on 8c. orange £250
Z902 5c. on 18c. lilac £200
Z903 10c. on 12c. blue £225
Z904 10c. on 16c. yellow £450
Z905 10c. on 24c. green £300

1880. Wmk Crown CC (Nos. 28/31).
Z906 2c. rose £100
Z907 5c. blue £110
Z908 10c. mauve £120

1882–96. Wmk Crown CA (Nos. 32/9).
Z910 2c. carmine .... 6·50
Z911 4c. slate-grey .... 21·00
Z912 5c. blue .... 7·00
Z913 10c. dull mauve .... 90·00
Z914 10c. green .... 9·00
Z915 10c. purple/*red* .... 6·50
Z916 30c. green .... 48·00

1885. (Nos. 40/2).
Z917 20c. on 30c. orange-red .... 16·00

1891. (Nos. 43/50).
Z919 7c. on 10c. green .... 27·00
Z920 14c. on 30c. mauve £110
Z920*a* 50c. on 48c. dull purple (No. 46) £375
Z921 $1 on 96c. purple/*red* (No. 47) £550
Z922 20c. on 30c. green .... 23·00
Z923 50c. on 48c. dull purple (No. 49) .... 24·00
Z924 $1 on 96c. purple/*red* (No. 50) .... 48·00

1891. *50th Anniv of Colony* (No. 51).
Z925 2c. carmine £950

1898. (No. 52).

Z926	$1 on 96c. black	75·00

1898. (No. 55).

Z927	10c. on 30c. green	£225

1900–01. Wmk Crown CA (Nos. 56/61).

Z928	2c. dull green	6·50
Z929	4c. carmine	5·00
Z930	5c. yellow	21·00
Z931	10c. ultramarine	5·50
Z932	12c. blue	£150
Z933	30c. brown	50·00

1903. Wmk Crown CA (Nos. 62/76).

Z934	1c. dull purple and brown	5·50
Z935	2c. dull green	5·50
Z936	4c. purple/*red*	4·00
Z937	5c. dull green and brown-orange	17·00
Z938	8c. slate and violet	10·00
Z939	10c. purple and blue/blue	5·50
Z940	12c. green and purple/*yellow*	15·00
Z941	20c. slate and chestnut	8·50
Z942	30c. dull green and black	42·00
Z943	50c. dull green and magenta	80·00
Z944	$1 purple and sage-green	70·00

1904–06. Wmk Mult Crown CA (Nos. 77/90).

Z949	2c. dull green	5·50
Z950	4c. purple/*red*	4·25
Z951	5c. dull green and brown-orange	17·00
Z952	8c. slate and violet	9·50
Z953	10c. purple and blue/*blue*	5·00
Z954	12c. green and purple/*yellow*	15·00
Z955	20c. slate and chestnut	9·50
Z956	30c. dull green and black	40·00
Z957	50c. green and magenta	27·00
Z958	$1 purple and sage-green	65·00
Z959	$2 slate and scarlet	£225
Z962	$10 slate and orange/*blue*	£1500

1907–11. Wmk Mult Crown CA (Nos. 91/9).

Z963	1c. brown	6·50
Z964	2c. green	6·50
Z965	4c. carmine-red	4·25
Z966	6c. orange-vermilion and purple	14·00
Z967	10c. bright ultramarine	4·75
Z969	30c. purple and orange-yellow	55·00
Z970	50c. black/*green*	38·00

1912–15. Wmk Mult Crown CA (Nos. 100/16).

Z972	1c. brown	4·75
Z973	2c. green	4·25
Z974	4c. red	3·75
Z975	6c. orange	7·00
Z976	8c. grey	21·00
Z977	10c. ultramarine	3·75
Z978	12c. purple/*yellow*	15·00
Z979	20c. purple and sage-green	5·00
Z980	25c. purple and magenta (Type A)	45·00
Z981	30c. purple and orange-yellow	20·00
Z982	50c. black/*green*	10·00
Z983	$1 purple and blue/*blue*	19·00

POSTCARD STAMP

1879. (Nos. P1/2).

ZP986	3c. on 16c. yellow	£950

POSTAL FISCAL STAMPS

1874–1902. Wmk Crown CC.

(a) P 15½×15 (Nos. F1/3).

ZF988	$2 olive-green	£130
ZF989	$3 dull violet	£110

(b) P 14.

ZF991	$2 dull bluish green	£425

TIENTSIN

Tientsin became a Treaty Port in 1860. A British consulate was established in 1861, but no formal postal agency was organised there until 1882. It was not, however, very successful and was closed during 1890. The British Post Office reopened on 1 October 1906 under the management of the Chinese Engineering and Mining Company.

British military post offices operated in Tientsin from 1927 until 1940.

Type **E** *used* 1906–13
Type **G** (*supplied* 1907) *used* 1907–22

Stamps of HONG KONG *cancelled at Tientsin between* 1906 *and* 1916 *with postmarks detailed above.*

1903. Wmk Crown CA (Nos. 62/76).

Z 998	1c. dull purple and brown	12·00
Z 999	5c. dull green and brown-orange	27·00
Z1000	8c. slate and violet	11·00
Z1000*a*	12c. green and purple/*yellow*	35·00

1904–06. Wmk Mult Crown CA (Nos. 77/90).

Z1001	2c. dull green	5·00
Z1002	4c. purple/*red*	4·00
Z1003	5c. dull green and brown-orange	15·00
Z1004	8c. slate and violet	12·00
Z1005	10c. purple and blue/*blue*	4·75
Z1006	12c. green and purple/*yellow*	18·00
Z1007	20c. slate and chestnut	12·00
Z1008	30c. dull green and black	38·00
Z1009	50c. green and magenta	28·00
Z1010	$1 purple and sage-green	50·00
Z1011	$2 slate and scarlet	£200
Z1012	$3 slate and dull blue	£550
Z1013	$5 purple and blue-green	£700
Z1014	$10 slate and orange/*blue*	£1900

1907–11. Wmk Mult Crown CA (Nos. 91/9).

Z1015	1c. brown	5·50
Z1016	2c. green	4·25
Z1017	4c. carmine-red	3·50
Z1018	6c. orange-vermilion and purple	18·00
Z1019	10c. bright ultramarine	4·25
Z1020	20c. purple and sage-green	80·00
Z1021	30c. purple and orange-yellow	65·00
Z1022	50c. black/green	45·00
Z1023	$2 carmine-red and black	£500

1912–15. Wmk Mult Crown CA (Nos. 100/16).

Z1024	1c. brown	4·75
Z1025	2c. green	4·25
Z1026	4c. red	3·25
Z1027	6c. orange	6·50
Z1028	8c. grey	27·00
Z1029	10c. ultramarine	4·75
Z1030	12c. purple/*yellow*	28·00
Z1031	20c. purple and sage-green	8·00
Z1033	30c. purple and orange-yellow	16·00
Z1034	50c. black/*green*	9·00
Z1035	$1 purple and blue/*blue*	13·00
Z1037	$3 green and purple	£160
Z1038	$5 green and red/*green*	£550

WEI HAI WEI

The territory of Wei Hai Wei was leased from the Chinese by the British Government from 24 May 1898 having been previously occupied by the Japanese. At that time there were no organised postal services from the area, although a private local post did operate between the port and Chefoo from 8 December 1898 until 15 March 1899. A Chinese Imperial post office opened in March 1899 to be followed by a British postal agency on the offshore island of Liu Kung Tau on 1 September 1899. A second British agency opened at Port Edward on 1 April 1904.

Liu Kung Tau oval *used* 1899–1901
Type **D** (inscr "LIU KUNG TAU") (*supplied* 1899) *used* 1901–30

Stamps of HONG KONG *cancelled at Liu Kung Tau between* 1899 *and* 1916 *with postmarks detailed above.*

1863–71. Wmk Crown CC (Nos. 8/19).

Z1039	12c. pale blue	

1882–96. Wmk Crown CA (Nos. 32/9).

Z1040	2c. carmine	55·00
Z1041	4c. slate-grey	70·00
Z1042	5c. blue	55·00
Z1043	10c. purple/*red*	38·00
Z1044	30c. green	65·00

1891. (Nos. 48/50).

Z1045	20c. on 30c. green	45·00
Z1046	50c. on 48c. dull purple	48·00

1898. (No. 52).

Z1047	$1 on 96c. black	90·00

1900–01. Wmk Crown CA (Nos. 56/61).

Z1049	2c. dull green	7·50
Z1050	4c. carmine	7·50
Z1051	5c. yellow	25·00
Z1052	10c. ultramarine	8·00
Z1053	12c. blue	£120
Z1054	30c. brown	75·00

1903. Wmk Crown CA (Nos. 62/76).

Z1055	1c. dull purple and brown	6·50
Z1056	2c. dull green	6·00
Z1057	4c. purple/*red*	5·00
Z1058	5c. dull green and brown-orange	18·00
Z1059	8c. slate and violet	14·00
Z1060	10c. purple and blue/*blue*	8·50
Z1061	12c. green and purple/*yellow*	27·00
Z1062	20c. slate and chestnut	14·00
Z1063	30c. dull green and black	48·00
Z1064	50c. dull green and magenta	85·00
Z1065	$1 purple and sage-green	70·00

1904–06. Wmk Mult Crown CA (Nos. 77/90).

Z1070	2c. dull green	6·50
Z1071	4c. purple/*red*	6·00
Z1073	8c. slate and violet	12·00
Z1076	20c. slate and chestnut	25·00
Z1077	30c. dull green and black	80·00
Z1078	50c. green and magenta	55·00

1907–11. Wmk Mult Crown CA (Nos. 91/9).

Z1084	1c. brown	7·00
Z1085	2c. green	7·00
Z1086	4c. carmine-red	5·00
Z1088	10c. bright ultramarine	6·00
Z1089	20c. purple and sage-green	85·00
Z1090	30c. purple and orange-yellow	70·00
Z1091	50c. black/*green*	55·00

1912–15. Wmk Mult Crown CA (Nos. 100/16).

Z1093	1c. brown	8·00
Z1094	2c. green	6·00
Z1095	4c. red	5·00
Z1096	6c. orange	11·00
Z1097	8c. grey	28·00
Z1098	10c. ultramarine	6·00
Z1104	$1 purple and blue/*blue*	28·00

POSTAL FISCAL STAMP

1874–1902. Wmk Crown CC. P 14 (Nos. F4/6).

Z1106	$2 dull bluish green	£850

Port Edward rectangle used 1904–08
Type **D** (inscr "WEI-HAI-WEI" at top and "PORT EDWARD" at foot) (*supplied* 1907) *used* 1907–30

Stamps of HONG KONG *cancelled at Port Edward between* 1904 *and* 1916 *with postmarks detailed above.*

1900–01. Wmk Crown CA (Nos. 56/61).

Z1109	2c. dull green	65·00
Z1110	10c. ultramarine	80·00

1903. Wmk Crown CA (Nos. 62/76).

Z1111	1c. dull purple and brown	26·00
Z1112	2c. dull green	26·00
Z1113	4c. purple/*red*	23·00
Z1114	5c. dull green and brown-orange	35·00
Z1115	8c. slate and violet	35·00
Z1116	10c. purple and blue/*blue*	27·00
Z1117	12c. green and purple/*yellow*	48·00
Z1118	20c. slate and chestnut	70·00
Z1119	30c. dull green and black	70·00
Z1120	50c. dull green and magenta	85·00
Z1121	$1 purple and sage-green	75·00

1904–06. Wmk Mult Crown CA (Nos. 77/90).

Z1126	2c. dull green	15·00
Z1127	4c. purple/*red*	13·00
Z1128	5c. dull green and brown-orange	22·00
Z1129	8c. slate and violet	17·00
Z1132	20c. slate and chestnut	65·00
Z1133	30c. dull green and black	60·00
Z1134	50c. green and magenta	65·00

1907–11. Wmk Mult Crown CA (Nos. 91/9).

Z1140	1c. brown	14·00
Z1141	2c. green	14·00
Z1142	4c. carmine-red	9·00
Z1143	6c. orange-vermilion and purple	27·00
Z1144	10c. bright ultramarine	10·00
Z1148	50c. black/*green*	45·00

1912–15. Wmk Mult Crown CA (Nos. 100/16).

Z1151	1c. brown	12·00
Z1152	2c. green	8·50
Z1153	4c. red	5·00
Z1155	8c. grey	26·00
Z1156	10c. ultramarine	6·00
Z1158	20c. purple and sage-green	17·00
Z1161	50c. black/*green*	20·00
Z1162	$1 purple and blue/*blue*	22·00

PRICES FOR STAMPS ON COVER

Nos. 1/14	*from* × 50
Nos. 15/17	—
Nos. 18/28	*from* × 30

The overprinted stamps Nos. 1/17 were introduced on 1 January 1917 to prevent currency speculation in the Treaty Ports. They were used in the then-existing agencies of Amoy, Canton, Chefoo, Foochow, Hankow, Hoihow, Ningpo,. Shanghai, Swatow, Tientsin and were also supplied to the British naval base of Wei Hai Wei.

CHINA
(1)

1917 (1 Jan)–**21**. *Stamps of Hong Kong, 1912–21* (wmk Mult Crown CA), *optd with T* **1**, *at Somerset House.*

1	1c. brown	7·00	1·50
	a. Black-brown	5·50	2·50
	b. Crown broken at right	£350	£400
	c. Wmk sideways	†	£3000
	w. Wmk inverted	†	£1400
2	2c. green	10·00	30
3	4c. carmine-red	7·00	30
4	6c. orange	7·00	60
5	8c. slate	15·00	1·25
6	10c. ultramarine	15·00	30
	y. Wmk inverted and reversed	†	£700
7	12c. purple/*yellow*	15·00	7·00
8	20c. purple and sage-green	15·00	60
9	25c. purple and magenta (A)	9·00	15·00
11	30c. purple and orange-yellow	42·00	6·50
12	50c. black/*blue-green* (*olive back*)	70·00	1·50
	a. Emerald surface (1917?)	55·00	8·50
	b. On emerald back (1919)	42·00	5·50
	c. On white back (1920)	£700	£130
13	$1 reddish purple and bright blue/*blue*	75·00	2·50
	a. Grey-purple and blue/blue (1921)	75·00	7·00
14	$2 carmine-red and grey-black	£225	70·00
15	$3 green and purple	£750	£225
16	$5 green and red/*blue-green* (*olive back*)	£350	£275

17	$10 purple and black/*red*	£950	£550
1/17 *Set of* 16		£2250	£1000
12s/17s H/S "Specimen" *Set of* 6		£2250	

1922 (Mar)–**27**. As last, but wmk Mult Script CA.

18	1c. brown	2·50	4·25
19	2c. green	5·00	2·25
	w. Wmk inverted	£275	
20	4c. carmine-rose	9·00	2·25
	a. Lower Chinese character at right broken at top	£250	£250
21	6c. orange-yellow	4·75	4·25
22	8c. grey	10·00	16·00
23	10c. bright ultramarine	12·00	4·25
	w. Wmk inverted	£180	
24	20c. purple and sage-green	17·00	5·00
25	25c. purple and magenta (B)	24·00	75·00
	a. Broken flower	£550	
26	50c. black/*emerald* (1927)	60·00	£200
	s. Handstamped "Specimen"	£275	
27	$1 purple and blue/*blue*	80·00	75·00
28	$2 carmine-red and grey-black	£200	£250
18/28 *Set of* 11		£375	£550

STAMP BOOKLETS

1917. *Black on red cover inscribed "*BRITISH POST OFFICE AGENCIES IN CHINA*". Stapled.*

SB1	$1 booklet containing eight 2c., six 4c. and six 10c. (Nos. 2/3, 6)	£5500

1922. *Cover as No. SB1. Stapled.*

SB2	$1 booklet containing eight 2c., six 4c., and six 10c. (Nos. 19/20, 23)	£5000

The British P.O.'s in the Treaty Ports closed by agreement with the Chinese on 30 November 1922, but the above over- printed issues continued in use at the Wei Hai Wei offices until they in turn closed on 30 September 1930. Under the terms of the Convention signed with China the Royal Navy continued to use the base at Wei Hai Wei until the mid-1930s.

BRITISH POST OFFICES IN JAPAN

Under the terms of the Anglo-Japanese Treaty of Yedo, signed on 26 August 1858, five Japanese ports were opened to British trade. British consulates were established at Decima (Nagasaki), Kanagawa (Yokohama), Hiogo (Kobe) and Hakodadi (Hakodate). The postage stamps of Hong Kong became available at the Yokohama and Nagasaki consulates during October 1864 and at Hiogo in 1869, although cancellation of mail did not commence until 1866 at Yokohama and Nagasaki or 1876 at Hiogo. Japan became a member of the U.P.U. on 1 June 1877 and all of the British Postal Agencies were closed by the end of 1879.

For illustrations of postmark types see BRITISH POST OFFICES IN CHINA.

HAKODATE

A British consular office existed at Hakodate, but it was never issued with a c.d.s. obliterator or Hong Kong stamps. No British covers are recorded from this consulate prior to opening of the Japanese Post Office.

HIOGO

The Port of Hiogo (Kobe) was first opened to foreigners on 1 January 1868. The British Consular mail service at Hiogo commenced during 1869 to serve the foreigners at Hiogo, Kobe and Osaka. The cities of Hiogo and Kobe later merged to become the single city of Kobe. The consular office at Hiogo closed on 30 November 1879.

Type **B** ("D30") (*supplied* 1876) *used* 1876–79
Type **D** (*supplied* 1876) *used* 1876–79

Stamps of HONG KONG *cancelled at Hiogo between* 1876 *and* 1879 *with postmarks detailed above.*

1863–71. Wmk Crown CC (Nos. 8/19).

Z1	2c. brown	£5500
Z2	4c. grey	£4000
Z3	6c. lilac	£4750
Z4	8c. orange	£4500
Z5	12c. blue	£5500
Z6	18c. lilac	
Z7	24c. green	£4000
Z8	30c. vermilion	
Z9	30c. mauve	£5500
Z10	48c. rose	£8000
Z12	96c. brownish grey	£8000

1877. (Nos. 20/1).

Z13	16c. on 18c. lilac	

1877. Wmk Crown CC (No. 22).

Z15	16c. yellow	£6500

NAGASAKI

The British Consulate opened in Nagasaki on 14 June 1859, but, with few British residents at the port, the consular staff found it inconvenient to carry out postal duties so that few Nagasaki c.d.s. or "N2" cancellations exist. The postal service was terminated on 30 September 1879.

Type **A** ("N2") (*supplied* 1866) *used* 1876–79
Type **D** (*supplied* 1866) *used* 1876–79

Stamps of HONG KONG *cancelled at Nagasaki between* 1876 *and* 1879 *with postmarks detailed above.*

1862. No wmk (Nos. 1/8).

Z15a	18c. lilac	£3000

1863–71. Wmk Crown CC (Nos. 8/19).

Z16	2c. brown	£2000
Z17	4c. grey	£1800
Z18	6c. lilac	£1700
Z19	8c. orange	£1800
Z20	12c. blue	£1900
Z21	18c. lilac	£3750
Z22	24c. green	£3250
Z24	30c. mauve	£2750
Z25	48c. rose	£3500
Z27	96c. brownish grey	

1876–77. (Nos. 20/1).

Z28	16c. on 18c. lilac	£2750
Z29	28c. on 30c. mauve	£2000

1877. Wmk Crown CC (No. 22).

Z30	16c. yellow	£3000

YOKOHAMA

The British Consulate opened in Kanagawa on 21 July 1859, but was relocated to Yokohama where it provided postal services from 1 July 1860 until a separate Post Office was established in July 1867. The British Post Office in Yokohama closed on 31 December 1879.

Type **A** ("Yl") (*supplied* 1866) *used* 1867–79
Type **D** (*supplied* 1866) *used* 1866–79

Stamps of HONG KONG *cancelled at Yokohama between* 1866 *and* 1879 *with postmarks detailed above.*

1862. No wmk (Nos. 1/8).

Z30*a*	8c. yellow-buff	£300
Z31	18c. lilac	£110

1863–71. Wmk Crown CC (Nos. 8/19).

Z32	2c. brown	19·00
Z33	4c. grey	20·00
	a. Perf 12½	£550
Z34	6c. lilac	25·00
Z35	8c. orange	25·00
Z36	12c. blue	19·00
Z37	18c. lilac	£650
Z38	24c. green	21·00
Z39	30c. vermilion	60·00
Z40	30c. mauve	19·00
Z41	48c. rose	50·00
Z42	96c. olive-bistre	£4000
Z43	96c. brownish grey	70·00

1876–77. (Nos. 20/1).

Z44	16c. on 18c. lilac	£300
Z45	28c. on 30c. mauve	85·00

1877. Wmk Crown CC (No. 22).

Z46	16c. yellow	£120

POSTAL FISCAL STAMPS

1874. Wmk Crown CC. P 15½×15 (Nos. F1/3).

ZF47	$2 olive-green	£130
ZF48	$3 dull violet	£120
ZF49	$10 rose-carmine	£1600

India

PRICES FOR STAMPS ON COVER TO 1945	
Nos. S1/3	*from* × 2
No. 1	†
Nos. 2/26	*from* × 3
Nos. 27/30	—
Nos. 31/4	*from* × 8
Nos. 35/49	*from* × 3
No. 50	†
Nos. 51/3	*from* × 4
Nos. 54/65	*from* × 2
Nos. 66/8	*from* × 5
Nos. 69/74	*from* × 3
Nos. 73/277	*from* × 2
Nos. O1/14	*from* × 6
Nos. O15/18	—
No. O19	*from* × 5
Nos. O20/30*a*	*from* × 10
No. O30*b*	†
Nos. O31/133	*from* × 6
Nos. O135/150	*from* × 2

(Currency. 12 pies = 1 anna; 16 annas = 1 rupee)

ISSUE FOR SIND PROVINCE

1

1852 (1 July). "Scinde Dawk." *Embossed.*

S1	**1**	½a. white	£5500	£950
S2		½a. blue	£15000	£4000
S3		½a. scarlet	£80000	£11000

These stamps were issued under the authority of Sir Bartle Frere, Commissioner in Sind.

No. S3 is on sealing wax (usually cracked). Perfect copies are very rare.

It is believed that examples in red were issued first followed, in turn, by those in white and blue. The latter, which shows an extra ring round the circumference, may have been produced by De La Rue. The Scinde Dawks were withdrawn in October 1854.

EAST INDIA COMPANY ADMINISTRATION

2 (*Much reduced*)

3

The ½a., 1a. and 4a. were lithographed in Calcutta at the office of the Surveyor-General. The die was engraved by Mr. Maniruddin (spelling uncertain). *Ungummed* paper watermarked as T **2** (the "No. 4" paper) with the Arms of the East India Co in the sheet. The watermark is sideways on the ½a. and 1a., and upright on the 4a. where the paper was trimmed so that only the central portion showing the oval and the arms was used. Imperforate.

1854 (1 April).

1	**3**	½a. vermilion	£950
		a. Deep vermilion	£1600

This stamp, with 9½ arches in the side border, was prepared for use and a supply was sent to Bombay, but was not officially issued.

The vermilion shade is normally found on toned paper and the deep vermilion on white.

ILLUSTRATIONS. Types **4/8** are shown twice actual size.

4

1854 (1 Oct)–**55**.
Die I.

2	**4**	½a. blue	75·00	18·00
		a. Printed on both sides	†	£11000
		b. Printed double	†	£9000
3		½a. pale blue	£100	26·00
4		½a. deep blue	85·00	23·00
5		½a. indigo	£275	70·00

We give the official date of validity. Stamps were on sale to the public from mid September. Actual usage at Toungoo, Burma, is known from mid August.

These stamps were printed between 5 May and 29 July 1854 (Printing 30 millions).

4a

Die II.

6	**4a**	½a. blue	65·00	80·00
7		½a. indigo	75·00	90·00

The bulk were printed between 1 and 12 August 1854, with some extra sheets on or before 2 November (Printing about 2 millions).

5

Die III (1855).

8	**5**	½a. pale blue	£950	42·00
8*a*		½a. blue	£900	40·00
9		½a. greenish blue	£1600	£160
10		½a. deep blue	£1200	80·00

These stamps were printed between 3 July and 25 August 1855 (Printing about 4¾ millions).

THE THREE DIES OF THE ½ ANNA

DIE I. *Chignon shading* mostly solid blobs of colour. *Corner ornaments*, solid blue stars with long points, always conspicuous. *Band below diadem* always heavily shaded. *Diadem and jewels*. The middle and right-hand jewels usually show a clearly defined cross. *Outer frame lines*. Stamps with white or faintly shaded chignons and weak frame lines are usually Die I (worn state).

DIE II. *Chignon* normally shows much less shading. A strong line of colour separates hair and chignon. *Corner ornaments*. The right blue star is characteristic (see illustration) but tends to disappear. It never obliterates the white cross. *Band below diadem*. As Die I but heavier, sometimes solid. *Diadem and jewels*. As Die I but usually fainter. *Outer frame lines*. Always strong and conspicuous.

DIE III. *Chignon shading* shows numerous fine lines, often blurred. *Corner ornaments* have a small hollow blue star with short points, which tends to disappear as in Die II. *Band below diadem*, shows light shading or hardly any shading. *Diadem and jewels*. Jewels usually marked with a solid squat star. The ornaments between the stars appear in the shape of a characteristic white "w". *Frame lines* variable.

The above notes give the general characteristics of the three Dies, but there are a few exceptions due to retouching, etc.

6 (*See note below No.* 14)

Die I.

11	**6**	1a. deep red	£475	60·00
12		1a. red	£325	40·00

Printing of these stamps commenced on 26 July 1854, and continued into August (Printing, see note below No. 14).

7

Die II: With more lines in the chignon than in Die I, and with white curved line where chignon joins head.*

13	**7**	1a. deep red	£170	60·00
14		1a. dull red	60·00	42·00

*Very worn printings of Die II may be found with chignon nearly as white as in Die I.

In stamps of Die I, however, the small blob of red projecting from the hair into the chignon is always visible.

These stamps were printed in August and September 1854 (Total printing, Dies I and II together, about 7¾ millions).

8

Die III. With pointed bust (1855).

15	**8**	1a. red	£1200	£140
16		1a. dull red	£1700	£180

These stamps were printed between 7 July and 25 August 1855 (Printing, about 1½ millions).

9

NOTE. Our catalogue prices for Four Annas stamps are for cut-square specimens, with clear margins and in good condition. Cut-to-shape copies are worth from 3% to 20% of these prices according to condition.

Four Dies of the Head:—

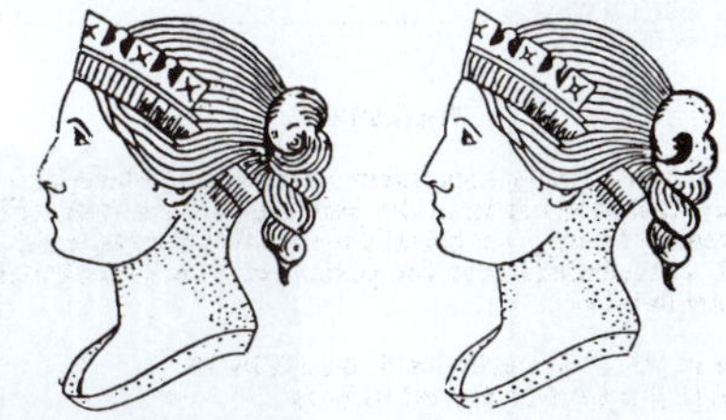

I II

DIE I. Band of diadem and chignon strongly shaded.

DIE II. Lines in band of diadem worn. Few lines in the upper part of the chignon, which, however, shows a strong drawn comma-like mark.

IIIA

III

DIE IIIA. Upper part of chignon partly redrawn, showing two short, curved vertical lines in the NE corner. "Comma" has disappeared.

DIE III. Upper part of chignon completely redrawn, but band of diadem shows only a few short lines.

Two Dies of the Frame:—

Die I. Outer frame lines weak. Very small dots of colour, or none at all, in the "R" and "A's". The white lines to the right of "INDIA" are separated, by a line of colour, from the inner white circle.

Die II. Outer frame lines strengthened. Dots in the "R" and "A's" strong. White lines to right of "INDIA" break into inner white circle.

(Des Capt. H. Thuillier)

1854 (15 Oct)–**55**. W **2** upright, central portion only. Imperf.

1st Printing. Head Die I. Frame Die I. Stamps widely spaced and separated by blue wavy line.

			Un	*Used*	*Us pr*
17	**9**	4a. indigo and red	£5000	£550	£2250
18		4a. blue and pale red	£5000	£450	£1900
		a. Head inverted	†	£38000/£150000	†

This printing was made between 13 and 28 Oct 1854 (Printing, 206,040).

Twenty-seven confirmed examples of No. 18a are now known, only three of which are cut-square. The range of prices quoted reflects the difference in value between a sound cut-to-shape stamp and the finest example known.

2nd Printing. Head Die II. Frame Die I. Stamps widely spaced and separated by blue wavy line.

19	**9**	4a. blue and red	£4750	£300	£1300
		a. Blue (head) printed double	†	£7500	†
20		4a. indigo and deep red	£4750	£350	£1500

This printing was made between 1 and 13 Dec 1854 (Printing, 393,960).

No. 19a is only known used cut-to-shape.

3rd Printing. Head Dies II, IIIA and III. Frame Dies I and II. Stamps, often in bright shades, widely spaced and separated by wavy line (1855).

21	**9**	4a. blue and red shades (Head III, Frame I)	£12000	£1200	£3750
		a. Head II, Frame I	—	£1700	£5500
		b. Head IIIA, Frame I	—	£1700	£6000
		c. Head III, Frame II	—	—	£12000

This printing was made between 10 March and 2 April 1855 (Printing, 138,960).

4th Printing. Head Die III. Frame Die II. Stamps closely spaced 2 to 2½ mm without separating line (1855).

22	**9**	4a. deep blue and red	£3000	£300	£1100
23		4a. blue and red	£2750	£250	£950
		a. Blue (head) printed double	†	£6000	†
24		4a. pale blue and pale red	£3000	£325	£1200

This printing was made between 3 April and 9 May 1855 (Printing, 540,960).

No. 23a is only known used cut-to-shape.

5th Printing. Head Die III. Frame Die II. Stamps spaced 4 to 6 mm without separating line (1855).

25	**9**	4a. blue and rose-red	£5500	£450	£2000
26		4a. deep blue and red	£5500	£450	£2000

This printing was made between 4 Oct and 3 Nov 1855 (Printing, 380,064).

Serrated perf about 18, or pin-perf.

27	½a. blue (Die I)	†	£4500
28	1a. red (Die I)	†	£2750
29	1a. red (Die II)	†	£2500
30	4a. blue and red (Die II)	†	£11000

This is believed to be an unofficial perforation. Most of the known specimens bear Madras circle postmarks (C122 to C126), but some are known with Bombay postmarks. Beware of fakes.

BISECTS. The bisected stamps for issues between 1854 and 1860 were used exclusively in the Straits Settlements during shortages of certain values. Prices quoted are for those with Singapore "B 172" cancellations. Penang marks are considerably rarer.

10

11

(Plate made at Mint, Calcutta. Typo Stamp Office)

1854 (4 Oct). Sheet wmk sideways, as W **2** but with "No. 3" at top left. Imperf.

31	**10**	2a. green (*shades*)	£100	26·00
		a. Bisected (1a.) (1857) (on cover)	†	£140000
34		2a. emerald-green	£1000	

The 2a. was also printed on paper with a sideways sheet watermark incorporating the words "STAMP OFFICE. One Anna" in double-ring circle, etc. (*Price* £500 *unused*, £375 *used*).

Apart from the rare emerald-green shade, there is a range of shades of No. 31 varying from bluish to yellowish green.

Many stamps show traces of lines external to the design shown in our illustration. Stamps with this frame on all four sides are scarce.

Many reprints of the ½, 1, 2, and 4a. exist.

PRINTERS. All Indian stamps from No. 35 to 200 were typographed by De La Rue & Co.

1855 (1 Oct). *Blue glazed paper.* No wmk. P 14.

35	**11**	4a. black	£600	19·00
		a. Imperf (pair)	£4000	£4000
		b. Bisected (2a.) (1859) (on cover)	†	£8500
36		8a. carmine (Die I)	£500	17·00
		a. Imperf (pair)	£2250	
		b. Bisected (4a.) (1859) (on cover)	†	£60000

The first supply of the 4a. was on white paper, but it is difficult to distinguish it from No. 45.

In the 8a. the paper varies from deep blue to almost white.

For difference between Die I and Die II in the 8a., see illustrations above No. 73.

1856–64. *Paper yellowish to white.* No wmk. P 14.

37	**11**	½a. blue (Die I)	80·00	4·00
		a. Imperf (pair)	£375	£1300
38		½a. pale blue (Die I)	75·00	2·25
39		1a. brown	50·00	3·25
		a. Imperf between (vert pair)		
		b. Imperf (pair)	£750	£1600
		c. Bisected (½a.) (1859) (on cover)	†	£65000
40		1a. deep brown	90·00	4·00
41		2a. dull pink (1860)	£600	32·00
		a. Imperf (pair)	£2000	
42		2a. yellow-buff (1859)	£350	32·00
		a. Imperf (pair)	£1300	£2500
43		2a. yellow (1863)	£450	35·00
44		2a. orange (1858)	£550	38·00
		a. Imperf (pair)		
45		4a. black	£350	10·00
		a. Bisected diagonally (2a.) (1859) (on cover)	†	£25000
		b. Imperf (pair)	£2250	£2250
46		4a. grey-black	£325	5·00
47		4a. green (1864)	£1300	40·00
48		8a. carmine (Die I)	£425	25·00
49		8a. pale carmine (Die I)	£475	25·00
		a. Bisected (4a.) (1859) (on cover)	†	£60000

Prepared for use, but not officially issued.

50	**11**	2a. yellow-green	£1000	£1100
		a. Imperf (pair)	£2250	

This stamp is known with trial obliterations, and a few are known postally used. It also exists *imperf*, but is not known used thus.

For difference between Die I and Die II in the ½a., see illustrations above No. 73.

CROWN COLONY

On the 1 November 1858, Her Majesty Queen Victoria assumed the government of the territories in India "heretofore administered in trust by the Honourable East India Company".

12

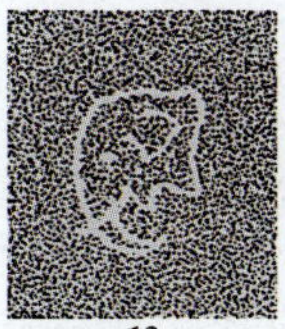
13

1860 (9 May). No wmk. P 14.

51	**12**	8p. purple/*bluish*	£225	90·00
52		8p. purple/*white*	48·00	6·00
		a. Bisected diagonally (4p.) (1862) (on cover)	†	£65000
		b. Imperf (pair)	£3000	£4000
53		8p. mauve	75·00	8·50

1865. *Paper yellowish to white.* W **13**. P 14.

54	**11**	½a. blue (Die I)	15·00	1·25
		a. Imperf	†	£900
		w. Wmk inverted	—	24·00
55		½a. pale blue (Die I)	15·00	1·25
56	**12**	8p. purple	9·00	11·00
		w. Wmk inverted	32·00	
57		8p. mauve	13·00	12·00
58	**11**	1a. pale brown	8·00	1·25
59		1a. deep brown	7·00	1·25
		w. Wmk inverted	65·00	30·00
60		1a. chocolate	11·00	1·50
61		2a. yellow	£130	7·00
62		2a. orange	60·00	2·75
		a. Imperf (pair)	†	£3500
63		2a. brown-orange	25·00	2·00
		w. Wmk inverted	75·00	40·00
64		4a. green	£400	25·00
		w. Wmk inverted	†	£120
65		8a. carmine (Die I)	£1500	80·00
		w. Wmk inverted	£2250	£225

The 8p. mauve, No. 57, is found variously surcharged "NINE" or "NINE PIE" by local postmasters, to indicate that it was being sold for 9 pies, as was the case during 1874. Such surcharges were made without Government sanction. (*Price, from* £500 *unused*).

The stamps of India, wmk Elephant's Head, surcharged with a crown and value in "cents", were used in the Straits Settlements.

14

(15)

(16)

1866 (28 June). *Fiscal stamps as T* **14** *optd.* Wmk Crown over "INDIA". P 14 (at sides only).

(a) As T **15**.

66	6a. purple (G.)	£800	£120
	a. Overprint inverted	†	£11000

There are 20 different types of this overprint.

(b) With T **16**.

68	6a. purple (G.)	£1500	£160

17

18

Die I

Die II

Two Dies of 4a.:—

Die I.—Mouth closed, line from corner of mouth downwards only. Pointed chin.

Die II.—Mouth slightly open; lips, chin, and throat defined by line of colour. Rounded chin.

1866 (1 Aug)–**78**. W **13**. P 14.

69	**17**	4a. green (Die I)	80·00	4·50
70		4a. deep green (Die I)	80·00	4·50
71		4a. blue-green (Die II) (1878)	25·00	3·25
72	**18**	6a.8p. slate (4.67)	55·00	25·00
		a. Imperf (pair)	£2250	

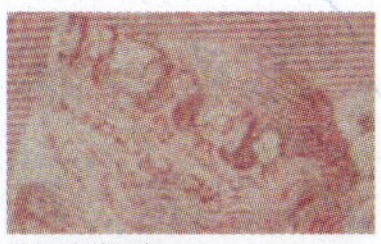
Die I (8a.)

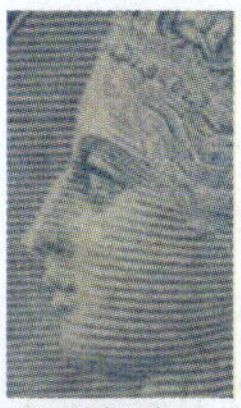
Die I (½a.)

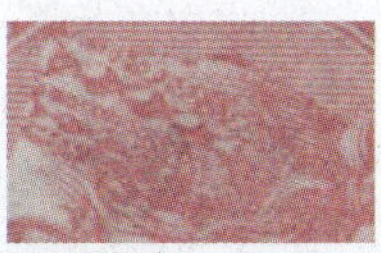
Die II (8a.)

Die II (½a.)

1868 (1 Jan). *Die II. Profile redrawn and different diadem.* W **13**. P 14.

73	**11**	8a. rose (Die II)	38·00	7·00
		w. Wmk inverted	60·00	
74		8a. pale rose (Die II)	38·00	7·00

1873. *Die II. Features, especially the mouth, more firmly drawn.* W **13**. P 14.

75	**11**	½a. deep blue (Die II)	6·00	1·00
76		½a. blue (Die II)	6·00	1·00
		w. Wmk inverted	55·00	
		y. Wmk inverted and reversed	†	95·00

19 20

1874 (18 July–1 Sept). W **13**. P 14.

77	**19**	9p. bright mauve (18.7.74)	17·00	16·00
78		9p. pale mauve	17·00	16·00
79	**20**	1r. slate (1.9.74)	50·00	29·00

21 22

1876 (19 Aug). W **13**. P 14.

80	**21**	6a. olive-bistre	8·50	2·50
		w. Wmk inverted	80·00	
81		6a. pale brown	7·50	1·50
82	**22**	12a. Venetian red	11·00	24·00

EMPIRE

Queen Victoria assumed the title of Empress of India in 1877, and the inscription on the stamps was altered from "EAST INDIA" to "INDIA".

23 24 25

26 27 28

29 30 31

32 33 34

1882 (1 Jan)–**90**. W **34**. P 14.

84	**23**	½a. deep blue-green (1883)	4·75	10
		w. Wmk inverted		
85		½a. blue-green	4·75	10
		a. Double impression	£550	£750
		w. Wmk inverted	—	85·00
86	**24**	9p. rose (1883)	1·00	2·50
87		9p. aniline carmine	1·00	2·50
		w. Wmk inverted	—	95·00
88	**25**	1a. brown-purple (1883)	5·50	30
89		1a. plum	5·50	30
		w. Wmk inverted	—	95·00
90	**26**	1a.6p. sepia	1·00	1·25
91	**27**	2a. pale blue (1883)	4·00	30
92		2a. blue	4·00	30
		a. Double impression	£1100	£1500
93	**28**	3a. orange	15·00	6·50
94		3a. brown-orange (1890)	10·00	2·00
		w. Wmk inverted	—	£110
95	**29**	4a. olive-green (6.85)	16·00	1·75
96		4a. slate-green	15·00	1·75
		w. Wmk inverted	—	85·00
97	**30**	4a.6p. yellow-green (1.5.86)	25·00	6·00
98	**31**	8a. dull mauve (1883)	29·00	2·00
99		8a. magenta	28·00	2·00
100	**32**	12a. purple/*red* (1.4.88)	7·50	3·25
		w. Wmk inverted	—	£110
101	**33**	1r. slate (1883)	21·00	5·50
		w. Wmk inverted	—	£100
84/101 *Set of* 11			£110	22·00
97s, 100s Handstamped "Specimen" *Set of* 2			80·00	

No. 92a is from a sheet of 2a. stamps with a very marked double impression issued in Karachi in early 1898.

(35) 36 37

1891 (1 Jan). *No. 97 surch with T* **35** *by Govt Press, Calcutta.*

102	**30**	2½a. on 4½a. yellow-green	4·25	60
		a. Surch double, one albino		

There are several varieties in this surcharge due to variations in the relative positions of the letters and figures.

1892 (Jan)–**97**. W **34**. P 14.

103	**36**	2a.6p. yellow-green	3·50	40
104		2a.6p. pale blue-green (1897)	4·50	80
105	**37**	1r. green and rose	29·00	6·50
106		1r. green and aniline carmine	16·00	2·00

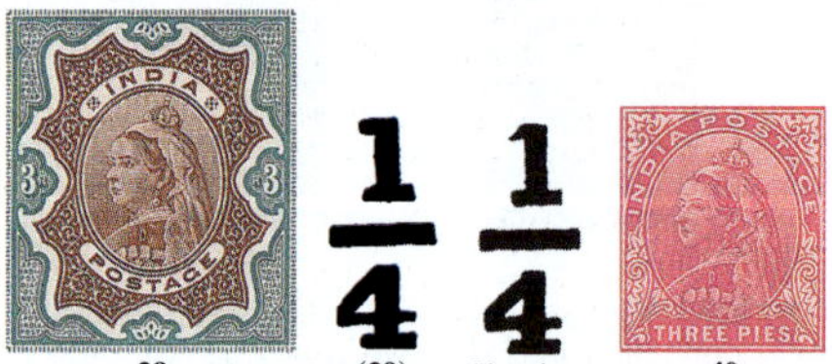

38 (39) Slanting serif (Lower pane R. 1/1) 40

USED HIGH VALUES. It is necessary to emphasise that used prices quoted for the following and all later high value stamps are for postally used copies.

(Head of Queen from portrait by von Angeli)

1895 (1 Sept). W **34**. P 14.

107	**38**	2r. carmine and yellow-brown	45·00	12·00
107*a*		2r. carmine and brown	50·00	14·00
108		3r. brown and green	38·00	10·00
109		5r. ultramarine and violet	48·00	32·00
107/9 *Set of* 3			£120	50·00

1898 (1 Oct). *No. 85 surch with T* **39** *by Govt Press, Calcutta.*

110	**23**	¼a. on ½a. blue-green	10	50
		a. Surch double	£275	
		b. Double impression of stamp	£275	
		c. Slanting serif on "1"	26·00	

1899. W **34**. P 14.

111	**40**	3p. aniline carmine	40	10

1900 (1 Oct)–**02**. W **34**. P 14.

112	**40**	3p. grey	75	1·50
113	**23**	½a. pale yellow-green	1·60	50
114		½a. yellow-green	3·25	70
		w. Wmk inverted	†	£200
115	**25**	1a. carmine	2·75	20
116	**27**	2a. pale violet	4·75	2·75
117		2a. mauve (1902)	8·50	3·50
118	**36**	2a.6p. ultramarine	4·00	4·25
112/18 *Set of* 5			12·50	8·25

41 42 43

44 45 46

47 48 49

50 51 52

1902 (9 Aug)–**11**. W **34**. P 14.

119	**41**	3p. grey	1·00	10
120		3p. slate-grey (1904)	1·00	10
121	**42**	½a. yellow-green	2·00	20
122		½a. green	2·00	20
123	**43**	1a. carmine	1·50	10
124	**44**	2a. violet (13.5.03)	4·75	40
125		2a. mauve	4·50	10
126	**45**	2a.6p. ultramarine (1902)	4·75	60
		w. Wmk inverted	†	£225
127	**46**	3a. orange-brown (1902)	4·75	60
128	**47**	4a. olive (20.4.03)	3·00	60
129		4a. pale olive	4·50	60
130		4a. olive-brown	10·00	3·00
131	**48**	6a. olive-bistre (6.8.03)	15·00	4·75
132		6a. maize	13·00	4·50
133	**49**	8a. purple (*shades*) (8.5.03)	8·50	1·00
134		8a. claret (1910)	16·00	1·00
135	**50**	12a. purple/*red* (1903)	9·50	2·00
136	**51**	1r. green and carmine (1903)	6·50	70
137		1r. green and scarlet (1911)	45·00	3·75
138	**52**	2r. rose-red and yellow-brown (1903)	48·00	4·00
139		2r. carmine and yellow-brown	48·00	4·00
		w. Wmk inverted	†	£275
140		3r. brown and green (1904)	32·00	21·00
141		3r. red-brown and green (1911)	45·00	23·00
142		5r. ultramarine and violet (1904)	75·00	35·00
143		5r. ultramarine and deep lilac (1911)	£130	50·00
144		10r. green and carmine (1909)	£140	30·00
146		15r. blue and olive-brown (1909)	£180	42·00
147		25r. brownish orange and blue (1909)	£950	£950
119/47 *Set of* 17			£1400	£1000

No. 147 can often be found with telegraph cancellation; these can be supplied at one third of the price given above.

1905 (2 Feb). *No.* 122 *surch with T* **39**.

148	**42**	¼ on ½a. green	55	10
		a. Surch inverted	—	£950

It is doubtful if No. 148a exists unused with genuine surcharge.

53 54

1906 (6 Dec)–**07**. W **34**. P 14.

149	**53**	½a. green	3·00	10
150	**54**	1a. carmine (7.1.07)	2·00	10

55 56 57

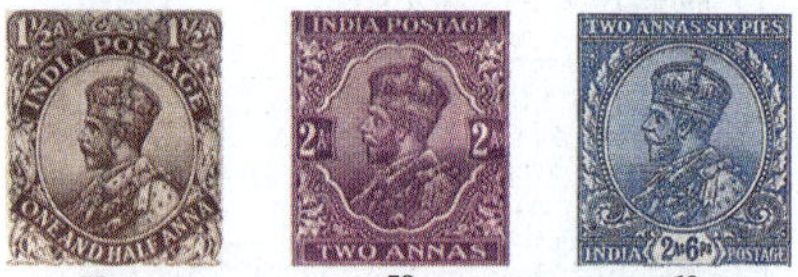

58 * 59 60

61 62 63

64 65 66

67 "Rs" flaw in right value tablet (R. 1/4)

*T **58**. Two types of the 1½a.; (A) As illustrated. (B) Inscribed "1½ As". "ONE AND A HALF ANNAS".

1911 (1 Dec)–**22**. W **34**. P 14.

151	**55**	3p. grey (1912)	1·40	20
		w. Wmk inverted		
152		3p. pale grey	2·00	20
153		3p. bluish grey (1922)	2·50	50
		w. Wmk inverted	16·00	
154		3p. slate	2·00	20
		a. "Rs" flaw	17·00	22·00
154*b*		3p. violet-grey	3·00	50
155	**56**	½a. light green (1912)	2·50	15
		w. Wmk inverted	45·00	
156		½a. emerald	3·25	15
		w. Wmk inverted	†	45·00
157		½a. bright green	3·25	15
159	**57**	1a. rose-carmine	3·25	20
160		1a. carmine	2·50	20
161		1a. aniline carmine	2·50	15
162		1a. pale rose-carmine (*chalk-surfaced paper*) (1918)	3·75	60

163	58	1½a. chocolate (Type A) (1919)	4·00	50
164		1½a. grey-brown (Type A)	8·00	2·75
165		1½a. chocolate (Type B) (1921)	3·75	5·00
		w. Wmk inverted	11·00	
166	59	2a. purple	3·50	40
167		2a. reddish purple	7·00	30
168		2a. deep mauve	6·00	40
		w. Wmk inverted	25·00	
169		2a. bright reddish violet	7·50	50
		a. Stop under "s" in right value tablet (R. 4/16)	£150	
170	60	2a.6p. ultramarine (1912)	2·75	3·00
171	61	2a.6p. ultramarine (1913)	2·75	20
172	62	3a. orange	4·00	20
173		3a. dull orange	8·50	45
174	63	4a. deep olive (1912)	6·00	60
175		4a. olive-green	6·00	60
		w. Wmk inverted	25·00	
177	64	6a. yellow-bistre (1912)	4·00	1·60
178		6a. brown-ochre	4·25	1·00
179	65	8a. deep magenta (1912)	6·00	2·00
180		8a. deep mauve	15·00	1·10
		w. Wmk inverted	70·00	
181		8a. bright mauve	42·00	8·00
182		8a. purple	18·00	2·00
183	66	12a. carmine-lake (1912)	6·00	2·25
184		12a. claret	18·00	2·50
185	67	1r. red-brown and deep blue-green (1913)	20·00	2·00
		w. Wmk inverted	55·00	
186		1r. brown and green (*shades*)	25·00	1·75
186*a*		1r. orange-brown and deep turquoise-green	42·00	4·25
187		2r. carmine and brown (1913)	22·00	1·75
		w. Wmk inverted	80·00	
188		5r. ultramarine and violet (1913)	55·00	6·50
189		10r. green and scarlet (1913)	85·00	13·00
190		15r. blue and olive (1913)	£120	27·00
191		25r. orange and blue (1913)	£200	38·00
151/91 *Set of* 19			£500	90·00

Examples of the ½a. printed double are now believed to be forgeries.

FORGERIES.—Collectors are warned against forgeries of all the later surcharges of India, and particularly the errors.

NINE

PIES

(68)

1921 (10 June). *T* **57** *surch with T* **68**.

192	9p. on 1a. rose-carmine	85	30
	a. Error. "NINE NINE"	80·00	£150
	b. Error. "PIES PIES"	80·00	£150
	c. Surch double	£180	£225
	w. Wmk inverted	†	85·00
193	9p. on 1a. carmine-pink	1·75	60
194	9p. on 1a. aniline carmine	12·00	4·50

In the initial setting of the surcharge No. 192a occurred on R. 2/13–16 of the fourth pane and No. 192b on R. 4/13-16 of the third. For the second setting No. 192a was corrected. Examples of No. 192b still occur but on R. 2/13-16 of the third pane. Later printings showed this corrected also.

1922. *T* **56** *surch with T* **39**.

195	¼a. on ½a. bright green	65	35
	a. Surch inverted	10·00	
	b. Surch omitted (in horiz pair with normal)	£250	
	c. Slanting serif on "1"	35·00	
	w. Wmk inverted		
196	¼a. on ½a. emerald	3·50	1·25
	w. Wmk inverted		

1922–26. W **34**. P 14.

197	57	1a. chocolate	1·75	10
		w. Wmk inverted	24·00	
198	58	1½a. rose-carmine (Type B) (1926)	3·00	30
199	61	2a.6p. orange (1926)	5·00	2·50
200	62	3a. ultramarine (1923)	13·00	60
197/200 *Set of* 4			20·00	3·25

69

70

71

PRINTERS. The following issues of postage and contemporary official stamps were all printed by the Security Printing Press, Nasik, *unless otherwise stated*.

1926–33. *Typo.* W **69**. P 14.

201	55	3p. slate	30	10
		w. Wmk inverted	1·60	30
202	56	½a. green	1·50	10
		w. Wmk inverted	2·75	30
203	57	1a. chocolate	60	10
		a. *Tête-bêche* (pair) (1932)	1·50	10·00
		w. Wmk inverted	60	10
204	58	1½a. rose-carmine (Type B) (1929)	3·75	10
		w. Wmk inverted	4·00	30
205	59	2a. bright purple	10·00	11·00
		a. Stop under "s" in right value tablet (R. 4/16)	£120	
		w. Wmk inverted	†	45·00
206	70	2a. purple	2·25	10
		a. *Tête-bêche* (pair) (1933)	9·00	40·00
		w. Wmk inverted	2·25	30
207	61	2a.6p. orange (1929)	2·75	10
		w. Wmk inverted	2·75	40
208	62	3a. ultramarine	12·00	1·00
209		3a. blue (1928)	11·00	10
		w. Wmk inverted	11·00	75
210	63	4a. pale sage-green	1·50	10
		w. Wmk inverted	—	8·50
211	71	4a. sage-green	6·00	10
		w. Wmk inverted	14·00	50
212	65	8a. reddish purple	4·00	10
		w. Wmk inverted	6·00	40
213	66	12a. claret	5·00	30
		w. Wmk inverted	7·00	80
214	67	1r. chocolate and green	5·50	45
		a. Chocolate (head) omitted	£6500	
		w. Wmk inverted	9·00	75
215		2r. carmine and orange	16·00	80
		w. Wmk inverted	16·00	1·50
216		5r. ultramarine and purple	32·00	1·25
		w. Wmk inverted	50·00	2·00
217		10r. green and scarlet (1927)	65·00	3·50
		w. Wmk inverted	£120	5·50
218		15r. blue and olive (1928)	50·00	30·00
		w. Wmk inverted	29·00	30·00
219		25r. orange and blue (1928)	£120	40·00
		w. Wmk inverted	£160	50·00
201/19 *Set of* 18			£275	80·00

Examples of the ½a. printed double are believed to be forgeries.

72 De Havilland D.H. 66 Hercules

Missing tree-top (R. 11/6 of 8a.)

Reversed serif on second "I" of "INDIA"

(Des R. Grant. Litho)

1929 (22 Oct). *Air.* W **69** (sideways*). P 14.

220	72	2a. deep blue-green	3·75	75
		w. Wmk stars pointing left	2·25	75
221		3a. blue	1·75	2·25
		a. "Q" for "O" in "Postage" (R.11/4)	£120	90·00
		w. Wmk stars pointing left	3·00	2·25
222		4a. olive-green	3·75	1·25
		w. Wmk stars pointing left	4·25	1·25
223		6a. bistre	2·25	1·00
		w. Wmk stars pointing left	2·50	1·00
224		8a. purple	4·00	1·00
		a. Missing tree-top	£150	90·00
		b. Reversed serif	£325	£160
		w. Wmk stars pointing left	4·25	1·00
225		12a. rose-red	15·00	6·00
		w. Wmk stars pointing left	15·00	6·00
220/5 *Set of* 6			26·00	11·00

*The normal sideways watermark shows the stars pointing right, *as seen from the back of the stamp.*

73 Purana Qila

74 War Memorial Arch

75 Council House

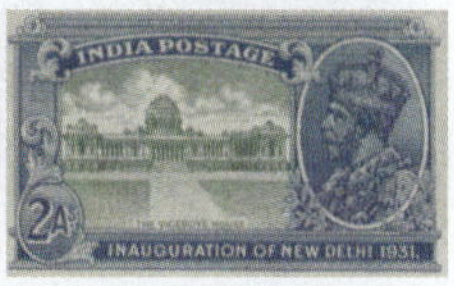

76 The Viceroy's House

77 Government of India Secretariat

78 Dominion Columns and the Secretariat

(Des H. W. Barr. Litho)

1931 (9 Feb). *Inauguration of New Delhi. T* **73/78**. W **69** (sideways*). P 13½×14.

226	73	¼a. olive-green and orange-brown	2·50	4·00
		a. "F" for "P" in "PURANA"	£130	£140
		w. Wmk stars pointing left	1·75	4·00
227	74	½a. violet and green	1·75	40
		w. Wmk stars pointing left	2·00	40
228	75	1a. mauve and chocolate	1·25	20
		w. Wmk stars pointing left	2·75	25
229	76	2a. green and blue	1·50	3·50
		w. Wmk stars pointing left	2·00	1·25
230	77	3a. chocolate and carmine	4·50	2·50
		w. Wmk stars pointing left	2·50	2·50
231	78	1r. violet and green	14·00	35·00
		w. Wmk stars pointing left	11·00	30·00
226/31 *Set of* 6			18·00	35·00

*The normal sideways watermark shows the stars pointing to the right, *as seen from the back of the stamp.*

79

80

81

82

83

9p. litho. Heavier and longer lines on face. King's nose often shows 6 horizontal lines and always has lowest line long and thin

9p. typo. Lines lighter and shorter. Always 5 lines on King's nose with the lowest short and thick

(T **82/3** des T. I. Archer. 9p. litho or typo; 1a.3p, 3a.6p. litho; others typo)

1932–36. W **69**. P 14.

232	79	½a. green (1934)	6·00	10
		w. Wmk inverted	—	1·75
233	80	9p. deep green (*litho*) (22.4.32)	2·75	10
		aw. Wmk inverted	4·00	1·75
233*b*		9p. deep green (*typo*) (27.8.34)	3·25	10
234	81	1a. chocolate (1934)	4·75	10
		w. Wmk inverted	12·00	1·75
235	82	1a.3p. mauve (22.4.32)	1·00	10
		w. Wmk inverted	1·50	30
236	70	2a. vermilion	12·00	4·00
		aw. Wmk inverted	18·00	8·00
236*b*	59	2a. vermilion (1934)	3·75	50
		bw. Wmk inverted	—	19·00
236*c*		2a. vermilion (*small die*) (1936)	6·00	30
		cw. Wmk inverted	—	8·50
237	62	3a. carmine	10·00	10
		w. Wmk inverted	—	2·25
238	83	3a.6p. ultramarine (22.4.32)	5·00	20
		w. Wmk inverted	5·00	30
239	64	6a. bistre (1935)	10·00	1·50
		w. Wmk inverted	—	16·00
232/9 *Set of* 9			50·00	5·50

No. 236*b* measures 19×22.6 mm and No. 236*c* 18.4×21.8 mm.

84 Gateway of India, Bombay

85 Victoria Memorial, Calcutta

86 Rameswaram Temple, Madras

87 Jain Temple, Calcutta

88 Taj Mahal, Agra

89 Golden Temple, Amritsar

90 Pagoda in Mandalay

"Bird" flaw (R. 9/3)

1935 (6 May). *Silver Jubilee. T* **84/90**. W **69** (sideways*). P 13½×14.

240	½a. black and yellow-green	1·50	20
	w. Wmk stars pointing left	1·00	15
241	9p. black and grey-green	2·00	20
	w. Wmk stars pointing left	1·50	65
242	1a. black and brown	3·00	20
	w. Wmk stars pointing left	2·25	10

243		1¼a. black and bright violet	75	10
		w. Wmk stars pointing left	1·00	15
244		2½a. black and orange	3·50	1·60
		w. Wmk stars pointing left	3·00	1·00
245		3½a. black and dull ultramarine	4·25	4·75
		a. "Bird" flaw	£170	£120
		w. Wmk stars pointing left	4·25	4·75
246		8a. black and purple	3·75	3·25
		w. Wmk stars pointing left	6·00	3·75
240/6 *Set of 7*			15·00	8·50

*The normal sideways watermark shows the stars pointing to the right, *as seen from the back of the stamp.*

91 King George VI

92 Dak Runner

93 Dak bullock cart

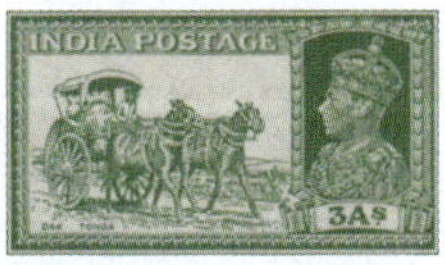
94 Dak tonga

95 Dak camel

96 Mail train

97 *Strathnaver* (liner)

98 Post truck

99 Armstrong Whitworth AW27 Ensign I mail plane (small head)

100 King George VI

1937 (23 Aug)–**40**. *T* **91/100**. *Typo.* W **69**. P 13½×14 or 14×13½ (T **93**).

247	**91**	3p. slate (15.12.37)	1·00	10
248		½a. red-brown (15.12.37)	6·00	10
		w. Wmk inverted		
249		9p. green	8·00	55
		w. Wmk inverted		
250		1a. carmine	1·25	10
		a. *Tête-bêche* (vert pair) (1940)	3·00	1·75
		w. Wmk inverted (from booklets)	1·75	1·50
251	**92**	2a. vermilion (15.12.37)	7·50	30
		w. Wmk inverted		
252	**93**	2a.6p. bright violet (15.12.37)	1·50	20
		w. Wmk inverted	—	25·00
253	**94**	3a. yellow-green (15.12.37)	8·50	30
		w. Wmk inverted	—	25·00
254	**95**	3a.6p. bright blue (15.12.37)	5·50	60
		w. Wmk inverted		
255	**96**	4a. brown (15.12.37)	13·00	20
		w. Wmk inverted	—	25·00
256	**97**	6a. turquoise-green (15.12.37)	14·00	80
257	**98**	8a. slate-violet (15.12.37)	7·50	50
		w. Wmk inverted		
258	**99**	12a. lake (15.12.37)	18·00	1·10
		w. Wmk inverted		
259	**100**	1r. grey and red-brown (15.12.37)	1·50	15
		w. Wmk inverted		
260		2r. purple and brown (15.12.37)	7·50	30
		w. Wmk inverted	38·00	
261		5r. green and blue (15.12.37)	29·00	50
		w. Wmk inverted	70·00	
262		10r. purple and claret (15.12.37)	22·00	80
		w. Wmk inverted	†	70·00
263		15r. brown and green (15.12.37)	95·00	70·00
		w. Wmk inverted	£160	£130
264		25r. slate-violet and purple (15.12.37)	£140	25·00
		w. Wmk inverted	—	£140
247/64 *Set of 18*			£350	90·00

No. 250a comes from surplus booklet sheets issued as normal stock following the rise in postal rates.

100a King George VI

101 King George VI

102 King George VI

103 Armstrong Whitworth A.W.27 Ensign I Mail Plane (large head)

(T **100a/102** des T. I. Archer. Typo (1½a. on 3a. litho also))

1940–43. W **69**. P 13½×14.

265	**100a**	3p. slate	30	10
		w. Wmk inverted	7·00	
266		½a. purple (1.10.42)	1·00	10
		w. Wmk inverted	—	15·00
267		9p. green	1·00	10
		w. Wmk inverted	—	18·00
268		1a. carmine (1.4.43)	1·50	10
		w. Wmk inverted	—	20·00
269	**101**	1a.3p. yellow-brown	1·00	10
		aw. Wmk inverted		
269*b*		1½a. dull violet (9.42)	1·50	10
		bw. Wmk inverted	—	16·00
270		2a. vermilion	1·50	10
		w. Wmk inverted	30·00	20·00
271		3a. bright violet (1942)	3·50	10
		w. Wmk inverted	—	12·00
272		3½a. bright blue	1·25	75
		w. Wmk inverted		
273	**102**	4a. brown	1·25	10
		w. Wmk inverted		
274		6a. turquoise-green	4·00	10
		w. Wmk inverted	†	40·00
275		8a. slate-violet	1·50	30
		w. Wmk inverted	—	48·00
276		12a. lake	6·50	1·00
277	**103**	14a. purple (15.10.40)	18·00	2·00
265/77 *Set of 14*			40·00	3·75

The 1½a. and 3a. were at first printed by lithography and were of finer execution and without Jubilee lines in the sheet margins. The two values exist with watermark inverted from both processes.

105 "Victory" and King George VI

= =

3 PIES

(**106**)

1946 (2 Jan). *Victory. Litho.* W **69**. P 13.

278	**105**	9p. yellow-green (8.2.46)	75	1·50
279		1½a. dull violet	30	30
		w. Wmk inverted	—	28·00
280		3½a. bright blue	1·00	1·25
281		12a. claret (8.2.46)	1·50	1·25
278/81 *Set of 4*			3·25	3·75

1946 (8 Aug). *Surch with T* **106**.

282	**101**	3p. on 1a.3p. yellow-brown	10	15

DOMINION

301 Asokan Capital (Inscr reads "Long Live India")

302 Indian National Flag

303 Douglas DC-4

"Teardrop" (R. 5/6)

(Des T. I. Archer. Litho)

1947 (21 Nov–15 Dec). *Independence.* W **69**. P 14×13½ (1½a.) or 13½×14 (others).

301	**301**	1½a. grey-green (15 Dec)	15	10
302	**302**	3½a. orange-red, blue and green	1·00	2·25
		a. Teardrop	28·00	
		w. Wmk inverted	16·00	16·00
303	**303**	12a. ultramarine (15 Dec)	2·00	2·75
301/3 *Set of 3*			2·75	4·50

304 Lockheed Constellation

(Des T. I. Archer. Litho)

1948 (29 May). *Air. Inauguration of India–U.K. Air Service.* W **69**. P 13½×14.

304	**304**	12a. black and ultramarine	1·50	3·00

305 Mahatma Gandhi

306 Mahatma Gandhi

(Photo Courvoisier)

1948 (15 Aug). *First Anniv of Independence.* P 11½.

305	**305**	1½a. brown	4·25	75
306		3½a. violet	5·50	2·75
307		12a. grey-green	7·50	2·50
308	**306**	10r. purple-brown and lake	£120	70·00
305/8 *Set of 4*			£130	70·00

307 Ajanta Panel

308 Konarak Horse

309 Trimurti

310 Bodhisattva

311 Nataraja

312 Sanchi Stupa, East Gate

313 Bodh Gaya Temple

314 Bhuvanesvara

315 Gol Gumbad, Bijapur

316 Kandarya Mahadeva Temple

317 Golden Temple, Amritsar

318 Victory Tower, Chittorgarh

319 Red Fort, Delhi

320 Taj Mahal, Agra

321 Qutb Minar, Delhi

322 Satrunjaya Temple, Palitana

(Des T. I. Archer and I. M. Das. Typo (low values), litho (rupee values))

1949 (15 Aug). W **69** (sideways* on 6p., 1r. and 10r.). P 14 (3p. to 2a.), 13½ (3a. to 12a.), 14×13½ (1r. and 10r.), 13½×14 (2r. and 5r.), 13 (15r.).

309	**307**	3p. slate-violet	15	10
		w. Wmk inverted		
310	**308**	6p. purple-brown	25	10
		w. Wmk star pointing right	1·50	1·25
311	**309**	9p. yellow-green	40	10
		w. Wmk inverted	†	65·00
312	**310**	1a. turquoise	60	10
		w. Wmk inverted		
313	**311**	2a. carmine	80	10
		w. Wmk inverted	25·00	1·75
314	**312**	3a. brown-orange	1·75	10
		w. Wmk inverted	†	85·00
315	**313**	3½a. bright blue	1·50	4·50
316	**314**	4a. lake	4·25	45
		w. Wmk inverted	28·00	3·25
317	**315**	6a. violet	2·25	30
		w. Wmk inverted	4·00	2·00
318	**316**	8a. turquoise-green	1·75	10
		w. Wmk inverted	—	65·00
319	**317**	12a. dull blue	2·50	30
		w. Wmk inverted	20·00	3·25
320	**318**	1r. dull violet and green	17·00	10
		w. Wmk star pointing left	32·00	1·25
321	**319**	2r. claret and violet	15·00	20
		w. Wmk inverted	75·00	3·25
322	**320**	5r. blue-green and red-brown	30·00	1·75
		w. Wmk inverted	95·00	4·25
323	**321**	10r. purple-brown and deep blue	70·00	11·00
		a. Purple-brown and blue	£110	6·00
		aw. Wmk star pointing left	£180	70·00
324	**322**	15r. brown and claret	18·00	25·00
309/24 *Set of* 16			£150	35·00

*The normal sideways watermark has the star pointing to the left on the 6p. value and to the right on the 1r. and 10r. (323*a*) *when seen from the back of the stamp*.

For T **310** with statue reversed see No. 333.

323 Globe and Asokan Capital

1949 (10 Oct). *75th Anniv of U.P.U. Litho.* W **69**. P 13.

325	**323**	9p. green	2·00	3·25
326		2a. rose	2·00	3·00
327		3½a. bright blue	2·00	3·00
328		12a. brown-purple	3·00	3·00
325/8 *Set of* 4			8·00	11·00

REPUBLIC

324 Rejoicing Crowds

325 Quill, ink-well and verse

326 Ear of corn and plough

327 Spinning-wheel and cloth

(Des D. J. Keymer & Co. Litho)

1950 (26 Jan). *Inauguration of Republic. T* **324/7**. W **69** (sideways on 3½a.). P 13.

329		2a. scarlet	1·75	50
		w. Wmk inverted	28·00	4·25
330		3½a. ultramarine	2·25	4·00
331		4a. violet	2·25	1·25
332		12a. maroon	3·75	2·50
		w. Wmk inverted	35·00	9·50
329/32 *Set of* 4			9·00	7·50

328 As T **310**, but statue reversed

329 *Stegodon ganesa*

1950 (15 July)–**51**. *Typo.* W **69**. P 14 (1a.), 13½ (others).

333	**328**	1a. turquoise	4·00	10
		aw. Wmk inverted	—	20·00
333*b*	**313**	2½a. lake (30.4.51)	3·00	3·25
333*c*	**314**	4a. bright blue (30.4.51)	6·00	10
333/*c Set of* 3			11·50	3·25

1951 (13 Jan). *Centenary of Geological Survey of India. Litho.* W **69**. P 13.

334	**329**	2a. black and claret	2·00	1·25

330 Torch

331 Kabir

1951 (4 Mar). *First Asian Games, New Delhi. Litho.* W **69** (sideways). P 14.

335	**330**	2a. reddish purple & brn-orge	1·00	1·00
336		12a. chocolate and light blue	4·50	2·25

PROCESS. All the following issues were printed in photogravure, *except where otherwise stated*.

1952 (1 Oct). *Indian Saints and Poets. T* **331** *and similar vert designs.* W **69**. P 14.

337		9p. bright emerald-green	30	55
338		1a. carmine	30	20
339		2a. orange-red	1·50	30
340		4a. bright blue	2·50	60
341		4½a. bright mauve	50	1·25
342		12a. brown	4·00	1·00
337/42 *Set of* 6			9·00	3·50

Designs:—1a. Tulsidas; 2a. Meera; 4a. Surdas; 4½a. Ghalib; 12a. Tagore.

332 Locomotives of 1853 and 1953

333 Mount Everest

1953 (16 Apr). *Railway Centenary.* W **69**. P 14½×14.

343	**332**	2a. black	1·00	10

1953 (2 Oct). *Conquest of Mount Everest.* W **69**. P 14½×14.

344	**333**	2a. bright violet	1·25	10
345		14a. brown	4·00	25

334 Telegraph Poles of 1851 and 1951

335 Postal Transport, 1854

1953 (1 Nov). *Centenary of Indian Telegraphs.* W **69**. P 14½×14.

346	**334**	2a. blue-green	1·50	10
347		12a. blue	3·50	40

1954 (1 Oct). *Stamp Centenary. T* **335** *and similar horiz designs.* W **69**. P 14½×14.

348		1a. reddish purple	50	20
349		2a. cerise	30	10
350		4a. orange-brown	4·00	1·50
351		14a. blue	1·50	40
348/51 *Set of* 4			5·75	2·00

Designs:—2, 14a. "Airmail"; 4a. Postal transport, 1954.

338 U.N. Emblem and Lotus

339 Forest Research Institute

1954 (24 Oct). *United Nations Day.* W **69** (sideways). P 13.

352	**338**	2a. turquoise-green	60	40

1954 (11 Dec). *Fourth World Forestry Congress, Dehra Dun.* W **69**. P 14½×14.

353	**339**	2a. ultramarine	35	10

340 Tractor

344 Woman Spinning

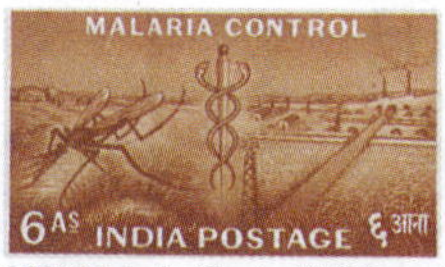

347 "Malaria Control" (Mosquito and Staff of Aesculapius)

1955 (26 Jan). *Five Year Plan. T* **340**, **344**, **347** *and similar designs.* W **69** (sideways on small horiz designs). P 14×14½ (small horiz) or 14½×14 (others).

354		3p. bright purple	30	10
355		6p. violet	30	10
356		9p. orange-brown	40	10
357		1a. blue-green	45	10
358		2a. light blue	30	10
359		3a. pale blue-green	50	10
360		4a. rose-carmine	50	10
361		6a. yellow-brown	1·50	10
362		8a. blue	7·00	10
363		10a. turquoise-green	3·75	2·75
364		12a. bright blue	3·25	10
365		14a. bright green	5·00	60
366		1r. deep dull green	4·00	10
367		1r.2a. grey	2·25	4·50
368		1r.8a. reddish purple	9·00	5·00
369		2r. cerise	4·25	10
370		5r. brown	14·00	70
371		10r. orange	15·00	4·75
354/71 *Set of* 18			65·00	17·00

Designs: *Horiz* (*as T* **340**)—6p. Power loom; 9p. Bullock-driven well; 1a. Damodar Valley Dam; 4a. Bullocks; 8a. Chittaranjan Locomotive Works; 12a. Hindustan Aircraft Factory, Bangalore; 1r. Telephone engineer; 2r. Rare Earth Factory, Alwaye; 5r. Sindri Fertiliser Factory; 10r. Steel plant. (*As T* **347**)—10a. Marine Drive, Bombay; 14a. Kashmir landscape; 1r.2a. Cape Comorin; 1r.8a. Mt Kangchenjunga. *Vert* (*as T* **344**)—3a. Naga woman weaving with hand loom.

For stamps as Nos. 366, 369/71 but W **374** see Nos. 413/16.

358 Bodhi Tree

359 Round Parasol and Bodhi Tree

(Des C. Pakrashi (2a.), R. D'Silva (14a.))

1956 (24 May). *Buddha Jayanti.* W **69** (sideways on 14a.). P 13×13½ (2a.) or 13½×13 (14a.)

372	**358**	2a. sepia	1·50	10
373	**359**	14a. vermilion	4·50	3·75

360 Lokmanya Bal Gangadhar Tilak

361 Map of India

1956 (23 July). *Birth Centenary of Tilak (journalist).* W **69**. P 13×13½.

374	**360**	2a. chestnut	20	10

(New Currency. 100 naye paise = 1 rupee)

1957 (1 Apr)–**58**. W **69** (sideways). P 14×14½.

375	**361**	1n.p. blue-green	10	10
376		2n.p. light brown	10	10
377		3n.p. deep brown	10	10
378		5n.p. bright green	4·25	10
379		6n.p. grey	10	10
379*a*		8n.p. light blue-green (7.5.58)	6·00	1·25
380		10n.p. deep dull green	4·25	10
381		13n.p. bright carmine-red	1·00	10
381*a*		15n.p. violet (16.1.58)	4·25	10
382		20n.p. blue	1·00	10
383		25n.p. ultramarine	60	10
384		50n.p. orange	3·00	10
385		75n.p. reddish purple	2·00	10
385*a*		90n.p. bright purple (16.1.58)	4·00	2·00
375/85a *Set of* 14			27·00	3·25

The 8, 15 and 90n.p. have their value expressed as "nP".

For similar stamps but W **374** see Nos. 399/412.

362 The Rani of Jhansi **363** Shrine

1957 (15 Aug). *Indian Mutiny Centenary.* W **69**. P 14½×14 (15n.p.) or 13×13½ (90n.p.)

386	**362**	15n.p. brown	40	10
387	**363**	90n.p. reddish purple	1·50	1·25

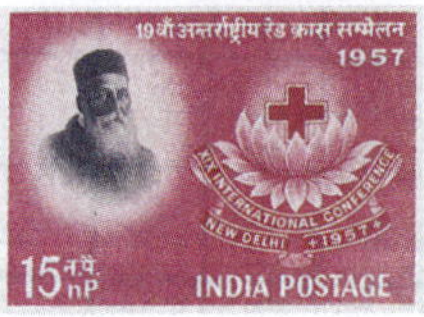

364 Henri Dunant and Conference Emblem **365** "Nutrition"

1957 (28 Oct). *19th International Red Cross Conference, New Delhi.* W **69** (sideways). P 13½×13.

388	**364**	15n.p. deep grey and carmine	10	10

1957 (14 Nov). *Children's Day. T* **365** *and similar designs.* W **69** (sideways on 90n.p.). P 14×13½ (90n.p.) or 13½×14 (others).

389	8n.p. reddish purple	10	25
390	15n.p. turquoise-green	20	10
391	90n.p. orange-brown	25	15
389/91	*Set of 3*	50	45

Designs: *Horiz*—15n.p. "Education". *Vert*—90n.p. "Re-creation".

368 Bombay University **369** Calcutta University

1957 (31 Dec). *Centenary of Indian Universities. T* **368/9** *and similar design.* W **69** (sideways on T **368**). P 14×14½ (No. 392) or 13½×14 (others).

392	10n.p. violet	15	60
393	10n.p. grey	15	60
394	10n.p. light brown	30	60
392/4	*Set of 3*	55	1·60

Design: *Horiz as T***369**—No. 394, Madras University.

371 J. N. Tata (founder) and Steel Plant **372** Dr. D. K. Karve

1958 (1 Mar). *50th Anniv of Steel Industry.* W **69**. P 14½×14.

395	**371**	15n.p. orange-red	10	10

1958 (18 Apr). *Birth Centenary of Karve (educationalist).* W **69** (sideways). P 14.

396	**372**	15n.p. orange-brown	10	10

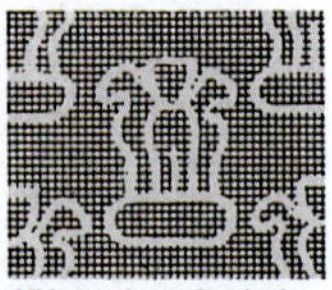

373 Westland Wapiti Biplane and Hawker Hunter **374** Asokan Capital

1958 (30 Apr). *Silver Jubilee of Indian Air Force.* W **69**. P 14½×14.

397	**373**	15n.p. blue	1·00	25
398		90n.p. ultramarine	1·25	2·00

1958–63. *As Nos. 366, 369/71 and 375/85a but W* **374**.

399	**361**	1n.p. blue-green (1960)	1·00	35
		a. Imperf (pair)	£200	
400		2n.p. light brown (27.10.58)	10	10
401		3n.p. deep brown (1958)	10	10
402		5n.p. bright green (27.10.58)	10	10
403		6n.p. grey (1963)	15	3·25
404		8n.p. light blue-green (1958)	1·00	10
405		10n.p. deep dull green (27.10.58)	15	10
		a. Imperf (pair)	†	—
406		13n.p. bright carmine-red (1963)	1·75	3·50
407		15n.p. violet (10.60)	60	10
408		20n.p. blue (27.10.58)	30	10
409		25n.p. ultramarine (27.10.58)	30	10
410		50n.p. orange (1959)	30	10
411		75n.p. reddish purple (1959)	40	10
412		90n.p. bright purple (1960)	5·50	10
413	–	1r. deep dull green (1959)	3·75	10
414	–	2r. cerise (1959)	7·00	10
415	–	5r. brown (1959)	9·00	40
416	–	10r. orange (1959)	29·00	6·00
399/416		*Set of 18*	55·00	12·00

The 5, 10, 15, 20, 25 and 50n.p. with serial numbers on the back are from coils of 810 stamps prepared from sheets for experimenting with vending machines. In the event the machines were not purchased and the stamps were sold over the counter.

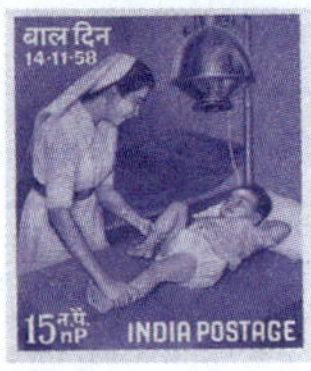

375 Bipin Chandra Pal **376** Nurse with Child Patient

1958 (7 Nov). *Birth Centenary of Pal (patriot).* W **374**. P 14×13½.

418	**375**	15n.p. deep dull green	10	10

1958 (14 Nov). *Children's Day.* W **374**. P 14×13½.

419	**376**	15n.p. violet	10	10

377 Jagadish Chandra Bose **378** Exhibition Gate

1958 (30 Nov). *Birth Centenary of Bose (botanist).* W **374**. P 14×13½.

420	**377**	15n.p. deep turquoise-green	20	10

1958 (30 Dec). *India 1958 Exhibition, New Delhi.* W **374** (sideways). P 14½×14.

421	**378**	15n.p. reddish purple	10	10

379 Sir Jamsetjee Jejeebhoy **380** "The Triumph of Labour" (after Chowdhury)

1959 (15 Apr). *Death Centenary of Jejeebhoy (philanthropist).* W **374**. P 14×13½.

422	**379**	15n.p. brown	10	10

1959 (15 June). *40th Anniv of International Labour Organization.* W **374** (sideways). P 14½×14.

423	**380**	15n.p. dull green	10	10

381 Boys awaiting admission to Children's Home **382** "Agriculture"

1959 (14 Nov). *Children's Day.* W **374**. P 14×14½.

424	**381**	15n.p. deep dull green	10	10
		a. Imperf (pair)	£800	

1959 (30 Dec). *First World Agricultural Fair, New Delhi.* W **374**. P 13½×13.

425	**382**	15n.p. grey	30	10

383 Thiruvalluvar (philosopher)

1960 (15 Feb). *Thiruvalluvar Commemoration.* W **374**. P 14×13½.

426	**383**	15n.p. reddish purple	10	10

384 Yaksha pleading with the Cloud (from the "Meghaduta") **385** Shakuntala writing a letter to Dushyanta (from the "Shakuntala")

1960 (22 June). *Kalidasa (poet) Commemoration.* W **374**. P 13.

427	**384**	15n.p. grey	65	10
428	**385**	1r.3n.p. pale yellow & brn	1·60	1·75

386 S. Bharati (poet) **387** Dr. M. Visvesvaraya

1960 (11 Sept). *Subramania Bharati Commemoration.* W **374**. P 14×13½.

429	**386**	15n.p. blue	10	10

1960 (15 Sept). *Birth Centenary of Dr. M. Visvesvaraya (engineer).* W **374**. P 13×13½.

430	**387**	15n.p. brown and bright carmine	10	10

388 "Children's Health"

1960 (14 Nov). *Children's Day.* W **374**. P 13½×13.

431	**388**	15n.p. deep dull green	10	10

389 Children greeting U.N. Emblem **390** Tyagaraja

1960 (11 Dec). *U.N.I.C.E.F. Day.* W **374**. P 13½×13.

432	**389**	15n.p. orange-brown & ol-brn	10	10

1961 (6 Jan). *114th Death Anniv of Tyagaraja (musician).* W **374**. P 14×13½.

433	**390**	15n.p. greenish blue	10	10

391 "First Aerial Post" cancellation

392 Air India Boeing 707 Airliner and Humber Sommer Biplane

1961 (18 Feb). *50th Anniv of First Official Airmail Flight, Allahabad-Naini. T* **391/2** *and similar design.* W **374**. P 14 (5n.p) or 13×13½ (others).

434	5n.p. olive-drab	1·10	30
435	15n.p. deep green and grey	1·10	30
436	1r. purple and grey	3·75	2·75
434/6	*Set of 3*	5·50	2·75

Design: *Horiz as T* **392**—1r. H. Pecquet flying Humber Sommer plane and "Aerial Post" cancellation.

394 Shivaji on horseback

395 Motilal Nehru (politician)

1961 (17 Apr). *Chatrapati Shivaji (Maratha ruler) Commemoration.* W **374**. P 13×13½.

437	**394**	15n.p. brown and green	80	40

1961 (6 May). *Birth Centenary of Pandit Motilal Nehru.* W **374**. P 14.

438	**395**	15n.p. olive-brown & brn-orge	30	10

396 Tagore (poet)

397 All India Radio Emblem and Transmitting Aerials

1961 (7 May). *Birth Centenary of Rabindranath Tagore.* W **374**. P 13×13½.

439	**396**	15n.p. yellow-orange & bl-grn	80	40

1961 (8 June). *Silver Jubilee of All India Radio.* W **374**. P 13½×13.

440	**397**	15n.p. ultramarine	10	10

398 Prafulla Chandra Ray

399 V. N. Bhatkande

1961 (2 Aug). *Birth Centenary of Ray (social reformer).* W **374**. P 14×13½.

441	**398**	15n.p. grey	10	20

1961 (1 Sept). *Birth Centenary of Bhatkande (composer) (1960).* W **374**. P 13×13½.

442	**399**	15n.p. olive-brown	10	10

400 Child at Lathe

401 Fair Emblem and Main Gate

1961 (14 Nov). *Children's Day.* W **374**. P 14×13½.

443	**400**	15n.p. brown	10	20

1961 (14 Nov). *Indian Industries Fair, New Delhi.* W **374**. P 14×14½.

444	**401**	15n.p. blue and carmine	10	10

402 Indian Forest

1961 (21 Nov). *Centenary of Scientific Forestry.* W **374**. P 13×13½.

445	**402**	15n.p. green and brown	40	30

403 Pitalkhora: Yaksha

404 Kalibangan Seal

1961 (14 Dec). *Centenary of Indian Archaeological Survey.* W **374**. P 14×13½ (15 n.p.) or 13½×14 (90n.p.).

446	**403**	15n.p. orange-brown	20	10
447	**404**	90n.p. yellow-olive & light brn	1·50	30

405 M. M. Malaviya

406 Gauhati Refinery

1961 (24 Dec). *Birth Centenary of Malaviya (educationist).* W **374**. P 14×13½.

448	**405**	15n.p. deep slate	10	20

1962 (1 Jan). *Inauguration of Gauhati Oil Refinery.* W **374**. P 13×13½.

449	**406**	15n.p. blue	40	20

407 Bhikaiji Cama

408 Village Panchayati and Parliament Building

1962 (26 Jan). *Birth Centenary of Bhikaiji Cama (patriot).* W **374**. P 14.

450	**407**	15n.p. reddish purple	10	10

1962 (26 Jan). *Inauguration of Panchayati System of Local Government.* W **374**. P 13×13½.

451	**408**	15n.p. bright purple	10	10

409 D. Saraswati (religious reformer)

410 G. S. Vidhyarthi (journalist)

1962 (4 Mar). *Dayanard Saraswati Commemoration.* W **374**. P 14.

452	**409**	15n.p. orange-brown	10	10

1962 (25 Mar). *Ganesh Shankar Vidhyarthi Commemoration.* W **374**. P 14×13½.

453	**410**	15n.p. red-brown	10	10

411 Malaria Eradication Emblem

412 Dr. R. Prasad

1962 (7 Apr). *Malaria Eradication.* W **374**. P 13×13½.

454	**411**	15n.p. yellow and claret	10	10

1962 (13 May). *Retirement of President Dr. Rajendra Prasad.* W **374**. P 13.

455	**412**	15n.p. bright purple (*shades*)	30	20

413 Calcutta High Court

416 Ramabai Ranade

1962. *Centenary of Indian High Courts. T* **413** *and similar horiz designs.* W **374**. P 14.

456		15n.p. dull green (1 July)	50	20
457		15n.p. red-brown (6 August)	50	20
458		15n.p. slate (14 August)	50	20
456/8		*Set of* 3	1·40	55

Designs:—No. 457, Madras High Court; No. 458, Bombay High Court.

1962 (15 Aug). *Birth Centenary of Ramabai Ranade (social reformer).* W **374**. P 14×13½

459	**416**	15n.p. orange-brown	10	20

417 Indian Rhinoceros

418 "Passing the Flag to Youth"

1962 (1 Oct). *Wild Life Week.* W **374**. P 13½×14.

460	**417**	15n.p. red-brown & dp turq	40	15

INSCRIPTIONS. From No. 461 onwards all designs except No. 463 are inscribed "BHARAT" in Devanagari in addition to "INDIA" in English.

1962 (14 Nov). *Children's Day.* W **374**. P 13½×13.

461	**418**	15n.p. orange-red & turq-grn	15	20

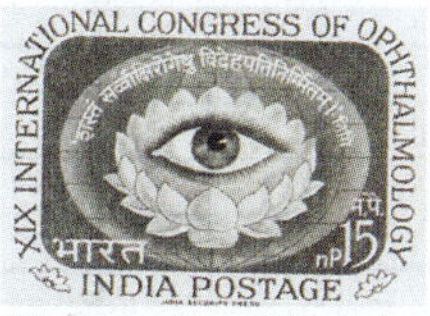

419 Human Eye within Lotus Blossom

420 S. Ramanujan

1962 (3 Dec). *19th International Ophthalmology Congress, New Delhi.* W **374**. P 13½×13.

462	**419**	15n.p. deep olive-brown	20	10

1962 (22 Dec). *75th Birth Anniv of Srinivasa Ramanujan (mathematician).* W **374**. P 13½×14.

463	**420**	15n.p. deep olive-brown	70	40

421 S. Vivekananda

Re.1

(**422**)

1963 (17 Jan). *Birth Centenary of Vivekananda (philosopher).* W **374**. P 14×14½.

464	**421**	15n.p. orange-brown & yell-ol	40	20

1963 (2 Feb). *No. 428 surch with T* **422**.

465	**385**	1r. on 1r.3n.p. pale yellow & brn	1·50	10

423 Hands reaching for F.A.O. Emblem

424 Henri Dunant (founder) and Centenary Emblem

1963 (21 Mar). *Freedom from Hunger.* W **374**. P 13.

466	**423**	15n.p. grey-blue	2·25	30

1963 (8 May). *Red Cross Centenary.* W **374**. P 13.

467	**424**	15n.p. red and grey	3·00	40
		a. Red (cross) omitted	£3000	

425 Artillery and Helicopter

1963 (15 Aug). *Defence Campaign. T* **425** *and similar horiz design.* W **374**. P 14.

468	15n.p. grey-green	1·25	10
469	1r. red-brown	1·50	65

Design:—1r. Sentry and parachutists.

427 D. Naoroji (parliamentarian)

428 Annie Besant (patriot and theosophist)

1963 (4 Sept). *Dadabhai Naoroji Commemoration.* W **374**. P 13.
470 **427** 15n.p. grey 10 10

1963 (1 Oct). *Annie Besant Commemoration.* W **374**. P 13½×14.
471 **428** 15n.p. turquoise-green 15 10
No. 471 is incorrectly dated "1837". Mrs. Besant was born in 1847.

429 Gaur

430 Lesser Panda

1963 (7 Oct). *Wild Life Preservation. T* **429/30** *and similar designs.* W **374**. P 13½×14 (10n.p.) or 13 (others)

472	10n.p. black and yellow-orange	1·00	1·50
473	15n.p. orange-brown and green	1·75	60
474	30n.p. slate and yellow-ochre	3·00	1·50
475	50n.p. orange and deep grey-green	3·25	80
476	1r. light brown and blue	2·00	50
472/6	*Set of 5*	10·00	4·50

Designs: *Vert*—30n.p. Indian elephant. *Horiz* (*as T***430**) 50n.p. Tiger; 1r. Lion.

434 "School Meals"

435 Eleanor Roosevelt at Spinning-wheel

1963 (14 Nov). *Children's Day.* W **374**. P 14×13½.
477 **434** 15n.p. bistre-brown 10 10

1963 (10 Dec). *15th Anniv of Declaration of Human Rights.* W **374**. P 13½×13.
478 **435** 15n.p. reddish purple 10 15

436 Dipalakshmi (bronze)

437 Gopabandhu Das (social reformer)

1964 (4 Jan). *26th International Orientalists Congress, New Delhi.* W **374**. P 13×13½.
479 **436** 15n.p. deep ultramarine 20 15

1964 (4 Jan). *Gopabandhu Das Commemoration.* W **374**. P 13×13½.
480 **437** 15n.p. deep dull purple 10 10

438 Purandaradasa

1964 (14 Jan). *400th Death Anniv of Purandaradasa (composer).* W **374**. P 13×13½.
481 **438** 15n.p. light brown 15 10

439 S. C. Bose and I. N. A. Badge

440 Bose and Indian National Army

1964 (23 Jan). *67th Birth Anniv of Subhas Chandra Bose (nationalist).* W **374**. P 13.
482 **439** 15n.p. yellow-bistre 50 20
483 **440** 55n.p. black, orange & orge-red 50 45

441 Sarojini Naidu

442 Kasturba Gandhi

1964 (13 Feb). *85th Birth Anniv of Sarojini Naidu (poetess).* W **374**. P 14.
484 **441** 15n.p. deep grey-green and purple 10 10

1964 (22 Feb). *20th Death Anniv of Kasturba Gandhi.* W **374**. P 14×13½.
485 **442** 15n.p. orange-brown 10 10

443 Dr. W. M. Haffkine (immunologist)

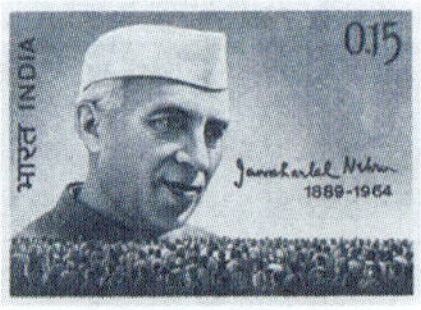

444 Jawaharlal Nehru (statesman)

1964 (16 Mar). *Haffkine Commemoration.* W **374**. P 13.
486 **443** 15n.p. deep purple-brown/*buff* 30 10

(Value expressed as paisa instead of naye paise.)

1964 (12 June). *Nehru Mourning Issue.* No wmk. P 13½×13.
487 **444** 15p. deep slate 10 10

445 Sir Asutosh Mookerjee

446 Sri Aurobindo

1964 (29 June). *Birth Centenary of Sir Asutosh Mookerjee (education reformer).* W **374**. P 13½×13.
488 **445** 15p. bistre-brown and yellow-olive 10 10

1964 (15 Aug). *92nd Birth Anniv of Sri Aurobindo (religious teacher).* W **374**. P 13×13½.
489 **446** 15p. dull purple 15 10

447 Raja R. Roy (social reformer)

448 I.S.O. Emblem and Globe

1964 (27 Sept). *Raja Rammohun Roy Commemoration.* W **374**. P 13×13½.
490 **447** 15n.p. brown 10 10

1964 (9 Nov). *Sixth International Organization for Standardization General Assembly, Bombay.* No wmk. P 13×13½.
491 **448** 15p. carmine 15 20

449 Jawaharlal Nehru (from 1r. commemorative coin)

450 St. Thomas (after statue, Ortona Cathedral, Italy)

1964 (14 Nov). *Children's Day.* No wmk. P 14×13½.
492 **449** 15p. slate 10 10

1964 (2 Dec). *St. Thomas Commemoration.* No wmk. P 14×13½.
493 **450** 15p. reddish purple 10 30
No. 493 was issued on the occasion of Pope Paul's visit to India.

451 Globe

452 J. Tata (industrialist)

1964 (14 Dec). *22nd International Geological Congress.* W **374**. P 14×13½.
494 **451** 15p. blue-green 40 30

1965 (7 Jan). *Jamsetji Tata Commemoration.* No wmk. P 13½×13.
495 **452** 15p. dull purple and orange 30 20

453 Lala Lajpat Rai

454 Globe and Congress Emblem

1965 (28 Jan). *Birth Centenary of Lala Lajpat Rai (social reformer).* No wmk. P 13×13½.
496 **453** 15p. light brown 20 10

1965 (8 Feb). *20th International Chamber of Commerce Congress, New Delhi.* No wmk. P 13½×13.
497 **454** 15p. grey-green and carmine 15 15

455 Freighter *Jalausha* and Visakhapatnam

456 Abraham Lincoln

1965 (5 Apr). *National Maritime Day.* W **374** (sideways). P 14½×14.
498 **455** 15p. blue 30 30

1965 (15 Apr). *Death Centenary of Abraham Lincoln.* W **374**. P 13.
499 **456** 15p. brown and yellow-ochre 15 10

457 I.T.U. Emblem and Symbols

458 "Everlasting Flame"

1965 (17 May). *I.T.U. Centenary.* W **374** (sideways). P 14½×14.
500 **457** 15p. reddish purple .... 1·00 30

1965 (27 May). *First Anniv of Nehru's Death.* W **374**. P 13.
501 **458** 15p. carmine and blue 15 10

459 I.C.Y. Emblem

460 Climbers on Summit

1965 (26 June). *International Co-operation Year.* P 13½×13.
502 **459** 15p. deep olive and yellow-brown .... 1·25 1·25

1965 (15 Aug). *Indian Mount Everest Expedition.* P 13.
503 **460** 15p. deep reddish purple 45 20

461 Bidri Vase

462 Brass Lamp

466 Electric Locomotive

474 Woman writing a Letter (medieval sculpture)

475 Dal Lake, Kashmir

1965–75. *T* **461/2**, **466**, **474/5** *and similar designs.*

(*a*) W **374** (sideways on 2, 3, 5, 6, 8, 30, 50, 60p., 2, 5, 10r.). P 14×14½ (4, 10, 15, 20, 40, 70p., 1r.) or 14½×14 (others)

504	2p. red-brown (16.10.67)	10	1·00
505	3p. brown-olive (16.10.67)	50	3·25
505*a*	4p. lake-brown (15.5.68)	10	3·25
506	5p. cerise (16.10.67)	10	10
	a. Imperf (pair)	£180	
507	6p. grey-black (1.7.66)	30	3·75
508	8p. red-brown (15.3.67)	30	4·25
509	10p. new blue (1.7.66)	40	10
510	15p. bronze-green (15.8.65)	4·50	10
511	20p. purple (16.10.67)	6·00	10
512	30p. sepia (15.3.67)	15	10
513	40p. maroon (2.10.68)	15	20
514	50p. blue-green (15.3.67)	20	10
515	60p. deep grey (16.10.67)	35	20
516	70p. chalky blue (15.3.67)	60	20
517	1r. red-brown and plum (1.7.66)	60	10
518	2r. new blue and deep slate-violet (15.3.67)	2·00	10
	w. Wmk capitals to right		
519	5r. deep slate-violet and brown (15.3.67)	2·50	90
520	10r. black and bronze-green (14.11.65)	21·00	80
504/20	*Set of* 18	35·00	16·00

(*b*) No wmk. P 14½×14

520*a*	5p. cerise (12.5.74)	75	10

(*c*) Wmk Large Star and "INDIA GOVT"† in sheet. P 14½×14.

521	2p. red-brown (1.3.75)	1·25	2·25
	aw. Wmk reversed	4·00	
521*b*	5p. cerise (1.3.75)	1·75	10

Designs: *Horiz* (*as T* **466**)—4p. Coffee berries; 15p. Plucking tea; 20p. Hindustan Aircraft Industries Ajeet jet fighter; 40p. Calcutta G.P.O.; 70p. Hampi Chariot (sculpture). (*As T* **475**)—5r. Bhakra Dam, Punjab; 10r. Atomic reactor, Trombay. *Vert* (*as T* **461/2**)—5p. "Family Planning"; 6p. Konarak Elephant; 8p. Spotted Deer ("Chital"); 30p. Indian dolls; 50p. Mangoes; 60p. Somnath Temple.

†The arrangement of this watermark in the sheet results in the words and the star appearing upright, inverted or sideways.

Two different postal forgeries exist of No. 511, both printed in lithography and without watermark. The cruder version is roughly perforated 15, but the more sophisticated is perforated 14×14½.

See also Nos. 721/38.

479 G. B. Pant (statesman)

480 V. Patel

1965 (10 Sept). *Govind Ballabh Pant Commemoration.* P 13.
522 **479** 15p. brown and deep green 10 20

1965 (31 Oct). *90th Birth Anniv of Vallabhbhai Patel (statesman).* P 14×13½.
523 **480** 15p. blackish brown 10 30

481 C. Das

482 Vidyapati (poet)

1965 (5 Nov). *95th Birth Anniv of Chittaranjan Das (lawyer and patriot).* P 13.
524 **481** 15p. yellow-brown.......................... 10 10

1965 (17 Nov). *Vidyapati Commemoration.* P 14×14½.
525 **482** 15p. yellow-brown.......................... 10 10

483 Sikandra, Agra

484 Soldier, Hindustan Aircraft Industries Ajeet jet fighters and Cruiser *Mysore*

1966 (24 Jan). *Pacific Area Travel Association Conference, New Delhi.* P 13½×14.
526 **483** 15p. slate.. 10 10

1966 (26 Jan). *Indian Armed Forces.* P 14
527 **484** 15p. violet.. 1·75 60

485 Lal Bahadur Shastri (statesman)

486 Kambar (poet)

1966 (26 Jan). *Shastri Mourning Issue.* P 13×13½.
528 **485** 15p. black 80 10

1966 (5 Apr). *Kambar Commemoration.* P 14×14½.
529 **486** 15p. grey-green 10 10

487 B. R. Ambedkar

488 Kunwar Singh (patriot)

1966 (14 Apr). *75th Birth Anniv of Dr. Bhim Rao Ambedkar (lawyer).* P 14×13½.
530 **487** 15p. purple-brown.......................... 10 10

1966 (23 Apr). *Kunwar Singh Commemoration.* P 14×13½.
531 **488** 15p. chestnut................................... 10 10

489 G. K. Gokhale

490 Acharya Dvivedi (poet)

1966 (9 May). *Birth Centenary of Gopal Krishna Gokhale (patriot).* P 13½×13.
532 **489** 15p. brown-purple and pale yellow 10 10

1966 (15 May). *Dvivedi Commemoration.* P 13½×14.
533 **490** 15p. drab.. 10 10

491 Maharaja Ranjit Singh (warrior)

492 Head Bhabha (scientist) and Nuclear Reactor

1966 (28 June). *Maharaja Ranjit Singh Commemoration.* P 14×13½.
534 **491** 15p. purple 60 20

1966 (4 Aug). *Dr. Homi Bhabha Commemoration.* P 14½×14.
535 **492** 15p. dull purple 15 30

493 A. K. Azad (scholar)

494 Swami Tirtha

1966 (11 Nov). *Abul Kalam Azad Commemoration.* P 13½×14.
536 **493** 15p. chalky blue 15 15

1966 (11 Nov). *60th Death Anniv of Swami Rama Tirtha (social reformer).* P 13×13½.
537 **494** 15p. turquoise-blue 30 30

495 Infant and Dove Emblem

496 Allahabad High Court

(Des C. Pakrashi)

1966 (14 Nov). *Children's Day.* P 13×13½.
538 **495** 15p. bright purple........................... 60 20

1966 (25 Nov). *Centenary of Allahabad High Court.* P 14½×14.
539 **496** 15p. dull purple 70 30

497 Indian Family

498 Hockey Game

1966 (12 Dec). *Family Planning.* P 13.
540 **497** 15p. brown.. 15 15

1966 (31 Dec). *India's Hockey Victory in Fifth Asian Games.* P 13.
541 **498** 15p. new blue.................................. 1·25 60

499 "Jai Kisan"

500 Voter and Polling Booth

1967 (11 Jan). *First Anniv of Shastri's Death.* P 13½×14.
542 **499** 15p. yellow-green 30 30

1967 (13 Jan). *Indian General Election.* P 13½×14.
543 **500** 15p. red-brown 15 15

501 Gurudwara Shrine, Patna

502 Taj Mahal, Agra

1967 (17 Jan). *300th Birth Anniv (1966) of Guru Gobind Singh (Sikh religious leader).* P 14×13½.
544 **501** 15p. bluish violet 50 15

1967 (19 Mar). *International Tourist Year.* P 14½×14.
545 **502** 15p. bistre-brown and orange......... 30 15

503 Nandalal Bose and "Garuda"

504 Survey Emblem and Activities

1967 (16 Apr). *First Death Anniv of Nandalal Bose (painter).* P 14×13½.
546 **503** 15p. bistre-brown 15 15

1967 (1 May). *Survey of India Bicentenary.* P 13½×13.
547 **504** 15p. reddish lilac 60 40

505 Basaveswara

506 Narsinha Mehta (poet)

1967 (11 May). *800th Death Anniv of Basaveswara (reformer and statesman).* P 13½×14.
548 **505** 15p. orange-red................................ 15 15

1967 (30 May). *Narsinha Mehta Commemoration.* P 14×13½.
549 **506** 15p. blackish brown 15 15

507 Maharana Pratap

508 Narayana Guru

1967 (11 June). *Maharana Pratap (Rajput leader) Commemoration.* P 14×14½.
550 **507** 15p. red-brown 15 15

1967 (21 Aug). *Narayana Guru (philosopher) Commemoration.* P 14.
551 **508** 15p. brown 30 20

509 President Radhakrishnan

510 Martyrs' Memorial, Patna

1967 (5 Sept). *75th Birth Anniv of Sarvepalli Radhakrishnan (former President).* P 13.
552 **509** 15p. claret 50 15

1967 (1 Oct). *25th Anniv of "Quit India" Movement.* P 14½×14.
553 **510** 15p. lake 15 15

511 Route Map

512 Wrestling

1967 (9 Nov). *Centenary of Indo-European Telegraph Service.* P 13½×14.
554 **511** 15p. black and light blue 70 20

1967 (12 Nov). *World Wrestling Championships, New Delhi.* P 13½×14.
555 **512** 15p. purple & lt orge-brn 50 20

513 Nehru leading Naga Tribesmen

514 Rashbehari Basu (nationalist)

1967 (1 Dec). *4th Anniv of Nagaland as a State of India.* P 13×13½.
556 **513** 15p. ultramarine 15 15

1967 (26 Dec). *Rashbehari Basu Commemoration.* P 14.
557 **514** 15p. maroon 15 20

515 Bugle, Badge and Scout Salute

1967 (27 Dec). *60th Anniv of Scout Movement in India.* P 14½×14.
558 **515** 15p. chestnut .... 1·00 60

516 Men embracing Universe

517 Globe and Book of Tamil

1968 (1 Jan). *Human Rights Year.* P 13.
559 **516** 15p. bronze-green 50 30

1968 (3 Jan). *International Conference-Seminar of Tamil Studies, Madras.* P 13.
560 **517** 15p. reddish lilac 60 15

518 U.N. Emblem and Transport

519 Quill and Bow Symbol

1968 (1 Feb). *United Nations Conference on Trade and Development, New Delhi.* P 14½×14.
561 **518** 15p. turquoise-blue 60 15

1968 (20 Feb). *Centenary of* Amrita Bazar Patrika *(newspaper).* P 13½×14.
562 **519** 15p. sepia and orange-yellow 15 15

520 Maxim Gorky

521 Emblem and Medal

1968 (28 Mar). *Birth Centenary of Maxim Gorky.* P 13½.
563 **520** 15p. plum 15 20

1968 (31 Mar). *First Triennale Art Exhibition, New Delhi.* P 13.
564 **521** 15p. orange, royal blue & lt bl 30 20
a. Orange omitted £800

522 Letter-box and "100,000"

523 Stalks of Wheat, Agricultural Institute and Production Graph

(Des C. Pakrashi)

1968 (1 July). *Opening of 100,000th Indian Post Office.* P 13.
565 **522** 20p. red, blue and black 40 15

1968 (17 July). *Wheat Revolution.* P 13.
566 **523** 20p. bluish green & orge-brn 30 15

524 "Self-portrait"

525 Lakshminath Bezbaruah

(Des from self-portrait)

1968 (17 Sept). *30th Death Anniv of Gaganendranath Tagore (painter).* P 13.
567 **524** 20p. brown-purple and ochre 50 15

1968 (5 Oct). *Birth Centenary of Lakshminath Bezbaruah (writer).* P 13½×14.
568 **525** 20p. blackish brown 30 15

526 Athlete's Legs and Olympic Rings

1968 (12 Oct). *Olympic Games, Mexico.* P 14½×14.
569 **526** 20p. brown and grey 15 15
570 1r. sepia and brown-olive 50 15

527 Bhagat Singh and Followers

528 Azad Hind Flag, Swords and Chandra Bose (founder)

1968 (19 Oct). *61st Birth Anniv of Bhagat Singh (patriot).* P 13.
571 **527** 20p. yellow-brown .... 1·00 50

1968 (21 Oct). *25th Anniv of Azad Hind Government.* P 14×14½.
572 **528** 20p. deep blue .... 1·25 15

529 Sister Nivedita

530 Marie Curie and Radium Treatment

1968 (27 Oct). *Birth Centenary of Sister Nivedita (social reformer).* P 14×14½.
573 **529** 20p. deep bluish green 30 30

1968 (6 Nov). *Birth Centenary of Marie Curie.* P 14½×14.
574 **530** 20p. slate-lilac .... 1·40 70

531 Map of the World

532 Cochin Synagogue

1968 (1 Dec). *21st International Geographical Congress, New Delhi.* P 13.
575 **531** 20p. new blue 15 15

1968 (15 Dec). *400th Anniv of Cochin Synagogue.* P 13.
576 **532** 20p. blue and carmine .... 1·00 40

533 I.N.S. *Nilgiri* (frigate)

534 Red-billed Blue Magpie

1968 (15 Dec). *Navy Day.* P 13.
577 **533** 20p. grey-blue .... 1·75 40

1968 (31 Dec). *Birds. T* **534** *and similar designs.* P 14×14½ (1r.) or 14½×14 (others).
578 20p. multicoloured .... 1·25 50
579 50p. scarlet, black and turquoise-green. 1·25 1·50
580 1r. dp blue, yellow-brown & pale bl ... 2·50 1·00
581 2r. multicoloured .... 1·75 1·50
578/81 *Set of* 4 .... 6·00 4·00

Designs: *Horiz*—50p. Brown-fronted Pied Woodpecker; 2r. Yellow-backed Sunbird. *Vert*—1r. Slaty-headed Scimitar Babbler.

538 Bankim Chandra Chatterjee

539 Dr. Bhagavan Das

1969 (1 Jan). *130th Birth Anniv of Bankim Chandra Chatterjee (writer).* P 13½.
582 **538** 20p. ultramarine 15 20

1969 (12 Jan). *Birth Centenary of Dr. Bhagavan Das (philosopher).* P 13½.
583 **539** 20p. pale chocolate 15 20

540 Dr. Martin Luther King

541 Mirza Ghalib and Letter Seal

1969 (25 Jan). *Martin Luther King Commemoration.* P 13½.
584 **540** 20p. deep olive-brown 60 20

1969 (17 Feb). *Death Centenary of Mirza Ghalib (poet).* P 14½×14.
585 **541** 20p. sepia, brown-red and flesh 15 15

542 Osmania University

1969 (15 Mar). *50th Anniv of Osmania University.* P 14½×14.
586 **542** 20p. olive-green 15 20

543 Rafi Ahmed Kidwai and Lockheed Constellation Mail Plane

1969 (1 Apr). *20th Anniv of "ALL-UP" Air Mail Scheme.* P 13.
587 **543** 20p. deep blue .... 1·50 30

544 I.L.O. Badge and Emblem

545 Memorial, and Hands dropping Flowers

1969 (11 Apr). *50th Anniv of International Labour Organisation.* P 14½×14.
588 **544** 20p. chestnut 15 20

1969 (13 Apr). *50th Anniv of Jallianwala Bagh Massacre, Amritsar.* P 14×13½.
589 **545** 20p. rose-carmine 15 20

546 K. Nageswara Rao Pantulu (journalist)

547 Ardaseer Cursetjee Wadia, and Ships

1969 (1 May). *Kasinadhuni Nageswara Rao Pantulu Commemoration.* P 13½×14.
590 **546** 20p. brown....................................... 15 20

1969 (27 May). *Ardaseer Cursetjee Wadia (ship-builder) Commemoration.* P 14½×14.
591 **547** 20p. turquoise-green 50 40

548 Serampore College

549 Dr. Zakir Husain

1969 (7 June). *150th Anniv of Serampore College.* P 13½.
592 **548** 20p. plum... 15 20

1969 (11 June). *President Dr. Zakir Husain Commemoration.* P 13.
593 **549** 20p. sepia... 15 20

550 Laxmanrao Kirloskar

1969 (20 June). *Birth Centenary of Laxmanrao Kirloskar (agriculturalist).* P 13.
594 **550** 20p. grey-black 15 15

551 Gandhi and his Wife

552 Gandhi's Head and Shoulders

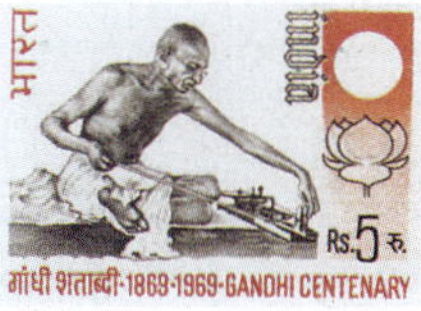

553 Gandhi walking (woodcut)

554 Gandhi with Charkha

(Des Suraj Sadan (20p.), P. Chitnis (75p.), Indian Security Press (1r.) and C. Pakrashi (5r.))

1969 (2 Oct). *Birth Centenary of Mahatma Gandhi.* P 13½×14 (20p), 14×14½ (1r.) or 13 (others).
595 **551** 20p. blackish brown 70 40
596 **552** 75p. cinnamon and drab................. 1·25 90
597 **553** 1r. blue .... 1·25 65
598 **554** 5r. greyish brown and red-orge ... 4·50 6·50
595/8 *Set of* 4 .... 7·00 7·50

555 *Ajanta* (bulk carrier) and I.M.C.O. Emblem

1969 (14 Oct). *10th Anniv of Inter-Governmental Maritime Consultative Organization.* P 13.
599 **555** 20p. violet-blue............................... 1·75 40

556 Outline of Parliament Building and Globe

557 Astronaut walking beside Space Module on Moon

1969 (30 Oct). *57th Inter-Parliamentary Conference, New Delhi.* P 14½×14.
600 **556** 20p. new blue................................... 15 20

1969 (19 Nov). *First Man on the Moon.* P 14×14½.
601 **557** 20p. olive-brown.............................. 50 30

558 Gurudwara Nankana Sahib (birthplace)

559 Tiger's Head and Hands holding Globe

1969 (23 Nov). *500th Birth Anniv of Guru Nanak Dev (Sikh religious leader).* P 13½.
602 **558** 20p. slate-violet 30 20

1969 (24 Nov). *International Union for the Conservation of Nature and Natural Resources Conference, New Delhi.* P 14½×14.
603 **559** 20p. orange-brown & bronze-grn .. 30 30

560 Sadhu Vaswani

561 Thakkar Bapa

1969 (25 Nov). *90th Birth Anniv of Sadhu Vaswani (educationist).* P 14×14½.
604 **560** 20p. grey... 15 15

1969 (29 Nov). *Birth Centenary of Thakkar Bapa (humanitarian).* P 13½.
605 **561** 20p. chocolate 15 20

562 Satellite, Television, Telephone and Globe

563 C. N. Annadurai

1970 (21 Jan). *12th Plenary Assembly of International Radio Consultative Committee.* P 13.
606 **562** 20p. Prussian blue 40 20

1970 (3 Feb). *First Death Anniv of Conjeevaram Natrajan Annadurai (statesman).* P 13.
607 **563** 20p. reddish purple and royal blue 30 15

564 M. N. Kishore and Printing Press

565 Nalanda College

1970 (19 Feb). *75th Death Anniv of Munshi Newal Kishore (publisher).* P 13.
608 **564** 20p. lake 15 20

1970 (27 Mar). *Centenary of Nalanda College.* P 14½×14.
609 **565** 20p. brown.. 60 50

566 Swami Shraddhanand (social reformer)

567 Lenin

1970 (30 Mar). *Swami Shraddhanand Commemoration.* P 14×13½.
610 **566** 20p. yellow-brown........................... 75 60

1970 (22 Apr). *Birth Centenary of Lenin.* P 13.
611 **567** 20p. orange-brown and sepia 40 20

568 New U.P.U. H.Q. Building

569 Sher Shah Suri (15th-century ruler)

1970 (20 May). *New U.P.U. Headquarters Building, Berne.* P 13.
612 **568** 20p. emerald, grey and black.......... 15 20

1970 (22 May). *Sher Shah Suri Commemoration.* P 13.
613 **569** 20p. deep bluish green.................... 30 30

570 V. D. Savarkar and Cellular Jail, Andaman Islands

571 "UN" and Globe

1970 (28 May). *Vinayak Damodar Savarkar (patriot) Commemoration.* P 13.
614 **570** 20p. orange-brown 50 30

1970 (26 June). *25th Anniv of United Nations.* P 13.
615 **571** 20p. light new blue.......................... 40 20

572 Symbol and Workers

1970 (18 Aug). *Asian Productivity Year.* P 14½×14.
616 **572** 20p. violet 20 20

573 Dr. Montessori and I.E.Y. Emblem

1970 (31 Aug). *Birth Centenary of Dr. Maria Montessori (educationist).* P 13.
617 **573** 20p. dull purple 30 30

574 J. N. Mukherjee (revolutionary) and Horse

575 V. S. Srinivasa Sastri

1970 (9 Sept). *Jatindra Nath Mukherjee Commemoration.* P 14½×14.
618 **574** 20p. chocolate .... 1·50 30

1970 (22 Sept). *Srinivasa Sastri (educationalist) Commemoration.* P 13×13½.
619 **575** 20p. yellow and brown-purple 30 30

576 I. C. Vidyasagar

577 Maharishi Valmiki

1970 (26 Sept). *150th Birth Anniv of Iswar Chandra Vidyasagar (educationalist).* P 13.
620 **576** 20p. brown and purple 40 30

1970 (14 Oct). *Maharishi Valmiki (ancient author) Commemoration.* P 13.
621 **577** 20p. purple 70 30

578 Calcutta Port

1970 (17 Oct). *Centenary of Calcutta Port Trust.* P 13½×13.
622 **578** 20p. greenish blue .... 1·50 70

579 University Building

1970 (29 Oct). *50th Anniv of Jamia Millia Islamia University.* P 14½×14.
623 **579** 20p. yellow-green 70 50

580 Jamnalal Bajaj

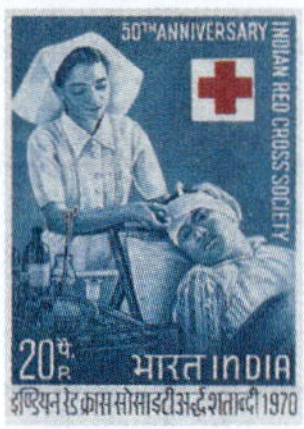

581 Nurse and Patient

1970 (4 Nov). *Jamnalal Bajaj (industrialist) Commemoration.* W **374**. P 13½×13.
624 **580** 20p. olive-grey 15 30

1970 (5 Nov). *50th Anniv of Indian Red Cross.* W **374** (sideways). P 13×13½.
625 **581** 20p. red and greenish blue 60 40

582 Sant Namdeo

583 Beethoven

1970 (9 Nov). *700th Birth Anniv of Sant Namdeo (mystic).* W **374**. P 13.
626 **582** 20p. orange 15 30

1970 (16 Dec). *Birth Bicentenary of Beethoven.* P 13.
627 **583** 20p. orange and greyish black .... 2·50 70

584 Children examining Stamps

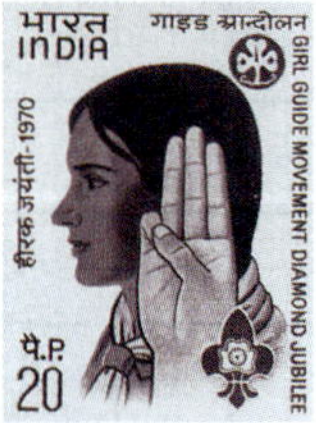

585 Girl Guide

1970 (23 Dec). *Indian National Philatelic Exhibition, New Delhi. T* **584** *and similar horiz design.* P 13.
628 20p. orange and myrtle-green 30 10
629 1r. orange-brown & pale yell-brn .... 2·50 1·00
Design:—1r. Gandhi commemorative through magnifier.

1970 (27 Dec). *Diamond Jubilee of Girl Guide Movement in India.* P 13.
630 **585** 20p. maroon 60 30

STAMP BOOKLETS

1904. *Black on green (No. SB1) or black on pink (No. SB2) covers. Stapled.*

SB1	12¼a. booklet containing twenty-four ½a. (No. 121) in blocks of 6	£1100
SB2	12¼a. booklet containing twelve 1a. (No. 123) in blocks of 6	£1100

1906–11. *Black on green (No. SB3), black on pink (No. SB4) or black on green and pink (No. SB5) match book type covers inscr* "Post Office of India" *and royal cypher of King Edward VII. Stapled.*

SB3	1r. booklet containing thirty-two ½a. (No. 149) in blocks of 4	£600
	a. Without "Post Office of India" inscr	£550
	b. Ditto and showing royal cypher of King George V (1911)	£500
SB4	1r. booklet containing sixteen 1a. (No. 150) in blocks of 4 (1907)	£550
	a. Without "Post Office of India" inscr	£500
	b. Ditto and showing royal cypher of King George V (1911)	£550
SB5	1r. booklet containing sixteen ½a. and eight 1a. (Nos. 149/50) in blocks of 4 (1907)	£1200
	a. Without "Post Office of India" inscr	£1000
	b. Ditto and showing royal cypher of King George V (1911)	£1000

1912–22. *Black on green (Nos. SB6/7, SB12), black on pink (No. SB8), black on green and pink (No. SB9), black on purple (No. SB10) or black on blue (No. SB11) match book type covers with foreign postage rates on back. Stapled.*

SB6	1r. booklet containing sixty-four 3p. (No. 152) in blocks of 4 (blank back cover)	£700
SB7	1r. booklet containing thirty-two ½a. (No. 155) in blocks of 4	£250
	a. Blank back cover	£250
	b. Advertisement contractor's notice on back cover	£350
	c. Advertisement on back (1922)	£325
SB8	1r. booklet containing sixteen 1a. (No. 159) in blocks of 4	£180
	a. Blank back cover	£180
	b. Advertisements on front flap and back cover (1922)	£225
SB9	1r. booklet containing sixteen ½a. and eight 1a. (Nos. 155, 159) in blocks of 4 (blank back cover)	£170
	a. Advertisement on back	£200
	b. Foreign postage rates on back	£180
SB10	1r.8a. booklet containing sixteen 1½a. (No. 163) in blocks of 4 (1919)	£400
	a. Blank back cover (1921)	£350
SB11	2r. booklet containing sixteen 2a. (No. 169) in blocks of 4 (blank back cover) (1921)	£600
	a. Black on purple cover with postage rates on back (1922)	£600
SB12	2r. booklet containing sixteen 2a. (No. 166) in blocks of 4 (1922)	£600
	a. Black on purple cover	£600

1921. *Black on buff match book type cover. Stapled.*

SB13	1r.2a. booklet containing twenty-four 9p. on 1a. (No. 192) in blocks of 4	£110

1922. *Black on brown (No. SB14) or black on green and pink (No. SB15) match book type covers with foreign postage rates on back. Stapled.*

SB14	1r. booklet containing sixteen 1a. (No. 197) in blocks of 4	£225
	a. Advertisement on back	£275
	b. Advertisements on front flap and back cover	
	c. Black on lilac cover with blank back	£250
	ca. Advertisements on front flap and back cover	£350
	d. Black on pink cover with blank back	£300
SB15	1r. booklet containing sixteen ½a. and eight 1a. (Nos. 155, 197) in blocks of 4 (blank back cover)	£600

1926–28. *Black on brown (No. SB16) or black on purple (No. SB17) match book type covers with foreign postage rates on back. Stapled.*

SB16	1r. booklet containing sixteen 1a. (No. 203) in blocks of 4	£130
SB17	2r. booklet containing sixteen 2a. (No. 205) in blocks of 4	£350
	a. Containing No. 206 (1928)	£450

1929. *Black on brown (No. SB18) or black on purple (No. SB19) separate leaf covers. Stitched.*

SB18	1r. booklet containing sixteen 1a. (No. 203) in blocks of 4 (blank back cover)	£130
	a. Advertisement contractor's notice on back cover	£120
	b. Advertisements on front flap and back cover	£150
	c. Advertisement on back cover	£150
SB19	2r. booklet containing sixteen 2a. (No. 205) in blocks of 4 (foreign postage rates on back cover)	£400
	a. Advertisement contractor's notice on back cover	£400
	b. Containing No. 206 (foreign postage rates on back cover)	£475
	ba. Advertisement contractor's notice on back cover	£475

1932. *Black on brown cover. Stitched.*

SB20	1r.4a. booklet containing sixteen 1¼a. (No. 235) in blocks of 4	£375

1934. *Black on buff cover. Stitched.*

SB21	1r. booklet containing sixteen 1a. (No. 234) in blocks of 4	£225

1937. *Black on red cover. Stamps with wmk upright or inverted. Stitched.*

SB22	1r. booklet containing sixteen 1a. (No. 250) in blocks of 4	£300

OFFICIAL STAMPS

Stamps overprinted "POSTAL SERVICE" or "I.P.N." were not used as postage stamps, and are therefore omitted.

Service.
(O 1)

(Optd by the Military Orphanage Press, Calcutta)

1866 (1 Aug)–**72**. *Optd with Type* O **1**. P 14.

(a) No wmk.

O1	11	½a. blue	–	£325
O2		½a. pale blue	£1400	£150
		a. Opt inverted		
O3		1a. brown	–	£200
O4		1a. deep brown	–	£150
O5		8a. carmine	26·00	65·00

(b) Wmk Elephant's Head, T **13**.

O6	11	½a. blue	£325	23·00
		w. Wmk inverted	†	£180
O7		½a. pale blue	£300	12·00
		a. Opt inverted		
		b. No dot on "i" (No. 50 on pane)	–	£350
		c. No stop (No. 77 on pane)	–	£300
O8	12	8p. purple (1.72)	24·00	60·00
		a. No dot on "i"	£325	£425
		b. No stop	£325	
O9	11	1a. brown	£275	18·00
O10		1a. deep brown	£300	40·00
		a. No dot on "i"	–	£550
		b. No stop	–	£450
O11		2a. orange	£200	95·00
O12		2a. yellow	£200	£100
		a. Opt inverted		
		b. Imperf		
		c. Raised stop between "c" and "e"	†	£1800
		w. Wmk inverted	£275	
		y. Wmk inverted and reversed	†	£400
O13		4a. green	£250	95·00
		a. Opt inverted		
O14	17	4a. green (Die 1)	£1100	£250

A variety with wide and more open capital "S" occurs six times in sheets of all values except No. O8. Price four times the normal.

Reprints exist of Nos. O6, O9 and O14; the latter is Die II instead of Die I.

Reprints of the overprint have also been made, in a different setting, on the 8 pies, purple, no watermark.

O 2

O 6

O 3

O 4

(No. O15 surch at Calcutta, others optd at Madras)

1866 (Oct). *Fiscal stamps, Nos. O15/18 with top and bottom inscrs removed, surch or optd.* Wmk Crown over "INDIA".

(a) Surch as in Type O **2**. *Thick blue glazed paper.* Imperf×perf 14.

O15	O 2	2a. purple	£300	£250

(b) Optd "SERVICE POSTAGE" *in two lines as in Types* O **3/4** *and similar type.* Imperf×perf 14.

O16	O 3	2a. purple (G.)	£1000	£550
O17	O 4	4a. purple (G.)	£4250	£1300
O18	–	8a. purple (G.)	£4000	£4500
		a. Optd on complete stamp (inscr "FOREIGN BILL")	†	£16000

(c) Optd "SERVICE POSTAGE" *in semi-circle.* Wmk Large Crown. P 15½×15.

O19	O 6	½a. mauve/*lilac* (G.)	£450	95·00
		a. Opt double	£3250	

So-called reprints of Nos. O15 to O18 are known, but in these the surcharge differs entirely in the spacing, etc., of the words; they are more properly described as Government imitations. The imitations of No. O15 have surcharge in *black* or in *green*. No. O19 exists with reprinted overprint which has a full stop after "POSTAGE".

PRINTERS. The following stamps up to No. O108 were overprinted by De La Rue and thereafter Official stamps were printed or overprinted by the Security Printing Press at Nasik.

Service.
(O 7)

On H. S. M.
(O 8)

On H. S. M.
(O 9)

1867–73. *Optd with Type* O **7**. Wmk Elephant's Head, T **13**. P 14.

O20	11	½a. blue (Die I)	48·00	50
		w. Wmk inverted	†	£100
O21		½a. pale blue (Die I)	60·00	2·25
O22		½a. blue (Die II) (1873)	£160	80·00
O23		1a. brown	50·00	50
		w. Wmk inverted	†	£130
O24		1a. deep brown	55·00	2·25
O25		1a. chocolate	60·00	2·25
O26		2a. yellow	30·00	2·50
O27		2a. orange	7·00	2·25
O28	17	4a. pale green (Die I)	19·00	2·00
O29		4a. green (Die I)	3·25	1·50
O30	11	8a. rose (Die II) (1868)	3·25	1·50
O30*a*		8a. pale rose (Die II)	3·75	1·50
		aw. Wmk inverted	45·00	28·00

Prepared for use, but not issued.

O30*b*	18	6a.8p. slate	£350	

1874–82. *Optd with Type* O **8**.

(a) In black.

O31	11	½a. blue (Die II)	15·00	20
O32		1a. brown	19·00	20
O33		2a. yellow	70·00	42·00
O33*a*		2a. orange	60·00	27·00
		aw. Wmk inverted	†	£130
O34	17	4a. green (Die I)	23·00	3·00
O35	11	8a. rose (Die II)	9·00	7·00

(b) Optd in blue-black.

O36	11	½a. blue (Die II) (1877)	£400	48·00
O37		1a. brown (1882)	£700	£150

1883–99. Wmk Star, T **34**. *Optd with Type* O **9**. P 14.

O37*a*	40	3p. aniline carmine (1899)	20	10
O38	23	½a. deep blue-green	3·00	10
		a. Opt double	†	£1600
		b. Opt inverted	†	£1100
		w. Wmk inverted	†	£110
O39		½a. blue-green	2·75	10
O40	25	1a. brown-purple	4·00	50
		a. Opt inverted	£375	£475
		aw. Wmk inverted	†	£600
		b. Opt double	†	£1700
		c. Opt omitted (in horiz pair with normal)	£2000	
O41		1a. plum	1·25	10
O42	27	2a. pale blue	8·50	60
O43		2a. blue	9·50	60
O44	29	4a. olive-green	26·00	50
O44*a*		4a. slate-green	26·00	50
O45	31	8a. dull mauve	25·00	1·25
O46		8a. magenta	10·00	50
O47	37	1r. green and rose (1892)	50·00	4·75
O48		1r. green and carmine (1892)	22·00	40
O37*a*/48 *Set of* 7			65·00	2·00

1900. *Colours changed. Optd with Type* O **9**.

O49	23	½a. pale yellow-green	3·00	90
O49*a*		½a. yellow-green	4·75	50
		ab. Opt double	£1200	
O50	25	1a. carmine	4·50	10
		a. Opt inverted	†	£1700
		b. Opt double	†	£1800
O51	27	2a. pale violet	45·00	1·50
O52		2a. mauve	50·00	50
O49/52 *Set of* 3			48·00	1·00

1902–09. *Stamps of King Edward VII optd with Type* O **9**.

O54	41	3p. grey (1903)	2·50	1·00
O55		3p. slate-grey (1905)	2·50	1·00
		a. No stop after "M" (R. 6/10)	£250	£160
O56	42	½a. green	1·25	30
O57	43	1a. carmine	1·00	10
O58	44	2a. violet	4·50	40
O59		2a. mauve	3·25	10
		w. Wmk inverted	†	£160
O60	47	4a. olive	13·00	30
O61		4a. pale olive	13·00	30
O62	48	6a. olive-bistre (1909)	1·50	15
O63	49	8a. purple (*shades*)	6·00	1·00
O64		8a. claret	8·00	85
O65	51	1r. green and carmine (1905)	4·00	80
O54/65 *Set of* 8			29·00	3·00

1906. *New types. Optd with Type* O **9**.

O66	53	½a. green	1·25	10
		a. No stop after "M" (R. 6/10)	£150	70·00
O67	54	1a. carmine	2·00	10
		a. No stop after "M" (R. 6/10)	£225	£100
		b. Opt albino (in pair with normal)	£1400	

On H. S. M.
(O 9a)

1909. *Optd with Type* O **9a**.

O68	52	2r. carmine and yellow-brown	11·00	1·50
O68*a*		2r. rose-red and yellow-brown	11·00	1·50
O69		5r. ultramarine and violet	14·00	1·50
O70		10r. green and carmine	32·00	20·00
O70*a*		10r. green and scarlet	90·00	8·00
O71		15r. blue and olive-brown	80·00	42·00
O72		25r. brownish orange and blue	£170	70·00
O68/72 *Set of* 5			£275	£110

NINE

SERVICE (O 10) (14 mm) **SERVICE** (O 11) (21½ mm) **PIES** (O 12)

1912–13. *Stamps of King George V (wmk Single Star, T* **34***) optd with Type* O **10** *or* O **11** *(rupee values).*

No.	Type	Description	Unused	Used
O73	**55**	3p. grey	40	10
O73*a*		3p. pale grey	30	10
O74		3p. bluish grey	1·50	10
		a. Opt omitted (in pair with normal)		
O75		3p. slate	1·25	30
		a. "Rs" Flaw		
O75*b*		3p. violet-grey	3·50	30
O76	**56**	½a. light green	50	10
O77		½a. emerald	70	15
O78		½a. bright-green	70	15
		a. Opt double	£100	
O80	**57**	1a. rose-carmine	1·00	10
O81		1a. carmine	1·60	10
O82		1a. aniline carmine	1·60	10
		a. Opt double	†	£1000
O83	**59**	2a. purple	75	30
O83*a*		2a. reddish purple	75	25
O84		2a. deep mauve	75	30
O84*a*		2a. bright reddish violet	3·50	55
		ab. Stop under "s" in right value tablet (R. 4/16)	£120	
O85	**63**	4a. deep olive	1·00	10
O86		4a. olive-green	1·00	10
O87	**64**	6a. yellow-bistre	1·50	2·75
O88		6a. brown-ochre	4·50	4·25
O89	**65**	8a. deep magenta	2·75	1·25
O89*a*		8a. deep mauve	3·25	1·25
O90		8a. bright mauve	25·00	4·00
O91	**67**	1r. red-brown and deep blue-grn (1913)	4·00	1·75
O91*a*		1r. brown and green	3·00	1·40
O92		2r. rose-carmine & brown (1913)	4·75	8·00
O93		5r. ultramarine and violet (1913)	21·00	29·00
O94		10r. green and scarlet (1913)	65·00	60·00
O95		15r. blue and olive (1913)	£120	£130
O96		25r. orange and blue (1913)	£275	£190
O73/96 *Set of* 13			£450	£375

1921. *No. O80 surch with Type* O **12**.

No.	Type	Description	Unused	Used
O97	**57**	9p. on 1a. rose-carmine	1·25	75

1922. *No. 197 optd with Type* O **10**.

No.	Type	Description	Unused	Used
O98	**57**	1a. chocolate	2·50	10

ONE RUPEE

ONE RUPEE (O **13**) (O **14**)

1925. *Official stamps surcharged.*

(a) Issue of 1909, as Type O **13**.

No.	Type	Description	Unused	Used
O99	**52**	1r. on 15r. blue and olive	4·25	4·00
O100		1r. on 25r. chestnut and blue	20·00	75·00
O101		2r. on 10r. green and scarlet	3·75	4·25
O101*a*		2r. on 10r. green and carmine	£250	65·00

(b) Issue of 1912 with Type O **14**.

No.	Type	Description	Unused	Used
O102	**67**	1r. on 15r. blue and olive	19·00	75·00
O103		1r. on 25r. orange and blue	5·50	11·00
		a. Surch inverted	£1000	

(c) Issue of 1912, as Type O **13**.

No.	Type	Description	Unused	Used
O104	**67**	2r. on 10r. green and scarlet	£1100	

Examples of the above showing other surcharge errors are believed to be of clandestine origin.

ONE ANNA (O **15**) SERVICE ONE ANNA (O **16**)

1926. *No. O62 surch with Type* O **15**.

No.	Type	Description	Unused	Used
O105	**48**	1a. on 6a. olive-bistre	30	30

1926. *Postage stamps of 1911–22 (wmk Single Star), surch as Type* O **16**.

No.	Type	Description	Unused	Used
O106	**58**	1a. on 1½a. chocolate (A)	20	10
O107		1a. on 1½a. chocolate (B)	3·75	4·50
		a. Error. On 1a. chocolate (197)	£180	
O108	**61**	1a. on 2a.6p. ultramarine	60	80

The surcharge on No. O108 has no bars at top.

Examples of Nos. O106/7 with inverted or double surcharges are believed to be of clandestine origin.

SERVICE (O **17a**) (13½ mm) **SERVICE** (O **17b**) (13½ mm) **SERVICE** (O **18**) (19½ mm)

Two types of the 13½ mm "SERVICE" opt.
Type **17a**: Small loop and long tail to "R"
Type **17b**: Large loop and shorter tail to "R"

1926–31. *Stamps of King George V (wmk Multiple Star, T* **69***) optd with Types* O **17a** *or* O **18** *(rupee values).*

No.	Type	Description	Unused	Used
O109	**55**	3p. slate (1.10.29)	55	10
		aw. Wmk inverted	3·00	1·00
		b. Opt Type **17b**		
O110	**56**	½a. green (1931)	11·00	60
		aw. Wmk inverted	—	2·00
		b. Opt Type **17b**		
O111	**57**	1a. chocolate	15	10
		aw. Wmk inverted	2·50	60
		b. Opt Type **17b**		
		bw. Wmk inverted		
O112	**70**	2a. purple	30	10
		w. Wmk inverted	2·75	50
O113	**71**	4a. sage-green	50	20
		w. Wmk inverted	2·75	1·25
O115	**65**	8a. reddish purple	2·50	10
		w. Wmk inverted	80	30
O116	**66**	12a. claret (1927)	70	2·50
		w. Wmk inverted	—	4·25
O117	**67**	1r. chocolate and green (1930)	6·00	1·00
		w. Wmk inverted	5·50	3·25
O118		2r. carmine and orange (1930)	11·00	11·00
		w. Wmk inverted	—	20·00
O120		10r. green and scarlet (1931)	90·00	48·00
O109/20 *Set of* 10			£110	55·00

1930. *As No. O111, but optd as Type* O **10** *(14 mm).*

No.	Type	Description	Unused	Used
O125	**57**	1a. chocolate	—	6·50
		w. Wmk inverted	£110	7·50

1932–36. *Stamps of King George V (wmk Mult Star, T* **69***) optd with Type* O **17**.

No.	Type	Description	Unused	Used
O126	**79**	½a. green (1935)	1·75	10
O127	**80**	9p. deep green (*litho*)	30	15
		aw. Wmk inverted	—	6·00
O127*b*		9p. deep green (*typo*)	2·50	15
O127*c*	**81**	1a. chocolate (1936)	2·50	10
		cw. Wmk inverted	5·00	80
O128	**82**	1a.3p. mauve	30	10
		w. Wmk inverted	60	40
O129	**70**	2a. vermilion	2·00	2·50
		w. Wmk inverted		
O130	**59**	2a. vermilion (1935)	4·00	1·25
		aw. Wmk inverted	—	12·00
O130*b*		2a. verm (*small die*) (1936)	1·25	10
		bw. Wmk inverted		
O131	**61**	2a.6p. orange (22.4.32)	50	10
		w. Wmk inverted	2·75	1·00
O132	**63**	4a. sage-green (1935)	2·25	10
		w. Wmk inverted		
O133	**64**	6a. bistre (1936)	22·00	10·00
O126/33 *Set of* 9			30·00	11·00

1937–39. *Stamps of King George VI optd as Types* O **17** *or* O **18** *(rupee values).*

No.	Type	Description	Unused	Used
O135	**91**	½a. red-brown (1938)	17·00	1·00
O136		9p. green (1937)	19·00	1·00
O137		1a. carmine (1937)	3·50	10
O138	**100**	1r. grey and red-brown (5.38)	50	50
O139		2r. purple and brown (5.38)	1·75	2·50
		w. Wmk inverted	—	35·00
O140		5r. green and blue (10.38)	6·00	7·00
		w. Wmk inverted	—	60·00
O141		10r. purple and claret (1939)	14·00	10·00
		w. Wmk inverted	90·00	60·00
O135/41 *Set of* 7			55·00	20·00

SERVICE 1A (O **19**)

O **20**

1939 (May). *Stamp of King George V, surch with Type* O **19**.

No.	Type	Description	Unused	Used
O142	**82**	1a. on 1¼a. mauve	12·00	20
		w. Wmk inverted	—	5·50

(Des T. I. Archer)

1939 (1 June)**–42.** *Typo.* W **69**. P 14.

No.	Type	Description	Unused	Used
O143	O **20**	3p. slate	60	10
O144		½a. red-brown	8·00	10
O144*a*		½a. purple (1942)	30	10
O145		9p. green	30	10
O146		1a. carmine	30	10
O146*a*		1a.3p. yellow-brown (1941)	3·75	70
		aw. Wmk inverted		
O146*b*		1½a. dull violet (1942)	65	10
		bw. Wmk inverted		
O147		2a. vermilion	60	10
		w. Wmk inverted		
O148		2½a. bright violet	75	1·25
O149		4a. brown	60	10
O150		8a. slate-violet	90	30
O143/50 *Set of* 11			15·00	2·00

1948 (15 Aug). *First Anniv of Independence. Nos. 305/8 optd as Type* O **17**.

No.	Type	Description	Unused	Used
O150*a*	**305**	1½a. brown	48·00	40·00
O150*b*		3½a. violet	£1100	£700
O150*c*		12a. grey-green	£3500	£2250
O150*d*	**306**	10r. purple-brown and lake	£25000	

Nos. O150*a/d* were only issued to the Governor-General's Secretariat.

O **21** Asokan Capital

O **22**

(Des T.I. Archer)

1950 (2 Jan)**–51.** *Typo* (O **21**) *or litho* (O **22**). W **69**. P 14.

No.	Type	Description	Unused	Used
O151	O **21**	3p. slate-violet (1.7.50)	15	10
O152		6p. purple-brown (1.7.50)	30	10
O153		9p. green (1.7.50)	1·25	10
O154		1a. turquoise (1.7.50)	1·25	10
O155		2a. carmine (1.7.50)	1·75	10
		w. Wmk inverted		
O156		3a. red-orange (1.7.50)	4·25	2·50
O157		4a. lake (1.7.50)	6·00	20
O158		4a. ultramarine (1.10.51)	50	10
O159		6a. bright violet (1.7.50)	4·00	2·00
O160		8a. red-brown (1.7.50)	2·00	10
		w. Wmk inverted	17·00	
O161	O **22**	1r. violet	3·00	10
		w. Wmk inverted		
O162		2r. rose-carmine	1·00	1·00
O163		5r. bluish green	2·00	2·00
O164		10r. reddish brown	3·50	24·00
O151/64 *Set of* 14			28·00	29·00

1957 (1 Apr)**–58.** *Values in naye paise. Typo (t) or litho (l).* W **69**. P 14.

No.	Type	Description	Unused	Used
O165	O **21**	1n.p. slate (*l*)	1·00	10
		a. Slate-black (l)	1·00	10
		b. Greenish slate (t)	10	10
		w. Wmk inverted	4·00	1·25
O166		2n.p. blackish violet (*t*)	10	10
		w. Wmk inverted		
O167		3n.p. chocolate (*t*)	20	10
O168		5n.p. green (*l*)	25	10
		a. Deep emerald (t)	1·50	10
O169		6n.p. turquoise-blue (*t*)	40	10
O170		13n.p. scarlet (*t*)	40	10
O171		15n.p. reddish violet (*l*) (6.58)	2·75	2·50
		a. Reddish violet (t)	3·00	2·75
O172		20n.p. red (*l*)	40	1·25
		a. Vermilion (t)	2·50	1·25
		aw. Wmk inverted		
O173		25n.p. violet-blue (*l*)	40	20
		a. Ultramarine (t)	2·75	30
O174		50n.p. red-brown (*l*)	1·75	10
		a. Reddish brown (t)	3·00	1·25
O165/74 *Set of* 10			6·00	3·75

1958–71. *As Nos. O165/74a and O161/4 but* W **374** *(upright). Litho (l) or typo (t).* P 14.

No.	Type	Description	Unused	Used
O175	O **21**	1n.p. slate-black (*t*) (1.59)	10	10
O176		2n.p. blackish violet (*t*) (1.59)	10	10
O177		3n.p. chocolate (*t*) (11.58)	10	10
		w. Wmk inverted	4·00	
O178		5n.p. deep emerald (*t*) (11.58)	10	10
O179		6n.p. turquoise-blue (*t*) (5.59)	10	10
O180		10n.p. dp grey-green (*l*) (1963)	50	50
		a. Dp grey-green (t) (1966?)	1·50	1·50
O181		13n.p. scarlet (*t*) (1963)	1·00	2·75
O182		15n.p. deep violet (*t*) (11.58)	10	10
		a. Light reddish violet (t) (1961)	2·75	10
O183		20n.p. vermilion (*t*) (5.59)	70	10
		a. Red (t) (1966?)	6·50	80
O184		25n.p. ultramarine (*t*) (7.59)	10	10
O185		50n.p. reddish brown (*t*) (6.59)	70	10
		a. Chestnut (l) (1966?)	7·50	1·50
O186	O **22**	1r. reddish violet (*l*) (2.59)	15	10
O187		2r. rose-carmine (*l*) (1960)	25	10
		a. Wmk sideways*. *Pale rose-carmine (l) (1969?)*	75	75
		aw. Wmk Capitals to right		
O188		5r. slate-green (*l*) (7.59)	40	60
		a. Wmk sideways*. *Deep grey-green (l) (1969?)*	90	90
O189		10r. brown-lake (*l*) (7.59)	90	1·00
		a. Wmk sideways* (*l*) (1971)	3·25	3·25
		ab. Printed on the gummed side	38·00	
		aw. Wmk capitals to right	3·25	
O175/89 *Set of* 15			4·50	5·25

*The normal sideways watermark shows the head of the capitals pointing left, *as seen from the back of the stamp.*

O **23**

1967 (20 Mar)**–73.** *Photo.* W **374** (sideways). P 15×14.

No.	Type	Description	Unused	Used
O190	O **23**	2p. violet (1973?)	2·00	1·25
O191		5p. green (1973?)	2·00	10
O192		10p. myrtle-green (2.7.73)	2·25	25
O193		15p. plum (2.7.73)	2·75	55
O194		20p. red (2.7.73)	8·00	6·50
O195		30p. ultramarine (1973)	8·00	1·25
O196		50p. chestnut (2.7.73)	4·25	3·00
O197		1r. dull purple (20.3.67)	85	10
		a. Deep slate-purple (1969)	2·00	10
O190/7 *Set of* 8			27·00	11·50

1967 (15 Nov)**–74.** *Wmk Large Star and* "INDIA GOVT" *in sheet*. Photo.* P 15×14. No gum.

No.	Type	Description	Unused	Used
O200	O **23**	2p. violet	10	1·00
O201		3p. chocolate	40	1·25
O202		5p. green	10	10
		a. Yellowish green (1969)	10	10
		w. Wmk reversed	4·00	
O203		6p. turquoise-blue	1·25	1·50
O204		10p. myrtle-green	10	30
		a. Bronze-green (1969)	1·00	1·00
		w. Wmk reversed	4·00	
O205		15p. plum	10	30
		w. Wmk reversed		
O206		20p. red	10	30
		w. Wmk reversed	4·00	
O207		25p. carmine-red (1974?)	15·00	3·75
		w. Wmk reversed	15·00	
O208		30p. ultramarine	10	60
O209		50p. chestnut	10	60
		w. Wmk reversed	4·50	
O200/9 *Set of* 10			15·00	8·75

*The arrangement of this watermark in the sheet results in the words and the star appearing upright, inverted or sideways.

INDIA USED ABROAD

In the years following 1858 the influence of the Indian Empire, political, military and economic, extended beyond its borders into neighbouring states, the Arabian Gulf, East Africa and the Far East. Such influence often led to the establishment of Indian civil post offices in the countries concerned where unoverprinted stamps of India were used.

Such offices operated in the following countries. An * indicates that details will be found under that heading elsewhere in the catalogue.

ADEN*

Unoverprinted stamps of India used from 1854 until 1937.

BAHRAIN*

Unoverprinted stamps of India used from 1884 until 1933.

BRITISH EAST AFRICA (KENYA, UGANDA AND TANGANYIKA)*

Unoverprinted stamps of India used during August and September 1890.

FRENCH INDIAN SETTLEMENTS

The first Indian post office, at Chandernagore, was open in 1784 to be followed by offices in the other four Settlements. By an agreement with the French, dating from 1814, these offices handled mail destined for British India, Great Britain, the British Empire and most other foreign destinations except France and the French colonies. In later years the system was expanded by a number of sub-offices and it continued to operate until the French territories were absorbed into India on 2 May 1950 (Chandernagore) or 1 November 1954.

Chandernagore. Opened 1784. Used numeral cancellations "B86" or "86".
- Sub-offices:
  - Gondalpara (opened 1906)
  - Lakhiganj (opened 1909)
  - Temata (opened 1891)

Karikal. Opened 1794. Used numeral cancellations in "C147", "147" or "6/M-21".
- Sub-offices:
  - Ambagarattur (opened 1904)
  - Kottuchari (opened 1901)
  - Nedungaon (opened 1903)
  - Puraiyar Road (opened 1901)
  - Settur (opened 1905)
  - Tirumalrayapatnam (opened 1875) – used numeral cancellation "6/M-21/1"
  - Tiramilur (opened 1898)

Mahe. Opened 1795. Used numeral cancellations "C192" or "9/M-14".

Pondicherry. Opened 1787. Used numeral cancellations "C111", "111" (also used elsewhere), "6/M-19" (also used elsewhere) or "6/M-20".
- Sub-offices:
  - Ariyankuppam (opened 1904)
  - Bahoor (opened 1885)
  - Mudaliarpet (opened 1897)
  - Muthialpet (opened 1885)
  - Pondicherry Bazaar (opened 1902)
  - Pondicherry Railway Station (opened 1895)
  - Olugarai (opened 1907)
  - Vallinur (opened 1875) – used numeral cancellation "M-19/1"

Yanam. Opened 1876. Used numeral cancellation "5/M-4".

IRAN

The British East India Company was active in the Arabian Gulf from the early years of the 17th century with their first factory (trading centre) being established at Jask in 1619. After 1853 this commercial presence was converted into a political arm of the Indian Government culminating in the appointment of a Political Resident to Bushire in 1862.

The first Indian post office in Iran (Persia) opened at Bushire on 1 May 1864 with monthly mail services operating to the Resident there and to the British Legation at Tehran. Further offices in the other Gulf ports followed, but, unless otherwise stated below, all were closed on 1 April 1923.

Details of the stamps known used from each post office are taken with permission, from the listing published by the Iran Philatelic Study Circle.

PERSIAN EXPEDITIONARY FORCE

Following the occupation of Herat, on the Afghan border, by Persia, Britain declared war on 1 Nov 1856 and the Indian Expeditionary Force took Bushire (occupied 12 Dec 1856 to 2 Oct 1857) and Mohammera (occupied 26 Mar 1857 to 16 May 1858) Kharg Island was used as a supply base (Dec 1856 to Feb 1858).

The expedition was accompanied by Field Post Offices using contemporary Indian stamps cancelled "131" in a diamond of lines. It should be noted that forgeries of this cancellation are known and the number was subsequently assigned to Billimoria in India.

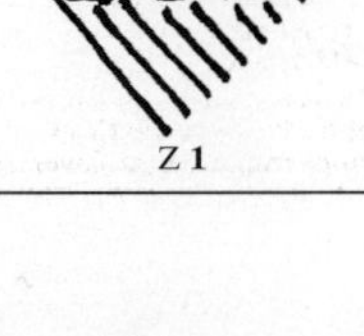

Z 1

Stamps of India cancelled with Type **Z1**.

1854–55. (Nos. 2/26).

Z1	½a. blue (Die I)	
Z2	1a. red (Die I)	
Z3	4a. blue and red (Head die III, frame die II)	

1854. (No. 31).

Z4	2a. green	

1856–64. (No. 37).

Z5	½a. blue (Die I)	

ABADAN

An island at the mouth of the Shatt-el-Arab, the Anglo-Persian Oil Co. established an oil pipeline terminus there in 1909. An Indian post office was opened in 1917 and closed in 1923.

Z 2

Z 3

Postmark type	*Approx period of use*
Z2	1917–23
Z3	1918–22

1911–22. (Nos. 151/91).

Z6	3p. grey	15·00
Z7	½a. green	10·00
Z8	1a. carmine	11·00
Z9	1½a. chocolate (Type A)	20·00
Z10	2a. purple	12·00
Z11	2a.6p. ultramarine (1913)	10·00
Z12	3a. orange	12·00
Z13	4a. olive-green	15·00
Z14	6a. brown-ochre	15·00
Z15	8a. mauve	12·00
Z16	12a. carmine-lake	18·00
Z17	1r. brown and green	15·00
Z18	2r. carmine and brown	20·00
Z19	5r. ultramarine and violet	25·00
Z20	10r. green and scarlet	35·00

AHWAZ

A city in south-west Iran, on the Karun River. An Indian post office was opened in 1915 and closed in 1923.

Z 4 25 mm large date

Z 5

Postmark type		*Approx period of use*
Z4	inscribed 'EXPERIMENTAL P.O./B504'	1915
Z2	inscribed "AHWAZ"	1915–21
Z5		1916–23

Stamps of India cancelled at Ahwaz

1911–22. (Nos. 151/91).

Z21	3p. grey	25·00
Z22	½a. green	10·00
Z23	1a. carmine	10·00
Z25	2a. purple	15·00
Z26	2a.6p. ultramarine (1913)	12·00
Z27	3a. orange	14·00
Z28	4a. olive-green	20·00
Z30	8a. mauve	25·00
Z32	1r. brown and green	35·00

OFFICIAL STAMPS

1903–09. (Nos. O54/65).

Z36	4a. olive	

1906. (Nos. O66/7).

Z38	½a. green	

1912–13. (Nos. O73/96).

Z43	2a. purple	

BANDAR ABBAS

Situated on the Strait of Hormuz, the British East India Company established a factory there in 1622. When a postal service between Bombay and Basra was established in 1862, Bandar Abbas was one of the regular ports of call but the Indian post office was not opened until 1 April 1867. It closed in 1923.

Z 6

Z 7

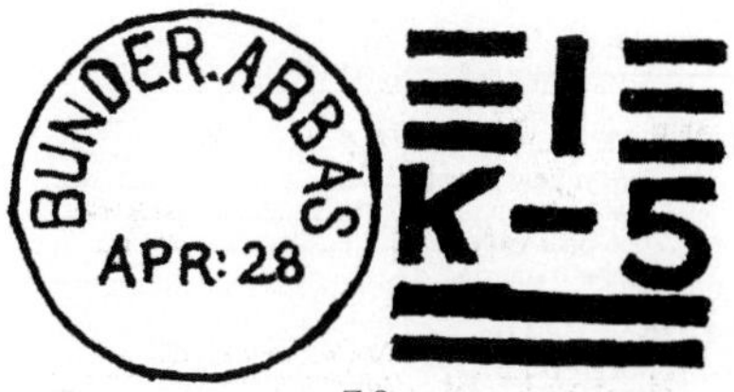

Z 8

Z 9 Nine lines in obliterator

Z 10 Eight lines in obliterator

Z 11

Z 12 Four thin lines in corners

Z 13

Postmark type		*Approx period of use*
Z6		1870
Z7		1871–1873
Z8		1874–1888
Z9	(inscr "BANDARABAS")	
Z10	(inscr "BANDAR-ABAS")	
Z11		1884
Z12	(inscr "BANDARABAS")	1886–1892
Z12	(inscr "BANDAR-ABAS")	1892–1893
Z4	(inscr "BANDARABAS/PAR")	
Z13		1907–1922
Z4*a*	(inscr "BANDAR-ABAS")	1905–1920

Stamps of India cancelled at Bandar Abbas

1865. (Nos. 54/65).
Z46 ½a. blue 15·00
Z48 1a. brown 15·00
Z49 2a. orange 30·00

1866–78. (Nos. 69/72).
Z50 4a. blue-green (Die II) 40·00

1868–73. (Nos. 73/6).
Z51 8a. rose (Die II) 40·00
Z52 ½a. blue (Die II) 8·00

1882–90. (Nos. 84/101).
Z53 ½a. blue-green 5·00
Z55 1a. plum 8·00
Z57 2a. blue 12·00
Z58 3a. orange 20·00
Z59 4a. olive-green 15·00
Z60 4a.6p. yellow-green 25·00
Z63 1r. slate 35·00

1892–97. (Nos. 103/6).
Z64 2a.6p. yellow-green 10·00

1899. (No. 111).
Z66 3p. aniline carmine 15·00

1900. (Nos. 112/8).
Z68 ½a. yellow-green 8·00
Z69 1a. carmine 8·00
Z70 2a. pale violet 14·00
Z71 2a. 6 p. ultramarine 11·00

1902–11. (Nos. 119/47).
Z72 3p. grey 7·00
Z73 ½a. green 5·00
Z74 1a. carmine 7·00
Z75 2a. mauve 6·00
Z76 2a.6p. ultramarine 5·00
Z78 4a. olive 15·00
Z82 1r. green and carmine 20·00
Z83 2r. carmine and yellow-brown 30·00

1906. (Nos. 149/50).
Z84 ½a. green 6·00
Z85 1a. carmine 7·00

1911–22. (Nos. 151/91).
Z86 3p. grey 9·00
Z87 ½a. green 5·00
Z88 1a. carmine 5·00
Z89 1½a. chocolate (Type A) 12·00
Z91 2a. purple 7·00
Z92 2a.6p. ultramarine (1912) 15·00
Z93 2a.6p. ultramarine (1913) 5·00
Z94 3a. orange 12·00
Z95 4a. olive-green 10·00
Z96 6a. brown-ochre 15·00

OFFICIAL STAMPS

1883–99. (Nos. O37a/48).
Z102 4a. olive-green 25·00

1900. (Nos. O49/52).
Z105 2a. mauve 25·00

1902–09. (Nos. O54/65).
Z108 1a. carmine 15·00
Z109 2a. mauve 15·00

1906. (Nos. O66/7).
Z112 1a. carmine 15·00

1912–13. (Nos. O73/96).
Z113 3p. grey 20·00
Z114 ½a. green 15·00
Z115 1a. carmine 12·00

1921. (No. O97).
Z118 9p. on 1a. rose-carmine 30·00

BUSHIRE

An Iranian Gulf port, the British East India Company's factory was transferred there from Bandar Abbas in 1762 and a political agency established. An Indian postal agency was established in 1857 and it was on the regular steamer service operated between Bombay and Basra in 1862. The Indian post office was opened on 1 May 1864 and closed in 1923.

Z 14 Three thick lines in corners

Z 15 (19 mm)

Z 16

Postmark type		*Approx period of use*
Z1	("308" in diamond of bars)	1865–70
Z7	("26")	1870–74
Z8	(inscr "BASHIR"/K-5)	1878–80
Z10	(inscr "BUSHIRE")	1880–82
Z11	(inscr "BUSHIRE")	1882–85
Z11	(c.d.s. only, inscr PAR/BUSHIRE)	?
Z11	(c.d.s. only, inscr DEP/BUSHIRE)	?
Z12	(inscr "BUSHIRE")	1884–99
Z13	(inscr "BUSHIRE")	1885–1904
Z15		1887–1892
Z14	(inscr "BUSHIRF")	1889–1892
Z16		1892–97
Z16		1897–1923
Z15	(inscr BUSHIRE/REG)	1892–1915
Z4	(inscr BUSHIRE)	1907–1915
Z4	(inscr BUSHIRE/REG)	1902–1921

Stamps of India cancelled at Bushire

1865. (Nos. 54/65).
Z119 ½a. blue 12·00
Z121 1a. brown 10·00
Z122 2a. orange 12·00
Z123 4a. green 75·00

1866–78. (Nos. 69/72).
Z125 4a. green (Die I) 25·00
Z126 4a. green (Die II) 12·00
Z127 6a.8p. slate 60·00

1868–73. (Nos. 73/6).
Z128 8a. rose (Die II) 25·00
Z129 ½a. blue (Die II) 5·00

1874–76. (Nos. 77/82).
Z130 1r. slate 75·00
Z131 6a. brown 20·00
Z132 12a. Venetian red 40·00

1882–90. (Nos. 84/101).
Z133 ½a. blue-green 3·00
Z135 1a. brown-purple 3·00
Z136 1½a. sepia 10·00
Z137 2a. blue 5·00
Z138 3a. orange 12·00
Z138*a* 3a. brown-orange 6·00
Z139 4a. olive-green 5·00
Z140 4a.6p. yellow-green 9·00
Z141 8a. magenta 7·00
Z142 12a. purple/*red* 20·00
Z143 1r. slate 20·00

1891. (No. 102).
Z144 2½a. on 4a.6p. yellow-green 8·00

1892–95. (Nos. 103/9).
Z145 2a.6p. yellow-green 4·00
Z146 1r. green and rose 15·00
Z147 2r. carmine and yellow-brown 40·00

1898. (No. 110).
Z148 ¼ on ½a. blue-green 15·00

1899. (No. 111).
Z149 3p. aniline carmine 8·00

1900. (Nos. 112/18).
Z151 ½a. yellow-green 5·00
Z152 1a. carmine 7·00
Z153 2a. pale violet 8·00
Z154 2a.6p. ultramarine 6·00

1902–11. (Nos. 119/47).
Z155 3p. grey 8·00
Z156 ½a. green 6·00
Z157 1a. carmine 6·00
Z158 2a. mauve 6·00
Z159 2a.6p. ultramarine 3·00
Z160 3a. orange-brown 10·00
Z161 4a. olive 9·00
Z162 6a. maize 12·00
Z163 8a. purple 9·00
Z165 1r. green and carmine 20·00
Z170 15r. blue and olive-brown 75·00

1905. (No. 148).
Z171 ¼ on ½a. 12·00

1906. (Nos. 149/50).
Z172 ½a. green 4·00
Z173 1a. carmine 4·00

1911–22. (Nos. 151/91).
Z174 3p. grey 8·00
Z175 ½a. green 3·00
Z176 1a. carmine 3·00
Z177 1½a. chocolate (Type A) 12·00
Z178 1½a. chocolate (Type B) 25·00
Z179 2a. purple 6·00
Z180 2a.6p. ultramarine (1912) 15·00
Z181 2a.6p. ultramarine (1913) 4·00
Z182 3a. orange 5·00
Z183 4a. olive-green 10·00
Z184 6a. brown-ochre 12·00
Z185 8a. mauve 15·00
Z186 12a. carmine-lake 20·00
Z187 1r. brown and green 18·00
Z191 15r. blue and olive 75·00

1921. (Nos. 192/4).
Z192 9p. on 1a. rose-carmine 12·00

OFFICIAL STAMPS

1867–73. (Nos. O20/30a).
Z193 ½a. blue (Die I) 20·00
Z194 1a. brown 20·00
Z195 8a. rose 15·00

1874–82. (Nos. O31/35).
Z196 ½a. blue 20·00
Z198 2a. orange 15·00
Z199 4a. green 15·00

1883–99. (Nos. O37a/48).
Z202 ½a. blue-green 12·00
Z203 1a. plum 12·00
Z204 2a. blue 15·00
Z205 4a. olive-green 15·00
Z207 1r. green and carmine 30·00

1900. (Nos. O49/52).
Z209 1a. carmine 15·00
Z210 2a. mauve 20·00

1902–09. (Nos. O54/65).
Z212 ½a. green 12·00
Z213 1a. carmine 8·00
Z214 2a. mauve 10·00
Z215 4a. olive 15·00

1906. (Nos. O66/67).
Z218 ½a. green 12·00
Z219 1a. carmine 10·00

1912–13. (Nos. O73/96).
Z221 ½a. green 10·00
Z222 1a. carmine 6·00
Z224 2a. purple 10·00

BUSHIRE CAMP

A sub-post office was opened in 1921 for troops of the South West Cordon Force. It closed in 1923.

Postmark type		*Approx period of use*
Z3	(inscr "BUSHIRE CAMP")	1921–22

Stamps of India cancelled at Bushire Camp

1911–22. (Nos. 151/91).
Z229 1a. carmine
Z232 2a.6p. ultramarine (1913)
Z233 3a. orange
Z235 6a. brown-ochre

OFFICIAL STAMPS

1902. (Nos. O54/65).
Z237 3p. grey

1912–13. (Nos. O73/96).
Z239 3p. grey
Z240 ½a. green
Z242 2a. mauve

CHAHBAR

A port on the Gulf of Oman, the Indian post office was opened on 20 August 1913 and closed on 31 March 1923.

Postmark type		*Approx period of use*
Z3	(inscr "CHAHBAR/B.O./PERSIAN GULF")	1914–1923

Stamps of India cancelled at Chahbar

1902–11. (Nos. 119/47).
Z244 3p. grey

1906. (Nos. 149/50).
Z247 1a. carmine

1911–22. (Nos. 151/91).
Z249 ½a. green
Z250 1a. carmine
Z252 2a. mauve

DUZDAB

A small town near the frontier with India, an Indian exchange post office was opened in 1921 and closed in 1925.

HENJAM

An island in the Straits of Hormuz, it was for a time a British Naval Station and telegraph relay station. The Indian post office opened on 21 June 1913 and closed in 1923.

Postmark type		*Approx period of use*
Z3	(Inscr "HENJAM/B.O./PERSIAN GULF")	1914–1922

Stamps of India cancelled at Henjam

1906. (Nos. 149/50).

Z254	½a. green	

1911–22. (Nos. 151/91).

Z256	3p. grey	55·00
Z257	½a. green	30·00
Z258	1a. carmine	50·00
Z260	2a. purple	55·00
Z261	2a.6p. ultramarine (1913)	60·00

OFFICIAL STAMPS

1912–13. (Nos. O73/96).

Z268	4a. olive-green	£100

JASK

A port on the Gulf of Oman and site of the British East India Company's first factory in 1619, the Indian post office opened on 1 September 1880 and closed on 20 March 1923.

Z **17** As Z9/10 but without obliterator

Postmark type		*Approx period of use*
Z17		1884–1888
Z14	(inscr JASK)	1889–1812
Z3	(inscr JASK/B.O.PERSIAN GULF)	1914–1920

Stamps of India cancelled at Jask

1865. (Nos. 54/65).

Z270	½a. blue	25·00

1866–78. (Nos. 69/72).

Z273	4a. green	50·00

1882–90. (Nos. 84/101).

Z276	½a. blue-green	12·00
Z278	1a. brown-purple	15·00
Z281	3a. orange	20·00
Z285	12a. purple/*red*	30·00

1891. (No. 102).

Z282	2½a. on 4a.6p. yellow-green	25·00

1892–97. (Nos. 103/09).

Z287	2a.6p. yellow-green	12·00

1898. (No. 110).

Z289	¼ on ½a. blue-green	30·00

1899. (No. 111).

Z290	3p. aniline-carmine	20·00

1900. (Nos. 112/18).

Z294	2a.6p. ultramarine	15·00

1902–11. (Nos. 119/47).

Z296	½a. green	15·00
Z297	1a. carmine	15·00
Z298	2a. mauve	15·00
Z299	2a.6p. ultramarine	10·00

1906–07. (Nos. 149/50).

Z303	½a. green	10·00
Z304	1a. carmine	10·00

1911–22. (Nos. 151/91).

Z306	½a. green	20·00
Z307	1a. carmine	15·00
Z310	2a. purple	15·00
Z311	2a.6p. ultramarine (1913)	20·00
Z315	8a. mauve	40·00
Z316	12a. carmine lake	40·00

OFFICIAL STAMPS

1902–09. (Nos. O54/69).

Z320	2a. mauve	25·00

1906. (Nos. O66/7).

Z322	½a. green	15·00
Z323	1a. carmine	20·00

KUH-MALIK-SIAH-ZIARAT

A few miles north of Duzdab, where the frontiers of Iran, India and Afghanistan meet, an Indian exchange post office was open by January 1906. It closed in mid–1924.

LINGA

A Persian Gulf port to the west of Bandar Abbas, the Indian post office there was opened on 1 April 1867. Linga was added to the regular ports of call of the Bombay–Basra steamer service in 1870. The post office closed in 1923.

Z **18** 25 mm small date

Postmark type		*Approx period of use*
Z7	(numeral "21")	1872–1875
Z8	(2/k-5)	1876–1880
Z11	(inscr LINGA)	1885
Z14	(inscr LINGA)	1882–1905
Z12	(inscr LINGA)	1900–1902
Z13	(inscr LINGA)	1905–1922
Z18		
Z2	(inscr LINGA)	1920–1923
Z12	(inscr LINGA)	1900–1902

Stamps of India cancelled at Linga.

1865. (Nos. 54/65).

Z327	½a. blue	15·00
Z328	1a. brown	15·00
Z329	2a. orange	25·00

1866–78. (Nos. 69/72).

Z330	4a. green (Die I)	35·00
Z331	4a. green (Die II)	30·00

1868–76. (Nos. 73/82).

Z332	8a. rose	40·00
Z333	½a. blue (Die II)	8·00
Z334	6a. pale brown	25·00
Z335	12a. Venetian red	50·00

1882–90. (Nos. 84/101).

Z336	½a. blue-green	4·00
Z338	1a. plum	6·00
Z340	2a. blue	7·00
Z341	3a. orange	9·00
Z342	4a. olive-green	12·00
Z343	4a.6p. yellow-green	15·00
Z344	8a. mauve	15·00
Z345	12a. purple-red	25·00
Z346	1r. slate	25·00

1891. (No. 102).

Z347	2½a. on 4a.6p. yellow-green	15·00

1892–97. (Nos. 103/9).

Z348	2a.6p. yellow-green	7·00
Z349	1r. green and rose	35·00
Z351	3r. brown and green	65·00

1899. (No. 111).

Z352	3p. aniline carmine	8·00

1900–02. (Nos. 112/18).

Z353	3p. grey	25·00
Z354	½a. yellow-green	6·00
Z355	1a. carmine	10·00
Z356	2a. mauve	11·00
Z357	2a.6p. ultramarine	10·00

1902–11. (Nos. 119/47).

Z358	3p. grey	10·00
Z359	½a. green	5·00
Z360	1a. carmine	6·00
Z361	2a. mauve	6·00
Z362	2a.6p. ultramarine	5·00
Z363	3a. orange-brown	10·00
Z364	4a. olive	10·00
Z368	1r. green and carmine	20·00
Z369	2r. carmine and yellow-brown	35·00

1906. (Nos. 149/50).

Z372	½a. green	6·00
Z373	1a. carmine	8·00

1911–22. (Nos. 151/91).

Z374	3p. grey	12·00
Z375	½a. green	4·00
Z376	1a. carmine	5·00
Z377	1½a. chocolate (Type A)	12·00
Z378	2a. purple	7·00
Z379	2a.6p. ultramarine (1912)	15·00
Z380	2a.6p. ultramarine (1913)	6·00
Z381	3a. orange	8·00
Z382	4a. olive-green	10·00
Z383	6a. brown-ochre	12·00

OFFICIAL STAMPS

1883–99. (Nos. O37a/48).

Z390	1a. plum	20·00

1906. (Nos. O66/7).

Z399	1a. carmine	20·00

1912–13. (Nos. O73/96).

Z401	½a. green	15·00
Z402	1a. carmine	15·00
Z403	2a. purple	20·00

MAIDAN-I-NAPHTUN

The site of the original oil find in Iran in the early part of the 20th century, an Indian post office was opened during World War 1. It was closed in 1923.

Z **19**

Postmark type		*Approx period of use*
Z18		1917–1920
Z3	(inscr "MAIDAN-I-NAPHTUN/REG")	1922–1923

Stamps of India cancelled at Maidan-i-Naphtun

1911–22. (Nos. 151/91).

Z406	½a. green	60·00
Z407	1a. carmine	70·00
Z409	2a. purple	80·00
Z410	2½a. ultramarine (1913)	75·00
Z411	3a. orange	85·00

MIRJAWA

On the border with India (now Pakistan), an Indian post office was opened in 1921 to service the needs of a railway construction project. It was closed by 1931.

Postmark type		*Approx period of use*
Z3	(inscr "MIRJAWA")	1926

Stamps of India cancelled at Mirjawa

1911–22. (Nos. 151/91).

Z418	2½a. ultramarine	
Z422	8a. mauve	

OFFICIAL STAMPS

1912–13. (Nos. O73/96).

Z428	1a. carmine	
Z429	2a. purple	

1922. (No. O98).

Z433	1a. chocolate	

MOHAMMERA

Now known as Khorramshahr, Mohammerah was the chief port of Iran, on the Shatt-el-Arab. The first Indian post office was opened in 1892 and closed in 1923.

Postmark type		*Approx period of use*
Z16	(inscr "MOHAMMERA")	1894–1900
Z16	(inscr "MOHAMMERAH")	1896–1904
Z4	(inscr "MOHAMMERA")	1904–1918
Z4*a*	(inscr "MOHAMMERA")	1910–1918
Z13	(inscr "MOHAMMERAH")	1905–1923
Z3	(inscr "MOHAMMERAH")	1919–1923

Stamps of India cancelled at Mohammera

1882–90. (Nos. 84/101).

Z434	½a. blue-green	7·00
Z435	1a. brown-purple	10·00
Z437	2a. blue	12·00
Z438	3a. brown-orange	20·00
Z439	1a. olive-green	20·00

1892–97. (Nos. 103/09).

Z440	2a.6p. yellow-green	7·00
Z441	1r. green and carmine	30·00
Z443	3r. brown and green	75·00

1899. (No. 111).

Z444	3p. aniline carmine	15·00

1900. (Nos. 112/18).

Z445	½a. yellow-green	8·00
Z446	1a. carmine	10·00
Z447	2a. pale violet	10·00
Z448	2a.6p. ultramarine	11·00

1902–11. (Nos. 119/47).

Z449	3p. grey	10·00
Z450	½a. green	6·00
Z451	1a. carmine	7·00
Z452	2a. mauve	7·00
Z453	2a.6p. ultramarine	4·00
Z454	3a. orange-brown	15·00
Z455	4a. olive	12·00
Z456	6a. olive-bistre	20·00
Z457	8a. purple	20·00
Z458	1r. green and carmine	25·00

1905. (No. 148).

Z459	¼ on ½a. green	10·00

1906. (Nos. 149/50).

Z460	½a. green	6·00
Z461	1a. carmine	6·00

1911–22. (Nos. 151/91).

Z462	3p. grey	10·00
Z463	½a. green	3·00
Z464	1a. carmine	3·00
Z465	1½a. chocolate (Type A)	10·00
Z466	2a. purple	5·00
Z467	2a.6p. ultramarine (1912)	12·00
Z468	2a.6p. ultramarine (1913)	4·00
Z469	3a. orange	6·00
Z470	4a. olive-green	7·00
Z471	6a. yellow-bistre	20·00
Z472	8a. mauve	12·00
Z474	1r. brown and green	12·00
Z475	2r. carmine and brown	25·00

1922–26. (Nos. 197/200).

Z481	1a. chocolate	9·00

OFFICIAL STAMPS

1883–99. (Nos. O37a/48).

Z482	1a. brown-purple	20·00

1902–09. (Nos. O54/65).

Z485	1a. carmine	
Z486	2a. mauve	
Z488	6a. olive-bistre	

1906. (Nos. O66/67).

Z490	½a. green	12·00

1912–13. (Nos. O73/96).

Z493	½a. green	12·00
Z494	1a. carmine	10·00
Z495	2a. purple	15·00

IRAQ*

Unoverprinted stamps of India used from 1868 until 1918.

KUWAIT*

Unoverprinted stamps of India used from 1904 until 1923.

MALAYA (STRAITS SETTLEMENTS)*

Unoverprinted stamps of India used from 1854 until 1867.

MUSCAT*

Unoverprinted stamps of India used from 1864 until 1947.

NEPAL

A post office was opened in the British Residency at Kathmandu in 1816 following the end of the Gurkha War. Stamps of India were used from 1854, initially with "B137", "137" or "C-37" numeral cancellations. The Residency Post Office continued to provide the overseas mail service after Nepal introduced its own issues in 1881.

In 1920 the Residency Post Office became the British Legation Post Office. On the independence of India in 1947 the service was transferred to the Indian Embassy and continued to function until 1965.

PORTUGUESE INDIA

A British post office was open in Damaun by 1823 and Indian stamps were used there until November 1883, some with "13" and "3/B-19" numeral cancellations.

No other British post offices were opened in the Portuguese territories, but from 1854 Indian stamps were sold by the local post offices. Between 1871 and 1877 mail intended for, or passing through, British India required combined franking of India and Portuguese India issues. After 1877 the two postal administrations accepted the validity of each other's stamps.

SOMALILAND PROTECTORATE*

Unoverprinted stamps of India used from 1887 until 1903.

TIBET

The first Indian post office in Tibet accompanied the Tibetan Frontier Commission in 1903. The Younghusband Military Expedition to Lhasa in the following year operated a number of Field Post Offices which were replaced by civil post offices at Gartok (opened 23 September 1906), Gyantse (opened March 1905), Pharijong (opened 1905) and Yatung (opened 1905). All Indian post offices in Tibet closed on 1 April 1955 except Gartok which, it is believed, did not operate after 1943. A temporary post office, C-622, operated at Gyantse between July 1954 and August 1955 following a flood disaster.

TRUCIAL STATES

Unoverprinted stamps of India used at Dubai from 19 August 1909 until 1947.

ZANZIBAR*

Unoverprinted stamps of India used from 1875 until 1895.

CHINA EXPEDITIONARY FORCE

Following the outbreak of the Boxer Rising in North China the Peking Legations were besieged by the rebels in June 1900. An international force, including an Indian Army division, was assembled for their relief. The Legations were relieved on 14 August 1900, but operations against the Boxers continued in North China with Allied garrisons at key cities and along the Peking–Tientsin–Shanhaikwan railway. The last Indian Army battalion, and accompanying Field Post Offices, did not leave North China until 1 November 1923.

Field Post Offices accompanied the Indian troops and commenced operations on 23 July 1900 using unoverprinted Indian postage and official stamps. The unoverprinted postage issues were replaced in mid-August by stamps overprinted "C.E.F." to prevent currency speculation. The use of unoverprinted official stamps continued as they were not valid for public postage.

PRICES FOR STAMPS ON COVER	
Nos. C1/10	*from* × 15
No. C10c	†
Nos. C11/22	*from* × 8
Nos. C23	*from* × 10
Nos. C24/5	*from* × 20
Nos. C26/8	*from* × 4
Nos. C29/34	*from* × 3

C. E. F.
(C 1)

Stamps of India overprinted with Type* C 1, *in black

1900 (16 Aug). *Stamps of Queen Victoria.*

C1	**40**	3p. carmine	40	1·25
		a. No stop after "C" (R. 1/2)		
		b. No stop after "F"	£180	
		c. Opt double, one albino		
C2	**23**	½a. blue-green	75	30
		a. Opt double		
		b. No stop after "F"	£180	
C3	**25**	1a. plum	4·25	1·50
		a. No stop after "F"	£275	
C4	**27**	2a. pale blue	3·00	9·00
		a. No stop after "F"	£275	
C5	**36**	2a.6p. green	2·75	13·00
		a. No stop after "F"	£375	
C6	**28**	3a. orange	2·75	16·00
		a. Opt double, one albino	£120	
		b. No stop after "F"	£375	
C7	**29**	4a. olive-green	2·75	7·50
		a. Opt double, one albino	£120	
		b. No stop after "F"	£375	
C8	**31**	8a. magenta	2·75	20·00
		a. No stop after "F"	£425	
		b. Opt double, one albino	£120	
C9	**32**	12a. purple/*red*	17·00	16·00
		a. Opt double, one albino	£160	
		b. No stop after "F"	£500	
C10	**37**	1r. green and carmine	27·00	29·00
		a. No stop after "F"	£550	£550
		b. Opt double, one albino	£180	
C1/10 *Set of* 10			55·00	£100

Prepared, but not issued.

C10*c*	**26**	1a.6p. sepia	£225	

The missing stop after "F" variety occurs in the ninth row of the upper pane.

1904 (27 Feb).

C11	**25**	1a. carmine	40·00	8·00

1905 (16 Sept)–**11**. *Stamps of King Edward VII.*

C12	**41**	3p. grey (4.11)	7·50	7·50
		a. Opt double, one albino	£120	
		b. Opt triple, one albino	£400	
		c. Slate-grey	7·50	7·50
C13	**43**	1a. carmine	7·50	70
		a. Opt double, one albino	£100	
C14	**44**	2a. mauve (11.3.11)	14·00	2·75
		a. Opt double, one albino	£130	
C15	**45**	2a.6p. ultramarine (11.3.11)	3·25	5·00
C16	**46**	3a. orange-brown (11.3.11)	3·75	4·00
C17	**47**	4a. olive-green (11.3.11)	8·50	17·00
C18	**49**	8a. claret (11.3.11)	8·00	7·50
		a. Purple	60·00	55·00
C19	**50**	12a. purple/*red* (1909)	11·00	19·00
		a. No stop after "E"	£600	
C20	**51**	1r. green and carmine (11.3.11)	16·00	28·00
C12/20 *Set of* 9			70·00	80·00

1908 (Dec)–**09**. "POSTAGE & REVENUE".

C21	**53**	½a. green (No. 149) (29.9.09)	1·75	1·50
		a. Opt double, one albino	£110	
C22	**54**	1a. carmine (No. 150)	3·25	30
		a. Opt double, one albino	£150	

1914 (5 May)–**22**. *Stamps of King George V. Wmk Star.*

C23	**55**	3p. grey (7.10.14)	8·00	30·00
		a. Opt double, one albino	£350	
C24	**56**	½a. light green	4·00	6·00
		a. Emerald	—	45·00
C25	**57**	1a. aniline carmine	5·00	4·00
C26	**58**	1½a. chocolate (Type A) (9.3.21)	29·00	90·00
		a. Opt double, one albino	£200	
C27	**59**	2a. purple (11.19)	21·00	80·00
		a. Deep mauve	28·00	90·00
		ab. Opt triple	£475	
C28	**61**	2a.6p. bright blue (2.19)	17·00	28·00
C29	**62**	3a. orange (5.22)	32·00	£275
C30	**63**	4a. olive-green (5.22)	29·00	£190
		a. Opt double, one albino	£375	
C32	**65**	8a. deep mauve (12.21)	28·00	£375
C33	**66**	12a. carmine-lake (8.20)	28·00	£130
C34	**67**	1r. brown and green (10.21)	75·00	£375
C23/34 *Set of* 11			£250	£1400

Most dates quoted for Nos. C23/34 are those of the earliest recorded postmarks.

On No. C27a two of the overprints are only lightly inked.

BRITISH RAILWAY ADMINISTRATION

As a vital communications link the North China Railway (Peking–Tientsin–Shanhaikwan) was captured by Russian forces during operations against the Boxers. Control of the line was subsequently, in February 1901, assigned to the China Expeditionary Force and a British Railway Administration was set up to run it. By international agreement the line was to provide postal services for the other national contingents and also, to a lesser extent, for the civilian population. Travelling post offices were introduced and, on 20 April 1901, a late letter service for which an additional fee of 5c. was charged.

Type **32** of China

B.R.A.
5
Five Cents
(BR **35**)

1901 (20 Apr). *No. 108 of China surch with Type* BR **35**.

BR133	**32**	5c. on ½c. brown (Bk.)	£325	£100
		a. Surch inverted	£8000	£2500
		b. Surch in green	£275	£140
		ba. Imperf between (horiz pair)	†	£16000

No. BR133 was used for the collection of the 5c. late letter fee and was affixed to correspondence by a postal official at the railway station. It was cancelled with a violet circular postmark showing "RAILWAY POST OFFICE" at top and the name of the station (PEKING, TIENTSIN, TONGKU, TONGSHAN or SHANHAIKWAN) at foot. With the exception of official mail it could only be used in combination with Indian stamps overprinted "C.E.F.", stamps from the other allied contingents or of the Chinese Imperial Post (*Price used on cover*: No. BR133 *from* £300. No. BR133b *from* £350).

It is suggested that stamps overprinted in black were used at Tientsin and Tongku with those in green being available at Peking, Tongshan and Shanhaikwan.

The late fee charge was abolished on 20 May 1901 and No. BR133 was then withdrawn. The British Railway Administration continued to run the line, and its travelling post offices, until it was returned to its private owners in September 1902.

INDIAN EXPEDITIONARY FORCES 1914–21

Nos. E1/13 were for use of Indian forces sent overseas during the First World War and its aftermath. Examples were first used in France during September 1914. Other areas where the stamps were used included East Africa, Mesopotamia and Turkey. "I.E.F." overprints ceased to be valid for postage on 15 October 1921.

PRICES FOR STAMPS ON COVER	
Nos. E1/13	*from* × 10

I. E. F.
(E **1**)

1914 (Sept). *Stamps of India (King George V) optd with Type* E **1**.

E1	**55**	3p. grey	15	30
		a. No stop after "F"	23·00	32·00
		b. No stop after "E"	£130	£130
		c. Opt double	42·00	40·00
E2	**56**	½a. light green	50	30
		a. No stop after "F"	85·00	85·00
		b. Opt double	£140	£275
E3	**57**	1a. aniline carmine	1·25	30
		a. No stop after "F"	32·00	42·00
E4		1a. carmine	4·50	4·50
E5	**59**	2a. purple	1·25	30
		a. No stop after "F"	65·00	80·00
		b. No stop after "E"	£300	£325
E6	**61**	2a.6p. ultramarine	1·50	3·50
		a. No stop after "F"	£190	£200
E7	**62**	3a. orange	1·00	1·50
		a. No stop after "F"	£180	£190
E8	**63**	4a. olive-green	1·00	1·50
		a. No stop after "F"	£300	£325
E9	**65**	8a. deep magenta	1·25	2·50
		a. No stop after "F"	£300	£325
E10		8a. deep mauve	11·00	16·00
E11	**66**	12a. carmine-lake	2·25	6·00
		a. No stop after "F"	£350	£350
		b. Opt double, one albino	55·00	
E12		12a. claret		
E13	**67**	1r. red-brown and deep blue-green	2·50	4·00
		a. Opt double, one albino	£100	
		b. Brown and green	3·50	5·00
E1/13 *Set of* 10			11·50	18·00

The "no stop after F" variety occurred on R. 4/12 of the upper pane, in one printing.

INDIAN CUSTODIAN FORCES IN KOREA

भारतीय
संरक्षा कटक
कोरिया
(K **1**)

1953 (17 Oct). *Stamps of India optd with Type* K **1**.

K1	**307**	3p. slate-violet	1·75	5·00
K2	**308**	6p. purple-brown	1·50	5·00
K3	**309**	9p. yellow-green	2·00	4·50
K4	**328**	1a. turquoise	1·50	4·50
K5	**311**	2a. carmine	1·50	4·50
K6	**313**	2½a. lake	1·50	4·75
K7	**312**	3a. brown-orange	1·50	5·00
K8	**314**	4a. bright blue	2·25	4·75
K9	**315**	6a. violet	9·00	9·00

K10	**316**	8a. turquoise-green	2·25	10·00
K11	**317**	12a. dull blue	2·25	17·00
K12	**318**	1r. dull violet and green	3·75	17·00
K1/12 *Set of* 12			28·00	80·00

INDIAN U.N. FORCE IN CONGO

U.N. FORCE
(INDIA)
CONGO
(U **1**)

1962 (15 Jan). *Stamps of India optd with Type* U **1**. W **69** (sideways) (13 n.p.) or W **374** (others).

U1	**361**	1n.p. blue-green	1·00	3·50
U2		2n.p. light brown	1·00	1·25
U3		5n.p. bright green	1·00	1·00
U4		8n.p. light blue-green	1·00	40
U5		13n.p. bright carmine-red	1·00	40
U6		50n.p. orange	1·00	70
U1/6 *Set of* 6			5·50	6·50

INDIAN U.N. FORCE IN GAZA (PALESTINE) UNEF

UNEF
(G **1**)

1965 (15 Jan). *No. 492 of India optd with Type* G **1**.

G1	**449**	15p. slate (C.)	2·50	7·50

INTERNATIONAL COMMISSION IN INDO-CHINA

The International Control Commissions for Indo-China were established in August 1954 as part of the Geneva Declaration which partitioned Vietnam and sought to achieve stable settlements in Cambodia and Laos. The three supervisory commissions were chaired by India with Canada and Poland as the other members. Joint inspection teams of servicemen from the three countries were also provided.

The Indian contingent included a postal unit which handled mail for the three commissions and the inspection teams. The unit arrived in Indo-China on 3 September 1954 and opened field post offices at Saigon (F.P.O. 742), Hanoi (F.P.O. 743), Vientiane (F.P.O. 744) and Phnom Penh (F.P.O. 745).

अन्तर्राष्ट्रीय आयोग कम्बोज (N **1**) — अन्तर्राष्ट्रीय आयोग लाओस (N **2**) — अन्तर्राष्ट्रीय आयोग वियत नाम (N **3**)

1954 (1 Dec). *Stamps of India*. W **69**.

(a) Optd as Type N **1**, *for use in Cambodia*

N1	**307**	3p. slate-violet	1·50	9·00
N2	**328**	1a. turquoise	1·00	1·00
N3	**311**	2a. carmine	1·00	1·00
N4	**316**	8a. turquoise-green	1·50	3·00
N5	**317**	12a. dull blue	1·50	3·00

(b) Optd as Type N **2**, *for use in Laos*

N6	**307**	3p. slate-violet	1·50	9·00
N7	**328**	1a. turquoise	1·00	1·00
N8	**311**	2a. carmine	1·00	1·00
N9	**316**	8a. turquoise-green	1·50	3·00
N10	**317**	12a. dull blue	1·50	3·00

(c) Optd as Type N **3**, *for use in Vietnam*

N11	**307**	3p. slate-violet	1·50	9·00
N12	**328**	1a. turquoise	1·00	1·00
N13	**311**	2a. carmine	1·00	1·00
N14	**316**	8a. turquoise-green	1·50	3·00
N15	**317**	12a. dull blue	1·50	3·00
N1/15 *Set of* 15			17·00	45·00

1957 (1 Apr). *Stamps of India*. W **69** (sideways).

(a) Optd as Type N **1**, *for use in Cambodia*

N16	**361**	2n.p. light brown	75	30
N17		6n.p. grey	50	30
N18		13n.p. bright carmine-red	70	40
N19		50n.p. orange	2·25	1·25
N20		75n.p. reddish purple	2·25	1·25

(b) Optd as Type N **2**, *for use in Laos*

N21	**361**	2n.p. light brown	75	30
N22		6n.p. grey	50	30
N23		13n.p. bright carmine-red	70	40
N24		50n.p. orange	2·25	1·25
N25		75n.p. reddish purple	2·25	1·25

(c) Optd as Type N **3**, *for use in Vietnam*

N26	**361**	2n.p. light brown	75	30
N27		6n.p. grey	50	30
N28		13n.p. bright carmine-red	70	40
N29		50n.p. orange	2·25	1·25
N30		75n.p. reddish purple	2·25	1·25
N16/30 *Set of* 15			17·00	9·50

F.P.O. 744 (Vientiane) was closed on 25 July 1958 and F.P.O. 745 (Phnom Penh) on 26 June 1958.

1960 (Sept)–**65**. *Stamps of India*. W **374**.

(a) Optd as Type N **2** *for use in Laos*

N38	**361**	2n.p. light brown (15.1.62)	15	2·50
N39		3n.p. deep brown (1.8.63)	10	20
N40		5n.p. bright green (1.8.63)	10	15
N41		50n.p. orange (1965)	4·00	4·25
N42		75n.p. reddish purple (1965)	4·00	4·50

(b) Optd as Type N **3**, *for use in Vietnam*

N43	**361**	1n.p. blue-green	10	20
N44		2n.p. light brown (15.1.62)	15	2·50
N45		3n.p. deep brown (1.8.63)	10	20
N46		5n.p. bright green (1.8.63)	10	15
N47		50n.p. orange (1965)	4·00	4·25
N48		75n.p. reddish purple (1965)	4·00	4·50
N38/48 *Set of* 11			15·00	21·00

F.P.O. 744 (Vientiane) re-opened on 22 May 1961.

Examples of the 2 n.p. value overprinted as Type N **1** for use in Cambodia exist, but were never placed on sale there as the Phnom Penh F.P.O. 745 was closed on 26 June 1958. Used examples appear to originate from unauthorised use of the F.P.O. 745 postmark which was in store at Saigon (*Price* 15p, *unused*).

अंनिआ
ICC
(N **4**)

ICC
(N **5**)

1965 (15 Jan). *No. 492 of India optd with Type* N **4**, *for use in Laos and Vietnam*.

N49	**449**	15p. slate (C.)	60	3·75

F.P.O. 743 (Hanoi) was closed on 13 July 1966.

1968 (2 Oct). *Nos. 504/5, 506, 509/10, 515 and 517/18 etc of India optd as Type* N **5**, *in red, for use in Laos and Vietnam*.

N50	2p. red-brown	10	3·25
N51	3p. brown-olive	10	3·25
N52	5p. cerise	10	1·50
N53	10p. new blue	2·25	2·50
N54	15p. bronze-green	60	2·50
N55	60p. deep grey	35	1·75
N56	1r. red-brown and plum	50	2·50
N57	2r. new blue and deep slate-violet	1·25	9·50
N50/7 *Set of* 8		4·50	24·00

INDIAN NATIONAL ARMY

The following were prepared for use in the Japanese occupied areas of India during the drive on Imphal.

Genuine examples are inscribed "PROVISIONAL GOVERNMENT OF FREE INDIA". Forgeries also exist inscribed "PROVISIONAL GOVT. OF FREE INDIA".

Typo in Rangoon. No gum. Perf 11½ or imperf. 1p. violet, 1p. maroon, 1a. green. *Price from* £65 *each unused*.

Ten stamps, sharing six different designs, inscribed "AZAD HIND", were produced in Germany during the Second World War, but did no postal duty.

JAPANESE OCCUPATION OF THE ANDAMAN AND NICOBAR ISLANDS

The Andaman Islands in the Bay of Bengal were occupied on the 23 March 1942 and the Nicobar Islands in July 1942. Civil administration was resumed in October 1945.

The following Indian stamps were surcharged with large figures preceded by a decimal point:—

Postage stamps—.3 on ½a. (No. 248), .5 on 1a. (No. 250), .10 on 2a. (No. 236*b*), .30 on 6a. (No. 274).

Official stamps—.10 on 1a.3p. (No. O146*a*), .20 on 3p. (No. O143), .20 in red on 3p. (No. O143).

Prices from £425 *each unused*.

INDIAN CONVENTION STATES

The following issues resulted from a series of postal conventions agreed between the Imperial Government and the state administrations of Patiala (1 October 1884), Gwalior, Jind and Nabha (1 July 1885), and Chamba and Faridkot (1 January 1887)

Under the terms of these conventions the British Indian Post Office supplied overprinted British India issues to the state administrations which, in turn, had to conform to a number of conditions covering the issue of stamps, rates of postage and the exchange of mail.

Such overprinted issues were valid for postage within the state of issue, to other "Convention States" and to destinations in British India.

Stamps of Chamba, Gwalior, Jind, Nabha and Patiala ceased to be valid for postage on 1 January 1951, when they were replaced by those of the Republic of India, valid from 1 April 1950.

RULERS OF INDIAN CONVENTION AND FEUDATORY STATES. Details of the rulers of the various states during the period when stamps were issued are now provided in a somewhat simplified form which omits reference to minor titles. Dates quoted are of the various reigns, extended to 1971 when the titles of the surviving rulers of the former princely states were abolished by the Indian Government.

During the absorption of the Convention and Feudatory States there was often an interim period during which the administration was handed over. In some instances it is only possible to quote the end of this interim period as the point of transfer.

STAMPS OF INDIA OVERPRINTED

In the Queen Victoria issues we omit varieties due to broken type, including the numerous small "A" varieties which may have come about through damaged type. We do, however, list the small "G", small "R" and tall "R" in "GWALIOR" as these were definitely the result of the use of type of the wrong size.

Variations in the length of the words due to unequal spacing when setting are also omitted.

CHAMBA

PRICES FOR STAMPS ON COVER	
Nos. 1/27	*from* × 20
Nos. 28/120	*from* × 12
Nos. O1/86	*from* × 25

Raja Sham Singh, 1873–1904

CHAMBA STATE (**1**) — CHAMBA (**2**)

1887 (1 Jan)–**95**. *Queen Victoria. Optd with T* **1**.

1	**23**	½a. blue-green	1·00	1·25
		a. "CHMABA"	£400	£650
		b. "8TATE"	£700	
		c. Opt double	£650	
2	**25**	1a. brown-purple	2·50	2·50
		a. "CHMABA"	£475	£650
		b. "8TATE"	£1500	
3		1a. plum	3·00	2·50
4	**26**	1a.6p. sepia (1895)	3·00	14·00
5	**27**	2a. dull blue	2·00	3·00
		b. "CHMABA"	£1900	£2750
		c. "8TATE"	£1900	
6		2a. ultramarine	1·25	2·25
7	**36**	2a.6p. green (1895)	35·00	£100
8	**28**	3a. orange (1887)	11·00	23·00
9		3a. brown-orange (1891)	3·00	6·00
		a. "CHMABA"	£5000	£7500
		b. Opt inverted		
10	**29**	4a. olive-green	5·50	9·50
		a. "CHMABA"	£1600	£2750
		b. "8TATE"	£4500	
11		4a. slate-green	4·50	8·00
		a. Opt double, one albino	85·00	
12	**21**	6a. olive-bistre (1890)	5·50	22·00
		a. Opt treble, two albino	£110	
13		6a. bistre-brown	20·00	23·00
14	**31**	8a. dull mauve (1887)	9·00	12·00
		a. "CHMABA"	£4000	£4250
15		8a. magenta (1895)	7·00	22·00
16	**32**	12a. purple/*red* (1890)	7·00	16·00
		a. "CHMABA"	£8500	
		b. First "T" in "STATE" inverted	£8500	
		c. Opt double, one albino	50·00	
17	**33**	1r. slate (1887)	48·00	£150
		a. "CHMABA"	£14000	
18	**37**	1r. green and carmine (1895)	9·50	17·00
		a. Opt double one albino	70·00	
19	**38**	2r. carmine and yellow-brown (1895)	£100	£400
20		3r. brown and green (1895)	£120	£350
21		5r. ultramarine and violet (1895)	£130	£550
		a. Opt double, one albino	£200	
1/21 *Set of* 15			£425	£1500

1900–04. *Colours changed*.

22	**40**	3p. carmine	60	90
		a. Opt double, one albino	45·00	
23		3p. grey (1904)	60	2·25
		a. Opt inverted	80·00	
24	**23**	½a. pale yellow-green (1902)	2·50	4·25
25		½a. yellow-green (1903)	75	1·75
26	**25**	1a. carmine (1902)	75	40
27	**27**	2a. pale violet (1903)	11·00	35·00
22/7 *Set of* 5			12·50	38·00

Raja Bhuri Singh, 1904–1919

1903–05. *King Edward VII. Optd with T* **1**.

28	**41**	3p. pale grey	25	1·60
29		3p. slate-grey (1905)	60	1·60
30	**42**	½a. green	80	60
31	**43**	1a. carmine	1·60	90
32	**44**	2a. pale violet (1904)	2·25	3·75
33		2a. mauve	1·90	3·50
34	**46**	3a. orange-brown (1905)	4·75	6·00
		a. Opt double, one albino	48·00	
35	**47**	4a. olive (1904)	7·00	22·00
36	**48**	6a. olive-bistre (1905)	4·50	24·00
		a. Opt double, one albino	48·00	
37	**49**	8a. purple (*shades*) (1904)	6·00	24·00
38		8a. claret	12·00	29·00
39	**50**	12a. purple/*red* (1905)	8·00	32·00
		a. Opt double, one albino	48·00	
40	**51**	1r. green and carmine (1904)	8·50	24·00
		a. Opt double, one albino	65·00	
28/40 *Set of* 10			38·00	£120

1907. *Nos. 149/50 of India optd with T* **1**.

41	**53**	½a. green	2·50	4·00
		a. Opt double, one albino	40·00	
42	**54**	1a. carmine	2·50	4·00

1913. *King George V optd with T* **1**.

43	**55**	3p. grey	40	1·25
		a. Pale grey	1·50	
		b. Bluish grey	1·50	
44	**56**	½a. light green	1·00	1·25
		a. Emerald	1·50	1·75
		b. Bright green	1·50	
		w. Wmk inverted		
45	**57**	1a. rose-carmine	10·00	12·00
		a. Aniline carmine	2·00	4·00
		ab. Opt double, one albino	45·00	
47	**59**	2a. purple	4·00	12·00
		a. Reddish purple	4·75	12·00
		b. Deep mauve	6·50	
		c. Bright reddish violet	8·50	
48	**62**	3a. orange	4·75	9·00
		a. Dull orange	—	9·00
49	**63**	4a. olive	4·00	5·50
50	**64**	6a. yellow-bistre	4·50	7·50
		a. Brown-ochre	5·50	7·00
51	**65**	8a. deep magenta	6·00	16·00
		a. Deep mauve	7·00	15·00
		b. Bright mauve	10·00	
		c. Purple	11·00	
52	**66**	12a. carmine-lake	5·50	13·00
		a. Claret	10·00	15·00
53	**67**	1r. red-brown and deep blue-green	18·00	32·00
		a. Opt double, one albino	42·00	
		b. Brown and green	18·00	30·00
		c. Orange-brown and deep turquoise-green	23·00	
43/53 *Set of* 10			45·00	90·00

Raja Ram Singh, 1919–1935

1921. *No. 192 of India optd with T* **2**.

54	**57**	9p. on 1a. rose-carmine	1·00	18·00

1923–27. *Optd with T* **1**. *New values, etc.*

55	**57**	1a. chocolate	3·50	5·50
56	**58**	1½a. chocolate (Type A)	27·00	£130
57		1½a. chocolate (Type B) (1924)	2·50	6·50
58		1½a. rose-carmine (Type B) (1927)	90	24·00
59	**61**	2a.6p. ultramarine	60	4·25
60		2a.6p. orange (1927)	2·75	23·00
61	**62**	3a. ultramarine (1924)	4·25	23·00
		a. Opt double, one albino	60·00	
55/61 *Set of 7*			38·00	£190

Nos. 58 and 60 with inverted overprint are of clandestine origin.

CHAMBA STATE (3) CHAMBA STATE (4)

1927–37. *King George V (Nasik printing, wmk Mult Star). Optd at Nasik with T* **3** *or* **4** *(1r.).*

62	**55**	3p. slate (1928)	20	1·75
		w. Wmk inverted	4·25	
63	**56**	½a. green (1928)	30	2·50
		w. Wmk inverted	2·50	
64	**80**	9p. deep green (*litho*) (1932)	5·00	22·00
64*a*		9p. deep green (*typo*)	10·00	22·00
65	**57**	1a. chocolate	1·75	1·50
		w. Wmk inverted	4·50	2·00
66	**82**	1a.3p. mauve (1932)	1·40	6·50
		w. Wmk inverted	4·50	6·50
67	**58**	1½a. rose-carmine (B) (1932)	6·50	7·50
		w. Wmk inverted	7·00	7·50
68	**70**	2a. purple (1928)	2·25	4·00
69	**61**	2a.6p. orange (1932)	3·25	20·00
		w. Wmk inverted	3·25	21·00
70	**62**	3a. bright blue (1928)	1·25	22·00
71	**71**	4a. sage-green (1928)	1·25	7·00
72	**64**	6a. bistre (*wmk inverted*) (1937)	26·00	£170
73	**65**	8a. reddish purple (1928)	1·60	12·00
		w. Wmk inverted	1·40	11·00
74	**66**	12a. claret (1928)	1·60	16·00
75	**67**	1r. chocolate and green (1928)	12·00	30·00
		w. Wmk inverted	13·00	30·00
62/75 *Set of 14*			60·00	£300

Raja Lakshman Singh, 1935–1971

1935–36. *New types and colours. Optd with T* **3**.

76	**79**	½a. green	1·10	11·00
77	**81**	1a. chocolate	2·25	1·25
78	**59**	2a. vermilion (No. 236*b*)	1·25	25·00
79		2a. vermilion (*small die, No. 236c*)	£120	£140
80	**62**	3a. carmine	2·25	12·00
81	**63**	4a. sage-green (1936)	5·50	17·00
76/81 *Set of 6*			£120	£190

CHAMBA STATE (5) CHAMBA (6) CHAMBA (7)

1938. *King George VI. Nos. 247/64 optd with T* **3** *(3p. to 1a.), T* **5** *(2a. to 12a.) or T* **4** *(rupee values).*

82	**91**	3p. slate	11·00	22·00
83		½a. red-brown	1·60	14·00
84		9p. green	10·00	38·00
85		1a. carmine	2·00	3·75
86	**92**	2a. vermilion	8·00	16·00
87	**93**	2a.6p. bright violet	8·50	32·00
88	**94**	3a. yellow-green	9·00	29·00
89	**95**	3a.6p. bright blue	9·00	30·00
90	**96**	4a. brown	23·00	30·00
91	**97**	6a. turquoise-green	26·00	70·00
92	**98**	8a. slate-violet	24·00	65·00
93	**99**	12a. lake	18·00	65·00
94	**100**	1r. grey and red-brown	35·00	75·00
95		2r. purple and brown	60·00	£350
96		5r. green and blue	95·00	£475
97		10r. purple and claret	£150	£750
98		15r. brown and green	£160	£1000
99		25r. slate-violet and purple	£225	£1100
82/99 *Set of 18*			£800	£3750

1942–47. *Optd with T* **6** *(to 12a.), "CHAMBA" only, as in T* **5** *(14a.) or T* **7** *(rupee values).*

(a) Stamps of 1937. W **69** (inverted on 15r.).

100	**91**	½a. red-brown	50·00	45·00
101		1a. carmine	75·00	60·00
102	**100**	1r. grey and red-brown	21·00	65·00
103		2r. purple and brown	24·00	£275
104		5r. green and blue	45·00	£300
105		10r. purple and claret	70·00	£475
106		15r. brown and green	£150	£850
		w. Wmk upright	£400	£1100
107		25r. slate-violet and purple	£140	£850
100/7 *Set of 8*			£500	£2500

(b) Stamps of 1940–43.

108	**100**	3p. slate	1·25	5·50
109		½a. purple (1943)	70	6·50
110		9p. green	1·10	20·00
111		1a. carmine (1943)	1·75	5·50
112	**101**	1½a. dull violet (1943)	2·00	14·00
113		2a. vermilion (1943)	8·50	16·00
114		3a. bright violet	21·00	48·00
115		3½a. bright blue	11·00	45·00
116	**102**	4a. brown	15·00	15·00
117		6a. turquoise-green	17·00	42·00
118		8a. slate-violet	18·00	50·00
119		12a. lake	24·00	65·00
120	**103**	14a. purple (1947)	14·00	3·00
108/120 *Set of 13*			£120	£300

The 3a. exists printed by lithography or typography.

OFFICIAL STAMPS

SERVICE

CHAMBA STATE (O 1)

1887 (1 Jan)–**98**. *Queen Victoria. Optd with Type* O **1**.

O1	**23**	½a. blue-green	75	20
		a. "CHMABA"	£250	£250
		b. "SERV CE"		
		c. "8TATE"	£800	
		d. Thin seriffed "I" in "SERVICE"	£180	
O2	**25**	1a. brown-purple	2·50	1·50
		a. "CHMABA"	£400	£400
		b. "SERV CE"	£3500	
		c. "8TATE"	£1800	
		d. "SERVICE" double	£2000	£1100
		e. "SERVICE" double, one albino	65·00	
O3		1a. plum	2·75	20
		a. Thin seriffed "I" in "SERVICE"	£225	
O4	**27**	2a. dull blue	3·00	2·00
		a. "CHMABA"	£1000	£2250
O5		2a. ultramarine (1887)	2·50	2·50
		a. Thin seriffed "I" in "SERVICE"	£350	
O6	**28**	3a. orange (1890)		
O7		3a. brown-orange (1891)	2·50	13·00
		a. "CHMABA"	£3000	£3500
		b. Thin seriffed "I" in "SERVICE"		
		c. Opt double, one albino		
O8	**29**	4a. olive-green	3·75	8·00
		a. "CHMABA"	£1100	£2250
		b. "SERV CE"	£4000	
		c. "8TATE"	£3250	
O9		4a. slate-green	2·25	10·00
		a. Thin seriffed "I" in "SERVICE"		
O10	**21**	6a. olive-bistre (1890)	5·00	15·00
		a. "SERVICE" double, one albino	65·00	
O11		6a. bistre-brown		
O12	**31**	8a. dull mauve (1887)	4·50	8·50
		a. "CHMABA"	£8000	£8000
O13		8a. magenta (1895)	3·75	3·00
		a. Thin seriffed "I" in "SERVICE"	£650	
O14	**32**	12a. purple/*red* (1890)	10·00	48·00
		a. "CHMABA"	£7500	
		b. First "T" in "STATE" inverted	£8500	
		c. Thin seriffed "I" in "SERVICE"		
		d. "SERVICE" double, one albino	65·00	
		e. "CHAMBA STATE" double, one albino	60·00	
O15	**33**	1r. slate (1890)	15·00	£150
		a. "CHMABA"	£5000	
O16	**37**	1r. green and carmine (1898)	6·00	42·00
		a. Thin seriffed "I" in "SERVICE"		
O1/16 *Set of 10*			45·00	£250

Printings up to and including that of December 1895 had the "SERVICE" overprint applied to sheets of stamps already overprinted with Type **1**. From the printing of September 1898 onwards both "SERVICE" and "CHAMBA STATE" were overprinted at the same time. Nos. O6, O8 and O12 only exist using the first method, and No. O16 was only printed using the second.

The thin seriffed "I" in "SERVICE" variety occurred on R. 19/12 of the September 1898 printing only.

1902–04. *Colours changed. Optd as Type* O **1**.

O17	**40**	3p. grey (1904)	60	80
O18	**23**	½a. pale yellow-green	1·25	4·00
O19		½a. yellow-green	5·00	2·75
O20	**25**	1a. carmine	1·50	60
O21	**27**	2a. pale violet (1903)	12·00	35·00
O17/21 *Set of 4*			14·00	35·00

1903–05. *King Edward VII. Stamps of India optd as Type* O **1**.

O22	**41**	3p. pale grey	35	15
		a. Opt double, one albino	40·00	
O23		3p. slate-grey (1905)	35	65
O24	**42**	½a. yellow-green	25	10
O25	**43**	1a. carmine	1·25	30
O26	**44**	2a. pale violet (1904)	3·00	2·00
O27		2a. mauve	1·25	1·50
O28	**47**	4a. olive (1905)	3·50	20·00
O29	**49**	8a. purple (1905)	8·50	20·00
O30		8a. claret	11·00	26·00
		a. Opt double, one albino	45·00	
O31	**51**	1r. green and carmine (1905)	1·75	14·00
O22/31 *Set of 7*			15·00	50·00

The 2a. mauve King Edward VII, overprinted "On H.M.S.", was discovered in Calcutta, but was not sent to Chamba, and is an unissued variety (*Price un.* £38).

1907. *Nos. 149/50 of India, optd with Type* O **1**.

O32	**53**	½a. green	40	75
		a. Opt inverted	£4500	£5500
		b. Opt double, one albino	42·00	
O33	**54**	1a. carmine	2·25	2·50

The inverted overprint, No. O32a, was due to an inverted cliché on R. 20/1 which was corrected after a few sheets had been printed.

1913–23. *King George V Official stamps (wmk Single Star) optd with T* **1**.

O34	**55**	3p. grey	20	40
		a. Pale grey	75	1·25
		b. Bluish grey	75	1·25
		c. Slate	50	1·25
O36	**56**	½a. light green	20	60
		a. Emerald	2·25	60
		b. Bright green	1·60	30
O38	**57**	1a. aniline carmine	20	10
		a. Rose-carmine	4·50	50
O40	**59**	2a. purple (1914)	1·10	15·00
		a. Reddish purple	9·50	
		b. Bright reddish violet (1923)	9·50	15·00
O41	**63**	4a. olive	1·10	20·00
O42	**65**	8a. deep magenta	1·75	21·00
		a. Deep mauve	4·75	21·00
O43	**67**	1r. red-brown and deep blue-green (1914)	5·50	32·00
		a. Opt double, one albino	42·00	
		b. Brown and green	7·00	32·00
O34/43 *Set of 7*			9·00	80·00

No. O36 with inverted overprint and No. O38*a* with double or inverted overprint (on gummed side) are of clandestine origin.

1914. *King George V. Optd with Type* O **1**.

O44	**59**	2a. purple	15·00	
O45	**63**	4a. olive	13·00	

1921. *No. O97 of India optd with T* **2** *at top.*

O46	**57**	9p. on 1a. rose-carmine	15	8·50

1925. *As 1913–14. New colour.*

O47	**57**	1a. chocolate	4·50	70

CHAMBA STATE SERVICE (O 2) CHAMBA STATE SERVICE (O 3)

1927–39. *King George V (Nasik printing, wmk Mult Star), optd at Nasik with Type* O **2** *or* O **3** *(rupee values).*

O48	**55**	3p. slate (1928)	50	40
		w. Wmk inverted	—	1·50
O49	**56**	½a. green (1928)	35	15
O50	**80**	9p. deep green (1932)	4·00	11·00
O51	**57**	1a. chocolate	20	10
		w. Wmk inverted	1·75	30
O52	**82**	1a.3p. mauve (1932)	6·00	1·00
		w. Wmk inverted		
O53	**70**	2a. purple (1928)	2·50	60
O54	**71**	4a. sage-green (1928)	1·50	2·75
O55	**65**	8a. reddish purple (1930)	8·00	11·00
		w. Wmk inverted	9·00	
O56	**66**	12a. claret (1928)	5·00	26·00
		w. Wmk inverted	14·00	
O57	**67**	1r. chocolate and green (1930)	15·00	48·00
O58		2r. carmine and orange (1939)	24·00	£250
O59		5r. ultramarine and purple (1939)	42·00	£300
O60		10r. green and scarlet (1939)	65·00	£300
O48/60 *Set of 13*			£160	£850

1935–39. *New types and colours. Optd with Type* O **2**.

O61	**79**	½a. green	5·50	50
O62	**81**	1a. chocolate	2·75	45
O63	**59**	2a. vermilion	5·50	1·25
O64		2a. vermilion (*small die*) (1939)	7·50	20·00
O65	**63**	4a. sage-green (1936)	8·00	7·50
O61/5 *Set of 5*			27·00	27·00

1938–40. *King George VI. Optd with Type* O **2** *or* O **3** *(rupee values).*

O66	**91**	9p. green	25·00	70·00
O67		1a. carmine	30·00	6·00
O68	**100**	1r. grey and red-brown (1940?)	£225	£750
O69		2r. purple and brown (1939)	42·00	£400
O70		5r. green and blue (1939)	60·00	£450
O71		10r. purple and claret (1939)	85·00	£800
O66/71 *Set of 6*			£425	£2250

CHAMBA SERVICE (O 4)

1940–43.

(a) Official stamps optd with T **6**.

O72	O **20**	3p. slate	70	1·25
O73		½a. red-brown	30·00	3·75
O74		½a. purple (1943)	70	3·75
O75		9p. green	7·00	12·00
		w. Wmk inverted	22·00	17·00
O76		1a. carmine (1941)	1·00	3·00
O77		1a.3p. yellow-brown (1941)	85·00	22·00
O78		1½a. dull violet (1943)	7·50	8·50
O79		2a. vermilion	7·50	8·50
O80		2½a. bright violet (1941)	4·50	24·00
O81		4a. brown	7·50	18·00
O82		8a. slate-violet	17·00	70·00
		w. Wmk inverted	17·00	70·00

(b) Postage stamps optd with Type O **4**.

O83	**100**	1r. grey and red-brown (1942)	20·00	£225
O84		2r. purple and brown (1942)	35·00	£300
O85		5r. green and blue (1942)	65·00	£425
O86		10r. purple and claret (1942)	75·00	£750
O72/86 *Set of 15*			£325	£1700

Chamba became part of Himachal Pradesh on 15 April 1948.

FARIDKOT

For earlier issues, see under INDIAN FEUDATORY STATES

PRICES FOR STAMPS ON COVER	
Nos. 1/17	*from* × 30
Nos. O1/15	*from* × 40

Raja Bikram Singh, 1874–1898

FARIDKOT STATE (1)

1887 (1 Jan)–**1900**. *Queen Victoria. Optd with T* **1**.

1	**23**	½a. deep green	2·50	1·75
		a. "ARIDKOT"		
		b. "FAR DKOT"	—	£2000
		c. Opt double, one albino	55·00	
2	**25**	1a. brown-purple	1·50	2·50
3		1a. plum	2·25	2·50
4	**27**	2a. blue	3·25	7·00
5		2a. deep blue	4·00	8·00
6	**28**	3a. orange	8·00	13·00
7		3a. brown-orange (1893)	3·75	6·00
8	**29**	4a. olive-green	8·50	18·00
		a. "ARIDKOT"	£1400	
9		4a. slate-green	8·50	25·00
10	**21**	6a. olive-bistre	38·00	70·00
		a. "ARIDKOT"	£1800	
		b. Opt double, one albino	60·00	
11		6a. bistre-brown	2·00	18·00
12	**31**	8a. dull mauve	15·00	45·00
		a. "ARIDKOT"	£3000	
13		8a. magenta	22·00	£150
		a. Opt double, one albino	45·00	
14	**32**	12a. purple/*red* (1900)	45·00	£425
15	**33**	1r. slate	45·00	£375
		a. "ARIDKOT"	£3500	
16	**37**	1r. green and carmine (1893)	40·00	£120
		a. Opt double, one albino	65·00	
1/16 *Set of* 10			£150	£900

The ½a., 1a., 2a., 3a., 4a., 8a. and 1r. (No. 16) are known with broken "O" (looking like a "C") in "FARIDKOT".

Raja Balbir Singh, 1898–1906

1900. *Optd with T* **1**.

17	**40**	3p. carmine	1·50	45·00

OFFICIAL STAMPS

SERVICE

FARIDKOT STATE

(O **1**)

1887 (1 Jan)–**98**. *Queen Victoria. Optd with Type* O **1**.

O1	**23**	½a. deep green	60	75
		a. "SERV CE"	£2500	
		b. "FAR DKOT"	£3000	
		c. Thin seriffed "I" in "SERVICE"	£250	
		d. "FARIDKOT STATE" double, one albino	48·00	
O2	**25**	1a. brown-purple	1·00	2·00
		a. Thin seriffed "I" in "SERVICE"	£275	
		b. Opt double, one albino	60·00	
O3		1a. plum	1·50	1·75
		a. "SERV CE"	£3750	
O4	**27**	2a. dull blue	2·00	11·00
		a. "SERV CE"	£3750	
O5		2a. deep blue	3·00	16·00
O6	**28**	3a. orange	6·50	11·00
		a. "SERVICE" double, one albino		
O7		3a. brown-orange (12.98)	4·00	38·00
		a. Thin seriffed "I" in "SERVICE"	£650	
O8	**29**	4a. olive-green	4·75	30·00
		a. "SERV CE"	£3250	
		b. "ARIDKOT"		
		c. "SERVICE" treble, two albino	95·00	
O9		4a. slate-green	15·00	48·00
		a. "SERVICE" double, one albino	42·00	
O10	**21**	6a. olive-bistre	38·00	£110
		a. "ARIDKOT"	£1400	
		b. "SERVIC"	£3000	
		c. "SERVICE" double, one albino	65·00	
		d. "FARIDKOT STATE" double, one albino	65·00	
O11		6a. bistre-brown	25·00	29·00
O12	**31**	8a. dull mauve	10·00	30·00
		a. "SERV CE"	£3000	
O13		8a. magenta	20·00	£150
O14	**33**	1r. slate	55·00	£275
		a. "SERVICE" double, one albino	95·00	
O15	**37**	1r. green and carmine (12.98)	90·00	£700
		a. Thin seriffed "I" in "SERVICE"		
O1/15 *Set of* 9			£170	£1000

The ½a., 1a., 2a., 3a., 4a., 8a. and 1r. (No. O15) are known with the broken "O".

Printings up to and including that of November 1895 had the "SERVICE" overprint applied to sheets already overprinted with Type **1**. From December 1898 onwards "SERVICE" and "FARIDKOT STATE" were overprinted at one operation to provide fresh supplies of Nos. O1/3, O7 and O15.

The thin seriffed "I" variety occurs on the December 1898 overprinting only.

This State ceased to use overprinted stamps after 31 March 1901.

GWALIOR

PRICES FOR STAMPS ON COVER	
Nos. 1/3	*from* × 10
Nos. 4/11	—
Nos. 12/66	*from* × 5
Nos. 67/128	*from* × 4
Nos. 129/37	*from* × 5
Nos. O1/94	*from* × 12

OVERPRINTS. From 1885 to 1926 these were applied by the Government of India Central Printing Press, Calcutta, and from 1927 at the Security Press, Nasik, *unless otherwise stated.*

Maharaja Jayaji Rao Sindhia, 1843–1886

गवालियर

GWALIOR (1)

GWALIOR गवालियर (2)

GWALIOR Small "G"

GWALIOR Small "R"

GWALIOR Tall "R" (original state)

GWALIOR Tall "R" (damaged state)

OVERPRINT VARIETIES OF TYPE 2.

Small "G" — Occurs on R. 7/11 from June 1900 printing of ½, 1, 2, 3, 4a. and 3p. (No. 38), and on R. 3/1 of a left pane from May 1901 printing of 2, 3 and 5r.

Small "R" — Occurs on R. 9/3 from June 1900 printing of 3p. to 4a. and on R. 2/3 from May 1901 printing of 2, 3 and 5r.

Tall "R" — Occurs on R. 20/2 from printings between June 1900 and May 1907. The top of the letter is damaged on printings from February 1903 onwards.

1885 (1 July)–**97**. *Queen Victoria.* I. *Optd with T* **1**.

(a) Space between two lines of overprint 13 mm. Hindi inscription 13 to 14 mm long (May 1885).

1	**23**	½a. blue-green	£150	30·00
2	**25**	1a. brown-purple	95·00	32·00
3	**27**	2a. dull blue	80·00	17·00
1/3 *Set of* 3			£300	70·00

A variety exists of the ½a. in which the space between the two lines of overprint is only 9½ mm but this is probably from a proof sheet.

(b) Space between two lines of overprint 15 mm on 4a. and 6a. and 16 to 17 mm on other values (June 1885). Hindi inscription 13 to 14 mm long.

4	**23**	½a. blue-green	60·00	
		a. Opt double, one albino	70·00	
		b. Hindi inscr 15 to 15½ mm long	£130	
		ba. Opt double, one albino	£180	
		c. Pair. Nos. 4/4b	£750	
5	**25**	1a. brown-purple	65·00	
		a. Opt double, one albino	75·00	
		b. Hindi inscr 15 to 15½ mm long	£130	
		ba. Opt double, one albino	£150	
		c. Pair. Nos. 5/5b	£750	
6	**26**	1a.6p. sepia	85·00	
		b. Hindi inscr 15 to 15½ mm long	£200	
		c. Pair. Nos. 6/6b	£850	
7	**27**	2a. dull blue	70·00	
		b. Hindi inscr 15 to 15½ mm long	£120	
		c. Pair. Nos. 7/7b	£425	
8	**17**	4a. green	95·00	
		b. Hindi inscr 15 to 15½ mm long	£180	
		c. Pair. Nos. 8/8b	£900	
9	**21**	6a. olive-bistre	95·00	
		a. Opt double, one albino	£100	
		b. Hindi inscr 15 to 15½ mm long	£225	
		ba. Opt double, one albino	£225	
		c. Pair. Nos. 9/9b	£900	
10	**31**	8a. dull mauve	75·00	
		b. Hindi inscr 15 to 15½ mm long	£160	
		c. Pair. Nos. 10/10b	£900	
11	**33**	1r. slate	75·00	
		b. Hindi inscr 15 to 15½ mm long	£160	
		c. Pair. Nos. 11/11b	£900	
4/11 *Set of* 8			£550	
4b/11b *Set of* 8			£1200	

The two types of overprint on these stamps occur in the same settings, with about a quarter of the stamps in each sheet showing the long inscription. Nos. 4/7 and 10/11 were overprinted in sheets of 240 and Nos. 8/9 in half-sheets of 160.

II. *Optd with T* **2**. *Hindi inscription 13 to 14 mm long.*

(a) In red (Sept 1885).

12	**23**	½a. blue-green	1·25	20
		b. Hindi inscr 15 to 15½ mm long	2·50	1·00
		c. Pair. Nos. 12/12b	16·00	18·00
13	**27**	2a. dull blue	23·00	18·00
		b. Hindi inscr 15 to 15½ mm long	42·00	42·00
		c. Pair. Nos. 13/13b	£425	£450
14	**17**	4a. green	28·00	16·00
		b. Hindi inscr 15 to 15½ mm long	£225	£100
		c. Pair. Nos. 14/14b	£800	
15	**33**	1r. slate	8·50	25·00
		aw. Wmk inverted	17·00	35·00
		b. Hindi inscr 15 to 15½ mm long	40·00	80·00
		bw. Wmk inverted	50·00	£100
		c. Pair. Nos. 15/15b	80·00	£140
		cw. Wmk inverted	95·00	
12/15 *Set of* 4			55·00	55·00
12b/15b *Set of* 4			£275	£200

No. 14 was overprinted in half-sheets of 160, about 40 stamps having the Hindi inscription 15 to 15½ mm long. The remaining three values were from a setting of 240 containing 166 13 to 14 mm long and 74 15 to 15½ mm long.

Reprints have been made of Nos. 12 to 15, but the majority of the specimens have the word "REPRINT" overprinted upon them.

(b) In black (1885–97).

16	**23**	½a. blue-green (1889)	2·25	2·25
		b. Opt double, one albino	24·00	
		c. Hindi inscr 15 to 15½ mm long	50	10
		ca. Opt double	†	£850
		cb. Opt double, one albino	85·00	
		cc. "GWALICR"	85·00	£100
		cd. Small "G"	65·00	48·00
		ce. Small "R"	80·00	
		cf. Tall "R"	90·00	90·00
		d. Pair. Nos. 16/16c	60·00	65·00
17	**24**	9p. carmine (1891)	32·00	55·00
		a. Opt double, one albino	55·00	
		c. Hindi inscr 15 to 15½ mm long	60·00	80·00
		ca. Opt double, one albino	85·00	
		d. Pair. Nos. 17/17c	£300	
18	**25**	1a. brown-purple	2·00	20
		c. Hindi inscr 15 to 15½ mm long	3·50	35
		d. Pair. Nos. 18/18c	17·00	18·00
19		1a. plum (*Hindi inscr 15 to 15½ mm long*)	3·25	10
		a. Small "G"	75·00	55·00
		b. Small "R"	90·00	
		c. Tall "R"	£120	
20	**26**	1a.6p. sepia	1·50	2·00
		c. Hindi inscr 15 to 15½ mm long	2·25	80
		d. Pair. Nos. 20/20c	17·00	20·00
21	**27**	2a. dull blue	8·00	1·00
		c. Hindi inscr 15 to 15½ mm long	2·75	10
		ca. "R" omitted	£500	£500
		d. Pair. Nos. 21/21c	£160	£170
22		2a. deep blue	13·00	3·00
		c. Hindi inscr 15 to 15½ mm long	4·00	75
		ca. Small "G"	£150	£160
		cb. Small "R"	£225	
		cc. Tall "R"	£250	£250
		d. Pair. Nos. 22/22c	£200	
23	**36**	2a.6p. yellow-green (*Hindi inscr 15 to 15½ mm long*) (1896)	9·00	20·00
		a. "GWALICR"	£700	
24	**28**	3a. orange	8·50	15·00
		a. Opt double, one albino	65·00	
		c. Hindi inscr 15 to 15½ mm long	65·00	48·00
		ca. Opt double, one albino		
		d. Pair. Nos. 24/24c	£325	
25		3a. brown-orange	35·00	6·50
		c. Hindi inscr 15 to 15½ mm long	4·25	15
		ca. Opt double, one albino	40·00	
		cb. Small "G"	£250	£275
		cc. Small "R"	£800	
		cd. Tall "R"	£200	£200
		d. Pair. Nos. 25/25c	£250	
26	**29**	4a. olive-green (1889)	10·00	1·75
		c. Hindi inscr 15 to 15½ mm long	14·00	4·00
		d. Pair. Nos. 26/26c	£130	
27		4a. slate-green	11·00	2·25
		c. Hindi inscr 15 to 15½ mm long	5·00	1·25
		ca. Opt double, one albino	70·00	
		cb. Small "G"	£500	£350
		cc. Small "R"	£500	
		cd. Tall "R"	£350	£350
		d. Pair. Nos. 27/27c	42·00	
28	**21**	6a. olive-bistre	10·00	20·00
		c. Hindi inscr 15 to 15½ mm long	5·00	19·00
		ca. Opt double, one albino	42·00	
		d. Pair. Nos. 28/28c	75·00	
29		6a. bistre-brown	3·50	8·50
		c. Hindi inscr 15 to 15½ mm long	5·00	13·00
		d. Pair. Nos. 29/29c	27·00	
30	**31**	8a. dull mauve	14·00	42·00
		c. Hindi inscr 15 to 15½ mm long	5·00	1·25
		d. Pair. Nos. 30/30c	£375	
31		8a. magenta (*Hindi inscr 15 to 15½ mm long*) (1897)	8·00	9·00
32	**32**	12a. purple/*red* (1891)	4·50	8·50
		c. Hindi inscr 15 to 15½ mm long	3·25	65
		ca. Pair, one without opt	£3750	
		cb. Tall "R"	£1300	£900
		d. Pair. Nos. 32/32c	80·00	
33	**33**	1r. slate (1889)	£120	£450
		c. Hindi inscr 15 to 15½ mm long	4·50	2·50
		d. Pair. Nos. 33/33c	£600	
34	**37**	1r. green and carmine (*Hindi inscr 15 to 15½ mm long*) (1896)	6·50	5·50
		a. Opt double, one albino	95·00	
		b. "GWALICR"	£900	£1400
35	**38**	2r. carmine and yellow-brown (*Hindi inscr 15 to 15½ mm long*) (1896)	5·50	3·00
		a. Small "G"	£375	£200
		b. Small "R"	£400	£225
		c. Opt double, one albino	85·00	
		d. Opt triple, two albino	£100	
36		3r. brown and green (*Hindi inscr 15 to 15½ mm long*) (1896)	7·50	3·50
		a. Small "G"	£425	£225
		b. Small "R"	£450	£250
37		5r. ultramarine and violet (*Hindi inscr 15 to 15½ mm long*) (1896)	14·00	6·50
		a. Small "G"	£425	£275
		b. Small "R"	£475	£300
16/37 *Set of* 16			£100	£100

Printings to 1891 continued to use the setting showing both types, but subsequently a new setting containing the larger overprint only was used.

The ½a., 1a., 2a. and 3a. exist with space between "I" and "O" of "GWALIOR".

The “GWALICR” error occurs on R. 1/5 in the May 1896 printing only.

Maharaja Madhav Rao Sindhia, 1886–1925

1899–1911.

(a) Optd with T 2 (B).

38	**40**	3p. carmine	50	20
		a. Opt inverted	£1100	£550
		b. Small “G”	60·00	60·00
		d. Small “R”	70·00	
		e. Tall “R”	50·00	
		f. Opt double, one albino	45·00	
39		3p. grey (1904)	7·50	60·00
		e. Tall “R”	£250	
		f. Opt double, one albino	60·00	
40	**23**	½a. pale yellow-green (1901)	1·40	1·60
		e. Tall “R”	90·00	
		f. Opt double, one albino	25·00	
40*g*		½a. yellow-green (1903)	3·75	1·60
		ge. Tall “R”	£130	
41	**25**	1a. carmine (1901)	1·25	35
		e. Tall “R”	95·00	
		f. Opt double, one albino	50·00	
42	**27**	2a. pale violet (1903)	2·75	5·50
		e. Tall “R”	£140	
43	**36**	2a.6p. ultramarine (1903)	1·50	6·50
		e. Tall “R”	£225	
38/43 *Set of 6*			13·50	70·00

(b) Optd as T 2, but “GWALIOR” 13 mm long. Opt spaced 2¾ mm.

44	**38**	3r. brown and green (1911)	£225	£225
45		5r. ultramarine and violet (1910)	65·00	55·00
		a. Opt double, one albino	£110	

1903–11. *King Edward VII. Optd as T 2.*

A. “GWALIOR” *14 mm long. Overprint spaced 1¾ mm (1903–06).*

46A	**41**	3p. pale grey	1·40	20
		e. Tall “R”	38·00	48·00
		f. Slate-grey (1905)	1·50	30
		fe. Tall “R”	42·00	50·00
48A	**42**	½a. green	20	10
		e. Tall “R”	38·00	48·00
49A	**43**	1a. carmine	20	10
		e. Tall “R”	42·00	55·00
		f. Opt double, one albino	45·00	
50A	**44**	2a. pale violet (1904)	2·00	1·00
		e. Tall “R”	95·00	
		f. Mauve	3·00	20
		fe. Tall “R”	£160	£130
52A	**45**	2a.6p. ultramarine (1904)	25·00	80·00
		e. Tall “R”	£1100	
53A	**46**	3a. orange-brown (1904)	2·00	35
		e. Tall “R”	£130	£150
54A	**47**	4a. olive	2·50	40
		e. Tall “R”	£225	£200
		f. Pale olive	12·00	3·25
		fe. Tall “R”	£425	
56A	**48**	6a. olive-bistre (1904)	2·75	3·50
		e. Tall “R”	£1000	
57A	**49**	8a. purple (*shades*) (1905)	5·00	1·60
		e. Tall “R”	£400	£325
59A	**50**	12a. purple/*red* (1905)	3·00	20·00
		e. Tall “R”	£1000	
60A	**51**	1r. green and carmine (1905)	3·00	1·75
		e. Tall “R”	£750	£800
61A	**52**	2r. carmine and yellow-brown (1906)	38·00	48·00
		a. Opt double, one albino	65·00	
46A/61A *Set of 12*			75·00	£140

B. “GWALIOR” *13 mm long. Overprint spaced 2¾ mm (1908–11).*

46B	**41**	3p. pale grey	3·00	10
		f. Slate-grey	3·00	40
49B	**43**	1a. carmine	5·00	1·50
50fB		2a. mauve	3·50	15
52B	**45**	2a.6p. ultramarine	1·25	8·50
53B	**46**	3a. orange-brown	4·00	20
54fB		4a. pale olive	3·75	60
56B	**48**	6a. olive-bistre	6·00	1·40
57B	**49**	8a. purple (*shades*)	9·00	1·60
		f. Claret	22·00	2·50
		fa. Opt double, one albino	65·00	
59B	**50**	12a. purple/*red*	3·75	3·25
		f. Opt double, one albino	80·00	
60B	**51**	1r. green and carmine	7·50	1·25
61B	**52**	2r. carmine and yellow-brown	9·00	11·00
		a. Opt double, one albino	65·00	
62B		3r. brown and green (1910)	28·00	50·00
		a. Red-brown and green	65·00	75·00
63B		5r. ultramarine and violet (1911)	19·00	27·00
46B/63B *Set of 13*			95·00	95·00

1907–08. *Nos. 149 and 150 of India optd as T 2.*

(a) “GWALIOR” *14 mm long. Overprint spaced 1¾ mm.*

64	**53**	½a. green	20	70
		e. Tall “R”	55·00	85·00

(b) “GWALIOR” *13 mm long. Overprint spaced 2¾ mm (1908).*

65	**53**	½a. green	1·50	20
66	**54**	1a. carmine	1·50	20

1912–14. *King George V. Optd as T 2.*

67	**55**	3p. grey	10	10
		a. Opt double	†	£1100
		b. Pale grey	70	10
		c. Bluish grey	—	50
		d. Slate	80	30
		da. “Rs” flaw	38·00	42·00
68	**56**	½a. light green	20	10
		a. Emerald	1·50	35
		b. Bright green	80	10
		ba. Opt inverted	†	£400
69	**57**	1a. aniline carmine	25	10
		a. Opt double	25·00	
70	**59**	2a. purple	80	10
		a. Reddish purple	90	10
		aw. Wmk inverted	†	£100
		b. Deep mauve	2·25	70
		c. Bright reddish violet	2·25	60
71	**62**	3a. orange	70	15
		a. Dull orange	80	25
72	**63**	4a. olive (1913)	60	60
73	**64**	6a. yellow-bistre	1·60	1·75
		a. Brown-ochre	1·25	1·40
74	**65**	8a. deep magenta (1913)	2·25	80
		a. Deep mauve	4·00	30
		b. Bright mauve	8·50	1·75
75	**66**	12a. carmine-lake (1914)	1·40	4·00
		a. Claret	—	5·00
76	**67**	1r. red-brown and deep blue-green (1913)	10·00	1·00
		a. Opt double, one albino	20·00	
		b. Brown and green	9·00	40
		ba. Opt double	£650	
		c. Orange-brown and deep turquoise-green	17·00	3·25
77		2r. carmine-rose and brown (1913)	5·00	4·50
		a. Opt double, one albino	50·00	
78		5r. ultramarine and violet (1913)	23·00	6·50
		a. Opt double, one albino	70·00	
67/78 *Set of 12*			40·00	17·00

GWALIOR
(3)

1921. *No. 192 of India optd with T 3.*

79	**57**	9p. on 1a. rose-carmine	10	50

No. 79 with inverted overprint is of clandestine origin.

1923–27. *Optd as T 2. New colours and values.*

80	**57**	1a. chocolate	1·10	10
		a. Opt double, one albino	48·00	
81	**58**	1½a. chocolate (B) (1925)	2·25	50
82		1½a. rose-carmine (B) (1927)	20	20
83	**61**	2a.6p. ultramarine (1925)	2·25	1·75
84		2a.6p. orange (1927)	35	50
85	**62**	3a. ultramarine (1924)	2·50	60
80/5 *Set of 6*			8·00	3·25

No. 82 with inverted overprint is of clandestine origin.

Maharaja George Jivaji Rao Sindhia, 1925–1961

GWALIOR
ग्वालियर
(4)

GWALIOR
ग्वालियर
(5)

1928–36. *King George V (Nasik printing, wmk Mult Star), optd at Nasik with T 4 or 5 (rupee values).*

86	**55**	3p. slate (1932)	1·00	15
		w. Wmk inverted	1·50	1·00
87	**56**	½a. green (1930)	1·50	10
		w. Wmk inverted		
88	**80**	9p. deep green (*litho*) (1932)	3·00	30
		aw. Wmk inverted	3·00	80
88*b*		9p. deep green (*typo*)	3·50	50
89	**57**	1a. chocolate	85	10
		w. Wmk inverted	—	1·40
90	**82**	1a.3p. mauve (1936)	50	15
91	**70**	2a. purple	75	30
		w. Wmk inverted	75	30
92	**62**	3a. bright blue	1·00	40
93	**71**	4a. sage-green	1·25	1·00
		w. Wmk inverted	2·00	2·50
94	**65**	8a. reddish purple (*wmk inverted*)	1·25	1·10
95	**66**	12a. claret	2·25	3·50
96	**67**	1r. chocolate and green	3·00	4·00
		w. Wmk inverted	6·00	3·50
97		2r. carmine and orange	12·00	6·50
		w. Wmk inverted	8·00	4·50
98		5r. ultramarine and purple (*wmk inverted*) (1929)	18·00	25·00
99		10r. green and scarlet (1930)	65·00	42·00
100		15r. blue & olive (*wmk inverted*) (1930)	£100	70·00
101		25r. orange and blue (1930)	£225	£160
86/101 *Set of 16*			£375	£275

1935–36. *New types and colours. Optd with T 4.*

102	**79**	½a. green (1936)	50	20
		w. Wmk inverted	5·00	3·00
103	**81**	1a. chocolate	20	10
104	**59**	2a. vermilion (1936)	3·00	3·50
102/4 *Set of 3*			3·25	3·50

1938–48. *King George VI. Nos. 247/50, 253, 255/6 and 259/64 optd with T 4 or 5 (rupee values).*

105	**91**	3p. slate	9·50	10
106		½a. red-brown	9·00	10
107		9p. green (1939)	48·00	4·00
108		1a. carmine	8·50	15
109	**94**	3a. yellow-green (1939)	28·00	5·00
110	**96**	4a. brown	45·00	3·50
111	**97**	6a. turquoise-green (1939)	4·00	11·00
112	**100**	1r. grey and red-brown (1942)	12·00	1·75
113		2r. purple and brown (1948)	50·00	9·50
114		5r. green and blue (1948)	32·00	40·00
115		10r. purple and claret (1948)	32·00	42·00
116		15r. brown and green (1948)	90·00	£170
117		25r. slate-violet and purple (1948)	80·00	£130
105/117 *Set of 13*			£400	£375

1942–45. *King George VI. Optd with T 4.*

118	**100a**	3p. slate	45	10
		w. Wmk inverted	—	18·00
119		½a. purple (1943)	1·00	10
120		9p. green	45	10
121		1a. carmine (1943)	1·00	10
		a. Opt double	—	£180
122	**101**	1½a. dull violet	7·00	20
123		2a. vermilion	1·50	20
124		3a. bright violet	16·00	2·00
		a. Opt double	—	£200
125	**102**	4a. brown	3·25	20
126		6a. turquoise-green (1945)	14·00	26·00
127		8a. slate-violet (1944)	3·75	2·75
128		12a. lake (1943)	5·50	23·00
118/28 *Set of 11*			50·00	50·00

The 1½a. and 3a. exist printed by lithography or typography.

GWALIOR
ग्वालियर
(6)

1949 (Apr). *King George VI. Optd with T 6 at the Alizah Printing Press, Gwalior.*

129	**100a**	3p. slate	2·00	50
130		½a. purple	2·00	50
131		1a. carmine	1·75	60
132	**101**	2a. vermilion	26·00	2·25
133		3a. bright violet	65·00	30·00
134	**102**	4a. brown	7·50	3·25
135		6a. turquoise-green	55·00	65·00
136		8a. slate-violet	£110	55·00
137		12a. lake	£425	£150
129/37 *Set of 9*			£650	£275

OFFICIAL STAMPS

गवालियर
सरविस
(O 1)

गवालियर
सरविस
(O 2)

1895–96. *Queen Victoria. Optd with Type O 1.*

O1	**23**	½a. blue-green	50	10
		a. Hindi characters transposed	26·00	28·00
		b. 4th Hindi character omitted	£475	40·00
		c. Opt double	†	£950
O2	**25**	1a. brown-purple	12·00	1·40
O3		1a. plum	2·00	10
		a. Hindi characters transposed	40·00	45·00
		b. 4th Hindi character omitted	£475	65·00
O4	**27**	2a. dull blue	3·25	40
O5		2a. deep blue	1·75	50
		a. Hindi characters transposed	65·00	90·00
		b. 4th Hindi character omitted	80·00	£110
O6	**29**	4a. olive-green	3·50	1·50
		a. Hindi characters transposed	£550	£600
		b. 4th Hindi character omitted	£3000	£1600
O7		4a. slate-green	2·75	1·40
		a. Hindi characters transposed	£300	£400
O8	**31**	8a. dull mauve	4·50	3·25
		a. Opt double, one albino	45·00	
O9		8a. magenta	4·00	2·75
		a. Hindi characters transposed	£1300	£1600
		b. 4th Hindi character omitted		
O10	**37**	1r. green and carmine (1896)	8·50	3·00
		a. Hindi characters transposed	£2750	
O1/10 *Set of 6*			18·00	7·00

In the errors listed above it is the last two Hindi characters that are transposed, so that the word reads “Sersiv”. The error occurs on R. 19/1 in the sheet from the early printings up to May 1896.

1901–04. *Colours changed.*

O23	**40**	3p. carmine (1902)	1·25	25
O24		3p. grey (1904)	2·50	3·50
O25	**23**	½a. pale yellow-green	5·00	15
O26		½a. yellow-green	75	10
O27	**25**	1a. carmine	6·00	10
O28	**27**	2a. pale violet (1903)	1·75	1·50
O23/8 *Set of 5*			11·00	5·00

1903–08. *King Edward VII. Optd as Type O 1.*

(a) Overprint spaced 10 mm (1903–5).

O29	**41**	3p. pale grey	70	10
		a. Slate-grey (1905)	70	10
O31	**42**	½a. green	3·00	10
O32	**43**	1a. carmine	1·10	10
O33	**44**	2a. pale violet (1905)	2·75	60
		a. Mauve	1·75	30
O35	**47**	4a. olive (1905)	17·00	1·75
		a. Opt double, one albino	65·00	
O36	**49**	8a. purple (1905)	7·50	70
		a. Claret	20·00	5·00
		ab. Opt double, one albino	50·00	
O38	**51**	1r. green and carmine (1905)	2·75	2·00
		a. Opt double, one albino	85·00	
O29/38 *Set of 7*			30·00	4·50

(b) Overprint spaced 8 mm (1907–8).

O39	**41**	3p. pale grey	6·00	15
		a. Slate-grey	10·00	1·50
O41	**42**	½a. green	4·00	15
O42	**43**	1a. carmine	2·50	10
O43	**44**	2a. mauve	17·00	75
O44	**47**	4a. olive	3·00	1·00
O45	**49**	8a. purple	4·00	3·75
O46	**51**	1r. green and carmine (1908)	42·00	13·00
O39/46 *Set of 7*			70·00	17·00

1907–08. *Nos. 149 and 150 of India optd as Type O 1.*

(a) Overprint spaced 10 mm (1908).

O47	**53**	½a. green	8·00	10
O48	**54**	1a. carmine	7·00	15
		a. Opt double, one albino	42·00	

(b) Overprint spaced 8 mm (1907).

O49	**53**	½a. green	1·75	15
O50	**54**	1a. carmine	65·00	3·00

1913–23. *King George V. Optd with Type O 1.*

O51	**55**	3p. grey	25	10
		a. Pair, one without opt	£1700	
		b. Pale grey	25	10
		c. Bluish grey	—	30
		d. Slate	40	10
		da. “Rs” flaw	85·00	
O52	**56**	½a. light green	20	10
		b. Emerald	—	10
		ba. Opt double	£110	£170
		c. Bright green	20	10

O53	57	1a. rose-carmine	12·00	50
		a. Aniline carmine	30	10
		ab. Opt double	65·00	
O54		1a. chocolate (1923)	3·75	15
O55	59	2a. purple	1·50	1·00
		a. Reddish purple	1·50	20
		b. Deep mauve	3·00	
		c. Bright reddish violet	1·60	30
O56	63	4a. olive	60	1·50
O57	65	8a. deep magenta	1·00	2·50
		a. Deep mauve	1·25	1·00
		b. Bright mauve	3·50	
O58	67	1r. red-brown and deep blue-green	30·00	25·00
		a. Opt double, one albino	75·00	
		b. Brown and green	27·00	24·00
		c. Orange-brown and deep turquoise-green	29·00	25·00
O51/8 *Set of* 8			32·00	25·00

1921. *No. O97 of India optd with T* **3**.

O59	57	9p. on 1a. rose-carmine	10	30

1927–35. *King George V (Nasik printing, wmk Mult Star), optd at Nasik as Type* O **1** *(but top line measures 13 mm instead of 14 mm) or with Type* O **2** *(rupee values).*

O61	55	3p. slate	30	10
		w. Wmk inverted	10	50
O62	56	½a. green	10	15
		w. Wmk inverted	3·00	
O63	80	9p. deep green (1932)	10	15
O64	57	1a. chocolate	10	10
		w. Wmk inverted	2·00	50
O65	82	1a.3p. mauve (1933)	50	15
		w. Wmk inverted	4·00	
O66	70	2a. purple	20	15
		w. Wmk inverted	3·25	
O67	71	4a. sage-green	75	30
		w. Wmk inverted	—	2·00
O68	65	8a. reddish purple (1928)	60	1·10
		w. Wmk inverted	2·50	2·25
O69	67	1r. chocolate and green	1·00	1·75
		w. Wmk inverted	1·90	3·25
O70		2r. carmine and orange (1935)	19·00	20·00
O71		5r. ultramarine and purple (1932)	23·00	£170
		w. Wmk inverted	24·00	
O72		10r. green and scarlet (1932)	£160	£450
O61/72 *Set of* 12			£180	£600

1936–37. *New types. Optd as Type* O **1** *(13 mm).*

O73	79	½a. green	15	15
		w. Wmk inverted	—	4·00
O74	81	1a. chocolate	15	15
O75	59	2a. vermilion	20	40
O76		2a. vermilion (*small die*)	2·50	1·25
O77	63	4a. sage-green (1937)	60	75
O73/7 *Set of* 5			3·25	2·40

1938. *King George VI. Optd as Type* O **1** *(13 mm).*

O78	91	½a. red-brown	6·50	30
O79		1a. carmine	1·50	20

(O 3) (O 4)

1940–42. *Official stamps optd with Type* O **3**.

O80	O 20	3p. slate	50	10
O81		½a. red-brown	4·50	25
O82		½a. purple (1942)	50	10
O83		9p. green (1942)	70	70
O84		1a. carmine	2·25	10
O85		1a.3p. yellow-brown (1942)	45·00	1·75
		w. Wmk inverted	—	22·00
O86		1½a. dull violet (1942)	1·25	30
O87		2a. vermilion	1·25	30
O88		4a. brown (1942)	1·25	3·25
O89		8a. slate-violet (1942)	4·75	9·50
O80/9 *Set of* 10			55·00	15·00

1941. *Stamp of 1932 (King George V) optd with Type* O **1** *and surch with Type* O **4**.

O90	82	1a. on 1a.3p. mauve	25·00	3·00
		w. Wmk inverted	35·00	8·00

1942–47. *King George VI. Optd with Type* O **2**.

O91	100	1r. grey and red-brown	10·00	22·00
O92		2r. purple and brown	18·00	95·00
O93		5r. green and blue (1943)	30·00	£550
O94		10r. purple and claret (1947)	80·00	£1100
O91/4 *Set of* 4			£120	£1600

Gwalior became part of Madhya Bharat by 1 July 1948.

JIND

For earlier issues, see under INDIAN FEUDATORY STATES

PRICES FOR STAMPS ON COVER	
Nos. 1/4	*from* × 20
Nos. 5/16	—
Nos. 17/40	*from* × 15
Nos. 41/149	*from* × 8
Nos. O1/86	*from* × 15

Raja Raghubir Singh, 1864–1887

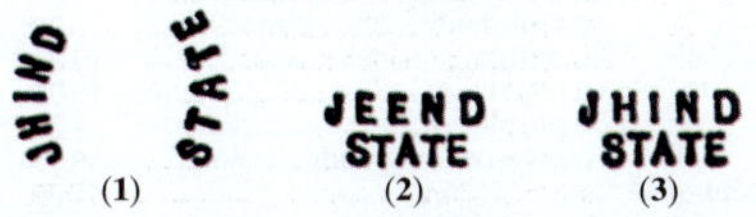

(1) (2) (3)

1885 (1 July). *Queen Victoria. Optd with T* **1**.

1	23	½a. blue-green	4·75	5·50
		a. Opt inverted	90·00	£110
2	25	1a. brown-purple	42·00	60·00
		a. Opt inverted	£950	£1000
3	27	2a. dull blue	19·00	21·00
		a. Opt inverted	£700	£800
4	17	4a. green	65·00	90·00
5	31	8a. dull mauve	£425	
		a. Opt inverted	£12000	
6	33	1r. slate	£475	
		a. Opt inverted	£14000	
1/6 *Set of* 6			£950	

The overprint inverted errors occurred on R. 10/8 in the setting of 120, although it is believed that one pane of the ½a. had the overprint inverted on the entire pane. Examples of inverted overprints on the ½a., 1a. and 2a. with the lines much less curved are thought to come from a trial printing.

All six values exist with reprinted overprint. This has the words "JHIND" and "STATE" 8 and 9 mm in length respectively, whereas in the originals the words are 9 and 9½ mm.

1885. *Optd with T* **2**.

7	23	½a. blue-green (R.)	£140	
8	25	1a. brown-purple	£140	
9	27	2a. dull blue (R.)	£140	
10	17	4a. green (R.)	£190	
		a. Opt double, one albino	£250	
11	31	8a. dull mauve	£190	
12	33	1r. slate (R.)	£190	
7/12 *Set of* 6			£900	

1886. *Optd with T* **3**, *in red.*

13	23	½a. blue-green	35·00	
		a. "JEIND" for "JHIND"	£1200	
14	27	2a. dull blue	38·00	
		a. "JEIND" for "JHIND"	£1200	
		b. Opt double, one albino	80·00	
15	17	4a. green	60·00	
		a. Opt double, one albino	60·00	
		b. Opt treble, two albino	95·00	
16	33	1r. slate	60·00	
		a. "JEIND" for "JHIND"	£1800	
13/16 *Set of* 4			£180	

Examples of No. 14a usually show an additional albino "SERVICE" overprint as Type O **16**.

1886–99. *Optd with T* **3**.

17	23	½a. blue-green	80	10
		a. Opt inverted	£200	
18	25	1a. brown-purple	2·50	20
		a. "JEIND" for "JHIND"	£500	
		b. Opt double, one albino	48·00	
19		1a. plum (1899)	4·50	1·00
20	26	1a.6p. sepia (1896)	2·50	3·75
		a. Opt double, one albino	55·00	
21	27	2a. dull blue	2·50	40
22		2a. ultramarine	2·50	75
		a. Opt double, one albino	55·00	
23	28	3a. brown-orange (1891)	3·25	75
24	29	4a. olive-green	4·00	2·25
25		4a. slate-green	6·00	4·00
26	21	6a. olive-bistre (1891)	8·50	22·00
		a. Opt double, one albino	42·00	
27		6a. bistre-brown	4·50	14·00
28	31	8a. dull mauve	8·50	20·00
		a. "JEIND" for "JHIND"	£1600	
29		8a. magenta (1897)	11·00	30·00
		a. Opt double, one albino	48·00	
30	32	12a. purple/*red* (1896)	7·00	25·00
		a. Opt double, one albino	48·00	
31	33	1r. slate	12·00	55·00
32	37	1r. green and carmine (1897)	11·00	60·00
33	38	2r. carmine and yellow-brown (1896)	£350	£1000
34		3r. brown and green (1896)	£500	£900
35		5r. ultramarine and violet (1896)	£500	£850
17/35 *Set of* 14			£1300	£2750

Varieties exist in which the word "JHIND" measures 10½ mm and 9¾ mm instead of 10 mm. Such varieties are to be found on Nos. 17, 18, 21, 24, 28 and 31.

Raja (Maharaja from 1911) Ranbir Singh, 1887–1959

1900–04. *Colours changed.*

36	40	3p. carmine	1·10	1·75
37		3p. grey (1904)	40	4·00
38	23	½a. pale yellow-green (1902)	4·75	7·00
39		½a. yellow-green (1903)	10·00	13·00
40	25	1a. carmine (1902)	1·25	7·00
		a. Opt double, one albino	40·00	
36/40 *Set of* 4			6·75	18·00

1903–09. *King Edward VII. Optd with T* **3**.

41	41	3p. pale grey	25	10
		a. Opt double, one albino	19·00	
42		3p. slate-grey (1905)	50	75
43	42	½a. green	2·00	1·75
44	43	1a. carmine	2·25	1·60
45	44	2a. pale violet	3·25	2·25
46		2a. mauve (1906)	2·75	80
		a. Opt double, one albino	42·00	
47	45	2a.6p. ultramarine (1909)	75	7·00
		a. Opt double, one albino	28·00	
48	46	3a. orange-brown	2·50	40
		a. Opt double	£120	£225
49	47	4a. olive	9·00	9·50
		a. Opt double, one albino	45·00	
50		4a. pale olive	9·50	11·00
51	48	6a. bistre (1905)	7·50	22·00
		a. Opt double, one albino	48·00	
52	49	8a. purple (*shades*)	3·00	22·00
53		8a. claret	17·00	35·00
54	50	12a. purple/*red* (1905)	3·25	12·00
55	51	1r. green and carmine (1905)	3·75	22·00
		a. Opt double, one albino	65·00	
41/55 *Set of* 11			34·00	90·00

1907–09. *Nos. 149/50 of India optd with T* **3**.

56	53	½a. green	40	20
57	54	1a. carmine (1909)	1·50	70

1913. *King George V. Optd with T* **3**.

58	55	3p. grey	10	2·25
59	56	½a. light green	10	75
60	57	1a. aniline carmine	10	45
61	59	2a. purple	15	4·25
62	62	3a. orange	1·50	14·00
63	64	6a. yellow-bistre	8·50	29·00
58/63 *Set of* 6			9·50	45·00

(4) (5) (6)

1914–27. *King George V. Optd with T* **4**.

64	55	3p. grey	1·00	50
		a. Pale grey	1·50	20
		b. Bluish grey	2·50	30
		c. Slate	2·50	
65	56	½a. light green	2·50	15
		a. Emerald	—	1·00
		b. Bright green	2·50	30
66	57	1a. aniline carmine	1·60	15
67	58	1½a. chocolate (Type A) (1922)	3·25	6·00
68		1½a. chocolate (Type B) (1924)	50	1·50
69	59	2a. purple	4·50	1·25
		a. Reddish purple	7·50	75
		b. Bright reddish violet (1922)	5·50	75
70	61	2a.6p. ultramarine (1922)	50	4·75
71	62	3a. orange	50	4·00
72	63	4a. olive	2·00	9·50
73	64	6a. yellow-bistre	4·50	18·00
		a. Brown-ochre	4·00	16·00
74	65	8a. deep magenta	5·50	16·00
		a. Deep mauve (1925)	9·50	14·00
		b. Bright mauve (1918)	—	24·00
75	66	12a. carmine-lake	5·00	20·00
76	67	1r. red-brown and deep blue-green	12·00	24·00
		a. Opt double, one albino	40·00	
		b. Brown and green	19·00	
77		2r. carmine and yellow-brown (1927)	6·50	£150
78		5r. ultramarine and violet (1927)	45·00	£300
64/78 *Set of* 15			85·00	£500

No. 71 with inverted overprint is of clandestine origin.

1922. *No. 192 of India optd "JIND" in block capitals.*

79	57	9p. on 1a. rose-carmine	1·25	15·00

1924–27. *Optd with T* **4**. *New colours.*

80	57	1a. chocolate	6·00	3·00
81	58	1½a. rose-carmine (Type B) (1927)	20	1·50
82	61	2a.6p. orange (1927)	1·25	8·00
83	62	3a. bright blue (1925)	2·00	5·00
80/3 *Set of* 4			8·50	16·00

Nos. 81/2 with inverted overprint are of clandestine origin.

1927–37. *King George V (Nasik printing, wmk Mult Star), optd at Nasik with T* **5** *or* **6** *(rupee values).*

84	55	3p. slate	10	10
		w. Wmk inverted	2·75	
85	56	½a. green (1929)	10	35
86	80	9p. deep green (1932)	2·25	40
87	57	1a. chocolate (1928)	15	10
		w. Wmk inverted	—	2·00
88	82	1a.3p. mauve (1932)	25	30
89	58	1½a. rose-carmine (Type B) (1930)	60	3·75
		w. Wmk inverted	1·25	3·75
90	70	2a. purple (1928)	3·25	40
		w. Wmk inverted	3·25	40
91	61	2a.6p. orange (1930)	1·60	
		w. Wmk inverted	1·25	11·00
92	62	3a. bright blue (1930)	6·50	18·00
		w. Wmk inverted	13·00	
93	83	3a.6p. ultramarine (1937)	4·00	24·00
		w. Wmk inverted	60	20·00
94	71	4a. sage-green (1928)	5·50	3·50
		w. Wmk inverted	1·75	3·50
95	64	6a. bistre (1937)	65	22·00
		w. Wmk inverted	6·50	
96	65	8a. reddish purple (1930)	6·00	2·25
		w. Wmk inverted	6·00	
97	66	12a. claret (1930)		
		w. Wmk inverted	8·00	22·00
98	67	1r. chocolate and green (1930)	5·00	6·00
		w. Wmk inverted		
99		2r. carmine and orange (1930)	42·00	£150
		w. Wmk inverted	26·00	
100		5r. ultramarine and purple (1928)	13·00	42·00
		w. Wmk inverted	45·00	
101		10r. green and carmine (1928)	15·00	18·00
102		15r. blue & olive (*wmk inverted*) (1929)	95·00	£700
103		25r. orange and blue (1929)	£150	£850
84/103 *Set of* 20			£300	£1700

1934. *New types and colours. Optd with T* **5**.

104	79	½a. green	30	25
105	81	1a. chocolate	2·00	30
		w. Wmk inverted	—	4·25
106	59	2a. vermilion	3·75	60
107	62	3a. carmine	3·25	40
108	63	4a. sage-green	3·25	1·50
104/8 *Set of* 5			11·50	2·75

1937–38. *King George VI. Nos. 247/64 optd with T* **5** *or T* **6** *(rupee values).*

109	91	3p. slate	10·00	2·50
110		½a. red-brown	75	5·00
111		9p. green (1937)	75	4·00
112		1a. carmine (1937)	75	60
113	92	2a. vermilion	1·75	19·00
114	93	2a.6p. bright violet	1·25	23·00
115	94	3a. yellow-green	6·50	20·00
116	95	3a.6p. bright blue	3·25	23·00
117	96	4a. brown	9·50	19·00
118	97	6a. turquoise-green	6·00	29·00
119	98	8a. slate-violet	5·00	23·00
120	99	12a. lake	2·75	30·00
121	100	1r. grey and red-brown	12·00	42·00
122		2r. purple and brown	15·00	£130
123		5r. green and blue	27·00	85·00
124		10r. purple and claret	48·00	80·00

125		15r. brown and green	£100	£800
126		25r. slate-violet and purple	£550	£950
109/26 *Set of* 18			£700	£2000

JIND

(7)

1941–43. *King George VI. Optd with T* **7**.

(a) Stamps of 1937. W **69** (inverted on 15r.).

127	**91**	3p. slate	14·00	22·00
128		½a. red-brown	1·00	2·50
129		9p. green	13·00	20·00
130		1a. carmine	1·00	6·00
131	**100**	1r. grey and red-brown	9·00	27·00
132		2r. purple and brown	18·00	35·00
133		5r. green and blue	40·00	95·00
134		10r. purple and claret	55·00	85·00
135		15r. brown and green	£130	£170
136		25r. slate-violet and purple	60·00	£350
127/36 *Set of* 10			£300	£750

(b) Stamps of 1940–43.

137	**100a**	3p. slate (1942)	50	1·40
138		½a. purple (1943)	50	2·25
139		9p. green (1942)	75	4·25
140		1a. carmine (1942)	1·00	1·50
141	**101**	1a.3p. yellow-brown	1·00	5·00
142		1½a. dull violet (1942)	8·00	5·00
143		2a. vermilion	1·75	5·00
144		3a. bright violet (1942)	25·00	6·00
145		3½a. bright blue	9·00	12·00
146	**102**	4a. brown	6·00	6·00
147		6a. turquoise-green	6·50	17·00
148		8a. slate-violet	4·25	15·00
149		12a. lake	14·00	18·00
137/149 *Set of* 13			70·00	90·00

The 1½a. and 3a. exist printed by lithography or typography.

OFFICIAL STAMPS

SERVICE

SERVICE (O 14) SERVICE (O 15) JHIND STATE (O 16)

1885 (1 July). *Queen Victoria. Nos. 1/3 of Jind optd with Type* O **14**.

O1	**23**	½a. blue green	2·00	40
		a. Opt Type **1** inverted	£100	60·00
O2	**25**	1a. brown-purple	70	10
		a. Opt Type **1** inverted	12·00	7·50
O3	**27**	2a. dull blue	40·00	48·00
		a. Opt Type **1** inverted	£1000	£1200

The three values have had the overprint reprinted in the same way as the ordinary stamps of 1885. See note after No. 6.

1885. *Nos. 7/9 of Jind optd with Type* O **15**.

O7	**23**	½a. blue-green (R.)	£100	
		a. "JEEND STATE" double, one albino	£170	
O8	**25**	1a. brown-purple	85·00	
O9	**27**	2a. dull blue (R.)	95·00	
O7/9 *Set of* 3			£250	

1886. *Optd with Type* O **16**, *in red*.

O10	**23**	½a. blue-green	28·00	
		a. "ERVICE"	£4000	
		b. "JEIND"	£700	
		c. "JHIND STATE" double, one albino	70·00	
O11	**27**	2a. dull blue	32·00	
		a. "ERVICE"	£2500	
		b. "JEIND"	£1200	
		c. "SERVICE" double, one albino	60·00	
		d. "JHIND STATE" double, one albino	60·00	

1886–1902. *Optd with Type* O **16**.

O12	**23**	½a. blue-green	2·00	10
		a. "JHIND STATE" double, one albino	48·00	
O13	**25**	1a. brown-purple	26·00	
		a. "ERVICE		
		b. "JEIND"	£500	
		c. "SERVICE" double, one albino	29·00	
O14		1a. plum (1902)	13·00	1·50
O15	**27**	2a. dull blue	3·25	1·00
		a. "SERVICE" double, one albino	45·00	
		b. "SERVICE" treble, two albino	50·00	
O16		2a. ultramarine	2·00	30
		a. "JHIND STATE" double, one albino	55·00	
O17	**29**	4a. olive-green (1892)	3·50	2·00
		a. "JHIND STATE" double, one albino	45·00	
O18		4a. slate-green	3·50	2·75
O19	**31**	8a. dull mauve (1892)	6·00	4·50
O20		8a. magenta (1897)	5·50	8·50
		a. "JHIND STATE" double, one albino	45·00	
O21	**37**	1r. green and carmine (1896)	6·50	50·00
		a. "SERVICE" double, one albino	65·00	
		b. "JHIND STATE" treble, two albino	70·00	
O12/21 *Set of* 6			29·00	55·00

Varieties mentioned in note after No. 35 exist on Nos. O12, O15, O17 and O20.

Printings up to and including that of October 1897 had the "SERVICE" overprint. Type O **15**, applied to sheets already overprinted with Type **3**. From the printing of December 1899 onwards "SERVICE" and "JHIND STATE" were overprinted at one operation, as Type O **16**, to provide fresh supplies of Nos. O12, O14 and O21.

1902. *Colour changed. Optd with Type* O **16**.

O22	**23**	½a. yellow-green	2·50	30
		a. "V" of "SERVICE" omitted	£160	80·00

No. O22a normally shows a tiny trace of the "V" remaining. Examples showing the letter completely missing are worth much more.

1903–06. *King Edward VII stamps of India optd with Type* O **16**.

O23	**41**	3p. pale grey	75	10
O24		3p. slate-grey (1906)	75	10
O25	**42**	½a. green	3·50	10
		a. "HIND"	£3000	£300
		b. Opt double, one albino	38·00	
		c. "SERV CE"	†	£300
O26	**43**	1a. carmine	3·00	10
		a. "HIND"	£3500	£275
		b. Opt double, one albino	38·00	
O27	**44**	2a. pale violet	3·00	1·00
O28		2a. mauve	2·00	10
O29	**47**	4a. olive	1·75	45
		a. Opt double, one albino	50·00	
O30	**49**	8a. purple (*shades*)	9·50	5·00
O31		8a. claret	6·00	1·50
O32	**51**	1r. green and carmine (1906)	2·50	2·25
O23/32 *Set of* 7			18·00	4·00

The "HIND" error Nos. O25a and O26a occurred on one position in the bottom row of the sheet.

1907. *Nos. 149/50 of India optd with Type* O **16**.

O33	**53**	½a. green	1·00	10
O34	**54**	1a. carmine	1·75	10

1914–27. *King George V. Official stamps of India optd with T* **4**.

O35	**55**	3p. grey	10	10
		a. "JIND STATE" double, one albino	48·00	
		b. Pale grey	10	10
		c. Bluish grey	—	30
O36	**56**	½a. light green	10	10
		a. Emerald	2·00	40
		b. Bright green	35	10
O37	**57**	1a. aniline carmine	75	10
		a. Pale rose-carmine	2·50	10
O39	**59**	2a. purple	25	30
		a. Reddish purple	—	15
		b. Deep mauve	2·25	40
O40	**63**	4a. olive	1·25	20
O41	**64**	6a. brown-ochre (1926)	1·75	2·25
O42	**65**	8a. deep magenta	70	1·00
		a. Deep mauve	2·25	1·75
O43	**67**	1r. red-brown and deep blue-green	2·50	1·75
		a. "JIND STATE" double, one albino	45·00	
		b. Brown and green	9·00	
O44		2r. carmine and yellow-brown (1927)	18·00	75·00
O45		5r. ultramarine and violet (1927)	24·00	£250
O35/45 *Set of* 10			45·00	£300

No. O40 with double overprint is of clandestine origin.

1924. *As 1914–27. New colour.*

O46	**57**	1a. chocolate	60	10

JIND STATE SERVICE (O 17) JIND STATE SERVICE (O 18) JIND SERVICE (O 19)

1927–37. *King George V (Nasik printing, wmk Mult Star), optd with Types* O **17** *or* O **18** *(rupee values).*

O47	**55**	3p. slate (1928)	10	20
O48	**56**	½a. green (1929)	10	1·00
O49	**80**	9p. deep green (*litho*) (1932)	60	15
O49*a*		9p. deep green (*typo*)	—	75
O50	**57**	1a. chocolate	10	10
		w. Wmk inverted	85	
O51	**82**	1a.3p. mauve (1932)	40	15
		w. Wmk inverted	1·60	80
O52	**70**	2a. purple (1929)	25	15
O53	**61**	2a.6p. orange (1937)	1·25	21·00
O54	**71**	4a. sage-green (1929)	35	25
		w. Wmk inverted	2·25	1·50
O55	**64**	6a. bistre (1937)	3·75	
		w. Wmk inverted	4·50	17·00
O56	**65**	8a. reddish purple (1929)	—	1·75
		w. Wmk inverted	60	1·75
O57	**66**	12a. claret (1928)	2·25	19·00
O58	**67**	1r. chocolate and green (1928)	5·00	5·50
O59		2r. carmine and orange (1930)	50·00	42·00
		w. Wmk inverted	38·00	
O60		5r. ultramarine and purple (1929)	13·00	£275
O61		10r. green and carmine (1928)	38·00	£150
		w. Wmk inverted	55·00	
O47/61 *Set of* 15			90·00	£475

1934. *Optd with Type* O **17**.

O62	**79**	½a. green	20	15
O63	**81**	1a. chocolate	20	15
O64	**59**	2a. vermilion	30	15
		w. Wmk inverted	1·25	2·50
O65	**63**	4a. sage-green	6·00	30
O62/5 *Set of* 4			6·25	65

1937–40. *King George VI. Optd with Types* O **17** *or* O **18** *(rupee values).*

O66	**91**	½a. red-brown (1938)	65·00	30
O67		9p. green	2·00	16·00
O68		1a. carmine	1·50	30
O69	**100**	1r. grey and red-brown (1940)	35·00	55·00
O70		2r. purple and brown (1940)	45·00	£250
O71		5r. green and blue (1940)	80·00	£400
O72		10r. purple and claret (1940)	£350	£1000
O66/72 *Set of* 7			£500	£1600

1939–43.

(a) Official stamps optd with T **7**.

O73	**O 20**	3p. slate	60	2·00
O74		½a. red-brown	2·00	1·25
O75		½a. purple (1943)	60	30
O76		9p. green	3·00	13·00
O77		1a. carmine	3·75	15
O78		1½a. dull violet (1942)	9·00	2·25
O79		2a. vermilion	8·00	30
		w. Wmk inverted	10·00	3·75
O80		2½a. bright violet	5·00	9·50
O81		4a. brown	8·50	4·75
O82		8a. slate-violet	9·00	8·00

(b) Postage stamps optd with Type O **19**.

O83	**93**	1r. grey and red-brown (1942)	18·00	55·00
O84		2r. purple and brown (1942)	42·00	£170
O85		5r. green and blue (1942)	70·00	£425
O86		10r. purple and claret (1942)	£140	£550
O73/86 *Set of* 14			£275	£1100

Jind was absorbed into the Patiala and East Punjab States Union by 20 August 1948.

NABHA

PRICES FOR STAMPS ON COVER	
Nos. 1/3	*from* × 15
Nos. 4/6	—
Nos. 10/36	*from* × 12
Nos. 37/117	*from* × 7
Nos. O1/68	*from* × 15

Raja Hira Singh, 1871–1911.

NABHA STATE (1) NABHA STATE (2)

1885 (1 July). *Queen Victoria. Optd with T* **1**.

1	**23**	½a. blue-green	4·25	6·00
2	**25**	1a. brown-purple	55·00	£190
3	**27**	2a. dull blue	25·00	65·00
4	**17**	4a. green	85·00	£250
5	**31**	8a. dull mauve	£325	
6	**33**	1r. slate	£375	
1/6 *Set of* 6			£800	

All six values have had the overprint reprinted. On the reprints the words "NABHA" and "STATE" both measure 9¼ mm in length, whereas on the originals these words measure 11 and 10 mm respectively. The varieties with overprint double come from the reprints.

1885 (Nov)–**1900.** *Optd with T* **2**.

(a) In red.

10	**23**	½a. blue-green	1·25	1·00
11	**27**	2a. dull blue	2·50	2·25
		a. Opt double, one albino	65·00	
12	**17**	4a. green	45·00	£225
13	**33**	1r. slate	£130	£300
		a. Opt double, one albino	£170	
10/13 *Set of* 4			£160	£475

(b) In black (Nov 1885–97).

14	**23**	½a. blue-green (1888)	60	10
15	**24**	9p. carmine (1892)	2·00	3·75
16	**25**	1a. brown-purple	3·00	1·00
17		1a. plum	2·75	1·25
18	**26**	1a.6p. sepia (1891)	1·75	4·00
		a. "ABHA" for "NABHA"	£300	
19	**27**	2a. dull blue (1888)	3·00	2·00
20		2a. ultramarine	3·00	2·25
21	**28**	3a. orange (1889)	11·00	24·00
		a. Opt double, one albino	40·00	
22		3a. brown-orange	4·00	2·25
23	**29**	4a. olive-green (1888)	6·00	3·25
24		4a. slate-green	6·50	2·50
25	**21**	6a. olive-bistre (1889)	8·50	16·00
26		6a. bistre-brown	3·75	4·50
27	**31**	8a. dull mauve	4·00	3·50
		a. Opt double, one albino	48·00	
28	**32**	12a. purple/*red* (1889)	4·75	5·50
		a. Opt double, one albino	42·00	
29	**33**	1r. slate (1888)	15·00	60·00
30	**37**	1r. green and carmine (1893)	14·00	7·50
		a. "N BHA" for "NABHA"		
		b. Opt double, one albino	60·00	
31	**38**	2r. carmine and yellow-brown (1897)	£140	£300
		a. Opt double, one albino	£250	
32		3r. brown and green (1897)	£140	£375
33		5r. ultramarine and violet (1897)	£150	£550
14/33 *Set of* 15			£450	£1200

(c) New value. In black (Nov 1900).

36	**40**	3p. carmine	30	20

1903–09. *King Edward VII. Optd with T* **2**.

37	**41**	3p. pale grey	75	15
		a. "NAB STA" for "NABHA STATE"	£900	
		b. Opt double, one albino	28·00	
37*c*		3p. slate-grey (1906)	75	15
38	**42**	½a. green	1·10	70
		a. "NABH" for "NABHA"	£1100	
39	**43**	1a. carmine	1·75	1·50
40	**44**	2a. pale violet	2·50	3·50
40*a*		2a. mauve	3·50	35
40*b*	**45**	2a.6p. ultramarine (1909)	19·00	90·00
		ba. Opt double, one albino	32·00	
41	**46**	3a. orange-brown	1·60	40
		a. Opt double, one albino	45·00	
42	**47**	4a. olive	4·75	1·75
43	**48**	6a. olive-bistre	4·00	20·00
		a. Opt double, one albino	32·00	
44	**49**	8a. purple	10·00	26·00
44*a*		8a. claret	15·00	26·00
45	**50**	12a. purple/*red*	4·50	27·00
46	**51**	1r. green and carmine	9·50	18·00
37/46 *Set of* 11			55·00	£170

1907. *Nos. 149/50 of India optd with T* **2**.

47	**53**	½a. green	1·50	1·25
48	**54**	1a. carmine	1·50	70

Maharaja Ripudaman (Gurcharan) Singh, 1911–1928.

1913. *King George V. Optd with T* **2**.

49 **55** 3p. grey ... 50 50
a. Pale grey ... 40 30
b. Bluish grey ... 1·50 50
c. Slate ... 1·00
50 **56** ½a. light green ... 50 40
a. Emerald ... 2·25 50
b. Bright green ... 50 30
51 **57** 1a. aniline carmine ... 1·10 10
52 **59** 2a. purple ... 1·00 1·25
a. Reddish purple ... 1·75 1·00
b. Deep mauve ... 2·00 90
53 **62** 3a. orange ... 50 35
a. Dull orange ... 1·50 50
54 **63** 4a. olive ... 75 2·00
55 **64** 6a. yellow-bistre ... 1·25 6·50
a. Brown-ochre ... 1·25 7·00
56 **65** 8a. deep magenta ... 7·00 6·50
a. Deep mauve ... 6·50 6·00
b. Bright mauve ... 8·00
57 **66** 12a. carmine-lake ... 3·00 24·00
58 **67** 1r. red-brown and deep blue-green ... 10·00 7·50
a. Opt double, one albino ... 45·00
b. Brown and green ... 18·00 7·00
c. Orange-brown and deep turquoise-green ... 20·00
49/58 *Set of* 10 ... 22·00 42·00

1924. *As 1913. New colour.*

59 **57** 1a. chocolate ... 7·00 4·00

No. 59 with inverted or double overprint is of clandestine origin.

NABHA STATE (3) NABHA STATE (4)

1927–36. *King George V (Nasik printing, wmk Mult Star), optd as T* **3** *or* **4** *(rupee values).*

60 **55** 3p. slate (1932) ... 1·75 15
w. Wmk inverted ... 3·50 1·75
61 **56** ½a. green (1928) ... 1·00 30
61*a* **80** 9p. deep green (*litho*) (1934) ... 11·00 12·00
61*b* 9p. deep green (*typo*) ... 2·50 1·10
62 **57** 1a. chocolate ... 1·50 15
w. Wmk inverted ... — 3·00
63 **82** 1a.3p. mauve (1936) ... 2·75 7·50
w. Wmk inverted ... 75
64 **70** 2a. purple (1932) ... 2·50 35
65 **61** 2a.6p. orange (1932) ... 1·50 9·50
66 **62** 3a. bright blue (1930) ... 3·00 1·40
67 **71** 4a. sage-green (1932) ... 4·50 2·50
71 **67** 2r. carmine and orange (1932) ... 32·00 £140
72 5r. ultramarine and purple (*wmk inverted*) (1932) ... 75·00 £400
60/72 *Set of* 11 ... £110 £500

Maharaja Partab Singh, 1928–1971

1936–37. *New types and colours. Optd as T* **3**.

73 **79** ½a. green ... 60 40
74 **81** 1a. chocolate ... 60 30
75 **62** 3a. carmine (1937) ... 4·00 17·00
76 **63** 4a. sage-green (1937) ... 6·00 5·00
73/6 *Set of* 4 ... 10·00 21·00

NABHA STATE (5) NABHA (6)

1938. *King George VI. Nos. 247/64 optd as T* **3** *(3p. to 1a.), T* **5** *(2a. to 12a.) or T* **4** *(rupee values).* W **69** *(inverted on 15r.).*

77 **91** 3p. slate ... 9·00 1·50
78 ½a. red-brown ... 7·00 1·75
79 9p. green ... 20·00 5·00
80 1a. carmine ... 3·00 1·00
81 **92** 2a. vermilion ... 1·25 8·00
82 **93** 2a.6p. bright violet ... 1·25 12·00
83 **94** 3a. yellow-green ... 1·40 6·00
84 **95** 3a.6p. bright blue ... 1·60 25·00
85 **96** 4a. brown ... 7·50 7·00
86 **97** 6a. turquoise-green ... 3·25 27·00
87 **98** 8a. slate-violet ... 2·25 25·00
88 **99** 12a. lake ... 2·50 25·00
89 **100** 1r. grey and red-brown ... 12·00 35·00
90 2r. purple and brown ... 30·00 £120
91 5r. green and blue ... 40·00 £200
92 10r. purple and claret ... 60·00 £400
93 15r. brown and green ... £190 £850
94 25r. slate-violet and purple ... £140 £850
w. Wmk inverted ... £250 £950
77/94 *Set of* 18 ... £450 £2250

1941–45. *King George VI. Optd with T* **6**.

(a) Stamps of 1937

95 **91** 3p. slate (1942) ... 40·00 6·00
96 ½a. red-brown (1942) ... 80·00 7·00
97 9p. green (1942) ... 11·00 16·00
98 1a. carmine (1942) ... 12·00 4·50
95/8 *Set of* 4 ... £130 30·00

(b) Stamps of 1940–43.

105 **100a** 3p. slate (1942) ... 1·25 1·00
106 ½a. purple (1943) ... 3·00 1·75
107 9p. green (1942) ... 2·50 1·75
108 1a. carmine (1945) ... 1·00 4·25
109 **101** 1a.3p. yellow-brown ... 1·00 3·75
110 1½a. dull violet (1942) ... 2·50 3·00
111 2a. vermilion (1943) ... 1·10 4·50
112 3a. bright violet (1943) ... 6·50 5·50
113 3½a. bright blue (1944) ... 17·00 65·00
114 **102** 4a. brown ... 1·75 1·00
115 6a. turquoise-green (1943) ... 14·00 55·00
116 8a. slate-violet (1943) ... 13·00 42·00
117 12a. lake (1943) ... 11·00 65·00
105/17 *Set of* 13 ... 70·00 £225

The 1½a. exists printed by lithography or typography.

OFFICIAL STAMPS

SERVICE

SERVICE (O 8) NABHA STATE (O 9)

1885 (1 July). *Nos. 1/3 of Nabha optd with Type* O **8**.

O1 **23** ½a. blue-green ... 5·00 1·50
O2 **25** 1a. brown-purple ... 70 20
a. Opt Type O **8** double ... † £2000
O3 **27** 2a. dull blue ... 85·00 £170
O1/3 *Set of* 3 ... 85·00 £170

The three values have had the overprint reprinted in the same way as the ordinary stamps of 1885.

1885 (Nov)–**97**. *Optd with Type* O **9**.

(a) In red.

O4 **23** ½a. blue-green ... 7·50 5·50
O5 **27** 2a. deep blue ... 1·60 55

(b) In black (Nov 1885–97).

O6 **23** ½a. blue-green (1888) ... 40 10
a. "SERVICE." with stop ... £130 2·25
b. "S ATE" for "STATE" ...
c. "SERVICE" double, one albino ... 42·00
O7 **25** 1a. brown-purple ... 2·00 60
O8 1a. plum ... 2·00 25
a. "SERVICE." with stop ... 9·00 75
ab. "SERVICE." with stop, and "NABHA STATE" double ... £1800 £250
O9 **27** 2a. dull blue (1888) ... 3·25 1·75
O10 2a. ultramarine ... 3·75 2·00
O11 **28** 3a. orange (1889) ... 25·00 95·00
O12 3a. brown-orange ... 29·00 95·00
a. "NABHA STATE" double, one albino ... 65·00
O13 **29** 4a. olive-green (1888) ... 3·50 1·50
O14 4a. slate-green ... 3·75 1·25
O15 **21** 6a. olive-bistre (1889) ... 22·00 35·00
a. "SERVICE" double, one albino ... 48·00
O16 6a. bistre-brown ... £700
O17 **31** 8a. dull mauve (1889) ... 2·75 1·50
O18 **32** 12a. purple/*red* (1889) ... 6·50 22·00
a. SERVICE" double, one albino ... 48·00
b. "NABHA STATE double, one albino ... 42·00
O19 **33** 1r. slate (1889) ... 42·00 £350
O20 **37** 1r. green and carmine (1.97) ... 32·00 85·00
O6/20 *Set of* 10 ... £120 £550

Printings up to and including that of August 1895 had the "SERVICE" overprint applied to sheets of stamps already overprinted with Type **2**. From the printing of January 1897 onwards the two parts of the overprint were applied at one operation. This method was only used for printings of the ½a., 1a. and 1r. (O20).

1903–06. *King Edward VII stamps of India optd with Type* O **9**.

O24 **41** 3p. pale grey (1906) ... 5·50 25·00
O25 3p. slate-grey (1906) ... 2·50 18·00
a. Opt double, one albino ... 38·00
O26 **42** ½a. green ... 80 35
O27 **43** 1a. carmine ... 80 10
O28 **44** 2a. pale violet ... 3·25 1·40
O29 2a. mauve ... 2·75 40
a. Opt double, one albino ... 48·00
O30 **47** 4a. olive ... 1·60 50
O32 **49** 8a. purple (*shades*) ... 1·75 1·50
a. Opt double, one albino ... 38·00
O33 8a. claret ... 12·00 5·50
O34 **51** 1r. green and carmine ... 1·75 2·50
O24/34 *Set of* 7 ... 11·00 21·00

1907. *Nos. 149/50 of India optd with Type* O **9**.

O35 **53** ½a. green ... 1·75 50
a. Opt double, one albino ... 22·00
O36 **54** 1a. carmine ... 75 30
a. Opt double, one albino ... 38·00

1913. *King George V. Optd with Type* O **9**.

O37 **63** 4a. olive ... 10·00 65·00
O38 **67** 1r. red-brown and deep blue-green ... 55·00 £500
a. Opt double, one albino ... £110

1913. *Official stamps of India optd with T* **2**.

O39 **55** 3p. grey ... 1·25 12·00
a. Pale grey ... 1·25 10·00
b. Bluish grey ... 1·10 10·00
c. Slate ... 1·10 10·00
O40 **56** ½a. light green ... 70 20
a. Emerald ... 1·50 10
b. Bright green ... 1·00 15
O41 **57** 1a. aniline carmine ... 60 10
O42 **59** 2a. purple ... 1·25 75
a. Reddish purple ... 2·25 50
b. Deep mauve ... 1·75 20
c. Bright reddish violet ...
O43 **63** 4a. olive ... 1·00 60
O44 **65** 8a. deep magenta ... 1·75 2·00
a. Deep mauve ... 3·50
b. Bright mauve ... 5·00
O46 **67** 1r. red-brown and deep blue-green ... 7·00 4·25
a. Brown and green ... 8·00 4·25
O39/46 *Set of* 7 ... 12·00 16·00

NABHA STATE SERVICE (O 10) NABHA SERVICE (O 11)

1932–42?. *King George V (Nasik printing, wmk Mult Star), optd at Nasik with Type* O **10**.

O47 **55** 3p. slate ... 10 15
O48 **81** 1a. chocolate (1935) ... 15 15
O49 **63** 4a. sage-green (1942?) ... 23·00 2·50
O50 **65** 8a. reddish purple (1937) ... 1·00 2·75
O47/50 *Set of* 4 ... 23·00 5·00

1938. *King George VI. Optd as Type* O **10**.

O53 **91** 9p. green ... 4·75 4·00
O54 1a. carmine ... 18·00 1·10

1940–43.

(a) Official stamps optd with T **6**.

O55 **O 20** 3p. slate (1942) ... 1·25 2·00
O56 ½a. red-brown (1942) ... 1·10 30
O57 ½a. purple (1943) ... 4·50 1·50
O58 9p. green ... 1·25 30
O59 1a. carmine (1942) ... 60 20
O61 1½a. dull violet (1942) ... 70 40
O62 2a. vermilion (1942) ... 2·25 1·50
w. Wmk inverted ... 5·00 2·50
O64 4a. brown (1942) ... 3·50 3·50
O65 8a. slate-violet (1942) ... 5·50 21·00

(b) Postage stamps optd with Type O **11**.

O66 **100** 1r. grey and red-brown (1942) ... 8·50 42·00
O67 2r. purple and brown (1942) ... 30·00 £190
O68 5r. green and blue (1942) ... £170 £550
O55/68 *Set of* 12 ... £200 £750

Nabha was absorbed into the Patiala and East Punjab States Union by 20 August 1948.

PATIALA

PRICES FOR STAMPS ON COVER	
Nos. 1/6	*from* × 10
Nos. 7/34	*from* × 6
Nos. 35/45	*from* × 8
Nos. 46/115	*from* × 4
Nos. O1/84	*from* × 15

Maharaja Rajindra Singh, 1876–1900

PUTTIALLA STATE (1) PUTTIALLA STATE (2) PATIALA STATE (3)

1884 (1 Oct). *Queen Victoria. Optd with T* **1**, *in red.*

1 **23** ½a. blue-green ... 4·00 4·75
a. Opt double, one sideways ... £3250 £800
b. Opt double, one albino ... 85·00
2 **25** 1a. brown-purple ... 50·00 75·00
a. Opt double ...
b. Optd in red and in black ... £700
3 **27** 2a. dull blue ... 13·00 16·00
4 **17** 4a. green ... 90·00 £100
5 **31** 8a. dull mauve ... £450 £1100
a. Opt inverted ... £11000
b. Optd in red and in black ... £130 £450
ba. Ditto. Opts inverted ... £8000
c. Opt double, one albino ... £500
6 **33** 1r. slate ... £150 £650
1/6 *Set of* 6 ... £700 £1800

Nos. 5a and 5ba each occur once in the setting of 120. The 8a. value also exists with a trial overprint (showing the words more curved) reading downwards (*Price £600 unused*), which should not be confused with No. 5a.

1885. *Optd with T* **2**.

(a) In red.

7 **23** ½a. blue-green ... 2·25 30
a. "AUTTIALLA" ... 16·00 35·00
b. "STATE" only ...
c. Wide spacing between lines ... 6·50 8·00
8 **27** 2a. dull blue ... 6·00 1·75
a. "AUTTIALLA" ... 42·00
b. Wide spacing between lines ... 28·00 30·00
ba. Ditto "AUTTIALLA" ... £850
9 **17** 4a. green ... 4·00 4·25
a. Optd in red and in black ... £250
b. Wide spacing between lines ... £450
c. Opt double, one albino ... 50·00
10 **33** 1r. slate ... 16·00 85·00
a. "AUTTIALLA" ... £450
b. Wide spacing between lines ... £450

(b) In black.

11 **25** 1a. brown-purple ... 60 30
a. Optd in red and in black ... 12·00 90·00
b. "AUTTIALLA" ... 70·00
ba. Ditto. Optd in red and in black ... £1700
c. Opt double ... £250 £275
d. Wide spacing between lines ... £325
12 **31** 8a. dull mauve ... 24·00 55·00
a. "AUTTIALLA" ... £375
b. Opt double, one albino ... 85·00
c. Wide spacing between lines ... £450
7/12 *Set of* 6 ... 48·00 £130

The ½, 2 and 4a. (T **29**), and 1r. (all overprinted in black), are proofs.

All six values exist with reprinted overprints, and the error "AUTTIALLA STATE" has been reprinted in complete sheets on all values and in addition in black on the ½, 2, 4a. and 1r. Nearly all these however, are found with the word "REPRINT" overprinted upon them. On the genuine "AUTTIALLA" errors, which occur on R. 9/12 in the setting of 120, the word "STATE" is 8½ mm long; on the reprints only 7¾ mm.

Nos. 7c, 8b, 9b, 10b, 11d and 12c show 1¼ mm spacing between the two lines of overprint. The normal spacing is ¾ mm.

Nos. 7/8 and 10/12 exist with error "PUTTILLA", but their status is uncertain (*Price, from £650, unused*).

1891–96. *Optd with T* **3**.

13 **23** ½a. blue-green (1892) ... 50 10
14 **24** 9p. carmine ... 1·00 2·25
15 **25** 1a. brown-purple ... 1·40 30

16 1a. plum 2·25 1·25
a. "PATIALA" omitted £200 £425
b. "PA" omitted
c. "PATIA" omitted
d. "PATIAL" omitted
17 26 1a.6p. sepia 1·40 2·00
18 27 2a. dull blue (1896) 1·60 30
19 2a. ultramarine 2·25 1·00
20 28 3a. brown-orange 2·50 75
21 29 4a. olive-green (1896) 2·50 75
a. "PATIALA" omitted £500 £250
22 4a. slate-green 2·75 75
23 21 6a. bistre-brown 2·50 15·00
24 6a. olive-bistre 5·50 22·00
a. Opt double, one albino 65·00
25 31 8a. dull mauve
26 8a. magenta (1896) 3·75 16·00
27 32 12a. purple/*red* 2·50 16·00
28 37 1r. green and carmine (1896) 4·50 55·00
29 38 2r. carmine and yellow-brown (1895) £140 £850
30 3r. brown and green (1895) £190 £900
a. Opt double, one albino £275
b. Opt treble, two albino £180
31 5r. ultramarine and violet (1895) £225 £950
13/31 *Set of* 14 £500 £2500

The errors on the 1a. plum and 4a. olive-green occur on R. 19/1 in the December 1898 printing. Nos. 16b/d are early stages of the error before the entire word was omitted.

1899–1902. *Colours changed and new value. Optd with T* **3**.
32 40 3p. carmine (1899) 30 15
a. Pair, one without opt £4000
b. Opt double, one albino 48·00
33 23 ½a. pale yellow-green 1·00 60
34 25 1a. carmine 2·50 1·75
32/4 *Set of* 3 3·50 1·75

Maharaja Bhupindra Singh, 1900–1938

1903–06. *King Edward VII. Optd with T* **3**.
35 41 3p. pale grey 40 10
a. Additional albino opt of Jind Type **3** £225
b. "S" in "STATE" sideways (R. 20/1) £900 £950
36 3p. slate-grey (1906) 75 10
37 42 ½a. green 1·10 15
38 43 1a. carmine 1·40 10
a. Horiz pair, one without opt £1000
39 44 2a. pale violet 1·60 65
a. Mauve 10·00 1·00
40 46 3a. orange-brown 1·60 35
41 47 4a. olive (1905) 2·75 1·50
42 48 6a. olive-bistre (1905) 3·25 10·00
43 49 8a. purple (1906) 3·75 3·00
44 50 12a. purple/*red* (1906) 7·50 26·00
45 51 1r. green and carmine (1905) 4·50 6·00
35/45 *Set of* 10 25·00 42·00

1912. *Nos. 149/50 of India optd with T* **3**.
46 53 ½a. green 40 25
47 54 1a. carmine 1·75 1·00

1912–26. *King George V. Optd with T* **3**.
48 55 3p. grey 25 10
a. Pale grey 1·00 15
b. Bluish grey 1·75
c. Slate 2·00 30
ca. "Rs" flaw 32·00
49 56 ½a. light green 70 20
a. Emerald 1·75 30
b. Bright green 1·50 35
50 57 1a. aniline carmine 1·60 20
51 58 1½a. chocolate (Type A) (1922) 30 55
52 59 2a. purple 1·50 1·50
a. Reddish purple 3·00
b. Deep mauve 2·75
c. Bright reddish violet 3·00
53 62 3a. orange 2·50 1·75
54 63 4a. olive 3·50 3·50
55 64 6a. yellow-bistre 2·00 4·50
a. Brown-ochre (1921) 3·75 6·00
56 65 8a. deep magenta 3·00 3·00
a. Purple (1921) 6·00 3·50
57 66 12a. carmine-lake 3·75 10·00
58 67 1r. red-brown and deep blue-green 9·50 15·00
a. Opt double, one albino 42·00
b. Brown and green (1924) 12·00
59 2r. carmine & yell-brn (1926) 14·00 £150
60 5r. ultramarine and violet (1926) 35·00 £200

1923–26. *As 1912–26. New colours.*
61 57 1a. chocolate 2·75 50
62 62 3a. ultramarine (1926) 3·25 9·50
48/62 *Set of* 15 75·00 £350

PATIALA STATE (4) PATIALA STATE (5)

1928–34. *King George V (Nasik printing, wmk Mult Star) optd at Nasik with T* **4** *or* **5** *(rupee values).*
63 55 3p. slate (1932) 2·00 10
w. Wmk inverted 3·50 1·25
64 56 ½a. green 25 10
w. Wmk inverted 2·75 1·25
65 80 9p. deep green (*litho*) (1934) 2·25 1·00
65*a* 9p. deep green (*typo*) 2·75 35
66 57 1a. chocolate 75 25
w. Wmk inverted 3·75 1·10
67 82 1a.3p. mauve (1932) 3·00 15
w. Wmk inverted 4·00 1·60
68 70 2a. purple 1·75 40
w. Wmk inverted 3·75
69 61 2a.6p. orange (1934) 4·75 2·75
w. Wmk inverted 3·50
70 62 3a. bright blue (1929) 3·00 2·75
71 71 4a. sage-green 5·00 2·00
w. Wmk inverted 8·00
72 65 8a. reddish purple (1933) 7·00 4·00
73 67 1r. chocolate and green (1929) 7·00 10·00
w. Wmk inverted 22·00 15·00
74 2r. carmine and orange 28·00
w. Wmk inverted 11·00 55·00
63/74w *Set of* 12 42·00 70·00

1935–37. *Optd with T* **4**.
75 79 ½a. blue-green (1937) 85 30
76 81 1a. chocolate (1936) 1·10 20
77 59 2a. vermilion (No. 236*b*) (1936) 40 1·50
78 62 3a. carmine 9·50 6·50
w. Wmk inverted 5·50 8·50
79 63 4a. sage-green 1·75 2·75
75/9 *Set of* 5 8·50 10·00

PATIALA STATE (6) PATIALA (7) PATIALA (8)

1937–38. *King George VI. Nos. 247/64 optd with T* **4** *(3p. to 1a.), T* **6** *(2a. to 12a.), or T* **5** *(rupee values).*
80 91 3p. slate 20·00 35
81 ½a. red-brown 8·00 50
82 9p. green (1937) 5·00 1·00
83 1a. carmine (1937) 2·75 20
84 92 2a. vermilion 1·50 9·50
85 93 2a.6p. bright violet 5·50 21·00
86 94 3a. yellow-green 6·00 9·00
87 95 3a.6p. bright blue 6·50 25·00
88 96 4a. brown 23·00 17·00
89 97 6a. turquoise-green 25·00 60·00
90 98 8a. slate-violet 27·00 42·00
91 99 12a. lake 25·00 70·00
92 100 1r. grey and red-brown 27·00 42·00
93 2r. purple and brown 29·00 £110
94 5r. green and blue 38·00 £250
95 10r. purple and claret 50·00 £400
96 15r. brown and green £120 £650
97 25r. slate-violet and purple £140 £650
80/97 *Set of* 18 £500 £2000

Maharaja Yadavindra Singh, 1938–1971

1941–46. *King George VI. Optd with T* **7** *or* **8** *(rupee value).*

(a) Stamps of 1937.
98 91 3p. slate 11·00 2·75
99 ½a. red-brown 6·50 2·25
100 9p. green £300 8·00
w. Wmk inverted
101 1a. carmine 25·00 2·50
102 100 1r. grey and red-brown (1946) 15·00 80·00
98/102 *Set of* 5 £325 90·00

(b) Stamps of 1940–43.
103 100a 3p. slate (1942) 4·00 15
104 ½a. purple (1943) 4·00 15
a. Pair, one without opt £7500
105 9p. green (1942) 1·50 15
a. Vert pair, one without opt £3750
106 1a. carmine (1944) 1·00 10
107 101 1a.3p. yellow-brown 1·60 3·50
108 1½a. violet (1942) 12·00 3·75
109 2a. vermilion (1944) 9·00 50
110 3a. bright violet (1944) 8·00 2·50
111 3½a. bright blue (1944) 19·00 38·00
112 102 4a. brown (1944) 9·00 4·50
113 6a. turquoise-green (1944) 3·50 30·00
114 8a. slate-violet (1944) 3·00 15·00
115 12a. lake (1945) 24·00 85·00
103/15 *Set of* 13 90·00 £160

The 1½a. exists printed by lithography or typography.

OFFICIAL STAMPS

SERVICE (O 2) SERVICE (O 3)

1884 (1 Oct). *Nos. 1/3 of Patiala optd with Type* O **2**, *in black.*
O1 23 ½a. blue-green 18·00 40
O2 25 1a. brown-purple 1·00 10
a. Opt Type **1** inverted £2000 £275
b. Opt Type **1** double † £120
c. "SERVICE" double £2000 £650
d. "SERVICE" inverted † £1700
w. Wmk inverted † £350
O3 27 2a. dull blue £5000 £120

Essays of No. O3 exist on which "STATE" measures 10 mm long (normal 9 mm) and the words of the Type **1** overprint are more curved. These are rare (*Price £950 unused*).

1885–90.

(a) No. 7 of Patiala optd with Type O **2**, *in black.*
O4 23 ½a. blue-green 1·50 25
a. "SERVICE" double † £700
b. "AUTTIALLA" 60·00 17·00
ba. "AUTTIALLA", and "SERVICE" double † £5500

(b) No. 11 of Patiala optd with Type O **2**, *in black.*
O5 25 1a. brown purple 1·50 10
a. "SERVICE" double £2000
b. "SERVICE" double, one inverted † £600
c. "AUTTIALLA" £700 48·00
d. "PUTTIALLA STATE" double † £1600

(c) As No. 7 of Patiala, but optd in black, and No. 8, optd with Type O **3**.
O6 23 ½a. blue-green (Bk.) (1890) 1·50 10
O7 27 2a. dull blue (R.) 75 40
a. "SERVICE" double, one inverted 30·00 £190

Stamps as Nos. O4/5, but with Type O **3** (in red on the ½a.), were prepared for use but not issued, although some were erroneously overprinted "REPRINT". No. O7 with overprint in black is a proof. The ½a "AUTTIALLA" has been reprinted in complete sheets, and can be found with "AUTTIALLA" double.

No. O7 exists with error "PUTTILLA", but its status is uncertain.

SERVICE

PATIALA STATE (O 4) PATIALA STATE SERVICE (O 5) PATIALA STATE SERVICE (O 6)

1891 (Nov)–**1900**. *Optd with Type* O **4**, *in black.*
O8 23 ½a. blue-green (9.95) 50 10
a. "SERVICE" inverted 60·00
b. "SERV CE" £1200
c. "STA E" £650 £550
d. "S ATE"
O9 25 1a. plum (10.1900) 6·00 10
a. "SERVICE" inverted 60·00
O10 27 2a. dull blue (12.98) 4·50 2·50
a. Deep blue 3·25 2·50
b. "SERVICE" inverted 60·00 £200
ba. "SERV CE" inverted £2500
c. Thin seriffed "I" in "SERVICE" £250
O12 28 3a. brown-orange 2·50 3·25
a. "SERV CE" £3250
O13 29 4a. olive-green 2·00 70
a. Slate-green (9.95) 2·00 30
b. "SERV CE"
O15 21 6a. bistre-brown 1·60 35
a. Olive-bistre £1200
O16 31 8a. dull mauve 3·50 1·75
a. Magenta (12.98) 3·50 2·25
b. "SERV CE" £4250
c. Thin seriffed "I" in "SERVICE" £475
O18 32 12a. purple/*red* 2·25 60
a. "SERV CE" £5500
O19 33 1r. slate 2·50 65
a. "SERV CE"
O8/19 *Set of* 9 22·00 8·50

Stamps from the first printing of November 1891 (Nos. O12/13, O15/16, O18/19) had the "SERVICE" overprint, as Type O **3**, applied to sheets already overprinted with Type **3**. Subsequent printings of Nos. O8/10*a*, O13*a* and O16*a* had both overprints applied at one operation as shown on Type O **4**.

The errors with "SERVICE" inverted occur from a trial printing, in two operations, during 1894, which was probably not issued. Some of the "SERV CE" varieties may also come from the same trial printing.

1902 (Jan)–**03**. *Optd with Type* O **4**.
O20 25 1a. carmine 90 10
O21 37 1r. green and carmine (5.03) 6·00 10·00

1903–10. *King Edward VII stamps of India optd with Type* O **4**.
O22 41 3p. pale grey 40 10
a. Slate-grey (1909) 50 15
O24 42 ½a. green 1·00 10
O25 43 1a. carmine 60 10
O26 44 2a. pale violet (1905) 80 25
a. Mauve 1·00 10
O28 46 3a. orange-brown 4·00 3·50
O29 47 4a. olive (1905) 2·75 20
a. Opt double, one albino 60·00
O30 49 8a. purple (*shades*) 1·75 75
a. Claret (1910) 5·50 2·75
O32 51 1r. green and carmine (1906) 2·00 80
O22/32 *Set of* 8 12·00 5·00

1907. *Nos. 149/50 of India optd with Type* O **4**.
O33 53 ½a. green 50 20
O34 54 1a. carmine 60 10

1913–26. *King George V. Official stamps of India optd with T* **3**.
O35 55 3p. grey 10 20
a. Pale grey 30 30
b. Slate (1926) 30 30
O36 56 ½a. light green 10 10
a. Emerald 2·25 50
b. Bright green 1·25 50
O37 57 1a. aniline carmine 10 10
O38 1a. chocolate (1925) 7·50 1·00
O39 59 2a. purple 90 75
a. Reddish purple — 1·25
b. Deep mauve 1·60 75
O40 63 4a. olive 50 35
O41 64 6a. brown-ochre (1926) 1·75 2·50
O42 65 8a. deep magenta 55 70
O43 67 1r. red-brown and deep blue-green 1·40 1·40
O44 2r. carmine and yellow-brown (1926) 18·00 50·00
a. Opt double, one albino 70·00
O45 5r. ultramarine and violet (1926) 12·00 24·00
O35/45 *Set of* 11 38·00 70·00

1927–36. *King George V (Nasik printing, wmk Mult Star), optd at Nasik with Type* O **5** *or Type* O **6** *(rupee values).*
O47 55 3p. slate 10 10
a. Blue opt 1·75 1·50
w. Wmk inverted 3·00 1·25
O48 56 ½a. green (1932) 1·00 55
w. Wmk inverted — 3·25
O49 57 1a. chocolate 15 10
w. Wmk inverted 1·75 50
O50 82 1a.3p. mauve (1932) 40 10
w. Wmk inverted 3·75 20
O51 70 2a. purple 20 30
w. Wmk inverted
O52 2a. vermilion (1933) 30 35
O53 61 2a.6p. orange (1933) 3·00 35
w. Wmk inverted 1·25 80
O54 71 4a. sage-green (1935) 50 30
w. Wmk inverted 3·00 1·50
O55 65 8a. reddish purple (1929) 1·25 65
w. Wmk inverted 1·25 80
O56 67 1r. chocolate and green (1929) 5·00 3·25
w. Wmk inverted 2·75 3·25
O57 2r. carmine and orange (1936) 16·00 42·00
O47/57 *Set of* 11 22·00 45·00

1935–39. *New types. Optd with Type* O **5**.

O58	**79**	½a. green (1936)	10	10
O59	**81**	1a. chocolate (1936)	35	30
O60	**59**	2a. vermilion	15	30
O61		2a. vermilion (*small die*) (1939)	17·00	5·00
O62	**63**	4a. sage-green (1936)	2·75	1·75
O58/62 *Set of* 5			19·00	6·50

1937–39. *King George VI. Optd with Type* O **5** *or* O **6** *(rupee values).*

O63	**91**	½a. red-brown (1938)	75	20
O64		9p. green (1938)	13·00	65·00
O65		1a. carmine	75	40
O66	**100**	1r. grey and red-brown (1939)	1·00	7·00
O67		2r. purple and brown (1939)	6·00	5·00
O68		5r. green and blue (1939)	17·00	65·00
O63/8 *Set of* 6			35·00	£130

(O **7**) (O **8**) (O **9**)

1939–40. *Stamp of 1932 (King George V).*

(a) Optd with Types O **5** *and* O **7**.

O69	**82**	1a. on 1a.3p. mauve	12·00	3·50
		w. Wmk inverted	11·00	3·25

(b) Optd with T **4** *and* O **8**.

O70	**82**	1a. on 1a.3p. mauve (1940)	10·00	3·25
		w. Wmk inverted	10·00	4·00

"SERVICE" measures 9¼ mm on No. O69 but only 8¾ mm on O70.

1939–44.

(a) Official stamps optd with T **7**.

O71	O **20**	3p. slate (1940)	1·75	10
O72		½a. red-brown	5·00	10
		w. Wmk inverted	—	18·00
O73		½a. purple (1942)	1·00	10
O74		9p. green	1·00	50
		w. Wmk inverted		
O75		1a. carmine	3·25	10
O76		1a.3p. yellow-brown (1941)	1·25	25
O77		1½a. dull violet (1944)	6·50	1·25
O78		2a. vermilion (1940)	10·00	35
		w. Wmk inverted	17·00	2·25
O79		2½a. bright violet (1940)	3·75	1·00
O80		4a. brown (1943)	1·75	2·50
O81		8a. slate-violet (1944)	5·00	6·00

(b) Postage stamps optd with Type O **9**.

O82	**100**	1r. grey and red-brown (1943)	5·00	11·00
O83		2r. purple and brown (1944)	13·00	65·00
O84		5r. green and blue (1944)	21·00	85·00
O71/84 *Set of* 14			70·00	£160

Patiala became part of the Patiala and East Punjab States Union by 20 August 1948.

INDIAN FEUDATORY STATES

These stamps were only valid for use within their respective states, *unless otherwise indicated.*

Postage stamps of the Indian States, current at that date, were replaced by those of the Republic of India on 1 April 1950.

Unless otherwise stated, all became obsolete on 1 May 1950 (with the exception of the "Anchal" stamps of Travancore-Cochin which remained current until 1 July 1951 or Sept 1951 for the Official issues).

ALWAR

PRICES FOR STAMPS ON COVER	
Nos. 1/2	*from* × 25
No. 3	*from* × 50
No. 4	—
No. 5	*from* × 50

Maharao Raja (Maharaja from 1889) Mangal Singh, 1874–1892.

1 (¼a.).

1877. *Litho. Rouletted.*

1	1	¼a. steel blue	16·00	8·00
		a. Bright greenish blue	9·50	7·00
		b. Ultramarine	4·75	1·10
		c. Grey-blue (shades)	4·75	1·10
2		1a. pale yellowish brown	11·00	5·50
		a. Brown (shades)	3·50	1·25
		b. Chocolate	10·00	8·00
		c. Pale reddish brown	3·25	1·50

Maharaja Jai Singh, 1892–1937

1899–1901. *Redrawn.* P 12.

(a) Wide margins between stamps.

3	1	¼a. slate-blue	8·50	3·00
		a. Imperf between (horiz pair)	£400	£500
		b. Imperf between (vert pair)	£800	£850
4		¼a. emerald-green	£550	

(b) Narrower margins (1901).

5	1	¼a. emerald-green	5·00	2·50
		a. Imperf between (horiz pair)	£300	£350
		b. Imperf between (vert pair)	£300	£350
		c. Imperf horiz (vert pair)	£325	
		d. Imperf (pair)	£375	
		e. Pale yellow-green	7·50	2·75
		ea. Imperf (pair)	£650	
		eb. Imperf between (horiz pair)	†	£650

In the redrawn type only the bottom outer frameline is thick, whereas in the original 1877 issue the left-hand frameline is also thick, as shown in Type **1**.

The stamps of Alwar became obsolete on 1 July 1902.

BAHAWALPUR
See after PAKISTAN

BAMRA

PRICES FOR STAMPS ON COVER	
Nos. 1/6	—
Nos. 8/40	*from* × 25

Raja Sudhal Deo, 1869–1903

GUM. The stamps of Bamra were issued without gum.

1 (¼a.)

1a

2 (½a.)

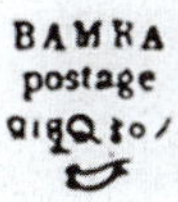

3 (1a.)

4 (2a.)

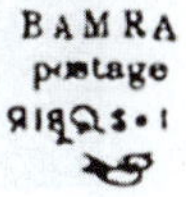

5 (4a.)

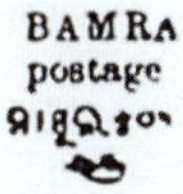

6 (8a.)

(illustrations actual size)

(Typo Jagannata Ballabh Press, Deogarh)

1888. Imperf.

1	1	¼a. black/*yellow*	£475	
		a. "g" inverted (R. 5/1)	£4750	
		b. Last native character inverted	£4750	
		c. Last native character as Type **1a**	£4750	
2	2	½a. black/*rose*	85·00	
		a. "g" inverted (R. 5/1)	£1600	
3	3	1a. black/*blue*	65·00	
		a. "g" inverted (R. 5/1)	£1400	
		b. Scroll inverted (R. 8/4)	£1200	
4	4	2a. black/*green*	90·00	£375
		a. "a" omitted (R. 8/3)	£1600	
		b. Scroll inverted (R. 8/4)	£1400	
5	5	4a. black/*yellow*	80·00	£375
		a. "a" omitted (R. 8/3)	£1500	
		b. Scroll inverted (R. 8/4)	£1300	
6	6	8a. black/*rose*	48·00	
		a. "a" omitted (R. 8/3)	£1300	
		b. Horiz pair, one printed on back	£800	
		c. Scroll inverted (R. 8/4)	£1100	

These stamps were all printed from the same plate of 96 stamps, 12×8, but for some values only part of the plate was used. There are 96 varieties of the ½, 4 and 8a., 72 of the 1a., 80 of the 2a. and not less than 88 of the ¼a.

The scroll ornament can be found pointing to either the right or the left.

There are two forms of the third native character. In the first five horizontal rows it is as in T **1** and in the last three rows as in T **4**.

These stamps have been reprinted: the ¼a. and ½a. in blocks of 8 varieties (all showing scroll pointing to right), and all the values in blocks of 20 varieties (all showing scroll pointing to left). On the reprints the fourth character is of a quite different shape.

8

1890 (July)–**93**. *Black on coloured paper. Nos. 24/5 and 39/40 show face value as "One Rupee".*

(a) "Postage" with capital "P".

8	8	¼a. on *rose-lilac*	4·75	6·00
		a. "Eudatory" (R. 2/4)	22·00	38·00
		b. "Quatrer" (R. 1/3)	22·00	38·00
		c. Inverted "e" in "Postage" (R. 2/3)	22·00	38·00
9		¼a. on *bright rose*	2·00	3·00
10		¼a. on *reddish purple*	2·00	2·75
		a. First "a" in "anna" inverted (R. 3/3)	48·00	55·00
		b. "AMRA" inverted (R. 4/4)	70·00	70·00
		c. "M" and second "A" in "BAMRA" inverted (R. 4/4)	95·00	95·00
11		½a. on *dull green*	3·50	3·50
		a. "Eudatory" (R. 2/4)	60·00	75·00
12		½a. on *blue-green*	5·50	4·25
13		1a. on *bistre-yellow*	4·50	3·25
		a. "Eudatory" (R. 2/4)	£130	£150
14		1a. on *orange-yellow*	48·00	48·00
		a. "annas" for "anna"	£200	£225
15		2a. on *rose-lilac*	20·00	38·00
		a. "Eudatory" (R. 2/4)	£180	£375
16		2a. on *bright rose*	4·50	4·75
17		2a. on *dull rose*	14·00	8·00
18		4a. on *rose-lilac*	£600	£900
		a. "Eudatory" (R. 2/4)	£4500	
19		4a. on *dull rose*	11·00	8·00
		a. "Eudatory" (R. 2/4)	£1100	£1200
		b. "BAMBA" (R. 2/1)	£1100	£1200
20		4a. on *bright rose*	6·50	8·50
20*a*		4a. on *deep pink*	18·00	15·00
21		8a. on *rose-lilac*	27·00	65·00
		a. "Foudatory" and "Postagc" (R. 1/2)	£250	£375
		b. "BAMBA" (R. 2/1)	£250	£375
22		8a. on *bright rose*	14·00	19·00
23		8a. on *dull rose*	29·00	19·00
24		1r. on *rose-lilac*	65·00	£110
		a. "Eudatory" (R. 2/4)	£550	£700
		b. "BAMBA" (R. 2/1)	£450	£550
		c. "Postagc" (R. 1/2)	£450	£550
25		1r. on *bright rose*	20·00	21·00
		a. Small "r" in "rupee"	£225	£225

(b) "postage" with small "p" (1891–93).

26	8	¼a. on *bright rose*	2·00	3·00
27		¼a. on *reddish purple*	2·00	2·75
28		½a. on *dull green*	4·50	4·25
		a. First "a" in "anna" inverted (R. 3/3)	40·00	42·00
29		½a. on *blue-green*	5·00	4·25
		a. First "a" in "anna" inverted (R. 3/3)	42·00	42·00
30		1a. on *bistre-yellow*	4·50	3·25
31		1a. on *orange-yellow*	48·00	48·00
32		2a. on *bright rose*	5·50	5·50
33		2a. on *dull rose*	13·00	9·00
34		4a. on *dull rose*	14·00	7·50
35		4a. on *bright rose*	8·00	10·00
35*a*		4a. on *deep pink*	19·00	15·00
36		8a. on *rose-lilac*	60·00	£110
37		8a. on *bright rose*	18·00	21·00
38		8a. on *dull rose*	29·00	19·00
39		1r. on *rose-lilac*	90·00	£160
40		1r. on *bright rose*	24·00	24·00
		a. Small "r" in "rupee"	£250	£250
		b. Small "r" in "rupee" and native characters in the order 2, 3, 1, 4, 5 (R. 4/4)	£1600	£1600

There are 10 settings of Type **8**. The first setting (of 20 (4×5)) has capital "P" throughout. The remaining settings (of 16 (4×4)) have capital "P" and small "p" mixed.

For the first setting the 8a. and 1r. values were printed within the same block, the ten left-hand stamps being 8a. values and the ten right-hand stamps 1r.

The various stamps were distributed between the settings as follows:

Setting I—Nos. 8/c, 11/a, 13/a, 15/a, 18/19a, 21, 24/a
Setting II—Nos. 19, 19b, 21/b, 24, 24b/c, 34, 36, 39
Setting III—Nos. 9, 11, 13, 16, 26, 28, 30, 32
Setting IV—Nos. 20, 22, 25, 35, 37, 40
Setting V—Nos. 10, 10b/c, 20*a*, 27, 35*a*
Setting VI—Nos. 11, 12, 28, 28a, 29/a
Setting VII—Nos. 10/a, 12, 17, 19, 23, 25a, 27, 29, 33/4, 38, 40a/b
Setting VIII—Nos. 17, 33
Setting IX—Nos. 10/a, 12, 14/a, 17, 19, 23, 27, 29, 31, 33/4, 38
Setting X—Nos. 19, 34

There are 4 sizes of the central ornament, which represents an elephant's trunk holding a stick:—*(a)* 4 mm long; *(b)* 5 mm; *(c)* 6½ mm; *(d)* 11 mm. These ornaments are found pointing to right or left, either upright or inverted.

Ornaments *(a)* are found in all settings; *(b)* in all settings from Settings III to X; *(c)* in Settings I and II; and *(d)* only in Setting I.

The stamps of Bamra have been obsolete since 1 January 1895.

BARWANI

PRICES FOR STAMPS ON COVER	
Nos. 1/43	*from* × 3

PROCESS. All Barwani stamps are typographed from clichés, and are in sheets of 4, *unless otherwise indicated*.

Issues to about 1930 were printed by the Barwani State Printing Press, and subsequently by the *Times of India* Press, Bombay.

GUM. Nos. 1/31 were issued without gum.

BOOKLET PANES. Those stamps which were printed in sheets of 4 were issued in stamp booklets, binding holes appearing in the side margin.

Rana Ranjit Singh, 1894–1930

1

2

3

1921 (Mar?). *Clear impression. Medium wove paper.* P 7 all round.

1	1	¼a. blue-green (dull *to* deep)	£150	£425
2		½a. dull blue	£325	£650
		a. Imperf (pair)	—	£2000

No. 1 also exists perforated on two sides only.

1921 (June?). *Blurred impression. Soft wove paper.* P 7 on two or three sides.

3	1	¼a. green (*shades*)	25·00	£130
4		½a. ultramarine (dull *to* pale)	17·00	£180

NOTE. As the small sheets of Barwani stamps were often not perforated all round, many of the earlier stamps are perforated on two or three sides only. Owing to the elementary method of printing, the colours vary greatly in depth, even within a single sheet.

1921. *Clear impression. Vertically laid bâtonné paper.* Imperf.

5	1	¼a. green (*shades*)	21·00	85·00
6		½a. green (*shades*)	5·50	
		a. Perf 11 at top or bottom only	4·75	

It is suggested that No. 5 may be an error due to printing from the wrong plate.

1922. *Clear impression. Thickish glazed wove paper.* P 7 on two or three sides.

7	1	¼a. dull blue	£110	

1922. *Smooth, soft medium wove paper.* P 7 on two or three sides.

(a) Clear impression.

8	1	¼a. deep grey-blue	65·00	£140

(b) Poor impression.

9	1	¼a. steel blue	17·00	

Examples of No. 9 exist with perforations on all four sides.

1922. P 11 on two or three sides.

(a) Thick, glazed white wove paper.

10	2	1a. vermilion (*shades*)	2·50	21·00
		a. Imperf between (vert pair)	£300	
		b. Doubly printed	£1000	
11		2a. purple (*to* violet)	2·25	25·00
		a. Doubly printed	£300	
		b. Imperf between (horiz pair)	£275	£425
		c. Imperf between (vert pair)	£180	

(b) Thick, toned wove paper.

12	2	2a. purple	19·00	60·00

1922. *Poor impression. Thin, poor wove paper.* Pin-perf 8½ on two or three sides.

13	1	¼a. grey (*to* grey-blue)	1·60	48·00
		a. Imperf (pair)	£450	
		b. Imperf between (vert pair)	£150	

1923. *Thin, smooth, unglazed wove paper.* P 11 on two or three sides.

14	1	½a. green (pale *to* deep)	1·25	21·00
		a. Imperf between (vert pair)	£650	
15	2	1a. brown-red	£2750	£3750

1923. *Poor impression. Thick, soft wove paper.* P 7.

16	1	½a. green (pale *to* deep)	26·00	

No. 16 also exists perforated on two or three sides.

1923 (Mar?). *Poor quality wove paper.* P 7 on two or three sides.

17	1	¼a. black	75·00	£375
		a. Imperf between (horiz pair)	£2500	

1923 (May?). *Horizontally laid bâtonné paper.* P 12.

18	1	¼a. rose (*shades*)	2·50	14·00
		a. Imperf between (vert pair)	£500	
		ab. Imperf between (horiz pair)	£1000	
		b. Pin perf 6	£170	85·00
		c. Perf compound of 12 and 6	55·00	80·00
		d. Perf 7	£900	£1000
		da. On wove paper	£3250	

No. 18 was issued in sheets of 12 (3 panes of 4) and was printed on paper showing a sheet watermark of Britannia and a double-lined inscription. No. 18d was only issued in booklet panes of 4.

1925. *Vertically laid bâtonné paper.* P 11.

19	1	¼a. blue (pale *to* deep)	1·50	11·00
		a. *Tête-bêche* (horiz pair)	£3000	

No. 19 was issued in sheets of 8 and was printed on paper with a sheet watermark of a shell and an inscription "SHELL" in double-lined capitals.

1927. *Very poor impression. Thin, brittle wove paper.* P 7.

20	1	¼a. milky blue (*shades*)	9·00	35·00
21		½a. yellow-green (*shades*)	10·00	75·00
		a. Imperf between (horiz pair)	£1200	
22	3	4a. orange-brown	95·00	£450
		a. Imperf between (horiz pair)	£1800	
20/2 *Set of* 3			£100	£500

1927. *Thick wove paper.* Sewing machine perf 6-10.

23	3	4a. yellow-brown	£120	
		a. Imperf between (horiz pair)	£3000	
		b. Perf 7	20·00	£275
		c. Orange-brown	£140	£475

1928–32? *Thick glazed paper.*

(a) P 7.

24	1	¼a. deep bright blue	11·00	
25		½a. bright yellow-green	25·00	

(b) P 10½ *(rough) (Nov 1928).*

26	1	¼a. ultramarine	6·50	
		a. *Tête-bêche* (horiz pair)	13·00	
		b. Horiz pair, one stamp printed on reverse	£2250	
27		½a. apple-green	4·75	
		a. *Tête-bêche* (vert pair)	9·00	

(c) P 11 *(clean-cut) (1929–32?).*

28	1	¼a. bright blue	2·25	14·00
		a. Indigo	1·75	13·00
		ab. Imperf between (horiz pair)	90·00	
		ac. Imperf between (horiz strip of 4)	£450	
		b. Deep dull blue	1·50	13·00
		ba. Imperf between (vert pair)	£350	
		c. Ultramarine	2·00	14·00
29		½a. myrtle-green	2·75	16·00
		a. Imperf between (horiz pair)	£300	
		b. Turquoise-green	3·50	17·00
		ba. Imperf between (vert pair)	£600	£700
30	2	1a. rose-carmine (1931)	16·00	45·00
		a. Imperf between (vert pair)	†	£2500
31	3	4a. salmon (*to* orange) (1931)	80·00	£225
		a. Imperf between (horiz pair)	£2750	
28/31 *Set of* 4			90·00	£275

No. 26 was printed in sheets of 8 (4×2) with the two centre pairs *tête-bêche* while No. 27, in similar sheets, had the two horizontal rows *tête-bêche*. Both sheets are always found with one long side imperforate.

Nos. 28/31 were printed in sheets of 8, the two lower values existing either 4×2 or 2×4 and the two higher values 4×2 only. No *tête-bêche* pairs were included in these printings. It is believed that a small printing of No. 31 was produced in sheets of 4, but details are uncertain.

Rana Devi Singh, 1930–1971

4 Rana Devi Singh

5 Rana Devi Singh

1932 (Oct)–**47**. *Medium to thick wove paper.*

A. Close setting *(2½–4½ mm).* P 11, 12 or compound *(1932–41).*

32A	4	¼a. slate	2·50	23·00
33A		½a. blue-green	4·00	23·00
34A		1a. brown	4·00	22·00
		a. Imperf between (horiz pair)	£1400	
35A		2a. purple (*shades*)	3·75	42·00
36A		4a. olive-green	6·00	42·00
32A/6A *Set of* 5			18·00	£140

B. Wide setting *(6–7 mm).* P 11 *(1945–47).*

32B	4	¼a. slate	5·00	32·00
33B		½a. blue-green	5·50	23·00
34B		1a. brown	13·00	23·00
		b. Chocolate. Perf 8½ (1947)	14·00	50·00
35aB		2a. rose-carmine	£350	£650
36B		4a. olive-green	25·00	48·00

The measurements given in the heading indicate the vertical spacing between impressions. There are eight settings of this interesting issue: four "Close" where the overall stamp dimensions from centre to centre of perfs vary in width from 21½ to 23 mm and in height from 25 to 27½ mm; three "Wide", width 23–23½ mm and height 29–30 mm and one "Medium" (26½×31 mm) (No. 34B*b* only).

1933–47. P 11.

A. *Close setting (3–4½ mm). Thick, cream-surfaced wove paper (1933 and 1941 (No. 38Aa)).*

37A	1	¼a. black	5·00	75·00
38A		½a. blue-green	10·00	32·00
		a. Yellowish green (1941)	10.00	28·00
39A	2	1a. brown (*shades*)	22·00	30·00
42A	3	4a. sage-green	40·00	£100

B. *Wide setting (7–10 mm). Medium to thick wove paper (1939–47).*

37B	1	¼a. black (1945)	4·75	38·00
38aB		½a. yellowish green (1945)	4·50	40·00
39B	2	1a. brown (*shades*)	15·00	28·00
		a. Perf 8½ (5 mm) (1947)	12·00	50·00
40B		2a. bright purple	£100	£325
41B		2a. rose-carmine (1945)	28·00	£130
42B	3	4a. sage-green (1941)	35·00	70·00
		a. Pale sage-green (1939)	15·00	45·00

There were two "Close" settings (over-all stamp size 25×29 mm) and five "Wide" settings with over-all sizes 26½–31½ × 31–36½ mm. There was also one "Medium" setting (26½×31 mm) but this was confined to the 1a. perf 8½, No. 39a.

1938. P 11.

43	5	1a. brown	40·00	75·00

Stamps printed in red with designs similar to Types **3** and **5** were intended for fiscal use.

STAMP BOOKLETS

Nos. 1/17, 18d/da and 20/5 are believed to have been issued in sewn or stapled booklets, usually containing thirty-two examples of one value in blocks of 4. All these early booklets had plain covers, often in shades of brown. Few complete booklets have survived from this period.

Nos. 32/47, produced by the *Times of India* Press in a series of nine printings between 1932 and 1947, were only issued in booklet form. Booklets from the 1932, 1933, 1937 and 1939 printings had plain card or paper covers in various colours, usually containing eight blocks of 4, except for the 1933 printing, which contained twenty blocks of 4. Booklets from the 1945 printing had plain white tissue covers from the same stock as the interleaving. All these booklets were stapled at left.

The following booklets, from a printing in 1941, and a series of three printings in 1947, had printed covers, produced by a handstamp in the case of Nos. SB14/15.

1941. *Buff, green (No.* SB3*) or blue (No.* SB7*) card covers inscribed "*BARWANI STATE POSTAGE STAMPS*", booklet value in brackets and number and value of stamps thus "(Rs 4) 32 2 Annas". Panes of 4 with margin at left only. Stapled.*

(a) Booklets 59×55 mm.

SB1	8a. booklet containing thirty-two ¼a. (No. 32A)	£1100
SB2	1r. booklet containing thirty-two ½a. (No. 33A)	£1300
SB3	2r. booklet containing thirty-two 1a. (No. 34A)	£1300
SB4	4r. booklet containing thirty-two 2a. (No. 35A)	£500
SB5	8r. booklet containing thirty-two 4a. (No. 36A)	£800

(b) Booklets 63×60 mm (No. SB6*) or 73×72 mm (No.* SB7*).*

SB6	1r. booklet containing thirty-two ½a. (No. 38A*a*)	£1200
SB7	8r. booklet containing thirty-two 4a. (No. 42B)	£1500

1947. *Grey tissue covers inscribed "32 STAMPS VALUE ...." Panes of 4 with margins all round. Stapled at left.*

(a) Booklets 70×95 mm.

SB8	1r. booklet containing thirty-two ½a. (No. 33B)	£700
SB9	2r. booklet containing thirty-two 1a. (No. 34B)	£1300
SB10	8r. booklet containing thirty-two 4a. (No. 36B)	£1200

(b) Booklets 76×95 mm.

SB11	8a. booklet containing thirty-two ¼a. (No. 37B)	£1000
SB12	4r. booklet containing thirty-two 2a. (No. 41B)	£1100
SB13	8r. booklet containing thirty-two 4a. (No. 42B*a*)	£550

1947. *Buff paper covers with violet handstamp inscribed "32 STAMPS VALUE Rs 2/-". Panes of 4 with margins all round, Sewn with twine at left.*

SB14	2r. booklets (71×69 *mm*) containing thirty-two 1a. (No. 34B*b*)	£600
SB15	2r. booklet (71×73 *mm*) containing thirty-two 1a. (No. 39B*a*)	£450

1947. *Grey tissue covers inscribed "32 STAMPS VALUE As 8". Panes of 4 with margins all round. Stapled at left.*

SB16	8a. booklet (70×75 *mm*) containing thirty-two ¼a. (No. 32B)	£275
SB17	8a. booklet (85×75 *mm*) containing thirty-two ¼a. (No. 37B)	£350

Barwani became part of Madhya Bharat by 1 July 1948.

BHOPAL

PRICES FOR STAMPS ON COVER	
Nos. 1/100	*from* × 10
Nos. O301/57	*from* × 15

The correct English inscription on these stamps is "H.H. NAWAB SHAH JAHAN BEGAM". In the case of Nos. 22 and 23 the normal stamps are spelt "BEGAN" and specimens with "BEGAM" are "errors".

As the stamps were printed from lithographic stones on which each unit was drawn separately by hand, numerous errors of spelling occurred. These are constant on all sheets and are listed. Some of our illustrations inadvertently include errors of spelling.

ILLUSTRATIONS. Types **1/3a** and **6/12a** are shown actual size.

EMBOSSING. Nos. 1/99 were only valid for postage when embossed with the device, in Urdu, of the ruling Begam. On T **1/3** and **6** to **12a**. this was intended to fill the central part of the design. Almost all varieties can be found with the embossing inverted or sideways, as well as upright.

Shah Jahan

Sultan Jahan

(actual size)

The various basic types were often in concurrent use but for greater convenience the following list is arranged according to types instead of being in strict chronological order.

GUM. Nos. 1/99 were issued without gum.

Nawab Shah Jahan Begam, 16 November 1868–15 June 1901

1 (¼a.)

1872. *Litho.*

(a) Double frame. Sheets of 20 (5×4).

1	1	¼a. black	£650	£475
		a. "BFGAM" (R. 3/1)	£1800	£1600
		b. "BEGAN" (R. 2/2, R. 4/4)	£1000	£850
		c. "EGAM" (R. 4/5)	£1800	£1600
2		½a. red	20·00	48·00
		a. "BFGAM" (R. 3/1)	75·00	£170
		b. "BEGAN" (R. 2/2, R. 4/4)	48·00	£110
		c. "EGAM" (R. 4/5)	75·00	£170

2 (½a.)

(b) Single frame. Sheets of 20 (4×5).

3	2	¼a. black	†	£6000
4		½a. red	35·00	75·00
		a. "NWAB" (R. 2/2)	£170	£325

3 (¼a.)

3a (¼a.)

1878 (1 Jan). *All lettered "EEGAM" for "BEGAM". Sheets of 20 (4×5).*

(a) Plate 1. Frame lines extend horiz and vert between stamps throughout sheet.

5	3	¼a. black	8·00	16·00

(b) Plate 2. Frame lines normal.

5*a*	3a	¼a. black	9·00	18·00

Apart from the frame line difference between Types **3** and **3a** the stamps can also be distinguished by the differences in the value tablets, notably the thin vertical line in the centre in Type **3a** compared with the slightly diagonal and heavier line in Type **3**.

4 (¼a.)

5 (½a.)

1878 (June?)–**79**. *Value in parenthesis (Nos. 6/7). Sheets of 32 (4×8).* Imperf.

6	4	¼a. green (1879)	14·00	27·00
7		¼a. green (*perf*) (1879)	11·00	19·00
8	5	½a. red	7·00	16·00
		a. "JAHN" (R. 5/2)	38·00	
		b. "NWAB" (R. 3/2, R. 4/2)	24·00	
		c. "EEGAM" (R. 1/3)	38·00	
9		½a. brown	28·00	45·00
		a. "JAHN" (R. 5/2)	£150	£190
		b. "NWAB" (R. 3/2, R. 4/2)	90·00	£130
		c. "EEGAM" (R. 1/3)	£150	£190

The ¼a. shows the "N" of "NAWAB" reversed on R. 6/4 and the "N" of "JAHAN" reversed on R. 1/2–4 and R. 2/2-4.

1880. *T* **5** *redrawn; value not in parenthesis. Sheets of 32 (4×8).*

(a) Imperf.

10 ¼a. blue-green .... 9·00
a. "NAWA" (R. 2/2–4) .... 28·00
b. "CHAH" (R. 8/3) .... 80·00
11 ½a. brown-red .... 18·00 24·00

(b) Perf.

12 ¼a. blue-green .... 12·00
a. "NAWA" (R. 2/2–4) .... 45·00
b. "CHAH" (R. 8/3) £110
13 ½a. brown-red .... 18·00

The ¼a. shows the "N" of "NAWAB" reversed on R. 8/4.
Nos. 12/13 sometimes come with gum.

1884. *T* **5** *again redrawn. Sheets of 32 (4×8), some with value in parenthesis, others not.* Perf.

14 ¼a. greenish blue .... 6·00 16·00
a. "ANAWAB" (R. 8/1–4) .... 15·00

In this plate there is a slanting dash under and to left of the letters "JA" of "JAHAN," instead of a character like a large comma, as on all previous varieties of this design. With the exception of R. 1/1 all stamps in the sheet show "N" of "JAHAN" reversed.

1895. *T* **5** *again redrawn. Sheets of 8 (2×4). Laid paper.*

15 ¼a. red *(imperf)* .... 7·00 3·25
16 ¼a. red *(perf)* .... — £800

In these cases where the same design has been redrawn several times, and each time in a number of varieties of type, it is not easy to distinguish the various issues. Nos. 6 and 7 may be distinguished from Nos. 10 and 12 by the presence or absence of the parenthesis marks (); 8, 9 and 11 differ principally in colour; 8 and 15 are very much alike, but differ in the value as well as in paper.

6 (2a.)

1881. *Sheets of 24 (4×6).* Imperf.

17 **6** ¼a. black .... 6·00 23·00
a. "NWAB" (R. 6/2–4) .... 15·00
18 ½a. red .... 5·00 17·00
a. "NWAB" (R. 6/2–4) .... 12·00
19 1a. brown .... 4·50 19·00
a. "NWAB" (R. 6/2–4) .... 9·50
20 2a. blue .... 3·25 19·00
a. "NWAB" (R. 6/2–4) .... 6·50
21 4a. buff .... 20·00 70·00
a. "NWAB" (R. 6/2–4) .... 55·00
17/21 *Set of 5* .... 35·00 £130

In this issue all values were produced from the same drawing, and therefore show exactly the same varieties of type. The value at foot in this and all the following issues is given in only one form.

7 (½a.)

1886. *Similar to T* **6** *but normally lettered (incorrectly) "BEGAN"; larger lettering. Sheets of 32 (4×8).*

(a) Imperf.

22 **7** ½a. pale red .... 2·75 10·00
a. "BEGAM" (R. 2/1) .... 12·00 32·00
b. "NWAB" (R. 3/4) .... 12·00

(b) Perf.

23 **7** ½a. pale red £750
a. "BEGAM" (R. 2/1) £1400
b. "NWAB" (R. 3/4) £1400

8 (4a.)

1886. *T* **8**. *T* **6** *redrawn. Sheets of 24 (4×6). The "M" of "BEGAM" is an inverted "W". The width of the stamps is rather greater than the height.*

(a) Wove paper. Imperf.

24 **8** 4a. yellow £1000
a. "EEGAM" (R. 2/3–4, R. 3/3–4, R. 4/2, R. 4/4, R. 6/1) £1300

(b) Laid paper.

25 **8** 4a. yellow *(imperf)* .... 12·00 38·00
a. "EEGAM" (R. 2/3–4, R. 3/3–4, R. 4/2, R. 4/4, R. 6/1) .... 16·00
26 4a. yellow *(perf)* .... 4·25 20·00
a. "EEGAM" (R. 2/3–4, R. 3/3–1, R. 4/2, R. 4/4, R. 6/1) .... 6·50 28·00

1889. *T* **6** *again redrawn. Sheets of 32 (4×8) lettered "BEGAN".*

27 ¼a. black *(perf)* .... 1·75 5·50
a. "EEGAN" (R. 7/3) .... 15·00 32·00
b. Imperf between (horiz pair) £275
28 ¼a. black *(imperf)* .... 2·25 5·50
a. "EEGAN" (R. 7/3) .... 18·00 32·00

9 (¼a.)

1889–90. *T* **9**. *T* **6** *again redrawn. Sheets of 24 (4×6), all with "M" like an inverted "W". Wove paper.*

(a) Imperf.

29 **9** ¼a. black .... 2·25 2·00
30 1a. brown .... 2·25 4·75
a. "EEGAM" (R. 2/3) .... 14·00 26·00
b. "BBGAM" (R. 3/1) .... 14·00 26·00
31 2a. blue .... 2·00 2·25
a. "BBEGAM" (R. 1/2) .... 8·50 14·00
b. "NAWAH" (R. 4/2) .... 8·50 14·00
32 4a. orange-yellow .... 2·50 3·75
29/32 *Set of 4* .... 8·00 11·50

(b) Perf.

33 **9** ¼a. black .... 3·00 4·25
a. Imperf between (horiz pair) .. £325
34 1a. brown .... 4·50 7·50
a. "EEGAM" (R. 2/3) .... 25·00 38·00
b. "BBGAM" (R. 3/1) .... 25·00 38·00
35 2a. blue .... 2·50 3·75
a. "BBEGAM" (R. 1/2) .... 9·50 18·00
b. "NAWAH" (R. 4/2) .... 9·50 18·00
36 4a. orange-yellow .... 3·00 8·00
33/6 *Set of 4* .... 11·50 21·00

Nos. 32 and 36 are nearly square, in many cases rather larger in height than in width.

1891. *As last, but sheets of 32 (4×8).*

37 **9** ½a. red *(imperf)* .... 2·00 3·75
38 ½a. red *(perf)* .... 1·75 4·75

1894–98. *T* **6** *again redrawn.*

(a) Sheets of 24 (4×6), almost all showing a character inside the octagon below, as in T **9**. *Wove paper.*

39 1a. deep brown *(imperf)* .... 7·50 4·25
a. Red-brown .... 35·00
b. Printed both sides .... — £600
41 1a. deep brown *(perf)* .... 8·00 5·00

10 (1a.)

(b) As Nos. 39/41, but printed from a new stone showing the lines blurred and shaky. Wove paper. Imperf (1898).

42 **10** 1a. purple-brown .... 3·25 4·25
a. "NAWAH" (R. 4/1) .... 18·00 24·00
43 1a. purple-brown/*buff* .... 3·25 4·25
a. "NAWAH" (R. 4/1) .... 18·00 24·00
b. Printed on both sides ....

The above are known without embossing.

11 (¼a.)

1895. *Sheets of 8 (2×4), lettered "EEGAM". White laid paper.*

44 **11** ¼a. black *(imperf)* .... 3·50 3·00
a. "A" inserted (R. 4/2) .... 8·50 7·00
45 ¼a. black *(perf)* .... 95·00 42·00
a. "NAW B" (R. 4/2) £325 £150

On the perf stamp the second "A" in "NAWAB" was missing on R. 4/2 in the setting. This letter was later inserted for the imperf printing varying progressively from small to large.

12 (½a.)

1895. *Narrow label at bottom. Sheets of 8 (2×4), lettered "W W" for "H H". Laid paper.*

46 **12** ½a. black *(imperf)* .... 1·50 1·75

12a

1896. *Sheets of 8 (2×4). Laid paper.*

47 **12a** ½a. red *(imperf)* .... 2·25 2·25

No. 47 is a combination of Types **1** and **6**, having the double outer frame to the octagon and the value in one form only.

13 (¼a.)

14 (¼a.)

1884. *Sheets of 32 (4×8).* Perf.

48 **13** ¼a. blue-green £150 £180
a. "JAN" (R. 2/1–2, R. 3/1, R. 3/3–4, R. 4/1–3, R. 5/1–3) £150 £180
b. "BEGM" (R. 2/3–4) £375 £425
c. "NWAB" and "JAN" (R. 3/2) £650
ca. "NWAB" and "JN" (R. 5/4) £650
d. "SHAHAN" (R. 4/4) £650
e. "JAHA" (R. 6/2–4) £300

1896. *T* **14**, *double-lined frame round each stamp. Sheets of 6 (2×3), lettered "JAN". Laid paper.*

49 **14** ¼a. bright green *(imperf)* .... 5·50 18·00

15 (½a.)

16 (¼a.)

1884. *Sheets of 32 (4×8). Laid paper.*

50 **15** ¼a. blue-green *(imperf)* £160 £180
a. "NWAB" (R. 1/1) £450
b. "SAH" (R. 1/4) £450
c. "NAWA" and "JANAN" (R. 3/2) £450
51 ¼a. blue-green *(perf)* .... 1·00 4·00
a. "NWAB" (R. 1/1) .... 4·00
b. "SAH" (R. 1/4) .... 4·00
c. "NAWA" and "JANAN" (R. 3/2) .... 4·00
d. Imperf between (vert pair) £300
52 ½a. black *(imperf)* .... 2·25 2·50
a. "NWAB" (R. 1/1) .... 10·00 12·00
b. "SAH" (R. 1/4) .... 10·00 12·00
c. "NAWA" and "JANAN" (R. 3/2) .... 10·00 12·00
53 ½a. black *(perf)* .... 90 3·25
a. "NWAB" (R. 1/1) .... 3·75 8·50
b. "SAH" (R. 1/4) .... 3·75 8·50
c. "NAWA" and "JANAN" (R. 3/2) .... 3·75 8·50

The ¼a. of this issue is in *blue-green*, or *greenish blue*. Both values were printed from the same stone, the value alone being altered. There are therefore the same varieties of each. These are the only stamps of this design on laid paper.

Both values show the "N" of "NAWAB" reversed on R. 1/1–4, R. 2/1–4, R. 3/1–4 and the "N" of "JAHAN" reversed on R. 1/1–4, R. 2/1–7, R. 3/4.

1886. *T* **15** *redrawn. Sheets of 32 (4×8). Wove paper.*

54 ¼a. green *(imperf)* .... 55 3·25
a. "NAWA" (R. 6/3–4) .... 2·00 7·00
b. "NWAB" (R. 1/1) .... 3·00 9·00
c. "NWABA" (R. 7/4) .... 3·00 9·00
d. "NAWAA" (R. 6/2) .... 3·00 9·00
e. "BEGAAM" and "NWABA" (R. 7/3) .... 3·00 9·00
55 ¼a. green *(perf)* .... 2·50 4·00
a. "NAWA" (R. 6/3–4) .... 8·00
b. "NWAB" (R. 1/1) .... 13·00
c. "NWABA" (R. 7/4) .... 13·00
d. "NAWAA" (R. 6/2) .... 13·00
e. "BEGAAM" and "NWABA" (R. 7/3) .... 13·00
f. Imperf between (horiz pair) £160
56 ½a. red *(imperf)* .... 65 1·75
a. "SAH" (R. 1/4) .... 4·00 6·50
b. "NAWABA" (R. 6/3–4) .... 3·00 5·00

The ¼a. varies from *yellow-green* to *deep green*.

All examples of the ¼a. value show the "N" of "NAWAB" reversed. On the same value the "N" of "JAHAN" is reversed on all positions except R. 3/2, R. 4/1, R. 4/3. On the ½a. both "N"s are always reversed.

1888. *T* **15** *again redrawn. Sheets of 32 (4×8), letters in upper angles smaller. "N" of "NAWAB" correct. Wove paper.*

57 ¼a. deep green *(imperf)* .... 1·00 2·00
a. "SAH" (R. 6/2) .... 4·50 7·00
b. "NAWA" (R. 4/4) .... 4·50 7·00

58 ¼a. deep green (*perf*) 2·00 2·75
a. "SAH" (R. 6/2) 7·50 9·00
b. "NAWA" (R. 4/4) 7·50 9·00
c. Imperf between (vert pair) £225

Nos. 50 to 58 have the dash under the letter "JA" as in No. 14.

1891. *T* **15** *again redrawn. Sheets of 32 (4×8), lettered "NWAB." Wove paper.*

(*a*) Imperf.

59 ½a. red 2·00 1·50
a. "SAH" (R. 2/4) 6·00

(*b*) P 3 to 4½, or about 7.

60 ½a. red 80 2·00
a. "SAH" (R. 2/4) 5·00

Nos. 59 and 60 have the comma under "JA". The "N" of "JAHAN" is reversed on R. 1/1–3, R. 2/1–2.

1894. *T* **15** *again redrawn; letters in corners larger than in 1888, value in very small characters. Sheets of 32 (4×8), all with "G" in left-hand lower corner. Wove paper.*

61 ¼a. green (*imperf*) 1·50 1·75
a. "NAWAH" (R. 4/4) 7·50 8·00
b. Value in brackets (R. 1/1) 7·50 8·00

62 ¼a. green (*perf*) 3·00 2·25
a. "NAWAH" (R. 4/4) 13·00 11·00
b. Value in brackets (R. 1/1) 13·00 11·00

Nos. 61 and 62 have neither the dash nor the comma under "JA".

1898. *T* **16**; *oval narrower, stops after "H.H.", space after "NAWAB". The line down the centre is under the first "H" of "SHAH" or between "HA" instead of being under the second "H" or between "AH". Sheets of 32 (4×8). Wove paper.* Imperf.

63 **16** ¼a. bright green 75 80
a. "SHAN" (R. 1/1) 3·50 3·50

64 ¼a. pale green 80 70
a. "SHAN" (R. 1/1) 3·50 3·50

65 ¼a. black 50 50
a. "SHAN" (R. 1/1) 3·25 3·25

1899. *T* **15** *redrawn. Sheets of 32 (4×8), the first "A" of "NAWAB" always absent. Numerous defective and malformed letters. Wove paper.* Imperf.

66 ½a. black 4·50 6·50
a. "NWASBAHJANNI" (R. 2/4) 22·00 29·00
b. "SBAH" (R. 3/3, R. 4/3–4, R.5/1–2, R. 6/4) 10·00 15·00
c. "SBAN" (R. 8/2) 22·00 29·00
d. "NWIB" (R. 3/2) 22·00 29·00
e. "BEIAM" (R. 4/4) 22·00 29·00
f. "SHH" (R. 6/3) 22·00 29·00
g. "SBAH" and "BBGAM" (R. 3/4) 22·00 29·00
h. "BBGAM" (R. 1/3) 22·00 29·00

17 (8a.)

18 (¼a.)

1890. *T* **17**. *Sheets of 10 (2×5). Single-line frame to each stamp.*

(*a*) *Wove paper.*

67 **17** 8a. slate-green (*imperf*) 65·00 £120
a. "HAH" (R. 3/1, R. 4/1, R. 5/1) 75·00 £130
b. "JABAN" (R. 2/2) 80·00

68 8a. slate-green (*perf*) 65·00 £120
a. "HAH" (R. 3/1, R. 4/1, R. 5/1) 75·00
b. "JABAN" (R. 2/2) 80·00

(*b*) *Thin laid paper.*

69 **17** 8a. green-black (*imperf*) 75·00 £150
a. "HAH" (R. 3/1, R. 4/1, R. 5/1) 85·00
b. "JABAN" (R. 2/2) 90·00

70 8a. green-black (*perf*) 75·00 £150
a. "HAH" (R. 3/1, R. 4/1, R. 5/1) 90·00 £170
b. "JABAN" (R. 2/2) 95·00

The "N" of "NAWAB" is reversed on R. 5/2 and the "N" of "JAHAN" on R. 1/1–2, R. 2/2, R. 3/2, R. 4/2 and R. 5/2.

1893. *T* **17** *redrawn. No frame to each stamp, but a frame to the sheet. Sheets of 10 (2×5).*

(*a*) *Wove paper.*

71 8a. green-black (*imperf*) 22·00 22·00
72 8a. green-black (*perf*) 30·00 40·00

(*b*) *Thin laid paper.* Imperf.

73 8a. green-black £200 £300

1898. *Printed from a new stone. Lettering irregular. Sheets of 10 (2×5). Wove paper.* Imperf.

74 8a. green-black 45·00 55·00
a. Reversed "E" in "BEGAM" (R. 1/2, R. 3/2) 90·00 £100

75 8a. black 42·00 55·00
a. Reversed "E" in "BEGAM" (R. 1/2, R. 3/2) 90·00 £100

1896–1901. *Sheets of 32 (4×8).*

(*a*) *Wove paper.* Imperf.

76 **18** ¼a. black 1·40 1·40

(*b*) *Printed from a new stone, lines shaky (1899).*

77 **18** ¼a. black 2·75 3·00

(*c*) *The same, on thick wove paper (1901).*

78 **18** ¼a. black £500 £600

Nawab Sultan Jahan Begam, 16 June 1901–17 May 1926

19 (¼a.)

20

1902. *T* **19**. *With the octagonal embossed device of the previous issues. Sheets of 16 (4×4) ¼a. or 8 (2×4) others. Thin, yellowish wove paper.* Imperf.

79 **19** ¼a. rose 5·50 9·00
80 ¼a. rose-red 3·75 6·00
81 ½a. black 4·00 7·00
a. Printed both sides £750 £750
82 1a. brown 7·00 17·00
83 1a. red-brown 5·00 15·00
84 2a. blue 8·50 15·00
85 4a. orange 75·00 £110
86 4a. yellow 38·00 85·00
87 8a. lilac £100 £190
88 1r. rose £275 £400
79/88 *Set of* 7 £400 £650

1903. *With a circular embossed device. Sheets of 16 (4×4) ¼a. (two plates) or 8 (2×4) (others). Wove paper.*

89 **19** ¼a. rose-red 1·50 5·00
a. Laid paper 1·00 8·00
90 ¼a. red 1·25 5·00
a. Laid paper 30 6·00
91 ½a. black 1·25 5·00
a. Laid paper 1·00 8·50
92 1a. brown 3·00 7·50
a. Laid paper 95·00
93 1a. red-brown 7·00
a. Laid paper
94 2a. blue 7·00 25·00
a. Laid paper £170 £225
95 4a. orange (*laid paper*) £325 £325
96 4a. yellow 18·00 50·00
a. Laid paper £140 £120
97 8a. lilac 55·00 £130
a. Laid paper £1600
98 1r. rose 85·00 £190
a. Laid paper £1300
89/98 *Set of* 7 £150 £375

1903. *No. 71 optd with initial of the new Begam, either 6 or 11 mm long, in red.*

99 8a. green-black £140 £150
a. Opt inverted £375 £400

Some of the previous stamps remained on sale (and probably in use) after the issue of the series of 1902, and some of these were afterwards put on sale with the new form of embossing; fresh plates were made of some of the old designs, in imitation of the earlier issues, and impressions from these were also sold with the new embossed device. We no longer list these doubtful items.

(Recess Perkins, Bacon & Co)

1908. P 13½.

100 **20** 1a. green 3·75 4·50
a. Printed both sides £120
b. Imperf (pair)

The ordinary postage stamps of Bhopal became obsolete on 1 July 1908.

OFFICIAL STAMPS

SERVICE
(O **1**)

SERVICE
(O **2**)

(Recess and optd Perkins, Bacon)

1908–11. *As T* **20**, *but inscribed* "H.H. BEGUM'S SERVICE" *at left.* No wmk. P 13 to 14. Overprinted.

(*a*) *With Type* O **1**.

O301 ½a. yellow-green 2·25 10
a. Imperf (pair) £160
b. Pair, one without overprint £650
c. Opt double, one inverted £110
ca. Ditto. Imperf (pair) £160
d. Opt inverted £180 £150
e. Imperf between (horiz pair) £800

O302 1a. carmine-red 4·25 40
a. Opt inverted £120 95·00
b. Imperf (pair) £140
c. *Red* 6·50 10

O303 2a. ultramarine 24·00 10
a. Imperf (pair) 55·00

O304 4a. brown (1911) 14·00 55
O301/4 *Set of* 4 40·00 75

(*b*) *With Type* O **2**.

O305 ½a. yellow-green 7·50 1·25
O306 1a. carmine-red 9·50 90
O307 2a. ultramarine 4·00 60
a. Opt inverted 25·00
O308 4a. brown (1911) 80·00 1·50
a. Opt inverted 20·00 70·00
b. Opt double £130
c. Imperf (pair) 85·00
d. Imperf (pair) and opt inverted 90·00
O305/8 *Set of* 4 90·00 3·75

The two overprints differ in the shape of the letters, noticeably in the "R".

Nawab Mohammad Hamidullah. Khan

17 May 1928 to transfer of administration to India, 1 June 1949

(O **4**)

(Des T. I. Archer. Litho Indian Govt Ptg Wks, Nasik)

1930 (1 July)–**31**. *Type* O **4** (*25½×30½ mm*). P 14.

O309 O **4** ½a. sage-green (1931) 12·00 1·75
O310 1a. carmine-red 11·00 15
O311 2a. ultramarine 9·50 45
O312 4a. chocolate 10·00 90
O309/12 *Set of* 4 38·00 3·00

The ½a., 2a. and 4a. are inscribed "POSTAGE" at left.

(Litho Perkins, Bacon)

1932–34. *As Type* O **4** (*21×25 mm*), *but inscr* "POSTAGE" *at left. Optd with Type* O **1**.

(*a*) *"BHOPAL STATE" at right.* P 13.

O313 ¼a. orange 2·50 50
a. Perf 11½ (1933) 7·50 20
b. Perf 14 (1934) 12·00 30
c. Perf 13½ (1934) 11·00 30
ca. Vert pair, one without opt £120

(*b*) *"BHOPAL GOVT" at right.* P 13½.

O314 ½a. yellow-green 7·50 10
O315 1a. carmine-red 11·00 15
a. Vert pair, one without opt £200
O316 2a. ultramarine 11·00 45
O317 4a. chocolate 11·00 1·00
a. Perf 14 (1934) 16·00 40
O313/17 *Set of* 5 38·00 1·10

No. O317 is comb-perforated and No. O317a line-perforated.

¼A
(O **5**)

THREE PIES
(O **6**)

ONE ANNA
(O **7**)

1935–36. *Nos. O314, O316 and O317 surch as Types* O **5** *to* O **7**.

O318 O **5** ¼a. on ½a. yellow-green (R.) 32·00 14·00
a. Surch inverted £200 85·00
b. Vert pair. Nos. O318/19 50·00 23·00
ba. Ditto. Surch inverted £450 £190

O319 O **6** 3p. on ½a. yellow-green (R.) 3·75 3·50
a. "THEEE PIES" (R. 7/10) 75·00 55·00
b. "THRFE" for "THREE" (R. 10/6) 75·00 55·00
c. Surch inverted 80·00 40·00

O320 O **5** ¼a. on 2a. ultramarine (R.) 29·00 20·00
a. Surch inverted £200 75·00
b. Vert pair. Nos. O320/1 45·00 30·00
ba. Ditto. Surch inverted £450 £180

O321 O **6** 3p. on 2a. ultramarine (R.) 4·50 4·50
a. Surch inverted 80·00 40·00
b. "THEEE PIES" (R. 7/10) 80·00 50·00
ba. Ditto. Surch inverted £700 £550
c. "THRFE" for "THREE" (R. 10/6) 80·00 50·00
ca. Ditto. Surch inverted £700 £550

O322 O **5** ¼a. on 4a. chocolate (R.) £1000 £325
a. Vert pair. Nos. O322 and O324 £1600 £550

O323 ¼a. on 4a. chocolate (No. O317a) (Blk.) (25.5.36) 80·00 26·00
a. Vert pair. Nos. O323 and O325 £120 55·00

O324 O **6** 3p. on 4a. chocolate (R.) £140 65·00
a. "THEEE PIES" (R. 7/10) £750 £500
c. "THRFE" for "THREE" (R. 10/6) £750 £500

O325 3p. on 4a. chocolate (No. O317a) (Blk.) (25.5.36) 2·50 3·25
a. "THRER" for "THREE" (R. 8/2) £375 £225
b. "FHREE" for "THREE" (R. 3/10, R. 10/1) £425 £325
c. "PISE" for "PIES" (R. 10/10) £700 £475
d. "PIFS" for "PIES" (R. 7/9) £375 £225

O326 O **7** 1a. on ½a. yellow-green (V.) 5·00 1·50
a. Surch inverted 70·00 45·00
b. First "N" in "ANNA" inverted (R. 4/5) 90·00 60·00
ba. Ditto. Surch inverted £700 £500

O327 1a. on 2a. ultramarine (R.) 2·25 2·00
a. Surch inverted 85·00 38·00
b. First "N" in "ANNA" inverted (R. 4/5) 80·00 55·00
ba. Ditto. Surch inverted £700 £500

O327*d* 1a. on 2a. ultramarine (V.) 50·00 55·00
da. Surch inverted 95·00 95·00
db. First "N" in "ANNA" inverted (R. 4/5) £650 £650
dc. Ditto. Surch inverted £1100 £1100

O328 1a. on 2a. ultram (Blk.) (25.5.36) 70 2·50
a. "ANNO" £2000

O329 1a. on 4a. chocolate (B.) 7·00 5·00
a. First "N" in "ANNA" inverted (R. 4/5) £120 85·00
b. Perf 14 13·00 6·00
ba. Ditto. First "N" in "ANNA" inverted (R. 4/5) £250 £100

Nos. O318 to O325 are arranged in composite sheets of 100 (10×10). The two upper horizontal rows of each value are surcharged as Type O **5** and the next five rows as Type O **6**. The remaining three rows are also surcharged as Type O **6** but in a slightly narrower setting.

The surcharge on No. O323 differs from Type O **5** in the shape of the figures and letter.

O 8

(Des T. I. Archer. Litho Indian Govt Ptg Wks, Nasik (No. O330). Typo Bhopal Govt Ptg Wks (others))

1935–39. *As Type* O **8**.

(a) Litho. Inscr "BHOPAL GOVT POSTAGE". *Optd* "SERVICE" *(13½ mm)*. P 13½.

O330		1a.3p. blue and claret	3·50	1·50

(b) Typo. Inscr "BHOPAL STATE POSTAGE". *Optd* "SERVICE" *(11 mm)*. P 12.

O331		1a.6p. blue and claret (1937)	2·50	1·00
		a. Imperf between (pair)	£200	£225
		b. Opt omitted	£180	£140
		c. Opt double, one inverted	£500	£500
		d. Imperf (pair)	†	£180
		e. Blue printing double	†	£170
O332		1a.6p. claret (1939)	6·00	1·75
		a. Imperf between (pair)	£200	£225
		b. Opt omitted	—	£425
		c. Opt double, one inverted	—	£425
		d. Opt double	—	£425

PRINTERS. From No. O333 all issues were printed by the Bhopal Govt Ptg Wks in typography.

O 9

O **10** The Moti Mahal

O **11** The Moti Masjid

O **12** Taj Mahal and Be-Nazir Palaces

O **13** Ahmadabad Palace

O **14** Rait Ghat

1936 (July)–**38**. *Optd* "SERVICE". P 12.

O333	O **9**	¼a. orange (Br.)	90	60
		a. Imperf between (vert pair)	£170	
		ab. Imperf between (horiz pair)	†	£375
		b. Opt inverted	£425	£325
		c. Black opt	8·50	75
		ca. Opt inverted	†	£400
		cb. Opt double	†	£300
O334		¼a. yellow (Br.) (1938)	4·25	1·50
O335		1a. scarlet	1·50	10
		a. Imperf between (horiz pair)	£160	£150
		b. Imperf between (vert pair)	†	£325
		c. Imperf between (block of four)	£425	£425
		d. Imperf vert (horiz pair)	†	£170

1936–49. *T* O **10/14**. P 12.

(a) Optd "SERVICE" *(13½ mm)*.

O336	O **10**	½a. purple-brown and yellow-green	70	80
		a. Imperf between (vert pair)	†	£225
		ab. Imperf between (horiz pair)	†	£225
		b. Opt double	£275	£170
		c. Frame double	£120	15·00
		d. Purple-brown and green (1938)	70	40

(b) Optd "SERVICE" *(11 mm)*.

O337	O **11**	2a. brown and blue (1937)	2·00	90
		a. Imperf between (vert pair)	†	£350
		ab. Imperf between (horiz pair)	†	£250
		b. Opt inverted	£300	£375
		c. Opt omitted	£400	
		d. Pair, one without opt	£650	
		e. As d. but opt inverted	£950	
O338		2a. green and violet (1938)	12·00	30
		a. Imperf between (vert pair)	†	£275
		b. Imperf between (vert strip of 3)	£160	£200
		c. Frame double	†	£300
		d. Centre double	†	£325
O339	O **12**	4a. blue and brown (1937)	3·75	50
		a. Imperf between (horiz pair)	†	£700
		b. Opt omitted	†	£325
		c. Opt double	†	£160
		d. Centre double	†	£400
		e. Blue and reddish brown (1938)	3·50	55
		ea. Frame double	†	£300
O340	O **13**	8a. bright purple and blue (1938)	5·50	2·25
		a. Imperf between (vert pair)	†	£425
		b. Opt omitted	†	£170
		c. Opt double	†	£160
		d. Imperf vert (horiz pair) and opt omitted	†	£325
		e. Imperf (pair) and opt omitted	†	£325
O341	O **14**	1r. blue and reddish purple (Br.) (1938)	22·00	8·50
		a. Imperf horiz (vert pair)	†	£1500
		b. Opt in black (1942)	17·00	4·50
		ba. Light blue and bright purple	40·00	29·00
		bb. Laid paper	£750	£800
O336/41*b* *Set of* 6			35·00	8·00

(c) Optd "SERVICE" *(11½ mm) with serifs.*

O342	O **14**	1r. dull blue and bright purple (Blk.) (1949)	45·00	90·00
		a. "SREVICE" for "SERVICE" (R. 6/6)	£130	£250
		b. "SERVICE" omitted	£900	

(d) Optd "SERVICE" *(13½ mm) with serifs.*

O343	O **13**	8a. bright purple and blue (1949)	80·00	£110
		a. "SERAICE" for "SERVICE" (R. 6/5)	£450	£550
		b. Fig "1" for "I" in "SERVICE" (R. 7/1)	£450	£550

The ½a. is inscr "BHOPAL GOVT" below the arms, other values have "BHOPAL STATE".

O **15** Tiger

O **16** Spotted Deer

1940. *T* O **15/16**. P 12.

O344	O **15**	¼a. bright blue	4·75	1·75
O345	O **16**	1a. bright purple	28·00	3·00

1941. *As Type* O **8** *but coloured centre inscr* "SERVICE"; *bottom frame inscr* "BHOPAL STATE POSTAGE". P 12.

O346		1a.3p. emerald-green	2·00	2·25
		a. Imperf between (pair)	£450	£475

O **17** The Moti Mahal

O **18** The Moti Masjid

O **19** Be-Nazir Palaces

1944–47. *T* O **17/19**. P 12.

O347	O **17**	½a. green	90	1·00
		a. Imperf (pair)	†	95·00
		b. Imperf between (vert pair)	†	£190
		c. Doubly printed	†	£160
O348	O **18**	2a. violet	11·00	4·00
		a. Imperf (pair)	†	£100
		c. Bright purple (1945)	3·50	3·75
		d. Mauve (1947)	11·00	15·00
		e. Error. Chocolate (imperf)	£250	£250
O349	O **19**	4a. chocolate	7·00	2·25
		a. Imperf (pair)	†	£130
		b. Imperf vert (horiz pair)	†	£275
		c. Doubly printed	†	£180
O347/9 *Set of* 3			10·25	6·25

O **20** Arms of Bhopal

2 As.

(O **21**)

2 As.

(O **22**)

1944–49. P 12.

O350	O **20**	3p. bright blue	1·00	85
		a. Imperf between (vert pair)	£140	£150
		b. Imperf between (horiz pair)	†	£300
		c. Stamp doubly printed	55·00	
O351		9p. chestnut (*shades*) (1945)	9·50	3·50
		a. Imperf (pair)	†	£190
		b. Orange-brown	2·00	4·25
O352		1a. purple (1945)	5·00	1·75
		a. Imperf horiz (vert pair)	†	£425
		b. Violet (1946)	9·00	3·25
O353		1½a. claret (1945)	1·50	1·25
		a. Imperf between (horiz pair)	†	£375
		b. Imperf between (vert pair)	†	£400
O354		3a. yellow	13·00	14·00
		a. Imperf (pair)	†	£190
		b. Imperf horiz (vert pair)	†	£250
		c. Imperf vert (horiz pair)		
		d. Orange-brown (1949)	£100	£110
O355		6a. carmine (1945)	19·00	50·00
		a. Imperf (pair)	†	£275
		b. Imperf horiz (vert pair)	†	£325
		c. Imperf vert (horiz pair)	†	£325
O350/5 *Set of* 6			38·00	65·00

1949 (July). *Surch with Type* O **21**. P 12.

O356	O **20**	2a. on 1½a. claret	2·50	7·50
		a. Stop omitted	13·00	32·00
		b. Imperf (pair)	£250	£300
		ba. Stop omitted (pair)	£650	£750
		c. "2" omitted (in pair with normal)	£1000	

The "stop omitted" variety occurs on positions 60 and 69 in the sheet of 81.

1949. *Surch with Type* O **22**. Imperf.

O357	O **20**	2a. on 1½a. claret	£1000	£1000
		a. Perf 12	£1100	£1100

Three different types of "2" occur in the setting of Type O **22**. This surcharge has been extensively forged, and should not be purchased without a reliable guarantee.

BHOR

PRICES FOR STAMPS ON COVER

Nos. 1/2	*from* × 40
No. 3	*from* × 6

GUM. The stamps of Bhor were issued without gum.

Pandit Shankar Rao, 1871–1922

1

2

1879. *Handstamped. Very thick to thin native paper.* Imperf.

1	**1**	½a. carmine (*shades*)	3·75	5·00
		a. *Tête-bêche* (pair)	£800	
2	**2**	1a. carmine (*shades*)	5·50	8·00

3

1901. *Typo. Wove paper.* Imperf.

3	**3**	½a. red	16·00	40·00

BIJAWAR

PRICES FOR STAMPS ON COVER
The stamps of Bijawar are very rare used on cover.

Maharaja Sarwant Singh, 1899–1941

1

2

(Typo Lakshmi Art Ptg Works, Bombay)

1935 (1 July)–**36**.

(a) P 11.

1	**1**	3p. brown	7·50	5·50
		a. Imperf (pair)	9·00	
		b. Imperf between (vert pair)	85·00	
		c. Imperf horiz (vert pair)	50·00	
2		6p. carmine	6·50	5·50
		a. Imperf (pair)	85·00	
		b. Imperf between (vert pair)	80·00	
		c. Imperf between (horiz pair)	85·00	£140
		d. Imperf horiz (vert pair)	90·00	

3		9p. violet	8·50	5·00
		a. Imperf (pair)	£140	
		b. Imperf between (vert pair)	95·00	
		c. Imperf between (horiz pair)	80·00	
		d. Imperf horiz (vert pair)	90·00	
4		1a. blue	9·50	5·50
		a. Imperf (pair)	85·00	
		b. Imperf between (vert pair)	90·00	
		c. Imperf between (horiz pair)	£150	
		d. Imperf horiz (vert pair)	£100	
		e. Imperf vert (horiz strip of 3)	£170	
5		2a. deep green	9·00	5·00
		a. Imperf (pair)	£100	
		b. Imperf horiz (vert pair)	12·00	
		c. Imperf between (vert pair)	35·00	
		d. Imperf between (horiz pair)	50·00	85·00
1/5 *Set of 5*			38·00	24·00

(b) Roul 7 (1936).

6	1	3p. brown	6·00	6·00
		a. Printed on gummed side	£550	
7		6p. carmine	8·00	22·00
8		9p. violet	6·00	£110
9		1a. blue	10·00	£120
10		2a. deep green	13·00	£130
6/10 *Set of 5*			38·00	£350

1937 (May). *Typo. P 9.*

11	2	4a. orange	15·00	80·00
		a. Imperf between (vert pair)	£140	
		b. Imperf (pair)	£200	
12		6a. lemon	15·00	80·00
		a. Imperf between (vert pair)	£150	
		b. Imperf (pair)	£200	
13		8a. emerald-green	16·00	£110
		a. Imperf (pair)	£225	
14		12a. greenish blue	16·00	£110
		a. Imperf (pair)	£250	
15		1r. bright violet	42·00	£170
		a. "1 Rs" for "1 R" (R. 1/2)	50·00	£325
		b. Imperf (pair)	£300	
		ba. "1 Rs" for "1 R" (R. 1/2)	£850	
11/15 *Set of 5*			95·00	£500

The stamps of Bijawar were withdrawn in 1941.

BUNDI

PRICES FOR STAMPS ON COVER	
No. 1	*from* × 2
No. 2	*from* × 4
Nos. 3/53	*from* × 10
Nos. 54/63	*from* × 5
Nos. 64/78	*from* × 2
Nos. 79/92	*from* × 10
Nos. O1/52	*from* × 15
Nos. O53/9	*from* × 20

GUM. Nos. 1/17 were issued without gum.

ILLUSTRATIONS. Types **1/10** and the tablet inscriptions for Type 11 are shown actual size.

In Nos. 1 to 17 characters denoting the value are below the dagger, except in Nos. 2a, 11 and 17.

All Bundi stamps until 1914 are lithographed and imperforate.

Maharao Raja Raghubir Singh, 1889–1927

1

1894 (May). *Each stamp with a distinct frame and the stamps not connected by the framing lines. Three vertical lines on dagger. Laid or wove paper.*

1	1	½a. slate-grey	£13000	£2250
		a. Last two letters of value below the rest	†	£6500

2 (Block of four stamps)

1894 (Dec). *Stamps joined together, with no space between them. Two vertical lines on dagger. Thin wove paper.*

2	2	½a. slate-grey	45·00	48·00
		a. Value at top, name below	£275	£350
		b. Right upper ornament omitted	£2500	£2750
		c. Last two letters of value below the rest	£1600	£1600
		d. Left lower ornament omitted	£2500	£2750

No. 2 was printed in sheets of 294, comprising two panes (10×14 and 11×14) side by side, in *tête-bêche* format. In the 10×14 pane No. 2a occurs on R1/1-10, No. 2b on R11/7 and No. 2d on R2/9. In the 11×14 pane No. 2c occurs on R2/11, 8/3 and 10/1.

3

1896 (Nov). *Dagger shorter, lines thicker. Stamps separate. Laid paper.*

3	3	½a. slate-grey	6·00	9·50
		a. Last two letters of value below the rest	£375	£500

No. 3 was printed in sheets of 168, comprising two panes (7×12) side by side.

4 (1 anna)

5 (2 annas)

6 (2 annas)

1897–98. *No shading in centre of blade of dagger. The stamps have spaces between them, but are connected by the framing lines, both vertically and horizontally. Laid paper.*

I. *Blade of dagger comparatively narrow, and either triangular, as in T* **4** *and* **6**, *or with the left-hand corner not touching the bar behind it, as in T* **5** *(1897–98).*

4	4	1a. Indian red	14·00	26·00
5	5	1a. red	12·00	18·00
6		2a. green	17·00	23·00
7	6	2a. yellow-green	14·00	27·00
8	5	4a. green	70·00	95·00
9		8a. Indian red	£110	£300
10		1r. yellow/*blue*	£325	£550
4/10 *Set of 5*			£475	£900

7

II. *Blade varying in shape, but as a rule not touching the bar; value above and name below the dagger, instead of the reverse (Jan 1898).*

11	7	4a. emerald-green	48·00	
		a. Yellow-green	28·00	70·00

8 (½ anna)

9 (1 anna)

III. *Blade wider and (except on the ½ a.) almost diamond shaped; it nearly always touches the bar (1898–1900).*

12	8	½a. slate-grey (5.2.98)	4·75	4·75
13	9	1a. Indian red (7.98)	3·75	3·75
14		2a. pale green (9.11.98)	13·00	17·00
		a. First two characters of value (= two) omitted	£2000	£2000
15		8a. Indian red (7.98)	14·00	18·00
16		1r. yellow/*blue* (7.98)	32·00	55·00
		a. On wove paper	16·00	27·00
12/16a *Set of 5*			45·00	65·00

10

IV. *Inscriptions as on No. 11; point of dagger to left (9.11.98).*

17	10	4a. green	38·00	45·00
		a. Yellow-green	18·00	25·00

All the above stamps are lithographed in large sheets, containing as many varieties of type as there are stamps in the sheets.

11 Raja protecting Sacred Cows

Type **11** was produced from separate clichés printed as a block of four. The same clichés were used for all values, but not necessarily in the same order within the block. The Devanagri inscriptions, "RAJ BUNDI" at top and the face value at bottom, were inserted into the basic clichés as required so that various differences exist within the 58 settings which have been identified.

The denominations may be identified from the following illustrations. The ½a., 3a. and rupee values can be easily distinguished by their colours.

Bottom tablets:—

¼a. 1a.

2a. 2½a.

4a. 6a.

8a. 10a.

12a. 1r.

The nine versions of the inscriptions are as follows:

A B

Top tablet

Type A. Top tablet has inscription in two separate words with a curved line over the first character in the second. The second word has three characters. Bottom tablet has short line above the first character in the second word.

Type B. Top tablet as Type A, but without the curved line over the first character in the second word. Bottom tablet as Type A.

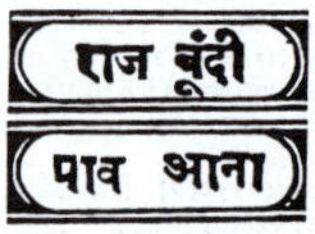

C

Type C. Top tablet as Type B, but with large loop beneath the first character in the second word. This loop is usually joined to the main character, but is sometimes detached as in the illustration. Bottom tablet as Type A.

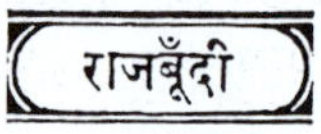

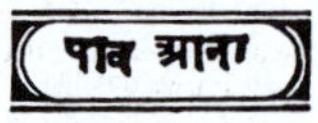

D E

Top tablet Bottom tablet

Type D. Top tablet in thinner lettering with the inscription shown as one word of six characters. The fourth character has a curved line above it, as in Type A, and a loop beneath, as in Type C. Bottom tablet as Type A, but thinner letters.

Type E. Top tablet as Type C. Bottom tablet shows a redrawn first character to the second word. This has the line at top extending over the entire character.

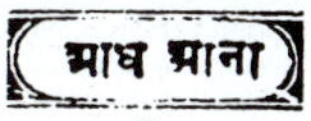

F

Bottom tablet

Type F. Top tablet as Type B. Bottom tablet as Type E, but first character in second word differs.

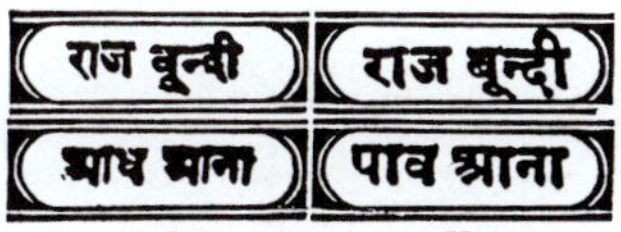

G H

Type G. Top tablet as Type C, but without dot over first character in second word. There are now four characters in the second word. Bottom tablet as Type E.

Type H. Top tablet as Type G, but with characters larger and bolder. Bottom tablet as Type E, but with characters larger and bolder.

I

Type I. Top tablet as Type H. Bottom tablet as Type E.

Some settings contained more than one inscription type within the block of four so that *se-tenant* examples are known of Type B with Type C (¼, 1, 2, 4, 8, 10 and 12a.), Type C with Type E (¼, ½ and 4a.) and Type E with Type F (½ and 4a.). Type F only exists from this mixed setting.

1914 (Oct)–**41**. *T* **11**. *Typo. Ungummed paper except for Nos. 73/8.*

I. *Rouletted in colour.*

(a) *Inscriptions as Type A. Thin wove paper (1916–23).*

18	½a. black	3·25	10·00
19	1a. vermilion	6·50	23·00
20	2a. emerald	6·00	42·00
	a. Deep green (coarse ptg on medium wove paper) (1923)	4·50	9·00
21	2½a. chrome-yellow (*shades*) (1917)	11·00	42·00
	a. Printed both sides	£1400	
22	3a. chestnut (1917)	27·00	42·00
23	4a. yellow-green	21·00	
24	6a. cobalt (1917)	23·00	£110
25	1r. reddish violet (1917)	27·00	£120

A special printing of the 1a. took place in late 1917 in connection with the "OUR DAY" Red Cross Society Fund. This had the "RAJ BUNDI" inscription in the bottom tablet with the face value below it. The top tablet carried four Devanagri characters for "OUR DAY". No evidence has been found to suggest that this 1a. stamp was used for postal purposes (*Price*, £200 *unused*).

(b) *Inscriptions as Type B. Thin wove or pelure paper (1914–23).*

25a	¼a. cobalt (1916)	4·25	22·00
	ab. Stamp doubly printed	£500	
26	¼a. ultramarine (*shades*) (1917)	1·90	4·25
	a. Indigo (1923)	4·25	8·50
	b. Error. Black (1923)		
27	½a. black	2·75	6·00
28	1a. vermilion (1915)	3·75	12·00
	a. Carmine (1923)	11·00	12·00
	b. Red (*shades*) (1923)	5·50	12·00
29	2a. emerald (*shades*) (1915)	7·50	23·00
30	2½a. olive-yellow (1917)	7·50	27·00
31	3a. chestnut (1917)	8·50	45·00
32	4a. apple-green (1915)	3·50	42·00
32a	4a. olive-yellow (1917)	£140	£190
33	6a. pale ultramarine (*shades*) (1917)	14·00	£110
	a. Deep ultramarine (1917)	7·00	£120
34	8a. orange (1915)	7·50	£110
35	10a. olive-sepia (1917)	£225	£550
	a. Yellow-brown	£300	
36	12a. sage-green (1917)	£650	
36a	1r. lilac (*shades*) (1915)	25·00	

(c) *Inscriptions as Type C. Thin to medium wove paper (1917–41).*

37	¼a. ultramarine (*shades*) (1923)	8·50	9·50
	a. Indigo (1923)	7·00	11·00
	b. Error. Black (1923)		
	c. Cobalt (medium wove paper) (1937)	23·00	20·00
38	½a. black	1·90	4·50
39	1a. orange-red	21·00	27·00
	a. Carmine (1923)	22·00	27·00
	b. Deep red (medium wove paper) (1936)	23·00	23·00
40	2a. emerald	14·00	27·00
	a. Sage-green	11·00	27·00
41	4a. yellow-green (*shades*)	65·00	£130
	a. Olive-yellow	£110	£170
	b. Bright apple-green (medium wove paper) (1936)	£550	£275
42	8a. reddish orange	9·00	70·00
43	10a. brown-olive	16·00	£100
	a. Olive-sepia	42·00	£150
	b. Yellow-brown	80·00	
44	12a. sage-green	13·00	95·00
45	1r. lilac	27·00	£170
46	2r. red-brown and black	85·00	£225
	a. Chocolate and black (medium wove paper) (1936)	70·00	£300
47	3r. blue and red-brown	£130	£300
	a. Grey-blue and chocolate (medium wove paper) (1941)	£120	
	ab. Chocolate (inscriptions) inverted	£25000	
48	4r. emerald and scarlet	£275	£375
49	5r. scarlet and emerald	£275	£375

(d) *Inscriptions as Type D. Thin wove paper (1918?).*

50	2½a. buff (*shades*)	14·00	50·00
51	3a. red-brown	23·00	27·00
	a. Semi-circle and dot omitted from 4th character	38·00	42·00
52	10a. bistre	35·00	£120
	a. 4th character turned to left instead of downwards	50·00	£170
53	12a. grey-olive	45·00	£120
	a. 4th character turned to left instead of downwards	65·00	
	b. Blackish green	70·00	
	ba. 4th character turned to left instead of downwards	£100	

(e) *Inscriptions as Type E.*

(i) *Medium wove paper (1930–37).*

54	¼a. deep slate	18·00	25·00
54a	¼a. indigo (*thin wove paper*) (1935)	22·00	25·00
	b. Cobalt (1937)	23·00	18·00
55	½a. black	17·00	15·00
56	1a. carmine-red	24·00	32·00
57	3a. chocolate (*shades*) (1936)	11·00	38·00
58	4a. yellow-olive (1935)	£650	£200
	a. Bright apple-green (1936)	£600	£200
	ab. No tail to 4th character	£900	£375

(ii) *Very thick wove paper (1930–32).*

59	¼a. indigo (1932)	25·00	30·00
60	½a. black	90·00	95·00
61	1a. bright scarlet (1931)	20·00	25·00
	a. Carmine-red	75·00	85·00

(iii) *Thin horizontally laid paper (1935).*

62	¼a. indigo	4·50	23·00
63	1a. scarlet-vermilion	10·00	30·00

Nos. 62 and 63 exist in *tête-bêche* blocks of four on the same or opposite sides of the paper.

(f) *Inscriptions as Type F. Medium wove paper (1935).*

63a	½a. black	£100	£160
63b	4a. yellow-olive	£1200	£700

(g) *Inscriptions as Type G.*

(i) *Horizontally laid paper (1935).*

64	½a. black	85·00	85·00
	a. Vert laid paper	80·00	80·00
65	1a. scarlet	70·00	50·00
66	4a. bright green	20·00	40·00

(ii) *Medium wove paper (1936).*

66a	½a. black	4·50	26·00
66b	4a. yellow-green	£1100	£550

(h) *Inscriptions as Type H. Medium wove paper (1935–41).*

67	¼a. ultramarine	2·00	7·00
68	½a. black (1938)	75·00	75·00
69	1a. deep red	8·50	38·00
	a. Rosine (1938)	18·00	40·00
70	4a. emerald (1938)	20·00	30·00
71	4r. yellow-green and vermilion (1941)	£190	
72	5r. vermilion and yellow-green (1941)	£250	

No. 70 shows the currency spelt as "ANE" with the last letter missing and an accent over the Devanagri "N".

II. P 11.

(a) *Inscriptions as Type H. Medium wove paper with gum (1939–41).*

73	¼a. ultramarine	25·00	38·00
	a. Greenish blue (1941)	1·75	48·00
74	½a. black	32·00	32·00
75	1a. scarlet-vermilion (1940)	£130	60·00
	a. Rose (1940)	12·00	50·00
76	2a. yellow-green (1941)	16·00	75·00

(b) *Inscriptions as Type I. Medium wove paper with gum (1940).*

77	½a. black	£170	£100
78	2a. bright apple-green	50·00	50·00

FISCAL USE. Collectors are warned that the low values of the later settings of Type **11** were extensively used for fiscal purposes. Stamps which have been fraudulently cleaned of pen-cancels, regummed or provided with forged postmarks are frequently met with. Particular care should be exercised with examples of Nos. 58/*a*, 64/5, 68/70, 74/5*a* and 77.

Maharao Raja Ishwari Singh, 1927–1945

20

1941–44. *Typo.* P 11.

79	**20**	3p. bright blue	2·75	5·00
80		6p. deep blue	4·25	8·50
81		1a. orange-red	6·50	10·00
82		2a. chestnut	8·50	18·00
		a. Deep brown (no gum) (1944)	15·00	20·00
83		4a. bright green	15·00	55·00
84		8a. dull green	20·00	£200
85		1r. deep blue	42·00	£300
79/85 *Set of 7*			90·00	£550

The first printing only of Nos. 79/85 is usually with gum; all further printings, including No. 82*a*, are without gum.

Maharao Raja Bahadur Singh, 1945–1971

21 Maharao Raja Bahadur Singh

22 Maharoa Raja Badahur Singh

23 Bundi

(Typo *Times of India* Press, Bombay)

1947. P 11.

86	**21**	¼a. blue-green	2·25	38·00
87		½a. violet	2·00	32·00
88		1a. yellow-green	2·00	32·00
89	**22**	2a. vermilion	1·90	65·00
90		4a. orange	2·25	90·00
91	**23**	8a. ultramarine	3·00	
92		1r. chocolate	15·00	
86/92 *Set of 7*			25·00	

OFFICIAL STAMPS

PRICES. Prices for Nos. O1/52 are for unused examples. Used stamps are generally worth a small premium over the prices quoted.

बूंदी BUNDI

सरविस SERVICE

(O 1) (O 2)

BUNDI

SERVICE

(O 3)

1915–41. *T* **11** *handstamped as Types* O **1/3**. *Ungummed paper except Nos. O47/52.*

A. Optd with Type O **1**. *B. Optd with Type* O **2**. *C. Optd with Type* O **3**.

I. *Rouletted in colour*

(a) *Inscriptions as Type A. Thin wove paper.*

		A	B	C
O1	½a. black	£375	†	†
	a. Red opt	£375	†	†
O1b	2a. emerald	4·25	£275	†
	ba. Deep green (coarse ptg on medium wove paper)	6·50	15·00	£325
	bb. Red opt	17·00	19·00	†
O2	2½a. chrome-yellow (*shades*)	4·00	20·00	£325
	a. Red opt	£275	£300	†
O3	3a. chestnut	3·75	23·00	†
	a. Green opt	£200	†	†
	b. Red opt	£300	£300	†
O4	6a. cobalt	27·00	30·00	£375
	a. Red opt	£350	£375	£400
O5	1r. reddish violet	60·00	55·00	†
	a. Red opt	£425	£450	†

(b) *Inscriptions as Type B. Thin wove or pelure paper.*

O6	¼a. ultramarine (*shades*)	1·60	1·75	7·50
	a. Red opt	1·25	4·00	£225
O7	½a. black	9·50	6·00	32·00
	a. Red opt	4·50	11·00	£225
	b. Green opt	£110	†	†
O8	1a. vermilion	4·00	†	†
	a. Red opt	—	†	†
	b. Carmine	29·00	16·00	85·00
	c. Red (*shades*)	5·50	7·00	£160
O9	2a. emerald (*shades*)	35·00	45·00	†
	a. Red opt	—	£160	†
O9b	3a. chestnut (R.)	—	†	†
O10	4a. apple-green	12·00	85·00	£300
	a. Red opt	£375	†	†
O10b	4a. olive-yellow	£275	£325	†
	ba. Red opt	—	£600	†
O11	6a. pale ultramarine (*shades*)	15·00	£300	†
	a. Red opt	£450	£450	†
	b. Deep ultramarine	65·00	80·00	†
	ba. Red opt	£225	£190	†
O12	8a. orange	55·00	75·00	£450
	a. Red opt	£400	†	†
O13	10a. olive-sepia	£190	£250	£700
	a. Red opt	£800	£850	£1000
O14	12a. sage-green	£150	£475	£750
	a. Red opt	†	†	£1000
O14b	1r. lilac	£325	†	†

(c) *Inscriptions as Type C. Thin to medium wove paper.*

O15	¼a. ultramarine (*shades*)	4·50	4·75	20·00
	a. Red opt	1·00	5·50	£325
	b. Green opt	5·00	60·00	†

c. *Cobalt (medium wove paper)* 65·00 65·00 £400
ca. Red opt 40·00 18·00 £120
O16 ½a. black 10·00 3·00 12·00
a. Red opt 75 8·00 £250
b. Green opt 3·00 † †
O17 1a. orange-red 1·25 — †
a. *Carmine* 28·00 11·00 23·00
b. *Deep red (medium wove paper)* 40·00 55·00 95·00
ba. Red opt † £180 †
O18 2a. emerald 6·50 19·00 95·00
a. Red opt † £140 †
b. *Sage-green* 13·00 13·00 95·00
O19 4a. yellow-green (*shades*) 12·00 80·00 †
b. Red opt — † †
c. *Olive-yellow* £140 £130 †
ca. Red opt £450 £450 †
O20 8a. reddish orange 15·00 35·00 £300
a. Red opt £350 £475 †
O21 10a. brown-olive 65·00 95·00 £475
a. Red opt £500 £500 £600
O22 12a. sage-green 50·00 £120 £600
a. Red opt £600 † £700
O23 1r. lilac £150 † †
a. Red opt £450 † †
O24 2r. red-brown and black £400 £190 †
a. Red opt † £1200 †
b. Green opt £1200
c. *Chocolate and black (medium wove paper)* £800 £800 †
O25 3r. blue and red-brown £350 £225 †
a. Red opt £1100 † †
b. *Grey-blue & chocolate (medium wove paper)* £1200 £1200 †
ba. Red opt £1300 † †
O26 4r. emerald and scarlet £300 £300 †
O27 5r. scarlet and emerald £325 £325 †

(d) Inscriptions as Type D. Thin wove paper.
O28 2½a. buff (*shades*) 15·00 19·00 †
b. Red opt £300 — †
O29 3a. red-brown 38·00 28·00 †
a. Variety as No. 51a 60·00 50·00 †
b. Red opt † £500 †
O30 10a. bistre 50·00 95·00 £600
a. Variety as No. 52a 85·00 £160 £850
b. Red opt £475 £550 †
ba. Variety as No. 52a £650 † †
O31 12a. grey-olive 70·00 £100 £600
a. Variety as No. 53a £100 £170 £850
b. Red opt £500 £650 †
ba. Variety as No. 53a £700 † †

(e) Inscriptions as Type E.
(i) Medium wove paper.
O32 ¼a. deep slate 35·00 18·00 †
a. Red opt 27·00 42·00 †
O32*b* ¼a. indigo (*thin wove paper*) 45·00 45·00 †
ba. Red opt 45·00 45·00 †
bb. Green opt £120 £150 †
c. *Cobalt* 65·00 65·00 £425
ca. Red opt 42·00 32·00 £120
O33 ½a. black 45·00 12·00 †
a. Red opt 25·00 10·00 †
b. Green opt £300 £250 †
O34 1a. carmine-red 42·00 45·00 £400
O35 3a. chocolate (*shades*) £180 £130 £250
a. Red opt £600 £600 †
O35*b* 4a. yellow-olive † £1500 †
ba. Bright apple-green £1600 £1600 †

(ii) Very thick wove paper.
O36 ¼a. indigo 11·00 13·00 †
a. Red opt 28·00 60·00 †
b. Green opt 95·00 † †
O37 ½a. black £150 £160 †
O38 1a. bright scarlet 15·00 20·00 £350
a. *Carmine-red* £110 90·00 †

(iii) Thin horizontally laid paper.
O39 ¼a. indigo 85·00 £100 †
a. Red opt 5·00 8·50 £250
O40 1a. scarlet-vermilion 48·00 29·00 †
a. Red opt £400 £425 †

Nos. O39/40a exist in *tête-bêche* blocks of four on the same or opposite sides of the paper.

(f) Inscriptions as Type F. Medium wove paper.
O40*b* ½a. black £550 £500 †
ba. Red opt £450 £500 †
bb. Green opt £600 † †
O40*c* 4a. yellow-olive † £1700 †

(g) Inscriptions as Type G.
(i) Horizontally laid paper.
O41 ½a. black £500 £650 †
a. Red opt £140 £150 †
b. Vert laid paper £150 £160 †
ba. Red opt £250 65·00 £475
O42 4a. bright green £225 £225 †
a. Red opt £300 £400 †

(ii) Medium wove paper.
O42*b* ½a. black £325 £325 †
ba. Red opt £375 £375 †

(h) Inscriptions as Type H. Medium wove paper.
O43 ¼a. ultramarine 25·00 75·00 †
a. Red opt £200 £450 †
O44 ½a. black 75·00 £120 †
a. Red opt 60·00 † £600
O45 1a. rosine £225 £180 £550
a. *Deep red* £400 £400 †
O46 4a. emerald £180 £250 £550
a. Red opt £550 † £600

II. P 11.

(a) Inscriptions as Type H. Medium wove paper with gum.
O47 ¼a. ultramarine 45·00 60·00 £130
a. Red opt 80·00 90·00 †
b. *Greenish blue* 70·00 70·00 £180
c. Ditto. Red opt £200 † †
O48 ½a. black 48·00 65·00 £400
a. Red opt 95·00 £375 £250
O49 1a. scarlet-vermilion £225 £250 £475
a. Stamp doubly printed † † £1200
b. *Rose* £160 £140 £375
O50 2a. yellow-green £550 £275 £425

(b) Inscriptions as Type I. Medium wove paper with gum.
O51 ½a. black £160 £325 £550
a. Red opt £475 £550 —
O52 2a. bright apple-green £550 £550 £1000

Until 1941 it was the general practice to carry official mail free but some of the above undoubtedly exist postally used.

1941. *Nos. 79 to 85 optd* "SERVICE".
O53 20 3p. bright blue (R.) 6·00 16·00
O54 6p. deep blue (R.) 16·00 16·00
O55 1a. orange-red 15·00 11·00
O56 2a. brown 16·00 13·00
O57 4a. bright green 48·00 £110
O58 8a. dull green £180 £550
O59 1r. deep blue (R.) £250 £650
O53/9 *Set of 7* £475 £1200

Two different types of "R" occur in the "SERVICE" overprint. On five positions in the sheet of 12 the "R" shows a larger loop and a pointed diagonal leg.

Bundi became part of the Rajasthan Union by 15 April 1948.

BUSSAHIR (BASHAHR)

PRICES FOR STAMPS ON COVER	
Nos. 1/21	*from* × 8
Nos. 22/23	*from* × 2
Nos. 24/43	*from* × 8

Raja Shamsher Singh, 1850–1914

1

2

3

4

5

6

7

8

(9)

The initials are those of the Tika Raghunath Singh, son of the then Raja, who was the organiser and former director of the State Post Office.

(Litho at the Bussahir Press by Maulvi Karam Bakhsh, Rampur)

1895 (20 June). *Laid paper. Optd with T* **9** *in pale greenish blue (B.), rose (R.), mauve (M.) or lake (L.). With or without gum.*

(a) Imperf.
1 1 ¼a. pink (M.) (1.9.95) £2500
a. Monogram in rose £3250
2 2 ½a. grey (R.) £500 £700
a. Monogram in mauve
3 3 1a. vermilion (M.) £200
4 4 2a. orange-yellow (M.) 75·00 £200
a. Monogram in rose £140 £225
b. Monogram in lake 95·00
c. Monogram in blue £250
5 5 4a. slate-violet (M.) £130
a. Monogram in rose £170
b. Monogram in lake £180
c. Without monogram £350
d. Thick paper £200
6 6 8a. red-brown (M.) £140 £250
a. Monogram in blue £170
b. Monogram in rose £200
c. Monogram in lake
d. Without monogram £275
e. Thick paper £150
7 7 12a. green (L.) £300
a. Monogram in mauve
8 8 1r. ultramarine (R.) £130
a. Monogram in mauve £190
b. Monogram in lake £170
c. Without monogram £375 £475

(b) Perf with a sewing machine; gauge and size of holes varying between 7 and 11½.
9 1 ¼a. pink (B.) 70·00 £100
a. Monogram in mauve — £180
b. Without monogram £375 £150
10 2 ½a. grey (R.) 23·00 £140
a. Without monogram £800
11 3 1a. vermilion (M.) 24·00 95·00
a. Without monogram
12 4 2a. orange-yellow (B.) 32·00 95·00
a. Monogram in rose
b. Monogram in mauve £130
c. Without monogram — £225
13 5 4a. slate-violet (B.) 25·00 95·00
a. Monogram in rose 35·00 £130
b. Monogram in mauve 50·00
c. Without monogram 45·00
14 6 8a. red-brown (M.) 24·00 £110
a. Monogram in blue 70·00 £180
b. Monogram in rose £100
c. Without monogram £130 £350
15 7 12a. green (R.) 80·00 £130
a. Monogram in mauve £140
b. Monogram in lake £130
c. Without monogram £225
16 8 1r. ultramarine (R.) 45·00 £120
a. Monogram in mauve £130
b. Without monogram £325 £425
9/16 *Set of 8* £300 £800

1899. *As 1895, but pin-perf or rouletted.*
17 3 1a. vermilion (M.) £180 £200
18 4 2a. orange-yellow (M.) 65·00 £160
a. Monogram in lake 70·00
b. Monogram in rose £110
c. Monogram in blue £180
d. Without monogram £400
19 5 4a. slate-violet (L.) £300
a. Monogram in blue
b. Monogram in rose £400
c. Monogram in mauve £375
20 7 12a. green (R.) £450 £550
21 8 1r. ultramarine (R.) £475

Nos. 1 to 21 were in sheets of 24. They seem to have been overprinted and perforated as required. Those first issued for use were perforated, but they were subsequently supplied imperf, both to collectors and for use. Nos. 17 to 21 were some of the last supplies. No rule seems to have been observed as to the colour of the overprinted monogram; pale blue, rose and mauve were used from the first. The pale blue varies to greenish blue or blue-green, and appears quite green on the yellow stamps. The lake is possibly a mixture of the mauve and the rose—it is a quite distinct colour and apparently later than the others. Specimens without overprint are either remainders left in the Treasury or copies that have escaped accidentally; they have been found sticking to the backs of others that bore the overprint.

Varieties may also be found doubly overprinted, in two different colours.

10

11

12

T **11**. Lines of shading above and at bottom left and right of shield.

T **12**. White dots above shield and ornaments in bottom corners.

13

14

15

16

(Printed at the Bussahir Press by Maulvi Karam Bakhsh)

1896–97. *Wove paper. Optd with monogram "R.S.", T* **9**, *in rose. Recess singly from line-engraved dies. With or without gum. Various perfs.*
22 10 ¼a. deep violet (1897) — £1000
23 11 ½a. grey-blue £800 £300
23*a* ½a. deep blue (1897) — £425

No. 23 exists sewing-machine perf about 10 and also perf 14½–16. Nos. 22 and 23*a* are pin-perf.

1896–1900. *As Nos. 22/3, but lithographed in sheets of various sizes. No gum.*

(a) Imperf.
24 10 ¼a. slate-violet (R.) 8·50
a. Monogram in mauve 10·00
b. Monogram in blue 14·00
c. Monogram in lake 21·00
25 11 ½a. blue (*shades*) (R.) 10·00 19·00
a. Monogram in mauve 10·00 19·00
b. Monogram in lake 11·00
c. Without monogram
d. Laid paper (B.) £170
da. Monogram in lake
26 13 1a. olive (*shades*) (R.) 18·00 42·00
a. Monogram in mauve 45·00
b. Monogram in lake 45·00

(b) Pin-perf or rouletted.
27 10 ¼a. slate-violet (R.) 21·00 19·00
a. Monogram in lake 25·00 22·00
b. Monogram in mauve — 32·00

28	11	½a. blue (*shades*) (R.)	14·00	32·00
		a. Monogram in mauve	18·00	35·00
		b. Monogram in lake	38·00	48·00
		c. Monogram in blue	£150	
		d. Laid paper (M.)		
29	13	1a. olive (*shades*) (R.)	26·00	
		a. Monogram in mauve	60·00	60·00
		b. Monogram in lake	55·00	55·00
30	14	2a. orange-yellow (B.)	£850	£900

Originally printings of the ¼a. and ½a. were in sheets of 8 (stone I), but this was subsequently increased to 24 (4×6). The 1a. and 2a. were always in sheets of 4.

Nos. 25d/da were printed from stone I and care is needed to distinguish this laid paper printing from some of the reprints on similar paper. Stamps from stone I are without marginal lines and are very clear impressions; reprints from stone IV have thick marginal lines and, in those shades similar to No. 25, show indistinct impressions.

1900–01. *¼a., 1a, colours changed; ½a. redrawn type; 2a. with dash before "STATE" and characters in lower left label; 4a. new value. No gum.*

(*a*) Imperf.

31	10	¼a. vermilion (M.)	5·00	11·00
		a. Monogram in blue	5·50	11·00
		b. Without monogram		
31*c*	12	½a. blue (M.)	10·00	26·00
		ca. Monogram in rose	35·00	
		cb. Without monogram	60·00	
32	13	1a. vermilion (M.)	4·75	16·00
		a. Monogram in blue	8·00	11·00
		b. Monogram in lake		
		c. Without monogram	55·00	
33	15	2a. ochre (M.) (9.00)	48·00	95·00
34		2a. yellow (M.) (11.00)	50·00	
		a. Monogram in blue	50·00	£100
		b. Without monogram	80·00	
35		2a. orange (B.) (1.01)	60·00	95·00
		a. Monogram in mauve	60·00	90·00
		b. Without monogram	65·00	
36	16	4a. claret (R.)	55·00	£120
		a. Monogram in mauve	75·00	£140
		b. Monogram in blue	95·00	£160
		c. Without monogram	35·00	

(*b*) *Pin-perf or rouletted.*

37	10	¼a. vermilion (M.)	4·25	11·00
		a. Monogram in blue	5·50	
		b. Without monogram		
37*c*	12	½a. blue (M.)	60·00	90·00
38	13	1a. vermilion (M.)	7·00	15·00
		a. Monogram in blue	10·00	12·00
39		1a. brown-red (M.) (3.01)	–	£200
40	15	2a. ochre (M.) (9.00)	65·00	
		a. Monogram in blue		
41		2a. yellow (M.) (11.00)	50·00	80·00
		a. Monogram in rose	65·00	£100
		b. Monogram in blue	85·00	£120
42		2a. orange (M.) (1.01)	65·00	75·00
		a. Monogram in blue	90·00	90·00
		b. Without monogram	–	£275
43	16	4a. claret (R.)	80·00	
		a. Monogram in blue	80·00	£170
		b. Monogram in mauve	£100	

The ¼a., ½a. and 1a. are in sheets of 24; the 2a. in sheets of 50 differing throughout in the dash and the characters added at lower left; the 4a. in sheets of 28.

(17)

The stamps formerly catalogued with large overprint "R.N.S." (T **17**) are now believed never to have been issued for use.

Remainders are also found with overprint "P.S.", the initials of Padam Singh who succeeded Raghunath Singh in the direction of the Post Office, and with the original monogram "R.S." in a damaged state, giving it the appearance of a double-lined "R."

The stamps of Bussahir have been obsolete since 1 April 1901. Numerous remainders were sold after this date, and all values were later reprinted in the colours of the originals, or in fancy colours, from the original stones, or from new ones. Printings were also made from new types, similar to those of the second issue of the 8a., 12a. and 1r. values, in sheets of 8.

Reprints are frequently found on laid paper.

Collectors are warned against obliterated copies bearing the Rampur postmark with date "19 MA 1900." Many thousand remainders and reprints were thus obliterated for export after the closing of the State Post Office.

CHARKHARI

PRICES FOR STAMPS ON COVER

Nos. 1/4	*from* × 2
Nos. 5/26	*from* × 20
Nos. 27/44	*from* × 3
Nos. 45/53	*from* × 100
Nos. 54/5	*from* × 5
No. 56	*from* × 2

Maharaja Malkhan Singh, 1880–1908

1

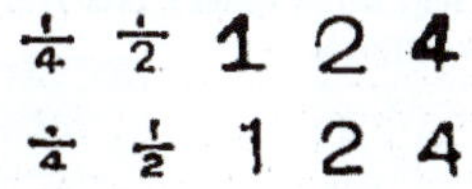

The top row shows the figures of value used in the stamps of 1894–97, and the bottom row those for the 1904 issue. In the 4a. the figure slopes slightly to the right in the first issue, and to the left in the second.

1894. *Typo from a single die. No gum.* Imperf.

1	1	¼ anna, rose	£1200	£700
2		1 annas, dull green	£1800	£2500
3		2 annas, dull green	£2250	
4		4 annas, dull green	£1400	

Nos. 1/2 are known pin-perforated.

1897. *Inscr* "ANNA". *No gum.* Imperf.

5	1	¼a. magenta	65·00	80·00
		a. Purple	4·25	4·25
		b. Violet	3·75	3·75
6		½a. purple	3·75	4·75
		a. Violet	2·50	3·00
7		1a. blue-green	6·00	9·50
		a. Turquoise-blue	4·50	6·50
		b. Indigo	15·00	23·00
		c. Figure of value inverted	£1500	
8		2a. blue-green	9·50	16·00
		a. Turquoise-blue	7·00	8·50
		b. Indigo	19·00	27·00
9		4a. blue-green	12·00	19·00
		a. Turquoise-blue	7·50	14·00
		b. Indigo	30·00	48·00
		ba. Figure of value sideways	£1500	
5/9 *Set of* 5			23·00	32·00

Minor varieties may be found with the first "A" in "ANNA" not printed.

All values are known on various coloured papers, but these are proofs or trial impressions.

1902–04. *Numerals changed as illustrated above. No gum.*

10	1	¼a. violet	1·75	2·50
11		½a. violet	4·50	3·50
12		1a. green	5·00	17·00
13		2a. green	35·00	35·00
14		4a. green	21·00	35·00
10/14 *Set of* 5			60·00	85·00

Stamps of this issue can be found showing part of the papermaker's watermark. "Mercantile Script Extra Strong John Haddon & Co."

Maharaja Jujhar Singh, 1908–1914

2 (Right-hand sword over left)

Type I

Type II

Type I. "P" of "POSTAGE" in same size as other letters. "E" small with long upper and lower arms. White dot often appears on one or both of the sword hilts.

Type II. "P" larger than the other letters. "E" large with short upper and lower arms. No dots occur on the hilts.

1909–19. *Litho in Calcutta. Wove paper.* P 11.

(*a*) *Type I.*

15	2	1p. chestnut	48·00	50·00
		a. Pale chestnut	4·75	38·00
		b. Orange-brown	4·75	38·00
		c. "CHARKHAPI"	38·00	
16		1p. turquoise-blue	60	45
		a. Imperf between (horiz pair)	£160	
		b. Greenish blue (1911)	1·00	1·00
		c. Pale turquoise-green	1·50	70
17		½a. vermilion	2·25	1·00
		a. Imperf (pair)	£950	
		b. Deep rose-red	1·00	1·25
18		1a. sage-green	3·50	2·25
		a. Yellow-olive	2·50	1·60
19		2a. grey-blue	3·25	3·25
		a. Dull violet-blue	3·00	3·50
20		4a. deep green	4·25	5·50
21		8a. brown-red	7·50	20·00
22		1r. pale chestnut	13·00	42·00
15*a*/22 *Set of* 8			32·00	£100

(*b*) *Type II.*

24	2	1p. turquoise-blue	4·75	4·50
25		½a. vermilion	2·25	1·60
		b. Deep rose-red	6·50	6·50
26		1a. yellow-olive (1919)	3·50	3·00
		a. Sage-green	2·75	1·60
24/6 *Set of* 3			9·00	7·00

No. 15, from the original printing, shows an upstroke to the "1", not present on other brown printings of this value.

See also Nos. 31/44.

3 "J" below Swords. Right sword overlaps left. Double framelines.

4 "JI" below Swords. Left sword overlaps right. Single frameline.

1912–17. *Handstamped. Wove paper. No gum.* Imperf.

27	3	1p. violet	£700	85·00
		a. Dull purple	–	95·00
28	4	1p. violet (1917)	7·00	5·00
		a. Dull purple	17·00	5·50
		b. *Tête-bêche* (pair)	75·00	75·00
		c. Laid paper	–	£600
		d. Pair, one stamp sideways	–	£130

Maharaja Ganga Singh, 1914–1920

Maharaja Arimardan Singh, 1920–1942

5 (actual size 63×25 mm)

6 (Left-hand sword over right)

1921. *Handstamped. No gum.*

(*a*) *Wove paper.* Imperf.

29	5	1a. violet	80·00	85·00
		a. Dull purple	90·00	£100

(*b*) *Laid paper.* P 11.

30	5	1a. violet	75·00	£140
		a. Imperf	£180	£190

(Typo State Ptg Press, Charkhari)

1930–45. *Wove paper. No gum.* Imperf.

31	6	1p. deep blue	60	14·00
		a. Vert pair, top ptd inverted on back, bottom normal upright	13·00	
		b. *Tête-bêche* (vert pair)	£400	
		c. Perf 11×imperf (horiz pair) (1939)	75·00	75·00
		d. Bluish slate	22·00	
		e. Laid paper (1944)	–	£400
32		1p. dull *to* light green (*pelure*) (1943)	60·00	£225
33		1p. violet (1943)	21·00	£160
		a. *Tête-bêche* (vert pair)	55·00	
34		½a. deep olive	2·50	14·00
35		½a. red-brown (1940)	6·00	25·00
		a. *Tête-bêche* (vert pair)	£500	
36		½a. black (*pelure*) (1943)	60·00	£190
37		½a. red (*shades*) (1943)	20·00	42·00
		a. *Tête-bêche* (vert pair)	42·00	
		b. Laid paper (1944)	–	£350
38		½a. grey-brown	70·00	85·00
39		1a. green	2·50	16·00
		a. Emerald (1938)	50·00	80·00
40		1a. chocolate (1940)	13·00	26·00
		a. *Tête-bêche* (vert pair)	80·00	
		b. Lake-brown	–	65·00
41		1a. red (1940)	£130	70·00
		a. Carmine	–	70·00
		b. Laid paper (1944)	–	£375
42		2a. light blue	1·25	17·00
		a. *Tête-bêche* (vert pair)	9·50	
43		2a. greenish grey (1941?)	60·00	80·00
		a. *Tête-bêche* (vert pair)	£120	
		b. Laid paper (1944)	–	£400
		c. Greyish green	90·00	£190
43*d*		2a. yellow-green (1945)	–	£950
44		4a. carmine	3·00	20·00
		a. *Tête-bêche* (vert pair)	14·00	

There are two different versions of No. 37a, one with the stamps *tête-bêche* base to base and the other showing them top to top.

7 The Lake

8 Imlia Palace

9 Industrial School

10 Bird's-eye view of City

11 The Fort

12 Guest House

13 Palace Gate

14 Temples at Rainpur

15 Goverdhan Temple

½ As.
(16)

(Typo Batliboi Litho Works, Bombay)

1931 (25 June). *T7/ 15*. P 11, 11½, 12 or compound.

45	**7**	½a. blue-green	2·25	10
		a. Imperf between (horiz pair)	38·00	12·00
		b. Imperf between (vert pair)	38·00	35·00
		c. Imperf horiz (vert pair)	38·00	
46	**8**	1a. blackish brown	1·60	10
		a. Imperf between (horiz pair)	11·00	8·50
		b. Imperf between (vert pair)	13·00	8·50
		c. Imperf horiz (vert pair)	13·00	
47	**9**	2a. violet	1·75	10
		a. Imperf between (horiz pair)	30·00	25·00
		b. Imperf between (vert pair)	30·00	25·00
		c. Imperf horiz (vert pair)	22·00	
		d. Doubly printed	10·00	
48	**10**	4a. olive-green	1·50	15
		a. Imperf between (vert pair)	65·00	65·00
49	**11**	8a. magenta	2·00	10
		a. Imperf between (horiz pair)	42·00	26·00
		b. Imperf between (vert pair)	42·00	42·00
		c. Imperf horiz (vert pair)	42·00	14·00
50	**12**	1r. green and rose	2·75	20
		a. Imperf between (vert pair)	£100	£100
		b. Green (centre) omitted	—	£170
		c. Imperf horiz (vert pair)	£120	
51	**13**	2r. red and brown	4·00	25
		a. Imperf horiz (vert pair)	£120	16·00
52	**14**	3r. chocolate and blue-green	15·00	40
		a. Imperf between (horiz pair)	—	£190
		b. *Tête-bêche* (pair)	£275	20·00
		c. Chocolate (centre) omitted	21·00	
53	**15**	5r. turquoise and purple	9·50	50
		a. Imperf between (horiz pair)	£190	
		b. Centre inverted	80·00	32·00
		c. Centre doubly printed	—	£110
45/53 *Set of* 9			35·00	1·60

Designs:—½a. The Lake; 1a. Imlia Palace, 2a. Industrial School; 4a. Bird's-eye view of City; 8a. The Fort; 1r. Guest House. 2r. Palace Gate; 3r. Temples at Rainpur.

This issue was the subject of speculative manipulation, large stocks being thrown on the market cancelled-to-order at very low prices and unused at less than face value. The issue was an authorized one but was eventually withdrawn by the State authorities.

1939 (1 Dec)–**40**. *Nos. 21/2 surch as T* **16**.

54	**2**	½a. on 8a. brown-red (1940)	35·00	£130
		a. No space between "½" and "As"	35·00	£130
		b. Surch inverted	£300	£400
		c. "1" of "½" inverted	£275	
55		1a. on 1r. chestnut (1940)	£120	£425
		a. Surch inverted	£325	
56		"1 ANNA" on 1r. chestnut	£1100	£1000

Maharaja Jaiendra Singh, 1942–1971

Charkhari became part of Vindhya Pradesh by 1 May 1948.

COCHIN

(6 puttans = 5 annas. 12 pies = 1 anna; 16 annas = 1 rupee)

Stamps of Cochin were also valid on mail posted to Travancore.

PRICES FOR STAMPS ON COVER

Nos. 1/3	*from* × 30
Nos. 4/5	*from* × 10
Nos. 6/6b	*from* × 3
Nos. 7/9	*from* × 20
Nos. 11/22	*from* × 15
Nos. 26/128	*from* × 8
Nos. O1/105	*from* × 15

HAVE YOU READ THE NOTES AT THE BEGINNING OF THIS CATALOGUE?
These often provide answers to the enquiries we receive.

Raja Kerala Varma I, 1888–1895

1

2

(Dies eng P. Orr & Sons, Madras; typo Cochin Govt, Ernakulam)

1892 (13 Apr). *No wmk, or wmk large Umbrella in the sheet.* P 12.

1	**1**	½ put. buff	2·50	3·00
		a. Orange-buff	2·75	2·75
		b. Yellow	3·25	3·50
		c. Imperf (pair)		
2		1 put. purple	3·00	2·75
		a. Imperf between (vert pair)	†	£2750
3	**2**	2 put. deep violet	2·00	2·25
1/3 *Set of* 3			6·75	7·00

1893. *Laid paper.* P 12.

4	**1**	½ put. orange-buff	£475	£130
		a. Orange	—	£130
		b. Yellow	—	£130

WATERMARKS. Prior to the 1911–23 issue, printed by Perkins, Bacon & Co, little attention was paid to the position of the watermark. Inverted and sideways watermarks are frequently found in the 1898 and 1902–03 issues.

1894. *Wmk small Umbrella on each stamp.* P 12.

5	**1**	½ put. buff	6·00	4·00
		a. Orange	2·50	1·50
		ab. Imperf (pair)		
		b. Yellow	4·25	1·00
6		1 put. purple	7·00	7·00
7	**2**	2 put. deep violet	4·25	4·50
		a. Imperf (pair)		
		b. Doubly printed	†	£1500
		c. Printed both sides	£1800	
		d. *Tête-bêche* (pair)	£4000	
5/7 *Set of* 3			12·50	11·50

The paper watermarked with a small umbrella is more transparent than that of the previous issue. The wmk is not easy to distinguish.

The 1 put. in deep violet was a special printing for fiscal use only.

Raja Rama Varma I, 1895–1914

1896 (End). *Similar to T* **1**, *but 28×33 mm.* P 12.

(a) Wmk Arms and inscription in sheet.

8	1 put. violet	95·00	95·00

(b) Wmk Conch Shell to each stamp.

9	1 put. deep violet	19·00	32·00

Nos. 8/9 were intended for fiscal use, but are also known used for postal purposes.

3

4

5

6

1898. *Thin yellowish paper. Wmk small Umbrella on each stamp. With or without gum.* P 12.

11	**3**	3 pies, blue	1·40	1·10
		a. Imperf between (horiz pair)	£500	
		b. Imperf between (vert pair)	£600	
		c. Doubly printed	£650	
12	**4**	½ put. green	1·75	1·50
		a. Imperf between (horiz pair)	£1100	£1100
		b. Stamp sideways (in pair)	†	£2500
13	**5**	1 put. pink	3·75	1·75
		a. *Tête-bêche* (pair)	£3500	£2250
		b. Laid paper (1905)	†	£1600
		ba. Laid paper. *Tête-bêche* (pair)	†	£8000
		c. Red	3·75	1·75
		d. Carmine-red	4·00	2·25
14	**6**	2 put. deep violet	3·25	2·25
		a. Imperf between (vert pair)	£550	
		b. Imperf between (vert strip of 3)	£700	
11/14 *Set of* 4			9·00	5·50

1902–03. *Thick white paper. Wmk small Umbrella on each stamp. With or without gum.* P 12.

16	**3**	3 pies, blue	1·50	10
		a. Doubly printed	—	£300
		b. Imperf between (horiz pair)	†	£800
17	**4**	½ put. green	1·25	40
		a. Stamp sideways (in pair)	£850	£850
		b. Doubly printed	—	£300
		c. Imperf between (horiz pair)	†	£1100
18	**5**	1 put. pink (1903)	1·75	10
		a. *Tête-bêche* (pair)	†	£3500
19	**6**	2 put. deep violet	2·50	50
		a. Doubly printed	£850	£300
16/19 *Set of* 4			6·00	1·00

2 (7) 2 (7a) 2 (7b)

1909. *T* **3** *(Paper and perf of 1903), surch with T* **7**. *Wmk is always sideways. No gum.*

22	**3**	2 on 3 pies, rosy mauve	15	50
		a. Surch Type **7** inverted	£100	£100
		b. Surch Type **7a**	£800	£400
		c. Surch Type **7b**	£150	
		d. Stamps *tête-bêche*	£170	£190
		e. Stamps and surchs *tête-bêche*.	£200	£250

Varieties a, d and e were caused by the inversion of one stamp (No. 7) in the plate and the consequent inversion of the corresponding surcharge to correct the error.

Types **7a** and **7b** were applied by handstamp to correct the omission of the surcharge on R. 3/2 in different settings. Other sheets show a handstamped version of Type **7**.

8 Raja Rama Varma I

8a

(Recess Perkins, Bacon & Co)

1911–13. *Currency in pies and annas.* W **8a**. P 14.

26	**8**	2p. brown	30	10
		a. Imperf (pair)		
27		3p. blue	1·50	10
		a. Perf 14×12½	27·00	2·00
		w. Wmk inverted	—	85·00
28		4p. green	1·75	10
		aw. Wmk inverted	—	£150
28*b*		4p. apple-green	2·50	40
		bw. Wmk inverted		
29		9p. carmine	1·40	10
		a. Wmk sideways		
30		1a. brown-orange	3·00	10
31		1½a. purple	7·50	45
32		2a. grey (1913)	7·50	40
33		3a. vermilion (1913)	38·00	38·00
26/33 *Set of* 8			55·00	38·00

No. 27a is line perforated. Nos. 27 and 33 exist perforated 14 either from comb or line machines. The other values only come from the comb machine.

Raja (Maharaja from 1921) Rama Varma II, 1914–1932

9 Raja Rama Varma II

10 Raja Rama Varma II

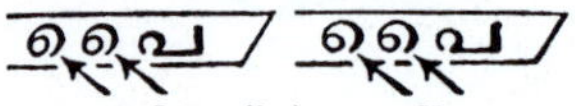
I (2p.) II

I (1a.) II

(Recess Perkins, Bacon & Co)

1916–30. W **8a**. P 13½ to 14.

35	**10**	2p. brown (Die I) *(a) (b) (c)*	8·00	10
		a. Imperf (pair)	£550	
		b. Die II *(b) (c)* (1930)	1·60	10
36		4p. green *(a) (b)*	1·00	10
37		6p. red-brown *(a) (b) (c)* (1922)	2·50	10
		w. Wmk inverted	—	£120
38		8p. sepia *(b)* (1923)	1·75	10
39		9p. carmine *(a)*	20·00	35
40		10p. blue *(b)* (1923)	6·00	10
41	**9**	1a. orange (Die I) *(a)*	18·00	3·00
		a. Die II *(a) (b)* (1922)	11·00	35
42	**10**	1½a. purple *(b)* (1923)	3·75	20
43		2a. grey *(a) (b) (d)*	4·25	10
44		2¼a. yellow-green *(a) (d)* (1922)	7·00	3·25
45		3a. vermilion *(a) (b)*	12·00	35
35/45 *Set of* 11			65·00	4·50

Four different perforating heads were used for this issue: *(a)* comb 13.9; *(b)* comb 13.6; *(c)* line 13.8; *(d)* line 14.2. Values on which each perforation occur are shown above. Stamps with perforation *(a)* are on hand-made paper, while the other perforations are on softer machine-made paper with a horizontal mesh.

2 2 2

Two pies (11) Two pies (12) Two pies (13)

2   2

Two Pies (14)   Two Pies (15)

1922–29. *T* 8 (P 14), *surch with T* **11/15**.

46	**11**	2p. on 3p. blue	40	30
		a. Surch double	£325	£325
47	**12**	2p. on 3p. blue	3·25	1·00
		a. Surch double	£750	
		b. "Pies" for "pies" (R. 4/8)	50·00	22·00
		ba. Surch double		
		c. Perf 12½ at foot		
48	**13**	2p. on 3p. blue (6.24)	7·00	35
		a. "Pies" for "pies" (R. 4/8)	65·00	16·00
		b. Perf 14×12½	14·00	18·00
		ba. Ditto. "Pies" for "pies" (R. 4/8)	£275	£325
49	**14**	2p. on 3p. blue (1929)	11·00	11·00
		a. Surch double	£375	
		b. Surch with Type **15**	75·00	£130
		ba. Ditto. Surch double	£2000	

There are four settings of these overprints. The first (July 1922) consisted of 39 stamps with Type **11**, and 9 with Type **12**, and in Type **11** the centre of the "2" is above the "o" of "Two". In the second setting (May 1924) there were 36 of Type **11** and 12 of Type **12**, and the centre of the figure is above the space between "Two" and "Pies". The third setting (June 1924) consists of stamps with Type **13** only.

The fourth setting (1929) was also in sheets of 48. No. 49b being the first stamp in the fourth row.

No. 47c is from the bottom row of a sheet and was re-perforated 12½ line at foot as the bottom line of 14 perforations were too far from the design.

ONE ANNA
ഒരു അണ

Three Pies
൩   3

ANCHAL & REVENUE (16)   മൂന്നു പൈ (17)

1928. *Surch with T* **16**.

50	**10**	1a. on 2¼a. yellow-green (*a*)	6·00	12·00
		a. "REVENUF" for "REVENUE"	55·00	85·00
		b. Surch double		

1932–33. *Surch as T* **17**. W **8a**. P 13½.

51	**10**	3p. on 4p. green (*b*)	1·25	1·40
		a. "r" in "Three" inverted	†	£375
52		3p. on 8p. sepia (*b*)	2·25	2·75
53		9p. on 10p. blue (*b*)	1·50	3·25
51/3 *Set of* 3			4·50	6·50

Maharaja Rama Varma III, 1932–1941

18 Maharaja Rama Varma III

18a

(Recess Perkins, Bacon & Co)

1933–38. *T* **18** (*but frame and inscription of* 1a. *as T* **9**). W **8a**. P 13×13½.

54	**18**	2p. brown (1936)	85	50
55		4p. green	60	10
56		6p. red-brown	70	10
57	**18a**	1a. brown-orange	85	20
58	**18**	1a.8p. carmine	3·00	6·50
59		2a. grey (1938)	6·00	1·60
60		2¼a. yellow-green	1·75	30
61		3a. vermilion (1938)	5·50	1·60
62		3a.4p. violet	1·75	1·40
63		6a.8p. sepia	1·75	15·00
64		10a. blue	3·00	17·00
54/64 *Set of* 11			23·00	40·00

For stamps in this design, but lithographed, see Nos. 67/71.

1934. *Surcharged as T* **14**. W **8a**. P 13½.

65	**10**	6p. on 8p. sepia (R.) (*b*)	75	60
66		6p. on 10p. blue (R.) (*b*)	1·75	2·00

"DOUBLE PRINTS". The errors previously listed under this description are now identified as blanket offsets, a type of variety outside the scope of this catalogue. Examples occur on issues from 1938 onwards.

SPACING OF OVERPRINTS AND SURCHARGES. The typeset overprints and surcharges issued from 1939 onwards show considerable differences in spacing. Except for specialists, however, these differences have little significance as they occur within the same settings and do not represent separate printings.

(Litho The Associated Printers, Madras)

1938. W **8a**. P 11.

67	**18**	2p. brown	1·00	40
		aw. Wmk inverted	£160	80·00
		b. Perf 13×13½	6·50	70
68		4p. green	1·00	35
		aw. Wmk inverted		
		b. Perf 13×13½	8·50	18·00
69		6p. red-brown	2·25	10
		aw. Wmk inverted	†	—
		b. Perf 13×13½	†	£3250
70	**18a**	1a. brown-orange	75·00	95·00
		aw. Wmk inverted		
		b. Perf 13×13½	£100	£140
71	**18**	2¼a. sage-green	6·00	25
		a. Perf 13×13½	17·00	7·00
67/71 *Set of* 5			80·00	95·00

Most examples of Nos. 70/b were used fiscally. Collectors are warned against examples which have been cleaned and regummed or provided with forged postmarks.

ANCHAL (19)   ANCHAL (19a)   THREE PIES ANCHAL (20)

SURCHARGED

ONE ANNA THREE PIES (21) ANCHAL   NINE PIES (22) ANCHAL

NINE PIES (23)   SURCHARGED NINE PIES (24)

1939 (Jan). *Nos. 57 and 70 optd with T* **19a**.

72	**18a**	1a. brown-orange (*recess*) (T **19**)	5·00	1·75
		w. Wmk inverted	†	£150
73		1a. brown-orange (*litho*) (T **19**)	£350	1·75
		aw. Wmk inverted	†	—
		b. Perf 13×13½	—	£350
74		1a. brown-orange (*litho*) (T **19a**)	75	1·60
		a. Perf 13×13½	13·00	60

In 1939 it was decided that there would be separate 1a. stamps for revenue and postal purposes. The "ANCHAL" overprints were applied to stamps intended for postal purposes.

1942–44. *T* **18a** *variously optd or surch.*

I. Recess-printed stamp. No. 58.

75	3p. on 1a.8p. carmine (T **20**)	£250	£100
76	3p. on 1a.8p. carmine (T **21**)	6·00	10·00
77	6p. on 1a.8p. carmine (T **20**)	3·50	21·00
78	1a.3p. on 1a.8p. carmine (T **21**)	1·00	50

II. Lithographed stamps. Nos. 68, 70 and 70b.

79	3p. on 4p. (T **21**)	7·00	4·00
	a. Perf 13×13½	15·00	4·00
80	6p. on 1a. (T **22**)	£475	£275
	a. "SIX PIES" double	†	£1200
81	6p. on 1a. (T **23**)	£250	£190
	a. Perf 13×13½	£160	70·00
82	9p. on 1a. (T **22**)	£140	£130
83	9p. on 1a. (T **23**) (P 13×13½)	£375	40·00
84	9p. on 1a. (T **24**) (P 13×13½)	25·00	8·00

Maharaja Kerala Varma II, 1941–1943

26 Maharaja Kerala Varma II

27 (The actual measurement of this wmk is 6¼ × 3⅝in.)

(Litho The Associated Printers, Madras)

1943. *Frame of* 1a. *inscr* "ANCHAL & REVENUE". P 13×13½.

(a) W **8a**.

85	**26**	2p. grey-brown	3·50	4·50
		a. Perf 11	†	£2000
85*b*		4p. green	£900	£375
85*c*		1a. brown-orange	95·00	£120
85/c *Set of* 3			£950	£450

(b) W **27**.

86	**26**	2p. grey-brown	30·00	3·75
		a. Perf 11	†	£3000
87		4p. green	7·00	22·00
		a. Perf 11	3·75	5·50
88		6p. red-brown	3·75	10
		a. Perf 11	8·00	1·60
89		9p. ultramarine (P 11)	45·00	1·25
		a. Imperf between (horiz pair)	£2000	
90		1a. brown-orange	£200	£200
		a. Perf 11	23·00	55·00
91		2¼a. yellow-green	27·00	2·50
		a. Perf 11	28·00	9·00

Part of W **27** appears on many stamps in each sheet, while others are entirely without wmk.

Although inscribed "ANCHAL (= Postage) & REVENUE" most examples of Nos. 85*c* and 90/a were used fiscally. Collectors are warned against examples which have been cleaned and regummed or provided with forged postmarks.

Maharaja Ravi Varma, 1943–1946

1943. *T* **26** *variously optd or surch.* P 13×13½.

(a) W **8a**.

92	3p. on 4p. (T **21**)	90·00	23·00
92*a*	9p. on 1a. (T **23**)	6·50	3·75
92*b*	9p. on 1a. (T **24**)	7·50	3·00
92*c*	1a.3p. on 1a. (T **21**)	†	£3750

(b) W **27**.

93	2p. on 6p. (T **20**)	75	4·00
	a. Perf 11	85	2·75
94	3p. on 4p. (T **20**) (P 11)	7·00	10
95	3p. on 4p. (T **21**)	5·50	10
96	3p. on 6p. (T **20**)	1·00	20
	a. Perf 11	85	85
97	4p. on 6p. (T **20**)	5·00	12·00

No. 92*c* is believed to be an error; a sheet of No. 85*b*, having been included in a stock of No. O52 intended to become No. O66.

28 Maharaja Ravi Varma

29 Maharaja Ravi Varma

I

II

(Litho The Associated Printers, Madras)

1944–48. W **27** *No gum*.

(a) Type I. P 11.

98	**28**	9p. ultramarine (1944)	16·00	4·00

(b) Type II. P 13.

98*a*	**28**	9p. ultramarine (1946)	16·00	18·00
		ab. Perf 13×13½	48·00	3·75
99		1a.3p. magenta (1948)	8·00	8·50
		a. Perf 13×13½	£300	60·00
100		1a.9p. ultramarine (*shades*) (1948)	9·50	16·00
98*a*/100 *Set of* 3			30·00	26·00

Nos. 98*a*/100 are line-perforated, Nos. 98ab and 99a comb-perforated.

Maharaja Kerala Varma III, 1946–48

(Litho The Associated Printers, Madras)

1946–48. *Frame of* 1a. *inscr* "ANCHAL & REVENUE". W **27**. *No gum* (*except for stamps perf 11*). P 13.

101	**29**	2p. chocolate	2·75	20
		a. Imperf horiz (vert pair)	£2500	£2500
		c. Perf 11	8·00	60
		d. Perf 11×13	£375	£140
102		3p. carmine	50	30
103		4p. grey-green	£2500	80·00
104		6p. red-brown (1947)	24·00	6·50
		a. Perf 11	£170	5·50
105		9p. ultramarine	1·50	10
		a. Imperf between (horiz pair)	†	£2250
106		1a. orange (1948)	9·00	32·00
		a. Perf 11	£500	
107		2a. black	£120	8·50
		a. Perf 11	£150	7·00
108		3a. vermilion	85·00	1·50
101/8 *Set of* 8			£2500	£120

Although inscribed "ANCHAL (=Postage) & REVENUE" most examples of No. 106 were used fiscally.

The 1a.3p. magenta, 1a.9p. ultramarine and 2¼a. yellow-green in Type **29** subsequently appeared surcharged or overprinted for official use. Examples of the 1a.3p. magenta exist without overprint, but may have not been issued in this state (*Price* £275 *unused*).

30 Maharaja Kerala Varma III

Die I

Die II

Two dies of 2p.:

Die I. Back of headdress almost touches value tablet. Narrow strip of tunic visible below collar.

Die II. Back of headdress further away from tablet. Wider strip of tunic visible below collar.

Die I

Die II

Two dies of 3a.4p.

Die I. Frame around head broken by value tablets. Two white lines below value inscription.

Die II. Continuous frame around head. Single white line below value inscription. (R. 6/1-2 on sheet 8×6).

Tail to turban flaw (R. 1/7)

(Litho The Associated Printers, Madras)

1948–50. W **27** (upright or inverted). P 11.

109	**30**	2p. grey-brown (I)	1·75	15
		a. Imperf vert (horiz pair)	†	£2250
		b. Die II	£150	2·25
110		3p. carmine	1·50	15
		a. Imperf between (vert pair)	—	£1700
111		4p. green	17·00	3·50
		a. Imperf vert (horiz pair)	£275	£325
112		6p. chestnut	18·00	25
		a. Imperf vert (horiz pair)	£800	
113		9p. ultramarine	2·50	50
114		2a. black	65·00	2·50
115		3a. orange-red	70·00	1·00
		a. Imperf vert (horiz pair)	£2500	
116		3a.4p. violet (1950)	70·00	£350
		a. Tail to turban flaw	£250	£700
		b. Die II	£200	
109/16 *Set of* 8			£225	£350

Maharaja Rama Varma IV, 1948–1964

31 Chinese Nets

32 Dutch Palace

(Litho The Associated Printers, Madras)

1949. W **27**. P 11.

117	**31**	2a. black	5·00	8·50
		a. Imperf vert (horiz pair)	£475	
118	**32**	2¼a. green	2·75	9·50
		a. Imperf vert (horiz pair)	£475	

A used example of a 2¼a. value in a slightly different design exists showing a larger portrait of the ruler, the conch shell at upper right pointing to the right and with shading below "DUTCH PALACE". This may have come from a proof sheet subsequently used for postal purposes.

SIX PIES

ആറു പൈ

(33)

പൈ

Normal

പൈ

Error

Due to similarities between two Malayalam characters some values of the 1948 provisional issue exist with an error in the second word of the Malayalam surcharge. On Nos. 119, 122 and O103 this occurs twice in the setting of 48. No. 125 shows four examples and No. O104b one. Most instances are as illustrated above, but in two instances on the setting for No. 125 the error occurs on the second character.

1949. *Surch as T* **33**.

		(i) On 1944–48 issue. P 13.		
119	**28**	6p. on 1a.3p. magenta	5·50	4·50
		a. Incorrect character	40·00	32·00
120		1a. on 1a.9p. ultramarine (R.)	2·25	1·40
		(ii) On 1946–48 issue.		
121	**29**	3p. on 9p. ultramarine	12·00	23·00
122		6p. on 1a.3p. magenta	16·00	15·00
		a. Surch double	†	£600
		b. Incorrect character	£100	95·00
123		1a. on 1a.9p. ultramarine (R.)	3·50	2·25
		a. Surch in black	†	£3000
		b. Black surch with smaller native characters 7½ mm instead of 10 mm long	†	£4000
		(iii) On 1948–50 issue.		
124	**30**	3p. on 9p. ultramarine	2·75	2·00
		a. Larger native characters 20 mm instead of 16½ mm long	2·75	50
		ab. Imperf between (vert pair)	†	£1800
		b. Surch double	£550	
		c. Surch both sides	£425	
125		3p. on 9p. ultramarine (R.)	5·50	2·75
		a. Incorrect character	30·00	25·00
126		6p. on 9p. ultramarine (R.)	1·75	40
119/26 *Set of* 8			45·00	45·00

The 9p. ultramarine (T **29**) with 6p. surcharge (T **33**) in red was prepared for use but not issued (*Price £225 unused*).

1949. *Surch as T* **20**. W **27**. P 13.

127	**29**	6p. on 1a. orange	65·00	£150
128		9p. on 1a. orange	95·00	£150

OFFICIAL STAMPS

On
C G
S
(O **1**)

ON
C G
S
(O **2** Small "ON")

ON
C G
S
(O **3** "G" without serif)

1913. *Optd with Type* O **1** *(3p.) or* O **2** *(others).*

O1	**8**	3p. blue (R.)	£120	10
		a. Black opt	†	£1200
		b. Inverted "S"	—	50·00
		c. Opt double	†	£550
O2		4p. green (*wmk sideways*)	9·00	10
		a. Opt inverted	—	£300
O3		9p. carmine	£110	10
		a. Wmk sideways	15·00	10
		w. Wmk inverted	†	£110
O4		1½a. purple	48·00	10
		a. Opt double	—	£700
O5		2a. grey	13·00	10
O6		3a. vermilion	55·00	45
O7		6a. violet	60·00	2·00
O8		12a. ultramarine	40·00	7·00
O9		1½r. deep green	35·00	75·00
O1/9 *Set of* 9			£350	80·00

1919–33. *Optd as Type* O **3**.

O10	**10**	4p. green (*a*) (*b*)	4·00	10
		a. Opt double	—	£500
O11		6p. red-brown (*a*) (*b*) (1922)	12·00	10
		a. Opt double	—	£450
		w. Wmk inverted	†	—
O12		8p. sepia (*b*) (1923)	11·00	10
O13		9p. carmine (*a*) (*b*)	65·00	10
O14		10p. blue (*b*) (1923)	14·00	10
		a. Opt double	†	£700
O15		1½a. purple (*a*) (*b*) (1921)	5·50	10
		a. Opt double	†	£700
O16		2a. grey (*b*) (1923)	42·00	30
O17		2¼a. yellow-green (*a*) (*b*) (1922)	13·00	10
		a. Opt double	†	£425
O18		3a. vermilion (*a*) (*b*) (*c*)	18·00	25
		a. Opt inverted	†	£450
O19		6a. violet (*a*) (*b*) (1924)	38·00	50
O19*a*		12a. ultramarine (*a*) (*b*) (1929)	15·00	5·00
O19*b*		1½r. deep green (*a*) (*b*) (1933)	25·00	£120
O10/19*b* *Set of* 12			£225	£120

All values exist showing a straight-backed "C" variety on R. 4/1.

8
Eight pies
(O **4** 27½ mm high)

ON
C G
S
(O **5** Straight back to "C")

ON
C G
S
(O **6** Circular "O"; "N" without serifs)

1923 (Jan)–**24**. *T* **8** *and* **10** *surch with Type* O **4**.

O20		8p. on 9p. carmine (No. O3)	£350	1·75
		a. "Pies" for "pies" (R. 4/8)	£1100	60·00
		b. Wmk sideways	£130	20
		ba. "Pies" for "pies" (R. 4/8)	£400	18·00
		c. Surch double	†	£350
O21		8p. on 9p. carm (*a*) (*b*) (No. O13) (11.24)	70·00	10
		a. "Pies" for "pies" (R. 4/8)	£190	12·00
		b. Surch double	†	£275
		c. Opt Type O **3** double	†	£300

Varieties with smaller "i" or "t" in "Eight" and small "i" in "Pies" are also known from a number of positions in the setting.

1925 (Apr). *T* **10** *surch as Type* O **4**.

O22		10p. on 9p. carmine (*b*) (No. O13)	80·00	1·00
		b. Surch double	†	£300
		c. Surch 25 mm high (*a*)	£225	1·25
		ca. Surch double	†	£325

1929. *T* **8** *surch as Type* O **4**.

O23		10p. on 9p. carmine (No. O3a)	£1200	15·00
		a. Surch double	†	£550
		b. Wmk upright	—	65·00

1929–31. *Optd with Type* O **5**.

O24	**10**	4p. green (*b*) (1931)	22·00	1·75
		a. Inverted "S"	£190	15·00
O25		6p. red-brown (*b*) (*c*) (*d*) (1930)	14·00	10
		a. Inverted "S"	£110	4·25
O26		8p. sepia (*b*) (1930)	7·00	10
		a. Inverted "S"	60·00	4·75
O27		10p. blue (*b*)	6·00	10
		a. Inverted "S"	55·00	5·00
O28		2a. grey (*b*) (1930)	40·00	25
		a. Inverted "S"	£250	8·50
O29		3a. vermilion (*b*) (1930)	8·50	20
		a. Inverted "S"	95·00	8·00
O30		6a. violet (*b*) (*d*) (1930)	£100	3·00
		a. Inverted "S"	£650	£100
O24/30 *Set of* 7			£180	5·00

1933. *Nos. O26/7 surch as T* **14**, *in red.*

O32	**10**	6p. on 8p. sepia (*b*)	2·50	10
		a. Inverted "S"	21·00	4·25
O33		6p. on 10p. blue (*b*)	4·00	10
		a. Inverted "S"	42·00	3·75

The inverted "S" varieties occur on R. 2/1 of one setting of this overprint only.

1933–38. *Recess-printed stamps of 1933–38 optd.*

		(a) With Type O **5**.		
O34	**18**	4p. green	4·25	10
O35		6p. red-brown (1934)	3·75	10
O36	**18a**	1a. brown-orange	16·00	10
O37	**18**	1a.8p. carmine	1·50	30
O38		2a. grey	18·00	10
O39		2¼a. yellow-green	6·00	10
O40		3a. vermilion	45·00	10
O41		3a.4p. violet	1·50	15
O42		6a.8p. sepia	1·50	20
O43		10a. blue	1·50	1·00
O34/43 *Set of* 10			90·00	2·00
		(b) With Type O **6** *(typo).*		
O44	**18a**	1a. brown-orange (1937)	40·00	60
O45	**18**	2a. grey-black (1938)	22·00	2·00
O46		3a. vermilion (1938)	11·00	2·50
O44/6 *Set of* 3			65·00	4·50

ON
C G
S
(O **7** Curved back to "c")

ON
C G
S
(O **8**)

ON
C G
S
(O **9** Circular "O"; N with serifs)

ON
C G
S
(O **10** Oval "O")

ON
C G
S
(O **11**)

1938–44. *Lithographed stamps of 1938.* W **8a**, optd.

		(a) With Type O **7** *or* O **8** *(1a).* P 11.		
O47	**18**	4p. green	28·00	2·75
		a. Inverted "S"	35·00	2·75
		b. Perf 13×13½	21·00	2·75
O48		6p. red-brown	27·00	40
		a. Inverted "S"	30·00	50
O49	**18a**	1a. brown-orange	£300	2·50
O50	**18**	2a. grey-black	20·00	1·00
		a. Inverted "S"	20·00	1·00
		(b) With Type O **9** *(litho) or* O **10** *(6p.).*		
O51	**18**	6p. red-brown (P 13×13½)	11·00	4·25
O52	**18a**	1a. brown-orange	1·00	10
O53	**18**	3a. vermilion	3·00	1·75
		(c) With Type O **11**.		
O53*a*	**18**	6p. red-brown	£850	£400

The inverted "S" varieties, Nos. O47a, O48a and O50a, occur 21 times in the setting of 48.

1942–43. *Unissued stamps optd with Type* O **10**. *Litho.* W **27**. P 11.

O54	**18**	4p. green	75·00	16·00
		a. Perf 13×13½	2·25	70
O55		6p. red-brown	£160	11·00
		a. Perf 13×13½	20·00	90
		ab. Optd both sides	†	£150

O56	**18a**	1a. brown-orange	12·00	5·00
		a. Perf 13×13½	1·60	4·25
		ab. Optd both sides	†	£150
O56*b*	**18**	2a. grey-black (1943)	75·00	80
		ba. Opt omitted	†	£1200
O56*c*		2¼a. sage-green (1943)	£1600	7·00
O56*d*		3a. vermilion (1943)	19·00	7·50

1943. *Official stamps variously surch with T* **20** *or* **21**.

(i) *On 1½a. purple of 1919–33.*

O57	**10**	9p. on 1½a. (*b*) (T **20**)	£650	27·00

(ii) *On recess printed 1a.8p. carmine of 1933–44 (Type O* **5** *opt).*

O58		3p. on 1a.8p. (T **21**)	5·50	3·00
O59		9p. on 1a.8p. (T **20**)	£130	30·00
O60		1a.9p. on 1a.8p. (T **20**)	2·75	2·75
O61		1a.9p. on 1a.8p. (T **21**)	1·50	40

(iii) *On lithographed stamps of 1938–44.* P 11. *(a)* W **8a**.

O62	**18**	3p. on 4p. (Types O **7** and **20**)(P 13×13½)	30·00	11·00
		a. Surch double	£425	£180
O63		3p. on 4p. (Types O **7** and **21**)(P 13×13½)	£170	60·00
O64	**18a**	3p. on 1a. (Types O **9** and **20**)	2·25	3·75
O65		9p. on 1a. (Types O **9** and **20**)	£275	55·00
O66		1a.3p. on 1a. (Types O **9** and **21**)	£300	£100

(b) W **27**.

O67	**18**	3p. on 4p. (Types O **10** and **20**)(P 13×13½)	£100	55·00
O67*a*		3p. on 4p. (Types O **10** and **21**)(P 13×13½)	£1600	
O67*b*	**18a**	3p. on 1a. (Types O **10** and **20**)	£160	80·00
		ba. Perf 13×13½	£110	75·00

1944. *Optd with Type* O **10**. W **27**. P 13×13½.

O68	**26**	4p. green	40·00	7·00
		a. Perf 11	£140	5·50
		b. Perf 13	£450	70·00
O69		6p. red-brown	2·75	10
		a. Opt double	—	75·00
		b. Perf 11	1·00	10
		ba. Opt double	—	75·00
		c. Perf 13	8·00	2·50
O70		1a. brown-orange	£3000	60·00
O71		2a. black	7·00	1·00
O72		2¼a. yellow-green	4·25	1·10
		a. Optd both sides	†	£130
O73		3a. vermilion	10·00	1·75
		a. Perf 11	9·50	40

Stamps perforated 13×13½ are from a comb machine; those perforated 13 from a line perforator.

1944. *Optd with Type* O **10** *and variously surch as Types* **20** *and* **21**. W **27**.

O74	**26**	3p. on 4p. (T **20**)	3·50	10
		a. Perf 11	8·00	60
		ab. Optd Type O **10** on both sides		£140
O75		3p. on 4p. (T **21**)	5·00	40
		a. Perf 11	£400	£170
O76		3p. on 1a. (T **20**)	26·00	7·50
O77		9p. on 6p. (T **20**)	11·00	3·50
		a. Stamp printed both sides	†	£475
O78		9p. on 6p. (T **21**)	4·50	40
O79		1a.3p. on 1a. (T **20**)	13·00	2·75
O80		1a.3p. on 1a. (T **21**)	3·75	10
O74/80 *Set of* 7			60·00	13·00

1946–47. *Stamps of 1944–48 (Head Type II) optd with Type* O **10**. P 13.

O81	**28**	9p. ultramarine	3·00	10
		a. Stamp printed both sides	†	£550
		b. Perf 13×13½	4·75	10
O82		1a.3p. magenta (1947)	1·60	20
		a. Opt double	20·00	12·00
		b. Optd on both sides		
		ba. Optd both sides, opt double and inverted on reverse	55·00	
O83		1a.9p. ultramarine (1947)	40	1·00
		a. Opt double		
		b. Pair, one without opt	†	£1700
O81/3 *Set of* 3			4·50	1·10

1946–48. *Stamps of 1946–48 and unissued values optd with Type* O **2**. P 13.

O84	**29**	3p. carmine	1·25	10
		a. Stamp printed both sides	†	£600
O85		4p. grey-green	30·00	7·00
O86		6p. red-brown	14·00	1·75
O87		9p. ultramarine	75	10
O88		1a.3p. magenta	4·00	1·40
O89		1a.9p. ultramarine	4·75	40
O90		2a. black	15·00	3·00
O91		2¼a. yellow-green	23·00	5·00
O84/91 *Set of* 8			85·00	17·00

1948–49. *Stamps of 1948–50 and unissued values optd with Type* O **7**.

O92	**30**	3p. carmine	1·25	15
		a. "C" for "G" in opt	15·00	3·25
O93		4p. green	1·50	40
		a. Imperf between (horiz pair)	†	£1600
		b. Imperf between (vert pair)	†	£1600
		c. Optd on both sides	75·00	75·00
		d. "C" for "G" in opt	16·00	5·00
O94		6p. chestnut	2·75	30
		a. Imperf between (vert pair)	†	£1800
		b. "C" for "G" in opt	26·00	4·00
O95		9p. ultramarine	3·25	10
		a. "C" for "G" in opt	27·00	3·75
O96		2a. black	2·75	15
		a. "C" for "G" in opt	27·00	4·25
O97		2¼a. yellow-green	3·25	6·50
		a. "C" for "G" in opt	30·00	55·00
O98		3a. orange-red	1·10	1·00
		a. "C" for "G" in opt	19·00	11·00
O99		3a.4p. violet (I)	45·00	45·00
		a. "C" for "G" in opt	£275	£300
		b. Tail to turban flaw	£275	
		c. Die II	£100	£100
O92/9 *Set of* 8			55·00	48·00

The "C" for "G" variety occurs on R. 1/4. Nos. O92/9, O103/4 and O104b also exist with a flat back to "G" which occurs twice in each sheet on R. 1/5 and R. 2/8.

No. O93 exists with watermark sideways, but can usually only be identified when in multiples.

1949. *Official stamps surch as T* **33**.

(i) *On 1944 issue.*

O100	**28**	1a. on 1a.9p. ultramarine (R.)	60	70

(ii) *On 1948 issue.*

O101	**29**	1a. on 1a.9p. ultramarine (R.)	23·00	17·00

(iii) *On 1949 issue.*

O103	**30**	6p. on 3p. carmine	1·25	75
		a. Imperf between (vert pair)	†	£1200
		b. Surch double	†	£350
		c. "C" for "G" in opt	15·00	10·00
		d. Incorrect character	15·00	10·00
O104		9p. on 4p. green (18 *mm long*)	75	3·00
		a. Imperf between (horiz pair)	£700	£800
		b. Larger native characters, 22 mm long	1·10	1·10
		ba. Ditto. Imperf between (horiz pair)	£650	£650
		bb. Incorrect character	20·00	17·00
		c. "C" for "G" in opt	18·00	27·00
		ca. Ditto. Larger native characters, 22 mm long	21·00	17·00
O100/4 *Set of* 4			24·00	18·00

No. O104 exists with watermark sideways, but can usually only be identified when in multiples.

1949. *No. 124a, but with lines of surch 17½ mm apart, optd* "SERVICE".

O105	**30**	3p. on 9p. ultramarine	60	80
		a. Imperf between (horiz pair)	†	£1900

From 1 July 1949 Cochin formed part of the new state of Travancore-Cochin. Existing stocks of Cochin issues continued to be used in conjunction with stamps of Travancore surcharged in Indian currency.

DHAR

PRICES FOR STAMPS ON COVER

Nos. 1/4	*from* × 50
No. 5	*from* × 30
No. 6	—
Nos. 7/9	*from* × 50
No. 10	—

Raja (Maharaja from 1877) Anand Rao Puar III, 1857–1898

1 (¼a.)

2

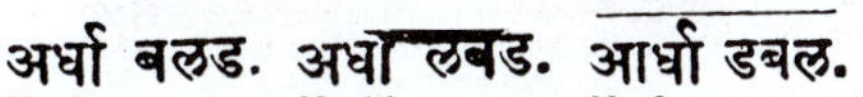

No. 1c No. 1d No. 2

1897–1900. *Type-set. Colour-fugitive paper. With oval handstamp in black. No gum.* Imperf.

1	**1**	½p. black/*red* (three characters at bottom left)	3·00	3·25
		a. Handstamp omitted	£325	
		b. Line below upper inscription (R. 2/2)	65·00	65·00
		c. Character transposed (R. 2/3)	28·00	28·00
		d. Character transposed (R. 2/5)	70·00	
2		½p. black/*red* (four characters at bottom left)	2·75	4·00
		a. Handstamp omitted	£225	
3		¼a. black/*orange*	3·75	5·00
		a. Handstamp omitted	£250	
4		½a. black/*magenta*	4·50	5·50
		a. Handstamp omitted	£275	£200
		b. Line below upper inscription (R. 2/2)	£100	£120
5		1a. black/*green*	8·50	17·00
		a. Handstamp omitted	£475	
		b. Printed both sides	£850	
		c. Line below upper inscription (R. 2/2)	£200	£275
6		2a. black/*yellow*	28·00	50·00
		e. Top right corner ornament transposed with one from top of frame (R. 2/5)	£110	£160
1/6 *Set of* 6			45·00	75·00

Nos. 1/6 were each issued in sheets of 10 (5×2), but may, on the evidence of a single sheet of the ½ price value, have been printed in sheets of 20 containing two of the issued sheets *tête-bêche*.

Research has identified individual characteristics for stamps printed from each position in the sheet.

The same research suggests that the type remained assembled during the entire period of production, being amended as necessary to provide the different values. Seven main settings have been identified with changes sometimes occurring during their use which form sub-settings.

The distribution of stamps between the main settings was as follows:

Setting I—½p.
Setting II—½a., 1a.
Setting III—1a.
Setting IV—½p., ½a., 1a.
Setting V—½p.
Setting VI—½p. (No. 2). ¼a.
Setting VII—2a.

The listed constant errors all occurred during Setting IV.

In No. 1c the three characters forming the second word in the lower inscription are transposed to the order (2) (3) (1) and in No. 1d to the order (3) (2) (1).

On Nos. 1b, 4b and 5c the line which normally appears above the upper inscription is transposed so that it appears below the characters.

All values show many other constant varieties including mistakes in the corner and border ornaments, and also both constant and non-constant missing lines, dots and characters.

Examples of complete forgeries and faked varieties on genuine stamps exist.

Raja (Maharaja from 1918) Udaji Rao Puar II, 1898–1926

(Typo at Bombay)

1898–1900. P 11 *to* 12.

7	**2**	½a. carmine	4·75	6·50
		a. Imperf (pair)	40·00	
		b. Deep rose	4·25	6·00
8		1a. claret	4·25	8·00
9		1a. reddish violet	4·25	15·00
		a. Imperf between (horiz pair)	£475	
		b. Imperf (pair)	£110	
10		2a. deep green	7·50	25·00
7/10 *Set of* 4			18·00	50·00

The stamps of Dhar have been obsolete since 31 March 1901.

DUNGARPUR

PRICES FOR STAMPS ON COVER

Nos. 1/15	*from* × 2

Maharawal Lakshman Singh, 1918–1971

1 State Arms

(Litho Shri Lakshman Bijaya Printing Press, Dungarpur)

1933–47. P 11.

1	**1**	¼a. bistre-yellow	—	£225
2		¼a. rose (1935)	£3000	£750
3		¼a. red-brown (1937)	—	£425
4		1a. pale turquoise-blue	—	£190
5		1a. rose (1938)	—	£2500
6		1a.3p. deep reddish violet (1935)	—	£300
7		2a. deep dull green (1947)	£1600	£400
8		4a. rose-red (1934)	—	£750

Nos. 2 and 5 are known in a *se-tenant* strip of 3, the centre stamp being the 1a. value.

2 **3** **4**

Maharawal Lakshman Singh

Three dies of ½a. (*shown actual size*):

Die I. Size 21×25½ mm. Large portrait (head 5 mm and turban 7½ mm wide), correctly aligned (sheets of 12 and left-hand stamps in subsequent blocks of four *se-tenant* horizontally with Die II)

Die II. Size 20×24½ mm. Large portrait (head 4¾ mm and turban 7 mm wide), but with less detail at foot and with distinct tilt to left (right-hand stamps in sheets of four horizontally *se-tenant* with Die I)

Die III. Size 21×25½ mm. Small portrait (head 4½ mm and turban 6½ mm wide) (sheets of 4)

(Typo L. V. Indap & Co, Bombay)

1939–46. *T* **2** *(various frames) and* **3/4**. Various perfs.

9	2	¼a. orange (P 12, 11, 10½ *or* 10)	£1000	90·00
10		½a. verm (Die I) (P 12, 11 *or* 10½) (1940)	£350	70·00
		a. Die II (P 10½) (1944)	£350	85·00
		ab. Horiz pair. Die I and Die II	£750	£225
		b. Die III (P 10) (1945)	£450	70·00
		c. Imperf between (vert pair)	†	£3500
11		1a. deep blue (P 12, 11, 10½ *or* 10)	£350	65·00
12	3	1a.3p. brt mauve (P 10½ *or* 10) (1944)	£1000	£275
13	4	1½a. deep violet (P 10) (1946)	£1100	£275
14	2	2a. brt green (P 12, *pin perf* 11½) (1943)	£1500	£500
15		4a. brown (P 12, 10½ *or* 10) (1940)	£1100	£225

Stamps perforated 12, 11 and 10½ were printed in sheets of 12 (4×3) which were imperforate along the top, bottom and, sometimes, at right so that examples exist with one or two adjacent sides imperforate. Stamps perforated 10 were printed in sheets of 4 either imperforate at top, bottom and right-hand side or fully perforated.

Dungarpur became part of Rajasthan by 15 April 1948.

DUTTIA (DATIA)

PRICES FOR STAMPS ON COVER

Nos. 1/7	—
Nos. 8/11	*from* × 5
Nos. 12/15	—
Nos. 16/40	*from* × 20

All the stamps of Duttia were impressed with a circular handstamp (as a rule in *blue*) before issue.

This handstamp shows the figure of Ganesh in the centre, surrounded by an inscription in Devanagari reading "DATIYA STET POSTAJ 1893". Stamps could not be used for postage without this control mark.

PROCESS. Nos. 1/15 were type-set and printed singly. Nos. 16/40 were typo from plates comprising 8 or more clichés.

GUM. The stamps of Duttia (*except* No. 25c) were issued without gum.

Maharaja Bhawani Singh, 1857–1907

Rectangular labels each showing a double hand-drawn frame (in black for the 1a. and in red for the others), face value in black and the Ganesh handstamp are known on thin cream (½a.), rose (1a.), orange (2a.) or pale yellow (4a.) paper. These are considered by some specialists to be the first stamps of Duttia, possibly issued during 1893, but the evidence for this is inconclusive.

1 (2a.)

2 (2a.) Ganesh

3 (¼a.)

1894? *Rosettes in lower corners. Control handstamp in blue.* Imperf.

1	1	½a. black/*green*	£16000	
2		2a. grey-blue/*yellow*	£3500	
		a. Handstamp in black	£4000	
		b. Handstamp in red	†	£27000

Only three examples of No. 1 have been reported. In each instance the Devanagari inscription was originally 8a., but was amended in manuscript to ½a.

1896. *Control handstamp in blue.* Imperf.

3	2	1a. red	£3250	£5000
		a. Handstamp in black	£3750	£5000
		b. Handstamp in brown	£4500	
		c. 2a. deep blue (handstamp in black)	£1500	
		d. Handstamp in brown	£15000	

1896. *Control handstamp in blue.* Imperf.

4	3	¼a. black/*orange*	£4250	
		a. Without handstamp	£3000	
5		½a. black/*blue-green*	£10000	
		a. Without handstamp	£3000	£6000
6		2a. black/*yellow*	£2500	
		a. Without handstamp	£11000	
7		4a. black/*rose*	£1300	
		a. Without handstamp	£15000	

Two types of centre:

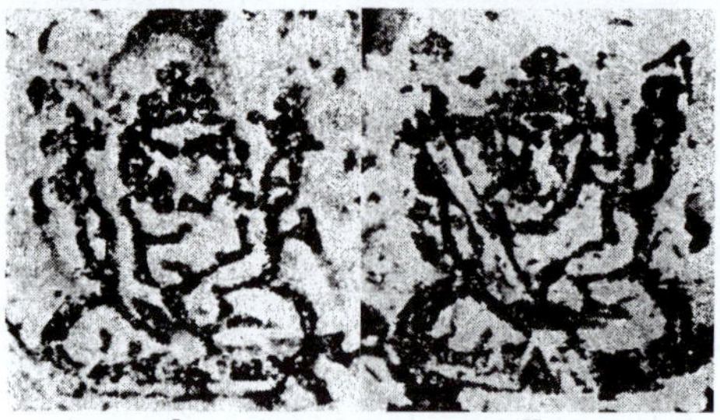
I II

Type I. Small Ganesh. Height 13 mm. Width of statue 11 mm. Width of pedestal 8 mm.

Type II. Large Ganesh. Height 13½ mm. Width of statue 11½ mm. Width of pedestal 11½ mm. "Flag" in god's right hand; "angle" above left. All stamps also show dot at top right corner.

1897–98. Imperf.

8	2	½a. black/*green* (I) (value in one group)	70·00	£450
		a. *Tête-bêche* (horiz pair)	£1300	
		b. Value in two groups	22·00	£300
		ba. *Tête-bêche* (vert pair)	£1300	
		bb. Doubly printed	£3250	
		bc. Type II (1898)	27·00	
9		1a. black/*white* (I)	£100	£350
		a. *Tête-bêche* (horiz pair)	£1300	
		b. Laid paper	22·00	
		ba. *Tête-bêche* (vert pair)	£1000	
		c. Type II (1898)	£120	
		ca. Laid paper	30·00	
10		2a. black/*yellow* (I)	28·00	£325
		a. *On lemon*	42·00	£350
		b. Type II (1898)	42·00	£375
11		4a. black/*rose* (I)	26·00	£225
		a. *Tête-bêche* (horiz pair)	£275	
		b. *Tête-bêche* (vert pair)	£150	£500
		c. Doubly printed	£3250	
		d. Type II (1898)	32·00	

A used example of the 4a. is known showing black roulettes at foot.

4 (2a.)

5 (2a.)

1897. *Name spelt "DATIA.".* Imperf.

12	4	½a. black/*green*	£100	£550
13		1a. black/*white*	£190	
14		2a. black/*yellow*	£120	£550
		a. *Tête-bêche* (vert pair)	£4750	
15		4a. black/*rose*	£120	£550
		a. *Tête-bêche* (vert pair)	£4750	
12/15 *Set of 4*			£475	

1899–1906.

(a) Rouletted in colour or in black, horizontally and at end of rows.

16	5	¼a. vermilion	3·25	
		a. Rose-red	3·00	
		b. Pale rose	2·75	
		c. Lake	3·75	21·00
		d. Carmine	3·75	
		e. Brownish red	8·50	
		ea. *Tête-bêche* (pair)	£3250	
17		½a. black/*blue-green*	2·75	21·00
		a. On deep green	6·00	
		b. On yellow-green (pelure)	5·00	22·00
		c. On dull green (1906)	3·25	
18		1a. black/*white*	3·00	21·00
19		2a. black/*lemon-yellow*	9·50	
		a. On orange-yellow	13·00	
		b. On buff-yellow	3·50	23·00
		ba. Handstamp in black	15·00	
		bb. Without handstamp	£425	
		c. On pale yellow (1906)	2·75	23·00
20		4a. black/*deep rose*	3·25	22·00
		a. *Tête-bêche* (pair)		
		b. Handstamp in black	20·00	
		c. Without handstamp	£325	

(b) Rouletted in colour between horizontal rows, but imperf at top and bottom and at ends of rows.

20*d*	5	¼a. brownish red	45·00	
21		1a. black/*white*	14·00	50·00
		a. Without handstamp	£650	
		b. Handstamp in black	£100	

One setting of 16 (8×2) of the ¼a. value (No. 16*e*) showed an inverted cliché at R. 1/2.

1904–05. *Without rouletting.*

22	5	¼a. red	3·75	32·00
		a. Without handstamp	£450	
23		½a. black/*green*	18·00	
24		1a. black (1905)	15·00	40·00

Maharaja Govind Singh, 1907–1955

1911. P 13½. *Stamps very wide apart.*

25	5	¼a. carmine	6·50	50·00
		a. Imperf horiz (vert pair)	£300	
		b. Imperf between (horiz pair)	£325	
		c. Stamps closer together (with gum)	8·50	42·00
		d. As c. Imperf vert (horiz pair)	£140	
25*e*		1a. black	£950	

No. 25*e* was mainly used for fiscal purposes (*Price on piece*, £90), but one example has been seen used on a registered postcard.

1912? *Printed close together.*

(a) Coloured roulette×imperf.

26	5	½a. black/*green*	7·50	35·00

(b) Printed wide apart. P 13½×coloured roulette (¼a.) or 13½×imperf (½a.).

27	5	¼a. carmine	5·50	42·00
		a. Without handstamp	£325	
28		½a. black/*dull green*	12·00	48·00

1916. *Colours changed. Control handstamp in blue (Nos. 29/33) or black (No. 34).* Imperf.

29	5	¼a. deep blue	5·50	26·00
30		½a. green	5·50	27·00
		a. Without handstamp	†	£1000
31		1a. purple	7·00	28·00
		a. *Tête-bêche* (vert pair)	24·00	
		ab. Without handstamp	£1000	
32		2a. brown	15·00	35·00
33		2a. lilac	7·50	27·00
		a. Handstamp in black	35·00	
		b. Without handstamp	£275	
34		4a. Venetian red (date?)	75·00	
		a. Without handstamp	£750	

1918. *Colours changed.*

(a) Imperf.

35	5	½a. blue	3·50	18·00
36		1a. pink	3·50	18·00
		a. Handstamp in black	10·00	
		b. Without handstamp	£275	

(b) P 11½.

37	5	¼a. black	5·00	25·00

1920. *Rouletted.*

38	5	¼a. blue	2·75	14·00
		a. Roul×perf 7	38·00	38·00
		b. Imperf between (vert pair)	£600	
		c. Without handstamp	£160	
		d. Handstamp in black	9·50	
39		½a. pink	3·50	16·00
		a. Roul×perf 7	£225	
		b. Without handstamp	£250	
		c. Handstamp in black		

1920. Rough perf about 7.

40	5	½a. dull red	16·00	42·00
		a. Handstamp in black	45·00	£100
		b. Without handstamp	£275	

The stamps of Duttia have been obsolete since 1 April 1921.

FARIDKOT

PRICES FOR STAMPS ON COVER

Nos. N1/4	*from* × 10
Nos. N5/6	*from* × 50
Nos. N7/8	—

GUM. The stamps of Faridkot (Nos. N1/8) were issued without gum.

Raja Bikram Singh, 1874–1898

N 1 (1 folus= ¼a.)

N 2 (1 paisa= ¼a.)

N 3

1879–86. *Rough, handstamped impression.* Imperf.

(a) Native thick laid paper.

N1	N 1	1f. ultramarine	45·00	48·00
N2	N 2	1p. ultramarine	£150	£150

(b) Ordinary laid paper.

N3	N 1	1f. ultramarine	14·00	16·00
N4	N 2	1p. ultramarine	85·00	£100

(c) Wove paper, thick to thinnish.

N5	N 1	1f. ultramarine	2·75	4·00
		a. *Tête-bêche* (pair)	£275	
		b. Pair, one stamp sideways	£1500	
N6	N 2	1p. ultramarine	5·00	11·00
		a. Pair, one stamp sideways	£1600	

(d) Thin wove whitey brown paper.

N7	N 2	1p. ultramarine	30·00	32·00

Faridkot signed a postal convention with the Imperial Government which led to the provision of India issues overprinted "FARIDKOT STATE" from 1 January 1887. These are listed in the Convention States section.

Although the previous issues were no longer valid for postal purposes the state authorities continued to sell them to collectors for many years after 1887. Initially remaining stocks of Nos. N1/7 were on offer, but these were soon supplemented by Type N 1 handstamped in other colours, examples of a ½a., handstamped in various colours, which had originally been prepared in 1877 and by a replacement 1p, as Type N 3, (*Price* £1.50 *unused, tête-bêche pair*, £225, *unused*) which had not done postal duty before the convention came into force. The sale of such items was clearly an important source of revenue as the 1f. as Type N 1, yet another version of the 1p. and the ½a. subsequently appeared printed in sheets by lithography for sale to stamp collectors.

HYDERABAD

PRICES FOR STAMPS ON COVER

Nos. 1/3	*from* × 10
Nos. 4/12	—
Nos. 13/60	*from* × 5
Nos. O1/53	*from* × 10

The official title of the State in English was The Dominions of the Nizam and in Urdu "Sarkar-i-Asafia" (State of the successors of Asaf). This Urdu inscription appears in many of the designs.

Nawab Mir Mahbub Ali Khan Asaf Jah VI, 1869–1911

1

2

(Eng Mr. Rapkin. Plates by Nissen & Parker, London. Recess Mint, Hyderabad)

1869 (8 Sept). P 11½.

1	1	1a. olive-green	18·00	7·50
		a. Imperf between (horiz pair)	£170	
		b. Imperf horiz (vert pair)	£600	£120
		c. Imperf (pair)	£450	£450
		d. Imperf vert (horiz pair)	†	£425

Reprints in the colour of the issue, and also in fancy colours, were made in 1880 on white wove paper, perforated 12½. Fakes of No. 1c are known created by the removal of the outer perforations from examples of Nos. 1a/b.

1870 (16 May). *Locally engraved; 240 varieties of each value; wove paper. Recess.* P 11½.

2	2	½a. brown	4·00	4·25
3		2a. sage-green	60·00	48·00

Stamps exist showing traces of lines in the paper, but they do not appear to be printed on true laid paper.

Reprints of both values were made in 1880 on white wove paper, perforated 12½: the ½a. in grey-brown, yellow-brown, sea-green, dull blue and carmine and the 2a. in bright green and in blue-green.

3

A Normal 2a. B Variety

In A the coloured lines surrounding each of the four labels join a coloured circle round their inner edge, in B this circle is missing.

C 3a. D

C. Normal

D. Character ^ omitted

Left side of central inscription omitted (Pl 4 R. 2/11)

Dot at top of central inscription omitted

Second dot in bottom label omitted

Centre dot in bottom label omitted

(Plates by Bradbury, Wilkinson & Co. Recess Mint, Hyderabad)

1871–1909.

(a) No wmk.

(i) Rough perf 11½.

4	3	½a. red-brown	18·00	20·00
		a. Dot at top of central inscription omitted	£170	
5		1a. purple-brown	£120	£130
		a. Imperf horiz (vert pair)	†	£1900
		b. Dot at top of central inscription omitted	£900	£900
6		2a. green (A)	£1300	
7		3a. ochre-brown	40·00	55·00
8		4a. slate	£150	£150
9		8a. deep brown		
10		12a. dull blue	£325	

(ii) Pin perf 8-9.

11	3	½a. red-brown	—	£475
12		1a. drab	£350	£170

(iii) P 12½.

13	3	½a. orange-brown	2·75	10
		a. Imperf vert (horiz pair)	†	85·00
		ab. Imperf horiz (vert pair)	†	£800
		b. Orange	2·75	10
		c. Red-brown	2·75	10
		d. Brick-red	2·75	10
		da. Imperf vert (horiz pair)	†	85·00
		db. Doubly printed	£450	£160
		e. Rose-red	2·75	20
		ea. Doubly printed	†	£225
		f. Error. Magenta	50·00	8·00
		g. Left side of central inscription omitted	£325	85·00
		h. Dot at top of central inscription omitted	65·00	2·75
14		1a. purple-brown	7·50	7·00
		a. Doubly printed	£450	
		b. Drab	1·25	15
		ba. Imperf (pair)	—	£375
		bb. Doubly printed	£200	
		c. Grey-black	2·00	10
		ca. Imperf (pair)	†	£900
		d. Black (1909)	2·25	10
		da. Doubly printed	£475	£250
		db. Imperf vert (horiz pair)	†	£900
		dc. Imperf horiz (vert pair)	†	£900
		e. Dot at top of central inscription omitted	—	£160
		f. Second dot in bottom label omitted	£120	42·00
15		2a. green (A)	3·75	15
		a. Deep green (A)	4·00	40
		b. Blue-green (A)	3·75	40
		ba. Blue-green (B)	£250	65·00
		c. Pale green (A)	3·75	15
		ca. Pale green (B)	£250	75·00
		d. Sage-green (A) (1909)	3·75	35
		da. Sage-green (B)	£170	48·00
		e. Dot at top of central inscription omitted	£375	£100
		f. Centre dot in bottom panel omitted	£160	45·00
16		3a. ochre-brown (C)	3·00	1·50
		a. Character omitted (D)	£225	75·00
		b. Chestnut (C)	3·00	1·50
		ba. Character omitted (D)	£180	60·00
17		4a. slate	7·50	3·50
		a. Imperf horiz (vert pair)	£900	£900
		b. Greenish grey	5·50	3·25
		ba. Imperf vert (horiz pair)	£1500	
		c. Olive-green	6·00	2·50
18		8a. deep brown	3·50	4·25
		a. Imperf vert (horiz pair)	£900	
19		12a. pale ultramarine	4·75	8·00
		a. Grey-green	5·00	5·00
13/19 *Set of 7*			22·00	12·50

(b) W 7. P 12½.

19*b*	3	1a. black (1909)	£130	16·00
19*c*		2a. sage-green (A) (1909)	£425	£110
19*d*		12a. bluish grey (1909)	£1200	

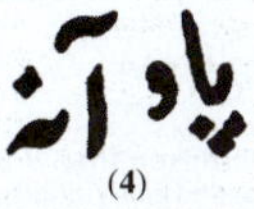
(4)

5

1898. *Surch with T* **4**. P 12½.

20	3	¼a. on ½a. orange-brown	50	85
		a. Surch inverted	38·00	24·00
		b. Pair, one without surcharge	£600	
		c. Left side of central inscription omitted	£180	

(Des Khusrat Ullah. Recess Mint, Hyderabad)

1900 (20 Sept). P 12½.

21	5	¼a. deep blue	5·50	3·50
		a. Pale blue	5·50	3·50

6

7

(Plates by Allan G. Wyon, London. Recess Mint, Hyderabad)

1905 (7 Aug). W 7. P 12½.

22	6	¼a. dull blue	2·50	60
		a. Imperf (pair)	32·00	£120
		b. Dull ultramarine	5·00	80
		ba. Perf 11×12½	32·00	25·00
		c. Pale blue-green	22·00	3·00
23		½a. orange	6·00	35
		a. Perf 11		
		b. Vermilion	4·00	25
		ba. Imperf (pair)	30·00	£120
		c. Yellow	85·00	17·00

1908–11. W 7. P 12½.

24	6	¼a. grey	1·00	10
		a. Imperf between (horiz pair)	£375	£375
		b. Imperf between (vert pair)	†	£375
		c. Perf 11½, 12	2·00	35
		d. Perf 11	75·00	21·00
25		½a. green	4·75	10
		a. Imperf between (vert pair)	£350	
		b. Perf 11½, 12	6·00	10
		c. Perf 13½	£130	40·00
		d. Pale green	4·75	20
		da. Perf 11½, 12	6·00	10
		e. Blue-green	7·00	1·00
26		1a. carmine	3·50	10
		a. Perf 11½, 12	7·00	1·00
		b. Perf 11	32·00	9·00
		c. Double impression (P 12½×11)		
27		2a. lilac	2·75	40
		a. Perf 11½, 12	3·50	1·10
		b. Perf 11	2·50	55
		c. Perf 13½	1·60	15
		ca. Imperf between (horiz pair)	†	£500
		cb. Rose-lilac	1·40	10
28		3a. brown-orange (1909)	2·75	1·00
		a. Perf 11½, 12	8·00	2·00
		b. Perf 11	1·25	60
		c. Perf 13½	2·50	30
29		4a. olive-green (1909)	3·00	1·25
		a. Perf 11½, 12	6·50	4·75
		b. Perf 11	35·00	12·00
		ba. Imperf between (pair)	£750	£750
		c. Perf 13½	1·10	30
30		8a. purple (1911)	4·50	6·00
		a. Perf 11½, 12		
		b. Perf 11	1·75	4·50
		c. Perf 13½	1·25	80
31		12a. blue-green (1911)	£130	80·00
		a. Perf 11½, 12	18·00	26·00
		b. Perf 11		
		c. Perf 13½	7·00	4·00
24/31c *Set of 8*			19·00	5·25

The above perforations also exist compound.

Nawab Mir Osman Ali Khan Asaf Jah VII, 1911–1967

1912. *New plates engraved by Bradbury, Wilkinson & Co.* W 7. P 12½.

32	6	¼a. grey-black	1·40	10
		a. Imperf horiz (vert pair)	†	£350
		b. Perf 11½, 12	80	35
		c. Perf 11	90	15
		ca. Imperf between (horiz pair)	†	£350
		cb. Imperf between (vert pair)	†	£350
		d. Perf 13½	60	10
33		¼a. brown-purple (*shades*) (P 13½)	1·75	10
		a. Imperf horiz (vert pair)	†	£350
34		½a. deep green	1·75	10
		a. Imperf between (pair)	†	£375
		b. Imperf (pair). Laid paper	£120	85·00
		c. Perf 11½, 12	7·50	55
		d. Perf 11	8·50	10
		e. Perf 13½		

The above perforations also exist compound.

In Wyon's ¼a. stamp the fraction of value is closer to the end of the label than in the B.W. issue. In the Wyon ¼a. and ½a. the value in English and the label below are further apart than in the B.W.

Wyon's ¼a. measures 19½×20 mm and the ½a. 19½×20½ mm; both stamps from the Bradbury plates measure 19¾×21½ mm.

8 Symbols

9

1915. *Inscr* "Post & Receipt". W **7**. P 13½.

35	**8**	½a. green	1·00	10
		a. Imperf between (pair)	85·00	90·00
		b. Emerald-green	3·50	20
		c. Perf 12½	6·50	35
		ca. Imperf between (pair)		
		d. Perf 11	60	10
		da. Imperf between (pair)	†	£300
		db. Imperf vert (horiz pair)	†	£300
		e. Imperf (pair)	£180	£120
36		1a. carmine	2·50	10
		a. Imperf between (pair)	£300	
		b. Scarlet	1·75	10
		ba. Imperf between (horiz pair)	†	£300
		bb. Imperf between (vert pair)	†	£300
		bc. Imperf vert (horiz pair)	†	£300
		c. Perf 12½	18·00	85
		ca. Imperf between (pair)		
		cc. Scarlet		
		d. Perf 11	1·25	20
		da. Scarlet	—	25·00
		e. Imperf (pair)	£250	£250

The above perforations also exist compound.

For ½a. claret, see No. 58.

1927 (1 Feb). As W **7**, but larger and sideways. P 13½.

37	**9**	1r. yellow	9·00	12·00

10 (4 pies)

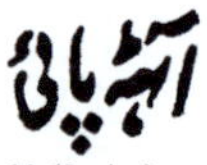
11 (8 pies)

1930 (6 May). *Surch as T* **10** *and* **11**. W **7**. P 13½.

38	**6**	4p. on ¼a. grey-black (R.)	80·00	22·00
		a. Perf 11	†	£200
		b. Perf 12½	†	80·00
		c. Perf 11½, 12	†	£450
39		4p. on ¼a. brown-purple (R.)	30	10
		a. Imperf between (pair)	£550	£550
		b. Surch double	†	£225
		c. Perf 11	†	£450
		d. Black surch	£450	£450
40	**8**	8p. on ½a. green (R.)	40	10
		a. Imperf between (horiz pair)	†	£275
		b. Perf 11	£275	£140
		c. Perf 12½	†	£275

12 Symbols

13 The Char Minar

14 High Court of Justice

15 Osman Sagar Resevoir

16 Entrance to Ajanta Caves

17 Bidar College

18 Victory Tower, Daulatabad

(Plates by De La Rue. Recess Stamps Office, Hyderabad)

1931 (12 Nov)–**47**. *T* **12/18**. W **7**. *Wove paper*. P 13½.

41	**12**	4p. black	30	10
		a. Laid paper (1947)	2·50	5·50
		b. Imperf (pair)	50·00	£110
42		8p. green	50	10
		a. Imperf between (vert pair)	—	£700
		b. Imperf (pair)	60·00	£120
		c. Laid paper (1947)	3·00	4·50
43	**13**	1a. brown (*shades*)	50	10
		a. Imperf between (horiz pair)	—	£750
		b. Perf 11	†	£850
44	**14**	2a. violet (*shades*)	3·00	10
		a. Imperf (pair)	£130	£275
45	**15**	4a. ultramarine	1·60	70
		a. Imperf (pair)	£140	£325
46	**16**	8a. orange	7·00	4·00
		a. Yellow-orange (1944)	75·00	32·00
47	**17**	12a. scarlet	7·50	12·00
48	**18**	1r. yellow	5·00	4·75
41/8 *Set of 8*			23·00	20·00

Nos. 41a and 42c have a large sheet watermark "THE NIZAM's GOVERNMENT HYDERABAD DECCAN" and arms within a circle, but this does not appear on all stamps.

19 Unani General Hospital

20 Osmania General Hospital

21 Osmania University

22 Osmania Jubilee Hall

(Litho Indian Security Printing Press, Nasik)

1937 (13 Feb). *T* **19/22**, *inscr* "H.E.H. THE NIZAM'S SILVER JUBILEE". P 14.

49	**19**	4p. slate and violet	60	2·25
50	**20**	8p. slate and brown	1·00	2·25
51	**21**	1a. slate and orange-yellow	1·40	1·40
52	**22**	2a. slate and green	1·75	4·50
49/52 *Set of 4*			4·25	9·50

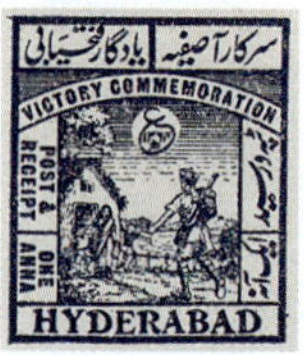

23 Family Reunion

24 Town Hall

(Des T. I. Archer. Typo)

1945 (6 Dec). *Victory*. W **7** (very faint). *Wove paper*. P 13½.

53	**23**	1a. blue	10	10
		a. Imperf between (vert pair)	£700	
		b. Laid paper	80	80

No. 53b shows the sheet watermark described beneath Nos. 41/8.

(Des. T. I. Archer. Litho Government Press)

1947 (17 Feb). *Reformed Legislature*. P 13½.

54	**24**	1a. black	1·60	1·90
		a. Imperf between (pair)	—	£950

25 Power House, Hyderabad

26 Kaktyai Arch, Warangal Fort

27 Golkunda Fort

(Des T. I. Archer. Typo)

1947–49. *As T* **25/27** *(inscr* "H. E. H. THE NIZAM'S GOVT. POSTAGE"*)*. W **7**. P 13½.

55	**25**	1a.4p. green	1·25	2·25
56	**26**	3a. greenish blue	2·00	4·25
		a. Bluish green	3·50	4·75
57	**27**	6a. sepia	4·50	18·00
		a. Red-brown (1949)	20·00	32·00
		ab. Imperf (pair)	£150	
55/7 *Set of 3*			7·00	22·00

1947. *As 1915 issue but colour changed*. P 13½.

58	**8**	½a. claret	3·00	75
		a. Imperf between (horizontal pair)	—	£350
		b. Imperf between (vert pair)	—	£650

An Independence commemorative set of four, 4p., 8p., 1a. and 2a., was prepared in 1948, but not issued.

1948. *As T* **12** *("POSTAGE" at foot). Recess.* W **7**. P 13½.

59		6p. claret	10·00	8·50

Following intervention by the forces of the Dominion of India during September 1948 the Hyderabad postal system was taken over by the Dominion authorities, operating as an agency of the India Post Office.

1949. *T* **12** *("POSTAGE" at top). Litho.* W **7**. P 13½.

60	**12**	2p. bistre-brown	2·50	3·00
		a. Imperf between (horizontal pair)	†	£850
		b. Imperf (pair)	£150	£475

No. 60 was produced from a transfer taken from a plate of the 4p., No. 41, with each impression amended individually.

OFFICIAL STAMPS

Official stamps became valid for postage within India from 1910.

(O **1**)

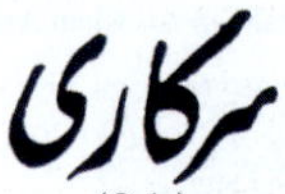
(O **1a**)

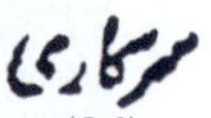
(O **2**)

1873.

I. *Handstamped as Type* O **1** *in red*.

O1	**1**	1a. olive-green	95·00	28·00
		a. Black opt	—	£350
O2	**2**	½a. brown	—	£750
		a. Black opt	—	£650
O3		2a. sage-green	—	£600
		a. Black opt	—	£200

At least ten different handstamps as Type O **1** were used to produce Nos. O1/17. These differ in the size, shape and spacing of the characters. The prices quoted are for the cheapest versions where more than one is known to exist on a particular stamp.

Imitations of these overprints on genuine stamps and on reprints are found horizontally or vertically in various shades of red, in magenta and in black.

II. *T* **3** *handstamped as Type* O **1** *in red*.

(a) Rough perf 11½.

O4		½a. red-brown		
		a. Black opt	—	£850
O5		1a. purple-brown	—	£1200
		a. Black opt	£130	£160
O6		2a. green (A)		
		a. Black opt	—	£1100
O7		4a. slate	—	£1400
		a. Black opt		
O8		8a. deep brown		
		a. Black opt	£1300	£1000
O8*b*		12a. dull blue	—	£1400

(b) Pin perf 8–9.

O8*c*		1a. drab (*black opt*)	8·00	95·00
		ca. Second dot in bottom label omitted	£170	

(c) P 12½.

O9		½a. red-brown	18·00	6·00
		a. Black opt	11·00	3·50
		ab. Left side of central inscription omitted	—	£225
		ac. Dot at top of central inscription omitted	—	65·00
O11		1a. purple-brown	£130	85·00
		a. Black opt	—	35·00
O12		1a. drab	23·00	24·00
		a. Black opt	3·00	2·50
		ab. Second dot in bottom label omitted	£110	£100
O13		2a. green (*to deep*) (A)	48·00	38·00
		a. Black opt	5·00	6·00
		ab. Inner circle missing (B)	£325	
		ac. Centre dot in bottom label omitted	£160	£160
O14		3a. ochre-brown	£170	£170
		a. Black opt	42·00	35·00
O15		4a. slate	80·00	48·00
		a. Black opt	21·00	20·00
O16		8a. deep brown	85·00	£150
		a. Imperf vert (horiz pair)	£750	
		b. Black opt	50·00	42·00
O17		12a. blue	£130	£160
		a. Black opt	60·00	90·00

The use of Official Stamps (Sarkari) was discontinued in 1878, but was resumed in 1909, when the current stamps were overprinted from a new die.

1909–11. *Optd with Type* O **1a**.

(a) On Type **3**. P 12½.

O18		½a. orange-brown	£120	5·50
		a. Opt inverted	†	£550
O19		1a. black	90·00	50
		a. Second dot in bottom label omitted	—	7·00
O20		2a. sage-green (A)	£100	1·00
		a. Optd on No. 15da (B)	—	11·00
		b. Stamp doubly printed	†	£160
		c. Centre dot in bottom label omitted	—	11·00
		d. Opt double	†	£225
O20*e*		3a. ochre-brown	7·50	3·00
		ea. Character omitted (D)	—	£450
O20*f*		4a. olive-green	£400	6·00
		fa. Perf 11½, 12	—	£325
O20*g*		8a. deep brown	—	42·00
O20*h*		12a. grey-green	—	85·00

(b) On Type **6** *(Wyon ptgs)*. P 12½.

O21		½a. orange	—	2·75
		a. Vermilion	£140	25
		ab. Opt inverted	†	£450
		ac. Imperf horiz (vert pair)	†	£450
O22		½a. green	21·00	10
		a. Pale green	21·00	10
		b. Opt inverted	†	85·00
		c. Imperf between (vert pair)	†	£350
		d. Imperf between (horiz pair)	†	£325
		e. Stamp doubly printed	†	£140
		f. Perf 11½, 12	19·00	30
		fa. Pale green	19·00	30
		fb. Opt inverted	†	85·00
		g. Perf 11		
		ga. Pale green		
		h. Perf 13½	—	90·00
O23		1a. carmine	65·00	15
		a. Opt double	£250	
		b. Perf 11½, 12	80·00	30
		ba. Stamp doubly printed	—	£150
		c. Perf 11	—	5·50
O24		2a. lilac	65·00	50
		a. Perf 11½, 12	£110	5·50
		b. Perf 11	£425	
O25		3a. brown-orange	£170	16·00
		b. Perf 11½, 12	£275	30·00

		ba. Opt inverted	†	£225
		c. Perf 11	£425	50·00
		d. Perf 13½	—	£100
O26		4a. olive-green (1911)	30·00	1·25
		a. Perf 11½, 12	£110	3·25
		b. Perf 11	—	21·00
O27		8a. purple (1911)	13·00	3·50
		a. Perf 11½, 12	£120	9·50
		b. Perf 11	£425	£130
O28		12a. blue-green (1911)	10·00	3·25
		a. Imperf between (horiz pair)	†	£1100
		b. Perf 11½, 12	32·00	4·50
		c. Perf 11	†	£400

(c) On Type **6** *(Bradbury Wilkinson ptgs).* P 11.

O28*d*	**6**	½a. deep green	£550	

1911–12. *Optd with Type* O **2**.

(a) Type **6** *(Wyon printings).* P 13½ (8a, 12a.) or 12½ (others).

O29		¼a. grey	60·00	1·00
		a. Perf 11½, 12	28·00	50
		ab. Imperf between (vert pair)	†	£400
		b. Perf 11	£110	42·00
		c. Perf 13½		
O30		½a. pale green	48·00	2·00
		a. Perf 11½, 12	—	30
		ab. Imperf between (vert pair)	†	£425
		b. Perf 13½		
O31		1a. carmine	2·00	15
		a. Opt inverted	—	42·00
		b. Imperf horiz (vert pair)	†	£400
		c. Perf 11½, 12	5·50	15
		d. Perf 11	1·25	15
		e. Perf 13½		
O32		2a. lilac	9·00	1·75
		a. Perf 11½, 12	24·00	3·75
		b. Perf 11	1·75	1·25
		c. Perf 13½	7·50	10
		ca. Imperf between (horiz pair)	†	£475
		cb. Rose-lilac	2·00	10
O33		3a. brown-orange	25·00	4·50
		a. Opt inverted	†	85·00
		b. Perf 11½, 12	18·00	3·75
		ba. Opt inverted	†	90·00
		c. Perf 11	32·00	4·50
		ca. Opt inverted	†	85·00
		d. Perf 13½	23·00	75
		da. Opt inverted	†	75·00
O34		4a. olive-green	18·00	3·00
		a. Opt inverted	—	85·00
		b. Perf 11½, 12	4·50	3·50
		ba. Opt inverted	—	90·00
		c. Perf 11	4·75	1·75
		d. Perf 13½	4·75	15
		da. Opt inverted	†	85·00
O35		8a. purple	7·50	20
		a. Perf 11½, 12		
		b. Perf 11	£425	55·00
		c. Perf 12½	—	£375
O36		12a. blue-green	24·00	2·50
		a. Perf 11½, 12		
		b. Perf 11		
		c. Perf 12½		

(b) Type **6** *(Bradbury, Wilkinson printings).* P 12½.

O37		¼a. grey-black	4·50	75
		a. Opt inverted	†	70·00
		b. Pair, one without opt		
		c. Imperf between (vert pair)	†	£325
		d. Perf 11½, 12	10·00	1·75
		da. Opt inverted	†	70·00
		db. Pair, one without opt		
		e. Perf 11	2·00	40
		ea. Opt sideways	†	75·00
		eb. Blue opt	†	75.00
		f. Perf 13½	4·50	10
		fa. Opt inverted	†	75·00
		fb. Pair, one without opt	†	£150
		fc. Imperf between (horiz pair)	†	£300
O38		¼a. brown-purple (*shades*) (P 13½)	3·75	10
		a. Imperf horiz (vert pair)	†	£325
		b. Imperf between (horiz pair)	†	£350
		c. Perf 11		
O39		½a. deep green	4·50	25
		a. Opt inverted	—	27·00
		b. Perf 11½, 12	11·00	2·00
		ba. Pair, one without opt	†	£150
		c. Perf 11	4·00	15
		ca. Opt inverted	—	30·00
		cb. Imperf horiz (vert pair)	†	£350
		d. Perf 13½	3·50	10
		da. Imperf between (horiz pair)	†	£275
		db. Imperf between (vert pair)	†	£350
		dc. Yellow-green	—	70

1917–20. *T* **8** *optd with Type* O **2**. P 13½.

O40		½a. green	3·50	10
		a. Opt inverted	†	24·00
		b. Pair, one without opt	†	£110
		c. Imperf between (horiz pair)	†	£180
		ca. Imperf vert (horiz pair)	†	£190
		d. Imperf between (vert pair)	†	£300
		e. Emerald-green	4·50	40
		f. Perf 12½	—	4·25
		g. Perf 11	9·00	30
		ga. Opt inverted	†	26·00
		gb. Pair, one without opt		
O41		1a. carmine	4·75	10
		a. Opt inverted	†	29·00
		b. Opt double	†	90·00
		c. Imperf horiz (vert pair)	†	£300
		d. Stamp printed double		
		e. Scarlet (1920)	2·75	10
		ea. Stamp printed double	†	£190
		eb. Imperf between (horiz pair)	†	£350
		ec. Imperf between (vert pair)	†	£250
		ed. Imperf horiz (vert pair)	†	£300
		ee. Opt inverted	†	£110
		f. Perf 12½	—	3·50
		g. Perf 11	14·00	15
		ga. Opt inverted	†	20·00
		gb. Scarlet (1920)	—	25·00

1930–34. *T* **6** *and* **8** *optd as Type* O **2** *and surch at top of stamp, in red, as T* **10** *or* **11**.

O42		4p. on ¼a. grey-black (O37*f*) (1934)	£425	17·00
O43		4p. on ¼a. brown-purple (O38)	2·25	10
		b. Imperf between (horiz pair)	†	£300
		c. Imperf between (vert pair)	†	£275
		d. Imperf horiz (vert pair)	†	£275
		e. Red surch double	†	£110
		f. Black opt double	†	£250
		g. Perf 11	†	£500
		h. Stamp doubly printed	†	£190
O44		8p. on ½a. green (O40)	1·50	10
		c. Imperf between (horiz pair)	†	£250
		ca. Imperf between (vert pair)	†	£300
		d. Red surch double	†	£110
		e. Stamp doubly printed	†	£190
		f. Black opt double	†	£250
O45		8p. on ½a. yellow-green (O39*db*)	35·00	48·00

For Nos. O42/5 the red surcharge was intended to appear on the upper part of the stamp, above the official overprint, Type O **2**, but surcharge and overprint are not infrequently found superimposed on one another.

1934–44. *Nos. 41/8 optd with Type* O **2**.

O46		4p. black	2·75	10
		a. Imperf (pair)	80·00	
		b. Imperf between (vert pair)	£700	£600
		c. Imperf between (horiz pair)	—	£600
O47		8p. green	1·25	10
		a. Opt inverted	†	£160
		b. Imperf between (horiz pair)	—	£600
		c. Opt double	†	£120
		d. Imperf (pair)	£170	£225
O48		1a. brown	2·00	10
		a. Imperf between (vert pair)	£600	£550
		b. Imperf between (horiz pair)	—	£500
		c. Imperf (pair)	£140	£190
		d. Opt double	—	£190
O49		2a. violet	7·50	10
		a. Imperf vert (horiz pair)	†	£1200
O50		4a. ultramarine	4·00	25
		a. Opt double	†	£500
		b. Imperf between (vert pair)	†	£1500
O51		8a. orange (1935)	14·00	60
		a. Yellow-orange (1944)	—	42·00
O52		12a. scarlet (1935)	13·00	1·75
O53		1r. yellow (1935)	20·00	2·50
O46/53 *Set of* 8			60·00	5·00

1947. *No. 58 optd with Type* O **2**.

O54	**8**	½a. claret	6·00	7·00

1949. *No. 60 optd with Type* O **2**.

O55	**12**	2p. bistre-brown	6·00	10·00

1950. *No. 59 optd with Type* O **2**.

O56		6p. claret	7·50	23·00

IDAR

PRICES FOR STAMPS ON COVER	
Nos. 1/2*b*	*from* × 2
Nos. 3/6	*from* × 3
Nos. F1/5	*from* × 2

Maharaja Himmat Singh, 1931–1960

1 Maharaja Himmat Singh

2 Maharaja Himmat Singh

(Typo M. N. Kothari & Sons, Bombay)

1932 (1 Oct)–**43**. P 11.

(a) White panels.

1	**1**	½a. light green	—	40·00
		a. Pale yellow-green (thick paper) (1939)	24·00	26·00
		b. Emerald (1941)	21·00	26·00
		ba. Imperf between (pair)	£2000	
		c. Yellow-green (1943)	17·00	25·00
		ca. Imperf between (horiz pair)	£1700	

(b) Coloured panels.

2	**1**	½a. pale yellow-green (*thick paper*) (1939)	38·00	32·00
		a. Emerald (1941)	26·00	28·00
		b. Yellow-green (1943)	14·00	26·00

In No. 2 the whole design is composed of half-tone dots. In No. 1 the dots are confined to the oval portrait.

(Typo P. G. Mehta & Co, Hitmatnagar)

1944 (21 Oct). P 12.

3	**2**	½a. blue-green	3·25	75·00
		a. Imperf between (vert pair)	£275	
		b. Yellow-green	3·75	75·00
		ba. Imperf between (vert pair)	12·00	
4		1a. violet	3·25	65·00
		a. Imperf (pair)	£200	
		b. Imperf vert (horiz pair)	£225	
5		2a. blue	3·50	£100
		a. Imperf between (vert pair)	80·00	
		b. Imperf between (horiz pair)	£200	
6		4a. vermilion	3·75	£110
		a. Doubly printed	£1200	
3/6 *Set of* 4			12·00	£325

Nos. 1 to 6 are from booklet panes of 4 stamps, producing single stamps with one or two adjacent sides imperf.

The 4a. violet is believed to be a colour trial (*Price* £400, *unused*).

POSTAL FISCAL STAMPS

F 1

F 2

1936 (?). *Typo.* P 11½ *on two or three sides.*

F1	**F 1**	1a. reddish lilac and bright green	—	£600

1940 (?)–**45**. *Typo.* P 12 *on two or three sides.*

F2	–	1a. violet	—	£160
		a. Perf 11	£140	£160
F3	**F 2**	1a. violet (1943)	£110	£160
F4		1¼a. on 1a. violet	£160	£350
F5		1¼a. yellow-green (1945)	20·00	
		a. Imperf between (vert pair)	42·00	
		b. Blue-green (1945)	80·00	£150

No. F2 shows the portrait as Type **1**. Used prices are for examples with postal cancellations. No. F4 shows a handstamped surcharge in Gujerati.

Idar became part of Bombay Province on 10 June 1948.

INDORE

(HOLKAR STATE)

PRICES FOR STAMPS ON COVER

Nos. 1/15	*from* × 20
Nos. 16/43	*from* × 6
Nos. S1/7	*from* × 40

Maharaja Tukoji Rao Holkar II, 1843–1886

1 Maharaja Tukoji Rao Holkar II

(Litho Waterlow & Sons)

1886 (6 Jan). P 15.

(a) Thick white paper.

1	1	½a. bright mauve	15·00	13·00

(b) Thin white or yellowish paper.

2	1	½a. pale mauve	3·75	2·25
		a. Dull mauve	4·00	3·00

Maharaja Shivaji Rao Holkar, 1886–1903

2 Type I 2a Type II

TYPES 2 AND 2a. In addition to the difference in the topline character (marked by arrow), the two Types can be distinguished by the difference in the angles of the 6-pointed stars and the appearance of the lettering. In Type I the top characters are smaller and more cramped than the bottom; in Type II both are in the same style and similarly spaced.

1889 (Sept). *Handstamped. No gum.* Imperf.

3	2	½a. black/*pink*	42·00	38·00
4	2a	½a. black/*pink*	3·50	3·75
		a. *Tête-bêche* (pair)	£250	

3 Maharaja Shivaji Rao Holkar 4 Maharaja Tukoji Holkar III 5 Maharaja Tukoji Holkar III

(Recess Waterlow)

1889–92. *Medium wove paper.* P 14 *to* 15.

5	3	¼a. orange (9.2.92)	1·50	80
		a. Imperf between (horiz pair)	†	£650
		b. Very thick wove paper	2·00	1·75
		c. Yellow	2·50	1·75
6		½a. dull violet	2·75	1·00
		a. Brown-purple	2·50	15
		b. Imperf between (vert pair)	£600	
7		1a. green (7.2.92)	3·00	1·25
		a. Imperf between (vert pair)	£1000	
		b. Very thick wove paper	75·00	
8		2a. vermilion (7.2.92)	7·00	2·00
		a. Very thick wove paper	8·00	3·50
5/8 *Set of* 4			12·50	3·75

Maharaja Tukoji Rao Holkar III, 1903–1926

(Recess Perkins, Bacon & Co)

1904–20. P 13½, 14.

9	4	¼a. orange	60	10
10	5	½a. lake (1909)	9·00	10
		a. Brown-lake (shades)	13·00	15
		b. Imperf (pair)	24·00	
11		1a. green	2·25	10
		a. Imperf (pair)	£120	
		b. Perf 12½ (1920)	£750	£140
12		2a. brown	15·00	1·00
		a. Imperf (pair)	80·00	
13		3a. violet	24·00	7·00
14		4a. ultramarine	18·00	3·75
		a. Dull blue	5·00	1·40
9/14a *Set of* 6			50·00	8·75

पाव आना.
(6)

7 Maharaja Yeshwant Rao Holkar II

1905 (June). *No. 6a surch "QUARTER ANNA" in Devanagari, as T* **6**.

15	3	¼a. on ½a. brown-purple	6·00	21·00

On 1 March 1908 the Indore State postal service was amalgamated with the Indian Imperial system. Under the terms of the agreement stamps showing the Maharaja would still be used for official mail sent to addresses within the state. Initially Nos. 9/14 were used for this purpose, the "SERVICE" overprints, Nos. S1/7, being withdrawn.

Maharaja Yeshwant Rao Holkar II, 1926–1961

(Recess Perkins, Bacon & Co)

1927–37. P 13 *to* 14.

16	7	¼a. orange *(a) (d) (e)*	60	20
17		½a. claret *(a) (d) (e)*	2·25	10
18		1a. green *(a) (d) (e)*	2·75	10
19		1¼a. green *(c) (d)* (1933)	4·00	85
20		2a. sepia *(a)*	8·50	2·50
21		2a. bluish green *(d)* (1936)	13·00	2·25
		a. Imperf (pair)	25·00	£180
22		3a. deep violet *(a)*	2·00	9·50
23		3a. Prussian blue *(d)* (1935?)	20·00	
		a. Imperf (pair)	32·00	£450
24		3½a. violet *(d)* (1934)	7·00	10·00
		a. Imperf (pair)	65·00	£450
25		4a. ultramarine *(a)*	7·00	5·00
26		4a. yellow-brown *(d)* (1937)	35·00	1·75
		a. Imperf (pair)	30·00	£325
27		8a. slate-grey *(a)*	6·50	4·50
28		8a. red-orange *(d)* (1937)	27·00	23·00
29		12a. carmine *(d)* (1934)	5·00	10·00
30	–	1r. black and light blue *(b)*	8·50	15·00
31	–	2r. black and carmine *(b)*	55·00	60·00
32	–	5r. black & brown-orange *(b)*	90·00	95·00

Nos. 30/32 are as Type **7**, but larger, size 23×28 mm.

Five different perforating heads were used for this issue: *(a)* comb 13.6; *(b)* comb 13.9; *(c)* line 13.2; *(d)* line 13.8; *(e)* line 14.2. Values on which each perforation occur are indicated above.

Nos. 21a, 23a, 24a and 26a were specifically ordered by the state government in 1933 and are known used for postage *circa* 1938–42. A plate proof of the 1r. in green and carmine is also known postally used (*Price of pair* £38 *unused*, £400 *used*).

Nos. 16/19 and 28/32 also exist as imperforate plate proofs, but these were never sent to India.

QUARTER ANNA
(8)

9

1940 (1 Aug). *Surch in words as T* **8** *by Times of India Press, Bombay.*

33	7	¼a. on 5r. black and brown-orange *(b)*	15·00	1·75
		a. Surch double (Blk.+G.)	†	£475
34		½a. on 2r. black and carmine *(b)*	25·00	3·25
35		1a. on 1¼a. green *(c) (d) (e)*	25·00	80
		b. Surch inverted *(d)*	90·00	
		c. Surch double *(c)*	£450	
33/5 *Set of* 3			60·00	5·25

(Typo "Times of India" Press, Bombay)

1940–46. P 11.

36	9	¼a. red-orange	2·00	10
37		½a. claret (1941)	3·75	10
38		1a. green (1941)	10·00	10
39		1¼a. yellow-green (1941)	16·00	2·25
		a. Imperf (pair)	£225	
40		2a. turquoise-blue (1941)	11·00	1·00
41		4a. yellow-brown (1946)	16·00	13·00
		Larger size (23×28 mm).		
42		2r. black and carmine (1943)	13·00	£170
43		5r. black and yellow-orange (1943)	12·00	£225
36/43 *Set of* 8			75·00	£375

OFFICIAL STAMPS

SERVICE SERVICE
(S 1) (S 2)

1904–06.

(a) Optd with Type S **1**.

S1	4	¼a. orange (1906)	75	1·25
S2	5	½a. lake	25	10
		a. Opt inverted	24·00	42·00
		b. Opt double	23·00	
		c. Imperf (pair)	75·00	
		d. Brown-lake	35	20
		da. Opt inverted	22·00	
		e. Pair, one without opt	£600	
S3		1a. green	15	20
S4		2a. brown (1905)	30	30
		a. Vert pair, one without opt	£900	
S5		3a. violet (1906)	2·00	3·75
		a. Imperf (pair)	£325	
S6		4a. ultramarine (1905)	5·00	1·50
		(b) Optd with Type S **2**.		
S7	5	½a. lake	10	1·50
		a. Opt double	£700	
S1/7 *Set of* 7			7·75	7·75

Types S **1** and S **2** differ chiefly in the shape of the letter "R".

Indore became part of Madhya Bharat by 1 July 1948.

JAIPUR

PRICES FOR STAMPS ON COVER

No. 1	*from* × 3
No. 2	*from* × 2
Nos. 3/5	*from* × 10

PRICES FOR STAMPS ON COVER

Nos. 6/70	*from* × 4
Nos. 71/80	*from* × 6
Nos. O1/34	*from* × 8

Maharaja Sawai Madho Singh II, 1880–1922

1 1a 2

Chariot of the Sun God, Surya

Type **1** – Value at sides in small letters and characters. "HALF ANNA", shown as one word except for R. 1/1 and 1/3, measuring between 13½ and 15 mm. Sheets of 12 (4×3) with stamps 2 to 2½ mm apart.

Type **1a** – Value in large letters and characters. "HALF ANNA", always with a gap between the two words, measuring between 14½ and 15½ mm. Sheets of 24 (4×6) with stamps 3 to 4 mm apart.

Type **2** – Value in large letters and characters. "HALF ANNA" measuring 16 to 17 mm. Both side inscriptions start below the inner frame line. Sheets of 24 (4×6) with stamps 1½ to 2 mm apart.

(Litho Durbar Press, Jaipur)

1904 (14 July). Roughly perf 14.

1	1	½a. pale blue	£140	£180
		a. Ultramarine	£190	£225
		b. Imperf, *ultramarine*	£375	
2	1a	½a. grey-blue	£2250	£200
		a. Imperf	£350	£600
		b. Ultramarine	–	£325
3	2	½a. pale blue	3·25	7·00
		a. Deep blue	3·50	7·00
		b. Ultramarine	3·75	7·00
		c. Imperf	£350	£350
4	1	1a. dull red	5·50	14·00
		a. Scarlet	5·50	14·00
5		2a. pale green	5·50	14·00
		a. Emerald-green	6·00	

Nos. 1b, 2a and 3c are on gummed paper. Imperforate plate proofs also exist for Nos. 1/5, but these are ungummed.

3 Chariot of the Sun God, Surya

(Recess Perkins, Bacon & Co)

1904. P 12.

6	3	½a. blue	6·50	9·00
		a. Perf 12½	28·00	20·00
		b. Perf comp of 12 and 12½	17·00	20·00
7		1a. brown-red	55·00	55·00
		a. Perf 12½	£150	£150
		b. Perf comp of 12 and 12½	£120	£120
		c. Carmine	2·50	4·50
		ca. Imperf between (vert pair)	£600	£800
		cb. Perf comp of 12 and 12½	10·00	17·00
8		2a. deep green	9·00	15·00
		a. Perf 12½	£190	£130
		b. Perf comp of 12 and 12½	27·00	40·00

Nos. 6b, 7b, 7cb and 8b occur on the bottom two rows of sheets otherwise perforated 12.

1905–08. Wmk "JAs WRIGLEY & SON Ld. 219" "SPECIAL POSTAGE PAPER LONDON" or "PERKINS BACON & Co Ld LONDON" in sheet. P 13½

9	3	¼a. olive-yellow (1906)	85	1·10
10		½a. blue (1906)	3·50	2·75
		a. Indigo	1·50	50
11		1a. brown-red (1906)	8·00	5·00
		a. Bright red (1908)	3·25	50
12		2a. deep green (1906)	3·50	1·50
13		4a. chestnut	7·50	2·25
14		8a. bright violet	4·00	2·75
15		1r. orange-yellow	23·00	21·00
		a. Yellow	24·00	16·00
		b. Yellow-ochre	24·00	27·00
9/15 *Set of* 7			38·00	22·00

4 Chariot of the Sun God, Surya

३ आना
(5)

(Typo Jaipur State Press)

1911. *Thin wove paper. No gum.* Imperf.

16	4	¼a. green	2·50	3·25
		a. Printed double	8·00	
		ab. Ditto, one inverted		
		b. "¼" inverted in right upper corner (R. 1/2)	6·00	
		c. No stop after "STATE" (R. 3/1)	6·00	
17		¼a. greenish yellow	30	1·00
		a. Printed double	2·00	
		b. "¼" inverted in right upper corner (R. 1/2)	1·50	
		c. No stop after "STATE" (R. 3/1)	1·50	

18		½a. ultramarine	30	1·00
		a. Printed double	2·00	
		b. No stop after "STATE" (R. 3/1)	75	
		c. Large "J" in "JAIPUR" (R. 1/2)	75	
		d. "⅓" for "½" at lower left (R. 3/1)	1·50	
		e. "1½a." at lower right (R. 3/2)	1·50	
19		½a. grey-blue	2·75	2·75
		a. No stop after "STATE" (R. 3/1)	4·25	
		b. Large "J" in "JAIPUR" (R. 1/2)	4·25	
		c. "⅓" for "½" at lower left (R. 3/1)	4·75	
		d. "1½a." at lower right (R. 3/2)	5·00	
20		1a. rose-red	50	1·00
		a. Printed double	£200	
21		2a. greyish green	2·75	5·50
		a. Deep green	2·00	6·50
		ab. Printed double	£250	

Issued in sheets of 6 (2×3). There are three recognised settings. Nos. 18d/e and 19c/d come from Setting B, and Nos. 16b/c, 17b/c, 18b/c and 19a/b from Setting C.

One sheet of the ¼a. is known in blue.

(Typo Jaipur State Press)

1912–22. Paper-maker's wmk "DORLING & CO. LONDON" in sheet. P 11.

22	3	¼a. pale olive-yellow	70	1·50
		a. Imperf horiz (vert pair)	£200	£200
		b. Imperf vert (horiz pair)	—	£160
23		¼a. olive	80	1·75
		a. Imperf between (horiz pair)	£190	
		b. Imperf vert (horiz pair)	£200	
		c. Imperf horiz (vert pair)	£200	
		d. *Tête-bêche* (pair)	£500	
24		¼a. bistre	40	1·75
		a. Imperf between (horiz pair)	£200	
		b. Imperf between (vert pair)	†	£375
		c. Imperf horiz (vert pair)	†	£375
		d. Doubly printed	†	£750
25		½a. pale ultramarine	1·50	1·25
		a. Imperf vert (horiz pair)	†	£600
		b. Blue	1·25	1·00
		ba. Imperf between (horiz pair)	£425	
26		1a. carmine (1918)	5·50	5·50
		a. Imperf between (vert pair)	†	£850
		b. Imperf horiz (vert pair)	†	£850
27		1a. rose-red	5·50	11·00
		a. Imperf between (vert pair)	£850	
28		1a. scarlet (1922)	4·00	3·75
		a. Imperf between (vert pair)	£900	£900
29		2a. green (1918)	4·00	5·00
30		4a. chocolate	7·00	10·00
31		4a. pale brown	7·50	11·00
		a. Imperf vert (horiz pair)	£600	
22/31 *Set of 5*			15·00	19·00

Maharaja Sawai Man Singh II 1922–1970

1926. *Surch with T* **5**.

32	3	3a. on 8a. bright violet (R.)	2·00	3·50
		a. Surch inverted	£180	£140
33		3a. on 1r. yellow (R.)	2·75	6·50
		a. Surch inverted	£550	£180
		c. Yellow-ochre	11·00	13·00

1928. *As 1913–18 issue.* Wmk "DORLING & CO. LONDON" (½a., 1a., 2a.) or "OVERLAND BANK" (all values) in sheet. *No gum.* P 12.

34	3	½a. ultramarine	3·00	4·00
		a. Perf comp of 12 and 11	16·00	9·00
35		1a. rose-red	27·00	17·00
		a. Imperf between (vert pair)	£600	
36		1a. scarlet	42·00	12·00
		a. Perf comp of 12 and 11	60·00	25·00
37		2a. green	90·00	30·00
		a. Perf comp of 12 and 11	£250	65·00
39		1r. orange-vermilion	£400	£550

The "OVERLAND BANK" paper has a coarser texture. The ½a. and 2a. values also exist on this paper perforated 11, but such stamps are difficult to distinguish from examples of Nos. 25 and 29.

6 Chariot of the Sun God, Surya

7 Maharaja Sawai Man Singh II

8 Elephant and State Banner

9 Sowar in Armour

10 Common Peafowl

11 Bullock carriage

12 Elephant carriage

13 Albert Museum

14 Sireh Deorhi Gate

15 Chandra Mahal

16 Amber Palace

17 Maharajas Jai Singh and Man Singh

(Des T. I. Archer. Litho Indian Security Printing Press, Nasik)

1931 (14 Mar). *Investiture of Maharaja. T* **6/17**. No wmk. P 14.

40	6	¼a. black and deep lake	3·00	2·75
41	7	½a. black and violet	50	20
42	8	1a. black and blue	9·00	9·50
43	9	2a. black and buff	9·00	9·50
44	10	2½a. black and carmine	32·00	60·00
45	11	3a. black and myrtle	19·00	45·00
46	12	4a. black and olive-green	19·00	55·00
47	13	6a. black and deep blue	6·00	55·00
48	14	8a. black and chocolate	20·00	90·00
49	15	1r. black and pale olive	40·00	£325
50	16	2r. black and yellow-green	42·00	£375
51	17	5r. black and purple	55·00	£400
40/51 *Set of 12*			£225	£1300

Eighteen of these sets were issued for presentation purposes with a special overprint "INVESTITURE-MARCH 14,1931" in red (*Price for set of 12 £3750 unused, £5000 used*).

18 Maharaja Sawai Man Singh II

One
Rupee
(19)

(Des T. I. Archer. Litho Indian Security Printing Press, Nasik)

1932–46. P 14.

(a) Inscr "POSTAGE & REVENUE".

52	18	1a. black and blue	3·25	1·75
53		2a. black and buff	4·50	2·75
54		4a. black and grey-green	4·50	12·00
55		8a. black and chocolate	6·00	15·00
56		1r. black and yellow-bistre	27·00	£120
57		2r. black and yellow-green	90·00	£475
52/7 *Set of 6*			£120	£550

(b) Inscr "POSTAGE".

58	7	¼a. black and brown-lake	50	50
59		¾a. black and brown-red (1943?)	8·00	4·25
60		1a. black and blue (1943?)	9·50	4·50
61		2a. black and buff (1943?)	9·50	5·00
62		2½a. black and carmine	4·50	3·25
63		3a. black and green	4·00	70
64		4a. black and grey-green (1943?)	48·00	£160
65		6a. black and deep blue	6·00	30·00
		a. Black and pale blue (1946)	9·00	80·00
66		8a. black and chocolate (1946)	28·00	£130
67		1r. black and yellow-bistre (1946)	20·00	£180
58/67 *Set of 10*			£120	£450

1936. *Nos. 57 and 51 surch with T* **19**.

68	18	1r. on 2r. black and yellow-green (R.)	10·00	£110
69	17	1r. on 5r. black and purple	10·00	85·00

पाव आना
(20)

21 Palace Gate

22 Maharaja and Amber Palace

23 Map of Jaipur

24 Observatory

25 Wind Palace

26 Coat of Arms

27 Amber Fort Gate

28 Chariot of the Sun

29 Maharaja's portrait between State Flags

1938 (Dec). *No. 41 surch "QUARTER ANNA" in Devanagari, T* **20**.

70	7	¼a. on ½a. black and violet (R.)	14·00	17·00

(Recess D.L.R.)

1947 (Dec)–**48**. *Silver Jubilee of Maharaja's Accession to Throne. T* **21/9**. P 13½×14.

71	21	¼a. red-brown and green (5.48)	1·50	5·00
72	22	½a. green and violet	50	4·50
73	23	¾a. black and lake (5.48)	1·50	6·00
74	24	1a. red-brown and ultramarine	1·00	4·75
75	25	2a. violet and scarlet	1·00	5·00
76	26	3a. green and black (5.48)	1·75	6·50
77	27	4a. ultramarine and brown	1·00	5·00
78	28	8a. vermilion and brown	1·00	6·00
79	29	1r. purple and green (5.48)	2·75	45·00
71/9 *Set of 9*			10·50	80·00

3 PIES

(30)

1947 (1 Dec). *No. 41 surch with T* **30**.

80	7	3p. on ½a. black and violet (R.)	17·00	27·00
		a. "PIE" for "PIES"	50·00	£110
		b. Bars at left vertical	75·00	£120
		c. Surch inverted	48·00	42·00
		d. Surch inverted and "PIE" for "PIES"	£250	£225
		e. Surch double, one inverted	75·00	55·00
		f. As variety e, but inverted surch showing "PIE" for "PIES"	£425	£400

There were three settings of Type **30**, each applied to quarter sheets of 30 (6×5). No. 80a occurs in two of these settings on R. 5/5 and one of these settings also shows No. 80b on R. 6/1.

OFFICIAL STAMPS

SERVICE
(O 1)

SERVICE
(O 2)

1928 (13 Nov)–**31**. *T* **3** *typographed. No gum (except for Nos. O6/a).* P 11, 12, or compound. Wmk "DORLING & CO. LONDON" (4a.) or "OVERLAND BANK" (others).

(a) Optd with Type O **1**.

O1		¼a. olive	2·50	2·75
		a. Bistre	2·50	2·25
O2		½a. pale ultramarine (Blk.)	1·25	20
		a. Imperf between (horiz pair)	£400	£400
		b. Imperf between (vert pair)	†	£800
		c. Opt inverted	†	£450
		d. Opt double (R. and Blk.)	†	£550
O3		½a. pale ultramarine (R.) (13.10.30)	2·75	30
		a. Imperf horiz (vert pair)	£800	
		b. Stamp doubly printed	†	£550
O3c		1a. rose-red	1·50	30
		d. Imperf between (horiz pair)	†	£800
O4		1a. scarlet	1·75	50
		a. Opt inverted	£900	£900
		b. Imperf between (horiz pair)	†	£850
O5		2a. green	1·50	40
		a. Imperf between (vert pair)	†	£950
		b. Imperf between (horiz pair)	£950	£950
O6		4a. pale brown (with gum)	5·50	1·75
		a. Chocolate (with gum)	2·00	1·75
O7		8a. bright violet (R.) (13.10.30)	17·00	55·00
O8		1r. orange-vermilion	38·00	£375

(b) Optd with Type O **2**.

O9		½a. ultramarine (Blk.) (11.2.31)	£180	15
		a. Imperf vert (horiz pair)	†	£900
O10		½a. ultramarine (R.) (15.10.30)	£200	15
		a. Imperf between (vert pair)	†	£900
O11		8a. bright violet (11.2.31)	£450	£200
O12		1r. orange-vermilion (11.2.31)	£475	£275

SERVICE
(O 3)

आध आना
(O 4)

1931–37. *Nos. 41/3 and 46 optd at Nasik with Type O* **3**, *in red.*

O13	7	½a. black and violet	30	10
O14	8	1a. black and blue	£275	3·00
O15	9	2a. black and buff (1936)	4·50	5·50
O16	12	4a. black and olive-green (1937)	48·00	40·00
O13/16 *Set of 4*			£300	45·00

1932. *No. O5 surch with Type* O **4**.

O17	**3**	½a. on 2a green	£150	2·00

1932–37. *Nos. 52/6 optd at Nasik with Type* O **3**, *in red.*

O18	**18**	1a. black and blue	4·50	15
O19		2a. black and buff	5·50	15
O20		4a. black and grey-green (1937)	£375	11·00
O21		8a. black and chocolate	12·00	1·10
O22		1r. black and yellow-bistre	30·00	26·00
O18/22 *Set of* 5			£400	35·00

1936–46. *Stamps of 1932–46, inscr* "POSTAGE".

(a) Optd at Nasik with Type O **3**, *in red.*

O23	**7**	¼a. black and brown-lake (1936)	40	10
O24		¾a. black and brown-red (1944)	1·50	50
O25		1a. black and blue (1941?)	4·50	30
O26		2a. black and buff (date?)	4·00	3·25
O27		2½a. black and carmine (1946)	11·00	£110
O28		4a. black and grey-green (1942)	6·00	7·50
O29		8a. black and chocolate (1943)	4·00	8·50
O30		1r. black and yellow-bistre (date?)	40·00	
O23/9 *Set of* 7			28·00	£120

(b) Optd locally as Type O **2** *(16 mm long), in black.*

O31	**7**	¼a. black and red-brown (1936)	90·00	75·00

9 PIES

(O 5)

1947. *No. O25 surch with Type* O **5**, *in red.*

O32	**7**	9p. on 1a. black and blue	3·75	3·75

1947 (Dec). *No. O13 surch as T* **30**, *but "3 PIES" placed higher.*

O33	**7**	3p. on ½a. black and violet (R.)	6·00	14·00
		a. Surch double, one inverted	48·00	48·00
		ab. "PIE" for "PIES" in inverted surcharge	£275	£300
		c. Surch inverted	—	£1500

1948 (Dec). *No. O13 surch "THREE-QUARTER ANNA" in Devanagari, as T* **20**, *but with two bars on each side.*

O34	**7**	¾a. on ½a. black and violet (R.)	19·00	20·00
		a. Surch double	£1500	£1400

There are three different types of surcharge in the setting of 30, which vary in one or other of the Devanagari characters.

Jaipur became part of Rajasthan by 7 April 1949.

JAMMU AND KASHMIR

PRICES FOR STAMPS ON COVER

Nos. 1/73	*from* × 3
Nos. 74/84	*from* × 2
No. 85	—
Nos. 86/9	*from* × 2
Nos. 90/101	*from* × 10
Nos. 101*b*/23	*from* × 5
Nos. 124/36	*from* × 10
Nos. 138/9	*from* × 100
Nos. 140/61*a*	*from* × 15
Nos. 162/8	*from* × 5
No. O1	*from* × 2
Nos. O2/4	*from* × 4
No. O5	—
Nos. O6/14	*from* × 30
Nos. O15/18	—

ILLUSTRATIONS. Designs of Jammu and Kashmir are illustrated actual size.

Maharaja Ranhir Singh, 1857–1885

1 (½a.)

2 (1a.)

3 (4a.)

Characters denoting the value (on the circular stamps only) are approximately as shown in the central circles of the stamps illustrated above.

These characters were taken from Punjabi merchants' notation and were not familiar to most of the inhabitants of the state. Type **1** was certainly the ½ anna value, but there has long been controversy over the correct face values of Types **2** and **3**.

The study of surviving material suggests that, to some extent, this confusion involved contemporary post office officials. Although covers posted at Jammu, where the stamps were in use for twelve years, show Type **2** used as the 1a. value and Type **3** as the 4a., those originating from Srinagar (Kashmir) during 1866–68 show both Types **2** and **3** used as 1a. stamps.

In the following listing we have followed contemporary usage at Jammu and this reflects the prevailing opinion amongst modern authorities.

GUM. The stamps of Jammu and Kashmir were issued without gum.

PRICES. Prices for the circular stamps, Nos. 1/49, are for cut-square examples. Cut-to-shape examples are worth from 10% to 20% of these prices, according to condition.

A. *Handstamped in watercolours*

1866 (23 Mar). *Native paper, thick to thin, usually having the appearance of laid paper and tinted grey or brown. For Jammu and Kashmir.*

1	**1**	½a. grey-black	£250	£100
2		½a. ultramarine	£3000	£3000
3	**2**	1a. royal blue	—	£500
3*a*		1a. ultramarine	£600	£120
4		1a. grey-black	£1600	£1400
5	**3**	4a. royal blue		
5*a*		4a. ultramarine	£850	£425

No. 4 may be an error of colour. It is only known used in Kashmir.

1867–76. *Reissued for use in Jammu only.*

6	**3**	4a. grey-black	£2250	
7		4a. indigo	£2500	£1400
8		4a. red (1869)	£100	£140
9		4a. orange-red (1872)	£225	£325
10		4a. orange (1872)		
11		4a. carmine-red (1876)	£1200	

1874–76. *Special Printings.*

12	**1**	½a. red	£100	£350
12*a*		½a. orange-red	£700	£750
13	**2**	1a. red	£200	£325
13*a*		1a. orange-red	£700	£750
13*b*		1a. orange	£900	
14	**1**	½a. deep black	26·00	£180
		a. *Tête-bêche* (pair)	£850	
15	**2**	1a. deep black	£325	
16	**3**	4a. deep black	£300	
17	**1**	½a. bright blue (1876)	£375	£450
18	**2**	1a. bright blue (1876)	£130	£375
		a. *Tête-bêche* (pair)	£1600	
19	**3**	4a. bright blue (1876)	£225	
20	**1**	½a. emerald-green	£120	£300
21	**2**	1a. emerald-green	£130	£300
22	**3**	4a. emerald-green	£300	£475
23	**1**	½a. yellow	£750	£950
24	**2**	1a. yellow	£950	
25	**3**	4a. yellow	£600	
25*a*		4a. deep blue-black (1876)	£1600	£900

These special printings were available for use, but little used.

B. *Handstamped in oil colours. Heavy blurred prints*

1877 (June)–**78**.

(a) Native paper.

26	**1**	½a. red	38·00	60·00
27	**2**	1a. red	48·00	£190
28	**3**	4a. red	£325	£550
29	**1**	½a. black	38·00	65·00
32		½a. slate-blue	£160	£275
34	**2**	1a. slate-blue	38·00	£300
35	**1**	½a. sage-green	£140	
36	**2**	1a. sage-green	£150	
37	**3**	4a. sage-green	£150	

(b) European laid paper, medium to thick.

38	**1**	½a. red	—	£1200
39	**3**	4a. red	£425	£500
41	**1**	½a. black	32·00	65·00
		a. Printed both sides	£950	
		b. *Tête-bêche* (pair)	£750	
44		½a. slate-blue	55·00	£300
45	**2**	1a. slate-blue	60·00	£400
46	**3**	4a. slate-blue	£900	£900
47		4a. sage-green	£1500	£1700
48	**1**	½a. yellow	£160	

(c) Thick yellowish wove paper.

49	**1**	½a. red (1878)	—	£950

Forgeries exist of the ½a. and 1a. in types which were at one time supposed to be authentic.

Reprints and imitations (of which some of each were found in the official remainder stock) exist in a great variety of fancy colours, both on native paper, usually thinner and smoother than that of the originals, and on various thin European *wove* papers, on which the originals were never printed.

The imitations, which do not agree in type with the above illustrations, are also to be found on *laid* paper.

All the reprints, etc. are in oil colours or printer's ink. The originals in oil colour are usually blurred, particularly when on native paper. The reprints, etc. are usually clear.

FOR USE IN JAMMU

4

T **4** to **11** have a star at the top of the oval band; the characters denoting the value are in the upper part of the inner oval. All are dated 1923, corresponding with A.D. 1866.

T **4**. *Printed in blocks of four, three varieties of ½ anna and one of 1 anna.*

1867 (Sept). *In watercolour on native paper.*

52	½a. grey-black	£1200	£425
53	1a. grey-black	£3000	£1800
54	½a. indigo	£425	£325
55	1a. indigo	£900	£425
56	½a. deep ultramarine	£325	£190
57	1a. deep ultramarine	£800	£425
58	½a. deep violet-blue	£225	£110
59	1a. deep violet-blue	£850	£425

1868 (May)–**72.** *In watercolour on native paper.*

60	½a. red (*shades*)	8·50	4·50
61	1a. red (*shades*)	20·00	13·00
62	½a. orange-red	£250	80·00
63	1a. orange-red	£850	£350
64	½a. orange (1872)	£130	£150
65	1a. orange (1872)	£3000	£1800

1874–76. *Special printings; in watercolour on native paper.*

66	½a. bright blue (1876)	£1600	£375
67	1a. bright blue (1876)	£475	£500
68	½a. emerald-green	£2500	£1300
69	1a. emerald-green	£3500	£2000
69*a*	½a. jet-black	£160	£190
69*b*	1a. jet-black	£2500	£1800

1877 (June)–**78.** *In oil colour.*

(a) Native paper.

70	½a. red	12·00	9·00
71	1a. red	38·00	27·00
72	½a. brown-red (1878)	—	45·00
73	1a. brown-red (1878)	—	£150
74	½a. black	†	£1200
75	1a. black	†	£2750
76	½a. deep blue-black	†	£1800
77	1a. deep blue-black	†	£4500

(b) Laid paper (medium or thick).

78	½a. red	—	£1100

(c) Thick wove paper.

79	½a. red	†	£475
80	1a. red		

(d) Thin laid, bâtonné paper.

84	½a. red	†	£1800
85	1a. red	£4500	

The circular and rectangular stamps listed under the heading "Special Printings" did not supersede those in *red*, which was the normal colour for Jammu down to 1878. It is not known for what reason other colours were used during that period, but these stamps were printed in 1874 or 1875 and were certainly put into use. The rectangular stamps were again printed in *black* (jet-black, as against the greyish black of the 1867 printings) at that time, and impressions of the two periods can also be distinguished by the obliterations, which until 1868 were in *magenta* and after that in *black*.

There are reprints of these, in *oil* colour, *brown-red* and *bright blue*, on native paper; they are very clearly printed, which is not the case with the originals in *oil* colour.

4a

1877 (Sept). *Provisional. Seal obliterator of Jammu handstamped in red watercolour on pieces of native paper, and used as a ½ anna stamp.*

86	**4a**	(½a.) rose-red	—	£1300

FOR USE IN KASHMIR

5

1866 (Sept(?)). *Printed from a single die. Native laid paper.*

87	**5**	½a. black	£3500	£450

Forgeries of this stamp are commonly found, copied from an illustration in *Le Timbre-Poste*.

6 (½a.)

7 (1a.)

1867 (Apr). *Native laid paper.*

88	**6**	½a. black	£1500	£200
89	**7**	1a. black	£2750	£500

Printed in sheets of 25 (5×5), the four top rows being ½a. and the bottom row 1a.

8 (¼a.)

9 (2a.)

10 (4a.)

11 (8a.)

1867–77. *Native laid paper.*

90	**8**	¼a. black	4·50	4·75
		a. *Tête-bêche* (vert pair)	£5500	
91	**6**	½a. ultramarine (6.67)	5·00	1·75
		a. Bisected (¼a.) (on cover) (1877)	†	£9000
92		½a. violet-blue (1870)	9·00	4·50
93	**7**	1a. ultramarine (6.67)	£4250	£1700
94		1a. orange (7.67)	15·00	12·00
95		1a. brown-orange (1868)	15·00	12·00
96		1a. orange-vermilion (1876)	19·00	13·00
97	**9**	2a. yellow	20·00	22·00
98		2a. buff	29·00	24·00
99	**10**	4a. emerald-green	50·00	48·00
		a. *Tête-bêche* (pair)	£1300	
		b. Stamp sideways (in pair)	£4500	
100		4a. sage-green	£350	£180
100*a*		4a. myrtle-green	£850	£850
101	**11**	8a. red (1868)	50·00	48·00
		a. *Tête-bêche* (pair)	£5000	£5000

Of the above, the ½a. and 1a. were printed from the same plate of 25 as Nos. 88/9, the ¼a. and 2a. from a new plate of 10 (5×2), the top row being ¼a. and the lower 2a., and the 4a. and 8a. from single dies. Varieties at one time catalogued upon European papers were apparently never put into circulation, though some of them were printed while these stamps were still in use.

Nos. 86 to 101 are in watercolour.

No. 91a was used at Srinagar, in conjunction with an India ½a., and was cancelled "KASHMIR 5/L-6".

FOR USE IN JAMMU AND KASHMIR

In the following issues there are 15 varieties on the sheets of the ⅛a., ¼a. and ½a.; 20 varieties of the 1a. and 2a. and 8 varieties of the 4a. and 8a. The value is in the lower part of the central oval.

12 (¼a.)

13 (½a.)

14 (1a.)

15 (2a.)

16 (4a.)

17 (8a.)

1878 (May)–**79**. *Provisional printings.*

I. *Ordinary white laid paper, of varying thickness.*

(*a*) *Rough perf 10 to 12 (i) or 13 to 16 (ii).*

101*b*	**12**	¼a. red (i)		
102	**13**	½a. red (i)	14·00	17·00
103	**14**	1a. red (i)	£1300	
104	**13**	½a. slate-violet (i)	75·00	75·00
104*a*	**14**	1a. violet (ii)		
104*b*	**15**	2a. violet (i)	£1800	

(*b*) Imperf.

105	**13**	½a. slate-violet (*shades*)	18·00	16·00
106	**14**	1a. slate-purple	27·00	28·00
107		1a. mauve	45·00	42·00
108	**15**	2a. violet	29·00	29·00
109		2a. bright mauve	40·00	38·00
110		2a. slate-blue	65·00	65·00
111		2a. dull blue	£120	£120
112	**12**	¼a. red	23·00	21·00
113	**13**	½a. red	10·00	11·00
114	**14**	1a. red	9·50	12·00
115	**15**	2a. red	90·00	90·00
116	**16**	4a. red	£225	£190

II. *Medium wove paper.*

(*a*) Rough perf 10 to 12.

117	**13**	½a. red	–	£325

(*b*) Imperf.

117*b*	**12**	¼a. red		
118	**13**	½a. red	18·00	10·00
119	**14**	1a. red	16·00	12·00
120	**15**	2a. red	70·00	

III. *Thick wove paper.* Imperf.

121	**13**	½a. red	32·00	60·00
122	**14**	1a. red	50·00	25·00
123	**15**	2a. red	22·00	26·00

Of the above stamps those in red were intended for use in Jammu and those in shades of violet and blue for use in Kashmir.

1879. *Definitive issue. Thin wove paper, fine to coarse.*

(*a*) Rough perf 10 to 12.

124	**13**	½a. red	£375	£275

(*b*) Imperf.

125	**12**	¼a. red	3·75	4·50
126	**13**	½a. red	1·00	1·00
		a. Bisected (¼a.) on cover or postcard		
127	**14**	1a. red	2·50	3·50
		a. Bisected (½a.) on cover	†	£5500
128	**15**	2a. red	3·25	4·75
129	**16**	4a. red	11·00	11·00
130	**17**	8a. red	12·00	13·00

The plates were transferred from Jammu to Srinagar in early 1881 when further printings in red and all orange stamps were produced.

1880 (Mar). *Provisional printing in watercolour on thin bâtonné paper.* Imperf.

130*a*	**12**	¼a. ultramarine	£900	£600

1881–83. *As Nos. 124 to 130. Colour changed.*

(*a*) Rough perf 10 to 12.

130*b*	**13**	½a. orange		

(*b*) Imperf.

131	**12**	¼a. orange	12·00	16·00
132	**13**	½a. orange	24·00	17·00
		a. Bisected (¼a.) on cover		
133	**14**	1a. orange	25·00	14·00
		a. Bisected (½a.) (on cover)	†	£9000
134	**15**	2a. orange	18·00	14·00
135	**16**	4a. orange	45·00	55·00
136	**17**	8a. orange	75·00	80·00

Nos. 126a and 133a were used at Leh between April and July 1883.

Nos. 125/30 and 132/6 were re-issued between 1890 and 1894 and used concurrently with the stamps which follow. Such re-issues can be identified by the "three circle" cancellations, introduced in December 1890.

18 (⅛a.)

1883–94. *New colours. Thin wove papers, toned, coarse to fine, or fine white (1889).* Imperf.

138	**18**	⅛a. yellow-brown	1·50	2·00
139		⅛a. yellow	1·50	2·00
140	**12**	¼a. sepia	1·25	1·00
141		¼a. brown	1·25	1·00
		a. Double impression	£1200	
142		¼a. pale brown	1·25	1·00
		a. Error. Green	75·00	
143	**13**	½a. dull blue	8·00	
144		½a. bright blue	55·00	
145		½a. vermilion	1·25	85
146		½a. rose	1·60	1·00
147		½a. orange-red	1·10	85
148	**14**	1a. greenish grey	1·00	1·00
149		1a. bright green	1·50	1·50
		a. Double impression		
150		1a. dull green	1·00	1·00
151		1a. blue-green	2·00	
152	**15**	2a. red/*yellow*	2·75	1·25
153		2a. red/*yellow-green*	3·75	4·00
154		2a. red/*deep green*	19·00	19·00
155	**16**	4a. deep green	4·00	4·75
156		4a. green	4·25	4·00
157		4a. pale green	4·25	3·25
158		4a. sage-green	4·75	
159	**17**	8a. pale blue	9·00	10·00
159*a*		8a. deep blue	13·00	15·00
160		8a. bright blue	12·00	14·00
161		8a. indigo-blue	14·00	16·00
161*a*		8a. slate-lilac	10·00	22·00

Well-executed forgeries of the ¼a. to 8a. have come from India, mostly postmarked; they may be detected by the type, which does not agree with any variety on the genuine sheets, and also, in the low values, by the margins being filled in with colour, all but a thin white frame round the stamp. The forgeries of the 8a. are in sheets of eight like the originals.

Other forgeries of nearly all values also exist, showing all varieties of type. All values are on thin, coarse wove paper.

In February 1890, a forgery, in watercolour, of the ½a. orange on thin wove or on thin laid paper appeared, and many have been found genuinely used during 1890 and 1891 (*Price* £5).

Nos. 143 and 144 were never issued.

Examples of the ¼a. brown, ½a. orange-red and 1a. green on wove paper exist with clean-cut perf 12.

There is a reference in the Jammu and Kashmir State Administration Report covering 1890–91 to the re-introduction of perforating and the machine-gumming of paper at the Jammu printing works.

The few known examples, the ¼a. being only recorded used, the others unused or used, would appear to date from this period, but there is, as yet, no direct confirmation as to their status.

Maharaja Partap Singh, 1885–1925

1887–94. *Thin creamy laid paper.* Imperf.

162	**18**	⅛a. yellow	60·00	70·00
163	**12**	¼a. brown	9·00	7·00
164	**13**	½a. brown-red (March 1887)	–	75·00
165		½a. orange-red	10·00	6·50
166	**14**	1a. grey-green	£100	£100
168	**17**	8a. blue (*Printed in watercolour*)	£150	£150
		a. On wove paper	£100	£100

19

T **19** represents a ¼a. stamp, which exists in sheets of twelve varieties, in *red* and *black* on thin wove and laid papers, also in *red* on native paper, but which does not appear ever to have been issued for use. It was first seen in 1886.

The ¼a. *brown* and the 4a. *green* both exist on ordinary white laid paper and the ½a. *red* on native paper. None of these are known to have been in use.

OFFICIAL STAMPS

1878.

I. *White laid paper.*

(*a*) Rough perf 10 to 12.

O1	**13**	½a. black	–	£2000

(*b*) Imperf.

O2	**13**	½a. black	£100	95·00
O3	**14**	1a. black	70·00	70·00
O4	**15**	2a. black	55·00	60·00

II. *Medium wove paper.* Imperf.

O5	**14**	1a. black	£350	

1880–94. *Thin wove papers, toned, coarse to fine, or fine white (1889).* Imperf.

O6	**12**	¼a. black	1·75	2·00
		a. Double print	£200	
O7	**13**	½a. black	15	75
		a. Printed both sides	£450	
O8	**14**	1a. black	20	1·00
O9	**15**	2a. black	30	45
O10	**16**	4a. black	1·25	1·75
O11	**17**	8a. black	2·50	1·10

1887–94. *Thin creamy laid paper.* Imperf.

O12	**12**	¼a. black	8·50	9·00
O13	**13**	½a. black	4·75	4·75
O14	**14**	1a. black	2·75	3·50
O15	**15**	2a. black	15·00	
O16	**16**	4a. black	55·00	65·00
O17	**17**	8a. black	28·00	50·00

1889. *Stout white wove paper.* Imperf.

O18	**12**	¼a. black	£250	£160

The stamps of Jammu and Kashmir have been obsolete since 1 November 1894.

JASDAN

PRICES FOR STAMPS ON COVER	
Nos. 1/2	*from* × 2
No. 3	*from* × 3
Nos. 4/6	*from* × 4

Darbar Ala Khachar, 1919–1971

1 Sun

(Typo L. V. Indap & Co, Bombay)

1942 (15 Mar)–**47**. *Stamps from booklet panes.* Various perfs.

1	**1**	1a. deep myrtle-green (P 10½)	£1300	£850
2		1a. light green (P 12)	£650	£650
3		1a. light green (P 10½) (1943)	£160	£190
4		1a. pale yellow-green (P 8½–9) (1946)	20·00	£160
5		1a. dull yellow-green (P 10) (1945)	30·00	£180
6		1a. bluish green (P 8½–9) (1947)	24·00	£160

Nos. 1/4 were issued in panes of four with the stamps imperforate on one or two sides; Nos. 5/6 were in panes of eight perforated all round.

A 1a. rose with the arms of Jasdan in the centre is a fiscal stamp.

Jasdan was merged with the United State of Kathiawar (later Saurashtra) by 15 April 1948.

JHALAWAR

PRICES FOR STAMPS ON COVER
Nos. 1/2 *from* × 30

Maharaj Rana Zalim Singh, 1875–1896

1 (1 paisa)

2 (¼ anna)

(Figure of an Apsara, "RHEMBA", a dancing nymph of the Hindu Paradise)

1886–90. *Typo in horizontal strips of 12. Laid paper. No gum.*

1	**1**	1p. yellow-green	4·75	15·00
		a. Blue-green	£120	55·00
2	**2**	¼a. green (*shades*)	1·25	2·50

The stamps formerly listed as on wove paper are from sheets on laid paper, with the laid paper lines almost invisible.

The Maharaj Rana was deposed in 1896 and much of the state's territory transferred to Kotah on 1 January 1899.

Raj (Maharaj from 1918) Rana Rhawani Singh, 1899–1929

The stamps of Jhalawar have been obsolete since 1 November 1900.

JIND

PRICES FOR STAMPS ON COVER
The stamps of Jind are very rare used on cover.

ILLUSTRATIONS. Designs of Jind are illustrated actual size.

Raja Raghubir Singh, 1864–1887

J **1** (½a.)

J **2** (1a.)

J **3** (2a.)

J **4** (4a.)

J **5** (8a.)

(Litho Jind State Rajah's Press, Sungroor)

1874. *Thin yellowish paper.* Imperf.

J1	J **1**	½a. blue	7·00	4·25
		a. No frame to value. (Retouched all over) (R. 4/7)	£375	£200
J2	J **2**	1a. rosy mauve	7·00	6·50
J3	J **3**	2a. yellow	1·00	4·50
J4		2a. brown-buff	£250	£140
J5	J **4**	4a. green	25·00	6·00
J6	J **5**	8a. dull purple	£650	£180
J6*a*		8a. bluish violet	£225	95·00
J7		8a. slate-blue	£190	85·00

Nos. J1/7 were produced from two sets of stones. Those from the first set had rather blurred impressions, but those from the second are clearer with a conspicuous white frame around the value. Nos. J4 and J6*a*/13 were only printed from the second set.

1876. *Bluish laid card-paper. No gum.* Imperf.

J8	J **1**	½a. blue	1·00	4·75
J9	J **2**	1a. purple	2·75	11·00
J10	J **3**	2a. brown	4·25	15·00
J11	J **4**	4a. green	3·75	15·00
J11*a*	J **5**	8a. bluish violet	9·00	22·00
J12		8a. slate-blue	7·50	11·00
J13		8a. steel-blue	9·00	16·00

Stocks of the ½a. (No. J8) and 2a. (No. J4) were perforated 12 in 1885 for use as fiscal stamps.

J **6** (¼a.)

J **7** (½a.)

J **8** (1a.)

J **9** (2a.)

J **10** (4a.)

J **11** (8a.)

(Litho Jind State Rajah's Press, Sungroor)

1882–85. *Types J* **6** *to J* **11**. *No gum.*

A. Imperf *(1882–4).*

(a) Thin yellowish wove paper.

J15	¼a. buff (*shades*)	30	1·50
J16	¼a. red-brown	30	1·50
	a. Doubly printed	50·00	
J17	½a. lemon	2·50	1·75
J18	½a. buff	2·00	1·50
J19	½a. brown-buff	80	60
J20	1a. brown (*shades*)	1·75	3·25
J21	2a. blue	2·00	9·00
J22	2a. deep blue	2·50	1·00
J23	4a. sage-green	1·50	1·00
J24	4a. blue-green	2·00	3·00
J25	8a. red	6·50	4·50

(b) Various thick laid papers.

J26	¼a. brown-buff	1·25	
J27	½a. lemon	1·25	
J28	½a. brown-buff		
J29	1a. brown	1·25	2·50
J30	2a. blue	18·00	21·00
J31	8a. red	2·50	11·00

(c) Thick white wove paper.

J32	¼a. brown-buff	18·00	
J33	½a. brown-buff	35·00	
J34	1a. brown	6·00	
J35	8a. red	4·75	11·00

B. Perf 12 *(1885).*

(a) Thin yellowish wove paper.

J36	¼a. buff (*shades*)	1·00	2·75
	a. Doubly printed	95·00	
J37	¼a. red-brown	3·50	
J38	½a. lemon	£160	£160
J39	½a. buff	60	3·75
J40	½a. brown-buff	3·00	5·50
J41	1a. brown (*shades*)	2·50	5·50
J42	2a. blue	3·75	10·00
J43	2a. deep blue	2·75	6·00
J44	4a. sage-green	5·00	11·00
J45	4a. blue-green	2·00	
	a. Imperf vert (horiz pair)	£600	
J46	8a. red	12·00	

(b) Various thick laid papers.

J47	¼a. brown-buff	8·50	
J48	½a. lemon	£130	26·00
J49	1a. brown	1·50	
J50	2a. blue	24·00	28·00
J51	8a. red	2·50	10·00

(c) Thick white wove paper.

J52	1a. brown		
J53	8a. red	10·00	

The perforated stamps ceased to be used for postal purposes in July 1885, but were used as fiscals to at least the mid-1920s. Other varieties exist, but they must either be fiscals or reprints, and it is not quite certain that all those listed above were issued as early as 1885.

Jind became a Convention State and from 1 July 1885 used overprinted Indian stamps.

KISHANGARH

PRICES FOR STAMPS ON COVER

Nos. 1/3	—
Nos. 4/91	*from* × 8
Nos. O1/32	*from* × 30

GUM. The stamps of Kishangarh were issued without gum, *except for* Nos. 42/50 and O17/24.

Maharaja Sardul Singh, 1879–1900

1

1899–1900. *Medium wove paper. Typo from a plate of 8 (4×2).*

1	**1**	1a. green (*imperf*)	22·00	60·00
2		1a. green (*pin-perf*) (1900)	75·00	

1900. *Thin white wove paper. Printed from a single die.* Imperf.

3	**1**	1a. blue	£400	

ILLUSTRATIONS. Types **2** to **10a** are shown actual size.

2 (¼a.)

3 (½a.)

4 (1a.)

5 (2a.) Maharaja Sardul Singh

6 (4a.)

7 (1r.)

8 (2r.)

9 (5r.)

1899 (Sept)–**1901**. *Thin white wove paper.*

(a) Imperf.

4	**2**	¼a. green (1900)	£550	£800
5		¼a. carmine	8·50	
		a. Rose-pink	1·25	2·75
6		¼a. magenta	5·00	5·00
		a. Doubly printed	£110	
7	**3**	½a. lilac (1900)	£160	£325
8		½a. red (1899)	£2500	£1300
9		½a. green (1899)	38·00	42·00
10		½a. pale yellow-olive	48·00	48·00
11		½a. slate-blue (1900)	42·00	42·00
		b. Deep blue	6·50	7·50
		c. Light blue	1·60	1·75
		ca. Pair, one stamp sideways	£1400	
12	**4**	1a. slate	5·00	5·00
		a. Laid paper	50·00	
12*b*		1a. pink	75·00	£200
13		1a. mauve	6·50	5·50
		a. Laid paper	40·00	
14		1a. brown-lilac	1·10	1·00
		a. Laid paper	32·00	
15	**5**	2a. dull orange	5·00	4·50
		a. Laid paper	£600	£500
16	**6**	4a. chocolate	6·00	
		a. Lake-brown	6·00	10·00
		b. Chestnut	6·00	10·00
		c. Laid paper (*shades*)	85·00	85·00
17	**7**	1r. dull green	24·00	35·00
18		1r. brown-lilac	20·00	25·00
19	**8**	2r. brown-red	85·00	£130
		a. Laid paper	65·00	
20	**9**	5r. mauve	80·00	£100
		a. Laid paper	80·00	

(b) Pin-perf 12½ or 14 *(from Nov 1899).*

21	**2**	¼a. green	£275	£475
		a. Imperf between (pair)	£1300	
22		¼a. carmine	6·00	7·00
		a. Rose-pink	25	40
		ab. *Tête-bêche* (horiz pair)	£1500	
		ac. Doubly printed	£110	
		ad. Trebly printed	£300	
		b. Rose		
23		¼a. magenta	5·00	7·00
		a. Bright purple		
		ab. Doubly printed		
24	**3**	½a. green	18·00	26·00
		a. Imperf between (pair)	£180	
25		½a. pale yellow-olive	13·00	16·00
		a. Imperf vert (horiz pair)	£180	
		b. Imperf between (horiz pair)	†	£425
26		½a. deep blue	2·50	3·25
		a. Light blue	1·00	50
		ab. Doubly printed	£140	£140
27	**4**	1a. slate	5·50	3·50
		a. Laid paper	50·00	24·00
27*b*		1a. pink	85·00	£250
28		1a. mauve	1·50	2·00
		a. Laid paper	42·00	13·00
29		1a. brown-lilac	75	1·00
		a. Laid paper	35·00	13·00
30	**5**	2a. dull orange	4·00	5·00
		a. Laid paper	£750	

31	6	4a. chocolate	2·25	5·50
		a. Lake-brown	2·50	5·50
		b. Chestnut	3·50	6·00
		c. Laid paper (*shades*)	70·00	65·00
32	7	1r. dull green	11·00	15·00
		a. Laid paper	90·00	
33		1r. pale olive-yellow	£850	
34	8	2r. brown-red	35·00	55·00
		a. Laid paper	45·00	
35	9	5r. mauve	35·00	55·00
		a. Laid paper	75·00	

All the above, both imperf and pin-perf, were printed singly, sometimes on paper with spaces marked in pencil. They exist in vertical *tête-bêche* pairs imperf between from the centre of the sheet. *Prices from 3×normal, unused.* No. 22ab is an error.

FISCAL STAMPS. Many of the following issues were produced in different colours for fiscal purposes. Such usage is indicated by the initials "M.C.", punched hole or violet Stamp Office handstamp.

Maharaja Madan Singh, 1900–1926

10 (¼a.)

10a (1r.)

1901. *Toned wove paper.* Pin-perf.

36	10	¼a. dull pink	8·00	6·00
37	4	1a. violet	48·00	27·00
38	10a	1r. dull green	14·00	16·00
36/8 *Set of 3*			65·00	45·00

Nos. 36/8 were printed in sheets of 24. Sheets of the 1r. were always torn to remove R. 5/4 where the cliché is believed to have been defective.

The 1a. (No. 37) differs from T **4** in having an inscription in native characters below the words "ONE ANNA".

11 (½a.)

12 Maharaja Sardul Singh

1903. *Litho. Thick white wove glazed paper.* Imperf.

39	11	½a. pink	13·00	3·00
		a. Printed both sides	†	£1400
40	12	2a. dull yellow	3·00	6·00

12a (8a.)

1904. *Printed singly. Thin paper.* Pin-perf.

41	12a	8a. grey	5·00	7·50
		a. *Tête-bêche* (vert pair)	26·00	
		b. Doubly printed	£140	

13 Maharaja Madan Singh

14 Maharaja Madan Singh

(Recess Perkins, Bacon & Co)

1904–10. *With gum.* P 12½.

42	13	¼a. carmine	45	75
		a. Perf 13½ (1910)	1·50	55
		b. Perf 12×12½	£120	
43		½a. chestnut	2·25	1·00
		a. Perf 13½ (1906)	1·25	30
44		1a. blue	5·50	2·75
		a. Perf 13½ (1906)	2·50	2·75
45		2a. orange-yellow	15·00	7·00
		a. Perf 13½ (1907)	22·00	19·00
46		4a. brown	20·00	20·00
		a. Perf 13½ (1907)	15·00	17·00
		b. Perf 12	75·00	55·00
47		8a. violet (1905)	13·00	25·00
48		1r. green	28·00	45·00
49		2r. olive-yellow	29·00	£170
50		5r. purple-brown	24·00	£200
42/50 *Set of 9*			£120	£425

Stamps in other colours, all perforated 13½, were produced by Perkins Bacon as business samples.

1912. *Printed from half-tone blocks. No ornaments to left and right of value in English; large ornaments on either side of value in Hindi. Small stop after "STATE".*

(a) Thin wove paper. Rouletted.

51	14	2a. deep violet ("TWO ANNA")	5·50	9·00
		a. *Tête-bêche* (vert pair)	12·00	40·00
		b. Imperf (pair)	£500	

No. 51 is printed in four rows, each inverted in respect to that above and below it.

(b) Thick white chalk-surfaced paper. Imperf.

52	14	2a. lilac ("TWO ANNA")	£1700	£800

(c) Thick white chalk-surfaced paper. Rouletted in colour (Medallion only in half-tone).

53	14	¼a. ultramarine	17·00	16·00

1913. *No ornaments on either side of value in English. Small ornaments in bottom label. With stop after "STATE". Thick white chalk-surfaced paper. Rouletted.*

54	14	2a. purple ("TWO ANNAS")	2·50	5·00

15

पाव आना

No. 59e. This occurs on R. 3/3 on one setting only

2 TWO ANNAS 2
No. 60. Small figures

2 TWO ANNAS 2
No. 60b. Large figures

(Typo Diamond Soap Works, Kishangarh)

1913 (Aug). *Thick surfaced paper. Half-tone centre. Type-set inscriptions. Rouletted. Inscr* "KISHANGARH".

59	15	¼a. pale blue	30	90
		a. Imperf (pair)	7·50	
		b. Roul×imperf (horiz pair)	27·00	
		ba. Imperf between (horiz pair)	45·00	
		c. "OUARTER" (R. 4/4)	5·00	7·00
		ca. As last, imperf (pair)	30·00	
		cb. As last, roul×imperf	60·00	
		d. "KISHANGAHR" (R. 2/3)	5·00	7·00
		da. As last, imperf (pair)	30·00	
		db. As last, roul×imperf	60·00	
		dc. As last, imperf between (horiz pair)	90·00	
		e. Character omitted	7·00	7·00
		ea. As last, imperf (pair)	35·00	
60		2a. purple	8·50	19·00
		a. "KISHANGAHR" (R. 2/3)	50·00	95·00
		b. Large figures "2"	32·00	60·00

1913–16. *Stamps printed far apart, horizontally and vertically, otherwise as No. 54, except as noted below.*

63	14	¼a. blue	20	45
64		½a. green (1915)	20	1·00
		a. Printed both sides	£225	
		b. Imperf (pair)	£150	£160
		c. Emerald-green (1916)	1·75	4·00
65		1a. red	1·25	2·50
		a. Without stop*	1·50	5·50
		ab. Imperf (pair)	£190	
66		2a. purple ("TWO ANNAS") (1915)	6·00	8·00
67		4a. bright blue	6·00	8·00
68		8a. brown	7·00	40·00
69		1r. mauve	16·00	£130
		a. Imperf (pair)	£300	
70		2r. deep green	£100	£350
71		5r. brown	40·00	£450
63/71 *Set of 9*			£160	£900

*For this issue, ornaments were added on either side of the English value (except in the ¼a.) and the inscription in the right label was without stop, except in the case of No. 65.

In Nos. 70 and 71 the value is expressed as "RUPIES" instead of "RUPEES".

Initial printings of the ¼a., 1a. and 4a. values were in sheets of 20 containing two panes of 10 separated by a central gutter margin. Stamps from these sheets measure 20×25½ mm and have heavier screening dots on the perforation margins than on the designs. Subsequent printings of these stamps, and of other values in the set, were from single pane sheets of 20 on which the designs measured 19½×23¾ mm and with the screening dots uniform across the sheet.

Maharaja Yagyanarayan Singh, 1926–1939

16 Maharaja Yagyanarayan Singh

17 Maharaja Yagyanarayan Singh

1928–36. *Thick surfaced paper. Typo.* Pin-perf.

72	16	¼a. light blue	1·25	2·00
73		½a. yellow-green	4·00	2·25
		a. Deep green	3·25	3·00
		ab. Imperf (pair)	£120	£120
		ac. Imperf between (vert or horiz pair)	£140	£140
74	17	1a. carmine	75	1·50
		a. Imperf (pair)	£200	£130
75		2a. purple	3·00	8·50
75*a*		2a. magenta (1936)	8·00	12·00
		ab. Imperf (pair)	£350	
76	16	4a. chestnut	1·75	1·75
		a. Imperf (pair)		
77		8a. violet	5·50	28·00
78		1r. light green	20·00	65·00
79		2r. lemon-yellow (1929)	28·00	£225
80		5r. claret (1929)	45·00	£275
		a. Imperf (pair)	£130	
72/80 *Set of 9*			95·00	£550

The 4a. to 5r. are slightly larger than, but otherwise similar to, the ¼a. and ½a. The 8a. has a dotted background covering the whole design.

Maharaja Samar Singh, 1939–1971

1943–47. *As last, but thick, soft, unsurfaced paper. Poor impression. Typo.* Pin-perf.

81	16	¼a. pale dull blue (1945)	5·00	13·00
		a. Imperf (pair)	35·00	
82		¼a. greenish blue (1947)	3·25	10·00
		a. Imperf (pair)	30·00	
83		½a. deep green (1944)	1·75	2·75
		a. Imperf (pair)	27·00	27·00
		b. Imperf between (vert or horiz pair)	55·00	
84		½a. yellow-green (1946)	7·50	10·00
		a. Imperf (pair)	38·00	38·00
		b. Imperf between (vert or horiz pair)	55·00	
85	17	1a. carmine-red (1944)	8·50	4·25
		a. Double print	£300	
		b. Imperf (pair)	38·00	38·00
		c. Imperf between (vert or horiz pair)	55·00	
		d. Red-orange (1947)	85·00	40·00
		da. Imperf (pair)	£150	£110
86		2a. bright magenta	13·00	13·00
		a. Imperf (pair)	80·00	85·00
87		2a. maroon (1947)	£100	20·00
		a. Imperf (pair)	50·00	55·00
		b. Imperf between (vert or horiz pair)	£140	
88	16	4a. brown (1944)	28·00	20·00
		a. Imperf (pair)		
89		8a. violet (1945)	48·00	£160
90		1r. green (1945)	60·00	£170
		a. Imperf (pair)	£225	£375
90*b*		2r. yellow (date?)		
		ba. Imperf (pair)	£600	
91		5r. claret (1945)	£700	£750
		a. Imperf (pair)	£400	

OFFICIAL STAMPS

ON
K S
D

(O 1)

1918. *Handstamped with Type* O **1**.

(a) Stamps of 1899–1901.

(i) Imperf.

O1	2	¼a. green	–	£170
O2		¼a. rose-pink	–	8·00
		a. Pair, one without opt	–	85·00
O3	4	1a. mauve	–	65·00
O3*a*		1a. brown-lilac	55·00	5·50
		ab. Pair, one without opt	£225	85·00
O4	6	4a. chocolate	–	£130

(ii) Pin-perf.

O5	2	¼a. green	–	£120
O6		¼a. rose-pink	2·25	60
		a. Pair, one without opt	95·00	45·00
		b. Stamp doubly printed	£100	70·00
O7	3	½a. light blue	£425	45·00
O8	4	1a. mauve	55·00	1·50
		a. Pair, one without opt	†	£120
O9		1a. brown-lilac	50·00	1·75
O10	5	2a. dull orange	–	£150
O11	6	4a. chocolate	65·00	16·00
		a. Pair, one without opt	–	95·00
O12	7	1r. dull green	£170	£120
O13	8	2r. brown-red	–	£950
O14	9	5r. mauve	–	£2000

(b) Stamp of 1901.

O14*a*	10a	1r. dull green	–	£900

(c) Stamps of 1903 and 1904.

O15	12	2a. dull yellow	85·00	5·00
		a. Stamp printed both sides	†	£900
		b. Red opt	£450	£275
O16	12a	8a. grey	90·00	24·00
		a. Red opt	–	£300

(d) Stamps of 1904–5. P 13½ (¼a. to 4a.) or 12½ (others).

O17	13	¼a. carmine	–	£300
O18		½a. chestnut	1·00	35
		a. Pair, one without opt	–	60·00
O19		1a. blue	11·00	4·00
		a. Red opt	24·00	7·00
		b. Pair, one without opt	–	80·00
O20		2a. orange-yellow	–	£1000
O21		4a. brown	60·00	18·00
		a. Red opt	90·00	42·00
O22		8a. violet	£400	£250
		a. Red opt	–	£275
O23		1r. green	£800	£750
		a. Red opt	–	£700
O24		5r. purple-brown		

(e) Stamps of 1913.

O25	15	¼a. pale blue	7·00	
		a. Imperf (pair)	90·00	
		b. Roul×imperf (horiz pair)	£170	
		c. "OUARTER"	25·00	
		ca. As last, imperf (pair)	£150	
		d. "KISAHNGAHR"	25·00	
		da. As last, imperf (pair)	£150	
		e. Character omitted	25·00	
		ea. As last, imperf (pair)	£150	
O26	14	2a. purple (No. 54)	–	£100
		a. Red opt	£160	20·00
O27	15	2a. purple	£550	£600
		a. "KISHANGAHR"	£1100	
		b. Large figures "2"	£750	£800

(f) Stamps of 1913–16.

O28 14 ¼a. blue 60 50
a. Red opt 2·00 1·75
O29 ½a. green 1·00 75
a. Pair, one without opt — 80·00
b. Red opt 4·50 1·60
ba. Pair, one without opt — £160
O30 1a. red 16·00 9·00
a. Without stop (No. 65a) 1·00 1·00
ab. Pair, one without opt £150
ac. Red opt £140 85·00
O31 2a. purple 8·50 4·00
a. Red opt £140 70·00
b. Pair, one without opt — 85·00
O32 4a. bright blue 28·00 15·00
a. Red opt — 35·00
O33 8a. brown £130 45·00
a. Red opt — 90·00
O34 1r. mauve £350 £325
O35 2r. deep green
O36 5r. brown £1800

This overprint is found inverted as often as it is upright; and many other "errors" exist.

Kishangarh became part of Rajasthan by 15 April 1948.

LAS BELA

PRICES FOR STAMPS ON COVER
Nos. 1/12 *from* × 8

Mir Kamal Khan, 1896–1926

1

2

(Litho Thacker & Co, Bombay)

1897–98. *Thick paper.* P 11½.
1 1 ½a. black on *white* 30·00 18·00

1898–1900. P 11½.
2 1 ½a. black on *greyish blue* (1898) 20·00 11·00
3 ½a. black on *greenish grey* (1899) 17·00 11·00
a. "BFLA" for "BELA" £180
b. Imperf between (horiz strip of 3)
4 ½a. black on *thin white surfaced paper* (1899) 30·00 48·00
5 ½a. black on *slate* (1900) 32·00 45·00
a. Imperf between (horiz pair) £950

1901–02. P 11½.
6 1 ½a. black on *pale grey* 16·00 11·00
a. "BFLA" for "BELA" £160 £200
7 ½a. black on *pale green* (1902) 24·00 26·00
8 2 1a. black on *orange* 24·00 26·00

There are at least 14 settings of the above ½a. stamps, the sheets varying from 16 to 30 stamps.

No. 6a occurred on R. 3/2 of the July 1901 printing in sheets of 16 (4×4).

1904 (Feb–Nov). *Stamps printed wider apart.* P 11½.
11 1 ½a. black on *pale blue* 16·00 9·00
a. Imperf between (pair) £800
b. Imperf between (horiz strip of 3) £1100
c. Perf 12½ (Nov) 22·00 13·00
12 ½a. black on *pale green* 16·00 9·00
c. Perf 12½ (Nov) 22·00 13·00

There are five plates of the above two stamps, each consisting of 18 (3×6) varieties.

All the coloured papers of the ½a. show coloured fibres, similar to those in granite paper.

The stamps of Las Bela have been obsolete since 1 April 1907.

MORVI

PRICES FOR STAMPS ON COVER
Nos. 1/17 *from* × 6
Nos. 18/19 *from* × 3

Thakur (Maharaja from 1926) Lakhdirji, 1922–48

1 Maharaja Lakhdirji

2 Maharaja Lakhdirji

3 Maharaja Lakhdirji

1931 (1 April). *Typo.* P 12.

(a) Printed in blocks of four. Stamps 10 mm apart (Nos. 1/2) or 6½ mm apart (No. 3). Perf on two or three sides.
1 1 3p. deep red 3·00 15·00
2 ½a. blue 26·00 45·00
3 2a. yellow-brown £110
1/3 *Set of 3* £130

(b) Printed in two blocks of four. Stamps 5½ mm apart. Perf on four sides.
4 1 3p. bright scarlet 6·00 24·00
a. Error. Dull blue 4·25 24·00
b. Ditto. Double print £650
c. Ditto. Printed on gummed side £650
5 ½a. dull blue 4·25 18·00
a. Chalk-surfaced paper 3·75 17·00
6 1a. brown-red 3·25 28·00
7 2a. yellow-brown 4·00 40·00
4/7 *Set of 4* 16·00 £100

Nos. 1/3 were supplied to post offices in panes of four sewn into bundles with interleaving.

1932–33. *Horizontal background lines wider apart and portrait smaller than in T* **1**. *Typo.* P 11.
8 2 3p. carmine-rose (*shades*) 5·00 14·00
9 6p. green 8·00 17·00
a. Imperf between (horiz pair) £1900
b. Emerald-green 6·50 14·00
10 1a. ultramarine (*to deep*) 4·50 14·00
a. Imperf between (vert pair) £1500
11 2a. bright violet (1933) 11·00 40·00
a. Imperf between (vert pair) £1500
8/11 *Set of 4* 24·00 75·00

1934. *Typo. London ptg.* P 14.
12 3 3p. carmine 3·00 3·50
13 6p. emerald-green 1·75 7·00
14 1a. purple-brown 2·25 14·00
a. Imperf between (horiz pair) † £1400
15 2a. bright violet 2·75 27·00
12/15 *Set of 4* 9·00 48·00

1935–48. *Typo. Morvi Press ptg.* Rough perf 11.
16 3 3p. scarlet (*shades*) 2·00 4·50
a. Imperf between (horiz pair) £1400
17 6p. grey-green 2·00 3·75
a. Emerald-green 9·00 30·00
b. Yellow-green 9·50
18 1a. brown 12·00 17·00
a. Pale yellow-brown 16·00 28·00
b. Chocolate 23·00 35·00
19 2a. dull violet (*to deep*) 2·50 20·00
16/19 *Set of 4* 17·00 40·00

Nos. 17*a*, 18*a* and 18*b* were issued between 1944 and 1948.

Maharaja Mahendra Singh, 1948–1957

Morvi was merged with the United State of Kathiawar (later Saurashtra) by 15 April 1948.

NANDGAON

PRICES FOR STAMPS ON COVER
The stamps of Nandgaon are very rare used on cover.

GUM. The stamps of Nandgaon were issued without gum.

Raja Mahant Balram Das, 1883–1897

1

2 (½a.)

(Litho at Poona)

1891. Imperf.
1 1 ½a. blue 7·00 £180
a. Dull blue 7·50
2 2a. rose 27·00 £550

The few covers in existence franked with Nos. 1/2 have undated manuscript cancellations, but other forms are known on loose examples.

The state was under Imperial administration from January 1888 to November 1891 and it is possible that Nos. 1/2 may have appeared in late 1887.

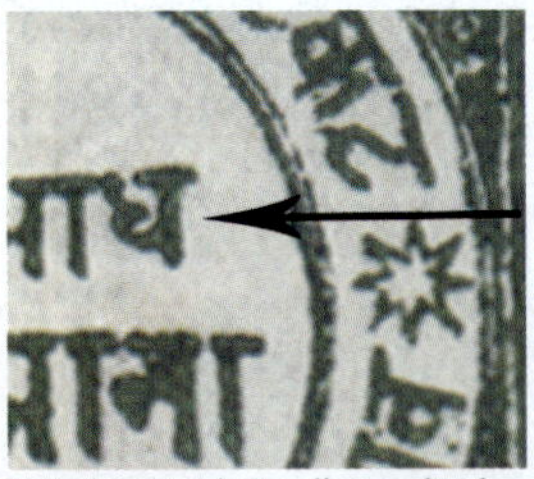
Last character in top line omitted

(Typo Balram Press, Raj-Nandgaon)

1893 (1 Jan)–**94.** *Printed in sheets of 16 (4×4).* Imperf.

(a) Stamps printed wide apart (8 to 10 mm) without wavy lines between them. Thin, toned wove paper.
3 2 ½a. dull *to* deep green 13·00 90·00
4 2a. red 13·00 90·00
b. Dull rose 13·00 90·00

(b) Stamps printed closer together (4 to 7 mm) with wavy lines between them. Thin, white wove paper (1894).
5 2 ½a. green 25·00 70·00
a. Last character in top line omitted (R. 4/3) 95·00
6 1a. rose 55·00 £120
ba. Laid paper £250

There were three settings of Type **2** with a number of separate printings made from the third:

Setting I - Nos. 3, 4, 4a, 4*b*, O2
Setting II - Nos. 5, 5b, 6, 6a, 6b
Setting III - Nos. 5, 6ba, O3, O3*a*, O4, O4a, O5 and subsequent reprints.

The same clichés were used for all values with the face value inscriptions changed. These exist in two different sizes with both occurring on the ½a., the small on the 1a. and the large on the 2a. except for No. O5 which has the small type.

The ordinary postage stamps of Nandgaon became obsolete on 1 July 1894.

OFFICIAL STAMPS

(O **1**) ("M.B.D." = Mahant Balram Das)

1893. *Handstamped with ruler's initials in oval. Type* O **1**, *in purple.*
O1 1 ½a. blue £375
O2 2a. rose £900

1894. *Handstamped with Type* O **1** *in purple.*

(a) Stamps printed wide apart (8 to 10 mm) without wavy lines between them. Thin, toned wove paper.
O2*a* 2 ½a. dull green £550
O3 2a. red 27·00 £150

(b) Stamps printed closer together (4 to 7 mm) with wavy lines between them. Thin, white wove paper.
O4 2 ½a. yellow-green 6·50 12·00
a. Sage-green 7·50
O5 1a. rose (*shades*) 12·00 38·00
a. Thin laid paper 11·00 85·00
O6 2a. rose (*shades*) 11·00 25·00

Further printings took place in 1895 after the Official stamps were withdrawn from postal use on 31 December 1894. These were all on thin, white wove paper with the ½a. and 2a. in slightly different shades and the 1a. in brown or ultramarine.

There is a forgery of the handstamp, Type O **1**, which shows 8 mm between the two ornaments below the initials instead of the normal 4 mm.

NAWANAGAR

PRICES FOR STAMPS ON COVER
No. 1 *from* × 20
No. 2 *from* × 8
Nos. 3/4 *from* × 2
No. 5 —
Nos. 6/12 —
Nos. 13/15 *from* × 100
Nos. 16/18 —

GUM. The stamps of Nawanagar were issued without gum.

Jam Vibhaji 1882–1895

1 (1 docra)

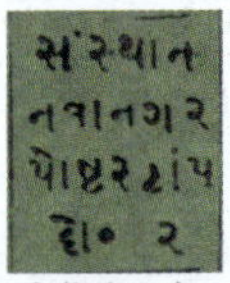
2 (2 docra)

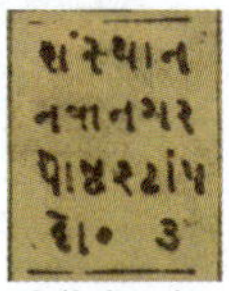
3 (3 docra)

1877. *Typo in sheets of 32 (4×8 or 8×4). Laid paper.*

(a) Imperf.
1 1 1doc. blue (*shades*) 75 25·00
a. *Tête-bêche* (pair) £1300
b. Doubly printed £100

(b) Perf 12½ (line).
2 1 1doc. slate-blue 80·00 £150
a. Perf 11 (harrow) 95·00
ab. *Tête-bêche* (pair) £1600

The inverted clichés which cause the *tête-bêche* pairs come from different settings and occur on R. 3/2 (No. 1a) or R. 4/4 (No. 2ab) of sheets of 32 (4×8).

1877. *T* **2** *and* **3**. *Type-set in black. Wove paper. Thick horizontal and vertical frame lines. Stamp 19 mm wide.*
3 1doc. *deep mauve* £3750 £225
a. Stamp 14½-15 mm wide † £400
b. Stamp 16 mm wide † £325
4 2doc. *green* £3750 £1800
5 3doc. *yellow* £3750 £1800

1880. *As last, but thin frame lines, as illustrated. Stamp 15 to 18 mm wide.*
6 1doc. *deep mauve* 3·75 11·00
a. On rose 3·75
ab. Stamp 14 mm wide 3·75 9·00
b. Error. Green
7 1doc. *magenta (stamp 14 mm wide)* 4·25
8 2doc. *yellow-green* 5·50 14·00
a. On blue-green 8·50
b. Error. Yellow £400
c. Stamp 14 mm wide 4·25 11·00
ca. On blue-green 10·00
9 3doc. *orange-yellow* 13·00
a. On yellow 6·00 20·00
ab. On laid paper £110
b. Stamp 14 mm wide. *On yellow* 6·00 13·00
ba. On laid paper 48·00

There are several different settings of each value of this series.

No. 8b occurs in the sheet of the 3 doc. value from one setting only.

4 (1 docra)

1893. *Typo in sheets of 36. P 12.*

(a) Thick paper.

10	4	1doc. black	4·25	
		a. Imperf (pair)	£600	
11		3doc. orange	5·00	

(b) Thick laid paper.

12	4	1doc. black	£700	

(c) Thin wove paper.

13	4	1doc. black *to* grey	1·75	6·00
		a. Imperf between (pair)	£475	
		b. Imperf (pair)	£475	
		c. Imperf horiz (vert pair)	£650	
		d. Imperf between (horiz strip of 6)	£1400	
14		2doc. green	2·25	8·00
		a. Imperf (pair)	£600	
		b. Imperf between (vert pair)	£650	
15		3doc. orange-yellow	2·75	13·00
		a. Imperf between (pair)	£650	
		b. Orange	2·25	12·00
		ba. Imperf (pair)	£550	
		bb. Imperf vert (horiz pair)	£600	
		bc. Imperf between (horiz pair)	£600	

(d) Thin, soft wove paper.

16	4	1doc. black		
17		2doc. deep green	3·75	
18		3doc. brown-orange	5·00	

Cancellations for postal purposes were intaglio seals, applied in black. Other forms of cancellation were only used on remainders.

The stamps of Nawanagar became obsolete on 1 January 1895.

NEPAL

Nepal being an independent state, its stamps will be found listed in Part 21 (*South-East Asia*) of this catalogue.

ORCHHA

PRICES FOR STAMPS ON COVER

Nos. 1/2	—
Nos. 3/7	*from* × 8
Nos. 8/30	*from* × 50
Nos. 31/45	*from* × 4

A set of four stamps, ½a. red, 1a. violet, 2a. yellow and 4a. deep blue-green, in a design similar to T **2**, was prepared in 1897 with State authority but not put into use. These exist both imperforate and pin-perforated. (*Price for set of* 4, *£18 unused or c.t.o.*)

Maharaja Partab Singh, 1874–1930

1

2

(T **1/2** litho Shri Pratap Prabhakar)

1913. *Background to arms unshaded, Very blurred impression. Wove paper. No gum.* Imperf.

1	1	½a. green	35·00	£100
2		1a. red	20·00	£180

1914–35. *Background shaded with short horizontal lines. Clearer impression. Wove paper. No gum.* Imperf.

3	2	¼a. bright ultramarine	2·00	5·00
		a. Grey-blue	40	4·50
		b. Deep blue	1·60	3·75
		ba. Laid paper	£600	
4		½a. green (*shades*)	55	6·50
		a. Dull green	1·50	7·00
		b. Apple-green	2·25	5·00
5		1a. scarlet	2·50	7·00
		a. Laid paper	—	£500
		b. Indian red	1·75	13·00
		c. Carmine	2·50	7·50
		ca. Laid paper (1935)	£200	£250
6		2a. red-brown (1916)	4·50	24·00
		a. Light brown	11·00	27·00
		b. Chestnut	19·00	28·00
7		4a. ochre (1917)	11·00	38·00
		a. Yellow-orange	8·00	38·00
		b. Yellow	11·00	38·00
3/7 *Set of* 5			13·50	70·00

There are two sizes of T **2** in the setting of 8 (4×2). In each value stamps from the upper row are slightly taller than those from the lower.

Maharaja Vir Singh II, 1930–1956

3 Maharaja Vir Singh II

4 Maharaja Vir Singh II

(Typo Lakshmi Art Ptg Wks, Bombay)

1935 (1 Apr). *Thick, chalk-surfaced wove paper.* P 9½, 10, 10×9½, 11, 11×9½, 11½, 11½×11, 11½×12, 12 *or* 12×11.

8	3	¼a. purple and slate	1·75	4·00
		a. Imperf between (vert pair)		
		b. Ordinary paper	50	3·50
		ba. Imperf between (vert pair)	11·00	
		bb. Imperf vert (horiz pair)	65·00	
		bc. Imperf horiz (vert pair)	65·00	
9		½a. olive-grey and emerald	50	3·00
		a. Imperf (pair)	75·00	
10		¾a. magenta and deep myrtle-green	50	3·00
		a. Imperf (pair)	75·00	
11		1a. myrtle-green and purple-brown	50	3·00
		a. Imperf (pair)	70·00	90·00
		b. Imperf horiz (vert pair)		
		c. Imperf vert (horiz pair)		
12		1¼a. slate and mauve	50	3·00
		a. Imperf (pair)	75·00	£300
		b. Imperf between (horiz pair)	75·00	
		c. Frame doubly printed	75·00	
13		1½a. brown and scarlet	50	3·00
		a. Imperf between (vert pair)	75·00	
		b. Imperf between (horiz pair)	75·00	
14		2a. blue and red-orange	50	3·00
		a. Imperf (pair)	14·00	
		b. Imperf between (horiz pair)	75·00	
15		2½a. olive-brown and dull orange	65	3·25
		a. Imperf (pair)	14·00	
		b. Imperf between (horiz pair)	75·00	
16		3a. bright blue and magenta	65	3·25
		a. Imperf between (horiz pair)	75·00	£120
		b. Imperf (pair)	75·00	
17		4a. deep reddish purple and sage-green	65	5·50
		a. Imperf (pair)	9·00	
		b. Imperf between (vert pair)	75·00	
		c. Imperf vert (horiz pair)	75·00	
18		6a. black and pale ochre	70	5·50
		a. Imperf (pair)	9·00	
19		8a. brown and purple	2·25	7·00
		a. Imperf (pair)	9·00	
		b. Imperf between (vert pair)	85·00	
20		12a. bright emerald and bright purple	1·00	7·00
		a. Imperf (pair)	9·00	
		b. Imperf between (vert pair)	85·00	
21		12a. pale greenish blue and bright purple	32·00	90·00
22		1r. chocolate and myrtle-green	80	8·00
		a. Imperf (pair)	9·50	
		b. Imperf between (horiz pair)	75·00	
23	4	1r. chocolate and myrtle-green	12·00	28·00
		a. Imperf (pair)	85·00	
		b. Imperf between (horiz pair)	£100	
24	3	2r. purple-brown and bistre-yellow	3·00	20·00
		a. Imperf (pair)	9·50	
25		3r. black and greenish blue	1·50	20·00
		a. Imperf (pair)	9·50	
26		4r. black and brown	3·00	23·00
		a. Imperf (pair)	9·50	
27		5r. bright blue and plum	3·00	24·00
		a. Imperf (pair)	9·50	
28		10r. bronze-green and cerise	7·00	32·00
		a. Imperf (pair)	13·00	
		b. Imperf between (horiz pair)	95·00	
29		15r. black and bronze-green	12·00	75·00
		a. Imperf (pair)	13·00	
30		25r. red-orange and blue	16·00	85·00
		a. Imperf (pair)	16·00	
8/20, 22/30 *Set of* 22			60·00	£325

Values to 5r. except the 1a., are inscribed "POSTAGE", and the remaining values "POSTAGE & REVENUE".

The central portrait of Type **3** is taken from a half-tone block and consists of large square dots. The portrait of Type **4** has a background of lines.

Owing to a lack of proper State control considerable quantities of these stamps circulated at below face value and the issue was subsequently withdrawn, supplies being exchanged for the 1939–42 issue. We are, however, now satisfied that the lower values at least did genuine postal duty until 1939.

Used prices are for stamps cancelled-to-order, postally used examples being worth considerably more.

5 Maharaja Vir Singh II

6 Maharaja Vir Singh II

(Litho Indian Security Printing Press, Nasik)

1939–42?. P 13½×14 (T **5**) *or* 14×13½ (T **6**).

31	5	¼a. chocolate	4·00	80·00
32		½a. yellow-green	3·75	65·00
33		¾a. bright blue	5·50	£100
34		1a. scarlet	3·75	20·00
35		1¼a. blue	4·50	£100
36		1½a. mauve	4·75	£130
37		2a. vermilion	3·75	80·00
38		2½a. turquoise-green	6·00	£225
39		3a. slate-violet	6·50	£120
40		4a. slate	7·50	28·00
41		8a. magenta	12·00	£225
42	6	1r. grey-green	21·00	£500
43		2r. bright violet	48·00	£700
44		5r. yellow-orange	£160	£1800
45		10r. turquoise-green (1942)	£550	£3000
46		15r. slate-lilac (date ?)	£15000	
47		25r. claret (date ?)	£10000	

Orchha became part of Vindhya Pradesh by 1 May 1948.

POONCH

PRICES FOR STAMPS ON COVER

No. 1	*from* × 3
Nos. 1a/2	*from* × 2
Nos. 3/63	*from* × 10
Nos. O1/10	*from* × 30

Poonch was ruled by a junior branch of the Jammu and Kashmir princely family and by treaty, was subject to the "advice and consent" of the Maharaja of that state.

The Poonch postal service operated an office at Kahuta in the Punjab which acted as the office of exchange between the state post and that of British India.

GUM. The stamps of Poonch were issued without gum, except for some examples of Nos. 7/10.

The stamps of Poonch are all imperforate, and handstamped in watercolours.

ILLUSTRATIONS. Designs of Poonch are illustrated actual size.

Raja Moti Singh, 1852–1892

1

2

1876. *T* **1** *(22×21 mm). Central face value in circle and five rosettes in outer frame. Yellowish white, wove paper.*

1		6p. red	£12000	£160
		a. Pair, one stamp sideways	†	—

1877. *As T* **1** *(19×17 mm). Central face value in oval and two rosettes in outer frame. Same paper.*

1*a*		½a. red	£15000	£5000

1879. *T* **2** *(21×19 mm). Central face value in oval and one rosette in outer frame. Same paper.*

2		½a. red	—	£5000

3 (½a.)

4 (1a.)

5 (2a.)

6 (4a.)

1880. *Yellowish white, wove paper.*

3	3	½a. red	50·00	20·00
4	4	1a. red	£120	70·00
5	5	2a. red	£225	£140
6	6	4a. red	£250	£170

1884. *Toned wove bâtonné paper.*

7	3	½a. red	4·50	4·50
8	4	1a. red	24·00	
9	5	2a. red	19·00	22·00
10	6	4a. red	48·00	48·00

These are sometimes found gummed.

7 (1 pice)

1884–87. *Various papers.*

(a) White laid bâtonné or ribbed bâtonné.

11	7	1p. red	26·00	26·00
		a. Pair, one stamp sideways	£300	
12	3	½a. red	2·75	3·50
		a. *Tête-bêche* (pair)	£3000	
13	4	1a. red	4·50	
		a. Pair, one stamp sideways	£1500	
14	5	2a. red	11·00	13·00
15	6	4a. red	17·00	

(b) Thick white laid paper.

22	7	1p. red	£130	
23	3	½a. red	80·00	
24	4	1a. red	85·00	
25	5	2a. red	90·00	
26	6	4a. red	£110	

(c) Yellow wove bâtonné.

27	7	1p. red	3·75	3·75
		a. Pair, one stamp sideways	42·00	
28	3	½a. red	6·50	6·50
29	4	1a. red	55·00	
30	5	2a. red	10·00	12·00
31	6	4a. red	5·00	5·00

(d) Orange-buff wove bâtonné.

32	7	1p. red	3·75	4·00
		a. Pair, one stamp sideways	30·00	38·00
		b. *Tête-bêche* (pair)	45·00	
33	3	½a. red	28·00	
34	5	2a. red	£100	

35	6	4a. red	25·00	

(e) Yellow laid paper.

36	7	1p. red	2·25	3·50
		a. Pair, one stamp sideways	20·00	
		b. *Tête-bêche* (pair)	30·00	
37	3	½a. red	4·00	
38	4	1a. red	55·00	
39	5	2a. red	60·00	65·00
40	6	4a. red	50·00	

(f) Yellow laid bâtonné.

41	7	1p. red	12·00	10·00

(g) Buff laid or ribbed bâtonné paper thicker than (d).

42	4	1a. red	75·00	
43	6	4a. red	80·00	

(h) Blue-green laid paper (1887).

44	3	½a. red	45·00	
45	4	1a. red	3·25	5·00
46	5	2a. red	45·00	
47	6	4a. red	70·00	

(i) Yellow-green laid paper.

48	3	½a. red		

(j) Blue-green wove bâtonné.

49	7	1p. red	48·00	45·00
49*a*	3	½a. red	£1300	
50	4	1a. red	3·00	3·75

(k) Lavender wove bâtonné.

51	4	1a. red	85·00	£110
52	5	2a. red	3·25	3·75
		a. Pair, one stamp sideways	£3250	

(l) Blue wove bâtonné.

53	7	1p. red	2·75	2·50
		a. Pair, one stamp sideways	30·00	40·00
		b. *Tête-bêche* (pair)	45·00	
54	4	1a. red	£400	£425

(m) Various coloured papers.

55	7	1p. red/*grey-blue laid*	9·00	6·00
		a. *Tête-bêche* (pair)	£325	
56		1p. red/*lilac laid*	50·00	55·00
		a. Pair, one stamp sideways	£375	£375
		b. *Tête-bêche* (pair)	£350	

1888. *Printed in aniline rose on various papers.*

57	7	1p. on *blue wove bâtonné*	6·00	
		a. *Tête-bêche* (pair)	85·00	
58		1p. on *buff laid*	16·00	
		a. *Tête-bêche* (pair)	£130	
59	3	½a. on *white laid*	25·00	
60	4	1a. on *green laid*	16·00	20·00
61		1a. on *green wove bâtonné*	9·00	10·00
62	5	2a. on *lavender wove bâtonné*	9·00	9·00
63	6	4a. on *yellow laid*	16·00	20·00
		a. Pair, one stamp sideways	£1000	
		b. *Tête-bêche* (pair)	£1000	

OFFICIAL STAMPS

Raja Baldeo Singh, 1892–1918

1887.

(a) White laid bâtonné paper.

O1	7	1p. black	2·75	3·00
		a. Pair, one stamp sideways	17·00	20·00
		b. *Tête-bêche* (pair)	20·00	
O2	3	½a. black	3·00	4·00
O3	4	1a. black	2·75	3·00
O4	5	2a. black	5·00	5·00
O5	6	4a. black	8·00	12·00

(b) White or toned wove bâtonné paper.

O6	7	1p. black	2·50	
		a. Pair, one stamp sideways	29·00	
		b. *Tête-bêche* (pair)	40·00	
O7	3	½a. black	3·00	3·50
		a. Pair, one stamp sideways	£2250	
O8	4	1a. black	15·00	14·00
O9	5	2a. black	6·50	6·50
O10	6	4a. black	10·00	

RAJASTHAN

Rajasthan was formed in 1948–49 from a number of States in Rajputana; these included Bundi, Jaipur and Kishangarh, whose posts continued to function more or less separately until ordered by the Indian Government to close on 1 April 1950.

PRICES FOR STAMPS ON COVER	
Nos. 1/7	*from* × 15
Nos. 8/10	—
Nos. 11/12	*from* × 5
Nos. 13/14	—
Nos. 15/25	*from* × 4
Nos. 26/42	*from* × 3
No. 43	*from* × 5
Nos. 44/60	*from* × 3
No. 61	*from* × 5
Nos. 62/5	—

BUNDI

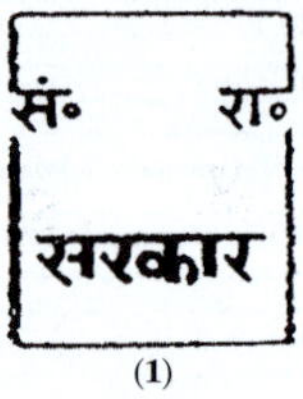

(1)

1948–49. *Nos. 86/92 of Bundi. (a) Handstamped with T* **1**.

A. In black. B. In violet. C. In blue.

		A	B	C
1	¼a. blue-green	5·50	6·00	35·00
	a. Pair, one without opt	£375	†	†
2	½a. violet	5·50	6·00	48·00
	a. Pair, one without opt	£400	£375	†
3	1a. yellow-green	4·75	16·00	45·00
	a. Pair, one without opt	†	£375	†
4	2a. vermilion	14·00	32·00	—
5	4a. orange	48·00	32·00	£130
6	8a. ultramarine	9·00	9·50	80·00
7	1r. chocolate	—	£275	95·00

The above prices are for unused, used stamps being worth about six times the unused prices. Most of these handstamps are known, sideways, inverted or double.

(b) Machine-printed as T 1 in black.

11	2a. vermilion	10·00	70·00
	a. Opt inverted	£300	
12	4a. orange	4·00	70·00
	a. Opt double	£275	
13	8a. ultramarine	18·00	
	a. Opt inverted	£650	
	b. Opt double	£400	
14	1r. chocolate	7·50	

JAIPUR

राजस्थान

RAJASTHAN
(2)

1950 (26 Jan). *T* **7** *of Jaipur optd with T* **2**.

15	¼a. black and brown-lake (No. 58) (B.)	8·00	22·00
16	½a. black and violet (No. 41) (R.)	6·50	23·00
17	¾a. black and brown-red (No. 59) (Blue-blk.)	10·00	27·00
	a. Opt in pale blue	16·00	45·00
18	1a. black and blue (No. 60) (R.)	7·50	48·00
19	2a. black and buff (No. 61) (R.)	8·50	65·00
20	2½a. black and carmine (No. 62) (B.)	9·00	30·00
21	3a. black and green (No. 63) (R.)	11·00	75·00
22	4a. black and grey-green (No. 64) (R.)	9·50	85·00
23	6a. black and pale blue (No. 65*a*) (R.)	9·50	£120
24	8a. black and chocolate (No. 66) (R.)	16·00	£170
25	1r. black and yellow-bistre (No. 67) (R.)	23·00	£250
15/25 *Set of* 11		£110	£800

KISHANGARH

1948 (Oct)–**49**. *Various stamps of Kishangarh handstamped with T* **1** *in red.*

(a) On stamps of 1899–1901.

26		¼a. rose-pink (No. 5*a*) (B.)	£250	
26*a*		¼a. rose-pink (No. 22*a*)	—	£250
27		½a. deep blue (No. 26)	£600	
29		1a. brown-lilac (No. 29)	14·00	42·00
		b. Imperf (pair)	40·00	95·00
		c. Violet handstamp	—	£450
		d. Black handstamp	—	£500
30		4a. chocolate (No. 31)	85·00	£110
		a. Violet handstamp	—	£600
31		1r. dull green (No. 32)	£300	£325
31*a*		2r. brown-red (No. 34)	£375	
32		5r. mauve (No. 35)	£350	£350

(b) On stamps of 1904–10.

33	13	½a. chestnut	—	£200
33*a*		1a. blue	—	£275
34		4a. brown	13·00	
		a. Blue handstamp	£250	
35	12a	8a. grey	£110	£180
36	13	8a. violet	11·00	
37		1r. green	12·00	
38		2r. olive-yellow	19·00	
39		5r. purple-brown	28·00	
		a. Blue handstamp	£450	

(c) On stamps of 1912–16.

40	14	½a. green (No. 64)	£450	£250
41		1a. red	—	£300
42		2a. deep violet (No. 51)	£550	
43		2a. purple (No. 66)	3·00	8·50
		a. Pair, one without handstamp	£425	
44		4a. bright blue		£550
45		8a. brown	5·00	
		a. Pair, one without handstamp	£425	
46		1r. mauve	10·00	
47		2r. deep green	10·00	
48		5r. brown	£450	

(d) On stamps of 1928–36.

49	16	½a. yellow-green	£200	
49*a*		2a. magenta	—	£600
50		4a. chestnut	£300	
51		8a. violet	6·00	60·00
		a. Pair, one without handstamp	£400	
52		1r. light green	21·00	
53		2r. lemon-yellow	16·00	
54		5r. claret	16·00	

(e) On stamps of 1943–47.

55	16	¼a. pale dull blue	£110	£110
56		¼a. greenish blue	50·00	50·00
		a. Imperf (pair)	£250	
57		½a. deep green	32·00	32·00
		a. Violet handstamp	—	£300
57*b*		½a. yellow-green	40·00	40·00
		ba. Imperf (pair)	£250	
		bb. Blue handstamp	—	£300
58	17	1a. carmine-red	75·00	75·00
		a. Violet handstamp	—	£300
58*b*		1a. orange-red (*imperf*)	£170	
		ba. Blue handstamp	£180	
59		2a. bright magenta	£225	£225
60		2a. maroon (*imperf*)	£250	
61	16	4a. brown	2·75	8·50
		a. Pair, one without handstamp	£300	
62		8a. violet	15·00	60·00
63		1r. green	6·50	
64		2r. yellow	95·00	
65		5r. claret	50·00	

A 1a. value in deep violet-blue was issued for revenue purposes, but is known postally used (*Price* £90 *used*).

RAJPIPLA

PRICES FOR STAMPS ON COVER	
No. 1	*from* × 50
Nos. 2/3	—

Maharana Ganbhir Singh, 1860–1897

The Rajpipla state post was opened to the public sometime in the late 1870s. Adhesive stamps were preceded by postal stationery lettersheets which were first reported in 1879.

1 (1 pice) **2** (2a.) **3** (4a.)

1880. *Litho. With or without gum (1p.) or no gum (others).* P 11 (1p.) or 12½.

1	1	1p. blue (1 June)	3·50	38·00
2	2	2a. green	30·00	£110
		a. Imperf between (horiz pair)	£600	£600
3	3	4a. red	16·00	70·00
1/3 *Set of* 3			45·00	£200

No. 1 was produced in sheets of 64 (8×8) and the higher values in sheets of 20 (5×4).

These stamps became obsolete in 1886 when the Imperial postal service absorbed the Rajpipla state post.

SHAHPURA

PRICES FOR STAMPS ON COVER	
Nos. 1/4	*from* × 2
No. F1	*from* × 2

DATES. Those quoted are of first known use.

Rajadhiraj Nahar Singh, 1870–1932

RAJ
SHAHPURA
Postage 1 pice
1

RAJ
SHAHPURA
1 pice
2

1914–17. *Typo.*

1	1	1p. carmine/*bluish grey* (P 11)	—	£750
2		1p. carmine/*drab* (*imperf*) (1917)	—	£1100

Some examples of No. 1 are imperforate on one side or on two adjacent sides.

1920–28. *Typo.* Imperf.

3	2	1p. carmine/*drab* (1928)	—	£1300
4		1a. black/*pink*	—	£1500

Nos. 3/4 were also used for fiscal purposes. Manuscript cancellations must be assumed to be fiscal, unless on cover showing other evidence of postal use.

POSTAL FISCAL

Rajadhiraj Umaid Singh, 1932–1947
Rajadhiraj Sudarshan Deo, 1947–1971

F 1

1932–47. *Typo.* P 11, 11½ or 12.

F1	F 1	1a. red (*shades*)	75·00	£250
		a. Pin-perf 7 (1947)		

Nos. F1/a were used for both fiscal and postal purposes. Manuscript cancellations must be assumed to be fiscal, unless on cover showing other evidence of postal use. The design was first issued for fiscal purposes in 1898.

Shahpura became part of Rajasthan by 15 April 1948.

SIRMOOR

PRICES FOR STAMPS ON COVER
The stamps of Sirmoor are very rare used on cover.

Raja Shamsher Parkash, 1886–1898

1 (1 pice) **2** **3** Raja Shamsher Parkash

1878 (June)–**80**. *Litho.* P 11½.

1	1	1p. pale green	16·00	£325

2		1p. blue (on *laid* paper) (1880)	4·50	£170
		a. Imperf between (pair)	£375	
		b. Imperf (pair)	£375	

(Litho at Calcutta)

1892. *Thick wove paper*. P 11½.

3	2	1p. yellow-green	1·10	1·10
		a. Imperf between (vert pair)	75·00	
		b. Deep green	75	75
		ba. Imperf between (vert pair)	75·00	75·00
4		1p. blue	1·25	80
		a. Imperf between (vert pair)	65·00	65·00
		b. Imperf between (horiz pair)	65·00	65·00
		c. Imperf vert (horiz pair)	65·00	
		d. Imperf (pair)	75·00	

These were originally made as reprints, about 1891, to supply collectors, but there being very little demand for them they were put into use. The design was copied (including the perforations) from an illustration in a dealer's catalogue.

A

B

C

D

There were seven printings of stamps as Type **3**, all in sheets of 70 (10×7) and made up from groups of transfers which can be traced through minor varieties.

Printings I to V and VII of the 3p. and 6p. are as Types A and C (both with large white dots evenly spaced between the ends of the upper and lower inscriptions).

Printing VI is as Type B (small white dots and less space) and Type D (large white dots unevenly positioned between the inscriptions).

(Litho Waterlow)

1885–96. P 14 to 15.

5	3	3p. chocolate (A)	75	40
		a. Brown (B) (1896)	30	35
6		3p. orange (A) (1888)	1·75	30
		a. Type B (1896)	30	20
		ab. Imperf (pair)	£600	
7		6p. blue-green (C)	4·50	4·00
		a. Green (C) (1888)	1·10	60
		b. Bright green (C) (1891)	65·00	65·00
		c. Deep green (C) (1894)	60	45
		d. Yellowish green (D) (1896)	40	1·50
8		1a. bright blue	2·75	3·75
		a. Dull blue (1891)	8·00	4·50
		b. Steel-blue (1891)	90·00	90·00
		c. Grey-blue (1894)	2·25	1·00
		d. Slate-blue (1896)	50	2·75
9		2a. pink	4·25	14·00
		a. Carmine (1894)	3·50	3·00
		b. Rose-red (1896)	3·25	4·00

Composition of the various printings was as follows:

Printing I	—	Nos. 5, 7, 8 and 9
Printing II	—	Nos. 6 and 7*a*
Printing III	—	Nos. 6, 7*b* and 8*a*
Printing IV	—	Nos. 5, 6, 7*a*, and 8*b*
Printing V	—	Nos. 6, 7*c*, 8*c* and 9*a*
Printing VI	—	Nos. 5*a*, 6a, 7*d*, 8*d* and 9*b*
Printing VII	—	Only exists overprinted "On S. S. S." (Nos. 78/81).

4 Indian Elephant

5 Raja Shamsher Parkash

(Recess Waterlow & Sons)

1894–99. P 12 to 15 and compounds.

22	4	3p. orange-brown	3·50	30
23		6p. green	75	30
		a. Imperf between (vert pair)	£3250	
24		1a. blue	4·50	2·25
25		2a. rose	3·50	1·50
26		3a. yellow-green	23·00	45·00
27		4a. deep green	16·00	23·00
28		8a. deep blue	19·00	28·00
29		1r. vermilion	38·00	75·00
22/9 *Set of 8*			95·00	£160

Raja Surindra Bikram Parkash, 1898–1911

(Recess Waterlow & Sons)

1899. P 13 to 15.

30	5	3a. yellow-green	4·25	22·00
31		4a. deep green	5·50	23·00
32		8a. deep blue	7·50	20·00
33		1r. vermilion	12·00	50·00
30/3 *Set of 4*			26·00	£100

OFFICIAL STAMPS

NOTE. The varieties occurring in the machine-printed "On S.S.S." overprints may, of course, also be found in the inverted and double overprints, and many of them are known thus.

Roman figures denote printings of the basic stamps (Nos. 7/21). Where more than one printing was overprinted the prices quoted are for the commonest.

I. MACHINE-PRINTED

On
S. S.
S.
(11)

1890. *Optd with T* **11**.

		(a) In black.		
50	3	6p. green (C)	£1200	£1200
		a. Stop before first "S"		
51		2a. pink	65·00	£180
		a. Stop before first "S"	£160	
		(b) In red.		
52	3	6p. green (C)	20·00	2·75
		a. Stop before first "S"	65·00	25·00
53		1a. bright blue	55·00	18·00
		a. Stop before first "S"	£140	65·00
		b. Opt inverted	£1400	£750
		(c) Doubly optd in red and in black.		
53*c*	3	6p. green (C)	£1100	£1100
		ca. Stop before first "S"	£2500	£2500

Nos. 50, 52 and 53*c* are from Printing II and the remainder from Printing I.

On S. S. S. (12)

On S. S. S. (13)

1891. *Optd with T* **12**.

		(a) In black.		
54	3	3p. orange (A)	3·00	35·00
		a. Opt inverted	£500	
55		6p. green (C)	1·50	1·50
		a. Opt double	£180	
		b. No stop after lower "S"	22·00	22·00
		c. Raised stop before lower "S".	£170	£130
56		1a. bright blue	£400	£475
57		2a. pink	19·00	70·00
		(b) In red.		
58	3	6p. green (C)	28·00	3·00
		a. Opt inverted	£250	£190
		b. Opt double	£250	£200
59		1a. bright blue	25·00	32·00
		a. Opt inverted	†	£600
		b. Opt double	†	£600
		c. No stop after lower "S"	£200	£225
		(c) In black and red.		
59*d*	3	6p. green (C)	£1300	

Nos. 54/5, 58 and 59*d* are from Printing II and the others from Printing I.

1892–97. *Optd with T* **13**.

		(a) In black.		
60	3	3p. orange (A)	60	50
		a. Type B	3·00	60
		b. Opt inverted	£250	
		c. First "S" inverted and stop raised	5·00	5·00
		d. No stop after lower "S"	5·00	5·00
		e. Raised stop after second "S".	38·00	16·00
		f. Vertical pair, Types **12** and **13**	£160	
61		6p. green (C)	8·00	2·25
		a. Deep green (C)	1·60	50
		b. First "S" inverted and stop raised	38·00	16·00
		c. Raised stop after second "S".	38·00	14·00
		d. No stop after lower "S"	48·00	19·00
		e. Opt double	£650	
62		1a. steel-blue		
		a. Grey-blue	12·00	1·00
		b. Opt double	£400	
		c. First "S" inverted and stop raised	45·00	10·00
		d. No stop after lower "S"	£180	70·00
		e. Raised stop after second "S".	80·00	12·00
63		2a. pink	15·00	22·00
		a. Carmine	7·00	7·00
		b. Opt inverted	£900	£900
		c. First "S" inverted and stop raised	40·00	40·00
		d. No stop after lower "S"	40·00	40·00
		e. Raised stop after second "S".	£170	£150
		(b) In red.		
64	3	6p. green (C)	5·50	50
		a. Bright green (C)	11·00	1·00
		b. Opt inverted	£140	£100
		c. First "S" inverted and stop raised	25·00	5·00
		d. Vertical pair, Types **12** and **13**	£160	£160
65		1a. bright blue	18·00	4·25
		a. Steel-blue	11·00	1·00
		b. Opt inverted	£325	£200
		c. Opt double	£325	
		d. First "S" inverted and stop raised	40·00	8·00
		e. No stop after lower "S"	40·00	8·00
		(c) Doubly overprinted in black and red.		
65*f*	3	6p. bright green (C)	—	£1200
		fa. Green (C). Red opt inverted	†	£1700

The printings used for this issue were as follows:

Printing I	—	Nos. 63 and 65
Printing II	—	Nos. 60, 64 and 65*fa*
Printing III	—	Nos. 60, 64*a* and 65*f*
Printing IV	—	Nos. 61, 62, 64 and 65*a*
Printing V	—	Nos. 60, 61*a*, 62*a* and 63*a*
Printing VI	—	No. 60a

There are seven settings of this overprint, the first of which was a composite setting of 20 (10×2), with examples of Type **12** in the upper row. The inverted "S" and the missing stop occur in the 3rd and 6th settings with the latter also including the raised stop after second "S".

On S. S. S. (14)

On S. S. S. (15)

1896–97. *Optd as T* **14**.

66	3	3p. orange (B) (1897)	13·00	1·25
		a. Comma after first "S"	55·00	30·00
		b. Opt inverted		
		c. Opt double	†	£700
67		6p. deep green (C)	5·50	60
		a. Yellowish green (D)	—	4·00
		b. Comma after first "S"	50·00	19·00
		c. Comma after lower "S"	£200	22·00
		d. "S" at right inverted	£200	45·00
68		1a. grey-blue	7·50	1·25
		a. Comma after first "S"	65·00	22·00
		b. Comma after lower "S"	£225	25·00
		c. "S" at right inverted	—	50·00
69		2a. carmine (1897)	17·00	14·00
		a. Comma after first "S"	£120	£120

Nos. 66 and 67*a* are from Printing VI and the remainder from Printing V.

There are four settings of this overprint, (1) 23 mm high, includes the comma after lower "S"; (2) and (3) 25 mm high, with variety, comma after first "S"; (4) 25 mm high, with variety, "S" at right inverted.

1898 (Nov). *Optd with T* **15**.

70	3	6p. deep green (C)	£225	11·00
		a. Yellowish green (D)	£200	8·50
		b. Small "S" at right	£375	25·00
		c. Comma after lower "S"	—	60·00
		d. Lower "S" inverted and stop raised	—	60·00
71		1a. grey-blue	£250	19·00
		a. Small "S" at right	£400	45·00
		b. Small "S" without stop	—	£190

No. 70*a* is from Printing VI and the others Printing V.

There are two settings of this overprint. Nos. 70b and 71a/b occur in the first setting, and Nos. 70c/d in the second setting.

On S. S. S. (16)

On S. S. S. (17)

1899 (July). *Optd with T* **16**.

72	3	3p. orange (B)	£325	8·50
73		6p. deep green (C)	—	25·00

No. 72 is from Printing VI and No. 73 from Printing V.

1899 (Dec)–**1900**. *Optd as T* **17**.

74	3	3p. orange (B)	—	9·50
		a. Raised stop after lower "S"	†	75·00
		b. Comma after first "S"	†	£275
		c. No stop after first "S"	†	£150
75		6p. deep green (C)	—	7·50
		a. Yellowish green (D)	†	8·50
		b. Raised stop after lower "S"	†	75·00
		c. Comma after first "S"	†	£225
		d. No stop after first "S"	†	£200
76		1a. bright blue	†	£180
		a. Grey-blue	†	12·00
		b. Slate-blue	—	15·00
		c. Raised stop after lower "S"	†	£110
		d. Comma after first "S"	†	£300
		e. No stop after first "S"	†	£160
77		2a. carmine	—	£140
		a. Raised stop after lower "S"	†	£550

There are two settings of this overprint: (1) 22 mm high, with raised stop variety; (2) 23 mm high, with "comma" and "no stop" varieties.

The printings used for this issue were as follows:

Printing I	—	No. 76
Printing V	—	Nos. 75, 76*a* and 77
Printing VI	—	Nos. 74, 75*a* and 76*b*

On S. S. S. (18)

On S S S (19)

(Optd by Waterlow & Sons)

1900. *Optd with T* **18**.

78	3	3p. orange	3·00	8·00
79		6p. green	50	45
80		1a. blue	35	60

81		2a. carmine	3·50	60·00

Nos. 78/81 were from Printing VII which was not issued without the overprint.

II. HANDSTAMPED

The words "On" and each letter "S" struck separately (except for Type **22** which was applied at one operation).

1894. *Handstamped with T* **19**.

		(a) In black.		
82	3	3p. orange (A)	3·25	3·75
		a. "On" only	75·00	
83		6p. green (C)	5·50	6·00
		a. Deep green (C)	13·00	15·00
		b. "On" only	70·00	70·00
84		1a. bright blue	65·00	48·00
		a. Dull blue	20·00	21·00
		b. Steel-blue		
		c. Grey-blue	22·00	20·00
		d. "On" only	—	£100
85		2a. carmine	19·00	18·00
		a. "On" only	£120	
		(b) In red.		
86	3	6p. green (C)	£140	£150
86*a*		1a. grey-blue	£450	£450

The printings used for this issue were as follows:
Printing I — No. 84
Printing III — No. 84*a*
Printing IV — Nos. 83, 84*b* and 86
Printing V — Nos. 82, 83*a*, 84*c*, 85 and 86*a*

1896. *Handstamped with letters similar to those of T* **13**, *with stops, but irregular.*

87	3	3p. orange (A)	95·00	75·00
		a. Type B		
88		6p. green (C)		
		a. Deep green (C)	85·00	70·00
		b. "On" omitted	£170	
88*c*		1a. grey-blue	£120	£120
89		2a. carmine	£225	

Printings used for this issue were as follows:
Printing II — No. 88
Printing III — No. 87
Printing IV — No. 88
Printing V — Nos. 87, 88*a*, 88*c* and 89
Printing VI — No. 87a

1897. *Handstamped with letters similar to those of T* **14**, *with stops, but irregular.*

90	3	3p. orange (B)	12·00	20·00
91		6p. deep green (C)	70·00	80·00
		a. "On" only	—	£110
92		1a. grey-blue	£350	£350
		a. "On" only	—	£110
93		2a. carmine	£140	£140

No. 90 was from Printing VI and the remainder from Printing V.

1897. *Handstamped with letters similar to those of T* **16**, *with stops, but irregular.*

93*a*	3	6p. deep green (C)	£180	£150

No. 93a is from Printing V.

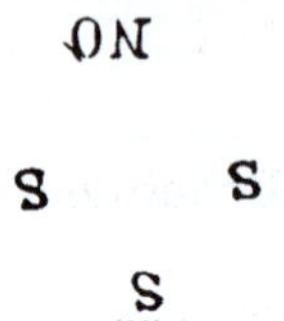
(20)

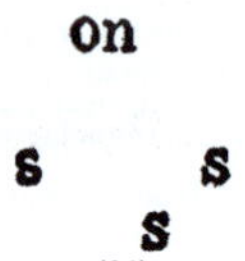
(21)

1896.

		(a) Handstamped with T **20**.		
94	3	3p. orange (A)	70·00	75·00
95		2a. carmine	75·00	80·00
		(b) Handstamped with T **21**.		
96	3	3p. orange (A)	£180	£190
97		6p. bright green (C)		
98		1a. bright blue	£325	
		a. Dull blue		
98*b*		2a. carmine	£350	

No. 98 comes from Printing 1, No. 98*a* from Printing III, No. 97 possibly from Printing IV and the remainder from Printing V.

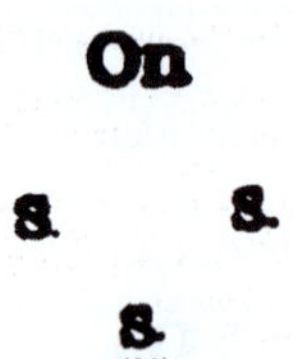
(22)

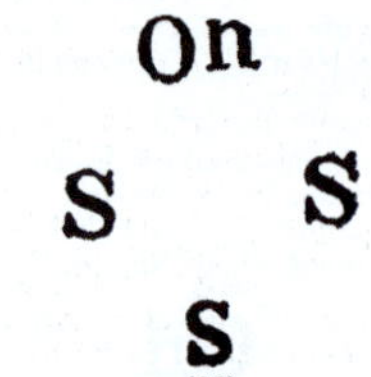
(23)

		(c) Handstamped with T **22**.		
99	3	3p. orange (B)	£130	
100		6p. deep green	£200	
101		1a. grey-blue	£250	
101*a*		2a. carmine	£400	

No. 99 is from Printing VI and the others from Printing V.

1899. *Handstamped with T* **23**.

102	3	3p. orange (A)	—	£200
		a. Type B	22·00	7·00
103		6p. green (C)		
		a. Deep green (C)	27·00	19·00
		b. Yellowish green (D)	15·00	16·00
104		1a. bright blue	—	£140
		a. Grey-blue	50·00	45·00
105		2a. pink		
		a. Carmine	60·00	30·00
		b. Rose-red	75·00	50·00
		c. "On" only	—	£150

Printings used for this issue were as follows:
Printing I — Nos. 104 and 105
Printing IV — Nos. 102 and 103
Printing V — Nos. 102, 103*a*, 104*a* and 105*a*
Printing VI — Nos. 102a, 103*b* and 105*b*

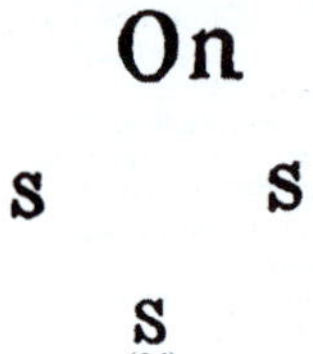
(24)

1901 (?). *Handstamped with T* **24**.

105*d*	3	6p. yellowish green (D)	—	£450

From Printing VI.

III. MIXED MACHINE-PRINTED AND HANDSTAMPED

1896.

		(i) Handstamped "On" as in T **19**, *and machine-printed opt T* **13** *complete.*		
106	3	6p. green (C)	—	£600
		(ii) Handstamped opt as T **14**, *and machine-printed opt T* **13** *complete.*		
107	3	6p. deep green (C)		

No. 106 is from Printing IV and No. 107 from Printing V.

Various other types of these handstamps are known to exist, but in the absence of evidence of their authenticity we do not list them. It is stated that stamps of T **4** were never officially overprinted.

The stamps of Sirmoor have been obsolete since 1 April 1902.

SORUTH

PRICES FOR STAMPS ON COVER	
Nos. 1/2	*from* × 5
Nos. 4/4*a*	—
Nos. 5/8	*from* × 1
No. 8*a*	*from* × 3
No. 9	*from* × 1
Nos. 10/11	*from* × 5
No. 11*e*	*from* × 1
No. 12	*from* × 4
No. 13	*from* × 5
Nos. 14/15	*from* × 3
Nos. 16/24	*from* × 20
Nos. 33/6	*from* × 50
Nos. 37/8	*from* × 10
Nos. 40/1	*from* × 50
Nos. 42/57	*from* × 10
Nos. O1/13	*from* × 20
No. 58	*from* × 15
No. 59	*from* × 6
No. 60	*from* × 10
No. 61	*from* × 6
Nos. O14/22	*from* × 10

The name "Saurashtra", corrupted to "Sorath" or "Soruth", was originally used for all the territory later known as Kathiawar. Strictly speaking the name should have been applied only to a portion of Kathiawar including the state of Junagadh. As collectors have known these issues under the heading of "Soruth" for so long, we retain the name.

GUM. Nos. 1/47 of Soruth were issued without gum.

JUNAGADH

Nawab Mahabat Khan II, 1851–1882

(Currency 40 dokras or 16 annas = 1 koree)

1 (="Saurashtra Post 1864–65")

1864 (Nov). *Handstamped in water-colour.* Imperf.

1	1	(1a.) black/*azure to grey* (laid)	£650	85·00
2		(1a.) black/*azure to grey* (wove)	—	£180
4		(1a.) black/*cream* (laid)	†	£1700
4*a*		(1a.) black/*cream* (wove)	—	£1000

ILLUSTRATIONS. Types **2** to **11** are shown actual size.

2 (1a.) (Devanagrinumeral)

3 (1a.) (Gujaratinumeral)

4 (4a.) (Devanagrinumeral)

5 (4a.) (Gujaratinumeral)

Differences in first character of bottom line on Nos. 8/*a*:

Type A "u" (error)

Type B "ka" (correct)

(Typeset Nitiprakash Ptg Press, Junagadh)

1868 (June)–**75**. *Designs as T* **2** *to* **5**. Imperf.

		A. Inscriptions in Gujarati characters. Wove paper.		
5		1a. black/*yellowish*	†	£25000
		B. Inscriptions in Devanagri characters (as in the illustrations).		
		I. Accents over first letters in top and bottom lines. Wove paper.		
6		1a. red/*green*	†	£11000
7		1a. red/*blue*	†	£8500
7*a*		1a. red/*yellow*	†	£14000
8		1a. black/*pink* (first character in bottom line as Type A)	†	£1800
8*a*		1a. black/*pink* (first character in bottom line as Type B)	£1100	£160
9		2a. black/*yellow* (1869)	†	£11000
		II. Accents over second letters in top and bottom lines.		
		(a) Wove paper.		
10	2	1a. black/*pink* (1869)	£550	75·00
		a. Printed both sides	†	—
		b. First two characters in last word of bottom line omitted (R. 4/1)	—	£800
		(b) Laid paper.		
11	2	1a. black/*azure* (1870)	90·00	9·00
		a. Final character in both top and bottom lines omitted (R. 1/1)	—	£200
		b. First two characters in last word of bottom line omitted (R. 4/1)	—	£150
		c. Doubly printed	†	£900
		d. *Se-tenant* pair. Nos. 11/12	£450	£160
11*e*		1a. black/*white*	†	£6500
12	3	1a. black/*azure* (1870)	£250	22·00
		a. Printed both sides	†	£1000
		b. Final character in bottom line omitted (R. 1/1)	£650	£150
		c. Accent omitted from last word in bottom line (R. 5/2, 5/4)	—	£110
		d. Large numeral (R. 4/1)	£800	£190
		e. First character in middle line omitted (R. 2/4)	—	£375
		f. Central two characters in middle line omitted (R. 2/4)	—	£600
13		1a. red/*white* (1875)	22·00	24·00
		a. First two characters in bottom line omitted (R. 5/1)	£100	£140
14	5	4a. black/*white*	£275	£450
		a. First two characters in last word of bottom line omitted (R. 4/1)	£1200	
		b. Final character in bottom line omitted (R. 5/2)	£2750	
15	4	4a. black/*white*	£150	£250
		a. Final character in bottom line omitted (R. 1/1)	£600	

The settings of Nos. 5/7*a* are unknown.

Nos. 10/15, and probably Nos. 8/9, were printed in sheets of 20 (4×5). The same type was used throughout, but changes occurred as the loose type was amended.

Specialists now recognise four main settings for the 1a., one of which was amended for the 2a. and another for the 4a. There are sub-settings within some of these groups:

1a. Setting I (pink wove paper) (No. 8)
Setting II (pink wove paper) (No. 8*a*)
Setting III (pink wove paper) (No. 10)
Setting IV (Devanagri numerals only) (pink wove paper) (Nos. 10/b)
Setting IVA (Devanagri numerals only) (azure vertical laid paper) (Nos. 11, 11b)
Setting IVB (Devanagri and Gujarati numerals mixed) (azure horizontal laid paper) (Nos. 11/a, 11d, 12)
Setting IVC (Devanagri and Gujarati numerals mixed) (azure or white vertical laid paper) (Nos. 11, 11c/d, 11*e*, 12/b 12e/f)
Setting IVD (Devanagri and Gujarati numerals mixed) (azure vertical laid paper) (Nos. 11, 11d, 12, 12d)
Setting IVE (Gujarati numerals only) (white vertical laid paper) (Nos. 13/a)

2a. Setting I (probably derived from 1a. Setting II) (yellow wove paper) (No. 9)

4a. Setting IA (Gujarati numerals only) (white vertical laid paper) (Nos. 14/a)
Setting IB (Devanagri numerals only) (white horizontal laid paper) (No. 15)
Setting IC (Devanagri numerals only) (white vertical laid paper) (Nos. 15/a)
Setting ID (only Gujarati numerals so far identified) (white vertical laid paper) (Nos. 14, 14b)

Settings IVA/D of the 1a. were subsequently adapted to form settings IA/D of the 4a.

The two known examples of No. 8 both come from the top row of the sheet. Marginal inscriptions indicate that No. 8*a* is from a separate setting.

Official imitations, consisting of 1a. carmine-red on white wove and white laid, 1a. black on blue wove, 4a. black on white wove, 4a. black on blue wove, 4a. red on white laid—all imperforate; 1a. carmine-red on white laid, 1a. black on blue wove, 4a. black on white laid and blue wove—all perforated 12, were made in 1890. Entire sheets of originals have 20 stamps (4×5), the imitations only 4 or 16.

6 7

(Typo Nitiprakash Ptg Press, Junagadh)

1878 (16 Jan)–**86**. *Laid paper with the lines wide apart. Imperf*

16	6	1a. green	1·00	50
		a. Printed both sides	£500	£550
		b. Laid lines close together (1886)	90	40
17	7	4a. vermilion	2·75	1·75
		a. Printed both sides	£650	
		b. Scarlet/bluish	3·75	3·25
18		4a. brown	14·00	

Nawab Bahadur Khan III, 1882–1892

1886. P 12. *(a) On toned laid paper with the lines close together.*

19	6	1a. green	40	15
		a. Imperf vert (horiz pair)	£140	
		b. Imperf between (vert pair)	†	£350
		c. Imperf horiz (vert pair)	†	£350
		d. Doubly printed	†	£475
		e. Error. Blue	£600	£600
		f. On bluish white laid paper	3·50	4·50
		fa. Imperf between (vert pair)	£225	£275
		fb. Imperf vert (horiz pair)	£225	
		g. Emerald-green	3·50	2·00
20	7	4a. red	2·75	1·25
		a. On bluish white laid paper	11·00	17·00
		ab. Printed both sides	£375	
		b. Carmine	4·50	3·50
21		4a. brown	12·00	
		(b) Wove paper.		
22	6	1a. green	3·50	1·50
		a. Imperf (pair)	80·00	£110
		b. Error. Blue	—	£600
		c. Imperf horiz (vert pair)	£160	
23	7	4a. red	5·00	12·00
		a. Imperf (pair)	£225	£300
		b. Imperf between (horiz pair)	£375	
		c. Imperf vert (horiz pair)	£375	
24		4a. brown	17·00	

There is a very wide range of colours in both values. The laid paper, on which imperforate printings continued to appear until 1912, is found both vertical and horizontal.

The 1a. was originally issued in sheets of 15 (5×3), but later appeared in sheets of 20 (5×4) with marginal inscriptions. Stamps were sometimes printed in double sheets showing two impressions of the plate printed *tête-bêche* on the same or opposite sides of the paper.

The 4a. was in horizontal strips of 5. No. 20 exists as a sheet of 10 (5×2), with two impressions of the plate printed *tête-bêche*, and No. 23 in a similar sized sheet but with both impressions upright.

Nawab Rasul Khan 1892–1911
Nawab Mahabat Khan III, 1911–1959

(Indian currency)

Three pies. ત્રણ પાઇ. (8) — One anna. એક આનો. (9)

1913 (1 Jan). *Surch in Indian currency with T* **8** *or* **9**. P 12.

		(a) On toned wove paper.		
33	6	3p. on 1a. emerald-green	15	20
		a. Imperf (pair)	£350	
		b. Imperf between (horiz pair)	£325	
		c. Imperf vert (horiz pair)	£325	
		d. Doubly printed	£225	
34	7	1a. on 4a. red	2·50	7·00
		a. Imperf (pair)	£650	
		b. Capital "A" in "Anna"	6·00	
		c. Surch inverted	£700	
		d. Imperf between (horiz pair)		
		(b) On white wove paper.		
35	6	3p. on 1a. emerald-green	15	20
		a. Imperf between vert (pair)	£500	
		b. Surch inverted	35·00	20·00
		c. Surch double	†	£450
36	7	1a. on 4a. carmine	2·25	7·00
		a. Imperf (pair)		
		b. Surch both sides	£750	
		c. Capital "A" in "Anna"	16·00	
		(c) On white laid paper.		
37	6	3p. on 1a. emerald-green	75·00	30·00
		a. Imperf (pair)	—	£475
		b. Larger English surch (21 mm long with capital "p" in "Pies") inverted	†	£2500
38	7	1a. on 4a. red	7·50	55·00
		a. Capital "A" in "Anna"	£400	
		b. Surch inverted	£700	
		c. Surch double	£700	
		d. Surch double, one inverted	£700	

The 1a. surcharge with capital "A" in "Anna" comes from a separate setting.

10 11

(Dies eng Thacker & Co, Bombay. Typo Junagadh State Press)

1914 (1 Sept). *New plates. T* **6/7** *redrawn as T* **10/11**. *Wove paper.* P 12.

40	10	3p. green	1·40	35
		a. Imperf (pair)	8·50	27·00
		b. Imperf vert (horiz pair)	£100	
		c. Laid paper	3·00	1·50
		ca. Imperf (pair)	21·00	40·00
		d. Error. Red (imperf)	†	£2750
41	11	1a. red	1·50	2·25
		a. Imperf (pair)	20·00	95·00
		b. Imperf horiz (vert pair)	£500	
		c. Laid paper	£250	£110

12 Nawab Mahabat Khan III

13 Nawab Mahabat Khan III

(Dies eng Popatlal Bhimji Pandya. Typo Junagadh State Press)

1923 (1 Sept). *Blurred impression. Laid paper.* Pin-perf 12.

42	12	1a. red	3·00	9·50

Sheets of 16 stamps (8×2).

This setting was later printed on wove paper, but single examples cannot readily be distinguished from No. 46b.

ત્રણ પાઇ (14) — ત્રણ પાઈ (14a)

1923 (1 Sept). *Surch with T* **14**.

43	12	3p. on 1a. red	5·00	7·00
		a. Surch with T **14a**	5·50	12·00

Four stamps in the setting have surch. T **14a**, i.e. with top of last character curved to right.

1923 (Oct). *Blurred impression. Wove paper.* Pin-perf 12, small holes.

44	13	3p. mauve	35	45

Sheets of 16 (4×4).

1924. *Clear impression. Wove paper.* P 12, large holes.

45	13	3p. mauve (1.24)	2·50	35
		a. Imperf (pair)	£300	
46	12	1a. red (4.24)	8·00	8·50
		a. Imperf (pair)	70·00	
		b. Pin perf	3·50	4·50

The first plate of the 3p., which printed No. 44, produced unsatisfactory impressions, so it was replaced by a second plate, producing two panes of 16 (4×4), from which No. 45 comes. Sheets printed from the first plate had very large margins.

The 1a. is also from a new plate, giving a clearer impression. Sheets of 16 stamps (4×4).

1929. *Clear impressions. Laid paper.* P 12, large holes.

47	13	3p. mauve	5·00	4·50
		a. Imperf (pair)	3·50	38·00
		b. Perf 11	14·00	10·00
		ba. Imperf between (horiz pair)	3·00	25·00

Sheets of two panes of 16 (4×4).

The laid paper shows several sheet watermarks.

No. 47ba was intentional to create a 6p. franking required by a rate change in October 1929.

15 Junagadh City

16 Gir Lion

17 Nawab Mahabat Khan III

18 Kathi Horse

(Des Amir Sheikh Mahamadbhai. Litho Indian Security Printing Press, Nasik)

1929 (1 Oct). *Inscr* "POSTAGE". P 14.

49	15	3p. black and blackish green	1·00	10
50	16	½a. black and deep blue	6·00	10
51	17	1a. black and carmine	5·00	1·00
52	18	2a. black and dull orange	13·00	2·00
		a. Grey and dull yellow	28·00	1·90
53	15	3a. black and carmine	6·00	13·00
54	16	4a. black and purple	13·00	28·00
55	18	8a. black and yellow-green	17·00	23·00
56	17	1r. black and pale blue	14·00	30·00
49/56 *Set of* 8			70·00	85·00

1935 (1 Jan). *As T* **17**, *but inscr* "POSTAGE AND REVENUE". P 14.

57	17	1a. black and carmine	10·00	1·00

OFFICIAL STAMPS

SARKARI
(O 1)

1929 (1 Oct). *Optd with Type* O **1**, *in vermilion, at Nasik.*

O1	15	3p. black and blackish green	2·00	15
		a. Red opt	1·75	10
O2	16	½a. black and deep blue	4·00	10
		a. Red opt	4·25	40
O3	17	1a. black and carmine (No. 51)	4·25	35
		a. Red opt	4·00	15
O4	18	2a. black and dull orange	2·50	1·25
		a. Grey and dull yellow	22·00	60
		b. Red opt	25·00	2·75
O5	15	3a. black and carmine	75	30
		a. Red opt	17·00	1·50
O6	16	4a. black and purple	4·25	45
		a. Red opt	21·00	3·00
O7	18	8a. black and yellow-green	3·75	3·00
O8	17	1r. black and pale blue	3·75	23·00
O1/8 *Set of* 8			22·00	25·00

SARKARI (O 2) — SARKARI (O 3)

1932 (Jan)–**35**. *Optd with Type* O **2**, *in red, at Junagadh State Press.*

O9	15	3a. black and carmine	22·00	18·00
		a. Optd with Type O **3** (1.35)	£100	5·00
O10	16	4a. black and purple	28·00	16·00
O11	18	8a. black and yellow-green	32·00	18·00
O12	17	1r. black and pale blue	35·00	95·00
		a. Optd with Type O **3** (1.35)	£160	£120
O9/12 *Set of* 4			£100	£120

1938. *No. 57 optd with Type* O **1**, *in vermilion.*

O13	17	1a. black and carmine	18·00	2·25
		a. Brown-red opt	14·00	1·50

The state was occupied by Indian troops on 9 November 1947 following the flight of the Nawab to Pakistan.

UNITED STATE OF SAURASHTRA

The administration of Junagadh state was assumed by the Government of India on 9 November 1947. An Executive Council took office on 1 June 1948.

Under the new Constitution of India the United State of Saurashtra was formed on 15 February 1948, comprising 221 former states and estates of Kathiawar, including Jasdan, Morvi, Nawanagar and Wadhwan, but excluding Junagadh. A referendum was held by the Executive Council of Junagadh which then joined the United State on 20 January 1949. It is believed that the following issues were only used in Junagadh.

The following issues were surcharged at the Junagadh State Press.

POSTAGE & REVENUE
ONE ANNA
(19)

Postage & Revenue
ONE ANNA
(20)

1949. *Stamps of 1929 surch.*

		(a) With T **19** *in red.*		
58	16	1a. on ½a. black and deep blue (5.49)	9·50	5·00
		a. Surch double	†	£550
		b. "AFNA" for "ANNA" and inverted "N" in "REVENUE"	£3000	
		c. Larger first "A" in "ANNA" (R. 2/5)	85·00	60·00
		(b) With T **20** *in green.*		
59	18	1a. on 2a. grey and dull yellow (2.49)	16·00	27·00
		a. "evenue" omitted	—	£750

No. 58b may have occurred on R. 2/5 with No. 58c being caused by its correction.

A number of other varieties occur on No. 58, including: small "V" in "REVENUE" (R. 2/3); small "N" in "REVENUE" (R. 2/4, 3/4); small "E" in "POSTAGE" (R. 3/2); thick "A" in "POSTAGE" (R. 4/4); inverted "N" in "REVENUE" and small second "A" in "ANNA" (R. 4/5); small "O" in "ONE" (R. 5/1); small "V" and "U" in "REVENUE" (R. 6/3); small "N" in "ONE" (R. 7/2).

In No. 59 no stop after "ANNA" is known on R. 1/4, 4/2, 7/4 and 8/3 and small "N" in "ONE" on R. 2/4.

21

(Typo Waterlow)

1949 (Sept). *Court Fee stamps of Bhavnagar state optd* "SAURASHTRA" *and further optd* "U.S.S. REVENUE & POSTAGE" *as in T* **21**, *in black.* P 11.

60	**21**	1a. purple	11·00	10·00
		a. "POSTAGE" omitted (R. 1/2)	£350	£250
		b. Opt double	£350	£400

The Court Fee stamps were in sheets of 80 (8×10) and were overprinted in a setting of 40 applied twice to each sheet.

Minor varieties include small "S" in "POSTAGE" (R. 2/1 of the setting); small "N" in "REVENUE" (R. 2/7); small "U" in "REVENUE" (R. 3/2); small "V" in "REVENUE" (R. 3/8, 5/5); and small O" in "POSTAGE" (R. 4/7).

Various missing stop varieties also occur.

POSTAGE & REVENUE
ONE ANNA
(22)

1950 (2 Mar). *Stamp of 1929 surch with T* **22**.

61	**15**	1a. on 3p. black and blackish green	40·00	55·00
		a. "P" of "POSTAGE" omitted (R. 8/1)	£500	£600
		b. "O" of "ONE" omitted (R. 6/1)	£750	

Other minor varieties include small second "A" in "ANNA" (R. 1/2); small "S" in "POSTAGE" with small "V" in "REVENUE" (R. 3/4, 6/1) and small "V" in "REVENUE" (R. 2/3, 3/1).

OFFICIAL STAMPS

1948 (July–Dec). *Nos. O4/O7 surch "ONE ANNA" (2¼ mm high) by Junagadh State Press.*

O14	**18**	1a. on 2a. grey & dull yellow (B.)	£14000	26·00
O15	**15**	1a. on 3a. black and carmine (Aug)	£3500	70·00
		a. Surch double	†	£3750
O16	**16**	1a. on 4a. black and purple (Dec)	£400	65·00
		a. "ANNE" for "ANNA" (R. 5/4)	£3000	£450
		b. "ANNN" for "ANNA" (R. 7/5)	£3000	£450
O17	**18**	1a. on 8a. black & yellow-green (Dec)	£350	48·00
		a. "ANNE" for "ANNA" (R. 5/4)	£3000	£350
		b. "ANNN" for "ANNA" (R. 7/5)	£3000	£350

Numerous minor varieties of fount occur in this surcharge.

1948 (Nov). *Handstamped "ONE ANNA" (4 mm high).*

O18	**17**	1a. on 1r. (No. O8)	£2250	48·00
O19		1a. on 1r. (No. O12)	£900	50·00
		a. Optd on No. O12a	–	80·00

A used copy of No. O12 is known surcharged in black as on Nos. O14/17. This may have come from a proof sheet.

1949 (Jan). *Postage stamps optd with Type* O **2**, *in red.*

O20	**15**	3p. black and blackish green	£250	17·00
O21	**16**	½a. black and deep blue	£600	15·00
O22	**18**	1a. on 2a. grey and dull yellow (No. 59)	85·00	24·00

Various wrong fount letters occur in the above surcharges.

MANUSCRIPT OVERPRINTS. Nos. 49, 50, 57, 58, 59 and 60 are known with manuscript overprints reading "Service" or "SARKARI" (in English or Gujerati script), usually in red. Such provisionals were used at Gadhda and Una between June and December 1949 (*Price from* £120 *each, used on piece*).

The United State of Saurashtra postal service was incorporated into that of India on 30 March 1950.

TRAVANCORE

PRICES FOR STAMPS ON COVER

Nos. 1/77	*from* × 10
Nos. O1/108	*from* × 15

(16 cash = 1 chuckram; 28 chuckrams = 1 rupee)

"Anchel" or "Anchal" = Post Office Department.

The stamps of Travancore were valid on mail posted to Cochin.

PRINTERS. All stamps of Travancore were printed by the Stamp Manufactory, Trivandrum, *unless otherwise stated.*

PRINTING METHODS. The dies were engraved on brass from which electrotypes were made and locked together in a forme for printing the stamps. As individual electrotypes became worn they were replaced by new ones and their positions in the forme were sometimes changed. This makes it difficult to plate the early issues. From 1901 plates were made which are characterised by a frame (or "Jubilee" line) round the margins of the sheets.

Up to the 6 cash of 1910 the dies were engraved by Dharmalingham Asari.

SHADES. We list only the main groups of shades but there are many others in view of the large number of printings and the use of fugitive inks. Sometimes shade variation is noticeable within the same sheet.

Maharaja Rama Varma X, 1885–1924

1 Conch or Chank Shell

1888 (16 Oct). *As T* **1**, *but each value differs slightly. Laid paper.* P 12.

1	**1**	1ch. ultramarine (*shades*)	4·75	4·25
2		2ch. red	6·00	11·00
3		4ch. green	20·00	17·00
1/3 *Set of* 3			28·00	29·00

The paper bears a large sheet watermark showing a large conch shell surmounted by "GOVERNMENT" in large outline letters, in an arch with "OF TRAVANCORE" at foot in a straight line. Many stamps in the sheet are without watermark.

These stamps on laid paper in abnormal colours are proofs.

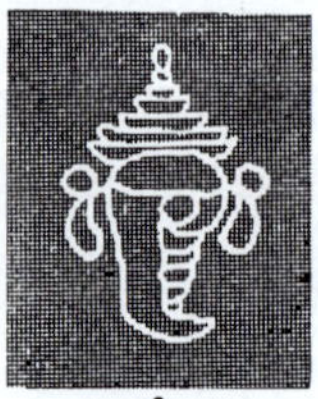

2

A B C

Three forms of watermark Type **2**.(*as seen from the back of the stamp*)

WATERMARKS AND PAPERS.

Type A appeared upright on early printings of the 1, 2 and 4ch. values on odd-sized sheets which did not fit the number of shells. Later it was always sideways with 15 mm between the shells on standard-sized sheets of 84 (14×6) containing 60 shells (10×6). It therefore never appears centred on the stamps and it occurs on hand-made papers only.

Type B is similar in shape but can easily be distinguished as it is invariably upright, with 11 mm between the shells, and is well centred on the stamps. It also occurs only on handmade papers. It was introduced in 1904 and from 1914, when Type A was brought back into use, it was employed concurrently until 1924.

Type C is quite different in shape and occurs on machine-made papers. There are two versions. The first, in use from 1924 to 1939, has 84 shells 11 mm apart and is always upright and well centred. The second, introduced in 1929 and believed not to have been used after 1930, has 60 shells (12×5) 15 mm apart and is invariably badly centred so that some stamps in the sheet are without watermark. This second version is normally found upright, but a few sideways watermark varieties are known and listed as Nos. 35g, 37c, O31j and O32i. We do not distinguish between the two versions of Type C in the lists, but stamps known to exist in the second version are indicated in footnotes. The machine-made paper is generally smoother and of more even texture.

NO WATERMARK VARIETIES. Some of these were formerly listed but we have now decided to omit them as they do not occur in full sheets. They arise in the following circumstances: (*a*) on sheets with wmk A; (*b*) on sheets with the wide-spaced form of wmk C; and (*c*) on late printings of the pictorial issues of 1939–46. They are best collected in pairs, with and without watermark.

DATES OF ISSUE. In the absence of more definite information the dates voted usually refer to the first reported date of new printings on different watermarks but many were not noted at the time and the dates of these are indicated by a query. Dated postmarks on single stamps are difficult to find.

3 **4** **5**

6 **7** **8**

1889–1904. *Wove paper.* Wmk A (upright or sideways). P 12 (sometimes rough).

4	**1**	½ch. slate-lilac (1894)	2·25	50
		a. Doubly printed	†	£300
		b. Reddish lilac	60	25
		ba. Imperf between (vert pair)	£300	£300
		bb. Doubly printed	†	£300
		c. Purple (1899)	1·25	25
		ca. Doubly printed	†	£300
		d. Dull purple (1904)	1·50	25
5	**5**	¾ch. black (14.3.01)	3·00	1·40
6	**1**	1ch. ultramarine	1·50	15
		a. *Tête-bêche* (pair)	£2500	£2250
		b. Doubly printed	†	£425
		c. Imperf vert (horiz pair)	†	£450
		d. Imperf between (vert pair)	†	£450
		e. Pale ultramarine (1892)	2·75	20
		f. Violet-blue (1901)	3·50	40
7		2ch. salmon (1890)	4·00	1·00
		a. Rose (1891)	3·50	30
		ab. Imperf (pair)	†	£475
		b. Pale pink (1899)	3·00	35
		ba. Imperf between (vert pair)	£180	
		bb. Doubly printed	£275	
		c. Red (1904)	3·00	15
		ca. Imperf between (horiz pair)	£375	£375
8		4ch. green	3·25	70
		a. Yellow-green (1901)	2·50	55
		b. Dull green (1904)	6·50	1·00
		ba. Doubly printed	†	£450

Nos. 6, 6*d*, 7 and 8 occur with the watermark upright and sideways. No. 7*a* is known only with the watermark upright. The remainder exist only with the watermark sideways.

The sheet sizes were as follows:

½ch. 56 (14×4) except for No. 4*d* which was 84 (14×6), initially without border, later with border.

¾ch. 84 (14×6) with border.

1ch. No. 6, 80 (10×8) and later 84 (14×6) without border and then with border; No. 6*d*, 96 (16×6); No. 6*e*, 84 (14×6) with border.

2ch. No. 7, 80 (10×8); No. 7*a*, 70 (10×7); Nos, 7*b*, 7*c*, 60 (10×6).

4ch. No. 8, 60 (10×6); Nos. 8*a*/*b*, 84 (14×6) with border.

After 1904 all stamps in Types **3** to **8** were in standard-sized sheets of 84 (14×6) with border.

For later printings watermarked Type A, see Nos. 23/30.

1904–20. Wmk B, upright (centred). P 12, sometimes rough.

9	**3**	4ca. pink (11.08)	30	10
		a. Imperf between (vert pair)	£275	£275
10	**1**	6ca. chestnut (2.10)	30	10
		a. Imperf between (horiz pair)	†	£275
11		½ch. reddish lilac	1·25	10
		a. Reddish violet (6.10)	1·25	10
		b. Lilac	1·25	30
		c. "CHUCRRAM" (R. 5/6)	6·50	3·75
		d. Imperf horiz (vert pair)	†	£190
12	**4**	10ca. pink (1920)	30·00	5·50
13	**5**	¾ch. black	1·50	25
14	**1**	1ch. bright blue		
		a. Blue	4·00	30
		b. Deep blue	4·00	30
		c. Indigo (8.10)	75	10
		d. Chalky blue (1912)	4·25	70
15		1¼ch. claret (*shades*) (10.14)	55	55
		a. Imperf between (horiz pair)	£325	£325
16		2ch. salmon	18·00	6·00
		a. Red (8.10)	60	10
17	**6**	3ch. violet (11.3.11)	2·75	20
		a. Imperf between (vert pair)	£275	£275
		b. Imperf between (vert strip of 3)	†	£350
18	**1**	4ch. dull green	14·00	5·00
		a. Slate-green	3·00	35
19	**7**	7ch. claret (1916)	2·25	50
		a. Error. Carmine-red	–	50·00
20	**8**	14ch. orange-yellow (1916)	2·75	2·50
		a. Imperf vert (horiz strip of 3)	£475	

1
—
4
(9)

1 C
(10)

1906. *Surch as T* **9**. Wmk B.

21	**1**	¼ on ½ch. reddish lilac	75	30
		a. Reddish violet	75	20
		b. Lilac	1·00	30
		c. "CHUCRRAM" (R. 5/6)	4·50	3·75
		d. Surch inverted	60·00	35·00
22		⅜ on ½ch. reddish lilac	40	35
		a. Reddish violet	40	35
		b. Lilac	50	35
		c. "CHUCRRAM" (R. 5/6)	4·00	4·00
		d. Surch inverted	–	50·00
		e. Surch double		
		f. "8" omitted	–	40·00

1914–22. Reversion to wmk A (sideways). P 12 (sometimes rough).

23	**3**	4ca. pink (1915)	8·00	60
24	**4**	5ca. olive-bistre (30.10.21)	80	20
		a. Imperf between (horiz pair)	48·00	55·00
		b. Imperf between (horiz strip of 3)	£110	£120
		c. "TRAVANCOPE"	–	8·00
25	**1**	6ca. orange-brown (2.15)	5·50	40
26		½ch. reddish violet (12.14)	3·00	40
		a. "CHUCRRAM" (R. 5/6)	11·00	4·00
		b. Imperf between (horiz pair)	£200	
27	**4**	10ca. pink (26.10.21)	40	10
28	**1**	1ch. grey-blue (5.22)	13·00	3·00
		a. Deep blue	13·00	3·00
29		1¼ch. claret (12.19)	13·00	35
		a. Imperf between (horiz pair)	†	£325
30	**6**	3ch. reddish lilac (8.22)	15·00	1·50

1921 (Mar). *Surch as T* **10**. Wmk A (sideways).

31	**3**	1c. on 4ca. pink	15	20
		a. Surch inverted	25·00	11·00
		b. On wmk B (upright)		
32	**1**	5c. on 1ch. grey-blue (R.)	1·00	10
		a. Deep blue	1·00	10
		b. Stamp printed both sides		
		c. Imperf between (vert pair)	†	£275
		d. Surch inverted	13·00	8·50

		e. Surch double	65·00	45·00
		f. On wmk B (upright). *Deep blue*	25·00	20·00
		fa. Surch inverted	†	£170

ALBINO OVERPRINT VARIETIES. Stamps with overprint double, one albino are frequently found in the provisional and official issues of Travancore, and are only worth a small premium over the normal prices.

Maharaja Bala Rama Varma XI, 1924–1971

1924–39. Wmk C. *Machine-made paper*. P 12.

33	4	5ca. olive-bistre (18.6.25)	11·00	2·75
		a. Imperf between (horiz pair)	£180	
		b. "TRAVANCOPE"	—	13·00
34		5ca. chocolate (1930)	2·75	20
		a. Imperf between (horiz pair)	38·00	
		b. Imperf between (vert pair)	†	£180
35	1	6ca. brown-red (3.24)	4·25	10
		a. Imperf between (horiz pair)	26·00	28·00
		b. Imperf between (vert pair)	£130	£130
		c. Printed both sides	50·00	
		d. Perf 12½	4·25	50
		e. Perf comp of 12 and 12½	6·00	4·00
		f. Perf 12½×11	—	£110
		g. Wmk sideways	—	22·00
36		½ch. reddish violet (date?)	4·25	4·25
		a. "CHUCRRAM" (R. 5/6)	32·00	
37	4	10ca. pink (8.24)	2·25	10
		a. Imperf between (horiz pair)	90·00	90·00
		b. Imperf between (vert pair)	26·00	29·00
		c. Wmk sideways (16.9.28)	—	8·50
38	5	¾ch. black (4.10.32)	9·00	50
39		¾ch. mauve (16.11.32)	35	10
		a. Imperf between (horiz pair)	†	£180
		b. Perf 12½ (8.37)	11·00	70
		ba. Imperf between (horiz pair)	£160	
		c. Perf comp of 12 and 12½	17·00	7·00
		ca. Imperf between (horiz pair)	£200	
40		¾ch. reddish violet (1939)	4·00	70
		a. Perf 12½	5·00	50
		b. Perf comp 12 and 12½	8·00	2·25
		c. Perf 11	—	£110
		d. Perf comp of 12 and 11	—	£110
41	1	1ch. slate-blue (8.26)	2·75	30
		a. Indigo	4·25	20
		b. Imperf between (horiz pair)	†	£275
		c. Imperf between (vert pair)	†	£275
		d. Perf 12½	10·00	1·10
42		1½ch. rose (1932)	2·75	10
		a. Imperf between (horiz strip of 3)	£225	
		b. Perf 12½	22·00	2·75
		c. Perf comp of 12 and 12½	—	40·00
43		2ch. carmine-red (4.6.29)	3·00	30
44	6	3ch. violet (4.25)	6·50	15
		a. Imperf between (vert pair)	90·00	90·00
		b. Perf 12½	—	11·00
		c. Perf comp of 12 and 12½	—	38·00
45	1	4ch. grey-green (5.4.34)	5·00	45
46	7	7ch. claret (1925)	11·00	1·75
		a. Doubly printed	†	£450
		b. Carmine-red (date?)	65·00	55·00
		c. Brown-purple (1932)	17·00	4·75
		ca. Perf 12½	8·50	17·00
		cb. Perf comb of 12 and 12½	7·50	17·00
46*d*	8	14ch. orange-yellow (date?)	40·00	
		da. Perf 12½	£180	

It is believed that the 12½ perforation and the perf 12 and 12½ compound were introduced in 1937 and that the 11 perforation came later, probably in 1939.

The 5ca. chocolate, 6ca., 10ca. and 3ch. also exist on the widespaced watermark (60 shells to the sheet of 84).

11 Sri Padmanabha Shrine

12 State Chariot

13 Maharaja Bala Rama Varma XI

(Des M. R. Madhawan Unnithan. Plates by Calcutta Chromotype Co. Typo Stamp Manufactory, Trivandrum)

1931 (6 Nov). *Coronation. Cream or white paper.* Wmk C. P 11½, 12.

47	11	6ca. black and green	1·60	1·60
		a. Imperf between (horiz pair)	£180	£200
48	12	10ca. black and ultramarine	1·25	70
		a. Imperf between (vert pair)	†	£475
49	13	3ch. black and purple	2·75	3·00
47/9 *Set of 3*			5·00	4·75

1 C (14) **1 C** (15)

1932 (14 Jan).

(i) Surch as T **14**.

(a) Wmk A (sideways).

50	1	1c. on 1¼ch. claret	15	50
		a. Imperf between (horiz pair)	£130	
		b. Surch inverted	4·25	7·50
		c. Surch double	32·00	32·00
		d. Pair, one without surch	£120	£140
		e. "c" omitted	45·00	45·00
51		2c. on 1¼ch. claret	15	20
		a. Surch inverted	4·25	7·00
		b. Surch double	28·00	
		c. Surch double, one inverted	60·00	
		d. Surch treble	70·00	
		e. Surch treble, one inverted	70·00	70·00
		f. Pair, one without surch	£120	£130
		g. "2" omitted	45·00	45·00
		h. "c" omitted	45·00	45·00
		i. Imperf between (horiz pair)	£130	
		j. Imperf between (vert pair)	£140	
		(b) Wmk B (upright).		
52	1	1c. on 1¼ch. claret	1·00	1·00
		a. Surch inverted	21·00	21·00
		b. Surch double	38·00	
53		2c. on 1¼ch. claret	6·50	6·50
		a. Imperf between (horiz pair)	£150	
		(c) Wmk C.		
54	1	1c. on 1¼ch. claret	14·00	20·00
		a. Surch inverted	65·00	70·00
55		2c. on 1¼ch. claret	30·00	20·00
		(ii) Surch as T **10**. Wmk B.		
56	1	2c. on 1¼ch. claret	4·00	15·00

1932 (5 Mar). *Surch as T* **15**. Wmk C.

57	4	1c. on 5ca. chocolate	15	15
		a. Imperf between (horiz pair)	£140	
		b. Surch inverted	7·50	10·00
		c. Surch inverted on back only	80·00	
		d. Pair, one without surch	£120	
		e. "1" omitted	38·00	
		f. "C" omitted	—	38·00
		g. "TRAVANCOPE"	8·50	
58		1c. on 5ca. slate-purple	1·25	20
		a. Surch inverted	†	£275
		b. "1" inverted	85·00	85·00
59		2c. on 10ca. pink	15	15
		a. Imperf between (horiz pair)	£140	
		b. Surch inverted	5·00	8·00
		c. Surch double	22·00	24·00
		d. Surch double, one inverted	80·00	80·00
		e. Surch double, both inverted	50·00	

No. 58 was not issued without the surcharge.

16 Maharaja Bala Rama Varma XI and Subramania Shrine

17 Sri Padmanabha

18 Mahadeva

19 Kanyakumari

(Plates by Indian Security Printing Press, Nasik. Typo Stamp Manufactory, Trivandrum)

1937 (29 Mar). *Temple Entry Proclamation. T* **16/19**. Wmk C. P 12.

60	16	6ca. carmine	2·50	1·25
		a. Imperf between (horiz strip of 3)	£550	
		b. Perf 12½	2·50	1·60
		c. Compound perf	40·00	40·00
61	17	12ca. bright blue	3·50	40
		a. Perf 12½	4·00	70
		ab. Imperf between (vert pair)	£475	
		b. Compound perf	65·00	
62	18	1½ch. yellow-green	1·50	2·00
		a. Imperf between (vert pair)	£375	
		b. Perf 12½	27·00	7·00
		c. Compound perf		
63	19	3ch. violet	4·25	2·25
		a. Perf 12½	5·00	3·50
60/3 *Set of 4*			10·50	5·25

COMPOUND PERFS. This term covers stamps perf compound of 12½ and 11, 12 and 11 or 12 and 12½, and where two or more combinations exist the prices are for the commonest. Such compounds can occur on values which do not exist, perf 12 all round.

20 Lake Ashtamudi

21 Maharaja Bala Rama Varma XI

22

23

24 Sri Padmanabha Shrine

25 Cape Comorin

26 Pachipari Reservoir

(Des Nilakantha Pellai. Plates by Indian Security Printing Press, Nasik. Typo Stamp Manufactory, Trivandrum)

1939 (9 Nov). *Maharaja's 27th Birthday. T* **20/26**. Wmk C. P 12½.

64	20	1ch. yellow-green	5·50	10
		a. Imperf between (horiz pair)	23·00	
		b. Perf 11	11·00	10
		ba. Imperf between (vert pair)	40·00	55·00
		bb. Imperf between (vert strip of 3)	23·00	45·00
		c. Perf 12	23·00	2·00
		ca. Imperf between (horiz pair)	22·00	
		cb. Imperf between (vert pair)	48·00	
		d. Compound perf	27·00	3·00
		da. Imperf between (vert pair)	£150	
65	21	1½ch. scarlet	3·50	4·50
		a. Doubly printed	£350	
		b. Imperf between (horiz pair)	30·00	
		c. Imperf between (vert pair)	26·00	
		d. Perf 11	4·50	23·00
		da. Imperf horiz (vert pair)	9·00	
		e. Perf 12	35·00	5·00
		f. Perf 13½	18·00	65·00
		g. Compound perf	50·00	7·50
		h. Imperf (pair)	32·00	
66	22	2ch. orange	7·00	2·25
		a. Perf 11	19·00	1·00
		b. Perf 12	£110	5·00
		c. Compound perf	£110	7·00
67	23	3ch. brown	6·50	10
		a. Doubly printed	—	£170
		b. Imperf between (horiz pair)	45·00	70·00
		c. Perf 11	21·00	30
		ca. Doubly printed	45·00	65·00
		d. Perf 12	40·00	3·75
		da. Imperf between (vert pair)	£140	£160
		e. Compound perf	40·00	1·00
68	24	4ch. red	8·50	40
		a. Perf 11	38·00	50
		b. Perf 12	35·00	8·00
		c. Compound perf	£180	£130
69	25	7ch. pale blue	11·00	19·00
		a. Perf 11	95·00	35·00
		ab. Blue	90·00	32·00
		b. Compound perf	£110	42·00
70	26	14ch. turquoise-green	7·00	65·00
		a. Perf 11	13·00	£110
64/70 *Set of 7*			45·00	80·00

27 Maharaja and Aruvikara Falls

2 CASH
(29)

28 Marthanda Varma Bridge, Alwaye

(Des Nilakantha Pellai. Plates by Indian Security Printing Press, Nasik. Typo Stamp Manufactory, Trivandrum)

1941 (20 Oct). *Maharaja's 29th Birthday. T* **27/28**. Wmk C. P 12½.

71	27	6ca. blackish violet	7·50	10
		a. Perf 11	6·50	10
		ab. Imperf between (vert pair)	20·00	
		ac. Imperf horiz (vert pair)	48·00	70·00
		b. Perf 12	25·00	1·75
		ba. Imperf between (horiz pair)	25·00	
		bb. Imperf between (vert pair)	55·00	
		bc. Imperf between (vert strip of 3)	22·00	
		c. Compound perf	8·50	1·25
72	28	¾ch. brown	8·50	20
		a. Perf 11	10·00	20
		ab. Imperf between (horiz pair)	£180	
		ac. Imperf between (vert pair)	32·00	50·00
		ad. Imperf between (vert strip of 3)	30·00	
		ae. Block of four imperf between (horiz and vert)	£250	
		b. Perf 12	55·00	10·00
		c. Compound perf	14·00	1·10

1943 (17 Sept). *Nos. 65, 71 (colour changed) and 72 surch as T* **29**. P 12½.

73		2ca. on 1½ch. scarlet	1·50	1·25
		a. Imperf between (vert pair)	48·00	
		b. "2" omitted	£325	£325
		c. "CA" omitted	£500	
		d. "ASH" omitted	£500	
		e. Perf 11	40	25

ea. "CA" omitted £500
f. Compound perf 75 1·25
fa. Imperf between (vert pair) £160
fb. "2" omitted £350
74 4ca. on ¾ch. brown 4·00 1·75
a. Perf 11 5·00 30
b. Perf 12 — £150
c. Compound perf 5·50 1·00
75 8ca. on 6ca. scarlet 4·75 10
a. Perf 11 4·00 10
ab. Imperf between (horiz pair) 42·00
b. Perf 12 — 85·00
c. Compound perf 16·00 7·50
73/5 *Set of 3* 7·50 60

30 Maharaja Bala Rama Varma XI

(31)

(Des Nilakantha Pellai. Plates by Indian Security Printing Press, Nasik. Typo Stamp Manufactory, Trivandrum)

1946 (24 Oct). *Maharaja's 34th Birthday.* Wmk C. P 12½.
76 **30** 8ca. carmine 28·00 4·00
a. Perf 11 1·25 2·00
b. Perf 12 40·00 2·50
ba. Imperf between (horiz pair) 40·00 60·00
bb. Imperf between (horiz strip of 3) 60·00
c. Compound perf

1946. *No. O103 revalidated for ordinary postage with opt T* **31**, *in orange.* P 12½.
77 **19** 6ca. blackish violet 6·50 3·00
a. Perf 11 40·00 6·50
b. Compound perf 6·50 6·50

OFFICIAL STAMPS

GUM. Soon after 1911 the Official stamps were issued without gum. Thus only the initial printings of the 1, 2, 3 and 4ch. values were gummed. As Nos. O38/9, O41/2 and O95 were overprinted on stamps intended for normal postage these, also, have gum.

PRINTINGS. Sometimes special printings of postage stamps were made specifically for overprinting for Official use, thus accounting for Official stamps appearing with watermarks or in shades not listed in the postage issues.

SETTINGS. These are based on the study of complete sheets of 84, and the measurements given are those of the majority of stamps on the sheet. Examples are known showing different measurements as each overprint was set individually in loose type, but these are not included in the listings.

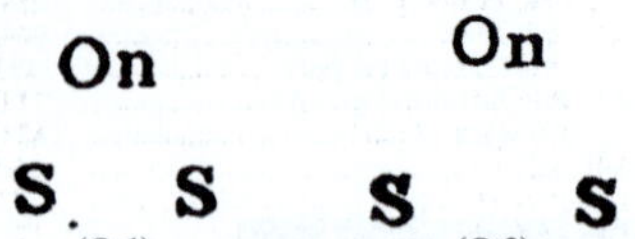

(O 1) (O 2)

Rounded "O"

1911 (16 Aug)–**30**. *Contemporary stamps optd with Type* O **1** *(13 mm wide).* P 12, sometimes rough.

(a) Wmk B (upright) *(16.8.11-21).*
O1 **3** 4ca. pink (1916) 20 10
a. Opt inverted † 80·00
b. Opt double £120 90·00
c. "S S" inverted 40·00 18·00
d. Imperf (pair) £300 £300
e. Stamp doubly printed † £300
f. Left "S" inverted — 19·00
O2 **1** 6ca. chestnut (date ?) 38·00 38·00
O3 ½ch. reddish lilac (R.) (1919) 1·50 35
a. "CHUCRRAM" (R. 5/6) 12·00 5·00
O4 **4** 10ca. pink (1921) 21·00 3·75
a. "O" inverted 60·00 11·00
b. Left "S" inverted 60·00 11·00
c. Right "S" inverted 60·00 11·00
d. Opt inverted † £130
O5 **1** 1ch. chalky blue (R.) 75 10
a. Imperf between (vert pair) † £190
b. Opt inverted 7·00 4·25
c. Opt double 65·00 50·00
d. "nO" for "On" 80·00 80·00
e. "O" inverted 8·00 2·25
f. Left "S" inverted 8·50 2·25
g. Right "S" inverted 9·00 2·50
h. "S S" inverted — 55·00
O6 2ch. red 35 10
a. Opt inverted 8·00 8·00
b. "O" inverted 9·00 1·25
c. Left "S" inverted 9·00 1·25
d. Right "S" inverted 10·00 2·50
O7 2ch. red (B.) (date ?) — £110
O8 **6** 3ch. violet 35 10
a. Imperf between (vert pair) £200 £200
b. Imperf vert (horiz pair) £160
c. Opt inverted 10·00 10·00
d. Opt double 80·00 65·00
e. Right "S" inverted 5·00 1·00
f. Right "S" omitted £130 £110
g. Left "S" omitted £130 £110
O9 3ch. violet (B.) (date ?) £160 80·00
O10 **1** 4ch. slate-green 55 10
a. Imperf between (horiz pair) — £300
b. Opt inverted 55·00 13·00
c. Opt double £130 90·00
d. "O" inverted 12·00 2·40
e. Left "S" inverted 13·00 3·75
f. Right "S" inverted 14·00 4·25
g. Left "S" omitted £130 £110
O11 4ch. slate-green (B.) (1921) — 70·00
a. "O" inverted — £160
b. Left "S" inverted — £160
c. Right "S" inverted — £160

(b) Wmk A(sideways) *(1919–25).*
O12 **3** 4ca. pink 4·00 15
a. Imperf (pair) £350 £350
b. Opt inverted 75·00 17·00
c. "O" inverted 40·00 8·50
d. Left "S" inverted 45·00 11·00
e. Right "S" inverted 45·00 13·00
O13 4ca. pink (B.) (1921) 55·00 75
a. "O" inverted — 24·00
O14 **4** 5ca. olive-bistre (1921) 90 10
a. Opt inverted 14·00 9·00
b. "O" inverted 6·00 1·75
c. Left "S" inverted 7·00 1·75
d. Right "S" inverted 7·00 1·75
O15 **1** 6ca. orange-brown (1921) 30 10
a. Imperf between (vert pair) † £225
b. Opt inverted 14·00 9·50
c. Opt double 80·00 80·00
d. "O" inverted 6·00 1·75
e. Left "S" inverted 8·00 2·00
f. Right "S" inverted 8·50 2·00
O16 6ca. orange-brown (B.) (1921) 13·00 1·75
a. Opt inverted £130 £120
b. "O" inverted 55·00 15·00
c. Left "S" inverted 55·00 15·00
d. Right "S" inverted 55·00 15·00
O17 ½ch. reddish violet (R.) (date?) 2·50 25
a. Reddish lilac (date?) 2·50 25
b. Imperf between (horiz pair) £170 £160
c. Imperf between (vert pair) 70·00 75·00
d. Stamp doubly printed 50·00
e. Opt inverted 13·00 3·50
f. Opt double, both inverted £160
g. "CHUCRRAM" (R. 5/6) 12·00 4·00
h. "On" omitted — £150
i. Right "S" inverted — 32·00
j. Right "S" omitted — £150
O18 **4** 10ca. pink (3.21) 75 10
a. Scarlet (1925?) — 12·00
b. Opt inverted — 19·00
c. Opt double 95·00 75·00
d. "O" inverted 10·00 3·25
e. Left "S" inverted 8·50 2·50
f. Right "S" inverted 10·00 3·25
g. Imperf between (vert pair) — £160
O19 10ca. pink (B.) (date?) 80·00 22·00
a. Opt inverted — 85·00
b. "O" inverted — 65·00
O20 **1** 1ch. grey-blue (R.) (date?) 5·00 60
a. Deep blue 5·00 80
b. "O" inverted 42·00 8·00
c. Left "S" inverted 45·00 11·00
d. "On" omitted
e. Opt inverted † 75·00
O21 1¼ch. claret (12.19) 40 10
a. Stamp doubly printed — £325
b. Opt inverted 9·50 8·00
c. Opt double 45·00
d. "O" inverted 13·00 2·00
e. Left "S" inverted 17·00 3·50
f. Right "S" inverted 17·00 4·25
g. Error. Carmine 50·00
O22 1¼ch. claret (B.) (1921) — 80·00
a. "O" inverted — £170
b. Left "S" inverted — £170
c. Right "S" inverted — £170

(c) Wmk C *(1925–30).*
O23 **4** 5ca. olive-bistre (1926) 40 40
a. Imperf between (horiz pair) £225 £225
b. Opt inverted 23·00 20·00
c. "O" inverted (R. 1/7) 6·00 3·50
d. Left "S" inverted (R. 6/1, 6/8) 4·75 2·75
e. Right "S" inverted (R. 6/7) 6·00 3·50
O23*f* 5ca. chocolate (1930) 55·00
fa. Opt inverted — £120
O24 10ca. pink (1926) 4·25 15
a. Imperf between (vert pair) — £200
b. Opt inverted 70·00 70·00
c. "O" inverted (R. 1/7) 28·00 3·00
d. Left "S" inverted (R. 6/1, 6/8) 23·00 2·75
e. Right "S" inverted (R. 6/7) 28·00 3·25
f. Stamp doubly printed
g. Opt double † £130
O25 **1** 1¼ch. claret (1926) 18·00 75
a. "O" inverted (R. 1/7) 65·00 8·00
b. Left "S" inverted (R. 6/1, 6/8) 55·00 6·00
c. Right "S" inverted (R. 6/7) 65·00 8·00
d. Opt double † £110
O26 **7** 7ch. claret 1·75 30
a. "O" inverted (R. 1/7) 17·00 4·00
b. Left "S" inverted (R. 6/1, 6/8) 15·00 3·50
c. Right "S" inverted (R. 6/7) 17·00 4·00
d. Error. Carmine-red 60·00
O27 **8** 14ch. orange-yellow 2·25 40
a. "O" inverted (R. 1/7) 17·00 4·00
b. Left "S" inverted (R. 6/1, 6/8) 14·00 3·00
c. Right "S" inverted (R. 6/7) 17·00 3·75

1926–30. *Contemporary stamps optd with Type* O **2** *(16½ mm wide).* Wmk C. P 12.
O28 **4** 5ca. olive-bistre 4·25 30
a. Right "S" inverted 21·00 4·50
b. Left "S" inverted 24·00 6·00
O29 5ca. chocolate (1930) 25 60
a. Imperf between (vert pair) † £300
b. Opt inverted 21·00
c. "O" inverted 4·50 6·00
d. Left "S" inverted 4·50 6·00
O30 **1** 6ca. brown-red (date?) 4·75 1·00
a. "O" inverted 23·00 7·50
b. Left "S" inverted 26·00 9·00
c. Opt double † £150
O31 **4** 10ca. pink 30 10
a. Imperf between (horiz pair) 80·00 80·00
b. Imperf between (vert pair) 65·00 65·00
c. Imperf vert (horiz strip of 3) † £170
d. Opt inverted 9·00 9·00
e. "Ou" for "On" 48·00 45·00
f. "O" inverted 5·00 2·00
g. Left "S" inverted 4·50 1·75
h. Right "S" inverted 4·25 1·25
i. Left "S" omitted 42·00 42·00
j. Wmk sideways 23·00 10·00
O32 **1** 1¼ch. claret (*shades*) 2·00 30
a. Imperf between (horiz pair) 95·00 £110
b. Imperf between (vert pair) £120 £130
c. Opt inverted 23·00 23·00
d. "O" inverted 21·00 4·50
e. Left "S" inverted 21·00 4·50
f. Right "S" inverted 21·00 4·50
g. Left "S" omitted £140 £120
h. Right "S" omitted £140 £120
i. Wmk sideways — 11·00
ia. Imperf between (vert pair) £150
O33 **6** 3ch. violet 11·00 80
a. Opt inverted † £130
b. "O" inverted 55·00 18·00
c. "O" omitted £110 85·00
d. "Ou" for "On" £150 £140
e. Left "S" inverted — 35·00
O34 **7** 7ch. claret (date?) £110 3·50
O35 **8** 14ch. orange-yellow 42·00 85
a. Imperf between (vert pair) £500
b. "O" inverted £110 9·50

The 5ca. olive-bistre, 3ch. and 7ch. exist only with the normal watermark spaced 11 mm; the 5ca. chocolate and 14ch. exist only with the wide 15 mm spacing; the 6ca., 10ca. and 1¼ch. exist in both forms.

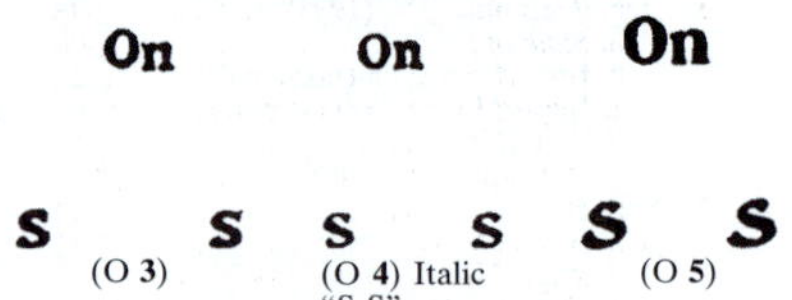

(O 3) (O 4) Italic "S S" (O 5)

1930. Wmk C. P 12.

(a) Optd with Type O **3**.
O36 **4** 10ca. pink £200 £150
O37 **1** 1¼ch. carmine-rose 4·75 3·25

(b) Optd with Type O **4**.
O38 **5** ¾ch. black (R.) 35 30
a. Left "S" omitted 95·00 95·00
b. Right "S" omitted 95·00
c. Large Roman "S" at left — £110

(c) Optd with Type O **5**.
O39 **5** ¾ch. black (R.) 35 15
a. Opt inverted † £225
b. "n" omitted £110 £110
O40 **1** 4ch. slate-green (R.) 30·00 16·00

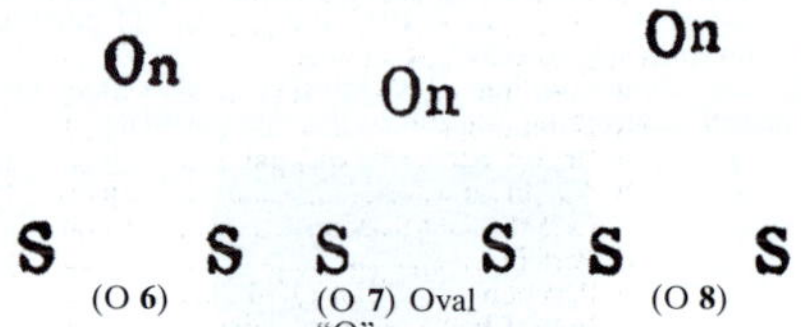

(O 6) (O 7) Oval "O" (O 8)

1930–39? *Contemporary stamps overprinted.* P 12.

(a) With Type O **6** *(16 mm high).*
(i) Wmk A.
O41 **3** 4ca. pink 27·00 65·00
a. Large right "S" as Type O **2** (R. 6/14) £140 £225

(ii) Wmk B.
O42 **3** 4ca. pink 20·00 65·00
a. Large right "S" as Type O **2** (R. 6/14) £120 £225

(iii) Wmk C.
O43 **1** 6ca. brown-red (1932) 35 10
a. Opt inverted 21·00
b. Opt double 48·00 48·00
c. "O" inverted (R. 5/11-12) 8·50 5·50
O44 **4** 10ca. pink 3·00 1·25
O45 **5** ¾ch. mauve (1933) 4·00 10
a. Imperf between (horiz pair) £110 80·00
b. Imperf between (horiz strip of 3) † £150
c. Imperf between (vert pair) † £130
d. Stamp doubly printed † £190
e. Perf 12½ 7·00 50
f. Perf comp of 12 and 12½ 18·00 2·50
g. Right "S" inverted — 29·00
O46 **1** 1¼ch. carmine-rose 15·00 1·75
a. Opt double £120 90·00
b. Large right "S" as Type O **2** (R. 6/14) £130 60·00
O47 4ch. grey-green 1·75 6·00
O48 4ch. grey-green (R.) (27.10.30) 70 20
a. Imperf between (horiz pair) £150 £130
b. Opt double 26·00 26·00
c. "O" inverted (R. 5/11-12) 50·00 22·00
d. Large right "S" as Type O **2** (R. 6/14) 50·00 30·00
e. Imperf between (vert pair) £150
O49 **8** 14ch. orange-yellow (1931) 9·50 1·75
a. Imperf between (vert pair) † £180

For the 1½ch. and 3ch., and for Nos. O43 and O48/9 but perf 12½, see Nos. O66/70 (new setting combining Types O **6** and O **8**).

(b) With Type O 7 (14 mm high). Wmk C.
O50 **3** 4ca. pink 12·00 40·00
a. "O" inverted 50·00 £110
O51 **4** 5ca. chocolate (1932) 24·00 9·50
a. Opt inverted 65·00 65·00
O52 **1** 6ca. brown-red 20 10
a. Imperf between (vert pair) 65·00 65·00
b. Opt inverted 26·00
c. Opt double † 70·00
d. "nO" for "On" £140 £140
e. Right "S" inverted 27·00 20·00
f. Left "S" omitted — 85·00
g. Large "n" as Type O 5 (R. 1/1, 1/14) 21·00 13·00
h. Large italic left "S" as Type O 5 24·00 15·00
i. Perf 12½ — 11·00
j. Perf compound of 12 and 12½ — 26·00
O53 ½ch. reddish violet (1932) 50 15
a. "CHUCRRAM" (R. 5/6) 9·00 6·00
b. "Ou" for "On" 70·00 70·00
c. Left "S" omitted — £140
d. "O" of "On" omitted £190
O54 ½ch. reddish violet (R.) (1935) 20 10
a. Imperf between (vert pair) £130 £130
b. "CHUCRRAM" (R. 5/6) 4·25 3·50
c. Left "S" inverted 28·00 25·00
O55 **4** 10ca. pink (date ?) 4·25 3·00
a. Imperf between (horiz pair) 13·00 24·00
b. Imperf between (vert pair) 10·00 22·00
c. "O" inverted 42·00 25·00
d. Right "S" inverted 42·00 25·00
O56 **5** ¾ch. mauve (1933?) 30 15
a. Imperf between (vert pair) † £160
b. "Ou" for "On" 75·00 70·00
c. "O" inverted 27·00 23·00
d. Right "S" inverted — 24·00
e. Opt double † £140
f. Perf comp of 12 and 12½ 30·00 20·00
O57 **1** 1ch. deep blue (R.) (1935) 1·75 40
a. Slate-blue 1·00 25
b. Imperf between (horiz pair) £140 £140
c. Imperf between (vert pair) 27·00 42·00
d. Perf 12½ 9·00 4·50
e. Perf comp of 12 and 12½ 25·00 9·50
O58 1¼ch. claret 1·40 1·60
O59 1½ch. rose (1933) 40 10
a. Imperf between (vert pair) † £170
b. Opt double 70·00 70·00
c. "O" inverted 5·00 2·75
e. Large "n" as Type O 5 (R. 1/1, 1/14) 50·00 23·00
f. Large italic left "S" as Type O 5 60·00 25·00
g. Left "S" inverted — 28·00
h. Perf 12½ — 12·00
i. Perf comp of 12 and 12½ — 26·00
ia. Stamp doubly printed — £225
O60 **6** 3ch. reddish violet (1933) 1·25 60
a. "O" inverted 25·00 11·00
b. Opt double † £110
O61 3ch. violet (R.) (1934) 80 10
a. Imperf between (horiz pair) £100 50·00
b. Imperf between (vert pair) 75·00 45·00
c. Opt inverted † 55·00
d. "O" inverted 23·00 14·00
e. Perf 12½ — 3·00
ea. Imperf between (vert pair) † £200
f. Perf comp of 12 and 12½ — 13·00
fa. Imperf between (horiz pair) † £200
g. "Ou" for "On" — 90·00
O63 4ch. grey-green (R.) (1935?) 1·50 20
a. "Ou" for "On" (R. 1/1) 70·00 45·00
O64 **7** 7ch. claret (*shades*) 1·25 30
a. Imperf between (vert pair) 32·00 42·00
b. "O" inverted 48·00 20·00
c. Left "S" inverted 55·00 27·00
d. Perf 12½ — 10·00
e. Perf comp of 12 and 12½ — 9·00
ea. Imperf between (vert pair) † £130
eb. Imperf between (vert strip of 3) £170 £170
O65 **8** 14ch. orange (1933) 1·75 40
a. Imperf between (horiz pair) 38·00 55·00
b. Imperf between (vert pair) £180
c. Opt inverted £375 £350

(c) New setting combining Type O 8 (18 mm high) in top row with Type O 6 (16 mm high) for remainder. Wmk C *(dates?).*

A. Type O 8.
O66A **1** 6ca. brown-red 8·00 4·50
a. Perf 12½ 8·50 4·50
b. Perf comp of 12 and 12½ — 50·00
O67A 1½ch. rose 50·00 7·00
a. Perf 12½ 80·00 9·00
O68A **6** 3ch. violet (R.) 70·00 9·00
a. Perf 12½ £100 28·00
b. Perf comp of 12 and 12½ £130 32·00
O69A **1** 4ch. grey-green (R.) 50·00 28·00
a. Perf 12½ 75·00 26·00
O70A **8** 14ch. orange-yellow 70·00 20·00
a. Perf 12½ 70·00 21·00

B. Type O 6.
O66Ba **1** 6ca. brown-red (P 12½) 3·50 1·00
ab. Imperf between (vert pair) £130 £130
ac. "O" inverted 18·00 9·00
g. Perf comp of 12 and 12½ — 21·00
O67B 1½ch. rose 13·00 35
a. Perf 12½ 23·00 65
ab. "O" inverted 75·00 21·00
c. Perf comp of 12 and 12½ — 27·00
O68B **6** 3ch. violet (R.) 13·00 1·00
a. Perf 12½ 24·00 1·25
b. Perf comp of 12 and 12½ 35·00 8·00
O69Ba **1** 4ch. grey-green (R.) (P 12½) 9·50 3·75
ab. Imperf between (horiz pair) † £225
ac. "O" inverted 90·00 40·00
O70Ba **8** 14ch. orange-yellow (P 12½) 16·00 1·00

Nos. O66/70A/B in vertical *se-tenant* pairs are very scarce. As with the postage issues it is believed that the 12½ and compound perforations were issued between 1937 and 1939.

1 ch

8 c
(O 9)

1 ch
Wrong fount "1 c" (R. 6/7)

1932. *Official stamps surch as T* **14** *or with Type* O **9**. P 12.
(a) With opt Type O **1**.
(i) Wmk A *(sideways).*
O71 **4** 6c. on 5ca. olive-bistre 60·00 26·00
a. "O" inverted £190 85·00
b. Left "S" inverted £180 80·00
c. Right "S" inverted £190 85·00
(ii) Wmk C.
O72 **4** 6c. on 5ca. olive-bistre 32·00 12·00
a. "O" inverted 80·00 27·00
b. Left "S" inverted 75·00 25·00
c. Right "S" inverted 80·00 27·00
O73 12c. on 10ca. pink £160
(b) With opt Type O **2**. Wmk C.
O74 **4** 6c. on 5ca. olive-bistre 1·75 2·00
a. Opt and surch inverted 55·00
b. Surch inverted 80·00
c. Left "S" inverted 16·00 8·50
d. Right "S" inverted 16·00 8·50
e. "6" omitted — 90·00
O75 6c. on 5ca. chocolate 20 25
a. Surch inverted 9·00 10·00
b. Surch double £110
c. Surch double, one inverted 95·00
d. "O" inverted 4·75 4·75
e. Left "S" inverted 4·75 4·75
f. Pair, one without surch £300
O76 12c. on 10ca. pink 2·00 1·50
a. Opt inverted 16·00 18·00
b. Surch inverted 7·00 7·00
c. Opt and surch inverted 40·00 42·00
d. Pair, one without surch £250
e. "O" inverted 9·00 5·50
f. Left "S" inverted 9·00 5·50
g. "Ou" for "On" £100 £100
h. Right "S" inverted 9·00 5·50
i. "c" omitted (R. 6/1) 65·00 65·00
O77 **1** 1ch.8c. on 1¼ch. claret 3·00 1·25
a. Surch inverted † £100
b. "O" inverted 13·00 4·75
c. Left "S" inverted 13·00 4·75
d. Right "S" inverted 13·00 4·75
e. Wrong fount "1 c" 32·00 20·00
(c) With opt Type O **3**. Wmk C.
O78 **4** 12c. on 10ca. pink † £425
O79 **1** 1ch.8c. on 1¼ch. carmine-rose 55·00 38·00
a. "n" omitted £250
b. Wrong fount "1 c" £200 £150
(d) With opt Type O **6**. Wmk C.
O80 **4** 12c. on 10ca. pink 95·00 29·00
O81 **1** 1ch.8c. on 1¼ch. carmine-rose £120 22·00
a. Wrong fount "1 c" £325 95·00
b. "h" omitted
c. Brown-red — 24·00
(e) With opt Type O **7**. Wmk C.
O82 **4** 6c. on 5ca. chocolate 20 30
a. Opt inverted 80·00 80·00
b. Surch inverted 11·00 13·00
c. Right "S" omitted £130 £130
d. Two quads for right "S" £500
e. Right "S" inverted 30·00
f. Surch double £120
O83 12c. on 10ca. pink 20 15
a. Opt inverted 8·00 9·00
b. Surch inverted 6·00 7·50
c. Opt and surch inverted 38·00 38·00
d. Opt double † 95·00
e. "O" inverted 19·00 19·00
f. Right "S" inverted 20·00 20·00
g. "On" omitted — £120
h. "n" omitted — £120
i. "c" omitted (R. 6/1) 38·00 38·00
j. Surch double † £110
O84 **1** 1ch.8c. on 1¼ch. claret 35 25
a. Imperf between (vert pair) † £350
c. Surch inverted 14·00 15·00
d. Surch double 65·00
e. "O" inverted 4·75 3·00
f. Wrong fount "1 c" 20·00 16·00

SERVICE
(O **10**) 13 mm ("R" with curved tail)

SERVICE
(O **11**) 13½ mm ("R" with straight tail)

SERVICE
8 CASH
(O **12**)

1939–41. *Nos. 35 and 40 with type-set opt, Type* O **10**. P 12½.
O85 **1** 6ca. brown-red (1941) 80 30
a. Perf 11 1·40 75
b. Perf 12 70 30
c. Compound perf 70 1·10
O86 **5** ¾ch. reddish violet £150 75·00
a. Perf 12 30·00 1·40
b. Compound perf £140 70·00

1939 (9 Nov). *Maharaja's 27th Birthday. Nos. 64/70 with type-set opt, Type* O **10**. P 12½.
O87 1ch. yellow-green 7·00 35
O88 1½ch. scarlet 7·50 1·25
a. "SESVICE" £110 29·00
b. Perf 12 55·00 11·00
ba. "SESVICE" — £170
bb. Imperf between (horiz pair) † £250
c. Compound perf 17·00 3·00
O89 2ch. orange 7·50 7·50
a. "SESVICE" £120 £140
b. Compound perf £130 £130
O90 3ch. brown 6·50 20
a. "SESVICE" 90·00 21·00
b. Perf 12 29·00 45
ba. "SESVICE" £275 50·00
c. Compound perf 12·00 4·50
O91 4ch. red 15·00 5·00
O92 7ch. pale blue 16·00 3·75
O93 14ch. turquoise-green 19·00 5·50
O87/93 *Set of 7* 70·00 21·00

1940 ((?))**–45.** *Nos. 40a and 42b optd with Type* O **11** *from stereos.* P 12½.
O94 **5** ¾ch. reddish violet 18·00 20
a. Imperf between (horiz pair) £150 £160
b. Perf 11 65·00 1·10
c. Perf 12 24·00 20
d. Compound perf 45·00 75
O95 **1** 1½ch. rose (1945) 14·00 8·00
a. Perf 12 4·50 1·00
b. Compound perf 23·00 13·00

1941 (?)**–42.** *Nos. 64/70 optd with Type* O **11** *from stereos.* P 12½.
O96 1ch. yellow-green 1·25 10
a. Imperf between (vert pair) 50·00 55·00
b. Opt inverted † 42·00
c. Opt double 23·00
d. Perf 11 75 10
da. Imperf between (vert pair) 42·00
db. Opt double £140 £140
e. Perf 12 3·25 50
ea. Imperf between (vert pair) £100 £100
eb. Stamp doubly printed £140
ec. Opt inverted † £140
ed. Opt double 24·00 32·00
f. Compound perf 8·00 1·25
fa. Imperf between (vert pair) † £180
O97 1½ch. scarlet 4·50 10
a. Imperf between (horiz pair) 70·00
b. Perf 11 2·50 15
ba. Imperf between (vert pair) £140 £140
bb. Imperf between (vert strip of 3) £100
bc. Imperf between (horiz pair) † £150
c. Perf 12 7·50 60
ca. Imperf between (vert strip of 3) £190
d. Compound perf 4·00 30
e. Imperf (pair) 26·00
O98 2ch. orange 2·75 30
a. Perf 11 11·00 2·00
ab. Imperf between (vert pair) † £600
b. Perf 12 £110 £110
ba. Imperf between (vert pair) £600 £600
c. Compound perf £110 £110
O99 3ch. brown 2·00 10
a. Imperf between (vert pair) † £600
b. Perf 11 3·50 10
c. Perf 12 6·50 2·25
ca. Imperf between (vert pair) £600 £600
d. Compound perf 21·00 75
O100 4ch. red 4·00 1·00
a. Perf 11 4·50 50
b. Perf 12 21·00 5·50
c. Compound perf 60·00 22·00
O101 7ch. pale blue 9·50 35
a. Perf 11 6·50 5·00
b. Perf 12 27·00 10·00
c. Compound perf 22·00 5·00
d. Blue (P 11) 14·00 7·00
da. Perf 12 11·00 6·50
db. Compound perf 30·00 20·00
O102 14ch. turquoise-green 16·00 70
a. Perf 11 16·00 1·50
b. Perf 12 11·00 2·40
c. Compound perf 75·00 10·00
O96/102 *Set of 7* 27·00 1·90

1942. *Maharaja's 29th Birthday. Nos 71/2 optd with Type* O **11**. P 12½.
O103 6ca. blackish violet 60 50
a. Perf 11 70 10
b. Perf 12 75·00 8·50
c. Compound perf 1·50 1·00
O104 ¾ch. brown 6·50 10
a. Imperf between (vert pair) † £425
b. Perf 11 8·50 10
c. Perf 12 75·00 3·00
d. Compound perf 11·00 85

1943. *Surch with Type* O **12**. P 12½.
O105 **27** 8ca. on 6ca. scarlet 3·50 30
a. Perf 11 1·25 10
ab. Surch inverted † £1200
b. Compound perf 8·50 1·25

1943–45. *Nos. 73/4 optd with Type* O **11**. P 12½.
O106 2ca. on 1½ch. scarlet 60 1·00
a. Perf 11 50 15
ab. Pair, one without surch £325
b. Compound perf 70 1·25
ba. "2" omitted £425 £425
c. Perf 12
O107 4ca. on ¾ch. brown (1945) 4·00 40
a. Perf 11 3·00 20
b. Compound perf 2·50 1·50

1946. *Maharaja's 34th Birthday. Optd with Type* O **11**. P 11.
O108 **30** 8ca. carmine 2·50 85
a. Imperf between (horiz pair) 45·00
ab. Imperf between (vert pair) † £225
b. Opt double † £275
c. Perf 12½ 3·50 1·10
ca. Stamp doubly printed 32·00
d. Perf 12 3·50 1·40
da. Stamp doubly printed 45·00

From 1 July 1949 Travancore formed part of the new State of Travancore-Cochin and stamps of Travancore surcharged in Indian currency were used.

TRAVANCORE-COCHIN

On 1 July 1949 the United State of Travancore and Cochin was formed ("U.S.T.C.") and the name was changed to State of Travancore-Cochin ("T.C.") by the new constitution of India on 26 January 1950.

PRICES FOR STAMPS ON COVER	
Nos. 1/13	*from* × 8
Nos. O1/17	*from* × 15

NO WATERMARK VARIETIES. These were formerly listed but we have now decided to omit them as they do not occur in full sheets. They are best collected in pairs, with and without watermarks.

COMPOUND PERFS. The notes above Type **17** of Travancore also apply here.

VALIDITY OF STAMPS. From 6 June 1950 the stamps of Travancore-Cochin were valid on mail from both Indian and state post offices to destinations in India and abroad.

ONE ANNA
ഒരണ
(**1**) 2p. on 6ca.

രണ്ടു പൈസ — Normal
രണ്ടു പൈസ — 1st character of 2nd group as 1st character of 1st group (Rt pane R. 14/2)

1949 (1 July). *Stamps of Travancore surch in "PIES" or "ANNAS" as T* **1**. P 12½.

1 **27** 2p. on 6ca. blackish violet (R.) 3·50 1·75
a. Surch inverted 45·00
b. Character error £170 £110
c. "O" inverted (Rt pane R. 13/1) 42·00 18·00
d. Perf 11 2·00 30
da. Imperf between (vert pair) £200 £200
db. Pair, one without surch £120
dc. Character error £160 £100
dd. "O" inverted (Rt pane R. 13/1) 42·00 20·00
e. Perf 12 50 20
ea. Imperf between (horiz pair) 75·00
eb. Imperf between (vert pair) 6·50 18·00
ec. Surch inverted £120
ed. Character error £160 £100
ee. Imperf between (vert strip of 3) 35·00
ef. Block of four imperf between (horiz and vert) 70·00
eg. "O" inverted (Rt pane R. 13/1) 38·00 20·00
eh. Imperf between (horiz strip of 3) 75·00
f. Perf 14 † £550
g. Imperf (pair) 9·00
ga. Character error £275
h. Compound perf — 38·00

2 **30** 4p. on 8ca. carmine 1·75 30
a. Surch inverted 55·00
b. "S" inverted (Rt pane R. 3/7) £100 48·00
c. Perf 11 2·75 30
ca. Imperf between (vert pair) £190 £190
cb. Surch inverted £120
cc. Pair, one without surch £150
cd. "FOUP" for "FOUR" £190 £110
ce. "S" inverted (Rt pane R. 3/7) £100 48·00
d. Perf 12 1·50 30
da. Imperf between (vert pair) 21·00
db. Pair, one without surch £140
dc. "FOUP" for "FOUR" £140 90·00
dd. "S" inverted (Rt pane R. 3/7) £110 55·00
de. Surch inverted £150
e. Imperf (pair) 75·00
f. Compound perf — 40·00
g. Perf 13½ † £650

3 **20** ½a. on 1ch. yellow-green 4·00 30
a. "NANA" for "ANNA" (Lt pane R. 3/3) £160 90·00
b. Inverted "H" in "HALF" — £120
c. Imperf between (vert pair) † £170
d. Perf 11 3·50 30
da. Imperf between (vert pair) 32·00
db. Surch inverted † £225
dc. "NANA" for "ANNA" (Lt pane R. 3/3) £200 £120
dd. Inverted "H" in "HALF" — £110
e. Perf 12 1·00 40
ea. Imperf between (horiz pair) 65·00 70·00
eb. Imperf between (vert pair) 6·50 15·00
ec. Surch inverted 5·00
ed. "NANA" for "ANNA" (Lt pane R. 3/3) £275 £130
ee. Block of four imperf between (horiz and vert) 55·00
f. Perf 14 † £450
g. Imperf (pair) 9·50 21·00
h. Compound perf — 38·00

4 **22** 1a. on 2ch. orange 4·00 30
a. Perf 11 75 30
ab. Surch double 50·00
b. Perf 12 4·25 50
ba. Imperf between (horiz pair) 8·50
bb. Imperf between (vert pair) 4·50 13·00
bc. Block of four imperf between (horiz and vert) 50·00
c. Perf 13½ £180 2·00
d. Imperf (pair) 9·00
e. Compound perf 42·00 24·00

5 **24** 2a. on 4ch. red (68) 4·25 60
a. Surch inverted † £300
b. "O" inverted 48·00 18·00
c. Perf 11 4·00 60
ca. "O" inverted — 20·00
d. Perf 12 3·25 55
da. "O" inverted 55·00 20·00
e. Compound perf 48·00 28·00

6 **25** 3a. on 7ch. pale blue (69) 13·00 6·00
a. Perf 11 6·00 3·75
ab. Blue 70·00 4·75
ac. "3" omitted † £700
b. Perf 12 13·00 3·00
c. Compound perf — 70·00
ca. Blue — 95·00

7 **26** 6a. on 14ch. turquoise-green (70) 19·00 35·00
a. Accent omitted from native surch (Rt pane R. 13/4) £325 £350
b. Perf 11 18·00 28·00
ba. Accent omitted from native surch (Rt pane R. 13/4) £325 £350
c. Perf 12 18·00 30·00
ca. Accent omitted from native surch (Rt pane R. 13/4) £350 £375
d. Compound perf 42·00 48·00
da. Accent omitted from native surch (Rt pane R. 13/4) £450
e. Imperf (pair)

1/7 *Set of* 7 28·00 30·00

There are two settings of the ½a. surcharge. In one the first native character is under the second downstroke of the "H" and in the other it is under the first downstroke of the "A" of "HALF". They occur on stamps perf 12½, 11 and 12 equally commonly and also on the Official stamps.

U. S. T. C. (**2**) T.-C. (**3**) SIX PIES (**4**)

1949. *No. 106 of Cochin optd with T* **2**.
8 **29** 1a. orange 6·00 70·00
a. No stop after "S" (R. 1/6) 80·00
b. Raised stop after "T" (R. 4/1) 80·00

1950 (1 Apr). *No. 106 of Cochin optd with T* **3**.
9 **29** 1a. orange 7·50 65·00
a. No stop after "T" 60·00 £275
b. Opt inverted £275
ba. No stop after "T" £1700

The no stop variety occurs on No. 5 in the sheet and again on No. 8 in conjunction with a short hyphen.

1950 (1 Apr). *No. 9 surch as T* **4**.
10 **29** 6p. on 1a. orange 4·50 55·00
a. No stop after "T" (R. 1/5) 22·00
b. Error. Surch on No. 8 15·00
ba. No stop after "S" £200
bb. Raised stop after "T" £200
11 9p. on 1a. orange 4·50 48·00
a. No stop after "T" (R. 1/5) 22·00
b. Error. Surch on No. 8 £160
ba. No stop after "S" £650
bb. Raised stop after "T" £650

5 Conch or Chank Shell

6 Palm Trees

(Litho Indian Security Printing Press, Nasik)

1950 (24 Oct). W **69** of India. P 14.
12 **5** 2p. rose-carmine 3·00 3·25
13 **6** 4p. ultramarine 3·75 16·00

The ordinary issues of Travancore-Cochin became obsolete on 1 July 1951.

OFFICIAL STAMPS

VALIDITY. Travancore-Cochin official stamps were valid for use throughout India from 30 September 1950.

SERVICE (O **1**) SERVICE (O **2**)

1949 (1 July)–**51**. *Stamps of Travancore surch with value as T* **1** *and optd "SERVICE". No gum. P 12½.*

(a) With Type O **1**.

(i) Wmk C of Travancore.

O1 **27** 2p. on 6ca. blackish violet (R.) 2·00 80
a. Imperf between (vert pair) £190 £190
b. Character error (Rt pane R. 14/2) 38·00 27·00
c. "O" inverted 26·00 14·00
d. Pair, one without surch £170
e. Perf 11 1·25 20
ea. Imperf between (vert pair) £190 £190
eb. Character error (Rt pane R. 14/2) 42·00 32·00
ec. "O" inverted 26·00 13·00
f. Perf 12 60 50
fa. Imperf between (horiz pair) 9·00 21·00
fb. Imperf between (vert pair) 6·50
fc. Character error (Rt pane R. 14/2) 40·00 30·00
fd. "O" inverted 26·00
fe. Block of four imperf between (horiz and vert) 28·00
g. Imperf (pair) 8·50 22·00
ga. Character error (Rt pane R. 14/2) £275
h. Compound perf 65·00

O2 **30** 4p. on 8ca. carmine 4·00 1·25
a. "FOUB" for "FOUR" (Lt pane R. 2/3) £200 £120
b. Perf 11 3·75 30
ba. "FOUB" for "FOUR" (Lt pane R. 2/3) £100 32·00
c. Perf 12 3·75 55
ca. "FOUB" for "FOUR" (Lt pane R. 2/3) £120 60·00
cb. "FOUR PIES" omitted (in pair with normal) £800
d. Compound perf 20·00 18·00

O3 **20** ½a. on 1ch. yellow-green 1·00 25
a. Pair, one without surch 95·00
b. Surch inverted 28·00
c. "NANA" for "ANNA" (Lt pane R. 3/3) £275 85·00
d. Perf 11 1·25 25
da. Pair, one without surch £170
db. Surch inverted 70·00
dc. "NANA" for "ANNA" (Lt pane R. 3/3) £275 £100
e. Perf 12 12·00 2·25
ea. "NANA" for "ANNA" (Lt pane R. 3/3) £450 £180
eb. Pair, one without surch £120
ec. Surch inverted on back only £325
f. Compound perf — 25·00

O4 **22** 1a. on 2ch. orange 18·00 7·00
a. Surch inverted 90·00
b. Pair, one without surch £650
c. Perf 11 16·00 7·50
ca. Pair, one without surch £700

O5 **24** 2a. on 4ch. red (68) 2·25 1·00
b. Perf 11 6·50 60
ba. Surch inverted £900
bb. "O" inverted — 45·00
c. Perf 12 6·50 5·50
ca. "O" inverted — 85·00
cb. Pair, one without surch £325
d. Compound perf — 35·00
e. Imperf (pair) 13·00

O6 **25** 3a. on 7ch. pale blue (69) 7·00 2·75
a. Imperf between (vert pair) 20·00
b. Blue 48·00 8·50
c. Perf 11 3·75 1·00
ca. Blue 48·00 8·50
d. Perf 12 4·50 5·50
da. Imperf between (horiz pair) 20·00
db. Imperf between (vert pair) 9·00
dc. Block of four imperf between (horiz and vert) 42·00
dd. Blue 48·00 5·00
dda. Imperf between (horiz pair) † £500
e. Imperf (pair) 12·00

O7 **26** 6a. on 14ch. turquoise-green (70) 18·00 11·00
a. Imperf between (vert pair) 30·00
b. Perf 11 16·00 11·00
c. Perf 12 50·00 11·00
ca. Imperf between (horiz pair) 27·00
cb. Imperf between (vert pair) 35·00
cc. Block of four imperf between (horiz and vert) 65·00
d. Imperf (pair) 15·00

O1/7 *Set of* 7 40·00 18·00

(ii) W **27** *of Cochin.*

O8 **27** 2p. on 6ca. blackish violet (R.) 40 1·75
a. Type O 1 double 18·00
b. Perf 11 50 1·75
c. Perf 12 1·25 1·75

O9 **24** 2a. on 4ch. red (68) 2·75 1·75
a. Perf 11 85 75
ab. Imperf between (vert pair) £300 £300
b. Perf 12 — 75·00
c. Compound perf 60·00 32·00

(b) With Type O **2**.

(i) Wmk C of Travancore.

O10 **30** 4p. on 8ca. carmine 1·00 20
a. "FOUB" for "FOUR" (Lt pane R. 2/3) £110 40·00
b. 2nd "E" of "SERVICE" in wrong fount £130 55·00
c. "S" in "PIES" inverted — 65·00
d. Imperf between (vert pair) † £170
e. Perf 11 50 20
ea. Imperf between (horiz pair) 5·00
eb. Imperf between (vert pair) 38·00
ec. "FOUB" for "FOUR" (Lt pane R. 2/3) £100 35·00
ed. 2nd "E" of "SERVICE" in wrong fount £130 65·00
ee. "S" in "PIES" inverted — 80·00
ef. Block of four imperf between (horiz and vert) 38·00
f. Perf 12 30 20
fa. Imperf between (horiz pair) 7·00
fb. Imperf between (vert pair) 2·25
fc. Block of four imperf between (horiz and vert) 16·00 28·00
fd. "FOUB" for "FOUR" (Lt pane R. 2/3) £120 42·00
ff. 2nd "E" of "SERVICE" in wrong fount £130 55·00
fg. "FOUK" for "FOUR" † £600
fh. Imperf between (vert strip of 3) 50·00
fi. Imperf between (horiz strip of 3) 55·00
g. Perf 13½ 4·50 1·25
h. Compound perf 8·50 8·50
i. Imperf (pair) 6·00
ia. 2nd "E" of "SERVICE" in wrong fount £190

O11 **20** ½a. on 1ch. yellow-green 1·00 20
a. "AANA" for "ANNA" (Rt pane R. 13/1) £200 65·00
b. Perf 11 50 20
ba. Imperf between (horiz pair) 85·00 85·00
bb. Imperf between (vert pair) 11·00
bc. Block of four imperf between (horiz and vert) 65·00
bd. "AANA" for "ANNA" (Rt pane R. 13/1) 80·00 40·00
c. Perf 12 1·25 15
ca. Imperf between (horiz pair) 3·50
cb. Imperf between (vert pair) 3·50 12·00

		cc. "AANA" for "ANNA" (Rt pane R. 13/1)	£110	55·00
		cd. Block of four imperf between (horiz and vert)	26·00	
		d. Compound perf	25·00	17·00
		da. "AANA" for "ANNA" (Rt pane R. 13/1)	–	£225
		e. Imperf (pair)	8·00	19·00
O12	22	1a. on 2ch. orange	40	30
		a. Imperf between (vert pair)	†	£180
		ab. Imperf between (horiz pair)	†	£180
		b. Perf 11	3·75	50
		ba. Imperf between (horiz pair)	8·50	21·00
		bb. Imperf between (vert pair)	£110	£110
		c. Perf 12	50	20
		ca. Imperf between (horiz pair)	7·50	
		cb. Imperf between (vert pair)	4·00	15·00
		cc. Block of four imperf between (horiz and vert)	23·00	
		d. Compound perf	29·00	20·00
		e. Imperf (pair)	16·00	
O13	24	2a. on 4ch. red (68)	4·25	80
		a. "O" inverted (Lt pane R. 14/3)	90·00	40·00
		b. Perf 11	1·50	1·10
		ba. "O" inverted (Lt pane R. 14/3)	80·00	42·00
		c. Perf 12	10·00	1·10
		ca. Imperf between (vert pair)	£130	£140
		cb. "O" inverted (Lt pane R. 14/3)	£140	40·00
		cc. Pair, one without surch	†	£900
		d. Compound perf	25·00	14·00
O14	25	3a. on 7ch. pale blue (69)	8·50	1·10
		a. "S" inverted in "SERVICE"(Lt pane R. 6/3)	75·00	32·00
		b. First "E" inverted (Lt pane R. 7/4)	£170	£130
		c. "C" inverted (Lt pane R.4/1 and 5/1)	90·00	75·00
		d. Second "E" inverted (Lt pane R. 3/2)	£160	£120
		e. Perf 11	1·50	1·10
		ea. "S" inverted in "SERVICE"(Lt pane R. 6/3)	50·00	32·00
		f. Perf 12	4·00	1·60
		fa. "S" inverted in "SERVICE"(Lt pane R. 6/3)	£130	80·00
		g. Compound perf	–	55·00
		h. Imperf (pair)	50·00	
O15	26	6a. on 14ch. turquoise-green (70)	1·50	4·50
		a. Accent omitted from native surch	16·00	13·00
		b. "S" inverted in "SERVICE"(Lt pane R. 11/4)	80·00	42·00
		c. Perf 11	14·00	4·00
		ca. Accent omitted from native surch	60·00	22·00
		cb. "S" inverted in "SERVICE"(Lt pane R. 11/4)	£140	50·00
		d. Perf 12	42·00	5·00
		da. Accent omitted from native surch	£130	30·00
		db. "S" inverted in "SERVICE"(Lt pane R. 11/4)	£275	65·00
		e. Compound perf	90·00	90·00
O10/15 *Set of* 6			5·25	5·75

(ii) W **27** of Cochin.

O16	20	½a. on 1ch. yellow-green	2·75	65
		a. Perf 11	40	40
		b. Perf 12	19·00	11·00
		c. Compound perf	12·00	3·00
O17	22	1a. on 2ch. orange	2·25	1·00
		a. Perf 11	50	40
		b. Perf 12	13·00	4·00
		c. Perf 13½	2·00	1·00
		d. Compound perf	5·50	3·00

Nos. O2, O10, O12 and O17 have the value at top in English and at bottom in native characters with "SERVICE" in between. All others have "SERVICE" below the surcharge.

Type O **2** was overprinted at one operation with the surcharges.

Nos. O10b, O10ed, O10ff and O10ia, show the second "E" of "SERVICE" with serifs matching those on the surcharge. The variety occurred on Right pane R. 10/6 and R. 11/6, but was soon corrected.

The "accent omitted" varieties on No. O15 occur on Left pane R. 5/1 and Right pane R. 1/4, 12/4, 14/1 and 13/4.

The Official stamps became obsolete in September 1951.

WADHWAN

PRICES FOR STAMPS ON COVER	
No. 1	*from* × 30
No. 2	–
Nos. 3/6	*from* × 30

Thakur Bal Singh, 1885–1910

1

(Litho Thacker & Co, Bombay)

1888–94.

(a) Thin toned wove paper.

1	1	½ pice, black (I, III) (P 12½ *large holes*)	19·00	70·00
		a. Imperf between (vert pair) (I)		
		b. Pin-perf 6½ irregular (I)	£110	
		c. Compound of 12½ and pin-perf 6½ (I)	£190	
2		½ pice, black (II) (P 12½ *irregular small holes*)	48·00	

(b) Medium toned wove paper.

3	1	½ pice, black (III) (P 12½)	13·00	50·00
4		½ pice, black (V) (P 12)	10·00	14·00

(c) Thick off-white or toned wove paper.

5	1	½ pice, black (IV, VI) (P 12) (7.92)	8·50	9·50
		a. Perf compound of 12 and 11 (IV)	21·00	50·00
6		½ pice, black (VII) (*fine impression*) (P 12) (1894)	8·50	23·00

Sheets from the Stone IV printing had at least one horizontal line of perforations gauging 11, normally between the bottom two rows of the sheet.

These stamps were lithographed from seven different stones taken from a single die. Brief details of the individual stones are as follows:

Stone I	– No. 1. Sheet size not known, but possibly 28 (4×7). Sheet margins imperforate
Stone II	– No. 2. Sheets of 42 (7×6) with imperforate margins
Stone III	– Nos. 1 (thin paper) and 3 (medium paper). Sheets of 40 (4×10) with imperforate margins
Stone IV	– Nos. 5/a. Sheets of 32 (4×8) with imperforate margins at top and right
Stone V	– No. 4. Sheets of 20 (4×5) with imperforate margins at top, right and bottom
Stone VI	– No. 5. Sheets of 30 (5×6) with all margins perforated
Stone VII	– No. 6. Sheets of 32 (4×8) with all margins perforated. Much finer impression than the other stones

Stamps from stones I and II come with or without the dot before "STATE". Those from the later stones always show the dot. The shading on the pennant above the shield can also be used in stone identification. Stamps from stones I to III show heavy shading on the pennant, but this is less evident on stone IV and reduced further to a short line or dot on stones V to VII. There is a ")" hairline after "HALF" on the majority of stamps from Stone III.

The stamps of Wadhwan became obsolete on 1 January 1895.

Ionian Islands

The British occupation of the Ionian Islands was completed in 1814 and the archipelago was placed under the protection of Great Britain by the Treaty of Paris of 9 November 1815. The United States of the Ionian Islands were given local self-government, which included responsibility for the postal services. Crowned-circle handstamps were, however, supplied in 1844, although it is believed these were intended for use on prepaid mail to foreign destinations.

Examples of the Great Britain 1855 1d. red-brown stamp are known used at Corfu, cancelled as No. CC2, but it is believed that these originate from mail sent by the British garrison.

For illustrations of the handstamp types see BRITISH POST OFFICES ABROAD notes, following GREAT BRITAIN.

CEPHALONIA

CROWNED-CIRCLE HANDSTAMPS

CC1 **CC 1** CEPHALONIA (19.4.1844)
Price on cover £1700

CORFU

CROWNED-CIRCLE HANDSTAMPS

CC2 **CC 1** CORFU (19.4.1844)
Price on cover £550

CC3 **CC 1** CORFU (G. or B.) (1844)
Price on cover –

ZANTE

CROWNED-CIRCLE HANDSTAMPS

CC4 **CC 1** ZANTE (G. or B.) (19.4.1844)
Price on cover £1300

Nos. CC1/2 were later, circa 1860/1, struck in green (Cephalonia) or red (Corfu).

It is believed that examples of No. CC4 in black are from an unauthorised use of this handstamp which is now on display in the local museum. A similar handstamp, but without "PAID AT" was introduced in 1861.

PRICES FOR STAMPS ON COVER	
Nos. 1/3	*from* × 10

PERKINS BACON "CANCELLED". For notes on these handstamps, showing "CANCELLED" between horizontal bars forming an oval, see Catalogue Introduction.

1

(Eng C. Jeens. Recess Perkins, Bacon & Co)

1859 (15 June). Imperf.

1	**1**	(½d.) orange (no wmk) (H/S "CANCELLED" in oval £11000)	95·00	£500
2		(1d.) blue (wmk "2") (H/S "CANCELLED" in oval £11000)	25·00	£180
3		(2d.) carmine (wmk "1") (H/S "CANCELLED" in oval £11000)	19·00	£180

On 30 May 1864, the islands were ceded to Greece, and these stamps became obsolete.

Great care should be exercised in buying used stamps, on or off cover, as forged postmarks are plentiful.

Iraq

(Currency. 16 annas = 1 rupee)

I. INDIAN POST OFFICES

Indian post offices were opened at Baghdad and Basra, then part of the Turkish Empire, on 1 January 1868. Unoverprinted stamps of India were used, cancels as detailed below.

Baghdad

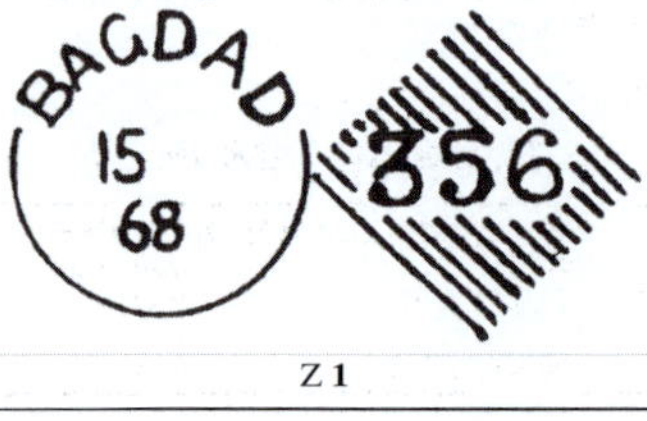

Z 1

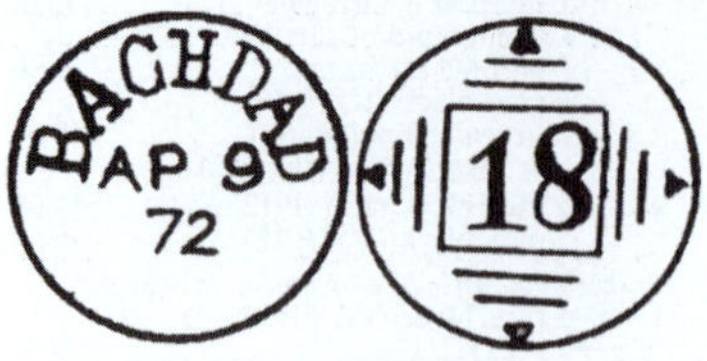

Z 2

Z 3

Z 4

Z 5

Z 6

Z 7

Postmark Type	*Approx period of use*
Z 1	1868–69
Z 2	1870–75
Z 3	1877–80
Z 4	1884–85
Z 5	1885–86
Z 6	1894–1914
Z 7	1901–1914

Between 1881 and 1887 stamps were often cancelled with a "B" in a square or circle of bars. Off cover, such stamps are indistinguishable from those used in other offices in the Bombay postal circle.

Type **Z1** may be found with the numeral obliterator and datestamp applied separately.

Type **Z4** exists with an acute accent over the first "A" of "BAGHDAD".

Stamps of India cancelled at Baghdad between 1868 and 1914 with postmarks detailed above.

1856–64. *(Nos. 37/49).*

Z1	2a. yellow-buff	80·00
Z2	4a. black	65·00

1865. *(Nos. 54/65).*

Z3	½a. blue (Die I)	11·00
Z4	1a. pale brown	13·00
Z5	2a. orange	21·00
Z7	8a. carmine (Die I)	£160

1866–78. *(Nos. 69/72).*

Z8	4a. green (Die I)	30·00
Z9	4a. blue-green (Die II)	32·00

1868. *(Nos. 73/4).*

Z10	8a. rose (Die II)	32·00

1873. *(Nos. 75/6).*

Z11	½a. blue (Die II)	8·50

1874. *(Nos. 77/9).*

Z12	9p. mauve	48·00

1876. *(Nos. 80/2).*

Z14	6a. olive-bistre	21·00
	a. Pale brown	21·00
Z15	12a. Venetian red	48·00

1882–90. *(Nos. 84/101).*

Z16	½a. blue-green	5·50
Z18	1a. brown-purple	5·50
Z19	1a.6p. sepia	11·00
Z20	2a. blue	6·50
Z21	3a. orange	13·00
	a. Brown-orange	7·50
Z22	4a. olive-green	7·50
Z23	4a.6p. yellow-green	21·00
Z24	8a. dull mauve	16·00
Z25	12a. purple/*red*	21·00
Z26	1r. slate	21·00

1891. *(No. 102).*

Z27	2½a. on 4a.6p. yellow-green	17·00

1892. *(Nos. 103/6).*

Z28	2a.6p. yellow-green	8·50
Z29	1r. green and aniline carmine	42·00

1895. *(Nos. 107/9).*

Z30	2r. carmine and yellow-brown	48·00
Z31	3r. brown and green	38·00
Z32	5r. ultramarine and violet	70·00

1899. *(No. 111).*

Z34	3p. aniline carmine	16·00

1900. *(Nos. 112/8).*

Z36	½a. yellow-green	7·50
Z37	1a. carmine	8·50
Z38	2a. pale violet	9·50
Z39	2a.6p. ultramarine	11·00

1902–11. *(Nos. 119/47).*

Z40	3p. grey	13·00
Z41	½a. yellow-green	7·50
Z42	1a. carmine	7·50
Z43	2a. violet	8·50
Z44	2a. mauve	6·50
Z45	2a.6p. ultramarine	5·50
Z46	3a. orange-brown	21·00
Z47	4a. olive	8·50
Z49	8a. purple	13·00
Z51	1r. green and carmine	27·00
Z52	2r. rose-red and yellow-brown	42·00
Z54	5r. ultramarine and violet	75·00

1905. *(No. 148).*

Z55	¼ on ½a. green	16·00

1906–07. *(Nos. 149/50).*

Z56	½a. green	5·50
Z57	1a. carmine	5·50

1911–22. *(Nos. 151/91).*

Z58	3p. grey	13·00
Z59	½a. light green	7·50
Z60	1a. carmine	7·50
Z61	2a. purple	8·50
Z62	2a.6p. ultramarine (No. 170)	11·00
Z63	2a.6p. ultramarine (No. 171)	10·00
Z64	3a. orange	15·00
Z67	8a. deep magenta	22·00
Z68	12a. carmine-lake	27·00

OFFICIAL STAMPS

1867–73. *(Nos. O20/30a).*

Z76	4a. green (Die I)	42·00
Z77	8a. rose (Die II)	55·00

1874–82. *(Nos. O31/5).*

Z80	2a. orange	38·00

1883–99. *(Nos. O37a/48).*

Z84	½a. blue-green	16·00
Z85	1a. brown-purple	17·00
Z86	2a. blue	20·00

1900. *(Nos. O49/51).*

Z90	½a. yellow-green	21·00
Z92	2a. pale violet	27·00

1902–09. *(Nos. O54/65).*

Z95	1a. carmine	16·00
Z96	2a. mauve	13·00
Z97	4a. olive	13·00
Z98	6a. olive-bistre	22·00
Z99	8a. purple	32·00

1906. *(Nos. O66/7).*

Z101	½a. green	13·00
Z102	1a. carmine	16·00

1912–13. *(Nos. O73/96).*

Z108	½a. light green	11·00
Z109	1a. carmine	13·00
Z112	6a. yellow-bistre	22·00

The post office at Baghdad closed on 30 September 1914.

Basra

Z 8

Z 9

Z 10

Postmark Type	*Approx period of use*
Z1 (inscr "BUSSORAH/357")	1868–73
Z2 (inscr "BUSREH/19")	1870–73
Z3 (inscr "BUSREH/1/K-6")	1877–79
Z8	1884
Z4 (inscr "BUSRAH")	1889–92
Z7	1905–18
Z9	1894–1916
Z10	1899–1903
Z12 (inscr "BUSRA")	1915–1918

Between 1881 and 1887 stamps were often cancelled with a "B" in a square or circle of bars. As at Baghdad, such stamps are indistinguishable from those used at other offices in the Bombay postal circle.

Stamps of India cancelled at Basra between 1868 and 1918 with postmarks detailed above.

1865. *(Nos. 54/65).*

Z121	½a. blue (Die I)	13·00
Z123	1a. pale brown	13·00
Z124	2a. orange	21·00
Z126	8a. carmine (Die I)	£160

1866–78. *(Nos. 69/72).*

Z127	4a. green (Die I)	26·00
Z128	4a. blue-green (Die II)	32·00

1868. *(Nos. 73/4).*

Z129	8a. rose (Die II)	55·00

1873. *(Nos. 75/6).*

Z130	½a. blue (Die II)	8·50

1876. *(Nos. 80/2).*

Z133	6a. pale brown	27·00
Z134	12a. Venetian red	60·00

1882–90. *(Nos. 84/101).*

Z135	½a. blue-green	5·50
Z136	9p. rose	32·00
Z137	1a. brown-purple	5·50
Z138	1a.6p. sepia	9·50
Z139	2a. blue	6·50
Z140	3a. orange	13·00
	a. Brown-orange	7·50
Z141	4a. olive-green	8·50
Z142	4a.6p. yellow-green	13·00
Z143	8a. dull mauve	13·00
Z145	1r. slate	26·00

1891. *(No. 102).*

Z146	2½a. on 4½a. yellow-green	11·00

1892–97. *(Nos. 103/6).*

Z147	2a.6p. yellow-green	6·50
Z148	1r. green and aniline carmine	55·00

1898.. *(No. 110).*

Z152	¼ on ½a. blue-green	22·00

1899. *(No. 111).*

Z153	3p. aniline carmine	9·50

1900. *(Nos. 112/8).*

Z155	½a. yellow-green	7·50
Z156	1a. carmine	7·50
Z157	2a. pale violet	9·50
Z158	2a.6p. ultramarine	9·50

1902–11. *(Nos. 119/47).*

Z159	3p. grey	16·00
Z160	½a. yellow-green	7·50
Z161	1a. carmine	8·50
Z162	2a. violet	8·50
	a. Mauve	8·50
Z163	2a.6p. ultramarine	5·50
Z165	4a. olive	11·00
Z167	8a. purple	15·00
Z169	1r. green and carmine	38·00

1905. *(No. 148).*

Z172	¼ on ½a. green	14·00

1906–07. *(Nos. 149/50).*

Z173	½a. green	7·50
Z174	1a. carmine	8·50

1911–22. *(Nos. 151/91).*

Z175	3p. grey	16·00
Z176	½a. light green	5·50
Z177	1a. carmine	5·50
Z178	2a. purple	6·50
Z179	2a.6p. ultramarine (No. 170)	11·00
Z180	2a.6p. ultramarine (No. 171)	7·50
Z181	3a. orange	16·00
Z182	4a. deep olive	11·00
Z186	1r. brown and green	27·00

OFFICIAL STAMPS

1867–73. *(Nos. 020/30a).*

Z196	4a. green (Die I)	55·00
Z197	8a. rose (Die II)	60·00

1874–82. *(Nos. 030/5).*

Z200	2a. orange	38·00

1883–99. *(Nos. 037a/48).*

Z204	½a. blue-green	16·00
Z205	1a. brown-purple	16·00
Z208	8a. dull mauve	38·00

The post office at Basra closed on 30 September 1914. In November Basra was captured by the invading Indian Expeditionary Force and the post office was reopened the following month.

Basra City

Z 11 Z 12

The office at Basra City opened in March 1915

Postmark Type	*Approx period of use*
Z **11**	1915
Z **12**	1915–18

1911–22. *(Nos. 151/91).*

Z222	½a. light green	11·00
Z223	1a. carmine	13·00
Z229	8a. deep mauve	27·00
Z230	12a. carmine-lake	30·00
Z231	1r. brown and green	26·00

The sale of Indian stamps by these offices was forbidden from 1 September 1918, being replaced by issues for Iraq, Nos. 1-14 (ex.4). The Indian post offices closed on 30 April 1919.

Other offices opened in Iraq after 1914 are believed to have been operated by the Indian Army, using stamps overprinted "I.E.F." Unoverprinted Indian stamps are also known cancelled at these offices (Amara, Ezra's Tomb, Fao, Magil and Naseriyeh) but their status is unclear.

II. ISSUES FOR BAGHDAD

PRICES FOR STAMPS ON COVER	
Nos. 1/25	*from* × 6

BRITISH OCCUPATION

British and Indian troops took Baghdad from the Turks on 11 March 1917.

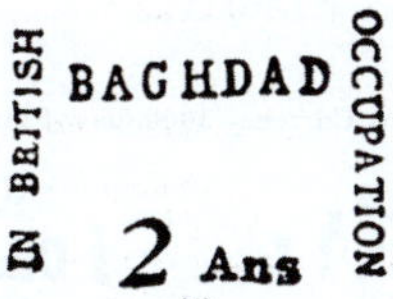

(1)

1917 (1 Sept). *Stamps of Turkey, surch as T* **1** *in three operations.*

(a) Pictorial designs of 1914. T **32**, *etc., and* **31**.

1	**32**	¼a. on 2pa. claret (Obelisk)	£180	£225
		a. "IN BRITISH" omitted	£9000	
2	**34**	¼a. on 5pa. dull purple (Leander's Tower)	£130	£140
		a. Value omitted	£8500	
3	**36**	½a. on 10pa. green (Lighthouse garden)	£750	£950
4	**31**	½a. on 10pa. green (Mosque of Selim)	£1300	£1500
5	**37**	1a. on 20pa. red (Castle)	£500	£600
		a. "BAGHDAD" double	£1700	
6	**38**	2a. on 1pi. bright blue (Mosque).	£225	£250

(b) As (a), but overprinted with small five-pointed Star.

7	**37**	1a. on 20pa. red (B.)	£350	£400
		a. "OCCUPATION" omitted	£7500	
		b. "BAGHDAD" double	£1700	
8	**38**	2a. on 1pi. bright blue (R.)	£4000	£4500

(c) Postal Jubilee stamps (Old G.P.O.). P 12½.

9	**60**	½a. on 10pa. carmine	£550	£650
		a. Perf 13½	£1200	£1300
10		1a. on 20pa. blue	£5500	
		a. Value omitted	£10000	
		b. Perf 13½	£1200	£1500
11		2a. on 1pi. black and violet	£325	£350
		a. "BAGHDAD" omitted	£7500	
		b. Perf 13½	£140	£150
		ba. "IN BRITISH" twice	†	£9000

(d) T **30** *(G.P.O., Constantinople) with opt T* **26**.

12	**30**	2a. on 1pi. ultramarine	£550	£700
		a. "IN BRITISH" omitted	£9500	

No. 11ba shows "BAGHDAD" superimposed on a second impression of "IN BRITISH" at the top of the stamp. The only known example is on cover.

(e) Stamps optd with six-pointed Star and Arabic date "1331" within Crescent. T **53** *(except No. 16, which has five-pointed Star and Arabic "1332", T* **57**).

13	**30**	½a. on 10pa. green (R.)	£130	£140
14		1a. on 20pa. rose	£500	£550
		a. Value omitted	£6000	£4750
		b. Optd with T **26** (Arabic letter "B") also	£6500	£6500
15	**23**	1a. on 20pa. rose (No. 554a)	£550	£650
		a. Value omitted	£9500	
16	**21**	1a. on 20pa. carmine (No. 732)	£4750	£6000
17	**30**	2a. on 1pi. ultramarine (R.)	£140	£160
		a. "BAGHDAD" omitted	†	£10000
18	**21**	2a. on 1pi. dull blue (No. 543) (R.)	£225	£275
		a. "OCCUPATION" omitted	£9500	

(f) Stamps with similar opt, but date between Star and Crescent (Nos. 19 and 22, T **54**; *others T* **55** *five-pointed Star).*

19	**23**	½a. on 10pa. grey-green (No. 609a) (R.)	£150	£180
		a. "OCCUPATION" omitted	£8000	
20	**60**	½a. on 10pa. carmine (P 12½) (B.)	£225	£250
		a. Perf 13½	£450	£500
21	**30**	1a. on 20pa. rose	£150	£180
22	**28**	1a. on 20pa. rose (Plate II) (No. 617)	£550	£600
23	**15**	1a. on 10pa. on 20pa. claret (No. 630)	£250	£275
		a. "OCCUPATION" omitted	£8500	£8500
24	**30**	2a. on 1pi. ultramarine (R.)	£225	£275
		a. "OCCUPATION" omitted	£9000	
		b. "BAGHDAD" omitted	£8000	
25	**28**	2a. on 1pi. ultramarine (Pl. II) (No. 645)	£1800	£2000

The last group *(f)* have the Crescent obliterated by hand in violet-black ink, as this included the inscription, "Tax for the relief of children of martyrs".

III. ISSUES FOR MOSUL

PRICES FOR STAMPS ON COVER	
Nos. 1/8	*from* × 50

BRITISH OCCUPATION

A British and Indian force occupied Mosul on 1 November 1918.

As the status of the vilayet was disputed stocks of "IRAQ IN BRITISH OCCUPATION" surcharges were withdrawn in early 1919 and replaced by Nos. 1/8.

POSTAGE

I.E.F. 'D'

1 Anna (1) **4** I **4** II

Two types of tougra in central design:
(a) Large "tougra" or sign-manual of El Ghazi 7 mm high.
(b) Smaller "tougra" of Sultan Rechad 5½ mm high.

Two types of 4a. surcharge:
I. Normal "4". Apostrophes on D 3½ mm apart.
II. Small "4". Apostrophes on D 4½ mm apart.

1919 (1 Feb). *Turkish Fiscal stamps surch as T* **1** *by Govt Press, Baghdad.* P 11½ (½a.), 12 (1a.), or 12½ (others).

1	½a. on 1pi. green and red	2·25	1·90
2	1a. on 20pa. black/*red* *(a)*	1·40	1·75
	a. Imperf between (horiz pair)	£700	
	b. Surch double	£550	
	c. "A" of "Anna" omitted	£250	
3	1a. on 20pa. black/*red* *(b)*	4·00	3·00
	b. Surch double	£650	
4	2½a. on 1pi. mauve and yellow *(b)*	1·50	1·50
	a. No bar to fraction (R. 2/4)	48·00	70·00
	b. Surch double	£1000	
5	3a. on 20pa. green *(a)*	1·60	4·00
6	3a. on 20pa. green and orange *(b)*	60·00	80·00
7	4a. on 1pi. deep violet *(a)* (I)	3·00	3·50
	a. "4" omitted	£1800	
	c. Surch double	£1000	
7*d*	4a. on 1pi. deep violet *(a)* (II)	10·00	17·00
	da. Surch double, one with "4" omitted	£3000	
8	8a. on 10pa. lake *(a)*	4·00	5·00
	a. Surch inverted	£750	£850
	b. Surch double	£650	£750
	c. No apostrophe after "D" (R. 1/5)	40·00	55·00
	d. Surch inverted. No apostrophe after "D"		
	e. "na" of "Anna" omitted	£300	
	f. Error. 8a. on 1pi. deep violet	£2500	

No. 4a occurs on some sheets only. No. 8c comes from the first setting only.

Nos. 1/8 were replaced by "IRAQ IN BRITISH OCCUPATION" surcharges during 1921.

In December 1925 the League of Nations awarded the vilayet of Mosul to Iraq.

IV. ISSUES FOR IRAQ

PRICES FOR STAMPS ON COVER	
Nos. 1/18	*from* × 6
Nos. 41/154	*from* × 2
Nos. O19/171	*from* × 4

BRITISH OCCUPATION

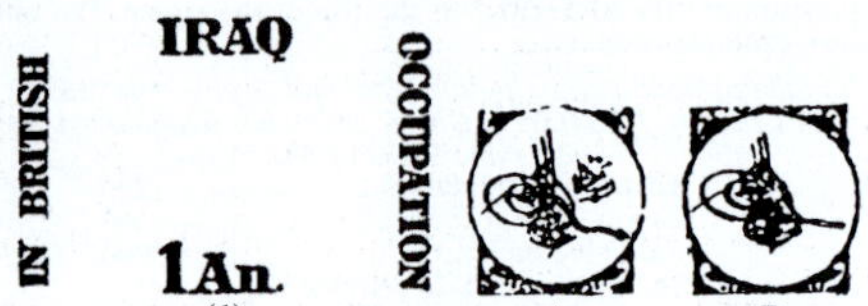

(1) A B

1918 (1 Sept)–**21**. *Turkish pictorial issue of 1914, surch as T* **1** *by Bradbury Wilkinson.* P 12.

(a) No wmk. Tougra as A (1 Sept 1918–20).

1	**34**	¼a. on 5pa. dull purple	50	1·00
2	**36**	½a. on 10pa. green	70	20
3	**37**	1a. on 20pa. red	50	10
4	**34**	1½a. on 5pa. dull purple (1920)	6·50	50
5	**38**	2½a. on 1pi. bright blue	1·25	1·40
		a. Surch inverted	£6000	
6	**39**	3a. on 1½pi. grey and rose	1·25	25
		a. Surch double (Bk. + R.)	£2750	£3500
7	**40**	4a. on 1¾pi. red-brown and grey	1·50	25
		a. Centre inverted	†	£22000
8	**41**	6a. on 2pi. black and green (32 mm surch)	1·60	1·75
		a. Centre omitted	£14000	
		b. Surch 27 mm wide	90·00	1·75
9	**42**	8a. on 2½pi. green and orange (30 mm surch)	1·50	1·50
		a. Surch inverted	†	£14000
		b. Surch 27 mm wide	14·00	70
10	**43**	12a. on 5pi. deep lilac	1·75	4·00
11	**44**	1r. on 10pi. red-brown	2·25	1·40
12	**45**	2r. on 25pi. yellow-green	7·50	2·50
13	**46**	5r. on 50pi. rose (32 mm surch)	22·00	26·00
		a. Surch 27 mm wide	38·00	30·00
14	**47**	10r. on 100pi. indigo	70·00	17·00
1/14 *Set of* 14			£110	50·00
1s/14s (ex 1½a. on 5pa.) Perf "Specimen" *Set of* 13			£450	

(b) No wmk. Tougra as B (one device instead of two) (1921).

15	**44**	1r. on 10pi. red-brown	£170	24·00

(c) Wmk Mult Script CA (sideways on ½a., 1½a.) (1921).

16	**36**	½a. on 10pa. green	2·00	2·00
17	**34**	1½a. on 5pa. dull purple	1·75	1·00
18	**45**	2r. on 25pi. yellow-green	15·00	11·00
16/18 *Set of* 3			17·00	12·50
16s/18s Optd "Specimen" *Set of* 3			95·00	

Designs: *Horiz*—5pa. Leander's Tower; 10pa. Lighthouse-garden, Stamboul; 20pa. Castle of Europe; 1pi. Mosque of Sultan Ahmed; 1½pi. Martyrs of Liberty Monument; 1¾pi. Fountains of Suleiman; 2pi. Cruiser *Hamidiye*; 2½pi. Candilli, Bosphorus; 5pi. Former Ministry of War; 10pi. Sweet Waters of Europe; 25pi. Suleiman Mosque; 50pi. Bosphorus at Rumeli Hisar; 100pi. Sultan Ahmed's Fountain.

The original settings of Nos. 1/18 showed the surcharge 27 mm wide, except for the 2½a. (24 mm), 4a. (26½ mm), 6a. (32 mm), 8a. (30½ mm), 12a. (33 mm), 1r. (31½ mm), 2r. (30 mm) and 5r. (32 mm). The 6a., 8a. and 5r. came from a subsequent setting with the surcharge 27 mm wide.

Nos. 2, 3, 5, 6 and 7/9 are known bisected and used on philatelic covers. All such covers have Makinah or F.P.O. 339 cancellations.

During January 1923 an outbreak of cholera in Baghdad led to the temporary use for postal purposes of the above issue overprinted "REVENUE".

LEAGUE OF NATIONS MANDATE

On 25 April 1920 the Supreme Council of the Allies assigned to the United Kingdom a mandate under the League of Nations to administer Iraq.

The Emir Faisal, King of Syria in 1920, was proclaimed King of Iraq on 23 August 1921.

King Faisal I

23 August 1921–8 September 1933

2 Sunni Mosque, Muadhdham

3 Gufas on the Tigris

4 Winged Cherub

5 Bull from Babylonian wall-sculpture

6 Arch of Ctesiphon

7 Tribal Standard, Dulaim Camel Corps

8 Shiah Mosque, Kadhimain

9 Allegory of Date Palm

(Des Miss Edith Cheesman (½a., 1a., 4a., 6a., 8a., 2r., 5r., 10r.), Mrs. C. Garbett (Miss M. Maynard) (others). Typo (1r.) or recess (others) Bradbury, Wilkinson)

1923 (1 June)–**25**. *T* **2/4** *and similar designs.* Wmk Mult Script CA (sideways on 2a., 3a., 4a., 8a., 5r.). P 12.

41	**2**	½a. olive-green	1·00	10
42	**3**	1a. brown	3·00	10
43	**4**	1½a. lake	1·25	10
44	**5**	2a. orange-buff	1·50	15
45	**6**	3a. grey-blue (1923)	1·50	15
46	**7**	4a. violet	3·00	30
		w. Wmk crown to left of CA	£250	£130
47	**8**	6a. greenish blue	1·50	30
48	**7**	8a. olive-bistre	3·00	30
49	**9**	1r. brown and blue-green	10·00	1·50
50	**2**	2r. black	16·00	7·50
51		2r. olive-bistre (1925)	60·00	3·25
52	**7**	5r. orange	32·00	13·00
53	**8**	10r. lake	40·00	20·00
41/53 *Set of* 13			£160	42·00
41s/53s Optd "Specimen" *Set of* 13			£425	

The normal sideways watermark on Nos. 44, 45, 46, 48 and 52 shows the crown to right of CA, *as seen from the back of the stamp.*

With the exception of Nos. 49 and 50, later printings of these stamps and of No. 78 are on a thinner paper.

10

11 King Faisal I

12

(Recess Bradbury, Wilkinson)

1927 (1 Apr). Wmk Mult Script CA. P 12.

78	**10**	1r. red-brown	8·50	50
		s. Optd "Specimen"	50·00	

See note below No. 53.

(Recess Bradbury Wilkinson)

1931 (17 Feb). Wmk Mult Script CA (sideways on 1r. to 25r.). P 12.

80	**11**	½a. green	1·50	30
81		1a. red-brown	1·50	30
82		1½a. scarlet	1·50	50
83		2a. orange	1·25	10
84		3a. blue	1·25	20
85		4a. slate-purple	1·25	2·50
86		6a. greenish blue	1·50	80
87		8a. deep green	1·50	3·00
88	**12**	1r. chocolate	3·75	2·50
89		2r. yellow-brown	7·50	6·50
90		5r. orange	26·00	40·00
91		10r. scarlet	85·00	£100
92	**10**	25r. violet	£850	£1000
80/91 *Set of* 12			£120	£140
80s/92s Perf "Specimen" *Set of* 13			£750	

(New Currency. 1000 fils = 1 dinar)

(**13**)

(**14**)

Normal "SIN"

Error "SAD" (R. 8/16 of second setting)

(Surcharged at Govt Ptg Wks, Baghdad)

1932 (1–21 Apr). *Nos. 80/92 and 46 surch in "Fils" or "Dinar" as T* **13** *or* **14**.

106	**11**	2f. on ½a. green (21.4.32) (R.)	50	10
		a. Wide space between "2" and "Fils"	26·00	26·00
107		3f. on ½a. green	50	10
		a. Surch double	£200	
		b. Surch inverted	£180	
		c. Arabic letter "SAD" instead of "SIN"	32·00	32·00
		d. Wide space between "3" and "Fils"	26·00	26·00
108		4f. on 1a. red-brown (21.4.32) (G.)	2·25	25
		a. Wide space between "4" and "Fils"	55·00	38·00
109		5f. on 1a. red-brown	75	10
		a. Inverted Arabic "5" (R. 8/11)	45·00	50·00
		b. Surch inverted	£325	
110		8f. on 1½a. scarlet	50	50
		a. Surch inverted	£170	
111		10f. on 2a. orange	50	10
		a. Inverted Arabic "1" (R. 8/13)	32·00	32·00
		b. No space between "10" and "Fils"	50	10
112		15f. on 3a. blue	1·50	1·00
113		20f. on 4a. slate-purple	1·75	1·75
		a. Surch inverted	£350	
114	–	25f. on 4a. violet (No. 46)	3·00	5·00
		a. "Flis" for "Fils" (R. 2/1, 10/8, 10/15)	£425	£550
		b. Inverted Arabic "5" (R. 10/7, 10/14)	£550	£750
		c. Vars a and b in *se-tenant* pair.	£1200	
		d. Error 20f. on 4a. violet (R. 10/1, 10/9)	£3250	
115	**11**	30f. on 6a. greenish blue	2·75	60
		a. Error 80f. on 6a. greenish blue	£3250	
116		40f. on 8a. deep green	2·50	4·25
117	**12**	75f. on 1r. chocolate	2·25	4·25
		a. Inverted Arabic "5"	50·00	75·00
118		100f. on 2r. yellow-brown	5·50	4·00
119		200f. on 5r. orange	21·00	28·00
120		½d. on 10r. scarlet	75·00	£100
		a. No bar in English "½"	£1000	£1200
		b. Scarlet-vermilion	80·00	£130
121	**10**	1d. on 25r. violet	£160	£250
106/121 *Set of* 16			£250	£350

Nos. 106/13 and 115/16 were in sheets of 160 (16×10) No. 114 sheets of 150 (15×10) and Nos. 117/21 sheets of 100 (10×10). There were three settings of the surcharge for the 3f. and two settings for the 5, 10, 25, 40, 100 and 200f. Nos. 109a and 111a come from the first setting and Nos. 107c, 111b and 114a/b come from the second.

The "wide space" varieties, Nos. 106a, 107a and 108a, show a 2 mm space between the numeral and "Fils" instead of 1 mm. On No. 106a it occurs R. 8/5 and R. 8/13, on 107d on R. 10/5 and R. 10/10 of the first setting and R. 6/6 of the second and on No. 108a on R. 7/1 and R. 7/9, although R. 7/9 is also known with normal spacing.

No. 109a occurs in the first setting and can be easily identified as it shows the point of the Arabic numeral at the foot of the surcharge.

All 10f. stamps from the second setting are as No. 111b except for R. 4/7–8 and 15–16 where the spacing is the same as for the first setting (Type **13**).

No. 114d shows "20" instead of "25". Many examples of this error were removed from the sheets before issue. The Arabic value "25" was unaltered.

No. 115a shows the error in the English face value only.

No. 117a occurs on R. 1/2, 1/7 and a third position in the first vertical row not yet identified.

No. 120a occurs on R. 1/2, R. 2/3 and R. 10/1.

No. 120b was a special printing of No. 91 which does not exist unsurcharged.

15

1932 (9 May–June). *T* **10** *to* **12**, *but with values altered to "FILS" or "DINAR" as in T* **15**. Wmk Mult Script CA (sideways on 50f. to 1d.). P 12.

138	**11**	2f. ultramarine (6.32)	50	20
139		3f. green	50	10
140		4f. brown-purple (6.32)	50	10
141		5f. grey-green	50	10
142		8f. scarlet	1·50	10
143		10f. yellow	1·50	10
144		15f. blue	1·50	10
145		20f. orange	2·00	50
146		25f. mauve	2·25	50
147		30f. bronze-green	2·25	15
148		40f. violet	1·50	1·00
149	**12**	50f. brown	1·50	20
150		75f. dull ultramarine	4·50	2·75
151		100f. deep green	7·00	70
152		200f. scarlet	13·00	3·25
153	**10**	½d. deep blue	50·00	45·00
154		1d. claret	£120	£120
138/54 *Set of* 17			£190	£150
138s/54s Perf "Specimen" *Set of* 17			£400	

OFFICIAL STAMPS

ON STATE SERVICE

(O **2**)

1920 (16 May)–**23**. *As Nos. 1/18, but surch includes additional wording "ON STATE SERVICE" as Type* O **2** *in black.*

(a) No wmk. Tougra as A.

O19	**36**	½a. on 10pa. blue-green	9·00	1·75
O20	**37**	1a. on 20pa. red	4·00	60
O21	**34**	1½a. on 5pa. purple-brown	25·00	2·50
O22	**38**	2½a. on 1pi. blue	4·00	4·25
O23	**39**	3a. on 1½pi. black and rose	21·00	80
O24	**40**	4a. on 1¾pi. red-brown and grey-blue	26·00	3·25
O25	**41**	6a. on 2pi. black and green	24·00	6·50
O26	**42**	8a. on 2½pi. yellow-green and orange-brown	24·00	4·00
O27	**43**	12a. on 5pi. purple	17·00	11·00
O28	**44**	1r. on 10pi. red-brown	23·00	9·00
O29	**45**	2r. on 25pi. olive-green	25·00	14·00
O30	**46**	5r. on 50pi. rose-carmine	48·00	40·00
O31	**47**	10r. on 100pi. slate-blue	75·00	95·00
O19/31 *Set of* 13			£300	£170

(b) No wmk. Tougra as B (No. 15) (1922).

O32	**44**	1r. on 10pi. red-brown	30·00	7·00

(c) Wmk Mult Script CA (sideways on ½a. to 8a.) (1921–23).

O33	**36**	½a. on 10pa. green	1·00	1·00
O34	**37**	1a. on 20pa. red	5·50	1·00
O35	**34**	1½a. on 5pa. purple-brown	2·75	65
O36	**40**	4a. on 1¾pi. red-brown and grey-blue	2·00	2·00
O37	**41**	6a. on 2pi. black and green (10.3.23)	23·00	£120
O38	**42**	8a. on 2½pi. yellow-green and orange-brown	3·25	2·00
O39	**43**	12a. on 5pi. purple (10.3.23)	23·00	75·00

O40	45	2r. on 25pi. olive-green (10.3.23).	70·00	£110
O33/40 *Set of* 8			£120	£275
O33s/40s Optd "Specimen" *Set of* 8			£250	

Nos. O25/6, O30 and O37/8 only exist from the setting with the surcharge 27½ mm wide.

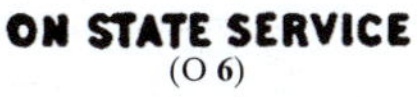

(O 6)

(O 7)

1923. *Optd with Types* O **6** *(horiz designs) or* O **7** *(vert designs).*

O54	2	½a. olive-green	1·50	1·25
O55	3	1a. brown	1·75	20
O56	4	1½a. lake	1·75	2·75
O57	5	2a. orange-buff	2·00	40
O58	6	3a. grey-blue	2·50	1·25
O59	7	4a. violet	4·25	1·25
O60	8	6a. greenish blue	3·75	1·25
O61	7	8a. olive-bistre	4·00	3·00
O62	9	1r. brown and blue-green	10·00	2·25
O63	2	2r. black (R.)	23·00	9·50
O64	7	5r. orange	50·00	30·00
O65	8	10r. lake	£100	48·00
O54/65 *Set of* 12			£180	90·00
O54s/65s Optd "Specimen" *Set of* 12			£400	

(O 8)

(O 9)

1924–25. *Optd with Types* O **8** *(horiz designs) or* O **9** *(vert designs).*

O66	2	½a. olive-green	1·25	10
O67	3	1a. brown	1·00	10
O68	4	1½a. lake	1·00	30
O69	5	2a. orange-buff	1·50	10
O70	6	3a. grey-blue	2·00	10
O71	7	4a. violet	4·00	30
O72	8	6a. greenish blue	1·75	20
O73	7	8a. olive-bistre	3·75	35
O74	9	1r. brown and blue-green	10·00	2·00
O75	2	2r. olive-bistre (1925)	35·00	3·75
O76	7	5r. orange	55·00	45·00
O77	8	10r. lake	£100	42·00
O66/77 *Set of* 12			£200	85·00
O66s/77s Optd "Specimen" *Set of* 12			£400	

1927 (1 Apr). *Optd with Type* O **9**.

O79	10	1r. red-brown	6·50	1·75
		s. Optd "Specimen"	50·00	

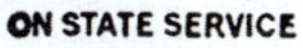

(O 12)

(O 13)

1931. *Optd.*

(a) As Type O **12**.

O93	11	½a. green	65	2·75
O94		1a. red-brown	80	10
O95		1½a. scarlet	4·50	23·00
O96		2a. orange	80	10
O97		3a. blue	85	1·25
O98		4a. slate-purple	1·00	1·50
O99		6a. greenish blue	4·50	23·00
O100		8a. deep green	4·75	23·00
		(b) As Type O **13**, *horizontally.*		
O101	12	1r. chocolate	14·00	21·00
O102		2r. yellow-brown	22·00	70·00
O103		5r. orange	42·00	£150
O104		10r. scarlet	£110	£250
		(c) As Type O **13**, *vertically upwards.*		
O105	10	25r. violet	£850	£1100
O93/104 *Set of* 12			£180	£500
O93s/105s Perf "Specimen" *Set of* 13			£750	

1932 (1 Apr). *Official issues of 1924–25 and 1931 surch in "FILS" or "DINAR", as T* **13** *or* **14**.

O122	11	3f. on ½a. green	4·00	3·50
		a. Pair, one without surch	£475	
O123		4f. on 1a. red-brown (G.)	2·50	10
O124		5f. on 1a. red-brown	2·50	10
		a. Inverted Arabic "5" (R. 8/11)	65·00	42·00
O125	4	8f. on 1½a. lake (No. O68)	7·50	50
O126	11	10f. on 2a. orange	3·25	10
		a. Inverted Arabic "1" (R. 8/13)	55·00	38·00
		b. "10" omitted	†	£2500
		c. No space between "10" and "Fils"	3·25	10
O127		15f. on 3a. blue	4·25	3·75
O128		20f. on 4a. slate-purple	4·25	3·75
O129		25f. on 4a. slate-purple	4·50	2·00
O130	8	30f. on 6a. greenish blue (No. O72)	7·00	1·75
O131	11	40f. on 8a. deep green	4·00	3·50
		a. "Flis" for "Fils" (R. 7/5, 7/13).	£425	£500
O132	12	50f. on 1r. chocolate	9·00	3·75
		a. Inverted Arabic "5" (R. 1/2) ..	£130	£140
O133		75f. on 1r. chocolate	7·00	7·00
		a. Inverted Arabic "5"	75·00	80·00
O134	2	100f. on 2r. olive-bistre (surch at top)	25·00	3·50
		a. Surch at foot	25·00	15·00
O135	7	200f. on 5r. orange (No. O76)	24·00	24·00
O136	8	½d. on 10r. lake (No. O77)	90·00	£110
		a. No bar in English "½" (R. 2/10)	£1100	£1400
O137	10	1d. on 25r. violet	£170	£275
O122/37 *Set of* 16			£325	£400

Nos. O122/4, O126/9 and O131 were in sheets of 160 (16×10), Nos. O130, O134 and O136 150 (10×15), No. O135 150 (15×10) and Nos. O125, O132/3 and O137 in sheets of 100 (10×10). There was a second setting of the surcharge for the 3f. (equivalent to the third postage setting), 10f. to 25f., 40f. to 100f. and 1d. Nos. O126c, O131a and O134a come from the second setting.

All 100f. stamps from the second setting are as No. O134a.

For notes on other varieties see below No. 121.

1932 (9 May). *Optd.*

(a) As Type O **12**.

O155	11	2f. ultramarine	1·50	10
O156		3f. green	1·50	10
O157		4f. brown-purple	1·50	10
O158		5f. grey-green	1·50	10
O159		8f. scarlet	1·50	10
O160		10f. yellow	2·25	10
O161		15f. blue	2·50	10
O162		20f. orange	2·50	15
O163		25f. mauve	2·50	15
O164		30f. bronze-green	3·50	20
O165		40f. violet	4·50	30
		(b) As Type O **13**, *horizontally.*		
O166	12	50f. brown	3·25	20
O167		75f. dull ultramarine	2·50	1·00
O168		100f. deep green	11·00	2·00
O169		200f. scarlet	20·00	6·50
		(c) As Type O **13**, *vertically upwards.*		
O170	10	½d. deep blue	12·00	26·00
O171		1d. claret	80·00	£110
O155/71 *Set of* 17			£140	£130
O155s/71s Perf "Specimen" *Set of* 17			£450	

The British Mandate was given up on 3 October 1932 and Iraq became an independent kingdom. Later issues will be found listed in Part 19 (*Middle East*) of this catalogue.

Ireland

All the issues of Ireland to 1970 are listed together here, in this section of the Gibbons Catalogue, purely as a matter of convenience to collectors.

PRICES FOR STAMPS ON COVER TO 1945	
Nos. 1/15	*from* × 5
Nos. 17/21	*from* × 3
Nos. 26/9*a*	*from* × 5
Nos. 30/43	*from* × 4
Nos. 44/6	—
Nos. 47/63	*from* × 5
Nos. 64/6	*from* × 3
Nos. 67/70	*from* × 6
Nos. 71/82	*from* × 2
Nos. 83/8	*from* × 3
Nos. 89/98	*from* × 2
Nos. 99/104	*from* × 3
Nos. 105/37	*from* × 2
Nos. D1/4	*from* × 7
Nos. D5/14	*from* × 6

PROVISIONAL GOVERNMENT

16 January—6 December 1922

Stamps of Great Britain overprinted.

T 104/8, W 100; T 109, W 110

(1)

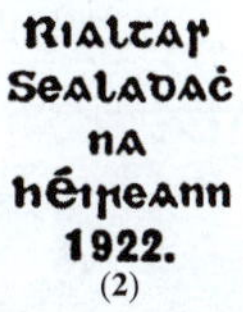

(2)

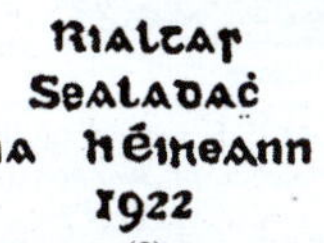

(3)

("Provisional Government of Ireland, 1922")

1922 (17 Feb–July). *T* **104** *to* **108** *(W* **100**) *and* **109** *of Great Britain overprinted in black.*

(a) With T **1**, *by Dollard Printing House Ltd. Optd in black*.*

1	105	½d. green	2·00	40
		a. Opt inverted	£450	£600
		w. Wmk inverted	—	£500
2	104	1d. scarlet	2·00	40
		a. Opt inverted	£275	£325
		b. Opt double, both inverted, one albino	£350	
		c. Opt double	†	£1100
		w. Wmk inverted	—	£350
3		1d. carmine-red	5·00	1·00
4		2½d. bright blue	2·25	6·00
		a. Red opt (1 Apr)	1·75	3·75
5	106	3d. bluish violet	4·75	4·50
6		4d. grey-green	4·75	16·00
		a. Red opt (1 Apr)	8·50	15·00
		b. Carmine opt (July)	45·00	65·00
7	107	5d. yellow-brown	4·75	8·50
		x. Wmk reversed	—	£400
8	108	9d. agate	13·00	23·00
		a. Opt double, one albino	£300	
		b. Red opt (1 Apr)	15·00	18·00
		c. Carmine opt (July)	85·00	90·00
9		10d. turquoise-blue	8·50	45·00
1/9 *Set of* 8			38·00	90·00

*All values except 2½d. and 4d. are known with greyish black overprint, but these are difficult to distinguish.

The carmine overprints on the 4d. and 9d. may have been produced by Alex Thom & Co. Ltd. There was a further overprinting of the 2½d. at the same time, but this is difficult to distinguish.

The ½d. with red overprint is a trial or proof printing (*Price* £160).

Bogus inverted *T* **1** overprints exist on the 2d., 4d., 9d and 1s. values.

(b) With T **2**, *by Alex Thom & Co Ltd.*

10	105	1½d. red-brown	2·75	1·25
		a. Error. ""PENCF"	£375	£300
		w. Wmk inverted	—	£300
		x. Wmk reversed	—	£300
12	106	2d. orange (Die I)	5·00	50
		a. Opt inverted	£190	£275
		w. Wmk inverted	—	£300
		x. Wmk reversed	£500	£300
13		2d. orange (Die II)	4·00	50
		a. Opt inverted	£325	£425
		w. Wmk inverted	—	£300
14	107	6d. reddish pur (*chalk-surfaced paper*)	17·00	16·00
15	108	1s. bistre-brown	13·00	9·50
10/15 *Set of* 5			38·00	25·00

Varieties occur throughout the *T* **2** overprint in the relative positions of the lines of the overprint, the "R" of "Rialtas" being over either the "Se" or "S" of "Sealadac" or intermediately.

(c) With T **3** *by Dollard Printing House Ltd.*

17	109	2s.6d. chocolate-brown	48·00	85·00
18		2s.6d. reddish brown	70·00	95·00
19		5s. rose-red	75·00	£160
21		10s. dull grey-blue	£150	£350
17/21 *Set of* 3			£250	£550

1922 (19 June–Aug). *Optd as T* **2**, *in black, by Harrison & Sons, for use in horiz and vert coils.*

26	105	½d. green	2·75	15·00
27	104	1d. scarlet	3·75	6·50
28	105	1½d. red-brown (21.6)	4·00	40·00
29	106	2d. bright orange (Die I)	21·00	42·00
29*a*		2d. bright orange (Die II) (August)	21·00	30·00
		ay. Wmk inverted and reversed	—	£325
26/9a *Set of* 5			48·00	£120

The Harrison overprint measures 15×17 mm (maximum) against the 14½×16 mm of *T* **2** (Thom printing) and is a much bolder black than the latter, while the individual letters are taller, the "i" of "Rialtas" being specially outstanding as it extends below the foot of the "R".

The "R" of "Rialtas" is always over the "Se" of "Sealadac".

1922. *Optd by Thom.*

(a) As T **2** *but bolder, in dull to shiny blue-black or red (June–Nov).*

30	105	½d. green	3·25	80
31	104	1d. scarlet	2·50	50
		a. "Q" for "O" (No. 357ab)	£1400	£1200
		b. Reversed "Q" for "O" (No. 357ac)	£350	£250
		w. Wmk inverted	†	£450
32	105	1½d. red-brown	3·50	3·50
33	106	2d. orange (Die I)	18·00	1·50
34		2d. orange (Die II)	3·50	50
		y. Wmk inverted and reversed	£150	£150
35	104	2½d. blue (R.)	6·00	22·00
36	106	3d. violet	3·75	2·00
		y. Wmk inverted and reversed	90·00	95·00
37		4d. grey-green (R.)	3·75	6·00
38	107	5d. yellow-brown	5·50	10·00
39		6d. reddish pur (*chalk-surfaced paper*)	8·50	3·50
		w. Wmk inverted	£160	95·00
40	108	9d. agate (R.)	14·00	18·00
41		9d. olive-green (R.)	6·00	38·00
42		10d. turquoise-blue	27·00	60·00
43		1s. bistre-brown	10·00	12·00
30/43 *Set of* 14			£100	£160

Both 2d. stamps exist with the overprint inverted but there remains some doubt as to whether they were issued.

These Thom printings are distinguishable from the Harrison printings by the size of the overprint, and from the previous Thom printings by the intensity and colour of the overprint, the latter being best seen when the stamp is looked through with a strong light behind it.

(b) As with T **3**, *but bolder, in shiny blue-black (Oct–Dec).*

44	109	2s.6d. chocolate-brown	£225	£325
45		5s. rose-red	£250	£350
46		10s. dull grey-blue	£950	£1300
44/6 *Set of* 3			£1300	£1700

The above differ from Nos. 17/21 not only in the bolder impression and colour of the ink but also in the "h" and "e" of "heireann" which are closer together and horizontally aligned.

(4)

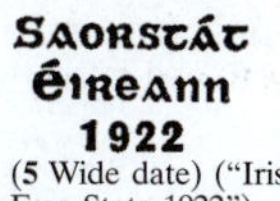

(5 Wide date) ("Irish Free State 1922")

1922 (21 Nov–Dec). *Optd by Thom with T* **4** *(wider setting) in shiny blue-black.*

47	105	½d. green	1·00	1·75
		a. Opt in jet-black	£100	90·00
48	104	1d. scarlet	6·00	2·50
		w. Wmk inverted	†	£180
49	105	1½d. red-brown (4 December)	3·00	12·00
50	106	2d. orange (Die II)	9·00	7·00
51	108	1s. olive-bistre (4 December)	45·00	60·00
47/51 *Set of* 5			55·00	75·00

The overprint *T* **4** measures 15¾ × 16 mm (maximum).

IRISH FREE STATE

6 December 1922—29 December 1937

1922 (Dec)–**23**.

(a) Optd by Thom with T **5**, *in dull to shiny blue-black or red.*

52 **105** ½d. green ... 2·00 30
a. No accent in "Saorstat" ... £1300 £1000
b. Accent inserted by hand ... 95·00 £120
53 **104** 1d. scarlet ... 2·00 50
aa. No accent in "Saorstat" ... £13000 £8500
a. No accent and final "t" missing £11000 £7000
b. Accent inserted by hand ... £150 £180
c. Accent and "t" inserted ... £225 £275
d. Accent and 'at' inserted ... £250 £300
e. Reversed "Q" for "O" (No. 357ac) ... £325 £250
54 **105** 1½d. red-brown ... 3·50 8·50
55 **106** 2d. orange (Die II) ... 1·50 1·00
56 **104** 2½d. bright blue (R.) (6.1.23) ... 7·00 9·00
a. No accent ... £160 £200
57 **106** 3d. bluish violet (6.1.23) ... 4·25 11·00
a. No accent ... £325 £400
58 4d. grey-green (R.) (16.1.23) ... 4·50 9·50
a. No accent ... £180 £225
59 **107** 5d. yellow-brown ... 5·00 4·75
60 6d. reddish pur (*chalk-surfaced paper*) ... 3·00 2·00
a. Accent inserted by hand ... £850 £850
y. Wmk inverted and reversed ... 75·00 42·00
61 **108** 9d. olive-green (R.) ... 5·00 5·50
a. No accent ... £275 £300
62 10d. turquoise-blue ... 21·00 60·00
63 1s. bistre-brown ... 7·00 11·00
a. No accent ... £9000 £9500
b. Accent inserted by hand ... £700 £750
64 **109** 2s.6d. chocolate-brown ... 42·00 60·00
a. Major Re-entry (R. 1/2) ... £1200 £1400
b. No accent ... £450 £550
c. Accent reversed ... £650 £800
65 5s. rose-red ... 80·00 £150
a. No accent ... £600 £850
b. Accent reversed ... £850 £1100
66 10s. dull grey-blue ... £180 £350
a. No accent ... £3000 £3750
b. Accent reversed ... £4250 £5000
52/66 *Set of* 15 ... £325 £600

The "no accent" and "accent inserted" varieties on the ½d. to 1s. values occur on R. 15/12. On the 2s.6d. to 10s. values the "no accent" varieties occur on R. 3/2 and R. 8/2, the "accent reversed" on R. 7/4.

The accents inserted by hand are in dull black. The reversed accents are grave (thus "à") instead of acute ("á"). A variety with "S" of "Saorstat" directly over "é" of "éireann", instead of to left, may be found in all values except the 2½d. and 4d. In the 2s.6d., 5s. and 10s. it is very slightly to the left in the "S" over "é" variety, bringing the "á" of "Saorstat" directly above the last "n" of "éireann".

(b) Optd with T **5**, *in dull or shiny blue-black, by Harrison, for use in horiz or vert coils (7.3.23).*

67 ½d. green ... 1·75 11·00
a. Long "1" in "1922" ... 20·00 50·00
y. Wmk inverted and reversed ... † —
68 1d. scarlet ... 4·00 13·00
a. Long "1" in "1922" ... 75·00 £140
69 1½d. red-brown ... 6·50 45·00
a. Long "1" in "1922" ... 85·00 £225
70 2d. orange (Die II) ... 8·50 12·00
a. Long "1" in "1922" ... 35·00 50·00
w. Wmk inverted ... — £200
67/70 *Set of* 4 ... 19·00 70·00

In the Harrison overprint the characters are rather bolder than those of the Thom overprint, and the foot of the "1" of "1922" is usually rounded instead of square. The long "1" in "1922" has a serif at foot. The second "e" of "eireann" appears to be slightly raised.

PRINTERS. The following and all subsequent issues to No. 148 were printed at the Government Printing Works, Dublin, *unless otherwise stated.*

6 "Sword of Light"

7 Map of Ireland

8 Arms of Ireland

9 Celtic Cross

10

(Des J. J. O'Reilly, *T* **6**; J. Ingram, *T* **7**; Miss M. Girling, *T* **8**; and Miss L. Williams, *T* **9**. Typo. Plates made by Royal Mint, London)

1922 (6 Dec)–**34**. W **10**. P 15×14.

71 **6** ½d. bright green (20.4.23) ... 2·25 90
a. Imperf × perf 14, Wmk sideways (11.34) ... 21·00 45·00
w. Wmk inverted ... 35·00 15·00
72 **7** 1d. carmine (23.2.23) ... 1·00 10
aw. Wmk inverted ... 35·00 8·00
b. Perf 15 × imperf (single perf) (1933) ... 90·00 £180
bw. Ditto. Wmk inverted ... £110 £180
c. Perf 15 × imperf (7.34) ... 12·00 42·00
d. Booklet pane. Three stamps plus three printed labels (21.8.31) ... £325
dw. Wmk inverted ... £325
73 1½d. claret (2.2.23) ... 2·25 2·50
w. Wmk inverted ... £1200
74 2d. grey-green (6.12.22) ... 1·50 10
a. Imperf × perf 14, Wmk sideways (11.34) ... 38·00 70·00
b. Perf 15 × imperf (1934) ... £10000 £1500
w. Wmk inverted ... 24·00 6·00
y. Wmk inverted and reversed ... 35·00 15·00
75 **8** 2½d. red-brown (7.9.23) ... 4·00 4·25
w. Wmk inverted ... 60·00 24·00
76 **9** 3d. ultramarine (16.3.23) ... 2·00 1·00
w. Wmk inverted ... 75·00 27·00
77 **8** 4d. slate-blue (28.9.23) ... 2·00 3·25
w. Wmk inverted ... £130 50·00
78 **6** 5d. deep violet (11.5.23) ... 8·00 9·50
79 6d. claret (21.12.23) ... 5·00 3·50
w. Wmk inverted ... £150 60·00
80 **8** 9d. deep violet (26.10.23) ... 15·00 8·00
81 **9** 10d. brown (11.5.23) ... 9·00 18·00
82 **6** 1s light blue (15.6.23) ... 17·00 5·50
71/82 *Set of* 12 ... 60·00 50·00

No. 72b is imperf vertically except for a single perf at each top corner. It was issued for use in automatic machines.

See also Nos. 111/22.

(**11** Narrow Date)

12 Daniel O'Connell

1925 (Aug)–**28**. *T* **109** *of Great Britain (Bradbury, Wilkinson printing) optd at the Government Printing Works, Dublin or by Harrison and Sons.*

(a) With T **11** *in black or grey-black (25.8.25).*

83 2s.6d. chocolate-brown ... 40·00 95·00
a. Wide and narrow date (pair) (1927) ... £275 £550
84 5s. rose-red ... 60·00 £150
a. Wide and narrow date (pair) (1927) ... £450
85 10s. dull grey-blue ... £140 £350
a. Wide and narrow date (pair) (1927) ... £1200
83/5 *Set of* 3 ... £225 £550

The varieties with wide and narrow date *se-tenant* are from what is known as the "composite setting," in which some stamps showed the wide date, as *T* **5**, while in others the figures were close together, as in *T* **11**.

Single specimens of this printing with wide date may be distinguished from Nos. 64 to 66 by the colour of the ink, which is black or grey-black in the composite setting and blue-black in the Thom printing.

The type of the "composite" overprint usually shows distinct signs of wear.

(b) As T **5** *(wide date) in black (1927–28).*

86 2s.6d. chocolate-brown (9.12.27) ... 48·00 60·00
a. Circumflex accent over "a" ... £275 £350
b. No accent over "a" ... £450 £500
c. Flat accent on "a" ... £500 £550
87 5s. rose-red (2.28) ... 75·00 £100
a. Circumflex accent over "a" ... £425 £550
c. Flat accent on "a" ... £700 £800
88 10s. dull grey-blue (15.2.28) ... £180 £225
a. Circumflex accent over "a" ... £1000 £1300
c. Flat accent on "a" ... £1600 £1800
86/8 *Set of* 3 ... £275 £350

This printing can be distinguished from the Thom overprints in dull black, by the clear, heavy impression (in deep black) which often shows in relief on the back of the stamp.

The variety showing a circumflex accent over the "a" occurred on R. 9/2. The overprint in this position finally deteriorated to such an extent that some examples of the 2s.6d. were without accent (No. 86b). A new cliché was then introduced with the accent virtually flat and which also showed damage to the "a" and the crossbar of the "t".

(Des L. Whelan. Typo)

1929 (22 June). *Catholic Emancipation Centenary.* W **10**. P 15×14.

89 **12** 2d. grey-green ... 70 45
90 3d. blue ... 4·25 8·50
91 9d. bright violet ... 4·25 4·00
89/91 *Set of* 3 ... 8·25 11·50

13 Shannon Barrage

14 Reaper

(Des E. L. Lawrenson. Typo)

1930 (15 Oct). *Completion of Shannon Hydro-Electric Scheme.* W **10**. P 15×14.

92 **13** 2d. agate ... 1·00 55

(*T* **14** and **15** des G. Atkinson. Typo)

1931 (12 June). *Bicentenary of the Royal Dublin Society.* W **10**. P 15×14.

93 **14** 2d. blue ... 75 30

15 The Cross of Cong

16 Adoration of the Cross

17 Hurler

1932 (12 May). *International Eucharistic Congress.* W **10**. P 15×14.

94 **15** 2d. grey-green ... 2·00 30
w. Wmk inverted ... † —
95 3d. blue ... 3·00 5·00

(*T* **16** to **19** des R. J. King. Typo)

1933 (18 Sept). *"Holy Year".* W **10**. P 15×14.

96 **16** 2d. grey-green ... 2·00 15
97 3d. blue ... 3·50 2·25

1934 (27 July). *Golden Jubilee of the Gaelic Athletic Association.* W **10**. P 15×14.

98 **17** 2d. green ... 1·75 55

1935 (Mar–July). *T* **109** *of Great Britain (Waterlow printings) optd as T* **5** *(wide date), at the Government Printing Works, Dublin.*

99 **109** 2s.6d. chocolate (No. 450) ... 45·00 60·00
a. Flat accent on "a" (R. 9/2) ... £300 £300
100 5s. bright rose-red (No. 451) ... 85·00 90·00
a. Flat accent on "a" (R. 9/2) ... £425 £425
101 10s. indigo (No. 452) ... £300 £325
a. Flat accent on "a" (R. 9/2) ... £1100 £1100
99/101 *Set of* 3 ... £375 £425

18 St. Patrick

19 Ireland and New Constitution

1937 (8 Sept). W **10**. P 14×15.

102 **18** 2s.6d. emerald-green ... £140 65·00
w. Wmk inverted ... £600 £250
103 5s. maroon ... £180 £120
w. Wmk inverted ... £500 £250
104 10s. deep blue ... £140 55·00
w. Wmk inverted ... £650
102/4 *Set of* 3 ... £425 £200

See also Nos. 123/5.

EIRE

29 December 1937–17 April 1949

1937 (29 Dec). *Constitution Day.* W **10**. P 15×14.

105 **19** 2d. claret ... 2·00 20
w. Wmk inverted ... — £200
106 3d. blue ... 4·75 3·75

For similar stamps see Nos. 176/7.

20 Father Mathew

(Des S. Keating. Typo)

1938 (1 July). *Centenary of Temperance Crusade.* W **10**. P 15×14.

107 **20** 2d. agate ... 2·50 50
w. Wmk inverted ... † —
108 3d. blue ... 12·00 6·50

21 George Washington, American Eagle and Irish Harp

22

(Des G. Atkinson. Typo)

1939 (1 Mar). *150th Anniv of U.S. Constitution and Installation of First U.S. President.* W **10**. P 15×14.

109 **21** 2d. scarlet ... 2·00 1·00
110 3d. blue ... 3·25 4·75

SIZE OF WATERMARK. *T* **22** can be found in various sizes from about 8 to 10 mm high. This is due to the use of two different dandy rolls supplied by different firms and to the effects of paper shrinkage and other factors such as pressure and machine speed.

White line above left value tablet joining horizontal line to ornament (R. 3/7)

1940–68. *Typo.* W **22**. P 15×14 or 14×15 (2s.6d. to 10s.).

111 **6** ½d. bright green (24.11.40) ... 2·00 40
w. Wmk inverted ... 60·00 9·00
112 **7** 1d. carmine (26.10.40) ... 30 10
aw. Wmk inverted ... 2·00 30
b. From coils. Perf 14 × imperf (9.40) ... 60·00 65·00
c. From coils. Perf 15 × imperf (20.3.46) ... 40·00 19·00
cw. Wmk inverted ... 40·00 19·00
d. Booklet pane. Three stamps plus three printed labels ... £2500
dw. Wmk inverted ... £2500

113		1½d. claret (1.40)	17·00	30
		w. Wmk inverted	40·00	9·50
114		2d. grey-green (1.40)	30	10
		w Wmk inverted	2·50	1·50
115	8	2½d. red-brown (3.41)	9·50	15
		w. Wmk inverted	20·00	4·75
116	9	3d. blue(12.40)	70	10
		w. Wmk inverted	3·75	1·00
117	8	4d. slate-blue (12.40)	55	10
		w. Wmk inverted	16·00	3·50
118	6	5d. deep violet (7.40)	65	10
		w. Wmk inverted	30·00	11·00
119		6d. claret (3.42)	2·25	50
		aw. Wmk inverted	24·00	7·00
		b. Chalk-surfaced paper (1967)..	1·25	20
		bw. Wmk inverted	13·00	2·50
119*c*		8d. scarlet (12.9.49)	80	80
		cw. Wmk inverted	45·00	18·00
120	8	9d. deep violet (7.40)	1·50	80
		w. Wmk inverted	10·00	3·00
121	9	10d. brown (7.40)	60	80
		aw. Wmk inverted	11·00	4·50
121*b*		11d. rose (12.9.49)	1·50	2·50
122	6	1s. light blue (6.40)	65·00	18·00
		w. Wmk inverted	£800	£170
123	18	2s.6d. emerald-green (10.2.43)	40·00	1·25
		aw. Wmk inverted	95·00	25·00
		b. Chalk-surfaced paper (1967)..	1·50	2·75
		bw. Wmk inverted	38·00	4·50
124		5s. maroon (15.12.42)	40·00	2·50
		a. Line flaw	£225	42·00
		bw. Wmk inverted	£200	42·00
		c. Chalk-surfaced paper (1968?)	13·00	4·25
		ca. Purple	4·00	8·50
		cb. Line flaw	95·00	50·00
		cw. Wmk inverted	38·00	10·00
125		10s. deep blue (7.45)	60·00	7·00
		aw. Wmk inverted	£225	85·00
		b. Chalk-surfaced paper (1968)..	19·00	12·00
		ba. Blue	4·00	16·00
		bw. Wmk inverted	£140	65·00
111/25ba *Set of* 17			£100	30·00

There is a wide range of shades and also variations in paper used in this issue.

See also Nos. 227/8.

(**23** Trans "In memory of the rising of 1916")

24 Volunteer and G.P.O., Dublin

1941 (12 Apr). *25th Anniv of Easter Rising (1916). Provisional issue. T* **7** *and* **9** *(2d. in new colour), optd with T* **23**.

126	7	2d. orange (G.)	2·00	85
127	9	3d. blue (V.)	25·00	11·00

(Des V. Brown. Typo)

1941 (27 Oct). *25th Anniv of Easter Rising (1916). Definitive issue.* W **22**. P 15×14.

128	24	2½d. blue-black	3·00	1·25

25 Dr. Douglas Hyde

26 Sir William Rowan Hamilton

27 Bro. Michael O'Clery

(Des S. O'Sullivan. Typo)

1943 (31 July). *50th Anniv of Founding of Gaelic League.* W **22**. P 15×14.

129	25	½d. green	1·25	30
130		2½d. claret	2·00	10

(Des S. O'Sullivan from a bust by Hogan. Typo)

1943 (13 Nov). *Centenary of Announcement of Discovery of Quaternions.* W **22**. P 15×14.

131	26	½d. green	40	70
132		2½d. brown	2·25	20

(Des R. J. King. Typo)

1944 (30 June). *Tercentenary of Death of Michael O'Clery. (Commemorating the "Annals of the Four Masters".* W **22** (sideways*). P 14×15.

133	27	½d. emerald-green	10	10
		w. Wmk facing right	55	20
134		1s. red-brown	1·25	10
		w. Wmk facing right	3·00	75

*The normal sideways watermark shows the top of the e facing left, *as seen from the back of the stamp.*

Although issued as commemoratives these two stamps were kept in use as part of the current issue, replacing Nos. 111 and 122.

28 Edmund Ignatius Rice

29 "Youth Sowing Seeds of Freedom"

(Des S. O'Sullivan. Typo)

1944 (29 Aug). *Death Centenary of Edmund Rice (founder of Irish Christian Brothers).* W **22**. P 15×14.

135	28	2½d. slate	1·75	45
		w. Wmk inverted	†	£170

(Des R. J. King. Typo)

1945 (15 Sept). *Centenary of Death of Thomas Davis (founder of Young Ireland Movement).* W **22**. P 15×14.

136	29	2½d. blue	1·50	75
		w. Wmk inverted	—	£170
137		6d. claret	6·00	6·00

30 "Country and Homestead"

(Des R. J. King. Typo)

1946 (16 Sept). *Birth Centenaries of Davitt and Parnell (land reformers).* W **22**. P 15×14.

138	30	2½d. scarlet	2·50	25
139		3d. blue	3·50	4·00

31 Angel Victor over Rock of Cashel

32 Over Lough Derg

33 Over Croagh Patrick

34 Over Glendalough

(Des R. J. King. Recess Waterlow (1d. to 1s.3d. until 1961), D. L. R. (8d., 1s.3d. from 1961 and 1s.5d.))

1948 (7 Apr)–**65**. *Air. T* **31** *and similar horiz designs.* W **22**. P 15 (1s.5d.) or 15×14 (others).

140	31	1d. chocolate (4.4.49)	2·50	4·25
141	32	3d. blue	3·00	2·75
142	33	6d. magenta	1·00	1·75
		aw. Wmk inverted		
142*b*	32	8d. lake-brown (13.12.54)	6·50	9·00
143	34	1s. green (4.4.49)	1·00	2·00
143*a*	31	1s.3d. red-orange (13.12.54)	8·00	1·25
		aw. Wmk inverted	£600	£300
143*b*		1s.5d. deep ultramarine (1.4.65)	3·50	2·00
140/3*b Set of* 7			23·00	21·00

35 Theobald Wolfe Tone

(Des K. Uhlemann. Typo)

1948 (19 Nov). 150th *Anniv of Insurrection.* W **22**. P 15×14.

144	35	2½d. reddish purple	1·00	10
		w. Wmk inverted	†	—
145		3d. violet	3·25	4·00

REPUBLIC OF IRELAND

18 April 1949

36 Leinster House and Arms of Provinces

37 J. C. Mangan

(Des Muriel Brandt. Typo)

1949 (21 Nov). *International Recognition of Republic.* W **22**. P 15×14.

146	36	2½d. reddish brown	1·75	10
		w. Wmk inverted	†	—
147		3d. bright blue	6·00	4·25

(Des R. J. King. Typo)

1949 (5 Dec). *Death Centenary of James Clarence Mangan (poet).* W **22**. P 15×14.

148	37	1d. green	1·50	35
		w. Wmk inverted	†	—

38 Statue of St. Peter, Rome

(Recess Waterlow & Sons)

1950 (11 Sept). *Holy Year.* W **22**. P 12½.

149	38	2½d. violet	1·00	40
150		3d. blue	8·00	12·00
151		9d. brown	8·00	12·00
149/51 *Set of* 3			15·00	22·00

PRINTERS. Nos. 152 to 200 were recess-printed by De La Rue & Co, Dublin, *unless otherwise stated.*

39 Thomas Moore

40 Ireland at Home

(Eng W. Vacek)

1952 (10 Nov). *Death Centenary of Thomas Moore (poet).* W **22**. P 13.

152	39	2½d. reddish purple	1·00	10
153		3½d. deep olive-green	1·75	4·00

(Des F. O'Ryan. Typo Government Printing Works, Dublin)

1953 (9 Feb). *"An Tostal" (Ireland at Home) Festival.* W **22** *(sideways).* P 14×15.

154	40	2½d. emerald-green	1·75	35
155		1s.4d. blue	15·00	25·00

41 Robert Emmet

42 Madonna and Child (Della Robbia)

43 Cardinal Newman (first Rector)

(Eng L. Downey)

1953 (21 Sept). 150*th Death Anniv of Emmet (patriot).* W **22**. P 13.

156	41	3d. deep bluish green	3·00	15
157		1s.3d. carmine	42·00	10·00

(Eng A. R. Lane)

1954 (24 May). *Marian Year.* W **22**. P 15.

158	42	3d. blue	1·00	10
159		5d. myrtle-green	2·00	3·25

(Des L. Whelan. Typo Govt Printing Works, Dublin)

1954 (19 July). *Centenary of Founding of Catholic University of Ireland.* W **22**. P 15×14.

160	43	2d. bright purple	1·50	10
		w. Wmk inverted	—	£200
161		1s.3d. blue	16·00	6·00

44 Statue of Commodore Barry

45 John Redmond

46 Thomas O'Crohan

(Des and eng H. Woyty-Wimmer)

1956 (16 Sept). *Barry Commemoration.* W **22**. P 15.

162	44	3d. slate-lilac	1·00	10
163		1s.3d. deep blue	4·50	8·00

1957 (11 June). *Birth Centenary of John Redmond (politician).* W **22**. P 14×15.

164	45	3d. deep blue	1·00	10
165		1s.3d. brown-purple	8·00	15·00

1957 (1 July). *Birth Centenary of Thomas O'Crohan (author).* W **22**. P 14×15.

166	46	2d. maroon	1·00	15
		a. Wmk sideways	†	£1000
167		5d. violet	1·00	4·50

47 Admiral Brown

48 "Father Wadding" (Ribera)

49 Tom Clarke

(Des S. O'Sullivan. Typo Govt Printing Works, Dublin)

1957 (23 Sept). *Death Centenary of Admiral William Brown.* W **22**. P 15×14.

168	47	3d. blue	2·25	20
169		1s.3d. carmine	24·00	16·00

1957 (25 Nov). 300*th Death Anniv of Father Luke Wadding (theologian).* W **22**. P 15.

170	48	3d. deep blue	2·00	10
171		1s.3d. lake	15·00	8·50

1958 (28 July). *Birth Centenary of Thomas J. ("Tom") Clarke (patriot).* W **22**. P 15.

172	**49**	3d. deep green	2·00	10
173		1s.3d. red-brown	4·00	11·00

50 Mother Mary Aikenhead

51 Arthur Guinness

(Eng Waterlow. Recess Imprimerie Belge de Securité, Brussels subsidiary of Waterlow & Sons)

1958 (20 Oct). *Death Centenary of Mother Mary Aikenhead (foundress of Irish Sisters of Charity).* W **22**. P 15×14.

174	**50**	3d. Prussian blue	2·00	10
175		1s.3d. rose-carmine	11·00	8·00

(Typo Govt Printing Works, Dublin)

1958 (29 Dec). *21st Anniv of the Irish Constitution.* W **22**. P 15×14.

176	**19**	3d. brown	1·00	10
177		5d. emerald-green	2·00	4·50

1959 (20 July). *Bicentenary of Guinness Brewery.* W **22**. P 15.

178	**51**	3d. brown-purple	3·00	10
179		1s.3d. blue	11·00	12·00

52 "The Flight of the Holy Family"

(Des K. Uhlemann)

1960 (20 June). *World Refugee Year.* W **22**. P 15.

180	**52**	3d. purple	40	10
181		1s.3d. sepia	60	3·25

53 Conference Emblem

(Des P. Rahikainen)

1960 (19 Sept). *Europa.* W **22**. P 15.

182	**53**	6d. light brown	12·00	3·00
183		1s.3d. violet	26·00	20·00

The ink of No. 183 is fugitive.

54 Dublin Airport, De Havilland D.H.84 Dragon Mk 2 *Iolar* and Boeing 720

55 St. Patrick

(Des J. Flanagan and D. R. Lowther)

1961 (26 June). *25th Anniv of Aer Lingus.* W **22**. P 15.

184	**54**	6d. blue	1·75	3·50
		w. Wmk inverted		
185		1s.3d. green	2·25	5·00

(Recess B.W.)

1961 (25 Sept). *Fifteenth Death Centenary of St. Patrick.* W **22**. P 14½.

186	**55**	3d. blue	1·00	10
187		8d. purple	3·00	5·50
188		1s.3d. green	3·00	1·60
186/8 *Set of 3*			6·25	6·50

56 John O'Donovan and Eugene O'Curry

(Recess B.W.)

1962 (26 Mar). *Death Centenaries of O'Donovan and O'Curry (scholars).* W **22**. P 15.

189	**56**	3d. carmine	30	10
190		1s.3d. purple	1·25	2·25

57 Europa "Tree"

(Des L. Weyer)

1962 (17 Sept). *Europa.* W **22**. P 15.

191	**57**	6d. carmine-red	90	1·00
192		1s.3d. turquoise	1·00	1·50

58 Campaign Emblem

(Des K. Uhlemann)

1963 (21 Mar). *Freedom from Hunger.* W **22**. P 15.

193	**58**	4d. deep violet	50	10
194		1s.3d. scarlet	2·75	2·75

59 "Co-operation"

(Des A. Holm)

1963 (16 Sept). *Europa.* W **22**. P 15.

195	**59**	6d. carmine	1·50	75
196		1s.3d. blue	4·00	3·75

60 Centenary Emblem

(Des P. Wildbur. Photo Harrison & Sons)

1963 (2 Dec). *Centenary of Red Cross.* W **22**. P 14½×14.

197	**60**	4d. red and grey	50	10
198		1s.3d. red, grey and light emerald	1·50	2·25

61 Wolfe Tone

(Des P. Wildbur)

1964 (13 Apr). *Birth Bicentenary of Wolfe Tone (revolutionary).* W **22**. P 15.

199	**61**	4d. black	50	10
200		1s.3d. ultramarine	1·90	2·00

62 Irish Pavilion at Fair

(Des A. Devane. Photo Harrison & Sons)

1964 (20 July). *New York World's Fair.* W **22**. P 14½×14.

201	**62**	5d. blue-grey, brown, violet and yellow-olive	50	10
		a. Brown omitted*	£5500	
202		1s.5d. blue-grey, brown, turquoise blue and light yellow-green	2·00	2·00

*No 201a comes from the top row of the sheet and shows part of the brown cross which would appear in the sheet margin. As the second horizontal row was normal it would appear that the brown cylinder was incorrectly registered.

63 Europa "Flower"

64 "Waves of Communication"

(Des G. Bétemps. Photo Harrison)

1964 (14 Sept). *Europa.* W **22** (sideways). P 14×14½.

203	**63**	8d. olive-green and blue	2·00	1·25
204		1s.5d. red-brown and orange	8·00	2·75

(Des P. Wildbur. Photo Harrison)

1965 (17 May). *I.T.U. Centenary.* W **22**. P 14½×14.

205	**64**	3d. blue and green	30	10
206		8d. black and green	1·25	1·60

PRINTERS Nos. 207 onwards were photogravure-printed by the Stamping Branch of the Revenue Commissioners, Dublin *unless otherwise stated*.

65 W. B. Yeats (poet)

66 I.C.Y. Emblem

(Des R. Kyne, from drawing by S. O'Sullivan)

1965 (14 June). *Yeats' Birth Centenary.* W **22** (sideways). P 15.

207	**65**	5d. black, orange-brown and deep green	30	10
208		1s.5d. black, grey-green and brown	2·25	1·75
		a. Brown omitted	£5500	

1965 (16 Aug). *International Co-operation Year.* W **22**. P 15.

209	**66**	3d. ultramarine and new blue	60	10
210		10d. deep brown and brown	1·00	3·00

67 Europa "Sprig"

(Des H. Karlsson)

1965 (27 Sept). *Europa.* W **22**. P 15.

211	**67**	8d. black and brown-red	2·50	1·00
212		1s.5d. purple and light turquoise-blue	10·00	3·50

68 James Connolly

69 "Marching to Freedom"

(Des E. Delaney (No. 216), R. Kyne, after portraits by S. O'Sullivan (others))

1966 (12 Apr). *50th Anniv of Easter Rising. T* **68/9** *and similar horiz portraits.* W **22**. P 15.

213	3d. black and greenish blue	50	10
	a. Horiz pair. Nos. 213/14	1·25	2·50
214	3d. black and bronze-green	50	10
215	5d. black and yellow-olive	50	10
	a. Horiz pair. Nos. 215/16	1·25	2·50
216	5d. black, orange and blue-green	50	10
217	7d. black and light orange-brown	50	2·25
	a. Horiz pair. Nos. 217/18	1·25	7·50
218	7d. black and blue-green	50	2·25
219	1s.5d. black and turquoise	50	1·50
	a. Horiz pair. Nos. 219/20	1·25	9·00
220	1s.5d. black and bright green	50	1·50
213/20 *Set of 8*		3·50	7·00

Designs:—No. 213, Type **68**; No. 214, Thomas J. Clarke; No. 215, P. H. Pearse; No. 216, Type **69**; No. 217, Eamonn Ceannt; No. 218, Sean MacDiarmada; No. 219, Thomas MacDonagh; No. 220, Joseph Plunkett.

Nos. 213/14, 215/16, 217/18 and 219/20 were each printed together, *se-tenant*, in horizontal pairs throughout the sheet.

76 R. Casement

77 Europa "Ship"

(Des R. Kyne)

1966 (3 Aug). *50th Death Anniv of Roger Casement (patriot).* W **22** (sideways). P 15.

221	**76**	5d. black	15	10
222		1s. red-brown	30	50

(Des R. Kyne, after G. and J. Bender)

1966 (26 Sept). *Europa.* W **22** (sideways). P 15.

223	**77**	7d. emerald and orange	1·00	40
224		1s.5d. emerald and light grey	2·00	1·00

78 Interior of Abbey (from lithograph)

79 Cogwheels

1966 (8 Nov). *750th Anniv of Ballintubber Abbey.* W **22**. P 15.

225	**78**	5d. red-brown	10	10
226		1s. black	20	25

1966–67. *As Nos.* 116, 118 *but photo. Smaller design* (17×21 *mm*). *Chalk-surfaced paper.* W **22**. P 15.

227	**9**	3d. blue (1.8.67)	40	15
228	**6**	5d. bright violet (1.12.66)	30	15
		w. Wmk inverted (from booklets)	1·75	1·25

No. 228 was only issued in booklets (Nos. SB16/17) at first but was released in sheets on 1.4.68 in a slightly brighter shade. In the sheet stamps the lines of shading are more regular.

(Des O. Bonnevalle)

1967 (2 May). *Europa.* W **22** (sideways). P 15.

229	**79**	7d. light emerald, gold and pale cream	1·00	40
230		1s.5d. carmine-red, gold and pale cream	3·00	1·00

80 Maple Leaves

(Des P. Hickey)

1967 (28 Aug). *Canadian Centennial.* W **22**. P 15.

231	**80**	5d. multicoloured	10	10
232		1s.5d. multicoloured	20	75

81 Rock of Cashel (from photo by Edwin Smith)

1967 (25 Sept). *International Tourist Year.* W **22** (inverted). P 15.

233	**81**	7d. sepia	15	20
234		10d. slate-blue	15	40

82 1c. Fenian Stamp Essay

83 24c. Fenian Stamp Essay

1967 (23 Oct). *Centenary of Fenian Rising.* W **22** (sideways). P 15.

235	**82**	5d. black and light green	10	10
236	**83**	1s. black and light pink	20	30

84 Jonathan Swift

85 Gulliver and Lilliputians

(Des M. Byrne)

1967 (30 Nov). *300th Birth Anniv of Jonathan Swift.* W **22** (sideways). P 15.

237	**84**	3d. black and olive-grey	10	10
238	**85**	1s.5d. blackish brown and pale blue	20	30

86 Europa "Key"

(Des H. Schwarzenbach and M. Biggs)

1968 (29 Apr). *Europa.* W **22**. P 15.

239	**86**	7d. brown-red, gold and brown	60	50
240		1s.5d. new blue, gold and brown	90	1·00

87 St. Mary's Cathedral, Limerick

(Des from photo by J. J. Bambury. Recess B.W.)

1968 (26 Aug). *800th Anniv of St. Mary's Cathedral, Limerick.* W **22**. P 15.

241	**87**	5d. Prussian blue	10	10
242		10d. yellow-green	20	60

88 Countess Markievicz

89 James Connolly

1968 (23 Sept). *Birth Centenary of Countess Markievicz (patriot).* W **22** (inverted on 1s.5d.). P 15.

243	**88**	3d. black	10	10
244		1s.5d. deep blue and blue	20	20

1968 (23 Sept). *Birth Centenary of James Connolly (patriot).* W **22** (sideways). P 15.

245	**89**	6d. deep brown and chocolate	20	75
246		1s. blackish grn, apple-grn & myrtle-grn	20	10

90 Stylised Dog (brooch)

91 Stag

92 Winged Ox (Symbol of St. Luke)

93 Eagle (Symbol of St. John The Evangelist)

(Des H. Gerl)

1968–70. *Pence values expressed with "p".* W **22** (sideways* on ½d. to 1s.9d). P 15.

247	**90**	½d. red-orange (7.6.69)	10	30
248		1d. pale yellow-green (7.6.69)	15	10
		a. Coil stamp. Perf 14×15 (8.70?)	1·00	3·00
249		2d. light ochre (14.10.68)	50	10
		a. Coil stamp. Perf 14×15 (8.70?)	1·00	4·25
250		3d. blue (7.6.69)	35	10
		a. Coil stamp. Perf 14×15 (8.70?)	1·00	3·75
251		4d. deep brown-red (31.3.69)	30	10
252		5d. myrtle-green (31.3.69)	1·25	75
253		6d. bistre-brown (24.2.69)	30	10
		w. Wmk e facing right	5·50	2·50
254	**91**	7d. brown and yellow (7.6.69)	45	3·50
255		8d. chocolate & orge-brown (14.10.68)	45	1·75
256		9d. slate-blue and olive-green (24.2.69)	50	10
257		10d. chocolate and bluish violet (31.3.69)	1·50	2·50
258		1s. chocolate and red-brown (31.3.69)	40	10
259		1s.9d. black & lt turquoise-bl (24.2.69)	4·00	2·75
260	**92**	2s.6d. multicoloured (14.10.68)	1·75	30
261		5s. multicoloured (24.2.69)	3·00	2·50
262	**93**	10s. multicoloured (14.10.68)	4·75	3·75
247/62 *Set of* 16			17·00	16·00

*The normal sideways watermark shows the top of the e facing left, *as seen from the back of the stamp.*

The 1d., 2d., 3d., 5d., 6d., 9d., 1s. and 2s.6d. exist with PVA gum as well as gum arabic. The coil stamps exist on PVA only, and the rest on gum arabic only.

Stamps in similar designs were issued from 1974 to 1983.

94 Human Rights Emblem

95 Dail Eireann Assembly

1968 (4 Nov). *Human Rights Year.* W **22** (sideways). P 15.

263	**94**	5d. yellow, gold and black	15	10
264		7d. yellow, gold and red	15	40

(Des M. Byrne)

1969 (21 Jan). *50th Anniv of Dail Eireann (First National Parliament).* W **22** (sideways). P 15×14½.

265	**95**	6d. myrtle-green	15	10
266		9d. Prussian blue	15	30

96 Colonnade

97 Quadruple I.L.O. Emblems

(Des L. Gasbarra and G. Belli; adapted Myra Maguire)

1969 (28 Apr). *Europa.* W **22**. P 15.

267	**96**	9d. grey, ochre and ultramarine	1·00	1·10
268		1s.9d. grey, gold and scarlet	1·25	1·40

(Des K. C. Dabczewski)

1969 (14 July). *50th Anniv of International Labour Organization.* W **22** (sideways). P 15.

269	**97**	6d. black and grey	20	10
270		9d. black and yellow	20	25

98 "The Last Supper and Crucifixion" (Evie Hone Window, Eton Chapel)

(Des R. Kyne)

1969 (1 Sept). *Contemporary Irish Art (1st issue).* W **22** (sideways). P 15×14½.

271	**98**	1s. multicoloured	30	1·50

See also No. 280.

99 Mahatma Gandhi

1969 (2 Oct). *Birth Centenary of Mahatma Gandhi.* W **22**. P 15.

272	**99**	6d. black and green	50	10
273		1s.9d. black and yellow	75	90

100 Symbolic Bird in Tree

(Des D. Harrington)

1970 (23 Feb). *European Conservation Year.* W **22**. P 15.

274	**100**	6d. bistre and black	20	10
275		9d. slate-violet and black	25	80

101 "Flaming Sun"

(Des L. le Brocquy)

1970 (4 May). *Europa.* W **22**. P 15.

276	**101**	6d. bright violet and silver	70	10
277		9d. brown and silver	1·10	1·25
278		1s.9d. deep olive-grey and silver	2·00	2·00
276/8 *Set of* 3			3·50	3·00

102 "Sailing Boats" (Peter Monamy)

103 "Madonna of Eire" (Mainie Jellett)

(Des P. Wildbur and P. Scott)

1970 (13 July). *250th Anniv of Royal Cork Yacht Club.* W **22**. P 15.

279	**102**	4d. multicoloured	15	10

1970 (1 Sept). *Contemporary Irish Art (2nd issue) (sideways).* W **22**. P 15.
280 **103** 1s. multicoloured 15 20

104 Thomas MacCurtain

106 Kevin Barry

(Des P. Wildbur)

1970 (26 Oct). *50th Death Anniversaries of Irish Patriots. T* **104** *and similar vert design. W* **22** *(sideways).* P 15.
281 9d. black, bluish violet and greyish black .... 1·00 25
a. Pair. Nos. 281/2 .... 2·00 2·50
282 9d. black, bluish violet and greyish black .... 1·00 25
283 2s.9d. black, new blue and greyish black. 1·75 1·50
a. Pair. Nos. 283/4 .... 3·50 11·00
284 2s.9d. black, new blue and greyish black. 1·75 1·50
281/4 *Set of* 4 .... 5·00 3·25

Designs:—Nos. 281 and 283, Type **104**; others, Terence MacSwiney.

Nos. 281/2 and 283/4 were each printed together, *se-tenant*, in horizontal and vertical pairs throughout the sheet.

(Des P. Wildbur)

1970 (2 Nov). *50th Death Anniv of Kevin Barry (patriot).* W **22** (inverted). P 15.
285 **106** 6d. olive-green 30 10
286 1s.2d. royal blue .... 40 1·10

STAMP BOOKLETS

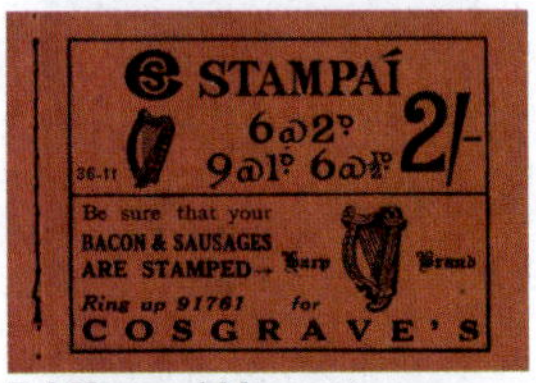

B **1** Harp and Monogram

B **2** Harp and "EIRE"

1931 (21 Aug)–**40**. *Black on red cover as Type* B **1**.
SB1 2s. booklet containing six ½d., six 2d. (Nos. 71, 74), each in block of 6, and nine 1d. (No. 72) in block of 6 and pane of 3 stamps and 3 labels (No. 72d or 72dw) *From* £3000
Edition Nos.:—31–1, 31–2, 32–3, 33–4, 33–5, 34–6, 34–7, 35–8, 35–9, 36–10, 36–11, 37–12, 37–13, 37–14, 15–38, 16–38, 17–38
a. Cover as Type B **2** .... *From* £3250
Edition Nos.:–18–39, 19–39, 20–39, 21–40, 22–40

1940. *Black on red cover as Type* B **2**.
SB2 2s. booklet containing six ½d., six 2d. (Nos. 71, 74), each in block of 6, and nine 1d. (No. 72) in block of 6 and pane of 3 stamps and 3 labels (No. 112d or 112dw)... £9500
Edition No.:—22–40

1940. *Black on red cover as Type* B **2**.
SB3 2s. booklet containing six ½d., six 2d. (Nos. 111, 114), each in block of 6, and nine 1d. (No. 112) in block of 6 and pane of 3 stamps and 3 labels (No. 112d or 112dw) £9500
Edition No.:—23–40

1941–44. *Black on red cover as Type* B **2**.
SB4 2s. booklet containing twelve ½d., six 1d. and six 2d. (Nos. 111/12, 114) in blocks of 6 *From* £1300
Edition Nos.:—24–41, 25–42, 26–44

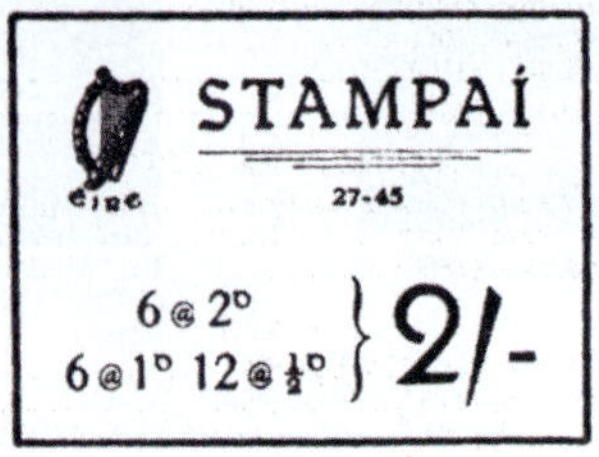

B **3**

1945. *Black on red cover as Type* B **3**.
SB5 2s. booklet containing twelve ½d., six 1d. and six 2d. (Nos. 111/12, 114) in blocks of 6...... £1300
Edition No.:—27–45

1946. *Black on buff cover as Type* B **2**.
SB6 2s. booklet containing twelve ½d., six 1d. and six 2d. (Nos. 111/12, 114) in blocks of 6...... £850
Edition No.:—28–46

1946–47. *Black on buff cover as Type* B **2**.
SB7 2s. booklet containing twelve ½d, six 1d. and six 2d. (Nos. 133, 112, 114) in blocks of 6 *From* £400
Edition Nos.:—29–46, 30–47

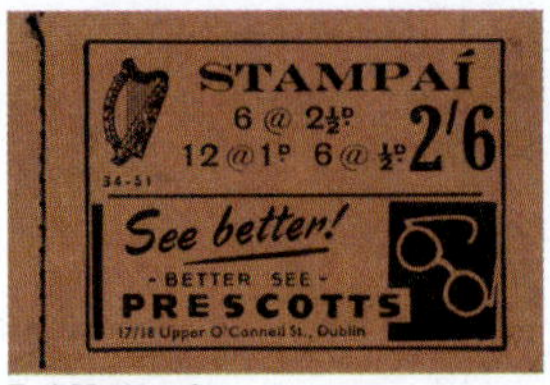

B **4** Harp only

1948–50. *Black on red cover as Type* B **4**.
SB8 2s.6d. booklet containing six ½d., twelve 1d. and six 2½d. (Nos. 133, 112, 115) in blocks of 6 *From* £200
Edition Nos.:—31–48, 32–49, 33–50

1951–53. *Black on buff cover as Type* B **4**.
SB9 2s.6d. booklet containing six ½d., twelve 1d. and six 2½d. (Nos. 133, 112, 115) in blocks of 6 *From* 60·00
Edition Nos.:—34–51, 35–52, 36–53

1954 (24 Nov). *Black on buff cover as Type* B **4**.
SB10 4s. booklet containing six ½d., six 1½d. and twelve 3d. (Nos. 133, 113, 116) in blocks of 6 .... £110
Edition No.:—37–54.

1956 (17 Dec). *Black on buff cover as Type* B **4**.
SB11 4s. booklet containing twelve 1d. and twelve 3d. (Nos. 112, 116) in blocks of 6.......... 65·00
Edition No.:—38–56.

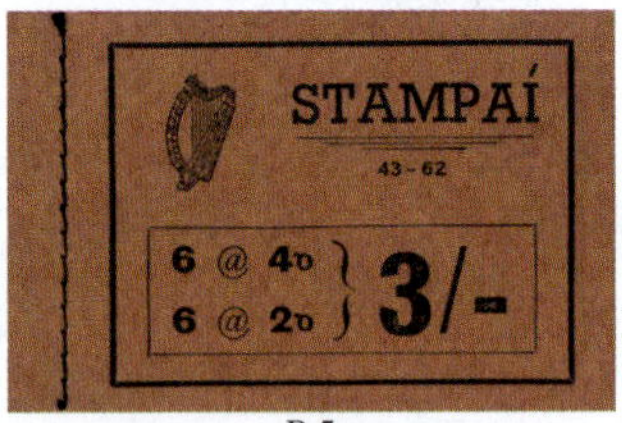

B **5**

1958–61. *Black on buff cover as Type* B **5**.
SB12 4s. booklet containing twelve 1d. and twelve 3d. (Nos. 112, 116) in blocks of 6.......... 60·00
Edition Nos.:—39–58, 40–59, 41–60, 42–61.

1962 (23 Oct)–**63**. *Black on buff cover as Type* B **5**.
SB13 3s. booklet containing six 2d. and six 4d. (Nos. 114, 117) in blocks of 6 .... *From* 50·00
Edition Nos.:—43–62, 44–63 (June).

B **6**

1964 (Sept). *Red on yellow cover as Type* B **6**.
SB14 3s. booklet containing twelve 1d. and six 4d. (Nos. 112, 117) in blocks of 6 .... 45·00

B **7**

1966 (1–9 Dec). *Covers as Type* B **7** *in red (No.* SB15*), blue (No.* SB16*) or green (No.* SB17*).*
SB15 2s.6d. booklet containing six 2d. and six 3d. (Nos. 114, 116) in blocks of 6 (9 Dec)........ 19·00
SB16 2s.6d. booklet containing six 5d. (No. 228) in block of 6 (9 Dec) .... 15·00
SB17 5s. booklet containing twelve 5d. (No. 228) in blocks of 6 .... 29·00

B **8**

1969 (12 Sept). *Plain blue-green cover as Type* B **8**.
SB18 6s. booklet containing twelve 6d. (No. 253) in blocks of six .... 45·00

POSTAGE DUE STAMPS

From 1922 to 1925 Great Britain postage due stamps in both script and block watermarks were used without overprint.

D **1**

(Des Ruby McConnell. Typo Govt Printing Works, Dublin)

1925 (20 Feb). W **10**. P 14×15.
D1 D **1** ½d. emerald-green .... 12·00 16·00
D2 1d. carmine .... 15·00 3·50
a. Wmk sideways £800 £400
w. Wmk inverted .... £350 75·00
y. Wmk inverted and reversed... £150 £150
D3 2d. deep green .... 38·00 5·50
a. Wmk sideways .... 50·00 17·00
w. Wmk inverted .... 90·00 35·00
D4 6d. plum .... 6·50 7·50
D1/4 *Set of* 4 .... 65·00 29·00

1940–70. W **22**. P 14×15.
D5 D **1** ½d. emerald-green (1942) .... 35·00 23·00
w. Wmk inverted .... — £375
D6 1d. carmine (1941) .... 1·50 70
w. Wmk inverted
D7 1½d. vermilion (1953) .... 2·75 7·00
w. Wmk inverted .... 17·00 25·00
D8 2d. deep green (1940) .... 2·75 70
w. Wmk inverted .... £325 80·00
D9 3d. blue (10.11.52) .... 3·00 3·25
w. Wmk inverted .... 7·00 5·00
D10 5d. blue-violet (3.3.43) .... 4·50 3·00
w. Wmk inverted .... 6·50 7·00
D11 6d. plum (21.3.60) .... 4·25 2·50
a. Wmk sideways (1968) .... 1·00 1·00
D12 8d. orange (30.10.62) .... 9·00 11·00
w. Wmk inverted .... 17·00 20·00
D13 10d. bright purple (27.1.65) .... 8·50 7·50
D14 1s. apple-green (10.2.69) .... 6·50 9·50
a. Wmk sideways (1970) .... 75·00 8·50
D5/14 *Set of* 10 .... 65·00 60·00

Stamps in these designs but in different colours were issued between 1971 and 1978.

Jamaica

Records show that the first local Postmaster for Jamaica on a regular basis was appointed as early as 1671, although a reasonably organised service did not evolve until 1687–8. In the early years of the 18th century overseas mail was carried by the British packets, but between 1704 and 1711 this service was run on a commercial basis by Edmund Dummer. Following the collapse of the Dummer scheme Jamaica was virtually without a Post Office until 1720 and it was not until 1755 that overseas mail was again carried by British packets.

Stamps of Great Britain were used in Jamaica from 8 May 1858, initially on overseas mail only, but their use was extended to mail sent to Jamaican addresses from 1 February 1859. The island assumed responsibility for the postal service on 1 August 1860 and the use of Great Britain stamps then ceased.

KINGSTON

Z 1

Stamps of GREAT BRITAIN *cancelled "A 01" as Type* Z **1**.

1858–60.

Z1	1d. rose-red (1857), *perf* 16	£500
Z2	1d. rose-red (1857), *perf* 14	70·00
Z4	4d. rose-carmine *or* rose (1857)	50·00
Z5	6d. lilac (1856)	50·00
Z6	1s. green (1856)	£225

Z 2

Stamps of GREAT BRITAIN *cancelled "A 01" as Type* Z **2**.

1859–60.

Z7	1d. rose-red (1857), *perf* 14	£275
Z9	4d. rose-carmine or rose (1857)	55·00
Z10	6d. lilac (1856)	55·00
Z11	1s. green (1856)	£550

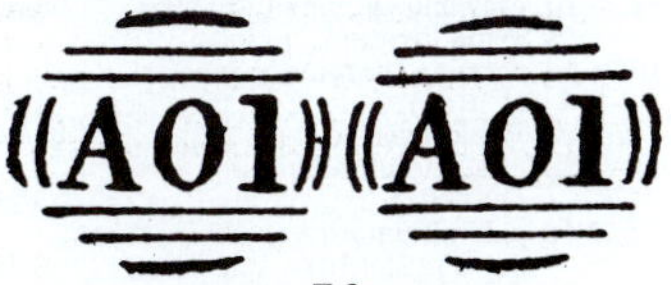

Z 3

Stamps of GREAT BRITAIN *cancelled "A 01" as Type* Z **3**.

1859–60.

Z12	1d. rose-red (1857), *perf* 14	£350
Z14	4d. rose-carmine *or* rose (1857)	£225
	a. Thick *glazed* paper	£450
Z15	6d. lilac (1856)	£225
Z16	1s. green (1856)	

Cancellation "A 01" was later used by the London, Foreign Branch Office.

OTHER JAMAICA POST OFFICES

British stamps were issued to several District post offices between 8 May 1858 and 1 March 1859 (i.e. before the Obliterators A 27—A 78 were issued). These can only be distinguished (off the cover) when they have the Town's date-stamp on them. They are worth about three times the price of those with an obliteration number.

Stamps of GREAT BRITAIN *cancelled "A 27" to "A 78" as Type* Z **1**.

1859–60.

"A 27". ALEXANDRIA

Z17	1d. rose-red (1857), *perf* 14	£650
Z17*a*	2d. blue (1855) Large Crown, *perf* 14 (Plate 6)	£850
Z18	4d. rose (1857)	£275
Z19	6d. lilac (1856)	£550

"A 28". ANNOTTO BAY

Z20	1d. rose-red (1857), *perf* 14	£450
Z21	4d. rose (1857)	£150
Z22	6d. lilac (1856)	£375

"A 29". BATH

Z23	1d. rose-red (1857), *perf* 14	£225
Z24	4d. rose (1857)	£150
Z25	6d. lilac (1856)	£475

"A 30". BLACK RIVER

Z26	1d. rose-red (1857), *perf* 14	£225
Z27	4d. rose (1857)	£110
Z28	6d. lilac (1856)	£200

"A31". BROWN'S TOWN

Z29	1d. rose-red (1857), *perf* 14	£350
Z30	4d. rose (1857)	£300
Z31	6d. lilac (1856)	£300

"A 32". BUFF BAY

Z32	1d. rose-red (1857), *perf* 14	£300
Z33	4d. rose (1857)	£225
Z34	6d. lilac (1856)	£225

"A 33". CHAPELTON

Z35	1d. rose-red (1857), *perf* 14	£325
Z36	4d. rose (1857)	£180
Z37	6d. lilac (1856)	£275

"A34". CLAREMONT

Z38	1d. rose-red (1857), *perf* 14	£475
Z39	4d. rose (1857)	£225
Z40	6d. lilac (1856)	£275

"A35". CLARENDON

Z41	1d. rose-red (1857), *perf* 14	£400
Z42	4d. rose (1857)	£180
Z43	6d. lilac (1856)	£300

"A 36". DRY HARBOUR

Z44	1d. rose-red (1857), *perf* 14	£550
Z45	4d. rose (1857)	£425
Z46	6d. lilac (1856)	£375

"A 37". DUNCANS

Z47	1d. rose-red (1857), *perf* 14	£600
Z48	4d. rose (1857)	£500
Z49	6d. lilac (1856)	£400

"A 38". EWARTON

A 38 was allocated to EWARTON but this office was closed towards the end of 1858 before the postmark arrived. A 38 was re-issued to Falmouth in 1862.

"A 39". FALMOUTH

Z53	1d. rose-red (1857), *perf* 14	£150
Z54	4d. rose (1857)	85·00
Z55	6d. lilac (1856)	£100
Z56	1s. green (1856)	£900

"A40". FLINT RIVER

Z57	1d. rose-red (1857), *perf* 14	£325
Z58	4d. rose (1857)	£200
Z59	6d. lilac (1856)	£250
Z60	1s. green (1856)	£950

"A 41". GAYLE

Z61	1d. rose-red (1857), *perf* 14	£600
Z62	4d. rose (1857)	£190
Z63	6d. lilac (1856)	£225
Z64	1s. green (1856)	£650

"A 42". GOLDEN SPRING

Z65	1d. rose-red (1857), *perf* 14	£425
Z66	4d. rose (1857)	£300
Z67	6d. lilac (1856)	£500
Z68	1s. green (1856)	£900

"A 43". GORDON TOWN

Z69	1d. rose-red (1857), *perf* 14	
Z70	4d. rose (1857)	
Z71	6d. lilac (1856)	£600

"A 44". GOSHEN

Z72	1d. rose-red (1857), *perf* 14	£200
Z73	4d. rose (1857)	£180
Z74	6d. lilac (1856)	95·00

"A 45". GRANGE HILL

Z75	1d. rose-red (1857), *perf* 14	£300
Z76	4d. rose (1857)	85·00
Z77	6d. lilac (1856)	£110
Z77*a*	1s. green (1856)	£800

"A 46". GREEN ISLAND

Z78	1d. rose-red (1857), *perf* 14	£450
Z79	4d. rose (1857)	£225
Z80	6d. lilac (1856)	£350
Z81	1s. green (1856)	£900

"A 47". HIGHGATE

Z82	1d. rose-red (1857), *perf* 14	£275
Z83	4d. rose (1857)	£180
Z84	6d. lilac (1856)	£350

"A 48". HOPE BAY

Z85	1d. rose-red (1857), *perf* 14	£550
Z86	4d. rose (1857)	£250
Z87	6d. lilac (1856)	£550

"A 49". LILLIPUT

Z88	1d. rose-red (1857), *perf* 14	£250
Z89	4d. rose (1857)	£250
Z90	6d. lilac (1856)	£130

"A 50". LITTLE RIVER

A 50 was allocated for use at LITTLE RIVER but this office was closed late in 1858, before the obliterator could be issued. Issued to Malvern in 1862.

"A 51". LUCEA

Z91	1d. rose-red (1857), *perf* 14	£400
Z92	4d. rose (1857)	£100
Z93	6d. lilac (1856)	£275

"A 52". MANCHIONEAL

Z94	1d. rose-red (1857), *perf* 14	£450
Z95	4d. rose (1857)	£250
Z96	6d. lilac (1856)	£450

"A 53". MANDEVILLE

Z97	1d. rose-red (1857), *perf* 14	£275
Z98	4d. rose (1857)	95·00
Z99	6d. lilac (1856)	£200

"A 54". MAY HILL

Z100	1d. rose-red (1857), *perf* 14	£140
Z101	4d. rose (1857)	£140
Z102	6d. lilac (1856)	95·00
Z102a	1s. green (1856)	£1100

"A 55". MILE GULLY

Z103	1d. rose-red (1857), *perf* 14	£375
Z104	4d. rose (1857)	£275
Z105	6d. lilac (1856)	£275

"A 56". MONEAGUE

Z106	1d. rose-red (1857), *perf* 14	£325
Z107	4d. rose (1857)	£300
Z108	6d. lilac (1856)	£550

"A 57". MONTEGO BAY

Z109	1d. rose-red (1857), *perf* 14	£250
Z110	4d. rose (1857)	75·00
Z111	6d. lilac (1856)	90·00
Z112	1s. green (1856)	£800

"A 58". MONTPELIER

Z113	1d. rose-red (1857), *perf* 14	
Z114	4d. rose (1857)	
Z115	6d. lilac (1856)	£850

"A 59". MORANT BAY

Z116	1d. rose-red (1857), *perf* 14	£475
Z117	4d. rose (1857)	95·00
Z118	6d. lilac (1856)	£110

"A 60". OCHO RIOS

Z119	1d. rose-red (1857), *perf* 14	
Z120	4d. rose (1857)	£130
Z121	6d. lilac (1856)	£275

"A 61". OLD HARBOUR

Z122	1d. rose-red (1857), *perf* 14	£250
Z123	4d. rose (1857)	£180
Z124	6d. lilac (1856)	£200

"A 62". PLANTAIN GARDEN RIVER

Z125	1d. rose-red (1857), *perf* 14	£200
Z126	4d. rose (1857)	£130
Z127	6d. lilac (1856)	£200

"A 63". PEAR TREE GROVE

No genuine specimen of A 63 has been found on a British stamp.

"A 64". PORT ANTONIO

Z131	1d. rose-red (1857), *perf* 14	£500
Z132	4d. rose (1857)	£325
Z133	6d. lilac (1856)	£350

"A 65". PORT MORANT

Z134	1d. rose-red (1857), *perf* 14	£375
Z135	4d. rose (1857)	£140
Z136	6d. lilac (1856)	£325

"A 66". PORT MARIA

Z137	1d. rose-red (1857), *perf* 14	£300
Z138	4d. rose (1857)	£100
Z139	6d. lilac (1856)	£350

"A 67". PORT ROYAL

Z140	1d. rose-red (1857), *perf* 14	£425
Z140*a*	2d. blue (1858) (plate 9)	
Z141	4d. rose (1857)	£475
Z142	6d. lilac (1856)	£425

"A 68". PORUS

Z143	1d. rose-red (1857), *perf* 14	£275
Z144	4d. rose (1857)	£120
Z145	6d. lilac (1856)	£425

"A 69". RAMBLE

Z146	1d. rose-red (1857), *perf* 14	£275
Z147	4d. rose (1857)	£225
	a. Thick glazed paper	£450
Z149	6d. lilac (1856)	£350

"A 70". RIO BUENO

Z150	1d. rose-red (1857), *perf* 14	£300
Z151	4d. rose (1857)	£250
Z152	6d. lilac (1856)	£150

"A 71". RODNEY HALL

Z153	1d. rose-red (1857), *perf* 14	£225
Z154	4d. rose (1857)	£140
Z155	6d. lilac (1856)	£180

"A 72". ST. DAVID

Z156	1d. rose-red (1857), *perf* 14	£275
Z157	4d. rose (1857)	£400
Z158	6d. lilac (1856)	

"A 73". ST. ANN'S BAY

Z159	1d. rose-red (1857), *perf* 14	£275
Z160	4d. rose (1857)	£130
Z161	6d. lilac (1856)	£225
Z161a	1s. green (1856)	£1000

"A 74". SALT GUT

Z162	1d. rose-red (1857), *perf* 14	£325
Z163	4d. rose (1857)	£200
Z164	6d. lilac (1856)	£275

"A 75". SAVANNAH-LA-MAR

Z165	1d. rose-red (1857), *perf* 14	£140
Z166	4d. rose (1857)	90·00
Z167	6d. lilac (1856)	£225
Z168	1s. green (1856)	£800

"A 76". SPANISH TOWN

Z169	1d. rose-red (1857), *perf* 14	£140
Z170	4d. rose (1857)	80·00
Z171	6d. lilac (1856)	£140
Z172	1s. green (1856)	£600

"A 77". STEWART TOWN

Z173	1d. rose-red (1857), *perf* 14	£500
Z174	4d. rose (1857)	£375
Z175	6d. lilac (1856)	£275

"A 78". VERE

Z176	1d. rose-red (1857), *perf* 14	£375
Z177	4d. rose (1857)	£130
Z178	6d. lilac (1856)	90·00
Z179	1s. green (1856)	£900

PRICES FOR STAMPS ON COVER

Nos. 1/6	*from* × 4
Nos. 7/15	*from* × 6
Nos. 16/26	*from* × 8
Nos. 27/9	*from* × 6
No. 30	*from* × 5
Nos. 31/2	*from* × 15
Nos. 33/6	*from* × 5
Nos. 37/56	*from* × 3
No. 57	*from* × 4
Nos. 58/67	*from* × 3
Nos. 68/77	*from* × 6
Nos. 78/89	*from* × 3
Nos. 90/103	*from* × 4
Nos. 104/7	*from* × 5
Nos. 108/17	*from* × 3
Nos. 118/20	*from* × 5
Nos. 121/33a	*from* × 4
Nos. 134/40	*from* × 8
Nos. F1/9	*from* × 3
Nos. O1/5	*from* × 3

CROWN COLONY

PRINTERS. Until 1923, all the stamps of Jamaica were typographed by De La Rue & Co, Ltd, London, *unless otherwise stated*.

The official dates of issue are given, where known, but where definite information is not available the dates are those of earliest known use, etc.

1

2

3

4

5

6

7

A

1860 (23 Nov)–**70**. W **7**. P 14.

1	1	1d. pale blue	60·00	15·00
		a. Pale greenish blue	80·00	19·00
		b. Blue	50·00	12·00
		c. Deep blue (1865)	£110	28·00
		d. Bisected (½d.) (20.11.61) (on cover)	†	£650
		w. Wmk inverted	£120	45·00
2	2	2d. rose	£190	50·00
		a. Deep rose	£130	50·00
		w. Wmk inverted	–	75·00
3	3	3d. green (10.9.63)	£130	25·00
		w. Wmk inverted	£160	40·00
4	4	4d. brown-orange	£200	50·00
		a. Red-orange	£200	22·00
		w. Wmk inverted		
5	5	6d. dull lilac	£180	22·00
		a. Grey-purple	£275	32·00
		b. Deep purple (1870)	£800	55·00
		w. Wmk inverted	–	85·00
6	6	1s. yellow-brown	£450	25·00
		a. Purple-brown (1862)	£550	23·00
		b. Dull brown (1868)	£180	27·00
		c. "$" for "S" in "SHILLING" (A)	£2500	£600
		w. Wmk inverted	–	60·00

The diagonal bisection of the 1d. was authorised by a P.O. notice dated 20 November 1861 to pay the ½d. rate for newspapers or book post. Specimens are only of value when on original envelope or wrapper. The authority was withdrawn as from 1 December 1872. Fakes are frequently met with. Other bisections were unauthorised.

The so-called "dollar variety" of the 1s. occurs once in each sheet of stamps in all shades and in later colours, etc, on the second stamp in the second row of the left upper pane. The prices quoted above are for the dull brown shade, the prices for the other shades being proportionate to their normal value.

All values except the 3d. are known imperf, mint only.

There are two types of watermark in the 3d. and 1s., one being short and squat and the other elongated.

8

9

10

1870–83. Wmk Crown CC.

(a) P 14.

7	8	½d. claret (29.10.72)	15·00	3·50
		a. Deep claret (1883)	19·00	5·50
		w. Wmk inverted	–	38·00
8	1	1d. blue (4.73)	75·00	75
		a. Deep blue	80·00	1·50
		w. Wmk inverted	£150	27·00
9	2	2d. rose (4.70)	80·00	70
		a. Deep rose	90·00	1·00
		w. Wmk inverted	£100	27·00
10	3	3d. green (1.3.70)	£100	8·50
		w. Wmk inverted	–	65·00
11	4	4d. brown-orange (1872)	£200	11·00
		a. Red-orange (1883)	£350	6·00
		w. Wmk inverted	–	60·00
12	5	6d. mauve (10.3.71)	70·00	5·50
		w. Wmk inverted	–	45·00
13	6	1s. dull brown (*to* deep) (23.2.73)	25·00	8·50
		a. "$" for "S" in "SHILLING" (A)	£1300	£600
		w. Wmk inverted	–	70·00
		(b) P 12½.		
14	9	2s. Venetian red (27.8.75)	40·00	21·00
		w. Wmk inverted	60·00	70·00
15	10	5s. lilac (27.8.75)	90·00	£140
		w. Wmk inverted	£120	£190
7/15 *Set of 9*			£600	£170

The ½d., 1d., 4d., 2s. and 5s. are known imperforate.

1883–97. Wmk Crown CA. P 14.

16	8	½d. yellow-green (2.85)	4·50	1·25
		a. Green	1·00	10
		w. Wmk inverted	–	30·00
		x. Wmk reversed	–	50·00
17	1	1d. blue (1884)	£325	4·75
18		1d. rose (*to* deep) (3.3.85)	70·00	1·25
		a. Carmine (1886)	50·00	60
		w. Wmk inverted	–	42·00
19	2	2d. rose (*to* deep) (17.3.84)	£200	4·00
		w. Wmk inverted	–	55·00
20		2d. grey (1885)	£130	5·00
		a. Slate (1886)	90·00	65
		w. Wmk inverted	–	28·00
21	3	3d. sage-green (11.86)	4·00	1·00
		a. Pale olive-green	2·50	1·50
22	4	4d. red-orange* (9.3.83)	£400	22·00
		aw. Wmk inverted		
		b. Red-brown (shades) (1885)	2·00	35
		bw. Wmk inverted	70·00	28·00
23	5	6d. deep yellow (4.10.90)	26·00	7·00
		a. Orange-yellow	4·00	3·50
24	6	1s. brown (*to* deep) (3.97)	5·50	6·00
		a. "$" for "S" in "SHILLING" (A)	£800	£500
		b. Chocolate	15·00	12·00
25	9	2s. Venetian red (2.97)	27·00	22·00
26	10	5s. lilac (2.97)	55·00	80·00
16/26 *Set of 11*			£650	£110
16s, 18s, 20s/3s Optd "Specimen" *Set of 6*			£500	

*No. 22 is the same colour as No. 11a.

The 1d. carmine, 2d. slate, and 2s. are known imperf. All values to the 6d. inclusive are known perf 12. These are proofs.

11

TWO PENCE
HALF-PENNY
(12)

1889 (8 Mar)–**91**. *Value tablet in second colour.* Wmk Crown CA. P 14.

27	11	1d. purple and mauve	5·00	20
		w. Wmk inverted	–	30·00
28		2d. green	22·00	3·75
		a. Deep green (brown gum)	12·00	6·00
		aw. Wmk inverted	70·00	
29		2½d. dull purple and blue (25.2.91)	5·50	50
		w. Wmk inverted	80·00	
27/9 *Set of 3*			20·00	4·00
27s/9s Optd "Specimen" *Set of 3*			£110	

A very wide range of shades may be found in the 1d. The headplate was printed in many shades of purple, and the dutyplate in various shades of mauve and purple and also in carmine, etc. There are fewer shades for the other values and they are not so pronounced.

1890 (4 June)–**91**. *No. 22b surch with T* **12** *by C. Vendyres, Kingston.*

30	4	2½d. on 4d. red-brown	28·00	11·00
		a. Spacing between lines of surch 1½ mm (2.91)	32·00	17·00
		b. Surch double	£325	£225
		c. "PFNNY" for "PENNY"	75·00	65·00
		ca. Ditto and broken "K" for "Y"	£130	£110
		w. Wmk inverted	75·00	38·00

This provisional was issued pending receipt of No. 29 which is listed above for convenience of reference.

Three settings exist. (1) Ten varieties arranged in a single vertical row and repeated six times in the pane. (2) Twelve varieties, in two horizontal rows of six, repeated five times, alternate rows show 1 and 1½ mm spacing between lines of surcharge. (3) Three varieties, arranged horizontally and repeated twenty times. All these settings can be reconstructed by examination of the spacing and relative position of the words of the surcharge and of the broken letters, etc, which are numerous.

A variety reading "PFNNK", with the "K" unbroken, is a forgery.

Surcharges misplaced either horizontally or vertically are met with, the normal position being central at the foot of the stamp with "HALF-PENNY" covering the old value.

13 Llandovery Falls, Jamaica (photo by Dr. J. Johnston)

14 Arms of Jamaica

(Recess D.L.R.)

1900 (1 May)–**01**. Wmk Crown CC (sideways*). P 14.

31	13	1d. red	5·00	20
		w. Wmk Crown to left of CC	5·50	50
		x. Wmk reversed	–	45·00
		y. Wmk sideways inverted and reversed		
32		1d. slate-black and red (25.9.01)	4·50	20
		a. Blued paper	£110	£100
		b. Imperf between (vert pair)	£10000	
		w. Wmk Crown to left of CC	12·00	11·00
		x. Wmk reversed	–	45·00
		y. Wmk sideways inverted and reversed		
31s/2s Optd "Specimen" *Set of 2*			£130	

*The normal sideways wmk shows Crown to right of CC, *as seen from the back of the stamp.*

Many shades exist of both centre and frame of the bi-coloured 1d. which was, of course, printed from two plates and the design shows minor differences from that of the 1d. red which was printed from a single plate.

(Typo D.L.R.)

1903 (16 Nov)–**04**. Wmk Crown CA. P 14.

33	14	½d. grey and dull green	1·50	30
		a. "SER.ET" for "SERVIET"	40·00	45·00
		w. Wmk inverted	30·00	30·00
34		1d. grey and carmine (24.2.04)	2·25	10
		a. "SER.ET" for "SERVIET"	32·00	35·00
35		2½d. grey and ultramarine	4·25	30
		a. "SER.ET" for "SERVIET"	60·00	75·00
36		5d. grey and yellow (1.3.04)	15·00	23·00
		a. "SER.ET" for "SERVIET"	£800	£1000
		w. Wmk inverted	95·00	
33/6 *Set of 4*			21·00	23·00
33s/6s Optd "Specimen" *Set of 4*			80·00	

The "SER.ET" variety occurs on R. 4/2 of the left upper pane. It was corrected by De La Rue in July 1905.

The centres of the above and later bi-coloured stamps in the Arms type vary in colour from grey to grey-black.

15 Arms type redrawn

16 Arms type redrawn

1905–11. Wmk Mult Crown CA. P 14.

(a) Arms types. Chalk-surfaced paper.

37	14	½d. grey and dull green (20.11.05)	4·50	20
		a. "SER.ET" for "SERVIET"	26·00	40·00
		w. Wmk inverted		
38	15	½d. yell-grn (*ordinary paper*) (8.11.06)	9·00	50
		aw. Wmk inverted	†	£110
		b. Dull green	3·75	20
		c. Deep green	4·50	20
39	14	1d. grey and carmine (20.11.05)	18·00	50
		w. Wmk inverted	–	90·00
40	16	1d. carmine (*ordinary paper*) (1.10.06)	1·50	10
		w. Wmk inverted	40·00	
41	14	2½d. grey and ultramarine (12.11.07)	3·25	4·75
42		2½d. pale ultramarine (*ordinary paper*) (21.9.10)	3·25	1·25
		a. Deep ultramarine	2·50	1·75
43		5d. grey and orange-yellow (24.4.07)	60·00	70·00
		a. "SER.ET" for "SERVIET"	£1200	£1400
44		6d. dull and bright purple (18.8.11)	13·00	13·00
45		5s. grey and violet (11.05)	45·00	45·00
37/45 *Set of 9*			£130	£120
38s, 40s, 42s, 44s/5s Optd "Specimen" *Set of 5*			£170	

See note below No. 36 concerning grey centres.

(b) Queen Victoria types. Ordinary paper.

46	3	3d. olive-green (3.8.05)	6·50	4·25
		a. Sage-green (1907)	5·00	3·00
47		3d. purple/*yellow* (10.3.10)	4·50	3·50
		a. Chalk-surfaced paper. *Pale purple/yellow* (11.7.10)	2·00	1·50
		aw. Wmk inverted	45·00	48·00
48	4	4d. red-brown (6.6.08)	75·00	75·00
49		4d. black/*yellow* (*chalk-surfaced paper*) (21.9.10)	7·50	48·00
50		4d. red/*yellow* (3.10.11)	1·50	8·00
51	5	6d. dull orange (27.6.06)	15·00	25·00
		a. Golden yellow (9.09)	26·00	55·00
52		6d. lilac (19.11.09)	27·00	48·00
		a. Chalk-surfaced paper. *Purple* (7.10)	10·00	22·00
53	6	1s. brown (11.06)	19·00	35·00
		a. Deep brown	28·00	50·00
		b. "$" for "S" in "SHILLING" (A)	£1300	£1400
54		1s. black/*green* (*chalk-surfaced paper*) (21.9.10)	5·50	8·50
		a. "$" for "S" in "SHILLING" (A)	£950	£1200
55	9	2s. Venetian red (11.08)	£100	£150
56		2s. pur/*bl* (*chalk-surfaced paper*) (21.9.10)	6·50	3·50
46/56 *Set of 11*			£200	£350
47s, 49s, 50s, 52s, 54s, 56s Optd "Specimen" *Set of 6*			£200	

No. 38 exists in coils constructed from normal sheets.

17

18

(T **17/18** typo D.L.R.)

1911 (3 Feb). Wmk Mult Crown CA. P 14.

57	**17**	2d. grey	4·00	13·00
		s. Optd "Specimen"	40·00	

1912–20. Wmk Mult Crown CA. *Chalk-surfaced paper (3d. to 5s.).* P 14.

58	**18**	1d. carmine-red (5.12.12)	1·50	10
		a. Scarlet (1916)	2·75	70
59		1½d. brown-orange (13.7.16)	1·00	60
		a. Yellow-orange	13·00	1·00
		b. Wmk sideways	†	£1500
60		2d. grey (2.8.12)	2·00	1·75
		a. Slate-grey	1·25	3·00
61		2½d. blue (13.2.13)	1·50	15
		a. Deep bright blue	65	1·00
62		3d. purple/*yellow* (6.3.12)	50	45
		a. White back (2.4.13)	55	40
		b. On lemon (25.9.16)	3·75	1·50
		bs. Optd "Specimen"	32·00	
		w. Wmk inverted		
63		4d. black and red/*yellow* (4.4.13)	50	3·50
		a. White back (7.5.14)	75	4·00
		b. On lemon (1916)	23·00	19·00
		bs. Optd "Specimen"	32·00	
		c. On pale yellow (1919)	22·00	15·00
64		6d. dull and bright purple (14.11.12)	4·50	9·00
		a. Dull purple and bright mauve (1915)	75	1·00
		b. Dull purple & bright magenta (1920)	3·75	2·25
65		1s. black/*green* (2.8.12)	2·25	2·00
		a. White back (4.1.15)	2·00	4·75
		b. On blue-green, olive back (1920)	2·25	5·50
66		2s. purple and bright blue/*blue* (10.1.19)	15·00	25·00
67		5s. green and red/*yellow* (5.9.19)	75·00	90·00
		a. On pale yellow (1920)	75·00	90·00
		b. On orange-buff (1920)	£140	£170
58/67 *Set of* 10			90·00	£110
58s/67s Optd "Specimen" *Set of* 10			£200	

No. 58 exists in coils constructed from normal sheets.

The paper of No. 67 is a bright yellow and the gum rough and dull. No. 67*a* is on practically the normal creamy "pale yellow" paper, and the gum is smooth and shiny. The paper of No. 67*b* approaches the "coffee" colour of the true "orange-buff", and the colours of both head and frame are paler, the latter being of a carmine tone.

For the ½d. and 6d. with Script wmk see Nos. 89*a*/90.

RED CROSS LABELS. A voluntary organization, the Jamaica War Stamp League later the Jamaica Patriotic Stamp League, was founded in November 1915 by Mr. Lewis Ashenheim, a Kingston solicitor. The aims of the League were to support the British Red Cross, collect funds for the purchase of aircraft for the Royal Flying Corps and the relief of Polish Jews.

One fund-raising method used was the sale, from 1 December 1915, of ½d. charity labels. These labels, which were available from post offices, depicted a bi-plane above a cross and were printed in red by Dennison Manufacturing Company, Framingham, U.S.A., the stamps being perforated 12 except for those along the edges of the sheet which have one side imperforate.

From 22 December 1915 supplies of the labels were overprinted "JAMAICA" in red, the colour of this overprint being changed to black from 15 January 1916. Copies sold from 11 March 1916 carried an additional "Half-Penny" surcharge, also in black.

Such labels had no postal validity when used by the general public, but, by special order of the Governor, were accepted for the payment of postage on the League's official mail. To obtain this concession the envelopes were to be inscribed "Red Cross Business" or "Jamaica Patriotic Stamp League" and the labels used endorsed with Mr. Ashenheim's signature. Such covers are rare.

WAR STAMP.
(19)

WAR STAMP.
(20)

WAR STAMP.
(21)

(T **19/21** optd Govt Printing Office, Kingston)

1916 (1 Apr–Sept). *Optd with T* **19**.

68	**15**	½d. yellow-green	10	35
		a. No stop after "STAMP" (R. 18/2)	11·00	25·00
		b. Opt double	£110	£130
		c. Opt inverted	95·00	£120
		d. Space between "W" and "A" (R. 20/1)	12·00	25·00
		e. Blue-green	10	60
		ea. No stop after "STAMP" (R. 3/11 or 11/1)	11·00	24·00
		eb. Space between "W" and "A" (R. 20/1)	16·00	32·00
		w. Wmk inverted		
69	**18**	3d. purple/*yellow* (white back)	18·00	32·00
		a. On lemon (6.16)	1·00	17·00
		ab. No stop after "STAMP" (R. 8/6 or 9/6)	25·00	80·00
		b. On pale yellow (9.16)	10·00	26·00

Minor varieties: ½d. (i) Small "P"; (ii) "WARISTAMP" (raised quad between words); (iii) Two stops after "STAMP". 3d. "WARISTAMP". There were several settings of the overprint used for each value. Where two positions are quoted for a variety these did not occur on the same sheet.

NOTE. The above and succeeding stamps with "WAR STAMP" overprint were issued for payment of a special war tax on letters and postcards or on parcels. Ordinary unoverprinted stamps could also be used for this purpose.

1916 (Sept–Dec). *Optd with T* **20**.

70	**15**	½d. blue-green (*shades*) (2.10.16)	10	30
		a. No stop after "STAMP" (R. 5/7)	12·00	35·00
		b. Opt omitted (in pair with normal)	£4250	£3750
		c. "R" inserted by hand (R. 1/10)	£1400	£1100
		w. Wmk inverted	45·00	
71	**18**	1½d. orange (1.9.16)	10	15
		aa. Wmk sideways	†	£1700
		a. No stop after "STAMP" (R. 4/12, 8/6, 10/10, 11/1, 18/12, 19/12)	5·00	7·50
		b. "S" in "STAMP" omitted (R. 6/12) (Dec)	£150	£160
		c. "S" inserted by hand	£400	
		d. "R" in "WAR" omitted (R. 1/10)	£2250	£2000
		e. "R" inserted by hand	£1100	£900
		f. Inverted "d" for "P"	£200	£160
		w. Wmk inverted	16·00	16·00
72		3d. purple/*lemon* (2.10.16)	3·00	1·00
		aa. Opt inverted	£300	
		a. No stop after "STAMP" (R. 5/7)	38·00	55·00
		b. "S" in "STAMP" omitted (R. 6/12) (Dec)	£600	£600
		c. "S" inserted by hand	£200	£200
		e. On yellow (12.16)	7·50	9·00
		ea. "S" in "STAMP" omitted (R. 6/12)	£750	£750
		eb. "S" inserted by hand	£425	£375

Nos. 70c, 71c, 71e, 72c and 72eb show the missing "R" or "S" inserted by handstamp. The 3d. is known with this "S" handstamp inverted or double.

Minor varieties, such as raised quads, small stop, double stop, spaced letters and letters of different sizes, also exist in this overprint. The setting was altered several times.

1917 (March). *Optd with T* **21**.

73	**15**	½d. blue-green (*shades*) (25.3.17)	65	30
		a. No stop after "STAMP" (R. 2/5, 8/11, 8/12)	10·00	22·00
		b. Stop inserted and "P" impressed a second time (R. 7/6)	£250	
		c. Optd on back only	£200	
		d. Opt inverted	17·00	42·00
74	**18**	1½d. orange (3.3.17)	20	10
		aa. Wmk sideways	†	£1500
		a. No stop after "STAMP" (R. 2/5, 8/11, 8/12)	3·00	18·00
		b. Stop inserted and "P" impressed a second time (R. 7/6)	£250	
		c. Opt double	80·00	85·00
		d. Opt inverted	80·00	75·00
		e. "WAP STAMP" (R. 6/2)		
		w. Wmk inverted	16·00	21·00
75		3d. purple/*yellow* (3.3.17)	1·00	1·40
		a. No stop after "STAMP" (R. 2/5, 8/11, 8/12)	18·00	40·00
		b. Stop inserted and "P" impressed a second time (R. 7/6)	£225	
		c. Opt inverted	£140	
		d. Opt sideways (reading up)	£375	
		da. Opt omitted (in horiz pair with No. 75d)	£3000	

Examples of No. 75d. exist showing parts of two or more overprints.

No. 75da shows the left-hand stamp as No. 75d and the right-hand stamp without overprint.

There are numerous minor varieties in this overprint with the setting being altered several times.

WAR STAMP
(22)

1919 (4 Oct)–**20**. *Optd with T* **22** *in red by D.L.R.*

76	**15**	½d. green	20	15
77	**18**	3d. purple/*yellow*	7·00	3·00
		a. Short opt (right pane R. 10/1)		
		b. Pale purple/buff (3.1.20)	4·00	1·25
		c. Deep purple/buff (1920)	9·00	6·50
76s/7s Optd "Specimen" *Set of* 2			70·00	

We list the most distinct variations in the 3d. The buff tone of the paper varies considerably in depth.

No. 77a shows the overprint 2 mm high instead of 2½ mm. The variety was corrected after the first overprinting. It is not found on the ½d.

23 Jamaica Exhibition, 1891

24 Arawak Woman preparing Cassava

25 War Contingent embarking, 1915

26 King's House, Spanish Town

Re-entry. Nos. 80a, 93a

The greater part of the design is re-entered, the hull showing in very solid colour and the people appear very blurred. There are also minor re-entries on stamps above (R. 7/4 and 6/4).

27 Return of War Contingent, 1919

A

B

28 Landing of Columbus, 1494

29 Cathedral, Spanish Town

30 Statue of Queen Victoria, Kingston

31 Admiral Rodney Memorial, Spanish Town

32 Sir Charles Metcalfe Statue, Kingston

33 Jamaican scenery

34

(Typo (½d., 1d.), recess (others) D.L.R.)

1919–21. *T* **23/29**, **34** *and similar vert designs.* Wmk Mult Crown CA (sideways* on 1d., 1½d. and 10s.). *Chalk-surfaced paper (½d., 1d.).* P 14.

78	**23**	½d. green and olive-green (12.11.20)	1·00	1·00
		w. Wmk inverted		
		x. Wmk reversed		
		y. Wmk inverted and reversed		
79	**24**	1d. carmine and orange (3.10.21)	1·75	1·75
		w. Wmk Crown to left of CA		
80	**25**	1½d. green (*shades*) (4.7.19)	40	1·00
		a. Major re-entry (R. 8/4)	80·00	
		b. "C" of "CA" missing from wmk	†	£250
		c. "A" of "CA" missing from wmk	£375	
		w. Wmk Crown to left of CA	22·00	
		y. Wmk sideways inverted and reversed	–	48·00
81	**26**	2d. indigo and green (18.2.21)	1·00	4·00
		w. Wmk inverted	35·00	
		y. Wmk inverted and reversed	38·00	
82	**27**	2½d. deep blue and blue (A) (18.2.21)	13·00	3·00
		a. Blue-black and deep blue	1·50	1·75
		b. "C" of "CA" missing from wmk	£250	£200
		c. "A" of "CA" missing from wmk	£200	
		w. Wmk inverted	25·00	
		x. Wmk reversed	32·00	
		y. Wmk inverted and reversed	32·00	
83	**28**	3d. myrtle-green and blue (8.4.21)	2·00	2·50
		w. Wmk inverted	32·00	35·00
		x. Wmk reversed	†	£100
84	**29**	4d. brown and deep green (21.1.21)	2·50	9·00
		w. Wmk inverted		
		x. Wmk reversed		
85	**30**	1s. orange-yell & red-orge (10.12.20)	3·75	5·50
		a. Frame inverted	£30000	£22000
		b. "C" of "CA" missing from wmk	£450	
		c. "A" of "CA" missing from wmk	£475	
		w. Wmk inverted		
		x. Wmk reversed		

86	31	2s. light blue and brown (10.12.20)	13·00	26·00
		b. "C" of "CA" missing from wmk	£600	
		c. "A" of "CA" missing from wmk		
		w. Wmk inverted	35·00	42·00
		x. Wmk reversed		
		y. Wmk inverted and reversed		
87	32	3s. violet-blue and orange (10.12.20)	20·00	£100
88	33	5s. blue and yellow-orange (15.4.21)	55·00	80·00
		a. Blue and pale dull orange	48·00	75·00
		w. Wmk inverted		
		x. Wmk reversed		
89	34	10s. myrtle-green (6.5.20)	75·00	£150
78/89 *Set of* 12			£150	£350
78s/89s Optd "Specimen" *Set of* 12			£250	

*The normal sideways wmk on Nos. 79/80 shows Crown to right of CA, *as seen from the back of the stamp*.

The 2½d. of the above series showed the Union Jack at left, incorrectly, as indicated in illustration A. In the issue on paper with Script wmk the design was corrected (Illustration B).

An example of No. 80 has been reported with the "A" inverted to the left of and above its normal position.

The "C" omitted variety has been reported on an example of No. 88 overprinted "Specimen".

A 6d. stamp showing the reading of the Declaration of Freedom from Slavery in 1836 was prepared and sent out in April 1921, but for political reasons was not issued and the stock was destroyed. Copies overprinted "Specimen" are known on both the Mult CA and Script CA papers, and are worth £700 each. The Mult CA "Specimen" exists with watermark reversed (*Price*, £900). Price without "Specimen" on Script CA £30000, on Mult CA £50000.

"Bow" flaw (R. 18/12)

1921 (21 Oct)–**27**. Wmk Mult Script CA. *Chalk-surfaced paper (6d.)*. P 14.

89*a*	18	½d. green (3.11.27)	1·75	10
		ab. Bow flaw	55·00	25·00
		as. Optd "Specimen"	45·00	
90		6d. dull purple and bright magenta	12·00	4·00
		s. Optd "Specimen"	40·00	

35 "POSTAGE & REVENUE" added

36 "Port Royal in 1853" (A. Duperly)

(Printing as before; the 6d. recess-printed)

1921–29. *As Nos. 78/89*. Wmk Mult Script CA (sideways* on 1d. and 1½d.). *Chalk-surfaced paper (½d., 1d.)*. P 14.

91	23	½d. green and olive-green (5.2.22)	50	50
		a. Green and deep olive-green	30	50
		w. Wmk inverted	30·00	30·00
92	35	1d. carmine and orange (5.12.22)	1·50	10
		w. Wmk Crown to right of CA	2·00	10
		x. Wmk reversed	—	50·00
93	25	1½d. green (*shades*) (2.2.21)	1·50	45
		a. Major re-entry (R. 8/4)	85·00	
		w. Wmk Crown to left of CA	—	22·00
		x. Wmk reversed	27·00	27·00
		y. Wmk sideways inverted and reversed	—	55·00
94	26	2d. indigo and green (4.11.21)	6·50	80
		a. Indigo and grey-green (1925)	9·00	1·00
		w. Wmk inverted	†	—
95	27	2½d. deep blue and blue (B) (4.11.21)	5·50	1·75
		a. Dull blue and blue (B)	6·00	60
		w. Wmk inverted	28·00	28·00
		x. Wmk reversed		
		y. Wmk inverted and reversed		
96	28	3d. myrtle-green and blue (6.3.22)	2·50	70
		a. Green and pale blue	1·25	15
		w. Wmk inverted		
		x. Wmk reversed		
97	29	4d. brown and deep green (5.12.21)	1·00	30
		a. Chocolate and dull green	1·00	30
		w. Wmk inverted	30·00	
		x. Wmk reversed	40·00	
98	36	6d. black and blue (5.12.22)	12·00	2·00
		a. Grey and dull blue	12·00	1·50
99	30	1s. orange and red-orange (4.11.21)	1·75	80
		a. Orange-yellow and brown-orange	1·75	65
		w. Wmk inverted		
		x. Wmk reversed	—	£130
100	31	2s. light blue and brown (5.2.22)	3·25	65
		w. Wmk inverted	30·00	30·00
101	32	3s. violet-blue and orange (23.8.21)	11·00	9·00
102	33	5s. blue and yellow-brown (8.11.23)	30·00	25·00
		a. Blue and pale dull orange	60·00	70·00
		b. Blue and yellow-orange (1927)	26·00	23·00
		c. Blue and pale bistre-brown (1929)	27·00	22·00
		w. Wmk inverted	—	£180
		x. Wmk reversed		
103	34	10s. myrtle-green (3.22)	50·00	70·00
91/103 *Set of* 13			£110	95·00
91s/103s Optd "Specimen" *Set of* 13			£250	

*The normal sideways wmk shows Crown to left of CA on No. 92 or Crown to right of CA on No. 93, *both as seen from the back of the stamp*.

The frame of No. 102*a* is the same colour as that of No. 88*a*.

The designs of all values of the pictorial series, with the exception of the 5s. and 10s. (which originated with the Governor, Sir Leslie Probyn), were selected by Mr. F. C. Cundall, F.S.A. The 1d. and 5s. were drawn by Miss Cundall, the 3d. by Mrs. Cundall, and the 10s. by De La Rue & Co. The 6d. is from a lithograph. The other designs are from photographs, the frames of all being the work of Miss Cundall and Miss Wood.

37

38

39

(Centres from photos by Miss V. F. Taylor. Frames des F. C. Cundall, F.S.A., and drawn by Miss Cundall. Recess B.W.)

1923 (1 Nov). *Child Welfare*. Wmk Mult Script CA. P 12.

104	37	½d. +½d.black and green	60	5·50
105	38	1d. +½d.black and scarlet	1·75	10·00
106	39	2½d. +½d.black and blue	11·00	18·00
104/6 *Set of* 3			12·00	30·00
104s/6s Optd "Specimen" *Set of* 3			£120	

Sold at a premium of ½d. for the Child Welfare League, these stamps were on sale annually from 1 November to 31 January, until 31 January 1927, when their sale ceased, the remainders being destroyed on 21 February 1927.

40

41

42

Die I

Die II

(Recess D.L.R.)

1929–32. Wmk Mult Script CA. P 14.

108	40	1d. scarlet (Die I) (15.3.29)	4·50	20
		a. Die II (1932)	7·00	10
109	41	1½d. chocolate (18.1.29)	3·50	15
110	42	9d. maroon (5.3.29)	4·50	1·00
108/10 *Set of* 3			11·00	1·10
108s/10s Perf "Specimen" *Set of* 3			80·00	

In Die I the shading below JAMAICA is formed of thickened parallel lines, and in Die II of diagonal cross-hatching.

43 Coco Palms at Don Christopher's Cove

44 Wag Water River, St. Andrew

45 Priestman's River, Portland

(Dies eng and recess Waterlow)

1932. Wmk Mult Script CA (sideways on 2d. and 2½d.). P 12½.

111	43	2d. black and green (4.11.32)	22·00	2·75
		a. Imperf between (vert pair)	£6500	
112	44	2½d. turquoise-blue & ultram (5.3.32)	5·50	1·50
		a. Imperf between (vert pair)	£15000	£15000
113	45	6d. grey-black and purple (4.2.32)	22·00	3·00
111/13 *Set of* 3			45·00	6·50
111s/13s Perf "Specimen" *Set of* 3			90·00	

1935 (6 May). *Silver Jubilee. As Nos. 91/4 of Antigua, but ptd by B.W.* P 11×12.

114	1d. deep blue and scarlet	50	15
	b. Short extra flagstaff	£1100	
	d. Flagstaff on right-hand turret	£100	
	e. Double flagstaff	£100	£120
115	1½d. ultramarine and grey-black	60	1·50
	a. Extra flagstaff	80·00	£110
	b. Short extra flagstaff	95·00	£120
	c. Lightning conductor	85·00	
116	6d. green and indigo	8·00	19·00
	a. Extra flagstaff	£180	£225
	b. Short extra flagstaff	£225	
	c. Lightning conductor	£170	
117	1s. slate and purple	5·50	12·00
	a. Extra flagstaff	£250	£325
	b. Short extra flagstaff	£300	
	c. Lightning conductor	£200	
114/17 *Set of* 4		13·00	29·00
114s/17s Perf "Specimen" *Set of* 4		£100	

For illustrations of plate varieties see Omnibus section following Zanzibar.

1937 (12 May). *Coronation. As Nos. 95/7 of Antigua, but printed by D.L.R.* P 14.

118	1d. scarlet	30	15
119	1½d. grey-black	65	30
120	2½d. bright blue	1·00	70
118/20 *Set of* 3		1·75	1·00
118s/20s Perf "Specimen" *Set of* 3		85·00	

46 King George VI

47 Coco Palms at Don Christopher's Cove

48 Bananas

49 Citrus Grove

50 Kingston Harbour

51 Sugar Industry

52 Bamboo Walk

53 King George VI

53a Tobacco Growing and Cigar Making

Extra branch (Centre plate (1) with frame Pl (1) to 7, R. 6/1)

Fishing rod (Centre plate (1) with frame Pl (1) to 7, R. 6/10)

Repaired chimney (Centre plate 1 R. 11/1)

(Recess D.L.R. (T **48**, 5s. and 10s.), Waterlow (others))

1938 (10 Oct)–**52**. *T* **46/53a** *and as Nos.* 88, 112/13, *but with inset portrait of King George VI, as in T* **49**. Wmk Mult Script CA. P 13½×14 (½d., 1d., 1½d.), 14 (5s., 10s.) or 12½ (others).

121	**46**	½d. blue-green (10.10.38)	1·75	10
		a. Wmk sideways	†	£4750
121*b*		½d. orange (25.10.51)	1·25	30
122		1d. scarlet	1·25	10
122*a*		1d. blue-green (25.10.51)	2·00	10
123		1½d. brown	1·25	10
124	**47**	2d. grey and green (10.12.38)	1·25	80
		a. Extra branch	30·00	15·00
		b. Fishing rod	30·00	15·00
		c. Perf 13×13½ (1939)	2·75	50
		cb. "C" of "CA" missing from wmk	£1100	
		d. Perf 12½×13 (1951)	1·25	10
125	**44**	2½d. greenish blue and ultram (10.12.38)	4·50	2·25
126	**48**	3d. ultramarine and green (10.12.38)	1·00	1·50
		a. "A" of "CA" missing from wmk	£1100	
126*b*		3d. greenish blue and ultram (15.8.49)	2·25	1·25
126*c*		3d. green and scarlet (1.7.52)	3·50	30
127	**49**	4d. brown and green (10.12.38)	50	10
128	**45**	6d. grey and purple (10.12.38)	6·50	30
		a. Perf 13½×13 (10.10.50)	2·25	10
129	**50**	9d. lake (10.12.38)	60	50
		a. "A" of "CA" missing from wmk		
130	**51**	1s. green and purple-brown (10.12.38)	7·50	20
		a. Repaired chimney	£550	£100
131	**52**	2s. blue and chocolate (10.12.38)	27·00	1·00
132	**33**	5s. slate-blue and yellow-orange (10.12.38)	14·00	3·75
		a. Perf 14, line (1941)	£4500	£190
		b. Perf 13 (24.10.49)	7·50	3·00
		ba. Blue and orange (10.10.50)	7·50	3·00
133	**53**	10s. myrtle-green (10.12.38)	11·00	9·50
		aa. Perf 13 (10.10.50)	15·00	7·00
133*a*	**53a**	£1 chocolate and violet (15.8.49)	42·00	30·00
121/33*a* *Set of* 18			£110	42·00
121s/33s Perf "Specimen" *Set of* 13			£275	

No. 130a occurred in conjunction with Frame plate 2 on printings between 1942 and 1951.

No. 132a shows the emergency use of a line perforation machine, giving an irregular gauge of 14–14.15, after the De La Rue works were damaged in December 1940. The normal comb measures 13.8×13.7.

Nos. 121 and 122 exist in coils constructed from normal sheets.

SELF-GOVERNMENT

54 Courthouse, Falmouth

55 King Charles II and King George VI

56 Institute of Jamaica

57 House of Assembly

58 "Labour and Learning"

59 Scroll, flag and King George VI

(Recess Waterlow)

1945 (20 Aug)–**46**. *New Constitution. T* **54/9**. Wmk Mult Script CA. P 12½.

134	**54**	1½d. sepia	20	30
		a. Perf 12½×13 (1946)	5·00	60
135	**55**	2d. green	11·00	90
		a. Perf 12½×13 (1945)	30	50
136	**56**	3d. ultramarine	20	50
		a. Perf 13 (1946)	2·50	2·75
137	**57**	4½d. slate	30	30
		a. Perf 13 (1946)	3·25	3·25
138	**58**	2s. red-brown	30	50
139	**59**	5s. indigo	1·75	1·00
140	**55**	10s. green	1·75	2·25
134/40 *Set of* 7			4·25	4·75
134s/40s Perf "Specimen" *Set of* 7			£150	

1946 (14 Oct). *Victory. As Nos.* 110/11 *of Antigua.* P 13½×14.

141		1½d. purple-brown	2·50	10
		a. Perf 13½	30	3·50
142		3d. blue	3·75	2·50
		a. Perf 13½	30	5·50
141s/2s Perf "Specimen" *Set of* 2			75·00	

1948 (1 Dec). *Royal Silver Wedding. As Nos.* 112/13 *of Antigua.*

143		1½d. red-brown (P 14×15)	30	10
144		£1 scarlet (P 11½×11)	27·00	65·00

1949 (10 Oct). *75th Anniv of Universal Postal Union. As Nos.* 114/17 *of Antigua.*

145		1½d. red-brown (P 13½–14)	20	15
146		2d. deep blue-green (P 11×11½)	1·25	4·25
147		3d. deep blue (P 11×11½)	50	1·50
148		6d. purple (P 13½–14)	50	2·50
145/8 *Set of* 4			2·25	7·50

(Recess Waterlow)

1951 (16 Feb). *Inauguration of B.W.I. University College. As Nos.* 118/19 *of Antigua.* P 14×14½.

149		2d. black and red-brown	30	50
150		6d. grey-black and purple	35	30

60 Scout Badge and Map of Caribbean

61 Scout Badge and Map of Jamaica

(Litho B.W.)

1952 (5 Mar). *First Caribbean Scout Jamboree.* Wmk Mult Script CA. P 13½×13 (2d.) or 13×13½ (6d.).

151	**60**	2d. blue, apple-green and black	30	10
152	**61**	6d. yellow-green, carmine-red and black	70	60

1953 (2 June). *Coronation. As No.* 120 *of Antigua.*

153		2d. black and deep yellow-green	1·50	10

62 Coco Palms at Don Christopher's Cove

(Recess Waterlow)

1953 (25 Nov). *Royal Visit.* Wmk Mult Script CA. P 12½×13.

154	**62**	2d. grey-black and green	55	10

63 HMS *Britannia* (ship of the line) at Port Royal

64 Old Montego Bay

65 Old Kingston

66 Proclamation of Abolition of Slavery, 1838

(Recess D.L.R.)

1955 (10 May). *Tercentenary Issue. T* **63/6**. Wmk Mult Script CA. P 12½.

155	**63**	2d. black and olive-green	85	10
156	**64**	2½d. black and deep bright blue	15	35
157	**65**	3d. black and claret	15	30
158	**66**	6d. black and carmine-red	30	20
155/8 *Set of* 4			1·25	80

67 Coconut Palms

68 Sugar Cane

69 Pineapples

70 Bananas

71 Mahoe

72 Breadfruit

73 Ackee

74 Streamertail

75 Blue Mountain Peak

76 Royal Botanic Gardens, Hope

77 Rafting on the Rio Grande

78 Fort Charles

79 Arms of Jamaica

80 Arms of Jamaica

(Recess B.W. (T **77/8**), D.L.R. (others))

1956 (1 May)–**58**. *T* **67/80**. Wmk Mult Script CA. P 13 (½d. to 6d.), 13½ (8d. to 2s.) or 11½ (3s. to £1).

159	**67**	½d. black and deep orange-red	10	10
160	**68**	1d. black and emerald	10	10
161	**69**	2d. black and carmine-red (2.8.56)	10	10
162	**70**	2½d. black and deep bright blue (2.8.56)	75	50
163	**71**	3d. emerald and red-brown (17.12.56)	20	10

164	72	4d. bronze-green and blue (17.12.56)	20	10
		w. Wmk inverted	£120	80·00
165	73	5d. scarlet and bronze-green (17.12.56)	20	2·25
166	74	6d. black and deep rose-red (3.9.56)	2·25	10
167	75	8d. ultramarine and red-orange (15.11.56)	50	10
168	76	1s. yellow-green and blue (15.11.56)	1·00	10
169	77	1s.6d. ultram and reddish purple (15.11.56)	80	10
170	78	2s. blue and bronze-green (15.11.56)	9·00	2·50
		a. *Grey-blue and bronze-green* (24.4.58)	13·00	2·50
171	79	3s. black and blue (2.8.56)	1·75	2·50
172		5s. black and carmine-red (15.8.56)	4·00	5·50
173	80	10s. black and blue-green (15.8.56)	30·00	19·00
174		£1 black and purple (15.8.56)	30·00	19·00
159/74 *Set of* 16			70·00	45·00

An earlier £1 value, in the design of No. 133*a* but showing the portrait of Queen Elizabeth II, was prepared, but not issued.

1958 (22 Apr). *Inauguration of British Caribbean Federation. As Nos. 135/7 of Antigua.*

175	2d. deep green	60	10
176	5d. blue	1·10	3·50
177	6d. scarlet	1·10	40
175/7 *Set of* 3		2·50	3·50

81 Bristol 175 Britannia 312 flying over *City of Berlin*, 1860

83 1s. Stamps of 1860 and 1956

82 Postal mule-cart and motor-van

(Recess Waterlow)

1960 (4 Jan). *Stamp Centenary. T* **81/83** *and similar design.* W w **12**. P 13×13½ (1s.) or 13½×14 (others).

178	81	2d. blue and reddish purple	45	10
179	82	6d. carmine and olive-green	45	50
180	83	1s. red-brown, yellow-green and blue	45	55
178/80 *Set of* 3			1·25	1·00

INDEPENDENT

1962
INDEPENDENCE
(84)

INDEPENDENCE
1962
(85)

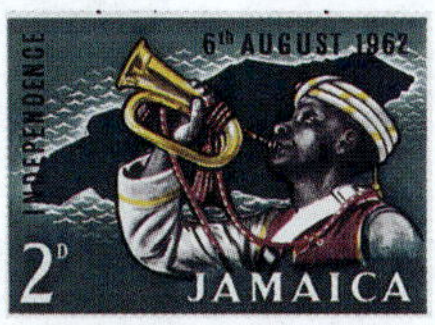

86 Military Bugler and Map

(Des V. Whiteley. Photo D.L.R. (2, 4d., 1s.6d., 5s.))

1962 (8 Aug)–**63**. *Independence.*

(a) *Nos. 159/60, 162, 171, 173/4 optd as T* **84** *and Nos. 163, 165/8, 170 optd with T* **85**.

181	67	½d. black and deep orange-red	10	1·00
182	68	1d. black and emerald	10	10
183	70	2½d. black and deep bright blue	10	1·00
184	71	3d. emerald and red-brown	10	10
185	73	5d. scarlet and bronze-green	20	60
186	74	6d. black and deep rose-red	2·50	10
187	75	8d. ultram and red-orge (opt at upper left)	20	10
		a. Opt at lower left (17.9.63?)	50	15
188	76	1s. yellow-green and blue	20	10
189	78	2s. blue and bronze-green	80	1·50
		a. *Dp blue and dp bronze-green* (20.8.63)	8·50	4·00
190	79	3s. black and blue	90	1·50
191	80	10s. black and blue-green	2·75	4·25
192		£1 black and purple	2·75	5·50

(b) *Horiz designs as T* **86**. W w **12**. P 13.

193	2d. multicoloured	1·50	10
194	4d. multicoloured	1·00	10
195	1s.6d. black and red	4·50	85
196	5s. multicoloured	5·50	4·00
181/96 *Set of* 16		21·00	19·00

Designs:—2, 4d. Type **86**; 1s.6d. Gordon House and banner; 5s. Map, factories and fruit.

For these overprints on stamps watermarked w **12** see Nos. 205/13.

89 Kingston Seal, Weightlifting, Boxing, Football and Cycling

93 Farmer and Crops

(Photo Harrison)

1962 (11 Aug). *Ninth Central American and Caribbean Games, Kingston. T* **89** *and similar horiz designs.* W w **12**. P 14½×14.

197	1d. sepia and carmine-red	20	10
198	6d. sepia and greenish blue	20	10
199	8d. sepia and bistre	20	10
200	2s. multicoloured	30	90
197/200 *Set of* 4		80	1·00

Designs:—6d. Kingston seal, diving, sailing, swimming and water polo; 8d. Kingston seal, pole-vaulting, javelin throwing, discus throwing, relay-racing and hurdling; 2s. Kingston coat of arms and athlete.

An imperf miniature sheet exists, but this was never available at face value or at any post office.

(Des M. Goaman. Litho D.L.R.)

1963 (4 June). *Freedom from Hunger.* P 12½.

201	93	1d. multicoloured	25	10
202		8d. multicoloured	1·00	60

1963 (4 Sept). *Red Cross Centenary. As Nos. 147/8 of Antigua.*

203	2d. red and black	15	10
204	1s.6d. red and blue	50	1·50

1963–64. *As Nos. 181/90, but wmk* w **12**.

205	67	½d. black and deep orange-red (3.12.63*)	10	15
206	68	1d. black and emerald (3.4.64)	10	1·60
207	70	2½d. black and deep bright blue (3.4.64)	25	2·75
208	71	3d. emerald and red-brown (17.12.63*)	15	15
209	73	5d. scarlet and bronze-green (3.4.64)	40	2·75
210	75	8d. ultramarine and red-orange (3.4.64)	20	75
211	76	1s. yellow-green and blue (21.12.63*)	35	75
212	78	2s. dp blue & dp bronze-green (3.4.64)	60	6·50
213	79	3s. black and blue (5.2.64)	2·00	5·00
205/13 *Set of* 9			3·50	18·00

The overprint on the 8d., 1s. and 2s. is at lower left, the others are as before.

*These are the earliest known dates recorded in Jamaica.

95 Carole Joan Crawford ("Miss World 1963")

(Des and photo D.L.R.)

1964 (14 Feb–25 May). *"Miss World 1963" Commemoration.* P 13.

214	95	3d. multicoloured	10	10
215		1s. multicoloured	15	10
216		1s.6d. multicoloured	20	50
214/16 *Set of* 3			40	60
MS216*a* 153×101 mm. Nos. 214/16. Imperf (25.5.64)			1·10	2·75

96 *Lignum Vitae*

97 Blue Mahoe

103 Gypsum Industry

109 Arms of Jamaica

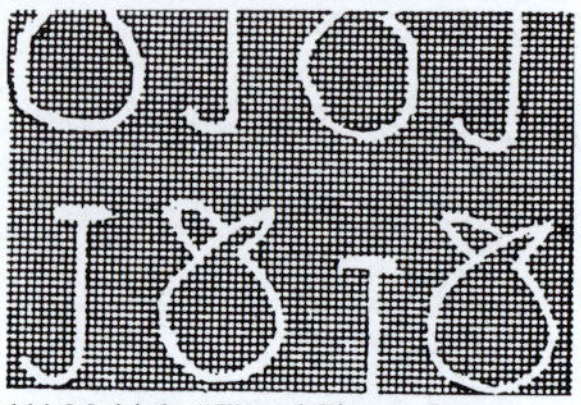

111 Multiple "J" and Pineapple

(Des V. Whiteley. Photo Harrison)

1964 (4 May)–**68**. *T* **96/7**, **103**, **109** *and similar designs.* W **111**. P 14½ (1d., 2d., 2½d., 6d., 8d.), 14×14½ (1½d., 3d., 4d., 10s.), 14½×14 (9d., 1s., 3s., 5s., £1) or 13½×14½ (1s.6d., 2s.).

217	1d. violet-blue, deep green and light brown (*shades*)	10	10
218	1½d. multicoloured	15	10
219	2d. red, yellow and grey-green	15	10
	w. Wmk inverted	7·00	
220	2½d. multicoloured	1·00	60
221	3d. yellow, black and emerald	15	10
222	4d. ochre and violet	50	10
223	6d. multicoloured	2·25	10
	a. Blue omitted	75·00	
	b. Value omitted	£1200	
	w. Wmk inverted	12·00	
224	8d. mult (yellowish green background)	2·50	1·50
	a. Red (beak) omitted	£150	
	b. *Greyish green background* (16.7.68)	7·50	4·25
225	9d. blue and yellow-bistre	1·50	10
226	1s. black and light brown	20	10
	a. Light brown omitted	£1800	
	ab. Value only omitted	£1000	
	b. Black omitted	£1500	
	ba. "NATIONAL STADIUM" etc omitted	£800	
227	1s.6d. black, light blue and buff	4·00	15
228	2s. red-brown, black and light blue	2·75	15
229	3s. blue and dull green	1·00	80
	aw. Wmk inverted	11·00	
	b. Perf 13½×14½	35	65
230	5s. black, ochre and blue	1·25	1·00
	w. Wmk inverted	85·00	
231	10s. multicoloured	1·25	1·25
	a. Blue ("JAMAICA", etc) omitted	£325	
232	£1 multicoloured	1·75	1·00
217/32 *Set of* 16		17·00	6·00

Designs: *Horiz.* (*As T* **96**)—1½d. Ackee; 2½d. Land shells; 3d. National flag over Jamaica; 4d. Antillean Murex (*Murex formosus*) (shell); 6d. *Papilio homerus* (butterfly); 8d. Streamertail. *As T* **103**—1s. National Stadium; 1s.6d. Palisadoes International Airport; 2s. Bauxite mining; 3s. Blue Marlin (sport fishing); 5s. Exploration of sunken city, Port Royal; £1 Queen Elizabeth II and national flag.

No. 223b. Two left half sheets are known with the black printing shifted downwards to such an extent that the value is omitted from the top row.

Nos. 226a/ab came from a sheet on which the two bottom rows had the colour omitted with the next row showing it missing from the lower third of the stamps.

No. 220b comes from the bottom row of one sheet and rows seven and eight of a second sheet; the latter also being the source of No. 220ba.

112 Scout Belt

113 Globe, Scout Hat and Scarf

114 Scout Badge and Alligator

(Photo Harrison)

1964 (27 Aug). *Sixth Inter-American Scout Conference, Kingston.* W **111**. P 14 (1s.) or 14½×14 (others).

233	112	3d. red, black and pink	10	10
234	113	8d. bright blue, olive and black	15	25
		w. Wmk inverted	27·00	
235	114	1s. gold, deep blue and light blue	20	45
		w. Wmk inverted	20	45
233/5 *Set of* 3			40	70

115 Gordon House, Kingston

118 Eleanor Roosevelt

(Des V. Whiteley. Photo Harrison)

1964 (16 Nov). *Tenth Commonwealth Parliamentary Conference, Kingston. T* **115** *and similar horiz designs.* W **111**. P 14½×14.

236	3d. black and yellow-green	10	10
237	6d. black and carmine-red	30	10

238 1s.6d. black and bright blue 50 30
236/8 *Set of* 3 .... 80 40
Designs:—6d. Headquarters House, Kingston; 1s.6d. House of Assembly, Spanish Town.

(Des V. Whiteley. Photo Harrison)

1964 (10 Dec). *16th Anniv of Declaration of Human Rights.* W **111**. P 14½×14.
239 **118** 1s. black, red and light green 10 10

119 Guides' Emblem on Map

120 Guide Emblems

(Photo Harrison)

1965 (17 May). *Golden Jubilee of Jamaica Girl Guides Association.* W **111** (sideways on 3d.). P 14×14½ (3d.) or 14 (1s.).
240 **119** 3d. yellow, green and light blue 10 10
241 **120** 1s. yellow, black and apple-green 20 40
w. Wmk inverted 20 40

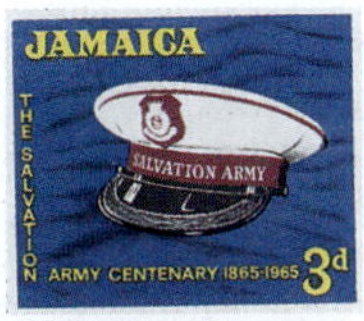

121 Uniform Cap

122 Flag-bearer and Drummer

(Photo Harrison)

1965 (23 Aug). *Salvation Army Centenary.* W **111**. P 14×14½ (3d.) or 14½×14 (1s.6d.).
242 **121** 3d. multicoloured 25 10
w. Wmk inverted .... 12·00
243 **122** 1s.6d. multicoloured 50 50
w. Wmk inverted .... 26·00

123 Paul Bogle, William Gordon and Morant Bay Court House

124 Abeng-blower, "Telstar", Morse Key and I.T.U. Emblem

(Photo Enschedé)

1965 (29 Dec). *Centenary of Morant Bay Rebellion.* No wmk. P 14×13.
244 **123** 3d. light brown, ultramarine and black 10 10
245 1s.6d. light brown, yellow-green and black 20 10
246 3s. light brown, rose and black 30 75
244/6 *Set of* 3 .... 55 85

(Photo Harrison)

1965 (29 Dec). *I.T.U. Centenary.* W **111**. P 14×14½.
247 **124** 1s. black, grey-blue and red 40 20

ROYAL VISIT
MARCH 1966
(**125**)

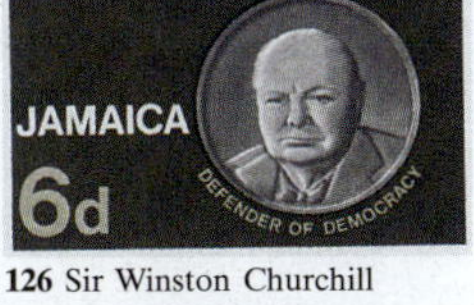

126 Sir Winston Churchill

1966 (3 Mar). *Royal Visit. Nos. 221, 223, 226/7 optd with T* **125**.
248 3d. yellow, black and emerald 15 10
249 6d. multicoloured .... 1·75 30
250 1s. black and light brown 55 10
251 1s.6d. black, light blue and buff .... 2·00 2·00
248/51 *Set of* 4 .... 4·00 2·25

(Des Jennifer Toombs. Photo Harrison)

1966 (18 April). *Churchill Commemoration.* W **111**. P 14.
252 **126** 6d. black and olive-green 65 30
253 1s. bistre-brown and deep violet-blue 85 80

127 Statue of Athlete and Flags

131 Bolivar's Statue and Flags of Jamaica and Venezuela

(Des V. Whiteley. Photo Harrison)

1966 (4 Aug). *Eighth British Empire and Commonwealth Games. T* **127** *and similar horiz designs.* W **111**. P 14½×14.
254 3d. multicoloured 10 10
255 6d. multicoloured 40 10
w. Wmk inverted .... 24·00
256 1s. multicoloured 10 10
257 3s. bright gold and deep blue 35 45
w. Wmk inverted .... 24·00
254/7 *Set of* 4 .... 80 55
MS258 128×103 mm. Nos. 254/7. Imperf .... 4·00 8·00
Designs:—6d. Racing cyclists; 1s. National Stadium, Kingston; 3s. Games emblem.
No. **MS**258 has been seen with the whole printing inverted except for the brown background.

(Des and photo Harrison)

1966 (5 Dec). *150th Anniv of "Jamaica Letter".* W **111**. P 14×15.
259 **131** 8d. multicoloured 20 10
w. Wmk inverted .... 24·00

132 Jamaican Pavilion

133 Sir Donald Sangster (Prime Minister)

(Des V. Whiteley. Photo Harrison)

1967 (28 Apr). *World Fair, Montreal.* W **111**. P 14½.
260 **132** 6d. multicoloured 10 15
261 1s. multicoloured 10 15
w. Wmk inverted .... 7·50

(Des and photo Enschedé)

1967 (28 Aug). *Sangster Memorial Issue.* P 13½.
262 **133** 3d. multicoloured 10 10
263 1s.6d. multicoloured 20 20

134 Traffic Duty

135 Personnel of the Force

(Des V. Whiteley. Photo Enschedé)

1967 (28 Nov). *Centenary of the Constabulary Force. T* **134/5** *and similar horiz design. Multicoloured.* W **111**. P 13½×14.
264 3d. Type **134** 40 10
a. Wmk sideways .... 1·00 2·25
265 1s. Type **135** 40 10
266 1s.6d. Badge and Constables of 1867 and 1967 (*as T* **134**) 50 75
264/6 *Set of* 3 .... 1·10 85

136 Wicket-keeping

137 Sir Alexander and Lady Bustamante

(Des V. Whiteley. Photo Harrison)

1968 (8 Feb). *M.C.C.'s West Indian Tour. T* **136** *and similar vert designs. Multicoloured.* W **111** (sideways*). P 14.
267 6d. Type **136** 50 65
a. Horiz strip of 3. Nos. 267/9 .... 1·50 1·75
w. Wmk top of J to right 50 65
268 6d. Batting 50 65
w. Wmk top of J to right 50 65
269 6d. Bowling 50 65
w. Wmk top of J to right 50 65
267/9 *Set of* 3 .... 1·50 1·75
*The normal sideways watermark shows the top of the "J" to left, *as seen from the back of the stamp*.
Nos. 267/9 were issued in small sheets of 9 comprising three *se-tenant* strips as No. 267a.
Nos. 267/9 exist on PVA gum as well as on gum arabic.

(Des and photo Harrison)

1968 (23 May). *Labour Day.* W **111**. P 14.
270 **137** 3d. rose and black 10 15
271 1s. olive and black 10 15

138 Human Rights Emblem over Map of Jamaica

(Photo Harrison)

1968 (3 Dec). *Human Rights Year. T* **138** *and similar multicoloured designs.* W **111**. P 14.
272 3d. Type **138** 10 10
a. Gold (flame) omitted £120
w. Wmk inverted .... 4·75
273 1s. Hands cupping Human Rights emblem (*vert*) 10 10
274 3s. Jamaican holding "Human Rights" 30 90
a. Gold (flame) omitted £150
272/4 *Set of* 3 .... 45 1·00
Three designs, showing 3d. Bowls of Grain, 1s. Abacus, 3s. Hands in Prayer, were prepared but not issued (*Price for set of 3 mint* £140).

141 ILO Emblem

142 Nurse, and Children being weighed and measured

(Des V. Whiteley. Litho Format)

1969 (23 May). *50th Anniv of International Labour Organization.* P 14.
275 **141** 6d. orange-yellow and blackish brown 10 10
276 3s. bright emerald and blackish brown 30 30

(Des and photo Harrison)

1969 (30 May). *20th Anniv of W.H.O. T* **142** *and similar designs.* W **111**. P 14.
277 6d. grey, brown and orange 10 15
278 1s. black, sepia and blue-green 10 15
279 3s. grey-black, brown and pale bright blue .... 20 1·25
277/9 *Set of* 3 .... 30 1·40
Designs: *Horiz*—1s. Malaria eradication. *Vert*—3s. Trainee nurse.

(New Currency. 100 cents = 1 Jamaica dollar)

C-DAY
8th September
1969
1c
(**145**)

146 "The Adoration of the Kings" (detail, Foppa)

1969 (8 Sept). *Decimal currency. Nos. 217, 219, 221/3 and 225/32 surch as T* **145**. *Sterling values unobliterated except 1c. to 4c. and 8c.*
280 1c. on 1d. violet-blue, deep green & light brown 10 10
281 2c. on 2d. red, yellow and grey-green 10 10
w. Wmk inverted .... 2·25
282 3c. on 3d. yellow, black and emerald 10 10
283 4c. on 4d. ochre and violet .... 1·25 10
a. "8t" of "8th" omitted (R. 10/1) .... 50·00
284 5c. on 6d. multicoloured .... 1·25 10
a. Blue omitted .... 90·00
285 8c. on 9d. blue and yellow-bistre 10 10
286 10c. on 1s. black and light brown 10 10
287 15c. on 1s.6d. black, light blue and buff 50 90
288 20c. on 2s. red-brown, black and light blue .... 1·50 1·50
a. "8th" omitted ....
289 30c. on 3s. blue and dull green .... 2·00 2·75
290 50c. on 5s. black, ochre and blue .... 1·25 3·00
291 $1 on 10s. multicoloured .... 1·25 6·50
w. Wmk inverted £120
292 $2 on £1 multicoloured .... 1·25 6·50
280/92 *Set of* 13 .... 9·00 19·00

No. 281 exists with PVA gum as well as gum arabic.

Unlike the positional No. 283a the similar variety on the 20c. on 2s. was caused by a paper fold.

(Des J. Cooter. Litho D.L.R.)

1969 (25 Oct). *Christmas. Paintings. T* **146** *and similar vert designs. Multicoloured.* W **111**. P 13.

293	2c. Type **146**	20	40
294	5c. "Madonna, Child and St. John" (Raphael)	25	40
295	8c. "The Adoration of the Kings" (detail, Dosso Dossi)	25	40
293/5 *Set of* 3		65	1·10

149 Half Penny, 1869

151 George William Gordon

(Des G. Drummond. Litho P.B.)

1969 (27 Oct). *Centenary of First Jamaican Coins. T* **149** *and similar horiz design.* W **111**. P 12½.

296	3c. silver, black and mauve	15	25
	b. Wmk sideways	60	80
297	15c. silver, black and light emerald	10	10

Design:—15c. One penny, 1869.

(Des G. Vasarhelyi. Litho Enschedé)

1970 (11 Mar). *National Heroes. T* **151** *and similar vert designs. Multicoloured.* P 12×12½.

298	1c. Type **151**	10	10
	a. Yellow (from flags) omitted	£250	
299	3c. Sir Alexander Bustamante	10	10
300	5c. Norman Manley	10	10
301	10c. Marcus Garvey	15	10
302	15c. Paul Bogle	30	25
298/302 *Set of* 5		50	40

156 "Christ appearing to St. Peter" (Carracci)

2c ■

(159)

(Des G. Drummond. Photo Enschedé)

1970 (23 Mar). *Easter. T* **156** *and similar vert designs. Multicoloured.* W **111**. P 12×12½.

303	3c. Type **156**	10	10
	w. Wmk inverted		
304	10c. "Christ Crucified" (Antonello da Messina)	10	10
	w. Wmk inverted		
305	20c. Easter Lily	20	60
303/5 *Set of* 3		30	70

1970 (16 July). *No. 219 surch with T* **159**.

306	2c. on 2d. red, yellow and grey-green	20	20

160 *Lignum Vitae*

161 Cable Ship *Dacia*

1970 (7 Sept–2 Nov). *Decimal Currency. Designs as Nos. 217/32 but inscr as T* **160** *in new currency.* W **111** (sideways on 2, 4, 15, 20c. and $1). P 14½ (1, 5c.), 14×14½ (4c., $1), 13½×14½ (15, 20c.) or 14½×14 (others).

307	1c. violet-blue, deep green & light brown	75	2·00
308	2c. red, yellow and grey-green (as 2d.)	30	10
309	3c. yellow, black and emerald (as 3d.)	50	1·00
310	4c. ochre and violet (as 4d.)	2·75	30
311	5c. multicoloured (as 6d.)	3·00	65
312	8c. blue and yellow-bistre (as 9d.)	2·25	10
	a. Wmk sideways	2·00	45
313	10c. black and light brown (as 1s.)	60	20
314	15c. black, light blue and buff (as 1s.6d.) (2.11)	2·75	3·00
315	20c. red-brown, black and lt blue (as 2s.) (2.11)	1·25	3·00
316	30c. blue and dull green (as 3s.) (2.11)	4·00	6·50
317	50c. black, ochre and blue (as 5s.) (2.11)	1·25	3·75
318	$1 multicoloured (as 10s.) (2.11)	1·00	5·50
319	$2 multicoloured (as £1) (2.11)	1·25	4·00
307/19 *Set of* 13		18·00	26·00

(Des G. Drummond. Litho J.W.)

1970 (12 Oct). *Centenary of Telegraph Service. T* **161** *and similar horiz designs.* W **111** (sideways). P 14½×14.

320	3c. yellow, red and black	15	10
321	10c. black and turquoise	20	10
322	50c. multicoloured	50	1·00
320/2 *Set of* 3		75	1·10

Designs:—10c. Bright's cable gear aboard *Dacia*; 50c. Morse key and chart.

164 Bananas, Citrus, Sugar-Cane and Tobacco

165 Locomotive *Projector* (1845)

(Des G. Drummond. Litho Questa)

1970 (2 Nov). *75th Anniv of Jamaican Agricultural Society.* W **111**. P 14.

323	**164**	2c. multicoloured	25	60
		w. Wmk inverted	7·50	
324		10c. multicoloured	45	10

(Des V. Whiteley. Litho Format)

1970 (21 Nov). *125th Anniv of Jamaican Railways. T* **165** *and similar horiz designs. Multicoloured.* W **111** (sideways). P 13½.

325	3c. Type **165**	30	10
326	15c. Steam locomotive No. 54 (1944)	65	30
327	50c. Diesel locomotive No. 102 (1967)	1·25	1·75
325/7 *Set of* 3		2·00	2·00

STAMP BOOKLETS

1912. *Black on red covers. Stapled.*

SB1	2s. booklet containing twenty-four 1d. (No. 40) in blocks of 6 (9 Mar)	
SB2	2s. booklet containing twelve ½d. and eighteen 1d. (Nos. 38, 58), each in blocks of 6 (5 Dec)	£1400

1923 (Dec). *Black on red cover. Stapled.*

SB3	2s. booklet containing twelve ½d. (No. 91) in blocks of 4 and eighteen 1d. (No. 92) in blocks of 6	£850

1928. *Black on red cover. Stapled.*

SB4	2s. booklet containing twelve ½d. and eighteen 1d. (Nos. 89*a*, 92) in blocks of 6	£1600

1928 (5 Sept). *Black on red cover. Stapled.*

SB5	1s.6d. booklet containing twelve ½d. and 1d. (Nos. 89*a*, 92), each in blocks of 6	

1929 (July)–**32**. *Black on red cover. Stapled.*

SB6	2s. booklet containing six ½d., twelve 1d. and six 1½d. (Nos. 89*a*, 108/9) in blocks of 6	£1200
	a. With 1d. Die II (No. 108a) (1932)	

1930–33. *Black on red cover. Stapled.*

SB7	2s. booklet containing twelve ½d. and eighteen 1d. (Nos. 89*a*, 108), each in blocks of 6	
	a. With 1d. Die II (No. 108a) (1933)	£900
	b. Black on blue cover (1933)	£1600

1935. *Silver Jubilee. Black on pink cover. Stapled.*

SB8	2s. booklet containing twenty-four 1d. (No. 114) in blocks of 6	£1400
	a. In blocks of 4	£2000

1938–40. *Black on green cover inscr "*JAMAICA POSTAGE STAMPS*" in one line. Inland Postage Rates on interleaf. Stapled.*

SB9	2s. booklet containing twelve ½d. and eighteen 1d. (Nos. 121/2), each in blocks of 6 (inland letter rate 1d. per oz)	£450
	a. Inland letter rate 1½d. for first 2 oz (1940)	£500

1942–47. *Black on blue cover inscr "*JAMAICA POSTAGE STAMPS*" in three lines. Inland Postage Rates on inside front cover. Stapled.*

SB10	2s. booklet containing twelve ½d. and eighteen 1d. (Nos. 121/2), each in blocks of 6 (Inland letter rate 1½d. for first 2 oz).	£225
	a. Black on yellow cover (1947)	£110

1946. *New Constitution. Black on blue cover. Stapled.*

SB12	2s. booklet containing sixteen 1½d. (No. 134a) in blocks of 4	£225

1952. *Black on yellow cover. Stapled.*

SB13	2s. booklet containing twelve ½d and eighteen 1d. (Nos. 121*b*, 122*a*), each in blocks of 6	25·00

1956. *Black on green cover. Stitched.*

SB14	3s. booklet containing ½d., 1d., 2d. and 2½d. (Nos. 159/62) in blocks of 6	11·00

1965 (15 Nov). *Black on green cover. Stitched.*

SB15	3s. booklet containing 1d., 2d. and 3d. (Nos. 217, 219, 221) in blocks of 6	5·00

POSTAL FISCALS

Revenue stamps were authorised for postal use by Post Office notice of 12 October 1887.

F 1

(Typo D.L.R.)

1865–73. P 14.

(a) Wmk Pineapple (T **7**).

F1	**F 1**	1d. rose (1865)	75·00	95·00
		a. Imperf (pair)	£500	

(b) Wmk Crown CC.

F2	**F 1**	1d. rose (1871)	55·00	55·00

(c) Wmk CA over Crown (Type w **7** *sideways, covering two stamps).*

F3	**F 1**	1d. rose (1873)	26·00	7·00
		a. Imperf		

F 2

F 3

(Typo D.L.R.)

1855–74. *(Issued). Glazed paper.* P 14.

(a) No wmk.

F4	**F 2**	1½d. blue/*blue* (1857)	55·00	48·00
		a. Imperf (1855)		
		b. Blue on white	60·00	60·00
F5		3d. purple/*blue* (1857)	55·00	55·00
		a. Imperf (1855)		
		b. Purple on lilac (1857)	55·00	55·00
		ba. Imperf (1855)		
		c. Purple on white (1857)	65·00	55·00

(b) Wmk Crown CC.

F6	**F 2**	3d. purple/*lilac* (1874)	20·00	21·00

All the above stamps *imperf* are exceedingly rare postally used.

1858 (1 Jan). *(Issued).* No wmk. P 15½×15.

F7	**F 3**	1s. rose/*bluish*	80·00	85·00
F8		5s. lilac/*bluish*	£375	£425
F9		10s. green/*bluish*	£450	£500

Telegraph stamps were also used postally, but no authority was given for such use.

OFFICIAL STAMPS

OFFICIAL (O 1)

OFFICIAL (O 2)

1890 (1 Apr)–**91**. *No. 16a optd with Type* O **1** *by C. Vendryes, Kingston.*

(a) "OFFICIAL" 17 to 17½ mm long.

O1	**8**	½d. green	13·00	2·25
		a. "O" omitted	£600	
		b. One "I" omitted		
		c. Both "I"s omitted	£650	£650
		d. "L" omitted	£700	£700
		e. Opt inverted	80·00	85·00
		f. Opt double	80·00	85·00
		g. Opt double, one inverted	£400	£400
		h. Opt double, one vertical	£650	
		j. Pair, overprints *tête-bêche*		

(b) "OFFICIAL" 15 to 16 mm long.

O2	**8**	½d. green (3.91)	30·00	27·00
		a. Opt double	£600	

There were five settings of the locally-overprinted Officials. No. O1 occurred from settings I (2×10), II (3×6), IV and V (horizontal row of 6 each). No. O2 came from setting III (2×6). There are numerous minor varieties, due to broken type, etc. (*e.g.* a broken "E" used for "F").

Stamps with the 17–17½ mm opt were reissued in 1894 during a temporary shortage of No. O3.

1890 (1 Apr)–**91**. *Optd with Type* O **2** *by* D.L.R. Wmk Crown CA. P 14.

O3	**8**	½d. green (1891)	10·00	1·75
O4	**11**	1d. rose	7·00	1·25
O5		2d. grey	15·00	1·25
O3/5 *Set of* 3			29·00	3·75
O3s/5s Optd "Specimen" *Set of* 3			£110	

Nos. O4/5 were not issued without overprint.

The use of Official stamps ceased from 1 January 1898.

Kenya

INDEPENDENT

(Currency. 100 cents = 1 East Africa, later Kenya Shilling)

1 Cattle Ranching

2 Wood-carving

3 National Assembly

(Des V. Whiteley. Photo Harrison)

1963 (12 Dec). *Independence. T* **1/3** *and similar designs.* P 14×15 (small designs) or 14½ (others).

1	5c. brown, deep blue, green and bistre	10	55
2	10c. brown	10	10
3	15c. magenta	1·00	10
4	20c. black and yellow-green	15	10
5	30c. black and yellow	15	10
6	40c. brown and light blue	15	30
	a. Printed on the gummed side	85·00	
7	50c. crimson, black and green	15	10
8	65c. deep turquise-green and yellow	55	65
9	1s. multicoloured	20	10
10	1s.30 brown, black and yellow-green	5·00	30
11	2s. multicoloured	1·25	40
12	5s. brown, ultramarine and yellow-green	1·25	50
13	10s. brown and deep blue	8·50	3·00
14	20s. black and rose	4·00	8·50
1/14	*Set of* 14	20·00	13·00

Designs: As *T* **1/2**—15c. Heavy industry; 20c. Timber industry; 30c. Jomo Kenyatta and Mt Kenya; 40c. Fishing industry; 50c. Kenya flag 65c. Pyrethrum industry. *As T* **3**—1s.30, Tourism (Treetops Hotel); 2s. Coffee industry; 5s. Tea industry; 10s. Mombasa Port; 20s. Royal College, Nairobi.

The 10c. was produced in coils of 1000 in addition to normal sheets.

4 Cockerel

(Des M. Goaman. Photo J. Enschedé)

1964 (12 Dec). *Inauguration of Republic. T* **4** *and similar vert designs. Multicoloured.* P 13×12½.

15	15c. Type **4**	15	15
16	30c. President Kenyatta	15	10
17	50c. Lion	15	10
18	1s.30 Hartlaub's Turaco	2·00	50
19	2s.50 Nandi flame	20	3·75
15/19	*Set of* 5	2·40	4·00

5 Thomson's Gazelle

6 Sable Antelope

7 Greater Kudu

(Des Rena Fennessy. Photo Harrison)

1966 (12 Dec)–**71**. *Various designs as T* **5/7**. *Chalk-surfaced paper.* P 14×14½ (5c. to 70c.) or 14½ (others).

20	5c. orange, black and sepia	20	20
21	10c. black and apple-green	10	10
	a. Glazed, ordinary paper (13.7.71)	1·00	4·00
22	15c. black and orange	10	10
	a. Glazed, ordinary paper (13.7.71)	1·00	1·00
23	20c. ochre, black and blue	10	15
	a. Glazed, ordinary paper (22.1.71)	1·00	1·50
24	30c. Prussian blue, blue and black	20	10
25	40c. black and yellow-brown	60	30
	a. Glazed, ordinary paper (19.2.71)	1·25	2·00
26	50c. black and red-orange	60	10
	a. Glazed, ordinary paper (19.2.71)	14·00	4·75
27	65c. black and light green	1·25	2·00
28	70c. black and claret (15.9.69)	5·00	1·50
	a. Glazed, ordinary paper (19.2.71)	21·00	13·00
29	1s. olive-brown, black and slate-blue	30	10
	a. Glazed, ordinary paper (22.1.71)	1·25	85
30	1s.30 indigo, light olive-green and black	4·00	20
31	1s.50 black, orange-brown and dull sage green (15.9.69)	3·00	2·25
	a. Glazed, ordinary paper (22.1.71)	3·50	6·00
32	2s.50 yellow, black and olive-brown	3·25	1·25
	a. Glazed, ordinary paper (22.1.71)	2·50	6·50
33	5s. yellow, black and emerald	75	70
	a. Glazed, ordinary paper (22.1.71)	2·50	12·00
34	10s. yellow-ochre, black and red-brown	1·75	3·00
35	20s. yellow-ochre, yellow-orange, black and gold	5·50	13·00
20/35	*Set of* 16	23·00	22·00
21a/33a	*Set of* 10	42·00	45·00

Designs: *As T* **5/6**—15c. Aardvark ("Ant Bear"); 20c. Lesser Bushbaby; 30c. Warthog; 40c. Common Zebra; 50c. African Buffalo; 65c. Black Rhinoceros; 70c. Ostrich. *As T* **7**—1s.30, African Elephant; 1s.50, Bat-eared Fox; 2s.50, Cheetah; 5s. Savanna Monkey ("Vervet Monkey"); 10s. Giant Ground Pangolin; 20s. Lion.

On chalk-surfaced paper, all values except 30c., 50c. and 2s.50 exist with PVA gum as well as gum arabic but the 70c. and 1s.50 exist with PVA gum only. The stamps on glazed, ordinary paper exist with PVA gum only.

Nos. 21 and 26 exist in coils constructed from normal sheets.

STAMP BOOKLETS

1964. *Black on blue cover. Stitched.*

SB1	5s. booklet containing 10c., 15c., 20c., 30c. and 50c. (Nos. 2/5, 7) in blocks of 4	16·00

1966 (12 Dec). *Black on bluish grey (No.* SB2*) or buff (No.* SB3*) covers. Stitched.*

SB2	3s. booklet containing four 5c., 10c. and eight 30c. (Nos. 20/1, 24), each in blocks of 4	14·00
SB3	5s. booklet containing four 5c., 10c., 50c. and eight 30c. (Nos. 20/1, 24, 26), each in blocks of 4	19·00

POSTAGE DUE STAMPS

The Postage Due stamps of Kenya, Uganda and Tanganyika were used in Kenya until 2 January 1967.

D **3**

1967 (3 Jan). *Chalk-surfaced paper.* P 14×13½.

D13 D **3**	5c. scarlet	15	2·75
	a. Perf 14. Ordinary paper. *Dull scarlet* (16.12.69)	40	5·50
D14	10c. green	20	2·50
	a. Perf 14. Ordinary paper (16.12.69)	55	4·25
D15	20c. blue	70	2·75
	a. Perf 14. Ordinary paper. *Deep blue* (16.12.69)	55	6·50
D16	30c. brown	80	3·25
	a. Perf 14. Ordinary paper. *Light red-brown* (16.12.69)	80	14·00
D17	40c. bright purple	65	5·00
	a. Perf 14. Ordinary paper. *Pale bright purple* (16.12.69)	65	14·00
D18	1s. bright orange	1·75	7·00
	a. Perf 14. Ordinary paper. *Dull bright orange* (18.2.70)	2·00	16·00
D13/18	*Set of* 6	3·75	21·00
D13a/18a	*Set of* 6	4·50	55·00

OFFICIAL STAMPS

Intended for use on official correspondence of the Kenya Government only but there is no evidence that they were so used.

OFFICIAL
(O **4**)

(15c. 30c. opt typo; others in photogravure)

1964 (1 Oct). *Nos. 1/5 and 7 optd with Type O* **4**.

O21	5c. brown, deep blue, green and bistre	10
O22	10c. brown	10
O23	15c. magenta	1·25
O24	20c. black and yellow-green	20
O25	30c. black and yellow	30
O26	50c. crimson, black and green	2·75
O21/26	*Set of* 6	4·00

Kenya, Uganda and Tanganyika

BRITISH EAST AFRICA

The area which became British East Africa had been part of the domain of the Zanzibari Sultans since 1794. In 1887 the administration of the province was granted to the British East Africa Association, incorporated as the Imperial British East Africa Company the following year.

Company post offices were established at Lamu and Mombasa in May 1890, British mails having been previously sent via the Indian post office on Zanzibar, opened in 1875.

A German postal agency opened at Lamu on 22 November 1888 and continued to operate until 31 March 1891, using German stamps. These can be identified by the "LAMU/OSTAFRIKA" cancellations and are listed under German East Africa in our Part 7 (*Germany*) catalogue.

PRICES FOR STAMPS ON COVER	
Nos. 1/3	*from* × 10
Nos. 4/19	*from* × 30
Nos. 20/6	*from* × 3
Nos. 27/8	*from* × 8
Nos. 29/30	*from* × 20
No. 31	*from* × 10
No. 32	—
Nos. 33/47	*from* × 10
No. 48	*from* × 15
Nos. 49/64	*from* × 12
Nos. 65/79	*from* × 15
Nos. 80/91	*from* × 8
Nos. 92/6	*from* × 12
Nos. 97/9	—

(Currency. 16 annas = 1 rupee)

BRITISH EAST AFRICA COMPANY ADMINISTRATION

BRITISH
EAST AFRICA
COMPANY

HALF ANNA
(1)

BRITISH
EAST AFRICA
COMPANY

1 ANNA
(2)

(Surch D.L.R.)

1890 (23 May). *Stamps of Great Britain (Queen Victoria) surch as T* **1** *or T* **2** *(1a. and 4a.).*

1 ½a. on 1d. deep purple (No. 173) £275 £200
2 1a. on 2d. grey-green and carmine (No. 200) £475 £275
3 4a. on 5d. dull purple and blue (No. 207*a*) £500 £300

The second stamp of each horizontal row of the 4a. on 5d. had the "BRITISH" shifted to the left, placing the "B" directly over the "S" of "EAST". In the normal overprint the "B" is over "ST" as shown in Type (**2**).

A copy of the ½a. with the short crossbar of "F" in "HALF" omitted exists in the Royal Collection but is the only known example.

Following the exhaustion of stocks of Nos. 1/3, stamps of India were used at Mombasa (and occasionally at Lamu) from late July 1890 until the arrival of Nos. 4/19. The following listing is for stamps clearly cancelled with the MOMBASA 21 mm circular date stamp (code "C"). Examples with LAMU circular date stamp are worth much more. Indian stamps used after October 1890, including other values, came from ship mail.

Stamps of INDIA 1882–90 (Nos. 84/101) cancelled at Mombasa between July and October 1890.

Z1 ½a. blue-green £500
Z2 1a. brown-purple £450
Z3 1a.6p. sepia £750
Z4 2a. blue £850
Z5 3a. orange £850
Z5*a* 4a. olive-green £900
Z6 4a.6p. yellow-green £275
Z7 8a. dull mauve £450
Z8 1r. slate £850

3

4

5
ANNAS.
(5)

(Litho B.W.)

1890 (13 Oct)–**95**. P 14.

4 **3** ½a. dull brown .... 4·25 8·00
a. Imperf (pair) £1400 £600
b. Deep brown (21.10.93) .... 70 6·50
ba. Imperf (pair) £900 £375
bb. Imperf between (horiz pair) .. £1600 £650
bc. Imperf between (vert pair) £1000 £500
c. Pale brown (16.1.95) .... 1·00 12·00
5 1a. blue-green .... 6·00 8·50
aa. "ANL" (broken "D") (R. 6/5) £750 £750
a. Imperf (pair) £2750 £700
ab. Ditto. "ANL" (broken "D") (R. 6/5) £16000
b. Deep blue-green (16.1.95) 75
6 2a. vermilion .... 3·00 4·25
a. Imperf (pair) £2250 £800
7 **3** 2½a. black/*yellow-buff* (9.91) .... 95·00 28·00
a. Imperf between (horiz pair) .. £5500
b. Black/pale buff (9.92) .... £100 9·00
c. Black/bright yellow (21.10.93) 4·75 5·00
cb. Imperf (pair) £1000 £400
cc. Imperf between (horiz pair) .. £1400 £450
cd. Imperf between (vert pair) £1400 £600
8 3a. black/*dull red* (30.3.91) .... 16·00 17·00
a. Black/bright red (21.10.93) .... 2·00 8·50
ab. Imperf (pair) £950 £400
ac. Imperf between (horiz pair) .. £900 £425
ad. Imperf between (vert pair) £700 £375
9 4a. yellow-brown .... 2·50 8·50
a. Imperf (pair) £2500 £1100
10 4a. grey (*imperf*) £1200 £1400
11 4½a. dull violet (30.3.91) .... 35·00 15·00
a. Brown-purple (21.10.93) .... 2·50 17·00
ab. Imperf (pair) £1600 £450
ac. Imperf between (horiz pair) .. £1400 £950
ad. Imperf between (vert pair) £1000 £500
12 8a. blue .... 5·50 9·50
a. Imperf (pair) £4750 £950
13 8a. grey £275 £225
14 1r. carmine .... 6·00 9·00
a. Imperf (pair) £12000 £1100
15 1r. grey £225 £225
16 **4** 2r. brick-red .... 14·00 35·00
17 3r. slate-purple .... 10·00 50·00
18 4r. ultramarine .... 12·00 50·00
19 5r. grey-green .... 30·00 70·00
4/9, 11/19 *Set of* 15 .... £500 £500

For the 5a. and 7½a. see Nos. 29/30.

The paper of Nos. 7, 7*b*, 7*c*, 8 and 8*a* is coloured on the surface only.

Printings of 1890/92 are on thin paper having the outer margins of the sheets imperf and bearing sheet watermark "PURE LINEN WOVE BANK" and "W. C. S. & Co." in a monogram, the trademark of the makers, Messrs. William Collins, Sons & Co.

1893/94 printings are on thicker coarser paper with outer margins perforated through the selvedge and without watermark. Single specimens cannot always be distinguished by lack of watermark alone. Exceptions are the 1893 printings of the 2½a. and 3a. which were on Wiggins Teape paper showing a sheet watermark of "1011" in figures 1 centimetre high.

Nos. 7 (coloured through) and 16/19 on thick unwatermarked paper are from a special printing made for presentation purposes.

The printings of the 4a., 8a. and 1r. values in grey were intended for fiscal purposes, but in the event, were made available for postal use.

Forgeries of the 4a., 8a., 1r. grey and 2 to 5r. exist. The latter are common and can be distinguished by the scroll above "LIGHT" where there are five vertical lines of shading in the forgeries and seven in the genuine stamps. Forged cancellations exist on the commoner stamps. Beware of "imperf" stamps made by trimming margins of stamps from marginal rows.

1891. *Mombasa Provisionals.*

(a) New value handstamped in dull violet, with original face value obliterated and initials added in black manuscript.

20 **3** "½ Anna" on 2a vermilion ("A.D.") (January) £8000 £850
a. "½ Anna" double .... † £8500
b. Original face value not obliterated .... † £2500
21 "1 Anna" on 4a brown ("A.B.") (February) £12000 £1900

(b) Manuscript value and initials in black.

22 **3** "½ Anna" on 2a. vermilion ("A.D.") (original face value not obliterated) (January) ..... † £2500
23 "½ Anna" on 2a. vermilion ("A.B.") (February) £8000 £850
a. Error. "½ Annas" ("A.B.") .... † £1000
24 "½ Anna" on 3a. black/*dull red* ("A.B.") (May) £12000 £2000
25 "1 Anna" on 3a. black/*dull red* ("V.H.M.") (June) £11000 £1200
26 "1 Anna" on 4a. brown ("A.B.") (March) £6500 £1500

A.D. = Andrew Dick, Chief Accountant.
A.B. = Archibald Brown, Cashier of the Company.
V.H.M. = Victor H. Mackenzie, Bank Manager.

Examples of Nos. 23 and 26 with a heavy manuscript surcharge, applied with a thicker nib, were used at Lamu. Such examples are worth a premium over the prices quoted.

(Surch B.W.)

1894 (1 Nov). *Surch as T* **5**.

27 **3** 5a. on 8a. blue .... 70·00 85·00
28 7½a. on 1r. carmine .... 70·00 85·00
27s/8s Handstamped "Specimen" *Set of* 2 .... 90·00

Forgeries exist.

1895 (16 Jan). No wmk. P 14.

29 **3** 5a. black/*grey-blue* .... 1·25 10·00
30 7½a. black .... 1·25 16·00
29s/30s Handstamped "Specimen" *Set of* 2 .... 75·00

The date quoted is that of earliest known use of stamps from this consignment.

These two stamps have "LD" after "COMPANY" in the inscription.

The paper of No. 29 is coloured on the surface only.

1895 (Feb). *No. 8 surch with manuscript value and initials ("T.E.C.R."). Original face value obliterated in manuscript.*

31 **3** "½ anna" on 3a. black/*dull red* (19.2) £425 50·00
32 "1 anna" on 3a. black/*dull red* (22.2) £1200 £3250

T.E.C.R. = T.E.C. Remington, Postmaster at Mombasa.

Similar manuscript surcharges on the black/*bright red* shade (No. 8*a*) are believed to be forgeries.

The Company experienced considerable financial problems during 1894 with the result that the British Government agreed to assume the administration of the territory, as a protectorate, on 1 July 1895.

IMPERIAL ADMINISTRATION

BRITISH
EAST
AFRICA
(6)

2½
(7)

(Handstamped at Mombasa)

1895 (9 July). *Handstamped with T* **6**.

33 **3** ½a. deep brown .... 75·00 26·00
a. Pale brown .... £110 48·00
b. Dull brown .... † £2500
c. Double £450 £425
d. Inverted £5500
34 1a. blue-green £160 £110
a. Double £500 £450
b. "ANL" (broken "D") (R. 6/5) £2750
35 2a. vermilion .... £180 95·00
a. Double £650 £475
36 2½a. black/*bright yellow* .... £180 55·00
a. Double £650 £425
37 3a. black/*dull red* .... 85·00 50·00
38 4a. yellow-brown .... 50·00 38·00
a. Double £475 £450
39 4½a. dull violet £200 £100
a. Double £700 £550
b. Brown-purple £1200 £950
ba. Double £2750 £2000
40 5a. black/*grey-blue* £225 £140
a. Double £900 £800
b. Inverted .... † £3750
41 7½a. black .... £120 80·00
a. Double £650 £550
42 8a. blue .... 95·00 75·00
a. Double £600 £600
b. Inverted £6000
43 1r. carmine .... 55·00 50·00
a. Double £550 £550
44 **4** 2r. brick-red £450 £250
45 3r. slate-purple £225 £130
a. Double £900 £900
b. Inverted ....
46 4r. ultramarine £200 £160
a. Double £800 £800
47 5r. grey-green £425 £250
a. Double £1300 £1300
33/47 *Set of* 15 .... £2250 £1400

Forgeries exist.

The ½a. stamps used for this issue were mainly from the 1893–94 printings on thicker paper, but two used examples are known on the 1890–92 thin paper printing with sheet watermark (No. 4).

1895 (29 Sept). *No. 39 surch with T* **7** *by The Zanzibar Gazette.*

48 **3** 2½a. on 4½a. dull violet (R.) .... £180 75·00
a. Opt (*T* **6**) double £1000 £850

British
East
Africa
(8)

British
East
Africa
(9)

SETTING OF TYPE 8. This consisted of 120 impressions in 10 horizontal rows of 12 stamps. This matched the size of the pane for all the Indian issues to 1r. with the exception of the 6a. The sheets of this value contained four panes, each 8×10, which meant that the outer vertical margins also received the overprint.

The setting of Type **9** is not known.

Although only the one setting was used for the low values it is known that some of the overprint errors occurred, or were corrected, during the course of the various printings.

(Overprinted at the offices of *The Zanzibar Gazette*)

1895 (27 Oct)–**96**. *Stamps of India (Queen Victoria) optd with T* **8** *or* **9** *(2r. to 5r.).* W **13** (Elephant Head) (6a.) or W **34** (Large Star) (others) of India.

49 ½a. blue-green (No. 85) (8.11.95) .... 7·00 5·50
a. "Br1tish" for "British" £6500 £6500
b. "Br1tish" for "British" (R. 10/12).. £400
c. "Afr1ca" for "Africa" (R. 1/11)...... £500
d. Opt double, one albino £225
e. "Briti" for "British" (R. 1/6) £1700
50 1a. plum (No. 89) (8.11.95) .... 6·50 6·00
a. "Br1tish" for "British" £8000 £4250
b. "Br1tish" for "British" (R. 10/12).. £475
c. "Afr1ca" for "Africa" (R. 1/11)...... £600
d. "Briti" for "British" (R. 1/6) £1700
51 1a.6p. sepia (No. 90) (23.11.95) .... 4·25 4·00
a. "Br1tish" for "British" (R. 10/12).. £500 £500
b. "Afr1ca" for "Africa" (R. 1/11)...... £650
52 2a. blue (No. 92) (28.10.95) .... 7·50 3·00
a. "Br1tish" for "British" £7000 £7000
b. "Br1tish" for "British" (R. 10/12).. £425 £275
c. "Afr1ca" for "Africa" (R. 1/11)...... £550 £350
53 2a.6p. yellow-green (No. 103) .... 8·50 2·50
c. "Br1tish" for "British" .... † £4500
d. "Eas" for "East" (R. 2/12) £1100 £1400
e. "Br1tish" for "British" (R. 10/12).. £550 £300
f. "Afr1ca" for "Africa" (R. 1/11)...... £700 £375
g. "Briti" for "British" (R. 1/6) £1700
54 3a. brown-orange (No. 94) (18.12.95) 15·00 11·00
a. "Br1tish" for "British (R. 10/12).... £550 £550
b. "Afr1ca" for "Africa" (R. 1/11)...... £750
c. Opt double, one albino £750
55 4a. olive-green (No. 95) (18.12.95) ...... 40·00 32·00
a. Slate-green .... 28·00 24·00
ab. "Br1tish" for "British" (R. 10/12).. £700 £550
ac. "Afr1ca" for "Africa" (R. 1/11)...... £850 £650
56 6a. pale brown (No. 81) (18.12.95) ...... 40·00 50·00
a. "Br1tish" for "British" (R. 10/8)...... £1400
b. "Afr1ca" for "Africa" (R. 1/7) £1600
c. "E st" for "East" .... † —
d. Opt double, one albino £450
57 8a. dull mauve (No. 98) (18.12.95) ...... 90·00 70·00
a. "Br1tish" for "British" (R. 10/12)..
b. "Afr1ca" for "Africa" (R. 1/11)......

		c. *Magenta* (1896)	28·00	50·00
		ca. "Br1tish" for "British" (R. 10/12)	£800	£700
		cb. "Afr1ca" for "Africa" (R. 1/11)	£850	£750
		cc. Inverted "a" for "t" of "East" (R. 2/12)	†	£18000
58		12a. purple/*red* (No. 100) (18.12.95)	22·00	35·00
		a. "Br1tish" for "British" (R. 10/12)	£750	£750
		b. "Afr1ca" for "Africa" (R. 1/11)	£900	
59		1r. slate (No. 101) (18.12.95)	95·00	65·00
		a. "Br1tish" for "British" (R. 10/12)		
		b. "Afr1ca" for "Africa" (R. 1/11)		
60		1r. green and aniline carmine (No. 106) (1896)	45·00	£130
		a. Inverted "a" for "t" of "East" (R. 2/12)	£12000	
		b. "Br1tish" for "British" (R. 10/12)	£1400	
		c. "Afr1ca" for "Africa" (R. 1/11)	£1400	
		d. Opt double, one sideways	£425	£900
		e. Opt double, one albino	£600	
61		2r. carm and yellow-brown (No. 107) (18.12.95)	90·00	£150
		a. "B" handstamped	£6500	£6500
62		3r. brown and green (No. 108) (18.12.95)	£110	£160
		a. "B" handstamped	£6500	£6500
		b. Opt double, one albino	£1400	
63		5r. ultramarine and violet (No. 109) (18.12.95)	£130	£160
		a. Opt double	£2500	
		b. "B" handstamped	£6000	£5500
		c. Opt double, one albino	£1400	
49/63 *Set of* 15			£550	£750

The relative horizontal positions of the three lines of the overprint vary considerably but the distance vertically between the lines of the overprint is constant.

In both the "Br1tish" and "Afr1ca" errors the figure one is in a smaller type size.

There are other varieties, such as inverted "s" in "British", wide and narrow "B", and inverted "V" for "A" in "Africa" (R. 1/1 and R. 6/7).

During the overprinting of Nos. 61/3 the "B" of "British" sometimes failed to print so that only traces of the letter appeared. It was replaced by a handstamped "B" which is often out of alignment with the rest of the overprint. The handstamp is known double.

The 2, 3 and 5r., normally overprinted in larger type than the lower values, are also known with a smaller overprint, for use as specimen stamps for the U.P.U. These were not issued for postal purposes (*Price* £450 *un per set*). The lower values were reprinted at the same time using similar type to the original overprint.

Forgeries exist.

2½

(10)

11

1895 (19 Dec). *No. 51 surch locally with T* **10** *in bright red.*

64		2½ on 1½a. sepia	95·00	50·00
		a. Inverted "1" in fraction (R. 5/7, 10/7)	£900	£600
		b. "Br1tish" for "British" (R. 10/12)	£1400	
		c. "Afr1ca" for "Africa" (R. 1/11)	£1400	

The setting of Type **10** was in 5 horizontal rows of 12 stamps, repeated twice for each pane.

No. 51 also exists surcharged with *T* **12**, **13** and **14** in brown-red. These stamps were sent to the Postal Union authorities at Berne, but were never issued to the public (*Price unused*: *T* **12** £85, *T* **13** £190, *T* **14** £140).

(Recess D.L.R.)

1896 (26 May)–**1901**. Wmk Crown CA. P 14.

65	**11**	½a. yellow-green	3·50	80
		x. Wmk reversed	†	£250
66		1a. carmine-rose	9·50	40
		a. Bright rose-red	7·50	40
		b. Rosine (1901)	22·00	4·00
		w. Wmk inverted	£150	£150
		x. Wmk reversed	£225	£170
67		2a. chocolate	7·50	5·00
		x. Wmk reversed	†	£200
68		2½a. deep blue	12·00	1·75
		a. Violet-blue	18·00	2·50
		b. Inverted "S" in "ANNAS" (R. 1/1)	£160	60·00
		w. Wmk inverted	†	£250
		x. Wmk reversed	£225	£180
69		3a. grey	6·00	9·00
		x. Wmk reversed	£150	£150
70		4a. deep green	7·00	3·50
71		4½a. orange-yellow	11·00	16·00
72		5a. yellow-bistre	7·50	5·00
73		7½a. mauve	7·00	22·00
		x. Wmk reversed	†	£275
74		8a. grey-olive	7·50	5·50
75		1r. pale dull blue	60·00	25·00
		a. Ultramarine	95·00	65·00
76		2r. orange	65·00	29·00
77		3r. deep violet	65·00	32·00
78		4r. carmine-lake	60·00	75·00
79		5r. sepia	55·00	40·00
		a. Thin "U" in "RUPEES" (R. 3/2)	£1600	£1300
		x. Wmk reversed	†	£500
65/79 *Set of* 15			£325	£225
65s/79s Optd "Specimen" *Set of* 15			£275	

Examples of some values exist apparently without watermark due to the paper being misplaced on the press.

(Overprinted at the offices of *The Zanzibar Gazette*)

1897 (2 Jan). *Nos. 156/7, 159 and 165/7 of Zanzibar optd with T* **8**. Wmk Single Rosette.

80		½a. yellow-green and red	55·00	45·00
81		1a. indigo and red	95·00	90·00
82		2a. red-brown and red	38·00	21·00
83		4½a. orange and red	50·00	30·00
		a. No right serif to left-hand "4"	£900	
		b. No fraction bar at right	£900	£600
84		5a. bistre and red	55·00	35·00
		a. "Bri" for "British"	£1800	£1800
85		7½a. mauve and red	50·00	35·00
		a. "Bri" for "British"	£2000	
		b. Optd on front and back		
80/5 *Set of* 6			£300	£225

Nos. 84a and 85a appear to have occurred when the type was obscured during part of the overprinting.

The above six stamps exist with an overprint similar to *T* **8** but normally showing a stop after "Africa". These overprints (in red on the 1a.) were made officially to supply the U.P.U. (*Price* £300 *un per set*). However, the stop does not always show. Pieces are known showing overprints with and without stop *se-tenant* (including the red overprint on the 1a.).

Stamps of Zanzibar, wmk "Multiple Rosettes" and overprinted with *T* **8** are forgeries.

2½ (12) 2½ (13) 2½ (14)

SETTING OF TYPES 12/14. The setting of 60 (6×10) contained 26 examples of Type **12**, 10 of Type **13** and 24 of Type **14**.

1897 (2 Jan). *Nos. 157 and 162 of Zanzibar optd with T* **8** *and further surch locally, in red.*

86	**12**	2½ on 1a. indigo and red	£110	65·00
		b. Opt Type **8** double	£6500	
87	**13**	2½ on 1a. indigo and red	£250	£110
88	**14**	2½ on 1a. indigo and red	£130	75·00
		a. Opt Type **8** double	£6500	
89	**12**	2½ on 3a. grey and red	£110	55·00
90	**13**	2½ on 3a. grey and red	£250	£100
91	**14**	2½ on 3a. grey and red	£130	60·00
86/91 *Set of* 6			£900	£400

Both the notes after No. 85 also apply here.

A special printing for U.P.U. requirements was made with the 2½ surcharge on the 1a. and 3a. stamps overprinted as *T* **8** but *with stop* after "Africa". It also included a "2" over "1" error in *T* **14**. (*Price*, £1600, either value).

15

(Recess D.L.R.)

1897 (Nov)–**1903**. Wmk Crown CC. P 14.

92	**15**	1r. grey-blue	90·00	35·00
		a. Dull blue (1901)	80·00	40·00
		b. Bright ultramarine (1903)	£400	£300
93		2r. orange	95·00	95·00
94		3r. deep violet	£130	£140
95		4r. carmine	£375	£450
		x. Wmk reversed	£600	£600
		y. Wmk inverted and reversed	£1000	
96		5r. deep sepia	£325	£400
97		10r. yellow-bistre	£350	£425
		s. Optd "Specimen"	65·00	
		x. Wmk reversed	£850	
98		20r. pale green	£800	£1700
		a. Optd "Specimen"	£125	
99		50r. mauve	£1600	
		s. Optd "Specimen"	£250	
		x. Wmk reversed	£1800	£6000
		xs. Optd "Specimen"	£275	
92s/6s Optd "Specimen" *Set of* 5			£180	

On 1 April 1901 the postal administrations of British East Africa and Uganda were merged. Subsequent issues were inscribed "EAST AFRICA AND UGANDA PROTECTORATES".

EAST AFRICA AND UGANDA PROTECTORATES

For earlier issues see BRITISH EAST AFRICA and UGANDA.

For the issues of the Mandated Territory of Tanganyika and the war-time issues that preceded them, see TANGANYIKA.

PRICES FOR STAMPS ON COVER TO 1945	
Nos. 1/43	*from* × 3
Nos. 44/75	*from* × 2
Nos. 76/95	*from* × 3
Nos. 96/105	—
Nos. 110/23	*from* × 2
Nos. 124/7	*from* × 3
Nos. 128/30	*from* × 5
Nos. 131/54	*from* × 3
Nos. D1/12	*from* × 8

PRINTERS. All the stamps issued between 1903 and 1927 were typographed by De La Rue & Co. Ltd, London.

USED HIGH VALUES. Beware of cleaned fiscally cancelled copies with faked postmarks.

1

2

1903 (24 July)–**04**. P 14.

(*a*) Wmk Crown CA.

1	**1**	½a. green (16.2.04)	4·00	14·00
2		1a. grey and red	1·75	1·25
3		2a. dull and bright purple (24.7.03)	8·50	2·50
		w. Wmk inverted	£160	£150
4		2½a. blue	12·00	48·00
5		3a. brown-purple and green	20·00	55·00
6		4a. grey-green and black	11·00	22·00
7		5a. grey and orange-brown	18·00	48·00
8		8a. grey and pale blue	21·00	40·00
		(*b*) Wmk Crown CC. *Ordinary paper.*		
9	**2**	1r. green	16·00	55·00
		a. Chalk-surfaced paper	55·00	95·00
10		2r. dull and bright purple	70·00	80·00
11		3r. grey-green and black	£100	£180
12		4r. grey and emerald-green	£110	£180
13		5r. grey and red	£110	£180
14		10r. grey and ultramarine	£250	£375
		a. Chalk-surfaced paper	£350	£425
		w. Wmk inverted	£550	
15		20r. grey and stone	£550	£1300
		s. Optd "Specimen"	£130	
16		50r. grey and red-brown	£1600	£3250
		s. Optd "Specimen"	£300	
		w. Wmk inverted	£3250	
1/13 *Set of* 13			£450	£800
1s/14s Optd "Specimen" *Set of* 14			£325	

1904–07. Wmk Mult Crown CA. *Ordinary paper (½a. to 8a.) or chalk-surfaced paper (1r. to 50r.).*

17	**1**	½a. grey-green	8·50	3·00
		a. Chalk-surfaced paper	9·50	3·25
18		1a. grey and red	3·75	80
		a. Chalk-surfaced paper	11·00	1·75
19		2a. dull and bright purple	3·25	2·75
		a. Chalk-surfaced paper	2·75	2·75
20		2½a. blue	8·00	30·00
21		2½a. ultramarine and blue	7·50	17·00
22		3a. brown-purple and green	3·75	32·00
		a. Chalk-surfaced paper	3·75	30·00
23		4a. grey-green and black	7·50	18·00
		a. Chalk-surfaced paper	7·50	18·00
24		5a. grey and orange-brown	8·00	15·00
		a. Chalk-surfaced paper	6·50	28·00
25		8a. grey and pale blue	7·00	8·50
		a. Chalk-surfaced paper	7·00	19·00
26	**2**	1r. green (1907)	27·00	60·00
		w. Wmk inverted	†	£450
27		2r. dull and bright purple (1906)	38·00	55·00
28		3r. grey-green and black (1907)	60·00	£100
29		4r. grey and emerald-green (1907)	85·00	£150
		w. Wmk inverted	£450	
30		5r. grey and red (1907)	£100	£120
31		10r. grey and ultramarine (1907)	£200	£250
		w. Wmk inverted	£550	£600
32		20r. grey and stone (1907)	£550	£1000
33		50r. grey and red-brown (1907)	£1800	£3250
17/30 *Set of* 13			£325	£500

(New Currency. 100 cents = 1 rupee)

1907–08. Wmk Mult Crown CA. *Chalk-surfaced paper (10, 12, 25, 50, 75c.).* P 14.

34	**1**	1c. brown	2·50	15
35		3c. grey-green	15·00	70
		a. Blue-green	18·00	3·00
36		6c. red	2·75	10
37		10c. lilac and pale olive	9·00	8·50
38		12c. dull and bright purple	10·00	2·75
39		15c. bright blue	24·00	8·50
40		25c. grey-green and black	12·00	7·00
41		50c. grey-green and orange-brown	12·00	12·00
42		75c. grey and pale blue (1908)	4·50	35·00
34/42 *Set of* 9			80·00	65·00
34s/42s Optd "Specimen" *Set of* 9			£180	

Original

Redrawn

1910. *T* **1** *redrawn. Printed from a single plate.* Wmk Mult Crown CA. P 14.

43		6c. red	15·00	30

In the redrawn type a fine white line has been cut around the value tablets and above the name tablet separating the latter from the leaves above, EAST AFRICA AND UGANDA is in shorter and thicker letters and PROTECTORATES in taller letters than in No. 36

3

4

4 cents

(5)

1912–21. Wmk Mult Crown CA. *Chalk-surfaced paper (25c. to 500r.).* P 14.

44	**3**	1c. black	30	1·75
45		3c. green	2·00	60
		a. Deep blue-green (1917)	4·50	1·50
		w. Wmk inverted	†	—
46		6c. red	1·25	40
		a. Scarlet (1917)	17·00	2·75
47		10c. yellow-orange	2·00	50
		a. Orange (1921)	10·00	3·50
48		12c. slate-grey	2·75	50
49		15c. bright blue	2·75	80
		w. Wmk inverted		
50		25c. black and red/*yellow*	50	1·25
		a. White back (5.14)	50	4·50
		as. Optd "Specimen"	35·00	
		b. On lemon (1916)	11·00	11·00

		bs. Optd "Specimen"	35·00	
		c. *On orange-buff* (1921)	45·00	17·00
		d. *On pale yellow* (1921)	11·00	5·00
51		50c. black and lilac	1·50	1·25
52		75c. black/*green*	1·50	17·00
		a. *White back* (5.14)	1·00	16·00
		as. Optd "Specimen"	35·00	
		b. *On blue-green, olive back*	6·00	7·50
		bs. Optd "Specimen"	35·00	
		c. *On emerald, olive back* (1919)	42·00	£150
		d. *On emerald back* (1921)	11·00	55·00
53	4	1r. black/*green*	1·75	4·25
		aw. Wmk inverted	£450	
		b. *On emerald back* (1919)	5·00	50·00
54		2r. red and black/*blue*	20·00	38·00
		w. Wmk inverted	£250	
55		3r. violet and green	20·00	90·00
56		4r. red and green/*yellow*	45·00	£100
		a. *On pale yellow*	£100	£170
57		5r. blue and dull purple	48·00	£140
58		10r. red and green/*green*	£150	£225
59		20r. black and purple/*red*	£350	£350
60		20r. purple and blue/*blue* (1918)	£400	£475
61		50r. dull rose-red and dull greyish green	£600	£650
		a. *Carmine and green*	£850	£900
		s. Optd "Specimen"	£160	
62		100r. purple and black/*red*	£5500	£2750
		s. Optd "Specimen"	£350	
63		500r. green and red/*green*	£22000	
		s. Optd "Specimen"	£700	
44/58 *Set of* 15			£275	£550
44s/60s Optd "Specimen" *Set of* 17			£600	

For values in this series overprinted "G.E.A." (German East Africa) see Tanganyika Nos. 45/62.

1919 (7 Apr). *No.* 46a *surch with T* **5** *by the Swift Press, Nairobi.*

64	3	4c. on 6c. scarlet (*shades*)	1·25	15
		a. Bars omitted	40·00	70·00
		b. Surch double	£120	£200
		c. Surch inverted	£275	£375
		d. Pair, one without surch	£1600	£1800
		e. Surch on back	£400	
		s. Handstamped "Specimen"	60·00	

1921–22. Wmk Mult Script CA. *Chalk-surfaced paper (50c. to 50r.).* P 14.

65	3	1c. black	80	1·75
		w. Wmk inverted	£325	£325
66		3c. green	6·00	8·50
		a. *Blue-green*	17·00	12·00
67		6c. carmine-red	7·50	12·00
68		10c. orange (12.21)	8·50	1·25
		w. Wmk inverted		
69		12c. slate-grey	7·50	£120
70		15c. bright blue	11·00	17·00
71		50c. black and dull purple	14·00	£110
72	4	2r. red and black/*blue*	70·00	£180
73		3r. violet and green	£120	£300
74		5r. blue and dull purple	£150	£250
75		50r. carmine and green	£2500	£5000
		s. Optd "Specimen"	£350	
65/74 *Set of* 10			£350	£900
65s/74s Optd "Specimen" *Set of* 10			£300	

For values in this series overprinted "G.E.A." see Tanganyika Nos. 63/73.

KENYA AND UGANDA

(New Currency. 100 cents = 1 East Africa shilling)

On 23 July 1920, Kenya became a Crown Colony with the exception of the coastal strip, previously part of the Sultan of Zanzibar's territories, which remained a protectorate.

The northern province of Jubaland was ceded to Italy on 29 June 1925 and later incorporated into Italian Somaliland.

6

7

1922 (1 Nov)–**27.** Wmk Mult Script CA. P 14.

(*a*) Wmk upright. *Ordinary paper.*

76	6	1c. pale brown	1·00	3·25
		a. *Deep brown* (1923)	1·50	3·50
		ax. Wmk reversed	£180	
77		5c. dull violet	3·75	75
		a. *Bright violet*	7·00	1·50
78		5c. green (1927)	2·00	50
79		10c. green	1·50	30
		w. Wmk inverted		
80		10c. black (5.27)	4·00	20
81		12c. jet-black	8·00	38·00
		a. *Grey-black*	6·00	26·00
82		15c. rose-carmine	1·25	10
83		20c. dull orange-yellow	3·25	10
		a. *Bright orange*	4·25	10
84		30c. ultramarine	3·00	50
85		50c. grey	2·50	10
86		75c. olive	5·50	9·00

(*b*) Wmk sideways*. *Chalk-surfaced paper.*

87	7	1s. green	4·25	2·50
88		2s. dull purple	8·00	12·00
		w. Wmk Crown to right of CA	£120	
89		2s.50 brown (1.10.25)	18·00	90·00
90		3s. brownish grey	17·00	6·50
		a. *Jet-black*	48·00	38·00
91		4s. grey (1.10.25)	26·00	90·00
		w. Wmk Crown to right of CA	50·00	£150
92		5s. carmine-red	23·00	22·00
93		7s.50 orange-yellow (1.10.25)	85·00	£180
94		10s. bright blue	50·00	50·00
		w. Wmk Crown to right of CA		
95		£1 black and orange	£170	£250
96		£2 green and purple (1.10.25)	£700	£1200
		s. Optd "Specimen"	£180	
97		£3 purple and yellow (1.10.25)	£950	
		s. Optd "Specimen"	£180	
98		£4 black and magenta (1.10.25)	£1900	
		s. Optd "Specimen"	£250	
99		£5 black and blue	£2250	
		s. Optd "Specimen"	£300	
		w. Wmk Crown to right of CA	£2750	
100		£10 black and green	£9000	
		s. Optd "Specimen"	£375	
		w. Wmk Crown to right of CA	£14000	
101		£20 red and green (1.10.25)	£20000	
		s. Optd "Specimen"	£600	
102		£25 black and red	£23000	
		s. Optd "Specimen"	£600	
		w. Wmk Crown to right of CA	£27000	
103		£50 black and brown	£30000	
		s. Optd "Specimen"	£700	
104		£75 purple and grey (1.10.25)	£85000	
		s. Optd "Specimen"	£1000	
105		£100 red and black (1.10.25)	£95000	
		s. Optd "Specimen"	£1200	
76/95 *Set of* 20			£375	£650
76s/95s Optd "Specimen" *Set of* 20			£475	

Nos. 87/94 were printed in two operations sometimes causing shade differences between the head and the frame.

*The normal sideways watermark shows Crown to left of CA, *as seen from the back of the stamp.*

KENYA, UGANDA AND TANGANYIKA

The postal administrations of Kenya, Tanganyika and Uganda were amalgamated on 1 January 1933. On the independence of the three territories the combined administration became the East African Posts and Telecommunications Corporation.

8 South African Crowned Cranes

9 Dhow on Lake Victoria

10 Lion

11 Kilimanjaro

12 Nile Railway Bridge, Ripon Falls

13 Mt. Kenya

14 Lake Naivasha

I II

(Des 1c., 20c., 10s., R. C. Luck, 10c., £1, A. Ross, 15c., 2s., G. Gill Holmes, 30c., 5s., R. N. Ambasana, 65c., L. R. Cutts. *T* **10** typo, remainder recess D.L.R.).

1935 (1 May)–**37.** Wmk Mult Script CA. *Chalk-surfaced paper (10c., £1).* P 12×13 (**10**), 14 (**9** and **14**) and 13 (remainder).

110	8	1c. black and red-brown	1·00	1·50
111	9	5c. black and green (I)	2·00	40
		a. Rope joined to sail (II) (1937)	22·00	5·00
		b. Perf 13×12 (I) (1936)	£6000	£650
		ba. Rope joined to sail (II) (1937)	£650	£200
112	10	10c. black and yellow	4·50	60
113	11	15c. black and scarlet	2·75	10
		a. Frame double, one albino	†	—
114	8	20c. black and orange	3·50	20
115	12	30c. black and blue	2·75	1·00
116	9	50c. bright purple and black (I)	3·00	10
117	13	65c. black and brown	4·25	2·00
118	14	1s. black and green	2·75	75
		a. Perf 13×12 (1936)	£1300	£120
119	11	2s. lake and purple	7·00	4·25
120	14	3s. blue and black	10·00	15·00
		a. Perf 13×12 (1936)	£2250	
121	12	5s. black and carmine	18·00	27·00
122	8	10s. purple and blue	75·00	95·00
123	10	£1 black and red	£190	£250
110/23 *Set of* 14			£300	£350
110s/23s Perf "Specimen" *Set of* 14			£350	

Line through "0" of 1910 (R. 4/2)

(Des H. Fleury. Recess D.L.R.)

1935 (6 May). *Silver Jubilee.* Wmk Mult Script CA. P 13½×14.

124		20c. light blue and olive-green	1·25	10
		f. Diagonal line by turret	85·00	45·00
		g. Dot to left of chapel	£160	80·00
		h. Dot by flagstaff	£160	80·00
		i. Dash by turret	£180	85·00
125		30c. brown and deep blue	2·50	3·00
		f. Diagonal line by turret	£150	£170
		g. Dot to left of chapel	£300	
		h. Dot by flagstaff	£300	
		i. Dash by turret	£325	
126		65c. green and indigo	1·75	2·75
		f. Diagonal line by turret	£160	
		g. Dot to left of chapel	£275	£325
127		1s. slate and purple	2·00	3·50
		f. Diagonal line by turret	£160	£180
		g. Dot to left of chapel	£325	
		h. Dot by flagstaff	£325	
		i. Line through "0" of 1910	£120	£140
124/7 *Set of* 4			6·75	8·50
124s/7s Perf "Specimen" *Set of* 4			£140	

For illustrations of the other plate varieties see Omnibus section following Zanzibar.

Broken leaf (R. 6/1)

(Des and recess D.L.R)

1937 (12 May). *Coronation. As Nos.* 95/7 *of Antigua.*

128		5c. green	20	10
129		20c. orange	40	30
		a. Broken leaf	48·00	
130		30c. bright blue	60	1·75
128/30 *Set of* 3			1·10	1·90
128s/30s Perf "Specimen" *Set of* 3			90·00	

15 Dhow on Lake Victoria

Damaged left-hand value tablet (Frame Pl 2–2, with Centre Pl 4A or 4B, R. 9/6)

Retouched value tablet (Frame Pl 2–2, with Centre Pls 4A, 4B, 5, 6 or 7, R. 9/6)

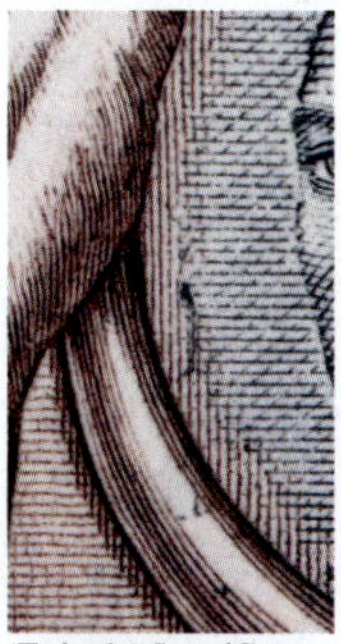
'Tadpole' flaw (Centre Pl 4B with Frame Pl 2–2 R. 10/8)

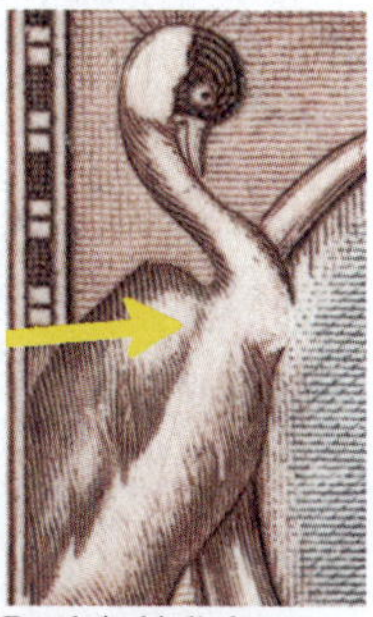
Break in bird's breast (Frame Pl 2–2, with Centre Pls 4A or 4B, R. 2/5)

Sky retouch (Pl 7A R. 10/6)

Damage on mountain (Pl 7B R. 6/7. August 1948 ptg. Retouched in June 1949 for 10c. and 1s.)

Mountain retouch (Pl 7B, R. 5/10 and 6/7. Ptgs from June 1949 onwards)

With dot

Dot removed

In the 50c. printing of 14 June 1950 using Frame-plate 3, the dot was removed by retouching on all but five stamps (R. 5/2, 6/1, 7/2, 7/4 and 9/1). In addition, other stamps show traces of the dot where the retouching was not completely effective.

PERFORATIONS. In this issue, to aid identification, the perforations are indicated to the nearest quarter.

(*T* **10** typo, others recess D.L.R.)

1938 (11 Apr)–**54**. *As T* **8** *to* **14** *(but with portrait of King George VI in place of King George V, as in T* **15**). Wmk Mult Script CA. *Chalk-surfaced paper (£1).*

131	**8**	1c. black & red-brown (P 13¼) (2.5.38)	2·50	85
		a. Perf 13¼×13¾. *Black and chocolate-brown* (1942)	30	50
		ab. "A" of "CA" missing from wmk	£300	
		ac. Damaged value tablet	90·00	
		ad. Retouched value tablet	45·00	65·00
		ae. Break in bird's breast	85·00	
		af. 'Tadpole' flaw	90·00	
		ag. Black and deep chocolate-brown (10.6.46)	2·25	2·25
		ah. Ditto. Retouched tablet	50·00	70·00
		ai. Black and red-brown (26.9.51)	3·75	3·75
132	**15**	5c. black and green (II) (P 13×11¾)	4·25	50
133		5c. reddish brown and orange (P 13×11¾) (1.6.49)	65	3·75
		a. Perf 13×12½ (14.6.50)	1·75	3·00
134	**14**	10c. red-brown and orange (P 13×11¾) (2.5.38)	2·25	10
		aw. Wmk inverted		
		b. Perf 14 (22.4.41)	£120	6·50
135		10c. black and green (P 13×11¾) (1.6.49)	30	1·50
		a. Mountain retouch	75·00	75·00
		b. Sky retouch		
		c. Perf 13×12½ (14.6.50)	2·50	10
136		10c. brown and grey (P 13×12½) (1.4.52)	1·25	55
137	**11**	15c. black and rose-red (P 13¼) (2.5.38)	26·00	55
		a. Perf 13¾×13¼ (2.43)	5·50	3·75
		ab. "A" of "CA" missing from wmk		
138		15c. black and green (P 13¾ × 13¼) (1.4.52)	2·25	5·50
139	**8**	20c. black and orange (P 13¼) (2.5.38)	40·00	30
		a. Perf 14 (19.5.41)	55·00	1·75
		b. Perf 13¼×13¾ (25.2.42)	8·00	10
		ba. Deep black and deep orange (21.6.51)	19·00	1·75
		bw. Wmk inverted	†	—
140	**15**	25c. black and carmine-red (P 13×12½) (1.4.52)	1·25	2·25
141	**12**	30c. black and dull violet-blue (P 13¼) (2.5.38)	50·00	40
		a. Perf 14 (3.7.41)	£140	11·00
		b. Perf 13¼×13¾ (10.5.42)	2·75	10
142		30c. dull purple and brown (P 13¼ × 13¾) (1.4.52)	1·50	40
143	**8**	40c. black and blue (P 13¼×13¾) (1.4.52)	1·75	3·25
144	**15**	50c. purple and black (II) (P 13×11¾) (2.5.38)	17·00	1·00
		a. Rope not joined to sail (I) (R. 2/5)	£250	£250
		b. Dull claret and black (29.7.47)	75·00	8·00
		c. Brown purple and black (4.48)	80·00	7·50
		d. Reddish purple and black (28.4.49)	40·00	5·00
		e. Ditto. Perf 13×12½ (10.49)	6·00	55
		ea. Dot removed (14.6.50)	21·00	55
		eb. Ditto. In pair with normal	£400	£130
		ew. Wmk inverted	†	£3750
145	**14**	1s. black and yellowish brown (P 13×11¾) (2.5.38)	24·00	30
		a. Black and brown (9.42)	11·00	30
		ab. Damage on mountain	—	£475
		ac. Mountain retouch	£1000	£275
		aw. Wmk inverted	†	£2750
		b. Perf 13×12½ (10.49)	12·00	60
		ba. Deep black and brown (clearer impression) (14.6.50)	26·00	2·25
146	**11**	2s. lake-brown & brown-purple (P 13¼) (2.5.38)	£110	2·25
		a. Perf 14 (1941)	70·00	12·00
		b. Perf 13¾×13¼ (24.2.44)	27·00	30
147	**14**	3s. dull ultramarine and black (P 13×11¾) (2.5.38)	42·00	4·50
		a. Deep violet-blue and black (29.4.47)	60·00	9·50
		ab. Damage on mountain	£2250	
		ac. Perf 13×12½ (14.6.50)	32·00	4·50
148	**12**	5s. black and carmine (P 13¼) (2.5.38)	£130	16·00
		a. Perf 14 (1941)	45·00	2·50
		b. Perf 13¼×13¾ (24.2.44)	32·00	1·50
149	**8**	10s. purple and blue (P 13¼) (2.5.38)	£120	22·00
		a. Perf 14. *Reddish purple and blue* (1941)	38·00	21·00
		b. Perf 13¼×13¾ (24.2.44)	42·00	4·50
150	**10**	£1 black and red (P 11¾ × 13) (12.10.38)	£350	£120
		a. Perf 14 (1941)	26·00	18·00
		ab. Ordinary paper (24.2.44)	28·00	19·00
		b. Perf 12½ (21.1.54)	13·00	35·00
131/50a (*cheapest*) *Set of* 20			£170	42·00
131s/50s Perf "Specimen" *Set of* 13			£650	

No. 131ab occurs once in some sheets, always in the sixth vertical row.

The first printing of the 50c. utilised the King George V centre plate on which each impression had been individually corrected to show the rope joined to sail. R. 2/5 was missed, however, and this continued to show Type I until replaced by a further printing from a new plate in September 1938.

Stamps perf 14, together with Nos. 131a, 137a, 139b, 141b, 146b, 148b and 149b, are the result of air raid damage to the De La Rue works which destroyed the normal perforators. Dates quoted for these stamps represent earliest known postmarks.

10c
KENYA
TANGANYIKA
UGANDA
(16)

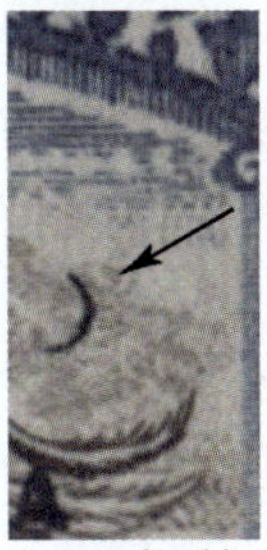

A screw head in the surcharging forme appears as a crescent moon (R. 20/4)

1941 (1 July)–**42**. *Pictorial Stamps of South Africa variously surch as T* **16** *by Government Printer, Pretoria. Inscr alternately in English and Afrikaans.*

		Unused pair	Used pair	Used single
151	5c. on 1d. grey and carmine (No. 56)	1·25	1·75	15
152	10c. on 3d. ultramarine (No. 59)	4·00	9·00	30
153	20c. on 6d. green and vermilion (No. 61*a*)	3·50	3·50	20
154	70c. on 1s. brown and chalky blue (No. 62) (20.4.42)	17·00	5·00	45
	a. Crescent moon flaw	65·00		
151/4 *Set of* 4		23·00	17·00	1·00
151s/4s Handstamped "Specimen" *Set of* 4		£250		

1946 (11 Nov). *Victory. As Nos. 110/11 of Antigua.*

155	20c. red-orange	30	10
156	30c. blue	30	75
155s/6s Perf "Specimen" *Set of* 2		80·00	

Examples of Nos. 155/6 were pre-released at Lindi on 15 October 1946.

1948 (1 Dec). *Royal Silver Wedding. As Nos. 112/13 of Antigua.*

157	20c. orange	15	20
158	£1 scarlet	42·00	70·00

1949 (10 Oct). *75th Anniv of Universal Postal Union. As Nos. 114/17 of Antigua.*

159	20c. red-orange	15	10
160	30c. deep blue	1·75	2·25
161	50c. grey	45	60
162	1s. red-brown	50	40
159/62 *Set of* 4		2·50	3·00

17 Lake Naivasha

(Recess D.L.R.)

1952 (1 Feb). *Visit of Princess Elizabeth and Duke of Edinburgh.* Wmk Mult Script CA. P 13×12½.

163	**17**	10c. black and green	30	1·50
164		1s. black and brown	1·10	2·00

1953 (2 June). *Coronation. As No 120 of Antigua.*

165	20c. black and red-orange	20	10

1954 (28 Apr). *Royal Visit. As No. 171 but inscr "*ROYAL VISIT 1954*" below portrait.*

166	30c. black and deep ultramarine	50	15

18 Owen Falls Dam

19 Giraffe

20 African Elephants

21 Lion

22 Mount Kilimanjaro

23 Royal Lodge, Sagana

24 Queen Elizabeth II

(Des G. Gill Holmes (10, 50c.), H. Grieme (15c., 1s.30, 5s.), R. McLellan Sim (10s.), De La Rue (65c., 2s., £1), O.C. Meronti (others). Recess D.L.R.)

1954 (1 June)–**59**. *Designs as T* **18/24**. Wmk Mult Script CA. P 13 (£1); others, 12½×13 (vert) or 13×12½ (horiz).

167	**18**	5c. black and deep brown	1·50	50
		a. Vignette inverted	†	£25000
168	**19**	10c. carmine-red	1·50	10
169	**20**	15c. black and light blue (28.3.58)	65	1·25
		a. Redrawn. Stop below "c" of "15 c" (29.4.59)	65	1·25
170	**21**	20c. black and orange	1·75	10
		a. Imperf (pair)	£1000	£1200
171	**18**	30c. black and deep ultramarine	1·25	10
		a. Vignette inverted	†	£17000
172	**20**	40c. bistre-brown (28.3.58)	1·25	75
		w. Wmk inverted		
173	**19**	50c. reddish purple	3·25	10
		a. Claret (23.1.57)	4·25	10
174	**22**	65c. bluish green & brown-purple (1.12.55)	2·75	1·50
175	**21**	1s. black and claret	3·00	10
176	**20**	1s.30 deep lilac and orange (1.12.55)	13·00	10
177	**22**	2s. black and green	11·00	80
		a. Black and bronze-green (19.4.56)	14·00	1·50
178	**20**	5s. black and orange	23·00	3·25
179	**23**	10s. black and deep ultramarine	27·00	4·25
180	**24**	£1 brown-red and black	17·00	16·00
		a. Venetian red and black (19.4.56)	45·00	22·00
167/80 *Set of* 14			95·00	26·00

Only one example of No. 167a and two of No. 171a have been found, all being used.

The 5, 10 and 50c. exist from coils made up from normal sheets.

25 Map of E. Africa showing Lakes

(Recess Waterlow)

1958 (30 July). *Centenary of Discovery of Lakes Tanganyika and Victoria by Burton and Speke.* W w **12**. P 12½.

181	**25**	40c. blue and deep green	65	40
182		1s.30c. green and violet	65	1·40

26 Sisal

27 Cotton

28 Mt Kenya and Giant Plants

29 Queen Elizabeth II

Serif at left of base of "Y" in "TANGANYIKA" (Pl. 1, R. 2/7). This was later retouched but traces still remain

1s. Re-entry. Whole of "TANGANYIKA" is doubled (Pl. 1-1 and 1-2, R. 9/4).

(Des M. Goaman. Photo (5c. to 65c.), recess (others) D.L.R.)

1960 (1 Oct)–**62**. *Designs as T* **26/9**. W w **12**. P 15×14 (5c. to 65c.), 13 (20s.) or 14 (others).

183		5c. Prussian blue	10	15
184		10c. yellow-green	10	10
185		15c. dull purple	30	10
		a. "Serif" variety	10·00	
		b. "Serif" retouched	10·00	
186		20c. magenta	20	10
187		25c. bronze-green	3·25	1·25
188		30c. vermilion	15	10
189		40c. greenish blue	15	20
190		50c. slate-violet	15	10
191		65c. yellow-olive	30	1·50
192		1s. deep reddish violet and reddish purple	80	10
		a. Blackish lilac and reddish purple (23.1.62)	5·00	30
		b. Re-entry	27·00	
193		1s.30 chocolate and brown-red	3·50	15
194		2s. deep grey-blue and greenish blue	5·00	40
195		2s.50 olive-green and deep bluish green	7·50	2·75
196		5s. rose-red and purple	3·75	60
197		10s. blackish green and olive-green	9·50	6·50
		a. Imperf (pair)	£1100	
198		20s. violet-blue and lake	20·00	27·00
183/98 *Set of 16*			48·00	35·00

Designs: *Vert as T* **26/7**—15c. Coffee; 20c. Blue Wildebeest; 25c. Ostrich; 30c. Thomson's Gazelle; 40c. Manta; 50c. Common Zebra; 65c. Cheetah. *Horiz as T* **28**—1s.30, Murchison Falls and Hippopotamus; 2s. Mt Kilimanjaro and Giraffe; 2s.50, Candelabra Tree and Black Rhinoceros; 5s. Crater Lake and Mountains of the Moon; 10s. Ngorongoro Crater and African Buffalo.

The 10c. and 50c. exist in coils with the designs slightly shorter in height, a wider horizontal gutter every eleven stamps and, in the case of the 10c. only, printed with a coarser 200 screen instead of the normal 250. (*Price for* 10c.10p. *unused*.) Plate 2 of 30c. shows coarser 200 screen. (*Price* 25p. *unused*.).

PRINTERS. All the following stamps were printed in photogravure by Harrison, unless otherwise stated.

30 Land Tillage

(Des V. Whiteley)

1963 (21 Mar). *Freedom from Hunger. T* **30** *and similar horiz design*. P 14½.

199	**30**	15c. blue and yellow-olive	25	10
200	–	30c. red-brown and yellow	40	10
201	**30**	50c. blue and orange-brown	50	10
202	–	1s.30 red-brown and light blue	95	1·75
199/202 *Set of 4*			1·90	1·75

Design:—30c., 1s.30, African with Corncob.

31 Scholars and Open Book

1963 (28 June). *Founding of East African University*. P 14½.

203	**31**	30c. lake, violet, black and greenish blue	10	10
204		1s.30 lake, blue, red and light yellow-brown	20	30

32 Red Cross Emblem

(Des V. Whiteley)

1963 (2 Sept). *Centenary of Red Cross*. P 14½.

205	**32**	30c. red and blue	1·40	30
206		50c. red and yellow-brown	1·60	1·25

33 Chrysanthemum Emblems

34

35 East African "Flags"

(Des V. Whiteley)

1964 (21 Oct). *Olympic Games. Tokyo*. P 14½.

207	**33**	30c. yellow and reddish violet	10	10
208	**34**	50c. deep reddish violet and yellow	15	10
209	**35**	1s.30 orange-yellow, deep green and light blue	40	10
210		2s.50 magenta, deep violet-blue and light blue	45	1·40
207/10 *Set of 4*			1·00	1·50

KENYA, UGANDA AND TANZANIA

The following stamps were issued by the East African Postal Administration for use in Uganda, Kenya and Tanzania, excluding Zanzibar.

36 Rally Badge

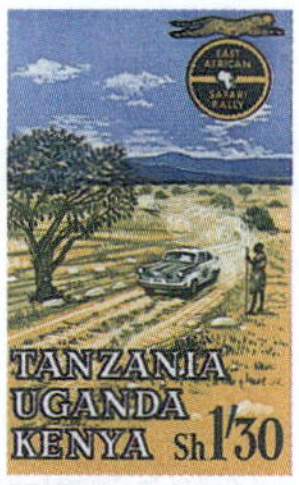

37 Cars *en route*

1965 (15 Apr*). 13*th East African Safari Rally*. P 14.

211	**36**	30c. black, yellow and turquoise	10	10
212		50c. black, yellow and brown	10	10
		a. Imperf (pair)	£800	
213	**37**	1s.30 deep bluish green, yellow-ochre and blue	25	10
214		2s.50 deep bluish green, brown-red and light blue	40	1·50
211/14 *Set of 4*			75	1·60

*This is the local release date. The Crown Agents in London issued the stamps the previous day.

38 I.T.U. Emblem and Symbols

1965 (17 May). *I.T.U. Centenary*. P 14½.

215	**38**	30c. gold, chocolate and magenta	15	10
216		50c. gold, chocolate and grey	15	10
217		1s.30 gold, chocolate and blue	40	10
218		2s.50 gold, chocolate and turquoise-green	75	2·25
215/18 *Set of 4*			1·75	2·25

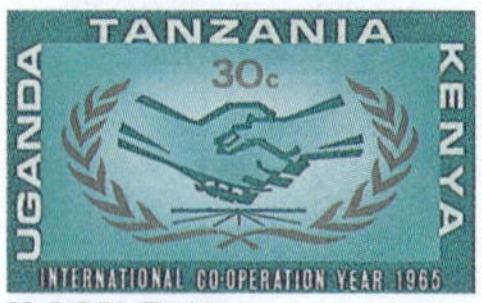

39 I.C.Y. Emblem

1965 (4 Aug). *International Co-operation Year*. P 14½×14.

219	**39**	30c. deep bluish green and gold	10	10
220		50c. black and gold	15	10
221		1s.30 ultramarine and gold	30	10
222		2s.50 carmine-red and gold	75	2·75
219/22 *Set of 4*			1·25	2·75

40 Game Park Lodge, Tanzania

(Des Rena Fennessy)

1966 (4 Apr). *Tourism. T* **40** *and similar horiz designs. Multicoloured*. P 14½.

223		30c. Type **40**	15	10
224		50c. Murchison Falls, Uganda	50	10
		a. Blue omitted	£350	
225		1s.30 Lesser Flamingoes, Lake Nakuru, Kenya	2·75	30
226		2s.50 Deep Sea Fishing, Tanzania	2·00	2·25
223/6 *Set of 4*			4·75	3·00

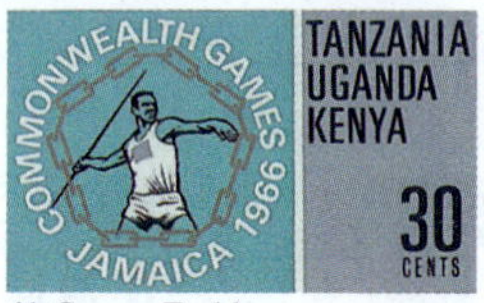

41 Games Emblem

(Des Harrison)

1966 (2 Aug). *Eighth British Empire and Commonwealth Games Jamaica*. P 14½.

227	**41**	30c. black, gold, turq-green & grey	10	10
228		50c. black, gold, cobalt and cerise	15	10
229		1s.30 black, gold, rosine and deep bluish green	20	10
230		2s.50 black, gold, lake and ultramarine	35	1·50
227/30 *Set of 4*			70	1·50

42 U.N.E.S.C.O. Emblem

(Des Harrison)

1966 (3 Oct). *20th Anniv of U.N.E.S.C.O.* P 14½×14.

231	**42**	30c. black, emerald and red	30	10
232		50c. black, emerald and light brown	35	10
233		1s.30 black, emerald and grey	1·00	15
234		2s.50 black, emerald and yellow	1·75	4·25
231/4 *Set of 4*			3·00	4·25

43 De Havilland D.H.89 Dragon Rapide

(Des R. Granger Barrett)

1967 (23 Jan). *21st Anniv of East African Airways. T* **43** *and similar horiz deseigns*. P 14½.

235		30c. slate-violet, greenish blue and myrtle-green	30	10
236		50c. multicoloured	40	10
		a. Red omitted	£425	
237		1s.30 multicoloured	85	30
238		2s.50 multicoloured	1·25	3·00
235/8 *Set of 4*			2·50	3·00

Designs:—50c. Vickers Super VC-10; 1s.30, Hawker Siddeley Comet 4B; 2s.50, Fokker F.27 Friendship.

44 Pillar Tomb

45 Rock Painting

(Des Rena Fennessy)

1967 (2 May). *Archaeological Relics. T* **44/5** *and similar designs*. P 14½.

239		30c. ochre, black and deep reddish purple	15	10
240		50c. orange-red, black and greyish brown	65	10
241		1s.30 black, greenish, yellow and deep yellow-green	85	15
242		2s.50 black, ochre and brown-red	1·40	2·50
239/42 *Set of 4*			2·75	3·00

Designs:—1s.30, Clay head; 2s.50, Proconsul skull.

48 Unified Symbols of Kenya, Tanzania, and Uganda

(Des Rena Fennessy)

1967 (1 Dec). *Foundation of East African Community*. P 14½×14.

243	**48**	5s. gold, black and grey	40	1·50

49 Mountaineering

(Des Rena Fennessy)

1968 (4 Mar). *Mountains of East Africa. T* **49** *and similar horiz designs. Multicoloured. P* 14.

244 30c. Type **49** ... 15 10
245 50c. Mount Kenya ... 30 10
246 1s.30 Mount Kilimanjaro ... 60 10
247 2s.50 Ruwenzori Mountains ... 90 2·25
244/7 *Set of* 4 ... 1·75 2·25

50 Family and Rural Hospital

(Des Rena Fennessy. Litho D.L.R.)

1968 (13 May). *20th Anniv of World Health Organization. T* **50** *and similar horiz designs. P* 13½.

248 30c. deep yellow-green, lilac and chocolate ... 10 10
249 50c. slate-lilac, lilac and black ... 15 10
250 1s.30 yellow-brown, lilac and chocolate ... 20 15
251 2s.50 grey, black and reddish lilac ... 30 1·90
248/51 *Set of* 4 ... 60 2·00

Designs:—50c. Family and nurse; 1s.30, Family and microscope; 2s.50, Family and hypodermic syringe.

51 Olympic Stadium, Mexico City

(Des V. Whiteley)

1968 (14 Oct). *Olympic Games, Mexico. T* **51** *and similar designs. P* 14.

252 30c. light green and black ... 10 10
253 50c. black and blue-green ... 15 10
254 1s.30 carmine-red, black and grey ... 25 15
255 2s.50 blackish brown and yellow-brown ... 35 1·50
252/5 *Set of* 4 ... 70 1·60

Designs: *Horiz*—50c. High-diving boards; 1s.30, Running tracks. *Vert*—2s.50, Boxing ring.

52 *Umoja* (railway ferry)

(Des A. Grosart)

1969 (20 Jan). *Water Transport. T* **52** *and similar horiz designs. P* 14.

256 30c. deep blue, light blue and slate-grey ... 30 10
a. Slate-grey omitted ... 55·00
257 50c. multicoloured ... 35 10
258 1s.30 bronze-grn, greenish blue & blue ... 60 20
259 2s.50 red-orange, dp blue & pale blue ... 1·10 3·25
256/9 *Set of* 4 ... 2·75 3·25

Designs:—50c. S.S. *Harambee*; 1s.30, M.V. *Victoria*; 2s.50, *St. Michael*.

53 I.L.O. Emblem and Agriculture

54 Pope Paul VI and Ruwenzori Mountains

(Des Rena Fennessy)

1969 (14 Apr). *50th Anniv of International Labour Organization. T* **53** *and similar horiz designs. P* 14.

260 30c. black, green and greenish yellow ... 10 10
261 50c. black, plum, cerise and rose ... 10 10
262 1s.30 black, orange-brown and yellow-orange ... 10 10
263 2s.50 black, ultramarine and turquoise-blue ... 20 90
260/3 *Set of* 4 ... 35 1·00

Designs:—50c. I.L.O. emblem and building work; 1s.30, I.L.O. emblem and factory workers; 2s.50, I.L.O. emblem and shipping.

(Des Harrison)

1969 (31 July). *Visit of Pope Paul VI to Uganda. P* 14.

264 **54** 30c. black, gold and royal blue ... 15 10
265 70c. black, gold and claret ... 20 10
266 1s.50 black, gold and deep blue ... 25 20
267 2s.50 black, gold and violet ... 30 1·40
264/7 *Set of* 4 ... 80 1·50

55 Euphorbia Tree shaped as Africa and Emblem

56 Marimba

(Des Rena Fennessy. Litho B.W.)

1969 (8 Dec). *Fifth Anniv of African Development Bank. P* 13½.

268 **55** 30c. deep bluish green, gold and blue-green ... 10 10
269 70c. deep bluish green, gold and reddish purple ... 15 10
270 1s.50 deep bluish green, gold and light turquoise-blue ... 30 10
271 2s.50 deep bluish green, gold and orange-brown ... 35 1·00
268/71 *Set of* 4 ... 75 1·10

(Des Rena Fennessy. Litho B.W.)

1970 (16 Feb). *Musical Instruments. T* **56** *and similar horiz designs. P* 11×12.

272 30c. buff, yellow-brown and bistre-brown ... 15 10
273 70c. olive-green, yellow-brown and yellow ... 25 10
274 1s.50 chocolate and yellow ... 50 10
275 2s.50 salmon, yellow and chocolate ... 75 2·50
272/5 *Set of* 4 ... 1·50 2·50

Designs:— 70c. Amadinda; 1s.50, Nzomari; 2s.50, Adeudeu.

57 Satellite Earth Station

58 Athlete

(Des V. Whiteley. Litho J.W.)

1970 (18 May). *Inauguration of East African Satellite Earth Station. T* **57** *and similar horiz designs. P* 14½×14.

276 30c. multicoloured ... 10 10
277 70c. multicoloured ... 15 10
278 1s.50 black, slate-violet and pale orange ... 25 10
279 2s.50 multicoloured ... 55 2·25
276/9 *Set of* 4 ... 90 2·25

Designs:— 70c. Transmitter in daytime; 1s.50, Transmitter at night; 2s.50, Earth and satellite.

(Des Rena Fennessy. Litho Walsall)

1970 (13 July). *Ninth Commonwealth Games. P* 14×14½.

280 **58** 30c. orange-brown and black ... 10 10
281 70c. olive-green and black ... 10 10
282 1s.50 slate-lilac and black ... 15 10
283 2s.50 turquoise-blue and black ... 20 1·25
280/3 *Set of* 4 ... 40 1·40

59 "25" and U.N. Emblem

(Des Rena Fennessy)

1970 (19 Oct). *25th Anniv of United Nations. P* 14½.

284 **59** 30c. multicoloured ... 10 10
285 70c. multicoloured ... 10 10
286 1s.50 multicoloured ... 20 10
287 2s.50 multicoloured ... 45 2·00
284/7 *Set of* 4 ... 70 2·00

STAMP BOOKLETS

1912–17. *Black on pink cover. Letter rate given as 6 cents per oz. Stapled.*

SB1 1r.80, booklet containing twelve 3c. and twenty four 6c. (Nos. 45/6), each in blocks of 6 ... £1500
a. Letter rate 6 cents per ½oz. Contains Nos. 45*a*/6*a* ...

SB2 2r. booklet containing six 3c. and thirty 6c. (Nos. 45/6), each in blocks of 6 ... £1500

1938. *Black on pink cover. Stapled.*

SB3 3s.40, booklet containing twelve 15c. and eight 20c. (Nos. 137, 139), each in blocks of 4 ... £200

1950–52. *Blue on yellow cover. Stapled.*

SB4 1s. booklet containing four 5c. and eight 10c. (Nos. 133a, 135c), each in blocks of 4 ... £140
a. Contents as SB4, but 10c. changed to No. 136. Stitched (1952) ... 38·00

1954 (3 Sept). *Blue on yellow cover. Stitched.*

SB6 1s. booklet containing four 5c. and eight 10c. (Nos. 167/8), each in blocks of 4 ... 3·00

1958 (16 Jan). *Black on yellow cover. Stitched.*

SB7 5s. booklet containing four 5c., 20c., 30c., 50c. and eight 10c. (Nos. 167/8, 170/1, 173), each in blocks of 4 ... 17·00

1958 (16 Dec)–**59**. *Black on rose-red cover. Stitched.*

SB8 5s. booklet containing 10c., 15c., 20c., 30c. and 50c. (Nos. 168/9, 170/1, 173), in blocks of 4. ... 48·00
a. Contents as No. SB8, but 15c. changed to No. 169a (20.4.59) ... 35·00

1961 (1 Feb). *Black on rose-red cover. Stitched.*

SB9 5s. booklet containing 10c., 15c., 20c., 30c. and 50c. (Nos. 184/6, 188, 190) in blocks of 4 ... 11·00

OFFICIAL STAMPS

For use on official correspondence of the Tanganyika Government.

OFFICIAL
(O **1**)

OFFICIAL
£1 Broken "O" in "OFFICIAL" (R. 1/6).

1959 (1 July). *Nos. 167/71, 173 and 175/80 optd as Type* O **1**.

O1 **18** 5c. black and deep brown ... 10 1·25
O2 **19** 10c. carmine-red ... 20 1·25
O3 **20** 15c. black and light blue (No. 169a) ... 30 1·25
O4 **21** 20c. black and orange ... 20 20
a. Opt double ... — £1300
O5 **18** 30c. black and deep ultramarine ... 15 80
O6 **19** 50c. reddish purple ... 1·00 20
O7 **21** 1s. black and claret ... 20 75
O8 **20** 1s.30 orange and deep lilac ... 5·50 2·00
O9 **22** 2s. black and bronze-green ... 1·25 1·00
O10 **20** 5s. black and orange ... 4·00 3·00
O11 **23** 10s. black and deep ultramarine ... 2·25 4·00
a. Opt at top ... 4·25 2·50
O12 **24** £1 brown-red and black ... 6·50 18·00
a. Broken "O" ... 55·00
O1/12 *Set of* 12 ... 19·00 29·00

The 30c., 50c. and 1s. exist with overprint double, but with the two impressions almost coincident.

OFFICIAL
(O **2**)

OFFICIAL
(O **3**)

1960 (18 Oct). *Nos. 183/6, 188, 190, 192 and 196 optd with Type* O **2** *(cents values) or* O **3**.

O13 5c. Prussian blue ... 10 2·00
O14 10c. yellow-green ... 10 2·00
O15 15c. dull purple ... 10 2·00
a. "Serif" variety ... 10·00
b. "Serif retouched ... 10·00
O16 20c. magenta ... 10 50
O17 30c. vermilion ... 10 10
O18 50c. slate-violet ... 30 1·00
O19 1s. deep reddish violet and reddish purple ... 30 10
a. Re-entry ... 20·00
O20 5s. rose-red and purple ... 17·00 65
O13/20 *Set of* 8 ... 17·00 7·25

The use of these overprints ceased on 8 December 1961.

POSTAGE DUE STAMPS

D **1**

D **2**

(Typo Waterlow)

1928 (Sept)–**33**. Wmk Mult Script CA. P 15×14.

D1 D **1** 5c. violet ... 2·50 50
D2 10c. vermilion ... 2·50 15
D3 20c. yellow-green ... 2·50 3·00
D4 30c. brown (1931) ... 17·00 14·00
D5 40c. dull blue ... 6·50 14·00
D6 1s. grey-green (1933) ... 70·00 £130
D1/6 *Set of* 6 ... 90·00 £150
D1s/6s Optd or Perf (30c., 1s.) "Specimen" *Set of* 6 ... £200

(Typo D.L.R.)

1935 (1 May)–**60**. Wmk Mult Script CA. P 14.

D7 D **2** 5c. violet ... 2·75 1·75
D8 10c. scarlet ... 30 50
D9 20c. green ... 40 50
D10 30c. brown ... 1·25 50
a. Bistre-brown (19.7.60) ... 3·00 8·50
D11 40c. ultramarine ... 1·50 3·00
D12 1s. grey ... 19·00 19·00
D7/12 *Set of* 6 ... 22·00 23·00
D7s/12s Perf "Specimen" *Set of* 6 ... £150

Kuwait

Kuwait, an independent Arab shaikhdom since 1756, placed itself under British protection in 1899 to counter the spread of Ottoman influence in the Arabian Gulf.

The first, somewhat limited, postal service, via Bushire, commenced with the appointment of a Political Agent to Kuwait in August 1904. Because of diplomatic problems this system continued until 21 January 1915 when a regular Indian post office was established.

Limited supplies of Indian stamps were used by the Political Agency postal service, but these became available to the general public from 21 January 1915. Stamps seen postally used from Kuwait before 1923 are usually ½a., 1a., 1r. or 5r. values, with the occasional Official issue. Much more common are values to 15r., both postage and Official, used telegraphically.

Before 1910 the name of the shaikhdom was spelt "KOWEIT" and this spelling appears on various circular postmarks used between 1915 and 1923. The more modern version of the name was first used for a postal cancellation in 1923.

1915 "KOWEIT"

1923 "KUWAIT"

On 1 August 1921 responsibility for the Kuwait postal service passed to the Iraq Post Office.

PRICES FOR STAMPS ON COVER TO 1945

Nos. 1/15	*from* × 5
Nos. 16/29	*from* × 3
Nos. 31/51	*from* × 2
Nos. 52/63	*from* × 4
Nos. O1/27	*from* × 10

USED HIGH VALUES. It is necessary to emphasize that used prices quoted for high value stamps are for postally used examples.

(Currency. 16 annas = 1 rupee)

KUWAIT (1) KUWAIT (2)

1923 (1 Apr)–**24**. *Stamps of India (King George V), optd with T* **1** *or* **2** *(rupee values, 15½ mm) by Indian Govt Ptg Wks.* W **34** (Large Star) of India. P 14.

1	½a. emerald (No. 156)	3·50	8·00
	a. Opt double	£250	
	b. Vert pair, one without opt	£650	
	c. Light green		
2	1a. chocolate (No. 197)	4·00	3·75
	a. Opt double	£350	
	b. Opt omitted (lower stamp of vert pair)	£1100	
3	1½a. chocolate (A) ("ANNA") (No. 163)	3·25	5·50
4	2a. bright reddish violet (No. 169)	3·75	6·00
	a. Reddish purple	6·50	
5	2a.6p. ultramarine (No. 171)	2·75	8·00
6	3a. dull orange (No. 173)	4·25	20·00
7	3a. ultramarine (No. 200) (1924)	9·00	3·00
8	4a. deep olive (No. 174)	8·00	24·00
	a. Olive-green	10·00	
9	6a. brown-ochre (No. 178)	8·50	13·00
10	8a. purple (No. 182)	8·00	38·00
11	12a. carmine-lake (No. 183)	14·00	45·00
	a. Claret	14·00	45·00
12	1r. brown and green (No. 186)	25·00	42·00
	a. Orange-brown and deep turquoise-green	27·00	48·00
13	2r. carmine and brown (No. 187)	48·00	£100
14	5r. ultramarine and violet (No. 188)	95·00	£250
15	10r. green and scarlet (No. 189)	£170	£500
1/15 *Set of* 15		£375	£900

Essays of the overprint using the obsolete spelling "KOWEIT" were prepared in 1923 and can be found on the original 14 values of the postage stamps and on the 13 stamps of the Official series. (*Price per set of 27 unused £25000*).

Nos. 1/4 and 6/7 are all known with inverted overprint (*Price, from £20 each, unused*) and the overprint is also known on examples of India No. 165 ("ANNAS"). It is doubtful if such errors were actually sold at the Kuwait Post Office, although some are known on registered or ordinary covers.

KUWAIT (3) KUWAIT (4)

1929–37. *Stamps of India (King George V, Nasik printing), optd with T* **3** *or* **4** *(rupee values).* W **69** (Mult Stars) of India. P 14.

16	½a. green (No. 202)	3·50	1·40
	aw. Wmk inverted	3·25	2·50
16*b*	½a. green (No. 232) (1934)	4·50	1·40
	bw. Wmk inverted	—	13·00
17	1a. chocolate (No. 203)	7·00	2·50
	aw. Wmk inverted	17·00	6·00
17*b*	1a. chocolate (No. 234) (1934)	7·00	1·25
18	2a. purple (No. 206)	3·25	1·25
19	2a. vermilion (No. 236)	20·00	85·00
	aw. Wmk inverted	20·00	90·00
19*b*	2a. vermilion (No. 236*b*) (1934)	16·00	6·50
19*c*	2a. vermilion (*small die*) (No. 236c) (1937)	4·75	2·50
20	3a. blue (No. 209)	2·75	2·25
21	3a. carmine (No. 237)	5·50	4·25
22	4a. sage-green (*wmk inverted*) (No. 211w)	25·00	80·00
	w. Wmk upright	48·00	
22*a*	4a. pale sage-green (No. 210) (1934)	6·50	14·00
22*b*	6a. bistre (No. 239) (1937)	22·00	55·00
23	8a. reddish purple (No. 212)	23·00	13·00
	w. Wmk inverted	9·00	22·00
24	12a. claret (*wmk inverted*) (No. 213w) (1933)	22·00	40·00
	w. Wmk upright	—	70·00
25	1r. chocolate and green (No. 214)	55·00	29·00
	a. Extended "T"	£425	
	w. Wmk inverted	15·00	
26	2r. carmine and orange (*wmk inverted*) (No. 215w)	15·00	65·00
	a. Extended "T"	£425	£850
	w. Wmk upright	£160	£160
27	5r. ultramarine and purple (No. 216) (1937)	95·00	£275
	a. Extended "T"	£700	
28	10r. green and scarlet (No. 217) (1934)	£200	£450
	a. Extended "T"	£1300	
29	15r. blue and olive (*wmk inverted*) (No. 218w) (1937)	£650	£850
	a. Extended "T"	£2500	
16/29 *Set of* 20		£1000	£1800

The "T" of "KUWAIT" shows a ¾ mm downward extension on R. 3/2, lower left pane.

Nos. 16, 17, 18/19 and 22 are inscribed "INDIA POSTAGE & REVENUE". The remainder are inscribed "INDIA POSTAGE".

No. 19*b* measures 19×22.6 mm and No. 19*c* 18.4×21.8 mm.

Examples of most values are known showing a forged Kuwait postmark dated "11 NOV 37".

1933 (1 Feb)–**34**. *Air. Nos. 220/3 of India optd as T* **2** *(16½ mm.).*

31	2a. deep blue-green	16·00	27·00
	w. Wmk stars to right	16·00	27·00
32	3a. blue	3·50	2·50
	w. Wmk stars to right	3·50	3·25
33	4a. olive-green	£120	£200
34	6a. bistre (2.34)	5·00	4·50
	w. Wmk stars to right	5·00	4·50
31/4 *Set of* 4		£130	£200

The normal sideways watermark on Nos. 31/4 shows stars pointing to left, *as seen from the back of the stamp*.

The 3a. value exists with a most pronounced lithography double print. *Price* £850 *un.*, £650 *used*. Examples of this and other stamps with slight double prints are of little additional value.

1939. *Nos. 248, 250/1, 253, 255/63 of India (King George VI) optd with T* **3** *or* **4** *(rupee values).*

36	½a. red-brown	7·00	1·75
38	1a. carmine	7·00	2·00
39	2a. vermilion	7·50	2·75
41	3a. yellow-green	7·50	2·00
43	4a. brown	38·00	19·00
44	6a. turquoise-green	25·00	11·00
45	8a. slate-violet	28·00	32·00
46	12a. lake	20·00	75·00
47	1r. grey and red-brown	20·00	4·25
	a. Extended "T"	£550	£425
	b. Opt triple, one inverted		
48	2r. purple and brown	5·00	16·00
	a. Extended "T"	£550	£600
49	5r. green and blue	17·00	22·00
	a. Extended "T"	£800	
50	10r. purple and claret	70·00	85·00
	a. Opt double	£550	
	b. Extended "T"	£1100	
51	15r. brown and green	£225	£300
	a. Extended "T"	£1500	
	w. Wmk inverted	£100	£180
36/51w *Set of* 13		£325	£400

On later printings the extended "T" variety was corrected in two stages.

Examples of most values are known showing a forged Kuwait postmark dated "17 NOV 39".

Following the rebellion in Iraq, control of the Kuwait postal service was assumed by the Indian authorities on 24 May 1941.

Unoverprinted stamps of INDIA were used in Kuwait between 1941 and 1945.

1945. *Nos. 265/8 and 269a of India (King George VI, on white background) optd with T* **3**.

52	3p. slate	3·25	6·00
53	½a. purple	1·75	4·00
54	9p. green	3·75	12·00
55	1a. carmine	2·25	2·25
56	1½a. dull violet	4·25	8·50
57	2a. vermilion	4·25	5·50
58	3a. bright violet	5·50	9·50
59	3½a. bright blue	4·25	10·00
60	4a. brown	5·50	3·75
60*a*	6a. turquoise-green	14·00	13·00
61	8a. slate-violet	7·00	7·50
62	12a. lake	8·50	5·50
63	14a. purple	15·00	18·00
52/63 *Set of* 13		70·00	95·00

Following a short period of Pakistani control, from August 1947 the Kuwait postal service passed to British administration on 1 April 1948.

KUWAIT 1 ANNA (5) KUWAIT 5 RUPEES (6)

NOTE. From 1948 onwards, for stamps with similar surcharges, but without name of country, see British Postal Agencies in Eastern Arabia.

1948 (1 Apr)–**49**. *Nos. 470, 475 476a/7 478a and 485/90 of Great Britain (King George VI), surch as T* **5** *or* **6** *(rupee values).*

64	½a. on ½d. pale green	2·25	2·25
65	1a. on 1d. pale scarlet	2·25	1·75
66	1½a. on 1½d. pale red-brown	2·50	1·75
67	2a. on 2d. pale orange	2·25	1·75
68	2½a. on 2½d. light ultramarine	2·50	1·00
69	3a. on 3d. pale violet	2·25	80
	a. Pair, one surch albino		
70	6a. on 6d. purple	2·25	75
71	1r. on 1s. bistre-brown	4·50	2·00
72	2r. on 2s. 6d. yellow-green	5·00	5·50
73	5r. on 5s. red	7·00	5·50
73*a*	10r. on 10s. ultramarine (4.7.49)	45·00	8·00
64/73*a* *Set of* 11		70·00	28·00

KUWAIT 2½ ANNAS (7) KUWAIT 15 RUPEES (8)

1948 (1 May). *Royal Silver Wedding. Nos. 493/4 of Great Britain surch with T* **7** *or* **8**.

74	2½a. on 2½d. ultramarine	2·25	2·50
75	15r. on £1 blue	35·00	38·00
	a. Short bars (R. 3/4)	£160	£180

No. 75a has the bars cancelling the original face value 3 mm long instead of the 3½ mm of the normal surcharge.

1948 (29 July). *Olympic Games. Nos. 495/8 of Great Britain surch as T* **7**, *but in one line (6a.) or two lines (others).*

76	2½a. on 2½d. ultramarine	1·25	3·00
77	3a. on 3d. violet	1·25	3·00
78	6a. on 6d. bright purple	1·50	3·00
79	1r. on 1s. brown	1·50	3·00
76/9 *Set of* 4		5·00	11·00

1949 (10 Oct). *75th Anniv of U.P.U. Nos. 499/502 of Great Britain surch "KUWAIT" and new values.*

80	2½a. on 2½d. ultramarine	1·25	3·25
	a. Lake in India	60·00	
81	3a. on 3d. violet	1·25	3·75
82	6a. on 6d. bright purple	1·25	3·75
83	1r. on 1s. brown	1·25	1·75
80/3 *Set of* 4		4·50	11·00

KUWAIT 2 RUPEES Type I — KUWAIT 2 RUPEES Type II

(8*a*)

KUWAIT 10 RUPEES — KUWAIT 10 RUPEES

(8*b*)

2r. Type I. Type-set surcharge. "2" level with "RUPEES". Surcharge sharp.

Type II. Plate-printed surcharge. "2" raised. Surcharge worn.

10r. Type I. Type-set surcharge. "1" and "O" spaced. Surcharge sharp and clean.

Type II. Plate-printed surcharge. "1" and "O" closer together. Surcharge appears heavy and worn, see especially "A", "R" and "P".

KUWAIT Extra bar in centre (R. 7/2) — KUWAIT Extra bar at top (R. 2/2)

1950 (2 Oct)–**54**. *Nos. 503/11 of Great Britain (King George VI) surch as T* **5** *or* **8a/b** *(rupee values).*

84	½a. on ½d. pale orange (3.5.51)	2·50	1·50
85	1a. on 1d. light ultramarine (3.5.51)	2·50	1·60
86	1½a. on 1½d. pale green (3.5.51)	2·50	2·25
87	2a. on 2d. pale red-brown (3.5.51)	2·50	1·50
88	2½a. on 2½d. pale scarlet (3.5.51)	2·50	2·75
89	4a. on 4d. light ultramarine	2·75	1·50

90 2r. on 2s. 6d. yellow-green (I) (3.5.51) 19·00 5·00
a. Extra bar in centre £750 £500
b. Type II surch (1954) £250 50·00
91 5r. on 5s. red (3.5.51) 27·00 6·00
a. Extra bar at top £500 £400
92 10r. on 10s. ultramarine (I) (3.5.51) 38·00 10·00
a. Type II surch (1952) £275 60·00
84/92 *Set of 9* 90·00 29·00

No. 92a is known with surch spaced 10 mm apart instead of 9 mm.

1952 (10 Dec)–**54**. *Nos. 515/21, 523 and 530/1 of Great Britain (Queen Elizabeth II.* W **153**), surch as T **5** (in two lines only on 2½ and 6a.).

93 ½a. on ½d. orange-red (31.8.53) 20 1·75
94 1a. on 1d. ultramarine (31.8.53) 20 10
95 1½a. on 1½d. green 15 1·75
96 2a. on 2d. red-brown (31.8.53) 35 10
97 2½a. on 2½d. carmine-red 15 1·75
98 3a. on 3d. deep lilac (B.) (18.1.54) 40 10
99 4a. on 4d. ultramarine (2.11.53) 1·25 1·00
100 6a. on 6d. reddish purple (18.1.54) 2·00 10
101 12a. on 1s.3d. green (2.11.53) 5·50 2·50
102 1r. on 1s.6d. grey-blue (2.11.53) 4·50 10
93/102 *Set of 10* 13·00 8·00

1953 (3 June). *Coronation. Nos. 532/5 (Queen Elizabeth) of Great Britain surch "KUWAIT" and new values.*

103 2½a. on 2½d. carmine-red 3·50 3·50
104 4a. on 4d. ultramarine 3·50 3·50
105 12a. on 1s.3d. deep yellow-green 5·00 5·50
106 1r. on 1s.6d. deep grey-blue 4·00 1·25
103/6 *Set of 4* 14·50 12·50

KUWAIT 2 RUPEES
I

KUWAIT 2 RUPEES
II
(9)

KUWAIT 5 RUPEES
I

KUWAIT 5 RUPEES
II
(10)

KUWAIT 10 RUPEES
I

KUWAIT 10 RUPEES
II
(11)

Type I (**9/11**). Type-set overprints by Waterlow. Bold (generally thicker) letters with sharp corners and straight edges. Bars close together and usually slightly longer than in Type II.

Type II (**9/11**). Plate-printed overprints by Harrison. Thinner letters, rounder corners and rough edges. Bars wider apart.

1955 (23 Sept)–**57**. *Nos. 536/8 of Great Britain ("Castles" high values) surch with T* **9/11**.

107 2r. o n 2s.6d.black-brown (I) 9·50 2·50
a. Type II (10.10.57) 75·00 7·00
108 5r. on 5s. rose-carmine (I) 9·50 7·00
a. Type II (10.10.57) £120 30·00
109 10r. on 10s. ultramarine (I) 9·50 4·75
a. Type II (10.10.57) £180 £120
107/9 *Set of 3* 26·00 13·00
107a/9a *Set of 3* £350 £140

1956. *Nos. 540/6, 548 and 555/6 of Great Britain (Queen Elizabeth II.* W **165**) surch as T **5** (in two lines only on 2½ and 6a.).

110 ½a. on ½d. orange-red 30 1·50
111 1a. on 1d. ultramarine 50 3·00
112 1½a. on 1½d. green 40 70
113 2a. on 2d. red-brown 40 50
114 2½a. on 2½d. carmine-red 60 3·50
116 4a. on 4d. ultramarine 4·75 3·25
117 6a. on 6d. reddish purple 2·25 40
118 12a. on 1s.3d. green 9·50 8·00
119 1r. on 1s.6d. grey-blue 7·00 30
110/19 *Set of 9* 23·00 19·00

KUWAIT NP 1 NP (12) KUWAIT NP 3 NP (13) KUWAIT 75 NP (14)

1957 (1 June)–**58**. *Nos. 540/2, 543a/8, 551 and 555 of Great Britain (Queen Elizabeth II.* W **165**) surch as T **12** (1, 15, 25, 40, 50n.p.), **14** (75n.p.) or **13** (others).

120 1n.p. on 5d. brown 10 70
121 3n.p. on ½d. orange-red 60 3·75
122 6n.p. on 1d. ultramarine 60 1·25
123 9n.p. on 1½d. green 60 2·75
124 12n.p. on 2d. light red-brown 60 3·75
125 15n.p. on 2½d. carmine-red (Type I) 60 4·25
a. Type II (11.58) 38·00 80·00
126 20n.p. on 3d. deep lilac (B.) 60 30
127 25n.p. on 4d. ultramarine 2·75 3·25
128 40n.p. on 6d. reddish purple 1·00 30
129 50n.p. on 9d. bronze-green 5·50 4·00
130 75n.p. on 1s.3d. green 6·00 4·75
120/30 *Set of 11* 17·00 26·00

20 Shaikh Abdullah

(Recess De La Rue)

1958 (1 Feb)–**59**. *T* **20/21** *and similar designs.* P 12½ (Nos. 131/6), 13½×13.

131 **20** 5n.p. bluish green 55 10
132 10n.p. rose-red 55 10
136 40n.p. maroon 2·10 65
131/6 *Set of 3* 3·00 75

Nos. 131/6 were only valid for internal use in Kuwait prior to 1 February 1959. Further values were added to this series following the closure of the British Agency Post Offices on 31 January 1959. Responsibility of the postal service then passed to the Kuwait Government and later issues are listed in Part 19 (*Middle East*) of this catalogue.

OFFICIAL STAMPS

KUWAIT SERVICE (O 1) KUWAIT SERVICE (O 2)

1923–24. *Stamps of India (King George V), optd with Type* O **1** *or* O 2 *(rupee values, 15½–16 mm).* W **34** (Large Star) of India. P 14.

O1 ½a. light green (No. 155) 3·50 30·00
a. Opt double, one albino 90·00
O2 1a. chocolate (No. 197) 3·25 19·00
a. Opt double, one albino 85·00
O3 1½a. chocolate (A) (No. 163) 3·50 48·00
O4 2a. bright reddish violet (No. 169) 6·50 32·00
a. Reddish purple 8·50
O5 2a.6p. ultramarine (No. 171) 4·50 75·00
O6 3a. dull orange (No. 173) 3·50 70·00
O7 3a. ultramarine (No. 200) (1924) 5·00 60·00
O8 4a. olive-green (No. 175) 3·50 65·00
O9 8a. purple (No. 182) 6·00 £110
O10 1r. brown and green (No. 186) 22·00 £180
a. Orange-brown and deep turquoise-green 26·00
b. Opt double, one albino £130
O11 2r. carmine and brown (No. 187) 22·00 £250
O12 5r. ultramarine and violet (No. 188) 90·00 £450
a. Opt double, one albino £150
O13 10r. green and scarlet (No. 189) £160 £375
O14 15r. blue and olive (No. 190) £225 £550
O1/14 *Set of 14* £500 £2000

1929–33. *Nos. 203, 206, 209 and 211/18w of India (King George V, Nasik printing) optd as Types* O **1** *(spaced 10 mm) or* O **2** *(14½ mm ×19–20 mm wide).* W **69** (Mult Stars) of India. P 14.

O16 1a. chocolate
w. Wmk inverted 4·50 29·00
O17 2a. purple 55·00 £190
O19 3a. blue 4·50 42·00
O20 4a. sage-green 4·25 80·00
w. Wmk inverted
O21 8a. reddish purple 5·00 £110
w. Wmk inverted 8·50
O22 12a. claret 29·00 £200
w. Wmk inverted 50·00
O23 1r. chocolate and green 6·50 £225
O24 2r. carmine and orange (*wmk inverted*) 11·00 £350
O25 5r. ultramarine and purple (*wmk inverted*) 32·00 £450
O26 10r. green and scarlet 65·00 £700
O27 15r. blue and olive (*wmk inverted*) £170 £1300
O16w/27 *Set of 11* £350 £3250

Labuan *see* **North Borneo**

Lagos *see* **Nigeria**

Leeward Islands

The Federal Colony of the Leeward Islands was constituted in 1871 formalising links between Antigua, British Virgin Islands, Dominica, Montserrat and St. Kitts-Nevis which stretched back to the 1670s. Issues for the individual islands were superseded by those inscribed "LEEWARD ISLANDS", but were in concurrent use with them from 1903 (British Virgin Islands from 1899). Dominica was transferred to the Windward Islands on 31 December 1939.

PRICES FOR STAMPS ON COVER TO 1945	
Nos. 1/8	*from* × 10
Nos. 9/16	*from* × 12
Nos. 17/19	*from* × 8
Nos. 20/8	*from* × 5
Nos. 29/35	*from* × 4
Nos. 36/45	*from* × 5
Nos. 46/57	*from* × 4
Nos. 58/87	*from* × 5
Nos. 88/91	*from* × 6
Nos. 92/4	*from* × 10
Nos. 95/114	*from* × 5

PRINTERS. All the stamps of Leeward Islands were typographed by De La Rue & Co, Ltd, London, *except where otherwise stated.*

1

2

1890 (31 Oct). *Name and value in second colour.* Wmk Crown CA. P 14.

1 **1** ½d. dull mauve and green 3·50 1·25
2 1d. dull mauve and rose 5·00 20
3 2½d. dull mauve and blue 6·50 20
w. Wmk inverted £325 £180
4 4d. dull mauve and orange 6·00 8·50
5 6d. dull mauve and brown 11·00 13·00
6 7d. dull mauve and slate 6·50 13·00
7 **2** 1s. green and carmine 23·00 50·00
8 5s. green and blue £120 £250
1/8 *Set of 8* £160 £300
1s/8s Optd "Specimen" *Set of 8* £200

The colours of this issue are fugitive.

(3)

One Penny (4) One Penny (5)

1897 (22 July) *Queen Victoria's Diamond Jubilee. Handstamped with T* **3**.

9 **1** ½d. dull mauve and green 5·00 17·00
a. Opt double £1400
10 1d. dull mauve and rose 6·00 17·00
a. Opt double £1000
b. Opt triple £3250
11 2½d. dull mauve and blue 6·50 17·00
a. Opt double £1200
12 4d. dull mauve and orange 45·00 75·00
a. Opt double £1200
13 6d. dull mauve and brown 50·00 £100
a. Opt double £1500
14 7d. dull mauve and slate 50·00 95·00
a. Opt double £1500
15 **2** 1s. green and carmine £120 £200
a. Opt double £2000
16 5s. green and blue £450 £750
a. Opt double £5500
9/16 *Set of 8* £600 £1100

Beware of forgeries.

1902 (11 Aug). *Nos. 4/6 surch locally.*

17 **4** 1d. on 4d. dull mauve and orange 4·00 7·00
a. Pair, one with tall narrow "O" in "One" 38·00 75·00
b. Surch double
18 1d. on 6d. dull mauve and brown 5·00 11·00
a. Pair, one with tall narrow "O" in "One" 55·00 £130
19 **5** 1d. on 7d. dull mauve and slate 4·50 9·00
17/19 *Set of 3* 12·00 24·00

The tall narrow "O" variety occurred on R. 1/1, 5/3, 5/5 and 7/4.

6

7

8

Wide "A" (R. 6/1 of both panes. Replaced in 1912)

Dropped "R" (R.1/1 of both panes from Pl 2 (1st ptg only))

1902 (1 Sept–Oct). Wmk Crown CA. P 14.

20 **6** ½d. dull purple and green 5·50 1·00
21 1d. dull purple and carmine 7·00 20
22 **7** 2d. dull purple and ochre (Oct) 2·75 4·25
23 **6** 2½d. dull purple and ultramarine 5·50 2·25
a. Wide "A" in "LEEWARD" £250 £160
24 **7** 3d. dull purple and black (Oct) 5·50 7·50
25 **6** 6d. dull purple and brown 2·50 8·00
26 **8** 1s. green and carmine 4·50 19·00
a. Dropped "R" in "LEEWARD" £375 £550
27 **7** 2s.6d. green and black (Oct) 27·00 75·00
28 **8** 5s. green and blue 50·00 80·00
20/8 *Set of 9* £100 £180
20s/8s Optd "Specimen" *Set of 9* £140

1905 (Apr)–**08**. Wmk Mult Crown CA. *Ordinary paper (½d., 3d.) or chalk-surfaced paper (others).*

29 **6** ½d. dull purple and green (2.06) 3·50 2·00
a. Chalk-surfaced paper (25.7.08) 24·00 15·00
30 1d. dull purple and carmine (29.8.06) 8·50 80
31 **7** 2d. dull purple and ochre (25.7.08) 6·50 18·00

32	**6**	2½d. dull purple and ultramarine (23.7.06)	65·00	42·00
		a. Wide "A" in "LEEWARD"	£600	£425
33	**7**	3d. dull purple and black	16·00	48·00
		a. Chalk-surfaced paper (18.4.08)	50·00	85·00
34	**6**	6d. dull purple and brown (15.7.08)	48·00	75·00
35	**8**	1s. green and carmine (15.7.08)	42·00	£110
29/35 *Set of* 7			£170	£275

1907 (14 Apr)–**11**. Wmk Mult Crown CA. *Chalk-surfaced paper (3d. to 5s.)*. P 14.

36	**7**	¼d. brown (7.8.09)	2·75	1·75
37	**6**	½d. dull green	3·50	1·25
38		1d. bright red (7.07)	10·00	80
		a. Rose-carmine (1910)	38·00	3·50
39	**7**	2d. grey (3.8.11)	3·50	7·50
40	**6**	2½d. bright blue (5.07)	7·50	4·25
		a. Wide "A" in "LEEWARD"	£275	£180
41	**7**	3d. purple/*yellow* (28.10.10)	3·50	7·50
42	**6**	6d. dull and bright purple (3.8.11)	8·50	7·00
43	**8**	1s. black/*green* (3.8.11)	5·50	21·00
44	**7**	2s.6d. black and red/*blue* (15.9.11)	40·00	48·00
45	**8**	5s. green and red/*yellow* (21.11.10)	42·00	65·00
36/45 *Set of* 10			£110	£150
36s/45s Optd "Specimen" *Set of* 10			£225	

10

11

12

13

1912 (23 Oct)–**22**. *Die I (¼d. to 3d., 6d., 1s., 2s.6d. 5s.) or Die II (4d., 2s.)*. Wmk Mult Crown CA. *Chalk-surfaced paper (3d. to 5s.)*. P 14.

46	**10**	¼d. brown	1·75	1·00
		a. Pale brown	3·50	2·00
47	**11**	½d. yellow-green (12.12)	5·50	2·00
		a. Deep green (1916)	5·50	1·50
48		1d. red	5·00	1·00
		a. Bright scarlet (8.15)	8·00	1·00
49	**10**	2d. slate-grey (9.1.13)	4·00	5·50
50	**11**	2½d. bright blue	3·25	7·00
		a. Deep bright blue (1914)	4·00	4·00
51	**10**	3d. purple/*yellow* (9.1.13)	1·75	14·00
		a. White back (11.13)	70·00	£150
		as. Optd "Specimen"	48·00	
		b. On lemon (11.14)	5·50	17·00
		c. On buff (1920)	35·00	50·00
		cs. Optd "Specimen"	45·00	
		d. On orange-buff (1920)	4·75	17·00
		dw. Wmk inverted	£375	
52		4d. black and red/*pale yellow* (Die II) (12.5.22)	5·00	22·00
53	**11**	6d. dull and bright purple (9.1.13)	3·00	8·00
54	**12**	1s. black/*green* (9.1.13)	3·00	8·00
		a. White back (11.13)	60·00	38·00
		as. Optd "Specimen"	50·00	
		b. On blue-green, olive back (1917)	10·00	8·00
		bs. Optd "Specimen"	50·00	
55	**10**	2s. purple and blue/*blue* (Die II) (12.5.22)	12·00	60·00
56		2s.6d. black and red/*blue* (11.13)	16·00	48·00
57	**12**	5s. green and red/*yellow* (9.14)	55·00	£100
		a. White back (11.13)	45·00	80·00
		as. Optd "Specimen"	60·00	
		b. On lemon (1915)	32·00	75·00
		c. On orange-buff (1920)	£110	£190
46/57*b* *Set of* 12			85·00	£225
46s/57s Optd "Specimen" *Set of* 12			£275	

Nos. 51a, 54a and 57a were only on sale from Montserrat.

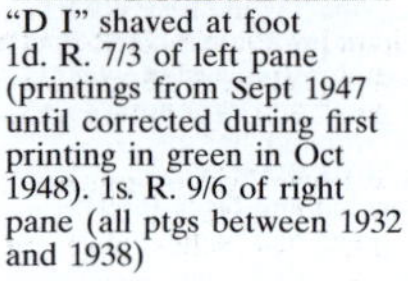

"D I" shaved at foot 1d. R. 7/3 of left pane (printings from Sept 1947 until corrected during first printing in green in Oct 1948). 1s. R. 9/6 of right pane (all ptgs between 1932 and 1938)

1921 (Oct)–**32**. Wmk Mult Script CA or Mult Crown CA (£1). *Chalk-surfaced paper (3d. to £1)*. P 14.

(a) Die II (1921–29).

58	**10**	¼d. brown (1.4.22)	2·25	1·00
59	**11**	½d. blue-green	1·25	75
60		1d. carmine-red	2·25	55
61		1d. bright violet (21.8.22)	2·25	1·00
62		1d. bright scarlet (1929)	11·00	2·25
63	**10**	1½d. carmine-red (10.9.26)	3·50	2·00
64		1½d. red-brown (1929)	1·25	10
65		2d. slate-grey (6.22)	2·00	80
		w. Wmk inverted	†	£225
		x. Wmk reversed		
66	**11**	2½d. orange-yellow (22.9.23)	7·00	55·00
67		2½d. bright blue (1.3.27)	3·50	1·25
68	**10**	3d. light ultramarine (22.9.23)	8·50	27·00
		a. Deep ultramarine (1925)	55·00	55·00
69		3d. purple/*yellow* (1.7.27)	2·00	6·50
70		4d. black and red/*pale yellow* (2.24)	3·00	21·00
71		5d. dull purple and olive-green (12.5.22)	2·50	4·25
72	**11**	6d. dull and bright purple (17.7.23)	12·00	30·00
73	**12**	1s. black/*emerald* (17.7.23)	8·00	8·00
74	**10**	2s. purple and blue/*blue* (12.5.22)	18·00	45·00
		a. Red-purple and blue/blue (1926)	7·50	48·00
		aw. Wmk inverted	£325	
75		2s.6d. black and red/*blue* (17.7.23)	6·50	23·00
76		3s. bright green and violet (12.5.22)	12·00	28·00
77		4s. black and red (12.5.22)	14·00	42·00
78	**12**	5s. green and red/*pale yellow* (17.7.23)	42·00	75·00
79	**13**	10s. green and red/*green* (1928)	70·00	£110
		a. Break in scroll	£275	
		b. Broken crown and scroll	£275	
		c. Nick in top right scroll	£275	
		e. Break in lines below left scroll	£275	
		f. Damaged leaf at bottom right	£275	
80		£1 purple and black/*red* (1928)	£225	£275
		a. Break in scroll	£475	
		b. Broken crown and scroll	£475	
		e. Break in lines below left scroll	£475	
		f. Damaged leaf at bottom right	£475	
58/80 *Set of* 22			£400	£700
58s/80s Optd or Perf (1d bright scarlet, 1½ red-brown, 10s. £1) "Specimen" *Set of* 23			£550	

(b) Reversion to Die I (Plate 23) (1931–32).

81	**10**	¼d. brown	9·00	16·00
82	**11**	½d. blue-green	27·00	40·00
83		1d. bright scarlet	35·00	1·00
84	**10**	1½d. red-brown	4·25	2·75
85	**11**	2½d. bright blue	7·00	3·50
86		6d. dull and bright purple	25·00	85·00
87	**12**	1s. black/*emerald*	55·00	75·00
		a. "D I" flaw	£500	
		b. "A" of "CA" missing from wmk	–	£2000
81/7 *Set of* 7			£140	£200

No. 68*a* was issued in St. Kitts-Nevis.

Nos. 59, 62 and 82/3 exist in coils, constructed from normal sheets. No. 82 was only issued in this form.

For illustrations of varieties on Nos. 79/80 see above No. 51*b* of Bermuda.

Nos. 81/7 result from the use, in error, of Die I which had previously been "retired" in late 1920, to produce Plate 23.

1935 (6 May). *Silver Jubilee. As Nos. 91/4 of Antigua, but printed by Waterlow.* P 11×12.

88		1d. deep blue and scarlet	1·60	2·00
89		1½d. ultramarine and grey	2·25	1·00
90		2½d. brown and deep blue	2·75	3·50
91		1s. slate and purple	17·00	24·00
		k. Kite and vertical log	£400	
		l. Kite and horizontal log	£425	
88/91 *Set of* 4			21·00	27·00
88s/91s Perf "Specimen" *Set of* 4			£120	

For illustrations of plate varieties see Omnibus section following Zanzibar.

1937 (12 May). *Coronation. As Nos. 95/7 of Antigua, but printed by D.L.R.*

92		1d. scarlet	80	75
93		1½d. buff	80	1·40
94		2½d. bright blue	90	1·40
92/4 *Set of* 3			2·25	3·25
92s/4s Perf "Specimen" *Set of* 3			90·00	

14

15

(Die A)

(Die B)

In Die B the figure "1" has a broader top and more projecting serif.

"ISI.ANDS" flaw (R. 1/2 of right pane) (Pl. 2 ptg of May 1944)

Broken second "E" in "LEEWARD" (R. 4/1 of right pane) (Pl. 2 and 3 ptgs from November 1942 until corrected in June 1949) (The similar variety on the 5s. shows traces of the top bar)

Broken top right scroll (R. 5/11) (1942 ptg of 10s. only. Corrected on £1 value from same period)

Broken lower right scroll (R. 5/12. 1942 ptgs only)

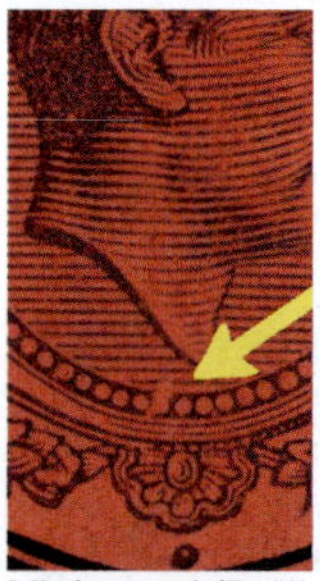

Missing pearl (R. 5/1. 1944 ptgs only)

Gash in chin (R. 2/5. 1942 ptgs only)

1938 (25 Nov)–**51**. *T* **14** *(and similar type, but shaded value tablet, ½d., 1d., 2½d., 6d.) and* **15** *(10s., £1). Chalk-surfaced paper (3d. to £1).* P 14.

(a) Wmk Mult Script CA.

95		¼d. brown	60	1·50
		a. Chalk-surfaced paper. *Deep brown* (13.6.49)	30	1·75
96		½d. emerald	70	70
		a. "ISIANDS" flaw	95·00	
97		½d. slate-grey (*chalk-surfaced paper*) (1.7.49)	1·50	1·50
98		1d. scarlet (Die A)	9·50	2·50
99		1d. scarlet (*shades*) (Die B) (1940)	2·25	1·75
		a. "D I" flaw (9.47)	£200	
		b. Carmine (9.42)	1·50	8·00
		c. Red (13.9.48)	6·00	4·00
		ca. "D I" flaw	£200	
100		1d. blue-green (*chalk-surfaced paper*) (1.7.49)	55	15
		a. "D I" flaw	£180	£180
101		1½d. chestnut	1·00	50
102		1½d. yellow-orange and black (*chalk-surfaced paper*) (1.7.49)	85	40
103		2d. olive-grey	3·00	1·50
		a. Slate-grey (11.42)	5·50	3·00
104		2d. scarlet (*chalk-surfaced paper*) (1.7.49)	1·40	1·25
105		2½d. bright blue	20·00	2·50
		a. Light bright blue (11.42)	80	1·25
106		2½d. black and purple (*chalk-surfaced paper*) (1.7.49)	55	15
107		3d. orange	35·00	2·75
		a. Ordinary paper. *Pale orange* (3.42)	50	85
108		3d. bright blue (1.7.49)	65	15
109		6d. deep dull purple and bright purple	23·00	5·50
		a. Ordinary paper (3.42)	8·00	2·75
		ab. Broken "E"	£425	£375
		b. Purple and deep magenta (29.9.47)	9·50	3·75
		ba. Broken "E"	£500	£425
110		1s. black/*emerald*	16·00	2·00
		a. "D I" flaw	£500	
		b. Ordinary paper (3.42)	4·25	1·00
		ba. Grey and black/emerald (8.42)	18·00	4·00
		bb. Black and grey/emerald (11.42)	£130	13·00
111		2s. reddish purple and blue/*blue*	21·00	2·75
		a. Ordinary paper (3.42)	10·00	2·00
		ab. Deep purple and blue/blue (29.9.47)	11·00	2·50
112		5s. green and red/*yellow*	48·00	18·00
		a. Broken "E" (R. 4/3 of left pane)	£1100	£700
		b. Ordinary paper (12.43)	32·00	15·00
		ba. Broken "E" (R. 4/3 of left pane)	£900	
		c. Bright green and red/yellow (24.10.51)	55·00	50·00
113		10s. bluish green and deep red/*green*	£200	£130
		a. Ordinary paper. *Pale green and dull red/green* (26.6.44*)	£650	£325
		ad. Broken top right scroll	£3750	
		ae. Broken lower right scroll	£3750	£3750
		af. Gash in chin	£3750	£3750
		b. Ordinary paper. *Green and red/green* (22.2.45*)	£150	80·00
		c. Ordinary paper. *Deep green and deep vermilion/green* (15.10.47*)	£120	80·00
		ca. Missing pearl	£1500	

(b) Wmk Mult Crown CA

114		£1 brown-purple and black/*red*	£350	£300
		a. Purple and black/carmine (21.9.42*)	85·00	48·00
		ae. Broken lower right scroll	£1400	£800
		af. Gash in chin	£1400	£800
		b. Brown-purple and black/salmon (5.2.45*)	38·00	25·00
		ba. Missing pearl	£1200	£850
		c. Perf 13. *Violet and black/scarlet* (4.1.52*)	32·00	38·00

		ca. Wmk sideways	£4500	
		cw. Wmk inverted	£4500	
95/114*b*		*Set of* 19	£190	£120
95s/114s		Perf "Specimen" *Set of* 13	£500	

*Dates quoted for Nos. 113a/14c are earliest known postmark dates. Nos. 113a and 114*a* were despatched to the Leeward Islands in March 1942, Nos. 113b and 114*b* in December 1943, No. 113c in June 1944 and No. 114c on 13 December 1951.

Nos. 96, 98 and 99 exist in coils constructed from normal sheets.

Printings of the 10s. in March 1942 (No. 113a) and of the £1 in February and October 1942 (No. 114*a*) were made by Williams Lea & Co. Ltd. following bomb damage to the De La Rue works in 1940.

For illustrations of Nos. 99a, 99ca, 100a and 110a see above No. 58.

1946 (1 Nov). *Victory. As Nos. 110/11 of Antigua.*

115		1½d. brown	15	75
116		3d. red-orange	15	75
115s/16s		Perf "Specimen" *Set of* 2	85·00	

1949 (2 Jan). *Royal Silver Wedding. As Nos. 112/13 of Antigua.*

117		2½d. ultramarine	10	10
118		5s. green	4·50	4·50

1949 (10 Oct). *75th Anniv of Universal Postal Union. As Nos. 114/17 of Antigua.*

119		2½d. blue-black	15	2·25
120		3d. deep blue	2·00	2·25
121		6d. magenta	15	2·25
122		1s. blue-green	15	2·25
119/22		*Set of* 4	2·25	8·25

(New Currency. 100 cents = 1 B.W.I. dollar)

1951 (16 Feb). *Inauguration of B.W.I. University College. As Nos. 118/19 of Antigua.*

123		3c. orange and black	30	1·75
124		12c. rose-carmine and reddish violet	70	1·75

1953 (2 June). *Coronation. As No. 120 of Antigua.*

125		3c. black and green	60	2·25

16 Queen Elizabeth II

17

1954 (22 Feb). *Chalk-surfaced paper.* Wmk Mult Script CA. P 14 (T **16**) or 13 (T **17**).

126	**16**	½c. brown	10	60
127		1c. grey	1·25	1·25
128		2c. green	1·75	10
129		3c. yellow-orange and black	2·50	1·00
130		4c. rose-red	1·75	10
131		5c. black and brown-purple	2·25	1·00
132		6c. yellow-orange	2·25	60
133		8c. ultramarine	2·50	10
134		12c. dull and reddish purple	2·00	10
135		24c. black and green	2·00	20
136		48c. dull purple and ultramarine	6·50	2·75
137		60c. brown and green	6·00	2·25
138		$1.20 yellow-green and rose-red	6·00	3·25
139	**17**	$2.40 bluish green and red	8·50	5·50
140		$4.80 brown-purple and black	10·00	8·50
126/40		*Set of* 15	50·00	24·00

The 3c., 4c., 6c., 8c., 24c., 48c., 60c. and $1.20 have their value tablets unshaded.

The stamps of Leeward Islands were withdrawn and invalidated on 1 July 1956 when the federal colony was dissolved.

Lesotho

INDEPENDENT KINGDOM

King Moshoeshoe II, 4 October 1966–November 1990 (deposed)

33 Moshoeshoe I and Moshoeshoe II

(Des and photo Harrison)

1966 (4 Oct). *Independence.* P 12½×13.

106	**33**	2½c. light brown, black and red	10	10
107		5c. light brown, black and new blue	10	10
108		10c. light brown, black and emerald	15	10
109		20c. light brown, black and bright purple	20	15
106/9		*Set of* 4	45	30

LESOTHO
(34)

35 "Education Culture and Science"

1966 (1 Nov). *Stamps of Basutoland optd as T* **34**.

A. On Nos. 69/71 and 73/9 (Script CA wmk)

110A		½c. grey-black and sepia	10	10
111A		1c. grey-black and bluish green	10	10
112A		2c. deep bright blue and orange	60	10
114A		3½c. indigo and deep ultramarine	30	10
115A		5c. chestnut and deep grey-green	10	10
116A		10c. bronze-green and purple	10	10
117A		12½c. brown and turquoise-green	4·50	35
118A		25c. deep ultramarine and crimson	30	20
119A		50c. black and carmine-red	80	1·00
120A		1r. black and maroon	1·00	4·00
		a. "LSEOTHO"	65·00	
		b. Opt double	£110	
		ba. Ditto. "LSEOTHO"		
110A/20A		*Set of* 10	7·00	5·00

B. On Nos. 84/92 and unissued 1r. (wmk w **12**).

111B		1c. grey-black and bluish green	10	10
113B		2½c. pale yellow-green and rose-red	50	10
115B		5c. chestnut and deep grey-green	20	10
117B		12½c. brown and turquoise-green	30	20
119B		50c. black and carmine-red	70	50
120B		1r. black and maroon	65	75
		a. "LSEOTHO"	42·00	50·00
111B/20B		*Set of* 6	2·00	1·40

(Des V. Whiteley. Litho D.L.R.)

1966 (1 Dec). *20th Anniv of U.N.E.S.C.O.* P 14½×14.

121	**35**	2½c. orange-yellow and emerald-green	10	10
122		5c. light green and olive	15	10
123		12½c. light blue and red	35	15
124		25c. red-orange and deep greenish blue	60	75
121/4		*Set of* 4	1·10	50

36 Maize

37 Moshoeshoe II

(Des and photo Harrison)

1967 (1 Apr). *Designs as T* **36/7**. No wmk. P 14½×13½ (2r.) or 13½×14½ (others).

125		½c. bluish green and light bluish violet	10	10
126		1c. sepia and rose-red	10	10
127		2c. orange-yellow and light green	10	1·00
128		2½c. black and ochre	10	10
129		3½c. chalky blue and yellow	10	30
130		5c. bistre and new blue	20	10
131		10c. yellow-brown and bluish grey	10	10
132		12½c. black and red-orange	20	10
133		25c. black and bright blue	55	20
134		50c. black, new blue and turquoise	4·50	1·50
135		1r. multicoloured	65	75
136		2r. black, gold and magenta	1·00	1·75
125/36		*Set of* 12	6·25	5·00

Designs: *Horiz as T* **36**—1c. Cattle; 2c. Agaves (wrongly inscr "Aloes"); 2½c. Basotho Hat; 3½c. Merino Sheep ("Wool"); 5c. Basotho Pony; 10c. Wheat; 12½c. Angora Goat ("Mohair"); 25c. Maletsunyane Falls; 50c. Diamonds; 1r. Arms of Lesotho.

See also Nos. 147/59 and 191/203.

46 Students and University

(Des V. Whiteley. Photo Harrison)

1967 (7 Apr). *First Conferment of University Degrees.* P 14×14½.

137	**46**	1c. sepia, ultramarine and light yellow-orange	10	10
138		2½c. sepia, ultramarine and light greenish blue	10	10
139		12½c. sepia, ultramarine and rose	10	10
140		25c. sepia, ultramarine and light violet	15	15
137/40		*Set of* 4	30	30

47 Statue of Moshoeshoe I

(Des and photo Harrison)

1967 (4 Oct). *First Anniv of Independence. T* **47** *and similar triangular designs.* P 14½×14.

141		2½c. black and light yellow-green	10	10
142		12½c. multicoloured	25	15
143		25c. black, green and light ochre	35	25
141/3		*Set of* 3	65	40

Designs:—12½c. Lesotho flag; 25c. Crocodile (national emblem).

50 Lord Baden-Powell and Scout Saluting

(Des V. Whiteley. Photo Harrison)

1967 (1 Nov). *60th Anniv of Scout Movement.* P 14×14½.

144	**50**	15c. multicoloured	20	10

51 W.H.O. Emblem and World Map

(Des G. Vasarhelyi. Photo Harrison)

1968 (7 Apr). *20th Anniv of World Health Organization. T* **51** *and similar horiz design.* P 14×14½.

145		2½c. blue, gold and carmine-red	15	10
		a. Gold (emblem) omitted		
146		25c. multicoloured	45	60

Design:—25c. Nurse and child.

53 Basotho Hat

54 Sorghum

1968–69. *As Nos. 125/36 and T* **54**, but wmk **53** (sideways on 2r.).

147		½c. bluish green and light bluish violet (26.11.68)	10	10
		a. Blue-green and violet (30.9.69)	1·75	1·75
148		1c. sepia and rose-red (26.11.68)	10	10
149		2c. orange-yellow and light green (26.11.68)	10	10
		a. Orange-yellow and yellow-green (30.9.69)	1·00	1·00
150		2½c. black and ochre (21.10.68)	15	10
		a. Black and yellow-ochre (30.9.69)	1·00	1·00
151		3c. chocolate, green and yellow-brown (1.8.68)	15	15
152		3½c. chalky blue and yellow (26.11.68)	15	10
153		5c. bistre and new blue (22.7.68)	60	10
154		10c. yellow-brown and pale bluish grey (26.11.68)	15	10
155		1½c. black and red-orange (30.9.69)	60	35
156		25c. black and bright blue (30.9.69)	1·50	1·00
157		50c. black, new blue and turquoise (30.9.69)	11·00	3·25
158		1r. multicoloured (26.11.68)	1·50	2·75
159		2r. black, gold and magenta (30.9.69)	8·00	13·00
147/59		*Set of* 13	21·00	18·00

55 Running Hunters

(Des Jennifer Toombs. Photo Harrison)

1968 (1 Nov). *Rock Paintings. T* **55** *and similar designs.* W **53** (sideways on 5c., 15c.). P 14×14½ (5c., 15c.) or 14½×14 (others).

160		3c. yellow-brown, light blue-green and blackish green	20	10
161		3½c. greenish yellow, yellow-olive and sepia	25	10
162		5c. Venetian red, yellow-ochre and blackish brown	25	10
163		10c. yellow, rose and deep maroon	35	10
164		15c. light buff, pale olive-yellow and blackish brown	50	30
165		20c. yellow-green, greenish yellow and blackish brown	60	55
166		25c. yellow, orange-brown and black	65	75
160/6		*Set of* 7	2·50	1·75

Designs: *Horiz*—3½c. Baboons; 10c. Archers; 20c. Eland; 25c. Hunting scene. *Vert*—5c. Javelin throwing; 15c. Blue Cranes.

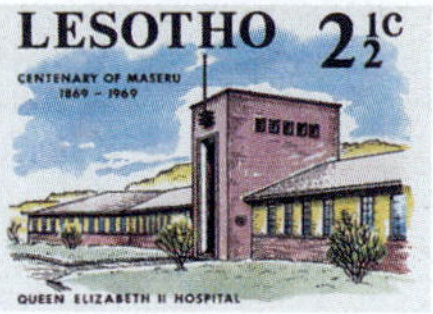

62 Queen Elizabeth II Hospital

(Des C. R. Househam and G. Drummond. Litho P.B.)

1969 (11 Mar). *Centenary of Maseru (capital). T* **62** *and similar horiz designs. Multicoloured.* W **53** (sideways). P 14×13½.

167 2½c. Type **62** 10 10
168 10c. Lesotho Radio Station 10 10
169 12½c. Leabua Jonathan Airport 35 10
170 25c. Royal Palace 25 15
167/70 *Set of* 4 65 30

66 Rally Car passing Mosotho Horseman

(Des P. Wheeler. Photo Harrison)

1969 (26 Sept). *Roof of Africa Car Rally. T* **66** *and similar horiz designs.* W **53**. P 14.

171 2½c. yellow, mauve and plum 15 10
172 12½c. cobalt, greenish yellow and olive-grey 20 10
173 15c. blue, black and mauve 20 10
174 20c. black, red and yellow 20 10
171/4 *Set of* 4 65 30

Designs:—12½c. Rally car on mountain road; 15c. Chequered flags and mountain scenery; 20c. Map of rally route and Rally Trophy.

71 Gryponyx and Footprints

75 Moshoeshoe I, when a Young Man

(Des Jennifer Toombs. Photo Harrison)

1970 (5 Jan). *Prehistoric Footprints (1st series). T* **71** *and similar designs.* W **53** (sideways*). P 14×14½ (3c.) or 14½×14 (others).

175 3c. pale brown, yellow-brown and sepia 90 70
176 5c. dull purple, pink and sepia 1·10 30
w. Wmk hat pointing right 3·25
177 10c. pale yellow, black and sepia 1·40 35
178 15c. olive-yellow, black and sepia 2·00 2·25
179 25c. cobalt and lack 2·75 2·25
175/9 *Set of* 5 7·25 5·25

Designs: (60×23 *mm*)—3c. Dinosaur footprints at Moyeni. (40×24 *mm*)—10c. Plateosauravus and footprints; 15c. Tritylodon and footprints; 25c. Massospondylus and footprints.

*The normal sideways watermark shows the hat pointing left, *when seen from the back of the stamp.*

See also Nos. 596/8.

(Des G. Vasarhelyi. Litho D.L.R.)

1970 (11 Mar). *Death Centenary of King Moshoeshoe I. T* **75** *and similar vert design.* W **53**. P 13½.

180 2½c. pale green and magenta 10 10
181 25c. pale blue and chesnut 20 20

Design:—25c. Moshoeshoe I as an old man.

77 U.N. Emblem and "25"

(Des V. Whiteley. Litho Questa)

1970 (26 June). *25th Anniv of United Nations. T* **77** *and similar horiz designs.* W **53** (sideways). P 14½×14.

182 2½c. light pink, light blue and maroon 10 10
183 10c. multicoloured 10 10
184 12½c. brown-red, cobalt and drab 10 25
185 25c. multicoloured 15 65
182/5 *Set of* 4 30 60

Designs:— 10c. U.N. Building; 12½c. "People of the World"; 25c. Symbolic Dove.

78 Basotho Hat Gift Shop, Maseru

(Des G. Drummond. Litho Questa)

1970 (27 Oct). *Tourism. T* **78** *and similar horiz designs. Multicoloured.* W **53** (sideways). P 14.

186 2½c. Type **78** 10 10
187 5c. Trout fishing 20 10
188 10c. Pony trekking 25 10
189 12½c. Skiing 50 10
190 20c. Holiday Inn, Maseru 40 50
186/90 *Set of* 5 1·25 70

POSTAGE DUE STAMPS

D 3

1966 (1 Nov). *Nos. D9/10 of Basutoland optd as T* **34** *but smaller.*

D11 D **2** 1c. carmine 30 75
a. "LSEOTHO" (R.4/7) 25·00
D12 5c. deep reddish violet 30 90
a. "LSEOTHO" (R.4/7) 45·00

No. D11 exists with the overprint centred near the foot of the stamp (just above "POSTAGE DUE") (price £50 mint). It is believed that this comes from a proof sheet which was issued in the normal way. It contains the "LSEOTHO" error, which only occurred in the first printing.

(Litho B.W.)

1967 (18 Apr). *No wmk.* P 13½.

D13 D **3** 1c. blue 15 3·00
D14 2c. brown-rose 15 3·50
D15 5c. emerald 20 3·50
D13/15 *Set of* 3 45 9·00

Long Island

PRICES FOR STAMPS ON COVER
Most covers from Long Island are philatelic, but these are worth from × 2 (Nos. 1/3) or from × 5 (Nos. 4/36).

The Turkish island of Chustan (or Keustan) in the Gulf of Smyrna was occupied by the Royal Navy during April 1916 and renamed Long Island.

The following stamps were provided by the Civil Administrator, Lieut-Cmdr H. Pirie-Gordon, for the postal service inaugurated on 7 May 1916.

USED STAMPS. Stamps of Long Island were cancelled by hand-drawn circular date stamps in blue crayon for the Northend post office ("N") or in red crayon for Nikola post office ("S").

QUANTITIES ISSUED. The figures quoted do not include the remainders subsequently recorded as having been destroyed.

(**1**)

2

1916 (7 May). *Turkish fiscal stamps surch by typewriter as in T* **1**. No wmk. P 12.

1 ½d. on 20pa. green and buff (new value in red, remainder of surch in black) £4000 £6000
2 1d. on 10pa. carmine and buff £4500 £6000
3 2½d. on 1pi. violet and buff (R.) £4000 £6000

Quantities issued: ½d. 25; 1d. 20; 2½d. 25.

1916 (7 May). *Typewritten as T* **2** *in various colours of ribbon and carbon. Each stamp initialled by the Civil Administrator. No gum.* Imperf.

(a) On pale green paper with horizontal grey lines. No wmk. *Sheets of 12 (4×3) or 16 (4×4) with stamps initialled in red ink.*

4 ½d. black £1600 £1300
a. "GRI" double £3000
b. "7" for "&" £4500
5 ½d. blue £1300
a. "G.R.I." double £3000
b. "7" for "&" £4500
6 ½d. mauve £550 £700
a. "G.R.I." double £1500
b. "7" for "&" £3500

Quantity issued: 140 in all.

(b) On thin horiz laid paper with sheet wmk of "Silver Linen" in double-lined letters. Sheets of 20 (4×5) or 16 (some ptgs of 1s.) with stamps initialled in red ink.

7 ½d. black £600 £800
a. "postage" for "Postage" £3250
b. "7" for "&" £3250
8 ½d. blue £900 £950
b. "7" for "&" £3250
9 ½d. mauve £325 £400
a. "postage" for "Postage" £1500
b. "7" for "&" £1800
10 1d. black £225 £425
a. "7" for "&" £1700
b. "Rvevue" for "Revenue" £1700
g. "Postagg" for "Postage" £3000
11 1d. blue £350 £500
a. "7" for "&" £3000
c. "postage" for "Postage" £3000
e. "G.R?I?" for "G.R.I." £3000
f. "ONR" for "ONE" £1500
12 1d. mauve £170 £350
a. "7" for "&" £2000
b. "Rvevue" for "Revenue" £3000
c. "postage" for "Postage" £3000
e. "G.R?I?" for "G.R.I." † £3000
f. "ONR" for "ONE" £1200 £1500
g. "Postagg" for "Postage" £1800
13 1d. red £200 £375
a. "7" for "&" £1800
c. "postage" for "Postage" £3000
f. "ONR" for "ONE" £1500 £1600
14 2½d. black £1300
15 2½d. blue £1300 £1600
16 2½d. mauve £3000 £1700
17 6d. black (inscr "SIX PENCE") £1800 £2500
a. "SIXPENCE" (one word) £3500
b. Without red ink initials † £3000
19 6d. mauve (inscr "SIX PENCE") £750 £1300
a. "SIXPENCE" (one word) £2750
20 1s. black £170 £450
a. "ISLANA" for "ISLAND" £3000
b. "Postge" for "Postage" £1500 £2250
c. "Rebenue" for "Revenue" £3000
21 1s. blue £1600
22 1s. mauve £160 £550
a. "ISLANA" for "ISLAND" £2000
b. "Postge" for "Postage" £3000
c. "Rebenue" for "Revenue" £3000

Quantities issued (all colours); ½d. 237; 1d. 881; 2½d. 80; 6d. 89; 1s. 383.

(c) On thin wove paper. No wmk. *Sheets of 24 with stamps initialled in indelible pencil.*

23 ½d. black £450 £600
25 ½d. mauve £950
26 1d. black £550 £700
27 1d. red £8000 £1400
30 2d. black £275 £650
b. Error. 1d. and 2d. *se-tenant* £7000
c. Initialled in red ink £1400 £1500
31 2d. mauve £275 £425
a. Error. 1d. and 2d. *se-tenant* £7000
32 2½d. black £550 £750
33 2½d. blue £1700
34 2½d. mauve £1500 £1400
35 6d. black £300 £650
a. "Rvenne &" for "Revenue" £3000
b. Error. 2d. and 6d. *se-tenant*, also "ISLND" for "ISLAND" £7000 £7000
c. "PENCC" £2500
36 6d. blue £1200
a. "Rvenne &" for "Revenue" £3500
b. Error. 2d. and 6d. *se-tenant*, also "ISLND" for "ISLAND" £7500
c. "PENCC" £3000

Quantities issued (all colours); ½d. 114; 1d. 120; 2d. 249; 2½d. 115; 6d. 200.

TOP SHEETS AND CARBONS. It is believed that the production sequence of the typewritten stamps was as follows:

½d. on pale green (Nos. 4/6)
Two black top sheets of 12 (4×3) and one of 16 (4×4)
Two blue carbon sheets of 12 (4×3) and one of 16 (4×4)
Five mauve carbon sheets of 12, two from one top sheet and three from the other
Varieties: "7" for "&" occurs on an unknown position from one of the sheets of 12 and "G.R.I." double occurs on R. 3/2-4 of the other

½d. on laid paper (Nos. 7/9) in sheets of 20 (4×5)
Three black top sheets
Three blue carbon sheets
Eight mauve carbon sheets, two or three from each top sheet
Varieties: "postage" occurs on R. 3/2 of one top sheet and "7" for "&" on R. 4/2 of another

1d. on laid paper (Nos. 10/13) in sheets of 20 (4×5)
Eleven red top sheets
Fifteen black carbon sheets, three each from five of the top sheets
Six blue carbon sheets, one each from six of the top sheets
Twenty-two mauve carbon sheets, probably two from each top sheet
Varieties: "7" for "&" on R. 3/3, "postage" on R. 3/3, "Rvevue" on R. 1/3 and "Postagg" on R. 2/4, all from different top sheets
The position of "G.R?I?" is not known. "ONR" occurs from three different top sheets on R. 5/1, R. 5/2 & 4 or R. 4/1 and 5/2

2½d. on laid paper (Nos. 14/16) in sheets of 20 (4×5)
One black top sheet
One blue carbon sheet
Two mauve carbon sheets

6d. on laid paper (Nos. 17/19) in sheets of 20 (4×5)
One black top sheet
One blue carbon sheet*
Three mauve carbon sheets
Variety: "SIXPENCE" occurs on R. 1/2-3

1s. on laid paper (Nos. 20/2)
Five black top sheets, four of 20 (4×5) and one of 16 (4×4)
Nine black carbon sheets three each from two of the top sheets of 20 and three from the top sheet of 16
Two blue carbon sheets, one each fom two of the top sheets of 20
Twelve mauve carbon sheets, nine from various top sheets of 20 and three from the top sheet of 16
Varieties: "ISLANA" occurs on R. 1/2 of one of the sheets of 20 and "Postge" on R. 1/3 of the sheet of 16. "Rebenue" comes from one of the other sheets of 20

½d. on wove paper (Nos. 23/5) in sheets of 24 (4×6)
One black top sheet
Three black carbon sheets
One blue carbon sheet*
One mauve carbon sheet

1d. on wove paper (Nos. 26/7) in sheets of 24 (4×6)
- One red top sheet
- Three black carbon sheets
- One blue carbon sheet*
- One mauve carbon sheet*

2d. on wove paper (Nos. 30/1) in sheets of 24 (4×6)
- Two black top sheets
- Six black carbon sheets, three from each top sheet. One initialled in red ink
- Four mauve carbon sheets, two from each top sheet
- Variety: the "1d." error occurs on R. 5/2 from one top sheet

2½d. on wove paper (Nos. 32/4) in sheets of 24 (4×6)
- One black top sheet
- Three black carbon sheets
- One blue carbon sheet
- One mauve carbon sheet

6d. on wove paper (Nos. 35/6) in sheets of 24 (4×6)
- Two black top sheets
- Six black carbon sheets, three from each top sheet
- Two blue carbon sheets, one from each top sheet
- Varieties: the "2d." error occurs on R. 5/3 from one top sheet which also showed "PENCC" on R. 3/2, and "Rvenne &" on R. 4/1 of the other

*These carbons are described in written records, but their existence has yet to be confirmed by actual examples.

Madagascar

PRICES FOR STAMPS ON COVER

Nos. 1/47	—
Nos. 50/6	*from* × 100
Nos. 57/62	*from* × 30

BRITISH CONSULAR MAIL

After May 1883 mail from the British community at Antananarivo, the capital, was sent by runner to the British Consulate at Tamatave for forwarding via the French Post Office.

In March of the following year the British Vice-Consul at Antananarivo, Mr. W. C. Pickersgill, reorganised this service and issued stamps for use on both local and overseas mail. Such stamps were only gummed at one of the top corners. This was to facilitate their removal from overseas mail where they were replaced by Mauritius stamps (at Port Louis) or by French issues (at the Vice-Consulate) for transmission via Tamatave and Reunion. Local mail usually had the stamps removed also, being marked with a "PAID" or a Vice-Consular handstamp, although a few covers have survived intact.

CONDITION. Due to the type of paper used, stamps of the British Consular Mail are usually found with slight faults, especially thins. Our prices are for average examples, really fine stamps being worth a premium.

USED STAMPS. Postmarks are not usually found on these issues. Cancellations usually take the form of a manuscript line or cross in crayon, ink or pencil or as five parallel horizontal bars in black, red or violet, approximately 15 mm long. Examples of Nos. 1/3, 5/8 and 11 showing a red diagonal line are believed to be cancelled-to-order.

1

2

1884 (Mar). *Typo locally. Rouletted vertically in colour. No gum, except on one upper corner. With circular consular handstamp reading* "BRITISH VICE-CONSULATE ANTANANARIVO" *around Royal arms in black.*

(a) Inscr "LETTER".

1	1	6d. (½ oz) magenta	£400	£425
		a. Violet handstamp	£2000	
2		1s. (1 oz) magenta	£400	£400
3		1s.6d. (1½ oz) magenta	£450	£450
4		2s. (2 oz) magenta	£650	£700

(b) Inscr "POSTAL PACKET".

5	1	1d. (1 oz) magenta	£450	£400
		a. Without handstamp	£6500	£6500
6		2d. (2 oz) magenta	£300	£300
7		3d. (3 oz) magenta	£350	£300
8		4d. (1 oz amended in ms to "4 oz") magenta	£750	£600
		a. Without manuscript amendment	£4250	£4000
		ab. Violet handstamp	£1400	
		ac. Without handstamp	£5500	£5500

Nos. 1/8 were printed in horizontal strips of four, each strip containing two impressions of the setting. Each strip usually contained two stamps with normal stops after "B.C.M." and two with a hollow stop after "B" (1d., 2d., 3d., 4d., 6d. and 2s.) or after "M" (1s. and 1s.6d.), although the 2d. and 3d. have also been seen with a hollow stop after "M" and the 6d. with hollow stops after both "B" and "C".

Several values are known with the handstamp either inverted or double.

1886. *Manuscript provisionals.*

(a) No. 2 with "SHILLING" *erased and* "PENNY" *written above in red ink.*

9	1	1d. on 1s. (1 oz) magenta		

(b) No. 2 surch "4½d." *and* "W.C.P." *in red ink with a line through the original value.*

10	1	4½d. on 1s. (1 oz) magenta		

1886. *As No. 1, but colour changed. Handstamped with circular* "BRITISH VICE-CONSULATE ANTANANARIVO" *in black.*

11	1	6d. (½ oz) rose-red	£900	£800

1886. *As No. 8a, but handstamped* "BRITISH CONSULAR MAIL ANTANANARIVO" *in black.*

12	1	4d. (1 oz) magenta	£1600	
		a. Violet handstamp	£5500	

1886. *Typo locally.* "POSTAGE" *and value in words printed in black. Rouletted vertically in colour. No gum, except on one upper corner.*

I. "POSTAGE" *29½ mm long. Stops after* "POSTAGE" *and value.*

(a) Handstamped "BRITISH VICE-CONSULATE ANTANANARIVO" *in black.*

14	2	1d. rose	£100	£150
		a. Violet handstamp	£300	
15		1½d. rose	£2000	£1000
		a. Violet handstamp	£1000	£750
16		2d. rose	£150	
		a. Violet handstamp	£300	
17		3d. rose	£2000	£950
		a. Violet handstamp	£400	£375
18		4½d. rose	£2500	£550
		a. Violet handstamp	£600	£325
19		8d. rose	£3500	£2750
		a. Violet handstamp	£1600	£1600
20		9d. rose	£3500	£2750
		a. Violet handstamp	£1200	

(b) Handstamped "BRITISH CONSULAR MAIL ANTANANARIVO" *in black.*

21	2	1d. rose	90·00	
22		1½d. rose	95·00	£150
23		2d. rose	£110	
24		3d. rose	£120	£170
		a. Handstamp in red	†	£12000
25		4½d. rose	£130	£160
		a. Handstamp in red	†	£7000
26		8d. rose	£150	
		a. Handstamp in violet	£1500	
27		9d. rose	£160	£225
		a. Without handstamp	£5000	
		b. Handstamp in violet	£400	

II. "POSTAGE" *29½ mm long. No stops after* "POSTAGE" *or value.*

(a) Handstamped "BRITISH VICE-CONSULATE ANTANANARIVO" *in violet.*

28	2	1d. rose	£1000	
29		1½d. rose	£2000	
30		3d. rose	£1200	
31		4½d. rose	£1800	
32		6d. rose	£1300	

(b) Handstamped "BRITISH CONSULAR MAIL ANTANANARIVO" *in black.*

33		1d. rose	85·00	£140
		a. Without handstamp	£3500	
		b. Violet handstamp	£110	
34		1½d. rose	90·00	£130
		a. Without handstamp	£3500	
		b. Violet handstamp	£180	
35		2d. rose	£100	£130
		b. Violet handstamp	£225	
36		3d. rose	£100	£140
		a. Without handstamp	£5000	
		b. Violet handstamp	£170	
37		4½d. rose	£100	£140
		a. Without handstamp	£5500	
		b. Violet handstamp	£170	
38		6d. rose	£110	£140
		a. Without handstamp	£6000	
		b. Violet handstamp	£350	

III. "POSTAGE" *24½ mm long. No stop after* "POSTAGE", *but stop after value.*

(a) Handstamped "BRITISH VICE-CONSULATE ANTANANARIVO" *in violet.*

39	2	4d. rose	£425	
40		8d. rose	£550	
40*a*		1s. rose	£15000	
41		1s.6d. rose	£7000	
42		2s. rose	£4250	
		a. Handstamp in black	£12000	

(b) Handstamped "BRITISH CONSULAR MAIL ANTANANARIVO" *in black.*

43		4d. rose	£300	
		a. Without handstamp	£4000	
		b. Violet handstamp	£425	
44		8d. rose	£1200	
		a. Without handstamp	£4000	
		b. Violet handstamp	£1100	
45		1s. rose	£500	
		a. Without handstamp	£5000	
		b. Violet handstamp	£1400	
46		1s.6d. rose	£600	
		a. Without handstamp	£4500	
		b. Violet handstamp	£1300	
47		2s. rose	£650	
		a. Without handstamp	£5000	
		b. Violet handstamp	£1500	

The above were also printed in horizontal strips of four.

The stamps of the British Consular Mail were suppressed in 1887, but the postal service continued with the charges paid in cash.

BRITISH INLAND MAIL

In January 1895 the Malagasy government agreed that a syndicate of British merchants at Antananarivo, including the Vice-Consul, should operate an inland postal service during the war with France. Mail was sent by runner to the port of Vatomandry and forwarded via Durban where Natal stamps were added.

Nos. 50/62 were cancelled with dated circular postmarks inscribed "BRITISH MAIL".

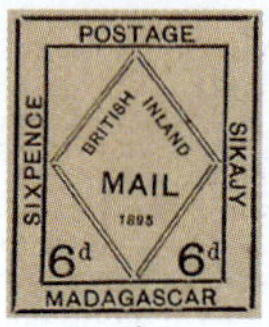

4

5 Malagasy Runners

(Typeset London Missionary Society Press, Antananarivo)

1895 (1 Jan). *Rouletted in black.*

(a) Thick laid paper.

50	4	4d. black	35·00	16·00
		a. "FUOR" for "FOUR" (R. 3/2)	—	£1000

(b) In black on coloured wove paper.

51	4	1d. *blue-grey*	35·00	13·00
52		6d. *pale yellow*	35·00	13·00
53		8d. *salmon*	32·00	13·00
54		1s. *fawn*	40·00	13·00
55		2s. *bright rose*	65·00	26·00
		a. Italic "2" at left (R. 1/2)	£150	65·00
56		4s. *grey*	65·00	13·00
50/6 *Set of 7*			£250	95·00

There are six types of each value, printed in blocks of 6 (2×3) separated by gutters, four times on each sheet; the upper and lower blocks being *tête-bêche*.

Nos. 51 and 56 have been reported on paper showing a sheet watermark.

(Typo John Haddon & Co, London)

1895 (Mar). *The inscription in the lower label varies for each value.* P 12.

57	5	2d. blue	8·50	50·00
		a. Imperf between (horiz pair)	£400	
58		4d. rose	8·50	50·00
		a. Imperf between (horiz pair)	£250	
		b. Imperf between (vert pair)	£275	
		c. Imperf vert (horiz pair)	£275	
59		6d. green	8·50	50·00
		a. Imperf between (horiz pair)	£700	
60		1s. slate-blue	8·50	80·00
		a. Imperf between (horiz pair)	£450	
61		2s. chocolate	20·00	£100
		a. Imperf between (horiz pair)	£500	
62		4s. bright purple	35·00	£150
		a. Imperf between (horiz pair)	£1900	
57/62 *Set of 6*			80·00	£425

This post was suppressed when the French entered Antananarivo on 30 September 1895.

Malawi

INDEPENDENT

44 Dr. H. Banda (Prime Minister) and Independence Monument

(Des M. Goaman. Photo Harrison)

1964 (6 July). *Independence.* T **44** *and similar horiz designs.* P 14½.

211	3d. yellow-olive and deep sepia	10	10
212	6d. red, gold, blue, carmine and lake	10	10
213	1s.3d. red, green, black and bluish violet	35	10
214	2s.6d. multicoloured	45	1·25
	a. Blue omitted	£1000	
211/14 *Set of 4*		90	1·40

Designs:—6d. Banda and rising sun; 1s.3d. Banda and Malawi flag; 2s.6d. Banda and Malawi coat of arms.

Six examples of No. 214a are known from the top horizontal row of an otherwise normal sheet.

48 Tung Tree

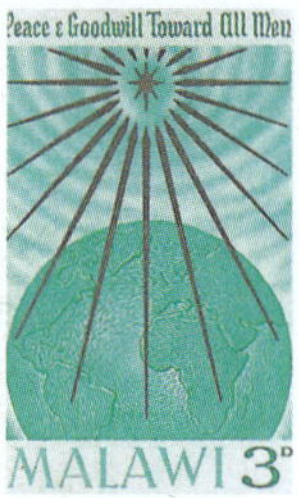

49 Christmas Star and Globe

(Des V. Whiteley. Photo Harrison)

1964 (6 July)–**65**. *As Nos. 199/210, but inscr* "MALAWI" *and T* **48** *(9d.).* No wmk. P 14½.

215	½d. reddish violet	10	60
216	1d. black and green	10	10
217	2d. light red-brown	10	10
218	3d. red-brown, yellow-green and bistre-brown	15	10

219		4d. black and orange-yellow	85	15
220		6d. bluish violet, yellow-green and light blue	75	10
221		9d. bistre-brown, green and yellow	30	15
222		1s. brown, turquoise-blue and pale yellow	25	10
223		1s.3d. bronze-green and chestnut	50	60
224		2s.6d. brown and blue	1·10	1·00
225		5s. blue, green, yellow and sepia	65	3·25
225*a*		5s. blue, green, yellow and sepia (1.6.65)	8·50	1·00
226		10s. green, orange-brown and black	1·50	2·00
227		£1 deep reddish purple and yellow	7·00	5·50
215/27 *Set of* 14			20·00	13·00

No. 225*a* is inscribed "LAKE MALAWI" instead of "LAKE NYASA".

See also Nos. 252/62.

(Des V. Whiteley. Photo Harrison)

1964 (1 Dec). *Christmas*. P 14½.

228	**49**	3d. blue-green and gold	10	10
		a. Gold (star) omitted	£250	
229		6d. magenta and gold	10	10
230		1s.3d. reddish violet and gold	10	10
231		2s.6d. blue and gold	20	50
228/31 *Set of* 4			45	70
MS231*a* 83×126 mm. Nos. 228/31. Imperf			1·00	1·75

No. 228a comes from a sheet on which 41 examples had the gold colour omitted due to a paper fold.

50 Coins

1/6

(51)

(Des V. Whiteley. Photo Enschedé)

1965 (1 Mar). *Malawi's First Coinage. Coins in black and silver.* P 13½.

232	**50**	3d. green	10	10
233		9d. magenta	20	10
		a. Silver omitted	†	—
234		1s.6d. purple	25	10
235		3s. blue	35	1·10
232/5 *Set of* 4			80	1·25
MS235*a* 126×104 mm. Nos. 232/5. Imperf			1·40	1·10

1965 (14 June). *Nos. 223/4 surch as T* **51**.

236		1s.6d. on 1s.3d. bronze-green and chestnut	10	10
237		3s. on 2s.6d. brown and blue	20	20

On No. 237 "3/-" occurs below the bars.

52 Chilembwe leading Rebels

(Des M. Goaman. Photo Harrison)

1965 (20 Aug). *50th Anniv of 1915 Rising.* P 14×14½.

238	**52**	3d. violet and light olive-green	10	10
239		9d. olive-brown and red-orange	10	10
240		1s.6d. red-brown and grey-blue	15	10
241		3s. turquoise-green and slate-blue	20	25
238/41 *Set of* 4			40	60
MS241*a* 127×83 mm. Nos. 238/41			5·00	6·00

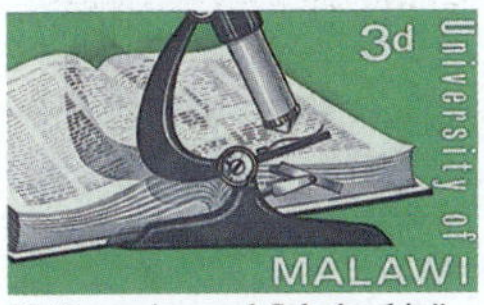

53 "Learning and Scholarship"

(Des H. E. Baxter. Photo Harrison)

1965 (6 Oct). *Opening of Malawi University.* P 14½.

242	**53**	3d. black and emerald	10	10
243		9d. black and magenta	10	10
244		1s.6d. black and reddish violet	10	10
245		3s. black and blue	15	40
242/5 *Set of* 4			30	50
MS246 127×84 mm. Nos. 242/5			2·50	2·50

54 *Papilio ophidicephalus*

(Des V. Whiteley. Photo Enschedé)

1966 (15 Feb). *Malawi Butterflies. T* **54** *and similar horiz designs. Multicoloured.* P 13½.

247		4d. Type **54**	80	10
248		9d. *Papilio desmondi (magdae)*	1·25	10
249		1s.6d. *Epamera handmani*	1·75	30
250		3s. *Amauris crawshayi*	2·75	6·00
247/50 *Set of* 4			6·00	6·00
MS251 130×100 mm. Nos. 247/50			17·00	11·00

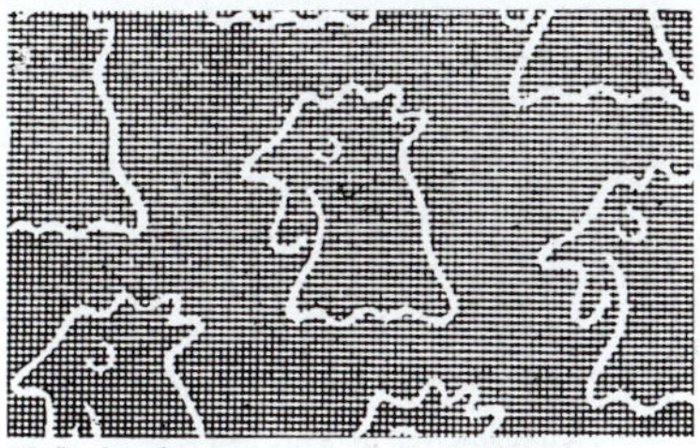

55 Cockerels

56 Burley Tobacco

57 *Cyrestis camillus* (butterfly)

(New values des V. Whiteley (1s.6d.), M. Goaman (£2). Photo Harrison)

1966–67. *As Nos. 215 etc.* but W **55** (sideways on ½d., 2d.), and new values and designs (1s.6d., £2). P 14½.

252	–	½d. reddish violet (1.4.66)	10	10
253	–	1d. black and green (1.4.66)	15	10
254	–	2d. light red-brown (4.6.66)*	15	10
255	–	3d. red-brown, yellow-green and bistre-brown (4.3.67)*	20	10
256	–	6d. bluish violet, yellow-green and light blue (2.7.66)*	2·00	85
257	**48**	9d. bistre-brown, green and yellow (5.12.66)*	1·75	10
258	–	1s. brown, turquoise-blue and pale yellow (1.4.66)	25	10
259	**56**	1s.6d. chocolate and yellow-green (15.11.66)	40	10
260	–	5s. blue, green, yellow and sepia (6.10.66)*	8·50	3·00
261	–	10s. green, orange-brown and black (6.10.66)*	17·00	22·00
262	**57**	£2 black, orange-yellow, pale yellow and slate-violet (7.9.66)	25·00	24·00
252/62 *Set of* 11			50·00	42·00

*These are local dates of issue. The Crown Agents, in London, did not distribute these printings until some time later.

No. 260 is inscribed "LAKE MALAWI".

The 2d. exists with both PVA gum and gum arabic.

58 British Central Africa 6d. Stamp of 1891

59 President Banda

(Des V. Whiteley. Photo Harrison)

1966 (4 May–10 June). *75th Anniv of Postal Services.* W **55**. P 14½.

263	**58**	4d. grey-blue and yellow-green	10	10
264		9d. grey-blue and claret	15	10
265		1s.6d. grey-blue and reddish lilac	20	10
266		3s. grey-blue and new blue	30	70
263/6 *Set of* 4			60	80
MS267 83×127 mm. Nos. 263/6 (10 June)			5·00	3·25

REPUBLIC

(Des M. Goaman. Photo Harrison)

1966 (6 July). *Republic Day.* W **55**. P 14×14½.

268	**59**	4d. brown, silver and emerald	10	10
269		9d. brown, silver and magenta	10	10
270		1s.6d. brown, silver and violet	15	10
271		3s. brown, silver and blue	25	15
268/71 *Set of* 4			50	30
MS272 83×127 mm. Nos. 268/71			2·00	3·00

60 Bethlehem

(Des and photo Harrison)

1966 (12 Oct). *Christmas.* W **55**. P 14½.

273	**60**	4d. myrtle-green and gold	10	10
274		9d. brown-purple and gold	10	10
275		1s.6d. orange-red and gold	15	10
276		3s. blue and gold	40	80
273/6 *Set of* 4			65	1·00

61 *Ilala I*

(Des Mrs. H. Breggar. Photo Harrison)

1967 (4 Jan). *Lake Malawi Steamers. T* **61** *and similar horiz designs.* W **55**. P 14½.

277		4d. black, yellow and bright green	40	10
		a. Yellow omitted	†	£475
278		9d. black, yellow and magenta	45	10
279		1s.6d. black, red and violet	65	20
280		3s. black, red and bright blue	1·25	1·75
277/80 *Set of* 4			2·50	1·90

Designs:—9d. *Dove*; 1s.6d. *Chauncy Maples I* (wrongly inscr "Chauncey"); 3s. *Gwendolen*.

No. 277a occurs on first day covers from Blantyre.

62 Golden Mbuna (female)

(Des R. Granger Barrett. Photo Enschedé)

1967 (3 May). *Lake Malawi Cichlids. T* **62** *and similar horiz designs. Multicoloured.* W **55** (sideways). P 12½×12.

281		4d. Type **62**	40	10
282		9d. Scraper-mouthed Mbuna	55	10
283		1s.6d. Zebra Mbuna	70	25
		a. Imperf (pair)	£150	
284		3s. Orange Mbuna	1·75	2·00
		a. Imperf (pair)	£190	
281/4 *Set of* 4			3·00	2·25

63 Rising Sun and Gearwheel

(Des Jennifer Toombs. Litho D.L.R.)

1967 (5 July). *Industrial Development.* P 13½×13.

285	**63**	4d. black and emerald	10	10
286		9d. black and carmine	10	10
287		1s.6d. black and reddish violet	10	10
288		3s. black and bright blue	15	30
285/8 *Set of* 4			30	50
MS289 134×108 mm. Nos. 285/8			75	1·40

64 Mary and Joseph beside Crib

(Des Jennifer Toombs. Photo Harrison)

1967 (21 Nov–1 Dec). *Christmas.* W **55**. P 14×14½.

290	**64**	4d. royal blue and turquoise-green	10	10
291		9d. royal blue and light red	10	10
292		1s.6d. royal blue and yellow	10	10
293		3s. royal blue and new blue	15	30
290/3 *Set of* 4			30	50
MS294 114×100 mm. Nos. 290/3. Wmk sideways. P 14×13½ (1 Dec)			1·00	3·00

65 *Calotropis procera*

(Des G. Drummond. Litho D.L.R.)

1968 (24 Apr). *Wild Flowers. T* **65** *and similar horiz designs. Multicoloured.* W **55** (sideways). P 13½×13.

295		4d. Type **65**	15	10
296		9d. *Borreria dibrachiata*	15	10
297		1s.6d. *Hibiscus rhodanthus*	15	10
298		3s. *Bidens pinnatipartita*	20	95
295/8 *Set of* 4			60	1·10
MS299 135×91 mm. Nos. 295/8			1·25	3·00

66 Bagnall Steam Locomotive No. 1, *Thistle*

(Des R. Granger Barrett. Photo Harrison)

1968 (24 July). *Malawi Locomotives. T* **66** *and similar horiz designs.* W **55**. P 14×14½.

300	4d. grey-green, slate-blue and red	25	10
301	9d. red, slate-blue and myrtle-green	30	15
302	1s.6d. multicoloured	40	30
303	3s. multicoloured	70	3·00
300/3 *Set of 4*		1·50	3·00
MS304 120×88 mm. Nos. 300/3. P 14½		2·00	6·00

Designs:—9d. Class G steam locomotive No. 49; 1s.6d. Class "Zambesi" diesel locomotive No. 202; 3s. Diesel railcar No. DR1.

67 "The Nativity" (Piero della Francesca)

(Des and photo Harrison)

1968 (6 Nov). *Christmas. Paintings. T* **67** *and similar horiz designs. Multicoloured.* W **55** (sideways on 4d.). P 14×14½.

305	4d. Type **67**	10	10
306	9d. "The Adoration of the Shepherds" (Murillo)	10	10
307	1s.6d. "The Adoration of the Shepherds" (Reni)	10	10
308	3s. "Nativity with God the Father and Holy Ghost" (Pittoni)	15	15
305/8 *Set of 4*		30	30
MS309 115×101 mm. Nos. 305/8. P 14×13½		35	1·60

68 Scarlet-chested Sunbird

69 Nyasa Lovebird

70 Carmine Bee Eater

(Des V. Whiteley. Photo Harrison)

1968 (13 Nov). *Birds. T* **68/70** *and similar designs. Multicoloured.* W **55** (sideways on 1d. to 4d. and 3s. to £1). P 14½.

310	1d. Type **68**	15	10
311	2d. Violet Starling	30	10
312	3d. White-browed Robin Chat	30	10
313	4d. Red-billed Fire Finch	50	40
	a. Red omitted	†	—
314	6d. Type **69**	2·00	15
315	9d. Yellow-rumped Bishop	2·00	60
316	1s. Type **70**	1·00	15
317	1s.6d. Grey-headed Bush Shrike	5·00	8·00
318	2s. Paradise Whydah	5·00	8·00
319	3s. African Paradise Flycatcher	8·00	4·25
320	5s. Bateleur	7·00	4·25
321	10s. Saddle-bill Stork	5·50	7·50
322	£1 Purple Heron	8·00	18·00
323	£2 Knysna Turaco ("Livingstone's Loerie")	42·00	48·00
310/23 *Set of 14*		75·00	90·00

Sizes:—2d. to 4d. as T **68**; 9d. as T **69**; 1s.6d., 2s, £2 as T **70**; 3s. to £1 as T **70** but vertical.

No. 310 exists in coils, constructed from normal sheets.

An example of No. 313a is known used on local cover from Limbe in September 1970.

71 I.L.O. Emblem

(Des G. Drummond. Photo, emblem die-stamped Harrison)

1969 (5 Feb). *50th Anniv of the International Labour Organization.* W **55** (sideways on No. **MS**328). P 14.

324	**71**	4d. gold and myrtle-green	10	10
325		9d. gold and chocolate	10	10
326		1s.6d. gold and blackish brown	10	10
327		3s. gold and indigo	15	15
324/7 *Set of 4*			30	30
MS328 127×89 mm. Nos. 324/7			1·00	4·75

72 White-fringed Ground Orchid

73 African Development Bank Emblem

(Des J.W. Litho B.W.)

1969 (9 July). *Orchids of Malawi. T* **72** *and similar horiz designs. Multicoloured.* W **55**. P 13½×13.

329	4d. Type **72**	15	10
330	9d. Red Ground orchid	20	10
331	1s.6d. Leopard Tree orchid	30	20
332	3s. Blue Ground orchid	60	2·00
329/32 *Set of 4*		1·10	2·00
MS333 118×86 mm. Nos. 329/32		1·10	3·75

(Des G. Vasarhelyi. Litho D.L.R.)

1969 (10 Sept). *Fifth Anniv of African Development Bank.* W **55**. P 14.

334	**73**	4d. yellow, yellow-ochre and chocolate	10	10
335		9d. yellow, yellow-ochre and myrtle-green	10	10
336		1s.6d. yellow, yellow-ochre and blackish brown	10	10
337		3s. yellow, yellow-ochre and indigo	15	15
334/7 *Set of 4*			30	30
MS338 102×137 mm. Nos. 334/7			50	90

74 Dove over Bethlehem

75 *Zonocerus elegans* (grasshopper)

(Des Jennifer Toombs. Photo Harrison)

1969 (5 Nov). *Christmas.* W **55**. P 14½×14.

339	**74**	2d. black and olive-yellow	10	10
340		4d. black and deep turquoise	10	10
341		9d. black and scarlet	10	10
342		1s.6d. black and deep bluish violet	10	10
343		3s. black and ultramarine	15	15
339/43 *Set of 5*			30	30
MS344 130×71 mm. Nos. 339/43			1·00	1·75
		a. Ultramarine (background of 3s.) omitted	£750	

(Des V. Whiteley. Litho Format)

1970 (4 Feb). *Insects of Malawi. T* **75** *and similar vert designs. Multicoloured.* W **55**. P 14.

345	4d. Type **75**	15	10
346	9d. *Mylabris dicincta* (beetle)	15	10
347	1s.6d. *Henosepilachna elaterii* (ladybird)	20	10
348	3s. *Sphodromantis speculabunda* (mantid)	35	65
345/8 *Set of 4*		75	75
MS349 86×137 mm. Nos. 345/8		1·25	2·25

Rand Easter Show
1970

(76)

1970 (18 Mar). *Rand Easter Show. No. 317 optd with T* **76**.

350	1s.6d. multicoloured	50	2·25

77 Runner

(Des J. Cooter. Litho B.W.)

1970 (3 June). *Ninth British Commonwealth Games, Edinburgh.* W **55**. P 13.

351	**77**	4d. royal blue and blue-green	10	10
352		9d. royal blue and carmine	10	10
353		1s.6d. royal blue and dull yellow	10	10
354		3s. royal blue and new blue	15	15
351/4 *Set of 4*			30	30
MS355 146×96 mm. Nos. 351/4			55	90

(New Currency, 100 tambalas = 1 kwacha)

10t

(78)

79 *Aegocera trimeni*

1970 (2 Sept). *Decimal Currency. Nos. 316 and 318 surch as T* **78**.

356	10t. on 1s. multicoloured	2·25	25
	a. Surch double	†	—
357	20t. on 2s. multicoloured	2·75	3·75

(Des R. Granger Barrett. Litho B.W.)

1970 (30 Sept). *Moths. T* **79** *and similar horiz designs. Multicoloured.* W **55**. P 11×11½.

358	4d. Type **79**	20	10
359	9d. *Faidherbia bauhiniae*	30	10
360	1s.6d. *Parasa karschi*	50	20
361	3s. *Teracotona euprepia*	1·25	3·50
358/61 *Set of 4*		2·00	3·50
MS362 112×92 mm. Nos. 358/61		4·25	6·00

80 Mother and Child

(Des Brother W. Meyer. Litho J.W.)

1970 (4 Nov). *Christmas.* W **55** (sideways). P 14.

363	**80**	2d. black and light yellow	10	10
364		4d. black and emerald	10	10
365		9d. black and orange-red	10	10
366		1s.6d. black and light purple	10	10
367		3s. black and blue	15	15
363/7 *Set of 5*			30	30
MS368 166×100 mm. Nos. 363/7			1·00	2·25

POSTAGE DUE STAMPS

D **2**

(Litho Bradbury, Wilkinson)

1967 (1 Sept). W **55**. P 11½.

D6	D **2**	1d. carmine	15	4·25
D7		2d. sepia	20	4·25
D8		4d. reddish violet	25	4·50
D9		6d. blue	25	4·75
D10		8d. emerald	35	5·00
D11		1s. black	45	5·50
D6/11 *Set of 6*			1·50	25·00

AFFIX
STAMP
HERE

Gibbons Stamp Monthly
7 Parkside
Christchurch Road
Ringwood
Hampshire
BH24 3SH

AFFIX
STAMP
HERE

Stanley Gibbons Publications
7 Parkside
Christchurch Road
Ringwood
Hampshire
BH24 3SH

Malaysia

The Federation of Malaya was formed on 1 February 1948 by the former Straits Settlements of Malacca and Penang, the four Federated Malay States and the five Unfederated States. It did not, however, issue any stamps until it became an independent member of the Commonwealth in 1957.

The philatelic history of the component parts of the federation is most complex.

The method adopted is to show the general issues for the area first, before dealing with the issues for the individual States. The section is divided as follows:

I. STRAITS SETTLEMENTS
II. FEDERATED MALAY STATES
III. MALAYAN POSTAL UNION
IV. MALAYA (BRITISH MILITARY ADMINISTRATION)
V. MALAYAN FEDERATION
VI. MALAYSIA
VII. MALAYAN STATES—Johore, Kedah, Kelantan, Malacca, Negri Sembilan (with Sungei Ujong), Pahang, Penang, Perak, Perlis, Sabah, Selangor, Trengganu
VIII. JAPANESE OCCUPATION OF MALAYA 1942–45
IX. THAI OCCUPATION OF MALAYA 1943–45

I. STRAITS SETTLEMENTS

The three original Settlements, Malacca, Penang (with Province Wellesley) and Singapore (with Christmas Island), were formed into a Crown Colony on 1 April 1867. The Cocos (Keeling) Islands were transferred to Straits Settlements on 7 February 1886. Labuan was attached to the Colony in 1896, becoming the fourth Settlement in 1906, but was transferred to North Borneo in 1946.

The first known prestamp cover with postal markings from Penang (Prince of Wales Island) is dated March 1806 and from Malacca, under British civil administration, February 1841. The civil post office at Singapore opened on 1 February 1823.

The stamps of India were used at all three post offices from late in 1854 until the Straits Settlements became a separate colony on 1 September 1867.

The Indian stamps were initially cancelled by dumb obliterators and their use in the Straits Settlements can only be identified from complete covers. In 1856 cancellations of the standard Indian octagonal type were issued, numbered "B 109" for Malacca, "B 147" for Penang and "B 172" for Singapore.

CURRENCY. Before 1867 official accounts of the East India Company administration for the Straits Settlements were kept in rupees, although the vast majority of commercial transactions used Spanish American silver dollars, supplies of which reached Malaya via the Philippines.

This confusing situation was rapidly amended when the Straits Settlements became a Crown Colony on 1 April 1867 and Spanish American dollars were declared to be the only legal currency. In 1874 American trade dollars and Japanese yen were also accepted, but in 1890 recognition of the Spanish American dollars was restricted to those from the Mexican mints. A shortage of silver coinage led to the introduction of silver British trade dollars in 1895 which also circulated in Hong Kong and Labuan.

Dollar banknotes first appeared in 1899, but Mexican dollars were not finally replaced until the issue of silver Straits Settlements dollars in 1903, the gold value of which was set at 2s.4d. in January 1906.

A

B

C

The Penang and Singapore octagonals were replaced by a duplex type, consisting of a double-ringed datestamp and a diamond-shaped obliterator containing the office number, in 1863 and 1865 respectively.

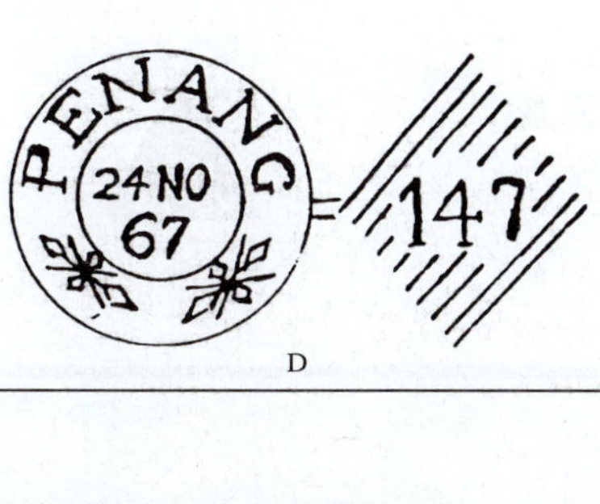

D

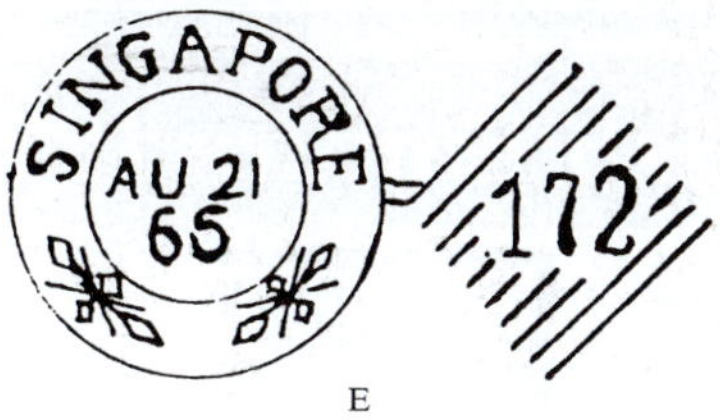

E

PRICES. Catalogue prices in this section are for stamps with clearly legible, if partial, examples of the postmarks.

EAST INDIA COMPANY ADMINISTRATION

MALACCA

Stamps of INDIA *cancelled with Type* A.

1854. (*Nos. 2/34*).

Z1	½a. blue (Die I)	£1400
Z2	1a. red (Die I)	£1100
Z3	1a. dull red (Die II)	£1200
Z4	2a. green	£1600
Z4*a*	4a. blue and pale red (Head Die I) (*cut-to-shape*)	£1700
Z5	4a. blue and red (Head Die II) (*cut-to-shape*)	£1700
Z5*a*	4a. blue and red (Head Die III) (*cut-to-shape*)	£1700

1855. (*Nos. 35/6*).

Z6	8a. carmine (Die I)/*blue glazed*	£550

1856–64. (*Nos. 37/49*).

Z7	½a. pale blue (Die I)	£375
Z8	1a. brown	£275
Z8*a*	2a. dull pink	£400
Z9	2a. yellow-buff	£300
Z10	2a. yellow	£325
Z10a	4a. black	£550
Z11	4a. green	£500
Z12	8a. carmine (Die I)	£375

1860. (*Nos. 51/3*).

Z13	8p. purple/*bluish*	£900
Z14	8p. purple/*white*	£450

1865. (*Nos. 54/65*).

Z15	4a. green	£500

PENANG

Stamps of INDIA *cancelled with Type* B.

1854. (*Nos. 2/34*).

Z20	½a. bluc (Die I)	£450
Z21	1a. red (Die I)	£180
Z21a	1a. red (Die II)	£1600
Z22	2a. green	£300
Z23	4a. blue and pale red (Head Die I)	£1700
Z24	4a. blue and red (Head Die II)	£1700
Z25	4a. blue and red (Head Die III)	£1100

1855. (*Nos. 35/6*).

Z26	4a. black/*blue glazed*	95·00
Z27	8a. carmine (Die I)/*blue glazed*	85·00
	a. Bisected (4a.) (1860) (on cover)	£60000

1856–64. (*Nos. 37/49*).

Z28	½a. pale blue (Die I)	90·00
Z29	1a. brown	55·00
Z30	2a. dull pink	80·00
Z31	2a. yellow-buff	75·00
Z32	2a. yellow	75·00
Z33	2a. orange	75·00
Z34	4a. black	55·00
Z35	8a. carmine (Die I)	70·00

1860. (*Nos. 51/3*).

Z36	8p. purple/*white*	£160

Stamps of INDIA *cancelled with Type* D.

1854. (*Nos. 2/34*).

Z38	1a. red (Die I)	£2750

1856–64. (*Nos. 37/49*).

Z39	½a. pale blue (Die I)	£200
Z40	1a. brown	60·00
Z40a	2a. yellow-buff	80·00
Z41	2a. yellow	70·00
Z42	4a. black	60·00
Z43	4a. green	£170
Z44	8a. carmine (Die I)	65·00

1860. (*Nos. 51/3*).

Z45	8p. purple/*white*	95·00
Z46	8p. mauve	95·00

1865. (*Nos. 54/65*).

Z47	8p. purple	
Z48	1a. deep brown	60·00
Z49	2a. yellow	70·00
Z50	4a. green	£180
Z51	8a. carmine (Die I)	

1866–67. (*Nos. 69/72*).

Z52	4a. green (Die 1)	£190

OFFICIAL STAMP

1866–67. (*No. O2*).

Z54	½a. pale blue	

SINGAPORE

Stamps of INDIA *cancelled with Type* C.

1854. (*Nos. 2/34*).

Z60	½a. blue (Die I)	£180
Z61	1a. red (Die I)	£120
Z62	1a. dull red (Die II)	£140
Z63	1a. red (Die III)	£1400
Z64	2a. green	85·00
	a. Bisected (1a.) (1857) (on cover)	£140000
Z65	4a. blue and pale red (Head Die I)	£1300
Z66	4a. blue and red (Head Die II)	£1300
Z67	4a. blue and red (Head Die III)	£800

1855. (*Nos. 35/6*).

Z68	4a. black/*blue glazed*	42·00
	a. Bisected (2a.) (1859) (on cover)	£8000
Z69	8a. carmine/*blue glazed*	42·00
	a. Bisected (4a.) (1859) (on cover)	£60000

1856–66. (*Nos. 37/49*).

Z70	½a. pale blue (Die I)	45·00
Z71	1a. brown	25·00
	a. Bisected (½a.) (1859) (on cover)	£65000
Z72	2a. dull pink	45·00
Z73	2a. yellow-buff	38·00
Z74	2a. yellow	40·00
Z75	2a. orange	45·00
Z76	4a. black	25·00
	a. Bisected (2a.) (1859) (on cover)	£24000
Z77	4a. green	£130
Z78	8a. carmine (Die I)	35·00
	a. Bisected (4a.) (1866) (on cover)	£60000

1860–61. (*Nos. 51/3*).

Z79	8p. purple/*bluish*	£550
Z80	8p. purple/*white*	70·00
	a. Bisected diagonally (4p.) (1861) (on cover)	£65000
Z81	8p. mauve	75·00

1865. (*Nos. 54/65*).

Z82	½a. blue (Die I)	55·00
Z83	8p. purple	£140
Z84	1a. deep brown	42·00
Z85	2a. yellow	45·00
Z86	2a. orange	45·00
Z87	4a. green	£120
Z88	8a. carmine (Die I)	£275

1866–67. (*Nos. 69/72*).

Z89	4a. green (Die I)	£150
Z90	6a.8p. slate	£325

OFFICIAL STAMPS

1866–67. (*Nos. O6/14*).

Z91	½a. pale blue	£450
Z92	2a. yellow	£600

Stamps of INDIA *cancelled with Type* E.

1856–64. (*Nos. 37/49*).

Z100	1a. brown	£300
Z101	2a. yellow	£375
Z102	4a. black	£375
Z103	8a. carmine (Die I)	£375

1860. (*Nos. 51/3*).

Z104	8p. purple/*white*	£400

1865. (*Nos. 54/65*).

Z105	2a. yellow	£350
Z106	2a. orange	£350
Z107	4a. green	£425

PRICES FOR STAMPS ON COVER

Nos. 1/9	*from* × 15
No. 10	—
Nos. 11/19	*from* × 8
Nos. 20/1	*from* × 20
Nos. 22/39	*from* × 10
Nos. 41/6	*from* × 20
No. 47	—
Nos. 48/9	*from* × 10
Nos. 50/62	*from* × 20
Nos. 63/71	*from* × 15
No. 72	—
Nos. 73/8	*from* × 20
No. 80	*from* × 30
Nos. 82/5	*from* × 10
Nos. 86/7	*from* × 20
Nos. 88/94	*from* × 15
Nos. 95/105	*from* × 8
Nos. 106/9	*from* × 20
Nos. 110/21	*from* × 6
No. 122	—
Nos. 123/6	*from* × 5
Nos. 127/38	*from* × 4
Nos. 139/40	—
Nos. 141/51	*from* × 15
Nos. 152/67	*from* × 4
Nos. 168/9	—
Nos. 193/212	*from* × 3
Nos. 213/15	—
Nos. 216/17	*from* × 10
Nos. 218/40*a*	*from* × 3
Nos. 240*b*/*d*	—
Nos. 241/55	*from* × 15
Nos. 256/9	*from* × 4
Nos. 260/98	*from* × 3
Nos. D1/6	*from* × 20

PRINTERS. All Straits Settlements issues were printed in typography by De La Rue & Co, Ltd, London, *unless otherwise stated*.

USED PRICES. The prices quoted for Nos. 1/9 are for fine used examples. Those showing parts of commercial "chops" are worth less.

CROWN COLONY

(Currency. 100 cents = 1 Spanish American dollar)

THREE HALF CENTS (1) — 32 CENTS (2)

1867 (1 Sept). *Nos. 54, 59, 61, 69 and 73 of India surch as T* **1** *or* **2** *(24c., 32c.) by De La Rue.* W **13** (Elephant's head) of India. P 14.

1		1½c. on ½a. blue (Die I) (R.)	90·00	£200
2		2c. on 1a. deep brown (R.)	£140	80·00
3		3c. on 1a. deep brown (B.)	£130	85·00
4		4c. on 1a. deep brown (Bk.)	£250	£250
5		6c. on 2a. yellow (P.)	£600	£250
6		8c. on 2a. yellow (G.)	£190	42·00
7		12c. on 4a. green (R.)	£950	£300
		a. Surch double	£2500	
8		24c. on 8a. rose (Die II) (B.)	£450	80·00
9		32c. on 2a. yellow (Bk.)	£350	90·00

The 32c. was re-issued for postal use in 1884.
No. 7a. is only known unused.

1869. (?) *No. 1 with* "THREE HALF" *deleted and* "2" *written above, in black manuscript.*

10		2 on 1½c. on ½a. blue	£15000	£5000

This stamp has been known from very early days and was apparently used at Penang, but nothing is known of its history.

5

6

7

8

9

1867 (Dec)–**72**. *Ornaments in corners differ for each value.* Wmk Crown CC. P 14.

11	**5**	2c. brown (6.68)	35·00	5·00
		a. Yellow-brown	38·00	5·00
		b. Deep brown	95·00	14·00
		w. Wmk inverted	£425	£150
12		4c. rose (7.68)	60·00	9·00
		a. Deep rose	75·00	12·00
		w. Wmk inverted	£170	
13		6c. dull lilac (1.68)	£100	17·00
		a. Bright lilac	£110	17·00
		w. Wmk inverted	†	£200
14	**6**	8c. orange-yellow	£170	13·00
		a. Orange	£170	13·00
		w. Wmk inverted	£375	£130
15		12c. blue	£140	6·50
		a. Ultramarine	£150	9·00
		w. Wmk inverted	£400	
16	**7**	24c. blue-green	£130	5·50
		a. Yellow-green	£275	21·00
		w. Wmk inverted	†	£225
17	**8**	30c. claret (12.72)	£250	12·00
		w. Wmk inverted	†	£375
18	**9**	32c. pale red	£475	65·00
		w. Wmk inverted	†	£275
19		96c. grey	£300	50·00
		a. Perf 12½ (6.71)	£2250	£225

Five Cents. (10) — Seven Cents. (11)

1879 (May). *Nos. 14a and 18 surch with T* **10** *and* **11**.

20	**6**	5c. on 8c. orange	£100	£150
		a. No stop after "Cents"	£850	£900
		b. "F i" spaced	£900	£950
21	**9**	7c. on 32c. pale red	£130	£160
		a. No stop after "Cents"	£1300	£1400

The no stop error occured once in the setting.

10 cents. (12)

10 (*a*) 10 (*b*) 10 (*c*) 10 (*d*)

10 (*e*) 10 (*f*) 10 (*g*) 10 (*h*)

10 (*i*) 10 (*j*) 10 (*jj*) 10 (*k*) 10 (*l*)

(*a*) "1" thin curved serif and thin foot, "0" narrow.
(*b*) "1" thick curved serif and thick foot: "0" broad. Both numerals heavy.
(*c*) "1" as (*a*); "0" as (*b*).
(*d*) "1" as (*a*) but thicker; "0" as (*a*).
(*e*) As (*a*) but sides of "0" thicker.
(*f*) "1" as (*d*); "0" as (*e*).
(*g*) As (*a*) but "0" narrower.
(*h*) "1" thin, curved serif and thick foot; "0" as (*g*).
(*i*) "1" as (*b*); "0" as (*a*).
(*j*) "1" as (*d*); "0" as (*g*) but raised.
(*jj*) "1" as (*a*) but shorter, and with shorter serif and thicker foot; "0" as (*g*) but level with "1".
(*k*) "1" as (*jj*); "0" as (*a*).
(*l*) "1" straight serif; "0" as (*g*).

1880 (Mar). *No. 17 surch with T* **12** *(showing numerals (a) to (jj)).*

22		10c. on 30c. claret (*a*)	£425	85·00
23		10c. on 30c. claret (*b*)	£400	80·00
24		10c. on 30c. claret (*c*)	£7500	£850
25		10c. on 30c. claret (*d*)	£3000	£275
26		10c. on 30c. claret (*e*)	£12000	£1700
27		10c. on 30c. claret (*f*)	£12000	£1700
28		10c. on 30c. claret (*g*)	£4500	£500
29		10c. on 30c. claret (*h*)	£12000	£1700
30		10c. on 30c. claret (*i*)	£12000	£1700
31		10c. on 30c. claret (*j*)	£12000	£1700
32		10c. on 30c. claret (*jj*)	£12000	£1700

Nos. 22/32 come from the same setting of 60 (6×10) containing twenty examples of No. 22 (R. 1/1-2, 1/4, 1/6, 2/1-6, 3/1, 3/3, 3/5, 4/1, 4/3-4, 10/1, 10/3-5), twenty-two of No. 23 (R. 4/6, 5/1-6, 6/1-6, 7/1, 8/2-4, 9/1-5), six of No. 25 (R. 1/5, 3/2, 3/4, 4/2, 4/5, 10/2), four of No. 28 (R. 7/2-5), two of No. 24 (R. 9/6, 10/6) and one each of Nos. 26 (R. 3/6), 27 (R. 1/3), 29 (R. 7/6), 30 (R. 8/1), 31 (R. 8/6) and 32 (R. 8/5).

No. 23 is known with large stop after "cents" and also with stop low.

1880 (Apr). *No. 17 surch as T* **12**, *but without "cents.", showing numerals (a) to (c), (g) to (i), (k) and (l).*

33		10. on 30c. claret (*a*)	£190	50·00
		w. Wmk inverted	†	£200
34		10 on 30c. claret (*b*)	£200	50·00
		w. Wmk inverted	†	£200
35		10 on 30c. claret (*c*)	£650	£110
		w. Wmk inverted	†	£425
36		10 on 30c. claret (*g*)	£1600	£325
		aw. Wmk inverted	†	£850
36*b*		10 on 30c. claret (*h*)	†	£15000
37		10 on 30c. claret (*i*)	£4500	£850
38		10 on 30c. claret (*k*)	£4500	£850
39		10 on 30c. claret (*l*)	£4500	£850

Nos. 33/9 were surcharged from an amended setting of 60 (6×10) of which 59 positions have been identified. Of those known No. 33 occurs on twenty-four (R. 6/1-6, 7/1-6, 8/1-6, 9/1-2, 9/6, 10/1-3), No. 34 on twenty-one (R. 1/2-6, 2/1-6, 3/1-6, 4/3-5, 5/6), No. 35 on eight (R. 1/1, 4/2, 4/6, 5/1-5), No. 36 on three (R. 9/3-5) and Nos. 37 (R. 10/6), 38 (R. 10/4) and 39 (R. 10/5) on one each. R. 4/1 remains unidentified.

The existence of No. 36*b*, known as a single example from the 6th vertical column, and a stamp in the Royal Collection with "1" as (*b*) and "0" as (*g*) suggests that there may have been another setting.

5 cents. (13) — 5 cents. (14) — 5 cents. (15)

1880 (Aug). *No. 14a surch with T* **13** *to* **15**.

41	**13**	5c. on 8c. orange	£140	£170
42	**14**	5c. on 8c. orange	£130	£160
43	**15**	5c. on 8c. orange	£500	£600

Surcharged in a setting of 60 (6×10) with *T* **13** on rows one to four, *T* **14** on rows five to nine and *T* **15** on row ten.

10 cents. (16) — 5 cents. (17)

1880–81. *Nos. 13, 15/a and 17 surch with T* **16**.

44		10c. on 6c. lilac (11.81)	65·00	6·00
		a. Surch double	—	£2750
45		10c. on 12c. ultramarine (1.81)	70·00	16·00
		a. Blue	50·00	9·00
46		10c. on 30c. claret (12.80)	£400	90·00

A second printing of the 10c. on 6c. has the surcharge heavier and the "10" usually more to the left or right of "cents".

1882 (Jan). *No. 12 surch with T* **17**.

47		5c. on 4c. rose	£275	£300

18

19

1882 (Jan). Wmk Crown CC. P 14.

48	**18**	5c. purple-brown	90·00	£100
49	**19**	10c. slate	£425	65·00
		s. Optd "Specimen"	£475	

1882. Wmk Crown CA. P 14.

50	**5**	2c. brown (Aug)	£300	45·00
51		4c. rose (April)	£120	8·00
52	**6**	8c. orange (Sept)	3·50	1·00
		w. Wmk inverted	†	£300
53	**19**	10c. slate (Oct)	7·50	1·25
		w. Wmk inverted		

For the 4c. in deep carmine see No. 98.

TWO CENTS — **20a** "S" wide
TWO CENTS — **20b** "E" and "S" wide
TWO CENTS — **20c** "N" wide
TWO CENTS — **20d** All letters narrow
TWO CENTS — **20e** "EN" and "S" wide
TWO CENTS — **20f** "E" wide

1883 (Apr). *Nos. 52 and 18 surch with T* **20a/f.**

54	**20a**	2c. on 8c. orange	£250	£110
55	**20b**	2c. on 8c. orange	£250	£110
56	**20c**	2c. on 8c. orange	£250	£110
57	**20d**	2c. on 8c. orange	£140	80·00
		a. Surch double	£3000	£1100
58	**20e**	2c. on 8c. orange	£1600	£600
59	**20a**	2c. on 32c. pale red	£800	£200
		a. Surch double	†	£2000
60	**20f**	2c. on 32c. pale red	£1100	£275
		a. Surch double		

The 8c. was surcharged using one of two triplet settings, either 54 + 55 + 56 or 57 + 57 + 57, applied to rows 2 to 10. A single handstamp, either No. 57 or No. 58, was then used to complete row 1. The 32c. was surcharged in the same way with a triplet of 59 + 60 + 59 and a single handstamp as No. 60.

2 Cents. (21) — 4 Cents (22) — 8 Cents (23)

1883 (June–July). *Nos. 51 and 15 surch with T* **21**.

61		2c. on 4c. rose	80·00	90·00
		a. "s" of "Cents" inverted	£1400	£1500
62		2c. on 12c. blue (July)	£325	£160
		a. "s" of "Cents" inverted	£5000	£2750

The inverted "S" error occurred once in the setting of 60.

Broken oval above "O" of "POSTAGE" (Lower right pane R. 10/5)

1883 (July)–**91**. Wmk Crown CA. P 14.

63	**5**	2c. pale rose	38·00	3·75
		a. Bright rose (1889)	10·00	85
64		4c. pale brown	35·00	2·50
		a. Broken oval	£325	70·00
		b. Deep brown	45·00	3·75
		ba. Broken oval	£450	£100
		w. Wmk inverted	£150	90·00
65	**18**	5c. blue (8.83)	14·00	1·00
		w. Wmk inverted	†	£275
66	**5**	6c. lilac (11.84)	25·00	12·00
		a. Violet	2·00	6·50
		w. Wmk inverted	—	£170
67	**6**	12c. brown-purple	65·00	14·00
68	**7**	24c. yellow-green (2.84)	75·00	8·00
		a. Blue-green	6·50	4·25
		w. Wmk inverted	†	£250
69	**8**	30c. claret (9.91)	14·00	15·00
		w. Wmk inverted	£100	75·00
70	**9**	32c. orange-vermilion (1.87)	9·00	3·25
		w. Wmk inverted	65·00	65·00
71		96c. olive-grey (7.88)	75·00	55·00
63*a*/71 *Set of* 9			£200	90·00
63s/5s, 67s Optd "Specimen" *Set of* 4			£1100	

Most examples of the 4c. in shades of olive-bistre are thought to be colour changelings.

For the 4c. in deep carmine and 12c. in claret see Nos. 98 and 102.

1884 (Feb–Aug). *Nos. 65, 15 and 67 surch with T* **22** *or* **23**.

72	**18**	4c. on 5c. blue (Aug)	£3250	£4000
73		4c. on 5c. blue (R.) (Aug)	£130	£100
74	**6**	8c. on 12c. blue	£650	£150
		w. Wmk inverted	†	£550
75		8c. on 12c. brown-purple (Aug)	£425	£140
		a. Inverted "8"	†	—
		b. "s" of "Cents" low (R. 5/1)	£4000	£1400

1884 (Aug). *No. 65 surch with T* **20d/f.**

76	**20d**	2c. on 5c. blue	£140	£150
77	**20e**	2c. on 5c. blue	£140	£150
		a. Pair, with and without surch		
		b. Surch double		
78	**20f**	2c. on 5c. blue	£140	£150

Surcharged as a triplet, 77 + 76 + 78. On No. 76 "TS" are dropped below the line.

8 (24) **3 CENTS** (25) **THREE CENTS** (26)

1884 (Sept). *No. 75 additionally surch with large numeral as T* **24** *in red.*

80 **6** 8 on 8c. on 12c. dull purple £350 £375
a. Surch *T* **24** double £5500
b. Surch *T* **23** in blue £9000
c. "s" of "Cents" low £3000 £3250

Examples as No. 75, but with Type **23** in blue, were further surcharged in error.

A similar "4" surcharge in red on No. 73 exists from a trial printing of which seven examples are known, all used on an official's correspondence (*Price £28000 used*).

1885. *No. 65 and T* **9** *in new colour,* wmk Crown CA, *surch with T* **25** *or* **26**.

82 **25** 3c. on 5c. blue (Sept) £140 £225
a. Surch double £2750
83 **26** 3c. on 32c. pale magenta (Dec) ... 4·00 4·00
a. Deep magenta .... 1·50 1·00

The surcharge on No. 82 was applied locally by a triplet setting. No. 83 was surcharged by De La Rue in complete panes.

3 cents (27) **2 Cents** (28)

1886 (Apr). *No. 48 surch with T* **27**.

84 **18** 3c. on 5c. purple-brown £200 £225

The surcharge on No. 84 was applied by a triplet setting.

1887 (July). *No. 65 surch with T* **28**.

85 **18** 2c. on 5c. blue .... 28·00 75·00
a. "C" of "Cents" omitted .... — £3750
b. Surch double £1200 £1100

The surcharge on No. 85 was applied by a triplet setting.

10 CENTS (29) **THIRTY CENTS** (30)

1891 (Nov). *Nos. 68 and 70 surch with T* **29** *and* **30**.

86 **7** 10c. on 24c. yellow-green .... 4·50 1·25
a. Narrow "0" in "10" (R. 4/6) .... 28·00 30·00
w. Wmk inverted .... 70·00 75·00
87 **9** 30c. on 32c. orange-vermilion .... 10·00 3·50
w. Wmk inverted

The "R" of "THIRTY" and "N" of "CENTS" are found wide or narrow and in all possible combinations.

ONE CENT (31) **ONE CENT** (32)

1892. *Stamps of 1882–91* (wmk Crown CA) *surch with* T **31**.

88 1c. on 2c. bright rose (Mar) .... 2·00 3·75
89 1c. on 4c. brown (Apr) .... 5·00 5·50
a. Surch double £1600
b. Broken oval £140 £150
w. Wmk inverted £180
90 1c. on 6c. lilac (Feb) .... 1·40 7·00
a. Surch double, one inverted £2000 £1800
w. Wmk inverted £180
91 1c. on 8c. orange (Jan) .... 1·00 1·50
92 1c. on 12c. brown-purple (Mar) .... 5·00 9·00
88/92 *Set of 5* .... 13·00 24·00

The three settings used for Nos. 88/92 contained various combinations of the following varieties: "ON" of "ONE" and "N" of "CENT" wide; "O" wide, "N" of "ONE" narrow and "N" of "CENT" wide; "O" narrow and both letters "N" wide; "ON" narrow and "N" of "CENT" wide; "O" wide and both letters "N" narrow; "ON" wide and "N" of "CENT" narrow; "ON" and "N" of "CENT" narrow; "O" narrow, "N" of "ONE" wide and "N" of "CENT" narrow. Antique "N" and "E" letters also occur.

1892–94. *Colours changed.* Wmk Crown CA. P 14. *Surch with T* **32** *and* **26** *by De La Rue.*

93 **6** 1c. on 8c. green (3.92) .... 1·00 1·50
94 **9** 3c. on 32c. carmine-rose (6.94) .... 2·25 70
a. Surch omitted £4000
93s/4s Optd "Specimen" *Set of 2* £130

No. 94a comes from a sheet found at Singapore on which all stamps in the upper left pane had the surcharge omitted. Five vertical inter-panneau pairs still exist with the surcharge omitted on the upper stamps (*Price £35000 unused*). The only used example of the error is on cover.

33

34

4 cents. (35)

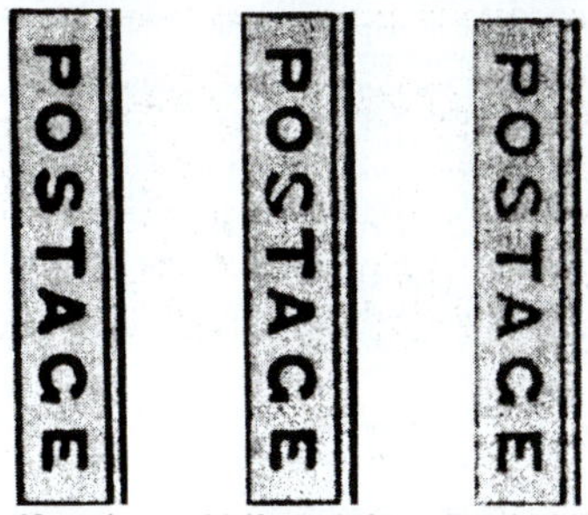

Normal Malformed "S" Repaired "S"

The malformed "S" occurs on R. 7/3 of the left pane from Key Plate 2. It is believed that the repair to it took place in mid-1898. Both states may occur on other stamps in Types **33** and **34**. Stamps subsequently printed from Key Plate 3 showed the "S" normal.

1892 (Mar)–**99**. Wmk Crown CA. P 14.

95 **33** 1c. green (9.92) .... 5·00 70
a. Malformed "S" £450 £150
b. Repaired "S" £425 £140
96 3c. carmine-rose (2.95) .... 11·00 40
a. Malformed "S" £600 £160
97 3c. brown (3.99) .... 9·00 60
a. Repaired "S" £500 £160
b. Yellow-brown .... 8·00 60
98 **5** 4c. deep carmine (7.99) .... 8·00 1·25
a. Broken oval .... £180 85·00
99 **18** 5c. brown (6.94) .... 9·00 1·00
100 5c. magenta (7.99) .... 2·25 2·00
101 **6** 8c. ultramarine (6.94) .... 4·50 50
a. Bright blue .... 7·50 80
102 12c. claret (3.94) .... 18·00 9·00
103 **33** 25c. purple-brown and green .... 30·00 7·00
a. Malformed "S" £950 £400
b. Repaired "S" £850 £375
c. Dull purple and green .... 30·00 6·50
104 50c. olive-green and carmine .... 21·00 2·50
a. Repaired "S" £900 £350
105 **34** $5 orange and carmine (10.98) ... £325 £250
a. Repaired "S" £3750 £3750
95/105 *Set of 11* £400 £250
95s/101s, 103s/5s Optd "Specimen" *Set of 10* £600

1898 (26 Dec). *T* **18** *and* **6** *surch with T* **35** *at Singapore.*

106 4c. on 5c. brown (No. 99) .... 2·75 4·75
107 4c. on 5c. blue (No. 65) .... 5·00 15·00
a. Surch double .... — £1600
108 4c. on 8c. ultramarine (No. 101) .... 1·60 2·75
a. Surch double £1300 £1200
b. Bright blue (No. 101*a*) .... 1·00 1·00
106/8*b* *Set of 3* .... 8·00 19·00

Nos. 107 and 108*b* exist with stop spaced 1½ mm from the "S" (R. 10/6).

FOUR CENTS (36)

37

38

1899 (Mar). *T* **18** (*wmk Crown CA. P 14*), *surch with T* **36** *by De La Rue.*

109 4c. on 5c. carmine .... 1·00 30
a. Surch omitted £30000
s. Optd "Specimen" .... 48·00
x. Wmk reversed .... 90·00

No. 109a is only known unused.

1902 (Apr)–**03**. Wmk Crown CA. P 14.

110 **37** 1c. grey-green (7.02) .... 2·75 3·00
a. Pale green .... 4·50 3·25
111 3c. dull purple and orange .... 3·50 20
w. Wmk inverted £600 £300
112 4c. purple/*red* (9.02) .... 4·75 30
113 **38** 5c. dull purple (8.02) .... 5·50 85
114 8c. purple/*blue* .... 4·50 20
115 10c. purple and black/*yellow* (9.02) .... 25·00 1·50
116 **37** 25c. dull purple and green (8.02) .. 14·00 6·00
117 **38** 30c. grey and carmine (7.02) .... 18·00 8·00
118 **37** 50c. deep green and carmine (9.02) .... 20·00 20·00
a. Dull green and carmine .... 23·00 23·00
119 **38** $1 dull green and black (9.02) .... 23·00 70·00
120 **37** $2 dull purple and black (9.02) ... 75·00 75·00
121 **38** $5 dull green and brown-orange (10.02) £200 £170
122 **37** $100 purple and green/*yellow* (3.03) (F.C. £225) £13000
s. Optd "Specimen" £600
110/21 *Set of 12* £350 £325
110s/21s Optd "Specimen" *Set of 12* £375

(Currency 100 cents = 1 Straits, later Malayan, dollar)

39

40

41

42

(Des N. Trotter and W. Egerton)

1903 (Dec)–**04**. Wmk Crown CA. P 14.

123 **39** 1c. grey-green .... 2·25 8·00
124 **40** 3c. dull purple (1.04) .... 11·00 4·50
125 **41** 4c. purple/*red* (4.04) .... 8·00 30
w. Wmk inverted .... † £300
126 **42** 8c. purple/*blue* (7.04) .... 50·00 1·25
123/6 *Set of 4* .... 65·00 12·50
123s/6s Optd "Specimen" *Set of 4* £160

1904 (Aug)–**10**. Wmk Multiple Crown CA. *Ordinary paper (1c. to $1 and $5) or chalk-surfaced paper ($2, $25, $100)*. P 14.

127 **39** 1c. deep green (9.04) .... 4·00 10
a. Chalk-surfaced paper (12.05). 13·00 1·50
aw. Wmk inverted .... £120 75·00
128 **40** 3c. dull purple .... 2·50 30
a. Chalk-surfaced paper (8.06) .. 13·00 1·50
aw. Wmk inverted .... £130 85·00
b. Plum (2.08) .... 9·00 1·75
129 **41** 4c. purple/*red* (11.04) .... 16·00 75
a. Chalk-surfaced paper (10.05). 16·00 1·25
aw. Wmk inverted .... 85·00 65·00
130 **38** 5c. dull purple (12.06) .... 16·00 2·25
a. Chalk-surfaced paper (12.06). 19·00 9·50
ay. Wmk inverted and reversed ... † £375
131 **42** 8c. purple/*blue* (8.05) .... 38·00 1·50
a. Chalk-surfaced paper (12.05). 35·00 2·75
132 **38** 10c. purple and black/*yellow* (8.05) .... 8·00 80
a. Chalk-surfaced paper (11.05). 12·00 3·00
133 **37** 25c. dull purple and green (1.05) ... 45·00 28·00
a. Chalk-surfaced paper (11.05). 50·00 27·00
134 **38** 30c. grey and carmine (3.05) .... 48·00 2·50
a. Chalk-surfaced paper (3.06) ... 55·00 2·75
135 **37** 50c. dull green and carmine (10.05) .... 60·00 16·00
a. Chalk-surfaced paper (11.06). 35·00 15·00
136 **38** $1 dull green and black (3.05) .... 60·00 26·00
a. Chalk-surfaced paper (3.06) ... 50·00 19·00
137 **37** $2 dull purple and black (10.05). £110 90·00
138 **38** $5 dull green and brown-orange (10.05) £275 £180
a. Chalk-surfaced paper (1.08) ... £225 £150
139 **37** $25 grey-green and black (7.06) ... £1900 £1900
s. Optd "Specimen" £300
140 $100 purple and green/*yellow* (6.10) (F.C. £350) £14000
127/38a *Set of 12* £500 £275

STRAITS SETTLEMENTS. (43) **Straits Settlements.** (44)

STRAITS SETTLEMENTS.

FOUR CENTS. (45)

1906 (20 Dec)–**07**. *T* **18** *of Labuan (Nos. 117 etc.) optd with T* **43** *or* **44** *(10c.) or additionally surch with T* **45**, *in black (No. 145), claret (No. 151) or brown-red (others) at Singapore.* P 13½–14.

141 1c. black and purple (P 14½–15) .... 70·00 £180
a. Perf 14 .... £375 £500
b. Line through "B" £750
142 2c. black and green £375 £450
a. Perf 14½–15 .... £180 £325
b. Perf 13½–14 comp 12–13 .... £1300 £1300
c. Line through "B" £1300
143 3c. black and sepia (1.07) .... 20·00 85·00
a. Line through "B" £400
144 4c. on 12c. black and yellow .... 2·75 7·50
a. No stop after "CENTS" (R. 1/8, 6/8) £500
b. Line through "B" £225 £325
145 4c. on 16c. green and brown (Blk.) ...... 7·00 8·00
a. "STRAITS SETTLEMENTS" in both brown-red and black £650 £750
b. Ditto. In vert pair with normal £7000
c. Line through "B" £250 £350
146 4c. on 18c. black and pale brown .... 2·75 7·50
a. No stop after "CENTS" (R. 1/8, 6/8) £375
b. "FOUR CENTS" and bar double. £9500
c. "FOUR CENTS" and bar 1½ mm below normal position (pair with normal) £2000
d. Line through "B" £225 £325
147 8c. black and vermilion .... 4·25 8·00
a. Line through "B" £225 £350
148 10c. brown and slate .... 8·50 8·50
a. No stop after "Settlements" (R. 1/4, 6/4) £450
b. Line through "B" £300 £325
149 25c. green and greenish blue (1.07) .... 23·00 42·00
a. Perf 14½–15 .... £100 £150
b. Perf 13½–14 comp 14½–15 .... £425
c. Line through "B" £425
150 50c. dull purple and lilac (1.07) .... 20·00 70·00
a. Line through "B" £450
151 $1 claret and orange (Claret) (1.07) .... 48·00 £120
a. Perf 14½–15 .... £800
b. Line through "B" £750 £1200
141/51 *Set of 11* £350 £750

Nos. 141/51 were overprinted by a setting of 50 (10×5) applied twice to the sheets of 100. The "FOUR CENTS" surcharges were applied separately by a similar setting.

No. 145a shows impressions of Type **43** in both brown-red and black. It is known from one complete sheet and the top half of another.

No. 146b occurred on row 5 from one sheet only. No. 146c occurred on R. 4/10 and 9/10 of the first printing.

The line through "B" flaw occurs on R. 5/10 of the basic stamp. For illustration see Labuan.

46

47

1906 (Sept)–**12**. Wmk Mult Crown CA. *Ordinary paper(1c. to 10c.) or chalk-surfaced paper (21c. to $500)*. P 14.

152	**39**	1c. blue-green (3.10)	23·00	1·10
153	**40**	3c. red (6.08)	5·50	10
154	**41**	4c. red (7.07)	7·50	2·50
155		4c. dull purple (2.08)	6·00	10
		a. Chalk-surfaced paper (1.12)	11·00	2·50
		as. Optd "Specimen"	£110	
156		4c. claret (9.11)	2·75	80
157	**38**	5c. orange (4.09)	2·75	2·50
158	**42**	8c. blue	4·25	60
159	**38**	10c. purple/*yellow* (7.08)	10·00	1·00
		a. Chalk-surfaced paper (5.12)	19·00	11·00
160	**46**	21c. dull purple and claret (11.10)	6·50	38·00
161	**37**	25c. dull and bright purple (7.09)	18·00	8·00
162	**38**	30c. purple and orange-yellow (11.09)	50·00	4·25
163	**46**	45c. black/*green* (11.10)	2·50	4·00
164	**37**	50c. black/*green* (4.10)	6·00	5·00
165	**38**	$1 black and red/*blue* (10.10)	15·00	5·50
166	**37**	$2 green and red/*yellow* (12.09)	24·00	24·00
167	**38**	$5 green and red/*green* (11.09)	£130	75·00
		w. Wmk inverted	£1100	
168	**47**	$25 purple and blue/*blue* (5.11)	£1800	£1500
		s. Optd "Specimen"	£475	
169		$500 purple and orange (5.10) (F.C. £750)	£110000	
		s. Optd "Specimen"	£2500	
152/67 *Set of* 16			£275	£160
153s/67s Optd "Specimen" *Set of* 15			£850	

Beware of dangerous forgeries of No. 169.

48

49

50

51

52

53

54

1912–23. *$25, $100 and $500 as T* **47**, *but with head of King George V. Die I (5, 10, 25, 30, 50c., $1, $2, $5)*. Wmk Mult Crown CA. *Ordinary paper (Nos. 193/6, 198/201, 203) or chalk-surfaced paper (others)*. P 14.

193	**48**	1c. green (9.12)	8·50	1·25
		a. Pale green (1.14)	8·00	1·25
		b. Blue-green (1917)	8·00	1·75
		bw. Wmk inverted	†	£375
194		1c. black (2.19)	2·25	1·00
		w. Wmk inverted	†	£375
195	**52**	2c. green (10.19)	1·75	50
		w. Wmk inverted	£500	
196	**49**	3c. red (2.13)	3·25	1·25
		a. Scarlet (2.17)	2·50	10
		y. Wmk inverted and reversed	£350	
197	**50**	4c. dull purple (3.13)	2·00	60
		a. Wmk sideways	†	£2500
		w. Wmk inverted	†	£375
198		4c. rose-scarlet (2.19)	2·25	15
		aw. Wmk inverted	†	£375
		b. Carmine	1·75	20
199	**51**	5c. orange (8.12)	2·00	50
		a. Yellow-orange	3·50	1·00
200	**52**	6c. dull claret (3.20)	2·00	50
		a. Deep claret	6·50	2·75
		aw. Wmk inverted	£275	£300
201		8c. ultramarine (3.13)	3·25	80
		w. Wmk inverted	†	£375
202	**51**	10c. purple/*yellow* (9.12)	1·50	1·00
		aw. Wmk inverted	†	£400
		b. White back (1913)	1·50	1·10
		bs. Optd "Specimen"	50·00	
		c. On lemon (1916)	18·00	1·25
		cs. Optd "Specimen"	75·00	
		d. Wmk sideways	†	£4000
203		10c. deep bright blue (1918)	7·00	50
		a. Bright blue (1919)	4·00	50
204	**53**	21c. dull and bright purple (11.13)	8·00	9·50
205	**54**	25c. dull purple and mauve (7.14)	16·00	12·00
		aw. Wmk inverted	£160	£180
		b. Dull purple and violet (1919)	70·00	15·00
207	**51**	30c. dull purple and orange (12.14)	8·00	3·50
208	**53**	45c. black/*green* (*white back*) (12.14)	6·50	18·00
		a. On blue-green, olive back (7.18)	3·75	22·00
		as. Optd "Specimen"	60·00	
		b. On emerald back (6.22)	3·25	13·00
209	**54**	50c. black/*green* (7.14)	5·50	3·50
		a. On blue-green, olive back (1918)	18·00	7·50
		b. On emerald back (1921)	12·00	9·50
		c. Die II. *On emerald back* (1922)	3·00	4·00
		cs. Optd "Specimen"	60·00	
210	**51**	$1 black and red/*blue* (10.14)	12·00	11·00
		w. Wmk inverted	£180	£190
211	**54**	$2 green and red/*yellow, white back* (1914)	13·00	45·00
		a. Green and red/yellow (1915)	11·00	45·00
		as. Optd "Specimen"	65·00	
		b. On orange-buff (1921)	60·00	75·00
		c. On pale yellow (1921)	65·00	85·00
212	**51**	$5 green and red/*green, white back* (11.13)	95·00	45·00
		a. Green and red/green (1915)	95·00	70·00
		as. Optd "Specimen"	95·00	
		b. On blue-green, olive back (1918)	£160	95·00
		bw. Wmk inverted		
		c. On emerald back (1920)	£200	£110
		d. Die II. *On emerald back* (1923)	£110	75·00
		ds. Optd "Specimen"	£100	
213	–	$25 purple and blue/*blue*	£1600	£450
		a. Break in scroll	£3250	
		b. Broken crown and scroll	£3250	
		e. Break in lines below scroll	£3250	
		f. Damaged leaf at bottom right	£3250	
		s. Optd "Specimen"	£400	
214	–	$100 black and carmine/*blue* (8.12) (F.C. £200)	£7000	
		a. Break in scroll	£12000	
		b. Broken crown and scroll	£12000	
		e. Break in lines below scroll		
		f. Damaged leaf at bottom right		
		s. Optd "Specimen"	£800	
215	–	$500 purple and orange-brown (8.12) (F.C. £500)	£70000	
		a. Break in scroll	£90000	
		b. Broken crown and scroll	£95000	
		f. Damaged leaf at bottom right		
		s. Optd "Specimen"	£2750	
193/212 *Set of* 19			£160	£130
193s/212s Optd "Specimen" *Set of* 19			£800	

The 6c. is similar to *T* **52**, but the head is in a beaded oval as in *T* **53**. The 2c., 6c. (and 12c. below) have figures of value on a circular ground while in the 8c. this is of oval shape.

For illustrations of the varieties on Nos. 213/15 see above No. 51*b* of Bermuda.

RED CROSS

2c.

(55)

MALAYA-
BORNEO
EXHIBITION.

(56)

1917 (1 May). *Surch with T* **55**.

216	**49**	3c. + 2c. scarlet	2·75	30·00
		a. No stop (R. 2/3)	£425	£800
217	**50**	4c. + 2c. dull purple	3·75	30·00
		a. No stop (R. 2/3)	£475	£800

Nos 216/17 were sold at face, plus 2c. on each stamp for Red Cross funds.

Nos. 216a and 217a occur in the first setting only.

Type I

Type II

The duty plate for the 25c. value was replaced in 1926. In Type II the solid shading forming the back of the figure 2 extends to the top of the curve; the upturned end of the foot of the 2 is short; two background lines above figure 5; c close to 5; STRAITS SETTLEMENTS in taller letters.

1921–33. Wmk Mult Script CA. *Ordinary paper (1c. to 6c., 10c. (No. 230), 12c.) or chalk-surfaced paper (others)*. P 14.

218	**48**	1c. black (3.22)	60	10
219	**52**	2c. green (5.21)	60	10
		w. Wmk inverted	40·00	
		x. Wmk reversed	†	—
		y. Wmk inverted and reversed		
220		2c. brown (3.25)	7·00	2·50
221	**49**	3c. green (9.23)	1·50	80
		w. Wmk inverted	40·00	50·00
222	**50**	4c. carmine-red (9.21)	2·00	4·50
		y. Wmk inverted and reversed	†	£300
223		4c. bright violet (8.24)	60	10
		w. Wmk inverted	40·00	
224		4c. orange (8.29)	1·00	10
225	**51**	5c. orange (Die I) (5.21)	1·75	15
		a. Wmk sideways	†	£3500
		bw. Wmk inverted	40·00	
		bx. Wmk reversed	†	—
		c. Die II (1922)	2·25	1·25
226		5c. brown (Die II) (1932)	2·75	10
		a. Die I (1933)	5·00	10
		ab. Face value omitted	£23000	
227	**52**	6c. dull claret (10.22)	2·00	15
		w. Wmk inverted	38·00	45·00
228		6c. rose-pink (2.25)	24·00	9·50
229		6c. scarlet (1.27)	2·50	10
230	**51**	10c. bright blue (Die I) (1921)	1·75	3·50
		w. Wmk inverted	40·00	65·00
231		10c. purple/*pale yellow* (Die I) (1923)	2·50	9·50
		a. Die II (11.26)	2·25	30
		b. Purple/bright yellow (Die II) (1932)	16·00	3·00
		ba. Die I (1933)	9·00	10
232	**52**	12c. bright blue (1.22)	1·25	20
		w. Wmk inverted	40·00	
233	**53**	21c. dull and bright purple (2.23)	6·00	50·00
234	**54**	25c. dull purple and mauve (Die I, Type I) (1921)	28·00	80·00
		a. Die II, Type I (1923)	12·00	3·75
		b. Die II, Type II (1927)	5·00	1·75
235	**51**	30c. dull purple and orange (Die I) (1921)	23·00	45·00
		a. Die II (1922)	2·00	1·25
236	**53**	35c. dull purple and orange-yellow (8.22)	12·00	6·00
		a. Dull purple and orange	3·50	4·50
237		35c. scarlet and purple (4.31)	10·00	5·50
238	**54**	50c. black/*emerald* (9.25)	1·75	40
239	**51**	$1 black and red/*blue* (Die II) (1921)	6·00	65
240	**54**	$2 green and red/*pale yellow* (Die II) (1923)	10·00	8·00
240*a*	**51**	$5 green and red/*green* (Die II) (1926)	90·00	32·00
240*b*	–	$25 purple and blue/*blue* (5.23)	£850	£150
		ba. Break in scroll	£1800	
		bb. Broken crown and scroll	£1800	£1100
		be. Break through lines below left scroll		
		bf. Damaged leaf at bottom right		
		bs. Optd "Specimen"	£275	
240*c*	–	$100 black and carmine/*blue* (5.23) (F.C. £150)	£6500	£2000
		ca. Break in scroll	£9500	
		cb. Broken crown and scroll	£9500	
		ce. Break through lines below left scroll		
		cf. Damaged leaf at bottom right		
		cs. Optd "Specimen"	£650	
240*d*	–	$500 purple and orange-brown (4.23) (F.C. £500)	£48000	
		da. Break in scroll	£60000	
		db. Broken crown and scroll	£65000	
		de. Break through lines below left scroll		
		df. Damaged leaf at bottom right		
		ds. Optd "Specimen"	£2250	
218/40*a* *Set of* 24			£160	£110
218s/40as (*ex* 6c. rose-pink) Optd or Perf (Nos. 224s, 226s, 237s) "Specimen" *Set of* 23			£650	

Nos. 240*b*/*d* are as Type **47**, but with portrait of George V.

No. 226ab was caused by a progressive inking failure, resulting in the value being completely omitted on R.10/10 of a single sheet.

The 2c. green was reissued in 1927, and exists with "Specimen" overprint 15.5×1.75 mm instead of the 14.5×2.5 mm of the original issue (*Price*, £65).

An 8c. in carmine was prepared but not issued (Optd "Specimen" £450).

The paper of Nos. 231*b*/ba is the normal *pale yellow* at the back, but with a bright yellow surface.

In 1926 new Key and Duty plates were made of 100 (10×10) instead of the usual 60 (6×10).

For illustrations of the varieties on Nos. 240*b*/*d* see above No. 51*b* of Bermuda.

SETTINGS OF TYPE 56. Nos. 241/55 were produced using a typeset block of 12 (6×2) overprints from which ten stereos were taken to provide a forme for the complete sheet of 120. Two such formes were prepared of which the second was only used for a limited number of Straits Settlements sheets in addition to the Kedah and Trengganu issues.

Several constant varieties occur on the original typeset block of 12 and so appear ten times on sheets printed from both Settings I and II. These include:

Oval last "O" in "BORNEO" (R. 1/3 of typeset block of 12)

Raised stop after "EXHIBITION" (R. 2/2 of typeset block of 12)

Small second "A" in "MALAYA" (R. 2/6 of typeset block of 12).

The two formes also produced constant varieties in each setting which include:

Setting I

No hyphen (Left pane. R. 7/1 or 9/2)

No stop (Left and right panes. Either on R. 10/4 (right pane) or, for some sheets, on other stamps from even numbered horizontal rows in the 4th vertical column (both panes))

Third "I" in "EXHIBITION" omitted (R. 8/5, 10/5 (left pane)). This must have occurred very late in the use of this setting and is only found on the 5c. and 10c.

Setting II

No stop (Left pane. R. 1/5)

"EXH.BITION" (Left pane. Stamps from even numbered horizontal rows in the 3rd vertical column)

1922 (31 Mar). *Malaya-Borneo Exhibition, Singapore. Optd with T* **56**.

(a) Wmk Mult Crown CA (Nos. 195, 198/9, 201, 205, 208a, 210, 211b and 212b).

241	**52**	2c. green	28·00	75·00
		b. Oval last "O" in "BORNEO"	60·00	£130
		c. Raised stop after "EXHIBITION"	60·00	£130
		d. Small second "A" in "MALAYA"	60·00	£130
		e. No hyphen	£200	
		f. No stop	75·00	£150
242	**50**	4c. rose-scarlet	8·50	23·00
		b. Oval last "O" in "BORNEO"	16·00	42·00
		c. Raised stop after "EXHIBITION"	16·00	42·00

		d. Small second "A" in "MALAYA"	16·00	42·00
		e. No hyphen	70·00	
		f. No stop	20·00	48·00
		h. "EXH.BITION"	70·00	
243	51	5c. orange	6·50	19·00
		b. Oval last "O" in "BORNEO"	12·00	35·00
		c. Raised stop after "EXHIBITION"	12·00	35·00
		d. Small second "A" in "MALAYA"	12·00	35·00
		e. No hyphen	48·00	
		f. No stop	14·00	40·00
		h. "EXH.BITION"	48·00	
244	52	8c. ultramarine	1·75	8·50
		b. Oval last "O" in "BORNEO"	4·75	16·00
		c. Raised stop after "EXHIBITION"	4·75	16·00
		d. Small second "A" in "MALAYA"	4·75	16·00
		e. No hyphen	32·00	
		f. No stop	5·50	18·00
		h. "EXH.BITION"	32·00	
245	54	25c. dull purple and mauve	3·25	40·00
		b. Oval last "O" in "BORNEO"	8·50	70·00
		c. Raised stop after "EXHIBITION"	8·50	70·00
		d. Small second "A" in "MALAYA"	8·50	70·00
		e. No hyphen	42·00	
		f. No stop	9·50	80·00
		h. "EXH.BITION"	42·00	
246	53	45c. black/*blue-green* (*olive back*)	3·00	32·00
		b. Oval last "O" in "BORNEO"	8·00	55·00
		c. Raised stop after "EXHIBITION"	8·00	55·00
		d. Small second "A" in "MALAYA"	8·00	55·00
		e. No hyphen	40·00	
		f. No stop	9·00	65·00
247	51	$1 black and red/*blue*	£325	£1000
		b. Oval last "O" in "BORNEO"	£550	
		c. Raised stop after "EXHIBITION"	£550	
		d. Small second "A" in "MALAYA"	£550	
		e. No hyphen		
		f. No stop	£650	
248	54	$2 green and red/*orange-buff*	26·00	£120
		a. *On pale yellow* (No. 211c)	65·00	£160
		b. Oval last "O" in "BORNEO"	50·00	£225
		c. Raised stop after "EXHIBITION"	50·00	£225
		d. Small second "A" in "MALAYA"	50·00	£225
		e. No hyphen	£225	
		f. No stop	60·00	£250
		h. "EXH.BITION"	£700	
249	51	$5 green and red/*blue-green* (*olive-back*)	£300	£500
		b. Oval last "O" in "BORNEO"	£450	
		c. Raised stop after "EXHIBITION"	£450	
		d. Small second "A" in "MALAYA"	£450	
		e. No hyphen	£1500	
		f. No stop	£500	

(*b*) Wmk Mult Script CA (*Nos. 218/19, 222, 225b, 230 and 239*).

250	48	1c. black	3·00	17·00
		b. Oval last "O" in "BORNEO"	7·00	26·00
		c. Raised stop after "EXHIBITION"	7·00	26·00
		d. Small second "A" in "MALAYA"	7·00	26·00
		e. No hyphen	40·00	
		f. No stop	8·50	29·00
		h. "EXH.BITION"	40·00	
251	52	2c. green	2·50	15·00
		b. Oval last "O" in "BORNEO"	5·50	25·00
		c. Raised stop after "EXHIBITION"	5·50	25·00
		d. Small second "A" in "MALAYA"	5·50	25·00
		e. No hyphen	32·00	
		f. No stop	6·50	27·00
		h. "EXH.BITION"	32·00	
252	50	4c. carmine-red	3·50	38·00
		b. Oval last "O" in "BORNEO"	8·00	70·00
		c. Raised stop after "EXHIBITION"	8·00	70·00
		d. Small second "A" in "MALAYA"	8·00	70·00
		e. No hyphen	40·00	
		f. No stop	9·00	75·00
253	51	5c. orange (Die II)	2·75	50·00
		b. Oval last "O" in "BORNEO"	7·00	85·00
		c. Raised stop after "EXHIBITION"	7·00	85·00
		d. Small second "A" in "MALAYA"	7·00	85·00
		e. No hyphen	40·00	
		f. No stop	8·50	95·00
		g. Third "I" in "EXHIBITION" omitted	£1800	
254		10c. bright blue	2·25	26·00
		b. Oval last "O" in "BORNEO"	6·00	48·00
		c. Raised stop after "EXHIBITION"	6·00	48·00
		d. Small second "A" in "MALAYA"	6·00	48·00
		e. No hyphen	32·00	
		f. No stop	7·00	55·00
		g. Third "I" in "EXHIBITION" omitted	£800	
255		$1 black and red/*blue* (Die II)	20·00	£130
		b. Oval last "O" in "BORNEO"	45·00	£250
		c. Raised stop after "EXHIBITION"	45·00	£250
		d. Small second "A" in "MALAYA"	45·00	£250
		e. No hyphen		
		f. No stop	50·00	£275
		h. "EXH.BITION"		
242/55 *Set of* 11			£325	£850

Examples of most values are known with part strikes of a forged Singapore postmark dated "AU 1 1910".

1935 (6 May). *Silver Jubilee. As Nos. 91/4 of Antigua. but ptd by Waterlow & Sons.* P 11×12.

256	5c. ultramarine and grey	3·00	30
257	8c. green and indigo	3·00	3·25
258	12c. brown and deep blue	3·00	6·00
	j. Damaged turret	£500	
259	25c. slate and purple	3·25	7·50
256/9 *Set of* 4		11·00	15·00
256s/9s Perf "Specimen" *Set of* 4		£190	

For illustration of plate variety see Omnibus section following Zanzibar.

57

58

1936 (1 Jan)–**37**. *Chalk-surfaced paper.* Wmk Mult Script CA. P 14.

260	57	1c. black (1.1.37)	1·25	20
261		2c. green (1.2.36)	1·50	70
262		4c. orange (15.6.36)	2·25	70
263		5c. brown (1.8.36)	1·00	30
264		6c. scarlet (1.2.36)	1·25	1·10
265		8c. grey	2·75	70
266		10c. dull purple (1.7.36)	2·25	60
267		12c. bright ultramarine (1.9.36)	2·00	2·50
268		25c. dull purple and scarlet (1.2.36)	1·25	50
269		30c. dull purple and orange	1·25	3·25
270		40c. scarlet and dull purple	1·25	2·50
271		50c. black/*emerald* (1.9.36)	4·50	1·25
272		$1 black and red/*blue* (1.7.36)	19·00	1·75
273		$2 green and scarlet (1.4.36)	50·00	10·00
274		$5 green and red/*emerald* (1.1.37)	£120	10·00
260/74 *Set of* 15			£190	32·00
260s/74s Perf "Specimen" *Set of* 15			£400	

1937 (12 May). *Coronation. As Nos. 95/7 of Antigua, but printed by D.L.R.*

275	4c. orange	55	10
276	8c. grey-black	1·00	10
277	12c. bright blue	2·50	1·00
275/7 *Set of* 3		3·50	1·10
275s/7s Perf "Specimen" *Set of* 3		£150	

1937–41. *Chalk-surfaced paper.* Wmk Mult Script CA. P 14 or 15×14 (15c.).

(*a*) *Die I (printed at two operations).*

278	58	1c. black (1.1.38)	8·50	10
279		2c. green (6.12.37)	18·00	20
280		4c. orange (1.1.38)	21·00	20
281		5c. brown (19.11.37)	20·00	30
282		6c. scarlet (10.1.38)	11·00	50
283		8c. grey (26.1.38)	38·00	10
284		10c. dull purple (8.11.37)	8·00	10
285		12c. ultramarine (10.1.38)	8·00	50
286		25c. dull purple and scarlet (11.12.37)	42·00	1·10
287		30c. dull purple and orange (1.12.37)	20·00	2·00
288		40c. scarlet and dull purple (20.12.37)	15·00	2·25
289		50c. black/*emerald* (26.1.38)	11·00	10
290		$1 black and red/*blue* (26.1.38)	15·00	20
291		$2 green and scarlet (26.1.38)	32·00	9·00
292		$5 green and red/*emerald* (26.1.38)	25·00	4·50

(*b*) *Die II (printed at one operation).*

293	58	2c. green (28.12.38)	50·00	40
294		2c. orange (6.10.41)	2·00	15·00
295		3c. green (*ordinary paper*) (5.9.41)	7·50	4·00
296		4c. orange (29.10.38)	80·00	10
297		5c. brown (18.2.39)	28·00	10
298		15c. ultramarine (*ordinary paper*) (6.10.41)	7·00	10·00
278/98 *Set of* 18			£275	45·00
278s/92s 294s/5s, 298s Perf "Specimen" *Set of* 18.			£500	

Die I. Lines of background outside central oval touch the oval and the foliage of the palm tree is usually joined to the oval frame. The downward-pointing palm frond, opposite the King's eye, has two points.

Die II. Lines of background are separated from the oval by a white line and the foliage of the palm trees does not touch the outer frame. The palm frond has only one point.

Nos. 295 and 298 were printed by Harrison and Sons following bomb damage to the De La Rue works on 29 December 1940.

The 6c. grey, 8c. scarlet and $5 purple and orange were only issued with the BMA overprint, but the 8c. without overprint is known although in this state it was never issued (*Price* £14).

STAMP BOOKLETS

1914–19. *Black on blue (No. SB1) or grey (No. SB1b) covers, Stapled.*

SB1	$1 booklet containing twenty-five 4c. dull purple (No. 197) in two blocks of 12 and one single	
	a. Containing 4c. rose-scarlet (No. 198) (1919)	
SB1*b*	$1 booklet containing four 1c., sixteen 3c. and twelve 4c. (Nos. 193, 196/7) in blocks of four	

1921. *Black on blue cover. Stapled.*

SB2	$1 booklet containing twenty-five 4c. (No. 222) in two blocks of 12 and one single	
	a. Contents as SB2, but four blocks of 6 and one single	

1922. *Black on red cover. Stapled.*

SB3	$1 booklet containing 5c. (No. 225) in block of 8 and 6c. (No. 227) in block of 10	£1700

1925–29. *Black on red cover. Stapled.*

SB4	$1.20 booklet containing thirty 4c. bright violet (No. 223) in blocks of 10	£3000
	a. Containing 4c. orange (No. 224) (1929)	£3250

1927. *Black on grey (No. SB5), green (No. SB6) or blue (No. SB7) covers. Stapled.*

SB5	$1 booklet containing 4c. and 6c. (Nos. 223, 229) in blocks of 10	£2250
SB6	$1.20 booklet containing twenty 6c. (No. 229) in blocks of 10	£2500
SB7	$1.20 booklet containing 2c., 4c. and 6c. (Nos. 219, 223, 229) in blocks of 10	£3250

1933. *Black on buff cover. Stapled.*

SB8	$1 booklet containing twenty 5c. (No. 226a) in blocks of 10	

1936. *Stapled.*

SB9	$1 booklet containing twenty 5c. (No. 263) in blocks of 10	
SB10	$1.30 booklet containing 5c. and 8c. (Nos. 263, 265) in blocks of 10	

1938. *Black on buff (No. SB11) or black on green (No. SB12) covers. Stapled.*

SB11	$1 booklet containing twenty 5c. (No. 281) in blocks of 10	£2250
SB12	$1.30 booklet containing 5c. and 8c. (Nos. 281, 283) in blocks of 10 and pane of airmail labels	£2500

POSTAGE DUE STAMPS

D 1

1924 (1 Jan)–**26**. Wmk Mult Script CA. P 14.

D1	D 1	1c. violet	5·00	5·50
D2		2c. black	3·25	1·00
D3		4c. green (5.26)	2·00	4·00
D4		8c. scarlet	4·50	55
D5		10c. orange	6·00	85
D6		12c. bright blue	7·00	65
D1/6 *Set of* 6			25·00	11·00
D1s/6s *Set of* 6			£250	

For later issues of Postage Due stamps, see MALAYAN POSTAL UNION.

POSTAL FISCAL STAMPS

1938. *T* **47** *but with head of King George VI and inscribed "REVENUE" at each side.* Wmk Mult Script CA. P 14.

F1	$25 purple and blue/*blue*	£600	£400

No. F1 was regularly used for postal purposes in 1941, although no specific authorisation for such use has been discovered.

The Straits Settlements were occupied by the Japanese in 1942. After the Second World War the stamps of MALAYA (BRITISH MILITARY ADMINISTRATION) were used. In 1946 Singapore became a separate Crown Colony and Labuan was transferred to North Borneo. Separate stamps were issued for Malacca and Penang, which both joined the Malayan Federation on 1 February 1948.

II. FEDERATED MALAY STATES

On 1 July 1896, the States of Negri Sembilan, Pahang, Perak and Selangor were organised on a federal basis to be known as the Federated Malay States. For the time being each State continued with individual issues, but stamps for the use of the Federation replaced these in 1900.

PRICES FOR STAMPS ON COVER

Nos. 1/13	*from* × 15
No. 14	—
Nos. 15/22	*from* × 10
Nos. 23/5	*from* × 3
No. 26	—
Nos. 27/50	*from* × 6
No. 51	—
Nos. 52/81	*from* × 5
No. 82	—
Nos. D1/6	*from* × 10

PRINTERS. All issues of the Federated Malay States were printed in typography by De La Rue & Co, Ltd, London, *unless otherwise stated.*

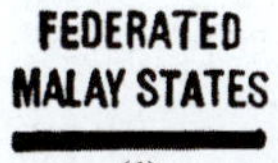

(1)

(2)

1900. *Optd with T* **1** *(cent values) or* **2** *(dollar values).*

(*a*) *Stamps of Negri Sembilan (T* **3**).

1	1c. dull purple and green	3·00	7·50
2	2c. dull purple and brown	29·00	65·00
3	3c. dull purple and black	2·75	4·00
4	5c. dull purple and olive-yellow	70·00	£170
5	10c. dull purple and orange	10·00	32·00
6	20c. green and olive	85·00	£100
7	25c. green and carmine	£250	£375
8	50c. green and black	90·00	£130
1/8 *Set of* 8		£475	£750
1s/8s Optd "Specimen" *Set of* 8		£190	

(*b*) *Stamps of Perak (T* **44** *and* **45**).

9	5c. dull purple and olive-yellow	22·00	60·00
10	10c. dull purple and orange	75·00	65·00
11	$1 green and pale green	£170	£250
	w. Wmk inverted	£900	

12	$2 green and carmine	£140	£250
13	$5 green and ultramarine	£450	£650
14	$25 green and orange	£9500	
	s. Optd "Specimen"	£400	
11s/13s Optd "Specimen" *Set of* 3		£150	

The Negri Sembilan 3c. dull purple and black does not exist without overprint Type **1**.

> The stamps of STRAITS SETTLEMENTS were used in Federated Malay States from 16 July 1900 until replaced by the 1900–1 issue.

3

4

1900–01. P 14.

(*a*) *T* **3**. Wmk Crown CA, sideways *(1901)*.

15	1c. black and green	12·00	8·00
	a. Grey and green	4·00	1·00
	b. Grey-brown and green	10·00	30
16	3c. black and brown	15·00	4·50
	a. Grey and brown	6·00	35
	b. Grey-brown and brown	7·00	20
17	4c. black and carmine	20·00	7·50
	a. Grey and carmine	8·50	4·75
	b. Grey-brown and carmine	25·00	2·25
18	5c. green and carmine/*yellow*	2·50	3·00
19	8c. black and ultramarine	48·00	21·00
	a. Grey and ultramarine	21·00	7·50
	b. Grey-brown and ultramarine	27·00	3·75
20	10c. black and claret	£120	48·00
	a. Grey and claret	75·00	9·00
	b. Black and purple	£150	42·00
	c. Grey and purple	80·00	14·00
	d. Grey-brown and purple	85·00	7·00
21	20c. mauve and black	18·00	11·00
22	50c. black and orange-brown	£160	£130
	a. Grey and orange-brown	£100	50·00
	b. Grey-brown and orange-brown	90·00	42·00
15/22b *Set of* 8		£200	60·00
15s/22s Optd "Specimen" *Set of* 8		£200	

Later printings in 1903–4 show the two upper lines of shading in the background at the corner nearest to the "S" of "STATE" blurred and running into one another, whereas in earlier printings these lines are distinct. Two plates were used for printing the central design of *T* **3**. In Plate 1 the lines of background are regular throughout, but in Plate 2 they are lighter around the head and back of the tiger. The 5c. was the only value with single wmk to be printed from Plate 2. Stamps with multiple wmk were printed for a short time from Plate 1, and show the two blurred lines of background near "S" of "STATE," but the majority of these stamps were printed from Plate 2 and later plates.

(*b*) *T* **4**. Wmk Crown CC *(1900)*.

23	$1 green and pale green	£120	£130
	w. Wmk inverted	†	—
24	$2 green and carmine	£130	£140
25	$5 green and bright ultramarine	£300	£325
	a. Green and pale ultramarine	£300	£300
26	$25 green and orange	£3000	£1600
	s. Optd "Specimen"	£300	
23s/5s Optd "Specimen" *Set of* 3		£160	

Two dies for 1c. green and 4c. scarlet

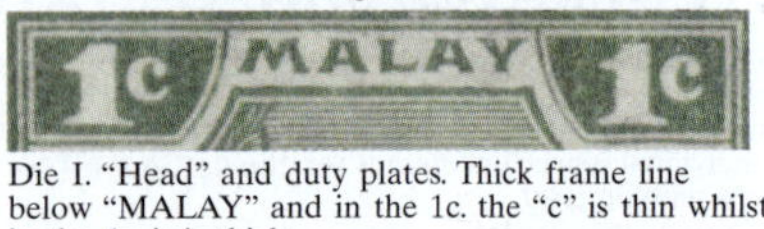

Die I. "Head" and duty plates. Thick frame line below "MALAY" and in the 1c. the "c" is thin whilst in the 4c. it is thick.

Die II. Single working plate. Thin frame line below "MALAY" and in the 1c. the "c" is thicker whilst in the 4c. it is thinner.

1904 (Aug)–**22**. *T* **3** *and T* **4** *(dollar values)*. Wmk Mult Crown CA (sideways* on *T* **3**). *Ordinary paper (1c. to 50c.) or chalk-surfaced paper ($1 to $25).*

27	1c. grey and green (8.04)	75·00	8·50
	a. Grey-brown and green	38·00	70
28	1c. green (Die I) (8.7.06)	15·00	30
29	1c. green (Die II) (1908)	8·50	20
	a. Yellow-green	20·00	2·25
	aw. Wmk Crown to right of CA	55·00	9·00
	b. Blue-green	26·00	1·75
30	1c. deep brown (21.1.19)	2·25	90
	w. Wmk Crown to right of CA	†	£200
31	2c. green (18.2.19)	2·50	30
	w. Wmk Crown to right of CA	55·00	13·00
32	3c. grey and brown (10.04)	70·00	1·00
	a. Grey-brown and brown (12.05)	48·00	1·75
	ab. Chalk-surfaced paper	45·00	2·75
33	3c. brown (11.7.06)	9·00	15
34	3c. carmine (2.2.09)	4·50	10
	aw. Wmk Crown to right of CA	10·00	40
	b. Scarlet (1.17)	17·00	50
	bw. Wmk Crown to right of CA	29·00	4·50
35	3c. grey (29.10.18)	2·50	20
	w. Wmk Crown to right of CA	50·00	13·00
36	4c. grey and scarlet (8.04)	55·00	5·50
	a. Chalk-surfaced paper. *Grey and rose*	25·00	3·00
	b. Grey-brown and scarlet	42·00	3·25
	c. Black and scarlet	24·00	2·50
	d. Black and rose	6·50	80
	dw. Wmk Crown to right of CA	11·00	80
	e. Black and deep rose (aniline) (1909)	50·00	5·00
	f. Jet black and rose (1914)	28·00	2·50
37	4c. scarlet (Die I) (11.2.19)	3·50	4·75
38	4c. scarlet (Die II) (15.4.19)	1·75	15
	aw. Wmk Crown to right of CA	55·00	6·00
	b. Wmk upright (2.22)	£800	£375
39	5c. green and carmine/*yellow* (5.06)	12·00	3·00
	aw. Wmk Crown to right of CA	70·00	19·00
	b. Chalk-surfaced paper	32·00	6·00
	c. Deep green and carmine/yellow	15·00	3·50
	d. On orange-buff (1921)	18·00	9·50
	e. On pale yellow (4.22)	13·00	7·50
40	6c. orange (11.2.19)	2·75	3·00
41	8c. grey and ultramarine (2.05)	75·00	22·00
	aw. Wmk Crown to right of CA		
	b. Grey-brown and ultramarine (12.05)	19·00	4·25
	ba. Chalk-surfaced paper	75·00	14·00
	bb. Wmk upright (3.07)	9·00	4·75
42	8c. ultramarine (8.3.10)	13·00	1·00
	aw. Wmk Crown to right of CA	90·00	30·00
	b. Deep blue (1918)	16·00	1·25
43	10c. grey-brown and claret (5.04)	80·00	7·50
	a. Chalk-surfaced paper (1905)	£110	13·00
	b. Black and claret	30·00	65
	bw. Wmk Crown to right of CA	45·00	1·50
	c. Grey-brown and purple (1905)	75·00	3·25
	d. Black and purple	30·00	2·75
	dy. Wmk Crown to right of CA and reversed	†	£300
	e. Jet-black and bright purple (1914)	95·00	5·00
44	10c. deep blue (3.6.19)	6·50	1·75
	a. Bright blue	6·50	1·00
	ab. Wmk inverted	†	—
	aw. Wmk Crown to right of CA	70·00	22·00
45	20c. mauve and black (3.05)	17·00	1·25
	a. Chalk-surfaced paper	13·00	3·00
	w. Wmk Crown to right of CA	85·00	22·00
46	35c. scarlet/*pale yellow* (25.8.22)	5·50	12·00
47	50c. grey and orange (3.05)	75·00	11·00
	aw. Wmk Crown to right of CA	£190	60·00
	b. Wmk inverted	†	—
	c. Grey-brown and orange-brown (1906)	50·00	10·00
	caw. Wmk Crown to right of CA	†	—
	cb. Chalk-surfaced paper. *Grey-brown and orange-brown*	55·00	7·50
	cbw. Wmk Crown to right of CA	†	80·00
	cc. Grey and orange-brown	65·00	10·00
	cd. Black and orange-brown	90·00	19·00
	ce. Jet-black and orange-brown (1914)	£120	23·00
48	$1 grey-green and green (10.07)	80·00	50·00
	a. Green and pale green	£100	50·00
	aw. Wmk inverted		
49	$2 green and carmine (4.12.07)	85·00	£120
	a. Printed on the gummed side		
	w. Wmk inverted		
	y. Wmk inverted and reversed	†	£750
50	$5 green and blue (1.08)	£200	£130
51	$25 green and orange (12.09)	£1300	£800
27/50 *Set of* 22		£550	£300
28s, 30s/1s, 33s/5s, 38s, 40s, 42s, 44s, 46s Optd "Specimen" *Set of* 11		£550	

*The normal sideways watermark shows Crown to left of CA, *as seen from the back of the stamp*. The watermark on No. 47b is vertical, inverted.

Nos. 29/*b*, 30, 31, 33, 34/*b* and 35 were printed from single working plates and all the rest from double plates.

Most examples of No. 47b have fiscal cancellations, but at least one is known postally used.

The 3c. scarlet (No. 34*b*) was surcharged '4/CENTS.' between horizontal lines in early 1918, but was never issued. The entire printing of five million stamps was sunk at sea, nevertheless a few examples do exist. (*Price*, £5000, *unused*).

1922–34. Wmk Mult Script CA (sideways* on *T* **3**). *Ordinary paper (1c. to 10c. (No. 66), 12c., 20c. (No. 69a), 35c. (No. 72)) or chalk-surfaced paper (others).*

52	**3**	1c. deep brown (1.8.22)	1·50	3·25
		w. Wmk Crown to right of CA	60·00	60·00
53		1c. black (12.6.23)	75	20
54		2c. brown (5.8.25)	6·50	8·50
55		2c. green (15.6.26)	3·00	10
		a. Wmk upright	£400	
56		3c. grey (27.12.22)	1·75	7·50
		w. Wmk Crown to right of CA	75·00	75·00
57		3c. green (22.1.24)	1·25	1·50
58		3c. brown (31.5.27)	2·75	50
		a. Wmk upright	£400	
59		4c. carmine-red (Die II) (27.11.23)	3·50	50
		w. Wmk Crown to right of CA	45·00	20·00
60		4c. orange (9.11.26)	1·50	10
		a. No watermark	£300	£200
		b. Wmk upright	£400	
		c. "A" of "CA" missing from wmk	†	£750
61		5c. mauve/*pale yellow* (17.3.22)	1·00	20
		w. Wmk Crown to right of CA	60·00	40·00
62		5c. brown (1.3.32)	3·50	10
63		6c. orange (2.5.22)	1·00	45
		w. Wmk Crown to right of CA	95·00	
64		6c. scarlet (9.11.26)	1·50	10
		a. Wmk upright		
65		10c. bright blue (23.10.23)	1·25	8·00
		w. Wmk Crown to right of CA		
66		10c. black and blue (18.1.24†)	2·00	75
67		10c. purple/*pale yellow* (14.7.31)	3·75	40
68		12c. ultramarine (12.9.22)	1·25	10
		w. Wmk Crown to right of CA	70·00	35·00
		x. Wmk sideways reversed	£200	
69		20c. dull purple and black (*chalk-surfaced paper*) (3.4.23)	4·00	1·75
		a. Ordinary paper (29.12.26)	42·00	3·00
		b. Wmk inverted	†	£250
70		25c. purple and bright magenta (3.9.29)	2·75	1·50
71		30c. purple and orange-yellow (3.9.29)	3·25	3·50
72		35c. scarlet/*pale yellow* (6.11.28)	3·25	23·00
73		35c. scarlet and purple (29.9.31)	13·00	14·00
74		50c. black and orange (24.4.24)	13·00	12·00
		aw. Wmk Crown to right of CA	£140	
		b. Black and orange-brown	30·00	5·00
75		50c. black/*green* (16.6.31)	4·00	2·50
76	**4**	$1 pale green and green (2.2.26)	22·00	95·00
		a. Grey-green and emerald (5.10.26)	19·00	50·00
77	**3**	$1 black and red/*blue* (10.3.31)	12·00	3·75
78	**4**	$2 green and carmine (17.8.26)	25·00	80·00
79	**3**	$2 green and red/*yellow* (6.2.34)	42·00	38·00
80	**4**	$5 green and blue (24.2.25)	£120	£190
		w. Wmk inverted	£900	
81	**3**	$5 green and red/*green* (7.34)	£180	£180
82	**4**	$25 green and orange (14.2.28)	£1000	£1200
		s. Optd "Specimen"	£275	
52/81 *Set of* 30			£450	£550
52s/81s Optd or Perf (No. 62s, 67s, 70s/1s, 73s, 77s, 79s, 81s) "Specimen" *Set of* 30			£1200	

*The normal sideways watermark shows Crown to left of CA, *as seen from the back of the stamp*.

†No. 66 was released in London by the Crown Agents some months earlier but this is the official date of issue in the States.

Nos. 52, 56 and 59 were printed from single working plates and the rest from double plates.

No. 55 exists in coils constructed from normal sheets.

The 5c. mauve on white Script paper is the result of soaking early printings of No. 61 in water.

STAMP BOOKLETS

1909. *Black on pink (Nos. SB1/2) or black on buff (No. SB3) covers. Stapled.*

SB1	25c. booklet containing twenty-four 1c. (No. 29) in blocks of 6	£2000
	a. Black on green cover (1917)	
	b. Black on blue cover	£2000
SB2	73c. booklet containing twenty-four 3c. (No. 34) in blocks of 6	£2000
	a. Black on red cover (1917)	
	b. Black on blue cover	£2000
SB3	97c. booklet containing twenty-four 4c. (No. 36*d*) in blocks of 6	£2250

1919. *Black on green (No. SB4) or black on pink (No. SB5) covers. Stapled.*

SB4	49c. booklet containing twenty-four 2c. (No. 31) in blocks of 6	£5000
SB5	97c. booklet containing twenty-four 4c. (No. 37) in blocks of 6	£1800

1922. *Black on buff cover (No. SB7). Stapled.*

SB6	$1.21 booklet containing twenty-four 5c. (No. 61) in blocks of 6	£2750
SB7	$1.45 booklet containing twenty-four 6c. (No. 63) in blocks of 6	£2250

1926. *As Nos. SB4, SB3 and SB7, but sold at face value without premium. Black on green (No. SB8), black on pink (No. SB9) or black on buff (No. SB10) covers. Stapled.*

SB8	48c. booklet containing twenty-four 2c. (No. 55) in blocks of 6	
SB9	96c. booklet containing twenty-four 4c. (No. 60) in blocks of 6	£2250
SB10	$1.44 booklet containing twenty-four 6c. (No. 64) in blocks of 6	£2250

1926. *Black on grey cover. Stapled.*

SB11	$1 booklet containing 4c. and 6c. (Nos. 60, 64) each in block of 10	£2250

1927. *Black on bluish green cover. Stapled.*

SB12	$1.50 booklet containing 2c., 3c., 4c. and 6c. (Nos. 55, 58, 60, 64) each in block of 10	£2750

1927–30. *Black on red (No. SB13), black on green (No. SB14) or black on blue (No. SB15) covers. Stapled.*

SB13	$1.20 booklet containing thirty 4c. (No. 60) in blocks of 10	£2500
	a. Black on orange cover (1930)	
SB14	$1.20 booklet containing twenty 6c. (No. 64) in blocks of 10 (1928)	£3000
SB15	$1.20 booklet containing 2c., 4c. and 6c. (Nos. 55, 60, 64) each in block of 10 (1928)	£2250
	a. Black on white cover (1930)	

1934. *Black on buff cover. Stapled.*

SB16	$1 booklet containing twenty 5c. (No. 62) in blocks of 10	£2750

POSTAGE DUE STAMPS

D 1

(Typo Waterlow)

1924 (1 Dec)–**26**. Wmk Mult Script CA (sideways*). P 15×14.

D1	D **1**	1c. violet	4·75	35·00
		w. Wmk Crown to left of CA (1926)	17·00	28·00
D2		2c. black	1·75	6·00
		w. Wmk Crown to left of CA (1926)	4·00	3·25
D3		4c. green (wmk Crown to left of CA) (27.4.26)	2·25	5·00
D4		8c. red	5·50	35·00
		w. Wmk Crown to left of CA (1926)	15·00	18·00
D5		10c. orange	9·00	17·00
		w. Wmk Crown to left of CA (1926)	26·00	21·00
D6		12c. blue	9·00	27·00
		w. Wmk Crown to left of CA (1926)	15·00	12·00
D1/6 *Set of* 6			29·00	75·00
D1s/6s Optd "Specimen" *Set of* 6			£190	

*The normal sideways watermark shows Crown to right of CA, *as seen from the back of the stamp*.

The issues of the Federated Malay States were replaced by stamps for the individual States from 1935 onwards.

III. MALAYAN POSTAL UNION

The Malayan Postal Union was organised in 1934 and, initially, covered the Straits Settlements and the Federated Malay States. Stamps of the Straits Settlements together with issues for the individual States continued to be used, but Malayan Postal Union postage due stamps were introduced in 1936.

Following the end of the Second World War the use of these postage dues spread throughout Malaya and to Singapore.

PRICES FOR STAMPS ON COVER TO 1945	
Nos. D1/6	*from* × 10
Nos. D7/13	*from* × 4

POSTAGE DUE STAMPS

D 1

10

cents

(D 2)

(Typo Waterlow until 1961, then D.L.R.)

1936 (June)–**38**. Wmk Mult Script CA. P 15×14.

D1	**D 1**	1c. slate-purple (4.38)	9·00	70
D2		4c. green (9.36)	23·00	1·00
D3		8c. scarlet	13·00	2·75
D4		10c. yellow-orange	19·00	30
D5		12c. pale ultramarine (9.36)	19·00	14·00
D6		50c. black (1.38)	28·00	4·50
D1/6 *Set of* 6			£100	21·00
D1s/6s Perf "Specimen" *Set of* 6			£225	

For use in Negri Sembilan, Pahang, Perak, Selangor and Straits Settlements including Singapore.

1945–49. *New values and colours.* Wmk Mult Script CA. P 15×14.

D7	**D 1**	1c. purple	3·25	2·00
D8		3c. green	6·00	5·00
D9		5c. scarlet	6·00	3·50
D10		8c. yellow-orange (1949)	13·00	14·00
		s. Perf "Specimen"	75·00	
D11		9c. yellow-orange	35·00	40·00
D12		15c. pale ultramarine	£110	28·00
D13		20c. blue (1948)	8·00	5·00
		s. Perf "Specimen"	75·00	
D7/13 *Set of* 7			£160	90·00

1951 (8 Aug)–**63**. Wmk Mult Script CA. P 14.

D14	**D 1**	1c. violet (21.8.52)	70	1·60
D15		2c. deep slate-blue (16.11.53)	1·25	2·25
		a. Perf 12½ (15.11.60)	1·50	18·00
		ab. Chalk-surfaced paper (10.7.62)	1·25	11·00
		ac. Ditto. Imperf horiz (vert pair)	†	£13000
D16		3c. deep green (21.8.52)	25·00	13·00
D17		4c. sepia (16.11.53)	70	7·00
		a. Perf 12½ (15.11.60)	1·50	20·00
		ab. Chalk-surfaced paper. *Bistre-brown* (10.7.62)	1·00	17·00
D18		5c. vermilion	48·00	12·00
D19		8c. yellow-orange	2·25	5·00
D20		12c. bright purple (1.2.54)	1·25	6·00
		a. Perf 12½. Chalk-surfaced paper (10.7.62)	2·00	25·00
D21		20c. blue	6·00	6·50
		a. Perf 12½. *Deep blue* (10.12.57)	7·00	26·00
		ab. Chalk-surfaced paper (15.10.63)	5·50	38·00
D14/21 *Set of* 8			75·00	48·00

Nos. D7 to D21ab were for use in the Federation and Singapore.

1964 (14 Apr)–**65**. *Chalk-surfaced paper.* Wmk w **12** (sideways on 1c.). P 12½.

D22	**D 1**	1c. maroon	30	17·00
		a. Perf 12. Wmk upright (4.5.65)	1·00	15·00
D23		2c. deep slate-blue	1·50	15·00
		a. Perf 12 (9.3.65)	1·00	20·00
D24		4c. bistre-brown	1·00	15·00
		a. Perf 12 (9.3.65)	1·50	15·00
D25		8c. yellow-orange (*p* 12) (4.5.65)	2·00	18·00
D27		12c. bright purple	1·50	19·00
		a. Perf 12 (4.5.65)	5·50	35·00
D28		20c. deep blue	2·50	35·00
		a. Perf 12 (4.5.65)	9·00	48·00
D22/8 Set of 6			7·50	£110

1964 (1 Dec). *As No. D19 surch locally with Type* D **2**.

D29	**D 1**	10c. on 8c. yellow-orange	60	3·00

First supplies of this stamp differed from No. D19 in that they had been climatically affected but later a fresh printing of No. D19 was surcharged.

1966. *Unsurfaced paper.* Wmk w **12**. P 15×14.

D30	**D 1**	50c. black	£1500	£1400

Nos. D22/9 were for use throughout Malaysia and Singapore. They were superseded on 15 August 1966 by the postage dues inscribed "MALAYSIA", but continued in use, together with No. D30, for Singapore until 31 January 1968 when they were replaced by Singapore Postage Dues.

IV. MALAYA (BRITISH MILITARY ADMINISTRATION)

Following the Japanese surrender on 2 September 1945 British troops landed in Malaya which was placed under a British Military Administration. The Director of Posts was ashore at Singapore on 6 September and had reached Kuala Lumpur by 13 September. Postal services in Singapore and Johore resumed on 17 September and had spread to the remainder of the country by 5 October. No stamps were initially available so all mail up to 1 oz. was carried free until the first overprinted stamps appeared on 19 October.

De La Rue had overprinted available stocks of pre-war Straits Settlements stamps earlier in 1945 and initial supplies of these London overprints were placed on sale from 19 October (Nos. 1, 2a, 4, 6a, 7 and 8a) with the 15c. and 25c. (Nos. 11 and 13a) issued later. A second consignment contained dollar values including the $5 purple and orange. Duplicate plates were subsequently sent to the Government Printing Office at Kuala Lumpur, where the overprinting of surviving local stocks of the 1c., 5c., 10c., 15c. (overprinted in black) and $5 green and red on emerald took place, and to Australia for those shipments which had been diverted there in 1941.

The stamps were used throughout all Malay States and in Singapore. From 1948 this general issue was gradually replaced by individual issues for each state. The last usage was in Kelantan where B M A overprints were not withdrawn until 10 July 1951.

B M A
MALAYA
(1)

1945 (19 Oct)–**48**. *T* **58** *of Straits Settlements from Die I (double-plate printing) or Die II (single-plate printing) optd with T* **1**. Wmk Mult Script CA. *Chalk-surfaced paper.* P 14 or 15×14 (No. 11).

1	1c. black (I) (R.)	4·50	70
	a. Ordinary paper	10	30
2	2c. orange (II) (8.7.47)	6·00	60
	a. Ordinary paper (19.10.45)	20	10
	w. Wmk inverted	†	£1600
3	2c. orange (I) (*ordinary paper*) (9.46)	27·00	4·25
4	3c. yellow-green (II) (*ordinary paper*)	1·75	50
	a. Blue-green (27.1.47)	6·00	4·00
	b. Chalk-surfaced paper. *Blue-green* (8.7.47)	16·00	1·00
5	5c. brown (II) (24.10.45)	70	1·00
6	6c. grey (II) (22.3.48)	21·00	4·00
	a. Ordinary paper (19.10.45)	30	20
7	8c. scarlet (II) (*ordinary paper*)	30	10
8	10c. purple (I) (12.45)	5·50	80
	a. Ordinary paper (19.10.45)	50	10
	b. Slate-purple (12.45)	5·00	30
	c. Magenta (22.3.48)	9·00	70
9	10c. purple (II) (28.7.48)	19·00	4·25
10	12c. bright ultramarine (I) (11.45)	1·75	10·00
11	15c. bright ultramarine (II) (*ordinary paper*) (11.45)	2·50	8·50
12	15c. bright ultramarine (II) (R.) (22.3.48)	35·00	1·00
	a. Ordinary paper (12.45)	75	20
	b. Blue (27.11.47)	65·00	85
	ba. Ordinary paper (8.7.47)	£130	15·00
13	25c. dull purple and scarlet (I) (22.3.48)	22·00	2·50
	a. Ordinary paper (12.45)	1·40	30
	ab. Opt double	£5000	
	ac. "A" of "CA" missing from watermark	†	£2500
14	50c. black/*emerald* (I) (R.) (12.45)	30·00	2·50
	a. Ordinary paper	75	10
15	$1 black and red (I) (*ordinary paper*) (12.45)	2·00	10
16	$2 green and scarlet (I) (*ordinary paper*) (12.45)	2·75	75
17	$5 green and red/*emerald* (I) (11.45)	90·00	£120
18	$5 purple and orange (I) (*ordinary paper*) (12.45)	3·75	3·00
1/18 *Set of* 15		95·00	£130
1s/11s, 13s/16s, 18s Perf "Specimen" *Set of* 14		£500	

The 8c. grey with "BMA" opt was prepared but not officially issued (*Price £375 unused*).

Nos. 3 and 9 do not exist without the overprint.

Initial printings on ordinary paper were produced by Harrison and Sons in 1941 following bomb damage to the De La Rue works on 29 December 1940.

No. 8 with reddish purple medallion and dull purple frame is from a 1947 printing with the head in fugitive ink which discolours with moisture.

Postal forgeries of the 50c. value exist made by dyeing examples of the 1c. and then altering the face value to 50c.

In 1946 8c. and 15c. stamps in the Crown Colony Victory design were prepared for the Malayan Union, but not issued. Examples of the 8c. carmine from this issue exist from unofficial leakages (*Price £425 unused*).

V. MALAYAN FEDERATION

The Malayan Federation, formed on 1 February 1948 by Malacca, Penang, the four Federated Malay States and the five Unfederated States, became an independent member of the BritishCommonwealth on 31 August 1957.

Commemoratives and a limited series of definitives were issued by the Federation and were used concurrently with the stamps from the individual States.

1 Tapping Rubber

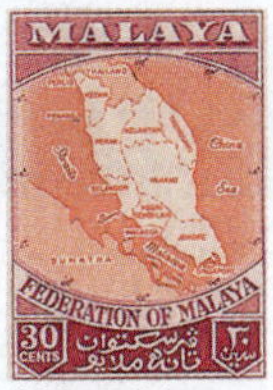

4 Map of the Federation

(Centre recess, frame litho (6c., 25c.); centre litho, frame recess (12c.); recess (30c.), D.L.R.)

1957 (5 May)–**63**. *T* **1**, **4** *and similar designs.* W w **12**. P 13×12½ (No. 4) or 13 (others).

1	6c. deep blue, red, yellow and grey-blue	50	10
	a. *Indigo, red, yellow and grey-blue* (20.6.61)	4·50	50
	b. *Indigo, red, yellow and slate-blue* (12.2.63)	4·00	50
	c. Yellow (star and crescent) omitted	65·00	
2	12c. red, yellow, blue, black and scarlet	1·00	1·00
3	25c. maroon, red, yellow and dull greenish blue	3·00	20
4	30c. orange-red and lake	1·00	20
	a. Perf 13. *Orange-red and deep lake* (20.6.61)	1·50	1·00
	ab. *Orange-red and lake* (10.7.62)	3·75	10
1/4 Set of 4		5·00	1·25

Designs: Horiz—12c. Federation coat of arms; 25c. Tin dredger.

5 Prime Minister Tunku Abdul Rahman and Populace greeting Independence

(Des A. B. Seeman. Recess Waterlow)

1957 (31 Aug). *Independence Day.* Wmk Mult Script CA. P 12½.

5	**5**	10c. bistre-brown	20	10

6 United Nations Emblem

7 United Nations Emblem

(Recess D.L.R.)

1958 (5 Mar). *U.N. Economic Commission for Asia and Far East Conference, Kuala Lumpur.* W w **12**. P 13½ (12c.) or 12½ (30c.).

6	**6**	12c. carmine-red	30	80
7	**7**	30c. maroon	40	80

8 Merdeka Stadium, Kuala Lumpur

9 The Yang di-Pertuan Agong (Tuanku Abdul Rahman)

(Photo Harrison)

1958 (31 Aug). *First Anniv of Independence.* W w **12**. P 13½×14½ (10c.) or 14½×13½ (30c.).

8	**8**	10c. green, yellow, red and blue	15	10
9	**9**	30c. red, yellow, violet-blue and green	40	70

10 "Human Rights"

11 Malayan with Torch of Freedom

(Des J. P. Hendroff. Litho (10c.), photo (30c.) D.L.R.)

1958 (10 Dec). *Tenth Anniv of Declaration of Human Rights.*

(a) W w **12**. *P 12½×13*

10	**10**	10c. blue, black, carmine and orange	15	10

(b) Wmk Mult Script CA. P 13×12½

11	**11**	30c. deep green	45	60

12 Mace and Malayan Peoples

(Photo Enschedé)

1959 (12 Sept). *Inauguration of Parliament.* No wmk. P 13×14.

12	**12**	4c. rose-red	10	10
13		10c. violet	10	10
14		25c. yellow-green	75	20
12/14 Set of 3			85	30

13

14

(Recess D.L.R.)

1960 (7 Apr). *World Refugee Year.* W w **12**. P 13½ (12c.) or 12½×13 (30c.)

15	**13**	12c. purple	10	60
16	**14**	30c. deep green	10	10

15 Seedling Rubber Tree and Map

16 The Yang di-Pertuan Agong (Tuanku Syed Putra)

(Photo Japanese Govt Ptg Wks)

1960 (19 Sept). *Natural Rubber Research Conference and 15th International Rubber Study Group Meeting, Kuala Lumpur. T* **15** *and similar vert design.* No wmk. P 13.

17		6c. yellow-green, black, orange and red-brown	20	1·25
18		30c. yellow-green, black, orange and bright blue	50	75

No. 18 is inscribed "INTERNATIONAL RUBBER STUDY GROUP 15th MEETING KUALA LUMPUR" at foot.

(Photo Harrison)

1961 (4 Jan). *Installation of Yang di-Pertuan Agong, Tuanku Syed Putra.* W w **12**. P 14×14½.

19	**16**	10c. black and blue	10	10

17 Colombo Plan Emblem

18 Malaria Eradication Emblem

(Photo Japanese Govt Ptg Works)

1961 (30 Oct). *Colombo Plan Conference, Kuala Lumpur.* P 13.

20	**17**	12c. black and magenta	35	2·75
21		25c. black and apple-green	80	2·25
22		30c. black and turquoise-blue	70	1·00
20/2 Set of 3			1·75	5·50

(Photo Harrison)

1962 (7 Apr). *Malaria. Eradication.* W w **13**. P 14×14½.

23	**18**	25c. orange-brown	20	40
24		30c. deep lilac	20	15
25		50c. ultramarine	40	80
23/5 Set of 3			70	1·25

19 Palmyra Palm Leaf

20 "Shadows of the Future"

(Photo Harrison)

1962 (21 July). *National Language Month.* W w **13** (upright or inverted). P 13½.

26	**19**	10c. light brown and deep reddish violet	15	10
27		20c. light brown and deep bluish green	50	1·25
28		50c. light brown and magenta	1·50	1·75
26/8 Set of 3			1·90	2·75

(Photo Enschedé)

1962 (1 Oct). *Introduction of Free Primary Education.* W w **13**. P 13½.

29	**20**	10c. bright purple	10	10
		w. Wmk inverted	42·00	
30		25c. ochre	50	1·25
31		30c. emerald	2·75	10
29/31 Set of 3			3·00	1·25

21 Harvester and Fisherman

22 Dam and Pylon

(Photo Courvoisier)

1963 (21 Mar). *Freedom from Hunger.* P 11½.

32	**21**	25c. carmine and apple-green	2·25	3·00
33		30c. carmine and crimson	2·50	1·50
34		50c. carmine and bright blue	2·50	3·00
32/4 Set of 3			6·50	6·75

(Photo Harrison)

1963 (26 June). *Cameron Highlands Hydro-Electric Scheme.* W w **13**. P 14.

35	**22**	20c. green and reddish violet	60	10
36		30c. blue-green and ultramarine	1·00	1·50

The definitive general issue for Malaysia and the low value sets for the individual states superseded the stamps of the Malayan Federation by 15 November 1965.

VI. MALAYSIA

On 16 September 1963, the Malayan Federation, Sabah (North Borneo), Sarawak and Singapore formed the Federation of Malaysia. Singapore left the Federation on 9 August 1965, and became an independent republic. Stamps of Singapore continued to be valid in Malaysia, and those of Malaysia in Singapore, until 1 February 1967.

Individual issues for the component States continued, but were restricted to low value definitives and the occasional "State" commemorative. The higher value definitives and the vast majority of commemoratives were issued on a "National" basis.

NATIONAL ISSUES

General issues for use throughout the Malaysian Federation.

1 Federation Map

2 Bouquet of Orchids

(Photo Harrison)

1963 (16 Sept). *Inauguration of Federation.* W w **13**. P 14½.

1	**1**	10c. yellow and bluish violet	40	10
		a. Yellow omitted	£200	
2		12c. yellow and deep green	1·00	60
3		50c. yellow and chocolate	1·40	10
1/3 *Set of* 3			2·50	65

(Photo Enschedé)

1963 (3 Oct). *Fourth World Orchid Conference, Singapore.* No wmk. P 13×14.

4	**2**	6c. multicoloured	1·25	1·25
5		25c. multicoloured	1·25	25

4 Parliament House, Kuala Lumpur

(Des V. Whiteley. Photo Harrison)

1963 (4 Nov). *Ninth Commonwealth Parliamentary Conference, Kuala Lumpur.* W w **13** (inverted). P 13½.

7	**4**	20c. deep magenta and gold	1·25	40
8		30c. deep green and gold	1·25	15

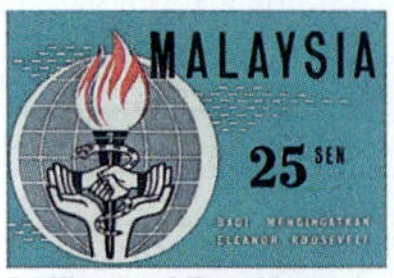

5 "Flame of Freedom" and Emblems of Goodwill, Health and Charity

6 Microwave Tower and I.T.U. Emblem

(Photo Harrison)

1964 (10 Oct). *Eleanor Roosevelt Commemoration.* W w **13**. P 14½×13½.

9	**5**	25c. black, red and greenish blue	20	10
10		30c. black, red and deep lilac	20	15
11		50c. black, red and ochre-yellow	20	10
9/11 *Set of* 3			55	30

(Photo Courvoisier)

1965 (17 May). *I.T.U. Centenary.* P 11½.

12	**6**	2c. multicoloured	40	1·50
13		25c. multicoloured	1·75	60
14		50c. multicoloured	2·25	10
12/14 *Set of* 3			4·00	2·00

7 National Mosque

8 Air Terminal

(Photo Harrison)

1965 (27 Aug). *Opening of National Mosque, Kuala. Lumpur.* W w **13**. P 14×14½.

15	**7**	6c. carmine	10	10
16		15c. red-brown	20	10
17		20c. deep bluish green	20	15
15/17 *Set of* 3			45	30

(Photo Harrison)

1965 (30 Aug). *Opening of International Airport, Kuala Lumpur.* W w **13**. P 14½×14.

18	**8**	15c. black, yellow-green and new blue	40	10
		a. Yellow-green omitted	27·00	
19		30c. black, yellow-green and magenta	60	20

9 Crested Wood Partridge

17 Sepak Raga (ball game) and Football

(Des A. Fraser-Brunner. Photo Harrison)

1965 (9 Sept). *T* **9** *and similar vert designs. Multicoloured.* W w **13**. P 14½.

20		25c. Type **9**	50	10
		w. Wmk inverted	3·50	
21		30c. Blue-backed Fairy Bluebird	60	10
		a. Blue (plumage) omitted	£200	
		w. Wmk inverted	6·00	
22		50c. Black-nailed Oriole	1·25	10
		a. Yellow omitted	£130	
		b. Imperf (pair)	£200	
		c. Scarlet (inscr and berries) omitted	75·00	
		w. Wmk inverted	13·00	
23		75c. Rhinoceros Hornbill	90	10
24		$1 Zebra Dove	1·50	10
		w. Wmk inverted	32·00	
25		$2 Great Argus Pheasant	4·25	30
		a. Imperf (pair)	£200	
		w. Wmk inverted	11·00	
26		$5 Asiatic Paradise Flycatcher	18·00	3·00
		w. Wmk inverted	35·00	
27		$10 Blue-tailed Pitta	48·00	13·00
		a. Imperf (pair)	£275	
20/7 *Set of* 8			65·00	14·00

All values except the 75c. and $10 exist with PVA gum as well as gum arabic.

(Des E. A. F. Anthony. Litho Japanese Govt Ptg Wks)

1965 (14 Dec). *Third South East Asian Peninsular Games. T* **17** *and similar vert designs.* P 13×13½.

28		25c. black and olive-green	40	1·25
29		30c. black and bright purple	40	20
30		50c. black and light blue	70	30
28/30 *Set of* 3			1·40	1·60

Designs:—30c. Running; 50c. Diving.

20 National Monument

21 The Yang di-Pertuan Agong (Tuanku Ismail Nasiruddin Shah)

(Photo Harrison)

1966 (8 Feb). *National Monument, Kuala Lumpur.* W w **13**. P 13½.

31	**20**	10c. multicoloured	50	10
		a. Blue omitted	85·00	
32		20c. multicoloured	1·00	40

(Photo Japanese Govt Ptg Wks)

1966 (11 Apr). *Installation of Yang di-Pertuan Agong, Tuanku Ismail Nasiruddin Shah.* P 13½.

33	**21**	15c. black and light yellow	10	10
34		50c. black and greenish blue	20	20

22 School Building

23 "Agriculture"

(Photo D.L.R.)

1966 (21 Oct). *150th Anniv of Penang Free School.* W w **13** (sideways). P 13.

35	**22**	20c. multicoloured	70	10
36		50c. multicoloured	90	10

The 50c. is also inscr "ULANG TAHUN KE-150" at foot and bears a shield at bottom left corner.

(Des Enche Ng Peng Nam. Photo Japanese Govt Ptg Wks)

1966 (1 Dec). *First Malaysia Plan. T* **23** *and similar horiz designs. Multicoloured.* P 13½.

37		15c. Type **23**	20	10
38		15c. "Rural Health"	20	10
39		15c. "Communications"	1·90	15
40		15c. "Education"	20	10
41		15c. "Irrigation"	20	10
37/41 *Set of* 5			2·50	50

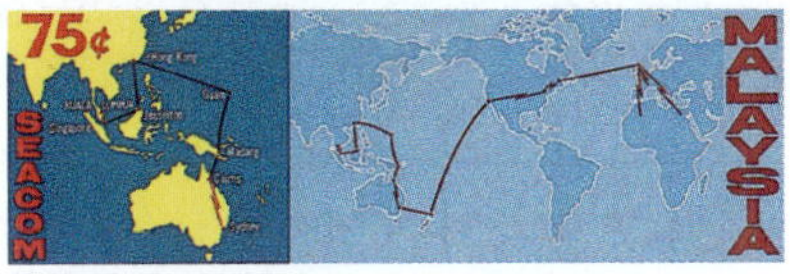

28 Cable Route Maps

(Des Enche Ng Peng Nam. Photo Japanese Govt Ptg Wks)

1967 (30 Mar). *Completion of Malaysia–Hong Kong Link of SEACOM Telephone Cable.* P 13½.

42	**28**	30c. multicoloured	80	50
43		75c. multicoloured	2·50	3·75

29 Hibiscus and Paramount Rulers

(Photo Harrison)

1967 (31 Aug). *Tenth Anniv of Independence.* W w **13**. P 14½.

44	**29**	15c. multicoloured	20	10
		w. Wmk inverted	4·00	
45		50c. multicoloured	1·25	80

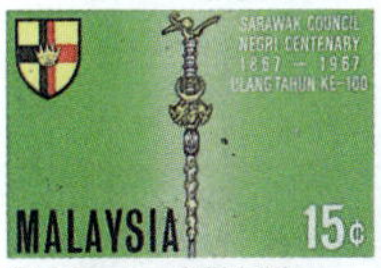

30 Mace and Shield

31 Straits Settlements 1867 8c. and Malaysia 1965 25c. Definitive

(Des Enche Ng Peng Nam. Photo Harrison)

1967 (8 Sept). *Centenary of Sarawak Council.* W w **13**. P 14½.

46	**30**	15c. multicoloured	10	10
47		50c. multicoloured	30	60

(Des Enche Ng Peng Nam. Photo Japanese Govt Ptg Works)

1967 (2 Dec). *Stamp Centenary. T* **31** *and similar shaped designs. Multicoloured.* P 11½.

48		25c. Type **31**	1·60	3·25
		a. *Tête-bêche* (horiz pair)	3·00	6·50
49		30c. Straits Settlements 1867 24c. and Malaysia 1965 30c. definitive	1·60	2·75
		a. *Tête-bêche* (horiz pair)	3·00	5·50
50		50c. Straits Settlements 1867 32c. and Malaysia 1965 50c. definitive	2·50	3·50
		a. *Tête-bêche* (horiz pair)	5·00	7·00
48/50 *Set of* 3			5·25	8·50

Nos. 48/50 were each printed in sheets with the stamps arranged horizontally *tête-bêche*.

34 Tapping Rubber, and Molecular Unit

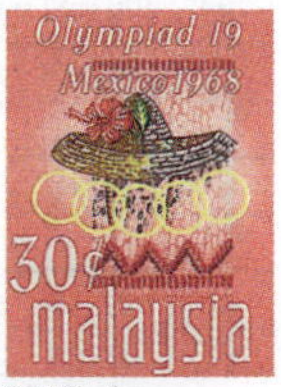

37 Mexican Sombrero and Blanket with Olympic Rings

(Litho B.W.)

1968 (29 Aug). *Natural Rubber Conference, Kuala Lumpur. T* **34** *and similar horiz designs. Multicoloured.* W w **13**. P 12.

51		25c. Type **34**	30	10
52		30c. Tapping rubber, and export consignment	40	20
53		50c. Tapping rubber, and aircraft tyres	40	10
51/3 *Set of* 3			1·00	35

(Litho B.W.)

1968 (12 Oct). *Olympic Games Mexico. T* **37** *and similar vert design. Multicoloured.* W w **13**. P 12×11½.

54		30c. Type **37**	20	10
55		75c. Olympic rings and Mexican embroidery	55	20

39 Tunku Abdul Rahman against background of Pandanus Weave

40 Tunku Abdul Rahman against background of Pandanus Weave

(Photo Japanese Govt Ptg Wks)

1969 (8 Feb). *Solidarity Week. T* **39/40** *and similar multicoloured design.* P 13½.

56		15c. Type **39**	15	10
57		20c. Type **40**	45	1·75
58		50c. Tunku Abdul Rahman with pandanus pattern (*horiz*)	50	20
56/8 *Set of* 3			1·00	1·40

42 Peasant Girl with Sheaves of Paddy

(Des Enche Hoessein Anas. Photo Harrison)

1969 (8 Dec). *National Rice Year.* W w **13**. P 13½.

59	**42**	15c. multicoloured	15	10
60		75c. multicoloured	55	1·50

43 Satellite tracking Aerial

44 "Intelsat III" in Orbit

(Photo Enschedé)

1970 (6 Apr). *Satellite Earth Station.* W w **13**. P 14×13 (15c.) or 13½×13 (30c.)

61	**43**	15c. multicoloured	1·00	15
		a. *Tête-Bêche* (horiz pair)	2·00	2·50
62	**44**	30c. multicoloured*	1·00	2·50
63		30c. multicoloured*	1·00	2·50
61/3 *Set of* 3			2·75	4·75

No. 61 was issued horizontally *tête-bêche* in the sheets.

*Nos. 62/3 are of the same design, differing only in the lettering colours (No. 62 white; No. 63 gold).

45 Euploea leucostictus

46 Emblem

(Des V. Whiteley. Litho B.W. (to 1976) or Harrison)

1970 (31 Aug). *Butterflies. T* **45** *and similar vert designs. Multicoloured.* P 13×13½.

64		25c. Type **45**	1·00	10
65		30c. *Zeuxidia amethystus*	1·50	10
66		50c. *Polyura athamas*	2·00	10
67		75c. *Papilio memnon*	2·00	10
68		$1 *Appias nero* (16.11)	2·50	10
69		$2 *Trogonoptera brookiana* (16.11)	3·50	10
70		$5 *Narathura centaurus* (16.11)	5·00	3·75
71		$10 *Terinos terpander* (16.11)	17·00	5·00
64/71 *Set of* 8			30·00	8·50

See also Nos. 144/5.

(Litho Harrison)

1970 (7 Sept). *50th Anniv of International Labour Organization.* P 14×13½.

72	**46**	30c. grey and new blue	10	20
73		75c. pink and new blue	20	30

47 U.N. Emblem encircled by Doves

(Des Enche Ng Peng Nam. Litho D.L.R.)

1970 (24 Oct). *25th Anniv of United Nations. T* **47** *and similar horiz designs.* P 13×12½.

74		25c. gold, black and brown	35	40
75		30c. multicoloured	35	35
76		50c. black and dull yellow-green	40	75
74/6 *Set of* 3			1·00	1·40

Designs:—30c. Line of doves and U.N. emblem; 50c. Doves looping U.N. emblem.

POSTAGE DUE STAMPS

Until 15 August 1966 the postage due stamps of MALAYAN POSTAL UNION were in use throughout MALAYSIA.

D 1

(Litho Harrison)

1966 (15 Aug)–**71**. *Ordinary paper.* W w **13** (upright). P 14½×14.

D1	D **1**	1c. rose	20	4·50
D2		2c. indigo	25	2·75
D3		4c. apple-green	1·00	8·00
D4		8c. blue-green	2·00	14·00
		a. Chalk-surfaced paper. *Bright blue green* (1.6.71)	4·50	15·00
D5		10c. bright blue	1·50	2·50
		a. Chalk-surfaced paper (1.6.71)	4·50	13·00
D6		12c. reddish violet	60	4·50
D7		20c. red-brown	2·00	4·75
		a. Chalk-surfaced paper. *Brown purple* (22.4.69)	2·75	15·00
D8		50c. brownish bistre	2·00	8·00
		a. Chalk-surfaced paper. *Olive-bistre* (1.6.71)	4·50	16·00
D1/8 *Set of* 8			8·50	42·00

Later issues in this design were printed on glazed or unwatermarked paper.

VII. MALAYSIAN STATES

PRINTERS. All Malaysian States stamps were printed in typography by De La Rue and Co. Ltd, London, *unless otherwise stated.*

JOHORE

A British adviser was appointed to Johore in 1914. The state joined the Federation of Malaya on 1 February 1948.

Until 1 January 1899 mail for addresses outside Malaya had the external postage paid by stamps of the STRAITS SETTLEMENTS.

PRICES FOR STAMPS ON COVER TO 1945	
Nos. 1/2	—
Nos. 3/5	*from* × 15
No. 6	*from* × 20
Nos. 7/8	—
Nos. 9/15	*from* × 25
No. 16	—
Nos. 17/20	*from* × 15
Nos. 21/31	*from* × 10
Nos. 32/8	*from* × 15
Nos. 39/53	*from* × 8
Nos. 54/60	*from* × 6
Nos. 61/74	*from* × 8
Nos. 75/7	—
Nos. 78/87	*from* × 8
No. 88	*from* × 10
Nos. 89/102	*from* × 6
Nos. 103/25	*from* × 5
Nos. 126/8	—
Nos. 129/30	*from* × 6
Nos. D1/5	*from* × 5

(1)

1876 (July). *No. 11 of Straits Settlements handstamped with T* **1**.

1		2c. brown	£17000	£5000

No. 1 is known with the handstamp double.

From September 1878 to August 1884 no overprinted stamps were supplied by Singapore to Johore.

JOHORE
(2)

JOHORE (3) ("H" and "E" wide. "J" raised. Opt 16 mm long)

JOHORE (4) ("H" wide, "E" narrow. Opt 16 mm long)

JOHORE (5) ("H" and "E" wide. Opt 16¾ mm long)

JOHORE. (6)

JOHORE (7)

JOHORE (8)

1884 (June)–**86**. *No.* 63 *of Straits Settlements optd with T* **2/8**.

2	**2**	2c. pale rose	£6500	
3	**3**	2c. pale rose (8.84)	£2000	£600
		a. Opt double	£3500	£1800
4	**4**	2c. pale rose (8.84)	£2500	£750
		a. Opt double		
5	**5**	2c. pale rose (8.84)	£2000	£600
		a. Opt double	–	£1900
6	**6**	2c. pale rose (3.85)	£180	£190
		a. Opt double	£1000	
7	**7**	2c. pale rose (1885)	£8000	
8	**8**	2c. pale rose (4.86)	£100	£110

Nos. 3 to 7 were from triplet settings, either 3+4+5 or three examples of the same overprint. Nos. 2 and 8 are probably single unit handstamps.

JOHOR (9) (All letters narrow)

JOHOR (10)

JOHOR (11) ("H" wide)

JOHOR (12)

JOHOR (13)

JOHOR. (14)

JOHOR (15)

JOHOR (16)

JOHOR Thin, narrow "J"

1884 (Aug)–**91**. *Nos.* 63/*a of Straits Settlements optd with T* **9/16**.

9	**9**	2c. pale rose	15·00	20·00
		a. Opt double	£800	
10	**10**	2c. pale rose (10.84)	15·00	12·00
		a. Thin, narrow "J" (R. 6/6)	£225	£180
		b. Opt double	£900	
		c. Bright rose (1890)	14·00	13·00
		ca. Thin, narrow "J" (R. 6/6)	£200	£200
		cb. Opt double	£1200	
11	**11**	2c. pale rose (2.85)	90·00	90·00
12	**12**	2c. pale rose (1886)	55·00	55·00
		a. Opt double	£750	
13	**13**	2c. pale rose (1886)	48·00	50·00
14	**14**	2c. pale rose (1888)	£160	60·00
		a. Thin, narrow "J"	£800	£375
		b. Opt double	£800	
15	**15**	2c. bright rose (9.90)	18·00	18·00
16	**16**	2c. bright rose (1891)	£9000	

Settings:

No. 9 – various triplets with the length of the overprint varying from 12 to 15 mm

No. 10 – triplet or 60 (6×10)

No. 11 – two types, length 13¼ mm and 14¼ mm, from separate printings, both triplets of 11+9+9

No. 12 – triplet

No. 13 – triplet

No. 14 – 30 (3×10)

No. 15 – 60 (6×10)

No. 16 – not known. As no used examples are known it is possible that this stamp was not issued.

JOHOR Two CENTS (17)

JOHOR Two CENTS (18)

JOHOR Two CENTS (19)

JOHOR Two CENTS (20)

1891 (May). *No.* 68 *of Straits Settlements surch as T* **17/20**.

17	**17**	2c. on 24c. green	27·00	40·00
		a. "CENST" (R. 5/4)	£900	£475
		b. Thin, narrow "J" (R. 5/6)	£425	£425
		w. Wmk inverted	£170	£170
18	**18**	2c. on 24c. green	£130	£140
		a. Thin, narrow "J" (R. 6/6)	£450	£450
		w. Wmk inverted	£450	
19	**19**	2c. on 24c. green	42·00	55·00
		w. Wmk inverted	£275	£275
20	**20**	2c. on 24c. green	£120	£130
		w. Wmk inverted	£450	£450

Nos. 17/20 come from the same setting of 60. Type **17** occurs on horizontal rows 1 to 5, Type **18** on row 6, Type **19** on rows 7, 8 and 9 and Type **20** on row 10.

The setting was altered to remove the "CENST" error and in doing so the thin, narrow "J" was moved from R. 5/6 to 6/6. Otherwise the two settings were the same.

21 Sultan Aboubakar

3 cents. (22)

KEMAHKOTAAN (23)

1891 (16 Nov)–**94**. No wmk. P 14.

21	**21**	1c. dull purple and mauve (7.94)	80	50
22		2c. dull purple and yellow	60	1·50
23		3c. dull purple and carmine (7.94)	60	50
24		4c. dull purple and black	2·75	20·00
25		5c. dull purple and green	7·00	21·00
26		6c. dull purple and blue	8·00	21·00
27		$1 green and carmine	75·00	£170
21/7 *Set of* 7			85·00	£200

1894 (Mar). *Surch with T* **22**.

28	**21**	3c. on 4c. dull purple and black	2·50	50
		a. No stop (R. 5/11)	95·00	70·00
29		3c. on 5c. dull purple and green	2·00	3·75
		a. No stop (R. 5/11)	£130	£160
		b. "3 cents." spaced 3½ mm from bar	£150	90·00
30		3c. on 6c. dull purple and blue	3·50	£450
		a. No stop (R. 5/11)	£180	£200
31		3c. on $1 green and carmine	12·00	75·00
		a. No stop (R. 5/11)	£425	£800
28/31 *Set of* 4			18·00	75·00

No. 29b shows the surcharge spaced 3½ mm from the bar instead of the normal 7½ mm. It appears to come from a separate setting as a cancelled-to-order block of eight is known.

1896 (Mar). *Coronation of Sultan Ibrahim. Optd with T* **23**.

32	**21**	1c. dull purple and mauve	50	1·00
		a. "KETAHKOTAAN"	3·75	5·00
33		2c. dull purple and yellow	50	1·00
		a. "KETAHKOTAAN"	5·00	7·00
34		3c. dull purple and carmine	55	1·00
		a. "KETAHKOTAAN"	9·00	12·00
35		4c. dull purple and black	80	2·25
		a. "KETAHKOTAAN"	2·75	13·00
36		5c. dull purple and green	5·50	7·50
		a. "KETAHKOTAAN"	3·50	7·50
37		6c. dull purple and blue	3·50	6·50
		a. "KETAHKOTAAN"	7·50	12·00
38		$1 green and carmine	50·00	£120
		a. "KETAHKOTAAN"	38·00	£170
32/8 *Set of* 7			55·00	£130
32a/8a *Set of* 7			60·00	£200

Stamps overprinted "KETAHKOTAAN" (= We mourn) come from the first overprinting. The overprint was subsequently changed to the intended "KEMAHKOTAAN" (= Coronation), but both were issued together some months after the Coronation of Sultan Ibrahim had taken place.

24 Sultan Ibrahim

25 Sultan Ibrahim

26

27

1896 (26 Aug)–**99**. W **27**. P 14.

39	**24**	1c. green	80	1·75
40		2c. green and blue	50	30
41		3c. green and purple	4·00	3·25
		a. Green and dull claret	4·00	2·75
42		4c. green and carmine	1·00	2·25
43		4c. yellow and red (1899)	1·50	1·25
44		5c. green and brown	2·00	3·25
45		6c. green and yellow	2·00	4·25
46	**25**	10c. green and black (1898)	7·00	48·00
47		25c. green and mauve (1898)	9·00	42·00
48		50c. green and carmine (1898)	16·00	45·00
49	**24**	$1 dull purple and green (1898)	32·00	75·00
50	**26**	$2 dull purple and carmine (1898)	40·00	80·00
51		$3 dull purple and blue (1898)	35·00	£110
52		$4 dull purple and brown (1898)	35·00	85·00
53		$5 dull purple and yellow (1898)	80·00	£130
39/53 *Set of* 15			£225	£550

Nos. 42 and 43 were reissued in 1918 to meet a shortage of 4c. stamps.

3 cents. (28)

10 cents. (29)

1903 (Apr). *Surch with T* **28** *or* **29**.

54	**24**	3c. on 4c. yellow and red	60	1·10
		a. Original value uncancelled	3·75	22·00
55		10c. on 4c. green and carmine	2·50	9·00
		a. Tall "1" in "10" (R. 9/12)	75·00	£130
		b. Original value uncancelled	20·00	70·00
		ba. As b, with tall "1" in "10" (R. 9/12)	£1300	£1800

The bars on these stamps were ruled by hand with pen and ink.

50 Cents. (30)

One Dollar (31)

1903 (Oct). *Surch with T* **30** *or* **31**.

56	**26**	50c. on $3 dull purple and blue	30·00	85·00
57		$1 on $2 dull purple and carmine	65·00	£120
		a. "e" of "One" inverted (R. 7/9)	£1700	

10 CENTS. (32)

1904. *Surch as T* **32**.

58	**24**	10c. on 4c. yellow and red (Apr)	20·00	40·00
		a. Surcharge double	£8000	
59		10c. on 4c. green and carmine (Aug)	9·50	55·00
60	**26**	50c. on $5 dull purple and yellow (May)	75·00	£170
58/60 *Set of* 3			95·00	£225

33

34

35 Sultan Sir Ibrahim

1904 (Sept)–**10**. W **27**. *Ordinary paper*. P 14.

61	**33**	1c. dull purple and green	2·00	40
		a. Chalk-surfaced paper (10.09)	9·50	9·50
62		2c. dull purple and orange	3·00	4·25
		a. Chalk-surfaced paper (10.10)	11·00	15·00
63		3c. dull purple and olive-black	4·75	60
		a. Chalk-surfaced paper	–	£100
64		4c. dull purple and carmine	8·00	3·25
65		5c. dull purple and sage-green	2·50	3·00
66	**35**	8c. dull purple and blue	4·25	11·00
67	**34**	10c. dull purple and black	50·00	11·00
		a. Chalk-surfaced paper (1910)	£100	80·00
68		25c. dull purple and green	8·50	40·00
69		50c. dull purple and red	45·00	17·00
70	**33**	$1 green and mauve	13·00	60·00
71	**35**	$2 green and carmine	26·00	50·00
72		$3 green and blue	30·00	80·00
73		$4 green and brown	30·00	£110
74		$5 green and orange	50·00	90·00
75	**34**	$10 green and black	80·00	£180
76		$50 green and ultramarine	£275	£400
77		$100 green and scarlet	£425	£700
61/75 *Set of* 15			£325	£600

1910–19. Wmk Mult Rosettes (vertical). *Chalk-surfaced paper*. P 14.

78	**33**	1c. dull purple and green (1912)	1·25	15
79		2c. dull purple and orange (1912)	6·00	1·00
80		3c. dull purple and olive-black (1912)	10·00	65
		a. Wmk horizontal (1910)	10·00	19·00
81		4c. dull purple and carmine (1912)	14·00	1·00
		a. Wmk horizontal (1910)	20·00	55·00
82		5c. dull purple and sage-green (1912)	7·00	2·75
83	**35**	8c. dull purple and blue (1912)	4·00	8·50
84	**34**	10c. dull purple and black (1912)	60·00	3·00
		a. Wmk horizontal (1911)	26·00	80·00
85		25c. dull purple and green (1912)	15·00	45·00
86		50c. dull purple and red (1919)	60·00	£130
87	**33**	$1 green and mauve (1918)	90·00	£120
78/87 *Set of* 10			£200	£275

3 CENTS. (36)

37 Sultan Sir Ibrahim and Sultana

1912 (Mar). *No.* 66 *surch with T* **36**.

88		3c. on 8c. dull purple and blue	5·50	9·00
		a. "T" of "CENTS" omitted	£1500	
		b. Bars double		

No. 88b shows the bars printed twice with the upper pair partly erased.

1918–20. Wmk Mult Crown CA. *Chalk-surfaced paper*. P 14.

89	**33**	2c. dull purple and green (1919)	50	1·00
		w. Wmk inverted	†	£300
90		2c. purple and orange (1919)	1·00	4·75
91		4c. dull purple and red	1·75	70
92		5c. dull purple and sage-green (1920)	2·00	8·50
		w. Wmk inverted	£170	
		ws. Ditto, optd "Specimen"	65·00	
93	**34**	10c. dull purple and blue	2·00	1·40
94		21c. dull purple and orange (1919)	2·25	2·50
95		25c. dull purple and green (1920)	8·00	27·00
96		50c. dull purple and red (6.18)	24·00	60·00
97	**33**	$1 green and mauve	14·00	75·00
98	**35**	$2 green and carmine	23·00	55·00
99		$3 green and blue	55·00	£130
100		$4 green and brown	70·00	£160
101		$5 green and orange	£110	£190
102	**34**	$10 green and black	£300	£450
89/102 *Set of* 14			£550	£1000
89s/102s Optd "Specimen" *Set of* 14			£550	

1922–40. Wmk Mult Script CA. *Chalk-surfaced paper*. P 14.

103	**33**	1c. dull purple and black	30	20
104		2c. purple and sepia (1924)	1·25	4·00
105		2c. green (1928)	50	40
106		3c. green (1925)	2·00	4·50
107		3c. purple and sepia (1928)	1·40	1·50
108		4c. purple and carmine (1924)	2·50	20
109		5c. dull purple and sage-green	50	30
		w. Wmk inverted		
110		6c. dull purple and claret	50	50
111	**34**	10c. dull purple and blue	16·00	32·00
		w. Wmk inverted	†	£300
112		10c. dull purple and yellow	50	25
113	**33**	12c. dull purple and blue	1·00	1·25
114		12c. ultramarine (1940)	48·00	2·25
115	**34**	21c. dull purple and orange (1928)	2·00	3·00
116		25c. dull purple and myrtle	3·75	1·00
117	**35**	30c. dull purple and orange (1936)	9·00	8·50
118		40c. dull purple and brown (1936)	9·00	9·50

119	34	50c. dull purple and red	3·75	1·60
120	33	$1 green and mauve	3·75	1·25
121	35	$2 green and carmine (1923)	7·50	4·00
122		$3 green and blue (1925)	65·00	90·00
123		$4 green and brown (1926)	£100	£180
		w. Wmk inverted	£750	
124		$5 green and orange	60·00	50·00
125	34	$10 green and black (1924)	£250	£375
126		$50 green and ultramarine	£1000	
		s. Optd "Specimen"	£190	
127		$100 green and scarlet	£1700	
		s. Optd "Specimen"	£300	
128	35	$500 blue and red (1926)	£20000	
		s. Optd "Specimen"	£850	
103/25 *Set of* 23			£550	£700
103s/25s Optd or Perf (12c. ultram, 30c., 40c.) "Specimen" *Set of* 23			£800	

Printings of the 1c., 2c., 6c., 10c., 50c., $1, $2, $5 and $10 were made in 1941 by Williams, Lea & Co. Ltd. following bomb damage to the De La Rue works on 29 December 1940.

(Recess Waterlow)

1935 (15 May). *50th Anniv of Treaty Relations with Great Britain.* Wmk Mult Script CA (sideways). P 12½.

129	37	8c. bright violet and slate	4·00	2·75
		s. Perf "Specimen"	65·00	

38 Sultan Sir Ibrahim

39 Sultan Sir Ibrahim

(Recess D.L.R.)

1940 (Feb). Wmk Mult Script CA. P 13½.

130	38	8c. black and pale blue	21·00	1·00
		s. Perf "Specimen"	70·00	

1948 (1 Dec). *Royal Silver Wedding. As Nos. 112/13 of Antigua.*

131	10c. violet	20	75
132	$5 green	25·00	42·00

1949 (2 May)–**55**. Wmk Mult Script CA. *Chalk-surfaced paper.* P 17½×18.

133	39	1c. black	50	10
134		2c. orange	20	20
		a. Orange-yellow (22.1.52)	1·50	2·25
135		3c. green	50	1·00
		a. Yellow-green (22.1.52)	19·00	3·50
136		4c. brown	1·00	10
136*a*		5c. bright purple (1.9.52)	70	30
137		6c. grey	60	20
		a. Pale grey (22.1.52)	60	50
		ac. Error. St. Edward's Crown W 9*b*	£2000	£1600
138		8c. scarlet	3·50	1·25
138*a*		8c. green (1.9.52)	5·50	2·25
139		10c. magenta	70	10
		aa. Imperf (pair)	£3000	
139*a*		12c. scarlet (1.9.52)	6·00	5·50
140		15c. ultramarine	3·50	10
141		20c. black and green	1·00	1·00
141*a*		20c. bright blue (1.9.52)	1·00	10
142		25c. purple and orange	3·00	10
142*a*		30c. scarlet and purple (4.9.55)	1·75	2·75
142*b*		35c. scarlet and purple (1.9.52)	6·50	1·25
143		40c. red and purple	5·50	13·00
144		50c. black and blue	3·50	10
145		$1 blue and purple	7·50	2·00
146		$2 green and scarlet	18·00	9·00
147		$5 green and brown	40·00	14·00
133/47 *Set of* 21			£100	48·00

1949 (10 Oct). *75th Anniv of U.P.U. As Nos. 114/17 of Antigua.*

148	10c. purple	30	40
149	15c. deep blue	2·00	1·25
150	25c. orange	65	3·50
151	50c. blue-black	1·25	3·75
148/51 *Set of* 4		3·75	8·00

1953 (2 June). *Coronation. As No. 120 of Antigua.*

152	10c. black and reddish purple	1·25	10

40 Sultan Sir Ibrahim

41 Sultan Sir Ismail and Johore Coat of Arms

(Recess D.L.R.)

1955 (1 Nov). *Diamond Jubilee of Sultan.* Wmk Mult Script CA. P 14.

153	40	10c. carmine-red	10	10

(Photo Courvoisier)

1960 (10 Feb). *Coronation of Sultan.* No wmk. P 11½.

154	41	10c. multicoloured	20	20

1960. *As T 9/19 of Kedah, but with portrait of Sultan Ismail.* P 13½ ($1); others 12½×13 (vert) or 13×12½ (horiz).

155	1c. black (7.10.60)	10	50
156	2c. orange-red (7.10.60)	10	1·25
157	4c. sepia (19.8.60)	10	10
158	5c. carmine-lake (7.10.60)	10	10
159	8c. myrtle-green (9.12.60)	1·50	3·00
160	10c. deep maroon (10.6.60)	30	10
161	20c. blue (9.12.60)	2·00	1·00
162	50c. black and bright blue (19.8.60)	50	20
163	$1 ultramarine and reddish purple (9.12.60)	2·50	5·00
164	$2 bronze-green and scarlet (9.12.60)	12·00	18·00
165	$5 brown and bronze-green (7.10.60)	30·00	38·00
155/65 *Set of* 11		45·00	60·00

In No. 161 there are only two figures in the boat, the steersman being missing. In the 20c. value for all the other dates there are three figures.

The 6, 12, 25 and 30c. values used with this issue were Nos. 1/4 of Malayan Federation.

42 *Vanda hookeriana* (Inset portrait of Sultan Ismail)

(Des A. Fraser-Brunner. Photo Harrison)

1965 (15 Nov). *T* **42** *and similar horiz designs.* W w **13** (upright). P 14½.

166	1c. Type **42**	10	30
	a. Black (orchid's name and part of flower) omitted	£275	
	w. Wmk inverted	2·50	
167	2c. *Arundina graminifolia*	10	1·00
168	5c. *Paphiopedilum niveum*	10	10
	b. Yellow (flower) omitted	85·00	
169	6c. *Spathoglottis plicata*	40	30
170	10c. *Arachnis flos-aeris*	40	20
171	15c. *Rhyncostylis retusa*	1·50	10
	b. Green (face value and leaves) omitted	£600	
172	20c. *Phalaenopsis violacea*	1·50	75
	a. Bright purple (blooms) omitted	£225	
166/72 *Set of* 7		3·50	2·25

The 2c. to 15c. exist with both PVA gum and gum arabic.

The 2c. with black (name of state, arms and head) omitted is listed under Sarawak No. 213a as there is some evidence that a sheet was issued there; if it also exists from any of the other states it would, of course, be identical.

The higher values used with this issue were Nos. 20/27 of Malaysia (National Issues).

1970. *As No. 166 and 170 but W w* **13** *(sideways).*

173	1c. multicoloured (20.11)	1·75	6·00
174	10c. multicoloured (27.5)	1·75	2·50

STAMP BOOKLETS

1928. *Black on white card. Interleaved with tissue. Stapled.*

SB1	$2 booklet containing ten 1c. and 2c. (Nos. 103, 105), twenty 4c. (No. 108), each in blocks of 10 and eighteen 5c. (No. 109) in blocks of 6	£2000

1929. *Black on pink cover. Stapled.*

SB2	$1 booklet containing 2c., 3c. and 5c. (Nos. 105, 107, 109) in blocks of 10	

1930. *Black on buff cover. Stapled.*

SB3	$1 booklet containing ten 1c. and 5c. (Nos. 103, 109) and twenty 2c. (Nos. 105) in blocks of 10	

POSTAGE DUE STAMPS

D 1

(Typo Waterlow)

1938 (1 Jan). Wmk Mult Script CA. P 12½.

D1	D 1	1c. carmine	16·00	42·00
D2		4c. green	40·00	40·00
D3		8c. orange	48·00	£140
D4		10c. brown	48·00	50·00
D5		12c. purple	55·00	£130
D1/5 *Set of* 5			£180	£350
D1s/5s Perf "Specimen" *Set of* 5			£150	

KEDAH

The Thai monarchy exercised suzerainty over Kedah and the other northern states of the Malay peninsula from the 16th century onwards. The extent of Thai involvement in its internal affairs was very variable, being dependent on the strength, or otherwise, of the Bangkok administration and the degree of co-operation of the local ruler.

The Thai postal service, which had been inaugurated in 1883, gradually extended into the north of the Malay penninsula and an office was opened at Alor Star in Kedah during 1887 with the earliest known postmark being dated 27 October. Further post offices at Kuala Muda (3 Oct 1907), Kulim (7 July 1907) and Langkawi (16 Feb 1908) followed.

A straight-line obliteration showing "Kedah" between short vertical dashes is not believed to be genuine.

Stamps of Thailand used in Kedah

Types of Thailand (Siam)

1

2

9

๑ อัฐ 1 (12) ๒ อัฐ 2 (17) ๒ อัฐ 2 (18)

4 atts (24) 4 atts (25)

1 Atts.

ราคา ๑ อัฐ (27) 2 Atts. (28) 2 (33)

1 Att. 1 Att.

ราคา ๑ อัฐ (34) ราคา ๑ อัฐ (35) 1 Att. (36)

2 Atts. 10 Atts.

ราคา ๒ อัฐ (37) 2 Atts. (38) ราคา ๑๐ อัฐ (39)

4 Atts. (40) 4 Atts. (41)

1 Att.

ราคา ๑ อัฐ (42) 2 Atts. (44) 3 Atts. (45) 4 Atts. (46)

2 Atts. (48a)

49

50

1 Att.

๑ อัฐ (51)

53

๔ อัฐ

1 att. (56) 9 Atts (59)

The following types of postmark were used on Siamese stamps from the Malay tributary states:

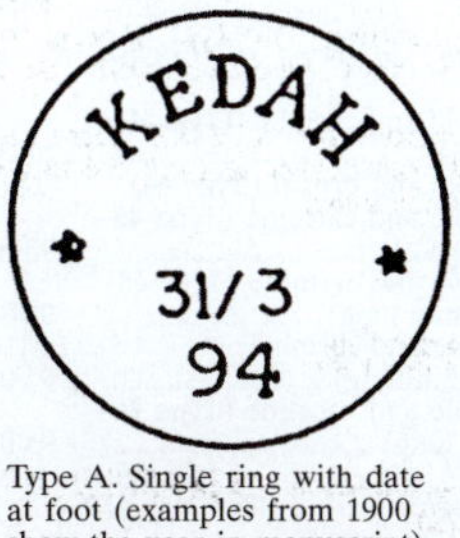

Type A. Single ring with date at foot (examples from 1900 show the year in manuscript)

Type B. Single ring with date in centre

Type C. Double ring. Bilingual

Type D. Double ring. English at top and ornament at foot

PRICES are for stamps showing a large part of the postmark with the inscription clearly visible.

The Siamese post office at Alor Star was opened during 1887 with the first known postmark being dated 27 October. Further post offices at Kuala Muda (3 Oct 1907), Kulim (7 July 1907) and Langkawi (16 Feb 1908) followed.

A straight-line obliteration showing "KEDAH" between short vertical dashes is not believed to be genuine.

Alor Star

Stamps of SIAM *cancelled as Type* A *inscribed* "KEDAH".

1883. *(Nos. 1/5).*
Z2 **1** 1att. rose-carmine £250
Z3 1sio. red £450
Z4 **2** 1sik. yellow £450

1897–91. *(Nos. 11/18).*
Z6 **9** 1a. green .... 85·00
Z7 2a. green and carmine .... 75·00
Z8 3a. green and blue .... 95·00
Z9 4a. green and brown .... 85·00
Z10 8a. green and yellow .... 85·00
Z11 12a. purple and carmine .... 75·00
Z12 24a. purple and blue .... 85·00
Z13 64a. purple and brown £140

1889–91. *Surch as T* **12** *(Nos. Z15, Z19), T* **17** *(No. Z21) or T* **18** *(No. Z22) (Nos. 20/30).*
Z15 **9** 1a. on 2a. rose-carmine .... 95·00
Z19 1a. on 3a. red £110
Z21 2a. on 3a. yellow £140
Z22 2a. on 3a. green and blue £170

1892. *Surch as T* **24/5** *(with or without stop) and Siamese handstamp (Nos. 33/6).*
Z28 **9** 4a. on 24a. purple and blue (Type **24**) .... 95·00
Z29 4a. on 24a. purple and blue (Type **25**) £120
Z30 4a. on 24a. purple and blue (Type **24** with stop) £120
Z31 4a. on 24a. purple and blue (Type **25** with stop) £120

1894. *Surch as T* **27** *with variations of English figures as T* **28** *and* **33** *(Nos. 37/44).*
Z34 **9** 2a. on 64a. purple and brown (Type **28**) .... 95·00
Z39 2a. on 64a. purple and brown (Type **33**) .... 95·00

1894. *Surch with T* **34** *(No. 45).*
Z41 **9** 1a. on 64a. purple and brown £120

1894–95. *Surch as T* **35** *with variations of English figures as T* **36/9** *(Nos. 46/50).*
Z42 **9** 1a. on 64a. purple and brown (Type **35**) .... 95·00
Z43 1a. on 64a. purple and brown (Type **36**) .... 95·00
Z44 2a. on 64a. purple and brown (Type **37**) .... 95·00
Z45 2a. on 64a. purple and brown (Type **38**) .... 95·00
Z46 10a. on 24a. purple and blue (Type **39**) .... 95·00

1896. *Surch as T* **39** *(Siamese) and T* **40** *(English) (No. 51).*
Z47 **9** 4a. on 12a. purple and carmine .... 95·00

1897. *Surch as T* **39** *(Siamese) and T* **41** *(English) (No. 52).*
Z48 **9** 4a. on 12a. purple and carmine .... 95·00

1898–99. *Surch as T* **42** *with variations of English section as T* **44/6** *(Nos. 53/62).*
Z49 **9** 1a. on 12a. purple and carmine (Type **42**–11½ mm long) £130
Z52 2a. on 64a. purple and brown (Type **44**) £110
Z53 3a. on 12a. purple and carmine (Type **45**–13½ mm long) .... 95·00
Z54 3a. on 12a. purple and carmine (Type **45**–11½ to 11¾ mm long) .... 95·00
Z55 4a. on 12a. purple and carmine (Type **46**–8 mm long) .... 95·00
Z56 4a. on 12a. purple and carmine (Type **46**–8½ to 9 mm long) .... 95·00

1899. *Surch in Siamese and English with T* **48a** *(Nos. 63/6).*
Z62 **9** 2a. on 64a. purple and brown £110

1899–1904. *(Nos. 67/81).*
Z63 **49** 1a. olive-green (wide Siamese characters in face value) .... 95·00
Z64 2a. grass-green .... 75·00
Z65 3a. red and blue .... 80·00
Z66 4a. carmine .... 75·00
Z67 8a. deep green and orange .... 75·00
Z69 12a. brown-purple and carmine £120
Z70 24a. brown-purple and blue £170
Z71 64a. brown-purple and chestnut £140

1899. *(Nos. 82/6).*
Z72 **50** 1a. green £300
Z73 2a. green and red £450

Stamps of SIAM *cancelled as Type* B *inscr* "KEDAH" *(from* March 1901).

1887–91. *(Nos. 11/18).*
Z74 **9** 12a. purple and carmine .... 75·00
Z75 24a. purple and brown .... 75·00

1898–99. *Surch with T* **42** *with variations of English section as T* **45/6** *(Nos. 53/62).*
Z76 **9** 1a. on 12a. purple and carmine (Type **42**–11½ mm long) .... 95·00
Z81 3a. on 12a. purple and carmine (Type **45**–11½ to 11¾ mm long) .... 75·00
Z83 4a. on 12a. purple and carmine (Type **46**–8½ to 9 mm long) .... 75·00
Z84 4a. on 24a. purple and blue (Type **46**) .... 80·00

1899–1904. *(Nos. 67/81).*
Z86 **49** 1a. olive-green (wide Siamese characters in face value) .... 75·00
a. Narrow Siamese characters in face value .... 70·00
Z87 2a. grass-green .... 60·00
Z88 2a. scarlet and pale blue .... 60·00
Z89 3a. red and blue .... 70·00
Z90 3a. deep green .... 70·00
Z91 4a. carmine .... 60·00
Z92 4a. chocolate and pink .... 65·00
Z93 8a. deep green and orange .... 60·00
Z94 10a. ultramarine .... 60·00
Z95 12a. brown-purple and carmine .... 70·00
Z96 24a. brown-purple and blue £140
Z97 64a. brown-purple and chestnut £130

1905–09. *(Nos. 92/105).*
Z102 **53** 1a. green and orange .... 60·00
Z103 2a. grey and deep violet .... 60·00
Z104 3a. green .... 70·00
Z105 4a. pale red and sepia .... 60·00
Z106 5a. carmine .... 70·00
Z107 8a. olive-bistre and dull black .... 60·00
Z108 12a. blue .... 70·00
Z109 24a. red-brown £170
Z110 1t. bistre and deep blue £170

Stamps of SIAM *cancelled as Type* C *inscr* "Kedah" *at foot (from* July 1907).

1887–91. *(Nos. 11/18).*
Z111 **9** 12a. purple and carmine .... 85·00

1899–1904. *(Nos. 67/81).*
Z112 **49** 1a. olive-green (wide Siamese characters in face value) .... 70·00
a. Narrow Siamese characters in face value .... 65·00
Z113 2a. scarlet and pale blue .... 60·00
Z114 3a. red and blue .... 70·00
Z116 8a. deep green and orange .... 70·00
Z117 10a. ultramarine .... 65·00
Z118 12a. brown-purple and carmine .... 65·00

1905–09. *(Nos. 95/105).*
Z128 **53** 1a. green and orange .... 60·00
Z129 2a. grey and deep violet .... 60·00
Z130 3a. green .... 70·00
Z131 4a. pale red and sepia .... 60·00
Z132 4a. scarlet .... 60·00
Z133 5a. carmine .... 70·00
Z134 8a. olive-bistre and dull black .... 60·00
Z135 9a. blue .... 60·00
Z136 18a. red-brown .... 95·00
Z137 24a. red-brown £170
Z138 1t. bistre and deep blue £170

1907. *Surch with T* **56** *(No. 109).*
Z139 **9** 1a. on 24a. purple and blue .... 70·00

Kuala Muda

Stamps of SIAM *cancelled as Type* B *inscr* "KUALA MUDA" *(from* July 1907).

1887–91. *(Nos. 11/18).*
Z143 **9** 12a. purple and carmine £350

1899–1904. *(Nos. 67/81).*
Z144 **49** 2a. scarlet and pale blue £350
Z145 24a. brown-purple and blue £400

1905–09. *(Nos. 92/105).*
Z146 **53** 1a. green and orange £350
Z147 2a. grey and deep violet £350
Z148 3a. green £375
Z150 5a. carmine £375
Z151 8a. olive-bistre and dull black £350

Stamps of SIAM *cancelled as Type* C *inscr* "Kwala Muda" *at foot (from* 1907).

1887–91. *(Nos. 11/18).*
Z155 **9** 12a. purple and carmine £160

1899–1904. *(Nos. 67/81).*
Z156 **49** 8a. deep green and orange £190
Z157 10a. ultramarine £190

1905–09. *(Nos. 92/105).*
Z158 **53** 1a. green and orange £190
Z159 2a. grey and deep violet £190
Z160 3a. green £200
Z161 4a. pale red and sepia £190
Z162 4a. scarlet £190
Z163 5a. carmine £225
Z164 8a. olive-bistre and dull black £190
Z165 9a. blue £160
Z166 24a. red-brown £400

1907. *Surch with T* **56** *(No. 109).*
Z167 **9** 1a. on 24a. purple and blue £160

Kulim

Stamps of SIAM *cancelled as Type* D *inscr* "KULIM" *(from* July 1907).

1887–91. *(Nos. 11/18).*
Z173 **9** 12a. purple and carmine £350

1899–1904. *(Nos. 67/81).*
Z174 **49** 8a. deep green and orange £350

1905–09. *(Nos. 92/105).*
Z175 **53** 1a. green and orange £375
Z176 2a. grey and deep violet £375
Z177 3a. green £400
Z178 4a. pale red and sepia £350
Z179 4a. scarlet £350
Z180 5a. carmine £375
Z181 8a. olive-bistre and dull black £350
Z182 9a. blue £350

1907. *Surch with T* **56** *(No. 109).*
Z184 **9** 1a. on 24a. purple and blue £350

Stamps of SIAM *cancelled as Type* C *inscr* "Kulim" *at foot (from* Feb 1908).

1887–91. *(Nos. 11/18).*
Z190 **9** 12a. purple and carmine £140

1899–1904. *(Nos. 67/81).*
Z191 **49** 8a. deep green and orange £140
Z192 10a. ultramarine £150

1905–09. *(Nos. 92/105).*
Z196 **53** 4a. pale red and sepia £140
Z197 4a. scarlet £140
Z198 5a. carmine £150
Z199 9a. blue £150
Z200 24a. red-brown £350
Z201 1t. bistre and deep blue £350

1907. *Surch with T* **56** *(No. 109).*
Z202 **9** 1a. purple and blue £150

Langkawi

Stamps of SIAM *cancelled as Type* D *inscr* "LANGKAWI" *(from* Feb 1908).

1899–1904. *(Nos. 67/81).*
Z208 **49** 8a. deep green and orange £350
Z209 10a. ultramarine £350

1905–09. *(Nos. 92/105).*
Z212 **53** 3a. green £375
Z213 4a. pale red and sepia £350
Z215 8a. olive-bistre and dull black £350

Stamps of SIAM *cancelled as Type* C *inscr* "Langkawi" *at foot (from* Nov 1908).

1887–91. *(Nos. 11/18).*
Z219 **9** 12a. purple and carmine £150

1899–1904. *(Nos. 67/81).*
Z220 **49** 1a. olive-green (Type B) £160
Z221 8a. green and orange £150

1905–09. *(Nos. 92/105).*
Z222 **53** 2a. grey and deep violet £150
Z223 3a. green £200
Z224 4a. pale red and sepia £150
Z225 4a. scarlet £160
Z226 8a. olive-bistre and dull black £150
Z228 24a. red-brown £400
Z229 1t. bistre and deep blue £400

1907. *Surch with T* **56** *(No. 109).*
Z230 **9** 1a. on 24a. purple and blue £160

Suzerainty over Kedah was transferred by Thailand to Great Britain on 15 July 1909 and the following day stamps of the FEDERATED MALAY STATES were placed on sale in post offices in the state.

A Treaty of Friendship between Great Britain and Kedah was signed on 1 November 1923 and the state joined the Federation of Malaya on 1 February 1948.

Stamps of the Federated Malay States used in Kedah

Alor Star

Cancelled as Type C inscribed "Kedah"

1909–12. *(Nos. 29/49).*
Z231 **3** 1c. green (Die II) .... 35·00
Z232 3c. carmine .... 40·00
Z233 4c. black and rose .... 40·00
Z234 5c. green and carmine/*yellow* .... 90·00
Z235 8c. grey-brown and ultramarine .... 90·00
a. Wmk upright .... 55·00
Z236 10c. black and purple .... 70·00
Z237 20c. mauve and black (chalk-surfaced paper) .... 75·00
Z238 50c. grey-brown and orange-brown (chalk-surfaced paper) .... 80·00
Z239 **4** $1 grey-green and green £180

Type F

Cancelled as Type F

1909–12. *(No. 34).*

Z241	3	3c. carmine	60·00

Type G

Cancelled as Type G

1909–12. *(Nos. 34/47cc).*

Z242	3	1c. green (Die II)	50·00
Z243		3c. carmine	50·00
Z244		4c. balck and rose	75·00
Z245		8c. grey-brown and ultramarine	
		a. Wmk upright	75·00
Z246		10c. black and purple	75·00
Z247		50c. grey-brown and orange-brown (chalk-surfaced paper)	85·00

Kulim

Type H

Cancelled as Type H

1909–12. *(Nos. 34/45a).*

Z248	3	1c. green (Die II)	60·00
Z249		3c. carmine	55·00
Z250		4c. black and rose	60·00
Z251		5c. green and carmine/yellow	85·00
Z252		10c. black and purple	85·00
Z253		20c. mauve and black (chalk-surfaced paper)	75·00

Type I

Cancelled as Type I

1909–12. *(Nos. 34/36d).*

Z254	3c. carmine	55·00
Z255	4c. black and rose	65·00

Langkawi

Cancelled as Type H inscribed "LANGKAWI"

1909–12. *(Nos. 34/49).*

Z256	3	3c. carmine	85·00
Z257		8c. grey-brown and ultramarine (wmk upright)	85·00
Z258	4	$1 grey-green and green	£200
Z259		$2 green and carmine	£300

Cancelled as Type I inscribed "LANGKAWI"

1909–12. *(Nos. 29/43d).*

Z260	3	1c. green (Die II)	85·00
Z261		3c. carmine	45·00
Z262		10c. black and purple	85·00

Kuala Muda

Cancelled as Type B inscribed "KUALA MUDA"

1909–12. *(Nos. 29/41bb).*

Z263	3	1c. green (Die II)	70·00
Z264		3c. carmine	45·00
Z265		4c. black and rose	80·00
Z266		5c. green and carmine/*yellow*	80·00
Z267		8c. grey-brown and ultramarine (wmk upright)	80·00

Jitra

The post office in Jitra was opened in 1910.

Type J

Cancelled as Type J

1910–12. *(No. 34).*

Z268	3	3c. carmine	70·00

Cancelled as Type I inscribed "JITRA"

1910–12. *(Nos. 29/34).*

Z269	3	1c. green Die II	45·00
Z270		3c. carmine	40·00

Lunas

The post office in Lunas was opened in 1910.

Type K

Cancelled as Type K

1910–12. *(No. 34).*

Z271	3	3c. carmine	90·00

Cancelled as Type I inscribed "LUNAS"

1910–12. *(Nos. 29/36d).*

Z272	3	1c. green (Die II)	60·00
Z273		3c. carmine	60·00
Z274		4c. black and rose	85·00

Semiling

The post office in Semiling was opened in 1910.

Cancelled as Type I inscribed "SEMILING"

1910–12. *(Nos. 29/41b).*

Z275	3	1c. green (Die II)	45·00
Z276		3c. carmine	80·00
Z277		4c. black and rose	80·00
Z278		8c. grey-brown and ultramarine (wmk upright)	80·00

Sungei Patani

The post office in Sungei Patani was opened in 1911.

Cancelled as Type I inscribed "SUNGEI PATANI"

1911–12. *(Nos. 29/34).*

Z279	3	1c. green (Die II)	95·00
Z280		3c. carmine	95·00

Yen

The post office in Yen was opened in 1910.

Cancelled as Type I inscribed "YEN"

1910–12. *(Nos. 29/34).*

Z281	3	1c. green (Die II)	£100
Z282		3c. carmine	£100

PRICES FOR STAMPS ON COVER TO 1945

Nos. 1/14	*from* × 15
Nos. 15/23	*from* × 10
Nos. 24/40	*from* × 8
Nos. 41/8	*from* × 12
Nos. 49/51	—
Nos. 52/9	*from* × 4
Nos. 60/8	*from* × 3
Nos. 68*a*/9	*from* × 4

1 Sheaf of Rice

2 Malay ploughing

3 Council Chamber, Alor Star

(Recess D.L.R.)

1912 (16 June). Wmk Mult Crown CA (sideways* on 10c. to $5). P 14.

1	1	1c. black and green	60	25
		y. Wmk inverted and reversed	£750	£350
2		3c. black and red	4·50	30
3		4c. rose and grey	10·00	25
4		5c. green and chestnut	2·25	3·00
5		8c. black and ultramarine	3·75	3·50
6	2	10c. blue and sepia	2·25	1·00
		w. Wmk Crown to left of CA	†	—
		y. Wmk Crown to left of CA and reversed	†	£325
7		20c. black and green	4·75	4·00
		x. Wmk reversed	£200	
8		30c. black and rose	3·00	11·00
9		40c. black and purple	3·50	16·00
10		50c. brown and blue	9·00	13·00
11	3	$1 black and red/*yellow*	16·00	22·00
		w. Wmk Crown to left of CA	50·00	
		x. Wmk reversed	£325	
		y. Wmk Crown to left of CA and reversed		
12		$2 green and brown	22·00	85·00
13		$3 black and blue/*blue*	90·00	£170
		a. "A" of "CA" missing from wmk	£1700	
14		$5 black and red	95·00	£170
1/14 *Set of* 14			£225	£450
1s/14s Optd "Specimen" *Set of* 14			£300	

*The normal sideways watermark shows the Crown to right of CA, *as seen from the back of the stamp.*

Due to an increase in postal rates 1c. and 4c. stamps of STRAITS SETTLEMENTS were used in Kedah for some months from March 1919.

Short sheaf (R. 10/1)

(i)

(ii)

DOUBLE AND SINGLE PLATES. (i) Printed from separate plates for frame and centre, with dotted shading extending close to the central sheaf. Soft impression of centre with little clear detail.

(ii) Printed from single plate, with white space around sheaf. Centre more deeply etched with sharp image.

1919 (June)–**21**. *New colours and values.* Wmk Mult Crown CA (sideways* on 21c., 25c.). P 14.

15	1	1c. brown (i) (18.8.19)	55	50
		w. Wmk inverted	£120	£150
		y. Wmk inverted and reversed	†	£350
18		2c. green (ii)	50	30
19		3c. deep purple (i) (1920)	65	1·75
		x. Wmk reversed	£350	
		y. Wmk inverted and reversed	80·00	£130
20		4c. rose (i)	4·50	30
21		4c. red (ii) (18.8.19)	3·50	1·00
		a. Short sheaf	£130	60·00
		w. Wmk inverted		
22	2	21c. mauve and purple (18.8.19)	5·50	60·00
		a. "A" of "CA" missing from wmk	—	£700
		w. Wmk Crown to left of CA	£150	£180
		ws. Ditto, optd "Specimen"		
		x. Wmk reversed	£325	
		y. Wmk Crown to left of CA and reversed	£300	
23		25c. blue and purple (1921)	1·75	28·00
		a. "A" of "CA" missing from wmk	£600	
15/23 *Set of* 6			11·00	80·00
15s/23s Optd "Specimen" *Set of* 6			£150	

*The normal sideways watermark shows Crown to right of CA, *as seen from the back of the stamp.*

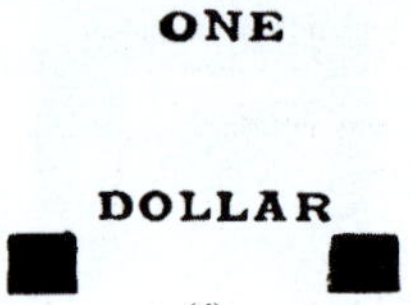

(4)

(5)

(Surch by Ribeiro & Co, Penang)

1919 (Mar). *Surch as T* **4**.

24 **3** 50c. on $2 green and brown 70·00 75·00
a. "C" of "CENTS" inserted by handstamp (R. 6/4) £1300 £1400
25 $1 on $3 black and blue/*blue* 20·00 90·00

Nos. 24/5 were surcharged from settings of 30 (5×6).

Two types of centre plate for Type **2** wmkd Mult Script CA:

Type I (Plate 1) (produced by electrotyping)

Type II (Plate 2) (produced by transfer die)

A new common centre plate, 2, was prepared from the original die in 1926. Stamps from Plate 2, produced using a transfer die, show considerably more detail of the ground and have the oxen, ploughman's hat and his clothing much more deeply cut as illustrated in Type II above.

1921–32. Wmk Mult Script CA (sideways* on 10c. to $5). P 14.

26 **1** 1c. brown (ii) 80 20
w. Wmk inverted † £325
y. Wmk inverted and reversed † £325
27 2c. dull green (ii) (Type I) 1·50 20
28 3c. deep purple (ii) 80 70
w. Wmk inverted £325
29 4c. deep carmine (ii) 5·00 20
a. Short sheaf £170 32·00
30 **2** 10c. blue and sepia (I) 2·75 75
ax. Wmk reversed £350
ay. Wmk Crown to left of CA and reversed £120
b. Type II (wmk Crown to left of CA) (1927) 55·00 2·75
by. Wmk Crown to right of CA and reversed £400 £275
31 20c. black and yellow-green (I) 4·00 2·00
32 21c. mauve and purple (I) 2·25 13·00
33 25c. blue and purple (I) 2·25 9·00
a. Type II (wmk Crown to left of CA) (1932) 90·00 4·00
34 30c. black and rose (I) (1922) 3·00 11·00
a. Type II (wmk Crown to left of CA) (1927) 50·00 3·00
35 40c. black and purple (I) 4·25 55·00
aw. Wmk Crown to left of CA (1924) 42·00 48·00
b. Type II (wmk Crown to left of CA) (1932) 90·00 26·00
36 50c. brown and grey-blue (I) 2·75 18·00
aw. Wmk Crown to left of CA (1924) 38·00 20·00
b. Type II (wmk Crown to left of CA) (1932) £100 9·00
37 **3** $1 black and red/*yellow* (1924) 65·00 70·00
w. Wmk Crown to left of CA 6·50 9·50
38 $2 myrtle and brown 13·00 £100
w. Wmk Crown to left of CA (1924) 32·00 90·00
39 $3 black and blue/*blue* 70·00 £100
w. Wmk Crown to left of CA (1924) £100 85·00
40 $5 black and deep carmine 85·00 £160
w. Wmk Crown to left of CA (1926) £120 £160
26/40 *Set of* 15 £180 £350
26s/40s Optd "Specimen" *Set of* 15 £300

*The normal sideways watermark shows Crown to right of CA, *as seen from the back of the stamp*.

Nos. 26/40 were produced by De La Rue using the "wet" method of recess-printing during which the stamps contracted when they were dried before gumming. From 1933 the firm adopted the "dry" method, using pre-gummed paper, with the result that stamps were up to 0.5 mm larger in size. Of the low values as Type **1** in this series only the 2c. was still current when the "dry" method was introduced.

Stamps as Type **1** can be found perforated either comb or line. The 1c. and 4c. come comb only, the 3c. line only and the 2c. either way.

Examples of Nos. 37/40 are known with part strikes of a forged Sungei Patang postmark dated "14 JY 1920".

For the 2c. Type II see No. 69.

OVERPRINT SETTINGS FOR NOS. 41/51. The low values in Type **1** were overprinted using Setting II as detailed under Straits Settlements. The three listed constant varieties from the original typeset block of 12 occur in the same positions for these Kedah stamps as does the No Stop variety from R. 1/5 of the left pane.

For the higher values in Type **2**, which were in sheets of 60 (5×12), a further setting was prepared using the first four vertical rows of the typeset block with each horizontal row completed by a single random impression of the overprint. This means that, in addition to their positions in the truncated typeset block, the Oval last "O" additionally occurs on R. 11/5 and the Raised stop on R. 5/5 of the sheet. In this setting, as for the low values, "BORNEO" was 14 mm long.

Further supplies were subsequently required of the 21, 25 and 50c. values and these were produced using a completely different setting of 20 (5×4), applied three times to each sheet, on which "BORNEO" was 15–15½ mm long.

1922 (Apr). *Malaya-Borneo Exhibition, Singapore. Optd as T* **5** *at Singapore*.

I. "BORNEO" 14 mm long.

(*a*) Wmk Mult Crown CA (*Nos. 10, 18 and 22/3*).

41 **1** 2c. green (ii) 3·50 25·00
b. Oval last "O" in "BORNEO" 8·00 45·00
c. Raised stop after "EXHIBITION" 8·00 45·00
d. Small second "A" in "MALAYA" 8·00 45·00
f. No stop 38·00
42 **2** 21c. mauve and purple 30·00 80·00
b. Oval last "O" in "BORNEO" 50·00 £130
c. Raised stop after "EXHIBITION" 50·00 £130
43 25c. blue and purple 30·00 80·00
a. Opt inverted £1500
b. Oval last "O" in "BORNEO" 50·00 £130
c. Raised stop after "EXHIBITION" 50·00 £130
44 50c. brown and blue 30·00 95·00
b. Oval last "O" in "BORNEO" 50·00 £150
c. Raised stop after "EXHIBITION" 50·00 £150

(*b*) *Wmk Mult Script CA* (*Nos. 26 and 28/30*).

45 **1** 1c. brown (ii) 4·50 22·00
b. Oval last "O" in "BORNEO" 9·00 40·00
c. Raised stop after "EXHIBITION" 9·00 40·00
d. Small second "A" in "MALAYA" 9·00 40·00
f. No stop 40·00
46 3c. deep purple (ii) 3·00 42·00
b. Oval last "O" in "BORNEO" 7·00 65·00
c. Raised stop after "EXHIBITION" 7·00 65·00
d. Small second "A" in "MALAYA" 7·00 65·00
f. No stop 35·00
47 4c. deep carmine (ii) 3·00 25·00
a. Short sheaf £130
b. Oval last "O" in "BORNEO" 7·00 45·00
c. Raised stop after "EXHIBITION" 7·00 45·00
d. Small second "A" in "MALAYA" 7·00 45·00
f. No stop 35·00
48 **2** 10c. blue and sepia (I) 5·50 45·00
b. Oval last "O" in "BORNEO" 11·00 70·00
c. Raised stop after "EXHIBITION" 11·00 70·00
41/8 *Set of* 8 £100 £375

II. "BORNEO" 15–15½ mm long. Wmk Mult Crown CA (*Nos. 10 and 22/3*).

49 **2** 21c. mauve and purple 23·00 £100
50 25c. blue and purple 23·00 £120
51 50c. brown and blue 50·00 £170
49/51 *Set of* 3 85·00 £350

Examples of all values are known with part strikes of the forged postmark mentioned after Nos. 26/40.

1922–40. *New colours, etc.* Wmk Mult Script CA (sideways* on 12, 35c.). P 14.

52 **1** 1c. black (ii) (Type I) 1·00 10
53 3c. green (ii) (1924) 2·25 90
54 4c. violet (ii) (1926) 1·00 10
a. Short sheaf 55·00 10·00
55 5c. yellow (ii) 1·75 10
w. Wmk inverted 85·00 £100
x. Wmk reversed † £225
y. Wmk inverted and reversed † £225
56 6c. carmine (ii) (1926) 2·25 65
a. Carmine-red (1940) 12·00 48·00
57 8c. grey-black (ii) (10.36) 15·00 10
58 **2** 12c. black and indigo (II) (1926) 6·00 3·50
59 35c. purple (II) (1926) 10·00 35·00
52/9 *Set of* 8 35·00 35·00
52s/9s Optd or Perf (8c.) "Specimen" *Set of* 8 £325

*The normal sideways watermark shows Crown to left of CA, *as seen from the back of the stamp*.

With the exception of the 6c. and 8c. the printing plates for the Type **1** values listed above were, as for the previous issue, produced by electrotyping with the face values added to the plates by pantograph. The plates for the 6c. and 8c. values were constructed by the more modern method of using a transfer die to enter each impression.

Printings after November 1933 were normally produced by the "dry" method as described beneath Nos. 26/40. There were late "wet" printings of the 1c. (No. 68*a*) and 2c. (No. 27) in August 1938. The 3c. only exists from a "wet" printing, the 6c. (No. 56*a*) and 8c. from dry printings and the remainder from either method.

Stamps as Type **1** can be found perforated either comb or line. The 3c. and 6c. (No. 56) come comb only, the 6c. (No. 56*a*) and 8c. line only and the 1, 4 and 5c. either way.

For the 1c. Type II see No. 68*a*.

6 Sultan Abdul Hamid Halimshah

(Recess Waterlow)

1937 (30 June). Wmk Mult Script CA. P 12½.

60 **6** 10c. ultramarine and sepia 4·75 1·75
61 12c. black and violet 48·00 4·50
a. "A" of "CA" missing from wmk
62 25c. ultramarine and purple 9·50 4·50
63 30c. green and scarlet 8·50 10·00
64 40c. black and purple 4·25 16·00
65 50c. brown and blue 9·00 4·50
66 $1 black and green 4·00 10·00
67 $2 green and brown £130 75·00
68 $5 black and scarlet 32·00 £170
60/8 *Set of* 9 £225 £275
60s/8s Perf "Specimen" *Set of* 9 £300

I II I II

1938 (May)–**40**. *As Nos. 52 and 27, but face values redrawn as Types II.*

68*a* **1** 1c. black £130 3·00
69 2c. bright green (1940) £275 6·50

1c. Type II. Figures "1" have square-cut corners instead of rounded, and larger top serif. Larger "C". Line perf. Produced from a new electrotyped Plate 2 with different engraved face values. Printings exist from either the "wet" or "dry" methods.

2c. Type II. Figures "2" have circular instead of oval drops and the letters "c" are thin and tall instead of thick and rounded. Produced from a new plate, made from a transfer die, and printed by the "dry" method.

1948 (1 Dec). *Royal Silver Wedding. As Nos. 112/13 of Antigua.*

70 10c. violet 20 40
71 $5 carmine 28·00 42·00

1949 (10 Oct). *75th Anniv of U.P.U. As Nos. 114/17 of Antigua.*

72 10c. purple 25 1·25
73 15c. deep blue 2·00 1·50
74 25c. orange 65 2·25
75 50c. blue-black 1·00 3·75
a. "A" of "CA" missing from watermark £800
72/5 *Set of* 4 3·50 8·00

7 Sheaf of Rice

8 Sultan Badlishah

1950 (1 June)–**55**. Wmk Mult Script CA. *Chalk-surfaced paper.* P 17½×18.

76 **7** 1c. black 50 30
77 2c. orange 50 15
78 3c. green 2·00 1·00
79 4c. brown 75 10
79*a* 5c. bright purple (1.9.52) 2·75 2·50
ab. Bright mauve (24.9.53) 2·75 1·00
80 6c. grey 70 15
81 8c. scarlet 1·75 3·75
81*a* 8c. green (1.9.52) 2·00 1·75
ab. Deep green (24.9.53) 16·00 15·00
82 10c. magenta 70 10
82*a* 12c. scarlet (1.9.52) 2·25 2·50
83 15c. ultramarine 2·50 35
84 20c. black and green 2·25 2·50
84*a* 20c. bright blue (1.9.52) 1·50 10
85 **8** 25c. purple and orange 1·50 30
85*a* 30c. scarlet and purple (4.9.55) 3·75 1·25
85*b* 35c. scarlet and purple (1.9.52) 3·00 1·50
86 40c. red and purple 3·75 6·50
87 50c. black and blue 3·00 35
88 $1 blue and purple 3·25 5·50
89 $2 green and scarlet 20·00 26·00
90 $5 green and brown 42·00 55·00
76/90 *Set of* 21 90·00 £100

1953 (2 June). *Coronation. As No. 120 of Antigua.*

91 10c. black and reddish purple 2·00 60

9 Copra

10 Pineapples

11 Ricefield

12 Masjid Alwi Mosque, Kangar

13 East Coast Railway "Golden Blowpipe" Express

14 Tiger

15 Fishing Prau

16 Aborigines with Blowpipes

17 Government Offices

18 Bersilat

19 Weaving

(Recess D.L.R.)

1957. *Inset portrait of Sultan Badlishah.* W w **12**. P 13×12½ (1c. to 8c.), 12½×13 (10c., 20c.), 12½ (50c., $2, $5) or 13½ ($1).

92	**9**	1c. black (21.8)	10	60
93	**10**	2c. orange-red (25.7)	30	1·75
94	**11**	4c. sepia (21.8)	30	1·00
95	**12**	5c. carmine-lake (21.8)	30	75
96	**13**	8c. myrtle-green (21.8)	2·00	8·00
97	**14**	10c. deep brown (4.8)	80	40
98	**15**	20c. blue (26.6)	2·75	2·50
99	**16**	50c. black and blue (25.7)	3·00	3·50
100	**17**	$1 ultramarine and reddish purple (25.7)	7·50	13·00
101	**18**	$2 bronze-green and scarlet (21.8)	27·00	38·00
102	**19**	$5 brown and bronze-green (26.6)	45·00	40·00
92/102 *Set of* 11			80·00	£100

The 6, 12, 25 and 30c. values used with this issue were Nos. 1/4 of Malayan Federation.

20 Sultan Abdul Halim Mu'Adzam Shah

21 Sultan Abdul Halim Shah

(Photo Harrison)

1959 (20 Feb). *Installation of the Sultan.* W w **12**. P 14×14½.

103	**20**	10c. multicoloured	40	10

1959 (1 July)–**62**. *As Nos. 92/102 but with inset portrait of Sultan Abdul Halim Shah as in T* **21**.

104	**21**	1c. black	10	75
105	**10**	2c. orange-red	10	2·00
106	**11**	4c. sepia	10	75
107	**12**	5c. carmine-lake	10	10
108	**13**	8c. myrtle-green	3·50	3·50
109	**14**	10c. deep brown	1·00	10
109*a*		10c. deep maroon (19.12.61)	7·50	55
110	**15**	20c. blue	1·00	1·00
111	**16**	50c. black and blue (p 12½)	30	1·75
		a. Perf 12½×13 (14.6.60)	30	60
112	**17**	$1 ultramarine and reddish purple	1·75	2·25
113	**18**	$2 bronze-green and scarlet	13·00	18·00
114	**19**	$5 brown and bronze-green (p 12½)	16·00	19·00
		a. Perf 13×12½ (26.11.62)	30·00	16·00
104/14 *Set of* 12			40·00	40·00

22 Vanda hookeriana

1965 (15 Nov). *As Nos. 166/72 of Johore but with inset portrait of Sultan Abdul Halim Shah as in T* **22**. W w **13** (upright).

115	1c. multicoloured	10	1·50
	a. Black omitted (orchid's name and part of flower)	£225	
116	2c. multicoloured	10	1·75
	b. Yellow (flower) omitted	£180	
117	5c. multicoloured	10	20
	a. Black (country name and head) omitted	£250	
118	6c. multicoloured	15	60
119	10c. multicoloured	30	20
	a. Red omitted	£600	
	b. Green (leaves) omitted	£700	
120	15c. multicoloured	1·50	10
121	20c. multicoloured	1·75	1·00
	a. Bright purple (blooms) omitted	£450	
	b. Yellow (leaves) omitted	48·00	
115/21 *Set of* 7		3·50	4·50

The 1c. to 15c. exist with PVA gum as well as gum arabic.

The 6c. value exists with black (country name, arms and head) omitted and is listed under Sarawak where it was issued.

The higher values used with this issue were Nos. 20/27 of Malaysia (National Issues).

1970 (27 May). *As Nos. 115 and 119 but W w* **13** *(sideways).*

122	**22**	1c. multicoloured	2·50	5·50
123	–	10c. multicoloured	1·00	4·00

KELANTAN

The Thai monarchy exercised suzerainty over Kelantan and the other northern states of the Malay peninsula from the 16th century onwards.

The first Siamese post office in Kelantan opened at Kota Bharu in 1895. It appears that in the early years this office only accepted letters franked with stamps for delivery within Kelantan.

The initial cancellation, of which no complete example has been discovered, showed Thai characters only. Partial examples have been reported on the 1887–91 8a. and 1896 4a. on 12a.

The operations of the Duff Development Company in Kelantan from 1903 led to a considerable expansion of the postal service based on the company's river steamers. A further post office opened at Batu Mengkebang in 1908, but may have been preceded by manuscript endorsements of "B.M." and date known from early 1907 onwards.

Type E. Double ring. English at top and bottom

For other stamps and postmark types, See under Kedah.

Kota Bharu

Stamps of SIAM *cancelled as Type* B *inscr* "KALANTAN" *(from* March 1898).

1887–91. *(Nos. 11/18).*

Z301	**9**	2a. green and carmine	£100
Z302		3a. green and blue	£110
Z303		4a. green and brown	£110
Z304		8a. green and yellow	£110
Z305		12a. purple and carmine	95·00
Z306		24a. purple and blue	£100

1894. *Surch as T* **27** *with variation of English figures as T* **33** *(Nos. 37/44).*

Z307	**9**	2a. on 64a. purple and brown	£150

1894–95. *Surch as T* **35** *with variation of English figures as T* **36** *(Nos. 46/50).*

Z308	**9**	1a. on 64a. purple and brown	£130

1896. *Surch as T* **39** *(Siamese) and T* **40** *(English) (No. 51).*

Z309	**9**	4a. on 12a. purple and carmine	£130

1897. *Surch as T* **39** *(Siamese) and T* **41** *(English) (No. 52).*

Z310	**9**	4a. on 12a. purple and carmine	£130

1898–99. *Surch as T* **42** *with variation of English section as T* **46** *(Nos. 53/62).*

Z311	**9**	3a. on 12a. (11½–11¾ mm long)	£140
Z312		4a. on 12a. purple and carmine (8 mm long)	£130

1899–1904. *(Nos. 67/81).*

Z313	**49**	1a. olive-green (wide Siamese characters in face value)	£100
Z314		2a. grass-green	95·00
Z315		2a. scarlet and pale blue	95·00
Z316		3a. red and blue	£110
Z317		4a. carmine	95·00
Z318		4a. chocolate and pink	£110
Z319		8a. deep green and orange	95·00
Z320		10a. ultramarine	£100
Z321		12a. brown-purple and carmine	£100
Z322		64a. brown-purple and chestnut	£225

1905–09. *(Nos. 92/105).*

Z323	**53**	1a. green and orange	95·00
Z324		2a. grey and deep violet	95·00
Z325		4a. pale red and sepia	95·00
Z326		4a. scarlet	95·00
Z327		5a. carmine	£120
Z328		8a. olive-bistre and dull black	95·00
Z329		12a. blue	£120
Z330		24a. red-brown	£300
Z331		1t. bistre and deep blue	£300

1907. *Surch with T* **56** *(No. 109).*

Z332	**9**	1a. on 24a. purple and blue	£130

Stamps of SIAM *cancelled as Type* E *inscr* "Kota Bahru/Kelantan" *(from* July 1908).

1887–91. *(Nos. 11/18).*

Z333	**9**	12a. purple and carmine	95·00
Z334		24a. purple and blue	£130

1899–1904. *(Nos. 67/81).*

Z335	**49**	8a. deep green and orange	£100
Z336		64a. brown-purple and chestnut	£150

1905–09. *(Nos. 92/105).*

Z337	**53**	1a. green and orange	£100
Z338		2a. grey and deep violet	£100
Z339		2a. pale yellow-green	£100
Z340		4a. pale red and sepia	£100
Z341		4a. scarlet	£100
Z342		8a. olive-bistre and dull black	95·00
Z343		9a. blue	£110
Z344		18a. red-brown	£170

1907. *Surch with T* **56** *(No. 109).*

Z345	**9**	1a. on 24a. purple and blue	£100

1908. *Surch as T* **59** *(Nos. 110/12).*

Z346	**9**	2a. on 24a. purple and blue	£150
Z347	**53**	4a. on 5a. carmine	£180
Z348	**49**	9a. on 10a. ultramarine	£120

Batu Mengkebang

Stamps of SIAM *cancelled as Type* E *inscr* "Batu Menkebang/ Kelantan" *(from* July 1908).

1887–91. *(Nos. 11/18).*

Z349	**9**	12a. purple and carmine	£180
Z349*a*		24a. purple and blue	£375

1899–1904. *(Nos. 67/81).*

Z350	**49**	8a. deep green and orange	£190

1905–09. *(Nos. 92/105).*

Z351	**53**	1a. green and orange	£180
Z352		2a. grey and deep violet	£180
Z353		2a. pale yellow-green	£190
Z354		4a. pale red and sepia	£190
Z355		4a. scarlet	£180
Z356		8a. olive-bistre and dull black	£150
Z357		9a. blue	£150
Z358		12a. blue	£225
Z359		24a. red-brown	£350
Z360		1t. bistre and deep blue	£375

1907. *Surch with T* **56** *(No. 109).*

Z361	**9**	1a. on 24a. purple and blue	£150

1908. *Surch as T* **59** *(Nos. 110/12).*

Z362	**49**	9a. on 10a. ultramarine	£225

Suzerainty over Kelantan was transferred by Thailand to Great Britain on 15 July 1909.

Siamese stamps were withdrawn from sale and replaced the following day by stamps of the Federated Malay States.

Stamps of the Federated Malay States used in Kelantan

Kota Bahru

Type M

Cancelled as Type F

1909–11. *(Nos. 29/49).*

Z367	**3**	1c. green (Die II)	80·00
Z368		3c. carmine	70·00
Z369		4c. black and rose	80·00
Z370		8c. grey-brown and ultramarine	70·00
		a. Wmk upright	85·00
Z373	**4**	$2 green and carmine	£275

Cancelled as Type M

1909–11. *(Nos. 29/45a).*

Z375	**3**	1c. green (Die II)	60·00
Z376		3c. carmine	60·00
Z377		4c. black and rose	60·00
Z378		5c. green and carmine/yellow	90·00
Z379		8c. grey-brown and ultramarine	80·00
		a. Wmk upright	90·00
Z380		10c. black and purple	£100
Z381		20c. mauve and black (chalk-surfaced paper)	£100

Batu Menkebang

Cancelled as Type I inscribed "Batu Menkebang"

1909–11. *(Nos. 34/43d).*

Z385	**3**	3c. carmine	£100
Z386		5c. green and carmine/yellow	£120
Z387		10c. black and purple	£120

Cancelled as Type M inscribed "BATU MENKEBANG" at top

1909–11. *(Nos. 29/45a).*

Z391	**3**	1c. green (Die II)	80·00
Z392		3c. carmine	50·00
Z393		4c. black and rose	70·00
Z394		5c. green and carmine/*yellow*	£110
Z395		8c. grey-brown and ultramarine (wmk upright)	90·00
Z396		20c. mauve and black (chalk-surfaced paper)	£110

Federated Malay States stamps were replaced by those of Kelantan in January 1911.

A British adviser was appointed to Kelantan in 1923 and the state joined the Federation of Malaya on 1 February 1948.

PRICES FOR STAMPS ON COVER TO 1945

Nos. 1/11	*from* × 30
No. 12	—
Nos. 14/23	*from* × 30
Nos. 30/8	*from* × 15

PRICES FOR STAMPS ON COVER TO 1945	
Nos. 39/*a*	*from* × 10
Nos. 40/8	*from* × 30
Nos. 49/52	*from* × 20
No. 53	*from* × 3
No. 54	—

1

MALAYA
BORNEO
EXHIBITION
(2)

1911 (Jan)–**15**. Wmk Mult Crown CA. *Ordinary paper* (1c. to 10c.) *or chalk-surfaced paper* (30c. to $25). P 14.

1	1	1c. yellow-green	7·00	1·00
		a. Blue-green	6·00	30
2		3c. red	4·25	15
3		4c. black and red	1·50	15
4		5c. green and red/*yellow*	10·00	1·00
		w. Wmk inverted	†	£500
5		8c. ultramarine	5·50	1·00
6		10c. black and mauve	30·00	75
7		30c. dull purple and red	11·00	2·50
		a. Purple and carmine	27·00	14·00
8		50c. black and orange	8·50	2·50
9		$1 green and emerald	48·00	40·00
9*a*		$1 green and brown (5.15)	65·00	2·00
10		$2 green and carmine	1·50	2·75
11		$5 green and blue	4·00	5·00
12		$25 green and orange	50·00	90·00
1/12 *Set of* 13			£225	£130
1s/12s Optd "Specimen" *Set of* 13			£275	

1921 (5 May)–**28**. Wmk Mult Script CA. *Ordinary paper* (1c. to 10c.) *or chalk-surfaced paper* (30c. to $1). P 14.

14	1	1c. dull green (7.21)	4·25	60
15		1c. black (24.2.23)	1·00	50
16		2c. brown (29.7.22)	7·00	3·75
16*a*		2c. green (24.7.26)	5·00	40
16*b*		3c. brown (5.3.27)	4·75	1·00
		ba. "C" of "CA" missing from wmk		
17		4c. black and red (15.7.22)	3·25	10
18		5c. green and red/*pale yellow* (12.22)	1·75	10
19		6c. claret (29.7.22)	3·50	1·00
19*a*		6c. scarlet (26.5.28)	4·00	4·50
20		10c. black and mauve	3·00	10
21		30c. purple and carmine (24.7.26)	4·00	5·00
22		50c. black and orange (21.3.25)	6·50	45·00
23		$1 green and brown (9.2.24)	85·00	85·00
14/23 *Set of* 13			65·00	£130
14s/23s Optd "Specimen" *Set of* 13			£375	

Examples of Nos. 22/3 are known showing part strikes of a forged Kota Bharu postmark dated "27 JUL 11".

For the 4c., 5c. and 6c. surcharged, see issues under "Japanese Occupation".

OVERPRINT SETTINGS FOR NOS. 30/8. All values were overprinted using a triplet of three slightly different types. It is not known if this was applied to the sheets three stamps at a time or if a forme to overprint a pane of 60 was constructed from it.

On the normal setting "MALAYA" is 13 mm long. The1c and 5c. only is also known with "MALAYA" 14 mm from a different triplet setting. It has been suggested that this was a trial overprint on one sheet which was subsequently included in postal stocks.

1922 (31 Mar). *Malaya-Borneo Exhibition, Singapore. Optd with T* **2** ("MALAYA" *13 mm long) by Govt Survey Office, Kkota Bharu.*

(a) Wmk Mult Crown CA.

30	1	4c. black and red	6·00	50·00
		a. Opt double	£3000	
31		5c. green and red/*pale yellow*	6·00	50·00
		a. "MALAYA" 14 mm long	£250	
32		30c. dull purple and red	6·00	80·00
33		50c. black and orange	9·50	85·00
34		$1 green and brown	32·00	£110
35		$2 green and carmine	85·00	£250
36		$5 green and blue	£200	£450

(b) Wmk Mult Script CA.

37	1	1c. green	3·50	55·00
		a. Opt double	£3000	
		b "MALAYA" 14 mm. long		
38		10c. black and mauve	6·00	75·00
30/8 *Set of* 9			£325	£1100

Nos. 30a and 37a show all three lines of the overprint double.

Examples of all values are known showing part strikes of the forged postmark mentioned below Nos. 14/23.

3 Sultan Ismail

4 Sultan Ismail

(Recess Harrison (No. 39) or D.L.R. (No. 39a))

1928–35. Wmk Mult Script CA. P 12.

39	3	$1 blue	15·00	80·00
		a. Perf 14 (1935)	50·00	42·00
		s. Perf "Specimen"	95·00	

(Recess B.W.)

1937 (July)–**40**. Wmk Mult Script CA. P 12.

40	4	1c. grey-olive and yellow	1·75	55
41		2c. green	6·00	20
42		4c. scarlet	6·00	1·00
43		5c. red-brown	4·75	10
44		6c. lake (10.37)	12·00	10·00
45		8c. grey-olive	4·75	10
46		10c. purple (10.37)	23·00	2·75
47		12c. blue	6·00	6·00
48		25c. vermilion and violet	7·00	3·50
49		30c. violet and scarlet (10.37)	48·00	21·00
50		40c. orange and blue-green	8·50	30·00
51		50c. grey-olive and orange (10.37)	75·00	8·50
52		$1 violet and blue-green (10.37)	48·00	13·00
53		$2 red-brown and scarlet (3.40)	£225	£180
54		$5 vermilion and lake (3.40)	£475	£600
40/54 *Set of* 15			£800	£800
40s/54s Perf "Specimen" *Set of* 15			£650	

For above issue surcharged see issues under "Japanese Occupation".

1948 (1 Dec). *Royal Silver Wedding. As Nos. 112/13 of Antigua.*

55	10c. violet	75	2·75
56	$5 carmine	28·00	48·00

1949 (10 Oct). *75th Anniv of U.P.U. As Nos. 114/17 of Antigua.*

57	10c. purple	25	30
58	15c. deep blue	2·25	1·75
59	25c. orange	40	4·50
60	50c. blue-black	70	3·00
57/60 *Set of* 4		3·25	8·75

Due to the exhaustion of certain B.M.A. values PERAK 2c., 3c., 4c., 6c., 15c., 20c. black and green, 25c., 40c. and 50c. stamps were used in Kelantan from 27 November 1950 until the issue of Nos. 61/81.

5 Sultan Ibrahim

Normal

No. 62a Tiny stop (R. 1/2)

1951 (11 July)–**55**. *Chalk-surfaced paper.* Wmk Mult Script CA. P 17½×18.

61	5	1c. black	50	30
62		2c. orange	1·25	35
		a. Tiny stop	28·00	
		b. Orange-yellow (11.5.55)	6·00	3·00
63		3c. green	4·25	1·25
64		4c. brown	1·25	15
65		5c. bright purple (1.9.52)	1·50	50
		a. Bright mauve (9.12.53)	2·75	1·00
66		6c. grey	75	20
67		8c. scarlet	3·50	3·50
68		8c. green (1.9.52)	2·50	1·75
69		10c. magenta	50	10
70		12c. scarlet (1.9.52)	3·50	2·25
71		15c. ultramarine	5·00	60
72		20c. black and green	3·00	9·00
73		20c. bright blue (1.9.52)	1·50	25
74		25c. purple and orange	1·50	55
75		30c. scarlet and purple (4.9.55)	1·25	3·50
76		35c. scarlet and purple (1.9.52)	1·50	1·50
77		40c. red and purple	12·00	16·00
78		50c. black and blue	5·00	40
79		$1 blue and purple	8·00	9·00
80		$2 green and scarlet	28·00	38·00
81		$5 green and brown	50·00	55·00
		a. Green and sepia (8.12.53)	£100	£110
61/81 *Set of* 21			£120	£130

1953 (2 June). *Coronation. As No. 120 of Antigua.*

82	10c. black and reddish purple	1·25	1·40

1957 (26 June)–**63**. *As Nos. 92/102 of Kedah but with inset portrait of Sultan Ibrahim.*

83	**9**	1c. black (21.8.57)	10	30
84	**10**	2c. orange-red (25.7.57)	75	1·50
		a. Red-orange (17.11.59)	9·00	6·00
85	**11**	4c. sepia (21.8.57)	40	10
86	**12**	5c. carmine-lake (21.8.57)	40	10
87	**13**	8c. myrtle-green (21.8.57)	1·00	3·00
88	**14**	10c. deep brown (4.8.57)	2·50	10
89		10c. deep maroon (19.4.61)	11·00	7·50
90	**15**	20c. blue	2·50	30
91	**16**	50c. black and blue (*p* 12½) (25.7.57)	50	50
		a. Perf 12½×13 (28.6.60)	1·00	30
92	**17**	$1 ultramarine and reddish purple (25.7.57)	7·00	1·50
93	**18**	$2 bronze-green and scarlet (*p* 12½) (21.8.57)	13·00	6·50
		a. Perf 13×12½ (9.4.63)	15·00	26·00
94	**19**	$5 brown and bronze-green (*p* 12½)	18·00	12·00
		a. Perf 13×12½ (13.8.63)	26·00	32·00
83/94 *Set of* 12			50·00	30·00

The 6, 12, 25 and 30c. values used with this issue were Nos. 1/4 of Malayan Federation.

(Photo Harrison)

1961 (17 July). *Coronation of the Sultan.* W w **12**. P 15×14.

95	**6**	10c. multicoloured	40	70

7 Sultan Yahya Petra

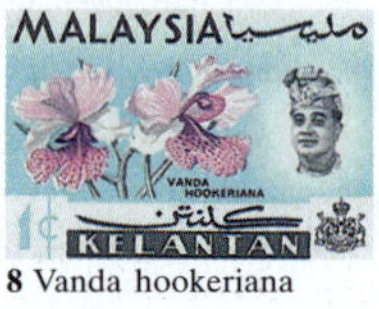
8 Vanda hookeriana

(Recess D.L.R.)

1961–63. *As Nos. 92/8 of Kedah but with inset portrait of Sultan Yahya Petra as in T* **7**. W w **13**. P 12½×13 (vert) or 13×12½ (horiz).

96	1c. black (1.3.62)	10	2·50
97	2c. orange-red (1.3.62)	30	2·50
98	4c. sepia (1.3.62)	1·25	1·75
99	5c. carmine-lake (1.3.62)	1·00	20
100	8c. myrtle-green (1.3.62)	11·00	13·00
	a. Deep green (15.1.63)	12·00	12·00
101	10c. deep maroon (2.12.61)	1·75	25
102	20c. blue (1.3.62)	7·50	2·00
96/102 *Set of* 7		20·00	19·00

1965 (15 Nov). *As Nos. 166/72 of Johore but with inset portrait of Sultan Yahya Petra as in T* **8**. W w **13** (upright).

103	1c. multicoloured	10	1·25
	b. Magenta omitted	£225	
104	2c. multicoloured	10	1·75
105	5c. multicoloured	15	30
106	6c. multicoloured	70	2·25
107	10c. multicoloured	30	25
	a. Red omitted	£130	
108	15c. multicoloured	1·50	25
109	20c. multicoloured	1·50	1·75
	a. Bright purple (blooms) omitted	£225	
	b. Yellow (leaves) omitted	60·00	
103/9 *Set of* 7		3·75	7·00

The 5c. and 10c. exist with PVA as well as gum arabic.

The higher values used with tissue were Nos. 20/27 of Malaysia (National Issues).

1970 (20 Nov). *As Nos. 103 and 107 but* W w **13** (sideways).

110	**8**	1c. multicoloured	1·50	7·50
111	–	10c. multicoloured	3·75	4·50

STAMP BOOKLETS

1927 (June). *Black on white (No. SB1) or black on grey (No. SB2) covers. Stapled.*

SB1	36c. booklet containing thirty-six 1c. (No. 15) in blocks of 6	£2750
SB2	96c. booklet containing twenty-four 4c. (No. 17) in blocks of 6	£2750

1927 (Dec). *Black on white (No. SB3) or on grey (No. SB4) covers. Stapled.*

SB3	40c. booklet containing forty 1c. (No. 15) in blocks of 10	£2750
SB4	80c. booklet containing twenty 4c. (No. 17) in blocks of 10	£2750

MALACCA

One of the Straits Settlements which joined the Federation of Malaya on 1 February 1948.

1948 (1 Dec). *Royal Silver Wedding. As Nos. 112/13 of Antigua.*

1	10c. violet	30	1·75
2	$5 brown	29·00	40·00

1949 (1 Mar)–**52**. *As T* **58** *of Straits Settlements, but inscr* "MALACCA" *at foot.* Wmk Mult Script CA. *Chalk-surfaced paper.* P 17½×18.

3	1c. black	30	70
4	2c. orange	80	45
5	3c. green	30	1·75
6	4c. brown	30	10
6*a*	5c. bright purple (1.9.52)	60	1·50
7	6c. grey	75	85
8	8c. scarlet	75	6·00
8*a*	8c. green (1.9.52)	4·00	4·75
9	10c. purple	30	10
9*a*	12c. scarlet (1.9.52)	4·00	7·50
10	15c. ultramarine	2·75	60
11	20c. black and green	75	7·00
11*a*	20c. bright blue (1.9.52)	6·00	2·50
12	25c. purple and orange	75	70
12*a*	35c. scarlet and purple (1.9.52)	3·75	3·00
13	40c. red and purple	1·50	11·00
14	50c. black and blue	1·50	1·25
15	$1 blue and purple	11·00	24·00
16	$2 green and scarlet	21·00	23·00
17	$5 green and brown	50·00	40·00
3/17 *Set of* 20		£100	£120

1949 (10 Oct). *75th Anniv of U.P.U. As Nos. 114/17 of Antigua.*

18	10c. purple	30	50
19	15c. deep blue	2·00	2·75
20	25c. orange	40	6·50
21	50c. blue-black	60	4·75
18/21 *Set of* 4		3·00	13·00

1953. *Coronation. As No. 120 of Antigua.*

22	10c. black and reddish purple	1·00	1·50

1 Queen Elizabeth II

2 Copra

1954 (9 June)–**57**. *Chalk-surfaced paper.* Wmk Mult Script CA. P 17½×18.

23	1	1c. black (27.4.55)	10	60
24		2c. yellow-orange (27.4.55)	30	1·25
25		4c. brown	1·00	10
		a. Pale brown (24.4.57)	11·00	4·25
26		5c. bright purple (12.7.54)	30	2·50
27		6c. grey	10	40
28		8c. green (5.1.55)	40	2·75
29		10c. brown-purple (1.7.54)	1·75	10
		a. Reddish purple (27.3.57)	3·75	1·50
30		12c. rose-red (5.1.55)	30	3·00
31		20c. bright blue (5.1.55)	20	1·25

32	25c. brown-purple and yellow-orge (27.4.55)	20	1·50
33	30c. rose-red and brown-purple (5.9.55)	20	30
34	35c. rose-red and brown-purple (8.9.54)	20	1·50
35	50c. black and bright blue (5.1.55)	2·00	2·50
36	$1 bright blue and brown-purple (8.9.54)	7·00	9·00
37	$2 emerald and scarlet (27.4.55)..	23·00	40·00
38	$5 emerald and brown (27.4.55)..	23·00	45·00
23/38 *Set of* 16		55·00	£100

1957. *As Nos. 92/102 of Kedah but with inset portrait of Queen Elizabeth II.*

39	**9**	1c. black (21.8)	10	40
40	**10**	2c. orange-red (25.7)	10	40
41	**11**	4c. sepia (21.8)	40	10
42	**12**	5c. carmine-lake (21.8)	40	10
43	**13**	8c. myrtle-green (21.8)	1·25	2·50
44	**14**	10c. deep brown (4.8)	30	10
45	**15**	20c. blue (26.6)	1·50	30
46	**16**	50c. black and blue (25.7)	30	1·00
47	**17**	$1 ultramarine & reddish purple (25.7)	4·00	4·00
48	**18**	$2 bronze-green and scarlet (21.8)	15·00	24·00
49	**19**	$5 brown and bronze-green (26.6)	17·00	45·00
39/49 *Set of* 11			35·00	70·00

The 6, 12, 25 and 30c. values used with this issue were Nos. 1/4 of Malayan Federation.

(Recess D.L.R.)

1960 (15 Mar)–**62**. *As Nos. 39/49, but with inset picture of Melaka tree and Pelandok (mouse deer) as in T* **2**. W w **12**. P 13×12½ (1c. to 8c., $2, $5), 12½×13 (10c. to 50c.) or 13½ ($1).

50	1c. black	10	30
51	2c. orange-red	10	65
52	4c. sepia	10	10
53	5c. carmine-lake	10	10
54	8c. myrtle-green	3·00	3·00
55	10c. deep maroon	30	10
56	20c. blue	1·50	80
57	50c. black and blue	1·25	80
	a. *Black and ultramarine* (9.1.62)	3·00	80
58	$1 ultramarine and reddish purple	3·25	2·50
59	$2 bronze-green and scarlet	7·00	14·00
60	$5 brown and bronze-green	11·00	14·00
50/60 *Set of* 11		25·00	32·00

3 *Vanda hookeriana*

1965 (15 Nov)–**68**. *As Nos. 166/72 of Johore but with Arms of Malacca inset and inscr "MELAKA" as in T* **3**. W w **13** (upright).

61	1c. multicoloured	10	1·75
62	2c. multicoloured	10	1·50
63	5c. multicoloured	10	40
	b. Yellow (flower) omitted	65·00	
	c. Red omitted	£110	
64	6c. multicoloured	30	1·00
65	10c. multicoloured	20	10
66	15c. multicoloured	1·75	40
67	20c. multicoloured (purple-brown background)	2·25	1·00
	a. *Red-brown background* (2.4.68)	3·50	2·50
61/7 *Set of* 7		4·00	5·00

The 5c., 6c., 10c. and 20c. exist with PVA gum as well as gum arabic.

The higher values used with this issue were Nos. 20/27 of Malaysia (National Issues).

1970. *As Nos. 61 and 65 but W w* **13** (sideways).

68	**3**	1c. multicoloured (27.5.70)	1·75	8·00
69	–	10c. multicoloured (20.11.70)	5·50	8·00

NEGRI SEMBILAN

A federation of smaller states reconstituted in 1886. Sungei Ujong, taken under British protection in 1874, was absorbed into Negri Sembilan by Treaty of 8 August 1895. The Negri Sembilan federation joined the Federated Malay States in 1896.

A. SUNGEI UJONG

Until 1 January 1899, when the Federated Malay States joined the U.P.U., mail for addresses outside Malaya was franked with the stamps of the STRAITS SETTLEMENTS.

PRICES FOR STAMPS ON COVER

Nos. 1/14	—
Nos. 15/27	*from* × 25
Nos. 28/36	*from* × 8
Nos. 37/49	*from* × 10
Nos. 50/5	*from* × 25

(1)

1878. *No. 11 of Straits Settlements handstamped with T* **1**.

1	2c. brown	£3250	£3500

This overprint on India No. 54 is bogus.

SUNGEI (**2**) (Narrow letters) SUNGEI (**3**) ("N" wide) SUNGEI (**4**) ("S" wide)

UJONG (**5**) ("N" wide) UJONG (**6**) (Narrow letters, "UJ" close together) UJONG (**7**) (Narrow letters, evenly spaced)

1881. *No. 11 of Straits Settlements optd with T* **2/7**.

2	**2+5**	2c. brown	£5000	£3750
3	**3+5**	2c. brown	£3500	£2750
4	**2+6**	2c. brown	£325	
		a. Opt Type **6** double	£1800	
5	**4+6**	2c. brown	£1200	
6	**2+7**	2c. brown	£400	

The two lines of this surcharge were applied as separate operations. On Nos. 2/3 "SUNGEI" was printed as a triplet, probably 2+3+3 "UJONG" being added by a single unit handstamp. Nos. 4 and 5 come from a similar triplet, 4+4+5, completed by another single unit handstamp. No. 6 comes from a single type triplet with the second line added as a triplet instead of by a single unit handstamp.

The 10c. slate overprinted Types **2** + **7** is bogus.

SUNGEI (**8**) ("N" and "E" wide) SUNGEI (**9**) ("SUN" and "E" wide) SUNGEI (**10**) ("SUN" wide)

SUNGEI (**11**) ("S" wide) SUNGEI (**12**) (Narrow letters)

UJONG (**13**) ("U" and "NG" wide) UJONG (**14**) (Narrow letters)

1881. *No. 11 of Straits Settlements optd with T* **8/14**.

7	**8+13**	2c. brown	£350	
8	**9+13**	2c. brown	£375	
9	**10+13**	2c. brown	£350	
10	**11+14**	2c. brown	£350	
		a. "S" inverted	£3750	
11	**12+14**	2c. brown	£225	

Nos. 7/11 also had the two lines of the overprint applied at separate operations. "SUNGEI" as a triplet, either 7+8+9 or 10+11+11, and "UJONG" as a single unit.

S.U.

(**15**)

1882. *Nos. 50/1 of Straits Settlements optd as T* **15**.

12	2c. brown (with stops)	£300	
	a. Opt double	£3250	
13	2c. brown (without stops)	£275	£325
14	4c. rose (with stops)	£3750	£4250

Each of the above was applied by a triplet setting.

Examples of Straits Settlements No. 11 with a similar overprint, including stops, are trials which were not issued.

SUNGEI (**16**) ("S" and "E" wide) SUNGEI (**17**) ("E" wide) UJONG (**18**) ("N" wide)

1882 (Dec)–**84**. *Nos. 12, 50, 52/3 and 63 of Straits Settlements optd with T* **11/12**, **14** *and* **16/18**.

15	**12+14**	2c. brown	£1100	£475
16	**11+14**	2c. brown	£1600	£700
17	**12+14**	2c. pale rose (1884)	£200	£200
18	**11+14**	2c. pale rose (1884)	£200	£200
		a. Opt Type **14** double		
19	**16+14**	2c. pale rose (1884)	£110	£110
		a. Opt Type **16** double	†	£1000
20	**17+14**	2c. pale rose (1884)	£120	£130
21	**12+18**	2c. pale rose (1884)	£120	£130
		a. Opt Type **18** double	£1100	
22	**12+14**	4c. rose	£1700	£1800
		a. Opt Type **12** double	†	£4000
23	**11+14**	4c. rose	£2750	£3000
24	**12+14**	8c. orange	£1900	£1400
25	**11+14**	8c. orange	£3250	£2750
26	**12+14**	10c. slate	£600	£475
27	**11+14**	10c. slate	£850	£750

Nos. 15/27 had the two lines of the overprint applied by separate triplets. Settings so far identified are Nos. 15+16+15, 17+18+19, 19+20+21, 22+23+22, 24+25+24 and 26+27+26.

The 4c. rose overprinted Types **16** + **14** is now believed to be a trial.

UJONG. (**19**) (With stop. Narrow letters) UJONG. (**20**) (With stop. "N" wide) UJONG (**21**) (Without stop. Narrow letters)

1883–84. *Nos. 50 and 63/4 of Straits Settlements optd with T* **12**, **16/17** *and* **19/21**.

28	**12+19**	2c. brown	48·00	£130
29	**16+19**	2c. brown	48·00	£130
30	**12+20**	2c. brown	48·00	£130
		a. Opt Type **12** double	£1200	
31	**16+21**	2c. pale rose (1884)	£100	£110
32	**17+21**	2c. pale rose (1884)	£100	£110
33	**12+21**	2c. pale rose (1884)	£100	£110
		a. Opt Type **21** double	£1200	
34	**16+21**	4c. brown (1884)	£275	£350
		a. Opt Type **16** double		
		b. Opt Type **21** double	£2250	
35	**17+21**	4c. brown (1884)	£275	£350
36	**12+21**	4c. brown (1884)	£275	£350
		a. Opt Type **21** double	£4000	

Nos. 28/36 had the two lines of the overprint applied by separate triplets. Settings were Nos. 28+29+30, 31+32+33 and 34+35+36.

The 8c. orange overprinted Types **12** + **19** is now believed to be a trial (*Price* £900 *unused*).

Sungei Ujong (**22**) SUNGEI UJONG (**23**) SUNGEI UJONG (**24**)

SUNGEI UJONG (**25**) SUNGEI UJONG (**26**) SUNGEI UJONG (**27**)

SUNGEI UJONG (**28**) SUNGEI UJONG. (**29**) SUNGEI UJONG (**30**)

Antique "G" in "SUNGEI" (R. 6/1)

1885–90. *Nos. 63/a of Straits Settlements optd with T* **22/30**.

37	**22**	2c. pale rose	75·00	85·00
		a. Opt double	£650	£650
38	**23**	2c. pale rose	40·00	60·00
		a. Opt double	£650	
39	**24**	2c. pale rose (1886)	95·00	£110
40	**25**	2c. pale rose (1886)	£140	£150
		a. Opt double		
41	**26**	2c. pale rose (1886)	90·00	£100
		a. Opt double		
42	**27**	2c. pale rose (1887)	19·00	42·00
43	**28**	2c. pale rose (1889)	12·00	15·00
		a. Narrow "E" (2 mm wide) (R. 3/4 and 4/3)	£120	
		c. Opt double	£1400	
		d. *Bright rose* (1890)	15·00	12·00
		da. Narrow "E" (2 mm wide) (R. 3/4 and 4/3)	£140	
		db. Antique "N" in "UJONG" (R. 10/6)	£225	
44	**29**	2c. pale rose (1889)	90·00	70·00
		a. "UNJOG" (R. 7/3)	£5000	£3500
45	**30**	2c. bright rose (1890)	45·00	19·00
		a. Antique "G" in "SUNGEI" (R. 6/1)	£600	
		b. Antique "G" in "UJONG" (R. 8/3)	£600	
		c. *Pale rose*		

All the above overprints had both lines applied at the same operation. Nos. 37/42 were from different triplet settings. The first printing of Type **28** was from a triplet (No. 43) but this was followed by two further settings of 60 (6×10), the first containing No. 43a and the second Nos. 43*d*/db. Nos. 44/5 were both from settings of 60.

The antique letter varieties on Types **28** and **30** are similar in style to those on Types **25** and **26**.

SUNGEI UJONG Two CENTS (**31**) SUNGEI UJONG Two CENTS (**32**) SUNGEI UJONG Two CENTS (**33**)

SUNGEI UJONG Two CENTS (**34**)

1891. *No. 68 of Straits Settlements surch with T* **31/4**.

46	**31**	2c. on 24c. green	£1000	£1000
47	**32**	2c. on 24c. green	£400	£400
		w. Wmk inverted	£750	£800
48	**33**	2c. on 24c. green	£1000	£1000
49	**34**	2c. on 24c. green	£225	£225
		a. Antique "G" in "SUNGEI" (R. 6/1)	£1200	
		b. Antique "G" in "UJONG" (R. 8/3)	£1200	
		w. Wmk inverted	£475	£550

Nos. 46/9 come from the same setting of 60 on which "SUNGEI UJONG" was from the same type as No. 45. No. 46 occurs in row 1. No. 47 from rows 2 to 4, No. 48 from row 5 and No. 49 from rows 6 to 10.

35

3 CENTS

(**36**)

37

1891 (Nov)–**94**. Wmk Crown CA. P 14.

50	**35**	2c. rose	32·00	27·00
51		2c. orange (12.94)	1·75	4·25
52		5c. blue (3.93)	5·50	6·50
50/2 *Set of* 3			35·00	35·00
50s/2s Optd "Specimen" *Set of* 3			65·00	

1894 (Dec). *Surch as T* **36** *by De La Rue*. Wmk Mult Crown CA. P 14.

53	**35**	1c. on 5c. green	1·00	70
54		3c. on 5c. rose	2·50	5·00

1895 (Oct). Wmk Crown CA. P 14.

55	**37**	3c. dull purple and carmine	14·00	4·25
53s/5s Optd "Specimen" *Set of* 3			65·00	

B. NEGRI SEMBILAN

Stamps of the STRAITS SETTLEMENTS were used in Negri Sembilan during 1891, until replaced by the stamps listed below. Until the Federated Malay States joined the U.P.U. on 1 January 1899 Straits Settlements stamps continued to be used for mail to addresses outside Malaya.

PRICES FOR STAMPS ON COVER TO 1945

No. 1	*from* × 200
Nos. 2/4	*from* × 10
Nos. 5/14	*from* × 8
Nos. 15/20	*from* × 10
Nos. 21/49	*from* × 4

Negri Sembilan
(1)

2

3

1891 (Aug?). *No. 63a of Straits Settlements optd with T* **1**.
1 2c. bright rose .... 3·00 7·00

Short "N" in "SEMBILAN" (Top left pane R. 8/3)

1891 (Nov)–**94**. Wmk Crown CA. P 14.
2 **2** 1c. green (6.93) .... 3·25 1·00
3 2c. rose .... 3·25 9·50
a. Short "N" .... 80·00
4 5c. blue (11.94) .... 30·00 40·00
2/4 *Set of* 3 .... 32·00 45·00
2s/4s Optd "Specimen" *Set of* 3 .... 85·00

1895–99. Wmk Crown CA. P 14.
5 **3** 1c. dull purple and green (1899) .... 16·00 7·50
6 2c. dull purple and brown (1898) .... 35·00 £120
7 3c. dull purple and carmine .... 15·00 1·25
8 5c. dull purple and olive-yellow (1897) .... 8·50 10·00
9 8c. dull purple and ultramarine (1898) .... 29·00 18·00
10 10c. dull purple and orange (1897) 27·00 14·00
11 15c. green and violet (1896) .... 42·00 80·00
12 20c. green and olive (1897) .... 65·00 38·00
13 25c. green and carmine (1896) .... 70·00 95·00
14 50c. green and black (1896) .... 75·00 70·00
5/14 *Set of* 10 .... £350 £400
5s/14s Optd "Specimen" *Set of* 10 .... £225

Four cents.
(4)

Four cents.
(5)

1898 (Dec)–**1900**.

(a) Surch as T **4**.
15 **3** 1c. on 15c. green and violet (1900) £100 £300
a. Raised stop (R. 5/1 and R. 10/1 of each pane) £425 £1100
b. Surch double, one albino £400
16 **2** 4c. on 1c. green .... 2·50 18·00
17 **3** 4c. on 3c. dull purple and carmine .... 3·25 20·00
a. Horiz pair, one without surch £11000 £5500
b. Surch double £2250 £1000
ba. Ditto. "Four cents" albino .... † £1000
c. Surch inverted £1800 £1300
d. "cents" repeated at left £2750 £2500
e. "Four" repeated at right £2750 £2500
f. Without bar £800 £650
g. Bar double .... † £800
18 **2** 4c. on 5c. blue .... 1·25 15·00

On Nos. 15 and 17 the bar is at the top of the stamp.
The surcharges were applied as a setting of 30 (6×5).

(b) Surch as T **5**.
19 **3** 4c. on 8c. dull purple & ultram (G.) (12.98) .... 7·00 4·25
a. Vert pair, one without surch .. £6500 £4000
b. Surch double £2500 £2250
c. Surch double (G.+R.) £850 £900
20 4c. on 8c. dull purple & ultramarine (Bk.) £1300 £1400

Care should be taken in distinguishing the true black surcharge, No. 20, from very deep shades of the green surcharge, No. 19.

Pending the arrival of the permanent Federated Malay States issue the stamps of SELANGOR, FEDERATED MALAY STATES provisional overprints, STRAITS SETTLEMENTS and PERAK were used at various times between October 1899 and April 1901.
The general issues for FEDERATED MALAY STATES were used in Negri Sembilan from 29 April 1901 until 1935.

6 Arms of Negri Sembilan

7 Arms of Negri Sembilan

1935 (2 Dec)–**41**. Wmk Mult Script CA. *Ordinary paper* (6c. grey, 15c.) *or chalk-surfaced paper (others)*. P 14.
21 **6** 1c. black (1.1.36) .... 1·00 20
22 2c. green (1.1.36) .... 1·00 20
23 2c. orange (11.12.41) .... 4·25 65·00
24 3c. green (*ordinary paper*) (21.8.41) .... 18·00 8·00
a. Chalk-surfaced paper (12.41). 8·00 9·00
25 4c. orange .... 1·75 10
26 5c. brown (5.12.35) .... 1·75 10
27 6c. scarlet (1.1.37) .... 16·00 2·75
a. Stop omitted at right (R. 10/4) £550 £150
28 6c. grey (18.12.41) .... 4·75 75·00
a. Stop omitted at right (R. 10/4) £225 £950
29 8c. grey .... 2·00 10
30 10c. dull purple (1.1.36) .... 1·25 10
31 12c. bright ultramarine (1.1.36) ...... 3·00 50
32 15c. ultramarine (1.10.41) .... 10·00 50·00
33 25c. dull purple and scarlet (1.4.36) .... 1·50 70
34 30c. dull purple and orange (1.1.36) .... 3·50 2·00
35 40c. scarlet and dull purple .... 3·00 2·00
36 50c. black/*emerald* (1.2.36) .... 6·00 2·25
37 $1 black and red/*blue* (1.4.36) .... 4·50 4·25
38 $2 green and scarlet (16.5.36) ..... 38·00 17·00
39 $5 green and red/*emerald* (16.5.36) .... 23·00 70·00
21/39 *Set of* 19 .... £120 £250
21s/39s Perf "Specimen" *Set of* 19 .... £400

The stamps issued in 1941 were printed by Harrison and Sons following bomb damage to the De La Rue works on 29 December 1940. The used prices quoted for Nos. 23, 28 and 32 are for examples with clearly identifiable 1941 cancellations.
An 8c. scarlet was issued but only with opt during Japanese Occupation of Malaya. Unoverprinted specimens result from leakages.

During shortages in 1941 stamps of STRAITS SETTLEMENTS (2c. green, 25c., 30c.), SELANGOR (2c. green, 2c. orange (both perfs), 8c. grey, 25c.), PERAK (2c. orange, 25c., 50c.) and PAHANG (8c. scarlet) were issued in Negri Sembilan.

1948 (1 Dec). *Royal Silver Wedding. As Nos. 112/13 of Antigua.*
40 10c. violet 40 50
41 $5 green .... 20·00 29·00

1949 (1 Apr)–**55**. *Chalk-surfaced paper.* Wmk Mult Script CA. P 17½×18.
42 **7** 1c. black .... 1·00 10
43 2c. orange 50 10
44 3c. green 50 30
45 4c. brown 30 10
46 5c. bright purple (1.9.52) .... 1·00 50
a. Bright mauve (25.8.53) 50 45
47 6c. grey .... 1·75 10
a. Pale grey (25.8.53) .... 6·00 1·50
48 8c. scarlet 50 75
49 8c. green (1.9.52) .... 3·50 1·60
50 10c. purple 30 10
51 12c. scarlet (1.9.52) .... 3·50 2·75
52 15c. ultramarine .... 3·25 10
53 20c. black and green .... 1·00 1·25
54 20c. bright blue (1.9.52) .... 1·25 10
55 25c. purple and orange .... 1·00 10
56 30c. scarlet and purple (4.9.55) ...... 1·25 2·50
57 35c. scarlet and purple (1.9.52) ...... 1·75 1·00
58 40c. red and purple .... 3·25 4·75
59 50c. black and blue .... 3·75 20
60 $1 blue and purple .... 4·50 2·25
61 $2 green and scarlet .... 13·00 23·00
62 $5 green and brown .... 50·00 65·00
42/62 *Set of* 21 .... 85·00 95·00

1949 (10 Oct). *75th Anniv of U.P.U. As Nos. 114/17 of Antigua.*
63 10c. purple 20 20
64 15c. deep blue .... 1·40 3·00
a. "A" of "CA" missing from wmk £800
65 25c. orange .... 30 2·50
66 50c. blue-black .... 60 3·25
63/6 *Set of* 4 .... 2·25 8·00

1953 (2 June). *Coronation. As No. 120 of Antigua.*
67 10c. black and reddish purple .... 1·25 50

1957 (26 June)–**63**. *As Nos. 92/102 of Kedah but with inset Arms of Negri Sembilan.*
68 **9** 1c. black (21.8.57) 10 10
69 **10** 2c. orange-red (25.7.57) 10 10
70 **11** 4c. sepia (21.8.57) 10 10
71 **12** 5c. carmine-lake (21.8.57) 10 10
72 **13** 8c. myrtle-green (21.8.57) .... 1·00 1·40
73 **14** 10c. deep brown (4.8.57) .... 2·00 10
74 10c. deep maroon (10.1.61) .... 6·50 10
75 **15** 20c. blue .... 1·00 10
76 **16** 50c. black and blue (*p* 12½) (25.7.57) .... 30 1·40
a. Perf 12½×13 (19.7.60) 75 10
77 **17** $1 ultramarine & reddish pur (25.7.57) .... 2·50 2·00
78 **18** $2 bronze-green & scarlet (*p* 12½) (21.8.57) .... 9·00 16·00
a. Perf 13×12½ (15.1.63) .... 17·00 27·00
79 **19** $5 brown and bronze-green (*p* 12½) .... 11·00 21·00
a. Perf 13×12½ (6.3.62) .... 26·00 22·00
ab. Perf 13×12½. Brown and yellow olive (13.11.62) .... £275 85·00
68/79 *Set of* 12 .... 30·00 35·00

The 6, 12, 25 and 30c. values used with this issue were Nos. 1/4 of Malayan Federation.

8 Tuanku Munawir

9 Vanda hookeriana

(Photo Enschedé)

1961 (17 Apr). *Installation of Tuanku Munawir as Yang di-Pertuan Besar of Negri Sembilan.* No wmk. P 14×13.
80 **8** 10c. multicoloured 30 70

1965 (15 Nov)–**69**. *As Nos. 166/72 of Johore but with Arms of Negri Sembilan inset and inscr "NEGERI SEMBILAN" as in T* **9**. W w **13** (upright).
81 1c. multicoloured .... 10 1·60
82 2c. multicoloured .... 10 1·60
w. Wmk inverted .... 3·00
83 5c. multicoloured 40 10
b. Yellow omitted .... 65·00
84 6c. multicoloured 40 60
85 10c. multicoloured 40 10
86 15c. multicoloured 80 10
87 20c. jet-black and multicoloured .... 1·25 1·00
a. Blackish brown & mult (19.12.69) 5·50 1·50
81/7 *Set of* 7 .... 3·00 4·50

The 2c., 6c., 15c. and 20c. exist with PVA gum as well as gum arabic.
The higher values used with this issue were Nos. 20/27 of Malaysia (National Issues).
See also No. 90.

10 Negri Sembilan Crest and Tuanku Ja'afar

(Des Z. Noor. Photo Japanese Govt Ptg Wks)

1968 (8 Apr). *Installation of Tuanku Ja'afar as Yang di-Pertuan Besar of Negri Sembilan.* P 13.
88 **10** 15c. multicoloured 15 70
89 50c. multicoloured .... 30 1·40

1970 (27 May). *As No. 81 but with W w* **13** *(sideways).*
90 **9** 1c. multicoloured .... 2·75 7·00

STAMP BOOKLETS

1935. *Stapled.*
SB1 $1 booklet containing twenty 5c. (No. 26) in blocks of 10 ....
SB2 $1.30 booklet containing 5c. and 8c. (Nos. 26, 29), each in block of 10 ....

PAHANG

The first British Resident was appointed in 1888. Pahang joined the Federated Malay States in 1896.

Until 1 January 1899, when the Federated Malay States joined the U.P.U., mail for addresses outside Malaya was franked with stamps of the STRAITS SETTLEMENTS.

PRICES FOR STAMPS ON COVER TO 1945

No. 1	*from* × 50
Nos. 2/3	—
No. 4	*from* × 100
No. 5	—
No. 6	*from* × 100
Nos. 7/10	*from* × 8
Nos. 11/13	*from* × 25
Nos. 14/16	*from* × 20
Nos. 17/a	—
Nos. 18/d	*from* × 6
Nos. 19/24	*from* × 8
No. 25	*from* × 20
Nos. 26/7	—
No. 28	*from* × 15
Nos. 29/46	*from* × 6

PAHANG (1) PAHANG (2) PAHANG (2a) (Antique letters)

1889 (Jan). *Nos. 52/3 and 63 of Straits Settlements optd with T* **1**.
1 2c. pale rose .... £110 50·00
2 8c. orange £1800 £1800
3 10c. slate £225 £250

All three values were overprinted from a triplet setting, but the 2c. also exists from a similar setting of 30 or 60.

1889. *No. 63 of Straits Settlements optd with T* **2**.
4 2c. pale rose .... 16·00 20·00
a. Bright rose .... 8·00 9·00
ab. Opt Type **2a**. Antique letters £850

No. 4 was overprinted from a setting of 60. No. 4ab usually occurs on R. 10/1, but has also been found on R. 8/1 as the result of revision of the setting.

PAHANG (3) PAHANG (4)

1890. *No. 63a of Straits Settlements optd.*
5 **3** 2c. bright rose £7000 £2000
6 **4** 2c. bright rose .... £110 14·00
w. Wmk inverted ....

No. 5 may have been overprinted from a triplet setting. No. 6 was from a setting of 60.

PAHANG Two CENTS (5)

PAHANG Two CENTS (6)

PAHANG Two CENTS (7) PAHANG Two CENTS (8)

1891. *No. 68 of Straits Settlements surch with T* **5/8**.

7	**5**	2c. on 24c. green	£190	£225
8	**6**	2c. on 24c. green	£900	£1100
9	**7**	2c. on 24c. green	£350	£400
10	**8**	2c. on 24c. green	£900	£1100

Nos. 7/10 come from one setting used to surcharge the panes of sixty. No. 7 occurs in rows 1 to 5, No. 8 on row 6, No. 9 on rows 7 to 9 and No. 10 on row 10.

9

10

1891 (Nov)**–95.** Wmk Crown CA. P 14.

11	**9**	1c. green (3.95)	4·25	3·25
12		2c. rose	4·50	3·25
13		5c. blue (6.93)	11·00	42·00
11/13 *Set of* 3			18·00	45·00
11s/13s Optd "Specimen" *Set of* 3			80·00	

Following an increase of postage rates on 1 March 1894 1 cent stamps of STRAITS SETTLEMENTS were used in Pahang until the autumn of the following year.

1895–99. Wmk Crown CA. P 14.

14	**10**	3c. dull purple and carmine	8·50	2·75
15		4c. dull purple and carmine (1899)	17·00	13·00
16		5c. dull purple and olive-yellow (1897)	30·00	21·00
14/16 *Set of* 3			50·00	32·00
14s/16s Optd "Specimen" *Set of* 3			65·00	

1897 (2 Aug). *No. 13 bisected, surch in red manuscript at Kuala Lipis and initialled "JFO".*

(a) Bisected horizontally.

17	2c. on half of 5c. blue (surch "2" and bar across "5")	—	£2250
17*a*	3c. on half of 5c. blue (surch "3")	£5500	£2250

(b) Bisected diagonally.

18	2c. on half of 5c. blue (surch "2" and bar across "5")	£1500	£400
	a. Unsevered pair. Nos. 18 and 18d	£11000	£4000
	b. Se-tenant pair. Nos. 18 and 18d	£4500	£1100
	c. Surch in black manuscript	£9000	£3250
18*d*	3c. on half of 5c. blue (surch "3")	£1500	£400
	dc. Surch in black manuscript	£9000	£3250

The initials are those of John Fortescue Owen, the District Treasurer at Kuala Lipis.

Nos. 17 and 18 only occur on the bottom half of the 5c. and Nos. 17*a* and 18*d* on the top half. No. 18a is a complete example of No. 13 showing the two surcharges. No. 18b is a *se-tenant* pair of bisects from adjoining stamps.

Pahang. (11) Pahang. (12)

1898–99.

(a) Nos. 72/5 of Perak optd with T **11**.

19	10c. dull purple and orange (3.98)	22·00	25·00
20	25c. green and carmine	85·00	£160
21	50c. dull purple and greenish black	£450	£500
22	50c. green and black (1899)	£275	£350

(b) Nos. 76 and 79 of Perak optd with T **12**.

23	$1 green and pale green	£375	£500
24	$5 green and ultramarine	£1400	£2250

Pahang Four cents (13) Four cents. (14)

1898.

(a) No. 71 of Perak surch with T **13**.

25	4c. on 8c. dull purple and ultramarine	6·00	6·00
	a. Surch inverted	£3750	£1500
	b. Surch double	£950	

(b) T **13** *on plain paper (no stamp), but issued for postage. Imperf.*

26	4c. black	—	£4000
27	5c. black	£2500	

No. 26 also exists pin-perforated.

1899. *No. 16 surch with T* **14**.

28	**10**	4c. on 5c. dull purple and olive-yellow	19·00	60·00

Pending the arrival of the permanent Federated Malay States issue the stamps of SELANGOR, FEDERATED MALAY STATES provisional overprints and PERAK were used at various times between November 1899 and July 1902.

The general issues for the FEDERATED MALAY STATES were used in Pahang from July 1902 until 1935.

15 Sultan Sir Abu Bakar

16 Sultan Sir Abu Bakar

1935 (2 Dec)**–41.** *Chalk-surfaced paper.* Wmk Mult Script CA. P 14.

29	**15**	1c. black (1.1.36)	20	40
30		2c. green (1.1.36)	2·00	50
31		3c. green (*ordinary paper*) (21.8.41)	45·00	4·25
		a. Chalk-surfaced paper	17·00	16·00
32		4c. orange	70	50
33		5c. brown (5.12.35)	70	10
34		6c. scarlet (1.1.37)	20·00	1·75
35		8c. grey	60	10
36		8c. scarlet (11.12.41)	4·00	60·00
37		10c. dull purple (1.1.36)	1·50	10
38		12c. bright ultramarine (1.1.36)	3·00	1·25
39		15c. ultram (*ordinary paper*) (1.10.41)	20·00	55·00
40		25c. dull purple and scarlet (1.4.36)	2·00	1·50
41		30c. dull purple and orange (1.1.36)	1·25	1·10
42		40c. scarlet and dull purple	1·00	2·00
43		50c. black/*emerald* (1.2.36)	4·00	1·50
44		$1 black and red/*blue* (1.4.36)	3·50	8·00
45		$2 green and scarlet (16.5.36)	24·00	35·00
46		$5 green and red/*emerald* (16.5.36)	9·00	70·00
29/46 *Set of* 18			£100	£225
29s/46s Perf "Specimen" *Set of* 18			£425	

The stamps issued during 1941 were printed by Harrison and Sons following bomb damage to the De La Rue works on 29 December 1940. The used prices quoted for Nos. 36 and 39 are for examples with clearly identifiable 1941 cancellations.

A 2c. orange and a 6c. grey were prepared but not officially issued. (*Price mint £4 each*).

During shortages in 1941 stamps of STRAITS SETTLEMENTS (2c., 25c.), SELANGOR (2c. orange, 3c., 8c.), NEGRI SEMBILAN (6c.) and PERAK (2c. orange) were issued in Pahang.

1948 (1 Dec). *Royal Silver Wedding. As Nos. 112/13 of Antigua.*

47	10c. violet	15	60
48	$5 green	25·00	40·00

1949 (10 Oct). *75th Anniv of U.P.U. As Nos. 114/17 of Antigua.*

49	10c. purple	30	25
50	15c. deep blue	1·10	1·50
51	25c. orange	35	2·00
52	50c. blue-black	70	2·50
49/52 *Set of* 4		2·25	5·50

1950 (1 June)**–56.** Wmk Mult Script CA. *Chalk-surfaced paper.* P 17½×18.

53	**16**	1c. black	10	10
54		2c. orange	20	10
55		3c. green	30	80
56		4c. brown	1·75	10
		a. Chocolate (24.3.54)	11·00	2·50
57		5c. bright purple (1.9.52)	50	70
		a. Bright mauve (10.9.53)	50	15
58		6c. grey	50	30
59		8c. scarlet	50	1·50
60		8c. green (1.9.52)	1·00	75
61		10c. magenta	25	10
62		12c. scarlet (1.9.52)	1·00	1·25
63		15c. ultramarine	75	10
64		20c. black and green	50	2·75
65		20c. bright blue (1.9.52)	1·50	10
		a. Ultramarine (8.3.56)	7·50	2·75
66		25c. purple and orange	50	10
67		30c. scarlet and brown-purple (4.9.55)	1·25	35
		a. Scarlet and purple (8.3.56)	21·00	5·50
68		35c. scarlet and purple (1.9.52)	60	25
69		40c. red and purple	1·50	7·50
70		50c. black and blue	1·50	10
71		$1 blue and purple	2·75	3·25
72		$2 green and scarlet	13·00	23·00
73		$5 green and brown	55·00	80·00
		a. Green and sepia (24.3.54)	£100	£100
53/73 *Set of* 21			75·00	£110

1953 (2 June). *Coronation. As No. 120 of Antigua.*

74	10c. black and reddish purple	1·75	10

1957 (26 June)**–62.** *As Nos. 92/102 of Kedah but with inset portrait of Sultan Sir Abu Bakar.*

75	**9**	1c. black (21.8.57)	10	10
76	**10**	2c. orange-red (25.7.57)	10	10
77	**11**	4c. sepia (21.8.57)	10	10
78	**12**	5c. carmine-lake (21.8.57)	10	10
79	**13**	8c. myrtle-green (21.8.57)	1·00	2·25
80	**14**	10c. deep brown (4.8.57)	1·25	10
81		10c. deep maroon (21.2.61)	3·50	30
82	**15**	20c. blue	2·25	20
83	**16**	50c. black and blue (*p* 12½) (25.7.57)	45	75
		a. Perf 12½×13 (17.5.60)	1·00	20
84	**17**	$1 ultramarine & reddish pur (25.7.57)	7·00	2·00
85	**18**	$2 bronze-grn & scar (*p* 12½) (21.8.57)	4·00	9·00
		a. Perf 13×12½ (13.11.62)	7·50	19·00
86	**19**	$5 brown and bronze-green (*p* 12½)	11·00	15·00
		a. Perf 13×12½ (17.5.60)	11·00	19·00
		b. Perf 13×12½. Brown and yellow olive (23.10.62)	35·00	38·00
75/86 *Set of* 12			27·00	26·00

The 6, 12, 25 and 30c. values used with this issue were Nos. 1/4 of Malayan Federation.

17 Vanda hookeriana

1965 (15 Nov). *As Nos. 166/72 of Johore but with inset portrait of Sultan Sir Abu Bakar as in T* **17**. W w **13** (upright).

87		1c. multicoloured	10	1·25
		c. Grey (flower name, etc) omitted	75·00	
		w. Wmk inverted	6·00	
88		2c. multicoloured	10	1·25
89		5c. multicoloured	15	10
		c. Red (leaves, etc) omitted	90·00	
90		6c. multicoloured	30	1·25
91		10c. multicoloured	20	10
		a. Red omitted	90·00	
92		15c. multicoloured	1·00	10
93		20c. multicoloured	1·60	40
87/93 *Set of* 7			3·00	3·75

The 2c., 5c. and 6c. exist with PVA gum as well as gum arabic.

The higher values used with this issue were Nos. 20/27 of Malaysia (National Issues).

1970 (27 May). *As Nos. 87 and 91 but W w* **13** *(sideways).*

94	**17**	1c. multicoloured	2·50	7·00
95	–	10c. multicoloured	1·00	3·50

STAMP BOOKLETS

1935. *Black on buff covers. Stapled.*

SB1	$1 booklet containing twenty 5c. (No. 33) in blocks of 10	
SB2	$1.30 booklet containing 5c. and 8c. (Nos. 33, 35) each in block of 10 and pane of airmail labels	£2500

PENANG

One of the Straits Settlements which joined the Federation of Malaya on 1 February 1948.

1948 (1 Dec). *Royal Silver Wedding. As Nos. 112/13 of Antigua.*

1	10c. violet	30	20
2	$5 brown	35·00	35·00

1949 (21 Feb)**–52.** *As T* **58** *of Straits Settlements, but inscr* "PENANG" *at foot.* Wmk Mult Script CA. *Chalk-surfaced paper.* P 17½×18.

3	1c. black	1·00	20
4	2c. orange	1·25	20
5	3c. green	40	1·00
6	4c. brown	40	10
7	5c. bright purple (1.9.52)	3·25	3·00
8	6c. grey	1·00	20
9	8c. scarlet	1·00	4·50
10	8c. green (1.9.52)	2·50	2·00
11	10c. purple	40	10
12	12c. scarlet (1.9.52)	3·25	7·50
13	15c. ultramarine	1·50	30
14	20c. black and green	1·75	1·25
15	20c. bright blue (1.9.52)	1·75	1·25
16	25c. purple and orange	2·25	75
17	35c. scarlet and purple (1.9.52)	2·00	1·25
18	40c. red and purple	3·25	13·00
19	50c. black and blue	4·50	20
20	$1 blue and purple	20·00	2·50
21	$2 green and scarlet	23·00	2·00
22	$5 green and brown	48·00	3·00
3/22 *Set of* 20		£110	40·00

1949 (10 Oct). *75th Anniv of U.P.U. As Nos. 114/17 of Antigua.*

23	10c. purple	20	10
24	15c. deep blue	2·25	3·50
25	25c. orange	45	3·50
26	50c. blue-black	1·50	3·50
23/6 *Set of* 4		4·00	9·50

1953 (2 June). *Coronation. As No. 120 of Antigua.*

27	10c. black and reddish purple	1·50	10

1954 (9 June)**–57.** *As T* **1** *of Malacca (Queen Elizabeth II) but inscr "PENANG" at foot. Chalk-surfaced paper.* Wmk Mult Script CA. P 17½×18.

28	1c. black (5.1.55)	10	70
29	2c. yellow-orange (8.9.54)	50	30
30	4c. brown (1.9.54)	70	10
	a. Yellow-brown (17.7.57)	7·00	7·00
31	5c. bright purple (1.10.54)	2·00	3·75
	a. Bright mauve (17.7.57)	7·00	7·00
32	6c. grey	20	80
33	8c. green (5.1.55)	20	3·50
34	10c. brown-purple (1.9.54)	20	10
35	12c. rose-red (5.1.55)	30	3·50
36	20c. bright blue (1.9.54)	50	10
37	25c. brown-purple & yellow-orange (1.12.54)	30	10
38	30c. rose-red and brown-purple (5.9.55)	30	10
39	35c. rose-red and brown-purple (8.9.54)	70	60
40	50c. black and bright blue (1.12.54)	50	10
41	$1 bright blue and brown-purple (1.10.54)	2·50	30
42	$2 emerald and scarlet (1.10.54)	11·00	3·75
43	$5 emerald and brown (5.1.55)	48·00	3·75
28/43 *Set of* 16		60·00	18·00

1957. *As Nos. 92/102 of Kedah, but with inset portrait of Queen Elizabeth II.*

44	**9**	1c. black (21.8)	10	1·50
45	**10**	2c. orange-red (25.7)	10	1·00
46	**11**	4c. sepia (21.8)	10	10
47	**12**	5c. carmine-lake (21.8)	10	30
48	**13**	8c. myrtle-green (21.8)	1·25	2·25
49	**14**	10c. deep brown (4.8)	30	10
50	**15**	20c. blue (26.6)	1·00	40
51	**16**	50c. black and blue (25.7)	1·25	70

52	17	$1 ultramarine and reddish purple (25.7)	6·50	1·00
53	18	$2 bronze-green and scarlet (21.8)	19·00	15·00
54	19	$5 brown and bronze-green (26.6)	23·00	13·00
44/54 *Set of* 11			45·00	32·00

The note after No. 86 of Pahang also applies here.

1 Copra

2 Vanda hookeriana

(Recess D.L.R.)

1960 (15 Mar). *As Nos. 44/54, but with inset Arms of Penang as in T* **1**. W w **12**. P 13×12½ (1c. to 8c., $2, $5), 12½×13 (10c. to 50c.) or 13½ ($1).

55		1c. black	10	1·60
56		2c. orange-red	10	1·60
57		4c. sepia	10	10
58		5c. carmine-lake	10	10
59		8c. myrtle-green	2·75	4·50
60		10c. deep maroon	30	10
61		20c. blue	55	10
62		50c. black and blue	30	30
		a. Imperf (pair)	£700	
63		$1 ultramarine and reddish purple	5·50	1·75
64		$2 bronze-green and scarlet	5·50	6·00
65		$5 brown and bronze-green	11·00	8·50
55/65 *Set of* 11			23·00	22·00

No. 62a comes from a sheet purchased at the Penang Post Office which had the upper five horizontal rows imperforate.

1965 (15 Nov)–**68**. *As Nos. 166/72 of Johore but with Arms of Penang inset and inscr "PULAU PINANG" as in T* **2**. W w **13** (upright).

66		1c. multicoloured	10	1·25
67		2c. multicoloured	10	1·25
68		5c. multicoloured	30	10
		b. Yellow (flower) omitted	60·00	
		c. Red omitted	£110	
		d. Blue (background and inscr) omitted	£450	
		da. Blue and yellow omitted	£750	
		w. Wmk inverted	1·75	
69		6c. multicoloured	30	1·25
		b. Yellow omitted	60·00	
70		10c. grey and multicoloured	20	10
		a. *Jet-black and multicoloured* (12.11.68)	20	10
71		15c. multicoloured	1·00	10
		b. Green (value and leaves) omitted	£550	
72		20c. multicoloured	1·60	30
		a. Bright purple (blooms) omitted	£650	
		b. Yellow (leaves) omitted	£700	
66/72 *Set of* 7			3·00	3·75

The 2c., 5c., 6c., 10c. and 20c. exist with PVA gum as well as gum arabic.

No. 70 with black (country name and arms) omitted is listed under Perak (No. 168a).

The higher values used with this issue were Nos. 20/27 of Malaysia (National Issues).

1970. *As Nos. 66 and 70 but W w* **13** *(sideways)*.

73	2	1c. multicoloured (27.5.70)	1·60	6·00
74	–	10c. multicoloured (20.11.70)	7·00	4·00

PERAK

Perak accepted a British Resident in 1874, although he was later murdered.

The state joined the Federated Malay States in 1896.

> The stamps of the STRAITS SETTLEMENTS were used in Perak during 1877/8.
>
> Until 1 January 1899, when the Federated Malay States joined the U.P.U., mail for addresses outside Malaya was franked with stamps of the STRAITS SETTLEMENTS

PRICES FOR STAMPS ON COVER TO 1945

No. 1	—
Nos. 2/9	*from* × 60
Nos. 10/13	*from* × 30
Nos. 14/16	*from* × 8
Nos. 17/22	*from* × 20
No. 23	—
Nos. 24/5	—
Nos. 26/8	*from* × 15
No. 29	*from* × 75
No. 30	*from* × 20
Nos. 31/2	—
Nos. 33/40	*from* × 15
Nos. 43/60	*from* × 6
Nos. 61/5	*from* × 20
Nos. 66/79	*from* × 12
No. 80	—
Nos. 81/7	*from* × 8
Nos. 88/102	*from* × 4
Nos. 103/21	*from* × 3

The Official stamps of Perak are rare used on cover.

(**1**)

1878. *No. 11 of Straits Settlements handstamped with T* **1**.

1		2c. brown	£2000	£1600

PERAK (**2**) (14½ mm long) PERAK (**3**) (11 mm long) PERAK (**4**) (10¼ mm long)

PERAK (**5**) (17 mm long) PERAK (**6**) ("RA" narrow) PERAK (**7**) ("R" narrow)

PERAK (**8**) ("P" and "K" wide) PERAK (**9**) (12 to 13½ mm long)

1880–81. *No. 11 (wmk Crown CC) of Straits Settlements optd with T* **2/9**.

2	2	2c. brown	£2750	£1100
3	3	2c. brown	£2250	£750
4	4	2c. brown	£1000	£700
5	5	2c. brown (1881)	35·00	65·00
		w. Wmk inverted	†	£500
6	6	2c. brown (1881)	£275	£300
7	7	2c. brown (1881)	£170	£190
8	8	2c. brown (1881)	£600	£550
		a. Opt double	†	£2500
9	9	2c. brown (1881)	£160	£170

Of the above No. 2 is from a single unit overprint, No. 5 from a setting of sixty and the remainder from settings applied as horizontal strips of three. Nos. 6/8 come from mixed triplets, either 6+7+7 or 7+7+8. No. 4 is believed to come from a single unit overprint in addition to a triplet.

PERAK (**10**) ("A" wide) PERAK (**11**) ("E" wide)

1882–83. *Nos. 50 (wmk Crown CA) and 63 of Straits Settlements optd with T* **9/11**.

10	9	2c. brown	19·00	60·00
		a. Opt double	£650	
11		2c. pale rose (1883)	29·00	50·00
		a. Opt double	£700	
12	10	2c. pale rose (1883)	29·00	85·00
13	11	2c. pale rose (1883)	29·00	65·00
		a. Opt double	£700	

The above were all overprinted as triplet settings. Those for the 2c. rose were 11+12+13, 13+11+11 and 13+11+12.

2 CENTS PERAK (**12**) 2 CENTS (**13**)

1883 (July). *No. 51 (wmk Crown CA) of Straits Settlements surch*.

(a) Surch with T **12**.

14		2c. on 4c. rose	£3250	
		a. On Straits Settlements No. 12 (wmk Crown CC)	£8000	

(b) Optd as T **9** *or* **11** *and surch with T* **13**.

15	11	2c. on 4c. rose	£1100	£425
16	9	2c. on 4c. rose	£650	£250

It is believed that No. 14 occurred on the top row of the sheet with the remaining nine rows surcharged with a triplet containing 15+16+16.

Only one unused example, with defects, of No. 14a is recorded.

PERAK (**14**) ("E" wide) PERAK (**15**) ("E" narrow) PERAK (**16**) (12½–13 mm long)

PERAK (**17**) (12–12½ mm long) PERAK (**18**) (10½ mm long) PERAK (**19**) (10 mm long)

PERAK (**20**) (13 mm long)

1884–91. *Nos. 63/a of Straits Settlements optd with T* **14/20**.

17	14	2c. pale rose	5·00	3·75
		a. Opt double	£650	£650
		b. Opt inverted	£425	£550
		c. Bright rose	6·50	2·75
18	15	2c. pale rose	65·00	65·00
		b. Opt inverted	£1500	£1600
		c. Opt triple	£1500	
		d. Bright rose		
19	16	2c. pale rose (1886)	£150	32·00
		a. Bright rose (1891)	2·25	7·50
		ab. Optd "FERAK"	£375	£500
20	17	2c. pale rose (1886)	8·50	30·00
		a. Opt double	£1600	
21	18	2c. pale rose (1886)	£140	£150
		a. Bright rose		
22	19	2c. bright rose (1890)	18·00	50·00
23	20	2c. bright rose (1891)	£3500	

Settings:

Nos. 17/18	– triplets (either 17 + 17 + 17 or 18 + 17 + 17) 30 (3×10) (containing twenty-eight as No. 17 and two as No. 18) 60 (6×10) (containing either fifty-seven as No. 17 and three as No. 18 or all as No. 17)
No. 19	– 60 (6×10) (No. 19a occurs on one position of the setting, it is often found amended in manuscript)
No. 20	– triplet
No. 21	– triplet
No. 22	– 60 (6×10)
No. 23	– not known

1 CENT (**21**)

1886. *No. 17 surch with T* **21**.

24	14	1c. on 2c. pale rose	£2750	£2250

ONE CENT PERAK (**22**) ONE CENT PERAK. (**23**) ONE CENT PERAK. (**24**) ("N" wide in "ONE" and "CENT")

1886. *No. 63 of Straits Settlements surch with T* **22/4**.

25	22	1c. on 2c. pale rose	£650	£700
26	23	1c. on 2c. pale rose	65·00	85·00
		a. Surch double	£1100	
27	24	1c. on 2c. pale rose	£110	£130

Nos. 26/7 are from a triplet setting, Types **23-24-23**, in which the two Type **23**'s can be differentiated by the height of the right upright of the "N" of "CENT", which is short on one. This triplet was used for the top nine rows of the sheet. Type **22** may have been used on the bottom row.

1 CENT PERAK (**25**) One CENT PERAK (**26**) ONE CENT PERAK (**27**)

1886. *No. 63 of Straits Settlements surch with T* **25**.

28	1c. on 2c. pale rose	£140	£140
	a. Surch double	£1800	£1800

No. 28 comes from a triplet setting.

1886. *No. 63 of Straits Settlements surch with T* **26**.

29	1c. on 2c. pale rose	4·00	12·00
	a. "One" inverted	£3000	
	b. Surch double	£1200	

No. 29 comes from a triplet setting. It is believed that No. 29a occurred when the type was dropped and "One" replaced upside down.

1887. *No. 63 of Straits Settlements surch with T* **27** *in blue*.

30	1c. on 2c. pale rose	50·00	50·00
	a. Optd in black	£1900	£1400

No. 30 was printed from a setting of 60.

1 CENT PERAK (**28**) 1 CENT PERAK (**29**)

1887. *No. 63 of Straits Settlements surch with T* **28**.

31	1c. on 2c. pale rose	£950	£700

No. 31 comes from a triplet setting.

1887. *No. 63 of Straits Settlements surch with T* **29**.

32	1c. on 2c. pale rose	£2250	£2250

The size of setting used for No. 32 is not known.

One CENT PERAK (**30**) One CENT PERAK (**31**) One CENT PERAK (**32**) One CENT PERAK (**33**)

One CENT PERAK (**34**) One CENT PERAK (**35**) One CENT PERAK (**36**) One CENT PERAK (**37**)

1887–89. *No. 63 of Straits Settlements surch with T* **30/7**.

33	30	1c. on 2c. pale rose	3·75	7·00
		a. Surch double	£1200	
		b. Bright rose	2·75	3·25
34	31	1c. on 2c. pale rose (1889)	£130	£150
		b. Bright rose	£180	
35	32	1c. on 2c. pale rose (1889)	16·00	45·00
		a. "PREAK" (R. 6/1)	£700	£8500
		b. Bright rose	20·00	45·00
		ba. "PREAK" (R. 6/1)	£850	£1200
		w. Wmk inverted	£300	
36	33	1c. on 2c. pale rose (1889)	9·00	17·00
		b. Bright rose	4·50	17·00
37	34	1c. on 2c. pale rose (1889)	11·00	19·00
		b. Bright rose	4·50	19·00
38	35	1c. on 2c. bright rose (1889)	£650	£800
39	36	1c. on 2c. bright rose (1889)	£350	£450
40	37	1c. on 2c. pale rose (1889)	20·00	40·00
		b. Bright rose	18·00	32·00

Settings. No. 33 originally appeared as a triplet, then as a block of 30 (3×10) and, finally, as part of a series of composite settings of 60. Specialists recognise four such composite settings:

Setting I contained No. 33 in Rows 1 to 4, R. 5/1 to 5/5 and Row 7; No. 34 on R. 5/6, 6/1 and 6/2; No. 35 on R. 6/3–6; No. 36 on Row 8; No. 37 on Rows 9 and 10.

Setting II was similar, but had the example of No. 33 on R. 3/5 replaced by No. 38 and those on R. 7/4 and R. 7/6 by No. 39.

Setting III contained No. 33 in Rows 1 to 5; No. 35 in Row 6 with the "PREAK" error on the first position; No. 36 in Row 7; No. 37 in Rows 8 and 9; No. 40 in Row 10.

Setting IV was similar, but showed the "PREAK" error on R. 6/1 corrected.

ONE CENT. (**38**) ONE CENT (**39**)

1889–90. *No. 17 surch with T* **38/9**.

41	38	1c. on 2c. bright rose	£300	£130
42	39	1c. on 2c. bright rose (1890)	–	£250

PERAK Two CENTS (40) PERAK One CENT (41)

1891. *Nos. 63a, 66 and 68 of Straits Settlements surch.*

(a) As T **30**, **32/4** *and* **37**, *but with "PERAK" at top and a bar through the original value.*

43	**30**	1c. on 6c. lilac	50·00	28·00
44	**32**	1c. on 6c. lilac	£180	£160
45	**33**	1c. on 6c. lilac	£180	£160
46	**34**	1c. on 6c. lilac	85·00	75·00
47	**37**	1c. on 6c. lilac	£180	£160

(b) With T **40** *and as T* **32/4** *and* **37** *but with "PERAK" at top, all with a bar through the original value.*

48	**40**	2c. on 24c. green	21·00	13·00
		w. Wmk inverted	£300	
49	**32**	2c. on 24c. green	£110	65·00
		w. Wmk inverted		
50	**33**	2c. on 24c. green	£110	65·00
51	**34**	2c. on 24c. green	70·00	35·00
52	**37**	2c. on 24c. green	£110	65·00

(c) With T **41** *and as T* **30**, **34** *and* **37**, *but with "PERAK" at top.*

(i) Without bar over original value.

53	**30**	1c. on 2c. bright rose	£180	
		a. Narrow "O" in "One" (R. 3/3)	£2500	
54	**41**	1c. on 2c. bright rose	£850	
55	**34**	1c. on 2c. bright rose	£375	
56	**37**	1c. on 2c. bright rose	£850	

(ii) With bar through original value.

57	**30**	1c. on 2c. bright rose	2·25	9·00
		a. Narrow "O" in "One" (R. 3/3)	25·00	70·00
58	**41**	1c. on 2c. bright rose	8·50	32·00
59	**34**	1c. on 2c. bright rose	2·25	13·00
60	**37**	1c. on 2c. bright rose	8·50	32·00

Settings. Nos. 43/7 were arranged as Setting IV described under Nos. 33/40.

Nos. 48/52 were similar except that Type **40** replaced Type **30** on the first five rows.

The first printing of the 1c. on 2c. was without a bar through the original face value. Both printings, Nos. 53/60, were from the same setting with Type **30** on Rows 1 to 5, **41** on Row 6, **34** on Rows 7 to 9 and **37** on Row 10.

42

3 CENTS (43)

1892 (1 Jan)–**95**. Wmk Crown CA. P 14.

61	**42**	1c. green	2·25	15
62		2c. rose	1·75	30
63		2c. orange (9.9.95)	50	3·75
64		5c. blue	3·25	7·50
61/4 *Set of* 4			7·00	10·50
61s/4s Optd "Specimen" *Set of* 4			£110	

1895 (26 Apr). *Surch with T* **43**. Wmk Crown CA. P 14.

65	**42**	3c. on 5c. rose	3·75	3·00
		s. Optd "Specimen"	30·00	

44

45

Malformed "C" in left value tablet (R. 9/3, left pane)

1895 (2 Sept)–**99**. P 14.

(a) Wmk Crown CA.

66	**44**	1c. dull purple and green	2·75	50
		a. Malformed "C"	£140	65·00
67		2c. dull purple and brown	3·25	50
68		3c. dull purple and carmine	3·25	50
69		4c. dull purple and carmine (1899)	12·00	5·00
70		5c. dull purple and olive-yellow	4·50	55
71		8c. dull purple and ultramarine	45·00	65
72		10c. dull purple and orange	15·00	50
73		25c. green and carmine (1897)	£170	12·00
74		50c. dull purple and greenish black	48·00	38·00
75		50c. green and black (12.98)	£225	£170

(b) Wmk Crown CC.

76	**45**	$1 green and pale green (1896)	£200	£200
77		$2 green and carmine (1896)	£350	£325
78		$3 green and ochre (1898)	£400	£400
79		$5 green and ultramarine (1896)	£500	£500
80		$25 green and orange (1899?)	£9000	£3250
		s. Optd "Specimen"	£275	
66/76 *Set of* 11			£650	£375
66s/79s Optd "Specimen" *Set of* 14			£425	

Pending the arrival of the permanent Federated Malay States issue the stamps of FEDERATED MALAY STATES provisional overprints, SELANGOR and STRAITS SETTLEMENTS were used at various times between June 1900 and February 1901.

The general issues for the FEDERATED MALAY STATES were used in Perak from 1901 until 1935.

One Cent. (46) ONE CENT. (47)

Three Cent. (48) Three Cent. (49)

Three Cent.
Thinner "t" in "Cent"

1900. *Stamps of 1895–99 surch.*

81	**46**	1c. on 2c. dull purple & brown (13 July*)	60	2·25
		a. Antique "e" in "One" (R. 5/2)	60·00	£130
		b. Antique "e" in "Cent" (R. 9/4)	60·00	£130
82	**47**	1c. on 4c. dull purple and carmine	1·00	13·00
		a. Surch double	£1100	
83	**46**	1c. on 5c. dull purple & ol-yell (30 June*)	2·75	13·00
		a. Antique "e" in "One" (R. 5/2)	95·00	£275
		b. Antique "e" in "Cent" (R. 9/4)	95·00	£275
84	**48**	3c. on 8c. dull purple & ultram (26 Sept*)	6·00	11·00
		a. Antique "e" in "Cent" (R. 9/4)	£170	£275
		b. No stop after "Cent" (R. 9/5)	£170	£275
		c. Surch double	£500	£550
85		3c. on 50c. green and black (31 Aug*)	4·00	7·50
		a. Antique "e" in "Cent" (R. 9/4)	£130	£200
		b. No stop after "Cent" (R. 9/5)	£130	£200
86	**49**	3c. on $1 green and pale green (21 Oct*)	55·00	£140
		a. Thinner "t" in "Cent"	£300	£500
		b. Surch double	£1500	
		w. Wmk inverted	£400	£550
87		3c. on $2 green and carmine (24 Oct*)	35·00	85·00
81/7 *Set of* 7			90·00	£225

*Earliest known postmark date.

With exception of No. 86a, whose sheet position is not known, the remaining surcharge varieties all occur in the left-hand pane.

No. 86b is also known showing the thinner "t" in "Cent" variety. (*Price* £4250 *unused*).

50 Sultan Iskandar

51 Sultan Iskandar

Malformed "2c." (R. 10/10)

1935 (2 Dec)–**37**. *Chalk-surfaced paper.* Wmk Mult Script CA. P 14.

88	**50**	1c. black (1.1.36)	1·75	10
89		2c. green (1.1.36)	1·75	10
90		4c. orange	2·00	10
91		5c. brown (5.12.35)	75	10
92		6c. scarlet (1.1.37)	11·00	4·25
93		8c. grey	1·00	10
94		10c. dull purple (1.1.36)	80	15
95		12c. bright ultramarine (1.1.36)	3·50	1·00
96		25c. dull purple and scarlet (1.4.36)	2·75	1·00
97		30c. dull purple and orange (1.1.36)	3·75	1·50
98		40c. scarlet and dull purple	5·50	4·50
99		50c. black/*emerald* (1.2.36)	6·00	1·25
100		$1 black and red/*blue* (1.4.36)	2·50	1·25
101		$2 green and scarlet (16.5.36)	26·00	7·00
102		$5 green and red/*emerald* (16.5.36)	£120	35·00
88/102 *Set of* 15			£170	50·00
88s/102s Perf "Specimen" *Set of* 15			£375	

No. 91 exists in coils constructed from normal sheets in 1936.

1938 (2 May)–**41**. Wmk Mult Script CA. *Chalk-surfaced paper.* P 14.

103	**51**	1c. black (4.39)	12·00	10
104		2c. green (13.1.39)	7·00	10
105		2c. orange (30.10.41)	3·50	6·00
		a. Malformed "2c"	80·00	£110
		b. Ordinary paper	5·00	18·00
		ba. Malformed "2c"	£110	£275
106		3c. green (*ordinary paper*) (21.8.41)	—	7·00
		a. Chalk-surfaced paper (10.41)	2·75	6·50
107		4c. orange (5.39)	38·00	10
108		5c. brown (1.2.39)	6·50	10
109		6c. scarlet (12.39)	27·00	10
110		8c. grey (1.12.38)	28·00	10
111		8c. scarlet (18.12.41)	1·00	65·00
112		10c. dull purple (17.10.38)	30·00	10
113		12c. bright ultramarine (17.10.38)	23·00	1·00
114		15c. brt ultram (*ordinary paper*) (8.41)	4·25	13·00
115		25c. dull purple and scarlet (12.39)	50·00	3·25
116		30c. dull purple and orange (17.10.38)	9·50	2·25
117		40c. scarlet and dull purple	50·00	2·00
118		50c. black/*emerald* (17.10.38)	32·00	75
119		$1 black and red/*blue* (7.40)	£140	19·00
120		$2 green and scarlet (9.40)	£160	65·00
121		$5 green and red/*emerald* (1.41)	£275	£350
103/21 *Set of* 19			£800	£475
103s/21s perf "Specimen" *Set of* 19			£450	

No. 108 exists in coils constructed from normal sheets.

The stamps issued during 1941 were printed by Harrison and Sons following bomb damage to the De La Rue works on 29 December 1940. The used price quoted for No. 111 is for an example with clearly identifiable 1941 cancellation.

During shortages in 1941 stamps of STRAITS SETTLEMENTS (2c. green) and SELANGOR (2c. orange (both perfs), 3c.) were issued in Perak.

1948 (1 Dec). *Royal Silver Wedding. As Nos. 112/13 of Antigua.*

122	10c. violet	15	10
123	$5 green	23·00	32·00

1949 (10 Oct). *75th Anniv of U.P.U. As Nos. 114/17 of Antigua.*

124	10c. purple	15	10
125	15c. deep blue	1·50	2·00
126	25c. orange	30	4·00
127	50c. blue-black	1·25	3·50
124/7 *Set of* 4		2·75	8·50

52 Sultan Yussuf 'Izzuddin Shah

53 Sultan Idris Shah

1950 (17 Aug)–**56**. *Chalk-surfaced paper.* Wmk Mult Script CA. P 17½×18.

128	**52**	1c. black	10	10
129		2c. orange	20	10
130		3c. green	3·00	10
		a. Yellowish green (15.11.51)	13·00	7·00
131		4c. brown	50	10
		a. Yellow-brown (20.6.56)	9·00	20
132		5c. bright purple (1.9.52)	50	2·25
		a. Bright mauve (10.11.54)	1·25	2·25
133		6c. grey	30	10
134		8c. scarlet	65	2·25
135		8c. green (1.9.52)	1·00	1·00
136		10c. purple	20	10
		a. Brown-purple (20.6.56)	9·00	55
137		12c. scarlet (1.9.52)	1·00	4·50
138		15c. ultramarine	1·00	10
139		20c. black and green	1·50	65
140		20c. bright blue (1.9.52)	75	10
141		25c. purple and orange	60	10
142		30c. scarlet and purple (4.9.55)	1·75	20
143		35c. scarlet and purple (1.9.52)	1·00	25
144		40c. red and purple	4·50	6·00
145		50c. black and blue	4·50	10
146		$1 blue and purple	7·00	1·00
147		$2 green and scarlet	13·00	7·00
148		$5 green and brown	38·00	17·00
128/48 *Set of* 21			70·00	38·00

1953 (2 June). *Coronation. As No. 152 of Johore.*

149	10c. black and reddish purple	1·50	10

1957 (26 June)–**61**. *As Nos. 92/102 of Kedah but with inset portrait of Sultan Yussuf 'Izzuddin Shah.*

150	1c. black (21.8.57)	10	20
151	2c. orange-red (25.7.57)	30	1·00
	a. *Red-orange* (15.12.59)	1·75	3·25
152	4c. sepia (21.8.57)	20	10
153	5c. carmine-lake (21.8.57)	20	10
154	8c. myrtle-green (21.8.57)	2·00	3·50
155	10c. deep brown (4.8.57)	1·50	10
156	10c. deep maroon (21.2.61)	3·50	10
157	20c. blue	2·25	10
158	50c. black and blue (*p* 12½) (25.7.57)	40	1·00
	a. Perf 12½×13 (24.5.60)	40	10
159	$1 ultramarine and reddish purple (25.7.57)	6·50	40
160	$2 bronze-green & scar (*p* 12½) (21.8.57)	3·75	4·00
	a. Perf 13×12½ (21.2.61)	4·00	3·00
161	$5 brown and bronze-green (*p* 12½)	11·00	10·00
	a. Perf 13×12½ (24.5.60)	9·00	8·00
150/61 *Set of* 12		27·00	14·50

The 6, 12, 25 and 30c. values used with this issue were Nos. 1/4 of Malayan Federation.

(Photo Harrison)

1963 (26 Oct). *Installation of the Sultan of Perok.* W w **13**. P 14½.

162	**53**	10c. red, black, blue and yellow	10	10

54 Vanda hookeriana

1965 (15 Nov)–**68**. *As Nos. 166/72 of Johore but with inset portrait of Sultan Idris as in T* **54**. W w **13** (upright).

163	1c. multicoloured	10	50
	w. Wmk inverted	4·25	
164	2c. multicoloured	10	70
	w. Wmk inverted	9·00	
165	5c. pale black and multicoloured	10	10
	a. *Grey-black and multicoloured* (2.4.68)	1·50	30
	b. Yellow (flower) omitted	70·00	
166	6c. multicoloured	15	40
167	10c. multicoloured	15	10
168	15c. multicoloured	80	10
	a. Black (country name and head) omitted	£1100	
	c. Magenta (background) omitted	£1000	

169 20c. multicoloured 1·25 10
a. Bright purple (blooms) omitted £130
163/9 Set of 7 2·40 1·60

No. 168a comes from a horizontal strip of three, the centre stamp having the black completely omitted. The two outer stamps show the colour partly omitted.

The 2c. to 15c. exist with PVA gum as well as gum arabic.

The higher values used with this issue were Nos. 20/27 of Malaysia (National Issues).

1970. *As Nos. 163 and 167, but W w* **13** *(sideways).*

170 **54** 1c. multicoloured (27.5.70) 2·50 7·00
171 – 10c. multicoloured (20.11.70) 7·00 3·25

STAMP BOOKLETS

1935.

SB1 $1 booklet containing twenty 5c. (No. 91) in blocks of 10
SB2 $1.30 booklet containing 5c. and 8c. (Nos. 91, 93), each in block of 10

1938.

SB3 $1 booklet containing twenty 5c. (No. 108) in blocks of 10
SB4 $1.30 booklet containing 5c. and 8c. (Nos. 108, 110), each in block of 10

OFFICIAL STAMPS

P.G.S. (O 1) Service. (O 2)

1889 (1 Nov). *Stamps of Straits Settlements optd Type* O **1**. Wmk Crown CC (Nos. O6 and O8) or Crown CA (others).

O1 2c. bright rose 4·75 6·50
a. Opt double £850 £850
b. Wide space between "G" and "S". 70·00 85·00
c. No stop after "S" 70·00 85·00
O2 4c. brown 15·00 24·00
a. Wide space between "G" and "S". 95·00 £130
b. No stop after "S" £160 £180
c. Broken oval £300
w. Wmk inverted £100
O3 6c. lilac 27·00 50·00
a. Wide space between "G" and "S". £150 £190
O4 8c. orange 38·00 65·00
a. Wide space between "G" and "S". £170 £275
O5 10c. slate 75·00 75·00
a. Wide space between "G" and "S". £325 £325
O6 12c. blue (CC) £200 £250
a. Wide space between "G" and "S". £750
O7 12c. brown-purple (CA) £250 £325
a. Wide space between "G" and "S". £850
O8 24c. green (CC) £750 £850
a. Wide space between "G" and "S". £2250
O9 24c. green (CA) £190 £225
a. Wide space between "G" and "S". £700

Nos. O1/9 were overprinted from a setting of 30 (3×10). The variety "wide space between G and S" occurs on R. 10/3 and R. 10/6 of the original printing. A later printing of the 2c. and 4c. values had this variety corrected, but was without a stop after "S" on R. 10/1 and R. 10/4.

The broken oval flaw occurs on R. 10/5 (lower right pane) of the basic stamp. For illustration see Straits Settlements.

1894 (1 June). *No. 64 optd with Type* O **2**.

O10 5c. blue 75·00 1·00
a. Overprint inverted £1000 £475

1897. *No. 70 optd with Type* O **2**.

O11 5c. dull purple and olive-yellow 2·75 50
a. Overprint double £650 £400

PERLIS

The Thai monarchy exercised suzerainty over Perlis and the other northern states of the Malay peninsula from the 16th century onwards.

The Siamese post office at Kangar is recorded as opening during 1894. It is believed that the initial cancellation showed Thai characters only, but no complete example has so far been discovered.

Stamps of SIAM *cancelled as Type* B *inscr* "PERLIS" *(from* July 1904).

1887–91. *(Nos. 11/18).*

Z401 **9** 12a. purple and carmine £225
Z402 24a. purple and blue £325

1897. *Surch as T* **39** *(Siamese) and T* **41** *(English) (No. 52).*

Z403 **9** 4a. on 12a. purple and carmine £400

1899–1904. *(Nos. 67/81).*

Z404 **49** 1a. olive-green (wide Siamese characters in face value) £250
Z405 2a. grass-green £225
Z406 2a. scarlet and pale blue £225
Z407 3a. red and blue £375
Z408 4a. carmine £225
Z409 4a. chocolate and pink £225
Z410 8a. deep green and orange £225
Z411 10a. ultramarine £225
Z412 12a. brown-purple and carmine £200
Z413 24a. brown-purple and blue £425

1905–09. *(Nos. 97/105).*

Z416 **53** 1a. green and orange £200
Z417 2a. grey and deep violet £200
Z418 3a. green £225
Z419 4a. pale red and sepia £200
Z420 5a. carmine £225
Z421 8a. olive-bistre and dull black £200
Z422 12a. blue £250
Z423 24a. red-brown £375

Stamps of SIAM *cancelled as Type* C *inscr* "Perlis" *at foot (from* Sept. 1907).

1887–91. *(Nos. 11/18).*

Z425 **9** 12a. purple and carmine £250

1899–1904. *(Nos. 67/81).*

Z426 **49** 1a. olive-green (narrow Siamese characters in face value) £250
Z427 8a. deep green and orange £250
Z428 10a. ultramarine £250

1905–09. *(Nos. 92/105).*

Z429 **53** 1a. green and orange £250
Z430 2a. grey and deep violet £225
Z431 3a. green £250
Z432 4a. pale red and sepia £225
Z433 4a. scarlet £250
Z434 5a. carmine £250
Z435 8a. olive-bistre and dull black £250
Z436 9a. blue £225
Z437 24a. red-brown £425

1907. *Surch with T* **56** *(No. 109).*

Z438 **9** 1a. on 24a. purple and blue £250

Suzerainty over Perlis was transferred by Thailand to Great Britain on 15 July 1909, although the use of Siamese stamps appears to have extended into early August. Stamps of the Federated Malay States were used there until 1912.

Stamps of the Federated Malay States used in Perlis

Cancelled as Type C inscribed "Perlis" at foot.

1909–12. *(Nos. 29/34).*

Z341 **3** 1c. green Die II £160
Z342 3c. carmine £160

Cancelled as Type B inscribed "PERLIS".

1909–12. *(Nos. 29/36d).*

Z343 **3** 1c. green Die II £150
Z344 3c. carmine 90·00
Z345 4c. black and rose £150

Federated Malay States stamps were withdrawn on 15 June 1912.

The stamps of Kedah were in use in Perlis between 1912 and 1941.

A Treaty of Friendship between Great Britain and Perlis was signed on 28 April 1930 and the state joined the Federation of Malaya on 1 February 1948.

1948 (1 Dec). *Royal Silver Wedding. As Nos. 112/13 of Antigua.*

1 10c. violet 30 2·75
2 $5 brown 29·00 48·00

1949 (10 Oct). *75th Anniv of U.P.U. As Nos. 114/17 of Antigua.*

3 10c. purple 30 1·75
4 15c. deep blue 1·25 4·00
5 25c. orange 45 2·50
6 50c. blue-black 1·00 3·75
3/6 Set of 4 2·75 11·00

1 Raja Syed Putra

1951 (26 Mar)–**55**. *Chalk-surfaced paper.* Wmk Mult Script CA. P 17½×18.

7 **1** 1c. black 20 1·00
8 2c. orange 75 50
9 3c. green 1·50 3·50
10 4c. brown 1·50 1·00
11 5c. bright purple (1.9.52) 50 3·00
12 6c. grey 1·50 1·75
13 8c. scarlet 2·50 6·00
14 8c. green (1.9.52) 1·00 3·50
15 10c. purple 70 40
a. Error. St. Edward's Crown W 9b £16000
16 12c. scarlet (1.9.52) 1·00 4·25
17 15c. ultramarine 4·25 6·00
18 20c. black and green 3·00 9·00
19 20c. bright blue (1.9.52) 1·25 1·00
20 25c. purple and orange 1·75 3·00
21 30c. scarlet and purple (4.9.55) 1·75 12·00
22 35c. scarlet and purple (1.9.52) 1·25 5·50
23 40c. red and purple 4·00 24·00
24 50c. black and blue 4·25 5·50
25 $1 blue and purple 7·50 25·00
26 $2 green and scarlet 16·00 48·00
27 $5 green and brown 55·00 £120
7/27 Set of 21 £100 £250

1953 (2 June). *Coronation. As No. 120 of Antigua.*

28 10c. black and reddish purple 1·25 3·00

1957 (26 June)–**62**. *As Nos. 92/102 of Kedah but with inset portrait of Raja Syed Putra.*

29 **9** 1c. black (21.8.57) 10 30
30 **10** 2c. orange-red (25.7.57) 10 30
31 **11** 4c. sepia (21.8.57) 10 30
32 **12** 5c. carmine-lake (21.8.57) 10 10
33 **13** 8c. myrtle-green (21.8.57) 2·00 1·75
34 **14** 10c. deep brown (4.8.57) 1·50 2·25
35 10c. deep maroon (14.3.61) 6·50 3·25
36 **15** 20c. blue 2·50 4·00
37 **16** 50c. black and blue (p 12½) (25.7.57) 60 3·75
a. Perf 12½×13 (8.5.62) 3·00 4·00
38 **17** $1 ultram & reddish purple (25.7.57) 8·00 11·00
39 **18** $2 bronze-green and scarlet (25.7.57) 8·00 8·00
40 **19** $5 brown and bronze-green (21.8.57) 11·00 11·00
29/40 Set of 12 35·00 42·00

The 6, 12, 25 and 30c. values used with this issue were Nos. 1/4 of Malayan Federation.

1965 (15 Nov). *As Nos. 166/72 of Johore but with inset portrait of Raja Syed Putra as in T* **2**.

41 1c. multicoloured 10 1·00
w. Wmk inverted 15·00
42 2c. multicoloured 10 1·50
43 5c. multicoloured 15 40
44 6c. multicoloured 65 1·50
45 10c. multicoloured 65 40
46 15c. multicoloured 1·00 40
47 20c. multicoloured 1·00 1·75
41/7 Set of 7 3·25 6·25

The 6c. exists with PVA gum as well as gum arabic.

The higher values used with this issue were Nos. 20/27 of Malaysia (National Issues).

SABAH

SABAH (136) SABAH (137)

1964 (1 July)–**65**. *Nos. 391/406 of North Borneo (D.L.R. printings), optd with T* **136** *(Nos. 408/19) or T* **137** *(Nos. 420/3).*

408 1c. emerald and brown-red 10 10
409 4c. bronze-green and orange 15 50
410 5c. sepia and violet 30 10
a. Light sepia and deep violet (17.8.65) 4·50 2·75
411 6c. black and blue-green 1·00 10
412 10c. green and red 2·00 10
413 12c. brown and grey-green 20 10
414 20c. blue-green and ultramarine 4·00 10
415 25c. grey-black and scarlet 1·00 90
416 30c. sepia and olive 30 10
417 35c. slate-blue and red-brown 30 20
418 50c. emerald and yellow-brown 30 10
419 75c. grey-blue and bright purple 3·75 65
420 $1. brown and yellow-green 8·50 1·25
421 $2. brown and slate 15·00 2·25
422 $5. emerald and maroon 15·00 12·00
423 $10. carmine and blue 15·00 28·00
408/23 Set of 16 60·00 42·00

Old stocks bearing Waterlow imprints of the 4c., 5c., 20c. and 35c. to $10 were used for overprinting, but in addition new printings of all values by De La Rue using the original plates with the De La Rue imprint replacing the Waterlow imprint were specially made for overprinting.

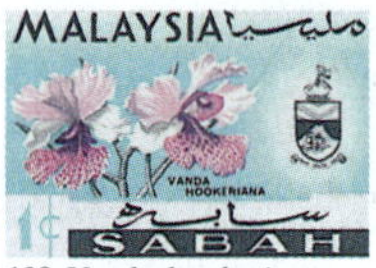

138 *Vanda hookeriana*

1965 (15 Nov)–**68**. *As Nos. 166/72 of Johore, but with Arms of Sabah inset as in T* **138**. W w **13** (upright).

424 1c. multicoloured 10 1·25
425 2c. multicoloured 10 1·75
426 5c. multicoloured 10 10
427 6c. multicoloured 30 1·50
428 10c. multicoloured 30 10
429 15c. multicoloured (pale black panel) 2·00 10
a. Brown-black panel (20.2.68) 3·00 25
430 20c. multicoloured 2·75 75
424/30 Set of 7 5·00 5·00

The 5c. to 15c. exist with PVA gum as well as gum arabic.

The higher values used with this issue were Nos. 20/27 of Malaysia (National Issues).

1970 (20 Nov). *As No. 428, but* W w **13** (sideways).

431 10c. multicoloured 5·00 5·00

SARAWAK

Sarawak joined the Federation of Malaysia at its formation on 16 September 1963. For the convenience of collectors, stamps issued after this date continue to be listed with earlier issues of Sarawak.

SELANGOR

The first British Resident was appointed in 1874. Selangor joined the Federated Malay States in 1896.

The stamps of the STRAITS SETTLEMENTS were used in Selangor from 1879 until 1881.

Until 1 January 1899, when the Federated Malay States joined the U.P.U., mail for addresses outside Malaya was franked with stamps of the STRAITS SETTLEMENTS.

PRICES FOR STAMPS ON COVER TO 1945	
Nos. 1/8	—
Nos. 9/19	from × 10
Nos. 20/30	from × 12
Nos. 31/3	from × 25
Nos. 34/6	from × 20
Nos. 37/8	from × 15
Nos. 38a/40	—
Nos. 41/2	from × 8
Nos. 43	—
Nos. 44/8	from × 8
Nos. 49/53	from × 30
Nos. 54/66	from × 10
Nos. 66a/7	from × 4
Nos. 68/85	from × 3
Nos. 86/7	from × 4

The Straits Settlements 1867 2c. brown with Crown CC watermark (No. 11) has been known since 1881 overprinted in black with a crescent and star over a capital S, all within an oval, similar in style to the overprints listed for Perak and Sungei Ujong.

The status of this item remains unclear, but it may well represent the first issue of distinctive stamps for Selangor. A similar overprint in red on the Straits Settlements 2c. brown with Crown CA watermark also exists and may have been produced for sale to collectors (*Price* £325, *unused*).

This overprint should not be confused with a somewhat similar cancellation used on Selangor stamps of the same period. This cancellation differs in having a circular frame with the capital S shown above the crescent and star. It is usually struck in red.

SELANGOR (1) ("S" inverted and narrow letters) | SELANGOR (2) ("S" wide) | SELANGOR (3) (narrow letters)

SELANGOR (4) ("N" wide) | SELANGOR (5) ("SE" and "AN" wide) | SELANGOR (6) ("SEL" and "N" wide)

SELANGOR (7) ("SELAN" wide)

1881–82. *No.* 11 (wmk Crown CC) *of Straits Settlements optd with T* **1/7**.

1	**1**	2c. brown	£550	£600
2	**2**	2c. brown	£190	£225
3	**3**	2c. brown	£120	£120
4	**4**	2c. brown	£8000	£3000
5	**5**	2c. brown (1882)	£225	£275
6	**6**	2c. brown (1882)	£225	£275
7	**7**	2c. brown (1882)	£225	£275

Nos. 1/3 and 5/7 have been identified as coming from triplet settings, either Nos. 1+2+3, 2+3+3 or 5+6+7. The setting for No. 4 is unknown.

S.
(8)

1882. *No.* 50 (wmk Crown CA) *of Straits Settlements optd with T* **8**.

8	**8**	2c. brown	—	£2750

SELANGOR (9) ("SEL" and "NG" wide) | SELANGOR (10) ("E" and "ANG" wide) | SELANGOR (11) ("ELANG" wide)

SELANGOR (12) ("S" and "L" wide) | SELANGOR (13) ("S" and "A" wide) | SELANGOR (14) ("E" wide)

SELANGOR (15) ("EL" wide) | SELANGOR (16) ("SE" and "N" wide) | SELANGOR (17) ("S" and "N" wide)

1882–83. *No.* 50 (wmk Crown CA) *of Straits Settlements optd with T* **2/3** *and* **9/17**.

9	**9**	2c. brown	£275	£375
10	**10**	2c. brown	£275	£375
11	**11**	2c. brown	£275	£375
12	**2**	2c. brown (1883)	£160	£130
13	**3**	2c. brown (1883)	£300	£130
14	**12**	2c. brown (1883)	—	£3500
15	**13**	2c. brown (1883)	£700	£600
16	**14**	2c. brown (1883)	£450	£350
17	**15**	2c. brown (1883)	£450	£350
18	**16**	2c. brown (1883)	£180	£170
		a. Opt double	£1100	
19	**17**	2c. brown (1883)	£180	£170

The above were all printed from triplet settings. Those so far identified are Nos. 9+10+11, 12 (with defective "G") +13+13, 15+16+17 and 18+12+19. No. 14 occurs as the first position of a triplet, but the second and third units are not yet known.

SELANGOR (18) ("E" and "A" wide) | SELANGOR (19) ("A" wide) | SELANGOR (20) ("L" wide)

SELANGOR (21) ("L" narrow) | SELANGOR (22) ("A" narrow) | SELANGOR (23) (wide letters)

1883–85. *No.* 63 *of Straits Settlements optd with T* **2**, **4**, **12**, **14/15** *and* **18/23**.

20	**12**	2c. pale rose	£225	£170
21	**14**	2c. pale rose	£130	£110
		a. Opt double		
22	**4**	2c. pale rose (1884)	£200	£170
23	**15**	2c. pale rose (1884)	£110	95·00
		a. Opt double	£1000	
		b. Opt triple		
24	**2**	2c. pale rose (1884)	£140	£110
25	**18**	2c. pale rose (1884)	£140	£110
26	**19**	2c. pale rose (1884)	£425	£180
27	**20**	2c. pale rose (1884)	£550	£250
28	**21**	2c. pale rose (1885)	£110	90·00
29	**22**	2c. pale rose (1885)	£190	£160
30	**23**	2c. pale rose (1885)	£500	£250

The above come from triplet settings with Nos. 20+21+21, 22+22+23, 23+26 (with defective "A") +26, 24+25+23 and 28+29+28 so far identified. The triplets for Nos. 27 and 30 are not known.

SELANGOR (24) | Selangor (25) | SELANGOR (26)

SELANGOR (27) | SELANGOR (28) | SELANGOR (29) | SELANGOR (30)

SELANGOR (31) | SELANGOR (32) | SELANGOR (33) | SELANGOR (34)

1885–91. *Nos.* 63/a *of Straits Settlements optd with T* **24/34**.

31	**24**	2c. pale rose	14·00	25·00
		a. Opt double	£1100	£900
		w. Wmk inverted	—	£500
32	**25**	2c. pale rose	£1500	£1600
33	**26**	2c. pale rose	35·00	45·00
34	**27**	2c. pale rose (1886)	55·00	60·00
		a. Opt double	†	£800
35	**28**	2c. pale rose (horiz opt without stop) (1887)	14·00	2·75
		a. Opt double	£800	
		b. Bright rose	14·00	2·25
36		2c. pale rose (horiz opt with stop) (1887)	£120	75·00
		a. Bright rose		
37	**29**	2c. pale rose (1889)	£275	85·00
38	**30**	2c. pale rose (vert opt) (1889)	80·00	6·00
		a. Bright rose		
38*b*		2c. bright rose (horiz opt) (1889)	£4000	
39	**31**	2c. pale rose (diagonal opt) (1889)	£3000	
40	**32**	2c. pale rose (1889)	£650	35·00
41	**28**	2c. brt rose (vert opt without stop) (1890)	20·00	35·00
42	**33**	2c. bright rose (1890)	£120	3·00
		a. Opt double		
43	**34**	2c. bright rose (1891)	£350	£150

Settings:
Nos. 31/4 – each in triplet containing three examples of the same stamp
No. 35 – triplet or 60 (6×10)
No. 36 – 60 (6×10)
Nos. 37/8 – 60 (6×10) containing both overprints in an unknown combination, but with No. 38 predominating
Nos. 38*b*/9 – not known
Nos. 40/3 – each in 60 (6×10)

SELANGOR Two CENTS (35) | SELANGOR Two CENTS (36) | SELANGOR Two CENTS (37)

SELANGOR Two CENTS (38) | SELANGOR Two CENTS (39)

1891. *No.* 68 *of Straits Settlements, surch with T* **35/9**, *each with bar obliterating old value.*

44	**35**	2c. on 24c. green	35·00	65·00
45	**36**	2c. on 24c. green	£190	£250
46	**37**	2c. on 24c. green	£190	£250
47	**38**	2c. on 24c. green	£100	£140
		a. "SELANGCR"		
48	**39**	2c. on 24c. green	£190	£250

Nos. 44/8 come from the one setting used to surcharge the panes of sixty. No. 44 occurs in rows 1 to 5, No. 45 on row 6, No. 46 on row 7, No. 47 on rows 8 and 9, and No. 48 on row 10.

The error, No. 47a, occurs in the first printing only and is No. 45 (R. 8/3) on the pane.

40

3 CENTS
(41)

1891 (1 Nov)–**95.** Wmk Crown CA. P 14.

49	**40**	1c. green (5.93)	1·50	25
50		2c. rose	3·50	1·00
51		2c. orange (27.5.95)	2·50	1·00
52		5c. blue (8.92)	24·00	4·75
49/52 *Set of* 4			28·00	6·25
49s/52s Optd "Specimen" *Set of* 4			95·00	

1894 (Dec). *Surch with T* **41**. Wmk Crown CA. P 14.

53	**40**	3c. on 5c. rose	3·75	50
		s. Optd "Specimen"	35·00	

42

43

Dented frame above "A" of "SELANGOR" (left pane R. 4/5)

1895–99. Wmk Crown CA or Crown CC (dollar values). P 14.

54	**42**	3c. dull purple and carmine	6·50	30
55		5c. dull purple and olive-yellow	8·00	30
56		8c. dull purple and ultramarine (1898)	48·00	7·00
57		10c. dull purple and orange	12·00	2·00
58		25c. green and carmine (1896)	80·00	55·00
59		50c. dull purple and greenish black (1896)	70·00	25·00
		a. Dented frame	£475	
60		50c. green and black (1898)	£425	£120
		a. Dented frame		
61	**43**	$1 green and yellow-green	50·00	£130
62		$2 green and carmine (1897)	£225	£250
63		$3 green and ochre (1897)	£550	£450
64		$5 green and blue	£250	£325
65		$10 green and purple (1899)	£700	£900
		s. Optd "Specimen"	£140	
66		$25 green and orange (1897)	£3500	£3500
		s. Optd "Specimen"	£275	
54/62 *Set of* 9			£850	£500
54s/64s Optd "Specimen" *Set of* 11			£400	

Pending the arrival of the permanent Federated Malay States issue the stamps of STRAITS SETTLEMENTS and PERAK were used at various times between July 1900 and March 1901.

The general issues for the FEDERATED MALAY STATES were used in Selangor from 1901 until 1935.

One cent. (44) | Three cents. (45)

Antique "t" (R. 3/4 and 8/4)

1900 (Oct). *Nos.* 55 *and* 59 *surch with T* **44** *or* **45**.

66*a*	**42**	1c. on 5c. dull purple & ol-yell (31 Oct*)	60·00	£130
66*b*		1c. on 50c. green and black (22 Oct*)	3·00	25·00
		bc. "cent" repeated at left	£3000	
		bd. Dented frame	£130	
67		3c. on 50c. green and black (30 Oct*)	4·00	24·00
		a. Antique "t" in "cents"	£375	£550
		b. Dented frame	£375	

*Earliest known postmark date.

It is believed that these stamps were surcharged from settings of 30, repeated four times to complete the sheet of 120.

No. 66bc occurred on two separate vertical strips of five stamps where two impressions of the setting overlapped.

46 Mosque at Palace, Klang

47 Sultan Suleiman

Joined script (R. 2/1)

(Des E. J. McNaughton)

1935 (2 Dec)–**41.** Wmk Mult Script CA (sideways on *T* **46**). *Chalk-surfaced paper.* P 14 or 14×14½ (No. 70).

68	**46**	1c. black (1.1.36)	30	10
69		2c. green (1.1.36)	90	10
		a. Joined script	50·00	20·00
70		2c. orange (*ordinary paper*) (P 14×14½) (21.8.41)	3·50	75
		aa. Joined script	£120	30·00
		a. Perf 14. Ordinary paper (9.41)	20·00	1·50
		ab. Joined script	£300	55·00
71		3c. green (*ordinary paper*) (21.8.41)	1·25	8·00
		a. chalk-surfaced paper (10.41)	18·00	2·75
72		4c. orange	50	10
73		5c. brown (5.12.35)	70	10
74		6c. scarlet (1.1.37)	5·50	10
75		8c. grey	60	10
76		10c. dull purple (1.1.36)	60	10
77		12c. bright ultramarine (1.1.36)	1·50	10
78		15c. brt ultram (*ordinary paper*) (1.10.41)	12·00	32·00
79		25c. dull purple and scarlet (1.4.36)	1·00	60
80		30c. dull purple and orange (1.1.36)	1·00	85
81		40c. scarlet and dull purple	1·50	1·00
82		50c. black/*emerald* (1.2.36)	1·00	15
83	**47**	$1 black and rose/*blue* (1.4.36)	8·00	90
84		$2 green and scarlet (16.5.36)	28·00	9·00
85		$5 green and red/*emerald* (16.5.36)	85·00	23·00
68/85 *Set of* 18			£140	60·00
68s/85s Perf "Specimen" *Set of* 18			£450	

The stamps issued during 1941 were printed by Harrison and Sons following bomb damage to the De La Rue works on 29 December 1940.

No. 69 exists in coils constructed from normal sheets.

Supplies of an unissued 8c. scarlet were diverted to Australia in 1941. Examples circulating result from leakages of this supply (*Price* £750).

48 Sultan Hisamud-din Alam Shah

49 Sultan Hisamud-din Alam Shah

1941. Wmk Mult Script CA. *Chalk-surfaced paper*. P 14.

86	**48**	$1 black and red/*blue* (15.4.41)	19·00	6·00
87		$2 green and scarlet (7.7.41)	48·00	32·00
		s. Perf "Specimen"	70·00	

A $5 green and red on emerald, *T* **48**, was issued overprinted during the Japanese occupation of Malaya. Unoverprinted examples are known, but were not issued (*Price* £120).

> During shortages in 1941 stamps of STRAITS SETTLEMENTS (2c.) and PERAK (25c.) were issued in Selangor.

1948 (1 Dec). *Royal Silver Wedding. As Nos. 112/13 of Antigua.*

88	10c. violet	20	30
89	$5 green	27·00	20·00

1949 (12 Sept)–**55**. Wmk Mult Script CA. *Chalk-surfaced paper*. P 17½×18.

90	**49**	1c. black	10	60
91		2c. orange	30	1·00
92		3c. green	3·00	1·50
93		4c. brown	40	10
94		5c. bright purple (1.9.52)	40	2·25
		a. Bright mauve (17.9.53)	30	80
95		6c. grey	30	40
96		8c. scarlet	1·00	1·00
97		8c. green (1.9.52)	80	1·75
98		10c. purple	20	10
99		12c. scarlet (1.9.52)	80	3·50
		w. Wmk inverted	£500	
100		15c. ultramarine	6·50	10
101		20c. black and green	3·75	35
102		20c. bright blue (1.9.52)	80	10
103		25c. purple and orange	2·00	20
104		30c. scarlet and purple (4.9.55)	2·00	2·25
105		35c. scarlet and purple (1.9.52)	80	1·50
106		40c. scarlet and purple	9·00	6·50
107		50c. black and blue	3·00	10
108		$1 blue and purple	3·00	60
109		$2 green and scarlet	13·00	60
110		$5 green and brown	45·00	2·25
90/110 *Set of* 21			85·00	22·00

1949 (10 Oct). *75th Anniv of U.P.U. As Nos. 114/17 of Antigua.*

111	10c. purple	30	10
112	15c. deep blue	2·25	2·50
113	25c. orange	35	4·25
114	50c. blue-black	1·00	4·25
111/14 *Set of* 4		3·50	10·00

1953 (2 June). *Coronation. As No. 120 of Antigua.*

115	10c. black and reddish purple	1·50	10

1957 (26 June)–**61**. *As Nos. 92/102 of Kedah but with inset portrait of Sultan Hisamud-din Alum Shah.*

116	1c. black (21.8.57)	10	2·25
117	2c. orange-red (25.7.57)	30	1·00
	a. Red-orange (10.11.59)	6·50	4·75
118	4c. sepia (21.8.57)	10	10
119	5c. carmine-lake (21.8.57)	10	10
120	8c. myrtle-green (21.8.57)	1·75	3·00
121	10c. deep brown (4.8.57)	1·75	10
122	10c. deep maroon (9.5.61)	6·50	10
123	20c. blue	2·50	20
124	50c. black and blue (*p* 12½) (25.7.57)	40	10
	a. Perf 12½×13 (10.5.60)	65	10
125	$1 ultramarine and reddish purple (25.7.57)	3·50	10
126	$2 bronze-green and scarlet (*p* 12½) (21.8.57)	4·00	2·00
	a. Perf 13×12½ (6.12.60)	4·50	2·00
127	$5 brown and bronze-green (*p* 12½)	10·00	2·25
	a. Perf 13×12½ (10.5.60)	10·00	1·50
116/27 *Set of* 12		28·00	9·00

The 6, 12, 25 and 30c. values used with this issue were Nos. 1/4 of Malayan Federation.

50 Sultan Salahuddin Abdul Aziz Shah

51 Sultan Salahuddin Abdul Aziz Shah

(Photo Harrison)

1961 (28 June). *Coronation of the Sultan.* W w **12**. P 15×14.

128	**50**	10c. multicoloured	20	10

A sheet exists showing the black printing so misplaced as to produce an effect of a "Double-headed" Sultan (*Priced* £160 *un.*).

1961–62. *As Nos. 92/8 of Kedah but with inset portrait of Sultan Salahuddin Abdul Aziz as in T* **51**. W w **13**. P 12½×13 (vert) or 13×12½ (horiz).

129	1c. black (1.3.62)	50	1·50
130	2c. orange-red (1.3.62)	75	1·90
131	4c. sepia (1.3.62)	1·25	10
132	5c. carmine-lake (1.3.62)	1·00	10
133	8c. myrtle-green (1.3.62)	4·50	4·50
134	10c. deep maroon (1.11.61)	75	10
135	20c. blue (1.3.62)	7·50	1·00
129/35 *Set of* 7		14·50	8·00

52 *Vanda hookeriana*

1965 (15 Nov). *As Nos. 166/72 of Johore but with inset portrait of Sultan Salahuddin Abdul Aziz Shah as in T* **52**.

136	1c. multicoloured	10	20
	b. Magenta omitted	£120	
	w. Wmk inverted	1·00	
137	2c. multicoloured	10	1·75
	b. Yellow (flower) omitted	50·00	
138	5c. multicoloured	25	10
	b. Yellow (flower) omitted	55·00	
	c. Red (leaves, etc) omitted	£325	
139	6c. multicoloured	15	10
140	10c. multicoloured	15	10
	a. Red omitted	£120	
141	15c. multicoloured	1·25	10
	b. Green (value and leaves) omitted	£550	
142	20c. multicoloured	1·90	70
	a. Bright purple (blooms) omitted	£130	
	b. Yellow (leaves) omitted	60·00	
136/42 *Set of* 7		3·50	2·50

The 2c. to 20c. values exist with PVA gum as well as gum arabic.

The higher values used with this issue were Nos. 20/27 of Malaysia (National Issues).

1970 (20 Nov). *As Nos.* 136 *etc. but* W w **13** (sideways).

143	**52**	1c. multicoloured	1·75	7·50
144		10c. multicoloured	5·00	2·00
145	–	20c. multicoloured	9·00	10·00
143/5 *Set of* 3			14·00	18·00

STAMP BOOKLETS

1935. *Stapled.*

SB1 $1 booklet containing twenty 5c. (No. 73) in blocks of 10

SB2 $1.30 booklet containing 5c. and 8c. (Nos. 73, 75), each in block of 10

TRENGGANU

Suzerainty over Trengganu was transferred by Thailand to Great Britain in 1909. A British adviser was appointed in 1919.

The state joined the Federation of Malaya on 1 February 1948.

PRICES FOR STAMPS ON COVER TO 1945	
Nos. 1/15	*from* × 12
No. 16/18	—
Nos. 19/22	*from* × 10
Nos. 23/33	*from* × 12
Nos. 34/6	—
Nos. 37/47	*from* × 15
Nos. 48/60	*from* × 6
Nos. D1/4	—

1 Sultan Zain ul ab din

2 Sultan Zain ul ab din

RED CROSS

2c.

(**3**)

1910 (14 Dec)–**19**. Wmk Mult Crown CA. *Ordinary paper* (1c. to 10c.) *or chalk-surfaced paper* (20c. to $25). P 14.

1	**1**	1c. blue-green	1·75	1·00
		a. Green	2·75	1·25
2		2c. brown and purple (1915)	1·00	90
3		3c. carmine-red	2·25	2·25
4		4c. orange	3·50	5·50
5		4c. red-brown and green (1915)	2·00	3·75
5*a*		4c. carmine-red (1919)	1·25	1·75
6		5c. grey	1·25	3·75
7		5c. grey and brown (1915)	2·25	2·00
8		8c. ultramarine	1·25	10·00
9		10c. purple/*yellow*	5·00	14·00
		a. On pale yellow	3·25	8·00
10		10c. green and red/*yellow* (1915)	1·25	2·25
11		20c. dull and bright purple	3·50	5·00
12		25c. green and dull purple (1915)	8·00	35·00
13		30c. dull purple and black (1915)	6·50	60·00
14		50c. black/*green*	4·50	9·50
15		$1 black and carmine/*blue*	17·00	24·00
16		$3 green and red/*green* (1915)	£190	£450
17	**2**	$5 green and dull purple (1912)	£200	£600
18		$25 rose-carmine and green (1912)	£1000	£2500
		s. Optd "Specimen"	£300	
1/17 *Set of* 18			£400	£1100
1s/17s Optd "Specimen" *Set of* 18			£600	

The 8c. is known used bisected at Kretai in December 1918. Such use was not officially authorised.

1917 (June)–**18**. *Surch with T* **3**.

19	**1**	3c. + 2c. carmine-red	50	8·50
		a. Comma after "2c."	10·00	40·00
		b. "SS" in "CROSS" inverted	£425	£500
		c. "CSOSS" for "CROSS"	95·00	£200
		d. "2" in thick block type	22·00	70·00
		e. Surch inverted	£1000	£1100
		f. Pair, one without surch	£4500	£4000
		g. "RED CROSS" omitted	£450	
		h. "RED CROSS" twice	£550	
		i. "2c." omitted	£450	
		j. "2c." twice	£550	
20		4c. + 2c. orange	1·50	15·00
		a. Comma after "2c."	18·00	70·00
		b. "SS" in "CROSS" inverted	£2000	£1600
		c. "CSOSS" for "CROSS"	£170	£400
		d. Surch double	£1300	
		e. "RED CROSS" omitted	£500	
		f. "RED CROSS" twice	£750	
		g. "2c." omitted	£500	
		h. "2c." twice	£700	
21		4c. + 2c. red-brown and green (1918)	3·75	42·00
		a. Pair, one without surch	£3750	
		b. "RED CROSS" omitted	£950	
		c. "RED CROSS" twice	£950	
22		8c. + 2c. ultramarine (1917)	1·25	30·00
		a. Comma after "2c."	11·00	85·00
		b. "SS" in "CROSS" inverted	£1000	£1100
		c. "CSOSS" for "CROSS"	£150	£425
		d. "RED CROSS" omitted	£500	
		e. "RED CROSS" twice	£650	
		f. "2c." omitted	£500	
		g. "2c." twice	£600	

Nos. 19/22 were sold at face, plus 2c. on each stamp for Red Cross funds.

The surcharges on Nos. 19/22 were arranged in settings of 18 (6×3) applied three times to cover the top nine rows of the sheet with the tenth row completed by a further impression so that "RED CROSS" from the centre row of the setting appears on the bottom sheet margin. Specialists recognise six different settings:

Setting I – Shows comma after "2" on both R. 1/3 and 1/5, "SS" inverted on R. 1/6 and "CSOSS" for "CROSS" on R. 2/1. Used for 4c. orange and 8c.

Setting Ia – Inverted "SS" on R. 1/6 corrected. Other varieties as Setting I. Used for 3c., 4c. orange and 8c.

Setting II – "CSOSS" on R. 2/1 corrected. Comma varieties as Setting I. Used for 3c., 4c. orange and 8c.

Setting III – Both comma varieties now corrected. Used for 3c., both 4c. and 8c.

Setting IIIa – "SS" inverted on R. 2/5. Used for 3c. only

Setting IV – Thick block "2" on R. 2/2. Inverted "SS" on R. 2/5 corrected. Used for 3c. only.

Nos. 19g/j, 20e/h and 22d/g result from the misplacement of the surcharge.

> During a temporary shortage between March and August 1921 2c., 4c. and 6c. stamps of the STRAITS SETTLEMENTS were authorised for use in Trengganu.

4 Sultan Suleiman

5 Sultan Suleiman

2 CENTS

(**6**)

1921–41. *Chalk-surfaced paper*. P 14.

(*a*) Wmk Mult Crown CA.

23	**4**	$1 purple and blue/*blue*	12·00	23·00
24		$3 green and red/*emerald*	£120	£250
25	**5**	$5 green and red/*pale yellow*	£120	£350
23/5 *Set of* 3			£225	£600
23s/5s Optd "Specimen" *Set of* 3			£150	

(*b*) Wmk Mult Script CA.

26	**4**	1c. black (1926)	1·75	1·50
		a. Ordinary paper (1941)	—	70·00
27		2c. green	1·50	2·00
		a. Ordinary paper (1941)	—	70·00
28		3c. green (1926)	2·00	1·00
29		3c. reddish brown (1938)	27·00	14·00
		a. Ordinary paper. *Chestnut* (1941)	—	20·00
30		4c. rose-red	2·25	1·25
		a. Ordinary paper. *Scarlet-vermilion* (1941)	£275	32·00
31		5c. grey and deep brown	2·00	5·00
32		5c. purple/*yellow* (1926)	1·75	1·25
		a. Deep reddish purple/brt yellow (1939)	£250	5·00
33		6c. orange (1924)	4·00	50
		a. Ordinary paper (1941)	—	£170
34		8c. grey (1938)	35·00	6·00
		a. Ordinary paper (1941)	—	30·00
35		10c. bright blue	2·00	1·00
36		12c. bright ultramarine (1926)	4·25	3·25
37		20c. dull purple and orange	2·25	1·50
38		25c. green and deep purple	2·25	3·00
39		30c. dull purple and black	3·25	3·75
40		35c. carmine/*yellow* (1926)	4·75	6·00
41		50c. green and bright carmine	9·00	3·25
42		$1 purple and blue/*blue* (1929)	9·00	3·75
43		$3 green and lake/*green* (1926)	55·00	£170
		a. Green and brown-red/green (1938)	£150	
44	**5**	$5 green and red/*yellow* (1938)	£475	£2750
45		$25 purple and blue	£800	£1600
		s. Optd "Specimen"	£180	
46		$50 green and yellow	£1900	£3500
		s. Optd "Specimen"	£400	
47		$100 green and scarlet	£6000	£7000
		s. Optd "Specimen"	£750	
26/43 *Set of* 18			£150	£200
26s/44s Optd or Perf (3c. reddish brown, 8c., $1, $5) "Specimen" *Set of* 19			£800	

The used price quoted for No. 44 is for an example with an identifiable cancellation from 1938–41.

Printings of the 2c. yellow-orange, 3c. blue-green, 4c. purple/*yellow*, 6c. slate-grey, 8c. rose, 15c. ultramarine and $1 black and red/*blue* on ordinary paper were despatched to Malaya in late 1941, but did not arrive before the Japanese occupation. Unused examples are known of the 2, 3, 6, 8 and 15c. (*Prices*, 3c. £750, *others* £250 *each, unused*).

The 12c. bright ultramarine was also printed on ordinary paper, and exists overprinted during the Japanese occupation. See No. J107b.

OVERPRINT SETTINGS FOR NOS. 48/58. The low values in Types **1** and **4** were overprinted using Setting II as detailed under Straits Settlements. The three listed constant varieties from the original typeset block of 12 occur in the same positions for these Trengganu stamps as does the No stop variety from R. 1/5 of the left pane.

A separate setting, believed to be of 30 (6×5), was required for the $5 in the larger design. This was constructed by duplicating the second horizontal row of the original typeset block five times so that the raised stop after "EXHIBITION" variety occurs on all stamps in the second vertical row and the small second "A" in "MALAYA" on all stamps in the sixth.

1922 (Apr). *Malaya-Borneo Exhibition, Singapore. Optd as T* **56** *of Straits Settlements at Singapore.*

48	**4**	2c. green	4·75	27·00
		b. Oval last "O" in "BORNEO"	9·50	48·00
		c. Raised stop after "EXHIBITION"	9·50	48·00
		d. Small second "A" in "MALAYA"	9·50	48·00
		f. No stop		
49		4c. rose-red	6·50	42·00
		b. Oval last "O" in "BORNEO"	13·00	75·00
		c. Raised stop after "EXHIBITION"	13·00	75·00
		d. Small second "A" in "MALAYA"	13·00	75·00
		f. No stop		
50	**1**	5c. grey and brown	3·25	45·00
		b. Oval last "O" in "BORNEO"	7·00	75·00
		c. Raised stop after "EXHIBITION"	7·00	75·00
		d. Small second "A" in "MALAYA"	7·00	75·00
		f. No stop		
51		10c. green and red/*yellow*	5·50	32·00
		b. Oval last "O" in "BORNEO"	11·00	55·00
		c. Raised stop after "EXHIBITION"	11·00	55·00
		d. Small second "A" in "MALAYA"	11·00	55·00
		f. No stop		
52		20c. dull and bright purple	5·50	35·00
		b. Oval last "O" in "BORNEO"	11·00	60·00
		c. Raised stop after "EXHIBITION"	11·00	60·00
		d. Small second "A" in "MALAYA"	11·00	60·00
		f. No stop		
53		25c. green and dull purple	4·75	35·00
		b. Oval last "O" in "BORNEO"	9·50	60·00
		c. Raised stop after "EXHIBITION"	9·50	60·00
		d. Small second "A" in "MALAYA"	9·50	60·00
		f. No stop		
54		30c. dull purple and black	5·50	35·00
		b. Oval last "O" in "BORNEO"	11·00	60·00
		c. Raised stop after "EXHIBITION"	11·00	60·00
		d. Small second "A" in "MALAYA"	11·00	60·00
		f. No stop		
55		50 c. black/*green*	5·50	45·00
		b. Oval last "O" in "BORNEO"	11·00	75·00
		c. Raised stop after "EXHIBITION"	11·00	75·00
		d. Small second "A" in "MALAYA"	11·00	75·00
		f. No stop		
56		$1 black and carmine/*blue*	14·00	70·00
		b. Oval last "O" in "BORNEO"	26·00	£130
		c. Raised stop after "EXHIBITION"	26·00	£130
		d. Small second "A" in "MALAYA"	26·00	£130
		f. No stop		
57		$3 green and red/*green*	£170	£400
		b. Oval last "O" in "BORNEO"	£300	£700
		c. Raised stop after "EXHIBITION"	£300	£700
		d. Small second "A" in "MALAYA"	£300	£700
		f. No stop		
58	**2**	$5 green and dull purple	£275	£650
		c. Raised stop after "EXHIBITION"	£425	£1000
		d. Small second "A" in "MALAYA"	£425	£1000
48/58 *Set of* 11			£450	£1300

1941 (1 May). *Nos. 32a and 35 surch as T* **6**.

59	**4**	2c. on 5c. deep reddish purple/*bright yellow*	6·50	3·50
60		8c. on 10c. bright blue	7·00	4·00

1948 (2 Dec). *Royal Silver Wedding. As Nos. 112/13 of Antigua.*

61	10c. violet	15	1·75
62	$5 carmine	25·00	42·00

1949 (10 Oct). *75th Anniv of U.P.U. As Nos. 114/17 of Antigua.*

63	10c. purple	30	75
64	15c. deep blue	1·90	3·75
65	25c. orange	40	2·50
66	50c. blue-black	1·00	3·50
	a. "C" of "CA" missing from wmk	£800	
63/6 *Set of* 4		3·25	9·50

7 Sultan Ismail

8 Sultan Ismail

1949 (27 Dec)–**55**. Wmk Mult Script CA. *Chalk-surfaced paper.* P 17½×18.

67	**7**	1c. black	65	75
68		2c. orange	65	75
69		3c. green	2·50	3·50
70		4c. brown	30	60
71		5c. bright purple (1.9.52)	30	1·75
72		6c. grey	1·75	60
73		8c. scarlet	60	2·50
74		8c. green (1.9.52)	80	1·75
		a. Deep green (11.8.53)	12·00	13·00
75		10c. purple	30	30
76		12c. scarlet (1.9.52)	80	2·75
77		15c. ultramarine	3·50	30
78		20c. black and green	4·00	3·75
79		20c. bright blue (1.9.52)	80	40
80		25c. purple and orange	2·25	2·00
81		30c. scarlet and purple (4.9.55)	1·25	2·25
82		35c. scarlet and purple (1.9.52)	85	2·25
83		40c. red and purple	7·00	17·00
84		50c. black and blue	2·00	2·25
85		$1 blue and purple	7·00	9·00
86		$2 green and scarlet	29·00	28·00
87		$5 green and brown	50·00	60·00
67/87 *Set of* 21			£100	£130

1953 (2 June). *Coronation. As No. 120 of Antigua.*

88	10c. black and reddish purple	1·75	1·25

1957 (26 June)–**83**. *As Nos. 92/102 of Kedah, but with inset portrait of Sultan Ismail.*

89	1c. black (21.8.57)	10	20
90	2c. orange-red (25.7.57)	1·50	30
	a. *Red-orange* (21.2.61)	26·00	12·00
91	4c. sepia (21.8.57)	10	10
92	5c. carmine-lake (21.8.57)	10	10
93	8c. myrtle-green (21.8.57)	4·00	60
94	10c. deep brown (4.8.57)	1·50	10
94*a*	10c. deep maroon (21.2.61)	5·00	30
95	20c. blue	1·75	1·60
96	50c. black and blue (*p* 12½) (25.7.57)	55	2·50
	a. Perf 12½×13 (17.5.60)	55	1·60
	ab. *Black and ultramarine* (20.3.62)	2·00	1·75
97	$1 ultramarine and reddish purple (25.7.57)	7·50	7·00
98	$2 bronze-green and scarlet (21.8.57)	17·00	7·00
99	$5 brown and bronze-green	19·00	22·00
	a. Perf 13×12½ (13.8.63)	25·00	24·00
89/99 *Set of* 12		50·00	35·00

The 6, 12, 25 and 30c. values used with this issue were Nos. 1/4 of Malayan Federation.

1965 (15 Nov). *As Nos. 166/72 of Johore but with inset portrait of Sultan Ismail Nasiruddin Shah as in T* **8**.

100	1c. multicoloured	10	2·00
101	2c. multicoloured	10	2·00
102	5c. multicoloured	15	70
	w. Wmk inverted		
103	6c. multicoloured	15	2·00
104	10c. multicoloured	20	25
105	15c. multicoloured	1·50	10
106	20c. multicoloured	1·50	1·25
	a. Bright purple (blooms) omitted	£170	
100/6 *Set of* 7		3·25	7·50

The 5c. value exists with PVA gum as well as gum arabic.

No. 101a, formerly listed here, is now listed as Sarawak No. 213a.

The higher values used with this issue were Nos. 20/27 of Malaysia (National Issues).

9 Sultan of Trengganu

(Des Enche Nik Zainal Abidin. Photo Harrison)

1970 (16 Dec). *25th Anniv of Installation of H.R.H. Tuanku Ismail Nasiruddin Shah as Sultan of Trengganu.* P 14½×13½.

107	**9**	10c. multicoloured	1·00	2·25
108		15c. multicoloured	60	1·25
109		50c. multicoloured	1·00	2·75
107/9 *Set of* 3			2·40	5·50

POSTAGE DUE STAMPS

D 1

1937 (10 Aug). Wmk Mult Script CA (sideways). P 14.

D1	**D 1**	1c. scarlet	7·50	55·00
D2		4c. green	9·50	60·00
D3		8c. yellow	55·00	£325
D4		10c. brown	£110	95·00
D1/4 *Set of* 4			£160	£475
D1s/4s Perf "Specimen" *Set of* 4			£150	

VIII. JAPANESE OCCUPATION OF MALAYA

PRICES FOR STAMPS ON COVER

Nos. J1/55	*from* × 10
Nos. J56/76	*from* × 12
Nos. J77/89	*from* × 20
Nos. J90/1	*from* × 15
Nos. J92/115	*from* × 6
Nos. J116/18	—
Nos. J119/32	*from* × 12
Nos. J133/45	*from* × 10
Nos. J146/223	*from* × 6
Nos. J224/58	*from* × 12
No. J259	*from* × 15
Nos. J260/96	*from* × 12
Nos. J297/310	*from* × 20
Nos. J311/17	—
Nos. JD1/10	*from* × 30
Nos. JD11/16	*from* × 12
Nos. JD17/20	*from* × 30
Nos. JD21/7	*from* × 20
Nos. JD28/33	*from* × 30
Nos. JD34/41	*from* × 60

Japanese forces invaded Malaya on 8 December 1941 with the initial landings taking place at Kota Bharu on the east coast. Penang fell, to a force which crossed the border from Thailand, on 19 December, Kuala Lumpur on 11 January 1942 and the conquest of the Malay peninsula was completed by the capture of Singapore on 15 February.

During the Japanese Occupation various small Dutch East Indies islands near Singapore were administered as part of Malaya. Stamps of the Japanese Occupation of Malaya were issued to the post offices of Dabo Singkep, Puloe Samboe, Tanjong Balei, Tanjong Batu, Tanjong Pinang and Terempa between 1942 and 1945. The overprinted issues were also used by a number of districts in Atjeh (Northern Sumatra) whose postal services were administered from Singapore until the end of March 1943.

Malayan post offices were also opened in October 1943 to serve camps of civilians working on railway construction and maintenance in Thailand. Overprinted stamps of the Japanese Occupation of Malaya were used at these offices between October 1943 and the end of the year after which mail from the camps was carried free. Their postmarks were inscribed in Japanese Katakana characters, and, uniquely, showed the Japanese postal symbol.

JOHORE

The postal service in Johore was reconstituted in mid-April 1942 using Nos. J146/60 and subsequently other general issues. Stamps of Johore overprinted "DAI NIPPON 2602" were, however, only used for fiscal purposes. Overprinted Johore postage due stamps were not issued for use elsewhere in Malaya.

POSTAGE DUE STAMPS

(1) (Upright)

(2)

Second character sideways (R. 6/3)

1942 (1 Apr). *Nos. D1/5 of Johore optd as T* **1** *in brown.*

JD1	**D 1**	1c. carmine	50·00	85·00
		a. Black opt	20·00	70·00
JD2		4c. green	80·00	95·00
		a. Black opt	65·00	80·00
JD3		8c. orange	£140	£150
		a. Black opt	80·00	95·00
JD4		10c. brown	50·00	70·00
		a. Black opt	16·00	50·00
JD5		12c. purple	90·00	£100
		a. Black opt	42·00	50·00

1943. *Nos. D1/5 of Johore optd with T* **2**.

JD6	**D 1**	1c. carmine	9·50	29·00
		a. Second character sideways	£325	£650
JD7		4c. green	8·00	32·00
		a. Second character sideways	£375	£650
JD8		8c. orange	9·50	32·00
		a. Second character sideways	£425	£700
JD9		10c. brown	9·00	42·00
		a. Second character sideways	£400	£800
JD10		12c. purple	11·00	60·00
		a. Second character sideways	£475	£900
JD6/10 *Set of* 5			42·00	£180

KEDAH

Postal services resumed by 31 January 1942 using unoverprinted Kedah values from 1c. to 8c. which were accepted for postage until 13 May 1942.

During the Japanese occupation Perlis was administered as part of Kedah.

DAI NIPPON

2602

(3)

DAI NIPPON

2602

(4)

1942 (13 May)–**43**. *Stamps of Kedah* (Script wmk) *optd with T* **3** (1c. to 8c.) *or* **4** (10c. to $5), *both in red.*

J1	**1**	1c. black (No. 68*a*)	6·00	9·00
J2		2c. bright green (No. 69)	27·00	30·00
J3		4c. violet	7·00	4·00
		a. Short sheaf	£190	£150
J4		5c. yellow	5·50	4·75
		a. Black opt (1943)	£200	£225
J5		6c. carmine (No. 56) (Blk.)	4·25	16·00
		a. *Carmine-red* (No. 56a)	50·00	75·00
J6		8c. grey-black	4·25	3·00
J7	**6**	10c. ultramarine and sepia	15·00	16·00
J8		12c. black and violet	32·00	45·00
J9		25c. ultramarine and purple	10·00	17·00
		a. Black opt (1943)	£300	£275
J10		30c. green and scarlet	70·00	80·00
J11		40c. black and purple	35·00	50·00
J12		50c. brown and blue	35·00	50·00
J13		$1 black and green	£140	£150
		a. Opt inverted	£700	£800
J14		$2 green and brown	£170	£170

J15		$5 black and scarlet	65·00	95·00
		a. Black opt (1943)	£1100	£1000
J1/15 *Set of* 15			£550	£650

Nos. J1/15 were gradually replaced by issues intended for use throughout Malaya. Kedah and Perlis were ceded to Thailand by the Japanese on 19 October 1943.

KELANTAN

Postal services resumed on 1 June 1942. Stamps used in Kelantan were overprinted with the personal seals of Sunagawa, the Japanese Governor, and of Handa, the Assistant Governor.

(**5**) Sunagawa Seal

(**6**) Handa Seal

40 CENTS
(**7**)

$1.00
(**8**)

1 Cents
(**9**)

1942 (June). *Stamps of Kelantan surch.*

(a) As T **7** *or* **8** *(dollar values). Optd with T* **5** *in red.*

J16	**4**	1c. on 50c. grey-olive and orange	£275	£180
J17		2c. on 40c. orange and blue-green	£750	£300
J18		4c. on 30c. violet and scarlet	£2000	£1200
J19		5c. on 12c. blue (R.)	£275	£190
J20		6c. on 25c. vermilion and violet	£325	£190
J21		8c. on 5c. red-brown (R.)	£425	£140
J22		10c. on 6c. lake	80·00	£120
		a. "CENST" for "CENTS"	£8000	
J23		12c. on 8c. grey-olive (R.)	55·00	£110
J24		25c. on 10c. purple (R.)	£1400	£1300
J25		30c. on 4c. scarlet	£2000	£2000
J26		40c. on 2c. green (R.)	65·00	85·00
		a. Surch double (B.+R.)	£4000	
J27		50c. on 1c. grey-olive and yellow	£1600	£1300
J28	**1**	$1 on 4c. black and red (R., bars Blk.)	50·00	80·00
J29		$2 on 5c. green and red/*yellow*	50·00	80·00
J30		$5 on 6c. scarlet	50·00	80·00
		a. Surch double	£475	

(b) As T **7**. *Optd with T* **6** *in red.*

J31	**4**	12c. on 8c. grey-olive	£200	£325
		a. Type **6** omitted (in horiz pair with normal)	£4000	

(c) As T **9**. *Optd with T* **5** *in red.*

J32	**4**	1c. on 50c. grey-olive and orange	£190	£100
		a. "Cente" for "Cents" (R. 5/1)	£2500	£1200
J33		2c. on 40c. orange and blue-green	£200	£120
		a. "Cente" for "Cents" (R. 5/1)	£2500	£1300
J34		5c. on 12c. blue (R.)	£170	£150
		a. "Cente" for "Cents" (R. 5/1)	£2000	
J35		8c. on 5c. red-brown (R.)	£130	75·00
		a. "Cente" for "Cents" (R. 5/1)	£1700	£1000
J36		10c. on 6c. lake	£425	£450
		a. "Cente" for "Cents" (R. 5/1)	£3750	

(d) As T **9**. *Optd with T* **6** *in red.*

J41	**4**	1c. on 50c. grey-olive and orange	£130	£170
		a. "Cente" for "Cents" (R. 5/1)	£1600	
J42		2c. on 40c. orange and blue-green	£140	£180
		a. "Cente" for "Cents" (R. 5/1)	£1700	
J43		8c. on 5c. red-brown (R.)	70·00	£130
		a. "Cente" for "Cents" (R. 5/1)	£1300	
J44		10c. on 6c. lake	£100	£170
		a. "Cente" for "Cents" (R. 5/1)	£1500	

As stamps of the above series became exhausted the equivalent values from the series intended for use throughout Malaya were introduced. Stamps as Nos. J28/30, J32/3 and J35/6, but without Type **5** or **6**, are from remainders sent to Singapore or Kuala Lumpur after the state had been ceded to Thailand (*Price from* £16 *each unused*). Nos. J19, J21, J23 and J25/6 have also been seen without Type **5** (*Price from* £80 *each unused*).

The 12c. on 8c., 30c. on 4c., 40c. on 2c. and 50c. on 1c. surcharged with Type **9**, formerly listed as Nos. J37/40, are now believed to exist only as remainders without the Type **5** red handstamp (*Price from* £20 *each, unused*).

Kelantan was ceded to Thailand by the Japanese on 19 October 1943.

MALACCA

Postal services from Malacca resumed on 21 April 1942, but there were no stamps available for two days.

PRICES. Those quoted are for single stamps. Blocks of four showing complete handstamp are worth from five times the price of a single stamp.

(**10**) "Military Administration Malacca State Government Seal"

1942 (23 Apr). *Stamps of Straits Settlements handstamped as T* **10**, *in red, each impression covering four stamps.*

J45	**58**	1c. black	£110	85·00
J46		2c. orange	65·00	70·00
J47		3c. green	70·00	80·00
J48		5c. brown	£160	£160
J49		8c. grey	£250	£130
J50		10c. dull purple	£100	£110
J51		12c. ultramarine	£110	£120
J52		15c. ultramarine	80·00	95·00
J53		40c. scarlet and dull purple	£600	£650
J54		50c. black/*emerald*	£950	£950
J55		$1 black and red/*blue*	£1100	£1000

The 30c., $2 and $5 also exist with this overprint, but these values were not available to the public. (*Price for set of* 3 £11000 *unused*).

POSTAGE DUE STAMPS

1942 (23 Apr). *Postage Due stamps of Malayan Postal Union handstamped as T* **10**, *in red, each impression covering four stamps.*

JD11	**D 1**	1c. slate-purple	£225	£180
JD12		4c. green	£225	£225
JD13		8c. scarlet	£3000	£1900
JD14		10c. yellow-orange	£475	£450
JD15		12c. ultramarine	£700	£650
JD16		50c. black	£2750	£1700

Nos. J45/55 and JD11/16 were replaced during May 1942 by the overprinted issues intended for use throughout Malaya.

PENANG

Postal services on Penang Island resumed on 30 March 1942 using Straits Settlements stamps overprinted by Japanese seals of the Government Accountant, Mr. A. Okugawa, and his assistant, Mr. Itchiburi.

(**11**) Okugawa Seal

(**12**) Itchiburi Seal

DAI NIPPON
2602
PENANG
(**13**)

1942 (30 Mar). *Straits Settlements stamps optd.*

(a) As T **11** *(three forms of the seal).*

J56	**58**	1c. black	9·50	12·00
J57		2c. orange	24·00	23·00
		a. Pair, one without handstamp	£1400	
J58		3c. green	20·00	23·00
J59		5c. brown	24·00	27·00
J60		8c. grey	26·00	38·00
J61		10c. dull purple	50·00	50·00
J62		12c. ultramarine	40·00	50·00
J63		15c. ultramarine	50·00	50·00
J64		40c. scarlet and dull purple	95·00	£110
J65		50c. black/*emerald*	£225	£225
J66		$1 black and red/*blue*	£250	£275
J67		$2 green and scarlet	£850	£700
J68		$5 green and red/*emerald*	£2500	£1500

(b) With T **12**.

J69	**58**	1c. black	£160	£130
J70		2c. orange	£160	£110
J71		3c. green	£100	£100
J72		5c. brown	£2500	£2500
J73		8c. grey	90·00	95·00
J74		10c. dull purple	£160	£170
J75		12c. ultramarine	£100	£120
J76		15c. ultramarine	£120	£130

Straits Settlements 1, 2, 3, 4 and 5c. values exist with a similar but circular seal containing four characters, but these were not available to the public.

1942 (15 Apr). *Straits Settlements stamps optd with T* **13** *by Penang Premier Press.*

J77	**58**	1c. black (R.)	6·00	3·00
		a. Opt inverted	£500	£500
		b. Opt double	£300	£300
J78		2c. orange	5·00	4·00
		a. "PE" for "PENANG"	£110	85·00
		b. Opt inverted	£160	
		c. Opt double	£500	
J79		3c. green (R.)	5·00	5·00
		a. Opt double, one inverted	£400	
J80		5c. brown (R.)	3·00	8·00
		a. "N PPON"	£190	
		b. Opt double	£500	£425
J81		8c. grey (R.)	2·25	1·40
		a. "N PPON"	55·00	60·00
		b. Opt double, one inverted	£475	
J82		10c. dull purple (R.)	1·50	2·25
		a. Opt double	£450	£450
		b. Opt double, one inverted	£400	£400
J83		12c. ultramarine (R.)	4·00	17·00
		a. "N PPON"	£550	
		b. Opt double	£400	
		c. Opt double, one inverted	£600	£600
J84		15c. ultramarine (R.)	1·75	3·75
		a. "N PPON"	£100	£110
		b. Opt inverted	£400	£400
		c. Opt double	£550	£550
J85		40c. scarlet and dull purple	5·00	17·00
J86		50c. black/*emerald* (R.)	3·75	29·00
J87		$1 black and red/*blue*	6·00	40·00
		a. Opt inverted	£1100	
J88		$2 green and scarlet	60·00	90·00
J89		$5 green and red/*emerald*	£600	£650
J77/89 *Set of* 13			£650	£800

Nos. J77/89 were replaced by the overprinted issues intended for use throughout Malaya.

SELANGOR

Postal services resumed in the Kuala Lumpur area on 3 April 1942 and gradually extended to the remainder of the state. Stamps of the general overprinted issue were used, but the following commemorative set was only available in Selangor.

SELANGOR
EXHIBITION
DAI NIPPON
2602
MALAYA
(**14**)

1942 (3 Nov). *Selangor Agri-horticultural Exhibition. Nos.* 294 *and* 283 *of Straits Settlements optd with T* **14**.

J90	**58**	2c. orange	12·00	24·00
		a. "C" for "G" in "SELANGOR" (R. 1/9)	£400	£450
		b. Opt inverted	£300	£400
J91		8c. grey	13·00	24·00
		a. "C" for "G" in "SELANGOR" (R. 1/9)	£400	£450
		b. Opt inverted	£300	£400

SINGAPORE

The first post offices re-opened in Singapore on 16 March 1942.

(**15**) "Malaya Military Government Division Postal Services Bureau Seal"

(Handstamped at Singapore)

1942 (16 Mar). *Stamps of Straits Settlements optd with T* **15** *in red.*

J92	**58**	1c. black	15·00	18·00
J93		2c. orange	13·00	13·00
		a. Pair, one without handstamp	£2000	
J94		3c. green	50·00	70·00
J95		8c. grey	24·00	18·00
J96		15c. ultramarine	17·00	15·00
J92/6 *Set of* 5			£110	£120

The overprint Type **15** has a double-lined frame, although the two lines are not always apparent, as in the illustration. Three chops were used, differing slightly in the shape of the characters, but forgeries also exist. It is distinguishable from Type **1**, used for the general issues, by its extra width, measuring approximately 14 mm against 12½ mm.

The 6, 10, 30, 40, 50c., $2 and $5 also exist with this overprint, but were not sold to the public.

Nos. J92/6 were replaced on the 3 May 1942 by the stamps overprinted with Type **1** which were intended for use throughout Malaya.

TRENGGANU

Postal services resumed in Trengganu on 5 March 1942 using unoverprinted stamps up to the 35c. value. These remained in use until September 1942.

1942 (Sept). *Stamps of Trengganu* (Script wmk) *optd as T* **1** *at Kuala Lumpur.*

J97	**4**	1c. black (No. 26a)	90·00	90·00
		a. Chalk-surfaced paper (No. 26)	–	£170
		b. Red opt	£225	£225
		c. Brown opt (chalk-surfaced paper)	£475	£275
J98		2c. green (No. 27a)	£140	£140
		a. Chalk-surfaced paper (No. 27)	–	£275
		b. Red opt	£275	£300
		c. Brown opt	£500	£325
J99		2c. on 5c. deep reddish purple/*bright yellow* (No. 59)	40·00	40·00
		a. Red opt	60·00	75·00
J100		3c. chestnut (No. 29a)	95·00	85·00
		a. Brown opt	£750	£450
J101		4c. scarlet-vermilion (No. 30a)	£180	£140
J102		5c. dp reddish purple/*bright yellow* (No. 32*a*)	10·00	19·00
		a. Purple/yellow (No. 32)	£140	£150
		b. Red opt	28·00	
J103		6c. orange (No. 33a)	9·50	25·00
		a. Red opt	£250	
		b. Brown opt	£750	£750
J104		8c. grey (No. 34a)	9·00	13·00
		a. Chalk-surfaced paper (No. 34)	£170	
		b. Brown to red opt	55·00	70·00
J105		8c. on 10c. bright blue (No. 60)	13·00	50·00
		a. Red opt	21·00	
J106		10c. bright blue	27·00	48·00
		a. Red opt	£250	
		b. Brown opt	£800	£800
J107		12c. bright ultramarine (No. 36)	8·00	48·00
		a. Red opt	28·00	60·00
		b. Ordinary paper	30·00	
J108		20c. dull purple and orange	8·50	42·00
		a. Red opt	22·00	
J109		25c. green and deep purple	7·50	50·00
		a. Red opt	23·00	
		b. Brown opt	£850	£850
J110		30c. dull purple and black	11·00	42·00
		a. Red opt	35·00	55·00
J111		35c. carmine/*yellow*	28·00	50·00
		a. Red opt	32·00	
J112		50c. green and bright carmine	85·00	£100
J113		$1 purple and blue/*blue*	£4250	£4250
J114		$3 green and brown-red/*green* (No. 43*a*)	70·00	£120
		a. Green and lake/green (No. 43)	£250	
		b. Red opt	70·00	

J115 5 $5 green and red/*yellow* £190 £250
J116 $25 purple and blue £1500
a. Red opt £5500
J117 $50 green and yellow £13000
J118 $100 green and scarlet £1600

DAI NIPPON
2602
MALAYA
(**16**)

1942 (Sept). *Stamps of Trengganu* (Script wmk) *optd with T* **16**.
J119 4 1c. black (No. 26a) 15·00 12·00
J120 2c. green (No. 27a) £250 £225
J121 2c. on 5c. deep reddish purple/*bright yellow* (No. 59) 6·00 8·00
J122 3c. chestnut (No. 29a) 14·00 26·00
J123 4c. scarlet-vermilion (No. 30a) 14·00 11·00
J124 5c. dp reddish purple/*bright yellow* (No. 32*a*) 5·50 13·00
J125 6c. orange (No. 33a) 6·00 13·00
J126 8c. grey (No. 34a) 80·00 27·00
J127 8c. on 10c. bright blue (No. 60) 6·00 10·00
J128 12c. bright ultramarine (No. 36) 5·50 30·00
J129 20c. dull purple and orange 17·00 17·00
J130 25c. green and deep purple 7·50 42·00
J131 30c. dull purple and black 8·00 38·00
J132 $3 green and brown-red/*green* (No. 43*a*) 85·00 £160
J119/32 *Set of* 14 £450 £550

1943. *Stamps of Trengganu* (Script wmk) *optd with T* **2**.
J133 4 1c. black (No. 26a) 17·00 19·00
a. Chalk-surfaced paper 45·00
J134 2c. green (No. 27a) 15·00 35·00
J135 2c. on 5c. bright reddish purple/*bright yellow* (No. 59) 9·50 23·00
J136 5c. bright reddish purple/*bright yellow* (No. 32*a*) 13·00 35·00
J137 6c. orange (No. 33a) 14·00 40·00
J138 8c. grey (No. 34a) 65·00 £110
J139 8c. on 10c. bright blue (No. 60) 27·00 55·00
J140 10c. bright blue 95·00 £250
J141 12c. bright ultramarine (No. 36) 17·00 50·00
J142 20c. dull purple and orange 22·00 50·00
J143 25c. green and deep purple 19·00 55·00
J144 30c. dull purple and black 23·00 55·00
J145 35c. carmine/*yellow* 23·00 75·00
J133/45 *Set of* 13 £325 £750

POSTAGE DUE STAMPS

1942 (Sept). *Nos. D1/4 of Trengganu optd with T* **1** *sideways*.
JD17 D 1 1c. scarlet 50·00 85·00
JD18 4c. green 90·00 £130
a. Brown opt 50·00 90·00
JD19 8c. yellow 14·00 50·00
JD20 10c. brown 14·00 50·00

The Trengganu 8c. postage due also exists overprinted with Type **16**, but this was not issued (*Price* £600 *unused*).

Trengganu was ceded to Thailand by the Japanese on 19 October 1943.

GENERAL ISSUES

The following stamps were produced for use throughout Malaya, except for Trengganu.

1942 (3 Apr). *Stamps optd as T* **1**.

(a) On Straits Settlements.
J146 58 1c. black (R.) 3·25 3·25
a. Black opt £400 £400
b. Violet opt £1100 £700
J147 2c. green (V.) £3000 £2000
J148 2c. orange (R.) 3·00 2·25
a. Black opt £130 £140
b. Violet opt £250 £225
c. Brown opt £900 £650
J149 3c. green (R.) 2·75 2·25
a. Black opt £400 £400
b. Violet opt £1100 £750
J150 5c. brown (R.) 24·00 28·00
a. Black opt £550 £550
J151 8c. grey (R.) 4·75 2·25
a. Pair, one without handstamp † £2250
b. Black opt £275 £275
J152 10c. dull purple (R.) 55·00 45·00
a. Brown opt £1000 £750
J153 12c. ultramarine (R.) 80·00 £130
J154 15c. ultramarine (R.) 3·50 3·75
a. Violet opt £750 £550
J155 30c. dull purple and orange (R.) £3000 £3000
J156 40c. scarlet and dull purple (R.) £110 95·00
a. Brown opt £800 £400
J157 50c. black/*emerald* (R.) 60·00 48·00
J158 $1 black and red/*blue* (R.) 85·00 75·00
J159 $2 green and scarlet (R.) £150 £180
J160 $5 green and red/*emerald* (R.) £180 £200

The 2c. green is known with the overprint in red, but this was not available to the public (*Price*, £350 *unused*).

(b) On Negri Sembilan.
J161 6 1c. black (R.) 19·00 13·00
a. Violet opt 22·00 20·00
b. Brown opt 13·00 17·00
c. Black opt 55·00 38·00
d. Pair. Nos. J161/a £275
e. Pair. Nos. J161 and J161b £350
J162 2c. orange (R.) 28·00 20·00
a. Violet opt 50·00 27·00
b. Black opt 38·00 28·00
c. Brown opt 65·00 55·00
J163 3c. green (R.) 40·00 20·00
a. Violet opt 24·00 29·00
c. Brown opt £170 60·00
d. Black opt 65·00 50·00
J164 5c. brown 40·00 21·00
a. Pair, one without opt £1900
b. Brown opt 17·00 15·00
c. Red opt 16·00 11·00
d. Violet opt 55·00 40·00
e. Pair. Nos. J164c/d £375
J165 6c. grey £150 £120
a. Brown opt £325 £325
J166 8c. scarlet £150 £130
J167 10c. dull purple £250 £225
a. Red opt £450 £325
b. Brown opt £600 £425
J168 12c. bright ultramarine (Br.) £1800 £1800
J169 15c. ultramarine (R.) 24·00 8·00
a. Violet opt £100 30·00
b. Brown opt 29·00 12·00
J170 25c. dull purple and scarlet 28·00 38·00
a. Red opt 65·00 80·00
b. Brown opt £550 £425
J171 30c. dull purple and orange £250 £200
a. Brown opt £1400 £1100
J172 40c. scarlet and dull purple £1500 £1100
a. Brown opt £1200 £1000
J173 50c. black/*emerald* £1300 £1300
J174 $1 black and red/*blue* £225 £250
a. Red opt £180 £200
b. Brown opt £425 £425
J175 $5 green and red/*emerald* £600 £700
a. Red opt £1200 £1200

Nos. J161a and J163a exist with the handstamped overprint sideways.

(c) On Pahang.
J176 15 1c. black 55·00 48·00
a. Red opt 55·00 50·00
b. Violet opt £375 £275
c. Brown opt £300 £225
J177 3c. green £450 £325
a. Red opt £225 £275
b. Violet opt £650 £475
J178 5c. brown 15·00 12·00
a. Red opt £225 £110
b. Brown opt £300 £110
c. Violet opt £500 £275
d. Pair. Nos. J178/b £850
J179 8c. grey £1100 £850
J180 8c. scarlet 21·00 8·00
a. Red opt £110 50·00
b. Violet opt £100 55·00
c. Brown opt £110 65·00
d. Pair. Nos. J180a/c £450
J181 10c. dull purple £375 £150
a. Red opt £325 £225
b. Brown opt £400 £250
J182 12c. bright ultramarine £2000 £2000
a. Red opt £1200 £1200
J183 15c. ultramarine £150 £110
a. Red opt £425 £250
b. Violet opt £750 £500
c. Brown opt £550 £325
J184 25c. dull purple and scarlet 21·00 29·00
J185 30c. dull purple and orange 13·00 28·00
a. Red opt £140 £170
J186 40c. scarlet and dull purple 22·00 35·00
a. Brown opt £475 £325
b. Red opt 85·00 90·00
J187 50c. black/*emerald* £1300 £1300
a. Red opt £1400 £1400
J188 $1 black and red/*blue* (R.) £150 £160
a. Black opt £300 £300
b. Brown opt £700 £700
J189 $5 green and red/*emerald* £700 £850
a. Red opt £1000 £1100

(d) On Perak.
J190 51 1c. black 60·00 38·00
a. Violet opt £275 £110
b. Brown opt 80·00 80·00
J191 2c. orange 30·00 20·00
a. Violet opt 70·00 70·00
b. Red opt 60·00 40·00
c. Brown opt 55·00 55·00
J192 3c. green 27·00 28·00
a. Violet opt £500 £325
b. Brown opt £180 £150
c. Red opt £350 £250
J193 5c. brown 8·00 6·00
a. Pair, one without opt £1200
b. Brown opt 42·00 30·00
c. Violet opt £300 £200
d. Red opt £225 £200
J194 8c. grey 80·00 48·00
a. Red opt £450 £225
b. Brown opt £400 £250
J195 8c. scarlet 42·00 42·00
a. Violet opt £550 £300
J196 10c. dull purple 26·00 24·00
a. Red opt £375 £225
J197 12c. bright ultramarine £250 £225
J198 15c. ultramarine 24·00 32·00
a. Red opt £250 £200
b. Violet opt £500 £325
c. Brown opt £400 £275
J199 25c. dull purple and scarlet 14·00 26·00
a. Red opt £300
J200 30c. dull purple and orange 17·00 32·00
a. Pair, one without opt £1900
b. Brown opt £750 £450
c. Red opt 38·00 55·00
ca. Pair, one without opt £2500
J201 40c. scarlet and dull purple £550 £375
a. Brown opt £550 £450
J202 50c. black/*emerald* 42·00 50·00
a. Red opt 55·00 60·00
b. Brown opt £475 £350
J203 $1 black and red/*blue* £475 £400
a. Brown opt £450 £375
J204 $2 green and scarlet £4000 £4000
J205 $5 green and red/*emerald* £500
a. Brown opt £1900

(e) On Selangor.
J206 46 1c. black, S 12·00 26·00
a. Red opt, SU 45·00 38·00
b. Violet opt, SU 48·00 45·00
J207 2c. green, SU £1800 £1300
a. Violet opt, SU £2250 £1300
J208 2c. orange (P 14×14½), S 95·00 60·00
a. Red opt, U £200 £170
b. Violet opt, U £225 £160
c. Brown opt, S 85·00 80·00
J209 2c. orange (P 14), S £120 80·00
a. Red opt, U £225 £170
b. Violet opt, U £400 £170
c. Brown opt, S — £170
J210 3c. green, SU 23·00 15·00
a. Red opt, SU 19·00 15·00
b. Violet opt, SU 70·00 50·00
c. Brown opt, SU 18·00 15·00
J211 5c. brown, SU 6·00 5·50
a. Red opt, SU 14·00 16·00
b. Violet opt, SU 21·00 22·00
c. Brown opt, SU 60·00 50·00
J212 6c. scarlet, SU £425 £425
a. Red opt, S £200 £250
b. Brown opt, S £950 £950
J213 8c. grey, S 20·00 17·00
a. Red opt, SU 60·00 40·00
b. Violet opt, U 38·00 35·00
c. Brown opt, S £180 75·00
J214 10c. dull purple, S 14·00 21·00
a. Red opt, S 80·00 60·00
b. Brown opt, S £170 90·00
J215 12c. bright ultramarine, S 65·00 75·00
a. Red opt, S £120 £130
b. Brown opt, S £130 £120
J216 15c. ultramarine, S 16·00 22·00
a. Red opt, SU 60·00 60·00
b. Violet opt, U £160 95·00
c. Brown opt, S £110 65·00
J217 25c. dull purple and scarlet, S 85·00 £110
a. Red opt, S 65·00 85·00
J218 30c. dull purple and orange, S 11·00 24·00
a. Brown opt, S £475 £275
J219 40c. scarlet and dull purple, S £150 £150
a. Brown opt, S £400 £200
b. Red opt, S £325
J220 50c. black/*emerald*, S £150 £160
a. Red opt, S £160 £170
b. Brown opt, S £600 £425
J221 48 $1 black and red/*blue* 32·00 45·00
a. Red opt £120 £150
J222 $2 green and scarlet 35·00 60·00
a. Pair, one without opt £1900
b. Red opt £800 £850
J223 $5 green and red/*emerald* 70·00 90·00

On *T* **46** the overprint is normally sideways (with "top" to either right or left), but on *T* **48** it is always upright.

S = Sideways.
U = Upright.
SU = Sideways or upright (our prices being for the cheaper).

Specialists recognise nine slightly different chops as Type **1**. Initial supplies with the overprint in red were produced at Singapore. Later overprintings took place at Kuala Lumpur in violet, red or brown and finally, black. No. J155 was from the Kuala Lumpur printing only. Except where noted, these overprints were usedwidely in Malaya and, in some instances, Sumatra.

The following stamps also exist with this overprint, but were not available to the public:
Straits Settlements (in red) 6, 25c.
Kelantan (in black) 10c.
Negri Sembilan 2c. green (Blk. or Brn.), 4c. (Blk.), 6c. scarlet (Blk.), 8c. grey (Blk.), 12c. (Blk.), $2 (Blk. or Brn.).
Pahang (in black, 2c. also in brown) 2, 4, 6c., $2.
Perak 2c. green (R.), 6c. (Blk.).
Selangor 4c. (Blk.).

1942 (May). *Optd with T* **16**.

(a) On Straits Settlements.
J224 58 2c. orange 2·50 60
a. Opt inverted 14·00 23·00
b. Opt double, one inverted 55·00 65·00
J225 3c. green 50·00 65·00
J226 8c. grey 7·50 3·50
a. Opt inverted 20·00 35·00
J227 15c. blue 18·00 11·00
J224/7 *Set of* 4 70·00 70·00

(b) On Negri Sembilan.
J228 6 1c. black 2·50 60
a. Opt inverted 9·00 25·00
b. Opt double, one inverted 35·00 50·00
J229 2c. orange 8·50 50
J230 3c. green 6·50 50
J231 5c. brown 1·75 3·50
J232 6c. grey 4·00 2·75
a. Opt inverted † £1600
b. Stop omitted at right (R. 10/4) £120 £130
J233 8c. scarlet 8·00 1·25
J234 10c. dull purple 3·25 2·50
J235 15c. ultramarine 18·00 2·50
J236 25c. dull purple and scarlet 6·50 18·00
J237 30c. dull purple and orange 8·50 3·00
J238 $1 black and red/*blue* 80·00 95·00
J228/38 *Set of* 11 £130 £110

(c) On Pahang.
J239 15 1c. black 3·25 3·75
a. Opt omitted (in pair with normal) £550
J240 5c. brown 1·25 70
J241 8c. scarlet 27·00 2·75
a. Opt omitted (in pair with normal) £1500
J242 10c. dull purple 12·00 8·00
J243 12c. bright ultramarine 3·50 17·00
J244 25c. dull purple and scarlet 6·00 24·00
J245 30c. dull purple and orange 3·50 12·00
J239/45 *Set of* 7 50·00 60·00

(d) On Perak.
J246 51 2c. orange 4·00 3·00
a. Opt inverted 50·00 50·00
J247 3c. green 1·25 1·50
a. Opt inverted 17·00 27·00
b. Opt omitted (in pair with normal) £550
J248 8c. scarlet 70 50
a. Opt inverted 4·50 7·00
b. Opt double, one inverted £225 £250

		c. Opt omitted (in horiz pair with normal)	£400	
J249		10c. dull purple	17·00	7·50
J250		15c. ultramarine	8·50	2·00
J251		50c. black/*emerald*	3·75	5·50
J252		$1 black and red/*blue*	£500	£550
J253		$5 green and red/*emerald*	48·00	75·00
		a. Opt inverted	£300	£375
J246/53 *Set of* 8			£550	£600

(e) On Selangor.

J254	**46**	3c. green	2·00	4·00
J255		12c. bright ultramarine	1·25	16·00
J256		15c. ultramarine	8·00	1·50
J257		40c. scarlet and dull purple	2·00	5·50
J258	**48**	$2 green and scarlet	10·00	45·00
J254/8 *Set of* 5			21·00	65·00

On *T* **46** the overprint is sideways, with "top" to left or right.

The following stamps also exist with this overprint, but were not available to the public.

Perak 1, 5, 30c. (*Price for set of* 3 *£400 unused*).

Selangor 1, 5, 10, 30c., $1, $5 (*Price for set of* 6 *£750 unused*).

(17)

(18) "Japanese Postal Service"

1942 (Nov). *No. 108 of Perak surch with T* **17**.

J259	**51**	2c. on 5c. brown	1·50	3·75
		a. Inverted "s" in "Cents" (R. 3/5)	60·00	85·00

1942 (Nov). *Perak stamps surch or opt only, as in T* **18**.

J260	**51**	1c. black	6·50	11·00
		a. Opt inverted	19·00	40·00
J261		2c. on 5c. brown	2·00	6·50
		a. "DAI NIPPON YUBIN" inverted	17·00	38·00
		b. Ditto and "2 Cents" omitted	45·00	65·00
		c. Inverted "s" in "Cents" (R. 3/5)	65·00	£120
J262		8c. scarlet	6·50	2·50
		a. Opt inverted	12·00	24·00
J260/2 *Set of* 3			13·50	18·00

A similar overprint exists on the Selangor 3c. but this was not available to the public (*Price £350 unused*).

On 8 December 1942 contemporary Japanese 3, 5, 8 and 25s. stamps were issued without overprint in Malaya and the 1, 2, 4, 6, 7, 10, 30 and 50s. and 1y. values followed on 15 February 1943.

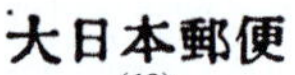

(19)

(20)

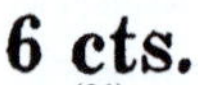

(21)

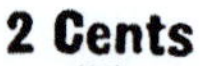

(22)

(23)

(24)

1942 (4 Dec)–**44**. *Stamps of various Malayan territories optd "Japanese Postal Service" in Kanji characters as T* **2** *or* **19**, *some additionally surch as T* **20** *to* **24**.

(a) Stamps of Straits Settlements optd with T **2**.

J263	**58**	8c. grey (Blk.) (1943)	1·40	50
		a. Opt inverted	55·00	70·00
		b. Opt omitted (in pair with normal)	£850	
		c. Red opt	2·50	3·50
J264		12c. ultramarine (1943)	1·50	12·00
J265		40c. scarlet and dull purple (1943)	3·00	5·50
J263/5 *Set of* 3			5·50	16·00

(b) Stamps of Negri Sembilan optd with T **2** *or surch also.*

J266	**6**	1c. black	50	3·00
		a. Opt inverted	11·00	27·00
		b. Sideways second character	32·00	35·00
		ba. Opt inverted with sideways second character	£750	
J267		2c. on 5c. brown (surch as *T* **20**)	80	1·75
J268		6c. on 5c. brown (surch *T* **21**) (1943)	40	2·00
		a. Opt Type **2** and surch as Type **21** both inverted	£225	£225
J269		25c. dull purple and scarlet (1943)	1·10	17·00
J266/9 *Set of* 4			2·50	21·00

(c) Stamp of Pahang optd with T **2** *and surch also.*

J270	**15**	6c. on 5c. brown (surch *T* **20**) (1943)	50	75
J271		6c. on 5c. brown (surch *T* **21**) (1943)	1·00	1·75

(d) Stamps of Perak optd with T **2** *or surch also.*

J272	**51**	1c. black	1·00	70
		a. Sideways second character	£225	£250
J273		2c. on 5c. brown (surch as *T* **20**)	75	50
		a. Opt Type **2** and surch Type **20** both inverted	18·00	32·00
		b. Opt Type **2** inverted	18·00	32·00
		c. Sideways second character	50·00	50·00
J274		2c. on 5c. brown (surch T **22**)	60	50
		a. Surch Type **22** inverted	18·00	32·00
		b. Opt Type **2** and surch Type **22** both inverted	25·00	35·00
		c. Sideways second character	25·00	32·00
		ca. Surch Type **22** inverted	£1400	
		cb. Opt Type **2** with sideways second character and surch Type **22** both inverted	£1400	
J275		5c. brown	55	65
		a. Opt inverted	40·00	45·00
		b. Sideways second character	£550	£400
J276		8c. scarlet	65	2·50
		a. Opt inverted	16·00	28·00
		b. Sideways second character	50·00	70·00
		ba. Opt inverted with sideways second character	£750	
		c. Opt omitted (in pair with normal)	£1200	
J277		10c. dull purple (1943)	60	50
J278		30c. dull purple and orange (1943)	5·00	7·50
J279		50c. black/*emerald* (1943)	4·00	22·00
J280		$5 green and red/emerald (1943)	70·00	£120
J272/80 *Set of* 9			75·00	£140

(e) Stamps of Selangor optd with T **2** *(sideways on T* **46**).

J281	**46**	1c. black (1943)	1·00	3·25
J282		3c. green	40	45
		a. Sideways second character	17·00	26·00
J283		12c. bright ultramarine	45	1·60
		a. Sideways second character	65·00	80·00
J284		15c. ultramarine	4·00	3·25
		a. Sideways second character	50·00	55·00
J285	**48**	$1 black and red/*blue*	3·00	23·00
		a. Opt inverted	£225	£225
		b. Sideways second character	£375	£400
J286		$2 green and scarlet (1943)	10·00	48·00
J287		$5 green and red/*emerald* (1943)	22·00	80·00
		a. Opt inverted	£250	£300
J281/7 *Set of* 7			35·00	£140

(f) Stamps of Selangor optd with T **19** *or surch also.*

J288	**46**	1c. black (R.) (1943)	35	50
J289		2c. on 5c. brown (surch as *T* **21**) (R.) (1943)	1·50	50
J290		3c. on 5c. brown (surch as *T* **21**) (1943)	30	4·75
		a. "s" in "cts." inverted (R. 4/3)	30·00	70·00
		b. Comma after "cts" (R. 9/3)	30·00	70·00
J291		5c. brown (R.) (1944)	2·00	5·00
J292		6c. on 5c. brown (surch *T* **21**) (1944)	1·00	1·75
J293		6c. on 5c. brown (surch *T* **23**) (1944)	40	70
		a. "6" inverted (R. 7/8)	£900	
		b. Full stop between "6" and "cts" (R. 8/6)		
		c. Surch and opt double	£500	
J294		15c. ultramarine	4·00	4·00
J295		$1 on 10c. dull purple (surch *T* **24**) (18.12.1944)	40	1·25
J296		$1.50 on 30c. dull purple and orange (surch *T* **24**) (18.12.1944)	40	1·25
J288/96 *Set of* 9			9·50	18·00

The error showing the second character in Type **2** sideways occurred on R. 6/3 in the first of four settings only.

The 2c. orange, 3c. and 8c. grey of Perak also exist overprinted with Type **2**, but these stamps were not available to the public (*Price for set of* 3 *£100 unused*).

Examples of No. J275 are known postally used from the Shan States (part of pre-war Burma).

25 Tapping Rubber

26 Fruit

27 Tin dredger

28 War Memorial, Bukit Bartok, Singapore

29 Fishing village

30 Japanese shrine, Singapore

31 Sago Palms

32 Straits of Johore

33 Malay Mosque, Kuala

(Litho Kolff & Co, Batavia)

1943 (29 Apr–1 Oct). P 12½.

J297	**25**	1c. grey-green (1 Oct)	1·75	55
J298	**26**	2c. pale emerald (1 June)	1·00	20
J299	**25**	3c. drab (1 Oct)	70	20
J300	**27**	4c. carmine-rose	2·75	20
J301	**28**	8c. dull blue	50	20
J302	**29**	10c. brown-purple (1 Oct)	80	20
J303	**30**	15c. violet (1 Oct)	1·25	4·50
J304	**31**	30c. olive-green (1 Oct)	1·50	35
J305	**32**	50c. blue (1 Oct)	4·50	4·50
J306	**33**	70c. blue (1 Oct)	20·00	13·00
J297/306 *Set of* 10			32·00	22·00

The 2c. and 4c. values exist, printed by typography, in paler shades either imperforate or rouletted. It is suggested that these may have been available in Singapore at the very end of the Japanese Occupation.

34 Ploughman

35 Rice-Planting

1943 (1 Sept). *Savings Campaign. Litho.* P 12½.

J307	**34**	8c. violet	9·50	2·75
J308		15c. scarlet	6·50	2·75

(Des Hon Chin. Litho)

1944 (15 Feb). *"Re-birth" of Malaya.* P 12½.

J309	**35**	8c. rose-red	16·00	3·25
J310		15c. magenta	4·00	3·25

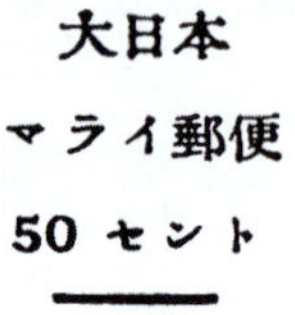

(36)

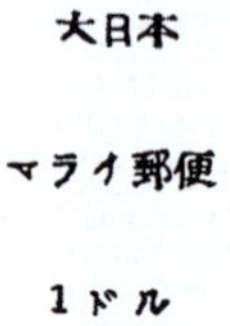

(37)

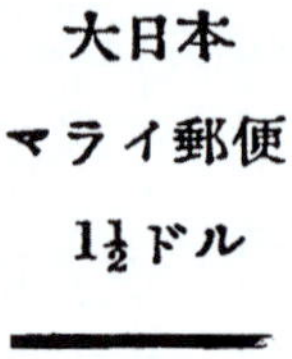

(38)

1944 (16 Dec). *Stamps intended for use on Red Cross letters. Surch with T* **36/8** *in red.*

(a) On Straits Settlements.

J311	**58**	50c. on 50c. black/*emerald*	10·00	24·00
J312		$1 on $1 black and red/*blue*	22·00	35·00
J313		$1.50 on $2 green and scarlet	32·00	70·00

(b) On Johore.

J314	**29**	50c. on 50c. dull purple and red	7·00	20·00
J315		$1.50 on $2 green and carmine	4·00	12·00

(c) On Selangor.

J316	**48**	$1 on $1 black and red/*blue*	3·50	14·00
J317		$1.50 on $2 green and scarlet	5·00	20·00
J311/17 *Set of* 7			75·00	£180

Nos. J311/17 were issued in Singapore but were withdrawn after one day, probably because supplies of Nos. J295/6 were received and issued on the 18 December.

A similar 6c. surcharge exists on the Straits Settlements 5c. but this was not available to the public (*Price £500 unused*).

STAMP BOOKLETS

1942. *Nos. SB3/4 of Perak and SB2 of Selangor with covers optd with T* **1**.

SB1	$1 booklet containing twenty 5c. (No. J193) in blocks of 10	£2750
SB2	$1.30 booklet containing 5c. and 8c. (Nos. J193/4), each in block of 10	£2750
SB3	$1.30 booklet containing 5c. and 8c. (Nos. J211 and J213), each in block of 10	£2750

POSTAGE DUE STAMPS

Postage Due stamps of the Malayan Postal Union overprinted.

1942 (3 Apr). *Handstamped as T* **1** *in black.*

JD21	D **1**	1c. slate-purple	12·00	28·00
		a. Red opt	£160	£160
		b. Brown opt	£140	£150
JD22		3c. green	70·00	75·00
		a. Red opt	£300	£325
JD23		4c. green	65·00	42·00
		a. Red opt	55·00	55·00
		b. Brown opt	£170	£170
JD24		8c. scarlet	£120	95·00
		a. Red opt	£170	£140
		b. Brown opt	£225	£225
JD25		10c. yellow-orange	29·00	50·00
		a. Red opt	£300	£300
		b. Brown opt	85·00	90·00
JD26		12c. ultramarine	25·00	50·00
		a. Red opt	£325	£325
JD27		50c. black	70·00	90·00
		a. Red opt	£500	£550

1942. *Optd with T* **16**.

JD28	D **1**	1c. slate-purple	3·25	10·00
JD29		3c. green	18·00	24·00
JD30		4c. green	16·00	11·00
JD31		8c. scarlet	26·00	21·00
JD32		10c. yellow-orange	2·00	17·00
JD33		12c. ultramarine	1·75	35·00
JD28/33 *Set of* 6			60·00	£110

The 9c. and 15c. also exist with this overprint, but these were not issued (*Price £650 each unused*).

1943–45. *Optd with T* **2**.

JD34	D **1**	1c. slate-purple	2·25	4·75
JD35		3c. green	2·25	4·50
		a. Opt omitted (in pair with normal)	£800	
JD36		4c. green	60·00	48·00
JD37		5c. scarlet	1·50	5·00
JD38		9c. yellow-orange	80	8·50
		a. Opt inverted	22·00	28·00
JD39		10c. yellow-orange	2·25	9·00
		a. Opt inverted	80·00	80·00
JD40		12c. ultramarine	2·25	17·00
JD41		15c. ultramarine	2·25	9·00
JD34/41 *Set of* 8			65·00	95·00

IX. THAI OCCUPATION OF MALAYA

Stamps issued for use in the Malay States of Kedah (renamed Syburi), Kelantan, Perlis and Trengganu, ceded by Japan to Thailand on 19 October 1943. British rule was restored on 9 (Kelantan), 18 (Perlis), 22 (Kedah) and 24 September 1945 (Trengganu). Nos. TM1/6 continued to be used for postage until replaced by the overprinted B.M.A. Malaya issues on 10 October 1945.

PRICES FOR STAMPS ON COVER

Nos. TK1/5	*from* × 30
Nos. TM1/6	*from* × 25
Nos. TT1/35	–

KELANTAN

TK **1**

(Typo Kelantan Ptg Dept, Khota Baru)

1943 (15 Nov). *Handstamped with State arms in violet. No gum.* P 11.

TK1	TK **1**	1c. black	£200	£300
TK2		2c. black	£250	£250
		a. Handstamp omitted	£700	
TK3		4c. black	£250	£300
		a. Handstamp omitted	£850	
TK4		8c. black	£250	£250
		a. Handstamp omitted	£550	
TK5		10c. black	£350	£450
TK1/5 *Set of 5*			£1200	£1400

Nos. TK1/5 were printed in sheets of 84 (12×7) and have sheet watermarks in the form of "STANDARD" in block capitals with curved "CROWN" above and "AGENTS" below in double-lined capitals. This watermark occurs four times in the sheet.

Sheets were imperforate at top and left so that stamps exist imperforate at top, left or at top and left.

Genuine examples have a solid star at the top centre of the arms, as shown in Type TK **1**. Examples with a hollow outline star in this position are forgeries.

Similar stamps, but with red handstamps, were for fiscal use.

GENERAL ISSUE

TM **1** War Memorial

(Litho Defence Ministry, Bangkok)

1944 (15 Jan–4 Mar). *Thick opaque, or thin semi-transparent paper. Gummed or ungummed.* P 12½.

TM1	TM **1**	1c. yellow (4 Mar)	30·00	32·00
TM2		2c. red-brown	12·00	20·00
		a. Imperf (pair)	£900	
		b. Perf 12½×11	20·00	20·00
TM3		3c. green (4 Mar)	20·00	38·00
		a. Perf 12½×11	30·00	42·00
TM4		4c. purple (4 Mar)	14·00	28·00
		a. Perf 12½×11	20·00	35·00
TM5		8c. carmine (4 Mar)	14·00	20·00
		a. Perf 12½×11	20·00	20·00
TM6		15c. blue (4 Mar)	38·00	60·00
		a. Perf 12½×11	42·00	60·00
TM1/6 *Set of 6*			£110	£180

5c. and 10c. stamps in this design were prepared, but never issued.

TRENGGANU

TRENGGANU
(TT 1)

(Overprinted at Trengganu Survey Office)

1944 (1 Oct). *Various stamps optd with Type TT* **1**.

		(a) On Trengganu without Japanese opt.		
TT1	**4**	1c. black (26a)		
TT2		30c. dull purple and black (39)		
		(b) On Trengganu stamps optd as T **1** *of Japanese Occupation.*		
TT2*a*	**4**	1c. black (J97)	–	£2250
TT3		8c. grey (J104)	£700	£475
		(c) On stamps optd with T **16** *of Japanese Occupation.*		
		(i) Pahang.		
TT4	**15**	12c. bright ultramarine (J243)	£600	£160
		(ii) Trengganu.		
TT5	**4**	2c. on 5c. deep reddish purple/*bright yellow* (J121)*	£650	£650
TT6		8c. on 10c. bright blue (J127) (inverted)	£550	£550
TT7		12c. bright ultramarine (J128) (inverted)	£600	£600

*This is spelt "TRENGANU" with one "G".

		(d) On stamps optd with T **2** *of Japanese Occupation.*		
		(i) Straits Settlements.		
TT8	**58**	12c. ultramarine (J264)	£600	£600
TT9		40c. scarlet and dull purple (J265)	£600	£600
		(ii) Negri Sembilan.		
TT9*a*	**6**	25c. dull purple and scarlet (J269)	–	£2250
		(iii) Pahang.		
TT10	**15**	6c. on 5c. brown (J271)		
		(iv) Perak.		
TT11	**51**	1c. black (J272)		
TT12		10c. dull purple (J277)		
TT13		30c. dull purple and orange (J278)	£1100	£600
TT13*a*		50c. black/*emerald* (J279)	–	£2250
		(v) Selangor.		
TT14	**46**	3c. green (J282)	£425	£425
TT15		12c. brt ultramarine (J283) (L. to R.)	£190	£110
TT16		12c. brt ultramarine (J283) (R. to L.)	£180	£110
		a. Sideways second character	£2500	£2500
		(e) On Selangor stamps optd with T **19** *of Japanese Occupation.*		
TT16*b*	**46**	1c. black (J288)	–	£2250
TT17		2c. on 5c. brown (J289)	£600	£600
TT18		3c. on 5c. brown (J290)	£600	£600
		(f) On pictorials of 1943 (Nos. J297/306).		
TT19	**25**	1c. grey-green	£450	£375
TT20	**26**	2c. pale emerald	£450	£180
TT21	**25**	3c. drab	£250	£140
TT22	–	4c. carmine-rose	£400	£180
TT23	–	8c. dull blue	£650	£600
TT24	–	10c. brown-purple	£1400	£750
TT25	**27**	15c. violet	£400	£180
TT26	–	30c. olive-green	£600	£160
TT27	–	50c. blue	£600	£300
TT28	–	70c. blue	£1300	£850
		(g) On Savings Campaign stamps (Nos. J307/8).		
TT29	**28**	8c. violet	£650	£650
TT30		15c. scarlet	£450	£180
		(h) On stamps of Japan.		
TT31	–	3s. green (No. 319)		
TT32	–	5s. claret (No. 396)	£600	£450
TT33	–	25c. brown and chocolate (No. 329)	£425	£130
TT34	–	30c. blue-green (No. 330)	£600	£180
		(i) On Trengganu Postage Due stamp optd with T **1** *of Japanese Occupation.*		
TT35	D **1**	1c. scarlet (JD17)	£3250	£3250

Maldive Islands

PRICES FOR STAMPS ON COVER TO 1945

Nos. 1/6	*from* × 10
Nos. 7/10	*from* × 50
Nos. 11/20	*from* × 20

BRITISH PROTECTORATE

(Currency. 100 cents = 1 Ceylon rupee)

MALDIVES

(1)

2 Minaret, Juma Mosque, Malé

3

1906 (9 Sept). *Nos. 277/9, 280a and 283/4 of Ceylon optd with T* **1**. Wmk Mult Crown CA. P 14.

1	**44**	2c. red-brown	19·00	45·00
2	**45**	3c. green	26·00	45·00
3		4c. orange and ultramarine	45·00	90·00
4	**46**	5c. dull purple	4·00	6·50
5	**48**	15c. blue	90·00	£180
6		25c. bistre	£100	£190
1/6 *Set of* 6			£250	£500

The *T* **1** opt has been extensively forged.

Supplies of Nos. 1/6 were exhausted by March 1907 and the stamps of CEYLON were used until 1909.

(Recess D.L.R.)

1909 (May). *T* **2** (18½×22½ *mm*). W **3**. P 14×13½ (2c., 5c.) or 13½×14 (3c., 10c.).

7	**2**	2c. orange-brown	2·25	3·75
		a. Perf 13½×14	2·50	90
8		3c. deep myrtle	50	70
9		5c. purple	50	35
10		10c. carmine	7·50	80
7/10 *Set of* 4			9·50	2·50

These stamps perforated 14×13½ (14×13.7) are from a line machine and those perforated 13½×14 (13.7×13.9) from a comb machine.

4

(Photo Harrison)

1933. *T* **2** *redrawn (reduced to* 18×21½ *mm)*. W **4**. P 15×14.

A. Wmk upright.

11A	**2**	2c. grey	2·75	2·00
12A		3c. red-brown	70	2·75
14A		5c. mauve	27·00	10·00
15A		6c. scarlet	1·50	5·50
16A		10c. green	85	55
17A		15c. black	6·50	17·00
18A		25c. brown	6·50	17·00
19A		50c. purple	6·50	21·00
20A		1r. deep blue	11·00	19·00
11A/20A *Set of* 9			55·00	85·00

B. Wmk sideways.

11B	**2**	2c. grey	6·00	5·00
12B		3c. red-brown	5·00	1·75
13B		5c. claret	40·00	32·00
15B		6c. scarlet	10·00	5·50
16B		10c. green	3·75	6·50
17B		15c. black	15·00	20·00
18B		25c. brown	11·00	20·00
19B		50c. purple	16·00	20·00
20B		1r. deep blue	16·00	3·25
11B/20B *Set of* 9			£110	£100

(New Currency. 100 larees = 1 rupee)

5 Palm Tree and Dhow

(Recess B.W.)

1950 (24 Dec). P 13.

21	**5**	2l. olive-green	2·25	3·00
		a. *Olive-brown* (1952)	6·00	7·00
22		3l. blue	10·00	65
23		5l. emerald-green	10·00	65
24		6l. red-brown	1·25	1·25
25		10l. scarlet	1·25	1·00
26		15l. orange	1·25	1·00
27		25l. purple	1·25	2·25
28		50l. violet	1·25	3·00
29		1r. chocolate	12·00	32·00
21/9 *Set of* 9			35·00	40·00

7 Fish

8 Native Products

1952. P 13.

30	**7**	3l. blue	2·00	60
31	**8**	5l. emerald	1·00	2·00

SULTANATE

Sultan Mohamed Farid Didi

20 November 1953–10 November 1968

The Maldive Islands became a republic on 1 January 1953, but reverted to a sultanate on 29 November 1953.

9 Malé Harbour

10 Fort and Building

(Recess B.W.)

1956 (1 Feb). P 13½ (T **9**) or 11½×11 (T **10**).

32	**9**	2l. purple	10	10
33		3l. slate	10	10
34		5l. red-brown	10	10
35		6l. blackish violet	10	10
36		10l. emerald	10	10
37		15l. chocolate	10	85
38		25l. rose-red	10	10
39		50l. orange	10	10
40	**10**	1r. bluish green	15	10
41		5r. blue	1·25	30
42		10r. magenta	2·75	1·25
32/42 *Set of* 11			4·50	2·75

11 Cycling

12 Basketball

(Des C. Bottiau. Recess and typo B.W.)

1960 (20 Aug). *Olympic Games.* P 11½×11 (T **11**) or 11×11½ (T **12**).

43	**11**	2l. purple and green	15	25
44		3l. greenish slate and purple	15	25
45		5l. red-brown and ultramarine	15	25
46		10l. emerald-green and brown	15	25
47		15l. sepia and blue	15	25
48	**12**	25l. rose-red and olive	15	25
49		50l. orange and violet	20	40
50		1r. emerald and purple	40	1·25
43/50 *Set of* 8			1·40	2·75

13 Tomb of Sultan

14 Custom House

(Recess B.W.)

1960 (15 Oct). *T* **13**, **14** *and similar horiz designs.* P 11½×11.

51		2l. purple	10	10
52		3l. emerald-green	10	10
53		5l. orange-brown	3·75	4·00
54		6l. bright blue	10	10
55		10l. carmine	10	10
56		15l. sepia	10	10
57		25l. deep violet	10	10
58		50l. slate-grey	10	10
59		1r. orange	15	10
60		5r. deep ultramarine	6·50	60
61		10r. grey-green	12·00	1·25
51/61 *Set of* 11			21·00	6·00

Designs:—5l. Cowrie shells; 6l. Old Royal Palace; 10l. Road to Junin Mosque, Malé; 15l. Council house; 25l. New Government Secretariat; 50l. Prime Minister's office; 1r. Old Ruler's tomb; 5r. Old Ruler's tomb (distant view); 10r. Maldivian Port.

Higher values were also issued, intended mainly for fiscal use.

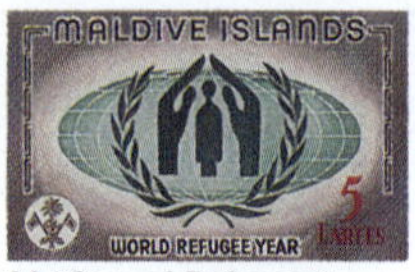

24 "Care of Refugees"

(Recess B.W.)

1960 (15 Oct). *World Refugee Year.* P 11½×11.

62	**24**	2l. deep violet, orange and green	10	15
63		3l. brown, green and red	10	15
64		5l. deep green, sepia and red	10	10
65		10l. bluish green, reddish violet and red	10	10
66		15l. reddish violet, grey-green and red	10	10
67		25l. blue, red-brown and bronze-green	10	10
68		50l. yellow-olive, rose-red and blue	10	10
69		1r. carmine, slate and violet	15	35
62/9 *Set of* 8			75	1·00

25 Coconuts

26 Map of Malé

(Photo Harrison)

1961 (20 Apr). P 14×14½ (Nos. 70/74) or 14½×14 (others).

70	**25**	2l. yellow-brown and deep green	10	50
71		3l. yellow-brown and bright blue	10	50
72		5l. yellow-brown and magenta	10	10
73		10l. yellow-brown and red-orange	15	10
74		15l. yellow-brown and black	20	15
75	**26**	25l. multicoloured	45	20
76		50l. multicoloured	45	40
77		1r. multicoloured	50	70
70/7 *Set of* 8			1·75	2·40

27 5c. Stamp of 1906

30 Malaria Eradication Emblem

(Des M. Shamir. Photo Harrison)

1961 (9 Sept). *55th Anniv of First Maldivian Stamp. T* **27** *and similar horiz designs.* P 14½×14.

78		2l. brown-purple, ultramarine and light green	10	85
79		3l. brown-purple, ultramarine and light green	10	85
80		5l. brown-purple, ultramarine and light green	10	15
81		6l. brown-purple, ultramarine and light green	10	1·00
82		10l. green, claret and maroon	10	15
83		15l. green, claret and maroon	15	15
84		20l. green, claret and maroon	15	20
85		25l. claret, green and black	15	20
86		50l. claret, green and black	25	80
87		1r. claret, green and black	40	2·00
78/87 *Set of* 10			1·40	5·50
MS87*a* 114×88 mm. No. 87 (block of four). Imperf			1·50	5·50

Designs:—2 to 6l. Type **27**; 10 to 20l. 1906 3c. and posthorn; 25l. to 1r. 1906 2c. and olive sprig.

(Recess B.W.)

1962 (7 Apr). *Malaria Eradication.* P 13½×13.

88	**30**	2l. chestnut	10	1·25
89		3l. emerald	10	1·25
90		5l. turquoise-blue	10	15
91		10l. red	10	15
92	–	15l. deep purple-brown	15	15
93	–	25l. deep blue	20	20
94	–	50l. deep green	25	55
95	–	1r. purple	55	80
88/95 *Set of* 8			1·40	4·00

Nos. 92/5 are as T **30**, but have English inscriptions at the side.

31 Children of Europe and America

33 Sultan Mohamed Farid Didi

(Des C. Bottiau. Photo Harrison)

1962 (9 Sept). *15th Anniv of U.N.I.C.E.F. T* **31** *and similar horiz design. Multicoloured.* P 14½×14.

96		2l. Type **31**	10	1·25
97		6l. Type **31**	10	1·25
98		10l. Type **31**	10	15
99		15l. Type **31**	10	15
100		25l. Children of Middle East and Far East	15	15
101		50l. As 25l.	20	15
102		1r. As 25l.	25	20
103		5r. As 25l.	1·25	4·50
96/103 *Set of* 8			2·00	7·00

(Photo Harrison)

1962 (29 Nov). *Ninth Anniv of Enthronement of Sultan.* P 14×14½.

104	**33**	3l. orange-brown and bluish green	10	65
105		5l. orange-brown and indigo	15	15
106		10l. orange-brown and blue	20	15
107		20l. orange-brown and olive-green	30	25
108		50l. orange-brown and deep magenta	35	45
109		1r. orange-brown and slate-lilac	45	65
104/9 *Set of* 6			1·40	2·00

34 Royal Angelfish

(Des R. Hegeman. Photo Enschedé)

1963 (2 Feb). *Tropical Fish. T* **34** *and similar triangular designs. Multicoloured.* P 13½.

110		2l. Type **34**	10	1·25
111		3l. Type **34**	10	1·25
112		5l. Type **34**	15	45
113		10l. Moorish Idol	25	45
114		25l. As 10l.	65	45
115		50l. Diadem Soldierfish	90	65
116		1r. Powder-blue Surgeonfish	1·25	75
117		5r. Racoon Butterflyfish	6·25	10·00
110/17 *Set of* 8			8·50	13·00

39 Fishes in Net

40 Handful of Grain

(Photo State Ptg Wks, Vienna)

1963 (21 Mar). *Freedom from Hunger.* P 12.

118	**39**	2l. brown and deep bluish green	30	1·50
119	**40**	5l. brown and orange-red	50	1·10
120	**39**	7l. brown and turquoise	70	1·10
121	**40**	10l. brown and blue	85	1·10
122	**39**	25l. brown and brown-red	2·50	4·00
123	**40**	50l. brown and violet	3·75	8·00
124	**39**	1r. brown and deep magenta	6·00	12·00
118/24 *Set of* 7			13·00	26·00

41 Centenary Emblem

42 Maldivian Scout Badge

(Photo Harrison)

1963 (1 Oct). *Centenary of Red Cross.* P 14×14½.

125	**41**	2l. red and deep purple	30	1·50
126		15l. red and deep bluish green	65	80
127		50l. red and deep brown	1·25	1·75
128		1r. red and indigo	1·75	2·00
129		4r. red and deep brown-olive	4·00	21·00
125/9 *Set of* 5			7·00	24·00

(Photo Enschedé)

1964. *World Scout Jamboree, Marathon (1963).* P 13½.

130	**42**	2l. green and violet	10	65
131		3l. green and bistre-brown	10	65
132		25l. green and blue	15	15
133		1r. green and crimson	55	1·50
130/3 *Set of* 4			80	2·50

43 Mosque, Malé

44 Putting the Shot

(Recess B.W.)

1964 (10 Aug). *"Maldives Embrace Islam".* W w **12**. P 11½.

134	**43**	2l. purple	10	60
135		3l. emerald-green	10	60
136		10l. carmine	10	10
137		40l. deep dull purple	30	25
138		60l. blue	50	40
139		85l. orange-brown	60	60
134/9 *Set of* 6			1·50	2·25

(Litho Enschedé)

1964 (1 Oct). *Olympic Games, Tokyo. T* **44** *and similar horiz design.* W w 12. P 14×13½.

140		2l. deep maroon and turquoise-blue	10	90
141		3l. crimson and chestnut	10	90
142		5l. bronze-green and deep green	15	20
143		10l. slate-violet and reddish purple	20	20
144		15l. sepia and yellow-brown	30	20
145		25l. indigo and deep blue	50	20
146		50l. deep olive-green and yellow-olive	75	35
147		1r. deep maroon and olive-grey	1·25	75
140/7 *Set of* 8			3·00	3·25
MS147*a* 126×140 mm. Nos. 145/7. Imperf			2·25	3·75

Designs:—2 to 10l. Type **44**; 15l. to 1r. Running.

46 Telecommunications Satellite

(Des M. Shamir. Photo Harrison)

1965 (1 July). *International Quiet Sun Years.* P 14½.

148	**46**	5l. blue	15	65
149		10l. brown	20	65
150		25l. green	40	65
151		1r. deep magenta	90	1·00
148/51 *Set of* 4			1·50	2·75

On 26 July 1965, Maldive Islands became independent and left the British Commonwealth.

47 Isis (wall carving, Abu Simbel)

48 President Kennedy and Doves

(Des M. and G. Shamir. Litho Harrison)

1965 (1 Sept). *Nubian Monuments Preservation. T* **47** *and similar vert design.* W w **12**. P 14½.

152	**47**	2l. bluish green and brown-purple	10	50
153	–	3l. lake and deep green	10	50
154	**47**	5l. dull green and brown-purple	15	10
155	–	10l. steel-blue and orange	20	10
156	**47**	15l. red-brown and deep violet	45	15
157	–	25l. reddish purple and deep blue	70	15
158	**47**	50l. yellow-green and sepia	85	40
159	–	1r. ochre and myrtle-green	1·25	55
152/9 *Set of* 8			3·25	2·00

Design:—3, 10, 25l., 1r. Rameses II on throne (wall carving, Abu Simbel).

(Photo State Ptg Wks, Vienna)

1965 (10 Oct). *Second Death Anniv of President Kennedy. T* **48** *and similar horiz design.* P 12.

160	**48**	2l. black and mauve	10	50
161		5l. bistre-brown and mauve	10	10
162		25l. indigo and mauve	10	10
163	–	1r. brt reddish purple, yellow and blue-green	25	25
164	–	2r. bronze-green, yellow and blue-green	40	70
160/4 *Set of* 5			85	1·50
MS164*a* 150×130 mm. No. 164 in block of four. Imperf			2·75	3·25

Design:—1r., 2r. Pres. Kennedy and hands holding olive-branch.

49 "XX" and U.N. Flag

50 I.C.Y. Emblem

(Des O. Adler. Photo State Ptg Wks, Vienna)

1965 (24 Nov). *20th Anniv of U.N.* P 12.

165	**49**	3l. turquoise-blue and red-brown	10	30
166		10l. turquoise-blue and violet	20	10
167		1r. turquoise-blue and bronze-green	1·10	35
165/7 *Set of* 3			1·25	65

(Des M. and G. Shamir. Photo State Ptg Wks, Vienna)

1965 (20 Dec). *International Co-operation Year.* P 12.

168	**50**	5l. brown and yellow-bistre	15	20
169		15l. brown and slate-lilac	20	20
170		50l. brown and yellow-olive	45	30
171		1r. brown and orange-red	1·25	1·50
172		2r. brown and new blue	1·75	4·00
168/72 *Set of* 5			3·50	5·50
MS173 101×126 mm. Nos. 170/2. Imperf			6·50	8·00

51 Princely Cone Shells

(Des M. and G. Shamir. Photo State Ptg Wks, Vienna)

1966 (1 June). *T* **51** *and similar multicoloured designs.* P 12.

174		2l. Type **51**	20	1·25
175		3l. Yellow flowers	20	1·25
176		5l. Reticulate Distorsio and Leopard Cone shells	30	15
177		7l. Camellias	30	15
178		10l. Type **51**	1·00	15
179		15l. Crab Plover and Seagull	3·75	30
180		20l. As 3l.	80	30
181		30l. Type **51**	2·75	35
182		50l. As 15l.	6·00	55
183		1r. Type **51**	4·00	55
184		1r. As 7l.	3·50	55
185		1r.50 As 3l.	3·75	3·50
186		2r. As 7l.	5·00	4·00
187		5r. As 15l.	23·00	14·00
188		10r. As 5l.	23·00	20·00
174/88 *Set of* 15			70·00	42·00

The 3l., 7l., 20l., 1r. (No. 184), 1r.50 and 2r. are diamond-shaped (43½×43½ *mm*); the others are horizontal designs as T **51**.

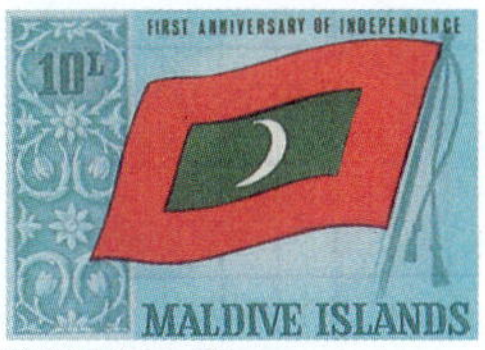

52 Maldivian Flag

(Des M. and G. Shamir. Litho Harrison)

1966 (26 July). *First Anniv of Independence.* P 14×14½.

189	**52**	10l. green, red and turquoise	2·00	50
190		1r. green, red, brown orange-yellow	5·00	90

53 "Luna 9" on Moon

(Des M. and G. Shamir. Litho Harrison)

1966 (1 Nov). *Space Rendezvous and Moon Landing. T* **53** *and similar horiz designs.* W w **12**. P 15×14.

191		10l. light brown, grey-blue and bright blue	25	10
192		25l. green and carmine	35	10
193		50l. orange-brown and green	50	15
194		1r. turquoise-blue and chestnut	80	35
195		2r. green and violet	1·75	65
196		5r. rose-pink and deep turquoise-blue	2·25	1·60
191/6 *Set of* 6			5·50	2·50
MS197 108×126 mm. Nos. 194/6. Imperf			3·50	5·00

Designs:—25l., 1r., 5r. "Gemini 6" and '7" rendezvous in space; 2r. "Gemini" spaceship as seen from the other spaceship; 50l. Type **53**.

54 U.N.E.S.C.O. Emblem, and Owl on Book

55 Sir Winston Churchill and Cortège

(Litho Harrison)

1966 (15 Nov). *20th Anniv of U.N.E.S.C.O. T* **54** *and similar vert designs.* W w **12**. *Multicoloured.* P 15×14.

198		1l. Type **54**	30	1·50
199		3l. U.N.E.S.C.O. emblem, and globe and microscope	30	1·50
200		5l. U.N.E.S.C.O. emblem, and mask, violin and palette	60	30
201		50l. Type **54**	4·50	65
202		1r. Design as 3l.	5·50	90
203		5r. Design as 5l.	15·00	18·00
198/203 *Set of* 6			24·00	21·00

(Des M. and G. Shamir. Litho Harrison)

1967 (1 Jan). *Churchill Commemoration. T* **55** *and similar horiz design. Flag in red and blue.* P 14½×13½.

204	**55**	2l. olive-brown	20	1·75
205	–	10l. turquoise-blue	1·25	25
206	**55**	15l. green	2·00	25
207	–	25l. violet	3·00	35
208	–	1r. brown	8·00	75
209	**55**	2r.50 crimson	15·00	14·00
204/9 *Set of* 6			26·00	16·00

Design:—10l., 25l.,1r. Churchill and catafalque.

IMPERFORATE STAMPS. From No. 210 onwards some sets and perforated miniature sheets exist imperforate from limited printings.

56 Footballers and Jules Rimet Cup

(Des M. and G. Shamir. Photo Govt Printer, Israel)

1967 (22 Mar). *England's Victory in World Cup Football Championship. T* **56** *and similar horiz designs. Multicoloured.* P 14×13½.

210		2l. Type **56**	20	1·00
211		3l. Player in red shirt kicking ball	20	1·00
212		5l. Scoring goal	20	20
213		25l. As 3l.	1·00	20
		a. Emerald (face value and inscr) omitted	£160	
214		50l. Making a tackle	1·75	30
215		1r. Type **56**	3·00	65
216		2r. Emblem on Union Jack	4·75	4·00
210/16 *Set of 7*			10·00	6·50
MS217		100×121 mm. Nos. 214/16. Imperf	12·00	8·50

57 Ornate Butterflyfish

(Des M. and G. Shamir. Photo Govt Printer, Israel)

1967 (1 May). *Tropical Fishes. T* **57** *and similar horiz designs. Multicoloured.* P 14.

218		2l. Type **57**	10	60
219		3l. Black-saddled Pufferfish	15	60
220		5l. Blue Boxfish	20	10
221		6l. Picasso Triggerfish	20	20
222		50l. Semicircle Angelfish	3·25	30
223		1r. As 3l.	4·50	75
224		2r. As 50l.	8·50	8·00
218/24 *Set of 7*			15·00	9·50

58 Hawker Siddeley H.S.748 over Hulule Airport Building

(Des M. and G. Shamir. Photo Govt Printer, Israel)

1967 (26 July). *Inauguration of Hulule Airport. T* **58** *and similar horiz design.* P 14×13½.

225		2l. reddish violet and yellow-olive	20	50
226		5l. deep green and lavender	25	10
227		10l. reddish violet and light turquoise-green	30	10
228		15l. deep green and yellow-ochre	50	10
229		30l. deep ultramarine and light blue	1·00	10
230		50l. deep brown and magenta	1·75	20
231		5r. deep ultramarine and yellow-orange	5·50	5·50
232		10r. deep brown and blue	7·50	9·00
225/32 *Set of 8*			15·00	14·00

Designs:—2l., 10l., 30l., 5r. T **58**; 5l., 15l., 50l., 10r. Airport building and Hawker Siddeley H.S.748. Higher values were also issued, intended mainly for fiscal use.

59 "Man and Music" Pavilion

International Tourist Year 1967

(60)

(Des M. and G. Shamir. Photo Govt Printer, Israel)

1967 (1 Sept). *World Fair Montreal. T* **59** *and similar horiz design. Multicoloured.* P 14×13½.

233		2l. Type **59**	10	60
234		5l. "Man and His Community" Pavilion	10	10
235		10l. Type **59**	10	10
236		50l. As 5l.	40	30
237		1r. Type **59**	75	50
238		2r. As 5l.	1·75	1·75
233/8 *Set of 6*			2·75	3·00
MS239		102×137 mm. Nos. 237/8. Imperf	2·25	3·50

1967 (1 Dec). *International Tourist Year. Nos. 225/32 optd as T* **60** *(in one or three lines), in gold.*

240		2l. reddish violet and yellow-olive	10	60
241		5l. deep green and lavender	15	15
242		10l. reddish violet and light turquoise-green	20	15
243		15l. deep green and yellow-ochre	20	15
244		30l. deep ultramarine and light blue	30	20
245		50l. deep brown and magenta	45	30
246		5r. deep ultramarine and yellow-orange	3·50	4·00
247		10r. deep brown and blue	5·00	6·50
240/7 *Set of 8*			9·00	11·00

61 Cub signalling and Lord Baden-Powell

62 French Satellite "A 1"

(Litho Harrison)

1968 (1 Jan). *Maldivian Scouts and Cubs. T* **61** *and similar vert design.* P 14×14½.

248	**61**	2l. brown, green and yellow	10	80
249	–	3l. carmine, bright blue and light blue	10	80
250	**61**	25l. bluish violet, lake and orange-red	1·50	40
251	–	1r. blackish green, chest & apple-green	3·50	1·60
248/51 *Set of 4*			4·50	3·25

Design:—3l., 1r. Scouts and Lord Baden-Powell.

(Des M. and G. Shamir. Photo Govt Printer, Israel)

1968 (27 Jan). *Space Martyrs. Triangular designs as T* **62**. P 14.

252		2l. magenta and ultramarine	10	40
253		3l. violet and yellow-brown	10	40
254		7l. olive-brown and lake	15	40
255		10l. deep blue, pale drab and black	15	15
256		25l. bright emerald and reddish violet	40	15
257		50l. blue and orange-brown	75	30
258		1r. purple-brown and deep bluish green	1·10	50
259		2r. deep brown, pale blue and black	1·75	2·00
260		5r. magenta, light drab and black	2·75	3·00
252/60 *Set of 9*			6·50	6·50
MS261		110×155 mm. Nos. 258/9. Imperf	4·50	4·75

Designs:—2l., 50l. Type **82**; 3l., 25l. "Luna 10"; 7l.,1r. "Orbiter" and "Mariner"; 10l., 2r. Astronauts White, Grissom and Chaffee; 5r. Cosmonaut V. M. Komarov.

63 Putting the Shot

64 "Adriatic Seascape" (Bonington)

(Des M. Shamir. Litho Harrison)

1968 (1 Feb). *Olympic Games, Mexico (1st issue). T* **63** *and similar vert design. Multicoloured.* P 14½.

262		2l. Type **63**	10	40
263		6l. Throwing the discus	10	40
264		10l. Type **63**	15	10
265		15l. As 6l.	20	10
266		1r. Type **63**	60	35
267		2r.50 As 6l.	1·50	2·00
262/7 *Set of 6*			2·40	3·00

See also Nos. 294/7.

(Des M. Shamir. Litho Govt Printer, Israel)

1968 (1 Apr). *Paintings. T* **64** *and similar horiz designs. Multicoloured.* P 14.

268		50l. Type **64**	1·75	30
269		1r. "Ulysses deriding Polyphemus" (Turner)	2·25	45
270		2r. "Sailing Boat at Argenteuil" (Monet)	3·00	2·50
271		5r. "Fishing Boats at Les Saintes-Maries" (Van Gogh)	5·00	6·00
268/71 *Set of 4*			11·00	8·25

65 LZ-130 *Graf Zeppelin II* and Montgolfier's Balloon

(Des M. Shamir. Photo Govt Printer, Israel)

1968 (1 June). *Development of Civil Aviation. T* **65** *and similar horiz designs.* P 14×13½.

272		2l. orange-brown, yellow-green and ultramarine	20	75
273		3l. turquoise-blue, violet orange-brown	20	75
274		5l. slate-green, crimson and turquoise-blue	20	20
275		7l. bright blue, purple and red-orange	1·75	1·00
276		10l. brown, turquoise-blue and bright purple	45	20
277		50l. crimson, slate-green and yellow-olive	1·50	30
278		1r. emerald, blue and vermilion	2·25	50
279		2r. maroon, bistre and bright blue	18·00	11·00
272/9 *Set of 8*			22·00	13·00

Designs:—3l., 1r. Boeing 707-420 and Douglas DC-3; 5l., 50l. Wright Type A and Lilienthal's glider; 7l., 2r. Projected Boeing 733 and Concorde; 10l. Type **65**.

66 W.H.O. Building, Geneva

International Boy Scout Jamboree, Farragut Park, Idaho, U.S.A. August 1-9, 1967

(67)

(Litho Harrison)

1968 (15 July). *20th Anniv of World Health Organisation.* P 14½×13½.

280	**66**	10l. violet, turquoise-blue and light greenish blue	60	10
281		25l. bronze-green, yellow-brown and orange-yellow	1·00	15
282		1r. deep brown, emerald and bright green	3·25	90
283		2r. bluish violet, magenta and mauve	5·25	5·50
280/3 *Set of 4*			9·00	6·00

1968 (1 Aug). *First Anniv of Scout Jamboree, Idaho. Nos. 248/51 optd with T* **67**.

284		2l. brown, green and yellow	10	50
285		3l. carmine, bright blue and light blue	10	50
286		25l. bluish violet, lake and orange-red	1·50	40
287		1r. blackish green, chestnut and apple-green	4·50	2·10
284/7 *Set of 4*			5·50	3·25

68 Curlew and Redshank

1968 (24 Sept). *T* **68** *and similar horiz designs. Photo. Multicoloured.* P 14×13½.

288		2l. Type **68**	50	75
289		10l. Pacific Grinning Tun and Papal Mitre shells	1·25	20
290		25l. Oriental Angel Wing and Tapestry Turban shells	1·75	25
291		50l. Type **68**	7·00	1·10
292		1r. As 10l.	4·50	1·10
293		2r. As 25l.	5·00	4·75
288/93 *Set of 6*			18·00	7·25

69 Throwing the Discus

(Des M. Shamir. Photo Govt Printer, Israel)

1968 (12 Oct). *Olympic Games, Mexico (2nd issue). T* **69** *and similar multicoloured designs.* P 14.

294		10l. Type **69**	10	10
295		50l. Running	20	10
296		1r. Cycling	4·25	60
297		2r. Basketball	5·00	2·50
294/7 *Set of 4*			8·50	3·00

INDEPENDENT REPUBLIC

11 November 1968

70 Fishing Dhow

71 "The Thinker" (Rodin)

(Photo Harrison)

1968 (11 Nov). *Republic Day. T* **70** *and similar horiz design.* P 14×14½.

298		10l. brown, ultramarine and light yellow-green	1·25	40
299		1r. green, red and bright blue	7·50	1·60

Design:—1r. National flag, crest and map.

(Des M. Shamir. Litho Rosenbaum Brothers, Vienna)

1969 (10 Apr). *U.N.E.S.C.O. "Human Rights". T* **71** *and similar vert designs, showing sculptures by Rodin. Multicoloured.* P 13½.

300	6l. Type **71**	30	15
301	10l. "Hands"	30	15
302	1r.50 "Eve"	2·00	2·25
303	2r.50 "Adam"	2·50	3·00
300/3 *Set of 4*		4·50	5·00
MS304 112×130 mm. Nos. 302/3. Imperf		9·00	9·00

72 Module nearing Moon's Surface

(Des M. Shamir. Litho Govt Printer, Israel)

1969 (25 Sept). *First Man on the Moon. T* **72** *and similar square designs. Multicoloured.* P 14.

305	6l. Type **72**	15	15
306	10l. Astronaut with hatchet	15	15
307	1r.50 Astronaut and module	2·25	1·40
308	2r.50 Astronaut using camera	2·50	2·00
305/8 *Set of 4*		4·50	3·25
MS309 101×130 mm. Nos. 305/8. Imperf		4·00	5·00

Gold Medal Winner
Mohamed Gammoudi
5000 m. run
Tunisia
REPUBLIC OF MALDIVES
(**73**)

1969 (1 Dec). *Gold-medal Winners, Olympic Games, Mexico (1968). Nos. 295/6 optd with T* **73**, *or similar inscr honouring P. Trentin (cycling) of France.*

310	50l. multicoloured	60	60
311	1r. multicoloured	1·40	90

74 Racoon Butterflyfish

(Des M. Shamir. Litho)

1970 (1 Jan). *Tropical Fish. T* **74** *and similar diamond-shaped designs. Multicoloured.* P 10½.

312	2l. Type **74**	40	70
313	5l. Clown Triggerfish	65	40
314	25l. Broad-barred Lionfish	1·75	40
315	50l. Long-nosed Butterflyfish	2·25	1·00
316	1r. Emperor Angelfish	3·00	1·00
317	2r. Royal Angelfish	4·00	6·50
312/17 *Set of 6*		11·00	9·00

75 Columbia Dauman Victoria, 1899

(Des M. Shamir. Litho)

1970 (1 Feb). *"75 Years of the Automobile". T* **75** *and similar horiz designs. Multicoloured.* P 12.

318	2l. Type **75**	20	50
319	5l. Duryea phaeton, 1902	25	30
320	7l. Packard S-24, 1906	30	30
321	10l. Autocar Runabout, 1907	35	30
322	25l. Type **75**	1·25	30
323	50l. As 5l.	2·25	55
324	1r. As 7l.	2·75	90
325	2r. As 10l.	3·25	5·50
318/25 *Set of 8*		9·50	7·75
MS326 95×143 mm. Nos. 324/5. P 11½		4·00	7·50

76 U.N. Headquarters, New York

77 Ship and Light Buoy

(Des M. Shamir. Litho Rosenbaum Brothers, Vienna)

1970 (26 June). *25th Anniv of United Nations. T* **76** *and similar horiz designs. Multicoloured.* P 13½.

327	2l. Type **76**	10	75
328	10l. Surgical operation (W.H.O.)	1·50	25
329	25l. Student, actress and musician (U.N.E.S.C.O.)	2·50	40
330	50l. Children at work and play (U.N.I.C.E.F.)	2·00	70
331	1r. Fish, corn and farm animals (F.A.O.)	2·00	1·00
332	2r. Miner hewing coal (I.L.O.)	6·00	6·50
327/32 *Set of 6*		12·50	8·75

(Des M. Shamir. Litho)

1970 (26 July). *10th Anniv of Inter-governmental Maritime Consultative Organization. T* **77** *and similar vert design. Multicoloured.* P 13½.

333	50l. Type **77**	50	40
334	1r. Ship and lighthouse	4·75	1·00

78 "Guitar-player and Masqueraders" (A. Watteau)

79 Australian Pavilion

(Des M. Shamir. Litho Govt Printer, Israel)

1970 (1 Aug). *Famous Paintings showing the Guitar. T* **78** *and similar vert designs. Multicoloured.* P 14.

335	3l. Type **78**	15	80
336	7l. "Spanish Guitarist" (E. Manet)	25	80
337	50l. "Costumed Player" (Watteau)	85	40
338	1r. "Mandolins-player" (Roberti)	1·40	55
339	2r.50 "Guitar-player and Lady" (Watteau)	3·00	3·50
340	5r. "Mandolins-player" (Frans Hals)	5·00	6·50
335/40 *Set of 6*		9·50	11·00
MS341 132×80 mm. Nos. 339/40. Roul		8·50	9·50

(Des M. Shamir. Litho Rosenbaum Brothers, Vienna)

1970 (1 Aug). *"EXPO 70" World Fair, Osaka, Japan. T* **79** *and similar vert designs. Multicoloured.* P 13½.

342	2l. Type **79**	10	80
343	3l. West German Pavilion	10	80
344	10l. U.S.A. Pavilion	55	10
345	25l. British Pavilion	1·75	15
346	50l. Soviet Pavilion	2·25	45
347	1r. Japanese Pavilion	2·50	65
342/7 *Set of 6*		6·50	2·50

80 Learning the Alphabet

(Des M. Shamir. Litho Govt Printer, Israel)

1970 (7 Sept). *International Education Year. T* **80** *and similar horiz designs. Multicoloured.* P 14.

348	5l. Type **80**	30	40
349	10l. Training teachers	40	20
350	25l. Geography lesson	1·75	30
351	50l. School inspector	2·00	55
352	1r. Education by television	2·25	75
348/52 *Set of 5*		6·00	2·00

Philympia
London 1970
(**81**)

82 Footballers

1970 (18 Sep). *"Philympia 1970" Stamp Exhibition, London. Nos. 306/***MS***309 optd with T* **81**, *in silver.*

353	10l. multicoloured	10	10
354	1r.50 multicoloured	65	75
355	2r.50 multicoloured	1·00	1·50
353/5 *Set of 3*		1·60	2·00
MS356 101×130 mm. Nos. 305/8 optd. Imperf		6·00	7·00

(Des M. Shamir. Litho Rosenbaum Brothers, Vienna)

1970 (1 Dec). *World Cup Football Championships, Mexico. T* **82** *and similar vert designs, each showing football scenes and outline of the Jules Rimet Trophy.* P 13½.

357	3l. multicoloured	15	40
358	6l. multicoloured	20	40
359	7l. multicoloured	20	30
360	25l. multicoloured	90	20
361	1r. multicoloured	2·50	90
357/61 *Set of 5*		3·50	2·00

Malta

Early records of the postal services under the British Occupation are fragmentary, but it is known that an Island Postmaster was appointed in 1802. A British Packet Agency was established in 1806 and it later became customary for the same individual to hold the two appointments together. The inland posts continued to be the responsibility of the local administration, but the overseas mails formed part of the British G.P.O. system.

The stamps of Great Britain were used on overseas mails from September 1857. Previously during the period of the Crimean War letters franked with Great Britain stamps from the Crimea were cancelled at Malta with a wavy line obliterator. Such postmarks are known between April 1855 and September 1856.

The British G.P.O. relinquished control of the overseas posts on 31 December 1884 when Great Britain stamps were replaced by those of Malta.

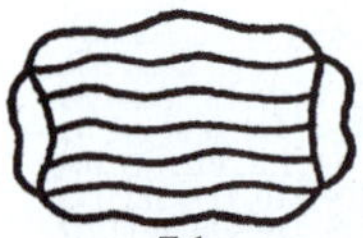

Z 1

Z 2

1855–56. *Stamps of* GREAT BRITAIN *cancelled with wavy lines obliteration, Type Z* **1**.

Z1	1d. red-brown (1854), Die I, wmk Small Crown, perf 16	£850
Z2	1d. red-brown (1855), Die II, wmk Small Crown, perf 14	£850
	a. Very blued paper	
Z3	1d. red-brown (1855), Die II, wmk Large Crown, perf 16	£850
Z3*a*	1d. red-brown (1855), Die II, wmk Large Crown, perf 14	£850
Z4	2d. blue (1855), wmk Large Crown, perf 14 Plate No. 5	
Z5	6d. (1854) embossed	£4250
Z6	1s. (1847) embossed	£4750

It is now established that this obliterator was sent to Malta and used on mail in transit emanating from the Crimea.

1857 (18 Aug)–**59**. *Stamps of* GREAT BRITAIN *cancelled "M", Type Z* **2**.

Z7	1d. red-brown (1841), imperf	£2000
Z8	1d. red-brown, Die I, wmk Small Crown, perf 16	£150
Z9	1d. red-brown, Die II, wmk Small Crown, perf 16	£950
Z10	1d. red-brown, Die II (1855), wmk Small Crown, perf 14	£250
Z11	1d. red-brown, Die II (1855), wmk Large Crown, perf 14	80·00
Z11*a*	1d. rose-red (1857) wmk Large Crown, perf 16	
Z12	1d. rose-red (1857), wmk Large Crown, perf 14	22·00
Z13	2d. blue (1841), imperf	£3500
Z14	2d. blue (1854) wmk Small Crown, perf 16 Plate No. 4	£800
Z15	2d. blue (1855), wmk Large Crown, perf 14 *From* Plate Nos. 5, 6	65·00
Z16	2d. blue (1858), wmk Large Crown, perf 16 Plate No. 6.	£325
Z17	2d. blue (1858) (Plate Nos. 7, 8, 9) *From*	45·00
Z18	4d. rose (1857)	40·00
	a. Thick glazed paper	£200
Z19	6d. violet (1854), embossed	£4000
Z20	6d. lilac (1856)	42·00
	a. Thick paper	£225
Z21	6d. lilac (1856) (*blued paper*)	£900
Z22	1s. green (1856)	£130
	a. Thick paper	£200

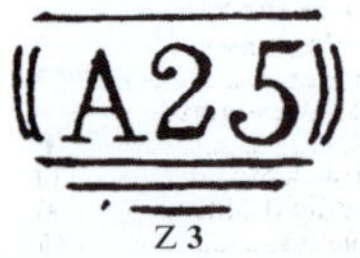

Z 3

Z 6

Z 4

Z 5

Z 7

1859–84. *Stamps of* GREAT BRITAIN *cancelled "A 25" as in Types Z 3/7.*

Z23	½d. rose-red (1870–79) *From* Plate Nos. 4, 5, 6, 8, 9, 10, 11, 12, 13, 14, 15, 19, 20.	27·00
Z24	1d. red-brown (1841), *imperf.*	£3250
Z25	1d. red-brown (1854), wmk Small Crown, perf 16	£375
Z26	1d. red-brown (1855), wmk Large Crown, perf 14	85·00
Z27	1d. rose-red (1857), wmk Large Crown, perf 14	8·50
Z28	1d. rose-red (1861), Alphabet IV	£475
Z30	1d. rose-red (1864–79) *From* Plate Nos, 71, 72, 73, 74, 76, 78, 79, 80, 81, 82, 83, 84, 85, 86, 87, 88, 89, 90, 91, 92, 93, 94, 95, 96, 97, 98, 99, 100, 101, 102, 103, 104, 105, 106, 107, 108, 109, 110, 111, 112, 113, 114, 115, 116, 117, 118, 119, 120, 121, 122, 123, 124, 125, 127, 129, 130, 131, 132, 133, 134, 135, 136, 137, 138, 139, 140, 141, 142, 143, 144, 145, 146, 147, 148, 149, 150, 151, 152, 153, 154, 155, 156, 157, 158, 159, 160, 161, 162, 163, 164, 165, 166, 167, 168, 169, 170, 171, 172, 173, 174, 175, 176, 177, 178, 179, 180, 181, 182, 183, 184, 185, 186, 187, 188, 189, 190, 191, 192, 193, 194, 195, 196, 197, 198, 199, 200, 201, 202, 203, 204, 205, 206, 207, 208, 209, 210, 211, 212, 213, 214, 215, 216, 217, 218, 219, 220, 221, 222, 223, 224.	18·00
Z31	1½d. lake-red (1870–79) (Plate Nos. 1, 3) *From*	£500
Z32	2d. blue (1841), *imperf.*	£4500
Z33	2d. blue (1855) wmk Large Crown perf 14	75·00
Z34	2d. blue (1858–69) *From* Plate Nos. 7, 8, 9, 12, 13, 14, 15.	18·00
Z35	2½d. rosy mauve (1875) (*blued paper*) *From* Plate Nos. 1, 2.	80·00
Z36	2½d. rosy mauve (1875–76) *From* Plate Nos. 1, 2, 3.	35·00
Z37	2½d. rosy mauve (Error of Lettering)	£2250
Z38	2½d. rosy mauve (1876–79) *From* Plate Nos. 3, 4, 5, 6, 7, 8, 9, 10, 11, 12, 13, 14, 15, 16, 17.	17·00
Z39	2½d. blue (1880–81) *From* Plate Nos. 17, 18, 19, 20.	11·00
Z40	2½d. blue (1881) (Plate Nos. 21, 22, 23). *From*	8·00
Z41	3d. carmine-rose (1862)	£120
Z42	3d. rose (1865) (Plate No. 4)	75·00
Z43	3d. rose (1867–73) *From* Plate Nos. 4, 5, 6, 7, 8, 9, 10.	28·00
Z44	3d. rose (1873–76) *From* Plate Nos. 11, 12, 14, 15, 16, 17, 18, 19, 20.	35·00
Z45	3d. rose (1881) (Plate Nos. 20, 21) *From*	£950
Z46	3d. on 3d. lilac (1883)	£500
Z47	4d. rose (or rose-carmine) (1857)	35·00
	a. Thick glazed paper	£130
Z48	4d. red (1862) (Plate Nos. 3, 4) *From*	32·00
Z49	4d. vermilion (1865–73) *From* Plate Nos. 7, 8, 9, 10, 11, 12, 13, 14.	17·00
Z50	4d. vermilion (1876) (Plate No. 15)	£190
Z51	4d. sage-green (1877) (Plate Nos. 15, 16) *From*	£100
Z52	4d. grey-brown (1880) wmk Large Garter Plate No. 17.	£160
Z53	4d. grey-brown (1880) wmk Crown *From* Plate Nos. 17, 18.	50·00
Z54	6d. violet (1854), embossed	£3000
Z55	6d. lilac (1856)	45·00
	a. Thick paper	
Z56	6d. lilac (1862) (Plate Nos. 3, 4) *From*	38·00
Z57	6d. lilac (1865–67) (Plate Nos. 5, 6) *From*	30·00
Z58	6d. lilac (1865–67) (Wmk error)	£1300
Z59	6d. lilac (1867) (Plate No. 6)	35·00
Z60	6d. violet (1867–70) (Plate Nos. 6, 8, 9) *From*	26·00
Z61	6d. buff (1872–73) (Plate Nos. 11, 12). *From*	£100
Z62	6d. chestnut (1872) (Plate No. 11)	32·00
Z63	6d. grey (1873) (Plate No. 12)	75·00
Z64	6d. grey (1873–80) *From* Plate Nos. 13, 14, 15, 16, 17.	35·00
Z65	6d. grey (1881–82) (Plate Nos. 17, 18) *From*	65·00
Z66	6d. on 6d. lilac (1883)	£130
Z67	8d. orange (1876)	£425
Z68	9d. straw (1862)	£650
Z69	9d. bistre (1862)	£600
Z70	9d. straw (1865)	£600
Z71	9d. straw (1867)	£750
Z72	10d. red-brown (1867)	£130
Z73	1s. (1847), embossed	£3250
Z74	1s. green (1856)	75·00
Z75	1s. green (1856) (*thick paper*)	£275
Z76	1s. green (1862)	65·00
Z77	1s. green ("K" *variety*)	£2250
Z78	1s. green (1865) (Plate No. 4)	42·00
Z79	1s. green (1867–73) (Plate Nos. 4, 5, 6, 7) *From*	30·00
Z80	1s. green (1873–77) *From* Plate Nos. 8, 9, 10, 11, 12, 13.	42·00
Z81	1s. orange-brown (1880) (Plate No. 13)	£275
Z82	1s. orange-brown (1881) *From* Plate Nos. 13, 14.	85·00
Z83	2s. blue (*shades*) (1867) *From*	£160
Z84	2s. brown (1880)	£3000
Z85	5s. rose (1867–74) (Plate Nos. 1, 2) *From*	£425
Z86	5s. rose (1882) (Plate No. 4), *blued paper*	£2000
Z87	5s. rose (1882) (Plate No. 4), *white paper*	£1700
Z88	10s. grey-green (1878)	£3000

1880.

Z89	½d. deep green	15·00
Z90	½d. pale green	15·00
Z91	1d. Venetian red	14·00
Z92	1½d. Venetian red	£450
Z93	2d. pale rose	40·00
Z94	2d. deep rose	42·00
Z95	5d. indigo	75·00

1881.

Z96	1d. lilac (14 *dots*)	28·00
Z97	1d. lilac (16 *dots*)	9·00

1883–84.

Z98	½d. slate-blue	16·00
Z99	1½d. lilac	
Z100	2d. lilac	£100
Z101	2½d. lilac	13·00
Z102	3d. lilac	
Z103	4d. dull green	£170
Z104	5d. dull green	£150
Z105	6d. dull green	
Z106	9d. dull green	
Z107	1s. dull green	£250
Z108	5s. rose (*blued paper*)	£1800
Z109	5s. rose (*white paper*)	£1100

POSTAL FISCALS

Z109*a*	1d. reddish lilac (Type F **8**) (1867) wmk Anchor	
Z110	1d. purple (Type F **12**) (1871) wmk Anchor	£800
Z111	1d. purple (Type F **12**) (1881) wmk Orb	£600

PRICES FOR STAMPS ON COVER TO 1945

Nos. 1/3	*from* × 4
Nos. 4/19	*from* × 5
Nos. 20/9	*from* × 6
No. 30	—
Nos. 31/3	*from* × 4
Nos. 34/7	*from* × 10
Nos. 38/88	*from* × 4
Nos. 92/3	*from* × 5
Nos. 97/103	*from* × 3
Nos. 104/5	—
Nos. 106/20	*from* × 3
No. 121	—
Nos. 122/38	*from* × 3
Nos. 139/40	—
Nos. 141/72	*from* × 4
Nos. 173/209	*from* × 3
Nos. 210/31	*from* × 2
Nos. D1/10	*from* × 30
Nos. D11/20	*from* × 15

CROWN COLONY

PRINTERS. Nos. 1/156. Printed by De La Rue; typographed *except where otherwise stated.*

1

Type 1

The first Government local post was established on 10 June 1853 and, as an experiment, mail was carried free of charge. During 1859 the Council of Government decided that a rate of ½d. per ½ ounce should be charged for this service and stamps in Type I were ordered for this purpose. Both the new rate and the stamps were introduced on 1 December 1860. Until 1 January 1885 the ½d stamps were intended for the local service only; mail for abroad being handled by the British Post Office on Malta, using G.B. stamps.

Specialists now recognise 29 printings in shades of yellow and one in green during the period to 1884. These printings can be linked to the changes in watermark and perforation as follows:

Ptg 1—Blued paper without wmk. P 14.
Ptgs 2 and 3—White paper without wmk. P 14.
Ptgs 4 to 9, 11, 13 to 19, 22 to 24—Crown CC wmk. P 14.
Ptg 10—Crown CC wmk. P 12½ (rough).
Ptg 12—Crown CC wmk. P 12½ (clean-cut).
Ptgs 20 and 21—Crown CC wmk. P 14×12½.
Ptgs 25 to 28, 30—Crown CA wmk. P 14.
Ptg 29—In green (No. 20).

(Des E. Fuchs)

1860 (1 Dec)–**63.** No wmk. P 14.

(a) Blued paper.

1	½d. buff (1.12.60)	£1000	£500

(b) Thin, hard white paper.

2	½d. brown-orange (11.61)	£1000	£425
3	½d. buff (1.63)	£700	£350
	a. *Pale buff*	£700	£350

No. 1 is printed in fugitive ink. It is known imperforate but was not issued in that state (*Price* £10000 *unused*).

The printing on No. 2 gives a very blurred and muddy impression; on Nos. 3/3*a* the impression is clear.

Specks of carmine can often be detected with a magnifying glass on Nos. 2/3*a*, and also on No. 4. Examples also exist on which parts of the design are in pure rose, due to defective mixing of the ink.

1863–81. Wmk Crown CC.

(a) P 14.

4	½d. buff (6.63)	95·00	60·00
	w. Wmk inverted	£375	£375
	x. Wmk reversed	£1000	
5	½d. bright orange (11.64)	£600	£160
	w. Wmk inverted	†	£800
6	½d. orange-brown (4.67)	£350	£100
7	½d. dull orange (4.70)	£225	80·00
	w. Wmk inverted	†	£500
	x. Wmk reversed	£1000	
8	½d. orange-buff (5.72)	£150	65·00
9	½d. golden yellow (aniline) (10.74)	£275	£325
10	½d. yellow-buff (9.75)	70·00	55·00
11	½d. pale buff (3.77)	£170	60·00
	w. Wmk inverted	†	£500
12	½d. bright orange-yellow (4.80)	£180	£100
13	½d. yellow (4.81)	£100	60·00
	w. Wmk inverted	†	£500

(b) P 12½ *rough (No. 14) or clean-cut (No. 15).*

14	½d. buff-brown (11.68)	£150	£110
15	½d. yellow-orange (5.71)	£300	£170

(c) P 14×12½.

16	½d. yellow-buff (7.78)	£180	95·00
	w. Wmk inverted	†	£1000
17	½d. yellow (2.79)	£200	£100

Examples of No. 4 from the 1863 printing are on thin, surfaced paper; later printings in the same shade were on unsurfaced paper.

The ink used for No. 5 is mineral and, unlike that on No. 9, does not stain the paper.

Some variations of shade on No. 6 may be described as chestnut. The ink of No. 6 is clear and never muddy, although some examples are over-inked. Deeper shades of No. 4, with which examples of No. 6 might be confused, have muddy ink.

It is believed that there are no surviving pairs of the buff-brown imperforate between variety previously listed.

The Royal Collection contains an unused horizontal pair of the yellow-buff perforated 12½×14.

1882 (Mar)–**84.** Wmk Crown CA. P 14.

18	½d. orange-yellow	40·00	35·00
19	½d. red-orange (9.84)	18·00	50·00

2

3

4

5

1885 (1 Jan)–**90.** Wmk Crown CA. P 14.

20	1	½d. green	3·25	50
		w. Wmk inverted	£110	85·00
21	2	1d. rose	85·00	26·00
		w. Wmk inverted	£1500	
22		1d. carmine (*shades*) (1890)	6·50	35
		w. Wmk inverted	†	£1200
23	3	2d. grey	6·50	1·75
24	4	2½d. dull blue	60·00	2·75
25		2½d. bright blue	45·00	1·00
26		2½d. ultramarine	45·00	1·00
27	3	4d. brown	11·00	3·00
		a. Imperf (pair)	£5000	£5000
		w. Wmk inverted	£1500	
28		1s. violet	42·00	11·00
29		1s. pale violet (1890)	60·00	20·00
		w. Wmk inverted	£750	£275
20/8		*Set of* 6	£100	16·00
20s/8s		Optd "Specimen" *Set of* 6	£3750	

Although not valid for postage until 1 January 1885 these stamps were available at the G.P.O., Valletta from 27 December 1884.

Three unused examples of the ½d. green, No. 20, are known line perforated 12. It is believed that these originated from proof books, the stamp not being issued for use with this perforation.

The Royal Collection includes an example of the 1d. carmine printed on the gummed side.

1886 (1 Jan). Wmk Crown CC. P 14.

30	5	5s. rose	£110	80·00
		s. Optd "Specimen"	£600	
		w. Wmk inverted	£150	£110

6 Harbour of Valletta

7 Gozo Fishing Boat

8 Galley of Knights of St. John

9 Emblematic figure of Malta

10 Shipwreck of St. Paul

(T **6/10** recess)

1899 (4 Feb)–**1901**. P 14.

(a) Wmk Crown CA (sideways* on ¼d).

31 **6** ¼d. brown (4.1.01) 6·00 2·50
a. Red-brown 1·50 40
w. Wmk Crown to left of CA 2·50 75
x. Wmk sideways reversed 38·00 20·00
y. Wmk Crown to left of CA and reversed 50·00 25·00
32 **7** 4½d. sepia 20·00 14·00
x. Wmk reversed £600
33 **8** 5d. vermilion 38·00 16·00
x. Wmk reversed £190 £190

(b) Wmk Crown CC.

34 **9** 2s.6d. olive-grey 42·00 12·00
35 **10** 10s. blue-black 90·00 65·00
x. Wmk reversed — £550
y. Wmk inverted and reversed £500 £425
31/5 *Set of* 5 £170 95·00
31s/5s Optd "Specimen" *Set of* 5 £225

*The normal sideways watermark shows Crown to right of CA, *as seen from the back of the stamp*.

One Penny
(11)

12

1902 (4 July). *Nos. 24 and 25 surch locally at Govt Ptg Office with T* **11**.

36 1d. on 2½d. dull blue 1·50 1·75
a. Surch double £15000 £3750
b. "One Pnney" (R. 9/2) 30·00 55·00
ba. Surch double, with "One Pnney" £30000
s. Optd "Specimen" 70·00
37 1d. on 2½d. bright blue 1·00 1·75
a. "One Pnney" (R. 9/2) 32·00 55·00

(Des E. Fuchs)

1903 (12 Mar)–**04**. Wmk Crown CA. P 14.

38 **12** ½d. green 8·50 85
39 1d. blackish brown and red (7.5.03) 15·00 40
40 2d. purple and grey 27·00 6·00
41 2½d. maroon and blue (9.03) 23·00 4·50
42 3d. grey and purple (26.3.03) 1·75 50
43 4d. blackish brown and brown (19.5.04) 26·00 16·00
44 1s. grey and violet (6.4.03) 22·00 7·00
38/44 *Set of* 7 £110 32·00
38s/44s Optd "Specimen" *Set of* 7 £150

1904–14. Wmk Mult Crown CA (sideways* on ¼d.). P 14.

45 **6** ¼d. red-brown (10.10.05) 8·00 1·50
a. Deep brown (2.4.10†) 4·00 10
w. Wmk Crown to left of CA 10·00 1·50
x. Wmk reversed
y. Wmk Crown to left of CA and reversed
47 **12** ½d. green (6.11.04) 5·50 30
aw. Wmk inverted
b. Deep green (1909) 5·00 10
bw. Wmk inverted
48 1d. black and red (24.4.05) 21·00 20
49 1d. red (2.4.07) 3·00 10
50 2d. purple and grey (22.2.05) 11·00 2·50
51 2d. grey (4.10.11) 3·50 5·50
52 2½d. maroon and blue (8.10.04) 24·00 60
53 2½d. bright blue (15.1.11) 5·50 3·50
54 4d. black and brown (1.4.06) 11·00 6·50
w. Wmk inverted
55 4d. black and red/*yellow* (21.11.11) 4·00 3·75
57 **7** 4½d. brown (27.2.05) 30·00 6·00
w. Wmk inverted £300 £225
58 4½d. orange (6.3.12†) 4·50 3·50
59 **8** 5d. vermilion (20.2.05) 30·00 5·50
60 5d. pale sage-green (1909) 4·25 3·50
a. Deep sage-green (1914) 11·00 14·00
61 **12** 1s. grey and violet (14.12.04) 50·00 2·00
62 1s. black/*green* (15.3.11) 7·50 3·75
63 5s. green and red/*yellow* (22.3.11) 65·00 75·00
45/63 *Set of* 17 £250 £110
45as, 47bs, 49s, 51s, 53s, 55s, 58s, 60s, 62s/3s Optd "Specimen" *Set of* 10 £400

*The normal sideways watermark shows Crown to right of CA, *as seen from the back of the stamp*.
†These are the earliest known dates of use.

13

14

15

1914–21. *Ordinary paper (¼d. to 2½d., 2s.6d.) or chalk-surfaced paper (others).* Wmk Mult Crown CA. P 14.

69 **13** ¼d. brown (2.1.14) 1·00 10
a. Deep brown (1919) 2·25 70
x. Wmk reversed † £750
71 ½d. green (20.1.14) 2·25 30
aa. Wmk sideways † £9500
a. Deep green (1919) 4·00 1·25
aw. Wmk inverted † £300
73 1d. carmine-red (15.4.14) 1·50 10
a. Scarlet (1915) 1·50 40
w. Wmk inverted † £300
75 2d. grey (12.8.14) 11·00 4·75
aw. Wmk inverted † £750
b. Deep slate (1919) 9·00 13·00
77 2½d. bright blue (11.3.14) 2·25 50
w. Wmk inverted † £160
78 **14** 3d. purple/*yellow* (1.5.20) 2·50 12·00
a. On orange-buff 65·00 45·00
79 **6** 4d. black (21.8.15) 15·00 5·00
a. Grey-black (28.10.16) 28·00 8·50
80 **13** 6d. dull and bright purple (10.3.14) 11·00 19·00
a. Dull purple and magenta (1918) 15·00 20·00
w. Wmk inverted
81 **14** 1s. black/*green* (*white back*) (2.1.14) 15·00 29·00
a. On green, green back (1915) 12·00 19·00
ab. Wmk sideways † £2250
as. Optd "Specimen" 50·00
b. On blue-green, olive back (1918) 19·00 25·00
c. On emerald surface (1920) 8·50 26·00
d. On emerald back (1921) 32·00 70·00
86 **15** 2s. purple and bright blue/*blue* (15.4.14) 50·00 30·00
a. Break in scroll £350
b. Broken crown and scroll £375
c. Nick in top right scroll £350 £350
d. Dull purple and blue/blue (1921) 90·00 60·00
da. Break in scroll £500
db. Broken crown and scroll £550
de. Break in lines below left scroll £550
df. Damaged leaf at bottom right £550
87 **9** 2s.6d. olive-green (1919) 70·00 80·00
a. Olive-grey (1920) 75·00 £100
88 **15** 5s. green and red/*yellow* (21.3.17) 90·00 £100
a. Break in scroll £475
b. Broken crown and scroll £500
c. Nick in top right scroll £500
e. Break in lines below left scroll £500
f. Damaged leaf at bottom right £500
69/88 *Set of* 12 £225 £250
69s/88s (*ex* 2s.6d.) Optd "Specimen" *Set of* 11 £450

The design of Nos. 79/*a* differs in various details from that of Type **6**.

We have only seen one copy of No. 71aa; it is in used condition.

A 3d. purple on yellow on white back, Type **14**, was prepared for use but not issued. It exists overprinted "Specimen" (*Price* £275).

An example of the 2s.6d. olive-grey with bottom margin attached exists with the "A" omitted from "CA" in the watermark on the margin.

For illustrations of the varieties on Nos. 86 and 88 see above No. 51*b* of Bermuda.

WAR TAX
(16)

17

18

1917–18. *Optd with T* **16** *by De La Rue.*

92 **13** ½d. deep green (14.12.17*) 1·75 15
w. Wmk inverted £475
y. Wmk inverted and reversed £800
93 **12** 3d. grey and purple (15.2.18*) 1·75 10·00
92s/3s Optd "Specimen" *Set of* 2 £140

*These are the earliest known dates of use.

(T **17** recess)

1919 (6 Mar). Wmk Mult Crown CA. P 14.

96 **17** 10s. black £3000 £4000
s. Optd "Specimen" £900

Dark flaw on scroll (R. 2/4 1st state)

Lines omitted from scroll (R. 2/4 2nd state)

1921 (16 Feb)–**22**. *Chalk-surfaced paper (6d., 2s.) or ordinary paper (others).* Wmk Mult Script CA. P 14.

97 **13** ¼d. brown (12.1.22) 4·25 30·00
98 ½d. green (19.1.22) 4·50 22·00
99 1d. scarlet (24.12.21) 4·75 1·75
w. Wmk inverted £750 £275
100 **18** 2d. grey 6·50 1·75
101 **13** 2½d. bright blue (15.1.22) 5·00 30·00
102 6d. dull purple and bright purple (19.1.22) 29·00 70·00
103 **15** 2s. purple and blue/*blue* (19.1.22) 65·00 £200
a. Break in scroll £300 £650
b. Broken crown and scroll £325
c. Dark flaw on scroll £2750
d. Lines omitted from scroll £475
e. Break in lines below left scroll £325
f. Damaged leaf at bottom right £325
g. Nick in top right scroll
104 **17** 10s. black (19.1.22) £350 £700
97/104 *Set of* 8 £425 £950
97s/104s Optd "Specimen" *Set of* 8 £425

For illustrations of other varieties on No. 103 see above No. 51*b* of Bermuda.

Examples of all values are known showing a forged G.P.O. Malta postmark dated "MY 10 22".

SELF-GOVERNMENT
(19)

SELF-GOVERNMENT
(20)

1922 (12 Jan–Apr). *Optd with T* **19** *or T* **20** *(large stamps), at Govt Printing Office, Valletta.*

(a) On No. 35. Wmk Crown CC.

105 **10** 10s. blue-black (R.) £190 £375

(b) On Nos. 71, 77, 78a, 80, 81d, 86c, 87a and 88. Wmk Mult Crown CA.

106 **13** ½d. green 1·00 2·00
w. Wmk inverted £120
107 2½d. bright blue 12·00 38·00
108 **14** 3d. purple/*orange-buff* 4·50 21·00
109 **13** 6d. dull and bright purple 3·50 20·00
x. Wmk reversed † £1000
110 **14** 1s. black/*emerald* 4·25 20·00
111 **15** 2s. purple and blue/*blue* (R.) £250 £475
a. Break in scroll £900
b. Broken crown and scroll £900
c. Nick in top right scroll £1100
e. Break in lines below left scroll £900
f. Damaged leaf at bottom right £900
112 **9** 2s.6d. olive-grey 26·00 45·00
a. "C" of "CA" missing from wmk £950
113 **15** 5s. green and red/*yellow* 50·00 80·00
a. Break in scroll £350
b. Broken crown and scroll £350
c. Lines omitted from scroll £350
e. Break in lines below left scroll £375
f. Damaged leaf at bottom right £375
106/13 *Set of* 8 £325 £650

(c) On Nos. 97/104. Wmk Mult Script CA.

114 **13** ¼d. brown 30 75
w. Wmk inverted
115 ½d. green (29.4) 3·00 7·00
116 1d. scarlet 1·00 20
117 **18** 2d. grey 3·50 45
118 **13** 2½d. bright blue (15.1) 1·10 1·25
119 6d. dull and bright purple (19.4) 18·00 42·00
120 **15** 2s. purple and blue/*blue* (R.) (25.1) 45·00 85·00
a. Break in scroll £250
b. Broken crown and scroll £250
c. Lines omitted from scroll £375
e. Break in lines below left scroll £300
f. Damaged leaf at bottom right £300
121 **17** 10s. black (R.) (9.3) £140 £225
x. Wmk reversed £2750
114/21 *Set of* 8 £190 £325

Examples of all values are known showing a forged G.P.O. Malta postmark dated "MY 10 22".

One Farthing
(21)

22

23

1922 (15 Apr.). *No. 100 surch with T* **21**, *at Govt Printing Office, Valletta.*

122 **18** ¼d. on 2d. grey 85 30
a. Dot to "i" of "Farthing" omitted £300

No. 122a occurred on R. 4/4 of the lower left pane during part of the printing only. Small or faint dots are found on other positions.

(Des C. Dingli (*T* **22**) and G. Vella (**23**))

1922 (1 Aug)–**26**. Wmk Mult Script CA (sideways* on *T* **22**, except No. 140). P 14.

(a) Typo. Chalk-surfaced paper.

123 **22** ¼d. brown (22.8.22) 2·50 60
a. Chocolate-brown 4·25 70
w. Wmk Crown to right of CA — 80·00
124 ½d. green 2·50 15
w. Wmk Crown to right of CA — 80·00

125		1d. orange and purple	4·25	20
		w. Wmk Crown to right of CA	—	60·00
126		1d. bright violet (25.4.24)	4·25	80
127		1½d. brown-red (1.10.23)	5·00	15
128		2d. bistre-brown and turquoise (28.8.22)	3·25	1·25
		w. Wmk Crown to right of CA	—	£110
129		2½d. ultramarine (16.2.26)	4·25	10·00
130		3d. cobalt (28.8.22)	4·75	1·75
		a. Bright ultramarine	4·00	1·50
131		3d. black/*yellow* (16.2.26)	4·25	17·00
132		4d. yellow and bright blue (28.8.22)	3·00	3·50
		w. Wmk Crown to right of CA	£180	
133		6d. olive-green and reddish violet	3·50	3·00
134	23	1s. indigo and sepia	9·00	2·50
135		2s. brown and blue	14·00	14·00
136		2s.6d. bright magenta and black (28.8.22)	11·00	15·00
137		5s. orange-yell and brt ultram (28.8.22)	21·00	48·00
138		10s. slate-grey and brown (28.8.22)	60·00	£160
		(b) Recess.		
139	22	£1 black and carmine-red (wmk sideways) (28.8.22)	£120	£300
140		£1 black and bright carmine (wmk upright) (14.5.25)	£100	£300
123/40 *Set of* 17			£225	£500
123s/39s Optd "Specimen" *Set of* 17			£500	

*The normal sideways watermark shows Crown to left of CA, *as seen from the back of the stamp.*

Two pence halfpenny (24) **POSTAGE** (25)

1925. *Surch with T* **24**, *at Govt Printing Office, Valletta.*

141	22	2½d. on 3d. cobalt (3 Dec)	1·75	4·25
142		2½d. on 3d. bright ultramarine (9 Dec)	1·75	4·00

1926 (1 Apr). *Optd with T* **25** *at Govt Printing Office, Valletta.*

143	22	¼d. brown	70	4·50
144		½d. green	70	15
		w. Wmk Crown to right of CA	90·00	
145		1d. bright violet	1·00	25
146		1½d. brown-red	1·25	60
147		2d. bistre-brown and turquoise	75	1·75
148		2½d. ultramarine	1·25	1·00
149		3d. black/*yellow*	75	80
		a. Opt inverted	£170	£475
150		4d. yellow and bright blue	11·00	23·00
		w. Wmk Crown to right of CA	£160	
151		6d. olive-green and violet	2·75	4·50
152	23	1s. indigo and sepia	5·50	15·00
153		2s. brown and blue	50·00	£140
154		2s.6d. bright magenta and black	17·00	45·00
155		5s. orange-yellow and bright ultramarine	9·50	45·00
156		10s. slate-grey and brown	7·00	18·00
143/56 *Set of* 14			95·00	£275

26

27 Valletta Harbour

28 St. Publius

29 Mdina (Notabile)

30 Gozo fishing boat

31 Neptune

32 Neolithic temple, Mnajdra

33 St. Paul

(*T* **26** *typo, others recess Waterlow*)

1926 (6 Apr)–**27**. *T* **26/33**. *Inscr* "POSTAGE". Wmk Mult Script CA. P 15×14 (*T* **26**) or 12½ (others).

157	26	¼d. brown	80	15
158		½d. yellow-green (5.8.26)	60	15
		a. Printed on the gummed side	£1100	
		w. Wmk inverted	†	£800
159		1d. rose-red (1.4.27)	3·00	1·00
160		1½d. chestnut (7.10.26)	2·00	10
161		2d. greenish grey (1.4.27)	4·50	12·00
162		2½d. blue (1.4.27)	4·00	1·50
162*a*		3d. violet (1.4.27)	4·25	3·50
163		4d. black and red	3·25	13·00
164		4½d. lavender and ochre	3·50	3·75
165		6d. violet and scarlet (5.5.26)	4·25	4·75
166	27	1s. black	6·50	6·50
167	28	1s.6d. black and green	6·50	15·00
168	29	2s. black and purple	6·50	19·00
169	30	2s.6d. black and vermilion	16·00	48·00
170	31	3s. black and blue	17·00	30·00
171	32	5s. black and green (5.5.26)	22·00	60·00
172	33	10s. black and carmine (9.2.27)	60·00	£100
157/72 *Set of* 17			£140	£275
157s/72s Optd "Specimen" *Set of* 17			£325	

AIR MAIL (34) **POSTAGE AND REVENUE** (35) **POSTAGE AND REVENUE.** (36)

1928 (1 Apr). *Air. Optd with T* **34**.

173	26	6d. violet and scarlet	1·75	1·00

1928 (1 Oct–5 Dec). *As Nos. 157/72, optd.*

174	35	¼d. brown	1·50	10
175		½d. yellow-green	1·50	10
176		1d. rose-red	1·75	3·25
177		1d. chestnut (5.12.28)	4·50	10
178		1½d. chestnut	2·00	85
179		1½d. rose-red (5.12.28)	4·25	10
180		2d. greenish grey	4·25	9·00
181		2½d. blue	2·00	10
182		3d. violet	2·00	80
183		4d. black and red	2·00	1·75
184		4½d. lavender and ochre	2·25	1·00
185		6d. violet and scarlet	2·25	1·50
186	36	1s. black (R.)	5·50	2·50
187		1s.6d. black and green (R.)	9·00	9·50
188		2s. black and purple (R.)	24·00	55·00
189		2s.6d. black and vermilion (R.)	17·00	21·00
190		3s. black and blue (R.)	19·00	24·00
191		5s. black and green (R.)	35·00	65·00
192		10s. black and carmine (R.)	65·00	95·00
174/92 *Set of* 19			£180	£250
174s/92s Optd "Specimen" *Set of* 19			£350	

1930 (20 Oct). *As Nos. 157/172, but inscr* "POSTAGE (&) REVENUE".

193		¼d. brown	60	10
194		½d. yellow-green	60	10
195		1d. chestnut	60	10
196		1½d. rose-red	70	10
197		2d. greenish grey	1·25	50
198		2½d. blue	2·00	10
199		3d. violet	1·50	20
200		4d. black and red	1·25	4·00
201		4½d. lavender and ochre	3·25	1·25
202		6d. violet and scarlet	2·75	1·25
203		1s. black	10·00	16·00
204		1s.6d. black and green	8·50	22·00
205		2s. black and purple	10·00	25·00
206		2s.6d. black and vermilion	17·00	50·00
207		3s. black and blue	32·00	55·00
208		5s. black and green	42·00	65·00
209		10s. black and carmine	90·00	£170
193/209 *Set of* 17			£200	£350
193s/209s Perf "Specimen" *Set of* 17			£350	

1935 (6 May). *Silver Jubilee. As Nos. 91/4 of Antigua, but printed by B.W.* P 11×12.

210		½d. black and green	50	70
		a. Extra flagstaff	25·00	42·00
		b. Short extra flagstaff	45·00	
		c. Lightning conductor	35·00	
211		2½d. brown and deep blue	2·50	4·50
		a. Extra flagstaff	£130	£160
		b. Short extra flagstaff	£180	£250
		c. Lightning conductor	£140	£200
212		6d. light blue and olive-green	7·00	7·00
		a. Extra flagstaff	£180	£225
		b. Short extra flagstaff	£300	
		c. Lightning conductor	£170	£225
213		1s. slate and purple	14·00	20·00
		a. Extra flagstaff	£425	£475
		b. Short extra flagstaff	£375	£450
		c. Lightning conductor	£300	
210/13 *Set of* 4			22·00	29·00
210s/13s Perf "Specimen" *Set of* 4			£160	

For illustrations of plate varieties see Omnibus section following Zanzibar.

Sheets from the second printing of the ½d., 6d. and 1s. in November 1935 had the extra flagstaff partially erased from the stamp with a sharp point.

1937 (12 May). *Coronation. As Nos. 95/7 of Antigua, but printed by D.L.R.* P 14.

214		½d. green	10	20
215		1½d. scarlet	1·25	65
		a. Brown-lake	£600	£600
216		2½d. bright blue	1·00	80
214/16 *Set of* 3			2·00	1·50
214s/16s Perf "Specimen" *Set of* 3			£100	

37 Grand Harbour, Valletta

38 H.M.S. *St. Angelo*

39 Verdala Palace

40 Hypogeum, Hal Saflieni

41 Victoria and Citadel, Gozo

42 De L'Isle Adam entering Mdina

43 St. John's Co-Cathedral

44 Ruins at Mnajdra

45 Statue of Manoel de Vilhena

46 Maltese girl wearing faldetta

47 St. Publius

48 Mdina Cathedral

49 Statue of Neptune

50 Palace Square, Valletta

51 St. Paul

Broken cross (Right pane R. 5/7)

Extra windows (R. 2/7) (corrected in 1945)

Flag on citadel (R. 5/8)

Damaged value tablet (R. 4/9)

Semaphore flaw (R. 2/7)

(Recess Waterlow)

1938 (17 Feb*)–**43**. *T* **37/51**. Wmk Mult Script CA (sideways on No. 217). P 12½.

217	**37**	¼d. brown	10	10
218	**38**	½d. green	2·75	30
218*a*		½d. red-brown (8.3.43)	55	30
219	**39**	1d. red-brown	4·25	40
219*a*		1d. green (8.3.43)	60	10
220	**40**	1½d. scarlet	1·25	30
		a. Broken cross	£150	65·00
220*b*		1½d. slate-black (8.3.43)	30	15
		ba. Broken cross	70·00	55·00
221	**41**	2d. slate-black	1·00	2·00
		a. Extra windows	65·00	
221*b*		2d. scarlet (8.3.43)	40	30
		ba. Extra windows	60·00	45·00
		bb. Flag on citadel	60·00	50·00
222	**42**	2½d. greyish blue	2·25	60
222*a*		2½d. dull violet (8.3.43)	60	10
223	**43**	3d. dull violet	1·50	80
223*a*		3d. blue (8.3.43)	30	20
224	**44**	4½d. olive-green and yellow-brown	50	30
225	**45**	6d. olive-green and scarlet	1·75	30
226	**46**	1s. black	1·75	30
227	**47**	1s.6d. black and olive-green	7·00	4·00
228	**48**	2s. green and deep blue	4·50	5·00
229	**49**	2s.6d. black and scarlet	8·50	5·50
		a. Damaged value tablet	£300	£150
230	**50**	5s. black and green	4·50	7·00
		a. Semaphore flaw	75·00	£110
231	**51**	10s. black and carmine	17·00	15·00
217/31 *Set of* 21			55·00	38·00
217s/31s Perf "Specimen" *Set of* 21			£425	

*This is the local date of issue but the stamps were released in London on 15 February.

1946 (3 Dec). *Victory. As Nos.* 110/11 *of Antigua, but inscr* "MALTA" *between Maltese Cross and George Cross.*

232		1d. green	15	10
		w. Wmk inverted	£850	
233		3d. blue	40	1·50
232s/3s Perf "Specimen" *Set of* 2			80·00	

SELF-GOVERNMENT

(**52**)

"NT" joined (R. 4/10)

Halation flaw (Pl 2 R. 2/5) (ptg of 8 Jan 1953)

Cracked plate (Pl 2 R. 5/1) (ptg of 8 Jan 1953)

(Optd by Waterlow)

1948 (25 Nov)–**53**. *New Constitution. As Nos.* 217/31 *but optd as T* **52**; *reading up on* ½d. *and* 5s., *down on other values, and smaller on* ¼d. *value.*

234	**37**	¼d. brown	30	20
235	**38**	½d. red-brown	30	10
		a. "NT" joined	19·00	25·00
236	**39**	1d. green	30	10
236*a*		1d. grey (R.) (8.1.53)	50	10
237	**40**	1½d. blue-black (R.)	1·25	10
		a. Broken cross	95·00	42·00
237*b*		1½d. green (8.1.53)	30	10
		ba. Albino opt	†	£13000
238	**41**	2d. scarlet	1·25	10
		a. Extra windows	£100	
		b. Flag on citadel	80·00	
238*c*		2d. yellow-ochre (8.1.53)	30	10
		ca. Halation flaw	£150	
		cc. Cracked plate	£140	
239	**42**	2½d. dull violet (R.)	80	10
239*a*		2½d. scarlet-vermilion (8.1.53)	50	1·50
240	**43**	3d. blue (R.)	2·50	15
240*a*		3d. dull violet (R.) (8.1.53)	50	15
241	**44**	4½d. olive-green and yellow-brown	2·50	1·50
241*a*		4½d. olive-grn and dp ultram (R.) (8.1.53)	50	90
242	**45**	6d. olive-green and scarlet	3·25	15
243	**46**	1s. black	3·25	40
244	**47**	1s.6d. black and olive-green	2·50	50
245	**48**	2s. green and deep blue (R.)	5·00	2·50
246	**49**	2s.6d. black and scarlet	12·00	2·50
		a. Damaged value tablet	£1000	
247	**50**	5s. black and green (R.)	23·00	3·50
		a. "NT" joined	£225	£120
		b. Semaphore flaw	—	£3000
248	**51**	10s. black and carmine	23·00	22·00
234/48 *Set of* 21			75·00	32·00

1949 (4 Jan). *Royal Silver Wedding. As Nos.* 112/13 *of Antigua, but inscr* "MALTA" *between Maltese Cross and George Cross and with* £1 *ptd in recess.*

249		1d. green	50	10
250		£1 indigo	38·00	38·00

1949 (10 Oct). *75th Anniv of U.P.U. As Nos.* 114/17 *of Antigua, but inscr* "MALTA" *in recess.*

251		2½d. violet	30	10
252		3d. deep blue	3·00	1·00
253		6d. carmine-red	60	1·00
254		1s. blue-black	60	2·50
251/4 *Set of* 4			4·00	4·25

53 Queen Elizabeth II when Princess

54 "Our Lady of Mount Carmel" (attrib Palladino)

(*T* **53/4**. Recess B.W.)

1950 (1 Dec). *Visit of Princess Elizabeth to Malta.* Wmk Mult Script CA. P 12×11½.

255	**53**	1d. green	10	15
256		3d. blue	20	20
257		1s. black	65	1·50
255/7 *Set of* 3			80	1·60

1951 (12 July). *Seventh Centenary of the Scapular.* Wmk Mult Script CA. P 12×11½.

258	**54**	1d. green	15	30
259		3d. violet	50	10
260		1s. black	1·10	1·60
258/60 *Set of* 3			1·60	1·75

1953 (3 June). *Coronation. As No.* 120 *of Antigua.*

261		1½d. black and deep yellow-green	60	10

55 St. John's Co-Cathedral

56 "Immaculate Conception" (Caruana) (altar-piece, Cospicua)

(Recess Waterlow)

1954 (3 May). *Royal Visit.* Wmk Mult Script CA. P 12½.

262	**55**	3d. violet	30	10

(Photo Harrison)

1954 (8 Sept). *Centenary of Dogma of the Immaculate Conception.* Wmk Mult Script CA. *Chalk-surfaced paper.* P 14×14.

263	**56**	1½d. emerald	15	10
264		3d. bright blue	15	10
265		1s. grey-black	35	20
263/5 *Set of* 3			60	35

57 Monument of the Great Siege, 1565

58 Wignacourt aqueduct horse trough

59 Victory Church

60 Second World War Memorial

61 Mosta Church

62 Auberge de Castile

63 The King's Scroll

64 Roosevelt's Scroll

65 Neolithic temples Tarxien

66 Vedette (tower)

67 Mdina gate

68 "Les Gavroches" (statue)

69 Monument of Christ the King

70 Grand Master Cottener's monument

71 Grand Master Perello's monument

72 St. Paul

73 Baptism of Christ

(Recess Waterlow (2s.6d. to £1). B.W.(others))

1956 (23 Jan)–**58**. *T* **57/73** *and similar designs.* Wmk Mult Script CA. P 14×13½ (2s.6d. to £1) or 11½ (others).

266	**57**	¼d. violet	20	10
267	**58**	½d. orange	50	10
268	**59**	1d. black (9.2.56)	1·25	10
269	**60**	1½d. bluish green (9.2.56)	30	10
270	**61**	2d. brown (9.2.56)	1·50	10
		a. Deep brown (26.2.58)	3·75	20
271	**62**	2½d. orange-brown	2·00	30
272	**63**	3d. rose-red (22.3.56)	1·50	10
		w. Wmk inverted	†	£750
273	**64**	4½d. deep blue	2·50	40
274	**65**	6d. indigo (9.2.56)	75	10
		w. Wmk inverted	£140	
275	**66**	8d. bistre-brown	4·25	1·00
276	**67**	1s. deep reddish violet	1·25	10
277	**68**	1s.6d. deep turquoise-green	12·00	20
278	**69**	2s. olive-green	12·00	3·25
279	**70**	2s.6d. chestnut (22.3.56)	9·50	2·50
280	**71**	5s. green (11.10.56)	15·00	3·00
281	**72**	10s. carmine-red (19.11.56)	38·00	13·00
282	**73**	£1 yellow-brown (5.1.57)	38·00	28·00
266/82 *Set of* 17			£120	45·00

See also Nos. 314/15.

74 "Defence of Malta"

75 Searchlights over Malta

(Des E. Cremona. Photo Harrison)

1957 (15 Apr). *George Cross Commemoration. Cross in silver. T* **74/5** *and similar design.* Wmk Mult Script CA. P 14½×14 (3d.) or P 14×14½ (others).

283	1½d. deep dull green	15	10
284	3d. vermilion	15	10
285	1s. reddish brown	15	10
283/5 *Set of 3*		40	25

Design: *Vert*—1s. Bombed buildings.

77 "Design"

(Des E. Cremona. Photo Harrison)

1958 (15 Feb). *Technical Education in Malta. T* **77** *and similar designs.* W w **12**. P 14×14½ (3d.) or 14½×14 (others).

286	1½d. black and deep green	15	10
287	3d. black, scarlet and grey	15	10
288	1s. grey, bright purple and black	15	10
286/8 *Set of 3*		40	25

Designs: *Vert*—3d. "Construction". *Horiz*—1s. Technical School, Paola.

80 Bombed-out Family

81 Sea Raid on Grand Harbour, Valletta

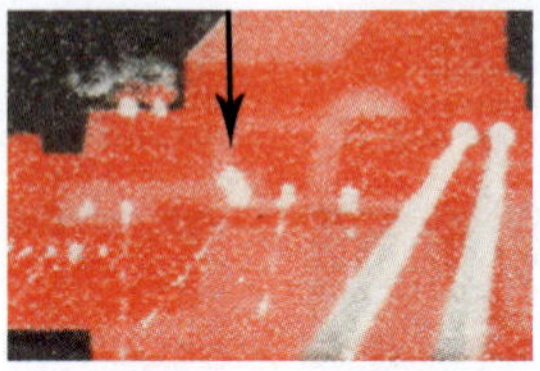

3d. White flaw on third gun from right appearing as larger gun-flash (Pl. 1A R. 5/7).

(Des E. Cremona. Photo Harrison)

1958 (15 Apr). *George Cross Commemoration. Cross in first colour, outlined in silver. T* **80/1** *and similar design.* W w **12**. P 14×14½ (3d.) or 14½×14 (others).

289	1½d. blue-green and black	15	10
290	3d. red and black	15	10
	a. "Gunflash" flaw	4·00	
291	1s. reddish violet and black	15	10
	a. Silver (outline) omitted	£500	
289/91 *Set of 3*		40	25

Design: *Horiz*—1s. Searchlight crew.

83 Air Raid Casualties

84 "For Gallantry"

(Des E. Cremona. Photo Harrison)

1959 (15 Apr). *George Cross Commemoration. T* **83/4** *and similar design.* W w **12**. P 14½×14 (3d.) or 14×14½ (others).

292	1½d. grey-green, black and gold	25	10
293	3d. reddish violet, black and gold	25	10
294	1s. blue-grey, black and gold	85	95
292/4 *Set of 3*		1·25	1·00

Design: *Vert*—1s. Maltese under bombardment.

86 Shipwreck of St. Paul (after Palombi)

87 Statue of St. Paul, Rabat, Malta

8d. Two white flaws in "PAUL" one giving the "P" the appearance of "R" and other a blob over the "L" (Pl. 1A-1A R.5/2).

(Des E. Cremona. Photo Harrison)

1960 (9 Feb). *19th Centenary of the Shipwreck of St. Paul. T* **86/7** *and similar designs.* W w **12**.

295	1½d. blue, gold and yellow-brown	15	10
	a. Gold (dates and crosses) omitted	60·00	
296	3d. bright purple, gold and blue	15	10
	a. Printed on the gummed side		
297	6d. carmine, gold and pale grey	25	10
298	8d. black and gold	30	50
	a. "RAUL" flaw	4·50	
299	1s. maroon and gold	25	10
300	2s.6d. blue, deep bluish green and gold	1·00	2·00
	a. Gold omitted	£600	£375
295/300 *Set of 6*		1·90	2·50

Designs: *Vert as T* **86**—3d. Consecration of St. Publius (first Bishop of Malta) (after Palombi); 6d. Departure of St. Paul (after Palombi). *Diamond shaped as T* **87**—1s. Angel with *Acts of the Apostles*; 2s.6d. St. Paul with *Second Epistle to the Corinthians*.

92 Stamp of 1860

(Centre litho; frame recess. Waterlow)

1960 (1 Dec). *Stamp Centenary.* W w **12**. P 13½.

301	**92**	1½d. buff, pale blue and green	25	10
		a. *Buff, pale bl & myrtle* (white paper)	3·00	1·75
		a. Blank corner	3·00	1·75
302		3d. buff pale blue and deep carmine	30	10
303		6d. buff, pale blue and ultramarine	40	1·00
301/3 *Set of 3*			85	1·10

Examples of the 1½d. apparently with the blue omitted are from sheets with a very weak printing of this colour.

No. 302a shows the right-hand bottom corner of the 1860 stamp blank. It occurs on R. 4/7 from early trial plates and sheets containing the error should have been destroyed, but some were sorted into good stock and issued at a post office.

93 George Cross

(Photo Harrison)

1961 (15 Apr). *George Cross Commemoration. T* **93** *and similar designs showing medal.* W w **12**. P 15×14.

304	1½d. black, cream and bistre	15	10
305	3d. olive-brown and greenish blue	30	10
306	1s. olive-green, lilac and deep reddish violet	75	2·00
304/6 *Set of 3*		1·10	2·00

96 "Madonna Damascena"

(Photo Harrison)

1962 (7 Sept). *Great Siege Commemoration. T* **96** *and similar vert designs.* W w **12** P 13×12.

307	2d. bright blue	10	10
308	3d. red	10	10
309	6d. bronze-green	30	10
310	1s. brown-purple	30	40
307/10 *Set of 4*		70	60

Designs:—3d. Great Siege Monument; 6d. Grand Master La Valette; 1s. Assault on Fort St. Elmo.

1963 (4 June). *Freedom from Hunger. As No. 146 of Antigua.*

311	1s.6d. sepia	1·75	2·50

1963 (2 Sept). *Red Cross Centenary. As Nos. 147/8 of Antigua.*

312	2d. red and black	25	15
313	1s. 6d. red and blue	1·75	4·25

1963 (15 Oct)–**64**. *As Nos. 268 and 270, but wmk.* w **12**.

314	**59**	1d. black	50	30
315	**61**	2d. deep brown (11.7.64*)	1·90	4·00

*This is the earliest known date recorded in Malta.

100 Bruce, Zammit and Microscope

101 Goat and Laboratory Equipment

(Des E. Cremona. Photo Harrison)

1964 (14 April). *Anti-Brucellosis Congress.* W w **12**. P 14.

316	**100**	2d. light brown, black and bluish green	10	10
		a. Black (microscope, etc) omitted	£350	
317	**101**	1s.6d. black and maroon	90	90

102 "Nicole Cotoner tending Sick Man" (M. Preti)

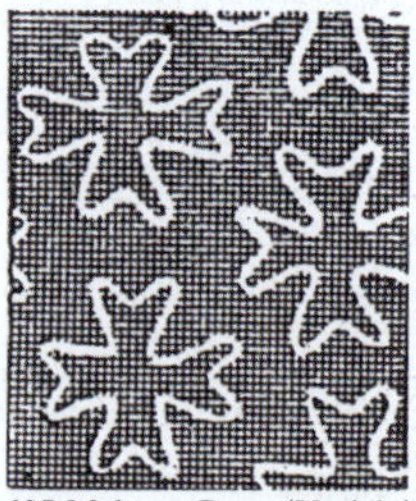

105 Maltese Cross (Upright)

In this illustration the points of the crosses meet in a vertical line. When the watermark is sideways they meet in a horizontal line.

(Des E. Cremona. Photo Harrison)

1964 (5 Sept). *First European Catholic Doctors' Congress, Vienna. T* **102** *and similar horiz designs. (sideways).* W **105**. P 13½×11½.

318	2d. red, black, gold and grey-blue	20	10
319	6d. red, black, gold and bistre	50	15
320	1s.6d. red, black, gold and reddish violet	1·10	1·90
318/20 *Set of 3*		1·60	1·90

Designs:—6d. St. Luke and Hospital; 1s.6d. Sacra Infermeria, Valletta.

INDEPENDENT

106 Dove and British Crown

109 "The Nativity"

(Des E. Cremona. Photo Harrison)

1964 (21 Sept). *Independence. T* **106** *and similar vert designs.* W w **105**. P 14½×13½.

321	2d. olive-brown, red and gold	30	10
	a. Gold omitted	70·00	
322	3d. brown-purple, red and gold	30	10
	a. Gold omitted	70·00	
323	6d. slate, red and gold	70	15
324	1s. blue, red and gold	70	15
325	1s.6d. indigo, red and gold	1·50	1·00
326	2s.6d. deep violet-blue, red and gold	1·50	2·25
321/6 *Set of 6*		4·50	3·25

Designs:—2d, 1s. Type **106**; 3d., 1s.6d. Dove and Pope's Tiara; 6d., 2s.6d. Dove and U.N. emblem.

(Des E. Cremona. Photo D.L.R.)

1964 (3 Nov). *Christmas.* W **105** (sideways). P 13×13½.

327	**109**	2d. bright purple and gold	10	10
328		4d. bright blue and gold	20	15
329		8d. deep bluish green and gold	45	45
327/9 *Set of 3*			65	60

110 Neolithic Era

117 Galleys of Knights of St. John

119 British Rule

(Des E. Cremona. Photo Harrison)

1965 (7 Jan)–**70**. *Chalk-surfaced paper. T* **110**, **117**, **119** *and similar designs.* W **105**. P 14×14½ (vert) or 14½ (horiz).

330		½d. multicoloured	10	10
		a. "½d." (white) printed twice†	10·00	
		ab. ditto, once inverted	†	£1600
		b. Rose-pink ("MALTA") printed twice	10·00	
		c. White (face value) omitted	50·00	
331		1d. multicoloured	10	10
		a. Gold (ancient lettering) omitted	80·00	
		b. White (Greek lettering and "PUNIC") omitted	85·00	
		c. White ptg double	22·00	
		d. "PUNIC" omitted	£110	
332		1½d. multicoloured	30	10
333		2d. multicoloured	10	10
		a. Gold omitted	26·00	
		b. Imperf (pair)	£275	
334		2½d. multicoloured	1·25	10
		a. Orange omitted*	85·00	
		b. Gold ("SARACENIC") omitted	55·00	
		c. Salmon printed twice†	65·00	
335		3d. multicoloured	10	10
		a. Gold (windows) omitted	95·00	
		b. "MALTA" (silver) omitted	26·00	
		c. "MALTA" (silver) printed twice	£325	
		d. Bright lilac ("SICULO NORMAN") omitted	£300	
		e. Imperf (pair)	£300	
336		4d. multicoloured	1·25	10
		a. "KNIGHTS OF MALTA" (silver) omitted	45·00	
		b. "MALTA" (silver) omitted	75·00	
		c. Black (shield surround) omitted	60·00	
		d. Imperf (pair)	£160	
		e. Gold ommited	£100	
337		4½d. multicoloured	1·50	75
		a. Silver ("MALTA", etc) omitted	£350	
337*b*		5d. multicoloured (1.8.70)	30	20
		ba. "FORTIFICATIONS" (gold) omitted	95·00	
338		6d. multicoloured	30	10
		a. "MALTA" (silver) omitted	45·00	
		b. Black omitted	90·00	
339		8d. multicoloured	70	10
		a. Gold (centre) omitted	42·00	
		b. Gold (frame) omitted	65·00	
339*c*		10d. multicoloured (1.8.70)	50	1·90
		ca. "NAVAL ARSENAL" (gold) omitted	£300	
340		1s. multicoloured	30	10
		a. Gold (centre) omitted	£170	
		b. Gold (framework) omitted	45·00	
341		1s. 3d. multicoloured	2·00	1·40
		a. Gold (centre) omitted	65·00	
		b. Gold (framework) omitted	£150	
		c. Imperf (pair)	£350	
342		1s.6d. multicoloured	60	20
		a. Head (black) omitted	£250	
		b. Gold (centre) omitted	48·00	
		c. Gold (frame) omitted	85·00	
343		2s. multicoloured	70	10
		a. Gold (centre) omitted	£170	
		b. Gold (framework) omitted	65·00	
344		2s.6d. multicoloured	70	50
345		3s. multicoloured	1·75	75
		a. Gold (framework) omitted	38·00	
		b. Gold ("1964") omitted	£200	
346		5s. multicoloured	6·00	1·00
		a. Gold (HAFMED emblem) omitted	95·00	
		b. Gold (framework) omitted	90·00	
347		10s. multicoloured	3·00	4·75
		a. Gold (centre) omitted	£190	
348		£1 multicoloured	4·00	5·00
		a. Pink omitted	28·00	
330/48 *Set of* 21			22·00	15·00

Designs: *Vert*—1d. Punic era; 1½d. Roman era; 2d. Proto Christian era; 2½d. Saracenic era; 3d. Siculo Norman era; 4d. Knights of Malta; 5d. Fortifications; 6d. French occupation. *Horiz*—10d. Naval arsenal; 1s. Maltese corps of the British army; 1s.3d. International Eucharistic congress, 1913; 1s.6d. Self-government, 1921; 2s. Gaza civic council; 2s.6d. State of Malta; 3s. Independence, 1964 5s. HAFMED (Allied forces, Mediterranean); 10s. The Maltese Islands (map); £1 Patron saints.

*The effect of this is to leave the Saracenic pattern as a pink colour. †On the ½d. the second impression is 6½ mm lower or 3 mm to the left, and on the 2½d. 1 mm lower so that it falls partly across "MALTA" and "2½d." Stamps with almost coincidental double impression are common The ½d. and 1d. had white printing plates. Two silver plates were used on the 4d., one for "KNIGHTS OF MALTA" and the other for "MALTA". Two gold plates were used for the 8d. to 10s., one for the framework and the other for the gold in the central part of the designs.

No. 337a comes from a sheet on which the silver printing was so misplaced that it missed the top horizontal row entirely.

The ½d. to 4d., 1s. and 1s.6d. to 5s. values exist with PVA gum as well as gum arabic and the 5d. and 10d. have PVA gum only.

129 "Dante" (Raphael)

(Des E. Cremona. Photo Govt Ptg Works, Rome)

1965 (7 July). *700th Birth Anniv of Dante.* P 14.

349	**129**	2d. indigo	10	10
350		6d. bronze-green	25	10
351		2s. chocolate	1·10	1·50
349/151 *Set of* 3			1·25	1·50

130 Turkish Camp

131 Turkish Fleet

(Des E. Cremona. Photo Harrison)

1965 (1 Sept). *400th Anniv of Great Siege. T* **130/1** *and similar designs.* W **105** (sideways). P 13 (6d., 1s.) or 14½×14 (others).

352		2d. olive-green, red and black	30	10
353		3d. olive-green, red, black and light drab	30	10
354		6d. multicoloured	40	10
		a. Gold (framework and dates) omitted	£275	
		b. Black (on hulls) omitted	£275	
355		8d. red, gold, indigo and blue	70	90
		a. Gold (flag and dates) omitted	£120	
356		1s. red, gold and deep grey-blue	40	10
357		1s.6d. ochre, red and black	75	30
358		2s.6d. sepia, black, red and yellow-olive	1·25	3·25
352/8 *Set of* 7			3·50	4·25

Designs: *Square (as T* **130**)—3d. Battle scene; 8d. Arrival of relief force; 1s.6d. "Allegory of Victory" (from mural by M. Preti); 2s.8d. Victory medal. *Vert (as T* **131**)—1s. Grand Master J. de La Valette's arms.

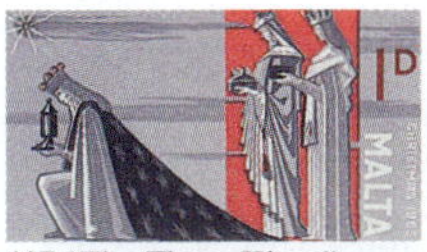

137 "The Three Kings"

138 Sir Winston Churchill

(Des E. Cremona. Photo Enschedé)

1965 (7 Oct). *Christmas.* W **105** (sideways). P 11×11½.

359	**137**	1d. slate-purple and red	10	10
360		4d. slate-purple and blue	30	25
361		1s.3d. slate-purple and bright purple	30	30
359/61 *Set of* 3			65	60

(Des E. Cremona. Photo Harrison)

1966 (24 Jan). *Churchill Commemoration. T* **138** *and similar square design.* W **105** (sideways). P 14½×14.

362	**138**	2d. black, red and gold	25	10
363	–	3d. bronze-green, yellow-olive and gold	25	10
364	**138**	1s. maroon, red and gold	40	10
		a. Gold (shading) omitted	£160	
365	–	1s.6d. chalky blue, violet-blue and gold	50	1·10
362/5 *Set of* 4			1·25	1·25

Design:—3d., 1s.6d. Sir Winston Churchill and George Cross.

140 Grand Master La Valette

145 President Kennedy and Memorial

(Des E. Cremona. Photo State Ptg Works, Vienna)

1966 (28 Mar). *400th Anniv of Valletta. T* **140** *and similar square designs. Multicoloured.* W **105** (sideways). P 12.

366		2d. Type 140	10	10
367		3d. Pope Pius V	15	10
		a. Gold omitted	£350	
368		6d. Map of Valletta	20	10
369		1s. Francesco Laparelli (architect)	20	10
370		2s.6d. Girolamo Cassar (architect)	50	50
366/70 *Set of* 5			1·00	80

(Des E. Cremona. Photo Harrison)

1966 (28 May). *President Kennedy Commemoration.* W **105** (sideways). P 15×14.

371	**145**	3d. olive, gold and black	10	10
		a. Gold inscr omitted	£160	
372		1s.6d. Prussian blue, gold and black	10	10

146 "Trade"

(Des E. Cremona. Photo D.L.R.)

1966 (16 June). *Tenth Malta Trade Fair.* W **105** (sideways). P 13½.

373	**146**	2d. multicoloured	10	10
374		8d. multicoloured	30	65
375		2s.6d. multicoloured	30	65
373/5 *Set of* 3			65	1·25

147 "The Child in the Manger"

148 George Cross

(Des E. Cremona. Photo D.L.R.)

1966 (7 Oct). *Christmas.* W **105**. P 13½.

376	**147**	1d. black, gold, turquoise-bl and slate-purple	10	10
377		4d. black, gold, ultramarine and slate-purple	10	10
378		1s.3d. black, gold, bright purple and slate purple	10	10
		a. Gold omitted	65·00	
376/8 *Set of* 3			25	25

(Des E. Cremona. Photo Harrison)

1967 (1 Mar). *25th Anniv of George Cross Award to Malta.* W **105** (sideways). P 14½×14.

379	**148**	2d. multicoloured	10	10
380		4d. multicoloured	10	10
381		3s. multicoloured	15	15
379/81 *Set of* 3			30	30

149 Crucifixion of St. Peter

150 Open Bible and Episcopal Emblems

(Des E. Cremona. Photo Harrison)

1967 (28 June). *1900th Anniv of Martyrdom of Saints Peter and Paul. T* **149/50** *and similar design.* W **105** (sideways). P 13½×14½ (8d.) or 14½ (others).

382		2d. chestnut, orange and black	10	10
383		8d. yellow-olive, gold and black	15	10
384		3s. blue, light blue and black	20	15
382/4 *Set of* 3			40	30

Design:—*Square as T* **149**—3s. Beheading of St. Paul.

152 "St. Catherine of Siena"

156 Temple Ruins, Tarxien

(Des E. Cremona. Photo Enschedé)

1967 (1 Aug). *300th Death Anniv of Melchior Gafa (sculptor). T* **152** *and similar horiz designs. Multicoloured.* W **105** (sideways). P 13½×13.

385		2d. Type **152**	10	10
386		4d. Thomas of Villanova"	10	10
387		1s.6d. "Baptism of Christ" (detail)	15	10
388		2s.6d. "St. John the Baptist" (from "Baptism of Christ")	15	10
385/8 *Set of* 4			45	35

(Des E. Cremona. Photo Harrison)

1967 (12 Sept). *15th International Historical Architecture Congress, Valletta. T* **156** *and similar square designs. Multicoloured.* W **105**. P 15×14½.

389		2d. Type **156**	10	10
390		6d. Facade of Palazzo Falzon, Notabile	10	10
391		1s. Parish Church, Birkirkara	10	10
392		3s. Portal, Auberge de Castille	25	25
389/92 *Set of* 4			50	50

160 "Angels" **161** "Crib" **162** "Angels"

(Des E. Cremona. Photo D.L.R.)

1967 (20 Oct). *Christmas.* W **105** (sideways). P 14.

393	**160**	1d. multicoloured	10	10
		a. Horiz strip of 3. Nos. 393/5	40	25
		b. White stars (red omitted)	85·00	
394	**161**	8d. multicoloured	20	10
395	**162**	1s.4d. multicoloured	20	10
393/5 *Set of 3*			45	25

Nos. 393/5 were issued in sheets of 60 of each value (arranged *tête-bêche*), and also in sheets containing the three values *se-tenant*, thus forming a triptych of the Nativity.

163 Queen Elizabeth II and Arms of Malta

(Des E. Cremona. Photo Harrison)

1967 (13 Nov). *Royal Visit.* *T* **163** *and similar designs.* W **105** (sideways on 2d., 3s.). P 14×15 (4d.) or 15×14 (others).

396		2d. multicoloured	10	10
		a. Grey-brown omitted*		
397		4d. black, brown-purple and gold	10	10
398		3s. multicoloured	20	25
396/8 *Set of 3*			35	40

Designs: *Vert*—4d. Queen in Robes of Order of St. Michael and St. George. *Horiz*—3s. Queen and outline of Malta.

*This affects the Queen's face.

166 Human Rights Emblem and People **167**

(Des E. Cremona. Photo Harrison)

1968 (2 May). *Human Rights Year.* W **105**. P 12½ (6d.) or 14½ (others).

399	**166**	2d. multicoloured	10	10
400	**167**	6d. multicoloured	10	10
401	–	2s. multicoloured	10	10
399/401 *Set of 3*			25	25

The design of the 2s. value is a reverse of Type **166**.

169 Fair "Products"

(Des E. Cremona. Photo Harrison)

1968 (1 June). *Malta International Trade Fair.* W **105** (sideways). P 14½×14.

402	**169**	4d. multicoloured	10	10
403		8d. multicoloured	10	10
404		3s. multicoloured	15	10
402/4 *Set of 3*			30	25

170 Arms of the Order of St. John and La Valette

171 "La Valette" (A. de Favray)

172 La Valette's Tomb

173 Angels and Scroll bearing Date of Death

(Des E. Cremona. Photo Govt Printer, Israel)

1968 (1 Aug). *Fourth Death Centenary of Grand Master La Valette.* W **105** (upright, 1s.6d.; sideways, others). P 13×14 (1d., 1s.6d.) or 14×13 (others).

405	**170**	1d. multicoloured	10	10
406	**171**	8d. multicoloured	15	10
407	**172**	1s.6d. multicoloured	15	10
408	**173**	2s.6d. multicoloured	20	20
405/8 *Set of 4*			55	45

174 Star of Bethlehem and Angel waking Shepherds

177 "Agriculture"

(Des E. Cremona. Photo Harrison)

1968 (3 Oct). *Christmas. T* **174** *and similar shaped designs. Multicoloured.* W **105** *(sideways)*. P 14½×14.

409		1d. Type **174**	10	10
410		8d. Mary and Joseph with shepherd watching over cradle	15	10
411		1s.4d. Three Wise Men and Star of Bethlehem	15	20
409/11 *Set of 3*			35	35

The shortest side at top and the long side at the bottom both gauge 14½, the other three sides are 14. Nos. 409/11 were issued in sheets of 60 arranged in ten strips of six, alternately upright and inverted.

(Des E. Cremona. Photo Enschedé)

1968 (21 Oct). *Sixth Food and Agricultural Organization Regional Conference for Europe. T* **177** *and similar vert designs. Multicoloured.* W **105** (sideways). P 12½×12.

412		4d. Type **177**	10	10
413		1s. F.A.O. emblem and coin	10	10
414		2s.6d. "Agriculture" sowing seeds	10	15
412/14 *Set of 3*			25	30

180 Mahatma Gandhi **181** I.L.O. Emblem

(Des E. Cremona. Photo Enschedé)

1969 (24 Mar). *Birth Centenary of Mahatma Gandhi.* W **105**. P 12×12½.

415	**180**	1s.6d. blackish brown, black and gold	15	10

(Des E. Cremona. Photo Harrison)

1969 (26 May). *50th Anniv of International Labour Organization.* W **105** (sideways). P 13½×14½.

416	**181**	2d. indigo, gold and turquoise	10	10
417		6d. sepia gold and chestnut	10	10

182 Robert Samut

(Des E. Cremona. Photo D.L.R.)

1969 (26 July). *Birth Centenary of Robert Samut (composer of Maltese National Anthem).* W **105** (sideways). P 13.

418	**182**	2d. multicoloured	10	10

183 Dove of Peace, U.N. Emblem and Sea-Bed

(Des E. Cremona. Photo D.L.R.)

1969 (26 July). *United Nations Resolution on Oceanic Resources.* W **105** (sideways). P 13.

419	**183**	5d. multicoloured	10	10

184 "Swallows" returning to Malta

(Des E. Cremona. Photo D.L.R.)

1969 (26 July). *Maltese Migrants' Convention.* W **105** (sideways). P 13.

420	**184**	10d. black, gold and yellow-olive	10	10

185 University Arms and Grand Master de Fonseca (founder)

(Des E. Cremona. Photo D.L.R.)

1969 (26 July). *Bicentenary of University of Malta.* W **105** (sideways). P 13.

421	**185**	2s. multicoloured	15	20

186 1919 Monument **187** Flag of Malta and Birds

(Des E. Cremona. Photo Enschedé)

1969 (20 Sept). *Fifth Anniv of Independence. T* **186/7** *and similar designs.* W **105** (upright on 5d., sideways others). P 13½×12½ (2d.), 12×12½ (5d.), or 12½×12 (others).

422		2d. multicoloured	10	10
423		5d. black, red and gold	10	10
424		10d. black, turquoise-blue and gold	10	10
425		1s.6d. multicoloured	20	40
426		2s.6d. black, olive-brown and gold	25	50
422/6 *Set of 5*			65	1·10

Designs:—*Vert as T* **187**—10d. "Tourism"; 1s.6d. U.N. and Council of Europe emblems; 2s.6d. "Trade and Industry".

191 Peasants playing Tambourine and Bagpipes

(Des E. Cremona. Litho D.L.R.)

1969 (8 Nov). *Christmas. Children's Welfare Fund. T* **191** *and similar horiz designs. Multicoloured.* W **105** (sideways). P 12½.

427		1d. +1d.Type **191**	10	20
		a. Gold omitted	£110	
		b. Horiz strip of 3. Nos. 427/9	30	75
428		5d. +1d.Angels playing trumpet and harp	15	20
429		1s.6d. +3d.Choirboys singing	15	45
427/9 *Set of 3*			35	75

Nos. 427/9 were issued in sheets of 60 of each value, and also in sheets containing the three values *se-tenant*, thus forming the triptych No. 427b.

194 "The Beheading of St. John" (Caravaggio)

(Des E. Cremona. Photo Enschedé)

1970 (21 Mar). *13th Council of Europe Art Exhibition. T* **194** *and similar multicoloured designs.* W **105** (upright, 10d., 2s.; sideways, others). P 14×13 (1d., 8d.), 12 (10d., 2s.) or 13×13½ (others).

430		1d. Type **194**	10	10
431		2d. "St. John the Baptist" (M. Preti) (45×32 *mm*)	10	10
432		5d. Interior of St. John's Co-Cathedral, Valletta (39×39 *mm*)	10	10
433		6d. "Allegory of the Order" (Neapolitan School) (45×32 *mm*)	10	10
434		8d. "St. Jerome" (Caravaggio)	15	50
435		10d. Articles from the Order of St. John in Malta (63×21 *mm*)	15	10
436		1s.6d. "The Blessed Gerard receiving Godfrey de Bouillon" (A. de Favray) (45×35 *mm*)	20	40
437		2s. Cape and Stolone (16th-century) (63×21 *mm*)	20	55
430/37 *Set of 8*			1·00	1·75

202 Artist's Impression of Fujiyama

(Des E. Cremona. Photo D.L.R.)

1970 (29 May). *World Fair, Osaka.* W **105** (sideways). P 15.

438	**202**	2d. multicoloured	10	10
439		5d. multicoloured	10	10
440		3s. multicoloured	15	15
438/40 *Set of 3*			30	30

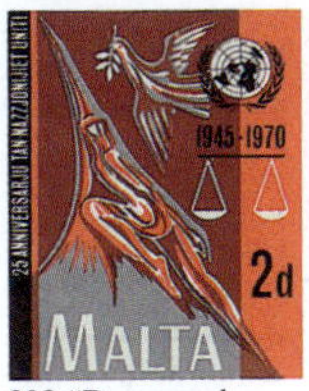

203 "Peace and Justice"

204 Carol-Singers, Church and Star

(Des J. Casha. Litho Harrison)

1970 (30 Sept). *25th Anniv of United Nations.* W **105**. P 14×14½.

441	**203**	2d. multicoloured	10	10
442		5d. multicoloured	10	10
443		2s.6d. multicoloured	15	15
441/3 *Set of* 3			30	30

(Des E. Cremona. Photo Govt Printer, Israel)

1970 (7 Nov). *Christmas. T* **204** *and similar vert designs. Multicoloured.* W **105** (sideways). P 14×13.

444	1d. +½d.Type **204**	10	10
445	10d. +2d.Church, star and angels with Infant	15	20
446	1s.6d. +3d.Church, star and nativity scene	20	35
444/6 *Set of* 3		40	60

STAMP BOOKLETS

B **1**

1970 (16 May). *Brownish black on brownish grey cover as Type* B **1** *depicting G.P.O. Palazzo Parisio, Valletta. Stitched.*

SB1 2s.6d. booklet containing six 1d. and twelve 2d. (Nos. 331, 333) in blocks of 6 ...... 4·50

1970 (18 May). *Black on pink cover as Type* B **1** *depicting Magisterial Palace, Valletta. Stitched.*

SB2 2s.6d. booklets containing six 1d. and twelve 2d. (Nos. 331, 333) in blocks of 6 ...... 4·00

POSTAGE DUE STAMPS

D **1**

D **2**

1925 (16 Apr). *Typeset by Govt Printing Office, Valletta.* Imperf.

D1	D **1**	½d. black	1·25	7·50
		a. *Tête-bêche* (horiz pair)	5·00	20·00
D2		1d. black	3·25	3·00
		a. *Tête-bêche* (horiz pair)	10·00	12·00
D3		1½d. black	3·00	3·75
		a. *Tête-bêche* (horiz pair)	10·00	15·00
D4		2d. black	9·50	17·00
		a. *Tête-bêche* (horiz pair)	24·00	45·00
D5		2½d. black	2·75	2·75
		a. "2" of "½" omitted	£900	£1300
		b. *Tête-bêche* (horiz pair)	12·00	15·00
D6		3d. black/*grey*	9·00	15·00
		a. *Tête-bêche* (horiz pair)	30·00	48·00
D7		4d. black/*buff*	5·00	9·50
		a. *Tête-bêche* (horiz pair)	17·00	38·00
D8		6d. black/*buff*	5·00	19·00
		a. *Tête-bêche* (horiz pair)	17·00	50·00
D9		1s. black/*buff*	7·50	22·00
		a. *Tête-bêche* (horiz pair)	25·00	60·00
D10		1s.6d. black/*buff*	14·00	55·00
		a. *Tête-bêche* (horiz pair)	40·00	£140
D1/10 *Set of* 10			55·00	£130

Nos. D1/10 were each issued in sheets containing 4 panes (6×7) printed separately, the impressions in the two right-hand panes being inverted. Fourteen horizontal *tête-bêche* pairs occur from the junction of the left and right-hand panes.

No. D5a occurred on R. 4/4 of the last 2½d. pane position to be printed. Forgeries exist, but can be detected by comparison with a normal example under ultra-violet light. They are often found in pair with normal, showing forged cancellations of "VALLETTA AP 20 25" or "G.P.O" MY 7 25".

(Typo B.W.)

1925 (20 July). Wmk Mult Script CA (sideways). P 12.

D11	D **2**	½d. green	1·25	60
D12		1d. violet	1·25	45
D13		1½d. brown	1·50	80
D14		2d. grey	11·00	1·00
D15		2½d. orange	2·00	1·25
		x. Wmk reversed	90·00	
D16		3d. blue	3·75	1·25
D17		4d. olive-green	12·00	16·00
D18		6d. purple	3·50	4·50
D19		1s. black	6·50	13·00
D20		1s.6d. carmine	8·50	32·00
D11/20 *Set of* 10			45·00	65·00
D11s/20s Optd "Specimen" *Set of* 10			£200	

1953–63. *Chalk-surfaced paper.* Wmk Mult Script CA (sideways). P 12.

D21	D **2**	½d. emerald	70	2·00
D22		1d. purple	70	1·25
		a. *Deep purple* (17.9.63)	75	3·50
D23		1½d. yellow-brown	2·50	10·00
D24		2d. grey-brown (20.3.57)	5·00	9·50
		a. *Blackish brown* (3.4.62)	22·00	13·00
D25		3d. deep slate-blue	1·00	2·00
D26		4d. yellow-olive	3·00	7·00
D21/6 *Set of* 6			11·50	29·00

1966 (1 Oct). *As No.* D24, *but wmk* w **12** *(sideways).*

D27	D **2**	2d. grey-brown	16·00	25·00

1967–70. *Ordinary paper.* W **105** (sideways).

(a) P 12, line (9.11.67)

D28	D **2**	½d. emerald	4·00	9·00
D29		1d. purple	4·00	9·00
D30		2d. blackish brown	4·00	9·00
D31		4d. yellow-olive	45·00	95·00
D28/31 *Set of* 4			50·00	£110

(b) P 12½, comb (30.5.68–70)

D32	D **2**	½d. emerald	35	2·00
D33		1d. purple	30	1·50
D34		1½d. yellow-brown	35	3·25
		a. *Orange-brown* (23.10.70)	90	3·00
D35		2d. blackish brown	85	70
		a. *Brownish black* (23.10.70)	2·00	3·00
D36		2½d. yellow-orange	60	70
D37		3d. deep slate-blue	60	60
D38		4d. yellow-olive	1·00	80
D39		6d. purple	75	1·50
D40		1s. black	90	1·50
D41		1s.6d. carmine	2·75	7·00
D32/41 *Set of* 10			7·00	16·00

The above are the local release dates. In the 12½ perforation the London release dates were 21 May for the ½d. to 4d. and 4 June for the 6d. to 1s.6d.

Nos. D34*a* and D35*a* are on glazed paper.

Mauritius

GREAT BRITAIN STAMPS USED IN MAURITIUS. We no longer list the Great Britain stamps with obliteration "B 53" as there is no evidence that British stamps were available from the Mauritius Post Office.

See under SEYCHELLES for stamps of Mauritius used at Victoria with "B 64" cancellations between 1861 and 1890.

A similar "B 65" cancellation was used on the island of Rodrigues, a dependency of Mauritius, from 11 December 1861 onwards.

PRICES FOR STAMPS ON COVER TO 1945

Nos. 1/5	*from* × 2
Nos. 6/9	*from* × 3
Nos. 10/15	*from* × 4
Nos. 16/25	*from* × 5
Nos. 26/9	*from* × 3
Nos. 30/1	—
Nos. 32/5	*from* × 4
Nos. 36/44	*from* × 5
Nos. 46/72	*from* × 3
Nos. 76/82	*from* × 5
Nos. 83/91	*from* × 6
Nos. 92/100	*from* × 4
Nos. 101/11	*from* × 3
Nos. 117/24	*from* × 8
Nos. 127/32	*from* × 7
No. 133	*from* × 4
Nos. 134/5	*from* × 10
No. 136	*from* × 8
Nos. 137/56	*from* × 6
Nos. 157/63	*from* × 5
Nos. 164/221	*from* × 3
No. 222	—
Nos. 223/41	*from* × 3
Nos. 242/4	*from* × 10
Nos. 245/8	*from* × 3
Nos. 249/63	*from* × 2
Nos. E1/6	*from* × 10
Nos. D1/7	*from* × 40
Nos. R1/3	*from* × 15

CROWN COLONY

Nos. 1/25*b* and 36/44 were printed in Mauritius.

1 ("POST OFFICE")

2 ("POST PAID")

(Engraved on copper by J. O. Barnard)

1847 (21 Sept). *Head of Queen on groundwork of diagonal and perpendicular lines. Imperf.*

1 **1** 1d. orange-red ... — £600000
2 2d. deep blue ... — £700000

A single plate contained one example of each value.

It is generally agreed that fifteen examples of No. 1 have survived (including two unused) and twelve of No. 2 (including four unused). Most are now in permanent museum collections.

NOTE. Our prices for early Mauritius are for stamps in very fine condition. Exceptional copies are worth more, poorer copies considerably less.

(Engraved on copper by J. O. Barnard)

1848 (June)–**59**. *Imperf.*

A. Earliest impressions. Design deep, sharp and clear. Diagonal lines predominate. Thick paper (Period of use: 1d. 1853–54, 2d. 1848–49).

3 **2** 1d. orange-vermilion/*yellowish* ... £45000 £14000
4 2d. indigo-blue/*grey to bluish* ... £40000 £16000
a. "PENOE" for "PENCE" (R. 3/1) ... £80000 £25000
5 2d. deep blue/*grey to bluish* ... £40000 £16000
a. "PENOE" for "PENCE" (R. 3/1) ... £80000 £28000

B. Early impressions. Design sharp and clear but some lines slightly weakened. Paper not so thick, grey to yellowish white or bluish (Period of use: 1d. 1853–55, 2d. 1849–54).

6 **2** 1d. vermilion ... £20000 £6000
7 1d. orange-vermilion ... £21000 £5500
8 2d. blue ... £22000 £6500
a. "PENOE" for "PENCE" (R. 3/1) ... £38000 £10000
9 2d. deep blue ... £26000 £7000

C. Intermediate impressions. White patches appear where design has worn. Paper yellowish white, grey or bluish, of poorish quality (Period of use: 1d and 2d. 1854–57).

10 **2** 1d. bright vermilion ... £13000 £2250
11 1d. dull vermilion ... £13000 £2250
12 1d. red ... £13000 £2250
13 2d. deep blue ... £17000 £3250
14 2d. blue ... £13000 £2500
a. "PENOE" for "PENCE" (R. 3/1) *from* ... £20000 £5000
15 2d. light blue ... £13000 £2500

D. Worn impressions. Much of design worn away but some diagonal lines distinct. Paper yellowish, grey or bluish, of poorish quality (Period of use: 1d. 1857–59, 2d. 1855–58).

16 **2** 1d. red/*yellowish or grey* ... £4750 £600
17 1d. red-brown/*yellowish or grey* ... £4750 £600
18 1d. red/*bluish* ... £3750 £550
a. Doubly printed ...
19 1d. red-brown/*bluish* ... £3750 £550
20 2d. blue (*shades*)/*yellowish or grey* ... £5500 £1100
a. "PENOE" for "PENCE" (R. 3/1) ... *from* — £1900
21 2d. grey-blue/*yellowish or grey* ... £6000 £1000
22 2d. blue (shades)/*bluish* ... £5500 £1000
a. Doubly printed ...

E. Latest impressions. Almost none of design showing except part of Queens's head and frame. Paper yellowish, grey or bluish, of poorish quality (Period of use: 1d. 1859, 2d. 1856–58)

23 **2** 1d. red ... £3250 £475
24 1d. red-brown ... £3250 £475
25 2d. grey-blue/*bluish* ... £4000 £475
a. "PENOE" for "PENCE" (R. 3/1) ... £7000 £1300

Earliest known use of the 2d. value is on 19 June 1848, but the 1d. value is not known used before 27 September 1853.

There were separate plates for the 1d. and 2d. values, each of 12 (3×4).

3

FOUR-PENCE

(4)

5

(Eng G. Fairman. Recess P.B.)

1858*. *Surch with T* **4**. *Imperf.*

26 **3** 4d. green ... £1300 £425

*Although originally gazetted for use from 8 April 1854, research into the archives indicates that No. 26 was not actually issued until 1858, when the stamps were mentioned in an ordinance of 30 April. The earliest dated postmark known is 27 March 1858.

PERKINS BACON "CANCELLED". For notes on these handstamps, showing "CANCELLED" between horizontal bars forming an oval, see Catalogue Introduction.

1858–62. *No value expressed. Imperf.*

27 **3** (4d.) green ... £450 £200
28 (6d.) vermilion ... 42·00 85·00
29 (9d.) dull magenta (1859) ... £700 £200
a. Reissued as (1d.) value (11.62) ... † £160

Prepared for use but not issued.

30 **3** (No value), red-brown ... 21·00
31 (No value), blue (H/S "CANCELLED" in oval £13000) ... 6·50

Use of the dull magenta as a 1d. value can be confirmed by the presence of the "B 53" cancellation which was first introduced in 1861.

Remainders of Nos. 30/1, overprinted "L.P.E. 1890" in red, were perforated at the London Philatelic Exhibition and sold as souvenirs.

(Recess P.B.)

1859–61. *Imperf.*

32 **5** 6d. bl (H/S "CANCELLED" in oval £14000) ... £650 48·00
33 6d. dull purple-slate (1861) ... 27·00 50·00
34 1s. vermilion (H/S "CANCELLED" in oval £10000) ... £2750 48·00
35 1s. yellow-green (1861) ... £550 £120

The 1859 printings had the colours transposed by mistake.

6

7

8

(Engraved on copper by J. Lapirot)

1859 (Mar–Nov). Imperf.

(a) Early impressions.

36 **6** 2d. deep blue ... £9000 £2500
37 2d. blue ... £7500 £2000

(b) Intermediate prints. Lines of background, etc, partly worn away (July).

38 **6** 2d. blue ... £4750 £900

(c) Worn impressions, bluish-paper (Oct).

39 **6** 2d. blue ... £3000 £600

(d) Retouched impression (Nov).

39*a* **6** 2d. blue ... † —
ab. "MAURITUIS" (R. 2/4) ... † £100000
ac. "MAURITUS" (R. 3/1) ... † £100000

Nos. 36/9*a* were printed from a plate of 12 (4×3).

Research by Mr A. Rudge has established the existence of an initial state of the plate, before the lines were deepened to produce the "Early impression". Only one stamp from this state has so far been identified.

The plate became worn through use, and was eventually extensively re-engraved. Only two pairs (one on cover) have been recorded from this re-touched impression. The errors made in the re-engraving of the inscriptions probably resulted in it being withdrawn from use.

(1848 plate re-engraved by R. Sherwin)

1859 (Oct). *Bluish paper. Imperf.*

40 **7** 2d. deep blue ... £140000 £4750

The 1d. plate was also re-engraved, but was not put into use. Reprints in black were made in 1877 from both 1d. and 2d. re-engraved plates. Coloured autotype illustrations were prepared from these reprints and 600 were included in the R.P.S.L. handbook on *British Africa* in 1900. Further reprints in black were made in 1911 after the plates had been presented to the R.P.S.L. and defaced.

(Lithographed by L. A. Dardenne)

1859 (12 Dec). *White laid paper. Imperf.*

41 **8** 1d. deep red ... £8500 £1700
41*a* 1d. red ... £6500 £1200
42 1d. dull vermilion ... £5000 £950
43 2d. slate-blue ... £5000 £900
43*a* 2d. blue ... £3250 £700
44 2d. pale blue ... £3000 £550
a. Heavy retouch on neck ... — £1500
b. Retouched below "TWO" ... — £800

The neck retouch shows a prominent curved white line running from the base of the chignon to the nape of the neck. No. 44b shows several diagonal lines in the margin below "TWO".

9

10

(Typo D.L.R.)

1860 (7 Apr)–**63**. No wmk. P 14.

46 **9** 1d. purple-brown ... £250 27·00
47 2d. blue ... £275 48·00
48 4d. rose ... £275 30·00
49 6d. green (1862) ... £800 £140
50 6d. slate (1863) ... £300 95·00
51 9d. dull purple ... £140 42·00
52 1s. buff (1862) ... £300 85·00
53 1s. green (1863) ... £650 £170

1862. Intermediate perf 14 to 16.

54 **5** 6d. slate ... 25·00 80·00
a. Imperf between (horiz pair) ... £7000
55 1s. deep green ... £2500 £325

1863–72. Wmk Crown CC. P 14.

56 **9** 1d. purple-brown ... 70·00 15·00
w. Wmk inverted ... 90·00 28·00
y. Wmk inverted and reversed ...
57 1d. brown ... 90·00 9·00
58 1d. bistre (1872) ... £130 12·00
w. Wmk inverted ...
59 2d. pale blue ... 70·00 10·00
a. Imperf (pair) ... £1700 £2000
w. Wmk inverted ... £160 28·00
x. Wmk reversed ...
y. Wmk inverted and reversed ...
60 2d. bright blue ... 90·00 10·00
61 3d. deep red ... £170 28·00
61*a* 3d. dull red ... 70·00 15·00
aw. Wmk inverted ... £140 38·00
62 4d. rose ... 85·00 3·50
w. Wmk inverted ... £170 22·00
63 6d. dull violet ... £300 35·00
w. Wmk inverted ...
x. Wmk reversed ...
y. Wmk inverted and reversed ... † £110
64 6d. yellow-green (1865) ... £190 15·00
65 6d. blue-green ... £170 6·50
w. Wmk inverted ... £275 38·00
y. Wmk inverted and reversed ...
66 9d. yellow-green (1872) ... £160 £250
w. Wmk inverted ...
67 **10** 10d. maroon (1872) ... £300 45·00
w. Wmk inverted ...
68 **9** 1s. yellow ... £250 25·00
w. Wmk inverted ... £350 50·00
69 1s. blue (1866) ... £130 25·00
w. Wmk inverted ... — 55·00
x. Wmk reversed ... — £150
70 1s. orange (1872) ... £225 12·00
w. Wmk inverted ... £375 50·00
y. Wmk inverted and reversed ...
71 5s. rosy mauve ... £190 55·00
w. Wmk inverted ... £375
72 5s. bright mauve (1865) ... £250 55·00
w. Wmk inverted ... £375

Most values of the above set, including the 2d. bright blue, exist imperforate, but these are from proof sheets. The 2d. pale blue imperforate (No. 59a) was issued in error.

HALF PENNY

(11)

½ d

HALF PENNY

(12)

1876.

(a) Nos. 51 and 67 surch with T **11** *locally.*

76 **9** ½d. on 9d. dull purple ... 15·00 17·00
a. Surch inverted ... £600
b. Surch double ... — £1800
77 **10** ½d. on 10d. maroon ... 2·50 22·00
y. Wmk inverted and reversed ...

(b) Prepared for use, but not issued. No. 51 surch with T **12**.

78 **9** ½d. on 9d. dull purple (R.) ... £2250
a. "PRNNY" ...
b. Black surch ... £3750

HALF PENNY

(13)

One Penny

(14)

One Shilling

(15)

Shill
Wrong fount "S"

1877 (Apr–Dec). *Nos. 62, 67 (colour changed) and 71/2 surch T* **13** *by D.L.R. or T* **14/15** *locally.*
79 **10** ½d. on 10d. rose .... 7·00 35·00
w. Wmk inverted .... 80·00
80 **9** 1d. on 4d. rose-carmine (6 Dec) .. 15·00 18·00
w. Wmk inverted .... 95·00 75·00
81 1s. on 5s. rosy mauve (6 Dec) £275 £100
w. Wmk inverted £375 £150
82 1s. on 5s. bright mauve (6 Dec) ... £250 £120
a. Wrong fount "S" ....
w. Wmk inverted ....

(New Currency. 100 cents = 1 rupee)

"CANCELLED" OVERPRINTS. Following the change of currency in 1878 various issues with face values in sterling were overprinted "CANCELLED" in serifed type and sold as remainders. The stamps involved were Nos. 51, 56/62, 65, 67/8, 71/2, 76, 78/b, 79 and 81/2. Examples of such overprints on stamps between Nos. 51 and 72 are worth about the same as the prices quoted for used, on Nos. 78/b they are worth 6% of the unused price, on No. 79 65% and on Nos. 81/2 20%.

2 CENTS (16) **2 Rs.50 C.** (17)

1878 (3 Jan). *Surch as T* **16** *or* **17** *(No. 91).* Wmk Crown CC. P 14.
83 **10** 2c. dull rose (lower label blank).. 11·00 7·00
w. Wmk inverted .... 80·00 50·00
84 **9** 4c. on 1d. bistre .... 19·00 7·00
85 8c. on 2d. blue .... 75·00 3·00
w. Wmk inverted ....
86 13c. on 3d. orange-red .... 16·00 32·00
87 17c. on 4d. rose .... £160 3·50
88 25c. on 6d. slate-blue .... £225 7·00
89 38c. on 9d. pale violet .... 28·00 80·00
90 50c. on 1s. green .... 85·00 3·75
w. Wmk inverted ....
91 2r.50 on 5s. bright mauve .... 16·00 20·00
83/91 *Set of 9* £550 £150

18

19

20

21

22

23

24

25

26

(Typo D.L.R.)

1879 (Mar)–**80**. Wmk Crown CC. P 14.
92 **18** 2c. Venetian red (1.80) .... 48·00 19·00
93 **19** 4c. orange .... 60·00 3·50
w. Wmk inverted ....
94 **20** 8c. blue (1.80) .... 26·00 3·50
w. Wmk inverted .... — £100
95 **21** 13c. slate (1.80) £140 £200
96 **22** 17c. rose (1.80) .... 75·00 7·00
w. Wmk inverted .... — £150
97 **23** 25c. olive-yellow .... £375 12·00
98 **24** 38c. bright purple (1.80) £160 £275
99 **25** 50c. green (1.80) .... 3·75 3·75
w. Wmk inverted £110
100 **26** 2r.50 brown-purple (1.80) .... 45·00 65·00
92/100 *Set of 9* £850 £550

27

(Typo D.L.R.)

1883–94. Wmk Crown CA. P 14.
101 **18** 1c. pale violet (1893) .... 1·75 45
102 2c. Venetian red .... 32·00 4·75
103 2c. green (1885) .... 3·00 60
104 **19** 4c. orange .... 70·00 4·00
w. Wmk inverted ....
105 4c. carmine (1885) .... 2·75 1·00
w. Wmk inverted ....
x. Wmk reversed .... † £180
106 **20** 8c. blue (1891) .... 2·50 1·50
w. Wmk inverted ....
x. Wmk reversed ....
107 **27** 15c. chestnut (1893) .... 5·50 1·25
w. Wmk inverted .... — £110
108 15c. blue (1894) .... 6·00 1·25
109 16c. chestnut (1885) .... 5·50 2·25
110 **23** 25c. olive-yellow .... 7·50 2·75
w. Wmk inverted £300 £150
111 **25** 50c. orange (1887) .... 32·00 13·00
w. Wmk inverted ....
101/11 *Set of 11* .... £150 29·00
101s, 103s, 105s, 107s/9s, 111s Optd "Specimen" *Set of 7* £550

16 CENTS (28) **16 CENTS** (28a)

1883 (26 Feb). *No. 96 surch with T* **28/a** *locally.*
112 **22** 16c. on 17c. rose (surch *T* **28**– 14½ mm long) .... £150 50·00
a. Surch double .... † £2250
b. Horiz pair. Nos. 112/13 .... £600 £550
113 16c. on 17c. rose (surch *T* **28**– 15½ mm long) .... £160 50·00
a. Surch double .... — £2500
114 16c. on 17c. rose (surch *T* **28a**) £300 £110

These stamps were surcharged using two different settings, each of which produced three horizontal rows at a time.

The length of the surcharge in the first setting (Type **28**) is either 14½ mm or 15½ mm and these exist in horizontal *se-tenant* pairs. In Type **28** the height of the surcharge is 3.25 mm. On the second setting (Type **28a**) the type differs, especially the numerals and "S", with the surcharge measuring 15-15½ mm long and 3 mm high.

SIXTEEN CENTS (29) **2 CENTS** (30) **2 CENTS** (31)

1883 (14 July). *Surch with T* **29** *by D.L.R.* Wmk Crown CA. P 14.
115 **22** 16c. on 17c. rose .... 90·00 2·00
w. Wmk inverted ....

1886 (11 May). *No. 98 surch with T* **30** *locally.*
116 **24** 2c. on 38c. bright purple .... £130 35·00
a. Without bar .... — £225
b. Surch inverted £900 £850
c. Surch double £950

1887 (6 July). *No. 95 surch with T* **31** *locally.*
117 **21** 2c. on 13c. slate (R.) .... 60·00 £100
a. Surch inverted £190 £200
b. Surch double £850 £750
c. Surch double, one on back of stamp £850
d. Surch double, both inverted ... † £1400

TWO CENTS (32) **TWO CENTS** (33)

1891 (10–16 Sept). *Nos. 88, 96, 98 and 105 surch locally as T* **32** *(Nos. 118/19, 121) or T* **33** *(No. 120).*
118 **19** 2c. on 4c. carmine (No. 105) (12 Sept) .... 1·50 70
a. Surch inverted .... 75·00
b. Surch double .... 80·00 75·00
c. Surch double, one inverted ..... 80·00 75·00
119 **22** 2c. on 17c. rose (No. 96) (16 Sept) £100 £110
a. Surch inverted £425
b. Surch double £750 £750
120 **9** 2c. on 38c. on 9d. pale violet (No. 89) (16 Sept) .... 5·00 4·75
a. Surch inverted £450
b. Surch double £750 £750
c. Surch double, one inverted £170 £180
w. Wmk inverted .... † £250
121 **24** 2c. on 38c. bright purple (No. 98) 6·50 8·00
a. Surch inverted £900
b. Surch double £190 £200
c. Surch double, one inverted £200 £225

Minor varieties are also known with portions of the surcharge missing, due to defective printing.

ONE CENT (34) **ONE CENT** (35)

1893 (1–7 Jan). *Surch with T* **34** *by D.L.R. or T* **35** *locally.* Wmk Crown CA. P 14.
123 **18** 1c. on 2c. pale violet .... 2·25 1·00
s. Optd "Specimen" .... 28·00
124 **27** 1c. on 16c. chestnut (7 Jan) .... 2·25 3·50
w. Wmk inverted .... 50·00

36

37

(Typo D.L.R.)

1895–99. Wmk Crown CA. P 14.
127 **36** 1c. dull purple and ultramarine (8.7.97) .... 75 1·50
128 2c. dull purple and orange (8.7.97) .... 5·00 50
129 3c. dull purple and deep purple ... 70 50
130 4c. dull purple and emerald (8.7.97) .... 3·75 50
131 6c. green and rose-red (1899) ..... 4·50 4·00
132 18c. green and ultramarine (8.7.97) .... 14·00 3·50
127/32 *Set of 6* .... 26·00 9·50
127s/32s Optd "Specimen" *Set of 6* £110

(Des L. Duvergé. Typo D.L.R.)

1898 (15 Apr). *Diamond Jubilee.* Wmk CA over Crown (sideways). P 14.
133 **37** 36c. orange and ultramarine .... 11·00 21·00
s. Optd "Specimen" .... 48·00

6 CENTS (38) **15 CENTS** (39)

1899 (23–28 May). *Nos. 132/3 surcharged with T* **38/9** *locally.*
134 **36** 6c. on 18c. green and ultramarine (R.) .... 1·00 1·00
a. Surch inverted £600 £300
135 **37** 15c. on 36c. orge and ultram (B) (28 May) .... 1·75 1·75
a. Bar of surch omitted £450

The space between "6" and "CENTS" varies from 2½ to 4 mm.

40 Admiral Mahé de Labourdonnais, Governor of Mauritius, 1735–46

4 Cents (41)

(Recess D.L.R.)

1899 (13 Dec). *Birth Bicentenary of Labourdonnais.* Wmk Crown CC. P 14.
136 **40** 15c. ultramarine .... 18·00 4·00
s. Optd "Specimen" .... 75·00
w. Wmk inverted £100

1900. *No. 109 surch with T* **41** *locally.*
137 **27** 4c. on 16c. chestnut .... 6·50 17·00

42

12 CENTS (43)

(Typo D.L.R.)

1900–05. *Ordinary paper.* Wmk Crown CC (1r.) or Crown CA (others) (sideways on 2r.50, 5r.). P 14.
138 **36** 1c. grey and black (1901) 50 10
139 2c. dull purple and bright purple (4.01) 75 20
140 3c. green and carmine/*yellow* (1902) .... 3·75 1·25
141 4c. purple and carmine/*yellow* ..... 1·50 40
w. Wmk inverted ....
142 4c. grey-green and violet (1903) .. 1·00 2·00
w. Wmk inverted ....
143 4c. black and carmine/*blue* (14.10.04) .... 9·50 60
w. Wmk inverted .... 20·00 17·00
144 5c. dull purple and brt pur/*buff* (8.10.02) .... 6·50 55·00
145 5c. dull purple and black/*buff* (2.03) .... 2·50 2·50
146 6c. purple and carmine/*red* (1902) .... 2·00 80
a. Wmk sideways £2250
w. Wmk inverted .... 25·00 17·00
147 8c. green and black/*buff* (16.7.02) 3·00 9·00
148 12c. grey-black and carmine (16.7.02) .... 1·75 2·25
149 15c. green and orange .... 16·00 7·00
w. Wmk inverted ....
150 15c. black and blue/*blue* (1905) ..... 55·00 1·25
151 25c. green and carmine/*green* (1902) .... 16·00 29·00
a. Chalk-surfaced paper .... 4·50 18·00
152 50c. dull green and deep green/*yellow* (1902) .... 17·00 55·00
153 **42** 1r. grey-black and carmine (1902) .... 50·00 50·00
w. Wmk inverted £120 £130
154 2r.50 green and black/*blue* (1902) ... 26·00 £120
155 5r. purple and carmine/*red* (1902) .... 80·00 £120
138/55 *Set of 18* £250 £400
138s/55s Optd "Specimen" *Set of 18* £300

Examples of Nos. 144 and 151/5 are known showing a forged Port Louis postmark dated "SP 29 10".

1902. *No. 132 surch with T* **43**.
156 **36** 12c. on 18c. green and ultramarine 2·00 6·50

The bar cancelling the original value seems in some cases to be one thick bar and in others two thin ones.

NEW INFORMATION
The editor is always interested to correspond with people who have new information that will improve or correct the catalogue

(44)

1902 (7 July). *Various stamps optd with T* **44** *locally.*

157 **36** 4c. purple and carmine/*yellow* (No. 141) ... 1·25 20
158 6c. green and rose-red (No. 131) . 1·25 2·75
159 15c. green and orange (No. 149).... 4·00 1·00
160 **23** 25c. olive-yellow (No. 110) ... 5·50 2·75
161 **25** 50c. green (No. 99) ... 8·50 4·25
162 **26** 2r.50 brown-purple (No. 100) ... £100 £170
157/62 *Set of* 6 ... £110 £170

Nos. 157/62 were overprinted to make surplus stocks of postage stamps available for revenue (fiscal) purposes also.

1902 (22 Sept). *No.* 133 *surch as T* **43**, *but with longer bar.*

163 **37** 12c. on 36c. orange and ultramarine ... 1·25 1·25
a. Surch inverted ... £650 £450

The note below No. 156 also applies to No. 163.

Forged double surcharge errors show a straight, instead of a curved, serif to the "1" of "12".

1904–07. *Ordinary paper (2c., 4c., 6c.) or chalk-surfaced paper (others).* Wmk Mult Crown CA. P 14.

164 **36** 1c. grey and black (1907)... 8·00 4·25
165 2c. dull and bright purple (1905). 29·00 3·00
a. Chalk-surfaced paper... 29·00 1·75
166 3c. green and carmine/*yellow* ... 21·00 9·00
167 4c. black and carmine/*blue* ... 24·00 1·50
a. Chalk-surfaced paper... 7·00 10
168 6c. purple and carmine/*red* ... 14·00 30
a. Chalk-surfaced paper... 8·00 10
171 15c. black and blue/*blue* (1907) ... 35
174 50c. green and deep green/*yellow* . 2·00 3·25
175 **42** 1r. grey-black and carmine (1907)... 32·00 50·00
164/75 *Set of* 8 ... £100 60·00

46

47

(Typo D.L.R.)

1910 (17 Jan). *Ordinary paper (1c. to 15c.) or chalk-surfaced paper (25c. to 10r.).* Wmk Mult Crown CA. P 14.

181 **46** 1c. black ... 2·75 30
182 2c. brown... 2·75 10
183 3c. green... 3·00 10
a. "A" of "CA" missing from wmk ... † —
w. Wmk inverted ... 32·00
184 4c. pale yellow-green and carmine... 3·50 10
w. Wmk inverted ... — 55·00
185 **47** 5c. grey and carmine ... 2·75 3·00
186 **46** 6c. carmine-red... 3·00 20
a. Pale red ... 4·50 1·50
ab. "A" of "CA" missing from wmk ... † —
187 8c. orange... 3·00 1·25
188 **47** 12c. greyish slate ... 2·50 2·75
189 **46** 15c. blue... 17·00 20
190 **47** 25c. black and red/*yellow*... 2·00 12·00
191 50c. dull purple and black ... 2·25 18·00
192 1r. black/*green*... 9·00 12·00
193 2r.50 black and red/*blue* ... 17·00 70·00
194 5r. green and red/*yellow* ... 27·00 95·00
195 10r. green and red/*green*... £120 £190
181/95 *Set of* 15... £190 £375
181s/95s Optd "Specimen" *Set of* 15... £300

On Nos. 185, 191, 192, 193 and 194 the value labels are as in *T* **48**.

48

49

(Typo D.L.R.)

1913–22. *Die I. Ordinary paper (5c., 12c.) or chalk-surfaced paper (others).* Wmk Mult Crown CA. P 14.

196 **48** 5c. grey and carmine (1913)... 1·75 4·00
a. Slate-grey and carmine... 10·00 10·00
198 **49** 12c. greyish slate (1914)... 6·50 1·00
199 25c. black and red/*yellow* (1913) ... 40 1·40
a. White back (1914) ... 80 17·00
aw. Wmk inverted and reversed... 38·00
b. On orange-buff (1920)... 35·00 60·00
c. On pale yellow (1921) ... 35·00 40·00
cs. Optd "Specimen"... 40·00
cw. Wmk inverted ... £120
d. Die II. *On pale yellow* (1921) ... 80 20·00
ds. Optd "Specimen"... 38·00
200 **48** 50c. dull purple and black (1920).. 48·00 95·00
201 1r. black/*blue-green (olive back)* (1917)... 3·75 17·00
a. On emerald (olive back) (1921)... 8·00 48·00
b. Die II. *On emerald (emerald back)* (1921)... 2·25 7·50
bs. Optd "Specimen"... 40·00
202 2r.50 black and red/*blue* (1916) ... 26·00 70·00
203 5r. green and red/*orange-buff* (1921)... 95·00 £150
a. On pale yellow (1921) ... 85·00 £150
b. Die II. *On pale yellow* (1922) ... 60·00 £170
204 **49** 10r. grn & red/*grn (bl-grn back)* (1913)... 80·00 £160
a. On blue-green (olive back) (1919)... £900
b. On emerald (olive back) (1921)... £100 £170
c. On emerald (emerald back) (1921)... 60·00 £160
d. Die II. *On emerald (emerald back)* (1922)... 35·00 £130
ds. Optd "Specimen"... 50·00
196/204d *Set of* 8... £160 £425
196s/202s, 203as, 204s Optd "Specimen" *Set of* 8. £250

Examples of Nos. 200/4d are known showing part strikes of the forged Port Louis postmark mentioned after Nos. 138/55.

49a

1921–26. *Chalk-surfaced paper (50r).* Wmk Mult Script CA. P 14.

205 **46** 1c. black ... 1·00 1·00
w. Wmk inverted ... 28·00
206 2c. brown... 1·00 10
w. Wmk inverted ...
207 2c. purple/*yellow* (1926)... 1·75 75
w. Wmk inverted ... 24·00
208 3c. green (1926)... 2·75 2·25
209 4c. pale olive-green and carmine. 1·50 1·75
x. Wmk reversed ... 80·00
210 4c. green (1922)... 1·00 10
w. Wmk inverted ...
x. Wmk reversed...
211 4c. brown (1926) ... 2·75 1·50
212 6c. carmine... 12·00 6·50
x. Wmk reversed... 75·00
213 6c. bright mauve (1922) ... 1·25 10
214 8c. orange (1925) ... 2·25 19·00
215 10c. grey (1922)... 2·00 3·25
216 10c. carmine-red (1926) ... 7·00 3·00
217 12c. carmine-red (1922) ... 1·50 40
218 12c. grey (1926)... 1·75 3·75
219 15c. blue... 5·50 4·75
ax. Wmk reversed... 90·00
b. Cobalt (1926)... 75 25
220 20c. blue (1922)... 2·00 80
221 20c. purple (1926)... 8·50 11·00
222 **49a** 50r. dull purple and green (1924).. £750 £2000
s. Optd "Specimen"... £225
205/21 *Set of* 17... 45·00 48·00
205s/21s Optd "Specimen" *Set of* 17... £350

Normal

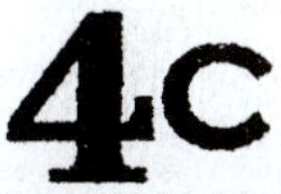

Open "C" (R. 9/6 of right pane)

A

B

Two types of duty plate in the 12c. In Type B the letters of "MAURITIUS" are larger; the extremities of the downstroke and the tail of the "2" are pointed, instead of square, and the "c" is larger.

1921–34. *Die II. Chalk-surfaced paper (25c. to 10r.).* Wmk Mult Script CA. P 14.

223 **49** 1c. black (1926)... 1·50 2·25
224 2c. brown (1926) ... 1·00 10
225 3c. green (1926)... 1·50 40
226 4c. sage-green and carmine (1926)... 1·75 30
a. Open "C"... 60·00
b. Die I (1932) ... 9·00 50·00
ba. Open "C"... £140
226*c* 4c. green (Die I) (1932) ... 8·00 45
ca. Open "C"... £130
227 **48** 5c. grey and carmine (1922)... 90 10
a. Die I (1932) ... 6·00 6·00
228 **49** 6c. sepia (1927) ... 4·00 60
229 8c. orange (1926) ... 1·25 11·00
230 10c. carmine-red (1926) ... 2·00 20
a. Die I (1932) ... 10·00 12·00
231 12c. grey (Type A) (1922)... 1·40 19·00
232 12c. carmine-red (Type A) (1922). 30 3·50
232*a* 12c. pale grey (Type A) (1926) ... 2·25 18·00
as. Optd "Specimen"... 40·00
232*b* 12c. grey (Type B) (1934)... 9·00 20
233 15c. Prussian blue (1926)... 2·75 20
234 20c. purple (1926)... 2·75 40
235 20c. Prussian blue (Die I) (1932) .. 10·00 1·50
a. Die II (1934)... 19·00 40
236 25c. black and red/*pale yellow* (1922)... 70 15
a. Die I (1932) ... 4·50 48·00
237 **48** 50c. dull purple and black (1921).. 7·50 3·50
238 1r. black/*emerald* (1924) ... 3·75 50
a. Die I (1932) ... 17·00 48·00
239 2r.50 black and red/*blue* (1922)... 20·00 11·00
240 5r. green and red/*yellow* (1924)... 32·00 75·00
241 **49** 10r. green and red/*emerald* (1924) £100 £250
223/41 *Set of* 20... £180 £325
223s/41s Optd or Perf (Nos. 226cs, 235s) "Specimen" *Set of* 20... £450

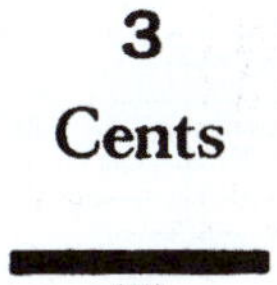

(50)

51

1925 (25 Nov). *Nos.* 210, 217 *and* 220 *surch locally as T* **50**.

242 **46** 3c. on 4c. green... 4·00 4·00
243 10c. on 12c. carmine-red ... 35 1·00
244 15c. on 20c. blue... 55 60
242/4 *Set of* 3... 4·50 5·00
242s/4s Optd "Specimen" *Set of* 3 ... 80·00

1935 (6 May). *Silver Jubilee. As Nos.* 91/4 *of Antigua.* P 13½×14.

245 5c. ultramarine and grey... 50 10
f. Diagonal line by turret ... 60·00 25·00
g. Dot to left of chapel... £110 50·00
h. Dot by flagstaff... £110 50·00
246 12c. green and indigo ... 4·50 10
f. Diagonal line by turret ... £130 40·00
g. Dot to left of chapel... £250 60·00
247 20c. brown and deep blue ... 5·50 20
f. Diagonal line by turret ... £160 50·00
g. Dot to left of chapel... £250 70·00
248 1r. slate and purple ... 29·00 50·00
h. Dot by flagstaff ... £400 £500
245/8 *Set of* 4... 35·00 50·00
245s/8s Perf "Specimen" *Set of* 4 ... £120

For illustrations of plate varieties see Omnibus section following Zanzibar.

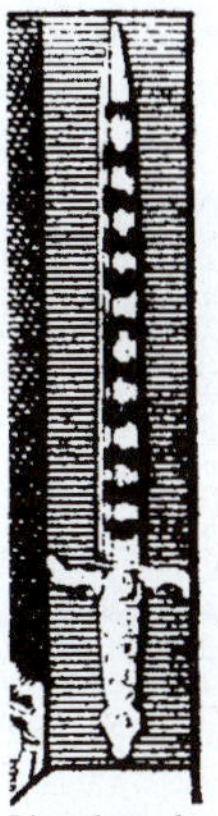

Line through sword (R. 2/2)

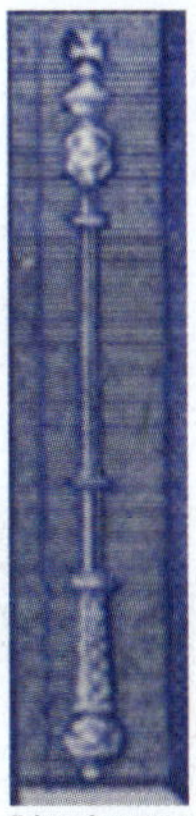

Line by sceptre (R. 5/3)

1937 (12 May). *Coronation. As Nos.* 95/7 *of Antigua.*

249 5c. violet... 40 20
250 12c. scarlet ... 50 2·25
251 20c. bright blue ... 1·40 30
a. Line through sword ... 80·00 35·00
b. Line by sceptre... 80·00 35·00
249/51 *Set of* 3... 2·10 2·50
249s/51s Perf "Specimen" *Set of* 3 ... 85·00

Sliced "S" at right (R. 2/2, 3/2, right pane)

Split frame (R. 7/6, right pane, Key Plate 1)

Sliced "S" at top (R. 4/1, left pane and R. 8/4, right pane)

Broken frame under "A" of "MAURITIUS" (R. 9/3 left pane, Key Plate 2)

"IJ" flaw (R. 3/6 of right pane)

Battered "A" (R. 6/1 of right pane)

(Typo D.L.R.)

1938–49. *T* **51** *and similar types. Chalk-surfaced paper (25c. to 10r.).* Wmk Mult Script CA. P 14.

252 2c. olive-grey (9.3.38)... 30 10
a. Perf 15×14 (1942)... 1·00 10
253 3c. reddish purple and scarlet (27.10.38)... 2·00 2·00
a. Sliced "S" at right ... 85·00 85·00
b. Split frame ... £120
c. Reddish lilac and red (4.43)... 4·00 3·50
ca. Sliced "S" at right ... £150 £150
254 4c. dull green (26.2.38)... 4·00 2·00
a. Open "C"... £150 85·00
b. Deep dull green (4.43)... 2·00 2·00
ba. Open "C"... £100 85·00
255 5c. slate-lilac (23.2.38)... 13·00 85
a. Pale lilac (shades) (4.43)... 3·25 20
b. Perf 15×14 (1942)... 55·00 10
256 10c. rose-red (9.3.38)... 2·75 30
a. Sliced "S" at top... £150 40·00
b. Deep reddish rose (shades) (4.43) . 2·50 20

No.	Type	Description	Unused	Used
		ba. Sliced "S" at top	£140	30·00
		c. Perf 15×14. *Pale reddish rose* (1942)	30·00	1·75
		ca. Sliced "S" at top	£475	£100
257		12c. salmon (*shades*) (26.2.38)	1·00	20
		a. Perf 15×14 (1942)	55·00	1·00
258		20c. blue (26.2.38)	1·00	10
		a. Broken frame	£300	£100
259		25c. brown-purple (2.3.38)	16·00	20
		a. "IJ" flaw	£400	50·00
		b. Ordinary paper (8.4.43)	8·00	10
		ba. "IJ" flaw	£225	40·00
260		1r. grey-brown (2.3.38)	32·00	2·50
		a. Battered "A"	£600	£150
		b. Ordinary paper (8.4.43)	19·00	1·25
		ba. Battered "A"	£475	£110
		c. *Drab* (4.49)	40·00	8·50
		ca. Battered "A"	£600	£225
261		2r.50 pale violet (2.3.38)	45·00	19·00
		a. Ordinary paper (8.4.43)	30·00	18·00
		ab. Broken frame	£800	£425
		b. *Slate-violet* (4.48)	55·00	35·00
262		5r. olive-green (2.3.38)	48·00	29·00
		a. Ordinary paper. *Sage-green* (8.4.43)	27·00	29·00
263		10r. reddish purple (*shades*) (2.3.38)	60·00	45·00
		a. Ordinary paper (8.4.43)	12·00	29·00
252/63a		*Set of* 12	95·00	70·00
252s/63s		Perf "Specimen" *Set of* 12	£275	

The broken frame on the 2r.50 (No. 261ab) differs slightly from that on the 20c. being an earlier state of the variety, but the distorted frame above "AU" is the same.

The stamps perf 15×14 were printed by Bradbury, Wilkinson from De La Rue plates and issued only in the colony in 1942. De La Rue printings of the 2c. to 20c. in 1943–45 were on thin, whiter paper. 1943–45 printings of the 25c. to 10r. were on unsurfaced paper.

1946 (20 Nov). *Victory. As. Nos. 110/11 of Antigua.*

No.	Description	Unused	Used
264	5c. lilac	10	75
265	20c. blue	20	25
264s/5s	Perf "Specimen" *Set of* 2	80·00	

52 1d. "Post Office" Mauritius and King George VI

(Recess B.W.)

1948 (22 Mar). *Centenary of First British Colonial Postage Stamp.* Wmk Mult Script CA. P 11½×11.

No.	Type	Description	Unused	Used
266	**52**	5c. orange and magenta	10	50
267		12c. orange and green	15	25
268	–	20c. blue and light blue	15	10
269	–	1r. blue and red-brown	25	30
266/9		*Set of* 4	60	1·00
266s/9s		Perf "Specimen" *Set of* 4	£130	

Design:—20c., 1r. As *T* **52** but showing 2d. "Post Office" Mauritius.

1948 (25 Oct). *Royal Silver Wedding. As Nos. 112/13 of Antigua.*

No.	Description	Unused	Used
270	5c. violet	10	10
271	10r. magenta	16·00	32·00

1949 (10 Oct). *75th Anniv of U.P.U. As Nos. 114/17 of Antigua.*

No.	Description	Unused	Used
272	12c. carmine	50	1·75
273	20c. deep blue	2·25	2·50
274	35c. purple	60	1·50
275	1r. sepia	50	20
272/5	*Set of* 4	3·50	5·50

53 Labourdonnais Sugar Factory

54 Grand Port

55 Aloe Plant

56 Tamarind Falls

57 Rempart Mountain

58 Transporting cane

59 Mauritius Dodo and map

60 Legend of Paul and Virginie

61 Labourdonnais Statue

62 Government House, Reduit

63 Pieter Both Mountain

64 Timor Deer

65 Port Louis

66 Beach scene

67 Arms of Mauritius

(Photo Harrison)

1950 (1 July). *T* **53/67**. *Chalk-surfaced paper.* Wmk Mult Script CA. P 13½×14½ (horiz), 14½×13½ (vert).

No.	Type	Description	Unused	Used
276	**53**	1c. bright purple	10	50
277	**54**	2c. rose-carmine	15	10
278	**55**	3c. yellow-green	60	3·75
279	**56**	4c. green	20	2·50
280	**57**	5c. blue	15	10
281	**58**	10c. scarlet	30	75
282	**59**	12c. olive-green	1·50	2·75
283	**60**	20c. ultramarine	1·00	15
284	**61**	25c. brown-purple	2·00	40
285	**62**	35c. violet	40	10
		w. Wmk inverted	†	£2000
286	**63**	50c. emerald-green	2·75	50
287	**64**	1r. sepia	7·00	10
288	**65**	2r.50 orange	15·00	14·00
289	**66**	5r. red-brown	16·00	15·00
290	**67**	10r. dull blue	15·00	28·00
276/290		*Set of* 15	55·00	60·00

The latitude is incorrectly shown on No. 282 and No. 283 is incorrectly inscribed "VIRGINIA".

1953 (2 June). *Coronation. As No. 120 of Antigua.*

No.	Description	Unused	Used
291	10c. black and emerald	1·25	15

68 Tamarind Falls

69 Historical Museum, Mahebourg

(Photo Harrison)

1953 (3 Nov)–**58**. *Designs previously used for King George VI issue but with portrait of Queen Elizabeth II as in T* **68/9**. *Chalk-surfaced paper.* Wmk Mult Script CA. P 13½×14½ (horiz) or 14½×13½ (vert).

No.	Type	Description	Unused	Used
293	**54**	2c. bright carmine (1.6.54)	10	10
294	**55**	3c. yellow-green (1.6.54)	30	40
295	**53**	4c. bright purple	10	1·00
		w. Wmk inverted	42·00	
296	**57**	5c. Prussian blue (1.6.54)	10	10
297	**68**	10c. bluish green	20	10
		a. *Yellowish green* (9.2.55)	20	10
298	**69**	15c. scarlet	10	10
299	**61**	20c. brown-purple	15	20
		w. Wmk inverted	6·00	
300	**60**	25c. bright ultramarine	1·50	10
		a. *Bright blue* (19.6 57)	5·50	60
301	**62**	35c. reddish violet (1.6.54)	20	10
		w. Wmk inverted	£150	
302	**63**	50c. bright green	55	85
302*a*	**59**	60c. deep green (2.8.54)	10·00	10
		ab. *Bronze-green* (27.8.58)	11·00	10
303	**64**	1r. sepia	30	10
		a. *Deep grey-brown* (19.6.57)	2·50	65
		w. Wmk inverted	£200	
304	**65**	2r.50 orange (1.6.54)	14·00	9·00
305	**66**	5r. red-brown (1.6.54)	16·00	10·00
		a. *Orange-brown* (19.6.57)	35·00	11·00
306	**67**	10r. deep grey-blue (1.6.54)	13·00	2·00
293/306		*Set of* 15	50·00	21·00

Nos. 296 and 300 exist in coils, constructed from normal sheets.

See also Nos. 314/16.

70 Queen Elizabeth II and King George III (after Lawrence)

(Litho Enschedé)

1961 (11 Jan). *150th Anniv of British Post Office in Mauritius.* W w **12**. P 13½×14.

No.	Type	Description	Unused	Used
307	**70**	10c. black and brown-red	10	10
		w. Wmk inverted	40·00	16·00
308		20c. ultramarine and light blue	30	50
		w. Wmk inverted	48·00	35·00
309		35c. black and yellow	40	50
310		1r. deep maroon and green	60	30
		w. Wmk inverted	£100	
307/10		*Set of* 4	1·25	1·25

1963 (4 June). *Freedom from Hunger. As No. 146 of Antigua.*

No.	Description	Unused	Used
311	60c. reddish violet	40	10

1963 (2 Sept). *Red Cross Centenary. As No. 147/8 of Antigua.*

No.	Description	Unused	Used
312	10c. red and black	15	10
313	60c. red and blue	60	20

1963 (12 Nov)–**65**. *As Nos. 297, 302ab and 304 but wmk w* **12**.

No.	Type	Description	Unused	Used
314	**68**	10c. bluish green (1964)	15	10
		a. *Yellowish green* (21.1.65)	25	10
315	**59**	60c. bronze-green (28.5.64)	3·25	10
316	**65**	2r.50 orange	9·50	8·50
314/16		*Set of* 3	11·50	8·50

71 Bourbon White Eye

(Des D. M. Reid-Henry. Photo Harrison)

1965 (16 Mar). *Horiz designs as T* **71**. *W w* **12** *(upright). Multicoloured; background colours given.* P 14½×14.

No.	Description	Unused	Used
317	2c. lemon	40	15
	a. Grey (leg) omitted	£225	
	w. Wmk inverted	11·00	
318	3c. brown	1·00	15
	a. Black (eye and beak) omitted	£225	
	w. Wmk inverted	42·00	
319	4c. light reddish purple	30	15
	a. Mauve-pink omitted	60·00	
	b. Pale grey omitted	£225	
	c. Orange omitted	£275	
	w. Wmk inverted	4·75	4·00
320	5c. grey-brown	3·25	10
	w. Wmk inverted	75·00	
321	10c. light grey-green	30	10
	w. Wmk inverted	8·00	
322	15c. pale grey	2·00	40
	a. Red (beak) omitted	£170	
	w. Wmk inverted	42·00	
323	20c. light yellow-bistre	2·00	10
	w. Wmk inverted	15·00	
324	25c. bluish grey	2·00	30
	w. Wmk inverted	9·50	
325	35c. greyish blue	3·25	10
	w. Wmk inverted	80·00	
326	50c. light yellow-buff	50	40
	w. Wmk inverted	55·00	
327	60c. light greenish yellow	60	10
	w. Wmk inverted	1·50	75
328	1r. light yellow-olive	6·00	10
	a. Pale orange omitted	£190	
	b. Light grey (ground) omitted	£275	
329	2r.50 pale stone	5·00	7·50
330	5r. pale grey-blue	14·00	13·00
	a. Brown-red omitted	£275	
331	10r. pale bluish green	30·00	30·00
317/31	*Set of* 15	60·00	45·00

Designs:—3c. Rodriguez Fody; 4c. Mauritius Olive White Eye; 5c. Mascarene Paradise Flycatcher; 10c. Mauritius Fody; 15c. Mauritius Parakeet; 20c. Mauritius Greybird; 25c. Mauritius Kestrel; 35c. Pink Pigeon; 50c. Reunion Bulbul; 60c. Mauritius Blue Pigeon (extinct); 1r. Mauritius Dodo (extinct); 2r.50, Rodriguez Solitaire (extinct); 5r. Mauritius Red Rail (extinct); 10r. Broad-billed Parrot (extinct).

*On the 4c. the background is printed in two colours so that in No. 319a the background colour is similar to that of the 5c.

On No. 317a it is the deep grey which is missing, affecting the leg, beak and part of the branch. On No. 319c the missing orange affects the under breast of the bird, which appears much paler. On No. 328a the omission affects the legs and part of the body and on No. 330a the whole of the bird appears in the same colour as the legs.

The 50c. and 2r.50 exist with PVA gum as well as gum arabic.

Nos. 320 and 324 exist in coils, constructed from normal sheets.

See also Nos. 340/1 and 370/5.

1965 (17 May). *I.T.U. Centenary. As No. 166/7 of Antigua.*

No.	Description	Unused	Used
332	10c. red-orange and apple-green	20	10
333	60c. yellow and bluish violet	70	20

1965 (25 Oct). *International Co-operation Year. As No. 168/9 of Antigua.*

No.	Description	Unused	Used
334	10c. reddish purple and turquoise-green	15	10
335	60c. deep bluish green and lavender	30	20

1966 (24 Jan). *Churchill Commemoration. As No. 170/3 of Antigua.*

No.	Description	Unused	Used
336	2c. new blue	10	3·25
	w. Wmk inverted	50·00	
337	10c. deep green	30	10
	w. Wmk inverted	32·00	
338	60c. brown	1·25	20

w. Wmk inverted ... 11·00
339 1r. bluish violet ... 1·40 20
336/9 *Set of 4* ... 2·75 3·25

1966–67. *As Nos. 320, 325 but wmk w* **12** *sideways**.
340 5c. grey-brown (1966) ... 70 15
w. Wmk Crown to right of CA ... 40·00
341 35c. greyish blue (27.6.67) ... 30 15
*The normal sideways watermark shows Crown to left of CA, *as seen from the back of the stamp*.
No. 340 exists in coils, constructed from normal sheets.

1966 (1 Dec). *20th Anniv of U.N.E.S.C.O. As No. 196/8 of Antigua*.
342 5c. slate-violet, red, yellow and orange ... 25 30
343 10c. orange-yellow, violet and deep olive ... 30 10
344 60c. black, bright purple and orange ... 1·40 15
342/4 *Set of 3* ... 1·75 50

86 Red-tailed Tropic Bird

(Des D. M. Reid-Henry. Photo Harrison)

1967 (1 Sept). *Self-Government. T* **86** *and similar horiz designs. Multicoloured.* W w **12**. P 14½.
345 2c. Type **86** ... 20 2·50
w. Wmk inverted ... 13·00
346 10c. Rodriguez Brush Warbler ... 60 10
347 60c. Rose-ringed Parakeet (extinct) ... 70 10
348 1r. Grey-rumped Swiftlet ... 70 10
345/8 *Set of 4* ... 2·00 2·50

SELF GOVERNMENT 1967
(**90**)

1967 (1 Dec). *Self-Government. As Nos. 317/31 but wmk sideways* on Nos. 352/3 and 357. Optd with T* **90**. P 14×14½.
349 2c. lemon ... 10 50
w. Wmk inverted ... 9·00
350 3c. brown ... 10 50
w. Wmk inverted ... 13·00
351 4c. light reddish purple ... 10 50
a. Orange omitted ... £150
352 5c. grey-brown ... 10 10
353 10c. light grey-green ... 10 10
w. Wmk Crown to right of CA ... 13·00
354 15c. pale grey ... 10 30
355 20c. light yellow-bistre ... 15 10
w. Wmk inverted ... 9·50
356 25c. bluish grey ... 15 10
357 35c. greyish blue ... 20 10
w. Wmk Crown to right of CA ... 70·00
358 50c. light yellow-buff ... 30 15
359 60c. light greenish yellow ... 30 10
w. Wmk inverted ... 6·00
360 1r. light yellow-olive ... 1·50 10
361 2r.50 pale stone ... 1·00 2·25
362 5r. pale grey-blue ... 6·00 3·25
363 10r. pale bluish green ... 8·00 15·00
349/63 *Set of 15* ... 16·00 21·00
*The normal sideways watermark shows Crown to the left of CA, *as seen from the back of the stamp*.

91 Flag of Mauritius

(Litho D.L.R.)

1968 (12 Mar). *Independence. T* **91** *and similar horiz design.* P 13½×13.
364 **91** 2c. multicoloured ... 10 1·50
365 – 3c. multicoloured ... 20 1·50
366 **91** 15c. multicoloured ... 20 10
367 – 20c. multicoloured ... 60 10
368 **91** 60c. multicoloured ... 70 10
369 – 1r. multicoloured ... 1·10 10
364/9 *Set of 6* ... 2·50 3·00
Design:—3c., 20c. and 1r. Arms and Mauritius Dodo emblem.

1968 (12 July). *As Nos. 317/18, 322/3 and 327/8 but background colours changed as below.*
370 2c. olive-yellow ... 20 3·50
a. Black printed double ... £130
b. Grey printed double ... 85·00
371 3c. cobalt ... 1·75 7·00
w. Wmk inverted ... 70·00
372 15c. cinnamon ... 55 20
a. Greenish blue omitted ... £250
373 20c. buff ... 3·50 4·00
374 60c. rose ... 1·50 1·00
w. Wmk inverted ... 35·00
375 1r. reddish purple ... 3·25 1·50
370/5 *Set of 6* ... 9·50 15·00

93 Dominique rescues Paul and Virginie

(Des V. Whiteley, from prints. Litho Format)

1968 (2 Dec). *Bicentenary of Bernardin de St. Pierre's Visit to Mauritius. Multicoloured designs as T* **93**. P 13½.
376 2c. Type **93** ... 10 1·25
377 15c. Paul and Virginia crossing the river ... 35 10
378 50c. Visit of Labourdonnais to Madame de la Tour (*horiz*) ... 50 10
379 60c. Meeting of Paul and Virginie in Confidence (*vert*) ... 50 10
380 1r. Departure of Virginie for Europe (*horiz*) ... 50 20
381 2r.50 Bernardin de St. Pierre (*vert*) ... 1·50 3·75
376/81 *Set of 6* ... 3·00 5·00

99 Black-spotted Emperor

(Des J. Vinson (3c., 20c., 1r.) R. Granger Barrett (others). Photo Harrison)

1969 (12 Mar)–**73**. *W w* **12** *(sideways* on 2, 3, 4, 5, 10, 15, 60 and 75c). Chalk-surfaced paper.* P 14.
382 2c. multicoloured ... 10 2·75
a. Pale green printed double** ... 70·00
383 3c. multicoloured ... 10 3·50
w. Wmk Crown to right of CA ... £100
384 4c. multicoloured ... 2·25 4·25
w. Wmk Crown to right of CA ... 13·00
385 5c. multicoloured ... 30 10
386 10c. scarlet, black and flesh ... 2·00 10
w. Wmk Crown to right of CA ... 11·00
387 15c. ochre, black and cobalt ... 30 10
w. Wmk Crown to right of CA ... 2·25
388 20c. multicoloured ... 65 70
a. Glazed ordinary paper (20.2.73) ... 45 7·50
389 25c. red, black and pale apple-green ... 30 3·50
a. Glazed ordinary paper (22.1.71) ... 3·75 6·50
w. Wmk inverted ... 4·00
390 30c. multicoloured ... 1·50 1·75
a. Glazed, ordinary paper (20.3.73) ... 7·50 13·00
391 35c. multicoloured ... 1·75 1·25
a. Glazed ordinary paper (3.2.71) ... 1·00 3·50
aw. Wmk inverted ... 2·50
392 40c. multicoloured ... 35 1·25
a. Glazed ordinary paper (20.2.73) ... 7·50 13·00
aw. Wmk inverted ... 14·00
393 50c. multicoloured ... 1·00 10
a. Red omitted ... £140
b. Glazed ordinary paper (22.1.71) ... 1·50 75
ba. Red printed double
bw. Wmk inverted ... 1·50 20
394 60c. black, rose and ultramarine ... 1·50 10
395 75c. multicoloured ... 1·50 2·75
w. Wmk Crown to right of CA ... 24·00
396 1r. multicoloured ... 60 10
a. Glazed ordinary paper (22.1.71) ... 2·25 15
aw. Wmk inverted ... 70·00
397 2r. 50 multicoloured ... 3·00 8·50
a. Glazed ordinary paper (20.2.73) ... 2·00 12·00
398 5r. multicoloured ... 8·00 10·00
a. Glazed ordinary paper (22.1.71) ... 12·00 5·50
aw. Wmk inverted ... 38·00
399 10r. multicoloured ... 2·50 4·75
w. Wmk inverted (26.1.72) ... 1·50 1·50
382/99 *Set of 18* ... 24·00 40·00
388a/98a *Set of 9* ... 35·00 55·00
Designs:—3c. Red Reef Crab; 4c. Episcopal Mitre (*Mitra mitra*); 5c. Black-saddled Pufferfish ("Bourse"); 10c. Starfish; 15c. Sea Urchin; 20c. Fiddler Crab 25c. Spiny Shrimp; 30c. Single Harp Shells and Double Harp Shell; 35c. Common Paper Nautilus (*Argonauta argo*); 40c. Spanish Dancer (*Hexabranchus sanguineus*); 50c. Orange Spider Conch (*Lambis crocata*) and Violet Spider Conch (*Lambis violacea*); 60c. Blue Marlin; 75c. *Conus clytospira*; 1r. Dolphin (fish); 2r.50, Spiny Lobster; 5r. Ruby Snapper ("Sacre Chien Rouge"); 10r. Yellowedged Lyretail ("Croissant Queue Jaune").
*The normal sideways watermark shows Crown to left of CA, *as seen from the back of the stamp*.
**No. 382a occurs from a sheet on which a second printing of the pale green appears above the normal.
Nos. 385/6 and 389 exist in coils constructed from normal sheets.
This set was re-issued between 1972 and 1974 with watermark w **12** upright on 2c. to 15c., 60c. and 75c. and sideways on other values. Between 1974 and 1977 it was issued on Multiple Crown CA Diagonal watermark paper.

117 Gandhi as Law Student

124 Frangourinier Cane-crusher (18th cent)

(Des J. W. Litho Format)

1969 (1 July). *Birth Centenary of Mahatma Gandhi. T* **117** *and similar vert designs. Multicoloured.* W w **12**. P 13½.
400 2c. Type **117** ... 20 20
401 15c. Gandhi as stretcher-bearer during Zulu Revolt ... 55 10
402 50c. Gandhi as Satyagrahi in South Africa ... 70 50
403 60c. Gandhi at No. 10 Downing Street, London ... 70 10
404 1r. Gandhi in Mauritius, 1901 ... 80 10
405 2r. 50 Gandhi, the "Apostle of Truth and Non-Violence" ... 3·75 2·00
400/5 *Set of 6* ... 1·90 2·75
MS406 153×153 mm. Nos. 400/5 ... 4·50 8·00

(Des V. Whiteley. Photo Enschedé)

1969 (22 Dec*). *150th Anniv of Telfair's Improvements to the Sugar Industry. T* **124** *and similar multicoloured designs.* W w **12** (sideways on 2c. to 1r.), P 11½×11 (2r.50) or 11×11½ (others).
407 2c. Three-roller Vertical Mill ... 10 20
408 15c. Type **124** ... 10 10
409 60c. Beau Rivage Factory, 1867 ... 10 10
410 1r. Mon Desert-Alma Factory, 1969 ... 10 10
411 2r.50 Dr. Charles Telfair (*vert*) ... 25 1·25
407/11 *Set of 5* ... 60 1·60
MS412 159×88 mm. Nos. 407/11†. Wmk sideways. P 11×11½ ... 1·25 2·25
*This was the local release date but the Crown Agents issued the stamps on 15 December.
†In the miniature sheet the 2r.50 is perf 11 at the top and imperf on the other three sides.

EXPO '70' OSAKA
(**128**)

129 Morne Plage, Mountain and Boeing 707

1970 (7 Apr). *World Fair, Osaka. Nos. 394 and 396 optd with T* **128** *by Harrison & Sons.*
413 60c. black, rose and ultramarine ... 10 10
w. Wmk Crown to right of CA ... 65·00
414 1r. multicoloured ... 20 20

(Des H. Rose. Litho G. Gehringer, Kaiserslautern, Germany)

1970 (2 May). *Inauguration of Lufthansa Flight, Mauritius Frankfurt. T* **129** *and similar multicoloured design.* P 14.
415 25c. Type **129** ... 20 10
416 50c. Boeing 707 and Map (*vert*) ... 20 10

131 Lenin as a Student

133 2d. "Post Office" Mauritius and original Post Office

(Photo State Ptg Works, Moscow)

1970 (15 May). *Birth Centenary of Lenin. T* **131** *and similar vert design.* P 12×11½.
417 15c. blackish green and silver ... 10 10
418 75c. blackish brown and gold ... 20 20
Design:—75c. Lenin as Founder of U.S.S.R.

(Des and litho D.L.R.)

1970 (15 Oct). *Port Louis, Old and New. T* **133** *and similar horiz designs. Multicoloured.* W w **12** (sideways). P 14.
419 5c. Type **133** ... 10 10
420 15c. G.P.O. Building (built 1870) ... 10 10
421 50c. Mail Coach (c. 1870) ... 50 10
422 75c. Port Louis Harbour (1970) ... 65 10
423 2r.50 Arrival of Pierre A. de Suffren (1783) ... 80 70
419/23 *Set of 5* ... 1·90 1·00
MS424 165×95 mm. Nos. 419/23 ... 3·25 8·00

138 U.N. Emblem and Symbols

(Des Jennifer Toombs. Litho Format)

1970 (24 Oct). *25th Anniv of United Nations.* W w **12** (sideways). P 14½.
425 **138** 10c. multicoloured ... 10 10
426 60c. multicoloured ... 40 10

STAMP BOOKLETS

1953 (10 Oct). *Black on white cover. Stapled.*
SB1 5r. booklet containing four 5c., eight 10c. and 50c. (Nos. 280, 286, 291) in blocks of 4 and one pane of 4 air mail labels ... £180

1954 (23 Sept). *Black on white or grey cover. Stapled.*
SB2 5r. booklet containing four 5c., eight 10c. and 50c. (Nos. 296, 297, 302) in blocks of 4 and one pane of 4 air mail labels ... 35·00

1955. *Black on grey cover. Stapled.*
SB3 5r. booklet containing four 5c., eight 10c. and 50c. (Nos. 296, 297a, 302) in block of 4 and one pane of 4 air mail labels ... 42·00

EXPRESS DELIVERY STAMPS

(E 1)

(E 2)

(E 3)

(E 4)

Type E **2**. "(INLAND)" was inserted at a second printing on stamps already surcharged with Type E **1** (No. E1).
Type E **3**. New setting made at one printing. More space above and below "(INLAND)".
Type E **4**. New setting with smaller "15c" and no stop.

1903 (10 Aug)–**04**. *No. 136 surch locally in red.*

E1	E **1**	15c. on 15c. ultramarine	9·50	27·00
E2	E **2**	15c. on 15c. ultramarine (28.3.04)	50·00	70·00
		a. "A" inverted	£1400	£950
		b. "(INLAND)" inverted	†	£2750
E3	E **3**	15c. on 15c. ultramarine (4.04)	7·50	3·00
		a. Surch inverted	£950	£600
		aw. Surch and wmk inverted	—	£700
		b. Surch double, both inverted	£1600	£1600
		c. Imperf between (vert pair)	£4500	
		w. Wmk inverted		
E4	E **4**	15c. on 15c. ultramarine (1904)	£700	£650
		a. Surch inverted	—	£1500
		b. Surch double	—	£3000
		c. Surch double, both inverted	—	£4750
		d. "c" omitted	—	£2250

(E 5)

1904. *T* **42** *(without value in label), surch with Type* E **5** *locally.* Wmk Crown CC. P 14.

E5		18c. green	2·25	27·00
		a. Exclamation mark for "I" in "FOREIGN"	£600	

1904. *T* **42** *(without value in label) surch with Type* E **3** *locally.*

E6		15c. grey-green (R.)	7·50	5·00
		a. Surch inverted	£800	£700
		b. Surch double	£600	£600
		c. Surch double, one "LNIAND"	£700	£600

POSTAGE DUE STAMPS

D 1

(Typo Waterlow)

1933–54. Wmk Mult Script CA. P 15×14.

D1	D **1**	2c. black	1·25	50
D2		4c. violet	50	65
D3		6c. scarlet	60	80
D4		10c. green	70	1·25
D5		20c. bright blue	50	1·50
D6		50c. deep magenta (1.3.54)	55	16·00
D7		1r. orange (1.3.54)	70	16·00
D1/7 *Set of* 7			4·25	32·00
D1s/5s Perf "Specimen" *Set of* 5			80·00	

Stamps in a similar design on Block CA paper were issued between 1966 and 1972.

(Typo D.L.R.)

1966–72. *Chalk-surfaced paper.* Wmk w **12**. P 13½×14 (2c.) or 15×14 (others).

D8	D **1**	2c. black (11.7.67)	2·50	2·75
D9		4c. slate-lilac (7.1.69)	1·75	8·00
D10		6c. red-orange (7.1.69)	6·50	21·00
		a. Perf 13½×14	22·00	45·00
D11		10c. yellow-green (16.2.67)	30	2·00
D12		20c. blue (3.1.66)	2·25	4·50
		a. Deep blue (7.1.69)	2·25	14·00
D13		50c. deep magenta (7.1.69)	75	12·00
		a. Magenta (10.1.72)	2·00	16·00
D8/13 *Set of* 6			12·50	45·00

FISCALS USED FOR POSTAGE

(F 1)

(F 2)

F 3

1889. *T* **19**, *wmk Crown CA, optd.* P 14.

R1	F **1**	4c. carmine	20·00	5·00
R2	F **2**	4c. lilac	5·50	12·00

(Typo D.L.R.)

1896. Wmk Crown CA. P 14.

R3	F **3**	4c. dull purple	30·00	48·00

Montserrat

A local post office operated on Montserrat from 1702, although the first recorded postal marking does not occur until 1791. A branch of the British G.P.O. was established at Plymouth, the island capital, in 1852.

The stamps of Great Britain were used from 1858 until the overseas postal service reverted to local control on 1 April 1860.

In the interim period between 1860 and the introduction of Montserrat stamps in 1876 No. CC1 and a similar "uncrowned" handstamp were again used.

PLYMOUTH

CROWNED-CIRCLE HANDSTAMPS

C 1

CC1 C **1** MONTSERRAT (R.) (15.7.1852) *Price on cover* £4500

No. CC1 was used as an emergency measure, struck in black, during 1886.

Stamps of GREAT BRITAIN *cancelled* "A 08" *as Type* Z **1** *of Jamaica.*

1858 (8 May)–**60**.

Z1	1d. rose-red (1857), *perf* 14	£1300
Z2	4d. rose (1857)	
Z3	6d. lilac (1856)	£550
Z4	1s. green (1856)	£2000

PRICES FOR STAMPS ON COVER TO 1945

Nos. 1/2	*from* × 50
No. 3	†
Nos. 4/5	*from* × 10
Nos. 6/13	*from* × 12
Nos. 14/22	*from* × 4
No. 23	—
Nos. 24/33	*from* × 4
Nos. 35/47	*from* × 3
No. 48	—
Nos. 49/59	*from* × 3
Nos. 60/2	*from* × 15
Nos. 63/83	*from* × 3
Nos. 84/93	*from* × 4
Nos. 94/7	*from* × 3
Nos. 98/100	*from* × 8
Nos. 101/12	*from* × 5

1

(2)

3 (Die I)

(T **1** recess D.L.R.)

1876 (Sept)–**83**. *Stamps of Antigua optd with T* **2**. Wmk Crown CC. P 14.

1	**1**	1d. red	24·00	17·00
		a. Bisected (½d.) (1883) (on cover)	†	£1400
		b. Inverted "S"	£1000	£750
		w. Wmk inverted	50·00	
		x. Wmk reversed	28·00	22·00
		y. Wmk inverted and reversed	45·00	50·00
2		6d. green	70·00	45·00
		a. Trisected (used as 2d.) (12.83) (on cover)	†	£6000
		b. Inverted "S"	£1900	£1200
		x. Wmk reversed	—	£100
3		6d. blue-green	£1200	
		a. Inverted "S"	£11000	

Nos. 1/3 were overprinted either from a setting of 120 (12×10) or from a setting of 60 (6×10) applied twice to each sheet. This setting of 60 had an inverted "S" on R. 2/3. The same setting was subsequently used for some sheets of Nos. 6 and 8.

No. 1 was bisected and used for a ½d. in 1883. This bisected stamp is found surcharged with a small "½" in *black* and also in *red*; both were unofficial and they did not emanate from the Montserrat P.O. (*Price on cover, from* £500).

The 6d. in blue-green is only known unused.

(T **3** typo D.L.R.)

1880 (Jan). Wmk Crown CC. P 14.

4	**3**	2½d. red-brown	£250	£180
5		4d. blue	£150	40·00
		w. Wmk inverted	—	£180
		x. Wmk reversed	£425	

1883 (Mar). Wmk Crown CA. P 12.

6	**1**	1d. red	70·00	55·00
		a. Inverted "S"	£2000	£1300
		b. Bisected (½d.) (on cover)	†	£1600
		x. Wmk reversed	—	50·00

Top left triangle detached
(Pl 2 R. 3/3 of right pane)

1884–85. Wmk Crown CA. P 14.

7	**3**	½d. dull green	1·00	9·00
		a. Top left triangle detached	£160	
8	**1**	1d. red	19·00	19·00
		a. Inverted "S"	£1000	£1000
		bx. Wmk reversed	—	26·00
		c. *Rose-red* (1885)	20·00	15·00
		ca. Bisected vert (½d.) (on cover)	†	£1300
		cb. Inverted "S"	£1100	£1000
		ex. Wmk reversed	23·00	21·00
9	**3**	2½d. red-brown	£250	65·00
10		2½d. ultramarine (1885)	24·00	21·00
		a. Top left triangle detached	£475	£425
		w. Wmk inverted	£120	
11		4d. blue	£1800	£250
12		4d. mauve (1885)	5·50	3·00
		a. Top left triangle detached	£300	
10s, 12s Optd "Specimen" *Set of* 2			£450	

The stamps for Montserrat were superseded by the general issue for Leeward Islands in November 1890, but the following issues were in concurrent use with the stamps inscribed "LEEWARD ISLANDS" until 1 July 1956, when Leeward Islands stamps were withdrawn and invalidated.

4 Device of the Colony

5

(Typo D.L.R.)

1903 (Aug).

(a) Wmk Crown CA. P 14.

14	**4**	½d. grey-green and green	75	15·00
15		1d. grey-black and red	75	40
		w. Wmk inverted		
16		2d. grey and brown	5·50	40·00
17		2½d. grey and blue	1·50	1·75
18		3d. dull orange and deep purple	5·00	42·00
19		6d. dull purple and olive	6·00	48·00
20		1s. green and bright purple	10·00	17·00
21		2s. green and brown-orange	28·00	18·00
22		2s.6d. green and black	21·00	45·00

(b) Wmk Crown CC. P 14.

23	**5**	5s. black and scarlet	£130	£180
14/23 *Set of* 10			£190	£375
14s/23s Optd "Specimen" *Set of* 10			£180	

1904–08. *Ordinary paper (½d., 2d., 3d., 6d.) or chalk-surfaced paper (others).* Wmk Mult Crown CA. P 14.

24	**4**	½d. grey-green and green	7·00	2·00
		a. Chalk-surfaced paper (3.06)	1·00	1·25
25		1d. grey-black and red (11.07)	17·00	24·00
26		2d. grey and brown	1·25	8·00
		a. Chalk-surfaced paper (5.06)	2·25	1·25
27		2½d. grey and blue (12.05)	2·50	6·50
28		3d. dull orange and deep purple	7·00	7·50
		a. Chalk-surfaced paper (5.08)	9·50	2·50
29		6d. dull purple and olive	4·50	28·00
		a. Chalk-surfaced paper (5.08)	11·00	5·50
30		1s. green and bright purple (5.08)	11·00	7·00
31		2s. green and orange (5.08)	42·00	42·00
32		2s.6d. green and black (5.08)	50·00	48·00
33	**5**	5s. black and red (9.07)	£120	£130
24/33 *Set of* 10			£225	£225

1908 (June)–**14**. *Ordinary paper (½d. to 2½d.) or chalk-surfaced paper (3d. to 5s.).* Wmk Mult Crown CA. P 14.

35	**4**	½d. deep green (4.10)	7·00	1·00
36		1d. rose-red	1·40	30
38		2d. greyish slate (9.09)	1·75	16·00
39		2½d. blue	2·25	3·50
40		3d. purple/*yellow* (9.09)	1·00	18·00
		a. White back (1.14)	4·00	38·00
		as. Optd "Specimen"	28·00	
43		6d. dull and deep purple (9.09)	6·50	55·00
		a. Dull and bright purple (1914)	11·00	55·00
44		1s. *black/green* (9.09)	8·50	45·00

45		2s. purple and bright blue/*blue* (9.09)	38·00	55·00
46		2s.6d. black and red/*blue* (9.09)	35·00	70·00
47	5	5s. red and green/*yellow* (9.09)	50·00	75·00
35/47 *Set of* 10			£140	£300
35s/47s Optd "Specimen" *Set of* 10			£250	

Examples of most values are known showing forged Montserrat postmarks dated "OC 16 1909" or "NO 26 1910".

7

8

WAR STAMP
(9)

(T **7/8** typo D.L.R.)

1914. *Chalk-surfaced paper.* Wmk Mult Crown CA. P 14.

48	**7**	5s. red and green/*yellow*	70·00	£110
		s. Optd "Specimen"	75·00	

1916 (10 Oct)–**22**. *Ordinary paper (½d. to 2½d.) or chalk-surfaced paper (3d. to 5s.).* Wmk Mult Crown CA. P 14.

49	**8**	½d. green	30	2·50
50		1d. scarlet	1·50	75
		a. Carmine-red	24·00	8·50
51		2d. grey	2·00	4·00
52		2½d. bright blue	1·50	22·00
53		3d. purple/*yellow*	1·25	18·00
		a. On pale yellow (13.7.22)	75	15·00
		as. Optd "Specimen"	27·00	
54		4d. grey-black and red/*pale yellow* (13.7.22)	5·50	38·00
55		6d. dull and deep purple	2·75	25·00
56		1s. black/*blue-green (olive back)*	3·00	28·00
57		2s. purple and blue/*blue*	14·00	40·00
58		2s.6d. black and red/*blue*	27·00	70·00
59		5s. green and red/*yellow*	42·00	70·00
49/59 *Set of* 11			90·00	£275
49s/59s Optd "Specimen" *Set of* 11			£200	

1917 (8 Oct)–**18**. *No. 49 optd with T* **9**.

60	**8**	½d. green (R.)	10	1·50
		a. Short opt (right pane R. 10/1)	10·00	
		y. Wmk inverted and reversed	55·00	
61		½d. green (Blk.) (5.18)	1·50	3·50
		a. Short opt (right pane R. 10/1)	20·00	
		b. Deep green (10.18)	15	1·75
		ba. "C" and "A" missing from wmk	£1200	
		bb. Short opt (right pane R. 10/1)	10·00	
		w. Wmk inverted	£110	

Nos. 60a, 61a, and 61bb show the overprint 2 mm high instead of 2½ mm.

No. 61ba shows the "C" omitted from one impression and the "A" missing from the next. The price quoted is for a horizontal pair.

1919 (4 Mar). T **8**. *Special printing in orange. Value and "WAR STAMP" as T* **9** *inserted in black at one printing.*

62		1½d. black and orange	10	30
60s/2s Optd "Specimen" *Set of* 3			90·00	

1922 (13 July)–**29**. *Ordinary paper (¼d. to 3d.) (No. 73) or chalk-surfaced paper (others).* Wmk Mult Script CA. P 14.

63	**8**	¼d. brown	15	5·50
64		½d. green (5.4.23)	30	30
65		1d. bright violet (5.4.23)	30	60
66		1d. carmine (1929)	75	1·50
67		1½d. orange-yellow	1·75	9·50
68		1½d. carmine (5.4.23)	30	4·00
69		1½d. red-brown (1929)	2·25	50
70		2d. grey	50	2·00
71		2½d. deep bright blue	8·50	16·00
		a. Pale bright blue (17.8.26)	60	90
		as. Optd "Specimen"	35·00	
72		2½d. orange-yellow (5.4.23)	1·25	19·00
73		3d. dull blue (5.4.23)	75	16·00
74		3d. purple/*yellow* (2.1.27)	1·10	4·75
75		4d. black and red/*pale yellow*	75	12·00
76		5d. dull purple and olive	3·75	10·00
77		6d. pale and bright purple (5.4.23)	3·00	7·50
78		1s. black/*emerald* (5.4.23)	3·00	7·00
79		2s. purple and blue/*blue*	7·00	17·00
80		2s.6d. black and red/*blue* (5.4.23)	12·00	55·00
81		3s. green and violet	12·00	19·00
82		4s. black and scarlet	15·00	38·00
83		5s. green and red/*pale yellow* (6.23)	27·00	50·00
63/83 *Set of* 21			85·00	£250
63s/83s Optd or Perf (Nos. 66s, 69s) "Specimen" *Set of* 21			£350	

10 Plymouth

(Recess D.L.R.)

1932 (18 Apr). *300th Anniv of Settlement of Montserrat.* Wmk Mult Script CA. P 14.

84	**10**	½d. green	75	9·50
85		1d. scarlet	75	5·50
86		1½d. red-brown	1·25	2·50
87		2d. grey	1·50	17·00
88		2½d. ultramarine	1·25	16·00
89		3d. orange	1·50	20·00
90		6d. violet	2·25	32·00
91		1s. olive-brown	12·00	45·00
92		2s.6d. purple	48·00	75·00
93		5s. chocolate	£100	£170
84/93 *Set of* 10			£150	£350
84s/93s Perf "Specimen" *Set of* 10			£225	

Examples of all values are known showing a forged G.P.O. Plymouth postmark dated "MY 13 32".

1935 (6 May). *Silver Jubilee. As Nos. 91/4 of Antigua, but ptd by Waterlow & Sons.* P 11×12.

94		1d. deep blue and scarlet	85	3·25
95		1½d. ultramarine and grey	2·00	3·50
96		2½d. brown and deep blue	2·25	4·00
97		1s. slate and purple	3·00	15·00
94/7 *Set of* 4			7·00	23·00
94s/7s Perf "Specimen" *Set of* 4			95·00	

1937 (12 May). *Coronation. As Nos. 95/7 of Antigua, but printed by D.L.R.* P 14.

98		1d. scarlet	30	1·50
99		1½d. yellow-brown	60	40
100		2½d. bright blue	50	1·50
98/100 *Set of* 3			1·25	3·00
98s/100s Perf "Specimen" *Set of* 3			70·00	

11 Carr's Bay

12 Sea Island cotton

13 Botanic Station

(Recess D.L.R.)

1938 (2 Aug)–**48**. Wmk Mult Script CA. P 12 (10s., £1) or 13 (others).

101	**11**	½d. blue-green	3·75	1·75
		a. Perf 14 (1942)	15	20
102	**12**	1d. carmine	3·75	40
		a. Perf 14 (1943)	50	30
103		1½d. purple	19·00	50
		a. Perf 14 (1942)	50	50
		ab. "A" of "CA" missing from wmk		
104	**13**	2d. orange	19·00	60
		a. Perf 14 (1942)	1·50	70
105	**12**	2½d. ultramarine	2·25	1·00
		a. Perf 14 (1943)	50	30
106	**11**	3d. brown	4·75	1·50
		a. Perf 14. *Red-brown* (1942)	2·00	40
		ab. Deep brown (1943)	1·75	5·50
107	**13**	6d. violet	20·00	80
		a. Perf 14 (1943)	2·50	60
108	**11**	1s. lake	20·00	70
		a. Perf 14 (1942)	2·25	30
109	**13**	2s.6d. slate-blue	35·00	80
		a. Perf 14 (1943)	19·00	2·50
110	**11**	5s. rose-carmine	45·00	8·00
		a. Perf 14 (1942)	24·00	3·00
111	**13**	10s. pale blue (1.4.48)	13·00	19·00
112	**11**	£1 black (1.4.48)	15·00	29·00
101a/12 *Set of* 12			70·00	50·00
101s/12s Perf "Specimen" *Set of* 12			£300	

Nos. 101/2 exist in coils constructed from normal sheets.

1946 (1 Nov). *Victory. As Nos. 110/11 of Antigua.*

113		1½d. purple	15	15
114		3d. chocolate	15	15
113s/14s Perf "Specimen" *Set of* 2			70·00	

1949 (3 Jan). *Royal Silver Wedding. As Nos. 112/13 of Antigua.*

115		2½d. ultramarine	10	10
116		5s. carmine	4·75	11·00

1949 (10 Oct). *75th Anniv of U.P.U. As Nos. 114/17 of Antigua.*

117		2½d. ultramarine	15	1·25
118		3d. brown	1·75	75
119		6d. purple	30	60
120		1s. purple	30	75
117/20 *Set of* 4			2·25	3·00

(New Currency. 100 cents = 1 West Indies, later Eastern Caribbean dollar)

1951 (16 Feb). *Inauguration of B.W.I. University College. As Nos. 118/19 of Antigua.*

121		3c. black and purple	20	1·25
122		12c. black and violet	20	1·25

14 Government House

15 Sea Island cotton: cultivation

16 Map of colony

17 Picking tomatoes

17a St Anthony's Church

18 Badge of Presidency

19 Sea Island cotton: ginning

19a Government House

(Recess B.W.)

1951 (17 Sept). *T* **14/19a**. Wmk Mult Script CA. P 11½×11.

123	**14**	1c. black	10	2·00
124	**15**	2c. green	15	70
125	**16**	3c. orange-brown	30	70
126	**17**	4c. carmine	30	1·75
127	**17a**	5c. reddish violet	30	1·00
128	**18**	6c. olive-brown	30	30
129	**19**	8c. deep blue	2·00	20
130	**17a**	12c. blue and chocolate	1·00	30
131	**17**	24c. carmine and yellow-green	1·25	30
132	**19**	60c. black and carmine	7·00	3·75
133	**15**	$1.20 yellow-green and blue	7·00	6·00
134	**19a**	$2.40 black and green	12·00	16·00
135	**18**	$4.80 black and purple	20·00	20·00
123/135 *Set of* 13			45·00	48·00

In the 4c. and 5c. the portrait is on the left and on the 12c. and 24c. it is on the right.

1953 (2 June). *Coronation. As No. 120 of Antigua.*

136		2c. black and deep green	60	40

20 Government House

Two Types of ½c., 3c., 6c. and $4.80: I. Inscr "PRESIDENCY". II. Inscr "COLONY".

1953 (15 Oct)–**62**. *As King George VI issue, but with portrait of Queen Elizabeth II as in T* **19**. Wmk Mult Script CA. P 11½×11.

136*a*	**16**	½c. deep violet (I) (3.7.56)	50	10
136*b*		½c. deep violet (II)(1.9.58)	80	10
137	**19**	1c. black	10	10
138	**15**	2c. green	15	10
139	**16**	3c. orange-brown (I)	50	10
139*a*		3c. orange-brown(II) (1.9.58)	80	2·00
140	**17**	4c. carmine-red (1.6.55)	30	20
141	**17a**	5c. reddish lilac (1.6.55)	30	1·00
142	**18**	6c. deep bistre-brown (I) (1.6.55)	30	10
142*a*		6c. deep bistre-brown (II) (1.9.58)	55	15
		ab. Deep sepia-brown (30.7.62)	8·50	5·50
143	**19**	8c. deep bright blue (1.6.55)	1·00	10
144	**17a**	12c. blue and red-brown (1.6.55)	1·50	10
145	**17**	24c. carmine-red and green (1.6.55)	1·50	20
145*a*	**15**	48c. yellow-olive and purple (15.10.57)	12·00	3·75
146	**19**	60c. black and carmine (1.6.55)	8·50	2·25
147	**15**	$1.20 green and greenish blue (1.6.55)	15·00	9·50
148	**19a**	$2.40 black and bluish green (1.6.55)	14·00	16·00
149	**18**	$4.80 black and deep purple (I) (1.6.55)	5·00	10·00
149*a*		$4.80 black and deep purple (II) (1.9.58)	18·00	7·50
136a/49 *Set of* 15			55·00	35·00

See also No. 157.

1956 (22 Apr). *Inauguration of British Caribbean Federation. As Nos. 135/7 of Antigua.*

150		3c. deep green	55	20
151		6c. blue	75	60
152		12c. scarlet	90	15
150/2 *Set of* 3			2·00	85

1963 (8 July). *Freedom from Hunger. As No. 146 of Antigua.*

153		12c. reddish violet	30	15

1963 (2 Sept). *Red Cross Centenary. As Nos. 147/8 of Antigua.*

154		4c. red and black	15	20
155		12c. red and blue	35	50

1964 (23 Apr). *400th Birth Anniv of William Shakespeare. As No. 164 of Antigua.*

156		12c. indigo	10	10

1964 (29 Oct). *As No. 138 but wmk w* **12**.

157		2c. green	60	20

1965 (17 May). *I.T.U. Centenary. As Nos. 166/7 of Antigua.*

158		4c. vermilion and violet	15	10
159		48c. light emerald and carmine	30	20

21 Pineapple

22 Avocado

(Des Sylvia Goaman. Photo Harrison)

1965 (16 Aug). *T* **21/2** *and similar vert designs showing vegetables, fruit or plants. Multicoloured.* W w **12** (upright). P 15×14.

160	1c. Type **21**	10	10
	w. Wmk inverted	1·00	1·25
161	2c. Type **22**	10	10
162	3c. Soursop	10	10
163	4c. Pepper	10	10
164	5c. Mango	10	10
165	6c. Tomato	10	10
166	8c. Guava	10	10
167	10c. Ochro	10	10
168	12c. Lime	50	40
	w. Wmk inverted	—	28·00
169	20c. Orange	30	10
170	24c. Banana	20	10
171	42c. Onion	75	60
172	48c. Cabbage	2·00	75
173	60c. Pawpaw	3·00	1·10
174	$1.20 Pumpkin	2·00	5·00
175	$2.40 Sweet potato	6·50	8·50
176	$4.80 Egg plant	6·50	11·00
160/76	*Set of 17*	20·00	25·00

See also Nos. 213/22.

1965 (25 Oct). *International Co-operation Year. As Nos. 168/9 of Antigua.*

177	2c. reddish purple and turquoise-green	10	20
178	12c. deep bluish green and lavender	25	10

1966 (26 Jan). *Churchill Commemoration. As Nos. 170/3 of Antigua.*

179	1c. new blue	10	1·50
	a. Cerise (sky) omitted	£375	
180	2c. deep green	20	20
181	24c. brown	70	10
182	42c. bluish violet	85	75
179/82	*Set of 4*	1·60	2·25

1966 (4 Feb). *Royal Visit. As No. 174 of Antigua.*

183	14c. black and ultramarine	85	15
184	24c. black and magenta	1·40	15

1966 (20 Sept). *Inauguration of W.H.O. Headquarters, Geneva. As Nos. 178/9 of Antigua.*

185	12c. black, yellow-green and light blue	15	25
186	60c. black, light purple and yellow-brown	35	75

1966 (1 Dec). *20th Anniv of U.N.E.S.C.O. As Nos. 196/8 of Antigua.*

187	4c. slate-violet, red, yellow and orange	10	10
	a. Orange omitted	£100	
188	60c. orange-yellow, violet and deep olive	45	10
189	$1.80 black, bright purple and orange	1·60	70
187/9	*Set of 3*	1·90	80

On No. 187a the omission of the orange only affects the squares of the lower case letters so that they appear yellow, the same as the capital squares.

25 Yachting

$1.00

(26)

(Des and photo Harrison)

1967 (29 Dec). *International Tourist Year. T* **25** *and similar multicoloured designs.* W w **12** (sideways on 15c.). P 14.

190	5c. Type **25**	15	10
191	15c. Waterfall near Chance Mountain (*vert*)	20	10
192	16c. Fishing, skin-diving and swimming	25	70
193	24c. Playing golf	1·60	45
190/3	*Set of 4*	2·00	1·25

1968 (6 May). *Nos. 168, 170, 172 and 174/6 surch as T* **26**. W w **12** (upright).

194	15c. on 12c. Lime	20	15
195	25c. on 24c. Banana	25	15
196	50c. on 48c. Cabbage	45	15
197	$1 on $1.20 Pumpkin	80	40
198	$2.50 on $2.40 Sweet potato	1·00	4·25
199	$5 on $4.80 Egg plant	1·10	4·25
194/9	*Set of 6*	3·50	8·50

See also Nos. 219 etc.

27 Sprinting

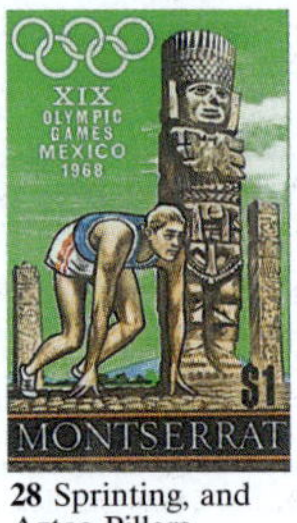

28 Sprinting, and Aztec Pillars

(Des G. Vasarhelyi. Photo Harrison)

1968 (31 July). *Olympic Games, Mexico. T* **27/8** *and similar designs.* W w **12** (sideways on $1). P 14.

200	15c. deep claret, emerald and gold	10	10
201	25c. blue, orange and gold	15	10
202	50c. green, red and gold	25	10
203	$1 multicoloured	35	30
200/3	*Set of 4*	75	55

Designs: *Horiz as T* **27**—25c. Weightlifting; 50c. Gymnastics.

31 Alexander Hamilton

(Des and photo Harrison)

1968 (6 Dec*). *Human Rights Year. T* **31** *and similar horiz designs. Multicoloured.* W w **12**. P 14×14½.

204	5c. Type **31**	10	10
205	15c. Albert T. Marryshow	10	10
206	25c. William Wilberforce	10	10
207	50c. Dag Hammarskjöld	10	15
208	$1 Dr. Martin Luther King	25	30
204/8	*Set of 5*	60	65

*Although first day covers were postmarked 2 December, these stamps were not put on sale in Montserrat until 6 December.

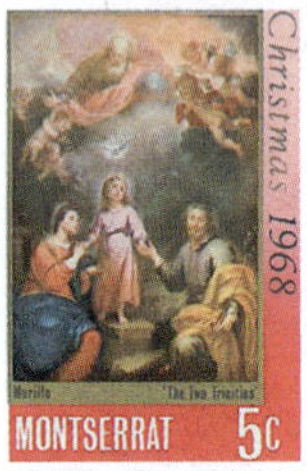

32 "The Two Trinities" (Murillo)

33 "The Adoration of the Kings" (detail, Botticelli)

(Des and photo Harrison)

1968 (16 Dec). *Christmas.* W w **12** (sideways). P 14½×14.

209	**32**	5c. multicoloured	10	10
210	**33**	15c. multicoloured	10	10
211	**32**	25c. multicoloured	10	10
212	**33**	50c. multicoloured	25	20
209/12		*Set of 4*	50	45

1969–70. *As Nos. 160/4, 167, 167 and 194/6 but wmk w* **12** *sideways**.

213	1c. Type **21** (24.6.69)	10	10
214	2c. Type **22** (23.4.70)	1·00	85
215	3c. Soursop (24.6.69)	30	15
	w. Wmk Crown to right of CA	18·00	
216	4c. Pepper (24.6.69)	60	15
217	5c. Mango (23.4.70)	1·75	85
218	10c. Ochro (24.6.69)	50	15
	w. Wmk Crown to right of CA	70·00	
219	15c. on 12c. Lime (24.6.69)	60	20
220	20c. Orange (17.3.69)	75	20
221	25c. on 24c. Banana (24.6.69)	90	25
222	50c. on 48c. Cabbage (24.6.69)	4·50	10·00
213/22	*Set of 10*	10·00	11·50

*The normal sideways watermark shows Crown to left of CA, *as seen from the back of the stamp.*

The 1c., 3c., 4c., 10c., 15c. and 20c. exist with PVA gum as well as gum arabic, but the 2c. and 5c. exist with PVA gum only.

34 Map showing "CARIFTA" Countries

35 "Strength in Unity"

(Des J. Cooter. Photo Harrison)

1969 (27 May). *First Anniv of CARIFTA (Caribbean Free Trade Area).* W w **12** (sideways* on T **34**). P 14.

223	**34**	15c. multicoloured	10	10
224		20c. multicoloured	10	10
		w. Wmk Crown to right of CA	1·60	
225	**35**	35c. multicoloured	10	20
226		30c. multicoloured	15	20
223/6		*Set of 4*	40	55

*The normal sideways watermark shows Crown to left of CA, *as seen from the back of the stamp.*

36 Telephone Receiver and Map of Montserrat

40 Dolphin (fish)

(Des R. Reid, adapted by V. Whiteley. Litho P.B.)

1969 (29 July). *Development Projects. T* **36** *and similar vert designs. Multicoloured.* W w **12**. P 13½.

227	15c. Type **36**	10	10
228	25c. School symbols and map	10	10
229	50c. Hawker Siddeley H.S.748 aircraft and map	15	20
230	$1 Electricity pylon and map	25	75
227/30	*Set of 4*	55	1·00

(Des Harrison. Photo Enschedé)

1969 (1 Nov). *Game Fish. T* **40** *and similar horiz designs. Multicoloured.* P 13×13½.

231	5c. Type **40**	35	10
232	15c. Atlantic Sailfish	50	10
233	25c. Black-finned Tuna	60	10
234	40c. Spanish Mackerel	80	55
231/4	*Set of 4*	2·00	75

41 King Caspar before the Virgin and Child (detail) (Norman 16th-cent stained glass window)

42 "Nativity" (Leonard Limosin)

(Des J. Cooter. Litho D.L.R.)

1969 (10 Dec). *Christmas. Paintings multicoloured; frame colours given.* W w **12** (sideways on 50c.). P 13.

235	**41**	15c. black, gold and violet	10	10
236		25c. black and vermilion	10	10
237	**42**	50c. black, ultramarine and yellow-orange	15	15
235/7		*Set of 3*	30	30

43 "Red Cross Sale"

(Des and litho J. W.)

1970 (13 Apr). *Centenary of British Red Cross. T* **43** *and similar horiz designs. Multicoloured.* W w **12** (sideways). P 14½×14.

238	3c. Type **43**	10	25
239	4c. School for deaf children	10	25
240	15c. Transport services for disabled	10	20
241	20c. Workshop	10	60
238/41	*Set of 4*	35	1·10

44 Red-footed Booby

45 "Madonna and Child with Animals" (Brueghel the Elder, after Dürer)

(Des V. Whiteley. Photo Harrison)

1970 (2 July)–**74**. *Birds. T* **44** *and similar multicoloured designs.* W w **12** *(sideways* on vert designs and upright on horiz designs). Glazed ordinary paper ($10) or chalk-surfaced paper (others).* P 14×14½ (horiz) or 14½×14 (vert).

242	1c. Type **44**	10	10
	w. Wmk inverted	17·00	
243	2c. American Kestrel (*vert*)	15	15
	a. Glazed, ordinary paper (22.1.71)	1·25	3·00
244	3c. Magnificent Frigate Bird (*vert*)	15	15
	w. Wmk Crown to right of CA		
245	4c. Great Egret (*vert*)	1·00	15
246	5c. Brown Pelican (*vert*)	2·00	10
	aw. Wmk Crown to right of CA	2·50	

	b. Glazed, ordinary paper (22.1.71)	1·50	2·00
	bw. Wmk Crown to right of CA		
247	10c. Bananaquit (*vert*)	40	10
	a. Glazed, ordinary paper (22.1.71)	1·50	2·00
248	15c. Smooth-billed Ani	30	15
	a. Glazed, ordinary paper (22.1.71)	4·50	5·00
	aw. Wmk inverted	4·50	
249	20c. Red-billed Tropic Bird	35	15
	a. Glazed, ordinary paper (22.1.71)	1·50	2·00
250	25c. Montserrat Oriole	50	50
	a. Glazed, ordinary paper (22.1.71)	5·00	6·00
251	50c. Green-throated Carib (*vert*)	5·00	1·50
	a. Glazed, ordinary paper (22.1.71)	4·00	4·50
252	$1 Antillean Crested Hummingbird	7·50	1·00
	aw. Wmk inverted	23·00	
	b. Glazed, ordinary paper (22.1.71)	4·25	5·00
253	$2.50 Little Blue Heron (*vert*)	5·50	12·00
	a. Glazed, ordinary paper (22.1.71)	8·00	10·00
254	$5 Purple-throated Carib	7·50	16·00
	a. Glazed, ordinary paper (22.1.71)	13·00	18·00
254*c*	$10 Forest hrush (30.10.74)	15·00	15·00
242/54*c*	*Set of* 14	40·00	42·00

*The normal sideways watermark shows Crown to left of CA, *as seen from the back of the stamp.*

Eight values in this set were subsequently reissued with the watermark sideways on horizontal designs and upright on vertical designs.

(Des G. Drummond. Litho D.L.R.)

1970 (1 Oct*). *Christmas. T* **45** *and similar multicoloured design.* W w **12**. P 13½×14.

255	5c. Type **45**	10	10
	w. Wmk inverted	23·00	
256	15c. "The Adoration of the Shepherds" (Domenichino)	10	10
257	20c. Type **45**	10	10
	w. Wmk inverted	4·00	
258	$1 As 15c.	35	1·50
255/8	*Set of* 4	60	1·60

*This was the local date of issue but the stamps were released by the Crown Agents on 21 September.

46 War Memorial

47 Girl Guide and Badge

(Des V. Whiteley. Litho JW.)

1970 (30 Nov). *Tourism. T* **46** *and similar horiz designs. Multicoloured.* W w **12** (sideways*). P 14½×14.

259	5c. Type **46**	10	10
260	15c. Plymouth from Fort St. George	10	10
261	25c. Carr's Bay	15	15
262	50c. Golf Fairway	1·00	2·25
	w. Wmk Crown to right of CA	6·00	
259/62	*Set of* 4	1·25	2·40
MS263	135×109 mm. Nos. 259/62	2·50	2·25

*The normal sideways watermark shows Crown to left of CA, *as seen from the back of the stamp.*

(Des V. Whiteley. Litho Questa)

1970 (31 Dec). *Diamond Jubilee of Montserrat Girl Guides. T* **47** *and similar vert design. Multicoloured.* W w **12**. P 14.

264	10c. Type **47**	10	10
265	15c. Brownie and Badge	10	10
266	25c. As 15c.	15	15
267	40c. Type **47**	20	80
264/7	*Set of* 4	50	1·00

Morocco Agencies (British Post Offices)

With the growth of trade and commerce during the 19th century European powers opened post offices or postal agencies in various ports along the Moroccan coast from the early 1850's onwards. French and, in the north, Spanish influence eventually became predominant, leading to the protectorates of 1912. The British, who had inaugurated a regular postal service between Gibraltar and Tangier or Tetuan in May 1778, established their first postal agency in 1857. German offices followed around the turn of the century.

Before 1892 there was no indigenous postal service and those towns where there was no foreign agency were served by a number of private local posts which continued to flourish until 1900. In November 1892 the Sultan of Morocco established the Cherifian postal service, but this was little used until after its reorganization at the end of 1911. The Sultan's post was absorbed by the French postal service on 1 October 1913. Issues of the local posts and of the Sultan's post can occasionally be found used on cover in combination with stamps of Gibraltar or the Morocco Agencies.

In 1857 the first British postal agency was established at Tangier within the precincts of the Legation and was run by the official interpreter. From 1 March 1858 all letters for Great Britain sent via the British mail packets from Gibraltar required franking with Great Britain stamps.

In 1872 the Tangier office was relocated away from the Legation and the interpreter was appointed British Postal Agent. At the same time the agency was placed under the control of the Gibraltar postmaster. When the colonial posts became independent of the British G.P.O. on 1 January 1886 Gibraltar retained responsibility for the Morocco Agencies. Further offices, each under the control of the local Vice-Consul, were opened from 1886 onwards.

I. GIBRALTAR USED IN MOROCCO

Details of the various agencies are given below. Type C, the "A26" killer, is very similar to postmarks used at Gibraltar during this period. In addition to the town name, postmarks as Types A, B and D from Fez, Mazagan, Saffi and Tetuan were also inscribed "MOROCCO".

Postmark Types used on Gibraltar issues.

Type A Circular datestamp

Type C "A26" killer

Type B Duplex cancellation

Type D Registered oval

BISECTS. The 10c., 40c. and 50c. values of the 1889 surcharges and of the 1889–96 issue are known bisected and used for half their value from various of the Morocco Agencies. These bisects were never authorised by the Gibraltar Post Office.

CASABLANCA

The British postal agency opened on 1 January 1887 and was initially supplied with ½d., 4d. and 6d. stamps from the Gibraltar 1886 overprinted on Bermuda issue and 1d., 2d. and 2½d. values from the 1886–87 set.

Stamps of GIBRALTAR *cancelled with Types* A (*without code or code* "C"), B (*without code or code* "A") *or* D.

1886. *Optd on Bermuda (Nos. 1/7).*

Z1	½d. dull green	80·00
Z2	4d. orange-brown	£375
Z3	6d. deep lilac	£375

1886–87. *Queen Victoria £sd issue (Nos. 8/14).*

Z4	½d. dull green	35·00
Z5	1d. rose	38·00
Z6	2d. brown-purple	85·00
Z7	2½d. blue	50·00
Z8	4d. orange-brown	£130
Z10	1s. bistre	£375

1889. *Surch in Spanish currency (Nos. 15/21).*

Z11	5c. on ½d. green	60·00
Z12	10c. on 1d. rose	48·00
Z13	25c. on 2d. brown-purple	75·00
Z14	25c. on 2½d. bright blue	45·00
Z15	40c. on 4d. orange-brown	£140
Z16	50c. on 6d. bright lilac	£130
Z17	75c. on 1s. bistre	£160

1889–96. *Queen Victoria Spanish currency issue (Nos. 22/33).*

Z18	5c. green	16·00
Z19	10c. carmine	15·00
Z20	20c. olive-green and brown	38·00
Z22	25c. ultramarine	15·00
Z23	40c. orange-brown	42·00
Z24	50c. bright lilac	32·00
Z25	75c. olive-green	95·00
Z26	1p. bistre	85·00
Z28	1p. bistre and ultramarine	42·00
Z29	2p. black and carmine	65·00

FEZ

The British postal agency in this inland town opened on 13 February 1892 and was initially supplied with stamps up to the 50c. value from the Gibraltar 1889–96 issue.

Stamps of GIBRALTAR *cancelled with Types* A (*without code*) *or* D.

1889–96. *Queen Victoria Spanish currency issue (Nos. 22/33).*

Z31	5c. green	35·00
Z32	10c. carmine	38·00
Z33	20c. olive-green and brown	70·00
Z35	25c. ultramarine	50·00
Z36	40c. orange-brown	90·00
Z37	50c. bright lilac	70·00

LARAICHE

The British postal agency at Laraiche opened in March 1886, although the first postmark, an "A26" killer, was not supplied until May.

Stamps of GIBRALTAR *cancelled with Types* B (*without code*) *or* D.

1886. *Optd on Bermuda (Nos. 1/7).*

Z39	½d. dull green	
Z40	1d. rose-red	
Z41	2½d. ultramarine	

1886–87. *Queen Victoria £sd issue (Nos. 8/14).*

Z42	½d. dull green	£110
Z43	1d. rose	£100
Z45	2½d. blue	£110

1889. *Surch in Spanish currency (Nos. 15/21).*

Z47	5c. on ½d. green	75·00
Z48	10c. on 1d. rose	
Z49	25c. on 2½d. bright blue	

It is believed that the other surcharges in this series were not supplied to Laraiche.

1889–96. *Queen Victoria Spanish currency issue (Nos. 22/33).*

Z50	5c. green	38·00
Z51	10c. carmine	48·00
Z52	20c. olive-green and brown	
Z54	25c. ultramarine	48·00
Z55	40c. orange-brown	
Z56	50c. bright-lilac	95·00
Z57	1p. bistre and ultramarine	

MAZAGAN

This was the main port for the inland city of Marrakesh. The British postal agency opened on 1 March 1888 and was initially supplied with stamps from the Gibraltar 1886–87 series.

Stamps of GIBRALTAR *cancelled with Types* A (*codes* "A" *or* "C") *or* D (*without code, code* "A" *or code* "C").

1886–87. *Queen Victoria £sd issue (Nos. 8/14).*

Z58	½d. dull green	38·00
Z59	1d. rose	38·00
Z60	2d. brown-purple	
Z61	2½d. blue	45·00
Z62	4d. orange-brown	£140
Z63	6d. lilac	£160

1889. *Surch in Spanish currency (Nos. 15/21).*

Z64	5c. on ½d. green	
Z65	10c. on 1d. rose	
Z66	25c. on 2½d. bright blue	

It is believed that the other surcharges in this series were not supplied to Mazagan.

1889–96. *Queen Victoria Spanish currency issue (Nos. 22/33).*

Z67	5c. green	22·00
Z68	10c. carmine	20·00
Z69	20c. olive-green and brown	65·00
Z70	25c. ultramarine	50·00
Z71	40c. orange-brown	90·00
Z72	50c. bright lilac	
Z74	1p. bistre and ultramarine	
Z75	2p. black and carmine	

MOGADOR

The British postal agency at this port opened on 1 April 1887 and was initially supplied with stamps from the Gibraltar 1886–87 series.

Stamps of GIBRALTAR *cancelled with Types* A (*code* "C"), B (*code* "C") *or* D.

1886–87. *Queen Victoria £sd issue (Nos. 8/14).*

Z76	½d. dull green	35·00
Z77	1d. rose	45·00
Z78	2d. brown-purple	85·00
Z79	2½d. blue	45·00

1889. *Surch in Spanish currency (Nos. 15/21).*

Z80	5c. on ½d. green	60·00
Z81	10c. on 1d. rose	60·00
Z82	25c. on 2½d. bright blue	60·00

It is believed that the other surcharges in this series were not supplied to Mogador.

1889–96. *Queen Victoria Spanish currency issue (Nos. 22/33).*

Z83	5c. green	16·00
Z84	10c. carmine	18·00
Z85	20c. olive-green and brown	
Z87	25c. ultramarine	22·00
Z88	40c. orange-brown	40·00
Z89	50c. bright lilac	40·00
Z90	1p. bistre and ultramarine	65·00

RABAT

The British postal agency at this port on the north-west coast of Morocco opened in March 1886, although the first cancellation, an "A26" killer, was not supplied until May. The initial stock of stamps was from the Gibraltar 1886 overprinted on Bermuda issue.

Stamps of GIBRALTAR *cancelled with Types* B (*code* "O") *or* D.

1886. *Optd on Bermuda (Nos. 1/7).*

Z92	½d. dull green	
Z93	1d. rose-red	
Z94	2½d. ultramarine	£160

1886–87. *Queen Victoria £sd issue (Nos. 8/14).*

Z95	½d. dull green	38·00
Z96	1d. rose	38·00
Z97	2d. brown-purple	85·00
Z98	2½d. blue	48·00
Z101	1s. bistre	£425

1889. *Surch in Spanish currency (Nos. 15/21).*

Z102	5c. on ½d. green	60·00
Z103	10c. on 1d. rose	50·00
Z104	25c. on 2½d. bright blue	60·00

It is believed that the other surcharges in this series were not supplied to Rabat.

1889–96. *Queen Victoria Spanish currency issue (Nos. 22/33).*

Z105	5c. green	23·00
Z106	10c. carmine	22·00
Z107	20c. olive-green and brown	48·00
Z108	25c. ultramarine	23·00
Z109	40c. orange-brown	55·00
Z110	50c. bright lilac	48·00

SAFFI

The British postal agency at this port opened on 1 July 1891 and was supplied with stamps from the Gibraltar 1889–96 series.

Stamps of GIBRALTAR *cancelled with Types* B (*code* "C") *or* D (*code* "C").

1889–96. *Queen Victoria Spanish currency issue (Nos. 22/33).*

Z111	5c. green	25·00
Z112	10c. carmine	25·00
Z113	20c. olive-green and brown	60·00
Z115	25c. ultramarine	27·00
Z116	40c. orange-brown	90·00
Z117	50c. bright lilac	70·00
Z118	1p. bistre and ultramarine	75·00
Z119	2p. black and carmine	85·00

TANGIER

The British postal agency in Tangier opened on 1 April 1857 and from 1 March of the following year letters from it sent via the packet service to Great Britain required franking with Great Britain stamps.

No identifiable postmark was supplied to Tangier until 1872 and all earlier mail was cancelled with one of the Gibraltar marks. In April 1872 a postmark as Type A was supplied on which the "N" of "TANGIER" was reversed. A corrected version, with code letter "A", followed in 1878, but both were used as origin or arrival marks and the Great Britain stamps continued to be cancelled with Gibraltar obliterators. The Type A postmarks generally fell into disuse after 1880 and very few identifiable marks occur on mail from Tangier until the introduction of Gibraltar stamps on 1 January 1886.

Stamps of GIBRALTAR *cancelled with Types* A (*codes* "A" *or* "C"), B (*code* "A") *or* D.

1886. *Optd on Bermuda (Nos. 1/7).*

Z120	½d. dull green	45·00
Z121	1d. rose-red	70·00
Z122	2d. purple-brown	£150
Z123	2½d. ultramarine	45·00
Z124	4d. orange-brown	£180
Z125	6d. deep lilac	£250
Z126	1s. yellow-brown	£550

1886–87. *Queen Victoria £sd issue (Nos. 8/14).*

Z127	½d. dull green	19·00
Z128	1d. rose	19·00
Z129	2d. brown-purple	50·00
Z130	2½d. blue	28·00
Z131	4d. orange-brown	85·00
Z132	6d. lilac	£130
Z133	1s. bistre	£300

1889. *Surch in Spanish currency (Nos. 15/21).*

Z134	5c. on ½d. green	30·00
Z135	10c. on 1d. rose	21·00
Z136	25c. on 2d. brown-purple	40·00
Z137	25c. on 2½d. on 2½d. bright blue	30·00
Z138	40c. on 4d. orange-brown	£100
Z139	50c. on 6d. bright lilac	95·00
Z140	75c. on 1s. bistre	£130

1889–96. *Queen Victoria Spanish currency issue (Nos. 22/33).*

Z141	5c. green	6·00
Z142	10c. carmine	6·00
Z143	20c. olive-green and brown	24·00
Z144	20c. olive-green	75·00
Z145	25c. ultramarine	8·50
Z146	40c. orange-brown	14·00
Z147	50c. bright lilac	13·00
Z148	75c. olive-green	55·00
Z149	1p. bistre	65·00
Z150	1p. bistre and ultramarine	22·00
Z151	2p. black and carmine	42·00
Z152	5p. slate-grey	£120

TETUAN

The British postal agency in this northern town opened on 1 April 1890 and was supplied with stamps from the Gibraltar 1889–96 series.

Stamps of GIBRALTAR *cancelled with Types* A (*code* "C"), B (*code* "C" *often inverted*) *or* D (*code* "C").

1889–96. *Queen Victoria Spanish currency issue (Nos. 22/33).*

Z153	5c. green	30·00
Z154	10c. carmine	35·00
Z155	20c. olive-green and brown	65·00
Z157	25c. ultramarine	40·00
Z158	40c. orange-brown	75·00
Z159	50c. bright lilac	75·00
Z161	1p. bistre and ultramarine	

PRICES FOR STAMPS ON COVER TO 1945

Nos. 1/16	*from* × 7
Nos. 17/30	*from* × 3
Nos. 31/74	*from* × 3
Nos. 75/6	*from* × 4
Nos. 112/24	*from* × 4
No. 125	—
Nos. 126/35	*from* × 5
Nos. 136/42	*from* × 2
Nos. 143/59	*from* × 3
Nos. 160/75	*from* × 8
Nos. 191/9	*from* × 5
Nos. 200/1	*from* × 3
Nos. 202/11	*from* × 4
Nos. 212/15	*from* × 5
Nos. 216/24	*from* × 8
Nos. 225/6	*from* × 2
Nos. 227/30	*from* × 8
Nos. 231/52	*from* × 6

The above prices apply to stamps used on cover from Morocco. Examples of Nos. 31/76 & 231/52 used on cover in G.B. after 1950 have little value.

II. GIBRALTAR ISSUES OVERPRINTED

With the reversion of Gibraltar to sterling in 1898 it became necessary to provide separate issues for the Morocco Agencies which continued to use Spanish currency.

The following were used in all the British postal agencies.

Morocco Agencies (1)	Morocco Agencies (2)
Agencies Inverted "V" for "A" (Right-hand pane R. 6/6)	Agencies Long tail to "S" (Right-hand pane R. 8/2)

Broken "M" (Pl 2 R. 4/5)

Flat top to "C" (Pl 2 R. 4/4)

1898 (1 June)–**1900**. *Nos. 22/8 and 31/2 (Queen Victoria) of Gibraltar optd Typographically (No. 2e) or by lithography (others) with T* **1** *(wide "M" and ear of "g" projecting upwards), in black at Gibraltar Chronicle office.*

1	5c. green	3·75	3·25
	a. Inverted "V" for "A"	42·00	50·00
	b. Long tail to "S"	45·00	55·00
	c. Broken "M" in "CENTIMOS"	70·00	
2	10c. carmine	6·00	1·00
	b. Bisected (5c.) (on cover)	†	£1100
	c. Inverted "V" for "A"	£225	£275
	d. Long tail to "S"	£225	
	e. Lines of opt 5 mm apart (6.00)	7·00	4·00
	ea. Opt double	£650	
3	20c. olive-green and brown	13·00	2·00
	a. Inverted "V" for "A"	80·00	85·00
	b. Long tail to "S"	85·00	90·00
3*c*	20c. olive-green	13·00	6·50
	ca. Opt double	£500	£650
	cb. Inverted "V" for "A"	90·00	£100
	cc. Long tail to "S"	95·00	£110
	cd. Flat top to "C" in "CENTIMOS"	£140	
4	25c. ultramarine	6·00	1·00
	a. Inverted "V" for "A"	£130	£130
	b. Long tail to "S"	£140	£140
5	40c. orange-brown (2.6.98)	6·00	3·25
	a. Inverted "V" for "A"	£170	£190
	b. Long tail to "S"	£180	£200
	c. Blue opt (7.98)	50·00	32·00
	ca. "Morocco" omitted (R. 1/1)	£1000	
6	50c. bright lilac (2.6.98)	17·00	23·00
	a. Inverted "V" for "A"	£250	£325
	b. Long tail to "S"	£300	£350
	c. Blue opt (7.98)	13·00	13·00
7	1p. bistre and ultramarine (2.6.98)	19·00	27·00
	a. Inverted "V" for "A"	£250	£350
	b. Long tail to "S"	£275	£375
	c. Blue opt (7.98)	£170	£250
8	2p. black and carmine (4.6.98)	26·00	27·00
	a. Inverted "V" for "A"	£325	£375
	b. Long tail to "S"	£350	£375
1/8 *Set of* 8		85·00	70·00

The blue overprint can be easily distinguished by looking through the stamp in front of a strong light.

The listed varieties of overprint occur from the first litho setting. They were corrected on the second setting of July 1898, which produced Nos. 5c, 6c, 7c and further supplies of No 8. The corrected type was subsequently used to produce additional stocks of Nos. 1/2. Numerous more minor varieties exist from these settings.

No. 2e comes from two further printings in 1900 using a third setting on which the two lines of the overprint were 5 mm apart instead of the 4 mm space used previously and applied typographically.

Agencies "CD" sideways flaw (Left-hand pane R. 1/5)	Morocco Broad top to "M" (Left-hand pane R. 7/3)	Agencies Hyphen between "nc" (Right-hand pane R. 3/5)

1899 (Feb)–**1902**. *Nos. 22/3, 25/8 and 31/2 (Queen Victoria) of Gibraltar optd typographically with T* **2** *(narrow "M" and ear of "g" horizontal), in black by D.L.R., London.*

9	5c. green (4.99)	1·00	1·25
	a. "CD" sideways	20·00	24·00
	b. Broad top to "M"	10·00	15·00
	c. Hyphen between "nc"	10·00	15·00
	d. Broken "M" in "CENTIMOS"	50·00	
10	10c. carmine	3·25	60
	a. "CD" sideways	32·00	24·00
	b. Broad top to "M"	14·00	15·00
	c. Hyphen between "nc"	14·00	15·00
	d. Opt double	£750	£750
11	20c. olive-green (5.02)	9·00	1·25
	b. Broad top to "M"	45·00	48·00
	c. Hyphen between "nc"	45·00	48·00
	d. Flat top to "C" in "CENTIMOS"	95·00	
12	25c. ultramarine (10.99)	11·00	90
	a. "CD" sideways	75·00	65·00
	b. Broad top to "M"	50·00	55·00
	c. Hyphen between "nc"	50·00	55·00
13	40c. orange-brown (3.02)	48·00	40·00
	b. Broad top to "M"	£225	£275
	c. Hyphen between "nc"	£225	£275
14	50c. bright lilac (4.99)	10·00	3·50
	b. Broad top to "M"	£120	£130
	c. Hyphen between "nc"	£120	£130
15	1p. bistre and ultramarine (4.99)	29·00	48·00
	b. Broad top to "M"	£160	£275
	c. Hyphen between "nc"	£160	£275
16	2p. black and carmine (3.01)	60·00	48·00
	b. Broad top to "M"	£350	£375
	c. Hyphen between "nc"	£350	£375
9/16 *Set of* 8		£150	£130
9s/16s Optd "Specimen" *Set of* 8		£225	

1903–05. *As Nos. 46/51 (King Edward VII) of Gibraltar, but with value in Spanish currency, optd with T* **2**. *Wmk Crown CA. P 14.*

17	5c. grey-green and green (1.03)	10·00	3·50
	a. "CD" sideways	70·00	60·00
	b. Broad top to "M"	60·00	65·00
	c. Hyphen between "nc"	60·00	65·00
18	10c. dull purple/*red* (8.03)	9·00	40
	a. "CD" sideways	65·00	42·00
	b. Broad top to "M"	60·00	42·00
	c. Hyphen between "nc"	60·00	42·00
	w. Wmk inverted	42·00	
19	20c. grey-green and carmine (9.04)	17·00	45·00
	a. "CD" sideways	£140	£225
	b. Broad top to "M"	£130	£225
	c. Hyphen between "nc"	£130	£225
20	25c. purple and black/*blue* (1.7.03)	8·00	30
	a. "CD" sideways	70·00	48·00
	b. Broad top to "M"	55·00	48·00
	c. Hyphen between "nc"	55·00	48·00
21	50c. purple and violet (3.7.05)	90·00	£170
	a. "CD" sideways	£400	£700
	b. Broad top to "M"	£375	£700
	c. Hyphen between "nc"	£375	£700
22	1p. black and carmine (19.11.05)	35·00	£160
	a. "CD" sideways	£275	£600
	b. Broad top to "M"	£225	£600
	c. Hyphen between "nc"	£225	£600
23	2p. black and blue (19.11.05)	50·00	£130
	a. "CD" sideways	£325	£550
	b. Broad top to "M"	£275	£550
	c. Hyphen between "nc"	£275	£550
17/23 *Set of* 7		£200	£450
17s/23s Optd "Specimen" *Set of* 7		£225	

Examples of Nos. 19 and 21/3 are known showing a forged Registered Mazagan postmark dated "15 SP 10".

1905 (Jan)–**06**. *As Nos. 17/23 but* wmk Mult Crown CA. *Ordinary paper (5, 10, 20c.) or chalk-surfaced paper (others).*

24	5c. grey-green and green (4.05)	13·00	4·50
	a. "CD" sideways	80·00	55·00
	b. Broad top to "M"	75·00	55·00
	c. Hyphen between "nc"	£900	£1100
	d. Chalk-surfaced paper (1.06)	8·50	6·50
	da. "CD" sideways	60·00	60·00
	db. Broad top to "M"	60·00	60·00
25	10c. dull purple/*red*	14·00	2·00
	a. "CD" sideways	80·00	40·00
	b. Broad top to "M"	75·00	40·00
	cw. Wmk inverted	27·00	20·00
	d. Chalk-surfaced paper (12.05)	6·00	2·00
	da. "CD" sideways	48·00	40·00
	db. Broad top to "M"	48·00	40·00
26	20c. grey-green and carmine (1.06)	6·00	32·00
	a. "CD" sideways	60·00	£170
	b. Broad top to "M"	60·00	£170
27	25c. purple and black/*blue* (6.06)	50·00	8·50
	a. "CD" sideways	£350	£160
	b. Broad top to "M"	£350	£160
28	50c. purple and violet (7.06)	7·50	55·00
	a. "CD" sideways	£160	£325
	b. Broad top to "M"	£150	£300
29	1p. black and carmine (11.05)	38·00	85·00
	a. "CD" sideways	£250	£375
	b. Broad top to "M"	£225	£375
30	2p. black and blue (11.05)	19·00	35·00
	a. "CD" sideways	£190	£250
	b. Broad top to "M"	£180	£250
24/30 *Set of* 7		£120	£200

Examples of Nos. 26 and 28/30 are known showing a forged Registered Mazagan postmark dated "15 SP 10".

Control of the British postal agencies in Morocco returned to the G.P.O., London, from 1 January 1907.

All the following issues are overprinted on Great Britain

III. BRITISH CURRENCY

Stamps overprinted "MOROCCO AGENCIES" only were primarily intended for use on parcels (and later, air-mail correspondence), and were on sale at British P.Os throughout Morocco including Tangier, until 1937.

PRICES. Our prices for used stamps with these overprints are for specimens used in Morocco. These stamps were valid for postal purposes in Great Britain from the summer of 1950 onwards. Examples with G.B. postmarks are worth 50 per cent of the used prices quoted.

MOROCCO AGENCIES (4) · MOROCCO AGENCIES (5) · MOROCCO AGENCIES (6)

1907 (30 Apr)–**13**. *King Edward VII optd as T* **4** *or* **5** *(2s.6d.).*

(a) De La Rue printings. Ordinary paper (½d., 1d., 4d. (No. 35a) or chalk-surfaced paper (others).

31	½d. pale yellowish green (1.6.07)	2·25	8·50
32	1d. scarlet (5.5.07)	9·50	5·50
33	2d. pale grey-green and carmine-red	10·00	5·50
34	4d. green and chocolate-brown (29.10.07)	3·75	4·25
35	4d. pale orange (3.12)	13·00	14·00
	a. Orange-red	10·00	12·00
36	6d. pale dull purple (5.5.07)	15·00	20·00
	a. Dull purple	19·00	24·00
37	1s. dull green and carmine (5.5.07)	26·00	17·00
38	2s.6d. pale dull purple (5.5.07)	95·00	£130
	a. Dull purple	95·00	£130
31/8 *Set of 8*		£150	£180
37s/8s Optd "Specimen" *Set of 2*		£140	

(b) Harrison printing. Ordinary paper.

40	4d. bright orange (No. 286) (1913)	27·00	26·00

(c) Somerset House printing. Ordinary paper.

41	2s.6d. dull greyish purple (No. 315) (1913)	£100	£200

1914–31. *King George V.*

(a) W **100** (Simple Cypher). Optd with *T* **4**.

42	½d. green	5·00	50
43	1d. scarlet	1·00	20
44	1½d. red-brown (1921)	3·75	12·00
45	2d. orange (Die I)	4·25	60
46	3d. bluish violet (1921)	1·25	35
47	4d. grey-green (1921)	3·75	1·50
48	6d. reddish purple (*chalk-surfaced paper*) (1921)	4·75	15·00
49	1s. bistre-brown (1917)	7·50	1·25
	a. Opt triple, two albino	£120	

(b) W **110** (Single Cypher). Optd with T **6**.

50	2s.6d. sepia-brown (*Waterlow ptg*) (No. 400) (1914)	45·00	55·00
	a. Re-entry (R. 2/1)	£800	£1000
	b. Opt double, one albino	£180	
51	2s.6d. yellow-brown (*D.L.R. ptg*) (No. 406) (1917)	48·00	30·00
	a. Opt double	£1600	£1400
	b. Opt triple, two albino	£225	
	c. Pale brown (No. 407)	40·00	50·00
53	2s.6d. chocolate-brown (*B.W. ptg*) (No. 414)	38·00	25·00
	a. Opt double, one albino*	£170	
54	5s. rose-red (*B.W. ptg*) (No. 416) (1931)	55·00	90·00
	a. Opt triple, two albino	£300	
42/54 *Set of 10*		£110	£130
49s/50s, 54s Optd "Specimen" *Set of 3*		£200	

*The albino overprint is quite clear, with "MOROCCO" appearing just below "AGENCIES" on the normal overprint and a little to the right as seen from the back. There is also a second faint albino impression just below the normal overprint.

MOROCCO AGENCIES S (7) · MOROCCO AGENCIES S (8)

Type **7**: Opt 14 mm long; ends of "s" cut off diagonally.
Type **8**: Opt 15½ mm long; ends of "s" cut off horizontally

1925–36. *King George V* (W **111** (Block Cypher)) *optd with T* **8** *(4d.) or* **7** *(others).*

55	½d. green	2·00	50
	aw. Wmk inverted	75·00	
	b. Optd with Type **8**	11·00	45·00
56	1½d. chestnut (1931)	12·00	13·00
57	2d. orange	2·25	1·00
58	2½d. blue	3·25	5·00
	a. Optd with Type **8**	£100	30·00
59	4d. grey-green (1.36)	8·00	38·00
60	6d. purple (1931)	2·00	8·50
	a. Opt double, one albino	£120	
	b. Optd with Type **8**	1·00	60
61	1s. bistre-brown	17·00	5·00
	as. Optd "Specimen"	65·00	
	b. Optd with Type **8**	55·00	50·00
55/61 *Set of 7*		40·00	55·00

1935 (8 May). *Silver Jubilee (Nos. 453/6) optd "MOROCCO AGENCIES" only, as in T* **17**.

62	½d. green (B.)	1·50	6·50
63	1d. scarlet (B.)	1·50	6·50
64	1½d. red-brown (B.)	3·25	14·00
65	2½d. blue (R.)	3·50	2·50
62/5 *Set of 4*		8·75	27·00

1935–37. *King George V.*

(a) Harrison photo ptgs (Nos. 440/5 and 449). W **111** (Block Cypher). *Optd with T* **8**.

66	1d. scarlet (4.35)	3·25	16·00
67	1½d. red-brown (28.4.36)	3·25	19·00
68	2d. orange (1.5.36)	1·25	9·50
69	2½d. ultramarine (11.2.36)	1·75	4·25
70	3d. violet (2.3.36)	50	30
71	4d. deep grey-green (14.5.36)	50	30
72	1s. bistre-brown (31.8.36)	80	4·50
	s. Optd "Specimen"	65·00	

(b) Waterlow re-engraved ptgs. W **110** (Single Cypher) optd with *T* **6**.

73	2s.6d. chocolate-brown (No. 450)	42·00	65·00
	s. Optd "Specimen"	75·00	
74	5s. bright rose-red (No. 451) (2.3.37)	24·00	£100
66/74 *Set of 9*		70·00	£200

1936 (26 Oct)–**37**. *King Edward VIII, optd "MOROCCO AGENCIES" only, as in T* **18** *with "MOROCCO" 14¼ mm long.*

75	1d. scarlet	10	40
	a. "MOROCCO" 15¼ mm long (5.1.37)	6·00	19·00
76	2½d. bright blue	10	15
	a. "MOROCCO" 15¼ mm long (5.1.37)	1·00	4·25

The first two printings of both values showed all the stamps with the short overprint, Nos. 75/6.

On 5 January 1937 a further printing of both values was placed on sale in London which had the 24 stamps from the bottom two horizontal rows (Rows 19 and 20) with the long overprint, Nos. 75a/6a. Subsequent printings increased the number of long overprints in the sheet to 25 by the addition of R. 8/9, and, finally, to 31 (R. 1/7, R. 7/1, R. 8/1, R. 13/3, 4 and 10, R. 14/6, but without R. 8/9).

For the 1d. value all sheets from cylinder 2 show the first setting. Sheets from cylinder 6 were also used for the first, and for all subsequent settings. The 2½d. value was overprinted on sheets from cylinder 2 throughout.

From 3 June 1937 unoverprinted stamps of Great Britain were supplied to the post offices at Tangier and Tetuan (Spanish Zone) as local stocks of issues overprinted "MOROCCO AGENCIES" were exhausted.

Type E

Type F

Stamps of GREAT BRITAIN *cancelled as Types* E *or* F *at Tangier.*

1937. *King George V.*

Z170	1½d. red-brown (No. 441)	
Z171	2d. orange (No. 442)	14·00
Z172	3d. violet (No. 444)	14·00
Z173	4d. deep grey-green (No. 445)	9·50
Z174	6d. purple (No. 426*a*)	9·50
Z175	1s. bistre-brown (No. 449)	35·00
Z176	2s.6d. chocolate-brown (No. 450)	80·00
Z177	5s. bright rose-red (No. 451)	

1937–39. *King George VI (Nos. 462/75).*

Z178	½d. green	14·00
Z179	1d. scarlet	14·00
Z180	1½d. red-brown	12·00
Z181	2d. orange	12·00
Z182	2½d. ultramarine	9·00
Z183	3d. violet	9·00
Z184	4d. grey-green	9·00
Z185	5d. brown	12·00
Z186	6d. purple	6·00
Z187	7d. emerald-green	9·50
Z188	8d. bright carmine	18·00
Z189	9d. deep olive-green	13·00
Z190	10d. turquoise-blue	18·00
Z191	1s. bistre-brown	6·00

1939–42. *King George VI (Nos. 476/8a).*

Z192	2s.6d. brown	48·00
Z193	2s.6d. yellow-green	14·00
Z194	5s. red	20·00
Z195	10s. dark blue	90·00
Z196	10s. ultramarine	38·00

1941–42. *King George VI pale colours (Nos. 485/90).*

Z197	½d. pale green	9·00
Z198	1d. pale scarlet	9·00
Z199	1½d. pale red-brown	9·00
Z200	2d. pale orange	9·00
Z201	2½d. light ultramarine	8·00
Z202	3d. pale violet	6·00

1946. *Victory (Nos. 491/2).*

Z203	2½d. ultramarine	8·00
Z204	3d. violet	8·00

Type G

Stamps of GREAT BRITAIN *cancelled as Type* G *at Tetuan.*

1937. *King George V.*

Z208	4d. deep grey-green (No. 445)	22·00
Z209	6d. purple (No. 426*a*)	22·00
Z210	1s. bistre-brown (No. 449)	

1937–39. *King George VI (Nos. 465/75).*

Z211	2d. orange	18·00
Z212	2½d. ultramarine	
Z213	3d. violet	
Z214	4d. grey-green	18·00
Z215	6d. purple	12·00
Z216	9d. deep olive-green	
Z217	1s. bistre-brown	12·00

1939–42. *King George VI (Nos. 476/7).*

Z218	2s.6d. brown	
Z219	2s.6d. yellow-green	40·00
Z220	5s. red	50·00

1941. *King George VI pale colours (Nos. 485/90).*

Z221	½d. pale green	
Z222	2d. pale orange	
Z223	2½d. light ultramarine	
Z224	3d. pale violet	12·00

Other unoverprinted stamps of Great Britain are known with Morocco Agencies postmarks during this period, but it is believed that only Nos. Z170/224 were sold by the local post offices.

The use of unoverprinted stamps in Tangier ceased with the issue of Nos. 261/75 on 1 January 1949. Stamps overprinted "MOROCCO AGENCIES" replaced the unoverprinted values at Tetuan on 16 August 1949.

MOROCCO AGENCIES (9) · MOROCCO AGENCIES (10)

1949 (16 Aug). *King George VI, optd with T* **9** *or* **10** *(2s.6d., 5s.).*

77	½d. pale green	1·75	7·00
78	1d. pale scarlet	2·75	9·00
79	1½d. pale red-brown	2·75	8·50
80	2d. pale orange	3·00	9·00
81	2½d. light ultramarine	3·25	10·00
82	3d. pale violet	1·50	1·75
83	4d. grey-green	50	1·25
84	5d. brown	3·00	15·00
85	6d. purple	1·50	1·50
86	7d. emerald-green	50	16·00
87	8d. bright carmine	3·00	6·50
88	9d. deep olive-green	50	11·00
89	10d. turquoise-blue	50	7·50
90	11d. plum	70	8·50
91	1s. bistre-brown	2·75	6·00
92	2s.6d. yellow-green	18·00	35·00
93	5s. red	32·00	60·00
77/93 *Set of 17*		70·00	£180

1951 (3 May). *King George VI (Nos. 503/7, 509/10), optd with T* **9** *or* **10** *(2s.6d., 5s.).*

94	½d. pale orange	2·00	1·00
95	1d. light ultramarine	2·00	1·40
96	1½d. pale green	2·00	3·50
97	2d. pale red-brown	2·25	4·00
98	2½d. pale scarlet	2·00	4·25
99	2s.6d. yellow-green (H.M.S. *Victory*)	13·00	21·00
100	5s. red (Dover)	13·00	23·00
94/100 *Set of 7*		32·00	50·00

1952–55. *Queen Elizabeth II.* W **153** (Tudor Crown). *Optd with T* **9**.

101	½d. orange-red (31.8.53)	10	10
102	1d. ultramarine (31.8.53)	15	1·75
103	1½d. green (5.12.52)	15	20
104	2d. red-brown (31.8.53)	20	2·00
105	2½d. carmine-red (5.12.52)	15	1·25
106	4d. ultramarine (1.3.55)	1·50	3·50
107	5d. brown (6.7.53)	60	60
108	6d. reddish purple (1.3.55)	85	3·50
109	8d. magenta (6.7.53)	60	70
110	1s. bistre-brown (6.7.53)	60	60
101/10 *Set of 10*		4·50	12·50

1956 (10 Sept). *Queen Elizabeth II.* W **165** (St. Edward's Crown). *Optd with T* **9**.

111	2½d. carmine-red (No. 544)	70	2·50

Stamps overprinted "MOROCCO AGENCIES" were withdrawn from sale on 31 December 1956.

IV. SPANISH CURRENCY

Stamps surcharged in Spanish currency were sold at British P.Os. throughout Morocco until the establishment of the French Zone and the Tangier International Zone, when their use was confined to the Spanish Zone.

During this period further British postal agencies were opened at Alcazar (1907–1916), Fez-Mellah (Jewish quarter) (1909), Marrakesh (1909), Marrakesh–Mellah (Jewish quarter) (1909–17) and Mequinez (1907–1916).

MOROCCO AGENCIES · MOROCCO AGENCIES

5 CENTIMOS (11) · 6 PESETAS (12)

1907 (1 Jan)–**12**. *King Edward VII surch as T* **11** *(5c. to 1p.) or* **12** *(3p. to 12p.).*

(a) De La Rue printings. Ordinary paper (Nos. 112/13, 116, 118, 122/3) or chalk-surfaced paper (others).

112	5c. on ½d. pale yellowish green	11·00	20
	a. Yellowish green	11·00	20
113	10c. on 1d. scarlet	15·00	10
	a. Bright scarlet	15·00	10
114	15c. on 1½d. pale dull purple and green	7·50	1·00
	a. Slate-purple and bluish green	4·25	20
	b. "1" of "15" omitted	£6000	
115	20c. on 2d. pale grey-green and carmine-red	3·50	40
	a. Pale grey-green and scarlet	4·75	85
116	25c. on 2½d. ultramarine	3·00	20
	a. Pale ultramarine	1·75	20
117	40c. on 4d. green and chocolate-brown (29.10.07)	1·75	3·25
	a. Deep green and chocolate-brown	2·50	1·75
118	40c. on 4d. pale orange (12.5.10)	2·50	1·25
	a. Orange-red	1·00	60
119	50c. on 5d. dull purple and ultramarine	4·75	4·25
	a. Slate-purple and ultramarine	3·50	4·00
120	1p. on 10d. dull purple and carmine	32·00	17·00
	a. Slate-purple and carmine	22·00	13·00
	b. No cross on crown		
121	3p. on 2s.6d. pale dull purple	21·00	25·00
	a. Dull purple	21·00	25·00

122	6p. on 5s. bright carmine	35·00	45·00
	a. Deep bright carmine	35·00	45·00
123	12p. on 10s. ultramarine (30.4.07)	80·00	75·00
112/23 *Set of* 12		£180	£150
117s, 123s Optd "Specimen" *Set of* 2		£150	

(b) Harrison printing Ordinary paper.

124	25c. on 2½d. bright blue (No. 283) (1912)	42·00	29·00
	a. Dull blue	26·00	29·00

(c) Somerset House printing. Ordinary paper.

125	12p. on 10s. blue (No. 319) (1912)	£190	£250

No. 114b occurred on stamps from the first vertical row of one sheet.

1912. *King George V (*W **49** (Imperial Crown)*) surch as T* **11**.

126	5c. on ½d. green (No. 339)	3·00	20
127	10c. on 1d. scarlet (No. 342)	1·00	10
	a. No cross on crown	£110	55·00

(13)

(14)

(15)

(16)

1914–26. *King George V.*

(a) W **100** (Simple Cypher)*. Surch as T* **11** *(5c.),* **13** *(3c. and 40c.)*,* **15** *(15c.) and* **14** *(remainder).*

128	3c. on ½d. green (1917)	1·25	6·00
129	5c. on ½d. green	75	10
130	10c. on 1d. scarlet	1·50	10
	y. Wmk inverted and reversed	—	£180
131	15c. on 1½d. red-brown (1915)	1·00	10
	a. Surch double, one albino	80·00	
132	20c. on 2d. orange (Die I)	1·00	25
	a. Surch double, one albino	80·00	
133	25c. on 2½d. blue (*shades*)	1·75	25
	a. Surch double, one albino	60·00	
	w. Wmk inverted		
134	40c. on 4d. grey-green (1917)	4·25	4·00
	a. Surch double, one albino		
135	1p. on 10d. turquoise-blue	4·25	8·50
	a. Surch double, one albino	85·00	

*The surcharge on Nos. 134, 148 and 158 is as *T* **13** for the value and *T* **15** for "MOROCCO AGENCIES".

(b) W **110** (Single Cypher)*. Surch as T* **16**.

(i) Waterlow printings.

136	6p. on 5s. rose-carmine	29·00	48·00
	a. Surch double, one albino	£140	
	b. Surch triple, two albino	£160	
137	6p. on 5s. pale rose-carmine	£140	£200
	a. Surch double, one albino	£190	
138	12p. on 10s. indigo-blue (R.)	£100	£170
	a. Surch double, one albino	£225	
	b. Surch triple, two albino		
136s, 138s Optd "Specimen" *Set of* 2		£180	

(ii) De La Rue printings.

139	3p. on 2s.6d. grey-brown (1918)	40·00	£130
	a. Surch double, one albino		
140	3p. on 2s.6d. yellow-brown	40·00	£150
	a. Surch double, one albino	£150	
141	12p. on 10s. blue (R.)	90·00	£160
	a. Surch double, one albino	£275	

(iii) Bradbury Wilkinson printings.

142	3p. on 2s.6d. chocolate-brown (1926)	23·00	75·00
128/42 *Set of* 11		£140	£275

1925–31. *King George V (*W **111** (Block Cypher)*), surch as T* **11**, **13**, **14** *or* **15**.

143	5c. on ½d. green (1931)	3·00	18·00
144	10c. on 1d. scarlet (1929)	22·00	29·00
145	15c. on 1½d. red-brown	7·50	23·00
146	20c. on 2d. orange (1931)	3·00	9·00
	a. Surch double, one albino	85·00	
147	25c. on 2½d. blue	2·50	2·50
	a. Surch double, one albino	60·00	
	w. Wmk inverted	60·00	
148	40c. on 4d. grey-green (1930)	3·00	2·50
	a. Surch double, one albino		
143/8 *Set of* 6		38·00	75·00

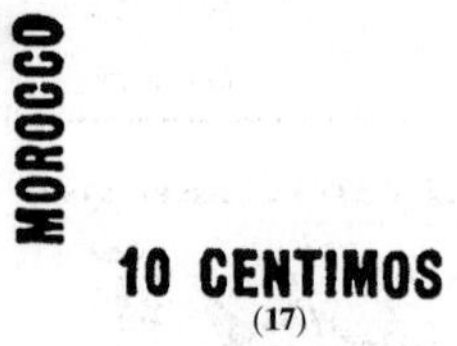

(17)

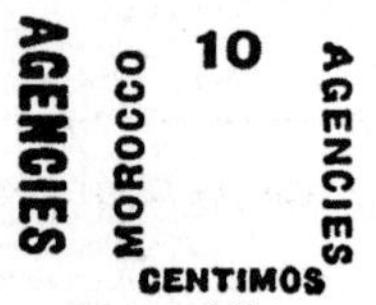

(18)

1935 (8 May). *Silver Jubilee (Nos. 453/6). Surch as T* **17**.

149	5c. on ½d. green (B.)	1·00	1·25
150	10c. on 1d. scarlet (B.)	2·75	2·25
	a. Pair, one with "CENTIMES"	£1500	£2250
151	15c. on 1½d. red-brown (B.)	5·50	19·00
152	25c. on 2½d. blue (R.)	3·50	2·25
149/52 *Set of* 4		11·50	22·00

No. 150a occurred on R. 5/4 of a small second printing made in June 1935. The error can only be identified when *se-tenant* with a normal No. 150. Beware of forgeries.

1935–37. *King George V (Harrison photo ptgs) (Nos. 439/43, 445 and 448). Surch as T* **11**, **13**, **14** *or* **15**. W **111** (Block Cypher).

153	5c. on ½d. green (9.6.36)	1·00	21·00
154	10c. on 1d. scarlet (11.36)	2·50	13·00
155	15c. on 1½d. red-brown (4.35)	6·50	3·25
156	20c. on 2d. orange (26.10.36)	50	25
157	25c. on 2½d. ultramarine (8.9.36)	1·25	5·50
158	40c. on 4d. deep grey-green (18.5.37)	50	3·75
159	1p. on 10d. turquoise-blue (14.4.37)	6·00	30
153/9 *Set of* 7		16·00	42·00

1936 (26 Oct)–**37**. *King Edward VIII surch as T* **18** *with* "MOROCCO" *14¼ mm long.*

160	5c. on ½d. green	10	10
161	10c. on 1d. scarlet	50	2·00
	a. "MOROCCO" 15¼ mm long (5.1.37)	2·75	15·00
162	15c. on 1½d. red-brown	10	15
163	25c. on 2½d. bright blue	10	10
160/3 *Set of* 4		65	2·00

The first three printings of the 10c. on 1d. (from cyls 4, 5 and 6) showed all stamps with the short surcharge (No. 161).

On 5 January 1937 a further printing was placed on sale in London which had 49 stamps in the sheet (R. 1/2 to 11, R. 2/1, 5 and 6, 8 and 9, R. 3/5, R. 4/5, R. 5/4 and 5, 10, R. 6/6 and 7, R. 7/8, R. 8/8, R. 9/8, R. 11/7, 9, R. 13/2 to 5, 7 and 8, R. 14/1, 7, R. 15/7, 11, R. 16/5, 10, R. 17/4, 10 and 11, R. 18/1, R. 19/2, R. 20/1 and 2, 3, 7, 9) with long surcharge (No. 161a). The next printing increased the number of long surcharges in the sheet to 50 (R. 10/2), but the final version, although retaining 50 long surcharges, showed them on R. 1/2 to 11, R. 17/5 to 8 and the entire rows 18, 19 and 20. The first two printings with long surcharges were from cylinder 6 and the last from cylinder 13.

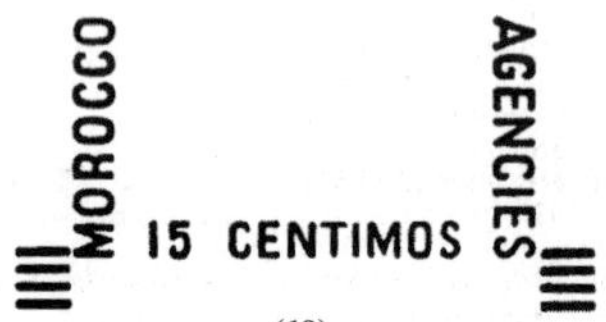

(19)

1937 (13 May). *Coronation (No. 461), surch as T* **19**.

164	15c. on 1½d. maroon (B.)	80	70

(20)

(21)

1937 (June)–**52**. *King George VI (Nos. 462/4, 466, 468, 471 and 474), surch as T* **20**.

165	5c. on ½d. green (B.)	1·25	30
166	10c. on 1d. scarlet	1·00	10
167	15c. on 1½d. red-brown (B.) (4.8.37)	1·50	25
168	25c. on 2½d. ultramarine	2·00	1·25
169	40c. on 4d. grey-green (9.40)	30·00	13·00
170	70c. on 7d. emerald-green (9.40)	1·75	15·00
171	1p. on 10d. turquoise-blue (16.6.52)	2·25	3·75
165/71 *Set of* 7		35·00	30·00

1940 (6 May). *Centenary of First Adhesive Postage Stamps (Nos. 479/81 and 483), surch as T* **21**.

172	5c. on ½d. green (B.)	30	2·75
173	10c. on 1d. scarlet	3·75	2·50
174	15c. on 1½d. red-brown (B.)	70	3·50
175	25c. on 2½d. ultramarine	80	2·50
172/5 *Set of* 4		5·00	10·00

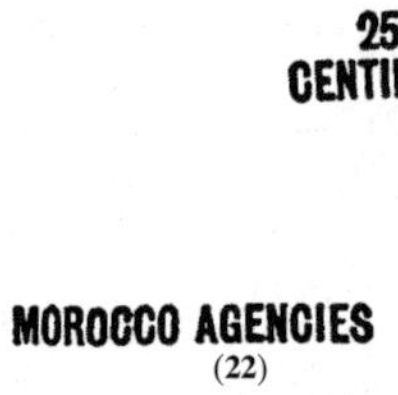

(22)

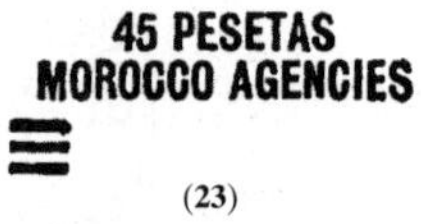

(23)

1948 (26 Apr). *Silver Wedding (Nos. 493/4), surch with T* **22** *or* **23**.

176	25c. on 2½d. ultramarine	1·25	30
177	45p. on £1 blue	17·00	22·00

1948 (29 July). *Olympic Games (Nos. 495/8), variously surch as T* **22**.

178	25c. on 2½d. ultramarine	50	1·50
179	30c. on 3d. violet	50	1·50
	a. Crown flaw	60·00	
180	60c. on 6d. bright purple	50	1·50
181	1p.20c. on 1s. brown	60	1·50
	a. Surch double	£950	
178/81 *Set of* 4		1·90	5·50

1951 (3 May)–**52**. *King George VI (Nos. 503/5 and 507/8), surch as T* **20**.

182	5c. on ½d. pale orange	2·00	6·00
183	10c. on 1d. light ultramarine	3·25	9·00
184	15c. on 1½d. pale green	1·75	20·00
185	25c. on 2½d. pale scarlet	1·75	13·00
186	40c. on 4d. light ultramarine (26.5.52)	60	13·00
182/6 *Set of* 5		8·50	55·00

1954–55. *Queen Elizabeth II.* W **153** (Tudor Crown)*. Surch as T* **20**.

187	5c. on ½d. orange-red (1.9.54)	20	2·75
188	10c. on 1d. ultrammarine (1.3.55)	50	1·00

1956. *Queen Elizabeth II.* W **165** (St. Edward's Crown)*. Surch as T* **20**.

189	5c. on ½d. orange-red (June)	15	3·00
190	40c. on 4d. ultramarine (15 Aug)	70	1·75

The British postal agency at Laraiche closed on 30 June 1938. Stamps surcharged in Spanish currency were withdrawn from sale when the Tetuan agency closed on 31 December 1956.

V. FRENCH CURRENCY

For use in the British postal agencies at Casablanca (closed 14.8.37), Fez (closed 8.1.38), Fez–Mellah (closed after 1930), Marrakesh (closed 14.8.37), Mazagan (closed 14.8.37), Mogador (closed 31.10.33), Rabat (closed 8.1.38) and Saffi (closed 14.8.37).

(24)

(25)

1917–24. *King George V (*W **100** (Simple Cypher)*), surch as T* **24** *or* **25** *(1f.).*

191	3c. on ½d. green (R.)	1·00	2·50
192	5c. on ½d. green	40	20
193	10c. on 1d. scarlet	2·75	40
194	15c. on 1½d. red-brown	2·00	20
195	25c. on 2½d. blue	1·50	20
196	40c. on 4d. slate-green	2·00	1·50
	a. Surch double, one albino		
197	50c. on 5d. yellow-brown (1923)	80	2·75
198	75c. on 9d. olive-green (1924)	1·00	75
	a. Surch double, one albino	£100	
199	1f. on 10d. turquoise-blue	6·00	3·00
	a. Surch double, one albino	85·00	
191/9 *Set of* 9		15·00	10·50

1924–32. *King George V (B.W. ptg).* W **110** (Single Cypher)*, surch as T* **25**, *but closer vertical spacing.*

200	3f. on 2s.6d. chocolate-brown	6·00	1·50
	a. Major re-entry (R. 1/2)	£475	£475
	b. Surch double, one albino		
	c. Reddish brown	10·00	10·00
201	6f. on 5s. rose-red (1932)	32·00	38·00
200s/1s Optd "Specimen" *Set of* 2		£140	

1925–34. *King George V (*W **111** (Block Cypher)*), surch as T* **24** *or* **25** *(1f.).*

202	5c. on ½d. green	30	6·50
203	10c. on 1d. scarlet	30	2·00
	a. Surch double, one albino	90·00	
204	15c. on 1½d. red-brown	1·00	1·75
205	25c. on 2½d. blue	1·50	50
206	40c. on 4d. grey-green	60	80
	a. Surch double, one albino	65·00	
207	50c. on 5d. yellow-brown	1·50	10
	w. Wmk inverted	75·00	
208	75c. on 9d. olive-green	5·00	15
	a. Surch double, one albino	£130	
	w. Wmk inverted	—	£140
209	90c. on 9d. olive-green	18·00	7·50
210	1f. on 10d. turquoise-blue	1·25	10
	a. Surch double, one albino	£100	
211	1f.50 on 1s. bistre-brown	10·00	2·25
	s. Optd "Specimen"	60·00	
202/11 *Set of* 10		35·00	19·00

1935 (8 May). *Silver Jubilee (Nos. 453/6), surch as T* **17**, *but in French currency.*

212	5c. on ½d. green (B.)	15	15
213	10c. on 1d. scarlet (B.)	3·50	60
214	15c. on 1½d. red-brown (B.)	45	1·00
215	25c. on 2½d. blue (R.)	30	25
212/15 *Set of* 4		4·00	1·75

1935–37. *King George V (Harrison photo ptgs.* W **111** (Block Cypher)*), surch as T* **24** *or* **25** *(1f.).*

216	5c. on ½d. green (10.35)	50	5·00
217	10c. on 1d. scarlet (2.3.36)	35	30
218	15c. on 1½d. red-brown	4·75	5·50
219	25c. on 2½d. ultramarine (25.9.36)	30	15
220	40c. on 4d. deep grey-green (2.12.36)	30	15
221	50c. on 5d. yellow-brown (15.9.36)	30	15
222	90c. on 9d. deep olive-green (15.2.37)	35	1·75
223	1f. on 10d. turquoise-blue (10.2.37)	30	30
224	1f.50 on 1s. bistre-brown (20.7.37)	75	3·25
	s. Optd "Specimen"	60·00	

1935–36. *King George V (Waterlow re-engraved ptgs.* W **100** (Single Cypher)*), surch as T* **25**, *but closer vertical spacing.*

225	3f. on 2s.6d. chocolate-brown (No. 450)	4·75	12·00
226	6f. on 5s. bright rose-red (No. 451) (17.6.36)	6·00	21·00
216/26 *Set of* 11		17·00	45·00
225s/6s Optd "Specimen" *Set of* 2		£140	

1936 (26 Oct). *King Edward VIII, surch as T* **18**, *but in French currency.*

227	5c. in ½d. green	10	15
	a. Bar through "POSTAGE"	£650	
228	15c. on 1½d. red-brown	10	15

No. 227a involved R. 18/10 to 12 on a total of eight sheets. The bar, probably a printers rule, became progressively longer so that on four of the sheets it extends over all three stamps. Price quoted is for an example with the bar through the entire word.

1937 (13 May). *Coronation (No. 461), surch as T* **19**, *but in French currency.*

229	15c. on 1½d. maroon (B.)	40	20

1937 (June). *King George VI, surch as T* **20**, *but in French currency.*

230	5c. on ½d. green (B.)	3·00	2·50

Stamps surcharged in French currency were withdrawn from sale on 8 January 1938.

VI. TANGIER INTERNATIONAL ZONE

By an agreement between Great Britain, France and Spain, Tangier was declared an international zone in 1924. Stamps overprinted "Morocco Agencies" or surcharged in Spanish currency were used there until replaced by Nos. 231/4.

PRICES. Our note *re* U.K. usage (at beginning of Section III) also applies to "TANGIER" optd stamps.

(26) (27)

1927. *King George V (*W **111** (Block Cypher)*), optd with T* **26**.

231	½d. green	4·25	20
	a. Opt double, one albino		
232	1d. scarlet	4·25	25
	a. Inverted "Q" for "O" (R. 20/3)	£800	
233	1½d. chestnut	6·00	4·25
234	2d. orange	3·25	20
	a. Opt double, one albino	80·00	
231/4 *Set of* 4		16·00	4·50

1934 (Dec)–**35**. *King George V (Harrison photo ptgs.* W **111** (Block Cypher)*), optd with T* **26**.

235	½d. green (2.35)	1·25	1·60
236	1d. scarlet	6·50	2·50
237	1½d. red-brown	75	20
235/7 *Set of* 3		7·75	3·75

1935 (8 May). *Silver Jubilee (Nos. 453/5), optd with T* **27** *in blue.*

238	½d. green	1·50	6·50
239	1d. scarlet	17·00	17·00
240	1½d. red-brown	1·25	1·25
238/40 *Set of* 3		18·00	22·00

1936 (26 Oct). *King Edward VIII, optd with T* **26**.

241	½d. green	10	20
242	1d. scarlet	10	10
243	1½d. red-brown	15	10
241/3 *Set of* 3		30	30

(28) (29)

1937 (13 May). *Coronation (No. 461), optd with T* **28**.

244	1½d. maroon (B.)	60	50

1937. *King George VI (Nos. 462/4), optd with T* **29**.

245	½d. green (B.) (June)	2·50	1·75
246	1d. scarlet (June)	11·00	1·75
247	1½d. red-brown (B.) (4 Aug)	2·50	40
245/7 *Set of* 3		14·50	3·50

(30) (31)

1940 (6 May). *Centenary of First Adhesive Postage Stamps (Nos. 479/81), optd with T* **30**.

248	½d. green (B.)	30	6·00
249	1d. scarlet	45	60
250	1½d. red-brown (B.)	2·00	7·50
248/50 *Set of* 3		2·50	12·50

1944. *King George VI pale colours (Nos. 485/6), optd with T* **29**.

251	½d. pale green (B.)	14·00	5·00
252	1d. pale scarlet	14·00	3·50

1946 (11 June). *Victory (Nos. 491/2), optd as T* **31**.

253	2½d. ultramarine	65	65
254	3d. violet	65	2·00

The opt on No. 254 is smaller (23×2½ mm).

1948 (26 Apr). *Royal Silver Wedding (Nos. 493/4), optd with T* **30**.

255	2½d. ultramarine	50	15
	a. Opt omitted (in vert pair with stamp optd at top)	£6000	
256	£1 blue	20·00	25·00

No. 255a comes from a sheet on which the overprint is misplaced downwards resulting in the complete absence of the opt from the six stamps of the top row. On the rest of the sheet the opt falls at the top of each stamp instead of at the foot (*Price* £250, *unused*, £350 *used*).

1948 (29 July). *Olympic Games (Nos. 495/8), optd with T* **30**.

257	2½d. ultramarine	1·00	2·00
258	3d. violet	1·00	2·25
	a. Crown flaw	70·00	
259	6d. bright purple	1·00	2·25
260	1s. brown	1·00	2·25
257/60 *Set of* 4		3·50	8·00

1949 (1 Jan). *King George VI, optd with T* **29**.

261	2d. pale orange	6·00	6·50
262	2½d. light ultramarine	2·50	6·50
263	3d. pale violet	70	1·25
264	4d. grey-green	11·00	11·00
265	5d. brown	3·75	24·00
266	6d. purple	70	30
267	7d. emerald-green	1·25	15·00
268	8d. bright carmine	3·75	13·00
269	9d. deep olive-green	1·50	13·00
270	10d. turquoise-blue	1·25	13·00
271	11d. plum	2·50	15·00
272	1s. bistre-brown	1·25	2·75
273	2s.6d. yellow-green	4·75	16·00
274	5s. red	13·00	38·00
275	10s. ultramarine	48·00	£130
261/75 *Set of* 15		90·00	£275

1949 (10 Oct). *75th Anniv of U.P.U. (Nos. 499/502), optd with T* **30**.

276	2½d. ultramarine	70	2·75
	a. Lake in India	60·00	
277	3d. violet	70	2·75
278	6d. bright purple	70	1·25
279	1s. brown	70	3·25
276/9 *Set of* 4		2·50	9·00

1950 (2 Oct)–**51**. *King George VI, optd with T* **29** *or* **30** *(shilling values).*

280	½d. pale orange (3.5.51)	85	1·50
281	1d. light ultramarine (3.5.51)	1·00	3·00
282	1½d. pale green (3.5.51)	1·00	14·00
283	2d. pale red-brown (3.5.51)	1·00	2·50
284	2½d. pale scarlet (3.5.51)	1·00	5·00
285	4d. light ultramarine	3·50	3·00
286	2s.6d. yell-grn (H.M.S. *Victory*) (3.5.51)	9·50	5·00
287	5s. red (Dover) (3.5.51)	15·00	17·00
288	10s. ultramarine (St. George) (3.5.51)	20·00	17·00
280/8 *Set of* 9		48·00	60·00

1952–54. *Queen Elizabeth II (*W **153** (Tudor Crown)*), optd with T* **29**.

289	1½d. orange-red (31.8.53)	10	50
290	1d. ultramarine (31.8.53)	15	40
291	1½d. green (5.12.52)	10	30
292	2d. red-brown (31.8.53)	20	1·25
293	2½d. carmine-red (5.12.52)	10	1·00
294	3d. deep lilac (B.) (18.1.64)	20	1·25
295	4d. ultramarine (2.11.53)	45	3·50
296	5d. brown (6.7.53)	60	1·00
297	6d. reddish purple (18.1.54)	45	15
298	7d. bright green (18.1.54)	80	3·00
299	8d. magenta (6.7.53)	60	1·50
300	9d. bronze-green (8.2.54)	1·40	1·00
301	10d. Prussian blue (8.2.54)	1·40	2·75
302	11d. brown-purple (8.2.54)	1·40	3·25
303	1s. bistre-brown (6.7.53)	50	70
304	1s.3d. green (2.11.53)	65	5·50
305	1s.6d. grey-blue (2.11.53)	1·00	2·00
289/305 *Set of* 17		9·00	26·00

1953 (3 June). *Coronation (Nos. 532/5), optd with T* **30**.

306	2½d. carmine-red	40	50
307	4d. ultramarine	1·00	50
308	1s.3d. deep yellow-green	1·00	1·25
309	1s.6d. deep grey-blue	1·00	1·25
306/9 *Set of* 4		3·00	3·00

1955 (23 Sept). *Queen Elizabeth II, Castle high values (*W **165** (St. Edward's Crown)*), optd with T* **30**.

310	2s.6d. black-brown	3·50	10·00
311	5s. rose-red	4·50	17·00
312	10s. ultramarine	16·00	22·00
310/12 *Set of* 3		21·00	45·00

1956. *Queen Elizabeth II (*W **165** St. Edward's Crown)*), optd with T* **29**.

313	½d. orange-red (21 March)	10	30
314	1d. ultramarine (13 April)	20	40
315	1½d. green (22 Oct)	40	1·75
316	2d. red-brown (25 July)	1·25	1·75
317	2d. light red-brown (10 Dec)	70	30
318	2½d. carmine-red (19 Dec)	40	30
319	3d. deep lilac (B) (22 Oct)	40	3·00
320	4d. ultramarine (25 June)	65	2·00
321	6d. reddish purple (22 Oct)	50	3·00
322	1s.3d. green (26 Nov)	1·75	12·00
313/22 *Set of* 10		5·75	22·00

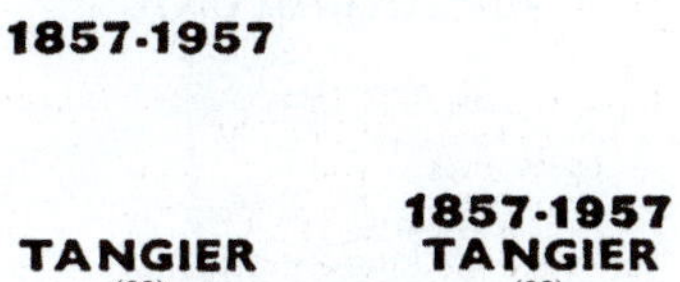

(32) (33)

1957 (1 Apr). *Centenary of British Post Office in Tangier.*

*(a) Nos. 540/2 and 543b/66 (*W **165** (St. Edward's Crown)*), optd as T* **32** *or* **33** *(7d)*

323	½d. orange-red	10	10
324	1d. ultramarine	10	10
325	1½d. green	10	10
326	2d. light red-brown	10	10
327	2½d. ermine-red	15	1·25
328	3d. deep lilac (B.)	15	40
329	4d. ultramarine	30	20
330	5d. brown	30	35
331	6d. reddish purple	30	35
332	7d. bright green	30	35
333	8d. magenta	30	1·00
334	9d. bronze-green	30	30
	a. "TANGIER" omitted	£5000	
335	10d. Prussian blue	30	30
336	11d. brown-purple	30	30
337	1s. bistro-brown	30	30
338	1s.3d. green	45	5·00
339	1s.6d. grey-blue	50	1·60

*(b) Nos. 536/8 (*W **165** (St. Edward's Crown)*), optd as T* **32**.

340	2s.6d. black-brown	2·00	4·25
	a. Hyphen omitted	65·00	£110
	b. Hyphen inserted	20·00	
341	5s. rose-red	2·75	7·00
	a. Hyphen omitted	65·00	£130
	b. Hyphen inserted	10·00	
342	10s. ultramarine	3·75	8·00
	a. Hyphen omitted	80·00	£150
	b. Hyphen inserted	15·00	
323/42 *Set of* 20		11·50	28·00

Nos. 340a/b, 341a/b and 342a/b occur on R.9/2 in the sheet of 40 (4×10). They are best collected in marginal blocks of four from the bottom left corner of the sheet. Specialists recognise two forms of No. 340b; one where the hyphen on R.9/2 was inserted separately to correct the error, No. 340a; the other from a later printing where a new and corrected overprinting plate was used. (*Price* £12 *un.*).

All stamps overprinted "TANGIER" were withdrawn from sale on 30 April 1957.

Muscat

An independent Arab Sultanate in Eastern Arabia with an Indian postal administration.

The Indian post office at Muscat town is officially recorded as having opened on 1 May 1864. Stamps of India were provided for its use, most surviving examples being of the ½a. value, although others to the 8a. are known.

The office was initially included in the Bombay Postal Circle and the first postmark, so far only recorded on stampless covers, was a single circle, 21½ mm in diameter, broken at the top by "MUSCAT" and with the date in two lines across the centre. This was followed by a cancellation showing the post office number, "309", within a diamond of 13, later 16, bars. It is believed that this was used in conjunction with a single ring date stamp inscribed "MUSCAT".

1864 Diamond

In 1869 the office was transferred to the Sind Circle, assigned a new number, "23", and issued with a duplex cancellation. Major reorganisation of the postal service in 1873 resulted in Muscat becoming office "K-4". For ten years from 1873 the cancellations do not, very confusingly, carry any indication of the year of use.

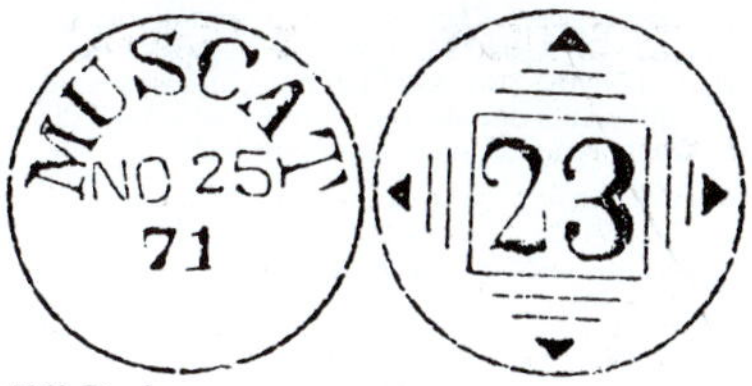

1869 Duplex

1873 Duplex

Muscat rejoined the Bombay Circle in 1879 and was issued with a cancellation showing a "B" within a square of horizontal bars. The date stamp used at this time was unique in that it carried the inscription "MASKAT", although the spelling reverted to the more usual form by 1882. The square cancellation had been replaced by a similar circular mark by 1884.

Subsequent postmarks were of various circular types, all inscribed "MUSCAT".

There was only one Indian post office in Muscat, but a further office did exist, from 12 April 1868, at the Muscat dependency of Guadur, a port on the Mekran coast of Baluchistan.

No cancellations have been reported from Guadur before its transfer to the Sind Circle in 1869. Cancellations are all similar in style to those for Muscat, Guadur being initially assigned number "24", although an office in Southern India is also known to have used this numeral. The 1869 duplex is interesting in that it is inscribed "GWADUR". Under the 1873 reorganisation the office became "4/K-1", this postmark using the "GUADUR" spelling.

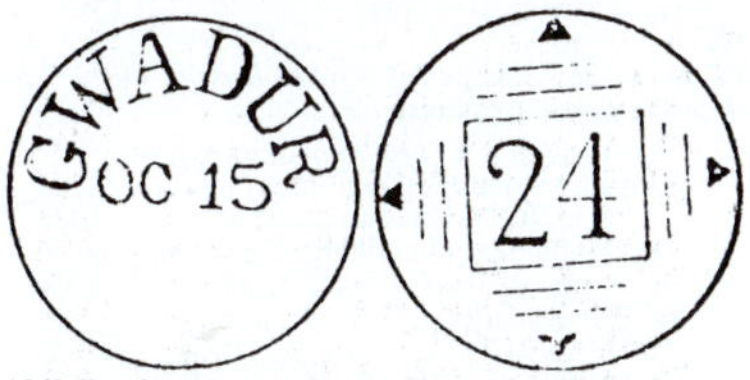

1869 Duplex

PRICES FOR STAMPS ON COVER	
Nos. 1/15	*from* × 50
Nos. O1/10	*from* × 75

(Currency 12 pies = 1 anna; 16 annas = 1 Indian rupee)

(1) (2)

1944 (20 Nov). *Bicentenary of Al-Busaid Dynasty. Nos. 259/60, 265/8 and 269a/77 (King George VI) of India optd ("*AL BUSAID 1363*" in Arabic script) as T* **1** *or* **2** *(rupee values).*

1	3p. slate	30	7·50
	w. Wmk inverted	5·00	
2	½a. purple	30	7·50

3	9p. green	30	7·50
4	1a. carmine	30	7·50
5	1½a. dull violet	30	7·50
6	2a. vermilion	40	7·50
	w. Wmk inverted		
7	3a. bright violet	1·00	7·50
	w. Wmk inverted	5·00	
8	3½a. bright blue	1·00	7·50
9	4a. brown	1·25	7·50
10	6a. turquoise-green	1·25	7·50
11	8a. slate-violet	1·50	7·50
12	12a. lake	1·50	7·50
13	14a. purple	4·00	12·00
14	1r. grey and red-brown	1·75	11·00
15	2r. purple and brown	4·50	17·00
1/15 *Set of* 15		18·00	£120

OFFICIAL STAMPS

1944 (20 Nov). *Bicentenary of Al-Busaid Dynasty. Nos. O138, O143, O144a/6 and 146b/50 of India optd as T* **1** *or* **2** *(1r.).*

O1	3p. slate	60	14·00
O2	½a. purple	80	14·00
O3	9p. green	70	14·00
O4	1a. carmine	70	14·00
O5	1½a. dull violet	1·00	14·00
O6	2a. vermilion	1·50	14·00
O7	2½a. bright violet	6·00	14·00
O8	4a. brown	2·50	14·00
O9	8a. slate-violet	4·50	16·00
O10	1r. grey and red-brown	3·50	24·00
O1/10 *Set of* 10		20·00	£140

Used prices quoted for Nos. 1/15 and O1/10 are for stamps cancelled with contemporary postmarks of the Indian postal administration. Those with cancellations of the subsequent British post office are worth considerably less. Collectors are warned against forged overprints and cancellations.

From December 1947 there was a Pakistani postal administration and stamps of Pakistan were used until 31 March 1948. The subsequent British administration operated from 1 April 1948 to 29 April 1966 when the stamps of the BRITISH POSTAL AGENCIES IN EASTERN ARABIA were used. Guadur, however, continued to use the stamps of Pakistan until the dependency was finally ceded to that country in 1953.

Natal *see* **South Africa**

Nauru

Stamps of MARSHALL ISLANDS were used in Nauru from the opening of the German Colonial Post Office on 14 July 1908 until 8 September 1914.

Following the occupation by Australian forces on 6 November 1914 the "N.W. PACIFIC ISLANDS" overprints on Australia (see NEW GUINEA) were used from 2 January 1915.

PRICES FOR STAMPS ON COVER TO 1945	
Nos. 1/12	*from* × 10
Nos. 13/16	*from* × 4
Nos. 17/25	—
Nos. 26/39	*from* × 6
Nos. 40/3	*from* × 10
Nos. 44/7	*from* × 15

BRITISH MANDATE

NAURU (1) NAURU (2) NAURU (3)

1916 (2 Sept)–**23**. *Stamps of Great Britain (1912–22) overprinted at Somerset House.*

(a) With T **1** *(12½ mm long) at foot.*

1	½d. yellow-green	2·25	8·50
	a. "NAUP.U"	£450	
	b. Double opt, one albino	60·00	
	c. Triple opt, two albino	£350	
2	1d. bright scarlet	1·75	8·00
	a. "NAUP.U"	£650	£1000
	b. Double opt, one albino	£325	
2*c*	1d. carmine-red	14·00	
	cb. Double opt, one albino	£225	
3	1½d. red-brown (1923)	55·00	80·00
4	2d. orange (Die I)	2·00	13·00
	a. "NAUP.U"	£400	£800
	b. Double opt, one albino	£110	
	c. Triple opt, two albino	£325	
	y. Wmk inverted and reversed	£120	
5	2d. orange (Die II) (1923)	70·00	£100
6	2½d. blue	2·75	7·00
	a. "NAUP.U"	£450	£850
	b. Double opt, one albino	£225	
7	3d. bluish violet	2·00	4·75
	a. "NAUP.U"	£475	£900
	b. Double opt, one albino	£325	
8	4d. slate-green	2·00	8·50
	a. "NAUP.U"	£650	£1300
	b. Double opt, one albino	£225	
9	5d. yellow-brown	2·25	10·00
	a. "NAUP.U"	£1600	
	b. Double opt, one albino	£160	
10	6d. purple (*chalk-surfaced paper*)	6·50	10·00
	a. "NAUP.U"	£1200	
	b. Double opt, one albino	£350	
11	9d. agate	8·50	23·00
	a. Double opt, one albino	£325	
12	1s. bistre-brown	7·00	19·00
	a. Double opt, one albino	£375	
	s. Optd "Specimen"	£130	
1/12 *Set of* 11		80·00	£170

(b) With T **2** *(13½ mm long) at centre (1923).*

13	½d. green	4·50	42·00
14	1d. scarlet	19·00	32·00
15	1½d. red-brown	26·00	42·00
	a. Double opt, one albino	£170	
16	2d. orange (Die II)	30·00	60·00
13/16 *Set of* 4		70·00	£160

The "NAUP.U" errors occur on R. 6/2 from Control I 16 only. The ink used on this batch of overprints was shiny jet-black.

There is a constant variety consisting of short left stroke to "N" which occurs at R. 1/8 on Nos. 1, 2, 4 (£30 *each*); 2*c* (£75); 3 (£175); 5 (£200); 6, 7 (£40 *each*); 8, 9, 10 (£60 *each*); 11, 12 (£85 *each*). All unused prices.

(c) With T **3**.

(i) Waterlow printing.

17	5s. rose-carmine	£2500	£2250
	s. Optd "Specimen"	£1700	
18	10s. indigo-blue (R.)	£11000	£5000
	a. Double opt, one albino	£13000	£7000
	s. Optd "Specimen"	£1000	
	sa. Ditto "NAURU" double, one albino	£2500	

(ii) De La Rue printing.

19	2s.6d. sepia-brown (*shades*)	£600	£1600
	a. Double opt, one albino	£1700	
	b. Treble opt, two albino	£1700	
	s. Optd "Specimen"	£325	
20	2s.6d. yellow-brown (*shades*)	65·00	£110
21	2s.6d. brown (*shades*)	70·00	£110
	a. Re-entry (R. 2/1)	£6000	
22	5s. bright carmine (*shades*)	£100	£140
	a. Treble opt, two albino	£1300	
	s. Optd "Specimen"	£300	
23	10s. pale blue (R.)	£250	£325
	a. Treble opt (Blk.+R.+albino)	£3250	
	b. Double opt, one albino	£1300	
	c. Treble opt, two albino	£1400	
23*d*	10s. deep bright blue (R.)	£500	£550

(iii) Bradbury, Wilkinson printing (1919).

24	2s.6d. chocolate-brown	90·00	£160
	b. Double opt, one albino	£475	
25	2s.6d. pale brown	80·00	£140
	a. Double opt, one albino	£475	

The initial printing of the 2s.6d. to 10s. values, made in Sept 1915 but not known to have been issued before 2 Sept 1916, comprised 1½ sheets each of the 2s.6d. (No. 19) and 10s. (No. 18) and 3 sheets of the 5s. (No. 17), as well as the supply of "Specimens", where the 5s. value was mostly from the De La Rue printing (No. 22).

The original supply of the 2s.6d. value (No. 19) included distinct shade variants, covered by "sepia-brown (*shades*)". The "Specimens" are mostly in a deeper shade than the issued stamp. One half-sheet of 20 was quite deep, and only appears to exist cancelled "SE 2 16", apart from a mint block of 4 in the Royal Collection. The full sheet of 40 was in a slightly paler shade and included 12 double, one albino and 8 treble, two albino varieties. A few sheets in sepia-brown shades were also included in later supplies of the 2s.6d. value, but these were mostly in shades of yellow-brown (No. 20) and brown (No. 21).

Examples of most values between Nos. 1 and 25 are known showing a forged P.O. Pleasant Island postmark dated "NO 2 21".

AUSTRALIAN MANDATE

4 *Century* (freighter)

(Des R. A. Harrison. Eng T. S. Harrison. Recess Note Printing Branch of the Treasury, Melbourne and from 1926 by the Commonwealth Bank of Australia)

1924–48. No wmk. P 11.

A. Rough surfaced, greyish paper (1924–34).

26A **4**	½d. chestnut	1·75	2·75
27A	1d. green	3·50	2·75
28A	1½d. scarlet	4·00	4·00
29A	2d. orange	4·00	11·00
30A	2½d. slate-blue	6·00	25·00
	c. Greenish blue (1934)	9·00	21·00
31A	3d. pale blue	4·00	13·00
32A	4d. olive-green	7·50	21·00
33A	5d. brown	4·25	7·00
34A	6d. dull violet	4·75	12·00
35A	9d. olive-brown	9·50	19·00
36A	1s. brown-lake	6·50	13·00
37A	2s.6d. grey-green	28·00	50·00
38A	5s. claret	50·00	£100
39A	10s. yellow	£130	£180
26A/39A *Set of* 14		£225	£400

B. Shiny surfaced, white paper (1937–48).

26B **4**	½d. chestnut	4·00	13·00
	c. Perf 14 (1947)	1·40	10·00
27B	1d. green	2·50	3·00
28B	1½d. scarlet	1·00	1·50
29B	2d. orange	2·25	8·00
30B	2½d. dull blue (1948)	3·00	4·00
	a. Imperf between (vert pair)	£12000	£18000
	b. Imperf between (horiz pair)	£12000	£18000
31B	3d. greenish grey (1947)	3·50	14·00
32B	4d. olive-green	4·25	13·00
33B	5d. brown	5·50	4·00
34B	6d. dull violet	5·50	5·00
35B	9d. olive-brown	7·50	21·00
36B	1s. brown-lake	7·50	2·75
37B	2s.6d. grey-green	30·00	35·00
38B	5s. claret	38·00	50·00
39B	10s. yellow	85·00	£100
26B/39B *Set of* 14		£170	£225

HIS MAJESTY'S JUBILEE.

1910 - 1935

(5)

6

1935 (12 July). *Silver Jubilee. T* **4** *(shiny surfaced, white paper) optd with T* **5**.

40	1½d. scarlet	75	80
41	2d. orange	1·50	4·25
42	2½d. dull blue	1·50	1·50
43	1s. brown-lake	5·00	3·50
40/3 *Set of* 4		8·00	9·00

Re-entry (R. 4/4)

(Recess John Ash, Melbourne)

1937 (10 May). *Coronation.* P 11.

44 **6**	1½d. scarlet	45	1·75
45	2d. orange	45	2·75
46	2½d. blue	45	1·75
	a. Re-entry	35·00	45·00
47	1s. purple	65	1·75
44/7 *Set of* 4		1·75	7·25

Japanese forces invaded Nauru on 26 August 1942 and virtually all the inhabitants were removed to Truk in the Caroline Islands.

The Australian army liberated Nauru on 13 September 1945. After an initial period without stamps Australian issues were supplied during October 1945 and were used from Nauru until further supplies of Nos. 26/39 became available. The deportees did not return until early in 1946

7 Nauruan Netting Fish

8 Anibare Bay

15 Map of Nauru

(Recess Note Printing Branch, Commonwealth Bank, Melbourne, and from 1960 by Note Ptg Branch, Reserve Bank of Australia, Melbourne)

1954 (6 Feb)–**65**. *T* **7/8**, **15** *and similar designs. Toned paper.* P 13½×14½ (horiz) or 14½×13½ (vert).

48	½d. deep violet	20	60
	a. Violet (8.5.61)	20	40
49	1d. bluish green	30	50
	a. Emerald-green (8.5.61)	20	40
	b. Deep green (1965)	85	50
50	3½d. scarlet	1·75	75
	a. Vermilion (1958)	3·50	60
51	4d. grey-blue	1·50	1·50
	a. Deep blue (1958)	7·50	2·50
52	6d. orange	70	20
53	9d. claret	60	20
54	1s. deep purple	30	30
55	2s.6d. deep green	2·50	1·00
56	5s. magenta	8·00	2·25
48/56 *Set of* 9		14·00	6·00

Designs: *Horiz*—3½d. Loading phosphate from cantilever; 4d. Great Frigate Bird; 6d. Nauruan canoe; 9d. Domaneab (meeting-house); 2s.6d. Buada lagoon. *Vert*—1s. Palm trees.

Nos. 48*a*, 49*a/b*, 50*a* and 51*a* are on white paper.

16 Micronesian Pigeon

17 Poison Nut

20 Capparis

21 White Tern

(Recess (10d., 2s.3d.) or photo (others) Note Ptg Branch, Reserve Bank of Australia, Melbourne)

1963–65. *T* **16/17**, **20/1** *and similar designs.* P 13½×13 (5d.), 13×13½ (8d.), 14×13½ (10d.), 15×14½ (1s.3d.) or 13½ (others).

57		2d. black, blue, red-brown and orange-yellow (3.5.65)	75	2·25
58		3d. multicoloured (16.4.64)	40	35
59		5d. multicoloured (22.4.63)	40	75
60		8d. black and green (1.7.63)	2·00	80
61		10d. black (16.4.64)	40	30
62		1s.3d. blue, black and yellow-green (3.5.65)	1·50	4·50
63		2s.3d. ultramarine (16.4.64)	2·75	55
64		3s.3d. multicoloured (3.5.65)	1·50	2·75
57/64 *Set of* 8			8·75	11·00

Designs: *Vert*—5d. "Iyo" (*calophyllum*). *Horiz*—8d. Black Lizard; 2s.3d. Coral pinnacles; 3s.3d. Finsch's Reed Warbler.

22 "Simpson and his Donkey"

(Des C. Andrew (after statue, Shrine of Remembrance, Melbourne. Photo Note Ptg Branch, Reserve Bank of Australia, Melbourne))

1965 (14 Apr). *50th Anniv of Gallipoli Landing.* P 13½.

65	22	5d. sepia, black and emerald	15	10

(New Currency. 100 cents = 1 Australian dollar)

24 Anibare Bay

25 "Iyo" (*calophyllum*)

(Recess (1, 2, 3, 5, 8, 19, 25c. and $1) or photo (others))

1966 (14 Feb–25 May). *Decimal Currency. Various stamps with values in cents and dollars as T* **24/5** *and some colours changed. Recess printed stamps on helecon paper.*

66	24	1c. deep blue	15	10
67	7	2c. brown-purple (25 May)	15	50
68	–	3c. bluish green (as 3½d.) (25 May)	30	2·00
69	25	4c. multicoloured	20	10
70	–	5c. deep ultramarine (as 1s.) (25 May)	25	60
71	–	7c. black and chestnut (as 8d.)	30	10
72	20	8c. olive-green	20	10
73	–	10c. red (as 4d.)	40	10
74	21	15c. blue, black and yellow-green (25 May)	60	2·25
75	–	25c. deep brown (as 2s.3d.) (25 May)	30	1·25
76	17	30c. multicoloured	45	30
77	–	35c. multicoloured (as 3s.3d.) (25 May)	75	35
78	16	50c. multicoloured	1·50	80
79	–	$1 magenta (as 5s.)	75	1·00
66/79 *Set of* 14			5·50	8·50

The 25c. is as No. 63, but larger, 27½×24½ mm.

REPUBLIC

Nauru became independent on 31 January 1968 and was later admitted into special membership of the Commonwealth.

REPUBLIC
OF
NAURU
(26)

1968 (31 Jan–15 May). *Nos. 66/79 optd with T* **26**.

80	24	1c. deep blue (R.)	10	30
81	7	2c. brown-purple	10	10
82	–	3c. bluish green	15	10
83	25	4c. multicoloured (15.5.68)	15	10
84	–	5c. deep ultramarine (R.)	10	10
85		7c. black and chestnut (R.) (15.5.68)	25	10
86	20	8c. olive-green (R.)	15	10
87	–	10c. red	60	15
88	21	15c. blue, black and yellow-green	1·25	2·50
89	–	25c. deep brown (R.)	20	15
90	17	30c. multicoloured (15.5.68)	55	15
91	–	35c. multicoloured (15.5.68)	1·25	30
92	16	50c. multicoloured	1·25	35
93		$1 magenta	75	50
80/93 *Set of* 14			6·00	4·00

27 "Towards the Sunrise"

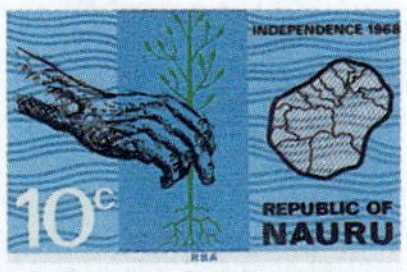

28 Planting Seedling, and Map

(Des H. Fallu (5c.), Note Ptg Branch (10c.). Photo Note Ptg Branch, Reserve Bank of Australia, Melbourne)

1968 (11 Sept). *Independence.* P 13½.

94	27	5c. black, slate-lilac, orange-yellow and yellow-green	10	10
95	28	10c. black, yellow-green and new blue	10	10

29 Flag of Independent Nauru

(Des J. Mason. Photo Note Ptg Branch, Reserve Bank of Australia, Melbourne)

1969 (31 Jan). P 13½.

96	29	15c. yellow, orange and royal blue	50	15

This is a definitive issue which was put on sale on the first anniversary of Independence.

Nevis *see* **St. Kitts-Nevis**

New Brunswick *see* **Canada**

Newfoundland *see* **Canada**

New Guinea *see after* **Australia**

New Hebrides

Stamps of NEW SOUTH WALES were used by various Postal Agencies in the New Hebrides from August 1891 onwards. From late 1892 the N.S.W. agency at Port Vila was run by the Australian New Hebrides Company who, from 1897, issued local 1d. and 2d. stamps for the carriage of mail on the Company's ships. These can be found used in combination with N.S.W. issues. Similar Postal Agencies supplying the stamps of NEW CALEDONIA were opened from 1903 onwards. The use of New South Wales and New Caledonia stamps was prohibited after 1 December 1908.

PRICES FOR STAMPS ON COVER TO 1945

Nos. 1/8 (F1/5)	*from* × 10
No. 9	*from* × 2
Nos. 10/16 (F6/10)	*from* × 8
Nos. 18/28 (F11/32)	*from* × 6
Nos. 30/4 (F33/7)	*from* × 4
No. 35 (F32*a*)	—
Nos. 36/9	*from* × 3
Nos. 40/2 (F38/41)	*from* × 4
Nos. 43/51 (F42/52)	*from* × 5
Nos. 52/63 (F53/64)	*from* × 3
Nos. D1/5 (FD53/7)	*from* × 100
Nos. D6/10 (FD65/9)	*from* × 8

ANGLO-FRENCH CONDOMINIUM

The New Hebrides, an island group in the south-west Pacific, were recognised as an area of joint Anglo-French influence in 1878. The position was regularised by the Convention of 20 October 1906 which created a Condominium, the two nations having equal rights and shares in the administration of the islands.

Stamps inscribed in English or French were issued concurrently and had equal validity throughout the islands. A common currency was reflected in the face values from 1938.

Where common designs were used, the main differences between stamps inscribed in English and those in French are as follows:

(a) Inscriptions in English or French.

(b) Position of cyphers. French issues normally have "RF" to the right or above the British royal cypher.

(c) French issues are without watermark, *unless otherwise stated.*

Inscriptions in English

Inscriptions in French

I. STAMPS INSCRIBED IN ENGLISH

NEW HEBRIDES.
CONDOMINIUM.
(1)

NEW HEBRIDES
CONDOMINIUM
(2)

1908 (29 Oct). *T* **23** *and* **24** *of Fiji optd with T* **1** *by Govt Printing Establishment, Suva. On the bicoloured stamps the word "FIJI" obliterated by a bar in the colour of the word.* P 14.

(a) Wmk Multiple Crown CA. Ordinary paper (½d., 1d.) or chalk-surfaced paper (1s.).

1		½d. green and pale green (No. 115)	7·00	16·00
1*a*		½d. green (No. 118)	40	7·00
2		1d. red	50	40
		a. Opt omitted (in vert pair with normal)	£7500	
3		1s. green and carmine	20·00	3·75
		(b) Wmk Crown CA.		
4		½d. green and grey-green	55·00	80·00
5		2d. dull purple and orange	60	70
6		2½d. dull purple and blue/*blue*	60	70
7		5d. dull purple and green	80	2·00
8		6d. dull purple and carmine	70	1·25
9		1s. green and carmine	£140	£300
1*a*/9 *Set of* 9			£200	£350

1910 (15 Dec). *Types as last optd with T* **2** *by D.L.R. Ordinary paper (½d. to 2½d.) or chalk-surfaced paper (5d., 6d., 1s.).* Wmk Multiple Crown CA. P 14.

10		½d. green	3·50	24·00
11		1d. red	11·00	8·50
12		2d. grey	70	3·00
13		2½d. bright blue	75	4·50
14		5d. dull purple and olive-green	2·00	5·50
15		6d. dull and deep purple	1·50	5·00
16		1s. black/*green* (R.)	1·50	7·50
10/16 *Set of* 7			19·00	50·00
10s/16s Optd "Specimen" *Set of* 7			£275	

3 Weapons and Idols

1d.
(4)

(Des J. Giraud. Recess D.L.R.)

1911 (25 July). Wmk Mult Crown CA. P 14.

18	3	½d. green	85	1·75
19		1d. red	3·75	2·00
20		2d. grey	8·00	4·00
21		2½d. ultramarine	3·25	5·50
24		5d. sage-green	4·50	7·00
25		6d. purple	3·00	5·00
26		1s. black/*green*	2·75	13·00
27		2s. purple/*blue*	26·00	22·00
28		5s. green/*yellow*	35·00	48·00
18/28 *Set of* 9			80·00	95·00
18s/28s Optd "Specimen" *Set of* 9			£200	

1920 (June)–**21**. *Surch with T* **4** *at Govt Printing Establishment, Suva.*

		(a) On Nos. 24 and 26/8.		
30	3	1d. on 5d. sage-green (10.3.21)	7·00	60·00
		a. Surch inverted	£3250	
31		1d. on 1s. black/*green*	2·00	13·00
32		1d. on 2s. purple/*blue*	1·00	10·00
33		1d. on 5s. green/*yellow*	1·00	10·00
		(b) On No. F16.		
34	3	2d. on 40c. red/*yellow*	1·00	19·00
		(c) On No. F27.		
35	3	2d. on 40c. red/*yellow*	£130	£700

1921 (Sept–Oct). Wmk Mult Script CA. P 14.

36	3	1d. scarlet	2·50	14·00
37		2d. slate-grey	4·25	38·00
39		6d. purple	14·00	75·00
36/9 *Set of* 3			19·00	£110
36s/9s Optd "Specimen" *Set of* 3			75·00	

1924 (1 May). *Surch as T* **4**, *at Suva.*

40	3	1d. on ½d. green (No. 18)	4·00	23·00
41		3d. on 1d. scarlet (No. 36)	4·00	11·00
42		5d. on 2½d. ultramarine (No. 21)	7·50	22·00
		a. Surch inverted	£2750	
40/2 *Set of* 3			14·00	50·00

5

(Recess D.L.R.)

1925 (June). Wmk Mult Script CA. P 14.

43	5	½d. (5c.) black	1·25	16·00
44		1d. (10c.) green	1·00	14·00
45		2d. (20c.) slate-grey	1·75	2·50
46		2½d. (25c.) brown	1·00	13·00
47		5d. (50c.) ultramarine	3·00	2·75
48		6d. (60c.) purple	3·50	14·00
49		1s. (1.25fr.) black/*emerald*	3·25	19·00
50		2s. (2.50fr.) purple/*blue*	6·00	22·00
51		5s. (6.25fr.) green/*yellow*	6·00	25·00
43/51 *Set of* 9			23·00	£110
43s/51s Optd "Specimen" *Set of* 9			£190	

(New Currency. 100 gold centimes = 1 gold franc)

The currency used for the face values of issues to 1977 was an artificial, rather than an actual, monetary unit. The actual currencies in use were Australian dollars and the local franc.

6 Lopevi Island and Outrigger Canoe

(Des J. Kerhor. Eng J. G. Hall. Recess B.W.)

1938 (1 June). *Gold Currency.* Wmk Mult Script CA. P 12.

52	6	5c. blue-green	2·50	4·50
53		10c. orange	1·25	2·25
54		15c. bright violet	3·50	4·50
55		20c. scarlet	1·60	3·00
56		25c. reddish brown	1·60	3·00
57		30c. blue	2·50	2·75
58		40c. grey-olive	4·50	6·50
59		50c. purple	1·60	2·75
60		1f. red/*green*	4·00	9·00
61		2f. blue/*green*	30·00	19·00
62		5f. red/*yellow*	70·00	48·00
63		10f. violet/*blue*	£200	75·00
52/63 *Set of* 12			£300	£160
52s/63s Perf "Specimen" *Set of* 12			£225	

(Recess Waterlow)

1949 (10 Oct). *75th Anniv of U.P.U. As No. 117 of Antigua.* Wmk Mult Script CA. P 13½×14.

64	10c. red-orange	30	1·00
65	15c. violet	30	1·00
66	30c. ultramarine	30	1·00
67	50c. purple	40	1·00
64/7 *Set of* 4		1·10	3·50

7 Outrigger Sailing Canoes

(Des C. Hertenberger (1f. to 5f.), R. Serres (others). Recess Waterlow)

1953 (30 Apr). *T* **7** *and similar horiz designs.* Wmk Mult Script CA. P 12½.

68	5c. green	75	45
69	10c. scarlet	75	20
70	15c. yellow-ochre	75	20
71	20c. ultramarine	75	20
72	25c. olive	60	20
73	30c. brown	60	20
74	40c. blackish brown	60	20
75	50c. violet	1·00	20
76	1f. orange	5·00	1·75
77	2f. reddish purple	5·00	8·50
78	5f. scarlet	7·00	22·00
68/78 *Set of* 11		20·00	30·00

Designs:—5 to 20c. Type **7**; 25 to 50c. Native carving; 1 to 5f. Two natives outside hut.

1953 (2 June). *Coronation. As No. 120 of Antigua.*

79	10c. black and carmine	60	50

10 *San Pedro y San Paulo* (Quiros)

(Photo Harrison)

1956 (20 Oct). *50th Anniv of Condominium. T* **10** *and similar horiz design.* Wmk Mult Script CA. P 14½×14.

80	5c. emerald	15	10
81	10c. scarlet	15	10
82	20c. deep bright blue	10	10
83	50c. deep lilac	15	15
80/3 *Set of* 4		50	40

Designs:—5, 10c. Type **10**; 20, 50c. "Marianne", "Talking Drum" and "Britannia".

12 Port Vila: Iririki Islet

13 River Scene and Spear Fisherman

(Des H. Cheffer (T **12**), P. Gandon (others). Recess Waterlow)

1957 (3 Sept). *Wmk Mult Script CA. T* **12/13** *and similar horiz design.* P 13½.

84	12	5c. green	40	1·50
85		10c. scarlet	30	10
86		15c. yellow-ochre	50	1·50
87		20c. ultramarine	40	10
88	13	25c. olive	45	10
89		30c. brown	45	10
90		40c. sepia	45	10
91		50c. violet	45	10
92	–	1f. orange	1·00	1·00
93	–	2f. mauve	4·00	3·00
94	–	5f. black	9·00	4·75
84/94 *Set of* 11			15·00	11·00

Design:—1 to 5f. Woman drinking from coconut.

1963 (2 Sept). *Freedom from Hunger. As No. 146 of Antigua.*

95	60c. green	50	15

15 Red Cross Emblem

(Des V. Whiteley. Litho B.W.)

1963 (2 Sept). *Red Cross Centenary.* W w **12**. P 13½.

96	15	15c. red and black	20	10
97		45c. red and blue	35	20

16 Exporting Manganese, Forari

17 Cocoa Beans

(Des V. Whiteley, from drawings by J. White (10c., 20c.), K. Penny (40c.), C. Robin (3f.). Photo Harrison. Des C. Robin (5c., 1f.), J. White (15c.), G. Vasarhelyi (25c., 5f.), A. Larkins, Turrell and Thomas (30c., 50c., 2f.). Recess Govt Printing Works, Paris)

1963 (25 Nov)–**72**. *T* **16/17** *and similar horiz designs.* W w **12** (10c., 20c., 40c., 3f.) or no wmk (others). P 14 (3f.), 12½ (10c., 20c., 40c.) or 13 (others).

98	5c. lake, purple-brown and greenish blue (15.8.66)	1·00	50
	a. Lake and greenish blue* (29.2.72)	38·00	30·00
99	10c. light brown, buff and emerald (16.8.65)	15	10
100	15c. yellow-bistre, red-brown and deep violet	15	10
101	20c. black, olive-green and greenish blue (16.8.65)	55	10
102	25c. reddish violet, orange-brown and crimson (15.8.66)	50	70
103	30c. chestnut, bistre and violet	75	10
104	40c. vermilion and deep blue (16.8.65)	80	1·40
105	50c. green, yellow and greenish blue	60	10
106	1f. red, black and deep bluish green (15.8.66)	2·00	3·25
107	2f. black, brown-purple and yellow-olive	2·00	1·75
108	3f. deep violet, orange-brown, emerald and black (16.8.65)	8·00	6·00
	w. Wmk inverted	10·00	
109	5f. blue, deep blue and black (24.1.67)	8·00	21·00
98/109 *Set of* 12		22·00	30·00

Designs:—15c. Copra; 20c. Fishing from Palikulo Point; 25c. Painted Triggerfish; 30c. New Caledonian Nautilus shell; 40c. Lionfish; 50c. Clown Surgeonfish; 1f. Cardinal Honeyeater; 2f. Buff-bellied Flycatcher; 3f. Thicket Warbler; 5f. White-collared Kingfisher.

*In No. 98*a* the globe is printed in the same colour as the centre, instead of in purple-brown.

See also No. 129.

28 I.T.U. Emblem

(Des M. Goaman. Litho Enschedé)

1965 (17 May). *I.T.U. Centenary.* W w **12**. P 11×11½.

110	28	15c. scarlet and drab	20	10
111		60c. blue and light red	35	20

29 I.C.Y. Emblem

(Des V. Whiteley. Litho Harrison)

1965 (24 Oct). *International Co-operation Year.* W w **12**. P 14½.

112	29	5c. reddish purple and turquoise-green	15	10
113		55c. deep bluish green and lavender	20	20

30 Sir Winston Churchill and St. Paul's Cathedral in Wartime

(Des Jennifer Toombs. Photo Harrison)

1966 (24 Jan). *Churchill Commemoration.* W w **12**. P 14.

114	30	5c. black, cerise, gold and new blue	20	10
115		15c. black, cerise, gold and deep green	50	10
116		25c. black, cerise, gold and brown	65	10
117		30c. black, cerise, gold and bluish violet	65	10
114/17 *Set of* 4			1·75	35

31 Footballer's Legs, Ball and Jules Rimet Cup

(Des V. Whiteley. Litho Harrison)

1966 (1 July). *World Cup Football Championships.* W w **12** (sideways). P 14.

118	31	20c. violet, yellow-green, lake and yellow-brown	30	15
119		40c. chocolate, blue-green, lake and yellow-brown	70	15

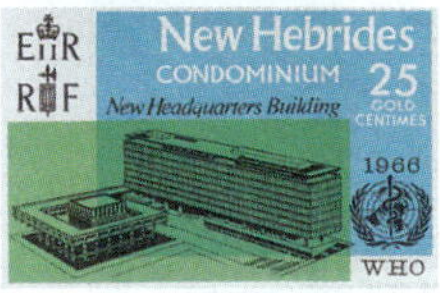

32 W.H.O. Building

(Des M. Goaman. Litho Harrison)

1966 (20 Sept). *Inauguration of W.H.O. Headquarters, Geneva.* W w **12** (sideways). P 14.

120	32	25c. black, yellow-green and light blue	15	10
121		60c. black, light purple and yellow-brown	40	20

33 "Education"

(Des Jennifer Toombs. Litho Harrison)

1966 (1 Dec). *20th Anniv of U.N.E.S.C.O.* W w **12** (sideways). *T* **33** *and similar horiz designs.* P 14.

122	15c. slate-violet, red, yellow and orange	25	10
123	30c. orange-yellow, violet and deep olive	65	10
124	45c. black, bright purple and orange	75	15
122/4 *Set of* 3		1·50	30

Designs:—30c. "Science"; 45c. "Culture".

36 The Coast Watchers

(Des R. Granger Barrett. Photo Enschedé)

1967 (26 Sept). *25th Anniv of the Pacific War. T* **36** *and similar horiz designs. Multicoloured.* W w **12**. P 14×13.

125	15c. Type **36**	20	10
126	25c. Map of war zone, U.S. marine and Australian soldier	45	20
127	60c. H.M.A.S. *Canberra* (cruiser)	50	30
128	1f. Boeing B-17 Flying Fortress	50	80
125/8 *Set of* 4		1·50	1·25

1967 (5 Dec). *New value with W w* **12** (sideways).

129	60c. vermilion and deep blue (as No. 104)	40	15

40 Globe and Hemispheres

(Des and eng J. Combet. Recess Govt Printing Works, Paris)

1968 (23 May). *Bicentenary of Bougainville's World Voyage. T* **40** *and similar horiz designs.* P 13.

130	15c. emerald, slate-violet and red	15	10
131	25c. deep olive, maroon and ultramarine	30	10
132	60c. bistre-brown, brown-purple and myrtle-green	35	10
130/2 *Set of* 3		70	25

Designs:—25c. Ships *La Boudeuse* and *L'Etoile*, and map; 60c. Bougainville, ship's figure-head and bougainvillea flowers.

43 Concorde and Vapour Trails

45 Kauri Pine

(Des S. W. Moss (25c.), R. Granger Barrett (60c.). Litho D.L.R.)

1968 (9 Oct). *Anglo-French Concorde Project. T* **43** *and similar horiz design.* W w **12** (sideways). P 14.

133 25c. light blue, orange-red and deep violet-blue ... 35 30
134 60c. red, black and bright blue ... 40 45
Design:—60c. Concorde in flight.

(Des V. Whiteley. Litho Format)

1969 (30 June). *Timber Industry.* W w **12**. P 14½.

135 **45** 20c. multicoloured (*shades*) ... 10 10

No. 135 was issued in small sheets of 9 (3×3) printed on a simulated wood-grain background and with a decorative border showing various stages of the local timber industry. There is a wide range of shades on the printing.

46 Cyphers, Flags and Relay Runner receiving Baton

48 Diver on Platform

(Des C. Haley. Photo Delrieu)

1969 (13 Aug). *Third South Pacific Games, Port Moresby. T* **46** *and similar horiz design. Multicoloured.* P 12½.

136 25c. Type **46** ... 10 10
137 1f. Cyphers, flags and relay runner passing baton ... 20 20

(Des V. Whiteley. Litho P.B.)

1969 (15 Oct). *Pentecost Island Land Divers. T* **48** *and similar vert designs. Multicoloured.* W w **12** (sideways). P 12½.

138 15c. Type **48** ... 10 10
139 25c. Diver jumping ... 10 10
140 1f. Diver at end of fall ... 20 20
138/40 *Set of* 3 ... 35 35

51 U.P.U. Emblem and New Headquarters Building

52 General Charles de Gaulle

(Des and eng J. Gauthier. Recess Govt Ptg Wks, Paris)

1970 (20 May). *Inauguration of New U.P.U. Headquarters Building.* P 13.

141 **51** 1f.05 slate, red-orange and bright purple ... 20 20

(Des V. Whiteley. Photo Govt Ptg Wks, Paris)

1970 (20 July). *30th Anniv of New Hebrides' Declaration for the Free French Government.* P 13.

142 **52** 65c. multicoloured ... 35 70
143 1f.10 multicoloured ... 45 70

35
≡
(**53**)

54 "The Virgin and Child" Bellini)

1970 (15 Oct). *As No. 101, but W w* **12** *(sideways) and surch with T* **53**.

144 35c. on 20c. black, olive-green and greenish black ... 30 30

(Des V. Whiteley. Litho Harrison)

1970 (30 Nov). *Christmas. T* **54** *and similar vert design. Multicoloured.* W w **12** (sideways). P 14½×14.

145 15c. Type **54** ... 10 10
146 50c. The Virgin and Child" (Cima) ... 20 20

POSTAGE DUE STAMPS

POSTAGE DUE (D 1) POSTAGE DUE (D 2) POSTAGE DUE (D 3)

1925 (June). *Optd with Type* D **1**, *by D.L.R.*

D1 **5** 1d. (10c.) green ... 30·00 1·00
D2 2d. (20c.) slate-grey ... 32·00 1·00
D3 3d. (30c.) red ... 32·00 2·50
D4 5d. (50c.) ultramarine ... 35·00 4·50
D5 10d. (1f.) carmine/*blue* ... 40·00 5·50
D1/5 *Set of* 5 ... £150 13·00
D1s/5s Optd "Specimen" *Set of* 5 ... £180

1938 (1 June). *Optd with Type* D **2**, *by B.W.*

D6 **6** 5c. blue-green ... 26·00 45·00
D7 10c. orange ... 26·00 45·00
D8 20c. scarlet ... 30·00 65·00
D9 40c. grey-olive ... 38·00 75·00
D10 1f. red/*green* ... 45·00 85·00
D6/10 *Set of* 5 ... £150 £275
D6s/10s Perf "Specimen" *Set of* 5 ... £140

1953 (30 Apr). *Nos. 68/9, 71, 74 and 76 optd with Type* D **3**, *by Waterlow.*

D11 5c. green ... 4·00 15·00
D12 10c. scarlet ... 1·75 12·00
D13 20c. ultramarine ... 5·00 21·00
D14 40c. blackish brown ... 10·00 32·00
D15 1f. orange ... 4·50 32·00
D11/15 *Set of* 5 ... 23·00 £100

1957 (3 Sept). *Nos. 84/5, 87, 90 and 92 optd with Type* D **3**, *by Waterlow.*

D16 **12** 5c. green ... 30 1·50
D17 10c. scarlet ... 30 1·50
D18 20c. ultramarine ... 75 1·75
D19 **13** 40c. sepia ... 1·00 2·50
D20 – 1f. orange ... 1·25 3·25
D16/20 *Set of* 5 ... 3·25 9·50

II. STAMPS INSCRIBED IN FRENCH

(Currency. 100 centimes = 1 French franc)

NOUVELLES HÉBRIDES (F 1) NOUVELLES-HÉBRIDES (F 2)

1908 (21 Nov). *T* **15/17** *of New Caledonia. optd with Types* F **1** *or* F **2** *(1f.), by Govt Ptg Wks, Paris.*

F1 5c. green ... 6·00 4·75
F2 10c. carmine ... 7·00 3·50
F3 25c. blue/*greenish* (R.) ... 7·00 2·25
F4 50c. red/*orange* ... 7·00 4·75
F5 1f. blue/*green* (R.) ... 17·00 20·00
F1/5 *Set of* 5 ... 40·00 30·00

CONDOMINIUM (F 3) 10c. (F 6)

1910 (Aug)–**11**. *Nos. F1/5 further optd with Type* F **3**, *or larger (1f.), by Govt Ptg Wks, Paris.*

F6 5c. green ... 3·75 3·00
F7 10c. carmine ... 3·75 1·25
F8 25c. blue/*greenish* (R.) (1911) ... 2·25 3·75
F9 50c. red/*orange* (1911) ... 6·50 9·75
F10 1f. blue/*green* (R.) ... 17·00 22·00
F6/10 *Set of* 5 ... 30·00 35·00

All the above were released in Paris on 16 March 1910. The 5c., 10c. and 1f. were issued in New Hebrides in August but the 25c. and 50c. were not received until 1911 after the issue of the definitive stamps and they were placed in reserve, although some may have been issued on request.

1911 (12 July). Wmk Mult Crown CA. P 14.

F11 **3** 5c. green ... 1·00 2·75
F12 10c. carmine ... 50 75
F13 20c. greyish slate ... 1·00 2·25
F14 25c. ultramarine ... 2·50 7·00
F15 30c. brown/*yellow* ... 6·50 5·25
F16 40c. red/*yellow* ... 1·40 4·00
F17 50c. sage-green ... 2·00 4·25
F18 75c. orange ... 7·00 23·00
F19 1f. red/*blue* ... 2·50 3·25
F20 2f. violet ... 8·50 22·00
F21 5f. red/*green* ... 12·00 35·00
F11/21 *Set of* 11 ... 40·00 95·00

1913. As last but wmk "R F" in sheet or without wmk.

F22 **3** 5c. green ... 1·25 5·00
F23 10c. carmine ... 1·00 4·00
F24 20c. greyish slate ... 1·00 2·40
F25 25c. ultramarine ... 1·25 5·50
F26 30c. brown/*yellow* ... 1·90 10·00
F27 40c. red/*yellow* ... 22·00 70·00
F28 50c. sage-green ... 11·00 27·00
F29 75c. orange ... 9·00 40·00
F30 1f. red/*blue* ... 6·00 10·00
F31 2f. violet ... 9·00 42·00
F32 5f. red/*green* ... 22·00 48·00
F22/32 *Set of* 11 ... 75·00 £225

The above were placed on sale in Paris on 29 April 1912.

1920–21. *Surch as Type* F **6**, *at Govt Printing Establishment, Suva, Fiji.*

(a) On stamps of 1908–11 (June 1920).

F32*a* 5c. on 50c. red/*orange* (F4) ... £500 £550
F33 5c. on 50c. red/*orange* (F9) ... 2·40 14·00
F33*a* 10c. on 25c. blue/*greenish* (F8) ... 50 1·50

(b) On stamps of 1911–13 (10.3.21).

F34 **3** 5c. on 40c. red/*yellow* (F27) ... 27·00 95·00
F35 20c. on 30c. brown/*yellow* (F15) ... 13·00 65·00
F36 20c. on 30c. brown/*yellow* (F26) ... 6·50 70·00

(c) On Inscr in English (10.3.21).

F37 **3** 10c. on 5d. sage-green (24) ... 11·00 50·00

1924 (1 May). *Stamps of 1911–13 surch as Type* F **6**, *at Suva.*

F38 **3** 5c. on 5c. green (F22) ... 1·00 7·00
F39 30c. on 10c. carmine (F23) ... 1·00 2·50
F40 50c. on 25c. ultramarine (F14) ... 38·00 90·00
F41 50c. on 25c. ultramarine (F25) ... 2·50 24·00
F38/41 *Set of* 4 ... 38·00 £110

F **7**

France Libre
(F **9**)

(Recess D.L.R.)

1925 (June). Wmk "R F" in sheet or without wmk. P 14.

F42 F **7** 5c. (½d.) black ... 75 10·00
F43 10c. (1d.) green ... 1·00 9·00
F44 20c. (2d.) greyish slate ... 1·75 2·75
F45 25c. (2½d.) brown ... 1·50 9·00
F46 30c. (3d.) red ... 1·50 11·00
F47 40c. (4d.) red/*yellow* ... 1·50 11·00
F48 50c. (5d.) ultramarine ... 1·50 1·75
F49 75c. (7½d.) yellow-brown ... 1·50 16·00
F50 1f. (10d.) carmine/*blue* ... 1·50 2·50
F51 2f. (1/8) violet ... 2·50 26·00
F52 5f. (4s.) carmine/*green* ... 3·50 26·00
F42/52 *Set of* 11 ... 17·00 £110
F42s/52s Optd "Specimen" *Set of* 11 ... £250

In July 1929 a batch of mail was carried by aircraft from Port Vila to the French cruiser *Tourville* for sorting and forwarding at Nouméa, New Caledonia. Stamps of the above issue (including those with English inscriptions) were affixed to covers and hand-stamped "PAR AVION" before cancellation.

(New Currency. 100 gold centimes = 1 gold franc)

1938 (1 June). *Gold Currency.* Wmk "R F" in sheet or without wmk. P 12.

F53 **6** 5c. blue-green ... 3·00 7·50
F54 10c. orange ... 2·75 2·25
F55 15c. bright violet ... 2·75 5·00
F56 20c. scarlet ... 3·00 4·00
F57 25c. reddish brown ... 6·50 5·50
F58 30c. blue ... 6·50 6·00
F59 40c. grey-olive ... 2·75 10·00
F60 50c. purple ... 2·75 3·75
F61 1f. lake/*pale green* (*shades*) ... 3·25 6·50
F62 2f. blue/*pale green* (*shades*) ... 35·00 35·00
F63 5f. red/*yellow* ... 55·00 60·00
F64 10f. violet/*blue* ... £130 £130
F53/64 *Set of* 12 ... £225 £250
F53s/64s Perf "Specimen" *Set of* 12 ... £350

1941 (15 Apr). *Adherence to General de Gaulle. Optd with Type* F **9**, *at Nouméa, New Caledonia.*

F65 **6** 5c. blue-green ... 2·00 25·00
F66 10c. orange ... 4·25 24·00
F67 15c. bright violet ... 7·50 40·00
F68 20c. scarlet ... 19·00 32·00
F69 25c. reddish brown ... 22·00 42·00
F70 30c. blue ... 22·00 38·00
F71 40c. grey-olive ... 22·00 40·00
F72 50c. purple ... 20·00 38·00
F73 1f. lake/*pale green* ... 21·00 38·00
F74 2f. blue/*pale green* ... 19·00 38·00
F75 5f. red/*yellow* ... 17·00 38·00
F76 10f. violet/*blue* ... 17·00 38·00
F65/76 *Set of* 12 ... £170 £375

1949 (10 Oct). *75th Anniv of U.P.U. As Nos. 64/7.* Wmk "R F" in sheet or without wmk. P 13½.

F77 10c. red-orange ... 3·00 6·50
F78 15c. violet ... 4·25 10·00
F79 30c. ultramarine ... 6·50 14·00
F80 50c. purple ... 7·50 17·00
F77/80 *Set of* 4 ... 19·00 42·00

1953 (30 Apr). *As Nos. 68/78.* Wmk "R F" in sheet or without wmk. P 12½.

F81 **7** 5c. green ... 2·25 3·25
F82 10c. scarlet ... 3·50 3·25
F83 15c. yellow-ochre ... 3·50 3·50
F84 20c. ultramarine ... 3·50 3·25
F85 – 25c. olive ... 1·25 3·25
F86 – 30c. brown ... 1·25 3·50
F87 – 40c. blackish brown ... 1·75 3·50
F88 – 50c. violet ... 1·25 3·00
F89 – 1f. orange ... 9·50 8·50
F90 – 2f. reddish purple ... 16·00 48·00
F91 – 5f. scarlet ... 18·00 85·00
F81/91 *Set of* 11 ... 55·00 £150

1956 (20 Oct). *Fiftieth Anniv of Condominium. As Nos. 80/3.* Wmk "R F" in sheet or without wmk. P 14½×14.

F92 **10** 5c. emerald ... 1·10 2·00
F93 10c. scarlet ... 1·10 2·25
F94 – 20c. deep bright blue ... 75 2·50
F95 – 50c. deep lilac ... 1·10 2·50
F92/5 *Set of* 4 ... 3·50 8·25

1957 (3 Sept). *As Nos. 84/94.* Wmk "R F" in sheet or without wmk. P 13½.

F96 **12** 5c. green ... 40 2·25
F97 10c. scarlet ... 1·25 2·25
F98 15c. orange-yellow ... 1·50 2·75
F99 20c. ultramarine ... 1·40 2·00
F100 **13** 25c. yellow-olive ... 1·25 1·75
F101 30c. brown ... 1·40 1·75
F102 40c. sepia ... 2·00 1·25
F103 50c. reddish violet ... 2·00 1·60
F104 – 1f. red-orange ... 6·00 4·00
F105 – 2f. mauve ... 11·00 21·00
F106 – 5f. black ... 28·00 48·00
F96/106 *Set of* 11 ... 50·00 80·00

F 14 Emblem and Globe

F 15 Centenary Emblem

(Des and eng J. Derrey. Recess Govt Ptg Wks, Paris)

1963 (2 Sept). *Freedom from Hunger.* P 13.
F107 **F 14** 60c. deep bluish green and chestnut ..... 15·00 17·00

(Des and eng J. Combet. Recess Govt Ptg Wks, Paris)

1963 (2 Sept). *Red Cross Centenary.* P 13.
F108 **F 15** 15c. red, grey and orange ..... 7·25 9·00
F109 45c. red, grey and yellow-bistre ..... 9·75 26·00

1963 (25 Nov)–**72**. *As Nos. 98/109 and 129.* No wmk. P 12½ (10, 20, 40, 60c.), 14 (3f.) or 13 (others).
F110 5c. lake, purple-brown and greenish blue (15.8.66) ..... 55 1·00
a. *Lake and greenish blue* (29.2.72) ..... 65·00 65·00
F111 10c. lt brown, buff and emerald* (16.8.65) ..... 2·00 2·75
F112 10c. light brown, buff and emerald (5.8.68) ..... 75 1·60
F113 15c. Yellow-bistre, red-brown and deep violet ..... 6·00 1·25
F114 20c. black, olive-green and greenish blue* (16.8.65) ..... 2·25 4·00
F115 20c. black, olive-green and greenish blue (5.8.68) ..... 1·50 1·60
F116 25c. reddish violet, orange-brown and crimson (15.8.6) ..... 70 1·10
F117 30c. chestnut, bistre and violet ..... 7·50 1·25
F118 40c. vermilion and deep blue* (16.8.65) ..... 3·25 7·50
F119 50c. green, yellow and greenish blue ..... 8·50 1·60
F120 60c. vermilion and deep blue (5.12.67) ..... 1·75 1·90
F121 1f. red, black and deep bluish green (15.8.66) ..... 2·00 5·00
F122 2f. black, brown purple and yellow-olive ..... 17·00 9·00
F123 3f. multicoloured* (16.8.65) ..... 9·50 26·00
F124 3f. multicoloured (5.8.68) ..... 8·50 12·00
F125 5f. blue, deep blue and black (24.1.67) ..... 25·00 29·00
F110/25 *Set of* 16 ..... 90·00 95·00

*Normally all French New Hebrides issues have the "RF" inscription on the right to distinguish them from the British New Hebrides stamps which have it on the left. The stamps indicated by an asterisk have "RF" wrongly placed on the left.

F 16a "Syncom" Communications Satellite, Telegraph Poles and Morse Key

(Des and eng J. Combet. Recess Govt Ptg Wks, Paris)

1965 (17 May). *Air. I.T.U. Centenary.* P 13.
F126 **F 16a** 15c. blue, chocolate and emerald ..... 8·50 9·00
F127 60c. carmine, deep bluish green and slate ..... 24·00 32·00

1965 (24 Oct). *International Co-operation Year. As Nos. 112/13.* P 14½.
F128 **29** 5c. deep reddish purple and turquoise-green ..... 2·50 6·00
F129 55c. deep bluish green and lavender ..... 9·50 12·00

1966 (24 Jan). *Churchill Commemoration. As Nos. 114/17.* P 14.
F130 **30** 5c. black, cerise, gold and new blue ..... 2·10 7·00
F131 15c. black, cerise, gold and deep green ..... 3·00 2·75
F132 25c. black, cerise, gold and brown ..... 3·50 8·50
F133 30c. black, cerise, gold and bluish violet ..... 4·25 9·00
F130/3 *Set of* 4 ..... 11·50 24·00

1966 (1 July). *World Cup Football Championship. As Nos. 118/19.* P 14.
F134 **31** 20c. violet, yellow-green lake and yellow-brown ..... 2·00 4·25
F135 40c. chocolate, blue-green, lake and yellow-brown ..... 3·50 4·25

1966 (20 Sept). *Inauguration of W.H.O. Headquarters, Geneva. As Nos. 120/1.* P 14.
F136 **32** 25c. black, yellow-green and light blue ..... 3·00 3·50
F137 60c. black, mauve and yellow-ochre ..... 4·50 7·50

1966 (1 Dec). *20th Anniv of U.N.E.S.C.O. As Nos. 122/4.* P 14.
F138 **33** 15c. slate-violet, red, yellow and orange ..... 1·50 2·75
F139 – 30c. orange-yellow, violet and deep olive ..... 2·25 4·25
F140 – 45c. black, bright purple and orange ..... 2·25 5·00
F138/40 *Set of* 3 ..... 5·50 11·00

1967 (26 Sept). *25th Anniv of the Pacific War. As Nos. 125/8.* P 14×13.
F141 15c. Type **36** ..... 1·25 1·50
F142 25c. Map of war zone, U.S. marine and Australian soldier ..... 1·60 3·00
F143 60c. H.M.A.S. *Canberra* (cruiser) ..... 1·75 2·50
F144 1f. Boeing B-17 Flying Fortress ..... 2·00 2·75
F141/4 *Set of* 4 ..... 6·00 8·75

1968 (23 May). *Bicentenary of Bougainville's World Voyage. As Nos. 130/2.* P 13.
F145 **40** 15c. emerald, slate-violet and red ..... 55 1·10
F146 – 25c. deep olive, maroon and ultramarine ..... 65 1·25
F147 – 60c. bistre-brown, brown-purple and myrtle-green ..... 1·10 1·50
F145/7 *Set of* 3 ..... 2·10 3·50

1968 (9 Oct). *Anglo-French Concorde Project. As Nos. 133/4.* P 14.
F148 **43** 25c. light blue, orange-red and deep violet-blue ..... 1·90 2·40
F149 – 60c. red, black and bright blue ..... 2·25 4·25

1969 (30 June). *Timber Industry. As No. 135.* P 14½.
F150 **45** 20c. multicoloured (*shades*) ..... 45 1·00

1969 (13 Aug). *3rd South Pacific Games, Port Moresby, Papua New Guinea. As Nos. 136/7. Multicoloured.* P 12½.
F151 25c. Type **46** ..... 50 1·40
F152 1f. Runner passing baton, and flags ..... 1·50 2·00

1969 (15 Oct). *Pentecost Island Land Divers. As Nos, 138/40. Multicoloured.* P 12½.
F153 15c. Type **48** ..... 55 1·25
F154 25c. Diver jumping ..... 45 1·25
F155 1f. Diver at end of fall ..... 1·10 2·00
F153/5 *Set of* 3 ..... 1·90 4·00

1970 (20 May). *Inauguration of New U.P.U. Headquarters Building, Berne. As No. 141.* P 13.
F156 **51** 1f.05 slate, red-orange and bright purple ..... 1·00 2·75

1970 (20 July). *30th Anniv of New Hebrides' Declaration for the Free French Government. As Nos. 142/3.* P 13.
F157 **52** 65c. multicoloured ..... 2·25 2·00
F158 1f.10 multicoloured ..... 2·50 2·25

1970 (15 Oct). *No. F115 surch with T* **53**.
F159 35c. on 20c. black, olive-green and greenish blue ..... 65 1·75

1970 (30 Nov). *Christmas. As Nos. 145/6. Multicoloured.* P 14½×14.
F160 15c. Type **54** ..... 25 1·00
F161 50c. "The Virgin and Child" (G. Cima) ..... 45 1·25

POSTAGE DUE STAMPS

CHIFFRE TAXE (FD 1) **CHIFFRE TAXE** (FD 2) **TIMBRE-TAXE** (FD 3)

1925 (June). *Optd with Type* FD **1**, *by D.L.R.*
FD53 **F 7** 10c. (1d.) green ..... 55·00 3·00
FD54 20c. (2d.) greyish slate ..... 55·00 3·00
FD55 30c. (3d.) red ..... 55·00 3·00
FD56 50c. (5d.) ultramarine ..... 55·00 3·00
FD57 1f. (10d.) carmine/*blue* ..... 55·00 3·00
FD53/7 *Set of* 5 ..... £250 13·50
FD53s/7s Optd "Specimen" *Set of* 5 ..... £250

Although on sale in Paris, the Postmaster would not issue any in unused condition for about a year and most copies are cancelled-to-order.

1938 (1 June). *Optd with Type* FD **2**, *by Bradbury, Wilkinson.*
FD65 **6** 5c. blue-green ..... 16·00 65·00
FD66 10c. orange ..... 19·00 65·00
FD67 20c. scarlet ..... 25·00 70·00
FD68 40c. grey-olive ..... 55·00 £140
FD69 1f. lake/*pale green* ..... 55·00 £140
FD65/9 *Set of* 5 ..... £150 £425
FD65s/9s Perf "Specimen" *Set of* 5 ..... £200

1941 (15 Apr). *Nos. FD65/9 optd with Type* F **9** *at Nouméa, New Caledonia.*
FD77 **6** 5c. blue-green ..... 16·00 38·00
FD78 10c. orange ..... 16·00 38·00
FD79 20c. scarlet ..... 16·00 38·00
FD80 40c. grey-olive ..... 20·00 38·00
FD81 1f. lake/*pale green* ..... 19·00 38·00
FD77/81 *Set of* 5 ..... 80·00 £170

1953 (30 Apr). *Optd with Type* FD **12**, *by Waterlow.*
FD92 **7** 5c. green ..... 9·00 23·00
FD93 10c. scarlet ..... 7·50 22·00
FD94 20c. ultramarine ..... 22·00 35·00
FD95 – 40c. blackish brown ..... 15·00 32·00
FD96 – 1f. orange ..... 17·00 55·00
FD92/6 *Set of* 5 ..... 65·00 £150

1957 (3 Sept). *Optd with Type* FD **12**, *by Waterlow.*
FD107 **12** 5c. green ..... 1·00 9·00
FD108 10c. scarlet ..... 1·40 9·00
FD109 20c. ultramarine ..... 2·75 13·00
FD110 **13** 40c. sepia ..... 6·50 26·00
FD111 – 1f. red-orange ..... 5·50 32·00
FD107/11 *Set of* 5 ..... 15·00 80·00

New Republic *see* **South Africa**

New South Wales *see* **Australia**

New Zealand

From 1831 mail from New Zealand was sent to Sydney, New South Wales, routed through an unofficial postmaster at Kororareka.

The first official post office opened at Kororareka in January 1840 to be followed by others at Auckland, Britannia, Coromandel Harbour, Hokianga, Port Nicholson, Russell and Waimate during the same year. New South Wales relinquished control of the postal service when New Zealand became a separate colony on 3 May 1841.

The British G.P.O. was responsible for the operation of the overseas mails from 11 October 1841 until the postal service once again passed under colonial control on 18 November 1848.

CC 1

CC 2

AUCKLAND

CROWNED-CIRCLE HANDSTAMPS

CC1 CC **1** AUCKLAND NEW ZEALAND (R.) (31.10.1846)......................... *Price on cover* £300

NELSON

CROWNED-CIRCLE HANDSTAMPS

CC2 CC **1** NELSON NEW ZEALAND (R.) (31.10.1846)......................... *Price on cover* £1100

NEW PLYMOUTH

CROWNED-CIRCLE HANDSTAMPS

CC3 CC **1** NEW PLYMOUTH NEW ZEALAND (R. or Black) (31.10.1846)........ *Price on cover* £2750

CC3*a* CC **2** NEW PLYMOUTH NEW ZEALAND (R. or Black) (1854)................ *Price on cover* £3250

OTAGO

CROWNED-CIRCLE HANDSTAMPS

CC4 CC **2** OTAGO NEW ZEALAND (R.) (1851) *Price on cover* £1900

PETRE

CROWNED-CIRCLE HANDSTAMPS

CC5 CC **1** PETRE NEW ZEALAND (R.) (31.10.1846)......................... *Price on cover* £1400

PORT VICTORIA

CROWNED-CIRCLE HANDSTAMPS

CC6 CC **2** PORT VICTORIA NEW ZEALAND (R.) (1851).................................. *Price on cover* £1200

RUSSELL

CROWNED-CIRCLE HANDSTAMPS

CC7 CC **1** RUSSELL NEW ZEALAND (R.) (31.10.1846)......................... *Price on cover* £7000

WELLINGTON

CROWNED-CIRCLE HANDSTAMPS

CC8 CC **1** WELLINGTON NEW ZEALAND (R.) (31.10.1846)......................... *Price on cover* £350

A similar mark for Christchurch as Type CC **2** is only known struck, in black, as a cancellation after the introduction of adhesive stamps.

No. CC3*a* is a locally-cut replacement with the office name around the circumference, but a straight "PAID AT" in the centre.

PRICES FOR STAMPS ON COVER TO 1945

Nos. 1/125	*from* × 2
Nos. 126/36	*from* × 3
Nos. 137/9	*from* × 2
No. 140	—
No. 141	*from* × 2
No. 142	—
Nos. 143/8	*from* × 2
Nos. 149/51	*from* × 10
Nos. 152/84	*from* × 2
Nos. 185/6	—
Nos. 187/203	*from* × 3
Nos. 205/7*e*	—
Nos. 208/13	*from* × 2
Nos. 214/16*j*	—
Nos. 217/58	*from* × 3
No. 259	—
Nos. 260/9	*from* × 3
No. 270	—
Nos. 271/6	*from* × 3
Nos. 277/307	*from* × 2
Nos. 308/16	*from* × 3
No. 317	—
Nos. 318/28	*from* × 3
Nos. 329/48	—
No. 349	*from* × 5
Nos. 350/1	—
No. 352	*from* × 5
Nos. 353/69	—
Nos. 370/86	*from* × 2
No. 387	*from* × 4
Nos. 388/99	*from* × 3
Nos. 400/666	*from* × 2
Nos. E1/5	*from* × 5
No. E6	*from* × 10

PRICES FOR STAMPS ON COVER TO 1945

Nos. D1/8	*from* × 3
Nos. D9/16	*from* × 5
Nos. D17/20	*from* × 3
Nos. D21/47	*from* × 6
Nos. O1/24	*from* × 12
Nos. O59/66	*from* × 4
Nos. O67/8	—
Nos. O69/81	*from* × 5
Nos. O82/7	—
Nos. O88/93	*from* × 20
Nos. O94/9	*from* × 12
Nos. O100/11	*from* × 5
Nos. O112/13	—
Nos. O115/19	*from* × 15
Nos. O120/33	*from* × 10
Nos. O134/51	*from* × 4
Nos. P1/7	*from* × 8
Nos. L1/9	*from* × 10
Nos. L9*a*/12	—
Nos. L13/20	*from* × 15
Nos. L21/3	—
Nos. L24/41	*from* × 12
No. F1	—
No. F2	*from* × 5
Nos. F3/144	—
Nos. F145/58	*from* × 3
Nos. F159/68	—
Nos. F169/79	*from* × 3
Nos. F180/6	—
Nos. F187/90	*from* × 2
Nos. F191/203	*from* × 3
Nos. F204/11	—
Nos. F212/18	*from* × 2
Nos. A1/3	*from* × 2

CROWN COLONY

PERKINS BACON "CANCELLED". For notes on these handstamps, showing "CANCELLED" between horizontal bars forming an oval, see Catalogue Introduction.

1

2

(Eng by Humphreys. Recess P.B.)

1855 (20 July). Wmk Large Star, W w **1**. Imperf.

1	**1**	1d. dull carmine *(white paper)* (H/S "CANCELLED" in oval £28000)................................	£70000	£14000
2		2d. dull blue *(blued paper)* (H/S "CANCELLED" in oval £29000)....................................	£35000	£650
3		1s. pale yellow-green *(blued paper)* (H/S "CANCELLED" in oval £25000)............................	£45000	£5500
		a. Bisected (6d.) (on cover)........	†	£42000

The 2d. and 1s. on white paper formerly listed are now known to be stamps printed on blued paper which have had the bluing washed out. Nos. 3a and 6a were used at Dunedin between March 1857, when the rate for ½ oz. letters to Great Britain was reduced to 6d., and August 1859. All known examples are bisected vertically.

(Printed by J. Richardson, Auckland, N.Z.)

1855 (Dec). *First printing. White paper.* Wmk Large Star. Imperf.

3*b*	**1**	1d. orange...	£32000	

1855 (Dec)–**57**. *Blue paper.* No wmk. Imperf.

4	**1**	1d. red..	£12000	£1800
5		2d. blue (3.56)................................	£3000	£300
		a. Without value............................		
6		1s. green (9.57)............................	£40000	£3750
		a. Bisected (6d.) (on cover)........	†	£26000

These stamps on blue paper may occasionally be found watermarked double-lined letters, being portions of the papermaker's name.

1857 (Jan). *White paper similar to the issue of July 1855.* Wmk Large Star.

7	**1**	1d. dull orange..................................	†	£30000

This stamp is in the precise shade of the 1d. of the 1858 printing by Richardson on *no wmk* white paper. An unsevered pair is known with Dunedin cancellation on a cover front showing an Auckland arrival postmark of 19.1.1857.

1857–63. *Hard or soft white paper.* No wmk.

(*a*) Imperf.

8	**1**	1d. dull orange (1858)...................	£3000	£650
8*a*		2d. deep ultramarine (1858).........	£2750	£900
9		2d. pale blue..................................	£1100	£180
10		2d. blue (12.57)............................	£1100	£180
11		2d. dull deep blue..........................	£1600	£275
12		6d. bistre-brown (8.59).................	£3500	£500
13		6d. brown...	£2000	£300
14		6d. pale brown................................	£2000	£300
15		6d. chestnut.....................................	£3750	£550
16		1s. dull emerald-green (1858)......	£16000	£1700
17		1s. blue-green.................................	£15000	£1700

(*b*) *Pin-roulette, about 10 at Nelson (1860).*

18	**1**	1d. dull orange................................	†	£5500
19		2d. blue..	†	£3500
20		6d. brown..	†	£4250
20*a*		1s. dull emerald-green..................	†	£7000
21		1s. blue-green.................................	†	£7000

(*c*) *Serrated perf about 16 or 18 at Nelson (1862).*

22	**1**	1d. dull orange................................	†	£5000
23		2d. blue..	†	£3500
24		6d. brown..	†	£3250
25		6d. chestnut.....................................	†	£7000
26		1s. blue-green.................................	†	£6500

(*d*) *Rouletted 7 at Auckland (April 1859).*

27	**1**	1d. dull orange................................	£8500	£4750
28		2d. blue..	£7500	£3250
29		6d. brown..	£7000	£2750
		a. Imperf between (pair)............	£25000	£12000
30		1s. dull emerald-green..................	†	£4750
31		1s. blue-green.................................	†	£4750

(*e*) P 13 *at Dunedin (1863).*

31*a*	**1**	1d. dull orange................................	†	£6500
31*b*		2d. pale blue...................................	£7000	£3500
32		6d. pale brown................................	†	£6500

(*f*) *"H" roulette 16 at Nelson.*

32*a*	**1**	2d. blue..	†	£4500
32*b*		6d. brown..	†	£4750

(*g*) *"Y" roulette 18 at Nelson.*

32*c*	**1**	1d. dull orange................................	†	£5500
32*d*		2d. blue..	†	£3750
32*e*		6d. brown..	†	£4500
32*f*		6d. chestnut.....................................	†	£4500
32*g*		1s. blue-green.................................	†	£7500

(*h*) *Oblique roulette 13 at Wellington.*

32*h*	**1**	1d. dull orange................................	†	£6000

The various separations detailed above were all applied by hand to imperforate sheets. The results were often poorly cut and badly aligned. Nos. 32*a*/*b* and 32*c*/*g* were produced using roulette wheels fitted with cutting edges in the shape of "H" or "Y".

(Printed by John Davies at the G.P.O., Auckland, N.Z.)

1862 (Feb–Dec). Wmk Large Star.

(*a*) Imperf.

33	**1**	1d. orange vermilion.......................	£800	£250
34		1d. vermilion....................................	£650	£250
35		1d. carmine-vermilion.....................	£425	£275
36		2d. deep blue (Plate I)..................	£700	85·00
		a. Double print.............................	—	£3250
37		2d. slate-blue (Plate I)...................	£1800	£200
37*a*		2d. milky blue (Plate I, worn)......	—	£225
38		2d. pale blue (Plate I, worn).........	£550	80·00
39		2d. blue (*to* deep) (Plate I, very worn)..	£550	80·00
40		3d. brown-lilac (Dec 1862)...........	£500	£150
41		6d. black-brown..............................	£1500	£130
42		6d. brown...	£1400	£110
43		6d. red-brown..................................	£1200	£100
44		1s. green..	£1600	£325
45		1s. yellow-green..............................	£1400	£350
46		1s. deep green................................	£1700	£375

The 2d. in a distinctive deep bright blue on white paper wmkd. Large Star is believed by experts to have been printed by Richardson in 1861 or 1862. This also exists doubly printed and with serrated perf.

No. 37 shows traces of plate wear to the right of the Queen's head. This is more pronounced on Nos. 37*a*/8 and quite extensive on No. 39.

(*b*) *Rouletted 7 at Auckland (5.62).*

47	**1**	1d. orange-vermilion......................	£4500	£800
48		1d. vermilion....................................	£3000	£800
48*a*		1d. carmine-vermilion.....................	£4500	£950
49		2d. deep blue...................................	£3250	£475
50		2d. slate-blue...................................	£4000	£800
51		2d. pale blue....................................	£2500	£600
52		3d. brown-lilac................................	£3000	£750
53		6d. black-brown..............................	£3250	£475
54		6d. brown...	£3000	£600
55		6d. red-brown..................................	£3000	£475
56		1s. green..	£3500	£850
57		1s. yellow-green..............................	£3500	£850
58		1s. deep green................................	£4500	£950

(*c*) *Serrated perf 16 or 18 at Nelson (8.62).*

59	**1**	1d. orange-vermilion......................	£9500	£2250
60		2d. deep blue...................................	†	£1200
		a. Imperf between (pair)............	£16000	£6500
61		2d. slate-blue...................................		
62		3d. brown-lilac................................	£4250	£1700
63		6d. black-brown..............................	†	£1800
64		6d. brown...	†	£2000
65		1s. yellow-green..............................	†	£4000

(*d*) *Pin-perf 10 at Nelson (8.62).*

66	**1**	2d. deep blue...................................	†	£3000
67		6d. black-brown..............................	†	£4000

(*e*) *"H" roulette 16 at Nelson.*

67*a*	**1**	2d. deep blue (Plate I).................	†	£2000
67*b*		6d. black-brown..............................	†	£2000
67*c*		1s. green..	—	£3750

(*f*) *"Y" roulette 18 at Nelson.*

67*d*	**1**	1d. orange-vermilion......................	†	£2500
67*e*		2d. deep blue (Plate I).................	†	£1900
67*f*		2d. slate-blue (Plate I)..................	†	£1900
67*g*		3d. brown-lilac................................	†	£2500
67*h*		6d. black-brown..............................	†	£1900
67*i*		6d. brown...	†	£1900
67*j*		1s. yellow-green..............................	†	£3750

(*g*) *Oblique roulette 13 at Wellington.*

67*k*	**1**	2d. deep blue (Plate I).................	†	£2250
67*l*		2d. slate-blue (Plate I)..................		
67*m*		3d. brown-lilac................................	†	£3000
67*n*		6d. black-brown..............................	†	£2250

(*h*) *Square roulette 14 at Auckland.*

67*o*	**1**	1d. orange-vermilion......................	†	£2500
67*p*		2d. deep blue (Plate I).................	†	£2000
67*q*		3d. brown-lilac................................	†	£3000
67*r*		6d. black-brown..............................	†	£2250

(*i*) *Serrated perf 13 at Dunedin.*

67*s*	**1**	1d. orange-vermilion......................	†	£3000
67*t*		2d. deep blue (Plate I).................	†	£1900
67*u*		3d. brown-lilac................................	£3750	£1800
67*v*		6d. black-brown..............................	†	£2000
67*w*		1s. yellow-green..............................	†	£3750

The dates put to above varieties are the earliest that have been met with.

1862. Wmk Large Star. P 13 (at Dunedin).

68	**1**	1d. orange-vermilion......................	£2250	£350
		a. Imperf between (horiz pair)..	†	£9500
69		1d. carmine-vermilion.....................	£2250	£350
70		2d. deep blue (Plate I)..................	£600	£100
71		2d. slate-blue (Plate I)...................	†	£600

72		2d. blue (Plate I)	£475	75·00
72a		2d. milky blue (Plate I)	—	£500
73		2d. pale blue (Plate I)	£475	75·00
74		3d. brown-lilac	£1900	£450
75		6d. black-brown	£1500	£225
		a. Imperf between (horiz pair) ..		
76		6d. brown	£1300	£150
77		6d. red-brown	£1200	£120
78		1s. dull green	£1900	£425
79		1s. deep green	£2000	£400
80		1s. yellow-green	£2000	£375

See also Nos. 110/25 and the note that follows these.

1862–63. *Pelure paper*. No wmk.

(a) Imperf.

81	1	1d. orange-vermilion (1863)	£9500	£2500
82		2d. ultramarine	£5500	£850
83		2d. pale ultramarine	£5000	£800
84		3d. lilac	£45000	†
85		6d. black-brown	£3000	£250
86		1s. deep green	£11000	£1100

The 3d. is known only unused.

(b) Rouletted 7 at Auckland.

87	1	1d. orange-vermilion	†	£6000
88		6d. black-brown	£3250	£475
89		1s. deep green	£12000	£1700

(c) P 13 at Dunedin.

90	1	1d. orange-vermilion	£14000	£3500
91		2d. ultramarine	£7000	£700
92		2d. pale ultramarine	£7000	£700
93		6d. black-brown	£5500	£400
94		1s. deep green	£12000	£1600

(d) Serrated perf 16 at Nelson.

95	1	6d. black-brown	—	£5500

(e) Serrated perf 13 at Dunedin.

95a	1	1d. orange-vermilion	†	£8500

1863 (early). *Thick soft white paper.* No wmk.

(a) Imperf.

96	1	2d. dull deep blue *(shades)*	£3000	£800

(b) P 13.

96a	1	2d. dull deep blue *(shades)*	£1800	£475

These stamps show slight beginnings of wear of the printing plate in the background to right of the Queen's ear, as one looks at the stamps. By the early part of 1864, the wear of the plate had spread, more or less, all over the background of the circle containing the head. The major portion of the stamps of this printing appears to have been consigned to Dunedin and to have been there perforated 13.

1864. Wmk "N Z", W **2**.

(a) Imperf.

97	1	1d. carmine-vermilion	£850	£350
98		2d. pale blue (Plate I worn)	£1300	£250
99		6d. red-brown	£4500	£700
100		1s. green	£1400	£275

(b) Rouletted 7 at Auckland.

101	1	1d. carmine-vermilion	£6000	£3000
102		2d. pale blue (Plate I worn)	£2000	£750
103		6d. red-brown	£6500	£3000
104		1s. green	£4250	£1100

(c) P 13 at Dunedin.

104a	1	1d. carmine-vermilion	£11000	£5500
105		2d. pale blue (Plate I worn)	£900	£180
106		1s. green	£1900	£500
		a. Imperf between (horiz pair) ..	£16000	
		aa. Perf 6½×13	†	£3750

(d) "Y" roulette 18 at Nelson.

106b	1	1d. carmine-vermilion	—	£6000

(e) P 12½ at Auckland.

106c	1	1d. carmine-vermilion	£11000	£4750
107		2d. pale blue (Plate I worn)	£400	70·00
108		6d. red-brown	£475	55·00
109		1s. yellow-green	£7500	£2500

The "NZ" watermark is frequently found inverted.

1864–67. Wmk Large Star. P 12½ (at Auckland).

110	1	1d. carmine-vermilion (1864)	£190	35·00
111		1d. pale orange-vermilion	£250	35·00
		a. Imperf (pair)	£4000	£2500
112		1d. orange	£550	90·00
113		2d. pale blue (Plate I worn) (1864)	£250	25·00
114		2d. deep blue (Plate II) (1866)	£190	22·00
		a. Imperf vert (horiz pair)	†	£4750
115		2d. blue (Plate II)	£190	22·00
		a. Retouched (Plate II) (1867)	£300	50·00
		c. Imperf (pair) (Plate II)	£2500	£1800
		d. Retouched. Imperf (pair)	£3750	£4000
116		3d. brown-lilac (1864)	£1900	£650
117		3d. lilac (1867)	£120	35·00
		a. Imperf (pair)	£4000	£1800
118		3d. deep mauve (1867)	£650	75·00
		a. Imperf (pair)	£4250	£1800
119		4d. deep rose (1865)	£2750	£250
120		4d. yellow (1865)	£225	£110
121		4d. orange	£2250	£1000
122		6d. red-brown (1864)	£275	28·00
122a		6d. brown	£300	40·00
		b. Imperf (pair)	£2250	£2250
123		1s. deep green (1864)	£1100	£350
124		1s. green	£500	£140
125		1s. yellow-green	£275	£110

The above issue is sometimes difficult to distinguish from Nos. 68/80 because the vertical perforations usually gauge 12¾ and sometimes a full 13. However, stamps of this issue invariably gauge 12½ horizontally, whereas the 1862 stamps measure a full 13.

Nos. 111a, 115c/d, 117a, 118a and 122b were issued during problems with the perforation machine which occurred in 1866–67, 1869–70 and 1871–73. Imperforate sheets of the 1s. were also released, but these stamps are very similar to Nos. 44/6.

The new plate of the 2d. showed signs of deterioration during 1866 and thirty positions in rows 13 and 16 to 20 were retouched by a local engraver.

The 1d., 2d. and 6d. were officially reprinted imperforate, without gum, in 1884 for presentation purposes. They can be distinguished from the errors listed by their shades which are pale orange, dull blue and dull chocolate-brown respectively, and by the worn state of the plates from which they were printed *(Prices £80 each unused)*.

1871. Wmk Large Star.

(a) P 10.

126	1	1d. brown	£800	£120

(b) P 12½×10.

127	1	1d. deep brown	†	£4000

(c) P 10×12½.

128	1	1d. brown	£275	55·00
		a. Perf 12½ comp 10 (1 side)	£600	£170
129		2d. deep blue (Plate II)	†	£12000
		a. Perf 10*	†	£20000
130		2d. vermilion	£250	35·00
		a. Retouched	£375	55·00
		b. Perf 12½ comp 10 (1 side)	£1800	£450
		c. Perf 10*	†	£20000
131		6d. deep blue	£2500	£800
		a. Blue	£1600	£550
		b. Imperf between (vert pair)	—	£8500
		c. Perf 12½ comp 10 (1 side)	£1400	£450
		ca. Imperf vert (horiz pair)	†	—

(d) P 12½.

132	1	1d. red-brown	£190	40·00
		a. Brown (shades, worn plate)	£190	40·00
		b. Imperf horiz (vert pair)	—	£5000
133		2d. orange	£160	29·00
		a. Retouched	£250	50·00
134		2d. vermilion	£200	32·00
		a. Retouched	£300	60·00
135		6d. blue	£275	60·00
136		6d. pale blue	£190	55·00

*Only one used copy each of Nos. 129a and 130c have been reported.

1872. No wmk. P 12½.

137	1	1d. brown	£900	£190
		a. Watermarked (script letters)*	£3750	£2250
		b. Watermarked (double-lined capitals)*	£1800	£550
138		2d. vermilion	£140	55·00
		a. Retouched	£200	85·00
		b. Watermarked (script letters)*	£3500	£1300
		c. Watermarked (double-lined capitals)*	£1700	£750
139		4d. orange-yellow	£180	£750
		a. Watermarked (double-lined capitals)*	£275	

*In or about 1872, 1d., 2d. and 4d. stamps were printed on paper showing sheet watermarks of either "W. T. & Co." (Wiggins Teape & Co.) in script letters or "T. H. Saunders" in double-lined capitals; portions of these letters are occasionally found on stamps.

1872. Wmk "N Z", W **2**. P 12½.

140	1	1d. brown	†	£6000
141		2d. vermilion	£1000	£325
		a. Retouched	£1500	£425

1872. Wmk Lozenges, with "INVICTA" in double-lined capitals four times in the sheet. P 12½.

142	1	2d. vermilion	£3000	£500
		a. Retouched	£4500	£750

3

4

(Des John Davies. Die eng on wood in Melbourne. Printed from electrotypes at Govt Ptg Office, Wellington)

1873 (1 Jan).

(a) Wmk "NZ", W **2**.

143	3	½d. pale dull rose (P 10)	£110	55·00
144		½d. pale dull rose (P 12½)	£180	85·00
145		½d. pale dull rose (P 12½×10)	£110	75·00
		a. Perf 10×12½	£150	80·00

(b) No wmk.

146	3	½d. pale dull rose (P 10)	£200	70·00
147		½d. pale dull rose (P 12½)	£250	£100
148		½d. pale dull rose (P 12½×10)	£150	85·00
		a. Perf 10×12½	£400	£150

As the paper used for Nos. 143/5 was originally intended for fiscal stamps which were more than twice as large, about one-third of the impressions fall on portions of the sheet showing no watermark, giving rise to varieties Nos. 146/8. In later printings of No. 151 a few stamps in each sheet are without watermark. These can be distinguished from No. 147 by the shade.

1875 (Jan). Wmk Star, W **4**.

149	3	½d. pale dull rose (P 12½)	22·00	3·00
		a. Imperf horiz (vert pair)	£800	£475
		b. Imperf between (horiz pair)	†	£750
		c. Perf compound of 12½ and 10	†	—
150		½d. dull pale rose (p *nearly* 12)	70·00	13·00

1892 (May). Wmk "NZ and Star", W **12b**. P 12½.

151	3	½d. bright rose (shades)	14·00	2·00
		a. No wmk	19·00	11·00
		w. Wmk inverted	65·00	42·00
		x. Wmk reversed	—	£140

5

6

7

8

9

10

11

12

12a 6 mm

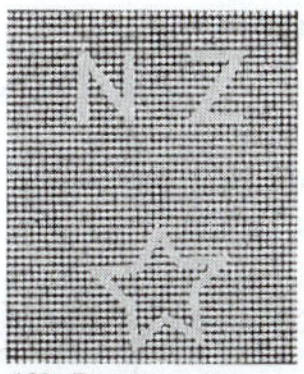

12b 7 mm

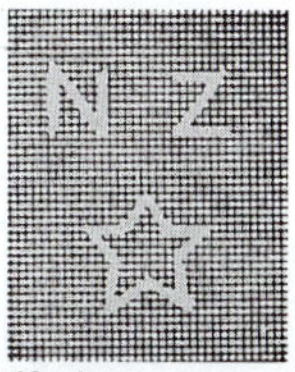

12c 4 mm

(*T* **5/10** eng De La Rue. *T* **11** and **12** des, eng & plates by W. R. Bock. Typo Govt Ptg Office, Wellington)

1874 (2 Jan)–**78**. *A. White paper.* W **12a**.

(a) P 12½.

152	5	1d. lilac	60·00	9·00
		a. Imperf	£450	
		w. Wmk inverted	†	60·00
		x. Wmk reversed	†	£200
		y. Wmk inverted and reversed	†	£550
153	6	2d. rose	60·00	7·00
154	7	3d. brown	£120	60·00
155	8	4d. maroon	£275	70·00
		w. Wmk inverted	£600	£170
156	9	6d. blue	£180	12·00
		w. Wmk inverted	—	65·00
		x. Wmk reversed	†	£250
157	10	1s. green	£550	30·00
		w. Wmk inverted	—	£300

(b) Perf nearly 12.

158	6	2d. rose (1878)	£600	£180

(c) Perf compound of 12½ and 10.

159	5	1d. lilac	£150	40·00
		w. Wmk inverted	—	75·00
160	6	2d. rose	£200	80·00
		w. Wmk inverted	—	£120
161	7	3d. brown	£160	65·00
162	8	4d. maroon	£550	£120
163	9	6d. blue	£250	48·00
		w. Wmk inverted	—	90·00
164	10	1s. green	£600	£120
		a. Imperf between (vert pair)	†	£5000
		bw. Wmk inverted	†	£375

(d) Perf nearly 12×12½.

164c	5	1d. lilac (1875)	£650	£250
165	6	2d. rose (1878)	£650	£225

B. Blued paper.

(a) P 12½.

166	5	1d. lilac	£110	32·00
167	6	2d. rose	£120	32·00
		w. Wmk inverted	—	65·00
		x. Wmk reversed	†	£110
168	7	3d. brown	£250	85·00
169	8	4d. maroon	£425	£110
170	9	6d. blue	£325	55·00
171		1s. green	£1000	£190

(b) Perf compound of 12½ and 10.

172	5	1d. lilac	£190	55·00
173	6	2d. rose	£550	85·00
174	7	3d. brown	£275	£850
175	8	4d. maroon	£550	£130
176	9	6d. blue	£325	95·00
177	10	1s. green	£1000	£225

1875. Wmk Large Star, W w **1**. P 12½.

178	5	1d. deep lilac	£850	£130
179	6	2d. rose	£375	25·00

1878. W **12a**. P 12×11½ (comb).

180	5	1d. mauve-lilac	50·00	7·00
181	6	2d. rose	50·00	7·00
182	8	4d. maroon	£150	48·00
183	9	6d. blue	90·00	12·00
184	10	1s. green	£150	42·00
		w. Wmk inverted	†	£400
185	11	2s. deep rose (1 July)	£350	£300
186	12	5s. grey (1 July)	£375	£300

This perforation is made by a horizontal "comb" machine, giving a gauge of 12 horizontally and about 11¾ vertically. Single specimens can be found apparently gauging 11½ all round or 12 all round, but these are all from the same machine. The perforation described above as "nearly 12" was from a single-line machine.

13

14

15

16

17

18

19

20

21

22

Description of Watermarks

W **12a**. 6 mm between "N Z" and star; broad irregular star; comparatively wide "N"; "N Z" 11½ mm wide.

W **12b**. 7 mm between "N Z" and star; narrower star; narrow "N"; "N Z" 10 mm wide.

W **12c**. 4 mm between "N Z" and star; narrow star; wide "N"; "N Z" 11½ mm wide.

Description of Papers

1882–88. Smooth paper with horizontal mesh. W **12a**.
1888–98. Smooth paper with vertical mesh. W **12b**.
1890–91. Smooth paper with vertical mesh. W **12c**.
1898. Thin yellowish toned, coarse paper with clear vertical mesh. W **12b**. Perf 11 only.

In 1899–1900 stamps appeared on medium to thick white coarse paper but we do not differentiate these (except where identifiable by shade) as they are more difficult to distinguish.

PAPER MESH. This shows on the back of the stamp as a series of parallel grooves, either vertical or horizontal. It is caused by the use of a wire gauze conveyor-belt during paper-making.

Description of Dies

1d.

Die 1

Die 2

Die 3

1882. Die 1. Background shading complete and heavy.
1886. Die 2. Background lines thinner. Two lines of shading weak or missing left of Queen's forehead.
1889. Die 3. Shading on head reduced; ornament in crown left of chignon clearer, with unshaded "arrow" more prominent.

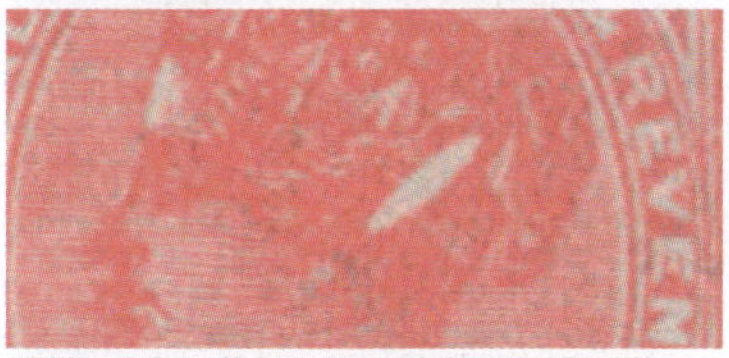

"Ellipse" flaw (Die 3, lower left pane, R. 9/2)

2d.

Die 1

Die 2

Die 3

1882. Die 1. Background shading complete and heavy.
1886. Die 2. Weak line of shading left of forehead and missing shading lines below "TA".
1889. Die 3. As Die 2 but with comma-like white notch in hair below "&".

6d.

Die 1

Die 2

1882. Die 1. Shading heavy. Top of head merges into shading. Second ornament from the right on the crown shows a line in its left portion.
1892. Die 2. Background lines thinner. Shading on head more regular with clear line of demarcation between head and background shading. Second ornament from the right in the crown has small dots in its left portion. Most examples also show a break in the back line of the neck immediately above its base.

Truebridge Miller

Sunlight Soap

STAMPS WITH ADVERTISEMENTS. During November 1891 the New Zealand Post Office invited tenders for the printing of advertisements on the reverse of the current 1d. to 1s. stamps. The contract was awarded to Messrs Miller, Truebridge & Reich and the first sheets with advertisements on the reverse appeared in February 1893. Different advertisements were applied to the backs of the individual stamps within the sheets of 240 (four panes of 60).

On the first setting those in a vertical format were inverted in relation to the stamps and each of the horizontal advertisements had its base at the left-hand side of the stamp when seen from the back. For the second and third settings the vertical advertisements were the same way up as the stamps and the bases of those in the horizontal format were at the right as seen from the back. The third setting only differs from the second in the order of the individual advertisements.

The experiment was not, however, a success and the contract was cancelled at the end of 1893.

(Des F. W. Sears (½d.), A. E. Cousins (2½d.), A. W. Jones (5d.); others adapted from 1874 issue by W. H. Norris. Dies eng A. E. Cousins (½d., 2½d., 5d.), W. R. Bock (others). Typo Govt Ptg Office)

1882–1900. *Inscr* "POSTAGE & REVENUE". *A. Paper with horiz mesh (1.4.82–86).* W **12a**.

(a) P 12×11½.

187	**14**	1d. rose *to* rose-red (Die 1)	45·00	7·00
		a. Imperf (pair)	£650	
		b. Imperf between (vert pair)	£700	
		cw. Wmk inverted		
		d. Die 2. *Pale rose to carmine-rose* (1886)	42·00	7·00
		dw. Wmk inverted	†	38·00
		dx. Wmk reversed	£110	42·00
188	**15**	2d. lilac *to* lilac-purple (Die 1)	55·00	4·00
		a. Imperf (pair)	£700	
		b. Imperf between (vert pair)	£700	
		cw. Wmk inverted	90·00	35·00
		d. Die 2. *Lilac* (1886)	60·00	14·00
189	**17**	3d. yellow	65·00	13·00
190	**18**	4d. blue-green	85·00	7·50
191	**20**	6d. brown (Die 1)	90·00	3·75
		w. Wmk inverted	£275	55·00
192	**21**	8d. blue (1885)	85·00	50·00
193	**22**	1s. red-brown	£120	16·00

(b) P 12½ (1884?).

193*a*	**14**	1d. rose *to* rose-red (Die 1)	£275	£110

B. Paper with vert mesh (1888–95). W **12b**.

(a) P 12×11½ (1888–95).

194	**13**	½d. black (1.4.95)	35·00	85·00
195	**14**	1d. rose *to* rosine (Die 2)	50·00	4·25
		aw. Wmk inverted	£170	18·00
		b. Die 3. *Rose to carmine* (1889)	50·00	4·00
		bb. Red-brown advert (1st setting) (2.93)	–	30·00
		bc. Red advert (1st setting) (3.93)	–	30·00
		bd. Blue advert (2nd setting) (4.93)	–	60·00
		be. Mauve advert (2nd setting) (5.93)	–	32·00
		bf. Green advert (2nd setting) (6.93)	†	–
		bg. Brown-red advert (3rd setting) (9.93)	–	32·00
		bh. "Ellipse" flaw	80·00	20·00
		bw. Wmk inverted	80·00	19·00
		bx. Wmk reversed	£120	38·00
196	**15**	2d. lilac (Die 2)	55·00	5·00
		a. Die 3. *Lilac to purple* (1889)	55·00	5·50
		ab. Red advert (1st setting) (3.93)	–	40·00
		ac. Mauve advert (2nd setting) (5.93)	–	40·00
		ad. Sepia advert (2nd setting) (5.93)	–	40·00
		ae. Green advert (2nd setting) (6.93)	–	£110
		af. Brown-red advert (3rd setting) (9.93)	–	40·00
		aw. Wmk inverted	90·00	11·00
197	**16**	2½d. pale blue (1891)	75·00	5·50
		a. Brown-red advert (2nd setting) (4.93)	–	75·00
		ax. Wmk reversed	–	£110
		b. Ultramarine (green advert. 2nd setting) (6.93)	–	75·00
198	**17**	3d. yellow	50·00	12·00
		a. Brown-red advert (2nd setting) (4.93)	–	85·00
		b. Sepia advert (2nd setting) (5.93)	–	£180
199	**18**	4d. green *to* bluish green	65·00	4·00
		a. Sepia advert (2nd setting) (5.93)	–	75·00
		aw. Wmk inverted	†	£180
200	**19**	5d. olive-black (1.2.91)	60·00	18·00
		a. Imperf (pair)	£650	
		b. Brown-purple advert (3rd setting) (9.93)	–	60·00
201	**20**	6d. brown (Die 1)	80·00	4·50
		a. Die 2 (1892)	£140	90·00
		ab. Sepia advert (2nd setting) (5.93)	–	£350
		ac. Brown-red advert (3rd setting) (9.93)	–	£200
		ax. Wmk reversed	†	–
202	**21**	8d. blue	70·00	48·00
203	**22**	1s. red-brown	£100	6·00
		a. Black advert (2nd setting) (5.93)	£450	£180
		b. Brown-purple advert (3rd setting) (9.93)	£275	40·00
		w. Wmk inverted	£275	50·00

(b) P 12×12½ (1888–91).

204	**14**	1d. rose (Die 2)	£225	£120
		a. Die 3 (1889)		

(c) P 12½ (1888–89).

205	**14**	1d. rose (Die 3) (1889)	£225	£130
		a. Mauve advert (2nd setting) (5.93)		
		x. Wmk reversed	†	–
206	**15**	2d. lilac (Die 2)	£200	£130
		a. Die 3. *Deep lilac* (1889)	£120	£120
		ab. Brown-red advert (3rd setting) (9.93)	–	£160
207	**16**	2½d. blue (1891)	£250	£140

(d) Mixed perfs 12×11½ and 12½ (1891–93).

207*a*	**14**	1d. rose (Die 3) (brn-red advert. 3rd setting)	†	£100
207*b*	**15**	2d. lilac (Die 3)	†	£375
		ba. Brown-red advert (3rd setting) (9.93)	†	–
207*c*	**18**	4d. green	†	£225
207*d*	**19**	5d. olive-black	†	£250
207*e*	**20**	6d. brown (Die 1)	†	£180
		ea. Die 2	†	£200

C. Paper with vert mesh (1890). W **12c**.

(a) P 12×11½.

208	**14**	1d. rose (Die 3)	£120	20·00
		a. "Ellipse" flaw	£325	65·00
209	**15**	2d. purple (Die 3)	80·00	14·00
		x. Wmk reversed		
210	**16**	2½d. ultramarine (27.12)	60·00	9·50
		x. Wmk reversed	†	£150
211	**17**	3d. yellow	85·00	25·00
		a. Lemon-yellow	85·00	29·00
212	**20**	6d. brown (Die 1)	£140	35·00
213	**22**	1s. deep red-brown	£190	£140

(b) P 12½.

214	**14**	1d. rose (Die 3)	£300	£160
215	**15**	2d. purple (Die 3)	£275	£160
216	**16**	2½d. ultramarine	£350	£160

(c) P 12×12½.

216*a*	**20**	6d. brown (Die 1)	£325	£200

D. Paper with vert mesh (1891–1900). Continuation of W **12b**.

(a) P 10×12½ (1891–94).

216*b*	**14**	1d. rose (Die 3)	£200	£150
		ba. Perf 12½×10	£225	£160
		baa. "Ellipse" flaw	£550	
		bb. Red-brown advert (1st setting) (2.93)	£425	£275
		bc. Brown-red advert (2nd setting) (4.93)	£425	£275
		bd. Mauve advert (2nd setting) (5.93)	£425	£275
		be. Green advert (2nd setting) (6.93)	£425	£275
216*c*	**15**	2d. lilac (Die 3)	£250	£100
216*d*	**16**	2½d. blue (1893)	£200	£100
		da. Perf 12½×10	£225	
216*e*	**17**	3d. yellow	£275	£150
		ea. Perf 12½×10		
216*f*	**18**	4d. green	£300	£225
216*g*	**19**	5d. olive-black (1894)	£200	£200
		ga. Perf 12½×10	£275	£200
216*h*	**20**	6d. brown (Die 1)	£350	£350
		i. Die 2 (1892)	£275	£275
		ia. Brown-purple advert (3rd setting) (9.93)	£450	£350
216*j*	**22**	1s. red-brown	£200	£190
		ja. Perf 12½×10	£250	

(b) P 10 (1891–95).

217	**13**	½d. black (1895)	6·00	1·75
218	**14**	1d. rose (Die 3)	9·00	1·00
		a. Carmine	10·00	1·50
		b. Imperf (pair)	£600	£600

		c. Imperf between (pair)	£650	
		d. Imperf horiz (vert pair)	£600	
		e. Mixed perfs 10 and 12½	£275	£150
		f. Red-brown advert (1st setting) (2.93)	22·00	4·75
		g. Red advert (1st setting) (3.93)	22·00	6·50
		h. Brown-red advert (2nd and 3rd settings) (4.93)	20·00	3·00
		i. Blue advert (2nd setting) (4.93)	75·00	32·00
		j. Mauve advert (2nd setting) (5.93)	20·00	3·00
		k. Green advert (2nd setting) (6.93)	65·00	17·00
		l. Brown-purple advert (3rd setting) (9.93)	20·00	4·00
		m. "Ellipse" flaw	35·00	10·00
		w. Wmk inverted	£110	35·00
		x. Wmk reversed	£150	£110
219	15	2d. lilac (Die 3)	18·00	1·50
		a. Purple	19·00	1·50
		b. Imperf between (pair)	£700	
		c. Mixed perfs 10 and 12½	£500	£350
		d. Red-brown advert (1st setting) (2.93)	32·00	9·00
		e. Red advert (1st setting) (3.93)	32·00	6·50
		f. Brown-red advert (2nd and 3rd settings) (4.93)	29·00	3·25
		g. Sepia advert (2nd setting) (5.93)	29·00	3·75
		h. Green advert (2nd setting) (6.93)	48·00	11·00
		i. Brown-purple advert (3rd setting) (9.93)	29·00	3·25
		x. Wmk reversed	£110	35·00
220	16	2½d. blue (1892)	55·00	3·50
		a. Ultramarine	55·00	4·00
		b. Mixed perfs 10 and 12½	£275	£160
		c. Mauve advert (2nd setting) (5.93)	£150	11·00
		d. Green advert (2nd setting) (6.93)	£160	13·00
		e. Brown-purple advert (3rd setting) (9.93)	£150	10·00
		ex. Wmk reversed	£170	48·00
221	17	3d. pale orange-yellow	55·00	10·00
		a. Orange	55·00	14·00
		b. Lemon-yellow	55·00	16·00
		c. Mixed perfs 10 and 12½	£350	£180
		d. Brown-red advert (2nd and 3rd settings) (4.93)	£110	20·00
		e. Sepia advert (2nd setting) (5.93)	£120	35·00
		f. Brown-purple advert (3rd setting) (9.93)	£110	18·00
222	18	4d. green (1892)	55·00	5·00
		a. Blue-green	55·00	5·00
		b. Mixed perfs 10 and 12½	£250	£150
		c. Brown-red advert (2nd setting) (4.93)	£110	6·00
		d. Brown-purple advert (3rd setting) (9.93)	£110	5·00
223	19	5d. olive-black (1893)	50·00	19·00
		a. Brown-purple advert (3rd setting) (9.93)	£150	30·00
		ab. Mixed perfs 10 and 12½	£250	£225
224	20	6d. brown (Die 1)	£100	32·00
		a. Mixed perfs 10 and 12½		
		b. Die 2 (1892)	60·00	9·00
		ba. Black-brown	60·00	9·00
		bb. Imperf (pair)	£700	
		bc. Mixed perfs 10 and 12½	£275	£160
		bd. Sepia advert (2nd setting) (4.93)	£300	15·00
		be. Brown-red advert (3rd setting) (9.93)	£300	15·00
		bf. Brown-pur advert (3rd setting) (9.93)	£300	15·00
		bx. Wmk reversed (with brown-purple advert)	†	55·00
225	21	8d. blue (brown-purple advert. 3rd setting) (9.93)	75·00	55·00
226	22	1s. red-brown	95·00	10·00
		a. Imperf between (pair)	£1000	
		b. Mixed perfs 10 and 12½	£300	£170
		c. Sepia advert (2nd setting) (5.93)	£200	30·00
		d. Black advert (2nd setting) (5.93)	£275	£120
		e. Brown-red advert (3rd setting) (9.93)	£200	30·00
		f. Brown-purple advert (3rd setting) (9.93)	£200	30·00

(*c*) P 10×11 (1895–97).

227	13	½d. black (1896)	3·25	60
		a. Mixed perfs 10 and 11	£120	75·00
		b. Perf 11×10	38·00	16·00
228	14	1d. rose (Die 3)	5·50	15
		a. Mixed perfs 10 and 11	£150	85·00
		b. Perf 11×10	60·00	11·00
		c. "Ellipse" flaw	30·00	11·00
		x. Wmk reversed	75·00	45·00
229	15	2d. purple (Die 3)	15·00	30
		a. Mixed perfs 10 and 11	80·00	60·00
230	16	2½d. blue (1896)	55·00	3·75
		a. Ultramarine	55·00	4·50
		b. Mixed perfs 10 and 11	—	£110
231	17	3d. lemon-yellow (1896)	65·00	15·00
232	18	4d. pale green (1896)	75·00	12·00
		a. Mixed perfs 10 and 11	—	£130
233	19	5d. olive-black (1897)	55·00	15·00
234	20	6d. deep brown (Die 2) (1896)	70·00	9·50
		a. Mixed perfs 10 and 11	†	£250
		b. Perf 11×10	£200	£120
235	22	1s. red-brown (1896)	85·00	9·50
		a. Mixed perfs 10 and 11	£200	£110

(*d*) P 11 (1895–1900).

236	13	½d. black (1897)	5·00	15
		aw. Wmk inverted	50·00	20·00
		ax. Wmk reversed	£110	60·00
		b. Thin coarse toned paper (1898)	29·00	4·25
		ba. Wmk sideways	—	£1200
237	14	1d. rose (Die 3)	4·00	10
		a. Deep carmine	5·50	1·50
		b. Imperf between (pair)	£650	
		c. Deep carmine/thin coarse toned (1898)	10·00	2·25
		ca. Wmk sideways	—	£1200
		d. "Ellipse" flaw	30·00	10·00
		w. Wmk inverted	38·00	25·00
		x. Wmk reversed	60·00	35·00
		y. Wmk inverted and reversed	90·00	60·00
238	15	2d. mauve (Die 3)	15·00	1·00
		a. Purple	15·00	1·00
		b. Deep purple/thin coarse toned (1898)	15·00	2·75
		ba. Wmk sideways	£350	£1200
		w. Wmk inverted	30·00	15·00
		x. Wmk reversed	£110	38·00
239	16	2½d. blue (1897)	50·00	3·75
		a. Thin coarse toned paper (1898)	80·00	19·00
240	17	3d. pale yellow (1897)	55·00	8·50
		a. Pale dull yellow/thin coarse toned (1898)	70·00	18·00
		b. Orange (1899)	45·00	12·00
		c. Dull orange-yellow (1900)	50·00	21·00
241	18	4d. yellowish green	50·00	4·75
		a. Bluish green (1897)	50·00	4·50
		w. Wmk inverted	£120	30·00
242	19	5d. olive-black/*thin coarse toned* (1899)	55·00	28·00
243	20	6d. brown (Die 2) (1897)	70·00	5·00
		a. Black-brown	70·00	5·00
		b. Brown/thin coarse toned (1898)	90·00	9·00
		x. Wmk reversed	†	65·00
244	21	8d. blue (1898)	70·00	50·00
245	22	1s. red-brown (1897)	85·00	7·00

Only the more prominent shades have been included.

Stamps perf compound of 11 and 12½ exist.

For the ½d. and 2d. with double-lined watermark, see Nos. 271/2.

23 Mount Cook or Aorangi

24 Lake Taupo and Mount Ruapehu

25 Pembroke Peak, Milford Sound

26 Lake Wakatipu and Mount Earnslaw, inscribed "WAKITIPU"

27 Lake Wakatipu and Mount Earnslaw, inscribed "WAKATIPU"

28 Huia

29 White Terrace, Rotomahana

30 Otira Gorge and Mount Ruapehu

31 Brown Kiwi

32 Maori War Canoe

33 Pink Terrace, Rotomahana

34 Kea and Kaka

35 Milford Sound

36 Mount Cook

(Des H. Young (½d.), J. Gaut (1d.), W. Bock (2d., 3d., 9d., 1s.), E. Howard (4d., 6d., 8d.), E. Luke (others). Eng A. Hill (2½d., 1s.), J. A. C. Harrison (5d.), Rapkin (others). Recess Waterlow)

1898 (5 Apr). No wmk. P 12 to 16.

246	23	½d. purple-brown	8·00	1·50
		a. Imperf between (pair)	£1500	£1200
		b. Purple-slate	8·00	1·50
		c. Purple-black	8·50	2·75
247	24	1d. blue and yellow-brown	6·00	60
		a. Imperf between (horiz pair)	£1100	
		b. Imperf vert (horiz pair)	£800	£850
		c. Imperf horiz (vert pair)	£800	£850
		d. Blue and brown	6·50	80
		da. Imperf between (pair)	£1100	
248	25	2d. lake	38·00	25
		a. Imperf vert (horiz pair)	£550	
		b. Rosy lake	38·00	25
		ba. Imperf between (vert pair)	£1100	
		bb. Imperf vert (horiz pair)	£550	
249	26	2½d. sky-blue (inscr "WAKITIPU")	11·00	38·00
		a. Blue	11·00	38·00
250	27	2½d. blue (inscr "WAKATIPU")	35·00	5·50
		a. Deep blue	35·00	5·50
251	28	3d. yellow-brown	25·00	7·50
252	29	4d. bright rose	16·00	19·00
		a. Lake-rose	18·00	22·00
		b. Dull rose	16·00	19·00
253	30	5d. sepia	75·00	£180
		a. Purple-brown	50·00	22·00
254	31	6d. green	65·00	40·00
		a. Grass-green	£150	£160
255	32	8d. indigo	48·00	42·00
		a. Prussian blue	50·00	42·00
256	33	9d. purple	50·00	38·00
257	34	1s. vermilion	75·00	26·00
		a. Dull red	75·00	26·00
		ab. Imperf between (pair)	£4000	
258	35	2s. grey-green	£140	£130
		a. Imperf between (vert pair)	£4000	£4000
259	36	5s. vermilion	£225	£425
246/59 *Set of* 13			£700	£700

37 Lake Taupo and Mount Ruapehu

(Recess Govt Printer, Wellington)

1899 (May)–**03**. *Thick, soft ("Pirie") paper.* No wmk. P 11.

260	27	2½d. blue (6.99)	15·00	3·50
		a. Imperf between (horiz pair)	£1100	
		b. Imperf horiz (vert pair)	£550	
		c. Deep blue	15·00	3·50
261	28	3d. yellow-brown (5.00)	23·00	2·25
		a. Imperf between (pair)	£1200	
		b. Imperf vert (horiz pair)	£550	
		c. Deep brown	23·00	2·25
		ca. Imperf between (pair)	£1200	
262	37	4d. indigo and brown (8.99)	5·50	3·00
		a. Bright blue and chestnut	5·50	3·00
		b. Deep blue and bistre-brown	5·50	3·00
263	30	5d. purple-brown (6.99)	28·00	3·50
		a. Deep purple-brown	28·00	3·50
		ab. Imperf between (pair)	£2000	
264	31	6d. deep green	65·00	70·00
		a. Yellow-green	85·00	£110
265		6d. pale rose (5.5.00)	38·00	4·50
		a. Imperf vert (horiz pair)	£500	
		b. Imperf between (horiz pair)	£1100	
		c. Rose-red	38·00	4·50
		ca. Printed double	£650	£700
		cb. Imperf between (vert pair)	£1200	
		cc. Imperf vert (horiz pair)	£375	
		cd. Showing part of sheet wmk(7.02)*	£100	90·00
		d. Scarlet	75·00	20·00
		da. Imperf vert (horiz pair)	£650	
266	32	8d. indigo	35·00	14·00
		a. Prussian blue	35·00	14·00
267	33	9d. deep purple (8.99)	45·00	25·00
		a. Rosy purple	42·00	11·00
268	34	1s. red (5.00)	60·00	8·50
		a. Dull orange-red	60·00	4·00
		b. Dull brown-red	60·00	10·00
		c. Bright red	65·00	32·00
269	35	2s. blue-green (7.99)	£130	45·00
		a. Laid paper (1.03)	£200	£225
		b. Grey-green	£130	55·00
270	36	5s. vermilion (7.99)	£225	£325
		a. Carmine-red	£275	£375
260/70 *Set of* 11			£600	£425

*No. 265cd is on paper without general watermark, but showing the words "LISBON SUPERFINE" wmkd once in the sheet; the paper was obtained from Parsons Bros, an American firm with a branch at Auckland.

38

1900. *Thick, soft ("Pirie") paper.* Wmk double-lined "NZ" and Star, W **38** (sideways*). P 11.

271	13	½d. black	9·00	14·00
		x. Wmk reversed	£180	£150
272	15	2d. bright purple	25·00	13·00
		w. Wmk sideways inverted	42·00	24·00
		y. Wmk sideways inverted and reversed	—	£150

*The normal sideways wmk on Nos. 271/2 shows the star to the right of NZ, *as seen from the back of the stamp.*

39 White Terrace, Rotomahana

41

40 Commemorative of the New Zealand Contingent in the South African War

(Des J. Nairn (1½d.). Recess Govt Printer, Wellington)

1900 (Mar–Dec). *Thick, soft ("Pirie") paper.* W **38**. P 11.

273	**23**	½d. pale yellow-green (7.3.00)	12·00	4·25
		a. Yellow-green	7·00	1·75
		b. Green	6·50	1·50
		ba. Imperf between (pair)	£425	
		c. Deep green	6·50	1·50
		w. Wmk inverted	27·00	14·00
		y. Wmk inverted and reversed	65·00	30·00
274	**39**	1d. crimson (7.3.00)	13·00	20
		a. Rose-red	13·00	20
		ab. Imperf between (pair)	£1300	£1200
		ac. Imperf vert (horiz pair)	£500	
		b. Lake	32·00	4·00
		w. Wmk inverted	†	£160
		x. Wmk reversed	†	—
		y. Wmk inverted and reversed	†	£300
275	**40**	1½d. khaki (7.12.00)	£1000	£650
		a. Brown	50·00	50·00
		ab. Imperf vert (horiz pair)	£1000	
		ac. Imperf (pair)	£1100	
		b. Chestnut	9·50	4·00
		ba. Imperf vert (horiz pair)	£1000	
		bb. Imperf horiz (vert pair)	£1400	
		c. Pale chestnut	9·50	4·00
		ca. Imperf (pair)	£1100	
276	**41**	2d. dull violet (3.00)	13·00	65
		a. Imperf between (pair)	£1200	
		b. Mauve	13·00	1·50
		c. Purple	10·00	75
		ca. Imperf between (pair)	£1100	

The above ½d. stamps are slightly smaller than those of the previous printing. A new plate was made to print 240 stamps instead of 120 as previously, and to make these fit the watermarked paper, the border design was redrawn and contracted, the centre vignette remaining as before. The 2d. stamp is also from a new plate providing smaller designs.

42

(Des G. Bach and G. Drummond. Eng J. A. C. Harrison. Recess Waterlow)

1901 (1 Jan). *Universal Penny Postage.* No wmk. P 12 to 16.

277	**42**	1d. carmine	3·50	4·25

All examples of No. 277 show a minute dot above the upper left corner of the value tablet which is not present on later printings.

(Recess Govt Printer, Wellington)

1901 (Feb–Dec). *Thick, soft ("Pirie") paper with vertical mesh.* W **38**.

(a) P 11.

278	**42**	1d. carmine	6·00	15
		a. Imperf vert (horiz pair)	£325	
		b. Deep carmine	6·00	15
		ba. Imperf vert (horiz pair)	£325	
		c. Carmine-lake	20·00	10·00
		x. Wmk reversed	†	45·00
		y. Wmk inverted and reversed	—	70·00

(b) P 14.

279	**23**	½d. green (11.01)	17·00	5·00
280	**42**	1d. carmine	55·00	15·00
		a. Imperf vert (horiz pair)	£275	
		y. Wmk inverted and reversed	£120	38·00

(c) P 14×11.

281	**23**	½d. green	8·00	10·00
		a. Deep green	8·00	10·00
		b. Perf 11×14	12·00	20·00
282	**42**	1d. carmine	£200	80·00
		a. Perf 11×14	£1400	£550

(d) P 11 and 14 mixed*.

283	**23**	½d. green	45·00	65·00
284	**42**	1d. carmine	£200	85·00

*The term "mixed" is applied to stamps from sheets which were at first perforated 14, or 14×11, and either incompletely or defectively perforated. These sheets were patched on the back with strips of paper, and re-perforated 11 in those parts where the original perforation was defective.

Nos. 278/84 were printed from new plates supplied by Waterlow. These were subsequently used for Nos. 285/307 with later printings on Cowan paper showing considerable plate wear.

WATERMARK VARIETIES. The watermark on the Basted Mills version of the W **38** paper used for Nos. 285/92 occurs indiscriminately normal, reversed, inverted etc.

(Recess Govt Printer, Wellington)

1901 (Dec). *Thin, hard ("Basted Mills") paper with vertical mesh.* W **38**.

(a) P 11.

285	**23**	½d. green	65·00	80·00
286	**42**	1d. carmine	85·00	£110

(b) P 14.

287	**23**	½d. green	26·00	28·00
		a. Imperf vert (horiz pair)	£350	
288	**42**	1d. carmine	14·00	5·00
		a. Imperf vert (horiz pair)	£275	
		b. Imperf horiz (vert pair)	£275	

(c) P 14×11.

289	**23**	½d. green	22·00	55·00
		a. Deep green	22·00	55·00
		b. Perf 11×14	20·00	50·00
290	**42**	1d. carmine	25·00	12·00
		a. Perf 11×14	10·00	3·50

(d) Mixed perfs.

291	**23**	½d. green	55·00	75·00
292	**42**	1d. carmine	75·00	75·00

(Recess Govt Printer, Wellington)

1902 (Jan). *Thin, hard ("Cowan") paper with horizontal mesh.* No wmk.

(a) P 11.

293	**23**	½d. green	£130	£170

(b) P 14.

294	**23**	½d. green	16·00	6·00
295	**42**	1d. carmine	12·00	3·25

(c) P 14×11.

296	**23**	½d. green	90·00	£160
		a. Perf 11×14	£130	£225
297	**42**	1d. carmine	£110	£120
		a. Perf 11×14	£120	£150

(d) Mixed perfs.

298	**23**	½d. green	£110	£150
299	**42**	1d. carmine	£120	£140

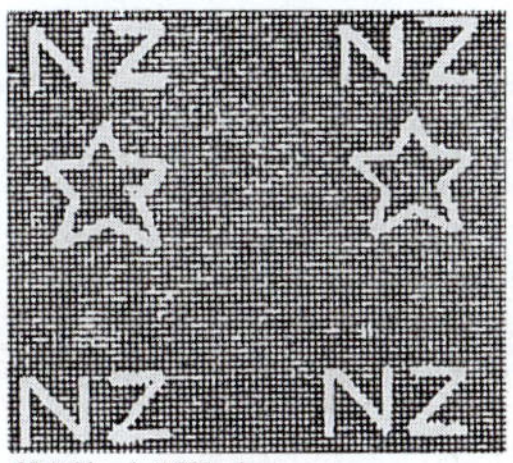

43 "Single" Wmk

SIDEWAYS WATERMARKS. In its sideways format the single NZ and Star watermark W **43**, exists indiscriminately sideways, sideways inverted, sideways reversed and sideways inverted plus reversed.

(Recess Govt Printer, Wellington)

1902 (Apr). *Thin, hard ("Cowan") paper.* W **43**.

(a) P 11.

300	**23**	½d. green	65·00	90·00
301	**42**	1d. carmine	£650	£550

(b) P 14.

302	**23**	½d. green	6·50	1·00
		a. Imperf vert (horiz pair)	£225	
		b. Deep green	6·50	1·00
		ba. Imperf vert (horiz pair)	£225	
		c. Yellow green	7·50	1·00
		d. Pale yellow-green	15·00	3·50
		w. Wmk inverted	32·00	15·00
		x. Wmk reversed	35·00	24·00
		y. Wmk inverted and reversed	60·00	32·00
303	**42**	1d. carmine	3·00	10
		a. Imperf horiz (vert pair)	£170	
		b. Booklet pane of 6 (21.8.02)	£250	
		c. Pale carmine	3·00	10
		ca. Imperf horiz (vert pair)	£170	
		cb. Booklet pane of 6	£250	
		*d. Deep carmine**	32·00	4·00
		w. Wmk inverted	70·00	35·00
		x. Wmk reversed	70·00	35·00
		y. Wmk inverted and reversed	55·00	18·00

(c) P 14×11.

304	**23**	½d. green	21·00	95·00
		a. Deep green	26·00	
		b. Perf 11×14	23·00	75·00
305	**42**	1d. carmine	£100	£120
		a. Perf 11×14	£130	£130
		*ab. Deep carmine**	£425	£425

(d) Mixed perfs.

306	**23**	½d. green	27·00	50·00
		a. Deep green	32·00	50·00
307	**42**	1d. carmine	26·00	48·00
		a. Pale carmine	26·00	48·00
		*b. Deep carmine**	£275	£300
		y. Wmk inverted and reversed		

*Nos. 303*d*, 305*ab* and 307*b* were printed from a plate made by Waterlow & Sons, known as the "Reserve" plate. The stamps do not show evidence of wearing and the area surrounding the upper part of the figure is more deeply shaded. This plate was subsequently used to produce Nos. 362, 364 and 366/9.

A special plate, made by W. R. Royle & Sons, showing a minute dot between the horizontal rows, was introduced in 1902 to print the booklet pane, No. 303b. A special characteristic of the booklet pane was that the pearl in the top left-hand corner was large. Some panes exist with the outer edges imperforate.

(Recess Govt Printer, Wellington)

1902 (28 Aug)–**09**. *Thin, hard ("Cowan") paper.* W **43** (sideways on 3d., 5d., 6d., 8d., 1s. and 5s.).

(a) P 11.

308	**27**	2½d. blue (5.03)	18·00	12·00
		a. Deep blue	20·00	12·00
		w. Wmk inverted	£130	65·00
		x. Wmk reversed	£150	35·00
		y. Wmk inverted and reversed	£200	55·00
309	**28**	3d. yellow-brown	28·00	1·75
		a. Bistre-brown	30·00	1·75
		b. Pale bistre	38·00	4·25
310	**37**	4d. deep blue and deep brown/*bluish* (27.11.02)	6·00	65·00
		a. Imperf vert (horiz pair)	£550	
311	**30**	5d. red-brown (4.03)	38·00	11·00
		a. Deep brown	30·00	7·00
		b. Sepia	45·00	16·00
312	**31**	6d. rose (9.02)	38·00	7·00
		a. Rose-red	38·00	7·50
		ab. Wmk upright	£1500	£1200
		b. Rose-carmine	42·00	7·50
		ba. Imperf vert (horiz pair)	£700	
		bb. Imperf horiz (vert pair)		
		c. Bright carmine-pink	50·00	8·00
		d. Scarlet	60·00	16·00
313	**32**	8d. blue (2.03)	38·00	11·00
		a. Steel-blue	38·00	11·00
		ab. Imperf vert (horiz pair)	£1300	
		ac. Imperf horiz (vert pair)	£1300	
314	**33**	9d. purple (5.03)	55·00	12·00
		w. Wmk inverted	£130	65·00
		x. Wmk reversed	£160	£130
		y. Wmk inverted and reversed	£180	£130
315	**34**	1s. brown-red (11.02)	55·00	13·00
		a. Bright red	55·00	14·00
		b. Orange-red	55·00	4·50
		ba. Error. Wmk W **12b** (inverted)	†	£1600
		c. Orange-brown	60·00	15·00
316	**35**	2s. green (4.03)	£110	60·00
		a. Blue-green	£100	45·00
		x. Wmk reversed	£450	
		w. Wmk inverted	£350	£130
317	**36**	5s. deep red (6.03)	£225	£275
		a. Wmk upright	£250	£300
		b. Vermilion	£225	£275
		ba. Wmk upright	£250	£300
		w. Wmk inverted	£800	£550

(b) P 14.

318	**40**	1½d. chestnut (2.07)	19·00	55·00
319	**41**	2d. grey-purple (12.02)	5·50	2·00
		a. Purple	5·50	2·00
		ab. Imperf vert (horiz pair)	£425	£650
		ac. Imperf horiz (vert pair)	£550	
		b. Bright reddish purple	6·50	2·75
320	**27**	2½d. blue (1906)	20·00	3·75
		a. Deep blue	20·00	3·75
		w. Wmk inverted	£120	90·00
		x. Wmk reversed	†	£180
		y. Wmk inverted and reversed	£225	£130
321	**28**	3d. bistre-brown (1906)	27·00	6·50
		a. Imperf vert (horiz pair)	£750	
		b. Bistre	27·00	6·50
		c. Pale yellow-bistre	50·00	16·00
322	**37**	4d. deep blue and deep brown/*bluish* (1903)	6·50	3·25
		a. Imperf vert (horiz pair)	£550	
		b. Imperf horiz (vert pair)	£550	
		c. Centre inverted	†	*
		d. Blue and chestnut/bluish	4·00	2·75
		e. Blue and ochre-brown/bluish	4·00	2·75
		w. Wmk inverted	30·00	13·00
		x. Wmk reversed	£120	70·00
		y. Wmk inverted and reversed	£150	£110
323	**30**	5d. black-brown (1906)	60·00	27·00
		a. Red-brown	32·00	13·00
324	**31**	6d. bright carmine-pink (1906)	55·00	9·50
		a. Imperf vert (horiz pair)	£650	
		b. Rose-carmine	55·00	9·50
325	**32**	8d. steel-blue (1907)	30·00	11·00
326	**33**	9d. purple (1906)	27·00	8·00
		w. Wmk inverted	£180	£120
327	**34**	1s. orange-brown (1906)	70·00	8·00
		a. Orange-red	65·00	8·00
		b. Pale red	£130	50·00
328	**35**	2s. green (1.06)	95·00	26·00
		a. Blue-green	£100	35·00
		aw. Wmk inverted	£550	£150
		ax. Wmk reversed	†	—
		ay. Wmk inverted and reversed	£550	£150
329	**38**	5s. deep red (1906)	£190	£225
		a. Wmk upright	£200	£300
		b. Dull red	£190	£225
		ba. Wmk upright	£200	£300

(c) Perf compound of 11 and 14.

330	**40**	1½d. chestnut (1907)	£1200	
331	**41**	2d. purple (1903)	£350	£325
332	**28**	3d. bistre-brown (1906)	£650	£550
333	**37**	4d. blue and yellow-brown (1903)	£325	£375
		x. Wmk reversed	—	£550
334	**30**	5d. red-brown (1906)	£1200	£1000
335	**31**	6d. rose-carmine (1907)	£350	£300
336	**32**	8d. steel-blue (1907)	£950	£1000
337	**33**	9d. purple (1906)	£1200	£1100
338	**36**	5s. deep red (1906)	£2500	£2500

(d) Mixed perfs.

339	**40**	1½d. chestnut (1907)	£1200	
340	**41**	2d. purple (1903)	£300	£300
341	**28**	3d. bistre-brown (1906)	£650	£550
342	**37**	4d. blue and chestnut/*bluish* (1904)	£275	£325
		a. Blue and yellow-brown/bluish	£275	£325
		w. Wmk inverted	£650	£550
		x. Wmk reversed	£650	£650
343	**30**	5d. red-brown (1906)	£900	£800
344	**31**	6d. rose-carmine (1907)	£325	£300
		a. Bright carmine-pink	£350	£300
345	**32**	8d. steel-blue (1907)	£900	£950
346	**33**	9d. purple (1906)	£1000	£1000
347	**35**	2s. blue-green (1906)	£1200	£1300
348	**36**	5s. vermilion (Wmk upright) (1906)	£1900	
		w. Wmk inverted		

Two sizes of paper were used for the above stamps:—

(1) A sheet containing 240 wmks, with a space of 9 mm between each.

(2) A sheet containing 120 wmks, with a space of 24 mm between each vertical row.

Size (1) was used for the ½d., 1d., 2d. and 4d., and size (2) for 2½d., 5d., 9d. and 2s. The paper in each case exactly fitted the plates, and had the watermark in register, though in the case of the 4d., the plate of which contained only 80 stamps, the paper was cut up to print it. The 3d., 6d., 8d. and 1s. were printed on variety (1), but with watermark sideways: by reason of this, specimens from the margins of the sheets show parts of the words "NEW ZEALAND POSTAGE" in large letters, and some copies have no watermark at all. For the 1½d. and 5s. stamps variety (1) was also used, but two watermarks appear on each stamp.

*The only known example of No. 322c, postmarked at Picton on 21 March 1904, was purchased for the New Zealand Post archive collection in 1998.

(Recess Govt Printer, Wellington)

1904 (Feb). *Printed from new "dot" plates made by W. R. Royle & Sons. Thin, hard ("Cowan") paper.* W **43**.

(a) P 14.

349	**42**	1d. rose-carmine	8·00	50
		a. Pale carmine	8·00	50
		w. Wmk inverted	80·00	30·00
		y. Wmk inverted and reversed	90·00	38·00

(b) P 11×14.

350	**42**	1d. rose-carmine	£140	£120

(c) Mixed perfs.

351	**42**	1d. rose-carmine	29·00	38·00
		a. Pale carmine	29·00	38·00

These plates have a dot in the margins between stamps, level with the small pearls at the side of the design, but it is frequently cut out by the perforations. However, they can be further distinguished by the notes below.

In 1906 fresh printings were made from four new plates, two of which, marked in the margin "W1" and "W2", were supplied by Waterlow Bros and Layton, and the other two, marked "R1" and "R2", by W. R. Royle & Son. The intention was to note which pair of plates wore the best and produced the best results. They can be distinguished as follows:—

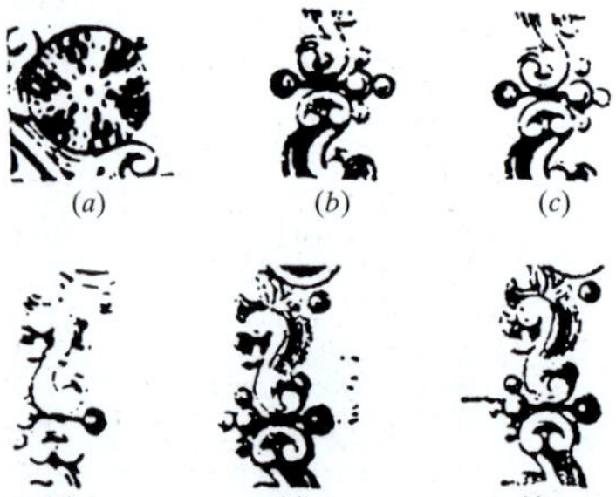

(*a*) (*b*) (*c*) (*d*) (*e*) (*f*)

(*a*) Four o'clock flaw in rosette at top right corner. Occurs in all these plates but not in the original Waterlow plates.
(*b*) Pearl at right strong.
(*c*) Pearl at right weak.
(*d*) Dot at left and S-shaped ornament unshaded.
(*e*) S-shaped ornament with one line of shading within.
(*f*) As (*e*) but with line from left pearl to edge of stamp.

"Dot" plates comprise (*a*) and (*d*).
Waterlow plates comprise (*a*), (*b*) and (*e*).
Royle plates comprise (*a*), (*c*) and (*e*) and the line in (*f*) on many stamps but not all.

(Recess Govt Printer, Wellington)

1906. *Thin, hard ("Cowan") paper.* W **43**.

(a) Printed from new Waterlow plates.

(i) P 14.

352	**42**	1d. deep rose-carmine	35·00	2·25
		a. Imperf horiz (vert pair)	£250	
		b. Aniline carmine	32·00	2·25
		ba. Imperf vert (horiz pair)	£250	
		c. Rose-carmine	32·00	2·25
		y. Wmk inverted and reversed		

(ii) P 11.

353	**42**	1d. aniline carmine	£600	£700

(iii) P 11×14.

354	**42**	1d. rose-carmine	£425	£750
		a. Perf 14×11	£425	£750

(iv) Mixed perfs.

355	**42**	1d. deep rose-carmine	£400	£550

(b) Printed from new Royle plates.

(i) P 14.

356	**42**	1d. rose-carmine	11·00	1·25
		a. Imperf horiz (vert pair)	£225	£250
		b. Bright rose-carmine	12·00	1·40
		w. Wmk inverted		
		y. Wmk inverted and reversed	—	£180

(ii) P 11.

357	**42**	1d. bright rose-carmine	£100	£180

(iii) P 11×14.

358	**42**	1d. rose-carmine	£100	£160
		a. Perf 14×11	£110	£160

(iv) Mixed perfs.

359	**42**	1d. rose-carmine	£100	£150

(v) P 14×14½ (comb).

360	**42**	1d. bright rose-carmine	65·00	55·00
		a. Rose-carmine	65·00	55·00

Nos. 360/*a* are known both with and without the small dot. See also No. 386.

1905 (15 June)–**06**. *Stamps supplied to penny-in-the-slot machines.*

(i) "Dot" plates of 1904.

(ii) Waterlow "reserve" plate of 1902.

(a) Imperf top and bottom; zigzag roulette 9½ on one or both sides, two large holes at sides.

361	**42**	1d. rose-carmine (*i*)	£150	
362		1d. deep carmine (*ii*)	£170	

(b) As last but rouletted 14½ (8.7.05).

363	**42**	1d. rose-carmine (*i*)	£160	
364		1d. deep carmine (*ii*)	£325	

(c) Imperf all round, two large holes each side (6.3.06).

365	**42**	1d. rose-carmine (*i*)	£130	
366		1d. deep carmine (*ii*)	£130	

(d) Imperf all round (21.6.06).

367	**42**	1d. deep carmine (*ii*)	£140	

(e) Imperf all round. Two small indentations on back of stamp (1.06).

368	**42**	1d. deep carmine (*ii*)	£170	£150

(f) Imperf all round; two small pin-holes in stamp (21.6.06).

369	**42**	1d. deep carmine (*ii*)	£150	£150

No. 365 *only* exists from strips of Nos. 361 or 363 (resulting from the use of successive coins) which have been separated by scissors. Similarly strips of Nos. 362 and 364 can produce single copies of No. 366 but this also exists in singles from a different machine.

Most used copies of Nos. 361/7 are forgeries and they should only be collected on cover.

44 Maori Canoe, *Te Arawa*

45 Maori art

46 Landing of Cook

46a Annexation of New Zealand

(Des L. J. Steele. Eng W. R. Bock. Typo Govt Printer, Wellington)

1906 (1–17 Nov). *New Zealand Exhibition, Christchurch. T* **44/46a**. W **43** (sideways). P 14.

370	½d. emerald-green	27·00	32·00
371	1d. vermilion	16·00	16·00
	a. Claret	£6500	£9500
372	3d. brown and blue	55·00	85·00
373	6d. pink and olive-green (17.11)	£190	£275
370/3 *Set of 4*		£250	£375

The 1d. in claret was the original printing, which was considered unsatisfactory.

47 (T **28** reduced)

48 (T **31** reduced)

49 (T **34** reduced)

(New plates (except 4d.), supplied by Perkins Bacon. Recess Govt Printer, Wellington).

1907–08. *Thin, hard ("Cowan") paper.* W **43**.

(a) P 14 (line).

374	**23**	½d. green (1907)	27·00	10·00
		a. Imperf (pair)	£250	
		b. Yellow-green	19·00	4·25
		c. Deep yellow-green	19·00	4·25
375	**47**	3d. brown (6.07)	65·00	25·00
376	**48**	6d. carmine-pink (3.07)	40·00	8·50
		a. Red	50·00	35·00

(b) P 14×13, 13½ (comb).

377	**23**	½d. green (1907)	17·00	11·00
		a. Yellow-green	8·00	4·50
		b. Imperf three sides (top stamp of vert pair)	£350	
378	**47**	3d. brown (2.08)	55·00	38·00
		a. Yellow-brown	55·00	38·00
379	**37**	4d. blue and yellow-brown/*bluish* (6.08)	30·00	42·00
380	**48**	6d. pink (2.08)	£325	£130
381	**49**	1s. orange-red (12.07)	£130	55·00

(c) P 14×15 (comb).

382	**23**	½d. yellow-green (1907)	8·00	1·00
		a. Imperf three sides (top stamp of vert pair)	£300	
		y. Wmk inverted and reversed	—	£170
383	**47**	3d. brown (8.08)	38·00	15·00
		a. Yellow-brown	38·00	15·00
384	**48**	6d. carmine-pink (8.08)	42·00	11·00
385	**49**	1s. orange-red (8.08)	£110	24·00
		a. Deep orange-brown	£325	£750

The ½d. stamps of this 1907–8 issue have a minute dot in the margin between the stamps, where not removed by the perforation. (See note after No. 351*a*). Those perforated 14 can be distinguished from the earlier stamps, Nos. 302/*d*, by the absence of plate wear. This is most noticeable on the 1902 printings as a white patch at far left, level with the bottom of the "P" in "POSTAGE". Such damage is not present on the new plates used for Nos. 374/*c*.

Stamps of *T* **47**, **48** and **49** also have a small dot as described in note after No. 351*a*.

TYPOGRAPHY PAPERS.

1908–30. De La Rue paper is chalk-surfaced and has a smooth finish. The watermark is as illustrated. The gum is toned and strongly resistant to soaking.

Jones paper is chalk-surfaced and has a coarser texture, is poorly surfaced and the ink tends to peel. The outline of the watermark commonly shows on the surface of the stamp. The gum is colourless or only slightly toned and washes off readily.

Cowan paper is chalk-surfaced and is white and opaque. The watermark is usually smaller than in the "Jones" paper and is often barely visible.

Wiggins Teape paper is chalk-surfaced and is thin and hard. It has a vertical mesh with a narrow watermark, whereas the other papers have a horizontal mesh and a wider watermark.

50

(Typo Govt Printer, Wellington, from Perkins Bacon plate).

1908 (1 Dec). *De La Rue chalk-surfaced paper.* W **43**. P 14×15 (comb).

386	**50**	1d. carmine	23·00	2·25
		w. Wmk inverted	—	65·00

The design of Type **50** differs from Type **42** by alterations in the corner rosettes and by the lines on the globe which are diagonal instead of vertical.

51

52

53

(Eng. P.B. Typo Govt Printer, Wellington)

1909 (8 Nov)–**12**. *De La Rue chalk-surfaced paper with toned gum.* W **43**. P 14×15 (comb).

387	**51**	½d. yellow-green	4·25	50
		aa. Deep green	4·25	50
		a. Imperf (pair)	£225	
		b. Booklet pane. Five stamps plus label in position 1 (4.10)	£650	
		c. Ditto, but label in position 6 (4.10)	£650	
		d. Booklet pane of 6 (4.10)	£190	
		e. Ditto, but with coloured bars on selvedge (5.12)	£180	
		w. Wmk inverted	†	£350

Stamps with blurred and heavy appearance are from booklets.

(Eng W. R. Royle & Son, London. Recess Govt Printer, Wellington)

1909 (8 Nov)–**16**. *T* **52** *and similar portraits.*

(a) W **43**. P 14×14½ (comb).

388	2d. mauve	9·50	6·50
	a. Deep mauve	18·00	6·50
	w. Wmk inverted	†	—
389	3d. chestnut	23·00	1·25
390	4d. orange-red	26·00	27·00
	a. Orange-yellow (1912)	6·00	8·00
	aw. Wmk inverted	£300	90·00
391	5d. brown (1910)	17·00	4·00
	a. Red-brown	17·00	4·00
	w. Wmk inverted	†	—
392	6d. carmine (1910)	40·00	1·25
	a. Deep carmine (29.10.13)	45·00	3·00
393	8d. indigo-blue	11·00	2·25
	a. Deep bright blue	13·00	2·25
	w. Wmk inverted	60·00	32·00
394	1s. vermilion (1910)	48·00	4·25
	w. Wmk inverted	£190	80·00
388/94 *Set of 8*		£160	48·00

(b) W **43**. P 14 (line)*.

395	3d. chestnut (1910)	48·00	17·00
396	4d. orange (1910)	20·00	15·00
397	5d. brown	26·00	4·50
	a. Red-brown (15.9.11)	26·00	5·00
	w. Wmk inverted		
398	6d. carmine	40·00	10·00
399	1s. vermilion	55·00	13·00
395/9 *Set of 5*		£170	55·00

(c) W **43** (sideways) *(paper with widely spaced wmk as used for Nos. 308 and 320 – see note below No. 348).* P 14 (line)*.

400	8d. indigo-blue (8.16)	30·00	65·00
	a. No wmk	95·00	£170

(d) W **43**. P 14×13½ (comb)†.

401	3d. chestnut (1915)	70·00	90·00
	a. Vert pair. P 14×13½ and 14×14½	£225	£300
	w. Wmk inverted	£180	£170
402	5d. red-brown (1916)	19·00	3·00
	a. Vert pair. P 14×13½ and 14×14½	55·00	£110
403	6d. carmine (1915)	75·00	£100
	a. Vert pair. P 14×13½ and 14×14½	£225	£375
404	8d. indigo-blue (3.16)	30·00	3·00
	a. Vert pair. P 14×13½ and 14×14½	55·00	£110
	b. Deep bright blue	35·00	3·25
	ba. Vert pair. P 14×13½ and 14×14½	65·00	£120
	w. Wmk inverted	80·00	42·00
401/4 *Set of 4*		£170	£180

*In addition to showing the usual characteristics of a line perforation, these stamps may be distinguished by their vertical perforation which measures 13.8. Nos. 388/94 generally measure vertically 14 to 14.3. An exception is 13.8 one vertical side but 14 the other.

†The 3d. and 6d. come in full sheets perf 14×13½. The 3d., 5d. and 6d. values also exist in two combinations: (*a*) five top rows perf 14×13½ with five bottom rows perf 14×14½ and (*b*) four top rows perf 14×13½ with six bottom rows perf 14×14½. The 8d. perf 14×13½ only exists from combination (*b*).

(Eng P.B. Typo Govt Printer, Wellington)

1909 (8 Nov)–**26**. P 14×15 (comb).

(a) W **43**. *De La Rue chalk-surfaced paper with toned gum.*

405	**53**	1d. carmine	1·75	10
		a. Imperf (pair)	£375	
		b. Booklet pane of 6 (4.10)	£160	
		c. Ditto, but with coloured bars on selvedge (5.12)	£120	
		w. Wmk inverted	35·00	25·00
		y. Wmk inverted and reversed		

(b) W **43**. *Jones chalk-surfaced paper with white gum.*

406	**53**	1d. deep carmine (6.24)	15·00	7·50
		a. On unsurfaced paper. *Pale carmine*	£375	
		b. Booklet pane of 6 with bars on selvedge (1.12.24)	£120	
		w. Wmk inverted	55·00	35·00

(c) W **43**. *De La Rue unsurfaced medium paper with toned gum.*

407	**53**	1d. rose-carmine (4.25)	35·00	£120

(d) W **43** (sideways). *De La Rue chalk-surfaced paper with toned gum.*

408	**53**	1d. bright carmine (4.25)	11·00	48·00
		a. No wmk	22·00	65·00
		b. Imperf (pair)	65·00	

(e) No wmk, but bluish "NZ" and Star lithographed on back. Art paper.
409 **53** 1d. rose-carmine (7.25) 2·00 4·75
a. "NZ" and Star in black 13·00
b. "NZ" and Star colourless 24·00
(f) W **43**. *Cowan thick, opaque, chalk-surfaced paper with white gum.*
410 **53** 1d. deep carmine (8.25) 8·00 1·10
a. Imperf (pair) £110 £140
b. Booklet pane of 6 with bars and adverts on selvedge £150
w. Wmk inverted 40·00 30·00
x. Wmk reversed (1926) 10·00 3·25
xa. Booklet pane of 6 with bars and adverts on selvedge (1927) £140
y. Wmk inverted and reversed (1926) 50·00 35·00
(g) W **43**. *Wiggins Teape thin, hard, chalk-surfaced paper with white gum.*
411 **53** 1d. rose-carmine (6.26) 32·00 23·00
w. Wmk inverted 48·00 30·00

Examples of No. 405 with a blurred and heavy appearance are from booklets.

No. 406a comes from a sheet on which the paper coating was missing from the right-hand half.

Many stamps from the sheets of No. 408 were without watermark or showed portions of "NEW ZEALAND POSTAGE" in double-lined capitals.

AUCKLAND EXHIBITION, 1913.
(59)

60

1913 (1 Dec). *Auckland Industrial Exhibition. Nos. 387aa, 389, 392 and 405 optd with T* **59** *by Govt Printer, Wellington.*
412 **51** ½d. deep green 18·00 55·00
413 **53** 1d. carmine 23·00 48·00
414 **52** 3d. chestnut £130 £250
415 6d. carmine £160 £300
412/15 *Set of 4* £300 £600

These overprinted stamps were only available for letters in New Zealand and to Australia.

(Des H. L. Richardson. Recess Govt Printer, Wellington, from plates made in London by P.B.)

1915 (30 July)–**30**. W **43**. P 14×13½ (comb) (see notes below).

(a) Cowan unsurfaced paper.
416 **60** 1½d. grey-slate 3·00 2·00
a. Perf 14×14½ (1915) 4·50 1·75
aw. Wmk inverted £140 £140
b. Vert pair. Nos. 416/a 35·00 95·00
417 2d. bright violet 9·00 50·00
a. Perf 14×14½ 7·00 40·00
b. Vert pair. Nos. 417/a 24·00 £160
418 2d. yellow (15.1.16) 7·50 32·00
a. Perf 14×14½ 7·00 32·00
b. Vert pair. Nos. 418/a 18·00 £250
419 2½d. blue 3·25 6·00
a. Perf 14×14½ (1916) 9·50 27·00
b. Vert pair. Nos. 419/a 40·00 £180
420 3d. chocolate 18·00 1·25
aw. Wmk inverted £140 £110
ax. Wmk reversed
b. Perf 14×14½ 13·00 2·00
bw. Wmk inverted £140 £110
bx. Wmk reversed £350
c. Vert pair. Nos. 420 and 420b 50·00 £140
cw. Wmk inverted
cx. Wmk reversed
421 4d. yellow 4·25 55·00
a. Re-entry (Pl 20 R. 1/6) 45·00
b. Re-entry (Pl 20 R. 4/10) 60·00
c. Perf 14×14½ 4·25 55·00
d. Vert pair. Nos. 421 and 421c 26·00 £250
422 4d. bright violet (7.4.16) 9·50 50
a. Imperf three sides (top stamp of vertical pair) £1500
b. Re-entry (Pl 20 R. 1/6) 48·00 25·00
c. Re-entry (Pl 20 R. 4/10) 65·00 30·00
dx. Wmk reversed
e. Perf 14×14½ 7·00 50
ex. Wmk reversed — £250
f. Vert pair. Nos. 422 and 422e 60·00 £150
fx. Wmk reversed
g. *Deep purple* (7.26) 35·00 15·00
h. Perf 14×14½ 7·00 50
ha. Imperf three sides (top stamp of vertical pair) £1500
hb. Vert pair. Nos. 422g/h £2000
hw. Wmk inverted † £1500
423 4½d. deep green 14·00 27·00
a. Perf 14×14½ (1915) 12·00 45·00
b. Vert pair. Nos. 423/a 50·00 £170
424 5d. light blue (4.22) 6·50 1·00
a. Imperf (pair) £140 £180
aa. Imperf (top stamp of vertical pair) £850
bw. Wmk inverted — £120
c. Perf 14×14½ 12·00 38·00
d. *Pale ultramarine* (5.30) 15·00 12·00
da. Perf 14×14½ 24·00 21·00
db. Vert pair. Nos. 424d/da 65·00 £180
425 6d. carmine 9·00 50
a. Imperf three sides (top stamp of vert pair) £1500
bw. Wmk inverted £130 75·00
bx. Wmk reversed — £130
by. Wmk inverted and reversed £1500
c. *Carmine-lake* (11.27) £500 £400
d. Perf 14×14½ (1915) 9·00 60
dw. Wmk inverted £100 45·00
e. Vert pair. Nos. 425 and 425d 65·00 £140
426 7½d. red-brown 12·00 23·00
a. Perf 14×14½ (10.20) 11·00 65·00
b. Vert pair. Nos. 426/a 50·00 £200
427 8d. indigo-blue (19.4.21) 13·00 50·00
a. Perf 14×14½ 11·00 50·00
b. Vert pair. Nos. 427/a 38·00 £180
428 8d. red-brown (3.22) 24·00 1·50
429 9d. sage-green 17·00 2·75
a. Imperf (pair) £1500
b. Imperf three sides (top stamp of vert pair) £1500
c. *Yellowish olive* (12.25) 20·00 18·00
d. Perf 14×14½ 17·00 20·00
e. Vert pair. Nos. 429 and 429d 75·00 £225
430 1s. vermilion 16·00 2·25
a. Imperf (pair) £2250
aa. Imperf (top stamp of vertical pair) £2000
bw. Wmk inverted £250 £180
c. Perf 14×14½ (1915) 14·00 50
ca. *Pale orange-red* (4.24) 30·00 22·00
cb. Imperf (pair) £325
cba. Imperf (top stamp of vertical pair) £750
cc. *Orange-brown* (1.2.28) £600 £450
cw. Wmk inverted £225
d. Vert pair. Nos. 430 and 430c 75·00 £250
dw. Wmk inverted
416/30 *Set of 15* £130 £200

(b) W **43** (sideways on 2d., 3d. and 6d.). *Thin paper with widely spaced watermark as used for Nos. 308 and 320 (see note below No. 348).* P 14×13½ (comb) (see notes below) (1½d.) or 14 (line) (others).
431 **60** 1½d. grey-slate (3.16) 3·00 8·50
a. No wmk 4·00 17·00
b. Perf 14×14½ 3·00 8·50
ba. No wmk 4·00 17·00
by. Wmk inverted and reversed £375 £375
c. Vert pair. Nos. 431 and 431b 23·00 £110
ca. Vert pair. Nos. 431a and 431ba 60·00 £180
432 2d. yellow (6.16) 6·50 55·00
a. No wmk 75·00 £150
433 3d. chocolate (6.16) 7·00 40·00
a. No wmk 75·00 £160
434 6d. carmine (6.16) 9·50 95·00
a. No wmk £100 £225
431/4 *Set of 4* 23·00 £180

The 1½d., 2½d., 4½d. and 7½d. have value tablets as shown in Type **60**. For the other values the tablets are shortened and the ornamental border each side of the crown correspondingly extended.

With the exception of Nos. 432/4 stamps in this issue were comb-perforated 14×13½, 14×14½ or a combination of the two.

The 1½d. (No. 416), 2½d., 4d. (both), 4½d., 5d., 6d., 7½d., 8d. red-brown, 9d. and 1s. are known to have been produced in sheets perforated 14×13½ throughout with the 4d. bright violet, 5d., 6d. and 1s. known perforated 14×14½ throughout.

On the sheets showing the two perforations combined, the top four rows are usually perforated 14×13½ and the bottom six 14×14½. Combination sheets are known to have been produced in this form for the 1½d. (Nos. 416 and 431), 2d. (both), 2½d., 3d., 4d. (both), 4½d., 6d., 7½d., 8d. indigo-blue, 9d. and 1s. On a late printing of the 4d. deep purple and 5d. pale ultramarine the arrangement is different with the top five rows perforated 14×14½ and the bottom five 14×13½.

With the exception of Nos. 432/4 any with perforations measuring 14×14 or nearly must be classed as 14×14½, this being an irregularity of the comb machine, and not a product of the 14-line machine.

During the laying-down of plate 20 for the 4d., from the roller-die which also contained dies of other values, an impression of the 4½d. value was placed on R. 1/6 and of the 2½d. on R. 4/10. These errors were subsequently corrected by re-entries of the 4d. impression, but on R. 1/6 traces of the original impression can be found in the right-hand value tablet and above the top frame line, while on R. 4/10 the foot of the "2" is visible in the left-hand value tablet with traces of "½" to its right.

61

62

★ ★
WAR STAMP
(63)

Type **62** (from local plates) can be identified from Type **61** (prepared by Perkins Bacon) by the shading on the portrait. This is diagonal on Type **62** and horizontal on Type **61**.

(Die eng W. R. Bock. Typo Govt Printer, Wellington, from plates made by P.B. (*T* **61**) or locally (*T* **62**))

1915 (30 July)–**33**. W **43**. P 14×15.

(a) De La Rue chalk-surfaced paper with toned gum.
435 **61** ½d. green 1·25 20
a. Booklet pane of 6 with bars on selvedge £130
b. *Yellow-green* 3·75 1·40
ba. Booklet pane of 6 with bars on selvedge £110
c. Very thick, hard, highly surfaced paper with white gum (12.15) 12·00 50·00
w. Wmk inverted 45·00 75·00
x. Wmk reversed — £100
y. Wmk inverted and reversed — £140
436 **62** 1½d. grey-black (4.16) 11·00 1·25
a. *Black* 11·00 1·40
y. Wmk inverted and reversed — £200
437 **61** 1½d. slate (5.9.16) 8·00 20
w. Wmk inverted — £250
438 1½d. orange-brown (9.18) 2·25 20
w. Wmk inverted £140 £100
x. Wmk reversed † —
y. Wmk inverted and reversed £200 £160
439 2d. yellow (9.16) 2·25 20
a. *Pale yellow* 3·75 70
w. Wmk inverted 95·00
440 3d. chocolate (5.19) 7·00 75
435/40 *Set of 6* 29·00 2·50

(b) W **43**. *Jones chalk-surfaced paper with white gum.*
441 **61** ½d. green (10.24) 9·00 10·00
a. Booklet pane of 6 with bars on selvedge (1.12.24) £120
w. Wmk inverted 60·00 35·00
442 2d. dull yellow (7.24) 7·00 38·00
w. Wmk inverted 45·00
443 3d. deep chocolate (3.25) 22·00 22·00
441/3 *Set of 3* 35·00 65·00

(c) No wmk, but bluish "NZ" and Star lithographed on back. Art paper.
444 **61** ½d. apple-green (4.25) 2·50 4·50
a. "NZ" and Star almost colourless 4·50
445 2d. yellow (7.25) 7·00 60·00

(d) W **43**. *Cowan thick, opaque, chalk-surfaced paper with white gum.*
446 **61** ½d. green (8.25) 1·50 30
a. Booklet pane of 6 with bars and adverts on selvedge £140
aa. Imperf three sides (top stamp of vertical pair) £850
ab. Booklet pane of 6 with bars on selvedge (1928) £325
bw. Wmk inverted 55·00 60·00
bx. Wmk reversed (1926) 5·00 2·75
bxa. Booklet pane of 6 with bars and adverts on selvedge (1927) £110
by. Wmk inverted and reversed (1926) 65·00 60·00
c. Perf 14 (1927) 1·75 35
ca. Booklet pane of 6 with bars on selvedge (1928) £100
cb. Booklet pane of 6 with bars and adverts on selvedge (1928) £100
cw. Wmk inverted 80·00 55·00
447 1½d. orange-brown (P 14) (8.29) 8·50 28·00
a. Perf 14×15 (7.33) 35·00 80·00
448 2d. yellow (8.25) 7·50 60
ax. Wmk reversed (1927) 16·00 95·00
ay. Wmk inverted and reversed (1927) £130
b. Perf 14 (1929) 2·75 20
bw. Wmk inverted 50·00 35·00
449 3d. chocolate (8.25) 7·50 1·00
aw. Wmk inverted 65·00
b. Perf 14 (1929) 7·50 2·75
446/9 *Set of 4* 18·00 28·00

(e) W **43**. *Wiggins Teape thin, hard, chalk-surfaced paper.*
450 **61** 1½d. orange-brown (P 14) (1930) 38·00 90·00
451 2d. yellow (5.26) 11·00 21·00
aw. Wmk inverted 35·00 35·00
b. Perf 14 (10.27) 9·50 21·00
bw. Wmk inverted 42·00 35·00

The designs of these stamps also differ as described beneath No. 434.

Stamps from booklet panes often have blurred, heavy impressions. Different advertisements can be found on the listed booklet panes.

Examples of No. 446cc, which occur in booklet panes, show the stamps perforated at top.

The ½d. and 2d. (Nos. 446c and 448b) are known showing ½d. and 1d. local surcharges from 1932 applied diagonally in blue to stamps previously stuck on to envelopes or cards at Christchurch (½d.) or Wellington (1d.).

1915 (24 Sept). *No. 435 optd with T* **63**.
452 **61** ½d. green 2·25 50

64 "Peace" and Lion

65 "Peace" and Lion

66

67

66a

67a

(Des and typo D.L.R. from plates by P.B., Waterlow and D.L.R.)

1920 (27 Jan). *Victory. T* **64/67a**. *De La Rue chalk-surfaced paper.* W **43** (sideways on ½d., 1½d., 3d. and 1s.). P 14.
453 ½d. green 3·00 2·50
a. *Pale yellow-green* 26·00 27·00
454 1d. carmine-red 4·50 60
a. *Bright carmine* 7·00 70
w. Wmk inverted 18·00 10·00
x. Wmk reversed 60·00 28·00
455 1½d. brown-orange 3·00 50
456 3d. chocolate 12·00 14·00
457 6d. violet 13·00 17·00
a. Wmk sideways † £600
x. Wmk inverted — £160
458 1s. orange-red 20·00 48·00
453/8 *Set of 6* 50·00 75·00

The above stamps were placed on sale in London in November, 1919.

2d. **2d.**

TWOPENCE

(68)

69

1922 (Mar). *No. 453 surch with T* **68**.

459	**64**	2d. on ½d. green (R.)	3·75	1·40

(Des and eng W. R. Bock, Typo Govt Printer, Wellington)

1923 (1 Oct)–**25**. *Restoration of Penny Postage.* W **43**. P 14×15.

		(a) De La Rue chalk-surfaced paper with toned gum.		
460	**69**	1d. carmine	3·00	60
		(b) Jones chalk-surfaced paper with white gum.		
461	**69**	1d. carmine (3.24)	9·50	6·50
		a. Wmk sideways	†	£425
		w. Wmk inverted	55·00	45·00
		(c) Cowan unsurfaced paper with very shiny gum.		
462	**69**	1d. carmine-pink (4.25)	32·00	27·00

The paper used for No. 462 is similar to that of Nos. 416/30.

70 Exhibition Buildings

(Des H. L. Richardson. Eng and typo Govt Printer, Wellington)

1925 (17 Nov). *Dunedin Exhibition. Cowan chalk-surfaced paper.* W **43**. P 14×15.

463	**70**	½d. yellow-green/*green*	3·00	12·00
		w. Wmk inverted	£150	£120
464		1d. carmine/*rose*	3·75	5·50
		w. Wmk inverted	£180	£120
465		4d. mauve/*pale mauve*	30·00	75·00
		a. "POSTAGF" at right (R. 1/2, R. 10/1)	£100	£180
463/5 *Set of 3*			32·00	85·00

71

72

(Des H. L. Richardson; plates by B.W. (1d. from sheets), P.B. (1d. from booklets), Royal Mint, London (others). Typo Govt Printer, Wellington)

1926 (12 July)–**34**. W **43**. P 14.

		(a) Jones chalk-surfaced paper with white gum.		
466	**72**	2s. deep blue	50·00	55·00
		w. Wmk inverted	55·00	60·00
467		3s. mauve	85·00	£170
		w. Wmk inverted	£100	£190
		(b) Cowan thick, opaque, chalk-surfaced paper with white gum.		
468	**71**	1d. rose-carmine (15.11.26)	75	20
		a. Imperf (pair)	£190	
		b. Booklet pane of 6 with bars on selvedge (1928)	£110	
		c. Booklet pane of 6 with bars and adverts on selvedge (1928)	90·00	
		dw. Wmk inverted	32·00	26·00
		e. Perf 14×15 (3.27)	65	50
		ea. Booklet pane of 6 with bars and adverts on selvedge (1934)	£100	
		ew. Wmk inverted	60·00	26·00
		ex. Wmk reversed	11·00	
469	**72**	2s. light blue (5.27)	60·00	27·00
470		3s. pale mauve (9.27)	£100	£170
468/70 *Set of 3*			£150	£180
		(c) Wiggins Teape thin, hard, chalk-surfaced paper with white gum.		
471	**71**	1d. rose-carmine (6.30)	21·00	13·00
		w. Wmk inverted	75·00	30·00

No. 468ex exists in a range of colours including scarlet and deep carmine to magenta but we have insufficient evidence to show that these were issued.

Following the reduction of the postage rate to ½d. on 1 June 1932 the firm of R. H. White & Co. Ltd. of Stratford returned a quantity of envelopes stamped with 1d. stamps (No. 468) to the New Plymouth post office who surcharged the stamps "HALFPENNY" in purple using a handstamp. The covers were then returned to the firm for normal use. Similar local surcharges were applied diagonally to 1d. stamps stuck onto postcards or lettercards at Dunedin, Greymouth and Invercargill in blue or at Palmerston North in purple. With the exception of the Greymouth provisional, where forty mint examples were acquired by a stamp dealer, these local surcharges are only found unused, no gum, or used.

73 Nurse

74 Smiling Boy

(Typo Govt Printing Office, Wellington)

1929–30. *Anti-Tuberculosis Fund. T* **73** *and similar design.* W **43**. P 14.

		(a) Inscribed "HELP STAMP OUT TUBERCULOSIS".		
544		1d.+1d. scarlet (11.12.29)	11·00	18·00
		w. Wmk inverted	£250	£180
		(b) Inscribed "HELP PROMOTE HEALTH".		
545		1d.+1d. scarlet (29.10.30)	20·00	40·00

(Des L. C. Mitchell. Dies eng and plates made Royal Mint, London (1d.), Govt Ptg Office, Wellington from W. R. Bock die (2d.). Typo Govt Ptg Office, Wellington)

1931 (31 Oct). *Health Stamps.* W **43** (sideways). P 14½×14.

546	**74**	1d.+1d. scarlet	75·00	75·00
547		2d.+1d. blue	75·00	60·00

75 New Zealand Lake Scenery

FIVE PENCE

(76)

(Des L. C. Mitchell. Plates, Royal Mint, London. Typo Govt Ptg Office)

1931 (10 Nov)–**35**. *Air.* W **43**. P 14×14½.

548	**75**	3d. chocolate	22·00	15·00
		a. Perf 14×15 (4.35)	£130	£425
549		4d. blackish purple	22·00	21·00
550		7d. brown-orange	22·00	9·00
548/50 *Set of 3*			60·00	40·00

1931 (18 Dec). *Air. Surch with T* **76**. W **43**. P 14×14½.

551	**75**	5d. on 3d. green (R.)	10·00	9·50

77 Hygeia, Goddess of Health

78 The Path to Health

(Des R. E. Tripe and W. J. Cooch. Eng H. T. Peat. Recess Govt Printing Office, Wellington)

1932 (18 Nov). *Health Stamp.* W **43**. P 14.

552	**77**	1d.+1d. carmine	20·00	27·00
		w. Wmk inverted	£250	£130
		x. Wmk reversed	†	£300

(Des J. Berry. Eng H. T. Peat. Recess Govt Printing Office, Wellington)

1933 (8 Nov). *Health Stamp.* W **43**. P 14.

553	**78**	1d.+1d. carmine	13·00	17·00
		w. Wmk inverted	£190	£130

TRANS-TASMAN
AIR MAIL
"FAITH IN AUSTRALIA."

(79)

80 Crusader

1934 (17 Jan). *Air. T* **75** *in new colour optd with T* **79**. W **43**. P 14×14½.

554	**75**	7d. light blue (B.)	35·00	40·00

(Des J. Berry. Recess D.L.R.)

1934 (25 Oct). *Health Stamp.* W **43** (sideways). P 14×13½.

555	**80**	1d.+1d. carmine	11·00	17·00

81 Collared Grey Fantail

82 Brown Kiwi

83 Maori Woman

84 Maori Carved House

85 Mt. Cook

86 Maori Girl

87 Mitre Peak

88 Striped Marlin

89 Harvesting

90 Tuatara Lizard

91 Maori Panel

92 Parson Bird

93 Capt. Cook at Poverty Bay

94 Mt. Egmont

Die I Die II

"CAPTAIN COQK" (R. 1/4)

(Des J. Fitzgerald (½d., 4d.), C. H. and R. J. G. Collins (1d.) M. Matthews (1½d.), H. W. Young (2d.), L. C. Mitchell (2½d., 3d., 8d., 1s., 3s.), W. J. Cooch and R. E. Tripe (5d.), T. I. Archer (6d.), I. F. Calder (9d.) and I. H. Jenkins (2s.). Litho Waterlow (9d.). Recess D.L.R. (remainder))

1935 (1 May)–**36**. W **43** (sideways on. 8d.).

556	**81**	½d. bright green, P 14×13½	1·75	1·50
		w. Wmk inverted	3·00	4·00
557	**82**	1d. scarlet (Die I), P 14×13½	1·75	1·25
		aw. Wmk inverted	5·50	4·50
		b. Perf 13½×14 (1936)	75·00	55·00
		c. Die II. Perf 14×13½ (1935)	7·50	3·50
		ca. Booklet pane of 6 with adverts on selvedge	60·00	
		cw. Wmk inverted	13·00	4·50
558	**83**	1½d. red-brown, P 14×13½	10·00	16·00
		a. Perf 13½×14 (1935)	6·50	9·00
		ay. Wmk inverted and reversed (2.36)	19·00	28·00
559	**84**	2d. orange, P 14×13½	3·75	1·75
		w. Wmk inverted	£250	85·00
560	**85**	2½d. chocolate and slate, P 13–14×13½	9·00	38·00
		aw. Wmk inverted	25·00	50·00
		b. Perf 13½×14 (11.35)	7·50	23·00
		bx. Wmk reversed	†	£900
561	**86**	3d. brown, P 14×13½	12·00	3·50
		w. Wmk inverted	£600	£250
562	**87**	4d. black and sepia, P 14	3·75	2·50
		w. Wmk inverted	£450	£180
563	**88**	5d. ultramarine, P 13–14×13½	23·00	35·00
		aw. Wmk inverted	†	£250
		b. Perf 13½×14	26·00	45·00
564	**89**	6d. scarlet, P 13½×14	9·00	8·50
		w. Wmk inverted	£325	£120
565	**90**	8d. chocolate, P 14×13½	9·50	15·00
566	**91**	9d. scarlet and black, P 14×14½	11·00	4·50
567	**92**	1s. deep green, P 14×13½	20·00	15·00
		w. Wmk inverted	—	£200
568	**93**	2s. olive-green, P 13–14×13½	45·00	45·00
		a. "CAPTAIN COQK"	£140	
		bw. Wmk inverted	£120	55·00
		c. Perf 13½×14 (1935)	55·00	50·00
		ca. "CAPTAIN COQK"	£150	
569	**94**	3s. chocolate and yellow-brown, P 13–14×13½	17·00	50·00
		a. Perf 13½×14 (11.35)	19·00	50·00
		aw. Wmk inverted	†	£250
		ay. Wmk inverted and reversed (1936)	£350	£375
556/69 *Set of 14*			£150	£190

Some stamps from sheets perforated 14×13½ by De La Rue sometimes show the horizontal perforations nearer 13½.

In the 2½d., 5d., 2s. and 3s. perf 13–14×13½ the horizontal perforations of each stamp are in two sizes, one half of each horizontal side measuring 13 and the other 14.

See also Nos. 577/90 and 630/1.

95 Bell Block Aerodrome

96 King George V and Queen Mary

(Des J. Berry. Eng Stamp Printing Office, Melbourne. Recess Govt Printing Office, Wellington)

1935 (4 May). *Air.* W **43**. P 14.

570	**95**	1d. carmine	1·00	70
		w. Wmk inverted	75·00	45·00
571		3d. violet	5·00	3·00
		w. Wmk inverted	£100	50·00
572		6d. blue	9·50	3·00
		w. Wmk inverted	£120	70·00
570/2 *Set of* 3			14·00	6·00

(Frame by J. Berry. Recess B.W.)

1935 (7 May). *Silver Jubilee.* W **43**. P 11×11½.

573	**96**	½d. green	75	1·00
574		1d. carmine	1·00	80
575		6d. red-orange	18·00	29·00
573/5 *Set of* 3			18·00	29·00

97 "The Key to Health"

98 "Multiple Wmk"

(Des S. Hall. Recess John Ash, Melbourne)

1935 (30 Sept). *Health Stamp.* W **43**. P 11.

576	**97**	1d.+1d. scarlet	2·50	2·75

WATERMARKS. In W **43** the wmk units are in vertical columns widely spaced and the sheet margins are unwatermarked or wmkd "NEW ZEALAND POSTAGE" in large letters.

In W **98** the wmk units are arranged alternately in horizontal rows closely spaced and are continued into the sheet margins.

Stamps with W **98** sideways show the star to the left of NZ, *as seen from the back*. Sideways inverted varieties have the star to right *as seen from the back*.

(Litho Govt Ptg Office, Wellington (9d). Recess Waterlow or D.L.R.(others))

1936–42. W **98**.

577	**81**	½d. bright green, P 14×13½	3·25	10
		w. Wmk inverted	5·50	3·50
578	**82**	1d. scarlet (Die II), P 14×13½ (4.36)	2·50	10
		w. Wmk inverted	7·00	4·50
579	**83**	1½d. red-brown, P 14×13½ (6.36)	12·00	5·50
580	**84**	2d. orange, P 14×13½ (3.36)	30	10
		aw. Wmk inverted	£225	90·00
		b. Perf 12½† (6.41)	6·00	20
		bw. Wmk inverted		
		c. Perf 14 (6.41)	26·00	1·25
		d. Perf 14×15 (6.41)	38·00	22·00
581	**85**	2½d. chocolate and slate, P 13–14×13½	8·50	21·00
		aw. Wmk inverted	35·00	65·00
		b. Perf 14 (11.36)	7·00	1·50
		bw. Wmk inverted	20·00	24·00
		c. Perf 14×13½ (11.42)	75	4·00
582	**86**	3d. brown, P 14×13½	35·00	1·25
		w. Wmk inverted	60·00	50·00
583	**87**	4d. black and sepia, P 14×13½	7·50	70
		aw. Wmk inverted	15·00	17·00
		b. Perf 12½* (1941)	32·00	15·00
		bw. Wmk inverted	†	—
		c. Perf 14, line (1941)	65·00	£110
		d. Perf 14×14½ comb (7.42)	1·00	20
		dw. Wmk inverted	£160	85·00
584	**88**	5d. ultramarine, P 13–14×13½ (8.36)	22·00	3·25
		aw. Wmk inverted	42·00	20·00
		b. Perf 12½*† (7.41)	15·00	4·00
		c. Perf 14×13½ (11.42)	2·00	2·00
		ca. Double print, one albino	£650	
		cw. Wmk inverted	£180	£130
585	**89**	6d. scarlet, P 13½×14 (8.36)	20·00	1·75
		aw. Wmk inverted	48·00	20·00
		b. Perf 12½* (10.41)	3·00	3·75
		c. Perf 14½×14 (6.42)	1·25	20
		cw. Wmk inverted	£350	£275
586	**90**	8d. chocolate, P 14×13½ (wmk sideways)	11·00	4·75
		aw. Wmk sideways inverted	30·00	40·00
		b. Wmk upright (7.39)	4·00	4·75
		bw. Wmk inverted		
		c. Perf 12½* (wmk sideways) (7.41)	3·75	1·50
		d. Perf 14×14½ (wmk sideways) (7.42)	3·75	1·50
		dw. Wmk sideways inverted	—	90·00
587	**91**	9d. red and grey, P 14×15 (wmk sideways)	48·00	3·25
		ay. Wmk sideways inverted and reversed	—	£160
		b. Wmk upright. *Red and grey-black*, P 13½×14 (1.3.38)	55·00	3·25
		bw. Wmk inverted	£140	70·00
588	**92**	1s. deep green, P 14×13½	2·50	70
		aw. Wmk inverted	65·00	42·00
		b. Perf 12½* (11.41)	65·00	23·00
589	**93**	2s. olive-green, P 13–14×13½ (8.36)	38·00	8·00
		a. "CAPTAIN COQK"	75·00	
		bw. Wmk inverted	£350	£170
		c. Perf 13½×14 (3.39)	£300	3·00
		ca. "CAPTAIN COQK"	£325	50·00
		d. Perf 12½*† (7.41)	19·00	9·00
		da. "CAPTAIN COQK"	70·00	
		e. Perf 14×13½ (10.42)	5·50	1·50
		ea. "CAPTAIN COQK"	£130	
		ew. Wmk inverted	—	£180
590	**94**	3s. chocolate and yellow-brown, P 13–14×13½	50·00	9·00
		aw. Wmk inverted	£120	38·00
		b. Perf 12½* (1941)	80·00	50·00
		c. Perf 14×13½ (1942)	3·50	2·75
577/90c *Set of* 14			£110	18·00

*†Stamps indicated with an asterisk were printed and perforated by Waterlow; those having a dagger were printed by D.L.R. and perforated by Waterlow. No. 580d was printed by D.L.R. and perforated by Harrison and No. 583c was printed by Waterlow and perforated by D.L.R. These are all known as "Blitz perfs" because De La Rue were unable to maintain supplies after their works were damaged by enemy action. All the rest, except the 9d., were printed and perforated by D.L.R.

On stamps printed and perforated by De La Rue the perf 14×13½ varies in the sheet and is sometimes nearer 13½. 2d. perf 14×15 is sometimes nearer 14×14½.

2½d., 5d., 2s. and 3s. In perf 13–14×13½ one half the length of each horizontal perforation measures 13 and the other 14. In perf 14×13½ the horizontal perforation is regular.

4d. No. 583c. is line-perf measuring 14 exactly and has a blackish sepia frame. No. 583d is a comb-perf measuring 14×14.3 or 14×14.2 and the frame is a warmer shade.

2s. No. 589c is comb-perf and measures 13.5×13.75.

For 9d. typographed, see Nos. 630/1.

99 N.Z. Soldier at Anzac Cove

100 Wool

101 Butter

102 Sheep

103 Apples

104 Exports

(Des L. C. Mitchell. Recess John Ash, Melbourne)

1936 (27 Apr). *Charity. 21st Anniv of "Anzac" Landing at Gallipoli.* W **43**. P 11.

591	**99**	½d.+½d. green	75	1·75
592		1d.+1d. scarlet	75	1·40

(Des L. C. Mitchell. Recess John Ash, Melbourne)

1936 (1 Oct). *Congress of British Empire Chambers of Commerce, Wellington. Industries Issue. T* **100/104**. W **43** (sideways). P 11½.

593		½d. emerald-green	30	30
594		1d. scarlet	30	20
595		2½d. blue	1·50	8·00
596		4d. violet	1·25	5·50
597		6d. red-brown	2·75	5·00
593/7 *Set of* 5			5·50	17·00

105 Health Camp

106 King George VI and Queen Elizabeth

(Des J. Berry. Recess John Ash, Melbourne)

1936 (2 Nov). *Health Stamp.* W **43** (sideways). P 11.

598	**105**	1d.+1d. scarlet	2·25	3·75

(Recess B.W.)

1937 (13 May). *Coronation.* W **98**. P 14×13½.

599	**106**	1d. carmine	30	10
600		2½d. Prussian blue	80	2·50
601		6d. red-orange	1·10	2·25
599/601 *Set of* 3			2·00	4·25

107 Rock climbing

108 King George VI

108a

(Des G. Bull and J. Berry. Recess John Ash, Melbourne)

1937 (1 Oct). *Health Stamp.* W **43**. P 11.

602	**107**	1d.+1d. scarlet	3·25	3·75

Broken ribbon flaw (R. 6/6 of Pl 8)

(Des W. J. Cooch. Recess B.W.)

1938–44. W **98**. P 14×13½.

603	**108**	½d. green (1.3.38)	7·50	10
		w. Wmk inverted	17·00	3·25
604		½d. orange-brown (10.7.41)	20	40
		w. Wmk inverted		
605		1d. scarlet (1.7.38)	5·00	10
		a. Broken ribbon	70·00	
		w. Wmk inverted	17·00	3·25
606		1d. green (21.7.41)	20	10
		w. Wmk inverted	60·00	23·00
607	**108a**	1½d. purple-brown (26.7.38)	26·00	3·25
		w. Wmk inverted	38·00	5·00
608		1½d. scarlet (1.2.44)	20	80
		w. Wmk inverted	—	70·00
609		3d. blue (26.9.41)	20	10
		w. Wmk inverted	—	90·00
603/9 *Set of* 7			35·00	4·00

For other values see Nos. 680/9.

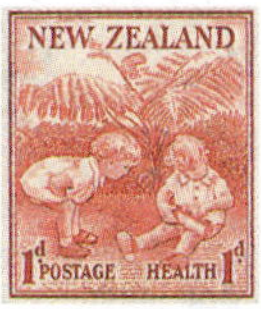
109 Children playing

110 Beach Ball

(Des J. Berry. Recess B.W.)

1938 (1 Oct). *Health Stamp.* W **98**. P 14×13½.

610	**109**	1d.+1d. scarlet	6·50	3·25

(Des S. Hall. Recess Note Printing Branch, Commonwealth Bank of Australia, Melbourne)

1939 (16 Oct). *Health Stamps. Surcharged with new value.* W **43**. P 11.

611	**110**	1d. on ½d.+½d. green	4·75	4·50
612		2d. on 1d.+1d. scarlet	5·50	4·50

111 Arrival of the Maoris, 1350

112 *Endeavour*, Chart of N.Z. and Capt. Cook

113 British Monarchs

114 Tasman with his ship and chart

115 Signing Treaty of Waitangi, 1840

116 Landing of immigrants, 1840

117 Road, rail, sea and air transport

118 H.M.S. *Britomar* at Akaroa, 1840

119 *Dunedin* and "frozen mutton route" to London

120 Maori council

121 Gold mining in 1861 and 1940

122 Giant Kauri tree

(Des L. C. Mitchell (½d., 3d., 4d.); J. Berry (others). Recess B.W.)

1940 (2 Jan–8 Mar). *Centenary of Proclamation of British Sovereignty. T* **111/122**. W **98**. P 14×13½ (2½d.), 13½×14 (5d.) or 13½ (others).

613	**111**	½d. blue-green	40	10
614	**112**	1d. chocolate and scarlet	3·00	10
615	**113**	1½d. light blue and mauve	30	60
616	**114**	2d. blue-green and chocolate	1·50	10
617	**115**	2½d. blue-green and blue	2·00	1·00
618	**116**	3d. purple and carmine	3·75	1·25
619	**117**	4d. chocolate and lake	13·00	1·50
620	**118**	5d. pale blue and brown	8·00	3·75
621	**119**	6d. emerald-green and violet	11·00	1·25
622	**120**	7d. black and red	1·75	4·00
623		8d. black and red (8.3)	11·00	3·25
624	**121**	9d. olive-green and orange	7·50	2·00
625	**122**	1s. sage-green and deep green	13·00	3·75
613/25 *Set of* 13			65·00	20·00

1940 (1 Oct). *Health Stamps. As T* **110**, *but without extra surcharge.* W **43**. P 11.

626	**110**	1d. +½d. blue-green	11·00	14·00
627		2d. +1d. brown-orange	11·00	14·00

1ᴰ 1ᴰ ■ ■ (123)   2ᴰ Inserted "2"   1941 (124)

1941. *Nos. 603 and 607 surch as T* **123**.

628	**108**	1d. on ½d. green (1.5.41)	1·75	10
629	**108a**	2d. on 1½d. purple-brown (4.41)	1·75	10
		a. Inserted "2"	£550	£325

The surcharge on No. 629 has only one figure, at top left, and there is only one square to obliterate the original value at bottom right.

The variety "Inserted 2" occurs on the 10th stamp, 10th row. It is identified by the presence of remnants of the damaged "2", and by the spacing of "2" and "D" which is variable and different from the normal.

(Typo Govt Printing Office, Wellington)

1941. *As T* **91**, *but smaller (17½×20½ mm). Chalk-surfaced paper.* P 14×15.

(a) W **43**.

630	**91**	9d. scarlet and black (5.41)	95·00	30·00
		w. Wmk inverted	†	£275

(b) W **98**.

631	**91**	9d. scarlet and black (29.9.41)	3·75	4·00
		w. Wmk inverted	£300	£200

1941 (4 Oct). *Health Stamps. Nos. 626/7 optd with T* **124**.

632	**110**	1d. +½d. blue-green	50	2·25
633		2d. +1d. brown-orange	50	2·25

125 Boy and Girl on Swing

126 Princess Margaret

127 Queen Elizabeth II as Princess

(Des S. Hall. Recess Note Printing Branch, Commonwealth Bank of Australia, Melbourne)

1942 (1 Oct). *Health Stamps.* W **43**. P 11.

634	**125**	1d. +½d. blue-green	30	1·25
635		2d. +1d. orange-red	30	1·25

(Des J. Berry. Recess B.W.)

1943 (1 Oct). *Health Stamps. T* **126/7**. W **98**. P 12.

636	1d. +½d. green	20	1·50
	a. Imperf between (vert pair)	£9000	
637	2d. +1d. red-brown	20	25
	a. Imperf between (vert pair)	£12000	£12000

✤ TENPENCE ✤
(128)

1944 (1 May). *No. 615 surch with T* **128**.

662	10d. on 1½d. light blue and mauve	15	30

129 Queen Elizabeth II as Princess and Princess Margaret

130 Statue of Peter Pan, Kensington Gardens

(Recess B.W.)

1944 (9 Oct). *Health Stamps.* W **98**. P 13½.

663	**129**	1d. +½d. green	30	40
664		2d. +1d. blue	30	30

(Des J. Berry. Recess B.W.)

1945 (1 Oct). *Health Stamps.* W **98**. P 13½.

665	**130**	1d. +½d. green and buff	15	20
		w. Wmk inverted	65·00	65·00
666		2d. +1d. carmine and buff	15	20
		w. Wmk inverted	£160	85·00

131 Lake Matheson

132 King George VI and Parliament House, Wellington

133 St. Paul's Cathedral

134 The Royal Family

135 R.N.Z.A.F. badge and aircraft

136 Army badge, tank and plough

137 Navy badge, H.M.N.Z.S. *Achilles* (cruiser) and *Dominion Monarch* (liner)

138 N.Z. coat of arms, foundry and farm

139 "St. George" (Wellington College War Memorial Window)

Printer's guide mark (R. 12/3)

Completed rudder (R. 2/4 of Pl 42883 and R. 3/2 of Pl 42796)

140 Southern Alps and Franz Joseph Glacier

141 National Memorial Campanile

Trailing aerial (R. 8/1 of Pl 42794)

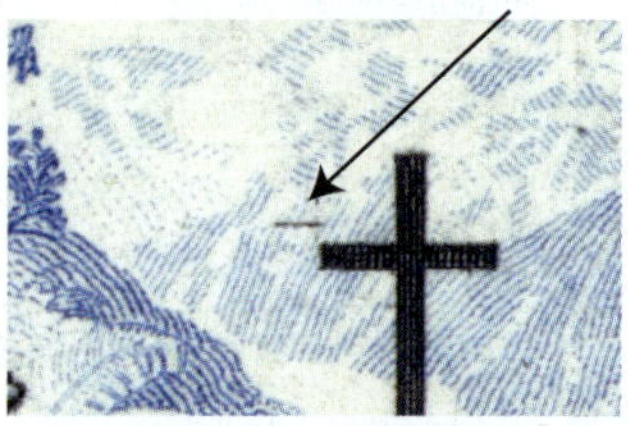

Guide mark (R. 3/3 of Pl 42723)

(Des J. Berry. Photo Harrison (1½d. and 1s.). Recess B.W. (1d. and 2d.) and Waterlow (others))

1946 (1 Apr). *Peace issue. T* **131/41**. W **98** (sideways on 1½d.). P 13 (1d., 2d.), 14×14½ (1½d., 1s.), 13½ (others).

667	**131**	½d. green and brown	20	65
		a. Printer's guide mark	18·00	
		w. Wmk inverted	80·00	50·00
668	**132**	1d. green	10	10
		w. Wmk inverted	50·00	30·00
669	**133**	1½d. scarlet	10	50
		w. Wmk sideways inverted	10	50
670	**134**	2d. purple	15	10
671	**135**	3d. ultramarine and grey	30	15
		a. Completed rudder	11·00	
		b. Ultramarine omitted		
672	**136**	4d. bronze-green and orange	20	20
		w. Wmk inverted	£140	55·00
673	**137**	5d. green and ultramarine	75	1·50
		a. Trailing aerial	18·00	
674	**138**	6d. chocolate and vermilion	15	30
675	**139**	8d. black and carmine	15	30
676	**140**	9d. blue and black	15	30
		a. Guide mark	18·00	
677	**141**	1s. grey-black	80	40
667/77 *Set of* 11			2·75	3·75

Only one example of No. 671b is known. It was caused by a paper fold.

142 Soldier helping Child over Stile

Feathers in hat (R. 8/8 of Pl 43010)

(Des J. Berry. Recess Waterlow)

1946 (24 Oct). *Health Stamps.* W **98**. P 13½.

678	**142**	1d. +½d. green and orange-brown	15	15
		a. *Yellow-green and orange-brown*	4·50	5·50
		w. Wmk inverted	42·00	32·00
679		2d. +1d. chocolate and orange-brown	15	15
		a. Feathers in hat	20·00	20·00

144 King George VI

145 Statue of Eros

Plate 1

Plate 2

(Des W. J. Cooch. Recess *T* **108a**, B.W.; *T* **144**, D.L.R.)

1947 (1 May)–**52**. W **98** (sideways on "shilling" values).

(a) P 14×13½.

680	**108a**	2d. orange	30	10
		w. Wmk inverted	£160	£160
681		4d. bright purple	80	1·00
682		5d. slate	1·00	1·00
683		6d. carmine	1·00	10
		w. Wmk inverted	£120	38·00
684		8d. violet	1·00	1·25
685		9d. purple-brown	2·00	60
		w. Wmk inverted	48·00	15·00
		(b) P 14.		
686	**144**	1s. red-brown and carmine (Plate 1)	2·00	1·50
		aw. Wmk sideways inverted	16·00	10·00
		b. Wmk upright (Plate 1)	50	80
		c. Wmk upright (Plate 2) (1950)	2·25	1·25
		cw. Wmk inverted	80·00	24·00
687		1s.3d. red-brown and blue (Plate 2)	1·50	1·25
		aw. Wmk sideways inverted	14·00	6·50
		b. Wmk upright (14.1.52)	2·25	4·50
		bw. Wmk inverted	†	—
688		2s. brown-orange and green (Plate 1)	4·25	2·50
		aw. Wmk sideways inverted	18·00	13·00
		b. Wmk upright (Plate 1)	6·00	11·00
689		3s. red-brown and grey (Plate 2)	4·50	3·50
		w. Wmk sideways inverted	35·00	17·00
680/9 *Set of* 10			15·00	11·00

In head-plate 2 the diagonal lines of the background have been strengthened and result in the upper corners and sides appearing more deeply shaded.

(Des J. Berry. Recess Waterlow)

1947 (1 Oct). *Health Stamps.* W **98** (sideways). P 13½.

690	**145**	1d. +½d. green	15	15
		w. Wmk sideways inverted	60·00	50·00
691		2d. +1d. carmine	15	15
		w. Wmk sideways inverted	80·00	75·00

146 Port Chalmers, 1848

147 Cromwell, Otago

148 First Church, Dunedin

149 University of Otago

(Des J. Berry. Recess B.W.)

1948 (23 Feb). *Centennial of Otago. T* **146/9**. W **98** (sideways on 3d.). P 13½.

692	1d. blue and green	25	35
	w. Wmk inverted	60·00	55·00
693	2d. green and brown	25	35
694	3d. purple	30	60
695	6d. black and rose	30	60
	w. Wmk inverted	—	£200
692/5 *Set of* 4		1·00	1·75

150 Boy Sunbathing and Children Playing

151 Nurse and Child

(Des E. Linzell. Recess B.W.)

1948 (1 Oct). *Health Stamps.* W **98**. P 13½.

696	**150**	1d. +½d. blue and green	15	20
		w. Wmk inverted	65·00	35·00
697		2d. +1d. purple and scarlet	15	20

1949 ROYAL VISIT ISSUE. Four stamps were prepared to commemorate this event: 2d. Treaty House, Waitangi; 3d. H.M.S. *Vanguard*; 5d. Royal portraits; 6d. Crown and sceptre. The visit did not take place and the stamps were destroyed, although a few examples of the 3d. later appeared on the market. A similar set was prepared in 1952, but was, likewise, not issued.

(Des J. Berry. Photo Harrison)

1949 (3 Oct). *Health Stamps.* W **98**. P 14×14½.

698	**151**	1d. +½d. green	25	20
699		2d. +1d. ultramarine	25	20
		a. No stop below "D" of "1D." (R. 1/2)	7·00	18·00

1½d.

POSTAGE

(152)

153 Queen Elizabeth II and Prince Charles

1950 (28 July). *As Type* F **6**, *but without value, surch with T* **152**. *Chalk-surfaced paper.* W **98** (inverted). P 14.

700	F **6**	1½d. carmine	40	30
		w. Wmk upright	3·50	4·25

(Des J. Berry and R. S. Phillips. Photo Harrison)

1950 (2 Oct). *Health Stamps.* W **98**. P 14×14½.

701	**153**	1d. +½d. green	25	20
		w. Wmk inverted	5·00	5·00
702		2d. +1d. plum	25	20
		w. Wmk inverted	55·00	55·00

154 Christchurch Cathedral

155 Cairn on Lyttleton Hills

156 John Robert Godley

157 Canterbury University College

158 Aerial view of Timaru

(Des L. C. Mitchell (2d.), J. A. Johnstone (3d.) and J. Berry (others). Recess B.W.)

1950 (20 Nov). *Centennial of Canterbury, N.Z. T* **154/8**. W **98** (sideways on 1d. and 3d.). P 13½.

703	1d. green and blue	50	65
704	2d. carmine and orange	50	65
705	3d. dark blue and blue	50	85
706	6d. brown and blue	60	85
707	1s. reddish purple and blue	60	1·10
703/7 *Set of* 5		2·40	3·50

159 "Takapuna" class Yachts

(Des J. Berry and R. S. Phillips. Recess B.W.)

1951 (1 Nov). *Health Stamps.* W **98**. P 13½.

708	**159**	1½d. +½d. scarlet and yellow	30	1·00
709		2d. +1d. deep green and yellow	30	25
		w. Wmk inverted	55·00	65·00

160 Princess Anne

161 Prince Charles

3D

(162)

(From photographs by Marcus Adams. Photo Harrison)

1952 (1 Oct). *Health Stamps.* W **98**. P 14×14½.

710	**160**	1½d. +½d. carmine-red	15	30
711	**161**	2d. +1d. brown	15	20

1952–53. *Nos.* 604 *and* 606 *surch as T* **162**.

712	**108**	1d. on ½d. brown-orange (11.9.53)	20	1·00
		a. "D" omitted	†	—
713		3d. on 1d. green (12.12.52*)	10	10

*Earliest known date used.

163 Buckingham Palace

164 Queen Elizabeth II

(Des L. C. Mitchell (1s.6d.), J. Berry (others). Recess D.L.R. (2d., 4d.), Waterlow (1s.6d.) Photo Harrison (3d., 8d.))

1953 (25 May). *Coronation. T* **163/4** *and similar designs.* W **98**. P 13 (2d., 4d.), 13½ (1s.6d.) or 14×14½ (3d., 8d.).

714	2d. deep bright blue	30	30
715	3d. brown	30	10
716	4d. carmine	1·25	2·50
717	8d. slate-grey	80	1·60
718	1s.6d. purple and ultramarine	2·00	2·75
714/18 *Set of* 5		4·25	6·50

Designs: *Horiz (as T* **163**)—4d. Coronation State Coach; 1s.6d. St. Edward's Crown and Royal Sceptre. *Vert* (*as T* **164**)—8d. Westminster Abbey.

168 Girl Guides

169 Boy Scouts

(Des J. Berry. Photo Harrison)

1953 (7 Oct). *Health Stamps.* W **98**. P 14×14½.

719	**168**	1½d. +½d. blue	15	10
720	**169**	2d .+1d. deep yellow-green	15	40
		a. Imperf 3 sides (block of 4)	£2000	

No. 720a shows the left-hand vertical pair imperforate at right and the right-hand pair imperforate at left, top and bottom.

170 Queen Elizabeth II

171 Queen Elizabeth II and Duke of Edinburgh

(Des L. C. Mitchell. Recess Waterlow)

1953 (9 Dec). *Royal Visit.* W **98**. P 13×14 (3d.) or 13½ (4d.).

721	**170**	3d. dull purple	10	10
		w. Wmk inverted	—	55·00
722	**171**	4d. deep ultramarine	10	60

172

173 Queen Elizabeth II

174

Die I

Die II

(Des L. C. Mitchell (T **172/3**), J. Berry (T **174**). Recess D.L.R. (T **173**), B.W. (others))

1953 (15 Dec)–**59**. W **98**. P 14×13½ (T **172**), 14 (T **173**) or 13½ (T **174**).

723	**172**	½d. slate-black (1.3.54)	15	30
724		1d. orange (1.3.54)	15	10
		w. Wmk inverted	40	1·25
725		1½d. brown-lake	20	10
		w. Wmk inverted	†	£350
726		2d. bluish green (1.3.54)	20	10
		w. Wmk inverted	†	£350
727		3d. vermilion (1.3.54)	20	10
		w. Wmk inverted	40	1·25
728		4d. blue (1.3.54)	40	50
729		6d. purple (1.3.54)	70	1·60
		w. Wmk inverted	£375	£200
730		8d. carmine (1.3.54)	60	60
		w. Wmk inverted	£700	£475
731	**173**	9d. brown and bright green (1.3.54)	60	60
		w. Wmk inverted	£375	£190
732		1s. black and carmine-red (Die 1) (1.3.54)	65	10
		aw. Wmk inverted	£375	£275
		b. Die II (1958)	£120	17·00
733		1s.6d. black and bright blue (1.3.54)	1·25	60
		aw. Wmk inverted	£325	£225
733*b*		1s.9d. black and red-orange (1.7.57)	5·50	1·50
		bw. Wmk inverted	£475	£300
		c. White opaque paper (2.2.59)	5·00	1·50
733*d*	**174**	2s.6d. brown (1.7.57)	18·00	8·00
734		3s. bluish green (1.3.54)	12·00	50
		w. Wmk inverted	£600	£375
735		5s. carmine (1.3.54)	19·00	4·50
736		10s. deep ultramarine (1.3.54)	42·00	19·00
723/36 *Set of* 16			90·00	35·00

1s. Dies I and II. The two dies of the Queen's portrait differ in the shading on the sleeve at right. The long lines running upwards from left to right are strong in Die I and weaker in Die II. In the upper part of the shading the fine cross-hatching is visible in Die I only between the middle two of the four long lines, but in Die II it extends clearly across all four lines.

In the lower part of the shading the strength of the long lines in Die I makes the cross-hatching appear subdued, whereas in Die II the weaker long lines make the cross-hatching more prominent.

Centre plates 1A, 1B and 2B are Die I; 3A and 3B are Die II.

For stamps as T **172** but with larger figures of value see Nos. 745/51.

WHITE OPAQUE PAPER. A new white opaque paper first came into use in August 1958. It is slightly thicker than the paper previously used, but obviously different in colour (white, against cream) and opacity (the previous paper being relatively transparent).

175 Young Climber and Mts Aspiring and Everest

(Des J. Berry. Recess; vignette litho B.W.)

1954 (4 Oct). *Health Stamps*. W **98**. P 13½.

737	**175**	1½d. +½d. sepia and deep violet	15	30
738		2d. + 1d. sepia and blue-black	15	30

176 Maori Mail Carrier

177 Queen Elizabeth II

178 Douglas DC-3 Airliner

(Des R. M. Conly (2d.), J. Berry (3d.), A. G. Mitchell (4d.). Recess D.L.R.)

1955 (18 July). *Centenary of First New Zealand Postage Stamps*. W **98**. P 14 (2d.) 14×14½ (3d.) or 13 (4d.)

739	**176**	2d. sepia and deep green	10	10
		w. Wmk inverted	—	£150
740	**177**	3d. brown-red	10	10
741	**178**	4d. black and bright blue	60	1·00
739/41 *Set of* 3			70	1·00

179 Children's Health Camps Federation Emblem

180

(Des E. M. Taylor. Recess B.W.)

1955 (3 Oct). *Health Stamps*. W **98** (sideways). P 13½×13.

742	**179**	1½d. +½d. sepia and orange-brown	10	60
743		2d. +1d. red-brown and green	10	35
744		3d. +1d. sepia and deep rose-red	15	15
		a. Centre omitted	£12000	
742/4 *Set of* 3			30	1·00

1955–59. *As Nos. 724/30 but larger figures of value with stars omitted from lower right corner and new colour* (8d.).

745	**180**	1d. orange (12.7.56)	50	10
		aw. Wmk inverted	1·50	2·25
		b. White opaque paper (2.6.59)	50	20
		bw. Wmk inverted	1·50	3·00
746		1½d. brown-lake (1.12.55)	60	60
747		2d. bluish green (19.3.56)	40	10
		a. White opaque paper (10.11.59)	55	10
748		3d. vermilion (1.5.56)	1·50	1·50
		aw. Wmk inverted	1·50	1·50
		b. White opaque paper (20.6.59)	50	10
		bw. Wmk inverted	2·00	3·00
749		4d. blue (3.2.58)	1·00	80
		a. White opaque paper (9.9.59)	2·00	1·50
750		6d. purple (20.10.55)	10·00	20
751		8d. chestnut (*white opaque paper*) (1.12.59)	6·50	8·00
745/51 *Set of* 7			18·00	8·50

See note *re* white opaque paper after No. 736.

181 "The Whalers of Foveaux Strait"

183 Takahe

(Des E. R. Leeming (2d.), L. C. Mitchell (3d.), M. R. Smith (8d.). Recess D.L.R.)

1956 (16 Jan). *Southland Centennial. T* **181**, **183** *and similar design*. W **98**. P 13½×13 (8d.) or 13×12½ (others)

752	2d. deep blue-green	30	15
753	3d. sepia	10	10
	w. Wmk inverted	—	£120
754	8d. slate-violet and rose-red	1·25	1·75
752/4 *Set of* 3		1·50	1·75

Design: Horiz—3d. "Farming".

184 Children picking Apples

(Des L. C. Mitchell, after photo by J. F. Louden. Recess B.W.)

1956 (24 Sept). *Health Stamps*. W **98**. P 13×13½.

755	**184**	1½d. +½d. purple-brown	15	70
		a. Blackish brown	2·00	6·50
756		2d. +1d. blue-green	15	55
757		3d. +1d. claret	15	15
755/7 *Set of* 3			40	1·25

185 New Zealand Lamb and Map

186 Lamb, *Dunedin* and *Port Brisbane* (refrigerated freighter)

(Des M. Goaman. Photo Harrison)

1957 (15 Feb). *75th Anniv of First Export of N.Z. Lamb*. W **98** (sideways inverted on 4d.). P 14×14½ (4d.) or 14½×14 (8d.).

758	**185**	4d. blue	50	1·00
		w. Wmk sideways	12·00	15·00
759	**186**	8d. deep orange-red	75	1·25

187 Sir Truby King

(Des M. R. Smith. Recess B.W.)

1957 (14 May). *50th Anniv of Plunket Society*. W **98**. P 13.

760	**187**	3d. bright carmine-red	10	10
		w. Wmk inverted	£100	

188 Life-savers in Action

189 Children on Seashore

(Des L. Cutten (2d.), L. C. Mitchell (3d.). Recess Waterlow)

1957 (25 Sept). *Health Stamps*. W **98** (sideways). P 13½.

761	**188**	2d. +1d. black and emerald	15	70
762	**189**	3d. +1d. ultramarine and rose-red	15	10
MS762*b*		Two sheets each 112×96 mm with Nos. 761 and 762 in blocks of 6 (2×3).. *Per pair*	9·00	25·00
MS762*c*		As last but with wmk upright .... *Per pair*	12·00	42·00

(190)

191 Girls' Life Brigade Cadet

192 Boys' Brigade Bugler

1958 (6 Jan–Mar). *No. 746 surch as T* **190**.

763	**180**	2d. on 1½d. brown-lake	70	10
		a. Smaller dot in surch	15	10
		b. Error. Surch on No. 725 (3.58)	£120	£160

Diameter of dot on No. 763 is 4¼ mm; on No. 763a 3¾ mm.

Forgeries of No. 763b are known.

(Des J. Berry. Photo Harrison)

1958 (20 Aug). *Health Stamps*. W **98**. P 14×14½.

764	**191**	2d. +1d. green	20	40
765	**192**	3d. +1d. blue	20	40
MS765*a*		Two sheets each 104×124 mm with Nos. 764/5 in blocks of 6 (3×2) .... *Per pair*	10·00	22·00

193 Sir Charles Kingsford-Smith and Fokker F.VIIa/3m *Southern Cross*

194 Seal of Nelson

(Des J. E. Lyle. Eng F. D. Manley. Recess Commonwealth Bank of Australia Note Ptg Branch)

1958 (27 Aug). *30th Anniv of First Air Crossing of the Tasman Sea*. W **98** (sideways). P 14×14½.

766	**193**	6d. deep ultramarine	50	75

(Des M. J. Macdonald. Recess B.W.)

1958 (29 Sept). *Centenary of City of Nelson*. W **98**. P 13½×13.

767	**194**	3d. carmine	10	10

195 "Pania" Statue, Napier

196 Australian Gannets on Cape Kidnappers

(Des M. R. Smith (2d.), J. Berry (3d.), L. C. Mitchell (8d.). Photo Harrison)

1958 (3 Nov). *Centenary of Hawke's Bay Province. T* **195/6** *and similar design*. W **98** (sideways on 3d.). P 14½×14 (3d.) or 13½×14½ (others).

768	2d. yellow-green	10	10
769	3d. blue	30	10
770	8d. red-brown	70	1·50
768/70 *Set of* 3		1·00	1·50

Design: Vert—8d. Maori sheep-shearer.

197 "Kiwi" Jamboree Badge

198 Careening H.M.S. *Endeavour* at Ship Cove

(Des Mrs. S. M. Collins. Recess B.W.)

1959 (5 Jan). *Pan-Pacific Scout Jamboree, Auckland*. W **98**. P 13½×13.

771	**197**	3d. sepia and carmine	30	10

(Des G. R. Bull and G. R. Smith. Photo Harrison)

1959 (2 Mar). *Centenary of Marlborough Province. T* **198** *and similar horiz designs*. W **98** (sideways). P 14½×14.

772	2d. green	30	10
773	3d. deep blue	30	10
774	8d. light brown	1·25	2·25
772/4 *Set of* 3		1·60	2·25

Designs:—3d. Shipping wool, Wairau Bar, 1857; 8d. Salt industry, Grassmere.

201 Red Cross Flag

(Photo Harrison)

1959 (3 June). *Red Cross Commemoration.* W **98** (sideways). P 14½×14.

775 **201** 3d. +1d. red and ultramarine 20 10
a. Red Cross omitted £1700

202 Grey Teal

203 New Zealand Stilt

(Des Display Section, G.P.O. Photo Harrison)

1959 (16 Sept). *Health Stamps.* W **98** (sideways). P 14×14½.

776 **202** 2d. +1d. greenish yellow, olive and rose-red 50 65
777 **203** 3d. +1d. black, pink and light blue 50 65
a. Pink omitted £120
bw. Wmk sideways inverted .... 18·00 20·00

MS777*c* Two sheets, each 95×109 mm with Nos. 776/7 in blocks of 6 (3×2) ....*Per pair* 9·00 26·00

204 "The Explorer"

205 "The Gold Digger"

(Des G. R. Bull and G. R. Smith. Photo Harrison)

1960 (16 May). *Centenary of Westland Province. T* **204/5** *and similar vert design.* W **98**. P 14×14½.

778 2d. deep dull green 20 10
779 3d. orange-red 30 10
780 8d. grey-black .... 90 3·00
778/80 *Set of* 3 .... 1·25 3·00

Design:—8d. "The Pioneer Woman".

207 Manuka (Tea Tree)

214 National Flag

216 Rainbow Trout

219 Taniwha (Maori Rock Drawing)

220 Butter Making

221 Tongariro National Park and Château

221a Tongariro National Park and Château

(Des Harrison (½d.), G. F. Fuller (1d., 3d., 6d.), A. G. Mitchell (2d., 4d., 5d., 8d., 3s., 10s., £1), P.O. Public Relations Division (7d.), P.O. Publicity Section (9d.), J. Berry (1s., 1s.6d.), R. E. Barwick (1s.3d.), J. C. Boyd (1s.9d.), D. F. Kee (2s.), L. C. Mitchell (2s.6d., 5s.). Photo D.L.R. (½d., 1d., 2d., 3d., 4d., 6d., 8d.) or Harrison (others))

1960 (11 July)–**66**. *T* **207**, **214**, **216**, **219/21a** *and similar designs. Chalk-surfaced paper (2½d., 5d., 7d., 1s.9d. (No. 795), 3s. (No. 799).* W **98** (sideways on 5d., 1s.3d., 1s.6d., 2s.6d., 3s. and 10s. or sideways inverted (2½d.)). P 14×14½ (1s.3d., 1s.6d., 2s., 5s., £1) or 14½×14 (others).

781 **207** ½d. grey, green and cerise (1.9.60) 10 10
a. Grey omitted £250 £200
b. Green omitted £325

782 – 1d. orange, green, lake and brown (1.9.60) 10 10
a. Orange omitted £475 £325
b. Coil. Perf 14½×13. Wmk sideways (11.63) .... 1·40 2·75
c. Chalk-surfaced paper (1965?) 10 75

783 – 2d. carmine, black, yellow and green 10 10
a. Black omitted £425
b. Yellow omitted £450

784 – 2½d. red, yellow, black and green (1.11.61) .... 1·00 10
a. Red omitted £650
b. Yellow omitted £250
c. Green omitted £250
d. Red and green omitted £750
w. Wmk sideways .... – 45·00

785 – 3d. yellow, green, yellow-brown and deep greenish blue (1.9.60) 30 10
a. Yellow omitted £170 £130
b. Green omitted £170 £130
c. Yellow-brown omitted £160
e. Coil. Perf 14½×13. Wmk sideways (3.10.63) .... 1·40 2·75
f. Chalk-surfaced paper (1965?) .... 30 1·00
fa. Yellow-brown omitted £350

786 – 4d. purple, buff, yellow-green and light blue 40 10
a. Purple omitted £400
b. Buff omitted £600
d. Chalk-surfaced paper (1965?) .... £700 12·00

787 – 5d. yellow, deep green, black and violet (14.5.62) .... 1·25 10
a. Yellow omitted £350
w. Wmk sideways inverted .... £120 45·00

788 – 6d. lilac, green and deep bluish green (1.9.60) 50 10
a. No wmk .... 30·00
ab. Lilac omitted £375
ac. Green omitted £375
c. Chalk-surfaced paper (1966?) .... 65 3·00

788*d* – 7d. red, green, yellow and pale red (16.3.66) .... 1·00 1·40
dw. Wmk inverted .... 4·50 8·50

789 – 8d. rose-red, yellow, green and grey (1.9.60) 40 10

790 **214** 9d. red and ultramarine (1.9.60) 40 10
a. Red omitted £325

791 – 1s. brown and deep green 30 10

792 **216** 1s.3d. carmine, sepia and bright blue .... 2·50 60
a. Carmine omitted £550
b. Carmine, sepia and greyish blue .... 2·00 25
w. Wmk sideways inverted £200 £110

793 – 1s.6d. olive-green and orange-brown 75 10

794 – 1s.9d. bistre-brown .... 10·00 15

795 – 1s.9d. orange-red, blue, green and yellow (4.11.63) .... 3·00 1·00
a. Wmk sideways £600
w. Wmk inverted .... † £550

796 **219** 2s. black and orange-buff .... 2·50 10
a. Chalk-surfaced paper (1966) .... 2·00 2·75

797 **220** 2s.6d. yellow and light brown .... 1·75 1·00
a. Yellow omitted £600 £350

798 **221** 3s. blackish brown .... 23·00 1·00

799 **221a** 3s. bistre, blue and green (1.4.64) .... 2·50 1·75
w. Wmk sideways inverted .... 55·00 55·00

800 – 5s. blackish green .... 2·25 80
a. Chalk-surfaced paper (1966) .... 1·50 5·00

801 – 10s. steel-blue .... 4·50 3·25
a. Chalk-surfaced paper (1966) .... 4·00 11·00

802 – £1 deep magenta .... 9·50 7·50

781/802 *Set of* 23 .... 55·00 16·00

Designs: *Vert* (*as T* **207**)—1d. Karaka; 2d. Kowhai Ngutu-kaka (Kaka Beak); 2½d. Titoki; 3d. Kowhai; 4d. Puarangi (Hibiscus); 5d. Matua Tikumu (Mountain Daisy); 6d. Pikiarero (Clematis); 7d. Koromiko; 8d. Rata. (*As T* **216**)—1s.6d. Tiki. (*As T* **219**)—5s. Sutherland Falls; £1 Pohutu Geyser. *Horiz* (*as T* **214**)—1s. Timber industry; 1s.9d. Aerial top dressing. (*As T* **221**)—10s. Tasman Glacier.

Nos. 782b and 785e were replaced by coils with upright watermark perf 14½×14 in 1966.

CHALKY PAPER. The chalk-surfaced paper is not only whiter but also thicker, making the watermark difficult to see. Examples of the 4d. value can be found on a thick surfaced paper. These should not be confused with the rare chalk-surfaced printing, No. 786d, which can be identified by its positive reaction to the silver test.

225 Sacred Kingfisher

226 New Zealand Pigeon

(Des Display Section, G.P.O. Recess B.W.)

1960 (10 Aug). *Health Stamps.* W **98**. P 13½.

803 **225** 2d. +1d. sepia and turquoise-blue 50 75
804 **226** 3d. +1d. deep purple-brown and orange 50 75

MS804*b* Two sheets each 95×107 mm with Nos. 803 and 804 in blocks of 6. P 11½×11 ....*Per pair* 26·00 38·00

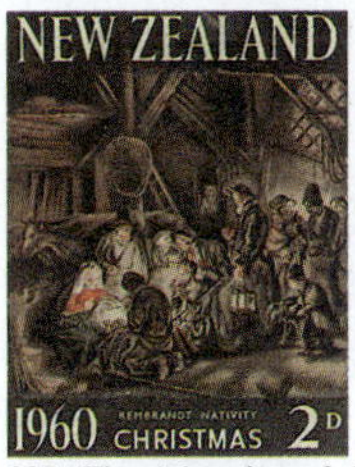

227 "The Adoration of the Shepherds" (Rembrandt)

(Photo Harrison)

1960 (1 Nov). *Christmas.* W **98**. P 12.

805 **227** 2d. red and deep brown/*cream* 15 10
a. Red omitted £350 £375

228 Great Egret

229 New Zealand Falcon

(Des Display Section, G.P.O. Recess B.W.)

1961 (2 Aug). *Health Stamps.* W **98**. P 13½.

806 **228** 2d. +1d. black and purple 50 70
807 **229** 3d. +1d. deep sepia and yellow-green 50 70

MS807*a* Two sheets each 97×121 mm with Nos. 806/7 in blocks of 6 (3×2) ....*Per pair* 26·00 32·00

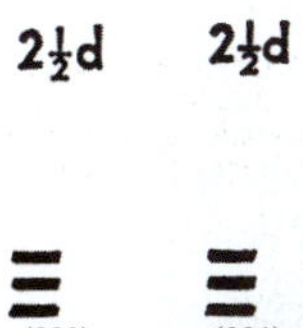

(**230**) (**231**)

232 "Adoration of the Magi" (Dürer)

1961 (1 Sept). *No. 748 surch with T* **230** *(wide setting).*

808 **180** 2½d. on 3d. vermilion 25 15
a. Narrow setting (T **231**) 15 15
b. Pair, wide and narrow .... 16·00 27·00

The difference in the settings is in the overall width of the new value, caused by two different spacings between the "2", "½" and "d".

(Photo Harrison)

1961 (16 Oct). *Christmas.* W **98** (sideways). P 14½×14.

809 **232** 2½d. multicoloured 10 10
w. Wmk sideways inverted .... 60·00 27·00

233 Morse Key and Port Hills, Lyttleton

(Des A. G. Mitchell (3d.) and L. C. Mitchell (8d.). Photo Harrison)

1962 (1 June). *Telegraph Centenary. T* **233** *and similar horiz design.* W **98** (sideways). P 14½×14.

810 3d. sepia and bluish green 10 10
a. Bluish green omitted £1500
811 8d. black and brown-red 90 90
a. Imperf (pair) £1700
b. Black omitted £1200

Design:—8d. Modern teleprinter.

No. 811a comes from a sheet with the two top rows imperforate and the third row imperforate on three sides.

235 Red-fronted Parakeet

236 Tieke Saddleback

(Des Display Section, G.P.O. Photo D.L.R.)

1962 (3 Oct). *Health Stamps.* W **98**. P 15×14.

812 **235** 2½d. +1d. multicoloured 50 70
a. Orange omitted
b. Printed on the gummed side .. £550
w. Wmk inverted .... 80·00 85·00
813 **236** 3d. +1d. multicoloured 50 70
a. Orange omitted £1700

MS813*b* Two sheets each 96×101 mm with Nos. 812/13 in blocks of 6 (3×2) ....*Per pair* 45·00 50·00

No. 812b comes from a miniature sheet.

237 "Madonna in Prayer" (Sassoferrato)

(Photo Harrison)

1962 (15 Oct). *Christmas.* W **98**. P 14½×14.
814 **237** 2½d. multicoloured 10 10

238 Prince Andrew

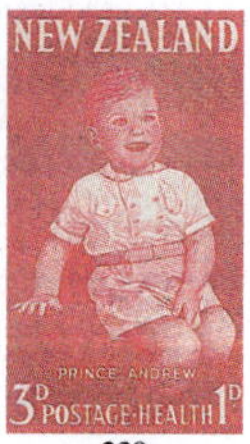

239

(Design after photographs by Studio Lisa, London. Recess D.L.R.)

1963 (7 Aug). *Health Stamps.* W **98**. P 14.
815 **238** 2½d. +1d. dull ultramarine 30 70
a. *Ultramarine* 40 80
b. *Deep blue* 30 40
816 **239** 3d. +1d. carmine 30 10
MS816*a* Two sheets each 93×100 mm with Nos. 815/16 in blocks of 6 (3×2) .... *Per pair* 25·00 40·00

240 "The Holy Family" (Titian)

(Photo Harrison)

1963 (14 Oct). *Christmas.* W **98** (sideways). P 12½.
817 **240** 2½d. multicoloured 10 10
a. Imperf (pair) £250
b. Yellow omitted £300
w. Wmk sideways inverted 40 40

241 Steam Locomotive *Pilgrim* (1863) and Class DG Diesel Locomotive

242 Diesel Express and Mt Ruapehu

(Des Commercial Art Section, N.Z. Railways. Photo D.L.R.)

1963 (25 Nov). *Railway Centenary.* W **98** (sideways on 3d., sideways inverted on 1s.9d). P 14.
818 **241** 3d. multicoloured 40 10
a. Blue (sky) omitted £475
819 **242** 1s.9d. multicoloured .... 1·50 1·50
a. Red (value) omitted £1700

243 "Commonwealth Cable"

(Des P. Morriss. Photo Note Printing Branch, Reserve Bank of Australia)

1963 (3 Dec). *Opening of COMPAC (Trans-Pacific Telephone Cable).* No wmk. P 13½.
820 **243** 8d. red, blue and yellow .... 50 1·25

244 Road Map and Car Steering-wheel

245 Silver Gulls

(Des L. C. Mitchell. Photo Harrison)

1964 (1 May). *Road Safety Campaign.* W **98**. P 15×14.
821 **244** 3d. black, ochre-yellow and blue . 30 10

(Des Display Section G.P.O., after Miss T. Kelly. Photo Harrison)

1964 (5 Aug). *Health Stamps. T* **245** *and similar horiz design. Multicoloured.* W **98**. P 14½.
822 2½d. +1d. Type **245** 40 50
a. Red (beak and legs) omitted £250 £180
w. Wmk inverted .... † £325
823 3d. +1d. Little Penguin 40 50
aw. Wmk inverted £150
MS823*b* Two sheets each 171×84 mm with Nos. 822/3 in blocks of 8 (4×2) .... *Per pair* 48·00 65·00
bw. Wmk inverted (No. 823 only) ....

246 Rev. S. Marsden taking first Christian service at Rangihoua Bay, 1814

7D
POSTAGE
(**247**)

(Des L. C. Mitchell. Photo Harrison)

1964 (12 Oct). *Christmas.* W **98** (sideways). P 14×13½.
824 **246** 2½d. multicoloured 10 10

1964 (14 Dec). *As Type F* **6**, *but without value, surch with T* **247**. W **98**. Unsurfaced paper. P 14×13½.
825 **F 6** 7d. carmine-red .... 50 1·50

248 Anzac Cove

(Des R. M. Conly. Photo Harrison)

1965 (14 Apr). *50th Anniv of Gallipoli Landing. T* **248** *and similar horiz design.* W **98**. P 12½.
826 4d. yellow-brown 10 10
827 5d. green and red 10 60
Design:—5d. Anzac Cove and poppy.

249 I.T.U. Emblem and Symbols

250 Sir Winston Churchill

(Photo Harrison)

1965 (17 May). *I.T.U. Centenary.* W **98**. P 14½×14.
828 **249** 9d. blue and pale chocolate 55 35

(Des P. Morriss from photograph by Karsh. Photo Note Ptg Branch, Reserve Bank of Australia)

1965 (24 May). *Churchill Commemoration.* P 13½.
829 **250** 7d. black, pale grey and light blue 30 50

251 Wellington Provincial Council Building

(Des from painting by L. B. Temple (1867). Photo Harrison)

1965 (26 July). *Centenary of Government in Wellington.* W **98** (sideways). P 14½×14.
830 **251** 4d. multicoloured 20 10

252 Kaka

253 Collared Grey Fantail (after Miss T. Kelly)

(Des Display Section, G.P.O. Photo Harrison)

1965 (4 Aug). *Health Stamps.* W **98**. P 14×14½.
831 **252** 3d. +1d. multicoloured 40 65
w. Wmk inverted .... † 70·00
832 **253** 4d. +1d. multicoloured 40 65
a. Green ("POSTAGE HEALTH" and on leaves) omitted £1000
bw. Wmk inverted .... 55·00 85·00
MS832*c* Two sheets each 100×109 mm with Nos. 831/2 in blocks of 6 (3×2) .... *Per pair* 38·00 48·00
cw. Wmk inverted (No. 831 only) .... † —

254 I.C.Y. Emblem

255 "The Two Trinities" (Murillo)

(Litho D.L.R.)

1965 (28 Sept). *International Co-operation Year.* W **98** (sideways inverted). P 14.
833 **254** 4d. carmine-red and light yellow-olive 20 10
w. Wmk sideways .... 4·25 2·25

(Photo Harrison)

1965 (11 Oct). *Christmas.* W **98**. P 13½×14.
834 **255** 3d. multicoloured 10 10
a. Gold (frame) omitted £1200

256 Arms of New Zealand

259 "Progress" Arrowhead

(Des Display Section, G.P.O. Photo D.L.R.)

1965 (30 Nov). *11th Commonwealth Parliamentary Conference. T* **256** *and similar horiz designs. Multicoloured.* P 14.
835 4d. Type **256** 25 20
a. Blue (incl value) omitted £750
b. Printed on the gummed side £600
836 9d. Parliament House, Wellington and Badge .... 65 1·25
837 2s. Wellington from Mt Victoria .... 4·75 6·50
a. Carmine omitted £700
835/7 *Set of* 3 .... 5·00 7·25

(Des Display Section, G.P.O. Photo Harrison)

1966 (5 Jan). *Fourth National Scout Jamboree, Trentham.* W **98**. P 14×15.
838 **259** 4d. gold and myrtle-green 15 10
a. Gold (arrowhead) omitted £900

260 New Zealand Bell Bird

262 "The Virgin with Child" (Maratta)

(Des Display Section, G.P.O. Photo Harrison)

1966 (3 Aug). *Health Stamps. T* **260** *and similar vert design. Multicoloured.* W **98** (sideways). P 14×14½.
839 3d. +1d. Type **260** 50 75
w. Wmk sideways inverted .... 90·00
840 4d. +1d. Weka Rail 50 75
a. Deep brown (values and date) omitted £1700
w. Wmk sideways inverted .... 90·00
MS841 Two sheets each 107×91 mm. Nos. 839/40 in blocks of 6 (3×2) .... *Per pair* 22·00 50·00
In No. 840a besides the value, "1966" and "Weka" are also omitted and the bird, etc. appears as light brown.

(Photo Harrison)

1966 (3 Oct). *Christmas.* W **98** (sideways). P 14½.
842 **262** 3d. multicoloured 10 10
a. Red omitted £325

263 Queen Victoria and Queen Elizabeth II

264 Half-sovereign of 1867 and Commemorative Dollar Coin

(Des Display Section, G.P.O. Photo Harrison)

1967 (3 Feb). *Centenary of New Zealand Post Office Savings Bank.* W **98** (sideways on 4d.). P 14×14½.
843 **263** 4d. black, gold and maroon 10 10
w. Wmk sideways inverted .... 65·00 23·00

844	**264**	9d. gold, silver, black, light blue and deep green	10	20
		w. Wmk inverted	£500	

(New Currency. 100 cents = 1 New Zealand Dollar)

265 Manuka (Tea Tree)

266 Pohutu Geyser

1967 (10 July). *Decimal Currency. Designs as 1960–66 issue, but with values inscr in decimal currency as T* **265/6**. *Chalky paper.* W **98** (sideways on 8c., 10c., 20c., 50c. and $2). P 13½×14 (½c. to 3c., 5c. and 7c.), 4½×4 (4c., 6c., 8c., 10c., 25c. and $1) or 14×14½ (15c., 20c., 50c. and $2).

845	**265**	½c. pale blue, yellow-green and cerise	10	10
846	–	1c. yellow, carmine, green and light brown (as 1d.)	10	10
		a. Booklet pane. Five stamps plus one printed label	2·25	
847	–	2c. carmine, black, yellow, and green (as 2d.)	10	10
848	–	2½c. yellow, green, yellow-brown and deep bluish green (as 3d.)	10	10
		a. Deep bluish green omitted*	£2500	
		b. Imperf (pair)†	£150	
849	–	3c. purple, buff, yellow-green and light greenish blue (as 4d.)	10	10
850	–	4c. yellow, deep green, black and violet (as 5d.)	30	10
851	–	5c. lilac, yellow-olive and bluish green (as 6d.)	50	50
852	–	6c. red, green, yellow and light pink (as 7d.)	50	1·00
853	–	7c. rose-red, yellow, green and grey (as 8d.)	60	1·00
		w. Wmk inverted		
854	**214**	8c. red and ultramarine	60	60
		a. Red omitted	£750	
855	–	10c. brown and deep green (as 1s.)	60	60
		w. Wmk sideways inverted		
856	–	15c. olive-green and orange-brown (as 1s.6d.)	2·00	1·75
		w. Wmk inverted	3·50	8·00
857	**219**	20c. black and buff	1·00	20
858	**220**	25c. yellow and light brown	1·25	2·00
859	**221a**	30c. olive-yellow, green and greenish blue	1·25	25
		w. Wmk inverted	£100	60·00
860	–	50c. blackish green (as 5s.)	1·75	50
861	–	$1 Prussian blue (as 10s.)	9·00	1·00
		w. Wmk inverted	£200	£120
862	**266**	$2 deep magenta	4·00	6·00
845/62 *Set of* 18			21·00	13·00

*This occurred on one horizontal row of ten, affecting the background colour so that the value is also missing. In the row above and the row below, the colour was partially omitted. The price is for a vertical strip.

The 2½c. value has been seen with the yellow omitted, but only on a used example.

†This comes from a sheet of which the six right-hand vertical rows were completely imperforate and the top, bottom and left-hand margins had been removed.

The 4c., 30c. and 50c. exist with PVA gum as well as gum arabic. No. 859a exists with PVA gum only.

For $4 to $10 in the "Arms" type, see under Postal Fiscal stamps.

For other versions of 15c., 30c. and $2 see Nos. 870/9.

268 Running with Ball

(Des L. C. Mitchell. Photo Harrison)

1967 (2 Aug). *Health Stamps. Rugby Football. T* **268** *and similar multicoloured design.* W **98** (sideways on 2½c.). P 14½×14 (2½c.) or 14×14½ (3c.)

867	2½c. +1c. Type **268**	15	15
868	3c. +1c. Positioning for a place-kick (*horiz*)	15	15
MS869	Two sheets; (a) 76×130 mm (867); (b) 130×76 mm (868). Containing blocks of six ... *Per pair*	23·00	38·00

270 *Kaita* (trawler) and Catch

271 Brown Trout

276 Dairy Farm, Mt Egmont and Butter Consignment

277 Fox Glacier, Westland National Park

(Des Display Section, G.P.O. (7, 8, 10, 18, 20, 25c. and 28c. from photo), R. M. Conly (7½c.). Litho B.W. (7, 8, 18, 20c.) or photo D.L.R. (7½c.) and Harrison (10, 25, 28c.). Others (15c., 30c., $2) as before)

1967–70. *T* **270/1**, **276/7** *and similar designs. Chalky paper (except 7, 8, 18, 20c.).* No wmk (7, 8, 20, 30c.) or W **98** (sideways inverted on 7½c., sideways on 10, 15, 25c., upright on 18, 28c., $2). P 13½ (7, 7½c.), 13×13½ (8, 18, 20c.), 14½×14 (10, 25, 30c.) or 14×14½ (15, 28c., $2).

870	**270**	7c. multicoloured (3.12.69)	1·00	1·00
871	**271**	7½c. multicoloured* (29.8.67)	50	70
		a. Wmk upright (10.68)	50	1·00
872	–	8c. multicoloured (8.7.69)	75	70
873	–	10c. multicoloured (2.4.68)	50	10
		a. Green (background) omitted	£600	
		w. Wmk sideways inverted	†	£1000
874	–	15c. apple-green, myrtle-green and carmine (as No. 856†) (19.3.68)	1·00	1·00
		w. Wmk sideways inverted	†	£130
875	–	18c. multicoloured (8.7.69)	1·00	55
		a. Printed on the gummed side	£500	
876	–	20c. multicoloured (8.7.69)	1·00	20
877	**276**	25c. multicoloured (10.12.68)	1·75	2·00
878	**277**	28c. multicoloured (30.7.68)	60	10
		aw. Wmk inverted	†	£1000
878*b*	**221a**	30c. olive-green, green and greenish blue (as No. 859) (2.6.70)	2·25	4·00
879	**266**	$2 black, ochre and pale blue (as No. 862) (10.12.68)	13·00	13·00
870/9 *Set of* 11			21·00	21·00

Designs: *Horiz*—8c. Apples and orchard; 10c. Forest and timber; 18c. Sheep and the "Woolmark"; 20c. Consignments of beef and herd of cattle.

*No. 871 was originally issued to commemorate the introduction of the brown trout into New Zealand.

†No. 874 is slightly larger than No. 856, measuring 21×25 mm and the inscriptions and numerals differ in size.

278 "The Adoration of the Shepherds" (Poussin)

279 Mount Aspiring, Aurora Australis and Southern Cross

280 Sir James Hector (founder)

(Photo Harrison)

1967 (3 Oct). *Christmas.* W **98** (sideways). P 13½×14.

880	**278**	2½c. multicoloured	10	10

(Des J. Berry. Litho D.L.R.)

1967 (10 Oct). *Centenary of the Royal Society of New Zealand.* W **98** (sideways on 4c.). P 14 (4c.) or 13×14 (8c.)

881	**279**	4c. multicoloured	25	20
		w. Wmk sideways inverted	8·00	7·00
882	**280**	8c. multicoloured	25	80

281 Open Bible

282 Soldiers and Tank

(Des Display Section, G.P.O. Litho D.L.R.)

1968 (23 Apr). *Centenary of Maori Bible.* W **98**. P 13½.

883	**281**	3c. multicoloured	10	10
		a. Gold (inscr etc.) omitted	£150	85·00
		w. Wmk inverted	28·00	25·00

(Des L. C. Mitchell. Litho D.L.R.)

1968 (7 May). *New Zealand Armed Forces. T* **282** *and similar horiz designs. Multicoloured.* W **98** (sideways). P 14×13½.

884	4c. Type **282**	25	15
	w. Wmk sideways inverted	9·00	12·00
885	10c. Airmen, Fairey Firefly and English Electric Canberra aircraft	35	70
886	28c. Sailors and H.M.N.Z.S. *Achilles*, 1939, and H.M.N.Z.S. *Waikato*, 1968	50	2·50
	w. Wmk sideways inverted	2·50	6·50
884/6 *Set of* 3		1·00	3·00

285 Boy breasting Tape, and Olympic Rings

287 Placing Votes in Ballot Box

(Des L. C. Mitchell. Photo Harrison)

1968 (7 May). *Health Stamps. T* **285** *and similar horiz design. Multicoloured.* P 14½×14.

887	2½c . +1c. Type **285**	20	15
888	3c. +1c. Girl swimming and Olympic rings	20	15
	a. Red (ring) omitted	£2250	
	b. Blue (ring) omitted	£1200	
MS889	Two sheets each 145×95 mm. Nos. 887/8 in blocks of six ... *Per pair*	16·00	42·00

No. 888a occurred in one miniature sheet. Six examples are known, one being used. No. 888b occurred from a second miniature sheet.

(Des J. Berry. Photo Japanese Govt Ptg Bureau, Tokyo)

1968 (19 Sept). *75th Anniv of Universal Suffrage in New Zealand.* P 13.

890	**287**	3c. ochre, olive-green and light blue	10	10

288 Human Rights Emblem

289 "Adoration of the Holy Child" (G. van Honthorst)

(Photo Japanese Govt Ptg Bureau, Tokyo)

1968 (19 Sept). *Human Rights Year.* P 13.

891	**288**	10c. scarlet, yellow and deep green	10	30

(Photo Harrison)

1968 (1 Oct). *Christmas.* W **98** (sideways). P 14×14½.

892	**289**	2½c. multicoloured	10	10

290 I.L.O. Emblem

(Photo Harrison)

1969 (11 Feb). *50th Anniv of International Labour Organization.* W **98** (sideways). P 14½×14.

893	**290**	7c. black and carmine-red	15	30

291 Supreme Court Building, Auckland

292 Law Society's Coat of Arms

(Des R. M. Conly. Litho B.W.)

1969 (8 Apr). *Centenary of New Zealand Law Society. T* **291/2** *and similar design.* P 13½×13 (3c.) or 13×13½ (others).

894	3c. multicoloured (*shades*)	10	10
895	10c. multicoloured	20	60
896	18c. multicoloured (*shades*)	30	1·50
894/6 *Set of* 3		55	2·00

Design: *Vert*—18c. "Justice" (from Memorial Window in University of Canterbury, Christchurch).

295 Student being conferred with Degree

(Des R. M. Conly. Litho B.W.)

1969 (3 June). *Centenary of Otago University. T* **295** *and similar multicoloured design.* P 13×13½ (3c.) or 13½×13 (10c.)

897	3c. Otago University (*vert*)	15	10
898	10c. Type **295**	30	25

296 Boys playing Cricket

298 Dr. Elizabeth Gunn (founder of First Children's Health Camp)

(Des R. M. Conly (4c.); L. C. Mitchell (others). Litho B.W.)

1969 (6 Aug). *Health Stamps. T* **296** *and similar horiz design and T* **298**. P 12½×13 (No. 901) or 13×12½ (others).

899	2½c. +1c. multicoloured	40	65
900	3c. +1c. multicoloured	40	65
901	4c. +1c. brown and ultramarine	40	2·00
899/901	*Set of 3*	1·10	3·00
MS902	Two sheets each 144×84 mm. Nos. 899/900 in blocks of six ... *Per pair*	16·00	50·00

Design:—3c. Girls playing cricket.

299 Oldest existing House in New Zealand, and Old Stone Mission Store, Kerikeri

(Litho D.L.R.)

1969 (18 Aug). *Early European Settlement in New Zealand, and 150th Anniv of Kerikeri. T* **299** *and similar horiz design. Multicoloured.* W **98** (sideways inverted). P 13×13½.

903	4c. Type **299**	20	25
904	6c. View of Bay of Islands	30	1·75

301 "The Nativity" (Federico Fiori (Barocci))

302 Captain Cook, Transit of Venus and "Octant"

(Photo Harrison)

1969 (1 Oct). *Christmas.* W **98**. P 13×14.

905	**301**	2½c. multicoloured	10	10
		a. No wmk	10	15

(Des Eileen Mayo. Photo; portraits embossed Harrison)

1969 (9 Oct). *Bicentenary of Captain Cook's Landing in New Zealand. T* **302** *and similar horiz designs.* P 14½×14.

906	4c. black, cerise and blue	75	35
	a. Imperf (pair)	£425	
907	6c. slate-green, purple-brown and black	1·00	2·50
908	18c. purple-brown, slate-green and black	1·75	2·50
909	28c. cerise, black and blue	2·75	4·00
906/9	*Set of 4*	5·50	8·50
MS910	109×90 mm. Nos. 906/9	18·00	35·00

Designs:—6c. Sir Joseph Banks (naturalist) and outline of H.M.S. *Endeavour*; 18c. Dr. Daniel Solander (botanist) and his plant; 28c. Queen Elizabeth II and Cook's chart 1769.

The miniature sheet exists additionally inscribed on the selvedge at bottom. "A SOUVENIR FROM NEW ZEALAND STAMP EXHIBITION, NEW PLYMOUTH 6TH–11TH OCTOBER. 1969". These were not sold from Post Offices.

306 Girl, Wheat Field and C.O.R.S.O. Emblem

307 Mother feeding her Child, Dairy Herd and C.O.R.S.O. Emblem

(Des L. C. Mitchell. Photo Japanese Govt Printing Bureau, Tokyo)

1969 (18 Nov). *25th Anniv of C.O.R.S.O. (Council of Organizations for Relief Services Overseas).* P 13.

911	**306**	7c. multicoloured	35	1·10
912	**307**	8c. multicoloured	35	1·25

308 "Cardigan Bay" (champion trotter)

(Des L. C. Mitchell. Photo Courvoisier)

1970 (28 Jan). *Return of "Cardigan Bay" to New Zealand.* P 11½.

913	**308**	10c. multicoloured	30	30

309 *Vanessa gonerilla* (butterfly)

310 Queen Elizabeth II and New Zealand Coat of Arms

(Des Enid Hunter (½c., 1c., 2c., 18c., 20c.), Eileen Mayo (2½c. to 7c.), D. B. Stevenson (7½c., 8c.), M. Cleverley (10c., 15c., 25c., 30c., $1, $2), M. V. Askew (23c., 50c.). Photo Harrison (½c. to 20c.), Enschedé (23c., 50c.), Courvoisier ($1, $2) or Litho B.W. (25c., 30c.))

1970 (12 Mar)–**76**. *Various designs as T* **309/10**. W **98** (sideways on 10c., or sideways inverted on 15c., 20c.) or No wmk (23c. to $2).

(a) Size as T **309**. P 13½×13.

914	½c. multicoloured (2.9.70)	10	20
	w. Wmk inverted	—	£120
915	1c. multicoloured (2.9.70)	10	10
	aw. Wmk inverted	45·00	30·00
	b. Wmk sideways inverted (booklets) (6.7.71)	80	1·75
	ba. Booklet pane. No. 915b×3 with three *se-tenant* printed labels	2·25	
	c. Blue omitted (booklets)	£225	£170
916	2c. multicoloured (2.9.70)	10	10
	a. Black (inscr, etc) omitted	£350	
	w. Wmk inverted	4·00	1·50
917	2½c. multicoloured (2.9.70)	30	20
918	3c. black, brown and orange (2.9.70)	15	10
	aw. Wmk inverted	2·50	2·75
	b. Wmk sideways inverted (booklets) (6.7.71)	55	1·50
	bw. Wmk sideways	28·00	28·00
919	4c. multicoloured (2.9.70)	15	10
	aw. Wmk inverted	3·00	1·75
	b. Wmk sideways inverted (booklets) (6.7.71)	55	1·50
	bw. Wmk sideways	75·00	65·00
	c. Bright green (wing veins) omitted	£250	
920	5c. multicoloured (4.11.70)	30	10
	w. Wmk inverted	†	—
921	6c. blackish green, yellow-green and carmine (4.11.70)	30	1·00
922	7c. multicoloured (4.11.70)	50	1·00
	w. Wmk inverted	—	50·00
923	7½c. multicoloured (4.11.70)	75	1·50
	w. Wmk inverted	†	—
924	8c. multicoloured (4.11.70)	50	1·00

(b) Size as T **310**. *Various perfs.*

925	10c. multicoloured (p 14½×14)	50	15
	w. Wmk sideways inverted	8·00	3·75
926	15c. black, flesh and pale brown (p 13½×13) (20.1.71)	75	50
	a. Pale brown omitted	£475	
	w. Wmk sideways	42·00	30·00
927	18c. chestnut, black and apple-green (p 13×13½) (20.1.71)	75	50
	w. Wmk inverted	48·00	30·00
928	20c. black and yellow-brown (p 13½×13) (20.1.71)	75	15
929	23c. multicoloured (p 13½×12½) (1.12.71)	60	30
930	25c. multicoloured (p 13×13½) (1.9.71)	1·00	40
	a. Printed on the gummed side	£550	
	b. Perf 14 (11.76?)	50	50
931	30c. multicoloured (p 13×13½) (1.9.71)	50	15
	a. Perf 14 (9.76?)	1·00	1·75
932	50c. multicoloured (p 13½×12½) (1.9.71)	50	20
	a. Apple green (hill) omitted	28·00	
	b. Buff (shore) omitted	55·00	
933	$1 multicoloured (p 11½) (14.4.71)	1·00	1·25
934	$2 multicoloured (p 11½) (14.4.71)	2·50	1·75
914/34	*Set of 21*	10·00	8·50

Designs: *Vert*—½c. *Lycaena salustius* (butterfly); 2c. *Argyrophenga antipodum* (butterfly); 2½c. *Nyctemera annulata* (moth); 3c. *Detunda egregia* (moth); 4c. *Charagia virescens* (moth); 5c. Scarlet Wrasse ("Scarlet Parrot Fish"); 6c. Big-bellied Sea Horses; 7c. Leather jacket (fish); 7½c. Intermediate Halfbeak ("Garfish"); 8c. John Dory (fish); 18c. Maori club; 25c. Hauraki Gulf Maritime Park; 30c. Mt Cook National Park. *Horiz*—10c. Type **310**: 15c. Maori fish hook; 20c. Maori tattoo Pattern, 23c. Egmont National Park; 50c. Abel Tasman National Park; $1 Geothermal Power; $2 Agricultural Technology.

Although issued as a definitive No. 925 was put on sale on the occasion of the Royal Visit to New Zealand.

Used examples of No. 931 are known showing the sky in light blue instead of the normal stone colour. It has been suggested by the printer involved that this was caused by a residue of ink used for another stamp remaining in the ink ducts when a printing of the 30c. commenced. Most authorities, however, agree that the "blue sky" stamps are colour changelings.

The 1c., 2c., 3c. to 7c. and 8c. to 20c. values were re-issued between 1973 and 1976 on unwatermarked paper.

311 Geyser Restaurant

312 U.N. H.Q. Building

(Des M. Cleverley. Photo Japanese Govt Printing Bureau, Tokyo)

1970 (8 Apr). *World Fair, Osaka. T* **311** *and similar horiz designs. Multicoloured.* P 13.

935	7c. Type **311**	20	75
936	8c. New Zealand Pavilion	20	75
937	18c. Bush Walk	40	75
935/7	*Set of 3*	70	2·00

(Des R. M. Conly (3c.), L. C. Mitchell (10c.). Litho D.L.R.)

1970 (24 June). *25th Anniv of United Nations. T* **312** *and similar vert design.* P 13½.

938	3c. multicoloured	10	10
939	10c. scarlet and yellow	20	20

Design:—10c. Tractor on horizon.

313 Soccer

(Des L. C. Mitchell. Litho D.L.R.)

1970 (5 Aug). *Health Stamps. T* **313** *and similar multicoloured design.* P 13½.

940	2½c. +1c. Netball (vert)	25	70
941	3c. +1c. Type **313**	25	70
MS942	Two sheets: (a) 102×125 mm (940); (b) 125×102 mm (941), containing blocks of six ... *Per pair*	18·00	48·00

314 "The Virgin adoring the Child" (Correggio)

315 "The Holy Family" (stained glass window, Invercargill Presbyterian Church)

(Litho D.L.R.)

1970 (1 Oct). *Christmas. T* **314/15** *and similar design.* P 12½.

943	2½c. multicoloured	10	10
944	3c. multicoloured	10	10
	a. Green (inscr and value) omitted	£275	
945	10c. black, orange and silver	30	75
943/5	*Set of 3*	35	75

Design: Horiz—10c. Tower of Roman Catholic Church, Sockburn.

No. 943 exists as an imperforate proof with the country inscription and face value omitted.

316 Chatham Islands Lily

(Des Eileen Mayo. Photo Japanese Govt Printing Bureau, Tokyo)

1970 (2 Dec). *Chatham Islands. T* **316** *and similar horiz design. Multicoloured.* P 13.

946	1c. Type **316**	10	35
947	2c. Shy Albatross	30	40

STAMP BOOKLETS

Nos. SB1 to SB19 are stapled.

Nos. SB1/6 were sold at ½d. above the face value of the stamps to cover the cost of manufacture.

1901 (1 Apr). *White card covers with postage rates.*

SB1	1s.½d. booklet containing twelve 1d. (No. 278) in blocks of 6	£2250
SB2	2s. 6½d. booklet containing thirty 1d. (No. 278) in blocks of 6	£3000

Original printings of Nos. SB1/2 showed the face value on the cover in small figures. Subsequent printings show large figures of value on the covers and the prices quoted are for this type.

1902 (21 Aug)–**05**. *White card covers with postage rates.*

SB3	1s.½d. booklet containing twelve 1d. in panes of 6 (Nos. 303b or 303cb)	£1800
SB4	2s.½d. booklet containing twenty-four 1d. in panes of 6 (Nos. 303b or 303cb) (21.3.05)	£2250
SB5	2s. 6½d. booklet containing thirty 1d. in panes of 6 (Nos. 303b or 303cb)	£2750

1910 (Apr). *White card cover with postage rates.*

SB6	2s. booklet containing eleven ½d. in pane of 5 with 1 label (Nos. 387b or 387c) and pane of 6 (No. 387d), and eighteen 1d. in three panes of 6 (No. 405b)	£3750

1912 (May). *White card cover.*

SB7	2s. booklet containing twelve ½d. and eighteen 1d. in panes of 6 with bars on the selvedge (Nos. 387e, 405c)	£2750

1915 (Feb). *Red card cover.*

SB8 2s. booklet containing twelve ½d. and eighteen 1d. in panes of 6 with bars on the selvedge (Nos. 435a or 435ba, 405c) £1500
a. Grey cover ....
b. Blue cover ....
c. Yellow-buff cover ....
d. Purple-buff cover ....

1924 (1 Dec)–**25**. *Cover inscription within frame.*

SB9 2s. booklet containing twelve ½d. and eighteen 1d. in panes of 6 with bars on the selvedge (Nos. 441a, 406b) (lilac cover) £1600
a. Grey cover ....
b. Pale blue cover £1800

SB10 2s. booklet containing twelve ½d. and eighteen 1d. in panes of 6 with bars and advertisements on the selvedge (Nos. 446a, 410b) (yellow-buff cover) (1925) £1800
a. Grey-green cover £1800
b. Grey-buff cover ....
c. Grey-pink cover £2000

1928–34.

SB11 2s. booklet containing twelve ½d. (P 14×15) and eighteen 1d. in panes of 6 with bars on the selvedge (Nos. 446ab, 468b) £2250
a. As No. SB11, but ½d. (P 14) (Nos. 446ca, 468b) £1500
b. As No. SB11 but panes with bars and advertisements on the selvedge (Nos. 446cb, 468c) £1700

SB12 2s. booklet containing twenty-four 1d. (P 14) in panes of 6 with bars and advertisements on the selvedge (No. 468c) (1930) £1500
a. As No. SB12, but 1d. (P 14×15) (No. 468ea) (1934) £1400

1935.

SB15 2s. booklet containing twenty-four 1d., in panes of 6 with advertisements on the selvedge (No. 557ca) £375

1936.

SB16 2s. booklet containing twenty-four 1d. (No. 578) in blocks of 6 .... £250

B 1

1938 (1 July). *Cream cover as Type* B **1**.

SB17 2s. booklet containing twenty-four 1d. (No. 605) in blocks of 6 .... £325

1938 (Nov). *Cream (No.* SB18*) or blue (No.* SB19*) covers as Type* B **1**.

SB18 2s. booklet containing twelve ½d. and eighteen 1d. (Nos. 603, 605) in blocks of 6 .... £425
SB19 2s.3d. booklet containing eighteen 1½d. (No. 607) in blocks of 6 .... £375

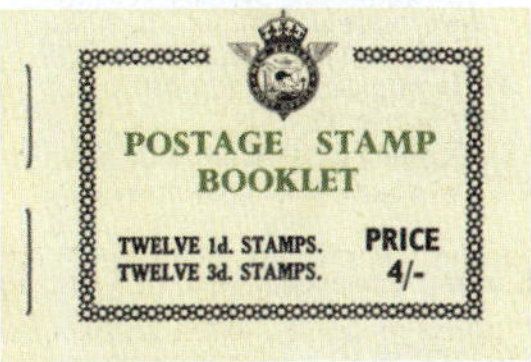

B 2

1954 (1 Apr). *Black and green on cream cover as Type* B **2**.

SB20 4s. booklet containing twelve 1d. and 3d. (Nos. 724, 727), each in blocks of 6 .... 4·00
a. Contents as SB20 but with one pane of air mail labels .... 19·00

1956 (1 May). *Black and green on cream cover as Type* B **2**.

SB21 4s. booklet containing twelve 1d. and 3d. (Nos. 724, 748), each in blocks of 6, and one pane of air mail labels .... 10·00

1957 (5 Sept). *Black and green on cream cover as Type* B **2**.

SB22 4s. booklet containing twelve 1d. and 3d. (Nos. 745, 748), each in blocks of 6, and one pane of air mail labels .... 9·00

B 3

1960 (1 Sept). *Black and red on cream cover as Type* B **3**.

SB23 4s. booklet containing twelve 1d. and 3d. (Nos. 782, 785), each in blocks of 6, and one pane of air mail labels .... 12·00

1962 (21 May). *Black and red on cream cover as Type* B **3**.

SB24 4s.6d. booklet containing twelve ½d., 1d. and 3d. (Nos. 781, 782, 785), each in blocks of 6, and one pane of air mail labels .... 48·00

1964. *Black and carmine on cream cover as Type* B **3**. *Stitched.*

SB25 4s.3d. booklet containing six ½d. and twelve 1d. and 3d. (Nos. 781/2, 785), each in blocks of 6, and one pane of air mail labels .... 18·00

B **4** Maori Art

1967 (10 July). *Black and carmine on pale lemon cover as Type* B **4**. *Stitched.*

SB26 50c. booklet containing ½c. (No. 845) in block of 6, eleven 1c. in block of 6 (No. 846) and pane of 5 stamps and 1 label (No. 846a), and twelve 3c. (No. 849) in blocks of 6 .... 7·50

EXPRESS DELIVERY STAMPS

E 1

(Typo Govt Printing Office, Wellington)

1903 (9 Feb). *Value in first colour.* W **43** (sideways). P 11.

E1	E 1	6d. red and violet	38·00	23·00

1926–36. *Thick, white, opaque chalk-surfaced "Cowan" paper.* W **43**.

(a) P 14×14½.

E2	E 1	6d. vermilion and bright violet	42·00	26·00
		w. Wmk inverted	£150	

(b) P 14×15 (1936).

E3	E 1	6d. carmine and bright violet	65·00	60·00

1937–39. *Thin, hard, chalk-surfaced "Wiggins Teape" paper.*

(a) P 14×14½.

E4	E 1	6d. carmine and bright violet	£100	50·00

(b) P 14×15 (1939).

E5	E 1	6d. vermilion and bright violet	£170	£300

E **2** Express Mail Delivery Van

(Des J. Berry. Eng Stamp Ptg Office, Melbourne Recess Govt Ptg Office, Wellington)

1939 (16 Aug). W **43**. P 14.

E6	E 2	6d. violet	1·50	1·75
		w. Wmk inverted	85·00	

No. E6 was withdrawn on 30 June 1948, when the Express Delivery Service ceased.

POSTAGE DUE STAMPS

D **1**

(I)

(II)

3D. *(a)* Large "D" **5D.** *(b)* Small "D"

(Typo Govt Printing Office, Wellington)

1899 (1 Dec). *Coarse paper.* W **12b**. P 11.

I. Type I. Circle of 14 ornaments 17 dots over "N.Z.", "N.Z." large.

(a) Large "D".

D1	D 1	½d. carmine and green	21·00	29·00
		a. No stop after "D" (Right pane R. 2/3)	£110	£160
D2		8d. carmine and green	60·00	85·00
		a. Carmine "8D." printed double		
D3		1s. carmine and green	65·00	90·00
D4		2s. carmine and green	£120	£150
D1/4 *Set of 4*		....	£225	£325

To avoid further subdivision the 1s. and 2s. are placed with the *pence* values, although the two types of "D" do not apply to the higher values.

(b) Small "D".

D6	D 1	5d. carmine and green	24·00	32·00
D7		6d. carmine and green	30·00	32·00
D8		10d. carmine and green	70·00	95·00
D6/8 *Set of 3*		....	£110	£140

II. Type II. Circle of 13 ornaments, 15 dots over "N.Z.", "N.Z." small.

(a) Large "D".

D9	D 1	½d. vermilion and green	3·00	16·00
		a. No stop after "D" (Right pane R. 2/3)	60·00	£100
D10		1d. vermilion and green	15·00	2·50
D11		2d. vermilion and green	50·00	9·00
D12		3d. vermilion and green	13·00	4·25
D9/12 *Set of 4*		....	75·00	29·00

(b) Small "D".

D14	D 1	1d. vermilion and green	15·00	2·25
D15		2d. vermilion and green	50·00	7·00
D16		4d. vermilion and green	32·00	14·00
D14/16 *Set of 3*		....	90·00	21·00

Nos. D9/16 were printed from a common frame plate of 240 (4 panes of 60) used in conjunction with centre plates of 120 (2 panes of 60) for the ½d. and 4d. or 240 for the other values. Sheets of the 1d. and 2d. each contained two panes with large "D" and two panes with small "D".

D **2**

D **3**

(Des W. R. Bock. Typo Govt Printing Office)

1902 (28 Feb). No wmk. P 11.

D17	D 2	½d. red and deep green	1·75	7·50

1904–08. *"Cowan" unsurfaced paper.* W **43** (sideways).

(a) P 11.

D18	D 2	½d. red and green (4.04)	1·75	3·00
		a. Imperf between (horiz pair)	£850	
D19		1d. red and green (5.12.05)	13·00	3·50
D20		2d. red and green (5.4.06)	90·00	£100
D18/20 *Set of 3*		....	90·00	£100

(b) P 14.

D21	D 2	1d. carmine and green (12.06)	16·00	1·50
		a. Rose-pink and green (9.07)	13·00	1·50
D22		2d. carmine and green (10.06)	9·00	8·00
		a. Rose-pink and green (6.08)	5·50	2·75

1919 (Jan)–**20**. *"De La Rue" chalky paper. Toned gum.* W **43**. P 14×15.

D23	D 2	½d. carmine and green (6.19)	3·25	3·75
D24		1d. carmine and green	7·00	50
		w. Wmk inverted	†	—
D25		2d. carmine and green (8.20)	17·00	3·25
D23/5 *Set of 3*		....	24·00	6·75

1925 (May). *"Jones" chalky paper. White gum.* W **43**. P 14×15.

D26	D 2	½d. carmine and green	35·00	45·00

1925 (July). No wmk, but bluish "N Z" and Star lithographed on back. P 14×15.

D27	D 2	½d. carmine and green	2·00	23·00
D28		2d. carmine and green	3·50	26·00

1925 (Nov)–**35**. *"Cowan" thick, opaque chalky paper.* W **43**.

(a) P 14×15.

D29	D 2	½d. carmine and green (12.26)	1·75	9·50
D30		1d. carmine and green	3·75	80
D31		2d. carmine and green (6.26)	19·00	4·25
		x. Wmk reversed	35·00	21·00
D32		3d. carmine and green (6.35)	48·00	55·00
D29/32 *Set of 4*		....	65·00	60·00

(b) P 14.

D33	D 2	½d. carmine and green (10.28)	50·00	30·00
D34		1d. rose and pale yellow-green (6.28)	4·00	1·25
D35		2d. carmine and green (10.29)	7·00	3·00
D36		3d. carmine and green (5.28)	15·00	42·00
D33/6 *Set of 4*		....	70·00	70·00

1937–38. *"Wiggins Teape" thin, hard chalky paper.* W **43**. P 14×15.

D37	D 2	½d. carmine and yellow-green (2.38)	30·00	40·00
D38		1d. carmine and yellow-green (1.37)	12·00	3·75
D39		2d. carmine and yellow-green (6.37)	48·00	15·00
D40		3d. carmine and yellow-green (11.37)	£100	70·00
D37/40 *Set of 4*		....	£170	£110

(Des J. Berry. Typo Govt Printing Office, Wellington)

1939–49. P 15×14.

(a) W **43** (sideways inverted) (16.8.39).

D41	D 3	½d. turquoise-green	5·00	5·00
D42		1d. carmine	2·75	1·75
		w. Wmk sideways	£150	6·00
D43		2d. bright blue	6·00	2·75
D44		3d. orange-brown	23·00	25·00
		w. Wmk sideways	£150	
D41/4 *Set of 4*		....	32·00	30·00

(b) W **98** (sideways (1d.), sideways inverted (2d.) or upright (3d.).

D45	D 3	1d. carmine (4.49)	17·00	5·50*
D46		2d. bright blue (12.46)	8·00	3·00
		w. Wmk sideways (4.49)	2·75	10·00
D47		3d. orange-brown (1943)	55·00	35·00
		a. Wmk sideways inverted (6.45)	22·00	8·50
		aw. Wmk sideways (28.11.49)	9·00	12·00
D45/7aw *Set of 3*		....	25·00	15·00*

*The use of Postage Due stamps ceased on 30 September 1951, our used price for No. D45 being for stamps postmarked after this date (*price for examples clearly cancelled* 1949–51, £27).

OFFICIAL STAMPS

1891 (Dec)–**1906**. *Contemporary issues handstamped "O.P.S.O." diagonally.*

(a) Stamps of 1873 type. W **12b**. P 12½.

O1 **3** ½d. rose (V.) — £650

(b) Stamps of 1882–97 optd in rose or magenta. W **12b**.

O2 **13** ½d. black (P 10) — £450
a. Violet opt — £550
O3 ½d. black (P 10×11) — £450
O4 **14** 1d. rose (P 12×11½) — £450
O5 1d. rose (P 11) — £450
O6 **15** 2d. purple (P 11) — £550
O7 2d. mauve-lilac (P 10) — £550
a. Violet opt
O8 **16** 2½d. blue (P 11) — £475
O9 2½d. ultramarine (P 10) — £475
O10 2½d. ultramarine (P 10×11) — £475
O11 **19** 5d. olive-black (P 12×11½) — £650
O12 **20** 6d. brown (P 12×11½) — £900

(c) Stamps of 1898–1903 optd in violet. P 11.

(i) No wmk.

O13 **23** ½d. green (P 14) (No. 294) — £450
O14 **26** 2½d. blue (P 12–16) (No. 249*a*) — £850
O15 **27** 2½d. blue (No. 260) — £650
O16 **37** 4d. indigo and brown (No. 262) — £750
O17 **30** 5d. purple-brown (No. 263) — £750
a. Green opt — £700
O18 **32** 8d. indigo (No. 266) — £900

(ii) W **38**.

O19 **42** 1d. carmine (No. 278) — £500

(iii) W **43** (sideways on 3d., 1s.).

O20 **42** 1d. carmine (P 14) (No. 303) — £500
a. Green opt — £500
O21 **27** 2½d. blue (No. 308) — £550
O22 **28** 3d. yellow-brown (No 309) — £750
O23 **34** 1s. orange-red (No. 315*b*) — £1800
O24 **36** 2s. green (No. 316) — £2750

The letters signify "On Public Service Only", and stamps so overprinted were used by the Post Office Department at Wellington on official correspondence to foreign countries.

Unused examples with the "O.P.S.O." handstamp are generally considered to be reprints.

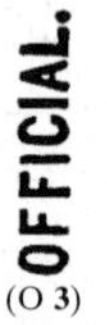

(O 3)

1907–11. *Stamps of 1902–6 optd with Type* O **3** *(vertically, upwards).* W **43** (sideways on 3d., 6d., 1s. and 5s.). P 14.

O59 **23** ½d. yellow-green 10·00 75
a. Perf 11×14 £170
b. Mixed perfs £170
O60 **42** 1d. carmine (No. 303) (1.7.07*) 9·50 14·00
a. Booklet pane of 6 55·00
ab. Imperf horiz (booklet pane of 6) £2500
O60*b* 1d. rose-carmine (Waterlow) (No. 352) 14·00 70
ba. Perf 11×14 — £375
bb. Mixed perfs — £375
O60*c* 1d. carmine (Royle) 30·00 70
ca. Perf 11×14 £275 £375
cb. Mixed perfs £275 £325
O61 **41** 2d. purple 11·00 1·75
a. Bright reddish purple 8·50 1·60
ab. Mixed perfs £325 £325
O63 **28** 3d. bistre-brown 48·00 1·75
a. Mixed perfs — £1100
O64 **31** 6d. bright carmine-pink £180 22·00
a. Imperf vert (horiz pair) £1000
b. Mixed perfs £700 £550
O65 **34** 1s. orange-red 95·00 17·00
O66 **35** 2s. blue-green 80·00 £110
a. Imperf between (pair) £3000
b. Imperf vert (horiz pair) £2250
w. Wmk inverted £425 £300
O67 **36** 5s. deep red £150 £180
a. Wmk upright (1911) £950 £1100

*Though issued in 1907 a large quantity of booklets was mislaid and not utilized until they were found in 1930.

1908–09. *Optd as Type* O **3**. W **43**.

O69 **23** ½d. green (P 14×15) 9·00 3·50
O70 **50** 1d. carmine (P 14×15) 65·00 3·50
O71 **48** 6d. pink (P 14×13, 13½) £180 45·00
O72 6d. pink (P 14×15) (1909) £160 35·00
O72*a* F **4** £1 rose-pink (P 14) (No. F89) £600 £450

1910. *No. 387 optd with Type* O **3**.

O73 **51** ½d. yellow-green 9·00 40
a. Opt inverted (reading downwards) † £2500

1910–16. *Nos. 389 and 392/4 optd with Type* O **3**. P 14×14½.

O74 **52** 3d. chestnut 14·00 80
a. Perf 14×13½ (1915) 65·00 £110
ab. Vert pair. Nos. O74/a £300 £550
O75 – 6d. carmine 19·00 5·50
a. Perf 14 (line) (No. 398) † —
b. Deep carmine 25·00 5·50
w. Wmk inverted
O76 – 8d. indigo-blue (R.) (5.16) 12·00 28·00
aw. Wmk inverted 55·00 70·00
b. Perf 14×13½ 12·00 28·00
bw. Wmk inverted 45·00 60·00
c. Vert pair, Nos. O76 and O76b 70·00 £130
cw. Wmk inverted £225 £250
O77 1s. vermilion 55·00 17·00
O74/7 *Set of* 4 90·00 42·00

1910–26. *Optd with Type* O **3**.

(a) W **43**. *De La Rue chalk-surfaced paper with toned gum.*

O78 **53** 1d. carmine (No. 405) 3·50 10
y. Wmk inverted and reversed

(b) W **43**. *Jones chalk-surfaced paper with white gum.*

O79 **53** 1d. deep carmine (No. 406) (1925) 11·00 6·50

(c) No wmk, but bluish "NZ" and Star lithographed on back. Art paper.

O80 **53** 1d. rose-carmine (No. 409) (1925) 6·00 20·00

(d) W **43**. *Cowan thick, opaque, chalk-surfaced paper with white gum.*

O81 **53** 1d. deep carmine (No. 410) (1925) 8·00 1·25
x. Wmk reversed (1926) 38·00 24·00

1913–25. *Postal Fiscal stamps optd with Type* O **3**.

(i) Chalk-surfaced De La Rue paper.

(a) P 14(1913–14).

O82 F **4** 2s. blue (30.9.14) 50·00 50·00
O83 5s. yellow-green (13.6.13) 80·00 £110
O84 £1 rose-carmine (1913) £600 £550
O82/4 *Set of* 3 £650 £650

(b) P 14½×14, comb (1915).

O85 F **4** 2s. deep blue (Aug) 55·00 50·00
a. No stop after "OFFICIAL" £150 £120
O86 5s. yellow-green (Jan) 80·00 £100
a. No stop after "OFFICIAL" £225 £275

(ii) Thick, white, opaque chalk-surfaced Cowan paper. P 14½×14 (1925).

O87 F **4** 2s. blue 80·00 80·00
a. No stop after "OFFICIAL" £200 £225

The overprint on these last, and on Nos. O69 and O72*a* is from a new set of type, giving a rather sharper impression than Type O **3**, but otherwise resembling it closely.

1915 (12 Oct)–**34**. *Optd with Type* O **3**. P 14×15.

(a) On Nos. 435/40 (De La Rue chalk-surfaced paper with toned gum).

O88 **61** ½d. green 1·25 20
O89 **62** 1½d. grey-black (6.16) 7·50 2·50
O90 **61** 1½d. slate (12.16) 5·50 1·00
O91 1½d. orange-brown (4.19) 5·00 30
O92 2d. yellow (4.17) 6·50 20
O93 3d. chocolate (11.19) 12·00 1·00
O88/93 *Set of* 6 35·00 4·75

(b) On Nos. 441 and 443 (Jones chalk-surfaced paper with white gum).

O94 **61** ½d. green (1924) 4·50 3·50
O95 3d. deep chocolate (1924) 38·00 9·50

(c) On Nos. 446/7 and 448a/9 (Cowan thick, opaque, chalk surfaced paper with white gum).

O96 **61** ½d. green (1925) 2·75 10
ax. Wmk reversed (1927) 21·00 18·00
ay. Wmk inverted and reversed (1927) £100 35·00
b. Perf 14 (1929) 3·75 50
ba. No stop after "OFFICIAL" 25·00 32·00
O97 1½d. orange-brown (P 14) (1929) 11·00 17·00
a. No stop after "OFFICIAL" 70·00 80·00
b. Perf 14×15 (1934) 38·00 35·00
O98 2d. yellow (P 14) (1931) 2·50 50
a. No stop after "OFFICIAL" 60·00 60·00
O99 3d. chocolate (1925) 6·50 70
a. No stop after "OFFICIAL" 70·00 50·00
b. Perf 14 (1930) 55·00 5·50
ba. No stop after "OFFICIAL" £160 £110
O96/9 *Set of* 4 21·00 17·00

1915 (Dec)–**27**. *Optd with Type* O **3**. P 14×13½.

(a) Nos. 420, 422, 425, 428 and 429/30 (Cowan unsurfaced paper).

O100 **60** 3d. chocolate 4·50 1·50
aw. Wmk inverted 25·00 5·50
b. Perf 14×14½ 4·50 1·75
bw. Wmk inverted 25·00 5·50
c. Vert pair, Nos. O100 and O100b 40·00 £110
cw. Wmk inverted £120 £180
d. Opt double † £1400
O101 4d. bright violet (4.25) 14·00 4·50
a. Re-entry (Pl 20 R. 1/6) 65·00 42·00
b. Re-entry (Pl 20 R. 4/10) 70·00 48·00
c. Perf 14×14½ *(Deep purple)* (4.27) 27·00 1·00
O102 6d. carmine (6.16) 5·00 75
aw. Wmk inverted £100
b. Perf 14×14½ 5·00 1·25
c. Vert pair, Nos. O102 and O102b 55·00 £140
O103 8d. red-brown (8.22) 65·00 £180
O104 9d. sage-green (4.25) 40·00 38·00
O105 1s. vermilion (9.16) 18·00 14·00
aw. Wmk inverted £180 £120
b. Perf 14×14½ 7·00 2·00
ba. Pale orange-red 15·00 20·00
bw. Wmk inverted £180 £180
c. Vert pair. Nos. O105 and O105b 65·00 £180
cw. Wmk inverted £500
O100/5 *Set of* 6 £120 £200

(b) No. 433 (Thin paper with widely spaced sideways wmk).

O106 **60** 3d. chocolate (P 14) (7.16) 3·00 15·00
a. No wmk 50·00 80·00

1927–33. *Optd with Type* O **3**. W **43**. P 14.

O111 **71** 1d. rose-carmine (No. 468) 2·00 20
a. No stop after "OFFICIAL" 28·00 85·00
bw. Wmk inverted † 38·00
c. Perf 14×15 4·25 20
O112 **72** 2s. light blue (No. 469) (2.28) 75·00 £120
O113 F **6** 5s. green (1933) £275 £325
O111/13 *Set of* 3 £325 £400

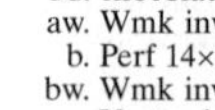

(O 4)

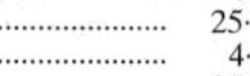

(O 5)

1936–61. *Pictorial issue optd horiz or vert (2s.) with Type* O **4**.

(a) W **43** (Single "N Z" and Star).

O115 **82** 1d. scarlet (Die I) (P 14×13½) 5·00 1·25
a. Perf 13½×14 £100 70·00
O116 **83** 1½d. red-brown (P 13½×14) 29·00 32·00
a. Perf 14×13½ £12000
O118 **92** 1s. deep green (P 14×13½) 38·00 55·00
w. Wmk inverted † £190
O119 F **6** 5s. green (P 14) (12.38) £130 50·00
O115/19 *Set of* 4 £180 £120

The watermark of No. O119 is almost invisible.

Only four examples of No. O116a exist. The error occurred when a sheet of No. 558a was found to have a block of four missing. This was replaced by a block of No. 558 and the sheet was then sent for overprinting.

(b) W **98** (Mult "N Z" and Star).

O120 **81** ½d. bright green, P 14×13½ (7.37) 7·50 4·50
O121 **82** 1d. scarlet (Die II), P 14×13½ (11.36) 8·50 50
w. Wmk inverted 32·00 35·00
O122 **83** 1½d. red-brown, P 14×13½ (7.36) 28·00 4·75
O123 **84** 2d. orange, P 14×13½ (1.38) 6·50 10
aw. Wmk inverted — £160
b. Perf 12½ (1942) £190 55·00
c. Perf 14 (1942) 55·00 15·00
O124 **85** 2½d. chocolate and slate, P 13-14×13½ (26.7.38) 65·00 95·00
a. Perf 14 (1938) 14·00 21·00
O125 **86** 3d. brown, P 14×13½ (1.3.38) 48·00 3·50
w. Wmk inverted — £140
O126 **87** 4d. black and sepia, P 14×13½ (8.36) 11·00 1·10
a. Perf 14 (8.41) 14·00 4·50
b. Perf 12½ (1941) 13·00 7·50
c. Perf 14×14½ (10.42) 4·75 1·00
cw. Wmk inverted — £180
O127 **89** 6d. scarlet, P 13½×14 (12.37) 28·00 80
aw. Wmk inverted † —
b. Perf 12½ (1941) 15·00 5·50
c. Perf 14½×14 (7.42) 14·00 40
O128 **90** 8d. chocolate, P 12½ (wmk sideways) (1942) 15·00 17·00
a. Perf 14×14½ (wmk sideways) (1945) 8·50 16·00
b. Perf 14×13½ † £2500
O129 **91** 9d. red and grey-black (G.) (No. 587*a*), P 13½×14 (1.3.38) 90·00 40·00
O130 9d. scarlet & black *(chalk-surfaced paper)* (Blk.) (No. 631), P 14×15 (1943) 20·00 22·00
O131 **92** 1s. deep green, P 14×13½ (2.37) 50·00 1·50
aw. Wmk inverted — £225
b. Perf 12½ (1942) 32·00 2·75
O132 **93** 2s. olive-green, P 13–14×13½ (5.37) 80·00 42·00
a. "CAPTAIN COQK" £160
b. Perf 13½×14 (1939) £225 7·00
ba. "CAPTAIN COQK" £275
c. Perf 12½ (1942) 80·00 22·00
ca. "CAPTAIN COQK" £150
d. Perf 14×13½ (1944) 42·00 10·00
da. "CAPTAIN COQK" £375
O133 F **6** 5s. green *(chalk-surfaced paper)*, P 14 (3.43) 42·00 6·00
aw. Wmk inverted 40·00 6·00
b. Perf 14×13½. Yellow-green *(ordinary paper)* (10.61) 17·00 32·00
O120/33 *Set of* 14 £300 £110

The opt on No. O127a was sometimes applied at the top of the stamp, instead of always at the bottom as on No. O127.

All examples of No. O128b were used by a government office in Whangerei.

The 5s. value on ordinary paper perforated 14×13½ does not exist without the "Official" overprint.

See notes on perforations after No. 590b.

1938–51. *Nos. 603 etc., optd with Type* O **4**.

O134 **108** ½d. green (1.3.38) 22·00 2·25
O135 ½d. brown-orange (1946) 2·00 4·00
O136 1d. scarlet (1.7.38) 24·00 15
O137 1d. green (10.7.41) 3·75 10
O138 **108a** 1½d. purple-brown (26.7.38) 75·00 19·00
O139 1½d. scarlet (2.4.51) 12·00 7·50
O140 3d. blue (16.10.41) 3·75 10
O134/40 *Set of* 7 £130 30·00

1940 (2 Jan–8 Mar). *Centennial. Nos. 613, etc., optd with Type* O **5**.

O141 ½d. blue-green (R.) 2·75 35
a. "ff" joined, as Type O **4** 50·00 60·00
O142 1d. chocolate and scarlet 7·00 10
a. "ff" joined, as Type O **4** 50·00 60·00
O143 1½d. light blue and mauve 4·00 2·00
O144 2d. blue-green and chocolate 6·50 10
a. "ff" joined, as Type O **4** 60·00 60·00
O145 2½d. blue-green and ultramarine 5·00 2·75
a. "ff" joined, as Type O **4** 50·00 65·00
O146 3d. purple and carmine (R.) 8·00 1·00
a. "ff" joined, as Type O **4** 42·00 48·00
O147 4d. chocolate and lake 40·00 1·50
a. "ff" joined, as Type O **4** £120 90·00
O148 6d. emerald-green and violet 27·00 1·50
a. "ff" joined, as Type O **4** 70·00 70·00
O149 8d. black and red (8.3) 30·00 17·00
a. "ff" joined, as Type O **4** 70·00 £100
O150 9d. olive-green and vermilion 13·00 4·00
O151 1s. sage-green and deep green 48·00 3·00
O141/51 *Set of* 11 £170 30·00

For this issue the Type O **4** overprint occurs on R. 4/3 of the 2½d. and on R. 1/10 of the other values.

1947 (1 May)–**51**. *Nos. 680, etc., optd with Type* O **4**.

O152 **108a** 2d. orange 3·50 10
O153 4d. bright purple 4·75 3·00
O154 6d. carmine 15·00 50
O155 8d. violet 8·00 6·50
O156 9d. purple-brown 9·00 6·50
O157 **144** 1s. red-brown and carmine (wmk upright) (Plate 1) 17·00 1·00
a. Wmk sideways (Plate 1) (1949) 8·50 9·00
aw. Wmk sideways inverted 40·00 17·00
b. Wmk upright (Plate 2) (4.51) 24·00 7·50
bw. Wmk inverted £100 32·00
O158 2s. brown-orange and green (wmk sideways) (Plate 1) 32·00 16·00
a. Wmk upright (Plate 1) 32·00 48·00
O152/8 *Set of* 7 70·00 30·00

O 6 Queen Elizabeth II

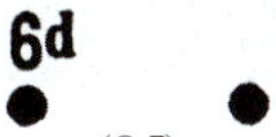
(O 7)

(Des J. Berry. Recess B.W.)

1954 (1 Mar)–**63**. W **98**. P 14×13½.

O159 **06** 1d. orange ... 75 40
a. White opaque paper (8.7.59) .. 50 20
O160 1½d. brown-lake ... 3·75 5·00
O161 2d. bluish green ... 50 50
a. White opaque paper (11.12.58) ... 40 30
O162 2½d. olive (*white opaque paper*) (1.3.63) ... 3·00 1·50
O163 3d. vermilion ... 70 10
a. White opaque paper (1960) ... 40 10
aw. Wmk inverted ... 25·00 16·00
O164 4d. blue ... 1·50 75
a. Printed on the gummed side .. £150
b. White opaque paper (1.9.61).. 1·00 50
O165 9d. carmine ... 7·00 2·50
O166 1s. purple ... 1·25 30
a. White opaque paper (2.10.61) 2·50 75
O167 3s. slate (*white opaque paper*) (1.3.63) ... 22·00 40·00
O159/67 *Set of* 9 ... 35·00 45·00

See note *re* white opaque paper after No. 736.
No. O164a shows the watermark inverted and reversed.

1959 (1 Oct). *No.* O160 *surch with Type* O **7**.
O168 O 6 6d. on 1½d. brown-lake ... 50 1·10

1961 (1 Sept). *No.* O161 *surch as Type* O **7**.
O169 O 6 2½d. on 2d. bluish green ... 1·25 1·50

Owing to the greater use of franking machines by Government Departments, the use of official stamps was discontinued on 31 March 1965, but they remained on sale at the G.P.O. until 31 December 1965.

STAMP BOOKLET

1907 (1 July). *White card cover.*
OB1 10s. booklet containing one hundred and twenty 1d. in panes of 6 (No. O60a) ... £1100

PROVISIONALS ISSUED AT REEFTON AND USED BY THE POLICE DEPARTMENT

1907 (Jan). *Current stamps of 1906, optd* "Official", *in red manuscript and handstamped with a circular "Greymouth—PAID—3".* P 14.

P1 **23** ½d. green ... £1100 £1300
P2 **40** 1d. carmine ... £1200 £1200
P3 **38** 2d. purple ... £1400 £1600
P4 **28** 3d. bistre ... £2000
P5 **31** 6d. pink ... £2000
P6 **34** 1s. orange-red ... £2750
P7 **35** 2s. green ... £8000

Only the ½d., 1d. and 2d. are known postally used, cancelled with the Reefton squared circle postmark. The 3d. and 6d. were later cancelled by favour at Wanganui.

LIFE INSURANCE DEPARTMENT

L 1 Lighthouse

L 2 Lighthouse

(Des W. B. Hudson and J. F. Rogers; Eng. A. E. Cousins. Typo Govt Printing Office, Wellington)

1891 (2 Jan)–**98**.

A. W **12c**. P 12×11½.

L1 L **1** ½d. bright purple ... 75·00 6·00
a. Mixed perf 12×11 and 12½..... † —
x. Wmk reversed ... † £110
L2 1d. blue ... 60·00 4·00
ax. Wmk reversed ...
ay. Wmk inverted and reversed... † 48·00
b. Wmk **12b** ... £110 22·00
bx. Wmk reversed ... † £225
L3 2d. brown-red ... 95·00 9·50
ax. Wmk reversed ... † 95·00
b. Wmk **12b** ... £110 17·00
L4 3d. deep brown ... £180 26·00
L5 6d. green ... £300 60·00
L6 1s. rose ... £500 £120
L1/6 *Set of* 6 ... £1100 £200

B. W **12b** (1893–98).

(a) P 10 (1893).

L7 L **1** ½d. bright purple ... 70·00 12·00
L8 1d. blue ... 60·00 1·75
L9 2d. brown-red ... 85·00 3·75
L7/9 *Set of* 3 ... £190 16·00

(b) P 11×10.

L10 L **1** ½d. bright purple (1896) ... 95·00 28·00
a. Perf 10×11 ... £190 75·00
L11 1d. blue (1897) ... † 50·00
a. Perf 10×11 ... 65·00 14·00

(c) Mixed perfs 10 and 11 (1897).

L12 L **1** 2d. brown-red ... £750 £750

(d) P 11 (1897–98).

L13 L **1** ½d. bright purple ... 60·00 4·00
a. Thin coarse toned paper (1898) ... 85·00 7·00
L14 1d. blue ... 60·00 75
a. Thin coarse toned paper (1898) ... 85·00 3·25

x. Wmk reversed ... £150 22·00
y. Wmk inverted and reversed... £150 35·00
L15 2d. brown-red ... 90·00 3·50
a. Chocolate ... £120 24·00
b. Thin coarse toned paper (1898) ... £150 5·00
L13/15 *Set of* 3 ... £190 7·50

1902–**04**. W **43** (sideways).

(a) P 11.

L16 L **1** ½d. bright purple (1903) ... 65·00 8·00
L17 1d. blue (1902) ... 60·00 2·00
L18 2d. brown-red (1904) ... £110 12·00
L16/18 *Set of* 3 ... £200 20·00

(b) P 14×11.

L19 L **1** ½d. bright purple (1903) ... £1600
L20 1d. blue (1904) ... £110 11·00

Nos. L16/17 and L20 are known without watermark from the margins of the sheet.

1905–**06**. *Redrawn, with "V.R." omitted.* W **43** (sideways).

(a) P 11.

L21 L **2** 2d. brown-red (12.05) ... £1100 95·00

(b) P 14.

L22 L **2** 1d. blue (7.06) ... £180 30·00

(c) P 14×11.

L23 L **2** 1d. blue (7.06) ... £550 £170
a. Mixed perfs ... † £450

Between January 1907 and the end of 1912 the Life Insurance Department used ordinary Official stamps.

1913 (2 Jan)–**37**. *New values and colours.* W **43**.

(a) "De La Rue" paper. P 14×15.

L24 L **2** ½d. green ... 17·00 2·50
a. Yellow-green ... 17·00 2·50
L25 1d. carmine ... 11·00 1·25
a. Carmine-pink ... 17·00 1·75
L26 1½d. black (1917) ... 42·00 8·50
L27 1½d. chestnut-brown (1919) ... 1·50 3·00
L28 2d. bright purple ... 50·00 29·00
w. Wmk inverted ... † £120
L29 2d. yellow (1920) ... 8·00 2·00
L30 3d. yellow-brown ... 48·00 30·00
L31 6d. carmine-pink ... 35·00 30·00
L24/31 *Set of* 8 ... £190 95·00

(b) "Cowan" paper.

(i) P 14×15.

L31*a* L **2** ½d. yellow-green (1925) ... 35·00 4·50
L31*b* 1d. carmine-pink (1925) ... 35·00 3·50
bw. Wmk inverted ... 50·00 18·00

(ii) P 14.

L32 L **2** ½d. yellow-green (1926) ... 12·00 3·50
w. Wmk inverted ... † 35·00
L33 1d. scarlet (1931) ... 7·50 2·00
w. Wmk inverted ... 18·00 8·00
L34 2d. yellow (1937) ... 7·00 8·00
w. Wmk inverted ... 35·00 50·00
L35 3d. brown-lake (1931) ... 18·00 24·00
L36 6d. pink (1925) ... 38·00 42·00
L32/6 *Set of* 5 ... 75·00 70·00

(c) "Wiggins Teape" paper. P 14×15.

L36*a* L **2** ½d. yellow-green (3.37) ... 8·00 12·00
L36*b* 1d. scarlet (3.37) ... 15·00 3·25
L36*c* 6d. pink (7.37) ... 35·00 40·00
L36*a*/*c* *Set of* 3 ... 50·00 50·00

For descriptions of the various types of paper, see after No. 385. In the 1½d. the word "POSTAGE" is in both the side-labels instead of at left only.

1944–**47**. W **98**. P 14×15.

L37 L **2** ½d. yellow-green (7.47) ... 6·50 9·00
L38 1d. scarlet (6.44) ... 3·25 2·00
L39 2d. yellow (1946) ... 17·00 22·00
L40 3d. brown-lake (10.46) ... 23·00 38·00
L41 6d. pink (7.47) ... 19·00 35·00
L37/41 *Set of* 5 ... 60·00 95·00

L 3 Castlepoint lighthouse

L 4 Taiaroa lighthouse

L 5 Cape Palliser lighthouse

L 6 Cape Campbell lighthouse

L 7 Eddystone lighthouse

L 8 Stephens Island lighthouse

L 9 The Brothers lighthouse

L 10 Cape Brett lighthouse

(Des J. Berry. Recess B.W.).

1947 (1 Aug)–**65**. *Type* L **3**/**10**. W **98** (sideways inverted on 1d., 2d., sideways on 2½d.). P 13½.

L42 L **3** ½d. grey-green and orange-red ... 2·00 70
L43 L **4** 1d. olive-green and pale blue ... 1·75 1·25
L44 L **5** 2d. deep blue and grey-black ... 1·75 1·00
L45 L **6** 2½d. black and bright blue (*white opaque paper*) (4.11.63) ... 9·50 13·00
L46 L **7** 3d. mauve and pale blue ... 3·75 1·00
L47 L **8** 4d. brown and yellow-orange ... 4·25 1·75
a. Wmk sideways (*white opaque paper*) (13.10.65) ... 3·50 14·00
L48 L **9** 6d. chocolate and blue ... 4·00 2·75
L49 L **10** 1s. red-brown and blue ... 4·00 3·50
L42/49 *Set of* 8 ... 28·00 22·00

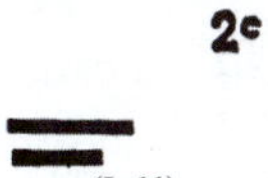
(L 11)

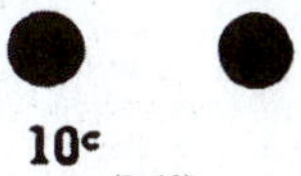
(L 12)

1967 (10 July)–**68**. *Decimal currency. Stamps of 1947–65, surch as Type* L **12** *or* L **11** *(2c.).*

L50 1c. on 1d. (No. L43) ... 2·25 4·25
a. Wmk upright (*white opaque paper*) (10.5.68) ... 1·00 4·50
L51 2c. on 2½d. (No. L45) ... 8·50 14·00
L52 2½c. on 3d. (No. L46) ... 1·25 4·00
a. Horiz pair, one without surcharge. £3250
b. Wmk sideways (*white opaque paper*) (4.68?) ... 2·40 4·75
L53 3c. on 4d. (No. L47a) ... 3·25 5·00
w. Wmk sideways inverted ... † £500
L54 5c. on 6d. (No. L48) ... 75 6·00
a. White opaque paper ... 1·50 6·50
L55 10c. on 1s. (No. L49) ... 1·50 10·00
a. Wmk sideways (*white opaque paper*) ... 75 4·00
aw. Wmk sideways inverted ... † —
L50/5a *Set of* 6 ... 14·00 32·00

See note *re* white paper below No. 736.

L 13 Moeraki Point lighthouse

L 14 Puysegur Point lighthouse

(Des J. Berry. Litho B.W.)

1969 (27 Mar)–**77**. *Types* L **13**/**14** *and similar designs. No wmk. Chalk-surfaced paper (8, 10c.), ordinary paper (others).* P 14 (8, 10c.) or 13½ (others).

L56 ½c. greenish yellow, red and deep blue 65 1·50
L57 2½c. ultramarine, green and pale buff ... 50 1·00
L58 3c. reddish brown and yellow ... 50 60
a. Chalk-surfaced paper (16.6.77)..... 50 2·25
L59 4c. light new blue, yellowish green and apple-green ... 50 75
a. Chalk-surfaced paper (16.6.77)..... 50 2·25
L60 8c. multicoloured (17.11.76) ... 40 2·00
L61 10c. multicoloured (17.11.76) ... 40 2·00
L62 15c. black, light yellow and ultramarine 40 1·25
a. Chalk-surfaced paper (3.75)... 20·00 22·00
ab. Perf 14 (24.12.76) ... 90 2·50
L56/62 *Set of* 7 ... 3·00 8·00

Designs: *Horiz*—4c. Cape Egmont Lighthouse. *Vert*—3c. Baring Head Lighthouse; 8c. East Cape; 10c. Farewell Spit; 15c. Dog Island Lighthouse.

POSTAL FISCAL STAMPS

As from 1 April 1882 fiscal stamps were authorised for postal use and conversely postage stamps became valid for fiscal use. Stamps in the designs of 1867 with "STAMP DUTY" above the Queen's head were withdrawn and although some passed through the mail quite legitimately they were mainly "philatelic" and we no longer list them. The issue which was specifically authorised in 1882 was the one which had originally been put on sale for fiscal use in 1880.

There is strong evidence that the authorities used up existing low value revenue stamps for postage, delaying the general release of the new "Postage and Revenue" low values (T **14**, **15** and **18**-**22**) to achieve this. Used prices for such stamps are for examples with 1882–3 postal cancellations.

Although all fiscal stamps were legally valid for postage only, values between 2s. and £1 were stocked at ordinary post offices. Other values could only be obtained by request from the G.P.O., Wellington or from offices of the Stamp Duties Department. Later the Arms types above £1 could also be obtained from the head post offices in Auckland, Christchurch, Dunedin and also a branch post office at Christchurch North where there was a local demand for them.

It seems sensible to list under Postal Fiscals the Queen Victoria stamps up to the £1 value and the Arms types up to the £5 because by 1931 the higher values were genuinely needed for postal purposes. Even the £10 was occasionally used on insured airmail parcels.

Although 2s. and 5s. values were included in the 1898 pictorial issue, it was the general practice for the Postal Department to limit the postage issues to 1s. until 1926 when the 2s. and 3s. appeared. These were then dropped from the fiscal issues and when in turn the 5s. and 10s. were introduced in 1953 and the £1 in 1960 no further printings of these values occurred in the fiscal series.

FORGED POSTMARKS. Our prices are for stamps with genuine postal cancellations. Beware of forged postmarks on stamps from which fiscal cancellations have been cleaned off.

Many small post offices acted as agents for government departments and it was the practice to use ordinary postal date-stamps on stamps used fiscally, so that when they are removed from documents they are indistinguishable from postally used specimens unless impressed with the embossed seal of the Stamp Duties Department.

Date-stamps very similar to postal date-stamps were sometimes supplied to offices of the Stamp Duties Department and it is not clear when this practice ceased. Prior to the Arms types the only sure proof of the postal use of off-cover fiscal stamps is when they bear a distinctive duplex, registered or parcel post cancellation, but beware of forgeries of the first two.

F 1

F 2

F 3

(Die eng W. R. Bock. Typo Govt Ptg Office)

1882 (Feb). W **12a**. P 12×11½.

F1	F 1	1d. lilac	£800	£475
F2		1d. blue	£180	35·00
		w. Wmk inverted		

The 1d. fiscal was specifically authorised for postal use in February 1882 owing to a shortage of the 1d. Type **5** and pending the introduction of the 1d. Type **14** on 1 April.

The 1d. lilac fiscal had been replaced by the 1d. blue in 1878 but postally used copies with 1882 duplex postmarks are known although most postally used examples are dated from 1890 and these must have been philatelic.

1882 (early). W **12a**. P 12×11½.

F3	F 2	1s. grey-green		
F4	F 3	1s. grey-green and red		
F4*a*		2s. rose and blue		

Examples of these are known postally used in 1882 and although not specifically authorised for postal use it is believed that their use was permitted where there was a shortage of the appropriate postage value.

WMK TYPE F 5. The balance of the paper employed for the 1867 issue was used for early printings of Type F **4** introduced in 1880 before changing over to the "N Z" and Star watermark. The values we list with this watermark are known with 1882–83 postal date stamps. Others have later dates and are considered to be philatelic but should they be found with 1882–83 postal dates we would be prepared to add them to the list.

F 4

F 5

The 12s.6d. value has the head in an oval (as Type **10**), and the 15s. and £1 values have it in a broken circle (as Type **7**).

(Dies eng W.R. Bock. Typo Govt Ptg Office)

1882 (1 Apr). *Type* F **4** *and similar types. "De La Rue" paper.*

A. W **12a** (6 mm).

(a) P 12 (1882).

F5	4d. orange-red (Wmk F **5**)	–	£325
F6	6d. lake-brown	–	£225
	a. Wmk F **5**	–	£650
F7	8d. green (Wmk F **5**)	–	£650
F8	1s. pink	–	£300
	a. Wmk F **5**		
F9	2s. blue	80·00	6·50
F10	2s.6d. grey-brown	£120	6·50
	a. Wmk F **5**		
F11	3s. mauve	£150	8·00
F12	4s. brown-rose	£160	14·00
	a. Wmk F **5**		
F13	5s. green	£190	15·00
	a. Yellow-green	£190	15·00
F14	6s. rose	£200	38·00
F15	7s. ultramarine	£225	70·00
F16	7s.6d. bronze-grey	£750	£160
F17	8s. deep blue	£250	75·00
F18	9s. orange	£300	80·00
F19	10s. brown-red	£190	25·00
	a. Wmk F **5**		
F20	15s. green	£600	£140
F21	£1 rose-pink	£300	70·00

(b) P 12½ (1886).

F22	2s. blue	80·00	6·50
F23	2s.6d. grey-brown	£120	6·50
F24	3s. mauve	£160	8·00
F25	4s. purple-claret	£160	14·00
	a. Brown-rose	£160	14·00
F26	5s. green	£190	15·00
	a. Yellow-green	£190	15·00
F27	6s. rose	£200	38·00
F28	7s. ultramarine	£225	70·00
F29	8s. deep blue	£250	75·00
F30	9s. orange	£300	80·00
F31	10s. brown-red	£190	25·00
F32	15s. green	£600	£140
F33	£1 rose-pink	£300	70·00

B. W **12b** (7 mm). P 12½ (1888).

F34	2s. blue	80·00	6·50
F35	2s.6d. grey-brown	£120	6·50
F36	3s. mauve	£150	8·00
F37	4s. brown-rose	£150	14·00
	a. Brown-red	£150	14·00
F38	5s. green	£180	15·00
	a. Yellow-green	£180	15·00
F39	6s. rose	£200	38·00
F40	7s. ultramarine	£225	70·00
F41	7s.6d. bronze-grey	£750	£160
F42	8s. deep blue	£250	75·00
F43	9s. orange	£300	80·00
F44	10s. brown-red	£190	24·00
	a. Maroon	£190	24·00
F45	£1 pink	£300	70·00

C. W **12c** (4 mm). P 12½ (1890).

F46	2s. blue	£110	14·00
F46*a*	2s.6d. grey-brown	£160	16·00
F47	3s. mauve	£200	38·00
F48	4s. brown-red	£170	22·00
F49	5s. green	£190	16·00
F50	6s. rose	£250	40·00
F51	7s. ultramarine	£275	75·00
F52	8s. deep blue	£300	85·00
F53	9s. orange	£350	£100
F54	10s. brown-red	£225	27·00
F55	15s. green	£650	£160

D. Continuation of W **12b**. P 11 (1895–1901).

F56	2s. blue	45·00	7·00
F57	2s.6d. grey-brown	£110	6·50
	a. Inscr "COUNTERPART" (1901)*	£170	£200
F58	3s. mauve	£150	8·00
F59	4s. brown-red	£150	13·00
F60	5s. yellow-green	£180	16·00
F61	6s. rose	£190	38·00
F62	7s. pale blue	£225	70·00
F63	7s.6d. bronze-grey	£750	£160
F64	8s. deep blue	£250	75·00
F65	9s. orange	£300	£100
	a. Imperf between (horiz pair)	£1500	
F66	10s. brown-red	£190	24·00
	a. Maroon	£190	24·00
F67	15s. green	£600	£140
F68	£1 rose-pink	£300	70·00

*The plate normally printed in yellow and inscribed "COUNTERPART" just above the bottom value panel, was for use on the counterparts of documents but was issued in error in the colour of the normal fiscal stamp and accepted for use.

E. W **43** *(sideways).*

(i) Unsurfaced "Cowan" paper.

(a) P 11 (1903).

F69	2s.6d. grey-brown	£120	6·50
F70	3s. mauve	£150	8·00
F71	4s. orange-red	£150	13·00
F72	6s. rose	£190	38·00
F73	7s. pale blue	£225	70·00
F74	8s. deep blue	£250	75·00
F75	10s. brown-red	£180	24·00
	a. Maroon	£180	24·00
F76	15s. green	£600	£140
F77	£1 rose-pink	£275	70·00

(b) P 14 (1906).

F78	2s.6d. grey-brown	£100	6·50
F79	3s. mauve	£130	8·00
F80	4s. orange-red	£130	11·00
F81	5s. yellow-green	£120	12·00
F82	6s. rose	£180	38·00
F83	7s. pale blue	£190	70·00
F84	7s.6d. bronze-grey	£700	£150
F85	8s. deep blue	£225	75·00
F86	9s. orange	£250	80·00
F87	10s. maroon	£170	24·00
F88	15s. green	£600	£140
F89	£1 rose-pink	£250	70·00

(c) P 14½×14, comb (clean-cut) (1907).

F90	2s. blue	45·00	6·00
F91	2s.6d. grey-brown	£120	6·50
F92	3s. mauve	£150	8·00
F93	4s. orange-red	£140	12·00
F94	6s. rose	£190	38·00
F95	10s. maroon	£180	22·00
F96	15s. green	£600	£140
F97	£1 rose-pink	£250	70·00

(ii) Chalk-surfaced "De la Rue" paper.

(a) P 14 (1913).

F98	2s. blue	40·00	5·50
F99	2s.6d. grey-brown	48·00	6·50
F100	3s. purple	£100	8·00
F101	4s. orange-red	£100	9·50
F102	5s. yellow-green	£100	11·00
F103	6s. rose	£160	22·00
F104	7s. pale blue	£170	40·00
F105	7s.6d. bronze-grey	£750	£160
F106	8s. deep blue	£200	45·00
F107	9s. orange	£275	80·00
F108	10s. maroon	£170	20·00
F109	15s. green	£600	£140
F110	£1 rose-carmine	£250	70·00

(b) P 14½×14, comb (1913–21).

F111	2s. deep blue	40·00	5·50
F112	2s.6d. grey-brown	48·00	6·50
F113	3s. purple	£100	8·00
F114	4s. orange-red	£100	9·50
F115	5s. yellow-green	£100	11·00
F116	6s. rose	£160	22·00
F117	7s. pale blue	£170	40·00
F118	8s. deep blue	£200	45·00
F119	9s. orange	£250	80·00
F120	10s. maroon	£170	20·00
F121	12s.6d. deep plum (1921)	£8000	£3250
F122	15s. green	£600	£140
F123	£1 rose-carmine	£225	70·00

The "De La Rue" paper has a smooth finish and has toned gum which is strongly resistant to soaking.

(iii) Chalk-surfaced "Jones" paper. P 14½×14, comb (1924).

F124	2s. deep blue	48·00	7·00
F125	2s.6d. deep grey-brown	55·00	7·50
F126	3s. purple	£120	8·50
F127	5s. yellow-green	£120	13·00
F128	10s. brown-red	£190	20·00
F129	12s.6d. deep purple	£8000	£3250
F130	15s. green	£550	£150

The "Jones" paper has a coarser texture, is poorly surfaced and the ink tends to peel. The outline of the watermark commonly shows on the surface of the stamp. The gum is colourless or only slightly toned and washes off readily.

(iv) Thick, opaque, chalk-surfaced "Cowan" paper. P 14½×14, comb (1925–30).

F131	2s. blue	42·00	6·50
F132	2s.6d. deep grey-brown	48·00	7·00
F133	3s. mauve	£140	13·00
F134	4s. orange-red	£100	13·00
F135	5s. yellow-green	£100	15·00
	x. Wmk reversed (1927)	£140	27·00
F136	6s. rose	£160	25·00
F137	7s. pale blue	£170	40·00
F138	8s. deep blue	£250	45·00
	a. *Blue* (1930)	£500	
F139	10s. brown-red	£170	20·00
	x. Wmk reversed (1927)	£225	£170
F140	12s.6d. blackish purple	£8000	£3250
F141	15s. green	£550	£150
F142	£1 rose-pink	£225	70·00

The "Cowan" paper is white and opaque and the watermark, which is usually smaller than in the "Jones" paper, is often barely visible.

(v) Thin, hard, chalk-surfaced "Wiggins Teape" paper. P 14½×14, comb (1926).

F143	4s. orange-red	£110	16·00
F144	£1 rose-pink	£250	£130

The "Wiggins Teape" paper has a horizontal mesh, in relation to the design, with narrow watermark, whereas other chalk-surfaced papers with this perforation have a vertical mesh and wider watermark.

F 6

35/-

(F 7)

(Des H. L. Richardson. Typo Govt Ptg Office)

1931–40. *As Type* F **6** *(various frames).* W **43**. P 14.

(i) Thick, opaque, chalk-surfaced "Cowan" paper, with horizontal mesh (1931–35).

F145	1s.3d. lemon (4.31)	6·00	40·00
F146	1s.3d. orange-yellow	8·50	10·00
F147	2s.6d. deep brown	15·00	4·50
F148	4s. red	15·00	7·00
F149	5s. green	22·00	14·00
F150	6s. carmine-rose	32·00	15·00
F151	7s. blue	28·00	26·00
F152	7s.6d. olive-grey	70·00	90·00
F153	8s. slate-violet	28·00	32·00
F154	9s. brown-orange	30·00	29·00
F155	10s. carmine-lake	24·00	9·50
F156	12s.6d. deep plum (9.35)	£130	£130
F157	15s. sage-green	70·00	40·00
F158	£1 pink	70·00	19·00
F159	25s. greenish blue	£425	£550
F160	30s. brown (1935)	£275	£150
F161	35s. orange-yellow	£3500	£4000
F162	£2 bright purple	£300	65·00
F163	£2 10s. red	£375	£450
F164	£3 green	£400	£250
F165	£3 10s. rose (1935)	£1500	£1600
F166	£4 light blue (1935)	£400	£170
F167	£4 10s. deep olive-grey (1935)	£1400	£1500
F168	£5 indigo-blue	£350	£110

(ii) Thin, hard 'Wiggins Teape" paper with vertical mesh (1936–40).

(a) Chalk-surfaced (1936–39).

F169	1s.3d. pale orange-yellow	25·00	3·75
F170	2s.6d. dull brown	80·00	3·75
F171	4s. pale red-brown	95·00	9·50
F172	5s. green	95·00	7·00
	w. Wmk inverted	–	£250
F173	6s. carmine-rose	95·00	35·00
F174	7s. pale blue	£140	38·00
F175	8s. slate-violet	£160	50·00
F176	9s. brown-orange	£170	75·00
F177	10s. pale carmine-lake	£160	7·00
F178	15s. sage-green	£250	55·00
F179	£1 pink	£180	27·00
F180	30s. brown (1.39)	£500	£180
F181	35s. orange-yellow	£4250	£4500
F182	£2 bright purple (1937)	£750	£110
	w. Wmk inverted		
F183	£3 green (1937)	£900	£350
F184	£5 indigo-blue (1937)	£1100	£225

(b) Unsurfaced (1940).

F185	7s.6d. olive-grey	£180	75·00

Not all values listed above were stocked at ordinary post offices as some of them were primarily required for fiscal purposes but all were valid for postage.

1939. *No.* F161 *surch with Type* F **7**.

F186	35/- on 35s. orange-yellow	£500	£275

Because the 35s. orange-yellow could so easily be confused with the 1s.3d. in the same colour, it was surcharged.

1940 (June). *New values surch as Type* F **7**. *"Wiggins Teape" chalk-surfaced paper.* W **43**. P 14.

F187	3/6 on 3s.6d. grey-green	55·00	23·00
F188	5/6 on 5s.6d. lilac	£100	55·00
F189	11/- on 11s. yellow	£180	£150
F190	22/- on 22s. scarlet	£475	£350
F187/90	*Set of* 4	£750	£500

These values were primarily needed for fiscal use.

1940–58. *As Type* F **6** *(various frames).* W **98**. P 14.

(i) "Wiggins Teape" chalk-surfaced paper with vertical mesh (1940–56).

F191	1s.3d. orange-yellow	16·00	2·75
	w. Wmk inverted	–	£180

F192 1s.3d. yellow and black (wmk inverted) (14.6.55) 5·00 1·75
aw. Wmk upright (9.9.55) 32·00 32·00
b. Error. Yellow and blue (wmk inverted) (7.56) 4·50 4·50
F193 2s.6d. deep brown 8·50 1·10
w. Wmk inverted (3.49) 8·50 1·00
F194 4s. red-brown 22·00 2·00
w. Wmk inverted (3.49) 25·00 2·00
F195 5s. green 22·00 1·00
w. Wmk inverted (1.5.50) 23·00 1·00
F196 6s. carmine-rose 35·00 3·25
w. Wmk inverted (1948) 35·00 3·25
F197 7s. pale blue 38·00 5·50
F198 7s.6d. olive-grey (wmk inverted) (21.12.50) 65·00 60·00
F199 8s. slate-violet 65·00 17·00
w. Wmk inverted (6.12.50) 65·00 18·00
F200 9s. brown-orange (1.46) 35·00 42·00
w. Wmk inverted (9.1.51) 65·00 42·00
F201 10s. carmine-lake 42·00 2·50
w. Wmk inverted (4.50) 45·00 2·50
F202 15s. sage-green 50·00 19·00
w. Wmk inverted (8.12.50) 75·00 26·00
F203 £1 pink 28·00 3·75
w. Wmk inverted (1.2.50) 45·00 4·50
F204 25s. greenish blue (1946) £475 £475
w. Wmk inverted (7.53) £600 £600
F205 30s. brown (1946) £325 £130
w. Wmk inverted (9.49) £300 £130
F206 £2 bright purple (1946) £120 26·00
w. Wmk inverted (17.6.52) £120 22·00
F207 £2 10s. red (wmk inverted) (9.8.51) £325 £350
F208 £3 green (1946) £180 48·00
w. Wmk inverted (17.6.52) £170 48·00
F209 £3 10s. rose (11.48) £2000 £1400
w. Wmk inverted (5.52) £2250 £1400
F210 £4 light blue (wmk inverted) (12.2.52) £180 £140
w. Wmk upright † £1000
F211 £5 indigo-blue £400 75·00
w. Wmk inverted (11.9.50) £250 55·00
F191/211 *Set of* 21 £3750 £2500

3s.6d.

Type I. Broad serifed capitals

Type II. Taller capitals, without serifs

Surcharged as Type F 7.

F212 3/6 on 3s.6d. grey-green (I) (1942) 20·00 7·00
w. Wmk inverted (12.10.50) 38·00 12·00
F213 3/6 on 3s.6d. grey-green (II) (6.53) 14·00 38·00
w. Wmk inverted (6.53) 45·00 45·00
F214 5/6 on 5s.6d. lilac (1944) 48·00 20·00
w. Wmk inverted (13.9.50) 60·00 18·00
F215 11/- on 11s. yellow (1942) 90·00 48·00
F216 22/- on 22s. scarlet (1945) £350 £160
w. Wmk inverted (1.3.50) £375 £170
F212/16 *Set of* 5 £475 £250

(ii) P 14×13½. "Wiggins Teape" unsurfaced paper with horizontal mesh (1956–58).

F217 1s.3d. yellow and black (11.56) 2·75 3·25
w. Wmk inverted 28·00 28·00
F218 £1 pink (20.10.58) 35·00 12·00

No. F192b had the inscription printed in blue in error but as many as 378,000 were printed.

From 1949–53 inferior paper had to be used and for technical reasons it was necessary to feed the paper into the machine in a certain way which resulted in whole printings with the watermark inverted for most values.

F 8

1967 (10 July)–**84**. *Decimal currency.* W **98** (sideways inverted). Unsurfaced paper. P 14 (line).

F219 **F 8** $4 deep reddish violet 8·00 7·00
a. Perf 14 (comb) (wmk sideways) (17.9.68) 2·50 1·50
aw. Wmk sideways inverted (6.7.84) 4·50 11·00
F220 $6 emerald 12·00 15·00
a. Perf 14 (comb) (wmk sideways) (17.9.68) 3·00 3·00
aw. Wmk sideways inverted (6.7.84) 4·50 13·00
F221 $8 light greenish blue 22·00 22·00
a. Perf 14 (comb) (wmk sideways) (20.6.68) 4·00 4·50
aw. Wmk sideways inverted (6.7.84)
F222 $10 deep ultramarine 25·00 20·00
a. Perf 14 (comb) (wmk sideways) (20.6.68) 4·00 3·75
aw. Wmk sideways inverted (6.7.84) 25·00 27·00
F219/22 *Set of* 4 60·00 60·00
F219a/22a *Set of* 4 12·00 11·50

The original printings were line perforated on paper with the watermark sideways ("N Z" to left of star, when viewed from the back). In 1968 the stamps appeared comb perforated with the watermark sideways inverted ("N Z" to right from back). A further comb perforated printing in July 1984 showed the normal sideways watermark.

ANTARCTIC EXPEDITIONS

VICTORIA LAND

These issues were made under authority of the New Zealand Postal Department and, while not strictly necessary, they actually franked correspondence to New Zealand. They were sold to the public at a premium.

1908 (15 Jan). *Shackleton Expedition. T* **42** *of New Zealand (P 14), optd* "King Edward VII Land", *in two lines, reading up, by Coulls, Culling and Co., Wellington.*

A1 1d. rose-carmine (No. 356 Royle) (G.) £450 38·00
a. Opt double † £1600
A1*b* 1d. rose-carmine (No. 352*c* Waterlow) (G.) £1400 £850

Nos. A1/1*b* were used on board the expedition ship, *Nimrod*, and at the Cape Royds base in McMurdo Sound. Due to adverse conditions Shackleton landed in Victoria Land rather than King Edward VII Land, the intended destination.

1911 (9 Feb)–**13**. *Scott Expedition. Stamps of New Zealand optd* "VICTORIA LAND.", *in two lines by Govt Printer, Wellington.*

A2 **51** ½d. deep green (No. 387*aa*) (18.1.13) £600 £700
A3 **53** 1d. carmine (No. 405) 55·00 £100
a. No stop after "LAND" (R. 7/5) £325 £750

Nos. A2/3 were used at the Cape Evans base on McMurdo Sound or on the *Terra Nova*.

ROSS DEPENDENCY

This comprises a sector of the Antarctic continent and a number of islands. It was claimed by Great Britain on 30 July 1923 and soon afterward put under the jurisdiction of New Zealand.

1 H.M.S. *Erebus*

2 Shackleton and Scott

3 Map of Ross Dependency and New Zealand

4 Queen Elizabeth II

(Des E. M. Taylor (3d.), L. C. Mitchell (4d.), R. Smith (8d.), J. Berry (1s.6d.). Recess D.L.R.)

1957 (11 Jan). W98 of New Zealand (Mult N Z and Star). P 13 (1s.6d.) or 14 (others).

1 **1** 3d. indigo 1·00 60
2 **2** 4d. carmine-red 1·00 60
3 **3** 8d. bright carmine-red and ultramarine 1·00 60
a. Bright carmine-red and blue 5·50 4·50
4 **4** 1s.6d. slate-purple 1·00 60
1/4 *Set of* 4 3·50 2·25

(New Currency. 100 cents = 1 New Zealand dollar)

5 H.M.S. *Erebus*

1967 (10 July). *Decimal currency. As Nos. 1/4 but with values inscr in decimal currency as T* **5**. *Chalky paper (except 15c.).* W98 of New Zealand (sideways on 7c.). P 13 (15c.) or 14 (others).

5 **5** 2c. indigo 8·50 6·00
a. Deep blue 14·00 7·50
6 **2** 3c. carmine-red 2·75 4·75
w. Wmk inverted 75·00
7 **3** 7c. bright carmine-red and ultramarine 2·75 6·00
8 **4** 15c. slate-purple 2·75 9·00
w. Wmk inverted £100
5/8 *Set of* 4 15·00 23·00

TOKELAU ISLANDS

Formerly known as the Union Islands, and administered as part of the Gilbert & Ellice Islands Colony, Tokelau was transferred to New Zealand on 4 November 1925 and administered with Western Samoa. The Islands were finally incorporated in New Zealand on 1 January 1949 and became a dependency. The name Tokelau was officially adopted on 7 May 1946.

Stamps of GILBERT AND ELLICE ISLANDS were used in Tokelau from Febuary 1911 until June 1926 when they were replaced by those of SAMOA. These were current until 1948.

The post office on Atafu opened in 1911, but the cancellations for the other two islands, Fakaofo and Nukunono, did not appear until 1926.

NEW ZEALAND ADMINISTRATION

1 Atafu Village and Map

2 Nukunono hut and map

3 Fakaofo village and map

(Des J. Berry from photographs by T. T. C. Humphrey. Recess B.W.)

1948 (22 June). *T* **1/3** *and similar horiz designs.* Wmk *T* **98** of New Zealand (Mult N Z and Star). P 13½.

1 **1** ½d. red-brown and purple 15 75
2 **2** 1d. chestnut and green 15 50
w. Wmk inverted £275
3 **3** 2d. green and ultramarine 15 50
1/3 *Set of* 3 40 1·60

Covers are known postmarked 16 June 1948, but this was in error for 16 July.

1953 (16 June*). *Coronation. As No. 715 of New Zealand, but inscr* "TOKELAU ISLANDS".

4 **164** 3d. brown 1·50 1·50

*This is the date of issue in Tokelau. The stamps were released in New Zealand on 25 May.

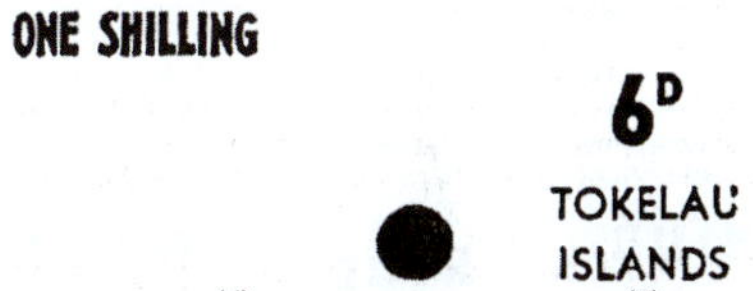

(4) (5)

1956 (27 Mar). *No. 1 surch with T* **4** *by Govt Printer, Wellington.*

5 **1** 1s. on ½d. red-brown and purple 75 1·25

1966 (8 Nov). *Postal fiscal stamps of New Zealand (Type F* **6**), *but without value, surch as T* **5** *by Govt Printer, Wellington.* W **98** of New Zealand. P 14.

6 6d. light blue 25 80
7 8d. light emerald 25 80
8 2s. light pink 30 80
6/8 *Set of* 3 70 2·25

(New Currency. 100 cents = 1 New Zealand dollar)

(6) (7)

1967 (4 Sept*). *Decimal currency.*

(a) Nos. 1/3 surch in decimal currency as T **6** *by Govt Printer, Wellington.*

9 1c. on 1d. 20 60
10 2c. on 2d. 30 1·00
11 10c. on ½d. 70 2·00

(b) Postal Fiscal stamps of New Zealand (Type F **6**), *but without value, surch as T* **7** *by Govt Printer, Wellington.* W **98** of New Zealand (sideways). P 14 (line or comb).

12 **F 6** 3c. reddish lilac 30 20
13 5c. light blue 30 20
14 7c. light emerald 30 20
15 20c. light pink 30 30
9/15 *Set of* 7 2·25 4·00

*This is the date of issue in Tokelau. The stamps were released in New Zealand on 10 July.

8 British Protectorate (1877)

(Des New Zealand P.O. artists from suggestions by Tokelau Administration. Litho B.W.)

1969 (8 Aug). *History of Tokelau. T* **8** *and similar horiz designs.* W **98** of New Zealand. P 13×12½.

16 5c. ultramarine, yellow and black 15 10
17 10c. vermilion, yellow and black 15 10
18 15c. green, yellow and black 20 15
19 20c. yellow-brown, yellow and black 25 15
16/19 *Set of* 4 65 45

Designs:—10c. Annexed to Gilbert and Ellice Islands, 1916; 15c. New Zealand Administration, 1925; 20c. New Zealand Territory, 1948.

1969 (14 Nov*). *Christmas. As T* **301** *of New Zealand, but inscr* "TOKELAU ISLANDS". W **98** of New Zealand. P 13½×14½.

20 2c. multicoloured 10 15

*This is the date of issue in Tokelau. The stamps were released in New Zealand on 1 October.

1970 (15 Nov*). *Christmas. As T* **314** *of New Zealand, but inscr* "TOKELAU ISLANDS". P 12½.
21 2c. multicoloured 10 20
*This is the date of issue in Tokelau. The stamps were released in New Zealand on 1 October.

NIUE

Niue became a British Protectorate on 20 April 1900 and was transferred to New Zealand control on 11 June 1901. There was considerable local resentment at attempts to incorporate Niue into the Cook Islands and, in consequence, the island was recognised as a separate New Zealand dependency from 1902.

PRICES FOR STAMPS ON COVER TO 1945	
No. 1	*from* × 3
Nos. 2/5	*from* × 8
Nos. 6/7	—
Nos. 8/9	*from* × 30
Nos. 10/12	—
Nos. 13/31	*from* × 3
Nos. 32/7c	—
Nos. 38/47	*from* × 5
Nos. 48/9	—
No. 50	*from* × 15
Nos. 51/4	—
Nos. 55/61	*from* × 8
Nos. 62/8	*from* × 12
Nos. 69/71	*from* × 3
Nos. 72/4	*from* × 10
Nos. 75/8	*from* × 8
Nos. 79/88	—
Nos. 89/97	*from* × 2

NEW ZEALAND DEPENDENCY

Stamps of New Zealand overprinted

NIUE
(1)

1902 (4 Jan). *Handstamped with T* **1** *in green or bluish green. Pirie paper.* Wmk double-lined "N Z" and Star, W **38** of New Zealand. P 11.
1 **42** 1d. carmine £300 £300
A few overprints were made with a *greenish violet* ink. These occurred only in the first vertical row and part of the second row of the first sheet overprinted owing to violet ink having been applied to the pad (*Price* £1400 *un*).

NIUE. ½ PENI. (2) — NIUE. TAHA PENI. (3) 1d. — NIUE. 2½ PENI. (4)

1902 (4 Apr). *Type-set surcharges. T* **2**, **3**, *and* **4**.
(i) Pirie paper. No wmk. P 11.
2 **27** 2½d. blue (R.) .... 1·50 4·00
a. No stop after "PENI" .... 26·00 50·00
b. Surch double £2500
(ii) Basted Mills paper. Wmk double-lined "N Z" and Star, W **38** of New Zealand.
(a) P 14.
3 **23** ½d. green (R.) .... 2·50 4·50
a. Spaced "U" and "E" (R. 3/3, 3/6, 8/3, 8/6) .... 15·00 23·00
b. Surch inverted £325 £550
c. Surch double £1100
4 **42** 1d. carmine (B.) .... 28·00 32·00
a. Spaced "U" and "E" (R. 3/3, 3/6, 8/6) £150 £160
b. No stop after "PENI" (R. 9/3) £400 £425
c. Varieties a. and b. on same stamp (R. 8/3) £400 £425
(b) P 11×14.
5 **42** 1d. carmine (B.) .... 1·75 2·50
b. Spaced "U" and "E" (R. 3/3, 3/6, 8/6) .... 12·00 16·00
c. No stop after "PENI (R. 9/3) .... 35·00 48·00
d. Varieties b. and c. on same stamp (R. 8/3) .... 35·00 48·00
(c) Mixed perfs.
6 **23** ½d. green (R.) £1600
7 **42** 1d. carmine (B.) £950

1902 (2 May). *Type-set surcharges, T* **2**, **3**. *Cowan paper.* Wmk single-lined "N Z" and Star, W **43** of New Zealand.
(a) P 14.
8 **23** ½d. green (R.) .... 1·00 1·00
a. Spaced "U" and "E" (R. 3/3, 3/6, 8/3, 8/6) .... 7·50 9·50
9 **42** 1d. carmine (B.) .... 60 1·00
a. Surch double £1700 £1800
b. Spaced "U" and "E" (R. 3/3, 3/6, 8/6) .... 9·50 16·00
c. No stop after "PENI" (R. 5/3, 7/3, 9/3, 10/3, 10/6) .... 9·00 15·00
d. Varieties b. and c. on same stamp (R. 8/3) .... 30·00 45·00
e. "I" of "NIUE" omitted (R. 6/5 from end of last ptg) .. £850
(b) P 14×11.
10 **23** ½d. green (R.) ....
(c) Mixed perfs.
11 **23** ½d. green (R.) £1600
12 **42** 1d. carmine (B.) £200
a. Spaced "U" and "E" (R. 3/3, 3/6, 8/3, 8/6) £600
b. No stop after "PENI" (R. 5/3, 7/3, 9/3, 10/3, 10/6) £550

NIUE. (5) — Tolu e Pene. (6) 3d. — Ono e Pene. (7) 6d. — Taha e Sileni. (8) 1s.

1903 (2 July). *Optd with name at top, T* **5**, *and values at foot, T* **6/8**, *in blue.* W **43** of New Zealand (sideways). P 11.
13 **28** 3d. yellow-brown .... 9·50 5·00
14 **31** 6d. rose-red .... 13·00 11·00
15 **34** 1s. brown-red ("Tahae" joined) ... £650
a. Surch double, one albino £850
16 1s. bright red .... 35·00 38·00
a. Orange-red .... 45·00 48·00
13/16 *Set of* 3 .... 50·00 48·00

NIUE. ½ PENI. (9) — NIUE. 2½ PENI. (9a) — NIUE. (10)

1911 (30 Nov). *½d. surch with T* **9**, *others optd at top as T* **5** *and values at foot as T* **7**, **8**. W **43** of New Zealand. P 14×15 (½d.) or 14×14½ (others).
17 **51** ½d. green (C.) 50 50
18 **52** 6d. carmine (B.) .... 2·00 7·00
19 1s. vermilion (B.) .... 6·50 48·00
17/19 *Set of* 3 .... 8·00 50·00

1915 (Sept). *Surch with T* **9a**. W **43** of New Zealand. P 14.
20 **27** 2½d. deep blue (C.) .... 19·00 42·00

1917 (Aug). *1d. surch as T* **3**, *3d. optd as T* **5** *with value as T* **6**. W **43** of New Zealand.
21 **53** 1d. carmine (P 14×15) (Br.) .... 16·00 5·50
a. No stop after "PENI" (R. 10/16) £650
22 **60** 3d. chocolate (P 14×14½) (B.) .... 45·00 85·00
a. No stop after "Pene" (R. 10/4) £800
b. Perf 14×13½ .... 55·00 95·00
c. Vert pair, Nos. 22/b £160

1917–21. *Optd with T* **10**. W **43** of New Zealand.
(a) P 14×15.
23 **61** ½d. green (R.) (2.20) .... 70 2·50
24 **53** 1d. carmine (B.) (10.17) .... 10·00 8·50
25 **61** 1½d. slate (R.) (11.17) .... 1·00 2·25
26 1½d. orange-brown (R.) (2.19) .... 70 5·00
27 3d. chocolate (B.) (6.19) .... 1·40 32·00
(b) P 14×13½
28 **60** 2½d. blue (R.) (10.20) .... 3·50 11·00
a. Perf 14×14½ .... 1·25 8·50
ab. Opt double, one albino £500
b. Vert pair, Nos. 28/a .... 18·00 65·00
29 3d. chocolate (B.) (10.17) .... 2·00 2·00
a. Perf 14×14½ .... 1·25 1·50
b. Vert pair, Nos. 29/a .... 22·00 50·00
30 6d. carmine (B.) (8.21) .... 8·00 24·00
a. Perf 14×14½ .... 4·75 24·00
b. Vert pair, Nos. 30/a .... 32·00 £110
31 1s. vermilion (B.) (10.18) .... 11·00 27·00
a. Perf 14×14½ .... 5·50 27·00
b. Vert pair, Nos. 31/a .... 42·00 £120
23/31a *Set of* 9 .... 24·00 £100

1918–29. *Postal Fiscal stamps as Type* F **4** *of New Zealand optd with T* **10**. W **43** of New Zealand (sideways).
(i) Chalk-surfaced "De La Rue" paper.
(a) P 14.
32 5s. yellow-green (R.) (7.18) £100 £110
(b) P 14½×14, comb.
33 2s. deep blue (R.) (9.18) .... 16·00 32·00
34 2s.6d. grey-brown (B.) (2.23) .... 21·00 48·00
35 5s. yellow-green (R.) (10.18) .... 25·00 50·00
36 10s. maroon (B.) (2.23) £120 £160
37 £1 rose-carmine (B.) (2.23) £150 £225
33/7 *Set of* 5 .... £300 £450
(ii) Thick, opaque, white chalk-surfaced "Cowan" paper. P 14½×14.
37*a* 5s. yellow-green (R.) (10.29) .... 27·00 60·00
37*b* 10s. brown-red (B.) (2.27) .... 90·00 £140
37*c* £1 rose-pink (B.) (2.28) £160 £225
37*a/c Set of* 3 .... £250 £375

11 Landing of Captain Cook

12 Landing of Captain Cook

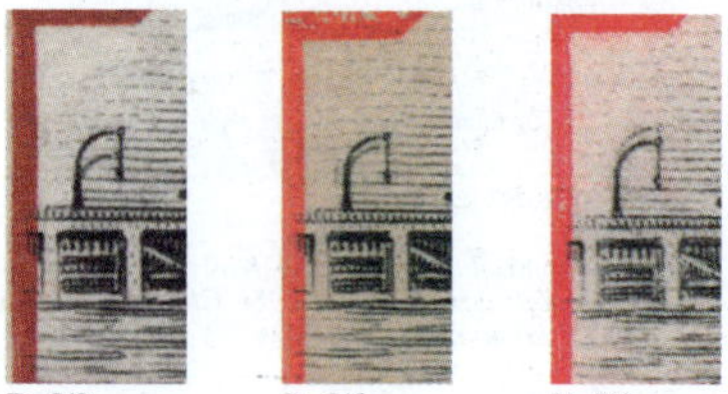
R. 2/8 R. 3/6 R. 5/2

Double derrick flaws

(Des, eng and recess P.B.)

1920 (23 Aug). *T* **11** *and similar designs.* No wmk. P 14.
38 ½d. black and green .... 3·75 3·75
39 1d. black and dull carmine .... 2·00 1·25
a. Double derrick flaw (R. 2/8, 3/6 or 5/2) .... 6·50 6·50
40 1½d. black and red .... 2·75 11·00
41 3d. black and blue .... 1·00 15·00
42 6d. red-brown and green .... 2·25 18·00
43 1s. black and sepia .... 2·25 18·00
38/43 *Set of* 6 .... 12·50 60·00
Designs: *Vert*—1d. Wharf at Avarua; 1½d. "Capt Cook (Dance)"; 3d. Palm tree. *Horiz*—6d. Huts at Arorangi; 1s. Avarua Harbour.
Examples of the 6d. with inverted centre were not supplied to the Post Office.

1925–27. *As Nos. 38/9 and new values.* W **43** of New Zealand (sideways on 4d.) P 14.
44 ½d. black and green (1927) .... 1·50 8·00
45 1d. black and deep carmine (1925) .... 1·75 1·00
a. Double derrick flaw (R. 2/8, 3/6 or 5/2) .... 5·50 4·50
46 2½d. black and blue (10.27) .... 4·25 11·00
47 4d. black and violet (10.27) .... 7·00 20·00
44/7 *Set of* 4 .... 13·00 35·00
Designs: *Vert*—2½d. Te Po, Rarotongan chief. *Horiz*—4d. Harbour, Rarotonga, and Mount Ikurangi.

1927–28. *Admiral type of New Zealand optd as T* **10**. W **43** of New Zealand. P 14.
(a) "Jones" paper (wmk inverted).
48 **72** 2s. deep blue (2.27) (R.) .... 15·00 48·00
(b) "Cowan" paper.
49 **72** 2s. light blue (R.) (2.28) .... 18·00 32·00

1931 (1 Apr). *No. 40 surch as T* **18** *of Cook Is.*
50 2d. on 1½d. black and red .... 3·75 1·00

1931 (12 Nov). *Postal Fiscal stamps as Type* F **6** *of New Zealand optd as T* **10**. W **43** of New Zealand. *Thick, opaque, chalk-surfaced "Cowan" paper.* P 14.
51 2s.6d. deep brown (B.) .... 4·00 11·00
52 5s. green (R.) .... 35·00 70·00
53 10s. carmine-lake (B.) .... 35·00 £100
54 £1 pink (B.) .... 70·00 £150
51/4 *Set of* 4 .... £130 £300
See also Nos. 79/82 for different type of overprint.

(Des L. C. Mitchell. Recess P.B.)

1932 (16 Mar). *T* **12** *and similar designs inscr "NIUE" and "COOK ISLANDS".* No wmk. P 13.
55 ½d. black and emerald .... 9·50 22·00
a. Perf 13×14×13×13 .... £250
56 1d. black and deep lake .... 1·00 50
57 2d. black and red-brown .... 2·50 4·00
a. Perf 14×13×13×13 .... £120 £170
58 2½d. black and slate-blue .... 8·00 75·00
59 4d. black and greenish blue .... 14·00 60·00
a. Perf 14 .... 16·00 55·00
60 6d. black and orange-vermilion .... 2·50 2·00
61 1s. black and purple (P 14) .... 2·25 5·00
55/61 *Set of* 7 .... 35·00 £150
Designs: *Vert*—1d. Capt. Cook; 1s. King George V. *Horiz*—2d. Double Maori canoe; 2½d. Islanders working cargo; 4d. Port of Avarua; 6d. R.M.S. *Monowai.*
Examples of the 2½d. with inverted centre were not supplied to the Post Office. (*Price*, £250, *unused*).
Nos. 55a and 57a are mixed perforations, each having one side perforated 14 where the original perforation, 13, was inadequate.

(Recess from Perkins Bacon's plates at Govt Ptg Office, Wellington, N.Z.)

1932–36. *As Nos. 55/61, but* W **43** of New Zealand. P 14.
62 ½d. black and emerald .... 50 3·50
63 1d. black and deep lake .... 50 1·75
w. Wmk inverted .... 45·00
64 2d. black and yellow-brown (1.4.36) .... 50 1·75
w. Wmk inverted .... 25·00 45·00
65 2½d. black and slate-blue .... 50 4·25
w. Wmk inverted .... 45·00
66 4d. black and greenish blue .... 1·75 4·25
w. Wmk inverted ....
67 6d. black and red-orange (1.4.36) 70 75
68 1s. black and purple (1.4.36) .... 8·50 24·00
62/8 *Set of* 7 .... 11·50 35·00
Imperforate proofs of No. 65 are known used on registered mail from Niue postmarked 30 August 1945 or 29 October 1945.
See also Nos. 89/97.

SILVER JUBILEE OF KING GEORGE V 1910-1935.
(13)

Normal Letters
B K E N
B K E N
Narrow Letters

1935 (7 May). *Silver Jubilee. Designs as Nos. 63, 65 and 67 (colours changed) optd with T* **13** *(wider vertical spacing on 6d.).* W **43** of New Zealand. P 14.
69 1d. red-brown and lake .... 60 3·50
a. Narrow "K" in "KING" .... 2·75 9·00
b. Narrow "B" in "JUBILEE" .... 3·75 13·00
70 2½d. dull and deep blue (R.) .... 3·75 9·50
a. Narrow first "E" in "GEORGE" .... 4·00 13·00
71 6d. green and orange .... 3·25 7·00
a. Narrow "N" in "KING" .... 15·00 35·00
69/71 *Set of* 3 .... 6·50 18·00
Examples of No. 70 imperforate horizontally are from proof sheets not issued through the Post and Telegraph Department (*Price* £250 *for vert pair*).

NIUE (14) — NIUE Short opt (R. 9/4)

1937 (13 May). *Coronation. Nos. 599/601 of New Zealand optd with T* **14**.
72 1d. carmine 30 10
a. Short opt .... 9·00
73 2½d. Prussian blue .... 40 1·50
a. Short opt .... 11·00
74 6d. red-orange 40 20
a. Short opt .... 11·00
72/4 *Set of* 3 .... 1·00 1·60

15 King George VI

16 Tropical Landscape

1938 (2 May). *T* **15** *and similar designs inscr* "NIUE COOK ISLANDS". W **43** of New Zealand. P 14.

75		1s. black and violet	12·00	8·00
76		2s. black and red-brown	12·00	17·00
77		3s. blue and yellowish green	35·00	17·00
75/7 *Set of* 3			55·00	38·00

Designs: *Vert*—2s. Island village. *Horiz*—3s. Cook Islands canoe.

1940 (2 Sept). *Unissued stamp surch as in T* **16**. W **98** of New Zealand. P 13½×14.

78		3d. on 1½d. black and purple	75	20

NIUE.
(17)

1941–67. *Postal Fiscal stamps as Type* F **6** *of New Zealand with thin opt, T* **17**. P 14.

(i) Thin, hard, chalk-surfaced "Wiggins Teape" paper with vertical mesh (1941–43).

(a) W **43** of New Zealand.

79		2s.6d. deep brown (B.) (4.41)	90·00	95·00
80		5s. green (R.) (4.41)	£350	£300
81		10s. pale carmine-lake (B.) (6.42)	£120	£225
82		£1 pink (B.) (2.43?)	£190	£400
79/82 *Set of* 4			£650	£900

(b) W **98** of New Zealand (1944 54).

83		2s.6d. deep brown (B.) (3.45)	3·50	10·00
		w. Wmk inverted (11.51)	15·00	21·00
84		5s. green (R.) (11.44)	8·50	11·00
		w. Wmk inverted (19.5.54)	7·50	14·00
85		10s. carmine-lake (B.) (11.45)	55·00	£110
		w. Wmk inverted	60·00	£110
86		£1 pink (B.) (6.42)	50·00	65·00
83/6 *Set of* 4			£100	£180

(ii) Unsurfaced "Wiggins Teape" paper with horizontal mesh. W **98** of New Zealand (1957–67).

87		2s.6d. deep brown (P 14×13½) (1.11.57)	9·50	10·00
88		5s. pale yellowish green (wmk sideways) (6.67)	16·00	75·00

No. 88 came from a late printing made to fill demands from Wellington, but no supplies were sent to Niue. It exists in both line and comb perf.

1944–46. *As Nos.* 62/7 *and* 75/7, *but W* **98** of New Zealand (sideways on ½d., 1d., 1s. and 2s.).

89	**12**	½d. black and emerald	50	2·75
90	–	1d. black and deep lake	50	2·00
91	–	2d. black and red-brown	6·50	7·50
92	–	2½d. black and slate-blue (1946)	60	1·25
93	–	4d. black and greenish blue	4·25	1·00
		w. Wmk inverted and reversed	17·00	
94	–	6d. black and red-orange	2·25	1·40
95	**15**	1s. black and violet	1·50	85
96	–	2s. black and red-brown (1945)	8·50	3·00
97	–	3s. blue and yellowish green (1945)	15·00	7·00
89/97 *Set of* 9			35·00	24·00

1946 (4 June). *Peace. Nos.* 668, 670, 674/5 *of New Zealand optd as T* **17** *without stop (twice, reading up and down on 2d.).*

98		1d. green (Blk.)	40	10
99		2d. purple (B.)	40	10
100		6d. chocolate and vermilion (Blk.)	40	80
		a. Opt double, one albino	£250	
101		8d. black and carmine (B.)	50	80
98/101 *Set of* 4			1·50	1·60

Nos. 102/112 are no longer used.

18 Map of Niue

19 H.M.S. *Resolution*

20 Alofi landing

20a Native hut

21 Arch at Hikutavake

21a Alofi Bay

22 Spearing fish

22a Cave, Makefu

23 Bananas

24 Matapa Chasm

(Des J. Berry. Recess B.W.)

1950 (3 July). *T* **18/24** *and similar designs.* W **98** of New Zealand (sideways inverted on 1d., 2d., 3d., 4d., 6d. and 1s.). P 13½×14 (horiz) or 14×13½ (vert).

113	**18**	½d. orange and blue	10	1·00
114	**19**	1d. brown and blue-green	2·25	2·25
115	**20**	2d. black and carmine	1·25	1·75
116	**20a**	3d. blue and violet-blue	10	20
117	**21**	4d. olive-green and purple-brown	10	20
118	**21a**	6d. green and brown-orange	1·00	1·25
119	**22**	9d. orange and brown	10	1·40
120	**22a**	1s. purple and black	10	20
121	**23**	2s. brown-orange and dull green	3·00	4·75
122	**24**	3s. blue and black	4·50	4·75
113/22 *Set of* 10			11·00	16·00

1953 (25 May). *Coronation. As Nos.* 715 *and* 717 *of New Zealand, but inscr* "NIUE".

123		3d. brown	65	40
124		6d. slate-grey	95	40

(New Currency. 100 cents = 1 New Zealand dollar)

(25)

26

1967 (10 July). *Decimal currency. (a) No.* 113/22 *surch as T* **25**.

125		½c. on ½d.	10	10
126		1c. on 1d.	1·10	15
127		2c. on 2d.	10	10
128		2½c. on 3d.	10	10
129		3c. on 4d.	10	10
130		5c. on 6d.	10	10
131		8c. on 9d.	10	10
132		10c. on 1s.	10	10
133		20c. on 2s.	35	1·00
134		30c. on 3s.	65	1·50
125/34 *Set of* 10			2·00	2·50

(b) Arms type of New Zealand without value, surch as in T **26**. W **98** of New Zealand (sideways). P 14.

135	**26**	25c. deep yellow-brown	30	55
		a. Rough perf 11	6·00	13·00
136		50c. pale yellowish green	70	80
		a. Rough perf 11	6·00	14·00
137		$1 magenta	45	1·25
		a. Rough perf 11	7·50	13·00
138		$2 light pink	50	2·00
		a. Rough perf 11	8·50	14·00
135/8 *Set of* 4			1·75	4·25
135a/8a *Set of* 4			25·00	48·00

The 25c., $1 and $2 perf 14 exist both line and comb perforated. The 50c. is comb perforated only. The perf 11 stamps resulted from an emergency measure in the course of printing.

1967 (3 Oct). *Christmas. As T* **278** *of New Zealand, but inscr* "NIUE". W **98** (sideways) of New Zealand. P 13½×14.

139		2½c. multicoloured	10	10
		w. Wmk sideways inverted	15	30

1969 (1 Oct). *Christmas. As T* **301** *of New Zealand, but inscr* "NIUE". W **98** of New Zealand. P 13½×14½.

140		2½c. multicoloured	10	10

27 "Pus"

37 Kalahimu

(Des Mrs. K. W. Billings. Litho Enschedé)

1969 (27 Nov). *T* **27** *and similar vert designs. Multicoloured.* P 12½×13½.

141		½c. Type **27**	10	10
142		1c. "Golden Shower"	10	10
143		2c. Flamboyant	10	10
144		2½c. Frangipani	10	10
145		3c. Niue Crocus	10	10
146		5c. Hibiscus	10	10
147		8c. "Passion Fruit"	10	10
148		10c. "Kampui"	10	10
149		20c. Queen Elizabeth II (after Anthony Buckley)	35	1·25
150		30c. Tapeu Orchid	1·10	1·75
141/150 *Set of* 10			1·60	3·00

For 20c. design as 5c. see No. 801.

(Des G. F. Fuller. Photo Enschedé)

1970 (19 Aug). *Indigenous Edible Crabs. T* **37** *and similar horiz designs. Multicoloured.* P 13½×12½.

151		3c. Type **37**	10	10
152		5c. Kalavi	10	10
153		30c. Unga	30	25
151/3 *Set of* 3			45	40

1970 (1 Oct). *Christmas. As T* **314** *of New Zealand, but inscr* "NIUE".

154		2½c. multicoloured	10	10

38 Outrigger Canoe and Fokker F.27 Friendship Aircraft over Jungle

(Des L. C. Mitchell. Litho B.W.)

1970 (9 Dec). *Opening of Niue Airport. T* **38** *and similar horiz designs. Multicoloured.* P 13½.

155		3c. Type **38**	10	20
156		5c. *Tofua II* (cargo liner) and Fokker F.27 Friendship over harbour	15	20
157		8c. Fokker F.27 Friendship over Airport	15	30
155/7 *Set of* 3			35	65

Nigeria

LAGOS

A British Consul was established at Lagos during 1853 as part of the anti-slavery policy, but the territory was not placed under British administration until occupied by the Royal Navy in August 1861. From 19 February 1866 Lagos was administered with Sierra Leone and from July 1874 as part of Gold Coast. It became a separate colony on 13 January 1886.

Although a postal service had been established by the British G.P.O. in April 1852 no postal markings were supplied to Lagos until 1859. The British G.P.O. retained control of the postal service until June 1863, when it became the responsibility of the colonial authorities.

CROWNED-CIRCLE HANDSTAMPS

CC 1

CC1 CC **1** LAGOS (19.12.1859) .... *Price on cover* £3500

First recorded use of No. CC**1** is 12 December 1871. It is later known used as a cancellation.

PRICES FOR STAMPS ON COVER	
Nos. 1/9	*from* × 10
Nos. 10/26	*from* × 8
Nos. 27/9	—
Nos. 30/8	*from* × 10
Nos. 39/41	—
No. 42	*from* × 20
Nos. 44/50	*from* × 8
Nos. 51/3	—
Nos. 54/60	*from* × 8
Nos. 61/3	—

PRINTERS. All the stamps of Lagos were typographed by D.L.R.

1

1874 (10 June)–**75**. Wmk Crown CC. P 12½.

1	1	1d. lilac-mauve	60·00	35·00
2		2d. blue	60·00	30·00
3		3d. red-brown (2.75)	90·00	42·00
5		4d. carmine	95·00	40·00
6		6d. blue-green	£100	15·00
8		1s. orange (value 15½ mm) (2.75)	£475	£140
		a. Value 16½ mm long (7.75)	£300	60·00
1/8a *Set of* 6			£600	£200

1876–79. Wmk Crown CC. P 14.

10	1	1d. lilac-mauve	38·00	18·00
11		2d. blue	55·00	13·00
12		3d. red-brown	£110	18·00
13		3d. chestnut	£120	35·00
14		4d. carmine	£200	11·00
		a. Wmk sideways	£1300	£130
15		6d. green	£100	6·00
16		1s. orange (value 16½ mm long) (1879)	£700	85·00
10/16 *Set of* 6			£1100	£130

1882 (June). Wmk Crown CA. P 14.

17	1	1d. lilac-mauve	21·00	14·00
18		2d. blue	£170	5·50
19		3d. chestnut	17·00	5·50
20		4d. carmine	£160	12·00
17/20 *Set of* 4			£325	32·00

1884 (Dec)–**86**. *New values and colours*. Wmk Crown CA. P 14.

21	1	½d. dull green (1885)	2·00	80
22		1d. rose-carmine	2·00	80
		w. Wmk inverted	£130	£100
23		2d. grey	75·00	6·50
24		4d. pale violet	£130	8·50
		w. Wmk inverted	—	£225
25		6d. olive-green	8·00	45·00
26		1s. orange (3.85)	9·00	20·00
27		2s.6d. olive-black (1886)	£325	£275
28		5s. blue (1886)	£600	£450
29		10s. purple-brown (1886)	£1600	£1000
21/9 *Set of* 9			£2500	£1600
27s/9s Optd "Specimen" *Set of* 3			£425	

We would warn collectors against clever forgeries of Nos. 27 to 29 on genuinely watermarked paper.

2½ PENNY

A

2½ PENNY

B

1887 (Mar)–**1902**. Wmk Crown CA. P 14.

30	1	2d. dull mauve and blue	4·50	2·00
31		2½d. ultramarine (A) (1891)	4·75	1·75
		a. Larger letters of value (B)	22·00	17·00
		b. Blue (A)	80·00	50·00
32		3d. dull mauve and chestnut (4.91)	2·50	3·25
33		4d. dull mauve and black	2·25	1·75
34		5d. dull mauve and green (2.94)	2·00	11·00
35		6d. dull mauve and mauve	4·75	3·00
		a. Dull mauve and carmine (10.02)	5·00	12·00
36		7½d. dull mauve and carmine (2.94)	2·25	30·00
37		10d. dull mauve and yellow (2.94)	3·25	13·00
38		1s. yellow-green and black	5·50	24·00
		a. Blue-green and black	5·00	28·00
39		2s.6d. green and carmine	23·00	80·00
40		5s. green and blue	40·00	£150
41		10s. green and brown	85·00	£200
30/41 *Set of* 12			£160	£475
30s/41s Optd "Specimen" *Set of* 12			£275	

HALF PENNY

(2)

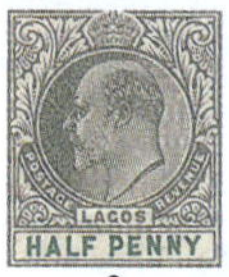

3

1893 (2 Aug). *No. 33 surch with T* **2** *locally*.

42	1	½d. on 4d. dull mauve and black	4·50	2·50
		a. Surch double	55·00	55·00
		b. Surch treble	£140	
		c. Error. ½d. on 2d. (No. 30)	—	£23000

There were two separate settings of No. 42. The most common, of which there were five separate printings, shows "HALF PENNY" 16 mm long and was applied as a horizontal pair or triplet. The scarcer setting, also applied as a triplet, shows "HALF PENNY" 16½ mm long.

Three examples of No. 42c are known, two unused and one used. Only the latter is in private hands.

1904 (22 Jan–Nov). Wmk Crown CA. P 14.

44	3	½d. dull green and green	1·50	5·50
45		1d. purple and black/*red*	1·00	15
46		2d. dull purple and blue	6·00	5·00
47		2½d. dull purple and blue/*blue* (B)	1·00	1·50
		aw. Wmk inverted	—	95·00
		b. Smaller letters of value as A	4·50	8·50
		bw. Wmk inverted	£140	£140
48		3d. dull purple and brown	2·25	1·75
49		6d. dull purple and mauve	35·00	10·00
50		1s. green and black	35·00	42·00
51		2s.6d. green and carmine	£120	£250
52		5s. green and blue	£130	£275
53		10s. green and brown (Nov)	£275	£750
44/53 *Set of* 10			£550	£1200
44s/53s Optd "Specimen" *Set of* 10			£190	

1904–06. *Ordinary paper*. Wmk Mult Crown CA. P 14.

54	3	½d. dull green and green (30.10.04)	7·50	2·50
		a. Chalk-surfaced paper (12.3.06)	10·00	1·75
		w. Wmk inverted		
55		1d. purple and black/*red* (22.10.04)	7·00	10
		a. Chalk-surfaced paper (21.9.05)	1·50	10
		aw. Wmk inverted	—	85·00
56		2d. dull purple and blue (2.05)	2·50	2·25
		a. Chalk-surfaced paper (25.9.06)	13·00	11·00
		aw. Wmk inverted	£130	
57		2½d. dull purple and blue/*blue* (B) (*chalk-surfaced paper*) (13.10.05)	1·75	16·00
		a. Smaller letters of value as A	55·00	£120
58		3d. dull purple and brown (274.05)	3·50	1·25
		a. Chalk-surfaced paper (2.8.06)	15·00	1·75
		w. Wmk inverted		
59		6d. dull purple and mauve (31.10.04)	6·50	3·00
		a. Chalk-surfaced paper (1.3.06)	4·25	1·50
60		1s. green and black (15.10.04)	13·00	22·00
		a. Chalk-surfaced paper (4.06)	23·00	2·25
		w. Wmk inverted		
61		2s.6d. green and carmine (3.12.04)	16·00	60·00
		a. Chalk-surfaced paper (21.10.06)	35·00	65·00
62		5s. green and blue (1.05)	22·00	£100
		a. Chalk-surfaced paper (21.10.06)	75·00	£180
63		10s. green and brown (3.12.04)	75·00	£225
		a. Chalk-surfaced paper (12.3.06)	85·00	£200
54/63 *Set of* 10			£130	£350

Lagos was incorporated into the Colony and Protectorate of Southern Nigeria, previously formed from Niger Coast Protectorate and part of the Niger Company territories, on 16 February 1906. Stamps of Lagos were then authorised for use throughout Southern Nigeria.

NIGER COAST PROTECTORATE

OIL RIVERS PROTECTORATE

A British consulate for the Bights of Benin and Biafra was established in 1849 on the off-shore Spanish island of Fernando Po. In 1853 the appointment was divided with a consul for the Bight of Benin at Lagos. The consulate for the Bight of Biafra was transferred to Old Calabar in 1882.

A British protectorate was proclaimed over the coastal area, with the exceptions of the colony of Lagos and the centre of the Niger delta, on 5 June 1885. It was not, however, until July 1891 that steps were taken to set up an administration with a consul-general at Old Calabar and vice-consuls at some of the river ports.

The consulate-general at Old Calabar and the vice-consulates at Benin, Bonny, Brass, Forcados and Opobo acted as collection and distribution centres for mail from November 1891, but were not recognised as post offices until 20 July 1892.

For a few months from July 1892 local administrative handstamps, as Type Z **1**, were in use either as obliterators or in conjunction with the c.d.s.

Z 1

These oval handstamps are usually found on the 1892 overprinted issue, but the following are known on unoverprinted stamps of Great Britain:

1892.

BENIN

Stamps of GREAT BRITAIN *cancelled with oval postmark, Type* **Z1**, *inscribed* "BENIN".

Z1	2½d. purple/*blue* (V.)	£1100

BONNY

Stamps of GREAT BRITAIN *cancelled with oval postmark, Type* **Z1**, *inscribed* "BONNY".

Z2	2½d. purple/*blue* (V.)	£1100

BRASS RIVER

Stamps of GREAT BRITAIN *cancelled with oval postmark, Type* **Z1**, *inscribed* "BRASS".

Z3	2½d. purple/*blue* (Blk.)	£800

OLD CALABAR RIVER

Stamps of GREAT BRITAIN *cancelled with oval postmark, Type* **Z1**, *inscribed* "OLD CALABAR".

Z4	2d. purple/*blue* (Blk.)	£800

Stamps of GREAT BRITAIN *cancelled* "BRITISH VICE-CONSULATE OLD CALABAR" *within double-lined circle*.

Z5	2½d. purple/*blue* (V.)	£500
Z6	5d. dull purple and blue (V.)	

For later use of Type Z **1** and the circular Vice-Consulate marks see note beneath No. 6.

Z 2

Unoverprinted stamps of Great Britain remained officially valid for postage in the Protectorate until 30 September 1892, but were available from post offices in the Niger Company Territories up to the end of 1899. The two areas were so closely linked geographically that offices in the Protectorate continued to accept letters franked with Great Britain stamps until the reorganisation of 1900. The listing below covers confirmed examples, known on cover or piece, the prices quoted being for the latter.

1892–99.

Stamps of GREAT BRITAIN *cancelled with circular postmarks as Type* **Z2**.

BENIN RIVER

Z7	2d. green and carmine	
Z8	2½d. purple/*blue*	£1000
Z9	3d. purple/*yellow*	£1000
Z10	5d. dull purple and blue	
Z11	1s. green	

BONNY RIVER

Z12	½d. vermilion	£400
Z12*a*	1d. lilac	£350
Z13	2½d. purple/*blue*	£300
Z14	5d. dull purple and blue	£400
Z15	6d. deep purple/*red*	£800

BRASS RIVER

Z16	1½d. dull purple and green	£900
Z17	2½d. purple/*blue*	£750
Z17*a*	2½d. purple/*blue* (squared-circle cancellation)	£900
Z18	6d. purple/*red*	£800

FORCADOS RIVER

Z19	1d. lilac	£650
Z20	2½d. purple/*blue*	
Z21	5d. dull purple and blue (m/s cancellation)	
Z22	10d. dull purple and carmine	

OLD CALABAR RIVER

Z23	½d. vermilion	£350
Z24	1d. lilac	£300
Z25	1½d. dull purple and green	£425
Z26	2d. green and vermilion	£425
Z27	2½d. purple/*blue*	£300
Z28	5d. dull purple and blue	£400
Z29	6d. purple/*red*	£400
Z30	1s. green	£600

OPOBO RIVER

Z31 2½d. purple/*blue* £350
Z32 10d. dull purple and carmine £650

Some later covers are known franked with G.B. stamps, but the origin of the stamps involved is uncertain.

PRICES FOR STAMPS ON COVER	
Nos. 1/6	*from* × 12
Nos. 7/36	*from* × 4
Nos. 37/44	—
Nos. 45/50	*from* × 10
Nos. 51/6	*from* × 12
Nos. 57/65	*from* × 3
Nos. 66/73	*from* × 12

(1)

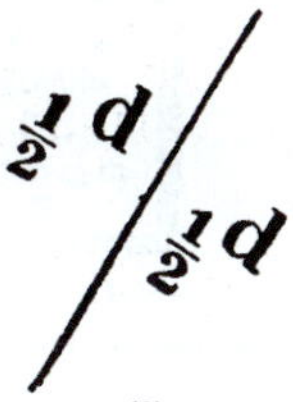
(2)

1892 (20 July)–**94**. *Nos. 172, 197, 200/1, 207a and 211 of Great Britain optd by D.L.R. with T* **1**.

1 ½d. vermilion .... 14·00 8·50
2 1d. lilac .... 8·50 8·50
a. Opt reversed "OIL RIVERS" at top £8500
b. Bisected (½d.) (on cover) .... † £2500
3 2d. grey-green and carmine .... 27·00 8·00
a. Bisected (1d.) (on cover) .... † £2500
4 2½d. purple/*blue* .... 6·50 2·25
5 5d. dull purple and blue (Die II (No. 207*a*)) .... 12·00 6·50
a. On Die I (No. 207) ....
6 1s. dull green .... 55·00 80·00
1/6 *Set of* 6 .... £110 £100
1s/6s H/S "Specimen" *Set of* 6 .... £300

Nos. 2b and 3a were used at Bonny River during August and September 1894.

Die II of the 5d. shows thin vertical lines to the right of "5d.". On Die I there are square dots in this position.

OVAL HANDSTAMPS. In addition to Nos. Z1/4 postmarks as Type Z **1** are also known used on the 1892–94 overprinted issue from the following offices:

Bakana (Nos. 2, 4/6)
Benin (Nos. 1/6)
Bonny (No. 2)
Brass (Nos. 3/5)
Buguma (Nos. 4 and 6)
Old Calabar (No. 4)
Opobo (Nos. 1/3)
Sombreiro River (Nos. 1/6)

The Vice-Consulate marks, as Nos. Z5/6, are also known struck on examples of No. 4 from Bonny, Forcados or Old Calabar.

Nos. 2 to 6 surcharged locally

1893 (3 Sept). *Issued at Old Calabar. Surch with T* **2** *and then bisected.*

7 ½d. on half of 1d. (R.) £150 £140
a. Unsevered pair £475 £450
ab. Surch inverted and dividing line reversed (unsevered pair) .... — £15000
b. Surch reversed (dividing line running from left to right) (unsevered pair) .... — £15000
c. Straight top to "1" in ½ £350 £350
d. "½" omitted ....
e. Surch double (unsevered pair with normal) .... — £1600
f. Vert *se-tenant* pair. Nos. 7a/8a .... — £20000
8 ½d. on half of 1d. (V.) £5000 £4500
a. Unsevered pair £15000 £14000
b. Surch double (pair) £21000

The surcharge was applied in a setting covering one horizontal row at a time. Violet ink was used for the top row in the first sheet, but was then replaced with red.

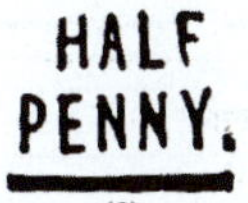

(3)

(4)

In T **3** "HALF" measures 9½ mm and "PENNY" 12½ mm with space 1½ mm between the words. Bar 14½ mm ending below the stop. The "F" is nearly always defective.

In T **4** "HALF" is 8½ mm, "PENNY" 12½ mm, spacing 2½ mm, and bar 16 mm, extending beyond the stop.

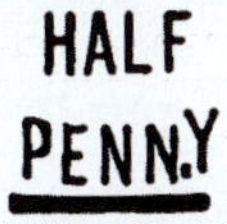

5 (Stop after "N")

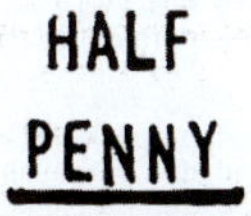

6 (No stop after "N")

In T **5** the "P" and "Y" are raised, and the space between the words is about 4 mm. Bar is short, approx 13½ mm. T **6** is similar but without the stop after "N".

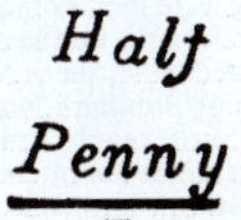

(7)

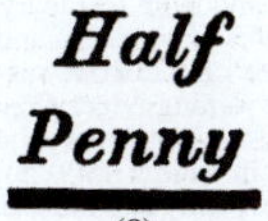

(8)

In T **7** the "a" and "e" are narrow and have a short upward terminal hook. The "1" has a very small hook. The letters "nny" have curved serifs, and the distance between the words is 5½ mm.

In T **8** the "a" and "e" are wider. The "1" has a wider hook. The letters "nny" have straight serifs, and the distance between the words is 4¼ mm.

(9)

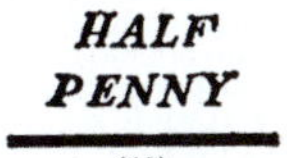

(10)

1893 (Dec). *Issue at Old Calabar. Nos. 3/4 handstamped.*

(a) With T **3**.

9 ½d. on 2d. (V.) £500 £325
a. Surch inverted £13000
b. Surch diagonal (up or down) £60000
c. Surch vertical (up or down) £7500
10 ½d. on 2½d. (Verm.) £13000
10*a* ½d. on 2½d. (C.) £30000

(b) With T **4**.

11 ½d. on 2½d. (G.) £300 £250
a. Surch double £2750 £2750
b. Surch diagonally inverted £13000
12 ½d. on 2½d. (Verm.) £1000 £300
13 ½d. on 2½d. (C.) £425 £425
a. Surch omitted (in pair) ....
14 ½d. on 2½d. (B.) £400 £450
15 ½d. on 2½d. (Blk.) £4000
a. Surch inverted £13000
b. Surch diagonal inverted (up or down) £11000
16 ½d. on 2½d. (B.-Blk.) £4750

(c) With T **5**.

17 ½d. on 2½d. (Verm.) £1200 £200
a. Surch double .... — £1800
b. Surch vertical (up) .... — £6000

(d) With T **6**.

18 ½d. on 2d. (V.) £850 £425
19 ½d. on 2½d. (Verm.) £425 £300
a. Surch inverted £7500
b. Surch double .... — £2250
c. Surch diagonal (up or down) £4250
d. Surch omitted (in strip of 3) £26000
e. Surch vertical (up or down) £13000
f. Surch diagonal, inverted (up or down) £6500

(e) With T **7**.

20 ½d. on 2d. (V.) £450 £250
a. Surch double .... — £6500
b. Surch vertical (up or down) £7500
c. Surch diagonal (up or down) £7500
d. Surch diagonal (inverted) £13000
e. Surch inverted ....
21 ½d. on 2½d. (Verm.) £350 £180
a. Surch double £4500
b. Surch vertical (up or down) £7500
c. Surch inverted £10000
d. Surch diagonal (up or down) £5500
e. Surch diagonal, inverted (up) £12000
22 ½d. on 2½d. (B.) £18000 £18000
23 ½d. on 2½d. (C.) £18000
24 ½d. on 2½d. (V.) £8500

(f) With T **8**.

25 ½d. on 2½d. (Verm) £500 £600
a. Surch diagonal (up) £7000
26 ½d. on 2½d. (B.) £30000
27 ½d. on 2½d. (G.) £425 £550
a. Surch double £5500
28 ½d. on 2½d. (C.) £22000 £22000

(g) With T **9**.

29 ½d. on 2d. (V.) £425 £325
30 ½d. on 2d. (B.) £1900 £700
a. Surch double ....
31 ½d. on 2½d. (Verm.) £600 £700
a. Surch double ....
32 ½d. on 2½d. (B.) £425 £375
33 ½d. on 2½d. (G.) £450 £475
a. Surch double (G.) £2000
b. Surch double (G. + Verm.) ....
34 ½d. on 2½d. (V.) £6500

(h) With T **10**.

35 ½d. on 2½d. (G.) £500 £450
36 ½d. on 2½d. (Verm.) £8500

Various types of surcharges on Nos. 9 to 36 were printed on the same sheet, and different types in different colours may be found *se-tenant* (*Prices, from £4250 per pair, unused*).

Unused examples of Nos. 11, 12 and 31 with surcharge omitted in pair with normal (No. 11) or as the first and third stamps in a strip of three (Nos. 12 and 31) exist in the Royal collection.

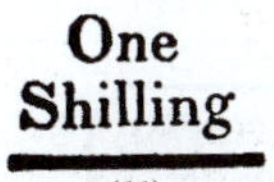

(11)

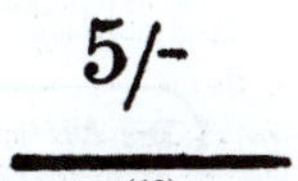

(12)

1893 (Dec). *Issued at Old Calabar. Nos. 3 and 5/6 handstamped.*

(a) With T **11**.

37 1s. on 2d. (V.) £450 £350
a. Surch inverted £9500
b. Surch vertical (up or down) £6500
c. Surch diagonal (up or down) £7500
d. Surch diagonal, inverted (up or down) £7500
e. Pair, Nos. 37 and 38 .... £5000
38 1s. on 2d. (Verm.) £600 £4000
a. Surch inverted £13000
b. Surch diagonal (up or down) £9500
c. Surch vertical (up or down) £13000
39 1s. on 2d. (Blk.) £5500
a. Surch inverted £18000
b. Surch vertical (up or down) £14000
c. Surch diagonal (up) £14000

(b) As T **12**.

40 5s. on 2d. (V.) £9000 £10000
a. Surch inverted £42000
b. Surch vertical (up or down) £38000 £38000
c. Surch diagonal (down) £35000
41 10s. on 5d. (Verm.) £6500 £8500
a. Surch inverted £38000
b. Surch vertical (up or down) £38000
c. Surch diagonal (down) ....
42 20s. on 1s. (V.) £120000
a. Surch inverted £160000
43 20s. on 1s. (Verm.) £120000
44 20s. on 1s. (Blk.) £120000

There are two main settings of the "One Shilling" surcharge:—

Type A. The "0" is over the "hi" of "Shilling" and the downstrokes on the "n" in "One", if extended, would meet the "ll" of "Shilling". The "g" is always raised. Type A is known in all three colours from one sheet of 120.

Type B. The "O" is over the first "i" of "Shilling" and the downstrokes of the "n" would meet the "li" of "Shilling". Type B is known in violet (two sheets) and vermilion (one sheet).

An example of No. 38 with surcharge diagonal, inverted exists on the Royal collection.

NIGER COAST PROTECTORATE

The protectorate was extended into the interior and the name changed to Niger Coast Protectorate on 12 May 1893.

PERFORATION. There are a number of small variations in the perforation of the Waterlow issues of 1893 to 1898 which were due to irregularity of the pins rather than different perforators.

In the following lists, stamps perf 12, 12½, 13 or compound are described as perf 12–13, stamps perf 13½, 14 or compound are described as perf 13½–14 and those perf 14½, 15 or compound are listed as perf 14½–15. In addition the 13½–14 perforation exists compound with 14½–15 and with 12–13, whilst perf 15½–16 comes from a separate perforator.

13

14

(Des G. D. Drummond. Recess Waterlow)

1894 (1 Jan). *T* **13** *(with "OIL RIVERS" obliterated and "NIGER COAST" in top margin). Various frames. Thick and thin papers.* No wmk. P 14½–15.

45 ½d. vermilion .... 5·50 5·50
a. Perf 13½–14 .... 7·00 9·00
46 1d. pale blue .... 6·00 3·50
a. Bisected (½d.) (on cover) .... † £650
b. Dull blue .... 4·50 3·25
ba. Bisected (½d.) (on cover) .... † £550
c. Perf 13½–14 .... 4·00 4·25
d. Perf 13½–14, comp 12–13 .... 24·00 21·00
e. Perf 12–13 .... — 75·00
47 2d. green .... 30·00 30·00
a. Imperf between (horiz pair) .... † £16000
b. Bisected (1d.) (on cover) .... † £800
c. Perf 14½–15, comp 12–13 ....
d. Perf 13½–14 .... 19·00 13·00
e. Perf 13½–14, comp 12–13 .... 50·00 30·00
f. Perf 12–13 ....
48 2½d. carmine-lake .... 9·00 3·50
a. Perf 13½–14 .... 17·00 12·00
b. Perf 13½–14, comp 12–13 .... 29·00 29·00
c. Perf 12–13 .... £130 £130
49 5d. grey-lilac .... 17·00 12·00
a. Lilac (1894) .... 14·00 18·00
b. Perf 13½–14 .... 14·00 13·00
c. Perf 13½–14, comp 12–13 .... 50·00
50 1s. black .... 14·00 12·00
a. Perf 14½–15, comp 12–13 .... 75·00
b. Perf 13½–14 .... 32·00 22·00
c. Perf 13½–14, comp 12–13 .... 32·00 27·00
d. Perf 14½–15, comp 13½–14 .... 55·00 38·00
45/50 *Set of* 6 .... 60·00 45·00

There were three printings of each value, in November 1893, Jan 1894 and March 1894.

Nos. 46a, 46ba and 47b were used at Bonny River during August and September 1894.

(Recess Waterlow)

1894 (May). *T* **14** *(various frames).* No wmk. P 14½–15.

51 ½d. yellow-green .... 4·75 5·00
a. Deep green .... 5·50 6·00
b. Perf 14½–15, comp 13½–14 ....
c. Perf 13½–14 .... 11·00 11·00
d. Perf 13½–14, comp 12–13 .... 26·00 22·00
52 1d. orange-vermilion .... 19·00 12·00
a. Vermilion .... 13·00 8·50
b. Bisected diagonally (½d.) (on cover) .... † £600
c. Perf 15½–16 .... — 60·00
d. Perf 13½–14 .... 26·00
e. Perf 13½–14, comp 12–13 .... — 20·00
53 2d. lake .... 32·00 6·50
a. Bisected diagonally (1d.) (on cover) ....
b. Perf 13½–14 .... 42·00 9·00
c. Perf 13½–14, comp 12–13 .... 60·00 21·00
54 2½d. blue .... 15·00 3·75
a. Pale blue .... 8·50 7·50
b. Perf 13½–14 .... 26·00 15·00
55 5d. purple .... 8·00 5·50
a. Deep violet .... 7·50 5·50
56 1s. black .... 55·00 19·00
a. Perf 13½–14 .... 55·00 7·00
b. Perf 13½–14, comp 12–13 .... 70·00 38·00
51/6 *Set of* 6 .... £110 32·00

Nos. 52b and 53a were used at Bonny River during August and September 1894.

(15) (16) (17)

1894. *Provisionals. Issued at Opobo.*

(a) Nos. 46b and 46 bisected vertically and surch with T **15** *(May–June).*

57 "½" on half of 1d. dull blue (R.) (May) £1600 £550
  a. Surch inverted (in strip of 3 with normals) £16000
58 "½" on half of 1d. pale blue (R.) (June) £900 £375
  a. Surch *tête-bêche* (pair)
  b. Surcharge inverted £5500
  c. Perf 13½–14 – £350
  d. Perf 13½–14, comp 12–13 – £400

(b) No. 3 bisected vertically and surch.

(i) With T **16** *(12 mm high) (June–Oct).*

59 "1" on half of 2d. (Verm.) £1700 £375
  a. Surch double £5500 £1200
  b. Surch inverted – £1600
  c. Unsevered pair † £3000

(ii) Smaller "1" (4¾ mm high).

60 "1" on half of 2d. (C.) – £9000

(iii) Smaller "1" (3¾ mm high).

61 "1" on half of 2d. (C.)

Nos. 60 and 61 exist *se-tenant*. *(Price £30,000 used).*

(c) No. 52a (Perf 14½–15) bisected, surch with T **15** *(Aug–Sept).*

62 "½" on half of 1d. vermilion (Blk.) £5000 £1000
63 "½" on half of 1d. vermilion (V.) £3750 £700
64 "½" on half of 1d. vermilion (B.) £3000 £450
  a. "½" double – £2500
  b. Perf 13½–14
  c. Perf 13½–14, comp 12–13

The stamp is found divided down the middle and also diagonally.

1894 (10 Aug). *Issued at Old Calabar. No. 54 surch with T* **17** *and two bars through value at foot.*

65 ½d. on 2½d. blue £375 £225
  a. Surch double £5500 £1800
  b. "OIE" for "ONE" £1800 £1100
  c. Ditto. Surch double – £8000

There are eight types in the setting of Type **17**, arranged as a horizontal row. No. 65b occurred on No. 8 in the setting at some point during surcharging.

(Recess Waterlow)

1897 (Mar)–**98**. *As T* **14** *(various frames).* Wmk Crown CA. P 14½–15.

66 ½d. green (7.97) 4·25 1·50
  a. Sage-green 4·50 2·25
  b. Perf 13½–14 3·25 3·00
  c. Perf 15½–16 13·00 6·50
  d. Perf 13½–14, comp 12–13 26·00 17·00
  x. Wmk reversed £100
67 1d. orange-vermilion 4·50 1·50
  a. Vermilion 4·50 1·50
  b. Imperf vert (horiz pair) £12000
  c. Perf 15½–16 9·50 7·50
  d. Perf 13½–14 2·50 2·75
  e. Perf 13½–14, comp 12–13 21·00 15·00
  f. Perf 13½–14, comp 14½–15 – 21·00
68 2d. lake (7.97) 1·75 2·00
  a. Perf 15½–16 4·25 2·75
  b. Perf 13½–14 4·25 3·75
  c. Perf 13½–14, comp 12–13 32·00
  x. Wmk reversed £110 £100
69 2½d. slate-blue (8.97) 7·50 2·00
  a. Deep bright blue 10·00 2·25
  b. Perf 13½–14 6·00 4·00
  c. Perf 15½–16 – 42·00
  w. Wmk inverted – £170
  x. Wmk reversed – £200
70 5d. red-violet (p 13½–14) (1898) 11·00 75·00
  a. Purple 9·00 80·00
  b. Perf 13½–14, comp 12–13 23·00 £130
  c. Perf 14½–15 – £150
71 6d. yellow-brown (6.98) 7·00 6·50
  a. Perf 13½–14 8·50 12·00
  b. Perf 15½–16 60·00 35·00
  x. Wmk reversed
72 1s. black (1898) 15·00 29·00
  a. Perf 13½–14 14·00 30·00
  b. Perf 13½–14, comp 12–13 50·00
73 2s.6d. olive-bistre (6.98) 70·00 £150
  a. Perf 15½–16 70·00 £160
  b. Perf 13½–14 22·00 90·00
74 10s. deep violet (6.98) £140 £225
  a. Bright violet £150 £250
  b. Perf 13½–14 £100 £190
  ba. Bright violet £100 £200
  bx. Wmk reversed £400
  c. Perf 13½–14, comp 12–13 £200 £325
66/74 *Set of* 9 £150 £350
71s, 73s/4s Optd "Specimen" *Set of* 3 £275

Owing to temporary shortages in Southern Nigeria, the above issue was again in use at various times from 1902 until 1907.

On 1 January 1900 the Niger Coast Protectorate together with the southern portion of the Niger Company Territories became the protectorate of Southern Nigeria.

NIGER COMPANY TERRITORIES

Following the development of trade along the Niger, British commercial interests formed the United African Company in 1879 which became the National African Company in 1882 and the Royal Niger Company in 1886. A charter was granted to the Company in the same year to administer territory along the Rivers Niger and Benue over which a British protectorate had been proclaimed in June 1885. The Company's territories extended to the Niger delta to provide access to the interior.

Post Offices were opened at Akassa (1887), Burutu (1896), Lokoja (1899) and Abutshi (1899). The stamps of Great Britain were used from 1888.

On the establishment of postal services in 1887 the Company arranged with the British G.P.O. that unstamped mail marked with their handstamps would be delivered in Great Britain, the recipients only being charged the normal rate of postage from West Africa. This system was difficult to administer, however, so the British authorities agreed in 1888 to the supply of G.B. stamps for use at the Company post offices.

Initially the stamps on such covers were left uncancelled until the mail arrived in the United Kingdom, the Company handstamp being struck elsewhere on the address side. This method continued to be used until early 1896, although a number of covers from the twelve months prior to that date do show the Company handstamp cancelling the stamps. Some of these covers were later recancelled on arrival in Great Britain. From May 1896 the postage stamps were cancelled in the Niger Territories.

In the following listings no attempt has been made to cover the use of the Company marks on the reverse of envelopes.

Dates given are those of earliest known postmarks. Colour of postmarks in brackets. Where two or more colours are given, price is for cheapest. Illustrations are reduced to two-thirds linear of the actual size.

Stamps of GREAT BRITAIN *cancelled as indicated below.*

ABUTSHI

1899. *Cancelled as T* **8**, *but inscribed "*THE ROYAL NIGER CO. C. & L. ABUTSHI*" with "*CUSTOMS (date) OFFICE*" in central oval.*

Z1 ½d. vermilion (V.) £800
Z2 1d. lilac (V.) £550
Z3 2½d. purple/*blue* (V.) £800
Z4 5d. dull purple and blue (V.) £850
Z5 10d. dull purple and carmine (V.) £1000
Z6 2s.6d. deep lilac (V.) £1100

AKASSA

The listings for Nos. Z7/15*a* are for *covers* on which the Akassa handstamp appears on the front, but is *not* used as a cancellation for the G.B. stamps. Examples of Nos. Z16/26 occur, from 1895–96, with the handstamp struck on the front of the cover away from the stamps, or, from 1896, used as a cancellation. The prices quoted are for *single stamps* showing the cancellation; covers from either period being worth considerably more. On Nos. Z29/42*b* the handstamp was used as a cancellation and the prices quoted are for *single stamps*.

1

2

1888–90. *Cancelled as T* **3**, *but with Maltese cross each side of "*AKASSA*". Size 36×22 mm.*

Z7 6d. deep purple/*red* (V.) £1500

1889–94. *Size 39×24 mm.*

Z8 **1** 2½d. purple/*blue* (V.) £700
Z9 3d. purple/*yellow* (V.)
Z10 5d. dull purple and blue (V.)
Z11 6d. deep purple/*red* (V.) £425
Z12 10d. dull purple and carmine (V.)
Z12*a* 1s. green (V.)
Z13 2s.6d. lilac (V.)

1894–95.

Z14 **2** 1d. lilac (V.) £550
Z15 2½d. purple/*blue* (V.) £500
Z15*a* 2s.6d. lilac (V.)

3

4

1895. *Size 39×25 mm.*

Z16 **3** 2½d. purple/*blue* (V.)

1895–99.

Z17 **4** ½d. vermilion (V.) £100
Z18 1d. lilac (V.) 90·00
Z19 2d. green and carmine (V.) £500
Z20 2½d. purple/*blue* (V.) 45·00
Z21 3d. purple/*yellow* (V.) £375
Z22 5d. dull purple and blue (V.) 75·00
Z23 6d. deep purple/*red* (V.) £375
Z24 9d. dull purple and blue (V.) £600
Z25 10d. dull purple and carmine (V.) £130
Z26 2s.6d. deep lilac (V.) £275

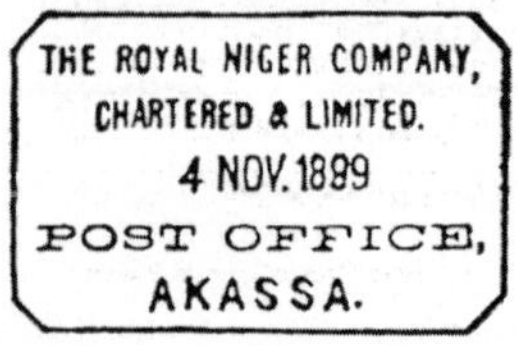

5

1897–99.

Z29 **5** ½d. vermilion (V.) 80·00
Z30 1d. lilac (V.) 60·00
  a. "RECD" for year in postmark £750
Z31 2d. green and carmine (V.) £300
Z32 2½d. purple/*blue* (V.) 75·00
  a. "RECD" for year in postmark (1898) £1100
Z33 3d. purple/*yellow* (V.) £275
Z34 4d. green and brown (V.) £375
Z35 4½d. green and carmine (V.) £1100
Z36 5d. dull purple and blue (V.) 85·00
Z37 6d. deep purple/*red* (V.) £325
Z38 9d. dull purple and blue (V.) £600
Z39 10d. dull purple and carmine (V.) £200
Z40 1s. green (V.) £1100
Z41 2s.6d. deep lilac (V.) £400

1899. *Cancelled as T* **7** *but inscribed "*AKASSA*".*

Z42 5d. dull purple and blue (V.) £1200

1899. *Cancelled as T* **4**, *but "*CUSTOMS DEPT*" in place of "*POST OFFICE*".*

Z42*a* 1d. lilac (V.) £850
Z42*b* 2½d. purple/*blue* (V.) £850

BURUTU

6

1896–99. *Cancelled as T* **6**, *"*BURUTU*" in sans-serif caps. Size 44×24 mm.*

Z43 **6** ½d. vermilion (V., Blk.) £120
Z44 1d. lilac (V.) 95·00
Z45 1½d. dull purple and green (V.) £500
Z46 2d. green and carmine (V., Blk.) £250
Z47 2½d. purple/*blue* (V., Blk.) 45·00
Z48 3d. purple/*yellow* (V., Blk.) £275
Z49 4d. green and brown (V. Blk.) £325
Z50 5d. dull purple and blue (V., Blk.) 90·00
Z51 6d. deep purple/*red* (V.) £350
Z52 9d. dull purple and blue (V.) £600
Z53 10d. dull purple and carmine (V., Blk.) £150
Z54 1s. green (V.) £950
Z55 2s.6d. lilac (V.) £325

1898–99. *Cancelled as T* **4**, *but inscribed "*BURUTU*" in serifed caps. Size 44×27 mm.*

Z56 ½d. vermilion (V., Blk.) 85·00
Z57 1d. lilac (V., Blk.) 55·00
Z58 2d. green and carmine (V.) £375
Z59 2½d. purple/*blue* (V., Blk.) 65·00
Z60 3d. purple/*yellow* (V.) £350
Z61 4d. green and brown (V.) £375
Z62 4½d. green and carmine (V.) £1100
Z63 5d. dull purple and blue (V.) 90·00
Z64 6d. deep purple/*red* (V.) £350
Z65 9d. dull purple and blue (V.) £600
Z66 10d. dull purple and carmine (V., Blk.) £140
Z67 2s.6d. lilac (V., Blk.) £375

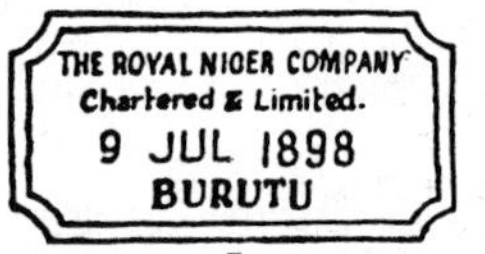

7

1898–99.

Z68 **7** 1d. lilac (V.)
Z69 2½d. purple/*blue* (V.) £350

1899. *Cancelled as T* **4**, *but inscribed "*CUSTOM DEPT. BURUTU*".*

Z70 1d. lilac (V.)

LOKOJA

8

1899.

Z71 **8** ½d. vermilion (V.) £140
Z72 1d. lilac (V.) 90·00
Z73 2½d. purple/*blue* (V.) £300
Z74 5d. dull purple and blue (V.) £500
Z75 10d. dull purple and carmine (V.) £600
Z76 2s.6d. deep lilac (V.) £750

AGENT GENERAL NIGER TERRITORIES

The listings for Nos. Z78/9 are for covers showing a handstamp struck on the address side, but *not* used as a cancellation for the G.B. stamp.

1894–99. *Cancelled as T* **8**, *but inscribed "*AGENT GENERAL NIGER TERRITORIES*".*

Z77 1d. lilac (V.)
Z78 2½d. purple/*blue* (V.) £1500

1895–96. *Cancelled as T* **7**, *but inscribed as Nos. Z77/8.*

Z79 2½d. purple/*blue* (V.) £1500
Z80 5d. dull purple and blue (V.)
Z81 10d. dull purple and carmine (V.)
Z82 2s.6d. deep lilac (V.)

It is now believed that these cancellations may have been used at Asaba. They all occur on covers with Akassa handstamps, often of different dates.

The British Government purchased the Royal Niger Company territories and from 1 January 1900 they were incorporated into the protectorates of Northern and Southern Nigeria. Of the post offices listed above, only Lokoja was then situated in Northern Nigeria, the remainder joining Niger Coast in forming Southern Nigeria.

Issues for Northern Nigeria did not reach Lokoja until sometime in March 1900 and the post office there continued to use unoverprinted stamps of Great Britain until these supplies arrived.

NORTHERN NIGERIA

The protectorate of Northern Nigeria was formed on 1 January 1900 from the northern part of the Niger Company Territories. Only one post office existed in this area, at Lokoja, and this continued to use unoverprinted stamps of GREAT BRITAIN until the arrival of Nos. 1/9 during April 1900.

PRICES FOR STAMPS ON COVER	
Nos. 1/7	from × 6
Nos. 8/9	—
Nos. 10/16	from × 5
Nos. 17/19	—
Nos. 20/6	from × 5
No. 27	—
Nos. 28/37	from × 5
Nos. 38/9	—
Nos. 40/9	from × 5
Nos. 50/2	—

PRINTERS. All issues were typographed by De La Rue & Co.

1

2

1900 (Apr). Wmk Crown CA. P 14.

1	1	½d. dull mauve and green	3·75	14·00
2		1d. dull mauve and carmine	3·75	3·75
3		2d. dull mauve and yellow	12·00	55·00
4		2½d. dull mauve and ultramarine	10·00	38·00
5	2	5d. dull mauve and chestnut	26·00	60·00
6		6d. dull mauve and violet	24·00	38·00
7	1	1s. green and black	24·00	75·00
8		2s.6d. green and ultramarine	£130	£475
9		10s. green and brown	£275	£750
1/9 *Set of* 9			£475	£1400
1s/9s Optd "Specimen" *Set of* 9			£200	

Examples of all values are known showing a forged Northern Nigeria postmark dated "AU 14 1900".

3

4

1902 (1 July). Wmk Crown CA. P 14.

10	3	½d. dull purple and green	2·00	1·00
		w. Wmk inverted	—	£275
11		1d. dull purple and carmine	2·25	75
12		2d. dull purple and yellow	2·00	3·00
13		2½d. dull purple and ultramarine	1·50	9·50
14	4	5d. dull purple and chestnut	3·50	5·00
15		6d. dull purple and violet	11·00	4·50
16	3	1s. green and black	3·75	6·00
17		2s.6d. green and ultramarine	8·50	60·00
18		10s. green and brown	48·00	55·00
10/18 *Set of* 9			75·00	£130
10s/18s Optd "Specimen" *Set of* 9			£160	

1904 (Apr). Wmk Mult Crown CA. P 14.

19	4	£25 green and carmine	£50000	

No. 19, although utilising the "POSTAGE & REVENUE" Key type, was intended to pay the fiscal fee for liquor licences.

1905 (Aug)–**07**. *Ordinary paper*. Wmk Mult Crown CA. P 14.

20	3	½d. dull purple and green (10.05)	24·00	8·00
		a. Chalk-surfaced paper (1906)	5·50	5·00
21		1d. dull purple and carmine	20·00	1·00
		a. Chalk-surfaced paper (1906)	5·50	1·25
22		2d. dull purple and yellow (10.05)	15·00	32·00
		a. Chalk-surfaced paper (1907)	19·00	29·00
23		2½d. dull purple and ultramarine (10.05)	6·50	8·00
24	4	5d. dull purple and chestnut (10.05)	24·00	70·00
		a. Chalk-surfaced paper (1907)	35·00	70·00
25		6d. dull purple and violet (10.05)	27·00	60·00
		a. Chalk-surfaced paper (1906)	42·00	42·00
26	3	1s. green and black (10.05)	60·00	95·00
		a. Chalk-surfaced paper (1906)	22·00	48·00
27		2s.6d. green and ultramarine (10.05)	48·00	50·00
		a. Chalk-surfaced paper (1906)	30·00	50·00
20a/7a *Set of* 8			£120	£225

1910 (30 Jan)–**11**. *Ordinary paper (½d. to 2½d.) or chalk-surfaced paper (others)*. Wmk Mult Crown. CA. P 14.

28	3	½d. green (15.4.10)	2·00	1·25
29		1d. carmine	2·00	1·25
30		2d. grey (26.10.11)	5·00	2·25
31		2½d. blue (10.10)	2·50	7·00
32	4	3d. purple/*yellow* (10.9.11)	3·75	75
34		5d. dull purple and olive-green (26.2.11)	4·00	13·00
35		6d. dull purple and purple (10.11.10)	6·00	17·00
		a. Dull and bright purple (1911)	5·00	6·00
36	3	1s. black/*green* (10.11.10)	2·75	75
37		2s.6d. black and red/*blue* (15.3.11)	10·00	32·00
38	4	5s. green and red/*yellow* (10.9.11)	23·00	75·00
39	3	10s. green and red/*green* (15.3.11)	45·00	48·00
28/39 *Set of* 11			95·00	£170
28s/39s Optd "Specimen" *Set of* 11			£275	

5

6

1912. *Ordinary paper (½d., 1d., 2d.) or chalk-surfaced paper (others)*. Wmk Mult Crown CA. P 14.

40	5	½d. deep green	2·25	60
41		1d. red	2·25	60
42		2d. grey	3·50	9·00
43	6	3d. purple/*yellow*	2·25	1·25
44		4d. black and red/*yellow*	1·25	2·25
45		5d. dull purple and olive-green	4·00	13·00
46		6d. dull and bright purple	4·00	4·25
47		9d. dull purple and carmine	2·00	12·00
48	5	1s. black/*green*	4·50	2·25
49		2s.6d. black and red/*blue*	7·00	45·00
50	6	5s. green and red/*yellow*	21·00	80·00
51	5	10s. green and red/*green*	38·00	48·00
52	6	£1 purple and black/*red*	£170	£110
40/52 *Set of* 13			£225	£275
40s/52s Optd "Specimen" *Set of* 13			£225	

Examples of most values are known showing forged postmarks of Lokoja dated "MR 22 12" or Minna dated "JN 16 1913". These forged postmarks have also been seen on examples of earlier issues.

On 1 January 1914 Northern Nigeria became part of Nigeria.

SOUTHERN NIGERIA

The Colony and Protectorate of Southern Nigeria was formed on 1 January 1900 by the amalgamation of Niger Coast Protectorate with the southern part of the Niger Territories. Lagos was incorporated into the territory on 1 May 1906.

The stamps of NIGER COAST PROTECTORATE were used in Southern Nigeria until the introduction of Nos. 1/9, and also during a shortage of these values in mid-1902. The issues of LAGOS were utilized throughout Southern Nigeria after 1 May 1906 until supplies were exhausted.

PRICES FOR STAMPS ON COVER	
Nos. 1/7	from × 8
Nos. 8/9	—
Nos. 10/18	from × 4
Nos. 19/20	—
Nos. 21/30	from × 4
Nos. 31/2	—
Nos. 33/42	from × 4
Nos. 43/4	—
Nos. 45/53	from × 4
Nos. 55/6	—

PRINTERS. All issues of Southern Nigeria were typographed by De La Rue & Co, Ltd, London.

1

2

3

1901 (Mar)–**02**. Wmk Crown CA. P 14.

1	1	½d. black and pale green	1·75	2·25
		a. Sepia and green (1902)	2·25	2·50
2		1d. black and carmine	1·40	1·50
		a. Sepia and carmine (1902)	2·50	1·75
3		2d. black and red-brown	3·25	4·00
4		4d. black and sage-green	2·75	21·00
5		6d. black and purple	2·75	6·50
6		1s. green and black	8·00	26·00
7		2s.6d. black and brown	48·00	85·00
8		5s. black and orange-yellow	55·00	£110
9		10s. black and purple/*yellow*	£100	£200
1/9 *Set of* 9			£200	£425
1s/9s Optd "Specimen" *Set of* 9			£170	

1903 (Mar)–**04**. Wmk Crown CA. P 14.

10	2	½d. grey-black and pale green	1·00	30
		w. Wmk inverted		
11		1d. grey-black and carmine	1·25	70
12		2d. grey-black and chestnut	8·50	1·50
13		2½d. grey-black and blue (1904)	2·00	1·00
14		4d. grey-black and olive-green	2·75	5·50
15		6d. grey-black and purple	4·75	8·00
16		1s. green and black	32·00	19·00
17		2s.6d. grey-black and brown	32·00	65·00
18		5s. grey-black and yellow	75·00	£170
19		10s. grey-black and purple/*yellow*	35·00	£110
20		£1 green and violet	£375	£800
10/20 *Set of* 11			£500	£1100
10s/20s Optd "Specimen" *Set of* 11			£250	

Two Dies of Head Plate:

A

B

In Head A the fifth line of shading on the king's cheek shows as a line of dots and the lines of shading up to the king's hair are broken in places. In Head B the lines of shading are more regular, especially the fifth line.

1904 (June)–**09**. *Head Die A. Ordinary paper*. Wmk Mult Crown CA. P 14.

21	2	½d. grey-black and pale green	60	10
		a. Chalk-surfaced paper (1905)	1·25	90
22		1d. grey-black and carmine	12·00	20
		a. Chalk-surfaced paper (1905)	12·00	10
23		2d. grey-black and chestnut (1905)	2·50	45
		a. Pale grey and chestnut (Head Die B) (1907)	4·50	40
24		2½d. grey-black and bright blue (9.09)	1·00	1·00
25		3d. orange-brown and bright purple (*chalk-surfaced paper*) (Head Die B) (18.8.07)	9·50	1·25
		s. Optd "Specimen"	22·00	
26		4d. grey-black and olive-green (12.05)	14·00	25·00
		a. Chalk-surfaced paper (1906)	26·00	30·00
		ab. Grey-black and pale olive-green (Head Die B) (1907)	38·00	38·00
27		6d. grey-black and bright purple (9.05)	13·00	3·50
		a. Chalk-surfaced paper (1906)	13·00	8·00
		ab. Head Die B (1907)	18·00	2·25
28		1s. grey-green and black (19.9.07)	3·25	3·50
		a. Chalk-surfaced paper (Head Die B) (1907)	38·00	3·25
29		2s.6d. grey-black and brown (30.4.06)	24·00	17·00
		a. Chalk-surfaced paper (1906)	38·00	13·00
		ab. Head Die B (1907)	45·00	20·00
30		5s. grey-black and yellow (10.12.07)	40·00	80·00
		a. Chalk-surfaced paper (Head Die B) (1908)	60·00	80·00
31		10s. grey-black and purple/*yellow* (*chalk-surfaced paper*) (Head Die B) (9.08)	£120	£180
32		£1 green and violet (19.3.06)	£275	£325
		a. Chalk-surfaced paper (1906)	£275	£350
		ab. Head Die B (1907)	£225	£300
21/32ab *Set of* 12			£425	£550

I

II

Die I. Thick "1", small "d". (double working plate).
Die II. Thinner "1", larger "d" (single working plate).

1907–11. *Colours changed. Head Die B. Ordinary paper (½d. to 2½d.) or chalk-surfaced paper (others)*. Wmk Mult Crown CA. P 14.

33	2	½d. pale green (1907)	3·00	20
		a. Head Die A	8·50	1·75
		b. Blue-green (1910)	2·25	20
34		1d. carmine (I) (12.8.07)	4·00	60
		a. Head Die A	15·00	2·00
		ab. Die II. *Carmine-red* (1910)	1·00	10
35		2d. greyish slate (9.09)	2·75	70
36		2½d. blue (9.09)	3·25	3·75
37		3d. purple/*yellow* (7.09)	2·00	30
38		4d. black and red/*yellow* (9.09)	2·25	80
39		6d. dull purple and purple (9.09)	32·00	3·25
		a. Dull purple and bright purple (1911)	26·00	3·25
		aw. Wmk inverted		
40		1s. black/*green* (7.09)	7·00	40
41		2s.6d. black and red/*blue* (9.09)	6·00	1·50
42		5s. green and red/*yellow* (9.09)	38·00	48·00
43		10s. green and red/*green* (9.09)	75·00	£110
44		£1 purple and black/*red* (9.09)	£225	£275
33/44 *Set of* 12			£350	£400
33s/44s Optd "Specimen" *Set of* 12			£300	

1912. Wmk Mult Crown CA. P 14.

45	3	½d. green	2·25	10
46		1d. red	2·25	10
		w. Wmk inverted	£170	£140
47		2d. grey	75	85
48		2½d. bright blue	3·00	2·75
49		3d. purple/*yellow*	1·00	30
50		4d. black and red/*yellow*	1·25	2·00
51		6d. dull and bright purple	1·50	1·25
52		1s. black/*green*	2·75	75
53		2s.6d. black and red/*blue*	8·00	40·00
54		5s. green and red/*yellow*	20·00	75·00
55		10s. green and red/*green*	45·00	90·00
56		£1 purple and black/*red*	£180	£225
45/56 *Set of* 12			£225	£400
45s/56s Optd "Specimen" *Set of* 12			£225	

STAMP BOOKLETS

1904. *Black on red cover. Stapled.*

SB1	2s.1d. booklet containing twenty-four 1d (No. 11) in blocks of 6	

1905 (1 June)–**06**. *Black on red cover. Stapled.*

SB2	2s.1d. booklet containing twenty-four 1d. (No. 22) in blocks of 6	£1800
	a. As No. SB2 but containing No. 22a (1906)	£1500

1907 (7 Oct). *Black on red cover. Stapled.*

SB3	2s.1d. booklet containing twenty-four 1d (No. 34) in blocks of 6	£2000

1910 (19 Sept). *Black on red cover. Stapled.*

SB4	2s. booklet containing eleven ½d. and eighteen 1d. (Nos. 33*b*, 34ab) in blocks of 6 or 5	

1912 (Oct). *Black on red cover. Stapled.*

SB5	2s. booklet containing twelve ½d. and eighteen 1d. (Nos. 45/6) in blocks of 6	£1500

On 1 January 1914 Southern Nigeria became part of Nigeria.

NIGERIA

Nigeria was formed on 1 January 1914 from the former protectorates of Northern and Southern Nigeria.

PRICES FOR STAMPS ON COVER TO 1945	
Nos. 1/10	*from* × 3
Nos. 11/12	—
Nos. 15/28	*from* × 3
Nos. 29/a	—
Nos. 30/3	*from* × 3
Nos. 34/59	*from* × 2

CROWN COLONY

1

2

(Typo D.L.R.)

1914 (1 June)–**29**. *Die I. Ordinary paper (½d. to 2½d.) or chalk-surfaced paper (others).* Wmk Mult Crown CA. P 14.

1	1	½d. green	5·50	70
2		1d. carmine-red	4·75	10
		a. Scarlet (1916)	8·50	20
		w. Wmk inverted	£110	£110
3		2d. grey	8·00	1·75
		a. Slate-grey (1918)	9·00	75
4		2½d. bright blue	8·50	3·50
		a. Dull blue (1915)	17·00	6·00
5	2	3d. purple/*yellow* (*white back*)	2·75	10·00
		a. Lemon back (19.8.15)	1·50	2·75
		b. On deep yellow (yellow back) (thick paper) (1915)	38·00	7·50
		bs. Optd "Specimen"	45·00	
		c. On orange-buff (1920)	9·00	22·00
		d. On buff (1920)	12·00	
		e. On pale yellow (1921)	12·00	15·00
6		4d. black and red/*yellow* (*white back*)	1·40	10·00
		a. Lemon back (19.8.15)	1·00	4·25
		b. On deep yellow (yellow back) (thick paper) (1915)	38·00	8·00
		bs. Optd "Specimen"	45·00	
		c. On orange-buff (1920)	11·00	10·00
		d. On buff (1920)	11·00	
		e. On pale yellow (1921)	10·00	18·00
7		6d. dull purple and bright purple	9·00	10·00
8	1	1s. black/*blue-green* (*white back*)	1·50	23·00
		a. On yellow-green (white back) (1915)	£150	
		b. Yellow-green back (19.8.15)	45·00	45·00
		c. Blue-green back (1915)	1·00	9·50
		cs. Optd "Specimen"	45·00	
		d. Pale olive back (1917)	28·00	32·00
		dw. Wmk inverted		
		e. On emerald (pale olive back) (1920)	8·00	40·00
		f. On emerald (emerald back) (1920)	1·25	15·00
9		2s.6d. black and red/*blue*	16·00	6·50
10	2	5s. green and red/*yellow* (*white back*)	15·00	55·00
		a. Lemon back (19.8.15)	21·00	55·00
		b. On deep yellow (yellow back) (thick paper) (1915)	55·00	70·00
		bs. Optd "Specimen"	48·00	
		c. On orange-buff (1920)	50·00	90·00
		d. On buff (1920)	60·00	
		e. On pale yellow (1921)	85·00	£150
11	1	10s. green and red/*blue-green* (*white back*)	48·00	£160
		a. Blue-green back (19.8.15)	55·00	90·00
		as. Optd "Specimen"	60·00	
		b. Pale olive back (1917)	£900	£1500
		c. On emerald (pale olive back) (1920)	£130	£180
		d. On emerald (emerald back) (1921)	35·00	£110
12	2	£1 deep purple and black/*red*	£190	£250
		a. Purple and black/red (1917)	£180	£225
		b. Die II. *Deep purple and black/red* (19.1.27)	£200	£325
		ba. Purple and black/red (1929)	£190	£300
1/12 *Set of* 12			£250	£375
1s/12s Optd "Specimen" *Set of* 12			£325	

The ½d. and 1d. were printed in sheets of 240 using two plates one above the other.

1921–32. *Ordinary paper (½d. to 3d.) or chalk-surfaced paper (others).* Wmk Mult Script CA. P 14.

15	1	½d. green (Die I) (1921)	1·25	40
		aw. Wmk inverted	95·00	95·00
		b. Die II (1925)	4·50	85
		c. Vert gutter pair. Die I and Die II. Nos. 15/b (1925)	£375	
16		1d. rose-carmine (Die I) (1921)	3·25	30
		aw. Wmk inverted	90·00	90·00
		b. Die II (1925)	1·75	35
		c. Vert gutter pair. Die I and Die II. Nos. 16/b (1925)	£350	
17	2	1½d. orange (Die II) (1.4.31)	5·50	15
18	1	2d. grey (Die I) (1921)	1·50	6·00
		a. Die II (1924)	8·00	40
19		2d. chestnut (Die II) (1.10.27)	4·50	1·00
20		2d. chocolate (Die II) (1.7.28)	2·25	15
		a. Die I (1932)	5·50	75
21		2½d. bright blue (Die I) (1921)	1·00	8·00
22	2	3d. bright violet (Die I) (1924)	5·00	3·25
		a. Die II (1925)	10·00	1·00
23		3d. bright blue (Die II) (1.4.31)	7·50	1·00
24		4d. black and red/*pale yellow* (Die II) (1923)	65	55
		a. Die I (1932)	4·00	5·50
25		6d. dull purple and bright purple (Die I) (1921)	12·00	26·00
		a. Die II (1923)	7·00	8·00
		aw. Wmk inverted	£120	
26	1	1s. black/*emerald* (Die II) (1924)	2·00	2·00
27		2s.6d. black and red/*blue* (Die II) (1925)	6·50	32·00
		a. Die I (1932)	40·00	80·00
28	2	5s. green and red/*pale yellow* (Die II) (1926)	15·00	70·00
		a. Die I (1932)	65·00	£200
29	1	10s. green and red/*green* (Die II) (1925)	60·00	£200
		a. Die I (1932)	£100	£450
15/29 *Set of* 15			£110	£300
15s/29s (ex 2d. chocolate) Optd or Perf (1½d., 3d. blue) "Specimen" *Set of* 14			£425	

The ½d. and 1d., together with the 1½d. from 1932, were printed in sheets of 240 using two plates one above the other. Nos. 15c and 16c come from printings in November 1924 which combined Key Plate No. 7 (Die I) above Key Plate No. 12 (Die II).

1935 (6 May). *Silver Jubilee. As Nos. 91/4 of Antigua, but ptd by Waterlow.* P 11×12.

30	1½d. ultramarine and grey	80	1·00
31	2d. green and indigo	1·50	1·00
	k. Kite and vertical log	95·00	85·00
32	3d. brown and deep blue	3·00	16·00
33	1s. slate and purple	4·00	32·00
30/3 *Set of* 4		8·50	45·00
30s/3s Perf "Specimen" *Set of* 4		95·00	

For illustration of plate variety see Omnibus section following Zanzibar.

3 Apapa Wharf

4 Cocoa

5 Tin dredger

6 Timber industry

7 Fishing Village

8 Cotton ginnery

9 Habe Minaret

10 Fulani cattle

11 Victoria-Buea Road

12 Oil Palms

13 River Niger at Jebba

14 Canoe Pulling

(Recess D.L.R.)

1936 (1 Feb). *T* **3**/**14**. Wmk Mult Script CA.

(a) P 11½×13.

34	3	½d. green	1·50	1·40
35	4	1d. carmine	50	40
36	5	1½d. brown	2·00	40
		a. Perf 12½×13½	70·00	4·00
37	6	2d. black	50	80
38	7	3d. blue	2·00	1·50
		a. Perf 12½×13½	£130	24·00
39	8	4d. red-brown	2·00	2·00
40	9	6d. dull violet	50	60
41	10	1s. sage-green	1·75	4·75

(b) P 14.

42	11	2s.6d. black and ultramarine	3·75	26·00
43	12	5s. black and olive-green	11·00	38·00
44	13	10s. black and grey	65·00	90·00
45	14	£1 black and orange	85·00	£160
34/45 *Set of* 12			£160	£300
34s/45s Perf "Specimen" *Set of* 12			£250	

1937 (12 May). *Coronation. As Nos. 95/7 of Antigua.* P 11×11½.

46	1d. carmine	1·00	2·50
47	1½d. brown	2·25	3·00
48	3d. blue	2·25	4·00
46/8 *Set of* 3		5·00	8·50
46s/8s Perf "Specimen" *Set of* 3		85·00	

15 King George VI

16 Victoria-Buea Road

(Recess B.W. (T **15**), D.L.R. (others))

1938 (1 May)–**51**. *Designs as T* **15**/**16**. Wmk Mult Script CA. P 12 (*T* **15**) or 13×11½ (others).

49	15	½d. green	10	10
		a. Perf 11½ (15.2.50)	1·75	55
50		1d. carmine	19·00	2·50
		a. Rose-red (shades) (1940)	75	30
		ab. "A" of "CA" missing from wmk		
50*b*		1d. bright purple (1.12.44)	10	20
		ba. Perf 11½ (15.2.50)	30	50
		bw. Wmk inverted (P 12)		
51		1½d. brown	20	10
		a. Perf 11½ (15.11.50)	10	10
52		2d. black	10	2·00
52*a*		2d. rose-red (1.12.44)	10	2·00
		ab. Perf 11½ (15.2.50)	10	50
52*b*		2½d. orange (4.41)	10	2·00
53		3d. blue	10	10
		a. Wmk sideways	†	£4250
53*b*		3d. black (1.12.44)	15	1·75
54		4d. orange	50·00	3·00
54*a*		4d. blue (1.12.44)	15	3·50
55		6d. blackish purple	40	10
		a. Perf 11½ (17.4.51)	1·50	60
56		1s. sage-green	60	10
		a. Perf 11½ (15.2.50)	55	10
57		1s.3d. light blue (1940)	90	30
		a. Perf 11½ (14.6.50)	1·75	70
		ab. Wmk sideways	†	£4000
58	16	2s.6d. black and blue	60·00	19·00
		a. Perf 13½ (6.42)	3·75	4·50
		ab. Black and deep blue (1947)	55·00	55·00
		b. Perf 14 (1942)	2·25	3·50
		bw. Wmk inverted	†	£4250
		c. Perf 12 (15.8.51)	2·00	4·50
59	13	5s. black and orange	£110	16·00
		a. Perf 13½ (8.42)	5·50	4·50
		b. Perf 14 (1948)	7·50	3·00
		c. Perf 12 (19.5.49)	5·50	4·00
49/59c *Set of* 16			55·00	18·00
49s/59s (*ex* 2½d.) Perf "Specimen" *Set of* 15			£300	

The 1d., No. 50ba, exists in coils constructed from normal sheets.

1946 (21 Oct). *Victory. As Nos. 110/11 of Antigua.*

60	1½d. chocolate	35	10
61	4d. blue	35	2·25
60s/1s Perf "Specimen" *Set of* 2		75·00	

1948 (20 Dec). *Royal Silver Wedding. As Nos. 112/13 of Antigua.*

62	1d. bright purple	35	30
63	5s. brown-orange	9·50	15·00

1949 (10 Oct). *75th Anniv of U.P.U. As Nos. 114/17 of Antigua.*

64	1d. bright reddish purple	15	30
65	3d. deep blue	1·25	3·50
66	6d. purple	30	3·50
67	1s. olive	50	2·00
64/7 *Set of* 4		2·00	8·50

1953 (2 June). *Coronation. As No. 120 of Antigua but ptd by B.W.*

68	1½d. black and emerald	40	10
	w. Wmk inverted	†	—

18 Old Manilla Currency

19 Bornu horsemen

Die I Flat-bed

Die Ia Rotary

Two types of 1d.:

The Belgian rotary printings have thicker lines of shading giving blotches of black colour instead of fine lines, particularly in the stirrups.

20 "Groundnuts"

21 "Tin"

Type A Gap in row of dots

Type B Unbroken row of dots

Two types of 2d. slate-violet:

Nos. 722c/cc. The original cylinder used was Type A (July 1956); later Type B (Sept 1957). The above illustrations will help classification, but two stamps per sheet of 60 of Type A show faint dots. However, one of these has the "2d." re-entry which does not exist in Type B sheets, and shades are distinctive.

22 Jebba Bridge and River Niger

23 "Cocoa"

Die I Flat-bed

Die Ia Rotary

Two types of 3d.:

As in the 1d. the Belgian rotary printings have thicker lines of shading and this is particularly noticeable in the dark hills in the background.

24 Ife Bronze

25 "Timber"

26 Victoria Harbour

27 "Palm-oil"

28 "Hides and skins"

29 New and Old Lagos

(Des M. Fievet. Recess Waterlow)

1953 (1 Sept)–**58**. *T* **18/29**. Wmk Mult Script CA. P 14.

69	**18**	½d. black and orange	15	30
70	**19**	1d. black and bronze-green (Die I)	20	10
		a. Die 1a (1.9.58)	20	10
71	**20**	1½d. blue-green	50	40
72	**21**	2d. black and yellow-ochre	4·00	30
		a. Black and ochre (18.8.54)	4·25	30
		b. Re-entry	£110	
72*c*		2d. slate-violet (Type A) (23.7.56)	3·00	1·75
		ca. Slate-blue (*shades*) (Type A)	8·50	40
		cb. Bluish grey (Type B) (25.9.57)	4·00	40
		cc. Grey (*shades*) (Type B)	5·50	30
73	**22**	3d. black and purple (Die II)	55	10
		a. Die 1a. *Black and reddish purple* (1.9.58)	55	10
		b. Imperf (pair)	£275	
74	**23**	4d. black and blue	2·50	20
75	**24**	6d. orange-brown and black	30	10
		a. Chestnut and black (18.8.54)	2·00	10
76	**25**	1s. black and maroon	40	10
77	**26**	2s.6d. black and green	7·50	50
		a. Black and deep green (18.8.54)	12·00	50
78	**27**	5s. black and red-orange	3·75	1·40
79	**28**	10s. black and red-brown	14·00	2·50
80	**29**	£1 black and violet	25·00	9·50
69/80 *Set of* 13			55·00	14·00

Nos. 70a, 72*c*/*cc* and 73a were printed on rotary machines by a subsidiary company, Imprimerie Belge de Securité, in Belgium.

No. 72b shows as a duplication in the steps of the terraces (Pl 3, R. 1/5).

Nos. 72*ca* and 72*cc* were only available in Nigeria.

The ½d. and 1d. (Die I) exist in coils constructed from sheets. Coils containing the 1d. (Die Ia) and 2d. (Type A) appeared in 1958 from continuously printed reels.

ROYAL VISIT 1956
(**30**)

31 Victoria Harbour

1956 (28 Jan). *Royal Visit. No. 72a optd with T* **30**.

81	**21**	2d. black and ochre	40	30
		a. Opt inverted	£200	

(Recess Waterlow)

1958 (1 Dec). *Centenary of Victoria.* W w **12**. P 13½×14.

82	**31**	3d. black and purple	20	30

32 Lugard Hall

(Recess Waterlow)

1959 (14 Mar). *Attainment of Self-Government, Northern Region of Nigeria. T* **32** *and similar horiz design.* W w **12**. P 13½ (3d.) or 13½×14 (1s.).

83	3d. black and purple	15	10
84	1s. black and green	55	60

Design:—1s. Kano Mosque.

INDEPENDENT FEDERATION

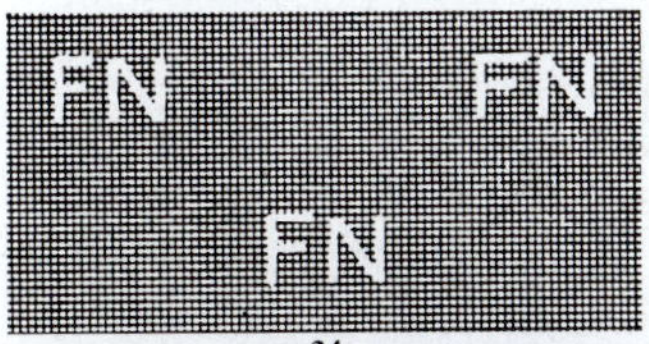

34

35 Legislative Building

38 Dove, Torch and Map

(Des L. J. Wittington (1d.), R. Crawford (3d.), R. D. Baxter (6d.), J. White (1s.3d.), Photo Waterlow)

1960 (1 Oct). *Independence. T* **35**, **38** *and similar horiz designs.* W **34**. P 13½ (1s.3d.) or 14 (others).

85	1d. black and scarlet	10	10
86	3d. black and greenish blue	15	10
87	6d. green and red-brown	20	20
88	1s.3d. bright blue and yellow	40	20
85/8 *Set of* 4		70	50

Designs: (*As T* **35**)—3d. African paddling canoe; 6d. Federal Supreme Court.

39 Groundnuts

48 Central Bank

1961 (1 Jan). *T* **39**, **48**, *and similar designs.* W **34**. P 15×14 (½d. to 1s.3d.) or 14½ (others).

89	½d. emerald	10	60
90	1d. reddish violet	80	10
91	1½d. carmine-red	80	2·25
92	2d. deep blue	30	10
93	3d. deep green	40	10
94	4d. blue	40	2·00
95	6d. yellow and black	80	10
	a. Yellow omitted	—	£750
96	1s. yellow-green	4·50	10
97	1s.3d. orange	1·50	10
98	2s.6d. black and yellow	2·75	15
99	5s. black and emerald	65	1·25
100	10s. black and ultramarine	3·50	4·25
101	£1 black and carmine-red	12·00	16·00
	w. Wmk inverted		
89/101 *Set of* 13		25·00	24·00

Designs: *Vert* (*as T* **39**)—1d. Coal mining; 1½d. Adult education; 2d. Pottery; 3d. Oyo carver; 4d. Weaving; 6d. Benin mask; 1s. Yellow-casqued Hornbill; 1s.3d. Camel train. *Horiz* (*as T* **48**)—5s. Nigeria Museum; 10s. Kano airport; £1 Lagos railway station.

PRINTERS. The above and all following issues to No. 206 were printed in phatogravure by Harrison & Sons, *except where otherwise stated.*

52 Globe and Diesel-electric Locomotive

56 Coat of Arms

(Des M. Goaman)

1961 (25 July). *Admission of Nigeria into U.P.U. T* **52** *and similar horiz designs.* W **34**. P 14½.

102	1d. red-orange and blue	30	10
103	3d. olive-yellow and black	30	10
104	1s.3d. blue and carmine-red	80	20
105	2s.6d. deep green and blue	85	2·00
102/5 *Set of* 4		2·00	2·00

Designs:—3d. Globe and mail-van; 1s.3d. Globe and Bristol 175 Britannia aircraft; 2s.6d. Globe and liner.

(Des S. Bodo (3d.), R. Hopeman (4d.), C. Adesina (6d.), M. Shamir (1s.6d), B. Enweonwu (2s.6d.))

1961 (1 Oct). *First Anniv of Independence. T* **56** *and similar designs.* W **34**. P 14½.

106	3d. multicoloured	10	10
107	4d. yellow-green and yellow-orange	20	10
108	6d. emerald-green	30	10
109	1s.3d. grey, emerald and blue	35	10
110	2s.6d. green and grey-blue	40	2·25
106/10 *Set of* 5		1·25	2·25

Designs: *Horiz*—4d. Natural resources and map; 6d. Nigerian Eagle; 1s.3d. Eagles in flight; 2s.6d. Nigerians and flag.

A used copy of No. 106 has been seen with both the silver (large "Y" appearing grey) and the yellow (appearing white) omitted.

61 "Health"

66 Malaria Eradication Emblem and Parasites

(Des M. Shamir)

1962 (25 Jan). *Lagos Conference of African and Malagasy States. T* **61** *and similar vert designs.* W **34**. P 14×14½.

111	1d. yellow-bistre	10	10
112	3d. deep reddish purple	10	10
113	6d. deep green	15	10
114	1s. brown	20	10
115	1s.3d. blue	25	20
111/15 *Set of* 5		65	40

Designs:—3d. "Culture"; 6d. "Commerce"; 1s. "Communications"; 1s.3d. "Co-operation".

1962 (7 Apr). *Malaria Eradication. T* **66** *and similar horiz designs.* W **34**. P 14½.

116	3d. green and orange-red	15	10
117	6d. blue and bright purple	20	10
118	1s.3d. magenta and violet-blue	20	10
119	2s.6d. blue and yellow-brown	30	90
116/19 *Set of* 4		75	1·00

Designs:—6d. Insecticide spraying; 1s.3d. Aerial spraying; 2s.6d. Mother, child and microscope.

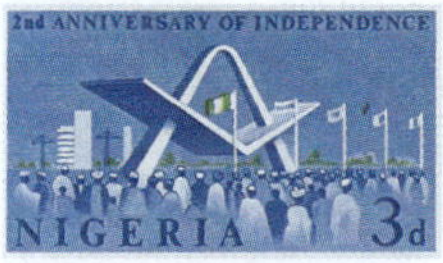

70 National Monument

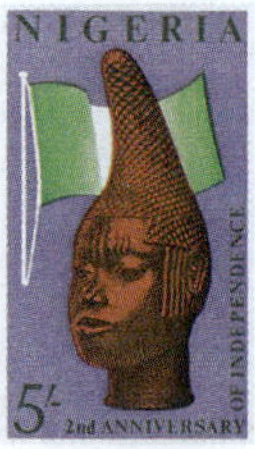

71 Benin Bronze

(Des S. Bodo (3d.), B. Enweonwu (5s.))

1962 (1 Oct). *Second Anniv of Independence.* W **34**. P 14½×14 (3d.) or 14×14½ (5s.).

120	**70**	3d. emerald and blue	10	10
		a. Emerald omitted	£500	£300
121	**71**	5s. red, emerald and violet	1·00	1·00

72 Fair Emblem

73 "Cogwheels of Industry"

(Des M. Goaman (1d., 2s.6d), J. O. Gbagbeolu and M. Goaman (6d), R. Hegeman (1s.))

1962 (27 Oct). *International Trade Fair, Lagos.* W **34**. *T* **72/3** *and similar designs.* P 14½.

122	1d. olive-brown and orange-red	10	10
123	6d. carmine-red and black	15	10
124	1s. orange-brown and black	15	10
125	2s.6d. ultramarine and yellow	60	20
122/5 *Set of 4*		85	30

Designs: *Horiz as T* **73**—1s. "Cornucopia of Industry"; 2s.6d. Oilwells and tanker.

76 "Arrival of Delegates"

77 Mace as Palm Tree

(Des S. Akosile (2½d.), M. Goaman (others))

1962 (5 Nov). *Eighth Commonwealth Parliamentary Conference, Lagos.* *T* **76/77** *and similar design.* W **34**. P 14½.

126	2½d. greenish blue	15	1·10
127	4d. indigo and rose-red	15	30
128	1s.3d. sepia and lemon	20	20
126/8 *Set of 3*		45	1·50

Design: *Horiz*—4d. National Hall.

80 Tractor and Maize

81 Mercury Capsule and Kano Tracking Station

(Des M. Goaman)

1963 (21 Mar). *Freedom from Hunger.* *T* **80** *and similar design.* W **34**. P 14.

129	3d. olive-green	1·50	20
130	6d. magenta	1·75	20

Design: *Vert*—3d. Herdsman.

(Des R. Hegeman)

1963 (21 June). *"Peaceful Use of Outer Space".* *T* **81** *and similar vert design.* W **34**. P 14½×14.

131	6d. blue and yellow-green	25	10
132	1s.3d. black and blue-green	35	20

Design:—1s.3d. Satellite and Lagos Harbour.

83 Scouts shaking Hands

(Des S. Apostolou (3d), G. Okiki (1s.))

1963 (1 Aug). *11th World Scout Jamboree, Marathon.* *T* **83** *and similar triangular-shaped design.* W **34**. P 14.

133	3d. red and bronze-green	30	20
134	1s. black and red	95	80
MS134*a*	93×95 mm. Nos. 133/4	1·75	1·75
	ab. Red omitted (on 3d. value)	£600	

Design:—1s. Campfire.

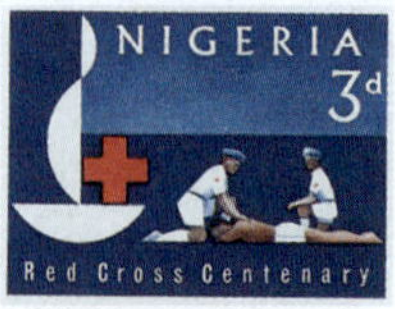

85 Emblem and First Aid Team

88 President Azikiwe and State House

(Des M. Goaman)

1963 (1 Sept). *Red Cross Centenary.* *T* **86** *and similar horiz designs.* W **34**. P 14½.

135	3d. red and deep ultramarine	50	10
136	6d. red and deep green	70	10
137	1s.3d. red and deep sepia	90	70
135/7 *Set of 3*		1·90	80
MS137*a*	102×102 mm. No. 137 (block of four)	8·50	11·00

Designs:—6d. Emblem and "Hospital Services"; 1s.3d. Patient and emblem.

(Des M. Shamir. Photo Govt Printer, Israel)

1963 (1 Oct). *Republic Day.* *T* **88** *and similar vert designs showing administrative buildings and President Azikiwe.* P 14×13.

138	3d. yellow-olive and grey-green	10	10
139	1s.3d. yellow-brown and sepia	10	10
	a. Yelow-brown (portrait) omitted		
140	2s.6d. turquoise-blue and deep violet-blue	15	15
138/40 *Set of 3*		30	30

Designs:—1s.3d. Federal Supreme Court Building; 2s.6d. Parliament Building.

89 Charter and Broken Whip

90 "Freedom of Worship"

(Des S. Apostolou (3d.), Mrs. F. P. Effiong (others). Photo D.L.R.)

1963 (10 Dec). *15th Anniv of Declaration of Human Rights.* *T* **89/90** *and similar designs.* W **34**. P 13.

141	3d. vermilion	10	10
142	6d. blue-green	15	10
143	1s.3d. ultramarine	30	10
144	2s.6d. bright purple	45	30
141/4 *Set of 4*		85	35

Designs: *Vert as T* **90**—1s.3d. "Freedom from want"; 2s.6d. "Freedom of speech".

93 Queen Nefertari

94 Rameses II

(Des M. Shamir)

1964 (8 Mar). *Nubian Monuments Preservation.* W **34**. P 14½.

145	**93**	6d. yellow-olive and emerald	50	10
146	**94**	2s.6d. brown, deep olive and emerald	1·75	2·25

95 President Kennedy

(Des M. Shamir (1s.3d), M. Goaman (2s.6d), Mr. Bottiau (5s.). Photo Govt Printer, Israel (1s.3d.); litho Lewin-Epstein, Bat Yam, Israel (others))

1964 (27 Aug). *President Kennedy Memorial Issue.* *T* **95** *and similar horiz designs.* P 13×14 (1s.3d.) or 14 (others).

147	1s.3d. light violet and black	30	15
148	2s.6d. black, red, blue and green	40	65
149	5s. black, deep blue, red and green	70	1·75
147/9 *Set of 3*		1·25	2·25
MS149*a*	154×135 mm. No. 149 (block of four). Imperf	7·00	12·00

Designs:—2s.6d. President Kennedy and flags; 5s. President Kennedy (U.S. coin head) and flags.

98 President Azikiwe

99 Herbert Macaulay

(Des S. Apostolou (3d), W. H. Irvine (others). Photo Govt Printer, Israel (3d); Harrison (others))

1964 (1 Oct). *First Anniv of Republic.* *T* **98** *or* **99** *and similar vert design.* P 14×13 (3d) or 14½ (others).

150	3d. red-brown	10	10
151	1s.3d. green	35	10
152	2s.6d. deep grey-green	70	90
150/2 *Set of 3*		1·00	1·00

Design:—2s.6d. King Jaja of Opobo.

101 Boxing Gloves

102 Hurdling

(Des A. Adalade (3d), S. Medahunsi (6d.), M. Shamir (1s.3d.), M. Goaman (2s.6d.))

1964 (10 Oct). *Olympic Games, Tokyo.* *T* **101** *and similar designs, and T* **102**. W **34**. P 14 (2s. 6d) or 14½ (others).

153	3d. sepia and olive green	45	10
154	6d. emerald and indigo	60	10
155	1s.3d. sepia and yellow-olive	1·00	15
156	2s.6d. sepia and chestnut	1·75	3·75
153/6 *Set of 4*		3·50	3·75
MS156*a*	102×102 mm. No. 156 (block of four). Imperf	3·00	4·25

Designs: *Horiz*—6d. High jumping. *Vert*—1s.3d. Running.

105 Scouts on Hill-top

(Des S. Apostolou (1d., 1s.3d), H. N. G. Cowham and Eagle Scout N. A. Lasisi (3d.), W. H. Irvine (6d.))

1965 (1 Jan). *50th Anniv of Nigerian Scout Movement.* *T* **105** *and similar vert designs.* P 14×14½.

157	1d. brown	10	10
158	3d. red, black and emerald	15	10
159	6d. red, sepia and yellow-green	25	20
160	1s.3d. bistre-brown, greenish yellow and black-green	40	85
157/60 *Set of 4*		75	1·10
MS160*a*	76×104 mm. No. 160 (block of four). Imperf	5·00	8·50

Designs:—3d. Scout badge on shield; 6d. Scout badges; 1s.3d. Chief Scout and Nigerian scout.

109 "Telstar"

110 Solar Satellite

(Des M. Shamir. Photo Govt Printer, Israel)

1965 (1 Apr). *International Quiet Sun Years.* P 14×13.

161	**109**	6d. reddish violet and turquoise-blue	15	15
162	**110**	1s.3d. green and reddish lilac	15	15

111 Native Tom-tom and Modern Telephone

(Des C. Botham (5s.), H. N. G. Cowham (others). Photo Enschedé)

1965 (2 Aug). *I.T.U. Centenary. T* **111** *and similar designs.* P 11½×11 (1s.3d.) or 11×11½ (others).

163 3d. black, carmine and yellow-brown .. 20 10
164 1s.3d. black, blue-green and chalky blue. 2·00 1·00
165 5s. black, carmine, blue and bright greenish blue .... 5·00 7·00
163/5 *Set of 3* .... 6·50 7·25

Designs: *Vert*—1s.3d. Microwave aerial. *Horiz*—5s. Telecommunications satellite and part of globe.

114 I.C.Y. Emblem and Diesel-hydraulic Locomotive

117 Carved Frieze

(Des W. H. Irvine. Photo D.L.R)

1965 (1 Sept). *International Co-operation Year. T* **114** *and similar horiz designs.* W **34**. P 14×15.

166 3d. green, red and orange .... 3·00 20
167 1s. black, bright blue and lemon .... 3·00 40
168 2s.6d. green, bright blue and yellow .... 9·00 7·00
166/8 *Set of 3* .... 13·50 7·00

Designs:—1s. Students and Lagos Teaching Hospital; 2s.6d. Kainji (Niger) Dam.

(Des S. Apostolou (3d.), W. H. Irvine (others). Photo D.L.R.)

1965 (1 Oct). *2nd Anniv of Republic. T* **117** *and similar designs.* P 14×15 (3d.) or 15×14 (others).

169 3d. black, red and orange-yellow 10 10
170 1s.3d. red-brown, deep green and light ultramarine 25 10
171 5s. brown, blackish brown and light green .... 60 1·25
169/71 *Set of 3* .... 85 1·25

Designs: *Vert*—1s.3d. Stone images at Ikom; 5s. Tada bronze.

120 Lion and Cubs

121 African Elephants

132 Hippopotamus

133 African Buffalo

(Des M. Fievet. Photo Harrison (1d., 2d., 3d., 4d. (No. 177a), 9d.) or Delrieu (others))

1965 (1 Nov)–**66**. *T* **120/1**, **132/3** *and similar designs. Without printer's imprint. Chalk-surfaced paper (1d., 2d., 3d., 4d., 9d.).* P 12×12½ (½d., 6d.), 12½×12 (1½d., 4d.), 14×13½ (1d., 2d., 3d., 9d.) or 12½ (others).

172 ½d. multicoloured (1.11.65) .... 1·00 2·75
173 1d. multicoloured (1.11.65) 50 15
174 1½d. multicoloured (2.5.66) .... 8·00 8·50
175 2d. multicoloured (1.4.66) .... 3·75 15
176 3d. multicoloured (17.10.66) .... 1·25 30
177 4d. multicoloured (2.5.66) .... 50 3·50
a. Perf 14×13½ (1966) 30 10
178 6d. multicoloured (2.5.66) .... 2·00 40
179 9d. Prussian blue and orange-red (17.10.66) .... 3·00 60
180 1s. multicoloured (2.5.66) .... 3·00 1·25
181 1s.3d. multicoloured (2.5.66) .... 8·50 1·50
182 2s.6d. orange-brown, buff and brown (2.5.66) .... 75 1·75
183 5s. chestnut, light yellow and brown (2.5.66) .... 1·75 3·00
a. Pale chestnut, yellow and brown-purple (1966) .... 2·75 3·25
184 10s. multicoloured (2.5.66) .... 6·50 3·25
185 £1 multicoloured (2.5.66) .... 17·00 9·00
172/85 *Set of 14* .... 50·00 29·00

Designs: *Horiz (as T* **121**)—1½d. Splendid Sunbird; 2d. Village Weaver and Red-headed Malimbe; 3d. Cheetah; 4d. Leopards; 9d. Grey Parrots. *(As T* **133**)—1s. Blue-breasted Kingfishers; 1s.3d. Crowned Cranes; 2s.6d. Kobs; 5s. Giraffes. *Vert (as T* **120**)—6d. Saddle-bill Stork.

The 2d. and 3d. exist with PVA gum as well as gum arabic.

See also Nos. 220, etc.

The 1d., 3d., 4d. (No. 177a), 1s., 1s.3d., 2s.6d., 5s. and £1 values exist overprinted "F.G.N." (Federal Government of Nigeria) twice in black. They were prepared during 1968 at the request of one of the State Governments for use as official stamps, but the scheme was abandoned and meter machines were used instead. Some stamps held at Lagos Post Office were sold over the counter in error and passed through the post in October 1968. The Director of Posts made limited stocks of all values, except the 1s., available from the Philatelic Bureau from 11 April 1969 "in order not to create an artificial scarcity", but they had no postal validity. Covers do, however, exist showing the 4d. value used by Lagos Federal Income Tax Office in April 1969, the 1s.3d. on commercial mail to Britain in May 1969 and others from the Office of the Secretary to the Military Government in 1973 carry the 3d., 4d. and 2s.6d. values.

COMMONWEALTH
P. M. MEETING
11. JAN. 1966
(**134**)

135 Y.M.C.A. Emblem and H.Q., Lagos

1966 (11 Jan). *Commonwealth Prime Ministers Meeting, Lagos. No. 98 optd with T* **134** *by the Nigerian Security Printing and Minting Co, Lagos, in red.*

186 **48** 2s.6d. black and yellow 30 30

(Des S. B. Ajayi. Litho Nigerian Security Printing & Minting Co Ltd)

1966 (1 Sept). *Nigerian Y.W.C.A.'s Diamond Jubilee.* P 14.

187 **135** 4d. yellow-orange, ultramarine, orange brown and yellow-green 15 10
188 9d. yellow-orange, ultramarine, brown and turquoise-green 15 60

137 Telephone Handset and Linesman

139 "Education, Science and Culture"

(Des S. B. Ajayi (4d.), N. Lasisi (1s.6d.), B. Enweonwu (2s.6d)

1966 (1 Oct). *Third Anniv of Republic. T* **137** *and similar designs.* W **34**. P 14½×14.

189 4d. green 10 10
190 1s.6d. black, brown and reddish violet..... 30 50
191 2s.6d. indigo, blue, yellow and green........ 1·00 2·25
189/91 *Set of 3* .... 1·25 2·50

Designs: *Vert*—4d. Dove and flag. *Horiz*—2s.6d. North Channel Bridge over Niger, Jebba.

(Des V. Whiteley from sketch by B. Salisu)

1966 (4 Nov). *20th Anniv of U.N.E.S.C.O.* W **34** (sideways). P 14½×14.

192 **139** 4d. black, lake and orange-yellow 40 10
193 1s.6d. black, lake and turquoise-green .... 1·75 2·75
194 2s.6d. black, lake and rose-pink........ 2·75 6·00
192/4 *Set of 3* .... 4·50 8·00

140 Children drinking

(Des V. Whiteley, after M. O. Afamefuna (4d.), I. U. Anawanti (1s.6d.) and S. Adeyemi (2s.6d.))

1966 (1 Dec). *Nigerian Red Cross. T* **140** *and similar designs.* W **34**. P 14×14½ (1s.6d.) or 14½×14 (others).

195 4d. +1d. black, reddish violet and red . 30 30
196 1s.6d. +3d. multicoloured.......... 55 3·75
197 2s.6d. +3d. multicoloured.......... 65 4·25
195/7 *Set of 3* .... 1·25 7·50

Designs: *Vert*—1s.6d. Tending patient. *Horiz*—2s.6d. Tending casualties, and badge.

143 Surveying

(Des M. Goaman)

1967 (1 Feb). *International Hydrological Decade. T* **143** *and similar multicoloured design.* W **34**. P 14½×14 (4d.) or 14×14½ (2s.6d.).

198 4d. Type **143** 10 10
199 2s.6d. Water gauge on dam (*vert*) .... 25 1·50

145 Globe and Weather Satellite

147 Eyo Masqueraders

(Des M. Shamir (4d.), S. Bodo (1s.6d.))

1967 (23 Mar). *World Meteorological Day. T* **145** *and similar horiz design.* W **34**. P 14½×14.

200 4d. magenta and blue 15 10
201 1s.6d. black, yellow and blue.......... 65 90

Design:—1s.6d. Passing storm and sun.

(Des G. A. Okiki (4d.), A. B. Saka Lawal (1s.6d.), S. Bodo (2s.6d.). Photo Enschedé)

1967 (1 Oct). *4th Anniv of Republic. T* **147** *and similar multicoloured designs.* P 11½×11 (2s.6d.) or 11×11½ (others).

202 4d. Type **147** 15 10
203 1s.6d. Crowd watching acrobat.......... 50 1·50
204 2s.6d. Stilt dancer (*vert*) .... 75 3·25
202/4 *Set of 3* .... 1·25 4·25

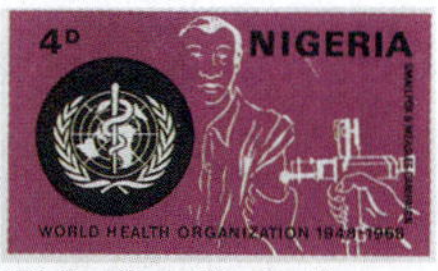

150 Tending Sick Animal

151 Smallpox Vaccination

(Des G. Drummond)

1967 (1 Dec). *Rinderpest Eradication Campaign.* P 14½×14.

205 **150** 4d. multicoloured 15 10
206 1s.6d. multicoloured .... 55 1·50

PRINTERS AND PROCESS. Nos. 207/89 were printed in photogravure by the Nigerian Security Printing and Minting Co Ltd, *unless otherwise stated.*

(Des J. Owei. Litho)

1968 (7 Apr). *20th Anniv of World Health Organization. T* **151** *and similar horiz design.* P 14.

207 4d. magenta and black 15 10
208 1s.6d. orange, lemon and black.......... 55 1·00

Design:—1s.6d. African and mosquito.

153 Chained Hands and Outline of Nigeria

155 Hand grasping at Doves of Freedom

(Des Jennifer Toombs)

1968 (1 July). *Human Rights Year. T* **153** *and similar design.* P 14.

209 4d. greenish blue, black and yellow..... 10 10
210 1s.6d. myrtle-green, orange-red and black .... 20 1·00

Design: *Vert*—1s.6d. Nigerian flag and Human Rights emblem.

(Des G. Vasarhelyi)

1968 (1 Oct). *5th Anniv of Federal Republic.* P 13½×14.

211 **155** 4d. multicoloured 10 10
212 1s.6d. multicoloured 20 20

156 Map of Nigeria and Olympic Rings

158 G.P.O.,Lagos

(Des J. Owei)

1968 (14 Oct). *Olympic Games, Mexico. T* **156** *and similar horiz design.* P 14.

213 4d. black, green and scarlet 20 10
214 1s.6d. multicoloured 80 30

Design:—1s.6d. Nigerian athletes, flag and Olympic rings.

(Des D.L.R.)

1969 (11 Apr). *Inauguration of Philatelic Service.* P 14.

215 **158** 4d. black and green.......... 10 10
216 1s.6d. black and blue.......... 20 50

159 Yakubu Gowon and Victoria Zakari

(Des adapted from photo by Jackie Phillips. Litho)

1969 (20 Sept). *Wedding of General Gowon.* P 13×13½.

217 **159** 4d. chocolate and emerald.......... 10 10
218 1s.6d. black and emerald.......... 90 30

1969–72. *(a) As No. 173 etc, but printed by Nigerian Security Printing and Minting Co Ltd. With printer's imprint* "N.S.P. & M. CO. LTD." P 13½ (6d.) or P 13×13½ (others).

220 1d. multicoloured .... 3·00 2·25
222 2d. multicoloured .... 3·00 1·50
a. Smaller imprint* (13.1.71) .... 1·00 1·75
223 3d. multicoloured (7.71) .... 65 2·00
a. Larger imprint* (22.10.71) .... 1·00 1·50

224 4d. multicoloured ... 8·00 10
a. Smaller imprint* ... 50·00
225 6d. multicoloured (1971) ... 2·25 20
226 9d. Prussian blue and orange-red (1970) ... 6·00 50
a. "TD" of "LTD" omitted from imprint (Pl. 1B, R. 10/2) ... 50·00
227 1s. multicoloured (8.71) ... 2·50 20
228 1s.3d. multicoloured (1971) ... 11·00 3·75
229 2s.6d. multicoloured (1972) ... 14·00 7·00
230 5s. multicoloured (1972) ... 3·00 16·00
220/30 *Set of* 10 ... 45·00 30·00

*On No. 222a the designer's name measures 4¾ mm. On No. 223a the imprints measure 9 and 8½ mm respectively. The normal imprints on Nos. 222/3 both measure 5½ mm.

The date given for Nos. 222a and 223a are for the earliest known used copies.

†No. 224 has the left-hand imprint 6 mm long and the right-hand 5½ mm. On No. 224a the imprints are 5½ mm and 4½ mm respectively. The width of the design is also ½ mm smaller.

Postal forgeries of the 2s.6d. exist printed by lithography and roughly perforated 11–12.

Imperforate proofs of similar 10s. and £1 values are known.

(b) As Nos. 222 and 224, but redrawn, and printed by Enschedé. No printer's imprint; designer's name at right. P 14½×13.
231 2d. multicoloured (9.70) ... 32·00 2·00
232 4d. multicoloured (3.71) ... 1·25 30

In the 2d. the face value is white instead of yellow, and in the 4d. the white lettering and value are larger.

160 Bank Emblem and "5th Anniversary"

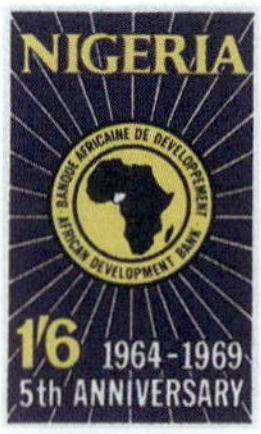

161 Bank Emblem and Rays

(Des J. Owei (4d.), B. Salisu (1s.6d.). Litho)

1969 (18 Oct). *Fifth Anniv of African Development Bank.* P 14.
233 **160** 4d. orange, black and blue ... 10 10
234 **161** 1s.6d. lemon, black and plum ... 20 1·25

162 I.L.O. Emblem

164 Olumo Rock

(Des D. West)

1969 (15 Nov). *50th Anniv of International Labour Organisation. T* **162** *and similar horiz design.* P 14.
235 4d. black and bright reddish violet ... 10 10
236 1s.6d. emerald and black ... 75 1·50
Design:—1s.6d. World map and I.L.O. emblem.

(Des A. Onwudimegwu)

1969 (30 Dec). *International Year of African Tourism. T* **164** *and similar designs.* P 14.
237 4d. multicoloured ... 15 10
238 1s. black and bright emerald ... 20 10
239 1s.6d. multicoloured ... 1·25 95
237/9 *Set of* 3 ... 1·40 1·00
Designs: *Vert*—1s. Traditional musicians; 1s.6d. Assob Falls.

167 Symbolic Tree

168 U.P.U. H.Q. Building

(Des E. Emokpae (4d., 1s., 2s.), B. Onobrakpeya (1s.6d.). Photo Enschedé)

1970 (28 May). *"Stamp of Destiny"; End of Civil War. T* **167** *and similar designs.* P 11×11½ (2s.) or 11½×11 (others).
240 4d. gold, new blue and black ... 10 10
241 1s. multicoloured ... 10 10
242 1s.6d. yellow-green and black ... 15 10
243 2s. multicoloured ... 20 20
240/3 *Set of* 4 ... 40 30
Designs: *Vert*—1s. Symbolic Wheel 1s.6d. United Nigerians supporting Map. *Horiz*—2s. Symbolic Torch.

(Des A. Onwudimegwu)

1970 (29 June). *New U. P. U. Headquarters Building.* P 14.
244 **168** 4d. reddish violet and greenish yellow ... 10 10
245 1s.6d. light greenish blue and deep blue ... 40 20

NEW INFORMATION

The editor is always interested to correspond with people who have new information that will improve or correct the catalogue

169 Scroll

170 Oil Rig

(Des A. Onwudimegwu)

1970 (1 Sept). *25th Anniv of United Nations. T* **169** *and similar vert design.* P 14.
246 4d. orange-brown, buff and black ... 10 10
247 1s.6d. steel-blue, cinnamon and gold ... 30 20
Design:—1s.6d. U.N. Building.

(Des E. Emokpae. Litho Enschedé)

1970 (30 Sept). *Tenth Anniv of Independence. T* **170** *and similar vert designs. Multicoloured.* P 13½×13.
248 2d. Type **170** ... 25 10
249 4d. University Graduate ... 15 10
250 6d. Durbar Horsemen ... 30 10
251 9d. Servicemen raising Flag ... 40 10
252 1s. Footballer ... 40 10
253 1s.6d. Parliament Building ... 40 40
254 2s. Kainji Dam ... 70 90
255 2s.6d. Agricultural Produce ... 70 1·10
248/55 *Set of* 8 ... 3·00 2·50

STAMP BOOKLETS

1915. *Black on crimson cover, inscribed* "NIGERIA".
SB1 2s. booklet containing twelve ½d. and eighteen 1d. (Nos. 1/2) in blocks of 6 ... £2000

1921–26. *Black on scarlet cover, inscribed* "NIGERIA".
SB2 4s. booklet containing twelve 1d. and eighteen 2d. grey (both Die I) (Nos. 16, 18) in blocks of 6 ... £2000
a. Containing Nos. 16 and 18a (1924) ... £1900
b. Containing Nos. 16b and 18a (1926) ... £1900

1926(?). *Black on scarlet cover, inscribed* "STAMPS BOOKLET/NIGERIA".
SB3 4s. booklet containing twelve 1d. and eighteen 2d. grey (both Die II) (Nos. 16b, 18a) in blocks of 6 ... £2000

1928. *Black on scarlet cover, inscribed* "STAMPS BOOKLET/NIGERIA".
SB5 4s. booklet containing twelve 1d. (Die II) and eighteen 2d. chestnut (Nos. 16b, 19) in blocks of 6 ... £2250

1929. *Black on scarlet cover, inscribed* "STAMPS BOOKLET/NIGERIA".
SB6 4s. booklet containing twelve 1d. (Die II) and eighteen 2d. chocolate (Nos. 16b, 20) in blocks of 6 ... £1800

1931 (Jan). *Black on scarlet cover, inscribed* "STAMPS BOOKLET/NIGERIA".
SB7 4s. booklet containing twelve 1d. and twenty-four 1½d. (Nos. 16a, 17) in blocks of 6 ... £2250

1957 (Aug). *Black on green cover. Stitched.*
SB8 2s. booklet containing four 1d. and eight ½d. and 2d. (Nos. 69/70, 72c) in blocks of 4 ... 24·00
a. Contents as No. SB8, but containing No. 72*cb* ... 50·00

1957 (Oct). *Black on buff cover. Stitched.*
SB9 10s. booklet containing eight 3d. and 1s. (Nos. 73, 76) in blocks of 4 and a pane of air mail labels ... 28·00

1963. *Black on green (No. SB10) or buff (No. SB11) covers. Stitched.*
SB10 2s. booklet containing 1d. and 3d. (Nos. 90, 93) in blocks of 6 ... 5·50
SB11 10s.6d. booklet containing six 1s.3d. and twelve 3d. (Nos. 93, 97) in blocks of 6 and two panes of air mail labels ... 15·00

1966. *Black on green cover. Stitched.*
SB12 3s. booklet containing four 1d. and 4d. and eight 2d. (Nos. 173, 175, 177a) in blocks of 4 ... 40·00

POSTAGE DUE STAMPS

D 1

(Litho BW.)

1959 (4 Jan). Wmk Mult Script CA. P 14½×14.
D1 **D 1** 1d. red-orange ... 15 1·00
D2 2d. red-orange ... 20 1·00
D3 3d. red-orange ... 25 1·50
D4 6d. red-orange ... 25 5·00
D5 1s. grey-black ... 50 6·50
D1/5 *Set of* 5 ... 1·25 13·50

1961 (1 Aug). W **34**. P 14½×14.
D6 **D 1** 1d. red ... 15 40
D7 2d. light blue ... 20 45
D8 3d. emerald ... 25 60
D9 6d. yellow ... 30 1·40
D10 1s. blue (*shades*) ... 50 2·25
D6/10 *Set of* 5 ... 1·25 4·50

BIAFRA

The Eastern Region of Nigeria declared its independence on 30 May 1967 as the Republic of Biafra. Nigerian military operations against the breakaway republic commenced in July 1967.

The Biafran postal service continued to use Nigerian stamps and when supplies of these became low in July 1967 "Postage Paid" cachets were used pending the issue of Nos. 1/3.

1 Map of Republic

2 Arms, Flag and Date of Independence

3 Mother and Child

(Typo and litho Mint, Lisbon)

1968 (5 Feb). *Independence.* P 12½.
1 **1** 2d. multicoloured ... 10 65
2 **2** 4d. multicoloured ... 10 65
3 **3** 1s. multicoloured ... 15 1·75
1/3 *Set of* 3 ... 40 2·75

(4)

1968 (1 Apr). *Nos. 172/5 and 177/85 of Nigeria optd as T* **4** *(without "SOVEREIGN" on 10s.) by Govt Printer at Enugu.*
4 ½d. multicoloured (No. 172) ... 1·50 4·75
5 1d. multicoloured (No. 173) ... 2·25 7·50
a. Opt double ... £200
b. Opt omitted (in pair with normal) ... £400
6 1½d. multicoloured (No. 174) ... 10·00 15·00
7 2d. multicoloured (No. 175) ... 27·00 50·00
8 4d. multicoloured (No. 177a) ... 17·00 50·00
9 6d. multicoloured (No. 178) ... 9·00 14·00
10 9d. Prussian blue and orange-red (No. 179) ... 3·00 3·50
11 1s. multicoloured (Blk.+R.) (No. 180) ... 60·00 £110
12 1s.3d. multicoloured (Blk.+R.) (No. 181) ... 35·00 50·00
a. Black opt omitted ... £300
b. Red opt omitted ... £300
13 2s.6d. orange-brown, buff and brown (Blk.+R.) (No. 182) ... 2·50 15·00
a. Red opt omitted ... £200
14 5s. chestnut, light yellow and brown (Blk.+R.) (No. 183) ... 2·50 14·00
a. Red opt omitted ... £200
b. Black opt omitted ... £200
c. Red opt double ... £300
d. Pale chestnut, yellow and brown-purple (No. 183*a*) ... 2·50 9·50
15 10s. multicoloured (No. 184) ... 10·00 38·00
16 £1 multicoloured (Blk.+R.) (No. 185) ... 10·00 38·00
a. Black ("SOVEREIGN BIAFRA") opt omitted ... £200
b. Red (coat of arms) opt omitted ... £200
4/16 *Set of* 13 ... £170 £375

Nos. 172/3 of Nigeria also exist surcharged "BIAFRA– FRANCE FRIENDSHIP 1968 SOVEREIGN BIAFRA", clasped hands and "+5/-" (½d.) or "+£1" (1d.). There is no evidence that these two surcharges were used for postage within Biafra (*Price for set of 2 £20 mint*).

5 Flag and Scientist

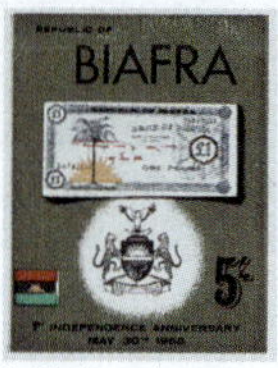

8 Biafran Arms and Banknote

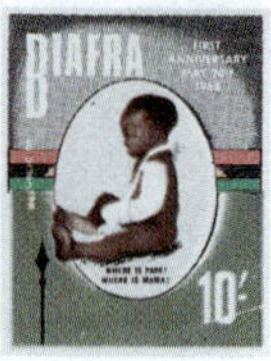

9 Orphaned Child

(Des S. Okeke. Litho Mint, Lisbon)

1968 (30 May). *First Anniv of Independence. T* **5**, **8/9** *and similar vert designs.* P 12½.
17 4d. multicoloured ... 20 10
18 1s. multicoloured ... 20 20
19 2s.6d. multicoloured ... 55 3·25
20 5s. multicoloured ... 60 3·75
a. Indigo (banknote) omitted ... 70·00
b. Red (from flag) omitted ... 65·00
21 10s. multicoloured ... 1·00 4·25
a. Bright green (from flag) omitted ... 40·00
17/21 *Set of* 5 ... 2·25 10·50
Designs:—1s. Victim of atrocity; 2s.6d. Nurse and refugees.

Nos. 17/21 also exist surcharged "HELP BIAFRAN CHILDREN" and different charity premium ranging from 2d. on the 4d. to 2s.6d. on the 10s. There is no evidence that these surcharges were used for postage within Biafra (*Price for set of 5 £2 mint*).

In September 1968 a set of four values, showing butterflies and plants, was offered for sale outside Biafra. The same stamps also exist overprinted "MEXICO OLYMPICS 1968" and Olympic symbol. There is no evidence that either of these issues were used for postage within Biafra (*Price for set of 4 £4 (Butterflies and Plants) or £3.50 (Olympic overprints), both mint*).

CANCELLED-TO-ORDER. Many issues of Biafra, including the three unissued sets mentioned above, were available cancelled-to-order with a special "UMUAHIA" handstamp. This was the same diameter as postal cancellations, but differed from them by having larger letters, 3 mm. high, and the year date in full. Where such cancellations exist on issued stamps the used prices quoted are for c-t-o examples. Postally used stamps are worth considerably more.

16 Child in Chains and Globe

17 Pope Paul VI, Map of Africa and Papal Arms

1969 (30 May). *Second Anniv of Independence. Multicoloured; frame colours given. Litho (in Italy).* P 13×13½.

35	**16**	2d. yellow-orange	1·25	4·25
36		4d. red-orange	1·25	4·25
		a. Green (wreath) and orange (Sun) omitted	£225	
37		1s. new blue	1·75	7·00
38		2s.6d. emerald	2·00	14·00
35/8 *Set of 4*			5·75	27·00

A miniature sheet with a face value of 10s. was also released.

1969 (1 Aug). *Visit of Pope Paul to Africa. T* **17** *and similar vert designs. Multicoloured. Litho (in Italy).* P 13×13½.

39	4d. Type **17**	40	3·00
40	6d. Pope Paul VI, map of Africa and arms of the Vatican	55	6·50
41	9d. Pope Paul VI, map of Africa and St. Peter's Basilica, Vatican	75	8·50
42	3s. Pope Paul VI, map of Africa and Statue of St. Peter	2·25	14·00
39/42 *Set of 4*		3·50	29·00

A miniature sheet with a face value of 10s. was also released.

No. 42 has a magenta background. This value is also known with the background in brown-red or brown.

On 17 December the French Agency released a Christmas issue consisting of Nos. 39/42 overprinted "CHRISTMAS 1969 PEACE ON EARTH AND GOODWILL TO ALL MEN" together with the miniature sheet overprinted "CHRISTMAS 1969" and surcharged £1. Later Nos. 35/38 were released overprinted in red "SAVE BIAFRA 9TH JAN 1970" with a premium of 8d., 1s.4d., 4s., and 10s. respectively together with the miniature sheet with a premium of £1. We have no evidence that these issues were actually put on sale in Biafra before the collapse, but it has been reported that the 4d. Christmas issue and 2d.+8d. Save Biafra exist genuinely used before capitulation.

Nos. 40/41 have been seen surcharged "+ 10/-HUMAN RIGHTS" and the United Nations emblem but it is doubtful if they were issued.

No. 81 of Nigeria has also been reported with the original "ROYAL VISIT 1956" overprint, together with "NIGERIA" from the basic stamp, obliterated and a "SERVICE" overprint added. Such stamps were not used for official mail in Biafra, although an example is known with the "UMUAHIA" c-t-o mark.

Biafra was overrun by Federal troops in January 1970 and surrender took place on 15 January.

Niue *see after* **New Zealand**

Norfolk Island *see after* **Australia**

North Borneo

PRICES FOR STAMPS ON COVER TO 1945

No. 1	*from* × 100
Nos. 2/3	*from* × 10
Nos. 4/5	—
Nos. 6/19	*from* × 10
Nos. 19*b*/21*b*	—
Nos. 22/8	*from* × 50
Nos. 29/35	—
Nos. 36/44	*from* × 100
Nos. 45/50	—
Nos. 51/2	*from* × 10
No. 54	—
Nos. 55/65	*from* × 10
Nos. 66/79	*from* × 4
Nos. 81/6	—
Nos. 87/91	*from* × 12
Nos. 92/111	*from* × 4
Nos. 112/26	*from* × 10
Nos. 127/40	*from* × 6
Nos. 141/5	—
Nos. 146/57	*from* × 5
Nos. 158/79	*from* × 8
Nos. 181/5	—
Nos. 186/8	*from* × 10
Nos. 189/230	*from* × 4
Nos. 231/4	—
Nos. 235/49	*from* × 3
Nos. 250/2	—
Nos. 253/75	*from* × 12
Nos. 276/92	*from* × 7
Nos. 293/4	—
Nos. 295/300	*from* × 6
Nos. 301/2	—
Nos. 303/17	*from* × 3
Nos. 318/19	*from* × 20
Nos. 320/34	*from* × 3
Nos. D1/30	*from* × 25
Nos. D31/6	*from* × 12
No. D37	—
Nos. D38/84	*from* × 40
Nos. D85/9	*from* × 8

BRITISH NORTH BORNEO COMPANY ADMINISTRATION

PRINTERS. The stamps of this country up to 1894 were designed by T. Macdonald and printed in lithography by Blades, East and Blades, London.

1

8 Cents.
(2)

EIGHT
CENTS
(3)

1883 (Mar). P 12.

1	**1**	2c. red-brown	30·00	65·00
		a. Imperf between (horiz pair)	£20000	

The figure "2" varies in size.

1883 (June). *No. 1 surch as T* **2** *or* **3**.

2	**2**	8c. on 2c. red-brown	£1300	£800
3	**3**	8c. on 2c. red-brown	£500	£190
		a. Surch double	†	£5000

Type **2** was handstamped and stamps without stop are generally forgeries. Type **3** was a setting of 50 (10×5) providing ten varieties; it normally has a stop which sometimes failed to print.

CANCELLED-TO-ORDER – Prices are separately indicated in a third price column, for stamps showing the recognisable black bars remainder cancellation. The issues since 1916 have not been thus cancelled.

It should be noted, however, that a postmark of this form was in use for postal purposes up to this period, and was used at one or two of the smaller post-offices until 1949. A small oval with five bars was used to mark railway mail during 1945/55 and also as a paquebot mark at Jesselton *c.* 1950.

4

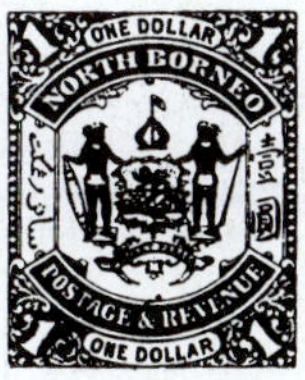
5

and
Revenue
(6)

1883. P 14.

4	**4**	50c. violet	£160	—	29·00
		a. Inverted "L" for first "F" in "FIFTY" (R. 5/2)	£1400	—	£250
5	**5**	$1 scarlet	£140	—	14·00

1883 (July). P 12.

6	**1**	4c. pink	55·00	60·00
		a. Imperf (horiz pair)	†	—
7		8c. green	80·00	60·00

1886. P 14.

8	**1**	½c. magenta	95·00	£180
9		1c. orange	£180	£325
		a. Imperf (pair)	£275	£275
		b. Imperf horiz (vert pair)	£1500	
10		2c. brown	32·00	28·00
		a. Imperf between (horiz pair)	£650	
11		4c. pink	17·00	50·00
12		8c. green	19·00	50·00
		a. Imperf between (horiz pair)	£850	
13		10c. blue	35·00	50·00
		a. Imperf (pair)	£350	
8/13 *Set of* 6			£325	£600

Imperforate examples of the 4c. pink are listed under No. 6a.

1886 (Sept). *Nos. 8 and 13 optd with T* **6**.

14		½c. magenta	£150	£250
15		10c. blue	£200	£250

3 CENTS (7) 5 CENTS (8) 3 CENTS Small "3" variety (R. 3/1, 3/4, 3/7)

(Surchd by *North Borneo Herald*, Sandakan)

1886 (Sept). *T* **1** *surch as T* **7/8**.

(a) P 12.

16	**7**	3c. on 4c. pink	£225	£300
		a. Small "3"	—	£7000
17	**8**	5c. on 8c. green	£250	£300

(b) P 14.

18	**7**	3c. on 4c. pink	£120	£130
		a. Small "3"	£1800	
19	**8**	5c. on 8c. green	£120	£130
		a. Surch inverted	£2500	

9

10

11

12

13

1886–87.

(a) P 14.

21*b*	**9**	½c. magenta	16·00	50·00
22		½c. rose	3·75	14·00
		a. Imperf (pair)	45·00	
23		1c. orange-yellow	14·00	30·00
		a. Imperf between (vert pair)	£400	
		b. Imperf (pair)	55·00	
24		1c. orange	2·00	10·00
		a. Imperf (pair)	42·00	
25		2c. brown	2·00	9·00
		a. Imperf (pair)	42·00	
26		4c. pink	3·50	14·00
		a. Imperf (pair)	45·00	
		b. Imperf between (horiz or vert pair)	£350	
		c. Imperf vert (horiz pair)	£325	
		d. Error. 1c. pink (R. 2/3) (centre stamp of strip of 3)	£300	£800
		da. Imperf between (pair)		
		db. Imperf (pair)	£4750	
27		8c. green	18·00	23·00
		a. Imperf (pair)	45·00	
28		10c. blue	8·50	30·00
		a. Imperf between (vert pair)	£425	
		b. Imperf (pair)	45·00	
29	**10**	25c. indigo	£300	18·00
		a. Imperf between (vert pair)		
		b. Imperf (pair)	£375	40·00
30	**11**	50c. violet	£375	20·00
		a. Imperf (pair)	£425	40·00
31	**12**	$1 scarlet	£350	19·00
		a. Imperf (pair)	£475	40·00
32	**13**	$2 sage-green	£450	25·00
		a. Imperf (pair)	£400	42·00
22/32 *Set of* 10			£1400	£160

(b) P 12.

34	**9**	½c. magenta	£225	£400
35		1c. orange	£180	£250

Nos. 21*b*/32 are known to have been sold as cancelled remainders, but these are difficult to distinguish from postally used. Values above 10c. are infrequently found postally used so that the used prices quoted are for the remainders.

14

15

16

17

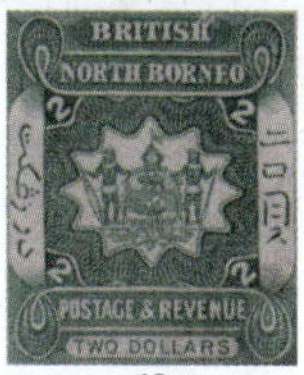
18

1888–92. *T* **14** *(as T* **9** *but inscr "POSTAGE & REVENUE") and T* **15/18** *(T* **10/13** *redrawn).* P 14.

36	**14**	½c. magenta (1889)	4·00	26·00	2·25
		a. Imperf vert (horiz pair)	†	†	£250
		b. Rose	1·50	5·50	60
		ba. Imperf between (horiz pair)	£400		
		c. Imperf (pair)	42·00	—	11·00
37		1c. orange (1892)	3·50	4·50	50
		a. Imperf vert (horiz pair)	£375		
		b. Imperf (pair)	42·00	—	9·50
38		2c. brown (1889)	11·00	18·00	90
		a. Imperf between (horiz pair)	†	†	£400
		b. Lake-brown	4·75	18·00	50
		c. Imperf (pair)	42·00	—	9·00
39		3c. violet (1889)	2·50	12·00	50
		b. Imperf (pair)	30·00	—	9·00
40		4c. rose-pink (1889)	7·50	35·00	50
		a. Imperf vert (horiz pair)	†	†	£250
		b. Imperf (pair)	45·00	—	9·50
41		5c. slate (1889)	2·75	24·00	50
		a. Imperf between (pair)			
		b. Imperf (pair)	45·00	—	9·50
42		6c. lake (1892)	10·00	24·00	50
		a. Imperf (pair)	45·00	—	12·00
43		8c. blue-green (1891)	30·00	38·00	1·00
		a. Yellow-green	22·00	28·00	50
		c. Imperf (pair)	45·00	—	12·00
44		10c. blue (1891)	8·00	29·00	1·00
		a. Imperf between (vert pair)	†	†	£275
		b. Dull blue	6·50	21·00	50
		ba. Imperf between (horiz pair)			
		d. Imperf (pair)	42·00	—	11·00
45	**15**	25c. indigo	70·00	85·00	75
		a. Imperf (pair)	£325	†	19·00
		b. Imperf vert (horiz pair)	†	†	£275
46	**16**	50c. violet	95·00	£130	75
		a. Imperf (pair)	£425	†	19·00
		b. Chalky blue	£110	£120	†
47	**17**	$1 scarlet	35·00	£110	75
		a. Imperf (pair)	£325	†	19·00
48	**18**	$2 dull green	£150	£190	1·50
		a. Imperf (pair)	£475	†	22·00
36*b*/48 *Set of* 13			£350	£600	7·50

Nos. 39, 43 and 44 showing stamps printed double or triple, one inverted, are from waste sheets subsequently sold by the British North Borneo Company to collectors.

These stamps to the 10c. value were forged on several occasions. Most forgeries of the ½c. value can be identified by the presence of a diagonal line joining the top two horizontal strokes of the uppermost Chinese character.

The new 25c. has the inscription "BRITISH NORTH BORNEO" in taller capitals. In the 50c. the "0" of the numerals "50" in the two upper corners is square-shaped at the top and bottom instead of being oval. The 1 dollar has 14 pearls instead of 13 at each side, and on the 2 dollars the word "BRITISH" measures 10½ to 11 mm in length in place of 12 mm.

19

20

1889. P 14.

49	**19**	$5 bright purple	£250	£275	8·50
		a. Imperf (pair)	£650	†	48·00
50	**20**	$10 brown	£300	£375	12·00
		a. Imperf (pair)	£850	†	55·00

		b. "DOLLAPS" for "DOLLARS" (R. 2/1)	£1500	£2000	£325
		ba. Ditto. Imperf (pair)	£3500	†	£750

Two Cents. (21) **6 cents.** (22) **1 cent.** (23)

1890 (Dec). *Surch as T* **21**, *in red.*

51	15	2c. on 25c. indigo	70·00	90·00
		a. Surch inverted	£450	£450
52		8c. on 25c. indigo	95·00	£110

The first printing of Nos. 51/2 had the two lines of the surcharge 3.5 mm apart. On a second printing of both values this gap widened to 5 mm.

1891–92. *Surch with T* **22**.

54	9	6c. on 8c. green (1892)	£9000	£4500
		a. Large "s" in "cents"	£16000	
55	14	6c. on 8c. yellow-green	25·00	10·00
		a. Surch inverted	£450	£500
		b. Inverted "c" in "cents" (R. 5/4)	£550	£650
		c. "cetns." for "cents" (R. 3/7)	£550	£650
		d. Large "s" in "cents" (R. 2/9 or 3/7)	£250	£200
56	9	6c. on 10c. blue	60·00	22·00
		a. Surch inverted	£300	£300
		b. Surch double		
		c. Surch treble	£550	
		d. Large "s" in "cents"	£300	£170
57	14	6c. on 10c. blue	£170	26·00
		a. Large "s" in "cents"	£700	£225

Unused examples of Nos. 55 and 57 are normally without gum.

There were three settings of the surcharge for No. 55. On the first two the large "s" in "cents" occurred on R. 2/9 with the other two listed varieties also included. Nos. 55b/c were corrected on the third setting and the large "s" in cents occurred on R. 3/7.

1892 (Mar–Nov). *Surch as T* **23** *("Cents." with capital "C" as in T* **21** *on No. 65), in red.*

63	14	1c. on 4c. rose-pink	23·00	14·00
		a. Surch double	£1500	
		b. Surch on back and on front	†	£600
		ba. As b, but with surch double on front		
64		1c. on 5c. slate (Nov)	7·00	6·00
65	15	8c. on 25c. indigo (date?)	£150	£160

Unused examples of Nos. 63/5 are normally without gum.

24 Dyak Chief

25 Sambar Stag (*Cervus unicolor*)

26 Sago Palm

27 Great Argus Pheasant

28 Arms of the Company

29 Malay Dhow

30 Estuarine Crocodile

31 Mount Kinabalu

32 Arms of the Company with Supporters

PERFORATION. There are a number of small variations in the perforation of the Waterlow issues of 1894 to 1922 which we believe were due to irregularity of the pins rather than different perforators.

In the following lists, stamps perf 12, 12½, 13 or compound are described as perf 12–13, stamps perf 13½, 14 or compound are described as perf 13½–14 and those perf 14½, 15 or compound are listed as perf 14½–15. In addition the 13½–14 perforation exists compound with 14½–15 and with 12–13, whilst perf 15½–16 comes from a separate perforator.

(Recess Waterlow)

1894 (Feb). P 14½–15.

66	24	1c. black and olive-bistre	1·25	9·50	50
		a. Imperf between (horiz or vert pair)	£850		
		b. Perf 13½–14	1·75	12·00	50
		c. Perf 13½–14, comp 14½–15	45·00	55·00	—
		d. Perf 13½–14, comp 12–13	24·00	50·00	—
		e. Perf 12–13			
67		1c. black and bistre-brown	2·00	16·00	50
		a. Perf 13½–14	2·75	16·00	50
		b. Perf 13½–14, comp 12–13	27·00	55·00	—
		c. Perf 12–13			
68	25	2c. black and rose-lake	5·50	4·75	50
		a. Imperf between (horiz or vert pair)	£850	£850	†
		b. Perf 13½–14	40·00	45·00	75
		c. Perf 13½–14, comp 14½–15			
69		2c. black and lake	5·50	4·75	50
		a. Perf 13½–14	40·00	40·00	1·50
		b. Perf 13½–14, comp 12–13	30·00	32·00	—
		c. Imperf between (horiz pair)			
70	26	3c. olive-green and dull purple	2·75	8·50	50
		a. Imperf between (horiz pair)	—	£850	†
		aa. Perf 13½–14, comp 14½–15			
		b. Bronze-green and dull purple	5·50	—	50
		c. Perf 13½–14			
71		3c. olive-green and violet (P 13½–14)	24·00	50·00	1·50
		a. Imperf between (horiz pair)			
72	27	5c. black and vermilion	14·00	11·00	60
		a. Imperf between (horiz or vert pair)	£750		
		b. Perf 13½–14	45·00	60·00	1·25
		c. Perf 13½–14, comp 12–13	—	65·00	5·50
		d. Perf 13½–14, comp 14½–15			
		e. Perf 12–13			
73	28	6c. black and bistre-brown	60·00	80·00	60
		a. Perf 13½–14	4·50	18·00	60
		b. Perf 13½–14, comp 12–13	—	65·00	5·50
		c. Perf 13½–14, comp 14½–15	60·00		
		d. Imperf between (horiz pair)			
74	29	8c. black and dull purple	6·50	11·00	60
		a. Imperf between (vert pair)	£750		
		b. Perf 13½–14	9·50	38·00	1·00
		ba. Imperf between (vert pair)	£500	†	£300
		d. Perf 13½–14, comp 12–13			
75	30	12c. black and blue	28·00	85·00	2·50
		a. Perf 13½–14	28·00	80·00	2·50
		b. Imperf between (horiz pair)	£1200	†	£650
		c. Perf 13½–14, comp 14½–15	—	—	5·00
76		12c. black and ultramarine	48·00	85·00	3·00
		a. Perf 13½–14	45·00	85·00	3·00
		b. Imperf between (pair)			
78	31	18c. black and deep green	27·00	50·00	2·00
		a. Perf 13½–14	32·00	50·00	2·00
		b. Perf 13½–14, comp 14½–15	—	—	5·00
		c. Perf 13½–14 comp 12–13	—	—	5·00
79	32	24c. blue and rose-lake	23·00	85·00	2·00
		a. Imperf between (vert pair)	—	—	£400
		b. Imperf between (vert strip of 3)	†	†	£550
		c. Perf 13½–14	23·00	70·00	2·00
		d. Perf 13½–14, comp 14½–15			
66/79 *Set of* 9			£100	£225	9·00

32a

32b

32c

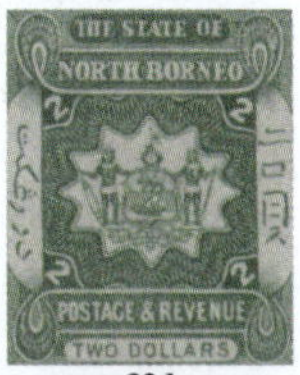
32d

32e

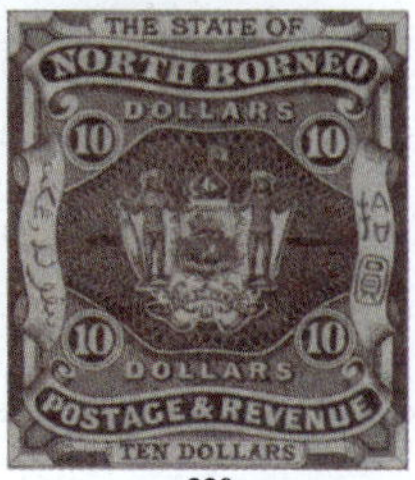
32f

(Litho Blades, East & Blades, London)

1894 (Feb). *T* **32a** *to* **32f**. P 14.

81	32a	25c. indigo	9·00	30·00	1·00
		a. Imperf (pair)	50·00	†	10·00
		b. Imperf between (horiz or vert pair)	£800	—	£100
82	32b	50c. deep slate-purple	30·00	60·00	2·00
		a. Imperf (pair)	—	†	10·00
		b. Imperf between (horiz pair)			
		d. Chalky blue	—	60·00	—
83	32c	$1 scarlet	12·00	25·00	1·25
		a. Perf 14×11	£300		
		b. Imperf (pair)	42·00	†	10·00
84	32d	$2 dull green	20·00	75·00	2·50
		a. Imperf (pair)	—	†	16·00
85	32e	$5 bright purple	£250	£300	16·00
		a. Imperf (pair)	£550	†	50·00
		b. Dull purple	£275	£300	10·00
86	32f	$10 brown	£275	£350	15·00
		a. Imperf (pair)	£550	†	50·00
81/6 *Set of* 6			£550	£700	29·00
81s/6s Optd "Specimen" *Set of* 6			£150		

For Nos. 81 to 83 in other colours, see Labuan 80*a*, 81*a* and 82*a*.

Nos. 81/4 showing stamps printed double, double, one inverted, or on both sides, are from waste sheets subsequently sold by the British North Borneo Company to collectors.

4 CENTS
(**33** (3½ mm between lines of surcharge))

(Surcharged by Waterlow)

1895 (June). *No.* **83** *surch as T* **33**.

87	32c	4 cents on $1 scarlet	7·00	1·50	50
		a. Surch double, one diagonal	£950		
88		10 cents on $1 scarlet	25·00	1·75	50
89		20 cents on $1 scarlet	42·00	17·00	50
90		30 cents on $1 scarlet	35·00	28·00	75
91		40 cents on $1 scarlet	38·00	48·00	75
87/91 *Set of* 5			£130	85·00	2·75
87s/91s Optd "Specimen" *Set of* 5			85·00		

For 4c. on $1 with wider spacing see No. 121.

No. 88 exists with the figures of the surcharge 2½ mm away from "CENTS". The normal setting has a space of 3½ mm. Examples of the narrow setting have, so far, only been seen on cancelled-to-order stamps.

34

35

36

37 Orang-Utan

38

39

40

41 Sun Bear

42

43 Borneo Railway Train

44

45

(Recess Waterlow)

1897 (Mar)–**1902**. *T* **34** *to* **45**. *New frames.* P 13½–14.

92	34	1c. black and bistre-brown	19·00	3·75	40
		aa. Perf 16			
		a. Perf 14½–15	11·00	2·75	40
		b. Perf 13½–14, comp 12–13	65·00	50·00	—
		c. Imperf between (horiz pair)	†	†	£550
		d. Perf 12–13	£150		
93		1c. black and ochre	50·00	15·00	50
		a. Perf 14½–15	38·00	14·00	50
		ab. Imperf between (horiz pair)	†	†	£550
		b. Perf 13½–14 comp 12–13			
94	35	2c. black and lake	45·00	3·50	40
		a. Perf 14½–15	22·00	2·00	40
		ab. Imperf between (horiz pair)	†	†	£600
		b. Perf 13½–14, comp 12–13	—	18·00	1·25
		c. Perf 12–13			

		d. Imperf between (vert pair)	†	†	£650
		e. Perf 13½–14, comp 14½–15	—	—	3·00
95		2c. black and green (1900)	50·00	2·00	60
		a. Perf 14½–15	95·00	18·00	2·00
		b. Perf 13½–14, comp 12–13.	£130	29·00	—
		c. Perf 12–13			
		d. Imperf between (horiz pair)	—	£1000	†
96	36	3c. green and rosy mauve	55·00	15·00	40
		a. Perf 14½–15	60·00	50·00	1·00
		b. Perf 13½–14, comp 12–13.	85·00	75·00	—
97		3c. green and dull mauve (P 14½–15)	20·00	3·00	50
98	37	4c. black and green (1900)	9·00	—	1·50
		a. Perf 13½–14, comp 12–13.			
99		4c. black and carmine (1900)	35·00	9·50	50
		a. Perf 16	85·00	48·00	50
		b. Perf 14½–15	60·00	2·25	50
		c. Perf 13½–14, comp 12–13.	38·00	45·00	2·00
		d. Perf 12–13			
100	38	5c. black and orange-vermilion	95·00	3·50	70
		a. Perf 14½–15	95·00	2·50	70
		ab. Imperf between (horiz pair)	†	£1600	†
		b. Perf 13½–14, comp 12–13.	£120	14·00	80
		c. Perf 12–13			
101	39	6c. black and bistre-brown	55·00	26·00	50
		a. Perf 14½–15	38·00	4·00	50
		b. Perf 13½–14, comp 12–13.	—	—	3·00
102	40	8c. black and brown-purple	75·00	50·00	—
		a. Perf 16	£110	20·00	70
		ab. Imperf between (vert pair)	£425	£425	—
		b. Perf 14½–15	45·00	2·75	60
103		8c. black and brown	12·00	30·00	75
		a. Perf 14½–15	65·00	80·00	—
		b. Perf 16			
104	41	10c. brown and slate-lilac (1902)	£110	45·00	2·75
		a. Imperf between (vert pair)			
105		10c. brown and slate-blue (1902)	£250	90·00	1·50
106	42	12c. black and dull blue	£150	48·00	1·75
		a. Imperf between (vert pair)	†	†	£650
		b. Perf 14½–15	£110	35·00	1·50
		c. Perf 13½–14, comp 12–13.	£180	55·00	—
		d. Perf 12–13			
107	43	16c. green and chestnut (1902)	£130	90·00	3·25
		a. Perf 14½–15	£180	£140	10·00
108	44	18c. black and green (P 16)	23·00	75·00	2·00
		a. Imperf vert (horiz pair)	†	†	85·00
		b. Imperf between (vert pair)	†	†	£350
		c. Imperf (pair)	†	†	£180
		d. Perf 14½–15	—	—	10·00
109	45	24c. blue and lake	21·00	90·00	2·50
		a. Perf 13½–14, comp 12–13.	50·00	£100	2·50
		b. Perf 12–13	£180		
92/109 (*one of each value*) *Set of* 12			£550	£300	12·50
92s/109s (*excl* 93, 97, 103, 105) Optd "Specimen" *Set of* 14			£300		

No. 98 was printed in an incorrect frame colour and it is doubtful if it was issued for postal purposes in North Borneo. Used examples come from dealers' stock sent to the territory for cancellation.

In the above the 18c. has "POSTAL REVENUE" instead of "POSTAGE AND REVENUE" and the 24c. has those words omitted. These stamps were replaced by others with corrected inscriptions; see Nos. 110 and 111.

46

47

1897. *Corrected inscriptions*. P 13½–14.

110	46	18c. black and green	£130	30·00	2·75
		a. Imperf between (horiz pair)	†	†	£600
		b. Perf 14½–15	90·00	12·00	1·50
		c. Perf 13½–14, comp 12–13	—	—	2·75
111	47	24c. blue and lake	90·00	50·00	2·25
		a. Perf 16	£150	£120	2·00
		b. Perf 14½–15	45·00	55·00	2·50
		c. Perf 13½–14, comp 12–13	—	—	3·75
		d. Perf 12–13			
110s/11s Optd "Specimen" *Set of* 2			50·00		

4 CENTS (48) (4½ mm between lines of surcharge)

BRITISH PROTECTORATE. (49)

4 cents (50)

1899 (22 July–Oct). *Surch with T* **48**. P 14½–15 (Nos. 112/17) or 14 (Nos. 118/26).

(a) 4½ mm between lines of surch.

112	4c. on 5c. (No. 100a)	48·00	48·00	
	a. Perf 13½–14	32·00	10·00	
	asa. Surch inverted, optd "Specimen"	£600		
	b. Perf 13½–14, comp 12–13	42·00	32·00	
113	4c. on 6c. (No. 101a) (date?)	19·00	24·00	
	a. Perf 13½–14	19·00	48·00	
	b. Perf 13½–14 comp 14½–15			
114	4c. on 8c. (No. 102b) (Oct)	15·00	10·00	
115	4c. on 12c. (No. 106b) (Oct)	25·00	13·00	
	a. Imperf between (horiz pair)	£750		
	b. Imperf between (vert pair)	—	£850	
	c. Perf 13½–14	45·00	50·00	
	d. Perf 12–13			
	e. Perf 13½–14, comp 12–13	42·00	40·00	
116	4c. on 18c. (No. 110a) (Oct)	14·00	14·00	
	a. Perf 13½–14	35·00	35·00	
117	4c. on 24c. (No. 111b) (Oct)	26·00	18·00	
	a. Perf 16	50·00	50·00	
	b. Perf 13½–14	23·00	38·00	
	c. Perf 13½–14, comp 12–13	38·00	38·00	
	d. Perf 12–13	£100	£110	
118	4c. on 25c. indigo (No. 81)	5·50	8·50	
	a. Imperf between (horiz strip of 3)	£1200		
119	4c. on 50c. deep slate-purple (No. 82)	13·00	16·00	
	a. Chalky blue	28·00	38·00	
121	4c. on $1 scarlet (No. 83)	5·50	12·00	
122	4c. on $2 dull green (No. 84)	5·50	13·00	
123	4c. on $5 bright purple (No. 85)	£150	£225	
	a. Dull purple	£250	£275	
124	4c. on $10 brown (No. 86)	£110	£225	
112/24 *Set of* 12		£350	£500	
112s/24s Optd "Specimen" *Set of* 12		£190		

(b) 8½ mm between lines of surch. P 14.

125	4c. on $5 (No. 85)	6·50	15·00	
126	4c. on $10 (No. 86)	6·50	15·00	

No. 121 differs only from No. 87 in having the "4" and "cents" wider apart.

Examples of the Kudat postmark dated "AU 15 1899" struck on Nos. 112/26 are generally considered to be faked.

A new setting of the surcharge, with 2½ mm between "4" and "CENTS" for values to $2 and 3½ mm on the $5 and $10, was used for the Specimen overprints, including unissued surcharges on the 1c., 2c. and 3c. values (*price* £110 *the set of three*).

(Optd by Waterlow)

1901 (8 Oct)–**05**. *Optd as T* **49**.

(a) P 13½–14.

127	1c. (No. 92) (R.)	3·50	1·50	30
	a. Perf 14½–15	2·50	1·75	30
128	2c. (No. 95) (R.)	4·00	1·25	30
	a. Perf 16	3·50	16·00	40
	b. Perf 14½–15	13·00	12·00	30
129	3c. (No. 96)	1·75	5·50	30
	a. Imperf between (vert pair)	†	†	£1100
	b. Perf 14½–15	9·00	2·75	30
	c. Perf 13½–14, comp 14½–15	50·00	—	75
130	4c. (No. 99) (G.)	9·00	1·50	30
	a. Perf 14½–15	25·00	1·50	50
131	5c. (No. 100) (G.)	50·00	3·50	30
	a. Perf 14½–15	14·00	2·50	30
132	6c. (No. 101) (R.)	50·00	65·00	1·25
	a. No stop after "Protectorate"	80·00	80·00	1·25
	b. Perf 16	4·00	15·00	70
133	8c. (No. 103) (B.)	3·75	3·75	50
	a. No stop after "Protectorate"	3·00	24·00	1·50
	b. Perf 13½–14, comp 12–13.	65·00	27·00	—
	c. Imperf horiz (vert pair)	†	†	£350
134	10c. (No. 104) (R.) (7.02)	65·00	5·00	1·00
	a. Perf 14½–15	£110	32·00	1·75
	c. Perf 13½–14. No stop after "Protectorate"	£200	—	9·00
	d. Opt double	£800	†	£300
	e. (No. 105)	£250	—	1·00
	f. Imperf vert (horiz pair)	†	†	£600
135	12c. (No. 106) (R.)	50·00	12·00	1·50
136	16c. (No. 107) (7.02)	£140	28·00	2·25
	a. Perf 14½–15	£140	55·00	2·25
	b. Perf 13½–14 comp 12–13	£250	85·00	—
137	18c. (No. 110) (R.)	12·00	25·00	1·25
	a. No stop after "Protectorate"			
	b. Perf 13½–14, comp 12–13.	55·00	—	1·50
138	24c. (No. 111)	16·00	40·00	1·50
	a. Perf 14½–15	65·00	95·00	1·75
	b. Imperf between (horiz pair)			

(b) P 14.

139	25c. (No. 81) (R.)	2·00	10·00	50
	a. No stop after "Protectorate"	£170	£200	24·00
	b. Overprints *tête-bêche* (horiz pair)			
	c. Overprint inverted	£600		
140	50c. (No. 82) (R.)	2·75	11·00	55
	a. No stop after "Protectorate"	90·00	£160	—
	b. Chalky blue			
141	$1 (No. 83) (R.) (1.04)	10·00	65·00	—
142	$1 (No. 83)	6·50	38·00	2·50
	a. Imperf horiz (vert pair)	£800		
	b. Opt double	†	†	£375
	c. Opt treble			
143	$2 (No. 84) (R.) (1903)	30·00	95·00	3·50
	a. Opt double	£1400	†	£450
144	$5 (No. 85*b*) (R.) (2.05)	£250	£475	8·00
145	$10 (No. 86) (R.) (2.05)	£450	£750	11·00
	a. Opt inverted	£2250	†	£450
127/45 *Set of* 18		£950	£1400	30·00
127s/40s Optd "Specimen" *Set of* 14		£275		

There was more than one setting of the overprint for some of the values. Full sheets of the 6c. and 8c. are known, without stop throughout.

1904–05. *Surch locally with T* **50**.

(a) P 14½–15.

146	4c. on 5c. (No. 100a)	42·00	48·00	12·00
	a. Surch omitted (in pair with normal)			
147	4c. on 6c. (No. 101a)	7·00	21·00	12·00
	a. Surch inverted	£225		
148	4c. on 8c. (No. 102b)	14·00	26·00	12·00
	a. Surch inverted	£300		
149	4c. on 12c. (No. 106b)	32·00	40·00	12·00
	a. Perf 13½–14	50·00	60·00	12·00
	b. Perf 13½–14 comp 12–13	32·00	60·00	—
	c. Surch omitted (in pair with normal)			
150	4c. on 18c. (No. 110b)	14·00	38·00	12·00
	a. Perf 13½–14			
151	4c. on 24c. (No. 111b)	26·00	50·00	12·00
	a. Perf 16	18·00	50·00	12·00
	b. Perf 13½–14	25·00	50·00	12·00
	c. Perf 12–13			

(b) P 14.

152	4c. on 25c. (No. 81)	4·50	25·00	12·00
153	4c. on 50c. (No. 82)	5·50	38·00	12·00
154	4c. on $1 (No. 83)	6·00	48·00	12·00
155	4c. on $2 (No. 84)	6·00	48·00	12·00
156	4c. on $5 (No. 85)	12·00	48·00	12·00
	a. Surch on No. 85*b*	30·00	50·00	—
157	4c. on $10 (No. 86)	12·00	48·00	12·00
	a. Surch inverted	£2500		
	b. Surch omitted (in pair with normal)			
146/57 *Set of* 12		£150	£425	£130

51 Malayan Tapir

52 Travellers' Tree

53 Jesselton Railway Station

54 The Sultan of Sulu, his staff and W. C. Cowie, Managing Director of the Company

55 Indian Elephant

56 Sumatran Rhinoceros

57 Ploughing with Buffalo

58 Wild Boar

59 Palm Cockatoo

60 Rhinoceros Hornbill

61 Banteng

62 Dwarf Cassowary

(Recess Waterlow)

1909 (1 July)–**23**. *Centres in black*. P 13½–14.

158	51	1c. chocolate-brown	7·00	2·00	30
		a. Perf 14½–15	48·00	14·00	40
159		1c. brown	22·00	1·60	30
		a. Perf 14½–15	42·00	4·50	30
		b. Imperf between (vert pair)	£1700		
160	52	2c. green	1·00	70	30
		a. Imperf between (pair)			
		b. Perf 14½–15	2·75	70	30
161	53	3c. lake	3·25	2·75	30
162		3c. rose-lake	3·00	2·75	50
		a. Perf 14½–15	38·00	—	55
163		3c. green (1923)	32·00	1·50	—
164	54	4c. scarlet	2·75	30	30
		a. Imperf between (vert pair)			
		b. Perf 14½–15	19·00	2·00	35
165	55	5c. yellow-brown	14·00	6·50	40
		a. Perf 14½–15			
166		5c. dark brown	26·00	5·50	—
167	56	6c. olive-green	13·00	2·25	30
		a. Perf 14½–15	80·00	6·50	60
168		6c. apple-green	38·00	3·50	60

169 **57** 8c. lake ... 4·00 1·75 60
a. Perf 14½–15 ... — — 10·00
170 **58** 10c. greyish blue ... 45·00 8·00 1·25
a. Perf 14½–15 ... 95·00 38·00 —
171 10c. blue ... 50·00 3·75 —
172 10c. turquoise-blue ... 42·00 2·00 2·00
a. Perf 14½–15 ... 65·00 5·50 —
173 **59** 12c. deep blue ... 35·00 3·50 1·00
a. Perf 14½–15 ... — — 10·00
b. Imperf between (horiz pair) ... † † £550
173*c* 12c. deep bright blue ...
174 **60** 16c. brown-lake ... 26·00 7·00 1·00
175 **61** 18c. blue-green ... £100 32·00 1·00
176 **62** 24c. deep rose-lilac ... 28·00 3·50 1·75
a. Deep lilac ... 40·00 6·00 —
158/76 *Set of* 13 ... £275 55·00 —
158s/76s Optd "Specimen" *Set of* 13 ... £275
For this issue perf 12½ see Nos. 277, etc.

20
CENTS
(63)

64

65

1909 (7 Sept). *No. 175 surch with T* **63** *by Waterlow.* P 13½–14.
177 20c. on 18c. blue-green (R.) ... 7·00 1·00 30
a. Perf 14½–15 ... £200 65·00 —
s. Optd "Specimen" ... 45·00

Re-entry. Doubled oars and dots behind lion (R. 4/5).

(Recess Waterlow)

1911 (7 Mar). P 13½–14.
178 **64** 25c. black and yellow-green ... 14·00 4·75 2·00
a. Perf 14½–15 ... 15·00 38·00 —
b. Imperf (pair) ... 50·00
c. Re-entry ... 50·00 25·00
178*d* 25c. black and blue-green ... 48·00
e. Re-entry ... £130
179 50c. black and steel-blue ... 14·00 4·50 2·25
a. Perf 14½–15 ... 22·00 22·00 —
ab. Imperf between (horiz pair) ... £3000
c. Imperf (pair) ... 85·00
d. Re-entry ... 50·00 25·00
180 $1 black and chestnut ... 17·00 4·00 3·50
a. Perf 14½–15 ... 55·00 15·00 7·00
b. Imperf (pair) ... £160
c. Re-entry ... 55·00 25·00
181 $2 black and lilac ... 65·00 17·00 4·75
a. Re-entry ... £180 60·00
182 **65** $5 black and lake ... £130 £130 32·00
a. Imperf (pair) ... £190
183 $10 black and brick-red ... £450 £500 80·00
a. Imperf (pair) ... £450
178/83 *Set of* 6 ... £650 £600 £110
178s/83s Optd "Specimen" *Set of* 6 ... £300

BRITISH
PROTECTORATE
(66)

2
cents
(67)

✠
(68)

1912 (July). *Nos. 85b and 86 optd with T* **66**.
184 $5 dull purple (R.) ... £1200 £1400 8·50
185 $10 brown (R.) ... £1800 — 8·50
a. Opt inverted ... † † —

1916 (Feb). *Nos. 162, 167 and 173 surch as T* **67** *by Govt Printing Office, Sandakan.* P 13½–14.
186 **53** 2c. on 3c. black and rose-lake ... 26·00 15·00
a. "s" inverted (R. 2/5) ... £100 95·00
b. Surch double ... £2000
187 **56** 4c. on 6c. black and olive-green (R.) ... 24·00 18·00
a. "s" inverted (R. 2/5) ... £100 £100
b. "s" inserted by hand ... — £1600
c. Perf 14½–15 ... £180 £180
ca. "s" inverted ...
188 **59** 10c. on 12c. black and deep blue (R.) ... 55·00 65·00
a. "s" inverted (R. 2/5) ... £170 £180
b. "s" inserted by hand ... £1400
186/8 *Set of* 3 ... 95·00 85·00
186s/8s Optd "Specimen" *Set of* 3 ... £120
Nos. 186/8 were surcharged from a setting of 25 (5×5) on which the required face values were inserted.

1916 (May). *Stamps of 1909–11 optd with T* **68** *by Waterlow. Centres in black.* P 13½–14.

(a) Cross in vermilion (thick shiny ink).
189 **51** 1c. brown ... 7·50 35·00
190 **52** 2c. green ... 50·00 80·00
a. Perf 14½–15 ... 32·00 80·00
ab. Opt double, one albino ... £325
191 **53** 3c. rose-lake ... 27·00 48·00
a. Nos. 191 and 204 *se-tenant* (vert pair) ... £3250
192 **54** 4c. scarlet ... 5·50 32·00
a. Perf 14½–15 ... £225 £160
193 **55** 5c. yellow-brown ... 45·00 55·00
a. Perf 14½–15 ...
194 **56** 6c. apple-green ... 65·00 70·00
a. Perf 14½–15 ... £225 £225
195 **57** 8c. lake ... 23·00 60·00
196 **58** 10c. blue ... 45·00 70·00
197 **59** 12c. deep blue ... 95·00 95·00
198 **60** 16c. brown-lake ... 95·00 95·00
199 **61** 20c. on 18c. blue-green ... 48·00 95·00
200 **62** 24c. dull mauve ... £120 £120
a. Imperf between (vert pair) ...
201 **64** 25c. green (P 14½–15) ... £350 £425
a. Re-entry ... £950
189/201 *Set of* 13 ... £800 £1100

(b) Cross in shades of carmine (matt ink).
202 **51** 1c. brown ... 26·00 65·00
a. Perf 14½–15 ... £225
203 **52** 2c. green ... 27·00 50·00
b. Perf 14½–15 ... £180
ba. Opt double ... † £1600
204 **53** 3c. rose-lake ... 48·00 65·00
204*a* **54** 4c. scarlet ... £700 £800
205 **55** 5c. yellow-brown ... 60·00 75·00
206 **56** 6c. apple-green ... 55·00 70·00
a. Perf 14½–15 ... £190 £225
207 **57** 8c. lake ... 29·00 55·00
208 **58** 10c. blue ... 50·00 70·00
209 **59** 12c. deep blue ... 90·00 £110
210 **60** 16c. brown-lake ... £100 £110
211 **61** 20c. on 18c. blue-green ... 90·00 £100
212 **62** 24c. dull mauve ... £110 £140
213 **64** 25c. green ... £800
a. Perf 14½–15 ... £425 £475
ab. Re-entry ... £1100
202/13a (*ex* 4c.) *Set of* 12 ... £900 £1200
The British North Borneo Company donated a proportion of the above issue to be sold by the National Philatelic War Fund for the benefit of the Red Cross and St. John's Ambulance Brigade.

RED CROSS
+
TWO CENTS
(69)

FOUR CENTS
(70)

1918 (Aug). *Stamps of 1909–11 surch as T* **69**. P 13½–14.

(a) Lines of surcharge 9 mm apart.
214 **51** 1c. +2c. brown ... 3·50 12·00
a. Imperf between (horiz pair) ... £2750
215 **52** 2c. +2c. green ... 1·00 8·50
a. Imperf between (horiz or vert pair) ... £3500
b. Imperf (pair) ...
c. Perf 14½–15 ...
216 **53** 3c. +2c. rose-red ... 14·00 19·00
a. Imperf between (horiz pair) ... £3500
b. Perf 14½–15 ... 27·00 65·00
217 3c. +2c. dull rose-carmine ... £150
a. Perf 14½–15 ... £190
218 **54** 4c. +2c. scarlet ... 70 5·00
a. Surch inverted ... £425
219 **55** 5c. +2c. deep brown ... 8·00 25·00
220 5c. +2c. pale brown ... 9·00 28·00
221 **56** 6c. +2c. olive-green ... 5·00 24·00
a. Perf 14½–15 ... £225 £250
221*b* 6c. +2c. apple-green ...
c. Perf 14½–15 ... £275
222 **57** 8c. +2c. lake ... 5·50 11·00
a. Inverted figure "3" for "C" in "CENTS" ...
223 **58** 10c. +2c. blue ... 8·00 24·00
224 **59** 12c. +2c. deep bright blue ... 21·00 48·00
a. Surch inverted ... £700
225 **60** 16c. +2c. brown-lake ... 22·00 45·00
226 **62** 24c. +2c. mauve ... 22·00 45·00

(b) Lines of surch 13–14 mm apart.
227 **52** 2c. +2c. green ... 85·00 £160
228 **56** 6c. +2c. olive-green ... £475 £850
229 **64** 25c. +2c. green ... 10·00 42·00
a. Re-entry ... 40·00
230 50c. +2c. steel-blue ... 12·00 42·00
a. Re-entry ... 48·00
231 $1 +2c. chestnut ... 45·00 50·00
a. Surcharge double, one albino ... £300
b. Re-entry ... £120
232 $2 +2c. lilac ... 75·00 95·00
a. Re-entry ... £200
233 **65** $5 +2c. lake ... £375 £600
234 $10 +2c. brick-red ... £400 £600
214/34 *Set of* 17 ... £900 £1500
The above stamps were dispatched from London in three consignments, of which two were lost through enemy action at sea.
No. 218a normally shows a second inverted albino surcharge.
Only one sheet was found of No. 228.
These stamps were sold at a premium of 2c. per stamp, which went to the Red Cross Society.

1918 (Oct). *Stamps of 1909–11 surch with T* **70**, *in red.* P 13½–14.
235 **51** 1c. +4c. chocolate ... 60 5·00
a. Imperf between (horiz pair) ... £2750
236 **52** 2c. +4c. green ... 65 8·00
237 **53** 3c. +4c. rose-lake ... 1·00 3·75
238 **54** 4c. +4c. scarlet ... 40 4·75
239 **55** 5c. +4c. brown ... 2·00 22·00
240 **56** 6c. +4c. apple-green ... 1·90 12·00
a. Imperf between (vert pair) ... £2500
241 **57** 8c. +4c. lake ... 1·25 9·50
242 **58** 10c. +4c. turquoise-blue ... 3·75 12·00
242*a* 10c. +4c. greenish blue ... 8·50 40·00
243 **59** 12c. +4c. deep blue ... 14·00 14·00
a. Surch double ... £1300
244 **60** 16c. +4c. brown-lake ... 8·00 16·00
245 **62** 24c. +4c. mauve ... 11·00 20·00
246 **64** 25c. +4c. yellow-green ... 6·00 50·00
a. Re-entry ... 30·00
247 25c. +4c. blue-green ... 29·00 75·00
a. Re-entry ... 85·00
248 50c. +4c. steel-blue ... 15·00 45·00
a. Perf 14½–15 ... 60·00
b. Re-entry ... 50·00
249 $1 +4c. chestnut ... 20·00 60·00
a. Perf 14½–15 ... £150
b. Re-entry ... 65·00
250 $2 +4c. lilac ... 50·00 80·00
a. Re-entry ... £130
251 **65** $5 +4c. lake ... £300 £400
252 $10 +4c. brick-red ... £325 £400
235/52 *Set of* 17 ... £700 £1000
Nos. 235/52 were sold at face, plus 4c. on each stamp for Red Cross Funds.
Examples of a double-ring "SANDAKAN N. BORNEO" postmark dated "1 NOV 1918" on these stamps are generally considered to be faked.

MALAYA-BORNEO
EXHIBITION
1922.
(71)

THREE
▬CENTS▬
(72)

1922 (31 Mar). *Malaya-Borneo Exhibition, Singapore. Stamps of 1909–22 some in different shades, optd as T* **71** *by Govt Printing Office, Sandakan.* P 13½–14.
253 **51** 1c. brown (R.) ... 16·00 65·00
a. "BORHEO" ... £325 £750
b. "BORNEQ" ... £500 £850
c. Stop after "EXHIBITION." ... 85·00
d. Raised stop after "1922" ... £850 £1100
e. "EXHIBITICN." with stop ... £850
f. Perf 14½–15 ... 35·00 70·00
fa. "BORHEO" ... £550
fb. "BORNEQ" ... £850 £1100
fc. Raised stop after "1922" ... £800
fd. "EXHIBITICN." with stop ... £800
fe. "MHLAYA" and "EXHIBITICN." with stop ... £6000
ff. Stop after "EXHIBITION." ... £150
253*g* 1c. brown (B.) (P 14½–15) ... £1400
ga. Vert pair, with and without opt ... £8000
gb. Raised stop after "1922." ... £6000
gc. "BORHEO" ... £4500
gd. "BORNEQ" ... £6000
gg. "MHLAYA" and "EXHIBITICN." with stop ... £6000
gh. "EXHIBITIOH" ... £6000
254 1c. orange-brown (R.) ... 35·00 65·00
255 **52** 2c. green (R.) ... 2·25 25·00
a. Stop after "EXHIBITION." ... 35·00
b. No hyphen ... 60·00
256 **53** 3c. rose-lake (B.) ... 16·00 60·00
a. Stop after "EXHIBITION." ... 80·00 £225
b. "EXHIBITICN." with stop ... £4500
c. Raised stop after "1922" ... £4500
257 **54** 4c. scarlet (B.) ... 3·75 40·00
a. Stop after "EXHIBITION." ... 40·00
b. Perf 14½–15 ... 90·00
ba. Stop after "EXHIBITION." ... £550
258 **55** 5c. orange-brown (B.) ... 9·50 60·00
a. Imperf between (vert pair) ... £1700 £2500
b. Stop after "EXHIBITION." ... 70·00 £250
c. Opt double ... £2500
d. Opt double (with stop) ... £8000
259 5c. chestnut (B.) ... 20·00 65·00
a. Stop after "EXHIBITION." ... £100
260 **56** 6c. apple-green (R.) ... 9·50 65·00
a. Stop after "EXHIBITION." ... 60·00
b. Opt double ... £2500
c. Opt double (with stop) ... £8000
261 **57** 8c. dull rose (B.) ... 8·00 42·00
a. Stop after "EXHIBITION." ... 80·00
262 8c. deep rose-lake (B.) ... 9·00 50·00
a. Stop after "EXHIBITION." ... 95·00
263 **58** 10c. turquoise-blue (R.) ... 16·00 60·00
a. Stop after "EXHIBITION." ... 95·00
b. Perf 14½–15 ... 40·00
ba. Stop after "EXHIBITION." ... £275
264 10c. greenish blue (R.) ... 17·00 75·00
a. Stop after "EXHIBITION." ... £100
265 **59** 12c. deep blue (R.) ... 10·00 21·00
a. Stop after "EXHIBITION." ... 95·00 £160
266 12c. deep bright blue (R.) ... 38·00
a. Stop after "EXHIBITION." ... £225
267 **60** 16c. brown-lake (B.) ... 22·00 65·00
a. Stop after "EXHIBITION." ... £120
b. Opt in red ... £11000
268 **61** 20c. on 18c. blue-green (B.) ... 23·00 80·00
a. Stop after "EXHIBITION." ... £200
269 20c. on 18c. blue-green (R.) ... 25·00 £140
a. Stop after "EXHIBITION." ... £300 £600
270 **62** 24c. mauve (R.) ... 42·00 70·00
a. Stop after "EXHIBITION." ... £190 £325
271 24c. lilac (R.) ... 42·00 70·00
a. Stop after "EXHIBITION." ... £190 £325
272 24c. reddish lilac (R.) ... 48·00 80·00
a. Stop after "EXHIBITION." ... £250

273	**64**	25c. blue-green (R.)	25·00	75·00
		a. Stop after "EXHIBITION."	£250	
		b. Re-entry	£150	
274		25c. yellow-green (R.)	9·00	60·00
		a. Stop after "EXHIBITION."	£140	
		b. Re-entry	85·00	
		c. Opt double	£3500	
		d. Perf 14½–15	14·00	70·00
		da. Stop after "EXHIBITION."	£225	
		db. Re-entry	£120	
275		50c. steel-blue (R.)	14·00	60·00
		a. Stop after "EXHIBITION."	£160	
		b. Re-entry	£120	
		c. Perf 14½–15	25·00	80·00
		ca. Stop after "EXHIBITION."	£200	
		cb. Re-entry	£150	
253/75 *Set of* 14			£180	£700
253s/75s Optd "Specimen" *Set of* 14			£450	

These overprints were applied from a number of settings covering 10, 20, 25 or 30 stamps at a time.

Of the ten settings known for the horizontal stamps the earliest were only used for the 1c. on which most of the varieties occur. Of the others the vast majority come from settings of 20 (10×2) with the stop after "EXHIBITION" variety on R. 2/7 or R. 2/9, or 25 (5×5) on which the same variety can be found on R. 5/4. In addition the 3c. comes from a different setting of 20 (10×2) on which there is a raised stop after "1922" on R. 2/8 and "EXHIBITICN." on R. 2/9.

The 1c. sequence is complicated, but additionally includes a setting of 10 with "BORHEO" on stamps 3 and 10, "BORNEQ" on stamp 4, raised stop on stamp 8 and "EXHIBITICN." on stamp 9. A setting of 20 repeats this sequence on its bottom line as does one of 30, although in this instance "MHLAYA" joins "EXHIBITICN" as the variety on stamp 9.

For the vertical stamps (2, 6, 10, 12, 16 and 20c. on 18c.) the settings were of 20 (10×2) or 25 (5×5). The stop after "EXHIBITION" occurs on R. 2/7 or R. 2/9 of the former and R. 5/4 of the latter.

The 25c. and 50c. high values were overprinted from a setting of 10×1 or 25 (5×5), with the stop after "EXHIBITION" on R. 5/4 of the letter.

1923 (Oct). *T* **54** *surch with T* **72**.

276		3c. on 4c. black and scarlet	1·50	6·00
		a. Surch double	£1300	
		s. Optd "Specimen"	50·00	

1925–28. *Designs as 1909–22 issue with centres in black and some frame colours changed*. P 12½.

277	**51**	1c. chocolate-brown	1·00	70
		a. Imperf between (horiz pair)	£1600	
278	**52**	2c. claret	85	60
		a. Imperf between (vert pair)	–	£1200
		b. Imperf between (horiz pair)		
279	**53**	3c. green	3·00	75
		a. Imperf between (horiz pair)	†	£1600
280	**54**	4c. scarlet	50	10
		a. Imperf between (vert pair)	£275	£425
		b. Imperf between (horiz pair)	£750	
		c. Imperf between (vert strip of three)	£1100	
281	**55**	5c. yellow-brown	6·00	2·75
		a. Imperf between (vert pair)	£1000	
282	**56**	6c. olive-green	8·50	90
283	**57**	8c. carmine	4·00	50
		a. Imperf between (vert pair)	£500	
		b. Imperf between (horiz pair)		
		c. Imperf between (vert strip of four)	£1600	
284	**58**	10c. turquoise-blue	4·00	90
		a. Imperf between (horiz pair)	£1000	£1400
		b. Imperf between (vert pair)		
285	**59**	12c. deep blue	22·00	80
286	**60**	16c. red-brown	30·00	£180
287	**61**	20c. on 18c. blue-green (R.)	13·00	3·00
288	**62**	24c. violet	60·00	£150
289	**64**	25c. green	13·00	4·25
		a. Re-entry	50·00	25·00
290		50c. steel-blue	20·00	14·00
		a. Re-entry	65·00	50·00
291		$1 chestnut	21·00	£450
		a. Re-entry	70·00	
292		$2 mauve	70·00	£500
		a. Re-entry	£170	
293	**65**	$5 lake (1928)	£170	£1000
294		$10 orange-red (1928)	£450	£1200
277/94 *Set of* 18			£800	£3250

Examples of No. 278 were supplied for U.P.U. distribution punched with a 3½ mm diameter hole.

Examples of the 16c., 24c., $1, $2, $5 and $10 in this perforation were not supplied to the territory for postal purposes. Used examples exist from covers prepared by stamp dealers.

73 Head of a Murut

74 Orang-Utan

75 Dyak warrior

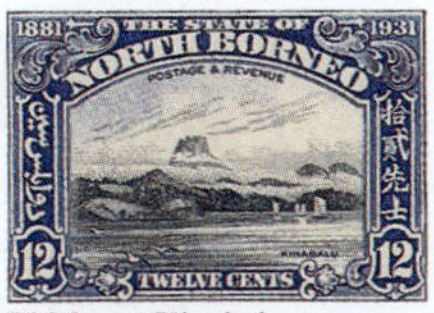
76 Mount Kinabalu

77 Clouded Leopard

78 Badge of the Company

79 Arms of the Company

80 Arms of the Company

(Eng J. A. C. Harrison. Recess Waterlow)

1931 (1 Jan). *50th Anniv of British North Borneo Company*. *T* **73/80**. P 12½.

295	**73**	3c. black and blue-green	1·25	80
296	**74**	6c. black and orange	16·00	3·25
297	**75**	10c. black and scarlet	4·25	13·00
298	**76**	12c. black and ultramarine	4·75	8·00
299	**77**	25c. black and violet	38·00	35·00
300	**78**	$1 black and yellow-green	27·00	£100
301	**79**	$2 black and chestnut	48·00	£110
302	**80**	$5 black and purple	£150	£450
295/302 *Set of* 8			£250	£650
295s/302s Optd "Specimen" *Set of* 8			£300	

Examples of all values are known showing a forged Jesselton postmark dated "22 AUG 1931".

81 Buffalo Transport

82 Palm Cockatoo

83 Native

84 Proboscis Monkey

85 Mounted Bajaus

86 Eastern Archipelago

87 Orang-Utan

88 Murut with blowpipe

89 Dyak

90 River scene

91 Native boat

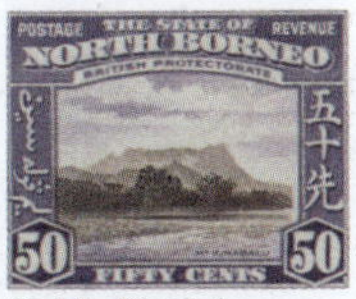
92 Mt. Kinabalu

93 Badge of the Company

94 Arms of the Company

95 Arms of the Company

(Eng J. A. C. Harrison. Recess Waterlow)

1939 (1 Jan). *T* **81/95**. P 12½.

303	**81**	1c. green and red-brown	3·50	1·75
304	**82**	2c. purple and greenish blue	5·00	1·75
305	**83**	3c. slate-blue and green	4·50	2·00
306	**84**	4c. bronze-green and violet	11·00	50
307	**85**	6c. deep blue and claret	10·00	11·00
308	**86**	8c. scarlet	14·00	1·50
309	**87**	10c. violet and bronze-green	38·00	6·00
310	**88**	12c. green and royal blue	35·00	6·50
		a. Green and blue	55·00	9·00
311	**89**	15c. blue-green and brown	28·00	10·00
312	**90**	20c. violet and slate-blue	20·00	5·00
313	**91**	25c. green and chocolate	25·00	13·00
		a. Vignette printed double, one albino	£190	
314	**92**	50c. chocolate and violet	28·00	11·00
315	**93**	$1 brown and carmine	95·00	20·00
316	**94**	$2 violet and olive-green	£150	£120
317	**95**	$5 indigo and pale blue	£425	£275
303/17 *Set of* 15			£800	£425
303s/17s Perf "Specimen" *Set of* 15			£475	

Examples of most values are known showing forged Jesselton postmarks dated "22 AUG 1941" or "15 JA 48".

No. 313a has the albino impression sideways.

WAR TAX
(**96**)

WAR
TAX
(**97**)

1941 (24 Feb). *Nos. 303/4 optd at Sandakan with T* **96/7**.

318		1c. green and red-brown	1·75	3·75
		a. Optd front and back	£500	
319		2c. purple and greenish blue	7·00	4·00

The 1c. was for compulsory use on internal mail and the 2c. on overseas mail, both in addition to normal postage.

BRITISH MILITARY ADMINISTRATION

North Borneo, including Labuan, was occupied by the Japanese in January 1942. Australian forces landed on Labuan on 10 June 1945 and by the end of the war against Japan on 14 August had liberated much of western North Borneo. The territory was placed under British Military Administration on 5 January 1946.

BMA
(**98**)

(**99**)

1945 (17 Dec). *Nos. 303/17 optd with T* **98**.

320	**81**	1c. green and red-brown	11·00	2·00
321	**82**	2c. purple and greenish blue	14·00	2·00
		a. Opt double	£7500	
322	**83**	3c. slate-blue and green	1·25	1·25
323	**84**	4c. bronze-green and violet	16·00	16·00
324	**85**	6c. deep blue and claret	1·25	1·25
325	**86**	8c. scarlet	3·00	75
326	**87**	10c. violet and bronze-green	3·00	40
327	**88**	12c. green and blue	6·00	3·00
		a. Green and royal blue	9·00	1·75
328	**89**	15c. blue-green and brown	1·50	1·00
329	**90**	20c. violet and slate-blue	5·50	1·75
330	**91**	25c. green and chocolate	6·50	1·50
331	**92**	50c. chocolate and violet	3·50	2·00
332	**93**	$1 brown and carmine	48·00	40·00
333	**94**	$2 violet and olive-green	50·00	35·00
		a. Opt double	£3750	
334	**95**	$5 indigo and pale blue	25·00	15·00
320/34 *Set of* 15			£170	£110

These stamps and the similarly overprinted stamps of Sarawak were obtainable at all post offices throughout British Borneo (Brunei, Labuan, North Borneo and Sarawak), for use on local and overseas mail.

CROWN COLONY

North Borneo became a Crown Colony on 15 July 1946.

Lower bar broken at right (R. 8/3)

Lower bar broken at left (R. 8/4 and R. 8/8)

1947 (1 Sept–22 Dec). *Nos. 303 to 317 optd with T* **99** *and bars obliterating words "THE STATE OF" and "BRITISH PROTECTORATE"*.

335	**81**	1c. green and red-brown (15.12)	15	1·00
		b. Lower bar broken at right	20·00	38·00
		c. Lower bar broken at left	18·00	35·00

336	**82**	2c. purple and greenish blue (22.12)	1·75	90
337	**83**	3c. slate-blue and green (R.) (22.12)	15	90
338	**84**	4c. bronze-green and violet	70	90
339	**85**	6c. deep blue and claret (R.) (22.12)	25	20
340	**86**	8c. scarlet	30	20
		b. Lower bar broken at right	22·00	22·00
341	**87**	10c. violet and bronze-green (15.12)	1·50	40
342	**88**	12c. green and royal blue (22.12)	2·50	2·75
		a. Green and blue	9·00	8·00
343	**89**	15c. blue-green and brown (22.12)	2·25	30
344	**90**	20c. violet and slate-blue (22.12)	3·25	85
		b. Lower bar broken at right	50·00	32·00
345	**91**	25c. green and chocolate (22.12)	3·00	50
		b. Lower bar broken at right	70·00	32·00
346	**92**	50c. chocolate and violet (22.12)	3·00	85
		b. Lower bar broken at right	70·00	32·00
		c. Lower bar broken at left	65·00	30·00
347	**93**	$1 brown and carmine (22.12)	8·50	1·75
348	**94**	$2 violet and olive-green (22.12)	17·00	17·00
349	**95**	$5 indigo and pale blue (R.) (22.12)	26·00	18·00
		b. Lower bar broken at right	£190	£170
335/49 *Set of* 15			65·00	42·00
335s/49s Perf "Specimen" *Set of* 15			£300	

1948 (1 Nov). *Royal Silver Wedding. As Nos. 112/13 of Antigua.*

350	8c. scarlet	30	80
351	$10 mauve	26·00	35·00

1949 (10 Oct). *75th Anniv of U.P.U. As Nos. 114/17 of Antigua.*

352	8c. carmine	60	30
353	10c. brown	3·25	1·75
354	30c. orange-brown	1·25	1·75
355	55c. blue	1·25	2·75
352/5 *Set of* 4		5·50	6·00

100 Mount Kinabalu

101 Native musical instrument

102 Coconut Grove

103 Hemp drying

104 Cattle at Kota Belud

105 Map

106 Log pond

107 Malay prau, Sandakan

108 Bajau Chief

109 Suluk river canoe, Lahad Datu

110 Clock Tower Jesselton

111 Bajau horsemen

112 Murut with blowpipe

113 Net-fishing

114 Arms of North Borneo

(Photo Harrison)

1950 (1 July)–**52**. *T* **100/114**. *Chalk-surfaced paper.* Wmk Mult Script CA. P 13½×14½ (horiz), 14½×13½ (vert).

356	**100**	1c. red-brown	15	1·25
357	**101**	2c. blue	15	50
358	**102**	3c. green	15	15
359	**103**	4c. bright purple	15	10
360	**104**	5c. violet	15	10
361	**105**	8c. scarlet	1·25	85
362	**106**	10c. maroon	1·50	15
363	**107**	15c. ultramarine	2·00	65
364	**108**	20c. brown	2·25	10
365	**109**	30c. olive-brown	5·00	20
366	**110**	50c. rose-carmine ("JESSLETON")	1·50	3·75
366*a*		50c. rose-carmine ("JESSELTON") (1.5.52)	12·00	3·00
367	**111**	$1 red-orange	4·75	1·00
368	**112**	$2 grey-green	9·50	16·00
369	**113**	$5 emerald-green	18·00	25·00
370	**114**	$10 dull blue	48·00	75·00
356/70 *Set of* 16			95·00	£110

1953 (3 June). *Coronation. As No. 120 of Antigua.*

371	10s. black and bright scarlet	1·75	70

115 Log Pond

(Photo Harrison)

1954 (1 Mar)–**59**. *Designs previously used for King George VI issue, but with portrait of Queen Elizabeth II as in T* **115**. *Chalk-surfaced paper.* Wmk Mult Script CA. P 14½×13½ (vert) or 13½×14½ (horiz).

372	**100**	1c. red-brown (1.10.54)	10	30
373	**101**	2c. blue (1.6.56)	75	15
374	**102**	3c. green (1.2.57)	2·50	2·00
		a. Deep green (14.1.59)	5·00	4·25
375	**103**	4c. bright purple (16.5.55)	1·00	20
376	**104**	5c. reddish violet (1.7.54)	75	10
377	**105**	8c. scarlet (1.10.54)	60	30
378	**115**	10c. maroon	30	10
379	**107**	15c. bright blue (16.5.55)	1·00	10
380	**108**	20c. brown (3.8.54)	30	15
381	**109**	30c. olive-brown (3.8.54)	2·25	20
382	**110**	50c. rose-carmine ("JESSELTON") (10.2.56)	5·00	20
		a. Rose (9.12.59)	17·00	1·50
		aw. Wmk inverted	—	£275
383	**111**	$1 red-orange (1.4.55)	6·50	20
384	**112**	$2 deep green (1.10.55)	12·00	1·25
		a. Grey-green (22.1.58)	27·00	6·50
385	**113**	$5 emerald-green (1.2.57)	10·00	28·00
386	**114**	$10 deep blue (1.2.57)	25·00	35·00
372/86 *Set of* 15			60·00	60·00

Plate 2 of the 30c., released 10 August 1960, had a finer, 250 screen, instead of the previous 200 (*price £3 mint*).

116 Borneo Railway, 1902

117 Malay prau

118 Mount Kinabalu

119 Arms of Chartered Company

(Recess Waterlow)

1956 (1 Nov). *75th Anniv of British North Borneo Co. T* **116/19**. Wmk Mult Script CA. P 13×13½ (horiz) or 13½×13 (vert).

387	**116**	10c. black and rose-carmine	1·00	40
388	**117**	15c. black and red-brown	30	30
389	**118**	35c. black and bluish green	30	1·50
390	**119**	$1 black and slate	65	2·50
387/90 *Set of* 4			2·00	4·25

120 Sambar Stag

121 Sun Bear

122 Clouded Leopard

123 Dusun woman with gong

124 Map of Borneo

125 Banteng

126 Butterfly orchid

127 Sumatran Rhinoceros

128 Murut with blow-pipe

129 Mount Kinabalu

130 Dusun and buffalo transport

131 Bajau horsemen

132 Orang-Utan

133 Rhinoceros Hornbill

134 Crested Wood Partridge

135 Arms of North Borneo

(Des Chong Yun Fatt. Recess Waterlow (until 1962), then D.L.R.)

1961 (1 Feb). *T* **120/35**. W w **12**. P 13.

391	**120**	1c. emerald and brown-red	20	10
392	**121**	4c. bronze-green and orange	20	90
393	**122**	5c. sepia and violet	30	10
394	**123**	6c. black and blue-green	50	40
395	**124**	10c. green and red	50	10
396	**125**	12c. brown and grey-green	30	10
397	**126**	20c. blue-green and ultramarine	3·50	10
398	**127**	25c. grey-black and scarlet	80	1·00
399	**128**	30c. sepia and olive	70	20
400	**129**	35c. slate-blue and red-brown	2·00	1·75
401	**130**	50c. emerald and yellow-brown	2·00	20
402	**131**	75c. grey-blue and bright purple	13·00	90
403	**132**	$1 brown and yellow-green	13·00	80
404	**133**	$2 brown and slate	32·00	3·00
405	**134**	$5 emerald and maroon	38·00	19·00
406	**135**	$10 carmine and blue	38·00	40·00
391/406 *Set of* 16			£130	60·00

(Des M. Goaman. Photo Harrison)

1963 (4 June). *Freedom from Hunger. As No. 14b of Antigua.*

407	12c. ultramarine	1·50	75

POSTAL FISCALS

Three
Cents.
Revenue

(F **1**) (Raised stop)

Ten
Cents.
Revenue

(F **2**)

1886. *Regular issues surch as Type* F **1** *or* F **2**.

F1	**1**	3c. on 4c. pink (No. 6)	£130	£180
		a. Raised stop after "Cents"	£110	£170

F2 5c. on 8c. green (No. 7) £130 £180
a. Raised stop after "Cents" £110 £170
F3 4 10c. on 50c. violet (No. 4) £170 £190
a. Surch double — £1300
b. No stop after "Cents" and stop after "Revenue." £475 £500
c. Inverted "L" for first "F" in "FIFTY" (R. 5/2) — £1000

It is believed that Nos. F1/2 were each surcharged from a horizontal setting of five so that the raised stop variety occurs on every stamp in the first, second, third, sixth, seventh and eighth vertical columns in the sheets of 50 (10×5).

POSTAGE DUE STAMPS

POSTAGE DUE
(D 1)

1895 (1 Aug)–**97**. *Nos. 68/79 optd with Type* D **1** *horizontally (8, 12, 18 and 24c.) or vertically, reading upwards (others).* P 14½–15.

D1 25 2c. black and rose-lake 26·00 40·00 2·75
a. Opt double* † † £300
b. Opt vertical, reading downwards* † † £425
D2 2c. black and lake 21·00 24·00 2·25
a. Perf 13½–14
b. Perf 13½–14, comp 12–13* † † 10·00
c. Opt omitted (in vert pair with normal)* † † £1900
D3 26 3c. olive-green and dull purple 6·00 16·00 1·00
a. Bronze-green and dull purple
b. Opt vertical, reading downwards* † † —
D4 3c. olive-green and violet
a. Perf 13½–14
b. Opt double* † † £425
D5 27 5c. black and vermilion 55·00 26·00 3·00
a. Printed double † — —
b. With stop after "DUE" in opt (1897) £225
c. Opt double £750 £800 †
d. Perf 13½–14 — 50·00 2·50
e. Perf 13½–14, comp 12–13 — 55·00 —
D6 28 6c. black and bistre-brown 60·00 70·00 2·50
a. Perf 13½–14 18·00 48·00 2·50
b. Perf 12–13* † † —
c. Perf 13½–14, comp 12–13
d. Opt vertical, reading downwards* † † —
D7 29 8c. black and dull purple 50·00 50·00 2·75
a. Opt double* † † £350
b. Perf 13½–14
ba. Opt inverted* † † £190
c. Perf 13½–14, comp 12–13 75·00
D8 30 12c. black and blue — 50·00 2·50
a. Opt double* † † £375
b. Perf 13½–14 70·00 50·00 2·50
c. Perf 13½–14, comp 14½–15 90·00
D9 12c. black and ultramarine (P 13½–14) 80·00 60·00 —
D10 31 18c. black and deep green 70·00 60·00 4·00
a. Opt inverted £375 £400 †
b. Perf 13½–14 80·00 80·00 4·00
ba. Opt double* † † £300
c. Opt vertical, reading upwards (1897) 75·00 95·00 4·75
ca. Opt vertical, reading downwards £475 £350 †
D11 32 24c. blue and rose-lake 75·00 85·00 4·00
a. Opt double* † † £325
b. Perf 13½–14 32·00 55·00 4·00
c. Perf 13½–14, comp 14½–15

D3s, D5s, D8s, D10cs, D11s Optd "Specimen" *Set of 5* £150

There were two local overprintings of these stamps which show variations in the distance between the two words. Further overprints were produced in London for sale to dealers by the British North Borneo Company. Those listings marked with an * only exist from the London overprinting and are usually only known cancelled-to-order.

No. D5b comes from at least one sheet which was included in a later overprinting.

1897–99. *Nos. 94/7, 99/103, 106, 108/11 optd with Type* D **1** *horizontally (8c.) or vertically reading upwards (others).* P 14½–15.

D12 35 2c. black and lake (1898) 8·50 9·00 1·50
a. Perf 13½–14 40·00
b. Opt horizontal* £160
s. Optd "Specimen" 27·00
D13 2c. black and green (P 13½–14)* 55·00 † 70
a. Perf 13½–14, comp 12–13* — † 90
b. Perf 16*
c. Perf 12–13*
d. Opt vertical, reading downwards*
e. Opt horizontal* £160
D14 36 3c. green and rosy mauve* 24·00 † 50
a. Perf 13½–14* 42·00 † 1·75
b. Perf 13½–14, comp 14½–15*
c. Opt double*
D15 3c. green and dull mauve 27·00 45·00 †
D16 37 4c. black and carmine* — † 1·00
a. Perf 13½–14 50·00 † 50
D17 38 5c. black and orange-vermilion (1899) 60·00 60·00 90
a. Perf 13½–14 21·00 50·00 1·75
D18 39 6c. black and bistre-brown 6·00 32·00 70
a. Perf 13½–14 — 40·00 50
b. Perf 13½–14, comp 12–13* — † 2·00
s. Optd "Specimen" 27·00
D19 40 8c. black and brown-purple (1898) 65·00 80·00 †
a. Opt vertical, reading upwards (P 16)* † † £325
s. Optd "Specimen" 27·00
D20 8c. black and brown (opt vert, reading upwards)* 7·50 † 50
a. Opt vertical, reading downwards* † † £600
b. Perf 13½–14*
D21 42 12c. black and dull blue* — † 5·00
a. Perf 13½–14* £110 † 4·00
D22 44 18c. black and green (P 16)* † † £850
D23 46 18c. black and green (P 13½–14)* 60·00 † 4·00
a. Perf 13½–14, comp 12–13* £100 † 4·00
D24 45 24c. blue and lake* — † £450
D25 47 24c. blue and lake* 35·00 † 2·25
a. Perf 13½–14*

In addition to local overprints, stamps from the 1897–1902 series were also overprinted by Waterlow on two occasions for sale by the British North Borneo Company to dealers from London. These Waterlow overprints were not supplied to North Borneo for postal purposes and are indicated by an * in the above listing.

1901–02. *Nos. 96/7, 100 and 102/3 optd locally as Type* D **1**, *but with stop after "DUE", horizontally (8c.) or vertically reading upwards (others).* P 13½–14.

D26 36 3c. green and rosy mauve (1902) 60·00 70·00
a. Opt double £300
D27 3c. green and dull mauve (P 14½–15) (1902) 55·00 70·00
a. Opt double £250 £275
D28 38 5c. black and orange-vermilion (P 14½–15) 70·00
D29 40 8c. black and brown-purple (P 14½–15) 23·00 75·00
D30 8c. black and brown (P 14½–15) £180 £200

1902 (10 Oct)–**12**. *Stamps of 1901–05 (optd "BRITISH PROTECTORATE") further optd with Type* D **1** *locally (No. D31) or by Waterlow (others).* P 13½–14.

(a) Optd horizontally showing stop after "DUE".

D31 34 1c. black and bistre-brown 4·50 55·00
a. With raised stop after "DUE" 4·75 60·00

(b) Optd vertically reading upwards.

D32 35 2c. black and green (P 16) £450 £225
D33 36 3c. green and rosy mauve £120 £130
D34 38 5c. black & orange-verm (P 14½–15) £200 £140
D35 40 8c. black and brown £170 £100
D36 47 24c. blue and lake £250 £120

(c) Optd horizontally at centre of stamp.

D37 34 1c. black and bistre-brown* — † 28·00
a. Perf 14½–15* £225 † 28·00
D38 35 2c. black and green (1909) 19·00 3·75 30
a. Perf 14½–15 (1903) 50·00 45·00 †
D39 36 3c. green and rosy mauve (1912) 6·00 3·25 30
a. Perf 14½–15 (1904) 50·00 40·00 †
ab. Type D **1** opt double £425
D40 37 4c. black and carmine (1912) 17·00 6·50 30
a. Type D **1** opt double £550 † £150
b. Perf 14½–15 (1.3.03) 8·50 19·00 1·50
D41 38 5c. black and orange-vermilion (1905) 32·00 4·50 30
a. Perf 14½–15 (1905) 75·00 30·00 †
D42 39 6c. black and bistre-brown (1912) 20·00 11·00 40
a. Type D **1** opt inverted* £475 † £110
b. Type D **1** opt double £700 — —
c. No stop after "PROTECTORATE" (1912)
d. Perf 16 (1906) 80·00 38·00 †
D43 40 8c. black and brown (1912) 21·00 4·25 40
a. No stop after "PROTECTORATE" (1903) 55·00 60·00 †
D44 41 10c. brown and slate-lilac (1906) £250 75·00 4·75
a. No stop after "PROTECTORATE" (1906) — — †
D45 10c. brown and slate-blue (1912) £100 22·00 1·40
D46 42 12c. black and dull blue (2.12.10) 32·00 19·00 3·00
D47 43 16c. green and chestnut (2.12.10) 60·00 24·00 3·00
D48 46 18c. black and green (2.12.10) 13·00 19·00 1·50
a. Type D **1** opt double* £500 † 70·00
b. Imperf between (vert pair) — † £800
D49 47 24c. blue and lake (1905) 12·00 28·00 3·00
a. Perf 14½–15 (1909) — — †
b. Type D **1** opt double* £350 † 90·00

(d) Optd horizontally at top of stamp.

D50 35 2c. black and green (P 16) (1906) 85·00 40·00
a. Perf 14½–15 (1908) 70·00 45·00
D51 37 4c. black and carmine (1906) 65·00 24·00

Items marked * only occur in stocks obtained from the British North Borneo Company in London.

POSTAGE DUE
(D 2)

POSTAGE DUE
(D 3)

Type D **2**. Thick letters. Ends of "S" and top of "G" straight. Pointed beard to "G".

Type D **3**. Thinner letters. Ends of "S" and top of "G" slanted. Square beard to "G".

1918–30. *Opt with Type* D **2** *locally.*

(a) On stamps of 1909–23. P 13½–14.

D52 52 2c. black and green (opt at foot) (1.24) 11·00 75·00
a. Perf 14½–15 23·00 80·00
s. Optd "Specimen" 28·00
D53 53 3c. black and green (opt at foot) (1.9.23) 4·50 45·00
D54 54 4c. black and scarlet (opt at top) (10.18) 90·00 17·00
D55 4c. black and scarlet (opt at foot) (1.22) 1·00 1·25
D56 4c. black and scarlet (opt in centre) (5.23) — 16·00
D57 55 5c. black and yellow-brown (opt at foot) (1.22) 9·50 26·00
D58 5c. black and yellow-brown (opt in centre) (1.23) 19·00 26·00
D59 56 6c. black and olive-green (opt at foot) (1.9.23) 12·00 14·00
D60 6c. black and olive-green (opt in centre) (6.23) 23·00 7·50
D61 – 6c. black and apple-green (opt at foot) (1.9.23) 10·00 16·00
D62 57 8c. black and rose-lake (opt at foot) (1.9.23) 1·50 1·50
a. Opt double £1000
D63 58 10c. black and turquoise-blue (opt at foot) (1.8.24) 14·00 19·00
a. Perf 14½–15 90·00 £170
D64 59 12c. black and deep blue (1.8.24) 60·00 50·00
a. Horiz pair, one without opt £13000
D65 60 16c. black and brown-lake (2.29)
a. Black and red-brown 20·00 50·00
s. Optd "Specimen" 30·00

(b) On stamps of 1925–28 with opt at foot. P 12½ (1928–30).

D66 52 2c. black and claret (3.30) 75 1·75
D67 53 3c. black and green (1926) 10·00 29·00
D68 54 4c. black and scarlet (1926) 1·50 2·00
D69 55 5c. black and yellow-brown (1926) 8·50 90·00
D70 56 6c. black and olive-green (3.28) 9·00 2·75
D71 57 8c. black and carmine (2.28) 5·50 20·00
D72 58 10c. black and turquoise-blue (1926) 11·00 90·00
D73 59 12c. black and deep blue (1926) 32·00 £160

Dates given as month and year only indicate first known postmark where recorded.

1930–38. *Optd with Type* D **3**, *locally, at foot of stamp.*

(a) On stamps of 1909–23. P 13½–14.

D74 57 8c. black and carmine (1931) — 1·50
D75 60 16c. black and brown-lake (11.31) 17·00 75·00
a. Black and red-brown 6·50

(b) On stamps of 1925–28. P 12½.

D76 52 2c. black and claret (5.31) 50 2·00
D77 53 3c. black and green (11.38) 8·00 29·00
D78 54 4c. black and scarlet (6.36) — 2·75
D79 55 5c. black and yellow-brown 16·00
D80 56 6c. black and olive-green (12.30) 7·50 2·50
D81 57 8c. black and carmine (9.31) 3·75 20·00
D82 58 10c. black and turquoise-blue (12.32) 17·00 90·00
D83 59 12c. black and deep blue 42·00
D84 60 16c. black and red-brown 65·00 £200

Dates given are those of earliest postmark where recorded.

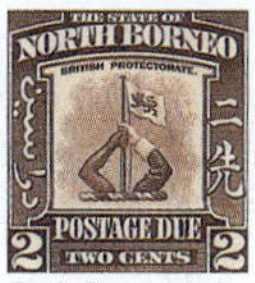

D **4** Crest of the Company

(Recess Waterlow)

1939 (1 Jan). P 12½.

D85 D 4 2c. brown 6·50 80·00
D86 4c. scarlet 6·50 £110
D87 6c. violet 24·00 £140
D88 8c. green 28·00 £250
D89 10c. blue 65·00 £400
D85/9 *Set of 5* £120 £900
D85s/9s Perf "Specimen" *Set of 5* £170

The stamps of North Borneo were withdrawn on 30 June 1964. For later issues see Malaysia/Sabah.

LABUAN

CROWN COLONY

The island of Labuan, off the northern coast of Borneo, was ceded to Great Britain by the Sultan of Brunei in December 1846.

Stamps of STRAITS SETTLEMENTS were used from 1867 until 1879. Covers of 1864 and 1865 are known from Labuan franked with stamps of INDIA or HONG KONG.

PRICES FOR STAMPS ON COVER

Nos. 1/4	—
Nos. 5/10	*from* × 50
Nos. 11/13	—
Nos. 14/21	*from* × 40
Nos. 22/5	—
Nos. 26/35	*from* × 50
Nos. 36/8	—

PRICES FOR STAMPS ON COVER

Nos. 39/47	*from* × 100
Nos. 49/50	*from* × 15
Nos. 51/7	*from* × 60
Nos. 62/74	*from* × 15
Nos. 75/9	*from* × 40
Nos. 80/8	*from* × 20
Nos. 89/97	*from* × 15
Nos. 98/116	*from* × 10
Nos. 117/28	*from* × 30
Nos. 129/37	*from* × 10
Nos. 138/42	—
Nos. D1/9	*from* × 30

1

8
(2)

8 8
(3)

(Recess D.L.R.)

1879 (May). Wmk CA over Crown, sideways. P 14.

1	1	2c. blue-green	£1200	£850
2		6c. orange-brown	£200	£180
		a. No dot at upper left (R. 2/4)	£450	£400
3		12c. carmine	£1600	£750
		a. No right foot to second Chinese character (R. 2/3)	£3500	£1400
4		16c. blue	65·00	£140

This watermark is always found sideways, and extends over two stamps, a single specimen showing only a portion of the Crown or the letters CA, these being tall and far apart. This paper was chiefly used for long fiscal stamps.

1880 (Jan)–**82**. Wmk Crown CC (reversed on 8c.). P 14.

5	1	2c. yellow-green	24·00	35·00
		w. Wnk inverted	£120	
		x. Wmk reversed	50·00	65·00
		y. Wmk inverted and reversed	90·00	90·00
6		6c. orange-brown	£110	£120
		a. No dot at upper left	£225	£225
		w. Wmk inverted	£200	
7		8c. carmine (4.82)	£110	£110
		a. No dot at lower left (R. 2/5)	£200	£200
		x. Wmk normal (not reversed)	£275	£275
8		10c. brown	£160	85·00
		w. Wmk inverted	£130	90·00
		x. Wmk reversed		
9		12c. carmine	£275	£325
		a. No right foot to second Chinese character	£475	£550
		w. Wmk inverted	£425	
		x. Wmk reversed	£300	£325
		y. Wmk inverted and reversed	£450	
10		16c. blue (1881)	85·00	85·00
		w. Wmk inverted	£180	£180
		x. Wmk reversed	£150	£160
		y. Wmk inverted and reversed	£250	
5/10 *Set of* 6			£650	£650

1880 (Aug).

(a) No. 9 surch with T **2** *in black and with the original value obliterated by manuscript bar in red or black.*

11		8c. on 12c. carmine	£1500	£850
		a. Type **2** inverted	£1800	£1000
		b. "12" not obliterated	£3000	£1700
		c. As b. with Type **2** inverted		
		d. No right foot to second Chinese character	£3000	£1500
		x. Wmk reversed	£1500	£850

(b) No. 4 surch with two upright figures and No. 9 surch with two at right angles as T **3**.

12		6c. on 16c. blue (R.)	£2750	£1000
		a. With one "6" only		
13		8c. on 12c. carmine	£1900	£1200
		a. Both "8's" upright		
		b. Upright "8" inverted	£2000	£1300
		c. No right foot to second Chinese character	£3250	£1900
		w. Wmk inverted	†	£1700
		x. Wmk reversed	£1900	£1200
		y. Wmk inverted and reversed		

EIGHT CENTS
(4)

Eight Cents
(5)

(6)

1881 (Mar). *No. 9 handstamped with T* **4**.

14		8c. on 12c. carmine	£375	£425
		a. No right foot to second Chinese character	£750	£850
		w. Wmk inverted	£475	
		x. Wmk reversed	£350	£400

1881 (June). *No. 9 surch with T* **5**.

15		8c. on 12c. carmine	£120	£130
		a. Surch double	£1700	£1700
		b. Surch inverted	£12000	
		c. "Eighr"	£18000	
		d. No right foot to second Chinese character	£275	£325
		w. Wmk inverted	£300	£300
		x. Wmk reversed	£120	£130

The error "Eighr" occurred on R. 2/1 of the first printing, but was soon corrected.

Only one sheet of 10 has been reported of No. 15b, which also shows wmk inverted and reversed.

1883. Wmk Crown CA (reversed on 8c.). P 14.

17	1	2c. yellow-green	22·00	30·00
		a. Imperf between (horiz pair)	£1300	
		w. Wmk inverted	60·00	
		x. Wmk reversed	23·00	45·00
		y. Wmk inverted and reversed		
18		8c. carmine	£300	£100
		a. No dot at lower left	£550	£190
19		10c. yellow-brown	38·00	48·00
		w. Wmk inverted	75·00	80·00
		x. Wmk reversed	75·00	80·00
20		16c. blue	£100	£190
21		40c. amber	20·00	£110
		x. Wmk reversed	29·00	£110
17/21 *Set of* 5			£425	£425

1883 (May). *No. 10 surch "One Dollar A.S.H." by hand as T* **6**.

22	1	$1 on 16c. blue (R.)	£4250	

The initials are those of the postmaster, Mr. A. S. Hamilton.

2 CENTS
(7)

2 Cents
(8)

2 Cents
(9)

1885 (June). *Nos. 18 and 10 handstamped as T* **7**.

23	1	2c. on 8c. carmine	£225	£425
		a. No dot at lower left	£400	
		x. Wmk normal (not reversed)	£350	
24		2c. on 16c. blue	£950	£900
		w. Wmk inverted	£1100	
		x. Wmk reversed	†	£900

1885 (July). *No. 20 surch as T* **8**.

25	1	2c. on 16c. blue	£110	£160
		a. Surch double	†	£6500
		b. "2" inserted	£1800	
		w. Wmk inverted		

No. 25b shows a second "2" applied by a separate handstamp to correct indistinct impressions of Type **8**.

1885 (Sept). *No. 18 handstamped diag as T* **9**.

26	1	2c. on 8c. carmine	65·00	£120
		a. No dot at lower left	£140	£275
		x. Wmk normal (not reversed)	£150	

1885 (Sept)–**86**. Wmk Crown CA. P 14.

30	1	2c. rose-red	3·50	13·00
		a. Pale rose-red (1886)	3·50	11·00
		x. Wmk reversed	10·00	
31		8c. deep violet	27·00	8·00
		a. No dot at lower left	60·00	21·00
		b. Mauve (1886)	29·00	9·00
		ba. No dot at lower left	65·00	23·00
		bw. Wmk inverted	80·00	
		bx. Wmk reversed	65·00	
32		10c. sepia (1886)	16·00	45·00
		w. Wmk inverted	42·00	
		x. Wmk reversed	28·00	
33		16c. grey (1886)	£140	
		x. Wmk reversed	£110	£160
30/3 *Set of* 4			£130	£190
30s/3s Optd "Specimen" *Set of* 4			£500	

ISSUES OF BRITISH NORTH BORNEO COMPANY

From 1 January 1890 while remaining a Crown Colony, the administration of Labuan was transferred to the British North Borneo Co, which issued the following stamps.

6 Cents
(10)

Two CENTS
(11)

Six CENTS
(12)

1891 (July)–**92**. *Handstamped with T* **10**.

34	1	6c. on 8c. deep violet (No. 31)	£150	£130
		a. Surch inverted	£275	£250
		b. Surch double	£500	
		c. Surch double, one inverted	£1000	
		d. "Cents" omitted	£450	£450
		f. Pair, one without surch, one surch inverted	£1800	
		g. No dot at lower left	£325	£300
35		6c. on 8c. mauve (No. 31*b*)	12·00	10·00
		a. Surch inverted	80·00	75·00
		b. Surch double, one inverted	£900	
		c. Surch double, both inverted	£900	
		d. "6" omitted	£500	
		e. Pair, one without surcharge	£1600	£1600
		f. Surch inverted with "Cents" omitted	£500	
		g. Pair, one without surch, one surch inverted	£1800	£1800
		h. Surch double	£325	
		i. No dot at lower left	26·00	26·00
		j. Imperf between (horiz pair)		
		w. Wmk inverted	60·00	60·00
		x. Wmk reversed	38·00	
36		6c. on 8c. mauve (R.) (No. 31*b*) (2.92)	£1100	£550
		a. Surch inverted	£1600	£700
		b. No. dot at lower left	£2250	
37		6c. on 16c. blue (No. 4) (3.92)	£2250	£1800
		a. Surch inverted	£9500	£7000
38		6c. on 40c. amber (No. 21)	£11000	£5000
		a. Surch inverted	£10000	£8000

There are two different versions of Type **10** with the lines of the surcharge either 1 mm or 2 mm apart.

(Recess D.L.R.)

1892–93. No wmk. P 14.

39	1	2c. rose-lake	6·50	3·50
40		6c. bright green	8·50	4·50
		a. No dot at upper left	21·00	15·00
41		8c. violet	7·00	12·00
		a. Pale violet (1893)	7·50	12·00
43		10c. brown	15·00	8·00
		a. Sepia-brown (1893)	15·00	14·00
45		12c. bright blue	8·00	6·50
		a. No right foot to second Chinese character	19·00	18·00
46		16c. grey	8·00	12·00
47		40c. ochre	21·00	35·00
		a. Brown-buff (1893)	45·00	25·00
39/47 *Set of* 7			65·00	65·00

The 6c., 12c., 16c. and 40c. are in sheets of 10, as are all the earlier issues. The other values are in sheets of 30.

1892 (Dec). *Nos. 47 and 46 surch locally as T* **11** *or* **12**.

49	1	2c. on 40c. ochre (13 December)	£170	90·00
		a. Surch inverted	£425	£550
50		6c. on 16c. grey (20 December)	£375	£150
		a. Surch inverted	£550	£300
		b. Surch sideways	£550	£300
		c. Surch "Six Cents"	£1900	

There are 10 slightly different versions of each of these surcharges which were applied in settings of 5×2, although instances of single handstamps are known.

A "SIX CENTS" handstamp with Roman "I" in "SIX" (without dot) is a clandestine surcharge, although it can be found with genuine postmarks. It also exists sideways or inverted.

The "Six Cents" surcharge of No. 50c was handstamped onto examples where the Type **12** surcharge had failed to print or where it was partially or completely albino.

CANCELLED-TO-ORDER. Prices are separately indicated, in a third price column, for stamps showing the recognisable black bars remainder cancellation. Earlier issues of the Company administration were also so treated, but, as postal cancellations were used, these cannot be identified.

(Litho D.L.R.)

1894 (Apr). No wmk. P 14.

51	1	2c. carmine-pink	1·60	14·00	50
52		6c. bright green	16·00	38·00	50
		a. Imperf between (horiz pair)	£7500		
		b. No dot at upper left	30·00	75·00	1·25
53		8c. bright mauve	16·00	38·00	50
54		10c. brown	48·00	50·00	50
55		12c. pale blue	23·00	70·00	70
		a. No right foot to second Chinese character	48·00	£120	1·40
56		16c. grey	27·00	£120	50
57		40c. orange-buff	50·00	£130	50
51/7 *Set of* 7			£160	£400	3·25
51s/7s H/S "Specimen" *Set of* 7			£120		

Collectors are warned against forgeries of this issue.

PERFORATION. There are a number of small variations in the perforation of the Waterlow issues of 1894 to 1905 which we believe to be due to irregularity of the pins rather than different perforators.

In the following lists, stamps perf 12, 12½, 13 or compound are described as perf 12–13, stamps perf 13½, 14 or compound are described as perf 13½–14 and those perf 14½, 15 or compound are listed as perf 14½–15. In addition the 13½–14 perforation exists compound with 14½–15 and with 12–13, whilst perf 16 comes from a separate perforator.

13

LABUAN
40
CENTS
(14)

1894 (May)–**96**. *T* **24/32** *of North Borneo (colours changed), with "LABUAN" engraved on vignette plate as T* **13** *(8, 12, 24c.) or horizontally (others). P 14½–15.*

(a) Name and central part of design in black.

62	24	1c. grey-mauve	1·50	10·00	50
		a. Imperf between (vert pair)	†	†	£650
		b. Perf 13½–14	11·00	10·00	—
		ba. Imperf between (vert pair)	£1100	—	£475
		c. Perf 13½–14, comp 14½–15	26·00		
		d. Perf 13½–14, comp 12–13	25·00	12·00	90
		e. Perf 12–13			
63	25	2c. blue	2·50	9·50	50
		a. Imperf (pair)	£600		
		b. Perf 13½–14	4·25	9·50	—
		c. Perf 13½–14, comp 14½–15	27·00		
		d. Perf 13½–14, comp 12–13			
		e. Perf 12–13	£120		
64	26	3c. ochre	3·75	18·00	50
		a. Perf 13½–14	11·00	9·00	—
		b. Perf 13½–14, comp 14½–15			
		c. Perf 13½–14, comp 12–13	40·00		
		d. Perf 12–13			
65	27	5c. green	32·00	27·00	65
		a. Perf 13½–14	38·00	17·00	—
		ab. Imperf between (horiz pair)	£1200		
		b. Perf 13½–14, comp 12–13	50·00		
		c. Perf 12–13	£140		
67	28	6c. brown-lake	2·50	17·00	50
		a. Imperf (pair)	£600	†	£300
		b. Perf 13½–14	—	—	1·50
		c. Perf 13½–14, comp 14½–15	—	—	1·00
		d. Perf 13½–14, comp 12–13			
		e. Perf 12–13			

68 **29** 8c. rose-red .... 25·00 29·00 80
a. Perf 13½–14 .... 29·00 48·00 —
69 8c. pink (1896).................. 7·00 25·00 50
a. Perf 13½–14 .... 30·00 32·00 60
70 **30** 12c. orange-vermilion........... 23·00 48·00 50
a. Imperf between (vert pair)............................ † † £3000
b. Perf 13½–14 .... 65·00 70·00 2·00
c. Perf 12–13 .... £200
d. Perf 13½–14, comp 12–13.......................... 80·00 85·00 —
71 **31** 18c. olive-brown.............. 22·00 55·00 50
a. Perf 13½–14 .... 70·00
72 18c. olive-bistre (1896)..... 55·00 70·00 50
a. Perf 13½–14 .... 27·00 65·00 —
b. Perf 13½–14, comp 12–13..........................
c. Imperf between (vert pair)............................ † † £1800
d. Perf 13½–14, comp 14½–15.......................... † † 1·50

(b) Name and central part in blue.

73 **32** 24c. pale mauve .... 25·00 55·00 50
a. Perf 13½–14 .... 24·00 50·00 —
b. Perf 13½–14 comp 14½–15..........................
74 24c. dull lilac (1896) .... 15·00 45·00 50
a. Perf 13½–14 .... 14·00 45·00 50
62/74 *Set of* 9 .... 95·00 £200 4·00
62s/74s Optd "Specimen" *Set of* 9........... £150

1895 (June). *No.* 83 *of North Borneo ($1 inscr "*STATE OF NORTH BORNEO*") surch as T* **14**.

75 **32c** 4c. on $1 scarlet .... 1·25 2·75 40
76 10c. on $1 scarlet .... 5·50 1·40 40
77 20c. on $1 scarlet .... 32·00 11·00 50
78 30c. on $1 scarlet .... 35·00 48·00 70
79 40c. on $1 scarlet .... 35·00 38·00 70
75/9 *Set of* 5 .... 95·00 90·00 2·40
75s/9s Optd "Specimen" *Set of* 5 .... 80·00

No. 76 exists with the figures of the surcharge 2½ mm away from "CENTS". The normal setting has a space of 4 mm. Examples of the narrow setting have, so far, only been seen on cancelled-to-order stamps (*Price* £20 *c.t.o.*).

LABUAN (15)

1846 JUBILEE 1896 (16)

4 CENTS (17)

1896. *T* **32***a to* **32***c of North Borneo (as Nos.* 81 *to* 83, *but colours changed) optd with T* **15**.

80 25c. green................................. 27·00 32·00 60
a. Opt omitted.......................... 24·00 — 1·25
b. Imperf (pair) .... — — 60·00
ba. Opt omitted.......................... 45·00
81 50c. maroon.............................. 27·00 32·00 60
a. Opt omitted.......................... 22·00 — 1·25
b. Imperf (pair) .... — — 60·00
ba. Opt omitted.......................... 42·00
82 $1 blue....................................... 65·00 60·00 60
a. Opt omitted.......................... 32·00 — 1·25
b. Imperf (pair) .... — — 60·00
ba. Opt omitted.......................... 48·00
80s/2s Optd "Specimen" *Set of* 3 .... 60·00

Nos. 80/1 showing stamps either printed double or double, one inverted, are from waste sheets subsequently sold by the British North Borneo Company to collectors.

1896 (24 Sept). *Jubilee of Cession of Labuan to Gt Britain. Nos.* 62 *to* 68 *optd with T* **16**. P 14½–15.

83 1c. black and grey-mauve ...... 20·00 22·00 80
b. Opt in orange..................... £200 £200 20·00
c. "JEBILEE" (R. 8/7)........... £1200 £550 £300
d. "JUBILE" (R. 3/10)........... £2250
e. Perf 13½–14 .... 26·00 22·00 —
ea. Opt double .... £375 £375 —
eb. Opt in orange..................... £275 £200 †
f. Perf 13½–14, comp 12–13. 32·00 20·00 —
fa. Opt in orange..................... — £200 †
g. Perf 12–13 ....
84 2c. black and blue................... 42·00 26·00 1·00
a. Imperf horiz (vert pair) ... £900 £1000 †
b. "JEBILEE" (R. 8/7)........... £1400 £1200 —
c. "JUBILE" (R. 3/10)........... £2500 £2500
d. Perf 13½–14 .... 42·00 20·00 —
e. Perf 13½–14, comp 14½–15.......................... — 40·00 —
f. Perf 13½–14 comp 12–13 . 45·00
85 3c. black and ochre................ 40·00 22·00 80
a. "JEBILEE" (R. 8/7)........... £1800 £1500 £700
b. "JUBILE" (R. 3/10)...........
d. Perf 13½–14 .... 45·00 28·00 90
db. Opt treble £650
e. Perf 13½–14, comp 14½–15..........................
f. Perf 13½–14, comp 12–13.
fa. Opt double £375 £375 £160
fb. Opt treble £650
86 5c. black and green................. 65·00 16·00 1·00
a. Opt double .... £750 £500 —
b. Perf 13½–14 .... 65·00 22·00 1·00
c. Perf 13½–14, comp 12–13.
d. Perf 13½–14, comp 14½–15.......................... — — 3·00
87 6c. black and brown-lake....... 30·00 23·00 80
a. Opt double .... £800 £500 †
b. "JUBILE" (R. 3/10)........... £3000
c. Perf 13½–14, comp 14½–15..........................
d. Perf 13½–14 .... — 80·00 —
88 8c. black and pink.................. 50·00 16·00 80
a. Opt double .... † £3000 †
b. Perf 13½–14 .... 45·00 15·00 80
c. Perf 13½–14, comp 14½–15.......................... 50·00 18·00 —
83/8 *Set of* 6 .... £200 £100 4·75
83s/8s Optd "Specimen" *Set of* 6 .... £150

The normal overprint on the 1c. varies in appearance from pure black to brownish black due to a mixing of the inks. The orange overprint on this value is in a clear, bright, unadulterated ink.

No. 84b is known in a vertical strip of 3 imperf horizontally except at the base of the bottom stamp (*Price* £6500 *unused*).

No. 87 also exists with error "JEBILEE", but only with additional "SPECIMEN" overprint. (*Price*, £1800).

1897 (Apr)–**1901**. *T* **34/45** *of North Borneo (colours changed), with "*LABUAN*" engraved on vignette plate as T* **13** *(8, 10, 12, 24c.) or horizontally (others). Name and central part in black (24c. in blue).* P 13½–14.

89 **34** 1c. dull claret (P 14½–15) 4·00 4·75 50
a. Perf 13½–14, comp 14½–15..........................
ab. Perf 16 .... — — 2·00
b. Brown (1901)............ 19·00 21·00 65
ba. Perf 14½–15 .... 3·00
bb. Perf 16 .... 15·00 13·00 —
90 **35** 2c. blue.............................. 18·00 4·50 65
a. Imperf between (vert pair)............................ † † £800
b. Imperf between (horiz pair) .... † † £850
c. Perf 14½–15 .... 25·00 — 75
d. Perf 13½–14, comp 12–13.......................... 45·00 20·00 —
e. Perf 16 .... — — 7·00
91 **36** 3c. ochre.......................... 8·50 23·00 50
a. Imperf between (vert pair)............................ £950 † £550
b. Perf 14½–15 .... 8·50 6·50 50
c. Perf 13½–14, comp 12–13.......................... 20·00 30·00 1·25
d. Perf 12–13 .... 85·00
92 **38** 5c. green.......................... 55·00 55·00 70
a. Perf 14½–15 .... 50·00 55·00 70
b. Perf 13½–14, comp 12–13..........................
93 **39** 6c. brown-lake................ 6·50 38·00 65
b. Perf 14½–15 .... 8·00 21·00 50
ba. Imperf between (vert pair)............................ † † £700
c. Perf 13½–14, comp 12–13.......................... — — 6·00
94 **40** 8c. rose-red .... 50·00 — 50
a. Perf 14½–15 .... 18·00 12·00 —
b. Perf 13½–14, comp 12–13.......................... 38·00 — 2·75
c. Vermilion.................... 12·00 — 50
ca. Perf 16 .... — — 5·00
95 **42** 12c. vermilion................... 90·00 £100 1·50
a. Perf 14½–15 .... 32·00 50·00 1·25
96 **44** 18c. olive-bistre .... 80·00 80·00 80
a. Perf 16 .... 12·00 45·00 50
ab. Imperf between (vert pair)............................ † † £3000
97 **45** 24c. grey-lilac................... 50·00 85·00 75
a. Perf 14½–15 .... 12·00 50·00 50
89/97 *Set of* 9 .... £140 £225 5·00
89s/97s Optd "Specimen" *Set of* 9 .... £160

The 12, 18 and 24c. above were errors; in the 12c., "LABUAN" is over the value at the top; the 18c. has "POSTAL REVENUE" instead of "POSTAGE AND REVENUE", and the 24c. is without "POSTAGE AND REVENUE".

1897 (Nov)–**98**.

*(a) Types of North Borneo (colours changed), with "*LABUAN*" engraved on the vignette plate as in T* **13**. P 13½–14.

98 **42** 12c. black and vermilion (3.98) .... † — 3·25
a. Perf 14½–15 .... 42·00 50·00 —
b. Perf 13½–14, comp 14½–15..........................
c. Perf 16 .... 55·00 60·00 —
99 **46** 18c. black and olive-bistre
a. Perf 14½–15 .... 80·00 60·00 2·00
b. Perf 13½–14, comp 12–13.......................... £100
c. Perf 16 .... † — 8·50
100 **47** 24c. blue and lilac-brown. 35·00 55·00 2·00
a. Perf 14½–15 .... 35·00 55·00 —
b. Perf 13½–14, comp 12–13.......................... — 65·00 —
c. Perf 16 .... 38·00
d. Blue and ochre (P 14½–15)............ — — 3·25

In the 12c. "LABUAN" is now correctly placed at foot of stamp. The 18c. and 24c. have the inscriptions on the stamps corrected, but the 18c. still has "LABUAN" *over* the value at foot, and was further corrected as follows.

*(b) As No. 99, but "*LABUAN*" at top.*

101 **46** 18c. black and olive-bistre (3.98) .... 60·00 60·00 —
a. Perf 14½–15 .... 29·00 70·00 2·75
b. Perf 13½–14, comp 12–13.......................... 42·00 55·00 —
c. Perf 12–13 ....
98s, 100s/1as Optd "Specimen" *Set of* 3 .. 70·00

1899 (July). *Surch with T* **17**.

(a) P 14½–15.

102 **38** 4c. on 5c. (No. 92a)........................ 40·00 26·00
103 **39** 4c. on 6c. (No. 93b)........................ 23·00 19·00
a. Perf 13½–14 .... 32·00 38·00
b. Perf 13½–14 comp 12–13 .... 50·00 60·00
104 **40** 4c. on 8c. (No. 94a)........................ 60·00 40·00
a. Perf 13½–14 .... 35·00 32·00
b. Perf 13½–14, comp 12–13........ 29·00 35·00
c. Perf 12–13 ....
105 **42** 4c. on 12c. (No. 98a)...................... 45·00 35·00
a. Perf 13½–14 .... 45·00 42·00
b. Perf 16 .... 45·00 40·00
c. Perf 13½–14, comp 12–13........ 55·00 65·00
106 **46** 4c. on 18c. (No. 101a).................... 27·00 18·00
a. Surch double £400 £500
107 **47** 4c. on 24c. (No. 100a).................... 27·00 30·00
a. Perf 13½–14 .... 22·00 25·00
b. Perf 13½–14, comp 12–13........ 32·00 30·00
c. Perf 16 .... 48·00 50·00

(b) P 14.

108 **32a** 4c. on 25c. (No. 80)......................... 6·00 7·50
109 **32b** 4c. on 50c. (No. 81)......................... 6·50 7·50
110 **32c** 4c. on $1 (No. 82) .... 6·50 7·50
102/10 *Set of* 9 .... £180 £160
102s/10s Optd "Specimen" *Set of* 9 .... £150

A new setting of the surcharge with closer spacing (2½ mm) between "4" and "CENTS" was used for the Specimen overprints, including unissued surcharges on the 1c., 2c. and 3c. values (*price* £140 *for the set of three*).

1900–02. *Types of North Borneo with "*LABUAN*" engraved on the vignette plate as in T* **13**, *in green on 16c.* P 13½–14.

111 **35** 2c. black and green......... 3·75 2·50 30
a. Imperf between (horiz pair)............................ £2750
b. Perf 13½–14, comp 12–13..........................
112 **37** 4c. black and yellow-brown........................ 8·50 48·00 60
a. Imperf between (vert pair)............................ £1200
b. Perf 13½–14, comp 12–13.......................... 38·00
113 4c. black and carmine (8.1900) .... 13·00 2·75 75
a. Perf 14½–15 .... 5·00 10·00 50
b. Perf 13½–14, comp 12–13.......................... 35·00 8·50 75
c. Perf 16 ....
114 **38** 5c. black and pale blue .. 20·00 18·00 65
a. Perf 13½–14, comp 12–13.......................... — 85·00 —
b. Perf 12–13 .... £140
115 **41** 10c. brown and slate-lilac (P 14½–15) (1902)..... 55·00 85·00 60
116 **43** 16c. green and chestnut (1902)........................ 50·00 £110 2·50
a. Perf 13½–14, comp 12–13.......................... 85·00 £110 —
b. Perf 12–13 .... £275
c. Perf 14½–15 .... £130
111/16 *Set of* 6 .... £120 £225 4·75
111s/16s Optd "Specimen" *Set of* 6.......... £150

No. 112 was printed in an incorrect frame colour and was not issued for postal purposes in Labuan. Used examples come from dealers' stock sent to the island for cancellation.

18

Line through "B" (R. 5/10)

(Recess Waterlow)

1902 (Sept)–**03**. P 13½–14.

117 **18** 1c. black and purple (10.03) .... 4·50 7·00 50
a. Perf 14½–15 .... 85·00 7·50 —
b. Perf 13½–14 comp 12–13.......................... 80·00 50·00
c. Line through "B"...... 65·00 90·00 8·00
118 2c. black and green......... 4·00 5·00 30
a. Perf 14½–15 .... £110 5·00 —
aa. Perf 13½–14, comp 12–13.......................... £110
b. Line through "B"...... 60·00 75·00 8·00
119 3c. black and sepia (10.03) .... 3·25 15·00 30
a. Line through "B"...... 60·00 £120 8·00
120 4c. black and carmine ..... 3·25 3·50 30
a. Perf 14½–15 .... 7·00 9·50 —
b. Perf 13½–14 comp 12–13.......................... 70·00 50·00 —
c. Line through "B"...... 60·00 65·00 8·00
121 8c. black and vermilion.. 13·00 9·00 50
a. Perf 14½–15 .... 8·00
b. Line through "B"...... 85·00 £100 8·00
122 10c. brown and slate-blue 3·25 15·00 30
b. Perf 14½–15 .... 6·50 17·00 50
ba. Imperf between (vert pair)............................ † † £700
c. Line through "B"...... 60·00 £140 8·00
123 12c. black and yellow........ 9·00 17·00 30
a. Imperf between (vert strip of 3) .... † † £3250
b. Perf 16 .... 9·00 21·00 50
c. Line through "B"...... 95·00 £160 8·00
124 16c. green and brown........ 4·75 22·00 30
a. Imperf between (vert pair)............................ † † £1900
b. Line through "B"...... 80·00 £180 8·00
125 18c. black and pale brown 3·25 25·00 30
a. Line through "B"...... 70·00 £200 8·00
126 25c. green and greenish blue........................... 7·50 20·00 50
a. Perf 14½–15 .... 15·00 35·00 60
b. Error. Black and greenish blue............ — † £500
c. Line through "B"...... 95·00 £200 9·00
127 50c. dull purple and lilac . 10·00 48·00 1·50
a. Perf 13½–14 comp 12–13.......................... 16·00 55·00 —
b. Line through "B"...... £170 £425 15·00
128 $1 claret and orange...... 8·50 50·00 1·50
a. Perf 14½–15 .... 10·00 — 1·50
b. Line through "B"...... £160 £450 15·00
117/28 *Set of* 12 .... 60·00 £225 6·00
117s/28s Optd "Specimen" *Set of* 12......... £190

4 cents (19)

1904 (Dec). *Issues of 1896, 1897–8 and 1897/1901 surch with T* **19**.

		(a) P 14½–15.			
129	**38**	4c. on 5c. (No. 92a)	48·00	40·00	14·00
130	**39**	4c. on 6c. (No. 93b)	12·00	38·00	14·00
131	**40**	4c. on 8c. (No. 94a)	25·00	42·00	14·00
132	**42**	4c. on 12c. (No. 98a)	24·00	42·00	14·00
		a. Perf 16	32·00	45·00	—
133	**46**	4c. on 18c. (No. 101) (P 13½–14)	23·00	45·00	14·00
		a. Perf 13½–14, comp 12–13	28·00	45·00	—
		b. Perf 12–13			
134	**47**	4c. on 24c. (No. 100a)	16·00	50·00	14·00
		a. Perf 13½–14	28·00	38·00	—
		b. Perf 13½–14, comp 12–13	40·00	48·00	—
		c. Perf 16	26·00	40·00	14·00
		(b) P 14.			
135	**32a**	4c. on 25c . (No. 80)	8·50	25·00	14·00
136	**32b**	4c. on 50c. (No. 81)	8·50	25·00	14·00
		a. Surch double	£325		
137	**32c**	4c. on $1 (No. 82)	8·50	25·00	14·00
129/37 *Set of* 9			£150	£300	£110

No. 136a usually shows one complete surcharge and parts of two further examples due to the position of the second impression.

The barred cancels can be found used on "philatelic" covers of this issue.

LABUAN (20) LABUAN (21)

1904 (12 Oct)–**05**. *Nos. 81, 83 (in Labuan colour), and 84/6 of North Borneo optd locally with T* **20** *(25c. $2) or* **21** *(others).*

138	**32a**	25c. indigo (2.05)	£1100	†	£900
139	**32c**	$1 blue (2.05)	†	†	£850
140	**32d**	$2 dull green	£3250	£3250	—
141	**14**	$5 bright purple (2.05)	£6000	£6500	£1400
142	**15**	$10 brown (11.05)	£28000	†	£10000

Dangerous forgeries exist.

The overprint on No. 140 is 12 mm long.

POSTAGE DUE STAMPS

POSTAGE DUE

(D 1)

1901. *Optd with Type* D **1**, *reading vertically upwards.* P 13½–14.

D1	**35**	2c. black and green (111)	19·00	30·00	50
		a. Opt double	£350		
		b. Perf 13½–14, comp 12–13	85·00	90·00	10·00
D2	**36**	3c. black and ochre (91)	24·00	£100	70
		a. Perf 13½–14, comp 12–13	80·00	—	2·50
D3	**37**	4c. black and carmine (113)	42·00	—	1·75
		a. Opt double	†	†	£700
		b. Perf 14½–15	42·00	95·00	50
D4	**38**	5c. black and pale blue (114)	50·00	£120	75
		a. Perf 14½–15	—	—	1·00
		b. Perf 13½–14, comp 12–13	90·00	£170	—
D5	**39**	6c. black and brown-lake (93)	38·00	£110	75
		a. Perf 14½–15	50·00	95·00	—
		b. Perf 16	65·00	—	65
D6	**40**	8c. black and vermilion (94c)	75·00	£110	1·50
		b. Perf 14½–15	85·00	£150	85
		ba. Frame inverted	†	†	£9500
		c. Perf 16	85·00	£110	—
		d. Black and rose-red (94)	90·00	£140	—
		da. Perf 14½–15	£120	—	7·50
		db. Perf 13½–14, comp 12–13	£120		
D7	**42**	12c. black and vermilion (98)	£110	—	4·50
		a. Opt reading downwards	†	†	£800
		b. Perf 14½–15	£100	£140	12·00
D8	**46**	18c. black and olive-bistre (101) (P 14½–15)	26·00	£120	1·25
D9	**47**	24c. blue and lilac-brown (100)	55·00	£130	5·50
		a. Perf 13½–14, comp 12–13	85·00		
		b. Perf 14½–15	38·00		
		ba. Blue and ochre	85·00	—	1·25
		c. Perf 16	60·00	£100	—
D1/9 *Set of* 9			£375	£850	10·00

No. D6ba only exists cancelled-to-order.

The administration of Labuan reverted to Colonial Office control, as part of an agreement with Brunei on 1 January 1906. By Letters Patent dated 30 October 1906 Labuan was incorporated with Straits Settlements and ceased issuing its own stamps. In 1946 it became part of the Colony of North Borneo.

JAPANESE OCCUPATION OF NORTH BORNEO

Japanese forces landed in Northern Borneo on 15 December 1941 and the whole of North Borneo had been occupied by 19 January 1942.

Brunei, North Borneo, Sarawak and, after a short period, Labuan, were administered as a single territory by the Japanese. Until 12 December 1942, previous stamp issues, without overprint, continued to be used in conjunction with existing postmarks. From November 1942 onwards unoverprinted stamps of Japan were made available and examples can be found used from the area for much of the remainder of the War. Japanese Occupation issues for Brunei, North Borneo and Sarawak were equally valid throughout the combined territory but not, in practice, equally available.

PRICES FOR STAMPS ON COVER	
Nos. J1/17	*from* × 5
Nos. J18/19	*from* × 6
Nos. J20/32	*from* × 25
Nos. J33/4	*from* × 2
Nos. J35/48	*from* × 12

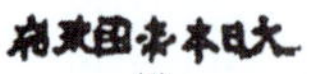
(1)

2 Mt. Kinabalu

3 Borneo Scene

1942 (30 Sept). *Stamps of North Borneo handstamped with T* **1**.

	(a) In violet on Nos. 303/17.		
J1	1c. green and red-brown	£160	£225
	a. Black opt	£275	£200
	ab. Pair, one without opt	£3500	
J2	2c. purple and greenish blue	£170	£225
	a. Black opt	£400	£225
J3	3c. slate-blue and green	£130	£225
	a. Black opt	£425	£325
J4	4c. bronze-green and violet	£200	£275
	a. Black opt	50·00	£130
J5	6c. deep blue and claret	£140	£275
	a. Black opt	£425	£350
J6	8c. scarlet	£190	£190
	a. Pair, one without opt	£3500	
	b. Black opt	£250	£190
J7	10c. violet and bronze-green	£180	£300
	a. Black opt	£400	£300
J8	12c. green and bright blue	£190	£450
	a. Black opt	£650	£450
J9	15c. blue-green and brown	£170	£450
	a. Pair, one without opt	£3500	
	b. Black opt	£700	£450
J10	20c. violet and slate-blue	£200	£550
	a. Black opt	£800	£550
J11	25c. green and chocolate	£200	£550
	a. Black opt	£800	£550
J12	50c. chocolate and violet	£275	£650
	a. Black opt	£900	£650
J13	$1 brown and carmine	£300	£800
	a. Black opt	£1000	£800
J14	$2 violet and olive-green	£475	£1000
	a. Pair, one without opt	£4750	
	b. Black opt	£1400	£950
J15	$5 indigo and pale blue	£600	£1100
	a. Black opt	£1800	£1300
	(b) In black on Nos. 318/19 ("WAR TAX").		
J16	1c. green and red-brown	£600	£300
	a. Pair, one without opt	†	£3500
	b. Violet opt	—	£800
J17	2c. purple and greenish blue	£1500	£550
	a. Pair, one without opt	†	£5500
	b. Violet opt	—	£1000

(Litho Kolff & Co., Batavia)

1943 (29 Apr). P 12½.

J18	**2**	4c. red	21·00	45·00
J19	**3**	8c. blue	17·00	45·00

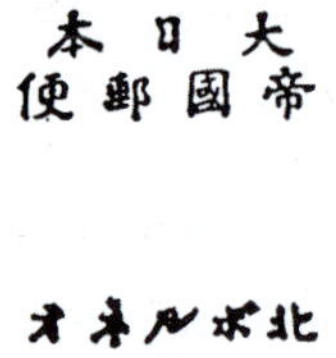
(4)

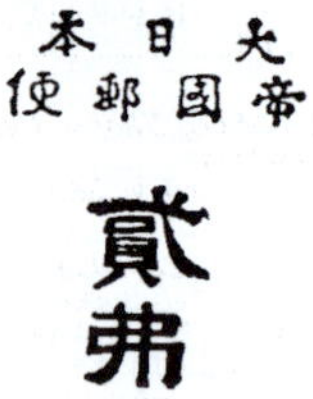
(5)

("Imperial Japanese Postal Service North Borneo")

1944 (30 Sept). *Nos. 303/15 of North Borneo optd with T* **4** *at Chinese Press, Kuching.*

J20	1c. green and red-brown	5·00	12·00
J21	2c. purple and greenish blue	7·50	9·00
	a. Optd on No. J2	£425	
J22	3c. slate-blue and green	5·50	10·00
	a. Optd on No. J3	£425	
J23	4c. bronze-green and violet	11·00	19·00
J24	6c. deep blue and claret	7·00	6·50
J25	8c. scarlet	9·50	17·00
	a. Optd on No. J6	£425	
J26	10c. violet and bronze-green	8·50	13·00
	a. Optd on No. J7	£425	
	b. Optd on No. J7a	£200	£400
J27	12c. green and bright blue	14·00	13·00
	a. Optd on No. J8	£425	
J28	15c. blue-green and brown	13·00	16·00
	a. Optd on No. J9	£425	
J29	20c. violet and slate-blue	26·00	45·00
	a. Optd on No. J10	£2000	
J30	25c. green and chocolate	26·00	45·00
	a. Optd on No. J11	£2000	
J31	50c. chocolate and violet	70·00	£120
	a. Optd on No. J12	£2750	
J32	$1 brown and carmine	90·00	£150
J20/32 *Set of* 13		£250	£425

The spacing between the second and third lines of the overprint is 12 mm on the horizontal stamps, and 15 mm on the upright.

1944 (11 May). *No. J1 surch with T* **5**.

J33	**81**	$2. on 1c green and red-brown	£4500	£3750

(6)

7 Girl War-worker

(**8**) ("North Borneo")

1944 (11 May). *North Borneo No. 315 surch with T* **6**.

J34	$5 on $1 brown and carmine	£4000	£3000
	a. Surch on No. J13	£7000	£4500

1944 (2 Oct)–**45**. *Contemporary stamps of Japan as T* **7** *(various subjects) optd with T* **8** *at Chinese Press, Kuching.*

J35	1s. red-brown (No. 391) (1.45)	8·50	26·00
J36	2s. scarlet (No. 392b) (10.44)	7·50	23·00
J37	3s. emerald-green (No. 316) (8.45)	8·00	26·00
J38	4s. yellow-green (No. 395) (10.44)	14·00	22·00
J39	5s. claret (No. 396) (1.45)	9·50	25·00
J40	6s. orange (No. 319) (8.45)	16·00	26·00
	a. Opt double, one inverted	£475	£475
J41	8s. violet (No. 321) (11.44)	6·50	26·00
	a. Opt double	£350	
J42	10s. carmine and pink (No. 399) (1.45)	8·50	26·00
J43	15s. blue (No. 401) (11.44)	11·00	26·00
J44	20s. blue-slate (No. 325) (11.44)	80·00	90·00
J45	25s. brown and chocolate (No. 326) (2.45)	55·00	75·00
J46	30s. turquoise-blue (No. 327)	£170	95·00
J47	50s. olive and bistre (No. 328) (8.45)	70·00	70·00
J48	1y. red-brown and chocolate (No. 329) (5.45)	70·00	£100
J35/48 *Set of* 14		£475	£600

Designs:—2s. General Nogi; 3s. Hydro-electric Works; 4s. Hyuga Monument and Mt Fuji; 5s. Admiral Togo; 6s. Garambi Lighthouse, Formosa; 8s. Meiji Shrine; 10s. Palms and map of S.E. Asia; 15s. Airman; 20s. Mt Fuji and cherry blossoms; 25s. Horyu Temple; 30s. Torii, Itsukushima Shrine at Miyajima; 50s. Kinkaku Temple; 1y. Great Buddha, Kamakura.

Examples of some values have been found with hand-painted forged overprints.

POSTAGE DUE STAMPS

1942 (30 Sept). *Nos. D85/6 and D88 of North Borneo handstamped with T* **1** *in black.*

JD1	D **2**	2c. brown	—	£3750
JD2		4c. scarlet	—	£3750
JD3		8c. green	—	£3750

Northern Nigeria *see* Nigeria

Northern Rhodesia

The north-eastern and north-western provinces of Rhodesia, previously administered by the British South Africa Company, became a Crown Colony on 1 April 1924.

The current stamps of Rhodesia (the "Admiral" design first issued in 1913) remained in use until 31 March 1925 and continued to be valid for postal purposes until 30 September of that year.

PRICES FOR STAMPS ON COVER TO 1945	
Nos. 1/21	*from* × 2
Nos. 22/4	*from* × 5
Nos. 25/45	*from* × 2
Nos. D1/4	*from* × 15

1

2

(Des W. Fairweather. Eng J. A. C. Harrison. Recess Waterlow)

1925 (1 April)–**29**. Wmk Mult Script CA. P 12½.

1	**1**	½d. green	1·75	80
2		1d. brown	1·75	10
3		1½d. carmine-red	2·75	30
4		2d. yellow-brown	2·75	10
5		3d. ultramarine	2·75	1·25
6		4d. violet	5·00	50
7		6d. slate-grey	5·00	40
8		8d. rose-purple	5·00	50·00
9		10d. olive-green	5·00	48·00
10	**2**	1s. yellow-brown and black	3·75	1·75
11		2s. brown and ultramarine	19·00	27·00
12		2s.6d. black and green	20·00	12·00
13		3s. violet and blue (1929)	27·00	20·00
14		5s. slate-grey and violet	40·00	17·00
15		7s.6d. rose-purple and black	£120	£180
16		10s. green and black	75·00	80·00
17		20s. carmine-red and rose-purple	£190	£225
1/17 *Set of* 17			£475	£600
1s/17s Optd or Perf (3s.) "Specimen" *Set of* 17			£800	

A used example of the 4d. exists imperforate between the stamp and a fragment of another below it.

1935 (6 May). *Silver Jubilee. As Nos. 91/4 of Antigua.* P 13½×14.

18	1d. light blue and olive-green	1·00	1·50
	f. Diagonal line by turret	70·00	85·00
	g. Dot to left of chapel	£170	
	h. Dot by flagstaff	£120	£150
	i. Dash by turret	£130	£160
19	2d. green and indigo	1·75	2·00
	f. Diagonal line by turret	85·00	£110
	g. Dot to left of chapel	£150	£180
20	3d. brown and deep blue	2·75	6·50
	f. Diagonal line by turret	£140	£200
	g. Dot to left of chapel	£250	£350
21	6d. slate and purple	6·00	1·50
	a. Frame printed double, one albino	£2250	£2500
	h. Dot by flagstaff	£325	£200
18/21 *Set of* 4		10·50	10·50
18s/21s Perf "Specimen" *Set of* 4		£160	

For illustrations of plate varieties see Omnibus section following Zanzibar.

Hyphen between "NORTHERN" AND "RHODESIA" (R. 9/6)

1937 (12 May). *Coronation. As Nos. 95/7 of Antigua.* P 11×11½.

22	1½d. carmine	30	35
23	2d. buff	40	35
24	3d. blue	60	1·25
	a. Hyphen flaw	£225	
22/4 *Set of* 3		1·10	1·75
22s/4s Perf "Specimen" *Set of* 3		£110	

3

4

"Tick bird" flaw (Pl 1 R. 7/1 of ptgs from Sept 1938 onwards)

(Recess Waterlow)

1938 (1 Mar)–**52**. Wmk Mult Script CA. P 12½.

25	**3**	½d. green	10	10
		a. "C" of "CA" missing from wmk		
26		½d. chocolate (15.11.51)	1·50	1·50
		a. Perf 12½×14 (22.10.52)	1·40	6·00
27		1d. brown	20	20
		a. Chocolate (1948)	1·75	75
28		1d. green (15.11.51)	75	2·00
29		1½d. carmine-red	45·00	75
		a. Imperf between (horiz pair)	£17000	
		b. "Tick bird" flaw	£5500	£400
30		1½d. yellow-brown (10.1.41)	30	10
		b. "Tick bird" flaw	£100	40·00
31		2d. yellow-brown	45·00	1·75
32		2d. carmine-red (10.1.41)	75	50
33		2d. purple (1.12.51)	45	1·50
34		3d. ultramarine	50	30
35		3d. scarlet (1.12.51)	50	2·75
36		4d. dull violet	40	40
37		4½d. blue (5.5.52)	2·00	8·00
38		6d. grey	40	10
39		9d. violet (5.5.52)	2·00	7·50
40	**4**	1s. yellow-brown and black	3·75	60
41		2s.6d. black and green	8·00	4·75
42		3s. violet and blue	17·00	13·00
43		5s. grey and dull violet	17·00	13·00
44		10s. green and black	21·00	20·00
45		20s. carmine-red and rose-purple	50·00	55·00
25/45 *Set of* 21			£200	£120
25s/45s Perf "Specimen" *Set of* 15			£400	

Nos. 26a and 28 exist in coils, constructed from normal sheets.

1946 (26 Nov). *Victory. As Nos. 110/11 of Antigua.* P 13½×14.

46	1½d. red-orange	75	75
	a. Perf 13½	14·00	12·00
47	2d. carmine	10	50
46s/7s Perf "Specimen" *Set of* 2		95·00	

The decimal perforation gauge for Nos. 46/7 is 13.7×14.1 and for No. 46a 13.7×13.4.

1948 (1 Dec). *Royal Silver Wedding. As Nos. 112/13 of Antigua, but 20s. ptd in recess.*

48	1½d. orange	30	10
49	20s. brown-lake	50·00	60·00

1949 (10 Oct). *75th Anniv of U.P.U. As Nos. 114/17 of Antigua.*

50	2d. carmine	20	30
51	3d. deep blue	2·00	2·50
52	6d. grey	1·00	1·75
53	1s. red-orange	75	1·00
50/3 *Set of* 4		3·50	5·00

5 Cecil Rhodes and Victoria Falls

(Recess D.L.R.)

1953 (30 May). *Birth Centenary of Cecil Rhodes.* Wmk Mult Script CA. P 12×11½.

54	**5**	½d. brown	50	1·00
55		1d. green	40	1·00
56		2d. mauve	40	30
57		4½d. blue	40	3·25
58		1s. orange and black	75	4·50
54/8 *Set of* 5			2·25	9·00

1953 (30 May). *Rhodes Centenary Exhibition. As No. 171 of Nyasaland.*

59	**6**	6d. violet	70	1·25

1953 (2 June). *Coronation. As No. 120 of Antigua but des and eng B.W. Recess D.L.R.*

60	1½d. black and yellow-orange	70	20

7

8

(Recess Waterlow)

1953 (15 Sept). Wmk Mult Script CA. P 12½×14 (pence values) or 12½×13½ (shilling values).

61	**7**	½d. deep brown	65	10
62		1d. bluish green	65	10
63		1½d. orange-brown	1·25	10
64		2d. reddish purple	1·25	10
65		3d. scarlet	80	10
66		4d. slate-lilac	1·25	2·00
67		4½d. deep blue	1·50	4·25
68		6d. grey-black	1·25	10
		w. Wmk inverted	£3000	£1300
69		9d. violet	1·25	4·25
70	**8**	1s. orange-brown and black	70	10
71		2s.6d. black and green	9·00	6·00
72		5s. grey and dull purple	10·00	12·00
73		10s. green and black	7·50	27·00
74		20s. rose-red and rose-purple	24·00	32·00
61/74 *Set of* 14			55·00	80·00

For issues from 1954 to 1963, see RHODESIA AND NYASALAND.

9 Arms

10 Arms

(Photo Harrison)

1963 (10 Dec). *Arms black, orange and blue; portrait and inscriptions black; background colours below.* P 14½ (T **9**) or 13½×13 (T **10**).

75	**9**	½d. bright violet	70	1·25
		a. Value omitted	£900	
76		1d. light blue	1·00	10
		a. Value omitted	12·00	
77		2d. brown	70	10
78		3d. yellow	30	10
		a. Value omitted	90·00	
		b. Value and orange (eagle) omitted	£200	
		c. Eagle printed double	£2750	
		d. Orange (eagle) omitted	£1200	
79		4d. green	70	30
		a. Value omitted	£110	
80		6d. light olive-green	1·00	10
		a. Value omitted	£650	
81		9d. yellow-brown	60	1·60
		a. Value omitted	£475	
		b. Value and orange (eagle) omitted	£375	
82		1s. slate-purple	50	10
83		1s.3d. bright purple	2·25	10
84	**10**	2s. orange	2·25	3·75
85		2s.6d. lake-brown	2·25	2·00
86		5s. magenta	8·50	8·00
		a. Value omitted	£1900	
87		10s. bright magenta	10·00	17·00
88		20s. blue	13·00	23·00
		a. Value omitted	£1000	
75/88 *Set of* 14			40·00	50·00

Nos. 75/6 exist in coils, constructed from normal sheets.

STAMP BOOKLET

B **1**

1964. *Black on blue cover as Type* B **1**. *Stitched.*

SB1	1s. booklet containing 3d. (No. 78) in block of 4	16·00

POSTAGE DUE STAMPS

D **1**

D **2**

(Typo D.L.R.)

1929 (June)–**52**. *Wmk Mult Script CA. Ordinary paper.* P 14.

D1	D **1**	1d. grey-black	2·50	2·50
		a. Chalk-surfaced paper. *Black* (22.1.52)	25·00	75·00
		ab. Error. St. Edward's Crown, W **9b**	£2750	
D2		2d. grey-black	4·00	3·00
		a Bisected (1d.) (on cover)	†	£650
D3		3d. grey-black	3·00	26·00
		a. Chalk-surfaced paper. *Black* (22.1.52)	7·00	65·00
		ab. Error. Crown missing, W **9a**	£375	
		ac. Error. St. Edward's Crown, W **9b**	£200	
D4		4d. grey-black	9·50	30·00
D1/4 *Set of* 4			17·00	55·00
D1s/4s Perf "Specimen" *Set of* 4			£130	

The 2d. is known bisected and used as a 1d. at Luanshya or Nkana on various dates between 1937 and 1951 and on understamped letters from South Africa at Chingola in May 1950.

Following an increase in the internal letter rate from 1½d. to 2d. on 1 July 1953 stocks of postage due stamps at Mkushi became exhausted. As an emergency measure the sub-postmaster was authorised to surcharge examples of No. 28 "POSTAGE DUE (or Postage Due, or "postage due") 1d." in red by typewriter. No. 55, the 1d. Rhodes Centenary stamp was also surcharged. Examples properly used on cover between 23 July and 15 September 1953 are of considerable scarcity (*Price on cover* £4000). No unused examples exist.

(Des D. Smith. Litho Govt Ptr, Lusaka)

1963 (10 Dec). P 12½.

D5	D **2**	1d. orange	1·75	4·75
D6		2d. deep blue	1·75	4·00
D7		3d. lake	1·75	6·50
D8		4d. ultramarine	1·75	11·00
D9		6d. purple	7·00	9·00
D10		1s. light emerald	8·00	26·00
		a. Imperf (vert pair)	£200	
		b. Block of four imperf horiz and imperf between vert	£850	
D5/10 *Set of* 6			20·00	55·00

In all values the stamps in the right-hand vertical row of the sheet are imperforate on the right.

The stamps of Northern Rhodesia were withdrawn on 23 October 1964 when the territory attained independence as the Republic of Zambia.

North-West Pacific Islands *see* New Guinea *after* Australia

Nova Scotia *see* Canada

Nyasaland

PRICES FOR STAMPS ON COVER TO 1945

Nos. 1/9*a*	*from* × 15
Nos. 10/19	—
No. 20	*from* × 10
Nos. 21/6	*from* × 5
Nos. 27/31	—
Nos. 32/7	*from* × 6
Nos. 38/42	—
Nos. 43/7	*from* × 12
Nos. 48/52	—
No. 53	*from* × 15
No. 54	*from* × 2
No. 55	*from* × 4
Nos. 55*b*/7*a*	*from* × 7
Nos. 57*d*/63	*from* × 6
Nos. 64/71	—
Nos. 72/9	*from* × 5
Nos. 80/2	—
Nos. 83/95	*from* × 4
Nos. 96/9	—
Nos. 100/57	*from* × 2

By 1891 the territory west of Lake Nyasa was recognised as being under British protection and the southern, eastern and northern borders had been delineated with the Portuguese and German governments.

BRITISH CENTRAL AFRICA

A protectorate under the name "Nyassaland Districts" was declared on 14 May 1891, the title being changed to the "British Central Africa Protectorate" on 22 February 1893. Such a description had been in use for some time previously and the handwritten notice of 20 July 1891, announcing the introduction of postal services, described the area as "British Central Africa".

Until 1895 the British South Africa Company contributed to the revenues of the protectorate administration which, in return governed North-eastern Rhodesia. Stamps of the British South Africa Company overprinted "B.C.A.", in addition to use in British Central Africa, were issued to post offices at Fife, Fort Rosebery, Katwe, Johnston Falls, Rhodesia (later Kalungwisi) and Tanganyika (later Abercorn) in North-eastern Rhodesia from 1893 until 1899.

B.C.A. (1) — B.C.A. FOUR SHILLINGS. (2) — ONE PENNY. (3)

1891 (20 July)–**95**. *Stamps of Rhodesia optd as T* **1**. P 14, 14½.

1	1	1d. black	9·00	6·50
2	4	2d. sea-green and vermilion	9·00	4·00
		a. Bisected (1d.) (on cover) (1895)	†	£3500
3		4d. reddish chestnut and black	9·50	5·50
4	1	6d. ultramarine	55·00	20·00
5		6d. deep blue	12·00	8·00
6	4	8d. rose-lake and ultramarine	16·00	29·00
6*a*		8d. red and ultramarine	29·00	45·00
7	1	1s. grey-brown	21·00	14·00
8		2s. vermilion	32·00	50·00
9		2s.6d. grey-purple	65·00	85·00
9*a*		2s.6d. lilac	65·00	85·00
10	4	3s. brown and green (1895)	65·00	65·00
11		4s. grey-black and vermilion (2.93)	70·00	85·00
12	1	5s. orange-yellow	80·00	80·00
13		10s. deep green	£160	£200
14	2	£1 deep blue	£800	£650
15		£2 rose-red	£1000	£1200
16		£5 sage-green	£1700	
17		£10 brown	£4000	£4750
1/14 *Set of* 13			£1200	£1100

The overprint varies on values up to 10s. Sets may be made with *thin* or *thick* letters.

The bisected 2d, No. 2a, was authorised for use at Blantyre, Chiromo and Zomba in July and October 1895.

1892 (Aug)–**93**. *Stamps of Rhodesia surch as T* **2**.

18	4	3s. on 4s. grey-black and vermilion (10.93)	£325	£325
19	1	4s. on 5s. orange-yellow	75·00	85·00

1895. *No. 2 surch at Cape Town with T* **3**.

20	4	1d. on 2d. sea-green and vermilion	16·00	42·00
		a. Surch double	£7000	£4750

Specimens are known with double surcharge, without stop after "PENNY". These are from a trial printing made at Blantyre, but it is believed that they were not issued to the public (*Price* £550 *un.*).

5 Arms of the Protectorate — **6** Arms of the Protectorate

(Des Sir Harry Johnston. Litho D.L.R.)

1895. No wmk. P 14.

21	5	1d. black	15·00	13·00
22		2d. black and green	30·00	12·00
23		4d. black and reddish buff	60·00	45·00
24		6d. black and blue	70·00	8·00
25		1s. black and rose	80·00	35·00
26	6	2s.6d. black and bright magenta	£225	£300
27		3s. black and yellow	£150	50·00
28		5s. black and olive	£180	£225
29		£1 black and yellow-orange	£950	£375
30		£10 black and orange-vermilion	£5500	£4000
31		£25 black and blue-green	£11000	
21/8 *Set of* 8			£700	£600
21s/9s Optd "Specimen" *Set of* 9			£375	

Cancellations inscribed "BRITISH CENTRAL AFRICA" within a double-circle and with the name of a town across the centre or at foot were intended for use on stamps presented for the payment of the hut tax. Such marks can be found in black, violet or blue and are without date. Stamps with such fiscal obliterations are of little value. Prices quoted are for postally used.

1896 (Feb). Wmk Crown CA (T **5**) or CC (sideways) (T **6**). P 14.

32	5	1d. black	3·25	6·50
		x. Wmk reversed	£550	£550
		y. Wmk inverted and reversed	†	£450
33		2d. black and green	15·00	5·00
34		4d. black and orange-brown	24·00	17·00
35		6d. black and blue	32·00	13·00
36		1s. black and rose	32·00	19·00
37	6	2s.6d. black and magenta	£150	£130
38		3s. black and yellow	£120	55·00
39		5s. black and olive	£170	£200
40		£1 black and blue	£900	£500
41		£10 black and orange	£7500	£4000
		s. Optd "Specimen"	£180	
42		£25 black and green	£15000	
		s. Optd "Specimen"	£325	
32/9 *Set of* 8			£500	£400
32s/40s Optd "Specimen" *Set of* 9			£375	

7 — **8**

(Typo D.L.R.)

1897 (Aug)–**1900**. T **7** (wmk Crown CA) and **8** (wmk Crown CC). P 14.

43	7	1d. black and ultramarine	3·25	1·25
		w. Wmk inverted	£170	£250
44		2d. black and yellow	2·00	2·00
45		4d. black and carmine	6·50	1·50
46		6d. black and green	48·00	4·25
47		1s. black and dull purple	11·00	7·00
48	8	2s.6d. black and ultramarine	65·00	42·00
49		3s. black and sea-green	£200	£250
50		4s. black and carmine	75·00	85·00
50*a*		10s. black and olive-green (1900)	£180	£190
51		£1 black and dull purple	£325	£180
52		£10 black and yellow	£5500	£1900
		s. Optd "Specimen"	£200	
43/51 *Set of* 10			£800	£700
43s/51s Optd "Specimen" *Set of* 10			£300	

ONE PENNY (9)

10

1897 (31 Dec). *No. 49 surch with T* **9**, *in red*.

53	8	1d. on 3s. black and sea-green	7·50	10·00
		a. "PNNEY" (R. 4/2)	£5000	£4000
		b. "PENN"	£2500	£2000
		c. Surch double	£500	£900

No. 53b shows an albino impression of the "Y".

1898 (11 Mar). Imperf.

(a) Setting I. The vertical frame lines of the stamps cross the space between the two rows of the sheet.

(i) With the initials "J.G." or "J.T.G." on the back in black ink.

54	10	1d. vermilion and grey-blue	£11000	£900
		a. Without the initials	£5500	
		b. Without the initials and centre inverted	£27000	

(ii) With a control number and letter or letters, printed in plain relief at the back.

55	10	1d. vermilion and grey-blue	—	£650

(b) Setting II. The vertical frame lines do not cross the space between the rows except at the extreme ends of the sheet. Control as No. 55.

55*b*	10	1d. vermilion and pale ultramarine	—	£130
		c. Control on face	—	£3500
		d. Centre omitted (vert pair with normal)	£27000	
56		1d. vermilion and deep ultramarine	—	£130
		a. Without Control at back	£4750	£180
		b. Control doubly impressed	—	£450

1898 (June). *Setting* II. *Control as No. 55*. P 12.

57	10	1d. vermilion and pale ultramarine	£3750	25·00
57*a*		1d. vermilion and deep ultramarine	—	38·00
		ab. Without Control at back	£3750	95·00
		ac. Two different Controls on back	—	£650
		ad. Control printed in black	£4500	

The two different settings of these stamps are each in 30 types, issued without gum.

1901. Wmk Crown CA. P 14.

57*d*	7	1d. dull purple and carmine-rose	2·50	50
57*e*		4d. dull purple and olive-green	8·50	11·00
58		6d. dull purple and brown	3·75	3·00
57*d*/8 *Set of* 3			13·00	13·00
57*d*s/8s Optd "Specimen" *Set of* 3			60·00	

11 — **12**

(Typo D.L.R.)

1903–04. T **11** (Wmk Crown CA) and **12** (Wmk Crown CC). P 14.

59	11	1d. grey and carmine	8·00	1·75
60		2d. dull and bright purple	3·50	1·00
61		4d. grey-green and black	2·50	9·00
62		6d. grey and reddish buff	3·25	2·00
		aw. Wmk inverted	£150	
62*b*		1s. grey and blue	4·00	12·00
63	12	2s.6d. grey-green and green	55·00	85·00
64		4s. dull and bright purple	70·00	80·00
		w. Wmk inverted	£900	
65		10s. grey-green and black	£150	£225
66		£1 grey and carmine	£300	£190
67		£10 grey and blue	£5500	£3750
		s. Optd "Specimen"	£400	
59/66 *Set of* 9			£550	£550
59s/66s Optd "Specimen" *Set of* 9			£350	

1907. *Chalk-surfaced paper*. Wmk Mult Crown CA. P 14.

68	11	1d. grey and carmine	8·00	2·75
69		2d. dull and bright purple	£14000	
70		4d. grey-green and black	£14000	
71		6d. grey and reddish buff	32·00	48·00

Nos. 69/70 were prepared, but not issued in Nyasaland due to the Protectorate's name being changed. It is estimated that no more than a dozen examples of each remain in collectors' hands.

NYASALAND PROTECTORATE

The title of the Protectorate was changed again from 6 July 1907.

13 — **14**

Serif on "G" (R. 4/5. All ptgs of £1 Duty plate)

(Typo D.L.R.)

1908 (22 July)–**11**. P 14.

(a) Wmk Crown CA. Chalk-surfaced paper.

72	13	1s. black/*green*	2·75	15·00

(b) Wmk Mult Crown CA. Ordinary paper (½d., 1d.) or chalk-surfaced paper (others).

73	13	½d. green	1·75	2·25
74		1d. carmine	4·75	1·00
75		3d. purple/*yellow*	1·50	4·25
		w. Wmk inverted	£275	£300
76		4d. black and red/*yellow*	1·50	1·50
		w. Wmk inverted	£120	£140
77		6d. dull purple and bright purple	3·75	11·00
78	14	2s.6d. brownish black and carmine-red/*blue*	60·00	90·00
		a. *Brownish black and deep rose-red/pale blue* (1911)	£200	£225
79		4s. carmine and black	85·00	£140
80		10s. green and red/*green*	£140	£275
81		£1 purple and black/*red*	£475	£600
		c. Serif on "G"	£2000	£2250
82		£10 purple and ultramarine	£9000	£6500
		s. Optd "Specimen"	£850	
72/81 *Set of* 10			£700	£1000
72s/81s Optd "Specimen" *Set of* 10			£550	

15

16

"Bullet holes" flaw (R. 5/2. March 1919 ptgs)

Triangle flaw (R. 3/5. March 1919 ptg of 4s.)

1913 (1 Apr)–**19**. Wmk Mult Crown CA. *Ordinary paper (½d. to 2½d.) or chalk-surfaced paper (others).* P 14.

83	**15**	½d. green	1·25	2·25
84		½d. blue-green (1918)	2·00	2·50
85		1d. carmine-red	2·00	2·00
86		1d. scarlet (1916)	2·75	1·00
87		2d. grey (1916)	4·25	1·00
88		2d. slate	10·00	2·75
89		2½d. bright blue	2·25	7·00
90		3d. purple/*yellow* (1914)	4·75	4·50
		a. On pale yellow	4·25	9·50
		w. Wmk inverted		
91		4d. black and red/*yellow* (*shades*)	2·00	2·50
		a. On pale yellow	6·00	8·00
92		6d. dull and bright purple	3·75	9·50
92*a*		6d. dull purple and bright violet	13·00	10·00
93		1s. black/*green*	1·75	8·50
		a. On blue-green, olive back	5·50	1·50
		aw. Wmk inverted	£150	£190
		b. On emerald back	3·75	6·50
		bs. Optd "Specimen"	60·00	
94	**16**	2s.6d. black and red/*blue*	11·00	17·00
		a. Break in scroll	£180	
		b. Broken crown and scroll	£250	
		c. Nick in top right scroll	£190	£250
		f. Damaged leaf at bottom right	£225	
		h. "Bullet-holes" flaw	£400	
		x. Wmk reversed	†	£1500
95		4s. carmine and black	22·00	60·00
		a. Break in scroll	£250	
		b. Broken crown and scroll	£300	
		d. Nick in top right scroll	£250	
		f. Damaged leaf at bottom right	£275	
		h. "Bullet-holes" flaw	£400	
		i. Triangle flaw	£400	
96		10s. pale green and deep scarlet/*green*	95·00	£120
		d. Nick in top right scroll	£500	
		e. Green and deep scarlet/green (1919)	95·00	£130
		ea. Break in scroll	£500	
		eb. Broken crown and scroll	£500	
		ef. Damaged leaf at bottom right	£550	
		eh. "Bullet holes" flaw	£700	
98		£1 purple and black/*red*	£180	£140
		a. Break in scroll	£800	£650
		b. Broken crown and scroll	£800	£650
		c. Nick in top right scroll	£850	
		e. Break in lines below left scroll	£900	
		f. Damaged leaf at bottom right	£800	
		h. "Bullet holes" flaw	£1300	
		i. Serif on "G"	£850	£650
		w. Wmk inverted		
99		£10 purple and dull ultramarine	£6000	
		c. Nick in top right scroll	£8000	
		e. Purple and royal blue (1919)	£3500	£1700
		ea. Break in scroll	£6000	£3000
		eb. Broken crown and scroll	£6000	
		ef. Damaged leaf at bottom right	£6500	
		eh. "Bullet holes" flaw	£6500	
		s. Optd "Specimen"	£450	
83/98 *Set of* 12			£300	£325
83s/98s Optd "Specimen" *Set of* 12			£500	

For illustrations of the other varieties on Nos. 94/9 see above Bermuda No. 51*b*.

For stamps overprinted "N.F." see TANZANIA.

Damaged crown (R. 4/1. 2s.6d. ptg of June 1924)

1921–33. Wmk Mult Script CA. *Ordinary paper (½d. to 2d.) or chalk-surfaced paper (others).* P 14.

100	**15**	½d. green	1·50	50
		w. Wmk inverted	—	£225
		y. Wmk inverted and reversed	—	£300
101		1d. carmine	2·25	50
102		1½d. orange	3·25	17·00
103		2d. grey	1·00	50
105		3d. purple/*pale yellow*	12·00	3·25
106		4d. black and red/*yellow*	3·00	11·00
107		6d. dull and bright purple	3·00	3·25
108		1s. black/*emerald* (1930)	9·00	4·50
109	**16**	2s. purple and blue/*pale blue* (1926)	15·00	12·00
		a. Break in scroll	£160	£160
		b. Broken crown and scroll	£160	£160
		e. Break in lines below left scroll	£160	£160
		f. Damaged leaf at bottom right	£160	£160
		g. Purple and blue/grey-blue (10.33)	32·00	25·00
		ga. Break in scroll	£325	£300
		gb. Broken crown and scroll	£325	£300
		gd. Break through scroll	£325	£300
		ge. Break in lines below left scroll	£325	£300
		gf. Damaged leaf at bottom right	£325	£300
		gg. Gash in fruit and leaf	£325	£300
		gh. Breaks in scrolls at right	£325	£300
110		2s.6d. black and carmine-red/*pale blue* (30.9.24)	21·00	21·00
		a. Break in scroll	£180	£190
		b. Broken crown and scroll	£180	£190
		c. Nick in top right scroll	£180	£190
		e. Break in lines below left scroll	£180	£190
		f. Damaged leaf at bottom right	£180	£190
		i. Damaged crown	£375	£375
		j. Grey-black and scarlet-vermilion/pale-blue (10.26)	28·00	17·00
		ja. Break in scroll	£250	£180
		jb. Broken crown and scroll	£250	£180
		je. Break in lines below left scroll	£250	£180
		jf. Damaged leaf at bottom right	£250	£180
		k. Black and scarlet-vermilion/grey-blue (10.33)	38·00	32·00
		ka. Break in scroll	£325	£325
		kb. Broken crown and scroll	£325	£325
		kd. Break through scroll	£350	£350
		ke. Break in lines below left scroll	£325	£325
		kf. Damaged leaf at bottom right	£325	£325
		kg. Gash in fruit and leaf	£350	£350
		kh. Breaks in scrolls at right	£350	£350
111		4s. carmine and black (1927)	19·00	30·00
		a. Break in scroll	£180	£250
		b. Broken crown and scroll	£180	
		c. Nick in top right scroll	£180	
		e. Break in lines below left scroll	£180	£250
		f. Damaged leaf at bottom right	£180	
112		5s. green and red/*yellow* (1929)	42·00	80·00
		a. Break in scroll	£300	
		b. Broken crown and scroll	£300	
		c. Nick in top right scroll	£300	
		e. Break in lines below left scroll	£300	
		f. Damaged leaf at bottom right	£300	
113		10s. green and red/*pale emerald* (1926)	95·00	£100
		a. Break in scroll	£450	£500
		b. Broken crown and scroll	£450	£500
		c. Nick in top right scroll	£450	£500
		e. Break in lines below left scroll	£450	£500
		f. Damaged leaf at bottom right	£450	£500
		g. Green and scarlet/emerald (1927)	£500	£650
		ga. Break in scroll	£1500	
		gb. Broken crown and scroll	£1500	
		ge. Break in lines below left scroll	£1500	£1800
		gf. Damaged leaf at bottom right	£1500	
100/13 *Set of* 13			£200	£250
100s/13s Optd or Perf (1s., 5s.) "Specimen" *Set of* 13			£450	

For illustrations of the other varieties on Nos. 109/13 see above Bermuda No. 51*b*.

17 King George V and Symbol of the Protectorate

(Des Major H. E. Green. Recess Waterlow)

1934 (June)–**35**. Wmk Mult Script CA. P 12½.

114	**17**	½d. green	75	1·25
115		1d. brown	75	75
116		1½d. carmine	75	3·00
117		2d. pale grey	80	1·25
118		3d. blue	2·50	1·75
119		4d. bright magenta (20.5.35)	2·50	3·50
120		6d. violet	2·50	50
121		9d. olive-bistre (20.5.35)	6·50	9·00
122		1s. black and orange	12·00	14·00
114/22 *Set of* 9			26·00	32·00
114s/22s Perf "Specimen" *Set of* 9			£225	

1935 (6 May). *Silver Jubilee. As Nos. 91/4 of Antigua, but ptd by Waterlow.* P 11×12.

123	1d. ultramarine and grey	1·00	2·00
	k. Kite and vertical log	£130	£170
	m. "Bird" by turret	£180	£200
124	2d. green and indigo	1·00	1·50
	m. "Bird" by turret	£180	£190
125	3d. brown and deep blue	7·00	17·00
	k. Kite and vertical log	£300	£400
126	1s. slate and purple	21·00	50·00
	k. Kite and vertical log	£375	£550
123/6 *Set of* 4		27·00	65·00
123s/6s Perf "Specimen" *Set of* 4		£130	

For illustrations of plate varieties see Omnibus section following Zanzibar.

1937 (12 May). *Coronation. As Nos. 95/7 of Antigua.* P 11×11½.

127	½d. green	30	2·00
128	1d. brown	50	1·25
129	2d. grey-black	50	3·00
127/9 *Set of* 3		1·10	5·50
127s/9s Perf "Specimen" *Set of* 3		95·00	

18 Symbol of the Protectorate

19

(T **18** recess Waterlow; T **19** typo D.L.R.)

1938 (1 Jan)–**44**. *Chalk-surfaced paper (2s. to £1).* P 12½ (T **18**) or 14 (T **19**).

(a) Wmk Mult Script CA.

130	**18**	½d. green	30	1·75
130*a*		½d. brown (12.12.42)	10	2·25
131		1d. brown	2·75	30
131*a*		1d. green (12.12.42)	30	1·75
132		1½d. carmine	5·00	5·00
132*a*		1½d. grey (12.12.42)	30	6·50
133		2d. grey	8·00	1·25
133*a*		2d. carmine (12.12.42)	30	1·75
		b. "A" of "CA" missing from wmk		
134		3d. blue	1·00	80
135		4d. bright magenta	2·75	1·75
136		6d. violet	2·75	1·75
137		9d. olive-bistre	2·75	3·75
138		1s. black and orange	3·50	2·50
139	**19**	2s. purple and blue/*blue*	10·00	14·00
140		2s.6d. black and red/*blue*	12·00	16·00
141		5s. pale green and red/*yellow*	50·00	25·00
		a. Ordinary paper. *Green and red/pale yellow* (3.44)	80·00	£120
142		10s. emerald and deep red/*pale green*	50·00	55·00
		a. Ordinary paper. *Bluish green and brown-red/pale green* (1.38)	£350	£325
		(b) Wmk Mult Crown CA.		
143	**19**	£1 purple and black/*red*	42·00	35·00
		c. Serif on "G"	£800	£600
130/43 *Set of* 18			£170	£160
130s/43s Perf "Specimen" *Set of* 18			£700	

No. 141a has a yellow surfacing often applied in horizontal lines giving the appearance of laid paper.

The printer's archives record the despatch of No. 142a to Nyasaland in January 1938, but no examples have been reported used before 1945. The paper coating on this printing varied considerably across the sheet. It is reported that some examples show a faint reaction to the silver test.

20 Lake Nyasa

21 King's African Rifles

22 Tea estate

23 Map of Nyasaland

24 Fishing village

25 Tobacco

25a Badge of Nyasaland

(Recess B.W.)

1945 (1 Sept). *T* **20/25a**. Wmk Mult Script CA (sideways on horiz designs). P 12.

144	**20**	½d. black and chocolate	50	10
145	**21**	1d. black and emerald	20	70
146	**22**	1½d. black and grey-green	30	50
147	**23**	2d. black and scarlet	1·50	85
148	**24**	3d. black and light blue	30	30
149	**25**	4d. black and claret	2·00	80
150	**22**	6d. black and violet	3·00	90
151	**20**	9d. black and olive	2·50	3·00
152	**23**	1s. indigo and deep green	2·50	20
153	**24**	2s. emerald and maroon	8·00	4·75
154	**25**	2s.6d. emerald and blue	8·50	5·50
155	**25a**	5s. purple and blue	4·50	6·50
156	**23**	10s. claret and emerald	18·00	15·00
157	**25a**	20s. scarlet and black	25·00	28·00
144/57 *Set of* 14			70·00	60·00
144s/57s Perf "Specimen" *Set of* 14			£350	

1946 (16 Dec). *Victory. As Nos. 110/11 of Antigua.*

158		1d. green	10	30
159		2d. red-orange	30	30
158s/9s Perf "Specimen" *Set of* 2			85·00	

26 Symbol of the Protectorate

27 Arms in 1891 and 1951

(Recess B.W.)

1947 (20 Oct). Wmk Mult Script CA. P 12.

160	**26**	1d. red-brown and yellow-green	50	20
		s. Perf "Specimen"	60·00	

1948 (15 Dec). *Royal Silver Wedding. As Nos. 112/13 of Antigua.*

161		1d. green	15	10
162		10s. mauve	16·00	26·00

1949 (21 Nov). *75th Anniv of U.P.U. As Nos. 114/17 of Antigua.*

163		1d. blue-green	30	20
		a. "A" of "CA" missing from wmk	£700	
164		3d. greenish blue	2·25	4·00
165		6d. purple	50	70
166		1s. ultramarine	30	50
163/6 *Set of* 4			3·00	4·75

(Des C. Twynam. Recess B.W.)

1951 (15 May). *Diamond Jubilee of Protectorate.* Wmk Mult Script CA. P 11×12.

167	**27**	2d. black and scarlet	1·25	1·50
168		3d. black and turquoise-blue	1·25	1·50
169		6d. black and violet	1·25	2·00
170		5s. black and indigo	4·00	7·00
167/70 *Set of* 4			7·00	11·00

28 Arms of Rhodesia and Nyasaland

(Recess Waterlow)

1953 (30 May). *Rhodes Centenary Exhibition.* Wmk Mult Script CA. P 14×13½.

171	**28**	6d. violet	50	30

1953 (2 June). *Coronation. As No. 120 of Antigua but des and recess B.W.*

172		2d. black and brown-orange	70	80

29 Grading Cotton

(Recess B.W.)

1953 (1 Sept)–**54**. *Designs previously used for King George VI issue, but with portrait of Queen Elizabeth II.* Wmk Mult Script CA. P 12.

173	**20**	½d. black and chocolate	10	1·50
		a. Perf 12×12½ (8.3.54)	10	1·50
174	**26**	1d. brown and bright green	65	40
175	**22**	1½d. black and deep grey-green	20	1·90
176	**23**	2d. black and yellow-orange	85	30
		a. Perf 12×12½ (8.3.54)	40	30
177	**29**	2½d. green and black	20	50
178	**25**	3d. black and scarlet	30	20
179	**24**	4½d. black and light blue	40	40
180	**22**	6d. black and violet	1·00	1·50
		a. Perf 12×12½ (8.3.54)	2·00	1·00
181	**20**	9d. black and deep olive	1·00	2·50
182	**23**	1s. deep blue and slate-green	2·75	50
183	**24**	2s. deep green and brown-red	2·00	3·75
184	**25**	2s.6d. deep emerald and deep blue	3·25	6·00
185	**25a**	5s. purple and Prussian blue	7·00	6·00
186	**23**	10s. carmine and deep emerald	4·75	19·00
187	**25a**	20s. red and black	18·00	29·00
173/87 *Set of* 15			38·00	65·00

Stamps perf 12×12½ come from sheets comb-perforated 11.8×12.25. They were also issued in coils of 480 stamps made up from sheets.

For issues between 1954 and 1963, see RHODESIA AND NYASALAND.

30

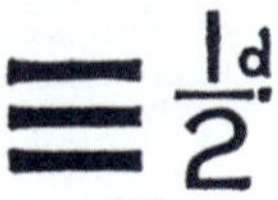
(31)

(Recess B.W.)

1963 (1 Nov). *Revenue stamps optd* "POSTAGE", *as in T* **30**, *or additionally surch as T* **31**. P 12.

188		½d. on 1d. greenish blue	30	30
189		1d. green	30	10
190		2d. scarlet	30	30
191		3d. blue	30	10
192		6d. brown-purple	30	10
193		9d. on 1s. cerise	40	25
194		1s. purple	45	10
195		2s.6d. black	1·25	2·75
196		5s. chocolate	3·25	1·50
197		10s. yellow-olive	4·50	7·50
		a. Greenish olive	14·00	16·00
198		£1 deep violet	5·00	7·50
188/98 *Set of* 11			14·50	18·00

32 Mother and Child

33 Chambo (fish)

34 Tea Industry

35 Nyala

(Des V. Whiteley. Photo Harrison)

1964 (1 Jan). *Designs as T* **32/5**. P 14½.

199		½d. reddish violet	10	30
200		1d. black and green	10	10
201		2d. light red-brown	10	10
202		3d. red-brown, yellow-green & bistre-brown	10	10
203		4d. indigo and orange-yellow	20	30
204		6d. purple, yellow-green and light blue	70	70
205		1s. brown, turquoise-blue and pale yellow	15	10
206		1s.3d. bronze-green and chestnut	3·50	10
207		2s.6d. brown and blue	3·25	50
208		5s. blue, green, yellow and black	1·50	1·75
209		10s. green, orange-brown and black	2·50	3·25
210		£1 deep reddish purple and yellow	7·00	12·00
199/210 *Set of* 12			17·00	17·00

Designs: As T **32/3**—2d. Zebu Bull; 3d. Groundnuts; 4d. Fishing. As T **34**—1s. Timber; 1s.3d. Turkish tobacco industry; 2s.6d. Cotton industry; 5s. Monkey Bay, Lake Nyasa; 10s. Forestry, Afzelia.

STAMP BOOKLETS

1954 (1 Jan). *Black on green cover, stitched (No.* SB1*) or buff cover, stapled (No.* SB2*). R.W. Gunson (Seeds) Ltd. advertisement on front.*

SB1	2s.6d. booklet containing four ½d., 1d., and twelve 2d. (Nos. 173/4, 176), each in blocks of 4	29·00
SB2	5s. booklet containing eight ½d., 1d., 6d. and twelve 2d. (Nos. 173/4, 176, 180), each in blocks of 4	35·00

POSTAGE DUE STAMPS

D 1

(Typo D.L.R.)

1950 (1 July). Wmk Mult Script CA. P 14.

D1	**D 1**	1d. scarlet	4·00	27·00
D2		2d. ultramarine	15·00	27·00
D3		3d. green	15·00	6·00
D4		4d. purple	25·00	55·00
D5		6d. yellow-orange	35·00	£150
D1/5 *Set of* 5			85·00	£225

Nyasaland attained independence on 5 July 1964 when the country was renamed Malawi.

Orange Free State *see* South Africa

Pakistan

(Currency. 12 pies = 1 anna; 16 annas = 1 rupee)

DOMINION

PAKISTAN (1) **PAKISTAN** (2)

1947 (1 Oct). *Nos. 259/68 and 269a/77 (King George VI) of India optd by litho at Nasik, as T* **1** *(3p. to 12a.) or* **2** *(14a. and rupee values).*

1		3p. slate	30	10
2		½a. purple	30	10
3		9p. green	30	10
4		1a. carmine	30	10
5		1½a. dull violet	60	10
		w. Wmk inverted	—	20·00
6		2a. vermilion	30	20
7		3a. bright violet	35	20
8		3½a. bright blue	1·00	2·25
9		4a. brown	35	20
10		6a. turquoise-green	1·00	1·25
11		8a. slate-violet	45	60
12		12a. lake	1·00	20
13		14a. purple	3·25	3·50
14		1r. grey and red-brown	3·00	1·25
		w. Wmk inverted	60·00	40·00
15		2r. purple and brown	3·25	2·50
16		5r. green and blue	4·50	4·00
17		10r. purple and claret	4·75	4·75
18		15r. brown and green	65·00	90·00
19		25r. slate-violet and purple	70·00	55·00
1/19 *Set of* 19			£140	£150

Numerous provisional "PAKISTAN" overprints, both handstamped and machine-printed, in various sizes and colours, on Postage and Official stamps, also exist.

These were made under authority of Provincial Governments, District Head Postmasters or Local Postmasters and are of considerable philatelic interest.

The 1a.3p. (India No. 269) exists only as a local issue (*Price*, Karachi opt £1.25 *unused*; £2 *used*).

The 12a., as No. 12 but overprinted at Karachi, exists with overprint inverted (*Price* £60 *unused*).

The 1r. value with Karachi local overprint exists with overprint inverted (*Price* £150 *unused*) or as a vertical pair with one stamp without overprint (*Price* £600 *unused*).

3 Constituent Assembly Building, Karachi

4 Karachi Airport entrance

5 Gateway to Lahore Fort

6 Crescent and Stars

(Des A. Chughtai (1r.). Recess D.L.R.)

1948 (9 July). *Independence. T* **3/6** . P 13½×14 or 11½ (1r.).

20		1½a. ultramarine	1·25	1·75
21		2½a. green	1·25	20
22		3a. purple-brown	1·25	35
23		1r. scarlet	1·25	70
		a. Perf 14×13½	4·75	20·00
20/3 *Set of* 4			4·50	2·75

7 Scales of Justice

8 Star and Crescent

9 Lloyds Barrage

10 Karachi Airport

11 Karachi Port Trust

12 Salimullah Hostel, Dacca

13 Khyber Pass

(Des M. Suharwardi (T **8**). Recess Pakistan Security Ptg Corp Ltd, Karachi (P 13 and 13½), D.L.R. (others))

1948 (14 Aug)–**56?**. *T* **7/13**. P 13½×14 or 11½ (1r.).

24	**7**	3p. red (P 12½)	10	10
		a. Perf 13½ (1954?)	1·50	1·00
25		6p. violet (P 12½)	1·25	10
		a. Perf 13½ (1954?)	3·50	2·75
26		9p. green (P 12½)	50	10
		a. Perf 13½ (1954?)	2·75	1·75
27	**8**	1a. blue (P 12½)	15	50
28		1½a. grey-green (P 12½)	15	10
29		2a. red (P 12½)	2·50	70
30	**9**	2½a. green (P 14×13½)	4·25	8·00
31	**10**	3a. green (P 14)	7·50	1·00
32	**9**	3½a. bright blue (P 14×13½)	4·25	5·50
33		4a. reddish brown (P 12½)	1·00	10
34	**11**	6a. blue (P 14×13½)	2·00	50
35		8a. black (P 12)	1·00	1·25
36	**10**	10a. scarlet (P 14)	6·00	9·00
37	**11**	12a. scarlet (P 14×13½)	7·50	1·00
38	**12**	1r. ultramarine (P 14)	8·50	10
		a. Perf 13½ (1954?)	16·00	6·00
39		2r. chocolate (P 14)	20·00	70
		a. Perf 13½ (1954?)	26·00	2·00
40		5r. carmine (P 14)	17·00	1·75
		a. Perf 13½ (7.53)	12·00	25
41	**13**	10r. magenta (P 14)	11·00	22·00
		a. Perf 12	95·00	7·50
		b. Perf 13 (1951)	18·00	2·00
42		15r. blue-green (P 12)	18·00	21·00
		a. Perf 14	18·00	55·00
		b. Perf 13 (1956?)	21·00	18·00
43		25r. violet (P 14)	55·00	80·00
		a. Perf 12	32·00	38·00
		b. Perf 13 (1954)	48·00	35·00
24/43a *Set of* 20			£120	75·00

Designs: *Vert (as T* **7**)—6a., 8a., 12a. Karachi Port Trust. (*As T* **10**)—1r., 2r., 5r. Salimullah Hostel, Dacca.

For 25r. with W **98**, see No. 210.

14 Star and Crescent

15 Karachi Airport

15a Karachi Port Trust

(Recess Pakistan Security Ptg Corp (P 13½), D.L.R. (others).

1949 (Feb)–**53?**. *Redrawn. Crescent moon with points to left as T* **14/15a**.

44	**14**	1a. blue (P 12½)	4·00	85
		a. Perf 13½ (1953?)	5·50	10
45		1½a. grey-green (P 12½)	3·75	85
		a. Perf 13½ (1952?)	3·50	10
		ab. Printed on the gummed side	55·00	
46		2a. red (P 12½)	4·50	10
		a. Perf 13½ (1953?)	4·50	10
47	**15**	3a. green (P 14)	15·00	1·00
48	**15a**	6a. blue (as No. 34) (P 14×13½)	14·00	2·00
49		8a. black (as No. 35) (P 12½)	14·00	2·50
50	**15**	10a. scarlet (P 14)	23·00	3·25
51	**15a**	12a. scarlet (as No. 37) (P 14×13½)	25·00	60
44/51 *Set of* 8			90·00	8·50

16

16a

(Recess D.L.R.)

1949 (11 Sept). *First Death Anniv of Mohammed Ali Jinnah. T* **16/a** . P 14.

52	**16**	1½a. brown	2·25	1·50
53		3a. green	2·25	1·50
54	**16a**	10a. black	6·50	8·00
52/4 *Set of* 3			10·00	10·00

17 Pottery

18 Aeroplane and Hourglass

Two Types of 3½a.:

I

II

19 Saracenic Leaf Pattern

20 Archway and Lamp

(Des A. Chughtai. Recess D.L.R., later printings, Pakistan Security Ptg Corp)

1951 (14 Aug)–**56**. *Fourth Anniv of Independence.* P 13.

55	**17**	2½a. carmine	1·75	1·25
56	**18**	3a. purple	1·00	10
57	**17**	3½a. blue (I)	1·25	5·50
57*a*		3½a. blue (II) (12.56)	3·50	5·00
58	**19**	4a. green	75	10
59		6a. brown-orange	1·00	10
60	**20**	8a. sepia	4·50	25
61		10a. violet	2·00	2·25
62	**18**	12a. slate	2·00	10
55/62 *Set of* 9			16·00	13·00

The above and the stamps issued on the 14 August 1954, 1955 and 1956, are basically definitive issues, although issued on the Anniversary date of Independence.

21 "Scinde Dawk" stamp and Ancient and Modern Transport

(Recess DLR)

1952 (14 Aug). *Centenary of "Scinde Dawk" Issue of India.* P 13.

63	**21**	3a. deep olive/*yellow-olive*	75	85
64		12a. deep brown/*salmon*	1·00	15

PRINTERS. All issues up to No. 219 were recess-printed by the Pakistan Security Printing Corporation, *unless otherwise stated.*

22 Kaghan Valley

23 Mountains, Gilgit

24 Tea Plantation, East Pakistan

1954 (14 Aug). *Seventh Anniv of Independence. T* **22/4** *and similar designs.* P 13½ (14a., 1r., 2r.) or 13 (others).

65		6p. reddish violet	10	10
66		9p. blue	3·25	2·25
67		1a. carmine	10	10
68		1½a. red	10	10
69		14a. deep green	2·00	10
70		1r. green	11·00	10
71		2r. red-orange	2·75	10
65/71 *Set of* 7			17·00	2·25

Designs: *As T* **22**—1½a. Mausoleum of Emperor Jehangir, Lahore. *As T* **23**—1a. Badshahi Mosque, Lahore. *As T* **24**—1r. Cotton plants, West Pakistan; 2r. Jute fields and river, East Pakistan.

29 View of K 2

1954 (25 Dec). *Conquest of K 2 (Mount Godwin-Austen).* P 13.

72	**29**	2a. deep violet	40	30

30 Karnaphuli Paper Mill, Type I (Arabic fraction on left)

Type II (Arabic fraction on right)

1955 (14 Aug)–**56**. *Eighth Anniv of Independence. T* **30** *and similar horiz designs.* P 13.

73	2½a. scarlet (I)	50	1·40
73*a*	2½a. scarlet (II) (12.56)	65	1·40
74	6a. deep ultramarine	1·00	10
75	8a. deep reddish violet	3·75	10
76	12a. carmine and orange	4·00	10
73/6 *Set of* 5		9·00	2·75

Designs:—6a. Textile mill, West Pakistan; 8a. Jute mill, East Pakistan; 12a. Main Sui gas plant.

TENTH
ANNIVERSARY
UNITED NATIONS

24.10.55.
(34)

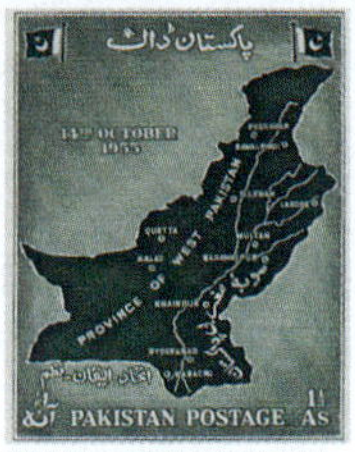

35 Map of West Pakistan

TENTH
ANNIVERSARY
UNITED NATIONS

24.10.55.
"UNITED NATIONS"
shifted 1 mm to left
(1½a. R. 7/10; 12a.
R. 1/8, 3/8, 5/8, 7/8, 9/8)

1955 (24 Oct). *Tenth Anniv of United Nations. Nos. 68 and 76 optd as T* **34**.

77	1½a. red (B.)	1·50	5·00
	a. "UNITED NATIONS" 1 mm to left	5·50	11·00
78	12a. carmine and orange (B.)	50	3·50
	a. "UNITED NATIONS" 1 mm to left	4·25	9·00

Forgeries exist of the overprint on No. 77. These are in very uneven thin type and measure 20×18 mm instead of the genuine 19½×19 mm.

1955 (7 Dec). *West Pakistan Unity.* P 13½.

79	**35**	1½a. myrtle-green	50	1·25
80		2a. sepia	65	10
81		12a. deep rose-red	1·50	50
79/81 *Set of* 3			2·40	1·60

REPUBLIC

36 Constituent Assembly Building, Karachi

(Litho D.L.R.)

1956 (23 Mar). *Republic Day.* P 13.

82	**36**	2a. myrtle-green	80	10

37

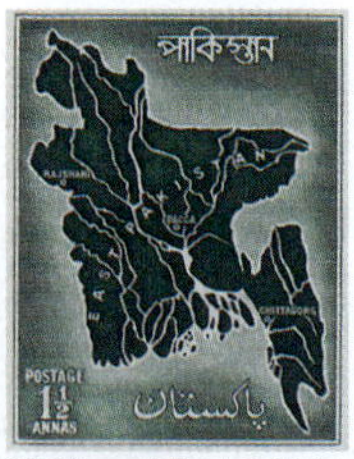

38 Map of East Pakistan

1956 (14 Aug). *Ninth Anniv of Independence.* P 13½.

83	**37**	2a. scarlet	65	10
		a. Printed on the gummed side	6·50	

1956 (15 Oct). *First Session of National Assembly of Pakistan at Dacca.* P 13½.

84	**38**	1½a. myrtle-green	40	1·50
85		2a. sepia	40	10
86		12a. deep rose-red	40	1·25
84/6 *Set of* 3			1·10	2·50

39 Karnaphuli Paper Mill, East Bengal

40 Pottery

41 Orange Tree

1957 (23 Mar). *First Anniv of Republic.* P 13.

87	**39**	2½a. scarlet	20	10
88	**40**	3½a. blue	30	10
89	**41**	10r. myrtle-green and yellow-orange	80	20
87/9 *Set of* 3			1·10	35

The above and No. 95 are primarily definitive issues, although issued on the Anniversary of Republic Day.
For 10r. with W **98**, see No. 208.

42 Pakistani Flag

43 Pakistani Industries

(Des Ahsan. Litho D.L.R.)

1957 (10 May). *Centenary of Struggle for Independence (Indian Mutiny).* P 13.

90	**42**	1½a. bronze-green	50	10
91		12a. light blue	1·25	10

(Litho D.L.R.)

1957 (14 Aug). *Tenth Anniv of Independence.* P 14.

92	**43**	1½a. ultramarine	20	30
93		4a. orange-red	45	1·50
94		12a. mauve	45	50
92/4 *Set of* 3			1·00	2·10

44 Coconut Tree

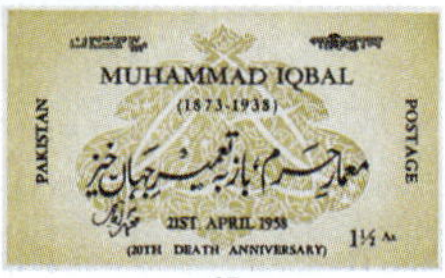

45

1958 (23 Mar). *Second Anniv of Republic.* P 13.

95	**44**	15r. red and deep reddish purple	3·50	3·00

This is a definitive issue, see note below No. 89.
See No. 209 for this stamp with W **98**.

(Photo Harrison)

1958 (21 Apr). *20th Death Anniv of Mohammed Iqbal (poet).* P 14½×14.

96	**45**	1½a. yellow-olive and black	55	1·00
97		2a. orange-brown and black	55	10
98		14a. turquoise-blue and black	90	10
96/8 *Set of* 3			1·75	1·00

46 UN Charter and Globe

PAKISTAN
BOY SCOUT
2nd NATIONAL
JAMBOREE

CHITTAGONG
Dec. 58—Jan. 59
(47)

1958 (10 Dec). *Tenth Anniv of Declaration of Human Rights.* P 13.

99	**46**	1½a. turquoise-blue	10	10
100		14a. sepia	45	10

1958 (28 Dec). *Second Pakistan Boy Scouts National Jamboree, Chittagong. Nos. 65 and 75 optd with T* **47**.

101	6p. reddish violet	20	10
102	8a. deep reddish violet	40	10

REVOLUTION
DAY
Oct. 27, 1959
(48)

49 "Centenary of An Idea"

1959 (27 Oct). *Revolution Day. No. 74 optd with T* **48** *in red.*

103	6a. deep ultramarine	80	10

1959 (19 Nov). *Red Cross Commemoration. Recess; cross typo.* P 13.

104	**49**	2a. red and green	30	10
105		10a. red and deep blue	55	10

50 Armed Forces Badge

51 Map of Pakistan

(Litho D.L.R.)

1960 (10 Jan). *Armed Forces Day.* P 13½×13.

106	**50**	2a. red, ultramarine and blue-green	50	10
107		14a. red and bright blue	1·00	10

1960 (23 Mar). P 13×13½.

108	**51**	6p. deep purple	40	10
109		2a. brown-red	60	10
110		8a. deep green	1·25	10
111		1r. blue	2·00	10
		a. Printed on the gummed side		
108/11 *Set of* 4			3·75	35

52 Uprooted Tree

53 Punjab Agricultural College

1960 (7 Apr). *World Refugee Year.* P 13.

112	**52**	2a. rose-carmine	20	10
113		10a. green	30	10

1960 (10 Oct). *Golden Jubilee of Punjab Agricultural College, Lyallpur. T* **53** *and similar horiz design.* P 12½×14.

114	2a. slate-blue and carmine-red	10	10
115	8a. bluish green and reddish violet	20	10

Design:—8a. College arms.

55 "Land Reforms, Rehabilitation and Reconstruction"

56 Caduceus

(Des M. Hanjra. Photo D.L.R.)

1960 (27 Oct). *Revolution Day.* P 13×13½.

116	**55**	2a. green, pink and brown	10	10
		a. Green and pink omitted	17·00	
		b. Pink omitted	5·00	
117		14a. green, yellow and ultramarine	50	75

(Photo D.L.R.)

1960 (16 Nov). *Centenary of King Edward Medical College, Lahore.* P 13.

118	**56**	2a. yellow, black and blue	50	10
119		14a. emerald, black and carmine	1·75	1·00

57 "Economic Co-operation"

58 Zam-Zama Gun, Lahore ("Kim's Gun," after Rudyard Kipling)

1960 (5 Dec). *International Chamber of Commerce CAFEA Meeting, Karachi.* P 13.

120	**57**	14a. orange-red	50	10

(Centre typo, background recess Pakistan Security Ptg Corp)

1960 (24 Dec). *Third Pakistan Boy Scouts National Jamboree, Lahore.* P 12½×14.

121	**58**	2a. carmine, yellow and deep bluish green	80	10

(New Currency. 100 paisa=1 rupee)

1 PAISA
(59)

1961 (1 Jan–14 Feb). *Nos. 24a, 67/8, 83 and 108/9, surch as T* **59**. *Nos. 123/4 and 126 surch by Pakistan Security Ptg Corp and others by the Times Press, Karachi.*

122	1p. on 1½a. red (10.1)	40	10
	a. Printed and surch on the gummed side	50·00	
123	2p. on 3p. red	10	10
124	3p. on 6p. deep purple	15	10
	a. "PASIA" for "PAISA"	5·00	
125	7p. on 1a. carmine (14.2)	40	10

126		13p. on 2a. brown-red (14.2)	40	10
		a. "PAIS" for "PAISA"	5·00	
127		13p. on 2a. scarlet (14.2)	30	10
122/7 *Set of 6*			1·60	55

No. 122. Two settings were used, the first with figure "1" 2½ mm tall and the second 3 mm.

On the 1p. with tall "1" and the 13p. (No. 127), the space between the figures of value and "P" of "PAISA" varies between 1½ mm and 3 mm.

See also Nos. 262/4.

ERRORS. In the above issue and the corresponding official stamps we have listed errors in the stamps surcharged by the Pakistan Security Printing Corp but have not included the very large number of errors which occurred in the stamps surcharged by the less experienced Times Press. This was a very hurried job and there was no time to carry out the usual checks. It is also known that some errors were not issued to the public but came on the market by other means.

NOTE. Stamps in the old currency were also *handstamped* with new currency equivalents and issued in various districts but these local issues are outside the scope of this catalogue.

60 Khyber Pass

61 Shalimar Gardens, Lahore

62 Chota Sona Masjid (gateway)

(*a*) (*b*) (*c*)

Types (*a*) and (*b*) show the first letter in the top right-hand inscription; (*a*) wrongly engraved, "SH" (*b*) corrected to "P".

On Nos. 131/2 and 134 the corrections were made individually on the plate, so that each stamp in the sheet may be slightly different.

Type (*c*) refers to No. 133a only.

1961–63. *No wmk*. P 13 (T **62**) or 14 (others).

		(*a*) *Inscribed* "SHAKISTAN" *in Bengali*		
128	**60**	1p. violet (1.1.61)	1·50	10
129		2p. rose-red (12.1.61)	1·50	10
130		5p. ultramarine (23.3.61)	3·00	10
		(*b*) *Inscribed* "PAKISTAN" *in Bengali*		
131	**60**	1p. violet	1·00	10
		a. Printed on the gummed side		
132		2p. rose-red	1·00	10
133		3p. reddish purple (27.10.61)	75	10
		a. Re-engraved. First letter of Bengali inscription as Type (*c*) (1963)	4·50	3·75
134		5p. ultramarine	5·00	10
		a. Printed on the gummed side		
135		7p. emerald (23.3.61)	2·00	10
136	**61**	10p. brown (14.8.61)	20	10
137		13p. slate-violet (14.8.61)	15	10
138		25p. deep blue (1.1.62)	5·50	10
139		40p. deep purple (1.1.62)	1·50	10
140		50p. deep bluish green (1.1.62)	35	10
141		75p. carmine-red (23.3.62)	40	70
142		90p. yellow-green (1.1.62)	70	70
143	**62**	1r. vermilion (7.1.63)	3·25	10
		a. Imperf (pair)		
144		1r.25 reddish violet (27.10.61)	75	80
144*a*		2r. orange (7.1.63)	5·50	15
144*b*		5r. green (7.1.63)	6·00	2·50
128/44b *Set of 19*			35·00	4·50

See also Nos. 170/81 and 204/7.

(**63**)

64 Warsak Dam and Power Station

1961 (12 Feb). *Lahore Stamp Exhibition. No. 110 optd with T* **63**.

145	**51**	8a. deep green (R.)	1·00	1·75

(Des A. Ghani)

1961 (1 July). *Completion of Warsak Hydro-Electric Project*. P 12½×14.

146	**64**	40p. black and blue	60	10

65 Narcissus

66 Ten Roses

(Des A. Ghani)

1961 (2 Oct). *Child Welfare Week*. P 14.

147	**65**	13p. turquoise-blue	50	10
148		90p. bright purple	1·25	20

(Des A. Ghani)

1961 (4 Nov). *Co-operative Day*. P 13.

149	**66**	13p. rose-red and deep green	40	10
150		90p. rose-red and blue	85	90

67 Police Crest and "Traffic Control"

68 Locomotive *Eagle*, 1861

(Photo D.L.R.)

1961 (30 Nov). *Police Centenary*. P 13.

151	**67**	13p. silver, black and blue	50	10
152		40p. silver, black and red	1·00	20

(Des M. Thoma. Photo D.L.R.)

1961 (31 Dec). *Railway Centenary. T* **68** *and similar horiz design*. P 14.

153	13p. green, black and yellow	75	80
154	50p. yellow, black and green	1·00	1·50

Design:—50p. Diesel locomotive No. 20 and tracks forming "1961".

(**70**)

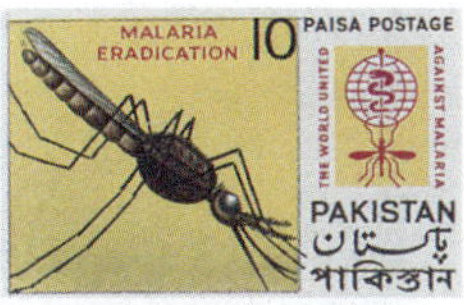
71 *Anopheles sp* (mosquito)

1962 (6 Feb). *First Karachi-Dacca Jet Flight. No. 87 surch with T* **70**.

155	**39**	13p. on 2½a. scarlet (R.)	1·75	1·25

(Photo D.L.R.)

1962 (7 Apr). *Malaria Eradication. T* **71** *and similar horiz design*. P 14.

156	10p. black, yellow and red	35	10
157	13p. black, greenish yellow and red	35	10

Design:—13p. Mosquito pierced by blade.

73 Pakistan Map and Jasmine

(Photo Courvoisier)

1962 (8 June). *New Constitution*. P 12.

158	**73**	40p. yellow-green, bluish green and grey	70	10

74 Football

78 Marble Fruit Dish and Bahawalpuri Clay Flask

(Des A. Ghani and M. Bhatti)

1962 (14 Aug). *Sports. T* **74** *and similar horiz designs*. P 12½×14.

159	7p. black and blue	10	10
160	13p. black and green	60	1·50
161	25p. black and purple	20	10
162	40p. black and orange-brown	2·00	2·50
159/62 *Set of 4*		2·50	3·75

Designs:—13p. Hockey; 25p. Squash; 40p. Cricket.

(Des A. Ghani and M. Bhatti)

1962 (10 Nov). *Small Industries. T* **78** *and similar vert designs*. P 13.

163	7p. brown-lake	10	10
164	13p. deep green	2·50	2·50
165	25p. reddish violet	10	10
166	40p. yellow-green	10	10
167	50p. deep red	10	10
163/7 *Set of 5*		2·50	2·50

Designs:—13p Sports equipment; 25p. Camel-skin lamp and brassware; 40p. Wooden powderbowl and basket-work; 50p. Inlaid cigarette-box and brassware.

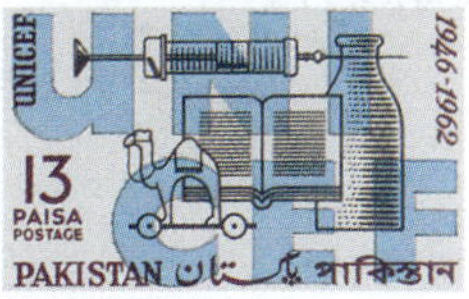
83 "Child Welfare"

(Des M. Thoma. Photo D.L.R.)

1962 (11 Dec). *16th Anniv of UNICEF*. P 14.

168	**83**	13p. black, light blue and maroon	35	10
169		40p. black, yellow and turquoise-blue	35	10

Nos. 170, etc.

Nos. 131/42

1962–70. *As T* **60/1** *but with redrawn Bengali inscription at top right. No wmk*.

170	**60**	1p. violet (1963)	10	10
171		2p. rose-red (1964)	1·75	10
		a. Imperf (pair)	3·00	
172		3p. reddish purple (1970)	8·00	3·75
173		5p. ultramarine (1963)	10	10
		a. Printed on the gummed side	12·00	
174		7p. emerald (1964)	7·00	3·50
175	**61**	10p. brown (1963)	10	10
		a. Printed on the gummed side	12·00	
176		13p. slate-violet	10	10
176*a*		15p. bright purple (31.12.64)	20	10
		ab. Imperf (pair)	4·50	
		ac. Printed on the gummed side		
176*b*	**61**	20p. myrtle-green (26.1.70)	30	10
		ba. Imperf (pair)	3·50	
		bb. Printed on the gummed side	15·00	
177		25p. deep blue (1963)	11·00	10
		a. Imperf (pair)		
178		40p. deep purple (1964)	15	30
		a. Imperf (pair)	6·50	
179		50p. deep bluish green (1964)	15	10
		a. Printed on the gummed side		
180		75p. carmine-red (1964)	30	70
		a. Printed on the gummed side	12·00	
181		90p. yellow-green (1964)	30	1·00
170/81 *Set of 14*			26·00	8·50

Other values in this series and the high values (Nos. 204/10) are known imperforate but we are not satisfied as to their status.

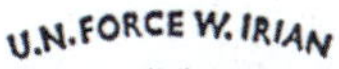

(**84**)

85 "Dancing" Horse, Camel and Bull

1963 (15 Feb). *Pakistan U.N. Force in West Irian. No. 176 optd with T* **84**.

182	**61**	13p. slate-violet (R.)	10	75

(Des S. Jahangir. Photo Courvoisier)

1963 (13 Mar). *National Horse and Cattle Show*. P 11½.

183	**85**	13p. blue, sepia and cerise	10	10

86 Wheat and Tractor

(Des B. Mirza)

1963 (21 Mar). *Freedom from Hunger. T* **86** *and similar horiz design*. P 12½×14.

184	13p. orange-brown	2·50	10
185	50p. bistre-brown	4·00	55

Design:—50p. Rice.

(**88**)

89 Centenary Emblem

1963 (23 Mar). *2nd International Stamp Exhibition, Dacca. No. 109 surch with T* **88**.

186	**51**	13p. on 2a. brown-red	50	50

1963 (25 June). *Centenary of Red Cross. Recess; cross typo*. P 13.

187	**89**	40p. red and deep olive	2·00	15

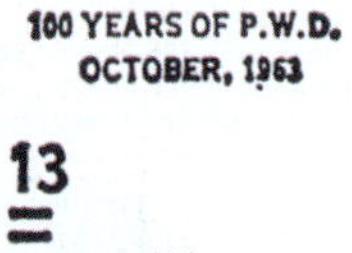

90 Paharpur **(94)**

(Des A. Ghani)

1963 (16 Sept). *Archaeological Series. T* **90** *and similar designs.* P 14×12½ (13p.) or 12½×15 (others).

188		7p. ultramarine	55	10
189		13p. sepia	55	10
190		40p. carmine	90	10
191		50p. deep reddish violet	95	10
188/91 *Set of 4*			2·75	35

Designs: *Vert*—13p. Moenjodaro; *Horiz*—40p. Taxila; 50p. Mainamati.

1963 (7 Oct). *Centenary of Public Works Department. No. 133 surch with T* **94** *by typography.*

192	**60**	13p. on 3p. reddish purple	10	10

Forged surcharges applied in *lithography* exist.

95 Ataturk's Mausoleum

(Des A. Ghani)

1963 (10 Nov). *25th Death Anniv of Kemal Ataturk.* P 13½.

193	**95**	50p. red	50	10

96 Globe and UNESCO Emblem

(Photo D.L.R.)

1963 (10 Dec). *15th Anniv of Declaration of Human Rights.* P 14.

194	**96**	50p. brown, red and ultramarine	40	10

97 Thermal Power Installations

(Des A. Ghani)

1963 (25 Dec). *Completion of Multan Thermal Power Station.* P 12½×14.

195	**97**	13p. ultramarine	10	10

98 Multiple Star and Crescent **99** Temple of Thot, Queen Nefertari and Maids

1963–79. *As Nos. 43b, 89, 95 and 143/4b, but* W **98** (sideways* on 15r.).

204	**62**	1r. vermilion	45	10
		a. Printed on the gummed side		
		b. Imperf (pair)	7·50	
		w. Wmk inverted	1·25	
205		1r.25 reddish violet (1964)	2·00	20
		aw. Wmk inverted	2·50	
		b. *Purple* (1975?)	2·50	20
		ba. Imperf (pair)	6·00	
206		2r. orange (1964)	1·00	15
		a. Imperf (pair)	8·00	
		w. Wmk inverted	2·00	
207		5r. green (1964)	5·50	65
		a. Imperf (pair)	11·00	
		w. Wmk inverted	5·50	
208	**41**	10r. myrtle-green and yellow-orange (1968)	4·50	4·75
		a. Imperf (pair)		
		bw. Wmk inverted		
		c. Wmk sideways	2·25	2·50
209	**44**	15r. red and deep reddish purple (20.3.79)	2·00	3·00
		a. Imperf (pair)	13·00	
		w. Wmk tips of crescent pointing downwards		
210	**13**	25r. violet (1968)	8·50	12·00
		aw. Wmk inverted	13·00	
		b. Wmk sideways	3·25	4·00
		ba. Imperf (pair)	15·00	
204/10b *Set of 7*			15·00	9·50

MULTIPLE STAR AND CRESCENT WATERMARKED PAPER. When viewed from the back with the stamp upright, upright and sideways reversed watermarks show the tips of the crescents pointing upwards and to the right; reversed and sideways watermarks show the tips pointing upwards to the left; inverted and sideways inverted and reversed watermarks show the tips pointing downwards and to the left, while sideways inverted and upright inverted and reversed watermarks show them pointing downwards and to the left. Upright and sideways reversed watermarks may be differentiated by the angle of the row of stars which is approximately 60° for the upright and 30° for the sideways reversed.

(Des A. Ghani)

1964 (30 Mar). *Nubian Monuments Preservation. T* **99** *and similar horiz design.* P 13×13½.

211		13p. turquoise-blue and red	30	10
212		50p. bright purple and black	70	10

Design:—50p. Temple of Abu Simbel.

101 "Unisphere" and Pakistan Pavilion **103** Shah Abdul Latif's Mausoleum

(Des A. Ghani)

1964 (22 Apr). *New York World's Fair. T* **101** *and similar design.* P 12½×14 (13p.) or 14×12½ (1r.25).

213		13p. ultramarine	10	10
214		1r.25 ultramarine and red-orange	40	20

Design: *Vert*—1r.25 Pakistan Pavilion on "Unisphere".

(Des A. Ghani)

1964 (25 June). *Death Bicentenary of Shah Abdul Latif of Bhit.* P 13½×13.

215	**103**	50p. bright blue and carmine-lake	1·00	10

104 Mausoleum of Quaid-i-Azam **105** Mausoleum

(Des A. Ghani)

1964 (11 Sept). *16th Death Anniv of Mohammed Ali Jinnah (Quaid-i-Azam).* P 13½ (15p.) or 13 (50p.).

216	**104**	15p. emerald-green	1·00	10
217	**105**	50p. bronze-green	2·25	10

106 Bengali and Urdu Alphabets **107** University Building

(Des N. Rizvi)

1964 (5 Oct). *Universal Children's Day.* P 13.

218	**106**	15p. brown	10	10

(Des N. Rizvi)

1964 (21 Dec). *First Convocation of the West Pakistan University of Engineering and Technology, Lahore.* P 12½×14.

219	**107**	15p. chestnut	10	10

PROCESS. All the following issues were lithographed by the Pakistan Security Printing Corporation, *unless otherwise stated.*

108 "Help the Blind" **109** ITU Emblem and Symbols

(Des A. Chughtai)

1965 (28 Feb). *Blind Welfare.* P 13.

220	**108**	15p. ultramarine and yellow	20	10

(Des N. Rizvi. Recess)

1965 (17 May). *ITU Centenary.* P 12½×14.

221	**109**	15p. reddish purple	1·50	30

NEW INFORMATION

The editor is always interested to correspond with people who have new information that will improve or correct the catalogue

110 ICY Emblem

1965 (26 June). *International Co-operation Year.* P 13×13½.

222	**110**	15p. black and light blue	50	15
223		50p. green and yellow	1·50	40

111 "Co-operation"

112 Globe and Flags of Turkey, Iran and Pakistan

1965 (21 July). *First Anniv of Regional Development Co-operation Pact.* P 13½×13 (15p.) or 13 (50p.)

224	**111**	15p. multicoloured	20	10
225	**112**	50p. multicoloured	1·10	10

113 Soldier and Tanks

(Des S. Ghori (7p.), N. Rizvi (15p.), A. Ghani (50p.))

1965 (25 Dec). *Pakistan Armed Forces. T* **113** *and similar horiz designs. Multicoloured.* P 13½×13.

226		7p. Type **113**	75	30
227		15p. Naval officer and *Tughril* (destroyer)	1·50	10
228		50p. Pilot and Lockheed F-104C Star fighters	2·50	30
226/8 *Set of 3*			4·25	60

116 Army, Navy and Air Force Crests **117** Atomic Reactor, Islamabad

(Des A. Ghani)

1966 (13 Feb). *Armed Forces Day.* P 13½×13.

229	**116**	15p. royal blue, dull green, bright blue and buff	1·00	10

(Des A. Ghani. Recess)

1966 (30 Apr). *Inauguration of Pakistan's First Atomic Reactor.* P 13.

230	**117**	15p. black	10	10

118 Bank Crest **119** Children

(Des A. Ghani)

1966 (25 Aug). *Silver Jubilee of Habib Bank.* P 12½×14.

231	**118**	15p. blue-green, yellow-orange and sepia	10	10

(Des S. Nagi)

1966 (3 Oct). *Universal Children's Day.* P 13½.

232	**119**	15p. black, red and pale yellow	10	10

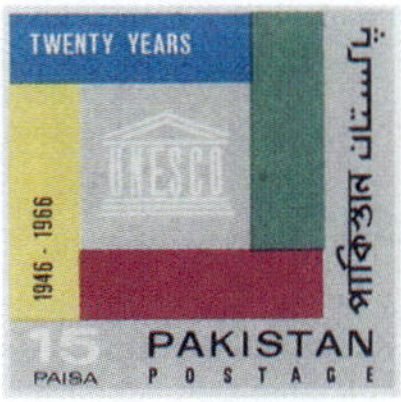

120 UNESCO Emblem

1966 (24 Nov). *20th Anniv of UNESCO.* P 14.
233 **120** 15p. multicoloured .... 3·75 30

121 Flag, Secretariat Building and President Ayub

(Des A. Ghani)

1966 (29 Nov). *Islamabad (new capital).* P 13.
234 **121** 15p. deep bluish green, chestnut, light blue and bistre-brown 35 10
235 50p. deep bluish green, chestnut, light blue and black 65 10

122 Avicenna **123** Mohammed Ali Jinnah

(Des A. Ghani)

1966 (3 Dec). *Foundation of Health and Tibbi Research Institute.* P 13×13½.
236 **122** 15p. dull green and salmon 40 10
a. Imperf (pair) .... 75·00

(Des A. Ghani. Recess and litho)

1966 (25 Dec). *90th Birth Anniv of Mohammed Ali Jinnah. T* **123** *and similar design bearing same portrait, but in different frame.* P 13.
237 **123** 15p. black, orange and greenish blue 15 10
238 – 50p. black, purple and ultramarine 35 10

124 Tourist Year Emblem **125** Emblem of Pakistan TB Association

(Des A. Ghani)

1967 (1 Jan). *International Tourist Year.* P 13½×13.
239 **124** 15p. black, light blue and yellow-brown 10 10

1967 (10 Jan). *Tuberculosis Eradication Campaign.* P 13½×13.
240 **125** 15p. red, sepia and chestnut 10 10

126 Scout Salute and Badge **127** "Justice"

(Des A. Rauf. Photo)

1967 (29 Jan). *4th National Scout Jamboree.* P 12½×14.
241 **126** 15p. light orange-brown and maroon 15 10

(Des A. Rauf)

1967 (17 Feb). *Centenary of West Pakistan High Court.* P 13.
242 **127** 15p. black, slate, light red and slate-blue 10 10

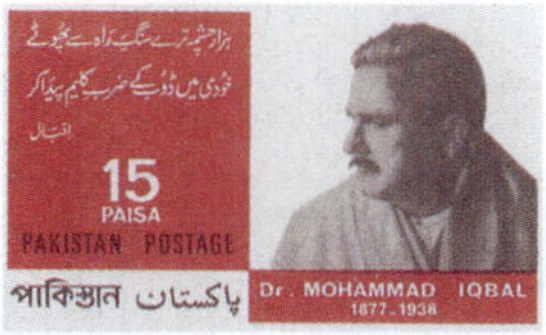

128 Dr. Mohammed Iqbal (philosopher)

(Des A. Rauf)

1967 (21 Apr). *Iqbal Commemoration.* P 13.
243 **128** 15p. sepia and light red 15 10
244 1r. sepia and deep green 35 10

129 Hilal-i-Isteqlal Flag

(Des A. Rahman)

1967 (15 May). *Award of Hilal-i-Isteqlal (for Valour) to Lahore, Sialkot, and Sargodha.* P 13.
245 **129** 15p. multicoloured 10 10

130 "20th Anniversary"

(Des F. Karim. Photo)

1967 (14 Aug). *20th Anniv of Independence.* P 13.
246 **130** 15p. red and deep bluish green 10 10

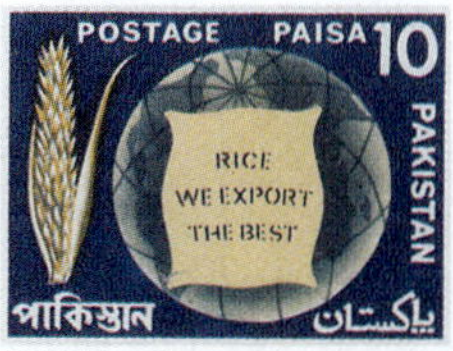

131 "Rice Exports" **132** Cotton Plant, Yarn and Textiles

(Des S. Nagi (10p.), F. Karim (others). Photo)

1967 (26 Sept). *Pakistan Exports. T* **131/2** *and similar design.* P 13×13½.
247 10p. yellow, deep bluish green and deep blue 10 15
248 15p. multicoloured 10 10
a. Pale orange (top panel) omitted ... 13·00
249 50p. multicoloured 20 15
247/9 *Set of 3* 35 35
Design: *Vert as T* **132**—50p. Raw jute, bale and bags.

134 Clay Toys

(Des F. Karim)

1967 (2 Oct). *Universal Children's Day.* P 13.
250 **134** 15p. multicoloured 10 10

135 Shah and Empress of Iran and Gulistan Palace, Teheran

(Des S. Ghori. Recess and litho)

1967 (26 Oct). *Coronation of Shah Mohammed Riza Pahlavi and Empress Farah of Iran.* P 13.
251 **135** 60p. purple, blue and light yellow-ochre .... 1·00 10

136 "Each For All—All For Each"

(Des A. Rauf)

1967 (4 Nov). *Co-operative Day.* P 13.
252 **136** 15p. multicoloured 10 10

137 Mangla Dam

(Des S. Nagi)

1967 (23 Nov). *Indus Basin Project.* P 13.
253 **137** 15p. multicoloured 10 10

138 Crab pierced by Sword **139** Human Rights Emblem

(Des F. Karim)

1967 (26 Dec). *The Fight against Cancer.* P 13.
254 **138** 15p. red and black 70 10

1968 (31 Jan). *Human Rights Year. Photo.* P 14×13.
255 **139** 15p. red and deep turquoise-blue .. 10 15
256 50p. red, yellow and silver-grey 10 15

140 Agricultural University, Mymensingh **141** WHO Emblem

(Des S. Ghori. Photo)

1968 (28 Mar). *First Convocation of East Pakistan Agricultural University.* P 13½×13.
257 **140** 15p. multicoloured 10 10

(Des A. Salahuddin. Photo)

1968 (7 Apr). *20th Anniv of World Health Organization.* P 14×13.
258 **141** 15p. green and orange-red 10 15
a. "PAIS" for "PAISA" (R. 4/5) . 2·50
259 50p. red-orange and indigo 10 15

142 Kazi Nazrul Islam (poet, composer and patriot)

(Des F. Karim. Recess and litho)

1968 (25 June). *Nazrul Islam Commemoration.* P 13.
260 **142** 15p. sepia and pale yellow 35 15
261 50p. sepia and pale rose-red 65 15
Nos. 260/1 with a two-line inscription giving the wrong date of birth ("1889") were prepared but not issued. Some are known to have been released in error.

4 PAISA
(143)

1968 (18 July–Aug). *Nos. 56, 74 and 61 surch as T* **143**.
262 4p. on 3a. purple .... 1·00 1·75
263 4p. on 6a. deep ultramarine (R.) (Aug) .... 1·25 1·75
264 60p. on 10a. violet (R.) .... 1·00 35
a. Surch in black .... 40 1·50
b. Surch triple .... 32·00
262/4 *Set of 3* .... 3·00 3·50

144 Children running with Hoops

(Des A. Rauf)

1968 (7 Oct). *Universal Children's Day.* P 13.
265 **144** 15p. multicoloured 10 10

145 "National Assembly"

(Des M. Khatoon)

1968 (27 Oct). *"A Decade of Development". T* **145** *and similar horiz designs.* P 13.
266 10p. multicoloured 10 10
267 15p. multicoloured 10 10
268 50p. multicoloured .... 2·00 20
269 60p. light blue, dull purple and vermilion 50 35
266/9 *Set of 4* .... 2·40 65

Designs:—15p. Industry and agriculture; 50p. Army, Navy and Air Force; 60p. Minaret and atomic reactor plant.

149 Chittagong Steel Mill

(Des M. Khatoon)

1969 (7 Jan). *Pakistan's First Steel Mill, Chittagong.* P 13.
270 **149** 15p. grey, light blue and pale yellow-olive 10 10

150 "Family" **151** Olympic Gold Medal and Hockey Player

(Des M. Khatoon)

1969 (14 Jan). *Family Planning.* P 13½×13.
271 **150** 15p. bright purple and pale greenish blue 10 10

(Des S. Ghori. Photo)

1969 (30 Jan). *Olympic Hockey Champions.* P 13½.
272 **151** 15p. black, gold, deep green and pale blue 75 50
273 1r. black, gold, deep green and flesh-pink .... 2·25 1·00

152 Mirza Ghalib and Lines of Verse

(Des A. Rauf)

1969 (15 Feb). *Death Centenary of Mirza Ghalib (poet).* P 13.
274 **152** 15p. multicoloured 20 15
275 50p. multicoloured 50 15

The lines of verse on No. 275 are different from those in T **152**.

153 Dacca Railway Station

(Des F. Karim)

1969 (27 Apr). *First Anniv of New Dacca Railway Station.* P 13.
276 **153** 15p. multicoloured 30 10

154 I.L.O. Emblem and "1919–1969" **155** "Lady on Balcony" (18th-cent Mogul)

(Des R-ud Din)

1969 (15 May). *50th Anniv of International Labour Organization.* P 13½.
277 **154** 15p. buff and bluish green 10 10
278 50p. cinnamon and cerise 40 10

(Des S. Ghori, A. Rauf, F. Karim, A. Salahuddin, N. Mohammad and M. Khatoon)

1969 (21 July). *Fifth Anniv of Regional Co-operation for Development. T* **155** *and similar vert designs showing miniatures. Multicoloured.* P 13.
279 20p. Type **155** 15 10
280 50p. "Kneeling Servant" (17th-cent Persian) 15 10
281 1r. "Suleiman the Magnificent holding Audience" (16th-cent Turkish) 20 10
279/81 *Set of 3* 45 25

158 Eastern Refinery, Chittagong

(Des M. Khatoon. Photo)

1969 (14 Sept). *First Oil Refinery in East Pakistan.* P 13½×13.
282 **158** 20p. multicoloured 10 10

159 Children playing outside "School"

(Des M. Khatoon. Photo)

1969 (6 Oct). *Universal Children's Day.* P 13.
283 **159** 20p. multicoloured 10 10

160 Japanese Doll and PIA Air Routes

(Des N. Mohammad)

1969 (1 Nov). *Inauguration of PIA Pearl Route, Dacca–Tokyo.* P 13½×13.
284 **160** 20p. multicoloured 40 10
a. Yellow and pink omitted .... 8·50
285 50p. multicoloured 60 40
a. Yellow and pink omitted .... 8·50

161 "Reflection of Light" Diagram

(Des A. Rauf. Photo)

1969 (4 Nov). *Millenary Commemorative of Ibn-al-Haitham (physicist).* P 13.
286 **161** 20p. black, lemon and light blue 10 10

162 Vickers Vimy and Karachi Airport **163** Flags, Sun Tower and Expo Site Plan

(Des N. Mohammad. Photo)

1969 (2 Dec). *50th Anniv of First England–Australia Flight.* P 13½×13.
287 **162** 50p. multicoloured 70 35

(Des R-ud Din)

1970 (15 Mar). *World Fair, Osaka.* P 13.
288 **163** 50p. multicoloured 20 30

164 New U.P.U. HQ Building

(Des R-ud Din)

1970 (20 May). *New U.P.U. Headquarters Building.* P 13½×13.
289 **164** 20p. multicoloured 15 10
290 50p. multicoloured 25 25

The above, in a miniature sheet, additionally inscr "U.P.U. Day 9th Oct, 1971", were put on sale on that date in very limited numbers.

165 U.N. HQ Building

(Des A. Rauf)

1970 (26 June). *25th Anniv of United Nations. T* **165** *and similar horiz design. Multicoloured.* P 13×13½.
291 20p. Type **165** 10 10
292 50p. U.N. emblem 15 20

167 IEY Emblem, Book and Pen

(Des M. Khatoon)

1970 (6 July). *International Education Year.* P 13.
293 **167** 20p. multicoloured 10 10
294 50p. multicoloured 20 20

168 Saiful Malook Lake (Pakistan)

1970 (21 July). *Sixth Anniv of Regional Co-operation for Development. T* **168** *and similar square designs. Multicoloured.* P 13.
295 20p. Type **168** 15 10
296 50p. Seeyo-Se-Pol Bridge, Esfahan (Iran) 20 10
297 1r. View from Fethiye (Turkey) 20 15
295/7 *Set of 3* 50 30

171 Asian Productivity Symbol

172 Dr. Maria Montessori

1970 (18 Aug). *Asian Productivity Year. Photo.* P 12½×14.

298	**171**	50p. multicoloured	20	20

(Des M. Khatoon)

1970 (31 Aug). *Birth Centenary of Dr. Maria Montessori (educationist).* P 13.

299	**172**	20p. multicoloured	15	10
300		50p. multicoloured	15	30

173 Tractor and Fertilizer Factory

1970 (12 Sept). *Tenth Near East FAO Regional Conference, Islamabad.* P 13.

301	**173**	20p. bright green and orange-brown	15	40

174 Children and Open Book

175 Pakistan Flagand Text

(Des F. Karim. Photo)

1970 (5 Oct). *Universal Children's Day.* P 13.

302	**174**	20p. multicoloured	15	10

(Des A. Salahuddin)

1970 (7 Dec). *General Elections for National Assembly.* P 13½×13.

303	**175**	20p. green and bluish violet	15	10

(Des A. Salahuddin)

1970 (17 Dec). *General Elections for Provincial Assemblies. As No. 303, but inscr* "PROVINCIAL ASSEMBLIES 17TH DEC., 1970".

304	**175**	20p. green and pale magenta	15	10

176 Conference Crest and burning Al-Aqsa Mosque

(Des R-ud Din)

1970 (26 Dec). *Conference of Islamic Foreign Ministers, Karachi.* P 13.

305	**176**	20p. multicoloured	15	15

STAMP BOOKLETS

1956 (23 Mar). *Black on green cover. Stapled.*

SB1	1r. 08 booklet containing twelve 6p. and 1½a. (Nos. 65, 68) in blocks of 4	9·00

OFFICIAL STAMPS

PAKISTAN
(O 1)

1947. *Nos. O138/41 and O143/50 (King George VI) of India, optd as Type* O **1** *(Nos. O1/9) or as T* **2** *(Nos. O10/13) both in litho by Nasik.*

O1		3p. slate	2·50	2·25
O2		½a. purple	40	10
O3		9p. green	5·00	3·75
O4		1a. carmine	40	10
		w. Wmk inverted	—	20·00
O5		1½a. dull violet	40	10
		w. Wmk inverted	20·00	10·00
O6		2a. vermilion	40	20
O7		2½a. bright violet	7·00	9·50
O8		4a. brown	1·25	1·50
O9		8a. slate-violet	1·75	3·00
O10		1r. grey and red-brown	80	2·50
O11		2r. purple and brown	6·50	5·50
O12		5r. green and blue	23·00	42·00
O13		10r. purple and claret	65·00	£120
O1/13 *Set of* 13			£100	£170

See note after No. 19. The 1a.3p. (India No. O146*a*) exists as a local issue (*Price*, Karachi opt, £7·50 *mint*, £23 *used*).

SERVICE (O 2) **SERVICE** (O 3) **SERVICE** (O 4)

NOTE. Apart from a slight difference in size, Types O **2** and O **3** can easily be distinguished by the difference in the shape of the "c". Type O **4** is taller and thinner in appearance.

PRINTERS. Type O **2** was overprinted by De La Rue and Type O **3** by the Pakistan Security Ptg Corp.

1948 (14 Aug)–**54?** *Optd with Type* O **2**.

O14	**7**	3p. red (No. 24)	10	10
O15		6p. violet (No. 25) (R.)	10	10
O16		9p. green (No. 26) (R.)	10	10
O17	**8**	1a. blue (No. 27) (R.)	3·75	10
O18		1½a. grey-green (No. 28) (R.)	3·50	10
O19		2a. red (No. 29)	1·50	10
O20	**10**	3a. green (No. 31)	26·00	12·00
O21	**9**	4a. reddish brown (No. 33)	1·75	10
O22	**11**	8a. black (No. 35) (R.)	2·50	10·00
O23	**12**	1r. ultramarine (No. 38)	1·25	10
O24		2r. chocolate (No. 39)	14·00	10·00
O25		5r. carmine (No. 40)	48·00	16·00
O26	**13**	10r. magenta (No. 41)	19·00	50·00
		a. Perf 12 (10.10.51)	24·00	55·00
		b. Perf 13 (1954?)	18·00	60·00
O14/26 *Set of* 13			£110	90·00

1949. *Optd with Type* O **2**.

O27		1a. blue (No. 44) (R.)	3·50	10
O28		1½a. grey-green (No. 45) (R.)	2·25	10
		a. Opt inverted	£275	45·00
O29		2a. red (No. 46)	2·50	10
		a. Opt omitted (in pair with normal)	—	£170
O30		3a. green (No. 47)	30·00	6·00
O31		8a. black (No. 49) (R.)	50·00	21·00
O27/31 *Set of* 5			80·00	24·00

1951 (14 Aug). *4th Anniv of Independence. As Nos. 56, 58 and 60, but inscr* "SERVICE" *instead of* "PAKISTAN POSTAGE".

O32	**18**	3a. purple	7·50	10·00
O33	**19**	4a. green	2·00	10
O34	**20**	8a. sepia	8·00	4·00
O32/4 *Set of* 3			16·00	12·50

1953. *Optd with Type* O **3**.

O35		3p. red (No. 24a)	10	10
O36		6p. violet (No. 25a) (R.)	10	10
O37		9p. green (No. 26a) (R.)	10	10
O38		1a. blue (No. 44a) (R.)	10	10
O39		1½a. grey-green (No. 45a) (R.)	10	10
O40		2a. red (No. 46a) (1953?)	15	10
O41		1r. ultramarine (No. 38a)	10·00	4·75
O42		2r. chocolate (No. 39a)	4·25	20
O43		5r. carmine (No. 40a)	50·00	22·00
O44		10r. magenta (No. 41b) (date?)	22·00	60·00
O35/44 *Set of* 10			80·00	80·00

1954 (14 Aug). *Seventh Anniv of Independence. Nos. 65/71 optd with Type* O **3**.

O45		6p. reddish violet (R.)	10	2·75
O46		9p. blue (R.)	1·50	7·50
O47		1a. carmine	15	2·50
O48		1½a. red	15	2·50
O49		14a. deep green (R.)	1·00	7·00
O50		1r. green (R.)	75	10
O51		2r. red-orange	3·00	15
O45/51 *Set of* 7			6·00	20·00

1955 (14 Aug). *Eighth Anniv of Independence. No. 75 optd with Type* O **3**.

O52		8a. deep reddish violet (R.)	1·00	10

1957 (Jan)–**59**. *Nos. 65/71 optd with Type* O **4**.

O53		6p. reddish violet (R.)	10	10
		a. Opt inverted	†	—
O54		9p. blue (R.) (1.59)	10	10
		a. Opt inverted	24·00	
O55		1a. carmine	10	10
		a. Opt inverted	—	60·00
		b. Printed on the gummed side		
O56		1½a. red	10	10
		a. Opt double		
		b. Printed on the gummed side		
O57		14a. deep green (R.) (2.59)	50	4·25
O58		1r. green (R.) (4.58)	50	10
O59		2r. red-orange (4.58)	5·50	10
O53/9 *Set of* 7			6·00	4·25

1958 (Jan)–**61**. *Optd with Type* O **4**.

O60	**7**	3p. red (No. 24a)	10	10
O61	–	5r. carmine (No. 40a) (7.59)	7·50	15
O62	**41**	10r. myrtle-green and yellow-orange (No. 89) (R.) (1961)	7·00	8·50
		a. Opt inverted	17·00	
O60/2 *Set of* 3			13·00	7·75

1958 (Jan)–**61**. *Nos. 74/5 optd with Type* O **4**.

O63		6a. deep ultramarine (R.) (4.61)	15	10
O64		8a. deep reddish violet (R.)	15	10

1959 (Aug). *No. 83 optd with Type* O **4**.

O65	**37**	2a. scarlet	10	10

1961 (Apr). *Nos. 110/11 optd with Type* O **4**.

O66	**51**	8a. deep green	20	10
O67		1r. blue	20	10
		a. Opt inverted	9·50	

NEW CURRENCY. In addition to the local handstamped surcharges mentioned in the note above No. 122, the following typographed surcharges were made at the Treasury at Mastung and issued in the Baluchi province of Kalat: 6p. on 1a. (No. O55), 9p. on 1½a. (No. O56) and 13p. on 2a. (No. O65). They differ in that the surcharges are smaller and "PAISA" is expressed as "Paisa". Being locals they are outside the scope of this catalogue.

1961. *Optd with Type* O **4**.

O68		1p. on 1½a. (No. 122)	10	10
		a. Optd with Type O **3**	4·25	1·75
O69		2p. on 3p. (No. 123) (1.1.61)	10	10
		a. Surch double		
		b. Optd with Type O **3**	7·00	3·75
O70		3p. on 6p. (No. 124)	10	10
O71		7p. on 1a. (No. 125)	10	10
		a. Optd with Type O **3**	7·50	9·00
O72		13p. on 2a. (No. 126)	10	10
O73		13p. on 2a. (No. 127)	10	10
O68/73 *Set of* 6			55	55

No. O68 exists with small and large "1" (see note below Nos. 122/7, etc.).

ERRORS. See note after No. 127.

SERVICE
(O 5)

1961–63. *Nos. 128/44b optd with Type* O **4** *(rupee values) or* O **5** *(others). (a) Inscribed* "SHAKISTAN".

O74		1p. violet (R.) (1.1.61)	10	10
O75		2p. rose-red (R.) (12.1.61)	10	10
O76		5p. ultramarine (R.) (23.3.61)	15	10
		a. Opt inverted		

(b) Inscribed "PAKISTAN"

O77		1p. violet (R.)	3·75	10
		a. Printed on the gummed side		
		b. Opt inverted		
O78		2p. rose-red (R.)	30	10
		a. Printed on the gummed side		
O79		3p. reddish purple (R.) (27.10.61)	10	10
O80		5p. ultramarine (R.)	7·50	10
O81		7p. emerald (R.) (23.3.61)	10	10
O82		10p. brown (R.)	10	10
		a. Opt inverted		
O83		13p. slate-violet (R.) (14.2.61)	10	10
O85		40p. deep purple (R.) (1.1.62)	10	10
O86		50p. deep bluish green (R.) (1.1.62)	15	10
		a. Opt double		
O87		75p. carmine-red (R.) (23.3.62)	20	10
		a. Opt double		
O88		1r. vermilion (7.1.63)	35	10
		a. Opt double	15·00	
		b. Opt as Type O **3**	16·00	16·00
		c. Opt inverted	12·00	
O89		2r. orange (7.1.63)	1·50	20
O90		5r. green (R.) (7.1.63)	4·25	7·00
O74/90 *Set of* 16			16·00	7·00

1963–78?. *Nos. 170, etc., optd with Type* O **5**, *in red.*

O91		1p. violet	10	10
O92		2p. rose-red (1965)	10	10
		a. Opt inverted	2·75	
		b. Albino opt		
		c. Opt double, one albino		
O93		3p. reddish purple (1967)	3·75	1·00
		a. Opt double	9·50	
		b. Opt inverted	3·75	
		c. Printed on the gummed side		
O94		5p. ultramarine	10	10
		a. Opt inverted	1·75	
		ab. Vert pair, top stamp without opt, lower with opt inverted		
O95		7p. emerald (date?)	17·00	12·00
O96		10p. brown (1965)	10	10
		a. Opt inverted	3·25	
O97		13p. slate-violet	10	10
O98		15p. bright purple (31.12.64)	10	2·00
O99		20p. myrtle-green (26.1.70)	10	40
		a. Opt double	24·00	
O100		25p. deep blue (1977)	12·00	3·75
O101		40p. deep purple (1972?)	15·00	6·50
O102		50p. deep bluish green (1965)	10	15
O103		75p. carmine-red (date?)	13·00	13·00
O104		90p. yellow-green (5.78?)	6·50	5·50
O91/104 *Set of* 14			60·00	40·00

1968?. *Nos. 204, 206 and 207 optd with Type* O **4**.

O105	**62**	1r. vermilion	3·25	70
		a. Opt inverted	13·00	
		b. Printed and overprinted on the gummed side	13·00	
		w. Wmk inverted	13·00	
O107		2r. orange (date?)	14·00	1·50
		a. Opt inverted	13·00	
O108		5r. green (R.) (date?)	21·00	7·00
		a. Opt inverted	17·00	
O105/8 *Set of* 3			35·00	8·25

BAHAWALPUR

Bahawalpur, a former feudatory state situated to the west of the Punjab, was briefly independent following the partition of India on 15 August 1947 before acceding to Pakistan on 3 October of the same year.

East India Company and later Indian Empire post offices operated in Bahawalpur from 1854. By a postal agreement of 1879 internal mail from the state administration was carried unstamped, but this arrangement was superseded by the issue of Official stamps in 1945.

These had been preceded by a series of pictorial stamps prepared in 1933–34 on unwatermarked paper. It was intended that these would be used as state postage stamps, but permission for such use was withheld by the Indian Government so they were used for revenue purposes. The same designs were utilised for the 1945 Official series, Nos. O1/6, on paper watermarked Star and Crescent. Residual stocks of the unwatermarked 1a., 8a., 1r. and 2r. were used for the provisional Officials, Nos. O7 and O11/13.

A commemorative 1a. Receipt stamp was produced to mark the centenary of the alliance with Great Britain. This may not have been ready until 1935, but an example of this stamp is known used on cover from Deh Rawal to Sadiq Garh and postmarked 14 August 1933. Both this 1a. and the same value from the unwatermarked set also exist with Official Arabic overprint in black. These were not issued for postal purposes although one used example of the latter has been recorded postmarked 22 February 1933 also from Deh Rawal.

Stamps of India were overprinted in the interim period between 15 August and 3 October 1947. After the state joined Pakistan postage stamps were issued for internal use until 1953.

PRICES FOR STAMPS ON COVER
The postage and Official stamps of Bahawalpur are rare used on cover.

Nawab (from 1947 Amir) Sadiq Mohammad Khan Abbasi V, 1907–1966

(1)

1947 (15 Aug). *Nos. 265/8, 269a/77 and 259/62 (King George VI) of India optd locally with T* **1**.

1	3p. slate (R.)	24·00
2	½a. purple	24·00
3	9p. green (R.)	24·00
4	1a. carmine	24·00
5	1½a. dull violet (R.)	24·00
6	2a. vermilion	24·00
	a. Opt double	£3000
7	3a. bright violet (R.)	24·00
8	3½a. bright blue (R.)	24·00
9	4a. brown	24·00
10	6a. turquoise-green (R.)	24·00
	a. Opt double	£3000
11	8a. slate-violet (R.)	24·00
12	12a. lake	24·00
13	14a. purple	65·00
14	1r. grey and red-brown	29·00
	a. Opt double, one albino	£350
15	2r. purple and brown (R.)	£1800
16	5r. green and blue (R.)	£1800
17	10r. purple and claret	£1800
1/17 *Set of* 17		£5500

Nos. 1/17 were issued during the interim period, following the implementation of the Indian Independence Act, during which time Bahawalpur was part of neither of the two Dominions created. The Amir acceded to the Dominion of Pakistan on 3 October 1947 and these overprinted stamps of India were then withdrawn.

The stamps of Bahawalpur only had validity for use within the state. For external mail Pakistan stamps were used.

PRINTERS. All the following issues were recess-printed by De La Rue & Co, Ltd, London.

2 Amir Muhammad Bahawal Khan I Abbasi

3

1947 (1 Dec). *Bicentenary Commemoration.* W **3** (sideways). P 12½×11½.

18	**2**	½a. black and carmine	3·00	4·25

4 H.H. the Amir of Bahawalpur

5 The Tombs of the Amirs

6 Mosque in Sadiq-Garh

7 Fort Derawar from the Lake

8 Nur-Mahal Palace

9 The Palace, Sadiq-Garh

10 H.H. the Amir of Bahawalpur

11 Three Generations of Rulers; H.H. the Amir in centre

1948 (1 Apr). W **3** (sideways on vert designs). P 12½ (T **4**), 11½×12½ (T **5**, **7**, **8** and **9**), 12½×11½ (T **6** and **10**) or 13½×14 (T **11**).

19	**4**	3p. black and blue	2·00	20·00
20		½a. black and claret	2·00	20·00
21		9p. black and green	2·00	20·00
22		1a. black and carmine	2·00	20·00
23		1½a. black and violet	3·00	16·00
24	**5**	2a. green and carmine	3·00	20·00
25	**6**	4a. orange and brown	3·00	20·00
26	**7**	6a. violet and blue	3·50	20·00
27	**8**	8a. carmine and violet	3·50	20·00
28	**9**	12a. green and carmine	3·75	30·00
29	**10**	1r. violet and brown	19·00	42·00
30		2r. green and claret	50·00	70·00
31		5r. black and violet	50·00	85·00
32	**11**	10r. scarlet and black	32·00	£100
19/32 *Set of* 14			£160	£450

12 H.H. The Amir of Bahawalpur and Mohammed Ali Jinnah

13 Soldiers of 1848 and 1948

1948 (3 Oct). *First Anniv of Union of Bahawalpur with Pakistan.* W **3**. P 13.

33	**12**	1½a. carmine and blue-green	1·50	4·00

1948 (15 Oct). *Multan Campaign Centenary.* W **3**. P 11½.

34	**13**	1½a. black and lake	1·25	10·00

1948. *As Nos. 29/32, but colours changed.*

35	**10**	1r. deep green and orange	1·75	18·00
36		2r. black and carmine	1·75	22·00
37		5r. chocolate and ultramarine	1·90	40·00
38	**11**	10r. red-brown and green	2·00	45·00
35/8 *Set of* 4			6·50	£110

14 Irrigation

15 Wheat

16 Cotton

17 Sahiwal bull

1949 (3 Mar). *Silver Jubilee of Accession of H.H. the Amir of Bahawalpur. T* **14/17**. W **3**. P 14.

39	3p. black and ultramarine	10	8·00
40	½a. black and brown-orange	10	8·00
41	9p. black and green	10	8·00
42	1a. black and carmine	10	8·00
39/42 *Set of* 4		35	29·00

Nos. 39/42 exist imperforate (*Prices, £20 per pair, unused*).

18 U.P.U. Monument, Berne

1949 (10 Oct). *75th Anniv of Universal Postal Union.* W **3**. P 13.

43	**18**	9p. black and green	20	1·25
		a. Perf 17½×17	1·25	18·00
44		1a. black and magenta	20	1·25
		a. Perf 17½×17	1·25	18·00
45		1½a. black and orange	20	1·25
		a. Perf 17½×17	1·25	18·00
46		2½a. black and blue	20	1·25
		a. Perf 17½×17	1·25	18·00
43/6 *Set of* 4			70	4·50
43a/6a *Set of* 4			4·50	60·00

Nos. 43/6 exist imperforate (*Prices, £10 per pair, unused*).

OFFICIAL STAMPS

O **1** Panjnad Weir

O **2** Dromedary and Calf

O **3** Blackbuck

O **4** Eastern White Pelicans

O **5** Friday Mosque, Fort Derawar

O **6** Temple at Pattan Munara

1945 (1 Mar). *Various horizontal pictorial designs, with red Arabic opt.* W **3**. P 14.

O1	O **1**	½a. black and green	5·50	14·00
O2	O **2**	1a. black and carmine	3·75	11·00
		a. Opt omitted	†	£1100
O3	O **3**	2a. black and violet	3·25	12·00
O4	O **4**	4a. black and olive-green	12·00	26·00
O5	O **5**	8a. black and brown	26·00	18·00
O6	O **6**	1r. black and orange	26·00	18·00
O1/6 *Set of* 6			70·00	90·00

Permission for the introduction of Nos. O1/6 was granted by the Imperial Government as from 1 January 1945, but the stamps were not used until 1 March. First Day covers exist showing the January date.

Examples of No. O2a come from a sheet used at Rahimya Khan.

It is believed that examples of Nos. O1/2 in different shades and with white gum appeared in 1949 and were included in the Silver Jubilee Presentation Booklet.

O **7** Baggage Camels

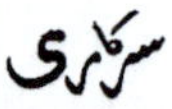

(O **8**)

1945 (10 Mar). *Revenue stamp with red Arabic opt.* No wmk. P 14.

O7	O **7**	1a. black and brown	55·00	65·00

1945 (Mar–June). *Surch as Type* O **8** *(at Security Printing Press, Nasik) instead of red Arabic opt.* No wmk. P 14.

O11	O **5**	½a. on 8a. black and purple	5·50	7·00
O12	O **6**	1½a. on 1r. black and orange	40·00	11·00
O13	O **1**	1½a. on 2r. black and blue (1 June)	£130	8·50
O11/13 *Set of* 3			£160	24·00

The stamps used as a basis for Nos. O7 and O11/13 were part of the Revenue series issued in 1933–34.

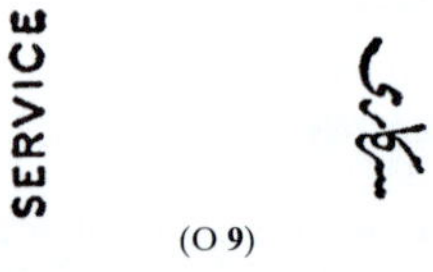
(O **9**)

O **10** H.H. the Amir of Bahawalpur

1945. *Optd with Type* O **9** *(by D.L.R.) instead of red Arabic opt.* No wmk. P 14.

O14	O **1**	½a. black and carmine	1·25	11·00
O15	O **2**	1a. black and carmine	2·00	13·00
O16	O **3**	2a. black and orange	3·25	45·00
O14/16 *Set of* 3			5·75	60·00

1945. P 14.

O17	O **10**	3p. black and blue	4·00	11·00
O18		1½a. black and violet	20·00	8·00

O **11** Allied Banners

(Des E. Meronti. Recess, background litho)

1946 (1 May). *Victory.* P 14.

O19	O **11**	1½a. green and grey	3·50	4·25

1948. *Nos. 19, 22, 24/5 and 35/8 optd as Nos. O1/6.*

O20	**4**	3p. black and blue (R.)	80	12·00
O21		1a. black and carmine (Blk.)	80	11·00
O22	**5**	2a. green and carmine (Blk.)	80	12·00
O23	**6**	4a. orange and brown (Blk.)	80	16·00
O24	**10**	1r. deep green and orange (R.)	80	18·00
O25		2r. black and carmine (R.)	80	24·00
O26		5r. chocolate and ultramarine (R.)	80	40·00
O27	**11**	10r. red-brown and green (R.)	80	40·00
O20/7 *Set of* 8			5·75	£150

1949 (10 Oct). *75th Anniv of Universal Postal Union. Nos. 43/6 optd as Nos. O1/6.*

O28	**18**	9p. black and green	15	4·50
		aw. Wmk inverted	†	£325
		b. Perf 17½×17	2·50	29·00
O29		1a. black and magenta	15	4·50
		b. Perf 17½×17	2·50	29·00
O30		1½a. black and orange	15	4·50
		b. Perf 17½×17	2·50	29·00
O31		2½a. black and blue	15	4·50
		b. Perf 17½×17	2·50	29·00
O28/31 *Set of* 4			55	16·00
O28b/31b *Set of* 4			9·00	£100

Nos. O28/31 exist imperforate (*Prices*, £10 *per pair, unused*).

From 1947 stamps of Pakistan were used on all external mail. Bahawalpur issues continued to be used on internal mail until 1953.

Palestine

The stamps of TURKEY were used in Palestine from 1865.

In addition various European Powers, and Egypt, maintained post offices at Jerusalem (Austria, France, Germany, Italy, Russia), Jaffa (Austria, Egypt, France, Germany, Russia) and Haifa (Austria, France) using their own stamps or issues specially prepared for Levant post offices. All foreign post offices had closed by the time of the British Occupation.

PRICES FOR STAMPS ON COVER TO 1945

No. 1	*from* × 6
No. 2	*from* × 4
Nos. 3/4	*from* × 5
Nos. 5/15	*from* × 4
Nos. 16/29	*from* × 3
Nos. 30/42	*from* × 2
No. 43	—
Nos. 44/57	*from* × 2
Nos. 58/9	—
Nos. 60/8	*from* × 3
Nos. 69/70	—
Nos. 71/89	*from* × 3
Nos. 90/103	*from* × 4
Nos. 104/11	*from* × 8
Nos. D1/5	*from* × 30
Nos. D6/20	*from* × 10

BRITISH MILITARY OCCUPATION

British and allied forces invaded Palestine in November 1917 capturing Gaza (7 November), Jaffa (16 November) and Jerusalem (9 December). The front line then stabilised until the second British offensive of September 1918.

Nos. 1/15 were issued by the British military authorities for use by the civilian population in areas they controlled previously, part of the Ottoman Empire. Before the issue of Nos. 1/2 in February 1918, civilian mail was carried free. In addition to Palestine the stamps were available from E.E.F. post offices in Syria (including what subsequently became Transjordan) from 23 September 1918 to 23 February 1922, Lebanon from 21 October 1918 to September 1920 and Cilicia from 2 September 1919 to 16 July 1920. Use in the following post offices outside Palestine is recorded in *British Empire Campaigns and Occupations in the Near East, 1914–1924* by John Firebrace:

Adana, Cilicia
Akkari ("Akkar"), Syria
Aleih ("Alie"), Lebanon
Aleppo ("Alep, Halep"), Syria
Alexandretta, Syria
Antakie, Syria
Baalbek, Lebanon
Bab, Syria
Babitoma, Syria
Ba'abda, Lebanon
Behamdoun, Lebanon
Beit Mery, Beyrouth Lebanon
Beit ed Dine, Lebanon
Bekaa, Lebanon
Beyrouth, Lebanon
Bouzanti, Syria
Broumana, Lebanon
Damascus ("Damas"), Syria
Damour ("Damor"), Lebanon
Der'a ("Deraa"), Syria
Deurt-Yol, Syria
Djey Han, Syria
Djezzin ("Djezzine"), Lebanon
Djon, Lebanon
Djounie, Lebanon
Djubeil, Lebanon
Douma, Syria
Edleb, Syria
Feke, Turkey
Habib Souk, Syria
Hajjin ("Hadjin"), Cilicia
Hama, Syria
Hasbaya, Lebanon
Hasine, Cilicia
Hommana, Lebanon
Homs, Syria
Kozan, Cilicia
Lattakia ("Laskie, Lattaquie"), Syria
Massel el Chouf ("Moussalc"), Lebanon
Merdjajoun Lebanon
Mersina ("Mersine"), Cilicia
Mounboudje, Syria
Nabatti, Lebanon
Nebk ("Nebik"), Syria
Payass, Syria
Racheya, Lebanon
Safita, Syria
Savour, Tyre, Lebanon
Selimie, Syria
Sidan ("Saida (Echelle)"), Lebanon
Suweidiya ("Suvedie"), Syria
Talia, Syria
Tarsous, Cilicia
Tartous, Syria
Tibnin, Lebanon
Tripoli, Syria
Zahle, Lebanon
Zebdani, Syria

This information is reproduced here by permission of the publishers, Robson Lowe Publications.

(Currency. 10 milliemes = 1 piastre)

1 (2) 3

"E.E.F." = Egyptian Expeditionary Force

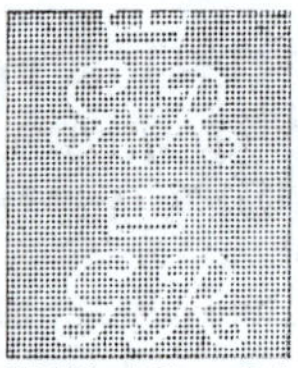

W **100** of Great Britain

(Des G. Rowntree. Litho Typographical Dept, Survey of Egypt, Giza, Cairo)

1918 (10 Feb). Wmk Royal Cypher in column (W **100** of Great Britain). *Ungummed. Roul 20.*

1	**1**	1p. indigo	£180	£100
		a. Deep blue	£150	90·00
		b. Blue	£150	90·00
		s. Optd "Specimen"	£300	

Control: A 18 (*Prices, corner block of 4*; No. 1 £850. No. 1*a*, £750. No. 1*b*, £850).

1918 (16 Feb). *As last (ungummed) surch with T* **2**.

2	**1**	5m. on 1p. cobalt-blue	£100	£475
		a. "MILLILMES" (R. 1/10)	£3250	£9000
		s. Optd "Specimen"	£300	
		w. Wmk inverted		

Control: B 18 A (*Corner block*, £1100).

1918 (5 Mar). *As No. 1 but colour changed. With gum.*

3	**1**	1p. ultramarine (*shades*)	2·00	2·00
		a. Crown missing from wmk	42·00	
		b. Printed on the gummed side		
		w. Wmk inverted	£180	£225

Control: C 18. (*Corner block*, £70).

1918 (5 Mar–13 May). *No. 3 surch with T* **2**.

4	**1**	5m. on 1p. ultramarine	5·50	2·25
		a. Arabic surch wholly or partly missing (R. 1/11)	£325	£400
		b. Crown missing from wmk	65·00	
		w. Wmk inverted	£250	

Controls: C 18 B (Mar). (*Corner block*, £700).
D 18 C (May). (*Corner block*, £200).

(Typo Stamping Dept, Board of Inland Revenue, Somerset House, London)

1918 (16 July–27 Dec). Wmk Royal Cypher in column (W **100** of Great Britain). P 15×14.

5	**3**	1m. sepia	30	40
		a. Deep brown	40	40
6		2m. blue-green	30	45
		a. Deep green	1·50	80
7		3m. yellow-brown (17 Dec)	35	35
		a. Chestnut	13·00	6·00
8		4m. scarlet	35	40
9		5m. yellow-orange (25 Sept)	3·25	50
		a. Orange	65	30
		b. Crown missing from wmk	£140	
		w. Wmk inverted	—	£1500
10		1p. deep indigo (9 Nov)	35	25
		a. Crown missing from wmk	£120	
		w. Wmk inverted	£150	£160
11		2p. pale olive	1·75	60
		a. Olive	2·25	1·10
12		5p. purple	2·50	2·25
13		9p. ochre (17 Dec)	6·50	6·00
14		10p. ultramarine (17 Dec)	6·50	3·75
		w. Wmk inverted	£400	
15		20p. pale grey (27 Dec)	13·00	17·00
		a. Slate-grey	18·00	23·00
5/15 *Set of* 11			29·00	28·00

There are two sizes of the design of this issue:
19×23 mm. 1, 2, and 4m., and 2 and 5p.
18×21½ mm. 3 and 5m., and 1, 9, 10 and 20p.

There are numerous minor plate varieties in this issue, such as stops omitted in "E.E.F.", malformed Arabic characters, etc.

CIVIL ADMINISTRATION UNDER BRITISH HIGH COMMISSIONER

Palestine was placed under civil administration by a British High Commissioner on 1 July 1920.

(4) (5) (6)

Differences:—
T **5**. 20 mm vert and 7 mm between English and Hebrew.
T **6**. 19 mm and 6 mm respectively.

Two settings of Type **4**:

Setting I (used for Nos. 16/26). This consisted of two horizontal rows of 12 of which the first setting row appeared on Rows 1, 3/7, 15, 17/18 and 20 of the sheet and the second on Rows 2, 8/14, 16 and 19.

On the first position in the top setting row the Arabic "t" (third character from the left) is incorrectly shown as an Arabic "z" by the addition of a dot to its right. On the eleventh position in the same row the first two letters in the Hebrew overprint were transposed so that " character appears first. On row 12 stamp 1 the final "E" of "PALESTINE" appears as a "B" on certain values. Once the errors were noticed vertical columns one and eleven were removed from the remaining sheets.

"PALESTINB"

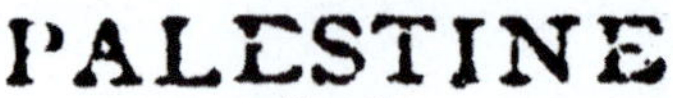

Normal

Setting II (used for Nos. 16/29). This consisted of a single horizontal row of 12 reproduced to overprint the complete sheet of 240. The order in which the horizontal rows were used was changed several times during overprinting. During one such re-arrangement a damaged impression was replaced by one from Setting I showing the Arabic "z" error. (R. 14/8 for 1, 2, 3, 4, 5m (P 14), 20p.). The "B" error also occurs in the second setting, once in each sheet on either R. 17/8, 18/8 or 19/8.

(Optd at Greek Orthodox Convent, Jerusalem)

1920 (1 Sept). *Optd with T* **4** *(Arabic 8 mm long).*

(*a*) P 15×14.

16	**3**	1m. sepia	5·50	1·90
		b. Arabic "z" (Settings I and II)	£1000	
		c. Hebrew characters transposed (I)	£1000	
		d. "PALESTINB" (II)	80·00	
17		2m. blue-green	8·50	4·50
		b. "Arabic "z" (Settings I and II)	£850	
		c. Hebrew characters transposed (I)	£850	
		d. "PALESTINB" (II)	90·00	
18		3m. chestnut	11·00	5·00
		a. Opt inverted	£475	£600
		b. Arabic "z" (Settings I and II)	£1500	
		c. Hebrew characters transposed (I)	£1500	
		d. "PALESTINB" (II)	50·00	
19		4m. scarlet	3·50	1·25
		b. Arabic "z" (Settings I and II)	£1500	
		c. Hebrew characters transposed (I)	£1500	
		d. PALESTINB" (II)	50·00	
20		5m. yellow-orange	18·00	4·25
		c. Hebrew characters transposed (I)	†	£2500
		d. "PALESTINB" (II)	95·00	
21		1p. deep indigo (Sil.)	4·25	80
		d. "PALESTINB" (II)	25·00	
		w. Wmk inverted	£120	£130
22		2p. deep olive	4·75	1·90
		a. Crown missing from wmk	£500	
		b. Arabic "z" (I)	£180	
		c. Hebrew characters transposed (I)	£180	
		d. "PALESTINB" (Settings I and II)	95·00	
23		5p. deep purple	22·00	23·00
		b. Arabic "z" (I)	£900	
		c. Hebrew characters transposed (I)	£500	
		d. "PALESTINB" (Setting I and II)	£150	
24		9p. ochre	11·00	20·00
		b. Arabic "z" (I)	£400	
		c. Hebrew characters transposed (I)	£450	
		d. "PALESTINB" (Settings I and II)	£170	
25		10p. ultramarine	11·00	17·00
		b. Arabic "z" (I)	£300	
		c. Hebrew characters transposed (I)	£400	
		d. "PALESTINB" (Settings I and II)	£225	
26		20p. pale grey	29·00	45·00
		b. Arabic "z" (Settings I and II)	£800	
		c. Hebrew characters transposed (I)	£900	
		d. "PALESTINB" (Settings I and II)	£1800	
16/26 *Set of* 11			£110	£110

(*b*) P 14.

27	**3**	2m. blue-green	2·25	1·40
		d. "PALESTINB" (II)	35·00	
28		3m. chestnut	60·00	55·00
29		5m. orange	3·75	45
		d. "PALESTINB" (II)	75·00	

Faulty registration of the overprint in this issue has resulted in numerous misplaced overprints, either vertically or horizontally, which are not of great importance with the exception of Nos. 21 and 29 which exist with the overprint out of sequence, i.e. Hebrew/Arabic/English or English/Arabic/Hebrew or English/Hebrew only. Also all values are known with Arabic/English only.

1920 (Dec)–**21**. *Optd with T* **5*** *(Arabic 10 mm long).*

(*a*) P 15×14.

30	**3**	1m. sepia (27.12.20)	2·25	1·00
		a. Opt inverted	£425	†
31		2m. blue-green (27.12.20)	8·00	4·00
		a. Opt double		
32		3m. yellow-brown (27.12.20)	3·50	1·00
33		4m. scarlet (27.12.20)	5·00	1·25
34		5m. yellow-orange	2·25	50
35		1p. deep indigo (Silver) (21.6.21)	£475	29·00
36		2p. olive (21.6.21)	65·00	28·00
37		5p. deep purple (21.6.21)	48·00	9·50

(*b*) P 14.

38	**3**	1m. sepia	£650	£750
39		2m. blue-green	4·00	4·00
40		4m. scarlet	60·00	75·00
41		5m. orange	85·00	9·00
		a. Yellow-orange	8·50	1·10
42		1p. deep indigo (Silver)	50·00	1·25
43		5p. purple	£200	£450

*In this setting the Arabic and Hebrew characters are badly worn and blunted, the Arabic "S" and "T" are joined (i.e. there is no break in the position indicated by the arrow in our illustration); the letters of "PALESTINE" are often irregular or broken; and the space between the two groups of Hebrew characters varies from 1 mm to over 1¾ mm. The " character in the left-hand Hebrew word extends above the remainder of the line (*For clear, sharp overprint, see Nos.* 47/59.).

The dates of issue given are irrespective of the perforations, i.e. one or both perfs could have been issued on the dates shown.

Nos. 31 and 39 exist with any one line of the overprint partly missing.

1920 (6 Dec). *Optd with T* **6**.

(*a*) P 15×14.

44	**3**	3m. yellow-brown	50·00	32·00
44*a*		5m. yellow-orange	£14000	£12000

(*b*) P 14.

45	**3**	1m. sepia	50·00	32·00
46		5m. orange	£375	30·00

(6a) (7) (8)

1921 (29 May–4 Aug). *Optd as T* **6a**.

(*a*) P 15×14.

47	**3**	1m. sepia (23.6)	13·00	3·50
48		2m. blue-green (18.6)	23·00	5·50
49		3m. yellow-brown (23.6)	30·00	3·00
50		4m. scarlet (23.6)	30·00	3·50
51		5m. yellow-orange	60·00	1·00
52		1p. deep indigo (Silver) (1.7)	18·00	75
53		2p. olive (4.8)	23·00	6·00
54		5p. purple (4.8)	25·00	8·00
55		9p. ochre (4.8)	50·00	90·00
56		10p. ultramarine (4.8)	60·00	14·00
57		20p. pale grey (4.8)	90·00	50·00
47/57 *Set of* 11			£375	£160

(b) P 14.

58 3 1m. sepia — £2000
59 20p. pale grey £12000 £2500

In this setting the Arabic and Hebrew characters are sharp and pointed and there is usually a break between the Arabic "S" and "T", though this is sometimes filled with ink. The space between the two groups of Hebrew characters is always 1¾ mm. The top of the " character in the Hebrew aligns with the remainder of the word.

The 3m. with "PALESTINE" omitted is an essay (*Price* £2500 *unused*).

1921 (26 Sept)–**22**. *Optd with T* **7** *("PALESTINE" in sans-serif letters) by Stamping Dept, Board of Inland Revenue, Somerset House, London.* Wmk Royal Cypher in column (W **100** of Great Britain). P 15×14.

60 3 1m. sepia (5.10.21) 1·25 30
61 2m. blue-green (11.10.21) 2·00 30
62 3m. yellow-brown (17.10.21) 2·25 30
63 4m. scarlet (15.10.21) 2·75 60
64 5m. yellow-orange 2·50 30
65 1p. bright turquoise-blue (14.11.21) 2·00 35
66 2p. olive (7.12.21) 3·25 40
67 5p. deep purple (11.12.21) 8·00 5·00
68 9p. ochre (10.3.22) 17·00 14·00
69 10p. ultramarine (10.3.22) 22·00 £500
w. Wmk inverted † —
70 20p. pale grey (10.3.22) 55·00 £1400
60/70 *Set of* 11 £100

Dates quoted are of earliest known postmarks.

(Printed and optd by Waterlow & Sons from new plates)

1922 (Sept–Nov). *T* **3** *(redrawn), optd with T* **8**. Wmk Mult Script CA.

(a) P 14.

71 3 1m. sepia 1·25 30
a. *Deep brown* 2·00 30
b. Opt inverted — £12000
c. Opt double £225 £425
w. Wmk inverted 38·00 27·00
72 2m. yellow 1·50 30
a. *Orange-yellow* 4·00 50
b. Wmk sideways † £1500
w. Wmk inverted 32·00 32·00
73 3m. greenish blue 2·25 15
w. Wmk inverted 32·00 32·00
74 4m. carmine-pink 2·25 20
w. Wmk inverted 40·00 40·00
75 5m. orange 2·50 30
w. Wmk inverted 55·00 40·00
76 6m. blue-green 2·00 30
w. Wmk inverted 42·00 42·00
77 7m. yellow-brown 2·00 30
w. Wmk inverted £200 £200
78 8m. scarlet 2·00 30
w. Wmk inverted 48·00 55·00
79 1p. grey 2·50 30
w. Wmk inverted 55·00 55·00
80 13m. ultramarine 2·75 15
w. Wmk inverted 32·00 22·00
81 2p. olive 3·00 35
a. Opt inverted £300 £500
b. *Ochre* £130 6·50
w. Wmk inverted £180 £140
82 5p. deep purple 4·75 1·25
aw. Wmk inverted † £550
82*b* 9p. ochre £900 £200
83 10p. light blue 70·00 13·00
a. "E.F.F." for "E.E.F." in bottom panel (R. 10/3) £700 £400
84 20p. bright violet £160 £110

(b) P 15×14.

86 3 5p. deep purple 55·00 4·00
87 9p. ochre 9·00 9·00
88 10p. light blue 7·50 2·50
a. "E.F.F." for "E.E.F." in bottom panel (R. 10/3) £400 £300
w. Wmk inverted £425 £225
89 20p. bright violet 9·00 5·50
71s/89s Optd "Specimen" *Set of* 15 £425

Most values can be found on thin paper.

In this issue the design of all denominations is the same size, 18×21½ mm. Varieties may be found with one or other of the stops between "E.E.F." missing.

BRITISH MANDATE TO THE LEAGUE OF NATIONS

The League of Nations granted a mandate to Great Britain for the administration of Palestine on 29 September 1923.

(New Currency. 1,000 mils = 1 Palestine pound)

9 Rachel's Tomb

10 Dome of the Rock

11 Citadel, Jerusalem

12 Sea of Galilee

(Des F. Taylor. Typo Harrison)

1927 (1 June)–**45**. Wmk Mult Script CA. P 13½×14½ (2m. to 20m.) or 14.

90 9 2m. greenish blue (14.8.27) 2·00 10
w. Wmk inverted † £500
91 3m. yellow-green 1·50 10
w. Wmk inverted † £250
92 10 4m. rose-pink (14.8.27) 6·50 1·25
93 11 5m. orange (14.8.27) 3·25 10
a. From coils. Perf 14½×14 (1936) 14·00 18·00
ac. Yellow. From coils. Perf 14½×14 (1945) 40·00 28·00
aw. Wmk inverted 17·00 25·00
b. Yellow (12.44) 3·75 15
w. Wmk inverted 27·00 28·00
94 10 6m. pale green (14.8.27) 4·75 1·75
a. *Deep green* 1·00 20
95 11 7m. scarlet (14.8.27) 9·00 60
96 10 8m. yellow-brown (14.8.27) 15·00 6·00
97 9 10m. slate (14.8.27) 1·50 10
a. *Grey*. From coils. Perf 14½×14 (11.38) 20·00 25·00
aw. Wmk inverted
b. Grey (1944) 1·50 10
98 10 13m. ultramarine 10·00 30
99 11 20m. dull olive-green (14.8.27) 2·75 15
a. *Bright olive-green* (12.44) 1·50 15
w. Wmk inverted † £350
100 12 50m. deep dull purple (14.8.27) 1·75 30
a. *Bright purple* (12.44) 4·00 30
x. Wmk reversed — £425
101 90m. bistre (14.8.27) 65·00 60·00
102 100m. turquoise-blue (14.8.27) 2·25 70
103 200m. deep violet (14.8.27) 8·00 5·00
a. *Bright violet* (1928) 35·00 16·00
b. *Blackish violet* (12.44) 10·00 3·50
90/103*b* *Set of* 14 £120 65·00
90s/103s Handstamped "Specimen" *Set of* 14 £375

Three sets may be made of the above issue; one on thin paper, one on thicker paper with a ribbed appearance, and another on thick white paper without ribbing.

2m. stamps in the grey colour of the 10m., including an example postmarked in 1935, exist as do 50m. stamps in blue, but it has not been established whether they were issued.

Nos. 90/1 and 93 exist in coils, constructed from normal sheets.

1932 (1 June)–**44**. *New values and colours*. Wmk Mult Script CA. P 13½×14½ (4m. to 15m.) or 14.

104 10 4m. purple (1.11.32) 1·50 10
w. Wmk inverted † £425
105 11 7m. deep violet 75 10
106 10 8m. scarlet 1·25 20
w. Wmk inverted † £550
107 13m. bistre (1.8.32) 2·00 10
108 15m. ultramarine (1.8.32) 4·75 10
a. *Grey-blue* (12.44) 4·25 40
b. *Greenish blue* 4·25 40
w. Wmk inverted † £550
109 12 250m. brown (15.1.42) 5·00 3·00
110 500m. scarlet (15.1.42) 5·00 3·00
111 £P1 black (15.1.42) 7·00 3·50
104/11 *Set of* 8 24·00 9·00
104s/11s Perf "Specimen" *Set of* 8 £425

No. 108 exists in coils, constructed from normal sheets.

STAMP BOOKLETS

1929. *Blue cover inscr* "PALESTINE POSTAGE STAMP BOOKLET" *and contents in English. Without advertisements on front. Stitched.*

SB1 150m. booklet containing twelve 2m., 3m. and eighteen 5m. (Nos. 90/1, 93) in blocks of 6 £2000
a. As No. SB1, but stapled £1600

1933. *Blue cover inscr* "PALESTINE POSTS & TELEGRAPHS POSTAGE STAMP BOOKLET" *and contents all in English, Arabic and Hebrew. Without advertisements on front. Stapled.*

SB2 150m. booklet. Contents as No. SB1

1937–38. *Red cover inscr* "POSTAGE STAMP BOOKLET" *and contents in English, Hebrew and Arabic. With advertisements on front. Stapled.*

SB3 150m. booklet containing 2m., 3m., 5m. and 15m. (Nos. 90/1, 93, 108) in blocks of 6 £1600
a. Blue cover (1938) £1600

1939. *Pink cover inscr* "POSTAGE STAMP BOOKLET" *and contents in English, Hebrew and Arabic. With advertisements on front. Stapled.*

SB4 120m. booklet containing six 10m. and twelve 5m. (Nos. 93, 97) in blocks of 6 £1500

POSTAL FISCALS

Type-set stamps inscribed "O.P.D.A." (= Ottoman Public Debt Administration) or "H.J.Z." (Hejaz Railway); British 1d. stamps of 1912–24 and Palestine stamps overprinted with one or other of the above groups of letters, or with the word "Devair", with or without surcharge of new value, are fiscal stamps. They are known used as postage stamps, alone, or with other stamps to make up the correct rates, and were passed by the postal authorities, although they were not definitely authorised for postal use.

POSTAGE DUE STAMPS

D 1

D 2 (MILLIEME)

D 3 (MIL)

(Typo Greek Orthodox Convent Press, Jerusalem)

1923 (1 Apr). P 11.

D1 D 1 1m. yellow-brown 18·00 26·00
a. Imperf (pair) £325
b. Imperf between (horiz pair) £1200
D2 2m. blue-green 14·00 10·00
a. Imperf (pair) £450
D3 4m. scarlet 10·00 10·00
D4 8m. mauve 7·00 7·00
a. Imperf (pair) £140
b. Imperf between (horiz pair) † £2250
D5 13m. steel blue 6·00 6·50
a. Imperf between (horiz pair) £1000
D1/5 *Set of* 5 50·00 55·00

Perfectly centred and perforated stamps of this issue are worth considerably more than the above prices, which are for average specimens.

(Types D **2/3**. Typo D.L.R.)

1924 (3 Oct). Wmk Mult Script CA. P 14.

D6 D 2 1m. deep brown 90 2·00
D7 2m. yellow 3·00 1·75
w. Wmk inverted † £475
D8 4m. green 2·00 1·25
D9 8m. scarlet 3·00 90
D10 13m. ultramarine 2·75 2·50
D11 5p. violet 10·00 1·75
D6/11 *Set of* 6 19·00 9·00
D6s/11s Optd "Specimen" *Set of* 6 £300

1928 (1 Feb)–**45**. Wmk Mult Script CA. P 14.

D12 D 3 1m. brown 1·50 85
a. Perf 15×14 (1944) 40·00 75·00
D13 2m. yellow 2·00 60
w. Wmk inverted † £475
D14 4m. green 2·50 1·60
a. Perf 15×14 (1945) 70·00 90·00
D15 6m. orange-brown (10.33) 18·00 5·00
D16 8m. carmine 2·25 1·00
D17 10m. pale grey 1·50 60
D18 13m. ultramarine 3·25 1·75
D19 20m. pale olive-green 3·25 1·25
D20 50m. violet 3·50 1·25
D12/20 *Set of* 9 35·00 14·00
D12s/20s Optd or Perf (6m.) "Specimen" *Set of* 9 £350

Nos. D12a and D14a were printed and perforated by Harrison and Sons following bomb damage to the De La Rue works on 29 December 1940.

The British Mandate terminated on 14 May 1948. Later issues of stamps and occupation issues will be found listed under Gaza, Israel and Jordan in Part 19 (*Middle East*) of this catalogue.

Papua *see after* **Australia**

Penrhyn Island
see after **Cook Islands**

Pitcairn Islands

CROWN COLONY

The settlement of Pitcairn Island by the *Bounty* mutineers in 1790 was not discovered until the American whaler *Topaz*, Capt. Mayhew Folger, called there in 1808. A visit by two Royal Navy frigates followed in 1814 and reports from their captains resulted in considerable interest being taken in the inhabitants' welfare by religious and philanthropic circles in Great Britain.

Due to overcrowding the population was resettled on Tahiti in 1831, but many soon returned to Pitcairn which was taken under British protection in 1838. The island was again evacuated in 1856, when the inhabitants were moved to Norfolk Island, but a number of families sailed back to their original home in 1859 and 1864.

The earliest surviving letter from the island is dated 1849. Before 1921 the mail service was irregular, as it depended on passing ships, and mail for the island was often sent via Tahiti. Some covers, purportedly sent from Pitcairn between 1883 and 1890 are known handstamped "Pitcairn Island" or "PITCAIRN ISLAND", but these are now believed to be forgeries.

In 1920 a regular mail service was introduced. As there were no stamps available, letters were allowed free postage as long as they carried a cachet, or manuscript endorsement, indicating their origin. Illustrations of Cachets I/VI, VIII, VIIIa, X and XIII are taken from *Pitcairn Islands Postal Markings 1883–1991*, published by the Pitcairn Islands Study Group, and are reproduced by permission of the author, Mr. Cy Kitching. Cachets I to XIII are shown three-quarter size.

Cachet I

Cat No. *Value on cover*
C1 **1920–25.** Cachet I (62×8 *mm*) (*violet or black*) £3250

Cachet II

C2 **1921–25.** Cachet II (*violet or red*) £2750

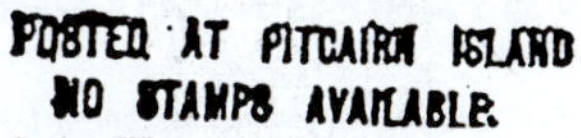

Cachet III

C3 **1922–28.** Cachet III (49×8½ *mm*) (*vio, pur or blk*) £2000

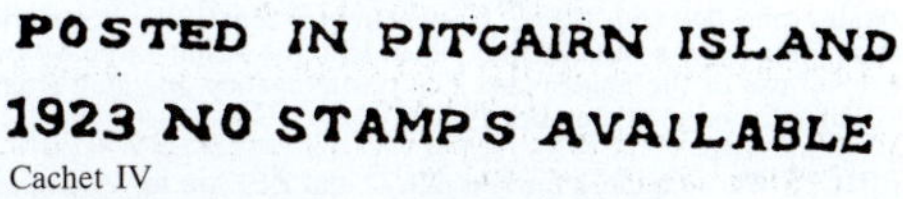

Cachet IV

C4 **1923.** Cachet IV (*black*) £2750

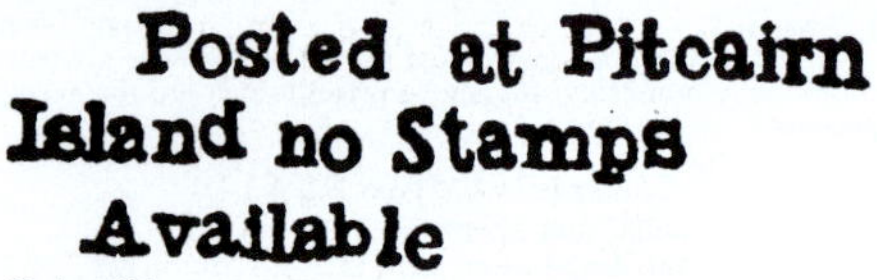

Cachet IVa

C4*a*	**1923.** Cachet IVa (73½×22 *mm*) (*red*)	£2750

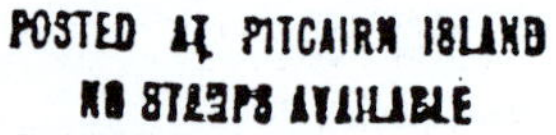

Cachet V

C5	**1923–28.** (Aug). Cachet V (47×9 *mm*) (*red, violet or black*)	£2500
C5*a*	**1925–26.** As Cachet V, but second line shown as "No Stamps Available" (*black*)	

Cachet VI

C6	**1923.** Cachet VI (*blue-green or red*)	
C7	**1923.** As Cachet V, but in three lines (*red*)	

Cachet VII

C8	**1923–27.** Cachet VII (*violet or black*)	£1900
C9	**1924.** As Cachet IV, but dated "1924" (*black*)	£2500

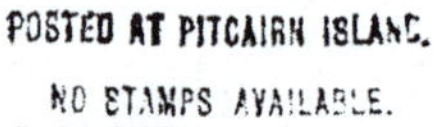

Cachet VIII

C10	**1924–26.** Cachet VIII (36×8 *mm*) (*vio, blk or red*)	£2500

Cachet VIIIa

C10*a*	**1924–26.** Cachet VIIIa (36×8¾ *mm*) (*vio or blk*)	£2000

Cachet IX

C11	**1924–26.** (Feb)–**25.** Cachet IX (63×7 *mm*) (*vio or blk*)	£2750

Cachet IXa

C11*a*	**1924.** Cachet IXa (58×8½ *mm*) (*vio or blk*)	
C12	**1925.** (Sept). As Cachet IV, but dated "1925" (*blk*)	£2500

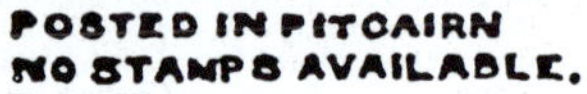

Cachet X

C13	**1925.** Cachet X (48×5 *mm*)	£2250

Cachet XI

C14	**1925–26.** Cachet XI (50×10 *mm*) (*violet or blk*)	£2500

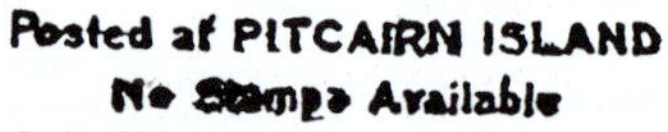

Cachet XII

C15	**1925.** Cachet XII (55×7½ *mm*) (*violet*)	
C15a	As Cachet XII but "POSTED AT" in capital letters	

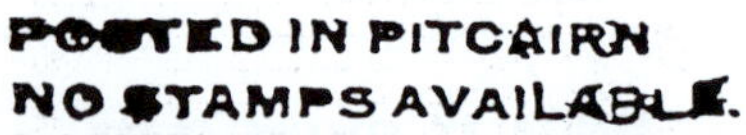

Cachet XIII

C16	**1926.** (Jan). Cachet XIII (64×8 *mm*) (*pur or blk*)	£3000

The New Zealand Government withdrew the free postage concession on 12 May 1926, but after representations from the islanders, opened a postal agency on Pitcairn using New Zealand stamps cancelled with Type Z **1**. Some impressions of this postmark appear to show a double ring, but this is the result of heavy or uneven use of the handstamp. The postal agency operated from 7 June 1927 until 14 October 1940.

PRICES. Those quoted for Nos. Z1/72 and ZF1 are for examples showing a virtually complete strike of Type Z **1**. Due to the size of the cancellation such examples will usually be on piece.

Z 1

Stamps of New Zealand cancelled with Type Z **1**.

1915–29. *King George V (Nos. 419, 422/6, 428/31 and 446/9).*

Z1	½d. green	28·00
Z2	1½d. grey-slate	65·00
Z3	1½d. orange-brown	50·00
Z4	2d. yellow	45·00
Z5	2½d. blue	85·00
Z6	3d. chocolate	90·00
Z7	4d. bright violet	85·00
Z8	4½d. deep green	£100
Z9	5d. light blue	85·00
Z10	6d. carmine	£100
Z11	7½d. red-brown	£110
Z12	8d. red-brown	£150
Z13	9d. yellowish olive	£150
Z14	1s. vermilion	£150

1925. *Dunedin Exhibition (No. 464).*

Z14a	1d. carmine/*rose*	

1926–27. *King George V in Admiral's uniform (Nos. 468/9).*

Z15	1d. rose-carmine	28·00
Z16	2s. light blue	£250

1929. *Anti-Tuberculosis Fund (No. 544).*

Z17	1d. +1d. scarlet	£140

1931. *Air (Nos. 548/9).*

Z18	3d. chocolate	£250
Z19	4d. blackish purple	£300

1932. *Health (No. 552).*

Z21	1d. +1d.carmine	£140

1935. *Pictorials (Nos. 556/8 and 560/9).* W **43**.

Z22	½d. bright green	65·00
Z23	1d. scarlet	40·00
Z24	1½d. red-brown	95·00
Z26	2½d. chocolate and slate	85·00
Z27	3d. brown	95·00
Z28	4d. black and sepia	£110
Z29	5d. ultramarine	£120
Z30	6d. scarlet	£110
Z31	8d. chocolate	£120
Z32	9d. scarlet and black	£120
Z33	1s. deep green	£100
Z34	2s. olive-green	£250
Z35	3s. chocolate and yellow-brown	£300

1935. *Silver Jubilee (Nos. 573/5).*

Z36	½d. green	45·00
Z37	1d. carmine	45·00
Z38	6d. red-orange	85·00

1935. *Health (No. 576).*

Z39	1d. +1d.scarlet	75·00

1936. *Pictorials (Nos. 577/82).* W **98**.

Z40	½d. bright green	50·00
Z41	1d. scarlet	17·00
Z42	1½d. red-brown	85·00
Z43	2d. orange	70·00
Z44	2½d. chocolate and slate	75·00
Z45	3d. brown	80·00

1936. *21st Anniv of "Anzac" Landing at Gallipoli (Nos. 591/2).*

Z46	½d. +½d.green	48·00
Z47	1d. +1d.scarlet	48·00

1936. *Congress of British Empire Chambers of Commerce (Nos. 593/7).*

Z48	½d. emerald-green	45·00
Z49	1d. scarlet	45·00
Z50	2½d. blue	50·00
Z51	4d. violet	80·00
Z52	6d. red-brown	80·00

1936. *Health (No. 598).*

Z53	1d. +1d. scarlet	75·00

1937. *Coronation (Nos. 599/601).*

Z54	1d. carmine	35·00
Z55	2½d. Prussian blue	38·00
Z56	6d. red-orange	38·00

1937. *Health (No. 602).*

Z57	1d. +1d. scarlet	75·00

1938. *King George VI (Nos. 603, 605, 607).*

Z58	½d. green	75·00
Z59	1d. scarlet	75·00
Z60	1½d. purple-brown	85·00

1940. *Centenary of British Sovereignty (Nos. 613/22, 624/5).*

Z61	½d. blue-green	38·00
Z62	1d. chocolate and scarlet	42·00
Z63	1½d. light blue and mauve	45·00
Z64	2d. blue-green and chocolate	45·00
Z65	2½d. blue-green and blue	48·00
Z66	3d. purple and carmine	48·00
Z67	4d. chocolate and lake	75·00
Z68	5d. pale blue and brown	80·00
Z69	6d. emerald-green and violet	80·00
Z70	7d. black and red	£100
Z71	9d. olive-green and orange	£100
Z72	1s. sage-green and deep green	£100

POSTAL FISCAL STAMPS

1932. *Arms (No. F147).*

ZF1	2s.6d. deep brown	£300

PRICES FOR STAMPS ON COVER TO 1945	
Nos. 1/8	*from* × 10

1 Cluster of Oranges

2 Christian on *Bounty* and Pitcairn Island

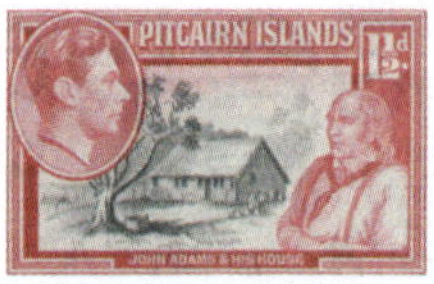

3 John Adams and his house

4 Lt. Bligh and H.M.S. *Bounty*

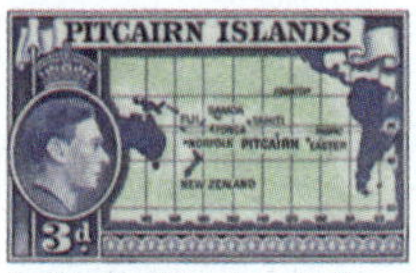

5 Pitcairn Islands and the Pacific Ocean

5a *Bounty* Bible

6 H.M.S. *Bounty*

6a School, 1949

7 Fletcher Christian and Pitcairn Island

8 Christian on H.M.S. *Bounty* and Pitcairn Coast

(Recess B.W. (1d., 3d., 4d., 8d. and 2s.6d.), and Waterlow (others))

1940 (15 Oct)–**51**. *T* **1/8**. Wmk Mult Script CA. P 11½×11 (1d., 3d., 4d., 8d. and 2s.6d.) or 12½ (others).

1	**1**	½d. orange and green	40	60
2	**2**	1d. mauve and magenta	55	80
3	**3**	1½d. grey and carmine	55	50
4	**4**	2d. green and brown	2·00	1·40
5	**5**	3d. yellow-green and blue	1·25	1·40
		aw. Wmk inverted	£3500	
5*b*	**5a**	4d. black and emerald-green (1.9.51)	18·00	11·00
6	**6**	6d. brown and grey-blue	5·00	1·50
6*a*	**6a**	8d. olive-green and magenta (1.9.51)	22·00	7·00
7	**7**	1s. violet and grey	4·00	2·50
8	**8**	2s.6d. green and brown	12·00	3·75
1/8 *Set of* 10			60·00	27·00
1s/8s (*ex* 4d., 8d.) Perf "Specimen" *Set of* 8			£1200	

Flagstaff flaw (R. 8/2)

1946 (2 Dec). *Victory. As Nos. 110/11 of Antigua.*

9	2d. brown	70	30
10	3d. blue	70	30
	a. Flagstaff flaw	40·00	38·00
9s/10s Perf "Specimen" *Set of* 2		£350	

1949 (1 Aug). *Royal Silver Wedding. As Nos. 112/13 of Antigua.*

11	1½d. scarlet	2·00	1·50
12	10s. mauve	40·00	50·00

1949 (10 Oct). *75th Anniv of U.P.U. As Nos. 114/17 of Antigua.*

13	2½d. red-brown	1·00	4·25
14	3d. deep blue	8·00	4·25
15	6d. deep blue-green	4·00	4·25
16	1s. purple	4·00	4·25
13/16 *Set of* 4		15·00	15·00

1953 (2 June). *Coronation. As No. of 120 Antigua, but ptd by B.W.*

17	4d. black and deep bluish green	2·00	3·50

9 *Cordyline terminalis*

10 Pitcairn Island Map

(Recess D.L.R.)

1957 (2 July)–**63**. *T* **9/10** *and similar designs.* Wmk Mult Script CA. P 13×12½ (horiz) or 12½×13 (vert).

18	½d. green and reddish lilac	80	1·50
	a. Green and reddish purple (9.3.63)	1·25	3·25
19	1d. black and olive-green	4·00	1·75
	a. Black and yellow-olive (19.2.59)	16·00	17·00
	b. Black and light olive-green (24.2.60)	42·00	19·00
20	2d. brown and greenish blue	2·25	60
21	2½d. deep brown and red-orange	50	40
22	3d. emerald and deep ultramarine	80	40
23	4d. scarlet and deep ultramarine (I)	90	40
23*a*	4d. carmine-red and deep ultramarine (II) (5.11.58)	3·50	1·50
24	6d. pale buff and indigo	2·75	55
25	8d. deep olive-green and carmine-lake	60	40
26	1s. black and yellowish brown	2·25	40
27	2s. green and red-orange	11·00	10·00
28	2s.6d. ultramarine and lake	23·00	10·00
	a. Blue and deep lake (10.2.59)	42·00	12·00
18/28 *Set of* 12		45·00	25·00

Designs: *Vert*—2d. John Adams and *Bounty* Bible; 2s. Island wheelbarrow. *Horiz*—2½d. Handicrafts: Bird model; 3d. Bounty Bay; 4d. Pitcairn School; 6d. Pacific Ocean map; 8d. Inland scene; 1s. Handicrafts: Ship model; 2s.6d. Launching new whaleboat.

Nos. 23/*a*. Type I is inscribed "PITCAIRN SCHOOL"; Type II "SCHOOL TEACHER'S HOUSE".

See also No. 33.

20 Pitcairn Island and Simon Young

(Des H. E. Maud. Photo Harrison)

1961 (15 Nov). *Centenary of Return of Pitcairn Islanders from Norfolk Island. T* **20** *and similar horiz designs.* W w **12**. P 14½×13½.

29	3d. black and yellow	50	45
30	6d. red-brown and blue	1·00	75
31	1s. red-orange and blue-green	1·00	75
29/31 *Set of* 3		2·25	1·75

Designs:—6d. Norfolk Island and Pitcairn Islands; 1s. Migrant brigantine *Mary Ann*.

1963 (4 June). *Freedom from Hunger. As No. 146 of Antigua.*

32	2s.6d. ultramarine	5·00	2·00

1963 (4 Dec). *As No. 18a, but wmk w* **12**.

33	**9** ½d. green and reddish purple	65	60

1963 (9 Dec). *Red Cross Centenary. As Nos. 147/8 of Antigua.*

34	2d. red and black	1·00	1·00
35	2s.6d. red and blue	2·00	4·00

23 Pitcairn Is Longboat

24 Queen Elizabeth II (after Anthony Buckley)

(Des M. Farrar Bell. Photo Harrison)

1964 (5 Aug)–**65**. *T* **23/4** *and similar horiz designs. Multicoloured.* W w **12**. P 14×14½.

36	½d. Type **23**	10	30
	a. Blue omitted	£450	
37	1d. H.M.S. *Bounty*	30	30
38	2d. "Out from Bounty Bay"	30	30
39	3d. Great Frigate Bird	75	30
40	4d. White Tern	75	30
41	6d. Pitcairn Warbler	75	30
42	8d. Red-footed Booby	75	30
	a. Pale blue (beak) omitted	£450	
	b. Pale blue (beak) printed double		
43	10d. Red-tailed Tropic Birds	60	30
44	1s. Henderson Island Crake	60	30
45	1s.6d. Stephen's Lory	2·00	1·25
46	2s.6d. Murphy's Petrel	2·00	1·50
47	4s. Henderson Island Fruit Dove	2·75	1·75
48	8s. Type **24** (5.4.65)	1·50	1·75
36/48 *Set of* 13		11·50	8·00

1965 (17 May). *I.T.U. Centenary. As Nos. 166/7 of Antigua.*

49	1d. mauve and orange-brown	75	40
50	2s.6d. turquoise-green and bright blue	3·00	3·50
	w. Wmk inverted	£140	

1965 (25 Oct). *International Co-operation Year. As Nos. 168/9 of Antigua.*

51	1d. reddish purple and turquoise-green	75	40
	a. "TRISTAN DA CUNHA" offset on back in reddish purple	£550	
52	1s.6d. deep bluish green and lavender	2·50	3·00

No. 51a was caused by the back of one sheet of stamps coming into contact with the blanket plate used for applying the Tristan da Cunha inscription to the same basic design.

1966 (24 Jan). *Churchill Commemoration. As Nos. 170/3 of Antigua.*

53	2d. new blue	1·00	85
54	3d. deep green	2·25	1·00
55	6d. brown	2·50	1·75
56	1s. bluish violet	3·00	2·50
53/6 *Set of* 4		7·75	5·50

1966 (1 Aug). *World Cup Football Championship. As Nos. 176/7 of Antigua.*

57	**25** 4d. violet, yellow-green, lake and yellow-brown	1·00	1·00
58	2s.6d. chocolate, blue-green, lake and yellow-brown	1·50	1·75

1966 (20 Sept). *Inauguration of W.H.O. Headquarters, Geneva. As Nos. 178/9 of Antigua.*

59	8d. black, yellow-green and light blue	2·00	3·25
60	1s.6d. black, light purple and yellow-brown	3·50	3·75

1966 (1 Dec). *20th Anniv of U.N.E.S.C.O. As Nos. 196/8 of Antigua.*

61	½d. slate-violet, red, yellow and orange	20	1·00
62	10d. orange-yellow, violet and deep olive	1·50	2·00
63	2s. black, bright purple and orange	3·00	3·25
61/3 *Set of* 3		4·25	5·75

36 Mangarevan Canoe, *circa* 1325

(Des V. Whiteley. Photo Harrison)

1967 (1 Mar). *Bicentenary of Discovery of Pitcairn Islands. T* **36** *and similar horiz designs. Multicoloured.* W w **12**. P 14½.

64	½d. Type **36**	10	20
65	1d. P. F. de Quiros and *San Pedro y San Pablo*, 1606	20	20
66	8d. *San Pedro y San Pablo* and *Los Tres Reyes*, 1606	25	20
67	1s. Carteret and H.M.S. *Swallow*, 1767	25	25
68	1s.6d. *Hercules*, 1819	25	25
64/8 *Set of* 5		1·00	1·00

(New Currency. 100 cents = 1 New Zealand dollar)

(**41** *Bounty Anchor*)

1967 (10 July). *Decimal currency. Nos. 36/48 surch in decimal currency by die-stamping in gold as T* **41**.

69	½c. on ½d. multicoloured	10	10
	a. Deep brown omitted	£1200	
	b. Surch double, one albino	£160	
70	1c. on 1d. multicoloured	30	1·25
71	2c. on 2d. multicoloured	25	1·25
72	2½c. on 3d. multicoloured	25	1·25
73	3c. on 4d. multicoloured	25	20
74	5c. on 6d. multicoloured	30	1·25
75	10c. on 8d. multicoloured	30	30
	a. "10c." omitted	£1400	
	b. Pale blue (beak) omitted	£650	
76	15c. on 10d. multicoloured	1·25	40
77	20c. on 1s. multicoloured	1·25	55
78	25c. on 1s.6d. multicoloured	1·50	1·25
79	30c. on 2s.6d. multicoloured	1·75	1·25
80	40c. on 4s. multicoloured	1·75	1·25
81	45c. on 8s. multicoloured	1·50	1·50
69/81 *Set of* 13		9·50	10·50

On No. 75a the anchor emblem is still present. Several examples of this variety have been identified as coming from R9/1.

The ½c. and 1c. exist with PVA gum as well as gum arabic.

42 Bligh and *Bounty*'s Launch

(Des Jennifer Toombs. Litho D.L.R.)

1967 (7 Dec). *150th Death Anniv of Admiral Bligh. T* **42** *and similar horiz designs.* P 13½×13.

82	1c. turquoise-blue, black and royal blue (*shades*)	10	10
83	8c. black, yellow and magenta	25	65
84	20c. black, brown and pale buff	25	70
82/4 *Set of* 3		55	1·25

Designs:—8c. Bligh and followers cast adrift; 20c. Bligh's tomb.

45 Human Rights Emblem

(Des G. Hamori. Litho D.L.R)

1968 (4 Mar). *Human Rights Year.* P 13½×13.

85	**45** 1c. multicoloured	10	10
86	2c. multicoloured	10	10
87	25c. multicoloured	35	35
85/7 *Set of* 3		50	50

46 Miro Wood and Flower

(Des Jennifer Toombs. Photo Harrison)

1968 (19 Aug). *Handicrafts (1st series). T* **46** *and similar designs.* W w **12** (sideways* on vert designs). P 14×13½ (5, 10c.) or 13½×14 (others).

88	5c. multicoloured	20	30
89	10c. bronze-green, brown and orange	20	40
90	15c. deep bluish violet, chocolate and salmon	25	40
91	20c. multicoloured	25	45
	w. Wmk Crown to right of CA	£200	
88/91 *Set of* 4		80	1·40

Designs: *Horiz*—10c. Flying Fish model. *Vert*—15c. "Hand" vases; 20c. Woven baskets.

*The normal sideways watermark shows Crown to left of CA, *as seen from the back of the stamp.*

50 Microscope and Slides

(Des Jennifer Toombs. Litho D.L.R.)

1968 (25 Nov). *20th Anniv of World Health Organisation. T* **50** *and similar horiz design.* W w **12** (sideways). P 14.

92	2c. black, turquoise-blue and ultramarine	10	20
93	20c. black, orange and bright purple	40	50

Design:—20c. Hypodermic syringe and jars of tablets.

52 Pitcairn Island

62 "Flying Fox" Cable System

(Des Jennifer Toombs. Litho Questa (50c., $1), D.L.R. (others))

1969 (17 Sept)–**75**. *T* **52**, **62** *and similar designs. Chalk-surfaced paper.* W w **12** (upright on 3c., 25c. sideways* on $1 and horiz designs). P 14½×14 (50c.), 14 ($1) or 13 (others).

94	1c. multicoloured	2·00	1·75
	a. Glazed, ordinary paper (9.8.71)	1·25	1·75
	aw. Wmk Crown to right of CA	2·25	2·75
95	2c. multicoloured	25	15
96	3c. multicoloured	25	15
97	4c. multicoloured	2·00	15
98	5c. multicoloured	70	15
	a. Gold (Queens head) omitted		
99	6c. multicoloured	30	20
100	8c. multicoloured	2·00	20
101	10c. multicoloured	2·50	85
	a. Glazed, ordinary paper (9.8.71)	2·00	3·50
	aw. Wmk Crown to right of CA	6·00	6·50
102	15c. multicoloured	2·25	1·50
	a. Queen's head omitted	£950	
103	20c. multicoloured	60	40
104	25c. multicoloured	70	40
	w. Wmk inverted		
105	30c. multicoloured	55	45
106	40c. multicoloured	75	60
106*a*	50c. multicoloured (*glazed, ordinary paper*) (2.1.73)	2·00	12·00
106*b*	$1 multicoloured (*glazed, ordinary paper*) (21.4.75)	5·50	17·00
94/106*b* *Set of* 15		20·00	32·00

Designs: *Horiz*—2c. Captain Bligh and *Bounty* chronometer; 4c. Plans and drawing of *Bounty*; 5c. Breadfruit containers and plant; 6c. Bounty Bay; 8c. Pitcairn longboat; 10c. Ship landing point; 15c. Fletcher Christian's Cave; 20c. Thursday October Christian's House; 30c. Radio Station, Taro Ground; 40c. *Bounty* Bible; 50c. Pitcairn Coat of Arms. *Vert*—3c. *Bounty* anchor; $1 Queen Elizabeth II.

*The normal sideways watermark shows Crown to left of CA, *as seen from the back of the stamp.*

The 1c. was reissued in 1974, W w **12** upright.

65 Lantana

69 Band-tailed Hind

(Des Jennifer Toombs. Litho D.L.R.)

1970 (23 Mar). *Flowers. T* **65** *and similar vert designs. Multicoloured.* W w **12**. P 14.

107	1c. Type **65**	15	50
108	2c. "Indian Shot"	20	65
109	5c. Pulau	25	75
110	25c. Wild Gladiolus	60	2·00
107/10 *Set of* 4		1·10	3·50

(Des Jennifer Toombs. Photo Harrison)

1970 (12 Oct). *Fishes. T* **69** *and similar horiz designs. Multicoloured.* W w **12**. P 14.

111	5c. Type **69**	1·50	70
	w. Wmk inverted	8·00	3·00
112	10c. High-finned Rudderfish	1·50	85
	w. Wmk inverted	10·00	3·50
113	15c. Elwyn's Wrasse	2·00	1·00
	w. Wmk inverted	9·00	3·50
114	20c. Yellow Wrasse ("Whistling Daughter")	2·50	1·25
	w. Wmk inverted	20·00	8·50
111/14 *Set of* 4		6·75	3·50

STAMP BOOKLET

1940 (15 Oct). *Black on deep green cover. Stapled.*

SB1 4s.8d. booklet containing one each ½d., 1d., 1½d., 2d., 3d., 6d., 1s. and 2s.6d. (Nos. 1/5, 6, 7/8) £2750

Genuine examples of No. SB1 are interleaved with ordinary kitchen wax-paper, which frequently tones the stamps, and are secured with staples 17 mm long.

The status of other booklets using different size staples or paper fasteners is uncertain although it is believed that some empty booklet covers were available on the island.

Prince Edward Island *see* Canada

Qatar

1957. 100 Naye Paise = 1 Rupee 1966. 100 Dirhams = 1 Riyal

The Arab Shaikhdom of Qatar consists of a large peninsula jutting into the Persian Gulf. In 1868, after Qatar had been invaded by Bahrain, a member of the leading Al Thani family was installed as Shaikh and an agreement was made by which he referred to the British Resident all disputes in which the shaikhdom was involved. Qatar was under nominal Turkish suzerainty, and Turkish troops were stationed there from 1871 until August 1915, when the Royal Navy forced them to abandon Doha, the capital, to the shaikh. On 3 November 1916 the shaikhdom entered into special treaty relations with the United Kingdom giving it British naval and military protection from attack. Oil was discovered on the peninsula in January 1940 and was first shipped to Europe at the end of 1949. On the withdrawal of British forces from the Gulf, Qatar declined to join the United Arab Emirates, terminated the Treaty with Great Britain and became fully independent on 3 September 1971.

There was no postal service from Qatar until 18 May 1950. Prior to this date the few foreign residents made their own arrangements for their mail to be carried to Bahrain for onward transmission through the postal service.

The first organised post from the capital, Doha, was an extension of the work in the state by the British Political Officer. From 18 May 1950 British residents were able to send mail via his office. The first three sendings had the Bahrain or British Postal Agencies in Eastern Arabia stamps cancelled by a circular office stamp, but later batches, up to the introduction of the first Doha postmark in July 1950, had the stamps cancelled on arrival at Bahrain.

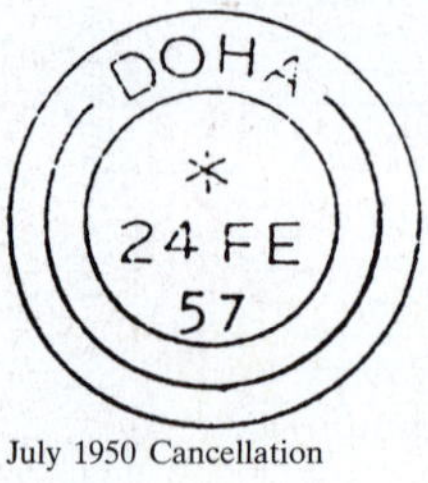

July 1950 Cancellation

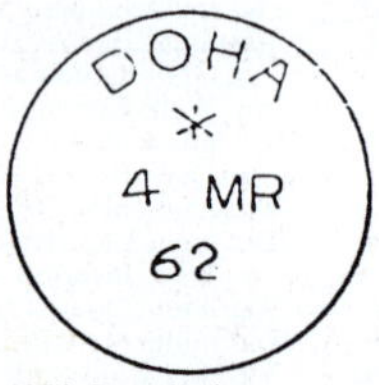

1956 Cancellation

The Post Office became a seperate entity in August 1950 when its services were made available to the general public. After initially using the Bahrain surcharges on Great Britain the supply of stamps for the Qatar office was switched to the British Postal Agencies in Eastern Arabia surcharges.

The circular cancellation, dating from July 1950, continued to be used until replaced by a slightly smaller version in early 1956.

A further post office was opened on 1 February 1956 at the Umm Said oil terminal, using its own cancellation.

Both offices were issued with standard oval Registered handstamps, Doha in 1950 and Umm Said in 1956.

1956. Umm Said Cancellation

All stamps to 1960 surcharged on Queen Elizabeth II issues of Great Britain.

QATAR NP 1 NP
(1)

QATAR NP 3 NP
(2)

QATAR 75 NP
(3)

1957 (1 Apr)–**59**.

(a) Nos. 540/2, 543b/8, 551 and 555/6 (St. Edwards's Crown wmk), surch as T **1** *to* **3**.

1	**1**	1n.p. on 5d. brown	10	10
2	**2**	3n.p. on ½d. orange-red	15	15
3		6n.p. on 1d. ultramarine	15	15
4		9n.p. on 1½d. green	15	10
5		12n.p. on 2d. light red-brown	20	2·75
6	**1**	15n.p. on 2½d. carmine-red (I)	15	10
7	**2**	20n.p. on 3d. deep lilac (B.)	15	10
8	**1**	25n.p. on 4d. ultramarine	40	1·75
9		40n.p. on 6d. reddish purple	15	15
		a. Deep claret (21.7.59)	30	10
10		50n.p. on 9d. bronze-green	40	1·50
11	**3**	75n.p. on 1s.3d. green	50	3·50
12		1r. on 1s.6d. grey-blue	11·00	10
1/12 *Set of* 12			12·00	9·00

Designs:—Nos. 1/12, Various portraits of Queen Elizabeth II.

QATAR 2 RUPEES
I

QATAR 2 RUPEES
(4) II

QATAR 5 RUPEES
I

QATAR 5 RUPEES
(5) II

QATAR 10 RUPEES
I

QATAR 10 RUPEES
(6) II

Type I (4/6). Type-set overprints. Bold thick letters with sharp corners and straight edges. Bars close together and usually slightly longer than in Type II.

Type II (4/6). Plate-printed overprints by Harrison. Thinner letters, rounded corners and rough edges. Bars wider apart.

(b) Nos. 536/8 (St. Edward's Crown wmk) surcharged with T **4/6**.

13	2r. on 2s.6d. black-brown (I) (1.4.57)	3·50	4·50
	a. Type II (18.9.57)	9·00	8·00
14	5r. on 5s. rose-red (1) (1.4.57)	5·00	6·00
	a. Type II (18.9.57)	9·00	19·00
15	10r. on 10s. ultramarine (I) (1.4.57)	5·50	16·00
	a. Type II (18.9.57)	50·00	£140
13/15 *Set of* 3		12·50	24·00
13a/15a *Set of* 3		60·00	£150

Designs:—No. 13, Carrickfergus Castle; 14, Caernarvon Castle; 15, Edinburgh Castle.

QATAR
15 NP
(7)

1957 (1 Aug). *World Scout Jubilee Jamboree. Nos. 557/9 surch in two lines as T* **7** *(15n.p.) or in three lines (others).*

16	15n.p. on 2½d. carmine-red	35	35
17	25n.p. on 4d. ultramarine	35	35
18	75n.p. on 1s.3d. green	40	40
16/18 *Set of* 3		1·00	1·00

Designs:—No. 16, Scout badge and "Rolling Hitch"; 17, "Scouts coming to Britain"; 18, Globe within a Compass.

1960 (26 Apr–28 Sept). *Nos. 570/5 and 579 (Mult Crown wmk) surcharged as T* **1** *or* **2**.

20	**2**	3n.p. on ½d. orange-red (28.9)	70	1·75
21		6n.p. on 1d. ultramarine (21.6)	2·00	2·75
22		9n.p. on 1½d. green (28.9)	75	1·50
23		12n.p. on 2d. light red-brown (28.9)	4·75	6·50
24	**1**	15n.p. on 2½d. carmine-red (11)	2·00	10
25	**2**	20n.p. on 3d. deep lilac (B.) (28.9)	50	10
26	**1**	40n.p. on 6d. deep claret (21.6)	1·75	1·50
20/6 *Set of* 7			11·00	12·50

Designs:—Various portraits of Queen Elizabeth II.

Shaikh Ahmad bin Ali al-Thani

24 October 1960–22 February 1972

8 Shaikh Ahmad bin Ali al-Thani

9 Peregrine Falcon

10 Dhow

11 Oil Derrick

12 Mosque

(Des O. C. Meronti (T **8**), M. Goaman (T **9**), M. Farrar Bell (T **10**), J. Constable and O. C. Meronti (T **11/12**). Photo Harrison, (T **8/10**). Recess D.L.R. (T **11/12**))

1961 (2 Sept). P 14½ (5n.p. to 75n.p.) or 13 (1r. to 10r.).

27	**8**	5n.p. carmine	15	15
28		15n.p. black	30	15
29		20n.p. reddish purple	30	15
30		30n.p. deep green	35	30
31	**9**	40n.p. red	2·40	30
32		50n.p. sepia	3·25	30
33	**10**	75n.p. ultramarine	1·60	2·50
34	**11**	1r. scarlet	2·75	35
35		2r. ultramarine	3·50	1·75
36	**12**	5r. bronze-green	20·00	5·00
37		10r. black	48·00	9·00
27/37 *Set of* 11			75·00	18·00

The Qatar Post Department took over the postal services on 23 May 1963.

Queensland *see* Australia

Rhodesia

Stamps of BECHUANALAND (see BOTSWANA) were used in Matabeleland on the runner post between Gubulawayo and Mafeking (Bechuanaland) from 9 August 1888 until 5 May 1894. Such stamps were cancelled "GUBULAWAYO" or by the barred oval "678" obliteration.

Between 27 June 1890 and 13 May 1892 external mail from Mashonaland sent via Bechuanaland was franked with that territory's stamps. A similar arrangement, using the stamps of MOZAMBIQUE existed for the route via Beira inaugurated on 29 August 1891. In both instances the stamps were cancelled by the post offices receiving the mail from Mashonaland. From 14 May until 31 July 1892 letters via Bechuanaland were franked with a combination of B.S.A Company and Bechuanaland issues.

Rhodesia joined the South African Postal Union on 1 August 1892 when its stamps became valid for international mail. Combination frankings with Mozambique stamps continued to be required until April 1894.

For the use of British Central Africa overprints in North-eastern Rhodesia from 1893 to 1899 see MALAWI (NYASALAND).

PRICES FOR STAMPS ON COVER TO 1945

Nos. 1/7	from × 5
Nos. 8/13	—
Nos. 14/17	from × 2
Nos. 18/24	from × 10
Nos. 25/6	—
Nos. 27/8	from × 7
Nos. 29/35	from × 10
Nos. 36/7	—
Nos. 41/6	from × 6
Nos. 47/50	—
Nos. 51/3	from × 2
Nos. 58/64	from × 3
Nos. 66/72	from × 8
Nos. 73/4	—
Nos. 75/87	from × 6
Nos. 88/93*a*	—
Nos. 94/9	from × 3
Nos. 100/10	from × 5
Nos. 111/13*e*	—
Nos. 114/18	from × 7
Nos. 119/60*a*	from × 10
Nos. 160*b*/6*b*	—
Nos. 167/78	from × 6
Nos. 179/81*a*	—
Nos. 182/5*a*	from × 4
Nos. 186/208	from × 8
Nos. 209/41	from × 8
Nos. 242/54*a*	—
Nos. 255/77	from × 8
Nos. 278/9*c*	—
Nos. 280/1	from × 15
Nos. 282/310	from × 8
Nos. 311/22	—

A. ISSUES FOR THE BRITISH SOUTH AFRICA COMPANY TERRITORY

1

2

½d.
(3)

(Recess B.W.)

1892 (2 Jan*)–**93**. *Thin wove paper.* P 14, 14½.

1	1	1d. black	10·00	2·75
2		6d. ultramarine	55·00	25·00
3		6d. deep blue (1893)	30·00	3·75
4		1s. grey-brown	45·00	10·00
5		2s. vermilion	55·00	29·00
6		2s.6d. grey-purple	35·00	48·00
7		2s.6d. lilac (1893)	50·00	45·00
8		5s. orange-yellow	70·00	50·00
9		10s. deep green	85·00	£100
10	2	£1 deep blue	£200	£130
11		£2 rose-red**	£450	£160
12		£5 sage-green	£1600	£450
13		£10 brown	£2750	£700
1/10 *Set of* 8			£450	£325

Great caution is needed in buying the high values in either used or unused condition, many stamps offered being revenue stamps cleaned and re-gummed or with forged postmarks.

*Printing of stamps in Types **1**, **2** and **4** commenced in 1890, although none were used for postal purposes before 2 January 1892 when the route to the East Coast was inaugurated.

**For later printings of the £2 see No. 74.

The following sheet watermarks are known on Nos. 1/26: (1) William Collins, Sons & Co's paper watermarked with the firm's monogram, and "PURE LINEN WOVE BANK" in double-lined capitals (1890 and 1891 ptgs). (2) As (1) with "EXTRA STRONG" and "139" added (1892 ptgs). (3) Paper by Wiggins Teape & Co, watermarked "W T & Co" in script letters in double-lined wavy border (1893 ptgs). (4) The same firm's paper, watermarked "1011" in double-lined figures (1894 ptgs except ½d.). (5) "WIGGINS TEAPE & CO LONDON" in double-lined block capitals (1894 ptg of No. 18). Many values can also be found on a slightly thicker paper without wmk, but single specimens are not easily distinguishable.

1892 (2 Jan). *Nos. 2 and 4 surch as T* **3**.

14	1	½d. on 6d. ultramarine	£120	£450
15		2d. on 6d. ultramarine	£140	£600
16		4d. on 6d. ultramarine	£170	£700
17		8d. on 1s. grey-brown	£170	£800
14/17 *Set of* 4			£550	£2250

Caution is needed in buying these surcharges as both forged surcharges and forged postmarks exist.

4

5 (ends of scrolls behind legs of springboks)

(T **4**. Centre recess; value B.W.)

1892 (2 Jan)–**94**. *Thin wove paper (wmks as note after No. 13).* P 14, 14½.

18	4	½d. dull blue and vermilion	2·50	3·75
19		½d. deep blue and vermilion (1893)	2·75	5·00
20		2d. deep dull green and vermilion	19·00	4·00
21		3d. grey-black and green (8.92)	15·00	5·50
22		4d. chestnut and black	27·00	3·50
23		8d. rose-lake and ultramarine	15·00	15·00
24		8d. red and ultramarine (1892)	13·00	15·00
25		3s. brown and green (1894)	£160	85·00
26		4s. grey-black and vermilion (1893)	38·00	50·00
18/26 *Set of* 7			£250	£150

(Recess P.B. from the Bradbury, Wilkinson plates)

1895. *Thick soft wove paper.* P 12½.

27	4	2d. green and red	25·00	14·00
28		4d. yellow-brown and black	25·00	16·00
		a. Imperf (pair)	£1800	

(Centre recess; value typo P.B.)

1896–97. *Wove paper.* P 14.

(a) Die I. Plates 1 and 2. Small dot to the right of the tail of the right-hand supporter in the coat of arms. Body of lion only partly shaded.

29	5	1d. scarlet and emerald	17·00	4·50
		a. Carmine-red and emerald		
30		2d. brown and mauve	26·00	2·00
31		3d. chocolate and ultramarine	6·50	1·75
32		4d. ultramarine and mauve	55·00	
		a. Imperf between (pair)		
		b. Blue and mauve	28·00	19·00
33		6d. mauve and pink	80·00	21·00
34		8d. green and mauve/*buff*	8·50	60
		a. Imperf between (pair)		
		b. Imperf (pair)	£3250	
35		1s. green and blue	15·00	2·75
36		3s. green and mauve/*blue*	65·00	35·00
		a. Imperf (pair)	£9000	
37		4s. orange-red and blue/*green*	55·00	2·75
29/37 *Set of* 9			£275	80·00

(b) Die II. Plates 3 and 4. No dot. Body of lion heavily shaded all over.

41	5	½d. slate and violet	3·50	3·25
42		1d. scarlet and emerald	6·00	3·75
43		2d. brown and mauve	13·00	4·75
44		4d. ultramarine and mauve	75·00	12·00
		a. Blue and mauve	13·00	50
46		6d. mauve and rose	11·00	75
47		2s. indigo and green/*buff*	29·00	8·50
48		2s.6d. brown and purple/*yellow*	75·00	55·00
49		5s. chestnut and emerald	50·00	9·00
50		10s. slate and vermilion/*rose*	£100	65·00
41/50 *Set of* 9			£275	£130

One Penny
(6)

THREE PENCE.
(7)

(Surchd by *Bulawayo Chronicle*)

1896 (April). *Matabele Rebellion provisionals. Surch with T* **6** *and* **7**.

51	6	1d. on 3d. (No. 21)	£550	£700
		a. "P" in "Penny" inverted	£40000	
		b. "y" in "Penny" inverted		
52		1d. on 4s. (No. 26)	£275	£300
		a. "P" in "Penny" inverted	£32000	
		b. "y" in "Penny" inverted	£32000	
		c. Single bar through original value	£1100	£1200
53	7	3d. on 5s. (No. 8)	£180	£225
		a. "R" in "THREE" inverted	£32000	
		b. "T" in "THREE" inverted	£40000	

Nos. 51 and 52 occur in two settings, one with 9¾ mm between value and upper bar, the other with 11 mm between value and upper bar.

BRITISH SOUTH AFRICA COMPANY.
(8)

9 (Ends of scrolls between legs of springboks)

1896 (22 May–Aug). *Cape of Good Hope stamps optd by Argus Printing Co, Cape Town, with T* **8**. Wmk Anchor (3d. wmk Crown CA). P 14.

58	6	½d. grey-black (No. 48*a*)	14·00	21·00
59	17	1d. rose-red (No. 58)	15·00	22·00
60	6	2d. deep bistre (No. 50*a*)	19·00	12·00
61		3d. pale claret (No. 40)	50·00	75·00
62		4d. blue (No. 51)	22·00	22·00
		a. "COMPANY," omitted	£9500	
63	4	6d. deep purple (No. 52*a*)	55·00	70·00
64	6	1s. yellow-ochre (No. 65) (Aug)	£140	£140
58/64 *Set of* 7			£275	£325

No. 62 also exists with "COMPANY" partially omitted. Examples with the word completely omitted, as No. 62a, are known from positions 1 to 6 of the setting.

Forgeries of this overprint show a narrow final "A" in "AFRICA" and have a rectangular full stop. On the genuine overprint both "As" are the same and the stop is oval.

(Eng J. A. C. Harrison (vignette), Bain or Rapkin (£1) (frames). Recess Waterlow)

1897. P 13½ to 16.

66	9	½d. grey-black and purple	3·75	6·50
67		1d. scarlet and emerald	4·00	6·00
68		2d. brown and mauve	11·00	2·75
69		3d. brown-red and slate-blue	3·50	50
		a. Imperf between (vert pair)	£3250	
70		4d. ultramarine and claret	14·00	2·75
		a. Imperf between (horiz pair)	£14000	£14000
71		6d. dull purple and pink	8·50	3·50
72		8d. green and mauve/*buff*	15·00	50
		a. Imperf between (vert pair)	†	£2750
73		£1 black and red-brown/*green*	£375	£225

(Recess Waterlow, from the Bradbury plate)

1897 (Jan). P 15.

74	2	£2 rosy red	£1700	£450

10

11

12

(Recess Waterlow)

1898–1908. P 13½ to 15½.

75	10	½d. dull bluish green	6·00	2·00
		a. Yellow green (1904)	3·25	2·00
		aa. Imperf vert (horiz pair)	£700	
		ab. Imperf (pair)	£750	
		ac. Imperf between (vert pair)	£1100	
76		½d. deep green (*shades*) (1908)	24·00	2·25
77		1d. rose (*shades*)	5·50	50
		a. Imperf (pair)	£650	£750
		b. Imperf between (vert pair)	£500	
		c. Imperf between (horiz pair)	—	£850
78		1d. red (*shades*) (1905)	6·50	50
		a. Imperf vert (horiz pair)	£350	£425
		ab. Imperf horiz (vert pair)	£950	
		b. Imperf (pair)	£500	£600
		c. Imperf between (horiz pair)	£750	£475
		d. Imperf between (vert strip of 4)	£2000	
79		2d. brown	3·75	60
80		2½d. dull blue (*shades*)	7·00	80
		a. Imperf vert (horiz pair)	£850	£1000
		b. Grey-blue (shades) (1903)	12·00	1·00
81		3d. claret	6·50	80
		a. Imperf between (vert pair)	£700	
82		4d. olive	6·00	30
		a. Imperf between (vert pair)	£700	
83		6d. reddish purple	14·00	1·75
		a. Reddish mauve (1902)	18·00	5·50
84	11	1s. bistre	19·00	3·25
		a. Imperf between (vert pair)	£2750	
		ab. Imperf between (horiz pair)	£3000	
		b. Deep olive-bistre (1907)	£275	
		bc. Imperf (pair)	£2750	
		bd. Imperf between (horiz pair)	£3750	
		c. Bistre-brown (1908)	55·00	14·00
		d. Brownish yellow (1908)	21·00	8·00
85		2s.6d. bluish grey (11.06)	48·00	1·00
		a. Imperf between (vert pair)	£1000	£500
86		3s. deep violet (1902)	19·00	2·75
		a. Deep bluish violet (1908)	65·00	12·00
87		5s. brown-orange	45·00	14·00
88		7s.6d. black (11.01)	75·00	25·00
89		10s. grey-green	35·00	1·00
90	12	£1 greyish red-purple (p 15½) (7.01)	£325	£110
		a. Perf 14. *Blackish purple* (1902)	£500	£120
91		£2 brown (5.08)	95·00	6·50
92		£5 deep blue (7.01)	£3250	£2500
93		£10 lilac (7.01)	£3250	£2250
93*a*		£20 yellow-bistre (1901?)	£14000	
75/90 *Set of* 14			£550	£140
80s/1s, 85s/6s, 88s/93s Perf "Specimen" *Set of* 10			£900	

A £100 cherry-red, perf 13½, was ordered in June 1901, a number of mint, together with several examples showing fiscal cancellations being known.

13 Victoria Falls

RHODESIA.
(14)

(Recess Waterlow)

1905 (13 July). *Visit of British Association and Opening of Victoria Falls Bridge.* P 14½ to 15 (5d.), 14 (others).

94	13	1d. red	5·50	6·00
		a. Perf 14½ to 15	13·00	14·00
95		2½d. deep blue	12·00	8·00
		a. Perf 14½ to 15	19·00	14·00
96		5d. claret	26·00	48·00
		a. Perf 14	48·00	65·00
		sa. Optd "Specimen"	£160	

97 1s. blue-green 29·00 48·00
a. Imperf (pair) £22000
b. Imperf between (horiz pair) .. £28000
c. Imperf between (vert pair) £30000
d. Imperf vert (horiz pair) £23000
e. Perf 14½ to 15 — £275
98 2s.6d. black £100 £150
99 5s. violet 90·00 40·00
a. Perf 14½ to 15 £325
94/9 *Set of* 6 £225 £275
94s/9s Optd or Perf (5d.) "Specimen" *Set of* 6 £400

1909 (15 Apr)–**12**. *Optd as T* **14**. P 13½ to 15.
100 **10** ½d. green *to* deep green 2·75 1·50
a. No stop 60·00 35·00
b. Yellow-green (1911) 35·00 27·00
101 1d. carmine-rose 4·75 1·00
a. No stop 70·00 27·00
b. Imperf between (horiz pair) .. £400
c. Deep carmine-rose £475 1·00
cd. Imperf between (horiz pair) .. £400
102 2d. brown 2·25 4·50
a. No stop £120 80·00
103 2½d. pale dull blue 1·50 80
a. No stop 45·00 26·00
104 3d. claret 1·60 1·00
a. No stop £170 75·00
b. Opt inverted † 15·00
c. Opt double † £1000
105 4d. olive 5·50 2·25
a. No stop 75·00 60·00
b. Opt inverted † 15·00
106 6d. reddish purple 5·00 5·50
a. No stop 70·00
b. Reddish mauve
c. Dull purple 18·00 5·50
ca. No stop 90·00 55·00
107 **11** 1s. bistre 21·00
a. No stop £170
b. Bistre-brown
ba. No stop
c. Deep brownish bistre 9·00 5·00
ca. No stop 90·00 48·00
108 2s.6d. bluish grey 23·00 11·00
a. No stop £100 65·00
b. Opt inverted † 20·00
109 3s. deep violet 17·00 11·00
110 5s. orange 32·00 48·00
a. No stop £120 £140
111 7s.6d. black 95·00 23·00
112 10s. dull green 45·00 16·00
a. No stop £300 £190
113 **12** £1 grey-purple £170 85·00
a. Vert pair, lower stamp without opt £30000
b. Opt in violet £375 £190
113*c* £2 brown £4000 £300
113*d* £2 rosy brown (*bluish paper*) (P 14½×15) (1912) £3250 £275
113*e* £5 deep blue (*bluish paper*) £7000 £4250
100/13 *Set of* 14 £350 £190
100s/13s Perf "Specimen" *Set of* 14 £350

In some values the no stop variety occurs on every stamp in a vertical row of a sheet, in other values only once in a sheet. Other varieties, such as no serif to the right of apex of "A", no serif to top of "E", etc., exist in some values.

No. 113a comes from a sheet with the overprint omitted from the bottom row.

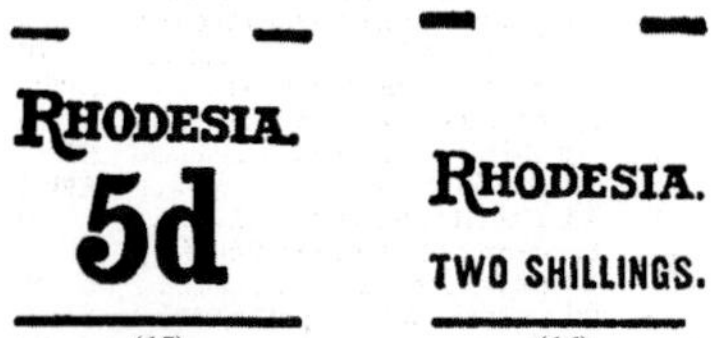

(15) (16)

1909 (April)–**11**. *Surch as T* **15** *and* **16** *(2s.) in black.*
114 **10** 5d. on 6d. reddish purple 8·00 14·00
a. Surcharge in violet 90·00
b. Reddish mauve
c. Dull purple 16·00 14·00
116 **11** 7½d. on 2s.6d. bluish grey 3·50 3·75
a. Surcharge in violet 18·00 9·00
ab. Surch double † £6500
117 10d. on 3s. deep violet 13·00 16·00
a. Surcharge in violet 4·50 3·75
118 2s. on 5s. orange 12·00 7·50
114s/18s Perf "Specimen" *Set of* 4 £180

In the 7½d. and 10d. surcharges the bars are spaced as in T **16**.

17 18

(Recess Waterlow)

1910 (11 Nov)–**13**.

(a) P 14.
119 **17** ½d. yellow-green 13·00 1·75
a. Imperf between (horiz pair) .. £22000
120 ½d. bluish green 22·00 3·50
a. Imperf (pair) £13000 £6500
121 ½d. olive-green 35·00 3·75
122 ½d. dull green 70·00 50·00
123 1d. bright carmine 27·00 3·25
a. Imperf between (vert pair) £19000 £12000
b. Imperf between (horiz pair) ..
124 1d. carmine-lake 60·00 3·00
125 1d. rose-red 28·00 2·75
126 2d. black and grey 50·00 11·00
127 2d. black-purple and slate-grey £160 £750
128 2d. black and slate-grey 55·00 7·50
129 2d. black and slate 70·00 9·00
130 2d. black and grey-black 80·00 16·00
131 2½d. ultramarine 26·00 7·50
131*a* 2½d. bright ultramarine 23·00 7·50
132 2½d. dull blue 27·00 9·00
133 2½d. chalky blue 22·00 17·00
134 3d. purple and ochre 38·00 38·00
135 3d. purple and yellow-ochre 45·00 15·00
136 3d. magenta and yellow-ochre £160 16·00
137 3d. violet and ochre £120 80·00
138 4d. greenish black and orange 90·00 90·00
139 4d. brown-purple and orange 70·00 60·00
140 4d. black and orange 45·00 18·00
141 5d. purple-brown and olive-green 32·00 50·00
141*a* 5d. purple-brown and olive-yellow 32·00 55·00
ab. Error. Purple-brown and ochre £600 £150
143 5d. lake-brown and olive £275 60·00
143*a* 5d. lake-brown and green (9.12).. £20000 £1600
144 6d. red-brown and mauve 40·00 40·00
145 6d. brown and purple 40·00 18·00
145*a* 6d. bright chestnut and mauve £700 65·00
146 8d. black and purple £5000
147 8d. dull purple and purple £170 95·00
148 8d. greenish black and purple £150 95·00
149 10d. scarlet and reddish mauve 40·00 48·00
150 10d. carmine and deep purple £650 60·00
151 1s. grey-black and deep blue-green 48·00 25·00
151*a* 1s. black and deep blue-green £150 35·00
152 1s. black and pale blue-green 55·00 16·00
152*a* 1s. purple-black and blue-green .. £250 60·00
153 2s. black and ultramarine 85·00 65·00
154 2s. black and dull blue £1100 75·00
154*a* 2s. purple-black and ultramarine £3000 £225
155 2s.6d. black and lake £325 £400
155*a* 2s.6d. black and crimson £325 £275
156 2s.6d. sepia and deep crimson £400 £350
156*a* 2s.6d. bistre-brown and crimson £1100 £650
157 2s.6d. black and rose-carmine £300 £375
158 3s. green and violet (*shades*) £180 £180
158*a* 3s. bright green and magenta £1200 £700
159 5s. vermilion and deep green £275 £375
160 5s. scarlet and pale yellow-green £275 £190
160*a* 5s. crimson and yellow-green £225 £190
160*b* 7s.6d. carmine and pale blue £600 £425
161 7s.6d. carmine and light blue £700 £900
162 7s.6d. carmine and bright blue £2500 £1000
163 10s. deep myrtle and orange £600 £275
164 10s. blue-green and orange £375 £450
165 £1 carmine-red and bluish black. £1100 £550
166 £1 rose-scarlet and bluish black.. £1200 £375
166*a* £1 crimson and slate-black £1400 £1100
b. Error. Scarlet and reddish mauve £10000

(b) P 15.
167 **17** ½d. blue-green £300 13·00
168 ½d. yellow-green £350 11·00
169 ½d. apple-green £600 27·00
170 1d. carmine £300 8·50
170*a* 1d. carmine-lake £450 16·00
170*b* 1d. rose-carmine £350 11·00
171 2d. black and grey-black £900 32·00
171*a* 2d. black and grey £900 32·00
171*b* 2d. black and slate £1000 32·00
172 2½d. ultramarine (*shades*) 70·00 35·00
173 3d. purple and yellow-ochre £7000 75·00
173*a* 3d. claret and pale yellow-ochre .. £3000 55·00
174 4d. black and orange (*shades*) 50·00 65·00
175 5d. lake-brown and olive £750 75·00
176 6d. brown and mauve £850 60·00
177 1s. black and blue-green (*shades*) £1100 55·00
178 2s. black and dull blue £2250 £350
179 £1 red and black £16000 £3000

(c) P 14×15 (½d., 3d., 1s.) or 15×14 (1d., 4d.).
179*a* **17** ½d. yellow-green † £2750
179*b* 1d. carmine † £6000
180 3d. purple and ochre £6000 £250
181 4d. black and orange £450
181*a* 1s. black and blue-green £25000 £2500

(d) P 13½.
182 **17** ½d. yellow-green £300 45·00
182*a* ½d. green £350 45·00
183 1d. bright carmine £2000 48·00
184 2½d. ultramarine (*shades*) 38·00 65·00
185 8d. black and purple (*shades*) 60·00 £250
185*a* 8d. grey-purple and dull purple £375 £450
119s/85s Optd "Specimen" (all perf 14 except 2½d. and 8d. perf 13½) *Set of* 18 £3500

Plate varieties in T **17** are:—½d., double dot below "D" in right-hand value tablet (R. 3/9) (*from* £500 *un*. £350 *used*); 2d. to £1 excluding 2½d., straight stroke in Queen's right ear known as the "gash in ear" variety (R. 1/2) (*from* 3 *to* 5 *times normal*).

Stamps from the above and the next issue are known compound perf with 14 or 15 on one side only or on adjoining sides but we no longer list them.

Examples of some values are known with a forged registered Bulawayo postmark dated "JA 10 11".

(Recess Waterlow)

1913 (1 Sept)–**22**. No wmk.

(i) From single working plates.

(a) P 14.
186 **18** ½d. blue-green 9·00 2·25
187 ½d. deep green 6·50 2·25
a. Imperf horiz (vert pair) £800
b. Imperf between (vert strip of 5) £3000
188 ½d. yellow-green 16·00 2·25
a. Imperf between (horiz pair) .. £850
188*b* ½d. dull green 11·00 2·25
ba. Imperf vert (horiz pair) £850 £850
bb. Imperf between (horiz pair) .. £1200
189 ½d. bright green 22·00 2·25
a. Imperf between (vert pair) £1500
190 1d. rose-carmine 6·50 2·25
a. Imperf between (horiz pair) .. £950 £800
191 1d. carmine-red (*shades*) 10·00 2·25
a. Imperf between (pair) £1400
192 1d. brown-red 4·00 2·25
193 1d. red 6·00 2·25
a. Imperf between (horiz pair) .. £900
194 1d. scarlet 17·00 2·50
a. Imperf between (horiz pair) .. £1100
195 1d. rose-red 10·00 2·25
a. Imperf between (horiz pair) .. £850 £850
b. Imperf between (vert pair) £2250
196 1d. rosine £500 20·00
197 1½d. brown-ochre (1919) 5·00 2·25
a. Imperf between (horiz pair) .. £750 £750
198 1½d. bistre-brown (1917) 5·00 2·25
a. Imperf between (horiz pair) .. £750 £750
199 1½d. drab-brown (1917) 6·00 2·25
a. Imperf between (horiz pair) .. £750
b. Imperf between (vert pair) £2000
200 2½d. deep blue 5·50 30·00
201 2½d. bright blue 5·50 28·00

(b) P 15.
202 **18** ½d. blue-green 8·50 19·00
203 ½d. green 14·00 17·00
204 1d. rose-red £550 22·00
a. Imperf between (horiz pair) .. £16000
205 1d. brown-red 4·50 7·00
206 1½d. bistre-brown (1919) 35·00 7·00
a. Imperf between (horiz pair) .. £21000
206*b* 1½d. brown-ochre (1917) 42·00 11·00
207 2½d. deep blue 20·00 50·00
208 2½d. bright blue 16·00 48·00

(c) P 14×15.
208*a* **18** ½d. green £6500 £190

(d) P 15×14.
208*b* **18** ½d. green £6500 £350
208*c* 1½d. drab-brown

(e) P 13½.
208*d* **18** 1d. red (1914) † £500

Die I Die II Die III

The remaining values were printed from double, i.e. head and duty, plates. There are at least four different head plates made from three different dies, which may be distinguished as follows:—

Die I. The King's left ear is neither shaded nor outlined; no outline to top of cap. Shank of anchor in cap badge is complete.

Die II. The ear is shaded all over, but has no outline. The top of the cap has a faint outline. Anchor as Die I.

Die III. The ear is shaded and outlined; a heavy continuous outline round the cap. Shank of anchor is broken just below the lowest line which crosses it.

(ii) Printed from double plates. Head Die I.

(a) P 14.
209 **18** 2d. black and grey 12·00 8·50
210 3d. black and yellow 75·00 12·00
211 4d. black and orange-red 8·50 32·00
212 5d. black and green 5·00 15·00
213 6d. black and mauve £200 24·00
213*a* 8d. violet and green £5000
214 2s. black and brown £110 80·00

(b) P 15.
215 **18** 3d. black and yellow 6·00 21·00
216 4d. black and orange-red £140 23·00
217 6d. black and mauve 7·00 8·00
217*a* 8d. violet and green £18000 £22000
218 2s. black and brown 11·00 42·00

(iii) Head Die II.

(a) P 14.
219 **18** 2d. black and grey 14·00 5·00
220 2d. black and brownish grey 55·00 8·50
221 3d. black and deep yellow 35·00 7·50
222 3d. black and yellow 75·00 7·50
223 3d. black and buff 8·50 7·00
224 4d. black and orange-red 22·00 9·50
225 4d. black and deep orange-red 15·00 9·50
226 5d. black and grey-green 17·00 38·00
227 5d. black and bright green 16·00 38·00
228 6d. black and mauve 32·00 4·00
229 6d. black and purple 80·00 5·00
230 8d. violet and green 14·00 65·00
231 10d. blue and carmine-red 20·00 48·00
232 1s. black and greenish blue 60·00 55·00
233 1s. black and turquoise-blue 13·00 13·00
234 2s. black and brown 85·00 12·00
235 2s. black and yellow-brown £325 35·00
236 2s.6d. indigo and grey-brown 60·00 40·00
236*a* 2s.6d. pale blue and brown £1000 65·00
236*b* 3s. brown and blue 95·00 £110
237 3s. chestnut and bright blue 95·00 £130
238 5s. blue and yellow-green £150 80·00
239 5s. blue and blue-green 65·00 70·00
240 7s.6d. blackish purple and slate-black £300 £325
241 10s. crimson and yellow-green £190 £325
242 £1 black and purple £400 £550
243 £1 black and violet £350 £600

(b) P 15.
244 **18** 2d. black and grey 8·50 10·00
245 4d. black and deep orange-vermilion £1100 £250
246 8d. violet and green £190 £170
247 10d. blue and red 10·00 32·00
248 1s. black and greenish blue 60·00 15·00
249 2s.6d. indigo and grey-brown 42·00 85·00
250 3s. chocolate and blue £700 £275
251 5s. blue and yellow-green £160 £170
251*a* 5s. blue and blue-green £1800
252 7s.6d. blackish purple and slate-black £140 £225
253 10s. red and green £180 £375
a. Frame double, one albino £550
254 £1 black and purple £1400 £1400
254*a* £1 black and deep purple £3000 £2500

186s, 190s, 198s, 208s, 209s, 211s/12s, 215s, 217s/18s, 230s, 232s, 237s/8s, 240s/2s, 247s, 249s Optd "Specimen" *Set of* 19 ..... £2250

(iv) Head Die III (1919). Toned paper, yellowish gum.

(a) P 14.

255 **18** 2d. black and brownish grey ..... 11·00 6·00
256 2d. black and grey-black ..... 9·00 3·50
a. Imperf between (horiz pair) .. £5000
b. Imperf between (horiz strip of 3) £12000
c. Imperf vert (horiz pair) £4750 £4750
257 2d. black and grey ..... 11·00 4·25
258 2d. black and sepia ..... 48·00 9·00
259 3d. black and yellow ..... 11·00 3·00
260 3d. black and ochre ..... 12·00 3·25
261 4d. black and orange-red ..... 15·00 7·00
262 4d. black and dull red ..... 14·00 9·00
263 5d. black and pale green ..... 7·50 35·00
a. Imperf between (horiz strip of 3) £27000
264 5d. black and green ..... 7·50 35·00
265 6d. black and reddish mauve ..... 7·50 7·50
a. Imperf between (horiz pair) .. £20000
266 6d. black and dull mauve ..... 7·50 7·50
267 8d. mauve and dull blue-green ..... 20·00 55·00
268 8d. mauve and greenish blue ..... 18·00 60·00
a. Imperf vert (horiz pair) £12000
269 10d. indigo and carmine ..... 16·00 50·00
270 10d. blue and red ..... 14·00 50·00
271 1s. black and greenish blue ..... 10·00 11·00
272 1s. black and pale blue-green ..... 9·00 8·50
272*a* 1s. black and light blue ..... 12·00 17·00
272*b* 1s. black and green ..... 70·00 35·00
273 2s. black and brown ..... 14·00 15·00
aa. Imperf between (vert pair) .... † £35000
273*a* 2s. black and yellow-brown £3250 £140
274 2s.6d. dp ultramarine & grey-brn ..... 40·00 70·00
274*a* 2s.6d. pale blue and pale bistre-brown (*shades*) ..... £110 75·00
274*b* 3s. chestnut and light blue £225 £160
275 5s. deep blue and blue-green (*shades*) ..... 90·00 60·00
276 5s. blue & pale yell-grn (*shades*). £120 65·00
276*a* 7s.6d. maroon and slate-black £800 £1200
277 10s. carmine-lake and yellow-green £325 £200
278 £1 black and bright purple £450 £600
279 £1 black and deep purple £500 £600
279*a* £1 black and violet-indigo £600 £700
279*b* £1 black and deep violet £650 £700

(b) P 15.

279*c* **18** 2d. black and brownish grey £5500 £400

Half Penny
(19)

Half- Penny.
(20)

1917 (15 Aug). *No. 190 surch at the Northern Rhodesian Administrative Press, Livingstone, with T* **19**, *in violet or violet-black.*

280 **18** ½d. on 1d. rose-carmine (*shades*) . 2·50 8·00
a. Surch inverted £1400 £1500
b. Letters "n n" spaced wider ..... 11·00 28·00
c. Letters "n y" spaced wider ..... 7·50 23·00

The setting was in two rows of 10 repeated three times in the sheet.

The two colours of the surcharge occur on the same sheet.

1917 (22 Sept). *No. 190 surch as T* **20** *(new setting with hyphen, and full stop after "Penny"), in deep violet.*

281 **18** ½d. on 1d. rose-carmine (*shades*) . 1·75 8·50

1922–24. *New printings on white paper with clear white gum.*

(i) Single working plates.

(a) P 14.

282 **18** ½d. dull green (1922) ..... 5·50 7·50
a. Imperf between (vert pair) £2500 £1700
283 ½d. deep blue-green (1922) ..... 5·50 8·00
284 1d. bright rose (1922) ..... 10·00 6·00
285 1d. bright rose-scarlet (1923) ..... 10·00 6·00
a. Imperf between (horiz pair) .. £1800
b. Imperf between (vert pair) £2250
286 1d. aniline red (8.24) (toned paper) ..... 20·00 10·00
287 1½d. brown-ochre (1923) ..... 8·50 7·50
a. Imperf between (vert pair) £2500 £1600

(b) P 15.

288 **18** ½d. dull green (1923) ..... 45·00
289 1d. bright rose-scarlet (1923) ..... 48·00
290 1½d. brown-ochre (1923) ..... 48·00

(ii) Double plates. Head Die III.

(a) P 14.

291 **18** 2d. black and grey-purple (1922) . 8·50 5·00
292 2d. black and slate-purple (1923) 7·50 7·00
293 3d. black and yellow (1922) ..... 10·00 28·00
294 4d. black and orange-vermilion (1922–3) ..... 15·00 40·00
295 6d. jet-black and lilac (1922–3) ..... 5·00 4·75
296 8d. mauve and pale blue-green (1922) ..... 35·00 80·00
297 8d. violet and grey-green (1923) .. 38·00 80·00
298 10d. bright ultramarine and red (1922) ..... 11·00 60·00
299 10d. bright ultramarine and carmine-red (1923) ..... 19·00 65·00
300 1s. black and dull blue (1922–3) .. 9·50 13·00
a. Imperf between (horiz pair) .. £18000
b. Imperf between (vert pair) £20000
301 2s. black and brown (1922–3) ..... 19·00 48·00
302 2s.6d. ultramarine and sepia (1922) . 48·00 85·00
303 2s.6d. violet-blue and grey-brown (1923) ..... 65·00 85·00
304 3s. red-brown and turquoise-blue (1922) ..... 95·00 £120
305 3s. red-brown and grey-blue (1923) £120 £150
306 5s. bright ultramarine and emerald (1922) £110 £150
307 5s. deep blue and bright green (1923) £130 £150
308 7s.6d. brown-purple and slate (1922) £200 £325
309 10s. crimson and bright yellow-green (1922) £180 £250
310 10s. carmine and yellow-green (1923) £200 £300
311 £1 black and magenta (1922) £550 £750
311*a* £1 black and deep magenta (1923) £650 £850

(b) P 15 (1923).

312 **18** 2d. black and slate-purple ..... 38·00
313 4d. black and orange-vermilion ... 42·00
314 6d. jet-black and lilac ..... 55·00
315 8d. violet and grey-green ..... 60·00
316 10d. bright ultramarine and carmine-red ..... 65·00
317 1s. black and dull blue ..... 75·00
318 2s. black and brown £110
319 2s.6d. violet-blue and grey-brown £120
320 3s. red-brown and grey-blue £160
321 5s. deep blue and bright green £225
322 £1 black and deep magenta £850

The 1922 printing shows the mesh of the paper very clearly through the gum. In the 1923 printing the gum is very smooth and the mesh of the paper is not so clearly seen. Where date is given as "(1922–23)" two printings were made, which do not differ sufficiently in colour to be listed separately.

Nos. 288/90 and 312/22 were never sent out to Rhodesia, but only issued in London. Any used copies could, therefore, only have been obtained by favour.

Southern Rhodesia, that part of the Company's territory south of the River Zambesi, became a self-governing colony on 1 October 1923. British South Africa Company rule continued in Northern Rhodesia until the administration was transferred to the Colonial Office on 1 April 1924.

The current stamps of Rhodesia, the Admiral series first issued in 1913, continued to be used in Southern Rhodesia until 1 April 1924 (invalidated 1 May 1924) and in Northern Rhodesia until 1 April 1925 (invalidated 30 September 1925).

For issues from 1924 to 1964 see Southern Rhodesia.

In October 1964 Southern Rhodesia was renamed Rhodesia.

RHODESIA

59 "Telecommunications"

60 Bangala Dam

(Des V. Whiteley. Photo Harrison)

1965 (17 May). *I.T.U. Centenary.* P 14½.

351 **59** 6d. violet and light yellow-olive ... 1·25 40
352 1s.3d. violet and lilac ..... 1·50 40
353 2s.6d. violet and light brown ..... 2·25 4·50
351/3 *Set of* 3 ..... 4·50 4·75

(Des V. Whiteley. Photo Harrison)

1965 (19 July). *Water Conservation. T* **60** *and similar vert designs. Multicoloured.* P 14.

354 3d. Type **60** 30 10
355 4d. Irrigation canal ..... 1·00 1·00
356 2s.6d. Cutting sugar cane ..... 2·25 3·50
354/6 *Set of* 3 ..... 3·25 4·25

63 Sir Winston Churchill, Quill, Sword and Houses of Parliament

(Des H. Baxter. Photo Harrison)

1965 (16 Aug). *Churchill Commemoration.* P 14½.

357 **63** 1s.3d. black and bright blue 70 35

UNILATERAL DECLARATION OF INDEPENDENCE

Independence was declared by Rhodesia on 11 November 1965 but this was not recognised by the British Government. Following a conference in London during 1979 it was agreed that the British Government should resume control, pending elections to be held in February 1980.

After the elections Rhodesia became an independent republic within the Commonwealth on 18 April 1980, as ZIMBABWE.

64 Coat of Arms

(Des Col. C. R. Dickenson. Litho Mardon Printers, Salisbury)

1965 (8 Dec). *"Independence".* P 11.

358 **64** 2s.6d. multicoloured 15 15
a. Imperf (pair) £750

INDEPENDENCE
11th November
1965
(65)

5/-
(66)

1966 (17 Jan).

(a) Nos. 92/105 of Southern Rhodesia optd with T **65** *or larger (5s. to £1) by Mardon Printers, Salisbury.*

359 ½d. yellow, yellow-green and light blue 10 10
a. Pair, one stamp without opt £3500
360 1d. reddish violet and yellow-ochre 10 10
361 2d. yellow and deep violet 10 10
362 3d. chocolate and pale blue 10 10
363 4d. yellow-orange and deep green 15 10
364 6d. carmine-red, yellow and deep dull green 15 10
365 9d. red-brown, yellow and olive-green 30 10
a. Opt double £500
366 1s. blue-green and ochre 40 10
a. Opt double £500
b. Pair, one stamp without opt £2750
367 1s.3d. red, violet and yellow-green 50 50
368 2s. blue and ochre ..... 60 3·25
369 2s.6d. ultramarine and vermilion ..... 60 1·00
370 5s. light brown, bistre-yellow and light blue ..... 1·50 5·50
a. Opt double £600
371 10s. black, yellow-ochre, light blue and carmine-red ..... 4·00 2·25
a. Extra "feather" ..... 22·00
372 £1 brown, yellow-green, buff and salmon-pink ..... 1·25 2·25

(b) No. 357 surch with T **66**.

373 5s. on 1s.3d. black and bright blue (R.) ... 3·50 9·50
a. "5/-" omitted .....
359/73 *Set of* 15 ..... 12·00 22·00

Owing to the existence of forgeries, No. 370a should only be purchased when accompanied by a certificate of genuineness. Other overprint errors exist from the clandestine use of the original settings.

67 Emeralds

68 Zeederberg Coach, *circa* 1895

(Des V. Whiteley. Photo Harrison)

1966 (9 Feb). *As Nos. 92/105, but inscr* "RHODESIA" *as T* **67**. *Some designs and colours changed.* P 14½ (1d. to 4d.), 13½×13 (6d. to 2s.6d) or 14½×14 (5s. to £1).

374 – 1d. reddish violet and yellow-ochre 10 10
375 – 2d. yellow-orange and deep green (as No. 96) 10 10
a. Yellow-orange omitted £1800
376 – 3d. chocolate and pale blue 10 10
a. Chocolate omitted £3750
b. Pale blue omitted £3000
377 **67** 4d. emerald and sepia ..... 1·50 10
378 **50** 6d. carmine-red, yellow and deep dull green 15 10
379 – 9d. yellow and deep violet (as No. 94) 30 20
380 **45** 1s. yellow, yellow-green and light blue 15 10
381 – 1s.3d. blue and ochre (as No. 101) ... 25 15
a. Ochre omitted £2750
382 – 1s.6d. red-brown, yellow and olive-green (as No. 98) ..... 2·25 25
383 – 2s. red, violet and yellow-green (as No. 100) 60 80
384 – 2s.6d. blue, vermilion and turquoise-blue ..... 1·50 20
385 **56** 5s. light brown, bistre-yellow and light blue 70 90
386 – 10s. black, yellow-ochre, light blue and carmine-red ..... 3·00 3·50
387 **58** £1 brown, yellow-green, buff and salmon-pink ..... 3·25 7·00
374/87 *Set of* 14 ..... 12·00 12·00

Nos. 379/80 are in larger format, as T **50**.

No. 374 exists in coils constructed from normal sheets. Coil-vending machines were withdrawn from service in 1967.

No. 375a occured on single rows from two separate sheets, No. 376a in the bottom row of a sheet, No. 376b in the top two rows of a sheet and No. 381a in the third vertical row on two sheets.

For stamps printed by lithography, see Nos. 397/407.

PRINTERS. All the following stamps were printed by lithography by Mardon Printers, Salisbury.

(Des V. Whiteley (Nos. 388/90))

1966 (2 May). *28th Congress of Southern Africa Philatelic Federation ("Rhopex"). T* **68** *and similar horiz designs.* P 14½.

388 3d. multicoloured 15 10
389 9d. grey-buff, sepia and grey-green 15 20
390 1s.6d. pale blue and black 25 30
391 2s.6d. salmon-pink, pale dull grn & blk ... 30 55
388/91 *Set of* 4 ..... 75 1·00
MS392 126×84 mm. Nos. 388/91 (*toned paper*) .... 5·00 11·00
a. White paper ..... 7·50 13·00

Designs:—9d. Sir Rowland Hill; 1s.6d. The Penny Black; 2s.6d. Rhodesian stamp of 1892 (No. 12).

The 3d., 2s.6d. and minature sheet exist imperforate from sheets prepared for presentation purposes.

69 De Havilland D.H.89 Dragon Rapide (1946)

70 Kudu

1966 (1 June). *20th Anniv of Central African Airways. T* **69** *and similar horiz designs.* P 14½×14.

393	6d. black, blue, yellow and green	75	35
394	1s.3d. blue, yellow-orange, black and green	1·00	40
395	2s.6d. black, blue, yellow and green	1·50	1·50
396	5s. black and blue	2·25	4·50
393/6 *Set of* 4		5·00	6·00

Aircraft:—1s.3d. Douglas DC-3 (1953); 2s.6d. Vickers Viscount 748 *Matopos* (1956); 5s. B.A.C. One Eleven 200.

The 6d., 2s.6d. and 5s. values exist imperforate from sheets prepared for presentation purposes.

1966–69. *As Nos. 374/87 but litho.* P 14½ (1d. to 2s.) or 14½×14 (others).

397	1d. reddish violet and yellow-ochre (*shades*) (2.6.66)	15	10
398	2d. orange and green (1.11.67)	85	65
399	3d. chocolate-brown and pale greenish blue (29.1.68)	1·50	10
400	4d. emerald, bistre-brown and drab (21.9.66)	65	10
401	6d. carmine-red, yellow and olive-grey (1.11.66)	60	50
402	9d. yellow and light violet (20.11.67)	30	10
403	1s.3d. blue and ochre (1.11.66)	1·50	30
404	2s. dull red, violet and sage-green (18.7.66)	1·50	4·00
405	5s. yellow-brown, deep bistre-yellow and light blue (25.6.66)	2·00	4·50
406	10s. black, buff, light blue and carmine-red (10.8.66)	8·00	14·00
407	£1 pale brown, yellow-green, brown-ochre and salmon (10.8.66)	8·00	15·00
397/407 *Set of* 11		22·00	35·00

In addition to the change in printing process from photogravure to lithography and the difference in perforation in the 6d. to 2s. values (14½ instead of 13½×13) and shade variations, the oval portrait frame is larger (and in some values thicker) in the 1d. to 2s., and in the 1s.3d. the Queen's head is also larger.

Trial printings, made in June 1966, exist of the 5s., 10s. and £1 values on a slightly thinner paper. These are rare.

The 1d., 3d. and 5s. values exist imperforate from sheets prepared for presentation purposes.

1967–68. *Dual Currency Issue. As Nos. 376, 380 and 382/4 but value in decimal currency in addition as in T* **70**. P 14½. *White gum (No. 408) or cream gum (others).*

408	3d./2½c. chocolate-brown and pale greenish blue (15.3.67)	50	15
409	1s./10c. yellow, green and greenish blue (1.11.67)	50	25
410	1s.6d./15c. red-brown, yellow and yellow-green (11.3.68)	3·50	70
411	2s./20c. dull red, violet and sage-green (11.3.68)	2·00	3·00
412	2s.6d./25c. ultramarine-blue, vermilion and bright turquoise-blue (9.12.68)	17·00	25·00
408/12 *Set of* 5		21·00	26·00

71 Dr. Jameson (administrator)

(Des from painting by F. M. Bennett)

1967 (17 May). *Famous Rhodesians (1st issue) and 50th Death Anniv of Dr. Jameson.* P 14½.

413	**71** 1s.6d. multicoloured	20	35

See also Nos. 426, 430 and 457. Further stamps in this series appeared after 1970.

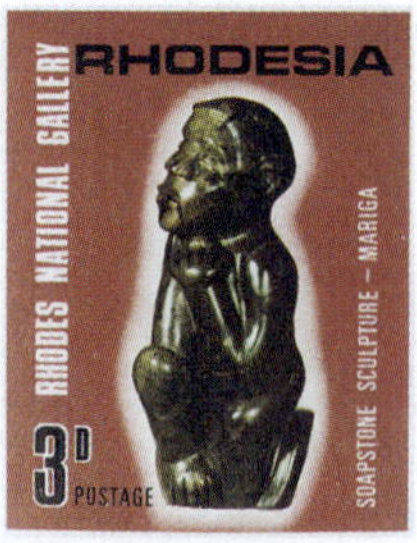

72 Soapstone Sculpture (Joram Mariga)

1967 (12 July). *Tenth Anniv of Opening of Rhodes National Gallery. T* **72** *and similar vert designs.* P 14½×14 (3d., 9d.) or 14 (others).

414	3d. reddish chestnut, yellow-olive and black	10	10
415	9d. light greenish blue, deep olive-brown and black	20	20
	a. Perf 13½	5·50	15·00
416	1s.3d. multicoloured	20	25
417	2s.6d. multicoloured	25	60
414/17 *Set of* 4		65	1·00

Designs: 9d. "The Burgher of Calais" (detail, Rodin); 1s.3d. "The Knight" (stamp design wrongly inscr) (Roberto Crippa); 2s.6d. "John the Baptist" (M. Tossini).

73 Baobab Tree

1967 (6 Sept). *Nature Conservation. T* **73** *and similar designs.* P 14½.

418	4d. light brown and black	10	20
419	4d. yellow-olive and black	25	20
420	4d. deep grey and black	25	20
421	4d. yellow-orange and black	10	20
418/21 *Set of* 4		60	70

Designs: *Horiz*—No. 418, Type **73**; 419, White Rhinoceros; 420, African Elephants. *Vert*—No. 421, Wild Gladiolus.

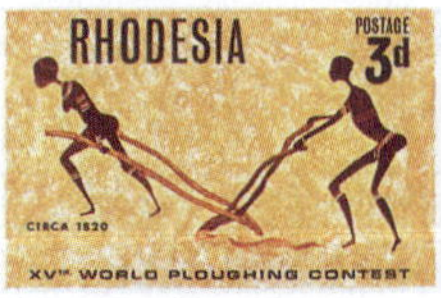

74 Wooden Hand Plough

(Des Rose Martin)

1968 (26 Apr). *15th World Ploughing Contest, Norton, Rhodesia. T* **74** *and similar horiz designs.* P 14½.

422	3d. pale orange, orange-vermilion and lake-brown	10	10
423	9d. multicoloured	15	20
424	1s.6d. multicoloured	20	55
425	2s.6d. multicoloured	20	75
422/5 *Set of* 4		60	1·40

Designs: 9d. Early wheel plough; 1s.6d. Steam powered tractor, and ploughs; 2s.6d. Modern tractor, and plough.

75 Alfred Beit (national benefactor)

76 Raising the Flag, Bulawayo, 1893

(Des from painting by A. Haywood)

1968 (15 July). *Famous Rhodesians (2nd issue).* P 14½.

426	**75** 1s.6d. pale orange, black and brown	20	30

(Des Rose Martin)

1968 (4 Nov). *75th Anniv of Matabeleland. T* **76** *and similar vert designs.* P 14½.

427	3d. pale orange, red-orange and black	15	10
428	9d. multicoloured	15	20
429	1s.6d. pale turquoise-green, deep emerald and blackish green	20	60
427/9 *Set of* 3		45	80

Designs:—9d. View and coat of arms of Bulawayo; 1s.6d. Allan Wilson (combatant in the Matabele War).

77 Sir William Henry Milton (administrator)

(Des from painting by S. Kendrick)

1969 (15 Jan). *Famous Rhodesians (3rd issue).* P 14½.

430	**77** 1s.6d. multicoloured	20	55

78 2 ft Gauge Steam Locomotive No. 15, 1897

(Des Rose Martin)

1969 (22 May). *70th Anniv of Opening of Beira-Salisbury Railway. T* **78** *and similar horiz designs showing locomotives. Multicoloured.* P 14½.

431	3d. Type **78**	40	10
432	9d. 7th Class steam locomotive No. 43, 1903	60	40
433	1s.6d. Beyer Peacock 15th Class steam locomotive No. 413, 1951	75	1·00
434	2s.6d. Class DE2 diesel-electric locomotive No. 1203, 1955	1·25	4·00
431/4 *Set of* 4		2·75	5·00

79 Low Level Bridge

(Des Rose Martin)

1969 (18 Sept). *Bridges of Rhodesia. T* **79** *and similar horiz designs. Multicoloured.* P 14½.

435	3d. Type **79**	30	10
436	9d. Mpudzi bridge	50	25
437	1s.6d. Umniati bridge	75	75
438	2s.6d. Birchenough bridge	1·00	1·50
435/8 *Set of* 4		2·25	2·25

(New Currency. 100 cents = 1 dollar)

80 Harvesting Wheat

81 Devil's Cataract, Victoria Falls

(Des from colour-transparencies (3, 6c.), Rose Martin (others))

1970 (17 Feb)–**73**. *Decimal Currency. T* **80/1** *and similar horiz designs.* P 14½.

439	1c. multicoloured	10	10
	a. Booklet pane of 4	30	
440	2c. multicoloured	10	10
441	2½c. multicoloured	10	10
	a. Booklet pane of 4	35	
441*c*	3c. multicoloured (1.1.73)	1·25	10
	ca. Booklet pane of 4	4·50	
442	3½c. multicoloured	10	10
	a. Booklet pane of 4	65	
442*b*	4c. multicoloured (1.1.73)	1·75	75
	ba. Booklet pane of 4	6·00	
443	5c. multicoloured	15	10
443*b*	6c. multicoloured (1.1.73)	4·00	3·75
443*c*	7½c. multicoloured (1.1.73)	7·00	60
444	8c. multicoloured	75	20
445	10c. multicoloured	60	10
446	12½c. multicoloured	1·25	10
446*a*	14c. multicoloured (1.1.73)	12·00	70
447	15c. multicoloured	1·25	15
448	20c. multicoloured	1·00	15
449	25c. multicoloured	4·00	60
450	50c. turquoise and ultramarine	1·25	55
451	$1 multicoloured	3·75	1·50
452	$2 multicoloured	7·00	15·00
439/52 *Set of* 19		42·00	22·00

Designs: *Size as T* **80**—2c. Pouring molten metal; 2½c. Zimbabwe Ruins; 3c. Articulated lorry; 3½c. and 4c. Statute of Cecil Rhodes; 5c. Mine headgear. *Size as T* **81**—6c. Hydrofoil *Seaflight*; 7½c. As 8c.; 10c. Yachting on Lake McIlwaine; 12½c. Hippopotamus in river; 14c. and 15c. Kariba Dam; 20c. Irrigation canal. *As T* **80/1** *but larger* (31×26 *mm*)—25c. Bateleurs; 50c. Radar antenna and Vickers Viscount 810; $1 "Air Rescue"; $2 Rhodesian flag.

Booklet panes Nos. 439a, 441a, 441ca, 442a and 442ba have margins all round.

82 Despatch Rider, *circa* 1890

(Des Rose Martin)

1970 (1 July). *Inauguration of Posts and Telecommunications Corporation. T* **82** *and similar horiz designs. Multicoloured.* P 14½.

453	2½c. Type **82**	30	10
454	3½c. Loading mail at Salisbury airport	40	50
455	15c. Constructing telegraph line, *circa* 1890	45	1·25
456	25c. Telephone and modern telecommunications equipment	50	2·00
453/6 *Set of* 4		1·50	3·50

83 Mother Patrick (Dominican nurse and teacher)

(Des Rose Martin from photograph)

1970 (16 Nov). *Famous Rhodesians (4th issue).* P 14½.

457	**83** 15c. multicoloured	60	50

STAMP BOOKLETS

1967 (Feb). *Black on orange cover, size 57×45 mm. Stitched.*

SB7	1s. booklet containing 3d. (No. 376) in block of 4	3·75

Although not issued in Rhodesia until February 1967, No. SB7 was released in London in June 1966.

1968 (21 Dec). *Black on yellow cover, size 51×94 mm. Stapled.*

SB8	5s. booklet containing twelve 1d. and 3d., and six 2d. (Nos. 397/9) in blocks of 6	18·00

1970 (17 Feb). *Red on yellow cover. Stapled.*

SB9	46c. booklet containing twelve 1c., eight 2½c. and four 3½c. in panes of 4 (Nos. 439a, 441a, 442a)	5·00

POSTAGE DUE STAMPS

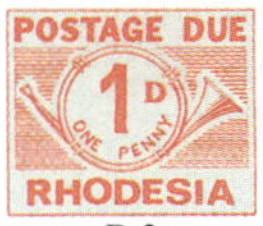

D **2**

D **3** Zimbabwe Bird (soapstone sculpture)

(Des E.W. Jones Typo Printing and Stationery Dept, Salisbury)

1965 (17 June). *Roul 9.*

D8	D **2**	1d. orange-red (*roul 5*)	50	12·00
		a. Roul 9	4·00	12·00
D9		2d. deep blue	40	8·00
D10		4d. green	50	8·00
D11		6d. plum	50	6·00
D8/11 *Set of* 4			1·75	30·00

The 2d. has a stop below the "D".

(Litho Mardon Printers, Salisbury)

1966 (15 Dec). P 14½.

D12	D **3**	1d. red	60	3·25
D13		2d. bluish violet	75	1·75
D14		4d. pale green	75	4·00
D15		6d. reddish violet	75	1·50
D16		1s. red-brown	75	1·50
D17		2s. black	1·00	4·75
D12/17 *Set of* 6			4·25	15·00

1970 (17 Feb)–**73**. *Decimal Currency. As Type D* **3**, *but larger (26×22½ mm).* P 14½.

D18	D **3**	1c. bright green	75	1·25
D19		2c. ultramarine	75	60
		a. Printed on the gummed side	65·00	
D20		5c. bright reddish violet	1·50	1·75
D21		6c. pale lemon (7.5.73)	4·50	4·00
D22		10c. cerise	1·50	4·00
D18/22 *Set of* 5			8·00	10·50

Rhodesia & Nyasaland

Stamps for the Central Africa Federation of Northern and Southern Rhodesia and Nyasaland Protectorate.

1

2

3 Queen Elizabeth II

(Recess Waterlow)

1954 (1 July)–**56**. P 13½×14 (T **1**), 13½×13 (T **2**) or 14½×13½ (T **3**).

1	**1**	½d. red-orange	15	10
		a. Coil stamp. Perf 12½×14 (6.2.56)	30	1·50
2		1d. ultramarine	15	10
		a. Coil stamp. Perf 12½×14. *Deep blue* (9.55)	1·50	16·00
		ab. Ultramarine (1.10.55)	4·00	15·00
3		2d. bright green	15	10
3*a*		2½d. ochre (15.2.56)	4·75	10
4		3d. carmine-red	20	10
5		4d. red-brown	60	20
6		4½d. blue-green	30	1·50
7		6d. bright reddish purple	2·25	10
		a. Bright purple (5.5.56)	4·50	10
8		9d. violet	2·00	1·00
9		1s. grey-black	2·00	10
10	**2**	1s.3d. red-orange and ultramarine	3·25	40
11		2s. deep blue and yellow-brown	7·50	4·00
12		2s.6d. black and rose-red	6·00	2·25
13		5s. violet and olive-green	17·00	6·50
14	**3**	10s. dull blue-green and orange	19·00	8·00
15		£1 olive-green and lake	30·00	26·00
1/15 *Set of* 16			85·00	45·00

Nos. 1a and 2a printed on rotary machines by subsidiary company, Imprimerie Belge de Securité, in Belgium.

4 De Havilland D.H.106 Comet 1 over Victoria Falls

5 Livingstone and Victoria Falls

Wing flaw (R. 3/3)

(Des J. E. Hughes 13d.), V. E. Horne (1s.). Recess Waterlow)

1955 (15 June). *Centenary of Discovery of Victoria Falls.* P 13½ (3d.) or 13 (1s.).

16	**4**	3d. ultramarine & dp turquoise-green	55	30
		a. Wing flaw	8·00	6·00
17	**5**	1s. purple and deep blue	55	70

6 Tea Picking

10 Rhodes's Grave

11 Lake Bangweulu

12a Rhodesian Railway Trains

19 Federal Coat of Arms

(Des M. Kinsella (9d.). Recess Waterlow (½d., 1d., 2d., 1s.) until 1962, then D.L.R. (2½d., 4d., 6d., 9d., 2s., 2s.6d.) and B.W. (others))

1959 (12 Aug)–**62**. *T* **6**, **10/11**, **12a**, **19** *and similar designs.* P 13½×14 (½d., 1d., 2d.), 14½ (2½d., 4d., 6d., 9d., 2s., 2s.6d.), 14×13½ (3d.), 13½×13 (1s.), 14 (1s.3d.) or 11 (others).

18	½d. black and light emerald	1·00	1·75
	a. Coil stamp. Perf 12½×14	3·25	5·50
19	1d. carmine-red and black	15	10
	a. Coil stamp. Perf 12½×14	3·25	8·50
	ab. Carmine-red and grey-black	5·50	10·00
	ac. Carmine-red (centre) omitted	£250	
20	2d. violet and yellow-brown	2·00	50
21	2½d. purple and grey-blue	1·75	1·00
22	3d. black and blue	40	10
	a. Black (centre) omitted	£17000	
	b. Printed on the gummed side	£425	
23	4d. maroon and olive	1·25	10
24	6d. ultramarine and deep myrtle-green	2·25	10
24*a*	9d. orange-brown and reddish violet (15.5.62)	8·00	3·00
25	1s. light green and ultramarine	1·25	10
26	1s.3d. emerald and deep chocolate	3·00	10
27	2s. grey-green and carmine	3·25	60
28	2s.6d. light blue and yellow-brown	4·50	40
29	5s. deep chocolate and yellow-green	9·00	2·25
30	10s. olive-brown and rose-red	25·00	19·00
31	£1 black and deep violet	45·00	55·00
18/31 *Set of* 15		95·00	75·00

Designs: *Vert* (*as T* **6**)—1d. V.H.F. mast; 2d. Copper mining; 2½d. Fairbridge Memorial. (*As T* **11**)—6d. Eastern Cataract, Victoria Falls. *Horiz* (*as T* **12a**)—1s. Tobacco; 1s.3d. Lake Nyasa; 2s. Chirundu Bridge; 2s.6d. Salisbury Airport. (*As T* **19**)—5s. Rhodes Statue; 10s. Mlanje.

Only three examples from two different sheets, all unused, are believed to exist of No. 22a, although further stamps from the same sheets can be found with the centre partially omitted.

20 Kariba Gorge, 1955

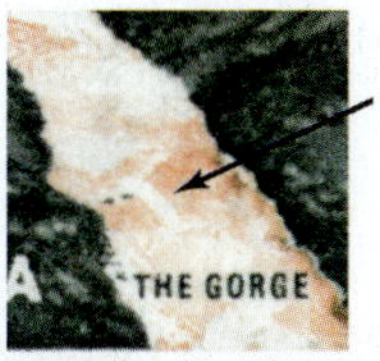

Gorge flaw (R. 4/6)

(Photo Harrison (3d., 6d.), D.L.R. (others))

1960 (17 May). *Opening of Kariba Hydro-Electric Scheme. T* **20** *and similar heriz designs.* P 14½×14 (3d., 6d.) or 13 (others).

32	3d. blackish green and red-orange	70	10
	a. Red-orange omitted	£4500	
	b. Gorge flaw	10·00	8·00
33	6d. brown and yellow-brown	70	20
34	1s. slate-blue and green	2·50	4·00
35	1s.3d. light blue and orange-brown	2·50	3·00
	a. Blue and deep orange-brown	9·00	7·00
36	2s.6d. deep slate-purple and orange-red	3·50	8·50
37	5s. reddish violet and turquoise-blue	8·50	11·00
32/7 *Set of* 6		16·00	24·00

Designs:—6d. 330 kV power lines; 1s. Barrage wall; 1s.3d. Barrage and lake; 2s.6d. Interior of power station; 5s. Barrage wall and Queen Mother (top left).

26 Miner Drilling

(Des V. Whiteley. Photo Harrison)

1961 (8 May). *Seventh Commonwealth Mining and Metallurgical Congress. T* **26** *and similar horiz design.* P 15×14.

38	6d. olive-green and orange-brown	50	20
39	1s.3d. black and light blue	50	80

Design:—1s.3d. Surface installations, Nchanga Mine.

Imperforate examples of the 6d. are believed to be printer's waste.

28 De Havilland D.H.66 Hercules *City of Basra* on Rhodesian Airstrip

31 Tobacco Plant

1962 (6 Feb). *30th Anniv of First London Rhodesia Airmail Service. T* **28** *and similar horiz designs.* P 14½×14.

40	6d. bronze-green and vermilion	35	50
41	1s.3d. light blue, black and yellow	1·50	50
42	2s.6d. rose-red and deep violet	4·00	5·50
40/2 *Set of* 3		5·25	6·00

Designs:—1s.3d. Short S.23 flying boat *Canopus* taking off from Zambesi; 2s.6d. Hawker Siddeley Comet 4 at Salisbury airport.

(Des V. Whiteley. Photo Harrison)

1963 (18 Feb). *World Tobacco Congress, Salisbury. T* **31** *and similar vert designs.* P 14×14½.

43	3d. green and olive-brown	30	10
44	6d. green, brown and blue	40	35
45	1s.3d. chestnut and indigo	60	45
46	2s.6d. yellow and brown	1·00	2·75
43/6 *Set of* 4		2·00	3·25

Designs:—6d. Tobacco field; 1s.3d. Auction floor; 2s.6d. Cured tobacco.

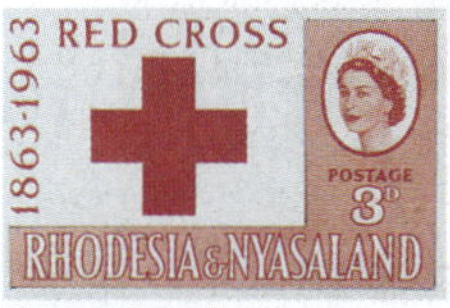

35 Red Cross Emblem

(Photo Harrison)

1963 (6 Aug). *Red Cross Centenary.* P 14½×14.

47	**35**	3d. red	1·00	10

36 African "Round Table" Emblem

(Des V. Whiteley. Photo Harrison)

1963 (11 Sept). *World Council of Young Men's Service Clubs, Salisbury.* P 14½×14.

48	**36**	6d. black, gold and yellow-green	50	1·50
49		1s.3d. black, gold, yellow-grn & lilac	50	1·00

STAMP BOOKLETS

1955 (1 Jan). *Black on yellow cover. Stitched.*

SB1	5s. booklet containing twelve ½d. and eighteen 1d. and 2d. (Nos. 1/3) in blocks of 6	35·00

1963 (4 Apr). *Black on yellow cover. Stitched.*

SB2	1s. booklet containing 3d. (No. 22) in block of 4	2·00

POSTAGE DUE STAMPS

After Federation in 1954 existing stocks of Postage Due Stamps from Northern Rhodesia, Nyasaland and Southern Rhodesia continued to be used and were sometimes distributed throughout the federation.

Increased postal rates in July 1956 and in 1959 led to the exhaustion of certain values, in particular the 1d., and various offices then used Rhodesia and Nyasaland postage issues for postage due purposes. There were isolated instances of such stamps being cancelled "POSTAGE DUE" from December 1956 onwards.

Some of these handstamps may have been applied at Bulawayo while others, in violet or black, originate from the Salisbury Delivery Room at Kingsway Post Office. Only the 1d. and 2d. (Nos. 2/3) are known with such handstamps. After mint examples began to appear the Postmaster General suppressed the use of the handstamps in August 1959.

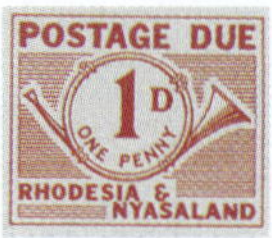

D 1

(Des E.W. Jones. Typo Federal Printing and Stationery Dept, Salisbury)

1961 (19 Apr). P 12½.

D1	D 1	1d. vermilion	3·75	5·50
		a. Imperf between (horiz pair)	£500	£600
D2		2d. deep violet-blue	3·00	3·00
D3		4d. green	3·00	9·50
D4		6d. purple	4·50	7·50
		a. Imperf between (horiz pair)	£1500	
D1/4 *Set of 4*			12·50	23·00

The 2d. has a stop below the "D".

The stamps of the Federation were withdrawn on 19 February 1964 when all three constituent territories had resumed issuing their own stamps.

St. Helena

CROWN COLONY

PRICES FOR STAMPS ON COVER TO 1945

Nos. 1/5	*from* × 12
Nos. 6/30	*from* × 10
Nos. 34/45	*from* × 15
Nos. 46/52	*from* × 6
Nos. 53/67	*from* × 5
No. 71	—
Nos. 72/86	*from* × 5
Nos. 87/8	*from* × 12
Nos. 89/95	*from* × 5
No. 96	—
Nos. 97/110	*from* × 5
Nos. 111/13	—
Nos. 114/40	*from* × 4

PERKINS BACON "CANCELLED". For notes on these handstamps, showing "CANCELLED" between horizontal bars forming an oval, see Catalogue Introduction.

1

ONE PENNY (2)

FOUR PENCE (3)

(Recess P.B.)

1856 (1 Jan). Wmk Large Star, W w **1**. Imperf.

1	1	6d. bl (H/S "CANCELLED" in oval £10000)	£500	£180

1861 (April (?)). Wmk Large Star, W w **1**.

(a) Clean-cut perf 14 to 16.

2	1	6d. blue	£1700	£275

(b) Rough perf 14 to 16.

2*a*	1	6d. blue	£425	£130

NOTE: The issues which follow consist of 6d. stamps, T **1**, printed in various colours and (except in the case of the 6d. values) surcharged with a new value, as T **2** to **10**, *e.g.* stamps described as "1d." are, in fact, 1d. on 6d stamps, and so on.

The numbers in the Type column below refer to the *types of the lettering* of the surcharged value.

(Printed by D.L.R. from P.B. plate)

Two Types of Bar on 1d. value:
A. Bar 16–17 mm long.
B. Bar 18½–19 mm long.

1863 (July). *Surch as T* **2/3** *with thin bar approximately the same length as the words.* Wmk Crown CC. Imperf.

3	2	1d. lake (Type A)	£130	£190
		a. Surch double	£6000	£3500
		b. Surch omitted	£20000	
		w. Wmk inverted	£400	
4		1d. lake (Type B)	£130	£200
		a. Vert pair. Nos. 3/4	£10000	
5	3	4d. carmine (*bar* 15½–16½ mm)	£500	£250
		a. Surch double	£14000	£6900

ONE PENNY (4 (A)) ONE PENNY (4 (B)) ONE PENNY (4 (C))

TWO PENCE (5) THREE PENCE (6) FOUR PENCE (7)

ONE SHILLING (8) FIVE SHILLINGS (9)

Three Types of Bar:
A. Thin bar (16½ to 17 mm) nearly the same length as the words.
B. Thick bar (14 to 14½ mm) much shorter than the words, except on the 2d. (Nos. 9, 22, 28) where it is nearly the same length.
C. Long bar (17 to 18 mm) same length as the words.

1864–80. *6d. as T* **1**, *without surcharge.* Wmk Crown CC.

(a) P 12½ (1864–73).

6	4	1d. lake (Type A) (1864)	55·00	29·00
		a. Surch double	£10000	
7		1d. lake (Type B) (1868)	£180	60·00
		a. Surch double		
		b. Imperf	£2750	
		w. Wmk inverted	—	£140
8	4	1d. lake (Type C) (1871)	£120	17·00
		a. Surch in blue-black	£1000	£550
		x. Wmk reversed	£180	
		y. Wmk inverted and reversed	£275	
9	5	2d. yellow (Type B) (1868)	£170	60·00
		a. Imperf	£10000	
		x. Wmk reversed	£350	
10		2d. yellow (Type C) (1873)	£120	45·00
		a. Surch in blue-black	£4000	£2250
		b. Surch double, one albino		
		x. Wmk reversed	£170	75·00
11	6	3d. deep dull purple (Type B) (1868)	95·00	50·00
		a. Surch double	—	£6500
		b. Imperf	£850	
		c. Light purple	£2750	£750
		x. Wmk reversed	£180	
12		3d. deep dull purple (Type A) (1873)	£120	60·00
13	7	4d. carmine (Type A) (*words 17 mm long*) (1864)	£160	50·00
		a. Surch double	†	£6000
14		4d. carmine (Type B) (*words 18 mm long*) (1868)	£110	60·00
		a. Surch double	†	£5500
		b. Surch double (18+19 *mm widths*)	£23000	£9500
		c. Imperf	£12000	
		x. Wmk reversed	£200	£100
15		4d. carmine-rose (Type B) (*words 19 mm long*) (1868)	£250	£120
		a. Surch omitted	†	£6000
16	–	6d. dull blue (1871)	£750	£100
		a. Ultramarine (1873)	£425	80·00
		x. Wmk reversed	£1300	£190
17	8	1s. deep yellow-green (Type A) (1864)	£350	28·00
		a. Surch double	†	£21000
		w. Wmk inverted	—	75·00
18		1s. deep yellow-green (Type B) (1868)	£650	£130
		a. Surch double	£17000	
		b. Imperf	£14000	
		c. Surch omitted*	£17000	
19		1s. deep green (Type C) (1871)	£550	16·00
		a. Surch in blue-black		
		x. Wmk reversed	£650	60·00
20	9	5s. orange (Type B) (1868)	55·00	65·00
		a. Yellow	£450	£425
		x. Wmk reversed	£140	£160

(b) P 14×12½ (1876).

21	4	1d. lake (Type B)	75·00	15·00
		w. Wmk inverted	£160	
22	5	2d. yellow (Type B)	£120	50·00
23		3d. purple (Type B)	£250	70·00
24		4d. carmine (Type B) (*words 16½ mm long*)	£130	60·00
		y. Wmk inverted and reversed	£130	70·00
25	–	6d. milky blue	£400	50·00
26	8	1s. deep green (Type C)	£750	24·00

(c) P 14 (1880).

27	4	1d. lake (Type B)	£100	20·00
28	5	2d. yellow (Type B)	£130	30·00
29	–	6d. milky blue	£425	50·00
		x. Wmk reversed	†	£130
30	8	1s. yellow-green (Type B)	21·00	12·00
		y. Wmk inverted and reversed	—	95·00

Two used examples of No. 15a are known, one being in the Royal Collection and the other damaged at bottom right. The price is for the latter.

*No. 18c is from a sheet of the 1s. with surcharge misplaced, the fifth row of 12 stamps being thus doubly surcharged and the tenth row without surcharge.

2½d (10)

11

12

1884–94. *T* **1** *surch. Bars similar to Type B above (except 2½d., T* **10**, *and the 1s., in which the bar is nearly the same length as the words). The 6d. as before without surcharge.* Wmk Crown CA. P 14.

34	–	½d. emerald (*words 17 mm*) (1884)	14·00	18·00
		a. "N" and "Y" spaced	£1100	
		b. Surch double	£1200	£1300
		ba. Ditto. "N" and "Y" spaced	£11000	
		w. Wmk inverted	—	42·00
		y. Wmk inverted and reversed	—	42·00
35	–	½d. green (*words 17 mm*) (1885)	11·00	18·00
		a. "N" and "Y" spaced	£475	£700
		x. Wmk reversed	12·00	20·00
36	–	½d. green (*words 14½ mm*) (1893)	2·50	2·75
		a. "N" and "Y" spaced	£1500	
37	4	1d. red (1887)	4·75	3·75
		x. Wmk reversed	5·50	4·50
38		1d. pale red (1890)	6·50	3·25
		x. Wmk reversed	8·50	5·00
39	5	2d. yellow (1894)	3·00	8·00
40	10	2½d. ultramarine (1893)	3·00	5·50
		a. Surch double	£20000	
		b. Stamp doubly printed	£9500	
		w. Wmk inverted	22·00	
41	6	3d. deep mauve (1887)	7·50	11·00
		a. Surch double	—	£9000
42		3d. deep reddish lilac (1887)	5·00	5·00
		a. Surch double	£10000	£6000
		w. Wmk reversed	8·00	5·00
43	7	4d. pale brown (*words 16½ mm*) (1890)	25·00	26·00
		a. Additional thin bar in surch (R. 7/2)	£750	
		by. Wmk inverted and reversed	35·00	
43*c*		4d. sepia (*words 17 mm*) (1894)	26·00	17·00
		cx. Wmk reversed	29·00	
44	–	6d. grey (1887)	25·00	5·00
		x. Wmk reversed	32·00	4·75
45	8	1s. yellow-green (1894)	50·00	25·00
		a. Surch double	£4750	
34/45 *Set of 8*			£110	65·00
40s/1s, 43bys, 44s Optd "Specimen" *Set of 4*			£190	

Examples of the above are sometimes found showing no watermark; these are from the bottom row of the sheet, which had escaped the watermark, the paper being intended for stamps of a different size to Type **1**.

Some are found without bar and others with bar at top of stamp, due to careless overprinting.

Nos. 34a and 35a occur on R. 18/12 and show a minimum space between the letters of 0.8 mm. Normal examples are spaced 0.5 mm, but some stamps show intermediate measurements due to loose type, On No. 34ba only one impression of the surcharge shows "N" and "Y" spaced. On the reset surcharge, No. 36, a similar variety occurs on R. 5/9.

Of the 2½d. with double surcharge only six copies exist, and of the 2½d. double printed, one row of 12 stamps existed on one sheet only.

CANCELLATIONS. Nos. 40/5 and No. 20 were sold as remainders in 1904 cancelled with a violet diamond-shaped grill with four interior bars extending over two stamps. These cannot be considered as *used* stamps, and they are consequently not priced in the list.

This violet obliteration is easily removed and many of these remainders have been cleaned and offered as unused; some are repostmarked with a date and name in thin type rather larger than the original, a usual date being "Ap.4.01."

(Typo D.L.R.)

1890–97. *Plate I for the 1½d. Plate II for the other values (for differences see Seychelles).* Wmk Crown CA. P 14.

46	11	½d. green (1897)	2·75	6·50
47		1d. carmine (1896)	17·00	2·00
48		1½d. red-brown and green (1890)	4·50	9·00
49		2d. orange-yellow (1896)	5·00	12·00
50		2½d. ultramarine (1896)	15·00	12·00
51		5d. mauve (1896)	11·00	30·00
52		10d. brown (1896)	24·00	60·00
46/52 *Set of 7*			70·00	£120
46s/52s Optd "Specimen" *Set of 7*			£300	

The note below No. 45a *re* violet diamond-shaped grill cancellation also applies to Nos. 48/52.

1902. Wmk Crown CA. P 14.

53	12	½d. green (Mar)	1·50	2·50
54		1d. carmine (24 Feb)	9·00	70
53s/4s Optd "Specimen" *Set of 2*			80·00	

13 Government House

14 The Wharf

(Typo D.L.R.)

1903 (May). Wmk Crown CC. P 14.

55	13	½d. brown and grey-green	2·00	3·25
		w. Wmk inverted	£150	£180
56	14	1d. black and carmine	1·50	35
57	13	2d. black and sage-green	6·50	1·25
58	14	8d. black and brown	22·00	32·00
59	13	1s. brown and brown-orange	23·00	40·00
60	14	2s. black and violet	50·00	85·00
55/60 *Set of 6*			95·00	£150
55s/60s Optd "Specimen" *Set of 6*			£225	

A printing of the 1d. value in Type **14** in red only on Mult Crown CA paper was made in 1911, but not sold to the public. Examples are known overprinted "SPECIMEN" (*Price* £325).

15

(Typo D.L.R.)

1908 (May)–**11.** *Ordinary paper (2½d.) or chalk-surfaced paper (4d., 6d.).* P 14.

(a) Wmk Mult Crown CA.

64	15	2½d. blue	1·75	1·50
66		4d. black and red/*yellow*	9·50	21·00
		a. Ordinary paper (1911)	3·25	18·00
67		6d. dull and deep purple	20·00	35·00
		a. Ordinary paper (1911)	7·00	14·00

(b) Wmk Crown CA. Chalk-surfaced paper.

71	15	10s. green and red/*green*	£200	£250
64/71 *Set of 4*			£200	£250
64s/71s Optd "Specimen" *Set of 4*			£250	

Examples of Nos. 58/60 and 66/71 are known showing a forged St. Helena postmark dated "JY 28 1".

16

17

(Typo D.L.R.)

1912–16. Wmk Mult Crown CA. P 14.

72	**16**	½d. black and green	2·25	10·00
73	**17**	1d. black and carmine-red	4·75	1·75
		a. Black and scarlet (1916)	10·00	20·00
74		1½d. black and dull orange (1913)	3·50	7·50
75	**16**	2d. black and greyish slate	4·50	1·75
76	**17**	2½d. black and bright blue	3·50	6·50
77	**16**	3d. black and purple/*yellow* (1913)	3·50	5·00
78	**17**	8d. black and dull purple	7·00	50·00
79	**16**	1s. black/*green*	9·00	35·00
80	**17**	2s. black and blue/*blue*	42·00	85·00
81		3s. black and violet (1913)	60·00	£140
72/81 *Set of* 10			£130	£300
72s/81s Optd "Specimen" *Set of* 10			£300	

No. 73*a* is on thicker paper than 73.

18

19

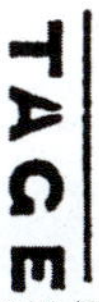

Split "A" (R. 8/3 of left pane)

(Typo D.L.R.)

1912. *Chalk-surfaced paper*. Wmk Mult Crown CA. P 14.

83	**18**	4d. black and red/*yellow*	12·00	25·00
84		6d. dull and deep purple	4·00	5·00
83s/4s Optd "Specimen" *Set of* 2			95·00	

1913. Wmk Mult Crown CA. P 14.

85	**19**	4d. black and red/*yellow*	8·00	2·75
		a. Split "A"	£300	£190
86		6d. dull and deep purple	14·00	28·00
		a. Split "A"	£450	
85s/6s Optd "Specimen" *Set of* 2			95·00	

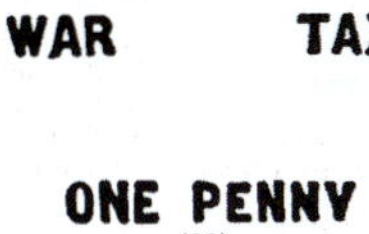

(20)

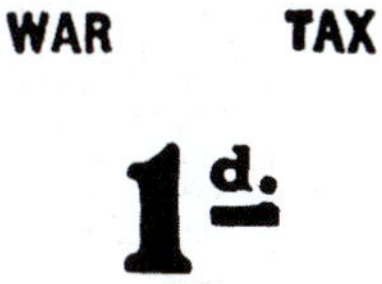

(21)

1916 (Sept). *As No. 73a, on thin paper, surch with T* **20**.

87	**17**	1d.+1d. black and scarlet	2·00	3·25
		a. Surch double	†	£17000
		s. Optd "Specimen"	55·00	

1919. *No. 73 on thicker paper, surch with T* **21**.

88	**17**	1d.+1d. black and carmine-red (*shades*)	1·75	4·50
		s. Optd "Specimen"	55·00	

1922 (Jan). *Printed in one colour*. Wmk Mult Script CA. P 14.

89	**17**	1d. green	1·75	35·00
		w. Wmk inverted	£250	
		y. Wmk inverted and reversed	£200	
90		1½d. rose-scarlet	10·00	35·00
91	**16**	3d. bright blue	20·00	65·00
		y. Wmk inverted and reversed	£200	
89/91 *Set of* 3			29·00	£120
89s/91s Optd "Specimen" *Set of* 3			£130	

22 Badge of St. Helena

PLATE FLAWS ON THE 1922–37 ISSUE. Many constant plate varieties exist on both the vignette and duty plates of this issue. The three major varieties are illustrated and listed below.

a. Broken mainmast. Occurs on R. 2/1 of all sheets from the second printing onwards. It does not appear on Nos. 93/6 and 111/13 as these stamps only exist from the initial printing invoiced in May 1922.

b. Torn flag. Occurs on R. 4/6 of all sheets from printings up to and including that invoiced in December 1922. The flaw was retouched for the printing invoiced in March 1925 and so does not occur on Nos. 97, 99*e*, "103/d", 107/10 and 111d.

c. Cleft rock. Occurs on R. 5/1 of all sheets from the second printing onwards. It does not appear on Nos. 93/6 and 111/13 as these stamps only exist from the initial printing invoiced in May 1922.

Damaged value tablet (R. 1/4 of first printing)

(Des T. Bruce. Typo D.L.R.)

1922 (June)–**37**. P 14

(*a*) Wmk Mult Crown CA. *Chalk-surfaced paper.*

92	**22**	4d. grey and black/*yellow* (2.23)	11·00	6·00
		a. Broken mainmast	£180	£190
		b. Torn flag	£180	£190
		c. Cleft rock	£160	£180
93		1s.6d. grey and green/*blue-green*	22·00	60·00
		b. Torn flag	£450	£750
94		2s.6d. grey and red/*yellow*	25·00	65·00
		b. Torn flag	£500	
95		5s. grey and green/*yellow*	42·00	95·00
		b. Torn flag	£700	£1000
96		£1 grey and purple/*red*	£425	£500
		b. Torn flag	£2250	
92/6 *Set of* 5			£475	£650
92s/6s Optd "Specimen" *Set of* 5			£500	

The paper of No. 93 is bluish on the surface with a full green back.

(*b*) Wmk Mult Script CA. *Ordinary paper (1s.6d., 2s.6d., 5s.) or chalk-surfaced paper (others).*

97	**22**	½d. grey and black (2.23)	2·50	2·50
		a. Broken mainmast	60·00	85·00
		b. Torn flag	£190	£275
		c. Cleft rock	50·00	85·00
		d. "A" of "CA" missing from wmk	†	—
		e. Damaged value tablet	£140	
		fw. Wmk inverted	£375	£425
		g. Grey-black and black (1937)	7·50	4·00
		ga. Broken mainmast	£150	£160
		ec. Cleft rock	£140	£150
98		1d. grey and green	2·50	1·60
		a. Broken mainmast	65·00	80·00
		b. Torn flag	£170	£200
		c. Cleft rock	55·00	80·00
99		1½d. rose-red (*shades*) (2.23)	2·75	13·00
		a. Broken mainmast	90·00	£160
		b. Torn flag	90·00	£160
		c. Cleft rock	80·00	£160
		dw. Wmk inverted	£900	
		dx. Wmk reversed	£1000	
		e. Deep carmine-red (1937)	80·00	85·00
		ea. Broken mainmast	£800	£900
		ec. Cleft rock	£800	£900
100		2d. grey and slate (2.23)	3·75	2·00
		a. Broken mainmast	£110	£130
		b. Torn flag	£225	£275
		c. Cleft rock	£100	£120
101		3d. bright blue (2.23)	2·00	4·00
		a. Broken mainmast	£100	£150
		b. Torn flag	£100	£150
		c. Cleft rock	85·00	£140
		x. Wmk reversed	£475	
103		5d. green and deep carmine/*green* (1927)	3·00	5·50
		a. Broken mainmast	£170	£225
		c. Cleft rock	£160	£225
		d. Green and carmine-red/green (1936)	3·00	5·50
		da. Broken mainmast	£190	£250
		dc. Cleft rock	£180	£250
104		6d. grey and bright purple	4·50	8·00
		a. Broken mainmast	£225	£325
		b. Torn flag	£225	£325
		c. Cleft rock	£190	£300
105		8d. grey and bright violet (2.23)	3·75	7·00
		a. Broken mainmast	£170	£275
		b. Torn flag	£170	£275
		c. Cleft rock	£150	£275
106		1s. grey and brown	6·50	9·00
		a. Broken mainmast	£275	£350
		b. Torn flag	£350	£400
		c. Cleft rock	£250	£325
107		1s.6d. grey and green/*green* (1927)	15·00	45·00
		a. Broken mainmast	£325	£600
		c. Cleft rock	£300	£600
108		2s. purple and blue/*blue* (1927)	20·00	42·00
		a. Broken mainmast	£350	
		c. Cleft rock	£325	
109		2s.6d. grey and red/*yellow* (1927)	14·00	65·00
		a. Broken mainmast	£325	£700
		c. Cleft rock	£300	£700
110		5s. grey and green/*yellow* (1927)	38·00	75·00
		a. Broken mainmast	£500	
		c. Cleft rock	£475	
111		7s.6d. grey-brown and yellow-orange	95·00	£150
		b. Torn flag	£750	£1600
		d. Brownish grey and orange (1937)	£750	£1000
		da. Broken mainmast	£7000	
		dc. Cleft rock	£7000	
112		10s. grey and olive-green	£130	£190
		b. Torn flag	£1300	
113		15s. grey and purple/*blue*	£900	£1600
		b. Torn flag	£4250	£7000
97/112 *Set of* 15			£300	£550
97s/113s Optd "Specimen" *Set of* 16			£1300	

Examples of all values are known showing a forged St. Helena postmark dated "DE 18 27".

23 Lot and Lot's Wife

24 The "Plantation"

25 Map of St. Helena

26 Quay at Jamestown

27 James Valley

28 Jamestown

29 Munden's Promontory

30 St. Helena

31 High Knoll

32 Badge of St. Helena

(Recess B.W.)

1934 (23 April). *Centenary of British Colonisation. T* **23**/ **32**. Wmk Mult Script CA. P 12.

114	**23**	½d. black and purple	1·00	80
115	**24**	1d. black and green	65	85
116	**25**	1½d. black and scarlet	2·50	3·25
117	**26**	2d. black and orange	2·50	1·25
118	**27**	3d. black and blue	1·40	4·50
119	**28**	6d. black and light blue	3·25	3·00
120	**29**	1s. black and chocolate	6·50	18·00
121	**30**	2s.6d. black and lake	38·00	50·00
122	**31**	5s. black and chocolate	80·00	80·00
123	**32**	10s. black and purple	£250	£250
114/23 *Set of* 10			£350	£375
114s/23s Perf "Specimen" *Set of* 10			£375	

Examples of all values are known showing a forged St. Helena postmark dated "MY 12 34".

1935 (6 May). *Silver Jubilee. As Nos. 91/4 of Antigua.* P 13½×14.

124		1½d. deep blue and carmine	1·00	5·50
		f. Diagonal line by turret	85·00	£170
125		2d. ultramarine and grey	2·25	90
		f. Diagonal line by turret	£110	£110
		g. Dot to left of chapel	£180	
126		6d. green and indigo	7·50	3·25
		a. Frame printed double, one albino	£2250	
		f. Diagonal line by turret	£250	
		h. Dot by flagstaff	£400	
127		1s. slate and purple	18·00	18·00
		h. Dot by flagstaff	£500	£500
		i. Dash by turret	£550	
124/7 *Set of* 4			26·00	25·00
124s/7s Perf "Specimen" *Set of* 4			£140	

For illustrations of plate varieties see Omnibus section following Zanzibar.

1937 (19 May). *Coronation. As Nos. 95/7 of Antigua, but ptd by D.L.R.* P 14.

128		1d. green	40	75
129		2d. orange	55	45
130		3d. bright blue	80	50
128/30 *Set of* 3			1·60	1·50
128s/30s Perf "Specimen" *Set of* 3			90·00	

33 Badge of St. Helena

(Recess Waterlow)

1938 (12 May)–**44**. Wmk Mult Script CA. P 12½.

131 **33** ½d. violet 15 65
132 1d. green .... 9·00 2·25
132*a* 1d. yellow-orange (8.7.40) 30 30
133 1½d. scarlet 30 40
134 2d. red-orange 30 15
135 3d. ultramarine .... 80·00 18·00
135*a* 3d. grey (8.7.40) 30 30
135*b* 4d. ultramarine (8.7.40) .... 2·00 1·75
136 6d. light blue .... 2·00 2·00
136*a* 8d. sage-green (8.7.40) .... 3·25 1·00
b. Olive-green (24.5.44) .... 4·50 4·00
137 1s. sepia .... 1·25 50
138 2s.6d. maroon .... 18·00 6·50
139 5s. chocolate .... 18·00 12·00
140 10s. purple .... 18·00 18·00
131/40 *Set of* 14 .... £140 55·00
131s/40s Perf "Specimen" *Set of* 14 .... £400
See also Nos. 149/51.

1946 (21 Oct). *Victory. As Nos. 110/11 of Antigua.*
141 2d. red-orange 40 50
142 4d. blue 40 30
141s/2s Perf "Specimen" *Set of* 2 .... 90·00

1948 (20 Oct). *Royal Silver Wedding. As Nos. 112/13 of Antigua.*
143 3d. black 30 30
144 10s. violet-blue .... 25·00 38·00

1949 (10 Oct). *75th Anniv of U.P.U. As Nos. 114/17 of Antigua.*
145 3d. carmine .... 25 1·00
146 4d. deep blue .... 3·00 1·60
147 6d. olive .... 45 2·25
148 1s. blue-black .... 35 1·10
145/8 *Set of* 4 .... 3·50 5·50

1949 (1 Nov). Wmk Mult Script CA. P 12½.
149 **33** 1d. black and green .... 1·25 1·50
150 1½d. black and carmine .... 1·25 1·50
151 2d. black and scarlet .... 1·25 1·50
149/51 *Set of* 3 .... 3·25 4·00

1953 (2 June). *Coronation. As No. 120 of Antigua.*
152 3d. black and deep reddish violet .... 1·00 1·50

34 Badge of St. Helena

34a Flax plantation

35 Heart-shaped Waterfall

35a Lace-making

36 Drying flax

37 St. Helena Sand Plover

38 Flagstaff and The Barn

39 Donkeys carrying flax

40 Island map

41 The Castle

42 Cutting flax

43 Jamestown

44 Longwood House

(Recess D.L.R.)

1953 (4 Aug)–**59**. *T* **34**/44. Wmk Mult Script CA. P 14.
153 **34** ½d. black and bright green 30 30
154 **34a** 1d. black and deep green 15 20
155 **35** 1½d. black and reddish purple .... 3·75 1·50
a. Black & deep reddish purple (14.1.59) .... 10·00 4·25
156 **35a** 2d. black and claret 50 30
157 **36** 2½d. black and red 40 30
158 **37** 3d. black and brown .... 3·25 30
159 **38** 4d. black and deep blue .... 40 1·00
160 **39** 6d. black and deep lilac 40 30
161 **40** 7d. black and grey-black .... 65 1·75
162 **41** 1s. black and carmine 40 70
163 **42** 2s.6d. black and violet .... 14·00 6·50
164 **43** 5s. black and deep brown .... 17·00 9·00
165 **44** 10s. black and yellow-orange .... 32·00 13·00
153/65 *Set of* 13 .... 65·00 30·00

45 Stamp of 1856

46 Arms of East India Company

(Recess D.L.R.)

1956 (3 Jan). *St. Helena Stamp Centenary.* Wmk Mult Script CA. P 11½.
166 **45** 3d. Prussian blue and carmine 10 10
167 4d. Prussian blue and reddish brown 10 20
168 6d. Prussian blue & dp reddish purple 15 25
166/8 *Set of* 3 .... 30 50

(Recess Waterlow)

1959 (5 May). *Tercentenary of Settlement. T* **46** *and similar horiz designs.* W w **12**. P 12½×13.
169 3d. black and scarlet 10 15
170 6d. light emerald and slate-blue 40 75
171 1s. black and orange 40 75
169/71 *Set of* 3 .... 80 1·50
Designs:—6d. East Indiaman *London* off James Bay; 1s. Commemoration Stone.

ST. HELENA
Tristan Relief
9d +
(**49**)

1961 (12 Oct). *Tristan Relief Fund. Nos. 46 and 49/51 of Tristan da Cunha surch as T* **49** *by Govt Printer, Jamestown.*
172 2½c. +3d.black and brown-red £1200 £500
173 5c. +6d.black and blue £1300 £550
174 7½c. +9d.black and rose-carmine £1800 £750
175 10c. +1s.black and light brown £2250 £900
172/5 *Set of* 4 .... £6000 £2500
The above stamps were withdrawn from sale on 19 October, 434 complete sets having been sold.

50 St. Helena Butterflyfish

51 Yellow Canary

53 Queen Elizabeth II

63 Queen Elizabeth II with Prince Andrew (after Cecil Beaton)

(Des V. Whiteley. Photo Harrison)

1961 (12 Dec)–**65**. *T* **50/1**, **53**, **63** *and similar designs.* W w **12**. P 11½×12 (horiz), 12×11½ (vert) or 14½×14 (£1).
176 1d. bright blue, dull violet, yellow and carmine 40 20
a. Chalk-surfaced paper (4.5.65) .... 1·75 30
177 1½d. yellow, green, black and light drab 50 20
178 2d. scarlet and grey 15 20
179 3d. light blue, black, pink and deep blue 70 20
a. Chalk-surfaced paper (30.11.65) .... 2·00 50
180 4½d. yellow-green, green, brown and grey 60 60
181 6d. red, sepia and light yellow-olive .... 5·50 70
a. Chalk-surfaced paper (30.11.65) .... 7·50 70
182 7d. red-brown, black and violet 35 70
183 10d. brown-purple and light blue 35 70
184 1s. greenish yellow, bluish green and brown .... 55 1·25
185 1s.6d. grey, black and slate-blue .... 11·00 4·75
186 2s.6d. red, pale yellow and turquoise (*chalk-surfaced paper*) .... 2·50 2·50
187 5s. yellow, brown and green .... 13·00 4·25
188 10s. orange-red, black and blue .... 13·00 10·00
189 £1 chocolate and light blue .... 14·00 14·00
a. Chalk-surfaced paper (30.11.65) .... 45·00 42·00
176/89 (*cheapest*) *Set of* 14 .... 55·00 35·00
Designs: *Horiz* (*as T* **50**)—2d. Brittle Starfish; 7d. Trumpetfish; 10d. Feather Starfish; 2s.6d. Orange Starfish; 10s. Deep-water Bullseye. *Vert* (*as T* **51**)—4½d. Red-wood Flower; 6d. Madagascar Red Fody; 1s. Gum-wood Flower; 1s.6d. White Tern; 5s. Night-blooming Cereus.

1963 (4 June). *Freedom from Hunger. As No. 146 of Antigua.*
190 1s. 6d. ultramarine 75 40

1963 (2 Sept). *Red Cross Centenary. As Nos. 147/8 of Antigua.*
191 3d. red and black 30 25
192 1s.6d. red and blue .... 70 1·75

FIRST LOCAL POST
4th JANUARY 1965
(**64**)

65 Badge of St. Helena

1965 (4 Jan). *First Local Post. Nos. 176, 179, 181 and 185 optd with T* **64**.
193 1d. bright blue, dull violet, yellow and carmine 10 25
194 3d. light blue, black, pink and deep blue 10 25
195 6d. red, sepia and light yellow-olive 40 30
196 1s.6d. grey, black and slate-blue 60 35
193/6 *Set of* 4 .... 1·10 1·00

1965 (17 May). *I.T.U. Centenary. As Nos. 166/7 of Antigua.*
197 3d. blue and grey-brown 25 25
198 6d. bright purple and bluish green 35 25

1965 (15 Oct). *International Co-operation. Year. As Nos. 168/9 of Antigua.*
199 1d. reddish purple and turquoise-green 30 15
200 6d. deep bluish green and lavender 30 15
w. Wmk inverted

1966 (24 Jan). *Churchill Commemoration. As Nos. 170/3 of Antigua.*
201 1d. new blue 15 20
202 3d. deep green 25 20
203 6d. brown 40 25
204 1s.6d. bluish violet 45 75
201/4 *Set of* 4 .... 1·10 1·25

1966 (1 July). *World Cup Football Championships. As Nos. 176/7 of Antigua.*
205 3d. violet, yellow-green, lake and yellow-brown 50 35
206 6d. chocolate, blue-green, lake and yellow-brown 75 35

1966 (20 Sept). *Inauguration of W.H.O. Headquarters, Geneva. As Nos. 178/9 of Antigua.*
207 3d. black, yellow-green and light blue 75 20
208 1s.6d. black, light purple and yellow-brown .... 2·25 1·00

1966 (1 Dec). *20th Anniversary of U.N.E.S.C.O. As Nos. 196/8 of Antigua.*
209 3d. slate-violet, red, yellow and orange 75 20
210 6d. orange-yellow, violet and deep olive .... 1·25 50
211 1s.6d. black, bright purple and orange .... 2·00 1·75
209/11 *Set of* 3 .... 3·50 2·25

(Des W. H. Brown. Photo Harrison)

1967 (5 May). *New Constitution.* W w **12** (sideways). P 14½×14.
212 **65** 1s. multicoloured 10 10
213 2s.6d. multicoloured 20 20
a. Red (ribbon, etc.) omitted £900

66 Fire of London

(Des M. Goaman. Recess D.L.R.)

1967 (4 Sept). *300th Anniv of Arrival of Settlers after Great Fire of London. T* **66** *and similar horiz designs.* W w **12**. P 13.
214 1d. carmine-red and black 15 10
a. Carmine and black .... 1·75 70
215 3d. ultramarine and black 20 10
216 6d. slate-violet and black 20 15
217 1s.6d. olive-green and black 20 20
214/17 *Set of* 4 .... 65 50
Designs:—3d. East Indiaman *Charles*; 6d. Settlers landing at Jamestown; 1s.6d. Settlers clearing scrub.

70 Interlocking Maps of Tristan and St. Helena

(Des Jennifer Toombs. Photo Harrison)

1968 (4 June). *30th Anniv of Tristan da Cunha as a Dependency of St. Helena. T* **70** *and similar horiz design.* W w **12**. P 14×14½.

218	**70**	4d. purple and chocolate	10	10
219	–	8d. olive and brown	10	30
220	**70**	1s.9d. ultramarine and chocolate	10	40
221	–	2s.3d. greenish blue and brown	15	40
218/21 *Set of 4*			40	1·10

Design:—8d., 2s.3d. Interlocking maps of St. Helena and Tristan.

72 Queen Elizabeth and Sir Hudson Lowe

(Des M. Farrar Bell. Litho D.L.R.)

1968 (4 Sept). *150th Anniv of the Abolition of Slavery in St. Helena. T* **72** *and similar horiz design. Multicoloured.* W w **12** (sideways). P 13×12½.

222	3d. Type **72**	10	15
223	9d. Type **72**	10	20
224	1s.6d. Queen Elizabeth and Sir George Bingham	15	30
225	2s.6d. As 1s. 6d	25	45
222/5 *Set of 4*		55	1·00

74 Blue Gum Eucalyptus and Road Construction

(Des Sylvia Goaman. Litho P.B.)

1968 (4 Nov). *Horiz designs as T* **74**. *Multicoloured.* W w **12** (sideways*). P 13½.

226	½d. Type **74**	10	10
227	1d. Cabbage-tree and electricity development	10	10
	w. Wmk Crown to right of CA	4·75	
228	1½d. St. Helena Redwood and dental unit	15	10
229	2d. Scrubweed and pest control	15	10
230	3d. Tree-fern and flats in Jamestown	30	10
231	4d. Blue gum Eucalyptus, pasture and livestock improvement	20	10
232	6d. Cabbage-tree and schools broadcasting	50	10
233	8d. St. Helena Redwood and country cottages	30	10
234	10d. Scrubweed and new school buildings	30	10
235	1s. Tree-fern and reafforestation	30	10
236	1s.6d. Blue gum Eucalyptus and heavy lift crane	70	3·00
237	2s.6d. Cabbage-tree and Lady Field Children's Home	70	3·50
238	5s. St. Helena Redwood and agricultural training	70	3·50
239	10s. Scrubweed and New General Hospital	2·00	4·50
240	£1 Tree-fern and lifeboat *John Dutton*	7·00	15·00
226/40 *Set of 15*		12·00	27·00

*The normal sideways watermark shows Crown to left of CA, *as seen from the back of the stamp.*

A distinct shade of the £1 value was issued in 1971, with the decimal currency definitives.

89 Brig *Perseverance*

93 W.O. and Drummer of the 53rd Foot, 1815

(Des Jennifer Toombs. Litho P.B.)

1970 (9 June). *Death Centenary of Charles Dickens. T* **97** *and similar horiz designs each incorporating a portrait of Dickens. Multicoloured. Chalk-surfaced paper.* W w **12** (sideways*). P 13½×13.

241	4d. Type **89**	20	20
242	8d. *Phoebe* (screw steamer)	25	40
243	1s.9d. *Llandovery Castle* (liner)	25	60
244	2s.3d. *Good Hope Castle* (cargo liner)	25	75
241/4 *Set of 4*		85	1·75

No. 242 is inscribed "DANE" in error.

(Des R. North. Litho Format)

1969 (3 Sept). *Military Uniforms. T* **93** *and similar vert designs. Multicoloured.* W w **12**. P 14.

245	6d. Type **93**	15	25
	w. Wmk inverted	90·00	
246	8d. Officer and Surgeon, 20th Foot, 1816	15	25
247	1s.8d. Drum Major, 66th Foot, 1816, and Royal Artillery Officer, 1820	20	45
248	2s.6d. Private, 91st Foot, and 2nd Corporal, Royal Sappers and Miners, 1832	20	55
245/8 *Set of 4*		65	1·40

97 Dickens, Mr. Pickwick and Job Trotter (*Pickwick Papers*)

(Des Jennifer Toombs. Litho P.B.)

1970 (9 June). *Death Centenary of Charles Dickens. T* **97** *and similar horiz designs each incorporating a portrait of Dickens. Multicoloured. Chalk-surfaced paper.* W w **12** (sideways*). P 13½×13.

249	4d. Type **97**	50	15
	a. Shiny unsurfaced paper	40	1·40
	b. Yellow omitted	£450	
	w. Wmk Crown to right of CA	30·00	
250	8d. Mr. Bumble and Oliver (*Oliver Twist*)	60	15
	a. Shiny unsurfaced paper	40	1·60
251	1s.6d. Sairey Gamp and Mark Tapley (*Martin Chuzzlewit*)	70	20
	a. Shiny unsurfaced paper	50	2·25
252	2s.6d. Jo and Mr. Turveydrop (*Bleak House*)	80	25
	a. Shiny unsurfaced paper	60	2·50
249/52 *Set of 4*		2·40	65
249a/52a *Set of 4*		1·75	7·00

*The normal sideways watermark shows Crown to left of CA, *as seen from the back of the stamp.*

Supplies sent to St. Helena were on paper with a dull surface which reacts to the chalky test and with PVA gum. Crown Agents supplies were from a later printing on shiny paper which does not respond to the chalky test and with gum arabic.

98 "Kiss of Life"

99 Officer's Shako Plate (20th Foot)

(Des Jennifer Toombs. Litho J.W.)

1970 (15 Sept). *Centenary of British Red Cross. T* **98** *and similar horiz designs.* W w **12** (sideways). P 14.

253	6d. bistre, vermilion and black	15	15
254	9d. turquoise-green, vermilion and black	15	20
255	1s.9d. pale grey, vermilion and black	20	30
256	2s.3d. pale lavender, vermilion and black	20	45
253/6 *Set of 4*		65	1·00

Designs:—9d. Nurse with girl in wheelchair; 1s.9d. Nurse bandaging child's knee; 2s.3d. Red Cross emblem.

(Des J.W. Litho Questa)

1970 (2 Nov). *Military Equipment (1st issue). T* **99** *and similar vert designs. Multicoloured.* W w **12**. P 12.

257	4d. Type **99**	20	20
258	9d. Officer's Breast-plate (66th Foot)	25	30
259	1s.3d. Officer's Full Dress Shako (91st Foot)	25	40
260	2s.11d. Ensign's Shako (53rd Foot)	30	60
257/60 *Set of 4*		90	1·40

See also Nos. 281/4, 285/8 and 291/4.

STAMP BOOKLETS

1962 (2 Mar). *Black on green cover. Stitched.*

SB1	4s.6d. booklet containing 1d., 1½d., 2d., 3d. and 6d. (Nos. 176/9, 181), each in block of 4	50·00

1969. *Black on grey-green cover. Stapled.*

SB2	5s.4d. booklet containing 1d., 2d., 3d., 4d. and 6d. (Nos. 227, 229/32), each in block of 4	30·00

St. Kitts-Nevis

ST. CHRISTOPHER

From 1760 the postal service for St. Christopher was organised by the Deputy Postmaster General on Antigua. It was not until May 1779 that the first postmaster was appointed to the island and the use of postmarks on outgoing mail commenced.

Stamps of Great Britain were used between May 1858 and the end of March 1860 when control of the postal services passed to the local authorities. In the years which followed, prior to the introduction of St. Christopher stamps in April 1870, a circular "PAID" handstamp was used on overseas mail.

BASSETERRE

Stamps of GREAT BRITAIN *cancelled* "A 12" *as Type* Z 1 *of Jamaica.*

1858–60.

Z1	1d. rose-red (1857), perf 14	£700
Z2	2d. blue (1858) (Plate No. 7)	£1100
Z3	4d. rose (1857)	£400
Z4	6d. lilac (1856)	£200
Z5	1s. green (1856)	£2000

PRICES FOR STAMPS ON COVER

Nos. 1/9	*from* × 25
Nos. 11/21	*from* × 30
Nos. 22/6	*from* × 25
No. 27	—
No. 28	*from* × 30
Nos. R1/6	—

1

Distorted "E" (R. 2/1)

1870 (1 Apr)–**79**. Wmk Crown CC.

(a) P 12½.

1	1	1d. dull rose	85·00	48·00
		a. Wmk sideways	£225	£160
		w. Wmk inverted		
2		1d. magenta (*shades*) (1871)	75·00	32·00
		a. Wmk sideways	†	£700
		w. Wmk inverted	£140	70·00
		x. Wmk reversed		
4		6d. yellow-green	£120	19·00
		w. Wmk inverted		
5		6d. green (1871)	£120	7·50
		w. Wmk inverted	—	£110

(b) P 14.

6	1	1d. magenta (*shades*) (1875)	70·00	7·00
		a. Bisected diag or vert (½d.) (on cover) (3.82)	†	£2500
		w. Wmk inverted		
7		2½d. red-brown (11.79)	£180	£250
8		4d. blue (11.79)	£200	15·00
		a. Wmk sideways	£1300	£170
		w. Wmk inverted	£375	50·00
9		6d. green (1876)	55·00	5·00
		a. Imperf between (pair)		
		b. Wmk sideways	£750	£170
		x. Wmk reversed	£250	

The magenta used for the 1d. was a fugitive colour which reacts to both light and water.

No. 6a was authorised for use between March and June 1882 to make up the 2½d. letter rate and for ½d. book post.

1882 (June)–**90**. Wmk Crown CA. P 14.

11	1	½d. dull green	2·50	2·00
		a. Wmk sideways	£300	
		x. Wmk reversed		
12		1d. dull magenta	£550	70·00
		a. Bisected diagonally (½d.) (on cover)		
13		1d. carmine-rose (2.84)	1·75	2·25
		a. Bisected (½d.) (on cover)		
		b. Distorted "E"	21·00	
		x. Wmk reversed		
14		2½d. pale red-brown	£180	60·00
15		2½d. deep red-brown	£190	65·00
16		2½d. ultramarine (2.84)	3·00	1·50
17		4d. blue	£500	20·00
		w. Wmk inverted		
18		4d. grey (10.84)	1·50	1·00
19		6d. olive-brown (3.90)	85·00	£375
		w. Wmk inverted		
20		1s. mauve (6.86)	95·00	65·00
		w. Wmk inverted	—	£150
21		1s. bright mauve (1890)	85·00	£160
19s/20s Optd "Specimen" *Set of 2*			£120	

FOUR PENCE (2) Halfpenny (3)

1884 (Dec). *No. 9 surch with T* **2** *by* The Advertiser Press.

22	1	4d. on 6d. green	65·00	50·00
		a. Full stop after "PENCE"	65·00	50·00
		b. Surch double	—	£2750

No. 22a occurred on alternate stamps.

1885 (Mar). *No. 13 bisected and each half diagonally surch with T* **3**.

23	1	½d. on half of 1d. carmine-rose	26·00	40·00
		a. Unsevered pair	£120	£120
		ab. Ditto, one surch inverted	£400	£275
		b. Surch inverted	£225	£110
		ba. Ditto, unsevered pair	£1000	
		c. Surch double		

ONE PENNY. (4) 4d. (5)

1886 (June). *No. 9 surch with T* **4** *or* **5** *each showing a manuscript line through the original value.*

24	1	1d. on 6d. green	20·00	32·00
		a. Surch inverted	£9000	
		b. Surch double	—	£1500
25		4d. on 6d. green	55·00	95·00
		a. No stop after "d"	£225	£300
		b. Surch double	£2500	£2750

No. 24b is only known penmarked with dates between 21 July and 3 August 1886, or with violet handstamp.

1887 (May). *No. 11 surch with T* **4** *showing a manuscript line through the original value.*

26	1	1d. on ½d. dull green	40·00	48·00

ONE PENNY. (7)

1888 (May). *No. 16 surch.*

(a) With T **4**. *Original value unobliterated.*

27	1	1d. on 2½d. ultramarine	£21000	£14000

(b) With T **7** *showing a manuscript line through the original value.*

28	1	1d. on 2½d. ultramarine	65·00	65·00
		a. Surch inverted	£25000	£11000

The 1d. of Antigua was used provisionally in St. Christopher between February and March 1890 during a shortage of 1d. stamps. Such use can be distinguished by the postmark, which is "A 12" in place of "A02" (*price from £130 used*).

REVENUE STAMPS USED FOR POSTAGE

Saint Christopher (R 1) SAINT KITTS NEVIS REVENUE (R 2)

1883. *Nos. F6 and F8 of Nevis optd with Type* R **1**, *in violet.* Wmk Crown CA. P 14.

R1	1d. lilac-mauve	£375	
R2	6d. green	95·00	£150

1885. *Optd with Type* R **2**. Wmk Crown CA. P 14.

R3	1	1d. rose	2·75	18·00
R4		3d. mauve	16·00	65·00
R5		6d. orange-brown	12·00	50·00
R6		1s. olive	3·00	42·00

Other fiscal stamps with overprints as above also exist, but none of these were ever available for postal purposes.

The stamps for St. Christopher were superseded by the general issue for Leeward Islands on 31 October 1890.

Stamps for St. Kitts, issued from 1980 onwards will be found listed after those for the combined colony.

NEVIS

Little is known concerning the early postal affairs of Nevis, although several covers exist from the island in the 1660s. It is recorded that the British G.P.O. was to establish a branch office on the island under an Act of Parliament of 1710, although arrangements may not have been finalised for a number of years afterwards. Nevis appears as "a new office" in the P.O. Accounts of 1787.

Stamps of Great Britain were used on the island from May 1858 until the colonial authorities assumed control of the postal service on 1 May 1860. Between this date and the introduction of Nevis stamps in 1861 No. CC1 was again used on overseas mail.

CHARLESTOWN

CROWNED-CIRCLE HANDSTAMPS

CC 1

CC1 CC **1** NEVIS (R.) (9.1852) *Price on cover* £4000

No. CC1, struck in black or red (1882) was later used on several occasions up to 1882 when there were shortages of adhesive stamps.

Stamps of GREAT BRITAIN *cancelled* "A 09" *as Type* Z 1 *of Jamaica.*

1858–60.

Z1	1d. rose-red (1857), perf 14	£600
Z2	2d. blue (1858) (Plate Nos. 7, 8)	£2000
Z3	4d. rose (1857)	£450
Z4	6d. lilac (1856)	£300
Z5	1s. green (1856)	

PRICES FOR STAMPS ON COVER

Nos. 5/22	*from* × 20
Nos. 23/4	*from* × 10
Nos. 25/34	*from* × 20
Nos. 35/6	*from* × 10
Nos. F1/8	*from* × 30

1

2

3

4

The designs on the stamps refer to a medicinal spring on the island

(Recess Nissen & Parker, London)

1862–(19 July). *Greyish paper.* P 13.

5	1	1d. dull lake	90·00	50·00
		a. On blued paper	£275	£120
6	2	4d. rose	£130	65·00
		a. On blued paper	£800	£170
7	3	6d. grey-lilac	£130	55·00
		a. On blued paper	£650	£225
8	4	1s. green	£325	75·00
		a. On blued paper	£950	£200

Nos. 5/8 and later printings of Types **1/4** were in sheets of 12 (3×4).

1866–76. *White paper.* P 15.

9	1	1d. pale red	50·00	48·00
10		1d. deep red	50·00	48·00
11	2	4d. orange	£130	23·00
12		4d. deep orange	£130	23·00
13	4	1s. blue-green	£275	35·00
14		1s. yellow-green (1876)	£850	£110
		a. Vertically laid paper	£21000	£6000
		b. No. 9 on sheet with crossed lines on hill	£3500	£500
		c. Ditto. On laid paper	†	£16000

Examples of the 4d. exist showing part of a papermakers watermark reading "A. COWAN & SONS EXTRA SUPERFINE".

(Lithographed by transfer from the engraved plates Nissen and Parker, London)

1876–78.

(a) P 15.

15	1	1d. pale rose-red	24·00	19·00
		a. Imperf (pair)	£1300	
16		1d. deep rose-red	32·00	27·00
17		1d. vermilion-red	29·00	29·00
		a. Bisected (½d.) (on cover)	†	£3000
18	2	4d. orange-yellow (1878)	£170	35·00
		a. Imperf between (vert pair)	£11000	
19	3	6d. grey (1878)	£225	£200
20	4	1s. pale green (1878)	90·00	£110
		a. Imperf		
		b. Imperf between (horiz strip of three)	£16000	
		c. No. 9 on sheet with crossed lines on hill	£250	
21		1s. deep green	£100	£140
		c. No. 9 on sheet with crossed lines on hill	£900	

(b) P 11½.

22	1	1d. vermilion-red (1878)	55·00	55·00
		a. Bisected (½d.) (on cover)	†	£3000
		b. Imperf (pair)	£650	
		c. Imperf between (horiz pair)		

No. 21c occurs on a small part of the deep green printing only.

RETOUCHES. 1d. Lithograph.

i.	No. 1 on sheet. Top of hill over kneeling figure redrawn by five thick lines and eight small slanting lines	£140	£150
ii.	No. 1 on sheet. Another retouch. Three series of short vertical strokes behind the kneeling figure	£140	£150
iii.	No. 3 on sheet. Right upper corner star and border below star retouched	£140	£150
iv.	No. 9 on sheet. Retouch in same position as on No. 3 but differing in detail	£160	£170
v.	No. 12 on sheet. Dress of standing figure retouched by a number of horizontal and vertical lines	£140	£150

5 (Die I) NEVIS. 4d. (6)

(Typo D.L.R.)

1879–80. Wmk Crown CC. P 14.

23	5	1d. lilac-mauve (1880)	75·00	40·00
		a. Bisected (½d.) (on cover)	†	£950
		w. Wmk inverted		
24		2½d. red-brown	£130	85·00

1882–90. Wmk Crown CA. P 14.

25	5	½d. dull green (11.83)	7·00	17·00
		a. Top left triangle detached	£275	
26		1d. lilac-mauve	£100	32·00
		a. Bisected (½d.) on cover (1883)	†	£700
27		1d. dull rose (11.83)	28·00	20·00
		a. *Carmine* (1884)	13·00	13·00
		ab. Top left triangle detached	£375	
28		2½d. red-brown	£120	50·00
29		2½d. ultramarine (11.83)	19·00	19·00
		a. Top left triangle detached	£650	

30		4d. blue	£325	50·00
31		4d. grey (1884)	14·00	5·00
		a. Top left triangle detached	£550	£375
32		6d. green (11.83)	£400	£350
33		6d. chestnut (10.88)	24·00	65·00
		a. Top left triangle detached	£750	
34		1s. pale violet (3.90)	£110	£180
		a. Top left triangle detached	£1500	
33s/4s Optd "Specimen" *Set of 2*			£110	

For illustration of the "top left triangle detached" variety, which occurs on Plate 2 R. 3/3 of the right pane, see below Montserrat No. 5.

1883 (4 Sept). *No. 26 bisected vertically and surch with T* **6**, *reading upwards or downwards.*

35		½d. on half 1d. lilac-mauve (V.)	£900	48·00
		a. Surch double	—	£325
		b. Surch on half "REVENUE" stamp No. F6	—	£550
36		½d. on half 1d. lilac-mauve	£1100	45·00
		a. Surch double	—	£325
		b. Unsevered pair	£6000	£700
		c. Surch on half "REVENUE" stamp No. F6	—	£550

FISCALS USED FOR POSTAGE

Revenue (F 1) REVENUE (F 2)

1882.

(a) Stamps of 1876–78 optd with Type F **1**. *by Nissen & Parker, London*

F1	1	1d. bright red	70·00	
F2	2	1d. rose	70·00	29·00
F3		4d. orange	£120	
F4	3	6d. grey	£200	
F5	4	1s. green	£225	
		a. No. 9 on sheet with crossed lines on hill		

(b) Nos. 26, 30 and 32 optd with Type F **2**. *by D.L.R.*

F6	5	1d. lilac-mauve	65·00	55·00
		a. Bisected (½d.) (on cover)		
F7		4d. blue	42·00	60·00
F8		6d. green	25·00	65·00

Nos. F1/5 were produced from fresh transfers. Similar "REVENUE" handstamps, both with and without stop, were also applied to postage issues.

The stamps of Nevis were superseded by the general issue for Leeward Islands on 31 October 1890.

ST. KITTS-NEVIS

CROWN COLONY

Stamps for the combined colony were introduced in 1903, and were used concurrently with the general issues of Leeward Islands until the latter were withdrawn on 1 July 1956.

PRICES FOR STAMPS ON COVER TO 1945	
Nos. 1/9	*from* × 3
No. 10	—
Nos. 11/20	*from* × 3
No. 21	—
Nos. 22/3	*from* × 15
Nos. 24/34	*from* × 3
Nos. 35/6	—
Nos. 37/47	*from* × 2
Nos. 47*a*/*b*	—
Nos. 48/57	*from* × 2
Nos. 58/60	—
Nos. 61/4	*from* × 2
Nos. 65/7	*from* × 5
Nos. 68/77	*from* × 2

1 Christopher Columbus

2 Medicinal Spring

(Typo D.L.R.)

1903. Wmk Crown CA. P 14.

1	1	½d. dull purple and deep green	1·75	70
2	2	1d. grey-black and carmine	4·75	20
3	1	2d. dull purple and brown	2·75	11·00
4		2½d. grey-black and blue	19·00	4·25
5	2	3d. deep green and orange	18·00	30·00
6	1	6d. grey-black and bright purple	5·50	42·00
7		1s. grey-green and orange	7·50	11·00
8	2	2s. deep green and grey-black	12·00	20·00
9	1	2s.6d. grey-black and violet	18·00	42·00
10	2	5s. dull purple and sage-green	55·00	55·00
1/10 *Set of 10*			£130	£190
1s/10s Optd "Specimen" *Set of 10*			£130	

1905–18. *Chalk-surfaced paper (1d. (No. 13), 5s.) or ordinary paper (others).* Wmk Mult Crown CA. P 14.

11	1	½d. dull purple and deep green	9·50	5·50
12		½d. grey-green (1907)	1·00	60
		a. Dull blue-green (1916)	50	1·75
13	2	1d. grey-black and carmine (1906)	3·00	25
14		1d. carmine (1907)	2·25	15
		a. Scarlet (1916)	80	20
15	1	2d. dull purple and brown	11·00	8·00
		a. Chalk-surfaced paper (1906)	6·50	8·00
16		2½d. grey-black and blue (1907)	16·00	3·25
17		2½d. bright blue (1907)	2·50	50
18	2	3d. deep green and orange	13·00	10·00
		a. Chalk-surfaced paper (1906)	2·75	2·75
19	1	6d. grey-black and deep violet	25·00	50·00
		a. Chalk-surfaced paper. *Grey-black and deep purple* (1908)	19·00	25·00
		ab. Grey-black and bright purple (1916)	6·50	26·00
20		1s. grey-green and orange (1909)	28·00	48·00
		a. Chalk-surfaced paper	3·50	30·00
21	2	5s. dull purple and sage-green (11.18)	38·00	85·00
11/21 *Set of 11*			80·00	£150
12s, 14s, 17s Optd "Specimen" *Set of 3*			60·00	

WAR TAX (3) **WAR STAMP** (3a)

1916 (Oct). *Optd with T* **3**. Wmk Mult Crown CA. P 14.

22	1	½d. dull blue-green (No. 12*a*)	1·25	50
		a. Deep green	1·00	50
		s. Optd "Specimen"	40·00	
		x. Wmk reversed	38·00	

No. 22*a* was a special printing produced for this overprint.

1918 (26 July). *Optd with T* **3a**. Wmk Mult Crown CA. P 14.

23	1	1½d. orange	80	80
		a. Short opt (right pane R. 10/1)	17·00	
		s. Optd "Specimen"	45·00	

No. 23 was a special printing produced for this overprint.
No. 23a shows the overprint 2 mm high instead of 2½ mm.

4

5

(Typo D.L.R.)

1920–22. *Ordinary paper (½d. to 2½d.) or chalk-surfaced paper (others).* Wmk Mult Crown CA (sideways*). P 14.

24	4	½d. blue-green	3·75	5·50
25	5	1d. scarlet	2·25	6·00
26	4	1½d. orange-yellow	1·25	1·75
		x. Wmk sideways reversed	90·00	
		y. Wmk sideways inverted and reversed		
27	5	2d. slate-grey	3·00	4·00
28	4	2½d. ultramarine	3·25	9·00
		a. "A" of "CA" missing from wmk	£450	
29	5	3d. purple/*yellow*	1·75	11·00
30	4	6d. dull purple and bright mauve	3·50	11·00
31	5	1s. grey and black/*green*	3·50	4·00
32	4	2s. dull purple and blue/*blue*	15·00	28·00
		x. Wmk sideways reversed	£200	
33	5	2s.6d. grey and red/*blue*	5·00	32·00
		y. Wmk sideways inverted and reversed	£200	
34	4	5s. green and red/*pale yellow*	5·00	40·00
		x. Wmk sideways reversed	£150	
35	5	10s. green and red/*green*	12·00	48·00
36	4	£1 purple and black/*red* (1922)	£225	£300
24/36 *Set of 13*			£250	£400
24s/36s Optd "Specimen" *Set of 13*			£325	

*The normal sideways watermark shows Crown to left of CA, *as seen from the back of the stamp.*

Examples of most values are known showing a forged St. Kitts postmark dated "8 DE 23".

1921–29. *Chalk-surfaced paper (2½d. (No. 44), 3d. (No. 45a) and 6d. to 5s.) or ordinary.* Wmk Mult Script CA (sideways*).

37	4	½d. blue-green	2·25	1·50
		a. Yellow-green (1922)	1·50	80
38	5	1d. rose-carmine	65	15
		sa. Perf "Specimen" (1929)	70·00	
39		1d. deep violet (1922)	6·50	1·00
		a. Pale violet (1929)	7·00	1·50
40	4	1½d. red (1925)	3·50	2·25
40*a*		1½d. red-brown (1929)	1·00	30
41	5	2d. slate-grey (1922)	50	60
42	4	2½d. pale bright blue (1922)	3·00	2·25
43		2½d. brown (1922)	2·25	9·00
44		2½d. ultramarine (1927)	1·50	1·50
45	5	3d. dull ultramarine (1922)	1·00	4·25
45*a*		3d. purple/*yellow* (1927)	75	4·50
46	4	6d. dull and bright purple (1924)	5·00	6·00
		aw. Wmk Crown to right of CA	4·00	6·00
46*b*	5	1s. black/*green* (1929)	3·75	5·50
47	4	2s. purple and blue/*blue* (1922)	8·00	23·00
47*a*	5	2s.6d. black and red/*blue* (1927)	15·00	29·00
47*b*	4	5s. green and red/*yellow* (1929)	40·00	75·00
37/47*b* *Set of 16*			85·00	£150
37s/47bs Optd or Perf (1½d. red-brown, 1s., 5s.) "Specimen" *Set of 16*			£375	

*The normal sideways watermark shows Crown to left of CA, *as seen from the back of the stamp.*

6 Old Road Bay and Mount Misery

(Typo D.L.R.)

1923. *Tercentenary of Colony. Chalk-surfaced paper.* P 14.

(a) Wmk Mult Script CA (sideways).

48	6	½d. black and green	2·25	7·00
49		1d. black and bright violet	4·50	1·50
50		1½d. black and scarlet	4·50	10·00
51		2d. black and slate-grey	3·75	1·50
52		2½d. black and brown	6·00	32·00
53		3d. black and ultramarine	3·75	15·00
54		6d. black and bright purple	9·50	32·00
55		1s. black and sage-green	14·00	32·00
56		2s. black and blue/*blue*	48·00	70·00
57		2s.6d. black and red/*blue*	50·00	85·00
58		10s. black and red/*emerald*	£300	£450

(b) Wmk Mult Crown CA (sideways).

59	6	5s. black and red/*pale yellow*	85·00	£190
60		£1 black and purple/*red*	£750	£1600
48/60 *Set of 13*			£1100	£2250
48s/60s Optd "Specimen" *Set of 13*			£700	

Examples of all values are known showing a forged St. Kitts postmark dated "8 DE 23".

1935 (6 May). *Silver Jubilee. As Nos. 91/4 of Antigua, but ptd by Waterlow.* P 11×12.

61		1d. deep blue and scarlet	1·00	70
		k. Kite and vertical log	£110	£120
		l. Kite and horizontal log	£140	£140
62		1½d. ultramarine and grey	75	75
		k. Kite and vertical log	85·00	95·00
63		2½d. brown and deep blue	1·00	80
64		1s. slate and purple	7·50	15·00
		k. Kite and vertical log	£325	
		l. Kite and horizontal log	£325	£400
61/4 *Set of 4*			9·25	15·00
61s/4s Perf "Specimen" *Set of 4*			95·00	

For illustrations of plate varieties see Omnibus section following Zanzibar.

1937 (12 May). *Coronation. As Nos. 95/7 of Antigua, but ptd by D.L.R.* P 14.

65		1d. scarlet	30	25
66		1½d. buff	40	10
67		2½d. bright blue	60	1·60
65/7 *Set of 3*			1·10	1·75
65s/7s Perf "Specimen" *Set of 3*			85·00	

Nos. 61/7 are inscribed "ST. CHRISTOPHER AND NEVIS".

7 King George VI

8 King George VI and Medicinal Spring

9 King George VI and Christopher Columbus

10 King George VI and Anguilla Island

Break in value tablet (R. 12/5) (1947 ptg only)

Break in oval (R. 12/1) (1938 ptg only)

Break in value tablet frame (R. 3/2)

Break in value tablet frame (R. 12/3) (ptgs between 1941 and 1945)

Break in frame above ornament (R. 2/4) (ptgs between 1941 and 1950)

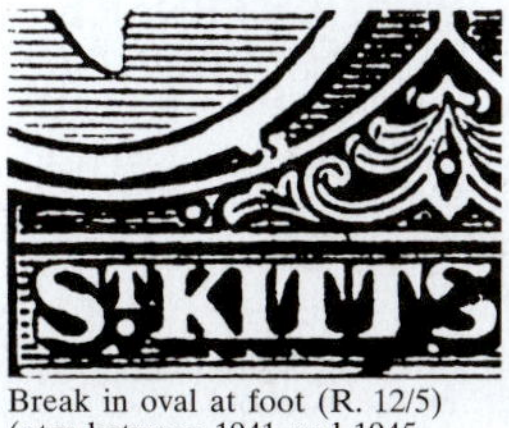

Break in oval at foot (R. 12/5) (ptgs between 1941 and 1945 only). Sometimes touched-in by hand painting

Break in oval at left (R. 7/1) (ptgs between 1941 and 1945 only)

(Typo; centre litho (T **10**). D.L.R.)

1938 (15 Aug)–**50**. *Chalk-surfaced paper (10s., £1).* Wmk Mult Script CA (sideways on T **8** and **9**). P 14 (T **7** and **10**) or 13×12 (T **8**/**9**).

68	7	½d. green	4·00	20
		a. Blue-green (5.4.43)	10	10
69		1d. scarlet	6·00	70
		a. Carmine (5.43)	1·50	50
		b. Carmine-pink (4.47)	60·00	16·00
		c. Rose-red (7.47)	1·50	80
70		1½d. orange	20	30

71 **8** 2d. scarlet and grey ... 25·00 2·75
a. Chalk-surfaced paper. *Carmine and deep grey* (18.2.41*) ... 55·00 10·00
b. Perf 14. *Scarlet and pale grey* (6.43*) ... 1·25 1·25
ba. Scarlet and deep grey (6.42*) ... 24·00 3·25
c. Perf 14. Chalk-surfaced paper. *Scarlet and pale grey* (2.50*) ... 4·25 3·50
72 **7** 2½d. ultramarine ... 5·00 30
a. Bright ultramarine (5.4.43) ... 70 30
73 **8** 3d. dull reddish purple and scarlet ... 21·00 6·00
a. Chalk-surfaced paper. *Brown-purple and carmine-red* (1940) ... 24·00 8·50
b. Perf 14. Chalk-surfaced paper. *Dull reddish purple and carmine-red* (6.43*) ... 35·00 4·75
c. Perf 14. Ordinary paper. *Reddish lilac and scarlet* (8.46*) ... 3·75 15·00
d. Perf 14. Ordinary paper. *Purple and bright scarlet* (1.46*) ... 13·00 9·00
da. Break in value tablet ... £190
e. Perf 14. Chalk-surfaced paper. *Deep purple and scarlet* (12.47*) ... 75·00 21·00
f. Perf 14. Ordinary paper. *Rose-lilac and bright scarlet* (1.49*) ... 11·00 11·00
g. Perf 14. Chalk-surfaced paper. *Deep reddish purple and bright scarlet* (8.50*) ... 7·50 8·00
74 **9** 6d. green and bright purple ... 6·50 2·25
a. Break in oval ... £160
b. Perf 14. Chalk-surfaced paper. *Green and deep claret* (17.5.43*) ... 55·00 11·00
c. Perf 14. Ordinary paper. *Green and purple* (10.44*) ... 7·00 1·50
d. Perf 14. Chalk-surfaced paper. *Green and purple* (11.48*) ... 6·00 4·00
75 **8** 1s. black and green ... 12·00 1·50
a. Break in value tablet frame ... £250
b. Perf 14 (8.43*) ... 4·00 85
ba. Break in value tablet frame ... £130 80·00
c. Perf 14. Chalk-surfaced paper (7.50*) ... 8·50 6·00
ca. Break in value tablet frame ... £170
76 2s.6d. black and scarlet ... 32·00 9·00
a. Perf 14. Chalk-surfaced paper (12.43*) ... 19·00 6·00
ab. Ordinary paper (5.45*) ... 12·00 3·75
77 **9** 5s. grey-green and scarlet ... 65·00 22·00
a. Perf 14. Chalk-surfaced paper (25.10.43*) ... £130 35·00
ab. Break in value tablet frame ... £750 £325
ac. Break in frame above ornament ... £750 £325
ad. Break in oval at foot ... £750 £325
ae. Break in oval at left ... £750 £325
b. Perf 14. Ordinary paper. *Bluish green and scarlet* (7.11.45*) ... 24·00 12·00
ba. Break in value tablet frame ... £325 £170
bb. Break in frame above ornament ... £350 £180
bc. Break in oval at foot ... £325 £160
bd. Break in oval at left ... £325 £170
c. Perf 14. Chalk-surfaced paper. *Green and scarlet-vermilion* (10.50*) ... 45·00 50·00
cb. Break in frame above ornament ... £425
77*e* **10** 10s. black and ultramarine (1.9.48) ... 13·00 19·00
77*f* £1 black and brown (1.9.48) ... 13·00 23·00
68*a*/77*f* *Set of* 12 ... 70·00 60·00
68*s*/77*fs* Perf "Specimen" *Set of* 10 ... £225

*Earliest postmark date. Many printings were supplied to St. Kitts-Nevis considerably earlier. Details of many of the dates are taken, with permission, from *A Study of the King George VI Stamps of St. Kitts-Nevis* by P. L. Baldwin (2nd edition 1997).

1946 (1 Nov). *Victory. As Nos. 110/11 of Antigua.*
78 1½d. red-orange ... 10 10
79 3d. carmine ... 10 10
78s/9s Perf "Specimen" *Set of* 2 ... 80·00

1949 (3 Jan). *Royal Silver Wedding. As Nos. 112/13 of Antigua.*
80 2½d. ultramarine ... 10 50
81 5s. carmine ... 7·00 4·25

1949 (10 Oct). *75th Anniv of U.P.U. As Nos. 114/17 of Antigua.*
82 2½d. ultramarine ... 15 30
83 3d. carmine-red ... 2·10 2·50
84 6d. magenta ... 20 1·75
85 1s. blue-green ... 20 40
a. "A" of "CA" missing from wmk ... — £500
82/5 *Set of* 4 ... 2·40 4·50

ANGUILLA   ANGUILLA

TERCENTENARY 1650-1950 (11)   TERCENTENARY 1650—1950 (12)

1950 (10 Nov). *Tercentenary of British Settlement in Anguilla. Nos. 69c, 70 and 72a (perf 14) optd as T* **11** *and new ptgs of T* **8/9** *on chalk-surfaced paper perf 13×12½ optd as T* **12**.
86 **7** 1d. rose-red ... 10 20
87 1½d. orange ... 10 50
a. Error. Crown missing, W **9a** ... £2250
b. Error. St. Edward's Crown, W **9b** ... £1100
88 2½d. bright ultramarine ... 15 20
89 **8** 3d. dull purple and scarlet ... 40 75
90 **9** 6d. green and bright purple ... 30 20
91 **8** 1s. black and green (R.) ... 1·00 25
a. Break in value tablet frame ... 15·00
86/91 *Set of* 6 ... 1·75 1·90

Nos. 87a/b occur on a row in the watermark, in which the crowns and letters "CA" alternate.

(New Currency. 100 cents = 1 West Indian dollar)

1951 (16 Feb). *Inauguration of B.W.I. University College. As Nos. 118/19 of Antigua.*
92 3c. black and yellow-orange ... 30 15
93 12c. turquoise-green and magenta ... 30 2·00

ST. CHRISTOPHER, NEVIS AND ANGUILLA

LEGISLATIVE COUNCIL

13 Bath House and Spa, Nevis

14 Warner Park

15 Map of the Islands

16 Brimstone Hill

17 Nevis from the Sea, North

18 Pinney's Beach

19 Sir Thomas Warner's Tomb

20 Old Road Bay

21 Sea Island Cotton

22 The Treasury

23 Salt Pond, Anguilla

24 Sugar Factory

(Recess Waterlow)

1952 (14 June). *Vert designs as T* **14** *(3c., $2.40) or horiz as T* **13/24**. Wmk Mult Script CA. P 12½.
94 **13** 1c. deep green and ochre ... 15 1·50
95 **14** 2c. green ... 1·00 1·00
96 **15** 3c. carmine-red and violet ... 30 1·25
97 **16** 4c. scarlet ... 20 20
98 **17** 5c. bright blue and grey ... 30 10
99 **18** 6c. ultramarine ... 30 15
100 **19** 12c. deep blue and reddish brown ... 1·25 10
101 **20** 24c. black and carmine-red ... 30 10
102 **21** 48c. olive and chocolate ... 2·25 2·75
103 **22** 60c. ochre and deep green ... 2·00 3·00
104 **23** $1.20 deep green and ultramarine ... 7·00 2·75
105 **24** $4.80 green and carmine ... 13·00 18·00
94/105 *Set of* 12 ... 25·00 28·00

1953 (2 June). *Coronation. As No. 120 of Antigua.*
106 2c. black and bright green ... 30 15

25 Sombrero Lighthouse

26 Map of Anguilla and Dependencies

(Recess Waterlow (until 1961), then D.L.R.)

1954 (1 Mar)–**63**. *Designs previously used for King George VI issue, but with portrait of Queen Elizabeth II as in T* **25/6** *or new values and designs (½c., 8c., $2.40).* Wmk Mult Script CA. P 12½.
106*a* **23** ½c. deep olive (3.7.56) ... 30 10
107 **13** 1c. deep green and ochre ... 20 10
a. Deep green and orange-ochre (13.2.62) ... 1·25 3·00
b. Imperf vert (horiz strip of three) ... † £7000
108 **14** 2c. green ... 50 10
a. Yellow-green (31.7.63) ... 4·50 6·50
109 **15** 3c. carmine-red and violet ... 65 10
a. Carmine and deep violet (31.7.63) ... 4·50 7·00
110 **16** 4c. scarlet ... 15 10
111 **17** 5c. bright blue and grey ... 15 10
112 **18** 6c. ultramarine ... 70 10
a. Blue (19.2.63) ... 1·25 30
112*b* **25** 8c. grey-black (1.2.57) ... 3·00 25
113 **19** 12c. deep blue and red-brown ... 15 10
114 **20** 24c. black and carmine-red (1.12.54) ... 15 10
115 **21** 48c. olive-bistre and chocolate (1.12.54) ... 1·00 60
116 **22** 60c. ochre and deep green (1.12.54) ... 5·50 5·50
117 **23** $1.20 deep green and ultramarine (1.12.54) ... 18·00 2·50
a. Deep green and violet-blue (19.2.63) ... 42·00 10·00
117*b* **26** $2.40 black and red-orange (1.2.57) ... 10·00 11·00
118 **24** $4.80 green and carmine (1.12.54) ... 13·00 11·00
106*a*/18 *Set of* 15 ... 48·00 28·00

27 Alexander Hamilton and View of Nevis

(Des Eva Wilkin. Recess Waterlow)

1957 (11 Jan). *Birth Bicentenary of Alexander Hamilton.* Wmk Mult Script CA. P 12½.
119 **27** 24c. green and deep blue ... 40 15

1958 (22 Apr). *Inauguration of British Caribbean Federation. As Nos. 135/7 of Antigua.*
120 3c. deep green ... 60 15
121 6c. blue ... 90 2·50
122 12c. scarlet ... 1·00 35
120/2 *Set of* 3 ... 2·25 2·75

MINISTERIAL GOVERNMENT

28 One Penny Stamp of 1861

(Recess Waterlow)

1961 (15 July). *Nevis Stamp Centenary. T* **28** *and similar horiz designs.* W w **12**. P 14.
123 2c. red-brown and green ... 20 20
124 8c. red-brown and deep blue ... 25 10
125 12c. black and carmine-red ... 30 15
126 24c. deep bluish green and red-orange ... 35 15
123/6 *Set of* 4 ... 1·00 55

Designs:—8c. Fourpence stamp of 1861; 12c. Sixpence stamp of 1861; 24c. One shilling stamp of 1861.

1963 (2 Sept). *Red Cross Centenary. As Nos. 147/8 of Antigua.*
127 3c. red and black ... 10 10
128 12c. red and blue ... 20 40

32 New Lighthouse, Sombrero

33 Loading Sugar Cane, St. Kitts

(Des V. Whiteley. Photo Harrison)

1963 (20 Nov)–**69**. *Vert designs as T* **32** *(2, 3, 15, 25, 60c., $1, $5) or horiz as T* **33** *(others) in sepia and light blue (½ c.), greenish yellow and blue ($1) or multicoloured (others).* W w **12** (upright). P 14.
129 ½c. Type **32** ... 10 10
w. Wmk inverted ... £225
130 1c. Type **33** ... 10 10
131 2c. Pall Mall Square, Basseterre ... 10 10
a. Yellow omitted (White fountain and church) ... £150
w. Wmk inverted
132 3c. Gateway, Brimstone Hill Fort, St. Kitts ... 10 10
w. Wmk inverted
133 4c. Nelson's Spring, Nevis ... 10 10
w. Wmk inverted
134 5c. Grammar School, St. Kitts ... 3·00 10
135 6c. Crater, Mt Misery, St. Kitts ... 10 10
w. Wmk inverted (19.12.69) ... 30 30
136 10c. Hibiscus ... 15 10
137 15c. Sea Island cotton, Nevis ... 55 10
w. Wmk inverted
138 20c. Boat building, Anguilla ... 20 10
139 25c. White-crowned Pigeon (turquoise-blue background) ... 2·00 10
a. Turquoise-green background (13.4.65) ... 4·75 1·50
w. Wmk inverted ... — 70·00

140		50c. St. George's Church Tower, Basseterre	40	25
141		60c. Alexander Hamilton	1·00	30
142		$1 Map of St. Kitts-Nevis	2·50	40
143		$2.50 Map of Anguilla	2·50	2·50
144		$5 Arms of St. Christopher, Nevis and Anguilla	5·50	4·00
129/44		*Set of* 16	16·00	7·75

The 1, 4, 5, 6, 10 and 20c. values exist with PVA gum as well as gum arabic.

See also Nos. 166/71.

ARTS
FESTIVAL
ST KITTS
1964
(48)

49 Festival Emblem

1964 (14 Sept). *Arts Festival. Nos. 132 and 139 optd as T* **48**.

145		3c. Gateway, Brimstone Hill Fort, St. Kitts	10	15
		a. Opt double	£275	
146		25c. White-crowned Pigeon	20	15
		a. "FESTIVAI" (R. 1/10)	70·00	
		w. Wmk inverted	–	8·00

1985 (17 May). *I.T.U. Centenary. As Nos. 166/7 of Antigua.*

147		2c. bistre-yellow and rose-carmine	10	10
148		50c. turquoise-blue and yellow-olive	40	50

1965 (15 Oct). *International Co-operation Year. As Nos. 168/9 of Antigua.*

149		2c. reddish purple and turquoise-green	10	20
150		25c. deep bluish green and lavender	20	10

1966 (24 Jan). *Churchill Commemoration. As Nos. 170/3 of Antigua.*

151		½c. new blue	10	2·50
		a. Value omitted	£225	
		b. Value at left instead of right	75·00	
152		3c. deep green	35	10
153		15c. brown	80	20
154		25c. bluish violet	85	20
151/4		*Set of* 4	1·75	2·75

1966 (4 Feb). *Royal Visit. As Nos. 174/5 of Antigua.*

155		3c. black and ultramarine	25	30
156		25c. black and magenta	55	30

1966 (1 July). *World Cup Football Championship. As Nos. 176/7 of Antigua.*

157		6c. violet, yellow-green, lake and yellow-brown	40	20
158		25c. chocolate, blue-green, lake and yellow-brown	60	10

(Photo Harrison)

1966 (15 Aug). *Arts Festival.* P 14×14½.

159	**49**	3c. black, buff, emerald-green and gold	10	10
160		25c. black, buff, emerald-green and silver	20	10

1966 (20 Sept). *Inauguration of W.H.O. Headquarters, Geneva. As Nos. 178/9 of Antigua.*

161		3c. black, yellow-green and light blue	10	10
162		40c. black, light purple and yellow-brown	30	20

1966 (1 Dec). *20th Anniv of U.N.E.S.C.O. As Nos. 196/8 of Antigua.*

163		3c. slate-violet, red, yellow and orange	10	10
164		6c. orange-yellow, violet and deep olive	10	10
165		40c. black, bright purple and orange	30	35
163/5		*Set of* 3	45	50

ASSOCIATED STATEHOOD

1967–69. *As Nos. 129, 13½, 137, 139 and 142 but wmk sideways.*

166	**20**	½c. sepia and light blue (9.1.69)	20	2·50
167	–	2c. multicoloured (27.6.67)	1·75	10
168	–	3c. multicoloured (16.7.68)	20	10
169	–	15c. multicoloured (16.7.68)	70	30
170	–	25c. multicoloured (16.7.68)	2·50	20
171	–	$1 greenish yellow and blue (16.7.68)	5·00	4·00
		a. Greenish yellow and ultramarine-blue (19.12.69)	11·00	6·00
166/71		*Set of* 6	9·25	6·50

The 2c. and $1 values exist with PVA gum as well as gum arabic.

Nos. 172/81 vacant.

50 Government Headquarters, Basseterre

53 John Wesley and Cross

(Des V. Whiteley. Photo Harrison)

1967 (1 July). *Statehood. T* **50** *and similar horiz designs. Multicoloured.* W w **12**. P 14½×14.

182		3c. Type **50**	10	10
183		10c. National flag	10	10
		w. Wmk inverted	20·00	
184		25c. Coat of arms	15	15
182/4		*Set of* 3	30	30

(Litho D.L.R.)

1967 (1 Dec). *West Indies Methodist Conference. T* **53** *and similar vert designs.* P 13×13½.

185		3c. black, cerise and reddish violet	10	10
186		25c. black, light greenish blue and blue	15	10
187		40c. black, yellow and orange	15	15
185/7		*Set of* 3	35	30

Designs:—25c. Charles Wesley and Cross; 40c. Thomas Coke and Cross.

56 Handley Page H.P.R.7 Dart Herald Aircraft over *Jamaica Producer* (freighter)

57 Dr. Martin Luther King

(Des and litho D.L.R.)

1968 (30 July). *Caribbean Free Trade Area.* W w **12** (sideways). P 13.

188	**56**	25c. multicoloured	40	10
189		50c. multicoloured	40	20

(Des G. Vasarhelyi. Litho Enschedé)

1968 (30 Sept). *Martin Luther King Commemoration.* W w **12**. P 12×12½.

190	**57**	50c. multicoloured	15	10

58 "Mystic Nativity" (Botticelli)

60 Tarpon Snook

(Des and photo Harrison)

1968 (27 Nov). *Christmas. Paintings. T* **58** *and similar vert design. Multicoloured.* W w **12** (sideways). P 14½×14.

191		12c. Type **58**	10	10
192		25c. "The Adoration of the Magi" (Rubens)	10	10
193		40c. Type **58**	15	10
194		50c. As 25c.	15	10
191/4		*Set of* 4	45	35

(Des G. Drummond. Photo Harrison)

1969 (25 Feb). *Fishes. T* **60** *and similar horiz designs.* W w **12**. P 14×14½.

195		6c. multicoloured	10	10
196		12c. black, turquoise-green and greenish blue	15	10
197		40c. multicoloured	25	10
198		50c. multicoloured	30	15
195/8		*Set of* 4	70	40

Designs:—12c. Needlefish; 40c. Horse-eyed Jack; 50c. Blackfinned Snapper.

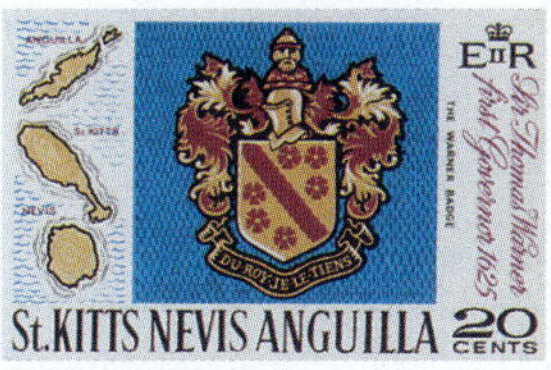

64 The Warner Badge and Islands

67 "The Adoration of the Kings" (Mostaert)

(Des V. Whiteley. Litho Format)

1969 (1 Sept). *Sir Thomas Warner Commemoration. T* **64** *and similar horiz designs. Multicoloured.* W w **12** (sideways). P 13½×14.

199		20c. Type **64**	10	10
200		25c. Sir Thomas Warner's tomb	10	10
201		40c. Charles I's commission	15	15
199/201		*Set of* 3	30	30

(Des Enschede. Litho B.W.)

1969 (17 Nov). *Christmas. Paintings. T* **67** *and similar vert design. Multicoloured.* W w **12** (sideways). P 13½.

202		10c. Type **67**	10	10
203		25c. Type **67**	10	10
204		40c. "The Adoration of the Kings" (Geertgen)	10	10
205		50c. As 40c.	10	10
202/5		*Set of* 4	35	35

(Des and litho J.W.)

1970 (2 Feb)–**74**. *Designs as T* **73** *in black, pale orange and emerald (½c.) or multicoloured (others).* W w **12** (upright on vert designs, sideways* on horiz designs). P 14.

206		½c. Pirates and treasure at Frigate Bay (*vert*)	10	10
		w. Wmk inverted (15.3.71)	20	20
207		1c. English two-decker warship, 1650 (*vert*)	30	10
208		2c. Naval flags of colonising nations (*vert*)	15	10
209		3c. Rapier hilt (17th-century) (*vert*)	15	10
210		4c. Type **73**	20	10
		w. Wmk Crown to right of CA (24.7.74)	55	15
211		5c. Sir Henry Morgan and fireships, 1669	30	10
		w. Wmk Crown to right of CA (24.7.74)	40	30
212		6c. L'Ollonois and pirate carrack (16th century)	30	10
		w. Wmk Crown to right of CA (24.7.74)	40	40
213		10c. 17th-century smugglers' ship	30	10
		w. Wmk Crown to right of CA (24.7.74)	40	15
214		15c. "Piece-of-eight" (*vert*) (I)	2·00	40
214*a*		15c. "Piece-of-eight" (*vert*) (II) (8.9.70)	3·00	10
215		20c. Cannon (17th-century)	35	10
		w. Crown to right of CA (24.7.74)	50	20
216		25c. Humphrey Cole's Astrolabe, 1574 (*vert*)	40	10
217		50c. Flintlock pistol (17th-century)	85	80
		w. Wmk Crown to right of CA (24.7.74)	1·25	80
218		60c. Dutch flute (17th-century) (*vert*)	1·50	70
219		$1 Captain Bartholomew Roberts and his crew's death warrant (*vert*)	1·50	75
220		$2.50 Railing piece (16th-century)	1·25	3·50
		w. Wmk Crown to right of CA (24.7.74)	2·00	3·25
221		$5 Drake, Hawkins and sea battle	1·50	4·50
		w. Wmk Crown to right of CA (24.7.74)	3·25	5·00
206/21		*Set of* 17	13·00	9·50

Nos. 214/*a*. Type I, coin inscribed "HISPANIANUM"; Type II corrected to "HISPANIARUM". No. 214*a* also differs considerably in shade from No. 214.

*The normal sideways watermark shows Crown to left of CA, *as seen from the back of the stamp.*

Values from this set were subsequantly reissued with W w **12** sideways on vertical designs and upright on horizontal designs. Later values were issued on paper watermarked W w **14**.

85 Graveyard Scene (Great Expectations)

(Des Jennifer Toombs. Litho B. W.)

1970 (1 May). *Death Centenary of Charles Dickens. T* **85** *and similar designs.* W w **12** (sideways on horiz designs). P 13.

222		4c. bistre-brown, gold and deep blue-green	10	60
223		20c. bistre-brown, gold and reddish purple	10	20
224		25c. bistre-brown, gold and olive-green	10	20
225		40c. bistre-brown, gold and ultramarine	15	35
222/5		*Set of* 4	40	1·25

Designs: *Horiz*—20c. Miss Havisham and Pip (*Great Expectations*). *Vert*—25c. Dickens's Birthplace; 40c. Charles Dickens.

86 Local Steel Band

(Des V. Whiteley. Litho Enschedé)

1970 (1 Aug). *Festival of Arts. T* **86** *and similar horiz designs. Multicoloured.* W w **12** (sideways). P 13½.

226		20c. Type **86**	10	10
227		25c. Local String Band	10	10
228		40c. Scene from *A Midsummer Night's Dream*	15	15
226/8		*Set of* 3	30	30

87 1d. Stamp of 1870 and Post Office, 1970

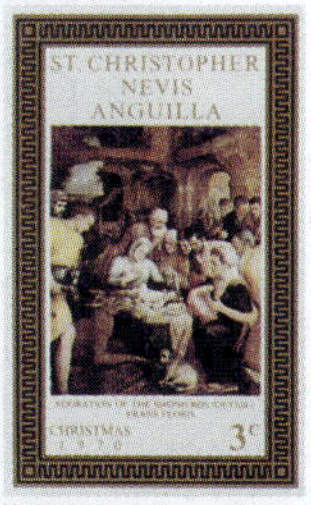

88 "Adoration of the Shepherds" (detail) (Frans van Floris)

(Des J. Cooter. Litho J.W.)

1970 (14 Sept). *Stamp Centenary. T* **87** *and similar horiz designs.* W w **12** (sideways). P 14½.

229		½c. green and rose	10	10
230		20c. deep blue, green and rose	10	10
231		25c. brown-purple, green and rose	10	10
232		50c. scarlet, green and black	30	45
229/32 *Set of* 4			55	65

Designs:—20c., 25c., 1d. and 6d. Stamps of 1870; 50c., 6d. Stamp of 1870 and early postmark.

(Des Enschede. Litho Format)

1970 (16 Nov). *Christmas. T* **88** *and similar vent design. Multicoloured.* W w **12**. P 14.

233		3c. Type **88**	10	10
234		20c. "The Holy Family" (Van Dyck)	10	10
235		25c. As 20c.	10	10
236		40c. Type **88**	15	50
235/6 *Set of* 4			40	70

St. Lucia

Although a branch office of the British G.P.O. was not opened at Castries, the island capital, until 1844 some form of postal arrangements for overseas mails existed from at least 1841 when the issue of a Ship Letter handstamp is recorded.

The stamps of Great Britain were used on the island from May 1858 until the end of April 1860 when the local authorities assumed responsibility for the postal service. No. CC1 was again used on overseas mail between 1 May and the introduction of St. Lucia stamps in December 1860.

CASTRIES

CROWN-CIRCLE HANDSTAMPS

CC 1

CC1 CC **1** ST. LUCIA (R.) (1.5.1844) ..... *Price on cover* £900

No. CC1 was utilised, struck in black, during a shortage of 1d. stamps in late April and early May 1904. *Price on cover* £325.

Stamps of GREAT BRITAIN *cancelled* "A 11" *as Type* Z **1** *of Jamaica.*

1858–60.

Z1	1d. rose-red (1857), *perf* 14	£1200
Z2	2d. blue (1855)	
Z3	4d. rose (1857)	£450
Z4	6d. lilac (1856)	£250
Z5	1s. green (1856)	£1900

PRICES FOR STAMPS ON COVER TO 1945

Nos. 1/3	*from* × 60
Nos. 5/8	*from* × 30
Nos. 9/10	†
Nos. 11/24	*from* × 15
Nos. 25/30	*from* × 10
Nos. 31/6	*from* × 6
Nos. 39/42	*from* × 10
Nos. 43/50	*from* × 15
Nos. 51/2	—
Nos. 53/62	*from* × 6
No. 63	*from* × 15
Nos. 64/75	*from* × 4
Nos. 76/7	—
Nos. 78/88	*from* × 3
No. 89	*from* × 4
No. 90	*from* × 20
Nos. 91/112	*from* × 3
Nos. 113/24	*from* × 2
Nos. 125/7	*from* × 10
Nos. 128/41	*from* × 2
Nos. D1/6	*from* × 10
Nos. F1/28	—

CROWN COLONY

PERKINS BACON "CANCELLED". For notes on these handstamps, showing "CANCELLED" between horizontal bars forming an oval, see Catalogue Introduction.

1

Half penny
(2)

(Recess P.B.)

1860 (18 Dec). Wmk Small Star, W w **2**. P 14 to 16.

1	**1**	(1d.) rose-red (H/S "CANCELLED" in oval £8000)	£100	65·00
		a. Imperf vert (horiz pair)		
		b. Double impression	£2500	
2		(4d.) blue (H/S "CANCELLED" in oval £9000)	£225	£150
		a. Deep blue		
		b. Imperf vert (horiz pair)		
3		(6d.) green (H/S "CANCELLED" in oval £12000)	£300	£200
		a. Imperf vert (horiz pair)		
		b. Deep green	£350	£225

(Recess D.L.R.)

1863. Wmk Crown CC. P 12½.

5	**1**	(1d.) lake	95·00	£110
		ax. Wmk reversed	70·00	90·00
		b. Brownish lake	£110	£110
		bx. Wmk reversed	85·00	90·00
7		(4d.) indigo	£120	£130
		x. Wmk reversed		
8		(6d.) emerald-green	£200	£200
		w. Wmk inverted		
		x. Wmk reversed	£180	£170

All three values exist imperforate from proof sheets.

Prepared for use, but not issued. Surch as T **2**.

9	**1**	½d. on (6d.)emerald-green	70·00	
		x. Wmk reversed	£100	
10		6d. on (4d.)indigo	£1100	

Nos. 9/10 were first recorded in 1885. They may have been prepared in 1876.

1864 (19 Nov)–**76**. Wmk Crown CC.

(a) P 12½.

11	**1**	(1d.) black	23·00	13·00
		a. Intense black	22·00	12·00
		x. Wmk reversed	29·00	16·00
		y. Wmk inverted and reversed	£110	
12		(4d.) yellow	£170	45·00
		b. Lemon-yellow	£1500	
		c. Chrome-yellow	£200	40·00
		d. Olive-yellow	£375	90·00
		w. Wmk inverted		
		x. Wmk reversed	£225	48·00
		y. Wmk inverted and reversed		
13		(6d.) violet	£130	38·00
		a. Mauve	£190	32·00
		b. Deep lilac	£160	38·00
		x. Wmk reversed	£160	
14		(1s.) brown-orange	£325	29·00
		b. Orange	£250	29·00
		c. Pale orange	£225	29·00
		ca. Imperf between (horiz pair)		
		x. Wmk reversed	£275	

(b) P 14.

15	**1**	(1d.) black (6.76)	32·00	20·00
		a. Imperf between (horiz pair)		
		x. Wmk reversed	35·00	20·00
16		(4d.) yellow (6.76)	£120	22·00
		a. Olive-yellow	£325	£100
		w. Wmk inverted		
		x. Wmk reversed	£120	22·00
17		(6d.) mauve (6.76)	£120	42·00
		a. Pale lilac	£120	22·00
		b. Violet	£250	70·00
		x. Wmk reversed	—	50·00
18		(1s.) orange (10.76)	£250	22·00
		a. Deep orange	£160	16·00
		w. Wmk inverted		
		x. Wmk reversed	£180	25·00

All four values exist imperforate from proof sheets.

HALFPENNY (3) 2½ PENCE (4)

5

1881 (Sept). *Surch with T* **3** *or* **4**. Wmk Crown CC. P 14.

23	**1**	½d. green	70·00	90·00
		x. Wmk reversed	—	£150
24		2½d. brown-red	40·00	23·00

The (1d.) black is known surcharged "1d." in violet ink by hand, but there is no evidence that this was done officially.

1882–84. *Surch as T* **3**. Wmk Crown CA.

(a) P 14.

25	**1**	½d. green (1882)	23·00	32·00
26		1d. black (C.)	30·00	13·00
		a. Bisected (on cover)	†	—
27		4d. yellow	£300	22·00
28		6d. violet	35·00	32·00
29		1s. orange	£275	£170

(b) P 12.

30	**1**	4d. yellow	£275	28·00

Deep blue stamps, wmk Crown CA, perf 14 or 12 are fiscals from which the overprint "THREE PENCE—REVENUE", or "REVENUE", has been fraudulently removed.

(Typo D.L.R.)

1883 (6 July)–**86**. *Die I.* Wmk Crown CA. P 14.

31	**5**	½d. dull green	10·00	6·00
		a. Top left triangle detached	£325	
32		1d. carmine-rose	45·00	13·00
33		2½d. blue	48·00	2·25
		a. Top left triangle detached	£750	£160
34		4d. brown (1885)	38·00	1·25
		a. Top left triangle detached	£700	£120
35		6d. lilac (1886)	£250	£200
36		1s. orange-brown (1885)	£375	£150
31/6 *Set of* 6			£700	£325

The 4d. and 6d. exist imperforate from proof sheets.

For illustration of "top left triangle detached" variety on this and the following issue see above No. 6 of Montserrat.

1886–87. *Die I.* Wmk Crown CA. P 14.

39	**5**	1d. dull mauve	9·00	6·00
		a. Top left triangle detached	£275	
40		3d. dull mauve and green	£120	17·00
		a. Top left triangle detached	—	£450
41		6d. dull mauve and blue (1887)	4·50	12·00
		a. Top left triangle detached	£250	£325
42		1s. dull mauve and red (1887)	£120	29·00
		a. Top left triangle detached	£1100	£700
39/42 *Set of* 4			£225	55·00
39s/42s Optd "Specimen" *Set of* 4			£190	

The 1d. exists imperforate from proof sheets.

1891–98. *Die II.* Wmk Crown CA. P 14.

43	**5**	½d. dull green	3·00	1·00
		w. Wmk inverted	£500	
44		1d. dull mauve	4·50	30
45		2d. ultramarine and orange (1898)	4·25	1·00
46		2½d. ultramarine	6·00	1·00
47		3d. dull mauve and green	5·00	5·50
48		4d. brown	4·00	2·25
49		6d. dull mauve and blue	24·00	24·00
50		1s. dull mauve and red	8·00	5·00
51		5s. dull mauve and orange	50·00	£140
52		10s. dull mauve and black	90·00	£150
43/52 *Set of* 10			£170	£300
45s, 51s/2s Optd "Specimen" *Set of* 3			£120	

For description and illustration of differences between Die I and Die II see Introduction.

ONE HALF PENNY (6) ½d (7) ONE PENNY (8)

N Normal "N" N Thick "N"

Three types of T **8**

I. All letters "N" normal.
II. Thick diagonal stroke in first "N" of "PENNY".
III. Thick diagonal stroke in second "N" of "PENNY".

1891–92.

(a) Stamps of Die I surch.

53	**6**	½d. on 3d. dull mauve and green	£140	70·00
		a. Small "A" in "HALF"	£350	£150
		b. Small "O" in "ONE"	£350	£150
		c. Top left triangle detached	£1000	
54	**7**	½d. on half 6d. dull mauve and blue	26·00	3·25
		a. No fraction bar	£300	£130
		b. Surch sideways	£1600	
		c. Surch double	£650	£650
		d. "2" in fraction omitted	£475	£500
		e. Thick "1" with sloping serif	£200	£120
		f. Surch triple	£1300	
		g. Figure "1" used as fraction bar	£475	£275
		h. Top left triangle detached	—	£325
55	**8**	1d. on 4d. brown (I) (12.91)	6·00	3·75
		a. Surch double	£250	
		b. Surch inverted	£950	£850
		c. Type II	26·00	21·00
		ca. Surch double	£450	
		cb. Surch inverted	—	£1500
		d. Type III	26·00	21·00
		e. Top left triangle detached	£225	£170

(b) Stamp of Die II surch.

56	**6**	½d. on 3d. dull mauve and green	80·00	26·00
		a. Surch double	£850	£650
		b. Surch inverted	£1900	£650
		c. Surch both sides	£1100	£750
		d. Small "O" in "ONE" (R. 2/6)	£225	90·00
		e. Small "A" in "HALF"	£225	90·00
		f. "ONE" misplaced ("O" over "H") (R. 4/6)	£225	90·00

Nos. 53 and 56 were surcharged with a setting of 30 (6×5). No. 55 was surcharged by a vertical setting of 10, repeated six times across each pane, with Type II (thick first "N") at pos. 1 and Type III (thick second "N") at pos. 9.

9

10

(Typo D.L.R.)

1902–03. Wmk Crown CA. P 14.

58	**9**	½d. dull purple and green	2·75	1·50
59		1d. dull purple and carmine	5·00	50
60		2½d. dull purple and ultramarine	27·00	5·50
61	**10**	3d. dull purple and yellow	7·00	8·50
62		1s. green and black	11·00	35·00
58/62 *Set of* 5			48·00	45·00
58s/62s Optd "Specimen" *Set of* 5			£110	

11 The Pitons

(Recess D.L.R.)

1902 (15 Dec). *400th Anniv of Discovery by Columbus.* Wmk Crown CC (sideways). P 14.

63	**11**	2d. green and brown	9·50	1·75
		s. Optd "Specimen"	60·00	

This stamp was formerly thought to have been issued on 16 December but it has been seen on a postcard clearly postmarked 15 December.

1904–10. *Chalk-surfaced paper (Nos. 71, 73/5 and 77) or ordinary paper (others).* Wmk Mult Crown CA. P 14.

64	**9**	½d. dull purple and green	5·00	60
		a. Chalk-surfaced paper	7·00	1·25
65		½d. green (1907)	1·75	1·00

66		1d. dull purple and carmine	6·00	1·25
		a. Chalk-surfaced paper	7·00	1·25
67		1d. carmine (1907)	4·25	30
68		2½d. dull purple and ultramarine	22·00	1·50
		a. Chalk-surfaced paper	13·00	4·50
69		2½d. blue (1907)	3·75	1·75
70	10	3d. dull purple and yellow	9·00	3·00
71		3d. purple/*yellow* (1909)	3·00	15·00
72		6d. dull purple and violet (1905)	19·00	22·00
		a. Chalk-surfaced paper	20·00	30·00
		ab. Dull purple and bright purple (1907)	8·50	30·00
73		6d. dull purple (1910)	70·00	85·00
74		1s. green and black (1905)	35·00	28·00
75		1s. black/*green* (1909)	4·75	8·00
76		5s. green and carmine (1905)	75·00	£180
77		5s. green and red/*yellow* (1907)	60·00	70·00
64/77 *Set of 14*			£250	£375
65s, 67s, 69s, 71s/2s, 72abs and 75s/7s Optd "Specimen" *Set of 9*			£300	

Examples of Nos. 71/7 are known with a forged Castries postmark dated "JA 21 09".

12

13

14

15

16

(Typo D.L.R.)

1912–21. *Die I. Chalk-surfaced paper (3d. to 5s.).* Wmk Mult Crown CA. P 14.

78	12	½d. deep green	70	50
		a. Yellow-green (1916)	1·25	30
79		1d. carmine-red	1·90	10
		a. Scarlet (1916)	5·00	10
		b. Rose-red	8·00	1·00
80	13	2d. grey	1·50	4·25
		a. Slate-grey (1916)	18·00	14·00
81	12	2½d. ultramarine	3·75	2·75
		a. Bright blue	2·75	2·75
		b. Deep bright blue (1916)	13·00	10·00
82	15	3d. purple/*yellow*	1·25	2·25
		b. Die II. *On pale yellow* (1921)	14·00	48·00
		bw. Wmk inverted		
83	14	4d. black and red/*yellow*	1·00	2·00
		a. White back	70	1·50
		as. Optd "Specimen"	28·00	
84	15	6d. dull and bright purple	2·00	15·00
		a. Grey-purple and purple (1918)	16·00	19·00
85		1s. black/*green*	3·50	5·00
		a. On blue-green (olive back) (1918)	11·00	11·00
86		1s. orange-brown (1920)	13·00	45·00
87	16	2s.6d. black and red/*blue*	23·00	45·00
88	15	5s. green and red/*yellow*	24·00	80·00
78/88 *Set of 11*			65·00	£180
78s/88s Optd "Specimen" *Set of 11*			£225	

(17)

(18)

1916 (1 June). *No. 79a optd locally with T* **17**.

89	12	1d. scarlet	13·00	14·00
		a. Opt double	£475	£475
		b. Carmine-red	60·00	48·00

For overprinting with Type **17** the sheets were vertically divided to the left of the centre margin and the top margin of the sheet was folded beneath the top row of stamps so that the marginal examples from this row show an inverted albino impression of the overprint in the top margin.

Examples are also recorded of similar albino overprints in the right-hand and bottom margins but it is unclear if some sheets had all margins folded under before overprinting.

1916 (Sept). *No. 79a optd in London with T* **18**.

90	12	1d. scarlet	1·25	30
		s. Optd "Specimen"	42·00	

1921–30. *Die II. Chalk-surfaced paper (3d. (No. 100) to 5s.).* Wmk Mult Script CA. P 14.

91	12	½d. green	85	50
92		1d. rose-carmine	12·00	17·00
93		1d. deep brown (1922)	1·40	15
94	14	1½d. dull carmine (1922)	75	2·50
95	13	2d. slate-grey	75	15
96	12	2½d. bright blue	4·75	2·75
97		2½d. orange (1925)	12·00	55·00
98		2½d. dull blue (1926)	4·75	2·75
99	15	3d. bright blue (1922)	6·00	16·00
		a. Dull blue (1924)	3·50	11·00
100		3d. purple/*pale yellow* (1926)	1·50	12·00
		a. Deep purple/pale yellow (1930)	20·00	12·00
101	14	4d. black and red/*yellow* (1924)	1·25	2·50
102	15	6d. grey-purple and purple	2·00	4·75
103		1s. orange-brown	3·25	3·25
104	16	2s.6d. black and red/*blue* (1924)	18·00	27·00
105	15	5s. green and red/*pale yellow* (1923)	50·00	85·00
91/105 *Set of 15*			£100	£200
91s/105s Optd "Specimen" *Set of 15*			£325	

1935 (6 May). *Silver Jubilee. As Nos. 91/4 of Antigua.* P 13½×14.

109	½d. black and green	20	1·50
	f. Diagonal line by turret	38·00	
110	2d. ultramarine and grey	1·00	1·25
	f. Diagonal line by turret	70·00	
111	2½d. brown and deep blue	1·00	1·25
	a. Frame printed double, one albino	†	—
	f. Diagonal line by turret	85·00	
	g. Dot to left of chapel	£130	£150
112	1s. slate and purple	12·00	12·00
	h. Dot by flagstaff	£375	
109/12 *Set of 4*		13·00	14·50
109s/12s Perf "Specimen" *Set of 4*		90·00	

For illustrations of plate varieties see Omnibus section following Zanzibar.

19 Port Castries

20 Columbus Square, Castries (inscr "COLOMBUS SQUARE" in error)

21 Ventine Falls

22 Fort Rodney, Pigeon Island

23 Inniskilling monument

24 Government House

25 The Badge of the Colony

(Recess D.L.R.)

1936 (1 Mar–Apr). *T* **19/**, **25**. Wmk Mult Script CA. P 14 or 13×12 (1s. and 10s.).

113	19	½d. black and bright green	30	50
		a. Perf 13×12 (8.4.36)	3·25	16·00
114	20	1d. black and brown	40	10
		a. Perf 13×12 (8.4.36)	4·50	3·00
115	21	1½d. black and scarlet	55	30
		a. Perf 12×13	9·00	2·25
116	19	2d. black and grey	50	20
117	20	2½d. black and blue	50	15
118	21	3d. black and dull green	1·25	70
119	19	4d. black and red-brown	50	1·00
120	20	6d. black and orange	1·00	1·00
121	22	1s. black and light blue	1·50	2·50
122	23	2s.6d. black and ultramarine	9·50	14·00
123	24	5s. black and violet	13·00	20·00
124	25	10s. black and carmine	50·00	75·00
113/24 *Set of 12*			70·00	£100
113s/24s Perf "Specimen" *Set of 12*			£200	

Examples of most values are known with a forged Castries postmark dated "1 MR 36".

1937 (12 May). *Coronation. As Nos. 95/7 of Antigua.* P 11×11½.

125	1d. violet	30	35
126	1½d. carmine	55	20
127	2½d. blue	55	1·25
125/7 *Set of 3*		1·25	1·60
125s/7s Perf "Specimen" *Set of 3*		85·00	

26 King George VI

27 Columbus Square

28 Government House

29 The Pitons

30 *Lady Hawkins* loading bananas

31 Device of St. Lucia

(Des E. Crafer (T **26**), H. Fleury (5s.). Recess Waterlow (½d. to 3½d., 8d., 3s., 5s., £1), D.L.R. (6d., 1s.) and B.W. (2s., 10s.))

1938 (22 Sept)–**48**. *T* **26/31** . Wmk Mult Script CA (sideways on 2s.).

128	26	½d. green (P 14½×14)	2·00	10
		a. Perf 12½ (1943)	10	10
129		1d. violet (P 14½×14)	3·50	75
		a. Perf 12½ (1938)	10	15
129*b*		1d. scarlet (P 12½) (1947)	1·00	10
		c. Perf 14½×14 (1948)	10	10
130		1½d. scarlet (P 14½×14)	2·00	40
		a. Perf 12½ (1943)	1·50	1·25
131		2d. grey (P 14½×14)	4·00	1·50
		a. Perf 12½ (1943)	10	10
132		2½d. ultramarine (P 14½×14)	4·25	15
		a. Perf 12½ (1943)	25	10
132*b*		2½d. violet (P 12½) (1947)	1·00	10
133		3d. orange (P 14½×14)	1·25	10
		a. Perf 12½ (1943)	10	10
133*b*		3½d. ultramarine (P 12½) (1947)	1·00	15
134	27	6d. claret (P 13½)	7·50	75
		a. Carmine-lake (P 13½) (1945)	3·50	35
		b. Perf 12. *Claret* (1948)	2·50	2·00
134*c*	26	8d. brown (P 12½) (1946)	3·50	30
135	28	1s. brown (P 13½)	1·50	30
		a. Perf 12 (1948)	75	30
136	–	2s. blue and purple (P 12)	4·50	1·25
136*a*	29	3s. bright purple (P 12½) (1946)	8·00	1·75
137	30	5s. black and mauve (P 12½)	14·00	11·00
138	31	10s. black/*yellow* (P 12)	10·00	9·00
141	26	£1 sepia (P 12½) (1946)	11·00	8·00
128a/41 *Set of 17*			55·00	30·00
128s/41s Perf "Specimen" *Set of 17*			£375	

1946 (8 Oct). *Victory. As Nos. 110/11 of Antigua.*

142	1d. lilac	10	10
143	3½d. blue	10	10
142s/3s Perf "Specimen" *Set of 2*		75·00	

1948 (26 Nov). *Royal Silver Wedding. As Nos. 112/13 of Antigua.*

144	1d. scarlet	15	10
145	£1 purple-brown	17·00	35·00

(New Currency. 100 cents = 1 West Indian dollar)

32 King George VI

33 Device of St. Lucia

(Recess Waterlow (**32**), B.W. (**33**))

1949 (1 Oct)–**50**. *Value in cents or dollars.* Wmk Mult Script CA. P 12½ (1c. to 16c.), 11×11½ (others).

146	32	1c. green	25	10
		a. Perf 14 (1949)	2·50	40
147		2c. magenta	1·00	10
		a. Perf 14½×14 (1949)	3·00	1·00
148		3c. scarlet	1·50	2·25
149		4c. grey	1·00	10
		a. Perf 14½×14	†	£14000
150		5c. violet	1·50	10
151		6c. orange	1·25	3·25
152		7c. ultramarine	3·50	2·75
153		12c. claret	5·50	3·75
		a. Perf 14½×14 (1950)	£650	£475
154		16c. brown	4·75	50
155	33	24c. light blue	50	10
156		48c. olive-green	1·50	1·25
157		$1.20 purple	2·25	8·00
158		$2.40 blue-green	3·25	17·00
159		$4.80 rose-carmine	9·50	18·00
146/159 *Set of 14*			32·00	50·00

Most examples of Nos. 146a and 147a were produced as coils, but a few sheets in these perforations were distributed and blocks of four are scarce.

No genuine mint example of No. 149a is known. Photographic forgeries do, however, exist.

1949 (10 Oct). *75th Anniv of U.P.U. As Nos. 114/17 of Antigua.*

160	5c. violet	15	70
161	6c. orange	1·60	2·25
	a. "A" of "CA" missing from wmk	£500	
162	12c. magenta	20	20
163	24c. blue-green	30	20
160/3 *Set of 4*		2·00	3·00

1951 (16 Feb). *Inauguration of B.W.I. University College. As Nos. 118/19 of Antigua.*

164	3c. black and scarlet	45	50
165	12c. black and deep carmine	65	50

34 Phoenix rising from Burning Buildings

NEW 1951
CONSTITUTION
(35)

(Flames typo, rest recess B.W.)

1951 (19 June). *Reconstruction of Castries.* Wmk Mult Script CA. P 13½×13.

166	**34**	12c. red and blue	25	1·00

1951 (25 Sept). *New Constitution. Nos. 147, 149/50 and 153 optd with T* **35** *by Waterlow.* P 12½.

167	**32**	2c. magenta	20	80
168		4c. grey	20	60
169		5c. violet	20	80
170		12c. claret	75	60
167/70 *Set of* 4			1·25	2·50

1953 (2 June). *Coronation. As No. 120 of Antigua.*

171		3c. black and scarlet	70	10

36 Queen Elizabeth II

37 Device of St. Lucia

(Recess Waterlow (T **36**), until 1960, then D.L.R. B.W. (T **37**))

1953 (28 Oct)–**63**. Wmk Mult Script CA. P 14½×14 (T **36**) or 11×11½ (T **37**).

172	**36**	1c. green (1.4.54)	10	10
173		2c. magenta	10	10
174		3c. red (2.9.54)	10	10
175		4c. slate (7.1.54)	10	10
176		5c. violet (1.4.54)	10	10
		a. Slate-violet (19.2.63)	17·00	3·00
177		6c. orange (2.9.54)	15	50
		a. Brown-orange (26.9.61)	16·00	1·25
178		8c. lake (2.9.54)	30	10
179		10c. ultramarine (2.9.54)	10	10
		a. Blue (14.8.62)	30	10
180		15c. red-brown (2.9.54)	30	10
		a. Brown (30.10.57)	70	10
181	**37**	25c. deep turquoise-blue (2.9.54)	30	10
182		50c. deep olive-green (2.9.54)	4·50	2·50
183		$1 bluish green (2.9.54)	4·00	3·75
184		$2.50 carmine (2.9.54)	5·00	6·50
172/84 *Set of* 13			13·50	12·50

1958 (22 Apr). *Inauguration of British Caribbean Federation. As Nos. 135/7 of Antigua.*

185		3c. deep green	40	20
186		6c. blue	65	1·75
187		12c. scarlet	90	80
185/7 *Set of* 3			1·75	2·50

MINISTERIAL GOVERNMENT

38 Columbus's *Santa Maria* off the Pitons

39 Stamp of 1860

(Recess Waterlow)

1960 (1 Jan). *New Constitution for the Windward and Leeward Islands.* W w **12**. P 13.

188	**38**	8c. carmine-red	30	45
189		10c. red-orange	30	45
190		25c. deep blue	50	50
188/90 *Set of* 3			1·00	1·25

(Eng H. Bard. Recess Waterlow)

1960 (18 Dec). *Stamp Centenary.* W w **12**. P 13½.

191	**39**	5c. rose-red and ultramarine	15	10
192		16c. deep blue and yellow-green	25	60
193		25c. green and carmine-red	25	15
191/3 *Set of* 3			60	75

1963 (4 June). *Freedom from Hunger. As No. 146 of Antigua.*

194		25c. bluish green	30	10

1963 (2 Sept). *Red Cross Centenary. As Nos. 147/8 of Antigua.*

195		4c. red and black	20	50
196		25c. red and blue	50	1·75

40 Queen Elizabeth II (after A.C. Davidson-Houston)

41

42 Fishing Boats

43 Castries Harbour

44 Vigie Beach

45 Queen Elizabeth II

(Des V. Whiteley. Photo Harrison)

1964 (1 Mar)–**69**. *Designs as T* **40/5**. W w **12**. P 14½ (T **40**), others 14½×14 (vert) or 14×14½ (horiz).

197	**40**	1c. crimson	10	10
		w. Wmk inverted	75	
198		2c. bluish violet	30	70
		w. Wmk inverted	—	5·50
199		4c. turquoise-green	1·00	30
		a. Deep turquoise (5.8.69)	3·00	1·50
		w. Wmk inverted	—	5·50
200		5c. Prussian blue	30	10
		w. Wmk inverted		
201		6c. yellow-brown	1·00	2·25
202	**41**	8c. multicoloured	10	10
203		10c. multicoloured	1·00	10
204	**42**	12c. multicoloured	50	1·25
205	–	15c. multicoloured	20	10
206	–	25c. multicoloured	20	10
207	**43**	35c. blue and buff	3·00	10
208	–	50c. multicoloured	2·50	10
209	**44**	$1 multicoloured	1·25	2·50
210	**45**	$2.50 multicoloured	2·50	2·00
197/210 *Set of* 14			12·50	9·00

Designs: *Horiz as T* **42/3**—15c. Pigeon Island; 25c. Reduit Beach; 50c. The Pitons.

See also No. 249.

1964 (23 Apr). *400th Birth Anniv of William Shakespeare. As No. 164 of Antigua.*

211		10c. blue-green	30	10

1965 (17 May). *I.T.U. Centenary. As Nos. 166/7 of Antigua.*

212		2c. mauve and magenta	10	10
213		50c. lilac and light olive-green	70	90

1965 (25 Oct). *International Co-operation Year. As Nos. 168/9 of Antigua.*

214		1c. reddish purple and turquoise-green	10	10
215		25c. deep bluish green and lavender	20	20

1966 (24 Jan). *Churchill Commemoration. As Nos. 170/3 of Antigua.*

216		4c. new blue	15	10
217		6c. deep green	35	1·75
218		25c. brown	55	15
219		35c. bluish violet	60	20
216/19 *Set of* 4			1·50	2·00

1966 (4 Feb). *Royal Visit. As Nos. 174/5 of Antigua.*

220		4c. black and ultramarine	50	25
221		25c. black and magenta	1·00	75

1966 (1 July). *World Cup Football Championship, England. As Nos. 176/7 of Antigua.*

222		4c. violet, yellow-green, lake and yellow-brown	25	10
223		25c. chocolate, blue-green, lake and yellow-brown	75	30

1966 (20 Sept). *Inauguration of W.H.O. Headquarters, Geneva. As Nos. 178/9 of Antigua.*

224		4c. black, yellow-green and light blue	15	30
225		25c. black, light purple and yellow-brown	45	40

1966 (1 Dec). *20th Anniv of U.N.E.S.C.O. As Nos. 196/8 of Antigua.*

226		4c. slate-violet, red, yellow and orange	15	10
227		12c. orange-yellow, violet and deep olive	25	65
228		25c. black, bright purple and orange	50	35
226/8 *Set of* 3			80	1·00

ASSOCIATED STATEHOOD

STATEHOOD
1st MARCH 1967
(49)

STATEHOOD
1st MARCH 1967
(50)

51 Map of St Lucia

(Optd by Art Printery,Castries from dies supplied by Harrison. Photo Harrison (No. 240))

1967 (7 Mar). *Statehood.*

(a) Postage. Nos. 198 and 200/9 optd with T **49** *(2, 5, 6c.) or T* **50** *(others) in red.*

229		2c. bluish violet	20	15
		a. Horiz pair, one without opt		
230		5c. Prussian blue	10	10
		a. Opt inverted	45·00	
231		6c. yellow-brown	10	10
232		8c. multicoloured	20	10
		a. Opt double	£1500	
233		10c. multicoloured	25	10
234		12c. multicoloured	20	10
235		15c. multicoloured	60	50
236		25c. multicoloured	30	50
237		35c. blue and buff	50	35
238		50c. multicoloured	50	55
239		$1 multicoloured	50	55
229/39 *Set of* 11			3·00	2·75

Overprinted 1c. and $2.50 stamps were prepared for issue but were not put on sale over the post office counter. Later, however, they were accepted for franking (*Price for set of* 2 £2 *mint*, £8 *used*).

The 1c., 6c. and $2.50 also exist with overprint in black, instead of red, and the 25c. U.N.E.S.C.O. value is also known with a similar overprint in blue or black.

(b) Air. P 14½×14.

240	**51**	15c. new blue	10	10

52 "Madonna and Child with the Infant Baptist" (Raphael)

53 Batsman and Sir Frederick Clarke (Governor)

(Des and photo Harrison)

1967 (16 Oct). *Christmas.* W w **12** (sideways). P 14½.

241	**52**	4c. multicoloured	10	10
242		25c. multicoloured	30	10

(Des V. Whiteley. Photo Harrison)

1968 (8 Mar). *M.C.C.'s West Indies Tour.* W w **12** (sideways). P 14½×14.

243	**53**	10c. multicoloured	20	30
244		35c. multicoloured	45	55

54 "The Crucified Christ with the Virgin Mary, Saints and Angels" (Raphael)

55 "Noli me tangere" (detail by Titian)

(Des and photo Harrison)

1968 (25 Mar). *Easter.* W w **12** (sideways). P 14×14½.

245	**54**	10c. multicoloured	10	10
246	**55**	15c. multicoloured	10	10
247	**54**	25c. multicoloured	15	10
248	**55**	35c. multicoloured	15	10
		a. Yellow (sunset) omitted	£160	
245/8 *Set of* 4			45	35

1968 (14 May). *As No.* 205 *but* W w **12** *(sideways).*

249		15c. multicoloured	30	30

*This is the London release date. Stamps from this printing were available some months earlier on St Lucia.

56 Dr. Martin Luther King

57 "Virgin and Child in Glory" (Murillo)

(Des V. Whiteley. Litho D.L.R.)

1968 (4 July). *Martin Luther King Commemoration.* W w **12**. P 13½×14.

250	**56**	25c. blue, black and flesh	15	15
251		35c. violet-black, black and flesh	15	15

(Des and photo Harrison)

1968 (17 Oct). *Christmas. Paintings. T* **57** *and similar vert design. Multicoloured.* W w **12** (sideways). P 14½×14.

252	5c. Type **57**	10	10
253	10c. "Madonna with Child" (Murillo)	10	10
254	25c. Type **57**	15	10
255	35c. As 10c.	15	10
252/5 *Set of 4*		45	35

59 Purple-throated Carib

(Des V. Whiteley. Litho Format)

1969 (10 Jan). *Birds. T* **59** *and similar horiz design. Multicoloured.* W w **12** (sideways). P 14.

256	10c. Type **59**	40	35
257	15c. St. Lucia Amazon	60	40
258	25c. Type **59**	70	45
259	35c. As 15c.	85	50
256/9 *Set of 4*		2·25	1·50

61 "Head of Christ Crowned with Thorns" (Rem)

62 "Resurrection of Christ" (Sodoma)

(Des and photo Harrison)

1969 (20 Mar). *Easter.* W w **12** (sideways). P 14½×14.

260	**61**	10c. multicoloured	10	10
261	**62**	15c. multicoloured	10	10
262	**61**	25c. multicoloured	15	15
263	**62**	35c. multicoloured	15	15
260/3 *Set of 4*			45	45

63 Map showing "CARIFTA" Countries

(Des J. Cooter. Photo Harrison)

1969 (29 May). *First Anniv of CARIFTA (Caribbean Free Trade Area). T* **63** *and similar horiz designs. Multicoloured.* W w **12**. P 14.

264	5c. Type **63**	10	15
265	10c. Type **63**	10	15
266	25c. Handclasp and names of CARIFTA countries	15	15
267	35c. As 25c.	15	15
264/7 *Set of 4*		45	55

65 Emperor Napoleon and Empress Josephine

66 "Virgin and Child" (P. Delaroche)

(Des and lithe Enschedé)

1969 (22 Sept). *Birth Bicentenary of Napoleon Bonaparte.* P 14×13.

268	**65**	15c. multicoloured	10	10
269		25c. multicoloured	10	10
270		35c. multicoloured	10	10
271		50c. multicoloured	15	55
268/71 *Set of 4*			40	75

(Des J. W. Photo Harrison)

1969 (27 Oct). *Christmas. Paintings. T* **66** *and similar vert design. Multicoloured.* W w **12** (sideways). P 14½×14.

272	5c. Type **66**	10	10
273	10c. "Holy Family" (Rubens)	10	10
274	25c. Type **66**	20	10
275	35c. As 10c.	20	10
272/5 *Set of 4*		55	35

68 House of Assembly

69 "The Sealing of the Tomb" (Hogarth)

(Des J. Cooter ($10), Sylvia and M. Goaman (others). Litho Questa ($10), Format (others))

1970 (2 Feb)–**73**. *T* **68** *and similar designs. Multicoloured.* W w **12** (sideways* on 1c. to 35c. and $10). P 14.

276	1c. Type **68**	10	10
277	2c. Roman Catholic Cathedral	15	10
278	4c. The Boulevard, Castries	1·00	10
	w. Wmk Crown to right of CA	6·50	
279	5c. Castries Harbour	1·50	10
280	6c. Sulphur springs	15	10
281	10c. Vigie Airport	2·00	10
282	12c. Reduit Beach	20	10
283	15c. Pigeon Island	30	10
284	25c. The Pitons and yacht	80	10
	w. Wmk Crown to right of CA	15·00	
285	35c. Marigot Bay	40	10
	w. Wmk Crown to right of CA	12·00	
286	50c. Diamond Waterfall (*vert*)	70	80
287	$1 Flag of St. Lucia (*vert*)	40	70
288	$2.50 St. Lucia Coat of Arms (*vert*)	55	1·75
289	$5 Queen Elizabeth II (*vert*)	1·00	4·00
289*a*	$10 Map of St. Lucia (*vert*) (3.12.73)	3·00	9·00
276/89a *Set of 15*		10·50	15·00

*The normal sideways watermark shows Crown to left of CA, *as seen from the back of the stamp.*

The 2c. and 4c. were subsequently reissued with W w **12** upright and the 4c., 5c., 10c. and 13c. on W w **14**.

(Des V. Whiteley. Litho Enschedé)

1970 (7 Mar). *Easter. Triptych by Hogarth. T* **69** *and similar multicoloured designs.* W w **12** (sideways). Roul. 9×P 12½.

290	25c. Type **69**	15	20
	a. Strip of 3. Nos. 290/2	55	
291	35c. "The Three Marys at the Tomb"	15	20
292	$1 "The Ascension (39×55 mm)	30	40
290/2 *Set of 3*		55	70

Nos. 290/2 were issued in sheets of 30 (6×5) containing the Hogarth Triptych spread over all three values of the set. This necessitated a peculiar arrangement with the $1 value (which depicts the centre portion of the triptych) 10 mm higher than the other values in the *se-tenant* strip.

72 Charles Dickens and Dickensian Characters

(Des V. Whiteley. Litho B.W.)

1970 (8 June). *Death Centenary ofCharles Dickens.* W w **12** (sideways). P 14.

293	**72**	1c. multicoloured	10	10
294		25c. multicoloured	20	10
295		35c. multicoloured	25	10
296		50c. multicoloured	35	1·25
293/6 *Set of 4*			80	1·40

73 Nurse and Emblem

(Des R. Granger Barrett. Litho J.W.)

1970 (18 Aug). *Centenary of British Red Cross. T* **73** *and similar horiz designs. Multicoloured.* W w **12** (sideways*). P 14.

297	10c. Type **73**	15	15
298	15c. Flags of Great Britain, Red Cross and St. Lucia	25	25
299	25c. Type **73**	35	40
300	35c. As 15c.	40	40
	w. Wmk Crown to right of CA	20·00	
297/300 *Set of 4*		1·00	1·10

*The normal sideways watermark shows Crown to left of CA, *as seen from the back of the stamp.*

74 "Madonna with the Lilies" (Luca della Robbie)

75 "Christ on the Cross" (Rubens)

(Des P. B. Litho and embossed Walsall)

1970 (16 Nov). *Christmas.* P 11.

301	**74**	5c. multicoloured	10	10
302		10c. multicoloured	15	10
303		35c. multicoloured	30	10
304		40c. multicoloured	30	30
301/4 *Set of 4*			75	55

POSTAGE DUE STAMPS

D 1

No. Normal — **No.** Wide fount

(Type-set Government Printing Office)

1930. *Each stamp individually handstamped with different number. No gum.* No wmk. Rough perf 12.

(a) Horizontally laid paper.

D1	D **1**	1d. black/*blue*	6·50	15·00
		b. Wide, wrong fount "No."	18·00	38·00
		c. Missing stop after "ST"	£180	£275
		d. Missing stop after "LUCIA"	£180	£275
		e. Handstamped number double	£800	
		f. Handstamped number triple		
		g. Incorrect number with correction above		
		h. Two different numbers on same stamp	£1000	
		i. Number omitted	£3000	

(b) Wove paper.

D2	D **1**	2d. black/*yellow*	15·00	40·00
		a. Imperf between (vert pair)	£7000	
		b. Wide, wrong fount "No."	35·00	95·00
		c. Missing stop after "ST"	£375	£600
		d. Missing stop after "LUCIA"	£550	
		e. Handstamped number double	–	£1200
		g. Incorrect number with correction above	£1400	£1500
		h. Two different numbers on same stamp	£1600	

Nos. D1/2 were produced in sheets of 60 (6×10) usually with imperforate outer edges at the top, at right and at foot. It would appear that the sheets were bound into books from which they could be detached using the line of perforations along the left-hand side.

There were three printings of each value, utilising the same basic type. The paper for the first two printings of the 1d. and the first printing of the 2d. showed papermaker's watermarks, that for the 1d. being "KINGSCLERE" in double-lined capitals below a crown with parts occurring on between ten and fourteen stamps in each sheet.

Details of the printings are as follows:

1d.

First printing. On paper with sheet watermark. Shows wide fount "No." on R. 10/3–6 and missing stop after "ST" on R. 5/3

Second printing. On paper with sheet watermark. Shows wide fount "No." on R. 10/2–6 and missing stop after "ST" on R. 5/3. The first two printings of the 1d. were numbered together as 1 to 12000.

Third printing. On paper without watermark. Shows wide fount "No." on all stamps in Row 10. Missing stop after "ST" on R. 5/3 corrected, but missing stop after "LUCIA" occurs on R. 9/2. Numbered 12001 to 24000.

2d.

First printing. On paper with sheet watermark. Shows wide fount "No." on R. 10/2–6 and missing stop after "ST" on R. 5/3 (as 1d. second printing). Numbered 1 to 4800.

Second printing. On paper without watermark. Shows wide fount "No." on all stamps in Row 10. Missing stop after "ST" corrected (printed *before* 1d. third printing). Numbered 4801 to 14820.

Third printing. On paper without watermark. Shows wide fount "No." on all stamps in Row 10. Missing stop after "ST" corrected, but missing stop after "LUCIA" occurs on R. 4/4 and 9/2 (printed *after* 1d. third printing). Numbered 14821 to 16800.

The handstamped numbers were applied at the Post Office using a numbering machine. Mistakes in the numbering on the 1d. were sometimes partially erased and then corrected with a second strike, either of the complete number or of incorrect digits, using a machine with a smaller font.

D 2

D 3

(Typo D.L.R.)

1933–47. Wmk Mult Script CA. P 14.

D3	D 2	1d. black	4·75	6·50
D4		2d. black	19·00	8·50
D5		4d. black (28.6.47)	7·00	45·00
D6		8d. black (28.6.47)	7·00	55·00
D3/6 *Set of* 4			35·00	£100
D3s/6s Perf "Specimen" *Set of* 4			£140	

1949 (1 Oct)–**52**. *Value in cents. Typo.* Wmk Mult Script CA. P 14.

D7	D 3	2c. black	1·75	27·00
		a. Chalk-surfaced paper (27.11.52)	10	9·00
		ab. Error. Crown missing, W **9a**	£150	
		ac. Error. St. Edward's Crown, W **9b**	32·00	
D8		4c. black	3·50	21·00
		a. Chalk-surfaced paper (27.11.52)	50	11·00
		ab. Error. Crown missing, W **9a**	£225	
		ac. Error. St. Edward's Crown, W **9b**	45·00	
D9		8c. black	3·25	25·00
		a. Chalk-surfaced paper (27.11.52)	3·00	40·00
		ac. Error. St. Edward's Crown, W **9b**	£325	
D10		16c. black	15·00	65·00
		a. Chalk-surfaced paper (27.11.52)	4·50	50·00
		ac. Error. St. Edward's Crown, W **9b**	£450	
D7/10 *Set of* 4			21·00	£120
D7a/10a *Set of* 4			7·25	£100

The 2c. and 4c. watermarked Block CA were issued in 1965.

1965 (9 Mar). *As Nos. D7/8, but wmk w* **12**. *Ordinary paper.* P 14.

D11	D 3	2c. black	35	9·00
D12		4c. black	45	9·00

Nos. D9a, D10a and D11/12 exist with a similar overprint to Type **49** in red (*Price for set of* 4 £100 *mint*).

POSTAL FISCAL STAMPS

Nos. F1/28 were authorised for postal use from 14 April 1885.

CANCELLATIONS. Many used examples of the Postal Fiscal stamps have had previous pen cancellations removed before being used postally.

SHILLING STAMP (F 1)   One Penny Stamp (F 2)   HALFPENNY Stamp (F 3)

1881. Wmk Crown CC. P 14.

(a) Surch as Type F **1**.

F1	1	ONE PENNY STAMP, black (C.)	75·00	50·00
		a. Surch inverted	£750	£750
		b. Surch double	£650	£700
F2		FOUR PENNY STAMP, yellow	£120	80·00
		a. Bisected (2d.) (on cover)	†	—
F3		SIX PENCE STAMP, mauve	£200	£150
F4		SHILLING STAMP, orange	£120	80·00
		a. "SHILEING"	£950	£700
		b. "SHILDING"	£700	£650

(b) Surch as Type F **2**.

F7	1	One Penny Stamp, black (R.)	75·00	55·00
		a. Surch double	£750	
		w. Wmk inverted		
F8		Four Pence Stamp, yellow	£110	65·00
		x. Wmk reversed		
F9		Six Pence Stamp, mauve	£120	65·00
F10		Shilling Stamp, orange	£130	85·00

(c) Surch as Type F **3**.

F11	1	Halfpenny Stamp, green	75·00	55·00
		a. "Stamp" double	£450	£450
F12		One Shilling Stamp, orange (wmk Crown CA)	£130	75·00
		a. "Stamp" double	£450	£500

A fiscally used example of No. F1b is known showing one red and one black surcharge.

FOUR PENCE REVENUE (F 4)   Revenue (F 5)   REVENUE (F 6)

1882. *Surch as Type F* **4**. Wmk Crown CA.

(a) P 14.

F13	1	1d. black (C.)	55·00	25·00
F14		2d. pale blue	35·00	12·00
F15		3d. deep blue (C.)	95·00	50·00
F16		4d. yellow	42·00	4·00
F17		6d. mauve	70·00	29·00

(b) P 12.

F18	1	1d. black (C.)	55·00	26·00
F19		3d. deep blue (C.)	75·00	20·00
F20		1s. orange	75·00	13·00

The 1d. and 2d. exist as imperforate proofs.

1883. *Nos. 25, 26, 30 and 32 optd locally as Type F* **5**.

(a) Word 11 mm long.

F21		1d. black (C.)	42·00	42·00
		a. Opt inverted		
		b. Opt double	£375	£350

(b) Word 13 mm

F22		1d. black (C.)	—	65·00

(c) Word 15½ mm

F23		½d. green	—	60·00
		a. "Revenue" double	—	£275
F24		1d. black (C.)	42·00	10·00
		a. "Revenue" double	£170	
		b. "Revenue" triple	£325	
		c. "Revenue" double, one inverted	£300	£300
F25		1d. rose (No. 32)	—	70·00
F26		4d. yellow	—	90·00

1884–85. *Optd with Type F* **6**. Wmk Crown CA. P 14.

F27	5	1d. slate (C.)	27·00	18·00
F28		1d. dull mauve (Die I) (1885)	27·00	9·50

No. F27 exists as an imperforate proof.

St. Vincent

Although postal markings for St. Vincent are recorded as early as 1793 it was not until 1852 that the British G.P.O. opened a branch office at Kingstown, the island's capital.

The stamps of Great Britain were used between May 1858 and the end of April 1860. From 1 May in that year the local authorities assumed responsibility for the postal services and fell back on the use of No. CC 1 until the introduction of St. Vincent stamps in 1861.6

KINGSTOWN

CROWNED-CIRCLE HANDSTAMPS

CC 1

CC1 CC **1** ST. VINCENT (R.) (30.1.1852) *Price on cover* £950

Stamps of GREAT BRITAIN *cancelled* "A 10" *as Type* Z **1** *of Jamaica.*

1858–60.

Z1	1d. rose-red (1857), perf 14	£650
Z2	2d. blue (1855)	
Z3	4d. rose (1857)	£400
Z4	6d. lilac (1856)	£300
Z5	1s. green (1856)	£1700

PRICES FOR STAMPS ON COVER TO 1945

No. 1	*from* × 50
No. 2	*from* × 15
Nos. 4/5	*from* × 40
Nos. 6/7	*from* × 20
No. 8	—
No. 9	*from* × 12
No. 10	—
No. 11	*from* × 15
Nos. 12/13	*from* × 20
No. 14	*from* × 10
No. 15	*from* × 50
No. 16	*from* × 15
No. 17	*from* × 10
No. 18	*from* × 100
No. 19	*from* × 20
Nos. 20/21	*from* × 7
No. 22	*from* × 100
No. 23	*from* × 25
No. 24	*from* × 15
No. 25	*from* × 25
No. 26	—
No. 26a	*from* × 50
Nos. 27/28	—
No. 29	*from* × 100
Nos. 30/31	*from* × 30
Nos. 32/34	—
No. 35	*from* × 30
Nos. 36/7	*from* × 50
No. 38	*from* × 10
Nos. 39/40	*from* × 100
No. 41	*from* × 25
Nos. 42/5	*from* × 8
No. 46	*from* × 15
Nos. 47/54	*from* × 4
Nos. 55/8	*from* × 8
No. 59	*from* × 10
No. 60	*from* × 6
Nos. 61/3	*from* × 8
Nos. 67/75	*from* × 3
Nos. 76/84	*from* × 2
Nos. 85/92	*from* × 3
No. 93	—
Nos. 94/8	*from* × 3
Nos. 99/107	*from* × 2
Nos. 108/19	*from* × 3
No. 120	—
No. 121	*from* × 3
No. 122	*from* × 5
No. 123	—
No. 124	*from* × 5
Nos. 126/9	*from* × 10
Nos. 131/45	*from* × 3
Nos. 146/8	*from* × 6
Nos. 149/59	*from* × 2

CROWN COLONY

1

(2)

3

(T **1**, **3** and **7** recess P.B)

1861 (8 May). No Wmk. Rough to intermediate perf 14 to 16.

1	1	1d. rose-red	50·00	14·00
		a. Imperf vert (horiz pair)	£350	
		b. Imperf (pair)	£275	
2		6d. deep yellow-green	£7500	£200

The perforations on the 1d. are usually rough, but individual examples can be found on which some, or all, of the holes have the appearance of the intermediate perforations. All examples of the 6d. show intermediate perforations.

Imperforate examples, possibly proofs, exist of the 1d. rose-red and 6d. deep green handstamped "CANCELLED" in oval of bars (see note on Perkins Bacon "CANCELLED" in Catalogue Introduction). (*Price* 1d. £8500, 6d. £9500).

1862 (Sept). No wmk. Rough perf 14 to 16.

4	1	6d. deep green	55·00	19·00
		a. Imperf between (horiz pair)	£13000	£14000
		b. Imperf (pair)	£1000	

1863–68. No wmk.

(a) P 11 to 12½.

5	1	1d. rose-red (3.63)	40·00	16·00
6		4d. deep blue (*shades*) (1866)	£275	£110
		a. Imperf between (horiz pair)	†	—
7		6d. deep green (7.68)	£225	75·00
8		1s. slate-grey (8.66)	£2500	£900

(b) P 14 to 16.

9	1	1s. slate-grey (*shades*) (8.66)	£375	£140

(c) P 11 to 12½×14 to 16.

10	1	1d. rose-red (1866)	£6000	£1100
11		1s. slate-grey (*shades*) (8.66)	£275	£120

1869 (Apr–Sep). *Colours changed.* No wmk. P 11 to 12½.

12	1	4d. yellow (9.69)	£350	£160
13		1s. indigo	£375	90·00
14		1s. brown (9.69)	£500	£160

1871 (Apr). Wmk Small Star, W w **2**. Rough perf 14 to 16.

15	1	1d. black	60·00	13·00
		a. Imperf between (vert pair)	£17000	
16		6d. deep green	£325	70·00
		a. Wmk sideways	—	90·00

1872 (June). *Colour changed.* W w **2** (sideways). P 11 to 12½.

17	1	1s. deep rose-red	£750	£140

1872–75. W w **2** (sideways).

(a) Perf about 15.

18	1	1d. black (*shades*) (11.72)	60·00	11·00
		a. Wmk upright	70·00	12·00
19		6d. dull blue-green (*shades*) (1873)	£2000	50·00
		b. Deep blue-green (1875)	£1500	50·00
		c. Wmk upright	£2250	

(b) P 11 to 12½×15.

20	1	1s. lilac-rose (1873)	£5500	£350

1875. *Colour changed.* W w **2** (sideways). P 11 to 12½.

21		1s. claret	£600	£250

1875–78. W w **2** (sideways).

(a) P 11 to 12½×15.

22	1	1d. black (*shades*) (4.75)	85·00	11·00
		a. Imperf between (horiz pair)	†	£23000
		b. Wmk upright	£150	50·00
23		6d. pale green (1877)	£650	50·00
24		1s. vermilion (2.77)	£950	85·00
		a. Imperf vert (horiz pair)		

(b) P 11 to 12½.

25	1	4d. deep blue (7.77)	£550	90·00

(c) Perf about 15.

26	1	6d. pale green (3.77)	£1600	£450
		a. Wmk upright. *Lt yellow-green* (1878)	£700	27·00
27		1s. vermilion (1878?)	†	£40000

Only two examples of No. 27 have been recorded. The 1s vermilion is also known apparently imperforate and used.

1880 (May). *No. 19b divided vertically by a line of perforation gauging 12, and surch locally with 1 2 in red.*

28	1	1d. on half 6d. deep blue-green	£550	£375
		a. Unsevered pair	£2000	£1200

1880 (June). W w **2** (sideways on 1d., 6d. and 1s.). P 11 to 12½.

29	1	1d. olive-green	£170	5·00
30		6d. bright green	£475	70·00
31		1s. bright vermilion	£800	55·00
		a. Imperf between (horiz pair)	£23000	
32	3	5s. rose-red	£1000	£1400
		a. Imperf	£7000	

(4)

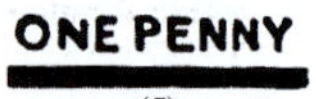

(5)

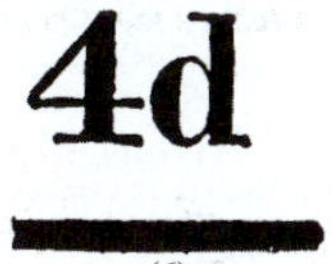

(6)

1881. *Nos. 30/1 surch locally. No. 33 is divided vertically as No. 28.*

33	4	½d. on half 6d. bright green (R.) (1.9)	£160	£170
		a. Unsevered pair	£450	£475
		b. Fraction bar omitted (pair with and without bar)	£4250	£5000
34	5	1d. on 6d. bright green (30.11)	£450	£350
35	6	4d. on 1s. bright vermilion (28.11)	£1600	£800

No. 33 exists showing the "1" of "½" with a straight serif. Some examples come from a constant variety on R. 6/20, but others are the result of faulty type.

It is believed that Type **4** was applied as a setting of 36 (6×6) surcharges repeated three times on each sheet across rows 1 to 9. The missing fraction bar occurs on R. 6/3 of the setting.

The tenth vertical row of stamps appears to have been surcharged from a separate setting of 12 (2×6) on which a constant "straight serif" flaw occurs on the bottom right half-stamp.

Three unused single copies of No. 33 are known with the surcharge omitted.

It is believed that Nos. 34 and 35 were surcharged in settings of 30 (10×3).

No. 34 was only on sale between the 30 November and 3 December when supplies of No. 37 became available.

7

(8)

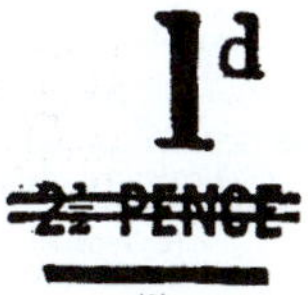

(9)

1881 (3 Dec). W w **2**. P 11 to 12½.

36	7	½d. orange (*shades*)	7·00	5·00
37	1	1d. drab (*shades*)	£700	11·00
38		4d. bright blue	£1200	£120
		a. Imperf between (horiz pair) ..		

(Recess D.L.R. from Perkins, Bacon plates)

1882 (Nov)–**83**. *No. 40 is surch with T* **8**. Wmk Crown CA. P 14.

39	1	1d. drab	55·00	3·00
		x. Wmk reversed	85·00	10·00
40		2½d. on 1d. lake (1883)	21·00	1·50
		w. Wmk inverted	65·00	10·00
		x. Wmk reversed	32·00	5·00
		y. Wmk inverted and reversed...		
41		4d. ultramarine	£650	75·00
		a. Dull ultramarine (wmk reversed)	£1000	£350
		w. Wmk inverted		
		x. Wmk reversed	£450	40·00
		y. Wmk inverted and reversed...		

1883–84. Wmk Crown CA. P 12.

42	7	½d. green (1884)	85·00	27·00
		x. Wmk reversed	—	£150
43	1	4d. ultramarine-blue	£750	42·00
		a. Grey-blue	£2250	£250
		w. Wmk inverted		
		x. Wmk reversed	£450	23·00
		y. Wmk inverted and reversed...		
44		6d. bright green	£150	£300
		x. Wmk reversed	£375	
45		1s. orange-vermilion	£140	60·00
		x. Wmk reversed	£325	£120

The ½d. orange, 1d. rose-red, 1d. milky blue (without surcharge) and 5s. carmine-lake which were formerly listed are now considered to be colour trials. They are, however, of great interest (*Prices un.* ½d. £950, 1d. red £1000, 1d. blue £1300, 5s. £2500).

1885 (Mar). *No. 40 further surch locally as in T* **9**.

46	1	1d. on 2½d. on 1d. lake	24·00	19·00
		w. Wmk inverted	65·00	
		x. Wmk reversed	25·00	21·00

Stamps with three cancelling bars instead of two are considered to be proofs.

1885–93. *No. 49 is surch with T* **8**. Wmk Crown CA. P 14.

47	7	½d. green	1·00	60
		a. Deep green	2·50	60
		w. Wmk inverted	38·00	16·00
		x. Wmk reversed	15·00	
48	1	1d. rose-red	3·00	1·00
		a. Rose (1886)	4·75	1·75
		b. Red (1887)	1·60	85
		c. Carmine-red (1889)	24·00	3·75
		w. Wmk inverted		
		x. Wmk reversed	5·00	1·50
49		2½d. on 1d. milky blue (1889)	23·00	6·00
		x. Wmk reversed		
50		4d. red-brown	£950	22·00
		x. Wmk reversed	—	80·00
51		4d. purple-brown (1886)	75·00	75
		a. Chocolate (1887)	75·00	1·40
		w. Wmk inverted		
		x. Wmk reversed	£160	10·00
		y. Wmk inverted and reversed...		
52		6d. violet (1888)	£160	£180
		w. Wmk inverted	£200	£250
		ws. Optd "Specimen"	80·00	
		x. Wmk reversed	£600	
53	3	5s. lake (1888)	27·00	50·00
		a. Printed both sides	£7000	
		b. Brown-lake (1893)	30·00	50·00
		w. Wmk inverted	£425	
49s, 51s/2s Optd "Specimen" *Set of* 3			£190	

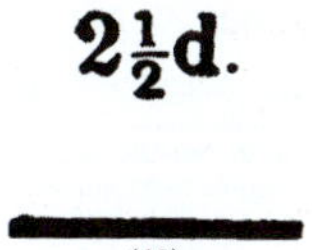

(10)

(11)

1890 (Aug). *No. 51a surch locally with T* **10**.

54	1	2½d. on 4d. chocolate	80·00	£110
		a. No fraction bar (R. 1/7, 2/4)	£400	£475

1890–93. *No. 55 is surch with T* **8**. *Colours changed*. Wmk Crown CA. P 14.

55	1	2½d. on 1d. grey-blue (1890)	21·00	55
		a. Blue (1893)	1·50	35
		w. Wmk inverted		
		x. Wmk reversed		
56		4d. yellow (1893)	1·60	9·00
		s. Optd "Specimen"	30·00	
57		6d. dull purple (1891)	2·25	17·00
58		1s. orange (1891)	5·50	11·00
		a. Red-orange (1892)	11·00	17·00

1892 (Nov). *No. 51a surch locally with T* **11**, *in purple.*

59	1	5d. on 4d. chocolate	23·00	38·00
		s. Optd "Specimen"	40·00	
		sa. Error. "Spicemen"	£1200	

Some letters are known double due to loose type, the best known being the first "E", but they are not constant.

(12)

13

14

Short "F" (R. 5/1)

1893–94. *Surch with T* **12**. Wmk Crown CA. P 14.

60	1	5d. on 6d. carmine-lake	20·00	30·00
		a. Deep lake (1893)	1·00	1·75
		b. Lake (1894)	2·00	4·25
		c. Surch double	£7000	£4000
		d. Short "F"	30·00	40·00
		s. Optd "Specimen"	45·00	

(Recess D.L.R.)

1897 (13 July). *New values*. Wmk Crown CA. P 14.

61	1	2½d. blue	5·50	1·75
62		5d. sepia	6·00	24·00
61s/2s Optd "Specimen" *Set of* 2			60·00	

1897 (6 Oct). *Surch as T* **12**. Wmk Crown CA. P 14.

63	1	3d. on 1d. mauve	5·00	19·00
		a. Red-mauve	11·00	32·00
		s. Optd "Specimen"	40·00	

(Typo D.L.R.)

1899 (1 Jan). Wmk Crown CA. P 14.

67	13	½d. dull mauve and green	2·75	2·50
68		1d. dull mauve and carmine	4·50	1·25
		w. Wmk inverted	£275	
69		2½d. dull mauve and blue	4·00	2·00
70		3d. dull mauve and olive	4·00	14·00
71		4d. dull mauve and orange	4·00	18·00
72		5d. dull mauve and black	7·00	14·00
73		6d. dull mauve and brown	13·00	42·00
74	14	1s. green and carmine	13·00	48·00
75		5s. green and blue	80·00	£140
67/75 *Set of* 9			£120	£250
67s/75s Optd "Specimen" *Set of* 9			£170	

15

16

(Typo D.L.R)

1902. Wmk Crown CA. P 14.

76	15	½d. dull purple and green	3·75	70
77		1d. dull purple and carmine	4·25	30
78	16	2d. dull purple and black	3·75	3·25
79	15	2½d. dull purple and blue	5·00	3·50
80		3d. dull purple and olive	5·00	4·00
81		6d. dull purple and brown	11·00	30·00
82	16	1s. green and carmine	24·00	55·00
83	15	2s. green and violet	25·00	55·00
84	16	5s. green and blue	70·00	£120
76/84 *Set of* 9			£130	£225
76s/84s Optd "Specimen" *Set of* 9			£120	

1904–11. *Ordinary paper (½d., 1d., 1s.) or chalk-surfaced paper (others).* Wmk Mult Crown CA. P 14.

85	15	½d. dull purple and green (1905)..	7·50	5·00
		a. Chalk-surfaced paper	1·25	1·25
86		1d. dull purple and carmine	24·00	1·50
		a. Chalk-surfaced paper	21·00	1·50
88		2½d. dull purple and blue (1906)	16·00	42·00
89		6d. dull purple and brown (1905)	16·00	42·00
90	16	1s. green and carmine (1906)	22·00	48·00
		a. Chalk-surfaced paper	11·00	55·00
91	15	2s. purple and bright blue/*blue* (3.09?)	23·00	42·00
92	16	5s. green and red/*yellow* (3.09?)..	17·00	50·00
93		£1 purple and black/*red* (22.7.11)	£275	£350
85/93 *Set of* 8			£350	£500

91s/3s Optd "Specimen" *Set of* 3			£190	

Examples of most values are known showing a forged Kingstown postmark code letter "O", dated "JA 7 10" or a forged Calliaqua postmark dated "SP 20 09". Both have also been seen on some values of the 1899 and 1902 issues.

17

18

(Recess D.L.R.)

1907–08. Wmk Mult Crown CA. P 14.

94	17	½d. green (2.7.07)	3·25	2·25
95		1d. carmine (26.4.07)	3·50	15
96		2d. orange (5.08)	1·50	6·50
97		2½d. blue (8.07)	32·00	8·50
98		3d. violet (1.6.07)	8·00	15·00
94/8 *Set of* 5			42·00	29·00
94s/8s Optd "Specimen" *Set of* 5			£120	

1909. *No dot below "d".* Wmk Mult Crown CA. P 14.

99	18	1d. carmine (3.09)	1·25	30
100		6d. dull purple (16.1.09)	5·50	35·00
101		1s. black/*green* (16.1.09)	4·25	8·50
99/101 *Set of* 3			10·00	40·00
99s/101s Optd "Specimen" *Set of* 3			75·00	

1909 (Nov)–**11**. *T* **18**, *redrawn (dot below "d", as in T* **17**). Wmk Mult Crown CA. P 14.

102		½d. green (31.10.10)	1·50	60
		w. Wmk inverted	£120	
103		1d. carmine	1·75	20
104		2d. grey (3.8.11)	4·00	9·00
105		2½d. ultramarine (25.7.10)	8·00	3·75
106		3d. purple/*yellow*	2·50	9·00
107		6d. dull purple	12·00	6·00
102/7 *Set of* 6			27·00	25·00
102s, 104s/6s Optd "Specimen" *Set of* 4			90·00	

19

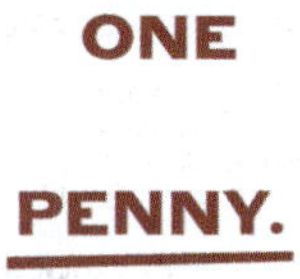

(20)

(Recess D.L.R.)

1913 (1 Jan)–**17**. Wmk Mult Crown CA. P 14.

108	19	½d. green	75	20
109		1d. red	80	75
		a. Rose-red	1·00	75
		b. Scarlet (1.17)	14·00	5·00
		w. Wmk inverted	£100	
		y. Wmk inverted and reversed...	£100	
110		2d. grey	7·00	35·00
		a. Slate	3·00	35·00
111		2½d. ultramarine	50	75
		x. Wmk reversed	£160	
112		3d. purple/*yellow*	80	5·00
		a. On lemon	2·75	12·00
		aw. Wmk inverted	£120	
		ax. Wmk reversed	£120	
		b. On pale yellow	2·50	9·00
113		4d. red/*yellow*	80	2·00
114		5d. olive-green (7.11.13)	2·25	14·00
		x. Wmk reversed	£130	
115		6d. claret	2·00	4·50
116		1s. black/*green*	1·50	3·75
117		1s. bistre (1.5.14)	4·00	26·00
118	18	2s. blue and purple	4·75	29·00
119		5s. carmine and myrtle	13·00	50·00
		x. Wmk reversed	£250	
120		£1 mauve and black	85·00	£160
108/20 *Set of* 13			£110	£275
108s/20s Optd "Specimen" *Set of* 13			£250	

Nos. 118/20 are from new centre and frame dies, the motto "PAX ET JUSTITIA" being slightly over 7 mm long, as against just over 8 mm in Nos. 99 to 107. Nos. 139/41 are also from the new dies.

Examples of several values are known showing part strikes of the forged postmarks mentioned below Nos. 85/93.

1915 (30 Jan). *No. 116 surch locally with T* **20**.

121	19	1d. on 1s. black/*green* (R.)	8·00	30·00
		a. "ONE" omitted	£1300	£1100
		b. "ONE" double	£650	
		c. "PENNY" and bar double	£650	£650
		d. "PENNY" and bar omitted	£1200	

The two lines of the surcharge were applied in separate operations, so that the spacing between them varies considerably.

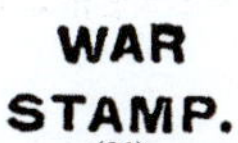

(21)

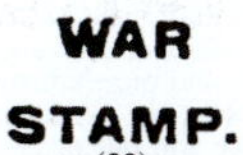

(22)

(24)

1916 (June). *No. 109 optd locally with T* **21**.

(a) First and second settings; words 2 to 2½ mm apart.

122	19	1d. red	9·00	12·00
		a. Opt double	£160	£160
		b. Comma for stop	9·00	20·00
		w. Wmk inverted		

In the first printing every second stamp has the comma for stop. The second printing of this setting has full stops only. These two printings can therefore only be distinguished in blocks or pairs.

(b) Third setting; words only 1½ mm apart.

123	19	1d. red	85·00	
		a. Opt double	£1100	

Stamps of the first setting are offered as this rare one. Care must be taken to see that the distance between the lines is not over 1½ mm.

(c) Fourth setting; optd with T **22**. *Words 3½ mm apart.*

124 **19** 1d. carmine-red ... 3·00 17·00
a. Opt double ... £225
w. Wmk inverted ...
y. Wmk inverted and reversed ...

1916 (Aug)–**18**. *T* **19**, *from new printings, optd with T* **24** *by De La Rue.*

126 1d. carmine-red ... 60 1·00
s. Optd "Specimen" ... 60·00
w. Wmk inverted ...
x. Wmk reversed ...
y. Wmk inverted and reversed ... £110
127 1d. pale rose-red ... 80 1·00
w. Wmk inverted ... 70·00
x. Wmk reversed ...
128 1d. deep rose-red ... 1·00 1·00
129 1d. pale scarlet (1918) ... 1·00 2·00

1921–32. Wmk Mult Script CA. P 14.

131 **19** ½d. green (3.21) ... 1·75 30
132 1d. carmine (6.21) ... 1·00 80
a. Red ... 2·50 15
132*b* 1½d. brown (1.12.32) ... 3·25 15
133 2d. grey (3.22) ... 2·50 80
133*a* 2½d. bright blue (12.25) ... 1·25 1·50
134 3d. bright blue (3.22) ... 1·00 6·00
135 3d. purple/*yellow* (1.12.26) ... 1·00 1·50
135*a* 4d. red/*yellow* (9.30) ... 1·75 6·00
136 5d. sage-green (8.3.24) ... 1·00 6·50
137 6d. claret (1.11.27) ... 1·50 3·50
138 1s. bistre-brown (9.21) ... 6·00 26·00
a. Ochre (1927) ... 3·25 17·00
139 **18** 2s. blue and purple (8.3.24) ... 7·50 13·00
140 5s. carmine and myrtle (8.3.24) ... 18·00 32·00
141 £1 mauve and black (9.28) ... 90·00 £130
131/41 *Set of* 14 ... £120 £200
131s/41s Optd or Perf (1½d., 4d., £1) "Specimen" *Set of* 14 ... £300

Examples of Nos. 140/1 are known with forged postmarks, including part strikes of those mentioned above, and others from Kingstown dated "6 MY 35" and "16 MY 41".

1935 (6 May). *Silver Jubilee. As Nos. 91/4 of Antigua, but ptd by Waterlow.* P 11×12.

142 1d. deep blue and scarlet ... 40 3·75
143 1½d. ultramarine and grey ... 1·00 4·25
144 2½d. brown and deep blue ... 1·90 4·25
145 1s. slate and purple ... 3·25 4·25
l. Kite and horizontal log ... £400
142/5 *Set of* 4 ... 6·00 15·00
142s/5s Perf "Specimen" *Set of* 4 ... 95·00

For illustration of plate variety see Omnibus section following Zanzibar.

1937 (12 May). *Coronation. As Nos. 95/7 of Antigua.* P 11×11½.

146 1d. violet ... 35 1·25
147 1½d. carmine ... 40 1·25
148 2½d. blue ... 45 2·25
146/8 *Set of* 3 ... 1·10 4·25
146s/8s Perf "Specimen" *Set of* 3 ... 75·00

25

26 Young's Island and Fort Duvernette

27 Kingstown and Fort Charlotte

28 Bathing Beach at Villa

29 Victoria Park, Kingstown

NEW CONSTITUTION 1951
(29a)

(Recess B.W.)

1938 (11 Mar)–**47**. Wmk Mult Script CA. P 12.

149 **25** ½d. blue and green ... 20 10
150 **26** 1d. blue and lake-brown ... 20 10
151 **27** 1½d. green and scarlet ... 20 10
152 **25** 2d. green and black ... 40 35
153 **28** 2½d. blue-black and blue-green ... 20 40
153*a* **29** 2½d. green and purple-brown (14.1.47) ... 40 20
154 **25** 3d. orange and purple ... 20 10
154*a* **28** 3½d. blue-black and blue-green (1.4.47) ... 55 2·50
155 **25** 6d. black and lake ... 1·25 40
156 **29** 1s. purple and green ... 1·25 80
157 **25** 2s. blue and purple ... 6·00 75
157*a* 2s.6d. red-brown and blue (14.1.47) ... 1·25 3·50
158 5s. scarlet and deep green ... 10·00 2·50
158*a* 10s. violet and brown (14.1.47) ... 4·00 9·00
aw. Wmk inverted ... £7000 £2500
159 £1 purple and black ... 22·00 15·00
149/59 *Set of* 15 ... 42·00 32·00
149s/59s Perf "Specimen" *Set of* 15 ... £300

1946 (15 Oct). *Victory. As Nos. 110/11 of Antigua.*

160 1½d. carmine ... 10 10
161 3½d. blue ... 10 10
160s/1s Perf "Specimen" *Set of* 2 ... 70·00

1948 (30 Nov). *Royal Silver Wedding. As Nos. 112/13 of Antigua.*

162 1½d. scarlet ... 10 10
163 £1 bright purple ... 22·00 25·00

No. 163 was originally printed in black, but the supply of these was stolen in transit. A few archive examples exist, some perforated "Specimen".

(New Currency. 100 cents = 1 West Indian dollar)

1949 (26 Mar)–**52**. *Value in cents and dollars.* Wmk Mult Script CA. P 12.

164 **25** 1c. blue and green ... 20 1·75
164*a* 1c. green and black (10.6.52) ... 30 2·50
165 **26** 2c. blue and lake-brown ... 15 50
166 **27** 3c. green and scarlet ... 50 1·00
166*a* **25** 3c. orange and purple (10.6.52) ... 30 2·50
167 4c. green and black ... 35 20
167*a* 4c. blue and green (10.6.52) ... 30 20
168 **29** 5c. green and purple-brown ... 15 10
169 **25** 6c. orange and purple ... 50 1·25
169*a* **27** 6c. green and scarlet (10.6.52) ... 30 2·25
170 **28** 7c. blue-black and blue-green ... 5·50 1·50
170*a* 10c. blue-black and blue-green (10.6.52) ... 50 20
171 **25** 12c. black and lake ... 35 15
172 **29** 24c. purple and green ... 35 55
173 **25** 48c. blue and purple ... 2·75 4·00
174 60c. red-brown and blue ... 2·00 4·25
175 $1.20, scarlet and deep green ... 4·25 4·25
176 $2.40, violet and brown ... 6·00 10·00
177 $4.80, purple and black ... 12·00 20·00
164/77 *Set of* 19 ... 32·00 48·00

1949 (10 Oct). *75th Anniv of U.P.U. As Nos. 114/17 of Antigua.*

178 5c. blue ... 20 20
179 6c. purple ... 1·50 2·25
180 12c. magenta ... 20 2·25
181 24c. blue-green ... 20 1·00
178/81 *Set of* 4 ... 1·90 5·25

1951 (16 Feb). *Inauguration of B.W.I. University College. As Nos. 118/19 of Antigua.*

182 3c. deep green and scarlet ... 30 65
183 12c. black and purple ... 30 1·75

1951 (21 Sept). *New Constitution. Optd with T* **29a** *by B.W.*

184 **27** 3c. green and scarlet ... 20 1·75
185 **25** 4c. green and black ... 20 60
186 **29** 5c. green and purple-brown ... 20 60
187 **25** 12c. black and lake ... 1·25 1·25
184/7 *Set of* 4 ... 1·60 3·75

1953 (2 June). *Coronation. As No. 120 of Antigua.*

188 4c. black and green ... 30 20

30

31

(Recess Waterlow (until 1961), then D.L.R.)

1955 (16 Sept)–**63**. Wmk Mult Script CA. P 13½×14 (T **30**) or 14 (T **31**).

189 **30** 1c. orange ... 10 10
a. Deep orange (11.12.62) ... 6·00 5·50
190 2c. ultramarine ... 10 10
a. Blue (26.9.61) ... 2·50 1·50
191 3c. slate ... 30 10
192 4c. brown ... 20 10
193 5c. scarlet ... 40 10
194 10c. reddish violet ... 20 20
a. Deep lilac (12.2.58) ... 1·25 10
195 15c. deep blue ... 1·25 40
196 20c. green ... 60 10
197 25c. black-brown ... 50 10
198 **31** 50c. red-brown ... 5·00 2·00
a. Chocolate (11.6.58) ... 5·50 1·50
199 $1 myrtle-green ... 8·00 1·00
a. Deep myrtle-green (11.6.58) ... 18·00 4·25
b. Deep yellowish green (15.1.63) ... 30·00 14·00
200 $2.50 deep blue ... 8·00 9·00
a. Indigo-blue (30.7.62) ... 38·00 15·00
189/200 *Set of* 12 ... 22·00 11·00

See also Nos. 207/20.

1958 (22 Apr). *Inauguration of British Caribbean Federation. As Nos. 135/7 of Antigua.*

201 3c. deep green ... 40 20
202 6c. blue ... 45 1·25
203 12c. scarlet ... 50 50
201/3 *Set of* 3 ... 1·25 1·75

MINISTERIAL GOVERNMENT

1963 (4 June). *Freedom from Hunger. As No. 146 of Antigua.*

204 8c. reddish violet ... 60 50

1963 (2 Sept). *Red Cross Centenary. As Nos. 147/8 of Antigua.*

205 4c. red and black ... 15 20
206 8c. red and blue ... 35 50

(Recess D.L.R.)

1964–65. *As 1955 but wmk w* **12**.

(a) P 12½ (14 Jan–Feb 1964).

207 **30** 10c. deep lilac ... 30 20
208 15c. deep blue ... 30 50
209 20c. green (24.26.41) ... 1·75 25
210 25c. black-brown ... 30 1·00
211 **31** 50c. chocolate ... 4·00 7·50
207/11 *Set of* 5 ... 6·00 8·50

(b) P 13×14 (T **30**) *or 14 (T* **31**).

212 **30** 1c. orange (15.12.64) ... 15 10
213 2c. blue (15.12.64) ... 15 10
214 3c. slate (15.12.64) ... 50 10
215 5c. scarlet (15.12.64) ... 15 10
216 10c. deep lilac (15.12.64) ... 15 10
217 15c. deep blue (9.11.64) ... 1·00 30
218 20c. green (1964) ... 45 10
w. Wmk inverted ...
219 25c. black-brown (20.10.64) ... 1·00 15
220 **31** 50c. chocolate (18.1.65) ... 6·50 7·00
212/20 *Set of* 9 ... 9·00 7·00

"This is the earliest known date recorded in St. Vincent although it may have been put on sale on 14.1.64.

32 Scout Badge and Proficiency Badges

33 Tropical Fruits

(Des V. Whiteley. Litho Harrison)

1964 (23 Nov). *50th Anniv of St. Vincent Boy Scouts Association.* W w **12**. P 14½.

221 **32** 1c. yellow-green and chocolate ... 10 10
222 4c. blue and brown-purple ... 10 10
223 20c. yellow and black-violet ... 30 10
224 50c. red and bronze-green ... 45 70
221/4 *Set of* 4 ... 85 90

(Des V. Whiteley. Photo Harrison)

1965 (23 Mar). *Botanic Gardens Bicentenary. T* **33** *and similar multicoloured designs.* W w **12**. P 14½×13½ (horiz) or 13½×14½ (vert).

225 1c. Type **33** ... 10 10
226 4c. Breadfruit and H.M.S. *Providence* (sloop), 1793 ... 10 10
227 25c. Doric Temple and pond (*vert*) ... 15 10
228 40c. Talipot Palm and Doric Temple (*vert*) ... 30 1·25
225/8 *Set of* 4 ... 60 1·40

1965 (17 May). *I.T.U. Centenary. As Nos. 166/7 of Antigua.*

229 4c. light blue and light olive-green ... 15 10
230 48c. ochre-yellow and orange ... 35 45

37 Boat-building, Bequia (inscr "BEOUIA")

(Des M. Goaman. Photo Harrison)

1965 (16 Aug)–**67**. *T* **37** *and similar multicoloured designs.* W w **12**. P 14½×13½ (horiz designs) or 13½×14½ (vert).

231 1c. Type **37** ("BEOUIA") ... 10 1·00
231*a* 1c. Type **37** ("BEQUIA") (27.6.67) ... 65 40
232 2c. Friendship Beach, Bequia ... 10 10
233 3c. Terminal Building, Amos Vale Airport ... 60 10
w. Wmk inverted ... 6·00
234 4c. Woman with bananas (*vert*) ... 1·00 30
w. Wmk inverted ...
235 5c. Crater Lake ... 15 10
236 6c. Carib Stone (*vert*) ... 15 40
237 8c. Arrowroot (*vert*) ... 30 10
238 10c. Owia Salt Pond ... 30 10
239 12c. Deep water wharf ... 70 10
w. Wmk inverted ... † —
240 20c. Sea Island cotton (*vert*) ... 30 10
w. Wmk inverted ... — 32·00
241 25c. Map of St. Vincent and islands (*vert*) ... 35 10
w. Wmk inverted ... 30·00
242 50c. Breadfruit (*vert*) ... 50 30
243 $1 Baleine Falls (*vert*) ... 3·00 30
244 $2.50 St. Vincent Amazon (*vert*) ... 18·00 9·50
245 $5 Arms of St. Vincent (*vert*) ... 3·00 13·00
231/45 *Set of* 16 ... 25·00 23·00

The 1c. (No. 231a), 2c., 3c., 5c. and 10c. exist with PVA gum as well as gum arabic.

See also No. 261.

1966 (24 June). *Churchill Commemoration. As Nos. 170/3 of Antigua.*

246 1c. new blue ... 10 10
247 4c. deep green ... 20 10
248 20c. brown ... 35 30
249 40c. bluish violet ... 55 1·00
246/9 *Set of* 4 ... 1·00 1·25

1966 (4 Feb). *Royal Visit. As Nos. 174/5 of Antigua.*

250 4c. black and ultramarine ... 50 20
251 25c. black and magenta ... 1·50 80

1966 (20 Sept). *Inauguration of W.H.O. Headquarters, Geneva. As Nos. 178/9 of Antigua.*

252 4c. black, yellow-green and light blue ... 25 10
253 25c. black, light purple and yellow-brown ... 50 80

1966 (1 Dec). *20th Anniv of U.N.E.S.C.O. As Nos. 196/8 of Antigua.*

254 4c. slate-violet, red, yellow and orange ... 20 10
255 8c. orange-yellow, violet and deep olive ... 40 10
256 25c. black, bright purple and orange ... 1·00 60
254/6 *Set of* 3 ... 1·40 70

38 Coastal View of Mount Coke Area

(Des and photo Harrison)

1967 (1 Dec). *Autonomous Methodist Church. T* **38** *and similar horiz designs. Multicoloured.* W w **12**. P 14×14½.

No.	Type	Description	Unused	Used
257		2c. Type **38**	10	10
258		8c. Kingstown Methodist Church	10	10
259		25c. First Licence to perform marriages	25	10
260		35c. Conference Arms	25	10
257/60		*Set of 4*	60	35

1968 (20 Feb). *As No. 234, but W w* **12** *sideways.*

No.	Type	Description	Unused	Used
261		4c. Woman with bananas	30	30

The above exists with PVA gum as well as gum arabic.

39 Meteorological Institute

(Des G. Vasarhelyi. Photo Harrison)

1968 (28 May). *World Meteorological Day.* W w **12**. P 14×14½.

No.	Type	Description	Unused	Used
262	**39**	4c. multicolored	10	10
263		25c. multicoloured	10	10
264		35c. multicoloured	15	15
262/4		*Set of 3*	30	30

40 Dr. Martin Luther King and Cotton Pickers

(Des V. Whiteley. Litho D.L.R.)

1968 (28 Aug). *Martin Luther King Commemoration.* W w **12** (sideways). P 13.

No.	Type	Description	Unused	Used
265	**40**	5c. multicoloured	10	10
266		25c. multicoloured	10	10
267		35c. multicoloured	15	15
265/7		*Set of 3*	30	30

41 Speaker addressing Demonstrators

42 Scales of Justice and Human Rights Emblem

(Des V. Whiteley. Photo Enschedé)

1968 (1 Nov). *Human Rights Year.* P 13×14 (3c.) or 14×13 (35c.).

No.	Type	Description	Unused	Used
268	**41**	3c. multicoloured	10	10
269	**42**	35c. royal blue and turquoise-blue	20	10

43 Male Masquerader

44 Steel Bandsman

(Des V. Whiteley. Litho Format)

1969 (17 Feb). *St. Vincent Carnival. T* **43/4** *and similar designs.* P 14.

No.	Type	Description	Unused	Used
270		1c. multicoloured	10	10
271		5c. red and deep chocolate	10	10
272		8c. multicoloured	10	10
273		25c. multicoloured	15	20
270/3		*Set of 4*	40	45

Designs: *Horiz*—8c. Carnival Revellers. *Vert*—25c. Queen of Bands.

METHODIST
CONFERENCE
MAY
1969
(47)

1969 (14 May). *Methodist Conference. Nos. 257/8, 241 and 260 optd with T* **47**.

No.	Type	Description	Unused	Used
274		2c. multicoloured	10	15
275		8c. multicoloured	15	25
276		25c. multicoloured	15	25
277		35c. multicoloured	75	2·00
274/7		*Set of 4*	1·00	2·40

48 "Strength in Unity"

49 Map of "CARTFTA" Countries

(Des J. Cooter. Litho D.L.R.)

1969 (1 July). *First Anniv of CARIFTA (Caribbean Free Trade Area).* W w **12** (sideways on T **48**). P 13.

No.	Type	Description	Unused	Used
278	**48**	2c. black, pale buff and red	10	10
279	**49**	5c. multicoloured	10	10
280	**48**	8c. black, pale buff and pale green	10	10
281	**49**	25c. multicoloured	35	15
278/81		*Set of 4*	60	40

ASSOCIATED STATEHOOD

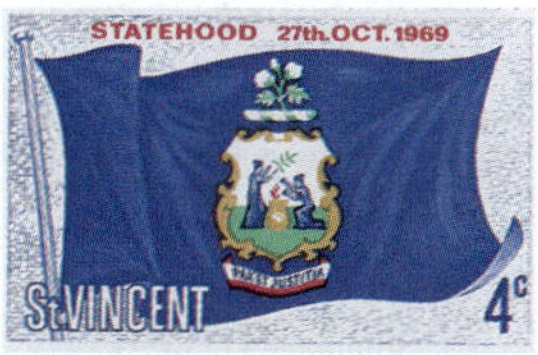

50 Flag of St. Vincent

(Des V. Whiteley, based on local designs. Photo Harrison)

1969 (27 Oct). *Statehood. T* **50** *and similar horiz designs.* W w **12**. P 14×14½.

No.	Type	Description	Unused	Used
282		4c. multicoloured	10	10
283		10c. multicoloured	10	10
284		50c. grey, black and orange	35	20
282/4		*Set of 3*	50	35

Designs: 10c. Battle scene with insets of Petreglyph and Carib chief Chatoyer; 50c. Carib House with maces and scales.

51 Green Heron

(Des J.W. Photo Harrison)

1970 (12 Jan)–**71**. *T* **51** *and similar multicoloured designs. Chalk-surfaced paper.* W w **12** (sideways* on 1, 2, 3, 6, 8, 20, 25c., $1, 2.50 and upright on others). P 14.

No.	Type	Description	Unused	Used
285		½c. House Wren (*vert*)	10	1·25
286		1c. Type **51**	35	3·00
		a. Glazed, ordinary paper (9.8.71)	30	1·50
		aw. Wmk Crown to right of CA	1·00	1·75
287		2c. Lesser Antillean Bullfinches	15	40
		w. Wmk Crown to right of CA	19·00	
288		3c. St. Vincent Amazons	15	30
289		4c. Rufous-throated Solitaire (*vert*)	20	30
290		5c. Red-necked Pigeon (*vert*)	2·50	30
		a. Glazed, ordinary paper (9.8.71)	1·00	30
291		6c. Bananaquits	30	40
292		8c. Purple-throated Carib	40	30
		w. Wmk Crown to right of CA	35·00	
293		10c. Mangrove Cuckoo (*vert*)	30	10
294		12c. Common Black Hawk (*vert*)	40	10
295		20c. Bare-eyed Thrush	40	15
296		25c. Hooded Tanager	50	20
297		50c. Blue Hooded Euphonia	2·00	75
		w. Wmk inverted	60·00	
298		$1 Barn Owl (*vert*)	5·00	2·00
299		$2.50 Yellow-bellied Elaenia (*vert*)	3·25	5·50
300		$5 Ruddy Quail Dove	3·50	6·50
285/300		*Set of 16*	16·00	17·00

*The normal sideways watermark shows Crown to left of CA, *as seen from the back of the stamp.*

Values in this set (and three additional values) were subsequently issued W w **12** upright on 2c., 3c., 6c., 20c. and 30c. and sideways on others.

52 De Havilland D.H.C.6 Twin Otter 100

(Des R. Granger Barrett. Litho Enschedé)

1970 (13 Mar). *20th Anniv of Regular Air Semices. T* **52** *and similar horiz designs. Multicoloured.* W w **12** (sideways). P 14×13.

No.	Type	Description	Unused	Used
301		5c. Type **52**	10	10
302		8c. Grumman G.21 Goose	15	10
303		10c. Hawker Siddeley H.S.748	20	10
304		25c. Douglas DC-3	65	30
301/4		*Set of 4*	1·00	55

53 "Children's Nursery"

54 "Angel and the Two Marys at the Tomb" (stained-glass window)

(Des R. Granger Barrett. Photo Harrison)

1970 (1 June). *Centenary of British Red Cross. T* **53** *and similar horiz designs. Multicoloured.* W w **12**. P 14.

No.	Type	Description	Unused	Used
305		3c. Type **53**	10	10
306		5c. "First Aid"	15	10
		w. Wmk inverted	60·00	
307		12c. "Voluntary Aid Detachment"	35	1·00
		w. Wmk inverted	2·25	
308		25c. "Blood Transfusion"	55	50
305/8		*Set of 4*	1·00	1·50

(Des L. Curtis. Litho J.W.)

1970 (7 Sept). *150th Anniv of St. George's Cathedral, Kingstown. T* **54** *and similar multicoloured designs.* W w **12** (sideways* on horiz designs). P 14.

No.	Type	Description	Unused	Used
309		½c. Type **54**	10	10
310		5c. St. George's Cathedral (*horiz*)	10	10
		w. Wmk Crown to right of CA		
311		25c. Tower, St. George's Cathedral	10	10
312		35c. Interior, St. George's Cathedral (*horiz*)	15	10
313		50c. Type **54**	20	30
309/13		*Set of 5*	60	60

*The normal sideways watermark shows Crown to left of CA, *as seen from the back of the stamp.*

55 "The Adoration of the Shepherds" (Le Nain)

(Des J. Cooter. Litho Questa)

1970 (23 Nov). *Christmas. T* **55** *and similar vert design. Multicoloured.* W w **12** (sideways* on 25c., 50c.). P 14.

No.	Type	Description	Unused	Used
314		8c. "The Virgin and Child" (Bellini)	10	10
315		25c. Type **55**	10	10
		w. Wmk Crown to right of CA	1·00	
316		35c. As 8c.	10	10
317		50c. Type **55**	15	20
		w. Wmk Crown to right of CA	1·50	
314/17		*Set of 4*	40	45

*The normal sideways watermark shows Crown to left of CA, *as seen from the back of the stamp.*

Samoa

PRICES FOR STAMPS ON COVER TO 1945

Nos. 1/20 are very rare used on cover.

Nos. 21/40	*from* × 20
Nos. 41/8	*from* × 100
Nos. 49/56	*from* × 4
Nos. 57/64	*from* × 12
Nos. 65/8	*from* × 2
Nos. 69/97	*from* × 20
Nos. 101/9	*from* × 3
Nos. 110/14	—
Nos. 115/21	*from* × 3
Nos. 122/32	—
Nos. 134/64	*from* × 3
Nos. 165/76	—
Nos. 177/214	*from* × 2

INDEPENDENT KINGDOM OF SAMOA

The first postal service in Samoa was organised by C. L. Griffiths, who had earlier run the *Fiji Times* Express post in Suva. In both instances the principal purpose of the service was the distribution of newspapers of which Griffiths was the proprietor. The first issue of the *Samoa Times* (later the *Samoa Times and South Sea Gazette*) appeared on 6 October 1877 and the newspaper continued in weekly publication until 27 August 1881.

Mail from the Samoa Express post to addresses overseas was routed via New South Wales, New Zealand or U.S.A. and received additional franking with stamps of the receiving country on landing.

Cancellations, inscribed "APIA SAMOA", did not arrive until March 1878 so that examples of Nos. 1/9 used before that date were cancelled in manuscript. the Samoa Express stamps may also be found cancelled at Fiji, Auckland and Sydney.

1

A 2nd State (Nos. 4/9)

B 3rd State (Nos. 10/19)

(Des H. H. Glover. Litho S. T. Leigh & Co, Sydney, N.S.W.)

1877 (1 Oct)–**80**.

A. 1st state: white line above "X" in "EXPRESS" not broken.

P 12½.

1	1	1d. ultramarine	£250	£160
2		3d. deep scarlet	£300	£150
3		6d. bright violet	£300	£150
		a. Pale lilac	£325	£150

B. 2nd state: white line above "X" usually broken by a spot of colour, and dot between top of "M" and "O" of "SAMOA".

P 12½ *(1878–79).*

4	1	1d. ultramarine	90·00	£160
5		3d. bright scarlet	£325	£450
6		6d. bright violet	£450	£550
7		1s. dull yellow	£200	90·00
		b. Perf 12 (1879)	80·00	£170
		c. Orange-yellow	£200	£100
8		2s. red-brown	£275	£400
		a. Chocolate	£300	£400
9		5s. green	£1700	£1100

C. 3rd state: line above "X" repaired, dot merged with upper right serif of "M" (1879).

(a) P 12½.

10	1	1d. ultramarine	£160	90·00
11		3d. vermilion	£275	£130
12		6d. lilac	£300	90·00
13		2s. brown	£250	£275
		a. Chocolate	£250	£275
14		5s. green	£1100	£600
		a. Line above "X" not repaired (R. 2/3)	£1300	

(b) P 12.

15	1	1d. blue	25·00	£300
		a. Deep blue	32·00	
		b. Ultramarine	28·00	£300
16		3d. vermilion	48·00	£300
		a. Carmine-vermilion	48·00	
17		6d. bright violet	40·00	£250
		a. Deep violet	40·00	
18		2s. deep brown	£160	
19		5s. yellow-green	£400	
		a. Deep green	£550	
		b. Line above "X" not repaired (R. 2/3)	£500	

D. 4th state: spot of colour under middle stroke of "M". P 12 *(1880).*

20	1	9d. orange-brown	60·00	£350

Originals exist imperf, but are not known used in this state.

On sheets of the 1d., 1st state, at least eight stamps have a stop after "PENNY". In the 2nd state, three stamps have the stop, and in the 3rd state, only one.

In the 1st state, all the stamps, 1d., 3d. and 6d., were in sheets of 20 (5×4) and also the 1d. in the 3rd state.

All values in the 2nd state, all values except the 1d. in the 3rd state and No. 20 were in sheets of 10 (5×2).

As all sheets of all printings of the originals were imperf at the outer edges, the only stamps which can have perforations on all four sides are Nos. 1 to 3*a*, 10 and 15 to 15*b*, all other originals being imperf on one or two sides.

The perf 12 stamps, which gauge 11.8, are generally very rough but later the machine was repaired and the 1d., 3d. and 6d. are known with clean-cut perforations.

Remainders of the 1d., unissued 2d. rose, 6d. (in sheets of 21 (7×3), 3d., 9d., 5s. (in sheets of 12 (4×3)) and of the 1s. and 2s. (sheet format unknown) were found in the Samoan post office when the service closed down in 1881. The remainders are rare in complete sheets.

Reprints of all values, in sheets of 40 (8×5), were made after the originals had been withdrawn from sale. These are practically worthless.

The majority of both reprints and remainders are in the 4th state as the 9d. with the spot of colour under the middle stroke of the "M", but a few stamps (both remainders and reprints) do not show this, while on some it is very faint.

There are six known types of forgery, one of which is rather dangerous, the others being crude.

The last mail despatch organised by the proprietors of the Samoa Express took place on 31 August 1881, although one cover is recorded postmarked 24 September 1881.

After the withdrawal of the Samoa Express service it would appear that the Apia municipality appointed a postmaster to continue the overseas post. Covers are known franked with U.S.A. or New Zealand stamps in Samoa, or routed via Fiji.

In December 1886 the municipal postmaster, John Davis, was appointed Postmaster of the Kingdom of Samoa by King Malietoa. Overseas mail sent via New Zealand was subsequently accepted without the addition of New Zealand stamps, although letters to the U.S.A. continued to require such franking until August 1891.

2 Palm Trees

3 King Malietoa Laupepa

4a 6 mm

4b 7 mm

4c 4 mm

Description of Watermarks

(These are the same as W **12a/c** of New Zealand)

W **4a**. 6 mm between "N Z" and star; broad irregular star; comparatively wide "N"; "N Z" 11½ mm wide, with horizontal mesh.

W **4b**. 7 mm between "N Z" and star; narrower star; narrow "N"; "N Z" 10 mm wide, with vertical mesh.

W **4c**. 4 mm between "N Z" and star; narrow star; wide "N"; "N Z" 11 mm wide, with vertical mesh.

(Des A. E. Cousins (*T* **3**). Dies eng W. R. Bock and A. E. Cousins (*T* **2**) or A. E. Cousins (*T* **3**). Typo Govt Ptg Office, Wellington)

1886–1900.

(i) W **4a**.

(a) P 12½(15 Oct–Nov 1886).

21	2	½d. purple-brown	25·00	55·00
22		1d. yellow-green	12·00	12·00
23		2d. dull orange	28·00	12·00
24		4d. blue	48·00	10·00
25		1s. rose-carmine	65·00	11·00
		a. Bisected (2½d.) (on cover)*	†	£325
26		2s.6d. reddish lilac	55·00	75·00

(b) P 12×11½(6 July–Nov 1887).

27	2	½d. purple-brown	70·00	80·00
28		1d. yellow-green	£100	28·00
29		2d. yellow	95·00	£140
30		4d. blue	£250	£200
31		6d. brown-lake	32·00	16·00
32		1s. rose-carmine	—	£190
33		2s.6d. reddish lilac	£1100	

(ii) W **4c**. P 12×11½ (9 May 1890).

34	2	½d. purple-brown	75·00	30·00
35		1d. green	55·00	40·00
36		2d. brown-orange	80·00	40·00
37		4d. blue	£140	5·00
38		6d. brown-lake	£300	11·00
39		1s. rose-carmine	£350	13·00
		x. Wmk reversed	£450	£110
40		2s.6d. reddish lilac	£450	8·50

(iii) W **4b**.

(a) P 12×11½ (9 May 1890–92).

41	2	½d. pale purple-brown	4·75	4·50
		a. Blackish purple	4·75	4·50
42		1d. myrtle-green	26·00	1·40
		a. Green	26·00	1·40
		b. Yellow-green	26·00	1·40
43		2d. dull orange	35·00	1·75
		x. Wmk reversed	£110	£110
44	3	2½d. rose (22.11.92)	75·00	4·50
		a. Pale rose	75·00	4·50
45	2	4d. blue	£225	20·00
46		6d. brown-lake	£110	9·50
47		1s. rose-carmine	£225	5·00
48		2s.6d. slate-lilac	—	9·00

(b) P 12½ (Mar 1891–92).

49	2	½d. purple-brown		
50		1d. green		
51		2d. orange-yellow	—	£375
52	3	2½d. rose (7.1.92)	26·00	4·50
53	2	4d. blue	£2750	£450
54		6d. brown-purple	£2750	£1300
55		1s. rose-carmine	£1200	£1000
56		2s.6d. slate-lilac	£3000	

(c) P 11 (May 1895–1900).

57	2	½d. purple-brown	3·25	1·75
		a. Deep purple-brown	2·25	1·75
		b. Blackish purple (1900)	2·25	35·00
58		1d. green	8·00	1·75
		a. Bluish green (1897)	7·50	1·75
		b. Deep green (1900)	2·75	25·00
59		2d. pale yellow	40·00	40·00
		a. Orange (1896)	20·00	20·00
		b. Bright yellow (1.97)	13·00	8·50
		c. Pale ochre (10.97)	5·00	8·50
		d. Dull orange (1900)	7·50	
60	3	2½d. rose	2·75	10·00
		a. Deep rose-carmine (1900)	2·25	42·00
61	2	4d. blue	16·00	8·00
		a. Deep blue (1900)	1·25	50·00
62		6d. brown-lake	11·00	3·00
		a. Brown-purple (1900)	1·75	60·00
63		1s. rose	10·00	3·75
		a. Dull rose-carmine/toned (5.98)	3·25	35·00
		b. Carmine (1900)	1·50	
64		2s.6d. purple	55·00	10·00
		a. Reddish lilac (wmk inverted) (1897)	11·00	9·00
		b. Deep purple/toned (wmk reversed) (17.5.98)	4·75	9·50
		ba. Imperf between (vert pair)	£450	
		c. Slate-violet	£120	

*Following a fire on 1 April 1895 which destroyed stocks of all stamps except the 1s. value perf 12½, this was bisected diagonally and used as a 2½d. stamp for overseas letters between 24 April and May 1895, and was cancelled in blue. Fresh supplies of the 2½d. did not arrive until July 1895, although other values were available from 23 May.

Examples of the 1s. rose perforated 11, No. 63, were subsequently bisected and supplied cancelled-to-order by the post office to collectors, often with backdated cancellations. Most of these examples were bisected vertically and all were cancelled in black (*Price* £7).

The dates given relate to the earliest dates of printing in the various watermarks and perforations and not to issue dates.

The perf 11 issues (including those later surcharged or overprinted), are very unevenly perforated owing to the large size of the pins. Evenly perforated copies are extremely hard to find.

For the 2½d. black, see Nos. 81/2 and for the ½d. green and 1d. red-brown, see Nos. 88/9.

(5)

(6)

(7)

1893 (Nov–Dec). *Handstamped singly, at Apia.*

(a) In two operations.

65	5	5d. on 4d. blue (37)	70·00	48·00
66		5d. on 4d. blue (45)	55·00	£100
67	6	5d. on 4d. blue (37)	£100	£110
68		5d. on 4d. blue (45)	70·00	

(b) In three operations (Dec).

69	7	5d. on 4d. blue (37) (R.)	27·00	50·00
70		5d. on 4d. blue (45) (R.)	30·00	32·00

In Types **5** and **6** the bars obliterating the original value vary in length from 13½ to 16½ mm and can occur with either the thick bar over the thin one or vice versa. Examples can be found with the bars omitted.

Double handstamps exist but we do not list them.

A surcharge as Type **7** but with stop after "d" is now considered to be a trial. It exists in black and in red. Where the "d" was applied separately its position in relation to the "5" naturally varies.

8

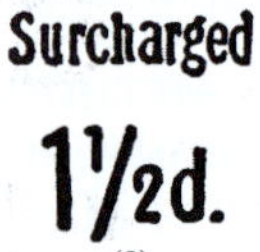

(9)

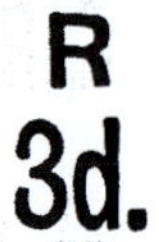

(10)

The "R" in Type **10** indicates use for registration fee.

(Des and die eng A. E. Cousins. Typo New Zealand Govt Ptg Office)

1894 (26 Feb)–**1900**. W **4***b* (sideways).

No.	Type	Description	Unused	Used
		(a) P 11½×12.		
71	8	5d. dull vermilion	20·00	2·75
		a. Dull red	20·00	3·75
		ab. Mixed perfs 11½×12 and 12½		
		(b) P 11.		
72	8	5d. dull red (1895)	27·00	9·50
		a. Deep red (1900)	3·50	16·00

1895–1900. W **4***b*.

No.	Type	Description	Unused	Used
		(i) Handstamped with T **9** *or* **10**.		
		(a) P 12×11½ (28.1.95).		
73	2	1½d. on 2d. dull orange (B.)	17·00	9·00
74		3d. on 2d. dull orange	48·00	15·00
		(b) P 11 (6.95).		
75	2	1½d. on 2d. orange (B.)	4·00	7·00
		a. Pair, one without handstamp .	£475	
		b. On 2d. yellow	7·50	7·00
76		3d. on 2d. orange	8·00	10·00
		a. On 2d. yellow	10·00	10·00
		(ii) Handstamped as T **9** *or* **10**. P 11 (1896).		
78	2	1½d. on 2d. orange-yellow (B.)	3·00	23·00
79		3d. on 2d. orange-yellow	3·75	48·00
		a. Imperf between (vert pair)	£475	
		b. Pair, one without handstamp .		
		(iv) Surch typo as T **10**. P 11 (7 Feb 1900).		
80	2	3d. on 2d. deep red-orange (G.)	1·50	£130

†In No. 78 the "2" has a serif and the handstamp is in pale greenish blue instead of deep blue. In No. 79 the "R" is slightly narrower. In both instances the stamp is in a different shade.

A special printing in a distinctly different colour was made for No. 80 and the surcharge is in green.

Most of the handstamps exist double.

1896 (Aug). *Printed in the wrong colour.* W **4***b*.

No.	Type	Description	Unused	Used
		(a) P 10×11.		
81	3	2½d. black	1·50	3·00
		(b) P 11.		
82	3	2½d. black	75·00	65·00
		a. Mixed perfs 10 and 11	£425	

Surcharged
2½d.
(11)

PROVISIONAL
GOVT.
(12)

1898–99. W **4***b*. P 11.

No.	Type	Description	Unused	Used
		(a) Handstamped as T **11** (10.98).		
83	2	2½d. on 1s. dull rose-carmine/*toned*	50·00	50·00
		(b) Surch as T **11** (1899).		
84	2	2½d. on 1d. bluish green (R.)	75	3·00
		a. Surch inverted	£750	£375
85		2½d. on 1s. dull rose-carmine/*toned* (R.)	8·50	13·00
		a. Surch double	£350	
86		2½d. on 1s. dull rose-carmine/*toned* (Blk.)	8·50	13·00
		a. Surch double	£450	
87		2½d. on 2s.6d. deep purple/*toned* *(wmk reversed)*	9·00	20·00

The typographed surcharge was applied in a setting of nine, giving seven types differing in the angle and length of the fractional line, the type of stop, etc.

1899 (18 July). *Colours changed.* W **4***b*. P 11.

No.	Type	Description	Unused	Used
88		½d. dull blue-green	2·25	3·50
		a. Deep green	2·25	3·50
89		1d. deep red-brown	3·00	3·25

1899 (20 Sept)–**1900**. *Provisional Government. New printings optd with T* **12** *(longer words and shorter letters on 5d.).* W **4***b*. P 11.

No.	Type	Description	Unused	Used
90	2	½d. dull blue-green (R.)	2·50	3·50
		a. Yellowish green (1900)	2·75	6·00
91		1d. chestnut (B.)	3·00	11·00
92		2d. dull orange (R.)	2·50	7·50
		a. Orange-yellow (1900)	2·50	9·00
93		4d. deep dull blue (R.)	70	15·00
94	8	5d. dull vermilion (B.)	3·50	9·00
		a. Red (1900)	3·25	9·00
95	2	6d. brown-lake (B.)	1·50	8·50
96		1s. rose-carmine (B.)	1·50	30·00
97		2s.6d. reddish purple (R.)	4·75	21·00
90/7 *Set of* 8			18·00	95·00

The Samoan group of islands was partitioned on 1 March 1900: Western Samoa (Upolu, Savaii Apolima and Manono) to Germany and Eastern Samoa (Tutuila, the Manu'a Is and Rose Is) to the United States. German issues of 1900–14 will be found listed in Part 7 (*Germany*) of this catalogue, there were no U.S. issues.

The Samoan Kingdom post office run by John Davis was suspended in March 1900.

NEW ZEALAND OCCUPATION

The German Islands of Samoa surrendered to the New Zealand Expeditionary Force on 30 August 1914 and were administered by New Zealand until 1962.

G.R.I.
1d.
(13)

G.R.I.
1 Shillings.
(14)

SETTINGS. Nos. 101/9 were surcharged by a vertical setting of ten, repeated ten times across the sheet. Nos. 110/14 were from a horizontal setting of four repeated five times in the sheet.

Nos. 101b, 102a and 104a occurred on position 6. The error was corrected during the printing of No. 102.

Nos. 101c, 102c, 104d and 105b are from position 10.

Nos. 101d, 102e and 104b are from position 1.

No. 108b is from position 9.

(Surch by *Samoanische Zeitung*, Apia)

1914 (3 Sept). *German Colonial issue (ship)* (no wmk) *inscr "SAMOA" surch as T* **13** *or* **14** *(mark values).*

No.	Type	Description	Unused	Used
101		½d. on 3pf. brown	45·00	12·00
		a. Surch double	£700	£550
		b. No fraction bar	75·00	35·00
		c. Comma after "I"	£700	£425
		d. "1" to left of "2" in "½"	75·00	35·00
102		½d. on 5pf. green	50·00	15·00
		a. No fraction bar	£130	60·00
		c. Comma after "I"	£425	£180
		d. Surch double	£700	£550
		e. "1" to left of "2" in "½"	£110	42·00
103		1d. on 10pf. carmine	95·00	40·00
		a. Surch double	£750	£600
104		2½d. on 20pf. ultramarine	48·00	11·00
		a. No fraction bar	80·00	40·00
		b. "1" to left of "2" in "½"	80·00	40·00
		c. Surch inverted	£950	£850
		d. Comma after "I"	£500	£850
		e. Surch double	£700	£600
105		3d. on 25pf. black and red/*yellow*	55·00	40·00
		a. Surch double	£1000	£750
		b. Comma after "I"	£5000	£1100
106		4d. on 30pf. black and orange/*buff*	£110	60·00
107		5d. on 40pf. black and carmine	£110	70·00
108		6d. on 50pf. black and purple/*buff*	60·00	35·00
		a. Surch double	£1000	£950
		b. Inverted "9" for "6"	£180	£100
109		9d. on 80pf. black and carmine/*rose*	£200	£100
110		"1 shillings" on 1m. carmine	£3250	£3500
111		"1 shilling" on 1m. carmine	£11000	£7000
112		2s. on 2m. blue	£3250	£2750
113		3s. on 3m. violet-black	£1400	£1200
		a. Surch double	£8500	£9500
114		5s. on 5m. carmine and black	£1100	£1000
		a. Surch double	£12000	£13000

No. 108b is distinguishable from 108, as the "d" and the "9" are not in a line, and the upper loop of the "9" turns downwards to the left.

UNAUTHORISED SURCHARGES. Examples of the 2d. on 20pf., 3d. on 30pf., 3d. on 40pf., 4d. on 40pf., 6d. on 80pf., 2s. on 3m. and 2s. on Marshall Islands 2m., together with a number of errors not listed above, were produced by the printer on stamps supplied by local collectors. These were not authorised by the New Zealand Military Administration.

SAMOA.
(15)

1914 (29 Sept)–**15**. *Stamps of New Zealand. T* **50**, **51**, **52** *and* **27**, *optd as T* **15**, *but opt only 14 mm long on all except 2½d.* Wmk "N Z" and Star, W **43** of New Zealand.

No.	Type	Description	Unused	Used
115		½d. yellow-green (R.) (P 14×15)	1·00	30
116		1d. carmine (B.) (P 14×15)	1·00	10
117		2d. mauve (R.) (P 14×14½) (10.14)	1·00	1·00
118		2½d. deep blue (R.) (P 14) (10.14)	1·75	1·75
		w. Wmk inverted		
119		6d. carmine (B.) (P 14×14½) (10.14)	1·75	1·75
		a. Perf 14×13½	17·00	23·00
		b. Vert pair. Nos. 119/a (1915)	50·00	95·00
120		6d. pale carmine (B.) (P 14×14½) (10.14)	10·00	10·00
121		1s. vermilion (B.) (P 14×14½) (10.14)	6·50	19·00
115/21 *Set of* 6			11·50	21·00

1914–24. *Postal Fiscal stamps as Type* F **4** *of New Zealand optd with T* **15**. W **43** of New Zealand (sideways). *Chalk-surfaced "De La Rue" paper.*

No.	Type	Description	Unused	Used
		(a) P 14 (Nov 1914–17).		
122		2s. blue (R.) (9.17)	£100	£100
123		2s.6d. grey-brown (B.) (9.17)	5·50	9·00
124		5s. yellow-green (R.)	15·00	11·00
125		10s. maroon (B.)	29·00	28·00
126		£1 rose-carmine (B.)	75·00	45·00
		(b) P 14½×14, comb (1917–24).		
127		2s. deep blue (R.) (3.18)	5·50	5·50
128		2s.6d. grey-brown (B.) (10.24)	£375	£160
129		3s. purple (R.) (6.23)	16·00	55·00
130		5s. yellow-green (R.) (9.17)	19·00	15·00
131		10s. maroon (B.) (11.17)	70·00	45·00
132		£1 rose-carmine (B.) (3.18)	80·00	70·00

We no longer list the £2 value as it is doubtful this was used for postal purposes.

See also Nos. 165/6*e*.

1916–19. *King George V stamps of New Zealand optd as T* **15**, *but 14 mm long.*

No.	Type	Description	Unused	Used
		(a) Typo. P 14×15.		
134	61	½d. yellow-green (R.)	60	1·25
135		1½d. slate (R.) (1917)	50	25
136		1½d. orange-brown (R.) (1919)	30	50
137		2d. yellow (R.) (14.2.18)	1·50	20
138		3d. chocolate (B.) (1919)	2·00	15·00
		(b) Recess. P 14×13½.		
139	60	2½d. blue (R.)	75	50
		a. Perf 14×14½	1·25	60
		b. Vert pair. Nos. 139/a	16·00	26·00
140		3d. chocolate (B.) (1917)	50	1·00
		a. Perf 14×14½	50	1·00
		b. Vert pair. Nos. 140/a	16·00	29·00
141		6d. carmine (B.) (5.5.17)	2·50	3·25
		a. Perf 14×14½	1·50	1·25
		b. Vert pair. Nos. 141/a	18·00	38·00
142		1s. vermilion (B.)	2·50	1·50
		a. Perf 14×14½	4·75	9·00
		b. Vert pair. Nos. 142/a	25·00	50·00
134/42 *Set of* 9			9·00	19·00

LEAGUE OF NATIONS MANDATE

Administered by New Zealand.

1920 (July). *Victory. Nos. 453/8 of New Zealand optd as T* **15**, *but 14 mm long.*

No.	Type	Description	Unused	Used
143		½d. green (R.)	5·00	12·00
144		1d. carmine (B.)	2·75	13·00
145		1½d. brown-orange (R.)	1·50	9·00
146		3d. chocolate (B.)	8·00	9·00
147		6d. violet (R.)	4·50	7·00
148		1s. orange-red (B.)	13·00	11·00
143/8 *Set of* 6			30·00	55·00

16 Native Hut

SILVER JUBILEE
OF
KING GEORGE V
1910-1935.
(17)

(Eng B.W. Recess-printed at Wellington, NZ)

1921 (23 Dec). W **43** of New Zealand.

No.	Type	Description	Unused	Used
		(a) P 14×14½.		
149	16	½d. green	3·00	9·50
150		1d. lake	4·50	40
151		1½d. chestnut	1·25	15·00
152		2d. yellow	2·25	2·00
149/52 *Set of* 4			10·00	24·00
		(b) P 14×13½.		
153	16	½d. green	4·50	1·75
154		1d. lake	5·00	20
155		1½d. chestnut	13·00	10·00
156		2d. yellow	13·00	80
157		2½d. grey-blue	1·75	8·00
158		3d. sepia	1·75	4·50
159		4d. violet	1·75	3·50
160		5d. light blue	1·75	7·00
161		6d. bright carmine	1·75	6·00
162		8d. red-brown	1·75	12·00
163		9d. olive-green	2·00	30·00
164		1s. vermilion	1·75	26·00
153/64 *Set of* 12			45·00	£100

1925–28. *Postal Fiscal stamps as Type* F **4** *of New Zealand optd with T* **15**. W **43** of New Zealand (sideways). P 14½×14.

No.	Type	Description	Unused	Used
		(a) Thick, opaque, white chalk-surfaced "Cowan" paper.		
165		2s. blue (R.) (12.25)	£190	£225
166		2s.6d. deep grey-brown (B.) (10.28)	55·00	£110
166*a*		3s. mauve (R.) (9.25)	65·00	£100
166*b*		5s. yellow-green (R.) (11.26)	23·00	45·00
		ba. Opt at top of stamp	£1900	
166*c*		10s. brown-red (B.) (12.25)	£190	£140
166*d*		£1 rose-pink (B.) (11.26)	85·00	£120
165/6*d* *Set of* 6			£550	£650
		(b) Thin, hard, chalk-surfaced "Wiggins Teape" paper.		
166*e*		£1 rose-pink (B.) (1928)	£1600	£900

1926–27. *T* **72** *of New Zealand, optd with T* **15**, *in red.*

No.	Type	Description	Unused	Used
		(a) "Jones" paper.		
167		2s. deep blue (11.26)	5·00	18·00
168		3s. mauve (10.26)	20·00	45·00
		w. Wmk inverted	20·00	48·00
		(b) "Cowan" paper.		
169		2s. light blue (10.11.27)	6·00	45·00
170		3s. pale mauve (10.11.27)	60·00	£100

1932 (Aug). *Postal Fiscal stamps as Type* F **6** *of New Zealand optd with T* **15**. W **43** of New Zealand. *Thick, opaque, white chalk-surfaced "Cowan" paper.* P 14.

No.	Type	Description	Unused	Used
171		2s.6d. deep brown (B.)	16·00	48·00
172		5s. green (R.)	26·00	50·00
173		10s. carmine-lake (B.)	48·00	£100
174		£1 pink (B.)	75·00	£140
175		£2 bright purple (R.)	£800	
176		£5 indigo-blue (R.)	£2250	

The £2 and £5 values were primarily for fiscal use.

1935 (7 May). *Silver Jubilee. Optd with T* **17**. P 14×13½.

No.	Type	Description	Unused	Used
177	16	1d. lake	30	30
		a. Perf 14×14½	95·00	£170
178		2½d. grey-blue	60	65
179		6d. bright carmine	2·75	3·25
177/9 *Set of* 3			3·25	3·75

18 Samoan Girl

19 Apia

20 River scene

21 Chief and Wife

22 Canoe and house

23 R. L. Stevenson's home "Vaillma"

24 Stevenson's tomb

25 Lake Lanuto'o

26 Falefa Falls

(Recess D.L.R.)

1935 (7 Aug). *T* **18/26**. W **43** of New Zealand ("N Z" and Star). P 14×13½ (½d., 2½d., 2s., 3s.), 14 (2d.) or 13½×14 (others).

180	½d. green	10	35
	w. Wmk inverted		
181	1d. black and carmine	10	10
182	2d. black and orange	3·50	3·25
	aw. Wmk inverted		
	b. Perf 13½×14	4·00	4·25
	bw. Wmk inverted		
183	2½d. black and blue	10	10
184	4d. slate and sepia	70	15
185	6d. bright magenta	50	10
186	1s. violet and brown	30	10
187	2s. green and purple-brown	80	50
188	3s. blue and brown-orange	1·50	3·50
180/8 *Set of* 9		6·50	7·00

See also Nos. 200/3.

WESTERN
SAMOA.
(27)

1935–42. *Postal Fiscal stamps as Type* F **6** *of New Zealand optd with T* **27**. W **43** of New Zealand. P 14.

(a) Thick, opaque chalk-surfaced "Cowan" paper (7.8.35).

189	2s.6d. deep brown (B.)	6·00	16·00
190	5s. green (B.)	15·00	25·00
191	10s. carmine-lake (B.)	60·00	75·00
192	£1 pink (B.)	60·00	£100
193	£2 bright purple (R.)	£160	£350
194	£5 indigo-blue (R.)	£225	£450

(b) Thin, hard chalk-surfaced "Wiggins Teape" paper (1941–42).

194*a*	5s. green (B.) (6.42)	£130	£140
194*b*	10s. pale carmine-lake (B.) (6.41)	£130	£150
194*c*	£2 bright purple (R.) (2.42)	£450	£800
194*d*	£5 indigo-blue (R.) (2.42)	£1700	£2000

The £2 and £5 values were primarily for fiscal use.
See also Nos. 207/14.

28 Coastal Scene

29 Map of Western Samoa

30 Samoan dancing party

31 Robert Louis Stevenson

(Des J. Berry (1d. and 1½d.). L. C. Mitchell (2½d. and 7d.). Recess B.W.)

1939 (29 Aug). *25th Anniv of New Zealand Control. T* **28, 31**. W **98** of New Zealand. P 13½×14 or 14×13½ (7d.).

195	1d. olive-green and scarlet	1·00	25
196	1½d. light blue and red-brown	1·75	75
197	2½d. red-brown and blue	1·50	1·00
198	7d. violet and slate-green	8·00	4·00
195/8 *Set of* 4		11·00	5·50

32 Samoan Chief

33 Apia Post Office

(Recess B.W.)

1940 (2 Sept). W **98** of New Zealand (Mult "N Z" and Star). P 14×13½.

199	**32**	3d. on 1½d. brown	75	20

T **32** was not issued without surcharge.

(*T* **33**. Des L. C. Mitchell. Recess B.W.)

1944–49. *As Nos. 180, 182/3 and T* **33**. W **98** of New Zealand (Mult "N Z" and Star) (sideways on 2½d.). P 14 or 13½×14 (5d.).

200	½d. green	30	19·00
202	2d. black and orange	3·50	6·00
203	2½d. black and blue (1948)	6·50	35·00
205	5d. sepia and blue (8.6.49)	2·25	50
200/5 *Set of* 4		11·00	55·00

1945–53. *Postal Fiscal stamps as Type* F **6** *of New Zealand optd with T* **27**. W **98** of New Zealand. *Thin hard, chalk-surfaced "Wiggins Teape" paper.* P 14.

207	2s.6d. deep brown (B.) (6.45)	7·50	18·00
	w. Wmk inverted	11·00	17·00
208	5s. green (B.) (5.45)	17·00	16·00
	w. Wmk inverted	17·00	18·00
209	10s. carmine-lake (B.) (4.46)	20·00	17·00
	w. Wmk inverted	30·00	32·00
210	£1 pink (B.) (6.48)	£110	£180
	w. Wmk inverted		
211	30s. brown (8.48)	£180	£300
	w. Wmk inverted		
212	£2 bright purple (R.) (11.47)	£190	£275
	w. Wmk inverted	£350	£450
213	£3 green (8.48)	£250	£375
	w. Wmk inverted		
214	£5 indigo-blue (R) (1946)	£350	£450
	w. Wmk inverted (5.53)	£375	£450
207/10 *Set of* 4		£140	£200

The £2 to £5 values were mainly used for fiscal purposes.

WESTERN
SAMOA
(34)

1946 (4 June). *Peace Issue. Nos. 668, 670 and 674/5 of New Zealand optd with T* **34** *(reading up and down at sides on 2d.).*

215	1d. green	40	15
	w. Wmk inverted	£150	
216	2d. purple (B.)	40	15
217	6d. chocolate and vermilion	40	15
218	8d. black and carmine (B.)	40	15
215/18 *Set of* 4		1·40	55

UNITED NATIONS TRUST TERRITORY

Administered by New Zealand.

35 Making Siapo Cloth

42 Thatching a Native Hut

43 Preparing Copra

44 Samoan Chieftainess

1952 (10 Mar). *T* **35, 42/4** *and similar designs.* W **98** of New Zealand (sideways on 1s. and 3s.). P 13 (½d., 2d. and 1s.) or 13½ (others).

219	½d. claret and orange-brown	10	1·75
220	1d. olive-green and green	10	30
221	2d. carmine-red	10	10
222	3d. pale ultramarine and indigo	40	20
223	5d. brown and deep green	7·00	70
224	6d. pale ultramarine and rose-magenta	1·00	10
225	8d. carmine	30	30
226	1s. sepia and blue	15	10
227	2s. yellow-brown	1·00	25
228	3s. chocolate and brown-olive	2·00	2·00
219/28 *Set of* 10		10·50	5·00

Designs: *Horiz* (*as* T **43**)—1d. Native houses and flags; 3d. Malifa Falls (wrongly inscribed "Aleisa Falls"); 6d. Bonito fishing canoe; 8d. Cacao harvesting. *Vert* (*as* T **35**)—2d. Seal of Samoa; 5d. Tooth-billed Pigeon.

1953 (25 May). *Coronation. Designs as Nos. 715 and 717 of New Zealand, but inscr "WESTERN SAMOA".*

229	2d. brown	1·00	15
230	6d. slate-grey	1·00	35

WESTERN

SAMOA
(45)

1955 (14 Nov). *Postal Fiscal stamps as Type* F **6** *of New Zealand optd with T* **45**. W **98** *(inverted). Chalk-surfaced "Wiggins, Teape" paper.* P 14.

232	5s. green (B.)	8·00	22·00
233	10s. carmine-lake (B.)	8·00	32·00
234	£1 pink (B.)	15·00	50·00
235	£2 bright purple (R.)	70·00	£160
232/5 *Set of* 4		90·00	£225

The £2 value was mainly used for fiscal purposes.

46 Native Houses and Flags

47 Seal of Samoa

(Recess B.W.)

1958 (21 Mar). *Inauguration of Samoan Parliament. T* **46/7** *and similar horiz design.* W **98** of New Zealand (sideways). P 13½×13 (6d.) or 13½ (others).

236	4d. cerise	25	30
237	6d. deep reddish violet	25	30
238	1s. deep ultramarine	75	50
236/8 *Set of* 3		1·10	1·00

Design:—1s. Map of Samoa, and the Mace.

INDEPENDENT

Samoa became independent on 1 January 1962.

49 Samoan Fine Mat

50 Samoa College

(Litho B.W.)

1962 (2 July). *Independence. T* **49/50** *and similar designs.* W **98** of New Zealand (sideways on horiz stamps). P 13½.

239	1d. brown and rose-carmine	10	10
240	2d. brown, green, yellow and red	10	10
241	3d. brown, blue-green and blue	10	10
242	4d. magenta, yellow, blue and black	15	20
243	6d. yellow and blue	80	20
244	8d. bluish green, yellow-green and blue	80	10
245	1s. brown and bluish green	20	10
246	1s.3d. yellow-green and blue	1·00	45
247	2s.6d. red and ultramarine	2·25	1·75
248	5s. ultramarine, yellow, red and drab	2·50	2·25
239/48 *Set of* 10		7·00	4·50

Designs: *Horiz*—3d. Public library; 4d. Fono House; 6d. Map of Samoa; 8d. Airport; 1s.3d. "Vailima"; 2s.6d. Samoan flag; 5s. Samoan seal. *Vert*—1s. Samoan orator.
See Nos. 257/62.

59 Seal and Joint Heads of State

60 Signing the Treaty

(Des L. C. Mitchell. Photo Harrison)

1963 (1 Oct). *First Anniv of Independence.* W **98** of New Zealand. P 14.

249	**59**	1d. deep sepia and green	10	10
250		4d. deep sepia and blue	10	10
251		8d. deep sepia and rose-pink	10	10
252		2s. deep sepia and orange	20	15
249/52 *Set of* 4			45	40

(Des L. C. Mitchell. Photo Enschedé)

1964 (1 Sept). *2nd Anniv of New Zealand-Samoa Treaty of Friendship.* P 13½.

253	**60**	1d. multicoloured	10	10
254		8d. multicoloured	10	10
255		2s. multicoloured	20	10
256		3s. multicoloured	20	30
253/6 *Set of* 4			55	55

61 Kava Bowl

1965 (4 Oct)–**66?**. *As Nos. 239, 241/5, but* W **61** (sideways on horiz designs).

257	1d. brown and rose-carmine	20	60
258	3d. brown, blue-green and blue (1966?)	27·00	3·75
259	4d. magenta, yellow, blue and black	25	60
260	6d. yellow and blue	75	50
261	8d. bluish green, yellow-green and blue	30	10
262	1s. brown and bluish green	25	60
257/62 *Set of* 6		27·00	5·50

62 Red-tailed Tropic Bird

63 Flyingfish

(Des L. C. Mitchell. Photo Harrison)

1965 (29 Dec). *Air.* W **61** (sideways). P 14½.

263	**62**	8d. black, red-orange and blue	50	10
264	**63**	2s. black and blue	75	20

64 Aerial View of Deep Sea Wharf

(Des Tecon Co (U.S.A.). Photo Enschedé)

1966 (3 Mar). *Opening of First Deep Sea Wharf Apia. T* **64** *and similar horiz design. Multicoloured.* W **61** (sideways). P 13½.

265	1d. Type **64**	10	10
266	8d. Aerial view of wharf and bay	15	10
267	2s. As 8d.	25	25
268	3s. Type **64**	30	35
265/8 *Set of* 4		70	70

66 W.H.O. Building

(Des M. Goaman. Photo D.L.R.)

1966 (4 July). *Inauguration of W.H.O. Headquarters. Geneva. T* **66** *and similar horiz design.* W **61** (sideways*). P 14.

269	3d. yellow-ochre, blue and light slate-lilac	35	10
270	4d. blue, yellow, green and light orange-brown	40	15
271	6d. reddish lilac, emerald and yellow-olive	45	20
	w. Wmk legs to left	1·75	
272	1s. blue, yellow, green and turquoise-green	80	25
269/72 *Set of* 4		1·75	60

Designs:—3d., 6d. Type **66**; 4d., 1s. W.H.O. Building on flag. *The normal sideways watermark has the legs of the bowl pointing to the right, *as seen from the back of the stamp*.

HURRICANE RELIEF
6d
(**68**)

1966 (1 Sept). *Hurricane Relief Fund. No. 261 surch with T* **68** *by Bradbury, Wilkinson.*

273	8d. +6d. bluish green, yellow-green and blue	10	10

69 Hon. Tuatagaloa L. S. (Minister of Justice)

(Des and photo Harrison)

1967 (16 Jan). *Fifth Anniv of Independence. T* **69** *and similar horiz designs.* W **61** (sideways). P 14½×14.

274	3d. sepia and bluish violet	10	10
275	8d. sepia and light new blue	10	10
276	2s. sepia and olive	10	10
277	3s. sepia and magenta	15	15
274/7 *Set of* 4		40	40

Designs:—8d. Hon F. C. F. Nelson (minister of Works, Marine and Civil Aviation); 2s. Hon To'omata T. L. (minister of Lands); Hon Fa'alava'au G. (minister of Post Office, Radio and Broadcasting).

73 Samoan Fales (houses), 1890

(Des V. Whiteley. Photo Harrison)

1967 (16 May). *Centenary of Mulinu'u as Seat of Government. T* **73** *and similar horiz design. Multicoloured.* W **61**. P 14½×14.

278		8d. Type **73**	15	10
279		1s. Fono (Parliament) House, 1967	15	10

(New Currency. 100 sene or cents=1 tala or dollar)

75 Carunculated Honeyeater

76 Black-breasted Honeyeater

(Des V. Whiteley. Litho Format ($2, $4). Photo Harrison (others))

1967 (10 July)–**69**. *Decimal currency Multicoloured designs as T* **75** *(1s. to $1) or 76 ($2, $4).* W **61** (sideways). P 13½ ($2, $4) or 14×14½ (others).

280	1s. Type **75**	10	10
281	2s. Pacific Pigeon	10	10
282	3s. Samoan Starling	10	10
283	5s. White-vented Flycatcher	10	10
284	7s. Red-headed Parrot Finch	10	10
285	10s. Purple Swamphen	15	10
286	20s. Barn Owl	1·25	40
287	25s. Tooth-billed Pigeon	50	15
288	50s. Island Thrush	50	30
289	$1 Samoan Fantail	75	1·75
289*a*	$2 Type **76** (14.7.69)	2·00	5·00
289*b*	$4 Savaii White Eye (6.10.69)	25·00	18·00
280/9b *Set of* 12		27·00	23·00

85 Nurse and Child

(Des G. Vasarhelyi. Photo D.L.R.)

1967 (1 Dec). *South Pacific Health Service. T* **85** *and similar horiz designs. Multicoloured.* P 14.

290	3s. Type **85**	15	15
291	7s. Leprosartum	20	15
292	20s. Mobile X-ray Unit	35	30
293	25s. Apia Hospital	40	35
290/3 *Set of* 4		1·00	85

89 Thomas Trood

93 Cocoa

(Des M. Farrar-Bell. Litho B.W.)

1968 (15 Jan). *6th Anniv of Independence. T* **89** *and similar horiz designs. Multicoloured.* P 13½.

294	2s. Type **89**	10	10
295	7s. Dr Wilhelm Solf	10	10
296	20s. J. C. Williams	10	10
297	25s. Fritz Marquardt	15	10
294/7 *Set of* 4		40	35

(Des Jennifer Toombs. Photo Enschedé)

1968 (15 Feb). *Agricultural Development. T* **93** *and similar vert designs.* W **61**. P 13×12½.

298	3s. deep red-brown, yellow-green and black	10	10
299	5s. myrtle-green, greenish yellow and light brown	10	10
300	10s. scarlet, blackish brown and olive-yellow	10	10
301	20s. yellow-bistre, yellow and blackish olive	15	15
298/301 *Set of* 4		40	40

Designs:— 5s. Breadfruit; 10s. Copra; 20s. Bananas.

97 Women weaving Mats

(Des G. Vasarhelyi. Photo Harrison)

1968 (22 Apr). *21st Anniv of the South Pacific Commission. T* **97** *and similar horiz designs. Multicoloured.* W **61**. P 14½×14.

302	7s. Type **97**	10	10
303	20s. Palm trees and bay	15	10
304	25s. Sheltered cove	15	15
302/4 *Set of* 3		35	30

1928-1968
KINGSFORD-SMITH
TRANSPACIFIC FLIGHT
20 SENE
(**100**)

1968 (13 June). *40th Anniv of Kingsford Smith's Trans-Pacific Flight. No. 285 surch with T* **100**.

305	20s. on 10s. Purple Swamphen	10	10

101 Bougainville's Route

(Des Jennifer Toombs. Litho B. W.)

1968 (17 June). *Bicentenary of Bougainville's Visit to Samoa. T* **101** *and similar horiz designs.* W **61** (sideways). P 14.

306	3s. new blue and black	10	20
307	7s. light ochre and black	15	20
308	20s. multicoloured	45	30
309	25s. multicoloured	60	40
306/9 *Set of* 4		1·10	1·00

Designs:—7s. Louis de Bougainville; 20s. Bougainvillea flower; 25s. Ships *La Boudeuse* and *L'Etoile*.

105 Globe and Human Rights Emblem

106 Dr. Martin Luther King

(Des G. Vasarhelyi. Photo Harrison)

1968 (26 Aug). *Human Rights Year.* W **61**. P 14.

310	**105**	7s. greenish blue, brown and gold	10	10
311		20s. orange, green and gold	10	15
312		25s. violet, green and gold	15	15
310/12 *Set of* 3			30	35

(Des and litho D.L.R.)

1968 (23 Sept). *Martin Luther King Commemoration.* W **61**. P 14½×14.

313	**106**	7s. black and olive-green	15	10
314		20s. black and bright purple	15	10

107 Polynesian Version of Madonna and Child

108 Frangipani-Plumeria acuminata

(Des and litho D.L.R.)

1968 (14 Oct). *Christmas.* W **61**. P 14.

315	**107**	1s. multicoloured	10	10
316		3s. multicoloured	10	10
317		20s. multicoloured	10	10
318		30s. multicoloured	15	15
315/18 *Set of* 4			40	40

(Des J.W. Litho Format)

1969 (20 Jan). *Seventh Anniv of Independence. T* **108** *and similar multicoloured designs.* P 14½.

319	2s. Type **108**	10	10
320	7s. Hibiscus (*vert*)	10	10
321	20s. Red-Ginger (*vert*)	15	10
322	30s. "Moso'oi"	20	80
319/22 *Set of* 4		50	1·00

109 R. L. Stevenson and *Treasure Island*

110 Weightlifting

(Des Jennifer Toombs. Litho D.L.R.)

1969 (21 Apr). *75th Death Anniv of Robert Louis Stevenson. Horiz designs, each showing portrait as in T* **109**. *Multicoloured.* W **61** (sideways). P 14.

323	3s. Type **109**	10	10
324	7s. *Kidnapped*	15	10
325	20s. *Dr. Jekyll and Mr. Hyde*	15	50
326	22s. *Weir of Hermiston*	15	50
323/6	*Set of* 4	50	1·10

(Des J. Mason. Photo Note Ptg Branch, Reserve Bank of Australia)

1969 (21 July). *Third South Pacifc Games, Port Moresby. T* **110** *and similar vert designs.* P 13½.

327	3s. black and sage-green	10	10
328	20s. black and light blue	10	10
329	22s. black and dull orange	15	15
327/9	*Set of* 3	30	30

Designs:—20s. Yachting; 22s. Boxing.

113 U.S. Astronaut on the Moon and the Splashdown near Samoan Islands

(Des J. Mason. Photo Note Ptg Branch, Reserve Bank of Australia)

1969 (24 July). *First Man on the Moon.* P 13½.

330	**113**	7s. multicoloured	15	15
331		20s. multicoloured	15	15

114 "Virgin with Child" (Murillo)

(Des and photo Heraclio Fournier)

1969 (13 Oct). *Christmas. T* **114** *and similar vert designs. Multicoloured.* P 14.

332	1s. Type **114**	10	10
333	3s. "The Holy Family" (El Greco)	10	10
334	20s. "The Nativity" (El Greco)	20	10
335	30s. "The Adoration of the Magi" (detail, Velazquez)	25	15
332/5	*Set of* 4	60	40
MS336	116×126 mm. Nos. 332/5	75	1·25

115 Seventh Day Adventists' Sanatorium, Apia

(Des V. Whiteley. Litho Format)

1970 (19 Jan). *Eighth Anniv of Independence. T* **115** *and similar designs.* W **61** (sideways on 2, 7 and 22s.). P 14.

337	2s. yellow-brown, pale slate and black	10	10
338	7s. violet, buff and black	10	10
339	20s. rose, lilac and black	15	10
340	22s. olive-green, cinnamon and black	15	15
337/40	*Set of* 4	45	40

Designs: *Horiz*—7s. Rev. Father Violette and Roman Catholic Cathedral, Apia; 22s. John Williams, 1797–1839 and London Missionary Society Church, Sapapali'l. *Vert*—20s. Mormon Church of Latter Day Saints, Tuasivi-on-Safotulafai.

119 Wreck of *Adler* (German steam gunboat)

(Des J.W. Litho Questa)

1970 (27 Apr). *(Great Apia Hurricane of 1889). T* **119** *and similar horiz designs. Multicoloured.* W **61** (sideways). P 13½.

341	5s. Type **119**	30	10
342	7s. U.S.S. *Nipsic* (steam sloop)	30	10
343	10s. H. M.S. *Calliope* (screw corvette)	30	25
344	20s. Apia after the hurricane	50	75
341/4	*Set of* 4	1·25	1·10

120 Sir Gordon Taylor's Short 825 Sandringham 7 Flying Boat *Frigate Bird III*

(Des R. Honisett. Photo Note Ptg Branch, Reserve Bank of Australia)

1970 (27 July). *Air. Aircraft. T* **120** *and similar horiz designs. Multicoloured.* P 13½×13.

345	3s. Type **120**	45	10
346	7s. Polynesian Airlines Douglas DC-3	55	10
347	20s. Pan-American Sikorsky S-42A flying boat *Samoan Clipper*	75	60
348	30s. Air Samoa Britten Norman Islander	75	1·75
	a. Pale purple omitted	£300	
345/8	*Set of* 4	2·25	2·25

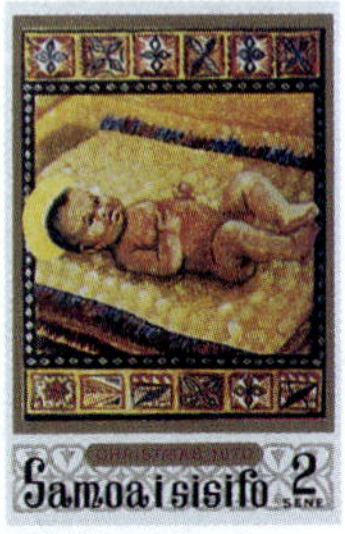

121 Kendal's Chronometer and Cook's Sextant

122 "Peace for the World" (F. B. Eccles)

(Des J. Berry, adapted J. Cooler. Litho Questa)

1970 (14 Sept). *Cook's Exploration of the Pacifc. T* **121** *and similar designs.* W **61** (sideways on 30s.). P 14.

349	1s. carmine, silver and black	15	15
350	2s. multicoloured	15	15
351	20s. black, bright blue and gold	35	25
352	30s. multicoloured	1·00	80
349/52	*Set of* 4	1·50	1·25

Designs: *Vert*—2s. Cook's statue, Whitby; 20s. Cook's head. *Horiz* (83×25 *mm*)—30s. Cook, H.M.S. *Endeavour* and island.

(Des from paintings. Photo Heraclio Fournier)

1970 (26 Oct). *Christmas. T* **122** *and similar vert designs. Multicoloured.* P 13.

353	2s. Type **122**	10	10
354	3s. "The Holy Family" (W. E. Jahnke)	10	10
355	20s. "Mother and Child" (F. B. Eccles)	15	10
356	30s. "Prince of Peace" (Meleane Fe'ao)	20	15
353/6	*Set of* 4	50	40
MS357	111×158 mm. Nos. 353/6	60	1·25

123 Pope Paul VI

(Des J. Cooter. Litho Format)

1970 (20 Nov). *Visit of Pope Paul to Samoa.* W **61**. P 14×14½.

358	**123**	8s. black and grey-blue	15	15
359		20s. black and plum	35	15

STAMP BOOKLETS

1958. *Blue on yellow (No. SB1) and blue (No. SB3) or black on pink (No. SB2). Stapled.*

SB1	2s.7d. booklet containing ½d. and 2d. (Nos. 219, 221), each in block of 6, 1d. and 3d. (Nos. 220, 222), each in block of 4	
SB2	6s. booklet containing 1d., 3d., 6d. and 8d. (Nos. 220, 222, 224/5), each in block of 4 ...	
SB3	9s.9d. booklet containing ½d., 2d., 5d. and 1s. (Nos. 219, 221, 223, 226), each in block of 6	
	Set of 3	£400

1960 (1 Apr). *Contents as Nos. SB1/3, but arms and inscription in black, and colour of covers changed. Stapled.*

SB4	2s.7d. Green cover	
	a. Buff cover	
SB5	6s. Grey cover	
	a. Blue cover	
SB6	9s.9d. Yellow cover	
	a. White cover	
	Set of 3 (Nos. SB4, SB5, SB6)	£160
	Set of 3 (Nos. SB4a, SB5a, SB6a)	£160

1962 (1 Sept). *Black on buff (No. SB7) or green (No. SB8) covers. Inscr "POSTAGE STAMP BOOKLET NO. 1" (1s.9d.) or "NO. 2" (6s.9d.). Stapled.*

SB7	6s.9d. booklet containing one each of 1d., 2d., 3d., 4d., 6d., 8d., 1s., 1s.3d. and 2s.6d. (Nos. 239/47) (loose in cellophane bag) ...	48·00
SB8	11s.9d. booklet containing one each of 1d., 2d., 3d., 4d., 6d., 8d., 1s., 1s.3d., 2s.6d. and 5s. (Nos. 239/48) (loose in cellophane bag) ...	48·00

1962 (1 Sept)–**64**. *Black on ink (No. SB9) or blue (No. SB10) covers. Inscr "POSTAGE STAMP BOOKLET NO. 3" (12s.) or "NO. 4" (6s.). Stapled.*

SB9	6s. booklet containing 1d., 3d., 6d. and 8d. (Nos. 239 241, 243/4), each in block of 4	42·00
SB10	12s. booklet containing 1d., 2d., 3d., 4d., 6d., 8d. and 1s. (Nos. 239/45), each in block of 4	42·00

1964 (1 Sept)–**67**. *As Nos. SB9/10 but containing stamps with mixed wmks (W* **98** *of New Zealand or W* **61** *of Samoa). Stapled.*

SB11	6s. As No. SB9 *From*	42·00
SB12	12s. As No. SB10 *From* *From*	48·00

1965 (1 Feb)–**67**. *As Nos. SB7/8, but containing stamps with mixed wmks (W* **98** *of New Zealand or W* **61** *of Samoa). Stapled.*

SB13	6s.9d. As No. SB7 *From*	42·00
SB14	11s.9d. As No. SB8 *From*	50·00

The composition of Nos. SB11/14 can vary as to the watermark and as it is possible to substitute stamps of one watermark for those of another, both in the cellophane bags and the blocks, we do not attempt to list them in greater detail. Prices will vary according to the contents.

Sarawak

Sarawak was placed under British protection in 1888. It was ceded to Great Britain on 1 July 1946 and was administered as a Crown Colony until 16 September 1963 when it became a state of the Federation of Malaysia.

From 1859 letters from Sarawak to overseas addresses, other than to other British possessions in Borneo and Singapore, were franked by stamps of INDIA and, after 1867, STRAITS SETTLEMENTS, a stock of which was kept by the Sarawak Post Office. The stamps of Sarawak continued to have this limited validity until 1 July 1897 when the country joined the U.P.U.

PRICES FOR STAMPS ON COVER TO 1945	
No. 1	—
Nos. 2/7	*from* × 50
Nos. 8/21	*from* × 8
Nos. 22/6	*from* × 6
No. 27	*from* × 40
Nos. 28/35	*from* × 6
Nos. 36/47	*from* × 8
No. 48	†
No. 49	*from* × 10
Nos. 50/61	*from* × 6
No. 62	†
Nos. 63/71	*from* × 4
Nos. 72/3	*from* × 8
Nos. 74/5	—
Nos. 76/90	*from* × 7
Nos. 91/105	*from* × 5
Nos. 106/25	*from* × 3
Nos. 126/45	*from* × 2

BROOKE FAMILY ADMINISTRATION

Sir James Brooke. 1842–11 June 1868

Sir Charles Brooke. 11 June 1868–17 May 1917

UNUSED PRICES. Nos. 1/7, 27 and 32/5 in unused condition are normally found without gum. Prices in the unused column are for stamps in this state. Examples of these issues with original gum are worth considerably more.

1 Sir James Brooke

2 Sir Charles Brooke

The initials in the corners of T **1** and **2** stand for "James (Charles) Brooke, Rajah (of) Sarawak".

(T **1** and **2**. Die eng Wm. Ridgeway. Litho Maclure, Macdonald & Co, Glasgow)

1869 (1 Mar). P 11.

1	**1**	3c. brown/*yellow*	50·00	£225

Similar stamps are known printed from the engraved die in orange-brown on orange surface-coloured paper, and perf 12. These are specimens submitted to the Sarawak authorities and exist both with and without obliterations.

1871 (1 Jan). P 11 (irregular).

2	**2**	3c. brown/*yellow*	1·75	3·50
		a. Stop after "THREE"	48·00	65·00
		b. Imperf between (vert pair)	£550	
		c. Imperf between (horiz pair) ..	£900	

The "stop" variety, No. 2a, which occurs on R. 10/7 of printing stone is of no more philatelic importance than any of the numerous other variations, such as narrow first "A" in "SARAWAK" (R. 2/7) and "R" with long tail in left lower corner (R. 9/10), but it has been accepted by collectors for many years, and we therefore retain it. The papermaker's wmk "L N L" appears once or twice in sheets of No. 2.

Specimens are known, recess-printed, similar to those mentioned in the note after No. 1.

TWO CENTS

Copies of No. 2 surcharged as above were first reported in 1876 but following the discovery of dies for forgeries and faked postmarks in 1891 it was concluded that the issue was bogus, especially as the availability of the 2c. of 1875 made it unnecessary to issue a provisional. It has now been established that a 2c. postal rate was introduced from 1 August 1874 for the carriage of newspapers. Moreover four examples are known with a stop after "CENTS." and showing other minor differences from the forgery illustrated. This version could be genuine and if others come to light we will reconsider listing it.

1875 (1 Jan). P 11½–12.

3	2	2c. mauve/*lilac* (*shades*)	13·00	17·00
4		4c. red-brown/*yellow*	3·75	3·00
		a. Imperf between (vert pair)	£800	£900
5		6c. green/*green*	3·75	3·75
6		8c. bright blue/*blue*	3·75	4·50
7		12c. red/*pale rose*	7·50	6·50
3/7 *Set of* 5			29·00	32·00

Nos. 3, 4, 6 and 7 have the watermark "L N L" in the sheet, as No. 2. No. 5 is watermarked "L N T".

All values exist imperf and can be distinguished from the proofs by shade and impression. Stamps rouletted, pin-perf, or roughly perf 6½ to 7 are proofs clandestinely perforated.

The 12c. "laid" paper, formerly listed, is not on a true laid paper, the "laid" effect being accidental and not consistent.

The lithographic stones for Nos. 3 to 7 were made up from strips of five distinct impressions hence there are five types of each value differing mainly in the lettering of the tablets of value. There are flaws on nearly every individual stamp, from which they can be plated.

4 Sir Charles Brooke

(Typo D.L.R.)

1888 (10 Nov)–**97**. No wmk. P 14.

8	4	1c. purple and black (6.6.92)	3·25	75
9		2c. purple and carmine (11.11.88)	4·00	2·50
		a. Purple and rosine (1897)	11·00	4·50
10		3c. purple and blue (11.11.88)	5·00	4·00
11		4c. purple and yellow	26·00	55·00
12		5c. purple and green (12.6.91)	20·00	3·50
13		6c. purple and brown (11.11.88)	20·00	55·00
14		8c. green and carmine (11.11.88)	14·00	4·00
		a. Green and rosine (1897)	23·00	15·00
15		10c. green and purple (12.6.91)	38·00	14·00
16		12c. green and blue (11.11.88)	13·00	9·50
17		16c. green and orange (28.12.97)	48·00	80·00
18		25c. green and brown (19.11 88)	50·00	45·00
19		32c. green and black (28.12.97)	38·00	60·00
20		50c. green (26.7.97)	50·00	95·00
21		$1 green and black (2.11.97)	85·00	90·00
8/21 *Set of* 14			£375	£475

Prepared for use but not issued.

21*a*	$2 green and blue	£900	
21*b*	$5 green and violet	£900	
21*c*	$10 green and carmine	£900	

On No. 21 the value is in black on an uncoloured ground.

The tablet of value in this and later similar issues is in the second colour given.

One Cent. (5) one cent. (6)

2c. (7) 5c (8) 5c. (9)

1889 (3 Aug)–**92**. *T* **4** *surch*. P 14.

22	5	1c. on 3c. purple and blue (12.1.92)	50·00	32·00
		a. Surch double	£750	£650
23	6	1c. on 3c. purple and blue (2.92)	3·00	2·75
		a. No stop after "cent" (R. 2/6)	£250	
24	7	2c. on 8c. green and carmine (3.8.89)	3·00	6·50
		a. Surch double	£450	
		b. Surch inverted	£3500	
		c. Surch omitted (in pair with normal)	£6500	
25	8	5c. on 12c. green and blue (with stop after "C") (17.2.91)	24·00	45·00
		a. No stop after "C"	30·00	50·00
		b. "C" omitted (in pair with normal)	£600	£650
		c. Surch double	£1200	
		d. Surch double, one vertical	£3750	
		e. Surch omitted (in pair with normal)	£10000	
26	9	5c. on 12c. green and blue (17.2.91)	£225	£250
		a. No stop after "C"	£110	£130
		b. "C" omitted (in pair with normal)	£800	£850
		c. Surch double	£1300	

ONE CENT

(10)

1892 (23 May). *No. 2 surch with T* **10**.

27	2	1c. on 3c. brown/*yellow*	1·40	2·00
		a. Stop after "THREE."	42·00	45·00
		b. Imperf between (vert pair)	£750	
		c. Imperf horiz (vert pair)	£700	
		d. Bar omitted (1st ptg)	£225	£250
		e. Bar at top and bottom (1st ptg)	£375	
		f. Surch double (2nd ptg)	£450	£500

No. 27 was surcharged with a setting of 100 (10×10). It was originally intended that there should be no bar at foot, but this was then added at a second operation before the stamps were issued. Subsequent supplies were surcharged with "ONE CENT" and bar at one operation.

Varieties with part of the surcharge missing are due to gum on the face of the unsurcharged stamps receiving part of the surcharge, which was afterwards washed off.

11

12

13 Sir Charles Brooke

14

(Die eng Wm. Ridgeway. Recess P.B.)

1895 (12 Feb–Sept). No wmk. P 11½–12.

28	11	2c. brown-red	11·00	9·00
		a. Imperf between (vert pair)	£500	
		b. Imperf between (horiz pair)	£425	
		c. Second ptg. Perf 12½ (Sept)	17·00	4·50
		ca. Perf 12½. Imperf between (horiz pair)	£600	
29	12	4c. black	11·00	3·50
		a. Imperf between (horiz pair)	£700	
30	13	6c. violet	14·00	9·00
31	14	8c. green	30·00	6·00
28/31 *Set of* 4			60·00	21·00

Stamps of these types, printed in wrong colours, are trials and these, when surcharged with values in "pence", are from waste sheets that were used by Perkins, Bacon & Co as trial paper when preparing an issue of stamps for British South Africa.

4 CENTS.

(15)

16

1899 (29 June–16 Nov). *Surch as T* **15**.

32	2	2c. on 3c. brown/*yellow* (19 Sept)	2·00	1·75
		a. Stop after "THREE"	65·00	65·00
		b. Imperf between (vert pair)	£900	
33		2c. on 12c. red/*pale rose*	3·00	3·00
		a. Surch inverted	£900	£1300
34		4c. on 6c. green/*green* (R.) (16 Nov)	35·00	80·00
35		4c. on 8c. bright blue/*blue* (R.)	4·50	9·00
32/5 *Set of* 4			40·00	85·00

A variety of surcharge with small "S" in "CENTS" may be found in the 2c. on 12c. and 4c. on 8c. and a raised stop after "CENTS" on the 4c. on 6c.

The omission of parts of the surcharge is due to gum on the surface of the stamps (see note after No. 27).

A block of 50 of No. 35 from the right of the pane is known line perforated 12.7 between the stamps and the margins at top and right.

(Typo D.L.R.)

1899 (10 Nov)–**1908**. *Inscribed* "POSTAGE POSTAGE". No wmk. P 14.

36	4	1c. grey-blue and rosine (1.1.01)	1·25	1·25
		a. Grey-blue and red	4·75	1·75
		b. Ultramarine and rosine	8·50	2·75
		c. Dull blue and carmine	15·00	4·50
37		2c. green (16.12.99)	2·00	90
38		3c. dull purple (1.2.08)	13·00	65
39		4c. rose-carmine (10.11.99)	11·00	2·50
		a. Aniline carmine	2·50	15
40		8c. yellow and black (6.12.99)	2·25	80
41		10c. ultramarine (10.11.99)	2·75	1·00
42		12c. mauve (16.12.99)	4·75	4·50
		a. Bright mauve (1905)	28·00	8·50
43		16c. chestnut and green (16.12.99)	4·75	1·75
44		20c. bistre and bright mauve (4.00)	5·50	4·75
45		25c. brown and blue (16.12.99)	6·50	5·00
46		50c. sage-green and carmine (16.12.99)	26·00	27·00
47		$1 rose-carmine and green (16.12.99)	70·00	£120
		a. Rosine and pale green	85·00	£130
36/47 *Set of* 12			£130	£150

Prepared for use but not issued.

48	4	5c. olive-grey and green	12·00	

The figures of value in the $1 are in colour on an uncoloured ground.

1902. *Inscribed* "POSTAGE POSTAGE". W **16**. P 14.

49	4	2c. green	30·00	16·00

Sir Charles Vyner Brooke. 17 May 1917–1 June 1946

17 Sir Charles Vyner Brooke

ONE cent

(18)

(Typo D.L.R.)

1918 (24 Mar–Apr). *Chalk-surfaced paper*. No wmk. P 14.

50	17	1c. slate-blue and red	2·25	2·75
		a. Dull blue and carmine	2·25	2·75
51		2c. green	2·50	1·50
52		3c. brown-purple (Apr)	3·25	2·75
53		4c. rose-carmine (Apr)	5·00	3·25
		a. Rose-red	6·50	3·00
54		8c. yellow and black (Apr)	12·00	60·00
55		10c. blue (*shades*) (Apr)	3·75	3·75
56		12c. purple (Apr)	14·00	32·00
57		16c. chestnut and green (Apr)	5·50	7·50
58		20c. olive and violet (*shades*) (Apr)	7·00	6·50
59		25c. brown and bright blue (Apr)	4·00	16·00
60		50c. olive-green and carmine (Apr)	10·00	15·00
61		$1 bright rose and green (Apr)	25·00	29·00
50/61 *Set of* 12			85·00	£160
50s/61s Optd "Specimen" *Set of* 12			£275	

Prepared for use but not issued.

62	17	1c. slate-blue and slate	22·00	

On the $1 the figures of value are in colour on an uncoloured ground.

Most values are known with part strikes of a forged Kuching postmark dated "12 MAR 90".

1922 (Jan)–**23**. *New colours and values. Chalk-surfaced paper*. No wmk. P 14.

63	17	2c. purple (5.3.23)	2·00	2·75
64		3c. dull green (23.3.22)	2·50	1·25
65		4c. brown-purple (10.4.23)	1·50	1·00
66		5c. yellow-orange	1·75	1·50
67		6c. claret	1·50	1·40
68		8c. bright rose-red (1922)	4·50	32·00
69		10c. black (1923)	2·75	4·25
70		12c. bright blue (12.22)	11·00	18·00
		a. Pale dull blue	11·00	21·00
71		30c. ochre-brown and slate	3·75	4·25
63/71 *Set of* 9			28·00	60·00

1923 (Jan). *Surch as T* **18**.

(a) First printing. Bars 1¼ mm apart.

72	17	1c. on 10c. dull blue	10·00	55·00
		a. "cnet" for "cent" (R. 9/5)	£400	£900
73		2c. on 12c. purple	6·50	42·00
		a. Thick, narrower "W" in "TWO"	20·00	95·00

(b) Second printing. Bars ¾ mm apart.

74	17	1c. on 10c. dull blue	£400	
		b. "cnet" for "cent" (R. 9/5)	£16000	
		c. Bright blue	£140	£400
		ca. "en" of "cent" scratched out and "ne" overprinted (R. 9/5)	£6000	
75		2c. on 12c. purple	80·00	£250
		a. Thick, narrower "W" in "TWO"	£150	

In the 2c. on 12c. the words of the surcharge are about 7½ mm from the bars.

The "cnet" error occurred on R. 9/5 of all sheets from the first printing of the 1c. on 10c. A single example of the error, No. 74*b*, is known from the second printing, but the error was then corrected, as shown by the evidence of a surviving plate block, only to have the correct spelling scratched out by a local employee, and "ne" substituted (No. 74ca).

The thick "W" variety occurs on all stamps of the last two horizontal rows of the first printing (12 stamps per sheet), and in the last two vertical rows of the second (20 stamps per sheet).

1928 (7 Apr)–**29**. *Chalk-surfaced paper*. W **16** (Multiple). P 14.

76	17	1c. slate-blue and carmine	1·50	35
77		2c. bright purple	2·25	1·25
78		3c. green	2·75	5·00
79		4c. brown-purple	1·75	10
80		5c. yellow-orange (7.8.29)	12·00	5·00
81		6c. claret	1·25	30
82		8c. bright rose-red	3·25	20·00
83		10c. black	1·75	1·25
84		12c. bright blue	3·25	27·00
85		16c. chestnut and green	3·25	4·00
86		20c. olive-bistre and violet	3·25	6·50
87		25c. brown and bright blue	5·50	8·50
88		30c. bistre-brown and slate	4·50	10·00
89		50c. olive-green and carmine	7·50	18·00
90		$1 bright rose and green	15·00	24·00
76/90 *Set of* 15			60·00	£120
76s/90s Optd or Perf (5c.) "Specimen" *Set of* 15			£275	

In the $1 the value is as before.

19 Sir Charles Vyner Brooke

20

(Recess Waterlow)

1932 (1 Jan). W **20**. P 12½.

91	19	1c. indigo	80	1·00
92		2c. green	1·00	1·75
93		3c. violet	4·00	1·00
94		4c. red-orange	5·00	75
95		5c. deep lake	6·50	1·25

96		6c. scarlet	7·00	9·50
97		8c. orange-yellow	9·00	8·50
98		10c. black	2·25	3·25
99		12c. deep ultramarine	4·00	9·50
100		15c. chestnut	6·50	8·50
101		20c. red-orange and violet	6·50	8·00
102		25c. orange-yellow and chestnut	10·00	22·00
103		30c. sepia and vermilion	9·50	28·00
104		50c. carmine-red and olive-green	14·00	13·00
105		$1 green and carmine	22·00	35·00
91/105 *Set of* 15			95·00	£130
91s/105s Perf "Specimen" *Set of* 15			£325	

21 Sir Charles Vyner Brooke

BMA
(22)

(Recess B.W.)

1934 (1 May)–**41**. No wmk. P 12.

106	**21**	1c. purple	1·25	10
107		2c. green	1·50	10
107*a*		2c. black (1.3.41)	3·75	1·60
108		3c. black	1·25	10
108*a*		3c. green (1.3.41)	7·00	4·50
109		4c. bright purple	2·00	15
110		5c. violet	2·00	10
111		6c. carmine	2·75	60
111*a*		6c. lake-brown (1.3.41)	7·50	8·00
112		8c. red-brown	2·25	10
112*a*		8c. carmine (1.3.41)	8·00	10
113		10c. scarlet	3·25	40
114		12c. blue	3·00	25
114*a*		12c. orange (1.3.41)	6·00	4·75
115		15c. orange	6·00	10·00
115*a*		15c. blue (1.3.41)	8·50	15·00
116		20c. olive-green and carmine	5·50	1·25
117		25c. violet and orange	5·50	1·50
118		30c. red-brown and violet	5·50	2·50
119		50c. violet and scarlet	7·00	75
120		$1 scarlet and sepia	2·25	75
121		$2 bright purple and violet	18·00	18·00
122		$3 carmine and green	38·00	40·00
123		$4 blue and scarlet	38·00	65·00
124		$5 scarlet and red-brown	48·00	65·00
125		$10 black and yellow	26·00	70·00
106/25 *Set of* 26			£225	£275
106s/25s Perf "Specimen" *Set of* 26			£550	

For the 3c. green, wmkd Mult Script CA, see No. 152a.

BRITISH MILITARY ADMINISTRATION

Following the Japanese surrender, elements of the British Military Administration reached Kuching on 11 September 1945. From 5 November 1945 current Australian 1d., 3d., 6d. and 1s. stamps were made available for civilian use until replaced by Nos. 126/45. Other Australian stamps were also accepted as valid for postage during this period.

1945 (17 Dec). *Optd with T* **22**.

126	**21**	1c. purple	1·25	60
127		2c. black (R.)	2·25	1·25
		a. Opt double	£7500	£7500
128		3c. green	1·25	1·50
129		4c. bright purple	2·25	30
		a. Opt double, one albino	£2000	
130		5c. violet (R.)	3·25	1·00
131		6c. lake-brown	3·00	75
132		8c. carmine	13·00	14·00
133		10c. scarlet	1·50	70
134		12c. orange	2·50	3·75
135		15c. blue	5·50	40
136		20c. olive-green and carmine	3·00	2·75
137		25c. violet and orange (R.)	3·50	2·75
138		30c. red-brown and violet	6·50	2·75
139		50c. violet and scarlet	1·25	35
140		$1 scarlet and sepia	2·50	3·00
141		$2 bright purple and violet	9·00	15·00
142		$3 carmine and green	23·00	75·00
143		$4 blue and scarlet	26·00	50·00
144		$5 scarlet and red-brown	£160	£225
145		$10 black and yellow (R.)	£150	£225
126/45 *Set of* 20			£375	£550

These stamps, and the similarly overprinted stamps of North Borneo, were obtainable at all post offices throughout British Borneo (Brunei, Labuan, North Borneo and Sarawak), for use on local and overseas mail.

The administration of Sarawak was returned to the Brooke family on 15 April 1946, but the Rajah, after consulting the inhabitants, ceded the territory to Great Britain on 1 June 1946. Values from the 1934–41 issue were used until replaced by Nos. 150/64.

23 Sir James Brooke, Sir Charles Vyner Brooke and Sir Charles Brooke

(24)

(Recess B.W.)

1946 (18 May). *Centenary Issue.* P 12.

146	**23**	8c. lake	2·00	1·00
147		15c. blue	2·25	2·00
148		50c. black and scarlet	2·25	2·50
149		$1 black and sepia	2·50	26·00
146/9 *Set of* 4			8·00	28·00
146s/9s Perf "Specimen" *Set of* 4			£160	

CROWN COLONY

1947 (16 Apr). *Optd with T* **24**, *typo by B.W. in blue-black or red.* Wmk Mult Script CA. P 12.

150	**21**	1c. purple	20	30
151		2c. black (R.)	25	15
152		3c. green (R.)	25	15
		a. Albino opt	£6500	
153		4c. bright purple	25	15
154		6c. lake-brown	30	90
155		8c. carmine	1·00	10
156		10c. scarlet	30	20
157		12c. orange	50	1·00
158		15c. blue (R.)	50	40
159		20c. olive-green and carmine (R.)	2·00	50
160		25c. violet and orange (R.)	65	30
161		50c. violet and scarlet (R.)	1·25	40
162		$1 scarlet and sepia	1·50	90
163		$2 bright purple and violet	2·75	3·25
164		$5 scarlet and red-brown	3·00	3·25
150/64 *Set of* 15			13·00	10·50
150s/64s Perf "Specimen" *Set of* 15			£300	

No. 152a shows an uninked impression of T **24**.

1948 (25 Oct). *Royal Silver Wedding. As Nos. 112/13 of Antigua.*

165	8c. scarlet	30	30
166	$5 brown	40·00	45·00

1949 (10 Oct). *75th Anniv of U.P.U. As Nos. 114/17 of Antigua.*

167	8c. carmine	1·25	60
168	15c. deep blue	3·50	2·50
169	25c. deep blue-green	2·00	1·50
170	50c. violet	2·00	6·50
167/70 *Set of* 4		8·00	10·00

25 *Trogonoptera brookiana*

26 Western Tarsier

27 Kayan tomb

28 Kayan girl and boy

29 Bead work

30 Dyak dancer

31 Malayan Pangolin

32 Kenyan boys

33 Fire making

34 Kelemantan rice barn

35 Pepper vines

36 Iban woman

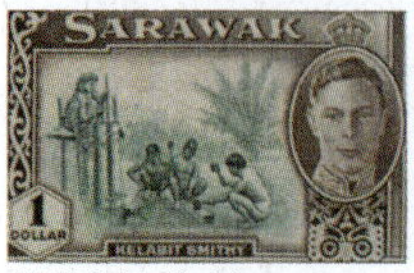

37 Kelabit Smithy

38 Map of Sawark

39 Arms of Sawark

(Recess; Arms typo B.W.)

1950 (3 Jan). *T* **25/39**. Wmk Mult Script CA. P 11½×11 (horiz) or 11×11½ (vert).

171	**25**	1c. black	40	30
172	**26**	2c. red-orange	30	40
173	**27**	3c. green	30	60
174	**28**	4c. chocolate	40	20
175	**29**	6c. turquoise-blue	40	15
176	**30**	8c. scarlet	70	30
177	**31**	10c. orange	1·75	4·50
178	**32**	12c. violet	3·50	1·50
179	**33**	15c. blue	2·50	15
180	**34**	20c. purple-brown and red-orange	2·50	30
181	**35**	25c. green and scarlet	3·50	30
182	**36**	50c. brown and violet	5·00	30
183	**37**	$1 green and chocolate	21·00	4·50
184	**38**	$2 blue and carmine	29·00	15·00
185	**39**	$5 black, yellow, red and puple	23·00	15·00
171/85 *Set of* 15			80.00	38.00

40 Map of Sarawak

(Recess B.W.)

1952 (1 Feb). Wmk Mult Script CA. P 11½×11.

186	**40**	10c. orange	1·75	50

1953 (3 June). *Coronation. As No. 152 of Johore.*

187	10c. black and deep violet-blue	1·25	1·50

41 Logging

44 Malabar Pied Hornbill

51 Queen Elizabeth II

52 Queen Elizabeth II (after Annigoni)

(Des M. Thoma (1, 2c.), R. Turrell (4c.), J. D. Hughes (6, 12c.) A. Hakim bin Moliti (8c.), J. Woodcock (10c.), J. Browning (15c.), G. Gundersen (20c.), K. Munich (25c.), Recess, Arms typo ($5). B.W.)

1955 (1 June)–**59**. *T* **41**, **44**, **51/2** *and similar designs.* Wmk Mult Script CA. P 11×11½ (1c., 2c., 4c.), 12×13 (30c., 50c., $1, $2) or 11½×11 (others).

188	**41**	1c. green (1.10.57)	10	30
189	–	2c. red-orange (1.10.57)	30	55
190	–	4c. lake-brown (1.10.57)	1·00	60
		a. *Brown-purple* (18.3.59)	9·00	6·50
191	**44**	6c. greenish blue (1.10.57)	3·25	3·00
192	–	8c. rose-red (1.10.57)	30	30
193	–	10c. deep green (1.10.57)	20	10
194	–	12c. plum (1.10.57)	3·75	55
195	–	15c. ultramarine (1.10.57)	1·00	30
196	–	20c. olive and brown (1.10.57)	1·00	10
197	–	25c. sepia and green (1.10.57)	6·50	20
198	**51**	30c. red-brown and deep lilac	7·50	30
199		50c. black and carmine (1.10.57)	2·50	30
200	**52**	$1 myrtle-green and orange-brown (1.10.57)	10·00	1·75
201		$2 violet and bronze-green (1.10.57)	17·00	3·75
202	–	$5 multicoloured (1.10.57)	24·00	16·00
188/202 *Set of* 15			70·00	25·00

Designs: *Horiz*—8c. Shield with spears; 10c. Kenyah ceremonial carving; 12c. Barong panau (sailing prau); 15c. Turtles; 20c. Melanau basket-making; 25c. Astana, Kuching; $5 Arms of Sarawak. *Vert* (as T **41**)—2c. Young Orang-Utan; 4c. Kayan dancing.

1963 (4 June). *Freedom from Hunger. As No. 407 of North Borneo.*

203	12c. sepia	1·50	1·00

STATE OF MALAYSIA

1964–65. *As 1955–57 but wmk w* **12**. Perfs as before.

204	**41**	1c. green (8.9.64)	10	75
205	–	2c. red-orange (17.8.65)	65	12·00
206	**44**	6c. greenish blue (8.9.64)	6·00	4·75
207	–	10c. deep green (8.9.64)	1·75	1·25
208	–	12c. plum (8.9.64)	2·25	9·50
209	–	15c. ultramarine (17.8.65)	1·25	14·00
210	–	20c. olive and brown (9.6.64)	50	1·00
211		25c. deep sepia and bluish green (8.9.64)	3·00	5·00
204/11 *Set of* 8			14·00	42·00

53 *Vanda hookeriana*

1965 (15 Nov). *As Nos. 166/72 of Johore but with Arms of Sarawak inset as in T* **53**.

212	1c. multicoloured	10	1·10
	c. Grey omitted	£100	
213	2c. multicoloured	30	2·00
	a. Black (country name and shield) omitted	£150	
	c. Yellow-olive (stems) omitted	£140	
214	5c. multicoloured	60	10
215	6c. multicoloured	60	2·00
	a. Black (country name and shield) omitted	£150	
216	10c. multicoloured	80	10
	a. Red omitted	£110	
217	15c. multicoloured	1·50	10
218	20c. multicoloured	2·00	50
212/18 *Set of 7*		5·25	5·25

The 1c., 6c., 10c. and 15c. exist with PVA gum as well as gum arabic.

No. 213a was formerly listed with Trengganu No. 101 but there is evidence that it was issued in Sarawak.

A used example of No. 218 is known with the bright purple (blooms) omitted.

The higher values used with this issue were Nos. 20/7 of Malaysia (National Issues).

JAPANESE OCCUPATION OF SARAWAK

Japanese forces landed in North Borneo on 16 December 1941 and Sarawak was attacked on 23 December 1941.

Brunei, North Borneo, Sarawak and after a short period, Labuan, were administered as a single territory by the Japanese. Until September–October 1942, previous stamp issues, without overprint, continued to be used in conjunction with existing postmarks. From 1 October 1942 onwards unoverprinted stamps of Japan were made available and examples can be found used from the area for much of the remainder of the War. Japanese Occupation issues for Brunei, North Borneo and Sarawak were equally valid throughout the combined territory but not, in practice, equally available.

PRICES FOR STAMPS ON COVER	
Nos. J1/21	*from* × 8
Nos. J22/6	—

(**1**) ("Imperial Japanese Government")

1942 (Oct). *Stamps of Sarawak handstamped with T* **1** *in violet.*

J1	**21**	1c. purple	32·00	80·00
		a. Pair, one without opt	£2750	
J2		2c. green	£130	£180
		a. Black opt	£110	
J3		2c. black	£120	£130
		a. Black opt	£180	£200
J4		3c. black	£425	£425
J5		3c. green	70·00	£100
		a. Black opt	£160	
J6		4c. bright purple	85·00	£100
		a. Black opt	£160	
J7		5c. violet	£100	£110
		a. Black opt	£160	
J8		6c. carmine	£160	£160
J9		6c. lake-brown	£100	£110
		a. Black opt	£150	£160
J10		8c. red-brown	£400	£400
		a. Black opt	£650	
J11		8c. carmine	75·00	£120
		a. Black opt	£300	£375
J12		10c. scarlet	95·00	£120
		a. Black opt	£160	
J13		12c. blue	£180	£190
		a. Black opt	£300	
J14		12c. orange	£180	£200
J15		15c. orange	£450	£450
		a. Black opt	£550	
J16		15c. blue	£130	£140
J17		20c. olive-green and carmine	75·00	£110
		a. Black opt	£160	
J18		25c. violet and orange	£120	£130
		a. Black opt	£170	
J19		30c. red-brown and violet	75·00	£110
		a. Black opt	£160	
J20		50c. violet and scarlet	70·00	£110
		a. Black opt	£300	
		b. Blue opt	£550	
J21		$1 scarlet and sepia	£120	£150
		a. Blue opt	£375	
J22		$2 bright purple and violet	£250	£325
		a. Blue opt	£425	
J23		$3 carmine and green	£2000	£2000
		a. Black opt	£2750	
J24		$4 blue and scarlet	£275	£400
J25		$5 scarlet and red-brown	£275	£400
J26		$10 black and yellow	£275	£400

The overprint, being handstamped, exists inverted or double on some values. Those on Nos. J20b, J21a and J22a are diagonal. The remainder are horizontal.

Stamps of T **21** optd with Japanese symbols within an oval frame are revenue stamps, while the same stamps overprinted with three Japanese characters between two vertical double rules, were used as seals.

"Nos. J1/26 have been extensively forged. Recent research indicates that complete or part sets on cover cancelled by Japanese circular postmarks in violet dated "17 11 21" (21 Nov 1942) or "18 3 1" (1 Mar 1943) have forged overprints."

Seychelles

Seychelles was administered as a dependency of Mauritius from 1810 until 1903, although separate stamp issues were provided from April 1890 onwards.

The first post office was opened, at Victoria on Mahé, on 11 December 1861 and the stamps of Mauritius were used there until 1890. No further post offices were opened until 1901.

Z 1

Stamps of MAURITIUS *cancelled with Type* Z **1**.

1848–59.

Z1	2d. blue (intermediate impression) (No. 14)	£11000

1859–61.

Z2	6d. blue (No. 32)	£900
Z3	6d. dull purple-slate (No. 33)	£2250
Z4	1s. vermilion (No. 34)	£1400

1860–63. *(Nos. 46/53).*

Z5	1d. purple-brown	£225
Z6	2d. blue	£275
Z7	4d. rose	£225
Z8	6d. green	£1000
Z9	6d. slate	£650
Z10	9d. dull purple	£120
Z11	1s. buff	£325
Z12	1s. green	£800

1862.

Z13	6d. slate (No. 54)	£800

1863–72. *(Nos. 56/72).*

Z14	1d. purple-brown	£120
Z14*a*	1d. brown	£100
Z15	1d. bistre	£110
Z16	2d. pale blue	£130
Z17	2d. bright blue	£130
Z18	3d. deep red	£160
Z19	3d. dull red	90·00
Z20	4d. rose	48·00
Z21	6d. dull violet	£250
Z22	6d. yellow-green	£110
Z23	6d. blue-green	75·00
Z24	9d. yellow-green	£1700
Z25	10d. maroon	£325
Z26	1s. yellow	£100
Z27	1s. blue	£300
Z28	1s. orange	£110
Z29	5s. rosy mauve	£950
Z30	5s. bright mauve	£950

1876. *(Nos. 76/7).*

Z31	½d. on 9d. dull purple	£325
Z32	½d. on 10d. maroon	£300

1877. *(Nos. 79/82).*

Z33	½d. on 10d. rose	£650
Z34	1d. on 4d. rose-carmine	
Z35	1s. on 5s. rosy mauve	
Z36	1s. on 5s. bright mauve	

1878. *(Nos. 83/91).*

Z37	2c. dull rose (lower label blank)	95·00
Z38	4c. on 1d. bistre	£375
Z39	8c. on 2d. blue	40·00
Z40	13c. on 3d. orange-red	£120
Z41	17c. on 4d. rose	40·00
Z42	25c. on 6d. slate-blue	£110
Z43	38c. on 9d. pale violet	£500
Z44	50c. on 1s. green	£110
Z45	2r.50 on 5s. bright mauve	£500

1879–80. *(Nos. 92/100).*

Z46	2c. Venetian red	£130
Z47	4c. orange	£130
Z48	8c. blue	40·00
Z49	13c. slate	£1400
Z50	17c. rose	90·00
Z51	25c. olive-yellow	£190
Z52	38c. bright purple	£1800
Z53	50c. green	£850
Z54	2r.50 brown-purple	£850

1883–90.

Z55	2c. Venetian red (No. 102)	95·00
Z56	2c. green (No. 103)	£200
Z57	4c. orange (No. 104)	65·00
Z58	4c. carmine (No. 105)	95·00
Z59	16c. chestnut (No. 109)	55·00
Z60	25c. olive-yellow (No. 110)	£110
Z61	50c. orange (No. 111)	£950

1883.

Z62	16c. on 17c. rose (No. 112)	£120

1883.

Z63	16c. on 17c. rose (No. 115)	45·00

1885.

Z64	2c. on 38c. bright purple (No. 116)	

1887.

Z65	2c. on 13c. slate (No. 117)	

POSTAL FISCAL

1889.

ZR1	4c. lilac (No. R2)	£1200

Mauritius stamps are occasionally found cancelled with the "SEYCHELLES" cds. Examples are known dated between 25 and 29 February 1884 when it seems that Type Z **1** may have been mislaid (*Price from* £425).

We no longer list the G.B. 1862 6d. lilac with this obliteration as there is no evidence that the stamps of Great Britain were sold by the Victoria post office.

PRICES FOR STAMPS ON COVER TO 1945

Nos. 1/8	*from* × 20
Nos. 9/24	*from* × 30
No. 25	*from* × 10
No. 26	*from* × 20
No. 27	*from* × 10
Nos. 28/32	*from* × 20
No. 33	*from* × 5
No. 34	*from* × 30
Nos. 35/6	—
Nos. 37/40	*from* × 40
Nos. 41/2	*from* × 25
Nos. 43/5	*from* × 10
Nos. 46/50	*from* × 30
Nos. 51/4	*from* × 10
Nos. 55/6	—
Nos. 57/9	*from* × 10
Nos. 60/7	*from* × 20
Nos. 68/70	—
Nos. 71/81	*from* × 10
Nos. 82/131	*from* × 5
Nos. 132/4	*from* × 10
Nos. 135/49	*from* × 3

(Currency: 100 cents = 1 Mauritius, later Seychelles rupee)

DEPENDENCY OF MAURITIUS

PRINTERS. Nos. 1 to 123 were typographed by De La Rue & Co.

1

Die I

Die II

In Die I there are lines of shading in the middle compartment of the diadem which are absent from Die II.

Normal

Malformed "S"

Repaired "S"

The malformed "S" occurs on R. 7/3 of the left pane from Key Plate 2. It is believed that the repair to it took place in mid-1898. Both states may occur on other stamps in Types **1** and **4**. Stamps subsequently printed from Key Plate 3 showed the "S" normal.

1890 (5 April)–**92**. Wmk Crown CA. P 14.

(i) Die I.

1	1	2c. green and carmine	4·00	12·00
2		4c. carmine and green	32·00	13·00
3		8c. brown-purple and blue	12·00	3·50
4		10c. ultramarine and brown	8·00	24·00
5		13c. grey and black	6·00	13·00
6		16c. chestnut and blue	8·00	4·25
7		48c. ochre and green	20·00	10·00
8		96c. mauve and carmine	65·00	48·00
1/8 *Set of* 8			£140	£110
1s/8s Optd "Specimen" *Set of* 8			£190	

(ii) Die II (1892).

9	1	2c. green and rosine	2·50	1·00
10		4c. carmine and green	2·50	1·75
11		8c. brown-purple and ultramarine	10·00	1·75
12		10c. bright ultramarine and brown	11·00	3·25
		a. Malformed "S"		
13		13c. grey and black	3·25	1·75
14		16c. chestnut and ultramarine	42·00	11·00
		a. Malformed "S"		
9/14 *Set of* 6			65·00	18·00

The 10c. Die I also exists in ultramarine and chestnut, but has so far only been found with "SPECIMEN" overprint (*Price* £750).

3
cents
(2)

18 CENTS
(3)

4

1893 (1 Jan). *Surch locally as T* **2**.

15		3c. on 4c. (No. 10)	1·10	1·50
		a. Surch inverted	£300	£375
		b. Surch double	£475	
		c. Surch omitted (in horiz pair with normal)	£13000	
16		12c. on 16c. (No. 6)	3·00	3·75
		a. Surch inverted	£475	
		b. Surch double	£15000	£9000
17		12c. on 16c. (No. 14)	18·00	2·50
		a. Surch double	£4500	£4500
		b. Surch omitted (in pair with normal)		
18		15c. on 16c. (No. 6)	10·00	13·00
		a. Surch inverted	£325	£300
		b. Surch double	£1300	£1300
19		15c. on 16c. (No. 14)	18·00	3·00
		a. Surch inverted	£900	£1000
		b. Surch double	£700	£750
		c. Surch triple	£4250	
20		45c. on 48c. (No. 7)	30·00	5·50
21		90c. on 96c. (No. 8)	60·00	35·00
		a. Wide "O" (3½ mm wide instead of 3 mm) (R. 1/1, 2/1 of setting)	£325	£300
15/21 *Set of* 7			£130	60·00

Nos. 15/21 were each produced from settings of 30.

Nos. 15, 16, 18, 19 and 20 exist with "cents" omitted and with "cents" above value due to misplacement of the surcharge.

Some examples of No. 15b occur in the same sheet as No. 15c with the double surcharge on stamps from the last vertical row of the left pane and the surcharge omitted on stamps from the last vertical row of the right pane.

Most examples of the inverted surcharge error No. 16a were officially defaced with a red vertical ink line (*Price* £200, *unused*). Similarly examples of No. 19a exist defaced with a horizontal ink line (*Price* £400, *unused*).

1893 (Nov). *New values. Die II.* Wmk Crown CA. P 14.

22	1	3c. dull purple and orange	1·50	50
23		12c. sepia and green	2·50	60
24		15c. sage-green and lilac	4·50	2·00
25		45c. brown and carmine	23·00	35·00
22/5 *Set of* 4			28·00	35·00
22s/5s Optd "Specimen" *Set of* 4			95·00	

1896 (1 Aug). *No. 25 surch locally as T* **3**.

26	1	18c. on 45c. brown and carmine	7·00	2·75
		a. Surch double	£1400	£1400
		b. Surch triple	£2000	
27		36c. on 45c. brown and carmine	8·50	55·00
		a. Surch double	£1700	
26s/7s Optd "Specimen" *Set of* 2			70·00	

1897–1900. *Colours changed and new values. Die II.* Wmk Crown CA. P 14.

28	1	2c. orange-brown and green (1900)	2·00	1·25
		a. Repaired "S"	£325	£300
29		6c. carmine (1900)	3·50	50
		a. Repaired "S"	£400	£300
30		15c. ultramarine (1900)	8·00	4·00
		a. Repaired "S"	£450	£350
31		18c. ultramarine	7·50	1·25
32		36c. brown and carmine	32·00	4·50
33	4	75c. yellow and violet (1900)	55·00	70·00
		a. Repaired "S"	£650	
34		1r. bright mauve and deep red	13·00	4·75
35		1r.50 grey and carmine (1900)	85·00	90·00
		a. Repaired "S"	£700	£900
36		2r.25 bright mauve and green (1900)	£110	85·00
		a. Repaired "S"	£900	
28/36 *Set of* 9			£275	£250
28s/36s Optd "Specimen" *Set of* 9			£250	

3 cents

(5)

6 cents
(5a)

1901 (21 June–Oct). *Surch locally with T* **5** *or* **5a**.

37		3c. on 10c. bright ultramarine and brown (No. 12) (9.01)	1·50	60
		a. Surch double	£900	
		b. Surch triple	£3000	
		c. Malformed "S"	£275	
38		3c. on 16c. chestnut and ultramarine (No. 14) (8.01)	3·50	5·50
		a. Surch inverted	£700	£700
		b. Surch double	£500	£550
		c. "3 cents" omitted	£550	£550
		d. Malformed "S"	£325	£375
39		3c. on 36c. brown and carmine (No. 32)	80	80
		a. Surch double	£750	£850
		b. "3 cents" omitted	£650	£700
40		6c. on 8c. brown-purple and ultramarine (No. 11) (7.01)	3·00	3·00
		a. Surch inverted	£650	£750
37/40 *Set of* 4			8·00	9·00
37s/40s H/S "Specimen" *Set of* 4			£100	

1902 (June). *Surch locally as T* **5**.

41	1	2c. on 4c. carmine and green (No. 10)	2·00	2·75
42	4	30c. on 75c. yellow and violet (No. 33)	1·75	4·25
		a. Narrow "0" in "30" (R. 3/6, 5/2-4)	8·00	45·00
		b. Repaired "S"	£325	

43		30c. on 1r. bright mauve and deep red (No. 34)	9·00	35·00
		a. Narrow "0" in "30" (R. 3/6, 5/2-4)	26·00	90·00
		b. Surch double	£1500	
44		45c. on 1r. bright mauve and deep red (No. 34)	4·00	38·00
45		45c. on 2r.25 bright mauve and green (No. 36)	45·00	£100
		a. Narrow "5" in "45" (R. 4/1)	£200	£375
		b. Repaired "S"	£700	£1000
41/5 *Set of 5*			55·00	£160
41s/5s Optd "Specimen" *Set of 5*			£130	

6

7

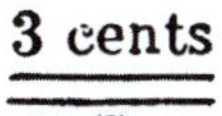

(8)

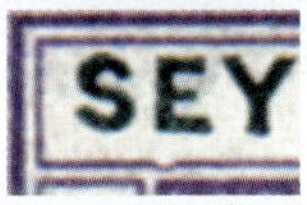
Dented frame (R. 1/6 of left pane)

1903 (26 May). Wmk Crown CA. P 14.

46	6	2c. chestnut and green	1·75	2·00
		a. Dented frame	£130	£160
47		3c. dull green	1·00	1·25
		a. Dented frame	£110	£140
48		6c. carmine	2·75	1·25
		a. Dented frame	£180	£150
49		12c. olive-sepia and dull green	2·75	2·50
		a. Dented frame	£180	£190
50		15c. ultramarine	4·00	2·50
		a. Dented frame	£250	£190
51		18c. sage-green and carmine	4·25	5·50
		a. Dented frame	£250	£325
52		30c. violet and dull green	7·00	11·00
		a. Dented frame	£300	£450
53		45c. brown and carmine	7·00	11·00
		a. Dented frame	£350	£450
		w. Wmk inverted	£375	£450
54	7	75c. yellow and violet	10·00	28·00
		a. Dented frame	£400	
55		1r.50 black and carmine	50·00	70·00
		a. Dented frame	£750	£950
56		2r.25 purple and green	35·00	85·00
		a. Dented frame	£700	£1000
46/56 *Set of 11*			£110	£200
46s/56s Optd "Specimen" *Set of 11*			£200	

1903. *Surch locally with T* **8**.

57	6	3c. on 15c. ultramarine (3.7)	1·00	3·25
		a. Dented frame	£200	
58		3c. on 18c. sage-green and carmine (2.9)	2·75	40·00
		a. Dented frame	£300	£850
59		3c. on 45c. brown and carmine (21.7)	3·00	3·25
		a. Dented frame	£300	
57/9 *Set of 3*			6·00	42·00
57s/9s H/S "Specimen" *Set of 3*			80·00	

CROWN COLONY

The Seychelles became a Separate Crown Colony by Letters Patent dated 31 August 1903.

1906. Wmk Mult Crown CA. P 14.

60	6	2c. chestnut and green	1·50	4·25
		a. Dented frame	£110	£190
61		3c. dull green	1·50	1·50
		a. Dented frame	£130	£150
62		6c. carmine	2·00	80
		a. Dented frame	£160	£120
63		12c. olive-sepia and dull green	3·00	3·25
		a. Dented frame	£200	£250
64		15c. ultramarine	3·00	2·00
		a. Dented frame	£190	£180
65		18c. sage-green and carmine	3·00	6·50
		a. Dented frame	£190	£325
66		30c. violet and dull green	6·00	8·00
		a. Dented frame	£250	£375
67		45c. brown and carmine	3·00	7·00
		a. Dented frame	£300	£375
68	7	75c. yellow and violet	8·50	55·00
		a. Dented frame	£400	
69		1r.50 black and carmine	55·00	60·00
		a. Dented frame	£750	£800
70		2r.25 purple and green	38·00	65·00
		a. Dented frame	£700	
60/70 *Set of 11*			£110	£190

9

10

Split "A"

1912 (Apr)–**16**. Wmk Mult Crown CA. P 14.

71	9	2c. chestnut and green	70	5·50
		a. Split "A"	95·00	£225
72		3c. green	3·00	60
		a. Split "A"	£130	£100
73		6c. Carmine-red (6.13)	4·25	1·00
		a. Aniline-carmine (1916)	13·00	4·50
		b. Split "A"	£200	£100
74		12c. olive-sepia and dull green (1.13)	1·25	4·00
		a. Split "A"	£140	£225
75		15c. ultramarine	3·75	1·50
		a. Split "A"	£200	£130
76		18c. sage-green and carmine (1.13)	3·25	6·50
		a. Split "A"	£180	£325
77		30c. violet and green (1.13)	7·00	1·25
		a. Split "A"	£275	£150
78		45c. brown and carmine (1.13)	2·75	40·00
		a. Split "A"	£200	
79	10	75c. yellow and violet (1.13)	2·75	5·50
		a. Split "A"	£225	£325
80		1r.50 black and carmine (1.13)	7·50	1·00
		a. Split "A"	£375	£130
81		2r.25 deep magenta and green (*shades*) (1.13)	60·00	2·50
		a. Split "A"	£750	£200
71/81 *Set of 11*			85·00	60·00
71s/81s Optd "Specimen" *Set of 11*			£225	

11

12

13

1917–22. *Die I. Chalk-surfaced paper (18c. to 5r.).* Wmk Mult Crown CA. P 14.

82	11	2c. chestnut and green	50	2·75
83		3c. green	2·00	1·25
84	12	5c. deep brown (1920)	2·25	7·00
85	11	6c. carmine	2·75	1·00
		a. Rose (1919)	5·50	2·50
86		12c. grey (1919)	1·75	1·00
87		15c. ultramarine	1·75	1·50
88		18c. purple/*yellow* (1919)	3·50	30·00
		a. On orange-buff (1920)	14·00	55·00
		b. On buff (1920)		
		c. Die II. *On pale yellow* (1922)	1·25	19·00
89	13	25c. black and red/*buff* (1920)	1·75	38·00
		a. On orange buff (1920)	40·00	75·00
		b. Die II. *On pale yellow* (1922)	1·75	10·00
90	11	30c. dull purple and olive (1918)	1·50	9·00
91		45c. dull purple and orange (1919)	3·00	35·00
92	13	50c. dull purple and black (1920)	6·00	35·00
93		75c. black/*blue-green* (*olive back*) (1918)	1·60	18·00
		a. Die II. *On emerald back* (1922)	1·40	20·00
94		1r. dull purple and red (1920)	12·00	50·00
95		1r.50 reddish purple and blue/*blue* (1918)	9·00	50·00
		a. Die II. *Blue-purple and blue/blue* (1922)	16·00	32·00
96		2r.25 yellow-green and violet (1918)	50·00	£140
97		5r. green and blue (1920)	£100	£250
82/97 *Set of 16*			£170	£550
82s/97s Optd "Specimen" *Set of 16*			£300	

Examples of most values are known showing forged postmarks. These include part strikes of Seychelles postmarks dated "24 AP 93" and "AU 6 1903", and Victoria postmarks dated "NO 27" or "MY 6 35".

1921–32. *Die II. Chalk-surfaced paper (18c. and 25c. to 5r.).* Wmk Mult Script CA. P 14.

98	11	2c. chestnut and green	25	15
99		3c. green	1·75	15
100		3c. black (1922)	1·00	30
101		4c. green (1922)	1·00	2·50
102		4c. sage-green and carmine (1928)	6·50	17·00
103	12	5c. deep brown	75	5·50
104	11	6c. carmine	2·75	9·00
		w. Wmk inverted	£180	
105		6c. deep mauve (1922)	1·25	10
106	13	9c. red (1927)	3·25	4·25
107	11	12c. grey	2·75	20
		a. Die I (1932)	17·00	65
108		12c. carmine-red (1922)	1·50	30
110		15c. bright blue	2·00	55·00
111		15c. yellow (1922)	1·00	2·75
112		18c. purple/*pale yellow* (1925)	2·50	12·00
113	13	20c. bright blue (1922)	1·50	35
		a. Dull blue (1924)	8·00	55
114		25c. black and red/*pale yellow* (1925)	2·75	19·00
115	11	30c. dull purple and olive	1·25	15·00
		w. Wmk inverted		
116		45c. dull purple and orange	1·25	5·00
117	13	50c. dull purple and black	2·50	2·25
118		75c. black/*emerald* (1924)	8·00	22·00
119		1r. dull purple and red	17·00	18·00
		a. Die I (1932)	12·00	35·00
121		1r.50 purple and blue/*blue* (1924)	14·00	22·00
122		2r.25 yellow-green and violet	16·00	14·00
123		5r. yellow-green and blue	95·00	£170
98/123 *Set of 24*			£160	£350
98s/123s Optd "Specimen" *Set of 24*			£400	

The 3c. green and 12c. grey (Die II) were reissued in 1927. "Specimen" overprints on these printings are 15.5×1.75 mm instead of the 14.5×2.5 mm of the original issue. (*Price*, 3c. £450, 12c. £110).

Examples of most values are known showing the forged postmarks mentioned above.

1935 (6 May). *Silver Jubilee. As Nos. 91/4 of Antigua, but ptd by B.W.* P 11×12.

128		6c. ultramarine and grey-black	1·25	2·00
		a. Extra flagstaff	£225	£375
		b. Short extra flagstaff	£250	£350
		c. Lightning conductor	£350	
		d. Flagstaff on right-hand turret	£400	£400
		e. Double flagstaff	£425	£425
129		12c. green and indigo	4·00	1·50
		a. Extra flagstaff	£3500	£3750
		b. Short extra flagstaff	£375	£275
		c. Lightning conductor	£2500	
		d. Flagstaff on right-hand turret	£600	£600
		e. Double flagstaff	£600	£600
130		20c. brown and deep blue	2·75	3·50
		a. Extra flagstaff	£350	£450
		b. Short extra flagstaff	£300	
		c. Lightning conductor	£450	£475
		d. Flagstaff on right-hand turret	£475	£550
		e. Double flagstaff	£475	
131		1r. slate and purple	7·50	20·00
		a. Extra flagstaff	£190	£350
		b. Short extra flagstaff	£400	
		c. Lightning conductor	£300	
		d. Flagstaff on right-hand turret	£550	
128/31 *Set of 4*			14·00	24·00
128s/31s Perf "Specimen" *Set of 4*			£150	

For illustrations of plate varieties see Omnibus section following Zanzibar.

Examples are known showing forged Victoria "B MY 6 35" postmarks.

1937 (12 May). *Coronation. As Nos. 95/7 of Antigua.*

132		6c. sage-green	45	15
133		12c. orange	65	50
134		20c. blue	70	1·00
132/4 *Set of 3*			1·60	1·50
132s/4s Perf "Specimen" *Set of 3*			90·00	

14 Coco-de-mer Palm

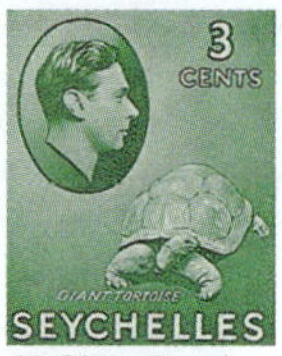

15 Giant Tortoise

16 Fishing Pirogue

"Handkerchief" on oar flaw (R. 6/2)

(Photo Harrison)

1938 (1 Jan)–**49**. Wmk Mult Script CA. *Chalk-surfaced paper.* P 14½×13½ (vert) or 13½×14½ (horiz).

135	14	2c. purple-brown (10.2.38)	1·50	40
		a. Ordinary paper (18.11.42)	30	1·75
136	15	3c. green	8·50	2·00
136*a*		3c. orange (8.8.41)	1·25	1·00
		ab. Ordinary paper (18.11.42)	55	1·50
137	16	6c. orange	12·00	3·50
137*a*		6c. greyish green (8.8.41)	4·00	1·25
		aw. Wmk inverted	£1100	
		b. Ordinary paper. *Green* (18.11.42)	55	2·25
		c. Green (5.4.49)	8·00	1·25
138	14	9c. scarlet (10.2.38)	14·00	2·75
138*a*		9c. grey-blue (8.8.41)	15·00	40
		ab. Ordinary paper (18.11.42)	15·00	1·50
		ac. Ordinary paper. *Dull blue* (19.11.45)	6·50	3·00
		ad. Dull blue (5.4.49)	18·00	6·00
		aw. Wmk inverted		
139	15	12c. reddish violet	48·00	1·25
139*a*		15c. brown-carmine (8.8.41)	19·00	40
		ab. Ordinary paper. *Brown-red* (18.11.42)	6·50	3·75
139*c*	14	18c. carmine-lake (8.8.41)	10·00	60
		ca. Ordinary paper (18.11.42)	7·00	2·75
		cb. Rose-carmine (5.4.49)	22·00	12·00
140	16	20c. blue	42·00	6·00
140*a*		20c. brown-ochre (8.8.41)	14·00	65
		ab. "Handkerchief" flaw		
		b. Ordinary paper (18.11.42)	2·50	3·00
		ba. "Handkerchief" flaw	£160	£100
141	14	25c. brown-ochre	50·00	14·00
142	15	30c. carmine (10.2.38)	50·00	10·00
142*a*		30c. blue (8.8.41)	15·00	50
		ab. Ordinary paper (18.11.42)	2·25	4·50
143	16	45c. chocolate (10.2.38)	21·00	2·50
		a. Ordinary paper. *Purple-brown* (18.11.42)	2·75	2·00
		b. Purple-brown (5.4.49)	25·00	13·00
144	14	50c. deep reddish violet (10.2.38)	13·00	60
		a. Ordinary paper (18.11.42)	1·75	3·25
144*b*		50c. bright lilac (13.6.49)	3·50	2·50
145	15	75c. slate-blue (10.2.38)	85·00	40·00
145*a*		75c. deep slate-lilac (8.8.41)	16·00	4·00
		ab. Ordinary paper (18.11.42)	2·50	4·00
146	16	1r. yellow-green (10.2.38)	£100	60·00
146*a*		1r. grey-black (8.8.41)	28·00	3·25
		ab. Ordinary paper (18.11.42)	2·00	4·00
147	14	1r.50 ultramarine (10.2.38)	26·00	4·50
		a. Ordinary paper (18.11.42)	4·50	9·50
		aw. Wmk inverted	£2750	
148	15	2r.25 olive (10.2.38)	50·00	11·00
		a. Ordinary paper (18.11.42)	24·00	25·00

149	**16**	5r. red (10.2.38)	17·00	9·00
		a. Ordinary paper (18.11.42)	23·00	32·00
135/49 *Set of* 25			£450	£160
135s/49s (*ex* 50c. bright lilac) Perf "Specimen" *Set of* 24			£550	

Examples of most values are known showing forged Victoria postmarks dated "NO 27", "SP 17 41", "DE 12 41", "SP 14 42", "DE 21 42" or "NO 16 43".

Lamp on mast flaw (R. 1/5)

1946 (23 Sept). *Victory. As Nos. 110/11 of Antigua.*

150	9c. light blue	10	10
151	30c. deep blue	30	20
	a. Lamp on mast flaw	30·00	
150s/1s Perf "Specimen" *Set of* 2		80·00	

Line by crown (R. 1/3)

1948 (5 Nov). *Royal Silver Wedding. As Nos 112/13 of Antigua.*

152	9c. ultramarine	15	60
	a. Line by crown	30·00	
153	5r. carmine	13·00	35·00

Examples are known showing forged Victoria "C 11 NOV 48" postmarks.

1949 (10 Oct). *75th Anniv of U.P.U. As Nos 1141/17 of Antigua, but inscribed "SEYCHELLES" in recess.*

154	18c. bright reddish purple	20	25
155	50c. purple	1·75	1·50
156	1r. grey	50	25
157	2r.25 olive	35	1·25
154/7 *Set of* 4		2·50	3·00

17 Sailfish

18 Map of Indian Ocean

(Photo Harrison)

1952 (3 Mar). *Various designs as T* **14/16** *but with new portrait and crown as in T* **17/18**. *Chalk-surfaced paper.* Wmk Mult Script CA. P 14½×13½ (vert) or 13½×14½ (horiz).

158	**17**	2c. lilac	60	70
		a. Error. Crown missing, W **9a**	£700	
		b. Error. St. Edward's Crown, W **9b**	£130	£180
159	**15**	3c. orange	60	30
		a. Error. Crown missing, W **9a**	£550	£550
		b. Error. St. Edward's Crown, W **9b**	£160	£160
160	**14**	9c. chalky blue	60	1·75
		a. Error. Crown missing, W **9a**	£1100	
		b. Error. St. Edward's Crown, W **9b**	£275	£350
161	**16**	15c. deep yellow-green	50	75
		a. Error. Crown missing, W **9a**	£700	
		b. Error. St. Edward's Crown, W **9b**	£250	£300
162	**18**	18c. carmine-lake	1·50	20
		a. Error. Crown missing, W **9a**	£1000	
		b. Error. St. Edward's Crown, W **9b**	£325	£275
163	**16**	20c. orange-yellow	1·25	1·50
		a. Error. Crown missing, W **9a**	£1200	£1000
		b. Error. St. Edward's Crown, W **9b**	£400	£425
164	**15**	25c. vermilion	70	1·75
		a. Error. Crown missing, W **9a**	£1400	
		b. Error. St. Edward's Crown, W **9b**	£400	
165	**17**	40c. ultramarine	1·00	1·50
		a. Error. Crown missing, W **9a**	£1500	
		b. Error. St. Edward's Crown, W **9b**	£650	
166	**16**	45c. purple-brown	1·00	30
		a. Error. Crown missing, W **9a**	£1500	
		b. Error. St. Edward's Crown, W **9b**	£475	£475
167	**14**	50c. reddish violet	1·25	1·75
		a. Error. Crown missing, W **9a**	£1600	£1500
		b. Error. St. Edward's Crown, W **9b**	£550	£650
168	**18**	1r. grey-black	3·75	3·50
		b. Error. St. Edward's Crown, W **9b**	£1300	
169	**14**	1r.50 blue	8·50	14·00
		b. Error. St. Edward's Crown, W **9b**	£2500	
170	**15**	2r.25 brown-olive	14·00	15·00
		b. Error. St. Edward's Crown, W **9b**	£1400	
171	**18**	5r. red	15·00	16·00
		b. Error. St. Edward's Crown, W **9b**	£1100	
172	**17**	10r. green	23·00	42·00
158/72 *Set of* 15			65·00	90·00

See *Introduction* re the watermark errors.

1953 (2 June). *Coronation. As No. 120 of Antigua.*

173	9c. black and deep bright blue	60	70

19 Sailfish

20 Seychelles Flying Fox

(Photo Harrison)

1954 (1 Feb)–**61**. *Designs previously used for King George VI issue, but with portrait of Queen Elizabeth II, as in T* **19** *and T* **20**. *Chalk-surfaced paper.* Wmk Mult Script CA. P 14½×13½ (vert) or 13½×14½ (horiz).

174	**19**	2c. lilac	10	10
175	**15**	3c. orange	10	10
175*a*	**20**	5c. violet (25.10.57)	2·25	30
176	**14**	9c. chalky blue	10	10
176*a*		10c. chalky blue (15.9.56)	50	2·25
		ab. Blue (11.7.61)	11·00	5·00
177	**16**	15c. deep yellow-green	1·50	30
178	**18**	18c. crimson	10	10
179	**16**	20c. orange-yellow	1·25	20
180	**15**	25c. vermilion	1·25	1·00
180*a*	**18**	35c. crimson (15.9.56)	5·00	1·75
181	**19**	40c. ultramarine	50	25
182	**16**	45c. purple-brown	20	15
183	**14**	50c. reddish violet	30	80
183*a*	**16**	70c. purple-brown (15.9.56)	6·00	2·00
184	**18**	1r. grey-black	1·00	40
185	**14**	1r.50 blue	5·00	8·50
186	**15**	2r.25 brown-olive	4·00	8·00
187	**18**	5r. red	18·00	9·00
188	**19**	10r. green	28·00	18·00
174/88 *Set of* 19			65·00	45·00

21 "La Pierre de Possession"

5
cents
(22)

(Photo Harrison)

1956 (15 Nov). *Bicentenary of "La Pierre de Possession".* Wmk Mult Script CA. P 14½×13½.

189	**21**	40c. ultramarine	15	15
190		1r. black	15	15

e	e	s	s	c	c
191	191a	191	191b	191	191c

1957 (16 Sept). *No. 182 surch with T* **22**.

191	5c. on purple-brown 45c.	15	10
	a. Italic "e"	7·50	7·50
	b. Italic "s"	4·75	4·75
	c. Italic "c"	3·75	3·75
	d. Thick bars omitted	£900	
	e. Surch double	£500	

There were two settings of this surcharge. The first setting contained No. 191a on R. 3/1, No. 191b on R. 5/3, No. 191c on R. 6/1 and 9/2, and No. 191d on R. 5/2. Nos. 191a and 191d did not occur on the second setting which shows No. 191b on R. 1/4, and No. 191c on R. 5/1 and R. 10/4.

23 Mauritius 6d. Stamp with Seychelles "B 64" Cancellation

(Recess: cancellation typo B.W.)

1961 (11 Dec). *Centenary of First Seychelles Post Office.* W w **12**. P 11½.

193	**23**	10c. blue, black and purple	25	10
194		35c. blue, black and myrtle-green	40	10
195		2r.25 blue, black and orange-brown	70	45
193/5 *Set of* 3			1·25	50

24 Black Parrot

29 Anse Royale Bay

40 Colony's Badge

(Des V. Whiteley. Photo Harrison)

1962 (21 Feb)–**68**. *T* **24**, **29**, **40** *and similar designs.* W w **12** (upright). P 13½×14½ (horiz designs and 10r.) or 14½×13½ (others).

196	5c. multicoloured	3·25	10
197	10c. multicoloured	1·50	10
198	15c. multicoloured	30	10
199	20c. multicoloured	30	10
200	25c. multicoloured	30	10
200*a*	30c. multicoloured (15.7.68)	6·50	5·00
201	35c. multicoloured	1·75	1·50
202	40c. multicoloured	20	1·50
203	45c. multicoloured (1.8.66)	3·50	5·00
204	50c. multicoloured	40	25
205	70c. ultramarine and light blue	6·00	3·00
206	75c. multicoloured (1.8.66)	2·25	4·25
207	1r. multicoloured	1·00	10
208	1r.50 multicoloured	5·50	6·50
209	2r.25 multicoloured	5·50	7·50
210	3r.50 multicoloured	2·25	6·50
211	5r. multicoloured	3·50	2·50
212	10r. multicoloured	12·00	4·00
196/212 *Set of* 18		48·00	42·00

Designs: *Vert* (*as T* **24**)—10c. Vanilla vine; 15c. Fisherman; 20c. Denis Island lighthouse; 25c. Clock Tower, Victoria; 50c. Cascade Church; 70c. Sailfish; 75c. Coco-de-Mer palm. *Horiz* (*as T* **29**)—30c.35c. Anse Royale Bay; 40c. Government House; 45c. Fishing pirogue; 1r. Cinnamon; 1r.50, Copra; 2r.25, Map; 3r.50, Land settlement; 5r. Regina Mundi Convent.

The 1r. exists with PVA gum as well as gum arabic, but the 30c. exists with PVA gum only.

See also Nos. 233/7.

For stamps of the above issue overprinted "B.I.O.T." see under British Indian Ocean Territory.

1963 (4 June). *Freedom from Hunger. As No. 146 of Antigua.*

213	70c. reddish violet	60	25

1963 (16 Sept). *Red Cross Centenary. As Nos. 147/8 of Antigua.*

214	10c. red and black	20	10
215	75c. red and blue	50	60

45
CENTS
(41)

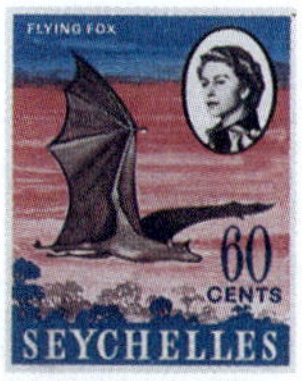

42 Seychelles Flying Fox

1965 (15 Apr). *Nos. 201 and 205 surch as T* **41**.

216	45c. on 35c. multicoloured	10	15
217	75c. on 70c. ultramarine and light blue	20	15

1965 (1 June). *I.T.U. Centenary. As Nos. 166/7 of Antigua.*

218	5c. orange and ultramarine	10	10
219	1r.50 mauve and apple-green	50	25

1965 (25 Oct). *International Co-operation Year. As Nos. 168/9 of Antigua.*

220	5c. reddish purple and turquoise-green	15	10
221	40c. deep bluish green and lavender	35	30

1966 (24 Jan). *Churchill Commemoration. As Nos. 170/3 of Antigua.*

222	5c. new blue	15	50
223	15c. deep green	40	10
224	75c. brown	1·00	25
225	1r.50 bluish violet	1·25	2·00
222/5 *Set of* 4		2·50	2·50

(Des V. Whiteley. Litho Harrison)

1966 (1 July). *World Cup Football Championship. As Nos. 176/7 of Antigua.*

226	15c. violet, yellow-green, lake and yellow-brown	20	25
	a. "50 c GRENADA" on front of stamp	£225	
227	1r. chocolate, blue-green, lake and yellow-brown	35	40

No. 226a shows a positive offset of the Grenada duty plate from the blanket on the front and a negative offset on the reverse.

Des M. Goaman. Litho Harrison.

1966 (20 Sept). *Inauguration of W.H.O. Headquarters, Geneva. As Nos. 178/9 of Antigua.*

228	20c. black, yellow-green and light blue	20	10
229	50c. black, light purple and yellow-brown	40	20

1966 (1 Dec). *20th Anniv of U.N.E.S.C.O. As Nos. 196/8 of Antigua.*

230	15c. slate-violet, red, yellow and orange	20	10
231	1r. orange-yellow, violet and deep olive	35	10
232	5r. black, bright purple and orange	80	1·00
230/2 *Set of* 3		1·25	1·00

1967–69. *As Nos. 196/7, 204 and new values as T* **42** *but* wmk w **12** (sideways).

233	5c. multicoloured (7.2.67)	35	2·25
234	10c. multicoloured (4.6.68)	30	15
235	50c. multicoloured (13.5.69)	1·75	3·75
236	60c. red, blue and blackish brown (15.7.68)	1·75	45
237	85c. ultramarine and light blue (as No. 205) (15.7.68)	1·00	40
233/7	*Set of* 5	4·50	6·50

The 10c. exists with PVA gum as well as gum arabic, but the 50c. to 85c. exist with PVA gum only.

UNIVERSAL
ADULT
SUFFRAGE
1967
(43)

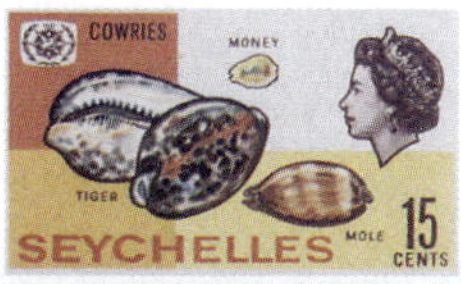

44 Money Cowrie, Mole Cowrie and Tiger Cowrie

1967 (18 Sept). *Universal Adult Suffrage. As Nos. 198 and 206, but* W w **12** (sideways), *and Nos. 203 and 210 (wmk upright), optd with T* **43**.

238	15c. multicoloured	10	10
	a. Opt double		
239	45c. multicoloured	10	10
240	75c. multicoloured	10	10
241	3r.50 multicoloured	20	50
238/41	*Set of* 4	30	65

(Des V. Whiteley. Photo Harrison)

1967 (4 Dec). *International Tourist Year. T* **44** *and similar horiz designs. Multicoloured.* W w **12**. P 14×13.

242	15c. Type **44**	20	10
243	40c. Beech Cone, Textile or Cloth of Gold Cone and Virgin Cone	25	10
244	1r. Arthritic Spider Conch	35	10
245	2r.25 Subulate Auger and Trumpet Triton Shells	60	1·25
242/5	*Set of* 4	1·25	1·25

= 30
(48)

49 Farmer with Wife and Children at Sunset

1968 (16 Apr). *Nos. 202/3 and as No. 206 surch as T* **48** *(30c.) or with "CENTS" added, and three bars (others).* W w **12** (sideways on No. 248)

246	30c. on 40c. multicoloured	10	20
247	60c. on 45c. multicoloured	15	20
248	85c. on 75c. multicoloured	20	25
246/8	*Set of* 3	40	60

(Des Mary Hayward. Litho Harrison)

1968 (2 Sept). *Human Rights Year.* W w **12**. P 14½×13½.

249	**49**	20c. multicoloured	10	10
250		50c. multicoloured	10	10
251		85c. multicoloured	10	10
252		2r.25 multicoloured	25	1·60
249/52		*Set of* 4	40	1·60

50 Expedition landing at Anse Possession

54 Apollo Launch

(Des Mary Hayward. Litho and die-stamped Harrison)

1968 (30 Dec). *Bicentenary of First Landing on Praslin. T* **50** *and similar multicoloured designs.* W w **12** (sideways on 50c., 85c.). P 14.

253	20c. Type **50**	35	10
254	50c. French warships at anchor (*vert*)	40	15
255	85c. Coco-de-Mer and Black Parrot (*vert*)	90	25
256	2r.25 French warships under sail	90	2·75
253/6	*Set of* 4	2·25	2·75

(Des V. Whiteley. Litho Format)

1969 (9 Sept). *First Man on the Moon. T* **54** *and similar horiz designs. Multicoloured.* W w **12** (sideways on horiz designs). P 13½.

257	5c. Type **54**	10	50
258	20c. Module leaving Mother-ship for Moon	15	10
259	50c. Astronauts and Space Module on Moon	20	15
260	85c. Tracking station	25	15
261	2r.25 Moon craters with Earth on the "Horizon"	45	1·60
257/61	*Set of* 5	1·00	2·25

59 Picault's Landing, 1742

60 Badge of Seychelles

(Des Mary Hayward. Litho Enschedé)

1969 (3 Nov)–**75**. *Horiz designs as T* **59/60**. *Multicoloured.* W w **12** (sideways*). *Slightly toned paper.* P 13×12½.

262	5c. Type **59**	10	10
	w. Wmk Crown to right of CA	1·75	
263	10c. U.S. satellite-tracking station	10	10
	a. Whiter paper (8.3.73)	70	60
264	15c. *Königsberg I* (German cruiser) at Aldabra, 1914†	3·00	2·00
	a. Whiter paper (8.3.73)	5·50	5·50
265	20c. Fleet re-fuelling off St. Anne, 1939–45	1·75	10
	a. Whiter paper (13.6.74)	1·25	1·75
266	25c. Exiled Ashanti King Prempeh	20	10
	a. Whiter paper (8.3.73)	65	2·50
267	30c. Laying Stone of Possession, 1756	1·00	4·00
268	40c. As 30c. (11.12.72)	3·25	1·25
	a. Whiter paper (13.6.74)	1·60	1·60
269	50c. Pirates and treasure	30	15
	a. Whiter paper (13.6.74)	1·50	1·75
270	60c. Corsairs attacking merchantman	1·00	1·50
271	65c. As 60c. (11.12.72)	6·00	8·00
	aw. Wmk Crown to left of CA	6·00	
	b. Whiter paper (13.8.75)	6·50	9·50
272	85c. Impression of proposed airport	3·50	1·75
273	95c. As 85c. (11.12.72)	6·50	4·25
	a. Whiter paper (13.6.74)	5·50	3·25
	ab. Wmk to left of CA		
274	1r. French Governor capitulating to British naval officer, 1794	35	15
	a. Whiter paper (8.3.73)	1·00	1·00
275	1r.50 H.M.S. *Sybille* (frigate) and *Chiffone* (French frigate) in battle, 1801	1·75	2·00
	a. Whiter paper (8.3.73)	3·50	9·00
276	3r.50 Visit of the Duke of Edinburgh, 1956	1·00	2·25
	a. Whiter paper (13.8.75)	2·50	14·00
277	5r. Chevalier Queau de Quincy	1·00	2·75
278	10r. Indian Ocean chart, 1574	2·75	8·00
279	15r. Type **60**	4·00	12·00
262/79	*Set of* 18	28·00	45·00
263a/76a	*Set of* 11	27·00	45·00

*The normal sideways watermark shows Crown to right of CA on the 40, 65 and 95c. and to left of CA on the others, *as seen from the back of the stamp*.

†The design is incorrect in that it shows *Königsberg II* and the wrong date ("1915").

The stamps on the whiter paper are highly glazed, producing shade variations and are easily distinguishable from the original printings on toned paper.

74 White Terns, French Warship and Island

(Des A. Smith; adapted V. Whiteley. Litho D.L.R.)

1970 (27 Apr). *Bicentenary of First Settlement, St. Anne Island. T* **74** *and similar horiz designs. Multicoloured.* W w **12** (sideways). P 14.

280	20c. Type **74**	70	10
281	50c. Spot-finned Flyingfish, ship and island	45	10
282	85c. Compass and chart	45	10
283	3r.50 Anchor on sea-bed	70	1·25
280/3	*Set of* 4	2·10	1·40

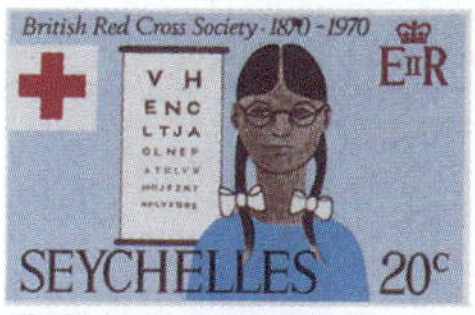

78 Girl and Optician's Chart

79 Pitcher Plant

(Des A. Smith. Litho Questa)

1970 (4 Aug). *Centenary of British Red Cross. T* **78** *and similar multicoloured designs.* W w **12** (sideways on horiz designs). P 14.

284	20c. Type **78**	30	10
285	50c. Baby, scales and milk bottles	30	10
286	85c. Woman with child and umbrella (*vert*)	30	10
287	3r.50 Red Cross local H.Q. building	1·25	2·75
284/7	*Set of* 4	2·00	2·75

(Des G. Drummond. Litho J.W.)

1970 (29 Dec). *Flowers. T* **79** *and similar vert designs. Multicoloured.* W w **12**. P 14.

288	20c. Type **79**	25	15
289	50c. Wild Vanilla	30	15
290	85c. Tropic-Bird Orchid	80	30
291	3r.50 Vare Hibiscus	1·00	2·25
288/91	*Set of* 4	2·10	2·50
MS292	81×133 mm. Nos. 288/91. Wmk inverted	2·75	13·00

POSTAGE DUE STAMPS

D 1

(Frame recess, value typo B.W.)

1951 (1 Mar). Wmk Mult Script CA. P 11½.

D1	D 1	2c. scarlet and carmine	80	1·50
D2		3c. scarlet and green	2·00	1·50
D3		6c. scarlet and bistre	2·00	1·25
D4		9c. scarlet and orange	2·00	1·25
D5		15c. scarlet and violet	1·75	12·00
D6		18c. scarlet and blue	1·75	12·00
D7		20c. scarlet and brown	1·75	12·00
D8		30c. scarlet and claret	1·75	7·50
D1/8		*Set of* 8	12·50	45·00

1964 (7 July)–**85**. *As 1951 but* W w **12**.

D9	D 1	2c. scarlet and carmine	2·50	12·00
D10		3c. scarlet and green (14.9.65)	1·25	14·00

Sierra Leone

PRICES FOR STAMPS ON COVER TO 1945

Nos. 1/15	*from* × 10
Nos. 16/26	*from* × 15
Nos. 27/34	*from* × 20
Nos. 35/7	*from* × 10
No. 38	—
No. 39	*from* × 15
Nos. 41/52	*from* × 8
No. 53	—
No. 54	*from* × 40
Nos. 55/63	*from* × 5
Nos. 64/71	—
Nos. 73/84	*from* × 4
No. 85	—
Nos. 86/97	*from* × 4
No. 98	—
Nos. 99/110	*from* × 4
No. 111	—
Nos. 112/26	*from* × 2
Nos. 127/30	—
Nos. 131/45	*from* × 2
Nos. 146/8	—
Nos. 155/66	*from* × 2
No. 167	—
Nos. 168/78	*from* × 2
Nos. 179/80	—
Nos. 181/4	*from* × 6
Nos. 185/7	*from* × 5
Nos. 188/200	*from* × 2

CROWN COLONY AND PROTECTORATE

The first settlement in Sierra Leone intended as a home for repatriated Africans, and subsequently those released by the Royal Navy from slave ships, was established in 1787. The Sierra Leone Company was created by Act of Parliment in 1791, but its charter was surrendered in 1808 and the coastal settlements then became a Crown Colony. The inland region was proclaimed a British protectorate on 21 August 1896.

A post office was established in 1843 but, until the inclusion of Freetown in the British Post Office packet system in 1850, overseas mail was carried at irregular intervals by passing merchant or naval vessels.

The stamps of GREAT BRITAIN were not sold at Sierra Leone post offices, although examples from ships of the West African Squadron do exist with local cancellations.

PRINTERS. All issues of Sierra Leone until 1932 were typographed by De La Rue & Co. Ltd, London.

1

2

HALF
PENNY

(3)

Dot after "SIX" and break in octagonal frame (R. 19/11)

1859 (21 Sept)–**74**. No wmk. P 14.

1	1	6d. dull purple	£225	50·00
		a. Dot after "SIX"	£1300	£450
2		6d. grey-lilac (1865)	£275	40·00
		a. Dot after "SIX"	—	£400
3		6d. reddish violet (P 12½) (1872)	£400	60·00
		a. Dot after "SIX"	—	£500
4		6d. reddish lilac (1874)	50·00	27·00
		a. Dot after "SIX"	£425	£225

Imperforate proofs exist.

The paper used for the 6d. value often shows varying degrees of blueing, caused by a chemical reaction.

The 6d. plate contained 240 stamps arranged in panes of 20 (4×5) with the sheets containing 12 such panes in four horizontal rows of three.

1872–73. Wmk Crown CC. P 12½.

		(a) Wmk sideways (April 1872).		
7	2	1d. rose-red	75·00	38·00
8		3d. buff	£140	38·00
9		4d. blue	£180	38·00
10		1s. green	£500	60·00
		(b) Wmk upright (Sept 1873).		
11	2	1d. rose-red	£130	30·00
		w. Wmk inverted	£250	95·00
12		2d. magenta	£130	50·00
13		3d. saffron-yellow	£500	85·00
14		4d. blue	£325	50·00
15		1s. green	£500	90·00

1876. Wmk Crown CC. P 14.

16	2	½d. brown	3·75	9·50
		w. Wmk inverted	£160	
17		1d. rose-red	50·00	15·00
18		1½d. lilac (Nov)	50·00	10·00
19		2d. magenta	65·00	4·00
20		3d. buff	50·00	5·00
		w. Wmk inverted		
21		4d. blue	£170	6·50
		w. Wmk inverted		
22		1s. green	65·00	6·50
16/22 *Set of 7*			£400	50·00

1883 (June–19 Sept). Wmk Crown CA. P 14.

23	2	½d. brown	27·00	55·00
24		1d. rose-red (13.9.83*)	£200	35·00
25		2d. magenta	50·00	8·50
26		4d. blue	£900	28·00

*Earliest known postmark date.

1884 SIERRA 5s. LEONE SURCHARGE. From 2 June 1884 the administration decided that, as a temporary measure, revenue and fiscal duties were to be paid with ordinary postage stamps. At that time there was no postage value higher than 1s., so a local surcharge, reading "SIERRA 5s. LEONE", was applied to No. 22 (*Price* £200 *unused*). Until withdrawal on 1 March 1885 this surcharge was valid for both fiscal and postal purposes, although no genuine postal cover or piece has yet been found. One mint example is known with overprint inverted (*Price* £850).

Remainders of the surcharge were cancelled by a horizontal red brush stroke (*Price* £32 *with upright surcharge*, £160 *with inverted surcharge*).

1884 (July)–**91**. Wmk Crown CA. P 14.

27	2	½d. dull green	3·00	1·75
		w. Wmk inverted	£200	£150
28		1d. carmine	7·00	1·00
		a. Rose-carmine (1885?)	28·00	8·50
		aw. Wmk inverted	†	£150
29		1½d. pale violet (1889)	3·50	6·50
30		2d. grey	42·00	2·75
31		2½d. ultramarine (1891)	13·00	1·50
		w. Wmk inverted	†	£180
32		3d. yellow (1889)	3·50	10·00
33		4d. brown	2·50	2·25
		w. Wmk inverted	£275	
		ws. Ditto, optd "Specimen"	£225	
34		1s. red-brown (1888)	25·00	14·00
27/34 *Set of 8*			90·00	35·00
27s/34s (*ex* 1½d., 3d.) Optd "Specimen" *Set of 6*.			£650	
27sa/8sa, 30sa, 33sa Optd "Specimen" (perf 12) *Set of 4*			£1500	

1885–96. Wmk Crown CC. P 14.

35	1	6d. dull violet (1885)	60·00	25·00
		a. Bisected (3d.) (on cover)	†	£2500
		b. Dot after "SIX"	—	£225
36		6d. brown-purple (1890)	20·00	14·00
		a. Dot after "SIX"	£225	£140
		s. Optd "Specimen"	70·00	
		w. Wmk inverted		
37		6d. purple-lake (1896)	2·75	7·00
		a. Dot after "SIX"	70·00	95·00

Proofs of the 6d. brown-purple exist from 1889 on Crown CA watermark and perforated 12 (*Price* £1500, *unused*).

1893 (8 Jan). *Surch with T* **3** *by Govt Printer, Freetown.*

		(a) On No. 18. Wmk Crown CC.		
38	2	½d. on 1½d. lilac	£475	£700
		a. "PFNNY"(R.3/1)	£3500	£4000
		(b) On No. 29. Wmk Crown CA.		
39	2	½d. on 1½d. pale violet	5·00	3·00
		a. Surch inverted	£110	£110
		b. "PFNNY" (R. 3/1)	80·00	75·00
		ba. Ditto. Surch inverted	£3500	£5000

On Nos. 38/9 the surcharge and the cancelling bars were often applied separately using a separate forme. When the bar missed its intended position across the value tablet, second, or even third bars were added, sometimes by pen or brush. No. 39a exists with the bars either normal or inverted with the rest of the surcharge.

Forged surcharges with "HALF PENNY" shown on one line were prepared by employees of the printer. It is believed that only a single example of this forgery still exists.

The 6d. fiscal, inscribed "STAMP DUTY" as Type **6** surcharged "ONE-PENNY" is known used for postage between May and August 1894, but no official sanction for such usage has been found.

4

5

1896–97. Wmk Crown CA. P 14.

41	4	½d. dull mauve and green (1897).	2·50	3·00
42		1d. dull mauve and carmine	5·00	1·75
43		1½d. dull mauve and black (1897)	4·00	22·00
44		2d. dull mauve and orange	2·50	5·00
45		2½d. dull mauve and ultramarine	2·50	1·25
46	5	3d. dull mauve and slate	8·50	7·00
47		4d. dull mauve and carmine (1897)	9·50	13·00
48		5d. dull mauve and black (1897)	13·00	15·00
49		6d. dull mauve (1897)	8·00	25·00
		w. Wmk inverted	—	£180
50		1s. green and black	6·00	21·00
51		2s. green and ultramarine	25·00	65·00
52		5s. green and carmine	80·00	£190
53		£1 purple/*red*	£190	£475
41/53 *Set of 13*			£325	£750
41s/53s Optd "Specimen" *Set of 13*			£225	

Examples of most values are known showing forged oval registered postmarks dated "16 JUL 11" or "4 SP 11".

6

POSTAGE
AND
REVENUE
(7)

2½d. (8) 2½d. (9) 2½d. (10)

2½d. (11) 2½d. (12) 2½d. (13)

POSTAGE AND REVENUE
(14)

REVENUE
Italic "N" (R. 3/4 of the setting)

1897. *Fiscal stamps as T* **6**. Wmk CA over Crown, w **7**. P 14.

		(a) Optd with T **7** *(26 Feb*).*		
54		1d. dull purple and green	4·75	3·50
		a. Opt double	£1900	£1900
		(b) Optd with T **7** *and surch T* **8**, **10**, **11** *(with square stop) or* **12** *with six thin bars across the original face value (27 Feb*).*		
55	8	2½d. on 3d. dull purple and green	11·00	15·00
		a. Surch double	£40000	
		b. Surch double (Types **8**+**10**)	£32000	
		c. Surch double (Types **8**+**11**)	£50000	
		d. Bars omitted		
56	10	2½d. on 3d. dull purple and green	55·00	65·00
57	11	2½d. on 3d. dull purple and green	£160	£180
58	12	2½d. on 3d. dull purple and green	£325	£425
59	8	2½d. on 6d. dull purple and green	8·50	15·00
60	10	2½d. on 6d. dull purple and green	45·00	55·00
61	11	2½d. on 6d. dull purple and green	£120	£140
62	12	2½d. on 6d. dull purple and green	£275	£325

*Earliest known postmark date.

Nos. 55/8 and 59/62 were surcharged from a setting of 30 (10×3) which contained 22 examples of Type **8** (including three with square stops), five of Type **10**, two of Type **11** and one of Type **12**.

Two examples are known of No. 55a, five of No. 55b (of which two are in the Royal Collection) and two of No. 55c (one in the Royal Collection). A unique example of a double surcharge on No. 55 showing Types **8**+**12** is also in the Royal Collection.

No. 55d comes from the top row of a setting and was caused by the downward displacement of the overprint. Stamps in the lower rows show the overprint transposed with the obliterating bars at the top of the stamp.

		(c) Optd with T **14** *and surch T* **8**, **9**, **10**, **11** *(with round stop) or* **13** *with five thin bars across the original face value (1 Mar).*		
63	8	2½d. on 1s. dull lilac	95·00	70·00
64	9	2½d. on 1s. dull lilac	£1500	£1300
65	10	2½d. on 1s. dull lilac	£850	£750
66	11	2½d. on 1s. dull lilac	£450	£425
		a. Italic "N"	£1400	£1300
66*b*	13	2½d. on 1s. dull lilac	£1500	£1300
67	8	2½d. on 2s. dull lilac	£1700	£2000
68	9	2½d. on 2s. dull lilac	£45000	£50000
69	10	2½d. on 2s. dull lilac	£18000	
70	11	2½d. on 2s. dull lilac	£10000	£12000
		a. Italic "N"	£45000	£45000
71	13	2½d. on 2s. dull lilac	£45000	

The setting of 30 (10×3) used for both Nos. 63/6*b* and 67/71 contained 22 examples of Type **8** (including one with square stop), one of Type **9**, two of Type **10**, four of Type **11** (including one with italic "N") and one of Type **13**.

Most examples of Nos. 63/6*b* are water-stained. Stamps in this condition are worth about 25% of the price quoted.

15

16

1903. Wmk Crown CA. P 14.

73	15	½d. dull purple and green	3·00	4·50
74		1d. dull purple and rosine	2·00	1·00
75		1½d. dull purple and black	1·25	14·00
76		2d. dull purple and brown-orange	3·75	16·00
77		2½d. dull purple and ultramarine	4·50	8·00
78	16	3d. dull purple and grey	10·00	13·00
79		4d. dull purple and rosine	7·00	15·00
80		5d. dull purple and black	8·00	35·00
81		6d. dull purple	11·00	22·00
82		1s. green and black	16·00	60·00
83		2s. green and ultramarine	50·00	70·00
84		5s. green and carmine	70·00	£110
85		£1 purple/*red*	£225	£250
73/85 *Set of 13*			£375	£550
73s/85s Optd "Specimen" *Set of 13*			£180	

1904–05. *Ordinary paper (1d.) or chalk-surfaced paper (others).* Wmk Mult Crown CA. P 14.

86	15	½d. dull purple and green (1905)	5·00	4·50
87		1d. dull purple and rosine	1·50	1·00
		a. Chalk-surfaced paper (1905)	4·50	1·50
88		1½d. dull purple and black (1905)	3·00	13·00
89		2d. dull purple and brown-orange (1905)	4·25	4·00
90		2½d. dull purple and ultramarine (1905)	4·75	2·00
91	16	3d. dull purple and grey (1905)	45·00	3·50
		w. Wmk inverted	40·00	32·00
92		4d. dull purple and rosine (1905).	8·00	7·00
		w. Wmk inverted	£120	
93		5d. dull purple and black (1905)	12·00	27·00
94		6d. dull purple (1905)	4·00	3·25
95		1s. green and black (1905)	7·50	9·00
96		2s. green and ultramarine (1905)	25·00	27·00
97		5s. green and carmine (1905)	35·00	55·00
98		£1 purple/*red* (1905)	£225	£250
86/98 *Set of 13*			£300	£325

1907–12. *Ordinary paper (½d. to 2½d.) or chalk-surfaced paper (others).* Wmk Mult Crown CA. P 14.

99	15	½d. green	1·00	50
100		1d. carmine	13·00	75
		a. Red	11·00	60
101		1½d. orange (1910)	1·50	2·00
102		2d. greyish slate (1909)	1·50	1·50
103		2½d. blue	3·75	3·00
104	16	3d. purple/*yellow* (1909)	7·50	2·75
		a. Ordinary paper (1912)	16·00	12·00
105		4d. black and red/*yellow* (1908)	2·25	1·60
106		5d. purple and olive-green (1908)	13·00	5·00
107		6d. dull and bright purple (1908).	13·00	8·00
108		1s. black/*green* (1908)	5·50	5·00
109		2s. purple and bright blue/*blue* (1908)	17·00	19·00
110		5s. green and red/*yellow* (1908)	40·00	60·00
111		£1 purple and black/*red* (1911)	£250	£180
99/111 *Set of 13*			£325	£250
99s/111s Optd "Specimen" *Set of 13*			£325	

Most values from the 1903, 1904–05 and 1907–12 issues are known with forged postmarks. These include oval registered examples dated "16 JUL 11" or "4 SP 11".

USED HIGH VALUES. The £2 and £5 values of the King George V series were intended for fiscal use only. Before the introduction of the airmail service at the end of 1926 there was no postal rate for which they could be used. Under the airmail rates used between 1926 and 1932 it is just possible that a very heavy letter may have required a £2 value. Postmarks on the £5 and on the £2 before December 1926 can only have been applied "by favour" or, in the case of the cds type, are on stamps removed from telegraph forms. Used prices quoted for Nos. 129/30 and 147/8 are for "by favour" cancellations.

17

18

19

20

1912–21. *Die I. Chalk-surfaced paper (3d. and 6d. to £5).* Wmk Mult Crown CA. P 14.

112	17	½d. blue-green	3·00	2·75
		a. Yellow-green (1914)	3·75	2·50
		aw. Wmk inverted	†	£225
		b. Deep green (1919)	5·50	3·25
113		1d. carmine-red	2·25	30
		a. Scarlet (1916)	6·00	1·00
		b. Rose-red (1918)	6·00	80
		bw. Wmk inverted	†	£160
		bx. Wmk reversed	£150	£150
114		1½d. orange (1913)	2·00	2·50
		a. Orange-yellow (1919)	5·00	1·00
115		2d. greyish slate	1·25	20
		a. "A" of "CA" missing from wmk		
		w. Wmk inverted	35·00	35·00
116		2½d. deep blue	13·00	2·75
		a. Ultramarine (1917)	1·00	1·00
116*b*	20	3d. purple/*yellow*	3·00	3·25
		ba. On pale yellow (1921)	3·25	3·25
117	18	4d. black and red/*yellow*	2·75	11·00
		a. On lemon (1915)	4·00	7·00
		b. Die II. *On pale yellow* (1921)	4·25	5·50
118		5d. purple and olive-green	1·25	7·00
119		6d. dull and bright purple	3·25	6·00
120	19	7d. purple and orange	3·00	9·00
121		9d. purple and black	5·00	12·00
122	18	10d. purple and red	3·00	18·00
124	20	1s. black/*green*	5·00	4·50
		a. On blue-green, green back	4·50	3·25
		w. Wmk inverted	55·00	55·00
125		2s. blue and purple/*blue*	14·00	5·50
126		5s. red and green/*yellow*	14·00	28·00
127		10s. red and green/*green*	70·00	£120
		a. Carmine and blue-green/green	95·00	£150
		b. Carmine and yellow-green/green	£110	£170
128		£1 black and purple/*red*	£170	£250
129		£2 blue and dull purple	£650	£900
		s. Optd "Specimen"	£130	
130		£5 orange and green	£1900	£2500
		s. Optd "Specimen"	£325	

112/28 *Set of* 17			£275	£425
112s/28s Optd "Specimen" *Set of* 17			£325	

Examples of Nos. 127/8 are known with part strikes of the forged postmarks mentioned after Nos. 99/111.

1921–27. *Die II. Chalk-surfaced paper (6d. to £5).* Wmk Mult Script CA. P 14.

131	**17**	½d. dull green	1·25	1·00
		a. Bright green	3·50	1·50
132		1d. bright violet (Die I) (1924)	2·00	2·25
		a. Die II (1925)	3·00	20
133		1½d. scarlet (1925)	1·75	1·25
134		2d. grey (1922)	1·25	20
135		2½d. ultramarine	1·75	13·00
136	**18**	3d. bright blue (1922)	1·25	1·25
137		4d. black and red/*pale yellow* (1925)	2·00	3·25
138		5d. purple and olive-green	1·25	1·25
139		6d. grey-purple and bright purple	1·25	2·50
		y. Wmk inverted and reversed		
140	**19**	7d. purple and orange (1927)	2·75	24·00
141		9d. purple and black (1922)	3·00	19·00
142	**18**	10d. purple and red (1925)	3·25	28·00
143	**20**	1s. black/*emerald* (1925)	9·50	7·00
144		2s. blue and dull purple/*blue*	9·50	10·00
		w. Wmk inverted	£150	£160
145		5s. red and green/*yellow* (1927)	9·50	55·00
146		10s. red and green/*green* (1927)	£110	£225
147		£2 blue and dull purple (1923)	£600	£850
		s. Optd "Specimen"	£130	
148		£5 orange and green (1923)	£1700	£2500
		s. Optd "Specimen"	£300	
131/46 *Set of* 16			£150	£350
131s/46s Optd "Specimen" *Set of* 16			£325	

21 Rice Field

22 Palms and Cola Tree

(Eng J.A.C. Harrison (T **21**))

1932 (1 Mar). Wmk Mult Script CA.

(a) Recess Waterlow. P 12½.

155	**21**	½d. green	20	40
156		1d. violet	30	30
157		1½d. carmine	30	1·50
		a. Imperf between (horiz pair)		
158		2d. brown	30	30
159		3d. blue	70	1·75
160		4d. orange	70	9·00
161		5d. bronze-green	1·00	4·75
162		6d. light blue	70	3·50
163		1s. lake	3·50	8·00

(b) Recess B.W. P 12.

164	**22**	2s. chocolate	5·00	5·50
165		5s. deep blue	13·00	20·00
166		10s. green	75·00	£130
167		£1 purple	£140	£225
155/67 *Set of* 13			£200	£375
155s/67s Perf "Specimen" *Set of* 13			£225	

23 Arms of Sierra Leone

23a "Freedom"

23b Map of Sierra Leone

24 Old Slave Market, Freetown

25 Native fruit seller

25a Government sanatorium

25b Bullom canoe

26 Punting near Banana

26a Government buildings, Freetown

26b Bunce Island

27 African Elephant

28 King George V

29 Freetown harbour

(Des Father F. Welsh. Recess B.W.)

1933 (2 Oct). *Centenary of Abolition of Slavery and of Death of William Wilberforce. T* **23/29**. Wmk Mult Script CA (sideways on horiz designs). P 12.

168	**23**	½d. green	1·00	1·25
169	**23a**	1d. black and brown	65	10
170	**23b**	1½d. chestnut	6·00	4·50
171	**24**	2d. purple	3·25	20
172	**25**	3d. blue	4·25	1·75
173	**25a**	4d. brown	6·50	10·00
174	**25b**	5d. green and chestnut	7·00	11·00
175	**26**	6d. black and brown-orange	8·50	7·00
176	**26a**	1s. violet	4·75	18·00
177	**26b**	2s. brown and light blue	30·00	42·00
178	**27**	5s. black and purple	£150	£170
179	**28**	10s. black and sage-green	£225	£325
180	**29**	£1 violet and orange	£425	£500
168/80 *Set of* 13			£800	£1000
168s/80s Perf "Specimen" *Set of* 13			£550	

1935 (6 May). *Silver Jubilee. As Nos. 91/4 of Antigua, but ptd by B.W.* P 11×12.

181		1d. ultramarine and grey-black	1·00	2·50
		a. Extra flagstaff	50·00	85·00
		b. Short extra flagstaff	£170	
		c. Lightning conductor	55·00	
182		3d. brown and deep blue	1·75	8·50
		a. Extra flagstaff	80·00	£130
		b. Short extra flagstaff	£400	
		c. Lightning conductor	95·00	
183		5d. green and indigo	2·50	21·00
		a. Extra flagstaff	£120	£225
		b. Short extra flagstaff	£450	
		c. Lightning conductor	£140	
184		1s. slate and purple	15·00	9·50
		a. Extra flagstaff	£350	£300
		b. Short extra flagstaff	£400	
		c. Lightning conductor	£325	£300
181/4 *Set of* 4			18·00	38·00
181s/4s Perf "Specimen" *Set of* 4			£120	

For illustrations of plate varieties see Omnibus section following Zanzibar.

1937 (12 May). *Coronation. As Nos. 95/7 of Antigua.* P 11×11½.

185		1d. orange	70	1·00
186		2d. purple	90	1·00
187		3d. blue	1·75	4·00
185/7 *Set of* 3			3·00	5·50
185s/7s Perf "Specimen" *Set of* 3			85·00	

30 Freetown from the Harbour

31 Rice Harvesting

(Recess Waterlow)

1938 (1 May)–**44**. Wmk Mult Script CA (sideways). P 12½.

188	**30**	½d. black and blue-green	15	40
189		1d. black and lake	40	60
		a. Imperf between (vert pair)	†	—
190	**31**	1½d. scarlet	20·00	1·00
190*a*		1½d. mauve (1.2.41)	30	60
191		2d. mauve	48·00	3·00
191*a*		2d. scarlet (1.2.41)	30	2·00
192	**30**	3d. black and ultramarine	55	50
193		4d. black and red-brown (20.6.38)	1·75	4·50
194	**31**	5d. olive-green (20.6.38)	3·25	4·00
195		6d. grey (20.6.38)	1·50	50
196	**30**	1s. black and olive-green (20.6.38)	2·25	70
196*a*	**31**	1s.3d. yellow-orange (1.7.44)	75	60
197	**30**	2s. black and sepia (20.6.38)	4·50	2·75
198	**31**	5s. red-brown (20.6.38)	10·00	12·00
199		10s. emerald-green (20.6.38)	23·00	14·00
200	**30**	£1 deep blue (20.6.38)	17·00	25·00
188/200 *Set of* 16			£120	65·00
188s/200s Perf "Specimen" *Set of* 16			£325	

1946 (1 Oct). *Victory. As Nos. 110/11 of Antigua.*

201		1½d. lilac	20	10
202		3d. ultramarine	20	30
201s/2s Perf "Specimen" *Set of* 2			80·00	

1948 (1 Dec). *Royal Silver Wedding. As Nos. 112/13 of Antigua.*

203		1½d. bright purple	15	15
204		£1 indigo	19·00	20·00

1949 (10 Oct). *75th Anniv of U.P.U. As Nos. 114/17 of Antigua.*

205		1½d. purple	20	50
206		3d. deep blue	2·00	5·50
207		6d. grey	50	6·50
208		1s. olive	35	1·00
205/8 *Set of* 4			2·75	12·00

1953 (2 June). *Coronation. As No. 120 of Antigua, but ptd by B.W.*

209		1½d. black and purple	30	30

32 Cape Lighthouse

33 Queen Elizabeth II Quay

34 Piassava workers

35 Cotton Tree, Freetown

36 Rice harvesting

37 Iron ore production

38 Whale Bay, York Village

39 Bullom canoe

40 Bristol 170 freighter Mk 31 aircraft and map

41 Orugu Railway Bridge

42 Kuranco Chief

43 Law Courts, Freetown

44 Government House

(Recess Waterlow)

1956 (2 Jan)–**61**. *T* **32/44**. Wmk Mult Script CA. P 13½×13 (horiz) or 14 (vert).

210	**32**	½d. black and deep lilac	1·00	2·50
211	**33**	1d. black and olive	90	40
212	**34**	1½d. black and ultramarine	1·60	6·50
213	**35**	2d. black and brown	70	40

214	**36**	3d. black and bright blue	1·25	10
		a. Perf 13×13½	1·75	9·50
215	**37**	4d. black and slate-blue	2·50	2·25
216	**38**	6d. black and violet	1·00	30
217	**39**	1s. black and scarlet	1·25	50
218	**40**	1s.3d. black and sepia	11·00	30
219	**41**	2s.6d. black and chestnut	14·00	11·00
220	**42**	5s. black and deep green	3·75	3·75
221	**43**	10s. black and bright reddish purple	3·50	2·75
		a. Black and purple (19.4.61)	10·00	26·00
222	**44**	£1 black and orange	15·00	29·00
210/22 *Set of* 13			50·00	50·00

Nos. 210/11 and 214 exist in coils, constructed from normal sheets.

INDEPENDENT

45 Palm Fruit Gathering

46 Licensed Diamond Miner

52

(Des K. Penny (½d., 1s.), Messrs Thorns, Turrell and Larkins (1d., 3d., 6d., 2s.6d.), W. G. Burnley (1½d., 5s.), J. H. Vandi (2d., 10s.), R. A. Sweet (4d., 1s 3d.), J. White (£1). Recess B. W.)

1961 (27 Apr). *Independence. T* **45/6** *and similar designs.* W **52**. P 13½.

223	½d. chocolate and deep bluish green	20	10
224	1d. orange-brown and myrtle-green	1·25	10
225	1½d. black and emerald	20	10
226	2d. black and ultramarine	20	10
227	3d. orange-brown and blue	20	10
228	4d. turquoise-blue and scarlet	20	10
229	6d. black and purple	20	10
230	1s. chocolate and yellow-orange	20	10
231	1s.3d. turquoise-blue and violet	20	10
232	2s.6d. deep green and black	2·75	30
233	5s. black and red	1·00	1·25
234	10s. black and green	1·00	1·25
235	£1 carmine-red and yellow	8·00	14·00
223/235 *Set of* 13		14·00	16·00

Designs: *Vert*—1½d., 5s. Bunda mask; 2d., 10s. Bishop Crowther and Old Fourah Bay College; 1s. Palm fruit gathering; £1, Forces Bugler. *Horiz*—3d., 6d. Sir Milton Margai; 4d., 1s.3d. Lumley Beach, Freetown; 2s.6d. Licensed diamond miner.

53 Royal Charter, 1799

55 Old House of Representatives, Freetown, 1924

(Des C. P. Rang (3d., 4d.), F. H. Burgess (1s.3d.). Recess B.W.)

1961 (25 Nov). *Royal Visit. T* **53, 55** *and similar designs.* W **52**. P 13½.

236	3d. black and rose-red	15	10
237	4d. black and violet	15	1·25
238	6d. black and yellow-orange	20	10
239	1s.3d. black and blue	3·00	1·75
236/9 *Set of* 4		3·00	2·75

Designs: *Vert*—4d King's Yard Gate, Freetown, 1817. *Horiz*—1s.3d. Royal Yacht *Britannia* at Freetown.

57 Campaign Emblem

(Recess B.W.)

1962 (7 Apr). *Malaria Eradication.* W **52**. P 11×11½.

240	**57**	3d. carmine-red	10	10
241		1s.3d. deep green	20	10

58 Fireball Lily

59 Jina-gbo

(Des M. Goaman. Photo Harrison)

1963 (1 Jan). *Flowers. Vert designs as T* **58** *(½d., 1½d., 3d., 4d., 1s., 2s.6d., 5s., 10s.) or horiz as T* **59** *(others). Multicoloured.* W **52** (sideways on vert designs). P 14.

242	½d. Type **58**	10	10
243	1d. Type **59**	10	10
244	1½d. Stereospermum	20	10
245	2d. Black-eyed Susan	20	10
246	3d. Beniseed	20	10
247	4d. Blushing Hibiscus	20	10
248	6d. Climbing Lily	30	10
249	1s. Beautiful Crinum	40	10
250	1s.3d. Blue Bells	1·50	20
251	2s.6d. Broken Hearts	1·25	30
252	5s. Ra-ponthi	1·25	80
253	10s. Blue Plumbago	3·00	1·50
254	£1 African Tulip Tree	6·00	7·00
242/254 *Set of* 13		13·00	9·50

71 Threshing Machine and Corn Bins

(Des V. Whiteley. Recess B.W.)

1963 (21 Mar). *Freedom from Hunger. T* **71** *and similar horiz design.* W **52**. P 11½×11.

255	3d. black and yellow-ochre	30	10
256	1s.3d. sepia and emerald-green	35	10

Design:—1s.3d. Girl with onion crop.

2ND YEAR OF INDEPENDENCE 19 PROGRESS 63 DEVELOPMENT 3d.
(73)

2nd Year Independence Progress Development 1963 10d.
(74)

(Optd by Govt Printer, Freetown)

1963 (27 Apr). *Second Anniv of Independence. Surch or optd as T* **73/4**. *(a) Postage.*

257	3d. on ½d. black and deep lilac (No. 210) (R.)	40	10
	a. Small "c" in "INDEPENDENCE"	4·75	5·50
258	4d. on ½d. black and ultramarine (No. 212) (Br.)	15	10
259	6d. on ½d. black and deep lilac (No. 210) (O.)	30	10
	a. Small "c" in "INDEPENDENCE"	5·50	6·00
260	10d. on 3d. black and bright blue (No. 214) (R.)	50	10
261	1s.6d. on 3d. black and bright blue (No. 214) (V.)	30	20
262	3s.6d. on 3d black and bright blue (No. 214) (Ult.)	40	20
	(b) Air. Additionally optd "AIR MAIL".		
263	7d. on 1½d. black and ultramarine (No. 212) (C.)	20	10
264	1s.3d. on 1½d. black and ultramarine (No. 212) (R.)	20	10
265	2s.6d. black and chestnut (No. 219) (V.)	2·25	40
266	3s.. on 3d black and bright blue (No. 214) (B.)	40	20
267	6s. on 3d. black and bright blue (No. 214) (R.)	1·00	20
268	11s. on 10s. black and bright reddish purple (No. 221) (C.)	1·40	85
269	11s. on £1 black and orange (No. 222) (C.)	£600	£200
257/268 *Set of* 12		6·75	2·40

75 Centenary Emblem

(Des M. Goaman. Recess B.W.)

1963 (1 Nov). *Centenary of Red Cross. T* **75** *and similar vert designs.* W **52**. P 11×11½.

270	3d. red and violet	50	10
271	6d. red and black	50	15
272	1s.3d. red and deep bluish green	65	20
270/2 *Set of* 3		1·50	40

Designs:—6d. Red Cress emblem; 1s.3d. Centenary emblem.

1853–1859–1963 Oldest Postal Service Newest G.P.O. in West Africa 1s.
(78)

1853–1859–1963 Oldest Postage Stamp Newest G.P.O. in West Africa AIRMAIL
(79)

1963 (4 Nov). *Postal Commemorations. Optd or surch by Govt Printer, Freetown. (a) Postage. As T* **78**.

273	3d. black and bright blue (No. 214)	10	10
	a. "1895" for "1859" (R. 3/3)	2·50	
	b. "1853/1859/1963" (R. 2/3)	2·50	
	ba. As No. 273b, but showing "S vice" also (R. 2/3)		
274	4d. on 1½d. black and ultramarine (No. 212) (C.)	10	10
	a. "1895" for "1859" (R. 1/2)	3·50	
	b. "1853*1859*1963" (R. 3/2, 11/4)	2·75	
	c. "1853 1859*1963" (R. 11/4)	3·75	
	d. No stop after "O", but stop after "Africa" (R. 10/1)	2·75	
275	9d. on ½d. black and ultramarine (No. 212) (V.)	10	10
	a. "1853*1859*1963"(R. 3/2,11/4)	2·40	
	b. No stop after "O" (R. 7/5)		
	c. No stop after "O", but stop after "Africa" (R. 10/1)	2·75	
276	1s. on 1s.3d. turquoise-blue and violet (No. 231) (C.)	10	10
	a. "1853*1859*1963" (R. 3/4, 10/2)	3·00	
277	1s.6d. on ½d. black and deep lilac (No. 210) (Mag.)	15	10
	a. "1853*1859*1963"(R. 11/1.)	4·50	
	b. "1853*1859 1963" (R. 4/5)	8·00	
278	2s. on 3d. black and bright blue (No. 214) (Br.)	15	10
	a. "1895" for "1859" (R. 4/10)	8·00	
	b. "1853/1859/1963" (R. 2/3)	6·00	
	(b) Air. As T **79**.		
279	7d. on 3d. black and rose-red (No. 236) (Br.)	20	50
	a. "1895" for "1859"(R.3/6, 4/4)	3·25	
	b. "1853·1859·1963" (R.2/3, 4/10)	2·50	
	c. No stop after "O" (R.1/2)	3·50	
280	1s.3d. black and blue (No. 239) (C.)	2·00	1·50
	a. "1895" for "1859" (R.7/3)	20·00	
	b. "1853*1859*1963" (R.3/2,10/4)	9·50	
	c. No stop after "O" (R.8/3)	13·00	
281	2s.6d. on 4d. turquoise-blue and scarlet (No. 228)	1·25	20
	a. "1895" for "1859" (R.7/3)	50·00	
	b. "1853*1859*1963" (R.3/2, 10/4)	6·00	
	c. No stop after "O" (R.8/3)	15·00	
282	3s. on 3d. black and rose-red (No. 236) (V.)	2·50	2·00
	a. "1895" for "1859" (R.3/3)	£350	
	b. "1853·1859·1963" (R.2/3, 4/10)	10·00	
	c. No stop after "O" (R.1/2)	14·00	
283	6s. on 6d. black and yellow-orange (No. 238) (Ult.)	1·00	1·00
	a. "1895" for "1859" (R.1/1)	50·00	
	b. "1853*1859*1963" (R.3/2, 10/4)	7·50	
	c. No stop after "O" (R.8/3)	12·00	
284	£1 black and orange (No. 222) (R.)	23·00	25·00
	a. "1895" for "1859" (R.11/4)	£300	
	b. "1853*1859*1963"(R.4/5, 11/1)	45·00	
273/84 *Set of* 12		27·00	27·00

The events commemorated are: 1853, "First Post Office"; 1859, "First Postage Stamps"; and 1963 "Newest G.P.O." in West Africa. Nos. 273, 278 have the overprint in five lines; Nos. 279, 282 in six lines (incl "AIRMAIL").

Some of the overprint varieties were corrected during printing.

80 Lion Emblem and Map

81 Globe and Map

Extended "A" in "SIERRA" (R. 3/3, later corrected on the 4d. value)

(Recess and litho Walsall Lithographic Co. Ltd)

1964 (10 Feb). *World's Fair, New York. Imperf. Self-adhesive.*

(a) Postage.

285	**80**	1d. multicoloured	10	10
286		3d. multicoloured	10	10
		a. Lion omitted	£450	
287		4d. multicoloured	10	10
		b. Extended "A"	2·00	
288		6d. multicoloured	10	10
		b. Extended "A"	2·00	
289		1s. multicoloured	10	10
		a. "POSTAGE 1/-" omitted	42·00	
		b. Extended "A"	2·00	
290		2s. multicoloured	30	20
		b. Extended "A"	3·00	
291		5s. multicoloured	50	50
		a. "POSTAGE 5/-" omitted	45·00	
		b. Extended "A"	5·00	

(b) Air.

292	**81**	7d. multicoloured	10	10
293		9d. multicoloured	10	10
		a. "AIR MAIL 9d." omitted		
294		1s.3d. multicoloured	20	10
		a. "AIR MAIL 1/3" omitted	45·00	
295		2s.6d. multicoloured	30	15
296		3s.6d. multicoloured	30	20
		a. "AIR MAIL 3/6" omitted		
297		6s. multicoloured	55	60
		a. "AIR MAIL 6/-" omitted	48·00	
298		11s. multicoloured	70	1·00
		a. "AIR MAIL 11/-" omitted	50·00	
285/98 *Set of 14*			3·25	3·00

Nos. 285/98 were issued in sheets of 30 (6×5) on green (postage) or yellow (airmail) backing paper with the emblems of Samuel Jones & Co. Ltd, self-adhesive paper-makers, on the back.

WARNING. These and later self-adhesive stamps should be kept on their backing paper except commercially used, which should be retained on cover or piece.

82 Inscription and Map

83 Pres Kennedy and Map

(Recess and litho Walsall)

1964 (11 May). *President Kennedy Memorial Issue. Imperf. Self-adhesive. (a) Postage. Green backing paper.*

299	**82**	1d. multicoloured	10	10
300		3d. multicoloured	10	10
301		4d. multicoloured	10	10
302		6d. multicoloured	10	10
		b. Extended "A"	2·00	
303		1s. multicoloured	10	10
		b. Extended "A"	2·00	
304		2s. multicoloured	30	35
		b. Extended "A"	3·00	
305		5s. multicoloured	50	1·00
		b. Extended "A"	5·00	
		(b) Air. Yellow backing paper.		
306	**83**	7d. multicoloured	10	10
307		9d. multicoloured	10	10
308		1s.3d. multicoloured	15	10
309		2s.6d. multicoloured	30	25
310		3s.6d. multicoloured	30	25
311		6s. multicoloured	55	1·25
312		11s. multicoloured	70	1·75
299/312 *Set of 14*			3·00	4·75

(New Currency. 100 cents = 1 leone)

(84) (85) (86)

1964–66. *Decimal currency. Various stamps surch locally.*

(i) First issue (4.8.64). (a) Postage. Surch as T **84**

313	–	1c. on 6d. multicoloured (No. 248) (R.)	10	10
314	**53**	2c. on 3d. black and rose-red	10	10
315	–	3c. on 3d. multicoloured (No. 246)	10	10
		a. Surch inverted	£140	
316	**45**	5c. on ½d. chocolate and deep bluish green (B.)	10	10
317	**71**	8c. on 3d. black and yellow-ochre (R.)	10	10
318	–	10c. on 1s.3d. mult (No. 250) (R.)	10	10
319	–	15c. on 1s. multicoloured (No. 249)	15	10
320	**55**	25c. on 6d. black and yellow-orange (V.)	30	25
321	–	50c. on 2s.6d. deep green and black (No. 232) (O.)	2·00	1·00
		(b) Air. As T **85** *or* **86** *(Nos. 326/7)*		
322	–	7c. on 1s.3d. sepia and emerald-green (No. 256) (B.)	10	10
		a. Surch omitted (in horiz pair with normal)		
		b. Surch double	70·00	
323	–	20c. on 4d. turquoise-blue and scarlet (No. 228)	25	20
324	–	30c. on 10s. black and green (No. 234) (R.)	40	45
325	–	40c. on 5s. black and red (No. 233) (B.)	50	60
326	**83**	1l. on 1s.3d. multicoloured (R.)	75	1·40
327		2l. on 11s. multicoloured	1·25	2·75
313/27 *Set of 15*			5·50	6·50

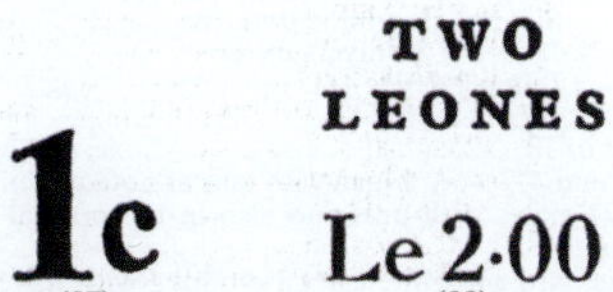

(87) (88)

(ii) Second issue (20.1.65). Surch as T **87** *or* **88** *(Nos. 332/3)*

(a) Postage.

328	–	1c. on 3d. orange-brown and blue (No. 227)	10	10
329	**82**	2c. on 1d. multicoloured	10	10
330		4c. on 3d. multicoloured	10	10
		a. Error. 4c. on 1d	£140	£225
		b. Stamp omitted (in pair with normal)		
331	–	5c. on 2d. multicoloured (No. 245)	10	10
332	–	1l. on 5s. multicoloured (No. 252) (Gold)	1·25	2·50
333	–	2l. on £1 carmine-red and yellow (No. 235) (B.)	2·25	4·00
		a. Surch double (B.+Blk.)	–	75·00
		(b) Air		
334	**83**	7c. on 7d. multicoloured (R.)	10	10
335		60c. on 9d. multicoloured	50	1·00
328/35 *Set of 8*			4·00	7·00

On No. 330b the stamp became detached before the surcharge was applied so that "4c" appears on the backing paper.

Normal — Small "c" (R. 3/3)

(iii) Third issue (4.65). Surch in figures (various sizes).

(a) Postage.

336	–	1c. on 1½d. black and emerald (No. 225) (R.)	10	10
		a. Small "c"	4·00	
337	**82**	2c. on 3d. multicoloured	10	10
338	**80**	2c. on 4d. multicoloured	10	10
		b. Extended "A"	2·00	
339	**59**	3c. on 1d. multicoloured	10	10
340	–	3c. on 2d. black and ultramarine (No. 226) (R.)	10	10
341	–	5c. on 1s.3d. turquoise-blue and violet (No. 231) (R.)	10	10
		a. Surch inverted		
342	**82**	15c. on 6d. multicoloured	80	50
		b. Extended "A"	7·00	
343		15c. on 1s. multicoloured (R.)	1·25	90
		b. Extended "A"	10·00	
344	–	20c. on 6d. black and purple (No. 229) (R.)	30	15
345	–	25c. on 6d. multicoloured (No. 248) (R.)	35	20
346	–	50c. on 3d. orange-brown and blue (No. 227) (R.)	80	55
347	**80**	60c. on 5s. multicoloured (V.)	3·50	2·00
		b. Extended "A"	27·00	
348	**82**	1l. on 4d. multicoloured (R.)	4·00	4·00
349	–	2l. on £1 carmine-red and yellow (No. 235) (B.)	9·00	9·00
		(b) Air.		
350	**81**	7c. on 9d. multicoloured	25	10
336/50 *Set of 15*			18·00	16·00

(89) (90)

(iv) Fourth issue (9.11.65). Surch as T **89**.

(a) Postage

351	**80**	1c. on 6d. multicoloured (V.)	2·50	7·00
		b. Extended "A"	20·00	
352		1c. on 2s. multicoloured (V.)	2·50	7·00
		b. Extended "A"	20·00	
353	**82**	1c. on 2s. multicoloured (V.)	2·50	7·00
		b. Extended "A"	20·00	
354		1c. on 5s. multicoloured (V.)	2·50	7·00
		b. Extended "A"	20·00	
		(b) Air.		
355	**81**	2c. on 1s.3d. multicoloured	2·50	7·00
356	**83**	2c. on 1s.3d. multicoloured	2·50	7·00
357		2c. on 3s.6d. multicoloured	2·50	7·00
358	**81**	3c. on 7d. multicoloured	2·50	7·00
359	**83**	3c. on 9d. multicoloured	2·50	7·00
360	**81**	5c. on 2s.6d. multicoloured	2·50	7·00
361	**83**	5c. on 2s.6d. multicoloured	2·50	7·00
362	**81**	5c. on 3s.6d. multicoloured	2·50	7·00
363		5c. on 6s. multicoloured	2·50	7·00
364	**83**	5c. on 6s. multicoloured	2·50	7·00
351/64 *Set of 14*			30·00	90·00

(v) Fifth issue (28.1.66). Air. No. 374 further surch with T **90**.

365	–	2l. on 30c. on 6d. multicoloured	1·75	1·50

91 Margai and Churchill

1965 (19 May). *Sir Milton Margai and Sir Winston Churchill Commemoration. Nos. 242/3, 245/50 and 252/4 surch as T* **91** *on horiz designs or with individual portraits on vert designs as indicated.*

(a) Postage.

366		2c. on 1d. Type **59**	35	10
		a. Horiz pair, one with "2 c" omitted	£400	
		b. Surch and portraits omitted (in horiz pair with normal)	£400	
367		3c. on 3d. Beniseed (Margai)	10	10
		a. Portrait and "3 c" double	£110	
		b. Portrait and "3 c" double, one inverted	£130	
		c. "3 c" omitted	£400	
368		10c. on 1s. Beautiful Crinum (Churchill)	75	10
		a. "10 c" omitted	£300	
369		20c. on 1s.3d. Blue Bells	90	10
		a. Portraits and "20 c" double, one inverted	£120	
		b. "20 c" omitted	£400	
		c. "20 c" double, one inverted	£120	
370		50c. on 4d. Blushing Hibiscus (Margai)	90	35
		a. Portrait inverted	£120	
		ab. Portrait inverted and "50 c" omitted	£140	
371		75c. on 5s. Ra-ponthi (Churchill)	3·50	90
		a. Surch value inverted	£200	
		(b) Air. Additionally optd "AIRMAIL".		
372		7c. on 2d. Black-eyed Susan	50	10
		a. "AIRMAIL" and "7c." omitted	£130	
		b. "AIRMAIL" and "7 c" double, one inverted	£130	
373		15c. on ½d. Type **58** (Margai)	35	10
		a. "AIRMAIL" and "15 c" double, one inverted	£140	
		b. Portrait double, one inverted	£120	
374		30c. on 6d. Climbing Lily (O. and W.)	1·75	25
		a. "AIRMAIL" and "30 c" double, one inverted	£120	
		b. "AIRMAIL" and "30 c" omitted	£120	
375		1l. on £1 African Tulip Tree	5·50	1·00
		a. "AIRMAIL" and "1 l" double, one inverted	£120	
		b. "AIRMAIL" and "1 l" omitted	£400	
376		2l. on 10s. Blue Plumbago (Churchill)	12·00	5·00
		a. Surch value omitted	£160	
366/76 *Set of 11*			23·00	7·00

On Nos. 366/76 the portraits and commemorative inscription were applied in a separate operation from the surcharge and, on Nos. 372/6, the word "AIRMAIL".

92 Cola Plant and Nut

93 Arms of Sierra Leone

94 Inscription and Necklace

(Des M. Meers. Manufactured by Walsall Lithographic Co, Ltd)

1965 (17 Dec*). *Imperf. Self-adhesive.*

A. Embossed on silver foil, backed with paper bearing advertisements. Emerald, olive-yellow and carmine; denominations in colours given. Postage.

377	**92**	1c. emerald	25	10
378		2c. carmine	25	10
379		3c. olive-yellow	25	10
380		4c. silver/*emerald*	30	10
381		5c. silver/*carmine*	30	10
		B. Typo and embossed on cream paper backed with advertisements.		
		(a) Postage.		
382	**93**	20c. multicoloured	2·00	60
383		50c. multicoloured	3·75	3·75
		(b) Air		
384	**93**	40c. multicoloured	3·50	3·75
		C. Die-stamped and litho, with advertisements on white paper backing (see footnote). Air.		
385	**94**	7c. multicoloured	80	15
		a. Bright green and gold (inscr and face value) omitted	£110	
386		15c. multicoloured	1·25	90

377/86 *Set of* 10		11·00	8·50

*It is believed that some values may have been released as early as 22 November.

The above stamps were issued in single form with attached tabs to remove the backing paper, with the exception of No. 385 which was in sheets of 25 bearing a single large advertisement on the back.

No. 385a shows the die-stamping omitted.

For other stamps in Type **92** see Nos. 421/31 and 435/42*a*.

For 10c. stamps in Type **93** see Nos. 433/6.

(95) (96)

1966 (27 Apr). *Fifth Anniv of Independence. Various stamps surch.*

(a) Postage. As T **95**.

387	1c. on 6d. multicoloured (No. 248)	10	10
388	2c. on 4d. multicoloured (No. 247)	10	10
389	3c. on 1½d. black and ultramarine (No. 212) (B.)	10	10
390	8c. on 1s. multicoloured (No. 249) (B.)	15	10
391	10c. on 2s.6d. multicoloured (No. 251) (B.)	15	10
392	20c. on 2d. black and brown (No. 213) (B.)	20	10
	(b) Air. As T **96**.		
393	7c. on 3d. red and violet (No. 270)	10	10
394	15c. on 1s. multicoloured (No. 249)	20	10
395	25c. on 2s.6d. multicoloured (No. 251)	65	60
396	50c. on 1½d. multicoloured (No. 244)	1·00	80
397	1l. on 4d. multicoloured (No. 247)	1·60	1·60
387/397 *Set of* 11		3·75	3·25

The inscription on No. 387 is in larger type.

97 Lion's Head

98 Map of Sierra Leone

(Des and embossed Walsall)

1966 (12 Nov). *First Sierra Leone Gold Coinage Commemoration. Circular designs, embossed on gold foil, backed with paper bearing advertisements. Imperf.*

(a) Postage. (i) *¼ golde coin. Diameter 1½ in.*

398	**97**	2c. magenta and yellow-orange	10	10
399	**98**	3c. emerald and bright purple	10	10
		(ii) ½ golde coin. Diameter 21/8in.		
400	**97**	5c. vermilion and ultramarine	10	10
401	**98**	8c. turquoise-blue and black	20	20
		(iii) 1 golde coin. Diameter 3¼ in.		
402	**97**	25c. violet and emerald	40	35
403	**98**	1l. orange and cerise	2·75	3·25
		(b) Air. (i) ¼ golde coin. Diameter 1½ in.		
404	**98**	7c. red-orange and cerise	15	10
405	**97**	10c. cerise and greenish blue	20	25
		(ii) ½ golde coin. Diameter 21/8in.		
406	**98**	15c. orange and cerise	35	35
407	**97**	30c. bright purple and black	50	60
		(iii) 1 golde coin. Diameter 3¼ in.		
408	**98**	50c. bright green and purple	1·00	1·00
409	**97**	2l. black and emerald	4·00	4·50
398/409 *Set of* 12			8·75	9·75

(99) (100) (101)

1967 (2 Dec). *Decimal Currency Provisionals. Surch as T* **99** *(Nos. 410/13), T* **100** *(Nos. 415/17) or T* **101** *(others).*

(a) Postage.

410	–	6½c. on 75c. on 5s. multicoloured (No. 371) (R.)	15	15
411	–	7½c. on 75c. on 5s. multicoloured (No. 371) (S.)	15	15
412	–	9½c. on 50c. on 4d. multicoloured (No. 370) (G.)	20	20
413	–	12½c. on 20c. on 1s.3d. multicoloured (No. 369) (V.)	30	25
414	**93**	1½c. on 50c. multicoloured	1·75	2·00
415	**82**	17½c. on 1l. on 4d. multicoloured (No. 348) (B.)	1·75	2·00
416		18½c. on 1l. on 4d. multicoloured (No. 348)	1·75	2·00
417	**80**	18½c. on 60c. on 5s. multicoloured (No. 347)	4·75	6·50
		b. Extended "A"	40·00	
418	**93**	25c. on 50c. multicoloured	70	80
		(b) Air.		
419	**93**	11½c. on 40c. multicoloured	25	25
420		25c. on 40c. multicoloured	70	80
410/20 *Set of* 11			11·00	13·50

102 Eagle

(Manufactured by Walsall)

1967 (2 Dec)–**69**. *Decimal Currency. Imperf. Self-adhesive.*

(a) Postage. As T **92**, *but embossed on white paper, backed with paper bearing advertisements. Background colours given first, and value tablet colours in brackets.*

421	**92**	½c. carmine-red (carmine/*white*)	10	30
422		1c. carmine (carmine/*white*)	15	10
423		1½c. orange-yellow (green/*white*)	20	15
424		2c. carmine-red (green/*white*)	35	10
425		2½c. apple-green (yellow/*white*)	60	50
426		3c. carmine-red (white/*carmine*)	35	10
427		3½c. reddish purple (white/*green*)	60	50
428		4c. carmine-red (white/*green*)	60	15
429		4½c. dull green (green/*white*)	60	50
430		5c. carmine (yellow/*white*)	60	15
431		5½c. brown-red (green/*white*)	60	70

(b) Air. T **102** *embossed on black paper, backed with paper bearing advertisements; or, (No. 433), as T* **93**, *typo and embossed on cream paper, also with advertisements.*

432	**102**	9½c. red and gold/*black*	70	70
432*a*		9½c. blue and gold/*black* (10.9.69)	7·00	7·00
433	**93**	10c. multicoloured (red frame)	70	70
		a. Face value omitted		
433*b*		10c. mult (black frame) (10.9.69)	8·00	8·00
434	**102**	15c. green and gold/*black*	1·00	1·00
434*a*		15c. red and gold/*black* (10.9.69)	8·50	8·50
421/34a *Set of* 17			27·00	26·00

The ½, 1½, 2, 2½, 3, 3½ and 5c. also exist without advertisements.

The footnote below Nos. 377/86 also applies here.

Although only released for collectors on 2 December, the 5c. was known to be in use locally in February and the 3c. in March. The 1c. and 2c. were also released locally some months earlier.

See also Nos. 538/44.

1968. *No advertisements on back, and colours in value tablet reversed. Background colours given first, and value tablet colours in brackets.*

435	**92**	½c. carmine-red (white/*green*)	10	10
436		1c. carmine (white/*carmine*)	15	10
437		2c. carmine (white/*green*)	5·00	5·50
438		2½c. apple-green (white/*yellow*)	5·50	6·00
439		3c. carmine-red (carmine/*white*)	2·25	75

On Nos. 435 and 438, the figure "½" is larger than in Nos. 421 and 425.

It is believed that the ½c. was released in February, the 2½c. in April and the others in March.

The 1c. also exists with advertisements on the backing paper.

The footnote below Nos. 377/86 also applies here.

1968–69. *No advertisements on back, colours changed and new value (7c.). Background colours given first, and value tablet colours in brackets. (a) Postage.*

440	**92**	2c. pink (white/*brown-lake*)	2·25	2·00
441		2½c. deep bluish green (white/ *orange*)	2·25	2·00
442		3½c. olive-yellow (blue/*white*)	2·50	2·25
		(b) Air		
442*a*	**92**	7c. yellow (carmine/*white*) (10.9.69)	7·50	3·75
435/42a *Set of* 9			24·00	20·00

On Nos. 441/2 the fraction "½" is larger than in Nos. 425 and 427.

It is believed that the 3½c. was released in March 1968 and the 2 and 2½c. in May 1968.

The 2c. also exists with advertisements on the backing paper.

The footnote below Nos. 377/86 also applies here.

103 Outline Map of Africa

(Litho Walsall)

1968 (25 Sept). *Human Rights Year. Each value comes in six types, showing different territories in yellow, as below. Imperf. self-adhesive.*

A. Portuguese Guinea. D. Rhodesia.
B. South Africa. E. South West Africa.
C. Mozambique. F. Angola.

To indicate yellow territory use above letters as suffix to the following catalogue numbers.

(a) Postage

443	**103**	½c. multicoloured	10	10
444		2c. multicoloured	10	10
445		2½c. multicoloured	10	10
446		3½c. multicoloured	10	10
447		10c. multicoloured	15	15
448		11½c. multicoloured	20	20
449		15c. multicoloured	25	25
		(b) Air.		
450	**103**	7½c. multicoloured	15	15
451		9½c. multicoloured	20	20
452		14½c. multicoloured	25	25
453		18½c. multicoloured	30	30
454		25c. multicoloured	40	40
455		1l. multicoloured	3·00	5·50
456		2l. multicoloured	9·00	12·00
443/56 Each territory *Set of* 14			12·50	18·00
443/56 Six territories *Set of* 84			65·00	£100

Nos. 443/56 were issued in sheets of 30 (6×5) on backing paper depicting diamonds or the coat of arms on the reverse. The six types occur once in each horizontal row.

(104)

1968 (30 Nov). *Mexico Olympics Participation.*

(a) Postage. No. 383 surch or optd (No. 461) as T **104**.

457	**93**	6½c. on 50c. multicoloured	35	30
458		17½c. on 50c. multicoloured	40	35
459		22½c. on 50c. multicoloured	60	50
		a. Surch double	£180	
460		28½c. on 50c. multicoloured	75	1·25
461		50c. multicoloured	1·10	2·25
		(b) Air. No. 384 surch or optd (No. 466) as T **104** *in red.*		
462	**93**	6½c. on 40c. multicoloured	35	30
		a. Surch double	£200	
463		17½c. on 40c. multicoloured	40	35
464		22½c. on 40c. multicoloured	60	50
465		28½c. on 40c. multicoloured	75	1·25
466		40c. multicoloured	1·00	2·25
457/66 *Set of* 10			5·50	8·50

105 1859 6d.

111 1965 15c. Self-adhesive

(Litho Walsall)

1969 (1 Mar). *Fifth Anniv of World's First Self-adhesive Postage Stamps. Reproductions of earlier issues. Multicoloured. Imperf. Self-adhesive.*

(a) Postage. Vert designs.

467	1c. Type **105**	10	10
468	2c. 1965 2c. self-adhesive	10	10
469	3½c. 1961 Independence £1	10	10
470	5c. 1965 20c. self-adhesive	10	10
471	12½c. 1948 Royal Silver Wedding £1	30	15
472	1l. 1923 £2	2·50	1·50
	(b) Air. Horiz designs.		
473	7½c. Type **111**	20	10
474	9½c. 1967 9½c. self-adhesive	20	10
475	20c. 1964 1s.3d. self-adhesive	40	25
476	30c. 1964 President Kennedy Memorial 6s. commemorative self-adhesive	55	35
477	50c. 1933 Centenary of Abolition of Slavery £1 commemorative	1·50	75
478	2l. 1963 2nd Anniversary of Independence 11s. commemorative	9·00	8·00
467/478 *Set of* 12		13·00	10·00

Nos. 467 and 473 were issued with tabs as note under Nos. 377/86 and No. 474 exists with tabs and also in the normal version on backing paper.

All values are on white backing paper with advertisements printed on the reverse.

117 Ore Carrier, Globe and Flags of Sierra Leone and Japan

118 Ore Carrier, Map of Europe and Africa and Flags of Sierra Leone and Netherlands

The 3½c., 9½c., 2l. and 10c., 50c., 1l. are as T **118** but show respectively the flags of Great Britain and West Germany instead of the Netherlands.

(Litho Walsall)

1969 (10 July). *Pepel Port Improvements.* Imperf. *Self-adhesive, backed with paper bearing advertisements. (a) Postage.*

479	**117**	1c. multicoloured	10	10
480	**118**	2c. multicoloured	10	10
481	–	3½c. multicoloured	10	10
482	–	10c. multicoloured	10	10
483	**118**	18½c. multicoloured	20	25
484	–	50c. multicoloured	80	85
		(b) Air.		
485	**117**	7½c. multicoloured	10	10
486	–	9½c. multicoloured	15	10
487	**117**	15c. multicoloured	20	25
488	**118**	25c. multicoloured	30	35
489	–	1l. multicoloured	1·50	1·75
490	–	2l. multicoloured	2·00	4·00
479/80 *Set of* 12			5·00	7·00

119 African Development Bank Emblem

120 Boy Scouts Emblem in "Diamond"

(Litho and embossed Walsall)

1969 (10 Sept). *Fifth Anniv of African Development Bank. Self adhesive, backed with paper bearing advertisements.* Imperf.

		(a) Postage.		
491	**119**	3½c. deep green, gold and blue	25	40
		(b) Air.		
492	**119**	9½c. bluish violet, gold and apple green	35	70

(Litho Walsall)

1969 (6 Dec). *Boy Scouts Diamond Jubilee. T* **120** *and similar design.* Imperf. *Self-adhesive, backed with paper bearing advertisements.*

		(a) Postage.		
493	**120**	1c. multicoloured	10	10
494		2c. multicoloured	10	10
495		3½c. multicoloured	15	10
496		4½c. multicoloured	15	15
497		5c. multicoloured	15	15
498		75c. multicoloured	5·50	2·75
		(b) Air.		
499	–	7½c. multicoloured	35	20
500	–	9½c. multicoloured	45	25
501	–	15c. multicoloured	70	50
502	–	22c. multicoloured	90	70
503	–	55c. multicoloured	4·00	2·00
504		3l. multicoloured	50·00	35·00
493/504 *Set of* 12			55·00	38·00

Design: *Octagonal Shape* (65×51 *mm*)—Nos. 499/504 Scout saluting, Baden-Powell and badge.

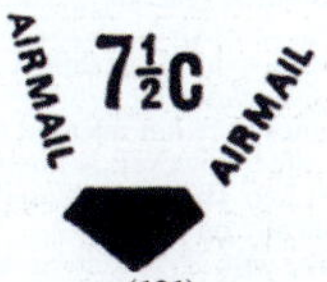

(121)

1970 (28 Mar). *Air. No. 443 surch as T* 121.

505	**103**	7½c. on ½c. multicoloured (G.)	30	10
506		9½c. on ½c. multicoloured (P.)	30	10
507		15c. on ½c. multicoloured (B.)	55	25
508		28c. on ½c. multicoloured (G.)	1·00	55
509		40c. on ½c. multicoloured (B.)	1·50	1·50
510		2l. on ½c. multicoloured (Sil.)	6·50	14·00
505/10 Each Territory *Set of* 6			9·00	15·00
505/10 Six Territories *Set of* 36			48·00	80·00

122 Expo Symbol and Maps of Sierra Leone and Japan

(Litho Walsall)

1970 (22 June). *World Fair, Osaka. T* **122** *and similar design.* Imperf. *Self-adhesive, backed with paper bearing advertisements.*

		(a) Postage.		
511	**122**	2c. multicoloured	10	10
512		3½c. multicoloured	10	10
513		10c. multicoloured	15	10
514		12½c. multicoloured	15	10
515		20c. multicoloured	20	10
516		45c. multicoloured	45	45
		(b) Air.		
517	–	7½c. multicoloured	10	10
518	–	9½c. multicoloured	15	10
519	–	15c. multicoloured	20	10
520	–	25c. multicoloured	40	20
521	–	50c. multicoloured	55	50
522		3l. multicoloured	1·75	5·50
511/22 *Set of* 12			3·75	6·50

Design: *Chrysanthemum shape* (43×42 *mm*)—Nos. 517/22 Maps of Sierra Leone and Japan.

123 Diamond

124 Palm Nut

(Litho and embossed Walsall)

1970 (3 Oct). Imperf. *Self-adhesive, backed with paper bearing advertisements.*

523	**123**	1c. multicoloured	25	20
524		1½c. multicoloured	25	20
525		2c. multicoloured	25	10
526		2½c. multicoloured	25	10
527		3c. multicoloured	30	10
528		3½c. multicoloured	30	10
529		4c. multicoloured	40	10
530		5c. multicoloured	50	10
531	**124**	6c. multicoloured	30	10
532		7c. multicoloured	35	15
533		8½c. multicoloured	50	15
534		9c. multicoloured	50	15
535		10c. multicoloured	55	15
536		11½c. multicoloured	70	20
537		18½c. multicoloured	1·60	55

1970 (3 Oct). *Air. As T* **102**, *but embossed on white paper. Backed with paper bearing advertisements.*

538	**102**	7½c. gold and red	45	10
539		9½c. rose and bright green	50	10
540		15c. pink and greenish blue	1·25	20
541		25c. gold and purple	2·25	50
542		50c. bright green and orange	4·50	2·75
543		1l. royal blue and silver	9·00	11·00
544		2l. ultramarine and gold	15·00	24·00
523/44 *Set of* 22			35·00	35·00

HAVE YOU READ THE NOTES AT THE BEGINNING OF THIS CATALOGUE?
These often provide answers to the enquiries we receive

126 "Jewellery Box" and Sewa Diadem

(Litho and embossed Walsall)

1970 (30 Dec). *Diamond Industry. T* **126** *and similar design. Imperf (backing paper roul 20). Self-adhesive, backed with paper bearing advertisements. (a) Postage.*

545	**126**	2c. multicoloured	35	10
546		3½c. multicoloured	35	10
547		10c. multicoloured	60	15
548		12½c. multicoloured	80	25
549		40c. multicoloured	2·25	1·00
550		1l. multicoloured	12·00	10·00
		(b) Air.		
551	–	7½c. multicoloured	60	10
552	–	9½c. multicoloured	70	10
553	–	15c. multicoloured	1·10	30
554	–	25c. multicoloured	1·50	60
555	–	75c. multicoloured	7·00	5·50
556		2l. multicoloured	27·00	24·00
545/556 *Set of* 12			48·00	38·00

Design: *Horiz* (63×61 *mm*)—Nos. 551/6, Diamond and curtain.

STAMP BOOKLETS

1929.

SB1	1s. booklet containing twelve 1d. (No. 132a)...
SB2	2s. booklet containing twelve 2d. (No. 134).....

Singapore

A Crown Colony until the end of 1957. From 1 August 1958, an internally self-governing territory designated the State of Singapore. From 16 September 1963, part of the Malaysian Federation until 9 August 1965, when it became an independent republic within the Commonwealth.

Stamps in the Crown Colony Victory design with face values of 8c. and 15c. were prepared for Singapore in 1946, but were not issued.

(Currency. 100 cents = 1 Malayan, dollar)

CROWN COLONY

(Typo D.L.R.)

1948 (1 Sept)–**52**. *As T* **58** *of Malaysia (Straits Settlements), but inscribed "SINGAPORE" at foot. Chalk-surfaced paper.* Wmk Mult Script CA.

	(a) P 14.		
1	1c. black	15	1·00
2	2c. orange	15	70
3	3c. green	50	1·50
4	4c. brown	20	1·50
5	6c. grey	40	1·00
6	8c. scarlet (1.10.48)	50	1·00
7	10c. purple	30	10
8	15c. ultramarine (1.10.48)	11·00	10
9	20c. black and green (1.10 48)	5·50	75
10	25c. purple and orange (1.10.48)	7·00	40
11	40c. red and purple (1.10.48)	9·50	5·00
12	50c. black and blue (1.10.48)	3·25	10
13	$1 blue and purple (1.10.48)	10·00	4·00
14	$2 green and scarlet (25.10.48)	48·00	5·00
15	$5 green and brown (1.10.48)	£110	6·00
1/15 *Set of* 15		£180	25·00
	(b) P 17½×18.		
16	1c. black (21.5.52)	1·50	4·25
17	2c. orange (31.10.49)	1·50	2·00
19	4c. brown (1.7.49)	1·50	10
19*a*	5c. bright purple (1.9.52)	3·00	2·00
21	6c. grey (10.12.52)	2·00	2·00
21*a*	8c. green (1.9.52)	7·50	4·00
22	10c. purple (9.2.50)	60	10
22*a*	12c. scarlet (1.9.52)	12·00	13·00
23	15c. ultramarine (9.2.50)	18·00	10
24	20c. black and green (31.10.49)	9·00	3·50
24*a*	20c. bright blue (1.9.52)	7·50	10
25	25c. purple and orange (9.2.50)	2·25	10
25*a*	35c. scarlet and purple (1.9.52)	7·00	1·00
26	40c. red and purple (30.4.51*)	45·00	18·00
27	50c. black and blue (9.2.50)	8·50	10
28	$1 blue and purple (31.10.49)	17·00	20
	a. Error. St. Edward's Crown, W **9***b*	£11000	£3750
29	$2 green and scarlet (24.5.51)	90·00	1·25
	a. Error. St. Edward's Crown. W **9***b*	£14000	
	w. Wmk inverted		
30	$5 green and brown (19.12.51)	£190	1·50
	w. Wmk inverted		
16/30 *Set of* 18		£375	48·00

*Earliest known postmark date.

Single-colour values were from single plate printings (Die II) and all bi-colour, except the 25c., from separate head and duty plates (Die I). For differences between the Dies see after Nos. 278/98 of Malaysia (Straits Settlements). The 25c. is unique in this series in that it combines a Die II frame with a separate head plate.

Nos. 28a and 29a occur on rows in the watermark in which the crowns and letters "CA" alternate.

Postal forgeries of the 50c., $1 and $2 exist on unwatermarked paper and perforated 14×14½.

1948 (25 Oct). *Royal Silver Wedding. As Nos. 112/13 of Antigua.*

31		10c. violet	75	1·00
32		$5. brown	£110	50·00

1949 (10 Oct). *75th Anniv of U.P.U. As Nos. 114/17 of Antigua.*

33		10c. purple	75	70
34		15c. deep blue	6·00	4·25
35		25c. orange	6·00	3·00
36		50c. blue-black	6·00	3·25
33/6 *Set of* 4			17·00	10·00

1953 (2 June). *Coronation. As No. 120 of Antigua.*

37		10c. black and reddish purple	2·00	30

1 Chinese Sampan

2 Malay kolek

3 Twa-kow lighter

4 Lombok sloop

5 Trengganu pinas

6 Palari schooner

7 Timber tongkong

8 Hainan junk

9 Cocos-Keeling schooner

10 Douglas DC-4M2 "Argonaut" aircraft

11 Oil tanker

12 *Chusan III* (liner)

13 Raffles Statue

14 Singapore River

15 Arms of Singapore

(Des Dr. C. A. Gibson-Hill, except 25c., 30c., 50c. and $5 (from photographs, etc.). Photo Harrison (1c. to 50a.). Recess (centre typo on $5) B.W. (others)

1955–59. *T* **1/15**. Wmk Mult Script CA. P 13½×14½ (1c. to 50c.) or 14 (others).

38	**1**	1c. black	10	1·00
39	**2**	2c. yellow-orange	2·00	1·25
40	**3**	4c. brown	1·00	15
		w. Wmk inverted	£225	£250
41	**4**	5c. bright purple	65	40
42	**5**	6c. deep grey-blue	65	70
43	**6**	8c. turquoise-blue	1·25	1·00
44	**7**	10c. deep lilac	3·00	10
45	**8**	12c. rose-carmine	4·00	2·75
46	**9**	20c. ultramarine	2·25	10
		a. *Blue* (13.3.58)	6·50	30
47	**10**	25c. orange-red and bluish violet	7·00	1·50
		a. *Orange-red and purple* (21.1.59)	27·00	3·75
48	**11**	30c. violet and brown-purple	3·75	10
49	**12**	50c. blue and black	2·25	10
50	**13**	$1 blue and deep purple	30·00	30
		a. Deep purple (Queen's head) omitted	£13000	
51	**14**	$2 blue-green and scarlet	42·00	1·75
52	**15**	$5 yellow, red, brown and slate-black	42·00	5·00
38/52 *Set of* 15			£120	14·50

Plate 2A and 2B of the 10c. (12 April 1960) and the blue "3A" and "3B" plates of the 50c. "3A-2A" "3B-2B" (part of the 24 January 1961 issue and later printings) were printed with a finer screen (250 dots per inch, instead of the normal 200) (*Price* 10c. £3.75 *un*, 20p *us*. 50c. £3.50 *un*, 10p *us*). No. 50a was caused by a paper fold.

INTERNAL SELF-GOVERNMENT

16 The Singapore Lion

17 State Flag

(Photo Harrison)

1959 (1 June). *New Constitution.* W w **12.** P 11½×12.

53	**16**	4c. yellow, sepia and rose-red	65	75
54		10c. yellow, sepia and reddish purple	1·00	40
55		20c. yellow, sepia and bright blue	2·25	3·00
56		25c. yellow, sepia and green	2·50	2·25
57		30c. yellow, sepia and violet	2·50	3·25
58		50c. yellow, sepia and deep slate	3·25	3·25
53/8 *Set of* 6			11·00	11·50

(Litho Enschede)

1960. *National Day.* W w **12** (sideways*). P 13½.

59	**17**	4c. red, yellow and blue	1·50	1·50
		w. Wmk Crown to right of CA	75·00	
60		10c. red, yellow and grey	2·75	30
		w. Wmk Crown to right of CA	70·00	

*The normal sideways watermark shows Crown to left of CA, *as seen from the back of the stamp.*

18 Clasped Hands

(Photo Enschedé)

1961 (3 June). *National Day.* W w **12** P 13½.

61	**18**	4c. black, brown and pale yellow	1·00	1·75
62		10c. black, deep green and pale yellow	1·25	10

19 *Arachnis "Maggie Oei"* (orchid)

20 Yellow Seahorse

21 Tiger Barb

24 *Vanda "Tan Chay Yan"* (orchid)

26a Black-naped Tern

30 White-rumped Shama

(Photo Harrison orchids, fish and 15c. bird) D.L.R. (birds, except 15c.)

1962 (31 Mar)–**66**. *T* **19/21**, **24**, **26a**, **30** *and similar designs.* W w **12** P 12½ (i), 14½×13½ (ii), 13½×14½ (iii), 13½×13 (iv) or 13×13½ (v).

63		1c. multicoloured	30	1·00
64		2c. brown and green	30	2·00
65		4c. black and orange-red	30	1·25
		a. Black omitted	£700	
66		5c. red and black	20	10
		a. Red omitted	£600	
67		6c. black and greenish yellow	55	1·25
68		8c. muticoloured (i) (10.3.63)	1·25	3·50
69		10c. red-orange and black (iii)	40	10
		a. Red-orange omitted	£375	£300
		b. Black omitted	£4000	
70		12c. multicoloured (i) (10.3.63)	1·25	3·50
70*a*		15c. multicoloured (i) (9.11.66)	4·00	10
		ab. Orange (eye) omitted	60·00	
		ac. Stone (shading in wings) omitted	£325	
		aw. Wmk inverted	23·00	
71		20c. orange and blue (ii)	40	10
		a. Orange omitted	£750	
72		25c. black and orange (iii)	75	10
		a. Black omitted	£700	
73		30c. multicoloured (i) (10.3.63)	1·25	10
		a. Yellow (flowers) omitted	£120	
		w. Wmk inverted	75·00	
74		50c. multicoloured (iv) (10.3.63)	1·25	10
75		$1 multicoloured (iv) (10.3.63)	18·00	60
76		$2 multicoloured (iv) (10.3.63)	9·00	1·00
77		$5 multicoloured (v) (10.3.63)	18·00	6·50
		w. Wmk inverted	£150	
63/77 *Set of* 16			50·00	19·00

Designs: Horiz (as *T* **21**)—5c. Orange Clownfish; 10c. Harlequinfish; 25c. Three-spotted Gorami. (As *T* **30**)—$1 White-breasted Kingfisher. Vert (as *T* **20**)—6c. Archerfish; 20c. Copper-banded Butterflyfish. (As *T* **24**)—12c. *Grammatophyllum speciosum* (orchid); 30c. *Vanda* "Miss Joaquim" (orchid). (As *T* **26a**)—$2 Yellow-bellied Sunbird; $5 White-bellied Sea Eagle.

The 10c. exists in coils, constructed from normal sheets.

The 15c., 30c., $2 and $5 exist with PVA gum as well as gum arabic.

See also Nos. 83/8.

34 "The Role of Labour in Nation-Building"

35 Blocks of Flats, Singapore

(Photo Courvoisier)

1962 (3 June). *National Day.* P 11½×12.

78	**34**	4c. yellow, rose-carmine and black	1·25	2·25
79		10c. yellow, blue and black	1·50	75

(Photo Harrison)

1963 (3 June). *National Day.* W w **12.** P 12½.

80	**35**	4c. orange-red, black, blue and turquoise-blue	50	80
81		10c. orange-red, black, yellow-olive and turquoise-blue	1·75	20
		w. Wmk inverted	50·00	

36 Dancers in National Costume

37 Workers

(Photo Harrison)

1963 (8 Aug). *South East Asia. Cultural Festival.* W w **12.** P 14×14½.

82	**36**	5c. multicoloured	50	50

INDEPENDENT REPUBLIC

1966 (1 Mar)–**67**. *As Nos* 63, 66, 69, 72, 74/5, *but W w* **12** *(sideways*)*.

83		1c. multicoloured (22.6.67)	10	2·00
84		5c. red and black (30.5.67)	3·50	2·75
85		10c. red-orange and black (19.5.67†)	1·75	1·25
86		25c. black and orange (9.66†)	70	2·00
		w. Wmk Crown to right of CA	3·75	
87		50c. multicoloured (11.1.66†)	4·50	3·00
		a. Imperf (pair)	£600	
88		$1 multicoloured (18.5.67)	16·00	12·00
83/8 *Set of* 6			23·00	21·00

*The normal sideways watermark show Crown to left of CA, *as seen from the back of the stamp.*

†The 25 and 50c. values were not released in London until 30.5.67 and 9.6.66. The 25c. value, however, is known used in September 1966 and the 50c. on 11.1.66. The 10c., released in London on 30 May 1967, is known used locally on 19 May.

The 1c. and 25c. exist with PVA gum as well as gum arabic.

(Photo D.L.R.)

1966 (9 Aug). *First Anniv of Republic. (30c.) or no wmk (others).* W w **12.** P 12½×13.

89	**37**	15c. multicoloured	75	30
90		20c. multicoloured	1·00	1·25
91		30c. multicoloured	1·25	2·00
89/91 *Set of* 3			2·75	3·25

38 Flag Procession

(Photo D.L.R.)

1967 (9 Aug). *National Day.* P 14×14½.

92	**38**	6c. rosine, brown and slate	50	90
93		15c. reddish purple, brown and slate	80	10
94		50c. bright blue, brown and slate	1·50	1·60
92/4 *Set of 3*			2·50	2·25

Nos. 92/4 are respectively inscribed "Build a Vigorous Singapore" in Chinese, Malay and Tamil in addition to the English inscription.

39 Skyscrapers and Afro-Asian Map

40 Symbolical Figure wielding Hammer, and Industrial Outline of Singapore

(Photo D.L.R.)

1967 (7 Oct). *2nd Afro-Asian Housing Congress.* P 14×13.

95	**39**	10c. multicoloured	30	10
		a. Opt omitted	£1100	£1100
96		25c. multicoloured	75	1·00
97		50c. multicoloured	1·40	1·60
95/7 *Set of 3*			2·25	2·40

The above were originally scheduled for release in 1966, and when finally issued were overprinted with the new date and a black oblong obliterating the old date.

(Photo Harrison)

1968 (9 Aug). *National Day. Inscription at top in Chinese* (6c.), *Malay* (15c.) *or Tamil* (50c.). P 13½×14.

98	**40**	6c. orange-red, black and gold	35	65
99		15c. apple-green, black and gold	45	15
100		50c. greenish blue, black and gold	1·00	1·25
98/100 *Set of 3*			1·60	1·90

41 Half check Pattern

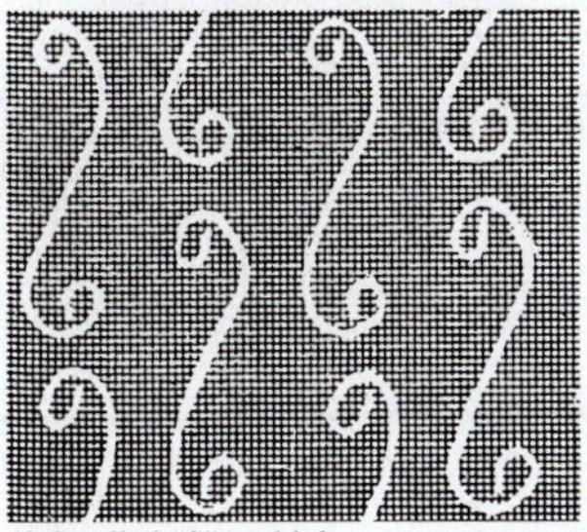

42 Scrolled "S" multiple

43 Mirudhangam

44 Pi Pa

45 Sword Dance

51 Dragon Dance

(Photo D.L.R. (5c. to $1), Japanese Govt Printing Bureau, Tokyo)

1968 (1 Dec)–**73**. *T* **43/5**, **51** *and similar designs.* (5c. *to* $1) *or* W **42** (*upright on* 1c., $5; *sideways on* 4c., $2, $10). *Chalk-surfaced paper* (5c. *to* $1). W **41**. P 14 (5c. to $1) or 13½ (others).

101	1c. multicoloured (10.11.69)	15	2·25
102	4c. multicoloured (10.11.69)	60	3·00
103	5c. multicoloured (29.12.68)	60	1·75
	a. Glazed unsurfaced paper (16.12.70)	14·00	13·00
	b. Perf 13 (27.6.73)	7·50	10·00
104	6c. black, lemon and orange	1·75	2·25
105	10c. multicoloured (29.12.68)	20	10
	a. Glazed unsurfaced paper (16.12.70)	15·00	10·00
	b. Perf 13 (14.7.73*)	15·00	8·50
106	15c. multicoloured (29.12.68)	60	10
107	20c. multicoloured	1·00	1·75
	a. Perf 13 (12.9.73)	12·00	17·00
108	25c. multicoloured (29.12.68)	1·25	1·75
	a. Perf 13 (27.6.73)	7·50	13·00
109	30c. multicoloured	40	1·50
	a. Perf 13 (12.9.73)	12·00	18·00
110	50c. black, orange-red and light yellow-brown	50	1·00
	a. Perf 13 (12.9.73)	12·00	32·00
111	75c. multicoloured	3·00	4·25
112	$1 multicoloured (29.12.68)	4·50	1·25
	a. Perf 13 (12.9.73)	22·00	25·00
113	$2 multicoloured (10.11.69)	3·50	1·00
114	$5 multicoloured (10.11.69)	13·00	1·50
115	$10 multicoloured (6.12.69)	38·00	15·00
101/15 *Set of 15*		60·00	35·00
103b/12a *Set of 7*		75·00	£110

Designs: Vert (as *T* **45**)—6c. Lion dance; 10c. Bharatha Natyam; 15c. Tari Payong; 20c. Kathak Kali; 25c. Lu Chih Shen and Lin Chung; 50c. Tari Lilin; 75c. Tarian Kuda Kepang; $1 Yao Chi. (As *T* **44**—$2, Rebab; $10 Ta Ku. Horiz (as *T* **43**)—$5 Vina.

*Earliest known date of use.

58 E.C.A.F.E. Emblem

59 "100000" and Slogan as Block of Flats

(Des Eng Sisk Loy. Photo Japanese Govt Ptg Bureau, Tokyo)

1969 (15 Apr). *25th Plenary Session of the U.N. Economic Commission for Asia and the Far East.* P 13.

116	**58**	15c. black, silver and pale blue	35	20
117		30c. black, silver and red	65	1·25
118		75c. black, silver and violet-blue	1·00	2·50
116/18 *Set of 3*			1·75	3·50

(Des Tay Siew Chiah. Litho B. W.)

1969 (20 July). *Completion of "100,000 Homes for the People" Project.* P 13½.

119	**59**	25c. black and emerald	1·00	50
120		50c. black and deep blue	1·25	1·25

60 Aircraft over Silhouette of Singapore Docks

61 Sea Shells

(Des Eng Siak Loy and Han Kuan Cheng. Litho B.W.)

1969 (9 Aug). *150th Anniv of Founding of Singapore. T* **60** *and similar vert designs.* P 14×14½.

121	15c. black, vermilion and yellow	2·50	70
122	30c. black, blue and new blue	2·50	1·00
123	75c. multicoloured	4·50	1·00
124	$1 black and vermilion	9·00	10·00
125	$5 vermilion and black	18·00	45·00
126	$10 black and bright green	27·00	45·00
121/6 *Set of 6*		55·00	90·00
MS127 120×120 mm. Nos. 121/6. P 13½		£450	£475

Designs:—30c. U.N. emblem and outline of Singapore; 75c. Flags and outline of Malaysian Federation; $1 Uplifted hands holding crescent and stars; $5 Tail of Japanese aircraft and searchlight beams; $10 Bust from statue of Sir Stamford Raffles.

(Des Tay Siew Chiah (15c.), Eng Siak Loy (others). Litho Rosenbaum Bros, Vienna)

1970 (15 Mar). *World Fair, Osaka. T* **61** *and similar vert designs. Multicoloured.* P 13½.

128	15c. Type **61**	1·25	15
129	30c. Veil-tailed Guppys	1·75	70
130	75c. Greater Flamingo and Helmeted Hornbill	5·00	2·75
131	$1 Orchid	5·00	5·50
128/31 *Set of 4*		11·50	8·25
MS132 94×154 mm. Nos. 128/31		24·00	24·00

62 "Kindergarten"

63 Soldier charging

(Des Choy Weng Yang. Litho B.W.)

1970 (1 July). *Tenth Anniv of People's Association. T* **62** *and similar square designs.* P 13½.

133	15c. agate and bright orange	85	20
134	50c. ultramarine and yellow-orange	2·25	2·75
135	75c. bright, purple and black	3·50	4·50
133/5 *Set of 3*		6·00	6·75

Designs:—50c. "Sport"; 75c. "Culture".

(Des Choy Weng Yang. Litho Rosenbaum Bros, Vienna)

1970 (9 Aug). *National Day. T* **63** *and similar vert designs. Multicoloured.* P 13½.

136	15c. Type **63**	1·25	20
137	50c. Soldier on assault course	3·75	3·50
138	$1 Soldier jumping	5·00	11·00
136/8 *Set of 3*		9·00	13·00

64 Sprinters

(Des Choy Weng Yang. Photo Japanese Govt Ptg Bureau, Tokyo)

1970 (23 Aug). *Festival of Sports. T* **64** *and similar horiz designs.* P 13×13½.

139	10c. magenta, black and ultramarine	2·00	3·25
	a. Horiz strip of 4. Nos. 139/42	9·00	13·00
140	15c. black, ultramarine and red-orange	2·50	3·50
141	25c. black, red-orange and bright green	2·75	3·75
142	50c. black, bright green and magenta	3·00	3·75
139/42 *Set of 4*		9·25	12·50

Designs:—15c. Swimmers; 25c. Tennis-players; 50c. Racing cars.

Nos. 139/42 were issued together *se-tenant* in horizontal strips of four within the sheet.

65 *Neptune Aquamarine* (freighter)

(Des W. Lee. Litho Rosenbaum Bros, Vienna)

1970 (1 Nov). *Singapore Shipping. T* **65** *and similar horiz designs.* P 12.

143	15c. multicoloured	2·75	65
144	30c. yellow-ochre and ultramarine	6·00	5·50
145	75c. yellow-ochre and vermillion	10·00	10·00
143/5 *Set of 3*		17·00	14·50

Designs:—30c. Container berth; 75c. Shipbuilding.

STAMP BOOKLET

1969 (1 Nov). *Black on green cover. Stapled.*

SB1	$1.80 booklet containing twelve 15c. (No. 106) in blocks of 4	50·00

POSTAGE DUE STAMPS

The postage due stamps of Malayan Postal Union were in use in Singapore until replaced by the following issues.

D 1

(Litho B.W.)

1968 (1 Feb)–**69**. *Toned paper.* W w **12**. P 9.

D1	**D 1**	1c. green	60	2·00
D2		2c. red	1·60	2·50
D3		4c. yellow-orange	2·00	5·50
D4		8c. chocolate	1·00	2·00
D5		10c. magenta	1·00	90
		a. White paper (16.12.69)	2·25	6·00
D6		12c. slate-violet	2·75	3·25
		a. White paper (16.12.69)	7·00	13·00
D7		20c. new blue	2·00	3·50
		a. White paper (16.12.69)	10·00	14·00
D8		50c. drab	11·00	5·50
D1/8 *Set of 8*			20·00	22·00

In 1973 the 10c. and 50c. were reissued on whiter paper, perf 13×13½. In 1977–8 the 1c., 4c., 10c., 20c. and 50c. were issued on unwatermarked paper, perf 13×13½.

Somaliland Protectorate

Egyptian post offices were opened in Somaliland during 1876 and the stamps of Egypt were used there until the garrisons were withdrawn in 1884.

Cancellations for these offices have been identified as follows (for illustrations of postmark types see SUDAN).

BARBARA (Berbera). Open 1876 to 1 November 1884. Circular datestamp as Sudan Type I.

ZEILA. Open 1876 to 1 November 1884. Circular datestamp as Sudan Types G and I, sometimes inscr ZEJLA. One example with seal type cancellation as Sudan Type B is also known.

Stamps of India were used at the two post offices from 1 January 1887 until 1903 usually cancelled with circular datestamps or the "B" obliterator used by all offices controlled from Bombay.

The Protectorate Post Office was established on 1 June 1903, when control of British Somaliland was transferred from the Indian Government to the British Foreign Office.

PRICES FOR STAMPS ON COVER TO 1945

Nos. 1/11	*from* × 25
Nos. 12/13	—
Nos. 18/22	*from* × 12
Nos. 23/4	—
Nos. 25/30	*from* × 30
Nos. 32/59	*from* × 12
Nos. 60/92	*from* × 6
Nos. 93/104	*from* × 3
Nos. 105/16	*from* × 4
Nos. O1/13	*from* × 8
Nos. O14/15	—

(Currency. 12 pies = 1 anna; 16 annas = 1 rupee)

BRITISH SOMALILAND
(1)

2

3

SETTINGS OF TYPE 1

In all printings the ½, 1, 2, 2½, 3, 4, 8, 12a. and 1r. values were overprinted from a setting of 240 (2 panes 12×10, one above the other), covering the entire sheet at one operation.

The 6a., which was in sheets of 320 (4 panes, each 8×10), had a modified setting of 160, applied twice to each sheet.

The high values were overprinted in sheets of 96 (8 panes, each 4×3).

The settings for the low value stamps contained two slightly different styles of overprint, identified by the position of "B" of "BRITISH". Type A shows this letter over the "M" of "SOMALILAND" and Type B over the "OM".

For the first printing with the overprint at the top of the design the 240 position setting showed all the stamps in the upper pane and 63 in the lower as Type A, with the remaining 57 as Type B. When the setting was used for the printing with overprint at foot it was amended slightly so that one of the Type A examples in the upper pane became a Type B.

The 6a. value with overprint at top shows 250 examples of Type A and 70 as Type B in each sheet. This proportion altered in the printing with overprint at foot to 256 as Type A and 64 as Type B.

OVERPRINT VARIETIES

Missing second "I" in "BRITISH"—Occurs on the stamps with overprint at top from R. 2/6 of the upper pane and R. 5/1 of the lower, although it is believed that the example on the 2½a. (No. 4a) only occurs from the second position. On the later printing with overprint at foot a similar error can be found on R. 7/12 of the upper pane. Some examples of both these errors show traces of the letter remaining, but the prices quoted are for stamps with it completely omitted.

Figure "1" for first "I" in "BRITISH"—Occurs on R. 6/4 of the upper pane for all printings of the 240 impression setting. In addition it has been reported from R. 7/12 of the Queen Victoria 2½, 12a. and 1r. with overprint at foot. Both versions of the 6a. show the variety on R. 6/4 of the upper left and upper right panes.

Curved overprint—Occurs on R. 3/4 of the top right-hand pane of the high values.

"SUMALILAND"—Occurs on R. 2/9 of the upper pane for all low values with the overprint at foot, except the 6a. A similar variety occurs on the high values from the same series on R. 1/3 of the top left pane.

"SOMAL.LAND"—Occurs on R. 7/5 of the lower pane from the 240 impression setting with the overprint at foot. In addition the Edwardian values of this series also have an example on R. 6/7. The 6a. has examples of the flaw on R. 6/9 and R. 7/5 of both the lower right and left panes. A similar variety occurs on the high values from the same series at R. 3/4 of the third pane in the right-hand column.

1903 (1 June). *Nos. 80, 94, 96, 98, 100, 106/9, 114/16 and 118 of India (Queen Victoria) optd with T* **1**, *at top of stamp, in Calcutta.* Wmk Elephant Head (6a.) or Star (others).

1		½a. yellow-green	2·75	4·25
		a. "BRIT SH"	£170	£250
		b. "BR1TISH"	£150	£225
2		1a. carmine	2·75	3·75
		a. "BRIT SH"	£200	£275
		b. "BR1TISH"	£150	
3		2a. pale violet	2·25	1·50
		a. "BRIT SH"	£375	£450
		b. "BR1TISH"	£300	
		c. Opt double	£800	
4		2½a. ultramarine	2·00	1·75
		a. "BRIT SH"	£550	
		b. "BR1TISH"	£350	
5		3a. brown-orange	3·25	3·00
		a. "BRIT SH"	£750	
		b. "BR1TISH"	£375	£400
6		4a. slate-green	3·50	2·75
		a. "BR1TISH"	£375	£400
7		6a. olive-bistre	6·00	4·50
		a. "BR1TISH"	£275	£300
8		8a. dull mauve	3·75	5·00
		a. "BR1TISH"	£375	
9		12a. purple/*red*	3·50	7·00
		a. "BR1TISH"	£375	£475
10		1r. green and aniline carmine	7·50	10·00
		a. "BR1TISH"	£450	
11		2r. carmine and yellow-brown	26·00	42·00
		a. Curved opt	£425	
12		3r. brown and green	22·00	50·00
		a. Curved opt	£425	
13		5r. ultramarine and violet	42·00	60·00
		a. Curved opt	£475	
1/13 *Set of* 13			£110	£180

1903 (1 Sept–2 Nov). *Stamps of India optd with T* **1**, *at bottom of stamp, in Calcutta.*

(a) On Nos. 80, 100, 106/9 and 118 (Queen Victoria).

18		2½a. ultramarine (2.11)	4·25	8·50
		a. "BR1TISH"	£190	
		b. "SUMALILAND"	£250	
		c. "SOMAL.LAND"	£250	
		d. "BRIT SH"	£1000	
19		6a. olive-bistre (2.11)	7·50	7·00
		a. "BR1TISH"	£275	
		b. "SOMAL.LAND"	£160	
20		12a. purple/*red* (2.11)	9·00	14·00
		a. "BR1TISH"	£275	
		b. "SUMALILAND"	£325	
		c. "SOMAL.LAND"	£325	
21		1r. green and aniline carmine (2.11)	5·00	11·00
		a. "BR1TISH"	£325	
		b. "SUMALILAND"	£425	
		c. "SOMAL.LAND"	£425	
22		2r. carmine and yellow-brown (2.11)	£100	£160
		a. Curved opt	£700	£1000
		b. "SUMALILAND"	£700	
		c. "SOMAL.LAND"	£700	
23		3r. brown and green (2.11)	£100	£160
		a. Opt double, both inverted with one albino	£750	
		b. Curved opt	£750	
		c. "SUMALILAND"	£750	
		d. "SOMAL.LAND"	£750	
24		5r. ultramarine and violet (2.11)	95·00	£140
		a. Curved opt	£650	
		b. "SUMALILAND"	£650	
		c. "SOMAL.LAND"	£650	

(b) On Nos. 122/4, 127/8 and 133 (King Edward VII).

25		½a. green	2·25	55
		a. "BRIT SH"	£400	
		b. "BR1TISH"	95·00	
		c. "SUMALILAND"	95·00	
		d. "SOMAL.LAND"	55·00	65·00
26		1a. carmine (8.10)	1·25	30
		a. "BRIT SH"	£275	
		b. "BR1TISH"	95·00	£100
		c. "SUMALILAND"	95·00	
		d. "SOMAL.LAND"	50·00	55·00
27		2a. violet (2.11)	1·75	2·50
		a. "BRIT SH"	£1100	
		b. "BR1TISH"	£190	
		c. "SUMALILAND"	£190	
		d. "SOMAL.LAND"	£100	
28		3a. orange-brown (2.11)	2·50	2·50
		a. "BR1TISH"	£200	£250
		b. "SUMALILAND"	£200	
		c. "SOMAL.LAND"	£100	£120
29		4a. olive (2.11)	1·50	4·00
		a. "BR1TISH"	£180	
		b. "SUMALILAND"	£180	
		c. "SOMAL.LAND"	£100	
30		8a. purple (2.11)	1·75	2·25
		a. "BR1TISH"	£275	
		b. "SUMALILAND"	£275	
		c. "SOMAL.LAND"	£150	
18/30 *Set of* 13			£300	£450

(Typo D.L.R.)

1904 (15 Feb–3 Sept).

(a) Wmk Crown CA. P 14.

32	**2**	½a. dull green and green	2·25	4·25
33		1a. grey-black and red (3.9)	14·00	3·25
34		2a. dull and bright purple (3.9)	2·25	2·25
35		2½a. bright blue (3.9)	5·50	3·75
36		3a. chocolate and grey-green (3.9)	2·50	2·75
37		4a. green and black (3.9)	2·75	4·75
38		6a. green and violet (3.9)	6·50	17·00
39		8a. grey-black and pale blue (3.9)	5·00	6·00
40		12a. grey-black and orange-buff (3.9)	8·00	11·00

(b) Wmk Crown CC. P 14.

41	**3**	1r. green (3.9)	12·00	40·00
42		2r. dull and bright purple (3.9)	48·00	75·00
43		3r. green and black (3.9)	48·00	95·00
44		5r. grey-black and red (3.9)	48·00	95·00
32/44 *Set of* 13			£180	£325
32s/44s Optd "Specimen" *Set of* 13			£180	

1905 (July)–**11**. *Ordinary paper.* Wmk Mult Crown CA. P 14.

45	**2**	½a. dull green and green	1·25	7·50
46		1a. grey-black and red (10.7.05)	17·00	7·00
		a. Chalk-surfaced paper (1906)	13·00	1·60
47		2a. dull and bright purple	7·50	13·00
		a. Chalk-surfaced paper (1909)	16·00	15·00
48		2½a. bright blue	3·00	10·00
49		3a. chocolate and grey-green	2·00	16·00
		a. Chalk-surfaced paper (1911)	11·00	35·00
50		4a. green and black	4·25	17·00
		a. Chalk-surfaced paper (1911)	16·00	42·00
51		6a. green and violet	3·00	25·00
		a. Chalk-surfaced paper (1911)	28·00	65·00
52		8a. grey-black and pale blue	7·50	11·00
		a. Chalk-surfaced paper. *Black and blue* (27.1.11)	27·00	70·00
53		12a. grey-black and orange-buff	6·50	10·00
		a. Chalk-surfaced paper. *Black and orange-brown* (9.11.11)	17·00	70·00

1909 (30 Apr–May). Wmk Mult Crown CA. P 14.

58	**2**	½a. bluish green (May)	29·00	29·00
59		1a. red	2·50	2·00
		s. Optd "Specimen"	28·00	
45/59 *Set of* 11			70·00	£130

4

5

(Typo D.L.R.)

1912 (Sept)–**19**. *Chalk-surfaced paper (2a. and 3a. to 5r.).* Wmk Mult Crown CA. P 14.

60	**4**	½a. green (11.13)	65	8·00
		w. Wmk inverted	15·00	60·00
61		1a. red	2·50	50
		a. Scarlet (1917)	3·00	1·25
62		2a. dull and bright purple (12.13)	3·50	16·00
		a. Dull purple and violet-purple (4.19)	24·00	40·00
63		2½a. bright blue (10.13)	1·00	8·50
64		3a. chocolate and grey-green (10.13)	2·25	6·50
		w. Wmk inverted	95·00	
65		4a. green and black (12.12)	2·50	10·00
66		6a. green and violet (4.13)	2·50	5·50
67		8a. grey-black and pale blue (10.13)	3·50	15·00
68		12a. grey-black and orange-buff (10.13)	3·50	21·00
69	**5**	1r. green (11.12)	14·00	17·00
70		2r. dull purple and purple (4.19)	23·00	75·00
71		3r. green and black (4.19)	65·00	£130
72		5r. black and scarlet (4.19)	60·00	£180
60/72 *Set of* 13			£160	£425
60s/72s Optd "Specimen" *Set of* 13			£225	

1921. *Chalk-surfaced paper (2a. and 3a. to 5r.).* Wmk Mult Script CA. P 14.

73	**4**	½a. blue-green	2·75	13·00
74		1a. carmine-red	3·50	70
75		2a. dull and bright purple	4·25	1·00
76		2½a. bright blue	1·00	6·00
77		3a. chocolate and green	2·50	7·50
78		4a. green and black	2·50	7·50
79		6a. green and violet	1·50	13·00
80		8a. grey-black and pale blue	2·00	5·50
81		12a. grey-black and orange-buff	8·50	15·00
82	**5**	1r. dull green	8·50	48·00
83		2r. dull purple and purple	23·00	55·00
84		3r. dull green and black	35·00	£110
85		5r. black and scarlet	75·00	£190
73/85 *Set of* 13			£150	£425
73s/85s Optd "Specimen" *Set of* 13			£200	

Examples of most values are known showing a forged Berbera postmark dated "21 OC 1932".

1935 (6 May). *Silver Jubilee. As Nos. 91/4 of Antigua, but ptd by Waterlow.* P 11×12.

86		1a. deep blue and scarlet	2·25	4·00
		m. "Bird" by turret	£110	£150
87		2a. ultramarine and grey	2·75	4·00
		k. Kite and vertical log	85·00	£130
88		3a. brown and deep blue	2·25	17·00
		k. Kite and vertical log	£120	£225
		l. Kite and horizontal log	£110	£225
89		1r. slate and purple	8·00	19·00
		k. Kite and vertical log	£150	
		l. Kite and horizontal log	£160	£250
86/9 *Set of* 4			14·00	40·00
86s/9s Perf "Specimen" *Set of* 4			95·00	

For illustrations of plate varieties see Omnibus section following Zanzibar.

1937 (13 May). *Coronation. As Nos. 95/7 of Antigua, but ptd by D.L.R.* P 14.

90		1a. scarlet	15	50
91		2a. grey-black	55	2·00
92		3a. bright blue	1·10	1·25
90/2 *Set of* 3			1·60	3·25
90s/2s Perf "Specimen" *Set of* 3			85·00	

6 Berbera Blackhead Sheep

7 Lesser Kudu

8 Somaliland Protectorate

(Des H. W. Claxton. Recess Waterlow)

1938 (10 May). *Portrait to left.* Wmk Mult Script CA. P 12½.

93	6	½a. green	70	5·00
94		1a. scarlet	50	2·00
95		2a. maroon	2·50	3·50
96		3a. bright blue	14·00	15·00
97	7	4a. sepia	5·50	10·00
98		6a. violet	11·00	12·00
99		8a. grey	4·25	12·00
100		12a. red-orange	11·00	24·00
101	8	1r. green	9·00	65·00
102		2r. purple	20·00	65·00
103		3r. bright blue	21·00	40·00
104		5r. black	25·00	40·00
		a. Imperf between (horiz pair)	£21000	
93/104 *Set of* 12			£110	£275
93s/104s Perf "Specimen" *Set of* 12			£225	

Examples of most values are known showing a forged Berbera postmark dated "15 AU 38".

Following the Italian Occupation, from 19 August 1940 until 16 March 1941, the stamps of ADEN were used at Berbera from 1 July 1941 until 26 April 1942.

9 Berbera Blackhead Sheep

5 Cents **(10)**   1 Shilling **(11)**

(Recess Waterlow)

1942 (27 Apr). *As T* **6/8** *but with full-face portrait of King George VI, as in T* **9**. Wmk Mult Script CA. P 12½.

105	9	½a. green	25	40
106		1a. scarlet	25	10
107		2a. maroon	70	20
108		3a. bright blue	2·25	20
109	7	4a. sepia	3·00	30
110		6a. violet	3·00	20
111		8a. grey	3·25	20
112		12a. red-orange	3·25	50
113	8	1r. green	2·50	1·75
114		2r. purple	2·75	6·50
115		3r. bright blue	5·50	12·00
116		5r. black	11·00	8·50
105/16 *Set of* 12			35·00	28·00
105s/16s Perf "Specimen" *Set of* 12			£225	

1946 (15 Oct). *Victory. As Nos. 110/11, of Antigua.*

117	1a. carmine	10	10
	a. Perf 13½	14·00	45·00
118	3a. blue	10	10
117s/18s Perf "Specimen" *Set of* 2		75·00	

1949 (28 Jan). *Royal Silver Wedding. As Nos. 112/13 of Antigua.*

119	1a. scarlet	10	10
120	5r. black	3·75	4·25

1949 (24 Oct*). *75th Anniv of U.P.U. As Nos. 114/17 of Antigua. Surch with face values in annas.*

121	1a. on 10c. carmine	20	40
122	3a. on 30c. deep blue (R.)	1·25	2·75
123	6a. on 50c. purple	35	2·75
124	12a. on 1s. red-orange	90	1·75
121/4 *Set of* 4		2·40	7·00

*This is the local date of issue. The Crown Agents released these stamps in London on 10 October.

(New Currency. 100 cents = 1 shilling)

1951 (1 Apr). *1942 issue surch as T* **10/11**.

125	5c. on ½a. green	30	2·00
126	10c. on 2a. maroon	30	1·00
127	15c. on 3a. bright blue	1·75	2·25
128	20c. on 4a. sepia	2·00	20
129	30c. on 6a. violet	1·75	1·00
130	50c. on 8a. grey	2·50	20
131	70c. on 12a. red-orange	4·00	6·00
132	1s. on 1r. green	2·00	1·25
133	2s. on 2r. purple	5·50	18·00
134	2s. on 3r. bright blue	9·00	7·00
135	5s. on 5r. black (R.)	13·00	11·00
125/35 *Set of* 11		38·00	45·00

1953 (2 June). *Coronation. As No. 120 of Antigua.*

136	15c. black and green	30	20

12 Camel and Gurgi

13 Sentry, Somaliland Scouts

14 Somali Stock Dove

15 Martial Eagle

16 Berbera Blackhead Sheep

17 Sheikh Isaaq's Tomb, Mait

18 Taleh Fort

(Recess B.W.)

1953 (15 Sept)–**58**. *T* **12/18**. Wmk Mult Script CA. P 12½.

137	12	5c. slate-black	15	50
138	13	10c. red-orange	2·25	60
		a. Salmon (20.3.58)	9·00	2·75
139	12	15c. blue-green	60	60
140		20c. scarlet	60	40
141	13	30c. reddish brown	2·25	40
142	14	35c. blue	5·50	1·75
143	15	50c. brown and rose-carmine	6·00	55
144	16	1s. light blue	1·00	30
145	17	1s.30 ultramarine and black (1.9.58)	13·00	3·25
146	14	2s. brown and bluish violet	28·00	6·00
147	15	5s. red-brown and emerald	32·00	7·00
148	–	10s. brown and reddish violet	22·00	24·00
137/48 *Set of* 12			£100	40·00

OPENING OF THE LEGISLATIVE COUNCIL 1957 **(19)**

LEGISLATIVE COUNCIL UNOFFICIAL MAJORITY. 1960 **(20)**

1957 (21 May). *Opening of Legislative Council. Nos. 140 and 144 optd with T* **19**.

149	20c. scarlet	10	15
150	1s. light blue	30	15

1960 (5 Apr). *Legislative Council's Unofficial Majority. Nos, 140 and 145 optd as T* **20**.

151	20c. scarlet	10	15
152	1s.30 ultramarine and black	1·50	15

OFFICIAL STAMPS

SERVICE

BRITISH SOMALILAND **(O 1)**   BRITISH SOMALILAND **(O 2)**   O.H.M.S. **(O 3)**

SETTING OF TYPE O 1

The 240 impression setting used for the Official stamps differs considerably from that on the contemporary postage issue with overprint at foot, although the "BR1TISH" error can still be found on R. 6/4 of the upper pane. The Official setting is recorded as consisting of 217 overprints as Type A and 23 as Type B.

OVERPRINT VARIETIES

Figure "1" for first "I" in "BRITISH"—Occurs on R. 6/4 of the upper pane as for the postage issue.

"BRITIS H"—Occurs on "R. 8/4" of the lower pane.

1903 (1 June). *Nos. O45, O48, O49a and O50/1 of India (Queen Victoria optd "O.H.M.S.") additionally optd with Type* O **1** *in Calcutta.*

O1	½a. yellow-green	6·50	48·00
	a. "BR1TISH"	£400	
	b. "BRITIS H"	£225	£650
O2	1a. carmine	15·00	10·00
	a. "BR1TISH"	£400	£450
	b. "BRITIS H"	£225	£375
O3	2a. pale violet	8·50	50·00
	a. "BR1TISH"	£475	
	b. "BRITIS H"	£275	
O4	8a. dull mauve	10·00	£400
	a. "BR1TISH"	£1300	
	b. "BRITIS H"	£750	
	c. Stop omitted after "M" of "O.H.M.S." (lower pane R. 10/12)	£3000	
O5	1r. green and carmine	10·00	£600
	a. "BR1TISH"	£1400	
	b. "BRITIS H"	£800	
O1/5 *Set of* 5		45·00	£1000

No. O4c was caused by an attempt to correct a minor spacing error of the "O.H.M.S." overprint which is known on the equivalent India Official stamp.

SETTING OF TYPE O 2

This 240 impression setting of "BRITISH SOMALILAND" also differs from that used to prepare the postage issue with overprint at foot, although many of the errors from the latter still occur in the same positions for the Official stamps. The setting used for Nos. O6/9*f* contained 180 overprints as Type A and 60 as Type B.

OVERPRINT VARIETIES

Missing second "I" in "BRITISH"—Occurs R. 7/12 of upper pane as for the postage issue.

Figure "1" for first "I" in "BRITISH"—Occurs R. 6/4 of upper pane as for the postage issue.

"SUMALILAND"—Occurs R. 2/9 of the upper pane as for the postage issue.

"SOMAL.LAND"—Occurs R. 6/7 of the lower pane as for the postage issue.

SERVICE **(O 2a)**

"SERVICE" in wrong fount (Type O **2a**)—Occurs R. 1/7 of lower pane.

1903. *Prepared for use but not issued. Nos. 106, 122/4 and 133 of India (1r. Queen Victoria, rest King Edward VII), optd with Type* O **2** *in Calcutta.*

O6	½a. green	40
	a. "BRIT SH"	70·00
	b. "BR1TISH"	65·00
	c. "SUMALILAND"	65·00
	d. "SOMAL.LAND"	65·00
	e. "SERVICE" as Type O **2a**	65·00
O7	1a. carmine	40
	a. "BRIT SH"	70·00
	b. "BR1TISH"	65·00
	c. "SUMALILAND"	65·00
	d. "SOMAL.LAND"	65·00
	e. "SERVICE" as Type O **2a**	65·00
O8	2a. violet	70
	a. "BRIT SH"	£100
	b. "BR1TISH"	90·00
	c. "SUMALILAND"	90·00
	d. "SERVICE" as Type O **2a**	90·00
O9	8a. purple	4·00
	a. "BRIT SH"	£2000
	b. "BR1TISH"	£1500
	c. "SUMALILAND"	£1500
	d. "SERVICE" as Type O **2a**	£1500
O9*f*	1r. green and aniline carmine	17·00
	fa. "BRIT SH"	£2000
	fb. "BR1TISH"	£1500
	fc. "SUMALILAND"	£1500
	fd. "SOMAL.LAND"	£1500
	fe. "SERVICE" as Type O **2a**	£1500
O6/9*f* *Set of* 5		20·00

Used examples of Nos. O6/9*f* are known, but there is no evidence that such stamps did postal duty.

SETTING OF TYPE O 3

The anna values were overprinted in sheets of 120 (2 panes 6×10) from a setting matching the pane size. The full stop after the "M" on the fifth vertical column was either very faint or completely omitted. The prices quoted are for stamps with the stop missing; examples with a partial stop are worth much less.

The 1r. value was overprinted from a separate setting of 60 which did not show the "missing stop" varieties.

1904 (1 Sept)–**05**. *Stamps of Somaliland Protectorate optd with Type* O **3**.

(*a*) Wmk Crown CA. P 14.

O10	2	½a. dull green and green	4·75	48·00
		a. No stop after "M"	£275	
O11		1a. grey-black and carmine	3·25	7·00
		a. No stop after "M"	£200	£300
O12		2a. dull and bright purple	£200	70·00
		a. No stop after "M"	£2250	£750
O13		8a. grey-black and pale blue	60·00	£140
		a. No stop after "M"	£600	£800
		(*b*) Wmk Mult Crown CA.		
O14	2	2a. dull and bright purple, **O** (7.05?)	90·00	£1000
		a. No stop after "M"	£2000	
		(*c*) Wmk Crown CC.		
O15	3	1r. green	£190	£650
O10s/13s , O15s Optd "Specimen" *Set of* 5			£130	

All Somaliland Protectorate stamps were withdrawn from sale on 25 June 1960 and until the unification on 1 July, issues of Italian Somalia together with Nos. 353/5 of Republic of Somalia were used. Later issues will be found listed in Part 14 (Africa since Independence N–Z) of this catalogue

South Africa

South Africa as a nation, rather than a geographical term, came into being with the creation of the Union of South Africa on 31 May 1910.

The development, both political and philatelic, of the area is very complex and the method adopted by the catalogue is to first list, in alphabetical order, the various colonies and republics which formed this federation, followed by stamps for the Union of South Africa.

The section is divided as follows:

I. CAPE OF GOOD HOPE. British Kaffraria. Mafeking Siege Stamps. Vryburg
II. GRIQUALAND WEST
III. NATAL
IV. NEW REPUBLIC
V. ORANGE FREE STATE. Orange River Colony
VI. TRANSVAAL. Pietersburg. Local British Occupation Issues
VII. ZULULAND
VIII. BRITISH ARMY FIELD OFFICES DURING SOUTH AFRICAN WAR
IX. UNION OF SOUTH AFRICA
X. REPUBLIC OF SOUTH AFRICA

I. CAPE OF GOOD HOPE

PRICES FOR STAMPS ON COVER

Nos. 1/4	*from* × 4
Nos. 5/14	*from* × 3
Nos. 18/21	*from* × 5
No. 22	—
Nos. 23/6	*from* × 5
Nos. 27/31	*from* × 8
Nos. 32/3	*from* × 10
No. 34	*from* × 25
No. 35	*from* × 20
No. 36	*from* × 10
Nos. 37/8	*from* × 25
Nos. 39/45	*from* × 10
Nos. 46/7	*from* × 12
Nos. 48/54	*from* × 10
Nos. 55/6	*from* × 25
No. 57	*from* × 50
Nos. 58/69	*from* × 10
Nos. 70/8	*from* × 6

PRICES. Our prices for early Cape of Good Hope are for stamps in very fine condition. Exceptional copies are worth more, poorer copies considerably less.

1 Hope

2

(Des Charles Bell, Surveyor-General. Eng W. Humphrys. Recess P.B.)

1853 (1 Sept). W **2**. Imperf.

(a) Paper deeply blued.

1	**1**	1d. pale brick-red	£3750	£325
		a. Deep brick-red	£5000	£350
		b. Wmk sideways	†	£425
2		4d. deep blue	£2500	£180
		a. Wmk sideways	£3250	£275

Plate proofs of the 4d. in a shade similar to the issued stamp exist on ungummed watermarked paper. (*Price* £275) The blueing on the reverse of these proofs is uneven giving a blotchy appearance.

(b) Paper slightly blued (blueing not pronounced at back).

3	**1**	1d. brick-red	£3000	£225
		a. Brown-red	£3250	£250
		b. Wmk sideways	†	£325
4		4d. deep blue	£1400	£120
		a. Blue	£1500	£160
		b. Wmk sideways	†	£275

PERKINS BACON "CANCELLED". For notes on these handstamps showing "CANCELLED" between horizontal bars forming an oval, see Catalogue Introduction.

1855–63. W **2**.

(a) Imperf.

5	**1**	1d. brick-red/*cream toned paper* (1857)	£5000	£900
		a. Rose (1858) (H/S "CANCELLED" in oval £18000)	£475	£200
		ab. Wmk sideways	—	£425
		b. Deep rose-red	£700	£250
		ba. Wmk sideways	—	£450
6		4d. deep blue/*white paper* (1855)	£700	55·00
		a. Blue (H/S "CANCELLED" in oval £18000)	£500	55·00
		b. Bisected (on cover)	†	£35000
		c. Wmk sideways	†	£180
7		6d. pale rose-lilac/*white paper* (18.2.58) (H/S "CANCELLED" in oval £14000)	£850	£225
		a. Wmk sideways	†	£950
		b. Deep rose-lilac/white paper	£1700	£325
		c. Slate-lilac/blued paper (1862)	£4250	£450
		d. Slate-purple/blued paper (1863)	£3500	£1000
		e. Bisected (on cover)	†	—
8		1s. bright yellow-green/*white paper* (18.2.58) (H/S "CANCELLED" in oval £18000)	£2750	£190
		a. Wmk sideways	†	£1100
		b. Deep dark green (1859)	£300	£500

The method adopted for producing the plate of the 4d., 6d and 1s. stamps involved the use of two dies, so that there are two types of each of these values differing slightly in detail, but produced in equal numbers.

The 1d. value in dull rose on ungummed watermarked paper with the watermark sideways is a plate proof. (*Price* £250).

The 4d. is known bisected in 1858 and used with two other 4d. values to pay the inland registered fee. The 6d. is known bisected and used with 1d. for 4d. rate.

The paper of No. 5 is similar to that of Nos. 1/4, but is without the blueing. It is much thicker than the white paper used for later printings of the 1d. The evolution of the paper on these Cape of Good Hope stamps is similar to that on the line-engraved issues of Great Britain. Examples of the 6d. slate-lilac apparently on white paper have had the blueing washed out.

The 4d. value is known printed in black on white watermarked paper. Twelve authenticated copies have been recorded, the majority of which show cancellations or, at least, some indication that they have been used.

It was, at one time, believed that these stamps came from a small supply printed in black to mark the death of the Prince Consort, but references to examples can be found in the philatelic press before news of this event reached Cape Town.

It is now thought that these stamps represent proof sheets, possibly pressed into service during a shortage of stamps in 1861.

There is, however, no official confirmation of this theory. (*Price* £35000 *un*, £30000 *with obliteration*).

(b) Unofficially rouletted.

9	**1**	1d. brick-red	†	£3000
10		4d. blue	†	£2250
11		6d. rose-lilac	†	£1500
12		1s. bright yellow-green	†	£3250
		a. Deep dark green	†	£3500

These rouletted stamps are best collected on cover.

3 Hope

(Local provisional (so-called "wood-block") issue. Engraved on steel by C. J. Roberts. Printed from stereotyped plates by Saul Solomon & Co, Cape Town)

1861 (Feb–Apr). *Laid paper.* Imperf.

13	**3**	1d. vermilion (27 February)	£14000	£2250
		a. Carmine (7 March)	£25000	£3000
		b. Brick-red (10 April)	£38000	£4250
		c. Error. Pale milky blue	£160000	£28000
		ca. Pale bright blue	—	£30000
14		4d. pale milky blue (23 February)	£21000	£1700
		aa. Retouch or repair to rt-hand corner	—	£6500
		a. Pale grey-blue (March?)	£22000	£1700
		b. Pale bright blue (March?)	£22000	£2000
		ba. Retouch or repair to rt-hand corner	—	£6500
		c. Deep bright blue (12 April)	£100000	£4500
		d. Blue	£27000	£3000
		e. Error. Vermilion	£160000	£40000
		ea. Carmine	—	£95000
		f. Sideways *tête-bêche* (pair)	†	£130000

Nos. 13/14 were each issued in *tête-bêche* pairs normally joined at edges bearing the same inscription ("POSTAGE" against "POSTAGE", etc). No. 14f, of which only one used example is known, comes from the first printing and shows the right-hand stamp misplaced so that "FOUR PENCE" adjoins "POSTAGE".

Nos. 13c/*ca* and 14e/*ea* were caused by the inclusion of incorrect clichés in the plates of the 1d. or 4d. values.

Both values were officially reprinted in March 1883, on wove paper. The 1d. is in deep red, and the 4d. in a deeper blue than that of the deepest shade of the issued stamp.

Specimens of the reprints have done postal duty, but their use thus was not intended. There are no reprints of the errors or of the retouched 4d.

Further reprints were made privately but with official permission, in 1940/41, in colours much deeper than those of any of the original printings, and on thick carton paper.

Examples of the 4d. are known unofficially rouletted.

Early in 1863, Perkins Bacon Ltd handed over the four plates used for printing the triangular Cape of Good Hope stamps to De La Rue & Co, Ltd, who made all the subsequent printings.

(Printed from the P.B. plates by D.L.R.)

1863–64. Imperf.

(a) W **2**.

18	**1**	1d. deep carmine-red (1864)	£180	£225
		a. Wmk sideways	£325	£300
		b. Deep brown-red	£400	£250
		ba. Wmk sideways	£500	£300
		c. Brownish red	£400	£225
		ca. Wmk sideways	£500	£275
19		4d. deep blue (1864)	£180	60·00
		a. Blue	£190	70·00
		b. Slate-blue	£2250	£500
		c. Steel-blue	£2000	£250
		d. Wmk sideways	£550	£190
20		6d. bright mauve (1864)	£250	£450
		a. Wmk sideways	†	£1300
21		1s. bright emerald-green	£425	£450
		a. Pale emerald-green	£1100	

(b) Wmk Crown CC (sideways).

22	**1**	1d. deep carmine-red	£24000	

No. 22 was a trial printing, and is only known unused.

Our prices for the 4d. blue are for stamps which are blue by comparison with the other listed shades. An exceptionally pale shade is recognised by specialists and is rare.

With the exception of the 4d., these stamps may be easily distinguished from those printed by Perkins Bacon by their colours, which are quite distinct.

The De La Rue stamps of all values are less clearly printed, the figure of Hope and the lettering of the inscriptions standing out less boldly, while the fine lines of the background appear blurred and broken when examined under a glass. The background as a whole often shows irregularity in the apparent depth of colour, due to wear of the plates.

For note regarding the two dies of the 4d., 6d., and 1s. values, see after No. 8.

All the triangular stamps were demonetised as from 1 October 1900.

4 "Hope" seated, with vine and ram. (With outer frame-line)

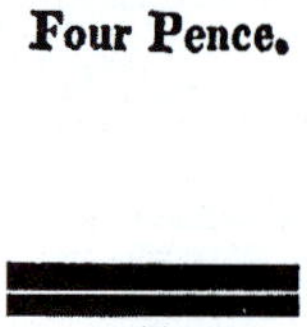

(5)

(Des Charles Bell. Die engraved on steel and stamps typo by D.L.R.)

1864–77. *With outer frame-line surrounding the design.* Wmk Crown CC. P 14.

23	**4**	1d. carmine-red (5.65)	90·00	27·00
		a. Rose-red	85·00	26·00
		w. Wmk inverted	£300	£140
24		4d. pale blue (8.65)	£120	3·75
		a. Blue	£120	3·75
		b. Ultramarine	£275	55·00
		c. Deep blue (1872)	£170	4·00
		w. Wmk inverted	£425	£160
25		6d. pale lilac (before 21.3.64)	£130	24·00
		a. Deep lilac	£225	7·50
		b. Violet (to bright) (1877)	£150	1·50
		w. Wmk inverted	†	£300
26		1s. deep green (1.64)	£550	20·00
		a. Green	£130	4·00
		ax. Wmk reversed		
		b. Blue-green	£140	5·00
		w. Wmk inverted	£650	£160

The 1d. rose-red, 6d. lilac, and 1s. blue-green are known imperf, probably from proof sheets.

The 1d. and 4d. stamps of this issue may be found with side and/or top outer frame-lines missing, due to wear of the plates.

See also Nos. 44 and 52/3.

(Surch by Saul Solomon & Co, Cape Town)

1868 (17 Nov). *No. 25a surch with T* **5**.

27	**4**	4d. on 6d. deep lilac (R.)	£300	16·00
		a. "Peuce" for "Pence"	£1800	£700
		b. "Fonr" for "Four"	—	£700
		w. Wmk inverted	—	£300

Specimens may also be found with bars omitted or at the top of the stamp, due to misplacement of the sheet.

The space between the words and bars varies from 12½ to 16 mm, stamps with spacing 15½ and 16 mm being rare. There were two printings, one of 120,000 in November 1868 and another of 1,000,000 in December. Stamps showing widest spacings are probably from the earlier printing.

6 (No outer frame-line)

(Die re-engraved. Typo D.L.R.)

1871–76. *Outer frame-line removed.* Wmk Crown CC. P 14.

28	**6**	½d. grey-black (*shades*) (12.75)	22·00	9·00
		w. Wmk inverted	—	£110
29		1d. carmine-red (*shades*) (2.72)	38·00	60
		w. Wmk inverted	£300	£130
30		4d. dull blue (*shades*) (12.76)	£110	75
		b. Ultramarine	£225	50·00
		w. Wmk inverted	£350	95·00
31		5s. yellow-orange (25.8.71)	£375	17·00
		w. Wmk inverted	†	£325

The ½d., 1d. and 5s. are known imperf, probably from proof sheets.

See also Nos. 36, 39, 40/3, 48/51, 54, 61/2 and 64/8.

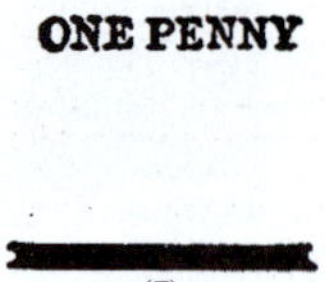

(7)

(8)

(Surch by Saul Solomon & Co, Cape Town)

1874–76. *Nos. 25a and 26a surch with T* **7**.

32	**4**	1d. on 6d. deep lilac (R.) (1.9.74)	£550	£100
		a. "E" of "PENNY" omitted	—	£1100
33		1d. on 1s. green (11.76)	95·00	60·00

These provisionals are found with the bar only, either across the centre of the stamp or at top, with value only; or with value and bar close together, either at top or foot. Such varieties are due to misplacement of sheets during surcharging.

1879 (1 Nov). *No. 30 surch with T* **8**.
34 **6** 3d. on 4d. blue (R.) £110 2·00
a. "PENCB" for "PENCE" £1900 £225
b. "THE.EE" for "THREE" £2250 £275
c. Surch double £9500 £3250
d. Variety b. double

The double surcharge must also have existed showing variety a. but only variety b. is known.

There are numerous minor varieties, including letters broken or out of alignment, due to defective printing and use of poor type.

The spacing between the bar and the words varies from 16½ to 18 mm.

THREEPENCE (9) — 3 (10) — 3 (11)

(Surch by D.L.R.)

1880 (Feb). *Special printing of the 4d. in new colour, surch, with T* **9**. Wmk Crown CC.
35 **6** 3d. on 4d. pale dull rose 75·00 2·25
w. Wmk inverted — £225

A minor constant variety exists with foot of "P" in "PENCE" broken off, making the letter appear shorter.

1880 (1 July). Wmk Crown CC. P 14.
36 **6** 3d. pale dull rose £200 27·00
w. Wmk inverted — £325

(Surch by Saul Solomon & Co, Cape Town)

1880 (Aug). *No. 36 surch.*
37 **10** "3" on 3d. pale dull rose 85·00 1·75
a. Surch inverted £1000 40·00
b. Vert pair. Nos. 37/8 £1100 £425
w. Wmk inverted — £160
38 **11** "3" on 3d. pale dull rose £225 8·00
a. Surch inverted £9000 £950
w. Wmk inverted — £425

The "3" (T **10**) is sometimes found broken. Vert pairs are known showing the two types of surcharge *se-tenant*, and vertical strips of three exist, the top stamp having surcharge T **10**, the middle stamp being without surcharge, and the lower stamp having surcharge T **11** (*Price for strip of* 3 £4250 *un.*).

1881 (Jan). Wmk Crown CC. P 14.
39 **6** 3d. pale claret £150 3·25
a. Deep claret £120 3·00
w. Wmk inverted

This was a definite colour change made at the request of the Postmaster-General owing to the similarity between the colours of the 1d. stamp and the 3d. in pale dull rose. Imperf copies are probably from proof sheets.

Proofs of this value were printed in brown, on unwatermarked wove paper and imperf, but the colour was rejected as unsuitable.

1882 (July)–**83**. Wmk Crown CA. P 14.
40 **6** ½d. black (1.9.82) 28·00 2·75
a. Grey-black 25·00 2·75
w. Wmk inverted — £150
41 1d. rose-red 65·00 2·00
a. Deep rose-red 60·00 2·00
w. Wmk inverted — £180
42 2d. pale bistre (1.9.82) £100 1·00
a. Deep bistre £110 1·00
w. Wmk inverted — £180
43 3d. pale claret 8·00 1·25
a. Deep claret 13·00 75
aw. Wmk inverted — £110
44 **4** 6d. mauve (to bright) (8.82) 95·00 80
45 **6** 5s. orange (8.83) £800 £225

Imperf pairs of the ½d., 1d. and 2d. are known, probably from proof sheets.

One Half-penny. (12)

13 "Cabled Anchor"

(Surch by Saul Solomon & Co, Cape Town)

1882 (July). *Nos. 39a and 43a surch with T* **12**.
46 **6** ½d. on 3d. deep claret (Wmk CC) £3750 £130
a. Hyphen omitted — £3500
47 ½d. on 3d. deep claret (Wmk CA) 35·00 4·25
a. "p" in "penny" omitted £2250 £750
b. "y" in "penny" omitted £1100 £650
c. Hyphen omitted £700 £350
w. Wmk inverted — £325

Varieties also exist with broken and defective letters, and with the obliterating bar omitted or at the top of the stamp.

1884–90. W **13**. P 14.
48 **6** ½d. black (1.86) 6·00 10
a. Grey-black 6·00 10
w. Wmk inverted — £400
49 1d. rose-red (12.85) 7·50 10
a. Carmine-red 7·50 10
w. Wmk inverted — £180
50 2d. pale bistre (12.84) 27·00 1·25
a. Deep bistre 8·00 10
w. Wmk inverted — £140
51 4d. blue (6.90) 14·00 50
a. Deep blue 14·00 50
52 **4** 6d. reddish purple (12.84) 60·00 1·60
a. Purple (shades) 13·00 20
b. Bright mauve 11·00 50
w. Wmk inverted — £300
53 1s. green (12.85) £150 5·00
a. Blue-green (1889) £100 50
w. Wmk inverted — £400
54 **6** 5s. orange (7.87) £100 6·50
48/54 *Set of* 7 £225 7·00

All the above stamps are known in imperf pairs, probably from proof sheets.

For later shade and colour changes, etc., see Nos. 61, etc.

2½d (14)

15

ONE PENNY. (16)

(Surch by D.L.R.)

1891 (Mar). *Special printing of the 3d. in new colour, surch with T* **14**.
55 **6** 2½d. on 3d. pale magenta 9·00 1·75
a. Deep magenta 4·50 20
b. "1" with horiz serif 60·00 32·00

No. 55b occurs on two stamps (Nos. 8 and 49) of the pane of 60.

Two types of "d" are found in the surcharge, one with square end to serif at top, and the other with pointed serif.

1892 (June). W **13**. P 14.
56 **15** 2½d. sage-green 15·00 10
a. Olive-green 15·00 55

See also No. 63.

(Surch by W. A. Richards & Sons, Cape Town)

1893 (Mar). *Nos. 50/a surch with T* **16**.
57 **6** 1d. on 2d. pale bistre 7·00 2·00
a. Deep bistre 3·75 50
b. No stop after "PENNY" 60·00 13·00
c. Surch double — £450

No. 57b occurs on stamp No. 42 of the upper left-hand pane, and on No. 6 of the lower right-hand pane.

Minor varieties exist showing broken letters and letters out of alignment or widely spaced. Also with obliterating bar omitted, due to misplacement of the sheet during surcharging.

17 "Hope" standing. Table Bay in background

18 Table Mountain and Bay with Arms of the Colony

(Des Mr. Mountford. Typo D.L.R.)

1893 (Oct)–**1902**. W **13**. P 14.
58 **17** ½d. green (9.98) 4·00 10
59 1d. rose-red 5·00 2·00
a. Carmine 1·50 10
aw. Wmk inverted † £130
60 3d. magenta (3.02) 4·00 1·75

The 1d. is known in imperf pairs, probably from proof sheets.

1893–98. *New colours, etc.* W **13**. P 14.
61 **6** ½d. yellow-green (12.96) 1·50 50
a. Green 2·75 50
62 2d. chocolate-brown (3.97) 2·00 1·25
63 **15** 2½d. pale ultramarine (3.96) 7·00 15
a. Ultramarine 7·00 10
64 **6** 3d. bright magenta (9.98) 11·00 1·00
65 4d. sage-green (3.97) 5·50 2·75
66 1s. blue-green (12.93) 70·00 5·50
a. Deep blue-green 85·00 10·00
67 1s. yellow-ochre (5.96) 12·00 2·00
68 5s. brown-orange (6.96) 80·00 3·50
61/8 *Set of* 8 £170 15·00

(Des E. Sturman. Typo D.L.R.)

1900 (Jan). W **13**. P 14.
69 **18** 1d. carmine 4·00 10
w. Wmk inverted — £130

19

20

21

22

23

24

25

26

27

(Typo D.L.R.)

1902 (Dec)–**04**. W **13**. P 14.
70 **19** ½d. green 2·25 10
71 **20** 1d. carmine 2·00 10
w. Wmk inverted
y. Wmk inverted and reversed
72 **21** 2d. brown (10.04) 14·00 80
w. Wmk inverted
73 **22** 2½d. ultramarine (3.04) 2·75 7·00
74 **23** 3d. magenta (4.03) 9·00 1·00
75 **24** 4d. olive-green (2.03) 12·00 65
76 **25** 6d. bright mauve (3.03) 19·00 30
77 **26** 1s. yellow-ochre 15·00 80
78 **27** 5s. brown-orange (2.03) £100 21·00
70/8 *Set of* 9 £160 28·00

All values exist in imperf pairs, from proof sheets.

The ½d. exists from coils constructed from normal sheets for use in stamp machines introduced in 1911.

STAMP BOOKLET

1905 (Dec). *Black on red cover. Stapled.*
SB1 2s.7d. booklet containing thirty 1d. (No. 71) in blocks of 6 £2000

OFFICIAL STAMPS

The following stamps, punctured with a double triangle device, were used by the Stationery and Printed Forms Branch of the Cape of Good Hope Colonial Secretary's Department between 1904 and 1906. Later South Africa issues may have been similarly treated, but this has not been confirmed.

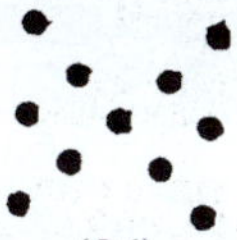

(O **1**)

1904. *Various issues punctured as Type* O **1**.

(a) Nos. 50 and 52a.
O1 **6** 2d. pale bistre 20·00
O2 **4** 6d. purple 24·00

(b) Nos. 58 and 60.
O3 **17** ½d. green 26·00
O4 3d. magenta 20·00

(c) Nos. 62 and 64/5.
O5 **6** 2d. chocolate-brown 20·00
O6 3d. bright magenta 26·00
O7 4d. sage-green 26·00

(d) No. 69.
O8 **18** 1d. carmine 20·00

(e) Nos. 70/2 and 74/8.
O9 **19** ½d. green 26·00
O10 **20** 1d. carmine 15·00
O11 **21** 2d. brown 24·00
O12 **23** 3d. magenta 19·00
O13 **24** 4d. olive-green 20·00
O14 **25** 6d. bright mauve 21·00
O15 **26** 1s. yellow-ochre 27·00
O16 **27** 5s. brown-orange 65·00

Nos. O1/16 are only known used.

Cape of Good Hope became a province of the Union of South Africa on 31 May 1910.

BRITISH KAFFRARIA

The history of the Cape eastern frontier was punctuated by a series of armed conflicts with the native population, known as the Kaffir Wars. After a particularly violent outbreak in 1846 the Governor, Sir Harry Smith, advanced the line of the Cape frontier to the Keikama and Tyumie Rivers. In the area between the new frontier and the Kei River a buffer state, British Kaffraria, was established on 17 December 1847. This area was not annexed to the Cape, but was administered as a separate Crown dependency by the Governor of Cape Colony in his capacity as High Commissioner for South Africa.

The territory, with its administration based on King William's Town, used the stamps of the Cape of Good Hope from 1853 onwards, the mail being sent via Port Elizabeth or overland from the Cape. Covers from British Kaffraria franked with the triangular issues are rare.

The first postal marking known from British Kaffraria is the 1849 type octagonal numeral No 47 from Port Beaufort. Oval post-marks of the 1853 type were used at Alice, Aliwal North, Bedford, Fort Beaufort, King William's Town and Queenstown. In 1864 numeral cancellations were issued to all post offices within the Cape system and it is known that the following numbers were initially assigned to post towns in Kaffraria: 4 (King William's Town), 7 (Bedford), 11 (Queenstown), 29 (East London), 32 (Fort Beaufort), 38 (Aliwal North) and 104 (Cathcart).

It is believed that post offices may have also existed at Adelaide, Barkly East, Sterkstoom and Stutterheim, but, to date, no examples of handstamps or cancellations are known from them during the British Kaffraria period.

Following the decimation by famine of the Xhosa tribes in 1857 British Kaffraria was annexed to Cape Colony in 1865. The area eventually formed the basis of the Ciskei independent "homeland".

MAFEKING SIEGE STAMPS

PRICES FOR STAMPS ON COVER	
Nos. 1/16	*from* × 12
Nos. 17/18	*from* × 25
Nos. 19/20	*from* × 15
Nos. 21/2	*from* × 12

23 MARCH to 17 MAY 1900

There are numerous forgeries of the Mafeking overprints, many of which were brought home by soldiers returning from the Boer War.

MAFEKING, 3d. BESIEGED. (1)

MAFEKING 3d. BESIEGED. (2)

(Surcharged by Townsend & Co, Mafeking)

1900 (23 Mar–28 Apr). *Various stamps surch as T* **1** *and* **2**.

(a) Cape of Good Hope stamps surch as T 1 (23 Mar).

1 **6** 1d. on ½d. green .... £225 70·00
2 **17** 1d. on ½d. green (24.3) .... £275 80·00
3 3d. on 1d. carmine .... £250 50·00
4 **6** 6d. on 3d. magenta (24.3) £38000 £250
5 1s. on 4d. sage-green (24.3) £7000 £350

A variety in the setting of each value exists without comma after "MAFEKING".

(b) Nos. 59 and 61/3 of Bechuanaland Protectorate (previously optd on Great Britain) surch as T **1**.

6 1d. on ½d. vermilion (28.3) .... £225 60·00
a. Surch inverted .... † £6000
b. Vert pair, surch *tête-bêche* .... † £32000
7 3d. on 1d. lilac (4.4) .... £900 95·00
a. Surch double .... † £27000
8 6d. on 2d. green and carmine (6.4) .... £2000 80·00
9 6d. on 3d. purple/*yellow* (30.3) £6000 £300
a. Surch inverted .... † £32000
b. Surch double

(c) Nos. 12 and 35 of British Bechuanaland (4d. previously optd on Great Britain) surch as T **1**.

10 6d. on 3d. lilac and black (27.3) .... £400 70·00
11 1s. on 4d. green and purple-brown (29.3) .... £1500 80·00
a. Surch double (both Type **1**) .... † £25000
ab. Surch double (Type **1** and Type **2**) £11000 £6500
b. Surch treble .... † £25000
c. Surch double, one inverted .... † £25000

(d) Nos. 61/2 and 65 of Bechuanaland Protectorate (previously optd on Great Britain) surch as T **2**.

12 3d. on 1d. lilac (1 Apr) .... £950 80·00
a. Surch double .... † £9500
13 6d. on 2d. green and carmine (25 Apr) .... £1200 80·00
14 1s. on 6d. purple/*rose-red* (12 Apr) .... £6000 95·00

(e) Nos. 36/7 of British Bechuanaland (previously optd on Great Britain) surch as T **2**.

15 1s. on 6d. purple/*rose-red* (28 Apr) £27000 £750
16 2s. on 1s. green (13 Apr) £12000 £450

On the stamps overprinted "BECHUANALAND PROTECTORATE" and "BRITISH BECHUANALAND" the local surcharge is so adjusted as not to overlap the original overprint.

Two used examples of British Bechuanaland No. 37 are known surcharged 2s. as T1 but their status is uncertain. (*Price* £35,000).

3 Cadet Sergt.-major Goodyear

4 General Baden-Powell

(Des Dr. W. A. Hayes (T **3**), Capt. H. Greener (T **4**))

1900 (6–11 Apr). *Produced photographically by Dr. D. Taylor. Horiz laid paper with sheet wmk* "OCEANA FINE". *P* 12.

(a) 18½ mm wide. (b) 21 mm wide.

17 **3** 1d. pale blue/*blue* (7.4) £900 £275
18 1d. deep blue/*blue* £900 £275
19 **4** 3d. pale blue/*blue* (*a*) £1300 £400
a. Reversed design £70000 £40000
20 3d. deep blue/*blue* (*a*) £1300 £350
a. Imperf between (horiz pair) .. † £70000
b. Double print .... † £18000
21 3d. pale blue/*blue* (*b*) (10.4) £9500 £900
a. Vert laid paper £14000
22 3d. deep blue/*blue* (*b*) (10.4) £11000 £1100

These stamps vary a great deal in colour from deep blue to pale grey.

No. 18 imperforate and without gum is believed to be a proof (*Price for unused pair* £20000).

No. 19a comes from a sheet of 12 printed in reverse of which ten, three mint and seven used, are known to have survived.

VRYBURG

PRICES FOR STAMPS ON COVER	
Nos. 1/4	*from* × 5
Nos. 11/12	*from* × 2

BOER OCCUPATION

Vryburg was occupied by Boer forces on 15 October 1899. Unoverprinted stamps of Transvaal were used initially. Nos. 1/4 were only available from 24 to 29 November. The Boers evacuated the town on 7 May 1900.

½ PENCE

Z.A.R.

(1)

1899 (24 Nov). *Cape stamps surch as T* **1**. *Surch 12 mm high on No. 3 and 10 mm on all other values.*

1 **6** ½ PENCE green .... £200 80·00
a. Italic "Z" £1700 £700
b. Surch 12 mm high £1700 £700
2 **17** 1 PENCE rose £225 £100
a. Italic "Z" £1900 £800
b. Surch 12 mm high £1900 £800
c. "I" for "1" £1200 £500
3 **4** 2 PENCE on 6d. mauve £2000 £500
a. Italic "Z" £11000 £4250
4 **15** 2½ PENCE on 2½d. blue £1700 £425
a. Italic "Z" £11000 £4250
b. Surch 12 mm high £11000 £4250

The "2 PENCE" on 6d. shows the surcharge 12 mm high. It is possible that this was the first value surcharged as the remaining three show the height reduced to 10 mm with the exception of one position in the second vertical row of the setting. The italic "Z" occurs on one position in the sixth vertical row. It is believed that the setting was of 60 (6×10).

BRITISH REOCCUPATION

V. R. SPECIAL POST

(2)

1900 (16 May). *Provisionals issued by the Military Authorities. Stamps of Transvaal handstamped with T* **2**.

11 **30** ½d. green .... — £2500
11*a* 1d. rose-red (No. 206) ....
12 1d. rose-red and green (No. 217) . £10000 £4500
13 2d. brown and green .... † £32000
14 2½d. dull blue and green .... † £32000

No. 11 is known used with double handstamp and Nos. 11/12 with the overprint reading downwards.

II. GRIQUALAND WEST

Griqualand West was situated to the North of Cape Colony, bounded on the north by what became British Bechuanaland and on the east by the Orange Free State.

The area was settled in the early nineteenth century by the Griqua tribal group, although many members of the tribe, including the paramount chief, migrated to Griqualand East (between Basutoland and the east coast of South Africa) in 1861–63. There was little European involvement in Griqualand West before 1866, but in that year the diamond fields along the Vaal River were discovered. Sovereignty was subsequently claimed by the Griqua Chief, the Orange Free State and the South African Republic (Transvaal). In 1871 the British authorities arbitrated in favour of the Griqua Chief who promptly ceded his territory to Great Britain. Griqualand West became a separate Crown Colony in January 1873.

During the initial stages of the prospecting boom, mail was passed via the Orange Free State, but a post office connected to the Cape Colony postal system was opened at Klip Drift (subsequently Barkly) in late 1870. Further offices at De Beer's New Rush (subsequently Kimberley), Douglas and Du Toit's Pan (subsequently Beaconsfield) were open by September 1873.

Cape of Good Hope stamps to the 5s. value were in use from October 1871, but those originating in Griqualand West can only be identified after the introduction of Barred Oval Diamond Numeral cancellations in 1873. Numbers known to have been issued in the territory are:

1 De Beers N.R. (New Rush) (subsequently Kimberley)
3 Junction R. & M. (Riet and Modder Rivers)
4 Barkly
6 or 9 Du Toit's Pan (subsequently Beaconsfield)
8 Langford (transferred to Douglas)
10 Thornhill

PRICES FOR STAMPS ON COVER. The stamps of Griqualand West are worth from ×10 the price quoted for used stamps, when on cover from the territory.

FORGED OVERPRINTS. Many stamps show forged overprints. Great care should be taken when purchasing the scarcer items.

***Stamps of the Cape of Good Hope,* Crown CC, perf 14, overprinted.**

1874 (Sept). *No. 24a of Cape of Good Hope surch "1d." in red manuscript by the Kimberley postmaster.*

1 1d. on 4d. blue £1500 £2500

G. W.

(1)

1877 (Mar). *Nos. 29/30 of Cape of Good Hope optd with T* **1**.

2 1d. carmine-red .... £550 90·00
a. Opt double .... † £2250
3 4d. dull blue (R.) .... £400 80·00
w. Wmk inverted £1300 £275

G (1a) G (2) G (3) G (4) G (5) G (6)

G (7) G (8) G (9) G (10) G (11)

G (12) G (13) G (14)

1877 (Mar)–**78**. *Nos. 24a, 25a, 26a and 28/31 Cape of Good Hope optd with capital "G".*

(a) First printing. Optd with T **1a/6** *and* **8** *in black (1d.) or red (others).*

4 ½d. grey-black
a. Opt Type **1a** .... 27·00 30·00
b. Opt Type **2** .... 65·00 80·00
c. Opt Type **3** .... 35·00 42·00
d. Opt Type **4** .... 65·00 80·00
e. Opt Type **5** .... 75·00 90·00
f. Opt Type **6** .... 32·00 38·00
g. Opt Type **8** £600 £650
5 1d. carmine-red
a. Opt Type **1a** .... 28·00 21·00
b. Opt Type **2** .... 70·00 45·00
c. Opt Type **3** .... 25·00 29·00
d. Opt Type **4** .... 70·00 45·00
e. Opt Type **5** .... 80·00 55·00
f. Opt Type **6** .... 28·00 21·00
g. Opt Type **8** .... *
6 4d. blue (with frame-line) (No. 24*a*)
a. Opt Type **1a** .... £300 45·00
b. Opt Type **2** £750 £130
c. Opt Type **3** .... £475 65·00
d. Opt Type **4** £750 £130
e. Opt Type **5** £850 £160
f. Opt Type **6** .... £375 60·00
g. Opt Type **8** £2500 £750
7 4d. dull blue (without frame-line) (No. 30)
a. Opt Type **1a** .... £225 29·00
b. Opt Type **2** .... £500 85·00
c. Opt Type **3** .... £350 38·00
d. Opt Type **4** .... £475 85·00
e. Opt Type **5** £600 £110
f. Opt Type **6** .... £325 35·00
g. Opt Type **8** £2000 £500
8 6d. deep lilac
a. Opt Type **1a** .... £150 32·00
b. Opt Type **2** .... £350 90·00
c. Opt Type **3** .... £225 45·00
cw. Wmk inverted .... † £350
d. Opt Type **4** .... £350 90·00
e. Opt Type **5** £425 £110
f. Opt Type **6** .... £200 42·00
g. Opt Type **8** £1800 £650
9 1s. green
a. Opt Type **1a** .... £190 27·00
ab. Opt inverted .... — £550
b. Opt Type **2** .... £425 65·00
ba. Opt inverted .... — £900
c. Opt Type **3** .... £325 35·00
d. Opt Type **4** .... £425 65·00
da. Opt inverted .... — £900
e. Opt Type **5** .... £500 80·00
f. Opt Type **6** .... £300 30·00
fa. Opt inverted .... — £650
g. Opt Type **8** £3250 £650
10 5s. yellow-orange
a. Opt Type **1a** .... £700 32·00
b. Opt Type **2** .... £1100 75·00
c. Opt Type **3** .... £900 42·00
cw. Wmk inverted .... † £850
d. Opt Type **4** .... £1100 75·00
dw. Wmk inverted .... † £1200
e. Opt Type **5** .... £1600 90·00
f. Opt Type **6** .... £850 38·00
g. Opt Type **8** £3250 £800

*The 1d. with overprint Type **8** from this setting can only be distinguished from that of the second printing when *se-tenant* with overprint Type **3**.

Nos. 4/10 were overprinted by a setting of 120 covering two panes of 60 (6×10). This setting contained 41 examples of Type **1a**, 10 of Type **2**, 23 of Type **3**, 10 of Type **4**, 8 of Type **5**, 27 of Type **6** and 1 of Type **8**. Sub-types of Types **1a** and **2** exist. The single example of Type **8** occurs on R.7/4 of the right-hand pane.

It is believed that there may have been an additional setting used for the 5s. which was in considerable demand to cover the postage and registration on diamond consignments. It is also possible that single panes of this value and of the 1s. were overprinted using the right-hand half of the normal 120 setting.

(b) Second printing. Optd with T **6/14** *in black (1878).*

11 1d. carmine-red
a. Opt Type **6** .... *
b. Opt Type **7** .... 30·00 21·00
c. Opt Type **8** .... 65·00 35·00
d. Opt Type **9** .... 32·00 22·00
e. Opt Type **10** .... 85·00 75·00
f. Opt Type **11** .... 75·00 48·00
g. Opt Type **12** .... 80·00 70·00
h. Opt Type **13** £130 £110
i. Opt Type **14** £425 £350
12 4d. dull blue (without frame-line) (No. 30)
a. Opt Type **6** .... £375 70·00
b. Opt Type **7** .... £140 27·00
c. Opt Type **8** .... £350 60·00
d. Opt Type **9** .... £160 28·00
e. Opt Type **10** .... £425 85·00
f. Opt Type **11** .... £375 75·00
g. Opt Type **12** .... £400 80·00
h. Opt Type **13** £600 £150
i. Opt Type **14** £2000 £475
13 6d. deep lilac
a. Opt Type **6** £500 £110
b. Opt Type **7** .... £275 60·00
ba. Opt double
c. Opt Type **8** .... £475 95·00
d. Opt Type **9** .... £325 70·00
da. Opt double .... — £900
e. Opt Type **10** £600 £150
ea. Opt double .... — £1100
f. Opt Type **11** £500 £110
g. Opt Type **12** £500 £140
h. Opt Type **13** £800 £225
i. Opt Type **14** £2500 £650

*The 1d. with overprint Type **6** from this setting can only be distinguished from that of the first printing when *se-tenant* with Types **11**, **12** or **13**.

Nos. 11/13 were overprinted by another double-pane setting of 120 in which only Types **6** and **8** were repeated from that used for the first printing. The second printing setting contained 12 examples of Type **6**, 30 of Type **7**, 13 of Type **8**, 27 of Type **9**, 9 of Type **10**, 11 of Type **11**, 11 of Type **12**, 6 of Type **13** and 1 of Type **14**. Sub-types of Types **7** and **12** exist.

G (15) G (16) G (17)

1878 (June). *Nos. 24a, 25a and 28/30 of Cape of Good Hope optd with small capital "G", T* **15/16**.

14 **15** ½d. grey-black (R.) .... 15·00 15·00
a. Opt inverted .... 17·00 17·00
b. Opt double .... 55·00 70·00
c. Opt double, both inverted £110 £130
d. Black opt £225 £130
da. Opt inverted £250

		db. Opt double, one inverted in red	£425	
		dc. Opt double, one inverted (Type **16**) in red	£200	
15	**16**	½d. grey-black (R.)	16·00	16·00
		a. Opt inverted	16·00	17·00
		b. Opt double	90·00	90·00
		c. Opt double, both inverted	75·00	85·00
		d. Black opt	55·00	55·00
		da. Opt inverted	£120	85·00
		db. Opt double, one inverted (Type **15**) in red	£200	
16	**15**	1d. carmine-red	16·00	13·00
		a. Opt inverted	16·00	16·00
		b. Opt double	£225	60·00
		c. Opt double, both inverted	£225	80·00
		d. Opt double, both inverted with one in red	45·00	48·00
		e. Opt double, both inverted with one (Type **16**) in red		
17	**16**	1d. carmine-red	16·00	14·00
		a. Opt inverted	95·00	35·00
		b. Opt double	–	£100
		c. Opt double, both inverted	–	£130
		d. Opt double, both inverted with one in red	95·00	95·00
18	**15**	4d. blue (with frame-line) (No. 24a)	–	£170
19	**16**	4d. blue (with frame-line) (No. 24a)	–	£170
20	**15**	4d. dull blue (without frame-line) (No. 30)	£150	35·00
		a. Opt inverted	£250	95·00
		b. Opt double	–	£250
		c. Opt double, both inverted	–	£325
		d. Red opt	£375	£110
		da. Opt inverted	£425	90·00
21	**16**	4d. dull blue (without frame-line) (No. 30)	£170	16·00
		a. Opt inverted	£275	35·00
		b. Opt double	–	£225
		c. Opt double, both inverted	–	£300
		d. Red opt	–	95·00
		da. Opt inverted	£400	95·00
22	**15**	6d. deep lilac	£150	30·00
23	**16**	6d. deep lilac	–	30·00

Nos. 14/23 were also overprinted using a double-pane setting of 120. Based on evidence from surviving ½d. and 1d. sheets all overprints in the left-hand pane were roman, Type **15**, and all those in the right-hand pane italic, Type **16**, except for R.1/6, 4/5, 6/6, 7/6, 8/6, 9/6 and 10/6 which were Type **15**. There is considerable evidence to suggest that after the ½d. value had been overprinted the setting was amended to show a Type **15**, instead of a Type **16**, on R.10/5 of the right-hand pane. Two strikes of the setting were required to overprint the sheets of 240 and it would appear that on many sheets the bottom two panes had the overprints inverted.

1879. *Nos. 25b, 26b and 28/31 of Cape of Good Hope optd with small capital "G", T* **17**.

24		½d. grey-black	19·00	8·50
		a. Opt double	£425	£300
25		1d. carmine-red	20·00	£6.50
		a. Opt inverted	–	95·00
		b. Opt double	–	£150
		c. Opt treble	–	£250
		w. Wmk inverted	†	£300
26		4d. dull blue	38·00	6·50
		a. Opt double	–	£130
27		6d. violet	£160	10·00
		a. Opt inverted	–	40·00
		b. Opt double	£750	£190
28		1s. green	£140	7·00
		a. Opt double	£400	£100
29		5s. yellow-orange	£475	16·00
		a. Opt double	£650	90·00
		b. Opt treble	–	£325

Nos. 24/9 were also overprinted using a setting of 120 which contained a number of minor type varieties.

Griqualand West was merged with Cape Colony in October 1880. The remaining stock of the overprinted stamps was returned from Kimberley to Cape Town and redistributed among various post offices in Cape Colony where they were used as ordinary Cape stamps.

III. NATAL

PRICES FOR STAMPS ON COVER

Nos. 1/7	*from* × 2
Nos. 9/25	*from* × 3
Nos. 26/56	*from* × 4
Nos. 57/8	–
Nos. 59/73	*from* × 5
Nos. 76/84	*from* × 4
Nos. 85/93	*from* × 3
Nos. 96/103	*from* × 6
Nos. 104/5	*from* × 5
Nos. 106/25	*from* × 6
Nos. 127/42	*from* × 4
Nos. 143/5a	–
Nos. 146/57	*from* × 4
No. 162	–
Nos. 165/71	*from* × 3
No. F1	–
Nos. O1/6	*from* × 10

1

2

3

4

5

(Embossed in plain relief on coloured wove paper)

1857 (26 May)–**61**. Imperf.

1	**1**	1d. blue (9.59)	–	£1200
2		1d. rose (1859)	–	£1800
3		1d. buff (1861)	–	£1100
4	**2**	3d. rose	–	£400
		a. *Tête-bêche* (pair)	–	£35000
5	**3**	6d. green	–	£1100
6	**4**	9d. blue	–	£7000
7	**5**	1s. buff	–	£5500

All the above have been reprinted more than once, and the early reprints of some values cannot always be distinguished with certainty from originals.

Stamps on surface-coloured paper with higher face values and perforated 12½ are fiscals.

NOTE. The value of the above stamps depends on their dimensions, and the clearness of the embossing, but our prices are for fine used.

PERKINS BACON "CANCELLED". For notes on these handstamps showing "CANCELLED" between horizontal bars forming an oval, see Catalogue Introduction.

6

7

(Eng C. H. Jeens. Recess P.B.)

1859–60. No wmk. P 14.

9	**6**	1d. rose-red (1860) (H/S "CANCELLED" in oval £12000)	£130	70·00
10		3d. blue	£170	42·00
		a. Imperf between (vert pair)	†	£8500

No. 10a is only known from a cover of 1867 franked with two such pairs.

The 3d. also exists with "CANCELLED" in oval, but no examples are believed to be in private hands.

1861. No wmk. Intermediate perf 14 to 16.

11	**6**	3d. blue	£225	65·00

1861–62. No wmk. Rough perf 14 to 16.

12	**6**	3d. blue	£120	32·00
		a. Imperf between (horiz pair)	£4250	
13		6d. grey (1862)	£200	55·00

1862. Wmk Small Star. Rough perf 14 to 16.

15	**6**	1d. rose-red	£150	65·00

The 1d. without watermark and the 3d. watermark Small Star, both imperforate, are proofs.

(Recess D.L.R.)

1863. *Thick paper*. No wmk. P 13.

18	**6**	1d. lake	95·00	27·00
19		1d. carmine-red	95·00	27·00

1863–65. Wmk Crown CC. P 12½.

20	**6**	1d. brown-red	£150	38·00
		y. Wmk inverted and reversed	–	£110
21		1d. rose	95·00	35·00
		x. Wmk reversed	95·00	35·00
22		1d. bright red	95·00	38·00
		x. Wmk reversed	95·00	38·00
23		6d. lilac	75·00	17·00
24		6d. violet	60·00	28·00
		x. Wmk reversed	60·00	28·00

(Typo D.L.R.)

1867 (Apr). Wmk Crown CC. P 14.

25	**7**	1s. green	£180	35·00
		w. Wmk inverted	–	£300

POSTAGE (7a) Postage. (7b) Postage. (7c)

Postage. (7d) POSTAGE. (7e)

1869 (23 Aug). *Optd horiz in Natal*. No wmk (3d.), wmk Crown CC (others). P 14 or 14–16 (3d.), 12½ (1d., 6d) or 14 (1s.).

(a) With T **7a** *(tall capitals without stop).*

26	**6**	1d. rose	£425	90·00
		x. Wmk reversed	£400	85·00
27		1d. bright red	£375	80·00
		x. Wmk reversed	–	75·00
28		3d. blue (No. 10)	£2500	£650
28*a*		3d. blue (No. 11)	£750	£275
28*b*		3d. blue (No. 12)	£550	95·00
29		6d. lilac	£600	75·00
30		6d. violet	£500	85·00
		x. Wmk reversed	£550	90·00
31	**7**	1s. green	£14000	£1300

(b) With T **7b** *(12¾ mm long).*

32	**6**	1d. rose	£375	80·00
33		1d. bright red	£350	75·00
		a. Opt double	†	£1500
		x. Wmk reversed	£325	70·00
34		3d. blue (No. 10)	–	£350
34*a*		3d. blue (No. 11)	£650	£225
34*b*		3d. blue (No. 12)	£475	85·00
35		6d. lilac	£500	70·00
36		6d. violet	£425	80·00
		x. Wmk reversed	£450	85·00
37	**7**	1s. green	£11000	£1000

(c) With T **7c** *(13¾ mm long).*

38	**6**	1d. rose	£750	£225
39		1d. bright red	£800	£200
		x. Wmk reversed	–	£190
40		3d. blue (No. 10)		
40*a*		3d. blue (No. 11)	–	£800
40*b*		3d. blue (No. 12)	£1800	£400
41		6d. lilac	£1900	£170
42		6d. violet	£1800	£160
		x. Wmk reversed	–	£180
43	**7**	1s. green	–	£2250

(d) With T **7d** *(14½ to 15½ mm long).*

44	**6**	1d. rose	£650	£180
45		1d. bright red	£650	£160
46		3d. blue (No. 10)		
46*a*		3d. blue (No. 11)	–	£500
46*b*		3d. blue (No. 12)	–	£300
47		6d. lilac	–	£110
48		6d. violet	£1400	£100
49	**7**	1s. green	£22000	£1600

(e) With T **7e** *(small capitals with stop).*

50	**6**	1d. rose	£110	45·00
		x. Wmk reversed	£110	45·00
51		1d. bright red	£160	45·00
		x. Wmk reversed	£160	45·00
52		3d. blue (No. 10)	£325	80·00
53		3d. blue (No. 11)	£170	50·00
54		3d. blue (No. 12)	£190	45·00
		a. Opt double	†	£1200
54*b*		6d. lilac	£190	65·00
55		6d. violet	£150	50·00
		x. Wmk reversed	£160	55·00
56	**7**	1s. green	£225	70·00

It is believed that there were two settings of these overprints. The first setting, probably of 240, contained 60 examples of Type **7a**, 72 of Type **7b**, 20 of Type **7c**, 28 of Type **7d** and 60 of Type **7e**. The second, probably of 60 (6×10), contained Type **7e** only.

POSTAGE (8)

1870. *No. 25 optd with T* **8** *by De La Rue.*

57	**7**	1s. green (C.)	†	£5500
58		1s. green (Blk.)	†	£1300
		a. Opt double	†	£2750
59		1s. green (G.)	£100	10·00

For 1s. orange, see No. 108.

POSTAGE POSTAGE (9) POSTAGE (10) POSTAGE POSTAGE (11)

1870–73. *Optd with T* **9** *by De La Rue.* Wmk Crown CC. P 12½.

60	**6**	1d. bright red	85·00	13·00
		x. Wmk reversed	85·00	13·00
61		3d. bright blue (R.) (1872)	90·00	13·00
		x. Wmk reversed	90·00	13·00
62		6d. mauve (1873)	£170	29·00
		x. Wmk reversed	£190	

1873 (July). *Fiscal stamp optd locally with T* **10**. Wmk Crown CC. P 14.

63	**7**	1s. purple-brown	£275	23·00
		w. Wmk inverted	–	£325

1874 (July). *No. 21 optd locally with T* **11**.

65	**6**	1d. rose	£275	75·00
		a. Opt double		
		x. Wmk reversed	–	75·00

12

13

14

15

16

(Typo D.L.R.)

1874 (Jan)–**99**. Wmk Crown CC (sideways on 5s.). P 14.

66	**12**	1d. dull rose	27·00	4·00
67		1d. bright rose	27·00	4·00

68	13	3d. blue	£120	25·00
		a. Perf 14×12½	£1700	£850
69	14	4d. brown (1878)	£130	13·00
		aw. Wmk inverted	£375	£120
		b. Perf 12½	£325	70·00
70	15	6d. bright reddish violet	65·00	7·50
		w. Wmk inverted	†	£170
71	16	5s. maroon (1882)	£225	55·00
		a. Perf 15½×15 (1874)	£400	95·00
72		5s. rose	95·00	35·00
73		5s. carmine (1899)	85·00	32·00
		s. Handstamped "Specimen"	£160	

POSTAGE (17) POSTAGE (18) ½ HALF (19)

1875–76. Wmk Crown CC. P 14 (1s.) or 12½ (others).

(a) Optd locally with T **17**.

76	6	1d. rose	£130	50·00
		a. Opt double	£1100	£475
		x. Wmk reversed	£130	50·00
77		1d. bright red	£120	65·00
		x. Wmk reversed	£120	65·00

(b) Optd locally with T **18** *(14½ mm long, without stop).*

81	6	1d. rose (1876)	95·00	65·00
		a. Opt inverted	£1200	£475
		x. Wmk reversed	95·00	65·00
82		1d. yellow (1876)	75·00	75·00
		a. Opt double, one albino	£200	
		x. Wmk reversed	85·00	85·00
83		6d. violet (1876)	65·00	8·00
		a. Opt double	—	£700
		b. Opt inverted	£700	£150
		w. Wmk inverted	—	£120
		x. Wmk reversed	65·00	8·00
84	7	1s. green (1876)	95·00	7·50
		a. Opt double	—	£325

TYPE 19. There are several varieties of this surcharge, of which T **19** is an example. They may be divided as follows:

(*a*) "½" 4½ mm high, "2" has straight foot.
(*b*) As last but "½" is 4 mm high.
(*c*) As last but "2" has curled foot.
(*d*) "½" 3½ mm. high, "2" has straight foot.
(*e*) As last but "2" has curled foot.
(*f*) As last but "2" smaller.

As the "½" and "HALF" were overprinted separately, they vary in relative position, and are frequently overlapping.

1877 (13 Feb). *No. 66 surch locally as T* **19**.

85	12	½d. on 1d. rose (*a*)	32·00	65·00
		a. "½" double		
86		½d. on 1d. rose (*b*)	£140	
87		½d. on 1d. rose (*c*)	£120	
88		½d. on 1d. rose (*d*)	70·00	90·00
89		½d. on 1d. rose (*e*)	75·00	
90		½d. on 1d. rose (*f*)	85·00	

POSTAGE Half-penny (21)

23

ONE HALF-PENNY. (24)

1877 (7 Oct)–**79**. *T* **6** (wmk Crown CC. P 12½) *surch locally as T* **21**.

91		½d. on 1d. yellow	8·50	17·00
		a. Surch inverted	£275	£190
		b. Surch double	£250	£180
		c. Surch omitted (lower stamp, vertical pair)	£2500	£1300
		d. "POSTAGE" omitted (in pair with normal)	£1700	
		e. "S" of "POSTAGE" omitted (R. 8/3)	£250	£190
		f. "T" of "POSTAGE" omitted	£250	£250
		x. Wmk reversed	8·50	17·00
92		1d. on 6d. violet (10.10.77)	55·00	11·00
		a. "S" of "POSTAGE" omitted (R. 8/3)	£400	£150
		x. Wmk reversed	—	11·00
93		1d. on 6d. rose (12.2.79)	£110	50·00
		a. Surch inverted	£600	£325
		b. Surch double	—	£250
		c. Surch double, one inverted	£275	£200
		d. Surch four times	£400	£225
		e. "S" of "POSTAGE" omitted (R. 8/3)	£600	£300
		x. Wmk reversed	—	50·00

No. 93c. is known with one surcharge showing variety "S" of "POSTAGE" omitted.

Other minor varieties exist in these surcharges.

(Typo D.L.R.)

1880 (13 Oct). Wmk Crown CC. P 14.

96	23	½d. blue-green	15·00	23·00
		a. Imperf between (vert pair)		

1882 (20 Apr)–**89**. Wmk Crown CA. P 14.

97	23	½d. blue-green (23.4.84)	95·00	16·00
		a. Dull green (10.4.85)	3·75	1·25
		aw. Wmk inverted	£225	
99	12	1d. rose (*shades*) (1.84)	3·75	25
		a. Carmine	4·25	35
		w. Wmk inverted	†	£170
100	13	3d. blue (23.4.84)	£110	17·00
101		3d. grey (11.89)	5·50	3·00
102	14	4d. brown	8·00	1·50
103	15	6d. mauve	6·50	2·00
		w. Wmk inverted	†	£120
97*a*/103 *Set of* 6			£120	22·00
97*as*, 99*as*, 101s/3s H/S "Specimen" *Set of* 5			£275	

1885 (26 Jan). *No. 99 surch locally with T* **24**.

104	12	½d. on 1d. rose	16·00	11·00
		a. No hyphen after "HALF"	75·00	45·00

TWO PENCE (25)

26

TWOPENCE HALFPENNY (27)

1886 (7 Jan). *No. 101 surch with T* **25** *by D.L.R.*

105	13	2d. on 3d. grey	20·00	5·50

(Typo D.L.R.)

1887 (Sept)–**89**. Wmk Crown CA. P 14.

106	26	2d. olive-green (Die I)	40·00	2·25
		a. Top left triangle detached	—	£225
		s. Optd "Specimen"	75·00	
107		2d. olive-green (Die II) (1889)	3·75	1·40
		s. Handstamped "Specimen"	60·00	

The differences between Dies I and II are shown in the introduction.

For illustration of "top left triangle detached" variety see above No. 21 of Antigua.

1888 (16 Mar). *As No. 25, but colour changed and* wmk Crown CA, *optd with T* **8** *by D.L.R.*

108	7	1s. orange (C.)	6·00	1·75
		a. Opt double	—	£1500
		s. Handstamped "Specimen"	£100	

1891 (22 Apr). *Surch locally with T* **27**.

109	14	2½d. on 4d. brown	12·00	15·00
		a. "TWOPENGE"	50·00	
		b. "HALFPENN"	£250	£200
		c. Surch double	£275	£200
		d. Surch inverted	£400	£325
		s. Handstamped "Specimen"	55·00	

(28)

POSTAGE. Half-Penny (29)

POSTAGE. Varieties of long-tailed letters

(Typo D.L.R.)

1891 (June). Wmk Crown CA. P 14.

113	28	2½d. bright blue	7·00	1·50
		s. Handstamped "Specimen"	60·00	

1895 (12 Mar). *No. 24 surch locally with T* **29** *in carmine.*

114		½d. on 6d. violet	2·50	5·00
		a. "Ealf-Penny"	20·00	38·00
		b. "Half-Pennv" and long "P"	18·00	38·00
		ba. "Half Pennv" and long "T" and "A"	18·00	38·00
		c. No stop after "POSTAGE" and long "P", "T" and "A"	18·00	38·00
		d. Long "P"	2·50	6·50
		e. Long "T"	2·50	6·50
		f. Long "A"	3·50	8·50
		g. Long "P" and "T"	2·50	6·50
		h. Long "P" and "A"	2·50	6·50
		i. Long "T" and "A"	3·00	8·00
		k. Long "P", "T" and "A"	3·25	8·00
		ka. Long "P", "T" and "A" with comma after "POSTAGE"	9·50	17·00
		l. Surch double	£275	
		la. Surch double, one vertical	£275	
		m. "POSTAGE" omitted	£1000	
		s. Handstamped "Specimen"	55·00	
		x. Wmk reversed	2·50	5·00

The surcharge was applied as a setting of 60 (12×5) which contained seventeen normals, one each of Nos. 114a, 114b, 114ba, 114c, six of No. 114d, six of 114e, three of 114f, six of 114g, seven of 114h, five of No. 114i, four of No. 114k and two of No. 114ka.

HALF (30)

31

32

1895 (18 Mar). *No. 99 surch locally with T* **30**.

125		HALF on 1d. rose (*shades*)	3·00	2·25
		a. Surch double	£375	£375
		b. "H" with longer left limb	30·00	
		c. Pair, one without surcharge		
		s. Handstamped "Specimen"	55·00	

No. 125b, in which the "A" also has a short right leg, occurs on the second, fourth, sixth etc., stamps of the first vertical column of the right-hand pane of the first printing only.

In the second printing what appears to be a broken "E" (with the top limb removed) was used instead of "L" in "HALF" on the last stamp in the sheet (*Price* £32), No. 125c also comes from this second printing.

(Typo D.L.R)

1902–03. *Inscr* "POSTAGE REVENUE". Wmk Crown CA. P 14.

127	31	½d. blue-green	3·25	50
128		1d. carmine	9·00	15
129		1½d. green and black	4·00	3·00
130		2d. red and olive-green	3·00	25
131		2½d. bright blue	1·50	3·75
132		3d. purple and grey	1·25	2·00
133		4d. carmine and cinnamon	5·50	20·00
134		5d. black and orange	2·75	2·75
		w. Wmk inverted	£150	80·00
135		6d. green and brown-purple	2·50	3·50
136		1s. carmine and pale blue	3·25	3·75
137		2s. green and bright violet	50·00	9·00
138		2s.6d. purple	40·00	12·00
139		4s. deep rose and maize	75·00	75·00
		a. Imperf between (horiz pair)		
127/39 *Set of* 13			£180	£120
127s/39s Optd "Specimen" *Set of* 13			£180	

No. 139a is also imperforate between stamp and left-hand margin.

(Typo D.L.R.)

1902. Wmk Crown CC. P 14.

140	32	5s. dull blue and rose	35·00	12·00
141		10s. deep rose and chocolate	75·00	28·00
142		£1 black and bright blue	£190	55·00
143		£1. 10s green and violet	£425	£100
		s. Optd "Specimen"	80·00	
144		£5 mauve and black	£3000	£650
		s. Optd "Specimen"	£130	
145		£10 green and orange	£8000	£3000
		as. Optd "Specimen"	£200	
145*b*		£20 red and green	£16000	£8500
		bs. Optd "Specimen"	£375	
140s/2s Optd "Specimen" *Set of* 3			£110	

USED HIGH VALUES. Collectors are warned against fiscally used high value Natal stamps with penmarks cleaned off and forged postmarks added.

1904–08. *Chalk-surfaced paper (£1 10s.).* Wmk Mult Crown CA. P 14.

146	31	½d. blue-green	7·00	15
147		1d. rose-carmine	7·00	15
		a. Booklet pane of 6, one stamp optd "NOT FOR USE" (1907)	£275	
148		1d. deep carmine	9·50	30
		w. Wmk inverted	†	80·00
149		2d. red and olive-green	11·00	3·25
152		4d. carmine and cinnamon	2·75	1·25
153		5d. black and orange (1908)	4·25	4·00
155		1s. carmine and pale blue	85·00	7·00
156		2s. dull green and bright violet	60·00	42·00
157		2s.6d. purple	55·00	42·00
162	32	£1. 10s. brown-orange and deep purple (1908)	£1200	£2000
		s. Optd "Specimen"	£225	
146/57 *Set of* 9			£225	90·00

1908–09. *Inscr* "POSTAGE POSTAGE". Wmk Mult Crown CA. P 14.

165	31	6d. dull and bright purple	4·50	3·00
166		1s. black/*green*	6·00	3·00
167		2s. purple and bright blue/*blue*	15·00	3·00
168		2s.6d. black and red/*blue*	25·00	3·00
169	32	5s. green and red/*yellow*	24·00	30·00
170		10s. green and red/*green*	85·00	90·00
171		£1 purple and black/*red*	£300	£275
165/71 *Set of* 7			£425	£375
165s/71s Optd "Specimen" *Set of* 7			£250	

STAMP BOOKLETS

1906. *Black on red cover. Stapled.*

SB1	2s.7d. booklet containing thirty 1d. (No. 147) in blocks of 6	£2000

1907. *Black on red cover. Stapled.*

SB2	2s.6d. booklet containing thirty 1d. (No. 147) in blocks of 6	£2000

The first stamp of the first pane in No. SB2 was overprinted "NOT FOR USE" (No. 147a), the additional penny being used to defray the cost of production.

FISCALS USED FOR POSTAGE

1869. *Embossed on coloured wove, surfaced paper.* P 12½.

F1	1	1d. yellow	50·00	80·00

Examples of 1d. yellow and 6d. rose values as Type **6**, 1s. purple-brown as Type **7** and various values between 5s, and £10 in the design illustrated above are believed to exist postally used, but, as such use was not authorised, they are not now listed.

OFFICIAL STAMPS

OFFICIAL (O 1)

1904. *T* **31**, wmk Mult Crown CA, *optd with Type* O **1**. P 14.

O1	½d. blue-green	3·00	35
O2	1d. carmine	6·00	80
O3	2d. red and olive-green	26·00	14·00
O4	3d. purple and grey	16·00	4·25
O5	6d. green and brown-purple	55·00	65·00
O6	1s. carmine and pale blue	£160	£200
O1/6 *Set of* 6		£225	£250

The use of stamps overprinted as above was discontinued after 30 May 1907. Stamps perforated with the letters "N.G.R." were for use on Government Railways.

Natal became a province of the Union of South Africa on 31 May 1910.

IV. NEW REPUBLIC

During the unrest following the death of Cetshwayo, the Zulu king, in 1884, a group of Boers from the Transvaal offered their support to his son, Dinizulu. The price for this support was the cession of a sizeable portion of Zulu territory to an independent Boer republic. The New Republic, centred on Vryheid, was proclaimed on 16 August 1884 with the remaining Zulu territory becoming a protectorate of the new administration. The first reference to an organised postal service occurs in December 1884.

Alarmed by these developments the British authorities annexed the southernmost part of the land grant, around St. Lucia Bay, to prevent access to the Indian Ocean. The remainder of the New Republic was, however, recognised as independent on 22 October 1886. Zululand was annexed by the British on 22 May 1887.

Difficulties beset the New Republic, however, and its Volksraad voted for union with the South African Republic (Transvaal). The two republics united on 21 July 1888. In 1903 the territory of the former New Republic was transferred to Natal.

Mail from Vryheid in 1884–85 was franked with issues of Transvaal (for dispatches made via Utrecht) or Natal (for those sent via Dundee from August 1885 onwards). Issues of the New Republic were never accepted as internationally valid by these administrations so that all external mail continued to show Transvaal or Natal stamps used in combination with those of the republic.

PRICES FOR STAMPS ON COVER

No. 1	—
Nos. 2/5	*from* × 50
Nos. 6/25	—
Nos. 26/9	*from* × 50
Nos. 30/47	—
Nos. 48/50	*from* × 50
No. 51	—
Nos. 52/3	*from* × 50
Nos. 72/5	*from* × 50
Nos. 76/7b	—
Nos. 78/80	*from* × 50
Nos. 81/95	—

1

Printed with a rubber handstamp on paper bought in Europe and sent out ready gummed and perforated.

1886 (7 Jan)–**87**. *Various dates indicating date of printing.* P 11½.

No.	Type	Description	Unused	Used
		A. Without Arms. (i) Yellow paper.		
1	**1**	1d. black (9.1.86)	—	£3000
2		1d. violet (9.1.86)	11·00	13·00
		a. "1d." omitted (in pair with normal) (24.4.86)	£2000	
3		2d. violet (9.1.86)	15·00	20·00
		a. "d" omitted (13.10.86)	£4000	
4		3d. violet (13.1.86)	30·00	35·00
		a. "d" omitted (13.10.86)	£4000	
		b. *Tête-bêche* (pair) (13.10.86)		
5		4d. violet (30.8.86)	45·00	
6		6d. violet (20.2.86)	40·00	45·00
		a. "6d." omitted (in pair with normal) (2.7.86)		
7		9d. violet (13.1.86)	75·00	
8		1s. violet (30.8.86)	75·00	
		a. "1s." omitted (in pair with normal) (6.9.86)		
9		1/s. violet (13.10.86)	£650	
10		1/6 violet (30.8.86)	80·00	
11		1s.6d. violet (13.1.86)	£450	
		a. *Tête-bêche* (pair) (6.9.86)		
		b. "d" omitted (13.10.86)	£100	
12		2s. violet (30.8.86)	42·00	
		a. *Tête-bêche* (pair) (6.9.86)	£750	
13		2/6 violet (13.1.86)	£150	
14		2s.6d. violet (1.86)	£120	
15		4/s. violet (17.1.87)	£450	
15*a*		4s. violet (17.1.87)		
16		5s. violet (1.86)	30·00	40·00
		a. "s" omitted (in pair with normal) (7.3.86)	£3000	
17		5/6 violet (20.2.86)	£140	
18		5s.6d. violet (13.1.86)	£300	
19		7/6 violet (13.1.86)	£180	
20		7s.6d. violet (24.5.86)	£120	
21		10s. violet (13.1.86)	£150	£160
		a. *Tête-bêche* (pair) (2.7.86)		
22		10s.6d. violet (1.86)	£170	
		a. "d" omitted (1.86)	£100	
23		13s. violet (24.11.86)	£450	
24		£1 violet (13.1.86)	£120	
		a. *Tête-bêche* (pair) (13.10.86)	£500	
25		30s. violet (13.1.86)	£100	
		a. *Tête-bêche* (pair) (24.11.86)	£500	
		(ii) Blue granite paper.		
26	**1**	1d. violet (20.1.86)	16·00	18·00
		a. "d" omitted (24.11.86)	£500	
		b. "1" omitted (in pair with normal) (24.11.86)		
27		2d. violet (24.1.86)	16·00	18·00
		a. "d" omitted (24.4.86)	£1000	
		b. "2d." omitted (in pair with normal) (24.4.86)		
28		3d. violet (30.8.86)	22·00	24·00
		a. *Tête-bêche* (pair) (13.10.86)	£300	
29		4d. violet (24.5.86)	30·00	35·00
30		6d. violet (20.2.86)	50·00	50·00
		a. "6" omitted in pair with normal (24.5.86)	£2000	
31		9d. violet (6.9.86)	£110	
32		1s. violet (1.86)	30·00	35·00
		a. *Tête-bêche* (pair) (21.5.86)	£325	
		b. "1s." omitted (in pair with normal) (29.4.86)	£2000	
33		1s.6d. violet (2.7.86)	£100	
		a. *Tête-bêche* (pair) (6.9.86)	£550	
		b. "d" omitted (13.10.86)		
34		1/6 violet (6.9.86)	£150	
35		2s. violet (21.5.86)	£120	
		a. "2s." omitted (in pair with normal) (24.5.86)	£2000	
36		2s.6d. violet (19.8.86)	£150	
37		2/6 violet (19.8.86)	£180	
38		4/s. violet (17.1.87)	£350	
39		5/6 violet (13.1.86)	£250	
		a. "/" omitted (13.1.87)		
40		5s.6d. violet (13.1.86)	£250	
41		7/6 violet (13.1.86)	£250	
41*a*		7s.6d. violet (13.1.86)	£300	
42		10s. violet (1.86)	£200	£200
		a. *Tête-bêche* (pair) (2.7.86)	£425	
		b. "s" omitted (13.1.86)		
43		10s.6d. violet (1.86)	£200	
		a. *Tête-bêche* (pair) (13.1.86)		
		b. "d" omitted (1.86)	£450	
44		12s. violet (13.1.86)	£300	
45		13s. violet (17.1.87)	£475	
46		£1 violet (13.1.86)	£275	
47		30s. violet (13.1.86)	£250	
		B. With embossed Arms of New Republic.		
		(i) Yellow paper.		
48	**1**	1d. violet (20.1.86)	14·00	16·00
		a. Arms inverted (20.1.86)	27·00	30·00
		b. Arms *tête-bêche* (pair) (14.4.86)	£100	£120
		c. *Tête-bêche* (pair) (3.11.86)	£800	
49		2d. violet (30.8.86)	16·00	18·00
		a. Arms inverted (24.11.86)	25·00	30·00
50		4d. violet (2.12.86)	50·00	60·00
		a. Arms inverted (12.86)	£100	70·00
		b. Arms *tête-bêche* (pair) (12.86)	£250	
51		6d. violet (2.12.86)	£200	
		(ii) Blue granite paper.		
52	**1**	1d. violet (20.1.86)	15·00	17·00
		a. Arms inverted (10.2.86)	38·00	42·00
		b. Arms *tête-bêche* (pair) (3.11.86)	£500	
53		2d. violet (24.5.86)	15·00	17·00
		a. Arms inverted (30.8.86)	50·00	60·00
		b. Arms *tête-bêche* (pair) (2.12.86)	£500	£500

Stamps as Type **1** were produced as and when stocks were required, each printing including in its design the date on which it was prepared. The dates quoted above for Nos. 1/53 are those on which the various stamps first appeared. Details of the various printing dates are given below. From these dates it can be seen that some values share common printing dates, and, it is believed, that the different values were produced *se-tenant* within the same sheet, at least in some instances. A reported proof sheet in the Pretoria Postal Museum, on yellow paper and embossed, contains 4 examples of the 6d. value and 3 each of the 3d., 4d., 9d., 1s., 1/6, 2/-, 2/6, 3s., 4s., 5s., 5/6, 7/6, 10/-, 10/6, £1 and 30/-.

The date on No. 1 measures 17 mm; on all others it is 15 mm.

The significance, if any, of the two coloured papers and the use of the embossing machine have never been satisfactorily explained. Both the different papers and the embossing machine were introduced in January 1886, and occur throughout the period that the stamps with dates were used.

PRINTINGS

Date	*Paper*	*Face value*	*Cat No.*	*Unused*	*Used*
Jan 86	*Yellow*	5s.	16	30·00	40·00
		10s.6d.	22	£200	
		10s.6	22a	£150	
	Blue	1s.	32		
		10s.	42	£200	£200
		10s.6d.	43	£200	
		10s.6	43b	£500	
7 Jan 86	*Yellow*	10s.6d.	22	£170	
	Blue	10s.	42		
		10s.6d.	43	£475	
9 Jan 86	*Yellow*	1d. blk	1	†	£3000
		1d. vio	2	11·00	13·00
		2d.	3	40·00	50·00
13 Jan 86	*Yellow*	1d.	2	38·00	
		2d.	3	35·00	38·00
		3d.	4	75·00	
		9d	7	£200	
		1s.6d.	11	£450	
		2/6	13	£160	
		2s.6d.	14	£200	
		5s.6d.	18		
		7/6	19	£180	
		10s.	21		
		£1	24	£150	
		30s.	25	£150	
	Blue	5/6	39	£250	
		5s.6d.	40	£250	
		7/6	41	£250	
		7s.6d.	41a	£300	
		10s.	42	£400	
		10s.	42b		
		10s.6d.	43	£200	
		10s.6d.	43a		
		12s.	44	£300	
		£1	46	£250	
		30s.	47	£250	
20 Jan 86	*Yellow*	1d.	2		
	Blue	1d.	26	£250	
	Yellow, embossed	1d.	48	75·00	
		1d.	48a	£100	
	Blue, embossed	1d.	52	£130	
Jan 20 86	*Blue*	1d.	26	25·00	
	Yellow, embossed	1d.	48a		
	Blue, embossed	1d.	52	£120	
24 Jan 86	*Blue*	1d.	26	30·00	
		2d.	27	50·00	
10 Feb 86	*Yellow*	1d.	2		
	Yellow, embossed	1d.	48		
		1d.	48a	75·00	
	Blue, embossed	1d.	52	£130	
		1d.	52a	45·00	
20 Feb 86	*Yellow*	6d.	6		
		1s.6d.	11		
		2s.6d.	14	£130	
		5/6	17	£140	
		5s.6d.	18		
	Blue	6d.	30		
7 Mar 86	*Yellow*	1d.	2	£110	
		2/6	13		
		2s.6d.	14	£120	
		5s.	16	£200	90·00
		5s.	16a	£3000	
		5/6	17	£140	
		5s.6d.	18	£300	
	Blue	2d.	27	£100	
		6d.	30		
		1s.	32		
17 Mar 86	*Yellow*	1d.	2	£100	
	Yellow, embossed	1d.	48	50·00	
	Blue, embossed	1d.	52	£130	
		1d.	52a	£110	
26 Mar 86	*Blue, embossed*	1d.	52a	£130	
14 Apr 86	*Yellow*	1d.	2		
	Yellow, embossed	1d.	48	30·00	
		1d.	48a	60·00	
		1d.	48b	£100	£120
	Blue, embossed	1d.	52	50·00	
		1d.	52a		
24 Apr 86	*Yellow*	1d.	2	£100	
		1d.	2a	£2000	
		5s.	16		
	Blue	2d.	27	75·00	
		2d.	27a	£1000	
		2d.	27b		
29 Apr 86	*Blue*	1s.	32	£110	
		1s.	32b		
21 May 86	*Yellow*	6d.	6	£130	
	Blue	1d.	26	90·00	
		1s.	32	30·00	35·00
		1s.	32a	£325	
		1s.	32b	£1500	
		2s.	35	£275	
23 May 86	*Blue, embossed*	1d.	52a	£100	
24 May 86	*Yellow*	1d.	2	£100	
		2d.	3	£120	
		5s.	16	£100	
		7/6	19	£180	
		7s.6d.	20	£120	
	Blue	1d.	26	35·00	38·00
		2d.	27	£300	£300
		4d.	29	£100	
		6d.	30	£120	
		6d.	30a	£2000	
		1s.	32	£200	
		1s.	32b	£2000	
		2s.	35	£150	
		2s.	35a	£2000	
	Blue, embossed	2d.	53	£100	
26 May 86	*Yellow*	1d.	2		
	Blue	1d.	26	£110	
	Yellow, embossed	1d.	48	£250	
		1d.	48a	£100	
	Blue, embossed	1d.	52	£130	
		1d.	52a	50·00	55·00
28 May 86	*Yellow, embossed*	1d.	48	£150	
Jun 30 86	*Blue*	1d.	26	16·00	18·00
	Yellow, embossed	1d.	48	18·00	20·00
		1d.	48a	27·00	30·00
		1d.	48b	£200	£225
	Blue, embossed	1d.	52	48·00	42·00
2 Jul 86	*Yellow*	6d.	6	£200	
		6d.	6a		
		9d	7	£200	£200
		10s.	21		
		10s.	21a		
	Blue	1s.6d.	33	£100	
		10s.	42	£200	
		10s.	42a	£425	
		10s.6d.	43		
		10s.6d.	43b	£450	
3 Jul 86	*Blue*	10s.	42		
Jul 7 86	*Yellow*	1d.	2		
	Blue	1d.	26		
	Yellow, embossed	1d.	48	75·00	
		1d.	48a	£100	£100
	Blue, embossed	1d.	52	18·00	20·00
		1d.	52a	60·00	42·00
4 Aug 86	*Yellow*	1d.	2		
	Yellow, embossed	1d.	48	60·00	
	Blue, embossed	1d.	52	60·00	
		1d.	52a		
19 Aug 86	*Yellow*	2/6	13		
		2s.6d.	14	£140	
	Blue	2s.6d.	36	£150	
		2/6	37	£180	
30 Aug 86	*Yellow*	1d.	2	11·00	13·00
		2d.	3	75·00	
		3d.	4	80·00	
		4d.	5	55·00	
		6d.	6	£100	
		9d.	7	75·00	
		1s.	8	75·00	
		1/6	10	80·00	
		2s.	12	£100	
		2/6	13	£150	
	Blue	2d.	27	16·00	18·00
		3d.	28		
	Yellow, embossed	2d.	49	£100	
	Blue, embossed	2d.	53	45·00	
		2d.	53a	£110	
6 Sep 86	*Yellow*	1d.	2	£100	
		2d.	3	35·00	40·00
		3d.	4	40·00	
		4d.	5	45·00	
		6d.	6	75·00	
		9d.	7	75·00	
		1s.	8	£100	
		1s.	8a		
		1/6	10	£140	
		1s.6d.	11	£450	

Date	Paper	Face value	Cat No.	Unused	Used
		1s.6d.	11a		
		2s.	12	£100	
		2s.	12a	£750	
		2/6	13	£150	
		2s.6d.	14		
		5s.	16	£140	
		7s.6d.	20	£200	
		10s.	21	£150	
		£1	24	£140	
	Blue	6d.	30	50·00	50·00
		9d.	31	£110	
		1s.	32	75·00	
		1s.6d.	33	£140	
		1s.6d.	33a	£550	
		1/6	34		
		2s.6d.	36		
		2/6	37	£400	
		7s.6d.	41a	£300	
		10s.6d.	43		
13 Sep 86	*Yellow*	1d.	2		
	Yellow, embossed	1d.	48	75·00	
		1d.	48a	75·00	
	Blue, embossed	1d.	52	£100	
6 Oct 86	*Yellow*	1d.	2		
	Blue	1d.	26	90·00	
	Yellow, embossed	1d.	48	75·00	60·00
		1d.	48a		
	Blue, embossed	1d.	52	48·00	20·00
		1d.	52a	90·00	
13 Oct 86	*Yellow*	1d.	2	25·00	25·00
		2d.	3	25·00	30·00
		2d.	3a	£4000	
		3d.	4	30·00	35·00
		3d.	4a	£4000	
		3d.	4b		
		4d.	5	50·00	
		6d.	6	40·00	45·00
		9d.	7	75·00	
		1s.	8	£150	
		1/s	9	£650	
		1/6	10	£150	
		1s 6.	11b	£100	
		2s.	12	42·00	
		2/6	13	£160	
		5s.	16	75·00	
		10s.	21	£150	£160
		10s.6.	22a	£100	
		£1	24	£120	
		£1	24a	£500	
	Blue	2d.	27	16·00	18·00
		3d.	28	22·00	24·00
		3d.	28a	£300	
		4d.	29	30·00	35·00
		1s.	32	50·00	
		1s 6.	33b		
		1/6	34	£150	
		2s.	35	£120	
3 Nov 86	*Yellow*	1d.	2	40·00	
	Blue	1d.	26		
	Yellow, embossed	1d.	48	14·00	16·00
		1d.	48a	27·00	30·00
		1d.	48b	£100	£120
		1d.	48c	£800	
	Blue, embossed	1d.	52	15·00	
		1d.	52a	38·00	42·00
		1d.	52b	£500	
13 Nov 86	*Yellow*	1d.	2	£120	
24 Nov 86	*Yellow*	1d.	2	£100	
		2d.	3	15·00	20·00
		3d.	4	35·00	40·00
		1/6	10	£150	
		10s.	21	£200	
		13s.	23	£450	
		30s.	25	£100	
		30s.	25a	£500	
	Blue	1d.	26	40·00	30·00
		1d.	26a	£500	
		1d.	26b		
		2d.	27	50·00	
		2d.	27a		
		4d.	29	30·00	35·00
		6d.	30	60·00	60·00
		9d.	31	£120	
		1s.	32	100·00	110·00
		1/6	34	£200	
		2s.	35	£150	
		2s.	35a	£3000	
	Yellow, embossed	2d.	49	£160	
		2d.	49a		
26 Nov 86	*Yellow*	1/6	10	£140	
2 Dec 86	*Yellow*	1d.	2		
		2d.	3		
	Blue	2d.	27		
	Yellow, embossed	1d.	48	25·00	30·00
		1d.	48a	£160	
		2d.	49	16·00	18·00
		2d.	49a	25·00	30·00
		4d.	50	£150	
		6d.	51	£150	
	Blue, embossed	1d.	52	35·00	
		1d.	52a	£160	
		2d.	53	15·00	17·00
		2d.	53a	50·00	60·00
		2d.	53b	£500	£500
3 Dec 86	*Yellow, embossed*	6d.	51		
Dec 86	*Yellow*	6d.	6		
	Blue	4d.	29		
	Yellow, embossed	4d.	50	50·00	60·00
		4d.	50a	£100	70·00
		4d.	50b	£250	
		6d.	51	£200	
4 Jan 87	*Yellow*	1d.	2	£100	
		2d.	3	40·00	
		13s.	23	£450	
	Blue	1d.	26	16·00	18·00
		2d.	27	20·00	20·00
	Blue, embossed	2d.	53	45·00	
13 Jan 87	*Yellow*	7/6	19		
	Blue	5/6	39	£450	
		5/6	39a		
		7/6	41	£500	
17 Jan 87	*Yellow*	1d.	2	75·00	
		2d.	3	75·00	
		3d.	4	75·00	
		4/s.	15	£450	
		4s.	15a		
	Blue	1d.	26	80·00	
		4/s.	38	£350	
		13s.	45	£475	
		30s.	47	£275	
20 Jan 87	*Blue*	2d.	27	38·00	
	Yellow, embossed	2d.	49	55·00	
		2d.	49a	£140	
	Blue, embossed	2d.	53	45·00	
		2d.	53a	£100	
Jan 20 87	*Yellow, embossed*	1d.	48a	£400	

1887 (Jan–Mar). *As T* **1**, *but without date. With embossed Arms.*

(a) Blue granite paper.

72	1d. violet	19·00	15·00
	b. Stamps *tête-bêche* (pair)	£475	
	c. Arms *tête-bêche* (pair)		
	d. Arms inverted	25·00	25·00
	e. Arms omitted	£110	£110
	f. Arms sideways		
73	2d. violet	11·00	11·00
	a. Stamps *tête-bêche* (pair)	£325	
	b. Arms inverted	28·00	28·00
	c. Arms omitted	£110	£100
	d. Arms *tête-bêche* (pair)		
74	3d. violet	19·00	19·00
	a. Stamps *tête-bêche* (pair)	£375	
	b. Arms *tête-bêche* (pair)		
	c. Arms inverted	50·00	50·00
75	4d. violet	15·00	15·00
	a. Stamps *tête-bêche* (pair)	£325	
	b. Arms *tête-bêche* (pair)	£275	
	c. Arms inverted	85·00	
76	6d. violet	19·00	19·00
	a. Arms inverted	85·00	
77	1/6 violet	26·00	24·00
	a. Arms inverted	£120	
	b. Arms *tête-bêche* (pair)	£400	
77*c*	2/6 violet	†	£750

(b) Yellow paper (March 1887).

78	2d. violet (*arms omitted*)	25·00	
79	3d. violet	16·00	17·00
	b. Stamps *tête-bêche* (pair)	£325	£375
	c. Arms *tête-bêche* (pair)	£200	
	d. Arms inverted	27·00	27·00
	e. Arms sideways	£300	
80	4d. violet	14·00	14·00
	a. Arms inverted	16·00	16·00
81	6d. violet	9·00	10·00
	a. Arms *tête-bêche* (pair)	£350	
	b. Arms inverted	45·00	45·00
	c. Arms omitted	80·00	
82	9d. violet	12·00	13·00
	a. Arms inverted	£200	
	b. Arms *tête-bêche* (pair)	£350	
83	1s. violet	12·00	12·00
	a. Arms inverted	70·00	
84	1/6 violet	24·00	22·00
85	2s. violet	19·00	18·00
	a. Arms inverted	55·00	50·00
	b. Arms omitted	£100	
86	2/6 violet	25·00	25·00
	a. Arms inverted	32·00	32·00
87	3s. violet	48·00	48·00
	a. Arms inverted	55·00	55·00
	b. Stamps *tête-bêche* (pair)	£450	
88	4s. violet	£300	
	a. Arms omitted		
88*b*	4/s violet	45·00	45·00
	ba. Arms omitted	£180	
89	5s. violet	40·00	40·00
	b. Arms inverted	—	£100
90	5/6 violet	16·00	17·00
91	7/6 violet	20·00	22·00
	a. Arms *tête-bêche* (pair)		
	b. Arms inverted	£100	
92	10s. violet	17·00	18·00
	b. Arms *tête-bêche* (pair)	£120	
	c. Arms inverted	27·00	
	d. Arms omitted	£100	48·00
93	10/6 violet	17·00	17·00
	b. Arms inverted	50·00	
94	£1 violet	55·00	55·00
	a. Stamps *tête-bêche* (pair)	£450	£500
	b. Arms inverted	60·00	
95	30s. violet	£140	

A £15 value as Nos. 78/95 exists, but is only known fiscally used (*Price* £4000).

Many values exist with double impressions of the handstamp.

New Republic united with the South African Republic (Transvaal) on 21 July 1888. In 1903 the territory of the former New Republic was transferred to Natal.

V. ORANGE FREE STATE

PRICES FOR STAMPS ON COVER

Nos. 1/9	*from* × 20
Nos. 10/13	*from* × 30
Nos. 18/19	*from* × 20
No. 20	—
Nos. 21/42	*from* × 40
Nos. 48/51	*from* × 25
Nos. 52/138	*from* × 10
Nos. 139/51	*from* × 7
Nos. F1/17	—
Nos. PF1/3	*from* × 20
No. M1	*from* × 20

Supplies of Cape of Good Hope stamps were available at Bloemfontein and probably elsewhere in the Orange Free State, from mid-1856 onwards for use on mail to Cape Colony and beyond. Such arrangements continued after the introduction of Orange Free State stamps in 1868. It is not known if the dumb cancellations used on the few surviving covers were applied in the Free State or at Cape Town.

1

(Typo D.L.R.)

1868 (1 Jan)–**94**. P 14.

1	**1**	1d. pale brown	21·00	1·50
2		1d. red-brown	14·00	45
3		1d. deep brown	22·00	45
4		6d. pale rose (1868)	50·00	8·00
5		6d. rose (1871)	23·00	5·50
6		6d. rose-carmine (1891)	23·00	12·00
7		6d. bright carmine (1894)	14·00	2·00
8		1s. orange-buff	80·00	6·50
9		1s. orange-yellow	45·00	1·50
		a. Double print	—	£3000

4 (**2**) (*a*) 4 (*b*) 4 (*c*) 4 (*d*)

1877. *No. 5 surcharged T* **2** *(a) to (d).*

10	**1**	4d. on 6d. rose (*a*)	£375	55·00
		a. Surch inverted	—	£550
		b. Surch double (*a* + *c*)		
		c. Surch double, one inverted (*a* + *c* inverted)	†	£3000
		d. Surch double, one inverted (*a* inverted + *c*)	†	£4750
11		4d. on 6d. rose (*b*)	£1300	£180
		a. Surch inverted	—	£1100
		b. Surch double (*b* + *d*)		
12		4d. on 6d. rose (*c*)	£200	28·00
		a. Surch inverted	—	£350
		b. Surch double		
13		4d. on 6d. rose (*d*)	£250	35·00
		a. Surch inverted	£1200	£375
		b. Surch double, one inverted (*d* + *c* inverted)	†	£3250

The setting of 60 comprised nine stamps as No. 10, four as No. 11, twenty-seven as No. 12 and twenty as No. 13.

1878 (July). P 14.

18	**1**	4d. pale blue	22·00	3·50
19		4d. ultramarine	4·00	2·75
20		5s. green	10·00	13·00

1d. (**3**) (*a*) 1d. (*b*) 1d. (*c*) 1d. (*d*) 1d. (*e*) 1d. (*f*)

Type **3**: (*a*) Small "1" and "d." (*b*) Sloping serif. (*c*) Same size as (*b*), but "1" with straighter horizontal serif. (*d*) Taller "1" with horizontal serif and antique "d". (*e*) Same size as (*d*) but with sloping serif and thin line at foot. (*f*) as (*d*) but with Roman "d".

1881 (19 May). *No. 20 surch T* **3** *(a) to (f) with heavy black bar cancelling the old value.*

21	**1**	1d. on 5s. green (*a*)	£100	23·00
22		1d. on 5s. green (*b*)	60·00	23·00
		a. Surch inverted	—	£800
		b. Surch double	—	£1100
23		1d. on 5s. green (*c*)	£225	75·00
		a. Surch inverted	—	£1200
		b. Surch double	—	£1400
24		1d. on 5s. green (*d*)	90·00	23·00
		a. Surch inverted	£1800	£800
		b. Surch double	—	£1100
25		1d. on 5s. green (*e*)	£550	£250
		a. Surch inverted	†	£2000
		b. Surch double	†	£2000
26		1d. on 5s. green (*f*)	85·00	23·00
		a. Surch inverted	—	£750
		b. Surch double	—	£800

No. 21 was the first printing in one type only. Nos. 22 to 25 constitute the second printing about a year later, and are all found on the same sheet; and No. 26 the third printing of which about half have the stop raised.

Owing to defective printing, examples of Nos. 22 and 24/5 may be found with the obliterating bar at the top of the stamps or, from the top row, without the bar.

½d (**4**)

1882 (Aug). *No. 20 surch with T* **4** *and with a thin black line cancelling old value.*

36	**1**	½d. on 5s. green	20·00	4·00
		a. Surch double	£425	£325
		b. Surch inverted	£1300	£800

3d (**5**) (*a*) 3d (*b*) 3d (*c*) 3d (*d*) 3d (*e*)

1882. *No. 19 surch with T* **5** *(a) to (e) with thin black line cancelling value.*

38	**1**	3d. on 4d. ultramarine (*a*)	85·00	27·00
		a. Surch double	†	£1200
39		3d. on 4d. ultramarine (*b*)	85·00	18·00
		a. Surch double	†	£1200
40		3d. on 4d. ultramarine (*c*)	38·00	18·00
		a. Surch double	†	£1200
41		3d. on 4d. ultramarine (*d*)	85·00	20·00
		a. Surch double	†	£1200
42		3d. on 4d. ultramarine (*e*)	£225	65·00
		a. Surch double	†	£2750

Examples of Nos. 39 and 41/2 exist without the cancelling bar due to the misplacement of the surcharge.

1883–84. P 14.

48 **1** ½d. chestnut 3·00 50
49 2d. pale mauve 16·00 75
50 2d. bright mauve 16·00 30
51 3d. ultramarine 3·50 2·00

For 1d. purple, see No. 68.

2d (**6**) (*a*) 2d (*b*) 2d (*c*)

1888 (Sept–Oct). *No. 51 surch with T* **6** *(a), (b) or (c).*

(a) Wide "2". (b) Narrow "2".

52 **1** 2d. on 3d. ultramarine (*a*) (Sept). 60·00 9·00
a. Surch inverted — £750
53 2d. on 3d. ultramarine (*b*) 40·00 2·00
a. Surch inverted — £300
b. "2" with curved foot (*c*) £1300 £500

1d (**7**) (*a*) 1d (*b*) Id (*c*)

1890 (Dec)–**91**. *Nos. 51 and 19 surch with T* **7** *(a) to (c).*

54 **1** 1d. on 3d. ultramarine (*a*) 8·50 60
a. Surch double 85·00 70·00
c. "1" and "d" wide apart £150 £110
d. Dropped "d" (Right pane R. 5/6) £160 £120
55 1d. on 3d. ultramarine (*b*) 23·00 2·75
a. Surch double £275 £250
57 1d. on 4d. ultramarine (*a*) 29·00 7·50
a. Surch double £140 £110
b. Surch double (*a* + *b*) £400
c. Surch triple — £1500
d. Raised "1" (Left pane R. 3/1)
58 1d. on 4d. ultramarine (*b*) 80·00 50·00
a. Surch double £425 £325
59 1d. on 4d. ultramarine (*c*) £1600 £500
a. Surch double

The settings of the 1d. on 3d. and on 4d. are not identical. The variety (*c*) does not exist on the 3d.

2½d. (**8**)

2½d.▪ Printer's quad after surcharge (Lower right pane No. 43)

1892 (Oct). *No. 51 surch with T* **8**.

67 **1** 2½d. on 3d. ultramarine 17·00 70
a. No stop after "d" 80·00 50·00
b. Printer's quad after surcharge — 50·00

1894 (Sept). *Colour changed.* P 14.

68 **1** 1d. purple 3·50 30

½d (**9**) (*a*) ½d (*b*) ½d (*c*)

½d (*d*) ½d (*e*) ½d (*f*) ½d (*g*)

Types (*a*) and (*e*) differ from types (*b*) and (*f*) respectively, in the serifs of the "1", but owing to faulty overprinting this distinction is not always clearly to be seen.

1896 (Sept). *No. 51 surch with T* **9** *(a) to (g).*

69 **1** ½d. on 3d. ultramarine (*a*) 6·00 10·00
70 ½d. on 3d. ultramarine (*b*) 13·00 13·00
71 ½d. on 3d. ultramarine (*c*) 12·00 2·50
72 ½d. on 3d. ultramarine (*d*) 12·00 2·25
73 ½d. on 3d. ultramarine (*e*) 12·00 2·25
74 ½d. on 3d. ultramarine (*f*) 13·00 14·00
75 ½d. on 3d. ultramarine (*g*) 7·50 4·00
a. Surch double 13·00 10·00
b. Surch triple 70·00 70·00

The double and triple surcharges are often different types, but are always type (*g*), or in combination with type (*g*).

Double surcharges in the same type, but without the "d" and bar, also exist, probably from a trial sheet prepared by the printer. Both mint and used examples are known.

Halve Penny. (**10**)

2½ (**11**)

1896. *No. 51 surch with T* **10**.

77 **1** ½d. on 3d. ultramarine 1·00 50

(i) Errors in setting.

78 **1** ½d. on 3d. (no stop) 17·00 28·00
79 ½d. on 3d. ("Peuny") 17·00 28·00

(ii) Surch inverted.

81 **1** ½d. on 3d. 55·00 60·00
81*a* ½d. on 3d. (no stop) £2000
81*b* ½d. on 3d. ("Peuny") £1500

(iii) Surch double, one inverted.

81*c* **1** ½d. on 3d. (Nos. 77 and 81) £180 £200
81*d* ½d. on 3d. (Nos. 77 and 81*a*) £800 £800
81*e* ½d. on 3d. (Nos. 77 and 81*b*) £900 £900
81*f* ½d. on 3d. (Nos. 81 and 78) — £900
82 ½d. on 3d. (Nos. 81 and 79) — £900

Examples from the top horizontal row can be found without the bar due to the surcharge being misplaced.

Nos. 69 to 75 also exist surcharged as last but they are considered not to have been issued with authority (*Prices from £30 each, unused*).

1897 (1 Jan). *No. 51 surch with T* **11**. *(a) As in illustration. (b) With Roman "1" and antique "2" in fraction.*

83 **1** 2½d. on 3d. ultramarine (*a*) 8·00 80
83*a* 2½d. on 3d. ultramarine (*b*) £170 90·00

1897. P 14.

84 **1** ½d. yellow (March) 2·00 35
85 ½d. orange 2·00 35
87 1s. brown (Aug) 23·00 1·50

The 6d. blue was prepared for use in the Orange Free State, but had not been brought into use when the stamps were seized in Bloemfontein. A few have been seen without the "V.R.I." overprint but they were not authorized or available for postage (*Price* £60).

BRITISH OCCUPATION

V. R. I. 4d (**31**) (Level stops)

V. R. I. ½d (**32**) Thin "V" (Raised stops)

V. R. I. ½d (**33**) Thick "V"

V. R I. Inserted "R"

(Surch by Curling & Co, Bloemfontein)

1900. *T* **1** *surch as T* **31**/**33** *(2½d. on 3d. optd "V.R.I." only).*

(a) First printings surch as T **31** *with stops level (March).*

101 ½d. on ½d. orange 3·50 4·00
a. No stop after "V" (R.10/3) 20·00 24·00
b. No stop after "I" (R.1/3) £160 £160
c. "½" omitted (R.7/5) £180 £180
d. "I" omitted £200 £200
e. "V.R.I." omitted £170
f. Value omitted £110
g. Small "½" 55·00 55·00
h. Surch double £180
102 1d. on 1d. purple 2·50 1·25
a. Surch on 1d. deep brown (No. 3) £600 £400
b. No stop after "V" (R. 10/3) 16·00 13·00
c. No stop after "R" £160 £170
d. No stop after "I"
e. "1" omitted (R. 7/5) £180 £190
f. "I" omitted (with stops present) £325 £325
g. "I" and stop after "R" omitted (R. 2/3) £250 £250
h. "V.R.I." omitted £160 £170
i. "d" omitted £325 £325
j. Value omitted 90·00 95·00
k. Inverted stop after "R" £225 £250
l. Wider space between "1" and "d" £100 £100
m. "V" and "R" close £160 £160
n. Pair, one without surch £475
o. "V" omitted £850
103 2d. on 2d. bright mauve 3·25 1·25
a. No stop after "V" (R. 10/3) 14·00 17·00
b. No stop after "R" £275 £275
c. No stop after "I" £275 £275
d. "V.R.I." omitted £300 £300
e. Value omitted £300
104 2½d. on 3d. ultramarine (*a*) 17·00 14·00
a. No stop after "V" (R. 10/3) 85·00 85·00
105 2½d. on 3d. ultramarine (*b*) £225 £225
106 3d. on 3d. ultramarine 2·75 2·75
a. No stop after "V" (R. 10/3) 19·00 19·00
b. Pair, one without surch £550
c. "V.R.I." omitted £250 £250
d. Value omitted £250 £250
107 4d. on 4d. ultramarine 8·50 17·00
a. No stop after "V" (R.10/3) 60·00 70·00
108 6d. on 6d. bright carmine 40·00 35·00
a. No stop after "V" (R. 10/3) £250 £275
b. "6" omitted (R. 7/5) £300 £300
109 6d. on 6d. blue 10·00 4·25
a. No stop after "V" (R. 10/3) 40·00 42·00
b. "6" omitted (R. 7/5) 75·00 80·00
c. "V.R.I." omitted £500 £300
110 1s. on 1s. brown 7·00 2·75
a. Surch on 1s. orange-yellow (No. 9) £3500 £2500
b. No stop after "V" (R. 10/3) 45·00 32·00
c. "1" omitted £130 £130
ca. "1" inserted by hand † £1000
d. "1" omitted and spaced stop after "s" £140 £150
e. "V.R.I." omitted £190 £190
f. Value omitted £190 £190
g. Raised stop after "s" 18·00 11·00
h. Wider space between "1" and "s" £150 £150
111 5s. on 5s. green 23·00 48·00
a. No stop after "V" (R. 10/3) £250 £300
b. "5" omitted £950 £1000
c. Inverted stop after "R" £700 £700
d. Wider space between "5" and "s" £130 £140
e. Value omitted £375 £400

All values are found with a rectangular, instead of an oval, stop after "R". Misplaced surcharges (upwards or sideways) occur.

No. 110ca shows the missing "1" replaced by a handstamp in a different type face.

(b) Subsequent printings.

(i) Surch as T **32**.

112 ½d. on ½d. orange 30 20
a. Raised and level stops mixed 2·00 2·00
b. Pair, one with level stops 11·00 15·00
c. No stop after "V" 2·75 3·00
d. No stop after "I" 27·00 28·00
e. "V" omitted £550
f. Small "½" 15·00 17·00
g. As a, and small "½" 15·00 17·00
i. Space between "V" and "R" 20·00 22·00
j. Value omitted £120 £120
113 1d. on 1d. purple 30 20
a. Raised and level stops mixed 1·60 2·25
b. Pair, one with level stops 20·00 21·00
c. No stop after "V" 3·25 6·00
d. No stop after "R" 16·00 17·00
e. No stop after "I" 16·00 17·00
f. No stops after "V" and "I" £300
g. Surch inverted £375
h. Surch double £110 £100
i. Pair, one without surch £250
j. Short figure "1" £110 £110
k. Space between "V" and "R" 50·00 55·00
l. Space between "R" and "I" £120 £130
m. Space between "1" and "d" £190 £190
n. Inserted "R" £325 £325
o. Inserted "V" £700
p. Stamp doubly printed, one impression inverted £2500
114 2d. on 2d. bright mauve 1·50 30
a. Raised and level stops mixed 4·75 4·75
b. Pair, one with level stops 8·50 9·00
c. Surch inverted £325 £325
d. "1" raised 75·00 75·00
e. Pair, one without surch £325 £325
f. No stop after "V" £1000
g. No stop after "I"
115 2½d. on 3d. ultramarine (*a*) £200 £180
a. Raised and level stops mixed £600
116 2½d. on 3d. ultramarine (*b*) £1200
117 3d. on 3d. ultramarine 60 30
a. Raised and level stops mixed 7·00 7·00
b. Pair, one with level stops 18·00 19·00
c. No stop after "V" £140 £140
d. No stop after "R" £375 £450
e. "I" omitted £400 £425
ea. "I" and stop inserted
f. Surch double £400
g. Surch double, one diagonal £375
h. Ditto, diagonal surch with mixed stops £6500
n. Inserted "R"
o. Space between "3" and "d" £140
118 4d. on 4d. ultramarine 3·75 3·00
a. Raised and level stops mixed 10·00 13·00
b. Pair, one with level stops 21·00 29·00
119 6d. on 6d. bright carmine 38·00 48·00
a. Raised and level stops mixed £140 £140
b. Pair, one with level stops £225 £275
120 6d. on 6d. blue 70 40
a. Raised and level stops mixed 8·00 8·00
b. Pair, one with level stops 20·00 22·00
c. No stop after "V" £500 £500
d. No stop after "R" £300
e. Value omitted £450
121 1s. on 1s. brown 5·50 45
a. Surch on 1s. orange-yellow (No. 9) £1300 £1300
b. Raised and level stops mixed 18·00 18·00
c. Pair, one with level stops 35·00 38·00
f. "s" omitted £250
g. "V.R.I." omitted £400
122 5s. on 5s. green 9·00 9·00
a. Raised and level stops mixed £325 £325
b. Pair, one with level stops £1000
c. Short top to "5" 60·00 70·00
s. Handstamped "Specimen" 55·00

(ii) Surch as T **33**.

123 ½d. on ½d. orange 4·75 3·25
124 1d. on 1d. purple 5·50 35
a. Inverted "1" for "I" 19·00 19·00
b. No stops after "R" and "I" 90·00 70·00
c. No stop after "R" 42·00 48·00
d. Surch double £325 £325
n. Inserted "R" £400 £400
p. Stamp doubly printed, one impression inverted £6000
125 2d. on 2d. bright mauve 12·00 12·00
a. Inverted "1" for "I" 27·00 30·00
126 2½d. on 3d. ultramarine (*a*) £650 £750
127 2½d. on 3d. ultramarine (*b*) £3750
128 3d. on 3d. ultramarine 6·00 13·00
a. Inverted "1" for "I" 65·00 75·00
b. Surch double £550
ba. Surch double, one diagonal £550
129 6d. on 6d. bright carmine £425 £425
130 6d. on 6d. blue 16·00 25·00
131 1s. on 1s. brown 24·00 8·50
132 5s. on 5s. green 55·00 48·00
s. Handstamped "Specimen" £160

Stamps with thick "V" occur in certain positions in *later* settings of the type with stops above the line (T **32**). *Earlier* settings with stops above the line have all stamps with thin "V".

Some confusion has previously been caused by the listing of certain varieties as though they occurred on stamps with thick "V" in fact they occur on stamps showing the normal thin "V", included in the settings which also contained the thick "V".

For a short period small blocks of unsurcharged Free State stamps could be handed in for surcharging so that varieties occur which are not found in the complete settings. Nos. 102a, 110a and 121a also occur from such stocks.

The inserted "R" variety occurs on positions 6 (T **32**) and 12 (T **33**) of the forme. The "R" of the original surcharge failed to print and the "R", but not the full stop, was added by the use of a handstamp. Traces of the original letter are often visible. The broken "V" flaw, also shown in the illustration, does not appear on No. 124n.

ORANGE RIVER COLONY

CROWN COLONY

E. R. I.

ORANGE RIVER COLONY. (**34**) 4d (**35**) 6d (**36**)

1900 (10 Aug)–**02**. *Nos. 58, 59a and 63a of Cape of Good Hope (wmk Cabled Anchor. P 14) optd with T* **34** *by W. A. Richards and Sons, Cape Town.*

133 ½d. green (13.10.00) 50 10
a. No stop 8·50 17·00
b. Opt double £650 £700
134 1d. carmine (May 1902) 2·00 10
a. No stop 18·00 22·00

135		2½d. ultramarine	2·25	35
		a. No stop	70·00	75·00
133/5 *Set of* 3			4·25	50

In the ½d. and 2½d., the "no stop" after "COLONY" variety was the first stamp in the left lower pane. In the 1d. it is the twelfth stamp in the right lower pane on which the stop was present at the beginning of the printing but became damaged and soon failed to print.

1902 (14 Feb). *Surch with T* **35** *by "Bloemfontein Express".*

136		4d. on 6d. on 6d. blue (No. 120) (R.)	1·50	75
		a. No stop after "R"	35·00	40·00
		b. No stop after "I"	£1200	
		c. Surch on No. 130 (Thick "V")	2·00	6·00
		ca. Inverted "1" for "I"	6·00	16·00

1902 (Aug). *Surch with T* **36**.

137	**1**	6d. on 6d. blue	4·00	13·00
		a. Surch double, one inverted		
		b. Wide space between "6" and "d" (R. 4/2)	60·00	90·00

One Shilling
*
(37)

38 King Edward VII, Springbok and Gnu

1902 (Sept). *Surch with T* **37**.

138	**1**	1s. on 5s. green (O.)	8·00	16·00
		a. Thick "V"	15·00	38·00
		b. Short top to "5"	70·00	80·00
		c. Surch double		

(Typo D.L.R.)

1903 (3 Feb)–**04**. Wmk Crown CA. P 14.

139	**38**	½d. yellow-green (6.7.03)	9·00	1·25
		w. Wmk inverted	£160	85·00
140		1d. scarlet	5·50	10
		w. Wmk inverted	£160	75·00
141		2d. brown (6.7.03)	8·00	80
142		2½d. bright blue (6.7.03)	2·50	50
143		3d. mauve (6.7.03)	9·00	90
144		4d. scarlet and sage-green (6.7.03)	35·00	2·25
		a. "IOSTAGE" for "POSTAGE"	£800	£450
145		6d. scarlet and mauve (6.7.03)	8·50	1·00
146		1s. scarlet and bistre (6.7.03)	35·00	1·75
147		5s. blue and brown (31.10.04)	85·00	24·00
139/47 *Set of* 9			£180	29·00
139s/47s Optd "Specimen" *Set of* 9			£180	

No. 144a occurs on R. 10/2 of the upper left pane.

The 2d. exists from coils constructed from normal sheets for use in stamp machines introduced in 1911.

Several of the above values are found with the overprint "C.S.A.R.", in black, for use by the Central South African Railways. Examples also exist perforated "CSAR" or "NGR".

1905 (Nov)–**09**. Wmk Mult Crown CA. P 14.

148	**38**	½d. yellow-green (28.7.07)	10·00	50
149		1d. scarlet	9·00	30
150		4d. scarlet and sage-green (8.11.07)	4·50	3·25
		a. "IOSTAGE" for "POSTAGE"	£180	£150
151		1s. scarlet and bistre (2.09)	55·00	18·00
148/51 *Set of* 4			70·00	20·00

POSTCARD STAMPS

From 1889 onwards the Orange Free State Post Office sold postcards franked with adhesives as Type **1**, some subsequently surcharged, over which the State Arms had been overprinted.

There are five known dies of the Arms overprint which can be identified as follows:

(a) Shield without flags. Three cows (two lying down, one standing) at left. Point of shield complete.
(b) Shield with flags. Four cows (two lying down, two standing) at left (*illustrated*).
(c) Shield with flags. Three cows (one lying down, two standing) at left.
(d) Shield without flags. Three cows (one lying down, two standing) at left.
(e) Shield without flags. Three cows (two lying down, one standing) at left. Point of shield broken.

There are also other differences between the dies.

PRICES. Those in the left-hand column are for unused examples on complete postcard; those on the right for used examples off card. Examples used on postcard are worth more.

1889 (Feb). *No. 2 (placed sideways on card) optd Shield Type (a).*

P1	**1**	1d. red-brown	90·00	40·00
		a. Optd Shield Type (b)	32·00	7·00

1891 (Aug). *No. 48 optd Shield Type (b).*

P2	**1**	½d. chestnut	5·50	1·75
		a. Optd Shield Type (c)	13·00	4·25
		b. Optd Shield Type (d)	6·00	2·25
		c. Optd Shield Type (e)	14·00	5·00

1892 (June). *No. 54 optd Shield Type (b).*

P3	**1**	1d. on 3d. ultramarine	90·00	48·00
		a. Optd Shield Type (c)	15·00	3·00

1½d. (P 1) 1½d. (P 2) 1½d. (P 3)

1892 (Sept)–**95**. *Nos. 50/1 optd Shield Type (b) or (d) (No. P6) and surch with Types* P **1**/**3**.

P4	**1**	1½d. on 2d. bright mauve (Type P **1**) (11.92)	8·00	3·75
P5		1½d. on 2d. bright mauve (Type P **2**) (9.93)	6·00	1·75
		a. Surch inverted		
P6		1½d. on 2d. bright mauve (Type P **3**) (R.) (6.95)	13·00	4·25
P7		1½d. on 3d. ultramarine (Type P **1**)	7·50	2·25

No. P5a shows the stamp affixed to the card upside down with the surcharge correctly positioned in relation to the card.

½d.
(P 4)

1895 (Aug). *No. 48 optd Shield Type (e) and surch with Type* P4.

P8	**1**	½d. on ½d. chestnut	13·00	2·75

1½d. (P 5) 1½d. (P 6)

1895 (Dec)–**97**. *No. 50 optd Shield Type (e) and surch with Types* P **5**/**6**.

P9	**1**	1½d. on 2d. bright mauve (Type P **5**)	6·50	2·75
P10		1½d. on 2d. bright mauve (Type P **6**) (12.97)	7·50	3·25
P11		1½d. on 2d. bright mauve (as Type P **6**, but without stop) (12.97)	7·50	3·25

1897 (Mar). *No. 85 optd Shield Type (d).*

P12	**1**	½d. orange	13·00	1·75
		a. Optd Shield Type (e)	14·00	2·75

V.R.I.
(P 7)

1900. *Nos. P10/11 optd as T* **31**/**2** *or with Type* P**7**.

P13	**1**	1½d. on 2d. bright mauve (No. P10) (T **31**)	28·00	5·50
P14		1½d. on 2d. bright mauve (No. P11) (T **31**)	28·00	5·50
P15		1½d. on 2d. bright mauve (No. P10) (T **32**)	28·00	5·50
P16		1½d. on 2d. bright mauve (No. P11) (T **32**)	28·00	5·50
P17		1½d. on 2d. bright mauve (No. P10) (Type P **7**)	40·00	10·00
P18		1½d. on 2d. bright mauve (No. P11) (Type P **7**)	40·00	10·00

POLICE FRANK STAMPS

The following frank stamps were issued to members of the Orange Free State Mounted Police ("Rijdende Dienst Macht") for use on official correspondence.

PF **1** (eight ornaments at left and right)

PF **2**

1896. P 12.

PF1	PF **1**	(–) Black	£225	£300

No. PF1 was printed in horizontal strips of 5 surrounded by wide margins.

1898. *As Type* PF **1**, *but with nine ornaments at left and right.* P 12.

PF2		(–) Black	£150	£200

No. PF2 was printed in blocks of 4 (2×2) surrounded by wide margins.

1899. P 12.

PF3	PF **2**	(–) Black/*yellow*	£130	£150
		a. No stop after "V"	£550	

No. PF3 was printed in sheets of 24 (6×4) with the edges of the sheet imperforate. It is believed that they were produced from a setting of 8 (2×4) repeated three times. No. PF3a occurs on R. 1/1 of the setting.

Examples of No. PF3 are known postmarked as late as 28 April 1900. The O.F.S. Mounted Police were disbanded by the British authorities at the end of the following month.

MILITARY FRANK STAMP

M **1**

(Typeset Curling & Co, Bloemfontein)

1899 (15 Oct). P 12.

M1	M **1**	(–) Black/*bistre-yellow*	20·00	55·00

Supplies of No. M1 were issued to members of the Orange Free State army on active service during the Second Boer War. To pass free through the O.F.S. fieldpost system, letters had to be franked with No. M1 or initialled by the appropriate unit commander. The franks were in use between October 1899 and February 1900.

No. M1 was printed in sheets of 20 (5×4) using a setting of five different types in a horizontal row. The colour in the paper runs in water.

Typeset forgeries can be identified by the appearance of 17 pearls, instead of the 16 of the originals, in the top and bottom frames. Forgeries produced by lithography omit the stops after "BRIEF" and "FRANKO".

FISCAL STAMPS USED FOR POSTAGE

The following were issued in December 1877 (Nos. F1 and F3 in 1882) and were authorised for postal use between 1882 and 1886.

F **1**

F **2**

F **3**

(Typo D.L.R.)

1882–86. P 14.

F1	F **1**	6d. pearl-grey	13·00	15·00
F2		6d. purple-brown	42·00	28·00
F3	F **2**	1s. purple-brown	14·00	20·00
F4		1s. pearl-grey	60·00	70·00
F5		1s.6d. blue	26·00	20·00
F6		2s. magenta	26·00	20·00
F7		3s. chestnut	32·00	70·00
F8		4s. grey		
F9		5s. rose	32·00	28·00
F10		6s. green	–	80·00
F11		7s. violet		
F12		10s. orange	75·00	45·00
F13	F **3**	£1 purple	85·00	45·00
		a. "VRY-STAAT" (R. 1/5)		
F14		£2 red-brown	95·00	£100
		a. "VRY-STAAT" (R. 1/5)		
F14*b*		£4 carmine		
		ba. "VRY-STAAT" (R. 1/5)		
F15		£5 green	£130	70·00
		a. "VRY-STAAT" (R. 1/5)		

Die proofs of Type F **3** showed a hyphen in error between "VRY" and "STAAT". This was removed from each impression on the plate before printing, but was missed on R. 1/5.

A fiscally used example of No. F2 exists showing "ZES PENCE" double, one inverted.

The 8s. yellow was prepared but we have no evidence of its use postally without surcharge Type F **3**.

ZES PENCE.
(F 4)

1886. *Surch with Type* F **4**.

F16	F **2**	6d. on 4s. grey		
F17		6d. on 8s. yellow	£350	

Postage stamps overprinted for use as Telegraph stamps and used postally are omitted as it is impossible to say with certainty which stamps were genuinely used for postal purposes.

Orange Free State became a province of the Union of South Africa on 31 May 1910.

VI. TRANSVAAL

(*formerly* South African Republic)

From 1852 mail from the Transvaal was forwarded to the Cape of Good Hope, via the Orange Free State, by a post office at Potchefstroom. In 1859 the Volksraad voted to set up a regular postal service and arrangements were made for letters sent to the Cape and for overseas to be franked with Cape of Good Hope stamps.

The Potchefstroom postmaster placed his first order for these on 23 August 1859 and examples of all four triangular values are known postmarked there. From 1868 mail via the Orange Free State required franking with their issues also.

A similar arrangement covering mail sent overseas via Natal was in operation from 9 July 1873 until the first British Occupation. Such letters carried combinations of Transvaal stamps, paying the rate to Natal, and Natal issues for the overseas postage. Such Natal stamps were sold, but not postmarked, by Transvaal post offices.

PRICES FOR STAMPS ON COVER

Nos. 1/6 are rare used on cover.	
Nos. 7/80	*from* × 20
Nos. 86/155	*from* × 3
Nos. 156/62	*from* × 6
Nos. 163/9	*from* × 5
Nos. 170/225	*from* × 10
Nos. 226/34	*from* × 20
Nos. 235/7	—
Nos. 238/43	*from* × 12
Nos. 244/55	*from* × 4
Nos. 256/7	*from* × 6
Nos. 258/9	—
Nos. 260/76	*from* × 20
Nos. F1/5	*from* × 5
Nos. D1/7	*from* × 20

The issues for Pietersburg, Lydenburg, Rustenburg, Schweizer Renecke and Wolmaransstad are very rare when on cover.

1 (Eagle with spread wings) 2 3

(Typo Adolph Otto, Gustrow, Mecklenburg-Schwerin)

1870 (1 May). *Thin paper, clear and distinct impressions.*

		(a) Imperf.		
1	1	1d. brown-lake	£450	
		a. Orange-red	£600	£600
2		6d. bright ultramarine	£200	£200
		a. Pale ultramarine	£225	£225
3		1s. deep green	£700	£700
		a. *Tête-bêche* (pair)		
		(b) Fine roulette, 15½ to 16.		
4	1	1d. brown-lake	£130	
		a. Brick-red	£110	
		b. Orange-red	£110	
		c. Vermilion	£110	
5		6d. bright ultramarine	95·00	95·00
		a. Pale ultramarine	£110	£110
6		1s. deep green	£200	£225
		a. Yellow-green	£160	£150
		b. Emerald-green	£120	£120

Examples of Nos. 1/6 may have been sold to dealers at some stage between their arrival in Transvaal during August 1869 and the sale of stamps to the public for postal purposes on 1 May 1870.

PLATES. The German printings of the 1d., 6d. and 1s. in Type **1** were from two pairs of plates, each pair printing sheets of 80 in two panes of five horizontal rows of eight.

One pair of plates, used for Nos. 4*a*, 4*c*, 5*a* and 6/*a*, produced stamps spaced 1¼ to 1½ mm apart with the rouletting close to the design on all four sides. The 1d. from these "narrow" plates shows a gap in the outer frame line at the bottom right-hand corner. The second pair, used for Nos. 1/3, 4, 4*b*, 5/*a* and 6*b*, had 2½ to 3½ mm between the stamps. These "wide" plates were sent to the Transvaal in 1869 and were used there to produce either single or double pane printings until 1883.

The 6d. and 1s. "wide" plates each had an inverted *cliché*. When printed these occurred on right-hand pane R. 4/1 of the 6d. and right-hand pane R. 1/1 of the 1s. These were never corrected and resulted in *tête-bêche* pairs of these values as late as 1883.

REPRINTS AND IMITATIONS. A number of unauthorised printings were made of these stamps by the German printer. Many of these can be identified by differences in the central arms, unusual colours or, in the case of the 1d., by an extra frame around the numeral tablets at top.

Genuine stamps always show the "D" of "EENDRAGT" higher than the remainder of the word, have no break in the border above "DR" and depict the flagstaff at bottom right, behind "MAGT", stopping short of the central shield. They also show the eagle's eye as a clear white circle. On the forgeries the eye is often blurred.

The most difficult of the reprints to detect is the 1s. yellow-green which was once regarded as genuine, but was subsequently identified, by J. N. Luff in *The Philatelic Record* 1911–12, as coming from an unauthorised plate of four. Stamps from this plate show either a white dot between "EEN" and "SHILLING" or a white flaw below the wagon pole.

(Typo M. J. Viljoen, Pretoria)

1870 (1 May–4 July).

I. Thin gummed paper from Germany. Impressions coarse and defective.

		(a) Imperf.		
8	1	1d. dull rose-red	95·00	
		a. Reddish pink	75·00	
		b. Carmine-red	65·00	75·00
9		6d. dull ultramarine	£325	70·00
		a. *Tête-bêche* (pair)		
		(b) Fine roulette, 15½ to 16.		
10	1	1d. carmine-red	£700	£275
11		6d. dull ultramarine	£200	90·00
		a. Imperf between (vert pair)	£800	
		(c) Wide roulette, 6½.		
12	1	1d. carmine-red	—	£950

II. Thick, hard paper with thin yellow smooth gum (No. 15) or yellow streaky gum (others).

		(a) Imperf.		
13	1	1d. pale rose-red	75·00	
		a. Carmine-red	75·00	85·00
14		1s. yellow-green	£120	£110
		a. *Tête-bêche* (pair)	£20000	
		b. Bisected (6d.) (on cover)	†	£1800
		(b) Fine roulette, 15½ to 16.		
15	1	1d. carmine-red (24 May)	95·00	
16		6d. ultramarine (10 May)	£110	£110
		a. *Tête-bêche* (pair)	£25000	£18000
17		1s. yellow-green	£650	£650

III. Medium paper, blotchy heavy printing and whitish gum. Fine roulette 15½ to 16 (4 July).

18	1	1d. rose-red	75·00	90·00
		a. Carmine-red	55·00	60·00
		b. Crimson. From over-inked plate	£140	£120
19		6d. ultramarine	95·00	70·00
		a. *Tête-bêche* (pair)		
		b. Deep ultramarine. From over-inked plate	£450	£160
20		1s. deep green	£140	80·00
		a. From over-inked plate	£500	£160

The rouletting machine producing the wide 6½ gauge was not introduced until 1875.

Nos. 18*b*, 19*b* and 20a were printed from badly over-inked plates giving heavy blobby impressions.

(Typo J. P. Borrius, Potchefstroom)

1870 (Sept)–**71**. *Stout paper, but with colour often showing through, whitish gum.*

		(a) Imperf.		
21	1	1d. black	£140	£120
		(b) Fine roulette, 15½ to 16.		
22	1	1d. black	20·00	29·00
		a. Grey-black	20·00	29·00
23		6d. blackish blue (7.71)	£140	60·00
		a. Dull blue	£100	80·00

(Typo Adolph Otto, Gustrow, Mecklenburg-Schwerin)

1871 (July). *Thin paper, clear and distinct impressions. Fine roulette, 15½ to 16.*

24	2	3d. pale reddish lilac	80·00	90·00
		a. Deep lilac	90·00	£100
		b. Vert laid paper		

No. 24 and later printings in the Transvaal were produced from a pair of plates in the same format as the 1869 issue. All genuine stamps have a small dot on the left leg of the eagle.

Imperforate examples in the issued shade, without the dot on eagle's leg, had been previously supplied by the printer, probably as essays, but were not issued for postal purposes. (*Price* £550 *unused*). They also exist *tête-bêche* (*Price for un pair* £3250).

Imperforate and rouletted stamps in other colours are reprints.

(Typo J. P. Borrius, Potchefstroom)

1872–74. *Fine roulette, 15½ to 16.*

		(a) Thin transparent paper.		
25	1	1d. black	£200	£650
26		1d. bright carmine	£170	55·00
27		6d. ultramarine	£120	45·00
28		1s. green	£150	60·00
		(b) Thinnish opaque paper, clear printing (Dec 1872).		
29	1	1d. reddish pink	70·00	42·00
		a. Carmine-red	70·00	42·00
30	2	3d. grey-lilac	£110	50·00
31	1	6d. ultramarine	70·00	30·00
		a. Pale ultramarine	80·00	32·00
32		1s. yellow-green	85·00	42·00
		a. Green	85·00	42·00
		aa. Bisected (6d.) (on cover)	†	£1800
		(c) Thickish wove paper (1873–74).		
33	1	1d. dull rose	£400	75·00
		a. Brownish rose	£500	£120
		b. Printed on both sides		
34		6d. milky blue	£150	48·00
		a. Deep dull blue	90·00	42·00
		aa. Imperf (pair)	£700	
		ab. Imperf between (horiz pair)	£750	
		ac. Wide roulette 6½		
		(d) Very thick dense paper (1873–74).		
35		1d. dull rose	£550	£130
		a. Brownish rose	£425	£110
36		6d. dull ultramarine	£180	65·00
		a. Bright ultramarine	£200	65·00
37		1s. yellow-green	£850	£650

(Typo P. Davis & Son, Pietermaritzburg)

1874 (Sept). P 12½.

		(a) Thin transparent paper.		
38	1	1d. pale brick-red	£110	40·00
		a. Brownish red	£110	40·00
39		6d. deep blue	£150	60·00
		(b) Thicker opaque paper.		
40	1	1d. pale red	£160	75·00
41		6d. blue	£140	55·00
		a. Imperf between (pair)		
		b. Deep blue	£140	55·00

(Typo Adolph Otto, Gustrow, Mecklenburg-Schwerin)

1874 (Oct). *Thin smooth paper, clearly printed. Fine roulette 15½ to 16.*

42	3	6d. bright ultramarine	60·00	24·00
		a. Bisected (3d.) (on cover)	†	£1400

Stamps in other shades of blue, brown or red, often on other types of paper, are reprints.

(Typo J. F. Celliers on behalf of Stamp Commission, Pretoria)

1875 (29 Apr)–**77**.

I. Very thin, soft opaque (semi-pelure) paper.

		(a) Imperf.		
43	1	1d. orange-red	£130	50·00
		a. Pin-perf	£750	£350
44	2	3d. lilac	95·00	50·00
45	1	6d. blue	90·00	42·00
		a. Milky blue	£130	45·00
		aa. *Tête-bêche* (pair)	£15000	
		ab. Pin-perf	—	£350
		(b) Fine roulette, 15½ to 16.		
46	1	1d. orange-red	£500	£140
47	2	3d. lilac	£550	£150
48	1	6d. blue	£500	£140
		(c) Wide roulette, 6½.		
49	1	1d. orange-red	—	£200
50	2	3d. lilac	£700	£300
51	1	6d. blue	—	£150
		a. Bright blue	—	£150
		b. Milky blue	—	£150

II. Very thin, hard transparent (pelure) paper (1875–76).

		(a) Imperf.		
52	1	1d. brownish red	60·00	32·00
		a. Orange-red	48·00	25·00
		b. Dull red	55·00	50·00
		ba. Pin-perf	£600	£375
53	2	3d. lilac	55·00	42·00
		a. Pin-perf	—	£400
		b. Deep lilac	65·00	42·00
54	1	6d. pale blue	55·00	50·00
		a. Blue	55·00	42·00
		ab. *Tête-bêche* (pair)		
		ac. Pin-perf	—	£350
		b. Deep blue	60·00	45·00
		(b) Fine roulette 15½ to 16.		
55	1	1d. orange-red	£350	£120
		a. Brown-red	£350	£120
56	2	3d. lilac	£400	£130
57	1	6d. blue	£160	95·00
		a. Deep blue	£160	£110
		(c) Wide roulette, 6½.		
58	1	1d. orange-red	£1000	£200
		a. Bright red	—	£180
59	2	3d. lilac	£900	£250
60	1	6d. deep blue	£1000	£100

III. Stout hard-surfaced paper with smooth, nearly white, gum (1876).

		(a) Imperf.		
61	1	1d. bright red	26·00	20·00
62	2	3d. lilac	£375	£120
63	1	6d. bright blue	£100	24·00
		a. *Tête-bêche* (pair)		
		b. Pale blue	£100	24·00
		c. Deep blue (deep brown gum)	60·00	20·00
		ca. *Tête-bêche* (pair)	—	£17000
		(b) Fine roulette, 15½ to 16.		
64	1	1d. bright red	£400	£150
65	2	3d. lilac	£350	
66	1	6d. bright blue	£750	£110
		a. Deep blue (deep brown gum)	£600	£275
		(c) Wide roulette, 6½.		
67	1	1d. bright red	£600	£150
68		6d. pale blue	—	£200
		a. Deep blue (deep brown gum)	£650	£250

IV. Coarse, soft white paper (1876–77).

		(a) Imperf.		
69	1	1d. brick-red	£130	50·00
70		6d. deep blue	£200	£550
		a. Milky blue	£350	95·00
71		1s. yellow-green	£375	£110
		a. Bisected (6d.) (on cover)	†	£1600
		(b) Fine roulette, 15½ to 16.		
72	1	1d. brick-red	—	£375
73		6d. deep blue	—	£160
74		1s. yellow-green	£700	£350
		(c) Wide roulette, 6½.		
75	1	1d. brick-red	—	£450
76		6d. deep blue	—	£1100
77		1s. yellow-green	—	£1200
		(d) Fine × wide roulette.		
78	1	1d. brick-red	£700	£350

V. Hard, thick, coarse yellowish paper (1876–77).

79	1	1d. brick-red (imperf)	—	£300
80		1d. brick-red (*wide roulette*)	—	£400

The pin-perforated stamps have various gauges and were probably produced privately or by one or more post offices other than Pretoria.

On Nos. 63*c*/*ca*, 66*a* and 68*a* the brown gum used was so intense that it caused staining of the paper which is still visible on used examples.

See also Nos. 171/4.

FIRST BRITISH OCCUPATION

By 1876 conditions in the Transvaal had deteriorated and the country was faced by economic collapse, native wars and internal dissension. In early 1877 Sir Theophilus Shepstone, appointed Special Commissioner to the South African Republic by the British Government, arrived in Pretoria and on 12 April annexed the Transvaal with the acquiescence of at least part of the European population.

V. R. V. R.

TRANSVAAL. TRANSVAAL.
(4) (5)

T **4** is the normal overprint, but Setting I No. 11 (R. 2/3) has a wider-spaced overprint as T **5**.

1877 (Apr). *Optd with T* **4** *in red.*

		(a) Imperf.		
86	2	3d. lilac (*semi-pelure*) (No. 44)	£1300	£300
		a. Opt Type **5**		
87		3d. lilac (*pelure*) (No. 53)	£1300	£180
		a. Opt Type **5**	£7000	£2500
		b. Opt on back	£3250	£3250
		c. Opt double, in red and in black	£6000	
88	1	6d. milky blue (No. 70)	£1600	£180
		a. Opt inverted	—	£5000
		b. Opt double	£4500	£1000
		c. Opt Type **5**	£7500	£3000
		d. Deep blue	—	£250
89		1s. yellow-green (No. 71)	£650	£180
		a. Bisected (6d.) (on cover)	†	£1800
		b. Opt inverted	—	£4500
		c. Opt Type **5**	£4750	£1500
		d. *Tête-bêche* (pair)		
		(b) Fine roulette, 15½ to 16.		
90	2	3d. lilac (*pelure*) (No. 56)	—	£1600
91	1	6d. deep blue (No. 73)	—	£1700
92		1s. yellow-green (No. 74)	£1600	£750
		a. Opt Type **5**		

(c) Wide roulette, 6½.

93 **2** 3d. lilac (*pelure*) (No. 59) — £2250
a. Opt Type **5**
94 **1** 6d. deep blue (No. 76) — £2250
a. Opt Type **5**
95 1s. yellow-green (No. 77) £4000 £2000
a. Opt inverted — £6000

Nos. 88a, 89b and 95a occurred on the inverted *cliché* of the basic stamps.

1877 (June). *Optd with T* **4** *in black.*

I. Very thin, hard transparent (pelure) paper.

96 **1** 1d. orange-red (imperf) (No. 52*a*) £275 £100
97 1d. orange-red (*fine roulette*) (No. 55) — £1000

II. Stout hard-surfaced paper with smooth, nearly white, gum.

98 **1** 1d. bright red (imperf) (No. 61) 27·00 22·00
a. Opt inverted £550 £500
b. Opt Type **5** £750 £800
99 1d. bright red (*fine roulette*) (No. 64) £160 50·00
a. Opt inverted
b. Opt double — £1100
c. Imperf between (horiz pair) £750
100 1d. bright red (*wide roulette*) (No. 67) £650 £200
100*a* 1d. bright red (*fine × wide roulette*) (No. 78)

III. New ptgs on coarse, soft white paper.

(a) Imperf.

101 **1** 1d. brick-red (5.77) 27·00 22·00
a. Opt double — £1200
b. Opt Type **5** £800
102 **2** 3d. lilac 85·00 42·00
a. Opt inverted
b. Deep lilac £170 85·00
103 **1** 6d. dull blue 95·00 32·00
a. Opt double £3500 £2000
b. Opt inverted £1400 £170
d. Opt Type **5** — £1100
da. Opt Type **5** inverted
e. Blue (bright to deep) £160 30·00
ea. Bright blue, opt inverted — £500
f. Pin-perf — £600
104 1s. yellow-green £110 50·00
a. Opt inverted £1200 £200
b. *Tête-bêche* (pair) £20000 £20000
c. Opt Type **5** £5000 £1500
d. Bisected (6d.) (on cover) † £1500

(b) Fine roulette, 15½ to 16.

105 **1** 1d. brick-red 80·00 75·00
a. Imperf horiz (vert strip of 3)
b. Imperf between (horiz pair) † £600
106 **2** 3d. lilac £190 65·00
107 **1** 6d. dull blue £225 55·00
a. Opt inverted — £750
b. Opt Type **5** £5000
108 1s. yellow-green £225 90·00
a. Opt inverted £1100 £450
b. Opt Type **5** — £2750

(c) Wide roulette, 6½.

109 **1** 1d. brick-red £650 £150
a. Opt Type **5** — £1000
110 **2** 3d. lilac — £750
111 **1** 6d. dull blue — £1200
a. Opt inverted — £4000
112 1s. yellow-green £475 £130
a. Opt inverted £1500 £600

1877 (31 Aug). *Optd with T* **4** *in black.*

113 **1** 6d. blue/*rose* (imperf) 90·00 48·00
a. Bisected (3d.) (on cover)
b. Opt inverted £120 48·00
c. *Tête-bêche* (pair)
d. Opt omitted £3500 £2500
114 6d. blue/*rose* (*fine roulette*) £200 70·00
a. Opt inverted £550 70·00
b. *Tête-bêche* (pair)
c. Opt omitted
d. Bisected (3d.) (on cover)
115 6d. blue/*rose* (*wide roulette*)
a. Opt inverted — £650
b. Opt omitted

Nos. 113/15 were overprinted from a setting of 40 which was applied upright to one pane in each sheet and inverted on the other.

V. R.   *V. R.*

Transvaal (**6**)   Transvaal (**7**)

1877 (28 Sept)–**79**. *Optd with T* **6** *in black.*

(a) Imperf.

116 **1** 1d. red/*blue* 60·00 30·00
a. "Transvral" (Right pane R. 2/3) £5500 £2500
b. Opt double £4000
c. Opt inverted £800 £400
d. Opt omitted
117 1d. red/*orange* (6.12.77) 22·00 20·00
a. Pin-perf
b. Printed both sides
c. Opt double £3500
d. Optd with Type **7** (15.4.78) 60·00 45·00
e. Pair. Nos. 117 and 117d £170
118 **2** 3d. mauve/*buff* (24.10.77) 55·00 27·00
a. Opt inverted — £750
b. Pin-perf
c. Bisected (1½d) (on cover) † —
d. Optd with Type **7** (15.4.78) 70·00 35·00
da. Pin-perf £750 £750
e. Pair. Nos. 118 and 118d £250
119 3d. mauve/*green* (18.4.79) £160 42·00
a. Pin-perf
b. Opt inverted — £2000
c. Opt double
d. Printed both sides † —
e. Optd with Type **7** £120 35·00
ea. Opt inverted — £2000
eb. Printed both sides — £1000
f. Opt omitted — £3500
g. Pair. Nos. 119 and 119e £550
120 **1** 6d. blue/*green* (27.11.77) 90·00 38·00
a. Deep blue/green £110 40·00
b. Broken "Y" for "V" in "V.R." (Left pane R. 3/7) — £750
c. Small "v" in "Transvaal" (Left pane R. 5/2) — £750
d. "V..R." (Right pane R. 3/4) — £750
e. *Tête-bêche* (pair) — £18000
f. Opt inverted — £1100
g. Pin-perf
h. Bisected (3d.) (on cover) † —
121 6d. blue/*blue* (20.3.78) 60·00 27·00
a. *Tête-bêche* (pair)
b. Opt inverted — £1100
c. Opt omitted — £2250
d. Opt double — £3250
e. Pin-perf
f. Bisected (3d.) (on cover) † £800
g. Optd with Type **7** £120 30·00
ga. *Tête-bêche* (pair) £15000
gb. Opt inverted — £700
gc. Bisected (3d.) (on cover) † —
h. Pair. Nos. 121 and 121g £400

(b) Fine roulette, 15½ to 16.

122 **1** 1d. red/*blue* 95·00 38·00
a. "Transvral" (Right pane R. 2/3) — £3000
123 1d. red/*orange* (6.12.77) 35·00 27·00
a. Imperf between (pair) £600
b. Optd with Type **7** (15.4.78) £150 £120
c. Pair. Nos. 123 and 123b £400
124 **2** 3d. mauve/*buff* (24.10.77) £100 27·00
a. Imperf horiz (vert pair) £750
b. Opt inverted — £3000
c. Optd with Type **7** (15.4.78) £160 £110
ca. Imperf between (pair)
d. Pair. Nos. 124 and 124c £600
125 3d. mauve/*green* (18.4.79) £650 £150
a. Optd with Type **7** £650 £150
b. Pair. Nos. 125 and 125a
126 **1** 6d. blue/*green* (27.11.77) 90·00 27·00
a. "V..R" (Right pane R. 3/4) — £1200
b. *Tête-bêche* (pair)
c. Opt inverted — £650
d. Opt omitted — £4000
e. Bisected (3d.) (on cover) † £700
127 6d. blue/*blue* (20.3.78) £250 55·00
a. Opt inverted — £900
b. Opt omitted — £3500
c. Imperf between (pair)
d. Bisected (3d.) (on cover) † £750
e. Optd with Type **7** £400 £110
ea. Opt inverted — £1100

(c) Wide roulette, 6¼.

128 **1** 1d. red/*orange* (15.4.78) £250 £100
a. Optd with Type **7** — £300
129 **2** 3d. mauve/*buff* (24.10.77) — £100
a. Optd with Type **7** (15.4.78) — £350
130 3d. mauve/*green* (18.4.79) £650 £275
a. Optd with Type **7** — £300
131 **1** 6d. blue/*green* (27.11.77) — £1000
132 6d. blue/*blue* (20.3.78) — £300
a. Opt inverted
b. Optd with Type **7** — £350
ba. Opt inverted

(d) Fine × wide roulette.

132*c* **1** 1d. red/*orange* £750

Nos. 116/32c were overprinted from various settings covering sheets of 80 or panes of 40 (8×5). Initially these settings contained Type **6** only, but from March 1878 settings also contained examples of Type **7**. Details of these mixed settings are as follows:
1d. red/*orange* (sheets of 80): all Type **6** except for 16 Type **7**.
3d. mauve/*buff* (panes of 40): 16 Type **7**.
3d. mauve/*green* (panes of 40): uncertain, some panes at least contained 27 Type **7**.
6d. blue/*blue* (sheets of 80): either 24 or 27 Type **7**.

9

(Recess B.W.)

1878 (26 Aug)–**80**. P 14, 14½.

133 **9** ½d. vermilion (1.9.80) 24·00 80·00
134 1d. pale red-brown 14·00 4·50
a. Brown-red 14·00 4·00
135 3d. dull rose (25 Nov) 17·00 5·50
a. Claret 21·00 7·00
136 4d. sage-green 24·00 7·00
137 6d. olive-black (25 Nov) 13·00 5·00
a. Black-brown 15·00 4·00
138 1s. green (25 Nov) £120 42·00
139 2s. blue (25 Nov) £170 80·00

The ½d. is printed on paper bearing the sheet watermark 'R TURNER/CHAFFORD MILLS' in double-lined block capitals. Other values are on unwatermarked paper.

The above prices are for specimens perforated on all four sides. Stamps from margins of sheets, with perforations absent on one or two sides, can be supplied for about 30% less.

The used price quoted for No. 139 is for an example with telegraphic cancel, a 23.5 mm circular datestamp of Pretoria (or more rarely Heidelberg or Standerton). Postally used examples are worth much more.

1 Penny (**10**)   1 Penny (**11**)   1 Penny (**12**)

1 Penny (**13**)   1 Penny (**14**)

1 PENNY (**15**)   *1 Penny* (**16**)

1879 (22 Apr). *No. 137a surch with T* **10** *to* **16** *in black.*

140 **10** 1d. on 6d. 80·00 42·00
a. Surch in red £250 £150
141 **11** 1d. on 6d. £190 80·00
a. Surch in red £600 £325
142 **12** 1d. on 6d. £190 80·00
a. Surch in red £600 £325
143 **13** 1d. on 6d. 85·00 48·00
a. Surch double
b. Surch in red £300 £170
144 **14** 1d. on 6d. £550 £160
a. Surch in red £6000 £1600
145 **15** 1d. on 6d. 42·00 23·00
a. Surch in red £150 75·00
146 **16** 1d. on 6d. £180 75·00
a. Surch in red £500 £300

Nos. 140/6 were surcharged from a setting of 60 containing eleven examples of Type **10**, four of Type **11**, four of Type **12**, nine of Type **13**, two of Type **14** (although there may have been only one in the first two ptgs), twenty-five of Type **15** and five of Type **16**.

The red surcharges may have been produced first.

V. R.   V. R.

Transvaal (**16a**)   Transvaal — Small "T" (R. 2/8, 3/8, 4/8, 5/8 on right pane of 1d. and left pane of 3d.)

1879 (Aug–Sept). *Optd with T* **16***a in black.*

(a) Imperf.

147 **1** 1d. red/*yellow* 48·00 38·00
a. Small "T" £325 £200
b. Red/orange 42·00 30·00
ba. Small "T" £275 £170
148 **2** 3d. mauve/*green* (Sept) 42·00 25·00
a. Small "T" £250 £100
149 3d. mauve/*blue* (Sept) 48·00 30·00
a. Small "T" £275 90·00

(b) Fine roulette 15½ to 16.

150 **1** 1d. red/*yellow* £350 £200
a. Small "T" £1000 £650
b. Red/orange £750 £375
ba. Small "T" £2000
151 **2** 3d. mauve/*green* £750 £250
a. Small "T" — £850
152 3d. mauve/*blue* — £180
a. Small "T" — £650

(c) Wide roulette 6½.

153 **1** 1d. red/*yellow* £650 £650
a. Small "T"
b. Red/orange — £1200
154 **2** 3d. mauve/*green* £1000 £650
a. Small "T"
155 3d. mauve/*blue* — £750

(d) Pin-perf about 17.

156 **1** 1d. red/*yellow* — £750
a. Small "T"
157 **2** 3d. mauve/*blue* — £850

SECOND REPUBLIC

Following the first Boer War the independence of the South African Republic was recognised by the Convention of Pretoria from 8 August 1881.

Nos. 133/9 remained valid and some values were available for postage until 1885.

EEN PENNY (**17**)

1882 (11 Aug). *No. 136 surch with T* **17**.

170 **9** 1d. on 4d. sage-green 15·00 5·00
a. Surch inverted £300 £200

Used examples of a similar, but larger, surcharge (width 20 mm) are known. These were previously considered to be forgeries, but it is now believed that some, at least, may represent a trial printing of the "EEN PENNY" surcharge.

(Typo J. F. Celliers)

1883 (20 Feb–3 Aug). *Re-issue of T* **1** *and* **2**. P 12.

171 **1** 1d. grey (*to* black) (5 Apr) 6·00 2·25
a. Imperf vert (horiz pair) £275
b. Imperf horiz (vert pair) £550 £350
172 **2** 3d. grey-black (*to* black)/*rose* 25·00 6·00
a. Bisected (1d.) (on cover) † £650
173 3d. pale red (7 May) 12·00 2·75
a. Bisected (1d.) (on cover) † £650
b. Imperf horiz (vert pair) † £1000
c. Chestnut 25·00 5·00
ca. Imperf between (horiz pair) † —
d. Vermilion 25·00 5·50
174 **1** 1s. green (*to* deep) (3 Aug) 60·00 4·50
a. Bisected (6d.) (on cover) † £475
b. *Tête-bêche* (pair) £950 £160

Reprints are known of Nos. 172, 173, 173*b* and 173*c*. The paper of the first is *bright rose* in place of *dull rose*, and the impression is brownish black in place of grey-black to deep black. The reprints on white paper have the paper thinner than the originals, and the gum yellowish instead of white. The colour is a dull deep orange-red.

The used price quoted for No. 174b is for an example with telegraphic cancel. Postally used examples are worth much more. (See note below No. 139).

18

PERFORATIONS. Stamps perforated 11½×12 come from the first vertical row of sheets of the initial printing otherwise perforated 12½×12.

REPRINTS. Reprints of the general issues 1885–93, 1894–95, 1895–96 and 1896–97 exist in large quantities produced using the original plates from 1911 onwards. They cannot readily be distinguished from genuine originals except by comparison with used stamps, but the following general characteristics may be noted. The reprints are all perf 12½, large holes; the paper is whiter and thinner than that usually employed for the originals and their colours lack the lustre of those of the genuine stamps.

Forged surcharges have been made on these reprints.

(Des J. Vurtheim. Typo Enschedé)

1885 (13 Mar)–**93**. P 12½.

175	18	½d. grey (30.3.85)	1·25	10
		a. Perf 13½	5·50	1·00
		b. Perf 12½×12	2·50	10
		ba. Perf 11½×12	25·00	7·00
176		1d. carmine	1·00	10
		a. Perf 12½×12	1·25	10
		aa. Perf 11½×12	16·00	2·75
		b. Rose	1·00	10
		ba. Perf 12½×12	1·25	10
177		2d. brown-purple (P 12½×12) (9.85)	2·25	3·25
178		2d. olive-bistre (14.4.87)	1·75	10
		a. Perf 12½×12	4·00	10
179		2½d. mauve (*to* bright) (8.93)	2·75	50
180		3d. mauve (*to* bright)	3·00	1·75
		a. Perf 12½×12	6·50	1·50
		aa. Perf 11½×12	28·00	17·00
181		4d. bronze-green	4·25	1·25
		a. Perf 13½	8·50	1·50
		b. Perf 12½×12	14·00	1·25
		ba. Perf 11½×12	£200	80·00
182		6d. pale dull blue	3·75	3·00
		a. Perf 13½	6·00	1·25
		b. Perf 12½×12	7·50	40
		ba. Perf 11½×12		
183		1s. yellow-green	3·00	1·00
		a. Perf 13½	26·00	6·00
		b. Perf 12½×12	9·50	75
184		2s.6d. orange-buff (*to* buff) (2.12.85)	9·50	2·75
		a. Perf 12½×12	17·00	7·00
185		5s. slate (2.12.85)	8·00	4·75
		a. Perf 12½×12	35·00	8·00
186		10s. dull chestnut (2.12.85)	30·00	9·00
		a. Yellow-brown (1891)		
187		£5 deep green (3.92)* (Optd "Monster" £150)	£3250	£180

Singles of the 6d. pale dull blue imperforate have been reported used in 1893.

*Most examples of No. 187 on the market are either forgeries or reprints.

HALVE PENNY

(19)

1885 (22 May–Aug). *Surch with T* **19**. *Reading up or down.*

188	2	½d. on 3d. (No. 173)	6·50	10·00
189	1	½d. on 1s. (No. 174) (Aug)	25·00	50·00
		a. *Tête-bêche* (pair)	£850	£350

Nos. 188/9 were surcharged by a setting of 40. After the left pane had been surcharged reading down, the sheets were turned so that the right pane had the surcharges reading up.

HALVE PENNY Z. A. R. (20) TWEE PENCE Z. A. R. (21) HALVE PENNY (22)

1885 (1 Sept). *No. 137a surch with T* **20/1** *in red.*

190	9	½d. on 6d. black-brown	65·00	95·00
191		2d. on 6d. black-brown	7·50	13·00

1885 (28 Sept). *No. 180a surch with T* **22**.

192	18	½d. on 3d. mauve	5·00	5·00
		a. "PRNNY" (R. 6/6)	42·00	60·00
		b. 2nd "N" inverted (R. 3/8)	90·00	£100
		c. Perf 11½×12	13·00	12·00

2d (23) 2d (24)

1887 (15 Jan). *No. 180a surch with T* **23/4**.

193	18	2d. on 3d. mauve (Type **23**)	8·50	8·50
		a. Surch double	—	£300
		b. Perf 11½×12	25·00	13·00
194		2d. on 3d. mauve (Type **24**)	2·00	3·75
		a. Surch double	£180	£180
		b. Perf 11½×12	7·00	9·00

Nos. 193/4 were surcharged from the same setting of 60 (10×6) which showed Type **24** on the top five horizontal rows and Type **23** on the sixth horizontal row.

Halve Penny (25) 1 Penny (26)

2½ Pence (27) 2½ Pence (28)

Two types of surcharge:
A. Vertical distance between bars 12½ mm.
B. Distance 13½ mm.

1893. *T* **18** *surch*. P 12½.

(a) In red.

195	25	½d. on 2d. olive-bistre (A) (27 May)	80	2·25
		a. Surch inverted	2·50	2·50
		b. Surch Type B	1·50	3·00
		ba. Surch inverted	5·00	10·00

(b) In black.

196	25	½d. on 2d. olive-bistre (A) (2 July)	85	2·25
		a. Surch inverted	4·50	5·00
		b. Extra surch on back inverted.	£160	
		c. Surch Type B	1·50	3·00
		ca. Surch inverted	20·00	15·00
		cb. Extra surch on back inverted.	£275	
197	26	1d. on 6d. blue (A) (26 Jan)	1·25	1·25
		a. Surch double	55·00	45·00
		b. Surch inverted	1·75	2·25
		c. Surch treble		
		d. Surch Type B	2·00	2·00
		da. Surch inverted	5·00	4·00
		db. Surch double	—	80·00
		e. Pair, one without surch	£225	
198	27	2½d. on 1s. green (A) (2 Jan)	1·75	4·50
		a. "2/½d" for "2½" (R. 1/10)	38·00	70·00
		b. Surch inverted	6·50	7·50
		ba. Surch inverted and "2/½d" for "2½"	£350	£300
		c. Extra surch on back inverted.	£450	£450
		d. Surch double, one inverted	£700	
		e. Surch Type B	2·75	6·00
		ea. Surch inverted	9·00	16·00
199	28	2½d. on 1s. green (A) (24 June)	6·00	5·00
		a. Surch double	45·00	40·00
		b. Surch inverted	7·50	7·50
		c. Surch Type B	9·00	9·50
		ca. Surch double	75·00	85·00
		cb. Surch inverted	19·00	19·00

Surcharge Types **25/8** all show a similar setting of the horizontal bars at top and bottom. On horizontal rows 1 to 4 and 6, the bars are 12½ mm apart and on row 5 the distance is 13½ mm.

29 (Wagon with shafts)

30 (Wagon with pole)

1894 (July). P 12½.

200	29	½d. grey	1·00	65
201		1d. carmine	1·75	10
202		2d. olive-bistre	1·75	10
203		6d. pale dull blue	2·50	40
204		1s. yellow-green	13·00	17·00

For note *re* reprints, see below T **18**.

1895 (16 Mar)–**96**. P 12½.

205	30	½d. pearl-grey (1895)	1·00	10
		a. Lilac-grey	1·00	10
206		1d. rose-red	1·00	10
207		2d. olive-bistre (1895)	1·25	20
208		3d. mauve (1895)	2·25	85
209		4d. olive-black (1895)	2·75	80
210		6d. pale dull blue (1895)	2·75	85
211		1s. yellow-green (18.3.95)	3·25	1·50
212		5s. slate (1896)	16·00	27·00
212*a*		10s. pale chestnut (1896)	16·00	6·00
205s/8s, 211s Optd "Monster" *Set of 5*			£150	

For note *re* reprints, see below T **18**.

Halve Penny (31)

1d. (32—Round dot) 1d. (32*a*—Square dot)

1895 (July–Aug). *Nos. 211 and 179 surch with T* **31/2**.

213	30	½d. on 1s. green (R.)	1·25	25
		a. Surch spaced	2·50	2·00
		b. "Pennij" for "Penny" (R. 6/6)	55·00	65·00
		c. Surch inverted	4·00	4·50
		d. Surch double	65·00	90·00
214	18	1d. on 2½d. bright mauve (G.)	50	30
		a. Surch inverted	20·00	14·00
		b. Surch double	65·00	65·00
		c. Surch on back only	75·00	
		d. Surch Type **32*a***	1·50	1·25
		da. Surch inverted	65·00	
		e. Surch treble	£550	

The normal space between "Penny" and the bars is 3 mm. On No. 213a, which comes from the fifth horizontal row of the setting, this is increased to 4 mm. Copies may be found in which one or both of the bars have failed to print.

Type **32*a*** with square stop occurred on R. 3/3-4, 3/6-8, 4/4-5, 4/7-8, 4/10, 6/3, 6/7-8 and 6/10 of the setting of 60.

33

34

1895 (July). *Fiscal stamp optd* "POSTZEGEL". P 11½.

215	33	6d. bright rose (G.)	2·00	2·00
		a. Imperf between (pair)		
		b. Opt inverted		

(Litho The Press Printing and Publishing Works, Pretoria)

1895 (6 Sept). *Introduction of Penny Postage.* P 11.

215*c*	34	1d. red (pale *to* deep)	2·00	2·25
		ca. Imperf between (pair)	£110	£120
		cb. Imperf vert (horiz pair)		
		cc. Imperf (pair)		

1896–97. P 12½.

216	30	½d. green (1896)	1·00	10
217		1d. rose-red and green (1896)	1·00	10
218		2d. brown and green (2.97)	1·00	20
219		2½d. dull blue and green (6.96)	1·75	20
220		3d. purple and green (3.97)	2·25	2·50
221		4d. sage-green and green (3.97)	2·25	2·50
222		6d. lilac and green (11.96)	1·50	1·50
223		1s. ochre and green (3.96)	2·00	70
224		2s.6d. dull violet and green (6.96)	2·25	2·75

For note *re* reprints, see below T **18**.

SECOND BRITISH OCCUPATION

The Second Boer War began on 11 October 1899 and was concluded by the Peace of Vereeniging on 31 May 1902. Pretoria was occupied by the British on 5 June 1900 and a civilian postal service began operating thirteen days later.

FORGERIES. The forgeries of the "V.R.I." and "E.R.I." overprints most often met with can be recognised by the fact that the type used is perfect and the three stops are always in alignment with the bottom of the letters. In the genuine overprints, which were made from old type, it is impossible to find all three letters perfect and all three stops perfect and in exact alignment with the bottom of the letters.

V. R. I. (35) E. R. I. (36) E. R. I. Half Penny (37)

1900 (18 June). *Optd with T* **35**.

226	30	½d. green	30	40
		a. No stop after "V"	12·00	12·00
		b. No stop after "R"	9·00	9·00
		c. No stop after "I"	7·50	7·50
		d. Opt inverted	10·00	12·00
		e. Opt double		
		f. "V.I.R." (R. 4/4)	£600	
227		1d. rose-red and green	30	30
		a. No stop after "V"	12·00	12·00
		b. No stop after "R"	9·00	9·00
		c. No stop after "I"	6·00	6·00
		d. Opt inverted	10·00	17·00
		e. Opt double	70·00	85·00
		f. No stops after "R" and "I"	75·00	75·00
		g. Opt omitted (in pair with normal)	£250	
228		2d. brown and green	3·00	2·25
		a. No stop after "V"	27·00	29·00
		c. No stop after "I"	32·00	32·00
		d. Opt inverted	17·00	19·00
		e. Opt double		
		f. "V.I.R." (R. 4/4)	£600	£650
		g. Opt albino		
229		2½d. dull blue and green	1·00	2·25
		a. No stop after "V"	19·00	23·00
		b. No stop after "R"	45·00	55·00
		c. No stop after "I"	15·00	18·00
		d. Opt inverted	11·00	12·00
230		3d. purple and green	1·00	2·00
		a. No stop after "V"	23·00	27·00
		b. No stop after "R"	45·00	55·00
		c. No stop after "I"	30·00	38·00
		d. Opt inverted	70·00	80·00
231		4d. sage-green and green	3·00	2·00
		a. No stop after "V"	42·00	42·00
		b. No stop after "R"	55·00	55·00
		c. No stop after "I"	38·00	38·00
		d. Opt inverted	25·00	28·00
		f. "V.I.R." (R. 4/4)	£600	
232		6d. lilac and green	3·00	1·75
		a. No stop after "V"	21·00	21·00

		b. No stop after "R"	27·00	27·00
		c. No stop after "I"	27·00	27·00
		d. Opt inverted	28·00	32·00
233		1s. ochre and green	3·00	3·25
		a. No stop after "V"	21·00	24·00
		b. No stop after "R"	21·00	24·00
		c. No stop after "I"	38·00	42·00
		d. Opt inverted	35·00	40·00
		e. Opt double	75·00	85·00
234		2s.6d. dull violet and green	3·75	10·00
		a. No stop after "V"	40·00	
		b. No stop after "R"	80·00	
		c. No stop after "I"	—	£425
235		5s. slate	7·00	14·00
		a. No stop after "V"	£110	
236		10s. pale chestnut	9·00	16·00
		a. No stop after "V"	95·00	
		c. No stop after "I"	95·00	
237	18	£5 deep green*	£2000	£800
		a. No stop after "V"		
234s/7s Optd "Specimen" *Set of* 4			£200	

*Many examples of No. 237 on the market are forgeries and the stamps should only be purchased if accompanied by a recent expert committee certificate.

The error "V.I.R." occurred on R. 4/4 in the first batch of stamps to be overprinted—a few sheets of the ½d., 2d. and 4d. The error was then corrected and stamps showing it are very rare.

A number of different settings were used to apply the overprint to Nos. 226/37. The missing stop varieties listed above developed during overprinting and occur on different positions in the various settings.

1901 (Jan)–**02**. *Optd with T* **36**.

238	30	½d. green	50	1·50
		a. Opt double		
239		1d. rose-red and green (20.3.01)	50	10
		a. "E" of opt omitted	75·00	
240		3d. purple and green (6.02)	2·25	3·25
241		4d. sage-green and green (6.02)	2·25	4·50
242		2s.6d. dull violet and green (10.02)	9·00	23·00

1901 (July). *Surch with T* **37**.

243	30	½d. on 2d. brown and green	65	75
		a. No stop after "E" (R. 4/6)	50·00	55·00

38 (POSTAGE REVENUE) **39** (POSTAGE POSTAGE)

(Typo D.L.R.)

1902 (1 Apr–17 Dec). Wmk Crown CA. P 14.

244	38	½d. black and bluish green	1·75	20
		w. Wmk inverted	90·00	60·00
245		1d. black and carmine	1·25	15
		w. Wmk inverted	70·00	50·00
246		2d. black and purple	3·75	70
247		2½d. black and blue	9·00	1·25
		w. Wmk inverted	65·00	38·00
248		3d. black and sage-green (17.12.02)	8·50	60
249		4d. black and brown (17.12.02)	7·00	1·50
250		6d. black and orange-brown	4·00	80
251		1s. black and sage-green	13·00	14·00
252		2s. black and brown	45·00	50·00
253	39	2s.6d. magenta and black	15·00	14·00
254		5s. black and purple/*yellow*	27·00	32·00
255		10s. black and purple/*red*	65·00	35·00
244/55 *Set of* 12			£180	£130
244s/55s (*inc* 247ws) Optd "Specimen" *Set of* 12			£150	

The colour of the "black" centres varies from brownish grey or grey to black.

1903 (1 Feb). Wmk Crown CA. P 14.

256	39	1s. grey-black and red-brown	13·00	3·75
257		2s. grey-black and yellow	15·00	14·00
258		£1 green and violet	£225	£140
259		£5 orange-brown and violet	£1400	£650
256s/9s Optd "Specimen" *Set of* 4			£225	

1904–09. *Ordinary paper*. Wmk Mult Crown CA. P 14.

260	38	½d. black and bluish green	8·00	2·75
		w. Wmk inverted	£110	65·00
		y. Wmk inverted and reversed	95·00	38·00
261		1d. black and carmine	5·50	40
262		2d. black and purple (*chalk-surfaced paper*) (1906)	11·00	1·75
263		2½d. black and blue (1905)	16·00	8·00
		aw. Wmk inverted	95·00	70·00
		b. Chalk-surfaced paper	14·00	3·75
264		3d. black and sage-green (*chalk-surfaced paper*) (1906)	3·50	50
265		4d. black and brown (*chalk-surfaced paper*) (1906)	4·75	70
		w. Wmk inverted	95·00	60·00
266		6d. black and orange (1905)	9·00	1·75
		a. Chalk-surfaced paper. *Black and brown-orange* (1906)	3·50	50
		w. Wmk inverted	£110	75·00
267	39	1s. black and red-brown (1905)	8·00	50
268		2s. black and yellow (1906)	22·00	8·00
269		2s.6d. magenta and black (1909)	48·00	7·00
270		5s. black and purple/*yellow*	23·00	1·50
271		10s. black and purple/*red* (1907)	60·00	2·75
272		£1 green and violet (1908)	£250	32·00
		a. Chalk-surfaced paper	£225	16·00
260/72 *Set of* 13			£400	42·00

There is considerable variation in the "black" centres as in the previous issue.

1905–09. Wmk Mult Crown CA. P 14.

273	38	½d. yellow-green	2·00	10
		a. *Deep green* (1908)	2·75	20
		w. Wmk inverted	£130	75·00
274		1d. scarlet	1·25	10
		aw. Wmk inverted	—	£275
		b. Wmk Cabled Anchor, T 13 of Cape of Good Hope	—	£325
275		2d. purple (1909)	3·50	60
276		2½d. bright blue (1909)	15·00	7·00
273/6 *Set of* 4			20·00	7·00
273s/6s Optd "Specimen" *Set of* 4			75·00	

A 2d. grey, T **38**, was prepared for use but not issued. It exists overprinted "Specimen", *price* £150.

The monocoloured ½d. and 1d. are printed from new combined plates. These show a slight alteration in that the frame does not touch the crown.

The ½d., 1d. and 2d. exist from coils constructed from normal sheets for use in stamp machines introduced in 1911. These coils were originally joined horizontally but the 1d. was subsequently issued joined vertically.

Many of the King's Head stamps are found overprinted or perforated "C.S.A.R.", for use by the Central South African Railways.

STAMP BOOKLETS

1905 (July). *Black on red cover showing arms. Stapled.*

SB1	2s.7d. booklet containing thirty 1d. (No. 261) in blocks of 6	£2000

1905. *Black on red cover. Stapled.*

SB2	2s.7d. booklet containing thirty 1d. (No. 274) in blocks of 6	£2250

1909. *Black on red cover. Stapled.*

SB3	2s.6d. booklet containing ten ½d. (No. 273) in block of 6 and block of 4, and twenty-four 1d. (No. 274) in blocks of 6	£2750

Stocks of No. SB3 were supplied containing twelve examples of the ½d., it being intended that the postal clerks would remove two stamps before the booklets were sold. In some instances this did not occur.

POSTAL FISCAL STAMPS

1900–02. *Fiscal stamps as in T* **33**, *but optd with T* **35**. P 11½.

F1	1d. pale blue	—	45·00
F2	6d. dull carmine	—	65·00
F3	1s. olive-bistre	—	80·00
F4	1s.6d. brown	—	95·00
F5	2s.6d. dull purple	—	£110

Nos. F1/5, previously listed as Nos. 1/5 of Volksrust, are fiscal issues which are known postally used from various Transvaal post offices between June 1900 and June 1902.

Other fiscal stamps are found apparently postally used, but these were used on telegrams not on postal matter.

POSTAGE DUE STAMPS

D 1

Inverted "p" for "d" (Right pane R. 10/6)

(Typo D.L.R.)

1907. Wmk Mult Crown CA. P 14.

D1	D 1	½d. black and blue-green	3·50	1·25
D2		1d. black and scarlet	4·00	85
D3		2d. brown-orange	4·75	1·25
D4		3d. black and blue	7·50	4·25
D5		5d. black and violet	2·00	12·00
		a. Inverted "p" for "d"	50·00	
D6		6d. black and red-brown	4·25	12·00
D7		1s. scarlet and black	11·00	8·50
D1/7 *Set of* 7			32·00	35·00

Transvaal became a province of the Union of South Africa on 31 May 1910.

PIETERSBURG

After the fall of Pretoria to the British in June 1900 the Transvaal government withdrew to the north of the country. Those post offices in areas not occupied by the British continued to function, but by early the following year supplies of stamps were exhausted. The following stamps were then authorised by the State Secretary and remained in use in some towns to early May 1901. Pietersburg itself was taken by British forces on 9 April.

PRICES. Genuinely used examples are very rare. Stamps cancelled by favour exist and are worth the same as the unused prices quoted.

The issued stamps are initialled by the Controller J. T. de V. Smit. All values exist without his signature and these are believed to come from remainders abandoned when the Boers evacuated Pietersburg.

P 1

P 2

P 3

TYPES P 1/3. Each value was printed in sheets of 24 (6×4) of which the first two horizontal rows were as Type P **1** (Large "P" in "POSTZEGEL" and large date), the third row as Type P **2** (Large "P" in "POSTZEGEL" and small date) and the fourth as Type P **3** (Small "P" in "POSTZEGEL" and small date). The stamps were issued to post offices in blocks of 12.

(Type-set *De Zoutpansberg Wachter* Press, Pietersburg)

1901 (20 Mar (1d.)–3 Apr (others)). A. Imperf.

(a) Controller's initials in black.

1	P 1	½d. black/*green*	15·00
		e. Controller's initials omitted	95·00
2	P 2	½d. black/*green*	45·00
		d. Controller's initials omitted	95·00
3	P 3	½d. black/*green*	45·00
		d. Controller's initials omitted	95·00
4	P 1	1d. black/*red*	3·50
5	P 2	1d. black/*red*	5·50
6	P 3	1d. black/*red*	7·00
7	P 1	2d. black/*orange*	6·00
8	P 2	2d. black/*orange*	14·00
9	P 3	2d. black/*orange*	22·00
10	P 1	4d. black/*blue*	5·50
11	P 2	4d. black/*blue*	9·50
12	P 3	4d. black/*blue*	32·00
13	P 1	6d. black/*green*	9·50
14	P 2	6d. black/*green*	15·00
15	P 3	6d. black/*green*	40·00
16	P 1	1s. black/*yellow*	8·00
17	P 2	1s. black/*yellow*	14·00
18	P 3	1s. black/*yellow*	25·00

(b) Controller's initials in red.

19	P 1	½d. black/*green*	15·00
20	P 2	½d. black/*green*	35·00
21	P 3	½d. black/*green*	40·00

B. P 11½.

(a) Controller's initials in red.

22	P 1	½d. black/*green*	5·50
		c. Imperf vert (horiz pair)	95·00
23	P 2	½d. black/*green*	17·00
		c. Imperf vert (horiz pair)	£120
24	P 3	½d. black/*green*	12·00
		b. Imperf vert (horiz pair)	£120

(b) Controller's initials in black.

25	P 1	1d. black/*red*	2·00
		m. Imperf vert (horiz pair)	55·00
		n. Imperf between (vert pair: No. 25 + No. 26)	75·00
		o. Imperf horiz (vert pair)	55·00
26	P 2	1d. black/*red*	2·75
		f. Imperf vert (horiz pair)	80·00
		g. Imperf horiz (vert pair: No. 26 + No. 27)	60·00
27	P 3	1d. black/*red*	4·00
		f. Imperf vert (horiz pair)	80·00
28	P 1	2d. black/*orange*	5·50
29	P 2	2d. black/*orange*	8·00
30	P 3	2d. black/*orange*	14·00

For the ½d. the First printing had initials in either black or red, those of the Second printing had them in black and all of the Third were in red.

CONSTANT VARIETIES

Rows 1 *and* 2 *are as Type* P **1**, *Row* 3 *as Type* P **2** *and Row* 4 *as Type* P **3**.

½d. value

First printing—Imperf

R.1/1	& 4 Top left "½" inverted, no stop after right "AFR"	(No. 19c)	70·00
R.1/2	Top right "½" inverted	(No. 19d)	90·00
R.1/3	"⅓" at lower right	(No. 19e)	90·00
R.1/5	"POSTZFGEL"	(No. 19f)	90·00
R.1/6	Left spray inverted, "AFB" at right	(No. 19g)	90·00
R.2/1	"REB" at left, left side of inner frame 3 mm too high	(No. 19h)	90·00
R.2/2	"BEP" at left	(No. 19i)	90·00
R.2/3	"POSTZEOEL"	(No. 19j)	90·00
R.2/4	"AER" at right, left side of inner frame 2 mm too high	(No. 19k)	90·00
R.2/5	No stop after date	(No. 19l)	90·00
R.2/6	No stop after "PENNY"	(No. 19m)	
R.3/1	"⅓" at top left, "PE" of "PENNY" spaced	(No. 20c)	90·00
R.3/2	Right spray inverted	(No. 20d)	90·00
R.3/3	Top left "½" inverted	(No. 20e)	90·00
R.3/4	No stop after "2" at left	(No. 20f)	
R.3/5	Centre figures "½" level	(No. 20g)	
R.3/6	"POSTZEGFL", no stop after right "AFR"	(No. 20h)	
R.4/3	"⅓" at top right	(No. 21b)	90·00
R.4/4	Lower left "½" inverted	(No. 21c)	90·00
R.4/5	"¼" at top left	(No. 21d)	90·00
R.4/6	Left spray inverted, "901" for "1901"	(No. 21e)	

This printing was produced first and was then adapted for the higher values.

Second printing

R.1/2	No stop after left "AFR"... Imperf	(No. 1a)	60·00
R.1/3	"⅓" at top left, no bar over lower right "½" ... Imperf	(No. 1b)	60·00
R.1/6	No stop after date ... Imperf	(No. 1c)	60·00
R.2/5	"BEP" at left, no stop after date Imperf	(No. 1d)	60·00

R.3/3 "AFB" at left .... Imperf (No. 2a) 60·00
Perf (No. 23a)
R.3/4 "POSTZEGEI" .... Imperf (No. 2b) 60·00
Perf (No. 23b)
R.3/6 No bar over lower right "½"
Imperf (No. 2c) 60·00
R.4/1 No stop after right "AFR". Imperf (No. 3a) 60·00
R.4/4 No stop after left "Z", no bar under top right "½" .... Imperf (No. 3b) 60·00
Perf (No. 23c)
R.4/5 "POSTZECEL AER" at left
Imperf (No. 3c) 60·00

Third printing

R.1/4 No stop after right "AFR". Imperf (No. 19a) 70·00
Perf (No. 22a) 40·00
R.2/1 Left side of inner frame too high
Imperf (No. 19b) 70·00
Perf (No. 22b) 40·00
R.3/5 Centre figures "½" level..... Imperf (No. 20a) 70·00
Perf (No. 23d) 40·00
R.3/6 No stop after right "AFR". Imperf (No. 20b) 70·00
Perf (No. 23e) 40·00
R.4/6 Hyphen between right "AFR" and "REP" .... Imperf (No. 21a) 70·00
Perf (No. 24a) 40·00

1*d. value*

First printing

R.1/2 Inverted "1" at lower left, first "1" of date dropped .... Imperf (No. 4a) 35·00
Perf (No. 25a) 22·00
R.1/3 No bar under top left "1".. Imperf (No. 4b) 35·00
.... Perf (No. 25b) 22·00
R.1/4 No bar over lower right "1"
Imperf (No. 4c) 35·00
Perf (No. 25c) 22·00
R.1/5 "POSTZFGEL" .... Imperf (No. 4d) 35·00
Perf (No. 25d) 22·00
R.1/6 "AFB" at right .... Imperf (No. 4e) 35·00
Perf (No. 25e) 22·00
R.2/1 "REB" at left .... Imperf (No. 4f) 35·00
Perf (No. 25f) 22·00
R.2/2 "BEP" at left .... Imperf (No. 4g) 35·00
Perf (No. 25g) 22·00
R.2/3 "POSTZEOEL" .... Imperf (No. 4h) 35·00
Perf (No. 25h) 22·00
R.2/4 "AER" at right .... Imperf (No. 4i) 35·00
Perf (No. 25i) 22·00
R.2/5 No stop after date .... Imperf (No. 4j) 35·00
Perf (No. 25j) 22·00
R.2/6 No stop after "PENNY".... Imperf (No. 4k) 35·00
Perf (No. 25k) 22·00
R.3/2 Right spray inverted .... Imperf (No. 5a) 35·00
Perf (No. 26a) 22·00
R.3/3 No bar over lower left "1" Imperf (No. 5b) 35·00
Perf (No. 26b) 22·00
R.3/4 No stop after left "Z" .... Imperf (No. 5c) 35·00
Perf (No. 26c) 22·00
R.3/6 "POSTZEGFL", no stop after right "AFR" .... Imperf (No. 5d) 35·00
Perf (No. 26d) 22·00
R.4/1 No stop after right "AFR". Imperf (No. 6a) 35·00
Perf (No. 27a) 22·00
R.4/2 & 6 Left spray inverted ..... Imperf (No. 6b) 22·00
Perf (No. 27b) 13·00
R.4/3 "POSTZEGEI" .... Imperf (No. 6c) 35·00
Perf (No. 27c) 22·00
R.4/4 No bar under top right "1" Imperf (No. 6d) 35·00
Perf (No. 27d) 22·00

Second printing

R.1/2 First "1" in date dropped... Imperf (No. 4l) 35·00
.... Perf (No. 25l) 22·00
R.3/6 No stop after right "AFR". Imperf (No. 5e) 35·00
.... Perf (No. 26e) 22·00
R.4/5 Dropped "P" in "PENNY" Imperf (No. 6e) 35·00
.... Perf (No. 27e) 22·00

It has been suggested that there may have been a third printing.

2*d. value*

First printing—Imperf

R.1/1 "1" at lower right .... (No. 7a) 45·00
R.1/2 No stop after left "AFR" (*on small part of printing*) .... (No. 7b) 90·00
R.1/3 No bar over lower right "2" (*on small part of printing*) .... (No. 7c) 90·00
R.1/3 "PENNY" for "PENCE" .... (No. 7d) 45·00
R.1/5 "POSTZFGEL" .... (No. 7e) 45·00
R.1/6 "AFB" at right .... (No. 7f) 45·00
R.2/1 "REB" at left .... (No. 7g) 45·00
R.2/2 "AFB" at left .... (No. 7h) 45·00
R.2/3 "POSTZEOEL" .... (No. 7i) 45·00
R.2/4 "AER" at right .... (No. 7j) 45·00
R.2/5 No stop after date .... (No. 7k) 45·00
R.2/6 No stop after date, vertical line after "POSTZEGEL" .... (No. 7l) 45·00
R.3/2 Right spray inverted .... (No. 8a) 45·00
R.3/3 No bar over lower left "2" .... (No. 8b) 45·00
R.3/4 Centre "2" inverted, no stop after left "Z" .... (No. 8c) 45·00
R.3/6 "POSTZEGFL", no stop after right "AFR" .... (No. 8d) 45·00
R.4/1 Centre "2" wider, no stop after right "AFR" (*occurs on second printing also*) .... (No. 9a) 38·00
R.4/2 Centre "2" wider, left spray inverted .... (No. 9b) 45·00
R.4/3 "POSTZEGEI" .... (No. 9c) 45·00
R.4/4 No bar under top right "2" .... (No. 9d) 45·00
R.4/5 "1" at lower left, "P" in "PENCE" dropped .... (No. 9e) 45·00
R.4/6 Left spray inverted .... (No. 9f) 45·00

Second printing

R.1/2 First "1" in date dropped... Imperf (No. 7m) 45·00
Perf (No. 28a) 30·00
R.2/1 No stop after left "REP"... Imperf (No. 7n) 45·00
Perf (No. 28b) 30·00
R.3/4 No stop after left "Z" .... Imperf (No. 8e) 45·00
R.3/6 No stop after right "AFR". Imperf (No. 8f) 45·00
Perf (No. 29a) 30·00
R.4/1 Centre 2 wider, no stop after right "AFR" (*occurs on first printing also*) .... Imperf (No. 9a) 38·00
Perf (No. 30a) 30·00
R.4/2 Centre "2" wider .... Imperf (No. 9g) 45·00
Perf (No. 30b) 30·00
R.4/5 "P" in "PENCE" dropped. Imperf (No. 9h) 45·00
Perf (No. 30c) 30·00

It has been suggested that there was a third printing of this value.

4*d. value*

First printing

R.1/2 No stop after left "AFR" .... (No. 10a) 45·00
R.1/3 No bar over lower right "4" .... (No. 10b) 45·00
R.1/3 "PENNY" for "PENCE" (*on small part of printing*) .... (No. 10c) 90·00
R.1/5 "POSTZFGEL" .... (No. 10d) 45·00
R.1/6 "AFB" at right .... (No. 10e) 45·00
R.2/1 "REB" at left .... (No. 10f) 45·00
R.2/2 "AFB" at left .... (No. 10g) 45·00
R.2/3 "POSTZEOEL" .... (No. 10h) 45·00
R.2/4 "AER" at right .... (No. 10i) 45·00
R.2/5 No stop after date .... (No. 10j) 45·00
R.3/2 Right spray inverted .... (No. 11a) 45·00
R.3/3 No bar over lower left "4" (*on small part of printing*) .... (No. 11b) 90·00
R.3/4 No stop after left "Z" .... (No. 11c) 45·00
R.3/6 "POSTZEGFL" .... (No. 11d) 45·00
R.4/1 Centre "4" wider, no stop after right "AFR" .... (No. 12a) 45·00
R.4/2 Centre "4" wider, left spray inverted .... (No. 12b) 45·00
R.4/3 "POSTZEGEI" .... (No. 12c) 45·00
R.4/4 No bar under top right "4" .... (No. 12d) 45·00
R.4/5 "AER" at left, "P" in "PENCE" dropped .... (No. 12e) 45·00
R.4/6 Left spray inverted .... (No. 12f) 45·00

Second printing

R.2/1 Left inner frame too high .... (No. 10k) 45·00
R.4/1–2 Centre "4" wider .... (No. 12g) 35·00
R.4/5 "P" in "PENCE" dropped .... (No. 12h) 45·00

6*d. value*

First printing

R.1/2 No stop after left "AFR" .... (No. 13a) 55·00
R.1/3 No bar over lower right "6" .... (No. 13b) 55·00
R.1/3 "PENNY" for "PENCE" (*on small part of printing*) .... (No. 13c) £110
R.1/5 "POSTZFGEL" .... (No. 13d) 55·00
R.1/6 "AFB" at right .... (No. 13e) 55·00
R.2/1 "REB" at left .... (No. 13f) 55·00
R.2/2 "AFB" at left .... (No. 13g) 55·00
R.2/3 "POSTZEOEL" .... (No. 13h) 55·00
R.2/4 "AER" at right .... (No. 13i) 55·00
R.2/5 No stop after date .... (No. 13j) 55·00
R.3/2 Right spray inverted .... (No. 14a) 55·00
R.3/4 Centre "6" inverted, no stop after left "Z" (*on small part of printing*) (No. 14b) £110
R.3/4 No stop after left "Z" .... (No. 14c) 55·00
R.3/6 "POSTZEGFL" .... (No. 14d) 55·00
R.4/1 Centre "6" wider, no stop after right "AFR" .... (No. 15a) 55·00
R.4/2 Centre "6" wider, left spray inverted .... (No. 15b) 55·00
R.4/3 "POSTZEGEI" .... (No. 15c) 55·00
R.4/4 No bar under top right "6" .... (No. 15d) 55·00
R.4/5 "AER" at left. "P" in "PENCE" dropped .... (No. 15e) 55·00
R.4/6 Left spray inverted .... (No. 15f) 55·00

Second printing

R.2/1 Left inner frame too high, no stop after left "REP" .... (No. 13k) 55·00
R.4/1–2 Centre "6" wider .... (No. 15g) 40·00
R.4/5 "P" in "PENCE" dropped .... (No. 15h) 55·00

1*s. value*

R.1/2 No stop after left "AFR" .... (No. 16a) 40·00
R.1/3 No bar over lower right "1" .... (No. 16b) 40·00
R.2/5 No stop after date .... (No. 16c) 40·00
R.3/3 Centre "1" inverted (*on small part of printing*) .... (No. 17a)
R.3/4 "POSTZEGEI", no stop after left "Z" .... (No. 17b) 40·00
R.4/1 No stop after right "AFR" .... (No. 18a) 40·00
R.4/4 No bar under top right "1" .... (No. 18b) 40·00
R.4/5 "AER" at left .... (No. 18c) 40·00

LOCAL BRITISH OCCUPATION ISSUES DURING THE SOUTH AFRICAN WAR 1900–2

Stamps of the Transvaal Republic, unless otherwise stated, variously overprinted or surcharged.

LYDENBURG

Lydenburg fell to the British on 6 September 1900.

V.R.I.
3d.
(L 1)

1900 (Sept). *Nos. 215b and 217 surch as Type* L **1**, *others optd "V.R.I" only.*

1	**30**	½d. green	£130	£130
2		1d. rose-red and green	£120	£110
2*a*	**34**	1d. on 1d. red		
3	**30**	2d. brown and green	£1200	£850
4		2½d. blue and green	£2250	£900
5		3d. on 1d. rose-red and green	£100	90·00
6		3d. purple and green		
7		4d. sage-green and green	£3000	£800
8		6d. lilac and green	£2500	£750
9		1s. ochre and green	£4250	£2750

The above were cancelled by British Army postal service postmarks. These overprints with Transvaal cancellations are believed to be forgeries.

RUSTENBURG

The British forces in Rustenburg, west of Pretoria, were besieged by the Boers during June 1900. When relieved on the 22 June 1900 no "V.R.I" stamps were available so a local handstamp was applied.

V.R.
(R 1)

1900 (23 June). *Handstamped with Type* R **1** *in violet.*

1	**30**	½d. green	£150	£110
2		1d. rose-red and green	£110	85·00
3		2d. brown and green	£325	£130
4		2½d. blue and green	£180	£110
5		3d. purple and green	£250	£140
6		6d. lilac and green	£1200	£350
7		1s. ochre and green	£1700	£750
8		2s.6d. dull violet and green	£9000	£4500
		a. Handstamp in black	†	£8000

Nos. 2 and 5 exist with the handstamp inverted.

SCHWEIZER RENECKE

BESIEGED
(SR 1)

1900 (Sept). *Handstamped with Type* SR **1** *in black, reading vert up or down.*

(*a*) *On stamps of Transvaal.*

1	**30**	½d. green	†	£250
2		1d. rose-red and green	†	£250
3		2d. brown and green	†	£325
4		6d. lilac and green	†	£950

(*b*) *On stamps of Cape of Good Hope.*

5	**17**	½d. green	†	£425
6		1d. carmine	†	£425

Schweizer Renecke, near the Bechuanaland border, was under siege from 1 August 1900 to 9 January 1901. The British commander authorised the above stamps shortly after 19 August. All stamps were cancelled with the dated circular town postmark ("Schweizer Renecke, Z.A.R."), usually after having been stuck on paper before use. Unused, without the postmark, do not exist.

No. 4 exists with double handstamp.

WOLMARANSSTAD

A British party occupied this town in the south-west of the Transvaal from 15 June to 27 July 1900. Transvaal stamps, to a face value of £5 2s.6d., were found at the local firm of Thos. Leask and Co. and surcharged as below. The first mail left on 24 June and the last on 21 July.

Cancelled
V-R-I.
(L 3)

Cancelled
V-R-I.
(L 4)

1900 (24 June). *Optd with Type* L **3**.

1	**30**	½d. green (B.)	£250	£375
		a. Opt inverted	£850	
		b. Opt in black		
1*c*		½d. on 1s. green (B.)		
2		1d. rose-red and green (B.)	£170	£275
		a. Opt in green	£1800	
		b. Opt in black		
3		2d. brown and green (B.)	£1800	£1800
		a. Opt in black	£3000	
4		2½d. blue and green (R.)	£1800	
		a. Opt in blue	£2750	£2750
		b. Opt in black		
5		3d. purple and green (B.)	£3000	£3250
6		4d. sage-green and green (B.)	£4000	£4500
7		6d. lilac and green (B.)	£4500	£5000
8		1s. ochre and green (B.)	—	£9000

The two lines of the overprint were handstamped separately. The ½d. exists with two impressions of the "Cancelled" handstamp, the 2½d. with two impressions of "V-R-I", one in red and one in blue and the 3d. with "Cancelled" in green and "V.R.I." in blue.

1900 (24 June). *Optd with Type* L **4**.

9	**34**	1d. red (B.)	£170	£300

The ½d., 1d. and 3d. in Type **30** are also known with this overprint.

VII. ZULULAND

Zululand remained an independent kingdom until annexed by Great Britain on 19 May 1887 when it was declared a Crown Colony.

The first European postal service was operated by a Natal postal agency at Eshowe opened in 1876 which cancelled Natal stamps with a "No. 56 P.O. Natal" postmark. The agency closed during the Zulu War of 1879 and did not re-open until 1885 when a Eshowe postmark was provided. "ZULULAND" was added to the cancellation in 1887 and stamps of Natal continued to be used until replaced by the overprinted series on 1 May 1888.

PRICES FOR STAMPS ON COVER	
Nos. 1/2	*from* × 100
Nos. 3/10	*from* × 20
No. 11	—
Nos. 12/16	*from* × 20
Nos. 20/3	*from* × 30
No. 24	*from* × 20
Nos. 25/6	*from* × 12
Nos. 27/9	—
No. F1	*from* × 100

(1)

(2)

1888 (1 May)–**93**.

(a) Nos. 173, 180, 197, 200/2, 205a, 207a/8, 209 and 211 of Great Britain (Queen Victoria) optd with T **1** *by D.L.R.*

1		½d. vermilion (11.88)	4·75	2·75
2		1d. deep purple	28·00	4·25
3		2d. grey-green and carmine	19·00	35·00
4		2½d. purple/*blue* (9.91)	26·00	21·00
5		3d. purple/*yellow*	25·00	22·00
6		4d. green and deep brown	48·00	70·00
7		5d. dull purple and blue (3.93)	95·00	£120
		w. Wmk inverted	†	—
8		6d. purple/*rose-red*	17·00	17·00
9		9d. dull purple and blue (4.92)	£100	£100
10		1s. dull green (4.92)	£120	£130
11		5s. rose (4.92)	£550	£650
1/11 *Set of* 11			£950	£1000
1s/11s (*ex* 1d.) H/S "Specimen" *Set of* 10			£600	

(b) No. 97a of Natal optd with T **2** *at Pietermaritzburg*

12		½d. dull green (with stop) (7.88)	55·00	85·00
		a. Opt double	£1100	£1200
		b. Opt inverted	£1300	
		d. Opt omitted (vert pair with normal)	£6000	
13		½d. dull green (without stop)	26·00	42·00
		a. Opt double	£1500	£1500

1893 (29 Nov*). *T* **15** *of Natal optd with T* **1** *by D.L.R.* (Wmk Crown CA. P 14).

16		6d. dull purple	60·00	55·00

*Earliest known date of use. No. 16 was, apparently, originally supplied in 1889 for fiscal purposes.

3

4

Shaved "Z" (R. 4/3 and R. 6/3)

(Typo D.L.R.)

1894 (18 Apr)–**96**. Wmk Crown CA. P 14.

20	**3**	½d. dull mauve and green	4·00	5·00
		w. Wmk inverted	£160	£190
21		1d. dull mauve and carmine	6·00	2·75
		a. Shaved "Z"	70·00	40·00
22		2½d. dull mauve and ultramarine	14·00	9·00
23		3d. dull mauve and olive-brown	8·00	3·00
24	**4**	6d. dull mauve and black	20·00	20·00
25		1s. green	40·00	38·00
26		2s.6d. green and black (2.96)	80·00	90·00
27		4s. green and carmine	£120	£160
28		£1 purple/*red*	£475	£550
29		£5 purple and black/*red*	£4500	£1500
		s. Optd "Specimen"	£450	
20/8 *Set of* 9			£700	£800
20s/8s Optd "Specimen" *Set of* 9			£425	

Dangerous forgeries exist of the £1 and £5.

FISCAL STAMP USED FOR POSTAGE

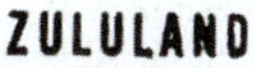

F 1

1891 (5 May*). F **1**, *Fiscal stamp of Natal optd with T* **1**. Wmk Crown CA. P 14.

F1		1d. dull mauve	3·75	3·00
		a. Top left triangle detached	£160	£140
		s. Handstamped "Specimen"	60·00	

*Earliest known date of postal use. A proclamation published in the *Natal Government Gazette* on 27 June 1891 authorised the use of this stamp for postal purposes, but it is clear from the wording that such use had already commenced.

For illustration of "top left triangle detached" variety see above No. 21 of Antigua.

Other values, 1s. to £20 as No. F1 exist apparently with postmarks, but, as these were never authorised for postal use, they are no longer listed.

Zululand was annexed to Natal on 31 December 1897 and its stamps were withdrawn from sale on 30 June 1898.

VIII. BRITISH ARMY FIELD OFFICES DURING SOUTH AFRICAN WAR, 1899–1902

Z 1

Z 2

Stamps of GREAT BRITAIN *used by British Army Field Offices in South Africa cancelled as Types* Z **1**, Z **2** *or similar postmarks.*

1881. *Stamp of Queen Victoria.*

Z1	1d. lilac (16 *dots*)	5·00

1883–84. *Stamps of Queen Victoria.*

Z1*a*	2s.6d lilac	£250
Z2	5s. rose	£275
Z2*a*	10s. ultramarine	£600

1887–92. *Stamps of Queen Victoria.*

Z3	½d. vermilion	6·00
Z4	1½d. dull purple and green	24·00
Z5	2d. grey-green and carmine	16·00
Z6	2½d. purple/*blue*	6·00
Z7	3d. purple/*yellow*	13·00
Z8	4d. green and brown	18·00
Z9	4½d. green and carmine	60·00
Z10	5d. dull purple and blue (Die II)	15·00
Z11	6d. purple/*rose-red*	12·00
Z12	9d. dull purple and blue	65·00
Z13	10d. dull purple and carmine	60·00
Z14	1s. dull green	90·00
Z15	£1 green	£900

1900. *Stamps of Queen Victoria.*

Z16	½d. blue-green	6·00
Z17	1s. green and carmine	£160

1902. *Stamps of King Edward VII.*

Z18	½d. blue-green	15·00
Z19	1d. scarlet	10·00
Z20	1½d. purple and green	
Z21	2d. yellowish green and carmine-red	
Z22	2½d. ultramarine	20·00
Z23	3d. purple/*orange-yellow*	
Z24	4d. green and grey-brown	
Z25	5d. dull purple and ultramarine	
Z26	6d. pale dull purple	35·00
Z27	9d. dull purple and ultramarine	
Z28	10d. dull purple and carmine	
Z29	1s. dull green and carmine	

ARMY OFFICIAL STAMPS

1896–1901. *Stamps of Queen Victoria optd "*ARMY OFFICIAL*".*

ZO1	½d. vermilion	£100
ZO2	½d. blue-green	£100
ZO3	1d. lilac (16 *dots*)	85·00
ZO4	6d. purple/*rose-red*	

IX. UNION OF SOUTH AFRICA

The province continued to use their existing issues until the introduction of Nos. 3/17. From 19 August 1910 the issues of any province were valid for use throughout the Union until they were demonetised on 31 December 1937.

PRICES FOR STAMPS ON COVER TO 1945

Nos. 1/15	*from* × 4
Nos. 16/17	—
Nos. 18/21	*from* × 6
Nos. 26/32	*from* × 2
No. 33	*from* × 4
Nos. 34/110	*from* × 1
Nos. D1/7	*from* × 4
Nos. D8/33	*from* × 6
Nos. O1/33	*from* × 4

1

(Des H. S. Wilkinson. Recess D.L.R.)

1910 (4 Nov). *Opening of Union Parliament. Inscribed bilingually.* Wmk Multiple Rosettes. P 14.

1	**1**	2½d. deep blue	3·00	3·00
		s. Handstamped "Specimen"	£350	
2		2½d. blue	1·75	1·40

The deep blue shade is generally accompanied by a blueing of the paper.

No. 1s. has the overprint in italic capital and lower case letters which measure 12½ mm in length.

2

3

4 Springbok's Head

(Typo D.L.R.)

1913 (1 Sept)–**24**. *Inscribed bilingually.* W **4**.

(a) P 14.

3	**2**	½d. green	1·50	30
		a. Stamp doubly printed	£10000	
		b. Blue-green	2·00	20
		c. Yellow-green	2·50	80
		d. Printed on the gummed side	£700	
		w. Wmk inverted	2·00	80
4		1d. rose-red (*shades*)	1·75	10
		a. Carmine-red	2·25	10
		b. Scarlet (*shades*)	2·75	75
		c. Printed on the gummed side	£750	
		w. Wmk inverted	2·50	70
5		1½d. chestnut (*shades*) (23.8.20)	80	10
		a. *Tête-bêche* (pair)	1·75	18·00
		b. Printed on the gummed side	£800	
		c. Wmk sideways	†	£1500
		w. Wmk inverted	80	10
6	**3**	2d. dull purple	1·75	10
		a. Deep purple	2·50	10
		b. Printed on the gummed side	£800	
		w. Wmk inverted	3·25	1·75
7		2½d. bright blue	3·75	1·25
		a. Deep blue	5·50	3·00
		w. Wmk inverted	£100	£100
8		3d. black and orange-red	12·00	30
		a. Black and dull orange-red	10·00	70
		w. Wmk inverted	18·00	8·00
9		3d. ultramarine (*shades*) (4.10.22)	3·50	1·75
		w. Wmk inverted	9·50	5·50
10		4d. orange-yellow and olive-green	9·00	55
		a. Orange-yellow and sage-green	6·50	55
		w. Wmk inverted	8·00	85
11		6d. black and violet	5·50	60
		a. Black and bright violet	9·50	1·00
		aw. Wmk inverted	16·00	9·50
12		1s. orange	13·00	80
		a. Orange-yellow	20·00	1·00
		w. Wmk inverted	18·00	1·25
13		1s.3d. violet (*shades*) (1.9.20)	13·00	7·00
		w. Wmk inverted	£100	£150
14		2s.6d. purple and green	55·00	1·50
15		5s. purple and blue	£110	8·00
		a. Reddish purple and light blue	£110	8·50
		w. Wmk inverted	£4250	£2500
16		10s. deep blue and olive-green	£180	7·50
		w. Wmk inverted	£4000	£1800
17		£1 green and red (7.16)	£600	£350
		a. Pale olive-green and red (1924)	£800	£1200
3/17 *Set of* 15			£900	£350
3s/8s, 10s/17s Optd or H/S (1½d. and 1s.3d. in violet, £1 in green) "Specimen" *Set of* 14			£1300	

(b) Coil stamps. P 14×imperf.

18	**2**	½d. green	6·00	1·00
		w. Wmk inverted	£550	£325
19		1d. rose-red (13.2.14)	14·00	3·75
		a. Scarlet	18·00	8·50
		w. Wmk inverted	£550	£325
20		1½d. chestnut (15.11.20)	11·00	15·00
		w. Wmk inverted	†	—
21	**3**	2d. dull purple (7.10.21)	14·00	4·75
18/21 *Set of* 4			40·00	22·00

The 6d. exists with "Z" of "ZUID" wholly or partly missing due to wear of plate (*Price wholly missing, £80 un, £38 us*).

5 De Havilland D.H.9 Biplane

(Eng A. J. Cooper. Litho *Cape Times* Ltd)

1925 (26 Feb). *Air. Inscr bilingually.* P 12.

26	**5**	1d. carmine	4·25	10·00
27		3d. ultramarine	7·00	10·00
28		6d. magenta	9·00	11·00
29		9d. green	23·00	55·00
26/9 *Set of* 4			38·00	75·00

Beware of forgeries of all values perforated 11, 11½ or 13.

INSCRIPTIONS. From 1926 until 1951 most issues were inscribed in English and Afrikaans alternately throughout the sheets.

PRICES for Nos. 30/135 are for unused horizontal pairs, used horizontal pairs and used singles (either inscription), *unless otherwise indicated.* Vertical pairs are worth between 25% and 40% of the prices quoted for horizontal pairs.

6 Springbok

7 *Dromedaris* (Van Riebeeck's ship)

8 Orange Tree

9

(Typo Waterlow until 1927, thereafter Govt Printer, Pretoria)

1926 (2 Jan)–**27**. W **9**. P 14½×14.

			Un pair	*Used pair*	*Used single*
30	**6**	½d. black and green	3·00	4·00	10
		a. Missing "1" in "½"	£2000		
		b. Centre omitted (in pair with normal)	£2000		
		cw. Wmk inverted	4·50	5·00	20
		d. Frame printed double	£2750		
		e. Perf 13½×14 (1927)	85·00	85·00	4·00
		ea. *Tête-bêche* (pair)	£1000		
		ew. Wmk inverted	80·00	80·00	4·00

31	7	1d. black and carmine	2·00	50	10
		a. Imperf (vert pair)*	£650		
		b. Imperf 3 sides (vert pair)*	£650	£700	
		cw. Wmk inverted	5·50	2·00	20
		d. Perf 13½×14 (1927)	£100	80·00	4·00
		da. *Tête-bêche* (pair)	£1100		
		dw. Wmk inverted	£100	80·00	4·00
		e. Wmk sideways	£2000	£2000	
32	8	6d. green and orange (1.5.26)	40·00	48·00	1·50
		w. Wmk inverted	70·00	75·00	
30/2 *Set of* 3			40·00	48·00	1·50

No. 30a exists in Afrikaans only. Nos. 30e and 31d were only issued in booklets.

No. 30d occurred on the bottom left-hand corner of one sheet and included the bottom four stamps in the first vertical row and the bottom two in the second. As listed No. 30d shows the left-hand stamp with the frame completely double and the right-hand stamp with two-thirds of the frame double.

*Both Nos. 31a and 31b occur in blocks of four with the other vertical pair imperforate at left.

For ½d. with pale grey centre, see No. 126.

For rotogravure printing see Nos. 42, etc.

10 "Hope"

(Recess B.W.)

1926 (2 Jan). *T* **10**. *Inscribed in English or Afrikaans.* W **9** (upright or inverted in equal quantities).

			Single stamps	
33		4d. grey-blue (English inscr) (*shades*)	1·75	1·25
		a. Inscr in Afrikaans	1·75	1·25

In this value the English and Afrikaans inscriptions are on separate sheets.

This stamp is known with private perforations or roulettes.

11 Union Buildings, Pretoria

12 Groot Schuur

12a A Native Kraal

13 Black and Blue Wildebeest

14 Ox-wagon inspanned

15 Ox-wagon outspanned

16 Cape Town and Table Bay

(Recess B.W.)

1927 (1 Mar)–**30**. W **9**. P 14.

			Un pair	*Used pair*	*Used single*
34	**11**	2d. grey and maroon	11·00	24·00	60
		aw. Wmk inverted	£550	£600	32·00
		b. Perf 14×13½ (2.30)	32·00	32·00	70
35	**12**	3d. black and red	15·00	26·00	60
		a. Perf 14×13½ (1930)	65·00	65·00	80
35*b*	**12a**	4d. brown (23.3.28)	27·00	50·00	1·00
		bw. Wmk inverted	£700	£650	38·00
		c. Perf 14×13½ (1930)	50·00	60·00	1·25
36	**13**	1s. brown and deep blue	30·00	55·00	1·00
		a. Perf 14×13½ (1930)	70·00	85·00	2·00
37	**14**	2s.6d. green and brown	£110	£350	17·00
		a. Perf 14×13½ (1930)	£325	£550	24·00
38	**15**	5s. black and green	£225	£650	35·00
		a. Perf 14×13½ (1930)	£400	£850	40·00
39	**16**	10s. bright blue and brown	£150	£130	10·00
		a. Centre inverted (*single stamp*)	£11000		
		b. Perf 14×13½ (1930)	£190	£180	12·00
34/9 *Set of* 7			£500	£1100	55·00
34s/9s H/S "Specimen" *Set of* 7			£900		

17 De Havilland D.H.60 Cirrus Moth

(Typo Govt Ptg Wks, Pretoria)

1929 (16 Aug). *Air. Inscribed bilingually.* No wmk. P 14×13½.

			Un single	*Us single*
40	**17**	4d. green	5·50	2·50
41		1s. orange	16·00	13·00

PRINTER. All the following issues, except *where stated otherwise*, are printed by rotogravure (the design having plain lines or a dotted screen) by the Government Printer, Pretoria.

I II

The two types of the 1d. differ in the spacing of the horizontal lines in the side panels:—Type I close; Type II wide. The Afrikaans had the spacing of the words POSSEEL-INKOMSTE close in Type I and more widely spaced in Type II.

"Cobweb" variety (retouch between horns) (Cyl. 1 R. 9/5)

"Dollar" variety (Cyl. 2 R. 10/9)

Airship flaw (Cyl 34 R. 9/4)

Window flaw (R. 20/4 on all ptgs before 1937)

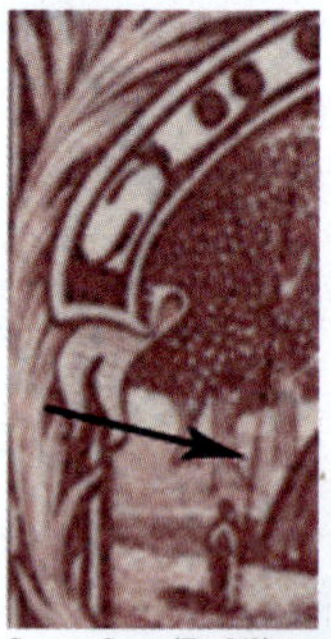

Spear flaw (R. 9/2)

"Monkey" in tree (R. 2/2)

Twisted horn (Cyl 7020 R. 1/5)

1930–45. *T* **6** *to* **8** *and* **11** *to* **14** *redrawn, "SUIDAFRIKA" (in one word) on Afrikaans stamps.* W **9**. P 15×14 (½d., 1d., and 6d.) or 14.

		Un pair	*Used pair*	*Used single*
42	½d. black and green (5.30)	3·75	3·00	10
	a. Two English or two Afrikaans stamps *se-tenant* (vert strip of 4)	40·00		
	b. *Tête-bêche*	£1000		
	c. "Cobweb" variety	40·00		
	d. "Dollar" variety	40·00		
	w. Wmk inverted	3·75	3·00	10
43	1d. black and carmine (I) (4.30)	4·75	3·00	10
	a. *Tête-bêche*	£1200		
	b. Frame omitted (*single stamp*)	£450		
	cw. Wmk inverted	4·75	3·00	10
43*d*	1d. black and carmine (II) (8.32)	48·00	3·75	10
	dw. Wmk inverted	40·00	4·00	10
44	2d. slate-grey and lilac (4.31)	24·00	21·00	30
	a. *Tête-bêche*	£4750		
	bw. Wmk inverted	17·00	9·00	20
	bwa. Frame omitted (*single stamp*)	£2750		
	c. Airship flaw	£100		
44*d*	2d. blue and violet (3.38)	£325	75·00	2·50
	da. Airship flaw	£750		
45	3d. black and red (11.31)	70·00	80·00	2·25
	aw. Wmk inverted	32·00	60·00	1·25
	b. Window flaw	£130		
45*c*	3d. blue (10.33)	19·00	7·00	20
	cw. Wmk inverted	6·00	6·00	10
	d. Window flaw	45·00		
	e. Centre omitted	£25000		
	f. Frame omitted (*single stamp*)	£12000		
46	4d. brown (19.11.32)	£180	£120	6·00
	aw. Wmk inverted	30·00	30·00	40
	b. Spear flaw	£120		
46*c*	4d. brown (*shades*) (*again redrawn*) (1936)	3·75	2·75	10
	ca "Monkey" in tree	38·00		
	cw. Wmk inverted	13·00	9·00	10
47	6d. green and orange (*wmk inverted*) (13.5.31)	13·00	4·50	10
	w. Wmk upright (8.32)	40·00	16·00	10
48	1s. brown and deep blue (14.9.32)	85·00	50·00	40
	aw. Wmk inverted	35·00	26·00	25
	b. Twisted horn flaw	£190		
49	2s.6d. green & brown (*shades*) (24.12.32)	£110	£110	3·25
	aw. Wmk inverted	£140	£150	3·25
49*b*	2s.6d. blue and brown (1945)	26·00	13·00	20
42/9*b* *Set of* 13		£500	£275	6·50

For similar designs with "SUID-AFRIKA" hyphenated, see Nos. 54 etc. and Nos. 114 etc.

Nos. 42/3, 43*d*/4 exist in coils.

No. 42a comes from the coil printing on the cylinder for which two horizontal rows were incorrectly etched so that two Afrikaans-inscribed stamps were followed by two English. This variety is normally without a coil join, although some examples do occur showing a repair join.

The 1d. (Type I) exists without watermark from a trial printing (*Price* £25 *un*).

Although it appears to be printed in one colour No. 45*c* was produced from vignette and frame cylinders in the same way as the bicoloured version. The clouds in the background, which are present on No. 45e, were printed from the frame cylinder.

Nos. 45b, 45d, 46b and 48b all occur on printings with either upright or inverted watermark. The price quoted is for the cheapest version in each instance.

The Rotogravure printings may be distinguished from the preceding Typographed and Recess printed issues by the following tests:—

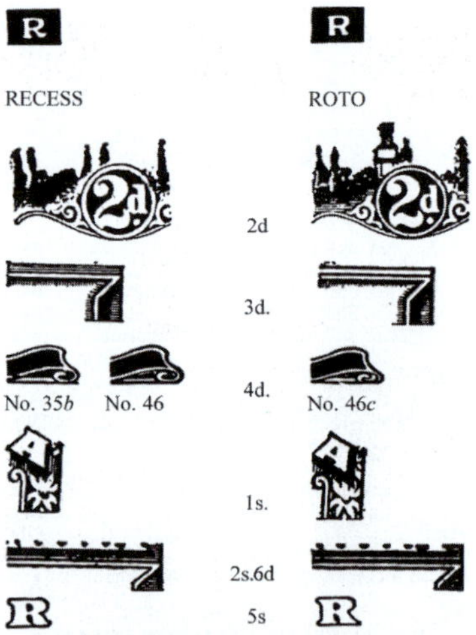

ROTOGRAVURE:

½d.	1d. and 6d. Leg of "R" in "AFR" ends squarely on the bottom line.
2d.	The newly built War Memorial appears to the left of the value.
3d.	Two fine lines have been removed from the top part of the frame.
4d.	No. 46. The scroll is in solid colour.
	No. 46*c*. The scroll is white with a crooked line running through it. (No. 35*b*. The scroll is shaded by the diagonal lines.)
1s.	The shading of the last "A" partly covers the flower beneath.
2s.6d.	The top line of the centre frame is thick and leaves only one white line between it and the name.
5s.	(Nos. 64/*b*). The leg of the "R" is straight.

Rotogravure impressions are generally coarser.

18 Church of the Vow

19 "The Great Trek" (C. Michell)

20 A Voortrekker

21 Voortrekker Woman

Blurred "SOUTH AFRICA" and red "comet" flaw (Cyls 6917/6922 R. 2/7)

(Des J. Prentice (½d., 2d., 3d.)

1933 (3 May)–**36**. *Voortrekker Memorial Fund.* W **9** (sideways). P 14.

50	**18**	½d. +½d. black and green (16.1.36)	3·75	5·50	50
51	**19**	1d. +½d. grey-black and pink	2·75	1·50	25
		a. Blurred "SOUTH AFRICA" and red "comet" flaw	48·00	50·00	
52	**20**	2d. +1d. grey-green and purple	3·75	4·00	55
53	**21**	3d. +1½d. grey-green and blue	6·00	5·00	70
50/3 *Set of* 4			15·00	14·50	1·75

22 Gold Mine

22a Groot Schuur

Dies of 6d.

I II III

23 Groot Constantia

Broken chimney and fainter headgear (Cyl 62 R. 11/6)

Flag on chimney at right (Cyl 62 R. 20/2)

"Falling ladder" flaw (R. 5/10)

1933–48. "SUID-AFRIKA" *(hyphenated) on Afrikaans stamps.* W **9**. P 15×14 (½d., 1d. and 6d.) or 14 (others).

54	**6**	½d. grey and green (*wmk inverted*) (9.35)	4·50	2·00	10
		aw. Wmk upright (1936)	9·00	7·50	10
		b. Coil stamp. Perf 13½×14 (1935)	40·00	65·00	1·00
		bw. Wmk upright	40·00	65·00	1·00
		c. Booklet pane of 6 (with adverts on margins) (*wmk upright*)	25·00		
56	**7**	1d. grey and carmine (*shades*) (19.4.34)	1·75	2·00	10
		a. Imperf (pair) (*wmk inverted*)	£160		
		b. Frame omitted (*single stamp*)	£275		
		cw. Wmk inverted	1·75	2·00	10
		d. Coil stamp. Perf 13½×14 (1935)	42·00	60·00	1·40
		dw. Wmk inverted	42·00	60·00	1·40
		e. Booklet pane of 6 (with adverts on margins) (1935)	19·00		
		f. Booklet pane of 6 (with blank margins) (1937)	19·00		
		h. Booklet pane of 6 (with postal slogans on margins) (1948)	4·00		
		i. Grey & brt rose-carm (7.48)	70	2·00	10
57	**22**	1½d. green and bright gold (12.11.36)	3·25	2·25	10
		a. Shading omitted from mine dump (in pair with normal)	£190	£140	
		b. Broken chimney and faint headgear	20·00		
		c. Flag on chimney at right	20·00		
		dw. Wmk inverted	1·50	1·75	10
		e. Blue-green and dull gold (8.40)	6·50	3·00	10
58	**11**	2d. blue and violet (11.38)	75·00	38·00	75
58*a*		2d. grey and dull purple (5.41)	50·00	85·00	1·50
59	**22a**	3d. ultramarine (2.40)	13·00	3·25	10
61	**8**	6d. green and vermilion (I) (10.37)	70·00	32·00	70
		a. "Falling ladder" flaw	£225	£250	
61*b*		6d. green and vermilion (II) (6.38)	40·00	1·00	10
61*c*		6d. green and red-orange (III) (11.46)	20·00	75	10
62	**13**	1s. brown and chalky blue (2.39)	50·00	15·00	20
		a. Frame omitted (*single stamp*)	£5000		
64	**15**	5s. black and green (10.33)	55·00	70·00	1·75
		aw. Wmk inverted	£120	£140	3·00
		b. Black and blue-green (9.44)	38·00	17·00	35
64*c*	**23**	10s. blue and sepia (*shades*) / (8.39)	65·00	14·00	70
		ca. Blue and charcoal (1944)	42·00	5·50	30
54/9, 61*c*/64*ca* *Set of* 10			£250	£150	2·75

The ½d. and 1d. coil stamps may be found in blocks emanating from the residue of the large rolls which were cut into sheets and distributed to Post Offices.

Nos. 54 and 56 also exist in coils.

1d. Is printed from Type II. Frames of different sizes exist due to reductions made from time to time for the purpose of providing more space for the perforations.

3d. In No. 59 the frame is unscreened and composed of solid lines. Centre is diagonally screened. Scrolls above "3d." are clear lined, light in the middle and dark at sides.

6d. Die I. Green background lines faint. "SUID-AFRIKA" 16¼ mm long.

Die II. Green background lines heavy. "SUID-AFRIKA" 17 mm long. "S" near end of tablet. Scroll open.

Die III. Scroll closed up and design smaller (18×22 mm).

Single specimens of the 1933–48 issue inscribed in English may be distinguished from those of 1930–45 as follows:–

½d. and 1d. Centres in grey instead of varying intensities of black.

2d. The letters of "SOUTH AFRICA" are narrower and thinner.

3d. The trees are taller and the sky is without lines.

6d. The frame is vermilion.

1s. The frame is chalky blue.

For similar designs, but printed in screened rotogravure, see Nos. 114 to 122a.

BOOKLET PANES. Booklets issued in 1935 contained ½d. and 1d. stamps in panes with advertisements in the top and bottom margins and no margin at right (Nos. 54b and 56d). These were replaced in 1937 by editions showing blank margins on all four sides (Nos. 56e and 75ba). Following a period when the booklet panes were without margins a further 3s. booklet was issued in 1948 which had four margins on the panes and postal slogans at top and bottom (Nos. 56h, 87b and 114a).

24

JIPEX 1936

(24a)

"Cleft skull" flaw (R. 14/2)

(Des J. Booysen)

1935 (1 May). *Silver Jubilee. Inscr bilingually.* W **9**. P 15×14.

65	**24**	½d. black and blue-green	2·75	12·00	10
		a. "Cleft skull" flaw	8·50	25·00	
66		1d. black and carmine	2·75	6·00	10
		a. "Cleft skull" flaw	8·50	18·00	
67		3d. blue	15·00	55·00	2·25
		a. "Cleft skull" flaw	48·00	£120	
68		6d. green and orange	30·00	75·00	3·25
		a. "Cleft skull" flaw	75·00	£170	
65/8 *Set of* 4			45·00	£130	5·00

In stamps with English at top the ½d., 3d. and 6d. have "SILWER JUBILEUM" to left of portrait, and "POSTAGE REVENUE" or "POSTAGE" (3d. and 6d.) in left value tablet. In the 1d., "SILVER JUBILEE" is to the left of portrait. In alternate stamps the positions of English and Afrikaans inscriptions are reversed.

1936 (2 Nov). *Johannesburg International Philatelic Exhibition. Optd with T* **24a**. W **9** (inverted).

	Un sheet	*Us sheet*
MS69 **6** ½d. grey and green (No. 54)	3·50	10·00
MS70 **7** 1d. grey and carmine (No. 56)	2·75	7·00

Issued each in miniature sheet of six stamps with marginal advertisements. Ten different arrangements of advertisements exist on the ½d. sheets, 21 different on the 1d.

25

"Mouse" flaw (R. 4/1)

(Des J. Prentice)

1937 (12 May). *Coronation.* W **9** (sideways*). P 14.

			Un pair	*Used pair*	*Used single*
71	**25**	½d. grey-black and blue-green	80	1·25	10
		w. Wmk horns pointing to left	80	1·25	10
72		1d. grey-black and carmine	80	1·00	10
		w. Wmk horns pointing to left	80	1·00	10
73		1½d. orange and greenish blue	80	80	10
		a. "Mouse" flaw	7·50		
		w. Wmk horns pointing to left	80	80	10
74		3d. ultramarine	1·50	3·00	10
		w. Wmk horns pointing to left	1·50	3·00	10
75		1s. red-brown and turquoise-blue	2·75	5·00	15
		a. Hyphen on Afrikaans stamp omitted (R. 2/13)	60·00		
		bw. Wmk horns pointing to left	2·75	5·00	15
71/5 *Set of* 5			6·00	10·00	40

*The normal sideways watermark shows the horns of the springbok pointing to the right, *as seen from the back of the stamp*.

No. 75a shows the hyphen completely omitted and the top of the "K" damaged. A less distinct flaw, on which part of the hyphen is still visible and with no damage to the "K", occurs on R. 4/17.

25a

"Tick" flaw on ear and spot on nose (multipositive flaw (occurring in 1947) (R. 3/4 or 3/1 on some ptgs of No. 114)

1937–40. W **9**. P 15×14.

75*c*	**25a**	½d. grey and green	10·00	2·25	10
		ca. Booklet pane of 6 (with blank margins) (1937)	55·00		
		cd. Grey and blue green (1940)	7·50	1·25	10
		ce. "Tick" flaw and spot on nose	60·00		

The lines of shading in T **25a** are all horizontal and thicker than in T **6**. In Nos. 75*c* and 75*cd* the design is composed of solid lines. For stamps with designs composed of dotted lines, see No. 114. Later printings of No. 75*cd* have a smaller design.

26 Voortrekker Ploughing

27 Wagon crossing Drakensberg

28 Signing of Dingaan–Retief Treaty

29 Voortrekker Monument

(Des W. Coetzer and J. Prentice)

1938 (14 Dec). *Voortrekker Centenary Memorial Fund.* W **9**. P 14 (Nos. 76/7) or 15×14 (others).

76	**26**	½d. +½d.blue and green..	14·00	4·75	30
77	**27**	1d. +1d.blue and carmine	17·00	5·50	40
78	**28**	1½d. +1½d. chocolate and blue-green	21·00	9·00	80
79	**29**	3d. +3d.bright blue	23·00	9·00	1·00
76/9 *Set of* 4			65·00	25·00	2·25

30 Wagon Wheel

31 Voortrekker Family

Three bolts in wheel rim (R. 15/5)

(Des W. Coetzer and J. Prentice)

1938 (14 Dec). *Voortrekker Commemoration.* W **9**. P 15×14.

80	**30**	1d. blue and carmine	7·00	3·50	30
		a. Three bolts in wheel rim	40·00	27·00	
81	**31**	1½d. greenish blue and brown	9·00	3·50	30

32 Old Vicarage, Paarl, now a museum

33 Symbol of the Reformation

34 Huguenot Dwelling, Drakenstein Mountain Valley

(Des J. Prentice)

1939 (17 July). *250th Anniv of Huguenot Landing in South Africa and Huguenot Commemoration Fund.* W **9**. P 14 (Nos. 82/3) or 15×14 (No. 84).

82	**32**	½d. +½d.brown and green	6·00	6·50	30
83	**33**	1d. +1d. green and carmine	13·00	7·00	30
84	**34**	1½d. +1½d. blue-green and purple	28·00	14·00	1·00
82/4 *Set of* 3			42·00	25·00	1·40

34a Gold Mine

1941 (Aug)–**48**. W **9** (sideways). P 14×15.

87	**34a**	1½d. blue-green and yellow-buff (*shades*)	3·00	1·50	10
		a. Yellow-buff (centre) omitted	£3750	£2000	
		b. Booklet pane of 6 (with postal slogans on margins) (1948)	8·00		

35 Infantry

36 Nurse and Ambulance

37 Airman

38 Sailor, Destroyer and Lifebelts

39 Women's Auxiliary Services

40 Artillery

41 Electric Welding

42 Tank Corps

42a Signaller

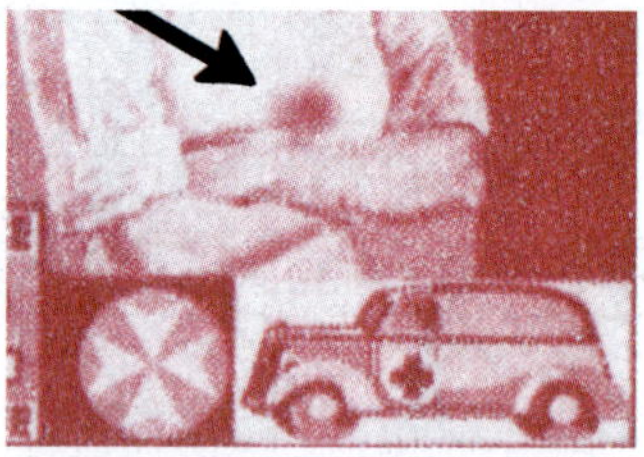
"Stain" on uniform (R. 14/11)

"Cigarette" flaw (R. 18/2)

1941–46. *War Effort.* W **9** (sideways on 2d., 4d., 6d.). P 14 (2d., 4d., 6d.) or 15×14 (others).

(a) Inscr alternately.

88	**35**	½d. green (19.11.41)	1·50	3·25	10
		a. Blue-green (7.42)	3·75	3·50	10
89	**36**	1d. carmine (3.10.41)	2·00	3·25	10
		a. "Stain" on uniform flaw	27·00		
90	**37**	1½d. myrtle-green (12.1.42)	1·50	3·00	10
91	**39**	3d. blue (1.8.41)	23·00	40·00	70
		a. "Cigarette" flaw	90·00		
92	**40**	4d. orange-brown (20.8.41)	22·00	25·00	15
		a. Red-brown (6.42)	35·00	38·00	1·25
93	**41**	6d. red-orange (3.9.41)	12·00	14·00	15
94	**42a**	1s.3d. olive-brown (2.1.43)	13·00	11·00	20
		a. Blackish brown (5.46)	5·00	8·00	20

(b) Inscr bilingually.

				Un single	*Us single*
95	**38**	2d. violet (15.9.41)		1·00	75
96	**42**	1s. brown (27.10.41)		3·75	1·00
88/96 *Set of 7 pairs and 2 singles*				65·00	90·00

43 Infantry

44 Nurse

45 Airman

46 Sailor

47 Women's Auxiliary Services

48 Electric Welding

49 Heavy Gun in Concrete Turret

50 Tank Corps

Unit (*pair*)

Unit (*triplet*)

Ear Flap flaw (Cyl 43 R. 13/3)

Apostrophe flaw (Cyl 6931 R. 19/1) (later corrected)

Line on Cap (Cyl 39 R. 12/11)

"Bursting Shell" (Cyl 46 R. 11/20)

Smoking "L" (Cyl 46 R. 8/2)

1942–44. *War Effort. Reduced sizes.* In pairs perf 14 (P) or strips of three, perf 15×14 (T), subdivided by roulette 6½. W **9** (sideways* on 3d., 4d. and 1s.).

(a) Inscr alternately.

			Un unit	*Us unit*	*Us single*
97	**43**	½d. blue-green (T) (10.42)	2·00	1·50	10
		a. Green (3.43)	3·00	2·25	10
		b. Greenish blue (7.44)	2·00	1·75	10
		c. Roulette omitted	£900	£650	
98	**44**	1d. carmine-red (T) (5.1.43)	1·50	1·50	10
		a. Bright carmine (3.44)	1·00	1·25	10
		b. Both roulettes omitted	£700	£700	
		ba. Left-hand roulette omitted	£900		
99	**45**	1½d. red-brown (P) (9.42)	65	2·25	10
		a. Roulette 13 (8.42)	1·50	4·25	15
		b. Roulette omitted	£300	£325	
		c. Ear flap flaw	15·00		
100	**46**	2d. violet (P) (2.43)	90	2·00	10
		a. Reddish violet (6.43)	1·50	1·00	10
		b. Roulette omitted	£800	£650	
		c. Apostrophe flaw	50·00		
		d. Line on cap	50·00		
101	**47**	3d. blue (T) (10.42)	7·00	18·00	10
102	**48**	6d. red-orange (P) (10.42)	2·00	2·00	10

(b) Inscr bilingually.

103	**49**	4d. slate-green (T) (10.42)	18·00	11·00	10
104	**50**	1s. brown (P) (11.42)	15·00	4·00	10
		a. "Bursting shell"	75·00		
		b. Smoking "L"	75·00		
97/104 *Set of* 8			40·00	38·00	65

*The sideways watermark shows springbok horns pointing to left on the 3d. and 1s., and to right on the 4d., *all as seen from the back of the stamp*.

52

53

1943. *Coil stamps. Redrawn. In single colours with plain background.* W **9**. P 15×14.

			Un pair	*Used pair*	*Used single*
105	**52**	½d. blue-green (18.2.43)	3·00	5·00	20
106	**53**	1d. carmine (9.43)	3·50	4·00	15

Quoted prices are for *vertical* pairs.

54 Union Buildings, Pretoria

1945–47. *Redrawn.* W **9**. P 14.

107	**54**	2d. slate and deep reddish violet (3.45)	16·00	2·50	10
		a. *Slate and deep lilac* (10.46)	16·00	5·00	10
		b. *Slate and bright violet* (1947)	4·00	10·00	15

In Nos. 107 to 107*b* the Union Buildings are shown at a different angle from Nos. 58 and 58*a*. Only the centre is screened i.e., composed of very small square dots of colour arranged in straight diagonal lines. For whole design screened and colours changed, see No. 116. No. 107*a/b* also show "2" of "2d." clear of white circle at top.

55 "Victory"

56 "Peace"

57 "Hope"

1945 (3 Dec). *Victory.* W **9**. P 14.

108	**55**	1d. brown and carmine	20	1·25	10
109	**56**	2d. slate-blue and violet	20	1·25	10
110	**57**	3d. deep blue and blue	20	1·50	10
108/10 *Set of* 3			55	3·50	25

58 King George VI

59 King George VI and Queen Elizabeth

60 Queen Elizabeth II as Princess, and Princess Margaret

"Bird" on "2" (Cyl 6912 R. 10/6)

"Black-eyed Princess" (R. 19/2)

(Des J. Prentice)

1947 (17 Feb). *Royal Visit.* W **9**. P 15×14.

111	**58**	1d. black and carmine	10	35	10
112	**59**	2d. violet	15	60	10
		a. "Bird" on "2" flaw	4·50	7·00	
113	**60**	3d. blue	15	60	10
		a. "Black-eyed Princess"	6·00	9·50	
111/13 *Set of* 3			35	1·40	20

"Flying saucer" flaw (Cyl 17 R. 17/2)

I

II 5s.

1947–54. *"SUID-AFRIKA" hyphenated on Afrikaans stamps. Printed from new cylinders with design in screened rotogravure.* W **9**. P 15×14 (½d., 1d. and 6d.) or 14 (others).

114	**25**	½d. grey and green (frame only screened) (1947)	2·00	4·00	10
		a. Booklet pane of 6 (with postal slogans on margins) (1948)	3·50		
		b. "Tick" flaw and spot on nose	38·00		
		c. Entire design screened (2.49)	2·00	4·00	10
		ca. Booklet pane of 6 (with margin at right) (1951)	3·75		
		cb. "Tick" flaw and spot on nose	38·00		
115	**7**	1d. grey and carmine (1.9.50)	2·25	4·00	10
		a. Booklet pane of 6 (with margin at right) (1951)	4·25		
116	**54**	2d. slate-blue and purple (3.50)	4·00	11·00	20
117	**22a**	3d. dull blue (4.49)	3·00	6·00	10
117*a*		3d. blue (3.51)	3·50	5·00	10
		ab. "Flying saucer" flaw	60·00	55·00	
118	**12a**	4d. brown (22.8.52)	4·50	11·00	20
119	**8**	6d. green and red-orange (III) (1.50)	3·75	1·50	10
		a. *Green and brown-orange* (III) (1951)	3·25	1·00	10
120	**13**	1s. brown and chalky blue (1.50)	10·00	10·00	10
		a. *Blackish brown and ultramarine* (4.52)	18·00	15·00	15
121	**14**	2s.6d. green and brown (8.49)	10·00	29·00	1·00
122	**15**	5s. black and pale blue-green (I) (9.49)	45·00	75·00	2·00
122*a*		5s. black and deep yellow-green (II) (1.54)	50·00	95·00	4·00
114/22 *Set of* 9			75·00	£130	3·25

In screened rotogravure the design is composed of very small squares of colour arranged in straight diagonal lines.

½d. Size 17¾×21¾ mm. Early printings have only the frame screened.

For the final printing of 114c, issued December 1951, the "Tick" flaw was removed, leaving a white "tick", but the spot on nose remained on R. 2/4.

1d. Size 18×22 mm. For smaller, redrawn design, see No. 135.

2d. For earlier issue with centre only screened, and in different colours, see Nos. 107/*a*.

3d. No. 117. Whole stamp screened with irregular grain. Scrolls above "3d." solid and toneless. Printed from two cylinders.

No. 117*a*. Whole stamp diagonally screened. Printed from one cylinder. Clouds more pronounced. Late printings were often in deep shades.

4d. Two groups of white leaves below name tablet and a clear white line down left and right sides of stamp.

61 Gold Mine

62 King George VI and Queen Elizabeth

1948 (1 Apr). Unit of four, perf 14, sub-divided by roulette 6½. W **9** (sideways).

			Un unit of 4	*Us unit*	*Used single*
124	**61**	1½d. blue-green and yellow-buff	3·25	5·00	10

(Des J. Booysen and J. Prentice)

1948 (26 Apr). *Silver Wedding.* W **9**. P 14.

			Un pair	*Used pair*	*Used single*
125	**62**	3d. blue and silver	50	1·25	10

(Typo Government Printer, Pretoria)

1948 (July). W **9**. P 14½×14.

126	**6**	½d. pale grey and blue-green	1·75	10·00	75

This was an economy printing made from the old plates of the 1926 issue for the purpose of using up a stock of cut paper. For the original printing in black and green, see No. 30.

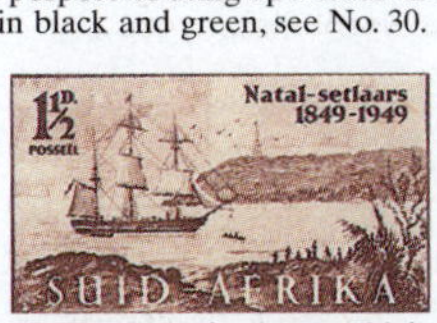
63 *Wanderer* (emigrant ship) entering Durban

Extended rigging on mainmast (R. 14/2)

"Pennant" flaw (R. 17/5)

(Des J. Prentice)

1949 (2 May). *Centenary of Arrival of British Settlers in Natal.* W **9**. P 15×14.

127	**63**	1½d. claret	80	80	10
		a. Extended rigging	11·00	11·00	
		b. "Pennant" flaw	11·00	11·00	

64 Hermes

Serif on "C" (R. 1/1)

"Lake" in East Africa (R. 2/19)

(Des J. Booysen and J. Prentice)

1949 (1 Oct). *75th Anniv of Universal Postal Union. As T* **64** *inscr* "UNIVERSAL POSTAL UNION" *and* "WERELDPOSUNIE" *alternately.* W **9** (sideways). P 14×15.

128	**64**	½d. blue-green	50	1·00	10
129		1½d. brown-red	50	1·00	10
130		3d. bright blue	60	1·00	10
		a. Serif on "C"	40·00		
		b. "Lake" in East Africa	40·00		
128/30 *Set of* 3			1·40	2·75	25

65 Wagons approaching Bingham's Berg

67 Bible, candle and Voortrekkers

66 Voortrekker Monument, Pretoria

(Des W. Coetzer and J. Prentice)

1949 (1 Dec). *Inauguration of Voortrekker Monument, Pretoria. T* **65** *and similar horiz designs.* W **9**. P 15×14.

		Un single	*Us single*
131	1d. magenta	10	10
132	1½d. blue-green	10	10
133	3d. blue	15	15
131/3 *Set of* 3		30	30

Designs:—1½d. Voortrekker Monument, Pretoria; 3d. Bible, candle and Voortrekkers.

68 Union Buildings, Pretoria

1950 (Apr)–**51**. W **9** (sideways). P 14×15.

			Un pair	*Used pair*	*Used single*
134	**68**	2d. blue and violet	40	1·00	10
		a. Booklet pane of 6 (with margin at right) (1951)	4·00		

1951 (22 Feb). *As No. 115, but redrawn with the horizon clearly defined. Size reduced to 17¼×21¼ mm.*

135	**7**	1d. grey and carmine	1·40	2·50	10

69 Seal and monogram

70 "Maria de la Quellerie" (D. Craey)

(Des Miss R. Reeves and J. Prentice (1d., 4½d.), Mrs. T. Campbell and J. Prentice (others))

1952 (14 Mar). *Tercentenary of Landing of Van Riebeeck. T* **69/70** *and similar designs.* W **9** (sideways on 1d. and 4½d.) P 14×15 (1d. and 4½d.) or 14×15 (others).

136	½d. brown-purple and olive-grey	10	10
137	1d. deep blue-green	10	10
138	2d. deep violet	50	10
139	4½d. blue	10	10
140	1s. brown	60	10
136/40 *Set of 5*		1·25	45

Designs: *Horiz*—2d. Arrival of Van Riebeeck's ships; 1s. "Landing at the Cape" (C. Davidson Bell). *Vert*—4½d. "Jan van Riebeeck" (D. Craey).

SATISE (74) SADIPU (75)

76 Queen Elizabeth II

1952 (26 Mar). *South African Tercentenary International Stamp Exhibition, Cape Town. No. 137 optd with T* **74** *and No. 138 with T* **75**.

141	1d. deep blue-green	20	1·75
142	2d. deep violet	50	1·25

(Des H. Kumst)

1953 (3 June). *Coronation.* W **9** (sideways). P 14×15.

143	**76**	2d. deep violet-blue	30	10
		a. *Ultramarine*	30	10

77 1d. "Cape Triangular" Stamp

(Des H. Kumst)

1953 (1 Sept). *Centenary of First Cape of Good Hope Stamp. T* **77** *and similar horiz design.* W **9**. P 15×14.

144	1d. sepia and vermilion	10	10
145	4d. deep blue and light blue	50	20

Design:—4d. Four pence "Cape Triangular" stamp.

79 Merino Ram

80 Springbok

81 Aloes

(Des A. Hendriksz and J. Prentice (4½d.))

1953 (1 Oct). W **9**. P 14.

146	**79**	4½s. slate-purple and yellow	20	10
147	**80**	1s.3d. chocolate	1·25	10
148	**81**	1s.6d. vermilion and deep blue-green	60	55
146/8 *Set of 3*			1·75	65

82 Arms of Orange Free State and Scroll

(Des H. Kumst)

1954 (23 Feb). *Centenary of Orange Free State.* W **9**. P 15×14.

149	**82**	2d. sepia and pale vermilion	10	10
150		4½d. purple and slate	20	50

83 Warthog

92 Springbok

93 Gemsbok

(Des H. Kumst)

1954 (14 Oct). *T* **83**, **92/3** *and similar designs.* W **9** (sideways on large vert designs). P 15×14 (½d. to 2d.), 14 (others).

151	½d. deep blue-green	10	10
152	1d. brown-lake	10	10
153	1½d. sepia	10	10
154	2d. plum	10	10
155	3d. chocolate and turquoise-blue	1·00	10
156	4d. indigo and emerald	1·00	20
157	4½d. blue-black and grey-blue	60	1·00
158	6d. sepia and orange	50	10
159	1s. deep brown and pale chocolate	1·25	10
160	1s.3d. brown and bluish green	2·75	10
161	1s.6d. brown and rose	1·75	60
162	2s.6d. brown-black and apple-green	3·50	20
163	5s. black-brown and yellow-orange	8·00	1·60
164	10s. black and cobalt	13·00	4·50
151/64 Set of 14		30·00	7·50

Designs: *Vert* (*as T* **83**)—1d. Black Wildebeest; 1½d. Leopard; 2d. Mountain Zebra. (*As T* **93**)—3d. White Rhinoceros; 4d. African Elephant; 4½d. Hippopotamus; 1s. Greater Kudu; 2s.6d. Nyala; 5s. Giraffe; 10s. Sable Antelope. *Horiz* (*as T* **92**)—6d. Lion.

No. 152 exists in coils.

See also Nos. 170/7 and 185/97.

97 President Kruger

98 President M. Pretorius

(Des H. Kumst)

1955 (21 Oct). *Centenary of Pretoria.* W **9** (sideways). P 14×15.

165	**97**	3d. slate-green	10	10
166	**98**	6d. maroon	10	30

99 A. Pretorius, Church of the Vow and Flag

100 Settlers' Block-wagon and House

(Des H. Kumst)

1955 (1 Dec). *Voortrekker Covenant Celebrations, Pietermaritzburg.* W **9**. P 14.

				Un pair	*Us pair*	*Us single*
167	**99**	2d. blue and magenta		45	3·25	10

(Des H. Kumst)

1958 (1 July). *Centenary of Arrival of German Settlers in South Africa.* W **9**. P 14.

168	**100**	2d. chocolate and pale purple	10	10

101 Arms of the Academy

(Des H. Kumst)

1959 (1 May). *50th Anniv of the South African Academy of Science and Art, Pretoria.* W **9**. P 15×14.

169	**101**	3d. deep blue and turquoise-blue	10	10
		a. Deep blue printing omitted	£3500	

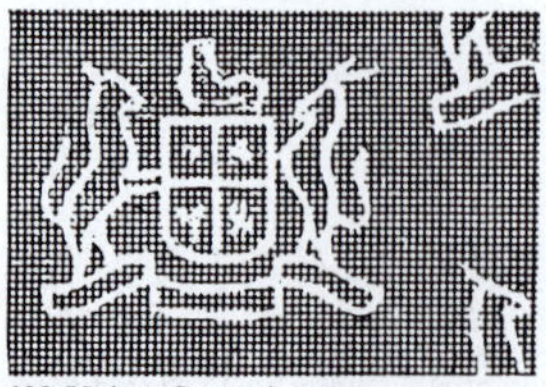

102 Union Coat of Arms

I II

1959–60. *As Nos. 151/2, 155/6, 158/9 and 162/3, but W* **102** *(sideways on Nos. 172/3 and 175/7).*

170	½d. deep greenish blue (12.60)	15	4·50
171	1d. brown-lake (I) (11.59)	10	10
	a. Redrawn. Type II (10.60)	20	10
172	3d. chocolate and turquoise-blue (9.59)	15	10
173	4d. indigo and emerald (1.60)	50	20
174	6d. sepia and orange (2.60)	70	1·50
175	1s. deep brown and pale chocolate (11.59)	6·00	65
176	2s.6d. brown-black and apple-green (12.59)	2·75	4·00
177	5s. black-brown and yellow-orange (10.60)	8·00	30·00
170/7 *Set of 8*		17·00	35·00

Nos. 171/a. In Type II "1d. Posgeld Postage" is more to the left in relation to "South Africa", with "1" almost central over "S" instead of to right as in Type I.

No. 171 exists in coils.

103 Globe and Antarctic Scene

(Des H. Kumst)

1959 (16 Nov). *South African National Antarctic Expedition.* W **102**. P 14×15.

178	**103**	3d. blue-green and orange	20	10

104 Union Flag

106 "Wheel of Progress"

(Des V. Ivanoff and H. Kumst (1s.), H. Kumst (others))

1960 (2 May). *50th Anniv of Union of South Africa. T* **104**, **106** *and similar designs.* W **102** (sideways on 4d. and 6d.). P 14×15 (4d., 6d.) or 15×14 (others).

179	4d. orange-red and blue	30	10
180	6d. red, brown and light green	30	10
181	1s. deep blue and light yellow	30	10
182	1s. 6d. black and light blue	70	2·25
179/82 *Set of 4*		1·40	2·25

Designs: *Vert*—6d. Union Arms. *Horiz*—1s.6d. Union Festival emblem.

See also No. 190, 192/3.

108 Steam Locomotives *Natal* (1860) and Class 25 (1950s)

(Des V. Ivanoff)

1960 (2 May). *Centenary of South African Railways.* W **102**. P 15×14.

183	**108**	1s.3d. deep blue	1·10	30

109 Prime Ministers Botha, Smuts, Hertzog, Malan, Strijdom and Verwoerd

1960 (31 May). *Union Day.* W **102**. P 15×14.

184	**109**	3d. brown and pale brown	15	10
		a. Pale brown omitted*	£5000	

*This is due to a rectangular piece of paper adhering to the background cylinder, resulting in R.2/1 missing the colour completely and six adjoining stamps having it partially omitted. The item in block of eight is probably unique.

(New Currency. 100 cents= 1 rand)

1961 (14 Feb). *As previous issues but with values in cents and rand.* W **102** (sideways on 3½ c., 7½ c., 20c., 50c., 1r.). P 15×14 (½ c., to 2½ c., 10c.), 14×15 (3½ c., 7½ c.) or 14 (others).

185	½c. deep bluish green (as 151)	10	10
186	1c. brown-lake (as 152)	10	10
187	1½c. sepia (as 153)	10	10
188	2c. plum (as 154)	10	1·00
189	2½c. brown (as 184)	20	10
190	3½c. orange-red and blue (as 179)	15	2·25
191	5c. sepia and orange (as 158)	20	10
192	7½c. red, brown and light green (as 180)	20	2·75
193	10c. deep blue and light yellow (as 181)	40	60
194	12½c. brown and bluish green (as 160)	1·00	1·25
195	20c. brown and rose (as 161)	2·25	2·75
196	50c. black-brown and orange-yellow (as 163)	4·50	10·00
197	1r. black and cobalt (as 164)	14·00	24·00
185/97 *Set of 13*		21·00	40·00

X. REPUBLIC OF SOUTH AFRICA

OUTSIDE THE COMMONWEALTH

110 African Pygmy Kingfisher

111 Kafferboom Flower

112 Afrikander Bull

113 Pouring Gold

114 Groot Constantia

115 Burchell's Gonolek

116 Baobab Tree

117 Maize

118 Cape Town Castle Entrance

119 Protea

120 Secretary Bird

121 Cape Town Harbour

122 Strelitzia

Two types of ½c.:

I

II

Type I from sheets. Spurs of branch indistinct.
Type II from coils. Spurs strengthened.

Three types of 1c.:

I

II

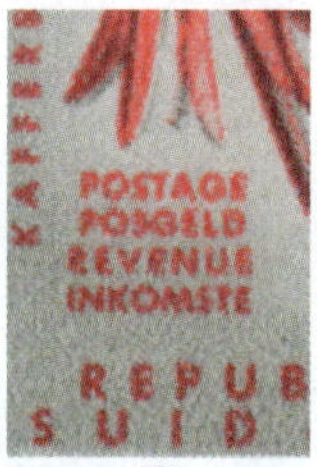

III

Type I. Lowest point of flower between "OS" of "POSTAGE". Right-hand petal over "E".

Type II. Flower has moved fractionally to the right so that lowest point is over "S" of "POSTAGE". Right-hand petal over "E".

Type III. Lowest point directly over "O". Right-hand petal over "G".

Two types of 2½c.

In Type I the lines of the building are quite faint. In Type II all lines of the building have been strengthened by re-engraving.

(Des Mrs. T. Campbell (½ c., 3c., 1r.); Miss N. Desmond (1c.); De La Rue (2½ c., 5c., 12½ c.); H. L. Prager (50c.); Govt. Ptg Dept artist (others))

1961 (31 May)–**63**. *Unsurfaced paper.* W **102** (sideways* on ½ c., 1½ c., 2½ c., 5c. to 20c.). P 14×15 (½ c., 1½ c.), 15×14 (1c.). or 14 (others).

198	**110**	½c. bright blue, carmine and brown (I)	10	10
		a. Perf 14 (3.63)	10	15
		b. Type II (coils) (18.5.63)	80	1·60
199	**111**	1c. red and olive-grey (I)	10	10
		a. Type II (1.62)	10	10
		b. Type III (coils) (5.63)	1·25	2·00
200	**112**	1½c. brown-lake and light purple	10	10
201	**113**	2c. ultramarine and yellow	2·00	10
202	**114**	2½c. violet and green (I)	15	10
		aw. Wmk top of arms to right	30	10
		b. Type II. *Dp violet & green* (9.61)	20	10
203	**115**	3c. red and deep blue	80	20
204	**116**	5c. yellow and greenish blue	30	10
205	**117**	7½c. yellow-brown and light green	60	10
206	**118**	10c. sepia and green	75	10
207	**119**	12½c. red, yellow and black-green	2·00	30
		a. Yellow omitted	£650	
		b. Red omitted	£750	
208	**120**	20c. turquoise-blue, carmine and brown orange	3·00	30
209	**121**	50c. black and bright blue	18·00	2·25
210	**122**	1r. orange, olive-green and light blue	10·00	2·25
198/210 *Set of* 13			32·00	4·50

*The normal sideways watermark shows the top of the arms to left, *as seen from the back of the stamp*.

1961–74 Definitives

Key to designs, perfs, watermarks, papers and phosphors

Value		*Type*	*Perf*	*W* **102** *Ordinary*	*No wmk Ordinary*	*W* **127** *Chalky*
½c.	**110**	(I)	14×15	198	—	—
		(I)	14	198a	—	—
		(II)	14×15	198b	—	—
1c.	**111**	(I)	15×14	199	211	—
		(II)		199a	211a	227
		(III)		199b	—	—
1½c.	**112**		14×15	200	—	228
2c.	**113**		14	201	212	229
2½c.	**114**	(I)	14	202	—	—
		(II)		202a	213/a	230/a
3c.	**115**		14	203	214	—
5c.	**116**		14	204	215	231
7½c.	**117**		14	205	216	232
10c.	**118**		14	206	217/b	233/a
12½c.	**119**		14	207	—	—
20c.	**120**		14	208	218	234/a
50c.	**121**		14	209	219	235
1r.	**122**		14	210	—	236

Redrawn Designs

Value	*Type*		*W* **127** *Upright or Tete-beche. Plain or phos*	*W* **127** *Tete-beche. Phos frame*	*No wmk. Phosphorised Glossy*	*No wmk. Phosphorised Chalky*
½c.	**130a**	14	238	—	—	—
		14×15	238b	—	—	—
		14	238c/d	—	—	—
1c.	**131**	15×14	239	—	—	—
		13½×14	239a	—	—	—
1½c.	**132**	14×15	240/b	284	—	—
		14×13½	240c	—	—	—
2c.	**133**	14	241/a	285/a	315a	—
		12½	—	—	315	315b
2½c.	**134**	14	242/a	286/a	—	—
3c.	**135**	14	243/a	287	—	—
		12½	—	—	316	316a
4c.	**134**	14	243b	288	—	—
5c.	**136**	14	244/a	289	318a	—
		12½	—	—	318	318b
6c.	**137**	14	—	290	—	—
		12½	—	—	—	319
7½c.	**137**	14	245	291	—	—
9c.	**139**	14	245a	292	—	—
		12½	—	—	320/a	—
10c.	**138**	14	246/a	293	321a	—
		12½	—	—	321	321b
12½c.	**139**	14	247/a	294	—	—
15c.	**140**	14	248	295	—	—
20c.	**141**	14	249/a	296/a	—	—
		12½	—	—	323	323a
50c.	**142**	14	250	—	—	—
		12½	—	—	324	324a
1r.	**143**	14	251	—	—	—
		12½	—	—	325	—

New Designs

			W **127** *Upright or Tete-beche. Plain or phos*	*W* **127** *Tete-beche. Phos frame*	*No wmk. Phosphorised Glossy*	*No wmk. Phosphorised Chalky*
½c.	**168**	14×13½	276	282	—	—
		14×14½	276a	—	313	—
		14×15	—	282a	—	—
1c.	**169**	13½×14	277	283	—	—
		14	—	—	314	—
4c.	**182**	14	310/a	—	—	—
		12½	—	—	317/b	317c
15c.	**182a**	14	311	—	—	—
		12½	—	—	—	322

1961 (1 Aug)–**63**. *As Nos. 199, 201/6 and 208/9 but without wmk.*

211	**111**	1c. red and olive-grey (I)	20	30
		a. Type II (9.62)	70	55
212	**113**	2c. ultramarine and yellow (8.63)	8·00	1·00
213	**114**	2½c. deep violet and green (II)	30	10
		a. *Violet and green* (12.61)	30	10
214	**115**	3c. red and deep blue (10.61)	45	10
		a. Deep blue (face value, etc) omitted	£1200	
215	**116**	5c. yellow and greenish blue (12.61)	50	10
216	**117**	7½c. yellow-brown and light green (3.62)	80	30
217	**118**	10c. sepia and green (11.61)	1·00	40
		a. *Sepia and emerald*	45·00	17·00
		b. *Sepia-brown and light green* (7.63)	2·25	55
218	**120**	20c. turquoise-blue carmine and brown-orange (4.63)	11·00	4·25
219	**121**	50c. black and bright blue (8.62)	11·00	4·25
211/19 *Set of* 9			30·00	9·00

123 Blériot XI Monoplane and Boeing 707 Airliner over Table Mountain

124 Folk-dancers

1961 (1 Dec). *50th Anniv of First South African Aerial Post.* W **102** (sideways). P 14×15.

220	**123**	3c. blue and red	50	10

(Des K. Esterhuysen)

1962 (1 Mar). *50th Anniv of Volkspele (folk-dancing) in South Africa.* W **102** (sideways). P 14×15.

221	**124**	2½c. orange-red and brown	15	10

125 *The Chapman* (emigrant ship)

1962 (20 Aug). *Unveiling of Precinct Stone, British Settlers Monument Grahamstown.* W **102**. P 15×14.

222	**125**	2½c. turquoise-green and purple	50	10
223		12½c. blue and deep chocolate	1·75	1·25

126 Red Disa (orchid), Castle Rock and Gardens

(Des M. F. Stern)

1963 (14 Mar). *50th Anniv of Kirstenbosch Botanic Gardens, Cape Town.* P 13½×14.

224 **126** 2½c. multicoloured 20 10
a. Red (orchid, etc) omitted £1700 £1000

127 (normal version)

128 Centenary Emblem and Nurse

129 Centenary Emblem and Globe

1963 (30 Aug). *Centenary of Red Cross. Chalk-surfaced paper.* Wmk **127** (sideways on 2½c.). P 14×13½ (2½c.) or 15×14 (12½c.)

225 **128** 2½c. red, black and reddish purple 20 10
w. Wmk reversed .... 3·00 1·40
226 **129** 12½c. red and indigo .... 2·25 1·00
a. Red cross omitted £1700 £1300

1963–67. *As 1961–3 but chalk-surfaced paper and W* **127** *(sideways on 1½c., 2½c., 5c., 7½c., 10c., 20c.).* P 15×14 (1c.) 14×15 (1½c.), or 14 (others).

227 **111** 1c. red and olive-grey (II) (9.63). 10 10
w. Wmk reversed 65 65
228 **112** 1½c. brown-lake and light purple (1.67) .... 1·75 2·25
229 **113** 2c. ultramarine and yellow (11.64) 15 20
230 **114** 2½c. violet and green (I) (10.63).... 10 10
a. *Bright reddish violet and emerald (II)* (3.66) 35 20
aw. Wmk inverted .... 2·50 90
231 **116** 5c. yellow and greenish blue (9.66) .... 1·25 30
232 **117** 7½c. yellow-brown and bright green (23.2.66) .... 7·50 6·50
233 **118** 10c. sepia-brown and light emerald (9.64) 40 10
a. *Sepia-brown and green* (1.67). 45 10
234 **120** 20c. turquoise-blue, carmine and brown orange (7.64) .... 1·00 1·00
a. *Deep turquoise-blue, carmine and flesh* (20.7.65) .... 1·75 80
235 **121** 50c. black and ultramarine (4.66).. 30·00 9·50
236 **122** 1r. orange, light green and pale blue (7.64) .... 48·00 45·00
227/36 *Set of* 10 .... 80·00 60·00

In the 2½c. (No. 230a), 5c., 7½c., 10c. (Jan 1967 printing only) and 50c. the watermark is indistinct but they can easily be distinguished from the stamps without watermark by their shades and the chalk-surfaced paper which is appreciably thicker and whiter.

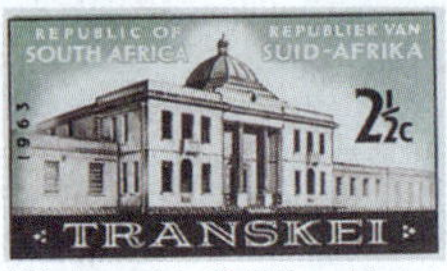

130 Assembly Building, Umtata

1963 (11 Dec). *First Meeting of Transkei Legislative Assembly. Chalk-surfaced paper.* W **127**. P 15×14.

237 **130** 2½c. sepia and light green 10 10
a. Light green omitted £1600

130a African Pygmy Kingfisher

131 Kafferboom Flower

132 Afrikander Bull

133 Pouring Gold

134 Groot Constantia

135 Burchell's Gonolek

136 Baobab Tree

137 Maize

138 Cape Town Castle Entrance

139 Protea

140 Industry

141 Secretary Bird

142 Cape Town Harbour

143 Strelitzia

(15c. des C. E. F. Skotnes)

Redrawn types.

½c. "½C" larger and REPUBLIEK VAN REPUBLIC OF" smaller.

3c. and 12½c. Inscriptions and figures of value larger.

Others. "SOUTH AFRICA" and SUID-AFRIKA larger and bolder. The differences vary in each design but are easy to see by comparing the position of the letters of the country name with "REPUBLIC OF" and "REPUBLIEK VAN".

1964–72. *As 1961–63 but designs redrawn and new values (4c., 9c. and 15c.). Chalk-surfaced paper.* W **127** (sideways on ½, 1½, 2½, 4, 5, 7½, 9, 10, 15 and 20c.). P 14×15 (1½c.), 15×14 (1c.) or 14 (others).

238 **130a** ½c. bright blue, carmine and brown (21.5.64) 10 10
a. Imperf (pair) £300
b. Perf 14×15. *Bright blue, carmine and yellow-brown* (6.7.67) 20 20
c. Perf 14. *Bright blue, lake and yellow-brown* (3.68) 60 70
d. Perf 14. *Bright blue, carmine lake and yellow-brown* (9.68) 30 10
239 **131** 1c. red and olive-grey (9.3.67) .. 10 10
a. Perf 13½×14 (7.68) 30 10
240 **132** 1½c. dull red-brown and light purple (21.9.67) 15 10
a. *Purple-brown and light purple* (1968) 15 10
b. *Bright red-brown and light purple* (5.68) 15 10
c. Perf 14×13½. *Red-brown and light purple* (14.8.69)..... 1·00 1·00
241 **133** 2c. ultramarine and yellow (8.1.68) 20 10
a. Yellow omitted £750
b. *Blue and yellow* (10.71) 60 10
242 **134** 2½c. violet and green (19.4.67).... 20 10
a. *Reddish violet and green* (8.67) 20 10
w. Wmk top of RSA to left...... £250 65·00
243 **135** 3c. red and deep blue (11.64).... 30 10
a. *Brown-red and deep blue* (3.72) .... 1·75 30
243*b* **134** 4c. violet and green (10.71)....... 75 30
244 **136** 5c. orange-yellow and greenish blue (14.2.68) 40 10
a. *Lemon and deep greenish blue* (10.71) .... 8·00 1·00
245 **137** 7½c. yellow-brown and bright green (26.7.67) 60 10
245*a* **139** 9c. red, yellow and slate-green (2.72) .... 7·50 4·00
246 **138** 10c. sepia and green (10.6.68)..... 1·75 30
a. *Brown and pale green* (7.68) 4·25 4·00
247 **139** 12½c. red, yellow and black-green (3.64) .... 1·00 40
a. *Red, pale yellow and blue-green* (2.2.66) .... 2·75 40
248 **140** 15c. black, light olive-yellow and red-orange (1.3.67) 85 25
249 **141** 20c. turquoise-blue, carmine and brown-orange (2.68) .... 6·00 15
a. *Turquoise-blue, carmine and orange-buff* (12.71) .... 5·50 1·25
250 **142** 50c. black and bright blue (17.6.68) .... 1·00 40
251 **143** 1r. orange, light green & lt bl (6.65) .... 1·00 1·00
w. Wmk inverted ....
238/51 *Set of* 16 .... 18·00 5·50

*The normal sideways watermark shows the top of RSA to right *as seen from the back of the stamp.*

WATERMARK. Two forms of the watermark Type **127** exist in the above issue: the normal Type **127** (sometimes indistinct), and a very faint *tête-bêche* watermark, i.e. alternately facing up and down, which was introduced in mid 1967. As it is extremely difficult to distinguish these on single stamps we do not list it. The ½ (both perfs), 1, 2, 2½, 3, 15c. and 1r. are known in both forms, the 1½, 4, 5, 7½, 9, 10, 20 and 50c. only in the *tête-bêche* form and the 12½ c. Type **127** only.

GUM. The 2, 3, 5, 20, 50c. and 1r. exist with PVA gum as well as gum arabic.

PHOSPHORISED PAPER. From October 1971 onwards phosphor bands (see Nos. 282/96) gave way to phosphorised paper which cannot be distinguished from non-phosphor stamps without the aid of a lamp. For this reason we do not distinguish these printings in the above issue, but some are slightly different shades and all have PVA gum. The 4c. and 9c. are on phosphorised paper only and differ from Nos. 288 and 292 by the lack of phosphor bands.

145 "Springbok" Badge of Rugby Board

147 Calvin

1964 (8 May). *75th Anniv of South African Rugby Board. Chalk-surfaced paper. T* **145** *and similar horiz design.* W **127** (sideways on 2½c.). P 14×15 (2½c.) or 15×14 (12½c.)

252 2½c. yellow-brown and deep green........ 15 10
253 12½c. black and light yellow-green .... 3·00 3·75

Design:—12½c. Rugby footballer.

1964 (10 July). *400th Death Anniv of Calvin (Protestant reformer). Chalk-surfaced paper.* W **127** (sideways). P 14×13½.

254 **147** 2½c. cerise, violet and brown 10 10

148 Nurse's Lamp

149 Nurse holding Lamp

I. Screened base to lamp

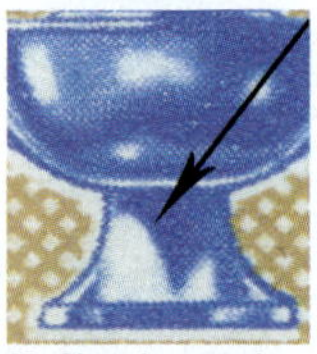

II. Clear base to lamp

1964 (12 Oct). *50th Anniv of South African Nursing Association. Chalk-surfaced paper.* W **127** (sideways on 2½ c.). P 14×15 (2½ c.) or 15×14 (12½c.)

255 **148** 2½c. ultramarine and dull gold (Type I) 10 10
256 2½c. bright blue and yellow-gold (Type II) 30 10
a. *Ultramarine and dull gold* 15 10
257 **149** 12½c. bright blue and gold .... 2·25 1·75
a. Gold omitted £1500
255/7 *Set of* 3 .... 2·25 2·25

150 I.T.U. Emblem and Satellites

1965 (17 May). *I.T.U. Centenary. T* **150** *and similar horiz design. Chalk-surfaced paper.* W **127**. P 15×14.

258 2½c. orange and blue 25 10
259 12½c. brown-purple and green .... 1·25 1·00

Design:—12½ c. I.T.U. emblem and symbols.

152 Pulpit in Groote Kerk, Cape Town

153 Church Emblem

1965 (21 Oct). *Tercentenary of Nederduites Gereformeerde Kerk (Dutch Reformed Church) in South Africa. Chalk-surfaced paper.* W **127** (sideways on 2½ c., inverted on 12½ c.). P 14×15 (2½ c.) or 15×14 (12½ c.).

260 **152** 2½c. brown and light yellow 15 10
261 **153** 12½c. black, light orange and blue... 70 85

154 Diamond

155 Bird in flight

(Des C.E.F. Skotnes)

1966 (31 May). *Fifth Anniv of Republic. T* **154/5** *and similar designs. Chalk-surfaced paper.* W **127** (sideways on 1c., 3c.). P 14×13½ (1c.), 13½×14 (2½c.), 14×15 (3c.) or 15×14 (7½c.).

		Un pair	Us pair	Us single
262	1c. black, bluish green and olive-yellow	45	45	10
263	2½c. blue, deep blue and yellow-green	85	1·25	10
264	3c. red, greenish yellow and red-brown	2·50	2·50	10
265	7½c. blue, ultramarine and yellow	3·25	3·25	10
262/5	*Set of* 4	6·25	6·75	35

Designs: *Vert*—3c. Maize plants. *Horiz*—7½c. Mountain landscape.

Nos. 262/5 exsist on Swiss made paper with *tête bêche* watermark from special printing made for use in presentation albums for delegates to the U.P.U. Congress in Tokyo in 1969 as supplies of the original Harrison paper were by then exhausted (*Set of* 4 *pairs price* £140 *mint*).

158 Verwoerd and Union Buildings, Pretoria

(Des from portrait by Dr. Henkel)

1966 (6 Dec). *Verwoerd Commemoration. T* **158** *and similar designs. Chalk-surfaced paper.* W **127** (sideways on 3c.). P 14×15 (3c.) or 15×14 (others).

266 2½ c. blackish brown and turquoise 10 10
267 3c. blackish brown and yellow-green .. 10 10
a. Blackish brown (portrait) omitted £3500
268 12½ c. blackish brown and greenish blue. 60 60
266/8 *Set of* 3 .... 70 60

Designs: *Vert*—3c. "Dr. H.F. Verwoerd" (I. Henkel). *Horiz*—12½c. Verwoerd and map of South Africa.

161 "Martin Luther" (Cranach the Elder)

162 Wittenberg Church Door

1967 (31 Oct). *450th Anniv of Reformation.* W **127** ((sideways), normal on 2½c., tête-bêche on 12½c.). P 14×15.

269 **161** 2½c. black and rose-red 10 10
270 **162** 12½c. black and yellow-orange .... 1·25 2·00

163 "Profile of Pres. Fouche" (I. Henkel)

164 Portrait of Pres. Fouche

1968 (10 Apr). *Inauguration of President Fouche.* W **127** (sideways). P 14×15.

271 **163** 2½c. chocolate and pale chocolate. 10 10
272 **164** 12½c. deep blue and light blue .... 60 1·00

No. 272 also exists with the watermark *tête-bêche* (*Price un* £1; *used* £1.50).

165 Hertzog in 1902

1968 (21 Sept). *Inauguration of General Hertzog Monument, Bloemfontein. T* **165** *and similar designs.* W **127** (tête-bêche on 2½c., inverted on 3c., sideways on 12½c.). P 14×13½ (12½c.) or 13½×14 (others).

273 2½c. black, brown and olive-yellow 10 10
274 3c. black, red-brown, red-orange and yellow 15 10
275 12½c. red and yellow-orange .... 1·50 1·50
273/5 *Set of* 3 .... 1·50 1·50

Designs: *Horiz*—3c. Hertzog in 1924. *Vert*—12½c. Hertzog Monument.

168 African Pygmy Kingfisher

169 Kafferboom Flower

1969. W **127** (tête-bêche, sideways on ½c.). P 14×13½ (½c.) or 13½×14 (1c.)

276 **168** ½c. new blue, carmine-red and yellow-ochre (1.69) 10 30
a. Coil. Perf 14×14½ (5.69) .... 2·25 3·25
277 **169** 1c. rose-red and olive-brown (1.69) 10 10

See also Nos. 282/3 and 313/14.

170 Springbok and Olympic Torch

171 Professor Barnard and Groote Schuur Hospital

1969 (15 Mar). *South African Games, Bloemfontein.* W **127** (tête-bêche, sideways). P 14×13½.

278 **170** 2½c. black, blue-black, red and sage-green 15 10
279 12½c. black, blue-black, red and cinnamon .... 70 1·50

1969 (7 July). *World's First Heart Transplant and 47th South African Medical Association Congress. T* **171** *and similar horiz design.* W **127** (tête-bêche). P 13½×14 (2½c.) or 15×14 (12½c.).

280 2½c. plum and rose-red 15 10
281 12½c. carmine-red and royal blue .... 1·25 2·00

Design:—12½c. Hands holding heart.

1969–72. *As 1964–72 issue, Nos. 276/7, and new value (6c.), but with phosphor bands printed horizontally and vertically between the stamp designs, over the perforations, producing a frame effect.* W **127** arranged tête-bêche (upright on 1, 2 and 3c., sideways on others). P 14×13½ (½, 1½c.), 13½×14 (1c.), or 14 (others).

282 **168** ½c. new blue, carmine-red and yellow-ochre (1.70) 15 70
a. Coil. Perf 14×15 (2.71) .... 3·25 4·00
w. Wmk reversed 65 85
283 **169** 1c. rose-red and olive-brown (12.69) 15 10
w. Wmk reversed 60 50
284 **132** 1½c. red-brown and light purple (12.69) 20 10
285 **133** 2c. ultramarine and yellow (11.69) 70 10
a. *Deep ultramarine and yellow* (8.70) .... 1·00 50
286 **134** 2½c. violet and green (1.70) 25 10
a. *Purple and green* (24.7.70) .... 1·75 10
w. Wmk reversed .... 20·00 17·00
287 **135** 3c. red and deep blue (30.9.69) ... 1·00 10
288 **134** 4c. violet and green (1.3.71) .... 40 1·00
289 **136** 5c. yellow and greenish blue (17.11.69) 85 10
290 **137** 6c. yellow-brown and bright green (3.5.71) 70 30
291 7½c. yellow-brown and bright green (17.11.69) .... 2·75 30
292 **139** 9c. red, yellow and black-green (17.5.71) .... 1·75 30
293 **138** 10c. brown and pale green (1.70) .. 1·50 10
294 **139** 12½c. red, yellow and black-green (2.5.70) .... 4·00 3·50
295 **140** 15c. black, light olive-yellow and red-orange (1.70) .... 1·50 2·25
296 **141** 20c. turquoise-blue, carmine and brown-orange 18.2.70) .... 8·00 2·25
a. *Turquoise-blue, carmine and orange-buff* (9.72) .... 11·00 1·75
282/96 *Set of* 15 .... 21·00 9·00

No. 286 exists on normal RSA wmk as well as RSA *tête-bêche* wmk. The 1, 2, 2½, 3, 10, 15 and 20c. exist with PVA gum as well as gum arabic, but the 4, 6 and 9c. exist with PVA gum only. Stamps without watermark in these designs were issued between 1972 and 1974.

173 Mail Coach

174 Transvaal Stamp of 1869

1969 (6 Oct). *Centenary of First Stamps of South African Republic (Transvaal). Phosphor bands on all four sides (2½c.).* W **127** (tête-bêche, sideways on 12½c.). P 13½×14 (2½c.) or 14×13½ (12½c.)

297 **173** 2½c. yellow, indigo and yellow-brown 15 10
298 **174** 12½c. emerald, gold and yellow-brown .... 2·75 3·50

PHOSPHOR FRAME. Nos. 299/306 have phosphor applied on all four sides as a frame.

175 "Water 70" Emblem

177 "The Sower"

1970 (14 Feb). *Water 70 Campaign. T* **175** *and similar design.* W **127** (tête-bêche (sideways on 2½c.)). P 14×13½ (2½c.) or 13½×14 (3c.)

299 2½c. green, bright blue and chocolate ... 30 10
300 3c. Prussian blue, royal blue and buff. 30 20

Design: *Horiz*—3c. Symbolic waves.

1970 (24 Aug). *150th Anniv of Bible Society of South Africa. T* **177** *and similar horiz design (gold die-stamped on 12½c.).* W **127** (tête-bêche, sideways on 2½c.). P 14×13½ (2½c.) or 13½×14 (12½c.)

301 2½c. multicoloured 15 10
302 12½c. gold, black and blue .... 1·50 2·00

Design:—12½ c. "Biblia" and open book.

STAMP BOOKLETS

1913. *Black on red cover. With "UNION OF SOUTH AFRICA" at top and "UNIE VAN ZUID AFRIKA" at foot. Stapled.*

SB1 2s.6d. booklet containing twelve ½d. and twenty-four 1d. (Nos. 3/4) in blocks of 6 .... £5500

1913–20. *Black on red cover with "UNION OF SOUTH AFRICA" and "UNIE VAN ZUID AFRIKA" both at top. Stapled.*

SB2 2s.6d. booklet containing twelve ½d. and twenty-four 1d. (Nos. 3/4) in blocks of 6 .... £5500
a. Black on pink cover (1920) £5500

1921. *Black on salmon-pink cover with "UNION OF SOUTH AFRICA" and "UNIE VAN ZUID AFRIKA" either side of arms and telegraph rates beneath. Stapled.*

SB3 3s. booklet containing twelve ½d., 1d. and 1½d. (Nos. 3/5) in blocks of 6 .... £475

1922. *Black on salmon-pink cover as No. SB3 surch. Stapled.*

SB4 3s.6d. on 3s. booklet containing twelve ½d., 1d. and 2d. (Nos. 3/4, 6) in blocks of 6 .... £1000

1926. *Black on salmon-pink cover as No. SB3. Stitched.*

SB5 2s.6d. booklet containing twelve ½d. and twenty-four 1d. (Nos. 30/1) £2000

1927. *Black on salmon-pink cover as No. SB3, but inscr "Union of South Africa" and "Unie van Suidafrika". Stitched.*

SB6 2s.6d. booklet containing twelve ½d. and twenty-four 1d. (Nos. 30e, 31d) £4750

1930. *Black on pink cover as No. SB6, but with advertisement at foot instead of telegraph rates. Stitched.*

SB7 2s.6d. booklet containing twelve ½d. and twenty-four 1d. (Nos. 42/3) in blocks of 6 .... £1800

1931. *Black on pink cover. Smaller inscr and advertisement on front cover. Stitched.*

SB8 3s. booklet containing twelve 1d. (No. 43) in blocks of 6 and twelve 2d. (No. 44) in blocks of 4 .... £1900

1935. *Black on lemon cover. Advertisement on front cover. Stitched.*

SB9 2s.6d. booklet containing two panes of six ½d. (No. 54c) and four panes of six 1d. (No. 56e), all with adverts on margins £250

1937. *Black on lemon cover. Advertisement on front cover. Stitched.*

SB10 2s.6d. booklet containing two panes of six ½d. (No. 75ba) and four panes of six 1d. (No. 56f), all with blank margins £600

1937. *Machine vended booklets. Red cover. Stitched.*

SB11 6d. booklet containing four ½d. and 1d. (Nos. 75c, 56) in pairs .... 7·00

1938. *Machine vended booklets. Blue cover. Stitched.*

SB12 3d. booklet containing ½d. and 1d. (Nos. 75c, 56), each in pair .... 40·00

1938. *Black on buff cover. Union arms at top left with advertisement at foot. Stitched.*

SB13 2s.6d. booklet containing twelve ½d. and twenty-four 1d. (Nos. 75c, 56) in blocks of 6 .... £600

1939. *Black on buff cover. Union arms centred at top with advertisement at foot. Stitched.*

SB14 2s.6d. booklet containing twelve ½d. and twenty-four 1d. (Nos. 75c, 56) in blocks of 6 .... £550

1939–40. *Green on buff cover. Union arms centred at top with large advertisement at bottom left. Stitched.*

SB15 2s.6d. booklet containing twelve ½d. and twenty-four 1d. (Nos. 75c, 56) in blocks of 6 .... £2250
a. Blue on buff cover (1940) £120

1941. *Blue on buff cover as No.* SB15. *Stitched.*

SB17 2s.6d. booklet containing twelve ½d. and 1d. (Nos. 75*c*, 56) in blocks of 6 and 1½d. (No. 57) in block of 4 .... £150

1948. *Black on buff cover. With advertisement. Stitched.*

SB18 3s. booklet containing two panes of six ½d., 1d. and 1½d. (Nos. 114a, 56h, 87b), all with postal slogans on margins, and pane of air mail labels .... 30·00

1951. *Black on buff cover. Stitched.*

SB19 3s.6d. booklet containing two panes of six ½d., 1d. and 2d. (Nos. 114ca, 115a, 134a), each with margins at right .... 13·00

POSTAGE DUE STAMPS

D 1

(A)

(B)

(Typo D.L.R.)

1914–22. *Inscribed bilingually. Lettering as* A. W **4**. P 14.

			Un single	Used single
D1	D **1**	½d. black and green (19.3.15)	2·25	3·75
D2		1d. black and scarlet (19.3.15)	2·25	15
		a. Black ptd double	£1700	
		w. Wmk inverted	90·00	
D3		2d. black and reddish violet (12.12.14)	6·50	50
		a. Black and bright violet (1922)	7·00	60
		w. Wmk inverted	£140	
D4		3d. black and bright blue (2.2.15)	2·25	60
		w. Wmk inverted	45·00	
D5		5d. black and sepia (19.3.15)	4·00	29·00
D6		6d. black and slate (19.3.15)	7·00	30·00
D7		1s. red and black (19.3.15)	60·00	£150
D1/7 *Set of* 7			75·00	£190

There are interesting minor varieties in some of the above values, e.g. ½d. to 3d., thick downstroke to "d"; 1d., short serif to "1"; raised "d"; 2d., forward point of "2" blunted; 3d., raised "d"; very thick "d".

(Litho Govt Printer, Pretoria)

1922. *Lettering as* A. No wmk. *Rouletted.*

D8	D **1**	½d. black and bright green (6.6.22)	1·50	15·00
D9		1d. black and rose-red (3.10.22)	1·00	1·00
D10		1½d. black and yellow-brown (3.6.22)	1·25	1·75
D8/10 *Set of* 3			3·25	16·00

(Litho Govt Printer, Pretoria)

1922–26. *Type* D **1** *redrawn. Lettering as* B. P 14.

D11	½d. black and green (1.8.22)	80	1·75
D12	1d. black and rose (16.5.23)	90	15
D13	1½d. black and yellow-brown (12.1.24)	1·00	1·25
D14	2d. black and pale violet (16.5.23)	1·00	70
	a. Imperf (pair)	£275	£375
	b. Black and deep violet	13·00	1·50
D15	3d. black and blue (3.7.26)	8·00	22·00
D16	6d. black and slate (9.23)	12·00	2·00
D11/16 *Set of* 6		21·00	25·00

The locally printed stamps, perf 14, differ both in border design and in figures of value from the rouletted stamps. All values except the 3d. and 6d. are known with closed "G" in "POSTAGE" usually referred to as the "POSTADE" variety. This was corrected in later printings.

D 2

D 3

D 4

Blunt "2" (R. 3/6, 8/6)

(Typo Pretoria)

1927–28. *Inscribed bilingually.* No wmk. P 13½×14.

D17	D **2**	½d. black and green	1·00	3·25
		a. Blunt "2"	11·00	
D18		1d. black and carmine	1·25	30
D19		2d. black and mauve	1·25	30
		a. Black and purple	20·00	80
D20		3d. black and blue	8·50	24·00
D21		6d. black and slate	21·00	3·50
D17/21 *Set of* 5			30·00	28·00

1932–42. *Type* D **2** *redrawn.* W **9**. P 15×14.

(a) Frame roto, value typo.

D22	½d. black and blue-green (1934)	2·75	1·75
	w. Wmk inverted	2·25	1·75
D23	2d. black and deep purple (10.4.33)	15·00	2·50
	w. Wmk inverted	15·00	2·50

(b) Whole stamp roto.

D25	1d. black and carmine (wmk inverted) (3.34)	2·25	10
D26	2d. black and deep purple (10.39)	30·00	10
	a. Thick (double) "2d." (R. 5/6, R. 18/2)	£350	27·00
	w. Wmk inverted	28·00	50
D27	3d. black and Prussian blue (3.8.32)	25·00	14·00
D28	3d. deep blue and blue (wmk inverted) (1935)	8·00	30
	a. Indigo and milky blue (wmk inverted) (1942)	80·00	3·25
	w. Wmk upright	55·00	3·00
D29	6d. green and brown-ochre (wmk inverted) (7.6.33)	25·00	5·00
	a. Green and bright orange (wmk inverted) (1938)	14·00	3·00
D22/9*a* *Set of* 7		85·00	19·00

In No. D26 the value is screened, whereas in No. D23 the black of the value is solid.

1943–44. *Inscr bilingually. Roto.* W **9**. In units of three, perf 15×14 subdivided by roulette 6½.

			Un unit	Us unit	Us single
D30	D **3**	½d. blue-green (1944)	15·00	50·00	40
D31		1d. carmine	10·00	5·50	10
D32		2d. dull violet	6·50	11·00	15
		a. Bright violet	16·00	50·00	65
D33		3d. indigo (1943)	55·00	80·00	1·25
D30/3 *Set of* 4			75·00	£130	1·90

Split "D" (R. 7/5 on every fourth sheet)

1948–49. *New figure of value and capital "D". Whole stamp roto.* W **9**. P 15×14.

D34	D **4**	½d. black and blue-green	6·00	13·00
D35		1d. black and carmine	16·00	5·50
D36		2d. black and violet (1949)	16·00	9·00
		a. Thick (double) "2D." (R. 15/5-6, R. 16/5-6)	75·00	38·00
D37		3d. deep blue and blue	15·00	17·00
		a. Split "D"	£225	£250
D38		6d. green and bright orange (1949)	25·00	8·00
D34/8 *Set of* 5			70·00	45·00

1950–58. *As Type* D **4**, *but "SUID-AFRIKA" hyphenated. Whole stamp roto.* W **9**. P 15×14.

D39	1d. black and carmine (5.50)	70	30
D40	2d. black and violet (4.51)	50	20
	a. Thick (double) "2D." (R. 15/5-6, R. 16/5-6)	8·00	8·00
	b. Black and reddish violet (12.52)	1·00	75
	ba. Thick (double) "2D."	10·00	10·00
	bb. Black (value) omitted	£3000	
D41	3d. deep blue and blue (5.50)	4·50	2·50
	a. Split "D"	£110	65·00
D42	4d. deep myrtle-green and emerald (2.58)	12·00	15·00
D43	6d. green and bright orange (3.50)	7·00	9·00
D44	1s. black-brown and purple-brown (2.58)	12·00	15·00
D39/44 *Set of* 6		32·00	38·00

No. D40bb occurs in horizontal pair with a normal.

D 5

D 6 Afrikaans at top

D 7 English at top

1961 (14 Feb). *Values in cents as Type* D **5**. *Whole stamp roto.* W **102**. P 15×14.

D45	1c. black and carmine	20	3·75
D46	2c. black and violet	35	3·75
D47	4c. deep myrtle-green and emerald	80	8·50
D48	5c. deep blue and blue	1·75	8·50
D49	6c. green and orange-red	6·50	8·50
D50	10c. sepia and brown-lake	7·00	10·00
D45/50 *Set of* 6		15·00	38·00

1961 (31 May)–**69**. *Roto.* W **102**. P 15×14.

D51	D **6**	1c. black and carmine	40	60
D52	D **7**	1c. black and carmine (6.62)	40	4·50
D53		2c. black and deep reddish violet	40	55
D54	D **6**	4c. deep myrtle-green and light emerald	2·25	2·25
D54*a*	D **7**	4c. deep myrtle-green and light emerald (6.69)	12·00	22·00
D55		5c. deep blue and grey-blue	2·00	4·25
D56		5c. black and grey-blue (6.62)	1·75	7·50
D57	D **6**	6c. deep green and red-orange	8·00	5·50
D58	D **7**	10c. sepia and purple-brown	2·75	1·75
D51/8 *Set of* 9			27·00	45·00

1967 (1 Dec)–**71**. *Roto.* W **127** (tête-bêche). P 15×14.

D59	D **6**	1c. black and carmine	20	55
D60	D **7**	1c. black and carmine	20	30
D61	D **6**	2c. black and deep reddish violet	30	1·50
D62	D **7**	2c. black and deep reddish violet	30	1·50
D62*b*		4c. deep myrtle-green and emerald (6.69)*	30·00	30·00
D62*c*	D **6**	4c. deep myrtle-green and emerald (6.69)*	£300	£300
D63		4c. black and pale green (4.71)	32·00	32·00
D64	D **7**	4c. black and pale green (4.71)	32·00	32·00
D65	D **6**	5c. black and deep blue	50	50
D66	D **7**	5c. black and deep blue	50	50
D67	D **6**	6c. green and orange-red (1968)	3·50	10·00
D68	D **7**	6c. green and orange-red (1968)	3·50	10·00
D69	D **6**	10c. black and purple-brown	1·00	2·75
		a. Black and brown-lake (12.69)	1·00	2·75
D70	D **7**	10c. black and purple-brown	1·00	2·75
		a. Black and brown-lake (12.69)	1·00	2·75
D59/70a *except* D62b/c *Set of* 12			70·00	90·00

Nos. D59/70 were printed in two panes, one with inscriptions as Type D **6** and the other as Type D **7**.

*Nos. D54a, D62b/c and further supplies of D54 were part of a printing released in June 1969. Most sheets were printed on paper with the Arms watermark, but some were printed on BSA paper with the watermark upright and faint. Of these many were spoilt, but a few sheets were issued in Types D **7** and D **6**, the latter being very scarce.

OFFICIAL STAMPS

(O **1**)

(O **2**)

(Approximate measurements of the space between the two lines of overprint are quoted in millimetres, either in the set headings or after individual listings)

1926 (1 Dec). *Optd with Type* O **1** *(reading upwards with stops and 12½ mm between lines of opt).*

(a) On 1913 issue (No. 6).

O1	**3**	2d. purple	21·00		1·75

(b) On 1926 issue (Nos. 30/2).

			Un pair	Us pair	Us single
O2	**6**	½d. black and green	8·00	18·00	1·50
O3	**7**	1d. black and carmine	4·00	8·00	50
O4	**8**	6d. green and orange	£550	75·00	10·00
		w. Wmk inverted	£1200	£400	32·00

The overprint occurs on both the London and Pretoria printings of Nos. 30/2. For the lower two values the overprinted London printings are scarcer than the Pretoria, but for the 6d. the ratio is reversed.

1928–30. *Nos.* 32 *and* 34 *optd as Type* O **1** *(reading upwards without stops).*

O5	**11**	2d. grey and maroon (P 14) (*17½ mm*)	6·00	23·00	2·00
		a. Lines of opt 19 mm apart (1929)	7·00	19·00	1·50
		ab. On No. 34a (P 14×13½) (1930)	50·00	50·00	5·50
O6	**8**	6d. green and orange (*11½–12 mm*)	21·00	45·00	2·75

1929–31. *Optd with Type* O **2**.

(a) On 1926 (Typo) issue (Nos. 30/2) (13½–15 mm between lines of opt).

O7	**6**	½d. black and green	2·50	4·50	35
		a. Stop after "OFFISIEEL" on English inscr stamp (1930)	38·00	45·00	3·25
		b. Ditto, but on Afrikaans inscr stamp (1930)	50·00	60·00	3·25
O8	**7**	1d. black and carmine	3·00	6·00	45
O9	**8**	6d. green and orange	8·00	40·00	3·25
		a. Stop after "OFFISIEEL" on English inscr stamp (1930)	70·00	£150	10·00
		b. Ditto, but on Afrikaans inscr stamp (1930)	80·00	£160	12·00

(b) On 1927 (Recess) issue (Nos. 36a/7) (17½–19 mm between lines of opt).

O10	**13**	1s. brown and deep blue (1931)	38·00	90·00	9·50
		a. Stop after "OFFICIAL" on Afrikaans inscr stamp (R. 10/1, 10/7)	£110	£225	
		b. Lines of opt 22 mm apart	£350	£500	
O11	**14**	2s.6d. green and brown (1931)	60·00	£150	19·00
		a. Stop after "OFFICIAL" on Afrikaans inscr stamp (R. 10/1)	£275	£500	
O7/11 *Set of* 5			£100	£250	29·00

The "stop" varieties for the ½d., and 6d. occur on R. 5/3, 5/11, 8/12, 15/3, 15/11, 18/12 with English inscriptions and R. 9/10, 9/12, 19/10, 19/12 with Afrikaans on the 1930 overprinting only.

As only the left-hand panes of the 2s.6d. were overprinted in 1931 the stop variety only occurs once. A further overprinting in 1932 was on both panes, but did not include No. O11a.

1930–47. *Nos.* 42/4 *and* 47/9 *("SUIDAFRIKA" in one word) optd with Type* O **2**.

O12	**6**	½d. black and green (9½–12½ mm) (1931)	2·25	5·00	40
		a. Stop after "OFFISIEEL" on English inscr stamp	38·00	60·00	4·00
		b. Ditto, but on Afrikaans inscr stamp	27·00	50·00	3·50
		c. "Cobweb" variety	42·00		
		d. "Dollar" variety	42·00		
		w. Wmk inverted (1934)	6·00	10·00	60
O13	**7**	1d. black and carmine (I) (12½ mm)	5·50	6·00	55
		a. Stop after "OFFISIEEL" on English inscr stamp	50·00	70·00	4·00
		b. Ditto, but on Afrikaans inscr stamp	35·00	50·00	3·50
		cw. Wmk inverted (1931)	5·50	6·00	55
		d. On Type II (No. 43d) (12½–13½ mm) (1933)	14·00	9·00	90
		da. Opt double	£275	£375	

O14	11	2d. slate-grey and lilac (20½–22½ mm) (1931)	7·50	11·00	1·50
		w. Wmk inverted (1934)	70·00	£110	8·00
O15		2d. blue and violet (20½–22½ mm) (1938)	£140	£100	9·00
O16	8	6d. green and orange (12½–13½ mm) (wmk inverted) (1931)	8·50	8·50	85
		a. Stop after "OFFISIEEL" on English inscr stamp	90·00	£100	6·50
		b. Ditto, but on Afrikaans inscr stamp	75·00	85·00	5·50
		c. "OFFISIEEL" reading upwards (R. 17/12, 18/12, 19/12, 20/12) (1933)	£700		
		w. Wmk upright (1935)	65·00	95·00	7·00
O17	13	1s. brown and deep blue (19 mm) (wmk inverted) (1932)	48·00	85·00	8·50
		a. Twisted horn flaw	£325		
		b. Lines of opt 21 mm apart (wmk inverted) (1933)	60·00	90·00	7·50
		ba. Twisted horn flaw	£325		
		bw. Wmk upright (1936)	65·00	£130	10·00
O18	14	2s.6d. green and brown (17½–18½ mm) (1933)	80·00	£140	15·00
		a. Lines of opt 21 mm apart (1934)	55·00	75·00	8·50
		aw. Wmk inverted (1937)	£400	£450	
O19		2s.6d. blue and brown (19½–20 mm) (11.47)	42·00	95·00	6·50
		a. Diaeresis over second "E" of "OFFISIEEL" on Afrikaans inscr stamp (R. 6/2)	£900	£1000	
		b. Ditto, but on English inscr stamp (R. 6/3)	£900	£1000	

The stop varieties for the ½d., 1d. and 6d. occur on R. 9/10, 9/12, 19/10, 19/12 with English inscriptions and R. 5/3, 5/11, 8/12, 15/3, 15/11, 18/12 with Afrikaans on the 1930 and 1931 overprintings only.

(O 3)

(O 4)

1935–49. *Nos. 54, 56/8, 61/2 and 64a/b ("SUID-AFRIKA" hyphenated) optd.*

(a) With Type O **2** *(reading downwards with "OFFICIAL" at right).*

O20	6	½d. grey and green (12½ mm) (wmk inverted) (1936)	25·00	35·00	1·75
		w. Wmk upright (1937)	7·00	29·00	1·75
O21	7	1d. grey and carmine (11½–13 mm) (wmk inverted)	4·75	6·00	35
		aw. Wmk upright (1937)	4·00	3·00	20
		b. *Grey and bright rose-carmine* (No. 56*i*) (1949)	4·00	5·00	30
O22	22	1½d. green and bright gold (20 mm) (wmk inverted) (1937)	50·00	32·00	1·75
		aw. Wmk upright (1939)	29·00	24·00	1·00
		b. *Blue-green and dull gold* (No. 57c) (1941)	50·00	11·00	1·10
O23	11	2d. blue and violet (20 mm) (1939)	£150	38·00	2·25
O24	8	6d. green and vermilion (I) (11½–13 mm) (1937)	80·00	45·00	3·75
		a. "Falling ladder" flaw	£800	£500	
		b. Die II (No. 61*b*) (1938)	14·00	10·00	1·25
		c. Die III *Green and red-orange* (No. 61c) (11.47)	4·00	8·50	85
O25	13	1s. brown and chalky blue (20 mm) (1939)	80·00	48·00	2·25
		a. Diaeresis over second "E" of "OFFISIEEL" on both English and Afrikaans inscr stamps (1941)	£2000	£1400	
		b. Ditto, but on English inscr stamp only (11.47)	£1400	£950	
O26	15	5s. black and blue-green (20 mm) (6.48)	65·00	£160	13·00
O27	23	10s. blue and blackish brown (No. 64ba) (20 mm) (6.48)	£100	£275	23·00

(b) With Type O **3** *(reading downwards with "OFFICIAL" at left and 18–19 mm between lines of opt).*

O28	15	5s. black and blue-green (1940)	£120	£140	12·00
O29	23	10s. blue and sepia (1940)	£475	£500	38·00

(c) With Type O **4** *(reading upwards with "OFFICIAL" at right and 18½ mm between lines of opt.*

O30	11	2d. grey and dull purple (No. 58*a*) (1941)	11·00	32·00	2·25

No. O25a first appeared in the 1941 overprinting where the variety occurs on stamps 5 and 6 of an unidentified row. The variety reappears in the November 1947 overprinting where the stamps involved are R. 6/1 and 2. No. O25b occurs on R. 6/3 of the same overprinting.

Horizontal rows of 6 of the 1s. exist with "OFFICIAL" twice on the first stamp and "OFFISIEEL" twice on the last stamp. Such rows are believed to come from two half sheets which were overprinted in 1947, but not placed into normal stock (*Price for row of 6, £2500, unused*).

(O 5)

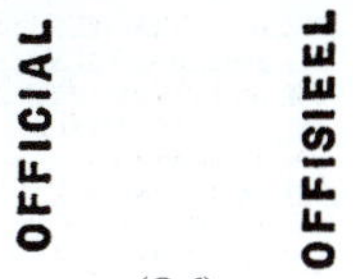

(O 6)

1937–44. *No. 75c (redrawn design) optd.*

(a) With Type O **2** *(reading downwards with "OFFICIAL" at right and 11–12½ mm between lines of opt).*

O31	25a	½d. grey and green	24·00	21·00	1·25
		a. *Grey and blue-green* (No. 75*cd*) (1944)	3·50	11·00	60

(b) With Type O **5** *(reading up and down with "OFFICIAL" at left and diaeresis over the second "E" of "OFFISIEEL". 10 mm between lines of opt).*

O32	25a	½d. grey and blue-green (No. 75*cd*) (1944)	45·00	30·00	2·00

1944–50. *Nos. 87 and 134 optd.*

(a) With Type O **2** *(reading downwards with "OFFICIAL" at right).*

O33	34a	1½d. blue-green and yellow-buff (14½ mm)	2·50	10·00	80
		a. With diaeresis over second "E" of "OFFISIEEL"	£600	£300	27·00
		b. Lines of opt 16½ mm apart (6.48)	2·25	12·00	60

(b) With Type O **6** *(reading upwards with "OFFICIAL" at left and 16 mm between lines of opt).*

O34	34a	1½d. blue-green and yellow-buff (1949)	80·00	85·00	4·00
O35	68	2d. blue and violet (1950)	£3000	£3500	£250

Two different formes were used to overprint Type **34a** between 1944 and 1946. The first, applied to the left halves of sheets only, had a diaeresis over the second "E" of "OFFISIEEL" on all positions of the setting, except for R. 1/2, 2/2 and 3/2. The second form, from which the majority of the stamps came, was applied twice to overprint complete sheets, had no diaeresis.

Examples of T**34a** overprinted with Type O2 *horizontally* exist, but their status is unclear. (*Price £750, unused pair*).

1947 (Nov)–**49**. *No. 107a optd with Type O* **2** *(reading downwards with "OFFICIAL" at right and 20 mm between lines of opt).*

O36	54	2d. slate and deep lilac	5·50	24·00	1·90
		a. With diaeresis over second "E" of "OFFISIEEL" (R. 1/5-6, 11/5-6)	£450	£700	
		b. Slate and bright violet (No. 107*b*) (1949)	8·00	16·00	1·60

1949–50. *Nos. 114 and 120 optd with Type O* **2** *(reading downwards with "OFFICIAL" at right).*

O37	25a	½d. grey and green (11 mm)	5·00	9·00	70
		a. "Tick" flaw and spot on nose	55·00		
		b. Entire design screened (No. 114c)	5·50	10·00	90
O38	13	1s. brown and chalky blue (17½–18½ mm) (1950)	11·00	28·00	2·50

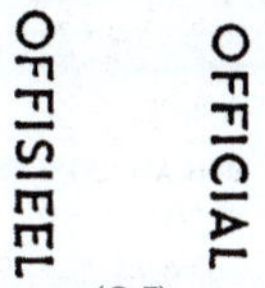

(O 7)

1950 (June)–**54**. *Optd as Type O* **7** *using stereo blocks measuring either 10 (½d., 1d., 6d.), 14½ (1½d., 2d.) or 19 mm (others) between the lines of opt.*

O39	25a	½d. grey and green (No. 114c) (6.51)	70	1·50	15
O41	7	1d. grey and bright rose-carmine (No. 56*i*)	1·00	6·00	50
O42		1d. grey and carmine (No. 115) (3.51)	1·00	3·25	20
O43		1d. grey and carmine (No. 135) (6.52)	1·25	2·00	20
O44	34a	1½d. blue-green and yellow-buff (No. 87) (3.51)	2·00	4·50	30
O45	68	2d. blue and violet (No. 134)	1·00	2·00	20
		a. Opt inverted	£1000		
O46	8	6d. green and red-orange (No. 119)	1·50	4·00	35
		a. Green and brown-orange (No. 119*a*) (6.51)	1·75	3·50	35
O47	13	1s. brown and chalky blue (No. 120)	5·50	18·00	2·00
		a. Blackish brown and ultram (No. 120*a*) (2.53)	£170	£190	18·00
O48	14	2s.6d. green and brown (No. 121)	8·50	35·00	3·50
O49	15	5s. black and blue-green (No. 64*a*) (3.51)	£180	£120	9·00
O50		5s. black and pale blue-green (I) (No. 122) (2.53)	65·00	85·00	6·50
		a. Black and deep yellow-green (II) (No. 122*a*) (1.54)	75·00	£100	9·00
O51	23	10s. blue and charcoal (No. 64*ca*)	75·00	£250	22·00

The use of the official stamps ceased in January 1955.

South Arabian Federation

Comprising Aden and most of the territories of the former Western Aden Protectorate plus one from the Eastern Aden Protectorate.

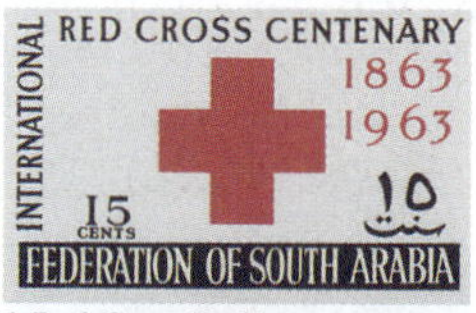

1 Red Cross Emblem

1963 (25 Nov). *Red Cross Centenary.* W w **12**. P 13½.

1	1	15c. red and black	30	30
2		1s.25 red and blue	70	95

2 Federal Crest

3 Federal Flag

(Des V. Whiteley. Photo Harrison)

1965 (1 Apr). P 14½×14 (T **2**) or 14½ (T **3**).

3	2	5f. blue	20	10
4		10f. violet-blue	20	10
5		15f. turquoise-green	20	10
6		20f. green	20	10
7		25f. yellow-brown	20	10
8		30f. yellow-bistre	20	10
9		35f. chestnut	20	10
10		50f. red	20	10
11		65f. yellow-green	30	30
12		75f. crimson	30	10
13		100f. multicoloured	50	10
14		250f. multicoloured	5·00	1·50
15		500f. multicoloured	9·00	1·50
16		1d. multicoloured	16·00	18·00
3/16 *Set of* 14			29·00	20·00

4 I.C.Y. Emblem

(Des V. Whiteley. Litho Harrison)

1965 (24 Oct). *International Co-operation Year.* W w **12**. P 14½.

17	4	5f. reddish purple and turquoise-green	20	10
18		65f. deep bluish green and lavender	80	20

5 Sir Winston Churchill and St. Paul's Cathedral in Wartime

(Des Jennifer Toombs. Photo Harrison)

1966 (24 Jan). *Churchill Commemoration.* No wmk. P 14.

19	5	5f. black, cerise, gold and new blue	15	10
20		10f. black, cerise, gold and deep green	55	10
21		65f. black, cerise, gold and brown	1·25	20
22		125f. black, cerise, gold and bluish violet	1·75	1·75
19/22 *Set of* 4			3·25	1·90

6 Footballer's Legs, Ball and Jules Rimet Cup

(Des V. Whiteley. Litho Harrison)

1966 (1 July). *World Cup Football Championship, England.* No wmk. P 14.

23	6	10f. violet, yellow-green, lake and yellow brown	50	10
24		50f. chocolate, blue-green, lake and yellow-brown	1·50	20

7 W.H.O. Building

(Des M. Goaman. Litho Harrison)

1966 (20 Sept). *Inauguration of W.H.O. Headquarters, Geneva.* No wmk. P 14.

25 **7** 10f. black, yellow-green and light blue 50 10
26 75f. black, light purple and yellow-brown 1·25 45

8 "Education"

9 "Science"

10 "Culture"

(Des Jennifer Toombs. Litho Harrison)

1966 (15 Dec). *20th Anniv of U.N.E.S.C.O.* No wmk. P 14.

27 **8** 10f. slate-violet, red, yellow and orange 30 20
28 **9** 65f. orange-yellow, vio & dp olive 1·25 1·40
29 **10** 125f. black, bright purple and orange 3·25 4·75
27/9 *Set of* 3 4·25 5·75

The South Arabian Federation became fully independent on 30 November 1967. Later issues for this area will be found listed in Part 19 (*Middle East*) of this catalogue under Yemen People's Democratic Republic.

KATHIRI STATE OF SEIYUN

19 (20) (21)

1966 (1 Apr). *New Currency. Nos. 29/41 surch as T* **19/21**.

42 5f. on 5c. (**19**) 25 20
a. Surch quadruple, one inverted 65·00
43 5f. on 10c. (**19**) (R.) 25 50
44 10f. on 15c. (**21**) (R.) 25 1·00
a. Surch inverted £110
45 15f. on 25c. (**20**) 25 80
w. Wmk inverted 50·00
46 20f. on 35c. (**20**) (R.) 25 30
47 25f. on 50c. (**21**) (R.) 25 75
48 35f. on 70c. (**20**) (R.) 25 2·00
49 50f. on 1s. (**21**) 25 20
50 65f. on 1s.25 (**21**) 25 20
51 75f. on 1s.50 (**21**) 25 30
52 100f. on 2s. (**20**) (R.) 38·00 48·00
53 250f. on 5s. (**21**) (R.) 1·40 3·75
54 500f. on 10s. (**20**) 1·75 3·75
42/54 *Set of* 13 40·00 55·00

(22) (23) (24)

1966 (13 Aug). *Nos. 29/41 surch with T* **22/4**.

55 5f. on 5c. (**22**) (B.) 1·50 30
a. Surch inverted 80·00
56 5f. on 10c. (**22**) (R.) 1·75 30
57 10f. on 15c. (**23**) (Y.) 2·00 70
a. Surch inverted 60·00
58 15f. on 25c. (**24**) (B.) 1·75 50
a. Surch inverted 70·00
59 20f. on 35c. (**24**) (Y.) 1·75 50
60 25f. on 50c. (**23**) (B.) 1·75 50
61 35f. on 70c. (**24**) (Br.) 2·25 60
62 50f. on 1s. (**23**) (G.) 2·00 1·00
a. Stop after FILS" 23·00
63 65f. on 1s.25 (**23**) (Y.) 2·25 1·50
64 75f. on 1s.50 (**23**) (G.) 2·75 2·75
a. Surch inverted 70·00
65 100f. on 2s. (**24**) (Y.) 3·75 2·50
a. Surch inverted 70·00
66 250f. on 5s. (**23**) (Y.) 3·00 4·00
a. Surch inverted 55·00
67 500f. on 10s. (**24**) (G.) 3·00 8·50
55/67 *Set of* 13 26·00 21·00

(25) (26)

1966 (13 Aug). *History of Olympic Games. Nos. 57, 59 and 61/7 optd as T* **25/6** *in red.*

68 10f. on 15c. deep bluish green (**25** ("LOS ANGELES 1932")) 35 35
a. Optd as T **25** inverted 27·00
69 20f. on 35c. deep blue (**25** ("BERLIN 1936")) 45 45
70 35f. on 70c. black (**26**) 45 45
a. Opt T **26** inverted 27·00
71 50f. on 1s. brown-orange (**25** ("LONDON 1948")) 50 55
a. Stop after "FILS" 14·00
72 65f. on 1s.25, blue-green (**25**) 50 1·00
73 75f. on 1s.50, deep reddish violet (**25** ("MELBOURNE 1956")) 60 1·50
74 100f. on 2s. deep yellow-green (**25** ("ROME 1960")) 70 1·75
75 250f. on 5s. deep blue and violet (**25** ("TOKYO 1964")) 1·00 3·50
a. Surch inverted 70·00
76 500f. on 10s. yellow-brown and violet (**25** ("MEXICO CITY 1968")) 1·25 4·00
68/76 *Set of* 9 5·25 12·00

CHAMPION: ENGLAND (27) FOOTBALL 1966 (28)

1966 (19 Sept). *World Cup Football Championships. Nos. 57, 59, 61/2, 65/7 optd with T 27/8.*

77 10f. on 15c. deep bluish green (**27**) 70 40
78 20f. on 35c. deep blue (**28**) 90 50
79 35f. on 70c. black (**28**) 1·25 50
80 50f. on 1s. brown-orange (**27**) 1·40 50
a. Stop after "FILS" 24·00
81 100f. on 2s. deep yellow-green (**28**) 2·75 2·25
82 250f. on 5s. deep blue and violet (**27**) 6·00 5·50
83 500f. on 10s. yellow-brown and violet (**28**) 7·50 8·50
77/83 *Set of* 7 18·00 16·00

29 "Telstar"

(Photo State Ptg Wks, Vienna)

1966 (25 Oct). *I.T.U. Centenary (1965). T* **29** *and similar vert designs.* P 13½.

84 5f. blackish green, black and reddish violet 1·60 15
85 10f. maroon, black and bright green 1·75 20
86 15f. Prussian blue, black and orange 2·25 20
87 25f. blackish green, black and orange-red 3·00 20
88 35f. maroon, black and deep olive-yellow 3·00 20
89 50f. Prussian blue, black and orange-brown 3·50 25
90 65f. blackish green, black and orange-yellow 4·00 30
84/90 *Set of* 7 17·00 1·25

Designs:—10, 35f. "Relay"; 15, 50f. "Ranger; others, Type **29**.

32 Churchill at Easel

(Photo State Ptg Wks, Vienna)

1966 (1 Dec). *Sir Winston Churchill's Paintings. T* **32** *and similar designs in black and gold (5f.) or multicoloured (others).* P 13½.

91 5f. Type **32** 1·75 15
92 10f. "Antibes" 2·00 15
93 15f. "Flowers" (*vert*) 2·00 20
94 20f. "Tapestries" 2·00 35
95 25f. "Village, Lake Lugano" 2·00 35
96 35f. "Church, Lake Como" (*vert*) 2·00 40
97 50f. "Flowers at Chartwell" (*vert*) 2·25 65
98 65f. Type **32** 2·75 90
91/8 *Set of* 8 15·00 2·75

WORLD PEACE PANDIT NEHRU (39)

40 "Master Crewe as Henry VIII" (Sir Joshua Reynolds)

1967 (1 Jan). *"World Peace". Nos. 67, 59 and 61/7 optd as T* **39** *in various sizes of type.*

99 10f. on 15c. deep bluish green (Type **39**) (R.) 2·50 1·75
100 20f. on 35c. deep blue ("WINSTON CHURCHILL") (R.) 5·00 2·50
101 35f. on 70c. black ("DAG HAMMAR SKJOLD") (B.) 50 80
102 50f. on 1s. brown-orange ("JOHN F. KENNEDY") (R.) 60 90
a. Stop after "FILS" 19·00
103 65f. on 1s.25 blue-green ("LUDWIG ERHARD") (Pk.) 70 1·10
104 75f. on 1s.50 deep reddish violet ("LYNDON JOHNSON") (B.) 80 1·25
105 100f. on 2s. deep yellow-green ("ELEANOR ROOSEVELT") (B.) 1·00 2·00
106 250f. on 5s. deep blue and violet ("WINSTON CHURCHILL") (R.) 14·00 11·00
107 500f. on 10s. yellow-brown and violet ("JOHN F. KENNEDY") (R.) 5·00 12·00
99/107 *Set of* 9 26·00 30·00

(Photo State Ptg Wks, Vienna)

1967 (1 Feb). *Paintings. T* **40** *and similar multicoloured designs.* P 13½.

108 5f. Type **40** 30 25
109 10f. "The Dancer" (Degas) 35 30
110 15f. "The Filet" (Manet) 40 35
111 20f. "Stag at Sharkey's" (boxing match, G. Bellows) 45 40
112 25f. Don Manuel Osorio" (Goya) 50 45
113 35f. "St. Martin distributing his Cloak" (A. van Dyck) 70 65
114 50f. The Blue Boy" (Gainsborough) 85 75
115 66f. "The White Horse" (Gauguin) 1·10 1·00
116 75f. "Mona Lisa" (Da Vinci) (45×62 *mm*) 1·40 1·25
108/16 *Set of* 9 5·50 4·75

(49)

50 Churchill Crown

1967. *American Astronauts. Nos. 57, 59, 61/2 and 65/6 optd as T* **49** *in various sizes of type, in red.*

117 10f. on 15c. deep bluish green ("ALAN SHEPARD, JR.") 55 1·25
118 20f. on 35c. deep blue ("VIRGIL GRISSOM") 70 1·25
119 35f. on 70c. black ("JOHN GLENN, JR.") 95 1·50
120 50f. on 1s. brown-orange (Type **49**) 95 1·50
a. Stop after "FILS" 22·00
121 100f. on 2s. deep yellow-green ("WALTER SCHIRRA, JR.") 1·75 3·50
122 250f. on 5s. deep blue and violet ("GORDON COOPER, JR.") 2·50 7·00
a. Opt (as T **49**) double £120
117/122 *Set of* 6 6·50 14·50

1967 (1 Mar). *Churchill Commemoration Photo.* P 13½.

123 **50** 75f. multicoloured 8·00 7·00

Appendix

The following stamps have either been issued in excess of postal needs, or have not been made available to the public in reasonable quantities at face value. Miniature sheets, imperforate stamps etc., are excluded from this section.

1967

Hunting. 20*f.*
Olympic Games, Grenoble. Postage 10, 25, 35, 50, 75*f. Air* 100, 200*f.*
Scout Jamboree, Idaho. Air 150*f.*
Paintings by Renoir. Postage 10, 35, 50, 65, 75*f. Air* 100, 200, 250*f.*
Paintings by Toulouse-Lautrec. Postage 10, 35, 50, 65, 75*f. Air* 100, 200, 250*f.*

The National Liberation Front is said to have taken control of Kathiri State of Seiyun on 1 October 1967.

QU'AITI STATE IN HADHRAMAUT

(New Currency. 1000 fils = 1 dinar)

1966 (1 Apr). *New currency. Nos. 41/52 surch as T* **20/21** *of Kathiri State of Setyun.*

53	5f. on 5c. greenish blue (**20**) (R.)	10	60
54	5f. on 10c. grey-black (**20**) (R.)	20	60
55	10f. on 15c. bronze-green (**20**) (R.)	10	30
56	15f. on 25c. carmine-red (**20**)	10	60
57	20f. on 35c. blue (**20**) (R.)	10	1·50
58	25f. on 50c. red-orange (**20**)	10	60
59	35f. on 70c. deep brown (**20**) (R.)	10	60
60	50f. on 1s. black and deep lilac (**21**) (R.)	10	30
61	65f. on 1s.25 black and red-orange (**21**) (R.)	1·00	30
62	100f. on 2s. black and indigo-blue (**21**) (R.)	2·50	75
63	250f. on 5s. black and bluish green (**21**) (R.)	1·50	1·50
64	500f. on 10s. black and lake (**21**) (R.)	22·00	3·00
53/64	*Set of* 12	25·00	9·50

(23)

(24)

1966 (1 Apr). *Churchill Commemoration. Nos. 54/6 optd with T* **23**.

65	5f. on 10c. grey-black (R.)	5·50	12·00
66	10f. on 15c. bronze-green (R.)	6·50	13·00
	a. Opt T **23** inverted	80·00	
67	15f. on 25c. carmine-red (B.)	8·50	14·00
65/7	*Set of* 3	18·50	35·00

1966 (1 Apr). *President Kennedy Commemoration. Nos. 57/9 optd with T* **24**.

68	20f. on 35c. blue (R.)	1·25	6·00
69	25f. on 50c. red-orange (B.)	1·25	6·50
70	35f. on 70c. deep brown (B.)	1·25	7·50
68/70	*Set of* 3	3·25	18·00

25 World Cup Emblem

(Photo State Ptg Wks, Vienna)

1966 (11 Aug). *World Cup Football Championship, England. T* **25** *and similar diamond-shaped designs.* P 13½.

71	5f. maroon and yellow-orange	2·00	25
72	10f. slate-violet and light green	2·25	25
73	15f. maroon and yellow-orange	2·50	30
74	20f. slate-violet and light green	2·75	30
75	25f. blackish green and orange-red	3·00	30
76	35f. blue and yellow	3·50	35
77	50f. blackish green and orange-red	4·00	40
78	65f. blue and yellow	4·75	40
71/8	*Set of* 8	22·00	2·25
MS78*a*	110×110 mm. Nos. 77/8	29·00	7·50

Designs:—10, 35f. Wembley Stadium; 15, 50f. Footballers; 20f. Jules Rimet Cup and football; 25, 65f. Type **25**.

29 Mexican Hat and Blanket

(Photo State Ptg Wks, Vienna)

1966 (25 Oct). *Pre-Olympic Games, Mexico (1968).* P 13½.

79	**29**	75f. sepia and light yellow-green	1·25	75

30 Telecommunications Satellite

(Photo State Ptg Wks, Vienna)

1966 (1 Dec). *International Co-operation Year (1965). T* **30** *and similar horiz designs.* P 13½.

80	5f. maroon, bright purple and emerald	2·75	35
81	10f. violet, orange, blue-green and new blue	3·00	35
82	15f. maroon, new blue and red	3·25	40
83	20f. Prussian blue, purple and red	3·50	45
84	25f. violet, olive-yellow, red and emerald	3·50	45
85	35f. maroon, rose-red and new blue	4·00	50
	a. New blue (face values) omitted	£250	
86	50f. maroon, green and red	4·75	55
87	65f. chocolate, bluish violet and red	5·50	55
80/87	*Set of* 8	27·00	3·25

Designs:—10f. Olympic runner (inscribed "ROME 1960"); 15f. Fishes; 25f. Olympic runner (inscribed "TOKIO 1964"); 50f. Tobacco plant; others, Type **30**.

Appendix

The following stamps have either been issued in excess of postal needs, or have not been made available to the public in reasonable quantities at face value. Miniature sheets, imperforate stamps etc. are excluded from this section.

1967

Stampex Stamp Exhibition, London. Postage 5, 10, 15, 20, 25*f. Air* 50, 65*f.*
Amphilex International Stamp Exhibition, Amsterdam. Air 75f.
Olympic Games, Mexico (1968). *75f.*
Paintings. Postage 5, 10, 15, 20, 25f. *Air* 50, 65*f.*
Scout Jamboree, Idaho. Air 35f.
Space Research. Postage 10, 25, 35, 50, 75f. *Air* 100, 250*f.*

The National Liberation Front is said to have taken control of Qu'aiti State in Hadhramaut on 17 September 1967.

MAHRA SULTANATE OF QISHN AND SOCOTRA

1 Mahra Flag

(Des and litho Harrison)

1967 (12 Mar). *Flag in green, black and vermilion; inscriptions in black; background colours given.* P 14×14½.

1	**1**	5f. mauve	2·25	40
2		10f. buff	2·25	40
3		15f. sage-green	2·25	40
4		20f. red-orange	2·25	40
5		25f. yellow-brown	2·25	40
6		35f. turquoise-green	2·25	40
7		50f. new blue	2·25	40
8		65f. blackish brown	2·25	40
9		100f. violet	2·25	40
10		250f. rose-red	2·25	40
11		500f. grey-green	2·25	40
1/11		*Set of* 11	22·00	4·00

Appendix

The following stamps have either been issued in excess of postal needs, or have not been made available to the public in reasonable quantities at face value. Miniature sheets, imperforate stamps etc., are excluded from this section.

1967

Scout Jamboree, Idaho. 15, 75, 100, 150*f.*
President Kennedy Commemoration. Postage 10, 15, 25, 50, 75, 100, 150*f. Air* 250, 500*f.*
Olympic Games, Mexico (1968). Postage 10, 25, 50*f. Air* 250, 500*f.*

The National Liberation Front is said to have taken control of Mabra Sultanate of Qishn and Socotra on 1 October 1967.

South Australia *see* **Australia**

Southern Cameroons *see* **Cameroon**

Southern Nigeria *see* **Nigeria**

Southern Rhodesia

PRICES FOR STAMPS ON COVER TO 1945

Nos. 1/61	*from* × 2

SELF-GOVERNMENT

The southern part of Rhodesia, previously administered by the British South Africa Company, was annexed by the British Government and granted the status of a self-governing colony from 1 October 1923.

The existing stamps of Rhodesia (the "Admiral" design first issued in 1913) remained in use until 31 March 1924 and continued to be valid for postal purposes until 30 April of that year.

1

2 King George V

3 Victoria Falls

(Recess Waterlow)

1924 (1 Apr)–**29**. P 14.

1	**1**	½d. blue-green	2·50	10
		a. Imperf between (horiz pair)	£900	£1000
		b. Imperf between (vert pair)	£900	£1000
		c. Imperf vert (horiz pair)	£1000	
2		1d. bright rose	1·75	10
		a. Imperf between (horiz pair)	£800	£900
		b. Imperf between (vert pair)	£1400	
		c. Perf 12½ (coil) (1929)	2·75	80·00
3		1½d. bistre-brown	2·25	80
		a. Imperf between (horiz pair)	£11000	
		b. Imperf between (vert pair)	£6500	
		c. Printed double, once albino	£375	
4		2d. black and purple-grey	3·50	1·00
		a. Imperf between (horiz pair)	£13000	
5		3d. blue	3·00	3·75
6		4d. black and orange-red	2·50	2·75
7		6d. black and mauve	2·00	4·75
		a. Imperf between (horiz pair)	£35000	
8		8d. purple and pale green	11·00	45·00
		a. Frame double, once albino	£500	
9		10d. blue and rose	14·00	50·00
10		1s. black and light blue	5·00	7·50
11		1s.6d. black and yellow	19·00	32·00
12		2s. black and brown	17·00	17·00
13		2s.6d. blue and sepia	30·00	60·00
14		5s. blue and blue-green	60·00	£160
1/14 *Set of* 14			£150	£350

Prices for "imperf between" varieties are for adjacent stamps from the same pane and not for those separated by wide gutter margins between vertical or horizontal pairs, which come from the junction of two panes.

(T **2** recess by B.W.; T **3** typo by Waterlow)

1931 (1 April)–**37**. *T* **2** *(line perf 12 unless otherwise stated and* **3** *(comb perf 16×14). (The 11½ perf is comb.).*

15	**2**	½d. green	85	1·00
		a. Perf 11½ (1933)	65	20
		b. Perf 14 (1935)	1·60	30
16		1d. scarlet	1·00	70
		a. Perf 11½ (1933)	2·00	20
		b. Perf 14 (1935)	50	20
16*c*		1½d. chocolate (3.3.33)	55·00	42·00
		d. Perf 11½ (1.4.32)	2·50	80
17	**3**	2d. black and sepia	4·25	1·40
18		3d. deep ultramarine	10·00	11·00
19	**2**	4d. black and vermilion	1·25	1·50
		a. Perf 11½ (1935)	17·00	5·00
		b. Perf 14 (10.37)	32·00	55·00
20		6d. black and magenta	2·25	3·00
		a. Perf 11½ (1933)	15·00	1·50
		b. Perf 14 (1936)	7·00	1·25
21		8d. violet and olive-green	1·75	3·25
		a. Perf 11½ (1934)	17·00	32·00
21*b*		9d. vermilion and olive-green (1.9.34)	6·50	9·00
22		10d. blue and scarlet	7·00	2·25
		a. Perf 11½ (1933)	6·00	13·00
23		1s. black and greenish blue	2·00	2·50
		a. Perf 11½ (1935)	£120	60·00
		b. Perf 14 (10.37)	£200	£140
24		1s.6d. black and orange-yellow	10·00	19·00
		a. Perf 11½ (1936)	55·00	£120
25		2s. black and brown	21·00	6·50
		a. Perf 11½ (1933)	35·00	32·00
26		2s.6d. blue and drab	35·00	35·00
		a. Perf 11½ (1933)	28·00	38·00
27		5s. blue and blue-green	48·00	48·00
		a. Printed on gummed side	£6000	
15/27 *Set of* 15			£130	£120

No. 16c was only issued in booklets.

PRINTERS. All stamps from Types **4** to **29** were recess-printed by Waterlow and Sons, Ltd, London, except where otherwise stated.

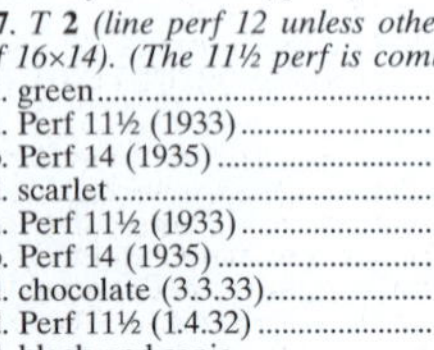

4

1932 (1 May). P 12½.

29	**4**	2d. green and chocolate	5·00	1·00
30		3d. deep ultramarine	5·00	1·75
		a. Imperf horiz (vert pair)	£9500	£12000
		b. Imperf between (vert pair)	£24000	

5 Victoria Falls

1935 (6 May). *Silver Jubilee.* P 11×12.

31	**5**	1d. olive and rose-carmine	3·50	2·75
32		2d. emerald and sepia	6·00	7·00
33		3d. violet and deep blue	5·50	10·00
34		6d. black and purple	8·50	18·00
31/4 *Set of* 4			21·00	35·00

1935–41. *Inscr* "POSTAGE AND REVENUE".

35	**4**	2d. green and chocolate (P 12½)	4·50	14·00
		a. Perf 14 (1941)	2·25	10
35*b*		3d. deep blue (P 14) (1938)	4·00	1·25

6 Victoria Falls and Railway Bridge

7 King George VI

1937 (12 May). *Coronation.* P 12½.

36	**6**	1d. olive and rose-carmine	60	1·00
37		2d. emerald and sepia	60	1·75
38		3d. violet and blue	3·25	9·00
39		6d. black and purple	1·75	3·75
36/9 *Set of* 4			5·50	14·00

1937 (25 Nov). P 14.

40	**7**	½d. green	50	10
41		1d. scarlet	50	10
42		1½d. red-brown	1·00	30
43		4d. red-orange	1·50	10
44		6d. grey-black	1·50	50
45		8d. emerald-green	2·00	3·25
46		9d. pale blue	1·50	1·00
47		10d. purple	2·25	2·75
48		1s. black and blue-green	2·75	10
		a. Frame double, one albino	£2250	
49		1s.6d. black and orange-yellow	12·00	2·50
50		2s. black and brown	20·00	55
51		2s.6d. ultramarine and purple	10·00	6·50
52		5s. blue and blue-green	18·00	2·50
40/52 *Set of* 13			65·00	18·00

Nos. 40/1 exist in coils, constructed from normal sheets. On No. 48a the frame appears blurred and over-inked.

8 British South Africa Co's Arms

9 Fort Salisbury, 1890

10 Cecil John Rhodes (after S. P. Kendrick)

11 Fort Victoria

12 Rhodes makes peace

13 Victoria Falls Bridge

14 Statue of Sir Charles Coghlan

15 Lobengula's Kraal and Govt House, Salisbury

Recut shirt collar (R. 6/1)

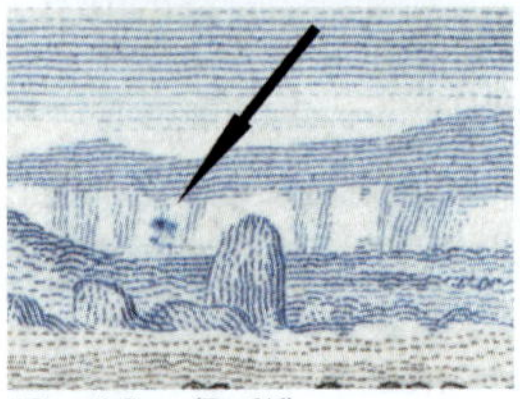

"Cave" flaw (R. 6/6)

(Des Mrs. L. E. Curtis (½d., 1d., 1½d., 3d.), Mrs I. Mount (others))

1940 (3 June). *British South Africa Company's Golden Jubilee. T* **8/15**. P 14.

53		½d. slate-violet and green	10	65
54		1d. violet-blue and scarlet	10	10
55		1½d. black and red-brown	15	80
		a. Recut shirt collar	24·00	40·00
56		2d. green and bright violet	30	70
57		3d. black and blue	30	1·50
		a. Cave flaw	55·00	90·00
58		4d. green and brown	2·25	2·75
59		6d. chocolate and green	1·25	2·75
60		1s. blue and green	1·25	2·00
53/60 *Set of* 8			5·00	10·00

16 Mounted Pioneer

Hat brim retouch (Pl 1B R. 1/8)

Line under saddlebag (Pl 1A R. 6/10)

(Roto South African Govt Printer, Pretoria)

1943 (1 Nov). *50th Anniv of Occupation of Matabeleland.* W **9** of South Africa (Mult Springbok) sideways. P 14.

61	**16**	2d. brown and green	20	1·00
		a. Hat brim retouch	21·00	25·00
		b. Line under saddlebag	21·00	25·00

17 Queen Elizabeth II when Princess and Princess Margaret

18 King George VI and Queen Elizabeth

1947 (1 Apr). *Royal Visit. T* **17/18**. P 14.

62		½d. black and green	30	60
63		1d. black and scarlet	30	60

19 Queen Elizabeth

20 King George VI

21 Queen Elizabeth II when Princess

22 Princess Margaret

Damage to right-hand frame (R. 1/10)

1947 (8 May). *Victory.* P 14.

64	**19**	1d. carmine	10	15
65	**20**	2d. slate	10	15
		a. Double print	£2250	
		b. Damaged frame	55·00	
66	**21**	3d. blue	85	1·60
67	**22**	6d. orange	30	1·40
64/7 *Set of 4*			1·25	3·00

(Recess B.W.)

1949 (10 Oct). *76th Anniv of U.P.U. As Nos. 115/16 of Antigua.*

68	2d. slate-green	70	25
69	3d. blue	80	4·00

23 Queen Victoria, Arms and King George VI

1950 (12 Sept). *Diamond Jubilee of Southern Rhodesia.* P 14.

70	**23**	2d. green and brown	50	1·25

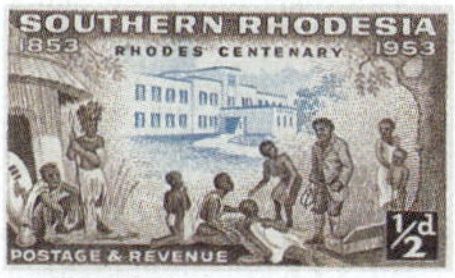

24 "Medical Services"

(Des A. R. Winter (2d.), Mrs. J. M. Enalim (others))

1953 (15 Apr). *Birth Centenary of Cecil Rhodes. T* **24** *and similar horiz designs.* P 14.

71	½d. pale blue and sepia	15	2·25
72	1d. chestnut and blue-green	15	10
73	2d. grey-green and violet	15	10
74	4½d. deep blue-green and deep ultramarine	75	2·75
75	1s. black and red-brown	3·00	1·50
71/5 *Set of 5*		3·75	6·00

Designs:—1d. "Agriculture"; 2d. "Building"; 4½d. "Water Supplies"; 1s. "Transport".

No. 74 also commemorates the Diamond Jubilee of Matabeleland.

1953 (30 May). *Rhodes Centenary Exhibition, Bulawayo. As No. 171 of Nyasaland, but without watermark.*

76	6d. violet	30	75

30 Queen Elizabeth II

(Recess D.L.R.)

1953 (1 June). *Coronation.* P 12×12½.

77	**30**	2s.6d. carmine	4·75	6·00

31 Sable Antelope

32 Tobacco planter

33 Rhodes's Grave

34 Farm Worker

35 Flame Lily

36 Victoria Falls

37 Baobab tree

38 Lion

39 Zimbabwe Ruins

40 Birchenough Bridge

41 Kariba Gorge

42 Basket Maker

43 Balancing Rocks

44 Coat of Arms

(Recess, centre typo (4d.), B.W.)

1953 (31 Aug). *T* **31/44** *and similar designs.* P 13½×14 (2d., 6d., 5s.), 14 (10s., £1) or 14×13½ (others).

78	½d. grey-green and claret	30	50
79	1d. green and brown	30	10
80	2d. deep chestnut and reddish violet	30	10
81	3d. chocolate and rose-red	55	2·25
82	4d. red, green and indigo	3·25	30
83	4½d. black and deep bright blue	2·50	4·00
84	6d. brown-olive & deep turquoise-green	3·25	1·25
85	9d. deep blue and reddish brown	3·00	4·00
86	1s. reddish violet and light blue	1·25	10
87	2s. purple and scarlet	12·00	4·75
88	2s.6d. yellow-olive and orange-brown	5·00	6·00
89	5s. yellow-brown and deep green	7·00	6·50
90	10s. red-brown and olive	9·50	21·00
91	£1 rose-red and black	15·00	27·00
78/91 *Set of 14*		55·00	70·00

For issues from 1954 to 1963 see under RHODESIA AND NYASALAND.

45 Maize

50 Flame Lily

56 Cattle

58 Coat of Arms

A large coloured flaw on the small guinea fowl gives the appearance of an extra feather (R. 2/2)

(Des V. Whiteley. Photo Harrison)

1964 (19 Feb). *T* **45**, **50**, **56**, **58** *and similar horiz designs.* P 14½ (½d. to 4d.), 13½×13 (6d. to 2s.6d.) or 14½×14 (others).

92	½d. yellow, yellow-green and light blue	20	2·25
93	1d. reddish violet and yellow-ochre	15	10
	a. Reddish violet omitted	£2500	
94	2d. yellow and deep violet	60	10
95	3d. chocolate and pale blue	20	10
96	4d. yellow-orange and deep green	30	10
97	6d. carmine-red, yellow and deep dull green	40	10
98	9d. red-brown, yellow and olive-green	2·50	1·50
99	1s. blue-green and ochre	3·25	30
	a. Blue-green (Queen and emeralds) omitted	£3250	
100	1s.3d. red, violet and yellow-green	3·00	10
101	2s. blue and ochre	2·50	3·25
102	2s.6d. ultramarine and vermilion	4·00	1·00
	a. Vermilion omitted	£3750	
	b. Ultramarine omitted	£8000	
103	5s. light brown, bistre-yellow and light blue	3·50	2·25
104	10s. black, yellow-ochre, light blue and carmine-red	11·00	6·50
	a. Extra "feather"	26·00	
105	£1 brown, yellow-green, buff and salmon-pink	6·00	16·00
92/105 *Set of 14*		32·00	30·00

Designs: (*As T* **45**)—1d. African Buffalo; 2d. Tobacco; 3d. Greater Kudu; 4d. Citrus. (*As T* **50**)—9d. Ansellia Orchid; 1s. Emeralds; 1s.3d. Aloe; 2s. Lake Kyle; 2s.6d. Tigerfish. (*As T* **56**)—10s. Helmet Guineafowl.

Nos. 92 and 93 exist in coils constructed from normal sheets.

Nos. 102a and 102b occur on different sheets and involve one vertical row of stamps in each instance. They were caused by the printing press being stopped and then restarted. Three such sheets showing No. 102a have been reported.

See also Nos. 359/72 of Rhodesia.

In October 1964 Southern Rhodesia was renamed Rhodesia.

STAMP BOOKLETS

1928 (1 Jan). *Black on blue cover. Stitched.*

SB1	2s.6d. booklet containing twelve ½d. and twenty-four 1d. (Nos. 1/2) in blocks of 6	£4250

1931. *Black on blue cover. Stitched.*

SB2	2s.6d. booklet containing twelve ½d. and twenty-four 1d. (Nos. 15/16) in blocks of 6	£5000

1933 (3 Mar). *Black on red cover, size 69×53 mm. Stitched.*

SB3	3s. booklet containing twelve ½d., 1d. and 1½d. (Nos. 15, 16, 16c) in blocks of 6	£3250

The 1½d. postage rate was reduced to 1d. eight weeks after No. SB3 was issued. Postal officials were instructed to detach the 1½d. panes and use them for other purposes. The remaining stocks of the booklet were then sold for 1s.6d.

1938 (Oct)–**45**. *Black on yellow cover. Stitched.*

SB4	2s.6d. booklet containing twenty-four ½d. and eighteen 1d. (Nos. 40/1) in blocks of 6 with postage rates on inside front cover	£275
	a. Label with new rates affixed to inside front cover (1945)	
	b. Inside front cover blank	£300

No. SB4b was issued sometime between 1945 and 1949.

1954 (Jan). *Black on yellow cover, size 71×54 mm. Stitched.*

SB5	2s.6d. booklet containing twelve ½d. and twenty-four 1d. (Nos. 78/9) in blocks of 6	70·00

1964 (19 Feb). *Black on orange cover, size 57×45 mm. Stitched.*

SB6	1s. booklet containing 3d. (No. 95) in block of 4	3·25

POSTAGE DUE STAMPS

SOUTHERN

RHODESIA

(D 1)

1951 (1 Oct). *Postage Due stamps of Great Britain optd with Type* D **1**.

D1	D **1**	½d. emerald (No. D27)	3·25	16·00
D2		1d. violet-blue (No. D36)	3·00	2·00
D3		2d. agate (No.D29)	2·50	1·75
D4		3d. violet (No. D30)	2·75	2·75
D5		4d. blue (No. D38)	1·75	3·50
D6		4d. dull grey-green (No. D31)	£225	£600
D7		1s. deep blue (No. D33)	2·50	4·50
D1/5, 7 *Set of 6*			14·00	27·00

No. D6 is reported to have been issued to Fort Victoria and Gwelo main post offices only.

South West Africa

The stamps of Germany were used in the colony from July 1886 until the introduction of issues for GERMAN SOUTH-WEST AFRICA in May 1897. Following occupation by South African forces in 1914–15 the issues of SOUTH AFRICA were used, being replaced by the overprinted issues in 1923.

Walvis (or Walfish) Bay, the major anchorage on the South West Africa coast, was claimed by Great Britain as early as 1796. In 1878 the 430 sq mile area around the port, together with a number of offshore islands, was annexed to Cape Province, passing to the Union of South Africa in 1910.

Stamps of the Cape of Good Hope and South Africa were used at Walfish Bay, often cancelled with numeral obliterator 300, until the enclave was transferred to the South West Africa administration on 1 October 1922.

The Walfish Bay territory reverted to South Africa on 30 August 1977 and from that date the stamps of South Africa were, once again, in use.

PRICES FOR STAMPS ON COVER TO 1945

Nos. 1/40*a*	*from* × 6
Nos. 41/133	*from* × 2
Nos. D1/5	*from* × 10
Nos. D6/51	*from* × 20
Nos. O1/4	*from* × 3
Nos. O5/20	*from* × 15
No. O21	*from* × 2
No. O22	*from* × 15

INSCRIPTIONS. Most of the postage stamps up to No. 140 are inscribed alternately in English and Afrikaans throughout the sheets and the same applies to all the Official stamps and to Nos. D30/33.

PRICES for Nos. 1/140 are for unused horizontal pairs, used horizontal pairs or used singles (either inscr), *unless otherwise indicated*.

OVERPRINT SETTINGS. Between 1923 and 1928 the King George V definitives of South Africa, Types **2** and **3**, and the various postage due stamps were issued overprinted for use in South West Africa. A number of overprint settings were used:

- Setting I – Overprint Types **1** and **2** ("Zuid-West Afrika"). 14 mm between lines of overprint. See Nos. 1/12 and D1/9
- Setting II – As Setting I, but 10 mm between lines of overprint. See Nos. 13/15 and D10/13
- Setting III – Overprint Types **3** ("Zuidwest Afrika") and **4**. "South West" 14 mm long. "Zuidwest" 11 mm long. 14 mm between lines of overprint. See Nos. 16/27 and D14/17
- Setting IV – As Setting III, but "South West" 16 mm long, "Zuidwest" 12 mm long and 14 mm between lines of overprint. See Nos. 28 and D17*a*/20
- Setting V – As Setting IV, but 12 mm between lines of overprint. See Nos. D21/4
- Setting VI – As Setting IV, but 9½ mm between lines of overprint. See Nos. 29/40 and D25/32.

South West — **Africa.** (**1**) **Zuid-West** — **Afrika.** (**2**)

1923 (1 Jan–17 June). *Nos. 3/4, 6 and 9/17 of South Africa optd alternately with T* **1** *and* **2** *by typography.*

(a) Setting I (14 mm between lines of opt).

		Un pair	*Us pair*	*Us single*
1	½d. green	2·50	9·00	1·00
	a. "Wes" for "West" (R. 20/8)	95·00	£150	
	b. "Afr ica" (R. 20/2)	£130		
	c. Litho opt in shiny ink (17 June)	10·00	60·00	4·75
2	1d. rose-red	3·75	9·50	1·00
	a. Opt inverted	£500		
	b. "Wes" for "West" (R. 12/2)	£170		
	c. "Af.rica" for "Africa" (R. 20/6)	£170	£275	
	d. Opt double	£950		
	e. "Afr ica" (R. 20/2)	£130		
	f. "Afrika" without stop (R. 17/8)	£350		
3	2d. dull purple	4·75	12·00	1·50
	a. Opt inverted	£650	£750	
	b. "Wes" for "West" (R. 20/8)	£275		
	c. Litho opt in shiny ink (30 Mar)	50·00	£120	10·00
4	3d. ultramarine	7·50	16·00	2·75
5	4d. orange-yellow and sage-green	13·00	45·00	4·00
	a. Litho opt in shiny ink (19 Apr)	35·00	70·00	8·00
6	6d. black and violet	8·00	45·00	4·00
	a. Litho opt in shiny ink (19 Apr)	30·00	75·00	7·50
7	1s. orange-yellow	18·00	48·00	5·00
	a. Litho opt in shiny ink (19 Apr)	60·00	£120	11·00
	b. "Afrika" without stop (R. 17/8)	£6000		
8	1s.3d. pale violet	32·00	55·00	5·50
	a. Opt inverted	£400		
	b. Litho opt in shiny ink (19 Apr)	75·00	£140	14·00
9	2s.6d. purple and green	60·00	£130	18·00
	a. Litho opt in shiny ink (19 Apr)	£130	£275	35·00
10	5s. purple and blue	£160	£350	50·00
11	10s. blue and olive-green	£1300	£2750	£400
12	£1 green and red	£700	£1900	£250
1/12 *Set of* 12		£2000	£4750	£650
1s/12s Optd "Specimen" *Set of* 12 *singles*		£1400		

Nos. 1/12 were overprinted in complete sheets of 240 (4 panes 6×10).

No. 3b shows traces of a type spacer to the right of where the "t" should have been. This spacer is not visible on Nos. 1a and 2b.

Minor varieties, such as broken "t" in "West", were caused by worn type. Stamps showing one line of overprint only or with the lower line above the upper line due to overprint misplacement may also be found. All values exist showing a faint stop after "Afrika" on R. 17/8, but only examples of the 1d. and 1s. have been seen with it completely omitted.

(b) Setting II (10 mm between lines of opt) (31 Mar).

13	5s. purple and blue	£140	£275	45·00
	a. "Afrika" without stop (R. 6/1)	£1100	£1300	£225
14	10s. blue and olive-green	£500	£850	£140
	a. "Afrika" without stop (R. 6/1)	£2250	£2750	£550
15	£1 green and red	£1000	£1400	£200
	a. "Afrika" without stop (R. 6/1)	£4250	£5000	£1000
13/15 *Set of* 3		£1500	£2250	£350

Nos. 13/15 were overprinted in separate panes of 60 (6×10).

Examples of most values are known showing a forged Windhoek postmark dated "30 SEP 24".

Zuidwest — **Afrika.** (**3**) **South West** — **Africa.** (**4**)

1923 (15 July)–**26**. *Nos. 3/4, 6 and 9/17 of South Africa optd as T* **3** *("Zuidwest" in one word, without hyphen) and* **4** *alternately.*

(a) Setting III ("South West" 14 mm long, "Zuidwest" 11 mm long, 14 mm between lines of opt).

16	½d. green (5.9.24)	8·50	38·00	4·00
	a. "outh" for "South" (R. 1/1)	£1700		
17	1d. rose-red (28.9.23)	5·50	9·00	1·40
	a. "outh" for "South" (R. 1/1)	£1600		
18	2d. dull purple (28.9.23)	8·00	9·00	1·25
	a. Opt double	£1000		
19	3d. ultramarine	5·00	10·00	1·25
20	4d. orange-yellow and sage-green	6·00	21·00	2·75
	w. Wmk inverted	†	†	—
21	6d. black and violet (28.9.23)	12·00	45·00	5·00
22	1s. orange-yellow	12·00	45·00	5·00
23	1s.3d. pale violet	20·00	45·00	5·50
24	2s.6d. purple and green	45·00	85·00	10·00
25	5s. purple and blue	60·00	£140	18·00
26	10s. blue and olive-green	£160	£250	40·00
27	£1 green and red (28.9.23)	£300	£400	60·00
16/27 *Set of* 12		£600	£1000	£140

Nos. 16/27 were overprinted in complete sheets of 240 (4 panes 6×10).

Two sets may be made with this overprint, one with bold lettering, and the other from September 1924, with thinner lettering and smaller stops.

(b) Setting IV ("South West" 16 mm long, "Zuidwest" 12 mm long, 14 mm between lines of opt).

28	2s.6d. purple and green (29.6.24)	80·00	£160	28·00

No. 28 was overprinted on two panes of 60 horizontally side by side.

(c) Setting VI ("South West" 16 mm long, "Zuidwest" 12 mm long, 9½ mm between lines of opt).

29	½d. green (16.12.25)	7·00	40·00	5·00
30	1d. rose-red (9.12.24)	3·25	10·00	1·40
	a. Opt omitted (in pair with normal)	£1600		
31	2d. dull purple (9.12.24)	4·00	22·00	1·75
32	3d. ultramarine (31.1.26)	4·50	29·00	2·75
	a. Deep bright blue (20.4.26)	42·00	£100	12·00
33	4d. orge-yellow & sage-grn (9.12.24)	5·50	45·00	4·00
34	6d. black and violet (9.12.24)	9·00	48·00	5·00
35	1s. orange-yellow (9.12.24)	8·50	48·00	5·00
36	1s.3d. pale violet (9.12.24)	11·00	48·00	5·00
37	2s.6d. purple and green (9.12.24)	32·00	75·00	10·00
38	5s. purple and blue (31.1.26)	45·00	£120	14·00
39	10s. blue and olive-green (9.12.24)	80·00	£160	20·00
40	£1 green and red (9.1.26)	£250	£400	55·00
	a. Pale olive-green and red (8.11.26)	£250	£450	65·00
29/40*a* *Set of* 12		£400	£900	£120
35s, 39s/40s H/S "Specimen" *Set of* 3		£500		

Nos. 29/40 were overprinted in complete sheets of 240 (4 panes of 6×10) with, initially, "South West Africa" 16½ mm long on the upper two panes and 16 mm long on the lower two. This order was subsequently reversed. For printings from 8 November 1926 all four panes showed the 16½ mm measurement. No. 40*a* only comes from this printing.

Examples of most values are known showing a forged Windhoek postmark dated "30 SEP 24".

Suidwes — **Afrika.** (**5**) **South West** — **Africa.** (**6**)

1926 (1 Jan–1 May). *Nos. 30/2 of South Africa optd with T* **5** *(on stamps inscr in Afrikaans) and* **6** *(on stamps inscr in English) sideways, alternately in black.*

41	½d. black and green	4·25	9·00	1·00
42	1d. black and carmine	3·50	8·00	80
43	6d. green and orange (1 May)	22·00	48·00	7·00
41/3 *Set of* 3		26·00	60·00	8·00

SOUTH WEST AFRICA (**7**) **SUIDWES-AFRIKA** (**8**)

1926. *No. 33 of South Africa, imperf optd.*

(a) With T **7** *(English).*

			Single Stamps
44A	4d. grey-blue	75	3·00
	(b) With T **8** *(Afrikaans).*		
44B	4d. grey-blue	75	3·00

1927. *As Nos. 41/3, but Afrikaans opt on stamp inscr in English and vice versa.*

45	½d. black and green	2·00	7·50	80
	a. "Africa" without stop (R. 13/8)	£160		
46	1d. black and carmine	2·50	2·50	50
	a. "Africa" without stop (R. 13/8)	£300		
47	6d. green and orange	9·00	32·00	3·00
	a. "Africa" without stop (R. 13/8)	£180		
45/7 *Set of* 3		12·00	38·00	3·75

SOUTH WEST AFRICA (**9**) **S.W.A.** (**10**) **S.W.A.** (**11**)

1927. *As No. 44A, but overprint T* **9**.

			Single Stamps
48	4d. grey-blue	6·00	19·00
	s. Handstamped "Specimen"	70·00	

1927 (Apr). *Nos. 34/9 of South Africa optd alternately as T* **5** *and* **6**, *in blue, but with lines of overprint spaced 16 mm.*

49	2d. grey and purple	4·75	16·00	1·75
50	3d. black and red	4·75	29·00	2·50
51	1s. brown and blue	15·00	32·00	4·00
52	2s.6d. green and brown	35·00	95·00	13·00
53	5s. black and green	75·00	£190	20·00
54	10s. blue and bistre-brown	65·00	£160	20·00
49/54 *Set of* 6		£180	£475	50·00
49s/51s, 54s H/S "Specimen" *Set of* 4		£375		

A variety of Nos. 49, 50, 51 and 54 with spacing 16½ mm between lines of overprint, occurs in the third vertical row of each sheet.

1927. *As No. 44, but perf 11½ by John Meinert Ltd, Windhoek.*

(a) Optd with T **7** *(English).*

			Single Stamps
55A	4d. grey-blue	1·00	5·00
	a. Imperf between (pair)	35·00	75·00
	s. Handstamped "Specimen"	70·00	
	(b) Optd with T **8** *(Afrikaans).*		
55B	4d. grey-blue	1·00	5·00
	a. Imperf between (pair)	38·00	75·00
	s. Handstamped "Specimen"	70·00	

1927 (Aug)–**30**. *Optd with T* **10**.

(a) On Nos. 13 and 17a of South Africa.

56	1s.3d. pale violet	1·25	6·50
	a. Without stop after "A" (R. 3/4)	£100	
	s. Handstamped "Specimen"	75·00	
57	£1 pale olive-green and red	90·00	£160
	a. Without stop after "A" (R. 3/4)	£1500	£2250

(b) On Nos. 30/2 and 34/9 of South Africa.

		Un pair	*Us pair*	*Us single*
58	½d. black and green	2·50	7·00	80
	a. Without stop after "A"	40·00	75·00	
	b. "S.W.A." opt above value	2·75	16·00	2·25
	c. As b, in vert pair, top stamp without opt	£550		
59	1d. black and carmine	1·25	3·75	55
	a. Without stop after "A"	40·00	75·00	
	b. "S.W.A." opt at top (30.4.30)	1·75	14·00	1·60
	c. As b, in vert pair, top stamp without opt	£600		
60	2d. grey and maroon	9·00	29·00	1·50
	c. Perf 14×13½	16·00	42·00	
	ca. Without stop after "A"	85·00	£140	
	cb. Opt double, one inverted	£750	£1000	
61	3d. black and red	5·00	24·00	3·25
	a. Without stop after "A"	75·00	£120	
	b. Perf 14×13½	11·00	45·00	
	ba. Without stop after "A"	90·00	£160	
	bb. Without stop after "W"	£170		
62	4d. brown (4.28)	12·00	40·00	7·00
	a. Without stop after "A"	90·00	£140	
	b. Perf 14×13½	28·00	60·00	
63	6d. green and orange	8·50	25·00	2·75
	a. Without stop after "A"	£120		
64	1s. brown and deep blue	13·00	48·00	5·00
	b. Perf 14×13½	50·00	90·00	
	ba. Without stop after "A"	£1400	£1800	£350
65	2s.6d. green and brown	42·00	85·00	12·00
	a. Without stop after "A"	£160	£275	
	b. Perf 14×13½	75·00	£140	
	ba. Without stop after "A"	£225	£350	
66	5s. black and green	60·00	£120	18·00
	a. Without stop after "A"	£250	£375	
	b. Perf 14×13½	£100	£170	
	ba. Without stop after "A"	£275	£425	
67	10s. bright blue and brown	£100	£200	28·00
	a. Without stop after "A"	£375	£600	
58/67 *Set of* 10		£225	£500	70·00
58s/61s, 63s/7s H/S "Specimen" *Set of* 9		£600		

On the ½d., 1d. and 6d. the missing stop variety occurs three times on each sheet, R. 1/7, 13/4 and one position not yet identified. For the other values it comes on R. 2/3 of the right pane and, for the 2s.6d., 5s. and 10s., on R. 8/1 of the left pane.

The missing stop after "W" on the 3d. occurs on R. 10/5 of the right pane.

The overprint is normally found at the base of the ½d., 1d., 6d., 1s.3d. and £1 values and at the top of the remainder.

Examples of all values are known showing a forged Windhoek postmark dated "20 MAR 31".

1930–31. *Nos.* 42 *and* 43 *of South Africa (rotogravure printing) optd with T* **10**.

68	½d. black and green (1931)	12·00	32·00	3·00
69	1d. black and carmine	9·00	27·00	2·75

1930 (27 Nov–Dec). *Air. Nos.* 40/1 *of South Africa optd.*

(a) As T **10**.

		Un single	*Us single*
70	4d. green (*first printing*)	8·00	28·00
	a. No stop after "A" of "S.W.A."........	70·00	£140
	b. Later printings....................................	4·50	28·00
71	1s. orange (*first printing*)	70·00	£120
	a. No stop after "A" of "S.W.A."........	£450	£650
	b. Later printings....................................	7·00	50·00

First printing: Thick letters, blurred impression. Stops with rounded corners.

Later printings: Thinner letters, clear impression. Clean cut, square stops.

(b) As T **11** *(12.30).*

72	4d. green..	1·25	6·00
	a. Opt double	£180	
	b. Opt inverted	£180	
73	1s. orange..	3·25	15·00
	a. Opt double	£500	

12 Kori Bustard

13 Cape Cross

14 Bogenfels

15 Windhoek

16 Waterberg

17 Luderitz Bay

18 Bush Scene

19 Elands

20 Mountain Zebra and Blue Wildebeests

21 Herero Huts

22 Welwitschia Plant

23 Okuwahaken Falls

24 Monoplane over Windhoek

25 Biplane over Windhoek

(Recess B.W.)

1931 (5 Mar). *T* **12** *to* **25** *(inscr alternately in English and Afrikaans).* W **9** of South Africa. P 14×13½.

(a) Postage.

74	½d. black and emerald...........	2·75	2·50	10
75	1d. indigo and scarlet	2·25	2·50	10
76	2d. blue and brown.................	70	5·00	15
	w. Wmk inverted	£450		
77	3d. grey-blue and blue............	70	4·25	15
78	4d. green and purple...............	1·50	7·00	20
79	6d. blue and brown.................	1·50	10·00	20
80	1s. chocolate and blue	2·25	13·00	25
81	1s.3d. violet and yellow............	6·00	11·00	50
82	2s.6d. carmine and grey............	20·00	24·00	1·75
83	5s. sage-green and red-brown	16·00	40·00	2·75
84	10s. red-brown and emerald	48·00	50·00	6·00
85	20s. lake and blue-green.........	70·00	80·00	10·00

(b) Air.

86	3d. brown and blue	27·00	32·00	2·50
87	10d. black and purple-brown...	42·00	75·00	7·00
74/87 *Set of* 14	....	£200	£300	28·00

Examples of most values are known showing a forged Windhoek postmark dated "20 MAR 31".

26

(Recess B.W.)

1935 (1 May). *Silver Jubilee. Inscr bilingually.* W **9** of South Africa. P 14×13½.

			Un single	*Us single*
88	**26**	1d. black and scarlet......................	1·00	25
89		2d. black and sepia	1·00	25
90		3d. black and blue.........................	7·50	24·00
91		6d. black and purple......................	3·00	14·00
88/91 *Set of* 4		....	11·00	35·00

1935–36. *Voortrekker Memorial Fund. Nos.* 50/3 *of South Africa optd with T* **10**.

92	½d. +½d.black and green........	1·50	5·50	75
	a. Opt inverted	£275		
93	1d. +½d.grey-black and pink .	1·50	3·25	40
	a. Blurred "SOUTH AFRICA" and red "comet" flaw....................	45·00		
94	2d. +1d.grey-green and purple	5·50	6·00	80
	a. Without stop after "A".....	£200	£225	
	b. Opt double	£225		
95	3d. +1½d.grey-green and blue	16·00	35·00	4·00
	a. Without stop after "A".....	£250	£325	
92/5 *Set of* 4	....	22·00	45·00	5·50

27 Mail Train

28

Re-entry (R. 6/3)

(Recess B.W.)

1937 (1 Mar). W **9** of South Africa. P 14×13½.

96	**27**	1½d. purple-brown............	26·00	4·00	35

(Recess B.W.)

1937 (12 May). *Coronation.* W **9** of South Africa (sideways). P 13½×14.

97	**28**	½d. black and emerald....	40	15	10
98		1d. black and scarlet.......	40	15	10
99		1½d. black and orange	40	15	10
100		2d. black and brown	40	15	10
101		3d. black and blue...........	50	15	10
102		4d. black and purple	50	20	10
		a. Re-entry	17·00	17·00	
103		6d. black and yellow	50	3·00	20
104		1s. black and grey-black	55	3·25	25
97/104 *Set of* 8		....	3·25	6·50	65

On. No. 102a the frame and leaves at lower left are doubled. The stamp is inscribed in Afrikaans.

1938 (14 Dec). *Voortrekker Centenary Memorial. Nos.* 76/9 *of South Africa optd as T* **11**.

105	½d. +½d.blue and green..........	9·50	24·00	2·00
106	1d. +1d.blue and carmine.......	24·00	19·00	1·40
107	1½d. +1½d. chocolate and blue-green	24·00	30·00	3·00
108	3d. +3d.bright blue.................	48·00	80·00	8·00
105/8 *Set of* 4	....	95·00	£140	13·00

1938 (14 Dec). *Voortrekker Commemoration. Nos.* 80/1 *of South Africa optd as T* **11**.

109	1d. blue and carmine	10·00	20·00	1·50
	a. Three bolts in wheel rim..	60·00		
110	1½d. greenish blue and brown .	15·00	25·00	2·00

1939 (17 July). *250th Anniv of Landing of Huguenots in South Africa and Huguenot Commemoration Fund. Nos.* 82/4 *of South Africa optd as T* **11**.

111	½d. +½d. brown and green	14·00	15·00	1·25
112	1d. +1d. green and carmine ...	19·00	15·00	1·25
113	1½d. +1½d. blue-green and purple	30·00	15·00	1·25
111/13 *Set of* 3	....	55·00	40·00	3·25

SWA (29) **SWA** (30) **SWA** (31) **S W A** (32)

1941 (1 Oct)–**43.** *War Effort. Nos.* 88/96 *of South Africa optd with T* **29** *or* **30** *(3d. and 1s.).*

(a) Inscr alternately.

114	½d. green (1.12.41)..................	75	4·50	25
	a. Blue-green (1942).............	65	2·50	15
115	1d. carmine (1.11.41)..............	55	3·50	20
	a. "Stain" on uniform	12·00		
116	1½d. myrtle-green (21.1.42)	55	3·75	20
117	3d. blue	22·00	23·00	1·00
	a. Cigarette flaw	80·00		
118	4d. orange-brown	6·50	17·00	1·00
	a. Red-brown	18·00	26·00	3·00
119	6d. red-orange..........................	7·00	8·00	50
120	1s.3d. olive-brown (15.1.43).......	13·00	22·00	1·25

(b) Inscr bilingually.

		Un single	*Us single*
121	2d. violet...	50	1·75
122	1s. brown (17.11.41)	1·60	2·00
114/22 *Set of 7 pairs and 2 singles*	....	48·00	75·00

1943–44. *War Effort (reduced sizes). Nos.* 97/104 *of South Africa, optd with T* **29** *(1½d. and 1s., No.* 130*), or T* **31** *(others).*

(a) Inscr alternately.

		Un unit	*Us unit*	*Us single*
123	½d. blue-green (T)..................	50	5·50	25
	a. Green	4·75	7·50	30
	b. Greenish blue	4·25	6·50	25
124	1d. carmine-red (T).................	3·50	5·50	20
	a. Bright carmine..................	3·50	5·50	20
125	1½d. red-brown (P)...................	50	1·50	15
126	2d. violet (P)...........................	8·50	5·50	20
	a. Reddish violet	11·00	5·50	20
	b. Apostrophe flaw	45·00		
127	3d. blue (T)	3·25	18·00	50
128	6d. red-orange (P)...................	6·00	3·00	30
	a. Opt inverted	£600		

(b) Inscr bilingually.

129	4d. slate-green (T)...................	2·00	21·00	60
	a. Opt inverted	£800	£475	55·00
130	1s. brown (opt T **29**) (P)........	12·00	26·00	2·00
	a. Opt inverted	£550	£350	
	b. Opt T **31**(1944).................	4·00	6·00	30
	c. Opt T **31** inverted	£500	£325	40·00
	d. "Bursting shell"................	35·00		
	e. Smoking "L"	35·00		
123/30*b Set of* 8	....	25·00	60·00	2·25

The "units" referred to above consist of pairs (P) or triplets (T).

No. 128 exists with another type of opt as Type **31**, but with broader "s", narrower "w" and more space between the letters.

1945. *Victory. Nos.* 108/10 *of South Africa optd with T* **30**.

131	1d. brown and carmine...........	25	75	10
	a. Opt inverted	£375	£400	
132	2d. slate-blue and violet.........	30	75	10
133	3d. deep blue and blue...........	1·50	1·75	10
131/3 *Set of* 3	....	1·75	3·00	20

1947 (17 Feb). *Royal Visit. Nos.* 111/13 *of South Africa optd as T* **31**, *but* 8½×2 *mm.*

134	1d. black and carmine	10	10	10
135	2d. violet..................................	10	60	10
	a. "Bird" on "2"......................	6·50		
136	3d. blue	15	40	10
	a. "Black-eyed Princess"......	8·00		
134/6 *Set of* 3	....	30	1·00	15

1948 (26 Apr). *Royal Silver Wedding. No.* 125 *of South Africa, optd as T* **31**, *but* 4×2 *mm.*

137	3d. blue and silver..................	1·00	35	10

1949 (1 Oct). *75th Anniv of U.P.U. Nos.* 128/30 *of South Africa optd as T* **30**, *but* 13×4 *mm.*

138	½d. blue-green.........................	75	2·25	25
139	1½d. brown-red	75	1·75	15
140	3d. bright blue	1·25	1·00	25
	a. Serif on "C"........................	40·00		
	b. "Lake" in East Africa.......	42·00		
138/40 *Set of* 3	....	2·50	4·50	60

1949 (1 Dec). *Inauguration of Voortrekker Monument, Pretoria. Nos.* 131/3 *of South Africa optd with T* **32**.

		Un single	*Us single*
141	1d. magenta..	10	10
142	1½d. blue-green..	10	10
143	3d. blue	15	60
141/3 *Set of* 3	....	30	70

1952 (14 Mar). *Tercentenary of Landing of Van Riebeeck. Nos.* 136/40 *of South Africa optd as T* **30**, *but* 8×3½ *mm (1d., 4½d.) or* 11×4 *mm (others).*

144	½d. brown-purple and olive-grey.........	10	50
145	1d. deep blue-green	10	10
146	2d. deep violet	50	10
147	4½d. blue	30	2·75
148	1s. brown..	75	20
144/8 *Set of* 5	....	1·50	3·25

33 Queen Elizabeth II and *Catophracties Alexandri*

1953 (2 June). *Coronation. T* **33** *and similar horiz designs.* W **9** of South Africa. P 14.

149	1d. bright carmine.................................	40	10
150	2d. deep bluish green............................	40	10
151	4d. magenta..	50	30
152	6d. dull ultramarine	50	60
153	1s. deep orange-brown..........................	65	20
149/53 *Set of* 5	....	2·25	1·10

Designs:—2d. *Bauhinia macrantha*, 4d. *Caralluma nebrownii*, 6d. *Gloriosa virescens*, 1s. *Rhigozum trieholotum*.

34 "Two Bucks" (rock painting)

36 "Rhinoceros Hunt" (rock painting)

38 Karakul Lamb

39 Ovambo Woman blowing Horn

(Des O. Schroeder (1d. to 4d.), M. Vandenschen (4½d. to 10s.))

1954 (15 Nov). *T* **34**, **36**, **38/9** *and similar designs.* W **9** of South Africa (sideways* on vert designs). P 14.

154		1d. brown-red	30	10
		w. Wmk horns of springbok to right..	15·00	7·00
155		2d. deep brown	35	10
156		3d. dull purple	1·25	10
157		4d. blackish olive	1·50	10
158		4½d. deep blue	70	40
159		6d. myrtle-green	70	70
		w. Wmk horns of springbok to right..	65·00	32·00
160		1s. deep mauve	70	50
161		1s.3d. cerise	2·00	1·00
162		1s.6d. purple	2·00	50
163		2s.6d. bistre-brown	4·50	70
164		5s. deep bright blue	6·00	2·75
165		10s. deep myrtle-green	32·00	15·00
154/65 *Set of* 12			48·00	20·00

Designs: *Vert* (*as T* **34**)—2d. "White Lady" (rock painting). (*As T* **38**)—2s.6d. Lioness; 5s. Gemsbok; 10s. African Elephant. (*As T* **39**)—1s. Ovambo woman; 1s.3d. Herero woman 1s.6d. Ovambo girl. *Horiz* (*as T* **36**)—1d. "White Elephant and Giraffe (rock painting).

*The normal sideways watermark shows the horns of the springbok pointing left, *as seen from the back of the stamp.*

1960. *As Nos.* 154/7, 162, *but* W **102** of South Africa (sideways on vert designs). P 14.

166		1d. brown-red	55	2·00
167		2d. deep brown	70	2·00
168		3d. dull purple	1·40	5·00
169		4d. blackish olive	2·75	4·75
169*a*		6d. myrtle-green	£750	£400
170		1s.6d. purple	20·00	15·00
166/70 (ex 169*a*) *Set of* 5			23·00	26·00

(New Currency. 100 cents = 1 South African rand)

46 G.P.O. Windhoek

47 Finger Rock

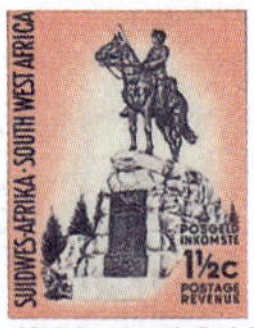

48 Mounted Soldier Monument

49 Quivertree

50 S.W.A. House, Windhoek

50a Greater Flamingoes and Swakopmund Lighthouse

51 Fishing Industry

52 Greater Flamingo

53 German Lutheran Church, Windhoek

54 Diamond

55 Fort Namutoni

55a Hardap Dam

56 Topaz

57 Tourmaline

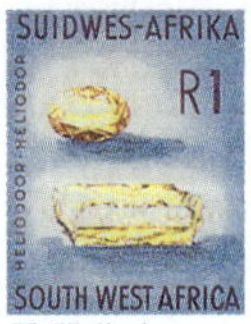

58 Heliodor

1961 (14 Feb)–**63**. *Unsurfaced paper.* W **102** of South Africa (sideways on vert designs). P 14.

171	**46**	½c. brown and pale blue	60	10
172	**47**	1c. sepia and reddish lilac	15	10
173	**48**	1½c. slate-violet and salmon	20	10
174	**49**	2c. deep green and yellow	75	1·40
175	**50**	2½c. red-brown and light blue	35	10
176	**50a**	3c. ultramarine and rose-red (1.10.62)	4·50	40
177	**51**	3½c. indigo and blue-green	1·00	15
178	**52**	5c. scarlet and grey-blue	7·50	10
179	**53**	7½c. sepia and pale lemon	70	15
180	**54**	10c. blue and greenish yellow	1·75	60
181	**55**	12½c. indigo and lemon	60	40
182	**55a**	15c. chocolate and light blue (16.3.63)	14·00	3·25
183	**56**	20c. brown and red-orange	4·00	30
184	**57**	50c. deep bluish green and yellow-orange	6·00	1·50
185	**58**	1r. yellow, maroon and blue	10·00	15·00
171/185 *Set of* 15			45·00	21·00

See also Nos. 186/91, 202/16, 224/6 and 240.

1962–66. *As No. 171, etc., but without watermark.*

186	**46**	½c. brown and pale blue (8.62)	50	1·75
187	**48**	1½c. slate-violet and salmon (9.62)	5·00	45
188	**49**	2c. deep green and yellow (5.62)	3·50	4·00
189	**50**	2½c. red-brown and light blue (1964)	6·50	6·00
190	**51**	3½c. indigo and blue-green (1966)	13·00	4·50
191	**52**	5c. scarlet and grey-blue (9.62)	7·00	1·50
186/91 *Set of* 6			32·00	16·00

59 "Agricultural Development"

60 Centenary Emblem and Map

61 Centenary Emblem and part of Globe

1963 (16 Mar). *Opening of Hardap Dam.* W **102** of South Africa (sideways). P 14.

192	**59**	3c. chocolate and light green	30	15

1963 (30 Aug). *Centenary of Red Cross.* P 14.

193	**60**	7½c. red, black and light blue	4·00	5·00
194	**61**	15c. red, black and orange-brown	6·00	8·00

62 Interior of Assembly Hall

63 Calvin

1964 (14 May). *Opening of Legislative Assembly Hall, Windhoek.* W **102** of South Africa. P 14.

195	**62**	3c. ultramarine and salmon	50	30

1964 (1 Oct). *400th Death Anniv of Calvin (Protestant reformer).* P 14.

196	**63**	2½c. brown-purple and gold	50	15
197		15c. deep bluish green and gold	2·25	3·75

64 Mail Runner of 1890

65 Kurt von Francois (founder)

66 Dr. H. Vedder

(Des D. Aschenborn)

1965 (18 Oct). *75th Anniv of Windhoek. Chalk-surfaced paper.* W **127** of South Africa (sideways). P 14.

198	**64**	3c. sepia and scarlet	50	15
199	**65**	15c. red-brown and blue-green	90	1·75

1966 (4 July). *90th Birth Anniv, of Dr. H. Vedder (philosopher and writer). Chalk-surfaced paper.* W **127** of South Africa (sideways). P 14.

200	**66**	3c. blackish green and salmon	30	15
201		15c. deep sepia and light blue	70	40

Nos. 200/1 exist on Swiss-made paper with *tête-bêche* watermark from a special printing made for use in presentation albums for delegates to the U.P.U. Congress in Tokyo in 1969, as supplies of the original Harrison paper were by then exhausted (*Set of* 2 *price £22 mint*).

1966–72. *As 1961–66 but chalk-surfaced paper and* W **127** of South Africa* (sideways† on vert designs).

202	**46**	½c. brown and pale blue (1967)	1·25	10
203	**47**	1c. sepia and light reddish lilac (1967)	1·50	10
		a. Grey-brown and lilac (9.72)	3·00	10
204	**48**	1½c. slate-violet and salmon (1968)	7·00	30
205	**49**	2c. deep bluish green and yellow	4·50	10
206	**50**	2½c. deep red-brown and light turquoise-blue	2·50	30
		a. Deep red-brown and pale blue (1967)	70	10
207	**50a**	3c. ultramarine and rose-red (1970)	8·50	1·50
208	**51**	3½c. indigo and blue-green (1967)	4·00	6·00
209	**50**	4c. deep red-brown and light turquoise-blue (1.4.71)	1·50	2·50
210	**52**	5c. scarlet and grey-blue (1968)	4·00	10
211	**53**	6c. sepia and greenish yellow (31.8.71)	7·00	9·00
212		7½c. sepia and pale lemon (1967)	3·50	30
		w. Wmk top of triangle to right..	3·50	30
213	**55**	9c. indigo and greenish yellow (1.7.71)	9·00	11·00
214	**54**	10c. bright blue and greenish yellow (6.70)	18·00	2·00
		a. Whiter background** (9.72)	18·00	2·75
215	**55a**	15c. chocolate and light blue (1.72)	23·00	7·00
216	**56**	20c. brown and red-orange (1968)	18·00	1·75
202/16 *Set of* 15			95·00	35·00

*The watermark in this issue is indistinct but the stamps can be distinguished from the stamps without watermark by their shades and the chalk-surfaced paper which is appreciably thicker and whiter. The 1 1½, 3 4 5, 6, 9 10 15 and 20c. are known only with the watermark *tête-bêche* but the ½ c. and 2½ c. exist with both forms, the remainder being as illustrated.

†The normal sideways watermark shows top of triangle pointing to left, *as seen from the back of the stamp.*

**No. 214a, printed from sheets, has a much whiter background around the value and behind "SOUTH WEST AFRICA" compared with No. 214, which was issued in coils only.

See also Nos. 224/6 and 240.

67 Camelthorn Tree

(Des D. Aschenborn (2½c., 3c.), Govt Printer, Pretoria (15c.))

1967 (6 Jan). *Verwoerd Commemoration. Chalk-surfaced paper. T* **67** *and similar designs.* W **127** of South Africa (sideways on vert designs). P 14.

217		2½c. black and emerald-green	15	10
218		3c. brown and new blue	15	10
219		15c. blackish brown and reddish purple	55	45
217/19 *Set of* 3			75	60

Designs: *Vert.*—3c. Waves breaking against rock; 15c. Dr. H. F. Verwoerd.

70 President Swart

71 President and Mrs. Swart

1968 (2 Jan). *Swart Commemoration. Chalk-surfaced paper.* W **127** of South Africa (tete-beche, sideways). P 14×15.

220	**70**	3c. orange-red, black and turquoise-blue		
		G. Inscribed in German	30	15
		A. Inscribed in Afrikaans	30	15
		E. Inscribed in English	30	15
221	**71**	15c. red, blackish olive and dull green		
		G. Inscribed in German	1·00	1·25
		A. Inscribed in Afrikaans	1·00	1·25
		E. Inscribed in English	1·00	1·25
		a. Red, brownish olive and bronze-green		
		G. Inscribed in German	1·00	1·25
		A. Inscribed in Afrikaans	1·00	1·25
		E. Inscribed in English	1·00	1·25
220/1 *Set of 2 values in strips of three*			11·00	9·00
Set of 6 singles			3·50	3·75

The three languages appear, *se-tenant*, both horizontally and vertically, throughout the sheet.

1970 (14 Feb). *Water 70 Campaign. As Nos. 299/300 of South Africa, but without phosphor band and inscr "SWA".*
222 2½c. green, bright blue and chocolate ... 50 30
223 3c. Prussian blue, royal blue and buff. 50 30

72 G.P.O., Windhoek

1970–71. *As Nos. 202 and 204/5 but "POSGELD INKOMSTE" omitted and larger figure of value as in T* **72**. W **127** of South Africa (tête-bêche, sideways on 1½ and 2c.).
224 **72** ½c. brown and pale blue (6.70) .... 1·50 30
225 – 1½c. slate-violet and salmon (1.6.71).. 13·00 16·00
226 – 2c. deep bluish green and lemon (11.70).. 5·00 40
224/6 *Set of* 3.. 18·00 16·00

1970 (24 Aug). *150th Anniv of Bible Society of South Africa. As Nos. 301/2 of South Africa, but inscr "SWA".*
228 2½c. multicoloured .... 1·50 10
229 12½c. gold, black and blue .... 5·00 6·00

No. 228 has a phosphor frame, probably added in error.

A mint example of No. 229 exists with a second, blind, impression of the die-stamped features.

POSTAGE DUE STAMPS

PRICES for Nos. D1/39 are for unused horizontal pairs, used horizontal pairs and used singles.

1923 (1 Jan–July). *Optd with T* **1** *and* **2** *alternately.*

(a) Setting I (14 mm between lines of overprint).

(i) On Nos. D5/6 of Transvaal.

		Un pair	Us pair	Us single
D1	5d. black and violet.................	4·00	50·00	11·00
	a. "Wes" for "West" (R. 8/6, 10/2 left pane)	£180		
	b. "Afrika" without stop (R. 6/1)	£120		
D2	6d. black and red-brown	17·00	50·00	11·00
	a. "Wes" for "West" (R. 10/2)	£375		
	b. "Afrika" without stop (R. 6/1, 7/2)	£200		
	c. 12 mm between lines of opt (R. 1/1)	£250		

(ii) On Nos. D3/4 and D6 of South Africa (De La Rue printing).

D3	2d. black and violet................	35·00	50·00	10·00
	a. "Wes" for "West" (R. 10/2)	£250	£375	
	b. "Afrika" without stop (R. 6/1, 7/2)	£225		
D4	3d. black and blue..................	19·00	50·00	10·00
	a. "Wes" for "West" (R. 8/6, 10/2).................................	£170		
	b. "Africa" without stop (R. 9/1)	£300		
D5	6d. black and slate (20 Apr)..	32·00	55·00	13·00
	a. "Wes" for "West" (R. 8/6)	£200		

(iii) On Nos. D9/10, D11 and D14 of South Africa (Pretoria printings).

D6	½d. black and green (P 14).....	6·00	29·00	5·50
	a. Opt inverted	£550		
	b. Opt double	£1200	£1300	
	c. "Wes" for "West" (R. 10/2)	£110		
	d. "Afrika" without stop (R. 6/1, 7/2)	£100		
D7	1d. black and rose (*roul*)........	7·00	30·00	6·00
	a. "Wes" for "West" (R. 10/2)	£120	£275	
	b. "Afrika" without stop (R. 6/1)	£120		
	c. Imperf between (horiz pair)	£1600		
D8	1½d. black and yellow-brown (*roul*)	1·25	14·00	2·75
	a. "Wes" for "West" (R. 8/6, 10/2).................................	90·00		
	b. "Afrika" without stop (R. 6/1)	95·00		
D9	2d. black and violet (P 14) (21 June)	3·50	25·00	5·00
	a. "Wes" for "West" (R. 8/6)	£110		
	b. "Afrika" without stop (R. 6/1)	£140		

Nos. D1/9 were initially overprinted as separate panes of 60, but some values were later done as double panes of 120.

A variety of Nos. D1, D4/5 and D9 with 15 mm between the lines of overprint occurs on four positions in each pane from some printings.

(b) Setting II (10 mm between lines of overprint).

(i) On No. D5 of Transvaal.

D10 5d. black and violet (20 Apr) 55·00 £170

(ii) On Nos. D3/4 of South Africa (De La Rue printing).

D11	2d. black and violet (20 Apr)	18·00	45·00	9·00
	a. "Afrika" without stop (R. 6/1)	£200		
D12	3d. black and blue (20 Apr)..	7·50	28·00	5·50
	a. "Afrika" without stop (R. 6/1)	£100		

(iii) On No. D9 of South Africa (Pretoria printing). Roul.

D13 1d. black and rose (July)........ £14000 – £1600

1923 (30 July)–**26**. *Optd as T* **3** *("Zuidwest" in one word without hyphen) and* **4**.

(a) Setting III ("South West" 14 mm long, "Zuidwest" 11 mm long and 14 mm between lines of overprint).

(i) On No. D6 of Transvaal.

D14 6d. black and red-brown .... 21·00 90·00 20·00

(ii) On Nos. D9 and D11/12 of South Africa (Pretoria printing).

D15	½d. black and green (P 14).....	14·00	32·00	5·50
D16	1d. black and rose (*roul*).......	7·00	32·00	5·50
D17	1d. black and rose (P 14) (2.8.23)	23·00	32·00	5·50

(b) Setting IV ("South West" 16 mm long, "Zuidwest" 12 mm long and 14 mm between lines of overprint).

(i) On No. D5 of Transvaal.

D17*a* 5d. black and violet (1.7.24) ... £600 £1100

(ii) On Nos. D11/12 and D16 of South Africa (Pretoria printing). P 14.

D18	½d. black and green (1.7.24) ...	7·50	30·00	5·50
D19	1d. black and rose (1.7.24)......	7·50	29·00	5·50
D20	6d. black and slate (1.7.24).....	2·25	42·00	9·00
	a. "Africa" without stop (R. 9/5)	£120	£275	

(c) Setting V (12 mm. between lines of overprint).

(i) On No. D5 of Transvaal.

D21 5d. black and violet (6.8.24) .. 6·00 50·00 9·00

(ii) On No. D4 of South Africa (De La Rue printing).

D22 3d. black and blue (6.8.24)..... 16·00 50·00 11·00

(iii) On Nos. D11 and D13 of South Africa (Pretoria printing). P 14.

D23	½d. black and green (6.8.24) ..	3·00	29·00	6·50
D24	1½d. black and yellow-brown (6.8.24)	5·00	45·00	7·50

(d) Setting VI (9½ mm between lines of overprint).

(i) On No. D5 of Transvaal.

D25	5d. black and violet (7.9.24) ...	2·75	20·00	3·50
	a. "Africa" without stop (R. 9/5)	80·00		

(ii) On No. D4 of South Africa (De La Rue printing).

D26 3d. black and blue (3.2.26)..... 9·00 55·00 11·00

(iii) On Nos. D11/16 of South Africa (Pretoria printing). P 14.

D27	½d. black and green (1.3.26)...	12·00	35·00	7·50
D28	1d. black and rose (16.3.25)...	2·00	12·00	1·60
	a. "Africa" without stop (R. 9/5 right pane)	85·00		
D29	1½d. black and yellow-brown (1.10.26)............................	4·50	32·00	6·50
	a. "Africa" without stop (R. 9/5 right pane)	90·00		
D30	2d. black and violet (7.9.24) ...	2·50	18·00	3·50
	a. "Africa" without stop (R. 9/5) right pane)..........	75·00		
D31	3d. black and blue (6.5.26).....	4·50	19·00	3·75
	a. "Africa" without stop (R. 9/5) right pane)..........	80·00		
D32	6d. black and slate (1.10.26) ..	12·00	50·00	14·00
	a. "Africa" without stop (R. 9/5 right pane)	£160		
D27/32 *Set of* 6	....	35·00	£150	32·00

For Setting VI the overprint was applied to sheets of 120 (2 panes of 60) of the 1d., 3d. and 6d., and to individual panes of 60 for the other values. The two measurements of "South West", as detailed under No. 40, also occur on the postage dues. Nos. D25 and D31/2 show it 16 mm long, No. 27 16½ mm long and the other stamps can be found with either measurement. In addition to the complete panes the 16½ mm long "South West" also occurs on R. 2/4 in the 16 mm left pane for Nos. D28 and D30/2.

Suidwes **Afrika.** (D **1**)

South West **Africa.** (D **2**)

1927 (14 May–27 Sept). *Optd as Types D* **1** *and D* **2**, *alternately, 12 mm between lines of overprint.*

(a) On No. D5 of Transvaal.

D33 5d. black and violet (27 Sept) 20·00 85·00 23·00

(b) On Nos. D13/16 of South Africa (Pretoria printing). P 14.

D34	1½d. black and yellow-brown...	1·00	20·00	3·50
D35	2d. black and pale violet (27 Sept)	4·75	16·00	3·25
	a. Black and deep violet	8·00	17·00	3·50
D37	3d. black and blue (27 Sept)..	14·00	45·00	11·00
D38	6d. black and slate (27 Sept) .	9·00	35·00	8·50

(c) On No. D18 of South Africa (Pretoria printing). P 14.

D39	1d. black and carmine	1·00	11·00	2·25
D33/9 *Set of* 6	....	45·00	£200	45·00

No. D33 was overprinted in panes of 60 and the remainder as complete sheets of 120.

Examples of all values can be found with very small or very faint stops from various positions in the sheet.

1928–29. *Optd with T* **10**.

(a) On Nos. D15/16 of South Africa.

		Un single	Us single
D40	3d. black and blue..................................	1·50	16·00
	a. Without stop after "A" (R. 3/6)......	38·00	
D41	6d. black and slate	6·00	28·00
	a. Without stop after "A" (R. 3/6)......	£130	

(b) On Nos. D17/21 of South Africa.

D42	½d. black and green................................	50	8·50
D43	1d. black and carmine	50	3·25
	a. Without stop after "A" (R. 3/6)......	40·00	
D44	2d. black and mauve	50	4·50
	a. Without stop after "A" (R. 3/6)......	55·00	
D45	3d. black and blue..................................	2·25	26·00
D46	6d. black and slate	1·50	21·00
	a. Without stop after "A" (R. 3/6)......	55·00	£190
D42/6 *Set of* 5	....	4·75	55·00

D 3

(Litho B.W.)

1931 (23 Feb). *Inscribed bilingually.* W **9** of South Africa. P 12.

D47	D **3**	½d. black and green..........................	1·00	7·50
D48		1d. black and scarlet........................	1·00	1·25
D49		2d. black and violet..........................	1·00	2·75
D50		3d. black and blue...........................	4·25	13·00
D51		6d. black and slate	13·00	25·00
D47/51 *Set of* 5		....	18·00	45·00

PRINTER. The following issues have been printed by the South African Government Printer, Pretoria.

1959 (18 May). *Centre typo; frame roto.* W **9** *of South Africa.* P 15×14.

D52	D **4**	1d. black and scarlet.......................	1·50	15·00
D53		2d. black and reddish violet...........	1·50	15·00
D54		3d. black and blue...........................	1·50	15·00
D52/4 Set of 3		....	4·00	40·00

1960 (1 Dec). *As Nos. D52 and D54 but* W **102** *of South Africa.*

D55	1d. black and scarlet	1·50	3·00
D56	3d. black and blue..................................	1·50	3·75

1961 (14 Feb). *As Nos. D52 etc, but whole stamp roto, and value in cents.* W **102** *of South Africa.*

D57	1c. black and blue-green.......................	70	3·75
D58	2c. black and scarlet..............................	70	3·75
D59	4c. black and reddish violet..................	70	6·00
D60	5c. black and light blue	1·00	4·25
D61	6c. black and green................................	1·25	6·50
D62	10c. black and yellow............................	4·00	9·00
D57/62 *Set of* 6	....	7·50	30·00

OFFICIAL STAMPS

OFFICIAL South West Africa. (O 1)

OFFISIEEL Suidwes Afrika. (O 2)

1926 (Dec). *Nos. 30, 31, 6 and 32 of South Africa optd with Type O* **1** *on English stamp and O* **2** *on Afrikaans stamp alternately.*

		Un pair	Us pair	Us single
O1	½d. black and green.................	80·00	£190	30·00
O2	1d. black and carmine	80·00	£190	30·00
O3	2d. dull purple	£180	£325	45·00
O4	6d. green and orange	£100	£190	30·00
O1/4 *Set of* 4	....	£400	£800	£120

OFFICIAL S.W.A. (O 3)

OFFISIEEL S.W.A. (O 4)

1929 (May). *Nos. 30, 31, 32 and 34 of South Africa optd with Type O* **3** *on English stamp and O* **4** *on Afrikaans stamp.*

O5	½d. black and green.................	1·00	15·00	2·75
O6	1d. black and carmine	1·00	15·00	2·75
	w. Wmk inverted	£300		
O7	2d. grey and purple..................	1·50	20·00	3·50
	a. Pair, one stamp without stop after "OFFICIAL"...	6·00	45·00	
	b. Pair, one stamp without stop after "OFFISIEEL".	6·00	45·00	
	c. Pair, comprising a and b ..	16·00	85·00	
O8	6d. green and orange	2·00	20·00	3·75
O5/8 *Set of* 4	....	5·00	65·00	11·50

Types O **3** and O **4** are normally spaced 17 mm between lines on all except the 2d. value, which is spaced 13 mm.

Except on No. O7, the words "OFFICIAL" or "OFFISIEEL" normally have no stops after them.

OFFICIAL S.W.A. (O 5)

OFFISIEEL S.W.A. (O 6)

OFFICIAL. S.W.A. (O 7)

OFFISIEEL. S.W.A. (O 8)

1929 (Aug). *Nos. 30, 31 and 32 of South Africa optd with Types O* **5** *and O* **6**, *and No. 34 with Types O* **7** *and O* **8**, *languages to correspond.*

O9	½d. black and green.................	75	15·00	2·75
O10	1d. black and carmine	1·00	15·00	2·75
O11	2d. grey and purple..................	1·00	15·00	3·25
	a. Pair, one stamp without stop after "OFFICIAL"...	3·75	40·00	
	b. Pair, one stamp without stop after "OFFISIEEL".	3·75	40·00	
	c. Pair, comprising a and b ..	18·00	90·00	
O12	6d. green and orange	2·50	27·00	6·50
O9/12 *Set of* 4	....	4·75	65·00	13·50

Examples of Nos. O1/12 are known showing forged Windhoek postmarks dated "30 SEP 24" or "20 MAR 31".

OFFICIAL (O 9)

OFFISIEEL (O 10)

1931. *English stamp optd with Type O* **9** *and Afrikaans stamp with Type O* **10** *in red.*

O13	**12**	½d. black and emerald....	11·00	21·00	3·75
O14	**13**	1d. indigo and scarlet	1·00	18·00	3·50
O15	**14**	2d. blue and brown	2·25	10·00	2·25
O16	**17**	6d. blue and brown	4·00	14·00	3·25
O13/16 *Set of* 4		....	16·00	55·00	11·50

OFFICIAL (O 11) **OFFISIEEL** (O 12)

1938 (1 July). *English stamp optd with Type* O **11** *and Afrikaans with Type* O **12** *in red.*

O17	**27**	1½d. purple-brown	27·00	48·00	6·00

OFFICIAL (O 13) **OFFISIEEL** (O 14)

1945–50. *English stamp optd with Type* O **13**, *and Afrikaans stamp with Type* O **14** *in red.*

O18	**12**	½d. black and emerald	13·00	30·00	5·00
O19	**13**	1d. indigo and scarlet (1950)	10·00	18·00	3·25
		a. Opt double	£500		
O20	**27**	1½d. purple-brown	35·00	50·00	7·00
O21	**14**	2d. blue and brown (1947?)	£600	£750	£100
O22	**17**	6d. blue and brown	22·00	60·00	8·00
O18/20, O22 *Set of* 4			70·00	£140	21·00

OFFICIAL (O 15) **OFFISIEEL** (O 16)

1951 (16 Nov)–**52**. *English stamp optd with Type* O **15** *and Afrikaans stamp with Type* O **16**, *in red.*

O23	**12**	½d. black and emerald (1952)	17·00	23·00	4·50
		a. Opts transposed	—	£2250	
O24	**13**	1d. indigo and scarlet	5·00	18·00	2·00
		a. Opts transposed	95·00	£200	
O25	**27**	1½d. purple-brown	24·00	29·00	5·00
		a. Opts transposed	75·00	95·00	
O26	**14**	2d. blue and brown	3·00	21·00	3·50
		a. Opts transposed	65·00	£200	
O27	**17**	6d. blue and brown	2·75	48·00	7·50
		a. Opts transposed	26·00	£150	
O23/7 *Set of* 5			45·00	£120	20·00

The above errors refer to stamps with the English overprint on Afrikaans stamp and *vice versa*.

The use of official stamps ceased in January 1955.

Sudan

ANGLO-EGYPTIAN CONDOMINIUM

An Egyptian post office was opened at Suakin in 1867 and the stamps of Egypt, including postage dues and the official (No. O64). were used in the Sudan until replaced by the overprinted "SOUDAN" issue of 1897.

Cancellations have been identified from eleven post offices, using the following postmark types:

A

B

C

D

E

F

G

H

I

J

K

L

BERBER (*spelt* BARBAR). *Open* 1 October 1873 *to* 20 May 1884. *Postmark type* G.

DABROUSSA. *Open* 1891 *onwards. Postmark as type* J *but with* 11 *bars in arcs.*

DONGOLA. *Open* 1 October 1873 *to* 13 June 1885 *and* 1896 *onwards. Postmark types* F, G, K, L.

GEDAREF. *Open* August 1878 *to* April 1884. *Postmark type* H.

KASSALA. *Open* 15 May 1875 *to* 30 July 1885. *Postmark type* G.

KHARTOUM. *Open* 1 October 1873 *to* 14 December 1885. *Postmark types* E (*spelt* KARTUM), G (*spelt* HARTUM), I (*with or without line of Arabic above date*).

KORTI. *Open* January *to* March 1885 *and* 1897. *Postmark type* K.

SUAKIN. *Open* November 1867 *onwards. Postmark types* A, B, C (*spelt* SUAKIM), D (*spelt* SUAKIM *and also with year replaced by concentric arcs*), I (*spelt* SOUAKIN), J (*spelt* SAWAKIN, *number of bars differs*).

TANI. *Open* 1885. *Postmark type* K.

TOKAR. *Open* 1891 *onwards. Postmark type* J (7 *bars in arcs*).

WADI HALFA. *Open* 1 October 1873 *onwards. Postmark types* F (*spelt* WADI HALFE), G (*spelt* WADI HALFE), I, J (*number of bars differs*).

WADI HALFA CAMP. *Open* 1896 *onwards. Postmark type* I.

Official records also list post offices at the following locations, but no genuine postal markings from them have yet been reported: Chaka, Dara, Debeira, El Abiad, El Fasher, El Kalabat, Faras, Fashoda, Fazogl, Ishkeit, Kalkal, Karkok, Mesellemia, Sara, Sennar and Taoufikia (not to be confused with the town of the same name in Egypt).

M

The post office at Kassala was operated by Italy from 1894 until 1896, using stamps of Eritrea cancelled with postmark type M.

From the last years of the nineteenth century that part of Sudan lying south of the 5 degree North latitude line was administered by Uganda (the area to the east of the Nile) (until 1912) or by Belgium (the area to the west of the Nile, known as the Lado Enclave) (until 1910).

Stamps of Uganda or East Africa and Uganda were used at Gondokoro and Nimuli between 1901 and 1911, usually cancelled with circular date stamps or, probably in transit at Khartoum, by a lozenge-shaped grid of 18×17 dots.

Stamps of Belgian Congo were used from the Lado Enclave between 1897 and 1910, as were those of Uganda (1901–10) and Sudan (1902–10), although no local postmarks were supplied, examples being initially cancelled in manuscript.

Stamps of Sudan were used at Gambeila (Ethiopia) between 1910 and 10 June 1940 and from 22 March 1941 until 15 October 1956. Sudan stamps were also used at Sabderat (Eritrea) between March 1910 and 1940.

PRICES FOR STAMPS ON COVER TO 1945

Nos. 1/9	*from* × 20
Nos. 10/17	*from* × 6
Nos. 18/29	*from* × 5
Nos. 30/95	*from* × 2
Nos. D1/11	*from* × 30
Nos. O1/3	*from* × 10
No. O4	*from* × 15
Nos. O5/10	*from* × 50
No. O11	*from* × 10
Nos. O12/31	*from* × 15
Nos. O32/42	*from* × 10
No. A1	*from* × 20
Nos. A2/5	—
Nos. A6/10	*from* × 50
Nos. A11	*from* × 15
Nos. A12/13	—
Nos. A14	*from* × 15
Nos. A15/16	—
Nos. A17/22	*from* × 20
Nos. A23/6	—
Nos. A27/8	*from* × 10

(Currency. 10 milliemes = 1 piastre. 100 piastres = £1 Sudanese)

السودان
SOUDAN
(1)

1897 (1 Mar). *Nos.* 54*b*, 55, 56*a*, 58/*a*, 59*a*, 6/*a*, 63 *and* 64 *of Egypt optd as T* **1** *by Govt Ptg Wks, Bûlaq, Cairo.*

1		1m. pale brown	3·25	2·00
		a. Opt inverted	£225	
		b. Opt omitted (in vert pair with normal)	£1300	
		c. Deep brown	3·25	2·25
		w. Wmk inverted		
3		2m. green	1·25	1·75
4		3m. orange-yellow	1·40	1·50
5		5m. rose-carmine	2·00	70
		a. Opt inverted	£225	£250
		b. Opt omitted (in vert pair with normal)	£1400	
6		1p. ultramarine	7·00	2·00
7		2p. orange-brown	70·00	16·00
8		5p. slate	65·00	22·00
		a. Opt double	£5000	
		b. Opt omitted (in vert pair with normal)	£5000	
9		10p. mauve	40·00	50·00
1/9 *Set of* 8			£170	85·00

Numerous forgeries exist including some which show the characteristics of the varieties mentioned below.

There are six varieties of the overprint on each value. Vertical strips of 6 showing them are worth a premium.

Four settings of the overprint were previously recognised by specialists, but one of these is now regarded as an unauthorised reprint from the original type. Here reprints can only be detected when in multiples. The 2p. with inverted watermark only exists with this unauthorised overprint so it is not listed.

In some printings the large dot is omitted from the left-hand Arabic character on one stamp in the pane of 60.

Only two examples, one unused and the other used (in the Royal Collection), are known of No. 8a. In both instances one impression is partially albino.

PRINTERS. All stamps of Sudan were printed by De La Rue & Co, Ltd, London, *except where otherwise stated.*

2 Arab Postman

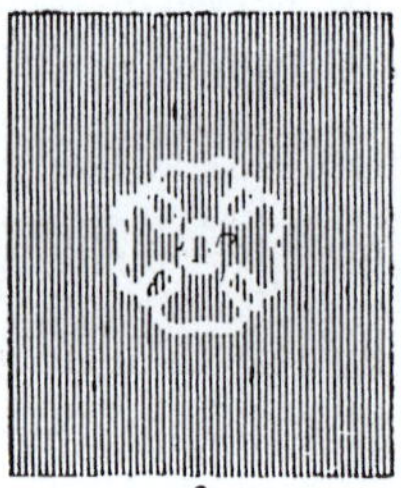
3

(Des E. A. Stanton. Typo)

1898 (1 Mar). W **3**. P 14.

10	**2**	1m. brown and pink	75	2·75
11		2m. green and brown	2·00	2·75
12		3m. mauve and green	2·00	2·25
13		5m. carmine and black	1·75	1·50
14		1p. blue and brown	9·50	3·50
15		2p. black and blue	30·00	6·50
16		5p. brown and green	40·00	15·00
17		10p. black and mauve	26·00	2·25
10/17 *Set of* 8			£100	32·00

4

5 Milliemes
(5)

1902–21. *Ordinary paper.* W **4**. P 14.

18	**2**	1m. brown and carmine (5.05)	1·25	65
19		2m. green and brown (11.02)	1·75	10
20		3m. mauve and green (3.03)	2·25	25
21		4m. blue and bistre (20.1.07)	1·50	2·50
22		4m. vermilion and brown (10.07)	1·50	75
23		5m. scarlet and black (12.03)	2·00	10
		w. Wmk inverted	—	£130
24		1p. blue and brown (12.03)	2·25	30
25		2p. black and blue (2.08)	27·00	1·75
26		2p. purple & orange-yellow (*chalk-surfaced paper*) (22.12.21)	6·00	10·00

27 | 5p. brown and green (2.08) | 27·00 | 30
a. Chalk-surfaced paper | 42·00 | 4·00
28 | 10p. black and mauve (2.11) | 27·00 | 3·75
a. Chalk-surfaced paper | 38·00 | 11·00
18/28 *Set of* 11 | 90·00 | 18·00

1903 (Sept). *No. 16 surch at Khartoum with T* **5**, *in blocks of 30.*

29 | **2** | 5m. on 5 pi. brown and green | 6·50 | 9·50
a. Surch inverted | £275 | £250

6

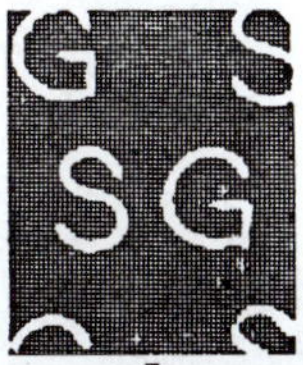
7

1921–23. *Chalk-surfaced paper. Typo.* W **4**. P 14.

30 | **6** | 1m. black and orange (4.2.22) | 80 | 4·25
31 | | 2m. yellow-orange and chocolate (1922) | 9·00 | 11·00
a. Yellow and chocolate (1923) | 12·00 | 12·00
32 | | 3m. mauve and green (25.1.22) | 2·50 | 9·00
33 | | 4m. green and chocolate (21.3.22) | 6·00 | 6·50
34 | | 5m. olive-brown and black (4.2.22) | 2·25 | 10
35 | | 10m. carmine and black (1922) | 4·00 | 10
36 | | 15m. bright blue and chestnut (14.12.21) | 3·00 | 1·00
30/36 *Set of* 7 | 25·00 | 29·00

1927–41. *Chalk-surfaced paper.* W **7**. P 14.

37 | **6** | 1m. black and orange | 70 | 10
a. Ordinary paper (1941) | 70 | 10
38 | | 2m. orange and chocolate | 75 | 10
a. Ordinary paper (1941) | 1·50 | 10
39 | | 3m. mauve and green | 70 | 10
a. Ordinary paper (1941) | 2·75 | 30
40 | | 4m. green and chocolate | 60 | 10
a. Ordinary paper (1941) | 3·50 | 40
aw. Wmk inverted | 75·00 | 75·00
41 | | 5m. olive-brown and black | 60 | 10
a. Ordinary paper (1941) | 2·50 | 10
42 | | 10m. carmine and black | 1·50 | 10
a. Ordinary paper (1941) | 3·50 | 10
43 | | 15m. bright blue and chestnut | 3·25 | 10
aw. Wmk inverted | † | £225
b. Ordinary paper (1941) | 2·50 | 10
44 | **2** | 2p. purple and orange-yellow | 4·00 | 10
a. Ordinary paper (1941) | 6·00 | 10
44*b* | | 3p. red-brown and blue (1.1.40) | 4·75 | 10
ba. Ordinary paper (1941) | 17·00 | 10
44*c* | | 4p. ultramarine and black (2.11.36) | 3·50 | 10
45 | | 5p. chestnut and green | 1·25 | 10
a. Ordinary paper (1941) | 6·50 | 2·75
45*b* | | 6p. greenish blue and black (2.11.36) | 8·50 | 1·75
ba. Ordinary paper (1941) | 42·00 | 3·00
45*c* | | 8p. emerald and black (2.11.36) | 8·50 | 3·50
ca. Ordinary paper (1941) | 50·00 | 5·00
46 | | 10p. black and reddish purple | 5·00 | 10
a. Ordinary paper. *Black and bright mauve* (1941) | 10·00 | 70
46*b* | | 20p. pale blue and blue (17.10.35) | 6·50 | 10
ba. Ordinary paper (1941) | 6·50 | 10
37/46*b Set of* 15 | 45·00 | 5·00

The ordinary paper of this issue is thick, smooth and opaque and was a wartime substitute for chalk-surfaced paper.

For similar stamps, but with different Arabic inscriptions, see Nos. 96/111.

AIR MAIL
(8)

AIR MAIL
(9)

AIR
Extended foot to "R" (R. 5/12)

1931 (15 Feb–Mar). *Air. Nos. 41/2 and 44 optd with T* **8** *or* **9** *(2p.).*

47 | **6** | 5m. olive-brown and black (Mar) | 35 | 70
48 | | 10m. carmine and black | 85 | 14·00
49 | **2** | 2p. purple and orange-yellow | 85 | 7·50
a. Extended foot to "R" | 29·00
47/9 *Set of* 3 | 1·90 | 20·00

2½ 2½

10 Statue of Gen. Gordon

AIR MAIL

(11)

1931 (1 Sept)–**37.** *Air. Recess.* W **7** (sideways*). P 14.

49*b* | **10** | 3m. green and sepia (1.1.33) | 2·50 | 6·50
50 | | 5m. black and green | 1·00 | 10
51 | | 10m. black and carmine | 1·00 | 20
52 | | 15m. red-brown and sepia | 40 | 10
aw. Wmk sideways inverted (top of G to right) | £160 | £140
b. Perf 11½×12½ (1937) | 4·50 | 10
53 | | 2p. black and orange | 30 | 10
ax. Wmk reversed | £180
ay. Wmk sideways inverted (top of G to right) and reversed | £180
b. Perf 11½×12½ (1937) | 4·50 | 15·00
53*c* | | 2½p. magenta and blue (1.1.33) | 3·50 | 10
d. Perf 11½×12½ (1936) | 3·00 | 10
da. Aniline magenta and blue | 8·50 | 3·50
dx. Wmk reversed | £140
dy. Wmk sideways inverted (top of G to right) and reversed | – | £200
54 | | 3p. black and grey | 60 | 15
a. Perf 11½×12½ (1937) | 85 | 35
55 | | 3½p. black and violet | 1·50 | 80
a. Perf 11½×12½ (1937) | 2·50 | 15·00
ay. Wmk sideways inverted (top of G to right) and reversed | † | –
56 | | 4½p. red-brown and grey | 10·00 | 15·00
57 | | 5p. black and ultramarine | 1·00 | 30
a. Perf 11½×12½ (1937) | 3·75 | 35
57*b* | | 7½p. green and emerald (17.10.35) | 9·50 | 5·00
bx. Wmk reversed | £180
by. Wmk sideways inverted (top of G to right) and reversed | £150 | £150
c. Perf 11½×12½ (1937) | 4·00 | 10·00
57*d* | | 10p. brown and greenish blue (17.10.35) | 9·00 | 1·75
e. Perf 11½×12½ (1937) | 4·00 | 23·00
ey. Wmk sideways inverted (top of G to right) and reversed | £190
49*b*/57*d Set of* 12 (P 14) | 35·00 | 26·00
52b/7e *Set of* 8 (P 11½×12½) | 24·00 | 55·00

*The normal sideways watermark shows the top of the G pointing left *as seen from the back of the stamp.*

1932 (18 July). *Air. No. 44 surch with T* **11**.

58 | **2** | 2½p. on 2p. purple and orange-yellow | 1·40 | 3·50

12 Gen. Gordon (after C. Ouless)

13 Gordon Memorial College, Khartoum

14 Gordon Memorial Service, Khartoum (after R. C. Woodville)

1935 (1 Jan). *50th Death Anniv of General Gordon. Recess.* W **7**. P 14.

59 | **12** | 5m. green | 35 | 10
60 | | 10m. yellow-brown | 85 | 25
61 | | 13m. ultramarine | 85 | 11·00
62 | | 15m. scarlet | 1·75 | 25
63 | **13** | 2p. blue | 1·50 | 20
64 | | 5p. orange-vermilion | 1·50 | 40
65 | | 10p. purple | 7·50 | 8·50
66 | **14** | 20p. black | 25·00 | 60·00
67 | | 50p. red-brown | 85·00 | £130
59/67 *Set of* 9 | £110 | £190

7½ PIASTRES
(15)

5 MILLIEMES
(16)

1935. *Air. Nos. 49b/51 and 56 surch as T* **15** *at Khartoum.*

68 | **10** | 15m. on 10m. black and carmine (Apr) | 40 | 10
a. Surch double | £900 | £1000
69 | | 2½p. on 3m. green and sepia (Apr) | 85 | 4·00
a. Second arabic letter from left missing | 50·00 | £110
b. Small "½" | 2·25 | 21·00
70 | | 2½p. on 5m. black and green (Apr) | 50 | 1·00
a. Second Arabic letter from left missing | 25·00 | 60·00
b. Small "½" | 1·25 | 6·00
c. Surch inverted | £950 | £1000
d. Ditto with variety a. | £7500
e. Ditto with variety b. | £2500 | £2750
71 | | 3p. on 4½p. red-brown and grey (Apr) | 1·75 | 18·00
72 | | 7½p. on 4½p. red-brown and grey (Mar) | 6·50 | 48·00
73 | | 10p. on 4½p. red-brown and grey (Mar) | 6·50 | 48·00
68/73 *Set of* 6 | 15·00 | £110

Nos. 69a and 70a occur in position 49 of the sheet of 50; the small "½" variety occurs in positions 17, 27, 32, 36, 41, 42 and 46.

The 15m. on 10m. surcharged in red (*Price*, £350) and the 2½p. on 3m. and 2½p. on 5m. in green are from proof sheets; the latter two items being known cancelled (*Price, £225 each, unused*).

There were four proof sheets of the 7½p. on 4½p, two in red and two in black. The setting on these proof sheets showed three errors subsequently corrected before No. 72 was surcharged. Twelve positions showed an Arabic "⅓" instead of "½", one an English "¼" for "½" and another one of the Arabic letters inverted. (*Price for red surcharge*, £350).

1938 (1 July). *Air. Nos. 53d, 55, 57b and 57d surch as T* **16** *by De La Rue.*

74 | **10** | 5m. on 2½p. magenta and blue (P 11½×12½) | 3·50 | 10
w. Wmk sideways inverted (top of G to right) | – | £120
x. Wmk reversed
75 | | 3p. on 3½p. black and violet (P 14) | 38·00 | 50·00
a. Perf 11½×12½ | £550 | £600
76 | | 3p. on 7½p. green and emerald (P 14) | 7·00 | 6·50
ax. Wmk reversed
ay. Wmk sideways inverted (top of G to right) and reversed | 70·00 | 70·00
b. Perf 11½×12½ | £550 | £600
77 | | 5p. on 10p. brown and greenish blue (P 14) | 1·75 | 4·75
ax. Wmk reversed | £120
b. Perf 11½×12½ | £550 | £600
74/7 *Set of* 4 | 45·00 | 55·00

A 5p. on 2½p., perf 11½×12½ exists either mint or cancelled from a trial printing (*Price £400 unused*).

5 Mills.

(17)

Normal ("Malime")

"Malmime" (Left-hand pane R. 5/1)

Short "mim" (Right-hand pane R. 3/1)

Broken "lam" (Right-hand pane R. 6/2)

5 M

Inserted "5" (Bottom right-hand pane R. 4/5)

1940 (25 Feb). *No. 42 surch with T* **17** *by McCorquodale (Sudan) Ltd, Khartoum.*

78 | **6** | 5m. on 10m. carmine and black | 1·25 | 75
a. "Malmime" | 60·00 | 75·00
b. Two dots omitted (Right-hand pane R. 8/6) | 60·00 | 75·00
c. Short "mim" | 60·00 | 75·00
d. Broken "lam" | 60·00 | 75·00
e. Inserted "5" | £170

4½ PIASTRES
(18)

4½ Piastres

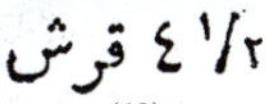
(19)

1940–41. *Nos. 41 and 45c surch as T* **18** *or* **19** *at Khartoum.*

79 | **6** | 4½p. on 5m. olive-brown & black (9.2.41) | 48·00 | 9·00
80 | **2** | 4½p. on 8p. emerald and black (12.12.40) | 42·00 | 9·00

20 Tuti Island, R. Nile, near Khartoum

21 Tuti Island, R. Nile near Khartoum

(Des Miss H. M. Hebbert. Litho Security Printing Press, Nasik, India)

1941 (25 Mar–10 Aug). P 14×13½ (T **20**) or P 13½×14 (T **21**).

81 | **20** | 1m. slate and orange (10.8) | 3·00 | 4·00
82 | | 2m. orange and chocolate (10.8) | 3·00 | 4·00
83 | | 3m. mauve and green (10.8) | 3·25 | 20
84 | | 4m. green and chocolate (10.8) | 80 | 60
85 | | 5m. olive-brown and black (10.8) | 30 | 10
86 | | 10m. carmine and black (10.8) | 13·00 | 3·50
87 | | 15m. bright blue and chestnut | 1·50 | 10
88 | **21** | 2p. purple and orange-yellow (10.8) | 6·50 | 60
89 | | 3p. red-brown and blue | 1·25 | 10
90 | | 4p. ultramarine and black | 3·50 | 10
91 | | 5p. chestnut and green (10.8) | 6·50 | 9·50
92 | | 6p. greenish blue and black (10.8) | 23·00 | 70
93 | | 8p. emerald and black (10.8) | 19·00 | 70
94 | | 10p. slate and purple (10.8) | 75·00 | 75
95 | | 20p. pale blue and blue (10.8) | 70·00 | 35·00
81/95 *Set of* 15 | £200 | 55·00

22

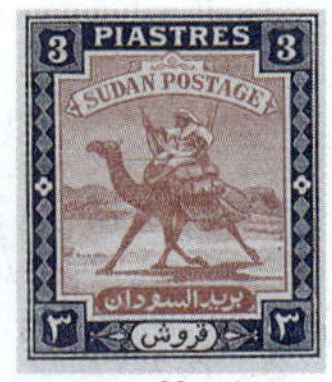
23

1948 (1 Jan–June). *Arabic inscriptions below camel altered. Typo. Ordinary paper (8, 10, 20p.) or chalk-surfaced paper (others).* W **7**. P 14.

96 | **22** | 1m. black and orange | 35 | 4·25
97 | | 2m. orange and chocolate | 80 | 4·50
98 | | 3m. mauve and green | 30 | 6·50
99 | | 4m. deep green and chocolate | 50 | 1·50
100 | | 5m. olive-brown and black | 7·00 | 2·25
w. Wmk inverted | 75·00
101 | | 10m. rose-red and black | 5·50 | 10
a. Centre inverted | † | –
102 | | 15m. ultramarine and chestnut | 5·00 | 10
103 | **23** | 2p. purple and orange-yellow | 8·50 | 2·50
104 | | 3p. red-brown and deep blue | 7·50 | 30

105 4p. ultramarine and black .... 4·00 1·75
106 5p. brown-orange and deep green .... 4·00 4·00
107 6p. greenish blue and black .... 4·50 3·25
108 8p. bluish green and black .... 4·50 3·50
109 10p. black and mauve .... 11·00 5·00
a. Chalk-surfaced paper (June).. 42·00 6·00
110 20p. pale blue and deep blue .... 4·50 50
a. Perf 13. Chalk-surfaced paper (June) .... 50·00 £190
111 50p. carmine and ultramarine .... 6·50 2·50
96/111 *Set of* 16 .... 65·00 38·00

A single used example is known of No. 101a.

For similar stamps, but with different Arabic inscriptions, see Nos. 37/46*b*.

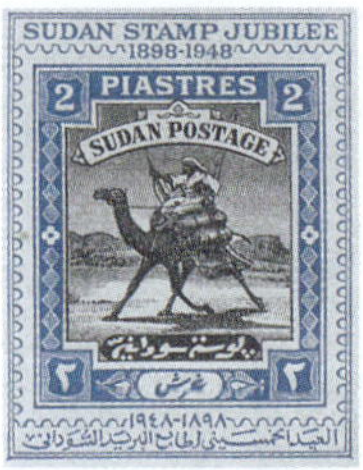
24

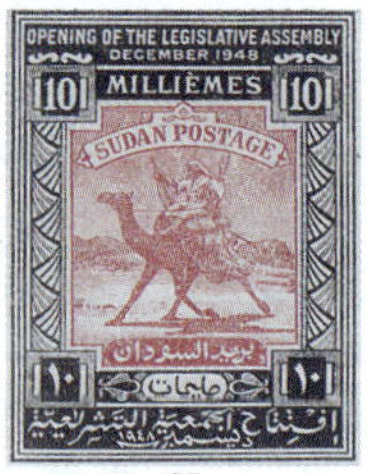
25

1948 (1 Oct). *Golden Jubilee of "Camel Postman" design. Chalk-surfaced paper. Typo.* W **7**. P 13.
112 **24** 2p. black and light blue 20 10

1948 (23 Dec). *Opening of Legislative Assembly, Chalk-surfaced paper. Typo.* W **7**. P 13.
113 **25** 10m. rose-red and black 50 10
114 5p. brown-orange and deep green .... 1·00 1·50

26 Blue Nile Bridge, Khartoum

27 Kassala Jebel

28 Sagia (water wheel)

29 Port Sudan

30 Gordon Memorial College

31 *Gordon Pasha* (Nile mail boat)

32 Suakin

33 G.P.O., Khartoum

(Des Col. W. L. Atkinson (2½p., 6p.), G. R. Wilson (3p.), others from photographs. Recess)

1950 (1 July). *Air. T* **26/33**. W **7**. P 12.
115 **26** 2p. black and blue-green .... 4·75 1·50
116 **27** 2½p. light blue and red-orange .... 1·00 1·25
117 **28** 3p. reddish purple and blue .... 3·75 1·25
118 **29** 3½p. purple-brown and yellow-brown .... 3·25 3·75
119 **30** 4p. brown and light blue .... 1·50 2·75
120 **31** 4½p. black and ultramarine .... 2·50 3·75
a. Black and steel-blue .... 13·00 7·50
121 **32** 6p. black and carmine .... 3·00 3·25
122 **33** 20p. black and purple .... 2·25 5·50
115/122 *Set of* 8 .... 20·00 21·00

34 Ibex

35 Whale-headed stork

36 Giraffe

37 Baggara girl

38 Shilluk warrior

39 Hadendowa

40 Policeman

41 Cotton Picking

42 Ambatch reed canoe

43 Nuba wrestlers

44 Weaving

45 Saluka farming

46 Gum tapping

47 Darfur chief

48 Stack Laboratory

49 Nile Lechwe

50 Camel postman

(Des Col. W. L. Atkinson (1m., 2m., 4m., 5m., 10m., 3p., 3½p., 20p.), Col. E. A. Stanton (50p.) others from photographs. Typo)

1951 (1 Sept)–**61**. *Designs as T* **34/50**. *Chalk-surfaced paper.* W **7**. P 14 (millieme values) or 13 (piastre values).
123 **34** 1m. black and orange .... 2·50 1·50
124 **35** 2m. black and bright blue .... 2·50 1·25
125 **36** 3m. black and green .... 8·00 4·00
126 **37** 4m. black and yellow-green .... 2·50 4·00
127 **38** 5m. black and purple .... 2·25 10
a. Black and reddish purple (8.6.59) .... 6·00 50
128 **39** 10m. black and pale blue 30 10
129 **40** 15m. black and chestnut .... 5·00 10
a. Black and brown-orange (1961*) .... 5·00 10
130 **41** 2p. deep blue and pale blue 30 10
a. Deep blue and very pale blue (9.58*) .... 4·50 30
131 **42** 3p. brown and dull ultramarine ... 11·00 10
a. Brown and deep blue (11.59) .. 10·00 1·75
132 **43** 3½p. bright green and red-brown ... 2·50 10
a. Light emerald and red-brown (11.61*) .... 4·25 10
133 **44** 4p. ultramarine and black .... 2·25 10
a. Deep blue and black (7.59*) ... 7·50 10
134 **45** 5p. orange-brown and yellow-green 75 10
135 **46** 6p. blue and black .... 8·50 2·50
a. Deep blue and black (8.61*) ... 16·00 7·00
136 **47** 8p. blue and brown .... 14·00 4·00
a. Deep blue and brown (5.60*). 16·00 4·00
137 **48** 10p. black and green .... 1·50 70
138 **49** 20p. blue-green and black .... 7·00 3·50
139 **50** 50p. carmine and black .... 15·00 3·50
123/39 *Set of* 17 .... 75·00 22·00

*Earliest known postmark date.

SELF-GOVERNMENT

51 Camel Postman

1954 (9 Jan). *Self-Government. Chalk-surfaced paper. Typo.* W **7**. P 13.
140 **51** 15m. orange-brown and bright green .... 50 1·25
141 3p. blue and indigo .... 50 3·00
142 5p. black and reddish purple .... 50 2·25
140/2 *Set of* 3 .... 1·40 6·00

Stamps as Type **51**, but dated "1953" were released in error at the Sudan Agency in London. They had no postal validity (*Price per set* £16 *un*).

Sudan became an independent republic on 1 January 1956. Later issues will be found in Part 14 *(Africa since Independence N-Z)* of this catalogue.

STAMP BOOKLETS

Nos. SB1/4 have one cover inscribed in English and one in Arabic. Listings are provided for booklets believed to have been issued, with prices quoted for those known to still exist.

1912 (Dec). *Black on pink cover, size 74×29 mm. Stapled.*
SB1 100m. booklet containing twenty 5m. (No. 23) in pairs £750

1924. *Black on pink cover, size 45×50 mm. Stapled.*
SB2 105m. booklet containing twenty 5m. (No. 34) in blocks of 4 ....

1930. *Black on pink cover, size 45×50 mm. Stapled.*
SB3 100m. booklet containing twenty 5m. (No. 41) in blocks of 4 .... £1300

Some supplies of No. SB3 included a page of air mail labels.

POSTAGE DUE STAMPS

1897 (1 Mar). *Type* D **24** *of Egypt, optd with T* **1** *at Bûlaq.*
D1 2m. green .... 1·75 5·00
a. Opt omitted (in horiz pair with normal) £3000
D2 4m. maroon .... 1·75 5·00
a. Bisected (2m.) (on cover).............. † —
D3 1p. ultramarine .... 10·00 3·50
D4 2p. orange .... 10·00 7·00
a. Bisected (1p.) (on cover)............... † £1200
D1/4 *Set of* 4 .... 21·00 18·00

In some printings the large dot is omitted from the left-hand Arabic character on one stamp in the pane.

No. D1 has been recorded used as a bisect.

D **1** Gunboat *Zafir*

D **2**

1901 (1 Jan)–**26**. *Typo. Ordinary paper.* W **4** (sideways). P 14.
D5 D **1** 2m. black and brown 55 60
a. Wmk upright (1912)............... £225 75·00
b. Chalk-surfaced paper (6.24*). 1·25 7·00
D6 4m. brown and green .... 2·00 90
a. Chalk-surfaced paper (9.26*). 7·00 4·00
D7 10m. green and mauve .... 5·00 3·75
a. Wmk upright (1912)................ £130 60·00
b. Chalk-surfaced paper (6.24*). 12·00 12·00
D8 20m. ultramarine and carmine .... 3·25 3·25
D5/8 *Set of* 4 .... 9·75 7·50

*Dates quoted for the chalk-surfaced paper printings are those of the earliest recorded postal use. These printings were despatched to the Sudan in March 1922 (10m.) or September 1922 (others).

The 4m. is known bisected at Khartoum or Omdurman in November/December 1901 and the 20m. at El Obeid in 1904–05.

1927–30. *Chalk-surfaced paper.* W **7**. P 14.
D9 D **1** 2m. black and brown (1930) .... 2·50 2·50
D10 4m. brown and green .... 1·00 80
D11 10m. green and mauve .... 1·25 1·60
a. Ordinary paper .... 20·00 8·00
D9/11 *Set of* 3 .... 4·25 4·50

1948 (1 Jan). *Arabic inscriptions at foot altered. Chalk-surfaced paper. Typo.* W **7**. P 14.
D12 D **2** 2m. black and brown-orange .... 1·75 40·00
D13 4m. brown and green .... 3·50 42·00
D14 10m. green and mauve .... 18·00 20·00
D15 20m. ultramarine and carmine .... 18·00 32·00
D12/15 *Set of* 4 .... 38·00 £120

The 10 and 20m. were reissued in 1979 on Sudan arms watermarked paper.

OFFICIAL STAMPS

1900 (8 Feb). *5 mils of 1897 punctured "S G" by hand. The "S" has 14 and the "G" 12 holes.*
O1 5m. rose-carmine .... 50·00 16·00

1901 (Jan). *1m. wmk Quatrefoil, punctured as No. O1.*
O2 1m. brown and pink .... 45·00 30·00

Nos. O1/2 are found with the punctured "SG" inverted, reversed or inverted and reversed.

O.S.G.S. (O 1) ("On Sudan Government Service")

O.S.G.S. (O 2) ("On Sudan Government Service")

1902. *No. 10 optd at Khartoum as Type* O **1** *in groups of 30 stamps.*

O3 **2** 1m. brown and pink ... 2·50 9·00
a. Oval "O" (No. 19) ... 40·00 £110
b. Round stops. (Nos. 25 to 30) ... 7·50 40·00
c. Opt inverted ... £275 £375
d. Ditto and oval "O" ... £3500 £4000
e. Ditto and round stops ... £750 £900
f. Opt double ... £400
g. Ditto and round stops ... £1100
h. Ditto and oval "O" ... £4000

1903–12. *T* **2** *optd as Type* O **2**, *by D.L.R. in sheets of 120 stamps.*

(i) W **3** *(Quatrefoil)*

O4 10p. black and mauve (3.06) ... 13·00 25·00
a. Malformed "O" ... £120

(ii) W **4** *(Mult Star and Cresent)*

O5 1m. brown and carmine (9.04) ... 50 10
a. Opt double ...
b. Malformed "O" ... 19·00 10·00
O6 3m. mauve and green (2.04) ... 2·50 15
a. Opt double ... £850 £850
b. Malformed "O" ... 42·00 12·00
O7 5m. scarlet and black (1.1.03) ... 2·50 10
a. Malformed "O" ... 42·00 10·00
O8 1p. blue and brown (1.1.03) ... 4·00 10
a. Malformed "O" ... 50·00 10·00
O9 2p. black and blue (1.1.03) ... 23·00 20
a. Malformed "O" ... £160 14·00
O10 5p. brown and green (1.1.03) ... 2·00 30
a. Malformed "O" ... 45·00 15·00
O11 10p. black and mauve (9.12) ... 4·00 60·00
a. Malformed "O" ... 65·00
O4/11 *Set of* 8 ... 45·00 75·00

The malformed "O" is slightly flattened on the left-hand side and occurs on position 7 of the lower pane.

1913 (1 Jan)–**22**. *Nos. 18/20 and 23/8 punctured "SG" by machine. The "S" has 12 holes and the "G" 13.*

O12 **2** 1m. brown and carmine ... 11·00 25
O13 2m. green and brown (1915) ... 10·00 7·50
O14 3m. mauve and green ... 17·00 70
O15 5m. scarlet and black ... 6·00 15
O16 1p. blue and brown ... 8·50 35
O17 2p. black and blue ... 18·00 65
O18 2p. purple and orange-yellow (*chalk-surfaced paper*) (1922) ... 6·50 8·00
O19 5p. brown and green ... 38·00 1·50
a. Chalk-surfaced paper ... 38·00 4·75
O20 10p. black and mauve (1914) ... 48·00 35·00
a. Chalk-surfaced paper ... 48·00 35·00
O12/20 *Set of* 9 ... £150 48·00

1922. *Nos. 32/5 punctured "SG" by machine. The "S" has 9 holes and the "G" 10.*

O21 **6** 3m. mauve and green ... 18·00 14·00
O22 4m. green and chocolate ... 24·00 9·00
O23 5m. olive-brown and black ... 4·00 1·50
O24 10m. carmine and black ... 4·00 1·50
O21/4 *Set of* 4 ... 45·00 23·00

1927–30. *Nos. 39/42, 44, 45 and 46 punctured "SG" by machine. Nos. O25/8 have 9 holes in the "S" and 10 in the "G"; Nos. O29/31 12 holes in the "S" and 13 in the "G".*

O25 **6** 3m. mauve and green (1928) ... 17·00 3·50
O26 4m. green and chocolate (1930) ... 80·00 48·00
O27 5m. olive-green and black ... 7·00 10
O28 10m. carmine and black ... 20·00 35
O29 **2** 2p. purple and orange-yellow ... 23·00 1·00
O30 5p. chestnut and green ... 20·00 3·50
O31 10p. black and reddish purple ... 45·00 10·00
O25/31 *Set of* 7 ... £190 60·00

The use of Nos. O25/31 on internal official mail ceased in 1932, but they continued to be required for official mail to foreign destinations until replaced by Nos. O32/46 in 1936.

S.G. (O **3**) **S.G.** (O **4**) **S.G.** (O **4a**)

1936 (19 Sept)–**46**. *Nos. 37a, 38a, 39/43 optd with Type* O **3**, *and 44, 44ba, 44c, 45, 45ba, 45ca, 46 and 46ba with Type* O **4**. W **7**. P 14.

O32 **6** 1m. black and orange (22.11.46) ... 2·50 10·00
a. Opt double ... † £180
O33 2m. orange and chocolate (*ordinary paper*) (4.45) ... 3·00 7·00
a. Chalk-surfaced paper ... — 70·00
O34 3m. mauve and green (*chalk-surfaced paper*) (1.37) ... 3·50 10
O35 4m. green and chocolate (*chalk-surfaced paper*) (6.46) ... 4·25 3·00
a. Ordinary paper ...
O36 5m. olive-brown and black (*chalk-surfaced paper*) (3.40) ... 3·75 10
a. Ordinary paper ... 22·00 40
O37 10m. carmine and black (*chalk-surfaced paper*) (6.46) ... 1·75 10
O38 15m. bright blue and chestnut (*chalk-surfaced paper*) (21.6.37) ... 8·50 30
a. Ordinary paper ... 55·00 3·00
O39 **2** 2p. purple and orange-yellow (*chalk-surfaced paper*) (4.37) ... 15·00 10
a. Ordinary paper ... 38·00 1·00
O39*b* 3p. red-brown and blue (4.46) ... 7·50 2·75
O39*c* 4p. ultramarine and black (*chalk-surfaced paper*) (4.46) ... 35·00 6·00
ca. Ordinary paper ... 65·00 4·00
O40 5p. chestnut and green (*chalk-surfaced paper*) ... 17·00 10
a. Ordinary paper ... 75·00 4·75
O40*b* 6p. greenish blue and black (4.46) ... 9·50 7·00
O40*c* 8p. emerald and black (4.46) ... 6·50 38·00
O41 10p. black and reddish purple (*chalk-surfaced paper*) (10.37) ... 35·00 16·00
a. Ordinary paper. *Black and bright mauve* (1941) ... 55·00 7·00
O42 20p. pale blue and blue (6.46) ... 30·00 27·00
O32/42 *Set of* 15 ... £160 95·00

1948 (1 Jan). *Nos. 96/102 optd with Type* O **3**, *and 103/111 with Type* O **4**.

O43 **22** 1m. black and orange ... 30 4·00
O44 2m. orange and chocolate ... 1·25 10
O45 3m. mauve and green ... 4·00 8·50
O46 4m. deep green and chocolate ... 3·75 4·50
O47 5m. olive-brown and black ... 3·50 10
O48 10m. rose-red and black ... 3·50 2·75
O49 15m. ultramarine and chestnut ... 4·00 10
O50 **23** 2p. purple and orange-yellow ... 4·00 10
O51 3p. red-brown and deep blue ... 4·00 10
O52 4p. ultramarine and black ... 3·25 10
a. Perf 13 (optd Type O **4a**) ... 13·00 15·00
O53 5p. brown-orange and deep green ... 5·00 10
O54 6p. greenish blue and black ... 3·50 10
O55 8p. bluish green and black ... 3·50 5·00
O56 10p. black and mauve ... 6·50 20
O57 20p. pale blue and deep blue ... 4·75 25
O58 50p. carmine and ultramarine ... 65·00 60·00
O43/58 *Set of* 16 ... £110 75·00

1950 (1 July). *Air. Optd with Type* O **4a**.

O59 **26** 2p. black and blue-green (R.) ... 15·00 3·25
O60 **27** 2½p. light blue and red-orange ... 1·50 1·75
O61 **28** 3p. reddish purple and blue ... 80 1·00
O62 **29** 3½p. purple-brown and yellow-brown ... 80 8·00
O63 **30** 4p. brown and light blue ... 80 7·50
O64 **31** 4½p. black and ultramarine (R.) ... 4·00 17·00
a. Black and steel-blue ... 12·00 21·00
O65 **32** 6p. black and carmine (R.) ... 1·00 4·25
O66 **33** 20p. black and purple (R.) ... 4·00 12·00
O59/66 *Set of* 8 ... 25·00 48·00

1951 (1 Sept)–**62?**. *Nos. 123/9 optd with Type* O **3**, *and 130/9 with Type* O **4a**.

O67 **34** 1m. black and orange (R.) ... 50 3·75
O68 **35** 2m. black and bright blue (R.) ... 50 1·00
O69 **36** 3m. black and green (R.) ... 8·50 15·00
O70 **37** 4m. black and yellow-green (R.) ... 10 5·50
O71 **38** 5m. black and purple (R.) ... 10 10
O72 **39** 10m. black and pale blue (R.) ... 10 10
O73 **40** 15m. black and chestnut (R.) ... 1·00 10
O74 **41** 2p. deep blue and pale blue ... 10 10
a. Opt inverted ... £850
b. Deep blue and very pale blue (9.61*) ... 1·75 10
O75 **42** 3p. brown and dull ultramarine ... 16·00 10
a. Brown and deep blue (8.60*) ... 16·00 2·00
O76 **43** 3½p. bright green and red-brown ... 25 10
a. Light emerald and red-brown (1962?) ... 4·50 3·00
O77 **44** 4p. ultramarine and black ... 3·00 10
a. Deep blue and black (1961) ... 3·50 10
O78 **45** 5p. orange-brown and yellow-green ... 25 10
O79 **46** 6p. blue and black ... 70 2·75
a. Deep blue and black (1962?) ... 10·00 8·00
O80 **47** 8p. blue and brown ... 1·00 10
a. Deep blue and brown (1962?) ... 6·00 3·50
O81 **48** 10p. black and green (R.) ... 70 10
O81*a* **49** 10p. black and green (Blk.) (1958) ... 16·00 3·00
O82 **50** 20p. blue-green and black ... 1·50 30
a. Opt inverted ... — £2750
O83 50p. carmine and black ... 3·50 1·25
O67/83 *Set of* 18 ... 48·00 27·00

The 5, 10 and 15m. values were reissued between 1957 and 1960 with a thinner overprint with smaller stops.

*Earliest known postmark date.

ARMY SERVICE STAMPS

ARMY OFFICIAL (A **1**) ARMY OFFICIAL (A **2**) Army Service (A **3**)

1905 (1 Jan). *T* **2** *optd at Khartoum as Types* A **1** *or* A **2**. W **4** (Mult Star and Crescent).

(i) "ARMY" reading up.

A1 1m. brown and carmine (A **1**) ... 4·25 2·25
a. "!" for "1" ... 70·00 40·00
b. Opt Type A **2** ... 50·00 25·00
c. Pair. Types A **1** and A **2** *se-tenant* ... 90·00 90·00

(ii) Overprint horizontal.

A2 1m. brown and carmine (A **1**) ... £350
a. "!" for "1" ... £4500
b. Opt Type A **2** ... £3000

The horizontal overprint exists with either "ARMY" or "OFFICIAL" reading the right way up. It did not fit the stamps, resulting in misplacements where more than one whole overprint appears, or when the two words are transposed.

(iii) "ARMY" reading down.

A3 1m. brown and carmine (A **1**) ... £110 75·00
a. "!" for "1" ... £950 £950
b. Opt Type A **2** ... £850 £550

1905 (Nov). *As No. A1*, W **3** *(Quatrefoil).*

A4 1m. brown and pink (A **1**) ... £170 £180
a. "!" for "1" ... £4000 £2500
b. Opt Type A **2** ... £2250 £2250
c. Pair. Types A **1** and A **2** *se-tenant* ... £3750

The setting used for overprinting Nos. A1/4 was 30 (6×5). The "!" for "1" variety occurs on R. 5/4 and overprint Type A **2** on R. 1/6 and 2/6 of the setting.

Two varieties of the 1 millieme.

A. 1st Ptg. 14 mm between lines of opt.
B. Later Ptgs. 12 mm between lines.
All other values are Type B.

1906 (Jan)–**11**. *T* **2** *optd as Type* A **3**.

(i) W **4** (Mult Star and Crescent).

A5 1m. brown and carmine (Type A) ... £450 £325
a. Opt double, one albino ... £475
A6 1m. brown and carmine (Type B) ... 1·75 20
a. Opt double, one diagonal ... † £1000
b. Opt inverted ... £500 £550
c. Pair, one without opt ... † £5500
d. "Service" omitted ... † £3750
A7 2m. green and brown ... 17·00 1·00
a. Pair, one without opt ... £3250
b. "Army" omitted ... £3500 £3500
A8 3m. mauve and green ... 19·00 40
a. Opt inverted ... £1900
A9 5m. scarlet and black ... 2·00 10
a. Opt. double ... £275 £200
ab. Opt double, one diagonal ... £250
b. Opt inverted ... † £275
c. "Amry" ... † £2500
e. Opt double, one inverted ... £1100 £475
f. "Armv" for "Army" (R. 4/9) ...
A10 1p. blue and brown ... 17·00 15
a. "Army" omitted ... — £2500
A11 2p. black and blue (1.09) ... 70·00 13·00
a. Opt double ... † £3000
A12 5p. brown and green (5.08) ... £140 65·00
A13 10p. black and mauve (5.11) ... £550 £650
A6s/10s Optd "Specimen" *Set of* 5 ... £110

There were a number of printings of these Army Service stamps; the earlier are as Type A **3**; the 1908 printing has a narrower "A" in "Army" and the 1910–11 printings have the tail of the "y" in "Army" much shorter.

A variety with no cross-bar to "A" of "Army" is known on some values, but does not appear to be constant.

(ii) W **3** (Quatrefoil).

A14 2p. black and blue ... 80·00 10·00
A15 5p. brown and green ... £110 £225
A16 10p. black and mauve ... £150 £425
A14/16 *Set of* 3 ... £300 £600
A14s/16s Optd "Specimen" *Set of* 3 ... £110

1913 (1 Jan)–**22**. *Nos. 18/20 and 23/8 punctured "AS" by machine. The "A" has 12 holes and the "S" 11.*

A17 **2** 1m. brown and carmine ... 35·00 3·75
A18 2m. green and brown ... 8·50 70
A19 3m. mauve and green ... 50·00 3·00
A20 5m. scarlet and black ... 13·00 50
a. On No. 13 ...
A21 1p. blue and brown ... 26·00 75
A22 2p. black and blue ... 65·00 5·00
A23 2p. purple and orange-yellow (*chalk-surfaced paper*) (1922) ... 70·00 55·00
A24 5p. brown and green ... 75·00 32·00
a. Chalk-surfaced paper ... 75·00 32·00
A25 10p. black and mauve (1914) ... £500 £275
A17/25 *Set of* 9 ... £750 £325

1922–24. *Nos. 31a and 34/5 punctured "AS" by machine. The "A" has 8 holes and the "S" 9.*

A26 **6** 2m. yellow and chocolate (1924) ... 80·00 45·00
A27 5m. olive-brown and black (4.2.22) ... 15·00 4·00
A28 10m. carmine and black ... 21·00 6·50
A26/8 *Set of* 3 ... £100 50·00

The use of Nos. A17/28 on internal Army mail ceased when the Egyptian units were withdrawn at the end of 1924, but existing stocks continued to be used on Army mail to foreign destinations until supplies were exhausted.

Swaziland

PRICES FOR STAMPS ON COVER TO 1945

Nos. 1/10	*from* × 40
Nos. 11/20	*from* × 4
Nos. 21/4	*from* × 5
Nos. 25/7	*from* × 10
Nos. 28/38	*from* × 4
Nos. 39/41	*from* × 5
Nos. D1/2	*from* × 30

TRIPARTITE GOVERNMENT

Following internal unrest and problems caused by the multitude of commercial concessions granted by the Swazi king the British and Transvaal governments intervened during 1889 to establish a tripartite administration under which the country was controlled by their representatives, acting with the agent of the Swazi king.

The Pretoria government had previously purchased the concession to run the postal service and, on the establishment of the tripartite administration, provided overprinted Transvaal stamps for use from a post office at Embekelweni and later at Bremersdorp and Darkton.

Swazieland (1)

1889 (18 Oct)–**90**. *Stamps of Transvaal (South African Republic) optd with T* **1**, *in black.*

(a) P 12½×12.

1 **18** 1d. carmine ... 17·00 19·00
a. Opt inverted ... £700 £650
2 2d. olive-bistre ... 85·00 25·00
a. Opt inverted ... — £1200
b. "Swazielan" ... £1100 £650
c. "Swazielan" inverted ...
3 1s. green ... 13·00 13·00
a. Opt inverted ... £800 £475

(b) P 12½.

4 18 ½d. grey 9·00 19·00
a. Opt inverted £900 £700
b. "Swazielan" £1500 £850
c. "Swazielan" inverted – £5500
5 2d. olive-bistre 21·00 15·00
a. Opt inverted £900 £450
b. "Swazielan" £475 £400
c. "Swazielan" inverted £5500 £4500
6 6d. blue 26·00 48·00
7 2s.6d. buff (20.10.90) £275 £325
8 5s. slate-blue (20.10.90) £160 £225
a. Opt inverted £1900 £2750
b. "Swazielan" £4500
c. "Swazielan" inverted
9 10s. dull chestnut (20.10.90) £6500 £4000

The variety without "d" occurs on R. 6/1 in each sheet of certain printings.

A printing of the ½d, 1d., 2d. and 10s. yellow-brown with stop after "Swazieland" was made in July 1894, but such stamps were not issued.

It is possible that the dates quoted above were those on which the overprinting took place in Pretoria and that the stamps were issued slightly later in Swaziland itself.

1892 (Aug). *Optd in carmine. P 12½.*

10 18 ½d. grey 7·50 16·00
a. Opt inverted £500
b. Opt double £475 £475
c. Pair, one without opt – £2000

No. 10 was overprinted in Pretoria during August 1892 when Swaziland was under quarantine due to smallpox. It is unlikely that it saw much postal use before all the overprints were withdrawn, although cancelled-to-order examples are plentiful.

It appears likely that no further supplies of stamps overprinted "Swazieland" were provided by Pretoria after December 1892, although stocks held at post offices were used up. The overprinted stamps were declared to be invalid from 7 November 1894. They were replaced by unoverprinted issues of the Transvaal (South African Republic).

Stamps of TRANSVAAL (SOUTH AFRICAN REPUBLIC) *used in Swaziland between* December 1892 *and* January 1900.

1885–93. *(Nos. 175/87).*

Z1 ½d. grey 35·00
Z2 1d. carmine 35·00
Z3 2d. olive-bistre 18·00
Z4 2½d. mauve 35·00
Z5 3d. mauve 35·00
Z6 4d. bronze-green 35·00
Z9 2s.6d. orange-buff

1893. *(Nos. 195/9).*

Z10 ½d. on 2d. olive-bistre (Type A surch in red)
a. Surch Type B
Z11 ½d. on 2d. olive-bistre (Type A surch in black)
Z12 1d. on 6d. blue (Type A surch) 38·00
a. Surch Type B 48·00
Z13 2½d. on 1s. green ("2½ Pence" in one line) (Type A surch) 38·00
a. Surch Type B 48·00

1894. *(Nos. 200/4).*

Z16 1d. carmine 35·00
Z17 2d. olive-bistre 35·00

1895–96. *(Nos. 205/12a).*

Z20 ½d. pearl-grey 35·00
Z21 1d. rose-red 18·00
Z22 2d. olive-bistre 18·00
Z25 6d. pale dull blue 35·00

1895. *(Nos. 213/14).*

Z27 ½d. on 1s. green

1895. *Introduction of Penny Postage (No. 215b).*

Z29 1d. red 50·00

1896–97. *(Nos. 216/24).*

Z30 ½d. green 35·00
Z31 1d. rose-red and green 18·00
Z35 4d. sage-green and green 35·00
Z36 6d. lilac and green 35·00
Z37 1s. ochre and green 70·00

Prices are for clear and fairly complete postmarks. Examples dated in 1892 and 1893 are worth a premium. For list of post offices open during this period see boxed note below. Most known examples are from Bremersdorp (squared circle inscr "SWAZIEL" later replaced by "Z.A.R." or c.d.s.) or Darkton (c.d.s.).

Shortly after the outbreak of the Boer War in 1899 the Transvaal administration withdrew from Swaziland, although the post office at Darkton, which was on the border, was still operating in early 1900. There was, however, no further organised postal service in Swaziland until the country became a British Protectorate in March 1902. From that date, until the introduction of the 1933 definitives, the stamps of Transvaal and subsequently South Africa were in use.

The following post offices or postal agencies existed in Swaziland before 1933. Dates given are those on which it is generally accepted that the offices were first opened. Some were subsequently closed before the end of the period.

Bremersdorp (1890)
Darkton (1891)
Dwaleni (1918)
Embabaan (1895)
Embekelweni (1889)
Ezulweni (1910)
Forbes Reef (1906)
Goedgegun (1925)
Hlatikulu (1903)
Hluti (1912)
Ivy (1912)
Kubuta (1926)
Mahamba (1899)
Malkerns (1914)
Malomba (1928)
Mankaiana (1913)
Mbabane (*previously* Embabaan) (1905)
M'dimba (1898)
Mhlotsheni (1910)
Mooihoek (1918)
Motshane (1929)
Nomahasha (1904)
Nsoko (1927)
Piggs Peak (1899)
Sandhlan (1903)
Sicunusa (1913)
Stegi (1910)
Umkwakweni (1898)
White Umbuluzi (1925)

BRITISH PROTECTORATE

2 King George V

3 King George VI

(Des Rev. C. C. Tugman. Recess D.L.R.)

1933 (3 Jan). Wmk Mult Script CA. P 14.

11 2 ½d. green 30 30
12 1d. carmine 30 20
13 2d. brown 30 45
14 3d. blue 45 3·00
15 4d. orange 2·75 3·50
16 6d. bright purple 1·25 1·00
17 1s. olive 1·50 2·75
18 2s.6d. bright violet 15·00 22·00
19 5s. grey 30·00 50·00
20 10s. sepia 95·00 £120
11/20 *Set of* 10 £130 £180
11s/20s Perf "Specimen" *Set of* 10 £250

The ½d., 1d., 2d. and 6d. values exist overprinted "OFFICIAL", but authority for their use was withdrawn before any were actually used. However, some stamps had already been issued to the Secretariat staff before instructions were received to invalidate their use (*Price* £25,000 *per set un*).

1935 (4 May). *Silver Jubilee. As Nos. 91/4 of Antigua, but ptd by B.W. P* 11×12.

21 1d. deep blue and scarlet 50 1·50
a. Extra flagstaff £300 £350
b. Short extra flagstaff £425
c. Lightning conductor £425
d. Flagstaff on right-hand turret £110
e. Double flagstaff £110
22 2d. ultramarine and grey-black 1·25 2·25
a. Extra flagstaff £110 £180
b. Short extra flagstaff £130 £190
c. Lightning conductor £110
23 3d. brown and deep blue 1·00 6·50
a. Extra flagstaff 80·00 £225
b. Short extra flagstaff £100 £200
c. Lightning conductor 90·00 £200
24 6d. slate and purple 1·25 3·00
a. Extra flagstaff 95·00 £170
b. Short extra flagstaff £110
c. Lightning conductor £120
21/4 *Set of* 4 3·50 12·00
21s/4s Perf "Specimen" *Set of* 4 £120

For illustrations of plate varieties see Omnibus section following Zanzibar.

1937 (12 May). *Coronation. As Nos. 95/7 of Antigua.* P 11×11½.

25 1d. carmine 50 2·50
26 2d. yellow-brown 50 25
27 3d. blue 50 75
25/7 *Set of* 3 1·40 3·25
25s/7s Perf "Specimen" *Set of* 3 90·00

(Recess D.L.R.)

1938 (1 Apr)–**54**. Wmk Mult Script CA. P 13½×13.

28 3 ½d. green 2·50 1·25
a. Perf 13½×14 (1.43) 30 2·75
b. Perf 13½×14. *Bronze-green* (2.50) 2·50 8·00
29 1d. rose-red 2·75 1·25
a. Perf 13½×14 (1.43) 1·00 1·75
30 1½d. light blue 4·25 75
a. Perf 14 (1941) 2·75 1·00
b. Perf 13½×14 (1.43) 30 1·00
ba. Printed on the gummed side £3250
31 2d. yellow-brown 2·50 1·25
a. Perf 13½×14 (1.43) 30 50
32 3d. ultramarine 11·00 1·75
a. Deep blue (10.38) 16·00 1·75
b. Perf 13½×14 *Ultramarine* (1.43) 6·00 8·00
c. Perf 13½×14 *Light ultram* (10.46) 22·00 17·00
d. Perf 13½×14 *Deep blue* (10.47) 13·00 12·00
33 4d. orange 7·00 2·25
a. Perf 13½×14 (1.43) 50 1·40
34 6d. deep magenta 18·00 2·75
a. Perf 13½×14 (1.43) 5·00 4·50
b. Perf 13½×14. *Reddish purple (shades)* (7.44) 4·50 1·50
c. Perf 13½×14. *Claret* (13.10.54) 7·50 6·50
35 1s. brown-olive 18·00 2·00
a. Perf 13½×14 (1.43) 1·25 65
36 2s.6d. bright violet 25·00 4·00
a. Perf 13½×14. *Violet* (1.43) 19·00 3·00
b. Perf 13½×14. *Reddish violet* (10.47) 18·00 11·00
37 5s. grey 55·00 15·00
a. Perf 13½×14. *Slate* (1.43) 55·00 50·00
b. Perf 13½×14. *Grey* (5.44) 35·00 15·00
38 10s. sepia 65·00 6·00
a. Perf 13½×14 (1.43) 6·50 6·00
28/38a *Set of* 11 65·00 29·00
28s/38s Perf "Specimen" *Set of* 11 £225

The above perforations vary slightly from stamp to stamp, but the average measurements are respectively: 13.3×13.2 comb (13½×13), 14.2 line (14) and 13.3×13.8 comb (13½×14).

Swaziland
(4)

1945 (3 Dec). *Victory. Nos. 108/10 of South Africa optd with T* **4**.

		Un pair	*Us pair*	*Us single*
39	1d. brown and carmine	65	80	10
40	2d. slate-blue and violet	65	80	10
41	3d. deep blue and blue	65	2·50	20
39/41 *Set of* 3		1·75	3·75	35

1947 (17 Feb). *Royal Visit. As Nos. 32/5 of Basutoland.*

		Un	*Us*
42	1d. scarlet	10	10
43	2d. green	10	10
44	3d. ultramarine	10	10
45	1s. mauve	10	10
42/5 *Set of* 4		35	35
42s/5s Perf "Specimen" *Set of* 4		£100	

1948 (1 Dec). *Royal Silver Wedding. As Nos. 112/13 of Antigua.*

46 1½d. ultramarine 50 70
47 10s. purple-brown 32·00 38·00

1949 (10 Oct). *75th Anniv of U.P.U. As Nos. 114/17 of Antigua.*

48 1½d. blue 15 20
a. "A" of "CA" missing from wmk
49 3d. deep blue 2·00 3·50
50 6d. magenta 30 70
51 1s. olive 30 1·75
48/51 *Set of* 4 2·25 5·50

1953 (3 June). *Coronation. As No. 120 of Antigua.*

52 2d. black and yellow-brown 20 20

5 Havelock Asbestos Mine

7 Swazi Married Woman

(Recess B.W.)

1956 (2 July). *T* **5**, **7** *and similar designs.* Wmk Mult Script CA. P 13×13½ (horiz) or 13½×13 (vert).

53 5 ½d. black and orange 10 10
54 – 1d. black and emerald 10 10
55 7 2d. black and brown 30 10
56 – 3d. black and rose-red 20 10
57 – 4½d. black and deep bright blue 60 10
58 – 6d. black and magenta 2·00 10
59 5 1s. black and deep olive 20 10
60 – 1s.3d. black and sepia 2·50 3·50
61 – 2s.6d. emerald and carmine-red 1·50 2·25
62 – 5s. deep lilac and slate-black 8·00 4·00
63 7 10s. black and deep lilac 18·00 17·00
64 – £1 black and turquoise-blue 50·00 30·00
53/64 *Set of* 12 75·00 50·00

Designs: *Horiz*—1d., 2s.6d. A Highveld view; *Vert*—3d., 1s.3d. Swazi courting couple; 4½d., 5s. Swazi warrior in ceremonial dress, 6d., £1. Greater Kudu.

(New Currency. 100 cents = 1 rand)

½c (11) 1c (12) 2c (13) 3½c (14)

2½c (I) 2½c (II) 4c (I) 4c (II)

5c (I) 5c (II) 25c (I) 25c (II)

50c (I) 50c (II) 50c (III)

R1 (I) R1 (II) R1 (III) R2 (I) R2 (II)

1961 (14 Feb). *Nos.* 53/64 *surch as T* **11** *to* **14**.

65 ½c. on ½d. 3·25 4·50
a. Surch inverted £950
66 1c. on 1d. 10 1·75
a. Surch double* £950
67 2c. on 2d. 10 2·00
68 2½c. on 2d. 10 1·25
69 2½c. on 3d. (Type I) 10 10
a. Type II 10 15
70 3½c. on 2d. (May) 10 1·25
71 4c. on 4½d. (Type I) 10 10
a. Type II 20 10
72 5c. on 6d. (Type I) 10 10
a. Type II 10 10
73 10c. on 1s. 25·00 4·00
a. Surch double* £1000
74 25c. on 2s.6d. (Type I) 30 65
a. Type II (central) 85 60
b. Type II (bottom left) £250 £275
75 50c. on 5s. (Type I) 30 60
a. Type II 4·50 2·25
b. Type III £450 £550
76 1r. on 10s. (Type I) 1·50 60
a. Type II 2·75 3·50
b. Type III 48·00 55·00
77 2r. on £1 (Type I) 9·00 9·50
a. Type II (middle left) 5·00 9·50
b. Type II (bottom) 60·00 £110
65/77a *Set of* 13 32·00 23·00

*On both Nos. 66a and 73a the second surcharge falls across the horizontal perforations.

No. 74b has the thin Type II surcharge at bottom left, in similar position to the thicker Type I, No. 74, with which it should not be confused.

No. 77b has the surcharge centrally placed at bottom. No. 77a has it at middle left, above "KUDU".

No. 66 with surcharge central (instead of bottom left) and No. 75a bottom left (instead of middle left) are believed to be from trial sheets released with the normal stocks. They do not represent separate printings. (No. 66 *price* £38 *un*, No. 75a *price* £120 *un*.).

(Recess B.W.)

1961. *As 1956 issue, but with values in cents and rands.* Wmk Mult Script CA. P 13×13½ (horiz) or 13½×13 (vert).

78	½c. black and orange (as ½d.) (14.2)	10	1·25
79	1c. black and emerald (as 1d.) (14.2)	10	10
80	2c. black and brown (as 2d.) (10.9)	10	2·50
81	2½c. black and rose-red (as 3d.) (14.2)	15	10
82	4c. black and deep bright blue (as 4½d.) (10.9)	15	1·50
83	5c. black and magenta (as 6d.) (10.9)	1·25	15
84	10c. black and deep olive (as 1s.) (14.2)	15	10
85	12½c. black and sepia (as 1s 3d.) (14.2)	1·25	40
86	25c. emerald and carmine-red (as 2s 6d.) (1.8)	3·00	4·50
87	50c. deep lilac and slate-black (as 5s.) (10.9)	2·50	1·40
88	1r. black and deep lilac (as 10s.) (10.9)	5·50	12·00
89	2r. black and turquoise-blue (as £1) (1.8)	13·00	11·00
78/89 *Set of* 12		24·00	32·00

15 Swazi Shields

16 Battle Axe

(Des Mrs. C. Hughes. Photo Enschedé)

1962 (24 Apr)–**66**. *Various designs as T* **15/16**. W w **12**. P 14×13 (horiz) or 13×14 (vert).

90	½c. black, brown and yellow-brown	10	10
	w. Wmk inverted	14·00	
91	1c. yellow-orange and black	10	10
	w. Wmk inverted	1·75	
92	2c. deep bluish green, black and yellow-olive	10	1·50
	w. Wmk inverted	23·00	
93	2½c. black and vermilion	10	10
	a. Black and dull red (5.66)	1·00	10
	w. Wmk inverted	2·25	
94	3½c. yellow-green and deep grey	10	40
	w. Wmk inverted	7·50	
95*a*	4c. black and turquoise-green	10	10
	a. Black and deep turquoise-green (5.66)	1·75	10
	w. Wmk inverted	7·50	
96	5c. black, red and orange-red	1·50	10
	w. Wmk inverted	8·00	
97	7½c. deep brown and buff	1·75	50
	a. Blackish brown and yellowish buff (5.66)	4·50	3·00
	w. Wmk inverted	9·50	
98	10c. black and light blue	4·50	20
	w. Wmk inverted	35·00	
99	12½c. carmine and grey-olive	1·75	3·25
	w. Wmk inverted		
100	15c. black and bright purple	1·50	70
101	20c. black and green	40	90
102	25c. black and bright blue	50	70
	w. Wmk inverted	28·00	
103	50c. black and rose-red	14·00	4·25
104	1r. emerald and ochre	2·50	2·25
105	2r. carmine-red and ultramarine	15·00	9·50
90/105 *Set of* 16		38·00	22·00

Designs: *Vert*—2c. Forestry; 2½c. Ceremonial headdress; 3½c. Musical instrument; 4c. Irrigation; 5c. Long-tailed Whydah; 7½c. Rock paintings; 10c. Secretary Bird; 12½c. Pink Arum; 15c. Swazi married woman; 20c. Malaria control; 25c. Swazi warrior; 1r. Aloes. *Horiz*—50c. Southern Ground Hornbill; 2r. Msinsi in flower.

1963 (4 June). *Freedom from Hunger. As No. 146 of Antigua.*

106	15c. reddish violet	50	15

1963 (2 Sept). *Red Cross Centenary. As Nos. 147/8 of Antigua.*

107	2½c. red and black	30	10
108	15c. red and blue	70	90

31 Goods Train and Map of Swaziland Railway

(Des R. A. H. Street. Recess B.W.)

1964 (5 Nov). *Opening of Swaziland Railway.* W w **12**. P 11½.

109	**31**	2½c. emerald-green and purple	55	10
110		3½c. turquoise-blue and deep yellow-olive	55	1·00
111		15c. red-orange and deep chocolate	70	70
112		25c. olive-yellow and deep ultramarine	85	80
109/12 *Set of* 4			2·40	2·25

1965 (17 May). *I.T.U. Centenary. As Nos. 166/7 of Antigua.*

113	2½c. light blue and bistre	15	10
114	15c. bright purple and rose	35	20

1965 (25 Oct). *International Co-operation Year. As Nos. 168/9 of Antigua.*

115	½c. reddish purple and turquoise-green	10	10
116	15c. deep bluish green and lavender	40	20

1966 (24 Jan). *Churchill Commemoration. As Nos. 170/3 of Antigua.*

117	½c. new blue	10	2·00
118	2½c. deep green	25	10
119	15c. brown	55	25
	w. Wmk inverted		
120	25c. bluish violet	80	70
117/20 *Set of* 4		1·50	2·75

1966 (1 Dec). *20th Anniv of U.N.E.S.C.O. As Nos. 196/8 of Antigua.*

121	2½c. slate-violet, red, yellow and orange	10	10
122	7½c. orange-yellow, violet and deep olive	40	60
123	15c. black, bright purple and orange	65	1·25
121/3 *Set of* 3		1·00	1·75

PROTECTED STATE

32 King Sobhuza II and Map

33 King Sobhuza II

(Des and photo Harrison)

1967 (25 Apr). *Protected State.* W w **12** (sideways on horiz designs). P 14½.

124	**32**	2½c. multicoloured	10	10
125	**33**	7½c. multicoloured	15	15
126	**32**	15c. multicoloured	20	30
127	**33**	25c. multicoloured	25	40
124/7 *Set of* 4			65	80

34 Students and University

(Des V. Whiteley. Photo Harrison)

1967 (7 Sept). *First Conferment of University Degrees.* P 14×14½.

128	**34**	2½c. sepia, ultramarine and light yellow-orange	10	10
129		7½c. sepia, ultramarine & light greenish blue	15	15
130		15c. sepia, ultramarine and rose	25	30
131		25c. sepia, ultramarine and light violet	30	35
128/31 *Set of* 4			65	75

35 Incwala Ceremony

36 Reed Dance

(Des Mrs. G. Ellison. Photo Harrison)

1968 (5 Jan). *Traditional Customs.* P 14.

132	**35**	3c. silver, vermilion and black	10	10
133	**36**	10c. silver, light brown, orange and black	10	10
134	**35**	15c. gold, vermilion and black	15	20
135	**36**	25c. gold, light brown, orange and black	15	20
132/5 *Set of* 4			40	50

3c

(**37**)

38 Cattle Ploughing

1968 (1 May). *No. 96 surch with T* **37**.

136	3c. on 5c. black, red and orange-red	1·50	10
	w. Wmk inverted	6·00	1·75

INDEPENDENT

(Des Mrs. G. Ellison. Photo Enschedé)

1968 (6 Sept). *Independence. T* **38** *and similar horiz designs.* W w **12** (sideways). P 14×12½.

137	3c. multicoloured	10	10
	a. Imperf (pair)	£140	
138	4½c. multicoloured	10	45
	a. Imperf (pair)	£140	
139	17½c. yellow, green, black and gold	15	70
140	25c. slate, black and gold	45	90
137/40 *Set of* 4		65	1·75
MS141	180×162 mm. Nos. 137/40 each×5	14·00	23·00
	a. Error Imperf	£1400	

Designs:—4½c. Overhead cable carrying asbestos; 17½c. Cutting sugar cane; 25c. Iron ore mining and railway map.

Nos. 137/40 were printed in sheets of 50, but also in miniature sheets of 20 (4×5) containing *se-tenant* strips of each value.

INDEPENDENCE
1968

(**42**)

43 Cape Porcupine

1968 (6 Sept). *Nos. 90/105 optd as T* **42**, *and No. 93 additionally surch 3c., by Enschedé. (a)* Wmk upright.

142	½c. black, brown and yellow-brown	10	10
	a. Brown omitted	£350	
	b. Albino opt	40·00	
143	1c. yellow-orange and black	10	10
	w. Wmk inverted	42·00	
144	2c. deep bluish green, black and yellow-olive	10	10
	w. Wmk inverted	—	35·00
145	2½c. black and vermilion	60	1·40
	a. Black and dull red	2·25	10
	w. Wmk inverted	38·00	
146	3c. on 2½c. black and vermilion	10	10
	a. Black and dull red	10	10
	w. Wmk inverted	38·00	
147	3½c. yellow-green and deep grey	15	10
	w. Wmk inverted	32·00	
148	4c. black and turquoise-green	10	10
	a. Black and deep turquoise-green	25	15
	b. Black and pale turquoise-green	20	1·50
149	5c. black, red and orange-red	4·25	10
	w. Wmk inverted	48·00	
150	7½c. deep brown and buff	50	10
151	10c. black and light blue	4·50	10
152	12½c. carmine and grey-olive	25	1·00
	w. Wmk inverted	2·00	3·00
153	15c. black and bright purple	25	1·25
154	20c. black and green	75	2·00
155	25c. black and bright blue	35	1·25
156	50c. black and rose-red	6·00	4·00
157	1r. emerald and ochre	2·00	4·50
158	2r. carmine-red and ultramarine	4·00	9·00
	(b) Wmk sideways		
159	50c. black and rose-red	3·50	7·00
160	2r. carmine-red and ultramarine	6·00	5·00
142/60 *Set of* 19		30·00	32·00

The 2½c., 3½c., 5c., 12½c., 50c. (No. 156) and 2r. (No. 158) exist with gum arabic only, the 1c., 2c., 3c., 4c., and 15c. with both gum arabic and PVA gum and the remainder with PVA gum only.

(Des and litho D.L.R.)

1969 (1 Aug)–**75**. *T* **43** *and similar designs showing animals. Multicoloured.* W w **12** (sideways on 3c., 3½c., 1r., 2r.). P 13×13½ (3, 3½c.), 12½×13 (1, 2r.) or 13×12½ (others).

161	½c. Caracal	10	10
162	1c. Type **43**	10	10
163	2c. Crocodile	20	10
	aw. Wmk inverted	4·00	
	b. Perf 12½×12 (29.9.75)	3·25	4·50
164	3c. Lion	60	10
165	3½c. African Elephant	75	10
166	5c. Bush Pig	30	10
167	7½c. Impala	35	10
168	10c. Charmer Baboon	45	10
169	12½c. Ratel	70	4·00
170	15c. Leopard	1·25	70
171	20c. Blue Wildebeest	95	60
172	25c. White Rhinoceros	1·40	1·75
	w. Wmk inverted	3·50	
173	50c. Common Zebra	1·50	3·25
174	1r. Waterbuck (*vert*)	3·00	6·50
175	2r. Giraffe (*vert*)	8·00	11·00
161/75 *Set of* 15		17·00	25·00

Nos. 161/73 are horizontal as Type **43** but the 3c. and 3½c. are larger, 35×24½ mm.

No. 163b was printed by the D.L.R. works in Bogota, Colombia.

Nos. 174 and 175 were reissued in new currency and No. 164 with Ww **12** upright in 1975.

44 King Sobhuza II and Flags

45 King Sobhuza II, U.N. Building and Emblem

(Des D.L.R. Litho P.B.)

1969 (24 Sept). *Admission of Swaziland to the United Nations.* W w **12** (sideways). P 13½.

176	**44**	3c. multicoloured	10	10
177	**45**	7½c. multicoloured	15	10
178	**44**	12½c. multicoloured	25	10
179	**45**	25c. multicoloured	40	40
176/9 *Set of* 4			75	55

46 Athlete, Shield and Spears

(Des L. Curtis. Litho Format)

1970 (16 July). *Ninth Commonwealth Games, Edinburgh. T* **46** *and similar vert designs. Multicoloured.* W w **12**. P 14.

180	3c. Type **46**	10	10
181	7½c. Runner	20	10
182	12½c. Hurdler	25	10
183	25c. Procession of Swaziland competitors	35	40
180/3 *Set of 4*		75	55

POSTAGE DUE STAMPS

D 1

Postage Due
2d
(D 2)

D 3

(Typo D.L.R.)

1933 (23 Jan)–**57**. Wmk Mult Script CA. P 14.

D1 D **1**	1d. carmine	40	12·00
	a. Chalk-surfaced paper. *Dp carmine* (24.10.51)	20	17·00
	ac. Error. St Edward's Crown, W **9b**	£300	
D2	2d. pale violet	2·50	28·00
	a. Chalk-surfaced paper (22.2.57)	4·75	42·00
	ab. Large "d"	50·00	
D1s/2s Perf "Specimen" *Set of 2*		45·00	

For illustrations of No. D2ab see above No. D1 of Basutoland.

1961 (8 Feb). *No. 55 surch with Type D* **2**.

D3 **7**	2d. on 2d.	1·25	2·75

Another 2d. on 2d. Postage Due, with small surcharge as Type D **5**, was produced *after the currency change*, to meet the philatelic demand (*Price 15p unused*).

(Typo D.L.R.)

1961 (14 Feb). *Chalk-surfaced paper.* Wmk Mult Script CA. P 14.

D4 D **3**	1c. carmine	15	1·10
D5	2c. violet	15	1·10
D6	5c. green	20	1·10
D4/6 *Set of 3*		45	3·00

Postage Due
1c
(D 4)

Postage Due
1c
(D 5)

1961. *No. 55 surcharged. A. As Type D* **4**. *(14 Feb).*

D7 **7**	1c. on 2d.	1·25	2·50
D8	2c. on 2d.	1·25	2·50
D9	5c. on 2d.	2·25	2·50
D7/9 *Set of 3*		4·25	6·75

B. As Type D 5. (Date?)

D10 **7**	1c. on 2d.	70	2·75
D11	2c. on 2d.	50	2·75
D12	5c. on 2d.	90	2·25
D10/12 *Set of 3*		1·90	7·00

Tanganyika

The stamps of GERMANY were used in the colony between October 1890 and July 1893 when issues for GERMAN EAST AFRICA were provided.

PRICES FOR STAMPS ON COVER TO 1945

The Mafia Island provisionals (Nos. M1/52) are very rare used on cover.

Nos. N1/5	*from* × 8
Nos. 45/59	*from* × 6
Nos. 60/2	—
Nos. 63/73	*from* × 6
Nos. 74/86	*from* × 8
Nos. 87/8	—
Nos. 89/92	*from* × 6
Nos. 93/106	*from* × 3
No. 107	—

MAFIA ISLAND

BRITISH OCCUPATION

Mafia Island was captured by the British from the Germans in January 1915. Letters were first sent out unstamped, then with stamps handstamped with Type M **1**. Later the military were supplied with handstamps by the post office in Zanzibar. These were used to produce Nos. M11/52.

(Currency. 100 heller = 1 rupee)

G.R.
MAFIA
(M 1)

(M 3)

1915 (Jan). *German East Africa Yacht types, handstamped with Type* M **1**. *Wmk Lozenges, or no wmk (1r., 2r.). A. In black (2½h. in blackish lilac). B. In deep purple. C. In reddish violet.*

		A	B	C
M1	2½h. brown	£850	†	£200
	a. Pair, one without handstamp	†	†	£3500
M2	4h. green	£750	£950	£300
	a. Pair, one without handstamp	†	†	£3500
M3	7½h. carmine	£450	£600	£100
	a. Pair, one without handstamp	£6000	†	£2500
M4	15h. ultramarine	£475	£750	£170
	a. Pair, one without handstamp	†	†	£3000
M5	20h. black and red/*yellow*	£700	£800	£325
	a. Pair, one without handstamp	†	£5500	£3500
M6	30h. black and carmine	£800	£1100	£375
	a. Pair, one without handstamp	£6500	†	£3500
M7	45h. black and mauve	£800	£1100	£475
	a. Pair, one without handstamp	£6500	†	£4000
M8	1r. carmine	£12000	†	£8000
M9	2r. green	£13000	†	£9000
M10	3r. blue-black and red	£14000	†	£10000

Prices are for unused examples.

A few contemporary Zanzibar stamps (1, 3, 6 and 15c.) and India – I.E.F. ½a and 1a are known with the above handstamp.

(Currency. 100 cents = 1 rupee)

1915 (May). *German East Africa Yacht types with handstamped four-line surcharge* "G.R.—POST—6 CENTS—MAFIA" *in black, green or violet.* Wmk Lozenges or no wmk (1r., 2r.).

M11	6c. on 2½h. brown	£1700	£1800
	a. Pair, one without handstamp	†	£7000
M12	6c. on 4h. green	£1800	£1900
	a. Pair, one without handstamp	£7000	
M13	6c. on 7½h. carmine	£1700	£1900
	a. Pair, one without handstamp	£7000	
M14	6c. on 15h. ultramarine	£1600	£1900
M15	6c. on 20h. black and red/*yellow*	£2500	£2500
M16	6c. on 30h. black and carmine	£3000	£3250
M17	6c. on 45h. black and mauve	£3000	£3000
	a. Pair, one without handstamp	£8000	
M18	6c. on 1r. carmine	£40000	
M19	6c. on 2r. green	£45000	
M20	6c. on 3r. blue-black and red	£50000	

The 5, 20 and 40 pesa values of the 1901 Yacht issue are also known with the above surcharge as are the contemporary 1c. and 6c. Zanzibar stamps.

1915 (Sept). *(a) German East African fiscal stamps.* "Statistik des Waaren-Verkehrs" *(Trade Statistical Charge) handstamped in bluish green or violet,* "O.H.B.M.S. Mafia" *in a circle, as Type* M **3**.

M21	24 pesa, vermilion/*buff*	£800	£1200
M22	12½ heller, drab	£850	£1300
	a. Pair, one without handstamp	£11000	
M23	25 heller, dull green	£850	£1300
M24	50 heller, slate	£850	£1300
	a. Pair, one without handstamp	£11000	
M25	1 rupee, lilac	£850	£1300

(b) German East African "Ubersetzungs- Gebühren" *(Fee) stamp, overprinted as before.*

M26	25 heller, grey	£850	£1300

G. R
POST
MAFIA
(M 4)

G. R.
Post
MAFIA.
(M 5)

(c) Stamps as above, but with further opt as Type M **4**, *in bluish green or violet.*

M27	24 pesa, vermilion/*buff*	£1200	
M28	12½ heller, drab	£1300	
M29	25 heller, dull green	£1300	
M30	50 heller, slate	£1300	
M31	1 rupee, lilac	£1300	
M32	25 heller, grey (No. M26)	£1300	
	a. Pair, one without handstamp Type M **4**	£8000	

Type M **3** is also known handstamped on the 7½h., 20h. and 30h. values of German East Africa 1905 Yacht issue and also on contemporary 1, 3, 6 and 25c. Zanzibar stamps.

(Currency. 12 pies = 1 anna. 16 annas = 1 rupee)

1915 (Sept). *Nos. E1/2, E4/9, E11 and E13 of Indian Expeditionary Forces (India King George V optd* "I.E.F.") *with a further opt Type* M **4** *handstruck in green, greenish black or dull blue.*

M33	3p. grey	40·00	90·00
	a. Pair, one stamp without handstamp	—	£1900
M34	½a. light green	55·00	90·00
	a. Pair, one stamp without handstamp	£2500	£1900
M35	1a. aniline carmine	60·00	90·00
M36	2a. purple	85·00	£150
M37	2½a. ultramarine	£120	£190
M38	3a. orange	£130	£190
	a. Pair, one stamp without handstamp	†	£3250
M39	4a. olive-green	£160	£250
M40	8a. deep magenta	£275	£400
	a. Pair, one stamp without handstamp	†	£3500
M41	12a. carmine-lake	£350	£500
M42	1r. red-brown and deep blue-green	£400	£550
	a. "I.E.F." opt double, one albino	£1000	
M33/42 *Set of 10*		£1500	£2250

All values exist with the overprint inverted, and several are known with overprint double or sideways.

1916 (Oct). *Nos. E1/2, E4/9, E11 and E13 of Indian Expeditionary Forces (India King George V optd* "I.E.F.") *with further opt Type* M **5** *handstruck in green, greenish black, dull blue or violet.*

M43	3p. grey	£140	£160
M44	½a. light green	£150	£150
	a. Pair, one without handstamp	†	£3500
M45	1a. aniline carmine	£120	£130
M46	2a. purple	£180	£180
M47	2½a. ultramarine	£200	£200
M48	3a. orange	£200	£200
M49	4a. olive-green	£300	£300
M50	8a. deep magenta	£400	£400
M51	12a. carmine-lake	£400	£475
M52	1r. red-brown and deep blue-green	£475	£550
M43/52 *Set of 10*		£2250	£2500

Stamps with handstamp inverted are known.

Used examples of Nos. M43/52 with black double-ring backdated postmarks of "JA 23 1915" are worth about 60% of the prices quoted.

NYASALAND-RHODESIAN FORCE

This issue was sanctioned for use by the Nyasaland-Rhodesian Force during operations in German East Africa, Mozambique and Nyasaland. Unoverprinted Nyasaland stamps were used by the Force prior to the introduction of Nos. N1/5 and, again, in 1918.

N. F.
(N 1)

1916 (7 Aug–18 Sept*). *Nos. 83, 86, 90/1 and 93 of Malawi (Nyasaland) optd with Type* N **1** *by Govt Printer, Zomba.*

N1	½d. green	1·50	8·00
N2	1d. scarlet	1·50	3·25
N3	3d. purple/*yellow* (15 Sept*)	13·00	17·00
	a. Opt double	†	£22000
N4	4d. black and red/*yellow* (13 Sept*)	35·00	40·00
N5	1s. black/*green* (18 Sept*)	45·00	50·00
N1/5 *Set of 5*		85·00	£110
N1s/5s Optd "Specimen" *Set of 5*		£225	

*Earliest known dates of use.

Of No. N3a only six copies were printed, these being the bottom row on one pane issued at M'bamba Bay F.P.O., German East Africa in March 1918.

This overprint was applied in a setting of 60 (10 rows of 6) and the following minor varieties occur on all values: small stop after "N" (R. 1/1); broken "F" (R. 4/3); very small stop after "F" (R. 6/5); no serifs at top left and bottom of "N" (R. 10/1).

TANGANYIKA

BRITISH OCCUPATION OF GERMAN EAST AFRICA

Following the invasion of German East Africa by Allied forces civilian mail was accepted by the Indian Army postal service, using Indian stamps overprinted "I.E.F." Some offices reverted to civilian control on 1 June 1917 and these used stamps of East Africa and Uganda until the "G.E.A." overprints were ready. The last field post offices, in the southern part of the country, did not come under civilian control until 15 March 1919.

(Currency. 100 cents = 1 rupee)

G.E.A. (1) G.E.A. (2) G.E.A. (3)

1917 (Oct)–**21**. *Nos. 44/5, 46a/51, 52b, 53/9 and 61 of Kenya, Uganda and Tanganyika optd with T* **1** *and* **2**. *Ordinary paper (1c. to 15c.) or chalk-surfaced paper (others).* Wmk Mult Crown CA.

45	1c. black (R.)	15	80
	aw. Wmk inverted	£200	
	ay. Wmk inverted and reversed	£130	
	b. Vermilion opt	20·00	16·00
47	3c. green	15	15
48	6c. scarlet	15	10
	a. Wmk sideways	£2000	£2500
	w. Wmk inverted	†	£225
49	10c. yellow-orange	50	60
	y. Wmk inverted and reversed	£170	
50	12c. slate-grey	50	2·25
	y. Wmk inverted and reversed	£150	
51	15c. bright blue	1·00	3·25
	w. Wmk inverted	£170	
52	25c. black and red/*yellow*	80	3·50
	a. On pale yellow (1921)	1·40	15·00
	as. Optd "Specimen"	40·00	
53	50c. black and lilac	1·00	3·25
54	75c. black/*blue-green, olive back* (R.)	1·00	4·50
	a. On emerald back (1921)	3·25	45·00
	as. Optd "Specimen"	50·00	
55	1r. black/*green* (R.)	3·00	7·00
	a. On emerald back (1919)	8·50	55·00
56	2r. red and black/*blue*	11·00	45·00
	x. Wmk reversed		

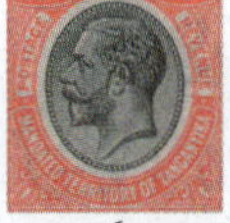

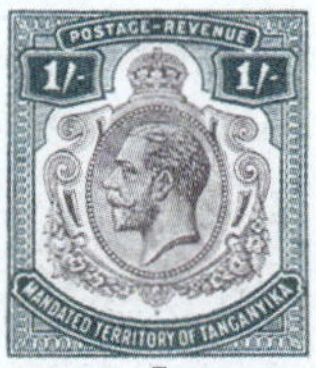

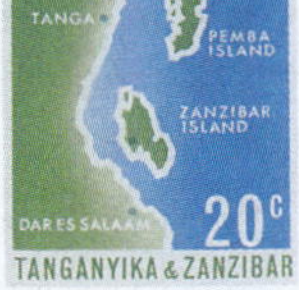

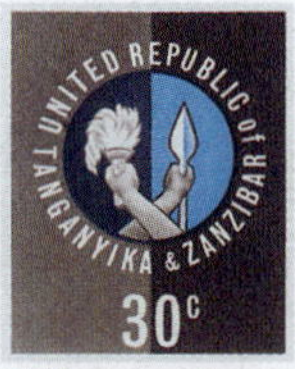

57		3r. violet and green	13·00	80·00
58		4r. red and green/*yellow*	17·00	90·00
59		5r. blue and dull purple	38·00	90·00
60		10r. red and green/*green*	95·00	£325
		a. On emerald back	£120	£400
61		20r. black and purple/*red*	£200	£425
62		50r. carmine and green	£500	£850
		s. Optd "Specimen"	£225	
45/61 *Set of* 16			£350	£1000
45s/61s Optd "Specimen" *Set of* 16			£400	

Early printings of the rupee values exist with very large stop after the "E" in "G.E.A." (R. 5/3). There are round stops after "E" varieties, which in one position of later printings became a small stop.

Examples of Nos. 45/55 can also be found handstamped with Type M **5**, but these were not issued.

1921. *Nos. 69/74 of Kenya, Uganda and Tanganyika optd with T* **1** *or* **2**. *Chalk-surfaced paper (50c. to 5r.).* Wmk Mult Script CA.

63		12c. slate-grey	6·50	95·00
64		15c. bright blue	4·00	7·00
65		50c. black and dull purple	11·00	85·00
66		2r. red and black/*blue*	32·00	£120
67		3r. violet and green	80·00	£200
68		5r. blue and dull purple	£110	£300
63/8 *Set of* 6			£200	£700
63s/8s Optd "Specimen" *Set of* 6			£225	

1922. *Nos. 65 and 68 of Kenya, Uganda and Tanganyika optd by the Government Printer at Dar-es-Salaam with T* **3**. Wmk Mult Script CA.

72		1c. black (R.)	1·00	20·00
73		10c. orange	1·25	14·00
		y. Wmk inverted and reversed	£140	

No. 73 is known with the overprint inverted, but this is of clandestine origin.

BRITISH MANDATED TERRITORY

(New Currency. 100 cents = 1 shilling)

4 Giraffe

5 Giraffe

(Recess B.W.)

1922–24. *Head in black.*

(a) Wmk Mult Script CA. P 15×14.

74	**4**	5c. slate-purple	2·25	20
75		10c. green	2·25	85
76		15c. carmine-red	2·00	10
77		20c. orange	2·50	10
78		25c. black	5·50	6·50
79		30c. blue	5·00	5·00
80		40c. yellow-brown	2·75	4·50
81		50c. slate-grey	2·75	1·50
82		75c. yellow-bistre	3·25	18·00
		(b) Wmk Mult Script CA (sideways). P 14.		
83	**5**	1s. green	5·50	16·00
		a. Wmk upright (1923)	3·25	11·00
84		2s. purple	5·50	18·00
		a. Wmk upright (1924)	4·50	27·00
85		3s. black	23·00	32·00
86		5s. scarlet	42·00	90·00
		a. Wmk upright (1923)	21·00	80·00
87		10s. deep blue	£140	£275
		a. Wmk upright (1923)	65·00	£130
88		£1 yellow-orange	£250	£400
		a. Wmk upright (1923)	£200	£375
74/88a *Set of* 15			£300	£600
74s/88s Optd "Specimen" *Set of* 15			£475	

On the £1 stamp the words of value are on a curved scroll running across the stamp above the words "POSTAGE AND REVENUE".

Nos. 83/8 are known showing a forged Dodoma postmark, dated "16 JA 22".

1925. *As 1922. Frame colours changed.*

89	**4**	5c. green	5·00	1·50
90		10c. orange-yellow	5·50	1·50
91		25c. blue	4·00	17·00
92		30c. purple	4·75	16·00
89/92 *Set of* 4			17·00	32·00
89s/92s Optd "Specimen" *Set of* 4			80·00	

6

7

(Typo D.L.R.)

1927–31. *Head in black. Chalk-surfaced paper (5s., 10s., £1).* Wmk Mult Script CA. P 14.

93	**6**	5c. green	1·75	10
94		10c. yellow	2·00	10
95		15c. carmine-red	1·75	10
96		20c. orange-buff	2·75	10
97		25c. bright blue	3·75	2·00
98		30c. dull purple	2·75	2·50
98*a*		30c. bright blue (1931)	25·00	30
99		40c. yellow-brown	2·00	5·00
100		50c. grey	2·50	1·00
101		75c. olive-green	2·00	17·00
102	**7**	1s. green	4·25	2·75
103		2s. deep purple	22·00	4·50
104		3s. black	29·00	65·00
105		5s. carmine-red	23·00	20·00
		a. Ordinary paper		
106		10s. deep blue	65·00	£110
107		£1 brown-orange	£170	£300
93/107 *Set of* 16			£325	£475
93s/107s Optd or Perf (No. 98as) "Specimen" *Set of* 16			£275	

Examples of Nos. 104/7 are known showing a forged Dar-es-Salaam postmark dated "20 NO 1928".

Tanganyika became part of the joint East African postal administration on 1 January 1933 and subsequently used the stamps of KENYA, UGANDA AND TANGANYIKA.

INDEPENDENT REPUBLIC

8 Teacher and Pupils

9 District Nurse and Child

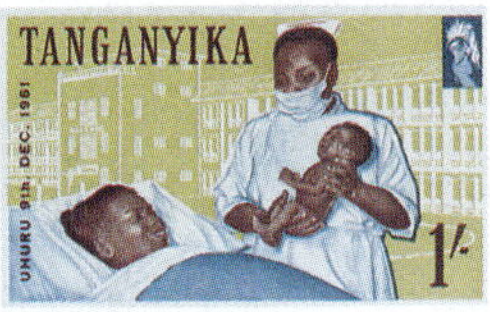

14 "Maternity"

15 Freedom Torch over Mt Kilimanjaro

(Des V. Whiteley. Photo Harrison)

1961 (9 Dec)–**64**. *Independence. T* **8/9**, **14/15** *and similar designs.* P 14×15 (5c., 30c.), 15×14 (10c.,15c., 20c., 50c.) or 14½ (others).

108		5c. sepia and light apple-green	10	10
109		10c. deep bluish green	10	10
110		15c. sepia and blue	10	10
		a. Blue omitted	£650	
111		20c. orange-brown	10	10
112		30c. black, emerald and yellow	10	10
		a. Inscr "UHURU 196"	£600	£180
		b. "1" inserted after "196"	20·00	
113		50c. black and yellow	10	10
114		1s. brown, blue and olive-yellow	15	10
115		1s.30 red, yellow, black, brown and blue	3·00	10
		a. Red, yellow, black, brown & deep blue (10.3.64)	5·00	80
116		2s. blue, yellow, green and brown	1·00	10
117		5s. deep bluish green and orange-red	1·00	50
118		10s. black, reddish purple and light blue	15·00	4·75
		a. Reddish purple (diamond) omitted	£160	£100
119		20s. red, yellow, black, brown and green	4·00	9·00
108/19 *Set of* 12			22·00	13·50

Designs: *Vert (as T* **9**)—15c. Coffee-picking; 20c. Harvesting maize; 50c. Serengeti lions. *Horiz (as T* **8**)—30c. Tanganyikan flag. *(As T* **14**)—2s. Dar-es-Salaam waterfront; 5s. Land tillage; 10s. Diamond and mine. *Vert*—20s. Type **15**.

No. 112a. The missing "1" in "1961" occurs on emerald Plate 1C, R. 10/10. The "1" was later inserted but it is, however, very slightly shorter and the figure is more solid than normal.

19 Pres. Nyerere inaugurating Self-help Project

20 Hoisting Flag on Mt Kilimanjaro

(Photo Harrison)

1962 (9 Dec). *Inauguration of Republic. Vert designs as T* **19/20**. P 14½.

120		30c. emerald	10	10
121		50c. yellow, black, green, red and blue	10	10
122		1s.30 multicoloured	10	10
123		2s.50 black, red and blue	30	50
120/3 *Set of* 4			55	70

Designs:—1s.30, Presidential emblem; 2s.50, Independence Monument.

23 Map of Republic

24 Torch and Spear Emblem

(Des M. Coaman. Photo Harrison)

1964 (7 July). *United Republic of Tanganyika and Zanzibar Commemoration.* P 14×14½.

124	**23**	20c. yellow-green and light blue	30	10
125	**24**	30c. blue and sepia	10	10
126		1s.30 orange-brown and ultramarine	10	10
127	**23**	2s.50 purple and ultramarine	1·50	1·25
124/7 *Set of* 4			1·75	1·25

Despite the inscription on the stamps the above issue was only on sale in Tanganyika and had no validity in Zanzibar.

STAMP BOOKLETS

1922–25. *Black on red cover.*

SB1 3s. booklet containing 5c., 10c., 15c. and 20c. (Nos. 74/7), each in block of 6 ..... £2000
a. As No. SB1, but contents changed (Nos. 89/90, 76/7) (1925)

1922–26. *Black on red cover. Stapled.*

SB2 3s. booklet containing six 10c., and twelve 5c. and 15c. (Nos. 74/6) in blocks of 6
a. As No. SB2, but contents changed (Nos. 74, 90, 76) (1925)
b. As No. SB2, but contents changed (Nos. 89/90, 76) (1926) £1400

1927. *Black on red covers. Stapled.*

SB3 3s. booklet containing six 10c., and twelve 5c. and 15c. (Nos. 93/5) in blocks of 6 ..... £1000
SB4 3s. booklet containing 5c., 10c. and 15c. (Nos. 93/5), each in block of 10 ..... £1500

1961 (9 Dec). *Black on blue-green cover, size 48×46 mm. Stitched.*

SB5 5s. booklet containing 10c., 15c., 20c., 30c. and 50c. (Nos. 109/13), each in block of 4 ..... 4·75

OFFICIAL STAMPS

OFFICIAL (O **1**)   **OFFICIAL** (O **2**) (3½ mm tall)

1961 (9 Dec). *Nos. 108/14 and 117 optd with Type O* **1** *(10, 15, 20, 50c. or larger (17 mm) 5, 30c.) or with Type O* **2** *(1s. or larger (22 mm) 5s.).*

O1		5c. sepia and light apple-green	10	10
O2		10c. deep bluish green	10	10
O3		15c. sepia and blue	10	10
O4		20c. orange-brown	10	10
O5		30c. black, emerald and yellow	10	10
O6		50c. black and yellow	10	10
O7		1s. brown, blue and olive-yellow	10	10
O8		5s. deep bluish green and orange-red	75	85
O1/8 *Set of* 8			1·00	1·00

Tanzania

The United Republic of Tanganyika and Zanzibar, formed 26 April 1964, was renamed the United Republic of Tanzania on 29 October 1964.

Issues to No. 176, except Nos. Z142/5, were also valid in Kenya and Uganda.

(Currency. 100 cents = 1 shilling)

25 Hale Hydro Electric Scheme

26 Tanzanian Flag

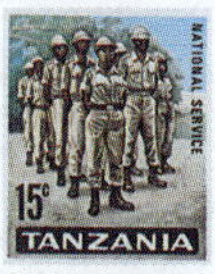

27 National Servicemen

33 Dar-es-Salaam Harbour

38 Arms of Tanzania

(Des V. Whiteley. Photo Harrison)

1965 (9 Dec). *T* **25/7**, **33**, **38** *and similar designs.* P 14×14½ (5c., 10c., 20c., 50c., 65c.), 14½×14 (15c., 30c., 40c.), or 14 (others).

128		5c. ultramarine and yellow-orange	10	10
129		10c. black, greenish yellow, green and blue	10	10
130		15c. multicoloured	10	10
131		20c. sepia, grey-green and greenish blue	10	10
132		30c. black and red-brown	10	10
133		40c. multicoloured	1·00	20
134		50c. multicoloured	1·00	10
135		65c. green, red-brown and blue	2·75	2·50
136		1s. multicoloured	1·50	10
137		1s.30 multicoloured	6·50	1·50
138		2s.50 blue and orange-brown	6·50	1·25
139		5s. lake-brown, yellow-green and blue	80	20
140		10s. olive-yellow, olive-green and blue	1·00	3·75
141		20s. multicoloured	7·00	18·00

Z142/5 … Z39/41 *Set of* 14 25·00 25·00

Designs: *Horiz (as T* **25**)—20c. Road-building; 50c. Common Zebras, Manyara National Park; 65c. Mt Kilimanjaro. *Vert (as T* **27**)—30c. Drum, spear, shield and stool; 40 c. Giraffes, Mikumi National Park. *Horiz (As T* **33**)—1s.30, Skull of *Zinjanthropus* and excavations, Olduvai Gorge, 2s.50, Fishing; 5s. Sisal industry; 10s. State House, Dar-es-Salaam.

Z **39** Pres, Nyerere and First Vice-Pres, Karume within Bowl of Flame

Z **40** Hands supporting Bowl of Flame

(Des J. Ahmed (Type Z **39**), G. Vasarhelyi (Type Z **40**). Photo Enschedé)

1966 (26 April). *2nd Anniv of United Republic.* P 14×13.

Z142 Z **39** 30c. multicoloured 20 45
Z143 Z **40** 50c. multicoloured 20 45
Z144 1s.30, multicoloured 30 45
Z145 Z **39** 2s.50, multicoloured 40 1·25
Z142/5 *Set of* 4 1·00 2·40

Nos. 2142/5 were on sale in Zanzibar only.

39 Black-footed Cardinalfish

40 Sobrinus Mudskipper

41 Lionfish

(Des Rena Fennesy. Photo Harrison)

1967 (9 Dec)–**73**. *Designs as T* **39/41**. *Chalk-surfaced paper.* P 14×15 (5c. to 70c.) or 14½ (others).

142 5c. magenta, yellow-olive and black 10 2·50
a. Glazed, ordinary paper (22.1.71) 30 2·00
143 10c. brown and bistre 10 10
a. Glazed, ordinary paper (27.9.72) 30 2·25
144 15c. grey, turquoise-blue and black 10 2·00
a. Glazed, ordinary paper (22.1.71) 30 3·75
145 20c. brown and turquoise-green 10 10
a. Glazed, ordinary paper (16.7.73) 30 6·00
146 30c. sage-green and black 20 10
a. Glazed, ordinary paper (3.5.71) 9·00 3·50
147 40c. yellow, chocolate and bright green 1·00 10
a. Glazed, ordinary paper (10.2.71) 1·00 60
148 50c. multicoloured 20 10
a. Glazed, ordinary paper (10.2.71) 50 2·25
149 65c. orange-yellow, bronze-green and black 2·00 4·50
150 70c. multicoloured (15.9.69) 1·00 2·75
a. Glazed, ordinary paper (22.1.71) 4·25 7·00
151 1s. orange-brown, slate-blue and maroon 30 10
a. Glazed ordinary paper (3.2.71) 1·00 10
152 1s.30 multicoloured 4·00 10
153 1s.50 multicoloured (15.9.69) 2·50 50
a. Glazed, ordinary paper (27.9.72) 2·25 10
154 2s.50 multicoloured 2·25 3·25
a. Glazed, ordinary paper (27.9.72) 12·00 10
155 5s. greenish yellow, black and turquoise-grn 5·00 2·75
a. Glazed, ordinary paper (12.12.70*) 3·25 10
156 10s. multicoloured 1·00 3·00
a. Glazed, ordinary paper (*dull blue-green background*) (12.12.70*) 1·00 10
ab. Deep dull green background (12.9.73) 1·75 50
157 20s. multicoloured 1·25 6·50
a. Glazed, ordinary paper (12.12.70*) 5·50 15
142/57 *Set of* 16 18·00 24·00
142a/57a *Set of* 14 35·00 24·00

*Earliest known postmark date.

Designs: *Horiz as T* **39/40**—15c. White-spotted Puffer; 20c. Thorny Seahorse; 30c. Dusky Batfish; 40c. Black-spotted Sweetlips 50c. Blue Birdwrasse; 65c. Bennett's Butterflyfish; 70c. Black-tipped Grouper. *Horiz as T* **41**:—1s.30, Powder-blue Surgeonfish; 1s.50, Yellow-finned Fusilier; 2s.50, Emperor Snapper; 5s. Moorish Idol; 10s. Painted Triggerfish; 20s. Horned Squirrelfish.

On chalk-surfaced paper all values except the 30c. exist with PVA gum as well as gum arabic, but the 70c. and 1s.50 exist with PVA gum only. Stamps on glazed, ordinary paper come only with PVA gum.

OFFICIAL STAMPS

(Opt photo Harrison)

1965 (9 Dec). *Nos. 128/32, 134, 136, 139 optd as Types* O **1** *(15c., 30c. or larger (17 mm) 5c., 10c., 20c., 50c.), or with* O **2** *of Tanganyika (1s., 5s.).*

O9 5c. ultramarine and yellow-orange 10 1·50
O10 10c. black, greenish yellow, green & blue 10 1·50
O11 15c. multicoloured 10 1·50
O12 20c. sepia, grey-green and greenish blue 10 1·50
O13 30c. black and red-brown 10 40
O14 50c. multicoloured 15 1·50
O15 1s. multicoloured 30 40
O16 5s. lake-brown, yellow-green and blue 1·75 8·00
O9/16 *Set of* 8 2·25 14·50

(Opt litho Govt Printer, Dar-es-Salaam)

1967 (10 Nov). *Nos. 134, 136 and 139 optd as No. O14 (50c.) or with Type* O **3** *(others).*

O17 50c. multicoloured (18.11) – 8·50
O18 1s. multicoloured (18.11) 17·00 5·50
O19 5s. lake-brown, yellow-green and blue 10·00 9·00

The issue dates given are for the earliest known postmarked copies.

Nos. O9/16 were overprinted by Harrison in photogravure and Nos. O17/19 have litho overprints by the Government Printer, Dar-es-Salaam. On No. O17 the overprint is the same size (17 mm long) as on No. O14.

1967 (9 Dec)–**71**. *Nos. 142/6, 148, 151 and 155 optd as Type* O **1**, *but larger (measuring 17 mm) (5c. to 50c.) or as Type* O **2** *of Tanganyika (1s. and 5s.). Chalk-surfaced paper.*

O20 5c. magenta, yellow-olive and black 10 3·00
a. Glazed, ordinary paper (22.1.71) 1·75 4·75
O21 10c. brown and bistre 10 50
a. Glazed, ordinary paper (1971) 5·00 4·00
O22 15c. grey turquoise-blue and black 10 3·50
a. Glazed, ordinary paper (22.1.71) 1·75 5·50
O23 20c. brown and turquoise-green 10 50
O24 30c. sage-green and black 10 30
O25 50c. multicoloured 15 1·60
a. Glazed, ordinary paper (22.1.71) 1·75 5·50
O26 1s. orange-brown, slate-blue and maroon 30 3·00
a. Glazed, ordinary paper (3.2.71) 10·00 5·50
O27 5s. greenish yellow, black and turquoise-greenn 2·50 17·00
a. Glazed, ordinary paper (3.2.71) 14·00 18·00
O20/7 *Set of* 8 3·00 25·00
O20a/7a *Set of* 6 30·00 38·00

The chalk-surfaced paper exists with both PVA gum and gum arabic, but the glazed, ordinary paper exists PVA gum only.

OFFICIAL (O **4**) **OFFICIAL** (O **5**)

1970 (10 Dec)–**73**. *Nos. 142/8, 151 and 155 optd locally by letterpress as Type* O **4** *(5 to 50c.) or as Type* O **2** *of Tanganyika, but measuring 28 mm (1s. and 5s.).*

(a) Chalk-surfaced paper.

O28 5c. magenta, yellow-olive and black 25 4·00
a. "OFFCIAL" (R.7/6)
O29 10c. brown and bistre 25 1·75
a. "OFFCIAL" (R.7/6)
O30 20c. brown and turquoise-green 50 2·00
O31 30c. sage-green and black 60 2·00
O28/31 *Set of* 4 1·40 8·75

(b) Glazed, ordinary paper (1973).

O32 5c. magenta, yellow-olive and black – 4·00
a. "OFFCIAL" (R.7/6) – 55·00
b. "OFFICIA" (R.10/9) – 60·00
O33 10c. brown and bistre – 4·00
a. "OFFCIAL" (R.7/6) – 60·00
O34 15c. grey, turquoise-blue and black – 4·00
a. "OFFCIAL" (R.7/6) – 60·00
O35 20c. brown and turquoise-green – 3·50
O36 40c. yellow, chocolate and bright green – 3·00
a. Opt double
b. "OFFICIA" (R.10/9) – 75·00
O37 50c. multicoloured – 3·00
a. "OFFCIAL" (R.7/6) – 65·00
O38 1s. orange-brown, slate-blue and maroon – 11·00
a. Opt double
O39 5s. greenish yellow, black and turquoise green – 30·00

The letterpress overprint can be distinguished from the photogravure by its absence of screening dots and the overprint showing through to the reverse, apart from the difference in length.

POSTAGE DUE STAMPS

Postage Due stamps of Kenya and Uganda wre issued for provisional use as such in Tanganyika on 1 July 1933. The postmark is the only means of identification.

The Postage Due stamps of Kenya, Uganda and Tanganyika were used in Tanganyika until 2 January 1967.

D **1**

(Litho D.L.R.)

1967 (3 Jan). P 14×13½.

D1 D **1** 5c. scarlet 35 7·50
D2 10c. green 45 7·50
D3 20c. deep blue 50 9·00
D4 30c. red-brown 50 10·00
D5 40c. bright purple 50 13·00
D6 1s. orange 80 12·00
D1/6 *Set of* 6 2·75 55·00

1969 (12 Dec)–**71**. *Chalk-surfaced paper.* P 14×15.

D7 D **1** 5c. scarlet 30 11·00
a. Glazed, ordinary paper (13.7.71) 4·00 8·00
D8 10c. green 65 6·00
a. Glazed, ordinary paper (13.7.71) 75 3·75
D9 20c. deep blue 40 12·00
a. Glazed, ordinary paper (13.7.71) 2·50 9·00
D10 30c. red-brown 50 18·00
a. Glazed, ordinary paper (13.7.71) 85 6·50
D11 40c. bright purple 2·00 18·00
a. Glazed, ordinary paper (13.7.71) 6·50 35·00
D12 1s. orange (*glazed, ordinary paper*) (13.7.71) 4·75 32·00
D7/12 *Set of* 6 7·75 70·00

The stamps on chalk-surfaced paper exist only with gum arabic, but the stamps on glazed paper exist only with PVA gum.

Togo

The stamps of GERMANY were used in the colony from March 1888 until June 1897 when issues for TOGO were provided.

PRICES FOR STAMPS ON COVER

Nos. H1/7	*from* × 6
No. H8	—
No. H9	*from* × 6
No. H10	*from* × 2
No. H11	—
Nos. H12/13	*from* × 6
Nos. H14/16	—
Nos. H17/19	*from* × 12
Nos. H20/6	—
Nos. H27/8	*from* × 20
No. H29	—
Nos. H30/1	*from* × 6
Nos. H32/3	—
Nos. H34/58	*from* × 6

ANGLO-FRENCH OCCUPATION

French forces invaded southern Togo on 8 August 1914 and the British landed at Lomé on 12 August. The German administration surrendered on 26 August 1914.

The territory was jointly administered under martial law, but was formally divided between Great Britain and France, effective 1 October 1920. League of Nations mandates were issued for both areas from 20 July 1922.

(Currency. 100 pfennig = 1 mark)

Stamps of German Colonial issue Yacht Types 1900 and 1909–14 (5pf. and 10pf.)

TOGO
Anglo-French
Occupation
(1)

Half penny
(2)

SETTINGS. Nos. H1/33 were all overprinted or surcharged by the Catholic Mission, Lomé.

The initial setting for the 3pf. to 80pf. was of 50 (10×5), repeated twice on each sheet of 100. Overprints from this setting, used for Nos. H1/9, had the lines of type 3 mm apart.

Nos. H1/2 were subsequently surcharged, also from a setting of 50, to form Nos. H12/13. The surcharge setting showed a thin dropped "y" with small serifs on R. 1/1–2, 2/1, 3/1, 4/1 and 5/1–2.

The type from the overprint and surcharge was then amalgamated in a new setting of 50 on which the lines of the overprint were only 2 mm apart. On this amalgamated setting, used for Nos. H27/8, the thin "y" varieties were still present and R. 4/7 showed the second "O" of "TOGO" omitted.

The surcharge was subsequently removed from this "2 mm" setting which was then used to produce Nos. H17/19. The missing "O" was spotted and corrected before any of the 30pf. stamps were overprinted.

The remaining low values of the second issue, Nos. H14/16 and H20/2, were overprinted from settings of 25 (5×5), either taken from the last setting of 50 or from an amended version on which there was no space either side of the hyphen. This slightly narrower overprint was subsequently used for Nos. H29/33. It shows the top of the second "O" broken so that it resembles a "U" on R. 1/5.

The mark values were overprinted from settings of 20 (5×4), showing the same differences in the spacing of the lines as on the low values.

It is believed that odd examples of some German colonial values were overprinted from individual settings in either spacing.

1914 (17 Sept*). *Optd with T* **1** *by Catholic Mission, Lomé. Wide setting. Lines 3 mm apart.*

H1 3pf. brown £110 95·00
H2 5pf. green £100 95·00
H3 10pf. carmine (Wmk Lozenges) £120 £100
a. Opt inverted £7500 £3000
b. Opt *tête-bêche* in vert pair † £8000
c. No wmk † £5500
H4 20pf. ultramarine 30·00 42·00
H5 25pf. black and red/*yellow* 30·00 35·00
H6 30pf. black and orange/*buff* 35·00 48·00
H7 40pf. black and carmine £225 £250
H8 50pf. black and purple/*buff* £10000 £8000
H9 80pf. black and carmine/*rose* £225 £275
H10 1m. carmine £5000 £2500
H11 2m. blue £8000 £9500
a. "Occupation" double £15000 £11000
b. Opt inverted £10000

*The post office at Lomé was open for four hours on 17 September, before closing again on instructions from Accra. It finally reopened on 24 September.

The *tête-bêche* overprint on the 10pf. is due to the sheet being turned round after the upper 50 stamps had been overprinted so that vertical pairs from the two middle rows have the overprint *tête-bêche*.

1914 (1 Oct). *Nos. H1 and H2 surch as T* **2**.

H12	½d. on 3pf. brown	£160	£140
	a. Thin "y" in "penny"	£400	£350
H13	1d. on 5pf. green	£160	£140
	a. Thin "y" in "penny"	£400	£350

TOGO
Anglo-French
Occupation
(3)

TOGO
Anglo-French
Occupation
Half penny
(4)

1914 (Oct). *(a) Optd with T* **3**. *Narrow Setting. Lines 2 mm apart. "*Anglo-French*" measures 16 mm.*

H14	3pf. brown	£5000	£900
H15	5pf. green	£1200	£700
H16	10pf. carmine	†	£2750
H17	20pf. ultramarine	22·00	12·00
	a. "TOG"	£3500	£2500
	b. Nos. H4 and H17 *se-tenant* (vert pair)	£8000	
H18	25pf. black and red/*yellow*	28·00	30·00
	a. "TOG"	£12000	
H19	30pf. black and orange/*buff*	19·00	29·00
H20	40pf. black and carmine	£5000	£1500
H21	50pf. black and purple/*buff*	†	£6000
H22	80pf. black and carmine/*rose*	£2250	£2000
H23	1m. carmine	£7000	£4000
H24	2m. blue	†	£9000
H25	3m. violet-black	†	£50000
H26	5m. lake and black	†	£50000

(b) Narrow setting, but including value, as T **4**.

H27	½d. on 3pf. brown	38·00	26·00
	a. "TOG"	£425	£300
	b. Thin y" in "penny"	60·00	60·00
H28	1d. on 5pf. green	4·75	4·25
	a. "TOG"	£130	£110
	b. Thin "y" in "penny"	12·00	15·00

In the 20pf. one half of a sheet was overprinted with the wide setting (3 mm), and the other half with the narrow setting (2 mm), so that vertical pairs from the middle of the sheet show the two varieties of the overprint.

TOGO
Anglo-French
Occupation
(6)

1915 (7 Jan). *Optd as T* **6**. *The words "*Anglo-French*" measure 15 mm instead of 16 mm as in T* **3**.

H29	3pf. brown	£8500	£2500
H30	5pf. green	£225	£130
	a. "Occupation" omitted	£12000	
H31	10pf. carmine	£200	£130
	a. No wmk	†	£7000
H32	20pf. ultramarine	£1400	£400
H32*a*	40pf. black and carmine	†	£8000
H33	50pf. black and purple/*buff*	£14000	£9500

This printing was made on another batch of German Togo stamps, found at Sansane-Mangu.

TOGO
ANGLO-FRENCH
OCCUPATION
(7)

OCCU — Accra opt
OCCU — London opt

Stamps of Gold Coast overprinted

1915 (May). *Nos. 70/81, 82a and 83/4 of Gold Coast (King George V) optd at Govt Press, Accra, with T* **7** *("*OCCUPATION*" 14½ mm long).*

H34	½d. green (*shades*)	30	2·25
	a. Small "F" in "FRENCH"	1·50	6·00
	b. Thin "G" in "TOGO"	3·25	11·00
	c. No hyphen after "ANGLO"	3·25	11·00
	e. "CUPATION" for "OCCUPATION"	£110	
	f. "CCUPATION" for "OCCUPATION"	65·00	
	g. Opt double		
H35	1d. red	30	60
	a. Small "F" in "FRENCH"	1·75	3·50
	b. Thin "G" in "TOGO"	6·00	11·00
	c. No hyphen after "ANGLO"	6·00	11·00
	f. "CCUPATION" for "OCCUPATION"	£180	
	g. Opt double	£350	£475
	h. Opt inverted	£170	£250
	ha. Ditto. "TOGO" omitted	£7500	
H36	2d. grey	30	1·25
	a. Small "F" in "FRENCH"	1·75	6·00
	b. Thin "G" in "TOGO"	5·50	15·00
	c. No hyphen after "ANGLO"	£170	
	d. Two hyphens after "ANGLO"	55·00	
	f. "CCUPATION" for "OCCUPATION"	£180	
H37	2½d. bright blue	2·50	4·00
	a. Small "F" in "FRENCH"	4·00	9·00
	b. Thin "G" in "TOGO"	11·00	27·00
	c. No hyphen after "ANGLO"	£110	
	d. Two hyphens after "ANGLO"	60·00	
	f. "CCUPATION" for "OCCUPATION"	£150	
H38	3d. purple/*yellow*	2·50	3·25
	a. Small "F" in "FRENCH"	4·00	8·00
	b. Thin "G" in "TOGO"	14·00	27·00
	c. No hyphen after "ANGLO"	55·00	
	f. "CCUPATION" for "OCCUPATION"	£180	
	g. White back	4·00	20·00
	ga. Small "F" in "FRENCH"	27·00	65·00
	gb. Thin "G" in "TOGO"	65·00	£120
H40	6d. dull and bright purple	2·25	1·75
	a. Small "F" in "FRENCH"	5·00	11·00
	b. Thin "G" in "TOGO"	16·00	27·00
	f. "CCUPATION" for "OCCUPATION"	£275	
H41	1s. black/*green*	2·50	7·00
	a. Small "F" in "FRENCH"	4·50	19·00
	b. Thin "G" in "TOGO"	17·00	50·00
	f. "CCUPATION" for "OCCUPATION"	£150	
	g. Opt double	£1200	
H42	2s. purple and blue/*blue*	12·00	15·00
	a. Small "F" in "FRENCH"	30·00	50·00
	b. Thin "G" in "TOGO"	70·00	95·00
	c. No hyphen after "ANGLO"	£190	
	f. "CCUPATION" for "OCCUPATION"	£425	
H43	2s.6d. black and red/*blue*	4·50	24·00
	a. Small "F" in "FRENCH"	18·00	80·00
	b. Thin "G" in "TOGO"	50·00	£160
	c. No hyphen after "ANGLO"	£190	
	f. "CCUPATION" for "OCCUPATION"	£600	
H44	5s. green and red/*yellow* (*white back*)	8·50	15·00
	a. Small "F" in "FRENCH"	50·00	80·00
	b. Thin "G" in "TOGO"	85·00	£170
	c. No hyphen after "ANGLO"	£250	
	f. "CCUPATION" for "OCCUPATION"	£450	
H45	10s. green and red/*green*	45·00	60·00
	a. Small "F" in "FRENCH"	95·00	
	b. Thin "G" in "TOGO"	£200	
	f. "CCUPATION" for "OCCUPATION"	£600	
H46	20s. purple and black/*red*	£150	£160
	a. Small "F" in "FRENCH"	£350	
	b. Thin "G" in "TOGO"	£650	
	f. "CCUPATION" for "OCCUPATION"	£850	
H34/46 *Set of* 12		£200	£250

Nos. H34/46 were overprinted in panes of 60 (6×10), using a setting of movable type. There were three printings:

1st printing (all values, 3d. No. H38 only).
2nd printing (all values, 3d. No. H38g only).
3rd printing (recorded on 1d., 3d. (H38), 2s., 2s.6d., 5s. only.)

Varieties occur as follows (Nos. indicate position in setting)

a. Small "F" in "FRENCH" (25, 58, 59). Present in all three printings on pos. 25, and on pos. 58 and 59 in 1st and 2nd printings.
b. Thin "G" in "TOGO" (24) Constant in all three printings. The letter is from a slightly smaller fount.
c. No hyphen after "ANGLO" (5, 28). Occurs on pos. 5 during the 1st printing (½d., 1d., 2d., 2½d., 3d. (No. H38), rare on the 2d. and 2½d.), and again on the 3rd printing (1d., 3d., (No. H38), 2s., 2s.6d., 5s.). It is also found on pos. 28 in the 1st printing (½d. and 1d. only).
d. Two hyphens after "ANGLO" (5). Occurs on pos. 5 during the 1st printing (2d., 2½d. only). The two hyphens vary in character. The same two values are also found with misplaced hyphen from this position.
e. "CUPATION" for "OCCUPATION" (33) ½d. value only, 1st printing.
f. "CCUPATION" for "OCCUPATION" (57). All values, 1st printing.

CHARACTERISTICS OF THE ACCRA OVERPRINT

Being set up from movable type, no two positions are exactly the same and there are many minor varieties of broken type. The two "C"s in "OCCUPATION" often differ slightly in shape and one or both usually have closed jaws. The word "OCCUPATION" is generally fractionally shorter (at 14½ to 14¾ mm) than in the subsequent London overprint, where the length is consistently 15 mm. The impression is variable, but usually appears weaker than the London overprint, which is normally bold and well-inked.

The position of the overprint on the stamp varies greatly, with the word "TOGO" often encroaching on the crown above the King's head (high position) or the word "OCCUPATION" encroaching on the value tablet (low position). The subsequent London overprint is invariably well-centred, leaving both crown and value tablet clear.

Note that the 3d. (No. H38g) and 5s. (No. H44) with white back do not occur with the London overprint.

The 1d. opt inverted (No. H35h) exists with small "F" (*Price* £1600 *unused*), thin "G" (*Price* £4250 *unused*) and "No hyphen" (*Price* £4250 *unused*).

Examples of all values, and especially the varieties, are known showing a forged Lomé postmark dated "22 1 15".

TOGO
ANGLO-FRENCH
OCCUPATION
8

1916 (Apr)–**20**. *Nos. 70/84 of Gold Coast (King George V) optd in London with T* **8** *("*OCCUPATION*" 15 mm long). Heavy type and thicker letters showing through on back.*

H47	½d. green	30	2·75
H48	1d. red	30	85
H49	2d. grey	60	1·25
H50	2½d. bright blue	70	1·50
H51	3d. purple/*yellow*	3·50	70
	a. *On buff-yellow* (1919)		
H52	6d. dull and bright purple	2·25	1·00
	w. Wmk inverted	£130	£180
H53	1s. black/*green*	3·50	8·00
	a. On blue-green (olive back) (1918)	7·50	17·00
	b. On emerald-green (olive back) (1920)	£700	
	c. On emerald-green (emerald-green back) (1920)	£325	£700
H54	2s. purple and blue/*blue*	4·50	8·50
	a. Wmk sideways	£2250	£2250
H55	2s.6d. black and red/*blue*	4·50	7·00
H56	5s. green and red/*yellow*	23·00	26·00
	a. On buff-yellow (1919)	19·00	50·00
H57	10s. green and red/*green*	24·00	65·00
	a. On blue-green (olive back) (1920)	18·00	75·00
H58	20s. purple and black/*red*	£150	£180
H47/58 *Set of* 12		£180	£275
H47s/58s Optd "Specimen" *Set of* 12		£350	

Nos. H47/58 were overprinted by De La Rue using a stereotype plate, probably of 120 (two panes, each 6×10). The overprint is much more consistent than the Accra printings and is usually bold and well-inked, with letters that appear thicker, particularly in the word "TOGO". "OCCUPATION" measures 15 mm in length. The two "C"s in "OCCUPATION" are identical in size and style, with open jaws.

The overprint is invariably well-centred, with the top of the word "TOGO" placed just below the top of the King's head on the 1d.and just below the base of the crown on the other values, leaving the value tablet completely clear.

Nos. H51a, 53*a/c*, 56/*a* and 57*a* are all shades which were overprinted only in London and do not exist with the Accra overprint. Nos. H51a and 56*a*, described as on "buff-yellow" paper, include second printings made in 1920, which are not easy to distinguish. Viewed from the back, the paper appears rather pale and dull, in comparison with the bright (almost lemon) yellow of Nos. H51 and 56.

Nos. H47/58 were withdrawn in October 1920 when Gold Coast stamps were introduced.

The mandates were transferred to the United Nations in January 1946. The inhabitants of the British mandate voted to join Ghana in 1957.

Tokelau *see after* New Zealand

Tonga

The Tongan Post Office was established in 1885 and FIJI 2d. and 6d. stamps are recorded in use until the arrival of Nos. 1/4.

PRICES FOR STAMPS ON COVER TO 1945	
Nos. 1/4	*from* × 60
Nos. 5/9	*from* × 20
Nos. 10/28	*from* × 8
Nos. 29/31	*from* × 7
Nos. 32/7	*from* × 6
Nos. 38/54	*from* × 5
Nos. 55/63	*from* × 6
Nos. 64/70	*from* × 3
Nos. 71/87	*from* × 2
Nos. O1/10	*from* × 25

PROTECTORATE KINGDOM

King George I, 1845–93

1 King George I

2

(Eng Bock and Cousins. Plates made and typo Govt Ptg Offi[ce] Wellington)

1886–88. W **2**. P 12½ (line) or 12×11½ (comb)*.

1	**1**	1d. carmine (P 12½) (27.8.86)	£400	6·
		a. Perf 12½×10		
		b. Perf 12×11½ (15.7.87)	10·00	3·
		ba. Pale carmine (P 12×11½)	16·00	8·
2		2d. pale violet (P 12½) (27.8.86)	50·00	10·
		a. Bright violet	70·00	3·
		b. Perf 12×11½ (15.7.87)	38·00	2·
		ba. Bright violet (P 12×11½)	45·00	3·
3		6d. blue (P 12½) (9.10.86)	60·00	2·
		a. Perf 12×11½ (15.10.88)	50·00	2·
		ab. Dull blue (P 12×11½)	28·00	2·
4		1s. pale green (P 12½) (9.10.86)	90·00	4·
		a. Deep green (P 12½)	£100	2·
		b. Perf 12×11½ (15.10.88)	55·00	6·
		ba. Deep green (P 12×11½)	55·00	3·

*See note after New Zealand, No. 186.

FOUR
PENCE.
(3)

EIGHT
PENCE.
(4)

(Surch Messrs Wilson & Horton, Auckland, N.Z.)

1891 (10 Nov). *Nos. 1b and 2b surch.*

5	**3**	4d. on 1d. carmine	3·00	11·
		a. No stop after "PENCE"	50·00	£1
6	**4**	8d. violet	35·00	90·
		a. Short "T" in "EIGHT"	£170	£3

No. 5a occurred on R. 6/8 and 9, R. 10/11, all from the rig[ht] hand pane.

1891 (23 Nov). *Optd with stars in upper right and lower le[ft] corners by lithography.* P 12½.

7	**1**	1d. carmine	48·00	55·
		a. Three stars	£400	
		b. Four stars	£500	
		c. Five stars	£750	
		d. Perf 12×11½	£300	
		da. Three stars	£500	
		db. Four stars	£650	
		dc. Five stars	£900	
8		2d. violet	70·00	38·
		a. Perf 12×11½	£375	

COMMONWEALTH STAMPS

PAGE NO.	CONDITION (mint/UM/used)	SG NO.	DESCRIPTION	PRICE
			SUB TOTAL	
			POSTAGE & PACKAGING	£5.00
			GRAND TOTAL	

Please complete payment, name and address details overleaf

COMMONWEALTH STAMPS

Priority order form

Four easy ways to place your order with us:

Phone:

Pauline MacBroom 0207 557 4450
Brian Lucas 0207 557 4446

Fax:

020 7557 4499

Email:

pmacbroom@stanleygibbons.co.uk
blucas@stanleygibbons.co.uk

Post:

Commonwealth Department
Stanley Gibbons Ltd, 399 Strand
London, WC2R 0LX.

Customer details

Account Number ______________________________

Name ______________________________

Address ______________________________

______________________________ Postcode ______________________________

Country ______________________________ Email ______________________________

Tel no ______________________________ Fax no ______________________________

Payment details

Registered Postage & Packing £5.00

I enclose my cheque/postal order for £..... .... in full payment. Please make cheques/postal orders payable to Stanley Gibbons Ltd. Cheques must be in £ sterling and drawn on a UK bank

Please debit my credit card for £....................... in full payment. I have completed the Credit Card section below.

Card Number

☐☐☐☐☐☐☐☐☐☐☐☐☐☐☐☐

CVC Number

☐☐☐

Start Date (Switch & Amex)

☐☐☐

Expiry Date

☐☐☐☐

Issue No (switch)

☐☐

Signature ______________________________ Date ______________________________

1892 (15 Aug). W **2**. P 12×11½.
9 **1** 6d. yellow-orange 16·00 26·00

5 Arms of Tonga

6 King George I

Damaged "O" in "TONGA" (R. 1/1, later corrected)

(Dies eng A. E. Cousins. Typo at Govt Printing Office, Wellington, N.Z.)

1892 (10 Nov). W **2**. P 12×11½.
10 **5** 1d. pale rose 14·00 22·00
a. Bright rose 12·00 22·00
b. Bisected diag (½d.) (1893) (on cover) † £850
c. Damaged "O" £100 £130
11 **6** 2d. olive 21·00 16·00
12 **5** 4d. chestnut 48·00 70·00
13 **6** 8d. bright mauve 55·00 £170
14 1s. brown 80·00 £110
10/14 *Set of 5* £190 £350

No. 10b was used from 31 May 1893 to provide a 2½d. rate before the arrival of No. 15, and on subsequent occasions up to 1895.

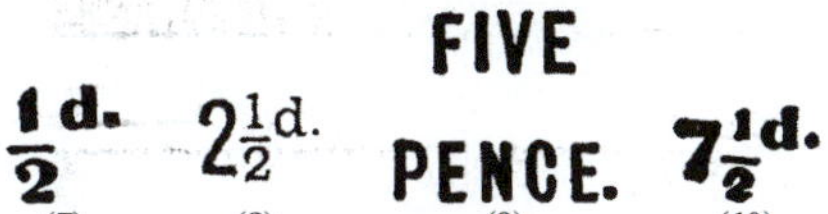
(7) (8) (9) (10)

1893. *Printed in new colours and surch with T* **7/10** *by Govt Printing Office, Wellington.*
(a) In carmine. P 12½ (21 Aug).
15 **5** ½d. on 1d. bright ultramarine 23·00 27·00
a. Surch omitted
16 **6** 2½d. on 2d. green 16·00 12·00
17 **5** 5d. on 4d. orange 4·00 6·50
18 **6** 7½d. on 8d. carmine 24·00 80·00
(b) In black. P 12×11½ (Nov).
19 **5** ½d. on 1d. dull blue 45·00 48·00
20 **6** 2½d. on 2d. green 17·00 17·00
a. Surch double £1800 £1800
b. Fraction bar completely omitted (R. 3/3)

King George II, 1893–1918

(11) (12) Small "F" in "HALF"

(Surch at the *Star* Office, Auckland, N.Z.)

1894 (June–Nov). *Surch with T* **11** *or* **12**.
21 **5** ½d. on 4d. chestnut (B.) (Nov) 2·00 7·00
a. "SURCHARCE" 9·00 21·00
b. Small "F" 9·00 21·00
22 **6** ½d. on 1s. brown 2·50 11·00
a. "SURCHARCE" 11·00 42·00
b. Small "F" 11·00 42·00
c. Surch double £275
d. Surch double with "SURCHARCE" £900
e. Surch double with small "F" £750
23 2½d. on 8d. mauve 5·50 8·00
a. No stop after "SURCHARGE" 32·00 55·00
24 2½d. on 1s. deep green (No. 4*a*) (Nov) 60·00 28·00
a. No stop after "SURCHARGE" £180
b. Perf 12×11½ 15·00 45·00
ba. No stop after "SURCHARGE" 55·00

Nos. 21/4 were surcharged in panes of 60 (6×10) with No. 21a occurring on R. 2/6, 4/6, 5/6, 8/6 and 10/6, No. 21b on R. 1/4, 3/4, 6/4, 7/4 and 9/4, No. 22a on R. 1/6, 3/6, 5/6, 8/6 and 10/6, No. 22b on R. 2/4, 4/4, 6/4, 7/4 and 9/4 (both after the setting had been rearranged), No. 23a on R. 3/1–3 and Nos. 24a and 24ba on R. 6/3 and R. 7/3 or R. 7/1–2.

Sheets used for these provisionals were surcharged with the remains of the tissue interleaving still in place. This sometimes subsequently fell away taking parts of the surcharge with it.

Deformed "E" in "PENI" (R. 2/2)

(Design resembling No. 11 litho and surch at *Star* Office Auckland, N.Z.)

1895 (22 May*). *As T* **6** *surch as T* **11** *and* **12**. No wmk. P 12.
25 **11** 1d. on 2d. pale blue (C.) 50·00 27·00
a. Deformed "E" £120 75·00
26 **12** 1½d. on 2d. pale blue (C.) 60·00 38·00
a. Deformed "E" £150 90·00
b. Perf 12×11 50·00 38·00
ba. Deformed "E" £120 90·00
27 2½d. on 2d. pale blue (C.)† 40·00 48·00
a. No stop after "SURCHARGE" £225 £225
b. Deformed "E" £110 £130
28 7½d. on 2d. pale blue (C.) £425
a. Deformed "E"
b. Perf 12×11 60·00 48·00
ba. Deformed "E" £150 £130

*Earliest known date of use.
†The 2½d. on 2d. is the only value which normally has a stop after the word "SURCHARGE".
No. 27a occurs on R. 1/3 of the right-hand pane.

12a King George II

13 King George II

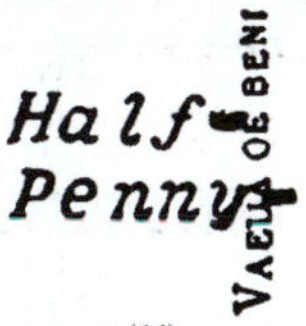
(**14**)

"BU" joined (R. 1/1)

Missing eyebrow (R. 2/4)

"7" for "1" in "½d." (R. 2/1)

1895 (20 June*). *Unissued stamp surch as in T* **12a**. No wmk. P 12.
29 **11** ½d. on 2½d. vermilion 40·00 32·00
a. "BU" joined 85·00 75·00
b. "SURCHARCE" 75·00 70·00
c. Missing eyebrow 85·00 75·00
d. Stop after "POSTAGE" (R. 2/5) 85·00 75·00
e. "7" for "1" in "½d." 85·00 75·00
30 1d. on 2½d. vermilion 80·00 45·00
a. "BU" joined £140 £100
c. Missing eyebrow £140 £100
d. Stop after "POSTAGE" (R. 2/5) £140 £100
e. "7" for "1" in "½d." £140 £100
31 **12** 7½d. on 2½d. vermilion 60·00 70·00
a. "BU" joined £110 £120
c. Missing eyebrow £110 £120
d. Stop after "POSTAGE" (R. 2/5) £110 £120
e. "7" for "1" in "½d." £110 £120

*Earliest known date of use.
No. 29b occurs on R. 1/6 and 3/6 of both the right and the left pane.
In the ½d. surcharge there is a stop after "SURCHARGE" and not after "PENNY". In the 1d. and 7½d. the stop is after the value only.

"Black Eye" flaw (Rt pane R. 2/4)

(Litho *Star* Office, Auckland, N.Z.)

1895 (9 July–Sept). No wmk. P 12.
32 **13** 1d. olive-green 24·00 26·00
a. Bisected diagonally (½d.) (on cover) (9.95) † £750
b. Imperf between (horiz pair) – £6500
33 2½d. rose 20·00 11·00
a. Stop (flaw) after "POSTAGE" (R. 4/5) 60·00 50·00
34 5d. blue 27·00 55·00
a. "Black eye" flaw 75·00
b. Perf 12×11 23·00 55·00
ba. "Black eye" flaw 70·00
c. Perf 11 £375
ca. "Black eye" flaw
35 7½d. orange-yellow 32·00 50·00
a. Yellow 32·00 50·00

1896 (May). *Nos. 26b and 28b with typewritten surcharge* "Half-Penny-", *in violet, and Tongan surcharge, in black, as T* **14**.
A. Tongan surch reading downwards (right panes).
36A **6** ½d. on 1½d. on 2d. £450
a. Perf 12 £425 £425
e. "Halef" £6500
f. "H" over "G"
g. "Pen?y" £5500
37A ½d. on 7½d. on 2d. 85·00 £110
a. "Hafl" for "Half" £2250 £2500
b. "Hafl" ("Penny" omitted) £4750
c. "PPenny" £750
d. Stops instead of hyphens £1100
e. "Halyf"
f. "Half-Penny-" inverted £2750
g. No hyphen after "Penny"
i. No hyphen after "Half" £1000
l. Capital "P" over small "p"
m. Hyphen after "Penny" over capital "Y" £2250
p. Perf 12 £800
pa. No hyphen after "Half"
B. Tongan surch reading upwards (left panes).
36B **6** ½d. on 1½d. on 2d. £450 £450
a. Perf 12 £475 £475
ab. "Haalf" £3000
c. "H" double
d. Tongan surch omitted £5500
e. "Penyny" £3000
37B ½d. on 7½d. on 2d. 85·00 £110
c. "PPenny" £950
d. Stops instead of hyphens £1100
f. "Half-Penny-" inverted £4000
g. Comma instead of hyphen after "Penny" £750
h. "Hwlf"
i. No hyphen after "Half" £1500
j. "Penny" double
k. "Penny" twice, with "Half" on top of upper "Penny" £4250
m. "Half H" £1000
n. Tongan surch double £1500
o. Two hyphens between "Half" and "Penny"
p. Perf 12 £800

Nos. 26b and 28b were in sheets of 48 (2 panes 6×4). The panes were separated before the surcharges were applied.
There are variations in the relative positions of the words "Half" and "Penny", both vertically and horizontally.

15 Arms

16 Ovava Tree, Kana-Kubolu

17 King George II

18 Prehistoric Trilith at Haamonga

19 Bread Fruit

20 Coral

21 View of Haapai

22 Red Shining Parrot

23 View of Vavau Harbour

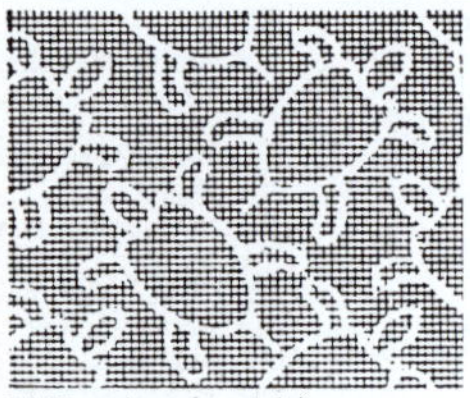

24 Tortoises (*upright*)

Types of Type **17**:

Type I. Top of hilt showing

Type II. No sword hilt

Normal

Lopped branch (R. 8/5) (ptgs from 1934 onwards)

Normal

Small "2" (R. 1/2, 1/4–5, 2/8, 4/4, 5/4 and 6/1)

Normal

Both "O"s small in "HOGOFULU" (R. 1/7)

Small second "O" in "HOGOFULU" (R. 2/7)

WATERMARKS. Stamps with W **24** upright show all the tortoise heads pointing upwards, or downwards if inverted. On stamps with sideways watermark the heads point upwards or downwards alternately. Stamps with inverted or sideways inverted watermarks are not separately listed.

(Recess D.L.R.)

1897 (1 June). W **24**. P 14.

38	**15**	½d. indigo	6·00	2·75
		a. Wmk sideways	70	3·00
39	**16**	1d. black and scarlet	80	80
		a. Wmk sideways	7·00	3·50
		b. Lopped branch	65·00	
40	**17**	2d. sepia and bistre (I)	21·00	6·00
		a. Wmk sideways	17·00	3·50
		b. Small "2"	42·00	15·00
41		2d. sepia and bistre (II)	38·00	9·00
		a. Wmk sideways	27·00	9·00
		b. Small "2"	60·00	25·00
42		2d. grey and bistre (II)	38·00	3·25
		a. Wmk sideways	20·00	3·50
		b. Small "2"	42·00	6·00
43		2½d. black and blue	6·00	1·40
		a. No fraction bar in "½" (R. 2/10)	£110	60·00
		b. Wmk sideways	6·00	1·60
		ba. No fraction bar in "½" (R. 2/10)	95·00	60·00
44	**18**	3d. black and yellow-green	3·50	13·00
		a. Wmk sideways	2·50	6·50
45	**19**	4d. green and purple	3·75	4·00
		a. Wmk sideways	4·00	4·50
46	**17**	5d. black with orange (II)	32·00	14·00
		a. Wmk sideways		
47	**20**	6d. red	13·00	6·00
		a. Wmk sideways	8·50	8·50
48	**17**	7½d. black and green (II)	18·00	23·00
		a. Centre inverted	£4750	
49		10d. black and lake (II)	45·00	48·00
		a. Wmk sideways		
		b. Both "O"'s small	£225	£225
		c. Small second "O"	£225	£225
50		1s. black and red-brown (II)	14·00	7·50
		a. No hyphen before "TAHA" (R. 3/5)	£160	£140
		b. Wmk sideways		
51	**21**	2s. black and ultramarine	75·00	80·00
		a. Wmk sideways	25·00	32·00
52	**22**	2s.6d. deep purple	50·00	30·00
		a. Wmk sideways	65·00	50·00
53	**23**	5s. black and brown-red	48·00	48·00
		a. Wmk sideways	26·00	32·00
38a/53a *Set of* 14			£225	£180

The 1d., 3d. and 4d. are known bisected and used for half their value.

T – L

1 June, 1899.

(**25**)

26 Queen Salote

1899 (1 June). *Royal Wedding. No. 39a optd with T* **25** *at "Star" Office, Auckland, N.Z.*

54	**16**	1d. black and scarlet (hyphen 2 mm long)	35·00	60·00
		a. "1889" for "1899" (R. 8/1, 8/4)	£225	£375
		b. Hyphen 3 mm long	50·00	80·00
		c. Wmk upright	55·00	85·00
		ca. "1889" for "1899" (R. 8/1, 8/4)	£425	£650
		cb. Hyphen 3 mm long	80·00	£130

The letters "T L" stand for Taufa'ahau, the King's family name, and Lavinia, the bride.

No. 54 was overprinted from a setting of 30 (3×10) applied twice to the sheets of 60. The setting contains twenty-one examples of the 2 mm hyphen and nine of the 3 mm.

Queen Salote, 1918–65

Dies of the 2d.:

Die I (As used for 1897 issue)

Die II

Normal

"2½" recut (note lines on "2" and different "½") (R. 1/1)

Retouched (small) hyphen (R. 3/5)

(Recess D.L.R.)

1920 (Apr)–**35**. W **24** (sideways). P 14.

55	**15**	½d. yellow-green (1934)	1·00	1·25
		a. Wmk upright	32·00	45·00
56	**26**	1½d. grey-black (1935)	50	3·00
57		2d. agate and aniline violet (Die I)	9·00	13·00
		a. Wmk upright	24·00	45·00
		b. Small "2"	60·00	85·00
		c. Black and slate-violet (1924)	12·00	2·25
		ca. Wmk upright		
		cb. Small "2"	55·00	20·00
		d. Black and deep purple (1925)	13·00	3·00
		db. Small "2"	65·00	25·00
57*e*		2d. black and blackish lilac (Die II) (1932)	4·75	8·50
58		2½d. black and blue (3.21)	6·50	40·00
59		2½d. bright ultramarine (1934)	3·00	1·00
		a. Recut "2½"	23·00	9·50
60		5d. black and orange-vermilion (1921)	3·25	4·75
61		7½d. black and yellow-green (1922)	1·75	1·75
62		10d. black and lake (1922)	2·50	4·75
		a. Both "O"'s small	28·00	45·00
		b. Small second "O"	28·00	45·00
		c. Black and aniline carmine (9.25)	7·00	
		ca. Both "O"'s small	75·00	
		cb. Small second "O"	75·00	
63		1s. black and red-brown (1922)	1·25	2·50
		a. Retouched (small) hyphen	15·00	24·00
		b. Wmk upright	32·00	32·00
		ba. Retouched (small) hyphen	£140	£140
55/63 *Set of* 10			30·00	55·00
55s/63s Optd or Perf (Nos. 55s/6s and 59s) "Specimen" *Set of* 9			£180	

In Die II the ball of the "2" is larger and the word "PENI-E-UA" is re-engraved and slightly shorter; the "U" has a spur on the left side.

For illustration of No. 62a see above No. 38.

TWO PENCE

PENI-E-UA

(**27**)

TWO PENCE

PENI-E-UA

(**28**)

1923 (20 Oct)–**24**. *Nos. 46, 48/9, 50, 51/2 and 53a surch as T* **27** *(vert stamps) or* **28** *(horiz stamps).*

64	**17**	2d. on 5d. black and orange (II) (B.)	1·00	85
		a. Wmk sideways	14·00	10·00
65		2d. on 7½d. black and green (II) (B.)	24·00	28·00
		a. Wmk sideways	75·00	85·00
66		2d. on 10d. black and lake (II) (B.)	16·00	50·00
		a. Wmk sideways	60·00	80·00
		b. Both "O"'s small	80·00	
		c. Small second "O"	80·00	
67		2d. on 1s. black and red-brown (II) (B.)	65·00	22·00
		a. No hyphen before "TAHA" (R. 3/5)	£350	£200
		b. Wmk sideways	85·00	65·00
68	**21**	2d. on 2s. black and ultramarine (R)	29·00	26·00
		a. Wmk sideways	11·00	7·00
69	**22**	2d. on 2s.6d. deep purple (R.)	32·00	6·50
		a. Wmk sideways	£120	65·00
70	**23**	2d. on 5s. black and brown-red (R.)	21·00	21·00
		a. Wmk sideways	3·25	2·50
64/70a *Set of* 7			£140	£100

29 Queen Salote

(Recess D.L.R.)

1938 (12 Oct). *20th Anniv of Queen Salote's Accession. Tablet at foot dated* "1918–1938". W **24** (sideways). P 13½.

71	**29**	1d. black and scarlet	1·00	4·75
72		2d. black and purple	11·00	4·25
73		2½d. black and ultramarine	11·00	5·50
71/3 *Set of* 3			21·00	13·00
71s/3s Perf "Specimen" *Set of* 3			80·00	

For Silver Jubilee issue in a similar design, see Nos. 83/7.

Further die of 2d.:

Die III

(Recess D.L.R.)

1942–49. Wmk Mult Script CA (sideways on 5s.). P 14.

74	**15**	½d. yellow-green	30	3·00
		a. "A" of "CA" missing from wmk	£600	
75	**16**	1d. black and scarlet	2·50	3·00
		a. Lopped branch	70·00	
76	**26**	2d. black and purple (Die II)	7·00	2·75
		a. Die III (4.49)	7·00	9·50
77		2½d. bright ultramarine	1·75	2·00
		a. Recut "2½"	32·00	
78	**18**	3d. black and yellow-green	65	4·50
79	**20**	6d. red	3·50	2·25
80	**26**	1s. black and red-brown	4·00	3·50
		a. Retouched (small) hyphen	42·00	38·00
81	**22**	2s.6d. deep purple (1943)	32·00	28·00
82	**23**	5s. black and brown-red (1943)	16·00	55·00
74/82 *Set of* 9			55·00	95·00
74s/82s Perf "Specimen" *Set of* 9			£180	

In Die III the foot of the "2" is longer than in Die II and extends towards the right beyond the curve of the loop; the letters of "PENI-E-UA are taller and differently shaped.

Damage to the "2" on R. 4/9 of No. 77 was frequently corrected by hand-painting.

For illustration of No. 75a see above No. 38 and of No. 77a see above No. 55.

The ½d. 1d., 3d. and 1s. exist perforated from either line or comb machines. The other values only come line perforated.

30

(Recess D.L.R.)

1944 (25 Jan). *Silver Jubilee of Queen Salote's Accession. As T* **29**, *but inscr* "1918–1943" *at foot, as T* **30**. Wmk Mult Script CA. P 14.

83		1d. black and carmine	15	1·25
84		2d. black and purple	15	1·25
85		3d. black and green	15	1·25
86		6d. black and orange	1·00	2·00
87		1s. black and brown	75	2·00
83/7 *Set of* 5			2·00	7·00
83s/7s Perf "Specimen" *Set of* 5			85·00	

1949 (10 Oct). *75th Anniv of U.P.U. As Nos. 114/17 of Antigua.*

88	2½d. ultramarine	20	1·00
89	3d. olive	2·00	3·50
90	6d. carmine-red	20	60
91	1s. red-brown	25	60
88/91 *Set of* 4		2·40	5·00

31 Queen Salote

33 Queen Salote

32 Queen Salote

(Photo Waterlow)

1950 (1 Nov). *Queen Salote's Fiftieth Birthday.* Wmk Mult Script CA. P 12½.

92	**31**	1d. carmine	80	2·50
93	**32**	5d. green	80	2·50
94	**33**	1s. violet	80	2·75
92/4 *Set of* 3			2·25	7·00

34 Map

35 Palace, Nuku'alofa

36 Beach scene

37 H.M.N.Z.S *Bellona*

38 Flag

39 Arms of Tonga and Great Britain

(Recess Waterlow)

1951 (2 July). *50th Anniv of Treaty of Friendship between Great Britain and Tonga. T* **34/9**. Wmk Mult Script CA. P 12½ (3d.), 13×13½ (½d.), 13½×13 (others).

95	½d. green	20	3·00
96	1d. black and carmine	15	3·50
97	2½d. green and brown	30	3·00
98	3d. yellow and bright blue	2·50	3·00
99	5d. carmine and green	2·75	1·00
100	1s. yellow-orange and violet	2·75	1·25
95/100 *Set of* 6		7·75	13·00

40 Royal Palace, Nuku'alofa

43 Swallows' Cave, Vava'u

52 Queen Salote

53 Arms of Tonga

(Des J. Berry. Centre litho, frame recess (£1), recess (others) B.W.)

1953 (1 July). *T* **40**, **43**, **52/3** *and similar designs.* W **24** (sideways). P 11×11½ (vert) or 11½×11 (horiz).

101	1d. black and red-brown	10	10
102	1½d. blue and emerald	20	10
103	2d. deep turquoise-green and black	1·00	20
104	3d. blue and deep bluish green	1·75	20
105	3½d. yellow and carmine-red	1·00	70
106	4d. yellow and deep rose-carmine	2·25	10
107	5d. blue and red-brown	60	10
108	6d. black and deep blue	1·00	30
109	8d. emerald and deep reddish violet	1·50	50
110	1s. blue and black	1·00	10
111	2s. sage-green and brown	8·00	60
112	5s. orange-yellow and slate-lilac	25·00	9·50
113	10s. yellow and black	8·00	9·50
114	£1 yellow, scarlet, ultramarine and deep bright blue	8·00	6·50
101/14 *Set of* 14		50·00	25·00

Designs: *Horiz (as T* **40***)*—1½d. Shore fishing with throw-net; 2d. *Hifofua* and *Aoniu* (ketches); 3½d. Map of Tongatapu; 4d. Vava'u Harbour; 5d. Post Office, Nuku'alofa; 6d. Aerodrome, Fua'amotu; 8d. *Matua* (inter-island freighter) at Nuku'alofa wharf; 2s. Lifuka, Ha'apai; 5s. Mutiny on the *Bounty*. *Vert (as T* **43***)*—1s. Map of Tonga Islands.

54 Stamp of 1886

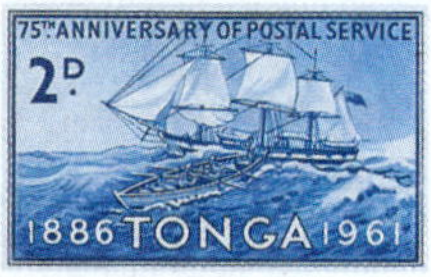

55 Whaling Ship and Whaleboat

(Des D. Bakeley. Photo Harrison)

1961 (1 Dec). *75th Anniv of Tongan Postal Service. T* **54/5** *and similar horiz designs.* W **24** (sideways). P 14½×13½.

115	1d. carmine and brown-orange	10	10
116	2d. ultramarine	1·25	45
117	4d. blue-green	20	45
118	5d. violet	1·25	45
119	1s. red-brown	1·25	45
115/19 *Set of* 5		3·50	1·60

Designs:—4d. Queen Salote and Post Office, Nuku'alofa; 5d. *Aoniu II* (inter-island freighter); 1s. Douglas DC-4 mailplane over Tongatapu.

1862
TAU'ATĀINA
EMANCIPATION
1962
(**59**)

60 "Protein Foods"

1962 (7 Feb). *Centenary of Emancipation. Nos. 101, 104, 107/10, 112, 117 optd with T* **59** *(No. 126 surch also), in red, by R. S. Wallbank Govt Printer.*

120	1d. black and red-brown	10	1·25
121	4d. blue-green	10	90
122	5d. blue and red-brown	15	90
123	6d. black and deep blue	20	1·25
124	8d. emerald and deep reddish violet	40	2·00
125	1s. blue and black	20	1·00
	a. Opt inverted	£400	£200
126	2s. on 3d. blue and deep bluish green	40	4·50
	a. Missing fraction-bar in surch	10·00	20·00
127	5s. orange-yellow and slate-lilac	6·00	4·50
	a. Opt inverted	£180	£275
120/127 *Set of* 8		6·50	14·50

(Des M. Goaman. Photo Harrison)

1963 (4 June). *Freedom from Hunger.* W **24**. P 14×14½.

128	**60**	11d. ultramarine	50	15

61 Coat of Arms

62 Queen Salote

63 Queen Salote

(Des Ida West. Die-cut Walsall)

1963 (17 June). *First Polynesian Gold Coinage Commemoration. Circular designs. Embossed on gold foil backed with paper, inscr overall* "TONGA THE FRIENDLY ISLANDS". Imperf.

(a) Postage. ¼ koula coin. Diameter 1⅝in.

129	**61**	1d. carmine	10	10
130	**62**	2d. deep blue	10	10
131	**61**	6d. blue-green	15	15
132	**62**	9d. bright purple	15	15
133	**61**	1s.6d. violet	30	30
134	**62**	2s. light emerald	40	40

(b) Air. (i) ½ koula coin. Diam 2⅛in.

135	**63**	10d. carmine	20	20
136	**61**	11d. blue-green	30	30
137	**63**	1s.1d. deep blue	30	30

(ii) 1 koula coin. Diam 3⅛in.

138	**63**	2s.1d. bright purple	45	45
139	**61**	2s.4d. light emerald	50	50
140	**63**	2s.9d. violet	50	50
129/140 *and* O17 *Set of* 13			12·00	13·00

Examples of a 9d. Postage value in the design of the 1s.6d. exists, but these have been identified as proofs.

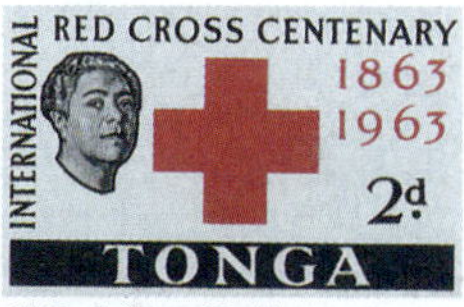

64 Red Cross Emblem

(Des V. Whiteley. Litho B.W.)

1963 (7 Oct). *Red Cross Centenary.* W **24** (sideways). P 13½.

141	**64**	2d. red and black	30	10
142		11d. red and blue	70	1·50

65 Queen Salote

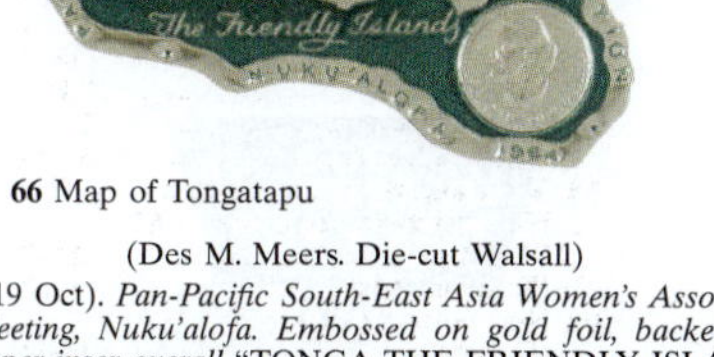

66 Map of Tongatapu

(Des M. Meers. Die-cut Walsall)

1964 (19 Oct). *Pan-Pacific South-East Asia Women's Association Meeting, Nuku'alofa. Embossed on gold foil, backed with paper inscr overall* "TONGA THE FRIENDLY ISLANDS". Imperf.

(a) Postage.

143	**65**	3d. pink	15	25
144		9d. light blue	20	30
145		2s. yellow-green	35	45
146		5s. lilac	65	1·00

(b) Air.

147	**66**	10d. blue-green	20	25
148		1s.2d. black	30	45
149		3s.6d. cerise	50	1·25
150		6s.6d. violet	85	2·00
143/150 *Set of* 8			2·75	5·25

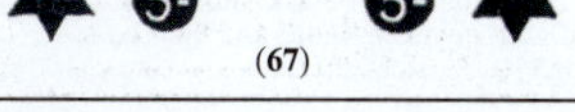

(**67**)

1965 (18 Mar). *"Gold Coin" stamps of 1963 surch as T* **67** *by Walsall Lithographic Co. New figures of value in gold; obliterating colours shown in brackets.*

(a) Postage.

151	**61**	1s.3d. on 1s.6d. violet (R.)	25	25
152	**62**	1s.9d. on 9d. bright purple (W.)	25	25
153	**61**	2s.6d. on 6d. blue-green (R.)	30	50
154		5s. on 1d. carmine	16·00	18·00
155	**62**	5s. on 2d. deep blue	2·75	3·75
156		5s. on 2s. light emerald	70	1·00
		(b) Air.		
157	**63**	2s.3d. on 10d. carmine	25	40
158	**61**	2s.9d. on 11d. blue-green (W.)	30	55
159	**63**	4s.6d. on 2s.1d. bright purple (R.)	13·00	14·00
160	**61**	4s.6d. on 2s.4d. light emerald (R.)	13·00	14·00
161	**63**	4s.6d. on 2s.9d. violet (R.)	7·50	8·50
151/161 and O18 *Set of* 12			48·00	55·00

King Taufa'ahau IV, 16 December 1965

1866-1966
TUPOU COLLEGE
& SECONDARY
EDUCATION
(68)

AIRMAIL
1866 CENTENARY 1966
TUPOU COLLEGE
&
SECONDARY EDUCATION
10d XX
(69)

OU COLLE
&
ARY EDUC
Misplaced "&"
(R. 5/5)

1966 (18 June). *Centenary of Tupou College and Secondary Education. Nos. 115/16 and 118/19 optd or surch.*

(a) Postage. As T **68**.

162	1d. carmine and brown-orange (P.)	10	10
163	3d. on 1d. carmine and brown-orange (P.)	10	10
	a. Misplaced "3d" (R. 2/5)	2·75	
	b. Surch inverted	†	£750
164	6d. on 2d ultramarine (R.)	15	10
165	1s.2d. on 2d. ultramarine (R.)	25	10
166	2s.. on 2d ultramarine (R.)	45	10
167	3s. on 2d. ultramarine (R.)	45	15
	(b) Air. As T **69.**		
168	5d. violet	15	10
	b. Misplaced "&"	2·75	
169	10d. on 1d. carmine and brown-orange	15	10
	b. Misplaced "&"	2·75	
170	1s. red-brown	40	10
	b. Misplaced "&"	2·75	
171	2s.9d. on 2d. ultramarine	50	15
	a. Sideways second "X" (R. 3/4)	9·00	
	b. Misplaced "&"	8·00	
172	3s.6d. on 5d. violet	55	15
	a. Sideways second "X" (R. 3/4)	9·00	
	b. Misplaced "&"	8·00	
173	4s.6d. on 1s. red-brown	85	15
	a. Sideways second "X" (R. 3/4)	9·00	
	b. Misplaced "&"	8·00	
162/173 and O19/20 *Set of* 14		5·25	1·75

On No. 163a the "d" is 20 mm from the "X" instead of the normal 22 mm.

(70)

(71)

1966 (16 Dec). *Queen Salote Commemoration. Nos. 143/4 and 147/8 optd as T* **70/1**, *or surch also, by Walsall Lithographic Co. Inscriptions and new figures of value in first colour and obliterating shapes in second colour given.*

(a) Postage. Optd as T **70**.

174	**65**	3d. (silver and ultramarine)	20	10
175		5d. on 9d. (silver and black)	25	10
176		9d. (silver and black)	40	15
177		1s.7d. on 3d. (silver and ultramarine)	1·00	80
178		3s.6d. on 9d. (silver and black)	1·25	1·00
179		6s.6d. on 3d. (silver and ultramarine)	1·75	2·25
		(b) Air. Optd as T **71**.		
180	**66**	10d. (silver and black)	40	10
181		1s.2d. (black and gold)	50	30
182		4s. on 10d. (silver and black)	1·50	1·10
183		5s.6d. on 1s.2d. (black and gold)	1·75	2·00
184		10s.6d. on 1s.2d. (gold and back)	2·25	2·75
174/184 *Set of* 11			10·00	9·50

(New Currency. 100 seniti = 1 pa'anga)

1 SENITI 1
(72)

10
Seniti
10
(73)

1967 (25 Mar). *Decimal currency. Various stamps surch as T* **72/3**.

185	1s. on 1d. (No. 101)	10	10
186	2s. on 4d. (No. 106)	20	10
187	3s. on 5d. (No. 107)	10	10
188	4s. on 5d. (No. 107)	30	30
189	5s. on 3½d. (No. 105)	10	10
190	6s. on 8d. (No. 109)	30	10
191	7s. on 1½d. (No. 102)	10	10
192	8s. on 6d. (No. 108)	30	10
193	9s. on 3d. (No. 104)	15	15
194	10s. on 1s. (No. 110)	15	15
195	11s. on 3d. on 1d. (No. 163)	30	20
	a. Misplaced "3d" (R. 2/5)	8·50	
196	21s. on 3s. on 2d. (No. 167)	25	35
197	23s. on 1d. (No. 101)	25	35
198	30s. on 2s. (No. 111)* (R.)	2·75	3·00
199	30s. on 2s. (No. 111)* (R.)	2·75	3·25
200	50s. on 6d. (No. 108) (R.)	1·25	1·75
201	60s. on 2d. (No. 103) (R.)	1·50	2·00
185/201 and O21 *Set of* 18		16·00	13·00

The above surcharges come in a variety of types and sizes.

*No. 198 has the surcharged value expressed horizontally; No. 199 has the figures "30" above and below "SENITI".

74 Coat of Arms (reverse)

75 King Taufa'ahau IV (obverse)

(Die-cut Walsall)

1967 (4 July). *Coronation of King Taufa'ahau IV. Circular designs. Embossed on palladium foil, backed with paper inscr overall* "The Friendly Islands Tonga", *etc.* Imperf.

Sizes
(a) Diameter 1½ in. *(d) Diameter 2³⁄₁₀ in.*
(b) Diameter 1⁷⁄₁₀in. *(e) Diameter 2⁷⁄₁₀ in.*
(c) Diameter 2 in. *(f) Diameter 2⁹⁄₁₀ in.*

(a) Postage.

202	**74**	1s. orange and greenish blue (*b*)	10	10
203	**75**	2s. greenish blue and deep magenta (*c*)	10	10
204	**74**	4s. emerald and bright purple (*d*)	15	10
205	**75**	15s. turquoise and violet (*e*)	40	25
206	**74**	28s. black and bright purple (*a*)	1·00	60
207	**75**	50s. carmine-red and ultramarine (*c*)	1·75	1·75
208	**74**	1p. blue and carmine (*f*)	2·50	3·00
		(b) Air.		
209	**75**	7s. carmine-red and black (*b*)	20	10
210	**74**	9s. brown-purple and emerald (*c*)	30	10
211	**75**	11s. greenish blue and orange (*d*)	35	15
212	**74**	21s. black and emerald (*e*)	65	30
213	**75**	23s. bright purple and light emerald (*a*)	75	45
214	**74**	29s. ultramarine and emerald (*c*)	1·00	60
215	**75**	2p. bright purple and orange (*f*)	3·50	4·25
202/15 *Set of* 14			11·50	10·50

The commemorative coins depicted in reverse (Type **74**) are inscribed in various denominations as follows: 1s.—"20 SENITI"; 4s.—"PA' ANGA"; 9s.—"50 SENITI"; 21s.—"TWO PA' ANGA"; 28s.—"QUARTER HAU"; 29s.—"HALF HAU"; 1p. "HAU".

The
Friendly Islands
welcome the
United States
Peace Corps
S
(76)

1967 (15 Dec). *Arrival of U.S. Peace Corps in Tonga. As Nos. 101/14, but imperf in different colours and surch as T* **76**.

(a) Postage.

216	1s. on 1d. black and orange-yellow	10	10
217	2s. on 2d. ultramarine and carmine-red	10	10
218	3s. on 3d. chestnut and yellow	10	10
219	4s. on 4d. reddish violet and yellow	10	10
220	5s. on 5d. green and yellow	10	10
221	10s. on 1s. carmine-red and yellow	10	10
222	20s. on 2s. claret and new blue	30	15
223	50s. on 5s. sepia and orange-yellow	2·75	1·25
224	1p. on 10s. orange-yellow	70	1·50
	(b) Air.		
225	11s. on 3½d. ultramarine (R.)	15	10
226	21s. on 1½d. emerald	30	20
227	23s. on 3½d. ultramarine	30	20
216/27 *and* O26/8 *Set of* 15		6·00	6·25

On Nos. 219 and 224 the opt is smaller, and in four lines instead of five. On Nos. 216/20 the surcharge takes the form of an alteration to the currency name as in T **76**.

2 SENITI 2
(77)

10
SENITI
10
(78)

1968 (6 Apr). *Various stamps surch as T* **77/8**.

(a) Postage.

228	1s. on 1d. (No. 101) (R.)	10	10
229	2s. on 4d. (No. 106)	10	20
230	3s. on 3d. (No. 104) (B.)	10	20
231	4s. on 5d. (No. 107) (R.)	10	20
232	5s. on 2d. (No. 103) (R.)	10	20
233	6s. on 6d. (No. 108) (R.)	10	20
234	7s. on 1½d.(No. 102) (R.)	10	15
235	8s. on 8d. (No. 109) (R.)	10	25
236	9s. on 3½d. (No. 105)	20	30
237	10s. on 1s. (No. 110) (R.)	20	20
238	20s. on 5s. (No. 112) (R.)	1·75	70
239	2p. on 2s. (No. 111) (R.)	1·50	2·75
	(b) Air. Surch as T **78** *with "AIRMAIL" added.*		
240	11s. on 10s. (No. 113) (R.)	25	30
241	21s. on 10s. (No. 113) (R.)	40	50
242	23s. on 10s. (No. 113) (R.)	40	50
228/42 *and* O22/5 *Set of* 19		8·75	12·50

(79)

Friendly Islands
Field & Track Trials
South Pacific Games
Port Moresby
1969
S
(80)

1968 (4 July). *50th Birthday of King Taufa'ahua IV. Nos. 202/15 optd as T* **79**. *(a) Postage.*

243	**74**	1s. orange and greenish blue (*b*) (R.)	10	40
244	**75**	2s. greenish blue & deep magenta (*b*) (B.)	20	40
245	**74**	4s. emerald and bright purple (*d*)	30	40
246	**75**	15s. turquoise and violet (*e*) (R.)	1·25	25
247	**74**	28s. black and bright purple (*a*) (R.)	2·00	30
248	**75**	50s. carmine-red and ultramarine (*c*) (B.)	2·75	1·40
249	**74**	1p. blue and carmine (*f*) (R.)	5·50	5·00
		(b) Air.		
250	**75**	7s. carmine-red and black (*b*) (B.)	50	20
251	**74**	9s. brown-purple and emerald (*c*) (R.)	55	20
252	**75**	11s. greenish blue and orange (*d*) (B.)	75	20
253	**74**	21s. black and emerald (*e*) (R.)	1·75	25
		a. Opt (gold only) double	£275	
254	**75**	23s. bright purple and light emerald (*a*) (B.)	1·75	25
255	**74**	29s. ultramarine and emerald (*c*) (R.)	2·00	35
256	**75**	2p. bright purple and orange (*f*) (B.)	9·00	9·00
243/56 *and* O29/32 *Set of* 18			42·00	30·00

The overprints vary in size, but are all crescent-shaped as Type **79** and inscribed "H.M'S BIRTHDAY 4 JULY 1968" (Type **79**) or "HIS MAJESTY'S 50th BIRTHDAY" (others).

1968 (19 Dec). *South Pacific Games Field and Track Trials, Port Moresby, Papua New Guinea. Nos. 101/13, but imperf, in different colours and surch as T* **80**. *(a) Postage.*

257	5s. on 5d green and yellow (R.)	10	15
258	10s. on 1s. carmine-red and yellow	10	15
259	15s. on 2s. claret and new blue	15	20
260	25s. on 2d. ultramarine and carmine-red	25	25
261	50s. on 1d. black and orange-yellow	35	55
262	75s. on 10s. orange-yellow (G.)	60	1·25
	(b) Air.		
263	6s. on 6d. black and yellow*	10	15
264	7s. on 4d. reddish violet and yellow	10	15
265	8s. on 8d. black and greenish yellow	10	15
	a. Surch 11½ mm as on 6d	£140	£100
266	9s. on 1½d. emerald	10	15
267	11s. on 3d. chestnut and yellow	15	15
268	21s. on 3½d. ultramarine	20	20
269	38s. on 5s. sepia and orange-yellow	2·25	1·00
270	1p. on 10s. orange-yellow	70	1·50
257/70 *and* O33/4 *Set of* 16		5·50	7·00

*On No. 263 the surcharge is smaller (11½ mm wide).

1s (81) *1s* (82)

1969. *Emergency Provisionals. Various stamps (Nos. 273/6 are imperf and in different colours) surch as T* **81** *or* **82**. *(a) Postage.*

271		1s. on 1s.2d. on 2d. ultramarine (No. 165)	1·75	2·75
272		1s. on 2s. on 2d. ultramarine (No. 166)	1·75	2·75
273		1s. on 6d. black and yellow (as No. 108)	60	70
274		2s. on 3½d. ultramarine (as No. 105)	65	70
275		3s. on 1½d. emerald (as No. 102)	65	70
276		4s. on 8d. black and greenish yellow (as No. 109)	90	1·00
		(b) Air. Nos. 171/3 surch with T **82**.		
277		1s. on 2s.9d. on 2d. ultramarine	1·75	2·75
		a. Sideways second "X" (R. 3/4)	21·00	
		b. Misplaced "&"	19·00	
278		1s. on 3s.6d. on 5d. violet	1·75	2·75
		a. Sideways second "X" (R. 3/4)	21·00	
		b. Misplaced "&"	19·00	
279		1s. on 4s.6d. on 1s. red-brown	1·75	2·75
		a. Sideways second "X" (R. 3/4)	21·00	
		b. Misplaced "&"	19·00	
271/9 *Set of* 9			10·00	15·00

SELF-ADHESIVE ISSUES. From No. 280 until No. 922 all stamps were manufactured by Walsall Security Printers Ltd and are self-adhesive. The backing paper is separated by roulette or perforations (from No. 780 onwards), and shows on its reverse the words "*TONGA where time begins*", or, from No. 568 onwards, various texts or illustrations. This also applies to the Official stamps.

83 Banana

1969 (21 Apr). *Coil stamps.*

280	**83**	1s. scarlet, black and greenish yellow	1·25	1·50
281		2s. bright green, black and greenish yellow	1·40	1·60
282		3s. violet, black and greenish yellow	1·50	1·75
283		4s. ultramarine, black and greenish yellow	1·60	2·00
284		5s. bronze-green, black and greenish yellow	1·75	2·00
280/4 *Set of* 5			6·75	8·00

Nos. 280/4 were produced in rolls of 200, each even stamp having a number applied to the front of the backing paper, with the usual inscription on the reverse.

See also Nos. 325/9, 413/17 and 675/89.

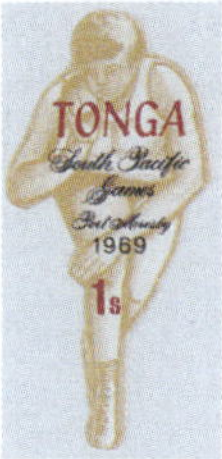

84 Putting the Shot

86 Oil Derrick and Map

1969 (13 Aug). *Third South Pacific Games, Port Moresby. T* **84** *and similar design. (a) Postage.*

285	**84**	1s. black, red and buff	10	15
286		3s. bright green, red and buff	10	15
287		6s. blue, red and buff	10	15
288		10s. bluish violet, red and buff	15	15
289		30s. blue, red and buff	30	30
		(b) Air.		
290	–	9s. black, violet and orange	15	15
291	–	11s. black, ultramarine and orange	15	15
292	–	20s. black, bright green and orange	25	25
293	–	60s. black, cerise and orange	75	1·25
294	–	1p. black, blue-green and orange	1·10	2·00
285/94 *and* O35/6 *Set of* 12			4·25	7·00

Design:—9, 11, 20, 60s., 1p. Boxing.

1969 (23 Dec). *First Oil Search in Tonga. T* **86** *and similar vert design.*

		(a) Postage.		
295	**86**	3s. multicoloured	15	15
296		7s. multicoloured	20	20
297		20s. multicoloured	50	50
298		25s. multicoloured	55	50
299		35s. multicoloured	80	80
		(b) Air.		
300	–	9s. multicoloured	30	25
301	–	10s. multicoloured	30	25
302	–	24s. multicoloured	60	50
303	–	29s. multicoloured	70	70
304	–	38s. multicoloured	80	80
295/304 *and* O37/8 *Set of* 12			10·50	13·00

Design:—Nos. 300/4, Oil derrick and island of Tongatapu.

87 Members of the British and Tongan Royal Families

1970 (7 Mar). *Royal Visit. T* **87** *and similar design. Multicoloured.*

		(a) Postage.		
305	**87**	3s. multicoloured	50	20
306		5s. multicoloured	55	20
307		10s. multicoloured	75	40
308		25s. multicoloured	2·00	75
309		50s. multicoloured	3·50	2·75
		(b) Air.		
310	–	7s. multicoloured	70	25
311	–	9s. multicoloured	75	30
312	–	24s. multicoloured	2·00	75
313	–	29s. multicoloured	2·25	80
314	–	38s. multicoloured	3·00	1·25
305/14 *and* O39/41 *Set of* 13			30·00	20·00

Design:—Nos. 310/14, Queen Elizabeth II and King Taufu'ahau Tupou IV.

89 Book, Tongan Rulers and Flag

1970 (4 June). *Entry into British Commonwealth. T* **89** *and similar design. (a) Postage.*

315	**89**	3s. multicoloured	20	15
316		7s. multicoloured	30	20
317		15s. multicoloured	55	30
318		25s. multicoloured	70	40
319		50s. multicoloured	1·25	1·50
		(b) Air.		
320	–	9s. turquoise-blue, gold and scarlet	20	20
321	–	10s. bright purple, gold and greenish blue	20	20
322	–	24s. olive-yellow, gold and green	50	30
323	–	29s. new blue, gold and orange-red	55	30
324	–	38s. deep orange-yellow, gold and bright emerald	70	55
315/24 *and* O42/4 *Set of* 13			17·00	14·00

Design: "*Star*" *shaped* (44×51 *mm*)—Nos. 320/4, King Taufa'ahau Tupou IV.

90 Coconut

1970 (9 June). *Coil stamps. (a) As T* **83** *but colours changed.*

325	**83**	1s. greenish yellow, bright purple and black	65	1·00
326		2s. greenish yellow, ultramarine and black	75	1·00
327		3s. greenish yellow, chocolate and black	75	1·00
328		4s. greenish yellow, emerald and black	75	1·00
329		5s. greenish yellow, orange-red and blue	80	1·00
		(b) T **90**. *Multicoloured; colour of face value given.*		
330	**90**	6s. rose-carmine	90	1·25
331		7s. bright purple	95	1·25
332		8s. bluish violet	1·10	1·25
333		9s. turquoise	1·25	1·25
334		10s. pale orange	1·25	1·25
325/34 *Set of* 10			8·25	10·00

Nos. 325/34 and O45/54 were produced in rolls of 200, each even stamp having a number applied to the front of the backing paper, with the usual inscription on the reverse.

91 "Red Cross"

(Litho (postage) or litho and die-stamped (air))

1970 (17 Oct). *Centenary of British Red Cross. T* **91** *and similar "cross" shaped design. (a) Postage.*

335	**91**	3s. vermilion, black and light green	20	30
336		7s. vermilion, black and ultramarine	30	20
337		15s. vermilion and bright purple	75	60
338		25s. vermilion, black and turquoise-blue	1·25	90
339		75s. vermilion and deep red-brown	5·50	6·00
		(b) Air.		
340	–	9s. vermilion and silver	35	20
341	–	10s. vermilion and bright purple	35	20
342	–	18s. vermilion and green	75	60
343	–	38s. vermilion and ultramarine	2·75	2·25
344	–	1p. vermilion and turquoise-blue	6·50	8·50
335/44 *and* O55/7 *Set of* 13			32·00	30·00

Design: *As T* **91**—Nos. 340/4 as Nos. 335/9 but with inscription rearranged and coat of arms omitted.

On Nos. 335/6 and 338 the black colour is produced as a composite of the other two colours used.

OFFICIAL STAMPS

G.F.B. (O 1) **1D/2** (O 2)

(G.F.B. = Gaue Faka Buleaga = On Government Service)

1893 (13 Feb). *Optd with Type* O **1** *by Govt Printing Office, Wellington, N.Z. W* **2**. *P* 12×11½.

O1	**5**	1d. ultramarine (C.)	16·00	50·00
		a. Bisected diagonally (½d.) (on cover)		
O2	**6**	2d. ultramarine (C.)	32·00	55·00
O3	**5**	4d. ultramarine (C.)	48·00	£100
O4	**6**	8d. ultramarine (C.)	90·00	£170
O5		1s. ultramarine (C.)	£110	£200
O1/5 *Set of* 5			£250	£500

Above prices are for stamps in good condition and colour. Faded and stained stamps from the remainders are worth much less.

1893 (Dec). *Nos. O1 to O5 variously surch with new value, sideways as Type* O **2**.

O6	**5**	½d. on 1d. ultramarine	23·00	50·00
O7	**6**	2½d. on 2d. ultramarine	28·00	45·00
O8	**5**	5d. on 4d. ultramarine	28·00	45·00
O9	**6**	7½d. on 8d. ultramarine	28·00	80·00
		a. "D" of "7½D." omitted	£1200	
		b. Surch double	£2000	
O10		10d. on 1s. ultramarine	32·00	85·00
O6/10 *Set of* 5			£120	£275

OFFICIAL AIR MAIL 1862 TAU'ATAINA EMANCIPATION 1962 (O 3)

OFFICIAL AIRMAIL 40 SENITI (O 4)

1962 (7 Feb). *Air. Centenary of Emancipation. Nos. 112/14, 116 and 118/19 optd with Type* O **3** *in red by R. S. Wallbank, Govt Printer.*

O11	–	2d. ultramarine	16·00	6·00
		a. "OFFICIAI"	25·00	11·00
		b. "MAII"	25·00	11·00
O12	–	5d. violet	17·00	6·50
		a. "OFFICIAI"	27·00	12·00
		b. "MAII"	27·00	12·00
O13	–	1s. red-brown	12·00	3·75
		a. "OFFICIAI"	30·00	11·00
		b. "MAII"	30·00	11·00
		c. Opt double	£350	
		ca. "OFFICIAI"	£750	
		cb. "MAII"	£750	
O14	–	5s. orange-yellow and slate-lilac	£130	70·00
		a. "MAII"	£275	£100
		b. "OFFICIAI"		
O15	**52**	10s. yellow and black	50·00	24·00
		a. "MAII"	£130	
O16	**53**	£1 yellow, scarlet, ultramarine and deep bright blue	75·00	40·00
		a. "MAII"	£180	
		b. "OFFICIAI"		
O11/16 *Set of* 6			£275	£130

SET PRICES. Official stamps from here onwards are included in the complete commemorative set prices given for any corresponding Postage issues

1963 (15 July). *Air. First Polynesian Gold Coinage Commemoration. As T* **63** *but inscr* "OFFICIAL AIRMAIL". *1 koula coin (diam 3⅛in.). Imperf.*

O17	**63**	15s. black	10·00	11·00

1965 (18 Mar). *No. O17 surch as T* **67**.

O18	**63**	30s. on 15s. black	3·25	4·25

1966 (18 June). *Air. Centenary of Tupou College and Secondary Education. No. 117 surch with* "OFFICIAL AIRMAIL" *and new value, with commemorative inscription as in T* **69** *but in italic capital letters.*

O19		10s. on 4d. blue-green	80	35
		a. Surch inverted	£300	£150
O20		20s. on 4d. blue-green	1·00	50

1967 (25 Mar). *Air. Decimal currency. No. 112 surch* "OFFICIAL AIRMAIL ONE PA' ANGA" *in three lines, in red.*

O21		1p. on 5s. yellow and lilac	7·00	2·50
		a. "AIRMAIL" above "OFFICIAL"	£170	

No. O21a occurred once in a number of sheets until it was corrected.

1967 (4 July). *Air. No. 114 surch in various denominations as Type* O **4**.

O22	**53**	40s. on £1 yellow, red and blue	60	75
O23		60s. on £1 yellow, red and blue	80	1·25
O24		1p. on £1 yellow, red and blue	1·10	2·25
O25		2p. on £1 yellow, red and blue	1·75	3·00

Nos. O22/5 were first used on 4 July 1967, but supplies of unused stamps were not made available until April 1968.

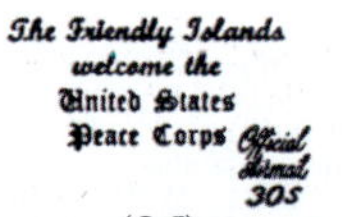

(O **5**)

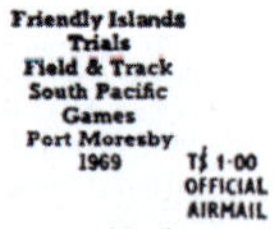

(O **6**)

1967 (15 Dec). *Air. Arrival of U.S. Peace Corps in Tonga. As No. 114, but imperf, and background colour changed, and surch as Type* O **5**.

O26	**53**	30s. on £1 yellow, scarlet, ultramarine and emerald-green	50	30
O27		70s. on £1 yellow, scarlet, ultramarine and emerald-green	70	1·25
O28		1p.50 on £1 yellow, scarlet, ultramarine and emerald-green	1·00	2·00

1968 (4 July). *Air. 50th Birthday of King Taufa'ahua IV. No. 207 surch* "HIS MAJESTY'S 50th BIRTHDAY" *(as T* **79**), "OFFICIAL AIRMAIL" *and new value.*

O29	**75**	40s. on 50s. (Turq.)	2·75	70
O30		60s. on 50s. (G.)	3·25	1·75
O31		1p. on 50s. (V.)	4·25	4·25
O32		2p. on 50s. (P.)	8·00	8·50

1968 (19 Dec). *Air. South Pacific Games Field and Track Trials, Port Moresby, New Guinea. As No. 114, but imperf, background colour changed and surch as Type* O **6**.

O33	**53**	20s. on £1 yellow, scarlet, ultramarine and emerald-green	20	25
O34		1p. on £1 yellow, scarlet, ultramarine and emerald-green	70	1·50

1969 (13 Aug). *Air. Third South Pacific Games, Port Moresby. Design as Nos. 290/4.*

O35		70s. carmine-red, bright green and turquoise	75	1·60
O36		80s. carmine-red, orange and turquoise	85	1·60

(O **7**)

(O **8**)

1969 (23 Dec). *Air. First Oil Search in Tonga. As No. 114 but imperf, background colour changed to emerald-green, and surch as Type* O **7**.

O37	**53**	90s. on £1 multicoloured	3·50	5·00
		a. "1966" for "1969" (R. 3/5)	£140	
O38		1p.10 on £1 multicoloured (R.)	3·50	5·00
		a. "1966" for "1969" (R. 3/5)	£140	

The "1966" error does not occur on every sheet. It is possible that Nos. O37/8 were surcharged in sheets of 120 containing two panes of 60 (6×10).

No. O38 is surch as Type O **7**, but without "OFFICIAL AIRMAIL".

1970 (7 Mar). *Royal Visit. As No. 110 but imperf colours changed, and surch as Type* O **8**.

O39		75s. on 1s. carmine-red and yellow	4·75	4·00
O40		1p. on 1s. carmine-red and yellow (B.)	5·50	4·50
O41		1p.25 on 1s. carmine-red & yellow (G.)	6·50	6·00

(O **9**)

1970 (4 June). *Air. Entry into British Commonwealth. As No. 112 but imperf, background colour changed, and surch as Type* O **9**.

O42		50s. on 5s. orange-yellow and sepia	4·00	1·75
O43		90s. on 5s. orange-yellow and sepia (R.)	5·00	3·50
O44		1p.50 on 5s. orange-yellow & sepia (G.)	6·00	6·50

1970 (4 June). *As Nos. 325/34, but inscr* "OFFICIAL POST". *Colour of* "TONGA" *given for 6 to 10s.*

O45	**83**	1s. greenish yellow, bright purple and black	65	1·00
O46		2s. greenish yellow, ultramarine and black	75	1·00
O47		3s. greenish yellow, chocolate and black	75	1·00
O48		4s. greenish yellow, emerald and black	75	1·00
O49		5s. greenish yellow, orange-red and black	80	1·00
O50	**90**	6s. ultramarine	90	1·25
O51		7s. deep mauve	95	1·25
O52		8s. gold	1·10	1·25
O53		9s. bright carmine	1·25	1·25
O54		10s. silver	1·25	1·25
O45/54 *Set of* 10			8·25	10·00

The note after No. 334 also applies here.

See also Nos. O82/91.

(O **10**)

1970 (17 Oct). *Centenary of British Red Cross. As Nos. 102 and 112 but imperf, colours changed and surch as Type* O **10**.

O55		30s. on 1½d. emerald (Blk. and R.)	1·75	2·00
O56		80s. on 5s. orange-yellow and sepia (B. & R.)	7·50	6·00
O57		90s. on 5s. orange-yellow and sepia (B. & R.)	7·50	6·00

Transjordan

PRICES FOR STAMPS ON COVER	
Nos. 1/88*a*	*from* × 10
Nos. 89/142	*from* × 5
Nos. 143/243	*from* × 3
Nos. D112/24	*from* × 5
Nos. D159/248	*from* × 3
Nos. O117	*from* × 5

Transjordan was part of the Turkish Empire from 1516 to 1918.

Turkish post offices are known to have existed at Ajlun ("Adjiloun"), Amman ("Omman"), Amman Station, Kerak ("Kerek"), Ma'an ("Mohan" or "Maan"), Qatrana, Salt and Tafila ("Tafile"). Stamps cancelled "Ibin" may have been used at Ibbin.

The area was overrun by British and Arab forces, organised by Colonel T. E. Lawrence, in September 1918, and as Occupied Enemy Territory (East), became part of the Syrian state under the Emir Faisal, who was king of Syria from 11 March to 24 July 1920. During 1920 the stamps of the Arab Kingdom of Syria were in use. On 25 April 1920 the Supreme Council of the Allies assigned to the United Kingdom a mandate to administer both Palestine and Transjordan, as the area to the east of the Jordan was called. The mandate came into operation on 29 September 1923.

E.E.F. post offices, using the stamps of Palestine, operated in the area from September 1918.

BRITISH MANDATED TERRITORY

(Currency. 1000 milliemes = 100 piastres = £1 Egyptian)

"EAST". Where the word "East" appears in Arabic overprints it is not used in its widest sense but as implying the land or government "East of Jordan".

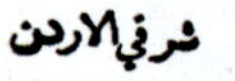

(**1**) ("East of Jordan")

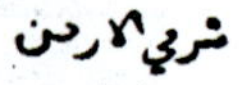

(**1a**)

(Optd at Greek Orthodox Convent, Jerusalem)

1920 (Nov). *T* **3** *of Palestine optd with T* **1**.

(a) P 15×14.

1	**1**	1m. sepia	1·75	2·75
		a. Opt inverted	£140	£275
2		2m. blue-green	14·00	15·00
		a. Silver opt		
3		3m. yellow-brown	2·00	2·25
		a. Opt Type **1a**	£1100	
4		4m. scarlet	2·25	2·25
5		5m. yellow-orange	4·50	2·25
5*a*		1p. deep indigo (Silver)	£2000	
6		2p. olive	7·00	9·50
		a. Opt Type **1a**	£850	
7		5p. deep purple	35·00	48·00
		a. Opt Type **1a**	£1400	
8		9p. ochre	£850	£1400
1/7 (*ex* 5*a*) *Set of* 7			55·00	70·00

(b) P 14.

9	**1**	1m. sepia	1·25	2·75
		a. Opt inverted	£170	
10		2m. blue-green	70	2·00
		a. Silver opt	£550	£600
11		3m. yellow-brown	18·00	21·00
12		4m. scarlet	15·00	28·00
13		5m. orange	2·00	2·00
14		1p. deep indigo (Silver)	1·50	2·75
15		2p. deep olive	6·00	6·00
16		5p. purple	3·50	8·50
17		9p. ochre	4·00	32·00
18		10p. ultramarine	10·00	32·00
19		20p. pale grey	12·00	50·00
9/19 *Set of* 11			65·00	£170

Nos. 1/9 were surcharged from five different settings of 120 (12×10) which produced eight sub-types of Type **1**. Type **1a** occurred on R. 8/12 from one setting. The 9p. also exists with this overprint, but no example appears to have survived without further overprint or surcharge.

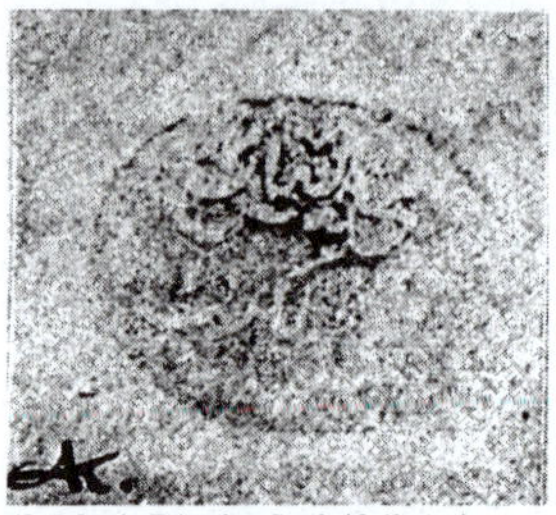

1b Moab District Seal (*full size*)

1920 (Nov). *Issued at Kerak. Handstamped. Manuscript initials* "AK" *in violet. Imperf.*

19*a*	**1b**	(1p.) pale blue	£3500	£4000

No. 19*a* was issued in November 1920 by the political officer for Moab District, Captain (later Sir) Alex Kirkbride, and was used until supplies of Nos. 1/19 reached the area in March 1921. The local Turkish canceller was used as a postmark.

Emir Abdullah, 1 April 1921–22 May 1946

Abdullah, a son of the King of the Hejaz, was made Emir of Transjordan in 1921. On 26 May 1923 Transjordan was recognised as an autonomous state and on 20 February 1928 it was accorded a degree of independence.

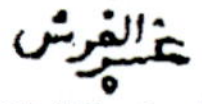

(**2**) ("Tenth of a piastre")

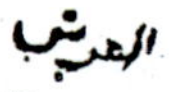

(**3**) ("Piastre")

(**4**) ("Arab Government of the East, April 1921")

1922 (Nov). *Nos. 1/19 additionally handstamped with steel dies at Amman as T* **2** *or* **3**.

(a) P 15×14.

20	**2**	1/10p. on 1m. sepia	25·00	45·00
		a. Red surch	70·00	70·00
		b. Violet surch	70·00	70·00
21		2/10p. on 2m. blue-green	28·00	28·00
		a. Error. Surch "3/10" for "2/10"	£110	£100
		b. Red surch	80·00	80·00
		c. Violet surch	£100	£100
		ca. Error. "3/10" for "2/10"		
22		3/10p. on 3m. yellow-brown	11·00	11·00
		a. Pair, one without surch	£800	
		b. Opt Type **1a**	£1200	£1200
		c. Error. "2/10" for "3/10"		
		d. Violet surch	£150	£150
		da. Opt Type **1a**	£2750	
23		4/10p. on 4m. scarlet	55·00	60·00
		a. Violet surch		
24		5/10p. on 5m. yellow-orange	£180	£100
		a. Pair, one without surch		
		b. Violet surch	£250	£225
25	**3**	2p. on 2p. olive	£250	75·00
		a. Opt Type **1a**	£1300	
		b. Red surch	£325	80·00
		ba. Opt Type **1a**		
		c. Violet surch	£300	90·00
26		5p. on 5p. deep purple	55·00	70·00
		a. Opt Type **1a**	£1600	
		b. Violet surch		
27		9p. on 9p. ochre	£300	£350
		a. Red surch	£130	£140
		b. Violet surch		

(b) P 14.

28	**2**	1/10p. on 1m. sepia	21·00	26·00
		a. Pair, one without surch	£1500	
		b. Red surch	60·00	60·00
		c. Violet surch	£250	£300
29		2/10p. on 2m. blue-green	25·00	25·00
		a. Pair, one without surch	£1500	
		b. Error. Surch "3/10" for "2/10"	£100	£100
		c. Red surch	80·00	80·00
		ca. Error. Surch "3/10" for "2/10"		
		d. Violet surch	80·00	80·00
30		5/10p. on 5m. orange	£225	£100
		a. Pair, one without surch	†	£2000
		b. Violet surch	£275	
31	**3**	1p. on 1p. deep indigo (R.)	£200	60·00
		a. Pair, one without surch	£1800	
		b. Violet surch	£400	
32		9p. on 9p. ochre (R.)	£550	£550
		a. Violet surch		
33		10p. on 10p. ultramarine	£850	£1000
		a. Violet surch inverted		
34		20p. on 20p. pale grey	£650	£850
		a. Violet surch	£900	£950

T **3** *of Palestine (perf 15×14) similarly surch.*

35	**3**	10p. on 10p. ultramarine	£1800	£2500
36		20p. on 20p. pale grey	£2500	£3000
		a. Violet surch		

T **2** reads "tenths of a piastre" and T **3** "the piastre", both with Arabic figures below. These surcharges were applied in order to translate the Egyptian face values of the stamps into the currency of the Arab Kingdom of Syria, but the actual face value of the stamps remained unchanged.

Being handstamped the surcharge may be found either at the top or bottom of the stamp, and exists double on most values.

1922 (Dec). *Stamps of 1920 handstamped with a steel die as T* **4** *in red-purple, violet or black*.*

(a) P 15×14.

37	4	1m. sepia (R.P.)	26·00	26·00
		a. Violet opt	29·00	29·00
		b. Black opt	23·00	23·00
38		2m. blue-green (R.P.)	23·00	23·00
		a. Violet opt	21·00	21·00
		b. Black opt	19·00	19·00
39		3m. yellow-brown (R.P.)	40·00	40·00
		a. Opt Type **1a**	£1600	
		b. Violet opt	7·50	7·50
		ba. Pair, one without opt	£1300	
		bb. Opt Type **1a**	£1500	£2000
		c. Black opt	8·50	8·50
		ca. Opt Type **1a**		
40		4m. scarlet (R.P.)	50·00	55·00
		b. Violet opt	50·00	55·00
		c. Black opt	50·00	55·00
41		5m. yellow-orange (R.P.)	38·00	10·00
		a. Violet opt	16·00	10·00
42		2p. olive (R.P.)	55·00	40·00
		a. Opt Type **1a**	£1500	
		b. Violet opt	22·00	16·00
		ba. Opt Type **1a**	£1500	£1300
		c. Black opt	13·00	10·00
43		5p. deep purple (R.P.)	£100	£120
		a. Pair, one without opt	£1600	
		b. Violet opt	60·00	80·00
		c. Black opt		
44		9p. ochre (R.P.)	£400	£450
		a. Violet opt	£200	£250
		ab. Opt Type **1a**	£2250	
		b. Black opt	65·00	80·00

(b) P 14.

45	4	1m. sepia (R.P.)	13·00	16·00
		a. Pair, one without opt	£1300	
		b. Violet opt	24·00	21·00
		c. Black opt	19·00	19·00
46		2m. blue-green (R.P.)	27·00	27·00
		a. Violet opt	8·00	8·00
		b. Black opt	11·00	11·00
46c		3m. yellow-brown (V.)	£800	£350
47		5m. orange (R.P.)	£300	75·00
		a. Violet opt	26·00	20·00
48		1p. deep indigo (R.P.)	26·00	15·00
		a. Violet opt	17·00	9·50
49		2p. deep olive (V.)	75·00	80·00
50		5p. purple (R.P.)	90·00	£100
		a. Violet opt	£100	£110
		b. Black opt		
51		9p. ochre (V.)	£900	£1000
52		10p. ultramarine (R.P.)	£1800	£1900
		a. Violet opt	£1100	£1600
		b. Black opt		
53		20p. pale grey (R.P.)	£1600	£2000
		a. Violet opt	£1100	£1800
		b. Black opt		

*The ink of the "black" overprint is not a true black, but is caused by a mixture of inks from different ink-pads. The colour is, however, very distinct from either of the others.

Most values are known with inverted and/or double overprints.

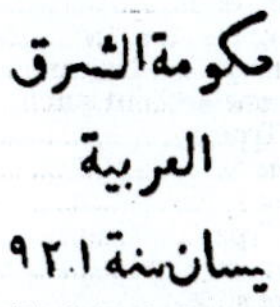

(**5**) ("Arab Government of the East, April 1921")

1923 (1 Mar). *Stamps of 1920, with typographed overprint, T* **5** *applied by Govt Printing Press, Amman.*

(a) P 15×14.

54	5	1m. sepia (Gold)	£1500	£1800
55		2m. blue-green (Gold)	21·00	23·00
56		3m. yellow-brown (Gold)	13·00	16·00
		a. Opt double	£500	
		b. Opt inverted	£550	
		c. Black opt	75·00	85·00
57		4m. scarlet	12·00	14·00
58		5m. yellow-orange	50·00	45·00
		a. Opt Type **1** albino	£1200	£1400
59		2p. olive (Gold)	17·00	17·00
		a. Opt Type **1a**	£1200	£1000
		b. Black opt	£250	£250
		ba. Opt Type **1a**		
60		5p. deep purple (Gold)	60·00	80·00
		a. Opt inverted	£225	
		b. Opt Type **1a**	£2000	
		ba. Opt inverted	£2500	
		c. Black opt inverted	£1500	

(b) P 14.

62	5	1m. sepia (Gold)	18·00	27·00
		a. Opt inverted	£750	
63		2m. blue-green (Gold)	15·00	19·00
		a. Opt inverted	£350	£350
		b. Opt double	£300	
		c. Black opt	£300	
		ca. Opt double	£1500	
64		5m. orange	11·00	13·00
65		1p. deep indigo (Gold)	11·00	15·00
		a. Opt double	£500	£550
		b. Black opt	£800	£850
66		9p. ochre	75·00	£100
		a. Gold opt	£3000	
67		10p. ultramarine (Gold)	70·00	£100
68		20p. pale grey (Gold)	70·00	£100
		a. Opt inverted	£375	
		b. Opt double	£450	
		c. Opt double, one inverted	£450	
		e. Opt double, one gold, one black, latter inverted	£750	
		f. Opt treble, one inverted	£1100	
		g. Black opt	£850	
		ga. Opt inverted	£1100	
		gb. Opt double, one inverted	£1300	

The gold overprints were created by sprinkling gold dust on wet black ink.

There are numerous constant minor varieties in this overprint in all values.

The 9p. perforated 15×14 was also prepared with this overprint, but the entire stock was used for No. 85.

The 20p. exists with top line of overprint only or with the lines transposed, both due to misplacement.

(**6**)

(**7**)

(**8**)

(**9**)

1923 (Apr–Oct). *Stamps of the preceding issues further surch by means of handstamps.*

(a) Issue of Nov 1920.

70	–	2½/10thsp. on 5m. (13) (B.–Blk.)	£160	£160
		a. Black surch	£160	£160
		b. Violet surch	£160	£160
70c	6	1/10p. on 3m. (3)	†	£5000
70d		1/10p. on 5m. (13)	£2500	
70e	9	2p. on 20p. (19)		

(b) Stamp of Palestine.

71	6	1/10p. on 3m. (P 15×14)	£3000	

(c) Issue of Nov 1922.

72	6	1/10p. on 3m. (22)	£7000	
		a. Pair, one without surch	£7500	
73		1/10p. on 5p. (26) (V.)	70·00	80·00
		a. Black surch		
		ab. Opt Type **3** omitted	£1200	
73b		1/10p. on 9p. (27a)	£1200	
74	7	½p. on 5p. (26)	70·00	80·00
		a. Pair, one without surch	£750	
75		½p. on 9p. (27)	£3500	
		a. On No. 27a	£350	£400
		ab. Opt Type **1a**	£3500	
76		½p. on 9p. (32)	—	£8000
77	8	1p. on 5p. (26)	80·00	£100

(d) Issue of Dec 1922.

78	6	1/10p. on 3m. (39) (V.)	85·00	£100
		a. Black surch	£750	
		ab. Opt Type **1a**		
		b. On No. 39v	45·00	55·00
		ba. Pair, one without surch	£1400	
		bb. Without numeral of value		
		bc. Black surch	£750	
79		1/10p. on 5p. (43b) (Blk.)	8·50	15·00
		a. Opt Type **1a**	£2000	
		b. Pair, one without surch	£500	
		c. Violet surch		
79d		1/10p. on 9p. (44b)	—	£1200
		da. On No. 44a. Violet surch	—	£1300
80	7	½p. on 2p. (42)	£100	£120
		a. Opt Type **1a**	£2000	
		b. On No. 42b	80·00	£110
		c. On No. 42c	60·00	£110
		ca. Pair, one without surch	£1000	
		w. Wmk inverted		
81		½p. on 5p. (43)	£3000	
		a. On No. 43b	£1000	
82		½p. on 5p. (50)	£2000	
		a. On No. 50a	£2500	
83	8	1p. on 5p. (43)	£3750	
		b. On No. 43b	£2000	£2250
83c		1p. on 5p. (50)	£2500	

(e) Issue of 1 March 1923.

84	6	1/10p. on 3m. (56)	26·00	35·00
		a. On No. 56c	£700	
85	7	½p. on 9p. (P 15×14)	90·00	£150
		a. Pair, one without surch	£5000	
86		½p. on 9p. (66)	£150	
87	9	1p. on 10p. (67)	£2250	£2500
		a. Violet surch	£2750	
88		2p. on 20p. (68)	60·00	80·00
88a		2p. on 20p. (68g)	£2000	

The handstamp on Nos. 70*c*, 88 and 88*a* has an Arabic "2" in place of the "1" shown in the illustration of Type **9**.

Being handstamped many of the above exist inverted or double.

TYPES OF SAUDI ARABIA. The following illustrations are repeated here for convenience from Saudi Arabia.

11

20

21

22

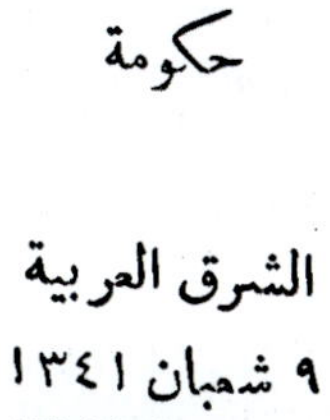

(**10**) ("Arab Government of the East, 9 Sha'ban 1341")

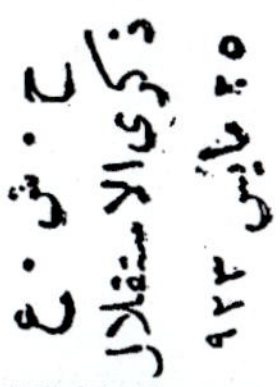

(**11**) ("Arab Government of the East. Commemoration of Independence, 25 May 1923")

It should be noted that as Arabic is read from right to left, the overprint described as reading downwards appears to the English reader as though reading upwards. Our illustration of Type **11** shows the overprint reading downwards

1923 (April). *Stamps of Saudi Arabia. T* **11**, *with typographed opt, T* **10**.

89	10	⅛p. chestnut	3·25	3·25
		a. Opt double	£200	
		b. Opt inverted	£110	
90		½p. scarlet	3·25	3·25
		a. Opt inverted		
91		1p. blue	2·25	1·00
		a. Opt inverted	£120	£140
92		1½p. lilac	2·50	2·00
		a. Opt double	£150	
		b. Top line omitted	—	£250
		c. Pair, one without opt	£250	
		d. Imperf between (horiz pair)	£160	
93		2p. orange	3·25	6·50
94		3p. brown	7·00	14·00
		a. Opt inverted	£225	
		b. Opt double	£225	£250
		c. Pair, one without opt	£375	
95		5p. olive	15·00	26·00
89/95 *Set of* 7			32·00	50·00

On same stamps, surcharged with new values (Saudi Arabia, Nos. 47 and 49).

96	10	¼p. on ⅛p. chestnut	8·00	7·00
		a. Opt and surch inverted	£150	
		b. Ditto but 2nd and 3rd lines of opt omitted	£200	
		c. Opt double	†	£200
97		10p. on 5p. olive	20·00	27·00
		a. Top line omitted	£350	

In this setting the third line of the overprint measures 19–21 mm. On 35 stamps out of the setting of 36 the Arabic "9" (right-hand character in bottom line) is widely spaced from the rest of the inscription. Minor varieties of this setting exist on all values.

For later setting, varying from the above, see Nos. 121/4.

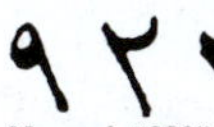

Normal. "923"

Error. "933"

An error reading "933" instead of "923" occurs as No. 3 in the setting of 24 on all values. Only 24 stamps are believed to have been overprinted for each of Nos. 103A, 108A, 105B and 107B so that for these stamps only one example of the error can exist. No example has yet been confirmed for Nos. 103A or 105B.

1923 (25 May). *T* **3** *of Palestine optd with T* **11**, *reading up or down, in black or gold by Govt Press, Amman, in a setting of 24 (12×2).*

A. Reading downwards.

98A	1m. (Blk)	18·00	18·00
	a. Opt double, one inverted (Blk.)	£650	£650
	b. Arabic "933"	85·00	
	c. Gold opt	£150	£160
	ca. Opt double, one inverted (Gold)	£900	
	cb. Opt double (Blk.+Gold)	£900	£900
	cc. Arabic "933"	£500	
99A	2m. (Blk)	30·00	40·00
	a. Arabic "933"	£160	
100A	3m. (Blk.)	11·00	13·00
	a. Arabic "933"	70·00	
101A	4m. (Blk.)	11·00	13·00
	a. Arabic "933"	70·00	
102A	5m. (Blk.)	55·00	65·00
	a. Arabic "933"	£325	
103A	1p. (Gold)	£650	£750
	a. Opt double	£750	£850
104A	2p. (Blk.)	55·00	75·00
	a. Arabic "933"	£300	
105A	5p. (Gold)	65·00	75·00
	a. Opt double (Gold)	£650	
	b. Arabic "933"	£325	
	c. Opt double (Blk.)	£1500	
106A	9p. (Blk.)	75·00	£100
	a. Arabic "933"	£350	
107A	10p. (Blk)	65·00	85·00
	a. Arabic "933"	£325	
108A	20p. (Blk.)	£750	£750
	a. Arabic "933"	£2750	

B. Reading upwards.

98B	1m. (Blk.)	90·00	£110
	b. Arabic "933"	£250	
	c. Gold opt	£150	£160
	cc. Arabic "933"	£350	
99B	2m. (Blk.)	48·00	55·00
	a. Arabic "933"	£250	

100B		3m. (Blk.)	90·00	£110
		a. Arabic "933"	£300	
101B		4m. (Blk.)	27·00	35·00
		a. Arabic "933"	£130	
103B		1p. (Gold)	55·00	70·00
		a. Opt double	£600	
		b. Black opt		
		c. Arabic "933"	£325	
105B		5p. (Gold)	£750	£600
		a. Opt double		
106B		9p. (Blk.)	55·00	70·00
		a. Arabic "933"	£300	
107B		10p. (Blk.)	£600	
		a. Arabic "933"	£2500	
108B		20p. (Blk.)	70·00	90·00
		a. Arabic "933"	£350	

The 9 and 10p. are perf 14, all the other values being perf 15×14.

No. 107A surch with T **9**.

109		1p. on 10p. ultramarine	£6000	

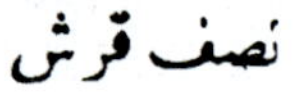

(12)

1923 (Sept). *No. 92 surch with T* **12**.

(a) Handstamped.

110	**12**	½p. on 1½p. lilac	8·50	9·00
		a. Surch and opt inverted	55·00	
		b. Opt double	75·00	
		c. Opt double, one inverted	90·00	£100
		d. Pair, one without opt	£150	

This handstamp is known inverted, double and double, one inverted.

(b) Typographed.

111	**12**	½p. on 1½p. lilac	50·00	50·00
		a. Surch inverted	£150	
		b. Surch double	£180	
		c. Pair, one without surch	£500	

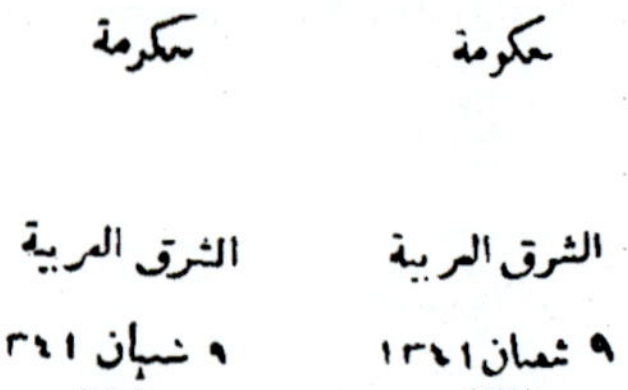

(13a) (13b)

("Arab Government of the East, 9 Sha'ban, 1341")

These two types differ in the spacing of the characters and in the position of the bottom line which is to the left of the middle line in T **13a** and centrally placed in T **13b**.

1923 (Oct). *T* **11** *of Saudi Arabia handstamped as T* **13a** *or* **13b**.

112	**13a**	½p. scarlet	11·00	12·00
113	**13b**	½p. scarlet	11·00	12·00

No. 112 exists with handstamp inverted.

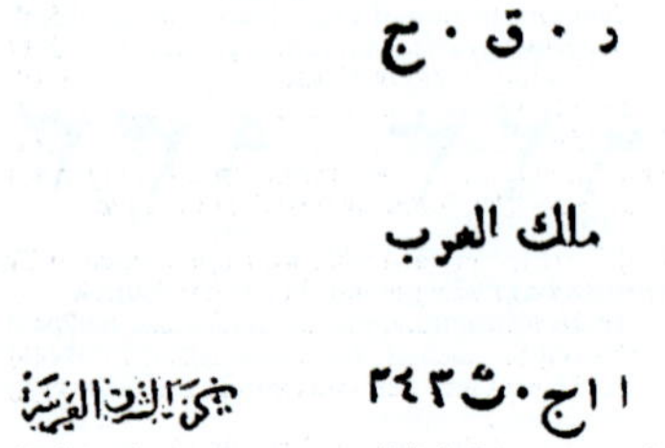

15 ("Arab Government of the East")

(**16**) ("Commemorating the coming of His Majesty the King of the Arabs" and date)

1924 (Jan). *T* **11** *of Saudi Arabia with typographed opt T* **15**.

114	**15**	½p. scarlet	14·00	13·00
		a. Opt inverted	£180	
115		1p. blue	£300	£200
116		1½p. lilac	£350	
		a. Pair, one without opt	£1500	

The ½p. exists with thick, brown gum, which tints the paper, and with white gum and paper.

The 2p. in the same design was also overprinted, but was not issued without the subsequent Type **16** overprint.

1924 (18 Jan). *Visit of King Hussein of Hejaz. Nos. 114/16 and unissued 2p. with further typographed opt T* **16** *in black.*

117	**16**	½p. scarlet	2·25	2·25
		a. Type **15** omitted	£150	
		b. Type **16** inverted	£150	
		c. Imperf between (pair)	£110	
		d. Type **16** in gold	2·50	2·50
		dc. Imperf between (pair)	£250	
118		1p. blue	2·50	2·75
		a. Type **15** omitted	£150	
		b. Both opts inverted	£200	
		c. Imperf between (pair)		
		d. Type **16** in gold	2·50	2·75
		db. Both opts inverted	£300	
		dc. Imperf between (pair)	£225	
119		1½p. lilac	3·25	3·50
		a. Type **15** omitted		
		b. Type **15** inverted	£130	
		d. Type **16** in gold	3·25	3·50
		da. Type **15** inverted	£150	
120		2p. orange	7·00	7·00
		d. Type **16** in gold	6·50	6·50

The spacing of the lines of the overprint varies considerably, and a variety dated "432" for "342" occurs on the twelfth stamp in each sheet (*Price £75 un*).

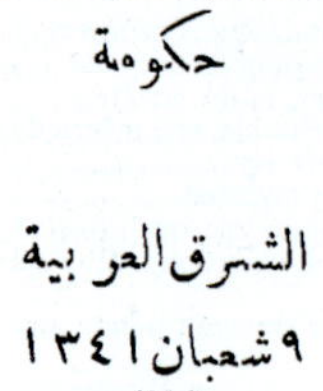

(16a)

"Shaban" (normal) "Shabal" (R. 4/6) "Shabn" (R. 5/3)

1924 (Mar–May). *T* **11** *of Saudi Arabia optd with T* **16a** *(new setting of Type* **10**).

121		1/8p. chestnut	27·00	16·00
		a. Opt inverted	£100	
122		½p. scarlet	7·00	3·75
		a. "Shabal"	50·00	
		b. "Shabn"	50·00	
		c. Opt inverted	£120	
123		1p. blue	13·00	2·00
		a. "Shabal"	75·00	
		b. "Shabn"	75·00	
		c. Opt double	£120	
		d. Imperf between (horiz pair) with opt double	£500	
124		1½p. lilac	18·00	18·00
		a. "Shabal"	90·00	
		b. "Shabn"	90·00	

This setting is from fresh type with the third line measuring 18¼ mm.

On all stamps in this setting (except Nos. 1, 9, 32 and 33) the Arabic "9" is close to the rest of the inscription.

The dots on the character "Y" (the second character from the left in the second line) are on many stamps vertical (:) instead of horizontal (..).

On some sheets of the ⅛p. and ½p. the right-hand character, "H", in the first line, was omitted from the second stamp in the first row of the sheet.

(**17**) ("Government of the Arab East, 1342") (**18**) ("Government of the Arab East, 1343")

"Hukumat" (normal) "Jakramat" (R. 2/1)

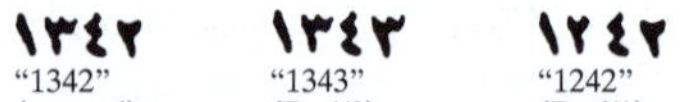

"1342" (normal) "1343" (R. 4/2) "1242" (R. 6/1)

1924 (Sept–Nov). *T* **11** *of Saudi Arabia with type-set opt as T* **17** *by Govt Press, Amman.*

125	**17**	⅛p. chestnut	70	70
		a. Opt inverted	£130	
		b. "Jakramat"	25·00	
		c. "1242"	25·00	
126		¼p. green	70	70
		a. *Tête-bêche* (pair, both opts normal)	7·50	10·00
		b. Opt inverted	85·00	
		c. *Tête-bêche* (pair, one with opt inverted)	£300	
		d. "Jakramat"	25·00	
		e. "1242"	25·00	
127		½p. bright scarlet	1·00	70
		a. Deep rose-red		
		b. "1343"	25·00	
129		1p. blue	6·00	1·50
		a. Imperf between (horiz pair)	£130	
		b. Opt inverted		
		c. "Jakramat"	35·00	
		d. "1242"	35·00	
130		1½p. lilac	3·75	4·50
		a. "1343"	50·00	
131		2p. orange	3·25	3·00
		a. Opt double		
		b. "1343"	50·00	
132		3p. brown-red	3·25	3·50
		a. Opt inverted	£100	
		b. Opt double	£100	
		c. "1343"	75·00	
133		5p. olive	4·00	4·50
		a. "Jakramat"	60·00	
		b. "1242"	60·00	
134		10p. brown-purple and mauve (R.)	8·50	11·00
		a. Centre inverted	£2500	
		b. Black opt	£250	
		c. "Jakramat"	90·00	
		d. "1242"	90·00	
125/34		*Set of 9*	28·00	27·00

Type **11** of Saudi Arabia was printed in sheets of 36 (6×6). The ¼p. value had the bottom three rows inverted, giving six vertical *tête-bêche* pairs. A few sheets were overprinted with the normal setting of Type **17**, with the result that the overprints on the bottom rows were inverted in relation to the stamp, including on one of the stamps in the *tête-bêche* pair (No. 126c). A corrected setting with the overprint inverted on the lower rows was used for the majority of the printing giving *tête-bêche* pairs with the overprints both normal in relation to the stamps (No. 126a).

1925 (2 Aug). *T* **20/2** *of Saudi Arabia with lithographed opt T* **18** *applied in Cairo.*

135	**18**	⅛p. chocolate	50	1·25
		a. Imperf between (horiz pair)	£120	£140
		b. Opt inverted	60·00	
136		¼p. ultramarine	1·00	2·00
		a. Opt inverted	60·00	
137		½p. carmine	70	60
		a. Opt inverted	60·00	
138		1p. green	70	1·25
139		1½p. orange	2·00	3·25
		a. Opt inverted	60·00	
140		2p. blue	2·75	4·25
		a. Opt treble	£150	£200
141		3p. sage-green (R.)	3·50	5·50
		a. Imperf between (horiz pair)	£120	£160
		b. Opt inverted	80·00	
		c. Black opt	£120	£150
142		5p. chestnut	4·50	9·50
		a. Opt inverted	80·00	
135/42		*Set of 8*	14·00	25·00

All values exist imperforate.

No. 141 imperforate with gold overprint comes from a presentation sheet for the Emir.

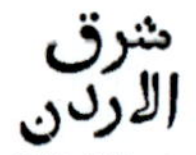

(**19**) ("East of the Jordan")

22 Emir Abdullah

23 Emir Abdullah

(Opt typo by Waterlow)

1925 (1 Nov)–**26**. *Stamps of Palestine, 1922 (without the three-line Palestine opt), optd with T* **19**. Wmk Mult Script CA. P 14.

143	**19**	1m. deep brown	25	2·00
144		2m. yellow	25	40
145		3m. greenish blue	1·25	1·00
146		4m. carmine-pink	1·25	2·25
147		5m. orange	1·75	50
		a. Yellow-orange	40·00	22·00
148		6m. blue-green	1·25	1·75
149		7m. yellow-brown	1·25	1·75
150		8m. scarlet	1·25	80
151		1p. grey	1·25	50
152		13m. ultramarine	1·75	2·00
153		2p. olive	2·75	3·00
		a. Olive-green	£120	35·00
154		5p. deep purple	5·00	7·50
155		9p. ochre	8·50	15·00
		a. Perf 15×14 (1926)	£900	£1300
156		10p. light blue	20·00	25·00
		a. Error. "E.F.F." in bottom panel (R.10/3)	£800	£900
		b. Perf 15×14 (1926)	80·00	90·00
157		20p. light violet	30·00	50·00
		a. Perf 15×14 (1926)	£850	£850
143/57		*Set of 15*	70·00	£100
143s/57s		Optd "Specimen" *Set of 15*	£250	

(New Currency. 1000 milliemes = £1 Palestinian)

(Recess Perkins, Bacon & Co)

1927 (1 Nov)–**29**. *New Currency.* Wmk Mult Script CA. P 14.

159	**22**	2m. greenish blue	75	30
160		3m. carmine-pink	2·50	2·00
161		4m. green	3·50	3·25
162		5m. orange	75	30
163		10m. scarlet	2·25	3·00
164		15m. ultramarine	1·75	30
165		20m. olive-green	1·75	2·25
166	**23**	50m. purple	2·50	7·50
167		90m. bistre	7·00	19·00
168		100m. blue	8·00	15·00
169		200m. violet	17·00	32·00
170		500m. brown (5.29)	60·00	85·00
171		1000m. slate-grey (5.29)	£100	£140
159/71		*Set of 13*	£180	£275
159s/71s		Optd or Perf (500, 1000m.) "Specimen" *Set of 13*	£275	

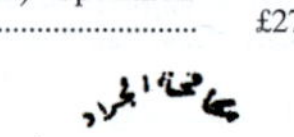

(**24**) ("Constitution")

(**27**)

1928 (1 Sept). *New Constitution of 20 February 1928. Optd with T* **24** *by Atwood, Morris & Co., Cairo.*

172	**22**	2m. greenish blue	3·25	3·50
173		3m. carmine-pink	3·50	6·50
174		4m. green	3·50	7·50
175		5m. orange	3·50	3·00
176		10m. scarlet	3·50	8·50
177		15m. ultramarine	3·50	3·50
178		20m. olive-green	7·50	15·00
179	**23**	50m. purple	11·00	15·00
180		90m. bistre	20·00	75·00
181		100m. blue	22·00	75·00
182		200m. violet	70·00	£170
172/82		*Set of 11*	£130	£350

1930 (1 Apr). *Locust Campaign. Optd as T* **27** *by Whitehead, Morris & Co, Alexandria.*

183	**22**	2m. greenish blue	2·75	5·50
		a. Opt inverted	£250	£550
184		3m. carmine-pink	2·00	6·50
185		4m. green	2·75	11·00
186		5m. orange	21·00	14·00
		a. Opt double	£400	£650
		b. Vert pair, top stamp opt double. Lower stamp without bottom line of opt	£1500	
187		10m. scarlet	2·25	4·25

188		15m. ultramarine	2·25	2·50
		a. Opt inverted	£225	£425
189		20m. olive-green	3·25	4·00
190	23	50m. purple	5·00	11·00
191		90m. bistre	10·00	45·00
192		100m. blue	12·00	45·00
193		200m. violet	32·00	85·00
194		500m. brown	75·00	£200
		a. "C" of "LOCUST" omitted (R. 5/3)	£800	£1100
183/94 *Set of* 12			£150	£375

No. 186a was sold at Kerak.

28

29

(Re-engraved with figures of value at left only. Recess Perkins, Bacon)

1930 (1 June)–**39**. Wmk Mult Script CA. P 14.

194*b*	28	1m. red-brown (6.2.34)	2·50	1·00
		c. Perf 13½×13 (1939)	8·50	4·00
195		2m. greenish blue	50	50
		a. Perf 13½×13. *Bluish green* (1939)	11·00	2·50
196		3m. carmine-pink	1·75	70
196*a*		3m. green (6.2.34)	3·25	85
		b. Perf 13½×13 (1939)	18·00	4·25
197		4m. green	1·50	3·25
197*a*		4m. carmine-pink (6.2.34)	2·75	1·00
		b. Perf 13½×13 (1939)	90·00	27·00
198		5m. orange	75	40
		a. Coil stamp. Perf 13½×14 (29.2.36)	24·00	18·00
		b. Perf 13½×13 (1939)	65·00	3·00
199		10m. scarlet	1·25	15
		a. Perf 13½×13 (1939)	£130	4·25
200		15m. ultramarine	1·75	20
		a. Coil stamp. Perf 13½×14 (29.2.36)	22·00	17·00
		b. Perf 13½×13 (1939)	42·00	4·50
201		20m. olive-green	1·75	35
		a. Perf 13½×13 (1939)	65·00	12·00
202	29	50m. purple	2·75	1·25
203		90m. bistre	2·50	4·25
204		100m. blue	3·75	4·25
205		200m. violet	13·00	14·00
206		500m. brown	25·00	50·00
207		£P1 slate-grey	60·00	90·00
194*b*/207 *Set of* 16			£110	£150
194*b*s/207s Perf "Specimen" *Set of* 16			£275	

For stamps perf 12 see Nos. 230/43, and for T **28** lithographed, perf 13½, see Nos. 222/9.

30 Mushetta

30a Nymphaeum, Jerash

30b Kasr Kharana

30c Kerak castles

30d Temple of Artemis, Jerash

31 Ajlun Castle

31a The Khazneh at Petra

31b Allenby Bridge over the Jordan

31c Threshing scene

31d Kasr Kharana

32 Temple of Artemis, Jerash

32a Ajlun Castle

32b The Khazneh at Petra

33 Emir Abdullah

(Vignettes from photographs; frames des Yacoub Sukker. Recess Bradbury, Wilkinson)

1933 (1 Feb). *As T* **30/3**. Wmk Mult Script CA. P 12.

208	1m. black and maroon	1·00	1·40
209	2m. black and claret	2·50	1·25
210	3m. blue-green	3·00	1·60
211	4m. black and brown	4·50	3·50
212	5m. black and orange	4·00	1·25
213	10m. carmine	6·50	4·00
214	15m. blue	3·75	1·25
215	20m. black and sage-green	4·75	5·00
216	50m. black and purple	22·00	16·00
217	90m. black and yellow	22·00	40·00
218	100m. black and blue	22·00	40·00
219	200m. black and violet	48·00	85·00
220	500m. scarlet and red-brown	£180	£250
221	£P1 black and yellow-green	£425	£700
208/21 *Set of* 14		£700	£1000
208s/21s Perf "Specimen" *Set of* 14		£550	

34

(Litho Survey Dept, Cairo)

1942 (18 May). *T* **28**, *but with Arabic characters above portrait and in top left circle modified as in T* **34**. No wmk. P 13½.

222	34	1m. red-brown	1·25	4·00
223		2m. green	2·25	2·00
224		3m. yellow-green	2·75	4·00
225		4m. carmine-pink	2·75	4·00
226		5m. yellow-orange	4·00	1·00
227		10m. scarlet	5·50	2·75
228		15m. blue	13·00	2·50
229		20m. olive-green	30·00	24·00
222/9 *Set of* 8			55·00	40·00

Forgeries of the above exist on whiter paper with rough perforations.

(Recess Bradbury, Wilkinson)

1943 (1 Jan)–**46**. Wmk Mult Script CA. P 12.

230	28	1m. red-brown	20	75
231		2m. bluish green	3·00	1·00
232		3m. green	2·00	1·25
233		4m. carmine-pink	1·75	1·25
234		5m. orange	1·75	20
235		10m. red	3·00	1·25
236		15m. blue	3·00	50
237		20m. olive-green (26.8.46)	3·00	1·00
238	29	50m. purple (26.8.46)	3·00	1·00
239		90m. bistre (26.8.46)	4·75	5·00
240		100m. blue (26.8.46)	5·00	1·75
241		200m. violet (26.8.46)	10·00	10·00
242		500m. brown (26.8.46)	13·00	12·00
243		£P1 slate-grey (26.8.46)	24·00	22·00
230/43 *Set of* 14			65·00	55·00

Nos. 237/43 were released in London by the Crown Agents in May 1944, but were not put on sale in Transjordan until 26 August 1946.

Printings of the 3, 4, 10, 15 and 20m. in changed colours, together with a new 12m. value, were released on 12 May 1947.

POSTAGE DUE STAMPS

(D 12 "Due")

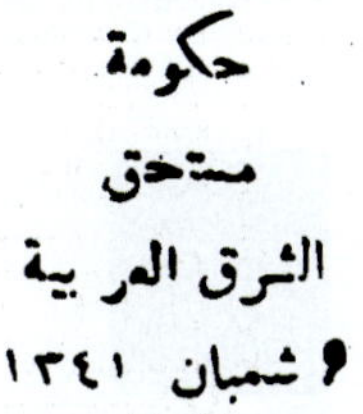
(D 13)

1923 (Sept). *Issue of April, 1923, with opt T* **10** *with further typographed opt Type* D **12** *(the 3p. with handstamped surch as T* **12** *at top).*

D112	½p. on 3p. brown	26·00	28·00
	a. "Due" inverted	50·00	55·00
	b. "Due" double	50·00	60·00
	ba. "Due" double, one inverted	£150	
	c. Arabic "t" & "h" transposed (R. 1/2)	£100	
	ca. As c, inverted	£350	
	d. Surch at foot of stamp	35·00	
	da. Ditto, but with var. c.	£120	
	e. Surch omitted	£200	
D113	1p. blue	14·00	16·00
	a. Type **10** inverted	80·00	
	b. "Due" inverted	45·00	40·00
	c. "Due" double	50·00	
	d. "Due" double, one inverted	£150	
	e. Arabic "t" & "h" transposed (R. 1/2)	70·00	
	f. "Due" omitted (in vertical pair with normal)	£200	
D114	1½p. lilac	20·00	21·00
	a. "Due" inverted	45·00	45·00
	b. "Due" double	50·00	
	ba. "Due" double, one diagonal	75·00	
	c. Arabic "t" & "h" transposed (R. 1/2)	70·00	
	ca. As c, inverted	£275	
	d. "Due" omitted (in pair with normal)	£200	
D115	2p. orange	22·00	23·00
	a. "Due" inverted	60·00	60·00
	b. "Due" double	65·00	
	ba. "Due" double, one diagonal	£100	
	c. "Due" treble	£150	
	d. Arabic "t" & "h" transposed (R. 1/2)	70·00	
	e. Arabic "h" omitted	90·00	

The variety, Arabic "t" and "h" transposed, occurred on R. 1/2 of all values in the first batch of sheets printed. The variety, Arabic "h" omitted, occurred on every stamp in the first three rows of at least three sheets of the 2p.

Handstamped in four lines as Type D **13** *and surch as on No. D112*

D116	½p. on 3p. brown	50·00	55·00
	a. Opt and surch inverted	£200	
	b. Opt double	£200	
	c. Surch omitted	£225	
	d. Opt inverted. Surch normal, but at foot of stamp	£150	
	e. Opt omitted and opt inverted (pair)	£300	
	f. "Due" double, one inverted	£160	
	h. Surch double	£250	

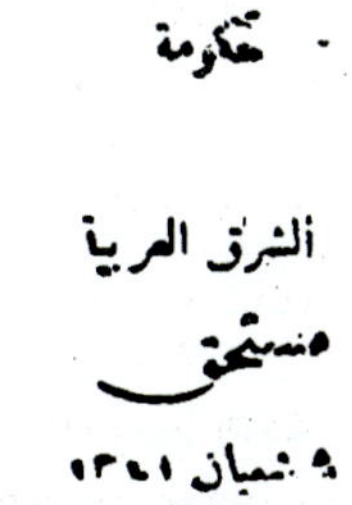
(D 14)

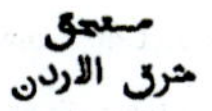
(D 20) ("Due. East of the Jordan")

1923 (Oct). *T* **11** *of Saudi Arabia handstamped with Type* D **14**.

D117	½p. scarlet	2·25	5·00
D118	1p. blue	4·75	5·00
	a. Pair, one without handstamp		
D119	1½p. lilac	3·75	6·00
D120	2p. orange	5·50	7·00
D121	3p. brown	12·00	15·00
	a. Pair, one without handstamp	£600	
D122	5p. olive	12·00	22·00
D117/22 *Set of* 6		35·00	55·00

There are three types of this handstamp, differing in some of the Arabic characters. They occur inverted, double etc.

1923 (Nov). *T* **11** *of Saudi Arabia with opt similar to Type* D **14** *but first three lines typo and fourth handstruck.*

D123	1p. blue	70·00	
D124	5p. olive	19·00	
	a. Imperf between (vert pair)	£750	

(Opt typo by Waterlow)

1925 (Nov). *Stamps of Palestine 1922 (without the three-line Palestine opt), optd with Type* D **20**. P 14.

D159	1m. deep brown	1·75	8·50
D160	2m. yellow	3·00	6·00
D161	4m. carmine-pink	3·25	12·00
D162	8m. scarlet	4·25	15·00
D163	13m. ultramarine	6·50	15·00
D164	5p. deep purple	7·50	20·00
	a. Perf 15×14	50·00	75·00
D159/64 *Set of* 6		23·00	70·00
D159s/64s Optd "Specimen" *Set of* 6		85·00	

Stamps as No. D164, but with a different top line to overprint Type D **20**, were for revenue purposes.

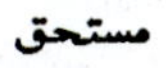

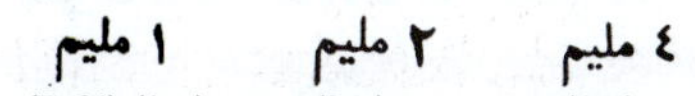
(D 21) (1m.) (2m.) (4m.)

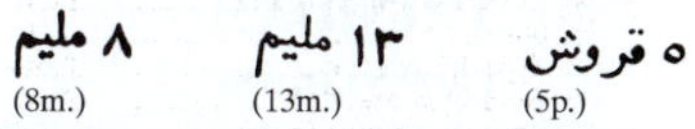
(8m.) (13m.) (5p.)

(Surch typo at Jerusalem)

1926 (Feb–May). *Postage stamps of 1 November 1925, surch "Due" and new value as Type* D **21** *by Greek Orthodox Printing Press, Jerusalem. Bottom line of surcharge differs for each value as illustrated.*

D165	1m. on 1m. deep brown	8·50	10·00
	a. Red opt	£130	
D166	2m. on 1m. deep brown	7·50	10·00
D167	4m. on 3m. greenish blue	8·00	12·00
D168	8m. on 3m. greenish blue	8·00	12·00
D169	13m. on 13m. ultramarine	12·00	13·00
D170	5p. on 13m. ultramarine	13·00	20·00
D165/70 *Set of* 6		50·00	70·00

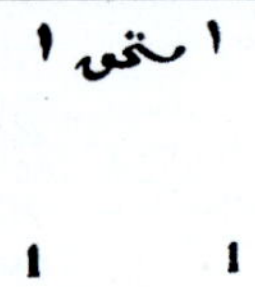

(D 25 "Due")

Extra Arabic character in opt (R. 4/10)

1929 (1 Jan). *Nos. 159 etc. optd only or surch in addition as Type* D **25** *by Whitehead, Morris & Co, Alexandria.*

D183	**22**	1m. on 3m. carmine-pink	1·00	7·00
		a. Extra Arabic character	25·00	
D184		2m. greenish blue	1·50	7·00
		a. Pair, one without opt	£350	
D185		4m. on 15m. ultramarine	1·50	8·00
		a. Surch inverted	£170	£250
D186		10m. scarlet	4·00	8·00
D187	**23**	20m. on 100m. blue	4·00	21·00
		a. Vert pair, one without surch	£550	
D188		50m. purple	4·75	22·00
		a. Horiz pair, one without opt	£550	
D183/8 *Set of* 6			15·00	65·00

D **26**

D **35**

(Recess Perkins, Bacon)

1929 (1 Apr)–**39**. Wmk Mult Script CA. P 14.

D189	D **26**	1m. red-brown	1·75	7·50
		a. Perf 13½×13 (1939)	£130	90·00
D190		2m. orange-yellow	2·50	5·50
D191		4m. green	3·25	9·00
D192		10m. scarlet	6·00	9·00
D193		20m. olive-green	9·50	16·00
D194		50m. blue	14·00	24·00
D189/94 *Set of* 6			32·00	65·00
D189s/94s Perf "Specimen" *Set of* 6			95·00	

(Litho Survey Dept, Cairo)

1942 (22 Dec). *Redrawn. Top line of Arabic in taller lettering.* No wmk. P 13½.

D230	D **35**	1m. red-brown	4·50	20·00
D231		2m. orange-yellow	12·00	9·50
D232		10m. scarlet	19·00	6·50
D230/2 *Set of* 3			32·00	32·00

Forgeries of the above exist on whiter paper with rough perforations.

(Recess Bradbury, Wilkinson)

1944–49. Wmk Mult Script CA. P 12.

D244	D **26**	1m. red-brown	1·00	4·00
D245		2m. orange-yellow	1·00	4·50
D246		4m. green	1·00	6·50
D247		10m. carmine	3·50	9·00
D248		20m. olive-green (1949)	75·00	90·00
D244/8 *Set of* 5			75·00	£100

OFFICIAL STAMP

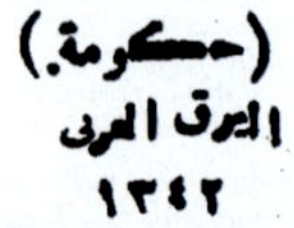

(O **16**) ("Arab Government of the East, 1342" = 1924)

1924. *T* **11** *of Saudi Arabia with typographed opt, Type* O **16**.

O117	½p. scarlet	26·00	£100
	a. Arabic "1242" (R. 2/2, 3/6, 4/5, 4/6)	£150	
	b. Imperf between (vert pair)		

By treaty of 22 March 1946 with the United Kingdom, Transjordan was proclaimed an independent kingdom on 25 May 1946.

Later issues are listed under JORDAN in Part 19 (*Middle East*) of this catalogue.

Transvaal *see* South Africa

Trinidad and Tobago

TRINIDAD

CROWN COLONY

The first post office was established at Port of Spain in 1800 to deal with overseas mail. Before 1851 there was no post office inland service, although a privately-operated one along the coast did exist, for which rates were officially fixed (see No. 1). During 1851 the colonial authorities established an inland postal system which commenced operation on 14 August. Responsibility for the overseas mails passed to the local post authorities in 1858.

No. CC1 is recorded in the G.P.O. Record Book on 21 March 1852, but no examples have been recorded used on cover before February 1858. The prepayment of postage on mail to Great Britain was made compulsory from 9 October 1858. From March 1859 it was used with the early Britannia 1d. stamps to indicate prepayment of the additional overseas rate in cash or, later, to show that letters were fully franked with adhesive stamps. This is the normal usage of the handstamp and commands little, if any premium over the cover price quoted below for the stamps involved. The use of the handstamp without an adhesive is rare.

PORT OF SPAIN

CROWNED-CIRCLE HANDSTAMPS

CC **1**

CC1 CC **1** TRINIDAD (R.) (*without additional adhesive stamp*) (21.3.52) ..... *Price on cover* £2750

PRICES FOR STAMPS ON COVER	
No. 1	*from* × 2
Nos. 2/12	*from* × 10
Nos. 13/20	*from* × 4
Nos. 25/9	*from* × 10
No. 30	—
Nos. 31/44	*from* × 4
No. 45	—
Nos. 46/59	*from* × 4
Nos. 60/3	*from* × 5
Nos. 64/8	*from* × 4
Nos. 69/74	*from* × 20
Nos. 75/8	*from* × 50
No. 79	—
No. 87	*from* × 20
Nos. 98/102	*from* × 6
No. 103	—
Nos. 104/5	*from* × 20
Nos. 106/12	*from* × 12
No. 113	—
Nos. 114/21	*from* × 4
Nos. 122/4	—
No. 125	*from* × 10
Nos. 126/30	*from* × 5
No. 131	—
Nos. 132/43	*from* × 3
Nos. 144/5	—
Nos. 146/8	*from* × 3
Nos. D1/17	*from* × 15

1

2 Britannia

1847 (16 Apr). *Litho.* Imperf.

1	**1**	(5c.) blue	£25000	£10000

The "LADY McLEOD" stamps were issued in April 1847, by David Bryce, owner of the S.S. *Lady McLeod*, and sold at five cents each for the prepayment of the carriage of letters by his vessel between Port of Spain and San Fernando.

The price quoted for used examples of No. 1 is for pen-cancelled. Stamps cancelled by having a corner skimmed-off are worth less.

(Recess P.B.)

1851 (14 Aug)–**56**. *No value expressed.* Imperf. *Blued paper.*

2	**2**	(1d.) purple-brown (1851)	17·00	75·00
3		(1d.) blue *to* deep blue (12.51)	17·00	60·00
4		(1d.) deep blue (1852)*	£150	80·00
5		(1d.) grey (11.52)	75·00	65·00
6		(1d.) brownish grey (1853)	50·00	75·00
7		(1d.) brownish red (1853)	£300	65·00
8		(1d.) brick-red (1856)	£170	70·00

No. 2 is known on paper bearing the sheet watermark "STACEY WISE/RUSH MILLS".

*No. 4 shows the paper deeply and evenly blued, especially on the back. It has more the appearance of having been printed on blue paper rather than on white paper that has become blued.

1854–57. Imperf. *White paper.*

9	**2**	(1d.) deep purple (1854)	28·00	90·00
10		(1d.) dark grey (1854)	48·00	85·00
12		(1d.) rose-red (1857)	£2500	65·00

PRICES. Prices quoted for the unused of most of the above issues and Nos. 25 and 29 are for "remainders" with original gum, found in London. Old colours that have been out to Trinidad are of much greater value.

3 Britannia

4 Britannia

The following provisional issues were lithographed in the Colony (from die engraved by Charles Petit), and brought into use to meet shortages of the Perkins Bacon stamps during the following periods:

(1) Sept 1852–May 1853; (2) March 1855–June 1855; (3) Dec 1856–Jan 1857; (4) Oct 1858–Jan 1859; (5) March 1860–June 1860.

1852–60. *No value expressed.* Imperf.

A. First Issue (Sept 1852). Fine impression; lines of background clear and distinct.

(i) Yellowish paper.

13	**3**	(1d.) blue	£8500	£1600

(ii) Bluish cartridge paper (Feb 1853).

14	**3**	(1d.) blue	—	£1800

B. Second issue (March 1855). Thinner paper. Impression less distinct than before.

15	**3**	(1d.) pale blue *to* greenish blue	—	£900

C. Third issue (August 1856). Background often of solid colour, but with clear lines in places.

16	**3**	(1d.) bright blue *to* deep blue	£4500	£1000

D. Fourth issue (October 1858). Impression less distinct, and rarely showing more than traces of background lines.

17	**3**	(1d.) very deep greenish blue	—	£650
18		(1d.) slate-blue	£4000	£650

E. Fifth issue (March 1860). Impression shows no (or hardly any) background lines.

19	**3**	(1d.) grey to bluish grey	£4000	£400
20		(1d.) red (*shades*)	14·00	£600

In the worn impression of the fourth and fifth issues, the impression varies according to the position on the stone. Generally speaking, stamps of the fifth issue have a flatter appearance and cancellations are often less well defined. The paper of both these issues is thin or very thin. In all issues except 1853 (Feb) the gum tends to give the paper a toned appearance.

Stamps in the slate-blue shade (No. 18) also occur in the fifth issue, but are not readily distinguishable.

PERKINS BACON "CANCELLED". For notes on these handstamps, showing "CANCELLED" between horizontal bars forming an oval, see Catalogue Introduction.

(Recess P.B.)

1859 (9 May). Imperf.

25	**4**	4d. grey-lilac (H/S "CANCELLED" in oval £8000)	£110	£325
28		6d. deep green (H/S "CANCELLED" in oval £8000)	£12000	£425
29		1s. indigo	£100	£350
30		1s. purple-slate	£7000	

"CANCELLED" examples of No. 25 are in lilac rather than grey-lilac.

No. 30 may be of unissued status.

1859 (Sept).

(a) Pin-perf 12½.

31	**2**	(1d.) rose-red	£1600	55·00
32		(1d.) carmine-lake	£1800	50·00
33	**4**	4d. dull lilac	—	£900
34		4d. dull purple	£6500	£900
35		6d. yellow-green	£2750	£200
36		6d. deep green	£2750	£200
37		1s. purple-slate	£7000	£1300

(b) Pin-perf 13½–14.

38	**2**	(1d.) rose-red	£225	29·00
39		(1d.) carmine-lake	£325	28·00
40	**4**	4d. dull lilac	£1200	80·00
40*a*		4d. brownish purple	£190	£110
41		4d. dull purple	£500	£110
42		6d. yellow-green	£600	75·00
43		6d. deep green	£600	70·00
43*a*		6d. bright yellow-green	£150	£110
		b. Imperf between (vert pair)	£6500	
44		1s. purple-slate	£7000	£800

(c) Compound pin-perf 13½–14×12½.

45	**2**	(1d.) carmine-lake	†	£3750
45*a*	**4**	4d. dull purple	†	—

PRICES. The Pin-perf stamps are very scarce with perforations on all sides and the prices quoted above are for good average specimens.

The note after No. 12 also applies to Nos. 38, 40*a*, 43*a*, 46, 47 and 50.

1860 (Aug). Clean-cut perf 14–16½.

46	**2**	(1d.) rose-red	£160	55·00
		a. Imperf vert (horiz pair)	£1100	
47	**4**	4d. brownish lilac	£170	80·00
48		4d. lilac	—	£300
49		6d. bright yellow-green	£425	90·00
50		6d. deep green	£275	£160

1861 (June). Rough perf 14–16½.

52	**2**	(1d.) rose-red (H/S "CANCELLED" in oval £8000)	£150	32·00
53		(1d.) rose	£150	28·00
54	**4**	4d. brownish lilac	£275	70·00
55		4d. lilac	£600	90·00
		a. Imperf		
56		6d. yellow-green	£275	80·00
57		6d. deep green	£400	70·00
58		1s. indigo	£850	£275
59		1s. deep bluish purple (H/S "CANCELLED" in oval £8000)	£1300	£425

(Recess D.L.R.)

1862–63. *Thick paper.*

(a) P 11½, 12.

60	**2**	(1d.) crimson-lake	£140	22·00
61	**4**	4d. deep purple	£190	60·00
62		6d. deep green	£1200	85·00
63		1s. bluish slate	£2250	95·00

(b) P 11½, 12, compound with 11.

63*a*	**2**	(1d.) crimson-lake	£1600	£500
63*b*	**4**	6d. deep green	—	£6500

(c) P 13 (1863).

64	**2**	(1d.) lake	45·00	22·00
65	**4**	6d. emerald-green	£500	55·00
67		1s. bright mauve	£4250	£275

(d) P 12½ (1863).

68	**2**	(1d.) lake	50·00	22·00

1863–80.

(a) Wmk Crown CC. P 12½.

69	**2**	(1d.) lake	55·00	7·00
		a. Wmk sideways	£120	18·00
		b. Rose	50·00	2·75
		ba. Imperf (pair)		
		c. Scarlet	55·00	3·00
		d. Carmine	55·00	3·25
		w. Wmk inverted	†	55·00

x. Wmk reversed 60·00 3·50
y. Wmk inverted and reversed... — 65·00
70 4 4d. bright violet £120 15·00
a. Pale mauve £200 18·00
b. Dull lilac £160 18·00
w. Wmk inverted £275 65·00
x. Wmk reversed £130 16·00
71 4d. grey (1872) £130 6·50
a. Bluish grey £120 7·00
ax. Wmk reversed £120 8·50
w. Wmk inverted — 65·00
72 6d. emerald-green 95·00 15·00
a. Deep green £400 8·00
b. Yellow-green 90·00 4·75
c. Apple-green 85·00 6·00
d. Blue-green £150 7·50
w. Wmk inverted — 60·00
x. Wmk reversed £100 6·00
73 1s. bright deep mauve £170 9·00
a. Lilac-rose £140 9·00
b. Mauve (aniline) £120 6·00
bw. Wmk inverted
bx. Wmk reversed — 7·50
74 1s. chrome-yellow (1872) £150 1·50
w. Wmk inverted — 70·00
x. Wmk reversed — 6·50

(*b*) P 14 (1876).
75 2 (1d.) lake 32·00 2·00
a. Bisected (½d.) (on cover) † £600
b. Rose-carmine 32·00 2·00
c. Scarlet 50·00 2·00
w. Wmk inverted — 50·00
x. Wmk reversed 35·00 2·00
76 4 4d. bluish grey £120 70
y. Wmk inverted and reversed... † 80·00
77 6d. bright yellow-green £100 2·25
a. Deep yellow-green £130 2·25
w. Wmk inverted † 70·00
x. Wmk reversed £110 3·25
78 1s. chrome-yellow £130 3·75

(*c*) P 14×12½ (1880).
79 4 6d. yellow-green † £6000

The 1s. perforated 12½ in purple-slate is a colour changeling.

5

(Typo D.L.R.)

1869. Wmk Crown CC. P 12½.
87 5 5s. rose-lake £170 75·00

HALFPENNY (6) **ONE PENNY** (7)

1879–82. *Surch with T* **6** *or* **7**. P 14.

(*a*) Wmk Crown CC (June 1879).
98 2 ½d. lilac 14·00 9·50
w. Wmk inverted £100 35·00
x. Wmk reversed 14·00 9·50
99 ½d. mauve 14·00 9·50
a. Wmk sideways 50·00 50·00
w. Wmk inverted † —

(*b*) Wmk Crown CA (1882).
100 2 ½d. lilac (wmk reversed) £180 75·00
101 1d. rosy carmine 45·00 2·00
a. Bisected (½d.) (on cover) † £550
x. Wmk reversed 45·00 2·25

1882. Wmk Crown CA. P 14.
102 4 4d. bluish grey £180 9·50
x. Wmk reversed

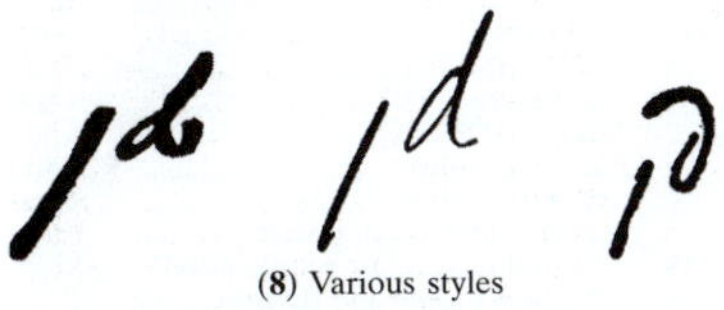
(**8**) Various styles

1882 (9 May). *Surch by hand in various styles as T* **8** *in red or black ink and the original value obliterated by a thick or thin bar or bars, of the same colour.*
103 1d. on 6d. (No. 77) (Bk.) — £1500
104 1d. on 6d. (No. 77) (R.) 11·00 6·50
x. Wmk reversed 15·00 9·50
105 1d. on 6d. (No. 77*a*) (R.) 11·00 6·50
a. Bisected (½d.) (on cover) † £300

10 **11** Britannia **12** Britannia

(Typo D.L.R.)

1883–94. P 14.

(*a*) Wmk Crown CA.
106 10 ½d. dull green 6·00 1·25
107 1d. carmine 12·00 50
a. Bisected (½d.) (on cover) † £900
w. Wmk inverted † £150
108 2½d. bright blue 15·00 60
110 4d. grey 2·75 60
w. Wmk inverted † £170
111 6d. olive-black (1884) 5·00 5·50
112 1s. orange-brown (1884) 6·50 4·00

(*b*) Wmk Crown CC.
113 5 5s. maroon (1894) 55·00 90·00
106/13 *Set of* 7 90·00 95·00
106s/12s Optd "Specimen" *Set of* 6 £650

Two types of 1d. value:

ONE PENNY (I) (round "o") **ONE PENNY** (II) (oval "o")

(Typo D.L.R.)

1896 (17 Aug)–**1906**. P 14.

(*a*) Wmk Crown CA.
114 11 ½d. dull purple and green 3·25 30
115 1d. dull purple and rose (I) 3·50 10
w. Wmk inverted
116 1d. dull purple and rose (II) (1900) £325 4·00
117 2½d. dull purple and blue 6·00 20
118 4d. dull purple and orange 6·50 18·00
119 5d. dull purple and mauve 8·00 14·00
120 6d. dull purple and black 7·50 5·50
121 1s. green and brown 7·00 6·50

(*b*) Wmk CA over Crown. *Ordinary paper.*
122 12 5s. green and brown 45·00 80·00
123 10s. green and ultramarine £225 £375
124 £1 green and carmine £160 £250
a. Chalk-surfaced paper (1906).. £300
114/24 *Set of* 10 £425 £700
114s/24s Optd "Specimen" *Set of* 10 £180

No. 119, surcharged "3d." was prepared for use in 1899 but not issued (*Price* £3000 *unused*). It also exists overprinted "Specimen" (*Price* £75).

Collectors are warned against apparently postally used copies of this issue which bear "REGISTRAR-GENERAL" obliterations and are of very little value.

13 Landing of Columbus

(Recess D.L.R.)

1898 (31 July). *400th Anniv of Discovery of Trinidad.* Wmk Crown CC. P 14.
125 13 2d. brown and dull violet 2·50 1·25
s. Optd "Specimen" 50·00

1901–06. *Colours changed. Ordinary paper.* Wmk Crown CA or CA over Crown (5s.). P 14.
126 11 ½d. grey-green (1902) 75 2·00
127 1d. black/*red* (II) 2·00 10
a. Value omitted £32000
w. Wmk inverted † £190
128 2½d. purple and blue/*blue* (1902) 18·00 25
129 4d. green and blue/*buff* (1902) 2·00 18·00
a. Chalk-surfaced paper 3·50 14·00
130 1s. black and blue/*yellow* (1903) 19·00 5·50
131 12 5s. lilac and mauve 55·00 70·00
a. Chalk-surfaced paper. *Deep purple and mauve* (1906) 80·00 90·00
126/31 *Set of* 6 85·00 80·00
126s/31s Optd "Specimen" *Set of* 6 £120

A pane of sixty of No. 127a was found at the San Fernando post office of which fifty-one were subsequently returned to London and destroyed. Only three mint examples, one of which is in the Royal Collection, are now thought to survive.

1904–09. *Ordinary paper (½d., 1d., 2½d. (No. 137)) or chalk-surfaced paper (others).* Wmk Mult Crown CA. P 14.
132 11 ½d. grey-green 4·00 1·00
a. Chalk-surfaced paper 7·00 2·25
133 ½d. blue-green (1906) 9·00 2·50
134 1d. black/*red* (II) 7·00 10
a. Chalk-surfaced paper 7·50 10
135 1d. rose-red (1907) 2·00 10
136 2½d. purple and blue/*blue* 23·00 90
137 2½d. blue (1906) 4·75 15
138 4d. grey and red/*yellow* (1906) 2·25 8·50
a. Black and red/yellow 9·00 21·00
139 6d. dull purple and black (1905).. 17·00 15·00
140 6d. dull and bright purple (1906). 7·00 11·00
141 1s. black and blue/*yellow* 20·00 8·00
142 1s. purple and blue/*golden yellow* 11·00 18·00
143 1s. black/*green* (1906) 1·75 1·25
144 12 5s. deep purple and mauve (1907) 50·00 90·00
145 £1 green and carmine (1907) £170 £275
132/45 *Set of* 13 £275 £375
135s/43s (*ex* Nos. 136, 139, 141) Optd "Specimen" *Set of* 6 £120

No. 135 is from a new die, the letters of "ONE PENNY" being short and thick, while the point of Britannia's spear breaks the uppermost horizontal line of shading in the background.

14 **15** **16**

(Typo D.L.R.)

1909. Wmk Mult Crown CA. P 14.
146 14 ½d. green 5·50 10
147 15 1d. rose-red 5·50 10
148 16 2½d. blue 17·00 3·25
146/8 *Set of* 3 25·00 3·25
146s/8s Optd "Specimen" *Set of* 3 70·00

TOBAGO

Although a Colonial Postmaster was appointed in January 1765 it was not until 1841 that the British G.P.O established a branch office at Scarborough, the island capital, to handle the overseas mail.

The stamps of Great Britain were in use from May 1858 to the end of April 1860 when the control of the postal service passed to the local authorities.

From April 1860 Nos. CC1/2 were again used on overseas mail, pending the introduction of Tobago stamps in 1879.

SCARBOROUGH

CROWNED-CIRCLE HANDSTAMPS

CC 1 CC 2

CC1 CC **1** TOBAGO (R.) (31.10.1851) *Price on cover* £1000
CC2 CC **2** TOBAGO (R.) (1875) *Price on cover* £4500

Stamps of GREAT BRITAIN *cancelled* "A 14" *as Type* Z **1** *of Jamaica.*

1858–60.
Z1 1d. rose-red (1857), perf 14 £900
Z2 4d. rose (1857) £375
Z3 6d. lilac (1856) £250
Z4 1s. green (1856) £1800

PRICES FOR STAMPS ON COVER	
Nos. 1/4	*from* × 30
Nos. 5/7	—
Nos. 8/12	*from* × 10
Nos. 13/19	*from* × 6
Nos. 20/4	*from* × 40
Nos. 26/33	*from* × 25

CANCELLATIONS. Beware of early stamps of Tobago with fiscal endorsements removed and forged wide "A 14" postmarks added.

1 **2** **2½ PENCE** (**3**)

(T **1** and **2** Typo D.L.R.)

1879 (1 Aug). *Fiscal stamps issued provisionally pending the arrival of stamps inscr* "POSTAGE". Wmk Crown CC. P 14.
1 1 1d. rose £110 85·00
2 3d. blue £110 70·00
3 6d. orange 48·00 75·00
w. Wmk inverted £100 £140
4 1s. green £400 75·00
a. Bisected (6d.) (on cover) † —
5 5s. slate £750 £750
6 £1 mauve £4250

The stamps were introduced for fiscal purposes on 1 July 1879.

Stamps of T **1**, watermark Crown CA, are fiscals which were never admitted to postal use.

1880 (Nov). *No.* 3 *bisected vertically and surch with pen and ink.*
7 1 1d. on half of 6d. orange £5500 £800
w. Wmk inverted £6000 £1000

1880 (20 Dec). Wmk Crown CC. P 14.
8 2 ½d. purple-brown 50·00 80·00
9 1d. Venetian red £120 65·00
a. Bisected (½d.) (on cover) † £2000
10 4d. yellow-green £300 30·00
a. Bisected (2d.) (on cover) † £2000
b. Malformed "CE" in "PENCE" £1900 £400
w. Wmk inverted — £170
11 6d. stone £375 £120
12 1s. yellow-ochre 75·00 85·00
w. Wmk inverted £200

For illustration of Nos. 10b, 18a, 22b, 30a, 31a and 33b see above No. 4 of Dominica.

1883 (Apr). *No.* 11 *surch with T* **3**.
13 2 2½d. on 6d. stone 70·00 70·00
a. Surch double £3750 £2000
b. Large "2" with long tail £160 £170

"SLASH" FLAW. Stamps as Type **2** were produced from Key and Duty plates. On the Key plate used for consignments between 2 October 1892 and 16 December 1896, damage in the form of a large cut or "slash" shows after the "E" of "POSTAGE" on R. 1/4.

After 1896 an attempt was made to repair the "slash". This resulted in its disappearance, but left an incomplete edge to the circular frame at right.

1882–84. Wmk Crown CA. P 14.
14 **2** ½d. purple-brown (1882) 2·00 14·00
15 1d. Venetian red (1882) 6·50 2·25
a. Bisected diag (½d.) (on cover)
16 2½d. dull blue (1883) 42·00 2·50
a. Bright blue 10·00 1·00
b. Ultramarine 10·00 1·00
c. "Slash" flaw 85·00 48·00
ca. "Slash" flaw repaired £140
18 4d. yellow-green (1882) £190 90·00
a. Malformed "CE" in "PENCE" £1400 £475
19 6d. stone (1884) £550 £475

1885–96. *Colours changed and new value.* Wmk Crown CA. P 14.
20 **2** ½d. dull green (1886) 2·75 1·25
a. "Slash" flaw 40·00 45·00
ab. "Slash" flaw repaired 75·00
w. Wmk inverted
21 1d. carmine (1889) 3·75 1·25
a. "Slash" flaw 55·00 48·00
ab. "Slash" flaw repaired 90·00
22 4d. grey (1885) 3·75 2·75
a. Imperf (pair) £2000
b. Malformed "CE" in "PENCE" 70·00 95·00
c. "Slash" flaw £130 £160
ca. "Slash" flaw repaired £160
23 6d. orange-brown (1886) 2·50 5·50
a. "Slash" flaw £140 £190
ab. "Slash" flaw repaired £170
24 1s. olive-yellow (1894) 3·00 20·00
a. Pale olive-yellow 7·00
b. "Slash" flaw £150 £325
ba. "Slash" flaw repaired £180
24*c* 1s. orange-brown (1896) 12·00 75·00
ca. "Slash" flaw £225
20s/3s (*ex* 4d.) Optd "Specimen" *Set of* 3 £170
No. 24*c* was printed in the colour of the 6d. by mistake.

½ PENNY (4) 2½ PENCE (5) ½d POSTAGE (6)

1886–89. *Nos. 16, 19 and 23 surch as T* **4**.
26 ½d. on 2½d. dull blue (4.86) 7·00 17·00
a. Figure further from word 30·00 65·00
b. Surch double £2250 £1800
c. Surch omitted. Vert pair with No. 26 £15000
d. Ditto with No. 26a £25000
27 ½d. on 6d. stone (1.86) 3·25 21·00
a. Figure further from word 26·00 £110
b. Surch inverted £2750
c. Surch double £3000
28 ½d. on 6d. orange-brown (8.87) £120 £160
a. Figure further from word £325 £375
b. Surch double — £2500
29 1d. on 2½d. dull blue (7.89) 85·00 18·00
a. Figure further from word £225 85·00
The surcharge is in a setting of 12 (two rows of 6) repeated five times in the pane. On Nos. 26/30a the "½" is 6 mm from the "P" (stamp 10 in the setting). The normal spacing is 3.75 mm. Stamps 7, 9 and 10 in the setting have a raised "P" in PENNY".

1891–92. *No. 22 surch with T* **4** *or* **5**.
30 ½d. on 4d. grey (3.92) 24·00 70·00
a. Malformed "CE" in "PENCE" £300 £550
b. Surch double £2750
31 2½d. on 4d. grey (8.91) 13·00 8·00
a. Malformed "CE" in "PENCE" £160 £200
b. Surch double £3000 £3000

1896. *Fiscal stamp (T* **1**, *value in second colour,* wmk Crown CA, P 14), *surch with T* **6**.
33 ½d. on 4d. lilac and carmine 80·00 42·00
a. Space between "½" and "d" £140 80·00
b. Malformed "CE" in "PENCE" £850 £650

Tobago became a ward of Trinidad on 1 January 1899. Stamps of Trinidad were used until issues inscribed "TRINIDAD AND TOBAGO" appeared in 1913.

TRINIDAD AND TOBAGO

PRICES FOR STAMPS ON COVER	
Nos. 149/55	*from* × 3
Nos. 156/7	—
Nos. 174/89	*from* × 10
Nos. 206/56	*from* × 2
Nos. D18/25	*from* × 12

17

18

(Typo D.L.R.)

1913–23. *Ordinary paper (½d. to 4d. and 1s.) or chalk-surfaced paper (others).* Wmk Mult Crown CA. P 14.
149 **17** ½d. green 3·00 10
a. Yellow-green (1915) 4·00 20
b. Blue-green (thick paper) (1917) 7·00 1·00
ba. Wmk sideways † £1700
c. Blue-green/bluish (3.18) 14·00 12·00
w. Wmk inverted
150 1d. bright red 1·50 10
a. Red (thick paper) (1916) 3·25 30
b. Pink (1918) 25·00 3·25
c. Carmine-red (5.18) 2·50 10
w. Wmk inverted
151 2½d. ultramarine 8·50 50
a. Bright blue (thick paper) (1916) 6·50 50
b. Bright blue (thin paper) (1918) 8·00 50
152 4d. black and red/*yellow*
a. Chalk-surfaced paper 70 6·00
b. White back (12.13) 1·75 10·00
bs. Optd "Specimen" 25·00
c. On lemon (1917) 10·00
d. On pale yellow (1923) 5·00 9·00
ds. Optd "Specimen" 30·00
153 6d. dull and reddish purple 9·50 8·50
a. Dull and deep purple (1918) 12·00 6·00
b. Dull purple and mauve (2.18) 10·00 8·00
154 1s. black/*green* 1·75 4·50
a. White back 1·00 9·00
as. Optd "Specimen" 25·00
b. On blue-green, olive back 9·00 9·00
c. On emerald back 1·50 3·00
cs. Optd "Specimen" 30·00
155 **18** 5s. dull purple and mauve (1914) 65·00 £100
a. Deep purple and mauve (1918) 65·00 £100
b. Lilac and violet 95·00 £140
c. Dull purple and violet £100 £150
d. Brown-purple and violet 60·00 £100
156 £1 grey-green and carmine (1914) £180 £250
a. Deep yellow-green and carmine (1918) £160 £225
149/56 *Set of* 8 £225 £300
149s/56s Optd "Specimen" *Set of* 8 £190
No. 156*a* is from a plate showing background lines very worn.

18a

1914 (18 Sept). *Red Cross Label authorised for use as ½d. stamp. Typo.* P 11–12.
157 **18a** (½d.) Red 17·00 £225
The above was authorised for internal postal use on one day only, to frank circular letters appealing for funds for the Red Cross. The used price is for stamp on cover cancelled on 18 Sep 1914. Labels affixed to earlier or later items of mail had no postal validity.

21.10.15.
(19)

19.10.16.

(19a)

1915 (21 Oct). *Optd with T* **19**. *Cross in red with outline and date in black.*
174 **17** 1d. red 1·50 2·50
a. Cross 2 mm to right 22·00 38·00
b. "1" of "15" forked foot 12·00 22·00
c. Broken "0" in "10" 12·00 22·00
The varieties occur in the following positions on the *pane* of 60: a. No. 11. b. No. 42. c. No. 45. Variety a. is only found on the right-hand pane.

1916 (19 Oct). *Optd with T* **19a**. *Cross in red with outline and date in black.*
175 **17** 1d. scarlet 50 2·00
a. No stop after "16" 11·00 30·00
b. "19.10.16" omitted
c. Red shading on cross omitted
No. 175a appears on stamp No. 36 on the right-hand pane only.

FORGERIES. Beware of forgeries of the "War Tax" errors listed below. There are also other unlisted errors which are purely fakes.

WAR TAX (19b) WAR TAX (20) WAR TAX (21) WAR TAX (22)

1917 (2 Apr). *Optd with T* **19b**.
176 **17** 1d. red 2·50 2·75
a. Opt inverted £225 £300
b. Scarlet 2·50 2·75
w. Wmk inverted

1917 (May). *Optd with T* **20**.
177 **17** ½d. green 20 20
a. Pair, one without opt £750
178 1d. red 1·50 1·75
a. Pair, one without opt £750 £1200
b. Scarlet 3·50 80
ba. Opt double £150
The varieties without overprint were caused by the type being shifted over towards the left so that one stamp in the lowest row of each pane escaped.

1917 (21 June). *Optd with T* **21**.
179 **17** ½d. yellow-green 2·25 15·00
a. Pale green 20 11·00
b. Deep green 1·25 11·00
180 1d. red 15 75
a. Pair, one without opt
No. 180a was caused by a shifting of the type to the left-hand side, but only a few stamps on the right-hand vertical row escaped the overprint and such pairs are very rare.

1917 (21 July–Sept). *Optd with T* **22**.
181 **17** ½d. yellow-green 4·25 7·00
a. Deep green 10 4·00
aw. Wmk inverted £110
182 1d. red (Sept) 4·00 1·00

WAR TAX (23) WAR TAX (24) WAR TAX (25)

1917 (1 Sept). *Optd with T* **23** *(closer spacing between lines of opt).*
183 **17** ½d. deep green 10 2·50
a. Pale yellow-green
184 1d. red 50·00 45·00

1917 (31 Oct). *Optd with T* **24**.
185 **17** 1d. scarlet 60 1·00
a. Opt inverted £150

1918 (7 Jan). *Optd with T* **25**.
186 **17** 1d. scarlet 1·50 15
a. Opt double £225 £225
b. Opt inverted £140 £140

War Tax (26) War Tax (26a)

27

1918 (13 Feb–May). *Optd with T* **26**.
187 **17** ½d. bluish green 10 2·25
a. Pair, one without opt £1400
y. Wmk inverted and reversed £100
188 1d. scarlet 1·75 1·25
a. Opt double £140
b. Rose-red (1.5.18) 10 60
Both values exist with "TAX" omitted, the ½d. due to a paper fold and the 1d. due to misplacement.

1918 (14 Sept). *New printing as T* **26**, *but 19 stamps on each sheet have the letters of the word "Tax" wider spaced, the "x" being to the right of "r" of "War" as T* **26a**. *Thick bluish paper.*
189 **17** 1d. scarlet ("Tax" spaced) 2·00 10·00
a. Opt double £225
b. Pair, one without opt £1300
c. Opt inverted on back £1300
The varieties 189b and 189c are caused by a paper fold.

1921–22. *Chalk-surfaced paper (6d. to £1).* Wmk Mult Script CA. P 14.
206 **17** ½d. green 3·00 2·25
207 1d. scarlet 60 30
208 1d. brown (17.2.22) 60 1·50
209 2d. grey (17.2.22) 1·00 1·25
210 2½d. bright blue 80 17·00
211 3d. bright blue (17.2.22) 4·50 3·00
212 6d. dull and bright purple 2·25 16·00
213 **18** 5s. dull purple and purple (1921) 55·00 £160
214 5s. deep purple and purple (1922) 70·00 £160
215 £1 green and carmine £120 £275
206/15 *Set of* 9 £170 £425
206s/15s Optd "Specimen" *Set of* 9 £250

(Typo D.L.R.)

1922–28. *Chalk-surfaced paper (4d. to £1).* P 14.
(a) Wmk Mult Crown CA.
216 **27** 4d. black and red/*pale yellow* 3·25 11·00
217 1s. black/*emerald* 3·50 9·50
(b) Wmk Mult Script CA.
218 **27** ½d. green 50 10
219 1d. brown 50 10
w. Wmk inverted 35·00 35·00
220 1½d. bright rose 2·25 20
aw. Wmk inverted 65·00 65·00
b. Scarlet 1·75 30
bw. Wmk inverted
222 2d. grey 50 1·25
w. Wmk inverted — £100
223 3d. blue 50 1·25
224 4d. black and red/*pale yellow* (1928) 3·25 3·25
225 6d. dull purple and bright magenta 2·25 25·00
226 6d. green and red/*emerald* (1924) 1·25 60
227 1s. black/*emerald* 5·50 1·75
228 5s. dull purple and mauve 22·00 38·00

229		£1 green and bright rose	£120	£225
216/29 *Set of* 13			£150	£275
216s/29s Optd "Specimen" *Set of* 13			£275	

(New Currency. 100 cents = 1 West Indian dollar)

28 First Boca

29 Imperial College of Tropical Agriculture

30 Mt. Irvine Bay, Tobago

31 Discovery of Lake Asphalt

32 Queen's Park, Savannah

33 Town Hall, San Fernando

34 Government House

35 Memorial Park

36 Blue Basin

(Recess B.W.)

1935 (1 Feb)–**37**. *T* **28/36**. Wmk Mult Script CA (sideways). P 12.

230	**28**	1c. blue and green	40	85
		a. Perf 13×12½ (1936)	30	10
231	**29**	2c. ultramarine and yellow-brown	1·00	1·00
		a. Perf 13×12½ (1936)	1·00	10
232	**30**	3c. black and scarlet	1·50	30
		a. Perf 13×12½ (1936)	2·75	30
233	**31**	6c. sepia and blue	4·25	2·50
		a. Perf 13×12½ (1937)	9·00	5·50
234	**32**	8c. sage-green and vermilion	3·75	3·50
235	**33**	12c. black and violet	3·25	1·75
		a. Perf 13×12½ (1937)	9·00	7·00
236	**34**	24c. black and olive-green	4·00	1·75
		a. Perf 13×12½ (1937)	14·00	12·00
237	**35**	48c. deep green	9·00	15·00
238	**36**	72c. myrtle-green and carmine	29·00	30·00
230/8 *Set of* 9			50·00	48·00
230s/8s Perf "Specimen" *Set of* 9			£150	

1935 (6 May). *Silver Jubilee. As Nos. 91/4 of Antigua, but ptd by B.W.* P 11×12.

239	2c. ultramarine and grey-black	30	75
	a. Extra flagstaff	35·00	55·00
	b. Short extra flagstaff	75·00	
	c. Lightning conductor	48·00	
	d. Flagstaff on right-hand turret	95·00	
240	3c. deep blue and scarlet	30	2·00
	a. Extra flagstaff	60·00	£120
	c. Lightning conductor	70·00	
241	6c. brown and deep blue	1·75	2·50
	a. Extra flagstaff	90·00	£150
	b. Short extra flagstaff	£160	
	c. Lightning conductor	£110	
242	24c. slate and purple	7·50	18·00
	a. Extra flagstaff	£150	£300
	c. Lightning conductor	£170	
	d. Flagstaff on right-hand turret	£250	
	e. Double flagstaff	£250	
239/42 *Set of* 4		9·00	21·00
239s/42s Perf "Specimen" *Set of* 4		£100	

For illustrations of plate varieties see Omnibus section following Zanzibar.

1937 (12 May). *Coronation. As Nos. 95/7 of Antigua, but ptd by D.L.R.* P 14.

243	1c. green	15	60
244	2c. yellow-brown	35	15
245	8c. orange	90	2·25
243/5 *Set of* 3		1·25	2·75
243s/5s Perf "Specimen" *Set of* 3		95·00	

37 First Boca

38 Imperial College of Tropical Agriculture

39 Mt. Irvine Bay, Tobago

40 Memorial Park

41 G.P.O. and Treasury

42 Discovery of Lake Asphalt

43 Queen's Park, Savannah

44 Town Hall, San Fernando

45 Government House

46 Blue Basin

47 King George VI

(Recess B.W.)

1938 (2 May)–**44**. *T* **37/47**. Wmk Mult Script CA (sideways on 1c. to 60c.).

(a) P 11½×11.

246	**37**	1c. blue and green	1·00	30
247	**38**	2c. blue and yellow-brown	1·25	20
248	**39**	3c. black and scarlet	11·00	1·00
248*a*		3c. green and purple-brown (1941)	30	20
		ab. "A" of "CA" missing from wmk		
249	**40**	4c. chocolate	26·00	1·75
249*a*		4c. scarlet (1941)	50	1·00
249*b*		5c. magenta (1.5.41)	50	15
250	**41**	6c. sepia and blue	2·75	80
251	**43**	8c. sage-green and vermilion	2·75	1·00
		a. "A" of "CA" missing from wmk	£850	
252	**44**	12c. black and purple	23·00	2·00
		a. Black and slate-purple (1944)	2·75	10
253	**45**	24c. black and olive-green	2·75	10
254	**46**	60c. myrtle-green and carmine	9·00	1·50

(b) T **47**. P 12.

255	**47**	$1.20 blue-green (1.40)	12·00	1·50
256		$4.80 rose-carmine (1.40)	27·00	45·00
246/56 *Set of* 14			90·00	48·00
246s/56s (*ex* 5c.) Perf "Specimen" *Set of* 13			£275	

1946 (1 Oct). *Victory. As Nos. 110/11 of Antigua.*

257	3c. chocolate	10	10
258	6c. blue	10	1·50
257s/8s Perf "Specimen" *Set of* 2		80·00	

1948 (22 Nov). *Royal Silver Wedding. As Nos. 112/13 of Antigua, but $4.80 in recess.*

259	3c. red-brown	10	10
260	$4.80 carmine	25·00	32·00

1949 (10 Oct). *75th Anniv of U.P.U. As Nos. 114/17 of Antigua.*

261	5c. bright reddish purple	35	1·00
262	6c. deep blue	2·00	2·25
263	12c. violet	55	1·50
264	24c. olive	55	1·25
261/4 *Set of* 4		3·00	5·50

1951 (16 Feb). *Inauguration of B.W.I. University College. As Nos. 118/19 of Antigua.*

265	3c. green and red-brown	20	1·25
266	12c. black and reddish violet	30	1·25

Nos. 265/6 are inscribed "TRINIDAD".

48 First Boca

49 Mt. Irvine Bay, Tobago

(Recess B. W.)

1953 (20 Apr)–**59**. *Designs previously used for King George VI issue, but with portrait of Queen Elizabeth II as is T* **48** *(1c., 2c., 12c.) or* **49** *(other values).* Wmk Mult Script CA. P 12 (dollar values) or 11½×11 (others).

267	1c. blue and green	20	40
	a. Blue and bluish green (10.6.59)	4·75	4·25
268	2c. indigo and orange-brown	20	40
269	3c. deep emerald and purple-brown	20	10
270	4c. scarlet	20	40
271	5c. magenta	30	30
272	6c. brown and greenish blue	50	30
273	8c. deep yellow-green and orange-red	2·50	30
274	12c. black and purple	30	10
275	24c. black and yellow-olive	2·50	30
	a. Black and olive (16.11.55)	3·50	55
	b. Black and greenish olive (12.12.56)	6·00	1·00
276	60c. blackish green and carmine	22·00	1·25
277	$1.20 bluish green	1·00	1·00
	a. Perf 11½ (19.1.55)	1·25	30
278	$4.80 cerise	7·00	21·00
	a. Perf 11½ (16.12.55)	9·00	14·00
267/78a *Set of* 12		32·00	16·00

Designs: *Horiz*—2c. Imperial College of Tropical Agriculture; 4c. Memorial Park; 5c. G.P.O. and Treasury; 6c. Discovery of Lake Asphalt; 8c. Queen's Park, Savannah; 12c. Town Hall, San Fernando; 24c. Government House; 60c. Blue Basin. *Vert* (18×21 *mm*)—$1.20, $4.80, Queen Elizabeth II.

1953 (3 June). *Coronation. As No. 120 of Antigua.*

279	3c. black and green	20	10

ONE CENT
(50)

1956 (20 Dec). *No. 268 surch with T* **50**.

280	1c. on 2c. indigo and orange-brown	1·25	1·75

1958 (22 Apr). *Inauguration of British Caribbean Federation. As Nos. 135/7 of Antigua.*

281	5c. deep green	20	10
282	6c. blue	25	1·50
283	12c. scarlet	25	10
281/3 *Set of* 3		60	1·50

PRINTERS. Nos. 284 to 354 were printed in photogravure by Harrison & Sons, unless otherwise stated.

51 Cipriani Memorial

52 Queen's Hall

53 Copper-rumped Hummingbird

54 Map of Trinidad and Tobago

(Des V. Whiteley (1, 2, 12, 35, 60c., $4.80), J. Matthews (5c.), H. Baxter (6, 8, 10, 15c.), M. Goaman (25c., 50c., $1.20))

1960 (24 Sept)–**67**. *Designs as T* **51/4**. W w **12** (upright). P 13½×14½ (1c., 60c., $1.20, $4.80) or 14½×13½ (others).

284	1c. stone and black	25	20
285	2c. bright blue	10	20
	a. Blue (23.6.64)	2·75	30
	b. New blue (18.4.67)	2·75	30
	w. Wmk inverted	4·25	
286	5c. chalky blue	10	10
	w. Wmk inverted	5·50	1·50
287	6c. red-brown	10	1·00
	a. Pale chestnut (13.4.67)	3·75	1·25
	w. Wmk inverted	28·00	
288	8c. yellow-green	10	1·50
289	10c. deep lilac	10	10
290	12c. vermilion	10	1·25
291	15c. orange	1·75	50
291*a*	15c. orange (15.9.64)	7·50	10
292	25c. rose-carmine and deep blue	80	10
	w. Wmk inverted	3·25	1·00
293	35c. emerald and black	3·75	10
	w. Wmk inverted	–	£180
294	50c. yellow, grey and blue	35	1·50
295	60c. vermilion, yellow-green and indigo	55	30
	a. Perf 14½ (17.7.65*)	£120	40·00
296	$1.20 multicoloured	15·00	2·75
297	$4.80 apple-green and pale blue	22·00	16·00
284/97 *Set of* 15		45·00	23·00

Designs: *Vert as T* **51**—60c. Anthurium Lilies. *Horiz as T* **52**—5c. Whitehall; 6c. Treasury Building; 8c. Governor General's House; 10c. General Hospital, San Fernando; 12c. Oil refinery; 15c. (No. 291), Crest; 15c. (No. 291*a*), Coat of arms; 25c. Scarlet Ibis; 35c. Pitch Lake; 50c. Mohammed Jinnah Mosque.

*This is the earliest date reported to us. It comes from an unannounced printing which was despatched to Trinidad on 3 December 1964.

The 2, 5, 6, 12 and 25c. exist with PVA gum as well as gum arabic.

See also No. 317.

65 Scouts and Gold Wolf Badge

1961 (4 Apr). *Second Caribbean. Scout Jamboree. Design multicoloured; background colours below.* W w **12**. P 13½×14½.

298	**65**	8c. light green	15	10
299		25c. light blue	15	10
		w. Wmk inverted	£150	60·00

INDEPENDENT

66 "Buccoo Reef" (painting by Carlisle Chang) **71** "Protein Foods"

1962 (31 Aug). *Independence. T* **66** *and similar horiz designs.* W w **12**. P 14½.

300		5c. bluish green	10	10
301		8c. grey	40	1·00
302		25c. reddish violet	15	10
303		35c. brown, yellow, green and black	2·25	15
304		60c. red, black and blue	2·75	3·75
300/4		*Set of* 5	5·00	4·50

Designs:—8c. Piarco Air Terminal; 25c. Hilton Hotel, Port-of-Spain; 35c. Greater Bird of Paradise and map; 60c. Scarlet Ibis and map.

(Des M. Goaman)

1963 (4 June). *Freedom from Hunger.* W w **12**. P 14×13½.

305	**71**	5c. brown-red	25	10
306		8c. yellow-bistre	30	85
307		25c. violet-blue	55	20
305/7		*Set of* 3	1·00	1·00

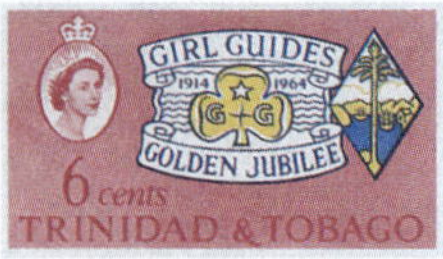

72 Jubilee Emblem

1964 (15 Sept). *Golden Jubilee of Trinidad and Tobago Girl Guides' Association.* W w **12**. P 14½×14.

308	**72**	6c. yellow, ultramarine and rose-red	10	70
309		25c. yellow, ultramarine and bright blue	15	20
310		35c. yellow, ultramarine and emerald-green	15	20
308/10		*Set of* 3	35	1·00

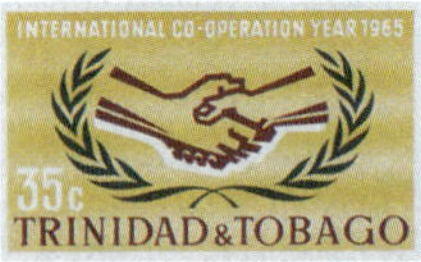

73 I.C.Y. Emblem

(Litho State Ptg Wks, Vienna)

1965 (15 Nov). *International Co-operation Year.* P 12.

311	**73**	35c. red-brown, deep green and ochre-yellow	65	20

74 Eleanor Roosevelt, Flag and U.N. Emblem

1965 (10 Dec). *Eleanor Roosevelt Memorial Foundation.* W w **12**. P 13½×14.

312	**74**	25c. black, red and ultramarine	15	10

FIFTH YEAR OF
INDEPENDENCE
31st AUGUST 1967

75 Parliament Building (**79**)

1966 (8 Feb). *Royal Visit. T* **75** *and similar horiz designs. Multicoloured.* W w **12** (sideways). P 13½×14½.

313		5c. Type **75**	15	10
314		8c. Map, Royal Yacht *Britannia* and Arms	1·50	1·00
315		25c. Map and flag	1·50	55
316		35c. Flag and panorama	1·50	70
313/16		*Set of* 4	4·25	2·00

1966 (15 Nov). *As No. 284 but* W w **12** (sideways*).

317		1c. stone and black	10	70
		w. Wmk Crown to right of CA		

*The normal sideways watermark shows Crown to left of CA, *as seen from the back of the stamp*.

No. 317 exists with PVA gum as well as gum arabic.

1967 (31 Aug). *Fifth Year of Independence. Nos. 288/9, 291a and 295 optd as T* **79**.

318		8c. yellow-green	10	10
319		10c. deep lilac	10	10
320		15c. orange	10	10
321		60c. vermilion, yellow-green and indigo	25	15
318/21		*Set of* 4	30	30

On No. 321 the overprint is in five lines.

80 Musical Instruments **81** Calypso King

1968 (17 Feb). *Trinidad Carnival. Horiz designs as T* **80** *(15 and 25c.), or vert designs as T* **81** *(35 and 60c.). Multicoloured.* P 12.

322		5c. Type **80**	10	10
323		10c. Type **81**	10	10
324		15c. Steel band	10	10
325		25c. Carnival procession	15	10
326		35c. Carnival King	15	10
327		60c. Carnival Queen	20	1·00
322/7		*Set of* 6	70	1·40

86 Doctor giving Eye-Test **87** Peoples of the World and Emblem

1968 (7 May). *20th Anniv of World Health Organization.* W w **12** (sideways). P 14.

328	**86**	5c. red, blackish brown and gold	15	10
329		25c. orange, blackish brown and gold	35	15
330		35c. bright blue, black and gold	40	25
328/30		*Set of* 3	80	45

1968 (5 Aug). *Human Rights Year.* W w **12** (sideways). P 13½×14.

331	**87**	5c. cerise, black and greenish yellow	10	10
332		10c. new blue, black and greenish yellow	15	10
333		25c. apple-green, black and greenish yellow	30	15
331/3		*Set of* 3	45	30

88 Cycling

(Des G. Vasarhelyi. Islands additionally die-stamped in gold (5c. to 35c.))

1968 (14 Oct). *Olympic Games, Mexico. T* **88** *and similar horiz designs. Multicoloured.* W w **12**. P 14.

334		5c. Type **88**	50	10
		w. Wmk inverted	†	£180
335		15c. Weightlifting	20	10
		w. Wmk inverted	9·00	
336		25c. Relay-racing	20	10
337		35c. Sprinting	20	10
338		$1.20 Maps of Mexico and Trinidad	1·00	45
334/8		*Set of* 5	1·90	65

93 Cocoa Beans **94** Green Hermit

(Des G. Vasarhelyi. Queen's profile die-stamped in gold (G.) or silver (S.), also the Islands on 20, 25c.)

1969 (1 Apr)–**72**. *Designs as T* **93/4**. W w **12** (sideways* on 1 to 8c., 40c., 50c.). *Chalk-surfaced paper.* P 14×14½ ($2.50, $5) or 14 (others).

339		1c. multicoloured (S.)	20	1·25
		a. Queen's head omitted	£100	
		bw. Wmk Crown to right of CA		
		c. Glazed, ordinary paper (24.3.72)	10	20
		cw. Wmk crown to right of CA		
340		3c. multicoloured (G.)	10	10
		aw. Wmk Crown to right of CA		
		b. Glazed, ordinary paper (24.3.72)	10	10
		bw. Wmk Crown to right of CA		
341		5c. multicoloured (G.)	2·75	10
		a. Glazed, ordinary paper (24.3.72)	2·00	10
		ab. Queen's head omitted	£150	
		ac. Imperf (pair)	£200	
		ad. Ditto and Queen's head omitted	£325	
		aw. Wmk Crown to right of CA	7·50	
342		6c. multicoloured (G.)	10	10
		a. Queen's head omitted	£150	
		b. Imperf (pair)	£250	
		c. Glazed, ordinary paper (24.3.72)	2·75	4·50
		cw. Wmk Crown to right of CA	4·75	
343		8c. multicoloured (S.)	2·25	3·00
344		10c. multicoloured (G.)	3·25	20
		a. Glazed, ordinary paper (24.3.72)	2·00	20
		aw. Wmk inverted	8·00	
345		12c. multicoloured (blue-green leaves) (S.)	15	3·00
		a. Myrtle-green leaves	4·25	4·75
		b. Glazed, ordinary paper (24.3.72)	50	3·50
346		15c. multicoloured (S.)	10	10
		a. Queen's head omitted	£375	
		b. Glazed, ordinary paper (24.3.72)	20	10
347		20c. scarlet, black and grey (G.)	30	10
		a. Glazed, ordinary paper (24.3.72)	50	1·25
348		25c. scarlet, black and new blue (S.)	30	75
		a. Glazed, ordinary paper (24.3.72)	3·50	2·50
		ab. Silver (Queen's head and island) omitted	£160	
349		30c. multicoloured (S.)	30	10
		a. Glazed, ordinary paper (24.3.72)	50	50
		aw. Wmk inverted	10·00	
350		40c. multicoloured (G.)	5·50	10
		a. Glazed, ordinary paper (24.3.72)	6·50	60
351		50c. multicoloured (S.)	30	4·00
		a. Glazed, ordinary paper (24.3.72)	1·50	5·00
		aw. Wmk Crown to right of CA	6·00	
352		$1 multicoloured (G.)	60	15
		a. Gold (Queen's head) omitted	£180	
		b. Glazed, ordinary paper (24.3.72)	1·50	4·50
		ba. Gold (Queen's head) omitted		
353		$2.50 multicoloured (G.)	1·00	4·50
		a. Perf 14 (1972)	7·50	15·00
		aw. Wmk inverted	38·00	
354		$5 multicoloured (G.)	1·00	4·50
		a. Gold (Queen's head) omitted	£375	
		b. Perf 14 (1972)	10·00	25·00
		bw. Wmk inverted	38·00	50·00
339/54		*Set of* 16	16·00	19·00
339c/352b		*Set of* 13	19·00	21·00

Designs: *Horiz as T* **93**—3c. Sugar refinery; 5c. Rufous vented Chachalaca; 6c. Oil refinery; 8c. Fertilizer plant 40c. Scarlet Ibis; 50c. Maracas Bay; $2.50, Fishing; $5 Red House. *Vert as T* **94**—12c. Citrus fruit; 15c. Arms of Trinidad and Tobago; 20c, 25c. Flag and outline of Trinidad and Tobago; 30c. Chaconia plant; $1, Poui tree.

*The normal sideways watermark shows the Crown to the left of CA, *as seen from the back of the stamp*.

The date quoted for the glazed, ordinary paper printings is that of receipt at the G.P.O.; the dates of issue are not known.

The listed missing die-stamped heads have the heads completely omitted and, except for No. 352a which results from a shift, show a blind impression of the die. They should not be confused with stamps from sheets containing a row of partially missing heads progressing down to mere specks of foil. The 20c. value also exists with the gold omitted from the map only. We have also seen stamps with an additional "blind" profile cutting into the rear of the head but without a second die-stamped impression. Varieties of this nature are outside the scope of this catalogue. See also Nos. 428/30 and 473.

Nos. 340/2 were later reissued with W w **12** upright and No. 344a with W w **14**.

108 Captain A. A. Cipriani (labour leader) and Entrance to Woodford Square

(Photo State Ptg Works, Vienna)

1969 (1 May). *50th Anniv of International Labour Organization. T* **108** *and similar horiz design.* P 12.

355		6c. black, gold and carmine-red	15	25
356		15c. black, gold and new blue	15	25

Design:—15c. Arms of Industrial Court and entrance to Woodford Square.

110 Cornucopia and Fruit **111** "CARIFTA" Countries

(Des and photo State Ptg Works, Vienna)

1969 (1 Aug). *First Anniv of CARIFTA (Caribbean Free Trade Area). T* **110/11** *and similar multicoloured designs.* P 13½.

357	6c. Type **110**	10	10
358	10c. British and member nations' flags (*horiz*)	10	10
359	30c. Type **111**	20	20
360	40c. Boeing 727-100 "Sunjet" in flight (*horiz*)	40	90
357/60 *Set of* 4		65	1·10

114 Space Module landing on Moon

(Des G. Vasarhelyi. Litho D.L.R.)

1969 (2 Sept). *First Man on the Moon. T* **114** *and similar multicoloured designs.* P 14.

361	6c. Type **114**	20	10
362	40c. Space module and astronauts on Moon (*vert*)	30	10
363	$1 Astronauts seen from inside space module	60	35
361/3 *Set of* 3		1·00	50

The above were released by the Philatelic Agency in the U.S.A. on 1 September, but not sold locally until 2 September.

117 Parliamentary Chamber, Flags and Emblems

(Photo Harrison)

1969 (23 Oct*). *15th Commonwealth Parliamentary Association Conference, Port-of-Spain. T* **117** *and similar horiz designs. Multicoloured.* W w **12**. P 14½×13½.

364	10c. Type **117**	10	10
365	15c. J.F. Kennedy College	10	10
366	30c. Parliamentary maces	25	50
367	40c. Cannon and emblem	25	50
364/7 *Set of* 4		60	1·00

*This was the local release date; the Philatelic Agency in New York released the stamps ten days earlier.

121 Congress Emblem

122 Emblem and Islands at Daybreak

(Photo Rosenbaum Bros, Vienna)

1969 (3 Nov). *International Congress of the Junior Chamber of Commerce. T* **121/2** *and similar vert design.* P 13½.

368	6c. black, red and gold	10	10
369	30c. gold, lake and light blue	25	40
370	40c. black, gold and ultramarine	25	40
368/70 *Set of* 3		50	75

Design:—40c. Emblem palm-trees and ruin.

The above were released by the Philatelic Agency in the U.S.A. on 2 November, but not sold locally until 3 November.

124 "Man in the Moon"

129 Statue of Gandhi

(Des V. Whiteley. Litho Questa)

1970 (6 Feb). *Carnival Winners. T* **124** *and similar multicoloured designs.* W w **12** (sideways on 40c.). P 14.

371	5c. Type **124**	10	10
372	6c. "City beneath the Sea"	10	10
373	15c. "Antelope" God Bambara	15	10
	w. Wmk inverted	—	15·00
374	30c. "Chanticleer" Pheasant Queen of Malaya	25	10
375	40c. Steel Band of the Year (*horiz*)	25	30
371/5 *Set of* 5		70	50

The above were released by the Philatelic Agency in the U.S.A. on 2 February, but not sold locally until 6 February.

(Photo State Printing Works, Vienna)

1970 (2 Mar). *Gandhi Centenary Year (1969). T* **129** *and similar multicoloured design.* P 12.

376	10c. Type **129**	25	10
377	30c. Head of Gandhi and Indian flag (*horiz*)	45	20

131 Symbols of Culture, Science, Arts and Technology

132 New U.P.U. H.Q. Building

(Des G. Lee. Photo State Printing Works, Vienna)

1970 (26 June). *25th Anniv of United Nations. T* **131/2** *and similar designs. Multicoloured.* P 12 (30c.) 13½×14 (10c.) or 13½ (others).

378	5c. Type **131**	10	10
379	10c. Children of different races, map and flag (34×25 *mm*)	20	10
380	20c. Noah's Ark, rainbow and dove (35×24 *mm*)	20	45
381	30c. Type **132**	25	30
378/81 *Set of* 4		65	75

NATIONAL
COMMERCIAL
BANK
ESTABLISHED
1.7.70

(**133**)

134 "East Indian Immigrants" (J. Cazabon)

1970 (1 July). *Inauguration of National Commercial Bank. No. 341 optd with T* **133**.

382	5c. multicoloured	30	10

(Des from paintings by Cazabon. Litho Questa)

1970 (1 Oct). *125th Anniv of San Fernando. T* **134** *and similar designs.* W w **12** (sideways on 5c. and 40c.). P 13½.

383	3c. multicoloured	10	90
	w. Wmk inverted	—	32·00
384	5c. black, blue and yellow-ochre	10	10
385	40c. black, blue and yellow-ochre	60	20
383/5 *Set of* 3		70	1·10

Designs: *Horiz*—5c. "San Fernando Town Hall"; 40c. "San Fernando Harbour, 1860".

135 "The Adoration of the Shepherds" (detail, School of Seville)

(Des G. Drummond. Litho Format)

1970 (8 Dec). *Christmas. Paintings. T* **135** *and similar vert designs. Multicoloured.* P 13½.

386	3c. Type **135**	10	10
387	5c. "Madonna and Child with Saints" (detail, Titian)	10	10
388	30c. "The Adoration of the Shepherds" (detail, Le Nain)	15	20
389	40c. "The Virgin and Child, St. John and an Angel" (Morando)	15	10
390	$1 "The Adoration of the Kings" (detail, Veronese)	35	2·50
386/90 *Set of* 5		75	2·75
MS391 114×153 mm. Nos. 386/9		1·00	1·25

STAMP BOOKLETS

1925.

SB1	2s. booklet containing eight ½d., 1d. and 1½d. (Nos. 218/20) in blocks of 4	

1931–32. *Black on pink covers.*

SB2	1s.8d. booklet containing eight ½d. and sixteen 1d. (Nos. 218/19) in blocks of 8	
SB3	2s. booklet containing eight ½d., 1d. and 1½d. (Nos. 218/20) in blocks of 8 (1932)	

1936.

SB4	48c. booklet containing eight 1, 2 and 3c. (Nos. 230a/2a) in blocks of 4	

1970 (8 Dec). *Christmas. Olive-green printed cover inscr* "CHRISTMAS GREETINGS".

SB5	$1.78 booklet containing six 3c., four 5c. and two 30c. and 40c. (Nos. 386/9) in pairs	4·50

POSTAGE DUE STAMPS

D 1

D 2

1/- Row 4   1/- Row 5

The degree of inclination of the stroke on the 1s. value varies for each vertical column of the sheet: Columns 1, 2 and 6 104°, Column 3 108°, Column 4 107° and Column 5 (Nos. D9a, D17a, D25a) 100°.

(Typo D.L.R.)

1885 (1 Jan). Wmk Crown CA. P 14.

D1	D 1	½d. slate-black	15·00	45·00
D2		1d. slate-black	7·50	20
D3		2d. slate-black	32·00	20
		w. Wmk inverted	†	£350
D4		3d. slate-black	50·00	40
D5		4d. slate-black	40·00	4·50
D6		5d. slate-black	23·00	60
D7		6d. slate-black	40·00	7·00
D8		8d. slate-black	55·00	3·75
D9		1s. slate-black	70·00	5·00
		a. Upright stroke	£130	15·00
D1/9 *Set of* 9			£275	60·00

1905–06. Wmk Mult Crown CA. P 14.

D10	D 1	1d. slate-black	4·75	20
D11		2d. slate-black	28·00	20
		w. Wmk inverted	†	£250
D12		3d. slate-black	14·00	2·75
		w. Wmk inverted	—	£140
D13		4d. slate-black	14·00	15·00
		w. Wmk inverted		
D14		5d. slate-black	15·00	15·00
D15		6d. slate-black	6·00	10·00
D16		8d. slate-black	12·00	14·00
D17		1s. slate-black	15·00	35·00
		a. Upright stroke	28·00	75·00
D10/17 *Set of* 8			95·00	85·00

1923–45. Wmk Mult Script CA. P 14.

D18	D 1	1d. black	1·60	2·75
D19		2d. black	4·00	1·50
D20		3d. black (1925)	4·25	4·00
D21		4d. black (1929)	4·25	24·00
D22		5d. black (1944)	35·00	£120
D23		6d. black (1945)	60·00	48·00
D24		8d. black (1945)	45·00	£180
D25		1s. black (1945)	75·00	£140
		a. Upright stroke	£140	£250
D18/25 *Set of* 8			£200	£450
D18s/25s Optd or Perf (5d. to 1s.) "Specimen" *Set of* 8			£160	

1947 (1 Sept)–**61**. *Values in cents. Ordinary paper.* Wmk Mult Script CA. P 14.

D26	D 1	2c. black	3·75	4·75
		a. Chalk-surfaced paper (20.1.53)	20	3·75
		ab. Error. Crown missing. W **9a**	£100	
		ac. Error. St. Edward's Crown. W **9b**	28·00	
D27		4c. black	1·25	3·00
		a. Chalk-surfaced paper (10.8.55)	4·75	4·50
D28		6c. black	3·50	7·00
		a. Chalk-surfaced paper (20.1.53)	30	7·50
		ab. Error. Crown missing. W **9a**	£325	
		ac. Error. St. Edward's Crown. W **9b**	75·00	
D29		8c. black	1·25	30·00
		a. Chalk-surfaced paper (10.9.58)	35	26·00
D30		10c. black	1·75	5·50
		a. Chalk-surfaced paper (10.8.55)	5·00	16·00
D31		12c. black	2·00	22·00
		a. Chalk-surfaced paper (20.1.53)	40	21·00
		ab. Error. Crown missing. W **9a**	£450	
		ac. Error. St. Edward's Crown. W **9b**	£140	
D32		16c. black	2·00	45·00
		a. Chalk-surfaced paper (22.8.61)	12·00	55·00
D33		24c. black	8·50	9·50
		a. Chalk-surfaced paper (10.8.55)	7·50	48·00
D26/33 *Set of* 8			22·00	£110
D26a/33a *Set of* 8			27·00	£160
D26s/33s Perf "Specimen" *Set of* 8			£140	

(Litho B.W.)

1969 (25 Nov)–**70**. *Size 19×24 mm.* P 14×13½.

D34	D 2	2c. pale blue-green	15	2·50
D35		4c. magenta (1970)	25	6·50
D36		6c. brown (1970)	50	4·50
D37		8c. slate-lilac (1970)	65	4·75
D38		10c. dull red (1970)	1·00	6·50
D39		12c. pale orange (1970)	80	4·75
D40		16c. bright apple-green (1970)	1·00	6·00
D41		24c. grey (1970)	1·00	8·00

D42		50c. grey-blue (1970)	1·00	4·50
D43		60c. sage-green (1970)	1·00	4·00
D34/43 *Set of* 10			6·50	45·00

Postage due stamps as T D2 but smaller (17×21 mm) were issued in 1976 and 1977.

"TOO LATE" STAMPS

A handstamp with the words "TOO LATE" was used upon letters on which a too-late fee had been paid, and was sometimes used for cancelling the stamps on such letters.

OFFICIAL STAMPS

O S (O 1) OFFICIAL (O 2) OFFICIAL (O 3)

1894. *Optd with Type* O **1**.

(a) On Nos. 106/12. Wmk Crown CA. P 14.

O1	**10**	½d. dull green	35·00	55·00
O2		1d. carmine	38·00	60·00
O3		2½d. bright blue	45·00	90·00
O4		4d. grey	48·00	£100
O5		6d. olive-black	48·00	£100
O6		1s. orange-brown	65·00	£140

(b) On No. 87. Wmk Crown CC. P 12½.

O7	**5**	5s. rose-lake	£160	£500

1909. *Nos. 133 and 135 optd with Type* O **2**. Wmk Mult Crown CA. P 14.

O8	**11**	½d. blue-green	1·50	8·00
O9		1d. rose-red	1·25	8·00
		a. Opt double	—	£325
		b. Opt vertical	£120	£140
		c. Opt inverted	£750	£225

1910. *No. 14b optd with Type* O **2**. Wmk Mult Crown CA. P 14.

O10	**14**	½d. green	7·00	9·00
		w. Wmk inverted	£160	

1913. *No. 149 optd with Type* O **3** *by lithography.*

O11	**17**	½d. green	1·25	10·00
		a. Opt vertical		

OFFICIAL (O 4) OFFICIAL (O 5) OFFICIAL (O 6)

1914. *No. 149 optd with Type* O **4**.

O12	**17**	½d. green	2·25	17·00

1914–17. *No. 149 optd with Type* O **5** *(without stop).*

O13	**17**	½d. green	3·75	16·00
		a. Blue-green (thick paper) (1917)	50	7·00

1916. *No. 149a optd with Type* O **5** *(with stop).*

O14	**17**	½d. yellow-green	2·75	4·50
		a. Opt double	40·00	

1917 (22 Aug). *No. 149 optd with Type* O **6**.

O15	**17**	½d. green	3·75	21·00
		a. Yellow-green	3·75	23·00
		b. Blue-green (thick paper)	1·50	21·00

Tristan da Cunha

Although first settled in 1817 no surviving mail is known from Tristan da Cunha until two whaler's letters written in 1836 and 1843, these being carried home in other whaling ships. Then there is a long gap until the late 1800's when other letters are known—surprisingly only some seven in number, up to 1908 when the first of the island cachet handstamps came into use.

The collecting of postal history material from 1908 to 1952, when Tristan's first stamps were issued, revolves around the numerous cachets of origin which were struck on mail from the island during these 44 years. The handstamps producing these cachets were supplied over the years by various people particularly interested in the island and the islanders, and were mostly used by the clergymen who volunteered to go and serve as the community's ministers.

The postal cachets are illustrated below. The use of the different cachets on mail frequently overlapped, at one period in 1930 there were five different types of handstamp in use. As there was no official source for providing them they appeared on the island from various donors; then disappeared without trace once they became worn out. Only one of these early rubber handstamps has apparently survived, Cachet Va.

Covers bearing the cachets are recognised collector's items, but are difficult to value in general terms. As elsewhere the value is discounted by poor condition of the cover, and may be increased by use on a scarce date or with additional postal markings.

Cachet Types V and VII on cover are the commonest, Type Va, used only for three months, and Type IVa are the scarcest, equalling the scarcest use of Type I examples. All cacheted covers, particularly if non-philatelic, are desirable forerunner items. Even a philatelic cover of Type V is, at present, worth in the region of £35.

Dates given are of the first recorded use.

Cachet I

Cachet II

Cat. No. — *Value on cover*

C1 **1908** (May). Cachet I ... *from* £4000
C2 **1919** (31 July). Cachet II ... *from* £425

Cachet III

C3 **1921** (8 Feb). Cachet III ... *from* £275

Cachet IVa

C4 **1927** (1 Oct). Cachet IV (*as* IVa, *but without centre label*) ... *from* £800
C5 **1928** (28 Oct). Cachet IVa ... *from* £5500

Cachet V

Cachet VI

C6 **1929** (24 Feb). Cachet V ... *from* 35·00
C7 **1929** (15 May). Cachet Va (*as* V, *but without break in inner ring. Shows* "T" "C" *and* "N" *damaged*) ... *from* £6500
C8 **1936** (Aug). Cachet VI ... *from* 60·00

Cachet VII

C9 **1936** (1 Feb). Cachet VII ... *from* 22·00

During World War II there was little mail from the island as its function as a meteorological station was cloaked by security. Such covers as are known are generally struck with the "tombstone" naval censor mark and postmarked "maritime mail" or have South African postal markings. A few philatelic items from early in the war bearing cachets exist, but this usage was soon stopped by the military commander and the handstamps were put away until peace returned. Covers from the period would be worth from £75 to at least £350.

Cachet VIII

C10 **1946** (8 May). Cachet VIII ... *from* 85·00

Cachet IX

C11 **1948** (2 Feb). Cachet IX ... *from* 45·00

This cachet with "A.B.C." below the date was in private use between 1942 and 1946.

Cachet X

C12 **1948** (29 Feb). Cachet X ... *from* 55·00

Cachet XI

Cachet XII

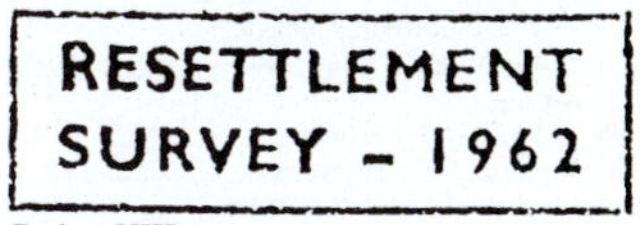

Cachet XIII

Cachets XI to XIII from the 1961/63 "volcano eruption" and "return to the island" period vary in value from £30 to £120, due to philatelic usage on the one hand and scarce mailings from the small survey parties on shore during this period on the other.

TRISTAN
DA CUNHA
(1)

1952 (1 Jan). *Nos. 131, 135a/40 and 149/51 of St. Helena optd with T* **1**.

1	½d. violet	15	3·00
2	1d. black and green	1·00	1·50
3	1½d. black and carmine	1·00	1·50
4	2d. black and scarlet	1·00	1·50
5	3d. grey	1·00	1·50
6	4d. ultramarine	5·00	2·50
7	6d. light blue	5·00	2·50
8	8d. olive-green	5·00	7·00
9	1s. sepia	5·00	2·00
10	2s.6d. maroon	20·00	13·00
11	5s. chocolate	24·00	20·00
12	10s. purple	48·00	32·00
1/12	*Set of* 12	£100	80·00

1953 (2 June). *Coronation. As No.* 120 *of Antigua.*

13	3d. black and grey-green	50	1·25

2 Tristan Crawfish

3 Carting Flax for Thatching

4 Rockhopper Penguin

5 Big Beach factory

6 Yellow-nosed Albatross

7 Island longboat

8 Tristan from the south-west

9 Girls on donkeys

10 Inaccessible Island from Tristan

11 Nightingale Island

12 St. Mary's Church

13 Southern Elephant seal at Gough Island

14 Inaccessible Island Rail

15 Island spinning wheel

(Recess D.L.R.)

1954 (2 Jan). *T* **2/15**. Wmk Mult Script CA. P 12½×13 (horiz) or 13×12½ (vert).

14	½d. red and deep brown	10	10
15	1d. sepia and bluish green	10	50
16	1½d. black and reddish purple	1·75	1·75
17	2d. grey-violet and brown-orange	30	20
18	2½d. black and carmine-red	1·50	60
19	3d. ultramarine and olive-green	60	1·75
20	4d. turquoise-blue and deep blue	60	70
21	5d. emerald and black	60	70
22	6d. deep green and violet	60	75
23	9d. reddish violet and Venetian red	60	45
24	1s. deep yellow-green and sepia	60	45
25	2s.6d. deep brown and light blue	17·00	8·00
26	5s. black and red-orange	50·00	11·00
27	10s. brown-orange and purple	21·00	12·00
14/27	*Set of* 14	85·00	35·00

16 Starfish

17 Concha Wrasse

18 Two-spined Thornfish

19 Atlantic Saury

20 Bristle Snipefish

21 Tristan Crawfish

22 False Jacopever

23 Five-fingered Morwong

24 Long-finned Scad

25 Christophersen's Medusafish

26 Blue Medusafish

27 Snoek

28 Blue Shark

29 Black Right Whale

(Des Mr. and Mrs. G. F. Harris. Recess Waterlow)

1960 (1 Feb). *Marine Life. T* **16/29**. W w **12**. P 13.

28	½d. black and orange	15	40
29	1d. black and bright purple	15	20
30	1½d. black and light turquoise-blue	20	70
31	2d. black and bluish green	30	1·00
32	2½d. black and sepia	55	60
33	3d. black and brown-red	1·25	1·50
34	4d. black and yellow-olive	1·25	60
35	5d. black and orange-yellow	1·50	60
36	6d. black and blue	1·75	60
37	9d. black and rose-carmine	1·75	60
38	1s. black and light brown	2·75	50
39	2s.6d. black and ultramarine	11·00	11·00
40	5s. black and light emerald	12·00	12·00
41	10s. black and violet	45·00	28·00
28/41	*Set of* 14	70·00	50·00

1961 (15 Apr). *As Nos. 28/30 and 32/41 but values in South African decimal currency.*

42	½c. black and orange (as ½d.)	10	1·25
43	1c. black and bright purple (as 1d.)	15	1·25
44	1½c. black and light turquoise-blue (as 1½d.)	35	1·25
45	2c. black and sepia (as 2½d.)	65	1·25
46	2½c. black and brown-red (as 3d.)	1·00	1·25
47	3c. black and yellow-olive (as 4d.)	1·00	1·25
48	4c. black and orange-yellow (as 5d.)	1·25	1·25
49	5c. black and blue (as 6d.)	1·25	1·25
50	7½c. black and rose-carmine (as 9d.)	1·25	1·25
51	10c. black and light brown (as 1s.)	2·00	1·25
52	25c. black and ultramarine (as 2s. 6d.)	8·00	7·50
53	50c. black and light emerald (as 5s.)	20·00	14·00
54	1r. black and violet (as 10s.)	48·00	27·00
42/54	*Set of* 13	75·00	55·00

Following a volcanic eruption the island was evacuated on 10 October 1961, but resettled in 1963.

TRISTAN DA CUNHA
RESETTLEMENT
1963
(30)

1963 (12 Apr). *Tristan Resettlement. As Nos. 176/88 of St. Helena, but Wmk Mult Script CA (sideways on 1d., 2d., 7d., 10d., 2s. 6d., 10s), optd with T* **30**.

55	1d. bright blue, dull violet, yellow and carmine	15	1·00
56	1½d. yellow, green, black and light drab	20	70
57	2d. scarlet and grey	25	1·00
58	3d. light blue, black, pink and deep blue	30	1·00
	a. Black printed double*	£275	
	w. Wmk inverted	£450	
59	4½d. yellow-green, green, brown and grey	50	60
60	6d. red, sepia and light yellow-olive	1·75	30
61	7d. red-brown, black and violet	50	30
62	10d. brown-purple and light blue	50	30
63	1s. greenish yellow, bluish green and brown	50	30
64	1s.6d. grey, black and slate-blue	4·75	1·00
65	2s.6d. red, pale yellow and turquoise	1·00	45
66	5s. yellow, brown and green	6·00	1·00
	w. Wmk inverted	85·00	70·00
67	10s. orange-red, black and blue	6·00	1·00
55/67	*Set of* 13	20·00	8·00

*No. 58a shows the outline round the Queen's head printed double.

1963 (2 Oct). *Freedom from Hunger. As No. 146 of Antigua.*

68	1s.6d. carmine	50	30

1964 (1 Feb). *Red Cross Centenary. As Nos. 147/8 of Antigua.*

69	3d. red and black	20	15
70	1s.6d. red and blue	30	20

31 South Atlantic Map

32 Flagship of Tristao da Cunha, 1506

33 *Heemstede* (Dutch East Indiaman), 1643

34 *Edward* (American Whaling ship), 1864

35 *Shenandoah* (Confederate warship), 1873

35a H.M.S *Challenger* (survey ship), 1873

36 H.M.S *Galatea* (screw frigate), 1867

37 H.M.S *Cilicia* (transport), 1942

38 Royal Yacht *Britannia*

39 H.M.S *Leopard* (frigate)

40 *Tjisadane* (liner)

41 *Tristania* (crayfish trawler)

42 *Boissevain* (cargo liner)

43 *Bornholm* (liner)

44 Queen Elizabeth II

44a *R.S.A.* (research vessel)

(Queen's portrait by Anthony Buckley. Des, eng and recess B.W.)

1965 (17 Feb)–**67**. *Designs as T* **31/44a**. W w **12** (sideways on £1). P 11½×11 (vert) or 11×11½ (horiz).

71	**31**	½d. black and ultramarine	15	30
72	**32**	1d. black and emerald-green	1·00	15
73	**33**	1½d. black and blue	1·00	15
74	**34**	2d. black and purple	1·00	15
75	**35**	3d. black and turquoise-blue	1·00	15
75*a*	**35a**	4d. black and orange (1.9.67)	4·00	4·00
76	**36**	4½d. black and brown	75	15
77	**37**	6d. black and green	1·00	15
78	**38**	7d. black and rose-red	1·00	30
79	**39**	10d. black and chocolate	1·00	55
80	**40**	1s. black and carmine	1·00	30
81	**41**	1s.6d. black and yellow-olive	4·50	2·50
82	**42**	2s.6d. black and orange-brown	2·75	2·75
83	**43**	5s. black and violet	6·00	3·50
84	**44**	10s. deep blue and carmine	1·75	1·25
84*a*	**44a**	10s. black and deep turquoise-blue (1.9.67)	13·00	9·00
84*b*	**44**	£1 deep blue and orange-brown (1.9.67)	13·00	11·00
71/84*b*		*Set of* 17	45·00	32·00

1965 (11 May*). *I.T.U. Centenary. As Nos. 166/7 of Antigua.*

85	3d. orange-red and grey	20	15
86	6d. reddish violet and yellow-orange	30	15

*This is the local date of issue; the stamps were not released in London until 17 May.

1965 (25 Oct). *International Co-operation Year. As Nos. 168/9 of Antigua.*

87	1d. reddish purple and turquoise-green	20	15
88	6d. deep bluish green and lavender	50	25

1966 (24 Jan). *Churchill Commemoration. As Nos. 170/3 of Antigua.*

89	1d. new blue	35	40
	a. Value omitted	£850	
90	3d. deep green	1·00	50
91	6d. brown	1·25	65
92	1s.6d. bluish violet	1·40	70
89/92	*Set of* 4	3·50	2·00

No. 89a was caused by misplacement of the gold and also shows the country inscription moved to the right.

45 H.M.S. *Falmouth* (frigate) at Tristan and Soldier of 1816

(Des V. Whiteley. Litho Harrison)

1966 (15 Aug). *150th Anniv of Tristan Garrison.* W w **12** (sideways*). P 14½.

93	**45**	3d. multicoloured	15	10
		w. Wmk Crown to right of CA	6·50	
94		6d. multicoloured	15	15
95		1s.6d. multicoloured	20	25
96		2s.6d. multicoloured	25	25
93/6		*Set of* 4	65	65

*The normal sideways watermark shows Crown to left of CA, *as seen from the back of the stamp.*

1966 (1 Oct*). *World Cup Football Championship. As Nos. 176/7 of Antigua.*

97		3d. violet, yellow-grn, lake & yellow-brown	20	10
98		2s.6d. chocolate, blue-green, lake and yellow-brown	50	20

*Released in St. Helena on 1 July in error.

1966 (1 Oct). *Inauguration of W.H.O. Headquarters, Geneva. As Nos. 178/9 of Antigua.*

99		6d. black, yellow-green and light blue	60	30
100		5s. black, light purple and yellow-brown	90	70

1966 (1 Dec). *20th Anniv of U.N.E.S.C.O. As Nos. 196/8 of Antigua.*

101		10d. slate-violet, red, yellow and orange	25	15
		w. Wmk Crown to right of CA	40·00	
102		1s.6d. orange-yellow, violet and deep olive	40	20
103		2s.6d. black, bright purple and orange	45	25
101/3 *Set of 3*			1·00	55

*The normal sideways watermark shows Crown to left of CA, *as seen from the back of the stamp.*

46 Calshot Harbour

(Des V. Whiteley. Litho D.L.R.)

1967 (2 Jan). *Opening of Calshot Harbour.* P 14×14½.

104	**46**	6d. multicoloured	10	10
105		10d. multicoloured	10	10
106		1s.6d. multicoloured	10	15
107		2s.6d. multicoloured	15	20
104/7 *Set of 4*			30	45

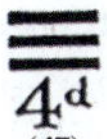

(**47**)

48 Prince Alfred, First Duke of Edinburgh

1967 (10 May). *No. 76 surch with T* **47**.

108		4d. on 4½d. black and brown	10	10

(Des M. Goaman. Litho Harrison)

1967 (10 July). *Centenary of First Duke of Edinburgh's Visit to Tristan.* W w **12**. P 14½.

109	**48**	3d. multicoloured	10	10
110		6d. multicoloured	10	10
111		1s.6d. multicoloured	10	10
112		2s.6d. multicoloured	15	15
109/12 *Set of 4*			30	30

49 Wandering Albatross

(Des V. Whiteley. Photo Harrison)

1968 (15 May). *Birds. T* **49** *and similar horiz designs. Multicoloured.* W w **12**. P 14×14½.

113		4d. Type **49**	30	30
114		1s. Wilkins's Finch	35	30
115		1s.6d. Tristan Thrush	40	55
116		2s.6d. Greater Shearwater	60	65
113/16 *Set of 4*			1·50	1·60

53 Union Jack and Dependency Flag

(Des Jennifer Toombs. Litho D.L.R.)

1968 (1 Nov). *30th Anniv of Tristan da Cunha as a Dependency of St. Helena. T* **53** *and similar horiz design.* W w **12** (sideways). P 14.

117	**53**	6d. multicoloured	10	30
118	–	9d. sepia, blue and turquoise-blue	10	35
119	**53**	1s.6d. multicoloured	15	40
120	–	2s.6d. carmine, blue and turquoise-blue	20	40
117/20 *Set of 4*			50	1·25

Design:—9d., 2s.6d. St. Helena and Tristan on chart.

55 Frigate

(Des and recess B.W.)

1969 (1 June). *Clipper Ships. T* **55** *and similar horiz designs.* W w **12**. P 11×11½.

121		4d. new blue	30	40
122		1s. carmine (full-rigged ship)	30	45
123		1s.6d. blue-green (barque)	35	90
124		2s.6d. chocolate (full-rigged clipper)	40	95
121/4 *Set of 4*			1·25	2·40

59 Sailing Ship off Tristan da Cunha

(Des Jennifer Toombs. Litho Format)

1969 (1 Nov). *United Society for the Propagation of the Gospel. T* **59** *and similar horiz designs. Multicoloured.* W w **12** (sideways). P 14½×14.

125		4d. Type **59**	40	30
126		9d. Islanders going to first Gospel service	15	30
127		1s.6d. Landing of the first minister	15	40
128		2s.6d. Procession outside St. Mary's Church	20	40
125/8 *Set of 4*			80	1·25

63 Globe and Red Cross Emblem

(Des and litho B.W.)

1970 (1 June). *Centenary of British Red Cross. T* **63** *and similar designs.* W w **12** (sideways on vert designs). P 13.

129	**63**	4d. light emerald, scarlet & deep bluish green	10	25
130		9d. bistre, scarlet and deep bluish green	15	30
131	–	1s.9d. light drab, scarlet and ultramarine	25	45
132	–	2s.6d. reddish purple, scarlet and ultramarine	30	55
129/32 *Set of 4*			70	1·40

Design: *Vert*—1s.9d., 2s.6d., Union Jack and Red Cross Flag.

64 Crawfish and Longboat

(Des Harrison. Litho Enschedé)

1970 (1 Nov). *Crawfish Industry. T* **64** *and similar horiz design. Multicoloured.* W w **12**. P 12½×13.

133		4d. Type **64**	20	30
134		10d. Packing and storing Crawfish	25	35
135		1s.6d. Type **64**	40	60
136		2s.6d. As 10d.	40	70
133/6 *Set of 4*			1·10	1·75

STAMP BOOKLETS

1957 (30 May)–**58**. *Black on blue cover. Postmarked "MY 30 57" on back cover. Stapled.*

SB1	3s.6d. booklet containing eight ½d. and four 1d., 1½d., 3d. and 4d. (Nos. 14/16, 19/20) in blocks of 4	£325
	a. Postmarked "JA 24 58" on back cover (24.1.58)	£275
	b. Without postmark	£250

1958 (Jan). *Black on red cover. Without postmark. Stapled.*

SB2	3s.6d. Contents as No. SB1	55·00

1960 (Feb). *Black on green cover. Stitched.*

SB3	3s.6d. booklet containing eight ½d. and four 1d., 1½d., 3d. and 4d. (Nos. 28/30, 33/4) in blocks of 4	30·00

1965 (17 Feb). *Black on green cover. Stapled.*

SB4	4s.2d. booklet containing eight ½d. and four 1d., 1½d., 3d. and 6d. (Nos. 71/3, 75, 77) in blocks of 4	6·00

The booklet covers were reprinted with amended postage rates and released by the Crown Agents on 21 September 1970.

POSTAGE DUE STAMPS

D 1

Normal

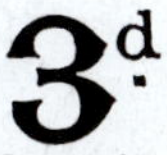

Large "d."
(R. 9/6, 10/6)

(Typo D.L.R.)

1957 (1 Feb). *Chalk-surfaced paper.* Wmk Mult Script CA. P 14.

D1	**D 1**	1d. scarlet	1·75	12·00
D2		2d. orange-yellow	2·50	4·75
		a. Large "d"	25·00	
D3		3d. green	2·50	5·50
		a. Missing serif	45·00	
D4		4d. ultramarine	4·50	7·00
D5		5d. lake	2·50	23·00
D1/5 *Set of 5*			12·00	48·00

For illustration of No. D2a see above No. D1 of Basutoland.

POSTAL FISCAL STAMPS

NATIONAL
SAVINGS
(F **1**)

1970 (15 May). *No. 77 optd with Type* F **1** *in red.*

F1		6d. black and green	20	30

No. F1 was originally intended as a National Savings Stamp, but also retained postal validity.

Trucial States

The Trucial States consisted of Abu Dhabi, Ajman (with Manama), Dubai, Fujeira, Ras al Khaima. Sharjah and Umm al Qiwain. However the following issue of stamps was only put into use in Dubai, despite the inscription "TRUCIAL STATES".

The first organised postal service in Dubai commenced on 19 August 1909 when an Indian Branch Office, administered from Karachi, was opened, using the unoverprinted stamps of India, principally the ½a. and 1a. values.

The initial cancellation was a single-ring type inscribed "DUBAI B.O. PERSIAN GULF", which remained in use until 1933.

1909 Cancellation

Its replacement was of the Indian double-circle type showing a similar inscription.

Dubai was upgraded to Sub-Post Office status on 1 April 1942 and this change was reflected in a new double-ring mark inscribed "DUBAI" only. At the same time the office was provided with a single-ring handstamp which also incorporated a cancelling device of seven wavy lines.

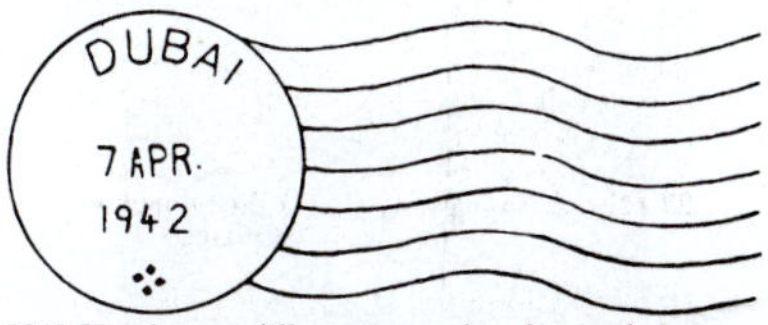

1942 Handstamp (*illustration reduced: actual size 65×27 mm*)

A further version of the double-ring type appeared in 1946, showing the "PERSIAN GULF" inscription restored to the lower segment of the postmark.

In October 1947 control of the Dubai Post Office passed to Pakistan whose stamps were used there until the end of March 1948.

On 1 April 1948 the post office was transferred, yet again, to British control and Great Britain stamps surcharged for use in the British Postal Agencies in Eastern Arabia were then sold in Dubai until 6 January 1961, being cancelled with British style single and double-ring postmarks.

(Currency. 100 naye paise = 1 rupee)

1 Palms

2 Dhow

(Des M. Goaman. Photo Harrison (T **1**). Des M. Farrar-Bell. Recess D.L.R. (T **2**))

1961 (7 Jan). P 15×14 (T **1**) or 13×12½ (T **2**).

1	**1**	5n.p. green	1·25	10
2		15n.p. red-brown	60	10
3		20n.p. bright blue	1·25	10
4		30n.p. orange-red	60	10
5		40n.p. reddish violet	60	10
6		50n.p. bistro	60	40
7		75n.p. grey	60	10
8	**2**	1r. green	6·00	3·50
9		2r. black	6·00	21·00
10		5r. carmine-red	8·50	23·00
11		10r. deep ultramarine	12·00	23·00
1/11 *Set of 11*			35·00	65·00

The Dubai Post Department took over the postal services on 14 June 1963. Later issues for Dubai will be found in Part 19 (*Middle East*) of this catalogue.

Turks and Caicos Islands

TURKS ISLANDS

DEPENDENCY OF JAMAICA

A branch of the British Post Office opened at Grand Turk on 11 December 1854 replacing an earlier arrangement under which mail for the islands was sorted by local R.M.S.P. agents.

No. CC 1 is known used between 22 October 1857 and 20 April 1862.

GRAND TURK

CROWNED-CIRCLE HANDSTAMPS

CC **1**

CC1 CC **1** TURKS-ISLANDS (Oct 1857)
Price on cover £5500

PRICES FOR STAMPS ON COVER TO 1945	
Nos. 1/5	*from* × 30
No. 6	—
Nos. 7/20	*from* × 50
Nos. 20*a*/48	—
Nos. 49/52	*from* × 12
Nos. 53/7	*from* × 10
Nos. 58/65	*from* × 20
Nos. 66/9	*from* × 5
Nos. 70/2	*from* × 10
Nos. 101/9	*from* × 8
Nos. 110/26	*from* × 6
Nos. 129/39	*from* × 4
Nos. 140/53	*from* × 12
Nos. 154/90	*from* × 3
Nos. 191/3	*from* × 10
Nos. 194/205	*from* × 2

1

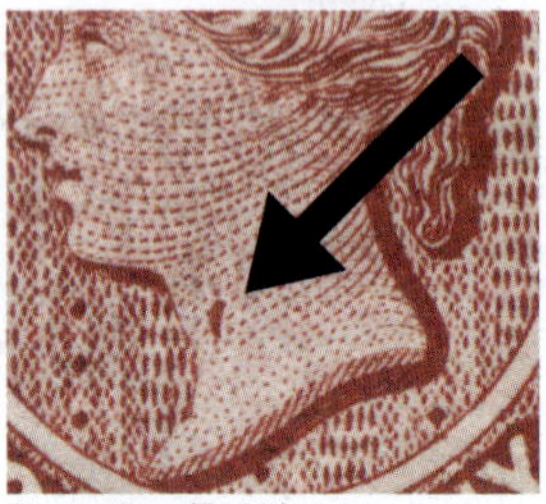

Throat flaw (R. 3/4)

(Recess P.B.)

1867 (4 Apr). No wmk. P 11–12.

1	**1**	1d. dull rose	60·00	60·00
		a. Throat flaw	£225	£250
2		6d. black	95·00	£120
3		1s. dull blue	90·00	60·00

1873–79. Wmk Small Star. W w **2** (sideways on Nos. 5 and 6). P 11–12×14½–15½.

4	**1**	1d. dull rose-lake (7.73)	50·00	50·00
		a. Throat flaw	£200	£225
		b. Wmk sideways	90·00	90·00
		ba. Throat flaw	£325	£350
5		1d. dull red (1.79)	55·00	60·00
		a. Imperf between (horiz pair)	£22000	
		b. Throat flaw	£225	£250
		c. Wmk upright		
6		1s. lilac (1.79)	£5000	£2000

1881 (1 Jan). *Stamps of the preceding issues surcharged locally, in black. Sheets of 30 (10×3).*

There are twelve different settings of the ½d., nine settings of the 2½d., and six settings of the 4d.

(2) (3)

Setting 1. *T* **2**. *Long fraction bar. Two varieties in a horizontal pair repeated fifteen times in the sheet.*

7	½. on 6d black	80·00	£130

Setting 2. *T* **3**. *Short fraction bar. Three varieties in a vertical strip repeated ten times in sheet.*

Setting 3. *Similar to setting* 2, *but the middle stamp of the three varieties has a longer bar.*

8	½ on 6d. black (*setting 2 only*)	75·00	£110
9	½ on 1s. dull blue	£100	£170
	a. Surch double	£6000	

(4) (5) (6)

Three varieties in a vertical strip repeated ten times in sheet.
Setting 4. *Types* **4**, **5**, **6**.
Setting 5. *Types* **4** (without bar), **5**, **6**.
Setting 6. *Types* **4**, **5**, **6** (without bar).
Setting 7. *Types* **4** (shorter thick bar), **6**, **6**.

10	½ on 1d. dull red (*setting 7 only*) (T **6**)		
	a. Type **4** (shorter thick bar)	£13000	
11	½ on 1s. dull blue (*setting 6 and 7*) (T **4**)	£1800	
	a. Type **4** (shorter thick bar)	£2250	
	b. Type **5**	£1100	
	c. Type **6**	£900	
	d. Type **6** (without bar)	£1900	
	e. Surch double (T **4**)	£9000	
	f. Surch double (T **5**)	£9000	
	g. Surch double (T **6** without bar)		
12	½ on 1s. lilac (T **4**)	£275	£400
	a. Without bar	£550	
	b. With short thick bar	£500	
	c. Surch double	£3500	
	cb. Surch double and short thick bar	£9000	
13	½ on 1s. lilac (T **5**)	£130	£225
	a. Surch double	£3250	
14	½ on 1s. lilac (T **6**)	£130	£225
	a. Without bar	£600	
	b. Surch double	£6000	
	ba. Surch double and without bar	£9000	

Care should be taken in the identification of Types **6** and **7** which are very similar. For the 1s. value some varieties of No. 9 are often confused with Nos. 11b/c.

(7) (8) (9) (10)

Setting 8. *T* **7**. *Three varieties in a vertical strip. All have a very short bar.*

15	½. on 1d dull red	65·00	£110
	a. Throat flaw	£275	
	b. Surch double	£6000	

Setting 9. *T* **8**. *Three varieties in a vertical strip. Bars long and thick and "1" leaning a little to left.*

16	½ on 1d. dull red	£190	£275
	a. Surch double	£4500	
	b. Throat flaw	£600	

Setting 10. *T* **9** *and* **10**. *Fifteen varieties repeated twice in a sheet. Ten are of T* **9** *(Rows 1 and 2), five of T* **10** *(Row 3).*

17	½ on 1d. dull red (T **9**)	55·00	£120
	a. Surch double	£5500	
18	½ on 1d. dull red (T **10**)	85·00	£170
	a. Surch double	£9000	
	b. Throat flaw	£300	
19	½ on 1s. lilac (T **9**)	95·00	£180
20	½ on 1s. lilac (T **10**)	£170	£350
20*a*	½. on 1s dull blue (T **9**)	£11000	
20*b*	½ on 1s. dull blue (T **10**)	£18000	

Types **9** and **11**. The difference is in the position of the "2" in relation to the "1". In setting 10 the "2" is to the left of the "1" except on No. 10 (where it is directly below the "1") and in setting 11 it is to the right except on No. 2 (where it is to the left, as in setting 10).

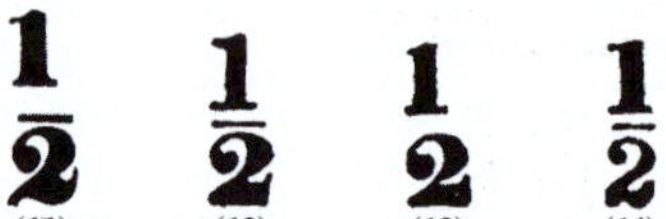

(11) (12) (13) (14)

Setting 11. *T* **9** and **11** to **14**. Fifteen varieties repeated twice in a sheet. Nine of T **11**, three of T **12**, and one each of T **9**, **13** and **14**.

Setting 12. *Similar to last, but T* **13** *replaced by another T* **12**.

21	½ on 1d. dull red (T **11**)	£100	£190
22	½ on 1d. dull red (T **12**)	£225	
	a. Throat flaw	£1100	
23	½ on 1d. dull red (T **13**)	£1100	
	a. Throat flaw	£1100	
24	½ on 1d. dull red (T **14**)	£600	
24*a*	½ on 1s. dull blue (T **11**)	£17000	

Type **9** from these settings, where it occurs on position 2, can only be distinguished from similar stamps from setting 10 when *se-tenant* with Type **11**.

In setting 11 Type **13** occupied R. 3/4 in the setting (5×3), corresponding to the position of the "Throat flaw" on the left half of each sheet of 30 (10×3). Nos. 23 and 23a therefore exist in equal quantities.

(15) (16)

Setting 1. *T* **15**. *Fraction in very small type.*

25	2½ on 6d. black	£13000	

Setting 2. *T* **16**. *Two varieties repeated fifteen times in a sheet. Large "2" on level with top of the "1", long thin bar.*

26	2½ on 6d. black	£350	£500
	a. Imperf between (horiz pair)	£38000	
	b. Surch double	£14000	

(17) (18) (19)

Setting 3. *T* **17**. *As T* **16**, *but large "2" not so high up.*

27	2½ on 1s. lilac	£3000	

Setting 4. *T* **18**. *Three varieties in a vertical strip repeated ten times in sheet. Large "2" placed lower and small bar.*

28	2½ on 6d. black	£170	£325
	a. Surch double	£12000	

Setting 5. *T* **19**. *Three varieties in a vertical strip repeated ten times in sheet "2" further from "½", small fraction bar.*

29	2½ on 1s. lilac	£550	£900

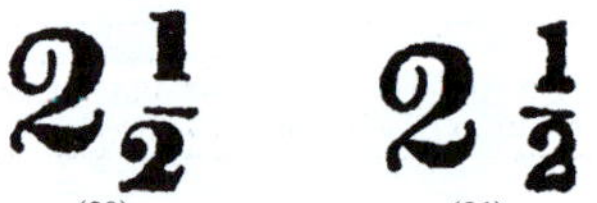

(20) (21)

Setting 6. *T* **20** *and* **21**. *Fifteen varieties. Ten of T* **20** *and five of T* **21**, *repeated twice in a sheet.*

30	2½ on 1s. lilac (T **20**)	£11000	
31	2½ on 1s. lilac (T **21**)	£18000	

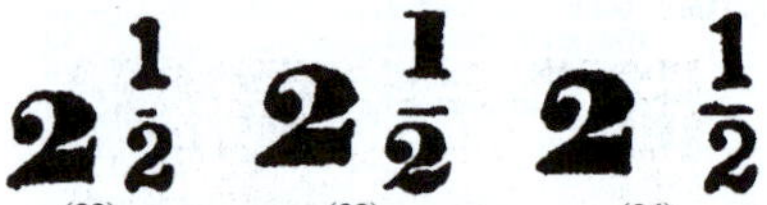

(22) (23) (24)

Setting 7. *T* **22**. *Three varieties in a vertical strip, repeated ten times in a sheet.*

32	2½ on 6d. black	£8500	
33	2½ on 1s. dull blue	£18000	

Setting 8. *T* **23** *and* **24**. *Fifteen varieties. Ten of T* **23** *and five of T* **24** *repeated twice in a sheet.*

34	2½ on 1d. dull red (T **23**)	£650	
35	2½ on 1d. dull red (T **24**)	£1400	
	a. Throat flaw	£3750	
36	2½ on 1s. lilac (T **23**)	£550	£750
	a. Surch "½" double	£3750	
37	2½ on 1s. lilac (T **24**)	£1200	
	a. Surch "½" double	£6500	

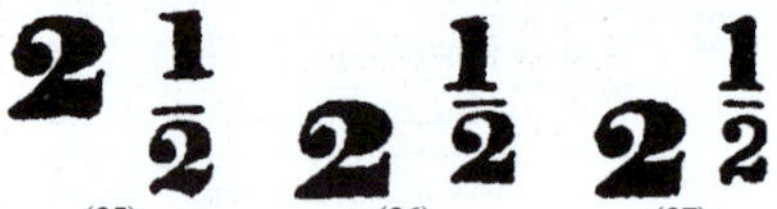

(25) (26) (27)

Setting 9. *T* **25**, **26**, *and* **27**. *Fifteen varieties. Ten of T* **25**, *three of T* **26**, *one of T* **26** *without bar, and one of T* **27**, *repeated twice in a sheet.*

38	2½ on 1s. dull blue (T **25**)	£850	
39	2½ on 1s. dull blue (T **26**)	£2750	
40	2½ on 1s. dull blue (T **26**) (without bar)	£10000	
41	2½ on 1s. dull blue (T **27**)	£10000	

(28) (29) (30)

Setting 1. *T* **28**. *"4" 8 mm high, pointed top.*

42	4 on 6d. black	£550	£325

Settings 2-6. *T* **29** *and* **30**.

43	4 on 6d. black (T **29**)	80·00	£110
44	4 on 6d. black (T **30**)	£350	£425
45	4 on 1s. lilac (T **29**)	£400	£600
	a. Surch double		
46	4 on 1s. lilac (T **30**)	£2500	
	a. Surch double		
47	4 on 1d. dull red (T **29**)	£750	£475
48	4 on 1d. dull red (T **28**)	£850	£550

The components of these settings can only be distinguished when in blocks. Details are given in the handbook by John J. Challis.

31

One Penny

(32)

(Typo D.L.R.)

1881. Wmk Crown CC (sideways* on T **1**). P 14.

49	**1**	1d. brown-red (Oct)	75·00	95·00
		a. Throat flaw	£275	£325
50	**31**	4d. ultramarine (Die I) (Aug)	£150	60·00
51	**1**	6d. olive-black (Oct)	£120	£170
52		1s. slate-green (Oct)	£180	£140

*The normal sideways watermark shows Crown to right of CC, *as seen from the back of the stamp*.

Nos. 49 and 51/2 also exist showing Crown to left of CC, but due to the position of the watermark such varieties are difficult to detect on single stamps.

1882–85. Wmk Crown CA (reversed on 1d.). P 14.
53 **31** ½d. blue-green (Die I) (2.82) .... 13·00 25·00
a. Pale green (12.85) .... 3·75 4·25
b. Top left triangle detached £250
55 **1** 1d. orange-brown (10.83) .... 85·00 30·00
a. Bisected (½d.) (on cover) .... † £5000
b. Throat flaw £300 £140
x. Wmk normal (not reversed) .. £140
56 **31** 2½d. red-brown (Die I) (2.82) .... 27·00 12·00
57 4d. grey (Die I) (10.84) .... 25·00 3·00
a. Bisected (2d.) (on cover) .... † £5000

For illustration of "top left triangle detached" variety see above No. 7 of Montserrat.

1887 (July)–**89**. Wmk Crown CA.

(a) P 12.
58 **1** 1d. crimson-lake .... 22·00 5·50
a. Imperf between (horiz pair) .. £22000
b. Throat flaw .... 60·00 14·00
x. Wmk reversed .... 16·00 3·75

(b) P 14.
59 **1** 6d. yellow-brown (2.89) .... 3·50 3·75
s. Optd "Specimen" .... 50·00
60 1s. sepia .... 5·00 3·50

During a shortage of 1d. stamps a supply of JAMAICA No. 27 was sent to the Turks and Caicos Islands in April 1889 and used until replaced by No. 61. *Price from £225 used.*

1889 (May). *Surch at Grand Turk with T* **32**.
61 **31** 1d. on 2½d. red-brown .... 11·00 13·00
a. "One" omitted £1600
b. Bisected (½d.) (on cover) .... † £5000

No. 61a was caused by misplacement of the surcharge. Stamps from the same sheet can be found with the surcharge reading "Penny One".

Neck flaw (R. 3/2)

1889–93. Wmk Crown CA. P 14.
62 **1** 1d. crimson-lake (7.89) .... 5·50 4·50
a. Bisected (½d.) (on cover) .... † £4750
b. Throat flaw .... 20·00 21·00
c. Neck flaw .... 29·00 30·00
x. Wmk reversed .... 55·00
63 1d. lake .... 4·25 3·25
a. Bisected (½d.) (on cover) .... † £4750
b. Throat flaw .... 15·00 14·00
c. Neck flaw .... 24·00 22·00
64 1d. pale rosy lake .... 4·25 5·00
b. Throat flaw .... 15·00 24·00
c. Neck flaw .... 24·00 32·00
65 **31** 2½d. ultramarine (Die II) (4.93) ..... 3·75 3·00
s. Optd "Specimen" .... 50·00

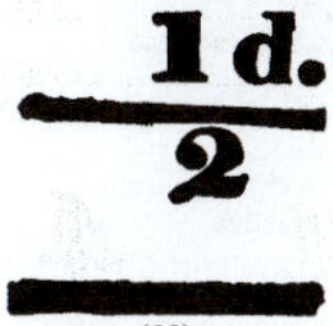

(33)

34

1893 (10 June). *No. 57 surch at Grand Turk with T* **33**.

Setting 1. Bars between "1d." and "2" separate, instead of continuous across the rows of stamps.
66 ½d. on 4d. grey £3000 £1300

Setting 2. Continuous bars. Thin and thick bar 10¾ mm apart. "2" under the "1".
67 ½d. on 4d. grey £200 £140

Setting 3. As last, but bars 11¾ mm apart.
68 ½d. on 4d. grey £160 £180

Setting 4. Bars 11 mm apart. Five out of the six varieties in the strip have the "2" below the space between the "1" and "d".
69 ½d. on 4d. grey £200 £170

There is a fifth setting, but the variation is slight.

(Typo D.L.R.)

1893–95. Wmk Crown CA. P 14.
70 **31** ½d. dull green (Die II) (12.93) ...... 3·50 2·75
71 4d. dull purple & ultramarine (Die II) (5.95) .... 15·00 17·00
72 **34** 5d. olive-green and carmine (6.94) .... 7·00 17·00
a. Bisected (2½d.) (on cover) ..... † £4750
70/2 *Set of* 3 .... 23·00 32·00
71s/2s Optd "Specimen" *Set of* 2 .... £100

TURKS AND CAICOS ISLANDS

35 Badge of the Islands

36 Badge of the Islands

The dates on the stamps have reference to the political separation from Bahamas.

(Recess D.L.R.)

1900 (10 Nov)–**04**. Wmk Crown CA (½d. to 1s.) or Wmk Crown CC (2s., 3s.). P 14.
101 **35** ½d. green .... 2·75 4·00
x. Wmk reversed ....
102 1d. red .... 3·50 75
w. Wmk inverted .... 95·00
103 2d. sepia .... 1·00 1·25
w. Wmk inverted ....
x. Wmk reversed £110
104 2½d. blue .... 8·00 16·00
a. Greyish blue (1904) .... 1·75 1·00
aw. Wmk inverted .... 90·00
ay. Wmk inverted and reversed ... — £160
105 4d. orange .... 3·75 7·00
106 6d. dull mauve .... 2·50 6·50
107 1s. purple-brown .... 3·25 19·00
108 **36** 2s. purple .... 40·00 60·00
109 3s. lake .... 55·00 80·00
101/9 *Set of* 9 .... £100 £160
101s/9s Optd "Specimen" *Set of* 9 .... £225

1905–08. Wmk Mult Crown CA. P 14.
110 **35** ½d. green .... 5·00 15
111 1d. red .... 16·00 50
w. Wmk inverted ....
112 3d. purple/*yellow* (1908) .... 2·25 6·00
s. Optd "Specimen" .... 50·00
w. Wmk inverted ....
110/12 *Set of* 3 .... 21·00 6·00

37 Turk's-head Cactus

38

(Recess D.L.R.)

1909 (2 Sept)–**11**. Wmk Mult Crown CA. P 14.
115 **37** ¼d. rosy mauve (1910) .... 1·75 1·00
w. Wmk inverted ....
116 ¼d. red (1911) 60 40
w. Wmk inverted ....
117 **38** ½d. yellow-green 75 40
w. Wmk inverted ....
x. Wmk reversed .... 60·00
y. Wmk inverted and reversed ...
118 1d. red .... 1·25 40
119 2d. greyish slate .... 3·50 1·40
120 2½d. blue .... 4·50 3·25
w. Wmk inverted ....
x. Wmk reversed .... 70·00 80·00
121 3d. purple/*yellow* .... 2·50 2·00
122 4d. red/*yellow* .... 3·25 7·00
123 6d. purple .... 7·00 5·00
124 1s. black/*green* .... 7·00 7·50
w. Wmk inverted ....
125 2s. red/*green* .... 35·00 50·00
126 3s. black/*red* .... 35·00 40·00
115/26 *Set of* 12 .... 90·00 £110
115s/26s Optd "Specimen" *Set of* 12 .... £250

See also Nos. 154 and 162.

39

WAR TAX
(40)

1913 (1 Apr)–**21**. Wmk Mult Crown CA. P 14.
129 **39** ½d. green .... 50 1·75
w. Wmk inverted ....
130 1d. red .... 1·00 2·25
a. Bright rose-scarlet .... 1·10 2·00
ax. Wmk reversed .... 60·00
b. Rose-carmine (1918) .... 3·75 6·00
131 2d. greyish slate .... 2·25 3·50
132 2½d. ultramarine .... 2·25 3·00
aw. Wmk inverted ....
b. Bright blue (1918) .... 4·00 2·75
133 3d. purple/*yellow* .... 2·25 11·00
a. On lemon .... 16·00
b. On yellow-buff .... 4·00 9·50
c. On orange-buff .... 1·75
cx. Wmk reversed .... 80·00
d. On pale yellow .... 2·25 9·00
134 4d. red/*yellow* .... 1·00 9·50
a. On orange-buff .... 1·60 7·50
ab. "A" of "CA" missing from wmk ....
as. Optd "Specimen" .... 48·00
b. Carmine on pale yellow .... 7·50 16·00
135 5d. pale olive-green (18.5.16) .... 6·50 22·00
136 6d. dull purple .... 2·50 3·50
w. Wmk inverted ....
x. Wmk reversed ....
137 1s. brown-orange .... 1·50 5·00
w. Wmk inverted ....
138 2s. red/*blue-green* .... 9·00 28·00
a. On greenish white (1919) .... 24·00 70·00
b. On emerald (3.21) .... 48·00 75·00
bs. Optd "Specimen" .... 50·00
bx. Wmk reversed £170
139 3s. black/*red* .... 15·00 26·00
129/39 *Set of* 11 .... 38·00 £100
129s/39s Optd "Specimen" *Set of* 11 .... £180

1917 (3 Jan). *Optd with T* **40** *at bottom of stamp.*
140 **39** 1d. red .... 10 1·50
a. Opt double £180 £250
ab. Opt double (in horiz pair with normal) £400
b. "TAX" omitted ....
c. "WAR TAX" omitted in vert pair with normal £600
d. Opt inverted at top .... 65·00 85·00
e. Opt double, one inverted £110
f. Opt inverted only, in pair with No. 140e £600
141 3d. purple/*yellow-buff* .... 1·25 6·00
a. Opt double .... 95·00
b. Purple/lemon .... 2·50 8·50
ba. Opt double .... 95·00 £120
bb. Opt double, one inverted £325

The overprint was in a setting of 60, applied twice to the sheets of 120. One sheet of the 1d. exists with the right-hand impression of the setting misplaced one row to the left so that stamps in vertical row 6 show a double overprint (No. 140ab). It appears that the right-hand vertical row on this sheet had the overprint applied at a third operation.

In Nos. 140e/f the inverted overprint is at foot and reads "TAX WAR" owing to displacement. No. 140e also exists with "WAR" omitted from the inverted overprint.

In both values of the first printings the stamp in the bottom left-hand corner of the sheet has a long "T" in "TAX", and on the first stamp of the sixth row the "X" is damaged and looks like a reversed "K". The long "T" was subsequently converted.

1917 (Oct). *Second printing with overprint at top or in middle of stamp.*
143 **39** 1d. red .... 10 1·25
a. Inverted opt at bottom or centre .... 50·00
c. Opt omitted (in pair with normal) £600
d. Opt double, one at top, one at bottom .... 65·00
e. As d., but additional opt in top margin £120
f. Pair, one as d., the other normal £300
g. Pair, one opt inverted, one normal £600
h. Double opt at top (in pair with normal) £275
i. Opt double .... 48·00 60·00
144 3d. purple/*yellow* .... 60 1·75
a. Opt double .... 45·00
b. Opt double, one inverted £325
c. Purple/lemon .... 3·50

1918. *Overprinted with T* **40**.
145 **39** 3d. purple/*yellow* (R.) .... 12·00 35·00
a. Opt double £325

WAR TAX (41)

WAR TAX (42)

WAR TAX (43)

1918. *Optd with T* **41** *in London by D.L.R.*
146 **39** 1d. rose-carmine .... 20 1·25
a. Bright rose-scarlet .... 15 1·25
aw. Wmk inverted .... 70·00
147 3d. purple/*yellow* .... 3·50 4·00
146/7 Optd "Specimen" *Set of* 2 .... 80·00

1919. *Optd with T* **41** *in London by D.L.R.*
148 **39** 3d. purple/*orange-buff* (R.) .... 10 3·50
s. Optd "Specimen" .... 40·00

1919. *Local overprint. T* **40**, *in violet.*
149 **39** 1d. bright rose-scarlet .... 30 3·75
a. "WAR" omitted £150
b. Opt double .... 21·00
c. Opt double in pair with normal £120
d. Opt double, one inverted ....
e. Rose-carmine .... 7·00 15·00
ea. Opt double ....
w. Wmk inverted .... 32·00

1919. *Optd with T* **42**.
150 **39** 1d. scarlet .... 10 1·00
a. Opt double £150 £180
b. Opt double, one albino and reversed ....
151 3d. purple/*orange-buff* .... 30 2·75
w. Wmk inverted .... 32·00
x. Wmk reversed .... 32·00

1919 (17 Dec). *Optd with T* **43**.
152 **39** 1d. scarlet .... 20 2·50
a. Opt inverted ....
153 3d. purple/*orange-buff* .... 50 2·75
w. Wmk inverted .... 32·00
x. Wmk reversed .... 25·00
y. Wmk inverted and reversed ... 12·00

The two bottom rows of this setting have the words "WAR" and "TAX" about 1 mm further apart.

1921 (23 Apr). Wmk Mult Script CA. P 14.

154	**37**	¼d. rose-red	2·75	17·00
155	**39**	½d. green	2·75	5·50
156		1d. carmine-red	1·00	5·50
157		2d. slate-grey	1·00	19·00
		y. Wmk inverted and reversed	70·00	
158		2½d. bright blue	1·75	7·50
		x. Wmk reversed	£100	
159		5d. sage-green	8·00	55·00
160		6d. purple	6·50	55·00
		w. Wmk inverted		
		x. Wmk reversed	75·00	
161		1s. brown-orange	7·50	30·00
154/61 *Set of* 8			28·00	£170
154s/61s Optd "Specimen" *Set of* 8			£140	

44

45

(Recess D.L.R.)

1922 (20 Nov)–**26**. P 14.

(a) Wmk Mult Script CA.

162	**37**	¼d. black (11.10.26)	80	1·00
163	**44**	½d. yellow-green	2·75	3·25
		a. Bright green	2·75	3·25
		b. Apple-green	5·50	10·00
164		1d. brown	50	3·25
165		1½d. scarlet (24.11.25)	6·50	17·00
166		2d. slate	50	5·00
167		2½d. purple/*pale yellow*	50	1·75
168		3d. bright blue	50	5·00
169		4d. red/*pale yellow*	1·25	16·00
		ax. Wmk reversed	70·00	
		b. Carmine/pale yellow	4·50	16·00
170		5d. sage-green	85	22·00
		y. Wmk inverted and reversed	80·00	
171		6d. purple	70	7·50
		x. Wmk reversed	80·00	
172		1s. brown-orange	80	20·00
173		2s. red/*emerald*	2·00	9·00

(b) Wmk Mult Crown CA.

174	**44**	2s. red/*emerald* (24.11.25)	25·00	75·00
175		3s. black/*red* (24.11.25)	5·00	28·00
162/75 *Set of* 14			42·00	£190
162s/75s Optd "Specimen" *Set of* 14			£200	

1928 (1 Mar). *Inscr* "POSTAGE & REVENUE". Wmk Mult Script CA. P 14.

176	**45**	½d. green	75	50
177		1d. brown	75	70
178		1½d. scarlet	75	3·25
179		2d. grey	75	50
180		2½d. purple/*yellow*	75	5·00
181		3d. bright blue	75	7·50
182		6d. purple	75	7·50
183		1s. brown-orange	3·75	7·50
184		2s. red/*emerald*	6·00	35·00
185		5s. green/*yellow*	11·00	35·00
186		10s. purple/*blue*	50·00	£100
176/86 *Set of* 11			70·00	£180
176s/86s Optd "Specimen" *Set of* 11			£170	

1935 (6 May). *Silver Jubilee. As Nos. 91/4 of Antigua, but ptd by Waterlow.* P 11×12.

187	½d. black and green	30	75
	k. Kite and vertical log	42·00	
	l. Kite and horizontal log	38·00	48·00
188	3d. brown and deep blue	2·75	4·50
	k. Kite and vertical log	90·00	£120
189	6d. light blue and olive-green	1·75	4·75
	k. Kite and vertical log	90·00	£120
190	1s. slate and purple	1·75	3·25
	k. Kite and vertical log	90·00	£130
187/90 *Set of* 4		6·00	12·00
187s/90s Perf "Specimen" *Set of* 4		95·00	

For illustrations of plate varieties see Omnibus section following Zanzibar.

1937 (12 May). *Coronation. As Nos. 95/7 of Antigua, but ptd by D.L.R.* P 14.

191	½d. myrtle-green	10	10
	a. Deep green	40·00	
192	2d. grey-black	65	65
193	3d. bright blue	65	65
191/3 *Set of* 3		1·25	1·25
191s/3s Perf "Specimen" *Set of* 3		85·00	

46 Raking Salt

47 Salt Industry

(Recess Waterlow)

1938 (18 June)–**45**. Wmk Mult Script CA. P 12½.

194	**46**	¼d. black	20	10
195		½d. yellowish green	4·25	15
		a. Deep green (6.11.44)	1·75	70
196		1d. red-brown	75	10
197		1½d. scarlet	75	15
198		2d. grey	1·00	30
199		2½d. yellow-orange	5·50	80
		a. Orange (6.11.44)	3·50	2·25
200		3d. bright blue	70	30
201		6d. mauve	16·00	2·25
201*a*		6d. sepia (9.2.45)	50	20
202		1s. yellow-bistre	4·75	9·00
202*a*		1s. grey-olive (9.2.45)	50	20
203	**47**	2s. deep rose-carmine	42·00	14·00
		a. Bright rose-carmine (6.11.44)	17·00	18·00
204		5s. yellowish green	50·00	22·00
		a. Deep green (6.11.44)	40·00	23·00
205		10s. bright violet	22·00	7·50
194/205 *Set of* 14			£100	50·00
194s/205s Perf "Specimen" *Set of* 14			£250	

1946 (4 Nov). *Victory. As Nos. 110/11 of Antigua.*

206	2d. black	10	15
207	3d. blue	15	15
206s/7s Perf "Specimen" *Set of* 2		75·00	

1948 (13 Sept). *Royal Silver Wedding. As Nos. 112/13 of Antigua.*

208	1d. red-brown	15	10
209	10s. mauve	9·50	14·00

50 Badge of the Islands

51 Flag of Turks and Caicos Islands

52 Map of islands

53 Queen Victoria and King George VI

(Recess Waterlow)

1948 (14 Dec). *Centenary of Separation from Bahamas. T* **50/53**. Wmk Mult Script CA. P 12½.

210	**50**	½d. blue-green	1·25	15
211		2d. carmine	1·25	15
212	**51**	3d. blue	1·75	15
213	**52**	6d. violet	1·25	30
214	**53**	2s. black and bright blue	1·25	2·00
215		5s. black and green	1·50	4·75
216		10s. black and brown	2·25	4·75
210/16 *Set of* 7			9·50	11·00

1949 (10 Oct). *75th Anniv of U.P.U. As Nos. 114/17 of Antigua.*

217	2½d. red-orange	20	1·60
218	3d. deep blue	2·25	60
219	6d. brown	30	75
220	1s. olive	20	35
217/20 *Set of* 4		2·75	3·00

54 Bulk Salt Loading

55 Salt Cay

56 Caicos mail

57 Grand Turk

58 Sponge diving

59 South Creek

60 Map

61 Grand Turk Light

62 Government House

63 Cockburn Harbour

64 Government offices

65 Loading salt

66 Dependency's Badge

(Recess Waterlow)

1950 (1 Aug). *T* **54/66**. Wmk Mult Script CA. P 12½.

221	**54**	½d. green	85	40
222	**55**	1d. red-brown	80	75
223	**56**	1½d. deep carmine	1·25	55
224	**57**	2d. red-orange	1·00	40
225	**58**	2½d. grey-olive	1·25	50
226	**59**	3d. bright blue	60	40
227	**60**	4d. black and rose	2·75	70
228	**61**	6d. black and blue	2·00	50
229	**62**	1s. black and blue-green	1·25	40
230	**63**	1s.6d. black and scarlet	10·00	3·25
231	**64**	2s. emerald and ultramarine	3·00	4·50
232	**65**	5s. blue and black	18·00	8·50
233	**66**	10s. black and violet	20·00	18·00
221/33 *Set of* 13			55·00	35·00

1953 (2 June). *Coronation. As No. 120 of Antigua, but ptd by B.W. & Co.*

234	2d. black and orange-red	60	1·25

67 M.V. *Kirksons*

(Recess Waterlow)

1955 (1 Feb). *T* **67** *and similar horiz design*. Wmk Mult Script CA. P 12½.

235	5d. black and bright green	60	70
236	8d. black and brown	2·50	70

Design:—8d. Greater Flamingoes in flight.

69 Queen Elizabeth II (after Annigoni)

70 Bonefish

82 Dependency's Badge

(Recess B.W.)

1957 (25 Nov). *T* **69/70**, **82** *and similar horiz designs as T* **70**. W w **12**. P 13½×14 (1d.), 14 (10s.) or 13½ (others).

237	1d. deep blue and carmine	30	20
238	1½d. grey-green and orange	15	30
239	2d. red-brown and olive	15	15
240	2½d. carmine and green	20	15
241	3d. turquoise-blue and purple	20	15
242	4d. lake and black	1·25	15
243	5d. slate-green and brown	1·25	40
244	6d. carmine-rose and blue	2·00	55
245	8d. vermilion and black	3·25	20
246	1s. deep blue and black	1·25	10
247	1s.6d. sepia and deep ultramarine	13·00	1·50
248	2s. deep ultramarine and brown	13·00	2·50
249	5s. black and carmine	7·00	2·00
250	10s. black and purple	18·00	8·00
237/250 *and* 253 *Set of* 15		90·00	29·00

Designs:—2d. Red Grouper; 2½d. Spiny Lobster; 3d. Albacore; 4d. Mutton Snapper; 5d. Permit; 6d. Queen or Pink Conch; 8d. Greater Flamingoes; 1s. Spanish Mackerel; 1s.6d. Salt Cay; 2s. *Uakon* (Caicos sloop); 5s. Cable Office.

83 Map of the Turks and Caicos Islands

(Photo D.L.R.)

1959 (4 July). *New Constitution*. Wmk Mult Script CA. P 13½×14.

251	**83**	6d. deep olive and light orange	50	70
252		8d. violet and light orange	50	40

84 Brown Pelican

(Des Mrs. S. Hurd. Photo Harrison)

1960 (1 Nov). W w **12**. P 14×14½.

253	**84**	£1 sepia and deep red	40·00	16·00

CROWN COLONY

1963 (4 June). *Freedom from Hunger. As No. 146 of Antigua.*

254	8d. carmine	30	15

1963 (2 Sept). *Red Cross Centenary. As Nos. 147/8 of Antigua.*

255	2d. red and black	15	50
256	8d. red and blue	30	50

1964 (23 Apr). *400th Birth Anniv of William Shakespeare. As No. 164 of Antigua.*

257	8d. green	30	10

1965 (17 May). *I.T.U. Centenary. As Nos. 166/7 of Antigua.*

258	1d. vermilion and brown	10	10
259	2s. light emerald and turquoise-blue	20	20

1965 (25 Oct). *International Co-operation Year. As Nos. 168/9 of Antigua.*

260	1d. reddish purple and turquoise-green	10	15
261	8d. deep bluish green and lavender	20	15

1966 (24 Jan). *Churchill Commemoration. As Nos. 170/3 of Antigua.*

262	1d. new blue	10	10
263	2d. deep green	20	10
264	8d. brown	35	10
	a. Gold ptg double	£130	
265	1s.6d. bluish violet	50	1·10
262/5 Set of 4		1·00	1·25

1966 (4 Feb). *Royal Visit. As Nos. 271/2 of Bahamas.*

266	8d. black and ultramarine	40	10
267	1s. 6d. black and magenta	60	20

85 Andrew Symmer going ashore

(Des V. Whiteley. Photo D.L.R.)

1966 (1 Oct). *Bicentenary of "Ties with Britain" T* **85** *and similar horiz designs.* P 13½.

268	1d. deep blue and orange	10	10
269	8d. red, blue and orange-yellow	20	15
270	1s.6d. multicoloured	25	20
268/70 *Set of 3*		50	40

Designs:—8d. Andrew Symmer and Royal Warrant; 1s.6d. Arms and Royal Cypher.

1966 (1 Dec). *20th Anniv of U.N.E.S.C.O. As Nos. 196/8 of Antigua.*

271	1d. slate-violet, red, yellow and orange	10	10
272	8d. orange-yellow, violet and deep olive	20	10
273	1s.6d. black, bright purple and orange	30	40
271/3 *Set of 3*		35	50

88 Turk's-head Cactus

89 Boat-building

90 Arms of Turks and Caicos Islands

91 Queen Elizabeth II

(Des V. Whiteley. Photo Harrison)

1967 (1 Feb). *Designs as T* **88/91**. W w **12**. P 14½×14 (vert) or 14×14½ (horiz).

274	1d. olive-yellow, vermilion and bright bluish violet	10	10
275	1½d. brown and orange-yellow	1·00	10
276	2d. deep slate and deep orange-yellow	20	10
277	3d. agate and dull green	20	10
278	4d. bright mauve, black and turquoise	2·50	10
279	6d. sepia and new blue	1·00	10
280	8d. yellow, turquoise-blue and deep blue	40	10
281	1s. maroon and turquoise	20	10
282	1s.6d. orange-yellow, lake-brown and deep turquoise-blue	50	20
283	2s. multicoloured	60	1·75
284	3s. maroon and turquoise-blue	75	40
285	5s. ochre, blue and new blue	1·25	2·75
286	10s. multicoloured	2·25	3·00
287	£1 Prussian blue, silver and crimson	3·50	7·00
274/287 *Set of 14*		13·00	14·00

Designs: *Vert as T* **88**—2d. Donkey; 3d. Sisal industry 6d. Salt industry; 8d. Skin-diving; 1s.6d. Water-skiing. *Horiz as T* **89**—4d. Conch industry; 1s. Fishing; 2s. Crawfish industry; 3s. Maps of Turks and Caicos Islands and West Indies; 5s. Fishing industry.

102 Turks Islands 1d. Stamp of 1867

(Des R. Granger Barrett. Photo Harrison)

1967 (1 May). *Stamp Centenary. T* **102** *and similar horiz designs.* W w **12**. P 14½.

288	1d. black and light magenta	15	10
	w. Wmk inverted	40·00	
289	6d. black and bluish grey	25	15
290	1s. black and turquoise-blue	25	15
288/90 *Set of 3*		60	30

Designs:—6d. Queen Elizabeth "stamp" and Turks Islands 6d. stamp of 1867; 1s. Turks Islands 1s. stamp of 1867.

104 Human Rights Emblem and Charter

(Des R. Granger Barrett. Photo Harrison)

1968 (1 Apr). *Human Rights Year.* W w **12**. P 14×14½.

291	**104**	1d. multicoloured	10	10
292		8d. multicoloured	15	15
293		1s.6d. multicoloured	15	15
291/3 *Set of 3*			30	30

105 Dr Martin Luther King and "Freedom March"

(Des V. Whiteley. Photo Harrison)

1968 (1 Oct). *Martin Luther King Commemoration.* W w **12**. P 14×14½.

294	**105**	2d. yellow-brown, blackish brown and deep blue	10	10
295		8d. yellow-brown, blackish brown and lake	15	15
296		1s.6d. yellow-brown, blackish brown and violet	15	15
294/6 *Set of 3*			30	30

(New Currency. 100 cents = 1 dollar)

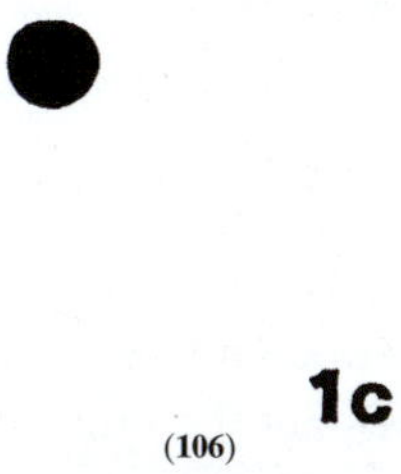

(106)

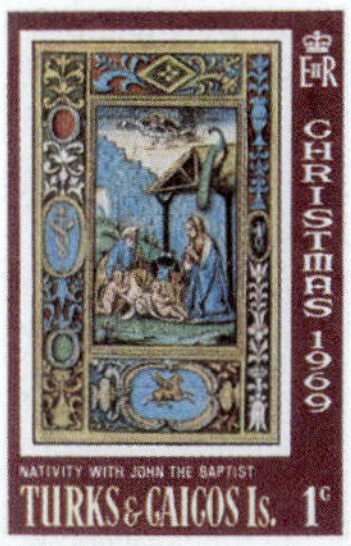

107 "The Nativity with John the Baptist"

1969 (8 Sept)–**71**. *Decimal currency. Nos. 274/87 surch as T* **106** *by Harrison & Sons, and new value (¼c.) as T* **90**.

297	¼c. pale greenish grey and multicoloured	10	10
	a. Bronze-green and multicoloured (2.2.71)	1·25	30
298	1c. on 1d.olive-yellow, vermillion and bright bluish violet	10	10
	a. Wmk sideways	10	10
299	2c. on 2d. deep slate and deep orange-yellow	10	10
	a. Wmk sideways	10	10
300	3c. on 3d. agate and dull green	10	10
	a. Wmk sideways	10	10
301	4c. on 4d. bright mauve, black and turquoise	1·50	10
302	5c. on 6d. sepia and new blue	10	10
	a. Wmk sideways	10	10
303	7c. on 8d. yellow, turquoise-blue and deep blue	10	10
	a. Wmk sideways	10	10
304	8c. on 1½d. brown and orange-yellow	10	10
	w. Wmk inverted	23·00	
305	10c. on 1s. maroon and turquoise	20	10
306	15c. on 1s.6d. orange-yellow, lake-brown and deep turquoise-blue	25	10
	a. Wmk sideways	20	25
307	20c. on 2s. multicoloured	30	25
308	30c. on 3s. maroon and turquoise-blue	55	35
309	50c. on 5s. ochre, blue and new blue	1·25	45
310	$1 on 10s. multicoloured	2·50	1·00
311	$2 on £1 Prussian blue, silver and crimson	2·75	11·00
	a. Wmk sideways	2·00	3·75
297/311 *Set of 15*		8·00	12·00
298a/311a *Set of 7*		2·25	3·25

The 4, 8, 10, 20, 30, 50c., and $1 exist with PVA gum as well as gum arabic.

No. 311 was only on sale through the Crown Agents.

(Des adapted by V. Whiteley. Litho D.L.R.).

1969 (20 Oct). *Christmas. Scenes from 16th-cent Book of Hours. T* **107** *and similar vert design. Multicoloured.* W w **12**. P 13×12½.

312	1c. Type **107**	10	10
313	3c. "The Flight into Egypt"	10	10
314	15c. Type **107**	15	10
315	30c. As 3c.	25	20
312/15 *Set of 4*		40	40

109 Coat of Arms

110 "Christ bearing the Cross"

(Des L. Curtis. Litho B.W.)

1970 (2 Feb). *New Constitution. Multicoloured; background colours given.* W w **12** (sideways). P 13×12½.

316	**109**	7c. brown	20	25
317		35c. deep violet-blue	35	25

For similar $10 design, but without commemorative inscription, see No. 946.

(Des, recess and lithe Enschedé)

1970 (17 Mar). *Easter. Details from the "Small Engraved Passion" by Dürer. T* **110** *and similar vert designs.* W w **12** (sideways). P 13×13½.

318	5c. olive-grey and blue	10	10
319	7c. olive-grey and vermilion	10	10
320	50c. olive-grey and red-brown	60	1·00
318/20 *Set of 3*		70	1·10

Designs:—7c. "Christ on the Cross"; 50c. "The Lamentation of Christ".

113 Dickens and Scene from Oliver Twist

(Des Sylvia Goaman. Recess and litho D.L.R.)

1970 (17 June). *Death Centenary of Charles Dickens. T* **113** *and similar horiz designs.* W w **12** (sideways). P 13.

321	1c. black and yellow-brown/*yellow*	10	50
322	3c. black and Prussian blue/*flesh*	10	40
323	15c. black and grey blue/*flesh*	20	20
324	30c. black and drab/*blue*	40	40
321/4 *Set of 4*		60	1·40

Designs (each incorporating portrait of Dickens as in T **113**, and a scene from one of his novels):—3c. *A Christmas Carol*; 15c. *Pickwick Papers*; 30c. *The Old Curiosity Shop*.

114 Ambulance—1870

(Des Harrison. Litho B.W.)

1970 (4 Aug). *Centenary of British Red Cross. T* **114** *and similar horiz design. Multicoloured.* W w **12**. P 13½×14.

325	1c. Type **114**	10	20
326	5c. Ambulance—1970	20	10
	a. Wmk sideways	20	10
	ab. Grey omitted	£325	
327	15c. Type **114**	40	15
	a. Wmk sideways	40	10
328	30c. As 5c.	50	20
	a. Wmk sideways	55	40
325/8 *Set of 4*		1·00	55

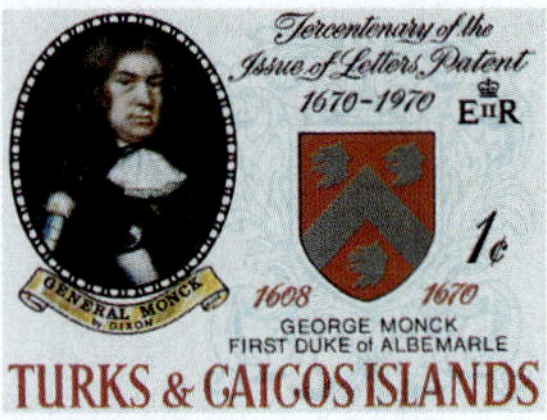

115 Duke of Albemarle and Coat of Arms

(Des V. Whiteley. Litho Enschedé)

1970 (1 Dec). *Tercentenary of Issue of Letters Patent. T* **115** *and similar horiz design. Multicoloured.* W w **12**. P 12½×13½.

329	1c. Type **115**	10	30
330	8c. Arms of Charles II and Elizabeth II	20	40
331	10c. Type **115**	20	15
332	35c. As 8c.	40	75
329/32	*Set of* 4	80	1·40

Uganda

PRICES FOR STAMPS ON COVER TO 1945

The type-written stamps of Uganda, Nos. 2/53, are very rare used on cover.

Nos. 54/60	*from* × 20
No. 61	—
Nos. 70/5	*from* × 12
No. 76	—
Nos. 84/90	*from* × 20
No. 91	—
Nos. 92/3	*from* × 40

PROTECTORATE

Following a period of conflict between Islamic, Protestant and Roman Catholic factions, Uganda was declared to be in the British sphere of influence by the Anglo-German Agreement of July 1890. The British East Africa Company exercised a variable degree of control until 27 August 1894 when the country was declared a British Protectorate.

Before the introduction of Nos. 84/91 the stamps of Uganda were only valid for internal postage. Letters for overseas were franked with British East Africa issues on arrival at Mombasa.

(Currency. 200 cowries = 1 rupee)

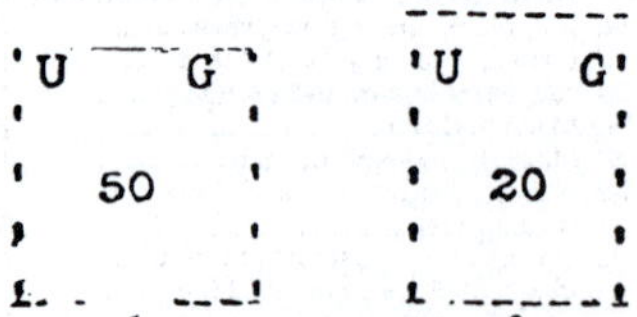

1 2

TYPE-WRITTEN STAMPS. Nos. 2/53 were type-written by the Revd. E. Millar at Mengo for the Uganda administration. For all "printings" a thin laid paper was used, and all issues were imperforate and ungummed. The laid lines are invariably horizontal, with the exception of No. 20a.

The original typewriter used had wide letters, but in late April, 1895 Millar obtained a new machine on which the type face was in a narrower fount.

Each sheet was made up of whatever values were required at the time, so that different values can be found *se-tenant* or *tête-bêche*. These last were caused by the paper being inverted in the machine so that space at the foot could be utilised.

For the first issue the sheets were of 117 (9×13), but with the introduction of the narrower width (Nos. 17 onwards) a larger number of stamps per sheet, 143 (11×13), was adopted.

The manuscript provisionals, Nos. 9*a*/16 come from the Mission at Ngogwe, most of the manuscript surcharges including the initials of the Revd. G. R. Blackledge stationed there.

1895 (20 Mar). *Wide letters. Wide stamps, 20 to 26 mm wide.*

2	1	10 (c.) black	£4000	£2250
4		20 (c.) black	£6500	£1800
		a. "U A" for "U G"	†	£5000
6		30 (c.) black	£1800	£1600
7		40 (c.) black	£5500	£2000
8		50 (c.) black	£1400	£1100
		a. "U A" for "U G"	†	£7000
9		60 (c.) black	£2500	£2250

It is now believed that the 5, 15 and 25 cowries values in this width, previously Nos. 1, 3 and 5, do not exist.

A strip of three of No. 2 is known on cover of which one stamp has the value "10" altered to "5" in manuscript and initialled "E.M."

1895 (May). *Wide stamps with pen-written surcharges, in black.*

9*a*	1	10 on 30 (c.) black	†	£70000
10		10 on 50 (c.) black	†	£70000
11		15 on 10 (c.) black	†	£50000
12		15 on 20 (c.) black	†	£70000
13		15 on 40 (c.) black	†	£60000
14		15 on 50 (c.) black	†	£70000
15		25 on 50 (c.) black	†	£70000
16		50 on 60 (c.) black	†	£70000

1895 (April). *Wide letters. Narrow stamps, 16 to 18 mm wide.*

17	1	5 (c.) black	£3250	£1300
18		10 (c.) black	£3250	£1600
19		15 (c.) black	£2000	£1500
20		20 (c.) black	£3250	£1500
		a. Vertically laid paper	†	£5000
21		25 (c.) black	£1500	£1500
22		30 (c.) black	£8500	£8500
23		40 (c.) black	£8000	£8000
24		50 (c.) black	£3750	£4250
25		60 (c.) black	£7500	£8500

A single used example of No. 20a has been seen. Nos. 2/53 otherwise show the laid lines horizontal.

1895 (May). *Narrow letters. Narrow stamps 16 to 18 mm wide.*

26	2	5 (c.) black	£1300
27		10 (c.) black	£1400
28		15 (c.) black	£1400
29		20 (c.) black	£1100
30		25 (c.) black	£1200
31		30 (c.) black	£1500
32		40 (c.) black	£1300
33		50 (c.) black	£1400
34		60 (c.) black	£1900

1895 (Nov). *Narrow letters. Narrow stamps, 16–18 mm wide. Change of colour.*

35	2	5 (c.) violet	£650	£650
36		10 (c.) violet	£600	£650
37		15 (c.) violet	£900	£600
38		20 (c.) violet	£425	£300
		a. "G U" for "U G"		
39		25 (c.) violet	£1500	£1500
40		30 (c.) violet	£2000	£1000
41		40 (c.) violet	£1800	£1400
42		50 (c.) violet	£1800	£1500
43		100 (c.) violet	£2500	£3000

Stamps of 35 (c.) and 45 (c.) have been recorded in violet, on vertically laid paper. They were never prepared for postal use, and did not represent a postal rate, but were type-written to oblige a local official. (*Price* £2750 *each, unused*)

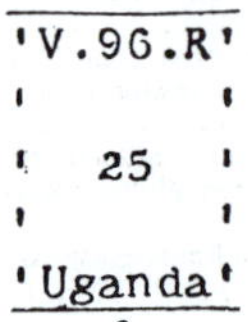

3

1896 (June).

44	3	5 (c.) violet	£650	£1000
45		10 (c.) violet	£750	£600
46		15 (c.) violet	£650	£750
47		20 (c.) violet	£300	£225
48		25 (c.) violet	£550	£900
49		30 (c.) violet	£600	£800
50		40 (c.) violet	£800	£850
51		50 (c.) violet	£650	£700
52		60 (c.) violet	£1500	£2000
53		100 (c.) violet	£1400	£2000

(New Currency. 16 annas = 1 rupee)

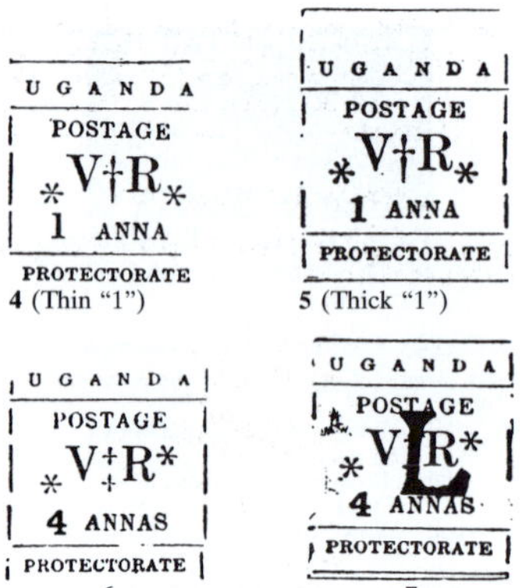

4 (Thin "1") 5 (Thick "1")

6 7

In the 2a. and 3a. the dagger points upwards; the stars in the 2a. are level with the top of "VR". The 8a. is as T **6** but with left star at top and right star at foot. The 1r. has three stars at foot. The 5r. has central star raised and the others at foot.

(Type-set by the Revd. F. Rowling at Lubwa's, in Usoga)

1896 (7 Nov). *Thick white wove paper (Nos. 54/8) or thin yellowish paper ruled with vertical lines 9 mm apart (Nos. 59/61).*

(a) Types **4/6**.

54	4	1a. black	£110	95·00
		a. Small "o" in "POSTAGE"	£600	£550
55	5	1a. black	20·00	25·00
		a. Small "o" in "POSTAGE"	80·00	£100
56	6	2a. black	26·00	30·00
		a. Small "o" in "POSTAGE"	£100	£120
57		3a. black	28·00	35·00
		a. Small "o" in "POSTAGE"	£120	£150
58		4a. black	28·00	32·00
		a. Small "o" in "POSTAGE"	£100	£120
59		8a. black	30·00	35·00
		a. Small "o' in "POSTAGE"	£130	£150
60		1r. black	75·00	95·00
		a. Small "o" in "POSTAGE"	£300	£425
61		5r. black	£250	£350
		a. Small "o" in "POSTAGE"	£800	£1000

(b) Optd "L", in black as in T **7** *for local use, by a postal official, R. R. Racey, at Kampala.*

70	4	1a. black	£190	£170
		a. Small "o" in "POSTAGE"	£1400	£1100
71	6	2a. black	£110	£120
		a. Small "o" in "POSTAGE"	£500	£550
72		3a. black	£250	£300
		a. Small "o" in "POSTAGE"	£1500	£1800
73		4a. black	£100	£160
		a. Small "o" in "POSTAGE"	£550	
74		8a. black	£190	£225
		a. Small "o" in "POSTAGE"	£1300	£1500
75		1r. black	£375	£425
		a. Small "o" in "POSTAGE"	£1800	
76		5r. black	£20000	£20000

Tête-bêche pairs of all values may be found owing to the settings of 16 (4×4) being printed side by side or above one another. They are worth a premium. The variety with small "O" occurs on R. 3/1.

8 9

UGANDA
(10)

(Recess D.L.R.)

1898 (Nov)–**1902**. P 14.

(a) Wmk Crown CA.

84	8	1a. scarlet	2·75	2·75
		a. Carmine-rose (1902)	2·00	1·25
86		2a. red-brown	4·50	7·50
87		3a. pale grey	14·00	30·00
		a. Bluish grey	15·00	15·00
88		4a. deep green	8·00	8·00
89		8a. pale olive	9·50	26·00
		a. Grey-green	18·00	38·00

(b) Wmk Crown CC.

90	9	1r. dull blue	45·00	48·00
		a. Bright blue	50·00	55·00
91		5r. brown	75·00	£110
84/91		*Set of* 7	£140	£190
84s/91s		Optd "Specimen" *Set of* 7	£160	

On 1 April 1901 the postal administrations of British East Africa and Uganda were merged. Subsequent issues to 1962 are listed under KENYA, UGANDA and TANGANYIKA.

1902 (Feb). *T* **11** *of British East Africa (Kenya, Uganda, and Tanganyika) optd with T* **10**.

92	½a. yellow-green	2·00	1·40
	a. Opt omitted (in pair with normal)	£4500	
	b. Opt inverted (at foot)	£2000	
	c. Opt double	£2250	
	x. Wmk reversed		
93	2½a. deep blue (R.)	2·75	3·00
	a. Opt double	£600	
	b. Inverted "S" (R. 1/1)	75·00	85·00
	x. Wmk reversed	£250	
	y. Wmk inverted and reversed	£250	

The Eastern Province of Uganda was transferred to British East Africa on 1 April 1902.

SELF-GOVERNMENT

(New Currency. 100 cents = 1 East African, later Uganda shilling)

11 Ripon Falls and Speke Memorial

(Des S. Scott. Recess B.W.)

1962 (28 July). *Centenary of Speke's Discovery of Source of the Nile.* W w **12**. P 14.

95	11	30c. black and red	15	25
96		50c. black and slate-violet	15	10
97		1s.30 black and green	30	25
98		2s.50 black and blue	2·25	2·25
95/8		*Set of* 4	2·50	2·50

INDEPENDENT

12 Murchison Falls

13 Tobacco-growing

14 Mulago Hospital

(Des V. Whiteley. Photo Harrison)

1962 (9 Oct)–**64**. *Independence. Various designs as T* **12/14**. P 15×14 (5c. to 50c.) or 14½ (others).

99	5c. deep bluish green	10	10
100	10c. reddish brown	10	10
	a. Brown (coil)	10	10
	b. Deep yellow-brown (17.10.64)	10	10
101	15c. black, red and green	10	10
102	20c. plum and buff	10	10
103	30c. blue	10	10
104	50c. black and turquoise-green	10	10
105	1s. sepia, red and turquoise-green	55	10

106	1s.30 yellow-orange and violet	20	10
107	2s. black, carmine and light blue	40	60
108	5s. vermilion and deep green	5·50	1·00
109	10s. slate and chestnut	2·75	3·00
110	20s. brown and blue	2·75	16·00
99/110 *Set of* 12		11·00	19·00

Designs: *As T* **12/13**—10c. Tobacco growing, 15c. Coffee growing; 20c. Ankole cattle; 30c. Cotton; 50c. Mountains of the Moon. *As T* **14**—1s.30, Cathedrals and Mosque; 2s. Makerere College; 5s. Copper mining; 10s. Cement industry; 20s. Parliament Buildings.

15 South African Crowned Crane

(Photo Harrison)

1965 (20 Feb). *International Trade Fair, Kampala.* P 14½×14.

111	**15**	30c. multicoloured	10	10
112		1s.30 multicoloured	20	10

16 Black Bee Eater

17 African Jacana

18 Ruwenzori Turaco

(Des Mrs. R. Fennessy. Photo Harrison)

1965 (9 Oct). *Birds. Various designs as T* **16/18**. P 15×14 (5c., 15c., 20c., 40c., 50c.), 14×15 (10c., 30c., 65c.) or 14½ (others).

113	5c. multicoloured	10	10
114	10c. chestnut, black and light blue	10	10
115	15c. yellow and sepia	20	10
116	20c. multicoloured	20	10
117	30c. black and brown-red	1·50	10
118	40c. multicoloured	1·00	1·75
119	50c. grey-blue and reddish violet	25	10
	a. White bird (grey-blue omitted)	£400	
120	65c. orange-red, black and light grey	2·50	2·75
121	1s. multicoloured	50	10
122	1s.30 chestnut, black and yellow	5·50	30
123	2s.50 multicoloured	4·25	65
124	5s. multicoloured	7·00	4·00
125	10s. multicoloured	11·00	11·00
126	20s. multicoloured	21·00	38·00
113/26 *Set of* 14		48·00	48·00

Designs: *Vert as T* **16**—15c. Orange Weaver; 20c. Narina Trogon; 40c. Blue-breasted Kingfisher; 50c. Whale-headed Stork. *Horiz as T* **17**—30c. Sacred Ibis; 65c. Red-crowned Bishop. *As T* **18**. *Vert*—1s.30, African Fish Eagle; 5s. Lilac-breasted Roller. *Horiz*—2s.50, Great Blue Turaco; 10s. Black-collared Lovebird; 20s. South African Crowned Crane.

The 15c., 40c., 65c., and 1s. exist with PVA gum as well as gum arabic.

19 Carved Screen

(Des Mrs. R. Fennessy. Photo Harrison)

1967 (26 Oct). *13th Commonwealth Parliamentary Association Conference. T* **19** *and similar horiz designs. Multicoloured.* P 14.

127	30c. Type **19**	10	10
128	50c. Arms of Uganda	10	10
129	1s.30 Parliamentary Building	10	10
130	2s.50 Conference Chamber	15	1·75
127/30 *Set of* 4		30	1·75

20 *Cordia abyssinica*

21 *Acacia drepanolobium*

(Des Mrs. R. Fennessy. Photo Harrison)

1969 (9 Oct)–**74**. *Flowers. Various designs as T* **20/1**. *Chalk-surfaced paper.* P 14½×14 (5c. to 70c.) or 14 (others).

131	5c. brown, green and light olive-yellow	10	85
	a. Glazed, ordinary paper (11.4.73)	40	10
132	10c. multicoloured	10	10
	a. Glazed, ordinary paper (27.9.72)	40	10
133	15c. multicoloured	40	10
134	20c. bluish violet, yellow-olive and pale sage-green	15	10
	a. Glazed, ordinary paper (27.9.72)	40	10
135	30c. multicoloured	20	10
136	40c. reddish violet, yellow-green and pale olive-grey	20	10
137	50c. multicoloured	20	10
138	60c. multicoloured	45	2·00
	a. Glazed, ordinary paper (9.5.73)	12·00	40
139	70c. multicoloured	25	30
	a. Glazed, ordinary paper (27.9.72)	1·00	45
140	1s. multicoloured	20	10
	a. Glazed, ordinary paper (22.1.71)	80	10
141	1s.50 multicoloured (cobalt background)	25	10
	a. Glazed, ordinary paper (3.2.71)	50	10
	b. Azure background (chalk-surfaced paper) (21.1.74)	55	20
142	2s.50 multicoloured	30	1·25
	a. Glazed, ordinary paper (3.2.71)	1·25	10
143	5s. multicoloured	40	1·60
	a. Glazed, ordinary paper (3.2.71)	1·75	10
144	10s. multicoloured	50	4·50
	a. Glazed, ordinary paper (3.2.71)	3·75	10
145	20s. multicoloured	1·00	5·50
	a. Glazed, ordinary paper (22.1.71)	11·00	15
131/45 *Set of* 15		3·50	14·00
131a/45a *Set of* 11		30·00	1·40

Designs: *As T* **20**—10c. *Grewia similis*; 15c. *Cassia. didymobotrya*; 20c. *Coleus barbatus*; 30c. *Ockna ovata*; 40c. *Ipomoea spathulata*; 50c. *Spathodea nilotica*; 60c. *Oncoba spinosa*; 70c. *Carissa edulis*. *As T* **21**—1s.50, *Clerodendrum myricoides*; 2s.50, *Acanthus arboreus*; 5s. *Kigelia aethiopium*; 10s. *Erythrina abyssinica*; 20s. *Monodora myristica*.

Some of the glazed ordinary paper printings were available in Uganda some time before the London release dates which are quoted in the listings.

STAMP BOOKLETS

1962 (9 Oct). *Black on buff cover. Stitched.*

SB1	5s. booklet containing 10c., 15c., 20c., 30c. and 50c. (Nos. 100/4), each in block of 4	6·50

1965. *Black on blue (No. SB2) or buff (No. SB3) covers. Stitched.*

SB2	3s. booklet containing four 15c. and eight 30c. (Nos. 115, 117) in blocks of 4	10·00
SB3	5s. booklet containing four 15c. and 50c., and eight 30c. Nos. 115, 117, 119) in blocks of 4	11·00

1970. *Black on blue (No. SB4) or buff (No. SB5) covers. Stitched.*

SB4	3s. booklet containing four 5c. and 10c., and eight 30c. (Nos. 131/2, 135) in blocks of 4	11·00
SB5	5s. booklet containing four 5c., 10c. and 50c., and eight 30c. (Nos. 131/2, 135, 137) in blocks of 4	11·00

POSTAGE DUE STAMPS

The Postage Due stamps of Kenya, Uganda and Tanganyika were used in Uganda until 2 January 1967.

D 1

(Litho D.L.R.)

1967 (3 Jan). *Chalk-surfaced paper.* P 14×13½.

D1	**D 1**	5c. scarlet	20	4·50
D2		10c. green	20	4·50
D3		20c. deep blue	35	4·50
D4		30c. red-brown	40	6·50
D5		40c. bright purple	60	11·00
D6		1s. orange	1·50	13·00
D1/6 *Set of* 6			3·00	40·00

1970 (31 Mar). *As Nos. D1/6, but on glazed ordinary paper.* P 14×15.

D7	**D 1**	5c. scarlet	15	2·75
D8		10c. green	15	2·50
D9		20c. deep blue	25	3·00
D10		30c. red-brown	35	4·25
D11		40c. bright purple	55	5·00
D7/11 *Set of* 5			1·25	16·00

Western Australia *see* **Australia**

Western Samoa *see* **Samoa**

Zambia

INDEPENDENT

11 Pres. Kaunda and Victoria Falls

12 College of Further Education, Lusaka

(Des M. Goaman (3d., 6d.), Gabriel Ellison (1s.3d.). Photo Harrison)

1964 (24 Oct). *Independence. T* **11/12** *and similar vert design.* P 13½×11½ (6d.) or 14½×13½ (others).

91	3d. sepia, yellow-green and blue	10	10
92	6d. deep violet and yellow	15	20
93	1s.3d. red, black, sepia and orange	20	25
91/3 *Set of* 3		40	50

Design:—1s.3d. Barotse dancer.

14 Maize-Farmer and Silo

15 Health—Radiographer

21 Fishing at Mpulungu

22 Tobacco Worker

(Des Gabriel Ellison. Photo Harrison)

1964 (24 Oct). *T* **14/15**, **21/2** *and similar designs.* P 14½ (½d. to 4d.), 14½×13½ (1s.3d., 2s. and £1) or 13½×14½ (others).

94	½d. red, black and yellow-green	10	1·50
95	1d. brown, black and bright blue	10	10
96	2d. red, deep brown and orange	10	10
97	3d. black and red	10	10
98	4d. black, brown and orange	15	10
99	6d. orange, deep brown and deep bluish green	30	10
100	9d. carmine, black and bright blue	15	10
101	1s. black, yellow-bistre and blue	15	10
102	1s.3d. light red, yellow, black and blue	20	10
103	2s. bright blue, black, deep brown and orange	25	30
104	2s.6d. black and orange-yellow	60	35
105	5s. black, yellow and green	1·00	75
106	10s. black and orange	3·75	3·75
107	£1 black, brown, yellow and red	2·00	5·50
94/107 *Set of* 14		8·00	11·50

Designs: *Vert* (*as T* **15**)—2d. Chinyau dancer; 3d. Cotton-picking. (*As T* **22**)—2s. Tonga basket-making; £1 Makishi dancer. *Horiz* (*as T* **14**)—4d. Angoni bull. (As T **21**)—6d. Communications, old and new; 9d. Zambezi sawmills and Redwood flower; 2s.6d. Luangwa Game Reserve; 5s. Education—student; 10s. Copper mining.

Nos. 94/5 and 97 exist in coils, constructed from normal sheets.

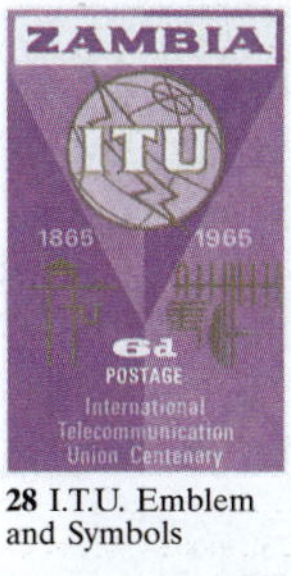

28 I.T.U. Emblem and Symbols

29 I.C.Y. Emblem

(Photo Harrison)

1965 (26 July). *I.T.U. Centenary.* P 14×14½.

108	**28**	6d. light reddish violet and gold	15	10
109		2s.6d. brownish grey and gold	85	1·50

(Photo Harrison)

1965 (26 July). *International Co-operation Year.* P 14½.

110	**29**	3d. turquoise and gold	15	10
111		1s.3d. ultramarine and gold	35	45

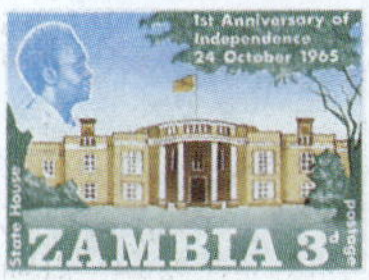

30 State House, Lusaka

34 W.H.O. Building and U.N. Flag

(Des Gabriel Ellison. Photo Harrison)

1965 (18 Oct). *First Anniv of Independence. T* **30** *and similar multicoloured designs.* No wmk. P 13½×14½ (3d.), 14×13½ (6d.) or 13½×14 (others).

112	3d. Type **30**	10	10
113	6d. Fireworks, Independence Stadium	10	10
	a. Bright purple (fireworks) omitted	£120	
114	1s.3d. Clematopsis (*vert*)	15	10
115	2s.6d. *Tithonia diversifolia* (*vert*)	30	1·25
112/15 *Set of* 4		50	1·25

(Des M. Goaman. Photo Harrison)

1966 (18 May). *Inauguration of W.H.O. Headquarters, Geneva.* P 14½.

116	**34**	3d. lake-brown, gold and new blue	40	10
		a. Gold omitted	£110	
117		1s.3d. gold, new blue and deep bluish violet	1·10	95

35 Proposed University Building

36 National Assembly Building

(Des Gabriel Ellison. Photo Harrison)

1966 (12 July). *Opening of Zambia University.* P 14½.

118	**35**	3d. blue-green and copper-bronze	10	10
119		1s.3d. reddish violet and copper-bronze	20	10

The building shown on Type **35** was never built.

(Des Gabriel Ellison. Photo Harrison)

1967 (2 May). *Inauguration of National Assembly Building.* P 14½.

120	**36**	3d. black and copper-bronze	10	10
121		6d. olive-green and copper-bronze	10	10

37 Airport Scene

(Des Gabriel Ellison. Photo Harrison)

1967 (2 Oct). *Opening of Lusaka International Airport.* P 13½×14½.

122	**37**	6d. violet-blue and copper-bronze	15	10
123		2s.6d. brown and copper-bronze	60	1·00

38 Youth Service Badge

39 "Co-operative Farming"

(Des Gabriel Ellison. Photo Harrison)

1967 (23 Oct). *National Development. T* **38/9** *and similar designs.* P 13½×14½ (6d., 1s.6d.) or 14½×13½ (others).

124	4d. black, red and gold	10	10
125	6d. black, gold and violet-blue	10	10
126	9d. black, grey-blue and silver	15	50
127	1s. multicoloured	50	10
128	1s.6d. multicoloured	70	2·25
124/8 *Set of* 5		1·40	2·75

Designs: *Vert*—9d. "Communications"; 1s. Coalfields. *Horiz*—1s.6d. Road link with Tanzania.

(New Currency. 100 ngwee = 1 kwacha)

43 Lusaka Cathedral

44 Baobab Tree

52 Chokwe Dancer

53 Kafue Railway Bridge

(Des Gabriel Ellison. Photo Harrison)

1968 (16 Jan). *Decimal Currency. T* **43/4**, **52/3** *and similar designs.* P 13½×14½ (1, 3, 15, 50n.) or 14½×13½ (others).

129	1n. multicoloured	10	10
	a. Copper-bronze (including value) omitted	£120	
	b. Ultramarine (windows) omitted	£120	
130	2n. multicoloured	10	10
131	3n. multicoloured	10	10
132	5n. bistre-brown and copper-bronze	10	10
133	8n. multicoloured	15	10
	a. Copper-bronze (background) omitted		
	b. Blue (of costumes) omitted	£110	
134	10n. multicoloured	25	10
135	15n. multicoloured	2·75	10
136	20n. multicoloured	4·50	10
137	25n. multicoloured	25	10
138	50n. chocolate, red-orange and copper-bronze	30	15
139	1k. royal blue and copper-bronze	4·50	20
140	2k. black and copper-bronze	2·25	1·25
129/40 *Set of* 12		14·00	1·75

Designs: *Horiz* (*as T* **43**)—3n. Zambia Airways Vickers VC-10 jetliner. (*As T* **53**)—15n. *Imbrasia zambesina* (moth); 2k. Eland. *Vert* (*as T* **44**)—5n. National Museum, Livingstone; 8n. Vimbuza dancer; 10n. Tobacco picking. (*As T* **52**)—20n. South African Crowned Cranes; 25n. Angoni warrior.

All values exist with PVA gum as well as gum arabic.

Nos. 129/30 and 132 exist in coils, constructed from normal sheets.

55 Ndola on Outline of Zambia

56 Human Rights Emblem and Heads

(Des Gabriel Ellison. Photo Harrison)

1968 (29 June). *Trade Fair, Ndola.* P 14.

141	**55**	15n. green and gold	10	10

(Des Gabriel Ellison. Photo and die-stamped (gold emblem) Harrison)

1968 (23 Oct). *Human Rights Year.* P 14.

142	**56**	3n. deep blue, pale violet and gold	10	10

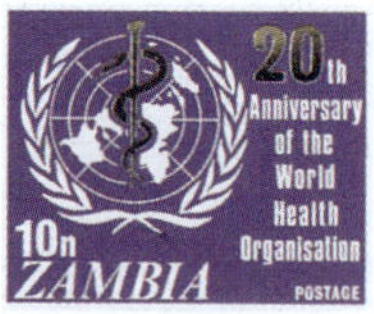

57 W.H.O. Emblem

58 Group of Children

(Des Gabriel Ellison. Photo and die-stamped (gold staff and "20") Harrison)

1968 (23 Oct). *20th Anniv of World Health Organization.* P 14.

143	**57**	10n. gold and bluish violet	10	10

(Des Gabriel Ellison. Photo and die-stamped (gold children) Harrison)

1968 (23 Oct). *22nd Anniv of UNICEF.* P 14.

144	**58**	25n. black, gold and ultramarine	15	70

59 Copper Miner

61 Zambia outlined on Map of Africa

(Des Gabriel Ellison. Photo Harrison)

1969 (18 June). *50th Anniv of International Labour Organization. T* **59** *and similar design.* P 14½×13½ (3n.) or 13½×14½ (25n.).

145	3n. copper-bronze and deep violet	25	10
146	25n. pale yellow copper-bronze and blackish brown	1·00	1·00

Design: *Horiz*—25n. Poling a furnace.

A used example of No. 145 exists with the copper-bronze omitted.

(Des Gabriel Ellison. Photo Harrison)

1969 (23 Oct). *International African Tourist Year. T* **61** *and similar multicoloured designs.* P 14×14½ (5n., 25n.) or 14½×14 (others).

147	5n. Type **61**	10	10
148	10n. Waterbuck (*horiz*)	15	10
149	15n. Kasaba Bay Golden Perch (*horiz*)	35	40
150	25n. Carmine Bee Eater	1·00	1·75
147/50 *Set of* 4		1·40	2·00

65 Satellite "Nimbus 3" orbiting the Earth

66 Woman collecting Water from Well

(Des Gabriel Ellison. Litho Enschedé)

1970 (23 Mar). *World Meteorological Day.* P 13×10½.

151	**65**	15n. multicoloured	20	50

(Des V. Whiteley (from local designs). Litho B.W.)

1970 (4 July). *Preventive Medicine. T* **66** *and similar vert designs.* P 13½×12.

152	3n. multicoloured	15	10
153	15n. multicoloured	30	30
154	25n. greenish blue, rosine and sepia	65	70
152/4 *Set of* 3		1·00	1·00

Designs:—15n. Child on scales; 25n. Child being immunized.

67 "Masks" (mural by Gabriel Ellison)

68 Ceremonial Axe

(Des Gabriel Ellison. Litho Harrison)

1970 (8 Sept). *Conference of Non-Aligned Nations.* P 14×14½.

155	**67**	15n. multicoloured	30	30

(Des Gabriel Ellison. Litho D.L.R.)

1970 (30 Nov). *Traditional Crafts. T* **68** *and similar multicoloured designs.* P 13½ (15n.), 12½ (25n.) or 14 (others).

156	3n. Type **68**	10	10
157	5n. Clay Smoking-Pipe Bowl	10	10
158	15n. Makishi Mask (30×47 *mm*)	25	30
159	25n. Kuomboka Ceremony (72×19 *mm*)	40	1·00
156/9 *Set of* 4		75	1·40
MS160 133×83 mm. Nos. 156/9. Imperf		6·00	13·00

STAMP BOOKLETS

B 2

1968. *Black on buff covers as Type* B **2** *(No.* SB2), *or size 82×58 mm (No.* SB3). *Stitched.*

SB2	20n. booklet containing eight 1n. and four 3n. (Nos. 129, 131) in blocks of 4	4·25
SB3	30n. booklet containing twelve 1n. and six 3n. (Nos. 129, 131) in blocks of 6	4·25

B 3

1970 (26 Aug). *Black on green cover as Type* B **3** *(No.* SB4) *or black on rose cover, size 82×58 mm (No.* SB5). *Stitched.*

SB4	20n. booklet containing eight 1n. and four 3n. (Nos. 129, 131) in blocks of 4	4·50
SB5	30n. booklet containing twelve 1n. and six 3n. (Nos. 129, 131) in blocks of 6	4·50

POSTAGE DUE STAMPS

D 3

(Des D. Smith. Litho Govt Printer, Lusaka)

1964 (24 Oct). P 12½.

D11	D **3**	1d. orange	30	2·50
D12		2d. deep blue	35	2·50

D13	3d. lake	45	1·75
D14	4d. ultramarine	45	2·25
D15	6d. purple	45	2·25
D16	1s. light emerald	55	4·25
D11/16 *Set of 6*		2·25	14·00

In all values the left-hand vertical row of the sheet is imperf at left and the bottom horizontal row is imperf at foot. The above were crudely perforated, resulting in variations in the sizes of the stamps.

The above were withdrawn on 15 January 1968 and thereafter decimal currency postage stamps were used for postage due purposes with appropriate cancellations.

Zanzibar

An Indian post office opened in Zanzibar in November 1868, but was closed for political reasons on 1 April of the following year. Little has survived from this period. Subsequently mail was forwarded via Seychelles or, later, Aden.

Stamps of INDIA were used in Zanzibar from 1 October 1875 until 10 November 1895, when the administration of the postal service was transferred from India to British East Africa. Separate cancellations for Zanzibar are known from 1 June 1878.

Z 1

Z 1a

Stamps of INDIA *cancelled with Type* Z **1** (1878–79)

1865. (*Nos. 54/65*).

Z1	1a. deep brown	£200
Z2	2a. orange	£200

1866–78. (*Nos. 69/72*).

Z3	4a. blue-green (Die II)	£190

1865. (*Nos. 54/65*).

Z4	½a. blue (Die II)	£180

Surviving covers show that Type Z **1** was normally used as a datestamp, struck clear of the stamps which were obliterated by a rhomboid of bars, but examples of the c.d.s. used as a cancel are known.

Stamps of INDIA *cancelled with Type* Z **1a**.

1873. (*Nos. 75/6*).

Z7	2a. orange	£225

In Type Z **1a** the word "ZANZIBAR" is shorter than in Types Z **1** and Z **3**. It was generally used as an arrival mark but cancellations on adhesives are known.

Z 2

Stamps of INDIA *cancelled with Type* Z **2** (1879–82).

1865. (*Nos. 54/65*).

Z10	8p. mauve	£200
Z11	1a. deep brown	18·00
Z12	2a. orange	18·00

1866–78. (*Nos. 69/72*).

Z13	4a. green (Die I)	£100
Z14	4a. blue-green (Die II)	28·00

1868. (*Nos. 73/4*).

Z15	8a. rose (Die II)	80·00

1873. (*Nos. 75/6*).

Z16	½a. blue (Die II)	18·00

1874. (*Nos. 77/9*).

Z17	1r. slate	£225

1876. (*Nos. 80/2*).

Z18	6a. pale brown	95·00
Z19	12a. Venetian red	£150

1882. (*No. 90*).

Z19*a*	1a.6p. sepia	£140

OFFICIAL STAMPS

1874–82. (*Nos. O31/7*).

Z19*b*	1a. brown	£225
Z20	2a. orange	£190
Z21	4a. green (Die I)	£250
Z22	8a. rose (Die II)	£250

Z 3

Stamps of INDIA *cancelled with Type* Z **3** (1882–84)

1865. (*Nos. 54/65*).

Z25	1a. deep brown	40·00
Z26	2a. brown-orange	35·00

1866–78. (*Nos. 69/72*).

Z26*a*	4a. green (Die I)	£100
Z27	4a. blue-green (Die II)	40·00

1868. (*Nos. 73/4*).

Z28	8a. rose (Die II)	65·00

1873. (*Nos. 75/6*).

Z29	½a. blue (Die II)	30·00

1874. (*Nos. 77/9*).

Z29*a*	1r. slate	£160

1876. (*Nos. 80/2*).

Z30	6a. pale brown	50·00
Z31	12a. Venetian red	£130

1882–83. (*Nos. 84/101*).

Z32	1a. brown-purple	35·00
Z33	1a.6p. sepia	38·00
Z34	3a. orange	42·00

OFFICIAL STAMPS

1867–73. (*Nos. O20/30a*).

Z35	2a. orange	£250
Z36	8a. rose	£275

Z 4

Z 5

Stamps of INDIA *cancelled with Type* Z **4** (June 1884–May 1887) (*between* January *and* September 1885 *the postmark was used without year numerals*).

1865. (*Nos. 54/65*).

Z39	1a. deep brown	95·00
Z40	2a. brown-orange	35·00

1866–78. (*Nos. 69/72*).

Z41	4a. green (Die I)	£140
Z41*a*	4a. blue-green (Die II)	32·00

1868. (*Nos. 73/4*).

Z42	8a. rose (Die II)	35·00

1873. (*Nos. 75/6*).

Z43	½a. blue (Die II)	30·00

1874. (*Nos. 77/9*).

Z44	1r. slate	£160

1876. (*Nos. 80/2*).

Z45	6a. pale brown	80·00
Z45*a*	12a. Venetian red	£150

1882–86. (*Nos. 84/101*).

Z46	½a. blue-green	15·00
Z47	1a. brown-purple	26·00
Z48	1a.6p. sepia	21·00
Z49	2a. blue	50·00
Z50	3a. orange	15·00
Z51	4a. olive-green	45·00
Z52	4a.6p. yellow-green	20·00
Z53	8a. dull mauve	48·00
Z54	1r. slate	42·00

OFFICIAL STAMPS

1867–73. (*Nos. O20/30a*).

Z55	2a. orange	£170

1874–82. (*Nos.O31/7*).

Z55*a*	½a. blue	£120
Z56	1a. brown	95·00
Z56*a*	2a. orange	£225

1883–95. (*Nos. O37a/48*).

Z57	1a. brown-purple	£110

Stamps of INDIA *cancelled with Type* Z **5** (1887–94).

1876. (*Nos. 80/2*).

Z60	6a. pale brown	18·00
Z61	12a. Venetian red	65·00

1882–90. (*Nos. 84/101*).

Z62	½a. blue-green	6·50
Z63	9p. aniline carmine	55·00
Z64	1a. brown-purple	6·00
Z65	1a.6p. sepia	9·00
Z66	2a. blue	7·00
Z67	3a. orange	9·00
Z68	3a. brown-orange	7·50
Z69	4a. olive-green	40·00
Z70	4a.6p. yellow-green	12·00
Z71	8a. dull mauve	20·00
Z72	12a. purple/*red*	50·00
Z73	1r. slate	16·00

1891. (*No. 102*).

Z74	2½a. on 4a.6p. yellow-green	8·00

1892–95. (*Nos. 103/6*).

Z75	2a.6p. yellow-green	6·00

OFFICIAL STAMPS

1867–73. (*Nos. O20/30a*).

Z75*a*	4a. green	£275

1874–82. (*Nos. O31/7I*).

Z76	½a. blue	90·00
Z77	1a. brown	£100
Z78	2a. yellow	£170

Z 6

Z 7

Stamps of INDIA *cancelled with Type* Z **6** (1888–95).

1876. (*Nos. 80/2*).

Z80	6a. pale brown	20·00
Z80*a*	12a. Venetian red	£150

1882–90. (*Nos. 84/101*).

Z81	½a. blue-green	32·00
Z82	9p. aniline carmine	65·00
Z83	1a. brown-purple	9·50
Z84	1a.6p. sepia	9·00
Z85	2a. blue	10·00
Z86	3a. orange	23·00
Z87	3a. brown-orange	17·00
Z88	4a. olive-green	17·00
Z89	4a.6p. yellow-green	19·00
Z90	8a. dull mauve	23·00
Z91	12a. purple/*red*	55·00
Z92	1r. slate	19·00

1891. (*No. 102*).

Z93	2½a. on 4a.6p. yellow-green	26·00

1892–95. (*Nos. 103/6*).

Z94	2a.6p. yellow-green	19·00

Stamps of INDIA *cancelled with Type* Z **7** (1894–95).

1876. (*Nos. 80/2*).

Z95	6a. pale brown	70·00

1882–90. (*Nos. 84/101*).

Z100	½a. blue-green	22·00
Z101	9p. aniline carmine	80·00
Z102	1a. brown-purple	30·00
Z103	1a.6p. sepia	50·00
Z104	2a. blue	22·00
Z105	3a. brown-orange	55·00
Z106	4a. olive-green	55·00
Z107	8a. dull mauve	70·00
Z108	12a. purple/*red*	75·00
Z109	1r. slate	70·00

1892–95. (*Nos. 103/6*).

Z110	2a.6p. yellow-green	14·00

1895. (*Nos. 107/9*).

Z111	2r. carmine and yellow-brown	£350

A French post office was opened on the island in January 1889 and this service used the stamps of FRANCE until 1894 when specific stamps for this office were provided. The French postal service on the island closed on 31 July 1904 and it is known that French stamps were again utilised during the final month.

A German postal agency operated in Zanzibar between 27 August 1890 and 31 July 1891, using stamps of GERMANY.

PRICES FOR STAMPS ON COVER TO 1945

Nos. 1/2	—
Nos. 3/16	*from* × 30
No. 17	*from* × 8
No. 18	*from* × 25
Nos. 19/21	—
No. 22	*from* × 40
Nos. 23/5	*from*×25
No. 26	*from* × 40
Nos. 27/40	—
Nos. 41/6	*from* × 25
Nos. 156/68	*from* × 15
Nos. 169/77	—
Nos. 178/87	*from* × 20
Nos. 188/204	*from* × 15
Nos. 205/9	*from* × 20
Nos. 210/38	*from* × 15
Nos. 239/45	—
Nos. 246/59	*from* × 8
Nos. 260/*f*	—
Nos. 261/330	*from* × 4
Nos. D1/3	*from* × 8
No. D4	*from* × 1
No. D5	*from* × 15

PRICES FOR STAMPS ON COVER TO 1945	
No. D6	—
No. D7	*from* × 1
Nos. D8/12	*from* × 15
No. D13	*from* × 1
No. D14	—
Nos. D15/16	*from* × 6
No. D17	*from* × 4
Nos. D18/24	*from* × 15
Nos. D25/30	*from* × 30

PROTECTORATE

(Currency. 12 pies = 1 anna. 16 annas = 1 rupee)

Zanzibar
(1)

1895 (14 Nov)–**96**. *Nos. 81, 85, 90/6, 98/101, 103 and 106/9 of India (Queen Victoria) optd with T* **1** *by Zanzibar Gazette.*

(a) In blue.

1		½a. blue-green	£18000	£5000
2		1a. plum	£2500	£500
		j. "Zanzidar" (R. 4/6, 8/5)	†	£25000

(b) In black.

3		½a. blue-green	4·50	3·75
		j. "Zanzidar" (R. 4/6, 8/5)	£1300	£700
		k. "Zanibar" (R. 7/2)	£1300	£1700
		l. Diaeresis over last "a" (R. 10/5)	£1800	£1800
		m. Opt double, one albino	£225	
4		1a. plum	4·75	3·75
		j. "Zanzidar" (R. 4/6, 8/5)	—	£3500
		k. "Zanibar" (R. 7/2)	£1700	£1900
		l. Diaeresis over last "a" (R. 10/5)	£4000	
5		1a.6p. sepia	5·00	4·00
		j. "Zanzidar" (R. 4/6, 8/5)	£3750	£1100
		k. "Zanibar" (R. 7/2)	£1600	£1700
		l. "Zanizbar" (R. 1/9)		
		m. Diaeresis over last "a" (R. 10/5)	£1600	
6		2a. pale blue	5·50	5·50
7		2a. blue	6·00	5·50
		j. "Zanzidar" (R. 4/6, 8/5)	£5500	£2500
		k. "Zanibar" (R. 7/2)	£5500	£2500
		l. Diaeresis over last "a" (R. 10/5)	£2500	
		m. Opt double	£250	
		n. Opt double, one albino	£250	
8		2½a. yellow-green	9·00	5·00
		j. "Zanzidar" (R. 4/6, 8/5)	£5500	£1700
		k. "Zanibar" (R. 7/2)	£650	£1300
		l. "Zapzibar"		
		n. Diaeresis over last "a" (R.10/5)	£2250	£1800
		o. Second "z" italic (R. 10/1)	£300	£425
		p. Opt double, one albino	£250	
10		3a. brown-orange	12·00	12·00
		j. "Zanzidar" (R. 4/6, 8/5)	£850	£1600
		k. "Zanizbar" (R. 1/9)	£5000	£5500
11		4a. olive-green	20·00	17·00
		j. "Zanzidar" (R. 4/6, 8/5)	£9000	£4250
12		4a. slate-green	15·00	17·00
		l. Diaeresis over last "a" (R. 10/5)	£4000	
13		6a. pale brown	20·00	11·00
		j. "Zanzidar" (R. 4/6, 8/5)	£9000	£4000
		k. "Zanibar" (R. 7/2)	£700	£1300
		l. "Zanzibarr"	£5500	£4250
		m. Opt double		
		n. Opt double, one albino	£150	
		o. Opt triple, two albino	£200	
14		8a. dull mauve	30·00	21·00
		j. "Zanzidar" (R 4/6, 8/5)	£8500	£7500
15		8a. magenta (6.96)	20·00	23·00
		l. Diaeresis over last "a" (R. 10/5)	£6000	
16		12a. purple/*red*	17·00	10·00
		j. "Zanzidar" (R.4/6, 8/5)	£8500	£4250
17		1r. slate	90·00	75·00
		j. "Zanzidar" (R 4/6, 8/5)	£8000	£4750
18		1r. green and aniline carmine (7.96)	20·00	28·00
		j. Opt vert downwards	£425	
19		2r. carmine and yellow-brown	90·00	95·00
		j. "r" omitted	£24000	
		k. "r" inverted	£3750	£4500
20		3r. brown and green	65·00	75·00
		j. "r" omitted	£24000	
		k. "r" inverted	£4500	£4750
		l. Opt double, one albino	£1000	
21		5r. ultramarine and violet	75·00	95·00
		j. "r" omitted	£24000	
		k. "r" inverted	£3750	£5500
		l. Opt double, one inverted	£850	
		m. Opt double, one albino	£1000	
3/21 *Set of* 15			£400	£425

Forged examples of the blue overprints, Nos. 1/2, can be found on piece with genuine cancellations as type Z 7, dated "13 FE 97".

There were a number of different settings for this overprint.

Values to 1r. were initially overprinted from settings of 120 (12×10) including one which showed "Zanzidar" on R. 4/6 and R. 8/5 (soon corrected) and "Zanizbar" on R. 1/9 (also soon corrected). Later supplies of these values were overprinted from settings of 80 (8×10) for the 6a. only or 60 (6×10) for the others. One of these settings included "Zanibar" on R. 7/2. Another late setting, size unknown, showed a diaeresis over last "a" on R. 10/5.

Many forgeries of this overprint exist and also bogus errors.

MINOR VARIETIES. The following minor varieties of type exist on Nos. 1/21:

A. First "Z" antique (sloping serifs) (all values)
B. Broken "p" for "n" (all values to 1r.)
C. Tall second "z" (all values)
D. Small second "z" (all values)
E. Small second "z" and inverted "q" for "b" (all values)
F. Second "z" Gothic (lower limb bent upwards) (½a. to 12a. and 1r.) (No. 18) (black opts only)
G. No dot over "i" (all values to 1r.)
H. Inverted "q" for "b" (all values to 1r.)
I. Arabic "2" for "r" (all values to 1r.) (black opts only)

Varieties D and E are worth the same as normal examples, A (2, 3, 5r.) and C normal plus 50%, G and I from 3 times normal, A (values to 1r.), F and H from 4 times normal and B from 5 times normal.

2½ (2) 2½ (3) 2½ (4) 2½ (5)

1895–98. *Provisionals. I. Stamps used for postal purposes.*

(a) No. 5 surch in red (30.11.95).

22	**2**	2½ on 1½a. sepia	55·00	45·00
		j. "Zanzidar"	£1400	£1300
		k. "Zanizbar"	£4000	£1900
		l. Inverted "1" in "½"	£1100	£900

(b) No. 4 surch in black (11.5.96).

23	**3**	2½ on 1a. plum	£160	£100
24	**4**	2½ on 1a. plum	£425	£275
		j. Inverted "1" in "½"	£2750	
25	**5**	2½ on 1a. plum	£170	£110

2½ (6) 2½ (7) 2½ (8)

(c) No. 6 surch in red (15.8.96).

26	**6**	2½ on 2a. pale blue	55·00	35·00
		j. Inverted "1" in "½"	£425	£275
		k. Roman "I" in "½"	£250	£160
		l. "Zanzibar" double, one albino	£140	
		m. "Zanzibar" triple, two albino	£300	
27	**7**	2½ on 2a. pale blue	£160	95·00
		j. "2" of "½" omitted	£12000	
		k. "2" for "2½"	£17000	
		l. "1" of "½" omitted	£12000	£6000
		m. Inverted "1" in "½"	£2750	£1700
		n. "Zanzibar" double, one albino	£400	
28	**8**	2½ on 2a. pale blue	£5000	£2500

No. 28 only exists with small "z" and occurs on R. 2/2 in the setting of 60.

(d) No. 5 surch in red (15.11.96).

29	**6**	2½ on 1½a. sepia	£140	£120
		j. Inverted "1 in "½"	£1300	£1100
		k. Roman "I" in "½"	£900	£900
		l. Surch double, one albino	£250	
30	**7**	2½ on 1½a. sepia	£400	£350
		l. Surch double, one albino	£700	
31	**8**	2½ on 1½a. sepia	£17000	£11000

No. 31 only exists with small "z" and occurs on R. 2/2 in the setting of 60.

II. Stamps prepared for official purposes. Nos. 4, 5 and 7 surch as before in red (1.98).

32	**3**	2½ on 1a. plum	£225	£600
33	**4**	2½ on 1a. plum	£425	£900
34	**5**	2½ on 1a. plum	£250	£600
35	**3**	2½ on 1½a. sepia	75·00	£190
		j. Diaeresis over last "a"	£6500	
36	**4**	2½ on 1½a. sepia	£190	£475
37	**5**	2½ on 1½a. sepia	£110	£275
38	**3**	2½ on 2a. dull blue	£110	£300
39	**4**	2½ on 2a. dull blue	£225	£500
40	**5**	2½ on 2a. dull blue	£130	£350

It is doubtful whether Nos. 32/40 were issued to the public.

1896. *Nos. 65/6, 68 and 71/3 of British East Africa (Queen Victoria), optd with T* **1**.

41		½a. yellow-green (23 May)	32·00	19·00
42		1a. carmine-rose (1 June)	30·00	17·00
		j. Opt double	£750	£850
		k. Opt double, one albino	£325	
43		2½a. deep blue (R.) (24 May)	75·00	45·00
44		4½a. orange-yellow (12 Aug)	45·00	50·00
45		5a. yellow-bistre (12 Aug)	50·00	32·00
		j. "r" omitted	—	£3250
46		7½a. mauve (12 Aug)	42·00	50·00
41/6 *Set of* 6			£250	£190

MINOR VARIETIES. The various minor varieties of type detailed in the note below No. 21 also occur on Nos. 22 to 46 as indicated below:

A. Nos. 23, 25, 27, 30, 35, 38, 41/6
B. Nos. 22/3, 26, 29/30, 32/3, 36, 39, 44/6
C. Nos. 22, 25/6, 32, 36, 38, 40/6
D. Nos. 22/46
E. Nos. 22/46
F. Nos. 22, 25/6, 29, 41/6
G. Nos. 25/6, 29, 35, 37/8, 40/6
H. Nos. 22, 41/6 (on the British East Africa stamps this variety occurs in the same position as variety C)
I. Nos. 26, 29, 35, 38, 41/6

The scarcity of these varieties on the surcharges (Nos. 22/40) is similar to those on the basic stamps, but examples on the British East Africa values (Nos. 41/6) are more common.

PRINTERS. All Zanzibar stamps up to Type **37** were printed by De La Rue & Co.

12

13

14 Sultan Seyyid Hamed-bin-Thwain

No right serif to left-hand "4" (R. 1/1)

1896 (Dec). *Recess. Flags in red on all values.* W **12**. P 14.

156	**13**	½a. yellow-green	4·00	1·75
157		1a. indigo	3·25	1·50
158		1a. violet-blue	5·50	4·25
159		2a. red-brown	2·75	75
160		2½a. bright blue	14·00	1·50
161		2½a. pale blue	15·00	1·50
162		3a. grey	12·00	6·50
163		3a. bluish grey	13·00	8·00
164		4a. myrtle-green	8·00	3·50
165		4½a. orange	5·50	5·50
		a. No right serif to left-hand "4"	£140	£150
		b. No fraction bar at right (R. 2/1)	£140	£150
166		5a. bistre	5·50	2·50
		a. Bisected (2½a.) (on cover)	†	£3750
167		7½a. mauve	3·75	3·75
168		8a. grey-olive	11·00	7·00
169	**14**	1r. blue	18·00	9·00
170		1r. deep blue	22·00	13·00
171		2r. green	26·00	9·50
172		3r. dull purple	27·00	9·50
173		4r. lake	23·00	13·00
174		5r. sepia	27·00	13·00
156/74 *Set of* 15			£170	80·00
156s/74s Optd "Specimen" *Set of* 15			£200	

The ½, 1, 2, 2½, 3 and 8a. are known without wmk, these being from edges of the sheets.

1897 (5 Jan). *No. 164 surch as before, in red.*

175	**3**	2½ on 4a. myrtle-green	70·00	45·00
176	**4**	2½ on 4a. myrtle-green	£225	£190
177	**5**	2½ on 4a. myrtle-green	85·00	60·00
175/7 *Set of* 3			£350	£250

18

1898 (Apr). *Recess.* W **18**. P 14.

178	**13**	½a. yellow-green	1·50	35
179		1a. indigo	3·50	65
		a. Greenish black	4·25	1·50
180		2a. red-brown	5·50	1·00
		a. Deep brown	7·00	1·75
181		2½a. bright blue	3·50	30
182		3a. grey	6·00	60
183		4a. myrtle-green	3·25	1·00
184		4½a. orange	9·00	1·00
		a. No right serif to left-hand "4"	£190	70·00
		b. No fraction bar at right (R. 2/1)	£190	70·00
185		5a. bistre	16·00	1·75
		a. Pale bistre	16·00	2·00
186		7½a. mauve	11·00	2·75
187		8a. grey-olive	15·00	2·25
178/87 *Set of* 10			65·00	10·00

19

20 Sultan Seyyid Hamoud-bin-Mohammed bin Said

1899 (June)–**1901**. *Recess. Flags in red.* W **18** (Nos. 188/99) or W **12** (others). P 14.

188	**19**	½a. yellow-green	2·25	60
		a. Wmk sideways	14·00	5·50
189		1a. indigo	4·50	20
		a. Wmk sideways	28·00	1·25
190		1a. carmine (1901)	2·25	20
191		2a. red-brown	2·75	50
192		2½a. bright blue	2·25	60
193		3a. grey	3·50	2·25
194		4a. myrtle-green	3·25	1·75
195		4½a. orange	14·00	5·50
196		4½a. blue-black (1901)	16·00	12·00
197		5a. bistre	3·25	1·25
198		7½a. mauve	3·25	4·50
199		8a. grey-olive	3·25	4·50
200	**20**	1r. blue	19·00	15·00
201		2r. green	19·00	18·00
202		3r. dull purple	32·00	35·00
203		4r. lake	50·00	55·00
204		5r. sepia	55·00	80·00
188/204 *Set of* 17			£200	£200
188s/204s Optd "Specimen" *Set of* 17			£225	

Two & One (21)

Two & Half (22)

Two & Half (22a) Thin open "w" (R. 2/2, 3/4)

Two & Half (22b) Serif to foot of "f" (R. 3/1)

1904. *Nos. 194/6 and 198/9 surch as T* **21** *and* **22**, *in black or lake (L.) by Zanzibar Gazette in setting of 30 (6×5).*

205	**19**	1 on 4½a. orange	4·00	5·50
206		1 on 4½a. blue/black (L.)	4·50	18·00
207		2 on 4a. myrtle-green (L.)	14·00	18·00

208 2½ on 7½a. mauve 13·00 20·00
a. Opt Type **22a** 85·00 £110
b. Opt Type **22b** £140 £190
c. "Hlaf" for "Half" £15000
209 2½ on 8a. grey-olive 23·00 32·00
a. Opt Type **22a** £140 £170
b. Opt Type **22b** £225 £300
c. "Hlaf" for "Half" £14000 £10000
205/9 *Set of 5* 50·00 80·00

23

24

Monogram of Sultan Seyyid Ali bin Hamoud bin Naherud

1904 (8 June). *Typo. Background of centre in second colour.* W **18**. P 14.
210 **23** ½a. green 2·00 90
211 1a. rose-red 2·00 10
212 2a. brown 2·75 45
213 2½a. blue 3·50 35
214 3a. grey 3·00 2·25
215 4a. deep green 2·50 1·60
216 4½a. black 3·00 2·50
217 5a. yellow-brown 4·50 1·25
218 7½a. purple 5·50 7·00
219 8a. olive-green 3·75 3·50
220 **24** 1r. blue and red 25·00 17·00
a. Wmk sideways 95·00 35·00
221 2r. green and red 30·00 45·00
a. Wmk sideways £190 £225
222 3r. violet and red 45·00 85·00
223 4r. claret and red 50·00 95·00
224 5r. olive-brown and red 50·00 £100
210/24 *Set of 15* £200 £325
210s/24s Optd "Specimen" *Set of 15* £150

25

26

27 Sultan Ali bin Hamoud

28 View of Port

1908 (May)–**09**. *Recess.* W **18** (sideways on 10r. to 30r.). P 14.
225 **25** 1c. pearl-grey (10.09) 2·25 30
226 3c. yellow-green 7·50 10
a. Wmk sideways 7·50 1·25
227 6c. rose-carmine 9·50 10
a. Wmk sideways 9·50 2·25
228 10c. brown (10.09) 4·25 2·00
229 12c. violet 17·00 3·25
a. Wmk sideways 13·00 1·25
230 **26** 15c. ultramarine 15·00 40
a. Wmk sideways 14·00 6·00
231 25c. sepia 5·00 1·00
232 50c. blue-green 8·00 4·50
233 75c. grey-black (10.09) 14·00 12·00
234 **27** 1r. yellow-green 29·00 12·00
a. Wmk sideways 70·00 10·00
235 2r. violet 18·00 14·00
a. Wmk sideways £180 70·00
236 3r. orange-bistre 25·00 50·00
237 4r. vermilion 50·00 80·00
238 5r. steel-blue 48·00 60·00
239 **28** 10r. blue-green and brown £170 £300
s. Optd "Specimen" 45·00
240 20r. black and yellow-green £400 £600
s. Optd "Specimen" 60·00
241 30r. black and sepia £450 £750
s. Optd "Specimen" 75·00
242 40r. black and orange-brown £600
s. Optd "Specimen" 95·00
243 50r. black and mauve £550
s. Optd "Specimen" 95·00
244 100r. black and steel-blue £750
s. Optd "Specimen" £160
245 200r. brown and greenish black £1200
s. Optd "Specimen" £200
225/38 *Set of 14* £225 £200
225s/38s Optd "Specimen" *Set of 14* £200

29 Sultan Kalif bin Harub

30 Sailing Canoe

31 Dhow

1913. *Recess.* W **18** (sideways on 75c. and 10r. to 200r.). P 14.
246 **29** 1c. grey 40 30
247 3c. yellow-green 75 50
248 6c. rose-carmine 1·50 20
249 10c. brown 1·10 2·50
250 12c. violet 1·00 30
251 15c. blue 1·75 30
252 25c. sepia 1·00 1·75
253 50c. blue-green 2·25 5·00
254 75c. grey-black 2·25 3·75
a. Wmk upright £150
as. Optd "Specimen" 95·00
255 **30** 1r. yellow-green 11·00 12·00
256 2r. violet 11·00 27·00
257 3r. orange-bistre 16·00 45·00
258 4r. scarlet 27·00 75·00
259 5r. steel-blue 40·00 45·00
260 **31** 10r. green and brown £150 £275
260*b* 20r. black and green £225 £450
bs. Optd "Specimen" 48·00
260*c* 30r. black and brown £225 £550
cs. Optd "Specimen" 60·00
260*d* 40r. black and vermilion £425 £750
ds. Optd "Specimen" 90·00
260*e* 50r. black and purple £400 £800
es. Optd "Specimen" 90·00
260*f* 100r. black and blue £500
fs. Optd "Specimen" £120
260*g* 200r. brown and black £800
gs. Optd "Specimen" £160
246/60 *Set of 15* £225 £450
246s/60as Optd "Specimen" *Set of 15* £200

1914–22. Wmk Mult Crown CA (sideways on 10r.). P 14.
261 **29** 1c. grey 80 25
262 3c. yellow-green 1·25 10
a. Dull green 6·50 15
w. Wmk inverted † £150
263 6c. deep carmine 85 10
a. Bright rose-carmine 85 10
aw. Wmk inverted † £150
264 8c. purple/*pale yellow* (1922) 75 4·50
265 10c. myrtle/*pale yellow* (1922) 75 30
266 15c. deep ultramarine 1·10 5·50
268 50c. blue-green 4·50 4·50
269 75c. grey-black 3·00 24·00
270 **30** 1r. yellow-green 4·00 3·50
271 2r. violet 6·00 8·50
272 3r. orange-bistre 18·00 38·00
273 4r. scarlet 16·00 85·00
y. Wmk inverted and reversed £150
274 5r. steel-blue 16·00 65·00
w. Wmk inverted £150
275 **31** 10r. green and brown £150 £500
261/75 *Set of 14* £200 £650
261s/75s Optd "Specimen" *Set of 14* £225

1921–29. Wmk Mult Script CA (sideways on 10r. to 30r.). P 14.
276 **29** 1c. slate-grey 20 7·50
277 3c. yellow-green 1·00 4·00
278 3c. yellow (1922) 30 10
w. Wmk inverted
279 4c. green (1922) 50 1·25
280 6c. carmine-red 30 50
281 6c. purple/*blue* (1922) 35 10
w. Wmk inverted † £250
282 10c. brown 70 10·00
283 12c. violet 40 30
w. Wmk inverted
284 12c. carmine-red (1922) 40 40
285 15c. blue 55 9·50
286 20c. indigo (1922) 1·00 30
287 25c. sepia 75 14·00
288 50c. myrtle-green 1·25 4·50
y. Wmk inverted and reversed £150 £160
289 75c. slate 2·50 55·00
290 **30** 1r. yellow-green 4·75 3·50
291 2r. deep violet 3·25 11·00
292 3r. orange-bistre 4·25 7·50
293 4r. scarlet 12·00 35·00
294 5r. Prussian blue 20·00 70·00
w. Wmk inverted £200
295 **31** 10r. green and brown £130 £350
296 20r. black and green £275 £550
s. Optd "Specimen" £100
297 30r. black and brown (1929) £225 £600
s. Perf "Specimen" 95·00
276/95 *Set of 20* £170 £500
276s/95s Optd "Specimen" *Set of 20* £275

32 Sultan Kalif bin Harub

33

1926–27. *T* **32** (*"CENTS" in serifed capitals*). *Recess.* Wmk Mult Script CA. P 14.
299 **32** 1c. brown 50 10
300 3c. yellow-orange 20 15
301 4c. deep dull green 20 30
302 6c. violet 20 10
303 8c. slate 1·00 4·50
304 10c. olive-green 1·00 40
305 12c. carmine-red 1·75 10
306 20c. bright blue 50 30
307 25c. purple/*yellow* (1927) 5·50 2·50
308 50c. claret 2·75 35
309 75c. sepia (1927) 21·00 28·00
299/309 *Set of 11* 30·00 32·00
299s/309s Optd "Specimen" *Set of 11* £130

(New Currency. 100 cents = 1 shilling)

1936 (1 Jan). *T* **33** (*"CENTS" in sans-serif capitals*), *and T* **30/1**, *but values in shillings. Recess.* Wmk Mult Script CA. P 14×13½–14.
310 **33** 5c. green 10 10
311 10c. black 10 10
312 15c. carmine-red 10 1·25
313 20c. orange 10 10
314 25c. purple/*yellow* 10 10
315 30c. ultramarine 10 10
316 40c. sepia 15 10
317 50c. claret 30 10
318 **30** 1s. yellow-green 50 10
319 2s. slate-violet 1·25 1·75
320 5s. scarlet 18·00 6·00
321 7s.50 light blue 28·00 26·00
322 **31** 10s. green and brown 29·00 22·00
310/22 *Set of 13* 70·00 50·00
310s/22s Perf "Specimen" *Set of 13* £150

Nos. 310/22 remained current until 1952 and the unused prices are therefore for unmounted examples.

36 Sultan Kalif bin Harub

1936 (9 Dec). *Silver Jubilee of Sultan. Recess.* Wmk Mult Script CA. P 14.
323 **36** 10c. black and olive-green 3·00 30
324 20c. black and bright purple 4·50 2·00
325 30c. black and deep ultramarine 14·00 35
326 50c. black and orange-vermilion 14·00 4·00
323/6 *Set of 4* 32·00 6·00
323s/6s Perf "Specimen" *Set of 4* 90·00

37 *Sham Alam* (Sultan's dhow)

VICTORY ISSUE
8TH JUNE 1946
(38)

1944 (20 Nov). *Bicentenary of Al Busaid Dynasty. Recess.* Wmk Mult Script CA. P 14.
327 **37** 10c. ultramarine 1·00 3·50
a. "C" of "CA" missing from wmk £600
328 20c. red 1·25 3·25
a. "C" of "CA" missing from wmk £600
329 50c. blue-green 1·25 30
330 1s. dull purple 1·25 65
a. "A" of "CA" missing from wmk
327/30 *Set of 4* 4·25 7·00
327s/30s Perf "Specimen" *Set of 4* 95·00

1946 (11 Nov). *Victory. Nos. 311 and 315 optd with T* **38**.
331 **33** 10c. black (R.) 20 50
332 30c. ultramarine (R.) 30 50
331s/2s Perf "Specimen" *Set of 2* 65·00

1949 (10 Jan). *Royal Silver Wedding. As Nos. 112/13 of Antigua.*
333 20c. orange 30 1·50
334 10s. brown 23·00 30·00

1949 (10–13 Oct). *75th Anniv of UPU. As Nos. 114/17 of Antigua.*
335 20c. red-orange (13 Oct) 30 3·00
336 30c. deep blue 1·75 1·50
a. "C" of "CA" missing from wmk £750
337 50c. magenta 1·00 3·00
338 1s. blue-green (13 Oct) 1·00 4·50
335/8 *Set of 4* 3·50 11·00

39 Sultan Kalif bin Harub

40 Seyyid Khalifa Schools, Beit-el-Ras

1952 (26 Aug)–**55**. Wmk Mult Script CA. P 12½ (cent values) or 13 (shilling values).
339 **39** 5c. black 10 10
340 10c. red-orange 10 10
341 15c. green 75 2·00
a. Yellow-green (12.11.53) 2·75 2·75
342 20c. carmine-red 60 70
343 25c. reddish purple 1·00 10
344 30c. deep bluish green 1·00 10
a. Deep green (29.3.55) 10·00 4·50
345 35c. bright blue 65 3·50
346 40c. deep brown 65 1·25
a. Sepia (12.11.53) 2·75 1·75

347		50c. violet	2·50	10
		a. Deep violet (29.3.55)	4·50	1·00
348	**40**	1s. deep green and deep brown	60	10
349		2s. bright blue and deep purple	2·25	2·50
350		5s. black and carmine-red	2·25	4·25
351		7s.50 grey-black and emerald	19·00	23·00
352		10s. carmine-red and black	10·00	12·00
339/52 *Set of* 14			35·00	45·00

41 Sultan Kalif bin Harub

(Photo Harrison)

1954 (26 Aug). *Sultan's 75th Birthday.* Wmk Mult Script CA. *Chalk-surfaced paper.* P 13×12.

353	**41**	15c. deep green	10	10
354		20c. rose-red	10	10
355		30c. bright blue	10	10
356		50c. purple	20	10
357		1s.25 orange-red	20	75
353/7 *Set of* 5			60	1·00

42 Cloves

43 *Urnmoja Wema* (dhow)

44 Sultan's Barge

45 Map of East African Coast

46 Minaret Mosque

47 Dimbani Mosque

48 Kibweni Palace

(Des W. J. Jennings (T **42**), A. Farhan (T **43**), Mrs. M. Broadbent (T **44**, **46**), R. A. Sweet (T **45**), A. S. B. New (T **47**), B. J. Woolley (T **48**). Recess B.W.)

1957 (26 Aug). W w **12**. P 11½ (5c., 10c.), 11×11½ (15c., 30c., 1s.25), 14×13½ (20c., 25c., 35c., 50c.,), 13½×14 (40c., 1s., 2s.) or 13×13½ (5s., 7s.50, 10s.).

358	**42**	5c. orange and deep green	10	40
359		10c. emerald and carmine-red	10	10
360	**43**	15c. green and sepia	20	2·75
361	**44**	20c. ultramarine	10	10
362	**45**	25c. orange-brown and black	10	1·25
363	**43**	30c. carmine-red and black	15	1·25
364	**45**	35c. slate and emerald	15	20
365	**48**	40c. brown and black	15	10
366	**45**	50c. blue and grey-green	15	30
367	**47**	1s. carmine and black	20	30
368	**43**	1s.25 slate and carmine	3·50	20
369	**47**	2s. orange and deep green	3·50	2·25
370	**48**	5s. deep bright blue	5·00	2·00
371		7s.50 green	10·00	4·00
372		10s. carmine	10·00	6·00
358/72 *Set of* 15			30·00	19·00

49 Sultan Seyyid Sir Abdulla bin Khalifa

50 "Protein Foods"

(Recess B.W.)

1961 (17 Oct). *As T* **42/8**, *but with portrait of Sultan Sir Abdulla as in T* **49**. W w **12**. P 13×13½ (20s.), others as before.

373	**49**	5c. orange and deep green	20	1·00
374		10c. emerald and carmine-red	20	10
375	**43**	15c. green and sepia	75	3·25
376	**44**	20c. ultramarine	30	30
377	**45**	25c. orange-brown and black	60	1·25
378	**43**	30c. carmine-red and black	2·75	2·00
379	**45**	35c. slate and emerald	2·50	4·25
380	**48**	40c. brown and black	30	20
381	**45**	50c. blue and grey-green	1·75	10
382	**47**	1s. carmine and black	40	1·25
383	**43**	1s.25 slate and carmine	2·50	4·25
384	**47**	2s. orange and deep green	70	3·25
385	**48**	5s. deep bright blue	3·25	8·00
386		7s.50 green	3·00	15·00
387		10s. carmine	3·00	9·00
388		20s. sepia	17·00	28·00
373/88 *Set of* 16			35·00	70·00

(Des M. Goaman. Photo Harrison)

1963 (4 June). *Freedom from Hunger.* W w **12**. P 14×14½.

389	**50**	1s.30 sepia	1·25	75

INDEPENDENT

51 Zanzibar Clove

53 "Religious Tolerance" (mosques and churches)

(Photo Harrison)

1963 (10 Dec). *Independence. Portrait of Sultan Seyyid Jamshid bin Abdulla. T* **51**, **53** *and similar vert designs.* P 12½.

390		30c. multicoloured	10	30
391		50c. multicoloured	10	30
392		1s.30, multicoloured	15	4·00
393		2s.50, multicoloured	20	4·75
		a. Green omitted	†	£550
390/3 *Set of* 4			50	8·50

Designs:—50c. "To Prosperity" (Zanzibar doorway); 2s.50, "Towards the Light" (Mangapwani Cave).

REPUBLIC

When the Post Office opened on 14 January 1964, after the revolution deposing the Sultan, the stamps on sale had the portrait cancelled by a manuscript cross. Stamps thus cancelled on cover or piece used between January 14 and 17 are therefore of interest.

JAMHURI 1964
(**55**= "Republic")

1964 (17 Jan). *Locally handstamped as T* **55** *in black.*

(i) Nos. 373/88.

394	**49**	5c. orange and deep green	1·00	65
395		10c. emerald and carmine-red	1·00	10
396	**43**	15c. green and sepia	1·25	2·75
397	**44**	20c. ultramarine	1·25	60
398	**45**	25c. orange-brown and black	1·75	20
399	**43**	30c. carmine-red and black	1·25	60
400	**45**	35c. slate and emerald	1·75	1·50
401	**46**	40c. brown and black	1·25	1·25
402	**45**	50c. blue and grey-green	1·75	10
403	**47**	1s. carmine and black	1·25	1·00
404	**43**	1s.25 slate and carmine	1·25	1·75
405	**47**	2s. orange and deep green	2·00	1·75
406	**48**	5s. deep bright blue	1·75	1·75
407		7s.50 green	2·00	1·75
408		10s. carmine	2·00	1·75
409		20s. sepia	2·50	5·50

(ii) Nos. 390/3 (Independence).

410		30c. multicoloured	30	1·00
411		50c. multicoloured	30	30
412		1s.30 multicoloured	60	80
413		2s.50 multicoloured	1·40	1·50
		a. Green omitted	£275	
394/413 *Set of* 20			25·00	24·00

T **55** occurs in various positions—diagonally, horizontally or vertically.

NOTE. Nos. 394 to 413 are the only stamps officially authorised to receive the handstamp but it has also been seen on Nos. 353/7, 389 and the Postage Dues. There are numerous errors but it is impossible to distinguish between cases of genuine oversight and those made deliberately at the request of purchasers.

JAMHURI 1964
(**56**)

JAMHURI
1964
(**57**)

1964 (28 Feb). *Optd by Bradbury, Wilkinson.*

(i) As T **56** *on Nos. 373/88.*

414	**49**	5c. orange and deep green	10	10
415		10c. emerald and carmine-red	10	10
416	**43**	15c. green and sepia	10	10
417	**44**	20c. ultramarine	10	10
418	**45**	25c. orange-brown and black	10	10
419	**43**	30c. carmine-red and black	10	10
420	**45**	35c. slate and emerald	10	10
421	**46**	40c. brown and black	10	10
422	**45**	50c. blue and grey-green	10	10
423	**47**	1s. carmine and black	10	10
424	**43**	1s.25 slate and carmine	1·50	20
425	**47**	2s. orange and deep green	50	20
426	**48**	5s. deep bright blue	50	35
427		7s.50 green	65	5·00
428		10s. carmine	1·25	5·00
429		20s. sepia	2·25	8·00

The opt T **56** is set in two lines on Types **46/8**.

(ii) As T **57** *on Nos. 390/3 (Independence).*

430		30c. multicoloured	10	10
431		50c. multicoloured	10	10
432		1s.30, multicoloured	10	10
433		2s.50, multicoloured	15	30
		a. Green omitted	£110	
414/33 *Set of* 20			7·25	18·00

The opt T **57** is set in one line on No. 432.

For the set inscribed "UNITED REPUBLIC OF TANGANYIKA AND ZANZIBAR" see Nos. 124/7 of Tanganyika.

58 Axe, Spear and Dagger

59 Zanzibari with Rifle

(Litho German Bank Note Ptg Co, Leipzig)

1964 (21 June). *T* **58/9** *and similar designs inscr. "JAMHURI ZANZIBAR 1964". Multicoloured.* P 13×13½ (vert) or 13½×13 (horiz).

434		5c. Type **58**	20	10
435		10c. Bow and arrow breaking chains	30	10
436		15c. Type **58**	30	10
437		20c. As 10c.	50	10
438		25c. Type **59**	50	10
439		30c. Zanzibari breaking manacles	30	10
440		40c. Type **59**	50	10
441		50c. As 30c.	30	10
442		1s. Zanzibari, flag and Sun	30	10
443		1s.30 Hands breaking chains (*horiz*)	30	1·00
444		2s. Hand waving flag (*horiz*)	30	30
445		5s. Map of Zanzibar and Pemba on flag (*horiz*)	55	3·25
446		10s. Flag on Map	4·25	4·00
447		20s. National flag (*horiz*)	3·75	20·00
434/47 *Set of* 14			11·00	26·00

68 Soldier and Maps

69 Building Construction

(Litho German Bank Note Ptg Co, Leipzig)

1965 (12 Jan). *First Anniv of Revolution.* P 13×13½ (vert) or 13½×13 (horiz).

448	**68**	20c. apple-green and deep green	10	10
449	**69**	30c. chocolate and yellow-orange	10	10
450	**68**	1s.30 light blue and ultramarine	10	10
451	**69**	2s.50 reddish violet and rose	10	15
448/51 *Set of* 4			35	40

Type **68** is inscribed "PEMPA" in error for "PEMBA".

70 Planting Rice

(Litho German Bank Note Ptg Co, Leipzig)

1965 (17 Oct). *Agricultural Development. T* **70** *and similar horiz design.* P 13×12½.

452	**70**	20c. sepia and blue	10	1·00
453	–	30c. sepia and magenta	10	1·00
454	–	1s.30 sepia and yellow-orange	20	2·00
455	**70**	2s.50 sepia and emerald	30	4·25
452/5 *Set of* 4			60	7·50

Design:—30c., 1s.30, Hands holding rice.

72 Freighter, Tractor, Factory, and Open Book and Torch

73 Soldier

(Litho German Bank Note Ptg Co, Leipzig)

1966 (12 Jan). *2nd Anniv of Revolution.* P 12½×13.

456	**72**	20c. multicoloured	20	20
457	**73**	50c. multicoloured	15	20
458	**72**	1s.30 multicoloured	15	20
459	**73**	2s.50 multicoloured	25	1·50
456/9 *Set of* 4			65	1·90

For stamps with similar inscription or inscribed "TANZANIA" only, and with commemorative date 26th April 1966, see Nos. 2142/5 of TANZANIA.

74 Tree-felling

75 Zanzibar Street

(Litho German Bank Note Ptg Co, Leipzig)

1966 (5 June). *Horiz designs as T* **74**, *and T* **75**. P 12½×13 (50c., 10s.) or 13×12½ (others).

460	5c. maroon and yellow-olive	70	80
461	10c. brown-purple and bright emerald	70	80
462	15c. brown-purple and light blue	70	80
463	20c. ultramarine and light orange	40	20
464	25c. maroon and orange-yellow	40	30
465	30c. maroon and ochre-yellow	70	20
466	40c. purple-brown and rose-pink	80	20
467	50c. green and pale greenish yellow	80	20
468	1s. maroon and bright blue	80	20
469	1s. 30 maroon and turquoise	80	2·25
470	2s. brown-purple and light blue-green	80	30
471	5s. rose-red and pale blue	1·25	4·25
472	10s. crimson and pale yellow	2·25	16·00
473	20s. deep purple-brown and magenta	4·25	26·00
460/473	*Set of* 14	14·00	48·00

Designs:—5c., 20s. Type **74**; 10c., 1s. Clove cultivation; 15, 40c. Chair-making; 20c., 5s. Lumumba College; 25c., 4s. 30, Agriculture; 30c., 2s. Agricultural workers; 50c.,10s. Type **75**.

81 "Education"

(Litho D.L.R.)

1966 (25 Sept). *Introduction of Free Education.* P 13½×13.

474	**81**	50c. black, light blue and orange	10	1·00
475		1s.30 black, Light blue and yellow-green	15	1·75
476		2s.50 black, light blue and pink	40	4·50
474/6		*Set of* 3	60	6·50

82 A.S.P. Flag

(Litho D.L.R.)

1967 (5 Feb). *Tenth Anniv of Afro-Shirazi Party (A.S.P.). T* **82** *and similar multicoloured design.* P 14.

477	30c. Type **82**	10	1·00
478	50c. Vice-President M. A. Karume of Tanzania, flag and crowd (*vert*)	10	1·00
479	1s.30 As 50c.	10	2·00
480	2s.50 Type **82**	30	3·25
477/80	*Set of* 4	55	6·50

84 Voluntary Workers

(Photo Delrieu)

1967 (20 Aug). *Voluntary Workers Brigade.* P 12½×12.

481	**84**	1s.30 multicoloured	15	2·25
482		2s.50 multicoloured	40	5·50

POSTAGE DUE STAMPS

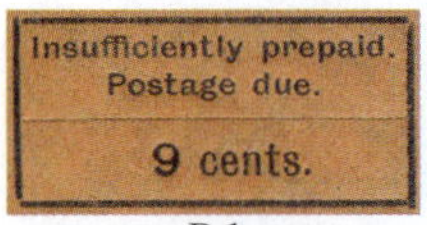

D 1

D 2

(Types D **1** and D **2** typo by the Government Printer)

1926–30. *Rouletted 10, with imperf sheet edges. No gum.*

D1	D **1**	1c. black/*orange*	11·00	£150
D2		2c. black/*orange*	4·50	70·00
D3		3c. black/*orange*	5·00	55·00
		a. "cent.s" for "cents."	£150	£400
D4		6c. black/*orange*	—	£7000
		a. "cent.s" for "cents."	—	£21000
D5		9c. black/*orange*	2·75	28·00
		a. "cent.s" for "cents."	25·00	£140
D6		12c. black/*orange*	£11000	£9500
D7		12c. black/*green*	£1500	£600
		a. "cent.s" for "cents."	£4000	£1700
D8		15c. black/*orange*	2·75	30·00
		a. "cent.s" for "cents."	25·00	£140
D9		18c. black/*salmon*	4·50	50·00
		a. "cent.s" for "cents."	48·00	£200
D10		18c. black/*orange*	22·00	85·00
		a. "cent.s" for "cents."	80·00	£300
D11		20c. black/*orange*	4·50	75·00
		a. "cent.s" for "cents."	48·00	£300
D12		21c. black/*orange*	3·50	42·00
		a. "cent.s" for "cents."	42·00	£190
D13		25c. black/*magenta*	£2750	£1300
		a. "cent.s" for "cents."	£7000	£4000
D14		25c. black/*orange*	£14000	£13000
D15		31c. black/*orange*	9·50	95·00
		a. "cent.s" for "cents."	60·00	
D16		50c. black/*orange*	21·00	£250
		a. "cent.s" for "cents."	£110	
D17		75c. black/*orange*	65·00	£550
		a. "cent.s" for "cents."	£275	

Initial printings, except the 1c. and 2c., contained the error "cent.s" for "cents" on R. 4/1 in the sheets of 10 (2×5). The error was corrected on subsequent supplies of the 3c., 9c. and 15c.

It is known that examples of these stamps used before early 1929 were left uncancelled on the covers. Uncancelled examples of Nos. D4, D6/7 and D13/14 which are not in very fine condition, must be assumed to have been used.

1930–33. *Rouletted 5. No gum.*

D18	D **2**	2c. black/*salmon*	17·00	35·00
D19		3c. black/*rose*	3·25	55·00
D21		6c. black/*yellow*	3·25	35·00
D22		12c. black/*blue*	4·50	28·00
D23		25c. black/*rose*	9·00	90·00
D24		25c. black/*lilac*	18·00	65·00
D18/24		*Set of* 6	50·00	£275

D 3

(Typo D.L.R.)

1936 (1 Jan)–**62**. Wmk Mult Script CA. P 14.

D25	D **3**	5c. violet	6·50	11·00
		a. Chalk-surfaced paper (18.7.56)	35	17·00
D26		10c. scarlet	5·50	2·75
		a. Chalk-surfaced paper (6.3.62)	35	8·00
D27		20c. green	2·25	5·50
		a. Chalk-surfaced paper (6.3.62)	35	22·00
D28		30c. brown	13·00	21·00
		a. Chalk-surfaced paper (18.7.56)	35	13·00
D29		40c. ultramarine	9·50	28·00
		a. Chalk-surfaced paper (18.7.56)	75	38·00
D30		1s. grey	12·00	30·00
		a. Chalk-surfaced paper (18.7.56)	1·00	23·00
D25/30		*Set of* 6	45·00	90·00
D25a/30a		*Set of* 6	2·75	£110
D25s/30s		Perf "Specimen" *Set of* 6	90·00	

All Zanzibar issues were withdrawn on 1 January 1968 and replaced by Tanzania issues. Zanzibar stamps remained valid for postage in Zanzibar for a limited period.

Zululand *see* South Africa

Set Prices for British Empire Omnibus Issues

The composition of these sets is in accordance with the tables on the following pages. Only such items considered basic stamps arc included; varieties such as shades, perforation changes and watermark changes are excluded.

Stamps issued in connection with any of the events by countries which are no longer in the British Commonwealth and which are not listed in the Part 1 Catalogue are omitted.

1935 SILVER JUBILEE

1935. *Silver Jubilee. Complete set of 250 stamps*

	PRICE	
	Un	*Used*
	£1100	£1500

Country	*Catalogue Nos.*	*Stamps*
Great Britain	453/6	4
Antigua	91/4	4
Ascension	31/4	4
Australia	156/8	3
Nauru	40/3	4
New Guinea	206/7	2
Papua	150/3	4
Bahamas	141/4	4
Barbados	241/4	4
Basutoland	11/14	4
Bechuanaland	111/14	4
Bermuda	94/7	4
British Guiana	301/4	4
British Honduras	143/6	4
British Solomon Islands	53/6	4
Canada	335/40	6
Newfoundland	250/3	4
Cayman Islands	108/11	4
Ceylon	379/82	4
Cyprus	144/7	4
Dominica	92/5	4
Egypt-British Forces	A10	1
Falkland Islands	139/42	4
Fiji	242/5	4
Gambia	143/6	4
Gibraltar	114/17	4
Gilbert and Ellice Islands	36/9	4
Gold Coast	113/16	4
Grenada	145/8	4
Hong Kong	133/6	4
India	240/6	7
Jamaica	114/17	4
Kenya, Uganda and Tanganyika	124/7	4
Leeward Islands	88/91	4
Malaya-Straits Settlements	256/9	4
Malta	210/13	4
Mauritius	245/8	4
Montserrat	94/7	4
Morocco Agencies		
British Currency	62/5	4
Spanish Currency	149/52	4
French Currency	212/15	4
Tangier	238/40	3
New Zealand	573/5	3
Cook Islands	113/15	3
Niue	69/71	3
Western Samoa	177/9	3
Nigeria	30/3	4
Northern Rhodesia	18/21	4
Nyasaland	123/6	4
St. Helena	124/7	4
St. Kitts-Nevis	61/4	4
St. Lucia	109/12	4
St. Vincent	142/5	4
Seychelles	128/31	4
Sierra Leone	181/4	4
Somaliland Protectorate	86/9	4
South Africa	65/8	4×2
Southern Rhodesia	31/4	4
South West Africa	88/91	4
Swaziland	21/4	4
Trinidad and Tobago	239/42	4
Turks and Caicos Islands	187/9	4
Virgin Islands	103/6	4
Total		250

The concept initiated by the 1935 Silver Jubilee omnibus issue has provided a pattern for a series of Royal commemoratives over the past 50 years which have introduced countless collectors to the hobby.

The Crown Colony Windsor Castle design by Harold Fleury is, surely, one of the most impressive produced to the 20th-century and its reproduction in the recess process by three of the leading stamp-printing firms of the era has provided a subject for philatelic research which has yet to be exhausted.

Each of the three, Bradbury, Wilkinson & Co. and Waterlow and Sons, who both produced fifteen issues, together with De La Rue & Co. who printed fourteen, used a series of vignette (centre) plates coupled with individual frame plates for each value. All were taken from dies made by Waterlow. Several worthwhile varieties exist on the frame plates but most interest has been concentrated on the centre plates, each of which was used to print a considerable number of different stamps.

Sheets printed by Bradbury, Wilkinson were without printed plate numbers, but research has now identified twelve centre plates which were probably used in permanent pairings. Stamps from some of these centre plates have revealed a number of prominent plate flaws, the most famous of which, the extra flagstaff, has been eagerly sought by collectors for many years.

Extra flagstaff (Plate "1" R. 9/1)

Short extra flagstaff (Plate "2" R. 2/1)

Lightning conductor (Plate "3" R. 2/5)

Flagstaff on right-hand turret (Plate "5" R. 7/1)

Double flagstaff (Plate "6" R. 5/2)

De La Rue sheets were initially printed with plate numbers, but in many instances these were subsequently trimmed off. Surviving examples do, however, enable a positive identification of six centre plates, 2A, 2B, (2A), (2B), 4 and 4/ to be made. The evidence of sheet markings and plate flaws clearly demonstrates that there were two different pairs of plates numbered 2A 2B. The second pair is designated (2A) (2B) by specialist collectors to avoid further confusion. The number of major plate flaws is not so great as on the Bradbury, Wilkinson sheets, but four examples are included in the catalogue.

Diagonal line by turret (Plate 2A R. 10/1 and 10/2)

Dot to left of chapel (Plate 2B R. 8/3)

Dot by flagstaff (Plate 4 R. 8/4)

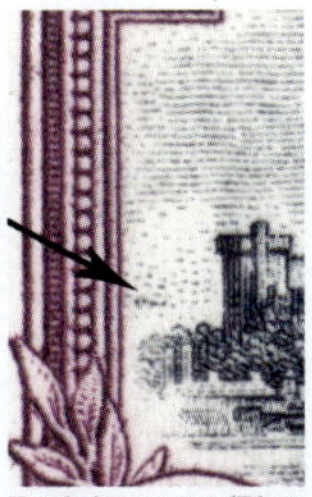

Dash by turret (Plate 4/ R. 3/6)

Much less is known concerning the Waterlow centre plate system as the sheets did not show plate numbers. Ten individual plates have. so far, been identified and it is believed that these were used in pairs. The two versions of the kite and log flaw from plate "2" show that this plate exists in two states.

Damaged turret (Plate "1" R. 5/6)

Kite and vertical log (Plate "2A" R. 10/6)

Kite and horizontal log (Plate "2B" R. 10/6)

Bird by turret (Plate "7" R. 1/5)

1937 CORONATION

1937. *Coronation*. .... Complete set of 202 stamps £180 £250

Country	*Catalogue Nos*	*Stamps*
Great Britain	461	1
Aden	13/15	3
Antigua	95/7	3
Ascension	35/7	3
Australia		
Nauru	44/7	4
New Guinea	208/11	4
Papua	154/7	4
Bahamas	146/8	3
Barbados	245/7	3
Basutoland	15/17	3
Bechuanaland	115/17	3
Bermuda	107/9	3
British Guiana	305/7	3
British Honduras	147/9	3
British Solomon Islands	57/9	3
Canada	356	1
Newfoundland	254/6, 257/67	14
Cayman Islands	112/14	3
Ceylon	383/5	3
Cyprus	148/50	3
Dominica	96/8	3
Falkland Islands	143/5	3
Fiji	246/8	3
Gambia	147/9	3
Gibraltar	118/20	3
Gilbert and Ellice Islands	40/2	3
Gold Coast	117/19	3
Grenada	149/51	3
Hong Kong	137/9	3
Jamaica	118/20	3
Kenya, Uganda and Tanganyika	128/30	3
Leeward Islands	92/4	3
Malaya-Straits Settlements	275/7	3
Malta	214/16	3
Mauritius	249/51	3
Montserrat	98/100	3
Morocco Agencies		
Spanish Currency	164	1
French Currency	229	1
Tangier	244	1
New Zealand	599/601	3
Cook Islands	124/6	3
Niue	72/4	3
Nigeria	46/8	3
Northern Rhodesia	22/4	3
Nyasaland	127/9	3
St. Helena	128/30	3
St. Kitts-Nevis	65/7	3
St. Lucia	125/7	3
St. Vincent	146/8	3
Seychelles	132/4	3
Sierra Leone	185/7	3
Somaliland Protectorate	911/2	3
South Africa	71/5	5×2
Southern Rhodesia	36/9	4
South West Africa	97/104	8×2
Swaziland	25/7	3

Country	Catalogue Nos	Stamps
Trinidad and Tobago	243/5	3
Turks and Caicos Islands	191/3	3
Virgin Islands	107/9	3
Total		202

1945–46 VICTORY

1945–46. *Victory*.......Complete set of 164 stamps 50·00 80·00

Country	Catalogue Nos.	Stamps
Great Britain	491/2	2
Aden	28/9	2
Seiyun	12/13	2
Shihr and Mukalla	12/13	2
Antigua	110/11	2
Ascension	48/9	2
Australia	213/15	3
Bahamas	176/7	2
Barbados	262/3	2
Basutoland	29/31	3×2
Bechuanaland	129/31	3×2
Bermuda	123/4	2
British Guiana	320/1	2
British Honduras	162/3	2
British Solomon Islands	73/4	2
Burma	64/7	4
Cayman Islands	127/8	2
Ceylon	400/1	2
Cyprus	164/5	2
Dominica	110/11	2
Falkland Islands	164/5	2
Falkland Islands Dependencies	G17/18	2
Fiji	268/9	2
Gambia	162/3	2
Gibraltar	132/3	2
Gilbert and Ellice Islands	55/6	2
Gold Coast	133/4	2
Grenada	164/5	2
Hong Kong	169/70	2
India	278/81	4
Hyderabad	53	1
Jamaica	141/2	2
Kenya, Uganda and Tanganyika	155/6	2
Leeward Islands	115/16	2
Malta	232/3	2
Mauritius	264/5	2
Montserrat	113/14	2
Morocco Agencies		
Tangier	253/4	2
New Zealand	667/77	11
Cook Islands	146/9	4
Niue	98/101	4
Western Samoa	215/18	4
Nigeria	60/1	2
Northern Rhodesia	46/7	2
Nyasaland	158/9	2
Pakistan		
Bahawalpur	O19	1
Pitcairn Islands	9/10	2
St. Helena	141/2	2
St. Kitts-Nevis	78/9	2
St. Lucia	142/3	2
St. Vincent	160/1	2
Seychelles	150/1	2
Sierra Leone	201/2	2
Somaliland Protectorate	117/18	2
South Africa	108/10	3×2
Southern Rhodesia	64/7	4
South West Africa	131/3	3×2
Swaziland	39/41	3×2
Trinidad and Tobago	257/8	2
Turks and Caicos Islands	206/7	2
Virgin Islands	122/3	2
Zanzibar	331/2	2
Total		164

1948 ROYAL SILVER WEDDING

1948–49. *Royal Silver Wedding*..............................
.... Complete set of 138 stamps £1800 £2000

Country	Catalogue Nos.	Stamps
Great Britain	493/4	2
Aden	30/1	2
Seiyun	14/15	2
Shihr and Mukalla	14/15	2
Antigua	112/13	2
Ascension	50/1	2
Bahamas	194/5	2
Bahrain	61/2	2
Barbados	265/62	2
Basutoland	36/7	2
Bechuanaland	136/7	2
Bermuda	125/6	2
British Guiana	322/3	2
British Honduras	164/5	2
British Postal Agencies in Eastern Arabia	25/6	2
British Solomon Islands	75/6	2
Cayman Islands	129/30	2
Cyprus	166/7	2
Dominica	112/13	2
Falkland Islands	166/7	2
Falkland Islands Dependencies	G19/20	2
Fiji	270/1	2
Gambia	164/5	2
Gibraltar	134/5	2
Gilbert and Ellice Islands	57/8	2
Gold Coast	147/8	2
Grenada	166/7	2
Hong Kong	171/2	2
Jamaica	143/4	2
Kenya, Uganda and Tanganyika	157/8	2
Kuwait	74/5	2
Leeward Islands	117/18	2
Malaya		
Johore	131/2	2
Kedah	70/1	2
Kelantan	55/6	2
Malacca	1/2	2
Negri Sembilan	40/1	2
Pahang	47/8	2
Penang	1/2	2
Perak	122/3	2
Perlis	1/2	2
Selangor	88/9	2
Trengganu	61/2	2
Malta	249/50	2
Mauritius	270/1	2
Montserrat	115/16	2
Morocco Agencies		
Spanish Currency	176/7	2
Tangier	255/6	2
Nigeria	62/3	2
North Borneo	350/1	2
Northern Rhodesia	48/9	2
Nyasaland	161/2	2
Pitcairn Islands	11/12	2
St. Helena	143/4	2
St. Kitts-Nevis	80/1	2
St. Lucia	144/5	2
St. Vincent	162/3	2
Sarawak	165/6	2
Seychelles	152/3	2
Sierra Leone	203/4	2
Singapore	31/2	2
Somaliland Protectorate	119/20	2
South Africa	125	1×2
South West Africa	137	1×2
Swaziland	46/7	2
Trinidad and Tobago	259/60	2
Turks and Caicos Islands	208/9	2
Virgin Islands	124/5	2
Zanzibar	333/4	2
Total		138

1949 75th ANNIVERSARY OF U.P.U.

1949. *U.P.U. 75th Anniversary*
Complete set of 310 stamps £300 £500

Country	Catalogue Nos.	Stamps
Great Britain	449/502	4
Aden	32/5	4
Seiyun	16/19	4
Shihr and Mukalla	16/19	4
Antigua	114/17	4
Ascension	52/5	4
Australia	232	1
Bahamas	196/9	4
Bahrain	67/70	4
Barbados	267/70	4
Basutoland	38/41	4
Bechuanaland	138/41	4
Bermuda	130/3	4
British Guiana	324/7	4
British Honduras	172/5	4
British Postal Agencies in Eastern Arabia	31/4	4
British Solomon Islands	77/80	4
Brunei	96/9	4
Cayman Islands	131/4	4
Ceylon	410/12	3
Cyprus	168/71	4
Dominica	114/17	4
Falkland Islands	168/71	4
Falkland Islands Dependencies	G31/4	4
Fiji	272/5	4
Gambia	166/9	4
Gibraltar	136/9	4
Gilbert and Ellice Islands	59/62	4
Gold Coast	149/52	4
Grenada	168/71	4
Hong Kong	173/6	4
India	325/8	4
Jamaica	145/8	4
Kenya, Uganda and Tanganyika	159/62	4
Kuwait	80/3	4
Leeward Islands	119/22	4
Malaya		
Johore	148/51	4
Kedah	72/5	4
Kelantan	57/60	4
Malacca	18/21	4
Negri Sembilan	63/6	4
Pahang	49/52	4
Penang	23/6	4
Perak	124/7	4
Perlis	3/6	4
Selangor	111/14	4
Trengganu	63/6	4
Malta	251/4	4
Mauritius	272/5	4
Montserrat	117/20	4
Morocco Agencies		
Tangier	276/9	4
New Hebrides	64/7, F77/80	4+4
Nigeria	64/7	4
North Borneo	352/5	4
Northern Rhodesia	50/3	4
Nyasaland	163/6	4
Pakistan		
Bahawalpur	43/6, O28/31	4+4
Pitcairn Islands	13/16	4
St. Helena	145/8	4
St. Kitts-Nevis	82/5	4
St. Lucia	160/3	4
St. Vincent	178/81	4
Sarawak	167/70	4
Seychelles	154/7	4
Sierra Leone	205/8	4
Singapore	33/6	4
Somaliland Protectorate	121/4	4
South Africa	128/30	3×2
Southern Rhodesia	68/9	2
South West Africa	138/40	3×2
Swaziland	48/51	4
Tonga	88/91	4
Trinidad and Tobago	261/4	4
Turks and Caicos Islands	217/20	4
Virgin Islands	126/9	4
Zanzibar	335/8	4
Total		310

1951 INAUGURATION OF B.W.I. UNIVERSITY COLLEGE

1951. *B.W.I. University College*
........................Complete set of 28 stamps 13·00 28·00

Country	Catalogue Nos.	Stamps
Antigua	118/19	2
Barbados	283/4	2
British Guiana	328/9	2
British Honduras	176/7	2
Dominica	118/19	2
Grenada	185/6	2
Jamaica	149/50	2
Leeward Islands	123/4	2
Montserrat	121/2	2
St. Kitts-Nevis	92/3	2
St. Lucia	164/5	2
St. Vincent	182/3	2
Trinidad and Tobago	265/6	2
Virgin Islands	130/1	2
Total		28

1953 CORONATION

1953. *Coronation.*
................................Complete set of 106 stamps £120 £100·00

1953–54 ROYAL VISIT

1953–54. *Royal Visit.*
................................Complete set of 13 stamps 5·00 3·50

1958 CARIBBEAN FEDERATION

1958. *Caribbean Federation.*
................................Complete set of 30 stamps 17·00 19·00

1963 FREEDOM FROM HUNGER

1963. *Freedom from Hunger.*
................................Complete set of 77 stamps £140 £100

1963 RED CROSS

1963. *Red Cross Centenary.*
..... Complete set of 108 stamps and 2 miniature sheets £170 £180

1964 SHAKESPEARE

1964. *Shakespeare. 400th Birth Anniversary.*
................................Complete set of 25 stamps 20·00 20·00

1965 I.T.U. CENTENARY

1965. *I.T.U. Centenary.*
..... Complete set of 112 stamps and 1 miniature sheet £140 £110

1965 I.C.Y.

1965. *I.C.Y.*
..... Complete set of 107 stamps and 2 miniature sheets £110 85·00

1965–67 CHURCHILL

1965–67. *Churchill.*
................................Complete set of 182 stamps £225 £170

1966 ROYAL VISIT

1966. *Royal Visit to the Caribbean.*
................................Complete set of 34 stamps 29·00 16·00

1966 FOOTBALL WORLD CUP

1966. *World Cup Football Championship.*
.... Complete set of 68 stamps and 2 miniature sheets £110 70·00

1966 W.H.O. HEADQUARTERS

1966. *W.H.O. New Headquarters.*
.... Complete set of 58 stamps and 1 miniature sheet 80·00 65·00

1966-67 U.N.E.S.C.O. ANNIVERSARY

1966–67. *U.N.E.S.C.O. 20th Anniversary.*
..... Complete set of 110 stamps and 1 miniature sheet £160 £130

1935 SILVER JUBILEE TO 1966 U.N.E.S.C.O.																			
Issuing countries	**1935** Silver Jubilee	**1937** Coronation	**1945–46** Victory	**1948** Silver Wedding	**1949** U.P.U.	**1951** B.W.I. Univ	**1953** Coronation	**1953–54** Royal Visit	**1958** Caribbean Federation	**1963** F.F.H.	**1963** Red Cross	**1964** Shakespeare	**1965** I.T.U.	**1965** I.C.Y.	**1965–66** Churchill	**1966** Royal Visit	**1966** Football Cup	**1966** W.H.O.	**1966** U.N.E.S.C.O.
Great Britain	4	1	2	2	4	—	4	—	—	2+2	3+3	5+4	2+2	2+2	2+2	—	3+3	—	—
Aden / South Arabian Federation	—	3	2	2	4	—	1	1	—	1	2	—	—	2	4	—	2	2	3
Seiyun	—	—	2	2	4	—	1	—	—	—	—	—	7	—	1	—	7	—	—
Shihr and Mukalla	—	—	2	2	4	—	1	—	—	—	—	—	—	8	3	—	8+**MS**	—	—
Antigua	4	3	2	2	4	2	1	—	3	1	2	1	2	2	4	2	2	2	3
Ascension	4	3	2	2	4	—	1	—	—	1	2	—	2	2	4	—	2	2	3
Australia	3	—	3	—	1	—	3	3	—	—	1	—	1	1	1	—	—	—	—
Bahamas	4	3	2	2	4	—	1	—	—	1	2	1	2	2	4	2	2	2	3
Bahrain	—	—	—	2	4	—	4	—	—	—	—	—	—	—	—	—	—	—	—
Barbados	4	3	2	2	4	2	1	—	3	—	—	—	2	—	4	2	—	—	3
Basutoland / Lesotho	4	3	3×2	2	4	—	1	—	—	1	2	—	2	2	4	—	—	—	4
Bechuanaland / Botswana	4	3	3×2	2	4	—	1	—	—	1	2	1	2	2	4	—	—	—	—
Bermuda	4	3	2	2	4	—	1	1	—	1	2	—	2	2	4	—	2	—	3
British Antarctic Territory	—	—	—	—	—	—	—	—	—	—	—	—	—	—	4	—	—	—	—
British Guiana / Guyana	4	3	2	2	4	2	1	—	—	1	2	—	2	2	2	2	—	—	—
British Honduras	4	3	2	2	4	2	1	—	—	1	2	—	2	2	4	—	—	—	—
British P.A's in Eastern Arabia	—	—	—	2	4	—	4	—	—	—	—	—	—	—	—	—	—	—	—
British Solomon Islands	4	3	2	2	4	—	1	—	—	1	2	—	2	2	4	—	2	2	3
British Virgin Islands	4	3	2	2	4	2	1	—	—	1	2	1	2	2	4	2	—	—	3
Brunei	—	—	—	—	4	—	—	—	—	1	—	—	2	2	4	—	2	2	3
Burma	—	—	4	—	—	—	—	—	—	—	—	—	—	—	—	—	—	—	—
Canada	6	1	—	—	—	—	1	—	—	—	—	—	—	1	1	—	—	—	—
Newfoundland	4	14	—	—	—	—	—	—	—	—	—	—	—	—	—	—	—	—	—
Cayman Islands	4	3	2	2	4	—	1	—	—	1	2	1	2	2	4	2	2	2	3
Ceylon	4	3	2	—	3	—	1	1	—	2	—	—	2	2	—	—	—	2	2
Cook Islands	3	3	4	—	—	—	2	—	—	—	—	—	—	—	6	—	—	—	—
Cyprus	4	3	2	2	4	—	1	—	—	2	2	4	3	2	—	—	—	—	1
Dominica	4	3	2	2	4	2	1	—	3	1	2	1	2	2	4	2	2	2	3
Egypt/ British Forces in Egypt	1	—	—	—	—	—	—	—	—	—	—	—	—	—	—	—	—	—	—
Falkland Islands	4	3	2	2	4	—	1	—	—	1	2	1	2	2	4	—	—	—	—
Falkland Island Dependencies	—	—	2	2	4	—	1	—	—	—	—	—	—	—	—	—	—	—	—
Fiji	4	3	2	2	4	—	1	1	—	1	2	—	2	2	4	—	2	2	—
Gambia	4	3	2	2	4	—	1	—	—	1	2	1	2	—	3	—	—	—	—
Gibraltar	4	3	2	2	4	—	1	1	—	1	2	1	2	2	4	—	2	2	3
Gilbert and Ellice Islands	4	3	2	2	4	—	1	—	—	1	2	—	2	2	4	—	2	2	3
Gold Coast / Ghana	4	3	2	2	4	—	1	—	—	3	4+**MS**	—	4+**MS**	4+**MS**	—	—	5+**MS**	4+**MS**	5+**MS**
Grenada	4	3	2	2	4	2	1	—	3	1	2	—	2	2	4	2	2	2	3
Hong Kong	4	3	2	2	4	—	1	—	—	1	2	—	2	2	4	—	—	2	3
India	7	—	4	—	4	—	—	—	—	1	1	—	1	1	—	—	—	—	—
Hyderabad	—	—	1	—	—	—	—	—	—	—	—	—	—	—	—	—	—	—	—
Ireland	—	—	—	—	—	—	—	—	—	2	2	—	2	2	—	—	—	—	—
Jamaica	4	3	2	2	4	2	1	1	3	2	2	—	1	—	2	4	—	—	—
K.U.T. / East Africa	4	3	2	2	4	—	1	1	—	4	2	—	4	4	—	—	—	—	4
Kuwait	—	—	—	2	4	—	4	—	—	1	—	—	—	—	—	—	—	—	—
Leeward Islands	4	3	2	2	4	2	1	—	—	—	—	—	—	—	—	—	—	—	—
Malayan States, etc.	4	3	—	22	44	—	11	—	—	3	—	—	3	—	—	—	—	—	—
North Borneo	—	—	—	2	4	—	1	—	—	1	—	—	—	—	—	—	—	—	—
Sarawak	—	—	—	2	4	—	1	—	—	1	—	—	—	—	—	—	—	—	—
Maldive Islands	—	—	—	—	—	—	—	—	—	7	5	—	—	5+**MS**	6	—	—	—	6
Malta	4	3	2	2	4	—	1	1	—	1	2	—	—	—	4	—	—	—	—
Mauritius	4	3	2	2	4	—	1	—	—	1	2	—	2	2	4	—	—	—	3
Montserrat	4	3	2	2	4	2	1	—	3	1	2	1	2	2	4	2	—	2	3
Morocco Agencies / Tangier	15	3	2	4	4	—	4	—	—	—	—	—	—	—	—	—	—	—	—
Nauru	4	4	—	—	—	—	—	—	—	—	—	—	—	—	—	—	—	—	—
New Hebrides / Vanuatu (English and French inscr)	—	—	—	—	4+4	—	1	—	—	1+1	2+2	—	2+2	2+2	4+4	—	2+2	2+2	3+3
New Zealand	3	3	11	—	—	—	5	2	—	—	—	—	1	1	1	—	—	—	—
Tokelau Islands	—	—	—	—	—	—	1	—	—	—	—	—	—	—	—	—	—	—	—
Nigeria	4	3	2	2	4	—	1	—	—	2	3+**MS**	—	3	3	—	—	—	—	3
Niue	3	3	4	—	—	—	2	—	—	—	—	—	—	—	—	—	—	—	—
Northern Rhodesia / Zambia	4	3	2	2	4	—	1	—	—	—	—	—	2	2	—	—	—	2	—
Nyasaland / Malawi	4	3	2	2	4	—	1	—	—	—	—	—	—	—	—	—	—	—	—
Pakistan	—	—	—	—	—	—	—	—	—	2	1	—	1	2	—	—	—	—	1
Bahawalpur	—	—	1	—	4+4	—	—	—	—	—	—	—	—	—	—	—	—	—	—
Papua New Guinea / Papua	4	4	—	—	—	—	—	—	—	—	1	—	—	—	—	—	—	—	—
New Guinea	2	4	—	—	—	—	—	—	—	—	—	—	—	—	—	—	—	—	—
Pitcairn Islands	—	—	2	2	4	—	1	—	—	1	2	—	2	2	4	—	2	2	3
Rhodesia and Nyasaland	—	—	—	—	—	—	—	—	—	—	1	—	—	—	—	—	—	—	—
St. Helena	4	3	2	2	4	—	1	—	—	1	2	—	2	2	4	—	2	2	3
St. Kitts-Nevis	4	3	2	2	4	2	1	—	3	—	2	—	2	2	4	2	2	2	3
St. Lucia	4	3	2	2	4	2	1	—	3	1	2	1	2	2	4	2	2	2	3
St. Vincent	4	3	2	2	4	2	1	—	3	1	2	—	2	—	4	2	—	2	3
Samoa	3	—	4	—	—	—	2	—	—	—	—	—	—	—	—	—	—	4	—
Seychelles	4	3	2	2	4	—	1	—	—	1	2	—	2	2	4	—	2	2	3
Sierra Leone	4	3	2	2	4	—	1	—	—	2	3	—	—	—	11	—	—	—	—
Singapore	—	—	—	2	4	—	1	—	—	—	—	—	—	—	—	—	—	—	—
Somaliland Protectorate	4	3	2	2	4	—	1	—	—	—	—	—	—	—	—	—	—	—	—
South Africa	4×2	5×2	3×2	1×2	3×2	—	1	—	—	—	2	—	2	—	—	—	—	—	—
Southern Rhodesia	4	4	4	—	2	—	1	—	—	—	—	—	3	—	1	—	—	—	—
South West Africa	4	8×2	3×2	1×2	3×2	—	5	—	—	—	2	—	—	—	—	—	—	—	—
Swaziland	4	3	3×2	2	4	—	1	—	—	1	2	—	2	2	4	—	—	—	3
Tonga	—	—	—	—	4	—	—	—	—	1	2	—	—	—	—	—	—	—	—
Trinidad and Tobago	4	3	2	2	4	2	1	—	3	3	—	—	—	1	—	4	—	—	—
Tristan da Cunha	—	—	—	—	—	—	1	—	—	1	2	—	2	2	4	—	2	2	3
Turks and Caicos islands	4	3	2	2	4	—	1	—	—	1	2	1	2	2	4	2	—	—	3
Zanzibar	—	—	2	2	4	—	—	—	—	1	—	—	—	—	—	—	—	—	—
Total number of stamps	250	202	164	138	310	28	106	13	30	77	108 +2**MS**	25	112 +**MS**	107 +2**MS**	182	34	68 +2**MS**	58 +**MS**	110 +**MS**

Index

R

S

T

U

V

W

Z

investment

How it can work for you:

Great Britain SG 137 1882 £5 Orange Plate 1

1998 Catalogue Price: £1,600
2008 Catalogue Price: £4,500

181% increase in 10 years.

Options

Option 1 Take the guaranteed minimum return on offer (60%) – Minimum return of £2,560 as per the 10 year contract.

Option 2 Stanley Gibbons repurchases at 75% of the catalogue price at the time - Sell to us at 75% of catalogue e.g. £3,375 (111% return).

Option 3 Sell through Stanley Gibbons Auctions, commission free.

Option 4 Roll over the contract for another term.

Option 5 Retain the items.

Option 6 Sell the items privately.

Breaking News

5 years ago we sold a superb mint example of the £5 Orange for £6,000 ($12,000).

That very same stamp recently set a world record price at auction in London. It sold for £15,270 ($30,540). £6,000 to £15,270 in 5 years... ***155% growth in value...***

Find out more about rare stamp and autograph investment.

Call us on 01481 708 274

Visit us at:
www.stanleygibbons.com/investment

Email us at:
investment@stanleygibbons.co.uk

Stanley Gibbons (Guernsey) Limited
18-20 Le Bordage, St Peter Port,
Guernsey, Channel Islands,
British Isles, GY1 1DE

investment

"If I could buy just one stamp..."

Investment Director Adrian Roose tackles the impossible question.

I'm often asked this question. "If you could buy just one stamp which would it be?"

Well... If you are looking for a single rare stamp to invest in then consider this item. It's returned almost 7.2% per annum over the last 10 years. There's no reason to suspect it won't offer the same returns over the next 10 years.

I've long been fascinated with the Great Britain SG121.

When I first joined Stanley Gibbons 14 years ago I followed the company training programme, working in different departments building up my knowledge.

I sat with the reference collection to study shade differences. I swotted up, reading reference books.

One of the first reference books I read was an invaluable little book stating how many of each Great Britain stamp had been printed.

It was worn and many pages were torn but in a supply and demand driven market the information it held was like the Holy Grail to me.

And one stamp always stood out. The Great Britain SG121.

It had, by far, the lowest print run of any Queen Victoria British stamp. Yet it wasn't the most expensive. Far from it, it looked distinctly undervalued.

I've watched over the years as this stamp has become more appreciated amongst collectors. They are beginning to realise how few of these stamps are available in top quality mint condition.

The Catalogue price is up from £7,500 to £20,000 in 10 years. A 166% increase in Catalogue prices.

If you'd bought the SG121 from us 10 years ago you wouldn't be taking the guaranteed minimum return of a 60% capital gain on your original investment (exit route 1).

We would have advised you to take exit route 2.

We'd be buying back the stamp for £15,000 (75% of Catalogue).

That equates to an almost 7.2% p.a. (compound) over 10 years.

Or (exit route 3) you could have placed it in our auction with 0% commission and potentially done even better.

I firmly believe this level of increase is just the start and the forthcoming years will see similar, if not better, increases.

How rare is this stamp? Approx 67,000 were printed. Compare that to a Penny Black, the world's first postage stamp. Probably the most famous stamp in the world. Over 68,000,000 Penny Blacks were printed.

We have staff scouring auctions the world over. They are permanently looking for rare stamps of the highest quality to offer to the collectors on our database.

Other staff travel the country on road-shows talking to the public and valuing their collections in the hope of finding quality stamps to offer to our clientele.

However despite our staff being permanently on the lookout this is the first Great Britain SG121 we have been able to offer in over 9 months...

This article is an extract from one of our investment newsletters. To subscribe *FREE* to this service visit: *www.stanleygibbons.com/fn*

Stanley Gibbons
One Country Albums

These albums have something the others do not... **Stanley Gibbons catalogue numbers**.

Ideal for the straightforward single country collection and the only Commonwealth one-country albums that feature **Stanley Gibbons catalogue numbers throughout.**

Available as separate volumes or in a great value set, all albums accommodate high-quality printed leaves featuring illustrations, Stanley Gibbons catalogue numbers and dates of issue. Supplements are produced annually to keep your collection up to date. Each volume is housed in a padded 4 or 22-ring maroon PVC binder, gold blocked on the spine and supplied with a self-adhesive title sheet. All album pages are 115gsm.

Great Britain Albums (with GB 4-ring binders)

R5250MAR	Volume 1 (1840-1970)	£32.97
R5252MAR	Volume 2 (1970-1990)	£33.97
R5254MAR	Volume 3 (1991-1999)	£33.97
R5255MAR	Volume 4 (2000-2007)	£36.97
R5250-SO	4 Volume Set Offer **Save £30.05**	£109.97

British Islands Albums (with 22-Ring binders)

R5524MAR	Guernsey Volume 1 (1941-1994)	£35.97
R5526MAR	Guernsey Volume 2 (1995-2004)	£35.97
R5529MAR	Guernsey Volume 3 (2005-2007)	£26.97
R5525MAR	Jersey Volume 1 (1941-1994)	£35.97
R5527MAR	Jersey Volume 2 (1995-2004)	£35.97
R5528MAR	Jersey Volume 3 (2005-2007)	£26.97
R5256MAR	Isle of Man Volume 1 (1958-1994)	£35.97
R5257MAR	Isle of Man Volume 2 (1995-2004)	£35.97
R5265MAR	Isle of Man Volume 3 (2005-2007)	£26.97
Guernsey, Jersey OR Isle of Man 3 Volume Set Offer	**Save £16.94**	£81.97

Commonwealth Albums (with 4-ring binders)

R5258MAR	Australia Vol. 1 (1913-1990)	£40.97
R5259MAR	Australia Vol. 2 (1991-2004)	£40.97
R5253MAR	Australia Vol. 3 (2005-2006)	£24.97
R5260MAR	Canada Vol. 1 (1851-1990)	£40.97
R5261MAR	Canada Vol. 2 (1991-2004)	£40.97
R5266MAR	Canada Vol. 3 (2005-2006)	£24.97
R5262MAR	New Zealand Vol. 1 (1855-1990)	£40.97
R5263MAR	New Zealand Vol. 2 (1991-2004)	£40.97
R5270MAR	New Zealand Vol. 3 (2005-2006)	£24.97
Australia, Canada OR New Zealand 3 Volume Set Offer	**Save £21.94**	£84.97

Stanley Gibbons Luxury Hingeless Albums

Featuring made-to-measure mounts designed to save you time and money

Our luxury hingeless album range offers the ultimate in quality, convenience and style. Handsomely bound in deeply padded navy blue leatherette, each album is richly embossed with the country's national crest on the cover and spine and presented in its own matching slipcase. Inside, the finest quality printed leaves have been expertly arranged with spaces for each stamp and selected illustrations and descriptions for your guidance. In addition, clear protective mounts are already in place to enable easy insertion of your stamps. Annual supplements help keep your album completely up to date.

GB

R5284	GB Volume 1 (1840-1970)	£99.95
R5285	GB Volume 2 (1971-1989)	£108.95
R5290	GB Volume 3 (1990-1999)	£88.95
R5295	GB Volume 4 (2000-2006)	£79.95
R5284-SO	GB 4-Vol Set Offer **Save £55.85**	£321.95

GB QEII

R5546	GB Q.E.II Volume 1 (1952-1989)	£110.95
R5581	GB Q.E.II Volume 2 (1990-1999)	£87.95
R5583	GB Q.E.II Volume 3 (2000-2006)	£84.95
R5546SO	GB Q.E.II Set Offer **Save £42.95**	£241.50
R5583-RB	Q.E. Volume 3 Binder only	£31.95

AUSTRALIA

R5280	Australia Volume 1 (1913-1965)	£75.95
R5281	Australia Volume 2 (1966-1985)	£89.95
R5291	Australia Volume 3 (1986-1999)	£99.95
R5297	Australia Volume 4 (2000-2006)	£72.95
R5280-SO	Australia Set Offer **Save £50.85**	£287.95

CANADA

R5282	Canada Volume 1 (1851-1969)	£90.95
R5283	Canada Volume 2 (1970-1985)	£100.95
R5293	Canada Volume 3 (1986-1999)	£110.95
R5298	Canada Volume 4 (2000-2006)	£80.95
R5282-SO	Canada Set Offer **Save £57.30**	£326.50

NEW ZEALAND

R5288	New Zealand Volume 1 (1855-1967)	£89.95
R5289	New Zealand Volume 2 (1967-1985)	£100.95
R5296	New Zealand Volume 3 (1986-1995)	£89.95
R5561	New Zealand Volume 4 (1996-2002)	£99.95
R5530	New Zealand Volume 5 (2003-2006)	£66.95
R5288-SO	New Zealand Set Offer **Save £66.80**	£380.95

Prices correct as of August 2008. Prices subject to change.

STANLEY GIBBONS

Unit 7 Parkside, Christchurch Road, Ringwood, BH24 3SH

Tel: +44 (0)1425 472363 Fax: 01425 470247 Email: info@stanleygibbons.co.uk

STANLEY GIBBONS
The Home of Philately since 1856

AN IMPORTANT MESSAGE TO YOU

Dear Catalogue User,

As a collector and Stanley Gibbons catalogue user for many years myself, I am only too aware of the need to provide you with the information you seek in an accurate, timely and easily accessible manner.

Naturally, I have my own views on where changes could be made, but one thing I learned long ago is that we all have different opinions and requirements.

I would therefore be most grateful if you would complete the form overleaf and return it to me (or send your answers on a separate sheet if you prefer not to cut the page out of your catalogue).

If you would like the form to be sent to you by email, let me know at hjefferies@stanleygibbons.co.uk

Very many thanks for your help.

Yours sincerely,

Hugh Jefferies,
Editor.

Questionnaire

Please complete and return it to:

Hugh Jefferies *(Catalogue Editor)*
Stanley Gibbons Limited
7 Parkside, Ringwood
Hampshire BH24 2LE
United Kingdom

or email: *hjefferies@stanleygibbons.co.uk*

2009 Commonwealth & British Empire Stamps 1840-1970

1. Level of detail
Do you feel that the level of detail in this catalogue is:
a) too specialised ☐
b) about right ☐
c) inadequate ☐

2. Frequency of issue
How often would you purchase a new edition of this catalogue?
a) Annually ☐
b) Every two years ☐
c) Every three to five years ☐
d) Less frequently ☐

3. Design and Quality
How would you describe the layout and appearance of this catalogue?
a) Excellent ☐
b) Good ☐
c) Adequate ☐
d) Poor ☐

4. *How important to you are the prices given in the catalogue*:
a) Important ☐
b) Quite important ☐
c) Of little interest ☐
d) Of no interest ☐

5. *Would you be interested in an electronic version of this catalogue?*
a) Yes ☐
b) Maybe ☐
c) No ☐

6. *Is there anything you would like to see in this catalogue that is not currently included?* ....

....

....

....

....

....

....

....

7. *Would you like us to let you know when the next edition of this catalogue is due to be published? If so please give your contact details below.*

Name: ....

Address:..

....

....

....

Email: ....

Telephone: ....

8. *Are there any other Stanley Gibbons Catalogues which you would like to be informed of when published.*
1.
2.
3.

Many thanks for your comments.

COLLECT
COMMONWEALTH STAMPS
STAMPS

From Stanley Gibbons, THE WORLD'S LARGEST STAMP STOCK

Condition (mint/UM/used)	Country	SG No.	Description	Price	Office use only
			POSTAGE & PACKAGING	£3.60	
			GRAND TOTAL		

Minimum price. The minimum catalogue price quoted is 10p. For individual stamps, prices between 10p and 95p are provided as a guide for catalogue users. The lowest price charged for individual stamps or sets purchased from Stanley Gibbons Ltd is £1

Please complete payment, name and address details overleaf